CONTENTS

Introduction and Acknowledgements 5
Utilita – Welcome 6
Team of the Season 2021–22 – Jonathan Taylor 8
Football Awards 2021–22 10
Review of the Season 2021–22 – Jonathan Wilson 18

THE FA PREMIER LEAGUE AND FOOTBALL LEAGUE: THE CLUBS
The English League Clubs 22
English League Players Directory 390
English League Players – Index 530

ENGLISH CLUBS STATISTICS
The FA Community Shield Winners 1908–2021 9
The FA Community Shield 2021 9
English League Tables and Leading Goalscorers 2021–22 12
Football League Play-offs 2021–22 16
Cups and Ups and Downs Diary 2021–22 537
Managers – In and Out 2021–22 538
English League Honours 1888–2022 540
English League Attendances 2021–22 550
League Attendances since 1946–47 552

THE LEAGUE CUP AND EFL TROPHY
League Cup Finals 1961–2022 553
Carabao Cup 2021–22 554
League Cup Attendances 1960–2022 561
Football League Trophy Finals 1984–2022 562
EFL Trophy Attendances 2021–22 562
Papa John's EFL Trophy 2021–22 563

THE FA CUP
FA Cup Finals 1872–2022 573
The Emirates FA Cup 2021–22 – Preliminary and Qualifying Rounds 575
The Emirates FA Cup 2021–22 – Competition Proper 580
FA Cup Attendances 1969–2022 591

NATIONAL LEAGUE
National League 2021–22 592
National League North 2021–22 594
National League South 2021–22 595
National League Clubs 596

SCOTTISH FOOTBALL
Scottish League Tables and Top Goalscorers 2021–22 642
The Scottish Football League Clubs 644
Scottish League Attendances 2021–22 728
Scottish League Honours 1890–2022 729
Scottish League Play-offs 2021–22 736
Scottish League Cup Finals 1946–2022 738
Premier Sports Scottish League Cup 2021–22 739
SPFL Trust Trophy 2021–22 746
Scottish FA Cup Finals 1874–2022 750
League Challenge Finals 1990–2022 751
Scottish FA Cup 2021–22 752

WOMEN'S FOOTBALL
Barclays FA Women's Super League 2021–22 758
FA Women's Championship 2021–22 758
FA Women's Continental Tyres League Cup 2021–22 759
FA Women's National League 2021–22 760
The Vitality Women's FA Cup 2020–21 762
The Vitality Women's FA Cup 2021–22 762
UEFA Women's Champions League 2021–22 766
UEFA Women's Champions League Finals 768
Women's European Championship Finals 768
FIFA Women's World Cup Finals 768
FIFA Women's World Cup 2021–23 – Qualifying Europe 769
England Women's Internationals 2021–22 771
England Women's International Matches 1972–2022 772

WELSH AND NORTHERN IRISH FOOTBALL

Welsh Football 2021–22 776
Northern Irish Football 2021–22 781

EUROPEAN FOOTBALL

European Cup Finals 1956–1992 786
UEFA Champions League Finals 1993–2022 786
UEFA Champions League 2021–22 787
European Cup-Winners' Cup Finals 1961–99 799
Inter-Cities Fairs Cup Finals 1958–71 799
UEFA Cup Finals 1972–97 800
UEFA Cup Finals 1998–2009 800
UEFA Europa League Finals 2010–22 800
UEFA Europa League 2021–22 801
UEFA Europa Conference League 2021–22 813
British and Irish Clubs in Europe – Summary of Appearances 829
FIFA Club World Cup 2021 831
European Super Cup 2021 831

INTERNATIONAL FOOTBALL

International Directory 832
Olympic Football 2021 – Tokyo 861
European Football Championship 1960–2020 862
UEFA Nations League 2020–21 862
FIFA World Cup 2022 Qualifying – Europe 863
FIFA World Cup 2022 – Qualified Teams 877
FIFA World Cup 2022 – Group Stage Draw 877
The World Cup 1930–2018 878
UEFA Nations League 2022–23 879
British and Irish International Results 1872–2022 887
Other British and Irish International Matches 2021–22 – Friendlies 910
British and Irish International Managers 911
British and Irish International Appearances 1872–2022 912
British and Irish International Goalscorers 1872–2022 942
South America 947
North America – Major League Soccer 2021 950
Africa – Africa Cup of Nations 2021 – Cameroon 951
UEFA Youth League 2021–22 952
UEFA Under-17 Championship 2021–22 953
UEFA Under-19 Championship 2021–22 956
UEFA Under-21 Championship 2021–23 – Qualifying 958
England Under-21 Results 1976–2022 960
British and Irish Under-21 Teams 2021–22 963
British Under-21 Appearances 1976–2022 966
England Youth Games 2021–22 981
University Football 2021–22 984

NON-LEAGUE FOOTBALL

Schools Football 2021–22 – Boodles Independent Schools FA Cup 2021–22 985
Non-League Tables 2021–22 – National League System Steps 3–4 986
The Buildbase FA Trophy 2021–22 990
England C 2021–22 992
The Buildbase FA Vase 2021–22 993
The FA Youth Cup 2021–22 997
The FA Sunday Cup 2019–20 1002
Premier League 2 2021–22 1003
Under-18 Professional Development League 2021–22 1004
Central League 2021–22 1005
Youth Alliance League 2021–22 1005

INFORMATION AND RECORDS

Important Addresses 1007
Football Club Chaplaincy 1008
Obituaries 1009
The Football Records 1025
International Records 1036
The Premier League and Football League Fixtures 2022–23 1037
National League Fixtures 2022–23 1047
The Scottish Premier League and Scottish League Fixtures 2022–23 1050
Stop Press 1054

INTRODUCTION

The 53rd edition of the *Football Yearbook* is sponsored for the second time by Utilita. The coverage in this edition is once again full and comprehensive. The post-COVID-19 era saw a new enthusiasm for the game with British clubs performing so well in Europe. We look forward to the World Cup in Qatar later in 2022, which will include both England and Wales. Wales defeated Ukraine in a play-off to reach the finals for the first time since 1958.

Coverage of the European Qualifying campaign for the FIFA World Cup 2022, including match line-ups and league tables from 2021–22, is included. Other international football at various levels is well covered in this edition.

At European club level, the Champions League, Europa League and the newly formed Europa Conference League all have comprehensive details included. For the preliminary and qualifying rounds all results are included with details of goalscorers, attendances, full line-ups and formations for all matches involving British and Irish clubs. From the Group Stage onwards, goalscorers, attendances, full line-ups and formations are included for all matches, together with all of the league tables from the respective group stages.

The 2021–22 Premier League season had an amzing finale with Manchester City crowned champions after a nail-biting final day. City were 14 points clear of Liverpool in January, although the Reds had two games in hand. That lead was reduced over the latter stages of the season, until the final day when either of these two giants could have won the league. City trailed 0-2 to Aston Villa but scored three late goals to secure the title from Liverpool who themselves trailed and then beat Wolverhampton Wanderers 3-1. Promoted clubs Norwich City and Watford were both relegated along with Burnley. Newcastle United were long-time favourites for the drop and failed to win any of their first 14 league matches. A much-publicised take-over by the Saudi PIF, together with the appointment of Eddie Howe as manager, saw the Magpies reach the dizzy heights of 11th. Promoted Brentford ended their first season in the top tier in a commendable 13th. Fulham returned to the Premier League at the first time of asking along with Bournemouth who had been in the Championship for two seasons and play-off winners Nottingham Forest who had been out of the Premier League for a long 23 years.

In League One, Wigan Athletic were promoted as champions and on the same day Rotherham United followed them into the Championship as runners-up. The League One Play-Off final saw Sunderland overcome Wycombe Wanderers 2-0 in a one-sided final at Wembley. League Two champions Forest Green Rovers made the leap to League One for the first time and were joined by Exeter City and Bristol Rovers. On the final day Rovers incredibly won 7-0 at home to Scunthorpe United to pip Northampton Town on goal difference. A 3-0 victory over Mansfield Town at Wembley saw Port Vale join the others in League One. Oldham Athletic became the first club who had played in the Premier League to be relegated to the National League. After 115 years in the Football League pyramid they finished second bottom of League Two with Scunthope United bottom and also relegated after 72 years in the Football League. Liverpool's Mohamed Salah won both the Football Writers' Footballer of the Year and the PFA Player of the Year awards. Phil Foden, after another brilliant season for both club and country, won the PFA Young Player of the Year for the second year in succession.

All of these statistics are reproduced in the pages devoted not only to the Premier League, but the three Football League competitions too, as well as all major allied cup competitions.

Women's football is also featured. The Women's Super League, Championship and National Leagues are included, together with the domestic cup competitions: Women's FA Cup and Continental Tyres League Cup. The UEFA Women's Champions League is also covered. England Women's Internationals since 1974 and all of the 2021–22 season's games are included. The UEFA Women's Euro 2022 finals were underway when the book went to press, with England Women performing well in the group stage.

In the club-by-club pages that contain the line-ups of all league matches, appearances are split into starting and substitute appearances. In the Players Directory the totals show figures combined.

The Players Directory and its accompanying A to Z index enable the reader to quickly find the club of any specific player.

Throughout the book players sent off are designated with ■; substitutes in the club pages are 12, 13 and 14. The Premier League and EFL recently voted to increase the number of substitutes to 5 for next season for their respective competitions.

In addition to competitions already mentioned there is full coverage of Scottish Premiership, Scottish Football League and Scottish domestic cup competitions. There are also sections devoted to Welsh and Northern Irish football, Under-21s and various other UEFA youth levels, schools, reserve team, academies and the leading non-league competitions as well as the work of club chaplains. The chief tournaments outside the UK at club and national level are not forgotten. The International Directory itself features Europe in some depth as well as every FIFA-affiliated country's international results for the year since July 2021; every reigning league and cup champion worldwide is listed.

Naturally there are international appearances and goals scored by players for England, Scotland, Northern Ireland, Wales and the Republic of Ireland. For easy reference, those players making appearances and scoring goals in the season covered are picked out in bold type.

The *Football Yearbook* would like to extend its appreciation to the publishers Headline for excellent support in the preparation of this edition, particularly Louise Rothwell for her continued help and Jonathan Taylor for the photographic selection throughout the book and his selection of the Team of the Season.

ACKNOWLEDGEMENTS

In addition the *Football Yearbook* is also keen to thank the following individuals and organisations for their co-operation. Special thanks to Jonathan Wilson for his Review of the Season.

Thanks are also due to Ian Nannestad for the Obituaries and the Did You Know? and Fact File features in the club section. Many thanks also to John English for his conscientious proof reading and compilation of the International Directory.

The *Football Yearbook* is grateful to the Football Association, the Scottish Professional Football League, the Football League, Rev. Nigel Sands for his contribution to the Chaplain's page and Bob Bannister, Paul Anderson, Kenny Holmes and Martin Cooper for their help.

Sincere thanks to George Schley and Simon Dunnington for their excellent work on the database, and to Andy Cordiner and the staff at Paperghosts for their much appreciated efforts in the production of the book throughout the year.

WELCOME

Welcome to the 2022–2023 edition of the *Football Yearbook*.

This will be a unique footballing year as we will see the FIFA World Cup take place in the winter for the first time in its 92-year history. It will be a World Cup featuring two home nations in England and Wales.

England have featured in all but three World Cups since their first appearance in 1950 and will enter Qatar 2022 as one of the favourites. For the Welsh, this will be only their second appearance following the 1958 tournament when they boasted a squad that contained the likes of Jack Kelsey, Ivor Allchurch, Cliff Jones and the famous Charles brothers, Mel and John. Let's hope both nations progress far into the competition.

Meanwhile, we have just experienced our first season with stadiums back to full capacity following the COVID-19 pandemic. Football's capacity to bounce back and endure is all too evident, with crowds continuing to increase, largely due to the outstanding quality of football on show.

Manchester City, again, proved just a fraction too good for closest rivals Liverpool as they won their fourth Premier League title in five seasons following a thrilling campaign that ebbed and flowed throughout.

Jurgen Klopp's Reds took both domestic knockout trophies – beating Chelsea on penalties in both League Cup and FA Cup finals – but were just edged out by Real Madrid in the UEFA Champions League final in Paris.

There was also British interest in the UEFA Europa League final after a phenomenal run of results took Glasgow Rangers to Seville to play Eintracht Frankfurt. But on a balmy Spanish evening, the Germans prevailed on penalties – where have we heard that before? – after the game ended in a 1-1 stalemate.

Rangers did secure the Scottish Cup a few days later but by then their great rivals Celtic had wrestled the Premiership title back to Glasgow's East End in Ange Postecoglou's debut season as manager – it was a remarkable tenth championship in 11 seasons for the Bhoys.

In the women's game, a record crowd of 49,094 saw Chelsea beat Manchester City in the FA Cup final to seal a famous Double, while in Scotland Rangers ended Glasgow City's remarkable run of 14 successive titles to record their first league success for the Light Blues. Celtic beat City 3-2 to win the Cup.

At Utilita, our commitment to this great game is as strong as ever, particularly for those who need more help than others. With inflation spiralling and the cost-of-living crisis becoming a grim reality for millions of households, we are mindful that squeezed finances will become an increasing problem from the grassroots right through to the Premier League.

Our 'Football Rebooted' campaign – designed to reallocate one million pairs of football boots to those who really need them – has been a huge success, but this is only just the start.

Everybody, regardless of social or financial status, deserves to take part in our national game. Having a 'kickabout' with pals has obvious physical and mental health benefits.

Our 'Price to Play' report, which studies the impact of COVID and the cost-of-living crisis on the grassroots game, gave cause for concern. Nearly half of parents said their child's club was adversely affected by the pandemic.

We know thousands of clubs fear for their very future. We know millions of families fear for their finances.

As former Liverpool and England star David James MBE – who holds the Premier League appearance record for a goalkeeper, and has fronted our 'Price to Play' report campaign – said: 'Without football, many young people's lives would no doubt have taken a far worse path – I'm sure mine would have been very different. The UK can ill afford the immediate burden that the closure of grassroots clubs will have on the NHS, policing and other social support. This study has identified affordability as the primary barrier stopping young people playing grassroots football – and there is no way this should happen in a country hosting the world's richest league.'

In my notes for last season's *Football Yearbook*, I said we want football to be a power for good. And it is. We should never underestimate that. But I see the role football plays in society becoming ever greater, ever more important, as we head into a period of austerity. It unifies, bringing people together, giving us hope and providing a welcome distraction from everyday life.

Whoever you support, I hope you enjoy the 2022–23 season, with all its inevitable twists and turns – it should be another belter.

Jem Maidment, Chief Marketing Officer, Utilita Energy

At the Memorial Stadium, Aaron Collins of Bristol Rovers celebrates his club's promotion from League Two. (Bradley Collyer/PA Images/Alamy)

TEAM OF THE SEASON 2021–22

JONATHAN TAYLOR

Alisson
(Liverpool)

Trent Alexander-Arnold *(Liverpool)* | **Ruben Dias** *(Manchester C)* | **Virgil van Dijk** *(Liverpool)* | **Andy Robertson** *(Liverpool)*

Bernardo Silva *(Manchester C)* | **Rodri** *(Manchester C)* | **Declan Rice** *(West Ham U)*

Mohamed Salah *(Liverpool)* | **Kevin De Bruyne** *(Manchester C)* | **Son Heung-min** *(Tottenham H)*

Manager: Jurgen Klopp
(Liverpool)

Alisson: Finished neck-and-neck with City's Ederson on 20 clean sheets in the league, but the Liverpool keeper arguably made fewer mistakes and continued to command the box with his trademark composure and assurance. A world-class presence between the sticks.

Trent Alexander-Arnold: A revelation going forward: 12 assists and countless first-rate set-piece deliveries contributed hugely to Liverpool's offensive threat. With greater maturity he seems to have improved his defensive capabilities, the Real Madrid goal in the Champions League final notwithstanding. One of the most exciting full-backs in Europe.

Ruben Dias: Last season's winner of the FWA's Footballer of the Year award delivered a rock-solid second season at the Etihad. With another long Champions League campaign and a second Premier League title under his belt, Dias has rapidly established himself as a defender of global repute.

Virgil van Dijk: The Rolls-Royce of central defenders: how Liverpool missed him for much of the previous season. But with 34 Premier League appearances, and 51 in total, VVD's almost continuous presence during the 2021–22 season was a significant factor in Liverpool's unlikely quadruple charge which only faltered at the final hurdles.

Andy Robertson: Like his young team-mate on the other flank, Robertson's attacking fair was much in evidence: a tally of 10 assists speaks for itself. But the Scotsman's defensive disciplines were as strong as ever, giving the Reds' left side enormous solidity.

Bernardo Silva: Occasionally overlooked, the Portuguese midfielder stepped up to deliver another fine season (his fifth at City) of consistently excellent performances. Perfectly suited to Guardiola's playing style, his wonderful passing, sublime balance and important goal threat (eight in the Premier League) marked him out as a vital component of the team's success.

Declan Rice: Played in all but two of West Ham's games in their highly impressive Premier League campaign and was a driving force in the club's progress to the Europa League semi-finals. Provided both the defensive shield and the link to those upfront – quite a double act. He is maturing into the complete central midfielder, though he perhaps needs to add more goals to his output. Will he remain with the Hammers for much longer?

Rodri: Like Rice, he was a pivotal figure in the middle of the park: a massive physical presence who both disrupted the opposition and dictated City's play. Missed only five Premier League games, scored seven goals, and provided a major aerial threat from set pieces. A vital cog in the wheel.

Mohamed Salah: Had to share the Golden Boot this time around but still matched last season's total of 23 Premier League goals. Enjoyed a discernibly more productive first half of the season, and perhaps finished the campaign in a relatively poor run of form, but his 31 goals from 51 games in all competitions hardly constitute a failure. He was named both the FWA Footballer of the Year and the PFA Player of the Year, and came within a whisker of winning the African Cup of Nations with Egypt in February.

Kevin De Bruyne: What more can be said about this most sublime of footballers? The Premier League Player of the Season found the net 15 times, provided eight assists and won his fourth title with City, yet the bare stats barely do him justice. The vision, the range of passing, the wicked set-piece delivery, the driving momentum from midfield, the eye for goal. I could go on. We are blessed to have him playing in this country. Simply exceptional.

Son Heung-min: The fact that he equalled Mo Salah's 23 goals to claim a share of the Golden Boot speaks volumes about his value to Spurs. The South Korean continued to link up superbly with Harry Kane: on the counter-attack it very often felt like a hot knife through butter, such was Son's pace, incisiveness and finishing prowess.

Manager: Jurgen Klopp: On the face of it, an FA Cup and a League Cup might feel like a slightly underwhelming return on a season that promised so much more. But don't underestimate the skill it took to deliver both of those trophies AND keep Liverpool in the running for the Premier League title until the last few minutes of a 38-game campaign AND get them to the Champions League final in which they narrowly lost to perennial winners Real Madrid. This was a managerial masterclass from Klopp which *could* have delivered a phenomenal quadruple. A close call, but the German gets the nod over Pep Guardiola.

THE FA COMMUNITY SHIELD WINNERS 1908–2021

CHARITY SHIELD 1908–2001

1908	Manchester U v QPR	1-1
Replay	Manchester U v QPR	4-0
1909	Newcastle U v Northampton T	2-0
1910	Brighton v Aston Villa	1-0
1911	Manchester U v Swindon T	8-4
1912	Blackburn R v QPR	2-1
1913	Professionals v Amateurs	7-2
1920	WBA v Tottenham H	2-0
1921	Tottenham H v Burnley	2-0
1922	Huddersfield T v Liverpool	1-0
1923	Professionals v Amateurs	2-0
1924	Professionals v Amateurs	3-1
1925	Amateurs v Professionals	6-1
1926	Amateurs v Professionals	6-3
1927	Cardiff C v Corinthians	2-1
1928	Everton v Blackburn R	2-1
1929	Professionals v Amateurs	3-0
1930	Arsenal v Sheffield W	2-1
1931	Arsenal v WBA	1-0
1932	Everton v Newcastle U	5-3
1933	Arsenal v Everton	3-0
1934	Arsenal v Manchester C	4-0
1935	Sheffield W v Arsenal	1-0
1936	Sunderland v Arsenal	2-1
1937	Manchester C v Sunderland	2-0
1938	Arsenal v Preston NE	2-1
1948	Arsenal v Manchester U	4-3
1949	Portsmouth v Wolverhampton W	1-1*
1950	English World Cup XI v FA Canadian Touring Team	4-2
1951	Tottenham H v Newcastle U	2-1
1952	Manchester U v Newcastle U	4-2
1953	Arsenal v Blackpool	3-1
1954	Wolverhampton W v WBA	4-4*
1955	Chelsea v Newcastle U	3-0
1956	Manchester U v Manchester C	1-0
1957	Manchester U v Aston Villa	4-0
1958	Bolton W v Wolverhampton W	4-1
1959	Wolverhampton W v Nottingham F	3-1
1960	Burnley v Wolverhampton W	2-2*
1961	Tottenham H v FA XI	3-2
1962	Tottenham H v Ipswich T	5-1
1963	Everton v Manchester U	4-0
1964	Liverpool v West Ham U	2-2*
1965	Manchester U v Liverpool	2-2*
1966	Liverpool v Everton	1-0
1967	Manchester U v Tottenham H	3-3*
1968	Manchester C v WBA	6-1
1969	Leeds U v Manchester C	2-1
1970	Everton v Chelsea	2-1
1971	Leicester C v Liverpool	1-0
1972	Manchester C v Aston Villa	1-0
1973	Burnley v Manchester C	1-0
1974	Liverpool v Leeds U *Liverpool won 6-5 on penalties.*	1-1
1975	Derby Co v West Ham U	2-0
1976	Liverpool v Southampton	1-0
1977	Liverpool v Manchester U	0-0*
1978	Nottingham F v Ipswich T	5-0
1979	Liverpool v Arsenal	3-1
1980	Liverpool v West Ham U	1-0
1981	Aston Villa v Tottenham H	2-2*
1982	Liverpool v Tottenham H	1-0
1983	Manchester U v Liverpool	2-0
1984	Everton v Liverpool	1-0
1985	Everton v Manchester U	2-0
1986	Everton v Liverpool	1-1*
1987	Everton v Coventry C	1-0
1988	Liverpool v Wimbledon	2-1
1989	Liverpool v Arsenal	1-0
1990	Liverpool v Manchester U	1-1*
1991	Arsenal v Tottenham H	0-0*
1992	Leeds U v Liverpool	4-3
1993	Manchester U v Arsenal *Manchester U won 5-4 on penalties.*	1-1
1994	Manchester U v Blackburn R	2-0
1995	Everton v Blackburn R	1-0
1996	Manchester U v Newcastle U	4-0
1997	Manchester U v Chelsea *Manchester U won 4-2 on penalties.*	1-1
1998	Arsenal v Manchester U	3-0
1999	Arsenal v Manchester U	2-1
2000	Chelsea v Manchester U	2-0
2001	Liverpool v Manchester U	2-1

COMMUNITY SHIELD 2002–21

2002	Arsenal v Liverpool	1-0
2003	Manchester U v Arsenal *Manchester U won 4-3 on penalties.*	1-1
2004	Arsenal v Manchester U	3-1
2005	Chelsea v Arsenal	2-1
2006	Liverpool v Chelsea	2-1
2007	Manchester U v Chelsea *Manchester U won 3-0 on penalties.*	1-1
2008	Manchester U v Portsmouth *Manchester U won 3-1 on penalties.*	0-0
2009	Chelsea v Manchester U *Chelsea won 4-1 on penalties.*	2-2
2010	Manchester U v Chelsea	3-1
2011	Manchester U v Manchester C	3-2
2012	Manchester C v Chelsea	3-2
2013	Manchester U v Wigan Ath	2-0
2014	Arsenal v Manchester C	3-0
2015	Arsenal v Chelsea	1-0
2016	Manchester U v Leicester C	2-1
2017	Arsenal v Chelsea *Arsenal won 4-1 on penalties.*	1-1
2018	Manchester C v Chelsea	2-0
2019	Manchester C v Liverpool *Manchester C won 5-4 on penalties.*	1-1
2020	Arsenal v Liverpool *Arsenal won 5-4 on penalties.*	1-1
2021	Leicester C v Manchester C	1-0

* *Each club retained shield for six months.*

THE FA COMMUNITY SHIELD 2021

Leicester C (0) 1 Manchester C (0) 0

Saturday, 7 August 2021

(at Wembley Stadium, attendance 45,502)

Leicester C: (4-2-3-1) Schmeichel; Pereira, Amartey, Soyuncu, Bertrand (Thomas 78); Ndidi, Tielemans (Soumare 70); Perez (Albrighton 70), Maddison (Dewsbury-Hall 70), Barnes (Iheanacho 78); Vardy (Daka 70).
Scorer: Iheanacho 89 (pen).

Manchester C: (4-3-3) Steffen; Cancelo, Dias, Ake, Mendy; Fernandinho, Gundogan (Rodri 64), Palmer (Bernardo 73); Mahrez, Torres (Knight 73), Edozie (Grealish 64).

Referee: Paul Tierney.

FOOTBALL AWARDS 2021–22

THE FOOTBALL WRITERS' FOOTBALLER OF THE YEAR 2022

The Football Writers' Association Sir Stanley Matthews Trophy for the Footballer of the Year was awarded to Mohamed Salah of Liverpool and Egypt. Kevin De Bruyne (Manchester C and Belgium) was runner-up and Declan Rice (West Ham U and England) came third.

Past Winners

1947–48 Stanley Matthews (Blackpool), 1948–49 Johnny Carey (Manchester U), 1949–50 Joe Mercer (Arsenal), 1950–51 Harry Johnston (Blackpool), 1951–52 Billy Wright (Wolverhampton W), 1952–53 Nat Lofthouse (Bolton W), 1953–54 Tom Finney (Preston NE), 1954–55 Don Revie (Manchester C), 1955–56 Bert Trautmann (Manchester C), 1956–57 Tom Finney (Preston NE), 1957–58 Danny Blanchflower (Tottenham H), 1958–59 Syd Owen (Luton T), 1959–60 Bill Slater (Wolverhampton W), 1960–61 Danny Blanchflower (Tottenham H), 1961–62 Jimmy Adamson (Burnley), 1962–63 Stanley Matthews (Stoke C), 1963–64 Bobby Moore (West Ham U), 1964–65 Bobby Collins (Leeds U), 1965–66 Bobby Charlton (Manchester U), 1966–67 Jackie Charlton (Leeds U), 1967–68 George Best (Manchester U), 1968–69 Dave Mackay (Derby Co) shared with Tony Book (Manchester C), 1969–70 Billy Bremner (Leeds U), 1970–71 Frank McLintock (Arsenal), 1971–72 Gordon Banks (Stoke C), 1972–73 Pat Jennings (Tottenham H), 1973–74 Ian Callaghan (Liverpool), 1974–75 Alan Mullery (Fulham), 1975–76 Kevin Keegan (Liverpool), 1976–77 Emlyn Hughes (Liverpool), 1977–78 Kenny Burns (Nottingham F), 1978–79 Kenny Dalglish (Liverpool), 1979–80 Terry McDermott (Liverpool), 1980–81 Frans Thijssen (Ipswich T), 1981–82 Steve Perryman (Tottenham H), 1982–83 Kenny Dalglish (Liverpool), 1983–84 Ian Rush (Liverpool), 1984–85 Neville Southall (Everton), 1985–86 Gary Lineker (Everton), 1986–87 Clive Allen (Tottenham H), 1987–88 John Barnes (Liverpool), 1988–89 Steve Nicol (Liverpool), 1989–90 John Barnes (Liverpool), 1990–91 Gordon Strachan (Leeds U), 1991–92 Gary Lineker (Tottenham H), 1992–93 Chris Waddle (Sheffield W), 1993–94 Alan Shearer (Blackburn R), 1994–95 Jurgen Klinsmann (Tottenham H), 1995–96 Eric Cantona (Manchester U), 1996–97 Gianfranco Zola (Chelsea), 1997–98 Dennis Bergkamp (Arsenal), 1998–99 David Ginola (Tottenham H), 1999–2000 Roy Keane (Manchester U), 2000–01 Teddy Sheringham (Manchester U), 2001–02 Robert Pires (Arsenal), 2002–03 Thierry Henry (Arsenal), 2003–04 Thierry Henry (Arsenal), 2004–05 Frank Lampard (Chelsea), 2005–06 Thierry Henry (Arsenal), 2006–07 Cristiano Ronaldo (Manchester U), 2007–08 Cristiano Ronaldo (Manchester U), 2008–09 Ryan Giggs (Manchester U), 2009–10 Wayne Rooney (Manchester U), 2010–11 Scott Parker (West Ham U), 2011–12 Robin van Persie (Arsenal), 2012–13 Gareth Bale (Tottenham H), 2013–14 Luis Suárez (Liverpool), 2014–15 Eden Hazard (Chelsea), 2015–16 Jamie Vardy (Leicester C), 2016–17 N'Golo Kanté (Chelsea), 2017–18 Mohamed Salah (Liverpool), 2018–19 Raheem Sterling (Manchester C), 2019–20 Jordan Henderson (Liverpool), 2020–21 Ruben Dias (Manchester C), 2021–22 Mohamed Salah (Liverpool).

THE FOOTBALL WRITERS' WOMEN'S FOOTBALLER OF THE YEAR 2022

Sam Kerr (Chelsea and Australia).

THE PFA AWARDS 2022

Player of the Year: Mohamed Salah (Liverpool and Egypt)
Young Player of the Year: Phil Foden (Manchester C and England)
Women's Player of the Year: Sam Kerr (Chelsea and Australia)
Women's Young Player of the Year: Lauren Hemp (Manchester C and England)
PFA Merit Award: Roy Hodgson.

PFA Premier League Team of the Year 2022
Alisson (Liverpool); Trent Alexander-Arnold (Liverpool),Virgil van Dijk (Liverpool), Antonio Rudiger (Chelsea), Joao Cancelo (Manchester C), Kevin De Bruyne (Manchester C), Thiago Alcantara (Liverpool), Bernardo Silva (Manchester C), Sadio Mane (Liverpool), Cristiano Ronaldo (Manchester U), Mohamed Salah (Liverpool).

PFA Championship Team of the Year 2022
Lee Nicholls (Huddersfield T); Djed Spence (Nottingham F), Tosin Adarabioyo (Fulham), Lloyd Kelly (Bournemouth), Tim Ream (Fulham), Philip Billing (Bournemouth), Fabio Carvalho (Fulham), Harry Wilson (Fulham), Ben Brereton Diaz (Blackburn R), Dominic Solanke (Bournemouth), Aleksandar Mitrovic (Fulham).

PFA League One Team of the Year 2022
Gavin Bazunu (Portsmouth); Ricardo Santos (Bolton W), Michael Ihiekwe (Rotherham U), Jack Whatmough (Wigan Ath), Harry Darling (Milton Keynes D), Cameron Brannagan (Oxford U), Scott Twine (Milton Keynes D), Barry Bannan (Sheffield W), Will Keane (Wigan Ath), Ross Stewart (Sunderland), Cole Stockton (Morecambe).

PFA League Two Team of the Year 2022
Liam Roberts (Northampton T); Kane Wilson (Forest Green R), Fraser Horsfall (Northampton T), Peter Clarke (Tranmere R), Jon Guthrie (Northampton T), Nicky Cadden (Forest Green R), Matt Jay (Exeter C), Ebrima Adams (Forest Green R), Jamille Matt (Forest Green R), Matt Stevens (Forest Green R), Dominic Telford (Newport Co).

PFA Women's Super League Team of the Year 2022
Ann-Katrin Berger (Chelsea); Ona Batlle (Manchester U), Leah Williamson (Arsenal), Millie Bright (Chelsea), Alex Greenwood (Manchester C), Kim Little (Arsenal), Caroline Weir (Manchester C), Guro Reiten (Chelsea), Lauren Hemp (Manchester C), Sam Kerr (Chelsea), Vivianne Miedema (Arsenal).

SCOTTISH AWARDS 2021–22

SCOTTISH PFA PLAYER OF THE YEAR AWARDS 2022

Player of the Year: Callum McGregor (Celtic and Scotland)
Young Player of the Year: Liel Abada (Celtic and Israel)
Manager of the Year: Ange Postecoglou (Celtic)
Championship Player of the Year: Michael McKenna (Arbroath)
League 1 Player of the Year: Dylan Easton (Airdrieonians)
League 2 Player of the Year: Joe Cardle (Kelty Hearts)
Women's Player of the Year: Priscilla Chincilla (Glasgow C and Costa Rica)
Women's Young Player of the Year: Jacynta Galabadaarachchi (Celtic and Australia)
Special Merit Award: Frank Reilly (Scotland administrator)

Scottish PFA Premiership Team of the Year 2022
Craig Gordon (Hearts); James Tavernier (Rangers), Cameron Carter-Vickers (Celtic), John Souttar (Hearts), Josip Juranovic (Celtic), Tom Rogic (Celtic), Callum McGregor (Celtic), Regan Charles-Cook (Ross Co), Jota (Celtic), Alfredo Morelos (Rangers), Kyogo Furuhashi (Celtic).

SCOTTISH FOOTBALL WRITERS' ASSOCIATION AWARDS 2022

Manager of the Year: Ange Postecoglou (Celtic)
Player of the Year: Craig Gordon (Hearts and Scotland)
Young Player of the Year: Calvin Ramsay (Aberdeen and Scotland)
International Player of the Year: John McGinn (Aston Villa and Scotland)
Women's International Player of the Year: Caroline Weir (Manchester C and Scotland)

PREMIER LEAGUE AWARDS 2021–22

	PLAYER OF THE MONTH AWARDS 2021–22	MANAGER OF THE MONTH AWARDS 2021–22
August	Michail Antonio (West Ham U)	Nuno Espirito Santo (Tottenham H)
September	Cristiano Ronaldo (Manchester U)	Mikel Arteta (Arsenal)
October	Mohamed Sala (Liverpool)	Thomas Tuchel (Chelsea)
November	Trent Alexander-Arnold (Liverpool)	Pep Guardiola (Manchester C)
December	Raheem Sterling (Manchester C)	Pep Guardiola (Manchester C)
January	David de Gea (Manchester U)	Bruno Lage (Wolverhampton W)
February	Joel Matip (Liverpool)	Eddie Howe (Newcastle U)
March	Harry Kane (Tottenham H)	Mikel Arteta (Arsenal)
April	Cristiano Ronaldo (Manchester U)	Mike Jackson (Burnley)

SKY BET LEAGUE AWARDS 2021–22

SKY BET FOOTBALL LEAGUE PLAYER OF THE MONTH AWARDS 2021–22

	Championship	*League One*	*League Two*
August	Sorba Thomas (Huddersfield T)	Cole Stockton (Morecambe)	Matt Stevens (Forest Green R)
September	Ben Brereton (Blackburn R)	Cole Stockton (Morecambe)	Nicky Cadden (Forest Green R)
October	Aleksandar Mitrovic (Fulham)	Michael Smith (Rotherham U)	Dom Telford (Newport Co)
November	Chris Willock (QPR)	Scott Twine (Milton Keynes D)	Dom Telford (Newport Co)
December	Isaiah Jones (Middlesbrough)	Dan Barlaser (Rotherham U)	Jake Beesley (Rochdale)
January	Antoine Semenyo (Bristol C)	Michael Smith (Rotherham U)	Luke McGee (Forest Green R)
February	Lucas João (Reading)	Alfie May (Cheltenham T)	Davis Keillor-Dunne (Oldham Ath)
March	Djed Spence (Nottingham F)	Barry Bannan (Sheffield W)	Ruel Sotiriou (Leyton Orient)
Season	Aleksandar Mitrovic (Fulham)	Scott Twine (Milton Keynes D)	Finn Azaz (Newport Co)

SKY BET FOOTBALL LEAGUE MANAGER OF THE MONTH AWARDS 2021–22

	Championship	*League One*	*League Two*
August	Marco Silva (Fulham)	Lee Johnson (Sunderland)	Rob Edwards (Forest Green R)
September	Scott Parker (Bournemouth)	Liam Manning (Milton Keynes D)	Darrell Clarke (Port Vale)
October	Scott Parker (Bournemouth)	Ryan Lowe (Plymouth Arg)	Darrell Clarke (Port Vale)
November	Mark Warburton (QPR)	Danny Cowley (Portsmouth)	Rob Edwards (Forest Green R)
December	Chris Wilder (Middlesbrough)	Lee Johnson (Sunderland)	Micky Mellon (Tranmere R)
January	Marco Silva (Fulham)	Liam Manning (Milton Keynes D)	Rob Edwards (Forest Green R)
February	Carlos Corberán (Huddersfield T)	Paul Warne (Rotherham U)	Matt Taylor (Exeter C)
March	Steve Morison (Cardiff C)	Steven Schumacher (Plymouth Arg)	Joey Barton (Bristol R)
April	Steve Cooper (Nottingham F)	Gareth Ainsworth (Wycombe W)	Matt Taylor (Exeter C)
Season	Nathan Jones (Luton T)	Leam Richardson (Wigan Ath)	Rob Edwards (Forest Green)

LEAGUE MANAGERS ASSOCIATION AWARDS 2021–22

SIR ALEX FERGUSON TROPHY FOR LMA MANAGER OF THE YEAR
Jurgen Klopp (Liverpool)

SKY BET CHAMPIONSHIP MANAGER OF THE YEAR
Marco Silva (Fulham)

SKY BET LEAGUE ONE MANAGER OF THE YEAR
Leam Richardson (Wigan Ath)

SKY BET LEAGUE TWO MANAGER OF THE YEAR
Matt Taylor (Exeter C)

FA WSL MANAGER OF THE YEAR
Emma Hayes (Chelsea)

FA WOMEN'S CHAMPIONSHIP MANAGER OF THE YEAR
Matt Beard (Liverpool)

LMA SPECIAL ACHIEVEMENT AWARD
Sally Harris (HCA Healthcare UK)

LMA SERVICE TO FOOTBALL AWARD
Kath Phipps (Manchester U)

KICK IT OUT AND SKY INCLUSION CHAMPION AWARD
Chris Ramsey MBE and Manisha Tailor MBE (QPR)

OTHER AWARDS

EUROPEAN FOOTBALLER OF THE YEAR 2021
Jorginho (Chelsea and Italy)

EUROPEAN WOMEN PLAYER OF THE YEAR 2021
Alexia Putellas (Barcelona and Spain)

FIFA BALLON D'OR PLAYER OF THE YEAR 2021
Lionel Messi (Paris Saint-Germain and Argentina)

FIFA BALLON D'OR WOMEN'S PLAYER OF THE YEAR 2021
Alexia Putellas (Barcelona and Spain)

FIFA BEST MEN'S PLAYER OF THE YEAR 2021
Robert Lewandowski (Bayern Munich and Poland)

FIFA BEST WOMEN'S PLAYER OF THE YEAR 2021
Alexia Putellas (Barcelona and Spain)

FIFA BEST MEN'S GOALKEEPER OF THE YEAR 2021
Edouard Mendy (Chelsea and Senegal)

FIFA BEST WOMEN'S GOALKEEPER OF THE YEAR 2021
Christiane Endler (Lyon and Chile)

FIFA BEST MEN'S COACH OF THE YEAR 2021
Thomas Tuchel (Chelsea)

FIFA BEST WOMEN'S COACH OF THE YEAR 2021
Emma Hayes (Chelsea)

FIFA PUSKAS AWARD GOAL OF THE YEAR 2021
Erik Lamela, Arsenal v Tottenham H, Premier League, 4 March 2021

FIFA FAIR PLAY AWARD 2021
Denmark

FIFPRO MEN'S WORLD XI 2021
(334) Gianluigi Donnarumma; David Alaba, Ruben Dias, Leonardo Bonucci; Jorginho, N'Golo Kante, Kevin De Bruyne; Cristiano Ronaldo, Erling Haaland, Robert Lewandowski, Lionel Messi.

PREMIER LEAGUE 2021–22

(P) *Promoted into division at end of 2020–21 season.*

			Home					Away					Total						
		P	*W*	*D*	*L*	*F*	*A*	*W*	*D*	*L*	*F*	*A*	*W*	*D*	*L*	*F*	*A*	*GD*	*Pts*
1	Manchester C	38	15	2	2	58	15	14	4	1	41	11	29	6	3	99	26	73	93
2	Liverpool	38	15	4	0	49	9	13	4	2	45	17	28	8	2	94	26	68	92
3	Chelsea	38	9	7	3	37	22	12	4	3	39	11	21	11	6	76	33	43	74
4	Tottenham H	38	13	1	5	38	19	9	4	6	31	21	22	5	11	69	40	29	71
5	Arsenal	38	13	2	4	35	17	9	1	9	26	31	22	3	13	61	48	13	69
6	Manchester U	38	10	5	4	32	22	6	5	8	25	35	16	10	12	57	57	0	58
7	West Ham U	38	9	5	5	33	26	7	3	9	27	25	16	8	14	60	51	9	56
8	Leicester C	38	10	4	5	34	23	4	6	9	28	36	14	10	14	62	59	3	52
9	Brighton & HA	38	5	7	7	19	23	7	8	4	23	21	12	15	11	42	44	–2	51
10	Wolverhampton W	38	7	3	9	20	25	8	3	8	18	18	15	6	17	38	43	–5	51
11	Newcastle U	38	8	6	5	26	27	5	4	10	18	35	13	10	15	44	62	–18	49
12	Crystal Palace	38	7	8	4	27	17	4	7	8	23	29	11	15	12	50	46	4	48
13	Brentford (P)	38	7	3	9	22	21	6	4	9	26	35	13	7	18	48	56	–8	46
14	Aston Villa	38	6	5	8	29	29	7	1	11	23	25	13	6	19	52	54	–2	45
15	Southampton	38	6	7	6	23	24	3	6	10	20	43	9	13	16	43	67	–24	40
16	Everton	38	9	2	8	27	25	2	4	13	16	41	11	6	21	43	66	–23	39
17	Leeds U	38	4	6	9	19	38	5	5	9	23	41	9	11	18	42	79	–37	38
18	Burnley	38	5	6	8	18	25	2	8	9	16	28	7	14	17	34	53	–19	35
19	Watford (P)	38	2	2	15	17	46	4	3	12	17	31	6	5	27	34	77	–43	23
20	Norwich C (P)	38	3	3	13	12	43	2	4	13	11	41	5	7	26	23	84	–61	22

PREMIER LEAGUE LEADING GOALSCORERS 2021–22

Qualification 7 league goals	*League*	*FA Cup*	*EFL Cup*	*Other*	*Total*
Mohamed Salah (Liverpool)	23	0	0	8	31
Harry Kane (Tottenham H)	17	3	1	6	27
Son Heung-Min (Tottenham H)	23	0	0	1	24
Cristiano Ronaldo (Manchester U)	18	0	0	6	24
Riyad Mahrez (Manchester C)	11	4	2	7	24
Sadio Mane (Liverpool)	16	2	0	5	23
Diogo Jota (Liverpool)	15	2	3	1	21
Kevin De Bruyne (Manchester C)	15	1	1	2	19
Jarrod Bowen (West Ham U)	12	2	1	3	18
James Maddison (Leicester C)	12	1	1	4	18
Jamie Vardy (Leicester C)	15	0	2	0	17
Raheem Sterling (Manchester C)	13	1	0	3	17
Wilfried Zaha (Crystal Palace)	14	1	0	0	15
Romelu Lukaku (Chelsea)	8	3	0	4	15
Ivan Toney (Brentford)	12	1	1	0	14
Phil Foden (Manchester C)	9	1	1	3	14
Kai Havertz (Chelsea)	8	0	2	4	14
Mason Mount (Chelsea)	11	1	0	1	13
Michail Antonio (West Ham U)	10	1	0	2	13
Bernardo Silva (Manchester C)	8	2	0	3	13
Gabriel Jesus (Manchester C)	8	1	0	4	13
Bukayo Saka (Arsenal)	11	0	1	0	12
Teemu Pukki (Norwich C)	11	0	0	0	11
Raphinha (Leeds U)	11	0	0	0	11
Ollie Watkins (Aston Villa)	11	0	0	0	11
Richarlison (Everton)	10	1	0	0	11
Emile Smith Rowe (Arsenal)	10	0	1	0	11
James Ward-Prowse (Southampton)	10	1	0	0	11
Said Benrahma (West Ham U)	8	0	0	3	11
Emmanuel Dennis (Watford)	10	0	0	0	10
Bruno Fernandes (Manchester U)	10	0	0	0	10
Ilkay Gundogan (Manchester C)	8	2	0	0	10
Jack Harrison (Leeds U)	8	0	2	0	10
Yoane Wissa (Brentford)	7	0	3	0	10
Maxwel Cornet (Burnley)	9	0	0	0	9
Neal Maupay (Brighton & HA)	8	1	0	0	9
Conor Gallagher (Crystal Palace)	8	0	0	0	8
Leandro Trossard (Brighton & HA)	8	0	0	0	8
Callum Wilson (Newcastle U)	8	0	0	0	8
Che Adams (Southampton)	7	0	1	0	8
Danny Ings (Aston Villa)	7	0	0	0	7
Martin Odegaard (Arsenal)	7	0	0	0	7
Rodri (Manchester C)	7	0	0	0	7

Other matches consist of UEFA Champions League, UEFA Europa League, UEFA Europa Conference League, FIFA Club World Cup, European Super Cup, FA Community Shield, EFL Cup.

SKY BET CHAMPIONSHIP 2021–22

(P) Promoted into division at end of 2020–21 season. (R) Relegated into division at end of 2020–21 season.

			Home					Away					Total						
		P	*W*	*D*	*L*	*F*	*A*	*W*	*D*	*L*	*F*	*A*	*W*	*D*	*L*	*F*	*A*	*GD*	*Pts*
1	Fulham (R)	46	14	4	5	56	20	13	5	5	50	23	27	9	10	106	43	63	90
2	Bournemouth	46	13	7	3	41	21	12	6	5	33	18	25	13	8	74	39	35	88
3	Huddersfield T	46	13	6	4	35	23	10	7	6	29	24	23	13	10	64	47	17	82
4	Nottingham F¶	46	13	4	6	43	22	10	7	6	30	18	23	11	12	73	40	33	80
5	Sheffield U (R)	46	13	5	5	38	15	8	7	8	25	30	21	12	13	63	45	18	75
6	Luton T	46	12	7	4	37	22	9	5	9	26	33	21	12	13	63	55	8	75
7	Middlesbrough	46	14	2	7	34	21	6	8	9	25	29	20	10	16	59	50	9	70
8	Blackburn R	46	12	5	6	36	26	7	7	9	23	24	19	12	15	59	50	9	69
9	Millwall	46	13	6	4	32	16	5	9	9	21	29	18	15	13	53	45	8	69
10	WBA (R)	46	12	8	3	33	16	6	5	12	19	29	18	13	15	52	45	7	67
11	QPR	46	10	6	7	30	25	9	3	11	30	34	19	9	18	60	59	1	66
12	Coventry C	46	10	5	8	32	26	7	8	8	28	33	17	13	16	60	59	1	64
13	Preston NE	46	9	10	4	33	28	7	6	10	19	28	16	16	14	52	56	–4	64
14	Stoke C	46	10	5	8	30	23	7	6	10	27	29	17	11	18	57	52	5	62
15	Swansea C	46	9	8	6	30	27	7	5	11	28	41	16	13	17	58	68	–10	61
16	Blackpool (P)	46	11	3	9	29	26	5	9	9	25	32	16	12	18	54	58	–4	60
17	Bristol C	46	8	8	7	33	29	7	2	14	29	48	15	10	21	62	77	–15	55
18	Cardiff C	46	7	4	12	22	29	8	4	11	28	39	15	8	23	50	68	–18	53
19	Hull C (P)	46	7	4	12	22	28	7	5	11	19	26	14	9	23	41	54	–13	51
20	Birmingham C	46	7	6	10	27	33	4	8	11	23	42	11	14	21	50	75	–25	47
21	Reading*	46	7	5	11	33	44	6	3	14	21	43	13	8	25	54	87	–33	41
22	Peterborough U (P)	46	6	7	10	27	33	3	3	17	16	54	9	10	27	43	87	–44	37
23	Derby Co*	46	11	7	5	30	22	3	6	14	15	31	14	13	19	45	53	–8	34
24	Barnsley	46	5	7	11	18	29	1	5	17	15	44	6	12	28	33	73	–40	30

**Derby Co deducted 21pts. *Reading deducted 6pts. ¶Nottingham F promoted via play-offs.*

SKY BET CHAMPIONSHIP LEADING GOALSCORERS 2021–22

Qualification 9 League Goals	*League*	*FA Cup*	*EFL Cup*	*Play-Offs*	*Total*
Aleksandar Mitrovic (Fulham)	43	0	0	0	43
Dominic Solanke (Bournemouth)	29	0	1	0	29
Joel Piroe (Swansea C)	22	1	1	0	24
Ben Brereton Diaz (Blackburn R)	22	0	0	0	22
Andreas Weimann (Bristol C)	22	0	0	0	22
Emil Riis Jakobsen (Preston NE)	16	0	4	0	20
Brennan Johnson (Nottingham F)	16	1	0	2	19
Karlan Ahearne-Grant (WBA)	18	0	0	0	18
Viktor Gyokeres (Coventry C)	17	1	0	0	18
Elijah Adebayo (Luton T)	16	1	0		16
Billy Sharp (Sheffield U)	14	0	1		15
Danny Ward (Huddersfield T)	14	0	0	0	14
Jacob Brown (Stoke C)	13	1	0	0	14
Benik Afobe (Millwall)	12	1	0	0	13
On loan from Stoke C.					
Harry Cornick (Luton T)	12	1	0		13
Lewis Grabban (Nottingham F)	12	1	0	0	13
Keane Lewis-Potter (Hull C)	12	0	1	0	13
Jonson Clarke-Harris (Peterborough U)	12	0	0	0	12
Matt Godden (Coventry C)	12	0	0	0	12
Chris Martin (Bristol C)	12	0	0	0	12
Michael Obafemi (Swansea C)	12	0	0	0	12
Morgan Gibbs-White (Sheffield U)	11	0	0	1	12
On loan from Wolverhampton W.					
Sam Surridge (Nottingham F)	9	1	2	0	12
(Includes 2 League goals and 2 EFL League Cup goals for Stoke C)					
Tom Lawrence (Derby Co)	11	0	0	0	11
John Swift (Reading)	11	0	0	0	11
Philip Billing (Bournemouth)	10	0	1	0	11
Fabio Carvalho (Fulham)	10	1	0	0	11
Matt Crooks (Middlesbrough)	10	1	0	0	11
Harry Wilson (Fulham)	10	1	0	0	11
Andre Gray (QPR)	10	0	0	0	10
On loan from Watford.					
Scott Hogan (Birmingham C)	10	0	0	0	10
Lucas Joao (Reading)	10	0	0	0	10
Tom Bradshaw (Millwall)	9	0	0	0	9
Ilias Chair (QPR)	9	0	0	0	9
Sam Gallagher (Blackburn R)	9	0	0	0	9
Neeskens Kebano (Fulham)	9	0	0	0	9
Gary Madine (Blackpool)	9	0	0	0	9
Jack Marriott (Peterborough U)	9	0	0	0	9
Kieffer Moore (Bournemouth)	9	0	0	0	9
(Includes 5 League goals for Cardiff C)					
Jamie Paterson (Swansea C)	9	0	0	0	9

SKY BET LEAGUE ONE 2021–22

(P) *Promoted into division at end of 2020–21 season.* (R) *Relegated into division at end of 2020–21 season.*

			Home					*Away*					*Total*						
		P	*W*	*D*	*L*	*F*	*A*	*W*	*D*	*L*	*F*	*A*	*W*	*D*	*L*	*F*	*A*	*GD*	*Pts*
1	Wigan Ath	46	13	5	5	36	22	14	6	3	46	22	27	11	8	82	44	38	92
2	Rotherham U (R)	46	15	3	5	43	22	12	6	5	27	11	27	9	10	70	33	37	90
3	Milton Keynes D	46	13	5	5	34	21	13	6	4	44	23	26	11	9	78	44	34	89
4	Sheffield W (R)	46	16	5	2	48	18	8	8	7	30	32	24	13	9	78	50	28	85
5	Sunderland¶	46	16	3	4	49	19	8	9	6	30	34	24	12	10	79	53	26	84
6	Wycombe W (R)	46	14	5	4	39	26	9	9	5	36	25	23	14	9	75	51	24	83
7	Plymouth Arg	46	14	4	5	32	19	9	7	7	36	29	23	11	12	68	48	20	80
8	Oxford U	46	13	6	4	47	27	9	4	10	35	32	22	10	14	82	59	23	76
9	Bolton W (P)	46	12	7	4	45	26	9	3	11	29	31	21	10	15	74	57	17	73
10	Portsmouth	46	14	5	4	46	25	6	8	9	22	26	20	13	13	68	51	17	73
11	Ipswich T	46	11	9	3	38	22	7	7	9	29	24	18	16	12	67	46	21	70
12	Accrington S	46	12	6	5	41	33	5	4	14	20	47	17	10	19	61	80	−19	61
13	Charlton Ath	46	10	4	9	32	28	7	4	12	23	31	17	8	21	55	59	−4	59
14	Cambridge U (P)	46	8	8	7	28	29	7	5	11	28	45	15	13	18	56	74	−18	58
15	Cheltenham T (P)	46	10	7	6	33	30	3	10	10	33	50	13	17	16	66	80	−14	56
16	Burton Alb	46	10	6	7	34	26	4	5	14	17	41	14	11	21	51	67	−16	53
17	Lincoln C	46	7	5	11	25	29	7	5	11	30	34	14	10	22	55	63	−8	52
18	Shrewsbury T	46	9	7	7	30	25	3	7	13	17	26	12	14	20	47	51	−4	50
19	Morecambe (P)	46	7	8	8	33	35	3	4	16	24	53	10	12	24	57	88	−31	42
20	Fleetwood T	46	5	8	10	33	37	3	8	12	29	45	8	16	22	62	82	−20	40
21	Gillingham	46	4	8	11	13	36	4	8	11	22	33	8	16	22	35	69	−34	40
22	Doncaster R	46	7	3	13	20	32	3	5	15	17	50	10	8	28	37	82	−45	38
23	AFC Wimbledon	46	2	14	7	27	34	4	5	14	22	41	6	19	21	49	75	−26	37
24	Crewe Alex	46	5	5	13	22	40	2	3	18	15	43	7	8	31	37	83	−4	29

¶*Sunderland promoted via play-offs.*

SKY BET LEAGUE ONE LEADING GOALSCORERS 2021–22

Qualification 9 League Goals	*League*	*FA Cup*	*EFL Cup*	*EFL Trophy*	*Play-Offs*	*Total*
Will Keane (Wigan Ath)	26	0	0	1	0	27
Ross Stewart (Sunderland)	24	0	0	0	2	26
Alfie May (Cheltenham T)	23	1	2	0	0	26
Cole Stockton (Morecambe)	23	1	2	0	0	26
Michael Smith (Rotherham U)	19	1	0	5	0	25
Matty Taylor (Oxford U)	20	2	0	0	0	22
Sam Smith (Cambridge U)	15	2	0	4	0	21
Scott Twine (Milton Keynes D)	20	0	0	0	0	20
Jayden Stockley (Charlton Ath)	13	4	0	3	0	20
Ryan Hardie (Plymouth Arg)	16	1	2	0	0	19
Callum Lang (Wigan Ath)	15	3	0	0	0	18
Lee Gregory (Sheffield W)	16	0	0	0	1	17
Sam Vokes (Wycombe W)	16	0	0	0	1	17
Daniel Udoh (Shrewsbury T)	13	1	2	0	0	16
Joe Ironside (Cambridge U)	14	1	0	0	0	15
George Hirst (Portsmouth)	13	0	0	2	0	15
On loan from Leicester C.						
Colby Bishop (Accrington S)	12	0	1	2	0	15
Freddie Ladapo (Rotherham U)	11	1	0	3	0	15
Anthony Scully (Lincoln C)	11	0	0	4	0	15
Cameron Brannagan (Oxford U)	14	0	0	0	0	14
Oladapo Afolayan (Bolton W)	12	0	0	2	0	14
Wes Burns (Ipswich T)	12	1	0	0	0	13
Amadou Bakayoko (Bolton W)	10	1	0	2	0	13
Ryan Bowman (Shrewsbury T)	10	3	0	0	0	13
Nathan Broadhead (Sunderland)	10	0	2	1	0	13
On loan from Everton.						
Macauley Bonne (Ipswich T)	12	0	0	0	0	12
On loan from QPR.						
Mohamed Eisa (Milton Keynes D)	12	0	0	0	0	12
Jack Rudoni (AFC Wimbledon)	12	0	0	0	0	12
Marcus Harness (Portsmouth)	11	1	0	0	0	12
Luke Jephcott (Plymouth Arg)	10	1	1	0	0	12
Garath McCleary (Wycombe W)	11	0	0	0	0	11
Conor Washington (Charlton Ath)	11	0	0	0	0	11
Vadaine Oliver (Gillingham)	10	0	1	0	0	11
Conor Chaplin (Ipswich T)	9	1	0	1	0	11
Christopher Long (Crewe Alex)	10	0	0	0	0	10
James McClean (Wigan Ath)	9	0	0	1	0	10
Barry Bannan (Sheffield W)	9	0	0	0	0	9
Daniel Barlaser (Rotherham U)	9	0	0	0	0	9
John Marquis (Lincoln C)	9	0	0	0	0	9
(Includes 4 League goals for Portsmouth).						
Callum Wright (Cheltenham T)	9	0	0	0	0	9
On loan from Leicester C.						

SKY BET LEAGUE TWO 2021–22

(P) *Promoted into division at end of 2020–21 season.* (R) *Relegated into division at end of 2020–21 season.*

			Home					*Away*					*Total*						
		P	*W*	*D*	*L*	*F*	*A*	*W*	*D*	*L*	*F*	*A*	*W*	*D*	*L*	*F*	*A*	*GD*	*Pts*
1	Forest Green R	46	14	4	5	34	18	9	11	3	41	26	23	15	8	75	44	31	84
2	Exeter C	46	14	6	3	37	19	9	9	5	28	22	23	15	8	65	41	24	84
3	Bristol R (R)	46	14	4	5	38	20	9	7	7	33	29	23	11	12	71	49	22	80
4	Northampton T (R)	46	13	5	5	32	15	10	6	7	28	23	23	11	12	60	38	22	80
5	Port Vale¶	46	11	6	6	35	22	11	6	6	32	24	22	12	12	67	46	21	78
6	Swindon T (R)	46	9	7	7	35	25	13	4	6	42	29	22	11	13	77	54	23	77
7	Mansfield T	46	15	4	4	40	24	7	7	9	27	28	22	11	13	67	52	15	77
8	Sutton U (P)	46	14	5	4	38	20	8	5	10	31	33	22	10	14	69	53	16	76
9	Tranmere R	46	16	3	4	36	16	5	9	9	17	24	21	12	13	53	40	13	75
10	Salford C	46	10	9	4	33	21	9	4	10	27	25	19	13	14	60	46	14	70
11	Newport Co	46	9	6	8	40	31	10	6	7	27	27	19	12	15	67	58	9	69
12	Crawley T	46	9	6	8	28	29	8	4	11	28	37	17	10	19	56	66	–10	61
13	Leyton Orient	46	9	5	9	36	22	5	11	7	26	25	14	16	16	62	47	15	58
14	Bradford C	46	6	10	7	29	29	8	6	9	24	26	14	16	16	53	55	–2	58
15	Colchester U	46	6	9	8	25	28	8	4	11	23	32	14	13	19	48	60	–12	55
16	Walsall	46	10	5	8	30	29	4	7	12	17	31	14	12	20	47	60	–13	54
17	Hartlepool U (P)	46	9	7	7	24	26	5	5	13	20	38	14	12	20	44	64	–20	54
18	Rochdale (R)	46	7	11	5	28	23	5	6	12	23	36	12	17	17	51	59	–8	53
19	Harrogate T	46	6	7	10	32	36	8	4	11	32	39	14	11	21	64	75	–11	53
20	Carlisle U	46	8	7	8	19	23	6	4	13	20	39	14	11	21	39	62	–23	53
21	Stevenage	46	9	6	8	29	30	2	8	13	16	38	11	14	21	45	68	–23	47
22	Barrow	46	5	9	9	25	28	5	5	13	19	29	10	14	22	44	57	–13	44
23	Oldham Ath	46	5	4	14	29	42	4	7	12	17	33	9	11	26	46	75	–29	38
24	Scunthorpe U	46	3	7	13	15	36	1	7	15	14	54	4	14	28	29	90	–61	26

¶*Port Vale promoted via play-offs.*

SKY BET LEAGUE TWO LEADING GOALSCORERS 2021–22

Qualification 9 League Goals	*League*	*FA Cup*	*EFL Cup*	*EFL Trophy*	*Play-Offs*	*Total*
Matt Stevens (Forest Green R)	23	1	0	3	0	27
Dominic Telford (Newport Co)	25	0	0	1	0	26
Harry McKirdy (Swindon T)	20	1	0	1	2	24
Jamille Matt (Forest Green R)	19	0	1	0	0	20
Aaron Collins (Bristol R)	16	2	0	0	0	18
Davis Keillor-Dunn (Oldham Ath)	15	1	0	1	0	17
Freddie Sears (Colchester U)	14	2	0	1	0	17
Matt Jay (Exeter C)	14	0	0	2	0	16
Aaron Drinan (Leyton Orient)	13	2	1	0	0	16
Luke Norris (Stevenage)	14	1	0	1	0	16
Harry Smith (Leyton Orient)	13	2	0	0	0	15
James Wilson (Port Vale)	9	3	0	0	3	15
Jack Diamond (Harrogate T)	13	1	0	0	0	14
On loan from Sunderland.						
Jack Payne (Swindon T)	13	1	0	0	0	14
Luke Armstrong (Harrogate T)	12	1	0	1	0	14
Timothee Dieng (Exeter C)	12	1	0	1	0	14
Jake Beesley (Rochdale)	11	1	2	0	0	14
(Includes 2 League goals for Blackpool).						
Josh Davison (Swindon T)	11	1	0	2	0	14
(Includes 2 League goals, 1 FA Cup goal and 1 EFL Trophy goal for Charlton Ath).						
On loan at from Charlton Ath.						
Sam Hoskins (Northampton T)	13	0	0	0	0	13
Kane Hemmings (Tranmere R)	12	0	0	1	0	13
(Includes 4 League goals and 1 EFL Trophy goal for Burton Alb).						
Jack Muldoon (Harrogate T)	12	0	0	1	0	13
Jamie Proctor (Port Vale)	12	0	1	0	0	13
Brandon Thomas-Asante (Salford C)	11	0	0	2	0	13
Elliott List (Stevenage)	9	1	2	1	0	13
Andy Cook (Bradford C)	12	0	0	0	0	12
Ben Garrity (Port Vale)	12	0	0	0	0	12
George Miller (Walsall)	12	0	0	0	0	12
On loan from Barnsley.						
Kwesi Appiah (Crawley T)	11	0	0	1	0	12
Ollie Banks (Barrow)	9	2	0	1	0	12
Rhys Oates (Mansfield T)	9	2	0	0	1	12
Anthony Evans (Bristol R)	10	1	0	0	0	11
Tyreece Simpson (Swindon T)	9	2	0	0	0	11
On loan from Ipswich T.						
Ruel Sotiriou (Leyton Orient)	9	0	0	2	0	11
Conor Wilkinson (Walsall)	10	0	0	0	0	10
Tom Nichols (Crawley T)	10	0	0	0	0	10
Alexander Pattison (Harrogate T)	9	0	0	1	0	10
Fraser Horsfall (Northampton T)	9	0	0	0	0	9
Ashley Nadesan (Crawley T)	9	0	0	0	0	9
Omari Patrick (Carlisle U)	9	0	0	0	0	9
Mitchell Pinnock (Northampton T)	9	0	0	0	0	9

FOOTBALL LEAGUE PLAY-OFFS 2021–22

▪ *Denotes player sent off.*

SKY BET CHAMPIONSHIP SEMI-FINALS FIRST LEG

Friday, 13 May 2022

Luton T (1) 1 *(Bradley 30)*

Huddersfield T (1) 1 *(Sinani 12)* 10,005

Luton T: (3142) Ingram; Burke (Hylton 80), Bradley, Naismith; Lansbury (Lockyer 67); Bree, Campbell, Clark, Bell; Jerome (Snodgrass 89), Cornick.
Huddersfield T: (343) Nicholls; Lees, Hogg, Sarr; Turton (Pipa 46), Russell, O'Brien, Toffolo; Sinani (Thomas 85), Ward (Rhodes 71), Holmes.
Referee: Robert Jones.

Saturday, 14 May 2022

Sheffield U (0) 1 *(Berge 90)*

Nottingham F (1) 2 *(Colback 10, Johnson 71)* 30,225

Sheffield U: (3412) Foderingham; Basham, Egan, Robinson; Osborn (Jebbison 82), Norwood (Baldock 69), Fleck, Stevens (Norrington-Davies 89); Berge; Gibbs-White, Ndiaye.
Nottingham F: (3412) Samba; Worrall, Cook, McKenna; Spence, Yates, Garner, Colback; Zinckernagel (Lolley 69); Johnson (Mighten 90), Surridge (Davis 77).
Referee: Andre Marriner.

SKY BET CHAMPIONSHIP SEMI-FINALS SECOND LEG

Monday, 16 May 2022

Huddersfield T (0) 1 *(Rhodes 82)*

Luton T (0) 0 23,407

Huddersfield T: (352) Nicholls; Lees, Hogg, Colwill; Pipa, Holmes (Sarr 86), Russell, O'Brien, Toffolo; Sinani (Thomas 61), Ward (Rhodes 41).
Luton T: (352) Ingram; Burke (Mendes Gomes 86), Bradley, Naismith; Bree, Campbell, Snodgrass, Clark, Bell; Cornick (Adebayo 90), Hylton (Jerome 65).
Huddersfield T won 2-1 on aggregate. Referee: Peter Bankes.

Tuesday, 17 May 2022

Nottingham F (1) 1 *(Johnson 19)*

Sheffield U (0) 2 *(Gibbs-White 47, Fleck 75)* 29,015

Nottingham F: (3412) Samba; Worrall, Cook, McKenna; Spence, Yates, Garner (Cafu 119), Colback; Zinckernagel (Lolley 71); Johnson, Surridge (Davis 75).
Sheffield U: (3412) Foderingham; Basham, Egan, Robinson; Baldock (Osborn 108), Norwood, Fleck (Hourihane 109), Norrington-Davies; Berge; Gibbs-White, Ndiaye.
aet; Nottingham F won 3-2 on penalties.
Referee: Michael Oliver.

SKY BET CHAMPIONSHIP FINAL

Wembley, Sunday, 29 May 2022

Huddersfield T (0) 0

Nottingham F (1) 1 *(Colwill 43 (og))* 80,019

Huddersfield T: (343) Nicholls; Lees, Sarr (Russell 57), Colwill; Pipa, Hogg, O'Brien, Toffolo; Sinani (Holmes 66), Ward (Rhodes 67), Thomas.
Nottingham F: (3412) Samba (Horvath 90); Worrall, Cook, McKenna; Spence, Yates, Garner, Colback; Zinckernagel (Lowe 74); Johnson, Davis (Surridge 66).
Referee: Jonathan Moss.

SKY BET LEAGUE ONE SEMI-FINALS FIRST LEG

Thursday, 5 May 2022

Wycombe W (1) 2 *(Tafazolli 38, Vokes 82)*

Milton Keynes D (0) 0 8987

Wycombe W: (4231) Stockdale; McCarthy, Stewart, Tafazolli, Jacobson; Gape (Wheeler 80), Scowen; McCleary, Horgan (Wing 77), Obita; Vokes (Akinfenwa 83).
Milton Keynes D: (352) Cumming; O'Hora, Darling, Lewington; Kesler, Coventry, Kasumu, McEachran▪, Harvie; Parrott (Wickham 90), Twine (Boateng 83).
Referee: Darren Bond.

Friday, 6 May 2022

Sunderland (1) 1 *(Stewart 45)*

Sheffield W (0) 0 44,742

Sunderland: (3412) Patterson; Wright, Batth, Cirkin; Gooch, Evans, O'Nien, Clarke (Doyle 90); Roberts (Embleton 81); Pritchard (Matete 80), Stewart.
Sheffield W: (3412) Peacock-Farrell; Storey, Dean, Hutchinson; Palmer, Byers (Dele-Bashiru 88), Luongo, Johnson; Bannan; Berahino (Windass 56), Gregory.
Referee: Matthew Donohue.

Huddersfield Town's unfortunate Levi Colwill scores an own goal for Nottingham Forest in the Championship Play-off Final at Wembley in May. Forest won the match 1-0 and will play in the Premier League for the first time in 23 years. (News Images/Alamy)

Sunderland's Ross Stewart scores against Wycombe Wanderers in the League One Play-off Final at Wembley, sending the Black Cats back up to the Championship. (Action Images via Reuters/Matthew Childs)

SKY BET LEAGUE ONE SEMI-FINALS SECOND LEG

Sunday, 8 May 2022

Milton Keynes D (1) 1 *(Parrott 26)*

Wycombe W (0) 0 13,012

Milton Keynes D: (541) Cumming; Kesler (Kemp 85), O'Hora, Darling, Lewington, Harvie (Watson 87); Corbeanu, Boateng (Wickham 75), Coventry, Parrott; Twine.
Wycombe W: (4231) Stockdale; McCarthy (Grimmer 85), Stewart, Tafazolli, Jacobson; Gape, Scowen; McCleary, Horgan (Wheeler 69), Obita; Vokes.
Wycombe W won 2-1 on aggregate. Referee: Thomas Bramall.

Monday, 9 May 2022

Sheffield W (0) 1 *(Gregory 74)*

Sunderland (0) 1 *(Roberts 90)* 32,978

Sheffield W: (3412) Peacock-Farrell; Storey, Dean, Hutchinson (Palmer 70); Hunt J (Mendez-Laing 71), Byers (Berahino 90), Luongo, Johnson; Bannan; Windass (Paterson 78), Gregory.
Sunderland: (3412) Patterson; Wright, Batth, Cirkin; Gooch, O'Nien, Evans, Clarke (Doyle 90); Pritchard (Matete 90); Roberts (Broadhead 90), Stewart.
Sunderland won 2-1 on aggregate. Referee: James Linington.

SKY BET LEAGUE ONE FINAL

Wembley, Saturday, 21 May 2022

Sunderland (1) 2 *(Embleton 12, Stewart 79)*

Wycombe W (0) 0 72,332

Sunderland: (4231) Patterson; Gooch, Wright, Batth, Cirkin; Evans, O'Nien; Roberts, Pritchard (Doyle 81), Embleton (Clarke 61); Stewart (Broadhead 88).
Wycombe W: (4231) Stockdale; McCarthy, Stewart, Tafazolli, Jacobson; Scowen, Horgan (Wing 55); McCleary, Gape (Akinfenwa 75), Obita (Hanlan 65); Vokes.
Referee: Simon Hooper.

SKY BET LEAGUE TWO SEMI-FINALS FIRST LEG

Saturday, 14 May 2022

Mansfield T (2) 2 *(Oates 13, Bowery 32)*

Northampton T (0) 1 *(Koiki 61)* 7469

Mansfield T: (4312) Bishop; Perch, O'Toole, Hawkins, McLaughlin; Longstaff (Wallace 60), Maris, Quinn (Stirk 77); Murphy (Akins 86); Bowery, Oates.
Northampton T: (4231) Maxted; Mills, Horsfall, Guthrie, Koiki; Sowerby, McWilliams; Kanu (Eppiah 56), Pinnock, Hoskins; Appere (Rose 66).
Referee: Anthony Backhouse.

Sunday, 15 May 2022

Swindon T (1) 2 *(McKirdy 26, 68)*

Port Vale (0) 1 *(Wilson 83)* 14,086

Swindon T: (433) Ward; Egbo (Odimayo 74), Baudry, Conroy, Iandolo; Payne, Reed, Williams (Gladwin 80); McKirdy, Davison, Barry (O'Brien 90).
Port Vale: (3412) Stone; Smith, Martin (Benning 78), Hall; Worrall, Pett, Garrity, Gibbons; Charsley (Taylor 46); Edmondson (Proctor 63), Wilson.
Referee: Ross Joyce.

SKY BET LEAGUE TWO SEMI-FINALS SECOND LEG

Wednesday, 18 May 2022

Northampton T (0) 0

Mansfield T (1) 1 *(McLaughlin 32)* 7619

Northampton T: (4231) Roberts; Mills (Rose 65), Horsfall, Guthrie, Koiki; Sowerby, McWilliams; Eppiah (Zimba 68), Pinnock, Hoskins; Appere.
Mansfield T: (433) Bishop; Hewitt, Hawkins, Perch, McLaughlin; O'Toole, Wallace (Clarke O 85), Quinn (Lapslie 82); Akins, Oates, Bowery.
Mansfield T won 3-1 on aggregate.
Referee: Robert Madley.

Thursday, 19 May 2022

Port Vale (1) 1 *(Wilson 8)*

Swindon T (0) 0 15,042

Port Vale: (3412) Stone; Gibbons, Smith, Hall; Worrall, Pett, Taylor (Charsley 60), Benning; Garrity; Wilson, Harratt (Edmondson 74).
Swindon T: (433) Ward; Egbo, Baudry, Conroy, Iandolo; Payne, Reed, Williams (O'Brien 106); McKirdy, Davison, Barry (Gladwin 81).
aet; Port Vale won 6-5 on penalties.
Referee: Sebastian Stockbridge.

SKY BET LEAGUE TWO FINAL

Wembley, Saturday, 28 May 2022

Mansfield T (0) 0

Port Vale (2) 3 *(Harratt 20, Wilson 24, Benning 85)* 37,303

Mansfield T: (4312) Bishop; Hewitt, Perch, Hawkins■, McLaughlin; Longstaff (Maris 65), O'Toole, Quinn (Akins 79); Murphy (Lapslie 54); Bowery, Oates.
Port Vale: (3412) Stone; Gibbons, Smith, Hall; Worrall (Martin 86), Pett, Taylor (Charsley 67), Benning; Garrity; Wilson, Harratt (Proctor 77).
Referee: Jarred Gillett.

REVIEW OF THE SEASON 2021–22

It was only in the 81st minute of the final game of the season that the league title was decided. Even after Ilkay Gundogan had scored Manchester City's third goal in five minutes to complete a comeback from 2-0 down against Aston Villa, a goal conceded would still have sent the title to Liverpool. Amid the drama of a crisp spring afternoon, it was possible to believe that all was well in football. Was the tensest final day since 2012 not evidence of the competitiveness of the league? Was the average Premier League attendance of 39,600, an all-time English top-flight record, not evidence of football's great popularity?

And this is the great paradox of modern football. It has never been so popular – third-flight average attendances topped 10,000 for the first time since 1960 – and the level has never been so high, and yet a number of clubs are in serious financial difficulty, an issue heightened by the pandemic, while ownership at the top level is the preserve of oligarchs, nation states, hedge funds, foreign billionaires and tax exiles. On the pitch this was a season defined by the rivalry between Manchester City and Liverpool; off it, it was dominated by issues of who football belongs to.

City are the model for incredibly rich owners looking to spend wisely. Sheikh Mansour's people identified Barcelona as the model and brought in two former Barcelona execs in Ferran Soriano and Txiki Begiristain even before appointing Pep Guardiola as coach. The result of that coherent vision – and a net transfer spend of around £600m over the past six seasons – was a fourth league title in five seasons.

The £100m purchase of Jack Grealish represented a deviation from their previous policy, although whether he was intended to add greater celebrity or a dash of unpredictability was not clear. He never fully convinced, but a lot of wide forwards have taken time to adjust to Guardiola's system and he admitted he was finding it difficult to know when to take a man on and when to retain possession with a simple pass. Joao Cancelo, Rodri, Phil Foden and, particularly, Kevin De Bruyne, were the obvious stand-outs.

But while City added the eighth league title in their history, success again eluded them in Europe. Their exit was simultaneously preposterous, as they conceded twice in injury time away to Real Madrid to take the semi-final to extra-time, and familiar. This was what Madrid had managed in the previous two rounds but, more significantly, it was how Guardiola sides often go out. They had dominated the first leg and spells of the second, but proved vulnerable on the break and again conceded a burst of goals in quick succession.

That Guardiola sides have suffered ill fortune in Champions League knockout games is undeniable (and City will point to the chances they missed, in particular the late Grealish chance that

Declan Rice of West Ham United pulls away from Tottenham's Emerson Royal in the Hammers' 1-0 victory at the London Stadium in October. (Zac Goodwin/PA Images/Alamy)

Son Heung-min of Tottenham Hotspur gets a shot away against Burnley at the Tottenham Hotspur Stadium in May. Spurs won the game 1-0. (Action Images via Reuters/Andrew Couldridge)

flicked just wide off the studs of Thibaut Courtois) but, equally, when a manager keeps losing games in the same way, it suggests a weakness in the method, at least against higher-grade sides. Guardiola's problem is that when he tries to adjust, he often seems to disrupt the rhythm of his side and then lays himself open to the charge of 'over-thinking'.

For Liverpool, the season ended with the two domestic cups but also an odd sense of disappointment. They came as near as any side ever has to a quadruple and their achievement in running City so close, despite spending £400m net less, is remarkable. They racked up 92 points; only once before has a side got that many and not won the title – and that was Liverpool in 2019. Those points tallies should themselves be a concern for the Premier League. It may be competitive between the top two, but they are at a level way beyond the rest of the division; the gap to third was 18 points.

And it's hard to avoid the sense that Liverpool are overperforming under Jurgen Klopp. They haven't wasted money on a major signing who didn't work out since the £32.5m spent on Christian Benteke in 2015. That is only sustainable for so long, particularly as the core of the team ages and the squad requires rejuvenation. A doubt, anyway, has begun to emerge about the high-octane approach against top opposition: although Liverpool did overcome a weakened City in the FA Cup semi-final, they failed to beat City in the league, Chelsea in four meetings including both Cup finals (although both were decided in their favour in shoot-outs), and Tottenham Hotspur.

That need for guile against the very best seemed to be acknowledged by Klopp as he started Thiago Alcantara against Madrid in the Champions League final, despite obvious fitness concerns. Liverpool controlled possession but once they went behind to Vinicius Junior's 59th-minute goal they threatened relatively infrequently and, when they did, they found Courtois in unbeatable form.

Kick-off had been delayed by events outside the stadium when a rail strike exposed dismal organisation which, coupled with problems with ticket scanners, caused a dangerous bottleneck of fans. French police responded with indiscriminate brutality while many without tickets, most seemingly local, took advantage of the chaos to scale fences. Although the problems were concentrated at the Liverpool end of the ground, Madrid supporters also reported issues, while fans from both clubs were attacked by gangs as they left the stadium. After an initial attempt to blame fans, Uefa initiated a full inquiry.

There had also been problems at the Europa League final, with water running out with temperatures over 30 degrees and poor signage leading to confusion. Given well over 100,000 fans travelled to Seville for the game, it was hard to avoid the sense that a serious incident was avoided more by luck than judgement. Eintracht Frankfurt beat Rangers on penalties.

Madrid's success was a victory for an old-fashioned kind of football rooted in individual ability. In the knockout stages they had often been second best but were carried through by the excellence of Karim Benzema, Luka Modric and Courtois. But it was also a victory for an old-fashioned model of club ownership. Certainly their president, Florentino Perez, delighted in pointing out how they had beaten the three major petroclubs – Paris Saint-Germain, Chelsea and City – in the previous rounds. But the inflationary impact of their effectively unlimited resources is still being felt, all the more so thanks to the pandemic, which is why he persists in his Super League aspirations.

The issue of ownership became a significant one in the Premier League as well. First the long-mooted Saudi takeover of Newcastle United went ahead after the league received 'legally binding assurances' that the Public Investment Fund of Saudi Arabia is a separate entity to the state of Saudi Arabia. £90m spent on four signings in January helped lift them from the bottom three to comfortable safety.

Then in March, Roman Abramovich was sanctioned by the UK government because of his ties to the Russian leader Vladimir Putin, leading to the forced sale of Chelsea. A US consortium led by Todd Boehly, who owns a stake in the LA Dodgers, completed a £4.5bn purchase in May. What was striking, though, was how the anger at the Super League proposals last year, when Chelsea fans took to the streets in protest, translated not into a desire for representation, but to a desperate hunt for the next billionaire to underwrite their transfer aspirations.

The team itself had already rather run out of steam by the time the transfer was announced, in no small part because Romelu Lukaku, signed for £100m, proved an oddly bad fit for Thomas Tuchel's system. But Chelsea were still good enough to take third, ahead of a Tottenham who acted swiftly to replace Nuno Espirito Santo with Antonio Conte and saw significant improvement by the end of the season. A young Arsenal showed sporadic potential, but faltered in the final weeks, while Manchester United's misery went on. Ole Gunnar Solskjaer was finally sacked after a humbling defeat at Watford, but the decision to appoint Ralf Rangnick as interim was wildly ill-conceived while the signing of Cristiano Ronaldo brought goals at the expense of cohesion.

West Ham, still buoyant under David Moyes, enjoyed their run to the Europa League semi-finals, and finally ending Manchester City's four-year reign as League Cup holders while Leicester took eighth despite a season ravaged by injuries. After a promising start under Bruno Lage, Wolves faded badly while Brighton impressed but again paid for the lack of a goalscorer.

Brentford, brisk and breezy under Thomas Frank, were by far the best of the promoted sides and headed off the threat of relegation with the signing of Christian Eriksen, happily recovered

Kevin De Bruyne of Manchester City shoots at goal against rivals United at the Etihad Stadium in March. City won 4-1, with KDB scoring twice. (REUTERS/Craig Brough)

Liverpool's Alisson denies Manchester City's Phil Foden in the 2-2 draw at Anfield in October. (Peter Byrne/PA Images/Alamy)

after his cardiac arrest. Aston Villa sacked Dean Smith and made a number of signings including Philippe Coutinho, but were only fleetingly impressive under Steven Gerrard. Patrick Vieira won a lot of praise for his work with a young squad at Crystal Palace, although the move to a more progressive approach earned only four more points than they had gained under Roy Hodgson, who finally retired after being unable to halt Watford's inevitable slide.

Everton struggled under both Rafa Benitez and Frank Lampard, but survived, as did Leeds United, who reluctantly dismissed Marcelo Bielsa and replaced him with a different kind of hard-pressing coach in Jesse Marsch. That left Burnley to go down, along with Norwich City and Watford, who had both seemed doomed from the start.

They will be replaced by Fulham, outstanding under Marco Silva, Bournemouth and, after a 23-year absence, Nottingham Forest. That two of last season's promoted clubs went down and two of last season's relegated clubs went up hints at a further problem in the financial structures of the modern game: the increasing gulfs between divisions. Peterborough United made an immediate return to League One, along with Barnsley and Derby County, who battled bravely under Wayne Rooney but couldn't overcome a 21-point deduction.

Rotherham made the return journey, bouncing straight back to the Championship, along with a resurgent Wigan and, thanks to a 16-game unbeaten run under their new manager Alex Neill, Sunderland, who took 46,000 to their play-off final victory over Wycombe, the most travelling fans from a single club in English history.

Forest Green continued their rise with a first ever promotion to League One. They were joined by Exeter and Bristol Rovers, who beat an already relegated Scunthorpe 7-0 on the final day to edge out Northampton on goal difference. Port Vale beat Mansfield in the play-off final. Joining Scunthorpe in relegation out of the league were Oldham, a sorry demise for a club that three decades ago was in the top flight but has been blighted by unsatisfactory ownership.

Stockport and Grimsby returned to the league as Wrexham, funded by the actors Ryan Reynolds and Rob McElhenney, suffered a remarkable 5-4 defeat in the play-off semi to go with an FA Trophy final defeat to Bromley – a dramatic if unsuccessful end to the first season of their documentary about the club. Reynolds and McElhenney seem benign enough, as does Peter Crouch, an unofficial board member at Dulwich Hamlet, but should it really be the fate of non-league clubs to become content for other people's documentaries?

It may be very different to the machinations of nation states and oligarchs, but in the National League as much as in the Premier League, 2021–22 was a season in which ownership took centre stage.

Jonathan Wilson

ACCRINGTON STANLEY

FOUNDATION

Accrington Football Club, founder members of the Football League in 1888, were not connected with Accrington Stanley. In fact both clubs ran concurrently between 1891 when Stanley were formed and 1895 when Accrington FC folded. Actually Stanley Villa was the original name, those responsible for forming the club living in Stanley Street and using the Stanley Arms as their meeting place. They became Accrington Stanley in 1893. In 1894–95 they joined the Accrington & District League, playing at Moorhead Park. Subsequently they played in the North-East Lancashire Combination and the Lancashire Combination before becoming founder members of the Third Division (North) in 1921, two years after moving to Peel Park. In 1962 they resigned from the Football League, were wound up, re-formed in 1963, disbanded in 1966 only to restart as Accrington Stanley (1968), returning to the Lancashire Combination in 1970.

Wham Stadium, Livingstone Road, Accrington, Lancashire BB5 5BX.

Telephone: (01254) 356 950.

Website: www.accringtonstanley.co.uk

Email: info@accringtonstanley.co.uk

Ground Capacity: 5,278.

Record Attendance: 13,181 v Hull C, Division 3 (N), 28 September 1948 (at Peel Park); 5,397 v Derby Co, FA Cup 4th rd, 26 January 2019.

Pitch Measurements: 102m × 66m (111.5yd × 72yd).

Chairman: Andy Holt. ***Managing Director:*** David Burgess.

Manager: John Coleman.

Assistant Manager: Jimmy Bell.

Colours: Red shirts with white trim, red shorts with white trim, red socks with white trim.

Year Formed: 1891, reformed 1968. ***Turned Professional:*** 1919.

Club Nickname: 'The Reds', 'Stanley'.

Previous Names: 1891, Stanley Villa; 1893, Accrington Stanley.

Grounds: 1891, Moorhead Park; 1897, Bell's Ground; 1919, Peel Park; 1970, Crown Ground (renamed Interlink Express Stadium, Fraser Eagle Stadium, Store First Stadium 2013; Wham Stadium 2015).

First Football League Game: 27 August 1921, Division 3 (N), v Rochdale (a) L 3–6 – Tattersall; Newton, Baines, Crawshaw, Popplewell, Burkinshaw, Oxley, Makin, Green (1), Hosker (2), Hartles.

Record League Victory: 8–0 v New Brighton, Division 3 (N), 17 March 1934 – Maidment; Armstrong (pen), Price, Dodds, Crawshaw, McCulloch, Wyper, Lennox (2), Cheetham (4), Leedham (1), Watson.

Record Cup Victory: 7–0 v Spennymoor U, FA Cup 2nd rd, 8 December 1938 – Tootill; Armstrong, Whittaker, Latham, Curran, Lee, Parry (2), Chadwick, Jepson (3), McLoughlin (2), Barclay; 7–0 v Leeds U U21, Football League Trophy, Northern Section Group G, 8 September 2020 – Savin; Sykes, Hughes, Burgess 1), Conneely, Allan, Sangare, Butcher (Sama), Uwakwe (3); Cassidy (2) (Scully), Charles (1) (Spinelli).

HONOURS

League Champions: FL 2 – 2017–18; Conference – 2005–06.
Runners-up: Division 3N – 1954–55, 1957–58.

FA Cup: 4th rd – 1927, 1937, 1959, 2010, 2017, 2019.

League Cup: 3rd rd – 2016–17.

FOOTBALL YEARBOOK FACT FILE

In the summer of 1975 the name of Accrington Stanley nearly disappeared from football just seven years after the club was reborn. Neighbouring club Great Harwood, looking to progress up the football pyramid, suggested the two should merge under the name of Hyndburn, the name of the local authority in which both were located. Nothing came of the proposal and Stanley lived on to eventually regain their place in the Football League.

Record Defeat: 1–9 v Lincoln C, Division 3 (N), 3 March 1951.

Most League Points (2 for a win): 61, Division 3 (N), 1954–55.

Most League Points (3 for a win): 93, FL 2, 2017–18.

Most League Goals: 96, Division 3 (N), 1954–55.

Highest League Scorer in Season: George Stewart, 35, Division 3 (N), 1955–56; George Hudson, 35, Division 4, 1960–61.

Most League Goals in Total Aggregate: George Stewart, 136, 1954–58.

Most League Goals in One Match: 5, Billy Harker v Gateshead, Division 3 (N), 16 November 1935; George Stewart v Gateshead, Division 3 (N), 27 November 1954.

Most Capped Player: Romuald Boco, 19 (51), Benin.

Most League Appearances: Sean McConville, 342, 2009–11; 2015–2022.

Youngest League Player: Ian Gibson, 15 years 358 days, v Norwich C, 23 March 1959.

Record Transfer Fee Received: £1,000,000 from Ipswich T for Kayden Jackson, August 2018.

Record Transfer Fee Paid: £85,000 (rising to £150,000) to Swansea C for Ian Craney, January 2008.

Football League Record: 1921 Original Member of Division 3 (N); 1958–60 Division 3; 1960–62 Division 4; 2006–18 FL 2; 2018– FL 1.

LATEST SEQUENCES

Longest Sequence of League Wins: 7, 24.2.2018 – 7.4.2018.

Longest Sequence of League Defeats: 9, 8.3.1930 – 21.4.1930.

Longest Sequence of League Draws: 4, 25.8.2018 – 15.9.2018.

Longest Sequence of Unbeaten League Matches: 15, 3.2.2018 – 21.4.2018.

Longest Sequence Without a League Win: 18, 17.9.1938 – 31.12.1938.

Successive Scoring Runs: 24 from 23.12.2017.

Successive Non-scoring Runs: 6 from 29.12.2018.

MANAGERS

William Cronshaw *c.*1894
John Haworth 1897–1910
Johnson Haworth *c.*1916
Sam Pilkingson 1919–24
(*Tommy Booth p-m 1923–24*)
Ernie Blackburn 1924–32
Amos Wade 1932–35
John Hacking 1935–49
Jimmy Porter 1949–51
Walter Crook 1951–53
Walter Galbraith 1953–58
George Eastham Snr 1958–59
Harold Bodle 1959–60
James Harrower 1960–61
Harold Mather 1962–63
Jimmy Hinksman 1963–64
Terry Neville 1964–65
Ian Bryson 1965
Danny Parker 1965–66
Jimmy Hinksman 1970–75
Don Bramley 1975–78
Dave Baron 1978–82
Mick Finn 1982
Dennis Cook 1982–83
Pat Lynch 1983–84
Gerry Keenan 1984–85
Frank O'Kane 1985–86
Eric Whalley 1986–88
Gary Pierce 1988–89
David Thornley 1989–90
Phil Staley 1990–93
Ken Wright 1993–94
Eric Whalley 1994–95
Stan Allan 1995–96
Tony Greenwood 1996–97
Leighton James 1997–98
Billy Rodaway 1998
Wayne Harrison 1998–99
John Coleman 1999–2012
Paul Cook 2012
Leam Richardson 2012–13
James Beattie 2013–14
John Coleman 2014–

TEN YEAR LEAGUE RECORD

		P	W	D	L	F	A	Pts	Pos
2012-13	FL 2	46	14	12	20	51	68	54	18
2013-14	FL 2	46	14	15	17	54	56	57	15
2014-15	FL 2	46	15	11	20	58	77	56	17
2015-16	FL 2	46	24	13	9	74	48	85	4
2016-17	FL 2	46	17	14	15	59	56	65	13
2017-18	FL 2	46	29	6	11	76	46	93	1
2018-19	FL 1	46	14	13	19	51	67	55	14
2019-20	FL 1	35	10	10	15	47	53	40	17§
2020-21	FL 1	46	18	13	15	63	68	67	11
2021-22	FL 1	46	17	10	19	61	80	61	12

§Decided on points-per-game (1.14)

DID YOU KNOW

Accrington Stanley played their 500th Football League game away to Plymouth Argyle on 1 April 2017. It was a successful day for the visitors with Jordan Clark's 8th-minute header giving them a 1-0 victory. The win meant that Stanley had now gone 12 games in League Two without defeat.

ACCRINGTON STANLEY – SKY BET LEAGUE ONE 2021–22 LEAGUE RECORD

Match No.	Date	Venue	Opponents	Result	H/T Score	Lg Pos.	Goalscorers	Attendance
1	Aug 7	A	Wycombe W	L 1-2	0-2	19	Butcher [86]	4551
2	14	H	Cambridge U	W 2-1	2-0	11	Butcher [14], Pell [30]	2077
3	17	H	Doncaster R	W 1-0	1-0	7	Dahlberg (og) [3]	2223
4	21	A	Crewe Alex	W 1-0	1-0	4	Nottingham [17]	4187
5	28	A	Milton Keynes D	L 0-2	0-1	9		6816
6	Sept 4	H	Shrewsbury T	W 1-0	1-0	2	Mumbongo [15]	2465
7	11	A	Sunderland	L 1-2	1-1	6	Nottingham [30]	29,830
8	18	H	Wigan Ath	L 1-4	0-2	11	Nottingham [52]	4517
9	25	A	Morecambe	D 3-3	2-2	7	Bishop 2 (1 pen) [19 (p), 68], Butcher [21]	4142
10	28	A	Oxford U	L 1-5	0-2	12	Hamilton [61]	5654
11	Oct 2	H	Ipswich T	W 2-1	0-1	10	Bishop [50], Pell [79]	2600
12	16	A	Cheltenham T	L 0-1	0-0	11		3437
13	19	A	Charlton Ath	W 3-2	1-1	10	Pell 2 [9, 57], Hamilton [66]	11,813
14	23	H	Portsmouth	D 2-2	0-1	11	Pell [50], Butcher [77]	2889
15	30	A	Gillingham	D 0-0	0-0	10		3609
16	Nov 13	H	Plymouth Arg	L 1-4	0-2	14	Leigh [50]	3130
17	20	H	Sheffield W	L 2-3	1-3	17	Mansell [33], Mumbongo [53]	4627
18	23	A	Burton Alb	L 0-4	0-2	17		1946
19	27	A	Lincoln C	W 1-0	0-0	14	Bishop [55]	8547
20	Dec 4	H	Fleetwood T	W 5-1	1-0	13	Hamilton 2 [29, 90], Bishop 2 [46, 78], Coyle [72]	1901
21	7	H	AFC Wimbledon	L 0-2	0-0	13		1746
22	11	H	Bolton W	W 1-0	1-0	10	Leigh [20]	4546
23	26	H	Rotherham U	W 1-0	0-0	10	McConville [75]	4870
24	29	A	Shrewsbury T	D 0-0	0-0	10		5817
25	Jan 8	H	Milton Keynes D	D 1-1	1-1	11	Bishop [9]	1880
26	15	H	Sunderland	D 1-1	0-0	10	Clark [84]	4498
27	22	A	Ipswich T	L 1-2	1-1	13	Hamilton [15]	20,126
28	29	H	Morecambe	D 2-2	2-2	13	Bishop [35], Nottingham [45]	3527
29	Feb 5	A	Rotherham U	L 0-1	0-0	15		8593
30	8	H	Oxford U	W 2-0	1-0	12	O'Sullivan [28], Hamilton [90]	1883
31	12	H	Crewe Alex	W 4-1	1-0	12	Sykes 2 [12, 60], Leigh [51], McConville [64]	2365
32	19	A	Cambridge U	L 0-2	0-0	13		5602
33	22	A	Doncaster R	L 0-2	0-0	14		5396
34	26	H	Wycombe W	W 3-2	1-2	12	Adedoyin [20], Sykes [48], Pell [64]	2242
35	Mar 5	A	Portsmouth	L 0-4	0-2	12		15,051
36	12	H	Charlton Ath	W 2-1	2-1	12	Longelo [28], Leigh [32]	2543
37	15	A	Sheffield W	D 1-1	0-0	12	Johnson (og) [83]	20,688
38	19	A	Plymouth Arg	L 0-4	0-2	13		13,076
39	26	H	Gillingham	L 1-2	0-0	13	Bishop (pen) [90]	2764
40	Apr 2	H	Cheltenham T	D 4-4	2-1	14	Leigh 2 [45, 48], McConville [45], Chapman (og) [87]	2181
41	5	A	Wigan Ath	L 0-3	0-2	14		9139
42	9	A	Fleetwood T	W 2-1	0-1	14	McConville [62], Nottingham [90]	2881
43	15	H	Burton Alb	D 0-0	0-0	13		2513
44	18	A	Bolton W	L 1-3	0-1	14	Rich-Baghuelou [50]	19,098
45	23	H	Lincoln C	W 2-1	1-0	13	Bishop 2 [34, 59]	3053
46	30	A	AFC Wimbledon	W 4-3	3-0	12	Rich-Baghuelou [18], Bishop [35], Nottingham [45], O'Sullivan [63]	7839

Final League Position: 12

GOALSCORERS

League (61): Bishop 12 (2 pens), Hamilton 6, Leigh 6, Nottingham 6, Pell 6, Butcher 4, McConville 4, Sykes 3, Mumbongo 2, O'Sullivan 2, Rich-Baghuelou 2, Adedoyin 1, Clark 1, Coyle 1, Longelo 1, Mansell 1, own goals 3.
FA Cup (1): Hamilton 1.
Carabao Cup (2): Bishop 1, Charles 1.
Papa John's Trophy (12): Bishop 2, Leigh 2, Nottingham 2, Pell 2, Hamilton 1, Malcolm 1, Nolan 1, O'Sullivan 1.

Trafford J 11	O'Sullivan J 13 + 12	Sykes R 38 + 1	Nottingham M 46	Burgess C 1	McConville S 45 + 1	Pell H 26 + 11	Butcher M 30 + 3	Pritchard J 5 + 5	Bishop C 41	Charles D 6	Mumbongo J 3 + 7	Rodgers H 20 + 2	Morgan D 13 + 1	Leigh T 17 + 7	Perritt H — + 2	Sherring S 9 + 1	Clark M 25	Savin T 33	Malcolm J 3 + 7	Hamilton E 38 + 3	Amankwah Y 20 + 4	Conneely S 19 + 3	Mansell L 5 + 1	Nolan J 1 + 4	Coyle L 13 + 6	Woods J 1 + 2	Longelo R 4 + 8	Rich-Baghuelou J 11 + 2	Adedoyin K 6 + 6	Lewis M 1 + 2	Isherwood L 2 + 2	*Match No.*
1	2[1]	3[2]	4	5	6	7	8	9	10	11	12	13																				1
1		2	3		9	7	8[1]	5	10	11		4	6	12																		2
1		2	3		9	6	8	5[1]	11	10[2]	12	4	7		13																	3
1		2	3[3]		9	8[1]	6	5	10	11[2]	12	4	7		14	13																4
1		2	3		9	6[2]	8		11	10	12	4	7	13			5[1]															5
		2	3		9	6	8[2]		11		10[1]		7			4	5	1	12	13												6
1		2	3		9	6[1]	8[3]		11	10	14		7			4	5[2]		13	12												7
1	13	2	3		9		6		10				7			4[1]	5		11[2]	8	12											8
1	5	2	3		9	12	8		11					14		4				6[1]		7[3]	10[2]	13								9
1	6	3	4		10	12	9		11							5				7	2[2]	8[1]		13								10
			3		5	10	8		11				7			4		1		9	2	6										11
	12	2	3		5[1]	10[3]	9		11				7[2]	14				1	13	8	4	6										12
			3		9	10	8		11				7			4		1		5	2	6										13
		12	3		9	10	8		11				7			4[1]		1		5	2	6										14
	5	2	3		9	10			11				7					1		8	4	6										15
		2	3		13	9[3]					12	5[2]		10				1	14	8	4	7	11[1]		6							16
1	14	2	3		8	9					12	4		10[3]					13	5		7	11[2]		6[1]							17
1	14	2	3		8	9[3]					10	5							13	7	4[1]	6	11[2]		12							18
	12	3	4		9	10[1]			11			5				2		1		6		7			8							19
	13	2	3[3]		10	7[2]			11		9[1]	5						1	14	8	4	6			12							20
	13	2	3		10	9			11			5						1		8	4[2]	7[1]		12	6							21
	12	3	4		10[1]		13		11			5		7[3]				1	6[2]	9	2				8	14						22
	13	2	3		10	14	12		11					7[3]			5	1	9[2]	8	4				6[1]							23
	9	3	4[2]		11	12	8		10			13		6[1]			2	1		5					7							24
	5[2]	3	4		10	13	6		11					9[1]			2	1		8	12				7■							25
	9[1]	4■	3		10[2]	8	6		11								2	1		7	5						12	13				26
	9[3]		4		11[1]	6[2]	7		10				13				2	1		8	5		14				12	3				27
	6	4	3		10	7	8		11[1]								2	1		9	5							12				28
		2	3		11	14	8							13			6	1		7	9[3]	5[2]	10[1]					4	12			29
	9[1]	3	4		11	13	7							6[2]			2	1		8	5						12		10			30
		3	4		11[3]		7[1]		10					6			2	1		8	5	12					13		9[2]	14		31
			3		10	13	7		11			4		6[1]			5	1		9		8[2]						2	12			32
			3		8	13			10			4[3]		6[2]			5	1		9		7					12	2	11[1]	14		33
		3	2		8	12	6		11			4	7[1]				5■	1		9						13			10[2]			34
		2	3		8	13	7		11			5[3]		14				1		9	4[1]	6[2]				10	12					35
		2	3		9	6			11			4		8■				1		12	14	13			7[1]		5[3]		10[2]			36
		3	4		6	8	7		11			5						1		9	12				13		2[2]			10[1]		37
		3	4		6	7[2]	8[1]		11			5[3]					2	1■		9					12		10		13		14	38
	12	2	3		9	6[3]		13	11			4					5			8[2]					7		14		10[1]		1	39
	12	2■	3		9	10[1]		13	11					6[2]			5	1		8					7			4				40
	10[2]		3		9		8	14	11					13			5	1		6[3]	2	7[1]						4	12			41
	6[2]		3		10		8[1]	12	11			5		7[3]			2	1		9					14			4	13			42
		4	3		9		7	6[1]	11					10[3]			2[2]	1		8				13			12	5	14			43
		3	4		10			12	11					7			2[1]	1		9		8[2]			13		6■	5				44
	13	3	4		6				11					10[2]			2	1■		8				9[1]	7			5			12	45
	6	3	4		10		12		11					7[1]			2			9		13			8[2]			5			1	46

FA Cup

First Round Port Vale (a) 1-5

Carabao Cup

First Round Rotherham U (a) 2-1

Second Round Oldham Ath (a) 0-0

(Oldham Ath won 5-4 on penalties)

Papa John's Trophy

Group G (N) Barrow (h) 2-2

(Accrington S won 5-4 on penalties)

Group G (N) Leicester C U21 (h) 5-0

Group G (N) Fleetwood T (a) 4-1

Second Round Wigan Ath (h) 1-1

(Wigan Ath won 5-4 on penalties)

AFC WIMBLEDON

FOUNDATION

While the history of AFC Wimbledon is straightforward since it was a new club formed in 2002, there were in effect two clubs operating for two years with Wimbledon connections. The other club was MK Dons, of course. In August 2001, the Football League had rejected the existing Wimbledon's application to move to Milton Keynes. In May 2002, they rejected local sites and were given permission to move by an independent commission set up by the Football League. AFC Wimbledon was founded in the summer of 2002 and held its first trials on Wimbledon Common. In subsequent years, there was considerable debate over the rightful home of the trophies obtained by the former Wimbledon football club. In October 2006, an agreement was reached between Milton Keynes Dons, its Supporters Association, the Wimbledon Independent Supporters Association and the Football Supporters Federation to transfer such trophies and honours to the London Borough of Merton.

Cherry Red Records Stadium, Plough Lane, London SW17 0NR.

Telephone: (0208) 547 3528.

Website: www.afcwimbledon.co.uk

Email: info@afcwimbledon.ltd.uk

Ground Capacity: 9,150.

Record Attendance: 8,502 v Wycombe W, FL 2, 18 April 2022.

Pitch Measurements: 104m × 66m (113.5yd × 72yd).

Chief Executive: Joe Palmer.

Head Coach: Johnnie Jackson.

Assistant Head Coach: Eddie Niedzwiecki.

Club Nickname: 'The Dons'.

Colours: Blue shirts with yellow trim, blue shorts with yellow trim, blue socks with yellow trim.

Year Formed: 2002.

Turned Professional: 2002.

Grounds: 2002, Kingsmeadow; 2020, Loftus Road (temporary groundshare with QPR); 2020, Plough Lane (renamed Cherry Reds Records Stadium 2021).

First Football League Game: 6 August 2011, FL 2 v Bristol R (h) L 2–3 – Brown; Hatton, Gwillim (Bush), Porter (Minshull), Stuart (1), Johnson B, Moore L, Wellard, Jolley (Ademeno (1)), Midson, Yussuff.

HONOURS

League: *Runners-up:* FL 2 – (7th) 2015–16 *(promoted via play-offs)*; Conference – (2nd) 2010–11 *(promoted via play-offs)*.

FA Cup: 5th rd – 2019.

League Cup: 3rd rd 2021.

FOOTBALL YEARBOOK FACT FILE

AFC Wimbledon wore a special commemorative kit for their first Football League fixture against Bristol Rovers in August 2011. The kit was based on the all-white strip worn by the original Wimbledon club for their own entry to the Football League back in 1977–78, although without the Adidas stripes and logo due to copyright reasons.

MANAGERS

Terry Eames 2002–04
Nicky English *(Caretaker)* 2004
Dave Anderson 2004–07
Terry Brown 2007–12
Neal Ardley 2012–18
Wally Downes 2018–19
Glyn Hodges 2019–21
Mark Robinson 2021–22
Mark Bowen 2022
Johnnie Jackson May 2022–

Record League Victory: 5–1 v Bury, FL 2, 19 November 2016 – Shea; Fuller, Robertson, Robinson (Taylor), Owens, Francomb (2 (1 pen)), Reeves, Parrett, Whelpdale (1), Elliott (1) (Nightingale), Poleon (1), (Barrett); 5–1 v Accrington S, FL 1, 10 April 2021 – Tzanev; O'Neill (Alexander), Heneghan', Nightingale, Guinness-Walker, Dobson (Oksanen), Woodyard, Rudoni, Assal (2) (Osew), Palmer (2) (McLoughlin), Pigott (1) (Longman).

Record Cup Victory: 5–0 v Bury, FA Cup 1st rd replay, 5 November 2016 – Shea; Fuller (Owens), Robertson, Robinson (1), Francomb. Parrett (1), Reeves, Bulman (Beere), Whelpdale, Barcham (Poleon (2)), Taylor (1).

Record Defeat: 0–5 v Oxford U, FL 2, 18 February 2020.

Most League Points (3 for a win): 75, FL 2, 2015–16.

Most League Goals: 64, FL 2, 2015–16.

Highest League Scorer in Season: Lyle Taylor, 20, 2015–16; Joe Pigott, 20, 2020–21.

Most League Goals in Total Aggregate: Kevin Cooper, 107, 2002–04.

Most League Goals in One Match: 3, Lyle Taylor v Rotherham U, FL 1, 17 October 2017; 3, Joe Pigott v Rochdale, FL 1, 19 February 2019; 3, Marcus Foss v Southend U, FL 1, 12 October 2019.

Most Capped Player: Shane Smeltz, 5 (58), New Zealand.

Most League Appearances: Barry Fuller, 205, 2013–18.

Youngest League Player: Jack Madelin, 17 years 186 days v Burton Alb, 22 October 2019.

Record Transfer Fee Received: £300,000 from Wrexham for Ollie Palmer, January 2022.

Record Transfer Fee Paid: £25,000 (in excess of) to Stevenage for Byron Harrison, January 2012.

Football League Record: 2011 Promoted from Conference Premier; 2011–16 FL 2; 2016–22 FL 1; 2022– FL 2.

LATEST SEQUENCES

Longest Sequence of League Wins: 5, 2.4.2016 – 23.4.2016.

Longest Sequence of League Defeats: 8, 2.10.2018 – 17.11.2018.

Longest Sequence of League Draws: 4, 6.4.2019 – 23.4.2019.

Longest Sequence of Unbeaten League Matches: 10, 7.4.2018 – 18.8.2018.

Longest Sequence Without a League Win: 27, 11.12.2021 – 30.4.2022.

Successive Scoring Runs: 11 from 24.10.2020.

Successive Non-scoring Runs: 6 from 1.4.2017.

TEN YEAR LEAGUE RECORD

		P	W	D	L	F	A	Pts	Pos
2012-13	FL 2	46	14	11	21	54	76	53	20
2013-14	FL 2	46	14	14	18	49	57	53*	20
2014-15	FL 2	46	14	16	16	54	60	58	15
2015-16	FL 2	46	21	12	13	64	50	75	7
2016-17	FL 1	46	13	18	15	52	55	57	15
2017-18	FL 1	46	13	14	19	47	58	53	18
2018-19	FL 1	46	13	11	22	42	63	50	20
2019-20	FL 1	35	8	11	16	39	52	35	20§
2020-21	FL 1	46	12	15	19	54	70	51	19
2021-22	FL 1	46	6	19	21	49	75	37	23

** 3 pts deducted. §Decided on points-per-game (1.00)*

DID YOU KNOW ?

AFC Wimbledon played their first-ever game against a Football League club on 26 July 2003 when they hosted a Watford XI in a charity match to raise funds for the Milly Dowler Fund. A crowd of over 2,000 saw the visitors win 4-1 with Wimbledon's goal being scored by Gavin Bolger. The match raised over £12,000 for the charity.

AFC WIMBLEDON – SKY BET LEAGUE ONE 2021–22 LEAGUE RECORD

Match No.	Date	Venue	Opponents	Result	H/T Score	Lg Pos.	Goalscorers	Attendance
1	Aug 7	A	Doncaster R	W 2-1	0-0	2	Assal[57], McCormick[74]	6419
2	14	H	Bolton W	D 3-3	1-2	7	Nightingale[20], Pressley (pen)[74], Mebude[75]	7728
3	17	H	Gillingham	D 1-1	0-0	10	Palmer[85]	7027
4	21	A	Sunderland	L 0-1	0-0	14		29,093
5	28	A	Ipswich T	D 2-2	0-0	15	Heneghan[58], Rudoni[90]	19,051
6	Sept 4	H	Oxford U	W 3-1	0-1	9	Rudoni 2[55, 81], Nightingale[78]	7542
7	11	A	Morecambe	W 4-3	1-0	4	Hartigan[5], Chislett[61], Nightingale[72], Assal[90]	3173
8	18	H	Plymouth Arg	L 0-1	0-0	7		7578
9	25	A	Shrewsbury T	L 1-2	1-1	8	Mebude[32]	5346
10	28	A	Rotherham U	L 0-3	0-2	14		8004
11	Oct 2	H	Burton Alb	D 1-1	0-0	14	McCormick[90]	7413
12	16	H	Sheffield W	D 2-2	0-1	17	Guinness-Walker[67], Rudoni[84]	8224
13	19	A	Lincoln C	W 1-0	1-0	14	Pressley (pen)[5]	7750
14	23	H	Wigan Ath	L 0-2	0-0	14		7979
15	30	A	Cambridge U	L 0-1	0-0	17		5609
16	Nov 20	A	Portsmouth	L 1-2	1-0	19	Palmer (pen)[24]	16,234
17	23	H	Crewe Alex	W 3-2	3-1	18	Rudoni[24], Palmer 2 (1 pen)[35, 44 (p)]	6943
18	27	H	Fleetwood T	D 2-2	0-1	17	Assal[53], McCormick[79]	7405
19	Dec 7	A	Accrington S	W 2-0	0-0	17	McCormick[59], Assal[76]	1746
20	11	A	Wycombe W	D 2-2	1-0	17	Rudoni 2[4, 90]	4915
21	29	A	Oxford U	L 0-3	0-2	18		7915
22	Jan 11	A	Milton Keynes D	L 0-1	0-1	20		7663
23	15	H	Morecambe	D 0-0	0-0	20		7128
24	18	H	Portsmouth	D 0-0	0-0	20		8086
25	22	A	Burton Alb	D 1-1	0-0	19	Palmer[70]	2768
26	25	H	Ipswich T	L 0-2	0-0	20		8117
27	29	H	Shrewsbury T	D 1-1	1-0	20	Assal[13]	7824
28	Feb 1	H	Cheltenham T	D 2-2	1-2	20	Assal[8], Cosgrave[80]	6138
29	5	A	Charlton Ath	L 2-3	2-2	20	Chislett[3], Heneghan[36]	22,486
30	8	H	Rotherham U	L 0-1	0-0	20		6387
31	12	H	Sunderland	D 1-1	1-1	20	McCormick (pen)[20]	8381
32	19	A	Bolton W	L 0-4	0-1	20		14,537
33	22	A	Gillingham	D 0-0	0-0	20		4151
34	26	H	Doncaster R	D 2-2	1-0	20	Rudoni[23], McCormick[49]	7912
35	Mar 5	A	Wigan Ath	L 0-1	0-1	20		9780
36	8	A	Plymouth Arg	L 0-2	0-1	20		11,247
37	12	H	Lincoln C	L 0-2	0-1	20		8174
38	19	A	Cheltenham T	L 1-3	1-0	21	Rudoni[26]	3836
39	26	H	Cambridge U	L 0-1	0-0	21		8463
40	Apr 2	A	Sheffield W	L 1-2	1-1	22	Assal[22]	22,374
41	5	H	Charlton Ath	D 1-1	0-0	22	Robinson[87]	8184
42	9	H	Milton Keynes D	D 1-1	1-0	22	Woodyard[19]	7841
43	15	A	Crewe Alex	L 1-3	1-0	22	Cosgrove[19]	4668
44	18	H	Wycombe W	D 1-1	1-0	22	Rudoni[21]	8502
45	23	A	Fleetwood T	D 1-1	1-0	22	McCormick[22]	5019
46	30	H	Accrington S	L 3-4	0-3	23	Assal[56], Rudoni 2[58, 66]	7839

Final League Position: 23

GOALSCORERS

League (49): Rudoni 12, Assal 8, McCormick 7 (1 pen), Palmer 5 (2 pens), Nightingale 3, Chislett 2, Heneghan 2, Mebude 2, Pressley 2 (2 pens), Cosgrave 1, Cosgrove 1, Guinness-Walker 1, Hartigan 1, Robinson 1, Woodyard 1.
FA Cup (5): Palmer 3, Assal 2.
Carabao Cup (2): Hartigan 1, Osew 1.
Papa John's Trophy (5): Pressley 2 (1 pen), Kalambayi 1, McCormick 1, Nightingale 1.

Tzanev N 46	Alexander C 21	Heneghan B 41	Nightingale W 33 + 2	Guinness-Walker N 20 + 8	Woodyard A 36	Hartigan A 26 + 8	Rudoni J 38 + 3	Assal A 38 + 4	McCormick L 34 + 6	Palmer O 16 + 2	Marsh G 21 + 6	Pressley A 9 + 12	Chislett E 11 + 18	Mebude D 12 + 13	Lawrence H 17 + 7	Kalambayi P 11 + 2	Csoka D 14 + 3	Osew P 22 + 5	Kaja E 1 + 4	Robinson Z 4 + 2	Cosgrave A 2 + 7	Ablade T 2 + 10	Brown L 14 + 1	Kalinauskas T 1 + 1	Cosgrove S 13 + 2	Osei Yaw D 1 + 5	Adjei-Hersey D 1 + 1	Bendle A 1	*Match No.*
1	2	3	4	5	6	7^1	8	9	10^3	11^2	12	13	14																1
1	2	3	4	5^3	6	7	10	9	8^2	11^1		13		12	14														2
1			3		6			9	12	14	7	10^1	13	11^3	5	2	4	8^2											3
1	5	3	4		6	7	12	8^3	10^2	11		13	9^1	14	2														4
1	5^2	3	4	13	7	8	14	6	9^3	10		11^1		12	2														5
1		3	4	5	7	8	9	13	6^2	10^3		14	12	11^1	2														6
1	2	3	4	12	6	7		8		11^3	13	14	9^2	10^1	5														7
1	2^1	3	4	12	6	7		10	9			11^3	8^2	13	5		14												8
1	2	3	4	5^2	6	7^1	14	8	9		12	11		10^3	13														9
1		3	2		6	14	11		13		7^3	10	9^2	12	5		4	8^1											10
1	2	3	4	12	6	7	8^1	10	9^3			11	14	13	5^2														11
1	2^3	4		5	6	7	11	8	13			12	9^2	10^1	14	3													12
1		4		5	6	7	8	10^2	9^1			11	12		2	3		13											13
1	2^1	4		5	6	7	8^3	10^2	9			11	12		13	3		14											14
1	5	3		12	6	7	10	8	9	13		11^2			2^1		4												15
1		3		5	6	7	10	8^3	9^1	11^2	12	13	14				4	2											16
1		3		5	6	7	10	8■	9^3	11^2	14	13			12		4	2^1											17
1		3		5	6	7	10	8	9^3	11^2		14	13		12		4	2^1											18
1		3		5	6	7	10	8	9	11							4	2											19
1		3		4	6	7	10	8^1	9	11^2		13			5			2	12										20
1		3		5	7	6^3	10		9	11^2	14			13			4	2	8^1	12									21
1	2	3	4	5■	6	7	10	8^2	9^1	11^3								12	13		14								22
1	2	3	4		6		10^1	8^2	9	11^3	7			12				5	13			14							23
1	2		3	14	6		8	12	9	11^2	7			10^1			4	5^3				13							24
1	2	3	4		6^3		8^2	12	9	11	7		14	10^1				5			13								25
1		3		5		12	10	9	6^3		7		8^1	14			4	2			11^2	13							26
1		3	4			12	8	10^3	6		7		9^1					2			13	11^2	5	14					27
1	2^3	3	4			7	8	10	9^2		6		13					14			12	11^1	5						28
1		3	4			6	8^2	10	13		7		9^3					2			12	14	5		11^1				29
1	5	3	12	8		6	9^3	11^2	14		7					2	4^1					13			10				30
1		3	4			12	8	10	6■		7		9^1					2			13		5		11^2				31
1		3	12	8							7		6^3	11		4		2			13	14	5	9^1	10^2				32
1	2	3	4						6		7	13	9^2	10				5			8^1	14	12		11^3				33
1	2		4		6		8	10^3	9^1		7	13	12	14		3							5		11^2				34
1			4		7	14	8^1	11^2	9		6^3					3	12	2				13	5		10				35
1	2		3		6	13	8^1	10	9^3		7^2					12	4					14	5		11				36
1	2^1	3	4		6	14	7	9^2	8^3					10				12		11		13	5						37
1		3	4	5	6	7	9	10^3						8^2	2	13				12					11^1	14			38
1		3	2	12	6	7	9^3	13					15	14	5			8^1					4		10^4	11^2			39
1		3	2		7	12	8	11^3			6^1			14	5		4	9		10^2						13			40
1		3	2	12	7		8	10			6		14	13	5^3		4^1	9^2		11									41
1		3	4	8	6		9	11^1	12		7		13		5	2^3				10^2					14				42
1		3	2	8^3	6		9	11^1	7^2				14		5				12				4		10	13			43
1		3	4		6^3		8	10	7^2		5		12		14	2							9		11^1	13			44
1		3	4			7^3	8^2	11	6		5		13			2							9		10^1	12	14		45
1		3	4^1				8	11	6				14	10			13	2					5		12		9^2	7^3	46

FA Cup

First Round	Guiseley	(h)	1-0
Second Round	Cheltenham T	(h)	4-3
Third Round	Boreham Wood	(a)	0-2

Carabao Cup

First Round	Charlton Ath	(a)	1-0
Second Round	Northampton T	(a)	1-0
Third Round	Arsenal	(a)	0-3

Papa John's Trophy

Group B (S)	Portsmouth	(h)	5-3
Group B (S)	Crystal Palace U21	(h)	0-2
Group B (S)	Sutton U	(a)	0-1

ARSENAL

FOUNDATION

Formed by workers at the Royal Arsenal, Woolwich in 1886, they began as Dial Square (name of one of the workshops), and included two former Nottingham Forest players, Fred Beardsley and Morris Bates. Beardsley wrote to his old club seeking help and they provided the new club with a full set of red jerseys and a ball. The club became known as the 'Woolwich Reds' although their official title soon after formation was Woolwich Arsenal.

Emirates Stadium, Highbury House, 75 Drayton Park, Islington, London N5 1BU.

Telephone: (020) 7619 5003.

Ticket Office: (020) 7619 5000.

Website: www.arsenal.com

Email: ask@arsenal.co.uk

Ground Capacity: 60,704.

Record Attendance: 73,295 v Sunderland, Div 1, 9 March 1935 (at Highbury); 73,707 v RC Lens, UEFA Champions League, 25 November 1998 (at Wembley); 60,383 v Wolverhampton W, Premier League, 2 November 2019 (at Emirates).

Pitch Measurements: 105m × 68m (115yd × 74.5yd).

Chief Executive: Vinai Venkatesham.

Manager: Mikel Arteta.

Assistant Coaches: Albert Stuiverberg, Steve Round.

Colours: Red shirts with white sleeves, white shorts with red trim, white socks with red trim.

Year Formed: 1886.

Turned Professional: 1891.

Previous Names: 1886, Dial Square; 1886, Royal Arsenal; 1891, Woolwich Arsenal; 1914, Arsenal.

Club Nickname: 'The Gunners'.

Grounds: 1886, Plumstead Common; 1887, Sportsman Ground; 1888, Manor Ground; 1890, Invicta Ground; 1893, Manor Ground; 1913, Highbury; 2006, Emirates Stadium.

HONOURS

League Champions: Premier League – 1997–98, 2001–02, 2003–04; Division 1 – 1930–31, 1932–33, 1933–34, 1934–35, 1937–38, 1947–48, 1952–53, 1970–71, 1988–89, 1990–91.
Runners-up: Premier League – 1998–99, 1999–2000, 2000–01, 2002–03, 2004–05, 2015–16; Division 1 – 1925–26, 1931–32, 1972–73; Division 2 – 1903–04.

FA Cup Winners: 1930, 1936, 1950, 1971, 1979, 1993, 1998, 2002, 2003, 2005, 2014, 2015, 2017, 2020.
Runners-up: 1927, 1932, 1952, 1972, 1978, 1980, 2001.

League Cup Winners: 1987, 1993.
Runners-up: 1968, 1969, 1988, 2007, 2011, 2018.

Double performed: 1970–71, 1997–98, 2001–02.

European Competitions
European Cup: 1971–72 *(qf)*, 1991–92.
UEFA Champions League: 1998–99, 1999–2000, 2000–01 *(qf)*, 2001–02, 2002–03, 2003–04 *(qf)*, 2004–05, 2005–06 *(runners-up)*, 2006–07, 2007–08 *(qf)*, 2008–09 *(sf)*, 2009–10 *(qf)*, 2010–11, 2011–12, 2012–13, 2013–14, 2014–15, 2015–16, 2016–17.
Fairs Cup: 1963–64, 1969–70 *(winners)*, 1970–71 *(qf)*.
UEFA Cup: 1978–79, 1981–82, 1982–83, 1996–97, 1997–98, 1999–2000 *(runners-up)*.
Europa League: 2017–18 *(sf)*, 2018–19 *(runners-up)*, 2019–20, 2020–21 *(sf)*.
European Cup-Winners' Cup: 1979–80 *(runners-up)*, 1993–94 *(winners)*, 1994–95 *(runners-up)*.
Super Cup: 1994 *(runners-up)*.

FOOTBALL YEARBOOK FACT FILE

Arsenal hosted the first FA Charity Shield (now the FA Community Shield) match to be played under floodlights. The Gunners played Blackpool under the Highbury lights on 12 October 1953, winning 3-1 with one goal from Tommy Lawton and two from Doug Lishman. The attendance of 39,853 was the best for the competition since the war.

MANAGERS

Sam Hollis 1894–97
Tom Mitchell 1897–98
George Elcoat 1898–99
Harry Bradshaw 1899–1904
Phil Kelso 1904–08
George Morrell 1908–15
Leslie Knighton 1919–25
Herbert Chapman 1925–34
George Allison 1934–47
Tom Whittaker 1947–56
Jack Crayston 1956–58
George Swindin 1958–62
Billy Wright 1962–66
Bertie Mee 1966–76
Terry Neill 1976–83
Don Howe 1984–86
George Graham 1986–95
Bruce Rioch 1995–96
Arsène Wenger 1996–2018
Unai Emery 2018–19
Mikel Arteta December 2019–

First Football League Game: 2 September 1893, Division 2, v Newcastle U (h) D 2–2 – Williams; Powell, Jeffrey; Devine, Buist, Howat; Gemmell, Henderson, Shaw (1), Elliott (1), Booth.

Record League Victory: 12–0 v Loughborough T, Division 2, 12 March 1900 – Orr; McNichol, Jackson; Moir, Dick (2), Anderson (1); Hunt, Cottrell (2), Main (2), Gaudie (3), Tennant (2).

Record Cup Victory: 11–1 v Darwen, FA Cup 3rd rd, 9 January 1932 – Moss; Parker, Hapgood; Jones, Roberts, John; Hulme (2), Jack (3), Lambert (2), James, Bastin (4).

Record Defeat: 0–8 v Loughborough T, Division 2, 12 December 1896.

Most League Points (2 for a win): 66, Division 1, 1930–31.

Most League Points (3 for a win): 90, Premier League, 2003–04.

Most League Goals: 127, Division 1, 1930–31.

Highest League Scorer in Season: Ted Drake, 42, 1934–35.

Most League Goals in Total Aggregate: Thierry Henry, 175, 1999–2007; 2011–12.

Most League Goals in One Match: 7, Ted Drake v Aston Villa, Division 1, 14 December 1935.

Most Capped Player: Thierry Henry, 81 (123), France.

Most League Appearances: David O'Leary, 558, 1975–93.

Youngest League Player: Jack Wilshere, 16 years 256 days v Blackburn R, 13 September 2008.

Record Transfer Fee Received: £40,000,000 from Liverpool for Alex Oxlade-Chamberlain, August 2017.

Record Transfer Fee Paid: £72,000,000 to Lille for Nicolas Pepe, August 2019.

Football League Record: 1893 Elected to Division 2; 1904–13 Division 1; 1913–19 Division 2; 1919–92 Division 1; 1992– Premier League.

LATEST SEQUENCES

Longest Sequence of League Wins: 14, 10.2.2002 – 18.8.2002.

Longest Sequence of League Defeats: 7, 12.2.1977 – 12.3.1977.

Longest Sequence of League Draws: 6, 4.3.1961 – 1.4.1961.

Longest Sequence of Unbeaten League Matches: 49, 7.5.2003 – 24.10.2004.

Longest Sequence Without a League Win: 23, 28.9.1912 – 1.3.1913.

Successive Scoring Runs: 55 from 19.5.2001.

Successive Non-scoring Runs: 6 from 25.2.1987.

TEN YEAR LEAGUE RECORD

		P	W	D	L	F	A	Pts	Pos
2012-13	PR Lge	38	21	10	7	72	37	73	4
2013-14	PR Lge	38	24	7	7	68	41	79	4
2014-15	PR Lge	38	22	9	7	71	36	75	3
2015-16	PR Lge	38	20	11	7	65	36	71	2
2016-17	PR Lge	38	23	6	9	77	44	75	5
2017-18	PR Lge	38	19	6	13	74	51	63	6
2018-19	PR Lge	38	21	7	10	73	51	70	5
2019-20	PR Lge	38	14	14	10	56	48	56	8
2020-21	PR Lge	38	18	7	13	55	39	61	8
2021-22	PR Lge	38	22	3	13	61	48	69	5

DID YOU KNOW ?

Arsenal wore their new colours of red shirts with white sleeves for the first time on 4 March 1933 when they lost 1-0 at home to Liverpool in a First Division fixture. The original shirts were innovative as they consisted of two parts, a white shirt with collar and a red sleeveless 'pullover' which was worn over the top.

ARSENAL – PREMIER LEAGUE 2021–22 LEAGUE RECORD

Match No.	*Date*	*Venue*	*Opponents*	*Result*		*H/T Score*	*Lg Pos.*	*Goalscorers*	*Atten-dance*
1	Aug 13	A	Brentford	L	0-2	0-1	20		16,479
2	22	H	Chelsea	L	0-2	0-2	19		58,729
3	28	A	Manchester C	L	0-5	0-3	20		52,276
4	Sept 11	H	Norwich C	W	1-0	0-0	16	Aubameyang ^{66}	59,337
5	18	A	Burnley	W	1-0	1-0	13	Odegaard ^{30}	21,944
6	26	H	Tottenham H	W	3-1	3-0	10	Smith Rowe ^{12}, Aubameyang ^{27}, Saka ^{34}	59,919
7	Oct 2	A	Brighton & HA	D	0-0	0-0	9		31,266
8	18	H	Crystal Palace	D	2-2	1-0	12	Aubameyang ^{8}, Lacazette ^{90}	59,475
9	22	H	Aston Villa	W	3-1	2-0	9	Thomas ^{23}, Aubameyang ^{45}, Smith Rowe ^{56}	59,496
10	30	A	Leicester C	W	2-0	2-0	6	Gabriel ^{5}, Smith Rowe ^{18}	32,209
11	Nov 7	H	Watford	W	1-0	0-0	5	Smith Rowe ^{56}	59,833
12	20	A	Liverpool	L	0-4	0-1	5		53,092
13	27	H	Newcastle U	W	2-0	0-0	5	Saka ^{56}, Martinelli ^{66}	59,886
14	Dec 2	A	Manchester U	L	2-3	1-1	5	Smith Rowe ^{13}, Odegaard ^{54}	73,123
15	6	A	Everton	L	1-2	1-0	7	Odegaard ^{45}	38,906
16	11	H	Southampton	W	3-0	2-0	6	Lacazette ^{21}, Odegaard ^{27}, Gabriel ^{62}	59,653
17	15	H	West Ham U	W	2-0	0-0	4	Martinelli ^{48}, Smith Rowe ^{87}	59,777
18	18	A	Leeds U	W	4-1	3-0	4	Martinelli 2 $^{16, 28}$, Saka ^{42}, Smith Rowe ^{84}	36,166
19	26	A	Norwich C	W	5-0	2-0	4	Saka 2 $^{6, 67}$, Tierney ^{44}, Lacazette (pen) ^{84}, Smith Rowe ^{90}	26,940
20	Jan 1	H	Manchester C	L	1-2	1-0	4	Saka ^{31}	59,757
21	23	H	Burnley	D	0-0	0-0	6		59,255
22	Feb 10	A	Wolverhampton W	W	1-0	1-0	5	Gabriel ^{25}	31,523
23	19	H	Brentford	W	2-1	0-0	6	Smith Rowe ^{48}, Saka ^{79}	60,015
24	24	H	Wolverhampton W	W	2-1	0-1	5	Pepe ^{82}, Jose Sa (og) ^{90}	59,888
25	Mar 6	A	Watford	W	3-2	2-1	4	Odegaard ^{5}, Saka ^{30}, Martinelli ^{52}	21,142
26	13	H	Leicester C	W	2-0	1-0	4	Thomas ^{11}, Lacazette (pen) ^{59}	60,111
27	16	H	Liverpool	L	0-2	0-0	4		59,968
28	19	A	Aston Villa	W	1-0	1-0	4	Saka ^{30}	41,956
29	Apr 4	A	Crystal Palace	L	0-3	0-2	5		25,149
30	9	H	Brighton & HA	L	1-2	0-1	5	Odegaard ^{89}	60,112
31	16	A	Southampton	L	0-1	0-1	6		31,465
32	20	A	Chelsea	W	4-2	2-2	5	Nketiah 2 $^{13, 57}$, Smith Rowe ^{27}, Saka (pen) ^{90}	32,249
33	23	H	Manchester U	W	3-1	2-1	4	Tavares ^{3}, Saka (pen) ^{32}, Xhaka ^{70}	60,223
34	May 1	A	West Ham U	W	2-1	1-1	4	Holding ^{38}, Gabriel ^{54}	59,959
35	8	H	Leeds U	W	2-1	2-0	4	Nketiah 2 $^{5, 10}$	60,108
36	12	A	Tottenham H	L	0-3	0-2	4		62,027
37	16	A	Newcastle U	L	0-2	0-0	5		52,274
38	22	H	Everton	W	5-1	2-1	5	Martinelli (pen) ^{27}, Nketiah ^{31}, Cedric Soares ^{56}, Gabriel ^{59}, Odegaard ^{82}	60,201

Final League Position: 5

GOALSCORERS

League (61): Saka 11 (2 pens), Smith Rowe 10, Odegaard 7, Martinelli 6 (1 pen), Gabriel 5, Nketiah 5, Aubameyang 4, Lacazette 4 (2 pens), Thomas 2, Cedric Soares 1, Holding 1, Pepe 1, Tavares 1, Tierney 1, Xhaka 1, own goal 1.
FA Cup (0).
Carabao Cup (16): Nketiah 5, Aubameyang 3, Lacazette 2 (1 pen), Pepe 2, Chambers 1, Patino 1, Saka 1, Smith Rowe 1.
Papa John's Trophy (12): Balogun 2, Hutchinson 2, Olayinka 2, Biereth 1, Flores 1, Ideho 1, Oulad M'hand 1, Sagoe Junior 1, own goal 1.

Leno B 4	Chambers C 2	White B 32	Pablo Mari V 2	Tierney K 22	Sambi Lokonga A 12 + 7	Xhaka G 27	Pepe N 5 + 15	Smith Rowe E 21 + 12	Martinelli G 21 + 8	Balogun F 1 + 1	Saka B 36 + 2	Nelson R — + 1	Tavares N 13 + 9	Cedric Soares R 16 + 5	Holding R 9 + 6	Aubameyang P 12 + 2	Kolasinac S 1 + 1	Odegaard M 32 + 4	Elneny M 8 + 6	Lacazette A 20 + 10	Maitland-Niles A 2 + 6	Ramsdale A 34	Tomiyasu T 20 + 1	Gabriel M 35	Thomas P 23 + 1	Nketiah E 8 + 13	Match No.
1	2^{3}	3	4	5	6	7	8	9	10^{2}	11^{1}	12	13	14														1
1			4	5^{2}	6	7	8	9	11^{3}	14	10^{1}		13	2	3	12											2
1	3			6		9■		10			7^{1}			2	4	11^{2}	5	8^{3}	12	13	14						3
		3		5	6^{1}		8	13			10			14		11		9			7^{3}	1	2^{2}	4	12		4
		3		5^{3}	12		7	8^{1}			10		14			11		9			13	1	2	4	6^{2}		5
		3		5	12	7^{1}		10^{3}			8^{2}		14			11		9			13	1	2	4	6		6
		3		5	7		12	10			8^{3}					11^{2}		9^{1}		13	14	1	2	4	6		7
		3		5	12		8	9	14		10^{1}					11		7^{2}		13		1	2	4	6^{3}		8
		3			7^{2}			9	14		6		5			11^{3}		12		10^{1}	13	1	2	4	8		9
		3			8		13	9^{3}			6^{2}		5			11	14	12		10^{1}		1	2	4	7		10
		3			7			9^{2}	14		6^{3}		5			11		12	13	10^{1}	8	1	2	4			11
		3			8^{1}			9			6		5			11		13	14	10^{2}	12	1	2	4	7^{3}		12
		3			8			9	12		6^{1}		5			11^{2}		10	14	13		1	2	4	7^{3}		13
		3						9^{1}	6		12		5			11^{3}		10^{2}	8	13		1	2	4	7	14	14
		3		5^{1}		7			10^{2}		8		12			14		9		11^{3}		1	2	4	6	13	15
		3		5	13	8^{2}	14		9		6				12			10		11^{3}		1	2	4^{1}	7		16
		3		5		8		12	9^{2}		6		14					10^{1}		11^{3}		1	2	4	7	13	17
		3		5		8		13	9		6^{2}		14	12				10^{3}		11		1	2^{1}	4	7		18
		2		5		7	13	14	10^{3}		8^{2}				3			9	12	11		1		4	6^{1}		19
		3		5		7		13	10		8^{3}				12			9^{1}	14	11^{2}		1	2	4■	6		20
		2		5	6			9^{1}	10		7				3			8		11		1		4		12	21
		3		5		7		12	10■		8^{2}			2	13			9^{1}		11^{3}		1		4	6	14	22
		3		5		7	12	10^{1}			8			2				9		11^{2}		1		4	6	13	23
		3		5^{3}		7	12		10^{1}		8		14	2^{2}				9		11		1		4	6	13	24
		3		5		7	12		10^{1}		8			2	14			9^{3}		11^{2}		1		4	6	13	25
		3		5		7	13	12	10^{1}		8^{2}			2				9		11^{3}		1		4	6	14	26
		3		5		7	13	12	10		8^{2}			2				9^{1}		11^{3}		1		4	6	14	27
1		3		5		8	12	11			9^{1}			2	14			6^{3}		10^{2}				4	7	13	28
		3			14	7		10	12		8		5^{1}	2^{2}				9		11		1		4	6^{3}	13	29
		3			7	5	13	8^{1}	11^{2}		9			2				6		10		1		4		12	30
		3			7	8	13	12	9		11		5^{2}	2^{1}				6				1		4		10	31
		2				7		10^{2}	12		8^{3}		5	13	3			9	6	14		1		4		11^{1}	32
		3				7		10^{1}	12		8^{2}		5	2^{3}	13			9	6			1	14	4		11	33
					14	8		13	11		9^{2}		5	12	3			6^{3}	7			1	2^{1}	4		10	34
						8	12	13	11^{2}		9^{1}			2	3			6	7	14		1	5	4		10^{3}	35
						7		12	10^{1}		8		14	2	3■			9	6	13		1	5	4^{3}		11^{2}	36
		3				7	15	10^{2}	13		8		5^{3}	12				9	6	14		1	2^{1}	4^{4}		11	37
					12	7^{1}	14		10		8^{3}		5	2	3			9	6	13		1		4		11^{2}	38

FA Cup

Third Round	Nottingham F	(a)	0-1

Carabao Cup

Second Round	WBA	(a)	6-0
Third Round	AFC Wimbledon	(h)	3-0
Fourth Round	Leeds U	(h)	2-0
Quarter-Final	Sunderland	(h)	5-1
Semi-Final 1st leg	Liverpool	(a)	0-0
Semi-Final 2nd leg	Liverpool	(h)	0-2

(Liverpool won 2-0 on aggregate)

Papa John's Trophy (Arsenal U21)

Group F (S)	Swindon T	(a)	1-2
Group F (S)	Newport Co	(a)	4-3
Group F (S)	Plymouth Arg	(a)	1-1

(Plymouth Arg won 5-4 on penalties)

Second Round	Ipswich T	(a)	2-2

(Arsenal U21 won 4-3 on penalties)

Third Round	Chelsea U21	(h)	4-1
Quarter-Final	Wigan Ath	(a)	0-1

ASTON VILLA

FOUNDATION

Cricketing enthusiasts of Villa Cross Wesleyan Chapel, Aston, Birmingham decided to form a football club during the winter of 1874–75. Football clubs were few and far between in the Birmingham area and in their first game against Aston Brook St Mary's rugby team they played one half rugby and the other soccer. In 1876 they were joined by Scottish soccer enthusiast George Ramsay who was immediately appointed captain and went on to lead Aston Villa from obscurity to one of the country's top clubs in a period of less than ten years.

Villa Park, Trinity Road, Birmingham B6 6HE.

Telephone: (0121) 327 2299.

Ticket Office: (0333) 323 1874.

Website: www.avfc.co.uk

Email: postmaster@avfc.co.uk

Ground Capacity: 42,749.

Record Attendance: 76,588 v Derby Co, FA Cup 6th rd, 2 March 1946.

Pitch Measurements: 105m × 68m (115yd × 74.5yd).

Executive Chairman: Nassef Sawiris.

Co-Chairman: Wes Edens.

Chief Executive: Christian Purslow.

Head Coach: Steven Gerrard.

Assistant Head Coaches: Gary McAllister, Neil Critchley.

Colours: Claret shirts with sky blue sleeves, white shorts with claret trim, sky blue socks with claret trim.

Year Formed: 1874.

Turned Professional: 1885.

Club Nickname: 'The Villans'.

Grounds: 1874, Wilson Road and Aston Park (also used Aston Lower Grounds for some matches); 1876, Wellington Road, Perry Barr; 1897, Villa Park.

First Football League Game: 8 September 1888, Football League, v Wolverhampton W (a) D 1–1 – Warner; Cox, Coulton; Yates, Harry Devey, Dawson; Albert Brown, Green (1), Allen, Garvey, Hodgetts.

Record League Victory: 12–2 v Accrington S, Division 1, 12 March 1892 – Warner; Evans, Cox; Harry Devey, Jimmy Cowan, Baird; Athersmith (1), Dickson (2), John Devey (4), Lewis Campbell (4), Hodgetts (1).

HONOURS

League Champions: Division 1 – 1893–94, 1895–96, 1896–97, 1898–99, 1899–1900, 1909–10, 1980–81; Division 2 – 1937–38, 1959–60; Division 3 – 1971–72.
Runners-up: Premier League – 1992–93; Division 1 – 1902–03, 1907–08, 1910–11, 1912–13, 1913–14, 1930–31, 1932–33, 1989–90; Football League 1888–89; Division 2 – 1974–75, 1987–88.

FA Cup Winners: 1887, 1895, 1897, 1905, 1913, 1920, 1957.
Runners-up: 1892, 1924, 2000, 2015.

League Cup Winners: 1961, 1975, 1977, 1994, 1996.
Runners-up: 1963, 1971, 2010, 2020.

Double Performed: 1896–97.

European Competitions
European Cup: 1981–82 *(winners)*, 1982–83 *(qf)*.
UEFA Cup: 1975–76, 1977–78 *(qf)*, 1983–84, 1990–91, 1993–94, 1994–95, 1996–97, 1997–98 *(qf)*, 1998–99, 2001–02, 2008–09.
Europa League: 2009–10, 2010–11.
Intertoto Cup: 2000 *(sf)*, 2001 *(winners)*, 2002 *(sf)*, 2008 *(qualified for UEFA Cup)*.
Super Cup: 1982 *(winners)*.
World Club Championship: 1982.

FOOTBALL YEARBOOK FACT FILE

Aston Villa were one of the first clubs to launch an official matchday programme, or journal as it was originally called. The club first produced a 12-page issue with the title *Villa News and Record* for the visit of Blackburn Rovers for the Division One fixture on 1 September 1906. The programme was priced at one penny, and included a player portrait, line-ups, results and fixtures, and interesting paragraphs of information about the club.

Record Cup Victory: 13–0 v Wednesbury Old Ath, FA Cup 1st rd, 30 October 1886 – Warner; Coulton, Simmonds; Yates, Robertson, Burton (2); Richard Davis (1), Albert Brown (3), Hunter (3), Loach (2), Hodgetts (2).

Record Defeat: 0–8 v Chelsea, Premier League, 23 December 2012.

Most League Points (2 for a win): 70, Division 3, 1971–72.

Most League Points (3 for a win): 83, FL C, 2017–18.

Most League Goals: 128, Division 1, 1930–31.

Highest League Scorer in Season: 'Pongo' Waring, 49, Division 1, 1930–31.

Most League Goals in Total Aggregate: Harry Hampton, 215, 1904–15.

Most League Goals in One Match: 5, Harry Hampton v Sheffield W, Division 1, 5 October 1912; 5, Harold Halse v Derby Co, Division 1, 19 October 1912; 5, Len Capewell v Burnley, Division 1, 29 August 1925; 5, George Brown v Leicester C, Division 1, 2 January 1932; 5, Gerry Hitchens v Charlton Ath, Division 2, 18 November 1959.

Most Capped Player: Steve Staunton, 64 (102), Republic of Ireland.

Most League Appearances: Charlie Aitken, 561, 1961–76.

Youngest League Player: Jimmy Brown, 15 years 349 days v Bolton W, 17 September 1969.

Record Transfer Fee Received: £100,000,000 from Manchester C for Jack Grealish, August 2021.

Record Transfer Fee Paid: £38,000,000 to Norwich C for Emiliano Buendia, June 2021.

Football League Record: 1888 Founder Member of the League; 1936–38 Division 2; 1938–59 Division 1; 1959–60 Division 2; 1960–67 Division 1; 1967–70 Division 2; 1970–72 Division 3; 1972–75 Division 2; 1975–87 Division 1; 1987–88 Division 2; 1988–92 Division 1; 1992–2016 Premier League; 2016–19 FL C; 2019– Premier League.

MANAGERS

George Ramsay 1884–1926 (*Secretary-Manager*)
W. J. Smith 1926–34 (*Secretary-Manager*)
Jimmy McMullan 1934–35
Jimmy Hogan 1936–44
Alex Massie 1945–50
George Martin 1950–53
Eric Houghton 1953–58
Joe Mercer 1958–64
Dick Taylor 1964–67
Tommy Cummings 1967–68
Tommy Docherty 1968–70
Vic Crowe 1970–74
Ron Saunders 1974–82
Tony Barton 1982–84
Graham Turner 1984–86
Billy McNeill 1986–87
Graham Taylor 1987–90
Dr Jozef Venglos 1990–91
Ron Atkinson 1991–94
Brian Little 1994–98
John Gregory 1998–2002
Graham Taylor OBE 2002–03
David O'Leary 2003–06
Martin O'Neill 2006–10
Gerard Houllier 2010–11
Alex McLeish 2011–12
Paul Lambert 2012–15
Tim Sherwood 2015
Remi Garde 2015–16
Roberto Di Matteo 2016
Steve Bruce 2016–18
Dean Smith 2018–21
Steven Gerrard November 2021–

LATEST SEQUENCES

Longest Sequence of League Wins: 10, 2.3.2019 – 22.4.2019.

Longest Sequence of League Defeats: 11, 14.2.2016 – 30.4.2016.

Longest Sequence of League Draws: 6, 12.9.1981 – 10.10.1981.

Longest Sequence of Unbeaten League Matches: 15, 12.3.1949 – 27.8.1949.

Longest Sequence Without a League Win: 19, 14.8.2015 – 2.1.2016.

Successive Scoring Runs: 35 from 10.11.1895.

Successive Non-scoring Runs: 6 from 26.12.2014.

TEN YEAR LEAGUE RECORD

		P	*W*	*D*	*L*	*F*	*A*	*Pts*	*Pos*
2012-13	PR Lge	38	10	11	17	47	69	41	15
2013-14	PR Lge	38	10	8	20	39	61	38	15
2014-15	PR Lge	38	10	8	20	31	57	38	17
2015-16	PR Lge	38	3	8	27	27	76	17	20
2016-17	FL C	46	16	14	16	47	48	62	13
2017-18	FL C	46	24	11	11	72	42	83	4
2018-19	FL C	46	20	16	10	82	61	76	5
2019-20	PR Lge	38	9	8	21	41	67	35	17
2020-21	PR Lge	38	16	7	15	55	46	55	11
2021-22	PR Lge	38	13	6	19	52	54	45	14

DID YOU KNOW ?

The last Football League match hosted by Aston Villa on Christmas Day took place in 1951 when local rivals Wolverhampton Wanderers were the visitors with an 11am kick-off. A crowd of 38,656 turned out to see Villa lead 2-0 and then 3-1 before two late goals earned the visitors a 3-3 draw.

ASTON VILLA – PREMIER LEAGUE 2021–22 LEAGUE RECORD

Match No.	Date	Venue	Opponents	Result		H/T Score	Lg Pos.	Goalscorers	Attendance
1	Aug 14	A	Watford	L	2-3	0-2	13	McGinn [70], Ings (pen) [90]	20,051
2	21	H	Newcastle U	W	2-0	1-0	9	Ings [45], El Ghazi (pen) [62]	41,964
3	28	H	Brentford	D	1-1	1-1	11	Emi [13]	42,045
4	Sept 11	A	Chelsea	L	0-3	0-1	12		39,969
5	18	H	Everton	W	3-0	0-0	10	Cash [66], Digne (og) [69], Bailey [75]	41,888
6	25	A	Manchester U	W	1-0	0-0	8	Hause [88]	72,922
7	Oct 3	A	Tottenham H	L	1-2	0-1	10	Watkins [67]	53,076
8	16	H	Wolverhampton W	L	2-3	0-0	12	Ings [48], McGinn [68]	41,951
9	22	A	Arsenal	L	1-3	0-2	13	Ramsey, J [82]	59,496
10	31	H	West Ham U	L	1-4	1-2	15	Watkins [34]	41,874
11	Nov 5	A	Southampton	L	0-1	0-1	15		30,178
12	20	H	Brighton & HA	W	2-0	0-0	15	Watkins [84], Mings [89]	41,925
13	27	A	Crystal Palace	W	2-1	1-0	11	Targett [15], McGinn [86]	25,203
14	Dec 1	H	Manchester C	L	1-2	0-2	13	Watkins [47]	41,400
15	5	H	Leicester C	W	2-1	1-1	10	Konsa 2 [17, 54]	41,572
16	11	A	Liverpool	L	0-1	0-0	12		53,093
17	14	A	Norwich C	W	2-0	1-0	9	Ramsey, J [34], Watkins [87]	26,836
18	26	H	Chelsea	L	1-3	1-1	11	James (og) [28]	41,907
19	Jan 2	A	Brentford	L	1-2	1-1	13	Ings [16]	16,876
20	15	H	Manchester U	D	2-2	0-1	13	Ramsey, J [77], Coutinho [81]	41,968
21	22	A	Everton	W	1-0	1-0	10	Emi [45]	38,203
22	Feb 9	H	Leeds U	D	3-3	3-2	11	Coutinho [30], Ramsey, J 2 [38, 43]	41,927
23	13	A	Newcastle U	L	0-1	0-1	12		52,207
24	19	H	Watford	L	0-1	0-0	12		41,936
25	26	A	Brighton & HA	W	2-0	1-0	12	Cash [17], Watkins [68]	31,475
26	Mar 5	H	Southampton	W	4-0	2-0	11	Watkins [9], Douglas Luiz [44], Coutinho [52], Ings [54]	41,855
27	10	A	Leeds U	W	3-0	1-0	9	Coutinho [22], Cash [65], Chambers [73]	36,400
28	13	A	West Ham U	L	1-2	0-0	9	Ramsey, J [90]	59,957
29	19	H	Arsenal	L	0-1	0-1	9		41,956
30	Apr 2	A	Wolverhampton W	L	1-2	0-2	10	Watkins (pen) [86]	31,012
31	9	H	Tottenham H	L	0-4	0-1	12		41,949
32	23	A	Leicester C	D	0-0	0-0	15		32,185
33	30	H	Norwich C	W	2-0	1-0	13	Watkins [41], Ings [90]	40,290
34	May 7	A	Burnley	W	3-1	2-0	11	Ings [7], Emi [31], Watkins [52]	20,891
35	10	H	Liverpool	L	1-2	1-1	11	Douglas Luiz [3]	41,919
36	15	H	Crystal Palace	D	1-1	0-0	13	Watkins [69]	41,136
37	19	H	Burnley	D	1-1	0-1	14	Emi [48]	40,468
38	22	A	Manchester C	L	2-3	1-0	14	Cash [37], Coutinho [69]	53,395

Final League Position: 14

GOALSCORERS

League (52): Watkins 11 (1 pen), Ings 7 (1 pen), Ramsey, J 6, Coutinho 5, Cash 4, Emi 4, McGinn 3, Douglas Luiz 2, Konsa 2, Bailey 1, Chambers 1, El Ghazi 1 (1 pen), Hause 1, Mings 1, Targett 1, own goals 2.
FA Cup (0).
Carabao Cup (7): Archer 4, El Ghazi 2 (1 pen), Guilbert 1.
Papa John's Trophy (12): Archer 6, Philogene-Bidace 2, Abldeen-Goodridge 1, Davis 1, Ramsey A 1, Thorndike 1.

Martinez D 36	Cash M 38	Konsa E 29	Mings T 35 + 1	Targett M 17	McGinn J 35	Nakamba M 10 + 6	El Ghazi A 4 + 5	Emi B 22 + 13	Young A 10 + 14	Ings D 22 + 8	Ramsey J 29 + 5	Bailey L 7 + 11	Traore B 1 + 8	Douglas Luiz d 31 + 3	Philogene-Bidace J — + 1	Tuanzebe A 6 + 3	Wesley M — + 1	Chukwuemeka Carney 2 + 10	Watkins O 33 + 2	Hause K 4 + 3	Steer J 1	Archer C — + 3	Davis K — + 1	Sanson M 3 + 7	Trezeguet M — + 1	Digne L 16	Coutinho P 16 + 3	Chambers C 9 + 2	Iroegbunam T 1 + 2	Olsen R 1	*Match No.*
1	2	3	4	5^{1}	6	7	8^{2}	9^{3}	10	11	12	13	14																		1
1	2	3	4		6		11	9^{1}	5	10^{3}	8			7^{2}	12	13	14														2
1	2	3^{3}		5		12	10	7	9^{2}	11				6		4		8^{1}	13	14											3
	2	3	5	6	9	14				10^{2}	7^{1}	12	13	8^{3}		4			11		1										4
1	2^{4}	3	5	6^{2}	9^{1}	12			14	10	7	13^{3}	15	8		4			11												5
1	5	2	4	9	6			12		10^{1}	7^{2}			8					11	3		13									6
1	5	2	4	9	6			12		11^{3}	8^{1}		13	7					10	3^{2}		14									7
1	5^{3}	2	4	9	6	12		8^{2}	14	11	13			7^{1}		3			10												8
1	5	2	4	8	6		14	9^{2}		10^{3}	13	12		7		3^{1}			11												9
1	2	3▮	13	5	6	7	14	9^{2}	12		8^{1}	11^{3}							10	4											10
1	2		4	5	6	7^{1}	10^{3}	9^{2}			12	8				3			11			13	14								11
1	2	3	4	5	6	7	14	9^{2}	13	10^{1}	8^{3}	12							11												12
1	2	3	4	5	6	7	13	14	11^{3}		8^{1}	9^{2}		12					10												13
1	2	3	4	5^{2}	6	7^{3}		11	12			9^{1}		8				13	10					14							14
1	2	3	4		6	7		11^{2}	5		9^{3}			8^{1}		14		13	10					12							15
1	2	3	4	5	6	7^{1}		13	11^{2}	14	9^{3}			8					10					12							16
1	2	3	4	5	6^{3}			9^{2}	11^{1}	12	8			7		14		13	10												17
1	2	3	4	5			14	9^{2}		10^{1}	8		12	7				13	11					6^{3}							18
1	2	3		5	6			11		10	8^{1}		9^{2}	7						4				12	13						19
1	2	3^{1}	4					11		10^{3}	8			7				14	9	12				6^{2}		5	13				20
1	2	3	4		6			9^{3}		13	8			7				12	10^{2}	14						5	11^{1}				21
1	2	3▮	4		6			9^{1}	13		8^{3}			7				12	10							5	11^{2}	14			22
1	2		4		6^{3}			9^{1}		12	8	13		7				14	10^{2}							5	11	3			23
1	2^{2}		4		6			9^{3}	13	10	8	14		7^{1}					12							5	11	3			24
1	2	3	4		6				13	10^{2}	8			7^{1}					9					12		5	11^{3}		14		25
1	2		4		6			14	5	9^{1}	8^{2}	13		7					10					12			11^{3}	3			26
1	2		4		6			13	14	10^{1}	8			7^{3}					11					12		5	9^{2}	3			27
1	2		4		6			14	12	10^{2}	8	13		7^{3}					11							5^{1}	9	3			28
1	2	3	4		6			9^{2}	5	14	8^{1}	13	12	7					10^{3}								11				29
1	2	3	4		7			14	12		8	10		13					11					6^{2}		5^{1}	9^{3}				30
1	2	3	4		6			13	14	10^{1}	8	12		7					11							5^{3}	9^{2}				31
1	2	3	4		6	14		13	5		8^{3}	9		7^{1}					11								10^{2}		12		32
1	2		4		8			14		12	9	7^{1}		13					11							5	10^{3}	3	6^{2}		33
1	2	3	4		7			9^{3}	13	10^{2}				8				12	11							5	14	6^{1}			34
1	2	3	4		8	7^{1}		13		11			14	6				12	10^{3}							5	9^{2}				35
1	2	3^{1}	4		8	7^{2}		14		11^{3}	13			6					10							5	9	12			36
1	2		4		9			6		14	8^{2}		12	7				10^{1}	11^{3}							5	13	3			37
	2		4		6	12		9^{3}	14	13	8^{2}			7					11							5	10^{1}	3		1	38

FA Cup

Third Round	Manchester U	(a)	0-1

Carabao Cup

Second Round	Barrow	(a)	6-0
Third Round	Chelsea	(a)	1-1

(Chelsea won 4-3 on penalties)

Papa John's Trophy (Aston Villa U21)

Group C (S)	Wycombe W	(a)	3-1
Group C (S)	Burton Alb	(a)	4-2
Group C (S)	Milton Keynes D	(a)	4-2
Second Round	Charlton Ath	(a)	1-2

BARNSLEY

FOUNDATION

Many clubs owe their inception to the Church and Barnsley are among them, for they were formed in 1887 by the Rev. T. T. Preedy, curate of Barnsley St Peter's, and went under that name until it was dropped in 1897 a year before being admitted to the Second Division of the Football League.

Oakwell Stadium, Grove Street, Barnsley, South Yorkshire S71 1ET.

Telephone: (01226) 211 211.

Ticket Office: (01226) 211 183.

Website: www.barnsleyfc.co.uk

Email: thereds@barnsleyfc.co.uk

Ground Capacity: 23,287.

Record Attendance: 40,255 v Stoke C, FA Cup 5th rd, 15 February 1936.

Pitch Measurements: 100.5m × 66.75m (110yd × 73yd).

Co-Chairmen: Chien Lee, Paul Conway.

Chief Executive: Khaled El-Ahmad.

Head Coach: Michel Duff.

Assistant Coaches: Martin Devaney, Tom Harban, Joseph Laumann.

Colours: Red shirts with white trim, white shorts with red trim, red socks with white trim.

Year Formed: 1887.

Turned Professional: 1888.

Previous Name: 1887, Barnsley St Peter's; 1897, Barnsley.

Club Nickname: 'The Tykes', 'The Reds', 'The Colliers'.

Ground: 1887, Oakwell.

First Football League Game: 1 September 1898, Division 2, v Lincoln C (a) L 0–1 – Fawcett; McArtney, Nixon; King, Burleigh, Porteous; Davis, Lees, Murray, McCullough, McGee.

Record League Victory: 9–0 v Loughborough T, Division 2, 28 January 1899 – Greaves; McArtney, Nixon; Porteous, Burleigh, Howard; Davis (4), Hepworth (1), Lees (1), McCullough (1), Jones (2). 9–0 v Accrington S, Division 3 (N), 3 February 1934 – Ellis; Cookson, Shotton; Harper, Henderson, Whitworth; Spence (2), Smith (1), Blight (4), Andrews (1), Ashton (1).

Record Cup Victory: 6–0 v Blackpool, FA Cup 1st rd replay, 20 January 1910 – Mearns; Downs, Ness; Glendinning, Boyle (1), Utley; Bartrop, Gadsby (1), Lillycrop (2), Tufnell (2), Forman. 6–0 v Peterborough U, League Cup 1st rd 2nd leg, 15 September 1981 – Horn; Joyce, Chambers, Glavin (2), Banks, McCarthy, Evans, Parker (2), Aylott (1), McHale, Barrowclough (1).

Record Defeat: 0–9 v Notts Co, Division 2, 19 November 1927.

Most League Points (2 for a win): 67, Division 3 (N), 1938–39.

Most League Points (3 for a win): 91, FL 1, 2018–19.

HONOURS

League Champions: Division 3N – 1933–34, 1938–39, 1954–55.
Runners-up: First Division – 1996–97; FL 1 – 2018–19; Division 3 – 1980–81; Division 3N – 1953–54; Division 4 – 1967–68.

FA Cup Winners: 1912.
Runners-up: 1910.

League Cup: quarter-final – 1982.

League Trophy Winners: 2016.

FOOTBALL YEARBOOK FACT FILE

It was common in the period before the First World War for the English and Scottish Cup holders to meet in a friendly the following season, the match often being promoted as a 'world championship' fixture. In September 1912, Barnsley, as FA Cup holders, travelled to play Celtic at Parkhead. The Reds came away with a 1-1 draw, Jimmy Moore scoring in front of a crowd estimated at 4,000.

Most League Goals: 118, Division 3 (N), 1933–34.

Highest League Scorer in Season: Cecil McCormack, 33, Division 2, 1950–51.

Most League Goals in Total Aggregate: Ernest Hine, 123, 1921–26 and 1934–38.

Most League Goals in One Match: 5, Frank Eaton v South Shields, Division 3 (N), 9 April 1927; 5, Peter Cunningham v Darlington, Division 3 (N), 4 February 1933; 5, Beau Asquith v Darlington, Division 3 (N), 12 November 1938; 5, Cecil McCormack v Luton T, Division 2, 9 September 1950.

Most Capped Player: Gerry Taggart, 35 (51), Northern Ireland.

Most League Appearances: Barry Murphy, 514, 1962–78.

Youngest League Player: Reuben Noble-Lazarus, 15 years 45 days v Ipswich T, 30 September 2008.

Record Transfer Fee Received: £3,000,000 (rising to £10,125,000) from Everton for John Stones, January 2013.

Record Transfer Fee Paid: £1,500,000 to Partizan Belgrade for Georgi Hristov, July 1997; £1,500,000 to QPR for Mike Sheron, January 1999.

Football League Record: 1898 Elected to Division 2; 1932–34 Division 3 (N); 1934–38 Division 2; 1938–39 Division 3 (N); 1946–53 Division 2; 1953–55 Division 3 (N); 1955–59 Division 2; 1959–65 Division 3; 1965–68 Division 4; 1968–72 Division 3; 1972–79 Division 4; 1979–81 Division 3; 1981–92 Division 2; 1992–97 Division 1; 1997–98 Premier League; 1998–2002 Division 1; 2002–04 Division 2; 2004–06 FL 1; 2006–14 FL C; 2014–16 FL 1; 2016–18 FL C; 2018–19 FL 1; 2019–22 FL C; 2022– FL 1.

LATEST SEQUENCES

Longest Sequence of League Wins: 10, 5.3.1955 – 23.4.1955.

Longest Sequence of League Defeats: 9, 14.3.1953 – 25.4.1953.

Longest Sequence of League Draws: 7, 28.3.1911 – 22.4.1911.

Longest Sequence of Unbeaten League Matches: 21, 1.1.1934 – 5.5.1934.

Longest Sequence Without a League Win: 26, 13.12.1952 – 26.8.1953.

Successive Scoring Runs: 44 from 2.10.1926.

Successive Non-scoring Runs: 6 from 27.11.1971.

MANAGERS

Arthur Fairclough 1898–1901 (*Secretary-Manager*)
John McCartney 1901–04 (*Secretary-Manager*)
Arthur Fairclough 1904–12
John Hastie 1912–14
Percy Lewis 1914–19
Peter Sant 1919–26
John Commins 1926–29
Arthur Fairclough 1929–30
Brough Fletcher 1930–37
Angus Seed 1937–53
Tim Ward 1953–60
Johnny Steele 1960–71 (*continued as General Manager*)
John McSeveney 1971–72
Johnny Steele (*General Manager*) 1972–73
Jim Iley 1973–78
Allan Clarke 1978–80
Norman Hunter 1980–84
Bobby Collins 1984–85
Allan Clarke 1985–89
Mel Machin 1989–93
Viv Anderson 1993–94
Danny Wilson 1994–98
John Hendrie 1998–99
Dave Bassett 1999–2000
Nigel Spackman 2001
Steve Parkin 2001–02
Glyn Hodges 2002–03
Gudjon Thordarson 2003–04
Paul Hart 2004–05
Andy Ritchie 2005–06
Simon Davey 2007–09 (*Caretaker from November 2006*)
Mark Robins 2009–11
Keith Hill 2011–12
David Flitcroft 2012–13
Danny Wilson 2013–15
Lee Johnson 2015–16
Paul Heckingbottom 2016–18
Jose Morais 2018
Daniel Stendel 2018–19
Gerhard Struber 2019–20
Valerien Ismael 2020–21
Markus Schopp 2021
Poya Asbaghi 2021–22
Michael Duff June 2022–

TEN YEAR LEAGUE RECORD

		P	W	D	L	F	A	Pts	Pos
2012-13	FL C	46	14	13	19	56	70	55	21
2013-14	FL C	46	9	12	25	44	77	39	23
2014-15	FL 1	46	17	11	18	62	61	62	11
2015-16	FL 1	46	22	8	16	70	54	74	6
2016-17	FL C	46	15	13	18	64	67	58	14
2017-18	FL C	46	9	14	23	48	72	41	22
2018-19	FL 1	46	26	13	7	80	39	91	2
2019-20	FL C	46	12	13	21	49	69	49	21
2020-21	FL C	46	23	9	14	58	50	78	5
2021-22	FL C	46	6	12	28	33	73	30	24

DID YOU KNOW ?

Mick Butler scored hat-tricks in consecutive games for Barnsley in the 1974–75 season. He netted three in a 4-3 win at Newport County on 15 March and seven days later he scored another three in the 5-3 home victory over Rochdale. He finished the campaign as the Reds' leading scorer with 19 goals.

BARNSLEY – SKY BET CHAMPIONSHIP 2021–22 LEAGUE RECORD

Match No.	Date	Venue	Opponents	Result		H/T Score	Lg Pos.	Goalscorers	Attendance
1	Aug 7	A	Cardiff C	D	1-1	0-0	8	Sibbick [69]	17,431
2	14	H	Coventry C	W	1-0	1-0	9	Frieser [39]	16,961
3	17	H	Luton T	L	0-1	0-1	13		12,999
4	21	A	QPR	D	2-2	2-0	13	Frieser [14], Woodrow [27]	11,882
5	28	H	Birmingham C	D	1-1	1-1	14	Styles [6]	13,950
6	Sept 11	A	Bournemouth	L	0-3	0-1	17		9486
7	15	A	Stoke C	D	1-1	1-1	17	Woodrow [38]	17,832
8	18	H	Blackburn R	D	0-0	0-0	19		13,640
9	25	A	Blackpool	L	0-1	0-1	20		12,698
10	29	H	Nottingham F	L	1-3	1-0	21	Woodrow (pen) [20]	13,657
11	Oct 2	H	Millwall	L	0-1	0-0	22		11,888
12	16	A	Reading	L	0-1	0-0	22		12,199
13	20	A	Middlesbrough	L	0-2	0-1	23		17,931
14	24	H	Sheffield U	L	2-3	0-0	23	Cole [78], Iseka [82]	15,720
15	30	A	Bristol C	L	1-2	1-2	23	Iseka [28]	18,347
16	Nov 3	H	Derby Co	W	2-1	1-1	22	Adeboyejo [39], Iseka [50]	13,786
17	6	H	Hull C	L	0-2	0-1	23		13,003
18	20	A	Fulham	L	1-4	0-2	23	Adeboyejo [78]	18,047
19	24	H	Swansea C	L	0-2	0-0	23		11,342
20	27	A	Peterborough U	D	0-0	0-0	23		12,264
21	Dec 4	H	Huddersfield T	D	1-1	1-1	23	Morris [45]	15,190
22	11	A	Preston NE	L	1-2	0-0	23	Woodrow [65]	11,106
23	17	H	WBA	D	0-0	0-0	23		12,086
24	29	A	Blackburn R	L	1-2	1-1	23	Morris [45]	14,228
25	Jan 22	A	Birmingham C	L	1-2	0-1	24	Adeboyejo [87]	15,742
26	25	A	Nottingham F	L	0-3	0-2	24		27,504
27	29	H	Bournemouth	L	0-1	0-1	24		11,972
28	Feb 2	H	Cardiff C	L	0-1	0-0	24		11,432
29	8	A	Luton T	L	1-2	1-1	24	Morris [44]	9101
30	12	H	QPR	W	1-0	0-0	24	Quina [74]	12,476
31	19	A	Coventry C	L	0-1	0-0	24		17,104
32	22	A	Hull C	W	2-0	2-0	24	Styles [27], Morris [45]	16,421
33	26	H	Middlesbrough	W	3-2	2-0	22	Andersen [7], Bassi 2 [16, 54]	16,107
34	Mar 5	A	Derby Co	L	0-2	0-1	23		25,891
35	8	H	Stoke C	D	1-1	0-0	23	Quina [70]	12,512
36	12	H	Fulham	D	1-1	1-0	22	Morris (pen) [44]	12,576
37	15	H	Bristol C	W	2-0	2-0	22	Morris [10], Helik [21]	11,322
38	19	A	Sheffield U	L	0-2	0-0	22		28,515
39	Apr 2	H	Reading	D	1-1	1-0	22	Morris [5]	14,149
40	9	A	Millwall	L	1-4	0-1	22	Palmer [49]	13,231
41	15	A	Swansea C	D	1-1	0-0	24	Gomes [54]	17,923
42	18	H	Peterborough U	L	0-2	0-1	24		12,197
43	22	A	Huddersfield T	L	1-2	0-2	24	Styles [90]	17,258
44	26	H	Blackpool	L	0-2	0-1	24		12,256
45	30	H	Preston NE	L	1-3	1-1	24	Marsh [16]	13,190
46	May 7	A	WBA	L	0-4	0-2	24		21,515

Final League Position: 24

GOALSCORERS

League (33): Morris 7 (1 pen), Woodrow 4 (1 pen), Adeboyejo 3, Iseka 3, Styles 3, Bassi 2, Frieser 2, Quina 2, Andersen 1, Cole 1, Gomes 1, Helik 1, Marsh 1, Palmer 1, Sibbick 1.
FA Cup (5): Morris 2, Andersen 1, Cole 1, Williams 1.
Carabao Cup (0).

Collins B 40	Sibbick T 11 + 1	Helik M 38	Kitching L 29 + 3	Brittain C 34 + 2	Styles C 40 + 3	Palmer R 24 + 9	Williams B 5	Morris C 26 + 2	Woodrow C 25 + 3	Frieser D 12 + 2	Benson J 14 + 11	Odour C 10 + 10	Moon J 18 + 7	Williams J 17 + 4	Cole D 8 + 16	Adeboyejo V 7 + 19	Halme A 2 + 3	Gomes C 28 + 3	Iseka A 14 + 11	Hondermarck W 3 + 6	Oulare O — + 2	Andersen M 28	Thompson C — + 1	Wolfe M 13 + 3	Bremang D — + 2	Vita R 18 + 1	Marsh A 2 + 2	Quina D 16	Bassi A 14 + 1	Walton J 6 + 1	Christie-Davies I 1 + 1	Sraha J 2	Helliwell J 1 + 1	Match No.
1	2	3	4	5	6	7^{1}	8^{3}	9	10	11^{2}	12	13	14																					1
1	2	3	4	5	6	7^{2}	8^{3}	9^{1}	11	10	13	12		14																				2
1	2	3	4	5	8	6^{3}			10	11^{2}	7	9^{1}			12	13	14																	3
1	2	3	4	5	8	6^{1}			10	9	7^{3}	11^{2}	12		13		14																	4
1	2^{2}	3	4	5	8	6			10	9^{1}	7	11	13			12																		5
1	2^{3}	3		5	7	6	8^{1}		10	9		11^{2}	4				14	12	13															6
1	5^{3}	3		7	8	6^{1}			9	11			4			12	2	13	10^{2}	14														7
1	5^{2}	3		6	8				11	12		9	4			14	2	7^{3}	10^{1}	13														8
1		3	4	5	7	14	8		10	9^{1}	6^{3}	12	2			11^{2}			13															9
1		3	4	5	7	6^{2}			11	9^{1}		10^{3}	2	8		12		14	13															10
1	12	3	4	5	7	6^{1}	8		10	14			2		11^{2}	13			9^{3}															11
1	2	3		5^{3}		6^{2}			11			12	4	8	14	9		7	10^{1}	13														12
1		3		5	7^{1}	12			11			9	4	8		13		6	10^{2}	2^{3}	14													13
1	2	3	4^{3}	5	8				10	11^{1}			7		13	9^{2}		6	12	14														14
1		3	4	5					10		12		7	8	9	13		6^{1}	11^{2}			2												15
1		3		5	8^{1}	14			11		7		4	12	13	9^{2}		6^{3}	10			2												16
1		3	4	5	13	14			11		6^{3}		2	8^{2}	10^{1}	12		7	9															17
1	2	3			6	9^{3}		10^{2}	11	8^{1}	7		14	5		13			12			4												18
1		3		2	8	6^{3}		12	10	9^{2}	7		4	5	11^{1}				13		14													19
1		3	5		8	12		11	10		6^{2}			2^{3}	9^{1}	13		7		14		4												20
1		2	4	5	8^{3}	6^{2}		11	10		13			14		12		7	9^{1}			3												21
1		2	4	5	8^{3}	6		11	10^{2}		13	9^{1}				14		7	12			3												22
1		2	4	8	9			11			7^{1}	13		5	12			6	10^{2}			3												23
1		3^{1}	5	2	9	6		10			7	8^{2}	12		13	14			11^{3}			4												24
1		3	5		8^{3}	6^{2}		10					13	2	12	9		7	11^{1}			4	14											25
1		3			8	7^{1}							2^{3}	5	11	9		6	10^{2}			4		12	13	14								26
1		3			8	6^{1}					12		2	5	10				11			4		7^{2}		9	13							27
1		3	4^{3}		10			12			6^{2}			5	11			7	13			2				9		8^{1}	14					28
1		3	4		5	14		11			6^{3}			13	12			7				2				8^{2}		10	9^{1}					29
1		3			6	12		10			7^{1}			2	13			5				4				9		8^{2}	11					30
1		3		5^{3}	9	6^{1}		10			12		14	2	13			7				4				8^{2}		11						31
1		3		12	8^{3}			11			13			2	14			6				4		7^{2}		5		10	9^{1}					32
1		3	12	13	8			11^{3}						2	14			7				4		6		5^{1}		10	9^{2}					33
1		3	14	2^{3}	8			11			12	13						6^{2}				4		7^{1}		5		10	9					34
1		3	4	5	6^{1}			10							13			7				2		12		8		11	9^{2}					35
1		4	5	2		12		11			13	14						7				3		6^{1}		8^{3}		10	9^{2}					36
1		3	13	2	8^{2}			11^{1}				14			12			7				4		6		5^{3}		10	9					37
1		3		2	9^{1}	13		11							14			6^{3}	12			4		7^{2}		5		10	8					38
1			4	2	8^{1}			11				12				13		6				3		7^{2}		5		10	9					39
1^{1}			4	2	8^{2}	7^{3}		11								13		6	14			3				5		10	9	12				40
			4	2	12	7^{1}		10	13									6				3		8^{2}		5		11	9	1				41
			4	2	8^{3}	6^{2}		11	12							14		7				3		13		5^{1}		10	9	1				42
			4	2	14	6		10	11^{3}										13			3		7^{1}		5		8^{2}	9	1	12			43
			4	5	9			11^{3}	10^{2}				2			12				13		3		7		8	14			1	6^{1}			44
			4		8	7^{1}		11	13			12	2			9				5^{3}				6			10^{2}			1		3	14	45
			4		8				11^{3}		12	9^{2}	2			14				5^{1}				7	13		10			1		3	6	46

FA Cup

Third Round (*aet*)	Barrow	(h)	5-4
Fourth Round	Huddersfield T	(a)	0-1

Carabao Cup

First Round	Bolton W	(a)	0-0

(Bolton W won 5-4 on penalties)

BARROW

FOUNDATION

Barrow was home to a number of junior soccer clubs at the start of the twentieth century before a public meeting was called to set up a senior team in the town. Almost 800 people attended the meeting held in the Drill Hall on the night of Tuesday 16 July 1901 which resulted in the formation of Barrow Association Football Club. A team was put together made up, in the main, of seasoned professionals, some of whom were described as 'bordering the veteran stage' and £300 was spent on laying out the club's new ground. The newly formed Barrow AFC were elected to the Lancashire League for the 1901–02 season and after making a promising start they eventually finished 10th out of 14 clubs.

The Dunes Hotel Stadium, Wilkie Road, Barrow-in-Furness, Cumbria LA14 5UW.

Telephone: (01229) 666010.

Website: www.barrowafc.com

Email: office@barrowafc.com

Ground Capacity: 5,449.

Record Attendance: 16,854 v Swansea T, FA Cup 3rd rd, 9 January 1954.

Pitch Measurements: 101m × 68m (110.5yd × 74.5yd).

Chairman: Paul Hornby.

Directors: Tony Shearer, Kristian Wilkes.

Chief Executive: Levi Gill.

Manager: Pete Wild.

Assistant Manager: Adam Temple.

Colours: Blue shirts with white trim, blue shorts with white trim, white socks with blue trim.

Year Formed: 1901.

Turned Professional: 1908.

Club Nickname: 'The Bluebirds'.

Grounds: 1901, The Strawberry Ground; 1904, Ainslie Street; 1905, Little Park, Roose; 1909, Holker Street (renamed The Progression Solicitors Stadium 2019; The Dunes Hotel Stadium 2021).

First Football League Game (since 2020): 12 September 2020, FL, v Lincoln C (a) L 0–1 – Dixon; Barry, Jones J, Hird, Ntlhe, Brown (Wilson), Jones M, Hardcastle, Beadling (Biggins), Hindle (James), Angus (1 pen).

Record League Victory: 12–1 v Gateshead, Division 3(N), 5 May 1934.

Record League Defeat: 1–10 v Hartlepools U, Division 4, 4 April 1966–67.

HONOURS

League Champions: National League – 2019–20.

FA Cup: 3rd rd – 1946, 1948, 1954, 1956, 1959, 1964, 1967, 1968, 1991, 2009, 2010, 2017, 2022.

League Cup: 3rd rd – 1963, 1968.

FA Trophy Winners: 1989–90, 2009–10.

FOOTBALL YEARBOOK FACT FILE

Barrow were one of the last Football League clubs to install floodlighting. It was not until the 1963–64 season that lights were installed at Holker Street. They were first used in a Division Four match with Doncaster Rovers on 21 October, and then formally inaugurated with a floodlit friendly against Dunfermline Athletic the following Monday, with the visitors winning 7-1.

Most League Points (2 for a win): 59, Division 4, 1966–67.

Most League Points (3 for a win): 50, FL 2, 2020–21.

Most League Goals: 116, Division 3(N), 1933–34.

Highest League Scorer in Season: 39, Jimmy Shankly, Division 3(N), 1933–34.

Most League Goals in One Match: 5, Jimmy Shankly v Gateshead, Division 3(N), 5 May 1934.

Most League Goals in Total Aggregate: Billy Gordon, 145, 1949–58.

Most Capped Player: Harry Panayiotou, 5 (29), Saint Kitts & Nevis.

Most League Appearances: Brian Arrowsmith, 378, 1952–71.

Youngest League Player (since 2020): Jayden Reid, 19 years 181 days v Bolton W, 20 October 2020.

Football League Record: 1921 Original Member of Division 3 (N); 1958–67 Division 4; 1967–70 Division 3; 1970–72 Division 4; 1972 Failed to gain re-election to Football League; 2020 Promoted from National League; 2020– FL 2.

LATEST SEQUENCES

Longest Sequence of League Wins: 4, 6.3.2021 – 20.3.2021.

Longest Sequence of League Defeats: 5, 24.11.2020 – 15.12.2020.

Longest Sequence of League Draws: 2, 5.3.2022 – 12.3.2022.

Longest Sequence of Unbeaten League Matches: 4, 18.9.2021 – 9.10.2021.

Longest Sequence Without a League Win: 9, 9.10.2021 – 27.11.2021.

Successive Scoring Runs: 12 from 21.8.2021.

Successive Non-scoring Runs: 4 from 13.11.2021.

MANAGERS

Jacob Fletcher 1901–04; **E. Freeland** 1904–05; **W. Smith** 1905–06; **Alec Craig** 1906–07; **Roger Charnley** 1907–08; **Jacob Fletcher** 1908–09; **Jas P. Phillips** 1909–13; **John Parker** 1913–20; **William Dickinson** 1920–22; **Jimmy Atkinson** 1922–23; **J. E. Moralee** 1923–26; **Robert Greenhalgh** 1926; **William Dickinson** 1926–27; **John S. Maconnachie** 1927–28; **Andrew Walker** 1929–30; **Thomas Miller** 1930; **John Commins** 1930–32; **Tommy Lowes** 1932–37; **James Y. Bissett** 1937; **Fred Pentland** 1938–40; **John Commins** 1945–47; **Andy Beattie** 1947–49; **Jack Hacking** 1949–55; **Joe Harvey** 1955–57; **Norman Dodgin** 1957–58; **Willie Brown** 1958–59; **Bill Rogers** 1959; **Ron Staniforth** 1959–64; **Don McEvoy** 1964–67; **Colin Appleton** 1967–69; **Fred Else** 1969; **Norman Bodell** 1969–70; **Don McEvoy** 1970–71; **Bill Rogers** 1971; **Jack Crompton** 1971–72; **Peter Kane** 1972–74; **Brian Arrowsmith** 1974–75; **Ron Yeats** 1975–77; **Alan Coglan and Billy McAdams** 1977; **David Hughes** 1977; **Brian McManus** 1977–79; **Micky Taylor** 1979–83; **Vic Halom** 1983–84; **Peter McDonnell** 1984; **Joe Wojciechowicz** 1984; **Brian Kidd** 1984–85; **John Cooke** 1985; **Bob Murphy** 1985; **Maurice Whittle** 1985; **David Johnson** 1985–86; **Glenn Skivington and Neil McDonald** 1986; **Ray Wilkie** 1986; **Neil McDonald** 1991; **John King** 1991–92; **Graham Heathcote** 1992; **Richard Dinnis** 1992–93; **Mick Cloudsdale** 1993–94; **Tony Hesketh** 1994–96; **Neil McDonald and Franny Ventre** 1996; **Mike Walsh** 1996; **Owen Brown** 1996–99; **Shane Westley** 1999; **Greg Challender** 1999; **Kenny Lowe** 1999–2003; **Lee Turnbull** 2003–05; **Darren Edmondson** 2005; **Phil Wilson** 2005–07; **Darren Sheridan and David Bayliss** 2007–12; **David Bayliss** 2012–13; **Alex Meechan** 2013; **Darren Edmondson** 2013–15; **Paul Cox** 2015–17; **Micky Moore** 2017; **Neill Hornby** 2017; **Ady Pennock** 2017–18; **Ian Evatt** 2018–20; **David Dunn** 2020; **Michael Jolly** 2020; **Mark Cooper** 2021–22; **Phil Brown** 2022; **Pete Wild** May 2022–

TEN YEAR LEAGUE RECORD

		P	W	D	L	F	A	Pts	Pos
2012-13	NL	46	11	13	22	45	83	46	22
2013-14	NLN	42	14	14	14	50	56	56	11
2014-15	NLN	42	26	9	7	81	43	87	1
2015-16	NL	46	17	14	15	64	71	65	11
2016-17	NL	46	20	15	11	72	53	75	7
2017-18	NL	46	11	16	19	51	63	49	20
2018-19	NL	46	17	13	16	52	51	64	11
2019-20	NL	37	21	7	9	68	39	70	1§
2020-21	FL 2	46	13	11	22	53	59	50	21
2021-22	FL 2	46	10	14	22	44	57	44	22

§Decided on points-per-game (1.89)

DID YOU KNOW ?

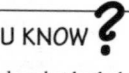

Barrow have played at both the 'old' and 'new' Wembley stadiums, both games being in the FA Trophy final. In May 1990 they defeated Leek Town in front of an attendance of 19,011 and 20 years later they beat Stevenage Borough 2-1 in extra time, with 21,223 fans present.

BARROW – SKY BET LEAGUE TWO 2021–22 LEAGUE RECORD

Match No.	Date	Venue	Opponents	Result		H/T Score	Lg Pos.	Goalscorers	Attendance
1	Aug 7	A	Stevenage	L	0-1	0-0	19		2536
2	14	H	Hartlepool U	W	3-2	1-1	12	Zanzala 3, Gordon 47, Sea 72	2846
3	17	H	Exeter C	D	0-0	0-0	10		2667
4	21	A	Harrogate T	L	1-2	1-0	16	Zanzala 17	1564
5	28	H	Bristol R	D	1-1	1-1	18	Banks 45	2116
6	Sept 4	A	Oldham Ath	W	3-0	1-0	9	Banks 15, Zanzala 53, Grayson 57	4232
7	10	H	Colchester U	L	2-3	1-2	10	Stevens 25, Banks (pen) 76	2430
8	18	A	Bradford C	D	1-1	1-0	15	Kay 21	15,403
9	24	H	Newport Co	W	2-1	0-1	8	Kay 63, Gordon 78	2427
10	Oct 2	A	Mansfield T	W	1-0	0-0	7	Banks (pen) 55	3951
11	9	H	Leyton Orient	D	1-1	0-0	11	Gotts 48	3374
12	16	A	Port Vale	L	1-3	1-0	13	Banks 33	5951
13	19	H	Scunthorpe U	D	1-1	0-1	11	Gotts 80	2739
14	23	A	Walsall	D	2-2	1-1	13	Williams 36, Gordon 90	4508
15	30	H	Rochdale	L	1-2	0-1	15	Banks 56	3366
16	Nov 13	A	Carlisle U	D	0-0	0-0	16		7470
17	20	H	Crawley T	L	0-1	0-0	19		3429
18	23	A	Forest Green R	L	0-2	0-0	20		1842
19	27	A	Sutton U	L	0-1	0-1	20		2678
20	Dec 11	H	Swindon T	W	2-0	0-0	19	Banks (pen) 62, Gordon (pen) 87	2863
21	26	A	Tranmere R	L	0-2	0-1	19		3500
22	29	H	Oldham Ath	D	0-0	0-0	19		3495
23	Jan 1	H	Bradford C	L	1-2	0-1	19	Gordon 52	3463
24	15	A	Colchester U	W	2-0	0-0	19	Dallison (og) 53, Kay 90	2297
25	22	H	Mansfield T	L	1-3	1-2	21	Jones, J 17	3224
26	25	H	Salford C	L	0-2	0-0	21		3510
27	29	A	Newport Co	L	1-2	0-2	21	Demetriou (og) 62	4080
28	Feb 1	A	Northampton T	W	1-0	0-0	20	Amadi-Holloway 51	4604
29	5	H	Tranmere R	D	1-1	0-1	19	Banks (pen) 58	3699
30	8	A	Hartlepool U	L	1-3	1-3	19	Rooney 17	4621
31	12	H	Stevenage	D	0-0	0-0	20		3001
32	26	H	Harrogate T	D	0-0	0-0	20		2974
33	Mar 1	A	Bristol R	L	0-1	0-0	22		6685
34	5	H	Walsall	D	1-1	1-0	22	Rooney 35	3439
35	12	A	Rochdale	D	0-0	0-0	21		2935
36	15	A	Scunthorpe U	W	1-0	1-0	21	Rooney 44	2009
37	19	H	Carlisle U	L	1-2	0-1	21	Banks 78	4658
38	26	A	Leyton Orient	L	0-2	0-0	21		6032
39	Apr 2	H	Port Vale	L	1-2	1-0	21	Kay 24	3215
40	9	A	Crawley T	L	0-1	0-0	21		2081
41	15	H	Forest Green R	W	4-0	2-0	21	Grayson 5, Rooney 38, Platt 53, Amadi-Holloway 90	3098
42	18	A	Salford C	D	2-2	0-1	21	Gordon 66, Amadi-Holloway 83	2575
43	23	H	Sutton U	W	1-0	0-0	21	Rooney 68	3019
44	26	A	Exeter C	L	1-2	1-1	21	Dawson (og) 11	7860
45	30	A	Swindon T	L	1-2	0-1	21	Platt 83	13,355
46	May 7	H	Northampton T	L	1-3	1-3	22	Kay 45	4603

Final League Position: 22

GOALSCORERS

League (44): Banks 9 (4 pens), Gordon 6 (1 pen), Kay 5, Rooney 5, Amadi-Holloway 3, Zanzala 3, Gotts 2, Grayson 2, Platt 2, Jones, J 1, Sea 1, Stevens 1, Williams 1, own goals 3.
FA Cup (10): Banks 2 (1 pen), Stevens 2, Driscoll-Glennon 1, Gordon 1, Gotts 1, Jones J 1, Kay 1, Zanzala 1.
Carabao Cup (1): Sea 1.
Papa John's Trophy (4): Arthur 1, Banks 1 (1 pen), Stevens 1, Zanzala 1.

Farman P 46	Platt M 24 + 4	Ellis M 14 + 2	Ntlhe K 3 + 2	Hutton R 37 + 7	Taylor J 10 + 2	Banks O 37 + 2	Grayson J 23 + 3	Brough P 40 + 1	Gordon J 29 + 7	Kay J 20 + 14	Arthur F 4 + 5	Devitt J — + 4	Sea D — + 10	White T 23 + 4	Williams G 5 + 13	Zanzala O 15 + 4	Brown C 19 + 2	James L 6 + 13	Jones J 19 + 6	Gotts R 34 + 1	Stevens J 16 + 3	Jones M 3	Beadling T 10 + 2	Driscoll-Glennon A 12 + 3	Harris W 5 + 4	Wakeling J 2 + 2	Amadi-Holloway A 14	Rooney J 19	Canavan N 17 + 1	Match No.
1	2^1	3	4	5	6	7	8^3	9	10	11^2	12	13	14																	1
1		3	4	5		7		9	10	13	2^3		12^4	6	8^2	11^1	14	15												2
1		3		5	14	6	4	8	9	11^1				7^3	12	10^2	2	13												3
1		3	12	5		6	4^4	8	9	11^3	15			7^2	13	10^1	2	14												4
1		3■	14	5		7	4	9	10	8^1				6	13	11^3	2^2		12											5
1				5	3	6	4	8	10	13	14			12		11^2			2	7^1	9^3									6
1				5	3^1	6	4	8	10^2	13			12			11			2■	7	9									7
1				2	7	4		5	8	10	3		12		13	11^1				6^2	9									8
1		3		5		2	4^3	8	9	10^2			12		13	11^1			14	7	6									9
1		3		5	13	6^2	4	8	10	11^1						12			2	7	9									10
1		3		5			4	8	10	12				6^1	13	11^2			2	7	9									11
1		3		5		7^1	4^2	8	11	14				6	12	13			2	10	9^3									12
1		3		5		6	4	8	10	12			14		13	11^3			2^1	7	9^2									13
1		3		2		7	4	5	10	11				12	9^1			13		8	6^2									14
1	12	3^3		5		6	4	8	11	10	14				9^2		2^1	13		7										15
1	3			13		6	4	8	10^1	12						11^3	5^2	14	2	7	9									16
1	3			5		7	4	9		13				12		11		10^1	2	8		6^2								17
1	3			5		6	4	8	9	11	12					10			2	7^1										18
1	3	13		12		6	4		5^2	8				7		11			2	10	9^1									19
1	12	3^1		14		6	4	8	13					7		11^2	5		2	10	9^3									20
1		3		5^3	2		4		11	13				6		12	8^1	14		10	9	7^2								21
1	3						4^2	8	11	13	2			6		12	5			10^3	9	7^1	14							22
1	4	14		6		7		5	11	9^3	3		12	8			2^2				13		10^1							23
1	3			5		6		4		12		13		7				9	2					8	10^2	11^1				24
1	3			5		6		4		14		12		7^1				10^2	2	9^3				8	11	13				25
1	3		8^2	5		6		4		10		14		7^3				13	2		9^1				11	12				26
1	3^1			5		6		4						7^2			12	11	2				9	8	13		10			27
1				5	7	6		4		13^3							2	11^2	14				3	8	12		10^1	9		28
1				5	7	6		4									2	11^2					3^1	8	13		10	9	12	29
1				5	7^1	6		4							14		2	13		12				8		11^2	10^3	9	3	30
1	14			13		6		4						7^1			5^2	12	2	9				8^3			11■	10	3	31
1				5		6		4	11^1					7					2	9				8	12			10	3	32
1	14			13	6	10		4	12					7^1					2	5				8^3	11^2			9	3■	33
1	4			12		6		8	10					7^2					2	5	13				11^1			9	3	34
1	3			2^2		6		5					14	7^1	10^3					8			13	12			11	9	4	35
1	2					6		4	11											5			7■	8			10	9	3	36
1	2			12		6		4	10				14	7^2						5	13			8^1			11^3	9	3	37
1	2			5	7^1	6		4	10^2	13				12						9^3				14			11	8	3	38
1	3			2		7	12		13	10^1								14		8			6	5^2			11	9^3	4	39
1	3			2		6	5		12	10^3								14	13	8^2			7				11	9^1	4	40
1	3			8^3			5^1	12	13	10^2					14		2			7			6				11	9	4	41
1	3			8^1				5	13	10^2					12		2^3		14	7			6				11	9	4	42
1	4			8			13	5	12	10■				7^2			2			6							11^1	9	3	43
1	3			8		13		5	11				14	7^2	10^1		2^3	12		6								9	4	44
1	3			9		12	13	5	10	11					14		2^1			6^3			8^2					7	4	45
1	3			8^2			5		11	9					13		2^3		14	7	10^1			12				6	4	46

FA Cup

First Round	Banbury U	(a)	4-0
Second Round	Ipswich T	(a)	0-0
Replay	Ipswich T	(h)	2-0
Third Round *(aet)*	Barnsley	(a)	4-5

Carabao Cup

First Round	Scunthorpe U	(h)	1-0
Second Round	Aston Villa	(h)	0-6

Papa John's Trophy

Group G (N)	Accrington S	(a)	2-2
(Accrington S won 5-4 on penalties)			
Group G (N)	Fleetwood T	(h)	1-3
Group G (N)	Leicester C U21	(h)	1-0

BIRMINGHAM CITY

FOUNDATION

In 1875, cricketing enthusiasts who were largely members of Trinity Church, Bordesley, determined to continue their sporting relationships throughout the year by forming a football club which they called Small Heath Alliance. For their earliest games played on waste land in Arthur Street, the team included three Edden brothers and two James brothers.

St Andrew's Trillion Trophy Stadium, Cattell Road, Birmingham B9 4RL.

Telephone: (0121) 772 0101.

Ticket Office: (0121) 772 0101 (option 2).

Website: www.bcfc.com

Email: reception@bcfc.com

Ground Capacity: 29,805.

Record Attendance: 66,844 v Everton, FA Cup 5th rd, 11 February 1939.

Pitch Measurements: 100m × 65m (109.5yd × 71yd).

Directors: Wenqing Zhao, Chun Kong Yiu, Gannan Zheng, Yao Wang.

Head Coach: John Eustace.

Assistant Head Coaches: Keith Downing, Matt Gardiner.

Colours: Blue shirts with white trim, white shorts with blue trim, blue socks.

Year Formed: 1875.

Turned Professional: 1885.

Previous Names: 1875, Small Heath Alliance; 1888, dropped 'Alliance'; 1905, Birmingham; 1945, Birmingham City.

Club Nickname: 'Blues'.

Grounds: 1875, waste ground near Arthur St; 1877, Muntz St, Small Heath; 1906, St Andrew's (renamed St Andrew's Trillion Trophy Stadium 2018).

First Football League Game: 3 September 1892, Division 2, v Burslem Port Vale (h) W 5–1 – Charsley; Bayley, Speller; Ollis, Jenkyns, Devey; Hallam (1), Edwards (1), Short (1), Wheldon (2), Hands.

Record League Victory: 12–0 v Walsall T Swifts, Division 2, 17 December 1892 – Charsley; Bayley, Jones; Ollis, Jenkyns, Devey; Hallam (2), Walton (3), Mobley (3), Wheldon (2), Hands (2). 12–0 v Doncaster R, Division 2, 11 April 1903 – Dorrington; Goldie, Wassell; Beer, Dougherty (1), Howard; Athersmith, Leonard (4), McRoberts (1), Wilcox (4), Field (1), (1 og).

Record Cup Victory: 9–2 v Burton W, FA Cup 1st rd, 31 October 1885 – Hedges; Jones, Evetts (1); Fred James, Felton, Arthur James (1); Davenport (2), Stanley (4), Simms, Figures, Morris (1).

Record Defeat: 1–9 v Blackburn R, Division 1, 5 January 1895; 1–9 v Sheffield W, Division 1, 13 December 1930; 0–8 v Bournemouth, FLC, 25 October 2014.

HONOURS

League Champions: Division 2 – 1892–93, 1920–21, 1947–48, 1954–55; Second Division – 1994–95.
Runners-up: FL C – 2006–07, 2008–09; Division 2 – 1893–94, 1900–01, 1902–03; 1971–72, 1984–85; Division 3 – 1991–92.

FA Cup: *Runners-up:* 1931, 1956.

League Cup Winners: 1963, 2011.
Runners-up: 2001.

League Trophy Winners: 1991, 1995.

European Competitions
Fairs Cup: 1955–58, 1958–60 *(runners-up)*, 1960–61 *(runners-up)*, 1961–62.
Europa League: 2011–12.

FOOTBALL YEARBOOK FACT FILE

Birmingham City were the first British club to reach the final of a European competition. They did so in the now defunct Inter-Cities Fairs Cup tournament for 1958–60, defeating a Cologne XI, a Zagreb XI and Union Saint-Gilloise before losing out to Barcelona in the final which was played over two legs.

Most League Points (2 for a win): 59, Division 2, 1947–48.

Most League Points (3 for a win): 89, Division 2, 1994–95.

Most League Goals: 103, Division 2, 1893–94 (only 28 games).

Highest League Scorer in Season: Walter Abbott, 34, Division 2, 1898–99 (Small Heath); Joe Bradford, 29, Division 1, 1927–28 (Birmingham City).

Most League Goals in Total Aggregate: Joe Bradford, 249, 1920–35.

Most League Goals in One Match: 5, Walter Abbott v Darwen, Division 2, 26 November, 1898; 5, John McMillan v Blackpool, Division 2, 2 March 1901; 5, James Windridge v Glossop, Division 2, 23 January 1915.

Most Capped Player: Maik Taylor, 58 (including 4 on loan at Fulham) (88), Northern Ireland.

Most League Appearances: Frank Womack, 491, 1908–28.

Youngest League Player: Jude Bellingham, 16 years 57 days v Swansea C, 25 August 2019.

Record Transfer Fee Received: £20,000,000 from Borussia Dortmund for Jude Bellingham, July 2020.

Record Transfer Fee Paid: £7,000,000 to Dinamo Zagreb for Ivan Sunjic, July 2019.

Football League Record: 1892 Elected to Division 2; 1894–96 Division 1; 1896–1901 Division 2; 1901–02 Division 1; 1902–03 Division 2; 1903–08 Division 1; 1908–21 Division 2; 1921–39 Division 1; 1946–48 Division 2; 1948–50 Division 1; 1950–55 Division 2; 1955–65 Division 1; 1965–72 Division 2; 1972–79 Division 1; 1979–80 Division 2; 1980–84 Division 1; 1984–85 Division 2; 1985–86 Division 1; 1986–89 Division 2; 1989–92 Division 3; 1992–94 Division 1; 1994–95 Division 2; 1995–2002 Division 1; 2002–06 Premier League; 2006–07 FL C; 2007–08 Premier League; 2008–09 FL C; 2009–11 Premier League; 2011– FL C.

LATEST SEQUENCES

Longest Sequence of League Wins: 13, 17.12.1892 – 16.9.1893.

Longest Sequence of League Defeats: 8, 28.9.1985 – 23.11.1985.

Longest Sequence of League Draws: 8, 18.9.1990 – 23.10.1990.

Longest Sequence of Unbeaten League Matches: 20, 3.9.1994 – 2.1.1995.

Longest Sequence Without a League Win: 17, 28.9.1985 – 18.1.1986.

Successive Scoring Runs: 24 from 24.9.1892.

Successive Non-scoring Runs: 6 from 18.9.2021.

MANAGERS

Alfred Jones 1892–1908 (*Secretary-Manager*)
Alec Watson 1908–10
Bob McRoberts 1910–15
Frank Richards 1915–23
Billy Beer 1923–27
William Harvey 1927–28
Leslie Knighton 1928–33
George Liddell 1933–39
William Camkin and Ted Goodier 1939–45
Harry Storer 1945–48
Bob Brocklebank 1949–54
Arthur Turner 1954–58
Pat Beasley 1959–60
Gil Merrick 1960–64
Joe Mallett 1964–65
Stan Cullis 1965–70
Fred Goodwin 1970–75
Willie Bell 1975–77
Sir Alf Ramsay 1977–78
Jim Smith 1978–82
Ron Saunders 1982–86
John Bond 1986–87
Garry Pendrey 1987–89
Dave Mackay 1989–91
Lou Macari 1991
Terry Cooper 1991–93
Barry Fry 1993–96
Trevor Francis 1996–2001
Steve Bruce 2001–07
Alex McLeish 2007–11
Chris Hughton 2011–12
Lee Clark 2012–14
Gary Rowett 2014–16
Gianfranco Zola 2016–17
Harry Redknapp 2017
Steve Cotterill 2017–18
Garry Monk 2018–19
Pep Clotet 2019–20
Aitor Karanka 2020–21
Lee Bowyer 2021–22
John Eustace July 2022–

TEN YEAR LEAGUE RECORD

		P	W	D	L	F	A	Pts	Pos
2012-13	FL C	46	15	16	15	63	69	61	12
2013-14	FL C	46	11	11	24	58	74	44	21
2014-15	FL C	46	16	15	15	54	64	63	10
2015-16	FL C	46	16	15	15	53	49	63	10
2016-17	FL C	46	13	14	19	45	64	53	19
2017-18	FL C	46	13	7	26	38	68	46	19
2018-19	FL C	46	14	19	13	64	58	52*	17
2019-20	FL C	46	12	14	20	54	75	50	20
2020-21	FL C	46	13	13	20	37	61	52	18
2021-22	FL C	46	11	14	21	50	75	47	20

** 9 pts deducted.*

DID YOU KNOW ?

Alex Govan scored three hat-tricks in a spell of 11 days for Birmingham City in the opening weeks of the 1956–57 campaign. He achieved this feat with strikes at Portsmouth and at home to Newcastle United and Preston North End, although he failed to score at Burnley in the middle of his sequence.

BIRMINGHAM CITY – SKY BET CHAMPIONSHIP 2021–22 LEAGUE RECORD

Match No.	Date	Venue	Opponents	Result	H/T Score	Lg Pos.	Goalscorers	Attendance
1	Aug 7	A	Sheffield U	W 1-0	1-0	5	Colin [19]	29,043
2	14	H	Stoke C	D 0-0	0-0	10		10,189
3	18	H	Bournemouth	L 0-2	0-0	14		9922
4	21	A	Luton T	W 5-0	2-0	8	Marc Roberts [7], Hogan 2 [26, 47], Gardner [84], Aneke [88]	10,014
5	28	A	Barnsley	D 1-1	1-1	8	Jutkiewicz [33]	13,950
6	Sept 10	H	Derby Co	W 2-0	1-0	4	Hogan [31], Bela [81]	14,912
7	15	H	Fulham	L 1-4	0-2	10	Deeney (pen) [87]	14,562
8	18	A	Peterborough U	L 0-3	0-2	11		12,199
9	25	H	Preston NE	D 0-0	0-0	12		14,925
10	28	A	QPR	L 0-2	0-1	13		12,257
11	Oct 2	H	Nottingham F	L 0-3	0-2	16		15,148
12	15	A	WBA	L 0-1	0-0	16		24,870
13	20	A	Huddersfield T	D 0-0	0-0	19		15,618
14	23	H	Swansea C	W 2-1	0-0	17	Deeney [47], McGree [82]	16,132
15	30	A	Middlesbrough	W 2-0	0-0	14	Marc Roberts [53], Hogan [56]	21,582
16	Nov 2	H	Bristol C	W 3-0	1-0	13	McGree [14], Hogan [68], Gardner [76]	16,143
17	6	H	Reading	L 1-2	1-0	15	Hogan [3]	17,535
18	20	A	Hull C	L 0-2	0-1	15		12,409
19	23	A	Coventry C	D 0-0	0-0	17		22,676
20	27	H	Blackpool	W 1-0	0-0	13	Jutkiewicz [81]	17,686
21	Dec 4	A	Millwall	L 1-3	0-2	16	Deeney [56]	14,324
22	11	H	Cardiff C	D 2-2	2-0	15	Deeney [29], Sunjic [45]	17,840
23	18	A	Blackburn R	L 0-4	0-1	17		12,148
24	Jan 2	H	QPR	L 1-2	0-1	18	Aneke [75]	18,279
25	15	A	Preston NE	D 1-1	0-1	18	Hogan [86]	12,821
26	18	A	Fulham	L 2-6	1-4	18	Sunjic [45], Gardner [74]	16,491
27	22	H	Barnsley	W 2-1	1-0	18	Hernandez [34], Hogan [51]	15,742
28	25	H	Peterborough U	D 2-2	0-1	18	Gardner [85], Hogan [88]	16,380
29	30	A	Derby Co	D 2-2	1-0	17	Taylor [7], Hogan [56]	32,211
30	Feb 4	H	Sheffield U	L 1-2	0-0	17	Taylor [61]	17,194
31	9	A	Bournemouth	L 1-3	0-2	18	Hernandez [69]	8708
32	12	H	Luton T	W 3-0	1-0	17	Bacuna [25], Taylor [46], Hernandez [69]	17,292
33	19	A	Stoke C	D 2-2	1-1	18	James [12], Gardner [58]	23,502
34	22	A	Reading	L 1-2	0-0	18	McIntyre (og) [82]	12,073
35	26	H	Huddersfield T	L 0-2	0-2	19		17,318
36	Mar 5	A	Bristol C	W 2-1	2-0	18	Chong [2], Gordon [13]	21,942
37	12	H	Hull C	D 0-0	0-0	19		17,231
38	15	H	Middlesbrough	L 0-2	0-1	19		15,852
39	19	A	Swansea C	D 0-0	0-0	19		18,620
40	Apr 3	H	WBA	W 1-0	0-0	18	Taylor (pen) [67]	17,936
41	9	A	Nottingham F	L 0-2	0-1	18		29,293
42	15	H	Coventry C	L 2-4	2-2	20	Pedersen [12], Gardner [39]	17,634
43	18	A	Blackpool	L 1-6	0-3	20	Sunjic [63]	13,993
44	23	H	Millwall	D 2-2	0-0	20	Bacuna [47], Taylor (pen) [79]	17,206
45	30	A	Cardiff C	D 1-1	1-0	20	Bela [22]	21,395
46	May 7	H	Blackburn R	L 1-2	0-2	20	Pedersen [78]	18,659

Final League Position: 20

GOALSCORERS

League (50): Hogan 10, Gardner 6, Taylor 5 (2 pens), Deeney 4 (1 pen), Hernandez 3, Sunjic 3, Aneke 2, Bacuna 2, Bela 2, Jutkiewicz 2, McGree 2, Pedersen 2, Marc Roberts 2, Chong 1, Colin 1, Gordon 1, James 1, own goal 1.
FA Cup (0).
Carabao Cup (1): Oakley 1.

Sarkic M 23	Roberts Marc 39	Dean H 14 + 1	Pedersen K 37	Colin M 31 + 2	Gardner G 31 + 4	Woods R 25 + 5	Chong T 18 + 2	Bela J 26 + 5	Hogan S 28 + 8	Jutkiewicz L 17 + 19	Leko J 1 + 3	Sunjic I 33 + 8	Castillo J 1 + 2	Aneke C 1 + 17	Ivan Sanchez A — + 2	Deeney T 15 + 6	Sanderson D 14 + 1	Friend G 11 + 3	McGree R 10 + 3	Graham J 18 + 6	James J 13 + 7	Roberts Mitchell 1	Oakley M 2	Etheridge N 21	Hall G 1 + 1	Mengi T 9	Hernandez O 21 + 1	Bellingham J — + 2	Bacuna J 16 + 1	Taylor L 14	Gordon N 11	Richards T 2 + 4	Trueman C — + 1	Jeacock Z 2	Match No.
1	2	3	4	5	6	7^{3}	8^{2}	9	10^{1}	11	12	13	14																						1
1	3	4	5	2	9	7		8	11^{1}	10^{2}	13	6		12																					2
1	2	3	4	5	6	7	9^{3}	8	13	11^{1}	10^{2}			12	14																				3
1	2	3	4	5	14	6	9^{2}	8	10^{1}	11^{3}		7		12	13																				4
1	2	3	4	5		6	9	8	10^{1}	11^{2}	13	7		12																					5
1	2	3	4	5	13	7	9	8	11^{2}	10^{1}		6				12																			6
1	2	3	4	5	13	7	9^{3}	8^{2}	11^{1}	10		6		14		12																			7
1	3^{2}	4	5	2	8■	7	6	9^{1}		11^{3}		13		14		10	12																		8
1		3		5		6	9	8	10^{1}	13		7		12		11^{2}	2	4																	9
1	2^{3}	3		5		6	9	8	11^{2}	12		7		13		10^{1}	4		14																10
1	2	3	4	5		6	9	8^{1}	10^{2}	11		7^{3}		12		14			13																11
1	3		8	5^{1}	6		9	12	11^{2}	10		7		13			2	4^{3}		14															12
1	3		9		6		11			10^{1}		8				12	2	4	7	5															13
1	3		8		6		10		9^{1}			7		13		11^{2}	2	4	12	5															14
1	3		8^{2}		7			13	10	12		6				11^{1}	2	4	9	5															15
1	3	12			6			8	11	13		7				10^{2}	2^{1}	4	9	5^{3}	14														16
1	3	2			7	12		8	10	13		6^{3}		14		11			9^{1}			4	5^{2}												17
1	3	4^{1}			9■	6		8	10^{3}	13		7		14		11^{2}	2		5		12														18
1	3	4				6■		8	10^{2}	13		7	12			11^{3}	2		9		14		5^{1}												19
1	3		4					9^{1}	10	13		7		12		11^{2}	2		8	5	6														20
	3		4					9^{1}	10^{2}	12		7		13		11	2		8	5	6			1											21
1	3		8						10^{1}	13		7		12		11^{2}	2	4	9	5	6														22
1	3^{1}		9	13				12		14		7		10^{3}		11	2	4	8	5^{2}	6														23
1			4	5	6^{2}	12			14			7	9^{1}	13		10	2	3			8				11^{3}										24
	3		4	5	6	12		9^{3}	14	11		8^{1}									7			1		2	10^{2}	13							25
	4^{2}		5	2	7	8		6	13	10^{1}		9						12			14			1		3	11^{3}								26
	4		5	2	6^{3}	7		13	10	11		12						14			8^{1}			1		3	9^{2}								27
	4		5^{1}	2	13	7		12	11	8		6^{2}								14	9^{3}			1		3	10								28
	4		5	2	8	7^{1}			11			12						13			14			1		3	9		6^{3}	10^{2}					29
	4		5	2	9	6			10^{2}	12										13				1		3	8^{1}		7	11					30
			4	2	7	14		8	11^{1}	12		6								5^{3}				1		3^{2}	13		9	10					31
			4	2	6	7		8^{3}		12		13								5	14			1		3	11		9^{2}	10^{1}					32
			4	3	8	7		5		12		13								2	6^{2}			1			11		9^{1}	10					33
			4	3	7	6		5		12										2	8^{1}			1			11		9	10					34
			4	3^{1}	7	8	13	5		10		12								2	9^{2}			1			11		6						35
	4		5		7		11		12			8								2				1			6^{1}		9	10	3				36
	3		4		6	12	10					8^{1}								5				1			9		7^{2}	11	2	13			37
	3		9■		8^{3}	7	13		12	10										5				1		4^{1}	11		14		2	6^{2}			38
	3			4	6		11		10			8								5				1			9		7^{1}		2	12			39
	3		8	2	7		9^{1}		10	14		13												1			5		6^{2}	11^{3}	4	12			40
	3		9	4	6				11^{3}	14		7				15				13				1^{1}			5^{2}		8		2	10^{4}	12		41
	3		4	5	7	6			11^{3}	14						12											8		9^{1}	10	2^{2}	13		1	42
	4		5	12		7			13			8				10^{2}				2^{1}	6						9			11	3			1	43
	3			5	6			8^{1}				7						4		12				1			11		9	10	2				44
	3			5	7			8^{2}				6						4		13	12			1			11		9^{1}	10	2				45
	3		5	2			7^{1}		14			6									8			1	12		10	13	9^{2}	11^{3}	4				46

FA Cup
Third Round *(aet)* Plymouth Arg (h) 0-1

Carabao Cup
First Round Colchester U (h) 1-0
Second Round Fulham (h) 0-2

BLACKBURN ROVERS

FOUNDATION

It was in 1875 that some public school old boys called a meeting at which the Blackburn Rovers club was formed and the colours blue and white adopted. The leading light was John Lewis, later to become a founder of the Lancashire FA, a famous referee who was in charge of two FA Cup finals, and a vice-president of both the FA and the Football League.

Ewood Park, Blackburn, Lancashire BB2 4JF.

Telephone: (01254) 372 001.

Ticket Office: (01254) 372 000.

Website: www.rovers.co.uk

Email: enquiries@rovers.co.uk

Ground Capacity: 31,363.

Record Attendance: 62,522 v Bolton W, FA Cup 6th rd, 2 March 1929.

Pitch Measurements: 105m × 66.84m (115yd × 72yd).

Chief Executive: Steve Waggott.

Manager: Jon Dahl Tomasson.

Assistant Manager: Remy Reijnierse.

Colours: Blue and white halved shirts with blue trim, white shorts with blue trim, blue socks with white trim.

Year Formed: 1875.

Turned Professional: 1880.

Club Nickname: 'Rovers'.

Grounds: 1875, all matches played away; 1876, Oozehead Ground; 1877, Pleasington Cricket Ground; 1878, Alexandra Meadows; 1881, Leamington Road; 1890, Ewood Park.

First Football League Game: 15 September 1888, Football League, v Accrington (h) D 5–5 – Arthur; Beverley, James Southworth; Douglas, Almond, Forrest; Beresford (1), Walton, John Southworth (1), Fecitt (1), Townley (2).

Record League Victory: 9–0 v Middlesbrough, Division 2, 6 November 1954 – Elvy; Suart, Eckersley; Clayton, Kelly, Bell; Mooney (3), Crossan (2), Briggs, Quigley (3), Langton (1).

Record Cup Victory: 11–0 v Rossendale, FA Cup 1st rd, 13 October 1884 – Arthur; Hopwood, McIntyre; Forrest, Blenkhorn, Lofthouse; Sowerbutts (2), Jimmy Brown (1), Fecitt (4), Barton (3), Birtwistle (1).

Record Defeat: 0–8 v Arsenal, Division 1, 25 February 1933; 0–8 v Lincoln C, Division 2, 29 August 1953.

HONOURS

League Champions: Premier League – 1994–95; Division 1 – 1911–12, 1913–14; Division 2 – 1938–39; Division 3 – 1974–75.
Runners-up: Premier League – 1993–94; FL 1 – 2017–18; First Division – 2000–01; Division 2 – 1957–58; Division 3 – 1979–80.

FA Cup Winners: 1884, 1885, 1886, 1890, 1891, 1928.
Runners-up: 1882, 1960.

League Cup Winners: 2002.

Full Members' Cup Winners: 1987.

European Competitions
European Cup: 1995–96.
UEFA Cup: 1994–95, 1998–99, 2002–03, 2003–04, 2006–07, 2007–08.
Intertoto Cup: 2007.

FOOTBALL YEARBOOK FACT FILE

Blackburn Rovers were badly affected by the 'Big Freeze' in the winter of 1962–63 and managed to play just one competitive fixture between 22 December and 5 March. To help the players retain match fitness two friendly fixtures were played at Morecambe in February, with Rovers beating both Bury and Huddersfield Town 1-0.

Most League Points (2 for a win): 60, Division 3, 1974–75.

Most League Points (3 for a win): 96, FL 1, 2017–18.

Most League Goals: 114, Division 2, 1954–55.

Highest League Scorer in Season: Ted Harper, 43, Division 1, 1925–26.

Most League Goals in Total Aggregate: Simon Garner, 168, 1978–92.

Most League Goals in One Match: 7, Tommy Briggs v Bristol R, Division 2, 5 February 1955.

Most Capped Player: Morten Gamst Pedersen, 69 (83), Norway.

Most League Appearances: Derek Fazackerley, 596, 1970–86.

Youngest League Player: Harry Dennison, 16 years 155 days v Bristol C, 8 April 1911.

Record Transfer Fee Received: £18,000,000 from Manchester C for Roque Santa Cruz, June 2009.

Record Transfer Fee Paid: £3,000,000 (rising to £10,000,000) to Arsenal for David Bentley, January 2006.

Football League Record: 1888 Founder Member of the League; 1936–39 Division 2; 1946–48 Division 1; 1948–58 Division 2; 1958–66 Division 1; 1966–71 Division 2; 1971–75 Division 3; 1975–79 Division 2; 1979–80 Division 3; 1980–92 Division 2; 1992–99 Premier League; 1999–2001 Division 1; 2001–12 Premier League; 2012–17 FL C; 2017–18 FL 1; 2018– FL C.

LATEST SEQUENCES

Longest Sequence of League Wins: 8, 1.3.1980 – 7.4.1980.

Longest Sequence of League Defeats: 7, 12.3.1966 – 16.4.1966.

Longest Sequence of League Draws: 5, 11.10.1975 – 1.11.1975.

Longest Sequence of Unbeaten League Matches: 23, 30.9.1987 – 27.2.1988.

Longest Sequence Without a League Win: 16, 11.11.1978 – 24.3.1979.

Successive Scoring Runs: 32 from 24.4.1954.

Successive Non-scoring Runs: 5 from 29.1.2022.

MANAGERS

Thomas Mitchell 1884–96
(*Secretary-Manager*)
J. Walmsley 1896–1903
(*Secretary-Manager*)
R. B. Middleton 1903–25
Jack Carr 1922–26
(*Team Manager under Middleton to 1925*)
Bob Crompton 1926–31
(*Hon. Team Manager*)
Arthur Barritt 1931–36
(*had been Secretary from 1927*)
Reg Taylor 1936–38
Bob Crompton 1938–41
Eddie Hapgood 1944–47
Will Scott 1947
Jack Bruton 1947–49
Jackie Bestall 1949–53
Johnny Carey 1953–58
Dally Duncan 1958–60
Jack Marshall 1960–67
Eddie Quigley 1967–70
Johnny Carey 1970–71
Ken Furphy 1971–73
Gordon Lee 1974–75
Jim Smith 1975–78
Jim Iley 1978
John Pickering 1978–79
Howard Kendall 1979–81
Bobby Saxton 1981–86
Don Mackay 1987–91
Kenny Dalglish 1991–95
Ray Harford 1995–96
Roy Hodgson 1997–98
Brian Kidd 1998–99
Graeme Souness 2000–04
Mark Hughes 2004–08
Paul Ince 2008
Sam Allardyce 2008–10
Steve Kean 2010–12
Henning Berg 2012
Michael Appleton 2013
Gary Bowyer 2013–15
Paul Lambert 2015–16
Owen Coyle 2016–17
Tony Mowbray 2017–22
Jon Dahl Tomasson June 2022–

TEN YEAR LEAGUE RECORD

		P	W	D	L	F	A	Pts	Pos
2012-13	FL C	46	14	16	16	55	62	58	17
2013-14	FL C	46	18	16	12	70	62	70	8
2014-15	FL C	46	17	16	13	66	59	67	9
2015-16	FL C	46	13	16	17	46	46	55	15
2016-17	FL C	46	12	15	19	53	65	51	22
2017-18	FL 1	46	28	12	6	82	40	96	2
2018-19	FL C	46	16	12	18	64	69	60	15
2019-20	FL C	46	17	12	17	66	63	63	11
2020-21	FL C	46	15	12	19	65	54	57	15
2021-22	FL C	46	19	12	15	59	50	69	8

DID YOU KNOW ?

Blackburn Rovers were defeated 2-1 at home by Chesterfield on 26 December 1972 with Tony Field scoring. However, the visitors were found to have fielded an ineligible player and the Football League ordered the match to be played again. Rovers were unable to improve on their earlier result, losing the replayed game 1-0.

BLACKBURN ROVERS – SKY BET CHAMPIONSHIP 2021–22 LEAGUE RECORD

Match No.	Date	Venue	Opponents	Result		H/T Score	Lg Pos.	Goalscorers	Attendance
1	Aug 7	H	Swansea C	W	2-1	1-0	4	Gallagher [36], Brereton (pen) [48]	10,260
2	14	A	Millwall	D	1-1	0-0	6	Brereton [76]	12,490
3	18	A	Nottingham F	W	2-1	0-0	6	Ayala [47], Lenihan [86]	23,964
4	21	H	WBA	L	1-2	0-2	9	Brereton [51]	11,926
5	28	A	Middlesbrough	D	1-1	1-1	10	Gallagher [17]	20,542
6	Sept 11	H	Luton T	D	2-2	2-0	9	Dolan [27], Pickering [31]	11,241
7	14	H	Hull C	W	2-0	0-0	7	Ayala [61], Brereton [65]	9140
8	18	A	Barnsley	D	0-0	0-0	6		13,640
9	25	H	Cardiff C	W	5-1	3-0	6	Gallagher [24], Brereton 3 (1 pen) [32, 45, 90 (p)], Dolan [53]	11,670
10	28	A	Huddersfield T	L	2-3	0-1	6	Brereton 2 (1 pen) [57, 65 (p)]	15,283
11	Oct 2	A	Blackpool	L	1-2	0-2	8	Brereton [50]	13,419
12	16	H	Coventry C	D	2-2	2-0	9	Rothwell [39], Gallagher [45]	14,110
13	19	A	QPR	L	0-1	0-0	11		11,771
14	23	H	Reading	W	2-0	0-0	12	Gallagher [61], Dolan [64]	10,517
15	30	A	Derby Co	W	2-1	2-0	7	Brereton 2 [8, 20]	22,098
16	Nov 3	H	Fulham	L	0-7	0-2	12		9326
17	6	H	Sheffield U	W	3-1	1-1	7	Khadra [37], Brereton [59], Poveda-Ocampo [70]	17,291
18	20	A	Bristol C	D	1-1	0-1	8	Brereton [75]	18,347
19	24	H	Peterborough U	W	4-0	3-0	7	Pickering [16], Brereton 2 [35, 60], Lenihan [45]	9038
20	27	A	Stoke C	W	1-0	0-0	4	Khadra [52]	21,739
21	Dec 4	H	Preston NE	W	1-0	0-0	4	Brereton [53]	18,487
22	11	A	Bournemouth	W	2-0	1-0	4	Pearson (og) [21], Van Hecke [65]	10,064
23	18	H	Birmingham C	W	4-0	1-0	3	Buckley [6], Khadra [52], Brereton 2 (1 pen) [60 (p), 79]	12,148
24	29	H	Barnsley	W	2-1	1-1	3	Rothwell [24], Brereton [65]	14,228
25	Jan 2	H	Huddersfield T	D	0-0	0-0	2		16,313
26	15	A	Cardiff C	W	1-0	1-0	3	Rothwell [14]	0
27	19	A	Hull C	L	0-2	0-1	3		13,950
28	24	H	Middlesbrough	W	1-0	0-0	2	Gallagher [76]	14,670
29	29	A	Luton T	D	0-0	0-0	2		9987
30	Feb 5	A	Swansea C	L	0-1	0-1	2		16,933
31	9	H	Nottingham F	L	0-2	0-1	3		13,869
32	14	A	WBA	D	0-0	0-0	3		20,680
33	23	A	Sheffield U	L	0-1	0-0	5		26,495
34	26	H	QPR	W	1-0	0-0	4	Khadra [77]	14,293
35	Mar 5	A	Fulham	L	0-2	0-2	4		19,343
36	8	H	Millwall	D	0-0	0-0	4		12,874
37	12	H	Bristol C	L	0-1	0-0	4		13,567
38	15	H	Derby Co	W	3-1	0-1	4	Wharton, S [53], Dolan [59], Gallagher [90]	12,406
39	19	A	Reading	L	0-1	0-0	6		12,805
40	Apr 2	A	Coventry C	D	2-2	0-1	6	Dack [46], Wharton, S [82]	19,939
41	9	H	Blackpool	D	1-1	1-0	7	Gallagher [10]	17,806
42	15	A	Peterborough U	L	1-2	0-0	8	Brereton [77]	9426
43	18	H	Stoke C	L	0-1	0-1	8		30,428
44	25	A	Preston NE	W	4-1	3-1	7	Gallagher [9], Buckley [12], Lenihan [37], Travis [52]	15,229
45	30	H	Bournemouth	L	0-3	0-1	9		21,396
46	May 7	A	Birmingham C	W	2-1	2-0	8	Buckley [29], Brereton [45]	18,659

Final League Position: 8

GOALSCORERS

League (59): Brereton 22 (4 pens), Gallagher 9, Dolan 4, Khadra 4, Buckley 3, Lenihan 3, Rothwell 3, Ayala 2, Pickering 2, Wharton, S 2, Dack 1, Poveda-Ocampo 1, Travis 1, Van Hecke 1, own goal 1.
FA Cup (2): Ayala 1, Khadra 1.
Carabao Cup (1): Dolan 1.

Kaminski T 44	Nyambe R 31	Lenihan D 41	Ayala D 16 + 5	Pickering H 31 + 1	Rothwell J 36 + 5	Travis L 45	Buckley J 39 + 3	Gallagher S 28 + 9	Dolan T 20 + 14	Brereton B 34 + 3	Davenport J 2 + 7	Butterworth D 1 + 10	Carter H 5 + 4	Chapman H — + 3	Clarkson L 4 + 3	Poveda-Ocampo I 4 + 6	Magliore T 1 + 3	Khadra R 18 + 9	Edun T 13 + 7	Van Hecke J 30 + 1	Johnson B 8 + 10	Rankin-Costello J 6 + 4	Wharton S 30	Pears A 2 + 1	Markanday D — + 2	Zeefuik D 4 + 2	Giles R 8 + 3	Hedges R 4 + 7	Vale J — + 2	Dack B — + 9	Brown J 1	*Match No.*
1	2	3	4	5	6	7	8^{2}	9^{1}	10^{3}	11	12	13	14																			1
1	2	3	4	6^{2}	5	8	10^{3}	7	11^{1}	9		13	12	14																		2
1		3	4	5	7^{2}	6	9	8	11^{1}	10	13		2	12																		3
1		3	4	5	7^{3}	6	8^{2}	11	13	10	12		2	14	9^{1}																	4
1		3	4	5	10^{1}	9	14	11	13	6			2■		8^{2}	7^{3}	12															5
1	2	3	4	5	7^{2}	6	9^{1}	11	8	10	12						13															6
1	2	3	4	5	9	7	8^{2}		10^{3}	11	14	12			6^{1}			13														7
1	2	3	4	5	9^{3}	6	7		10^{1}	11					12	8^{2}		13	14													8
1	2	3^{1}	4	5	7^{3}	6	10	8	9^{2}	11			12					13	14													9
1	2^{1}		4	5	7^{2}	6	9	8^{3}	11^{4}	10			3		14	13	12	15														10
1			3	5	7^{3}	6	9	8^{1}	11	10		14	4				2^{2}	13	12													11
1	2	5	4		9	8	7^{1}	10^{3}	11^{2}	14	12					13			6	3												12
1	5	4	3	9^{2}	13	7^{1}		14		11		10^{3}			6				8	2	12											13
1	2^{2}	4	3^{1}		8^{3}	7	6	10	9	11						13			5	12	14											14
1		4			8	6	2	10^{2}	9^{1}	11						13		12	5	3	7											15
1	2	3			8^{2}	6	10^{1}		9^{3}	11		14	12						5	4■	7	13										16
1	2	3			13	7	10		12	11	8^{2}	14				6^{3}		9^{1}	5				4									17
1	2^{3}	3	12		13	6	7			10	8^{2}				14	9^{1}		11	5				4									18
1	5	2	3^{1}	8	7	6	9^{3}		10	11^{2}		14						13			12		4									19
1^{1}	5	2		8	7^{3}	6	9		13	11	14							10^{2}		3			4	12								20
	5	2		8	7^{3}	6	9^{1}		13	10								11^{2}	14	3	12		4	1								21
	5^{3}	2	13	8	6	7	9	12		10								11^{1}		3	14		4^{2}	1								22
1	5	2		8	7^{3}	6	9^{1}	12		11		13						10^{2}		3	14		4									23
1	5	2		8	7^{2}	6	9^{3}	12	14	11								10^{1}	13	3			4									24
1	5	2		8^{2}	7	6	10^{3}	12	14	11								9^{1}	13	3			4									25
1	5■	2	13		6	7^{3}	9	12		11^{2}								10^{1}	8	3	14		4									26
1		2	14		6		7^{2}	9^{3}		10								11	8	3	13	5^{1}	4		12							27
1	5	2				6	9^{2}	11				12						10^{1}	8	3	7		4			13						28
1	5	2	14			6	9^{3}	11^{2}				13							8^{1}	3	7	12	4			10						29
1	5^{3}	2			7	6	11			12								13		3		14	4			8^{2}	9	10^{1}				30
1		2■			8	7	10^{1}	12	13	11								9^{2}		3			4			6^{3}	5	14				31
1	2				7	6	9^{3}	11	13	10^{1}								12		3	14	5^{2}	4				8					32
1	5^{1}	2		8	7	6	10	11	12									9		3			4									33
1	5^{1}	2		8^{3}		6		9^{2}	10									11		3	7		4			12	14	13				34
1		2		8	14	6		13	10^{3}									11^{2}		3	7	12	4			5^{1}	9					35
1		2		8	7	6	9^{2}	11^{3}	13											3		5	4				10^{1}	12	14			36
1		2		8	7	6	10^{2}	9	12									11		3		5^{1}	4							13		37
1		2		8	7	6		13	10									11^{3}		3	9^{2}	5^{1}	4				14			12		38
1		2		12	7	6	9^{2}	10	11^{3}									5^{1}		3			4				8	14		13		39
1	3			6	9	7	8^{3}	11		12										4		2^{1}	5				10^{2}	14		13		40
1	5^{1}	2		8	7	6	13	10^{4}	9^{2}	11										3			4^{3}				14	15		12		41
1	5^{1}	2				6	9^{3}	10^{2}	14	11									7■	3	12		4				8			13		42
1	5	2		8	12	6	13	10	9^{3}	11										3^{1}	7^{2}		4					14				43
1		2		5	7^{2}	6	9^{3}	11^{1}		10						12			13	3			4					8		14		44
1		2		5	7^{2}	6	9	10^{3}	12	11						13				3			4					8^{1}		14		45
1			3	5		6	9	11^{3}		10^{2}									7^{1}				4		13			8	14	12	2	46

FA Cup
Third Round Wigan Ath (a) 2-3

Carabao Cup
First Round Morecambe (h) 1-2

BLACKPOOL

FOUNDATION

Old boys of St John's School, who had formed themselves into a football club, decided to establish a club bearing the name of their town and Blackpool FC came into being at a meeting at the Stanley Arms Hotel in the summer of 1887. In their first season playing at Raikes Hall Gardens, the club won both the Lancashire Junior Cup and the Fylde Cup.

Bloomfield Road, Seasiders Way, Blackpool, Lancashire FY1 6JJ.

Telephone: (01253) 599 344.

Ticket Office: (01253) 599 745.

Website: www.blackpoolfc.co.uk

Email: via website.

Ground Capacity: 16,616.

Record Attendance: 38,098 v Wolverhampton W, Division 1, 17 September 1955.

Pitch Measurements: 103.6m × 64.5m (113.5yd × 70.5yd).

Owner: Simon Sadler.

Chief Executive: Ben Mansford.

Head Coach: Michael Appleton.

Assistant Head Coaches: David Kerslake, Richard O'Donnell.

Colours: Tangerine shirts with white trim, white shorts with tangerine trim, tangerine socks with white trim.

Year Formed: 1887.

Turned Professional: 1887.

Previous Name: 'South Shore' combined with Blackpool in 1899, twelve years after the latter had been formed on the breaking up of the old 'Blackpool St John's' club.

Club Nickname: 'The Seasiders'.

Grounds: 1887, Raikes Hall Gardens; 1897, Athletic Grounds; 1899, Raikes Hall Gardens; 1899, Bloomfield Road.

First Football League Game: 5 September 1896, Division 2, v Lincoln C (a) L 1–3 – Douglas; Parr, Bowman; Stuart, Stirzaker, Norris; Clarkin, Donnelly, Robert Parkinson, Mount (1), Jack Parkinson.

Record League Victory: 7–0 v Reading, Division 2, 10 November 1928 – Mercer; Gibson, Hamilton, Watson, Wilson, Grant, Ritchie, Oxberry (2), Hampson (5), Tufnell, Neal. 7–0 v Preston NE (away), Division 1, 1 May 1948 – Robinson; Shimwell, Crosland; Buchan, Hayward, Kelly; Hobson, Munro (1), McIntosh (5), McCall, Rickett (1). 7–0 v Sunderland, Division 1, 5 October 1957 – Farm; Armfield, Garrett, Kelly J, Gratrix, Kelly H, Matthews, Taylor (2), Charnley (2), Durie (2), Perry (1).

Record Cup Victory: 7–1 v Charlton Ath, League Cup 2nd rd, 25 September 1963 – Harvey; Armfield, Martin; Crawford, Gratrix, Cranston; Lea, Ball (1), Charnley (4), Durie (1), Oates (1).

HONOURS

League Champions: Division 2 – 1929–30.
Runners-up: Division 1 – 1955–56; Division 2 – 1936–37, 1969–70; Division 4 – 1984–85.

FA Cup Winners: 1953.
Runners-up: 1948, 1951.

League Cup: semi-final – 1962.

League Trophy Winners: 2002, 2004.

Anglo-Italian Cup Winners: 1971.
Runners-up: 1972.

FOOTBALL YEARBOOK FACT FILE

Eamonn Collins became the youngest player to appear in a senior competitive match in England when he came on as a second-half substitute for Blackpool against Kilmarnock in an Anglo Scottish Cup tie on 9 September 1980. Collins, who was just 14 years and 323 days old, never played for the Seasiders at first-team level again, moving on to Southampton in October 1983.

Record Defeat: 1–10 v Small Heath, Division 2, 2 March 1901 and v Huddersfield T, Division 1, 13 December 1930.

Most League Points (2 for a win): 58, Division 2, 1929–30 and Division 2, 1967–68.

Most League Points (3 for a win): 86, Division 4, 1984–85.

Most League Goals: 98, Division 2, 1929–30.

Highest League Scorer in Season: Jimmy Hampson, 45, Division 2, 1929–30.

Most League Goals in Total Aggregate: Jimmy Hampson, 248, 1927–38.

Most League Goals in One Match: 5, Jimmy Hampson v Reading, Division 2, 10 November 1928; 5, Jimmy McIntosh v Preston NE, Division 1, 1 May 1948.

Most Capped Player: Jimmy Armfield, 43, England.

Most League Appearances: Jimmy Armfield, 568, 1952–71.

Youngest League Player: Matty Kay, 16 years 32 days v Scunthorpe U, 13 November 2005.

Record Transfer Fee Received: £6,750,000 from Liverpool for Charlie Adam, July 2011.

Record Transfer Fee Paid: £1,250,000 to Leicester C for D.J. Campbell, August 2010.

Football League Record: 1896 Elected to Division 2; 1899 Failed re-election; 1900 Re-elected; 1900–30 Division 2; 1930–33 Division 1; 1933–37 Division 2; 1937–67 Division 1; 1967–70 Division 2; 1970–71 Division 1; 1971–78 Division 2; 1978–81 Division 3; 1981–85 Division 4; 1985–90 Division 3; 1990–92 Division 4; 1992–2000 Division 2; 2000–01 Division 3; 2001–04 Division 2; 2004–07 FL 1; 2007–10 FL C; 2010–11 Premier League; 2011–15 FL C; 2015–16 FL 1; 2016–17 FL 2; 2017–21 FL 1; 2021– FL C.

MANAGERS

Tom Barcroft 1903–33 (*Secretary-Manager*)
John Cox 1909–11
Bill Norman 1919–23
Maj. Frank Buckley 1923–27
Sid Beaumont 1927–28
Harry Evans 1928–33 (*Hon. Team Manager*)
Alex 'Sandy' Macfarlane 1933–35
Joe Smith 1935–58
Ronnie Suart 1958–67
Stan Mortensen 1967–69
Les Shannon 1969–70
Bob Stokoe 1970–72
Harry Potts 1972–76
Allan Brown 1976–78
Bob Stokoe 1978–79
Stan Ternent 1979–80
Alan Ball 1980–81
Allan Brown 1981–82
Sam Ellis 1982–89
Jimmy Mullen 1989–90
Graham Carr 1990
Bill Ayre 1990–94
Sam Allardyce 1994–96
Gary Megson 1996–97
Nigel Worthington 1997–99
Steve McMahon 2000–04
Colin Hendry 2004–05
Simon Grayson 2005–08
Ian Holloway 2009–12
Michael Appleton 2012–13
Paul Ince 2013–14
José Riga 2014
Lee Clark 2014–15
Neil McDonald 2015–16
Gary Bowyer 2016–18
Terry McPhillips 2018–19
Simon Grayson 2019–20
Neil Critchley 2020–22
Michael Appleton June 2022–

LATEST SEQUENCES

Longest Sequence of League Wins: 9, 21.11.1936 – 1.1.1937.

Longest Sequence of League Defeats: 8, 26.11.1898 – 7.1.1899.

Longest Sequence of League Draws: 5, 4.12.1976 – 1.1.1977.

Longest Sequence of Unbeaten League Matches: 17, 6.4.1968 – 21.9.1968.

Longest Sequence Without a League Win: 23, 7.2.2015 – 29.8.2015.

Successive Scoring Runs: 33 from 23.2.1929.

Successive Non-scoring Runs: 5 from 25.11.1989.

TEN YEAR LEAGUE RECORD

		P	W	D	L	F	A	Pts	Pos
2012-13	FL C	46	14	17	15	62	63	59	15
2013-14	FL C	46	11	13	22	38	66	46	20
2014-15	FL C	46	4	14	28	36	91	26	24
2015-16	FL 1	46	12	10	24	40	63	46	22
2016-17	FL 2	46	18	16	12	69	46	70	7
2017-18	FL 1	46	15	15	16	60	55	60	12
2018-19	FL 1	46	15	17	14	50	52	62	10
2019-20	FL 1	35	11	12	12	44	43	45	13§
2020-21	FL 1	46	23	11	12	60	37	80	3
2021-22	FL C	46	16	12	18	54	58	60	16

§*Decided on points-per-game (1.29)*

DID YOU KNOW ?

After winning at Chesterfield on 2 March 1907 Blackpool went 41 games without an away win, the run covering two full seasons. Their next victory on an opposition ground came in the first game of the 1909–10 campaign when they won 2-1 at Hyde Road against Manchester City.

BLACKPOOL – SKY BET CHAMPIONSHIP 2021–22 LEAGUE RECORD

Match No.	*Date*	*Venue*	*Opponents*	*Result*		*H/T Score*	*Lg Pos.*	*Goalscorers*	*Attendance*
1	Aug 7	A	Bristol C	D	1-1	0-1	8	Lavery [90]	18,729
2	14	H	Cardiff C	L	0-2	0-0	21		11,393
3	17	H	Coventry C	L	0-1	0-1	22		11,608
4	21	A	Bournemouth	D	2-2	0-2	22	Husband [57], Yates (pen) [60]	9187
5	28	A	Millwall	L	1-2	0-0	22	Lavery [56]	11,049
6	Sept 11	H	Fulham	W	1-0	0-0	19	Bowler [49]	11,268
7	14	H	Huddersfield T	L	0-3	0-0	22		11,277
8	18	A	Middlesbrough	W	2-1	0-1	20	Ekpiteta [62], Hall (og) [78]	21,022
9	25	H	Barnsley	W	1-0	1-0	14	Lavery [32]	12,698
10	28	A	Hull C	D	1-1	1-0	14	Lavery [42]	10,189
11	Oct 2	H	Blackburn R	W	2-1	2-0	12	Lavery [4], Yates [24]	13,419
12	16	A	Nottingham F	L	1-2	0-1	15	Yates [53]	27,946
13	20	A	Reading	W	3-2	0-2	12	Dale [69], Yates 2 (1 pen) [73, 85 (p)]	10,587
14	23	H	Preston NE	W	2-0	1-0	11	Anderson [27], Madine [68]	13,946
15	30	A	Sheffield U	W	1-0	0-0	6	Anderson [76]	28,304
16	Nov 3	H	Stoke C	L	0-1	0-0	10		12,297
17	6	H	QPR	D	1-1	0-1	10	Madine (pen) [54]	11,769
18	20	A	Swansea C	D	1-1	0-1	10	Anderson [86]	16,886
19	23	H	WBA	D	0-0	0-0	9		11,517
20	27	A	Birmingham C	L	0-1	0-0	11		17,686
21	Dec 4	H	Luton T	L	0-3	0-1	15		11,366
22	11	A	Derby Co	L	0-1	0-0	17		21,663
23	18	H	Peterborough U	W	3-1	1-1	12	Anderson [27], Carey [86], Yates [90]	9745
24	26	A	Huddersfield T	L	2-3	2-1	13	Yates [1], Madine [18]	18,968
25	29	H	Middlesbrough	L	1-2	0-0	13	Lavery [90]	13,428
26	Jan 1	H	Hull C	W	1-0	1-0	12	Madine (pen) [31]	11,300
27	22	H	Millwall	W	1-0	0-0	12	Lavery [55]	10,696
28	29	A	Fulham	D	1-1	0-1	14	Bowler [57]	19,092
29	Feb 5	H	Bristol C	W	3-1	2-0	13	Hamilton [36], Madine [39], Bowler [48]	11,026
30	8	A	Coventry C	D	1-1	1-1	14	Madine [24]	15,752
31	12	H	Bournemouth	L	1-2	1-0	14	Bowler [37]	11,141
32	19	A	Cardiff C	D	1-1	1-0	15	Ekpiteta [11]	19,025
33	23	A	QPR	L	1-2	0-1	15	Bowler [82]	12,042
34	26	H	Reading	W	4-1	1-1	14	Ekpiteta [27], Madine [61], Lavery [86], Bowler [90]	10,954
35	Mar 5	A	Stoke C	W	1-0	0-0	14	Bowler [86]	26,384
36	12	H	Swansea C	W	1-0	1-0	12	Madine [4]	12,344
37	16	H	Sheffield U	D	0-0	0-0	13		11,915
38	Apr 2	H	Nottingham F	L	1-4	0-3	14	Connolly [89]	13,986
39	5	A	Preston NE	L	0-1	0-1	16		18,740
40	9	A	Blackburn R	D	1-1	0-1	16	Ekpiteta [48]	17,806
41	15	A	WBA	L	1-2	0-1	16	Ekpiteta [53]	21,717
42	18	H	Birmingham C	W	6-1	3-0	16	Beesley 2 [3, 56], Hamilton [14], Dougall [40], Yates (pen) [85], Connolly [90]	13,993
43	23	A	Luton T	D	1-1	0-1	16	Madine (pen) [55]	9843
44	26	A	Barnsley	W	2-0	1-0	15	Dale [39], Casey [66]	12,256
45	30	H	Derby Co	L	0-2	0-0	16		15,298
46	May 7	A	Peterborough U	L	0-5	0-1	16		9118

Final League Position: 16

GOALSCORERS

League (54): Madine 9 (3 pens), Lavery 8, Yates 8 (3 pens), Bowler 7, Ekpiteta 5, Anderson 4, Beesley 2, Connolly 2, Dale 2, Hamilton 2, Carey 1, Casey 1, Dougall 1, Husband 1, own goal 1.
FA Cup (1): Anderson 1.
Carabao Cup (5): Lavery 2, Anderson 1, Bowler 1, Connolly 1.

Maxwell C 20 + 1	Connolly C 25 + 6	Keogh R 26 + 3	Husband J 28 + 3	Garbutt L 14 + 3	Hamilton C 17 + 7	James R 15 + 2	Ward G 4	Anderson K 29 + 3	John-Jules T 8 + 3	Yates J 23 + 16	Bowler J 30 + 12	Lavery S 20 + 17	Dougall K 37 + 3	Ekpiteta M 39 + 1	Stewart K 10 + 2	Lawrence-Gabriel J 19 + 2	Wintle R 18	Madine G 27 + 7	Sterling D 22 + 2	Mitchell D 6 + 7	Moore S — + 1	Grimshaw D 26	Carey S 5 + 6	Dale O 7 + 8	Gretarsson D 2 + 1	Thorniley J 12 + 2	Kirk C 7 + 2	Beesley J 4 + 2	Robson E 2	Casey O 3 + 3	Virtue M 1 + 2	Mariette L — + 1	Daniels J — + 1	Match No.
1	2	3	4	5	6^{2}	7	8	9	10^{1}	11	12	13																						1
1	2	3	4	5	6^{1}		7	9	11^{2}	10	12	13	8																					2
1	2	3	4	5	14	7^{2}	8	9^{3}	13	10^{1}	6	11	12																					3
1	2		4	5		12	8^{2}	9	11^{1}	10	6	13	7	3																				4
1	2■	4		5	13	7		9	14	10^{2}	6^{3}	11^{1}	8	3	12																			5
1		4	14	5				9	11^{3}	10^{1}	6	12	13	3	8	2	7^{2}																	6
1		4		5				12	9^{2}	11^{1}	6	10	7	3		2^{3}	8	13	14															7
1		4		5				9	11^{1}	13	6^{3}	10^{2}	8	3		14	7	12	2															8
1		4	14	5				9^{3}	11^{1}		6^{2}	10	8	3			7	12	2	13														9
1		4		5				9	14	13	12	11^{3}	8	3			7	10^{2}	2	6^{1}														10
1^{3}		4^{2}	13	5				9		12	6	10^{1}	7	3			8	11	2		14													11
		4		5					9^{1}	10	6		13	3	7^{2}	2	8	11^{3}		12		1	14											12
		4	5					9^{1}		11^{3}	13		8	3		2	7	14		6^{2}		1	10	12										13
	13	4	5					9		10^{1}	6^{3}		8^{2}	3		2	7	11		14		1	12											14
		4	5	14				9^{3}		10^{2}	6^{1}		8	3		2	7	11		12		1	13											15
		4^{1}	5	12				10		11^{2}	14		6	3		2	7	13		8^{3}		1	9											16
			4			5		10			6^{2}		8	3		2	7	11		13		1	12	9^{1}										17
	8^{3}		5			6		10		11^{2}	12	13		4		2	9		3	7^{1}		1		14										18
			4		13	5		9			6^{1}	11^{2}	8	3		2	7	10				1		12										19
	6		4			5		9		14	12	13	7	3				11^{3}	2	8^{1}		1		10^{2}										20
1			4			5		9		11	12	13	7^{3}	3			6		2	8^{1}			14	10^{2}										21
1	7	12	4			5^{1}		10		14	13	11		3			6		2				9^{2}	8^{3}										22
	14		4			5		9		12	6	10^{2}	8	3		2	7^{3}	11^{1}				1	13											23
		12	5					9		11^{1}	6^{2}	14	7	3		2■		10^{3}	13	15		1	8^{4}		4									24
	7	4^{3}	6					9		11^{1}	12	13	8	3				10	2	14		1			5^{2}									25
	13	4	5					9^{3}		12	6^{2}	11^{1}	8	3			7	10	2			1			14									26
	7	4		5^{1}	9^{3}					13	6	11^{2}	8	3		12		10	2			1		14										27
	8	4			10					12	7	11^{1}	9	3		2			6			1				5								28
	7	3			9^{2}					11	6^{1}		8			2		10^{3}	5			1		12		4	13	14						29
	13	4^{1}				5^{2}				11	6		8	3	14			10	2			1		9		12			7^{3}					30
	7				9					11^{2}	6	13		3^{1}	8	2		10	5			1				4				12				31
	8				13	5				10^{1}	6	12		3	7			11	2			1				4	9^{2}							32
	8				10^{2}	6^{1}				14	7	11^{3}	9			2		12	3			1		13		5				4				33
					9	12				10^{2}	6	13	7	3	8	2^{1}		11^{3}	5			1				4		14						34
	14				9	5				13	6^{3}	10^{2}	7	3	8			11	2			1				4^{1}				12				35
	3		5		13	6					7^{3}	12	9	4	8			11^{1}	2			1		14			10^{2}							36
	3^{2}		6		10^{1}					14	7	12	9	4	8			11^{3}	2			1				5	13							37
	12		5		9^{2}			13		11^{3}	6	14	8	3	7^{1}			10	2			1				4								38
12	2	4	5		10^{2}			9		14	8	13	6^{4}	3				11^{3}				1^{1}							7		15			39
1	7	14	5		6^{1}			13			12	10^{3}	8	3		2		11								4	9^{2}							40
1	7		5		14			9^{2}			6^{3}	11	8	3		2^{1}		10						13		4					12			41
1	2	4	5		6			7		12		10^{1}	8	3				13									9	11^{2}						42
1	2	4	5		6			7			12	13	8	3				11									9^{1}	10^{2}						43
1	2		5		12					13		11^{1}	8	3										6		14	9^{2}	10		4^{3}	7			44
1	2	3	5^{1}	12	6			8		14		10	7					11								4^{2}	9^{3}			13				45
1	2	4^{1}		5	6					10^{3}				12	7								8^{2}	9				11		3		13	14	46

FA Cup

Third Round Hartlepool U (a) 1-2

Carabao Cup

First Round Middlesbrough (h) 3-0

Second Round Sunderland (h) 2-3

BOLTON WANDERERS

FOUNDATION

In 1874 boys of Christ Church Sunday School, Blackburn Street, led by their master Thomas Ogden, established a football club which went under the name of the school and whose president was vicar of Christ Church. Membership was 6d (two and a half pence). When their president began to lay down too many rules about the use of church premises, the club broke away and formed Bolton Wanderers in 1877, holding their earliest meetings at the Gladstone Hotel.

University of Bolton Stadium, Burnden Way, Lostock, Bolton BL6 6JW.

Telephone: (01204) 673 673.

Ticket Office: (01204) 328 888.

Website: www.bwfc.co.uk

Email: reception@bwfc.co.uk (or via website).

Ground Capacity: 28,018.

Record Attendance: 69,912 v Manchester C, FA Cup 5th rd, 18 February 1933 (at Burnden Park); 28,353 v Leicester C, Premier League, 23 December 2003 (at The Reebok Stadium).

Pitch Measurements: 102m × 68m (111.5yd × 74.5yd).

Chairman: Sharon Brittan.

Directors: Michael James, Nick Luckcock.

Manager: Ian Evatt.

Assistant Manager: Peter Atherton.

Colours: White shirts with blue sleeves and blue and red trim, blue shorts with white and red trim, white socks with red and blue trim.

Year Formed: 1874.

Turned Professional: 1880.

Previous Name: 1874, Christ Church FC; 1877, Bolton Wanderers.

Club Nickname: 'The Trotters'.

Grounds: Park Recreation Ground and Cockle's Field before moving to Pike's Lane ground 1881; 1895, Burnden Park; 1997, Reebok Stadium (renamed Macron Stadium 2014; University of Bolton Stadium 2018).

First Football League Game: 8 September 1888, Football League, v Derby Co (h) L 3–6 – Harrison; Robinson, Mitchell; Roberts, Weir, Bullough, Davenport (2), Milne, Coupar, Barbour, Brogan (1).

Record League Victory: 8–0 v Barnsley, Division 2, 6 October 1934 – Jones; Smith, Finney; Goslin, Atkinson, George Taylor; George T. Taylor (2), Eastham, Milsom (1), Westwood (4), Cook, (1 og).

Record Cup Victory: 13–0 v Sheffield U, FA Cup 2nd rd, 1 February 1890 – Parkinson; Robinson (1), Jones; Bullough, Davenport, Roberts; Rushton, Brogan (3), Cassidy (5), McNee, Weir (4).

HONOURS

League Champions: First Division – 1996–97; Division 2 – 1908–09, 1977–78; Division 3 – 1972–73.
Runners-up: Division 2 – 1899–1900, 1904–05, 1910–11, 1934–35; Second Division – 1992–93; FL 1 – 2016–17.

FA Cup Winners: 1923, 1926, 1929, 1958.
Runners-up: 1894, 1904, 1953.

League Cup: *Runners-up:* 1995, 2004.

League Trophy Winners: 1989.
Runners-up: 1986.

European Competitions
UEFA Cup: 2005–06, 2007–08.

FOOTBALL YEARBOOK FACT FILE

Bolton Wanderers were selected as the visiting team to inaugurate the current Tynecastle Park when it was opened by Heart of Midlothian in 1886. The teams met on 10 April in front of a crowd of 6,000 with the home team winning 4-1. Wanderers' goal was scored by King, a 'guest' player who belonged to the Thistle club of Glasgow.

Record Defeat: 1–9 v Preston NE, FA Cup 2nd rd, 5 November 1887.

Most League Points (2 for a win): 61, Division 3, 1972–73.

Most League Points (3 for a win): 98, Division 1, 1996–97.

Most League Goals: 100, Division 1, 1996–97.

Highest League Scorer in Season: Joe Smith, 38, Division 1, 1920–21.

Most League Goals in Total Aggregate: Nat Lofthouse, 255, 1946–61.

Most League Goals in One Match: 5, Tony Caldwell v Walsall, Division 3, 10 September 1983.

Most Capped Player: Ricardo Gardner, 72 (111), Jamaica.

Most League Appearances: Eddie Hopkinson, 519, 1956–70.

Youngest League Player: Ray Parry, 15 years 267 days v Wolverhampton W, 13 October 1951.

Record Transfer Fee Received: £15,000,000 from Chelsea for Nicolas Anelka, January 2008.

Record Transfer Fee Paid: £8,250,000 to Toulouse for Johan Elmander, June 2008.

Football League Record: 1888 Founder Member of the League; 1899–1900 Division 2; 1900–03 Division 1; 1903–05 Division 2; 1905–08 Division 1; 1908–09 Division 2; 1909–10 Division 1; 1910–11 Division 2; 1911–33 Division 1; 1933–35 Division 2; 1935–64 Division 1; 1964–71 Division 2; 1971–73 Division 3; 1973–78 Division 2; 1978–80 Division 1; 1980–83 Division 2; 1983–87 Division 3; 1987–88 Division 4; 1988–92 Division 3; 1992–93 Division 2; 1993–95 Division 1; 1995–96 Premier League; 1996–97 Division 1; 1997–98 Premier League; 1998–2001 Division 1; 2001–12 Premier League; 2012–16 FL C; 2016–17 FL 1; 2017–19 FL C; 2019–20 FL 1; 2020–21 FL 2; 2021– FL 1.

LATEST SEQUENCES

Longest Sequence of League Wins: 11, 5.11.1904 – 2.1.1905.

Longest Sequence of League Defeats: 11, 7.4.1902 – 18.10.1902.

Longest Sequence of League Draws: 6, 25.1.1913 – 8.3.1913.

Longest Sequence of Unbeaten League Matches: 23, 13.10.1990 – 9.3.1991.

Longest Sequence Without a League Win: 26, 7.4.1902 – 10.1.1903.

Successive Scoring Runs: 24 from 22.11.1996.

Successive Non-scoring Runs: 11 from 9.4.2019.

MANAGERS

Tom Rawthorne 1874–85 (*Secretary*)
J. J. Bentley 1885–86 (*Secretary*)
W. G. Struthers 1886–87 (*Secretary*)
Fitzroy Norris 1887 (*Secretary*)
J. J. Bentley 1887–95 (*Secretary*)
Harry Downs 1895–96 (*Secretary*)
Frank Brettell 1896–98 (*Secretary*)
John Somerville 1898–1910
Will Settle 1910–15
Tom Mather 1915–19
Charles Foweraker 1919–44
Walter Rowley 1944–50
Bill Ridding 1951–68
Nat Lofthouse 1968–70
Jimmy McIlroy 1970
Jimmy Meadows 1971
Nat Lofthouse 1971 (*then Admin. Manager to 1972*)
Jimmy Armfield 1971–74
Ian Greaves 1974–80
Stan Anderson 1980–81
George Mulhall 1981–82
John McGovern 1982–85
Charlie Wright 1985
Phil Neal 1985–92
Bruce Rioch 1992–95
Roy McFarland 1995–96
Colin Todd 1996–99
Roy McFarland and Colin Todd 1995–96
Sam Allardyce 1999–2007
Sammy Lee 2007
Gary Megson 2007–09
Owen Coyle 2010–12
Dougie Freedman 2012–14
Neil Lennon 2014–16
Phil Parkinson 2016–19
Keith Hill 2019–20
Ian Evatt July 2020–

TEN YEAR LEAGUE RECORD

		P	*W*	*D*	*L*	*F*	*A*	*Pts*	*Pos*
2012-13	FL C	46	18	14	14	69	61	68	7
2013-14	FL C	46	14	17	15	59	60	59	14
2014-15	FL C	46	13	12	21	54	67	51	18
2015-16	FL C	46	5	15	26	41	81	30	24
2016-17	FL 1	46	25	11	10	68	36	86	2
2017-18	FL C	46	10	13	23	39	74	43	21
2018-19	FL C	46	8	8	30	29	78	32	23
2019-20	FL 1	34	5	11	18	27	66	14	23§
2020-21	FL 2	46	23	10	13	59	50	79	3
2021-22	FL 1	46	21	10	15	74	57	73	9

§*Decided on points-per-game (0.41)*

DID YOU KNOW ?

When Bolton Wanderers visited Maine Road for their First Division fixture on 21 March 1936, Fred Swift was in goal for the Trotters while his younger brother Frank was the keeper for the home team. Frank had much the better day as City romped to a 7-0 victory, although both teams finished the campaign in mid-table positions.

BOLTON WANDERERS – SKY BET LEAGUE ONE 2021–22 LEAGUE RECORD

Match No.	Date		Venue	Opponents	Result		*H/T Score*	*Lg Pos.*	*Goalscorers*	*Attendance*
1	Aug	7	H	Milton Keynes D	D	3-3	1-1	7	Sheehan ^{30}, Bakayoko ^{67}, Baptiste ^{90}	16,087
2		14	A	AFC Wimbledon	D	3-3	2-1	14	Doyle (pen) ^{23}, Sheehan ^{27}, Afolayan ^{48}	7728
3		17	A	Lincoln C	W	1-0	0-0	9	Sarcevic ^{76}	9130
4		21	H	Oxford U	W	2-1	1-1	7	Afolayan ^{45}, Doyle ^{63}	15,073
5		28	A	Cambridge U	L	0-1	0-1	13		6124
6	Sept	6	H	Burton Alb	D	0-0	0-0	12		13,305
7		11	A	Ipswich T	W	5-2	3-2	3	Afolayan 2 $^{10, 45}$, Doyle (pen) ^{18}, Sheehan ^{47}, Johnston ^{56}	19,267
8		18	H	Rotherham U	L	0-2	0-2	8		20,877
9		25	A	Sunderland	L	0-1	0-1	9		32,368
10		28	A	Charlton Ath	W	4-1	1-1	7	Afolayan ^{43}, Lee 2 $^{73, 81}$, Sarcevic ^{90}	12,707
11	Oct	2	H	Shrewsbury T	W	2-1	2-0	7	Sarcevic ^{18}, Afolayan ^{23}	14,124
12		9	A	Sheffield W	L	0-1	0-0	8		23,692
13		16	H	Wigan Ath	L	0-4	0-1	10		20,892
14		19	A	Plymouth Arg	L	0-3	0-2	11		12,813
15		23	H	Gillingham	D	2-2	0-2	12	Afolayan ^{86}, Lee ^{90}	13,807
16		30	A	Portsmouth	L	0-1	0-0	14		16,231
17	Nov	12	H	Crewe Alex	W	2-0	0-0	10	Sheehan (pen) ^{50}, Bakayoko ^{54}	13,804
18		20	A	Wycombe W	L	0-1	0-0	13		5710
19		23	H	Doncaster R	W	3-0	2-0	11	Doyle ^{37}, Kachunga ^{45}, Thomason ^{57}	12,501
20		27	H	Cheltenham T	D	2-2	1-2	12	Amaechi ^{26}, Kachunga ^{58}	13,145
21	Dec	7	A	Fleetwood T	L	0-3	0-1	16		3279
22		11	A	Accrington S	L	0-1	0-1	15		4546
23	Jan	1	A	Rotherham U	L	1-2	1-1	16	Doyle ^{42}	9736
24		11	H	Wycombe W	L	0-2	0-1	18		12,584
25		15	H	Ipswich T	W	2-0	0-0	17	Lee ^{74}, Afolayan ^{81}	14,020
26		22	A	Shrewsbury T	W	1-0	0-0	15	Charles ^{89}	8027
27		29	H	Sunderland	W	6-0	2-0	14	Charles 2 $^{19, 51}$, Afolayan ^{41}, Lee ^{59}, Batth (og) ^{85}, John ^{88}	20,059
28	Feb	1	H	Cambridge U	W	2-0	1-0	11	Bakayoko ^{39}, Afolayan ^{70}	13,334
29		5	A	Morecambe	D	1-1	0-0	10	Bakayoko ^{90}	5617
30		8	H	Charlton Ath	W	2-1	1-0	10	Charles ^{10}, Aimson ^{83}	13,523
31		12	A	Oxford U	W	3-2	2-2	10	John ^{10}, Fossey ^{38}, Bakayoko ^{86}	10,027
32		15	A	Burton Alb	L	1-3	0-3	10	Charles ^{90}	3487
33		19	H	AFC Wimbledon	W	4-0	1-0	10	Bodvarsson ^{36}, Afolayan ^{56}, Charles ^{67}, Bakayoko ^{87}	14,537
34		22	H	Lincoln C	W	3-1	0-0	10	Johnston ^{53}, Sadlier ^{76}, Bakayoko ^{83}	13,841
35		26	A	Milton Keynes D	L	0-2	0-1	10		10,388
36	Mar	5	A	Gillingham	W	3-0	1-0	11	Morley ^{31}, John ^{65}, Bodvarsson ^{86}	5109
37		8	H	Morecambe	D	1-1	0-1	11	Bodvarsson ^{90}	14,559
38		12	H	Plymouth Arg	L	0-1	0-1	11		16,078
39		19	A	Crewe Alex	W	1-0	0-0	11	Bakayoko ^{90}	5985
40	Apr	2	A	Wigan Ath	D	1-1	0-1	11	Bodvarsson ^{83}	15,279
41		5	H	Portsmouth	D	1-1	0-0	11	Sadlier (pen) ^{76}	13,809
42		9	H	Sheffield W	D	1-1	0-0	10	Williams ^{90}	19,164
43		15	A	Doncaster R	W	2-1	0-0	11	Bakayoko ^{47}, Sadlier ^{78}	8668
44		18	H	Accrington S	W	3-1	1-0	10	Afolayan ^{42}, Bodvarsson 2 $^{69, 89}$	19,098
45		23	A	Cheltenham T	W	2-1	0-0	10	Sadlier ^{57}, Bakayoko (pen) ^{76}	5228
46		30	H	Fleetwood T	W	4-2	1-1	9	Charles 2 $^{37, 86}$, John ^{53}, Bodvarsson ^{90}	16,886

Final League Position: 9

GOALSCORERS

League (74): Afolayan 12, Bakayoko 10 (1 pen), Charles 8, Bodvarsson 7, Doyle 5 (2 pens), Lee 5, John 4, Sadlier 4 (1 pen), Sheehan 4 (1 pen), Sarcevic 3, Johnston 2, Kachunga 2, Aimson 1, Amaechi 1, Baptiste 1, Fossey 1, Morley 1, Thomason 1, Williams 1, own goal 1.
FA Cup (5): Kachunga 2, Bakayoko 1, Doyle 1, own goal 1.
Carabao Cup (0).
Papa John's Trophy (11): Afolayan 2, Bakayoko 2 (1 pen), Delfouneso 2, Doyle 2 (1 pen), John 1, Lee 1, own goal 1.

Gilks M 1	Jones G 28 + 1	Baptiste A 6 + 6	Johnston G 38 + 5	John D 38 + 1	Sheehan J 12 + 3	Williams M 39 + 1	Bakayoko A 16 + 16	Sarcevic A 13 + 1	Afolayan O 38 + 6	Doyle E 20 + 1	Isgrove L 12 + 6	Kachunga E 15 + 17	Lee K 19 + 6	Dixon J 23	Santos R 37	Gordon L 10 + 3	Delfouneso N 2 + 9	Brockbank H 2 + 2	Thomason G 9 + 4	Aimson W 22 + 3	Amaechi X 2 + 8	Senior A 2	Fossey M 15	Charles D 21 + 2	Darcy R — + 1	Trafford J 22	Morley A 21	Bodvarsson J 10 + 11	Sadlier K 8 + 10	Dempsey K 5 + 6	Match No.
1	2	3	4	5	6^{3}	7	8	9	10^{2}	11^{1}	12	13	14																		1
	2	4	12	5^{1}	7	6	8^{3}	9	10^{2}	11	14	13		1	3																2
	2		4		7	6	8^{1}	9^{3}	10	11^{2}	12	13	14	1	3	5															3
	2	12	4	5^{1}	7	6		9^{3}	10	11	8^{2}	13	14	1	3																4
	2^{1}	13	4^{2}	5	7	6^{3}		9	10	11	8	12		1	3		14														5
	2		4			6		9	10^{2}	11^{1}	8	12	7	1	3	5	13														6
	2	14	4^{3}		7^{2}	6		9	10	11	8^{1}	12	13	1	3	5															7
	2		4		7^{1}	6		9^{2}	10	11	8	13	12	1	3	5															8
	2		4	13	7^{3}	6		9	10	11	8^{1}	12	14	1	3	5^{2}															9
	2	4^{2}	13	5^{1}		6		9	10	11^{3}		8	7	1	3	12	14														10
	2^{1}		4	5	14	6	13	9	10	11^{2}	12	8	7^{3}	1	3																11
	2		4	5	13	6	12	9^{2}	10	11^{1}	14	8^{3}	7	1	3																12
			4		7^{3}	6	8^{2}	9	10	11	12	13		1	3	5		2^{1}	14												13
		3	4		7	6	11^{3}	12	10	14	8^{2}	13	9^{1}	1		5		2													14
			4^{1}	5	7^{2}	6	13		10	11	2	8^{3}	9	1	3		14			12											15
			13	5	12	6			10	11	2^{3}	8	7	1	3		9^{1}	14		4^{2}											16
				5	7	6	11^{1}		10		2	8	9	1	3					4	12										17
		2^{2}	12	5		6^{1}			10		8	11	7	1	3				9	4	13										18
			12	5					10	11^{2}	8^{1}	9	7^{3}	1	4	2	14		6	3	13										19
		13	6	5						11		8	7	1	3	2^{2}	12		9	4	10^{1}										20
		13	4	8					11	10^{2}		9	7	1	3■	5			6	2^{1}	12										21
		3	4	5		6			10	11^{1}		8	7^{2}	1			13		9		12	2									22
			6	5^{3}			12		10	11^{1}		8		1	3	14	9	13	7	4		2^{2}									23
	12			5		6	8^{1}		10				7	1	3		13		9	4			2^{3}	11^{2}	14						24
	2^{2}		4	5		7	11^{3}		12				8		3		13			14			9	10^{1}		1	6				25
	2		4	8		6	11^{2}		12				9^{1}		3								5	10		1	7	13			26
	2		4	8		6	12		11^{2}				7^{1}		3								5	10^{3}		1	9	14	13		27
	2		4	8		6	11^{1}		9^{2}						3				14				5	10^{3}		1	7	12	13		28
			4	8		6	14		11^{2}				9^{1}		3■					2			5	10^{3}		1	7	12		13	29
	2			8		6	13		11^{1}						3					4			5	10^{3}		1	7	12	14	9^{2}	30
	2		4	8		6	11		13				9^{1}		3								5	10^{3}		1	7^{2}	14		12	31
			4	8^{3}		6	11^{1}		13						3					2	14		5	12		1		10	9^{2}	7	32
	2		4	8			12		9^{2}						3				14				5	10		1	6	11^{1}	13	7^{3}	33
	2		4	8^{1}		6	13		9^{3}											3			5	10		1	7	11^{2}	12	14	34
	2		4	8^{2}		6	11^{3}		12						3								5	10		1	7^{1}	14	13	9	35
			4	8		6^{3}	12		9^{1}						3				14	2			5	10^{2}		1	7	11	13		36
			4	8		6^{1}	11^{2}		9^{3}						3					2	14		5	10		1	7	13	12		37
			4^{1}	8		6	14		9			13			3					2			5	10^{3}		1	7	11^{2}	12		38
			4	8		6^{3}	12		9^{2}			13			3					2				10		1	7	11^{1}	5	14	39
	5		4			6^{2}	13		11			9^{1}			3					2				10^{3}		1	7	12	8	14	40
	2		4	8		14			9^{2}			13			3^{1}					12				10		1	6	11	5	7^{3}	41
	2		4	5^{2}		7	12					6				13				3	14			10		1	8	11^{1}	9^{3}		42
	2		4	5		6	10^{1}		13			14							9^{3}	3				12		1	7	11^{2}	8		43
	2		4	8		6	13		9			11^{3}								3	5^{1}			10^{2}		1	7	14	12		44
	2		4	5		7^{1}	14		9			13								3				11^{2}		1	8	10	6^{3}	12	45
	2	14	4	8			11^{2}		9			12							6^{3}	3				10		1	7	13	5^{1}		46

FA Cup

First Round	Stockport Co	(h)	2-2
Replay	Stockport Co	(a)	3-5
(aet)			

Carabao Cup

First Round	Barnsley	(h)	0-0
(Bolton W won 5-4 on penalties)			
Second Round	Wigan Ath	(a)	0-0
(Wigan Ath won 5-4 on penalties)			

Papa John's Trophy

Group D (N)	Port Vale	(h)	3-2
Group D (N)	Liverpool U21	(h)	4-1
Group D (N)	Rochdale	(a)	3-0
Second Round	Fleetwood T	(h)	1-0
Third Round	Hartlepool U	(a)	0-1

AFC BOURNEMOUTH

FOUNDATION

There was a Bournemouth FC as early as 1875, but the present club arose out of the remnants of the Boscombe St John's club (formed 1890). The meeting at which Boscombe FC came into being was held at a house in Gladstone Road in 1899. They began by playing in the Boscombe and District Junior League.

Vitality Stadium, Dean Court, Kings Park, Bournemouth, Dorset BH7 7AF.

Telephone: (01202) 726 300.

Ticket Office: (0344) 576 1910.

Website: www.afcb.co.uk

Email: enquiries@afcb.co.uk

Ground Capacity: 11,379.

Record Attendance: 28,799 v Manchester U, FA Cup 6th rd, 2 March 1957.

Pitch Measurements: 105m × 68m (115yd × 74.5yd).

Chairman: Jeff Mostyn.

Chief Executive: Neill Blake.

Manager: Scott Parker.

Assistant Manager: Matt Wells.

Colours: Red and black striped shirts, black shorts with red trim, black socks with red trim.

Year Formed: 1899.

Turned Professional: 1910.

Previous Names: 1890, Boscombe St John's; 1899, Boscombe FC; 1923, Bournemouth & Boscombe Ath FC; 1972, AFC Bournemouth.

Club Nickname: 'Cherries'.

Grounds: 1899, Castlemain Road, Pokesdown; 1910, Dean Court (renamed Fitness First Stadium 2001; Seward Stadium 2011; Goldsands Stadium 2012; Vitality Stadium 2015).

First Football League Game: 25 August 1923, Division 3 (S), v Swindon T (a) L 1–3 – Heron; Wingham, Lamb; Butt, Charles Smith, Voisey; Miller, Lister (1), Davey, Simpson, Robinson.

Record League Victory: 8–0 v Birmingham C, FL C, 25 October 2014 – Boruc; Francis, Elphick, Cook, Daniels; Ritchie (1), Arter (Gosling), Surman, Pugh (3); Pitman (1) (Rantie 2 (1 pen)), Wilson (1) (Fraser). 10–0 win v Northampton T at start of 1939–40 expunged from the records on outbreak of war.

Record Cup Victory: 11–0 v Margate, FA Cup 1st rd, 20 November 1971 – Davies; Machin (1), Kitchener, Benson, Jones, Powell, Cave (1), Boyer, MacDougall (9 incl. 1p), Miller, Scott (De Garis).

Record Defeat: 0–9 v Lincoln C, Division 3, 18 December 1982.

HONOURS

League Champions: FL C – 2014–15; Division 3 – 1986–87.
Runners-up: FL C – 2021–22; FL 1 – 2012–13; Division 3S – 1947–48; FL 2 – 2009–10; Division 4 – 1970–71.

FA Cup: 6th rd – 1957, 2021.

League Cup: quarter-final – 2015, 2018, 2019.

League Trophy Winners: 1984.
Runners-up: 1998.

FOOTBALL YEARBOOK FACT FILE

Bournemouth installed floodlights at their former ground, Dean Court, at the beginning of the 1961–62 campaign and they were first used during the game with Northampton Town on 27 September. The Cherries won 3-2 and the attendance of 14,112 was the highest of the season to date. The following month there was a formal inauguration of the lights when West German club SSV Reutlingen were the visitors.

Most League Points (2 for a win): 62, Division 3, 1971–72.

Most League Points (3 for a win): 97, Division 3, 1986–87.

Most League Goals: 98, FL C, 2014–15.

Highest League Scorer in Season: Ted MacDougall, 42, 1970–71.

Most League Goals in Total Aggregate: Ron Eyre, 202, 1924–33.

Most League Goals in One Match: 4, Jack Russell v Clapton Orient, Division 3 (S), 7 January 1933; 4, Jack Russell v Bristol C, Division 3 (S), 28 January 1933; 4, Harry Mardon v Southend U, Division 3 (S), 1 January 1938; 4, Jack McDonald v Torquay U, Division 3 (S), 8 November 1947; 4, Ted MacDougall v Colchester U, 18 September 1970; 4, Brian Clark v Rotherham U, 10 October 1972; 4, Luther Blissett v Hull C, 29 November 1988; 4, James Hayter v Bury, Division 2, 21 October 2000.

Most Capped Player: Josh King, 34 (62), Norway.

Most League Appearances: Steve Fletcher, 628, 1992–2007; 2008–13.

Youngest League Player: Jimmy White, 15 years 321 days v Brentford, 30 April 1958.

Record Transfer Fee Received: £41,000,000 from Manchester C for Nathan Aké, August 2020.

Record Transfer Fee Paid: £25,200,000 to Levante for Jefferson Lerma, August 2018.

Football League Record: 1923 Elected to Division 3 (S) and remained a Third Division club for record number of years until 1970; 1970–71 Division 4; 1971–75 Division 3; 1975–82 Division 4; 1982–87 Division 3; 1987–90 Division 2; 1990–92 Division 3; 1992–2002 Division 2; 2002–03 Division 3; 2003–04 Division 2; 2004–08 FL 1; 2008–10 FL 2; 2010–13 FL 1; 2013–15 FL C; 2015–20 Premier League; 2020–22 FL C; 2022– Premier League.

MANAGERS

Vincent Kitcher 1914–23 (*Secretary-Manager*)
Harry Kinghorn 1923–25
Leslie Knighton 1925–28
Frank Richards 1928–30
Billy Birrell 1930–35
Bob Crompton 1935–36
Charlie Bell 1936–39
Harry Kinghorn 1939–47
Harry Lowe 1947–50
Jack Bruton 1950–56
Fred Cox 1956–58
Don Welsh 1958–61
Bill McGarry 1961–63
Reg Flewin 1963–65
Fred Cox 1965–70
John Bond 1970–73
Trevor Hartley 1974–75
John Benson 1975–78
Alec Stock 1979–80
David Webb 1980–82
Don Megson 1983
Harry Redknapp 1983–92
Tony Pulis 1992–94
Mel Machin 1994–2000
Sean O'Driscoll 2000–06
Kevin Bond 2006–08
Jimmy Quinn 2008
Eddie Howe 2008–11
Lee Bradbury 2011–12
Paul Groves 2012
Eddie Howe 2012–20
Jason Tindall 2020–21
Jonathan Woodgate 2021
Scott Parker June 2021–

LATEST SEQUENCES

Longest Sequence of League Wins: 8, 12.3.2013 – 20.4.2013.

Longest Sequence of League Defeats: 7, 13.8.1994 – 13.9.1994.

Longest Sequence of League Draws: 5, 25.4.2000 – 19.8.2000.

Longest Sequence of Unbeaten League Matches: 18, 6.3.1982 – 28.8.1982.

Longest Sequence Without a League Win: 14, 6.3.1974 – 27.4.1974.

Successive Scoring Runs: 31 from 28.10.2000.

Successive Non-scoring Runs: 6 from 1.2.1975.

TEN YEAR LEAGUE RECORD

		P	W	D	L	F	A	Pts	Pos
2012-13	FL 1	46	24	11	11	76	53	83	2
2013-14	FL C	46	18	12	16	67	66	66	10
2014-15	FL C	46	26	12	8	98	45	90	1
2015-16	PR Lge	38	11	9	18	45	67	42	16
2016-17	PR Lge	38	12	10	16	55	67	46	9
2017-18	PR Lge	38	11	11	16	45	61	44	12
2018-19	PR Lge	38	13	6	19	56	70	45	14
2019-20	PR Lge	38	9	7	22	40	65	34	18
2020-21	FL C	46	22	11	13	73	46	77	6
2021-22	FL C	46	25	13	8	74	39	88	2

DID YOU KNOW ?

In the days before they turned professional, Boscombe, as AFC Bournemouth were then known, regularly entered the FA Amateur Cup. They reached the third qualifying round on three occasions (1907–08, 1910–11 and 1911–12) but never progressed into the competition proper.

AFC BOURNEMOUTH – SKY BET CHAMPIONSHIP 2021–22 LEAGUE RECORD

Match No.	Date	Venue	Opponents	Result		H/T Score	Lg Pos.	Goalscorers	Attendance
1	Aug 6	H	WBA	D	2-2	1-1	1	Marcondes [12], Billing [52]	9254
2	14	A	Nottingham F	W	2-1	1-0	5	Brooks [28], Billing [58]	25,035
3	18	A	Birmingham C	W	2-0	0-0	4	Solanke [77], Anthony [87]	9922
4	21	H	Blackpool	D	2-2	2-0	7	Solanke 2 [6, 19]	9187
5	28	A	Hull C	D	0-0	0-0	6		10,199
6	Sept 11	H	Barnsley	W	3-0	1-0	5	Zemura 2 [8, 82], Solanke [46]	9486
7	14	H	QPR	W	2-1	2-0	1	Anthony [12], Solanke [37]	10,495
8	18	A	Cardiff C	W	1-0	0-0	1	Billing [54]	19,090
9	25	H	Luton T	W	2-1	2-0	1	Billing [17], Solanke [31]	9737
10	29	A	Peterborough U	D	0-0	0-0	2		8971
11	Oct 2	H	Sheffield U	W	2-1	0-0	1	Solanke (pen) [62], Billing [65]	9349
12	16	A	Bristol C	W	2-0	2-0	1	Lowe [21], Zemura [45]	20,828
13	19	A	Stoke C	W	1-0	0-0	1	Solanke [51]	18,427
14	23	H	Huddersfield T	W	3-0	2-0	1	Solanke 2 (1 pen) [10 (p), 21], Kelly [64]	9253
15	30	A	Reading	W	2-0	1-0	1	Solanke [43], Lowe [59]	13,551
16	Nov 3	H	Preston NE	L	1-2	0-0	1	Billing [60]	8578
17	6	H	Swansea C	W	4-0	1-0	1	Solanke 2 [26, 49], Anthony 2 [64, 90]	9725
18	21	A	Derby Co	L	2-3	2-1	2	Anthony [19], Solanke [38]	20,764
19	24	A	Millwall	D	1-1	1-0	2	Solanke [44]	12,237
20	27	H	Coventry C	D	2-2	1-0	2	Anthony [45], Billing [66]	11,094
21	Dec 3	A	Fulham	D	1-1	0-0	2	Solanke [46]	19,020
22	11	H	Blackburn R	L	0-2	0-1	2		10,064
23	18	A	Middlesbrough	L	0-1	0-0	2		18,323
24	27	A	QPR	W	1-0	1-0	1	Solanke [41]	16,308
25	30	H	Cardiff C	W	3-0	1-0	1	Christie [25], Solanke [68], Smithies (og) [83]	8942
26	Jan 15	A	Luton T	L	2-3	0-2	2	Marcondes [51], Rogers [78]	9649
27	22	H	Hull C	L	0-1	0-0	2		8823
28	29	A	Barnsley	W	1-0	1-0	3	Billing [12]	11,972
29	Feb 9	H	Birmingham C	W	3-1	2-0	2	Christie [17], Solanke [31], Anthony [76]	8708
30	12	A	Blackpool	W	2-1	0-1	2	Lowe [86], Dembele [90]	11,141
31	26	H	Stoke C	W	2-1	0-1	2	Solanke [83], Lowe [89]	9613
32	Mar 5	A	Preston NE	L	1-2	0-0	3	Lowe [50]	12,173
33	8	H	Peterborough U	D	1-1	0-1	2	Christie [52]	8293
34	12	H	Derby Co	W	2-0	1-0	2	Solanke [45], Lowe [90]	9979
35	15	H	Reading	D	1-1	1-0	2	Solanke [8]	9085
36	19	A	Huddersfield T	W	3-0	2-0	2	Anthony [19], Lerma [31], Solanke [46]	20,336
37	Apr 2	H	Bristol C	W	3-2	1-1	2	Solanke [40], Cook, L [52], Dembele [81]	9937
38	6	A	WBA	L	0-2	0-2	2		20,501
39	9	A	Sheffield U	D	0-0	0-0	2		26,769
40	15	H	Middlesbrough	D	0-0	0-0	2		9903
41	18	A	Coventry C	W	3-0	2-0	2	Lowe [12], Solanke 2 [45, 55]	24,492
42	23	H	Fulham	D	1-1	0-0	2	Solanke (pen) [90]	10,352
43	26	A	Swansea C	D	3-3	0-2	2	Moore 2 [72, 90], Solanke (pen) [81]	17,780
44	30	A	Blackburn R	W	3-0	1-0	2	Solanke [21], Billing 2 [70, 79]	21,396
45	May 3	H	Nottingham F	W	1-0	0-0	2	Moore [83]	10,563
46	7	H	Millwall	W	1-0	0-0	2	Moore [81]	10,244

Final League Position: 2

GOALSCORERS

League (74): Solanke 29 (4 pens), Billing 10, Anthony 8, Lowe 7, Moore 4, Christie 3, Zemura 3, Dembele 2, Marcondes 2, Brooks 1, Cook, L 1, Kelly 1, Lerma 1, Rogers 1, own goal 1.
FA Cup (3): Marcondes 3.
Carabao Cup (5): Brooks 2, Billing 1, Saydee 1, Solanke 1.

Travers M 45	Smith A 20	Mepham C 12 + 10	Kelly L 40 + 1	Zemura J 32 + 1	Marcondes E 8 + 9	Billing P 37 + 3	Kilkenny G 13 + 1	Brooks D 7	Solanke D 46	Anthony J 38 + 7	Saydee C — + 2	Rossi Z 3 + 1	Davis L 7 + 5	Stanislas J 2 + 5	Pearson B 8 + 15	Nyland O 1	Stacey J 24 + 1	Lerma J 33 + 1	Rogers M 1 + 14	Cahill G 21 + 1	Christie R 36 + 2	Lowe J 9 + 25	Cook L 25 + 3	Cook S 3	Brady R 2 + 4	Hill J — + 1	Phillips N 17	Cantwell T 8 + 3	Dembele S 4 + 9	Moore K — + 4	Laird E 4 + 2	Match No.
1	2	3	4	5	6	7	8	9^1	10	11	12																					1
1		2	4	5	6^1	7	8	$9^{\blacksquare}$	10^2	11	13	3	12																			2
1		2	4	5	8^1	6	7		10	11		3	9^2	12	13																	3
1		2^3	4	5	12	8	7^2	9	10	11		3	14	6^1	13																	4
		3	4	5	11^2			6^1	10	9			13		8	1	2	7	12													5
1	2		4	5		9		8^1	11^3	10^2					7			6	13	3	12	14										6
1	2	14	4	5		7		9^1	10	11^2					12			8	13	3	6^3											7
1	2	14	4	5		8			10^2	11^3					7			6	12	3	9^1	13										8
1	2	13	4	5		8			10^3	11^1					6			7	12	3	9^2	14										9
1			4	5		10		6^3	11	12					13		2	8	9^1	3	7^2	14										10
1	2	12	4	5		8^1			10^3	11					6		14	7		3	9^2	13										11
1			4	5		9^2	6		11	10				13			2	12	14	3	8^3	7^1										12
1		13	4	5		8^2	7^1		10	11					12		2	6		3	9^3	14										13
1			4	5		8	7		10^3	11				12			2	6^2	14	3	9^1	13										14
1		14	4	5^3		8	7^1		10	11^2					12		2	6		3	9	13										15
1		5^2	4		14	8			10	12					7^1		2	6	13	3	9^3	11										16
1			4			9^2	7		11^3	10			5				2	6	14	3	8^1	12	13									17
1		4				9	12		11	10			5^2				2	6^3	14	3	8	13	7^1									18
1		4			13		7^1		11	10^3			5				2	6	14	3	9	8^2	12									19
1		2			14	8	6^2		11	9^3		13	12				5	$3^{\blacksquare}$			10^1		7	4								20
1	5^3	13			8^1	7			11	10^2					12		2			3	9		6	4	14							21
1			13		12				10	11^3					7^1		2		14	3	8	9	6	4^2	5							22
1			4	5		9	7		11	10^2				12			2			3	8^1	13	6^3		14							23
1		3		5		9			11	12				10^1	14		2	7		4	8^2	13	6^3									24
1			4	5	14	8			10^2	11^1				12^3			2	7		3	9	13	6									25
1			4		8				10	11^1			5				2	7	13	3	9	12	6^2									26
1		3^1	4		6	8			10	13			5^3				2	7	14	12	9	11^2										27
1			4	5		8			10	11^1					7		2	6		$3^{\blacksquare}$	9^2	12				13						28
1			4	5		8^3			10	11							2	$7^{\blacksquare}$			9^1		13				3	6^2	12	14		29
1			4	5^3	13	8^2			10	9			14				2^1					12	7				3	6	11			30
1	2^1	3	4	5	13	8			10						14							9	7^2					6	11^3		12	31
1	$2^{\blacksquare 1}$		4	5		8			10	11^2					14						13	9	7				3	6^3			12	32
1			4	5	14	8^3			10	12							2^1				9	13	7				3	6	11^2			33
1			4	12					10	11			5^1		14		2	8			9^3	13	7				3	6^2				34
1			4	5					10	11^3					13		2	6			9	12	7^2				3	8^1	14			35
1	2		4	5		8^1			10^3	11								6^2			9	13	7				3	12	14			36
1	2		4	5		8			10^3	11^1					13			6^2			9	14	7				3		12			37
1	2		4	5		8			10	11^3								6			9^1	14	7^2				3	13	12			38
1	2		4	5^2		9			11	12								6			8		7		13		3		10^1			39
1	5		4			9^2			11	12								6			8^3	13	7				3	10^1	14		2	40
1	5	13	4			12			11	10					14			6			8	9^1	7^3				3				2^2	41
1	5		4			10^1			11	9^2								8^3			7	12	6				3	14	13		2	42
1	5^1		4			12			11	10								6			9^3	8^2	7		14		3			13	2	43
1	2	13	4	5		9			11^3	10^1								6			8^2	14	7				3		12			44
1	2	14	4	5		9			11	10^3					13			6^1			8^2		7				3			12		45
1	2		4	5	9^2	14	7		11	10													6^3		8^1		3		12	13		46

FA Cup

Third Round	Yeovil T	(a)	3-1
Fourth Round	Boreham Wood	(h)	0-1

Carabao Cup

First Round	Milton Keynes D	(h)	5-0
Second Round	Norwich C	(a)	0-6

BRADFORD CITY

FOUNDATION

Bradford was a rugby stronghold around the turn of the 20th century but after Manningham RFC held an archery contest to help them out of financial difficulties in 1903, they were persuaded to give up the handling code and turn to soccer. So they formed Bradford City and continued at Valley Parade. Recognising this as an opportunity to spread the dribbling code in this part of Yorkshire, the Football League immediately accepted the new club's first application for membership of the Second Division.

The Utilita Energy Stadium, Valley Parade, Bradford, West Yorkshire BD8 7DY.

Telephone: (01274) 773 355.

Ticket Office: (01274) 770 012.

Website: www.bradfordcityafc.co.uk

Email: support@bradfordcityfc.co.uk

Ground Capacity: 24,433.

Record Attendance: 39,146 v Burnley, FA Cup 4th rd, 11 March 1911.

Pitch Measurements: 100m × 64m (109.5yd × 70yd).

Chairman: Stephan Rupp.

Director: Alan Biggin.

Manager: Mark Hughes.

Assistant Manager: Glyn Hodges.

Colours: White shirts with amber and claret trim, claret shorts with amber trim, white socks with amber and claret trim.

Year Formed: 1903.

Turned Professional: 1903.

Club Nickname: 'The Bantams'.

Ground: 1903, Valley Parade (renamed Bradford & Bingley Stadium 1999; Intersonic Stadium 2007; Coral Windows Stadium 2007; Northern Commercials Stadium 2016; The Utilita Energy Stadium 2019).

First Football League Game: 1 September 1903, Division 2, v Grimsby T (a) L 0–2 – Seymour; Wilson, Halliday; Robinson, Millar, Farnall; Guy, Beckram, Forrest, McMillan, Graham.

Record League Victory: 11–1 v Rotherham U, Division 3 (N), 25 August 1928 – Sherlaw; Russell, Watson; Burkinshaw (1), Summers, Bauld; Harvey (2), Edmunds (3), White (3), Cairns, Scriven (2).

Record Cup Victory: 11–3 v Walker Celtic, FA Cup 1st rd (replay), 1 December 1937 – Parker; Rookes, McDermott; Murphy, Mackie, Moore; Bagley (1), Whittingham (1), Deakin (4 incl. 1p), Cooke (1), Bartholomew (4).

Record Defeat: 1–9 v Colchester U, Division 4, 30 December 1961.

HONOURS

League Champions: Division 2 – 1907–08; Division 3 – 1984–85; Division 3N – 1928–29.
Runners-up: First Division – 1998–99; Division 4 – 1981–82.

FA Cup Winners: 1911.

League Cup: *Runners-up:* 2013.

European Competitions
Intertoto Cup: 2000 (*sf*).

FOOTBALL YEARBOOK FACT FILE

Centre-forward Bert Whitehurst joined Bradford City from Liverpool in February 1929 and became something of a goalscoring sensation for the Valley Parade club. They won 13 of the remaining 15 Division Three North fixtures to pip long-time leaders Stockport County for the divisional title, Whitehurst netting 24 goals including a club-record tally of seven against Tranmere Rovers.

Most League Points (2 for a win): 63, Division 3 (N), 1928–29.

Most League Points (3 for a win): 94, Division 3, 1984–85.

Most League Goals: 128, Division 3 (N), 1928–29.

Highest League Scorer in Season: David Layne, 34, Division 4, 1961–62.

Most League Goals in Total Aggregate: Bobby Campbell, 121, 1981–84, 1984–86.

Most League Goals in One Match: 7, Albert Whitehurst v Tranmere R, Division 3 (N), 6 March 1929.

Most Capped Player: Jamie Lawrence, 19 (24), Jamaica.

Most League Appearances: Cec Podd, 502, 1970–84.

Youngest League Player: Robert Cullingford, 16 years 141 days v Mansfield T, 22 April 1970.

Record Transfer Fee Received: £2,000,000 from Newcastle U for Des Hamilton, March 1997; £2,000,000 from Newcastle U for Andrew O'Brien, March 2001.

Record Transfer Fee Paid: £2,500,000 to Leeds U for David Hopkin, July 2000.

Football League Record: 1903 Elected to Division 2; 1908–22 Division 1; 1922–27 Division 2; 1927–29 Division 3 (N); 1929–37 Division 2; 1937–61 Division 3; 1961–69 Division 4; 1969–72 Division 3; 1972–77 Division 4; 1977–78 Division 3; 1978–82 Division 4; 1982–85 Division 3; 1985–90 Division 2; 1990–92 Division 3; 1992–96 Division 2; 1996–99 Division 1; 1999–2001 Premier League; 2001–04 Division 1; 2004–07 FL 1; 2007–13 FL 2; 2013–19 FL 1; 2019– FL 2.

LATEST SEQUENCES

Longest Sequence of League Wins: 10, 26.11.1983 – 3.2.1984.

Longest Sequence of League Defeats: 8, 21.1.1933 – 11.3.1933.

Longest Sequence of League Draws: 6, 30.1.1976 – 13.3.1976.

Longest Sequence of Unbeaten League Matches: 21, 11.1.1969 – 2.5.1969.

Longest Sequence Without a League Win: 16, 28.8.1948 – 20.11.1948.

Successive Scoring Runs: 30 from 26.12.1961.

Successive Non-scoring Runs: 7 from 18.4.1925.

MANAGERS

Robert Campbell 1903–05
Peter O'Rourke 1905–21
David Menzies 1921–26
Colin Veitch 1926–28
Peter O'Rourke 1928–30
Jack Peart 1930–35
Dick Ray 1935–37
Fred Westgarth 1938–43
Bob Sharp 1943–46
Jack Barker 1946–47
John Milburn 1947–48
David Steele 1948–52
Albert Harris 1952
Ivor Powell 1952–55
Peter Jackson 1955–61
Bob Brocklebank 1961–64
Bill Harris 1965–66
Willie Watson 1966–69
Grenville Hair 1967–68
Jimmy Wheeler 1968–71
Bryan Edwards 1971–75
Bobby Kennedy 1975–78
John Napier 1978
George Mulhall 1978–81
Roy McFarland 1981–82
Trevor Cherry 1982–87
Terry Dolan 1987–89
Terry Yorath 1989–90
John Docherty 1990–91
Frank Stapleton 1991–94
Lennie Lawrence 1994–95
Chris Kamara 1995–98
Paul Jewell 1998–2000
Chris Hutchings 2000
Jim Jefferies 2000–01
Nicky Law 2001–03
Bryan Robson 2003–04
Colin Todd 2004–07
Stuart McCall 2007–10
Peter Taylor 2010–11
Peter Jackson 2011
Phil Parkinson 2011–16
Stuart McCall 2016–18
Simon Grayson 2018
Michael Collins 2018
David Hopkin 2018–19
Gary Bowyer 2019–20
Stuart McCall 2020
Mark Trueman and Conor Sellars 2021
Derek Adams 2021–22
Mark Hughes February 2022–

TEN YEAR LEAGUE RECORD

		P	*W*	*D*	*L*	*F*	*A*	*Pts*	*Pos*
2012-13	FL 2	46	18	15	13	63	52	69	7
2013-14	FL 1	46	14	17	15	57	54	59	11
2014-15	FL 1	46	17	14	15	55	55	65	7
2015-16	FL 1	46	23	11	12	55	40	80	5
2016-17	FL 1	46	20	19	7	62	43	79	5
2017-18	FL 1	46	18	9	19	57	67	63	11
2018-19	FL 1	46	11	8	27	49	77	41	24
2019-20	FL 2	37	14	12	11	44	40	54	9§
2020-21	FL 2	46	16	11	19	48	53	59	15
2021-22	FL 2	46	14	16	16	53	55	58	14

§Decided on points-per-game (1.46)

DID YOU KNOW ?

Bradford City struggled badly in 1908–09, their first season in the old First Division, and were bottom of the table by the end of November. Fortunes improved after a bantam was introduced as the club mascot, and they finished the season strongly, losing just one of their last 10 League fixtures to avoid relegation. The Valley Parade club has continued to be known as 'the Bantams' from this time onwards.

BRADFORD CITY – SKY BET LEAGUE TWO 2021–22 LEAGUE RECORD

Match No.	Date	Venue	Opponents	Result	H/T Score	Lg Pos.	Goalscorers	Attendance
1	Aug 7	A	Exeter C	D 0-0	0-0	12		5609
2	14	H	Oldham Ath	W 2-1	1-0	6	Angol 2 (1 pen) [32, 90 (p)]	17,624
3	17	H	Stevenage	W 4-1	3-1	2	Cook 3 [1, 30, 38], Canavan [88]	14,257
4	21	A	Mansfield T	W 3-2	1-1	2	O'Connor [19], Vernam [61], Cook [87]	6058
5	28	A	Leyton Orient	L 0-2	0-0	3		4901
6	Sept 4	H	Walsall	D 1-1	1-1	3	Watt [14]	15,822
7	11	A	Salford C	L 0-1	0-0	6		2863
8	18	H	Barrow	D 1-1	0-1	9	Vernam [59]	15,403
9	25	A	Crawley T	L 1-2	0-1	11	Cooke [81]	2435
10	Oct 2	H	Rochdale	W 2-0	1-0	7	Gilliead [36], Cook (pen) [75]	15,809
11	9	A	Newport Co	D 0-0	0-0	12		4089
12	16	H	Bristol R	D 2-2	1-0	10	Vernam [42], Cook [49]	16,664
13	19	H	Hartlepool U	L 1-3	0-1	12	O'Connor [72]	14,344
14	23	A	Swindon T	W 3-1	2-0	11	Lavery [16], Sutton [40], Robinson [75]	9461
15	30	H	Forest Green R	D 1-1	1-0	12	Cook [10]	14,873
16	Nov 13	A	Port Vale	D 1-1	0-0	11	Angol [74]	7010
17	20	H	Northampton T	D 1-1	0-0	10	Vernam [67]	15,372
18	23	A	Tranmere R	L 1-2	1-0	12	Sutton [26]	5962
19	27	A	Scunthorpe U	D 1-1	0-1	12	Songo'o [67]	3823
20	Dec 8	H	Colchester U	D 0-0	0-0	13		14,658
21	11	H	Sutton U	D 2-2	1-1	14	Robinson [34], Angol [81]	14,658
22	Jan 1	A	Barrow	W 2-1	1-0	12	Angol [8], Cook [49]	3463
23	8	A	Carlisle U	L 0-2	0-1	14		4996
24	15	H	Salford C	W 2-1	0-1	10	Watson (og) [57], O'Connor [85]	14,671
25	22	A	Rochdale	D 0-0	0-0	12		4941
26	25	A	Walsall	W 2-1	1-0	11	Daly [37], Cook (pen) [88]	4097
27	29	H	Crawley T	L 1-2	1-0	11	Cook [31]	14,623
28	Feb 1	H	Leyton Orient	D 1-1	0-0	11	Watt [83]	13,646
29	5	A	Harrogate T	L 0-2	0-0	12		2778
30	8	A	Stevenage	W 1-0	0-0	11	Walker [55]	1953
31	12	H	Exeter C	L 0-1	0-1	11		15,058
32	19	A	Oldham Ath	L 0-2	0-2	13		7716
33	22	H	Harrogate T	L 1-3	1-1	15	Foulds [12]	14,512
34	26	H	Mansfield T	L 0-2	0-1	15		16,797
35	Mar 5	H	Swindon T	L 1-2	1-1	15	Evans [18]	15,008
36	12	A	Forest Green R	W 2-0	0-0	15	Cooke [64], Cook [90]	3339
37	15	A	Hartlepool U	W 2-0	0-0	13	Foulds [70], Songo'o [76]	5106
38	19	H	Port Vale	L 1-2	0-0	15	Vernam [70]	16,046
39	26	H	Newport Co	D 0-0	0-0	14		14,716
40	Apr 2	A	Bristol R	L 1-2	0-0	15	Pereira [46]	9186
41	9	A	Northampton T	D 0-0	0-0	15		5548
42	15	H	Tranmere R	D 1-1	1-0	16	Walker [19]	17,257
43	18	A	Colchester U	L 0-3	0-2	18		2893
44	23	H	Scunthorpe U	W 2-1	2-1	16	Walker [1], Vernam [5]	15,248
45	30	A	Sutton U	W 4-1	1-0	14	Vernam 2 [16, 77], Songo'o [85], Cook [90]	4010
46	May 7	H	Carlisle U	W 2-0	1-0	14	Angol [13], Walker [69]	18,283

Final League Position: 14

GOALSCORERS

League (53): Cook 12 (2 pens), Vernam 8, Angol 6 (1 pen), Walker 4, O'Connor 3, Songo'o 3, Cooke 2, Foulds 2, Robinson 2, Sutton 2, Watt 2, Canavan 1, Daly 1, Evans 1, Gilliead 1, Lavery 1, Pereira 1, own goal 1.
FA Cup (2): Angol 1, Robinson 1.
Carabao Cup (1): Cooke 1.
Papa John's Trophy (1): Robinson 1.

O'Donnell R 19	Threlkeld O 22	Canavan N 17	O'Connor P 45	Ridehalgh L 28 + 1	Watt E 41	Sutton L 23 + 9	Gilliead A 38 + 5	Cooke C 28 + 14	Angol L 14 + 4	Cook A 35 + 4	Vernam C 19 + 9	Crankshaw O — + 6	Cousin-Dawson F 8 + 3	Evans G 13 + 7	Lavery C 5 + 14	Songo'o Y 39 + 2	Kelleher F 6 + 3	Robinson T 5 + 18	Scales K — + 2	Foulds M 18 + 5	Eisa A 1 + 3	Hornby S 6	Walker J 15 + 4	Daly M 8 + 1	Bass A 21	Elliott T 2 + 5	Delfouneso N 4 + 2	Hendrie L 16	Staunton R 1	Pereira D 9 + 1	Match No.
1	2^{1}	3	4	5	6	7	8^{2}	9	10	11	12	13																			1
1		4	3	5	6		8	7	10	11	12		2	9^{1}																	2
1		4	3	5	8		6	7	11^{1}	10^{3}	9^{2}	12	2		13	14															3
1		4	3	5	7^{1}		8	9^{2}		11	10	13	2	12		6															4
1		4	3^{3}	5	7^{1}		8	9		11	10	12	2^{2}		13	6	14														5
1	2	4^{3}	3	5	7		8	6		11	10^{2}	12		9^{1}	13			14													6
1	2		3	5	7	12	8^{3}	6		11^{2}	10			9^{1}	13		4	14													7
1	2		3	5	7		8	6		11^{2}	10			9^{1}	12		4	13													8
1	2		4	5	6^{2}	14	8^{3}	9		11		12		10^{1}		7	3		13												9
1	2		4	5	6	7^{2}	8	9		11	10^{1}			13		3		12													10
1	2^{1}		4	5	6	7	8	9		11	10^{2}			13		3		12													11
1	2		4	5^{1}	6^{2}	7	8	9		11	10					3			13	12											12
1	2^{2}		3		6^{3}	7	8^{1}	9		11	10		13		12	4		14		5											13
1	2	3	4		8	7	9			11^{1}				13	10^{2}	5		12		6											14
1	2	5	3		8	9^{2}	7	13		11					10^{1}	4		12		6											15
1	5^{1}	4	2	12	7	6	9	14	13		10					3^{2}		11^{3}		8											16
1		3	4	5	6		8	9^{2}			10		2		12	7		11^{1}			13										17
1		4	3	5	9	7	12		11^{1}		10^{2}		2		6^{3}	8		13			14										18
1	2	4	3	5		6	8	9	11							7		12			10^{1}										19
	2	4	3	5	6	9	8^{3}	12	10					13	14	7^{2}		11^{1}				1									20
	5	4▪	2	8	7	6	9	12	10							3		11^{1}				1									21
	2		4	5	6	12	8	9	10^{3}	11^{1}						7^{2}	3	14		13		1									22
	2^{2}		4	5	7		8	9^{3}	10	11^{1}	12					6	3	14		13		1									23
		4	3	5	6	7	8	13	11	12	10^{2}		2^{1}			14						1	9^{3}								24
	2		3	5	6^{1}	7	8	12	11^{3}	13	14					4						1	9	10^{2}							25
	2	4	3	5^{1}		14	8	7		11	13					6				12			9^{2}	10^{3}	1						26
		4	3			14	12	7		11	10^{1}		2			6^{3}				5			8	9^{2}	1	13					27
	2		4		6	7	13	9^{3}		11						3		12		5			8^{2}	10^{1}	1	14					28
	5		3	9	6		14	7^{2}		11^{3}						2		13		4			8		1	10^{1}	12				29
			4	5^{1}	6	7	13			10^{3}						3				12			8^{2}	11	1	14	9	2			30
			4		6	7		14		11						3		13		5			10^{2}	9^{3}	1	12	8^{1}	2			31
			4▪		6	7	8	9^{2}		11^{3}			12			3		14							1	13	10	2	5^{1}		32
			2		8	7	9	14		10			13			3		12		4^{2}				6^{3}	1	11^{1}		5			33
			2		6	7^{3}	8	12		10				13	14	3		11^{2}		4				9^{1}	1			5			34
			4		6	13	8	9^{3}		11				7^{2}	10^{1}	3		12		5				14	1			2			35
			4		7	13	8^{2}	9^{3}		10				6	14	3				5			12		1			2		11^{1}	36
			4		6^{2}	10		8		11				9^{1}	14	3				5			13		1		12	2		7^{3}	37
			4			10^{2}		7		11	13			6		3				5			12		1		9^{1}	2		8	38
			4		6		8	9^{1}		10	12			7^{2}	14	3				5			11^{3}		1			2		13	39
			4		6		10^{3}	13		11	12			7^{2}	14	3				5			9^{1}		1			2		8	40
			4	5	7		10^{3}	14	13	11^{2}	12			6^{1}		3							9		1			2		8	41
			4	5	7▪		6	13	12	11^{1}	10^{2}			14		3							9^{3}		1			2		8	42
	2^{1}		4▪			10	7	9	13	11^{2}				6^{3}	8	3	14			5			12		1						43
				5	7^{3}	14	6	13	11^{1}		10				12	3	4						9^{2}		1			2		8	44
			4	5	7	14	6^{3}		11^{1}	12	10					3	13						9		1			2		8^{2}	45
			4		7		6	14	11^{1}	12	10^{2}					3				5	13		9^{3}		1			2		8	46

FA Cup

First Round	Exeter C	(h)	1-1
Replay	Exeter C	(a)	0-3
(aet)			
2nd Replay	Exeter C	(a)	1-2

Match replayed due to too many substitutes being played by Exeter C in the first replay.

Carabao Cup

First Round	Nottingham F	(a)	1-2

Papa John's Trophy

Group F (N)	Lincoln C	(h)	0-3
Group F (N)	Manchester U U21	(h)	0-3
Group F (N)	Sunderland	(a)	1-1

(Bradford C won 4-2 on penalties)

BRENTFORD

FOUNDATION

Formed as a small amateur concern in 1889 they were very successful in local circles. They won the championship of the West London Alliance in 1893 and a year later the West Middlesex Junior Cup before carrying off the Senior Cup in 1895. After winning both the London Senior Amateur Cup and the Middlesex Senior Cup in 1898 they were admitted to the Second Division of the Southern League.

Brentford Community Stadium, 166 Lionel Road North, Brentford, Middlesex TW8 9QT.

Telephone: (0208) 847 2511.

Ticket Office: (0333) 005 8521.

Website: www.brentfordfc.com

Email: enquiries@brentfordfc.com

Ground Capacity: 17,250.

Record Attendance: 38,678 v Leicester C, FA Cup 6th rd, 26 February 1949 (at Griffin Park).

Pitch Measurements: 105m × 66m (115yd × 72yd).

Chairman: Cliff Crown.

Chief Executive: Jon Varney.

Head Coach: Thomas Frank.

Assistant Head Coach: Brian Riemer.

Colours: Red and white striped shirts with black trim, black shorts with red trim, black socks with red and white trim.

Year Formed: 1889.

Turned Professional: 1899.

Club Nickname: 'The Bees'.

Grounds: 1889, Clifden Road; 1891, Benns Fields, Little Ealing; 1895, Shotters Field; 1898, Cross Road, S. Ealing; 1900, Boston Park; 1904, Griffin Park; 2020, Brentford Community Stadium.

First Football League Game: 28 August 1920, Division 3, v Exeter C (a) L 0–3 – Young; Hodson, Rosier, Jimmy Elliott, Levitt, Amos, Smith, Thompson, Spreadbury, Morley, Henery.

Record League Victory: 9–0 v Wrexham, Division 3, 15 October 1963 – Cakebread; Coote, Jones; Slater, Scott, Higginson; Summers (1), Brooks (2), McAdams (2), Ward (2), Hales (1), (1 og).

Record Cup Victory: 7–0 v Windsor & Eton (a), FA Cup 1st rd, 20 November 1982 – Roche; Rowe, Harris (Booker), McNichol (1), Whitehead, Hurlock (2), Kamara, Joseph (1), Mahoney (3), Bowles, Roberts; 7–0 v Oldham Ath (h), Carabao Cup, 21 September 2021 – Fernandez; Jorgensen, Goode, Thompson, Roerslev (Bidstrup 71), Ghoddos, Jensen, Onyeka (Peart-Harris 72), Fosu (Stevens 71), Wissa (2), Forss (4 (1 pen)), own goal (1). *N.B.* 8–0 v Uxbridge: Frail, Jock Watson, Caie, Bellingham, Parsonage (1), Jay, Atherton, Leigh (1), Bell (2), Buchanan (2), Underwood (2), FA Cup, 3rd Qual rd, 31 October 1903.

Record Defeat: 0–7 v Swansea T, Division 3 (S), 8 November 1924; v Walsall, Division 3 (S), 19 January 1957; v Peterborough U, 24 November 2007.

HONOURS

League Champions: Division 2 – 1934–35; Division 3 – 1991–92; Division 3S – 1932–33; FL 2 – 2008–09; Third Division – 1998–99; Division 4 – 1962–63.
Runners-up: FL 1 – 2013–14; Second Division – 1994–95; Division 3S – 1929–30, 1957–58.

FA Cup: 6th rd – 1938, 1946, 1949, 1989.

League Cup: semi-final 2021.

League Trophy: *Runners-up:* 1985, 2001, 2011.

FOOTBALL YEARBOOK FACT FILE

Although Brentford agreed to adopt professionalism from the summer of 1899, they remained nominally amateur before an FA Commission investigated and found they were in breach of the rules. The B's, as they were then known, were suspended from activities for a month. Once this had ended, three men – Bert Lane, Alfred Mattocks and Harry Thurston – became the first registered professionals with the club.

Most League Points (2 for a win): 62, Division 3 (S), 1932–33 and Division 4, 1962–63.

Most League Points (3 for a win): 94, FL 1, 2013–14.

Most League Goals: 98, Division 4, 1962–63.

Highest League Scorer in Season: Jack Holliday, 38, Division 3 (S), 1932–33.

Most League Goals in Total Aggregate: Jim Towers, 153, 1954–61.

Most League Goals in One Match: 5, Jack Holliday v Luton T, Division 3 (S), 28 January 1933; 5, Billy Scott v Barnsley, Division 2, 15 December 1934; 5, Peter McKennan v Bury, Division 2, 18 February 1949.

Most Capped Player: John Buttigieg, 22 (98), Malta; Henrik Dalsgaard, 22 (27), Denmark.

Most League Appearances: Ken Coote, 514, 1949–64.

Youngest League Player: Danis Salman, 15 years 248 days v Watford, 15 November 1975.

Record Transfer Fee Received: £28,000,000 from Aston Villa for Ollie Watkins, September 2020.

Record Transfer Fee Paid: £16,000,000 to Hull C for Keane Lewis-Potter, July 2022.

Football League Record: 1920 Original Member of Division 3; 1921–33 Division 3 (S); 1933–35 Division 2; 1935–47 Division 1; 1947–54 Division 2; 1954–62 Division 3 (S); 1962–63 Division 4; 1963–66 Division 3; 1966–72 Division 4; 1972–73 Division 3; 1973–78 Division 4; 1978–92 Division 3; 1992–93 Division 1; 1993–98 Division 2; 1998–99 Division 3; 1999–2004 Division 2; 2004–07 FL 1; 2007–09 FL 2; 2009–14 FL 1; 2014–21 FL C; 2021– Premier League.

LATEST SEQUENCES

Longest Sequence of League Wins: 9, 30.4.1932 – 24.9.1932.

Longest Sequence of League Defeats: 9, 20.10.1928 – 25.12.1928.

Longest Sequence of League Draws: 5, 16.3.1957 – 6.4.1957.

Longest Sequence of Unbeaten League Matches: 26, 20.2.1999 – 16.10.1999.

Longest Sequence Without a League Win: 18, 9.9.2006 – 26.12.2006.

Successive Scoring Runs: 26 from 4.3.1963.

Successive Non-scoring Runs: 7 from 7.3.2000.

MANAGERS

Will Lewis 1900–03 (*Secretary-Manager*)
Dick Molyneux 1902–06
W. G. Brown 1906–08
Fred Halliday 1908–12, 1915–21, 1924–26 (*only Secretary to 1922*)
Ephraim Rhodes 1912–15
Archie Mitchell 1921–24
Harry Curtis 1926–49
Jackie Gibbons 1949–52
Jimmy Bain 1952–53
Tommy Lawton 1953
Bill Dodgin Snr 1953–57
Malcolm Macdonald 1957–65
Tommy Cavanagh 1965–66
Billy Gray 1966–67
Jimmy Sirrel 1967–69
Frank Blunstone 1969–73
Mike Everitt 1973–75
John Docherty 1975–76
Bill Dodgin Jnr 1976–80
Fred Callaghan 1980–84
Frank McLintock 1984–87
Steve Perryman 1987–90
Phil Holder 1990–93
David Webb 1993–97
Eddie May 1997
Micky Adams 1997–98
Ron Noades 1998–2000
Ray Lewington 2000–01
Steve Coppell 2001–02
Wally Downes 2002–04
Martin Allen 2004–06
Leroy Rosenior 2006
Scott Fitzgerald 2006–07
Terry Butcher 2007
Andy Scott 2007–11
Nicky Forster 2011
Uwe Rosler 2011–13
Mark Warburton 2013–15
Marinus Dijkhuizen 2015
Dean Smith 2015–18
Thomas Frank October 2018–

TEN YEAR LEAGUE RECORD

		P	W	D	L	F	A	Pts	Pos
2012-13	FL 1	46	21	16	9	62	47	79	3
2013-14	FL 1	46	28	10	8	72	43	94	2
2014-15	FL C	46	23	9	14	78	59	78	5
2015-16	FL C	46	19	8	19	72	67	65	9
2016-17	FL C	46	18	10	18	75	65	64	10
2017-18	FL C	46	18	15	13	62	52	69	9
2018-19	FL C	46	17	13	16	73	59	64	11
2019-20	FL C	46	24	9	13	80	38	81	3
2020-21	FL C	46	24	15	7	79	42	87	3
2021-22	PR Lge	38	13	7	18	48	56	46	13

DID YOU KNOW ?

Brentford goalkeeper Chic Brodie suffered a suspected fractured leg when conceding a goal in the home game with Oxford United on 26 February 1966. Billy Cobb came on as a substitute with defender Mel Scott taking over in goal. The Bees still trailed 1-0 at the break but produced a fine second-half performance to end up 5-1 winners.

BRENTFORD – PREMIER LEAGUE 2021–22 LEAGUE RECORD

Match No.	Date	Venue	Opponents	Result		H/T Score	Lg Pos.	Goalscorers	Attendance
1	Aug 13	H	Arsenal	W	2-0	1-0	1	Canos [22], Norgaard [73]	16,479
2	21	A	Crystal Palace	D	0-0	0-0	4		23,091
3	28	A	Aston Villa	D	1-1	1-1	9	Toney [7]	42,045
4	Sept 11	H	Brighton & HA	L	0-1	0-0	10		16,518
5	18	A	Wolverhampton W	W	2-0	2-0	9	Toney (pen) [28], Mbeumo [34]	29,724
6	25	H	Liverpool	D	3-3	1-1	9	Pinnock [27], Janelt [63], Wissa [82]	16,876
7	Oct 3	A	West Ham U	W	2-1	1-0	7	Mbeumo [20], Wissa [90]	49,940
8	16	H	Chelsea	L	0-1	0-1	7		16,940
9	24	H	Leicester C	L	1-2	0-1	12	Jorgensen [60]	16,814
10	30	A	Burnley	L	1-3	0-3	12	Ghoddos [79]	18,821
11	Nov 6	H	Norwich C	L	1-2	0-2	14	Henry [60]	16,837
12	20	A	Newcastle U	D	3-3	2-2	14	Lascelles (og) [61], Toney [11], Henry [31]	52,131
13	28	H	Everton	W	1-0	1-0	12	Toney (pen) [24]	16,957
14	Dec 2	A	Tottenham H	L	0-2	0-1	12		54,202
15	5	A	Leeds U	D	2-2	0-1	12	Baptiste [54], Canos [61]	35,639
16	10	H	Watford	W	2-1	0-1	9	Jansson [84], Mbeumo (pen) [90]	16,861
17	26	A	Brighton & HA	L	0-2	0-2	13		30,141
18	29	H	Manchester C	L	0-1	0-1	14		17,009
19	Jan 2	H	Aston Villa	W	2-1	1-1	12	Wissa [42], Roerslev Rasmussen [83]	16,876
20	11	A	Southampton	L	1-4	1-2	13	Janelt [23]	27,383
21	16	A	Liverpool	L	0-3	0-1	14		52,824
22	19	H	Manchester U	L	1-3	0-0	14	Toney [85]	17,094
23	22	H	Wolverhampton W	L	1-2	0-0	14	Toney [71]	16,982
24	Feb 9	A	Manchester C	L	0-2	0-1	14		51,658
25	12	H	Crystal Palace	D	0-0	0-0	14		16,958
26	19	A	Arsenal	L	1-2	0-0	14	Norgaard [90]	60,015
27	26	H	Newcastle U	L	0-2	0-2	15		17,039
28	Mar 5	A	Norwich C	W	3-1	1-0	15	Toney 3 (2 pens) [32, 52 (p), 58 (p)]	26,887
29	12	H	Burnley	W	2-0	0-0	15	Toney 2 (1 pen) [85, 90 (p)]	16,984
30	20	A	Leicester C	L	1-2	0-2	15	Wissa [85]	31,830
31	Apr 2	A	Chelsea	W	4-1	0-0	14	Janelt 2 [50, 60], Eriksen [54], Wissa [87]	39,061
32	10	H	West Ham U	W	2-0	0-0	13	Mbeumo [48], Toney [64]	17,032
33	16	A	Watford	W	2-1	1-0	11	Norgaard [15], Jansson [90]	20,747
34	23	H	Tottenham H	D	0-0	0-0	11		17,072
35	May 2	A	Manchester U	L	0-3	0-1	14		73,482
36	7	H	Southampton	W	3-0	2-0	12	Jansson [13], Wissa [14], Ajer [79]	17,051
37	15	A	Everton	W	3-2	1-2	11	Coleman (og) [37], Wissa [62], Henry [64]	38,819
38	22	H	Leeds U	L	1-2	0-0	13	Canos [78]	16,957

Final League Position: 13

GOALSCORERS

League (48): Toney 12 (5 pens), Wissa 7, Janelt 4, Mbeumo 4 (1 pen), Canos 3, Henry 3, Jansson 3, Norgaard 3, Ajer 1, Baptiste 1, Eriksen 1, Ghoddos 1, Jorgensen 1, Pinnock 1, Roerslev Rasmussen 1, own goals 2.
FA Cup (5): Mbeumo 3 (1 pen), Forss 1, Toney 1 (1 pen).
Carabao Cup (12): Forss 5 (1 pen), Wissa 3, Canos 1, Mbeumo 1, Toney 1, own goal 1.

Raya D 24	Ajer K 23 + 1	Jansson P 37	Pinnock E 32	Canos S 25 + 6	Onyeka F 12 + 8	Norgaard C 35	Janelt V 27 + 4	Henry R 33 + 1	Mbeumo B 34 + 1	Toney I 32 + 1	Sorensen M 9 + 2	Bidstrup M — + 4	Forss M 1 + 6	Ghoddos S 4 + 13	Wissa Y 12 + 18	Jensen M 19 + 12	Baptiste S 9 + 13	Roerslev Rasmussen M 12 + 9	Jorgensen M 6 + 2	Fernandez A 12	Goode C 4 + 2	Thompson D 2	Stevens F — + 1	Lossl J 2	Da Silva J 2 + 7	Eriksen C 10 + 1	Fosu T — + 1	Young-Coombes N — + 1	*Match No.*
1	2^{1}	3	4	5	6^{2}	7	8	9	10^{3}	11	12	13	14																1
1	2	3	4	5	6^{1}	7	8^{3}	9	10^{2}	11		14		12	13														2
1	2	3	4	5		6	7^{3}	8	10^{2}	11				9^{1}	12	13	14												3
1	2	3	4	5^{1}	14	7	8^{2}	9	10	11						13	6^{3}	12											4
1	2	3^{3}	4	5^{1}	12	7	8	9^{2}	10	11							6▮	13	14										5
1	2	3	4^{1}	5	6^{2}	7^{3}	8	9	10	11					14		13		12										6
1		3	4	5	8^{2}	7		9	10^{3}	11		13			14	12	6^{1}		2										7
1		3	4	5^{2}	6^{1}	7		9	10	11			12	13		8			2										8
1	12	3	4^{1}	5	6^{3}	7		9	11^{2}	10			13	14		8			2										9
		3	4	5^{3}	6^{1}	7	13	9		11			10	12		8^{2}		14	2	1									10
		3	4	5		7	8^{2}	9^{3}	10	11			14	13		6			2^{1}	1	12								11
		3	4	5	12	7	6^{3}	8	9	10				11^{1}			14	2^{2}		1	13								12
		3	4	5^{3}	6	7^{1}	8	9^{2}	11	10					14		12	13		1	2								13
		3	4	5^{3}	6^{1}	7	8^{2}	9	11	10					14	13	12			1	2								14
		3	4	11^{2}	12	7	8^{3}	9	10						13	14	6^{1}	5		1	2								15
		3			14	7	4	9^{3}	10				12	13	11^{1}	8^{2}	6	5		1	2								16
		3	2	5	13	7			10^{1}	11	4			14	12	8^{2}	6			1		9^{3}							17
		3	2	12	8^{2}					11	4	13		14	10^{1}	7	6	5		1		9^{3}							18
		3	2	9^{1}	6^{3}	7	14			10	4			12	11	8^{2}	13	5		1									19
	2	3	4^{2}	9^{3}		7	6		10	11					12	13	8^{1}	5		1			14						20
	2	3	4	12		7	8	9^{1}	10^{3}	11					13	14	6^{2}	5		1									21
		3	2	9^{2}		7	8^{1}	13	10	11	4				14	6^{3}	12	5						1					22
	2	3	4	5^{5}		7	8	9^{1}	10	11			15	16	14	6^{2}	13^{4}	12^{3}						1					23
1	2	3	4	10^{1}	6^{3}	7		9	12					11^{2}	14	8		5							13				24
1	2	3	4	5^{3}		7	8^{1}	9	10					13	11^{2}	6	14								12				25
1	2	3	4	5^{3}		7	12	9	10					14	11	8^{1}	13								6^{2}				26
1	2^{3}	3	4	14		7	8	5	10	13					11^{2}	6^{1}									9▮	12			27
1	2^{2}	3	4	10^{3}	12	8^{1}	7	5	6	11					14			13								9			28
1	2	3	4	10^{1}	14	8^{2}	7	5	6^{3}	11					12	13										9			29
1	2^{2}	3	4			8	9^{1}	5^{3}	6	11					10	7	12	13									14		30
1	3	4	5	14		8	9^{1}	6^{3}	10^{2}	11					13	12		2								7			31
1	2^{3}		4	13		7	6^{1}	5	9^{2}	10					11	12		14	3							8			32
1	2	3	4^{1}			7	6^{3}	5	9	10	12			13	11^{2}	14										8			33
1		4					8	6	10	11	5			2^{2}	13	7^{1}		3							12	9			34
1	3	4				8^{2}	7^{1}	6	11^{3}	10	5				14	12		2							13	9			35
1	2	3				7		5	9^{2}	10	4				11^{1}	6^{3}	13								12	8		14	36
1	2^{2}	3				7	12	5	9	10	4^{1}				11^{3}	6		14							13	8			37
1	2	3		13▮			7	5^{2}	9	10	4^{3}				11	6^{1}	14								12	8			38

FA Cup

Third Round	Port Vale	(a)	4-1
Fourth Round	Everton	(a)	1-4

Carabao Cup

Second Round	Forest Green R	(h)	3-1
Third Round	Oldham Ath	(h)	7-0
Fourth Round	Stoke C	(a)	2-1
Quarter-Final	Chelsea	(h)	0-2

BRIGHTON & HOVE ALBION

FOUNDATION

A professional club Brighton United was formed in November 1897 at the Imperial Hotel, Queen's Road, but folded in March 1900 after less than two seasons in the Southern League at the County Ground. An amateur team Brighton & Hove Rangers was then formed by some prominent United supporters and after one season at Withdean, decided to turn semi-professional and play at the County Ground. Rangers were accepted into the Southern League but folded in June 1901. John Jackson, the former United manager, organised a meeting at the Seven Stars public house, Ship Street on 24 June 1901 at which a new third club Brighton & Hove United was formed. They took over Rangers' place in the Southern League and pitch at County Ground. The name was changed to Brighton & Hove Albion before a match was played because of objections by Hove FC.

American Express Community Stadium, Village Way, Falmer, Brighton BN1 9BL.

Telephone: (01273) 668 855.

Ticket Office: (0844) 327 1901.

Website: www.brightonandhovealbion.com

Email: supporter.services@bhafc.co.uk

Ground Capacity: 31,780.

Record Attendance: 36,747 v Fulham, Division 2, 27 December 1958 (at Goldstone Ground); 8,691 v Leeds U, FL 1, 20 October 2007 (at Withdean); 31,637 v Manchester U, Premier League, 7 May 2022 (at Amex).

Pitch Measurements: 105m × 68m (115yd × 74.5yd).

Chairman: Tony Bloom.

Chief Executive: Paul Barber.

Head Coach: Graham Potter.

Assistant Head Coach: Billy Reid.

Colours: Blue and white striped shirts with gold trim, blue shorts with gold trim, white socks.

Year Formed: 1901.

Turned Professional: 1901.

Club Nickname: 'The Seagulls'.

Grounds: 1901, County Ground; 1902, Goldstone Ground; 1997, Priestfield Stadium (groundshare with Gillingham); 1999, Withdean Stadium; 2011, American Express Community Stadium.

First Football League Game: 28 August 1920, Division 3, v Southend U (a) L 0–2 – Hayes; Woodhouse, Little; Hall, Comber, Bentley; Longstaff, Ritchie, Doran, Rodgerson, March.

Record League Victory: 9–1 v Newport Co, Division 3 (S), 18 April 1951 – Ball; Tennant (1p), Mansell (1p); Willard, McCoy, Wilson; Reed, McNichol (4), Garbutt, Bennett (2), Keene (1). 9–1 v Southend U, Division 3, 27 November 1965 – Powney; Magill, Baxter; Leck, Gall, Turner; Gould (1), Collins (1), Livesey (2), Smith (3), Goodchild (2).

HONOURS

League Champions: FL 1 – 2010–11; Second Division – 2001–02; Division 3S – 1957–58; Third Division – 2000–01; Division 4 – 1964–65.
Runners-up: FL C – 2016–17; Division 2 – 1978–79; Division 3 – 1971–72, 1976–77, 1987–88; Division 3S – 1953–54, 1955–56.

FA Cup: *Runners-up:* 1983.

League Cup: 5th rd – 1979.

FOOTBALL YEARBOOK FACT FILE

Brighton & Hove Albion finished in second place in Division Two of the Southern League for 1902–03 but then had to face Watford, who had finished second to bottom of the First Division, in a 'test match', an earlier version of the play-off system. The teams played at West Ham on 27 April with Brighton winning 5-3 in front of just a few hundred spectators to gain promotion.

Record Cup Victory: 10–1 v Wisbech, FA Cup 1st rd, 13 November 1965 – Powney; Magill, Baxter; Collins (1), Gall, Turner; Gould, Smith (2), Livesey (3), Cassidy (2), Goodchild (1), (1 og).

Record Defeat: 0–9 v Middlesbrough, Division 2, 23 August 1958.

Most League Points (2 for a win): 65, Division 3 (S), 1955–56 and Division 3, 1971–72.

Most League Points (3 for a win): 95, FL 1, 2010–11.

Most League Goals: 112, Division 3 (S), 1955–56.

Highest League Scorer in Season: Peter Ward, 32, Division 3, 1976–77.

Most League Goals in Total Aggregate: Tommy Cook, 114, 1922–29.

Most League Goals in One Match: 5, Jack Doran v Northampton T, Division 3 (S), 5 November 1921; 5, Adrian Thorne v Watford, Division 3 (S), 30 April 1958.

Most Capped Player: Shane Duffy, 50 (includes 9 on loan at Celtic) (55), Republic of Ireland.

Most League Appearances: Ernie 'Tug' Wilson, 509, 1922–36.

Youngest League Player: Ian Chapman, 16 years 259 days v Birmingham C, 14 February 1987.

Record Transfer Fee Received: £50,000,000 from Arsenal for Ben White, July 2021.

Record Transfer Fee Paid: £20,700,000 to RB Salzburg for Enoch Mwepu, July 2021.

Football League Record: 1920 Original Member of Division 3; 1921–58 Division 3 (S); 1958–62 Division 2; 1962–63 Division 3; 1963–65 Division 4; 1965–72 Division 3; 1972–73 Division 2; 1973–77 Division 3; 1977–79 Division 2; 1979–83 Division 1; 1983–87 Division 2; 1987–88 Division 3; 1988–96 Division 2; 1996–2001 Division 3; 2001–02 Division 2; 2002–03 Division 1; 2003–04 Division 2; 2004–06 FL C; 2006–11 FL 1; 2011–17 FL C; 2017– Premier League.

MANAGERS

John Jackson 1901–05
Frank Scott-Walford 1905–08
John Robson 1908–14
Charles Webb 1919–47
Tommy Cook 1947
Don Welsh 1947–51
Billy Lane 1951–61
George Curtis 1961–63
Archie Macaulay 1963–68
Fred Goodwin 1968–70
Pat Saward 1970–73
Brian Clough 1973–74
Peter Taylor 1974–76
Alan Mullery 1976–81
Mike Bailey 1981–82
Jimmy Melia 1982–83
Chris Cattlin 1983–86
Alan Mullery 1986–87
Barry Lloyd 1987–93
Liam Brady 1993–95
Jimmy Case 1995–96
Steve Gritt 1996–98
Brian Horton 1998–99
Jeff Wood 1999
Micky Adams 1999–2001
Peter Taylor 2001–02
Martin Hinshelwood 2002
Steve Coppell 2002–03
Mark McGhee 2003–06
Dean Wilkins 2006–08
Micky Adams 2008–09
Russell Slade 2009
Gus Poyet 2009–13
Óscar Garcia 2013–14
Sammi Hyypia 2014
Chris Hughton 2014–19
Graham Potter May 2019–

LATEST SEQUENCES

Longest Sequence of League Wins: 9, 2.10.1926 – 20.11.1926.

Longest Sequence of League Defeats: 12, 17.8.2002 – 26.10.2002.

Longest Sequence of League Draws: 6, 16.2.1980 – 15.3.1980.

Longest Sequence of Unbeaten League Matches: 22, 2.5.2015 – 15.12.2015.

Longest Sequence Without a League Win: 15, 21.10.1972 – 27.1.1973.

Successive Scoring Runs: 31 from 4.2.1956.

Successive Non-scoring Runs: 6 from 30.3.2019.

TEN YEAR LEAGUE RECORD

		P	W	D	L	F	A	Pts	Pos
2012-13	FL C	46	19	18	9	69	43	75	4
2013-14	FL C	46	19	15	12	55	40	72	6
2014-15	FL C	46	10	17	19	44	54	47	20
2015-16	FL C	46	24	17	5	72	42	89	3
2016-17	FL C	46	28	9	9	74	40	93	2
2017-18	PR Lge	38	9	13	16	34	54	40	15
2018-19	PR Lge	38	9	9	20	35	60	36	17
2019-20	PR Lge	38	9	14	15	39	54	41	15
2020-21	PR Lge	38	9	14	15	40	46	41	16
2021-22	PR Lge	38	12	15	11	42	44	51	9

DID YOU KNOW ?

Although Brighton & Hove Albion entered the Football League Cup from its inception in 1960–61, it was not until 1965–66 that they won a match in the competition at their home stadium, the Goldstone Ground. After a run of two defeats and two draws they beat Luton Town 2-0 in a first-round replay on 7 September 1965 with goals from Bobby Smith and Billy Cassidy.

BRIGHTON & HOVE ALBION – PREMIER LEAGUE 2021–22 LEAGUE RECORD

Match No.	*Date*	*Venue*	*Opponents*	*Result*		*H/T Score*	*Lg Pos.*	*Goalscorers*	*Attendance*
1	Aug 14	A	Burnley	W	2-1	0-1	7	Maupay [73], Mac Allister [78]	16,910
2	21	H	Watford	W	2-0	2-0	2	Duffy [10], Maupay [41]	29,485
3	28	H	Everton	L	0-2	0-1	7		30,548
4	Sept 11	A	Brentford	W	1-0	0-0	4	Trossard [90]	16,518
5	19	H	Leicester C	W	2-1	1-0	4	Maupay (pen) [35], Welbeck [50]	31,078
6	27	A	Crystal Palace	D	1-1	0-1	6	Maupay [90]	22,975
7	Oct 2	H	Arsenal	D	0-0	0-0	5		31,266
8	16	A	Norwich C	D	0-0	0-0	4		26,777
9	23	H	Manchester C	L	1-4	0-3	4	Mac Allister (pen) [81]	31,215
10	30	A	Liverpool	D	2-2	1-2	7	Mwepu [41], Trossard [65]	53,197
11	Nov 6	H	Newcastle U	D	1-1	1-0	6	Trossard (pen) [24]	31,267
12	20	A	Aston Villa	L	0-2	0-0	8		41,925
13	27	H	Leeds U	D	0-0	0-0	8		31,166
14	Dec 1	A	West Ham U	D	1-1	0-1	7	Maupay [89]	59,626
15	4	A	Southampton	D	1-1	0-1	9	Maupay [90]	28,706
16	15	H	Wolverhampton W	L	0-1	0-1	13		30,362
17	26	H	Brentford	W	2-0	2-0	9	Trossard [34], Maupay [42]	30,141
18	29	A	Chelsea	D	1-1	0-1	10	Welbeck [90]	40,080
19	Jan 2	A	Everton	W	3-2	2-0	8	Mac Allister 2 [3, 71], Burn [21]	38,203
20	14	H	Crystal Palace	D	1-1	0-0	8	Andersen (og) [87]	30,675
21	18	H	Chelsea	D	1-1	0-1	9	Webster [60]	30,880
22	23	A	Leicester C	D	1-1	0-0	9	Welbeck [82]	31,231
23	Feb 12	A	Watford	W	2-0	1-0	9	Maupay [44], Webster [83]	20,795
24	15	A	Manchester U	L	0-2	0-0	9		73,012
25	19	H	Burnley	L	0-3	0-2	9		29,921
26	26	H	Aston Villa	L	0-2	0-1	10		31,475
27	Mar 5	A	Newcastle U	L	1-2	0-2	13	Dunk [55]	52,214
28	12	H	Liverpool	L	0-2	0-1	13		31,474
29	16	H	Tottenham H	L	0-2	0-1	13		31,144
30	Apr 2	H	Norwich C	D	0-0	0-0	13		31,245
31	9	A	Arsenal	W	2-1	1-0	11	Trossard [28], Mwepu [66]	60,112
32	16	A	Tottenham H	W	1-0	0-0	10	Trossard [90]	58,685
33	20	A	Manchester C	L	0-3	0-0	10		52,226
34	24	H	Southampton	D	2-2	2-1	11	Welbeck [2], Salisu (og) [44]	31,335
35	30	A	Wolverhampton W	W	3-0	1-0	9	Mac Allister (pen) [42], Trossard [70], Bissouma [86]	31,243
36	May 7	H	Manchester U	W	4-0	1-0	9	Caicedo [15], Cucurella [49], Gross [57], Trossard [60]	31,637
37	15	A	Leeds U	D	1-1	1-0	10	Welbeck [21]	36,638
38	22	H	West Ham U	W	3-1	0-1	9	Veltman [50], Gross [80], Welbeck [90]	31,604

Final League Position: 9

GOALSCORERS

League (42): Maupay 8 (1 pen), Trossard 8 (1 pen), Welbeck 6, Mac Allister 5 (2 pens), Gross 2, Mwepu 2, Webster 2, Bissouma 1, Burn 1, Caicedo 1, Cucurella 1, Duffy 1, Dunk 1, Veltman 1, own goals 2.
FA Cup (3): Bissouma 1, Maupay 1, Moder 1.
Carabao Cup (6): Connolly 2, Moder 1, Mwepu 1, Webster 1, Zeqiri 1.
Papa John's Trophy (4): Tolaj 2, Ferguson 1, Miller 1.

Sanchez R 37	Webster A 16 + 6	Duffy S 15 + 3	Dunk L 29	Gross P 24 + 5	Alzate S 5 + 4	March S 17 + 14	Mwepu E 12 + 6	Bissouma Y 25 + 1	Trossard L 32 + 2	Maupay N 25 + 7	Lallana A 18 + 6	Moder J 19 + 9	Mac Allister A 22 + 11	Connolly A 1 + 3	Veltman J 33 + 1	Welbeck D 15 + 10	Richards T — + 2	Cucurella M 35	Burn D 12 + 1	Lamptey T 16 + 14	Steele J 1	Locadia J — + 1	Sarmiento J 1 + 4	Ferguson E — + 1	Caicedo M 8	*Match No.*
1	2	3	4	5	6^2	7	8^1	9	10^3	11	12	13	14													1
1	2	3	4	5		8	13	7	9^2	11^1	6^3	14	10	12												2
1	2	3	4	5				7	9	11	6^2	8^3	10^1		12	13	14									3
1	2^1	3	4			14		7	9	10	6	12	13		5	11^2		8^3								4
1		3	4			5^1	12	7^3	9	11	6	14			2	10^2		8	13							5
1		2	3	6	12^2				9	10	7	13		14	5	11^3		8	4^1							6
1		2	3	6^2		13			10	11	7	8^1	12		5			9	4							7
1		2	3	6		13			10	11	7	8^3	14		5^1			9^2	4	12						8
1			3	6^3		5	13		10	11^2	7	8	14		2			9	4^1	12						9
1		3	4	14		8	6	7^1	11		9^3	10^2	12		2			5		13						10
1■	14	3	4			10^2	8^1	6	11	13	9		12		2			5		7^3						11
	2	3	4	6^3		12		7	10	13	11	8	14					9^1		5^2	1					12
1	3		4	6		13		7	11	10^1		8^3			2			9		5^2		12	14			13
1	3^2	13	4			12		7	10	11	9	6			2^3			5		14			8^1			14
1		3		8^1		13	6	7	10	11		14		12	2^3			9	4	5^2						15
1						9	6^2	7^3	11		14	8	12	10^1	3		13	5	4	2						16
1	3			13	14		7		11^1	10	6^2	9	8^3			12		5	4	2						17
1					14	8	12	7		11	6	9^3	10^2		2	13		4	3	5^1						18
1	3	13					6	8	11^3	10	7^2	14	9		2^1			5	4	12						19
1	3			7^2		14			11	10	6^1	9	8		2^3	13		5	4	12						20
1	3			8^1	6	14			13	12		11	9		2	10^2		5	4	7^3						21
1	3			7^2	6^1	14			11	10		9	8		2^3	12		5	4	13						22
1	4	14	3	7^1				13		10	5^3	8	12		2	11^2		9		6						23
1	3		4■	7^1	12			6	11^2	10^3		9	8		2	14		5		13						24
1		3				13		8	12	10	7^1	6^2	9		4	11^3		5		2				14		25
1			3			9		7	11	10		6^1	8		2	12		4		5						26
1		3	4	6	7^3	13			11	12		8^1	14		2	10		5		9^2						27
1			4	13	6^1	8		7^3	10	11	12^2		9		3	14		5		2						28
1		3	4	6^2		8		7^1	10	11		13	9		2^3	12		5		14						29
1			3	5		9^2	12		7	10^1		13^3	8		2	11		4		6			14			30
1	14		3	5			6^2	7^1	9^3		12		10		2	11		4		13					8	31
1			3	6		14	10^1	7	9		13		11		2	12		4		5^3					8^2	32
1	12		3	10		9	6			14			7		2	11^3		4		5^1			13		8^2	33
1	3^1		4	12		13	6^2		9	10^3			7		2	11		5					14		8	34
1	12		3	14		5^2	9^1	6	8^3				10		2	11		4		13					7	35
1	12		3	9		5^2		6	8^3	14			10^1		2	11		4		13					7	36
1	12		3	9		5^1		6	8^3		13		10		2	11		4		14					7^2	37
1	3		4	9		5^2	14	6^1		12			10		2	11		8		13					7^3	38

FA Cup

Third Round	WBA	(a)	2-1
(aet)			
Fourth Round	Tottenham H	(a)	1-3

Carabao Cup

Second Round	Cardiff C	(a)	2-0
Third Round	Swansea C	(h)	2-0
Fourth Round	Leicester C	(a)	2-2

(Leicester C won 4-2 on penalties)

Papa John's Trophy (Brighton & HA U21)

Group D (S)	Walsall	(a)	0-1
Group D (S)	Forest Green R	(a)	2-2
(Forest Green R won 5-3 on penalties)			
Group D (S)	Northampton T	(a)	2-1

BRISTOL CITY

FOUNDATION

The name Bristol City came into being in 1897 when the Bristol South End club, formed three years earlier, decided to adopt professionalism and apply for admission to the Southern League after competing in the Western League. The historic meeting was held at the Albert Hall, Bedminster. Bristol City employed Sam Hollis from Woolwich Arsenal as manager and gave him £40 to buy players. In 1900 they merged with Bedminster, another leading Bristol club.

Ashton Gate Stadium, Ashton Road, Bristol BS3 2EJ.

Telephone: (0117) 963 0600.

Ticket Office: (0117) 963 0600 (option 1).

Website: www.bcfc.co.uk

Email: supporterservices@bristol-sport.co.uk

Ground Capacity: 26,459.

Record Attendance: 43,335 v Preston NE, FA Cup 5th rd, 16 February 1935.

Pitch Measurements: 105m × 66.8m (115yd × 73yd).

Chairman: Jon Lansdown CBE.

Chief Executive Officer: Richard Gould.

Manager: Nigel Pearson.

Assistant Manager: Curtis Fleming.

Colours: Red shirts with white trim, white shorts with red trim, red socks with white trim.

Year Formed: 1894.

Turned Professional: 1897.

Previous Name: 1894, Bristol South End; 1897, Bristol City.

Club Nickname: 'Robins'.

Grounds: 1894, St John's Lane; 1904, Ashton Gate.

First Football League Game: 7 September 1901, Division 2, v Blackpool (a) W 2–0 – Moles; Tuft, Davies; Jones, McLean, Chambers; Bradbury, Connor, Boucher, O'Brien (2), Flynn.

Record League Victory: 9–0 v Aldershot, Division 3 (S), 28 December 1946 – Eddols; Morgan, Fox; Peacock, Roberts, Jones (1); Chilcott, Thomas, Clark (4 incl. 1p), Cyril Williams (1), Hargreaves (3).

Record Cup Victory: 11–0 v Chichester C, FA Cup 1st rd, 5 November 1960 – Cook; Collinson, Thresher; Connor, Alan Williams, Etheridge; Tait (1), Bobby Williams (1), Atyeo (5), Adrian Williams (3), Derrick, (1 og).

Record Defeat: 0–9 v Coventry C, Division 3 (S), 28 April 1934.

Most League Points (2 for a win): 70, Division 3 (S), 1954–55.

HONOURS

League Champions: Division 2 – 1905–06; FL 1 – 2014–15; Division 3S – 1922–23, 1926–27, 1954–55.
Runners-up: Division 1 – 1906–07; Division 2 – 1975–76; FL 1 – 2006–07; Second Division – 1997–98; Division 3 – 1964–65, 1989–90; Division 3S – 1937–38.

FA Cup: *Runners-up:* 1909.

League Cup: semi-final – 1971, 1989, 2018.

League Trophy Winners: 1986, 2003, 2015.
Runners-up: 1987, 2000.

Welsh Cup Winners: 1934.

Anglo-Scottish Cup Winners: 1978.

FOOTBALL YEARBOOK FACT FILE

Goalkeeper Frank Coombs was one of the stars of Dartford's FA Cup first-round tie with Bristol City in November 1947, helping his team to a 0-0 draw, but then conceded nine goals in the replay. His form must have impressed the management at Ashton Gate, for in June 1949 he signed for the Robins and went on to make 24 first-team appearances before moving on to play for Southend United.

Most League Points (3 for a win): 99, FL 1, 2014–15.

Most League Goals: 104, Division 3 (S), 1926–27.

Highest League Scorer in Season: Don Clark, 36, Division 3 (S), 1946–47.

Most League Goals in Total Aggregate: John Atyeo, 314, 1951–66.

Most League Goals in One Match: 6, Tommy 'Tot' Walsh v Gillingham, Division 3 (S), 15 January 1927.

Most Capped Player: Billy Wedlock, 26, England.

Most League Appearances: John Atyeo, 596, 1951–66.

Youngest League Player: Marvin Brown, 16 years 105 days v Bristol R, 17 October 1999.

Record Transfer Fee Received: £20,000,000 from Brighton & HA for Adam Webster, August 2019.

Record Transfer Fee Paid: £8,000,000 to Chelsea for Tomas Kalas, July 2019.

Football League Record: 1901 Elected to Division 2; 1906–11 Division 1; 1911–22 Division 2; 1922–23 Division 3 (S); 1923–24 Division 2; 1924–27 Division 3 (S); 1927–32 Division 2; 1932–55 Division 3 (S); 1955–60 Division 2; 1960–65 Division 3; 1965–76 Division 2; 1976–80 Division 1; 1980–81 Division 2; 1981–82 Division 3; 1982–84 Division 4; 1984–90 Division 3; 1990–92 Division 2; 1992–95 Division 1; 1995–98 Division 2; 1998–99 Division 1; 1999–2004 Division 2; 2004–07 FL 1; 2007–13 FL C; 2013–15 FL 1; 2015– FL C.

LATEST SEQUENCES

Longest Sequence of League Wins: 14, 9.9.1905 – 2.12.1905.

Longest Sequence of League Defeats: 8, 10.12.2016 – 21.1.2017.

Longest Sequence of League Draws: 4, 6.11.1999 – 27.11.1999.

Longest Sequence of Unbeaten League Matches: 24, 9.9.1905 – 10.2.1906.

Longest Sequence Without a League Win: 21, 16.3.2013 – 22.10.2013.

Successive Scoring Runs: 25 from 26.12.1905.

Successive Non-scoring Runs: 6 from 20.12.1980.

MANAGERS

Sam Hollis 1897–99
Bob Campbell 1899–1901
Sam Hollis 1901–05
Harry Thickett 1905–10
Frank Bacon 1910–11
Sam Hollis 1911–13
George Hedley 1913–17
Jack Hamilton 1917–19
Joe Palmer 1919–21
Alex Raisbeck 1921–29
Joe Bradshaw 1929–32
Bob Hewison 1932–49
(*under suspension 1938–39*)
Bob Wright 1949–50
Pat Beasley 1950–58
Peter Doherty 1958–60
Fred Ford 1960–67
Alan Dicks 1967–80
Bobby Houghton 1980–82
Roy Hodgson 1982
Terry Cooper 1982–88
(*Director from 1983*)
Joe Jordan 1988–90
Jimmy Lumsden 1990–92
Denis Smith 1992–93
Russell Osman 1993–94
Joe Jordan 1994–97
John Ward 1997–98
Benny Lennartsson 1998–99
Tony Pulis 1999–2000
Tony Fawthrop 2000
Danny Wilson 2000–04
Brian Tinnion 2004–05
Gary Johnson 2005–10
Steve Coppell 2010
Keith Millen 2010–11
Derek McInnes 2011–13
Sean O'Driscoll 2013
Steve Cotterill 2013–16
Lee Johnson 2016–20
Dean Holden 2020–21
Nigel Pearson February 2021–

TEN YEAR LEAGUE RECORD

		P	W	D	L	F	A	Pts	Pos
2012-13	FL C	46	11	8	27	59	84	41	24
2013-14	FL 1	46	13	19	14	70	67	58	12
2014-15	FL 1	46	29	12	5	96	38	99	1
2015-16	FL C	46	13	13	20	54	71	52	18
2016-17	FL C	46	15	9	22	60	66	54	17
2017-18	FL C	46	17	16	13	67	58	67	11
2018-19	FL C	46	19	13	14	59	53	70	8
2019-20	FL C	46	17	12	17	60	65	63	12
2020-21	FL C	46	15	6	25	46	68	51	19
2021-22	FL C	46	15	10	21	62	77	55	17

DID YOU KNOW?

As the two teams in the 1909 FA Cup final wore red as their main colour, both were required to change for the big match. Bristol City turned out in royal blue shirts, which had the Bristol coat of arms woven in red silk on the left breast, with white shorts. City went down to a narrow 1-0 defeat to Manchester United and have never reached the final since.

BRISTOL CITY – SKY BET CHAMPIONSHIP 2021–22 LEAGUE RECORD

Match No.	*Date*	*Venue*	*Opponents*	*Result*		*H/T Score*	*Lg Pos.*	*Goalscorers*	*Attendance*
1	Aug 7	H	Blackpool	D	1-1	1-0	8	Martin [44]	18,729
2	14	A	Middlesbrough	L	1-2	0-1	17	King [60]	22,004
3	17	A	Reading	W	3-2	2-1	12	Weimann 2 [5, 52], Martin [14]	14,207
4	20	H	Swansea C	L	0-1	0-1	13		20,139
5	28	A	Cardiff C	W	2-1	1-0	11	Weimann 2 [21, 70]	20,891
6	Sept 11	H	Preston NE	D	0-0	0-0	11		17,967
7	15	H	Luton T	D	1-1	0-0	11	Baker [57]	16,878
8	18	A	QPR	W	2-1	1-0	9	Martin [45], Wells [90]	14,922
9	25	H	Fulham	D	1-1	0-0	8	Palmer [79]	19,326
10	29	A	Millwall	L	0-1	0-0	10		11,389
11	Oct 2	A	Peterborough U	W	3-2	2-2	9	Thompson (og) [34], Tanner [40], Martin [84]	8560
12	16	H	Bournemouth	L	0-2	0-2	11		20,828
13	19	H	Nottingham F	L	1-2	1-0	13	Scott [39]	18,325
14	23	A	WBA	L	0-3	0-2	16		23,845
15	30	H	Barnsley	W	2-1	2-1	15	Weimann 2 [42, 45]	18,347
16	Nov 2	A	Birmingham C	L	0-3	0-1	18		16,143
17	6	A	Coventry C	L	2-3	1-0	19	Martin (pen) [45], Weimann [68]	19,855
18	20	H	Blackburn R	D	1-1	1-0	18	O'Dowda [34]	18,347
19	24	H	Stoke C	W	1-0	1-0	18	Bakinson [38]	16,949
20	28	A	Sheffield U	L	0-2	0-1	18		25,615
21	Dec 4	H	Derby Co	W	1-0	1-0	17	Scott [16]	18,732
22	11	A	Hull C	D	2-2	0-1	18	Semenyo [54], James [90]	10,446
23	18	H	Huddersfield T	L	2-3	1-1	18	Weimann 2 [2, 90]	18,169
24	30	H	QPR	L	1-2	1-1	18	Scott [3]	19,543
25	Jan 2	H	Millwall	W	3-2	1-2	14	Weimann 3 [7, 73, 85]	18,033
26	15	A	Fulham	L	2-6	2-5	16	Semenyo 2 [7, 29]	17,810
27	22	H	Cardiff C	W	3-2	1-1	16	Martin 2 [33, 63], Weimann [77]	21,435
28	25	A	Luton T	L	1-2	0-1	16	Weimann [56]	9202
29	29	A	Preston NE	D	2-2	1-0	16	Martin [12], Semenyo [81]	11,936
30	Feb 5	A	Blackpool	L	1-3	0-2	17	Wells [86]	11,026
31	9	H	Reading	W	2-1	1-0	16	Semenyo [44], Morrison (og) [47]	17,798
32	13	A	Swansea C	L	1-3	1-0	17	Weimann [42]	19,162
33	19	H	Middlesbrough	W	2-1	1-0	16	Weimann [7], Semenyo [68]	20,148
34	22	H	Coventry C	L	1-2	0-1	16	Martin [62]	19,192
35	26	A	Nottingham F	L	0-2	0-1	16		28,506
36	Mar 5	H	Birmingham C	L	1-2	0-2	19	Scott [48]	21,942
37	12	A	Blackburn R	W	1-0	0-0	18	Weimann [90]	13,567
38	15	A	Barnsley	L	0-2	0-2	18		11,322
39	19	H	WBA	D	2-2	1-0	18	Wells [29], Weimann [85]	20,586
40	Apr 2	A	Bournemouth	L	2-3	1-1	18	Atkinson [4], Weimann [90]	9937
41	9	H	Peterborough U	D	1-1	1-0	19	Atkinson [43]	19,052
42	15	A	Stoke C	W	1-0	0-0	18	Dasilva [84]	20,298
43	18	H	Sheffield U	D	1-1	0-0	18	Martin [49]	18,934
44	23	A	Derby Co	W	3-1	2-0	17	Weimann [10], Semenyo [38], Klose [79]	22,753
45	30	H	Hull C	W	5-0	3-0	17	Weimann 2 [5, 82], Semenyo [33], Martin 2 [35, 54]	21,799
46	May 7	A	Huddersfield T	L	0-2	0-2	17		17,797

Final League Position: 17

GOALSCORERS

League (62): Weimann 22, Martin 12 (1 pen), Semenyo 8, Scott 4, Wells 3, Atkinson 2, Baker 1, Bakinson 1, Dasilva 1, James 1, King 1, Klose 1, O'Dowda 1, Palmer 1, Tanner 1, own goals 2.
FA Cup (0).
Carabao Cup (2): Janneh 2.

Bentley D 37 + 1	Vyner Z 19 + 3	Baker N 13 + 2	Atkinson R 29 + 5	Dasilva J 28 + 8	James M 31 + 2	King A 10 + 4	Weimann A 46	Scott A 35 + 3	O'Dowda C 16 + 4	Martin C 43 + 2	Palmer K 1 + 5	Williams J 13 + 9	Bell S 3 + 2	Wells N 7 + 25	Janneh S — + 1	Kalas T 34 + 1	Simpson D 2 + 1	Pring C 23 + 9	Massengo H 26 + 11	Semenyo A 24 + 7	Tanner G 11 + 2	Bakinson T 10 + 3	Benarous A 7 + 4	O'Leary M 9	Towler R 1	Conway T — + 4	Klose T 18	Cundy R 10 + 4	Idehen D — + 2	*Match No.*
1	2	3	4	5	6	7	8	9[2]	10[1]	11	12[3]	13	14																	1
1	2[3]	3	4	5	6	7	8	9[2]		11	10[1]			12	13	14														2
1		14	4	5	6	7[1]	9	8[2]		11	13					3	2	10[3]	12											3
1			4	5	6	14	9	8[1]		11				13		3	2[3]	10[2]	7	12										4
1	2	5	4	13	7	8[1]	10[3]	14		11						3		9[2]	6	12										5
1	2[3]	5	4	12	8	7[2]	10			11				14		3		9[1]	6	13										6
1	2[2]	5	4	13	7	14	11	6[1]		10				12		3		9[3]	8											7
1		4[1]	3	12	6		11			10[2]				13		2		8[3]	9	14	5	7								8
1		13	4	5	7		6			11	14	12		10		3		9[2]			2[3]	8[1]								9
1		4[1]	3	9[2]	7		10		13	11	14	6[3]				2		12			5	8								10
1			4		6	7	9	12	10[1]	11		8				3		5			2									11
1		4		13	7	8	10		9[2]	11		6[1]		12		3		5[3]			2	14								12
1		4	3	9	5		7	8[2]	14	10[1]	13			11[3]		2			12		6									13
1		4[1]	3	9[3]	5		7		14	10				11		2	13	12	8[4]		6[2]	15								14
1			4	12	7		9			10				11		3		5[1]	6		2	8[2]	13							15
1	3		4	9[2]	6[1]		7	14		10				11[3]		2		13	12		5	8								16
1	4			12			6	10[1]	9	11				13		3		5[2]	7		2	8								17
1	2	4					11	5[3]	9	10[2]		8		14		3			12	13		7	6[1]							18
1	2	4[2]	13				11	5	9[3]	10		6[1]				3		14	12			7	8							19
1	2	4[1]	12				10	5	9	11				13		3			8	14		7[3]	6[2]							20
1	2		4		12		9	5	8[2]	10				14		3		13	7	11[3]		6[1]								21
1	2		3[3]		6		9	5[1]	8	10[2]				13		4			7	11	12		14							22
1	2		4[1]		6		9	5		10				13		3		12	7[2]	11			8							23
	3		12		7	6	8	9	10					13		4		5		11[2]	2[1]			1						24
	2				6		7	8	10	13				14		3		5	12	11[3]			9[2]	1	4[1]					25
	3		12	5[1]		7	10	9	8[3]	13						2		4	6[2]	11		14		1						26
	12		3[1]	13		6[2]	11	5	8	9						2		4	7	10				1						27
	2			5[3]			9	7	8[2]	11		12		13		3		4	6	10[1]				1		14				28
	14			5[2]			9	7[3]	8[1]	11		12				2		4	6	10				1			3	13		29
				5			9[2]	7	8[1]	11		12		13		2		4	6	10				1			3			30
	2			5			9	7	13[3]	11		12				3		8[2]	6[1]	10				1			4	14		31
13	2			5			9	7		11		12		14		3		8[3]	6[1]	10				1[2]			4			32
1				8			9	7		10		3[2]	5[1]			2		12	6	11							4	13		33
1				5			9	6		11		12	2[2]			3		13	8	10			7[1]				4			34
1				2	14		9	7		11[2]		6		13		3		5[1]	8[3]	10							4	12		35
1			13	5	8[3]		9	6		10		7	2[1]	14		3		12		11							4[2]			36
1			5	6	9		2	7[1]		10		8		13					12	11[2]							4	3		37
1			5	6	8		2	7[1]		10		12[2]		13					9	11[3]						14	4	3		38
1			4	5	6		9			10				12				8	7	11[1]							3	2		39
1			4	5	6		9	7		11				10				8[1]	12							13	3	2[2]		40
1	12		4	8	6		9	5		11		7[2]		10[3]					13	14							3	2[1]		41
1			4	9	7		6	5		11		8[1]		13					12	10[2]							3	2		42
1			4	9[1]	6		7	5		10				13					8	11[2]			12				3	2		43
1			4		6	15	9	5[1]		10		7[4]	12[3]						14	11			8[2]				3	2	13	44
1			4	8	6		9[3]	5[1]		10		7		13						11[2]			12			14	3	2		45
1			4	8	6	14	9	5		10									7[1]	11	12						3[3]	2[2]	13	46

FA Cup
Third Round Fulham (h) 0-1
(aet)

Carabao Cup
First Round Forest Green R (a) 2-2
(Forest Green R won 6-5 on penalties)

BRISTOL ROVERS

FOUNDATION

Bristol Rovers were formed at a meeting in Stapleton Road, Eastville, in 1883. However, they first went under the name of the Black Arabs (wearing black shirts). Changing their name to Eastville Rovers in their second season in 1888–89, they won the Gloucestershire Senior Cup. Original members of the Bristol & District League in 1892, this eventually became the Western League and Eastville Rovers adopted professionalism in 1897.

The Memorial Stadium, Filton Avenue, Horfield, Bristol BS7 0BF.

Telephone: (0117) 909 6648.

Ticket Office: (0117) 909 8848.

Website: www.bristolrovers.co.uk

Email: admin@bristolrovers.co.uk

Ground Capacity: 10,697.

Record Attendance: 38,472 v Preston NE, FA Cup 4th rd, 30 January 1960 (at Eastville); 9,464 v Liverpool, FA Cup 4th rd, 8 February 1992 (at Twerton Park); 12,011 v WBA, FA Cup 6th rd, 9 March 2008 (at Memorial Stadium).

Pitch Measurements: 100m × 68m (109.5yd × 74.5yd).

Chief Executive: Martyn Starnes.

Manager: Joey Barton.

First-Team Coach: Kevin Bond.

HONOURS

League Champions: Division 3 – 1989–90; Division 3S – 1952–53.

Runners-up: Division 3 – 1973–74; Conference – (2nd) 2014–15 *(promoted via play-offs)*.

FA Cup: 6th rd – 1951, 1958, 2008.

League Cup: 5th rd – 1971, 1972.

League Trophy: *Runners-up:* 1990, 2007.

Colours: Blue and white quartered shirts with black trim, white shorts with black trim, blue socks with black and white trim.

Year Formed: 1883.

Turned Professional: 1897.

Previous Names: 1883, Black Arabs; 1884, Eastville Rovers; 1897, Bristol Eastville Rovers; 1898, Bristol Rovers. ***Club Nicknames:*** 'The Pirates', 'The Gas'.

Grounds: 1883, Purdown; Three Acres, Ashley Hill; Rudgeway, Fishponds; 1897, Eastville; 1986, Twerton Park; 1996, The Memorial Stadium.

First Football League Game: 28 August 1920, Division 3, v Millwall (a) L 0–2 – Stansfield; Bethune, Panes; Boxley, Kenny, Steele; Chance, Bird, Sims, Bell, Palmer.

Record League Victory: 7–0 v Brighton & HA, Division 3 (S), 29 November 1952 – Hoyle; Bamford, Fox; Pitt, Warren, Sampson; McIlvenny, Roost (2), Lambden (1), Bradford (1), Petherbridge (2), (1 og). 7–0 v Swansea T, Division 2, 2 October 1954 – Radford; Bamford, Watkins; Pitt, Muir, Anderson; Petherbridge, Bradford (2), Meyer, Roost (1), Hooper (2), (2 og). 7–0 v Shrewsbury T, Division 3, 21 March 1964 – Hall; Hillard, Gwyn Jones; Oldfield, Stone (1), Mabbutt; Jarman (2), Brown (1), Biggs (1p), Hamilton, Bobby Jones (2); 7–0 v Scunthorpe U (h), FL 2, 7 May 2022 – Belshaw; Anderson H, Taylor (1), Connolly, Clarke T (Nicholson), Whelan, Thomas, Evans (2) (Clarke L), Finley, Anderson E (1), Collins (2), own goal 1.

Record Cup Victory: 7–1 v Dorchester, FA Cup 4th qualifying rd, 25 October 2014 – Midenhall; Locyer, Trotman (McChrystal), Parkes, Monkhouse (2), Clarke, Mansell (1) (Thomas), Brown, Gosling, Harrison (3), Taylor (1) (White).

FOOTBALL YEARBOOK FACT FILE

At the start of the 1922–23 season Bristol Rovers signed a young engineering student from the local university, Mahmoud Saqr Mokhtar. Mokhtar played a number of games for Rovers' reserve team in the opening weeks of the season, proving to be a capable winger. He switched his studies to Liverpool University and played for the reserve teams of both Tranmere Rovers and Chester. Before coming to England, he had been a member of the Egypt squad at the 1920 Olympic Games.

Record Defeat: 0–12 v Luton T, Division 3 (S), 13 April 1936.

Most League Points (2 for a win): 64, Division 3 (S), 1952–53.

Most League Points (3 for a win): 93, Division 3, 1989–90.

Most League Goals: 92, Division 3 (S), 1952–53.

Highest League Scorer in Season: Geoff Bradford, 33, Division 3 (S), 1952–53.

Most League Goals in Total Aggregate: Geoff Bradford, 242, 1949–64.

Most League Goals in One Match: 4, Sidney Leigh v Exeter C, Division 3 (S), 2 May 1921; 4, Jonah Wilcox v Bournemouth, Division 3 (S), 12 December 1925; 4, Bill Culley v QPR, Division 3 (S), 5 March 1927; 4, Frank Curran v Swindon T, Division 3 (S), 25 March 1939; 4, Vic Lambden v Aldershot, Division 3 (S), 29 March 1947; 4, George Petherbridge v Torquay U, Division 3 (S), 1 December 1951; 4, Vic Lambden v Colchester U, Division 3 (S), 14 May 1952; 4, Geoff Bradford v Rotherham U, Division 2, 14 March 1959; 4, Robin Stubbs v Gillingham, Division 2, 10 October 1970; 4, Alan Warboys v Brighton & HA, Division 3, 1 December 1973; 4, Jamie Cureton v Reading, Division 2, 16 January 1999; 4, Ellis Harrison v Northampton T, FL 1, 7 January 2017.

Most Capped Player: Vitalijs Astafjevs, 30 (167), Latvia.

Most League Appearances: Stuart Taylor, 546, 1966–80.

Youngest League Player: Ronnie Dix, 15 years 173 days v Charlton Ath, 25 February 1928.

Record Transfer Fee Received: £2,000,000 from Fulham for Barry Hayles, November 1998; £2,000,000 from WBA for Jason Roberts, July 2000.

Record Transfer Fee Paid: £370,000 to QPR for Andy Tillson, November 1992.

Football League Record: 1920 Original Member of Division 3; 1921–53 Division 3 (S); 1953–62 Division 2; 1962–74 Division 3; 1974–81 Division 2; 1981–90 Division 3; 1990–92 Division 2. 1992–93 Division 1; 1993–2001 Division 2; 2001–04 Division 3; 2004–07 FL 2; 2007–11 FL 1; 2011–14 FL 2; 2014–15 Conference Premier; 2015–16 FL 2; 2016–21 FL 1; 2021–22 FL 2; 2022– FL 1.

LATEST SEQUENCES

Longest Sequence of League Wins: 12, 18.10.1952 – 17.1.1953.

Longest Sequence of League Defeats: 8, 26.10.2002 – 21.12.2002.

Longest Sequence of League Draws: 6, 4.2.2017 – 28.2.2017.

Longest Sequence of Unbeaten League Matches: 32, 7.4.1973 – 27.1.1974.

Longest Sequence Without a League Win: 20, 5.4.1980 – 1.11.1980.

Successive Scoring Runs: 26 from 26.3.1927.

Successive Non-scoring Runs: 6 from 14.10.1922.

MANAGERS

Alfred Homer 1899–1920 (*continued as Secretary to 1928*)
Ben Hall 1920–21
Andy Wilson 1921–26
Joe Palmer 1926–29
Dave McLean 1929–30
Albert Prince-Cox 1930–36
Percy Smith 1936–37
Brough Fletcher 1938–49
Bert Tann 1950–68 (*continued as General Manager to 1972*)
Fred Ford 1968–69
Bill Dodgin Snr 1969–72
Don Megson 1972–77
Bobby Campbell 1978–79
Harold Jarman 1979–80
Terry Cooper 1980–81
Bobby Gould 1981–83
David Williams 1983–85
Bobby Gould 1985–87
Gerry Francis 1987–91
Martin Dobson 1991
Dennis Rofe 1992
Malcolm Allison 1992–93
John Ward 1993–96
Ian Holloway 1996–2001
Garry Thompson 2001
Gerry Francis 2001
Garry Thompson 2001–02
Ray Graydon 2002–04
Ian Atkins 2004–05
Paul Trollope 2005–10
Dave Penney 2011
Paul Buckle 2011–12
Mark McGhee 2012
John Ward 2012–14
Darrell Clarke 2014–18
Graham Coughlan 2018–19
Ben Garner 2019–20
Paul Tisdale 2020–21
Joey Barton February 2021–

TEN YEAR LEAGUE RECORD

		P	W	D	L	F	A	Pts	Pos
2012-13	FL 2	46	16	12	18	60	69	60	14
2013-14	FL 2	46	12	14	20	43	54	50	23
2014-15	Conf P	46	25	16	5	73	34	91	2
2015-16	FL 2	46	26	7	13	77	46	85	3
2016-17	FL 1	46	18	12	16	68	70	66	10
2017-18	FL 1	46	16	11	19	60	66	59	13
2018-19	FL 1	46	13	15	18	47	50	54	15
2019-20	FL 1	35	12	9	14	38	49	45	14§
2020-21	FL 1	46	10	8	28	40	70	38	24
2021-22	FL 2	46	23	11	12	71	49	80	3

§Decided on points-per-game (1.29)

DID YOU KNOW ?

Bristol Rovers had a disastrous start to their home game with Leeds United on 29 August 1960 and found themselves 4-0 down at half-time. However, the Pirates staged a tremendous second-half comeback, with two goals from Peter Hooper and one each from George Petherbridge and Ian Hamilton to secure a 4-4 draw.

BRISTOL ROVERS – SKY BET LEAGUE TWO 2021–22 LEAGUE RECORD

Match No.	Date	Venue	Opponents	Result		H/T Score	Lg Pos.	Goalscorers	Atten-dance
1	Aug 7	A	Mansfield T	L	1-2	0-1	17	Harries [63]	6342
2	14	H	Stevenage	L	0-2	0-0	23		7071
3	17	H	Oldham Ath	W	1-0	1-0	15	Saunders [35]	6005
4	21	A	Exeter C	L	1-4	0-4	20	Finley [70]	5284
5	28	A	Barrow	D	1-1	1-1	22	Nicholson [44]	2116
6	Sept 4	H	Crawley T	W	1-0	0-0	16	Clarke, L [47]	6513
7	11	A	Hartlepool U	L	0-1	0-0	21		5193
8	18	H	Leyton Orient	L	1-3	0-3	22	Pitman (pen) [90]	6172
9	25	A	Walsall	W	2-1	0-1	18	Taylor [79], Spence [90]	5434
10	Oct 2	H	Swindon T	L	1-3	1-0	20	Anderson, H [17]	7625
11	9	H	Carlisle U	W	3-0	1-0	16	Evans [35], Nicholson [86], Saunders [90]	6302
12	16	A	Bradford C	D	2-2	0-1	16	Kilgour [48], Pitman [90]	16,664
13	19	A	Colchester U	D	1-1	0-0	17	Pitman [58]	2069
14	23	H	Newport Co	L	1-3	1-2	18	Pitman [45]	7500
15	30	A	Harrogate T	W	1-0	0-0	16	Anderton [64]	2614
16	Nov 13	H	Northampton T	W	2-1	0-1	14	Grant [53], Evans [59]	6884
17	20	H	Tranmere R	D	2-2	2-1	14	Grant [5], Nicholson [22]	7165
18	23	A	Salford C	D	1-1	1-0	14	Nicholson [14]	1740
19	27	A	Forest Green R	L	0-2	0-1	16		4128
20	Dec 7	H	Port Vale	L	1-2	0-2	16	Collins [56]	6071
21	11	H	Rochdale	W	4-2	1-0	15	Evans [10], Collins 2 [51, 89], Anderson, H [84]	6215
22	Jan 15	H	Hartlepool U	W	2-0	0-0	16	Collins [87], Evans [90]	7004
23	22	A	Swindon T	D	1-1	1-1	15	Finley [35]	12,695
24	25	A	Scunthorpe U	W	3-2	1-0	13	Grant [36], Evans (pen) [62], Clarke, L [78]	2403
25	29	H	Walsall	W	1-0	0-0	12	Collins [90]	8003
26	Feb 5	A	Sutton U	D	1-1	0-1	13	Evans (pen) [85]	3394
27	8	A	Oldham Ath	L	1-2	1-2	14	Nicholson [43]	5147
28	12	H	Mansfield T	D	0-0	0-0	14		7707
29	15	H	Sutton U	W	2-0	1-0	11	Anderson, H [4], Collins [46]	6700
30	19	A	Stevenage	W	4-0	1-0	11	Finley [36], Anderson, E [49], Anderson, H [54], Collins [74]	3538
31	22	A	Leyton Orient	W	2-0	2-0	9	Evans [34], Collins [37]	3840
32	26	H	Exeter C	D	1-1	1-1	10	Hoole [10]	9689
33	Mar 1	H	Barrow	W	1-0	0-0	9	Evans [81]	6685
34	5	A	Newport Co	L	0-1	0-1	9		6237
35	8	A	Crawley T	W	2-1	1-0	9	Anderson, H [41], Collins [65]	2223
36	12	H	Harrogate T	W	3-0	2-0	8	Collins 2 [33, 55], Anderson, E [39]	7884
37	15	H	Colchester U	W	1-0	0-0	7	Anderson, E [49]	7314
38	19	A	Northampton T	W	1-0	1-0	4	Anderson, H [1]	6405
39	26	A	Carlisle U	L	0-1	0-0	6		5884
40	Apr 2	H	Bradford C	W	2-1	0-0	5	Finley [57], Taylor [75]	9186
41	9	A	Tranmere R	D	1-1	0-0	6	Anderson, E [63]	6637
42	15	H	Salford C	W	1-0	0-0	5	Anderson, E [75]	9590
43	18	A	Port Vale	W	3-1	2-1	5	Anderson, E [10], Connolly [32], Loft [90]	10,840
44	23	H	Forest Green R	D	0-0	0-0	5		9690
45	30	A	Rochdale	W	4-3	0-2	4	Finley [54], Collins 3 [66, 89, 90]	4628
46	May 7	H	Scunthorpe U	W	7-0	2-0	3	Lobley (og) [18], Taylor [22], Collins 2 [53, 79], Evans 2 [61, 76], Anderson, E [85]	9790

Final League Position: 3

GOALSCORERS

League (71): Collins 16, Evans 10 (2 pens), Anderson, E 7, Anderson, H 6, Finley 5, Nicholson 5, Pitman 4 (1 pen), Grant 3, Taylor 3, Clarke, L 2, Saunders 2, Anderton 1, Connolly 1, Harries 1, Hoole 1, Kilgour 1, Loft 1, Spence 1, own goal 1.
FA Cup (9): Collins 2 (1 pen), Finley 2, Spence 2, Anderton 1, Coutts 1 (1 pen), Evans 1 (1 pen).
Carabao Cup (0).
Papa John's Trophy (6): Anderton 1, Jones 1, Nicholson 1, Saunders 1, Thomas 1, Westbrooke 1.

Jaakkola A 4	Hoole L 27 + 2	Hughes M 6	Anderton N 26 + 8	Harries C 15 + 1	Coutts P 35 + 4	Grant J 20 + 2	Anderson H 39 + 5	Thomas L 10 + 18	Clarke T 5 + 2	Saunders H 10 + 11	Westbrooke Z — + 3	Taylor C 41 + 1	Baldwin J 2 + 1	Finley S 34 + 2	Hargreaves C 1	Rodman A 3 + 1	Nicholson S 26 + 8	Collins A 36 + 9	Belshaw J 42	Pitman B 8 + 8	Hanlan B — + 1	Kilgour A 10 + 1	Evans A 34 + 1	Clarke L 2 + 9	Whelan G 19 + 12	Brown J 4 + 2	Spence S 1 + 5	Martinez P — + 1	Loft R 2 + 11	Connolly J 24	Anderson E 20 + 1	Nolan J — + 1	Match No.
1	2	3	4	5	6■	7	8^3	9^2	10^1	11	12	13	14																				1
1	2	3	4	5		7	10	8^1		11^3				6^2	9	12	13	14															2
		2	4	13		7	8^2	9^1		10^3			3	6		5	12	11	1	14													3
		3	4		9	7	8			11^2			2^1	6		5	12	10^3	1	14	13												4
		3	4^1		12	7	8	13		14		2		6		5	10^2	9^3	1	11													5
			14	4	13	6	5			8		3		7			10^3	11^1	1			2	9^2	12									6
		3	4			10	5			8^2		2		7				14	1	12			9	11^1	6^3	13							7
			4^1			5	13	14		12		3		6				10^2	1	11		2	9^3		7	8							8
				4	6		5			10^3		3		8				12	1	11		2	9^2		7^1	13	14						9
	14			4	6		5			12	15	3^3		9				13	1	11^4		2■	10^1		7^2	8							10
	2		12	4	6		8^2	13		10		3					14	11^3	1				9		7	5^1							11
	2^2		5		6^3		8	13		11^1		4					14	9	1	12		3	10		7								12
	14			4■	12		5	9^1	13■			3					8^2	10^3	1	11		2	7		6								13
			5		14		2^3	6			13	4		12			9	11^1	1	10		3	8		7^2								14
			13	4	6		2	9^3				3					11	14	1	10^1		12	8		7	5^2							15
			12	4	8	9^1	5	13				3		6			11^3	14	1			2	10^2		7■								16
			12	4	7	8	5^3					3		6			11	14	1			2^1	9		13		10^2						17
			5	4	6	2		13				3		8			9^2	10^1	1	12			11		7^3		14						18
			9	4	7	2^3	5^2	13				3		8				12	1	11			10		6^1		14						19
			5	4■	6^3		2		12			3		8■			9^2	11	1	14			10^1		7		13						20
	2		4		6		5	14	8^3			3^1					11^2	10	1				9		7		13	12					21
			12	4	5	9	6^3					3					8^2	10	1	13		2	7		14				11^1				22
	2				7	5	13	12				3		6			10^3	8^1	1				9	14					11^2	4			23
	2		12		6	5^1		10				4		7^2			8	11^3	1	14			9	13						3			24
	2■		5		7	6^3	12	8^2		13		3					10^1	11	1				9		14					4			25
1			5		7	2^3	14	8^2		13		3					10	11					9		6^1					4	12		26
1	2		5^2	4	6		14	13		9				8			12	11					10^1							3	7^3		27
	2		5		6		10^1			12		4		7			8	11	1											3	9		28
	2		5		7^1		8^2	13				3		6			10^3	11	1					14	12					4	9		29
	2		5		7^1		10	14				3		6^3			8^2	11	1						12				13	4	9		30
	2				7^2		5					3		6			8^3	11	1				10	14	13				12	4	9^1		31
	2				7		5	13				3		6^1			8^3	11^2	1				9		14				12	4	10		32
	2		5^1				10			14		3					8	12	1				6	11^3	7				13	4	9^2		33
	2		5				10					3^1		14			8	11	1				6^3		7^2				12	4	9	13	34
	2		5		6		8					3		7^1				11^2	1				10		12				13	4	9		35
	2		5		6^2		8^3			12		3		7^1				11	1				9		13				14	4	10		36
	2		5		6		8^1			12		3		7^2				11	1				9		13				14	4	10^3		37
	2		5		6		7					3		9				11	1				8							4	10		38
	2				8^3		5	14		12		3		9			7^1	11	1					13	6^2					4	10		39
	2				6		8	12	5^1			3		7			10^2	11	1					13						4	9		40
	2				6	13	8		5^1			3		7			10^2	11	1					12						4	9		41
	2				6	5^2	8	13				3		7^3			10^1	11	1				12		14					4	9		42
	2		12		6^3	5	8					3		7				11^1	1				9^2		14				13	4	10		43
	2		5^2		6		7	12		14		3		9^1				11	1				8^3						13	4	10		44
	2^3				6■	5^1	7	12				3^2		9			14	11	1				8						13	4	10		45
						14	2	7^3	5^1			3		9			12	11	1				8^2	13	6					4	10		46

FA Cup

First Round	Oxford U	(a)	2-2
Replay	Oxford U	(h)	4-3
(aet)			
Second Round	Sutton U	(h)	2-1
Third Round	Peterborough U	(a)	1-2

Carabao Cup

First Round	Cheltenham T	(h)	0-2

Papa John's Trophy

Group E (S)	Cheltenham T	(h)	2-0
Group E (S)	Chelsea U21	(h)	1-2
Group E (S)	Exeter C	(a)	3-5

BURNLEY

FOUNDATION

On 18 May 1882 Burnley (Association) Football Club was still known as Burnley Rovers as members of that rugby club had decided on that date to play Association Football in the future. It was only a matter of days later that the members met again and decided to drop Rovers from the club's name.

Turf Moor, Harry Potts Way, Burnley, Lancashire BB10 4BX.

Telephone: (01282) 446 800.

Ticket Office: (01282) 446 800 (option 2 or 3).

Website: www.burnleyfc.com

Email: info@burnleyfc.com

Ground Capacity: 21,744.

Record Attendance: 54,775 v Huddersfield T, FA Cup 3rd rd, 23 February 1924.

Pitch Measurements: 105m × 68m (115yd × 74.5yd).

Chairman: Alan Pace.

Manager: Vincent Kompany.

Assistant Manager: Simon Davies.

Colours: Claret shirts with sky blue sleeves, sky blue shorts with claret trim, sky blue socks with claret trim.

Year Formed: 1882.

Turned Professional: 1883.

Previous Name: 1882, Burnley Rovers; 1882, Burnley.

Club Nickname: 'The Clarets'.

Grounds: 1882, Calder Vale; 1883, Turf Moor.

First Football League Game: 8 September 1888, Football League, v Preston NE (a) L 2–5 – Smith; Lang, Bury, Abrahams, Friel, Keenan, Brady, Tait, Poland (1), Gallocher (1), Yates.

Record League Victory: 9–0 v Darwen, Division 1, 9 January 1892 – Hillman; Walker, McFettridge, Lang, Matthews, Keenan, Nicol (3), Bowes, Espie (1), McLardie (3), Hill (2).

Record Cup Victory: 9–0 v Crystal Palace, FA Cup 2nd rd (replay), 10 February 1909 – Dawson; Barron, McLean; Cretney (2), Leake, Moffat; Morley, Ogden, Smith (3), Abbott (2), Smethams (1). 9–0 v New Brighton, FA Cup 4th rd, 26 January 1957 – Blacklaw; Angus, Winton; Seith, Adamson, Miller; Newlands (1), McIlroy (3), Lawson (3), Cheesebrough (1), Pilkington (1). 9–0 v Penrith, FA Cup 1st rd, 17 November 1984 – Hansbury; Miller, Hampton, Phelan, Overson (Kennedy), Hird (3 incl. 1p), Grewcock (1), Powell (2), Taylor (3), Biggins, Hutchison.

Record Defeat: 0–11 v Darwen, FA Cup 1st rd, 17 October 1885.

Most League Points (2 for a win): 62, Division 2, 1972–73.

Most League Points (3 for a win): 93, FL C, 2013–14; FL C, 2015–16.

HONOURS

League Champions: Division 1 – 1920–21, 1959–60; FL C – 2015–16; Division 2 – 1897–98, 1972–73; Division 3 – 1981–82; Division 4 – 1991–92.
Runners-up: Division 1 – 1919–20, 1961–62; FL C – 2013–14; Division 2 – 1912–13, 1946–47; Second Division – 1999–2000.

FA Cup Winners: 1914.
Runners-up: 1947, 1962.

League Cup: semi-final – 1961, 1969, 1983, 2009.

League Trophy: *Runners-up:* 1988.

Anglo-Scottish Cup Winners: 1979.

European Competitions
European Cup: 1960–61 *(qf)*.
Fairs Cup: 1966–67 *(qf)*.
Europa League: 2018–19.

FOOTBALL YEARBOOK FACT FILE

George Beel, who holds the Burnley record both for individual goals scored in a season and career total goals, also holds the record for netting the most hat-tricks for the club. He scored a total of 11 trebles for the Clarets, four of which came in the 1928–29 season, including consecutive games away to Birmingham and at home to Portsmouth.

Most League Goals: 102, Division 1, 1960–61.

Highest League Scorer in Season: George Beel, 35, Division 1, 1927–28.

Most League Goals in Total Aggregate: George Beel, 179, 1923–32.

Most League Goals in One Match: 6, Louis Page v Birmingham C, Division 1, 10 April 1926.

Most Capped Player: Jimmy McIlroy, 51 (55), Northern Ireland.

Most League Appearances: Jerry Dawson, 522, 1907–28.

Youngest League Player: Tommy Lawton, 16 years 174 days v Doncaster R, 28 March 1936.

Record Transfer Fee Received: £25,000,000 (rising to £30,000,000) from Everton for Michael Keane, July 2017; £25,000,000 from Newcastle U for Chris Wood, January 2022.

Record Transfer Fee Paid: £15,000,000 to Leeds U for Chris Wood, August 2017; £15,000,000 to Middlesbrough for Ben Gibson, August 2018.

Football League Record: 1888 Original Member of the Football League; 1897–98 Division 2; 1898–1900 Division 1; 1900–13 Division 2; 1913–30 Division 1; 1930–47 Division 2; 1947–71 Division 1; 1971–73 Division 2; 1973–76 Division 1; 1976–80 Division 2; 1980–82 Division 3; 1982–83 Division 2; 1983–85 Division 3; 1985–92 Division 4; 1992–94 Division 2; 1994–95 Division 1; 1995–2000 Division 2; 2000–04 Division 1; 2004–09 FL C; 2009–10 Premier League; 2010–14 FL C; 2014–15 Premier League; 2015–16 FL C; 2016–22 Premier League; 2022– FL C.

LATEST SEQUENCES

Longest Sequence of League Wins: 10, 16.11.1912 – 18.1.1913.

Longest Sequence of League Defeats: 8, 2.1.1995 – 25.2.1995.

Longest Sequence of League Draws: 6, 21.2.1931 – 28.3.1931.

Longest Sequence of Unbeaten League Matches: 30, 6.9.1920 – 25.3.1921.

Longest Sequence Without a League Win: 24, 16.4.1979 – 17.11.1979.

Successive Scoring Runs: 27 from 13.2.1926.

Successive Non-scoring Runs: 6 from 21.3.2015.

MANAGERS

Harry Bradshaw 1894–99 (*Secretary-Manager from 1897*)
Club Directors 1899–1900
J. Ernest Mangnall 1900–03 (*Secretary-Manager*)
Spen Whittaker 1903–10 (*Secretary-Manager*)
John Haworth 1910–24 (*Secretary-Manager*)
Albert Pickles 1925–31 (*Secretary-Manager*)
Tom Bromilow 1932–35
Selection Committee 1935–45
Cliff Britton 1945–48
Frank Hill 1948–54
Alan Brown 1954–57
Billy Dougall 1957–58
Harry Potts 1958–70 (*General Manager to 1972*)
Jimmy Adamson 1970–76
Joe Brown 1976–77
Harry Potts 1977–79
Brian Miller 1979–83
John Bond 1983–84
John Benson 1984–85
Martin Buchan 1985
Tommy Cavanagh 1985–86
Brian Miller 1986–89
Frank Casper 1989–91
Jimmy Mullen 1991–96
Adrian Heath 1996–97
Chris Waddle 1997–98
Stan Ternent 1998–2004
Steve Cotterill 2004–07
Owen Coyle 2007–10
Brian Laws 2010
Eddie Howe 2011–12
Sean Dyche 2012–22
Vincent Kompany June 2022–

TEN YEAR LEAGUE RECORD

		P	*W*	*D*	*L*	*F*	*A*	*Pts*	*Pos*
2012-13	FL C	46	16	13	17	62	60	61	11
2013-14	FL C	46	26	15	5	72	37	93	2
2014-15	PR Lge	38	7	12	19	28	53	33	19
2015-16	FL C	46	26	15	5	72	35	93	1
2016-17	PR Lge	38	11	7	20	39	55	40	16
2017-18	PR Lge	38	14	12	12	36	39	54	7
2018-19	PR Lge	38	11	7	20	45	68	40	15
2019-20	PR Lge	38	15	9	14	43	50	54	10
2020-21	PR Lge	38	10	9	19	33	55	39	17
2021-22	PR Lge	38	7	14	17	34	53	35	18

DID YOU KNOW ?

In March 1891 Burnley hosted neighbours Nelson in a friendly fixture played under artificial lights. The match ended 4-2 to the Clarets with a crowd of over 4,000 turning out. The game kicked off at 7.15 with the pitch illuminated by 16 Wells' lamps.

BURNLEY – PREMIER LEAGUE 2021–22 LEAGUE RECORD

Match No.	Date	Venue	Opponents	Result		H/T Score	Lg Pos.	Goalscorers	Attendance
1	Aug 14	H	Brighton & HA	L	1-2	1-0	14	Tarkowski 2	16,910
2	21	A	Liverpool	L	0-2	0-1	18		52,591
3	29	H	Leeds U	D	1-1	0-0	16	Wood 61	18,665
4	Sept 13	A	Everton	L	1-3	0-0	18	Mee 53	38,354
5	18	H	Arsenal	L	0-1	0-1	19		21,944
6	25	A	Leicester C	D	2-2	2-1	19	Vardy (og) 12, Cornet 40	31,650
7	Oct 2	H	Norwich C	D	0-0	0-0	18		17,427
8	16	A	Manchester C	L	0-2	0-1	19		52,711
9	23	A	Southampton	D	2-2	1-1	18	Cornet 2 13, 57	29,145
10	30	H	Brentford	W	3-1	3-0	17	Wood 4, Lowton 32, Cornet 36	18,821
11	Nov 6	A	Chelsea	D	1-1	0-1	18	Vydra 79	39,798
12	20	H	Crystal Palace	D	3-3	2-3	18	Mee 19, Wood 27, Cornet 49	18,028
13	Dec 1	A	Wolverhampton W	D	0-0	0-0	18		30,328
14	4	A	Newcastle U	L	0-1	0-1	18		51,948
15	12	H	West Ham U	D	0-0	0-0	18		18,065
16	30	A	Manchester U	L	1-3	1-3	18	Lennon 38	73,121
17	Jan 2	A	Leeds U	L	1-3	0-1	18	Cornet 54	36,083
18	23	A	Arsenal	D	0-0	0-0	20		59,255
19	Feb 5	H	Watford	D	0-0	0-0	20		19,527
20	8	H	Manchester U	D	1-1	0-1	20	Rodriguez 47	21,233
21	13	H	Liverpool	L	0-1	0-1	20		21,239
22	19	A	Brighton & HA	W	3-0	2-0	19	Weghorst 21, Brownhill 40, Lennon 69	29,921
23	23	H	Tottenham H	W	1-0	0-0	18	Mee 71	19,488
24	26	A	Crystal Palace	D	1-1	0-1	18	Milivojevic (og) 46	24,203
25	Mar 1	H	Leicester C	L	0-2	0-0	18		17,825
26	5	H	Chelsea	L	0-4	0-0	18		19,439
27	12	A	Brentford	L	0-2	0-0	18		16,984
28	Apr 2	H	Manchester C	L	0-2	0-2	19		22,000
29	6	H	Everton	W	3-2	1-2	18	Collins 12, Rodriguez 57, Cornet 85	19,830
30	10	A	Norwich C	L	0-2	0-1	18		26,361
31	17	A	West Ham U	D	1-1	1-0	18	Weghorst 33	59,958
32	21	H	Southampton	W	2-0	2-0	18	Roberts 12, Collins 44	17,384
33	24	H	Wolverhampton W	W	1-0	0-0	17	Vydra 62	19,246
34	30	A	Watford	W	2-1	0-1	16	Cork 83, Brownhill 86	20,738
35	May 7	H	Aston Villa	L	1-3	0-2	16	Cornet 90	20,891
36	15	A	Tottenham H	L	0-1	0-1	18		61,729
37	19	A	Aston Villa	D	1-1	1-0	17	Barnes (pen) 45	40,468
38	22	H	Newcastle U	L	1-2	0-1	18	Cornet 69	21,361

Final League Position: 18

GOALSCORERS

League (34): Cornet 9, Mee 3, Wood 3, Brownhill 2, Collins 2, Lennon 2, Rodriguez 2, Vydra 2, Weghorst 2, Barnes 1 (1 pen), Cork 1, Lowton 1, Roberts 1, Tarkowski 1, own goals 2.
FA Cup (1): Rodriguez 1.
Carabao Cup (4): Rodriguez 4.

Pope N 36	Lowton M 20 + 5	Tarkowski J 35	Mee B 21	Taylor C 30 + 1	Gudmundsson J 13 + 5	Westwood A 26 + 1	Cork J 20	McNeil D 35 + 3	Wood C 17	Rodriguez J 13 + 16	Barnes A 8 + 15	Brownhill J 32 + 3	Vydra M 5 + 17	Pieters E 8 + 4	Lennon A 17 + 11	Cornet M 21 + 5	Collins N 18 + 1	Roberts C 19 + 2	Hennessey W 2	Stephens D 1 + 2	Weghorst W 17 + 3	Long K 4 + 2	*Match No.*
1	2	3	4	5	6	7	8^3	9^2	10	11^1	12	13	14										1
1	2	3	4	5	6^2		8	9	10^1	12	11	7		13									2
1	2	3	4	5	6^1	7		9	10		11^2	8	13		12								3
1	2	3	4	5	6^2	7		9	10^3	14	11^1	8	12		13								4
1	2	3	4	5	6^1	7		9	11^3	14	10^2	8	12			13							5
1	2	3	4	5	12	7		6^3	11		13	8	10^2		14	9^1							6
1	2	4		5	13	8		9	11^3	12	14	7	10^1		6^2		3						7
1	2	4			13	9	8^2	6	11^3	14	12	7		5		10^1	3						8
1	2	4		5	13	7	8^1	6	11^3	12		10	14			9^2	3						9
1	2	3	4	5	6	7		9	11			8	12			10^1							10
1	2	3	4	5	6^2	7		9	11^1	12		8	13	14		10^3							11
1	2	3	4	5	6	7		9	10^1	12		8	13			11^2							12
1	2		4	5	6^2		8	9	10^1	12		7	13		14	11^3	3						13
1	2^2	4		5	6^3	7		9	10	14		8	12			11^1	3	13					14
1	2	3	4	5	6	7^2	8	9^3	10^1	11		13	12		14								15
	2	3	4	5	9	7	8^1	6^3	11				13	14	10^2				1	12			16
	2	3	4	5	9^1	7	8	6	11^3	13			14		10^2	12			1				17
1		3	4		12	7		9		10^1		8	11	5	6			2					18
1		3	4			7		9		12				5	6^1	10		2		8	11		19
1		3	4			7		6		10^2	13	8		5	12	9^1		2			11		20
1		3	4			7		12		10^1	13	8		5	6	9		2			11^2		21
1	14		4				7	9		12	13	8		5	6^3	10^1	3	2			11^2		22
1		3	4				7	9		11	12	8		5	6			2			10^1		23
1		3	4	12		13	7^1	9		11^3	14	8		5^2	6			2			10		24
1		3	4^1	5		7^3		9		13	14	8			6	11^2	12	2			10		25
1		4		5		7		9		10^1	13	8			6	12	3	2			11^2		26
1		4		5		7		9		12		8			6	11	3■	2			10^1		27
1		4		5		7	8^2	10^1		13	14	9			6	12		2			11^3	3	28
1	12	4		5		7		14		10		8	13		6^3	9	3	2^1			11^2		29
1	2	4		5		7		13		10^3	14	8	12		6^2	9	3				11^1		30
1	2^2	4		5		7^1	8	6^3		10		12	14			9	3	13			11		31
1	14	4		5			8	6^3		10		7	13		12	9^1	3	2			11^2		32
1		4		5			7	6^3		9^1	12	8	11^2		13		3	2			10	14	33
1	13	4		5			7	6			12	8	10^3		9^2		3	2		14	11^1		34
1		4^1		5			7	6			10^3	8		14	9^2	13	3	2			11	12	35
1	5^1			6			8	9			11^2	7			12	10	4	2			13	3	36
1	14■	4		6			9	7^2			10^1	8			13	11^3	3	2			12	5	37
1		5		6			9	7			10	8^2			13	11	3	2^1			12	4	38

FA Cup

Third Round	Huddersfield T	(h)	1-2

Carabao Cup

Second Round	Newcastle U	(a)	0-0
(Burnley won 4-3 on penalties)			
Third Round	Rochdale	(h)	4-1
Fourth Round	Tottenham H	(h)	0-1

BURTON ALBION

FOUNDATION

Once upon a time there were three Football League clubs bearing the name Burton. Then there were none. In reality it had been two. Originally Burton Swifts and Burton Wanderers competed in it until 1901 when they amalgamated to form Burton United. This club disbanded in 1910. There was no senior club representing the town until 1924 when Burton Town, formerly known as Burton All Saints, played in the Birmingham & District League, subsequently joining the Midland League in 1935–36. When the Second World War broke out the club fielded a team in a truncated version of the Birmingham & District League taking over from the club's reserves. But it was not revived in peacetime. So it was not until a further decade that a club bearing the name of Burton reappeared. Founded in 1950 Burton Albion made progress from the Birmingham & District League, too, then into the Southern League and because of its geographical situation later had spells in the Northern Premier League. In April 2009 Burton Albion restored the name of the town to the Football League competition as champions of the Blue Square Premier League.

Pirelli Stadium, Princess Way, Burton-on-Trent, Staffordshire DE13 0AR.

Telephone: (01283) 565 938.

Ticket Office: (01283) 565 938.

Website: www.burtonalbionfc.co.uk

Email: office@burtonalbionfc.co.uk

Ground Capactiy: 7,088.

Record Attendance: 5,806 v Weymouth, Southern League Cup final 2nd leg, 1964 (at Eton Park); 6,746 v Derby Co, FL C, 26 August 2016 (at Pirelli Stadium).

Pitch Measurements: 100m × 67m (109.5yd × 73.5yd).

Chairman: Ben Robinson MBE DL.

Manager: Jimmy Floyd Hasselbaink.

Assistant Manager: Dino Maamria.

Colours: Yellow shirts with black trim, black shorts with yellow trim, yellow socks with black trim.

Year Formed: 1950.

Turned Professional: 1950.

Club Nickname: 'The Brewers'.

Grounds: 1950, Eton Park; 2005, Pirelli Stadium.

First Football League Game: 8 August 2009, FL 2, v Shrewsbury T (a) L 1–3 – Redmond; Edworthy, Boertien, Austin, Branston, McGrath, Maghoma, Penn, Phillips (Stride), Walker, Shroot (Pearson) (1).

HONOURS

League Champions: FL 2 – 2014–15; Conference – 2008–09.

Runners-up: FL 1 – 2015–16.

FA Cup: 4th rd – 2011.

League Cup: semi-final 2019.

FOOTBALL YEARBOOK FACT FILE

Stan Round and Richie Barker scored 115 goals between them in all games for Burton Albion in 1965–66 with Round setting a club record with his tally of 59. The Brewers won promotion to the Premier Division of the Southern League, netting a total of 121 league goals in the season, the highest of any club in the league that season.

Record League Victory: 6–1 v Aldershot T, FL 2, 12 December 2009 – Krysiak; James, Boertien, Stride, Webster, McGrath, Jackson, Penn, Kabba (2), Pearson (3) (Harrad) (1), Gilroy (Maghoma).

Record Cup Victory: 12–1 v Coalville T, Birmingham Senior Cup, 6 September 1954.

Record Defeat: 0–10 v Barnet, Southern League, 7 February 1970.

Most League Points (3 for a win): 94, FL 2, 2014–15.

Most League Goals: 71, FL 2, 2009–10; 2012–13.

Highest League Scorer in Season: Shaun Harrad, 21, 2009–10.

Most League Goals in Total Aggregate: Lucas Atkins, 65, 2014–22.

Most League Goals in One Match: 3, Greg Pearson v Aldershot T, FL 2, 12 December 2009; 3, Shaun Harrad v Rotherham U, FL 2, 11 September 2010; 3, Lucas Akins v Colchester U, FL 1, 23 April 2016; 3, Marcus Harness v Rochdale, FL 1, 5 January 2019; 3, Scott Fraser v Oxford U, FL 1, 20 August 2019; 3, Kane Hemmings v Crewe Alex, FL 1, 13 March 2021.

Most Capped Player: Liam Boyce, 11 (28), Northern Ireland.

Most League Appearances: Lucas Atkins, 307, 2014–22.

Youngest League Player: Sam Austin, 17 years 310 days v Stevenage, 25 October 2014.

Record Transfer Fee Received: £2,000,000 from Hull C for Jackson Irvine, August 2017.

Record Transfer Fee Paid: £500,000 to Ross Co for Liam Boyce, June 2017.

Football League Record: 2009 Promoted from Blue Square Premier; 2009–15 FL 2; 2015–16 FL 1; 2016–18 FL C; 2018– FL 1.

MANAGERS

Reg Weston 1953–57
Sammy Crooks 1957
Eddie Shimwell 1958
Bill Townsend 1959–62
Peter Taylor 1962–65
Alex Tait 1965–70
Richie Norman 1970–73
Ken Gutteridge 1973–74
Harold Bodle 1974–76
Ian Storey-Moore 1978–81
Neil Warnock 1981–86
Brian Fidler 1986–88
Vic Halom 1988
Bobby Hope 1988
Chris Wright 1988–89
Ken Blair 1989–90
Steve Powell 1990–91
Brian Fidler 1991–92
Brian Kenning 1992–94
John Barton 1994–98
Nigel Clough 1998–2009
Roy McFarland 2009
Paul Peschisolido 2009–12
Gary Rowett 2012–14
Jimmy Floyd Hasselbaink 2014–15
Nigel Clough 2015–20
Jake Buxton 2020
Jimmy Floyd Hasselbaink January 2021–

LATEST SEQUENCES

Longest Sequence of League Wins: 6, 23.2.2021 – 13.3.2021.

Longest Sequence of League Defeats: 8, 25.2.2012 – 24.3.2012.

Longest Sequence of League Draws: 6, 25.4.2011 – 16.8.2011.

Longest Sequence of Unbeaten League Matches: 13, 7.3.2015 – 8.8.2015.

Longest Sequence Without a League Win: 16, 31.12.2011 – 24.3.2012.

Successive Scoring Runs: 18 from 16.4.2011 – 8.10.2011.

Successive Non-scoring Runs: 5 from 19.3.2022.

TEN YEAR LEAGUE RECORD

		P	W	D	L	F	A	Pts	Pos
2012-13	FL 2	46	22	10	14	71	65	76	4
2013-14	FL 2	46	19	15	12	47	42	72	6
2014-15	FL 2	46	28	10	8	69	39	94	1
2015-16	FL 1	46	25	10	11	57	37	85	2
2016-17	FL C	46	13	13	20	49	63	52	20
2017-18	FL C	46	10	11	25	38	81	41	23
2018-19	FL 1	46	17	12	17	66	57	63	9
2019-20	FL 1	35	12	12	11	50	50	48	12§
2020-21	FL 1	46	15	12	19	61	73	57	16
2021-22	FL 1	46	14	11	21	51	67	53	16

§Decided on points-per-game (1.37)

DID YOU KNOW ?

Centre-forward Maurice Hodgkin was Burton Albion's record scorer during their time in Birmingham League football. He scored twice on his debut in August 1952 and in total netted 71 goals in his five-year spell with the Brewers.

BURTON ALBION – SKY BET LEAGUE ONE 2021–22 LEAGUE RECORD

Match No.	Date	Venue	Opponents	Result	H/T Score	Lg Pos.	Goalscorers	Attendance
1	Aug 7	A	Shrewsbury T	W 1-0	1-0	5	Brayford 31	5903
2	14	H	Ipswich T	W 2-1	1-1	4	Powell 19, Akins (pen) 86	3766
3	17	H	Sunderland	W 1-0	0-0	2	Smith 66	4239
4	21	A	Cambridge U	L 0-3	0-0	6		4468
5	27	H	Cheltenham T	D 1-1	0-1	4	Akins 67	2909
6	Sept 6	A	Bolton W	D 0-0	0-0	3		13,305
7	11	H	Gillingham	D 1-1	0-1	7	Hemmings 46	2555
8	18	A	Crewe Alex	L 0-2	0-1	10		4482
9	25	H	Lincoln C	L 1-2	0-1	15	Shaughnessy 86	3359
10	28	H	Portsmouth	W 2-1	1-0	10	O'Connor 32, Jebbison 60	2810
11	Oct 2	A	AFC Wimbledon	D 1-1	0-0	9	Hemmings 66	7413
12	9	A	Plymouth Arg	L 1-2	0-2	10	Akins 59	11,915
13	15	H	Morecambe	W 3-2	2-1	7	O'Connor 2 5, 49, Shaughnessy 14	2477
14	19	A	Fleetwood T	W 1-0	1-0	7	O'Connor 36	2226
15	23	H	Oxford U	L 1-3	0-2	8	Lakin 80	3391
16	30	A	Wigan Ath	L 0-2	0-1	9		9020
17	Nov 13	H	Charlton Ath	L 0-1	0-1	13		3555
18	20	A	Milton Keynes D	L 0-1	0-0	15		9770
19	23	H	Accrington S	W 4-0	2-0	12	Jebbison 2 28, 50, Smith 2 45, 49	1946
20	27	H	Doncaster R	W 2-0	0-0	10	O'Connor 55, Jebbison 75	2954
21	Dec 7	A	Wycombe W	L 1-2	0-2	10	Shaughnessy 54	3602
22	11	A	Rotherham U	L 1-3	1-1	13	Hemmings 44	9007
23	Jan 1	H	Crewe Alex	W 4-1	3-1	12	Chapman 6, Brayford 25, Hemmings 34, Jebbison 90	3119
24	8	A	Cheltenham T	D 1-1	0-1	12	Jebbison 51	3201
25	15	A	Gillingham	W 3-1	0-1	12	Haymer 50, Brayford 79, Smith 87	4198
26	22	H	AFC Wimbledon	D 1-1	0-0	11	Jebbison 77	2768
27	25	H	Milton Keynes D	L 0-1	0-0	11		2171
28	29	A	Lincoln C	W 2-1	0-0	10	Powell 56, Hughes 80	9159
29	Feb 5	H	Sheffield W	L 0-2	0-1	12		4763
30	8	A	Portsmouth	L 1-2	0-2	14	Ahadme 50	13,407
31	12	H	Cambridge U	D 2-2	1-1	13	Ahadme (pen) 2, Kokolo 62	2578
32	15	H	Bolton W	W 3-1	3-0	12	Powell 11, Brayford 2 14, 18	3487
33	19	A	Ipswich T	L 0-3	0-1	12		20,516
34	22	A	Sunderland	D 1-1	0-0	13	Borthwick-Jackson 53	30,237
35	26	H	Shrewsbury T	L 0-2	0-1	14		3258
36	Mar 1	A	Sheffield W	L 2-5	1-2	14	Guedioura 30, Niasse 53	20,309
37	5	A	Oxford U	L 1-4	1-4	15	Guedioura 45	7631
38	12	H	Fleetwood T	W 3-2	0-1	14	Niasse 2 61, 90, Moult 84	2648
39	19	A	Charlton Ath	L 0-2	0-2	14		11,348
40	Apr 2	A	Morecambe	L 0-3	0-2	17		5238
41	9	H	Plymouth Arg	D 0-0	0-0	17		3938
42	12	H	Wigan Ath	D 0-0	0-0	17		3589
43	15	A	Accrington S	D 0-0	0-0	16		2513
44	19	H	Rotherham U	W 2-0	1-0	16	Borthwick-Jackson 3, Brayford 69	3537
45	23	A	Doncaster R	L 0-2	0-1	16		6034
46	30	H	Wycombe W	L 1-2	0-1	16	Ahadme 72	4440

Final League Position: 16

GOALSCORERS

League (51): Jebbison 7, Brayford 6, O'Connor 5, Hemmings 4, Smith 4, Ahadme 3 (1 pen), Akins 3 (1 pen), Niasse 3, Powell 3, Shaughnessy 3, Borthwick-Jackson 2, Guedioura 2, Chapman 1, Haymer 1, Hughes 1, Kokolo 1, Lakin 1, Moult 1.
FA Cup (3): Jebbison 1, Leak 1, Powell 1.
Carabao Cup (1): own goal 1.
Papa John's Trophy (8): Holloway 3, Hemmings 1, Jebbison 1, Lakin 1, Smith 1, own goal 1.

Garratt B 40	Brayford J 33	Shaughnessy C 35 + 3	Leak R 14 + 2	Haymer T 45	Oshilaja A 30	O'Connor T 17 + 1	Smith J 23 + 6	Maddox J 8 + 8	Patrick O 5 + 2	Akins L 21 + 1	Powell J 29 + 5	Borthwick-Jackson C 33 + 4	Taylor T 12 + 4	Mancienne M 19 + 3	Bostwick M 8 + 2	Amadi-Holloway A 2 + 4	Rowe D — + 2	Morris B 1 + 6	Lakin C 12 + 15	Hemmings K 10 + 8	Chapman H 16 + 12	Blake-Tracy F 5 + 2	Jebbison D 14 + 6	Hughes S 21	Ahadme G 10 + 4	Gilligan C 7 + 1	Kokolo W 11 + 4	Moult L 3 + 7	Saydee C 7 + 11	Niasse O 7 + 5	Guedioura A 2 + 2	Kovar M 6	*Match No.*
1	2	3	4	5	6	7	8	9^{1}	10^{2}	11	12	13																					1
1	2	3	4	5		7	8^{2}		11	10	9		6^{1}	12	13																		2
1	2	3	4	5		7	8		11^{2}	10	9^{1}			6	12	13																	3
1	2	3	4	5		7^{1}	8^{2}		11	10	9^{3}	12		6		14	13																4
1	2	3	4	5			10		11^{2}	8	9	7		6^{1}		13	14	12^{3}															5
1	2■	4		5			8^{3}			10	9^{1}	7			3			13	6	11^{2}	12	14											6
1		4		2			8^{3}			10	14	7			3			13	6	11^{1}	9	5^{2}	12										7
1	2	4		5			8			10	14	7^{1}			3			12	6■	11^{2}	9^{3}		13										8
1	2	4		5	7		12	13		8	10^{1}				3			6^{2}		14	9		11^{3}										9
1	2	4	12	5	6	7	10	14		8					3^{1}				9^{3}	13			11^{2}										10
1	2^{1}	3	4	5	6	7	8	14		11								12	9^{2}	13	10^{3}												11
1		3	4^{3}	2	6	7	8^{2}	14		10		5							9	11^{1}	13		12										12
1		3		2	4	7	8			10		5	14	6^{3}					13	12	9^{2}		11^{1}										13
1		2		5	3	7				11		8	6						13	12	9^{2}	4	10^{1}										14
1		2		5	6	7	12			10^{2}		8^{3}			3				14	11	9	4^{1}	13										15
1		3		5	4	8^{1}	9■			10^{2}	6	14		7	2				12	13			11^{3}										16
1		2	3		4■	7				5^{3}	9	8^{1}		6^{2}		11			13	10	14	12											17
1		2	4	5				11^{1}	14		9^{3}	8	7	6^{2}	3				13	12			10										18
1		2	3	5		7^{1}	9^{3}		13	8		4	6					12	14	11			10^{2}										19
1		2	3	5		7	9^{1}			8		4	6^{2}	14					13	11	12		10^{3}										20
1		2		5	3	6	9^{3}	12		8^{2}		4		7		10			13	14			11^{1}										21
1		2	3	8	7					5^{2}		4	6			13			9^{1}	11	10		12										22
1	3	2	4	5	6	13		7			12	8^{2}							11^{1}	10	9^{3}		14										23
1	3	2		5	4	6	14	9		12	13	8	7^{2}						10^{1}				11^{3}										24
1	3			5	4	7^{1}	13				9	8	6						12				10^{2}	2	11								25
1	3			5	4						9	8	6^{1}						13				10	2	11	7^{2}	12						26
1	3	12		5	4			6			9	8^{2}	7^{1}										11	2	10^{3}		13	14					27
1	3	7		5	4						9^{3}		13	14									10	2	11^{1}	6^{2}	8	12					28
1	3	7		5	4^{1}			6^{3}			10	12									9			2	13		8	11^{2}	14				29
1		2	3	5							10	4	7^{1}	6^{2}							12				11^{3}	9	8	14	13				30
1	3	7		5							9^{2}	4^{1}							13		15	8		2	11	6^{4}	12	10^{3}	14				31
1	3	4	12	5				13			9^{2}		14	7^{1}										2	11^{3}	6	8		10				32
1	3	7		5			13	9			6										14	4		2	11^{1}		8^{3}		10^{2}	12			33
1	2	4		5			6^{2}				7	10		8					9		13			3					12	11^{1}			34
1	3	4		5			10^{1}				6	9		7^{3}					8^{2}		14			2					11	12	13		35
1	3			5	6		12				9	4							14					2	10^{1}		8		13	11^{2}	7^{3}		36
1	3			5	4^{1}		9	12			10	8	7^{2}											2			13		11^{3}	14	6		37
1	2^{3}	7		5	4		8							6^{2}					9^{1}		10			3		13		14	12	11			38
1	2	7		5	4		8^{1}				9^{2}	10									12			3		6^{3}			13	11	14		39
1	2	7■		5	4		8					10	13								12			3	14	6^{3}		11^{2}	9^{1}				40
	3			5	4		10^{1}	13			9	7		6^{2}							11^{3}			2			8	14	12			1	41
	3			5	4						9	7		6							11^{2}			2			8	13	10^{1}	12		1	42
	3			5	4						9^{1}	7		6					14		10^{3}			2	13		8		12	11^{2}		1	43
	3	13		5	4						9^{2}	7		6							11^{1}			2			8	14	12	10^{3}		1	44
	3			5	4						9	7		6^{2}					14		10			2	11^{1}		8^{3}		13	12		1	45
	4	13		5	2			9^{1}			8	7		6^{2}							12			3	14				10	11^{3}		1	46

FA Cup

First Round	Fleetwood T	(a)	2-1
Second Round	Port Vale	(h)	1-2

Carabao Cup

First Round	Oxford U	(h)	1-1

(Oxford U won 4-2 on penalties)

Papa John's Trophy

Group C (S)	Milton Keynes D	(h)	1-2
Group C (S)	Aston Villa U21	(h)	2-4
Group C (S)	Wycombe W	(a)	5-0

CAMBRIDGE UNITED

FOUNDATION

The football revival in Cambridge began soon after World War II when the Abbey United club (formed 1912) decided to turn professional in 1949. In 1951 they changed their name to Cambridge United. They were competing in the United Counties League before graduating to the Eastern Counties League in 1951 and the Southern League in 1958.

The Abbey Stadium, Newmarket Road, Cambridge CB5 8LN.

Telephone: (01223) 566 500.

Ticket Office: (01223) 566 500 (option 1).

Website: www.cambridge-united.co.uk

Email: info@cambridge-united.co.uk

Ground Capacity: 8,127.

Record Attendance: 14,000 v Chelsea, Friendly, 1 May 1970.

Pitch Measurements: 100.5m × 67.5m (110yd × 74yd).

Chairman: Shaun Grady.

Chief Executive: Ian Mather.

Head Coach: Mark Bonner.

Assistant Head Coach: Gary Waddock.

Colours: Amber shirts with black trim, black shorts with amber trim, black socks with amber trim.

Year Formed: 1912.

Turned Professional: 1949.

Ltd Co.: 1948.

Previous Name: 1919, Abbey United; 1951, Cambridge United.

Club Nickname: The 'U's'.

Grounds: 1932, Abbey Stadium (renamed R Costings Abbey Stadium 2009; Cambs Glass Stadium 2016; The Abbey Stadium 2017).

First Football League Game: 15 August 1970, Division 4, v Lincoln C (h) D 1–1 – Roberts; Thompson, Meldrum (1), Slack, Eades, Hardy, Leggett, Cassidy, Lindsey, McKinven, Harris.

Record League Victory: 7–0 v Morecambe, FL 2, 19 April 2016 – Norris; Roberts (1), Coulson, Clark, Dunne (Williams), Ismail (1), Berry (2 pens), Ledson (Spencer), Dunk (2), Williamson (1) (Simpson).

Record Cup Victory: 5–1 v Bristol C, FA Cup 5th rd second replay, 27 February 1990 – Vaughan; Fensome, Kimble, Bailie (O'Shea), Chapple, Daish, Cheetham (Robinson), Leadbitter (1), Dublin (2), Taylor (1), Philpott (1).

Record Defeat: 0–7 v Sunderland, League Cup 2nd rd, 1 October 2002; 0–7 v Luton T, FL 2, 18 November 2017.

HONOURS

League Champions: Division 3 – 1990–91; Division 4 – 1976–77.
Runners-up: FL 2 – 2020–21; Division 3 – 1977–78; Fourth Division – (6th) 1989–90 *(promoted via play-offs)*; Third Division – 1998–99; Conference – (2nd) 2013–14 *(promoted via play-offs)*.

FA Cup: 6th rd – 1990, 1991.

League Cup: quarter-final – 1993.

League Trophy: *Runners-up:* 2002.

FOOTBALL YEARBOOK FACT FILE

Cambridge United's first game against Football League opposition was in November 1953 when they faced Newport County at home in an FA Cup first-round tie. United, who won through four qualifying rounds, drew 2-2 in front of a record gate of 7,500 and then won the replay 2-1 before going out to Bradford Park Avenue in the second round of the competition.

Most League Points (2 for a win): 65, Division 4, 1976–77.

Most League Points (3 for a win): 86, Division 3, 1990–91.

Most League Goals: 87, Division 4, 1976–77.

Highest League Scorer in Season: Paul Mullin, 32, FL 2, 2020–21.

Most League Goals in Total Aggregate: John Taylor, 86, 1988–92; 1996–2001.

Most League Goals in One Match: 5, Steve Butler v Exeter C, Division 2, 4 April 1994.

Most Capped Player: Reggie Lambe, 12 (45), Bermuda.

Most League Appearances: Steve Spriggs, 416, 1975–87.

Youngest League Player: Andy Sinton, 16 years 228 days v Wolverhampton W, 2 November 1982.

Record Transfer Fee Received: £1,300,000 from Leicester C for Trevor Benjamin, July 2000.

Record Transfer Fee Paid: £190,000 to Luton T for Steve Claridge, November 1992.

Football League Record: 1970 Elected to Division 4; 1973–74 Division 3; 1974–77 Division 4; 1977–78 Division 3; 1978–84 Division 2; 1984–85 Division 3; 1985–90 Division 4; 1990–91 Division 3; 1991–92 Division 2; 1992–93 Division 1; 1993–95 Division 2; 1995–99 Division 3; 1999–2002 Division 2; 2002–04 Division 3; 2004–05 FL2; 2005–14 Conference Premier; 2014–21 FL 2; 2021– FL 1.

MANAGERS

Bill Whittaker 1949–55
Gerald Williams 1955
Bert Johnson 1955–59
Bill Craig 1959–60
Alan Moore 1960–63
Roy Kirk 1964–66
Bill Leivers 1967–74
Ron Atkinson 1974–78
John Docherty 1978–83
John Ryan 1984–85
Ken Shellito 1985
Chris Turner 1985–90
John Beck 1990–92
Ian Atkins 1992–93
Gary Johnson 1993–95
Tommy Taylor 1995–96
Roy McFarland 1996–2001
John Beck 2001
John Taylor 2001–04
Claude Le Roy 2004
Herve Renard 2004
Steve Thompson 2004–05
Rob Newman 2005–06
Jimmy Quinn 2006–08
Gary Brabin 2008–09
Martin Ling 2009–11
Jez George 2011–12
Richard Money 2012–15
Shaun Derry 2015–18
Joe Dunne 2018
Colin Calderwood 2018–20
Mark Bonner March 2020–

LATEST SEQUENCES

Longest Sequence of League Wins: 7, 19.2.1977 – 1.4.1977.

Longest Sequence of League Defeats: 7, 8.4.1985 – 30.4.1985.

Longest Sequence of League Draws: 6, 6.9.1986 – 30.9.1986.

Longest Sequence of Unbeaten League Matches: 14, 9.9.1972 – 10.11.1972.

Longest Sequence Without a League Win: 31, 8.10.1983 – 23.4.1984.

Successive Scoring Runs: 26 from 9.4.2002.

Successive Non-scoring Runs: 5 from 29.9.1973.

TEN YEAR LEAGUE RECORD

		P	W	D	L	F	A	Pts	Pos
2012-13	Conf P	46	15	14	17	68	69	59	14
2013-14	Conf P	46	23	13	10	72	35	82	2
2014-15	FL 2	46	13	12	21	61	66	51	19
2015-16	FL 2	46	18	14	14	66	55	68	9
2016-17	FL 2	46	19	9	18	58	50	66	11
2017-18	FL 2	46	17	13	16	56	60	64	12
2018-19	FL 2	46	12	11	23	40	66	47	21
2019-20	FL 2	37	12	9	16	40	48	45	16§
2020-21	FL 2	46	24	8	14	73	49	80	2
2021-22	FL 1	46	15	13	18	56	74	58	14

§Decided on points-per-game (1.22)

DID YOU KNOW ?

Cambridge United's Abbey Stadium was opened on 31 August 1932 when the U's, then members of the Cambridgeshire League, played a friendly against Cambridge University Press. The first competitive game was three days later when United were defeated 5-4 by Histon Institute in an FA Cup tie.

CAMBRIDGE UNITED – SKY BET LEAGUE ONE 2021–22 LEAGUE RECORD

Match No.	Date	Venue	Opponents	Result	H/T Score	Lg Pos.	Goalscorers	Attendance
1	Aug 7	H	Oxford U	D 1-1	0-1	11	Ironside (pen) [78]	6444
2	14	A	Accrington S	L 1-2	0-2	17	Ironside [79]	2077
3	17	A	Plymouth Arg	D 1-1	0-0	17	Ironside [76]	10,532
4	21	H	Burton Alb	W 3-0	0-0	12	Smith [53], Haymer (2 ogs) [73, 79]	4468
5	28	H	Bolton W	W 1-0	1-0	10	Tracey [16]	6124
6	Sept 11	H	Lincoln C	L 1-5	0-3	15	Ironside [59]	5833
7	18	A	Portsmouth	W 2-1	1-0	13	Ironside [38], O'Neil [69]	15,330
8	25	H	Fleetwood T	D 2-2	1-1	12	May [35], Tracey [51]	4429
9	28	H	Gillingham	L 0-2	0-1	15		4019
10	Oct 2	A	Crewe Alex	D 2-2	0-2	15	Jaaskelainen (og) [79], May [90]	4237
11	16	H	Ipswich T	D 2-2	1-2	18	Brophy [40], Ironside [88]	7944
12	19	H	Sheffield W	D 1-1	1-0	16	Williams [20]	7342
13	23	A	Shrewsbury T	L 1-4	0-1	18	Iredale [58]	5711
14	26	A	Doncaster R	D 1-1	1-0	17	Gardner (og) [7]	6146
15	30	H	AFC Wimbledon	W 1-0	0-0	15	Weir [47]	5609
16	Nov 2	A	Morecambe	W 2-0	1-0	10	Worman [28], Ironside (pen) [72]	3414
17	13	A	Milton Keynes D	L 1-4	0-3	12	Smith [82]	9904
18	20	A	Rotherham U	L 1-3	0-2	14	Smith [51]	9534
19	23	H	Wigan Ath	D 2-2	1-0	15	Ironside [44], May [53]	4101
20	27	H	Sunderland	L 1-2	1-2	16	Smith [27]	7174
21	Dec 7	A	Cheltenham T	W 5-0	1-0	15	Smith [37], Pollock (og) [52], Ironside 3 [63, 73, 88]	2762
22	11	A	Charlton Ath	L 0-2	0-1	16		24,886
23	18	H	Rotherham U	L 0-1	0-0	16		5323
24	Jan 3	H	Portsmouth	D 0-0	0-0	16		6832
25	15	A	Lincoln C	W 1-0	0-0	16	Ironside [90]	8507
26	18	H	Doncaster R	W 3-1	1-0	13	Knibbs [45], Dunk [62], Smith [90]	4575
27	22	H	Crewe Alex	W 1-0	1-0	12	May [42]	5428
28	29	A	Fleetwood T	D 1-1	0-0	12	Pilkington (og) [65]	2515
29	Feb 1	A	Bolton W	L 0-2	0-1	13		13,334
30	8	A	Gillingham	L 0-1	0-0	15		3824
31	12	A	Burton Alb	D 2-2	1-1	16	Knibbs [25], Smith [72]	2578
32	19	H	Accrington S	W 2-0	0-0	14	Smith [66], Hoolahan [90]	5602
33	22	H	Plymouth Arg	W 2-0	2-0	12	Smith [5], Lankester [42]	5286
34	26	A	Oxford U	L 2-4	1-1	13	Smith 2 [6, 56]	10,004
35	Mar 1	A	Wycombe W	L 0-3	0-2	13		4083
36	5	H	Shrewsbury T	D 0-0	0-0	13		5651
37	12	A	Sheffield W	L 0-6	0-4	15		22,646
38	19	H	Milton Keynes D	L 0-1	0-0	17		6325
39	26	A	AFC Wimbledon	W 1-0	0-0	16	May [46]	8463
40	Apr 2	A	Ipswich T	W 1-0	0-0	13	Ironside [56]	26,515
41	5	H	Wycombe W	L 1-4	0-1	13	Knibbs [79]	4751
42	9	H	Morecambe	W 2-1	1-0	13	Smith [42], Ironside (pen) [71]	5813
43	16	A	Wigan Ath	W 2-1	2-0	12	Knibbs [33], Smith [43]	10,576
44	19	H	Charlton Ath	L 0-2	0-0	12		5409
45	23	A	Sunderland	L 1-5	1-3	14	Digby [30]	32,500
46	30	H	Cheltenham T	D 2-2	1-1	14	Smith 2 [22, 50]	5880

Final League Position: 14

GOALSCORERS

League (56): Smith 15, Ironside 14 (3 pens), May 5, Knibbs 4, Tracey 2, Brophy 1, Digby 1, Dunk 1, Hoolahan 1, Iredale 1, Lankester 1, O'Neil 1, Weir 1, Williams 1, Worman 1, own goals 6.
FA Cup (8): Knibbs 2, Smith 2, Ironside 1, Masterson 1, May 1, Worman 1.
Carabao Cup (1): Williams 1.
Papa John's Trophy (10): Smith 4 (1 pen), Knibbs 3, Digby 1, Tracey 1, Yearn 1.

Mitov D 42	Williams G 40	Jones L 25	Taylor G 3	Iredale J 35	Digby P 43 + 1	O'Neil L 15 + 6	Tracey S 15 + 11	Hoolahan W 20 + 6	Brophy J 40 + 3	Ironside J 34 + 4	May A 32 + 6	Smith S 34 + 12	Weir J 10 + 5	Dunk H 26 + 8	Masterson C 15 + 1	Knibbs H 14 + 20	Lankester J 7 + 11	Okedina J 27 + 3	McKenzie-Lyle K — + 1	Holy T 2	Worman B 8 + 5	Sherring S 11 + 3	Tolaj L — + 4	Bennett L 4 + 1	Simper L 2	Mannion W 2	Yearn K — + 1	*Match No.*
1	2	3	4	5	6	7[1]	8[2]	9	10	11	12	13																1
1	2[3]		4	5	3	7	14	10	6	11	13	12	8[2]	9[1]														2
1	2	3	4[1]	5	7	9	6[2]		10	11	8[3]	13	14	12														3
1	2	3		5	7	8	12	9	6[1]	11		10[2]			4	13												4
1	2	3		5	6	7	8[2]	9	10[3]	11[1]		12		14	4	13												5
1	2	3		5	7[2]	8	6[1]	9[3]		11		10	13		4	14	12											6
1	2	3		5	8	9	6[2]		10	11[1]	7	12		13	4													7
1	2			5	9	7	6		10	11	8[1]	12			4			3										8
1	2	3		5	7[3]	8	6		9[1]	10	14	11[2]	13		4		12											9
1	2	3		5	9	7	13	12	10[3]	11	8	14			4[1]		6[2]											10
1	2	3		5	7		8[1]	9	10[2]	11[3]	6	12		14	4	13												11
1	2	3		5	8		12		10[2]	11	9	6[1]	7	13	4													12
1[1]	2	3		5	7		8[4]	9	10[2]	11	6■	14	13		4[3]	15			12									13
	2	4		8			6[1]		10	12		11[2]	9	5		13		3		1	7							14
	2	4[1]		5	6		10	9	13	11		8[2]	7		12			3		1								15
1				4	6		12		10[2]	11		13	8	5	3	7[1]		2			9							16
1	2			5	7			9	10	11	14	8[3]	6[2]	12	4[1]	13		3										17
1	2			4	7[2]			9[1]	10	11	6	8	13	5	3	12												18
1	2			4	7				10[1]	11	9[2]	8	6	5	3	12					13							19
1	2			4	7		13	9	10[2]	11	6[1]	8		5	3	12												20
1	2			4	7		10[1]		12	11	9	8[2]	6[3]	5		13	14	3										21
1	2			4	7				10	11	9	8[3]	6[1]	5[2]		12	13	3			14							22
1	2			4	7				10[1]	11	9	8[2]	6	5		13	12	3										23
1	2			4	6			13	10[2]	11	9	8■		5		12		3			7[1]							24
1				4	7			12	10[3]	11	9	8[2]		5		13	14	2			6[1]	3						25
1				4	7	13			10	11[1]	6	12		5		8[2]	9[3]	2			14	3						26
1	2			4	7			9	10[2]		6[3]	11		5		8[1]	12	13			14	3						27
1	2			4	7			10	9		8	11		5		12	6[1]	3										28
1	2			4[1]	6				10		9	11		5		8[2]	14	3			7[3]	12	13					29
1	2				6	7[1]			10		9	11		5		8[2]	12	3				4	13					30
1	2				6			9	10		7	11		5		8		3				4						31
1	2				6	12		9[1]	10		7	11		5		8		3				4						32
1	2				6	7[1]	13		10		9	11		14			8[2]	3			12	4		5[3]				33
1	2				7	12	13	9	10		6[2]	11		5[3]			8[1]	3				4	14					34
1	2	3			6		8[1]		10[3]	12	9	11		5			13				7[2]	4	14					35
1	2	4			7		12	9	10[1]	11	6	8[2]		5		13		3										36
1	2	4			7	12		9[2]	10	11	6[1]	8		5		13		14				3[3]						37
1	2	4			6	7[3]		12	10	11	14	8[2]		5		9[1]	13	3										38
1	2	4			6		13	12	10[3]	11	7	8[1]		5		9[2]		3				14						39
1	2	4			6				10[1]	11	7	8		5		9		3				12						40
1	2	4		10[1]	6				12	11	7	14		5		13	8[3]	3			9[2]							41
1		4		5[3]	6			12	10[1]	11		8		14		9		13				3[2]		2	7			42
1	2	4		5	7	12	13		10	11	6	8[2]				9[1]		3										43
		4		5	12	6[1]	8[3]	9		13		11				14	10[2]	3			7			2		1		44
1	2	4■		5	7	13			10	11	6	8[1]				9[2]		3						12				45
		4		5		7[1]	8[2]	9[3]		13	12	11				10		3						2	6	1	14	46

FA Cup

First Round	Northampton T	(a)	2-2
Replay	Northampton T	(h)	3-1
Second Round	Exeter C	(h)	2-1
Third Round	Newcastle U	(a)	1-0
Fourth Round	Luton T	(h)	0-3

Carabao Cup

First Round	Swindon T	(h)	0-0

(Cambridge U won 3-1 on penalties)

Second Round	Millwall	(a)	1-3

Papa John's Trophy

Group H (S)	Oxford U	(h)	4-1
Group H (S)	Tottenham H U21	(h)	1-0
Group H (S)	Stevenage	(a)	0-1
Second Round	Walsall	(h)	2-0
Third Round	Portsmouth	(h)	2-1
Quarter-Final	Rotherham U	(a)	1-1

(Rotherham U won 7-6 on penalties)

CARDIFF CITY

FOUNDATION

Credit for the establishment of a first class professional football club in such a rugby stronghold as Cardiff is due to members of the Riverside club formed in 1899 out of a cricket club of that name. Cardiff became a city in 1905 and in 1908 the South Wales and Monmouthshire FA granted Riverside permission to call themselves Cardiff City. The club turned professional under that name in 1910.

Cardiff City Stadium, Leckwith Road, Cardiff CF11 8AZ.

Telephone: (0333) 311 1927.

Ticket Office: (0333) 311 1920.

Website: www.cardiffcityfc.co.uk

Email: club@cardiffcityfc.co.uk

Ground Capacity: 33,280.

Record Attendance: 57,893 v Arsenal, Division 1, 22 April 1953 (at Ninian Park); 33,028 v Manchester U, Premier League, 22 December 2018 (at Cardiff City Stadium).

Ground Record Attendance: 62,634, Wales v England, 17 October 1959 (at Ninian Park); 33,280, Wales v Belgium, 12 June 2015 (at Cardiff City Stadium).

Pitch Measurements: 105m × 68m (115yd × 74.5yd).

Chairman: Mehmet Dalman.

Chief Executive: Ken Choo.

Manager: Steve Morison.

Assistant Manager: Tom Ramasut.

Colours: Blue shirts with black trim, blue shorts with black trim, blue socks with black trim.

Year Formed: 1899.

Turned Professional: 1910.

Previous Names: 1899, Riverside; 1902, Riverside Albion; 1908, Cardiff City.

Club Nickname: 'The Bluebirds'.

Grounds: Riverside, Sophia Gardens, Old Park and Fir Gardens; 1910, Ninian Park; 2009, Cardiff City Stadium.

First Football League Game: 28 August 1920, Division 2, v Stockport Co (a) W 5–2 – Kneeshaw; Brittan, Leyton; Keenor (1), Smith, Hardy; Grimshaw (1), Gill (2), Cashmore, West, Evans (1).

Record League Victory: 9–2 v Thames, Division 3 (S), 6 February 1932 – Farquharson; Eric Morris, Roberts; Galbraith, Harris, Ronan; Emmerson (1), Keating (1), Jones (1), McCambridge (1), Robbins (5).

Record Cup Victory: 8–0 v Enfield, FA Cup 1st rd, 28 November 1931 – Farquharson; Smith, Roberts; Harris (1), Galbraith, Ronan; Emmerson (2), Keating (3); O'Neill (2), Robbins, McCambridge.

HONOURS

League Champions: FL C – 2012–13; Division 3S – 1946–47; Third Division – 1992–93.
Runners-up: FL C – 2017–18; Division 1 – 1923–24; Division 2 – 1920–21, 1951–52, 1959–60; Division 3 – 1975–76, 1982–83; Third Division – 2000–01; Division 4 – 1987–88.

FA Cup Winners: 1927.
Runners-up: 1925, 2008.

League Cup: *Runners-up:* 2012.

Welsh Cup Winners: 22 times.

European Competitions
European Cup-Winners' Cup: 1964–65 *(qf)*, 1965–66, 1967–68 *(sf)*, 1968–69, 1969–70, 1970–71 *(qf)*, 1971–72, 1973–74, 1974–75, 1976–77, 1977–78, 1988–89, 1992–93, 1993–94.

FOOTBALL YEARBOOK FACT FILE

Cardiff City led the First Division table for most of the 1923–24 season and going into the final round of fixtures merely needed to equal the performance of their closest rivals, Huddersfield Town, to secure the title. The Bluebirds faced Birmingham at St Andrew's and midway through the second half were awarded a penalty, but Len Davies' shot was saved by the home keeper and the match ended 0-0, with Huddersfield winning 3-0 to become champions.

Record Defeat: 2–11 v Sheffield U, Division 1, 1 January 1926.

Most League Points (2 for a win): 66, Division 3 (S), 1946–47.

Most League Points (3 for a win): 90, FL C, 2017–18.

Most League Goals: 95, Division 3, 2000–01.

Highest League Scorer in Season: Robert Earnshaw, 31, Division 2, 2002–03.

Most League Goals in Total Aggregate: Len Davies, 128, 1920–31.

Most League Goals in One Match: 5, Hugh Ferguson v Burnley, Division 1, 1 September 1928; 5, Walter Robbins v Thames, Division 3 (S), 6 February 1932; 5, William Henderson v Northampton T, Division 3 (S), 22 April 1933.

Most Capped Player: Aron Gunnarsson, 62 (97), Iceland.

Most League Appearances: Phil Dwyer, 471, 1972–85.

Youngest League Player: Bob Adams, 15 years 355 days v Southend U, 18 February 1933.

Record Transfer Fee Received: £10,000,000 from Internazionale for Gary Medel, August 2014.

Record Transfer Fee Paid: £15,000,000 to Nantes for Emiliano Sala, January 2019.

Football League Record: 1920 Elected to Division 2; 1921–29 Division 1; 1929–31 Division 2; 1931–47 Division 3 (S); 1947–52 Division 2; 1952–57 Division 1; 1957–60 Division 2; 1960–62 Division 1; 1962–75 Division 2; 1975–76 Division 3; 1976–82 Division 2; 1982–83 Division 3; 1983–85 Division 2; 1985–86 Division 3; 1986–88 Division 4; 1988–90 Division 3; 1990–92 Division 4; 1992–93 Division 3; 1993–95 Division 2; 1995–99 Division 3; 1999–2000 Division 2; 2000–01 Division 3; 2001–03 Division 2; 2003–04 Division 1; 2004–13 FL C; 2013–14 Premier League; 2014–18 FL C; 2018–19 Premier League; 2019– FL C.

LATEST SEQUENCES

Longest Sequence of League Wins: 9, 26.10.1946 – 28.12.1946.

Longest Sequence of League Defeats: 8, 15.9.2021 – 23.10.2021.

Longest Sequence of League Draws: 6, 29.11.1980 – 17.1.1981.

Longest Sequence of Unbeaten League Matches: 21, 21.9.1946 – 1.3.1947.

Longest Sequence Without a League Win: 15, 21.11.1936 – 6.3.1937.

Successive Scoring Runs: 24 from 25.8.2012.

Successive Non-scoring Runs: 8 from 20.12.1952.

MANAGERS

Davy McDougall 1910–11
Fred Stewart 1911–33
Bartley Wilson 1933–34
B. Watts-Jones 1934–37
Bill Jennings 1937–39
Cyril Spiers 1939–46
Billy McCandless 1946–48
Cyril Spiers 1948–54
Trevor Morris 1954–58
Bill Jones 1958–62
George Swindin 1962–64
Jimmy Scoular 1964–73
Frank O'Farrell 1973–74
Jimmy Andrews 1974–78
Richie Morgan 1978–81
Graham Williams 1981–82
Len Ashurst 1982–84
Jimmy Goodfellow 1984
Alan Durban 1984–86
Frank Burrows 1986–89
Len Ashurst 1989–91
Eddie May 1991–94
Terry Yorath 1994–95
Eddie May 1995
Kenny Hibbitt (*Chief Coach*) 1995–96
Phil Neal 1996
Russell Osman 1996–97
Kenny Hibbitt 1997–98
Frank Burrows 1998–2000
Billy Ayre 2000
Bobby Gould 2000
Alan Cork 2000–02
Lennie Lawrence 2002–05
Dave Jones 2005–11
Malky Mackay 2011–13
Ole Gunnar Solskjaer 2014
Russell Slade 2014–16
Paul Trollope 2016
Neil Warnock 2016–19
Neil Harris 2019–21
Mick McCarthy 2021
Steve Morison November 2021–

TEN YEAR LEAGUE RECORD

		P	*W*	*D*	*L*	*F*	*A*	*Pts*	*Pos*
2012-13	FL C	46	25	12	9	72	45	87	1
2013-14	PR Lge	38	7	9	22	32	74	30	20
2014-15	FL C	46	16	14	16	57	61	62	11
2015-16	FL C	46	17	17	12	56	51	68	8
2016-17	FL C	46	17	11	18	60	61	62	12
2017-18	FL C	46	27	9	10	69	39	90	2
2018-19	PR Lge	38	10	4	24	34	69	34	18
2019-20	FL C	46	19	16	11	68	58	73	5
2020-21	FL C	46	18	14	14	66	49	68	8
2021-22	FL C	46	15	8	23	50	68	53	18

DID YOU KNOW ?

David Summerhayes became the first substitute used by Cardiff City in a Football League match when he replaced Colin Baker in the home game with Bury on the opening day of the 1965–66 season. The first substitute to score for the Bluebirds in a League fixture was George Johnston who netted shortly before the final whistle in the home defeat by Portsmouth on 16 October 1965.

CARDIFF CITY – SKY BET CHAMPIONSHIP 2021–22 LEAGUE RECORD

Match No.	*Date*	*Venue*	*Opponents*	*Result*		*H/T Score*	*Lg Pos.*	*Goalscorers*	*Attendance*
1	Aug 7	H	Barnsley	D	1-1	0-0	8	Pack [54]	17,431
2	14	A	Blackpool	W	2-0	0-0	3	Bacuna [52], Moore [86]	11,393
3	17	A	Peterborough U	D	2-2	0-0	5	Flint 2 [83, 90]	8534
4	21	H	Millwall	W	3-1	0-0	6	Flint 2 [66, 70], Morrison [83]	18,168
5	28	H	Bristol C	L	1-2	0-1	9	Bentley (og) [59]	20,891
6	Sept 12	A	Nottingham F	W	2-1	0-1	8	Colwill 2 [58, 73]	24,153
7	15	A	Coventry C	L	0-1	0-1	9		16,372
8	18	H	Bournemouth	L	0-1	0-0	10		19,090
9	25	A	Blackburn R	L	1-5	0-3	13	Morrison [58]	11,670
10	28	H	WBA	L	0-4	0-1	16		17,363
11	Oct 2	H	Reading	L	0-1	0-1	20		18,400
12	17	A	Swansea C	L	0-3	0-1	20		19,288
13	20	A	Fulham	L	0-2	0-0	21		15,789
14	23	H	Middlesbrough	L	0-2	0-1	21		17,513
15	30	A	Stoke C	D	3-3	0-2	21	Colwill [66], Harris [70], Moore [71]	21,413
16	Nov 3	H	QPR	L	0-1	0-1	21		16,882
17	6	H	Huddersfield T	W	2-1	0-1	20	Moore 2 [74, 90]	17,355
18	20	A	Preston NE	W	2-1	0-1	19	McGuinness [51], Collins [66]	10,749
19	24	H	Hull C	L	0-1	0-1	20		17,180
20	27	A	Luton T	W	2-1	1-0	20	Colwill [10], Morrison [77]	9987
21	Dec 4	H	Sheffield U	L	2-3	1-0	21	Harris [32], McGuinness [90]	18,310
22	11	A	Birmingham C	D	2-2	0-2	20	Moore [66], McGuinness [90]	17,840
23	30	A	Bournemouth	L	0-3	0-1	20		8942
24	Jan 2	A	WBA	D	1-1	1-0	20	Collins [34]	22,925
25	15	H	Blackburn R	L	0-1	0-1	20		0
26	22	A	Bristol C	L	2-3	1-1	20	Collins [31], Watters [90]	21,435
27	30	H	Nottingham F	W	2-1	1-0	20	Hugill [6], Davies, I [65]	18,866
28	Feb 2	A	Barnsley	W	1-0	0-0	20	Ikpeazu [71]	11,432
29	9	H	Peterborough U	W	4-0	2-0	20	Ralls [4], Flint [39], Hugill [57], Ikpeazu [85]	17,297
30	12	A	Millwall	L	1-2	0-0	20	Bagan [90]	12,710
31	15	H	Coventry C	W	2-0	0-0	19	Bagan [72], Harris [87]	18,660
32	19	H	Blackpool	D	1-1	0-1	19	Bagan [49]	19,025
33	23	A	Huddersfield T	L	1-2	0-0	19	Doyle [61]	20,167
34	26	H	Fulham	L	0-1	0-1	20		18,928
35	Mar 1	H	Derby Co	W	1-0	0-0	18	Ikpeazu [85]	18,767
36	5	A	QPR	W	2-1	0-1	17	Davies, I [70], Colwill [74]	16,170
37	12	H	Preston NE	D	0-0	0-0	17		19,743
38	16	H	Stoke C	W	2-1	2-1	17	Doyle [39], Hugill [43]	17,184
39	Apr 2	H	Swansea C	L	0-4	0-1	17		27,280
40	9	A	Reading	W	2-1	0-1	17	Doughty [59], Vaulks [85]	19,039
41	15	A	Hull C	L	1-2	0-2	17	Flint [81]	15,685
42	18	H	Luton T	L	0-1	0-0	17		19,381
43	23	A	Sheffield U	L	0-1	0-0	19		26,802
44	27	A	Middlesbrough	L	0-2	0-1	19		19,727
45	30	H	Birmingham C	D	1-1	0-1	19	Vaulks (pen) [82]	21,395
46	May 7	A	Derby Co	W	1-0	0-0	18	Hugill [55]	29,402

Final League Position: 18

GOALSCORERS

League (50): Flint 6, Colwill 5, Moore 5, Hugill 4, Bagan 3, Collins 3, Harris 3, Ikpeazu 3, McGuinness 3, Morrison 3, Davies, I 2, Doyle 2, Vaulks 2 (1 pen), Bacuna 1, Doughty 1, Pack 1, Ralls 1, Watters 1, own goal 1.
FA Cup (3): Colwill 1, Davies I 1, Harris 1.
Carabao Cup (3): Watkins 2, Murphy 1.

Phillips D 17	McGuinness M 33 + 1	Flint A 35 + 3	Nelson C 30	Ng P 39	Pack M 23 + 1	Ralls J 26 + 3	Bagan J 22 + 4	Bacuna L 13 + 2	Giles R 19 + 2	Collins J 13 + 13	Wintle R 20 + 3	Moore K 15 + 7	Harris M 17 + 17	Morrison S 16	Vaulks W 23 + 13	Colwill R 15 + 19	Sang T 3	Bowen S 3 + 1	Evans K 2 + 3	Brown C 5	Smithies A 29	King E 3 + 1	Davies I 10 + 18	Zimba C 1	Drameh C 22	Doyle T 17 + 2	Watters M 5 + 3	Doughty A 7 + 2	Hugill J 17 + 1	Ikpeazu U 1 + 12	Denham O 5	*Match No.*
1	2	3	4	5	6	7^{1}	8	9^{2}	10	11^{3}	12	13	14																			1
1		3	4	5	6	7^{2}	8	11	9	10^{1}		12		2	13																	2
1		3	4	5^{1}	6	7	8	9^{2}	11	10^{3}		12	13	2		14																3
1		3	4		6	7	8	13	12	14		10^{3}	11^{1}	2		9^{2}	5															4
1		4	5		8	9	6	7^{1}	10	13		11		3		12	2^{2}															5
1		4	5	2	6		9			10^{1}		12	11^{3}	3	8	13		7^{2}	14													6
1		4	5	2	8		6			13		11	10^{2}	3	9^{3}	7^{1}		12	14													7
1		4	5		9		14	7		12		11	10^{2}	3	8	13	2^{1}			6^{3}												8
1		3	4	5^{2}	6		8	10	12	14		11	13	2	7^{1}	9^{3}																9
1	5^{1}	3	4		7			9	10	11^{2}		12	13	2	6^{3}	14				8												10
	2	3	4		6	7^{3}		10^{1}	8	14		11			13	12		9^{2}		5	1											11
	2	4	5		9	8^{3}		7^{1}	10	12		11		3	14	13				6^{2}	1											12
	4	3		2	7		5		8^{3}	12		11	13		6	10^{2}		9^{1}	14		1											13
	4	3		2^{1}	7				8	11		12	10^{3}		6^{2}	9				5	1	13	14									14
	2	13	4	5				7	8			11	12	3^{2}	6	10			9^{1}		1											15
	2		4	5	7	13			8			11	12	3	6^{2}	9			10^{1}		1											16
	2^{2}	3	4	5	6	7		9^{3}	8			11	10^{1}		14	13					1		12									17
	2	3	4	5	7			14	8	12			13		6	11^{3}					1		9^{2}	10^{1}								18
	2^{4}	3	4	5	7	12		9^{2}	8	13		11	15		6^{1}	14					1		10^{3}									19
	2		4	5	6	7			8	10^{2}		11	12	3		9^{1}					1		13									20
	2	12	4	5	7	6			8	10^{2}		13	11^{1}	3■	14						1		9^{3}									21
	2	3	4^{2}	5	6^{3}	7			8	10^{1}		11	12		14	9					1		13									22
	2	3	4	5		7		10■	8	13		11^{2}	9^{1}		6	14					1		12^{3}									23
	2	3■	4	5	7	8			9	10			11^{2}		6^{1}	12					1		13									24
	3	4	5	6	13	9				10	8		11^{2}		7^{1}	14					1		12		2^{3}							25
	2^{3}	3	4	9	7	8				11^{2}	13		10								1		14		5	6^{1}	12					26
	5			3		9^{3}				13	8			4	14						1		12		2	7	11^{1}	6	10^{2}			27
	5	12		3							8			4^{1}	9						1		13		2	7	11^{2}	6^{3}	10	14		28
	5	4		3		9^{1}	6				8				12	14					1		10		2	7^{3}			11^{2}	13		29
	5	4		3		9	6				8		11^{1}		14						1		12		2	7^{3}			10^{2}	13		30
	5	4		3			6				8		14		9						1	7^{2}	11^{3}		2	13	10^{1}		12			31
	5	4		3			6				8		13		9						1		11^{2}		2	7			10^{1}	12		32
	5	4		3		13	6				8		12		9						1		10^{1}		2	7^{2}			11^{3}	14		33
	5	4		3		9	13			11	14				8^{3}	10^{1}					1		12		2	7		6^{2}				34
	5	4		3		9	6^{3}				8		13								1		11^{2}		2	7		14	10^{1}	12		35
	4	3		2		8	12				7				6^{1}	10					1		13		5			9^{2}	11^{3}	14		36
	5	4		3		9	14				8					13					1		10^{1}		2	7^{2}		6^{3}	11	12		37
	5	4		3		9	6				8		11^{1}		14						1		12		2	7^{3}			10^{2}	13		38
	5	4		3		9	6				8		11^{2}			13					1		12		2	7^{1}			10^{3}	14		39
1			4	3		7^{1}	5				6				12	8							13		2	9		10^{2}	11^{3}	14		40
1	2^{2}	3					8				7		11		6	13							9^{3}		5	12		14		10^{1}	4	41
1			4	3			5				7		13		6	8							12		2	9^{2}		10^{1}	11^{3}	14		42
1	13		3	2		7^{1}	8				6				12	14									5^{2}	9	11^{3}		10		4	43
1			3	5						13	7		12		8	9									2	6	10^{1}		11^{2}		4	44
1	3		4	6							8^{2}		11		12	13						9^{1}			2	7^{3}	14		10		5	45
1		4	5	8			6				9		10			12						7^{2}	13^{3}		2		14		11		3^{1}	46

FA Cup

Third Round *(aet)*	Preston NE	(h)	2-1
Fourth Round	Liverpool	(a)	1-3

Carabao Cup

First Round	Sutton U	(h)	3-2
Second Round	Brighton & HA	(h)	0-2

CARLISLE UNITED

FOUNDATION

Carlisle United came into being when members of Shaddongate United voted to change its name on 17 May 1904. The new club was admitted to the Second Division of the Lancashire Combination in 1905–06, winning promotion the following season. Devonshire Park was officially opened on 2 September 1905, when St Helens Town were the visitors. Despite defeat in a disappointing 3–2 start, a respectable mid-table position was achieved.

Brunton Park, Warwick Road, Carlisle, Cumbria CA1 1LL.

Telephone: (0330) 094 5930.

Ticket Office: (0330) 094 5930 (option 1).

Website: www.carlisleunited.co.uk

Email: enquiries@carlisleunited.co.uk

Ground Capacity: 17,030.

Record Attendance: 27,500 v Birmingham C, FA Cup 3rd rd, 5 January 1957 and v Middlesbrough, FA Cup 5th rd, 7 February 1970.

Pitch Measurements: 102m × 68m (111.5yd × 74.5yd).

Chairman: Andrew Jenkins.

Chief Executive: Nigel Clibbens.

Manager: Paul Simpson.

Assistant Manager: Gavin Skelton.

Colours: Blue shirts with white and red trim, blue shorts with red trim, blue socks.

Year Formed: 1904. ***Turned Professional:*** 1921.

Previous Name: 1904, Shaddongate United; 1904, Carlisle United.

Club Nicknames: 'The Cumbrians', 'The Blues'.

Grounds: 1904, Milholme Bank; 1905, Devonshire Park; 1909, Brunton Park.

First Football League Game: 25 August 1928, Division 3 (N), v Accrington S (a) W 3–2 – Prout; Coulthard, Cook; Harrison, Ross, Pigg; Agar (1), Hutchison, McConnell (1), Ward (1), Watson.

Record League Victory: 8–0 v Hartlepool U, Division 3 (N), 1 September 1928 – Prout; Smiles, Cook; Robinson (1) Ross, Pigg; Agar (1), Hutchison (1), McConnell (4), Ward (1), Watson. 8–0 v Scunthorpe U, Division 3 (N), 25 December 1952 – MacLaren; Hill, Scott; Stokoe, Twentyman, Waters; Harrison (1), Whitehouse (5), Ashman (2), Duffett, Bond.

Record Cup Victory: 6–0 v Shepshed Dynamo, FA Cup 1st rd, 16 November 1996 – Caig; Hopper, Archdeacon (pen), Walling, Robinson, Pounewatchy, Peacock (1), Conway (1) (Jansen), Smart (McAlindon (1)), Hayward, Aspinall (Thorpe), (2 og). 6–0 v Tipton T, FA Cup 1st rd, 6 November 2010 – Collin; Simek, Murphy, Chester, Cruise, Robson (McKenna), Berrett, Taiwo (Hurst), Marshall, Zoko (Curran) (2), Madine (4).

Record Defeat: 1–11 v Hull C, Division 3 (N), 14 January 1939.

HONOURS

League Champions: Division 3 – 1964–65; FL 2 – 2005–06; Third Division – 1994–95.
Runners-up: Division 3 – 1981–82; Division 4 – 1963–64; Conference – (3rd) 2004–05 *(promoted via play-offs)*.

FA Cup: 6th rd – 1975.

League Cup: semi-final – 1970.

League Trophy Winners: 1997, 2011.
Runners-up: 1995, 2003, 2006, 2010.

FOOTBALL YEARBOOK FACT FILE

Severe flooding has twice closed Carlisle United's Brunton Park ground in the last 20 years. The Carlisle floods of January 2005 led to a temporary move to Morecambe's Christie Park, while Storm Desmond, which hit in December 2015, saw the ground out of action again for several weeks when home games were played at Deepdale, Ewood Park and Bloomfield Road.

Most League Points (2 for a win): 62, Division 3 (N), 1950–51.

Most League Points (3 for a win): 91, Division 3, 1994–95.

Most League Goals: 113, Division 4, 1963–64.

Highest League Scorer in Season: Jimmy McConnell, 42, Division 3 (N), 1928–29.

Most League Goals in Total Aggregate: Jimmy McConnell, 124, 1928–32.

Most League Goals in One Match: 5, Hugh Mills v Halifax T, Division 3 (N), 11 September 1937; 5, Jim Whitehouse v Scunthorpe U, Division 3 (N), 25 December 1952.

Most Capped Player: Reggie Lambe, 6 (45), Bermuda; Hallam Hope, 6 (9) Barbados.

Most League Appearances: Allan Ross, 466, 1963–79.

Youngest League Player: John Slaven, 16 years 162 days v Scunthorpe U, 16 March 2002.

Record Transfer Fee Received: £1,000,000 from Crystal Palace for Matt Jansen, February 1998.

Record Transfer Fee Paid: £140,000 to Blackburn R for Joe Garner, August 2007.

Football League Record: 1928 Elected to Division 3 (N); 1958–62 Division 4; 1962–63 Division 3; 1963–64 Division 4; 1964–65 Division 3; 1965–74 Division 2; 1974–75 Division 1; 1975–77 Division 2; 1977–82 Division 3; 1982–86 Division 2; 1986–87 Division 3; 1987–92 Division 4; 1992–95 Division 3; 1995–96 Division 2; 1996–97 Division 3; 1997–98 Division 2; 1998–2004 Division 3; 2004–05 Conference; 2005–06 FL 2; 2006–14 FL 1; 2014– FL 2.

LATEST SEQUENCES

Longest Sequence of League Wins: 7, 18.2.2006 – 8.4.2006.

Longest Sequence of League Defeats: 12, 27.9.2003 – 13.12.2003.

Longest Sequence of League Draws: 6, 11.2.1978 – 11.3.1978.

Longest Sequence of Unbeaten League Matches: 19, 1.10.1994 – 11.2.1995.

Longest Sequence Without a League Win: 15, 12.4.2014 – 20.9.2014.

Successive Scoring Runs: 26 from 23.8.1947.

Successive Non-scoring Runs: 7 from 25.2.2017.

MANAGERS

Harry Kirkbride 1904–05 (*Secretary-Manager*)
McCumiskey 1905–06 (*Secretary-Manager*)
Jack Houston 1906–08 (*Secretary-Manager*)
Bert Stansfield 1908–10
Jack Houston 1910–12
Davie Graham 1912–13
George Bristow 1913–30
Billy Hampson 1930–33
Bill Clarke 1933–35
Robert Kelly 1935–36
Fred Westgarth 1936–38
David Taylor 1938–40
Howard Harkness 1940–45
Bill Clark 1945–46 (*Secretary-Manager*)
Ivor Broadis 1946–49
Bill Shankly 1949–51
Fred Emery 1951–58
Andy Beattie 1958–60
Ivor Powell 1960–63
Alan Ashman 1963–67
Tim Ward 1967–68
Bob Stokoe 1968–70
Ian MacFarlane 1970–72
Alan Ashman 1972–75
Dick Young 1975–76
Bobby Moncur 1976–80
Martin Harvey 1980
Bob Stokoe 1980–85
Bryan 'Pop' Robson 1985
Bob Stokoe 1985–86
Harry Gregg 1986–87
Cliff Middlemass 1987–91
Aidan McCaffery 1991–92
David McCreery 1992–93
Mick Wadsworth (*Director of Coaching*) 1993–96
Mervyn Day 1996–97
David Wilkes and John Halpin (*Directors of Coaching*), and **Michael Knighton** 1997–99
Nigel Pearson 1998–99
Keith Mincher 1999
Martin Wilkinson 1999–2000
Ian Atkins 2000–01
Roddy Collins 2001–02; 2002–03
Paul Simpson 2003–06
Neil McDonald 2006–07
John Ward 2007–08
Greg Abbott 2008–13
Graham Kavanagh 2013–14
Keith Curle 2014–18
John Sheridan 2018–19
Steven Pressley 2019
Chris Beech 2019–21
Keith Millen 2021–22
Paul Simpson February 2022–

TEN YEAR LEAGUE RECORD

		P	W	D	L	F	A	Pts	Pos
2012-13	FL 1	46	14	13	19	56	77	55	17
2013-14	FL 1	46	11	12	23	43	76	45	22
2014-15	FL 2	46	14	8	24	56	74	50	20
2015-16	FL 2	46	17	16	13	67	62	67	10
2016-17	FL 2	46	18	17	11	69	68	71	6
2017-18	FL 2	46	17	16	13	62	54	67	10
2018-19	FL 2	46	20	8	18	67	62	68	11
2019-20	FL 2	37	10	12	15	39	56	42	18§
2020-21	FL 2	46	18	12	16	60	51	66	10
2021-22	FL 2	46	14	11	21	39	62	53	20

§Decided on points-per-game (1.14)

DID YOU KNOW ?

Carlisle United were elected to the Football League at the annual general meeting in June 1928, the fourth occasion on which they had applied for membership of the League. They finished second in the ballot for the two places available in Division Three North with 33 votes, well clear of Durham City who recorded just 11 votes and thus lost their place in the competition.

CARLISLE UNITED – SKY BET LEAGUE TWO 2021–22 LEAGUE RECORD

Match No.	Date	Venue	Opponents	Result		H/T Score	Lg Pos.	Goalscorers	Attendance
1	Aug 7	H	Colchester U	D	0-0	0-0	12		6382
2	14	A	Swindon T	W	2-1	2-1	6	Riley[13], Abrahams[43]	9450
3	17	A	Port Vale	D	0-0	0-0	6		4943
4	21	H	Leyton Orient	D	1-1	1-0	9	Abrahams (pen)[8]	4597
5	28	A	Hartlepool U	L	1-2	1-1	12	Clough[38]	6112
6	Sept 4	H	Salford C	W	2-1	1-1	8	Dickenson[8], Mellish[59]	4671
7	11	A	Crawley T	L	1-2	0-1	12	Mellish[83]	2151
8	18	H	Scunthorpe U	D	2-2	0-2	13	Gibson[81], Dickenson[90]	4499
9	25	A	Sutton U	L	0-4	0-2	17		2873
10	Oct 2	H	Forest Green R	L	0-2	0-2	19		3963
11	9	A	Bristol R	L	0-3	0-1	22		6302
12	16	H	Tranmere R	L	0-1	0-0	23		4831
13	19	A	Newport Co	D	2-2	1-2	23	Riley[1], Clough (pen)[67]	2962
14	23	H	Oldham Ath	D	0-0	0-0	22		4274
15	30	A	Northampton T	L	0-3	0-1	23		4909
16	Nov 13	H	Barrow	D	0-0	0-0	22		7470
17	20	A	Exeter C	L	1-2	0-0	23	Gibson[84]	4796
18	23	H	Harrogate T	L	0-2	0-1	23		3172
19	27	H	Walsall	W	1-0	0-0	22	Abrahams[88]	3795
20	Dec 7	A	Mansfield T	L	0-1	0-1	22		3695
21	11	A	Stevenage	W	2-0	1-0	21	Mellish[44], Gibson (pen)[65]	2842
22	Jan 1	A	Scunthorpe U	W	1-0	1-0	21	McDonald[40]	3020
23	8	H	Bradford C	W	2-0	1-0	19	Gibson[45], Patrick[87]	4996
24	15	H	Crawley T	D	1-1	0-1	20	Alessandra[90]	4350
25	18	H	Hartlepool U	D	0-0	0-0	19		4570
26	22	A	Forest Green R	L	0-3	0-1	20		2864
27	29	H	Sutton U	L	0-2	0-2	20		4399
28	Feb 1	A	Salford C	L	1-2	0-0	22	Patrick[67]	2059
29	8	H	Port Vale	L	1-3	1-2	22	Windsor[21]	3379
30	12	A	Colchester U	D	2-2	0-0	22	Patrick[51], Sho-Silva[86]	2664
31	19	H	Swindon T	L	0-3	0-1	23		4345
32	26	A	Leyton Orient	W	1-0	1-0	22	Patrick[5]	5272
33	Mar 1	H	Rochdale	W	2-0	1-0	19	Patrick[25], Sho-Silva[89]	5360
34	5	A	Oldham Ath	W	2-1	0-1	18	Patrick[48], Feeney[90]	7327
35	12	H	Northampton T	W	2-1	0-0	17	Sho-Silva[74], Gibson (pen)[90]	8514
36	15	H	Newport Co	L	1-2	0-1	18	Patrick[80]	4445
37	19	A	Barrow	W	2-1	1-0	17	Gibson[32], Dennis[75]	4658
38	26	H	Bristol R	W	1-0	0-0	18	Dennis[72]	5884
39	29	A	Rochdale	L	0-2	0-1	18		2160
40	Apr 2	A	Tranmere R	D	2-2	0-1	18	Patrick[55], Sho-Silva[90]	6477
41	9	H	Exeter C	L	0-1	0-0	19		5132
42	15	A	Walsall	L	0-1	0-1	19		5114
43	18	H	Mansfield T	W	1-0	0-0	17	Patrick[56]	5496
44	23	A	Harrogate T	L	0-3	0-2	20		2707
45	30	H	Stevenage	W	2-1	0-0	18	Riley[52], Alessandra[63]	5701
46	May 7	A	Bradford C	L	0-2	0-1	20		18,283

Final League Position: 20

GOALSCORERS

League (39): Patrick 9, Gibson 6 (2 pens), Sho-Silva 4, Abrahams 3 (1 pen), Mellish 3, Riley 3, Alessandra 2, Clough 2 (1 pen), Dennis 2, Dickenson 2, Feeney 1, McDonald 1, Windsor 1.
FA Cup (3): Clough 1, Gibson 1, Young 1.
Carabao Cup (0).
Papa John's Trophy (8): Young 2, Abrahams 1, Armer 1, Charters 1, Gibson 1, Mampala 1, Mellor 1.

Norman M 10	Tanner G 5	Whelan C 30 + 5	McDonald R 30 + 1	Armer J 39 + 2	Riley J 27 + 4	Guy C 34	Mellish J 42	Alessandra L 15 + 9	Abrahams T 12 + 8	Dickenson B 35 + 4	Mampala M — + 8	Toure G 1 + 4	Feeney M 31 + 4	Charters T 1 + 8	Clough Z 10 + 7	Young B 7 + 7	Mellor K 17 + 4	Gibson J 33 + 6	Dinzeyi J 1	Bell L — + 1	Jensen L 1	Devine D 9 + 8	Howard M 35	Fishburn S 3 + 6	Omotoye T 7 + 6	Patrick O 22 + 2	Senior J 3 + 1	Simeu D 18	Windsor O 3	Sho-Silva O 4 + 9	Devitt J 4 + 3	Dennis K 12 + 5	Roberts M 3 + 3	Ellis J 2	Match No.
1	2	3	4	5	6	7	8^{1}	9	10	11^{2}	12	13																							1
1	2	3	4	5	6	7	8^{3}	9	10^{2}	11^{1}	13		12	14																					2
1	2	3	4	5^{3}	6	7	8	9^{1}	10^{2}	11			14		12	13																			3
1	2	3	4	5	6	7	8^{1}	9	10^{2}	11^{3}	13	14			12																				4
1	2	3	5	6	7	8	9	14	10^{2}	13			4^{1}		11^{3}	12																			5
1		3	4	5	6	7	8	13	10^{2}	11^{3}	14				9^{1}		2	12																	6
1		3	4	5^{1}	6	7	8	9	10^{3}	11^{2}					14	13	2	12																	7
1		3	4	5	6^{1}	7	8	14	11^{2}	12					10^{3}	13	2	9																	8
1		3	4	5^{2}	6	7	8	10		11	12▪				14	13	2^{1}	9^{3}																	9
1		6		5^{3}	2	7	8		12	11		9^{1}	4		13	10^{2}			3	14															10
		4		5^{3}		7	8	6^{1}	13	11			3	14	9	10^{2}		12			1	2													11
		2^{2}	4	5	12	7	8	11	13	9			3^{3}	14	10^{1}			6					1												12
			4	13	2	7	8^{1}	11^{2}		5			3	9	10^{3}	12		6					1	14											13
		3	4	5	2	7	6^{2}	11^{1}	14	9				13	10^{3}	12		8					1												14
		3	4	5	14	7	6	11^{2}	12	10^{1}	13				9		2^{3}	8					1												15
		3	4	5		8	7	14	10^{3}	12				15	9^{1}	11^{2}	2	6^{4}					1	13											16
		3	4	5^{1}			8▪		11^{3}	9			13	12		10^{2}	2	6				7	1	14											17
		4	3			8			11^{1}	5	13			14	9	10^{2}	2	6				7^{3}	1	12											18
		7	4	5	6^{1}	8			13		14		3	12		10^{2}	2	9					1	11^{3}											19
		2	4	5		7^{1}	8		10^{2}	9			3			11^{3}	12	6				14	1	13											20
		13	4	5		7	9^{1}		12	10			3				2	8				6	1	11^{2}											21
		7	4	5		8^{1}	11			9			3				2	6				12	1	10											22
		7	4	5		8	11			9			3				2	6					1		10^{1}	12									23
		8^{1}	4	5^{2}		7	10	13	14	9			3				2	6					1		11^{3}	12									24
			4	5		7	8	13		6			3				2^{1}	9					1		11^{2}	10	12								25
			4	5		7	8	13		6^{2}			3		14			9^{3}					1	12	11^{1}	10	2								26
		7^{3}	4	5		6	9	13		10^{2}					14			12					1		11^{1}	8	2	3							27
		13	4^{1}	5	14	7^{3}	8	10		9			12					6					1			11	2^{2}	3							28
		7		5	2								3					12				8^{1}	1		10^{2}	9		4	6^{3}	11	13	14			29
		7		8	5		6						3										1			11		2	9^{1}	10^{2}	13	12	4		30
		2			6	7	8^{2}						3					12					1			11		4	9^{1}	10^{3}	14	13	5		31
		12		5	2	7	8						3					6					1		13	10^{2}		4		14	9^{1}	11^{3}			32
		14		6	2	8^{3}	5						4					7				12	1			11		3		13	9^{1}	10^{2}			33
				6	2	8	5						4					7				12	1			10		3		13	9^{2}	11^{1}			34
				6	2	8	5			12			4					7					1			11		3		13	9^{1}	10^{2}			35
			5		2	8				9			4					7^{2}				13	1		12	10		3		11^{3}		14	6^{1}		36
		12		6^{2}	2	8^{1}	5			9			4					7				13	1			10		3				11			37
		8^{1}	14	6	2^{3}		5^{2}			9			4				13	7				12	1			10		3				11			38
		8^{2}		6^{3}	2		5			9			4					7				12	1		14	10		3		13		11^{1}			39
			5				9			6		12	4				2	7				8^{1}	1			11		3^{2}		13		10			40
			5				9			6^{2}		14	4				2	7				8	1			11^{3}		3		12		10^{1}	13		41
			4	14	12		7			8			3^{1}				5	6					1		11^{3}	9		2		13		10^{2}			42
				6^{1}	2		5	11^{2}		9			4					7				8	1			10		3		13			12		43
				6	2		5	11^{2}		9			4				14	7				8^{3}	1		12	10		3^{1}				13			44
		3		6	8^{1}		5	12		9			4				14	7					1		13	10						11^{2}		2^{3}	45
		3		6^{1}			5	8		9			4					7					1		13	10						11^{2}	12	2	46

FA Cup

First Round	Horsham	(h)	2-0
Second Round	Shrewsbury T	(h)	1-2

Carabao Cup

First Round	Sheffield U	(a)	0-1

Papa John's Trophy

Group A (N)	Hartlepool U	(h)	3-3
(Carlisle U won 4-3 on penalties)			
Group A (N)	Everton U21	(h)	2-0
Group A (N)	Morecambe	(a)	2-0
Second Round	Lincoln C	(h)	1-1
(Carlisle U won 4-3 on penalties)			
Third Round	Harrogate T	(a)	0-1

CHARLTON ATHLETIC

FOUNDATION

The club was formed on 9 June 1905, by a group of 14- and 15-year-old youths living in streets by the Thames in the area which now borders the Thames Barrier. The club's progress through local leagues was so rapid that after the First World War they joined the Kent League where they spent a season before turning professional and joining the Southern League in 1920. A year later they were elected to the Football League's Division 3 (South).

The Valley, Floyd Road, Charlton, London SE7 8BL.

Telephone: (020) 8333 4000.

Ticket Office: (03330) 144 444.

Website: www.cafc.co.uk

Email: info@cafc.co.uk

Ground Capacity: 27,111.

Record Attendance: 75,031 v Aston Villa, FA Cup 5th rd, 12 February 1938 (at The Valley).

Pitch Measurements: 102.4m × 67.7m (112yd × 74yd).

Owner, Chief Executive: Thomas Sandgaard.

Chief Operating Officer: Tony Keohane.

Manager: Ben Garner.

First-Team Coach: Jason Euell.

HONOURS

League Champions: First Division – 1999–2000; FL 1 – 2011–12; Division 3S – 1928–29, 1934–35.
Runners-up: Division 1 – 1936–37; Division 2 – 1935–36, 1985–86.

FA Cup Winners: 1947.
Runners-up: 1946.

League Cup: quarter-final – 2007.

Full Members' Cup:
Runners-up 1987.

Colours: Red shirts with white trim, white shorts with red trim, red socks with white trim.

Year Formed: 1905.

Turned Professional: 1920.

Club Nickname: 'The Addicks'.

Grounds: 1906, Siemen's Meadow; 1907, Woolwich Common; 1909, Pound Park; 1913, Horn Lane; 1920, The Valley; 1923, Catford (The Mount); 1924, The Valley; 1985, Selhurst Park (groundshare with Crystal Palace); 1991, Upton Park (groundshare with West Ham U); 1992, The Valley.

First Football League Game: 27 August 1921, Division 3 (S), v Exeter C (h) W 1–0 – Hughes; Johnny Mitchell, Goodman; Dowling (1), Hampson, Dunn; Castle, Bailey, Halse, Green, Wilson.

Record League Victory: 8–1 v Middlesbrough, Division 1, 12 September 1953 – Bartram; Campbell, Ellis; Fenton, Ufton, Hammond; Hurst (2), O'Linn (2), Leary (1), Firmani (3), Kiernan.

Record Cup Victory: 8–0 v Stevenage, FL Trophy, 9 October 2018 – Phillips; Marshall, Dijksteel, Sarr, Stevenson (3) (Reeves), Lapslie (1), Maloney, Ward (Morgan), Pratley (1), Vetokele (2), Ajose (1).

Record Defeat: 1–11 v Aston Villa, Division 2, 14 November 1959.

Most League Points (2 for a win): 61, Division 3 (S), 1934–35.

Most League Points (3 for a win): 101, FL 1, 2011–12.

FOOTBALL YEARBOOK FACT FILE

In April 1919 Charlton Athletic were recognised for their efforts in raising money for wounded soldiers and sailors. The club, who at the time were an amateur team, raised £800 from a series of games and further money from charity work. Thirty members of the club served in the forces during the First World War, with three losing their lives while another six were wounded.

Most League Goals: 107, Division 2, 1957–58.

Highest League Scorer in Season: Ralph Allen, 32, Division 3 (S), 1934–35.

Most League Goals in Total Aggregate: Stuart Leary, 153, 1953–62.

Most League Goals in One Match: 5, Wilson Lennox v Exeter C, Division 3 (S), 2 February 1929; 5, Eddie Firmani v Aston Villa, Division 1, 5 February 1955; 5, John Summers v Huddersfield T, Division 2, 21 December 1957; 5, John Summers v Portsmouth, Division 2, 1 October 1960.

Most Capped Player: Jonatan Johansson, 42 (106), Finland.

Most League Appearances: Sam Bartram, 579, 1934–56.

Youngest League Player: Jonjo Shelvey, 16 years 59 days v Burnley, 26 April 2008.

Record Transfer Fee Received: £16,500,000 from Tottenham H for Darren Bent, June 2007.

Record Transfer Fee Paid: £4,750,000 to Wimbledon for Jason Euell, January 2001.

Football League Record: 1921 Elected to Division 3 (S); 1929–33 Division 2; 1933–35 Division 3 (S); 1935–36 Division 2; 1936–57 Division 1; 1957–72 Division 2; 1972–75 Division 3; 1975–80 Division 2; 1980–81 Division 3; 1981–86 Division 2; 1986–90 Division 1; 1990–92 Division 2; 1992–98 Division 1; 1998–99 Premier League; 1999–2000 Division 1; 2000–07 Premier League; 2007–09 FL C; 2009–12 FL 1; 2012–16 FL C; 2016–19 FL 1; 2019–20 FL C; 2020– FL 1.

LATEST SEQUENCES

Longest Sequence of League Wins: 12, 26.12.1999 – 7.3.2000.

Longest Sequence of League Defeats: 10, 11.4.1990 – 15.9.1990.

Longest Sequence of League Draws: 6, 13.12.1992 – 16.1.1993.

Longest Sequence of Unbeaten League Matches: 15, 4.10.1980 – 20.12.1980.

Longest Sequence Without a League Win: 18, 18.10.2008 – 17.1.2009.

Successive Scoring Runs: 25 from 26.12.1935.

Successive Non-scoring Runs: 5 from 17.10.2015.

MANAGERS

Walter Rayner 1920–25
Alex Macfarlane 1925–27
Albert Lindon 1928
Alex Macfarlane 1928–32
Albert Lindon 1932–33
Jimmy Seed 1933–56
Jimmy Trotter 1956–61
Frank Hill 1961–65
Bob Stokoe 1965–67
Eddie Firmani 1967–70
Theo Foley 1970–74
Andy Nelson 1974–79
Mike Bailey 1979–81
Alan Mullery 1981–82
Ken Craggs 1982
Lennie Lawrence 1982–91
Steve Gritt and Alan Curbishley 1991–95
Alan Curbishley 1995–2006
Iain Dowie 2006
Les Reed 2006
Alan Pardew 2006–08
Phil Parkinson 2008–11
Chris Powell 2011–14
José Riga 2014
Bob Peeters 2014–15
Guy Luzon 2015
Karel Fraeye 2015–16
José Riga 2016
Russell Slade 2016
Karl Robinson 2016–18
Lee Bowyer 2018–21
Nigel Adkins 2021
Johnny Jackson 2021–22
Ben Garner June 2022–

TEN YEAR LEAGUE RECORD

		P	W	D	L	F	A	Pts	Pos
2012-13	FL C	46	17	14	15	65	59	65	9
2013-14	FL C	46	13	12	21	41	61	51	18
2014-15	FL C	46	14	18	14	54	60	60	12
2015-16	FL C	46	9	13	24	40	80	40	22
2016-17	FL 1	46	14	18	14	60	53	60	13
2017-18	FL 1	46	20	11	15	58	51	71	6
2018-19	FL 1	46	26	10	10	73	40	88	3
2019-20	FL C	46	12	12	22	50	65	48	22
2020-21	FL 1	46	20	14	12	70	56	74	7
2021-22	FL 1	46	17	8	21	55	59	59	13

DID YOU KNOW ?

When Charlton Athletic won the League One title in 2011–12 they topped the table from 17 September through to the end of the season. They were confirmed as champions with three games still to play and finished the campaign eight points clear of runners-up Sheffield Wednesday.

CHARLTON ATHLETIC – SKY BET LEAGUE ONE 2021–22 LEAGUE RECORD

Match No.	*Date*	*Venue*	*Opponents*	*Result*		*H/T Score*	*Lg Pos.*	*Goalscorers*	*Attendance*
1	Aug 7	H	Sheffield W	D	0-0	0-0	17		17,639
2	14	A	Oxford U	L	1-2	1-2	18	Washington (pen) 36	8440
3	17	A	Milton Keynes D	L	1-2	1-1	20	Stockley 15	7939
4	21	H	Wigan Ath	L	0-2	0-0	21		13,839
5	28	H	Crewe Alex	W	2-0	2-0	19	Jaiyesimi 36, Stockley 41	13,167
6	Sept 11	H	Cheltenham T	L	1-2	0-2	20	Leko 59	13,790
7	18	A	Wycombe W	L	1-2	0-1	23	Lavelle 90	5832
8	21	A	Gillingham	D	1-1	1-0	21	Lee 18	7301
9	25	H	Portsmouth	D	2-2	0-1	22	Clare 47, Davison 87	16,378
10	28	H	Bolton W	L	1-4	1-1	23	Davison 12	12,707
11	Oct 2	A	Fleetwood T	W	2-1	1-0	21	Leko 41, Stockley 69	3197
12	16	A	Lincoln C	L	1-2	0-0	22	Lavelle 63	9169
13	19	H	Accrington S	L	2-3	1-1	22	Morgan (og) 31, Stockley 78	11,813
14	23	A	Sunderland	W	1-0	0-0	22	Stockley 66	31,883
15	30	H	Doncaster R	W	4-0	2-0	20	Lee 21, Washington (pen) 34, Stockley 62, Purrington 71	16,449
16	Nov 2	H	Rotherham U	D	1-1	0-1	18	Washington 83	12,592
17	13	A	Burton Alb	W	1-0	1-0	17	Purrington 20	3555
18	20	H	Plymouth Arg	W	2-0	0-0	12	Purrington 61, Washington 84	26,090
19	23	A	Morecambe	D	2-2	2-1	14	Jaiyesimi 2, Washington 27	4009
20	27	A	Shrewsbury T	L	0-1	0-0	15		6158
21	Dec 7	H	Ipswich T	W	2-0	1-0	14	Stockley 26, Gilbey 88	26,376
22	11	H	Cambridge U	W	2-0	1-0	11	Washington 2 30, 89	24,886
23	18	A	Plymouth Arg	L	0-1	0-1	12		12,711
24	Jan 1	H	Wycombe W	L	0-1	0-1	13		18,895
25	12	A	Crewe Alex	L	1-2	0-2	14	Burstow 80	3556
26	15	A	Cheltenham T	D	1-1	0-1	14	Aneke 90	4709
27	22	H	Fleetwood T	W	2-0	0-0	14	Burstow 53, Morgan 90	21,811
28	31	A	Portsmouth	W	2-1	1-0	14	Washington 31, Robertson (og) 64	15,326
29	Feb 5	H	AFC Wimbledon	W	3-2	2-2	11	Inniss 18, Washington 31, Famewo 60	22,486
30	8	A	Bolton W	L	1-2	0-1	13	Aneke 76	13,523
31	12	A	Wigan Ath	L	1-2	1-1	14	Lee 7	9657
32	19	H	Oxford U	L	0-4	0-2	16		14,029
33	22	H	Milton Keynes D	L	0-2	0-1	16		8807
34	26	A	Sheffield W	L	0-2	0-2	16		21,845
35	Mar 5	H	Sunderland	D	0-0	0-0	16		13,716
36	12	A	Accrington S	L	1-2	1-2	17	Stockley (pen) 18	2543
37	15	H	Gillingham	W	1-0	1-0	16	Gilbey 40	9728
38	19	H	Burton Alb	W	2-0	2-0	15	Washington 12, Taylor 42	11,348
39	26	A	Doncaster R	W	1-0	0-0	14	Stockley 67	6350
40	Apr 2	H	Lincoln C	L	1-2	0-1	15	Stockley 88	10,091
41	5	A	AFC Wimbledon	D	1-1	0-0	15	Stockley 69	8184
42	9	A	Rotherham U	W	1-0	0-0	15	Dobson 55	9087
43	15	H	Morecambe	L	2-3	0-2	15	Stockley 53, Aneke 81	10,700
44	19	A	Cambridge U	W	2-0	0-0	13	Taylor 73, Washington 80	5409
45	23	H	Shrewsbury T	W	2-0	0-0	12	Stockley 64, Aneke 86	11,287
46	30	A	Ipswich T	L	0-4	0-2	13		26,002

Final League Position: 13

GOALSCORERS

League (55): Stockley 13 (1 pen), Washington 11 (2 pens), Aneke 4, Lee 3, Purrington 3, Burstow 2, Davison 2, Gilbey 2, Jaiyesimi 2, Lavelle 2, Leko 2, Taylor 2, Clare 1, Dobson 1, Famewo 1, Inniss 1, Morgan 1, own goals 2.
FA Cup (6): Stockley 4 (1 pen), Burstow 1, Davison 1.
Carabao Cup (0).
Papa John's Trophy (15): Burstow 3, Stockley 3 (2 pens), Davison 2, Blackett-Taylor 1, Gilbey 1, Lee 1, Leko 1, Pearce 1, Purrington 1, own goal 1.

MacGillivray C 43	Matthews A 28	Inniss R 12 + 3	Famewo A 34 + 3	Gunter C 17 + 1	Clare S 31 + 5	Morgan A 21 + 1	Dobson G 38	Jaiyesimi D 22 + 11	Stockley J 28 + 5	Washington C 28 + 7	Clayden C — + 2	Davison J 9 + 6	Watson B 6 + 3	Elerewe A — + 3	Kirk C 5 + 3	Taylor C 15 + 12	Lee E 26 + 8	Lavelle S 18 + 1	Leko J 15 + 10	Souare P 7 + 2	Pearce J 20 + 3	Arter H 4	Purrington B 24 + 3	Gilbey A 32 + 5	Burstow M 8 + 8	Henderson S 2	Aneke C 4 + 5	Fraser S 6 + 3	Castillo J 1 + 1	Kanu D — + 2	Campbell T — + 2	Forster-Caskey J 1 + 3	Harness N 1	*Match No.*
1	2	3	4	5	6	7	8	9	10	11^{1}	12																							1
1	2	3	4	5^{3}	6	7	8^{2}	9^{1}	10	11	14	12	13																					2
1	2	3^{1}	4	5	6	7	8^{3}	9	10	11^{2}			14	12	13																			3
1	2	3	4	5		7	8^{2}	9^{1}	10	13		14	6		11^{3}	12																		4
1	2	3^{1}	4	5	14	7		6^{3}	10	11			8	12	9^{2}		13																	5
1	2		4	5		8		6^{2}	11	13			7		9^{1}		10	3^{3}	12	14														6
1			4	5			7		10^{3}	11		14				13	12	2	9^{1}	8^{2}	3	6												7
1	2					8			14	9^{1}		11^{3}	7			6	10^{2}	3	12		4		5	13										8
1	2				12				10^{2}			14	7			13	11^{3}	3	9	5	4	6^{1}		8										9
1	2		4		7^{2}				14	12		11	8^{3}			6	10	3	9^{1}				5	13										10
1			4	2	14				12			11^{1}			9^{2}	13	10	3	6	5		7^{3}		8										11
1			4	2					13			11^{2}	14		9	12	10^{1}	3	6	5		7^{3}		8										12
1			4	2	6^{2}	7		14	10	12		13				9^{1}		3	11	5^{3}				8										13
1	2		4		13		5	14	10	11							9^{2}	3^{1}	6^{3}		12		8	7										14
1			4	2	13		6	12	10	11^{3}		14					9^{2}		7^{1}		3		5	8										15
1			4	2			5	6^{1}	10	11						12	8				3		9	7										16
1			4		2		5	6^{2}	11■			10^{1}		13		12	8				3		9	7										17
1			4	12	2		5	6^{3}		11		10^{2}				14	8				3^{1}		9	7	13									18
1			4	3^{2}	2		5	6^{1}		11		10^{3}			13	12	8						9	7	14									19
1			3		2		5	13		10		11^{1}				6^{2}	7		12	9			4	8										20
1			4		2		5	6^{1}	10	11							7		12		3		9	8										21
1			4		2		5	12	10	11							8		6^{1}	13	3		9^{2}	7										22
1		13			2^{2}		5	6	11						12		8		10^{3}	9^{1}	3		4	7	14									23
1		14	4		2		5^{3}	6^{2}		11		10^{1}					8		12		3		9	7	13									24
			4		2	14	7	5^{2}		11						12	9		10		3		8^{1}	6^{3}	13	1								25
	5^{2}	3	4		2	6	7^{3}	9^{1}								12	8		13					14	10	1	11							26
1		3	4		2	6	7	5		13						9^{3}	8^{1}						14	12	11^{2}		10							27
1	5	3^{1}	4		2	8	6			11						9^{3}			13		12		14	7			10^{2}							28
1	5	3	4		2	6^{3}	7	12		10						9^{1}								8	13		11^{2}	14						29
1	5		4		2	8	7	9		10								13			3^{1}			6^{3}	11^{2}		12	14						30
1	2^{1}	4			3		7	10									9		8				5	6	11^{2}				12	13				31
1	2	4	13		3■	9	7	10^{1}									8^{3}		11^{2}				5	6	12						14			32
1	5		4	2		8	7^{3}	12									13	3	10^{1}					6	11^{2}				9		14			33
1	5^{1}		4	2		8^{2}	7	12	13								11	3	14				9	6^{4}	10^{3}			15						34
1				4			7	5	10								8	2	13		3		9	12	11^{2}			6^{1}						35
1				4^{3}	5		7	13	10	12							8	2	11		3^{1}		9^{2}		14			6						36
1	5				2		7		11	10						9^{2}	12	3			13		4	6				8^{1}						37
1	5				2		7	12	11	10						9^{1}	13	3					4	6				8^{2}						38
1	5		12		2		7		11	10						9^{1}	13	3					4	6				8^{2}						39
1	5^{2}				2		7^{3}		11	10						9	14	3	13				4	6■				8^{1}				12		40
1	2	12■	13		3		7	6^{3}	10	11						14	9	4^{1}					5									8^{2}		41
1	5		4		2	8	7		11	10						9^{1}					3		12	6										42
1	5		4		2	8^{2}	7		11	12						9					3			6^{1}	10^{3}		14					13		43
1	5		4		2	6	7	13	11^{1}	10						9^{2}					3			8			12							44
1	5		4		2	8	7	9	10	11^{2}											3			6^{1}			12			13				45
	5	2	4			8^{2}	7		11	10^{3}						9	14				3			6^{1}			12					13	1	46

FA Cup

First Round	Havant & Waterlooville	(h)	4-0
Second Round	Gateshead	(a)	2-0
Third Round	Norwich C	(h)	0-1

Carabao Cup

First Round	AFC Wimbledon	(h)	0-1

Papa John's Trophy

Group G (S)	Crawley T	(h)	6-1
Group G (S)	Southampton U21	(h)	4-1
Group G (S)	Leyton Orient	(a)	0-1
Second Round	Aston Villa U21	(h)	2-1
Third Round	Milton Keynes D	(h)	1-0
Quarter-Final	Hartlepool U	(a)	2-2

(Hartlepool U won 5-4 on penalties)

CHELSEA

FOUNDATION

Chelsea may never have existed but for the fact that Fulham rejected an offer to rent the Stamford Bridge ground from Mr H. A. Mears who had owned it since 1904. Fortunately he was determined to develop it as a football stadium rather than sell it to the Great Western Railway and got together with Frederick Parker, who persuaded Mears of the financial advantages of developing a major sporting venue. Chelsea FC was formed in 1905 and applications made to join both the Southern League and Football League. The latter competition was decided upon because of its comparatively meagre representation in the south of England.

Stamford Bridge, Fulham Road, London SW6 1HS.

Telephone: (0371) 811 1955.

Ticket Office: (0371) 811 1905.

Website: www.chelseafc.com

Email: enquiries@chelseafc.com

Ground Capacity: 40,267.

Record Attendance: 82,905 v Arsenal, Division 1, 12 October 1935.

Pitch Measurements: 103m × 67.5m (112.5yd × 74yd).

Chairman: Bruce Buck.

Chief Executive: Guy Laurence.

Manager: Thomas Tuchel.

Assistant Managers: Arno Michels, Zsolt Low.

Colours: Rush blue shirts with black and yellow trim, rush blue shorts with black and yellow trim, white socks with rush blue and yellow trim.

Year Formed: 1905. ***Turned Professional:*** 1905.

Club Nickname: 'The Blues'.

Ground: 1905, Stamford Bridge.

First Football League Game: 2 September 1905, Division 2, v Stockport Co (a) L 0–1 – Foulke; Mackie, McEwan; Key, Harris, Miller; Moran, Jack Robertson, Copeland, Windridge, Kirwan.

Record League Victory: 8–0 v Wigan Ath, Premier League, 9 May 2010 – Cech; Ivanovic (Belletti), Ashley Cole (1), Ballack (Matic), Terry, Alex, Kalou (1) (Joe Cole), Lampard (pen), Anelka (2), Drogba (3, 1 pen), Malouda; 8–0 v Aston Villa, Premier League, 23 December 2012 – Cech; Azpilicueta, Ivanovic (1), Cahill, Cole, Luiz (1), Lampard (1) (Ramirez (2)), Moses, Mata (Piazon), Hazard (1), Torres (1) (Oscar (1)).

HONOURS

League Champions: Premier League – 2004–05, 2005–06, 2009–10, 2014–15, 2016–17; Division 1 – 1954–55; Division 2 – 1983–84, 1988–89.
Runners-up: Premier League – 2003–04, 2006–07, 2007–08, 2010–11; Division 2 – 1906–07, 1911–12, 1929–30, 1962–63, 1976–77.

FA Cup Winners: 1970, 1997, 2000, 2007, 2009, 2010, 2012, 2018.
Runners-up: 1915, 1967, 1994, 2002, 2017, 2020, 2021, 2022.

League Cup Winners: 1965, 1998, 2005, 2007, 2015.
Runners-up: 1972, 2008, 2019, 2022.

Full Members' Cup Winners: 1986, 1990.

European Competitions
Champions League: 1999–2000 *(qf)*, 2003–04 *(sf)*, 2004–05 *(sf)*, 2005–06, 2006–07 *(sf)*, 2007–08 *(runners-up)*, 2008–09 *(sf)*, 2009–10, 2010–11 *(qf)*, 2011–12 *(winners)*, 2012–13, 2013–14 *(sf)*, 2014–15, 2015–16, 2017–18, 2019–20, 2020–21 *(winners)*, 2021–22 *(qf)*.
Fairs Cup: 1958–60 *(qf)*, 1965–66 *(sf)*, 1968–69.
UEFA Cup: 2000–01, 2001–02, 2002–03.
Europa League: 2012–13 *(winners)*, 2018–19 *(winners)*. ***European Cup-Winners' Cup:*** 1970–71 *(winners)*, 1971–72, 1994–95 *(sf)*, 1997–98 *(winners)*, 1998–99 *(sf)*.
Super Cup: 1998 *(winners)*, 2012, 2013, 2019.
Club World Cup: 2012 *(runners-up)*, 2022 *(winners)*.

FOOTBALL YEARBOOK FACT FILE

Chelsea, leading the Second Division table in January 1907, were drawn to face struggling Lincoln City in round one of the FA Cup. The Blues led 2-0 at Sincil Bank only to concede twice in the final three minutes. The replay was even more sensational as Chelsea went down to defeat in extra time. The Blues were so impressed with Lincoln manager David Calderhead that they recruited him the following summer and he stayed at Stamford Bridge for over 25 years.

Record Cup Victory: 13–0 v Jeunesse Hautcharage, ECWC, 1st rd 2nd leg, 29 September 1971 – Bonetti; Boyle, Harris (1), Hollins (1p), Webb (1), Hinton, Cooke, Baldwin (3), Osgood (5), Hudson (1), Houseman (1).

Record Defeat: 1–8 v Wolverhampton W, Division 1, 26 September 1953; 0–7 v Nottingham F, Division 1, 20 April 1991.

Most League Points (2 for a win): 57, Division 2, 1906–07.

Most League Points (3 for a win): 99, Division 2, 1988–89.

Most League Goals: 103, Premier League, 2009–10.

Highest League Scorer in Season: Jimmy Greaves, 41, 1960–61.

Most League Goals in Total Aggregate: Bobby Tambling, 164, 1958–70.

Most League Goals in One Match: 5, George Hilsdon v Glossop, Division 2, 1 September 1906; 5, Jimmy Greaves v Wolverhampton W, Division 1, 30 August 1958; 5, Jimmy Greaves v Preston NE, Division 1, 19 December 1959; 5, Jimmy Greaves v WBA, Division 1, 3 December 1960; 5, Bobby Tambling v Aston Villa, Division 1, 17 September 1966; 5, Gordon Durie v Walsall, Division 2, 4 February 1989.

Most Capped Player: Frank Lampard, 104 (106), England.

Most League Appearances: Ron Harris, 655, 1962–80.

Youngest League Player: Ian Hamilton, 16 years 138 days v Tottenham H, 18 March 1967.

Record Transfer Fee Received: £88,500,000 from Real Madrid for Eden Hazard, June 2019.

Record Transfer Fee Paid: £97,500,000 to Internazionale for Romelu Lukaku, August 2021.

Football League Record: 1905 Elected to Division 2; 1907–10 Division 1; 1910–12 Division 2; 1912–24 Division 1; 1924–30 Division 2; 1930–62 Division 1; 1962–63 Division 2; 1963–75 Division 1; 1975–77 Division 2; 1977–79 Division 1; 1979–84 Division 2; 1984–88 Division 1; 1988–89 Division 2; 1989–92 Division 1; 1992– Premier League.

MANAGERS

John Tait Robertson 1905–07
David Calderhead 1907–33
Leslie Knighton 1933–39
Billy Birrell 1939–52
Ted Drake 1952–61
Tommy Docherty 1961–67
Dave Sexton 1967–74
Ron Suart 1974–75
Eddie McCreadie 1975–77
Ken Shellito 1977–78
Danny Blanchflower 1978–79
Geoff Hurst 1979–81
John Neal 1981–85 (*Director to 1986*)
John Hollins 1985–88
Bobby Campbell 1988–91
Ian Porterfield 1991–93
David Webb 1993
Glenn Hoddle 1993–96
Ruud Gullit 1996–98
Gianluca Vialli 1998–2000
Claudio Ranieri 2000–04
Jose Mourinho 2004–07
Avram Grant 2007–08
Luiz Felipe Scolari 2008–09
Guus Hiddink 2009
Carlo Ancelotti 2009–11
Andre Villas-Boas 2011–12
Roberto Di Matteo 2012
Rafael Benitez 2012–13
Jose Mourinho 2013–15
Guus Hiddink 2015–16
Antonio Conte 2016–18
Maurizio Sarri 2018–19
Frank Lampard 2019–21
Thomas Tuchel January 2021–

LATEST SEQUENCES

Longest Sequence of League Wins: 13, 1.10.2016 – 31.12.2016.

Longest Sequence of League Defeats: 7, 1.11.1952 – 20.12.1952.

Longest Sequence of League Draws: 6, 20.8.1969 – 13.9.1969.

Longest Sequence of Unbeaten League Matches: 40, 23.10.2004 – 29.10.2005.

Longest Sequence Without a League Win: 21, 3.11.1987 – 2.4.1988.

Successive Scoring Runs: 27 from 29.10.1988.

Successive Non-scoring Runs: 9 from 14.3.1981.

TEN YEAR LEAGUE RECORD

		P	W	D	L	F	A	Pts	Pos
2012-13	PR Lge	38	22	9	7	75	39	75	3
2013-14	PR Lge	38	25	7	6	71	27	82	3
2014-15	PR Lge	38	26	9	3	73	32	87	1
2015-16	PR Lge	38	12	14	12	59	53	50	10
2016-17	PR Lge	38	30	3	5	85	33	93	1
2017-18	PR Lge	38	21	7	10	62	38	70	5
2018-19	PR Lge	38	21	9	8	63	39	72	3
2019-20	PR Lge	38	20	6	12	69	54	66	4
2020-21	PR Lge	38	19	10	9	58	36	67	4
2021-22	PR Lge	38	21	11	6	76	33	74	3

DID YOU KNOW ?

Chelsea's game at Blackpool on 29 October 1932 was played in appalling conditions. The Blues trailed 3-0 at half-time by which time Willie Ferguson had left the field with exhaustion. The home team added a fourth 15 minutes from time, then four more Chelsea men left the field at short intervals leaving them to finish the match with just six men.

CHELSEA – PREMIER LEAGUE 2021–22 LEAGUE RECORD

Match No.	*Date*	*Venue*	*Opponents*	*Result*	*H/T Score*	*Lg Pos.*	*Goalscorers*	*Atten-dance*
1	Aug 14	H	Crystal Palace	W 3-0	2-0	2	Alonso [27], Pulisic [40], Chalobah [58]	38,965
2	22	A	Arsenal	W 2-0	2-0	1	Lukaku [15], James [35]	58,729
3	28	A	Liverpool	D 1-1	1-1	2	Havertz [22]	52,550
4	Sept 11	H	Aston Villa	W 3-0	1-0	2	Lukaku 2 [15, 90], Kovacic [49]	39,969
5	19	A	Tottenham H	W 3-0	0-0	1	Thiago Silva [49], Kante [57], Rudiger [90]	60,059
6	25	H	Manchester C	L 0-1	0-0	3		40,036
7	Oct 2	H	Southampton	W 3-1	1-0	1	Chalobah [9], Werner [84], Chilwell [89]	40,109
8	16	A	Brentford	W 1-0	1-0	1	Chilwell [45]	16,940
9	23	H	Norwich C	W 7-0	3-0	1	Mount 3 (1 pen) [8, 85 (p), 90], Hudson-Odoi [18], James [42], Chilwell [57], Aarons (og) [62]	40,113
10	30	A	Newcastle U	W 3-0	0-0	1	James 2 [65, 77], Jorginho (pen) [81]	52,208
11	Nov 6	H	Burnley	D 1-1	1-0	1	Havertz [33]	39,798
12	20	A	Leicester C	W 3-0	2-0	1	Rudiger [14], Kante [28], Pulisic [71]	32,192
13	28	H	Manchester U	D 1-1	0-0	1	Jorginho (pen) [69]	40,041
14	Dec 1	A	Watford	W 2-1	1-1	1	Mount [30], Ziyech [72]	20,388
15	4	A	West Ham U	L 2-3	2-1	3	Thiago Silva [28], Mount [44]	59,942
16	11	H	Leeds U	W 3-2	1-1	3	Mount [42], Jorginho 2 (2 pens) [58, 90]	39,959
17	16	H	Everton	D 1-1	0-0	3	Mount [70]	39,933
18	19	A	Wolverhampton W	D 0-0	0-0	3		30,631
19	26	A	Aston Villa	W 3-1	1-1	3	Jorginho 2 (2 pens) [34, 90], Lukaku [56]	41,907
20	29	H	Brighton & HA	D 1-1	1-0	2	Lukaku [28]	40,080
21	Jan 2	H	Liverpool	D 2-2	2-2	2	Kovacic [42], Pulisic [45]	40,072
22	15	A	Manchester C	L 0-1	0-0	2		53,319
23	18	A	Brighton & HA	D 1-1	1-0	3	Ziyech [28]	30,880
24	23	H	Tottenham H	W 2-0	0-0	3	Ziyech [47], Thiago Silva [55]	40,020
25	Feb 19	A	Crystal Palace	W 1-0	0-0	3	Ziyech [89]	25,109
26	Mar 5	A	Burnley	W 4-0	0-0	3	James [47], Havertz 2 [53, 55], Pulisic [69]	19,439
27	10	A	Norwich C	W 3-1	2-0	3	Chalobah [3], Mount [14], Havertz [90]	26,722
28	13	H	Newcastle U	W 1-0	0-0	3	Havertz [89]	40,026
29	Apr 2	H	Brentford	L 1-4	0-0	3	Rudiger [48]	39,061
30	9	A	Southampton	W 6-0	4-0	3	Alonso [8], Mount 2 [16, 54], Werner 2 [22, 49], Havertz [31]	31,359
31	20	H	Arsenal	L 2-4	2-2	3	Werner [17], Azpilicueta [32]	32,249
32	24	H	West Ham U	W 1-0	0-0	3	Pulisic [90]	32,231
33	28	A	Manchester U	D 1-1	0-0	3	Alonso [60]	73,564
34	May 1	A	Everton	L 0-1	0-0	3		39,256
35	7	H	Wolverhampton W	D 2-2	0-0	3	Lukaku 2 (1 pen) [56 (p), 58]	32,190
36	11	A	Leeds U	W 3-0	1-0	3	Mount [4], Pulisic [55], Lukaku [83]	36,549
37	19	H	Leicester C	D 1-1	1-1	3	Alonso [35]	31,478
38	22	H	Watford	W 2-1	1-0	3	Havertz [11], Barkley [90]	32,089

Final League Position: 3

GOALSCORERS

League (76): Mount 11 (1 pen), Havertz 8, Lukaku 8 (1 pen), Jorginho 6 (6 pens), Pulisic 6, James 5, Alonso 4, Werner 4, Ziyech 4, Chalobah 3, Chilwell 3, Rudiger 3, Thiago Silva 3, Kante 2, Kovacic 2, Azpilicueta 1, Barkley 1, Hudson-Odoi 1, own goal 1.
FA Cup (14): Lukaku 3, Werner 2, Ziyech 2 (1 pen), Alonso 1, Azpilicueta 1, Christensen 1, Hudson-Odoi 1, Loftus-Cheek 1, Mount 1, Saul 1.
Carabao Cup (7): Havertz 2, Jorginho 1 (1 pen), Rudiger 1, Werner 1, own goals 2.
UEFA Champions League (21): Werner 4, Havertz 3, Jorginho 2 (2 pens), Lukaku 2, Pulisic 2, Azpilicueta 1, Chalobah 1, Christensen 1, Hudson-Odoi 1, James 1, Mount 1, Rudiger 1, Ziyech 1.
Papa John's Trophy (5): Baker 1, Fiabema 1, Uwakwe 1, Wareham 1, own goal 1.

Mendy E 34	Chalobah T 17 + 3	Christensen A 17 + 2	Rudiger A 34	Azpilicueta C 24 + 3	Jorginho F 26 + 3	Kovacic M 16 + 9	Alonso M 25 + 3	Mount M 27 + 5	Pulisic C 13 + 9	Werner T 15 + 6	James R 22 + 4	Havertz K 22 + 7	Emerson d — + 1	Lukaku R 16 + 10	Kante N 21 + 5	Ziyech H 14 + 9	Thiago Silva E 28 + 4	Hudson-Odoi C 11 + 4	Saul N 5 + 5	Arrizabalaga K 4	Loftus-Cheek R 13 + 11	Chilwell B 6 + 1	Barkley R 1 + 5	Sarr M 6 + 2	Kenedy R 1	Match No.
1	2	3	4	5¹	6	7	8³	9	10²	11	12	13	14													1
1		3	4	2	6	7¹	8	9²		14	5	10³		11	12	13										2
1	14	3	4	2	7³	13	8	10			5■	9¹		11	6²		12									3
1	2		4	13	12	6	8			14		10²		11		9	3	5³	7¹							4
		2	4	5	6	7	8	9¹		13		10²		11	12		3			1						5
1		3	4	2	7³	8	9			11	5¹	13		10	6²		12				14					6
1	2		4	5	13	7²		12		9				11			3	10¹			6³	8	14			7
1	2	3		5³		8¹		12		10	14	13		11²	6						7	9		4		8
1	2		4		6¹	7		9			5	11²				14	3	10³			12	8	13			9
1		2	4		7						5	11			6²	9¹	3	10³	14		12	8	13			10
1		2	4		7			13	14		5	11			6²		3	10³			12	8	9¹			11
1	2		4		7³			9¹	12		5	11²			6	13	3	10			14	8				12
1	2		4		7		8¹	12	13	11³	5			14		9	3	10²			6					13
1	2²	3	4	5³			8	9	10			11		14		13	12		7¹		6					14
1		2	4		7		8³	10	14		5	11¹		12		9²	3	13			6					15
1		13	4	2¹	7		8³	9		11²	5	10		14			3	12			6					16
1	14		4	2³	7		8¹	9	11		5					10	3		12		6²		13			17
1	7¹		4	2		13	8	9	11		5				6	10²	3		12							18
1	2¹	13	4		7	14	8	9	11		5			12	6³		3²	10								19
1	13	3²	4	2	7	6	12	9	5		8¹			11	14			10³								20
1	2¹		4	5	12	7	8	9	10			11²			6		3	13								21
			2	5		7	8³	14	9¹	13				11	6	10²	3	12		1				4		22
			4	2	7³	14	5	9		12		13		11¹	6	8²	3	10		1						23
			3	2	6¹	9	13	8						11	12	7³	4	10²	14	1				5		24
1		2	4		7²	14	13		8			11		10	6¹	9	3				12			5³		25
1	2		4		7	13		9³	10	14	5²	11			6¹		3		8		12					26
1	2	4		5¹	6	7³		9		10²		11		13	14		3		8		12					27
1	2	3	4		7	13		8¹	14	11²		10		12	6	9								5³		28
1			4	2		13	5¹	6		11²	12	10		14	8³	9	3				7					29
1		2	4			7	8	9³	12	11	13	10¹			6	14	3²				5					30
1		3¹		5			8³	9		11	2	13		10²	7	14	12				6			4		31
1	2			4	7		8	9	12	11³		10¹		13	6	14	3				5²					32
1			4	2	6		8	9	13	10²	5	11¹		12	7³		3				14					33
1			4	2²	6¹	12	8	9	13	11³	5	10				14	3				7					34
1			4	2²		7	8¹		9	11	5	14		10³			3		12		6			13		35
1	2	3	4	13	6	7¹	8	9	10²		5³			11		14					12					36
1	2		4	13	6		8		10²		5	14		11³	7¹	9	3				12					37
1			4²	2				10³			5	11			6	9	3		7			14	13	12	8¹	38

FA Cup

Third Round	Chesterfield	(h)	5-1
Fourth Round	Plymouth Arg	(h)	2-1
(aet)			
Fifth Round	Luton T	(a)	3-2
Sixth Round	Middlesbrough	(a)	2-0
Semi-Final	Crystal Palace	(Wembley)	2-0
Final	Liverpool	(Wembley)	0-0
(aet; Liverpool won 6-5 on penalties)			

Carabao Cup

Third Round	Aston Villa	(h)	1-1
(Chelsea won 4-3 on penalties)			
Fourth Round	Southampton	(h)	1-1
(Chelsea won 4-3 on penalties)			
Quarter-Final	Brentford	(a)	2-0
Semi-Final 1st leg	Tottenham H	(h)	2-0
Semi-Final 2nd leg	Tottenham H	(a)	1-0
(Chelsea won 3-0 on aggregate)			
Final	Liverpool	(Wembley)	0-0
(aet; Liverpool won 11-10 on penalties)			

UEFA Champions League

Group H	Zenit St Petersburg	(h)	1-0
Group H	Juventus	(a)	0-1
Group H	Malmo	(h)	4-0
Group H	Malmo	(a)	1-0
Group H	Juventus	(h)	4-0
Group H	Zenit St Petersburg	(a)	3-3
Round of 16 1st leg	Lille	(h)	2-0
Round of 16 2nd leg	Lille	(a)	2-1
Quarter-Final 1st leg	Real Madrid	(h)	1-3
Quarter-Final 2nd leg	Real Madrid	(a)	3-2
(aet)			

Papa John's Trophy (Chelsea U21)

Group E (S)	Exeter C	(a)	1-1
(Chelsea U21 won 4-3 on penalties)			
Group E (S)	Bristol R	(a)	2-1
Group E (S)	Cheltenham T	(a)	0-0
(Cheltenham T won 5-4 on penalties)			
Second Round	Forest Green R	(a)	1-1
(Chelsea U21 won 4-1 on penalties)			
Third Round	Arsenal U21	(a)	1-4

CHELTENHAM TOWN

FOUNDATION

The origins of Cheltenham Town date back to around 1887. A key figure in the development of football in the town was Albert Close White who had learnt the game whilst studying at St Mark's Teacher Training College in Chelsea. He returned to Cheltenham in 1884 and for the next 40 years he was a teacher at Cheltenham Parish Boys' School, where he introduced a range of sporting activities including association football. He later recalled the formation of the Cheltenham Town club: 'The club was started somewhere between 1884–7, and its first matches were more or less practice or scratch games, and were played on the East Gloucestershire Cricket Ground.' A fixture list from 1894–95 gave the club's ground as Eldorado Road, with team colours of chocolate and blue.

The Jonny-Rocks Stadium, Whaddon Road, Cheltenham, Gloucestershire GL52 5NA.

Telephone: (01242) 573 558.

Ticket Office: (01242) 573 558 (option 1).

Website: www.ctfc.com

Email: info@ctfc.com

Ground Capacity: 7,036.

Record Attendance: 10,389 v Blackpool, FA Cup 3rd rd, 13 January 1934 (at Cheltenham Athletic Ground); 8,326 v Reading, FA Cup 1st rd, 17 November 1956 (at Whaddon Road).

Pitch Measurements: 100m × 65m (109.5yd × 71yd).

Chairman: David Bloxham.

Manager: Wade Elliott.

Assistant Manager: Russell Milton.

Colours: Red shirts with thin white stripes and white sleeves and black trim, black shorts, red socks.

Year Formed: 1887.

Turned Professional: 1932.

Club Nickname: 'The Robins'.

Grounds: Pre-1932, Agg-Gardner's Recreation Ground; Whaddon Lane; Carter's Lane; 1932, Whaddon Road (renamed The Abbey Business Stadium 2009; World of Smile Stadium 2015; LCI Rail Stadium 2016; The Jonny-Rocks Stadium 2019).

First Football League Game: 7 August 1999, Division 3, v Rochdale (h) L 0–2 – Book; Griffin, Victory, Banks, Freeman, Brough (Howarth), Howells, Bloomer (Devaney), Grayson, Watkins (McAuley), Yates.

Record League Victory: 5–0 v Mansfield T, FL 2, 6 May 2006 – Higgs; Gallinagh, Bell, McCann (1) (Connolly), Caines, Duff, Wilson, Bird (1p), Gillespie (1) (Spencer), Guinan (Odejayi (1)), Vincent (1).

Record Cup Victory: 12–0 v Chippenham R, FA Cup 3rd qual. rd, 2 November 1935 – Bowles; Whitehouse, Williams; Lang, Devonport (1), Partridge (2); Perkins, Hackett, Jones (4), Black (4), Griffiths (1).

HONOURS

League Champions: FL 2 – 2020–21; Conference – 1998–99, 2015–16.
Runners-up: Conference – 1997–98.

FA Cup: 5th rd – 2002.

League Cup: 3rd rd – 2022.

FOOTBALL YEARBOOK FACT FILE

Cheltenham Town, then an amateur team competing in the Gloucestershire Northern Senior League, lost 7-3 at league leaders Sharpness on 12 January 1924. The teams met again at Whaddon Road just five weeks later with Sharpness emerging as winners by an identical 7-3 scoreline. Cheltenham finished the season fifth from bottom with Sharpness winning the league by a clear six points.

Record Defeat: 1–8 v Crewe Alex, FL 2, 2 April 2011; 0–7 v Crystal Palace, League Cup 2nd rd, 2 October 2002. *N.B.* 1–10 v Merthyr T, Southern League, 8 March 1952.

Most League Points (2 for a win): 60, Southern League Division 1, 1963–64.

Most League Points (3 for a win): 82, FL 2, 2020–21.

Most League Goals: 67, FL 2, 2017–18.

Highest League Scorer in Season: Mo Eisa, 23, FL 2, 2017–18.

Most League Goals in Total Aggregate: Julian Alsop, 39, 2000–03; 2009–10.

Most League Goals in One Match: 4, Alfie May v Wycombe W, FL 1, 19 February 2022.

Most Capped Player: Grant McCann, 9 (39), Northern Ireland.

Most League Appearances: David Bird, 288, 2001–11.

Youngest League Player: Kyle Haynes, 17 years 85 days v Oldham Ath, 24 March 2009.

Record Transfer Fee Received: £1,400,000 from Bristol C for Mo Eisa, July 2018.

Record Transfer Fee Paid: £60,000 to Aldershot T for Jermaine McGlashan, January 2012.

Football League Record: 1999 Promoted to Division 3; 2002 Division 2; 2003–04 Division 3; 2004–06 FL 2; 2006–09 FL 1; 2009–15 FL 2; 2015–16 National League; 2016–21 FL 2; 2021– FL 1.

LATEST SEQUENCES

Longest Sequence of League Wins: 5, 11.2.2020 – 29.2.2020.

Longest Sequence of League Defeats: 7, 14.4.2018 – 18.8.2018.

Longest Sequence of League Draws: 5, 5.4.2003 – 21.4.2003.

Longest Sequence of Unbeaten League Matches: 16, 1.12.2001 – 12.3.2002.

Longest Sequence Without a League Win: 14, 20.12.2008 – 7.3.2009.

Successive Scoring Runs: 17 from 16.2.2008.

Successive Non-scoring Runs: 5 from 10.3.2012 – 30.3.2012.

MANAGERS

George Blackburn 1932–34
George Carr 1934–37
Jimmy Brain 1937–48
Cyril Dean 1948–50
George Summerbee 1950–52
William Raeside 1952–53
Arch Anderson 1953–58
Ron Lewin 1958–60
Peter Donnelly 1960–61
Tommy Cavanagh 1961
Arch Anderson 1961–65
Harold Fletcher 1965–66
Bob Etheridge 1966–73
Willie Penman 1973–74
Dennis Allen 1974–79
Terry Paine 1979
Alan Grundy 1979–82
Alan Wood 1982–83
John Murphy 1983–88
Jim Barron 1988–90
John Murphy 1990
Dave Lewis 1990–91
Ally Robertson 1991–92
Lindsay Parsons 1992–95
Chris Robinson 1995–97
Steve Cotterill 1997–2002
Graham Allner 2002–03
Bobby Gould 2003
John Ward 2003–07
Keith Downing 2007–08
Martin Allen 2008–09
Mark Yates 2009–14
Paul Buckle 2014–15
Gary Johnson 2015–18
Michael Duff 2018–22
Wade Elliott June 2022–

TEN YEAR LEAGUE RECORD

		P	W	D	L	F	A	Pts	Pos
2012-13	FL 2	46	20	15	11	58	51	75	5
2013-14	FL 2	46	13	16	17	53	63	55	17
2014-15	FL 2	46	9	14	23	40	67	41	23
2015-16	NL	46	30	11	5	87	30	101	1
2016-17	FL 2	46	12	14	20	49	69	50	21
2017-18	FL 2	46	13	12	21	67	73	51	17
2018-19	FL 2	46	15	12	19	57	68	57	16
2019-20	FL 2	36	17	13	6	52	27	64	4§
2020-21	FL 2	46	24	10	12	61	39	82	1
2021-22	FL 1	46	13	17	16	66	80	56	15

§*Decided on points-per-game (1.78)*

DID YOU KNOW ?

Gilbert Jessop, the renowned Gloucestershire and England cricketer, played for Cheltenham Town in the 1890s. Jessop, who played in 18 Test matches for England, mainly appeared as a full-back for Town and was elected the club vice-captain for 1897–98.

CHELTENHAM TOWN – SKY BET LEAGUE ONE 2021–22 LEAGUE RECORD

Match No.	*Date*	*Venue*	*Opponents*	*Result*	*H/T Score*	*Lg Pos.*	*Goalscorers*	*Attendance*
1	Aug 7	A	Crewe Alex	D 1-1	1-1	11	Williams, A [40]	5301
2	14	H	Wycombe W	L 1-3	1-1	20	Williams, A [45]	3860
3	17	H	Ipswich T	W 2-1	0-1	15	Wright [62], Boyle [81]	4746
4	21	A	Fleetwood T	L 2-3	1-1	18	Wright [8], May [87]	2392
5	27	A	Burton Alb	D 1-1	1-0	16	Wright [28]	2909
6	Sept 4	H	Milton Keynes D	D 1-1	1-0	16	Joseph [14]	3704
7	11	A	Charlton Ath	W 2-1	2-0	14	Blair [6], Perry [32]	13,790
8	18	H	Oxford U	W 1-0	0-0	9	May [68]	5004
9	25	A	Wigan Ath	L 0-2	0-1	14		8867
10	28	A	Sunderland	L 0-5	0-3	16		28,313
11	Oct 2	H	Rotherham U	L 0-2	0-0	17		3748
12	16	H	Accrington S	W 1-0	0-0	14	Vassell [79]	3437
13	19	H	Morecambe	W 3-1	1-1	12	Sercombe [26], Joseph 2 [65, 68]	2909
14	23	A	Doncaster R	L 2-3	0-2	13	May [68], Williams, A [90]	6101
15	30	H	Sheffield W	D 2-2	1-0	16	Vassell [14], Blair [90]	5582
16	Nov 2	A	Portsmouth	D 1-1	1-1	15	Freestone [6]	14,322
17	20	H	Shrewsbury T	W 2-1	1-1	11	Thomas (pen) [24], Joseph [66]	3914
18	23	A	Gillingham	W 2-0	1-0	10	Long [30], May [60]	3115
19	27	A	Bolton W	D 2-2	2-1	11	May 2 [14, 45]	13,145
20	Dec 7	H	Cambridge U	L 0-5	0-1	12		2762
21	11	H	Lincoln C	D 2-2	1-0	14	May [16], Blair [90]	3512
22	18	A	Shrewsbury T	L 1-3	1-1	14	Williams, A [16]	5741
23	26	H	Plymouth Arg	L 0-2	0-1	14		5703
24	Jan 1	A	Oxford U	D 1-1	0-0	14	Wright [48]	8351
25	8	H	Burton Alb	D 1-1	1-0	13	Wright [21]	3201
26	15	H	Charlton Ath	D 1-1	1-0	13	N'Lundulu [43]	4709
27	22	A	Rotherham U	L 0-1	0-1	17		9187
28	29	H	Wigan Ath	D 0-0	0-0	17		4405
29	Feb 1	A	AFC Wimbledon	D 2-2	2-1	16	May 2 (1 pen) [31, 34 (p)]	6138
30	8	H	Sunderland	W 2-1	0-1	16	Bonds [64], May [78]	5744
31	12	H	Fleetwood T	W 2-0	2-0	15	May [41], Raglan [45]	3517
32	19	A	Wycombe W	D 5-5	1-3	15	May 4 [3, 52, 71, 81], Etete [66]	5574
33	22	A	Ipswich T	D 0-0	0-0	15		21,318
34	26	H	Crewe Alex	L 1-2	0-1	15	Etete [48]	4227
35	Mar 5	H	Doncaster R	W 4-0	2-0	14	May 2 [16, 75], Williams, B [38], Pollock [84]	4212
36	8	A	Milton Keynes D	L 1-3	0-2	14	Boyle [89]	6894
37	12	A	Morecambe	W 3-1	1-0	13	Sercombe [44], Wright [46], May [80]	3733
38	19	H	AFC Wimbledon	W 3-1	0-1	12	Wright [81], Lloyd [83], May [90]	3836
39	22	A	Plymouth Arg	L 0-2	0-2	12		12,274
40	26	A	Sheffield W	L 1-4	1-1	12	May [4]	21,925
41	Apr 2	A	Accrington S	D 4-4	1-2	12	May [33], Boyle 2 [66, 90], Wright [90]	2181
42	9	H	Portsmouth	W 1-0	0-0	12	Sercombe [76]	5117
43	15	H	Gillingham	D 2-2	1-1	12	Wright [40], Etete [78]	4415
44	18	A	Lincoln C	L 0-3	0-3	13		8672
45	23	H	Bolton W	L 1-2	0-0	15	Ramsey [89]	5228
46	30	A	Cambridge U	D 2-2	1-1	15	May 2 [23, 90]	5880

Final League Position: 15

GOALSCORERS

League (66): May 23 (1 pen), Wright 9, Boyle 4, Joseph 4, Williams, A 4, Blair 3, Etete 3, Sercombe 3, Vassell 2, Bonds 1, Freestone 1, Lloyd 1, Long 1, N'Lundulu 1, Perry 1, Pollock 1, Raglan 1, Ramsey 1, Thomas 1 (1 pen), Williams, B 1.
FA Cup (5): Pollock 2, May 1, Williams A 1, own goal 1.
Carabao Cup (4): May 2, Vassell 2.
Papa John's Trophy (2): Chapman 1, Miles 1.

Evans O 27	Long S 37 + 2	Raglan C 25 + 3	Boyle W 29 + 2	Blair M 38 + 1	Sercombe L 33 + 8	Thomas C 21 + 3	Chapman E 19 + 6	Hussey C 23	Williams A 10 + 13	May A 40 + 6	Lloyd G 3 + 9	Wright C 29 + 5	Vassell K 10 + 6	Perry T 5 + 5	Tozer B 2	Flinders S 19	Freestone L 18 + 10	Joseph K 13 + 6	Pollock M 34	Norton C 1 + 8	Barkers D 1 + 4	Crowley D 9 + 3	Horton G 1 + 1	Bonds E 17 + 6	N'Lundulu D 4	Ramsey A 9 + 6	Etete K 10 + 3	Williams B 9 + 2	Hutchinson R 6	Colkett C 4 + 5	Brown C — + 3	*Match No.*
1	2	3	4	5	6	7	8	9	10	11^{1}	12																					1
1	2^{3}	3	4	5	8	13	7^{2}	9	10	11^{1}		6	12	14																		2
1	5	2	4		8	7	14	9	11^{2}	12	13	6^{3}	10^{1}		3																	3
	5	2^{3}	4	14	8^{2}	7		9	10^{1}	11	12	6		13	3	1																4
	2		3	5	8	14	7	9	11^{1}	10^{2}	12	6^{3}		13		1	4															5
	2		3	5	8	13	7^{2}	9	14	11^{1}		6		12		1	4	10^{3}														6
	2		4	5	12	6	7	8		11^{3}		9		10^{1}		1	13	14	3^{2}													7
	2		4	5		7	8	9		11			12	6^{2}		1	13	10^{1}	3													8
	2			5	6	7	8	9		10^{2}			13	12		1	4^{1}	11^{3}	3	14												9
	3			2	7	8	9	6		12				10^{3}		1	5	11^{2}	4^{1}	13	14											10
	3			2	9^{3}	8	14			10^{2}			12	7		1	5	11^{1}	4	13	6											11
	2		4	5		7	12	9		11^{2}			10	6^{1}		1		13	3		14	8^{3}										12
	4			2	7	6	8	5		14			10^{2}			1		11^{3}	3	13	12	9^{1}										13
	4			2	7	6^{2}	8	5	14	13			11^{3}			1		10	3	12		9^{1}										14
	4			2	7	6	8	5		12			10			1		11^{2}	3	13		9^{1}										15
	2			5	6	7	8^{2}	9		11			10^{3}			1	4	14	3^{1}			13	12									16
	2			5	6	7		9		12			11			1	4^{1}	13	3	10^{2}	14	8^{3}										17
	2				6		7	8	14	11^{2}		13	10^{3}			1	4	5	3	12		9^{1}										18
	3				6		7	8	14	11^{2}		12	10^{1}			1		5	4	13		9^{3}	2									19
	2	14		5	6		7	8		10		9^{2}	13			1	4^{1}	12	3			11^{3}										20
1	4	2		5	6		7	8^{1}	14	9			10^{3}				12	11^{2}	3			13										21
1	4	3		2	6		7	5	11	10		12						8^{1}				9										22
1	2	3^{3}		5		7		9	10^{1}	11		6	13				4	12				14		8^{2}								23
1	4	2	13	5	7	6			14	11		9^{1}					8	10^{3}	3^{2}					12								24
1	4	2^{1}	12	5	7^{2}	6		9	14	10		8							3					13	11^{3}							25
1	2	12	4	5	7^{2}	6			13	11		9^{1}					8		3					14	10^{3}							26
1	2^{1}	12	4	5	6	7				10^{2}		8					9		3						11^{3}	13	14					27
1		2	4	5	6	7^{2}				11^{3}		8					14		3					13	10^{1}		12	9▮				28
1		2	4	5	6					11		8^{3}					12		3					7		13	10^{2}		9^{1}	14		29
1		2	4	5	13					10		12					14		3					7		6^{2}	11	9^{3}		8^{1}		30
1		2	4	5						10		8							3					7		6	11	9				31
1		2	4	5	12				14	10		8					13		3					7		6^{1}	11^{3}	9^{2}				32
1	14	2		5					11	10		13					4		3					6		8^{2}		12	9^{1}	7^{3}		33
1		2	4	5	12				13	10		6							3^{2}					7		8^{1}	11	9				34
1		2	4	5	13				14	10		6							3					7^{2}		8^{1}	11^{3}	9		12		35
1	12	2	4	5^{3}	6				13	11		9							3^{1}					14		10^{2}		8		7		36
1	2	3	4	5	6				11^{3}	10	14	8					13							7^{1}				9^{2}		12		37
1	2	3	4	5	8^{3}				11^{1}	10	13	6												7^{2}		14		9		12		38
1	5	2	4	10	8^{3}		14			11	13	6					9		3^{2}					7^{1}						12		39
1	5	2^{2}	4	10^{1}	13		8^{3}			11	12	6							3					7			14		9			40
1	2	3	4	5	12		13			11	10^{3}	8					9							7^{2}		6^{1}					14	41
1	2		4	5	8^{2}		13			11	12	6							3					7			10^{1}		9			42
1	2		4		6	5^{1}				11		8					13		3					7		12	10		9^{2}			43
1	2	3	4		14		8^{2}			11		7					12							13		9^{1}	10		5	6^{3}		44
	2		4		6^{3}				12	11	5^{2}	8				1	9		3					7		14	10^{1}				13	45
	5^{1}	2	4▮		8					10	11	6				1	9^{2}		3					7^{3}		14		13			12	46

FA Cup

First Round	Gillingham	(a)	1-1
Replay	Gillingham	(h)	1-0
Second Round	AFC Wimbledon	(a)	3-4

Carabao Cup

First Round	Bristol R	(a)	2-0
Second Round	Gillingham	(a)	1-1
(Cheltenham T won 5-4 on penalties)			
Third Round	Preston NE	(a)	1-4

Papa John's Trophy

Group E (S)	Bristol R	(a)	0-2
Group E (S)	Exeter C	(h)	2-2
(Exeter C won 3-2 on penalties)			
Group E (S)	Chelsea U21	(h)	0-0
(Cheltenham T won 5-4 on penalties)			

COLCHESTER UNITED

FOUNDATION

Colchester United was formed in 1937 when a number of enthusiasts of the much older Colchester Town club decided to establish a professional concern as a limited liability company. The new club continued at Layer Road which had been the amateur club's home since 1909.

JobServe Community Stadium, United Way, Colchester, Essex CO4 5UP.

Telephone: (01206) 755 100.

Ticket Office: (01206) 755 161.

Website: www.cu-fc.com

Email: media@colchesterunited.net

Ground Capacity: 10,105.

Record Attendance: 19,072 v Reading, FA Cup 1st rd, 27 November 1948 (at Layer Road); 10,064 v Norwich C, FL 1, 16 January 2010 (at Community Stadium).

Pitch Measurements: 105m × 68m (115yd × 74.5yd).

Executive Chairman: Robbie Cowling.

Head Coach: Wayne Brown.

Assistant Head Coaches: Joe Dunne, Dave Huzzey.

Colours: Royal blue shirts with white trim, royal blue shorts with white trim, white socks with royal blue trim.

Year Formed: 1937.

Turned Professional: 1937.

Club Nickname: 'The U's'.

Grounds: 1937, Layer Road; 2008, Weston Homes Community Stadium (renamed JobServe Community Stadium 2018).

First Football League Game: 19 August 1950, Division 3 (S), v Gillingham (a) D 0–0 – Wright; Kettle, Allen; Bearryman, Stewart, Elder; Jones, Curry, Turner, McKim, Church.

Record League Victory: 9–1 v Bradford C, Division 4, 30 December 1961 – Ames; Millar, Fowler; Harris, Abrey, Ron Hunt; Foster, Bobby Hunt (4), King (4), Hill (1), Wright.

Record Cup Victory: 9–1 v Leamington, FA Cup 1st rd, 5 November 2005 – Davison; Stockley (Garcia), Duguid, Brown (1), Chilvers, Watson (1), Halford (1), Izzet (Danns) (2), Iwelumo (1) (Williams), Cureton (2), Yeates (1).

HONOURS

League Champions: Conference – 1991–92.
Runners-up: FL 1 – 2005–06; Division 4 – 1961–62; Conference – 1990–91.

FA Cup: 6th rd – 1971.

League Cup: 5th rd – 1975, 2020.

League Trophy: *Runners-up:* 1997.

FOOTBALL YEARBOOK FACT FILE

Colchester United did not enter the FA Cup until their second season of existence, in 1938–39. Their first-ever game in the competition was at Layer Road on 12 November 1938 when they faced Ilford in a fourth qualifying round tie. Although drawing 1-1 at half time, the U's went through to the first round proper with a 4-1 win in front of around 6,100 fans. Goalscorers were Arthur Pritchard, George Wallis, George Crisp and Jack Hodge.

Record Defeat: 0–8 v Leyton Orient, Division 4, 15 October 1988.

Most League Points (2 for a win): 60, Division 4, 1973–74.

Most League Points (3 for a win): 81, Division 4, 1982–83.

Most League Goals: 104, Division 4, 1961–62.

Highest League Scorer in Season: Bobby Hunt, 38, Division 4, 1961–62.

Most League Goals in Total Aggregate: Martyn King, 130, 1956–64.

Most League Goals in One Match: 4, Bobby Hunt v Bradford C, Division 4, 30 December 1961; 4, Martyn King v Bradford C, Division 4, 30 December 1961; 4, Bobby Hunt v Doncaster R, Division 4, 30 April 1962.

Most Capped Player: Luke Gambin 11 (includes 2 on loan at Newport Co) (35), Malta.

Most League Appearances: Micky Cook, 613, 1969–84.

Youngest League Player: Todd Miller, 16 years 166 days v Exeter C, 16 March 2019.

Record Transfer Fee Received: £2,500,000 from Reading for Greg Halford, January 2007.

Record Transfer Fee Paid: £400,000 to Cheltenham T for Steve Gillespie, July 2008.

Football League Record: 1950 Elected to Division 3 (S); 1958–61 Division 3; 1961–62 Division 4; 1962–65 Division 3; 1965–66 Division 4; 1966–68 Division 3; 1968–74 Division 4; 1974–76 Division 3, 1976–77 Division 4; 1977–81 Division 3; 1981–90 Division 4; 1990–92 Conference; 1992–98 Division 3; 1998–2004 Division 2; 2004–06 FL 1; 2006–08 FL C; 2008–16 FL 1; 2016– FL 2.

MANAGERS

Ted Fenton 1946–48
Jimmy Allen 1948–53
Jack Butler 1953–55
Benny Fenton 1955–63
Neil Franklin 1963–68
Dick Graham 1968–72
Jim Smith 1972–75
Bobby Roberts 1975–82
Allan Hunter 1982–83
Cyril Lea 1983–86
Mike Walker 1986–87
Roger Brown 1987–88
Jock Wallace 1989
Mick Mills 1990
Ian Atkins 1990–91
Roy McDonough 1991–94
George Burley 1994
Steve Wignall 1995–99
Mick Wadsworth 1999
Steve Whitton 1999–2003
Phil Parkinson 2003–06
Geraint Williams 2006–08
Paul Lambert 2008–09
Aidy Boothroyd 2009–10
John Ward 2010–12
Joe Dunne 2012–14
Tony Humes 2014–15
Kevin Keen 2015–16
John McGreal 2016–20
Steve Ball 2020–21
Hayden Mullins 2021–22
Wayne Brown January 2022–

LATEST SEQUENCES

Longest Sequence of League Wins: 7, 31.12.2005 – 7.2.2006.

Longest Sequence of League Defeats: 9, 31.10.2015 – 28.12.2015.

Longest Sequence of League Draws: 6, 21.3.1977 – 11.4.1977.

Longest Sequence of Unbeaten League Matches: 20, 22.12.1956 – 19.4.1957.

Longest Sequence Without a League Win: 20, 2.3.1968 – 31.8.1968.

Successive Scoring Runs: 24 from 15.9.1962.

Successive Non-scoring Runs: 5 from 6.3.2021.

TEN YEAR LEAGUE RECORD

		P	W	D	L	F	A	Pts	Pos
2012-13	FL 1	46	14	9	23	47	68	51	20
2013-14	FL 1	46	13	14	19	53	61	53	16
2014-15	FL 1	46	14	10	22	58	77	52	19
2015-16	FL 1	46	9	13	24	57	99	40	23
2016-17	FL 2	46	19	12	15	67	57	69	8
2017-18	FL 2	46	16	14	16	53	52	62	13
2018-19	FL 2	46	20	10	16	65	53	70	8
2019-20	FL 2	37	15	13	9	52	37	58	6§
2020-21	FL 2	46	11	18	17	44	61	51	20
2021-22	FL 2	46	14	13	19	48	60	55	15

§Decided on points-per-game (1.57)

DID YOU KNOW ?

Colchester United were unable to complete their Southern League fixtures for the 1946–47 season as their opponents Millwall Reserves were unable to raise a team. The league management committee ruled that the match would be classified as a draw and as a result the U's received a single point rather than the two they might have expected.

COLCHESTER UNITED – SKY BET LEAGUE TWO 2021–22 LEAGUE RECORD

Match No.	Date	Venue	Opponents	Result	H/T Score	Lg Pos.	Goalscorers	Attendance
1	Aug 7	A	Carlisle U	D 0-0	0-0	12		6382
2	14	H	Northampton T	L 0-1	0-1	17		2772
3	17	H	Mansfield T	D 1-1	0-0	17	Sears (pen) 90	2354
4	21	A	Oldham Ath	W 2-1	2-0	13	Sears (pen) 9, Chilvers 12	3496
5	27	A	Rochdale	D 1-1	1-0	10	Taylor (og) 40	3054
6	Sept 10	A	Barrow	W 3-2	2-1	8	Judge 35, Sears 38, Eastman 80	2430
7	18	H	Crawley T	L 0-1	0-1	16		2640
8	25	A	Swindon T	D 0-0	0-0	16		8436
9	Oct 2	H	Salford C	L 0-2	0-2	18		2566
10	8	A	Tranmere R	L 0-2	0-0	18		7324
11	16	H	Harrogate T	W 1-0	0-0	19	Jasper 88	2439
12	19	H	Bristol R	D 1-1	0-0	19	Chilvers 88	2069
13	23	A	Port Vale	L 0-3	0-2	19		5423
14	26	H	Sutton U	L 1-3	1-2	19	Sears 2	3013
15	30	H	Scunthorpe U	W 2-1	2-0	17	Sears 5, Dobra 14	2433
16	Nov 20	A	Stevenage	L 0-1	0-1	20		2683
17	23	H	Exeter C	W 3-1	2-0	19	Jasper 12, Chilvers 45, Sears 74	2028
18	26	H	Newport Co	D 1-1	0-1	17	Sears 78	2401
19	Dec 8	A	Bradford C	D 0-0	0-0	18		14,658
20	11	A	Walsall	L 0-3	0-2	20		4065
21	Jan 1	A	Crawley T	L 1-3	0-2	20	Sears 79	2022
22	11	A	Forest Green R	L 0-2	0-1	22		1829
23	15	H	Barrow	L 0-2	0-0	22		2297
24	18	A	Sutton U	L 2-3	2-1	22	Edwards 3, Sears (pen) 44	2532
25	22	A	Salford C	W 3-0	2-0	22	Chambers 30, Kenlock 33, Andrews 82	1759
26	29	H	Swindon T	D 1-1	0-0	22	Huws 90	3327
27	Feb 1	H	Rochdale	D 1-1	0-0	21	Judge 53	2298
28	5	A	Leyton Orient	W 1-0	1-0	20	Sears 4	5641
29	8	A	Mansfield T	L 1-2	0-1	20	Judge 90	4815
30	12	H	Carlisle U	D 2-2	0-0	21	Smith 69, Wright 74	2664
31	19	A	Northampton T	L 0-3	0-1	21		5309
32	22	H	Hartlepool U	L 1-2	1-0	21	Chilvers 22	2115
33	26	H	Oldham Ath	D 1-1	0-1	21	Clarke (og) 52	2983
34	Mar 1	H	Leyton Orient	D 2-2	0-0	20	Kenlock 75, Edwards 79	3415
35	5	H	Port Vale	W 1-0	0-0	19	Dallison 85	2772
36	12	A	Scunthorpe U	W 3-1	0-1	19	Chilvers 2 60, 76, Edwards 67	2427
37	15	A	Bristol R	L 0-1	0-0	19		7314
38	21	H	Forest Green R	L 0-1	0-1	20		6140
39	26	H	Tranmere R	W 1-0	0-0	19	Tchamadeu 90	2459
40	Apr 2	A	Harrogate T	W 2-1	2-1	19	Sears 21, Chilvers 45	1615
41	9	H	Stevenage	L 0-2	0-1	20		3094
42	15	A	Exeter C	L 0-2	0-1	20		7549
43	18	H	Bradford C	W 3-0	2-0	19	Kenlock 16, Sarpeng-Wiredu 33, Sears 75	2893
44	22	A	Newport Co	W 2-1	0-1	15	Akinde 68, Chilvers 77	5989
45	30	H	Walsall	D 2-2	1-1	19	Sears 2 (1 pen) 24, 56 (p)	3520
46	May 7	A	Hartlepool U	W 2-0	1-0	15	Akinde 9, Cooper 53	5375

Final League Position: 15

GOALSCORERS

League (48): Sears 14 (4 pens), Chilvers 8, Edwards 3, Judge 3, Kenlock 3, Akinde 2, Jasper 2, Andrews 1, Chambers 1, Cooper 1, Dallison 1, Dobra 1, Eastman 1, Huws 1, Sarpeng-Wiredu 1, Smith 1, Tchamadeu 1, Wright 1, own goals 2.
FA Cup (5): Sears 2, Jasper 1, McCoulsky 1, Sarpong-Wiredu 1.
Carabao Cup (0).
Papa John's Trophy (4): Chambers 2, Dobra 1, Sears 1.

George S 30	Eastman T 21 + 7	Chambers L 42 + 1	Smith T 29 + 3	Coxe C 23 + 8	Sarpeng-Wiredu B 35 + 3	Skuse C 41	Judge A 27 + 5	Clampin R 4 + 1	Sears F 43 + 2	Nouble F 14 + 5	Jasper S 11 + 7	Hannant L 26 + 11	Chilvers N 29 + 9	Welch-Hayes M 7 + 5	Daniels C 16 + 2	Kennedy G 2 + 4	Tchamadeu J 21 + 5	Dobra A 7 + 4	Tovide S 1 + 5	Turner J 8 + 1	McCoulsky S — + 4	Andrews C 3 + 8	Dallison T 9	Huws E 10 + 2	Edwards O 9 + 4	Kenlock M 19 + 1	Akinde J 6 + 9	Collins T — + 1	Hornby S 8	Wright T 5 + 7	Thomas D — + 1	Cooper C — + 1	Bennet K — + 1	Ihionvien B — + 1	*Match No.*
1	2	3	4	5	6	7	8	9	10^1	11	12																								1
1	2	3	4	5^1	6^2	7	9	8	12	10	11^3	13	14																						2
1	4^1	3		12		7	6	8^2	10	11	14	5^3	9	2	13																				3
1		3	4	14	6		7		8^1	11	10^3	12	9^2	2	5	13																			4
1		3	4	14	6	7^2			8	11	10^1	12	9^3	2	5	13																			5
1	12	3■	4	2	6	7	9^1		10^3	11		8^2	13		5		14																		6
1	3		4	2^3	6^1	7	8		9	10	11^2	14	13		5			12																	7
1		3	4	2	7^3	6	9		10^2	11	12	8^1	14		5			13																	8
1	12	3	4	2^1	13	6	7		8	11	14		10^3		5			9^2																	9
1	4	3		2	6	7	9^1	5	10	11^3	13	8^2	12						14																10
1	4	3	14		6	7			9	11^2	12	8	10^1		5		2^3		13																11
1	4	3			8	7^1			11	10	9^2	6^3	12		5		2■	13	14																12
1	3^1	2	4		7	8^3			11^2	10		6	9	12	5	14			13																13
1		3	4	12		8			10	13		6^1	9	2	5	7^2			11■																14
1	4	3			8	7		13	10^2	12	9^1	14	6	2	5			11^3																	15
1^1	4^2	3	13			7			10	11^3	9		8		5		2	6		12	14														16
	13	3	4	12		6			11^3		8	10^2	7		5		2^1	9		1	14														17
	14	3	4	2		6	12		11		8^1	10^3	7		5			9^2		1	13														18
		3	4	13	12	7	9^3		11		8^1	14	6		5		2	10^2		1															19
		3	4		7	6	9^1		11		8	10^2			5		2	12		1	13														20
	3	12	4	5	7^3	6	9		11		13	14	8^2				2	10^1		1															21
	2	3	4	8	7	6	9^3					13	10^2		12		5^1		14	1		11													22
		3		8	6^2	7	9		11	14		12	13	2^1			5			1		10^3	4												23
	13	3	4^2		9	7			11	12		10		2						1			5	6	8^1										24
1		3			9	7^1	10^2		11	14		8	12				2					13^3	4	6		5									25
1■		3■			9^1	7	10^2		11			8^3					2						4	6	14	5	12	13							26
	3				12	6^1	10		9								2					13	4	7	8	5	11^2		1						27
	3		4		7	6^1			9			8		13		12	2					11^3			14	5			1	10^2					28
	12	3	4		6		9		11			8^1				7^3	2					14			13	5			1	10^2					29
	2^1	3	4		7^2	6	11		10								5							13	9	8			1	12					30
	2^1	3	4			6	11		10^3				13				5					12		7^2	9	8			1	14					31
		3	4	2	7^2	6	13		10				9^3									12			8	5	11^1		1	14					32
1		3	4	2		7	8		12			11^2	6										5^3		9	14	10^1			13					33
1		3		2		6^1	7		11			10^2	9				14						4	12	8^3	5	13								34
1		3	14	2	6				11^3			8	9				12						4	7^2		5	13			10^1					35
1		3	4	2	6	7			11			8^1	9	14											10^3	5^2	13			12					36
1	4	3		2	7	6^2			11			8^1	9									13			10	5	12								37
1	4	3		2	7^3	6			9				8				13					12				5	11^1			10^2	14				38
1	13	3		2	7	6	12		9			8^3	10				14						4^2			5	11^1								39
1	4	3		2	7	6^2	12		11			10	9	13			8^1									5									40
1	4	3		2	6	7^2	10		11				9									13				5	12			8^1					41
1	4	3	5	2	7	6	12		11			8^2	10^3											9^1			13			14					42
1		3	4		8	6^1	7		11^2			12	9	14			2^3							10	13	5									43
1		3	4	12	8	6	7^3		11			14	9				2							10^2		5^1	13								44
		3	4	12	8		7^3		11			10	9				2							6^2		5^1	13		1	14					45
		3	4	2	7^2		6^1		11			9	8				5										10^3		1			12	13	14	46

FA Cup

First Round	AFC Sudbury	(a)	4-0
Second Round	Wigan Ath	(h)	1-2

Carabao Cup

First Round	Birmingham C	(a)	0-1

Papa John's Trophy

Group A (S)	Gillingham	(h)	0-1
Group A (S)	West Ham U U21	(h)	1-0
Group A (S)	Ipswich T	(a)	0-0
(Ipswich T won 4-3 on penalties)			
Second Round	Swindon T	(a)	2-1
Third Round	Sutton U	(a)	1-2

COVENTRY CITY

FOUNDATION

Workers at Singers' cycle factory formed a club in 1883. The first success of Singers FC was to win the Birmingham Junior Cup in 1891 and this led in 1894 to their election to the Birmingham & District League. Four years later they changed their name to Coventry City and joined the Southern League in 1908 at which time they were playing in blue and white quarters.

The Coventry Building Society Arena, Jimmy Hill Way, Foleshill, Coventry CV6 6GE.

Postal Address: Sky Blue Lodge, Leamington Road, Coventry CV8 3FL.

Telephone: (02476) 991 987.

Ticket Office: (02476) 991 987.

Website: www.ccfc.co.uk

Email: info@ccfc.co.uk

Ground Capacity: 32,609.

Record Attendance: 51,455 v Wolverhampton W, Division 2, 29 April 1967 (at Highfield Road); 31,407 v Chelsea, FA Cup 6th rd, 7 March 2009 (at Ricoh Arena).

Pitch Measurements: 100m × 65m (109.5yd × 71yd).

Chairman: Tim Fisher.

Chief Executive: David Boddy.

Manager: Mark Robins.

Assistant Manager: Adi Viveash.

Colours: Sky blue shirts with navy blue trim, sky blue shorts with navy blue trim, sky blue socks with navy blue trim.

Year Formed: 1883.

Turned Professional: 1893.

Previous Name: 1883, Singers FC; 1898, Coventry City.

Club Nickname: 'Sky Blues'.

Grounds: 1883, Binley Road; 1887, Stoke Road; 1899, Highfield Road; 2005, Ricoh Arena; 2013, Sixfields Stadium (groundshare with Northampton T); 2014, Ricoh Arena; 2019, St Andrew's Trillion Trophy Stadium (groundshare with Birmingham C); 2021, The Coventry Building Society Arena.

First Football League Game: 30 August 1919, Division 2, v Tottenham H (h) L 0–5 – Lindon; Roberts, Chaplin, Allan, Hawley, Clarke, Sheldon, Mercer, Sambrooke, Lowes, Gibson.

Record League Victory: 9–0 v Bristol C, Division 3 (S), 28 April 1934 – Pearson; Brown, Bisby; Perry, Davidson, Frith; White (2), Lauderdale, Bourton (5), Jones (2), Lake.

Record Cup Victory: 8–0 v Rushden & D, League Cup 2nd rd, 2 October 2002 – Debec; Caldwell, Quinn, Betts (1p), Konjic (Shaw), Davenport, Pipe, Safri (Stanford), Mills (2) (Bothroyd (2)), McSheffery (3), Partridge.

Record Defeat: 2–10 v Norwich C, Division 3 (S), 15 March 1930.

HONOURS

League Champions: Division 2 – 1966–67; FL 1 – 2019–20.
Division 3 – 1963–64; Division 3S – 1935–36.
Runners-up: Division 3S – 1933–34; Division 4 – 1958–59.

FA Cup Winners: 1987.

League Cup: semi-final – 1981, 1990.

League Trophy Winners: 2017.

European Competitions
Fairs Cup: 1970–71.

FOOTBALL YEARBOOK FACT FILE

When Coventry City moved up to the Southern League for the 1908–09 season, they had no club nickname apart from 'City' or 'the Cits'. The issue was discussed in the column written by Nemo in the local *Midland Daily Telegraph* newspaper and several names were suggested including 'the Pedallers', 'the Cyclists' and 'the Sinners'. In November 1908 'the Bantams' was adopted as their first nickname on account of the fact the team was both lightweight and combative.

Most League Points (2 for a win): 60, Division 4, 1958–59 and Division 3, 1963–64.

Most League Points (3 for a win): 75, FL 2, 2017–18.

Most League Goals: 108, Division 3 (S), 1931–32.

Highest League Scorer in Season: Clarrie Bourton, 49, Division 3 (S), 1931–32.

Most League Goals in Total Aggregate: Clarrie Bourton, 173, 1931–37.

Most League Goals in One Match: 5, Clarrie Bourton v Bournemouth, Division 3 (S), 17 October 1931; 5, Arthur Bacon v Gillingham, Division 3 (S), 30 December 1933.

Most Capped Player: Magnus Hedman, 44 (58), Sweden.

Most League Appearances: Steve Ogrizovic, 507, 1984–2000.

Youngest League Player: Ben Mackey, 16 years 167 days v Ipswich T, 12 April 2003.

Record Transfer Fee Received: £13,000,000 from Internazionale for Robbie Keane, July 2000.

Record Transfer Fee Paid: £6,500,000 to Norwich C for Craig Bellamy, August 2000.

Football League Record: 1919 Elected to Division 2; 1925–26 Division 3 (N); 1926–36 Division 3 (S); 1936–52 Division 2; 1952–58 Division 3 (S); 1958–59 Division 4; 1959–64 Division 3; 1964–67 Division 2; 1967–92 Division 1; 1992–2001 Premier League; 2001–04 Division 1; 2004–12 FL C; 2012–17 FL 1; 2017–18 FL 2; 2018–20 FL 1; 2020– FL C.

LATEST SEQUENCES

Longest Sequence of League Wins: 6, 25.4.1964 – 5.9.1964.

Longest Sequence of League Defeats: 9, 30.8.1919 – 11.10.1919.

Longest Sequence of League Draws: 6, 1.11.2003 – 29.11.2003.

Longest Sequence of Unbeaten League Matches: 25, 26.11.1966 – 13.5.1967.

Longest Sequence Without a League Win: 19, 30.8.1919 – 20.12.1919.

Successive Scoring Runs: 25 from 10.9.1966.

Successive Non-scoring Runs: 11 from 11.10.1919.

MANAGERS

H. R. Buckle 1909–10
Robert Wallace 1910–13
(*Secretary-Manager*)
Frank Scott-Walford 1913–15
William Clayton 1917–19
H. Pollitt 1919–20
Albert Evans 1920–24
Jimmy Kerr 1924–28
James McIntyre 1928–31
Harry Storer 1931–45
Dick Bayliss 1945–47
Billy Frith 1947–48
Harry Storer 1948–53
Jack Fairbrother 1953–54
Charlie Elliott 1954–55
Jesse Carver 1955–56
George Raynor 1956
Harry Warren 1956–57
Billy Frith 1957–61
Jimmy Hill 1961–67
Noel Cantwell 1967–72
Bob Dennison 1972
Joe Mercer 1972–75
Gordon Milne 1972–81
Dave Sexton 1981–83
Bobby Gould 1983–84
Don Mackay 1985–86
George Curtis 1986–87
(*became Managing Director*)
John Sillett 1987–90
Terry Butcher 1990–92
Don Howe 1992
Bobby Gould 1992–93
(*with Don Howe, June 1992*)
Phil Neal 1993–95
Ron Atkinson 1995–96
(*became Director of Football*)
Gordon Strachan 1996–2001
Roland Nilsson 2001–02
Gary McAllister 2002–04
Eric Black 2004
Peter Reid 2004–05
Micky Adams 2005–07
Iain Dowie 2007–08
Chris Coleman 2008–10
Aidy Boothroyd 2010–11
Andy Thorn 2011–12
Mark Robins 2012–13
Steven Pressley 2013–15
Tony Mowbray 2015–16
Russell Slade 2016–17
Mark Robins March 2017–

TEN YEAR LEAGUE RECORD

		P	W	D	L	F	A	Pts	Pos
2012-13	FL 1	46	18	11	17	66	59	55*	15
2013-14	FL 1	46	16	13	17	74	77	51*	18
2014-15	FL 1	46	13	16	17	49	60	55	17
2015-16	FL 1	46	19	12	15	67	49	69	8
2016-17	FL 1	46	9	12	25	37	68	39	23
2017-18	FL 2	46	22	9	15	64	47	75	6
2018-19	FL 1	46	18	11	17	54	54	65	8
2019-20	FL 1	34	18	13	3	48	30	67	1§
2020-21	FL C	46	14	13	19	49	61	55	16
2021-22	FL C	46	17	13	16	60	59	64	12

** 10 pts deducted. §Decided on points-per-game (1.97)*

DID YOU KNOW?

When Singers FC applied to change their title to Coventry City in May 1898 the local rugby union club (Coventry Football Club) objected but were overruled. City first played a competitive game under their new name on 3 September 1898 when they visited Wellington Town for a Birmingham League fixture. Wearing their new kit of blue and black quarters, they slumped to a 5-0 defeat.

COVENTRY CITY – SKY BET CHAMPIONSHIP 2021–22 LEAGUE RECORD

Match No.	*Date*	*Venue*	*Opponents*	*Result*		*H/T Score*	*Lg Pos.*	*Goalscorers*	*Attendance*
1	Aug 8	H	Nottingham F	W	2-1	0-1	4	Gyokeres [81], McFadzean [90]	20,843
2	14	A	Barnsley	L	0-1	0-1	14		16,961
3	17	A	Blackpool	W	1-0	1-0	4	Gyokeres [45]	11,608
4	21	H	Reading	W	2-1	0-1	4	Allen [62], Godden [90]	16,464
5	28	A	QPR	L	0-2	0-0	7		14,774
6	Sept 11	H	Middlesbrough	W	2-0	0-0	6	Gyokeres [71], Waghorn [90]	18,515
7	15	H	Cardiff C	W	1-0	1-0	4	Gyokeres [15]	16,372
8	18	A	Millwall	D	1-1	1-1	4	Gyokeres [9]	12,516
9	24	H	Peterborough U	W	3-0	0-0	2	Hamer [57], Gyokeres 2 [61, 64]	20,652
10	29	A	Luton T	L	0-5	0-4	4		9805
11	Oct 2	H	Fulham	W	4-1	0-1	3	Gyokeres 2 [47, 70], Godden (pen) [51], Maatsen [61]	18,497
12	16	A	Blackburn R	D	2-2	0-2	4	Walker [62], Kaminski (og) [68]	14,110
13	20	A	Preston NE	L	1-2	1-0	4	Walker [45]	10,837
14	23	H	Derby Co	D	1-1	1-0	4	Godden (pen) [20]	23,829
15	30	A	Hull C	W	1-0	1-0	4	Godden [9]	11,901
16	Nov 2	H	Swansea C	L	1-2	1-2	4	McFadzean [27]	16,514
17	6	H	Bristol C	W	3-2	0-1	4	Godden 2 (1 pen) [51 (p), 90], O'Hare [74]	19,855
18	20	A	Sheffield U	D	0-0	0-0	5		28,075
19	23	H	Birmingham C	D	0-0	0-0	4		22,676
20	27	A	Bournemouth	D	2-2	0-1	5	Godden [85], Kane [90]	11,094
21	Dec 4	H	WBA	L	1-2	0-2	6	McFadzean [83]	23,755
22	11	A	Huddersfield T	D	1-1	0-1	7	Godden [90]	16,493
23	29	H	Millwall	L	0-1	0-0	10		18,500
24	Jan 15	A	Peterborough U	W	4-1	2-1	8	Hamer [15], Godden 2 [25, 90], Thompson (og) [81]	10,282
25	22	H	QPR	L	1-2	0-1	10	Shipley [50]	20,942
26	25	H	Stoke C	W	1-0	0-0	9	Gyokeres [68]	16,860
27	29	A	Middlesbrough	L	0-1	0-0	9		22,940
28	Feb 8	H	Blackpool	D	1-1	1-1	12	Gyokeres [42]	15,752
29	12	A	Reading	W	3-2	1-1	12	Hyam [45], Rose [47], Maatsen [65]	22,692
30	15	A	Cardiff C	L	0-2	0-0	12		18,660
31	19	H	Barnsley	W	1-0	0-0	10	Hyam [90]	17,104
32	22	A	Bristol C	W	2-1	1-0	8	Maatsen [25], Gyokeres [89]	19,192
33	26	H	Preston NE	D	1-1	0-0	10	Tavares [90]	19,743
34	Mar 5	A	Swansea C	L	1-3	0-2	11	Hamer [84]	18,405
35	8	H	Luton T	L	0-1	0-1	11		16,996
36	12	H	Sheffield U	W	4-1	1-1	10	Gyokeres [20], O'Hare 2 [52, 59], Godden [68]	21,732
37	16	H	Hull C	L	0-2	0-2	11		15,587
38	19	A	Derby Co	D	1-1	1-0	11	Godden [28]	24,264
39	Apr 2	H	Blackburn R	D	2-2	1-0	11	Pickering (og) [8], Gyokeres [90]	19,939
40	6	A	Nottingham F	L	0-2	0-1	12		28,977
41	10	A	Fulham	W	3-1	2-0	10	Ream (og) [20], Gyokeres [24], O'Hare [90]	19,401
42	15	A	Birmingham C	W	4-2	2-2	9	Sheaf 2 [40, 45], Rose [71], O'Hare [90]	17,634
43	18	H	Bournemouth	L	0-3	0-2	11		24,492
44	23	A	WBA	D	0-0	0-0	10		22,160
45	30	H	Huddersfield T	L	1-2	0-1	11	Gyokeres [90]	23,828
46	May 7	A	Stoke C	D	1-1	1-1	12	Gyokeres [14]	23,086

Final League Position: 12

GOALSCORERS

League (60): Gyokeres 17, Godden 12 (3 pens), O'Hare 5, Hamer 3, Maatsen 3, McFadzean 3, Hyam 2, Rose 2, Sheaf 2, Walker 2, Allen 1, Kane 1, Shipley 1, Tavares 1, Waghorn 1, own goals 4.
FA Cup (2): Gyokeres 1, Hyam 1.
Carabao Cup (1): Walker 1.

Moore S 41	Dabo F 26 + 3	McFadzean K 35 + 2	Hyam D 41 + 2	Da Costa J 2 + 2	Hamer G 37 + 2	Sheaf B 33 + 2	Maatsen I 35 + 5	O'Hare C 43 + 2	Waghorn M 11 + 16	Gyokeres V 41 + 4	Rose M 24 + 5	Walker T 4 + 15	Jones J — + 9	Allen J 29 + 9	Clarke-Salter J 27 + 2	Godden M 17 + 7	Kane T 23 + 6	Kelly L 8 + 8	Wilson B 5	Shipley J 8 + 3	Eccles J 3 + 2	Bidwell J 13 + 3	Tavares F — + 7	Howley R — + 1	*Match No.*
1	2	3	4	5^{1}	6	7	8^{3}	9	10^{2}	11	12	13	14												1
1	5	3	2		6	7^{3}	8	9	12	10	4^{2}	11^{1}		13	14										2
1	5	3	2	14	6	7	8^{3}	10	12	11	13			9^{1}	4^{2}										3
1	2	3	4	5^{1}	6	7	8	9	10^{2}	11				12		13									4
1	5	3	2		6	7	8	9	10^{2}	11^{1}		13		14	4^{3}	12									5
1	5	3	2		6		8^{2}	9	10^{3}	11	12			7	4^{1}	14	13								6
1	5■	3	2		7		8^{1}	9	10^{2}	11				6	4	13	12								7
1		3	2		6	7	8	9^{2}		10	12	14		13	4^{1}	11^{3}	5								8
1		3	2		6^{1}		8^{3}	9	11	10^{2}		13	14	7	4		5	12							9
1		3^{3}	2		7^{1}	12	8	9	11	10^{2}	13	14		6	4		5								10
1	5	3	2			7	8	9		11^{1}		12			4	10		6							11
1	5	3	2		12	7^{1}		9	13	11	4	10^{2}					8	6							12
1	5	3	2		7	14	8	9^{3}	12	10^{1}	4	11		13				6^{2}							13
1	5	3	2		6	7^{1}	8	9		11^{2}		13			4	10		12							14
1	5	3	2		6^{3}	7	8	9		11^{2}		13		12	4	10^{1}		14							15
1	5	3	2		7		8	9		11		13	12	6^{1}	4	10^{2}									16
1	5	3			6^{3}	7	8■	9		10^{2}	2	13			4^{1}	11	12	14							17
1	8	3	2		6^{1}	7^{3}		10		11^{2}	4	13		9		12	5	14							18
1	5	3	2		6^{1}		8	9^{2}		10	4	13		12		11		7							19
1	2	3	4			7^{2}	8^{3}	9		12		14	13	10^{1}		11	5	6							20
1	2	3	13		6^{1}	7	8^{2}	9^{3}		11	4	14				10	5	12							21
1	8^{1}	3	2			7^{2}	12	9^{3}			4	13	14	10		11	5	6							22
		3	2			7	8	9		13	4^{3}	11	14	12		10^{1}	5	6^{2}	1						23
			2		7^{1}	6		10		12	3			9	4	11	5		1	8^{2}	13				24
1		3	2		6	7		10	13	11			14	9^{2}	4		5^{3}			8^{1}		12			25
1		3	2	14	7^{1}	6		12	13	11				9	4					10^{2}	5^{3}	8			26
1		3	2		12	7	14	9	13	11				6^{1}	4					10^{2}	5	8^{3}			27
1			2		6	7	8	9	12	11	3				4		5^{2}			10^{1}		13			28
1			2		6	7	10	9^{2}		11	3			13	4		5			12		8^{1}			29
1		3	2			6	14	9	13	11	4^{1}			7	12		5^{3}			10^{2}		8			30
1	13	3	2			6	8	9	11^{1}	10				7	4		5^{2}						12		31
1	12	3	2		7		10^{2}	9		11				6	4		5^{1}			13		8			32
1	12■		2		6	7	8	9^{3}	10^{1}	11	3				4		5^{2}					13	14		33
1		3			7	6	10		13	11^{2}	2			9	4	12	5					8^{1}			34
1		3			7		8	12	9^{1}	10	2			6	4	11^{2}	5						13		35
1	5^{2}	3^{1}	12		7		8	9	14	10	2			6	4	11^{3}	13								36
1	5		2		7^{3}	3	8	9	14	11				6^{2}	4	10^{1}				13			12		37
1	5		3		7	2	12	9^{3}	14	13				6	4^{1}	11				10^{2}		8			38
1	5		3		7		8	9		10	2			6		11						4^{1}	12		39
1	9		2		6^{3}	7^{1}	13	10		11	3			8			5^{2}					4	12	14	40
1	5		3		8	7	9	10		11	2			6								4			41
1	5^{1}	13	3		8^{2}	7	9^{3}	10	14	11	2			6			12					4			42
1		12	3		8^{3}	7	9	10	13	11	2			6^{2}			5	14				4^{1}			43
		3	4		8^{2}	7	9	10^{1}	12	11	2			6			5	13	1						44
		3	4		6^{3}			9	10^{2}	11	2		14	7			5^{1}		1		12	8	13		45
		3	2				8	9^{3}		11			13	6	4	14	12	7	1	10^{2}	5^{1}				46

FA Cup

Third Round	Derby Co	(h)	1-0
Fourth Round	Southampton	(a)	1-2
(aet)			

Carabao Cup

First Round	Northampton T	(h)	1-2

CRAWLEY TOWN

FOUNDATION

Formed in 1896, Crawley Town initially entered the West Sussex League before switching to the mid-Sussex League in 1901, winning the Second Division in its second season. The club remained at such level until 1951 when it became members of the Sussex County League and five years later moved to the Metropolitan League while remaining as an amateur club. It was not until 1962 that the club turned semi-professional and a year later, joined the Southern League. Many honours came the club's way, but the most successful run was achieved in 2010–11 when they reached the fifith round of the FA Cup and played before a crowd of 74,778 spectators at Old Trafford against Manchester United. Crawley Town spent 48 years at the Town Mead ground before a new site was occupied at Broadfield in 1997, ideally suited to access from the neighbouring motorway. History was also made on 9 April when the team won promotion to the Football League after beating Tamworth 3-0 to stretch their unbeaten League record to 26 games. They finished the season with a Conference record points total of 105 and at the same time, established another milestone for the longest unbeaten run, having extended it to 30 matches by the end of the season.

The People's Pension Stadium, Winfield Way, Crawley, West Sussex RH11 9RX.

Telephone: (01293) 410 000.

Ticket Office: (01293) 410 000.

Website: www.crawleytownfc.com

Email: feedback@crawleytownfc.com

Ground Capacity: 5,907.

Record Attendance: 5,880 v Reading, FA Cup 3rd rd, 5 January 2013.

Pitch Measurements: 103.5m × 66m (113yd × 72yd).

Chairman: Ziya Eren.

Managing Director: Selim Gaygusuz.

Head Coach: Kevin Betsy.

Assistant Head Coach: Dan Micciche.

Colours: Red shirts with white and black trim, red shorts with white trim, red socks with white trim.

Year Formed: 1896. ***Turned Professional:*** 1962.

Club Nickname: 'The Red Devils'.

Grounds: Up to 1997, Town Mead; 1997 Broadfield Stadium (renamed Checkatrade.com Stadium 2013; The People's Pension Stadium 2018).

HONOURS

League Champions: Conference – 2010–11.
FL 2 – (3rd) 2011–12 *(promoted).*

FA Cup: 5th rd – 2011, 2012.

League Cup: 4th rd – 2020.

FOOTBALL YEARBOOK FACT FILE

Crawley Town (then known as Crawley) struggled with financial problems during the 1930s and at the end of the 1934–35 season suspended playing activities. The club was revived in June 1938 with the assistance of another local side, Crawley Rangers, and was admitted to Division Two of the Brighton and District League for the 1938–39 campaign.

First Football League Game: 6 August 2011, FL 2 v Port Vale (a) D 2–2 – Shearer; Hunt, Howell, Bulman, McFadzean (1), Dempster (Thomas), Simpson, Torres, Tubbs (Neilson), Barnett (1) (Wassmer), Smith.

Record League Victory: 5–1 v Barnsley, FL 1, 14 February 2015 – Price; Dickson, Bradley (1), Ward, Fowler (Smith); Young, Elliott (1), Edwards, Wordsworth (Morgan), Pogba (Tomlin); McLeod (3).

Record League Defeat: 0–6 v Morecambe, FL 2, 10 September 2011.

Most League Points (3 for a win): 84, FL 2, 2011–12.

Most League Goals: 76, FL 2, 2011–12.

Highest League Scorer in Season: James Collins, 20, FL 2, 2016–17.

Most League Goals in Total Aggregate: Ollie Palmer, 27, 2018–20.

Most League Goals in One Match: 3, Izale McLeod v Barnsley, FL 1, 14 February 2015; 3, Jimmy Smith v Colchester U, FL 2, 14 February 2017; 3, Max Watters v Barrow, FL 2, 12 December 2020.

Most Capped Player: Ricky German, 3, Grenada.

Most League Appearances: Glenn Morris, 257, 2016–22.

MANAGERS

John Maggs 1978–90
Brian Sparrow 1990–92
Steve Wicks 1992–93
Ted Shepherd 1993–95
Colin Pates 1995–96
Billy Smith 1997–99
Cliff Cant 1999–2000
Billy Smith 2000–03
Francis Vines 2003–05
John Hollins 2005–06
David Woozley, Ben Judge and John Yems 2006–07
Steve Evans 2007–12
Sean O'Driscoll 2012
Richie Barker 2012–13
John Gregory 2013–14
Dean Saunders 2014–15
Mark Yates 2015–16
Dermot Drummy 2016–17
Harry Kewell 2017–18
Gabriele Cioffi 2018–19
John Yems 2019–22
Kevin Betsy June 2022–

Youngest League Player: Brian Galach, 17 years 353 days v Tranmere R, 4 May 2019.

Record Transfer Fee Received: £1,100,000 from Peterborough U for Tyrone Barnett, July 2012.

Record Transfer Fee Paid: £220,000 to York C for Richard Brodie, August 2010.

Football League Record: 2011 Promoted from Conference Premier; 2011–12 FL 2; 2012–15 FL 1; 2015– FL 2.

LATEST SEQUENCES

Longest Sequence of League Wins: 7, 17.9.2011 – 25.10.2011.

Longest Sequence of League Defeats: 8, 28.3.2016 – 7.5.2016.

Longest Sequence of League Draws: 5, 25.10.2014 – 29.11.2014.

Longest Sequence of Unbeaten League Matches: 13, 17.9.2011 – 17.12.2011.

Longest Sequence Without a League Win: 13, 25.10.2014 – 27.1.2015.

Successive Scoring Runs: 21 from 6.4.2019.

Successive Non-scoring Runs: 4 from 14.10.2017.

TEN YEAR LEAGUE RECORD

		P	*W*	*D*	*L*	*F*	*A*	*Pts*	*Pos*
2012-13	FL 1	46	18	14	14	59	58	68	10
2013-14	FL 1	46	14	15	17	48	54	57	14
2014-15	FL 1	46	13	11	22	53	79	50	22
2015-16	FL 2	46	13	8	25	45	78	47	20
2016-17	FL 2	46	13	12	21	53	71	51	19
2017-18	FL 2	46	16	11	19	58	66	59	14
2018-19	FL 2	46	15	8	23	51	68	53	19
2019-20	FL 2	37	11	15	11	51	47	48	13§
2020-21	FL 2	46	16	13	17	56	62	61	12
2021-22	FL 2	46	17	10	19	56	66	61	12

§Decided on points-per-game (1.30)

DID YOU KNOW ?

Although Crawley Town only joined the EFL in 2010–11 they first took part in an EFL competition in 2005–06. One of 12 Football Conference sides that were allowed to enter the EFL Trophy that season, the Red Devils were drawn away to Gillingham in the first round. The match went to extra time before the Gills went through 2-0 in front of a crowd of 1,988.

CRAWLEY TOWN – SKY BET LEAGUE TWO 2021–22 LEAGUE RECORD

Match No.	Date	Venue	Opponents	Result	H/T Score	Lg Pos.	Goalscorers	Attendance
1	Aug 7	A	Hartlepool U	L 0-1	0-0	19		5184
2	17	H	Salford C	W 2-1	1-1	14	Nadesan 38, Hessenthaler 75	2167
3	21	A	Forest Green R	L 3-6	2-2	19	Hessenthaler 2 14, 30, Appiah 86	1922
4	28	H	Northampton T	D 0-0	0-0	20		2254
5	Sept 4	A	Bristol R	L 0-1	0-0	22		6513
6	11	H	Carlisle U	W 2-1	1-0	19	Nichols 32, Tsaroulla 90	2151
7	18	A	Colchester U	W 1-0	1-0	14	Payne 22	2640
8	21	H	Harrogate T	D 2-2	2-1	12	Lynch 42, Ashford 45	1791
9	25	H	Bradford C	W 2-1	1-0	8	Ferry 39, Tsaroulla 73	2435
10	Oct 2	A	Tranmere R	L 1-2	0-1	14	Appiah 64	6046
11	9	A	Rochdale	W 1-0	1-0	9	Appiah 14	2268
12	16	H	Sutton U	L 0-1	0-0	12		3572
13	19	H	Exeter C	L 1-3	1-0	14	Appiah 31	1960
14	23	A	Scunthorpe U	L 1-2	0-1	16	Appiah 73	2112
15	30	H	Port Vale	L 1-4	1-0	18	Appiah 44	2234
16	Nov 20	A	Barrow	W 1-0	0-0	18	Tilley 56	3429
17	23	H	Newport Co	D 1-1	0-0	17	Appiah 55	1483
18	27	H	Mansfield T	L 1-2	0-1	19	Tilley 48	1824
19	Dec 7	A	Walsall	D 1-1	1-1	18	Nichols 45	3609
20	11	A	Leyton Orient	W 2-1	1-0	16	Francomb 32, Appiah 66	5142
21	Jan 1	H	Colchester U	W 3-1	2-0	14	Nadesan 2 15, 55, Lynch 37	2022
22	8	A	Northampton T	W 1-0	1-0	11	Nichols 41	4714
23	15	A	Carlisle U	D 1-1	1-0	11	Nadesan 25	4350
24	18	A	Stevenage	L 1-2	1-1	12	Nichols 45	1942
25	22	H	Tranmere R	L 0-1	0-0	14		2803
26	29	A	Bradford C	W 2-1	0-1	13	Nichols 71, Craig 90	14,623
27	Feb 1	A	Swindon T	D 1-1	1-0	13	Powell (pen) 41	7306
28	5	H	Stevenage	D 2-2	1-0	14	Nichols 2 34, 46	2214
29	8	A	Harrogate T	W 3-1	0-0	12	Oteh 48, Tsaroulla 79, Nichols 84	1785
30	12	H	Hartlepool U	L 0-1	0-1	12		2228
31	26	H	Forest Green R	W 2-1	2-0	13	Nadesan 24, Tunnicliffe 32	2086
32	Mar 1	H	Oldham Ath	D 2-2	0-0	12	Nadesan 2 58, 61	1927
33	5	H	Scunthorpe U	D 0-0	0-0	13		2144
34	8	H	Bristol R	L 1-2	0-1	13	Hessenthaler 69	2223
35	12	A	Port Vale	L 1-4	1-2	13	Smith (og) 9	5131
36	15	A	Exeter C	L 1-2	1-2	15	Appiah 45	4042
37	19	H	Swindon T	W 3-1	1-0	13	Appiah 29, Nichols 72, Hutchinson 90	2977
38	26	H	Rochdale	W 1-0	1-0	12	Nadesan 18	2164
39	29	A	Salford C	L 1-2	0-1	13	Nichols 82	1290
40	Apr 9	H	Barrow	W 1-0	0-0	12	Appiah 57	2081
41	15	A	Newport Co	W 2-1	2-0	12	Nadesan 15, Francillette 21	5137
42	18	H	Walsall	W 1-0	0-0	12	Hutchinson 69	2258
43	23	A	Mansfield T	L 0-2	0-1	12		5022
44	26	A	Sutton U	L 0-3	0-2	12		3109
45	30	H	Leyton Orient	L 0-2	0-1	12		3372
46	May 7	A	Oldham Ath	D 3-3	2-2	12	Francomb 39, Tilley 44, Oteh 69	4591

Final League Position: 12

GOALSCORERS

League (56): Appiah 11, Nichols 10, Nadesan 9, Hessenthaler 4, Tilley 3, Tsaroulla 3, Francomb 2, Hutchinson 2, Lynch 2, Oteh 2, Ashford 1, Craig 1, Ferry 1, Francillette 1, Payne 1, Powell 1 (1 pen), Tunnicliffe 1, own goal 1.
FA Cup (0).
Carabao Cup (2): Ashford 1, Davies 1.
Papa John's Trophy (1): Appiah 1 (1 pen).

Morris G 46	Davies A 19 + 14	Tunnicliffe J 17 + 1	Craig T 32 + 3	Gallacher O 1 + 2	Matthews S 6 + 2	Hessenthaler J 31 + 1	Payne J 31 + 4	Powell J 37	Frost T 9 + 5	Nadesan A 30 + 9	Dallison T 11 + 1	Ferry W 27 + 9	Tilley J 23 + 7	Francomb G 37 + 1	Francillette L 24 + 2	Appiah K 17 + 9	Ashford S 7 + 5	Tsaroulla N 24 + 3	Nichols T 35 + 4	Battle A — + 1	Lynch J 21 + 3	Marshall M 1 + 18	Bansal-McNulty A 2 + 2	Rodari D — + 1	Grego-Cox R 2 + 8	Watts C — + 1	Hutchinson I 11 + 8	Oteh A 5 + 3	Kastrati F — + 1	Match No.
1	2	3^{1}	4	5^{2}	6^{3}	7	8	9	10	11	12	13	14																	1
1	13		4			7	8	6	10^{1}	11^{2}	5	9^{3}	14	2	3	12														2
1	14		4			7	8	9	10^{2}	11^{3}	5	6	12	2	3^{1}	13														3
1	2		4			8	13	7	9^{1}	11	5^{3}	6^{2}			3	12	10	14												4
1	2		4			7	8	6	9^{1}	13				3		12	10^{3}	5	11^{2}	14										5
1						7	8	6	12	13	3	9^{1}		2		14	10^{2}	5	11^{3}		4									6
1						8	7	9		12	3	6		2		13	11^{1}	5	10^{2}		4									7
1	12					7	8	6		13■	3	9		2^{1}			10^{3}	5	11		4^{2}	14								8
1	2					7	8	9			3	6^{1}			4	12	11^{2}	5	10			13								9
1	6^{2}		12			7	8	9			4			2	3^{1}	13	11^{3}	5	10			14								10
1			4			6	7	9			3			2		10^{2}	13	5	11			12	8^{1}							11
1			4			6	8	7^{1}		12	3	9^{2}		2	13	10		5	11											12
1			4			6^{1}	7	8		10■	3	12		2^{3}		11		5^{2}	9		13	14								13
1			4			6	7	9				14		2^{3}		11	13	5	10^{1}		3		8^{2}	12						14
1	13		4			7	14	8	6^{1}			9^{2}		2^{3}		11		5	10		3■	12								15
1	2		4			7		8	6^{2}	10^{1}		12	9^{3}	5	3	11	14		13											16
1	2		4			8		7	6^{1}	10		12^{3}	9^{2}	5	3	11			14						13					17
1	2		4			7		8	6^{1}	10^{2}			9^{3}	5	3	11			12		14				13					18
1	2		4			7^{1}		8	13	11		12	9^{3}	5	3				10			6^{2}	14							19
1	5		3					7		10^{1}		8	13	6	2	9^{2}			11		4				12					20
1			3					7		10^{1}		8^{3}	5	6	2	11	13		9^{2}		4		12		14					21
1	13		3		9^{1}		12	7		11^{3}			5	6	2		14	8^{2}	10		4									22
1	14		3		9^{1}		7	6		11			5	2				8	10^{2}		4				13	12^{3}				23
1	5^{1}		3		9^{2}		6	7	13	10			8^{3}	2				12	11		4				14					24
1	5	2	3		9^{1}		14	7		12			11	6^{3}				8^{2}	10		4	13								25
1	5	2	3				7	6		9			8					12	10		4^{1}	13			11^{2}					26
1	2^{1}	3	4				6	7	13	10^{3}			8		12			5	9			14			11^{2}					27
1		4	3				7	6		12		14	5^{3}	13	2			9	10								8^{2}	11^{1}		28
1		3	4				7	8		13		6^{3}	12	2				5	10						14		9^{1}	11^{2}		29
1	14	3	4		12		8^{3}	7		10		9^{1}	6^{2}	2				5							15		13	11^{4}		30
1	14	3	4				8	9		12		2		7^{3}				6	13		5						10^{2}	11^{1}		31
1	12	2	3				7	6		10		5						8^{1}	11		4	13					9^{2}			32
1	12	3	4				8	9^{1}	13	10		2^{2}		7				6			5	14					11^{3}			33
1		3^{1}	4			12	8	7		11		2	14	9^{3}		13		6			5						10^{2}			34
1	2		4^{3}	14^{4}		6	7^{1}	8				9	12		3^{2}	11		5	10			15					13			35
1						4	7	6		10		12	5	3	2^{2}	9		8^{1}	11								13			36
1	13					2	6	7^{1}		10^{3}		8	5^{2}	4	3	9			11			14					12			37
1	12	3				7	6			10^{2}		8^{1}	5	4	2	9			11								13			38
1	5^{3}	3^{1}				7	6			10		12	8^{2}	4	2	9			11			13					14			39
1				12		2	7			10^{3}		8^{1}	5	4	3	9			11		13	14					6^{2}			40
1		13			12	7	6			10^{3}		8	5	2	3	9^{1}			11		4^{2}						14			41
1	13	3	14		9^{1}	7				10^{3}		8	5^{2}		2				11		4	12					6			42
1	5^{1}	3				6						9	10■	7^{2}	2				11		4	13					8	12		43
1	5	2	3^{2}			7				9		8		6					10		4	13					12	11^{1}		44
1	13	3^{2}	12			7				10		8	5	6	2				11		4^{1}						9^{3}	14		45
1	2^{1}		4			7				5		8	10^{2}	6	3				11								9	12	13	46

FA Cup

First Round	Tranmere R	(h)	0-1

Carabao Cup

First Round	Gillingham	(h)	2-2

(Gillingham won 10-9 on penalties)

Papa John's Trophy

Group G (S)	Charlton Ath	(a)	1-6
Group G (S)	Leyton Orient	(h)	0-4
Group G (S)	Southampton U21	(h)	0-4

CREWE ALEXANDRA

FOUNDATION

The first match played at Crewe was on 1 December 1877 against Basford, the leading North Staffordshire team of that time. During the club's history they have also played in a number of other leagues including the Football Alliance, Football Combination, Lancashire League, Manchester League, Central League and Lancashire Combination. Two former players, Aaron Scragg in 1899 and Jackie Pearson in 1911, had the distinction of refereeing FA Cup finals. Pearson was also capped for England against Ireland in 1892.

The Mornflake Stadium, Gresty Road, Crewe, Cheshire CW2 6EB.

Telephone: (01270) 213 014.

Ticket Office: (01270) 252 610.

Website: www.crewealex.net

Email: info@crewealex.net

Ground Capacity: 10,109.

Record Attendance: 20,000 v Tottenham H, FA Cup 4th rd, 30 January 1960.

Pitch Measurements: 100.5m × 67m (110yd × 73yd).

Chairman: Charles Grant.

Manager: Alex Morris.

Assistant Manager: Lee Bell.

HONOURS

League: *Runners-up:* Second Division – 2002–03; FL 2 – 2019–20.

FA Cup: semi-final – 1888.

League Cup: 3rd rd – 1975, 1976, 1979, 1993, 1999, 2000, 2002, 2005, 2009, 2020.

League Trophy Winners: 2013.

Welsh Cup Winners: 1936, 1937.

Colours: Red shirts with white trim, white shorts with red trim, red socks with white trim.

Year Formed: 1877. ***Turned Professional:*** 1893. ***Club Nickname:*** 'The Railwaymen'.

Ground: 1898, Gresty Road (renamed The Mornflake Stadium 2021).

First Football League Game: 3 September 1892, Division 2, v Burton Swifts (a) L 1–7 – Hickton; Moore, Cope; Linnell, Johnson, Osborne; Bennett, Pearson (1), Bailey, Barnett, Roberts.

Record League Victory: 8–0 v Rotherham U, Division 3 (N), 1 October 1932 – Foster; Pringle, Dawson; Ward, Keenor (1), Turner (1); Gillespie, Swindells (1), McConnell (2), Deacon (2), Weale (1).

Record Cup Victory: 8–0 v Hartlepool U, Auto Windscreens Shield 1st rd, 17 October 1995 – Gayle; Collins (1), Booty, Westwood (Unsworth), Macauley (1), Whalley (1), Garvey (1), Murphy (1), Savage (1) (Rivers (1p)), Lennon, Edwards, (1 og). 8–0 v Doncaster R, LDV Vans Trophy 3rd rd, 10 November 2002 – Bankole; Wright, Walker, Foster, Tierney; Lunt (1), Brammer, Sorvel, Vaughan (1) (Bell); Ashton (3) (Miles), Jack (2) (Jones (1)).

FOOTBALL YEARBOOK FACT FILE

Crewe Alexandra's home Fourth Division game against bottom-of-the-league Lincoln City on 19 October 1966 was abandoned after 38 minutes when the floodlights failed. The visitors, who had won just one of their opening 11 League games, were leading 1-0 at the time. Crewe won the rearranged game the following April 3-0.

Record Defeat: 2–13 v Tottenham H, FA Cup 4th rd replay, 3 February 1960.

Most League Points (2 for a win): 59, Division 4, 1962–63.

Most League Points (3 for a win): 86, Division 2, 2002–03.

Most League Goals: 95, Division 3 (N), 1931–32.

Highest League Scorer in Season: Terry Harkin, 35, Division 4, 1964–65.

Most League Goals in Total Aggregate: Bert Swindells, 126, 1928–37.

Most League Goals in One Match: 5, Tony Naylor v Colchester U, Division 3, 24 April 1993.

Most Capped Player: Clayton Ince, 38 (79), Trinidad & Tobago.

Most League Appearances: Tommy Lowry, 436, 1966–78.

Youngest League Player: Steve Walters, 16 years 119 days v Peterborough U, 6 May 1988.

Record Transfer Fee Received: £3,000,000 (rising to £6,000,000) from Manchester U for Nick Powell, June 2012.

Record Transfer Fee Paid: £650,000 to Torquay U for Rodney Jack, July 1998.

Football League Record: 1892 Original Member of Division 2; 1896 Failed re-election; 1921 Re-entered Division (N); 1958–63 Division 4; 1963–64 Division 3; 1964–68 Division 4; 1968–69 Division 3; 1969–89 Division 4; 1989–91 Division 3; 1991–92 Division 4; 1992–94 Division 3; 1994–97 Division 2; 1997–2002 Division 1; 2002–03 Division 2; 2003–04 Division 1; 2004–06 FL C; 2006–09 FL 1; 2009–12 FL 2; 2012–16 FL 1; 2016–20 FL 2; 2020–22 FL 1; 2022– FL 2.

LATEST SEQUENCES

Longest Sequence of League Wins: 7, 30.4.1994 – 3.9.1994.

Longest Sequence of League Defeats: 10, 16.4.1979 – 22.8.1979.

Longest Sequence of League Draws: 5, 18.9.2010 – 9.10.2010.

Longest Sequence of Unbeaten League Matches: 17, 25.3.1995 – 16.9.1995.

Longest Sequence Without a League Win: 30, 22.9.1956 – 6.4.1957.

Successive Scoring Runs: 26 from 7.4.1934.

Successive Non-scoring Runs: 9 from 6.11.1974.

MANAGERS

W. C. McNeill 1892–94 (*Secretary-Manager*)
J. G. Hall 1895–96 (*Secretary-Manager*)
R. Roberts (*1st team Secretary-Manager*) 1897
J. B. Blomerley 1898–1911 (*Secretary-Manager, continued as Hon. Secretary to 1925*)
Tom Bailey (*Secretary only*) 1925–38
George Lillycrop (*Trainer*) 1938–44
Frank Hill 1944–48
Arthur Turner 1948–51
Harry Catterick 1951–53
Ralph Ward 1953–55
Maurice Lindley 1956–57
Willie Cook 1957–58
Harry Ware 1958–60
Jimmy McGuigan 1960–64
Ernie Tagg 1964–71 (*continued as Secretary to 1972*)
Dennis Viollet 1971
Jimmy Melia 1972–74
Ernie Tagg 1974
Harry Gregg 1975–78
Warwick Rimmer 1978–79
Tony Waddington 1979–81
Arfon Griffiths 1981–82
Peter Morris 1982–83
Dario Gradi 1983–2007
Steve Holland 2007–08
Gudjon Thordarson 2008–09
Dario Gradi 2009–11
Steve Davis 2011–17
David Artell 2017–22
Alex Morris April 2022–

TEN YEAR LEAGUE RECORD

		P	*W*	*D*	*L*	*F*	*A*	*Pts*	*Pos*
2012-13	FL 1	46	18	10	18	54	62	64	13
2013-14	FL 1	46	13	12	21	54	80	51	19
2014-15	FL 1	46	14	10	22	43	75	52	20
2015-16	FL 1	46	7	13	26	46	83	34	24
2016-17	FL 2	46	14	13	19	58	67	55	17
2017-18	FL 2	46	17	5	24	62	75	56	15
2018-19	FL 2	46	19	8	19	60	59	65	12
2019-20	FL 2	37	20	9	8	67	43	69	2§
2020-21	FL 1	46	18	12	16	56	61	66	12
2021-22	FL 1	46	7	8	31	37	83	29	24

§Decided on points-per-game (1.86)

DID YOU KNOW ?

On Christmas Day 1940 Crewe Alexandra played Tranmere Rovers twice on the same day. In the morning game at Prenton Park the Alex won 2-1 and they retained nine of their line-up for the 3.15pm kick off at Gresty Road. That game ended 2-2 with both fixtures watched by estimated attendances of just 1,000.

CREWE ALEXANDRA – SKY BET LEAGUE ONE 2021–22 LEAGUE RECORD

Match No.	Date	Venue	Opponents	Result	H/T Score	Lg Pos.	Goalscorers	Attendance
1	Aug 7	H	Cheltenham T	D 1-1	1-1	11	Mandron 28	5301
2	14	A	Portsmouth	L 0-2	0-0	21		11,470
3	17	A	Oxford U	L 0-1	0-1	21		6757
4	21	H	Accrington S	L 0-1	0-1	22		4187
5	28	A	Charlton Ath	L 0-2	0-2	23		13,167
6	Sept 11	A	Shrewsbury T	D 1-1	1-1	23	Mandron 44	5867
7	18	H	Burton Alb	W 2-0	1-0	21	Bostwick (og) 10, Bennett 87	4482
8	21	H	Morecambe	L 1-3	0-2	22	Mandron 49	3542
9	25	A	Rotherham U	D 1-1	0-0	23	Porter (pen) 90	8747
10	28	A	Plymouth Arg	D 1-1	1-0	22	Kashket 3	11,138
11	Oct 2	H	Cambridge U	D 2-2	2-0	22	Finney 10, Robertson 26	4237
12	16	A	Fleetwood T	L 0-3	0-0	23		2917
13	19	H	Sunderland	L 0-4	0-2	23		5618
14	23	A	Wycombe W	L 1-2	0-1	24	Lowery 77	4813
15	30	H	Milton Keynes D	L 1-4	0-1	24	Long 52	4512
16	Nov 2	H	Doncaster R	D 1-1	1-1	24	Porter 33	3392
17	12	A	Bolton W	L 0-2	0-0	24		13,804
18	20	H	Gillingham	W 2-0	1-0	24	Long 11, Lowery 90	4047
19	23	A	AFC Wimbledon	L 2-3	1-3	24	Long 11, Porter 89	6943
20	28	A	Ipswich T	L 1-2	0-2	24	Long 73	18,883
21	Dec 7	H	Lincoln C	W 2-0	0-0	23	Mandron 2 (2 pens) 48, 52	3285
22	11	H	Sheffield W	L 0-2	0-1	24		6325
23	29	A	Morecambe	W 2-1	0-1	22	Porter 52, Murphy 58	3831
24	Jan 1	A	Burton Alb	L 1-4	1-3	23	Lowery 19	3119
25	12	H	Charlton Ath	W 2-1	2-0	22	Finney 38, Mandron 45	3556
26	15	H	Shrewsbury T	D 0-0	0-0	22		5587
27	22	A	Cambridge U	L 0-1	0-1	22		5428
28	29	H	Rotherham U	L 0-2	0-1	22		5014
29	Feb 1	A	Gillingham	L 0-1	0-1	22		4917
30	8	H	Plymouth Arg	L 1-4	1-0	23	Long 19	3874
31	12	A	Accrington S	L 1-4	0-1	23	Agyei 90	2365
32	15	A	Wigan Ath	L 0-2	0-0	24		8509
33	22	H	Oxford U	L 0-1	0-0	24		3968
34	26	A	Cheltenham T	W 2-1	1-0	24	Long 18, Porter 83	4227
35	Mar 5	H	Wycombe W	L 1-3	0-1	24	Porter 58	4031
36	8	H	Portsmouth	L 1-3	0-2	24	Long 90	4307
37	12	A	Sunderland	L 0-2	0-0	24		30,036
38	15	H	Wigan Ath	L 0-2	0-1	24		5310
39	19	H	Bolton W	L 0-1	0-0	24		5985
40	Apr 2	H	Fleetwood T	L 1-3	1-1	24	Long 45	3813
41	5	A	Milton Keynes D	L 1-2	0-2	24	Sambou 90	7315
42	9	A	Doncaster R	L 0-2	0-1	24		5912
43	15	H	AFC Wimbledon	W 3-1	0-1	24	Mandron 60, Long 62, Sambou 90	4668
44	19	A	Sheffield W	L 0-1	0-0	24		22,566
45	23	H	Ipswich T	D 1-1	0-1	24	Lowery 86	4986
46	30	A	Lincoln C	L 1-2	1-0	24	Long 21	9147

Final League Position: 24

GOALSCORERS

League (37): Long 10, Mandron 7 (2 pens), Porter 6 (1 pen), Lowery 4, Finney 2, Sambou 2, Agyei 1, Bennett 1, Kashket 1, Murphy 1, Robertson 1, own goal 1.
FA Cup (0).
Carabao Cup (1): Ainley 1.
Papa John's Trophy (10): Mandron 3, Finney 2, Knight 2, Robbins 1, Robertson 1, own goal 1.

Richards D 32	Ramsey K 12 + 3	Daniels D 11	Offord L 43 + 1	Adebisi R 22	Murphy L 28 + 10	Finney O 18 + 10	Lundstram J 15 + 7	Dale O 2	Mandron M 26 + 7	Ainley C 24 + 7	MacDonald S 2 + 1	Porter C 20 + 16	Jaaskelainen W 14	Long C 29 + 3	Thomas T 12 + 1	Knight B 4 + 2	Griffiths R 10 + 11	McFadzean C 6 + 4	Robertson S 16 + 4	Kashket S 15 + 3	Bennett J 8 + 1	Sass-Davies B 21 + 1	Johnson T 14 + 6	Gomes M 4 + 4	Lowery T 31 + 1	Williams M 18 + 1	Tabiner J — + 1	Onyeka T — + 1	O'Riordan C 9 + 2	Sambou B 6 + 10	Alebiosu R 6	Uwakwe T 7 + 1	Agyei D 8 + 1	Harper R 12 + 3	Salisbury C — + 4	Lawton S — + 2	Billington L 1	*Match No.*
1	2	3	4	5	6	7[1]	8	9	10	11[2]	12	13																										1
	2	3	4	5	8	13	6	9[1]	10[3]	11	7[2]	14	1	12																								2
1	2		3	5	7	8[1]	6[2]		10	11		12			4	9	13																					3
1	2[2]		4■	5	8	12			11	6	7[3]	10			3	9[1]	14	13																				4
	12		3	2	7	8[2]	6		11	10		13	1		4	9[1]	14	5[3]																				5
	5	3	2	8[3]	7	13			10			12	1		4			14	6	9[1]	11[2]																	6
	2	3	13	5	6[1]		12		10	8[3]		14	1		4[2]				7	11	9																	7
	2	3		5		13	6		10	8[2]		12	1		4				7	9[1]	11																	8
	5	3	4	8	6		12		10	11[1]		13	1						7	9[2]		2																9
	2[1]	4	3[3]	6	9		13		11			14	1		5				8	7	10[2]		12															10
	2	3	4	5	6	8[2]	13		12			10	1					14	7	9[1]	11[3]																	11
			3	2	7[3]	8			13			10[2]	1	12	4			5	6	9[1]	11			14														12
	5	3	2		7				10				1	8[2]	4[3]			9	6	12	11[1]	14		13														13
		4	5	2	8[1]				13			11[2]	1	10[3]				6	7	14		3		9	12													14
		3	4	2	6[1]				10[2]			13	1	9		12		5	7		11			14	8[3]													15
1			3	2	8				13			10		9[1]	5				7[2]	11[3]	14	4		12	6													16
1			3	2					10[2]			13		11[1]	4			6	8	12				9	7	5												17
1			3	6	7	12			13			11		10[2]	14					2[3]		4		8[1]	9	5												18
1				6	8[3]	12						11		10	3[2]		14	13		2		4		9[1]	7	5												19
1			3	6		7			12			11		10		13	9[2]			2[1]		4			8	5												20
1			3	6	13	8[3]			10	2[2]						11	9[1]		14			4	12		7	5												21
1	14		3	6	12	9				2		10					11[1]		8[2]			4	13		7	5[3]												22
1	12		3	6[1]	8	9[3]			11	2[2]		10							14			4	13		7	5												23
1	2[3]		3		8[2]	9			11	6[1]		10							12			4	14		7	5	13											24
1			3		12	8[2]			2			10		11			13		7[1]			4	6		9	5												25
1			5		9[1]	8	13		2	6[2]		11		10[3]			12					4	3		7			14										26
1			3		12	9[3]			6[2]	13		11		10			14		8[1]			4	2		7	5												27
1			5		8	9[2]			2	13		11[3]		10					12■			4	6[1]		7				3	14								28
			4		7	8[3]			10[2]	14		13	1	11[1]								3			6					12	2	5	9					29
			4		6[1]					13			1	10			12					3			7					11[3]	2	5	9	8[2]	14			30
1			5		14					12		11[2]		13			8		7				3						4		2[3]	6	10	9[1]				31
1			4		7[3]					13		14		10			8[2]						12		6				3	11	2[1]	5	9					32
1			4				12			8				10			7[2]						2		6				3	11[3]		5[1]	9	13	14			33
1			4				5					10		11[2]			8						2		7				3	12			9[1]	6	13			34
1			4			12	5[3]					10		11			9						2		7				3	13			8[2]	6[1]	14			35
1			4		6		9			14		10		11			7[1]						2[2]		8	12			3				5[3]	13				36
1			2			13	5			10[2]				11			7						4		8	9[3]			3	12				6[1]		14		37
1			2		13		5[3]			7		14		11			12						9		8	4[2]			3	10				6[1]				38
1			3		12	9[1]	5			8[3]		13		11			14						2		7	4				10				6[2]				39
1			4		6[3]	8				5		10		11						9[1]			2		7	3[2]			13	12				14				40
1			2		7[1]		6		13	5				11						8[3]			3		10	4[2]			12	14				9				41
1			2		12		6		10[2]	5		13		11								3			7					8[1]				9		14	4[3]	42
1			4			12	2		11	9				10[2]						8[1]		3			7	5				13				6				43
1			4		14		2[3]		11	9				10						8[1]		3			7	5				13		12		6[2]				44
1			4		8[2]	12			11	9				10			13					3			6	5[3]				14	2[1]	7						45
1			4		14	9[2]	12		11	8				10								3			7						2[1]	5	13	6[3]				46

FA Cup

First Round	Swindon T	(h)	0-3

Carabao Cup

First Round	Hartlepool U	(a)	1-0
Second Round	Leeds U	(a)	0-3

Papa John's Trophy

Group C (N)	Shrewsbury T	(a)	1-0
Group C (N)	Wigan Ath	(h)	2-0
Group C (N)	Wolverhampton W U21	(h)	3-0
Second Round	Doncaster R	(h)	2-0
Third Round	Rotherham U	(h)	2-4

CRYSTAL PALACE

FOUNDATION

There was a Crystal Palace club as early as 1861 but the present organisation was born in 1905 after the formation of a club by the company that controlled the Crystal Palace (building) had been rejected by the FA, who did not like the idea of the Cup Final hosts running their own club. A separate company had to be formed and they had their home on the old Cup Final ground until 1915.

Selhurst Park Stadium, Whitehorse Lane, London SE25 6PU.

Telephone: (020) 8768 6000.

Ticket Office: (0871) 200 0071.

Website: www.cpfc.co.uk

Email: info@cpfc.co.uk

Ground Capacity: 25,486.

Record Attendance: 51,482 v Burnley, Division 2, 11 May 1979 (at Selhurst Park).

Pitch Measurements: 101m × 68m (110.5yd × 74.5yd).

Chairman: Steve Parish.

Chief Executive: Phil Alexander.

Manager: Patrick Vieira.

First-Team Coach: Kristian Wilson.

HONOURS

League Champions: First Division – 1993–94; Division 2 – 1978–79; Division 3S – 1920–21.
Runners-up: Division 2 – 1968–69; Division 3 – 1963–64; Division 3S – 1928–29, 1930–31, 1938–39; Division 4 – 1960–61.

FA Cup: *Runners-up:* 1990, 2016.

League Cup: semi-final – 1993, 1995, 2001, 2012.

Full Members' Cup Winners: 1991.

European Competition
Intertoto Cup: 1998.

Colours: Red and blue diagonal striped shirts, blue shorts with red trim, blue socks with red trim.

Year Formed: 1905.

Turned Professional: 1905.

Club Nickname: 'The Eagles'.

Grounds: 1905, Crystal Palace; 1915, Herne Hill; 1918, The Nest; 1924, Selhurst Park.

First Football League Game: 28 August 1920, Division 3, v Merthyr T (a) L 1–2 – Alderson; Little, Rhodes; McCracken, Jones, Feebury; Bateman, Conner, Smith, Milligan (1), Whibley.

Record League Victory: 9–0 v Barrow, Division 4, 10 October 1959 – Rouse; Long, Noakes; Truett, Evans, McNichol; Gavin (1), Summersby (4 incl. 1p), Sexton, Byrne (2), Colfar (2).

Record Cup Victory: 8–0 v Southend U, Rumbelows League Cup 2nd rd (1st leg), 25 September 1990 – Martyn; Humphrey (Thompson (1)), Shaw, Pardew, Young, Thorn, McGoldrick, Thomas, Bright (3), Wright (3), Barber (Hodges (1)).

Record Defeat: 0–9 v Burnley, FA Cup 2nd rd replay, 10 February 1909; 0–9 v Liverpool, Division 1, 12 September 1990.

FOOTBALL YEARBOOK FACT FILE

Crystal Palace scored a total of 20 goals in two matches within the space of a week in October 1959. They beat Barrow 9-0 in a Third Division game on 10 October with Roy Summersby scoring four. The following Wednesday they defeated a touring Caribbean XI 11-1 in a friendly, with Tommy Barnett contributing four and Ray Colfar three of their goals.

Most League Points (2 for a win): 64, Division 4, 1960–61.

Most League Points (3 for a win): 90, Division 1, 1993–94.

Most League Goals: 110, Division 4, 1960–61.

Highest League Scorer in Season: Peter Simpson, 46, Division 3 (S), 1930–31.

Most League Goals in Total Aggregate: Peter Simpson, 153, 1930–36.

Most League Goals in One Match: 6, Peter Simpson v Exeter C, Division 3 (S), 4 October 1930.

Most Capped Player: Wayne Hennessey, 55 (104), Wales.

Most League Appearances: Jim Cannon, 571, 1973–88.

Youngest League Player: John Bostock, 15 years 287 days v Watford, 29 October 2007.

Record Transfer Fee Received: £45,000,000 from Manchester U for Aaron Wan-Bissaka, July 2019.

Record Transfer Fee Paid: £27,000,000 to Liverpool for Christian Benteke, August 2016.

Football League Record: 1920 Original Members of Division 3; 1921–25 Division 2; 1925–58 Division 3 (S); 1958–61 Division 4; 1961–64 Division 3; 1964–69 Division 2; 1969–73 Division 1; 1973–74 Division 2; 1974–77 Division 3; 1977–79 Division 2; 1979–81 Division 1; 1981–89 Division 2; 1989–92 Division 1; 1992–93 Premier League; 1993–94 Division 1; 1994–95 Premier League; 1995–97 Division 1; 1997–98 Premier League; 1998–2004 Division 1; 2004–05 Premier League; 2005–13 FL C; 2013– Premier League.

LATEST SEQUENCES

Longest Sequence of League Wins: 8, 21.5.2017 – 30.9.2017.

Longest Sequence of League Defeats: 8, 10.1.1998 – 14.3.1998.

Longest Sequence of League Draws: 5, 21.9.2002 – 19.10.2002.

Longest Sequence of Unbeaten League Matches: 18, 22.2.1969 – 13.8.1969.

Longest Sequence Without a League Win: 20, 3.3.1962 – 8.9.1962.

Successive Scoring Runs: 24 from 27.4.1929.

Successive Non-scoring Runs: 9 from 19.11.1994.

MANAGERS

John T. Robson 1905–07
Edmund Goodman 1907–25 (*Secretary 1905–33*)
Alex Maley 1925–27
Fred Mavin 1927–30
Jack Tresadern 1930–35
Tom Bromilow 1935–36
R. S. Moyes 1936
Tom Bromilow 1936–39
George Irwin 1939–47
Jack Butler 1947–49
Ronnie Rooke 1949–50
Charlie Slade and Fred Dawes (*Joint Managers*) 1950–51
Laurie Scott 1951–54
Cyril Spiers 1954–58
George Smith 1958–60
Arthur Rowe 1960–62
Dick Graham 1962–66
Bert Head 1966–72 (*continued as General Manager to 1973*)
Malcolm Allison 1973–76
Terry Venables 1976–80
Ernie Walley 1980
Malcolm Allison 1980–81
Dario Gradi 1981
Steve Kember 1981–82
Alan Mullery 1982–84
Steve Coppell 1984–93
Alan Smith 1993–95
Steve Coppell (*Technical Director*) 1995–96
Dave Bassett 1996–97
Steve Coppell 1997–98
Attilio Lombardo 1998
Terry Venables (*Head Coach*) 1998–99
Steve Coppell 1999–2000
Alan Smith 2000–01
Steve Bruce 2001
Trevor Francis 2001–03
Steve Kember 2003
Iain Dowie 2003–06
Peter Taylor 2006–07
Neil Warnock 2007–10
Paul Hart 2010
George Burley 2010–11
Dougie Freedman 2011–12
Ian Holloway 2012–13
Tony Pulis 2013–14
Neil Warnock 2014
Alan Pardew 2015–16
Sam Allardyce 2016–17
Frank de Boer 2017
Roy Hodgson 2017–21
Patrick Vieira July 2021–

TEN YEAR LEAGUE RECORD

		P	W	D	L	F	A	Pts	Pos
2012-13	FL C	46	19	15	12	73	62	72	5
2013-14	PR Lge	38	13	6	19	33	48	45	11
2014-15	PR Lge	38	13	9	16	47	51	48	10
2015-16	PR Lge	38	11	9	18	39	51	42	15
2016-17	PR Lge	38	12	5	21	50	63	41	14
2017-18	PR Lge	38	11	11	16	45	55	44	11
2018-19	PR Lge	38	14	7	17	51	53	49	12
2019-20	PR Lge	38	11	10	17	31	50	43	14
2020-21	PR Lge	38	12	8	18	41	66	44	14
2021-22	PR Lge	38	11	15	12	50	46	48	12

DID YOU KNOW ?

Crystal Palace competed in the emergency Football League competitions throughout the Second World War with some success. In 1940–41 they won the League South title, despite losing seven of their 27 fixtures. The competition was decided on goal average and Palace topped the table on 1.954, well ahead of their closest rivals, West Ham United.

CRYSTAL PALACE – PREMIER LEAGUE 2021–22 LEAGUE RECORD

Match No.	Date	Venue	Opponents	Result		H/T Score	Lg Pos.	Goalscorers	Attendance
1	Aug 14	A	Chelsea	L	0-3	0-2	18		38,965
2	21	H	Brentford	D	0-0	0-0	13		23,091
3	28	A	West Ham U	D	2-2	0-1	14	Gallagher 2 [58, 70]	59,751
4	Sept 11	H	Tottenham H	W	3-0	0-0	11	Zaha (pen) [76], Edouard 2 [84, 90]	22,740
5	18	A	Liverpool	L	0-3	0-1	14		52,985
6	27	H	Brighton & HA	D	1-1	1-0	15	Zaha (pen) [45]	22,975
7	Oct 3	H	Leicester C	D	2-2	0-2	14	Olise [61], Schlupp [72]	22,445
8	18	A	Arsenal	D	2-2	0-1	14	Benteke [50], Edouard [73]	59,475
9	23	H	Newcastle U	D	1-1	0-0	15	Benteke [56]	24,609
10	30	A	Manchester C	W	2-0	1-0	13	Zaha [6], Gallagher [88]	53,014
11	Nov 6	H	Wolverhampton W	W	2-0	0-0	9	Zaha [61], Gallagher [78]	24,390
12	20	A	Burnley	D	3-3	3-2	9	Benteke 2 [8, 36], Guehi [41]	18,028
13	27	H	Aston Villa	L	1-2	0-1	10	Guehi [90]	25,203
14	30	A	Leeds U	L	0-1	0-0	12		35,558
15	Dec 5	A	Manchester U	L	0-1	0-0	13		73,172
16	12	H	Everton	W	3-1	1-0	12	Gallagher 2 [41, 90], Tomkins [62]	24,066
17	15	H	Southampton	D	2-2	1-2	11	Zaha [2], Ayew [65]	22,861
18	26	A	Tottenham H	L	0-3	0-2	12		40,539
19	28	H	Norwich C	W	3-0	3-0	10	Edouard (pen) [8], Mateta [38], Schlupp [42]	24,433
20	Jan 1	H	West Ham U	L	2-3	0-3	11	Edouard [83], Olise [90]	24,351
21	14	A	Brighton & HA	D	1-1	0-0	11	Gallagher [69]	30,675
22	23	H	Liverpool	L	1-3	0-2	13	Edouard [55]	25,002
23	Feb 9	A	Norwich C	D	1-1	0-1	13	Zaha [60]	26,652
24	12	A	Brentford	D	0-0	0-0	12		16,958
25	19	H	Chelsea	L	0-1	0-0	13		25,109
26	23	A	Watford	W	4-1	2-1	11	Mateta [15], Gallagher [42], Zaha 2 [85, 90]	20,012
27	26	H	Burnley	D	1-1	1-0	11	Schlupp [9]	24,203
28	Mar 5	A	Wolverhampton W	W	2-0	2-0	10	Mateta [19], Zaha (pen) [34]	31,395
29	14	H	Manchester C	D	0-0	0-0	11		25,309
30	Apr 4	H	Arsenal	W	3-0	2-0	9	Mateta [16], Ayew [24], Zaha (pen) [74]	25,149
31	10	A	Leicester C	L	1-2	0-2	10	Zaha [66]	31,896
32	20	A	Newcastle U	L	0-1	0-1	14		51,938
33	25	H	Leeds U	D	0-0	0-0	14		25,357
34	30	A	Southampton	W	2-1	0-1	12	Eze [60], Zaha [90]	31,359
35	May 7	H	Watford	W	1-0	1-0	10	Zaha (pen) [31]	24,622
36	15	A	Aston Villa	D	1-1	0-0	12	Schlupp [81]	41,136
37	19	A	Everton	L	2-3	2-0	13	Mateta [21], Ayew [36]	40,000
38	22	H	Manchester U	W	1-0	1-0	12	Zaha [37]	25,434

Final League Position: 12

GOALSCORERS

League (50): Zaha 14 (5 pens), Gallagher 8, Edouard 6 (1 pen), Mateta 5, Benteke 4, Schlupp 4, Ayew 3, Guehi 2, Olise 2, Eze 1, Tomkins 1.
FA Cup (10): Guehi 2, Mateta 2, Olise 2, Hughes 1, Kouyate 1, Riedewald 1, Zaha 1.
Carabao Cup (0).
Papa John's Trophy (2): Rak-Sakyi 1, Street 1.

Guaita V 30	Ward J 27 + 1	Kouyate C 23 + 4	Guehi M 36	Mitchell T 35 + 1	Ayew J 23 + 8	Riedewald J 1 + 2	McArthur J 15 + 6	Schlupp J 20 + 12	Zaha W 31 + 2	Mateta J 13 + 9	Benteke C 11 + 14	Andersen J 32 + 2	Rak-Sakyi J 1 + 1	Gallagher C 33 + 1	Milivojevic L 9 + 6	Edouard O 18 + 10	Olise M 12 + 14	Tomkins J 6 + 2	Eze E 6 + 7	Hughes W 13 + 3	Clyne N 15 + 1	Butland J 8 + 1	Ferguson N — + 1	*Match No.*
1	2	3	4	5	6	7^{3}	8	9^{2}	10	11^{1}	12	13	14											1
1	2	7	4	5	12		8	11^{1}	9		10	3		6										2
1	2	7	4	5	11		8^{1}	12	9		10	3		6										3
1	2	7^{1}	4	5	9^{3}		8		11		10^{2}	3		6	12	13	14							4
1	2	7^{3}	4	5	9	13	8^{2}		11		10^{1}	3		6		12	14							5
1	2	12	4	5	9^{3}		8	14	11		13	3		6	7^{1}	10^{2}								6
1	2		4	5	9^{1}		8	13	11		14	3		6^{2}	7	10^{3}	12							7
1	2	12	4	5	8^{2}		7				11	3		9	6^{1}	10^{3}	13	14						8
1	2		4	5			7	13	12	14	11	3		9^{3}	6^{2}	10	8^{1}							9
1	2	7^{3}	4	5	9^{1}		8	13	10		12	3		6		11^{2}	14							10
1	2	7	4	5	14		8^{1}	13	9		10^{3}	3		6		11^{2}	12							11
1	2	7	4	5	8^{1}			13	10		11	3		9^{2}	6^{3}	14	12							12
1	2	7	4	5	14				10^{2}		11			9	6^{1}	13	8^{3}	3	12					13
1	2	7	4	5	9^{3}			6^{2}	10		12			8		11^{1}	14	3		13				14
1		7^{2}	4	5	9^{3}			6	11		10^{1}			8		12	14	3	13		2			15
1	2	8	4	5^{3}	9			12	11		13			6		10^{2}		3		7^{1}	14			16
	2	8^{1}	4	5	9^{2}				11		12	14		6		10	13	3^{3}		7		1		17
	2	8		5^{3}	9			13	11■	12		3		6^{2}		10^{1}		4		7		1	14	18
1	2	7	4	5	9			6		10^{2}	13	3^{3}			12	11		14		8^{1}				19
1	2		4	5	9	14		6		12	10^{2}	3			7^{1}	11	13			8^{3}				20
	2		4	5				8		13	14	3		6	12	10^{2}	9^{3}		11^{1}	7		1		21
1	2		4	5	14			8		10^{3}	13	3		6		11^{1}	9		12	7^{2}				22
1	2		4	5	12			8^{2}	11	10^{3}		3		6		14	9^{1}		13	7				23
1	2		4	5	9^{3}		12	8	11	13		3		6		10^{2}	14			7^{1}				24
1^{1}		6	4	5	8^{2}		7^{3}	10	11	14		3					9		13		2	12		25
		7	4	5	12		13		11	10^{3}		3		6		14	9^{1}			8^{2}	2	1		26
		13	4	5			8	11^{2}	10	12		3		6	7^{1}		9				2	1		27
1		7^{2}	4	5				8	11	10^{1}	13	3		6	12		9^{3}			14	2			28
1		7	4	5	12			8	11	10^{2}		3		6		13	9^{1}				2			29
1		7^{3}	4	5	9^{2}		12	8	11	10^{1}		3		6	14	13					2			30
1	12	6^{3}	4	5^{1}	8		14	7	10	11		3		9^{2}					13		2			31
1		6^{3}	4	5	12		13	7	10	14		3		9^{2}		11	8^{1}				2			32
1	5		4		9^{1}		7	13	11	10^{3}	14	3		6			12		8^{2}		2			33
1	5		4		9		7	8^{2}	12	10^{1}		3		6			13		11^{3}	14	2			34
	5		4^{2}	13				12	11^{3}	14		3		6^{1}		10	9		8	7	2	1		35
		3	5	6				14	11	10^{1}	13	4		7	8^{2}	12			9^{3}		2	1		36
			4	5	9			8^{2}	11	10^{3}	14	3		13	12				6	7^{1}	2	1		37
1	4	12		5			14	7	10			3	8^{1}	9		11^{2}			13	6^{3}	2			38

FA Cup

Third Round	Millwall	(a)	2-1
Fourth Round	Hartlepool U	(h)	2-0
Fifth Round	Stoke C	(h)	2-1
Sixth Round	Everton	(h)	4-0
Semi-Final	Chelsea	(Wembley)	0-2

Carabao Cup

Second Round	Watford	(a)	0-1

Papa John's Trophy (Crystal Palace U21)

Group B (S)	Sutton U	(a)	0-3
Group B (S)	AFC Wimbledon	(a)	2-0
Group B (S)	Portsmouth	(a)	0-3

DERBY COUNTY

FOUNDATION

Derby County was formed by members of the Derbyshire County Cricket Club in 1884, when football was booming in the area and the cricketers thought that a football club would help boost finances for the summer game. To begin with, they sported the cricket club's colours of amber, chocolate and pale blue, and went into the game at the top immediately entering the FA Cup.

Pride Park Stadium, Pride Park, Derby DE24 8XL.

Telephone: (0871) 472 1884.

Ticket Office: (0871) 472 1884 (option 1).

Website: www.dcfc.co.uk

Email: derby.county@dcfc.co.uk

Ground Capacity: 32,956.

Record Attendance: 41,826 v Tottenham H, Division 1, 20 September 1969 (at Baseball Ground); 33,378 v Liverpool, Premier League, 18 March 2000 (at Pride Park).

Stadium Record Attendance: 33,597, England v Mexico, 25 May 2001 (at Pride Park).

Pitch Measurements: 105m × 68m (115yd × 74.5yd).

Executive Chairman: Mel Morris CBE.

Chief Executive Officer: Stephen Pearce.

Manager: Liam Rosenior (caretaker).

Colours: White shirts with black trim, black shorts with white trim, white socks with black trim.

Year Formed: 1884.

Turned Professional: 1884.

Club Nickname: 'The Rams'.

Grounds: 1884, Racecourse Ground; 1895, Baseball Ground; 1997, Pride Park (renamed The iPro Stadium 2013; Pride Park Stadium 2016).

First Football League Game: 8 September 1888, Football League, v Bolton W (a) W 6–3 – Marshall; Latham, Ferguson, Williamson; Monks, Walter Roulstone; Bakewell (2), Cooper (2), Higgins, Harry Plackett, Lol Plackett (2).

Record League Victory: 9–0 v Wolverhampton W, Division 1, 10 January 1891 – Bunyan; Archie Goodall, Roberts; Walker, Chalmers, Walter Roulstone (1); Bakewell, McLachlan, Johnny Goodall (1), Holmes (2), McMillan (5). 9–0 v Sheffield W, Division 1, 21 January 1899 – Fryer; Methven, Staley; Cox, Archie Goodall, May; Oakden (1), Bloomer (6), Boag, McDonald (1), Allen, (1 og).

Record Cup Victory: 12–0 v Finn Harps, UEFA Cup 1st rd 1st leg, 15 September 1976 – Moseley; Thomas, Nish, Rioch (1), McFarland, Todd (King), Macken, Gemmill, Hector (5), George (3), James (3).

Record Defeat: 2–11 v Everton, FA Cup 1st rd, 1889–90.

HONOURS

League Champions: Division 1 – 1971–72, 1974–75; Division 2 – 1911–12, 1914–15, 1968–69, 1986–87; Division 3N – 1956–57.
Runners-up: Division 1 – 1895–96, 1929–30, 1935–36; First Division – 1995–96; Division 2 – 1925–26; Division 3N – 1955–56.

FA Cup Winners: 1946.
Runners-up: 1898, 1899, 1903.

League Cup: semi-final – 1968, 2009.

Texaco Cup Winners: 1972.

Anglo-Italian Cup: *Runners-up:* 1992–93, 1993–94, 1994–95.

European Competitions
European Cup: 1972–73 *(sf)*, 1975–76.
UEFA Cup: 1974–75, 1976–77.

FOOTBALL YEARBOOK FACT FILE

Derby County set a new club record during the 1945–46 season when they won 14 consecutive League and Cup games. The run started with a 5-2 away win at Tottenham on Christmas Day and it was not ended until 23 February when Leicester held the Rams to a 1-1 draw at Filbert Street. Highlights of the run included 8-1 victories over both Millwall and Southampton at the Baseball Ground.

Most League Points (2 for a win): 63, Division 2, 1968–69 and Division 3 (N), 1955–56 and 1956–57.

Most League Points (3 for a win): 85, FL C, 2013–14.

Most League Goals: 111, Division 3 (N), 1956–57.

Highest League Scorer in Season: Jack Bowers, 37, Division 1, 1930–31; Ray Straw, 37 Division 3 (N), 1956–57.

Most League Goals in Total Aggregate: Steve Bloomer, 292, 1892–1906 and 1910–14.

Most League Goals in One Match: 6, Steve Bloomer v Sheffield W, Division 1, 2 January 1899.

Most Capped Player: Deon Burton, 42 (61), Jamaica.

Most League Appearances: Kevin Hector, 486, 1966–78 and 1980–82.

Youngest League Player: Mason Bennett, 15 years 99 days v Middlesbrough 22 October 2011.

Record Transfer Fee Received: £8,500,000 (rising to £11,000,000) from Huddersfield T for Tom Ince, July 2017.

Record Transfer Fee Paid: £7,500,000 (rising to £10,000,000) to Arsenal for Krystian Bielik, August 2019.

Football League Record: 1888 Founder Member of the Football League; 1907–12 Division 2; 1912–14 Division 1; 1914–15 Division 2; 1915–21 Division 1; 1921–26 Division 2; 1926–53 Division 1; 1953–55 Division 2; 1955–57 Division 3 (N); 1957–69 Division 2; 1969–80 Division 1; 1980–84 Division 2; 1984–86 Division 3; 1986–87 Division 2; 1987–91 Division 1; 1991–92 Division 2; 1992–96 Division 1; 1996–2002 Premier League; 2002–04 Division 1; 2004–07 FL C; 2007–08 Premier League; 2008–22 FL C; 2022– FL 1.

LATEST SEQUENCES

Longest Sequence of League Wins: 9, 15.3.1969 – 19.4.1969.

Longest Sequence of League Defeats: 8, 12.12.1987 – 10.2.1988.

Longest Sequence of League Draws: 6, 26.3.1927 – 18.4.1927.

Longest Sequence of Unbeaten League Matches: 22, 8.3.1969 – 20.9.1969.

Longest Sequence Without a League Win: 36, 22.9.2007 – 30.8.2008.

Successive Scoring Runs: 29 from 3.12.1960.

Successive Non-scoring Runs: 8 from 30.10.1920.

MANAGERS

W. D. Clark 1896–1900
Harry Newbould 1900–06
Jimmy Methven 1906–22
Cecil Potter 1922–25
George Jobey 1925–41
Ted Magner 1944–46
Stuart McMillan 1946–53
Jack Barker 1953–55
Harry Storer 1955–62
Tim Ward 1962–67
Brian Clough 1967–73
Dave Mackay 1973–76
Colin Murphy 1977
Tommy Docherty 1977–79
Colin Addison 1979–82
Johnny Newman 1982
Peter Taylor 1982–84
Roy McFarland 1984
Arthur Cox 1984–93
Roy McFarland 1993–95
Jim Smith 1995–2001
Colin Todd 2001–02
John Gregory 2002–03
George Burley 2003–05
Phil Brown 2005–06
Billy Davies 2006–07
Paul Jewell 2007–08
Nigel Clough 2009–13
Steve McClaren 2013–15
Paul Clement 2015–16
Darren Wassall 2016
Nigel Pearson 2016
Steve McClaren 2016–17
Gary Rowett 2017–18
Frank Lampard 2018–19
Phillip Cocu 2019–20
Wayne Rooney 2020–22
Liam Rosenior (caretaker) June 2022–

TEN YEAR LEAGUE RECORD

		P	W	D	L	F	A	Pts	Pos
2012-13	FL C	46	16	13	17	65	62	61	10
2013-14	FL C	46	25	10	11	84	52	85	3
2014-15	FL C	46	21	14	11	85	56	77	8
2015-16	FL C	46	21	15	10	66	43	78	5
2016-17	FL C	46	18	13	15	54	50	67	9
2017-18	FL C	46	20	15	11	70	48	75	6
2018-19	FL C	46	20	14	12	69	54	74	6
2019-20	FL C	46	17	13	16	62	64	64	10
2020-21	FL C	46	11	11	24	36	58	44	21
2021-22	FL C	46	14	13	19	45	53	34*	23

** 21 pts deducted.*

DID YOU KNOW ?

Inside-forward Eddie Thomas made a sensational start to his career with Derby County after signing shortly after the start of the 1964–65 season, scoring in each of his first six appearances, including a double at Norwich. He continued to find the net regularly and finished the campaign as the Rams' joint-top scorer with Alan Durban on 22 goals.

DERBY COUNTY – SKY BET CHAMPIONSHIP 2021–22 LEAGUE RECORD

Match No.	*Date*	*Venue*	*Opponents*	*Result*		*H/T Score*	*Lg Pos.*	*Goalscorers*	*Attendance*
1	Aug 7	H	Huddersfield T	D	1-1	1-1	8	Davies [39]	16,249
2	14	A	Peterborough U	L	1-2	0-0	17	Stretton [77]	10,477
3	18	A	Hull C	W	1-0	0-0	12	Baldock [57]	10,451
4	21	H	Middlesbrough	D	0-0	0-0	14		16,123
5	28	H	Nottingham F	D	1-1	1-0	15	Lawrence [11]	22,991
6	Sept 10	A	Birmingham C	L	0-2	0-1	16		14,912
7	14	A	WBA	D	0-0	0-0	14		21,636
8	18	H	Stoke C	W	2-1	2-0	12	Bird [31], Davies [34]	20,545
9	25	A	Sheffield U	L	0-1	0-0	24		27,905
10	29	H	Reading	W	1-0	1-0	24	Forsyth [33]	18,769
11	Oct 2	H	Swansea C	D	0-0	0-0	24		21,640
12	16	A	Preston NE	D	0-0	0-0	24		18,092
13	19	H	Luton T	D	2-2	1-0	24	Lawrence [20], Knight [60]	20,258
14	23	A	Coventry C	D	1-1	0-1	24	Shinnie [78]	23,829
15	30	H	Blackburn R	L	1-2	0-2	24	Davies [89]	22,098
16	Nov 3	A	Barnsley	L	1-2	1-1	24	Baldock [24]	13,786
17	6	A	Millwall	D	1-1	1-1	24	Ebosele [44]	14,372
18	21	H	Bournemouth	W	3-2	1-2	24	Knight [13], Lawrence 2 (1 pen) [62, 69 (p)]	20,764
19	24	A	Fulham	D	0-0	0-0	24		16,468
20	29	H	QPR	L	1-2	1-0	24	Lawrence [10]	20,003
21	Dec 4	A	Bristol C	L	0-1	0-1	24		18,732
22	11	H	Blackpool	W	1-0	0-0	24	Plange [51]	21,663
23	27	H	WBA	W	1-0	0-0	24	Kazim-Richards [58]	24,846
24	30	A	Stoke C	W	2-1	1-0	24	Plange [16], Kazim-Richards [85]	22,235
25	Jan 3	A	Reading	D	2-2	0-1	24	Kazim-Richards [86], Davies [90]	12,512
26	15	H	Sheffield U	W	2-0	0-0	23	Lawrence 2 [69, 78]	24,597
27	22	A	Nottingham F	L	1-2	0-0	23	Lawrence (pen) [88]	29,256
28	30	H	Birmingham C	D	2-2	0-1	23	Plange [87], Bielik [90]	32,211
29	Feb 2	A	Huddersfield T	L	0-2	0-0	23		16,231
30	8	H	Hull C	W	3-1	2-0	23	Forsyth [19], Lawrence [37], Ebosele [47]	22,595
31	12	A	Middlesbrough	L	1-4	1-3	23	Bird [39]	26,266
32	19	H	Peterborough U	W	1-0	0-0	22	Sibley [90]	30,251
33	23	H	Millwall	L	1-2	0-2	22	Cooper (og) [88]	23,943
34	26	A	Luton T	L	0-1	0-0	23		10,070
35	Mar 1	A	Cardiff C	L	0-1	0-0	23		18,767
36	5	H	Barnsley	W	2-0	1-0	22	Morrison 2 [22, 47]	25,891
37	12	A	Bournemouth	L	0-2	0-1	23		9979
38	15	A	Blackburn R	L	1-3	1-0	23	Morrison [28]	12,406
39	19	H	Coventry C	D	1-1	0-1	23	Lawrence (pen) [67]	24,264
40	Apr 2	H	Preston NE	W	1-0	0-0	23	Morrison [80]	23,600
41	9	A	Swansea C	L	1-2	1-2	23	Lawrence (pen) [22]	18,374
42	15	H	Fulham	W	2-1	0-1	22	Plange [50], Adarabioyo (og) [73]	23,773
43	18	A	QPR	L	0-1	0-0	23		15,298
44	23	H	Bristol C	L	1-3	0-2	23	Forsyth [61]	22,753
45	30	A	Blackpool	W	2-0	0-0	22	Ebiowei [73], Cashin [82]	15,298
46	May 7	H	Cardiff C	L	0-1	0-0	23		29,402

Final League Position: 23

GOALSCORERS

League (45): Lawrence 11 (4 pens), Davies 4, Morrison 4, Plange 4, Forsyth 3, Kazim-Richards 3, Baldock 2, Bird 2, Ebosele 2, Knight 2, Bielik 1, Cashin 1, Ebiowei 1, Shinnie 1, Sibley 1, Stretton 1, own goals 2.
FA Cup (0).
Carabao Cup (4): Hutchinson 1, Kazim-Richards 1 (1 pen), Morrison 1, Sibley 1.

Roos K 17 + 1	Byrne N 41	Stearman R 10 + 4	Davies C 46	Forsyth C 23 + 3	Bird M 41 + 1	Shinnie G 21	Jozwiak K 13 + 4	Lawrence T 37 + 1	Watson L 3 + 1	Kazim-Richards C 5 + 18	Sibley L 11 + 15	Ebosele F 18 + 17	Hutchinson I — + 1	Morrison R 25 + 11	Stretton J 1 + 8	Jagielka P 20	Buchanan L 24 + 6	Baldock S 12 + 1	Williams D 2 + 4	Knight J 31 + 7	Allsop R 29 + 1	Aghatise O — + 3	Thompson L 19 + 4	Plange L 19 + 7	Cashin E 14 + 4	Bielik K 12 + 3	Ebiowei M 11 + 5	Cybulski B 1 + 3	Richards C — + 1	Robinson D — + 1	*Match No.*
1	2	3	4	5	6	7	8^{2}	9^{3}	10^{1}	11	12	13	14																		1
1	2	3	4	5	6	7	14	9		11^{1}	13	8^{2}		10^{3}	12																2
1	2	14	4	12	6	7	10				8			9^{3}	13	3	5^{1}	11^{2}													3
1	2		4	5	6	7	10^{3}		13		8^{1}			9	12	3	14	11^{2}													4
1	2		4	5	6	7	8^{2}	11^{1}			10			9	12	3	13														5
1	2		4		8	7^{1}		11^{3}			9^{2}			6	12	3	5	10	13	14											6
1	5		2		14	6	10^{1}	12			9				13	3	4	11^{2}	8	7^{3}											7
1	2	14	4		6	7	13	10			8^{2}			9^{1}		3	5	11^{3}		12											8
1■	2		4		6	7	14	11			8^{1}			9^{2}		3	5	10^{3}		13	12										9
	2	3	4	5	6	7		10						9^{3}	12		13	11^{1}	14	8^{2}	1										10
	2	3^{1}	4	5	6	7		10				14		9^{2}	11^{3}		12		13	8	1										11
			4		6	7		10		13	12^{2}	2		9		3	5	11^{1}		8	1										12
	2		4		7	8	11^{2}	10		12		14		6^{1}		3	5		13	9^{3}	1										13
1	2		4		7	8	11^{1}	10		13	12	9^{2}		6		3	5														14
1	2		4	5	7	8^{3}	10^{2}	11		12	9^{1}	14		6		3		13													15
1	2		4	5^{1}	7			11		10^{2}	14	13		6		3	12	9^{3}		8											16
1	2■		4		6	7		9^{3}		12	13	8^{1}				3	5	11^{2}		10		14									17
1		13	4	14	8	9		10		12		2^{2}				3	5^{3}	11^{1}		6			7								18
1	2		4	5^{2}	6	8		10		12		9^{1}		13		3				11			7								19
1	2		4	5	7	8^{3}	12	11		13		14		10^{1}		3				9^{2}			6								20
	2		4	5^{3}	7	8		10		12		9		14		3				11^{1}	1		6^{2}	13							21
			3	4	7^{1}	8	5	11								2			9^{2}	6	1	14	12	10^{3}	13						22
	2	3	4	8	7					12		5^{3}		13				11^{1}		9	1		6	10^{2}	14						23
	2		4	5	6		8^{1}	9^{3}		12		13		14		3				10	1		7	11^{2}							24
	2		4	5^{2}	7		6	10		12		13		14		3				9^{3}	1		8	11^{1}							25
	2	3	4	12	7		9^{1}	11^{3}		13		5								6	1		8	10^{2}	14						26
	2	3	4		7			10		11^{2}	14	6^{1}		12■			5			9	1		8^{3}	13							27
	2	3	4	5^{2}	6		8^{1}	9		13		12								10	1		7^{3}	11		14					28
	2	3■	4					10			9^{2}	6			14		5			7	1		8^{3}	11^{1}	13	12					29
	2		3	5	7			10			12	8^{1}					4			9	1		13	11^{3}		6^{2}	14				30
	2		3	5^{3}	7			9				12		13			4			8	1		10^{1}	11		6^{2}	14				31
	2		3	5^{1}	6			10■			12	8		13						9^{3}	1			11	4	7^{2}		14			32
	2		3		7					12	10^{2}	8^{1}		13			5			9	1			11	4	6^{3}	14				33
	5		2	8^{2}	10^{1}					11		12		6			4			9^{3}	1			13	3	7	14				34
	2		3		8					12	14	6		10			5			9^{3}	1			11^{2}	4	7^{1}	13				35
	2		3		7			10				5		9^{2}			12			13	1		14	11	4	6^{3}	8^{1}				36
	2		3		7			10		12		13		9			5			14	1			11^{1}	4	6^{2}	8^{3}				37
	2		3		6			10		12		14		11			5^{3}			9^{2}	1		7	13	4		8^{1}				38
	2		3		6			11			14	13		10^{3}			5				1		8^{1}	12	4^{2}	7	9				39
	2	14	4		7■			9				10^{1}		13			5			6	1			11^{3}	3	12	8^{2}				40
	2		4					10				12		9			5^{1}			13	1		7^{3}	11^{2}	3	6	8	14			41
	2		3					9			13	12					5			10	1		7^{1}	11	4	6^{2}	8^{3}		14		42
	2		3					9■			13			12			5^{3}			10^{2}	1		7	11	4	6^{1}	8	14			43
	2	3	4	5	7^{3}				10^{4}		12			9						14	1		6^{1}	13			8	11^{2}		15	44
1			3	5	7				6^{2}		12	2		9						10		14	13	11^{1}	4		8^{3}				45
14			3	5^{2}	6			11^{1}			10	13		9						2	1^{3}		7	12	4		8				46

FA Cup

Third Round	Coventry C	(a)	0-1

Carabao Cup

First Round	Salford C	(h)	3-3
(Derby Co won 5-3 on penalties)			
Second Round	Sheffield U	(a)	1-2

DONCASTER ROVERS

FOUNDATION

In 1879, Mr Albert Jenkins assembled a team to play a match against the Yorkshire Institution for the Deaf. The players remained together as Doncaster Rovers, joining the Midland Alliance in 1889 and the Midland Counties League in 1891.

Eco-Power Stadium, Stadium Way, Lakeside, Doncaster, South Yorkshire DN4 5JW.

Telephone: (01302) 764 664.

Ticket Office: (01302) 762 576.

Website: www.doncasterroversfc.co.uk

Email: reception@doncasterroversfc.co.uk

Ground Capacity: 15,148.

Record Attendance: 37,149 v Hull C, Division 3 (N), 2 October 1948 (at Belle Vue); 15,001 v Leeds U, FL 1, 1 April 2008 (at Keepmoat Stadium).

Pitch Measurements: 100m × 66m (109.5yd × 72yd).

Chairman: David Blunt.

Chief Executive: Gavin Baldwin.

Manager: Gary McSheffrey.

Assistant Manager: Frank Sinclair.

Colours: Red shirts with thin white hoops, red shorts with white trim, red socks with black and white trim.

Year Formed: 1879.

Turned Professional: 1885.

Club Nickname: 'Rovers', 'Donny'.

Grounds: 1880–1916, Intake Ground; 1920, Benetthorpe Ground; 1922, Low Pasture, Belle Vue; 2007, Keepmoat Stadium (renamed Eco-Power Stadium 2021).

First Football League Game: 7 September 1901, Division 2, v Burslem Port Vale (h) D 3–3 – Eggett; Simpson, Layton; Longden, Jones, Wright, Langham, Murphy, Price, Goodson (2), Bailey (1).

Record League Victory: 10–0 v Darlington, Division 4, 25 January 1964 – Potter; Raine, Meadows, Windross (1), White, Ripley (2), Robinson, Booth (2), Hale (4), Jeffrey, Broadbent (1).

Record Cup Victory: 7–0 v Blyth Spartans, FA Cup 1st rd, 27 November 1937 – Imrie; Shaw, Rodgers, McFarlane, Bycroft, Cyril Smith, Burton (1), Killourhy (4), Morgan (2), Malam, Dutton; 7–0 v Chorley, FA Cup 1st rd replay, 20 November 2018 – Lawlor; Mason, Butler, Anderson T■, Andrew, Whiteman (Rowe), Coppinger (Taylor), Kane (1) (Crawford), May (4), Marquis (1), Blair (1).

Record Defeat: 0–12 v Small Heath, Division 2, 11 April 1903.

HONOURS

League Champions: FL 1 – 2012–13; Division 3N – 1934–35, 1946–47, 1949–50; Third Division – 2003–04; Division 4 – 1965–66, 1968–69.
Runners-up: Division 3N – 1937–38, 1938–39; Division 4 – 1983–84; Conference – (3rd) 2002–03 *(promoted via play-offs (and golden goal)).*

FA Cup: 5th rd – 1952, 1954, 1955, 1956, 2019.

League Cup: 5th rd – 1976, 2006.

League Trophy Winners: 2007.

FOOTBALL YEARBOOK FACT FILE

Centre-forward Ron Morgan scored a hat-trick on his senior debut for Doncaster Rovers in October 1937 when he was brought into the starting line-up to replace Eddie Perry who was on international duty with Wales. Morgan scored his goals in a 7-2 Division Three North Cup game against Lincoln City but was given only a handful of further first-team chances before moving on to sign for Accrington Stanley.

Most League Points (2 for a win): 72, Division 3 (N), 1946–47.

Most League Points (3 for a win): 92, Division 3, 2003–04.

Most League Goals: 123, Division 3 (N), 1946–47.

Highest League Scorer in Season: Clarrie Jordan, 42, Division 3 (N), 1946–47.

Most League Goals in Total Aggregate: Tom Keetley, 180, 1923–29.

Most League Goals in One Match: 6, Tom Keetley v Ashington, Division 3 (N), 16 February 1929.

Most Capped Player: Len Graham, 14, Northern Ireland.

Most League Appearances: James Coppinger, 614, 2004–21.

Youngest League Player: Alick Jeffrey, 15 years 229 days v Fulham, 15 September 1954.

Record Transfer Fee Received: £2,000,000 from Reading for Matthew Mills, July 2009.

Record Transfer Fee Paid: £1,150,000 to Sheffield U for Billy Sharp, August 2010.

Football League Record: 1901 Elected to Division 2; 1903 Failed re-election; 1904 Re-elected; 1905 Failed re-election; 1923 Re-elected to Division 3 (N); 1935–37 Division 2; 1937–47 Division 3 (N); 1947–48 Division 2; 1948–50 Division 3 (N); 1950–58 Division 2; 1958–59 Division 3; 1959–66 Division 4; 1966–67 Division 3; 1967–69 Division 4; 1969–71 Division 3; 1971–81 Division 4; 1981–83 Division 3; 1983–84 Division 4; 1984–88 Division 3; 1988–92 Division 4; 1992–98 Division 3; 1998–2003 Conference; 2003–04 Division 3; 2004–08 FL 1; 2008–12 FL C; 2012–13 FL 1; 2013–14 FL C; 2014–16 FL 1; 2016–17 FL 2; 2017–22 FL 1; 2022– FL 2.

LATEST SEQUENCES

Longest Sequence of League Wins: 10, 22.1.1947 – 4.4.1947.

Longest Sequence of League Defeats: 9, 14.1.1905 – 1.4.1905.

Longest Sequence of League Draws: 4, 1.1.2018 – 23.1.2018.

Longest Sequence of Unbeaten League Matches: 20, 26.12.1968 – 12.4.1969.

Longest Sequence Without a League Win: 20, 9.8.1997 – 29.11.1997.

Successive Scoring Runs: 27 from 10.11.1934.

Successive Non-scoring Runs: 7 from 27.9.1947.

MANAGERS

Arthur Porter 1920–21
Harry Tufnell 1921–22
Arthur Porter 1922–23
Dick Ray 1923–27
David Menzies 1928–36
Fred Emery 1936–40
Bill Marsden 1944–46
Jackie Bestall 1946–49
Peter Doherty 1949–58
Jack Hodgson and Sid Bycroft (*Joint Managers*) 1958
Jack Crayston 1958–59 (*continued as Secretary-Manager to 1961*)
Jackie Bestall 1959–60
Norman Curtis 1960–61
Danny Malloy 1961–62
Oscar Hold 1962–64
Bill Leivers 1964–66
Keith Kettleborough 1966–67
George Raynor 1967–68
Lawrie McMenemy 1968–71
Maurice Setters 1971–74
Stan Anderson 1975–78
Billy Bremner 1978–85
Dave Cusack 1985–87
Dave Mackay 1987–89
Billy Bremner 1989–91
Steve Beaglehole 1991–93
Ian Atkins 1994
Sammy Chung 1994–96
Kerry Dixon (*Player-Manager*) 1996–97
Dave Cowling 1997
Mark Weaver 1997–98
Ian Snodin 1998–99
Steve Wignall 1999–2001
Dave Penney 2002–06
Sean O'Driscoll 2006–11
Dean Saunders 2011–13
Brian Flynn 2013
Paul Dickov 2013–15
Darren Ferguson 2015–18
Grant McCann 2018–19
Darren Moore 2019–21
Andy Butler 2021
Richie Wellens 2021
Gary McSheffrey December 2021–

TEN YEAR LEAGUE RECORD

		P	W	D	L	F	A	Pts	Pos
2012-13	FL 1	46	25	9	12	62	44	84	1
2013-14	FL C	46	11	11	24	39	70	44	22
2014-15	FL 1	46	16	13	17	58	62	61	13
2015-16	FL 1	46	11	13	22	48	64	46	21
2016-17	FL 2	46	25	10	11	85	55	85	3
2017-18	FL 1	46	13	17	16	52	52	56	15
2018-19	FL 1	46	20	13	13	76	58	73	6
2019-20	FL 1	34	15	9	10	51	33	54	9§
2020-21	FL 1	46	19	7	20	63	67	64	14
2021-22	FL 1	46	10	8	28	37	82	38	22

§*Decided on points-per-game (1.59)*

DID YOU KNOW ?

Alick Jeffrey is the only Doncaster Rovers player to win an England Amateur international cap. He made his debut against France in May 1955 and later the same year played against Northern Ireland and West Germany. Alick also appeared for the Great Britain amateur team in an Olympic Games qualifying match against Bulgaria in the same year.

DONCASTER ROVERS – SKY BET LEAGUE ONE 2021–22 LEAGUE RECORD

Match No.	Date	Venue	Opponents	Result		H/T Score	Lg Pos.	Goalscorers	Attendance
1	Aug 7	H	AFC Wimbledon	L	1-2	0-0	19	Seaman 46	6419
2	14	A	Sheffield W	L	0-2	0-0	23		24,738
3	17	A	Accrington S	L	0-1	0-1	23		2223
4	21	H	Portsmouth	D	0-0	0-0	22		6660
5	28	A	Rotherham U	L	0-2	0-2	23		9748
6	Sept 11	A	Wigan Ath	L	1-2	1-1	24	Rowe 22	8975
7	18	H	Morecambe	W	1-0	0-0	24	Rowe 81	5651
8	25	A	Plymouth Arg	L	1-2	0-0	24	Hiwula 54	11,003
9	28	A	Ipswich T	L	0-6	0-2	24		18,111
10	Oct 2	H	Milton Keynes D	W	2-1	1-1	24	Rowe 6, Cukur 79	5927
11	16	H	Wycombe W	L	0-2	0-2	24		6134
12	19	A	Gillingham	L	0-1	0-0	24		3713
13	23	H	Cheltenham T	W	3-2	2-0	23	Dodoo 23, Anderson 45, Vilca 54	6101
14	26	H	Cambridge U	D	1-1	0-1	23	Galbraith 68	6146
15	30	A	Charlton Ath	L	0-4	0-2	23		16,449
16	Nov 2	A	Crewe Alex	D	1-1	1-1	23	Olowu 45	3392
17	20	H	Lincoln C	D	0-0	0-0	23		8129
18	23	A	Bolton W	L	0-3	0-2	23		12,501
19	27	A	Burton Alb	L	0-2	0-0	23		2954
20	Dec 7	H	Oxford U	L	1-2	0-1	24	Horton 74	5785
21	11	H	Shrewsbury T	W	1-0	0-0	23	Olowu 79	5697
22	27	H	Sunderland	L	0-3	0-2	23		10,751
23	Jan 2	A	Morecambe	L	3-4	3-0	24	Barlow 7, Gardner 26, Olowu 29	4001
24	8	H	Fleetwood T	L	0-1	0-0	24		5648
25	15	H	Wigan Ath	L	1-2	0-1	24	Bogle 60	7169
26	18	A	Cambridge U	L	1-3	0-1	24	Dodoo 71	4575
27	22	A	Milton Keynes D	W	1-0	1-0	23	Dodoo 41	7229
28	29	H	Plymouth Arg	L	1-3	1-1	24	Horton 10	6493
29	Feb 1	H	Rotherham U	L	0-5	0-2	24		9255
30	5	A	Sunderland	W	2-1	2-0	24	Griffiths 22, Rowe 45	38,395
31	8	H	Ipswich T	L	0-1	0-1	24		6383
32	12	A	Portsmouth	L	0-4	0-0	24		14,767
33	15	A	Lincoln C	W	1-0	0-0	23	Gardner (pen) 80	9237
34	19	H	Sheffield W	L	1-3	1-0	23	Gardner (pen) 45	11,217
35	22	H	Accrington S	W	2-0	0-0	22	Martin 67, Olowu 87	5396
36	26	A	AFC Wimbledon	D	2-2	0-1	23	Rowe 2 63, 66	7912
37	Mar 5	A	Cheltenham T	L	0-4	0-2	23		4212
38	12	H	Gillingham	L	0-1	0-1	23		6920
39	19	A	Fleetwood T	D	0-0	0-0	23		3146
40	26	H	Charlton Ath	L	0-1	0-0	23		6350
41	Apr 2	A	Wycombe W	L	0-2	0-1	23		5943
42	9	H	Crewe Alex	W	2-0	1-0	23	Rowe 10, Martin 47	5912
43	15	H	Bolton W	L	1-2	0-0	23	Odubeko 77	8668
44	18	A	Shrewsbury T	D	3-3	0-3	23	Odubeko 54, Griffiths 77, Knoyle 90	6556
45	23	H	Burton Alb	W	2-0	1-0	23	Dodoo 36, Martin 75	6034
46	30	A	Oxford U	D	1-1	0-1	22	Martin 67	9139

Final League Position: 22

GOALSCORERS

League (37): Rowe 7, Dodoo 4, Martin 4, Olowu 4, Gardner 3 (2 pens), Griffiths 2, Horton 2, Odubeko 2, Anderson 1, Barlow 1, Bogle 1, Cukur 1, Galbraith 1, Hiwula 1, Knoyle 1, Seaman 1, Vilca 1.
FA Cup (3): Rowe 2, Horton 1.
Carabao Cup (0).
Papa John's Trophy (5): Dodoo 4, Vilca 1.

Dahlberg P 18	Knoyle K 42 + 3	Williams R 32	Anderson T 19	Rowe T 42 + 1	Smith Matthew 37 + 6	Close B 14	Gardner D 12 + 8	Seaman C 9 + 5	Cukur T 10 + 11	Barlow A 13 + 15	Bostock J 17 + 4	John C 2 + 3	Bogle O 2 + 8	Galbraith E 27 + 6	Williams E — + 1	Horton B 14 + 6	Olowu J 33 + 2	Dodoo J 26 + 7	Hiwula J 18 + 2	Vilca R 7 + 3	Taylor J 2 + 1	Jones L 10	Hasani L 4 + 3	Blythe B 2	Ravenhill L 1 + 2	Agard K 4 + 4	Greaves A — + 1	Martin J 18 + 2	Younger O 12 + 4	Odubeko A 8 + 8	Jackson B 12 + 3	Clayton A 9 + 3	Mitchell J 18	Griffiths R 12 + 4	*Match No.*
1	2	3	4	5	6	7	8[1]	9	10[3]	11[2]	12	13	14																						1
1	2	3	4	5		7[3]	8[2]		10[1]	11	6		12	9	13	14																			2
1	2	3	4	5		7	11[1]		10	9[2]	6[3]	12	13	8		14																			3
1	2	4	3[1]	11	13	7	14	9	10[3]		6[2]	5		8		12																			4
1	2	3		11	9	7		10	12	13	6[2]	4		8		5[1]																			5
1	2	3		5	10[3]	6	13	8[1]			14			7[2]			4	9	11	12															6
1	2	4	3	5	6	7		13	12					8				10	9[1]	11[2]															7
1	2	3	4	5	6[2]	7			10[1]	13				8				9	11	12															8
1	2	3	4	5	7	6	8[2]		10[3]	14							13	9	11[1]	12															9
1	2	4	3	5	13	6			14	12	7[2]			8				10[3]	9	11[1]															10
1	2	3	4	5	13	7			11		6[2]			12				9[3]	8	10[1]	14														11
1	2[3]	4[2]	3	5	12	6			10[1]	14	7			8			13	11	9																12
1		3	2	8[1]	12	6			13	14	7			5			4	10	11[3]	9[2]															13
1	12	3	4		7		8[1]		13		6[2]			5			2	10	11	9															14
1	2[1]	3	4	12	8				14		7			6		13	5	10	11[2]	9[3]															15
1	2	4	3	9	7				11		12			6			5	8	10[1]																16
	2		3	9					13	12	7[1]			6		5	4	11		10[3]	8[2]	1	14												17
	2		3	9	6				12	10				7		5	4■	11			8[1]	1													18
1	2		3	4	6	9[1]			13	8				7		5[2]		11	10				12												19
	2		3	10	6				11[1]	9[3]			14	7		8		13	12			1	5	4[2]											20
	2		3	9	6[2]					12				7		8	4	10	11			1	5[1]		13										21
	2			11	7		13			14			12			5	4	10[3]	9			1	6[1]	3	8[2]										22
	2			4	6		9[2]		14	5[3]			10[1]	8		7	3	12	11			1			13										23
1	5	3		4	7			13	14	8[1]			11	6		9[3]	2	12	10[2]																24
	3			8[3]	6			13		11[1]			12	7		5	4	10				1	2[2]			9	14								25
	3			8	6[3]			2[1]		14			12	7		5	4	10				1	13			9		11[2]							26
	2			8	6			12		14			13	7[1]		5	4	10				1				9[2]		11[3]	3						27
	2			8	6[3]			14						7		5[2]	4	9				1				12		11[1]	3	10[4]	13	15			28
	2			8	6			9						12		5[1]	4	11[3]											3	10	13	7[2]	1	14	29
	14	3		7	6		12	8									4	13										9[1]	2	11[2]	5		1	10[3]	30
	12	3[1]		7[2]	6		13	8[3]		14							4											9	2	11	5		1	10	31
	2			8	6		7			14							4	10[1]								13		11[3]	3	12	5[2]		1	9	32
	5	3		8	6		7										4	12										10[2]	2	13	9		1	11[1]	33
	5	3		8[1]	6		7										4	13								14		12	2	10[3]	9		1	11[2]	34
	5[1]	3		8	6		7[2]									14	4											10	2	12	9	13	1	11[3]	35
	5	3[1]		8	6		7[2]			14							4											10[3]	2	12	9	13	1	11	36
	2			9	6		8[2]							13			4									14		11[1]	3	10[3]	5	7■	1	12	37
	2	3		7	12			5[2]		14				6			4	10[3]	13									9		11	8[1]		1		38
	2	3		8	6		14			5				7			4		11[3]							10[1]		9[2]			13		1	12	39
	2	3		8	6[3]					5[1]	14						4	10	11									13	12		9[2]	7	1		40
	2[3]	4		9[2]	8						6			14		13	5											10	3	12		7[1]	1	11	41
	2[1]	3		5	6[3]					9	7			14			4											11	12	13		8	1	10[2]	42
	2	3		5	9[3]					8[1]	6[2]			12			4	14										10		13		7	1	11	43
	2	3[2]		5	8						6			9[1]			4											10	13	11		7	1	12	44
	2	3			6		13				7	14					4[1]	9										11	12		5[3]	8	1	10[2]	45
	2	3			6[2]		13				7						4	9										11		12	5	8	1	10[1]	46

FA Cup

First Round	Scunthorpe U	(a)	1-0
Second Round	Mansfield T	(h)	2-3

Carabao Cup

First Round	Walsall	(a)	0-0
(Doncaster R won 4-3 on penalties)			
Second Round	Stoke C	(a)	0-2

Papa John's Trophy

Group E (N)	Rotherham U	(h)	0-6
Group E (N)	Manchester C U21	(h)	2-1
Group E (N)	Scunthorpe U	(a)	3-2
Second Round	Crewe Alex	(a)	0-2

EVERTON

FOUNDATION

St Domingo Church Sunday School formed a football club in 1878 which played at Stanley Park. Enthusiasm was so great that in November 1879 they decided to expand membership and changed the name to Everton, playing in black shirts with a scarlet sash and nicknamed the 'Black Watch'. After wearing several other colours, royal blue was adopted in 1901.

Goodison Park, Goodison Road, Liverpool L4 4EL.

Telephone: (0151) 556 1878.

Ticket Office: (0151) 556 1878.

Website: www.evertonfc.com

Email: everton@evertonfc.com

Ground Capacity: 39,414.

Record Attendance: 78,299 v Liverpool, Division 1, 18 September 1948.

Pitch Measurements: 100.48m × 68m (110yd × 74.5yd).

Chairman: Bill Kenwright CBE.

Chief Executive: Dr Denise Barrett-Baxendale MBE.

Manager: Frank Lampard.

Assistant Manager: Joe Edwards.

Colours: Blue shirts with yellow and white trim, white shorts with yellow and blue trim, white socks with blue trim.

Year Formed: 1878.

Turned Professional: 1885.

Previous Name: 1878, St Domingo FC; 1879, Everton.

Club Nickname: 'The Toffees'.

Grounds: 1878, Stanley Park; 1882, Priory Road; 1884, Anfield Road; 1892, Goodison Park.

First Football League Game: 8 September 1888, Football League, v Accrington (h) W 2–1 – Smalley; Dick, Ross; Holt, Jones, Dobson; Fleming (2), Waugh, Lewis, Edgar Chadwick, Farmer.

Record League Victory: 9–1 v Manchester C, Division 1, 3 September 1906 – Scott; Balmer, Crelley; Booth, Taylor (1), Abbott (1); Sharp, Bolton (1), Young (4), Settle (2), George Wilson; 9–1 v Plymouth Arg, Division 2, 27 December 1930 – Coggins; Williams, Cresswell; McPherson, Griffiths, Thomson; Critchley, Dunn, Dean (4), Johnson (1), Stein (4).

HONOURS

League Champions: Division 1 – 1914–15, 1927–28, 1931–32, 1938–39, 1962–63, 1969–70, 1984–85, 1986–87; Football League 1890–91; Division 2 – 1930–31.
Runners-up: Division 1 – 1894–95, 1901–02, 1904–05, 1908–09, 1911–12, 1985–86; Football League 1889–90; Division 2 – 1953–54.

FA Cup Winners: 1906, 1933, 1966, 1984, 1995.
Runners-up: 1893, 1897, 1907, 1968, 1985, 1986, 1989, 2009.

League Cup: *Runners-up:* 1977, 1984.

League Super Cup: *Runners-up:* 1986.

Full Members' Cup: *Runners-up:* 1989, 1991.

European Competitions
European Cup: 1963–64, 1970–71 *(qf)*.
Champions League: 2005–06.
Fairs Cup: 1962–63, 1964–65, 1965–66.
UEFA Cup: 1975–76, 1978–79, 1979–80, 2005–06, 2007–08, 2008–09.
Europa League: 2009–10, 2014–15, 2017–18.
European Cup-Winners' Cup: 1966–67, 1984–85 *(winners)*, 1995–96.

FOOTBALL YEARBOOK FACT FILE

Centre-forward Bert Freeman scored in 10 consecutive Football League matches for Everton between 10 October and 12 December 1908. He finished the season as the Toffees' leading scorer with 38 goals from 38 League and Cup appearances, with his tally including four hat-tricks, two of which were against Sheffield United.

Record Cup Victory: 11–2 v Derby Co, FA Cup 1st rd, 18 January 1890 – Smalley; Hannah, Doyle (1); Kirkwood, Holt (1), Parry; Latta, Brady (3), Geary (3), Edgar Chadwick, Millward (3).

Record Defeat: 4–10 v Tottenham H, Division 1, 11 October 1958.

Most League Points (2 for a win): 66, Division 1, 1969–70.

Most League Points (3 for a win): 90, Division 1, 1984–85.

Most League Goals: 121, Division 2, 1930–31.

Highest League Scorer in Season: William Ralph 'Dixie' Dean, 60, Division 1, 1927–28 (All-time League record).

Most League Goals in Total Aggregate: William Ralph 'Dixie' Dean, 349, 1925–37.

Most League Goals in One Match: 6, Jack Southworth v WBA, Division 1, 30 December 1893.

Most Capped Player: Tim Howard, 93 (121), USA.

Most League Appearances: Neville Southall, 578, 1981–98.

Youngest League Player: Jose Baxter, 16 years 191 days v Blackburn R, 16 August 2008.

Record Transfer Fee Received: £75,000,000 from Manchester U for Romelu Lukaku, July 2017.

Record Transfer Fee Paid: £40,000,000 (rising to £45,000,000) to Swansea C for Gylfi Sigurdsson, August 2017.

Football League Record: 1888 Founder Member of the Football League; 1930–31 Division 2; 1931–51 Division 1; 1951–54 Division 2; 1954–92 Division 1; 1992– Premier League.

MANAGERS

W. E. Barclay 1888–89
(Secretary-Manager)
Dick Molyneux 1889–1901
(Secretary-Manager)
William C. Cuff 1901–18
(Secretary-Manager)
W. J. Sawyer 1918–19
(Secretary-Manager)
Thomas H. McIntosh 1919–35
(Secretary-Manager)
Theo Kelly 1936–48
Cliff Britton 1948–56
Ian Buchan 1956–58
Johnny Carey 1958–61
Harry Catterick 1961–73
Billy Bingham 1973–77
Gordon Lee 1977–81
Howard Kendall 1981–87
Colin Harvey 1987–90
Howard Kendall 1990–93
Mike Walker 1994
Joe Royle 1994–97
Howard Kendall 1997–98
Walter Smith 1998–2002
David Moyes 2002–13
Roberto Martinez 2013–16
Ronald Koeman 2016–17
Sam Allardyce 2017–18
Marco Silva 2018–19
Carlo Ancelotti 2019–21
Rafael Benitez 2021–22
Frank Lampard January 2022–

LATEST SEQUENCES

Longest Sequence of League Wins: 12, 24.3.1894 – 13.10.1894.

Longest Sequence of League Defeats: 6, 27.8.2005– 15.10.2005.

Longest Sequence of League Draws: 5, 4.5.1977 – 16.5.1977.

Longest Sequence of Unbeaten League Matches: 20, 29.4.1978 – 16.12.1978.

Longest Sequence Without a League Win: 14, 6.3.1937 – 4.9.1937.

Successive Scoring Runs: 40 from 15.3.1930.

Successive Non-scoring Runs: 6 from 27.8.2005.

TEN YEAR LEAGUE RECORD

		P	W	D	L	F	A	Pts	Pos
2012-13	PR Lge	38	16	15	7	55	40	63	6
2013-14	PR Lge	38	21	9	8	61	39	72	5
2014-15	PR Lge	38	12	11	15	48	50	47	11
2015-16	PR Lge	38	11	14	13	59	55	47	11
2016-17	PR Lge	38	17	10	11	62	44	61	7
2017-18	PR Lge	38	13	10	15	44	58	49	8
2018-19	PR Lge	38	15	9	14	54	46	54	8
2019-20	PR Lge	38	13	10	15	44	56	49	12
2020-21	PR Lge	38	17	8	13	47	48	59	10
2021-22	PR Lge	38	11	6	21	43	66	39	16

DID YOU KNOW ?

In the 1930–31 season Everton defeated Charlton Athletic 7-1 at Goodison and 7-0 at The Valley in their Second Division fixtures. In the away game the Toffees led 6-0 at the half-time break with all five forwards having scored within a 17-minute spell.

EVERTON – PREMIER LEAGUE 2021–22 LEAGUE RECORD

Match No.	*Date*	*Venue*	*Opponents*	*Result*		*H/T Score*	*Lg Pos.*	*Goalscorers*	*Attendance*
1	Aug 14	H	Southampton	W	3-1	0-1	4	Richarlison ^{47}, Doucoure ^{76}, Calvert-Lewin ^{81}	38,487
2	21	A	Leeds U	D	2-2	1-1	3	Calvert-Lewin (pen) ^{30}, Gray ^{50}	36,293
3	28	A	Brighton & HA	W	2-0	1-0	4	Gray ^{41}, Calvert-Lewin (pen) ^{58}	30,548
4	Sept 13	H	Burnley	W	3-1	0-0	4	Keane ^{60}, Townsend ^{65}, Gray ^{66}	38,354
5	18	A	Aston Villa	L	0-3	0-0	5		41,888
6	25	H	Norwich C	W	2-0	1-0	5	Townsend (pen) ^{29}, Doucoure ^{77}	38,821
7	Oct 2	A	Manchester U	D	1-1	0-1	4	Townsend ^{65}	73,128
8	17	H	West Ham U	L	0-1	0-0	8		39,132
9	23	H	Watford	L	2-5	1-1	8	Davies ^{3}, Richarlison ^{63}	38,834
10	Nov 1	A	Wolverhampton W	L	1-2	0-2	10	Iwobi ^{66}	30,617
11	7	H	Tottenham H	D	0-0	0-0	11		39,059
12	21	A	Manchester C	L	0-3	0-1	11		52,571
13	28	A	Brentford	L	0-1	0-1	14		16,957
14	Dec 1	H	Liverpool	L	1-4	1-2	14	Gray ^{38}	39,641
15	6	H	Arsenal	W	2-1	0-1	12	Richarlison ^{80}, Gray ^{90}	38,906
16	12	A	Crystal Palace	L	1-3	0-1	14	Rondon ^{70}	24,066
17	16	A	Chelsea	D	1-1	0-0	14	Branthwaite ^{74}	39,933
18	Jan 2	H	Brighton & HA	L	2-3	0-2	15	Gordon 2 $^{53, 76}$	38,203
19	15	A	Norwich C	L	1-2	0-2	15	Richarlison ^{60}	26,629
20	22	H	Aston Villa	L	0-1	0-1	16		38,203
21	Feb 8	A	Newcastle U	L	1-3	1-1	16	Lascelles (og) ^{36}	52,186
22	12	H	Leeds U	W	3-0	2-0	16	Coleman ^{10}, Keane ^{23}, Gordon ^{78}	39,150
23	19	A	Southampton	L	0-2	0-0	16		31,312
24	26	H	Manchester C	L	0-1	0-0	17		39,105
25	Mar 7	A	Tottenham H	L	0-5	0-3	17		59,647
26	13	H	Wolverhampton W	L	0-1	0-0	17		39,112
27	17	H	Newcastle U	W	1-0	0-0	17	Iwobi ^{90}	39,068
28	Apr 3	A	West Ham U	L	1-2	0-1	17	Holgate ^{53}	59,953
29	6	A	Burnley	L	2-3	2-1	17	Richarlison 2 (2 pens) $^{18, 41}$	19,830
30	9	H	Manchester U	W	1-0	1-0	17	Gordon ^{27}	39,080
31	20	H	Leicester C	D	1-1	0-1	17	Richarlison ^{90}	39,153
32	24	A	Liverpool	L	0-2	0-0	18		53,213
33	May 1	H	Chelsea	W	1-0	0-0	18	Richarlison ^{46}	39,256
34	8	A	Leicester C	W	2-1	2-1	16	Mykolenko ^{6}, Holgate ^{30}	32,001
35	11	A	Watford	D	0-0	0-0	16		20,653
36	15	H	Brentford	L	2-3	2-1	16	Calvert-Lewin ^{10}, Richarlison (pen) ^{45}	38,819
37	19	H	Crystal Palace	W	3-2	0-2	16	Keane ^{54}, Richarlison ^{75}, Calvert-Lewin ^{85}	40,000
38	22	A	Arsenal	L	1-5	1-2	16	van de Beek ^{45}	60,201

Final League Position: 16

GOALSCORERS

League (43): Richarlison 10 (3 pens), Calvert-Lewin 5 (2 pens), Gray 5, Gordon 4, Keane 3, Townsend 3 (1 pen), Doucoure 2, Holgate 2, Iwobi 2, Branthwaite 1, Coleman 1, Davies 1, Mykolenko 1, Rondon 1, van de Beek 1, own goal 1.
FA Cup (9): Rondon 2, Townsend 2, Andre Gomes 1, Gray 1, Holgate 1, Mina 1, Richarlison 1.
Carabao Cup (4): Townsend 2, Digne 1, Iwobi 1.
Papa John's Trophy (1): McAllister 1.

Pickford J 35	Coleman S 30	Holgate M 23 + 2	Keane M 31 + 1	Digne L 13	Allan M 25 + 3	Doucoure A 29 + 1	Townsend A 17 + 4	Gray D 28 + 6	Richarlison d 28 + 2	Calvert-Lewin D 15 + 2	Iwobi A 22 + 6	Mina Y 11 + 2	Gordon A 25 + 10	Delph F 8 + 3	Kean M — + 1	Andre Gomes F 7 + 7	Godfrey B 23	Rondon J 8 + 12	Begovic A 3	Kenny J 11 + 4	Davies T 2 + 4	Dobbin L — + 3	Gbamin J 1 + 2	Onyango T — + 3	Tosun C — + 1	Branthwaite J 4 + 2	Simms E 1	Mykolenko V 12 + 1	Alli B 1 + 10	van de Beek D 5 + 2	El Ghazi A — + 2	Price I — + 1	Match No.
1	2	3	4	5	6	7	8^{1}	9^{2}	10^{3}	11	12	13	14																				1
1	2		4	5	8	7	12	9^{2}	10	11^{3}	6^{1}	3		13	14																		2
1	2	3	4	5	7	8	6	9^{2}	10	11^{1}	12					13																	3
1	5		4	8	7	6	9	11^{3}	10^{2}		14	2				12	3^{1}	13															4
			4	5	8^{2}	7	6	10			9^{4}	3	13			12	2^{3}	11^{1}	1	14	15												5
1			4	5	8	7	6^{1}	10^{2}			9^{3}	3	12				2	11			13	14											6
1			4	5	8	7	6	10^{2}				3	9^{1}				2	11			12	13											7
1	2		4	5	8	7	6	10			9^{1}		12				3	11															8
1	2		3	5	8		6	10^{2}	12		13		9^{1}				4	11			7												9
1	2	4	3		8		6	11^{3}	10		9^{2}		13	12			5	14					7^{1}										10
1	2	13■	4	5	8^{2}		10	9^{3}	11				6	7^{1}			3				12		14										11
1	2		4	5	8^{3}		10	9^{1}	11		12		6	7^{2}			3	13						14									12
1	2		4	5	8	7	6^{1}	12			10		9				3	11															13
1	2		4	5	8	7	6^{2}	9^{3}	10				12	13			3	11^{1}							14								14
1	2	12	4		8	7	10^{2}	9	11		14	3^{1}	6^{3}			13	5																15
1	2	3	4			8	7	10	11^{2}				13	6^{1}		9	5	12															16
1		3	4			8					7		10^{3}			9^{2}	6			2		12	13	14		5	11^{1}						17
1	6	5	4		9^{2}	8		10		11			7			13	3	12		2^{1}													18
1	2^{2}		4			7		9	13	11		12	6			8	3	10^{1}										5					19
1		4			12	7^{3}	6^{2}	9	10	11		3	13			8^{1}	5			2				14									20
1	5	4	3		6		8	10^{1}	11			2^{2}	9			7^{3}										13			12	14			21
1	2	3	4		7				11^{3}	10^{1}	9		6^{2}					14		5									12	8	13		22
1	2	3	4		7^{1}		13		11	10	6^{2}		9^{3}			12				5									14	8			23
1	2	3	4		6	7		13	11		8^{3}		10^{2}							5									12	9^{1}	14		24
1	2	3	4^{1}		7	6			11	10^{3}			5							9						12		13	14	8^{2}			25
1	5	3				6	13	11^{2}	10				9				4			2■								8^{1}	12	7			26
	2	3	4		7■	6	14	10^{1}	11^{2}	12	8		9^{3}			13	5		1														27
1		7	3■			6		9	11	10^{1}	8		12				4			2								5					28
1		7^{2}				6		12	11	10	8		9^{1}				3	13		2						4		5					29
1	2		3		6	13		12	11	10^{1}	8		9	7^{2}			4											5					30
1	2				6^{1}			11^{2}	10		8	3	9	7			4	13										5	12				31
1	2	3	4		7^{1}	6		9^{2}	10		8		11					13										5	12				32
1	3	5			12	8		10^{3}	11^{2}		2	4	7	9^{1}				13										6	14				33
1	3	5	12			8		10^{3}	11		2	4^{1}	7	9				14		13								6^{2}					34
1	3	5	4		13	8		10^{1}	11	12	2		7	9^{2}														6					35
1	2^{3}	4				6		13	11	10	5		9^{2}			7^{1}		14■		12						3■		8					36
1	2	4	3			6		13	10^{3}	11	5		9^{2}			7^{1}				14								8	12				37
		3	4			9^{1}		7		11	2		13						1	6	8^{3}					5			10^{2}	12		14	38

FA Cup

Third Round	Hull C	(a)	3-2
(aet)			
Fourth Round	Brentford	(h)	4-1
Fifth Round	Boreham Wood	(h)	2-0
Sixth Round	Crystal Palace	(a)	0-4

Carabao Cup

Second Round	Huddersfield T	(a)	2-1
Third Round	QPR	(a)	2-2

(QPR won 8-7 on penalties)

Papa John's Trophy (Everton U21)

Group A (N)	Morecambe	(a)	1-0
Group A (N)	Carlisle U	(a)	0-2
Group A (N)	Hartlepool U	(a)	0-1

EXETER CITY

FOUNDATION

Exeter City was formed in 1904 by the amalgamation of St Sidwell's United and Exeter United. The club first played in the East Devon League and then the Plymouth & District League. After an exhibition match between West Bromwich Albion and Woolwich Arsenal, which was held to test interest as Exeter was then a rugby stronghold, it was decided to form Exeter City. At a meeting at the Red Lion Hotel in 1908, the club turned professional.

St James Park, Stadium Way, Exeter, Devon EX4 6PX.

Telephone: (01392) 411 243.

Ticket Office: (01392) 413 952.

Website: www.exetercityfc.co.uk

Email: reception@ecfc.co.uk

Ground Capacity: 8,714.

Record Attendance: 20,984 v Sunderland, FA Cup 6th rd (replay), 4 March 1931.

Pitch Measurements: 103m × 64m (112.5yd × 70yd).

Club Board Chairman: Richard Pym.

Chief Operating Officer: Justin Quick.

Manager: Matt Taylor.

Assistant Manager: Wayne Carlisle.

Colours: Red and white striped shirts with white sleeves and black trim, red shorts, red socks.

Year Formed: 1904.

Turned Professional: 1908.

Club Nickname: 'The Grecians'.

Ground: 1904, St James Park.

First Football League Game: 28 August 1920, Division 3, v Brentford (h) W 3–0 – Pym; Coleburne, Feebury (1p); Crawshaw, Carrick, Mitton; Appleton, Makin, Wright (1), Vowles (1), Dockray.

Record League Victory: 8–1 v Coventry C, Division 3 (S), 4 December 1926 – Bailey; Pollard, Charlton; Pullen, Pool, Garrett; Purcell (2), McDevitt, Blackmore (2), Dent (2), Compton (2). 8–1 v Aldershot, Division 3 (S), 4 May 1935 – Chesters; Gray, Miller; Risdon, Webb, Angus; Jack Scott (1), Wrightson (1), Poulter (3), McArthur (1), Dryden (1), (1 og).

Record Cup Victory: 14–0 v Weymouth, FA Cup 1st qual rd, 3 October 1908 – Fletcher; Craig, Bulcock; Ambler, Chadwick, Wake; Parnell (1), Watson (1), McGuigan (4), Bell (6), Copestake (2).

Record Defeat: 0–9 v Notts Co, Division 3 (S), 16 October 1948. 0–9 v Northampton T, Division 3 (S), 12 April 1958.

HONOURS

League Champions: Division 4 – 1989–90.
Runners-up: Division 3S – 1932–33; FL 2 – 2008–09, 2021–22; Division 4 – 1976–77; Conference – (4th) 2007–08 *(promoted via play-offs)*.

FA Cup: 6th rd replay – 1931; 6th rd – 1981.

League Cup: 4th rd – 1974, 1979, 1980, 1990.

FOOTBALL YEARBOOK FACT FILE

Exeter City had a good start to the 1939–40 season, drawing their opening games against Torquay United and defeating Northampton Town and Port Vale before the campaign ended due to the outbreak of war. When football resumed normal activities again in 1946–47 the fixture lists were the same as for the abandoned season. The Grecians had exactly the same results from their first three fixtures, and in both seasons they scored five goals and conceded three.

Most League Points (2 for a win): 62, Division 4, 1976–77.

Most League Points (3 for a win): 89, Division 4, 1989–90.

Most League Goals: 88, Division 3 (S), 1932–33.

Highest League Scorer in Season: Fred Whitlow, 33, Division 3 (S), 1932–33.

Most League Goals in Total Aggregate: Tony Kellow, 129, 1976–78, 1980–83, 1985–88.

Most League Goals in One Match: 4, Harold 'Jazzo' Kirk v Portsmouth, Division 3 (S), 3 March 1923; 4, Fred Dent v Bristol R, Division 3 (S), 5 November 1927; 4, Fred Whitlow v Watford, Division 3 (S), 29 October 1932.

Most Capped Player: Joel Grant, 2 (14), Jamaica.

Most League Appearances: Arnold Mitchell, 495, 1952–66.

Youngest League Player: Ethan Ampadu, 15 years 337 days v Crawley T, 16 August 2016.

Record Transfer Fee Received: £1,800,000 (rising to £5,730,000) from Brentford for Ollie Watkins, July 2017.

Record Transfer Fee Paid: £100,000 to Aberdeen for Jayden Stockley, August 2017.

Football League Record: 1920 Elected to Division 3; 1921–58 Division 3 (S); 1958–64 Division 4; 1964–66 Division 3; 1966–77 Division 4; 1977–84 Division 3; 1984–90 Division 4; 1990–92 Division 3; 1992–94 Division 2; 1994–2003 Division 3; 2003–08 Conference; 2008–09 FL 2; 2009–12 FL 1; 2012–22 FL 2; 2022– FL 1.

MANAGERS

Arthur Chadwick 1910–22
Fred Mavin 1923–27
Dave Wilson 1928–29
Billy McDevitt 1929–35
Jack English 1935–39
George Roughton 1945–52
Norman Kirkman 1952–53
Norman Dodgin 1953–57
Bill Thompson 1957–58
Frank Broome 1958–60
Glen Wilson 1960–62
Cyril Spiers 1962–63
Jack Edwards 1963–65
Ellis Stuttard 1965–66
Jock Basford 1966–67
Frank Broome 1967–69
Johnny Newman 1969–76
Bobby Saxton 1977–79
Brian Godfrey 1979–83
Gerry Francis 1983–84
Jim Iley 1984–85
Colin Appleton 1985–87
Terry Cooper 1988–91
Alan Ball 1991–94
Terry Cooper 1994–95
Peter Fox 1995–2000
Noel Blake 2000–01
John Cornforth 2001–02
Neil McNab 2002–03
Gary Peters 2003
Eamonn Dolan 2003–04
Alex Inglethorpe 2004–06
Paul Tisdale 2006–18
Matt Taylor June 2018–

LATEST SEQUENCES

Longest Sequence of League Wins: 7, 31.12.2016 – 4.2.2017.

Longest Sequence of League Defeats: 7, 14.1.1984 – 25.2.1984.

Longest Sequence of League Draws: 6, 13.9.1986 – 4.10.1986.

Longest Sequence of Unbeaten League Matches: 15, 17.8.2021 – 20.11.2021.

Longest Sequence Without a League Win: 18, 21.2.1995 – 19.8.1995.

Successive Scoring Runs: 22 from 15.9.1958.

Successive Non-scoring Runs: 6 from 17.1.1986.

TEN YEAR LEAGUE RECORD

		P	W	D	L	F	A	Pts	Pos
2012-13	FL 2	46	18	10	18	63	62	64	10
2013-14	FL 2	46	14	13	19	54	57	55	16
2014-15	FL 2	46	17	13	16	61	65	64	10
2015-16	FL 2	46	17	13	16	63	65	64	14
2016-17	FL 2	46	21	8	17	75	56	71	5
2017-18	FL 2	46	24	8	14	64	54	80	4
2018-19	FL 2	46	19	13	14	60	49	70	9
2019-20	FL 2	37	18	11	8	53	43	65	5§
2020-21	FL 2	46	18	16	12	71	50	70	9
2021-22	FL 2	46	23	15	8	65	41	84	2

§Decided on points-per-game (1.76)

DID YOU KNOW 

Exeter City have played in four play-off finals at the 'new' Wembley Stadium. In 2006–07 they lost out to Morecambe in the Conference play-off final, but 12 months later they returned to defeat Cambridge United 1-0 and regain their place in the Football League. They also reached the League Two play-off final in both 2017 and 2018, but on both occasions failed to secure promotion.

EXETER CITY – SKY BET LEAGUE TWO 2021–22 LEAGUE RECORD

Match No.	Date	Venue	Opponents	Result		H/T Score	Lg Pos.	Goalscorers	Attendance
1	Aug 7	H	Bradford C	D	0-0	0-0	12		5609
2	14	A	Leyton Orient	L	0-3	0-2	20		4860
3	17	A	Barrow	D	0-0	0-0	20		2667
4	21	H	Bristol R	W	4-1	4-0	12	Jay 2 [3, 15], Dieng [22], Kite [24]	5284
5	28	A	Harrogate T	D	1-1	0-1	11	Key [79]	1883
6	Sept 4	H	Forest Green R	D	0-0	0-0	13		4008
7	11	A	Scunthorpe U	W	4-0	1-0	8	Jay 2 [41, 46], Key [57], Dieng [75]	2443
8	18	H	Sutton U	W	2-0	0-0	5	Goodliffe (og) [68], Nombe [84]	4511
9	25	A	Hartlepool U	D	1-1	1-1	6	Nombe [41]	5194
10	Oct 2	H	Walsall	D	2-2	1-1	6	Dieng [5], Nombe [61]	4839
11	9	A	Stevenage	D	2-2	1-1	10	Nombe [10], Jay [49]	3186
12	16	H	Newport Co	D	2-2	1-2	9	Jay [22], Nombe [55]	5078
13	19	A	Crawley T	W	3-1	0-1	7	Jay [54], Atangana [56], Nombe [90]	1960
14	23	H	Mansfield T	W	2-1	0-0	4	Dieng [61], Jay [83]	4329
15	30	A	Salford C	W	2-1	0-0	4	Jay [53], Ripley (og) [90]	1892
16	Nov 13	H	Oldham Ath	W	2-1	1-0	3	Jay [17], Brown, J [50]	5103
17	20	H	Carlisle U	W	2-1	0-0	2	Nombe [60], Caprice [80]	4796
18	23	A	Colchester U	L	1-3	0-2	2	Amond [69]	2028
19	27	A	Rochdale	D	1-1	0-0	3	Ray [59]	2102
20	Dec 7	H	Northampton T	L	1-2	0-1	4	Amond [50]	3823
21	11	H	Tranmere R	L	0-1	0-1	5		4850
22	Jan 1	A	Sutton U	L	1-2	1-1	8	Dieng [9]	3278
23	4	A	Forest Green R	D	0-0	0-0	8		2631
24	15	H	Scunthorpe U	W	2-0	0-0	8	Brown, J [63], Zanzala [76]	4676
25	22	A	Walsall	W	2-0	1-0	8	Dieng [44], Diabate [84]	4750
26	29	H	Hartlepool U	D	0-0	0-0	8		5121
27	Feb 5	A	Swindon T	W	2-1	0-0	7	Brown, J [84], Dieng [88]	10,642
28	8	H	Leyton Orient	W	1-0	0-0	6	Diabate [90]	4111
29	12	A	Bradford C	W	1-0	1-0	4	Phillips [44]	15,058
30	15	H	Harrogate T	W	4-3	1-2	3	Brown, J (pen) [37], Grounds [71], Dieng [81], Sparkes [90]	3852
31	26	A	Bristol R	D	1-1	1-1	4	Brown, J [24]	9689
32	Mar 4	A	Mansfield T	L	1-2	0-1	5	Jay [90]	6702
33	8	H	Swindon T	W	3-1	2-0	3	Brown, J [17], Grounds [26], Jay [81]	5958
34	12	H	Salford C	D	0-0	0-0	5		5775
35	15	H	Crawley T	W	2-1	2-1	5	Dieng 2 [31, 44]	4042
36	19	A	Oldham Ath	W	2-0	0-0	2	Taylor, K [52], Brown, J [90]	5111
37	22	A	Port Vale	D	0-0	0-0	2		5301
38	26	H	Stevenage	W	2-1	2-1	2	Stubbs 2 [28, 44]	5923
39	Apr 2	A	Newport Co	W	1-0	0-0	2	Dieng [72]	5697
40	9	A	Carlisle U	W	1-0	0-0	2	Amond [89]	5132
41	15	H	Colchester U	W	2-0	1-0	2	Sparkes [32], Zanzala [63]	7549
42	18	A	Tranmere R	L	0-2	0-1	2		6666
43	23	H	Rochdale	W	2-0	1-0	2	Dieng [34], Jay [60]	6935
44	26	H	Barrow	W	2-1	1-1	2	Phillips [35], Jay [78]	7860
45	30	A	Northampton T	D	1-1	0-1	1	Nombe [71]	7764
46	May 7	H	Port Vale	L	0-1	0-1	2		8147

Final League Position: 2

GOALSCORERS

League (65): Jay 14, Dieng 12, Nombe 8, Brown, J 7 (1 pen), Amond 3, Diabate 2, Grounds 2, Key 2, Phillips 2, Sparkes 2, Stubbs 2, Zanzala 2, Atangana 1, Caprice 1, Kite 1, Ray 1, Taylor, K 1, own goals 2.
FA Cup (4): Nombe 2 (1 pen), Dieng 1, own goal 1.
Carabao Cup (0).
Papa John's Trophy (10): Amond 2, Coley 2, Collins 2, Jay 2 (1 pen), Daniel 1, Dieng 1.

Dawson C 45	Sweeney P 42 + 1	Ray G 18 + 1	Grounds J 7 + 8	Key J 44	Atangana N 4 + 12	Dieng T 39 + 3	Sparkes J 15 + 6	Jay M 41 + 4	Brown J 42 + 1	Nombe S 19 + 9	Kite H 12 + 2	Seymour B 1 + 5	Rowe C 4 + 4	Amond P 8 + 18	Hartridge A 27 + 1	Caprice J 29 + 5	Edwards O 3 + 7	Taylor K 6 + 8	Collins A 36 + 2	Coley J 4 + 14	Daniel C 4	Brown S 1	Stubbs S 21 + 1	Diabate C 16 + 2	Dyer J — + 1	Zanzala O 12 + 3	Phillips K 6 + 5	Match No.
1	2	3	4	5	6	7^1	8	9	10^2	11	12	13																1
1	2	3	4■	5	7	6^1	8^2	9^3	10		12	11	13	14														2
1	2	3		5	12	6^1		9	10		7	13		11^2	4	8												3
1	2	3		5	13^3	6^2		9	10	12	7			11^1	4	8	14											4
1	2	3		5		7^2		9	10	13	6■			11^1	4	8	12											5
1	2	3		5	12	6^1		9		10				11^2	4	8	13	7										6
1	2	3		5	12	7		9^3	10^2	11	6^1	13			4	8		14										7
1	2^2	3		5	14	7^3		9	10	11	6^1				4	8	13	12										8
1	2	3		5^3	13	6^2		9	10	11					4	8	14	7^1	12									9
1	2^1	3		5	14	7^3		9	10	11	6^2				4	8			13	12								10
1	2	3^1		5	13	7^2		9	10^3	11					4	8	12		6	14								11
1	3		13	2		8		10	6^3	11					4	12	9^1	14	7		5^2							12
1	2	3		5	7^1	12		9		11				13	4	8		10^2	6									13
1	3	14		2		7		9^3	13	11				12	4		10^2	8^1	6		5							14
1	2	3		5	12	6		9^1	10^2	11				13	4	8			7									15
1	2	3		5	13			9^2	10^1	11	7			12	4	8			6									16
1	3		12	2		7		9	8	11^3				14	4	13			6	10^2	5^1							17
1	2	3^1		5		7		9^2	10^3	11				12	4	8	14		6	13								18
	2	3		5^2		6	13	9	10^1	11				12	4	8			7			1						19
1	2	3^2		5				9	10		7^3	14		11^1	4	8		12	6	13								20
1	12	3^3		2				9	11		7			14	4^1	13		8	6	10^2	5							21
1			13	2		9^2		14	8		7			11		5	10^3		6				3	4^1	12			22
1			4^2	5		8^3		10	6		2	12		11^1		9		14	7				13	3				23
1	2			5		7	13	9	10^2					12		8			6				3	4		11^1		24
1	2			5		6		9	11					12		8			7				3	4		10^1		25
1	2		13	5		7	12	9	11^3					10^1		8		14	6				3^2	4				26
1	2^3			5		6	13	9	11	12						8^2			7	14			3	4			10^1	27
1	2			5		7^3	8	9^1	10	12				13				14	6				3	4			11^2	28
1	2			5	14	9		12	10^3	13	6^1					8			7				3	4			11^2	29
1	2		14		6^2	13	8	9	10	11						5			7	12			3^3	4^1				30
1	2		12	5		7		9	10^3	11^2						8			6	14			3	4^1			13	31
1	2		4^2	5		7	13	9		12						8			6	10^3			3			14	11^1	32
1	2		4^1	5		7	8	9	10^3	11^2					12				6	14			3				13	33
1	2			5		7	8	9	10^2	11^1					4				6	13			3			12		34
1	3			2		7	5	10^3	9						4			14	6	8^1				12		11^2	13	35
1	2				12■	8^1	9	14	10						4	5		6^3	7				3			13	11^2	36
1				5			13	9	10				7	12	4	8^2			6				3	2		11^1		37
1	2			5		14	8	9^2	10				7^3		4				6	13			3			11^1	12	38
1	2			5		9^2	8		10				7		4				6	13			3			11^1	12	39
1	2			5		7	8^2	9^3	10					12	4	14			6	13			3			11^1		40
1	2			5		7	8	9^3	10				14	13	4^1				6				3	12		11^2		41
1	2			5		9	8	13	10				7^2	14					6	12			3	4^1		11^3		42
1	2		4	5		7		9^2	10				13	12		8			6					3		11^1		43
1	2		13	5		7	8	9^3	10	12			14						6				3	4^1			11^2	44
1	2		4	5		7	8^2	9^1	10	14						13			6	12				3		11^3		45
1	2		12	5		7		9^2	10	13				14		8			6				3^1	4		11^3		46

FA Cup

First Round	Bradford C	(a)	1-1
Replay	Bradford C	(h)	3-0
(aet; match declared void)			
2nd Replay	Bradford C	(h)	2-1
Match replayed due to too many substitutes being played by Exeter C in the first replay.			
Second Round	Cambridge U	(a)	1-2

Carabao Cup

First Round	Wycombe W	(h)	0-0
(Wycombe W won 4-3 on penalties)			

Papa John's Trophy

Group E (S)	Chelsea U21	(h)	1-1
(Chelsea U21 won 4-3 on penalties)			
Group E (S)	Cheltenham T	(a)	2-2
(Exeter C won 3-2 on penalties)			
Group E (S)	Bristol R	(h)	5-3
Second Round	Portsmouth	(h)	2-3

FLEETWOOD TOWN

FOUNDATION

Originally formed in 1908 as Fleetwood FC, it was liquidated in 1976. Re-formed as Fleetwood Town in 1977, it folded again in 1996. Once again, it was re-formed a year later as Fleetwood Wanderers, but a sponsorship deal saw the club's name immediately changed to Fleetwood Freeport through the local retail outlet centre. This sponsorship ended in 2002, but since then local energy businessman Andy Pilley took charge and the club has risen through the non-league pyramid until finally achieving Football League status in 2012 as Fleetwood Town.

Highbury Stadium, Park Avenue, Fleetwood, Lancashire FY7 6TX.

Telephone: (01253) 775 080.

Ticket Office: (01253) 775 080.

Website: www.fleetwoodtownfc.com

Email: info@fleetwoodtownfc.com

Ground Capacity: 5,137.

Record Attendance: (Before 1997) 6,150 v Rochdale, FA Cup 1st rd, 13 November 1965; (Since 1997) 5,194 v York C, FL 2 Play-Off semi-final 2nd leg, 16 May 2014.

Pitch Measurements: 100.5m × 65m (110yd × 71yd).

Chairman: Andy Pilley.

Chief Executive: Steve Curwood.

Head Coach: Scott Brown.

Assistant Head Coach: Steven Whittaker.

Colours: Red shirts with white sleeves and red and black trim, white shorts with red and black trim, red socks with white and black trim.

Year Formed: 1908 (re-formed 1997).

Previous Names: 1908, Fleetwood FC; 1977, Fleetwood Town; 1997, Fleetwood Wanderers; 2002 Fleetwood Town.

Club Nicknames: 'The Trawlermen', 'The Cod Army'.

Grounds: 1908, North Euston Hotel; 1934, Memorial Park (now Highbury Stadium).

First Football League Game: 18 August 2012, FL 2, v Torquay U (h) D 0–0 – Davies; Beeley, Mawene, McNulty, Howell, Nicolson, Johnson, McGuire, Ball, Parkin, Mangan.

HONOURS

League Champions: Conference – 2011–12.

FA Cup: 3rd rd – 2012, 2017, 2018, 2019, 2020.

League Cup: 3rd rd – 2021.

League Trophy: 3rd rd – 2020.

FOOTBALL YEARBOOK FACT FILE

The legendary Manchester City and England goalkeeper Frank Swift began his senior career playing for Fleetwood Reserves in the West Lancashire League. Frank was an amateur player which meant no transfer fee could be paid when he made the switch, but City later donated £10 to Fleetwood in recognition of the move.

Record League Victory: 13–0 v Oldham T, North West Counties Div 2, 5 December 1998.

Record Defeat: 0–7 v Billingham T, FA Cup 1st qual rd, 15 September 2001.

Most League Points (3 for a win): 82, FL 1, 2016–17.

Most League Goals: 66, FL 2, 2013–14.

Highest League Scorer in Season: Ched Evans, 17, FL 1, 2018–19.

Most League Goals in Total Aggregate: Paddy Madden, 43, 2018–21.

Most League Goals in One Match: 3, Steven Schumacher v Newport Co, FL 2, 2 November 2013; 3, Paddy Madden v Burton Alb, FL 1, 19 October 2019.

Most Capped Player: Conor McLaughlin, 25 (43), Northern Ireland.

Most League Appearances: Alex Cairns, 209, 2016–22.

Youngest League Player: Barry Baggley, 17 years 26 days v Walsall, 9 March 2019.

Record Transfer Fee Received: £1,000,000 (rising to £1,700,000) from Leicester C for Jamie Vardy, May 2012; £1,000,000 from Bournemouth for James Hill, January 2022.

Record Transfer Fee Paid: £300,000 to Kidderminster H for Jamille Matt, January 2013; £300,000 to Huddersfield T for Kyle Dempsey, May 2017.

Football League Record: 2012 Promoted from Conference Premier; 2012–14 FL 2; 2014– FL 1.

MANAGERS

Alan Tinsley 1997
Mark Hughes 1998
Brian Wilson 1998–99
Mick Hoyle 1999–2001
Les Attwood 2001
Mark Hughes 2001
Alan Tinsley 2001–02
Mick Hoyle 2002–03
Tony Greenwood 2003–08
Micky Mellon 2008–12
Graham Alexander 2012–15
Steven Pressley 2015–16
Uwe Rosler 2016–18
John Sheridan 2018
Joey Barton 2018–21
Simon Grayson 2021
Stephen Crainey 2021–22
Scott Brown May 2022–

LATEST SEQUENCES

Longest Sequence of League Wins: 5, 1.2.2020 – 22.2.2020.

Longest Sequence of League Defeats: 6, 20.1.2018 – 20.2.2018.

Longest Sequence of League Draws: 4, 25.1.2022 – 8.2.2022.

Longest Sequence of Unbeaten League Matches: 18, 19.11.2016 – 4.3.2017.

Longest Sequence Without a League Win: 13, 22.1.2022 – 19.3.2022.

Successive Scoring Runs: 24 from 2.5.2016.

Successive Non-scoring Runs: 4 from 23.1.2021.

TEN YEAR LEAGUE RECORD

		P	*W*	*D*	*L*	*F*	*A*	*Pts*	*Pos*
2012-13	FL 2	46	15	15	16	55	57	60	13
2013-14	FL 2	46	22	10	14	66	52	76	4
2014-15	FL 1	46	17	12	17	49	52	63	10
2015-16	FL 1	46	12	15	19	52	56	51	19
2016-17	FL 1	46	23	13	10	64	43	82	4
2017-18	FL 1	46	16	9	21	59	68	57	14
2018-19	FL 1	46	16	13	17	58	52	61	11
2019-20	FL 1	35	16	12	7	51	38	60	6§
2020-21	FL 1	46	16	12	18	49	46	60	15
2021-22	FL 1	46	8	16	22	62	82	40	20

§Decided on points-per-game (1.71)

DID YOU KNOW ?

Centre-forward Tommy Ross scored more than 50 goals in each of his first three seasons with Fleetwood after signing from Lancaster in 1930. He continued to score regularly throughout his seven years with the Cod Army and in total netted over 350 goals for the club.

FLEETWOOD TOWN – SKY BET LEAGUE ONE 2021–22 LEAGUE RECORD

Match No.	Date	Venue	Opponents	Result		H/T Score	Lg Pos.	Goalscorers	Attendance
1	Aug 7	H	Portsmouth	L	0-1	0-0	22		4562
2	14	A	Lincoln C	L	1-2	1-0	22	Andrew ^{32}	8241
3	17	A	Sheffield W	L	0-1	0-1	22		21,130
4	21	H	Cheltenham T	W	3-2	1-1	19	Clarke ^{33}, Johnson, D ^{80}, Morris ^{90}	2392
5	28	A	Plymouth Arg	D	1-1	1-1	18	Camps ^{34}	10,453
6	Sept 11	A	Rotherham U	W	4-2	1-2	17	Morton ^{24}, Garner, G ^{54}, Andrew ^{61}, Camps ^{69}	8463
7	18	H	Sunderland	D	2-2	0-1	16	Morton ^{81}, Garner, G (pen) ^{90}	4250
8	25	A	Cambridge U	D	2-2	1-1	18	Hill ^{2}, Lane ^{76}	4429
9	28	A	Milton Keynes D	D	3-3	2-2	20	Garner, G 2 $^{12, 32}$, Batty ^{88}	6564
10	Oct 2	H	Charlton Ath	L	1-2	0-1	20	Andrew ^{51}	3197
11	16	H	Crewe Alex	W	3-0	0-0	19	Johnson, C ^{60}, Andrew ^{72}, Garner, G ^{90}	2917
12	19	H	Burton Alb	L	0-1	0-1	20		2226
13	23	A	Ipswich T	L	1-2	0-0	21	Morton ^{81}	20,099
14	30	H	Wycombe W	D	3-3	1-2	22	Andrew ^{5}, Garner, J ^{60}, Morris ^{64}	2657
15	Nov 2	H	Wigan Ath	L	2-3	1-0	22	Andrew ^{8}, Morton (pen) ^{52}	3246
16	20	H	Morecambe	L	1-2	0-1	22	Johnson, C ^{82}	3545
17	23	A	Oxford U	L	1-3	1-2	22	Matete ^{40}	5708
18	27	A	AFC Wimbledon	D	2-2	1-0	22	Garner, G ^{35}, Johnson, C ^{84}	7405
19	Dec 4	A	Accrington S	L	1-5	0-1	22	Biggins ^{57}	1901
20	7	H	Bolton W	W	3-0	1-0	21	Garner, G ^{6}, Biggins 2 $^{77, 79}$	3279
21	11	H	Gillingham	W	2-1	1-0	19	Biggins ^{38}, Clarke ^{65}	2313
22	18	A	Morecambe	D	0-0	0-0	18		4018
23	26	H	Shrewsbury T	L	0-3	0-0	19		2878
24	Jan 8	A	Doncaster R	W	1-0	0-0	20	Harrison ^{50}	5648
25	15	H	Rotherham U	W	1-0	0-0	19	Pilkington ^{90}	3385
26	22	A	Charlton Ath	L	0-2	0-0	20		21,811
27	25	H	Plymouth Arg	D	3-3	1-1	19	Lane ^{24}, Harrison ^{89}, Johnson, C ^{90}	2584
28	29	H	Cambridge U	D	1-1	0-0	19	Lane ^{72}	2515
29	Feb 5	A	Shrewsbury T	D	1-1	1-0	19	Pilkington ^{21}	5808
30	8	H	Milton Keynes D	D	1-1	0-1	19	Lane ^{51}	3227
31	12	A	Cheltenham T	L	0-2	0-2	19		3517
32	26	A	Portsmouth	D	3-3	3-1	19	Pilkington ^{7}, Biggins ^{15}, Lane ^{41}	15,224
33	Mar 1	A	Wigan Ath	L	0-2	0-2	19		8627
34	5	H	Ipswich T	L	0-2	0-0	19		4190
35	8	A	Sunderland	L	1-3	1-0	19	Harrison ^{28}	28,017
36	12	A	Burton Alb	L	2-3	1-0	19	Oshilaja (og) ^{18}, Butterworth ^{57}	2648
37	15	A	Wycombe W	L	0-1	0-0	19		3391
38	19	H	Doncaster R	D	0-0	0-0	19		3146
39	Apr 2	A	Crewe Alex	W	3-1	1-1	19	Macadam ^{18}, Pilkington ^{64}, Harrison ^{72}	3813
40	5	H	Lincoln C	D	1-1	1-0	19	Batty ^{31}	3341
41	9	H	Accrington S	L	1-2	1-0	19	Harrison ^{45}	2881
42	15	H	Oxford U	L	2-3	1-3	21	Harrison (pen) ^{39}, Hayes ^{53}	2589
43	18	A	Gillingham	D	0-0	0-0	21		8436
44	23	H	AFC Wimbledon	D	1-1	0-1	20	Garner, J ^{88}	5019
45	26	H	Sheffield W	L	2-3	2-1	20	Camps ^{18}, Garner, J ^{34}	3901
46	30	A	Bolton W	L	2-4	1-1	20	Baggley ^{17}, Garner, J ^{79}	16,886

Final League Position: 20

GOALSCORERS

League (62): Garner, G 7 (1 pen), Andrew 6, Harrison 6 (1 pen), Biggins 5, Lane 5, Garner, J 4, Johnson, C 4, Morton 4 (1 pen), Pilkington 4, Camps 3, Batty 2, Clarke 2, Morris 2, Baggley 1, Butterworth 1, Hayes 1, Hill 1, Johnson, D 1, Macadam 1, Matete 1, own goal 1.
FA Cup (1): Garner J 1.
Carabao Cup (1): own goal 1.
Papa John's Trophy (8): Morton 3, Edmondson 2, Garner G 1 (1 pen), Matete 1, McMillan 1.

Cairns A 42	Clarke T 35	Hill J 13	Andrew D 39	Halliday B 3	Biggins H 26 + 6	Rossiter J 10	Clark M 8 + 2	Morris S 13 + 13	Morton C 15 + 3	Garner G 23 + 5	Pilkington A 9 + 17	Batty D 23 + 7	Edmondson R 4 + 7	Matete J 18 + 2	Holgate H 5 + 1	Camps C 29 + 2	Johnson D 3	Johnson C 32 + 3	Lane P 30 + 7	Garner J 4 + 14	Conn-Clarke C — + 4	McLaughlin C 7 + 2	Johnston C 15 + 2	Hayes C 17 + 7	Baggley B 5 + 2	Boyle D 6 + 4	Harrison E 16 + 2	Jules Z 19 + 1	Nsiala A 18 + 2	Harrop J 3 + 2	Butterworth D 5 + 7	Macadam H 7 + 3	Thiam C — + 3	O'Hara K 4	Match No.
1	2	3	4	5	6^{2}	7	8^{3}	9	10	11^{1}	12	13	14																						1
1	3	2	4	5	13	7	8	9^{2}	11	10^{3}	14	12		6^{1}																					2
1	3	2^{1}	8	5	7	6		12	10^{2}	11	13		14		4	9^{3}																			3
1	3		5		8	7		6	12	14	11^{3}	13	10^{1}		4	9^{2}	2																		4
1	3		5		6	7		9^{3}	11^{2}	10	12		14	13	4	8^{1}	2																		5
1	3	2	9		6	7	12^{2}		11^{3}	10			14			8	4^{1}	5	13																6
1	3	2	4		6^{2}	7	8^{1}		11	10						9		5	13	12															7
1	3	2	4		6^{3}	7	8^{2}			10			11^{1}			9		5	13	12	14														8
1	4	3	5		9^{2}	6				11		13		7		10^{1}		2	8	12															9
1	4	3	5		9^{3}	6				11		12	14	7^{1}		10^{2}		2	8	13															10
1		3	4		5		9^{1}		13	10		6^{3}	11^{2}	8		7		2	12			14													11
1		3	4		5^{2}		9		12	11		8	10^{1}	7		6^{3}		2	13	14															12
1		3	4		8		5^{1}		10	11^{2}	12	6		7				9	13			2^{3}	14												13
1	3	4	9		7^{2}			13	11		10^{1}	6		8				5	14	12		2^{3}													14
1	3	2	4					12	11	13		8		6^{2}		7		5	9^{1}	10															15
1	3^{2}		5		14			6	10	11^{1}	13■	7		8^{3}	4			2	9	12															16
1	3^{3}		4		5		9^{2}	12	11	13		7		6	14			2	8	10^{1}															17
1	3		5^{2}		13			9^{3}	11	10		7	14	8	4^{1}			2	6			12													18
1	3		5		12			13	11	10^{1}		7■		8				2^{3}	6^{2}		14	4		9											19
1	3		5		6				11	10				7^{3}				12	8^{2}			4	2	9^{1}	13	14									20
1	3		5		9		14	6^{2}	10^{1}	11^{3}			13	8				12	7			4	2												21
1	3		5		9^{2}			6^{1}		11				8		13			7		12	4	2	10											22
1	3		5		9			13		11^{1}				8		7^{2}		14	6		12	4	2	10^{3}											23
1	3		5		9			13			12	8^{3}				7		4	6				2	10^{2}		14	11^{1}								24
1	3		5								13	7		14		8^{3}		6	11				2^{1}	9^{2}			10	4	12						25
1	3		5					12			13	7^{2}		6		8			9				2^{3}	11^{1}			10	4	14						26
1			5					14			13	7^{1}		6^{2}		8		2	9				11^{3}	12			10	4	3						27
1	3		5					9^{3}			13	6^{2}				7		2	8				12	14			10	4		11^{1}					28
1	4		6		14			13			10^{2}	8^{3}				9■		2	7								11	5	3^{1}		12				29
1	4		5		8			9^{1}			13	7						2	6								10		3		11^{2}	12			30
1			5		8^{1}						9^{2}	7^{3}						2	6					13		14	10	4	3		11	12			31
1	4		6		9						10^{1}					8			7^{3}	13			2		14		11^{2}	5	3		12				32
1	3		5		9^{2}			7								6		2		13■			8	12			11	4			10^{1}				33
1	3		9					14			10^{1}					7		5	6^{2}				8	12			11^{3}	4	2		13				34
1			5					7^{3}		12								2	9				10	13	8^{2}	6	11^{1}	4■	3				14		35
			5^{1}		12			7^{3}		11^{2}								4	9				2	10	8	6			3		13		14	1	36
					9													4	7	12			2^{2}	10	8	6		5	3		11^{1}		13	1	37
					9					12						13		4	7	14			2	10	8^{1}	6^{3}		5	3		11^{2}			1	38
1	3				7^{3}					11^{2}	12	14				6		5	8					10^{1}			13	4	2			9			39
1	3									10	13	7^{1}				6		5	8					11^{2}			12	4	2^{3}		14	9			40
1■	3									9^{2}	10^{1}	6				7		5	8					13			11^{3}	4	2		14	12			41
	3										12	7				8		5	9^{2}	14				11			10^{3}	4	2	13		6^{1}		1	42
1											12	7^{2}				8		4	6■	13				9^{3}		14	10	5	3	11^{1}		2			43
1			5					13			8	6				7				14				9			10^{1}	4	3	11^{2}	12^{3}	2			44
1	3		8								12	6^{1}				9				10				11		7		4^{2}	2	13		5			45
1	4^{2}		5					14			11	12				8				10				9	6^{1}	7^{3}		13	3			2			46

FA Cup

First Round	Burton Alb	(h)	1-2

Carabao Cup

First Round	Stoke C	(a)	1-2

Papa John's Trophy

Group G (N)	Leicester C U21	(h)	4-1
Group G (N)	Barrow	(a)	3-1
Group G (N)	Accrington S	(h)	1-4
Second Round	Bolton W	(a)	0-1

FOREST GREEN ROVERS

FOUNDATION

A football club was recorded at Forest Green as early as October 1889, established by Rev Edward Peach, a local Congregationalist minister. This club joined the Mid-Gloucestershire League for 1894–95 but disappeared around 1896 and was reformed as Forest Green Rovers in 1898. Rovers affiliated to the Gloucestershire county FA from 1899–1900 and competed in local leagues, mostly the Stroud & District and Dursley & District Leagues before joining the Gloucestershire Senior League North in 1937, where they remained until 1968. They became founder members of the Gloucestershire County League in 1968 and progressed to the Hellenic League in 1975. Success over Rainworth MW in the 1982 FA Vase final at Wembley was the start of the club's rise up the pyramid, firstly to the Southern League for the 1982–83 season and then the Football Conference from 1998–99. Rovers reached the play-offs in 2014–15 and 2015–16, losing to Bristol Rovers and Grimsby Town respectively, before finally achieving their goal of a place in the Football League with their 3-1 Play-Off victory over Tranmere Rovers on 14 May 2017.

The Fully Charged New Lawn Stadium, Another Way, Nailsworth, GL6 0FG.

Telephone: (01453) 834 860.

Ticket Office: (0333) 123 1889.

Website: fgr.co.uk

Email: reception@fgr.co.uk

Ground Capacity: 5,009.

Record Attendance: 4,836 v Derby Co, FA Cup 3rd rd, 3 January 2009.

Pitch Measurements: 100m × 66m (109.5yd × 72yd).

Chairman: Dale Vince.

Chief Executive: Henry Staelens.

Head Coach: Ian Burchnall.

Assistant Head Coach: Michael Doyle.

Colours: Green and black patterned shirts, green shorts with black patterned trim, green socks with black patterned trim.

Year Formed: 1889.

Previous Names: 1889, Forest Green; 1898, Forest Green Rovers; 1911, Nailsworth & Forest Green United; 1919 Forest Green Rovers; 1989, Stroud; 1992, Forest Green Rovers.

Club Nicknames: Rovers, The Green, FGR, The Little Club on the Hill, Green Army, The Green Devils.

HONOURS

League Champions: FL 2 – 2021–22.

FA Cup: 3rd rd – 2009, 2010.

League Cup: 2nd rd – 2018, 2020, 2022.

FA Trophy: *Runners-up:* 1998–99, 2000–01.

FA Vase: *Winners:* 1981–82.

FOOTBALL YEARBOOK FACT FILE

When Forest Green Rovers won the FA Vase in 1982, they defeated three former finalists of the competition on their way to Wembley with victories over Almondsbury Greenway, Willenhall Town and Blue Star. They overcame Rainworth Miners' Welfare in the final to take the trophy for the only time in their history.

Grounds: 1890, The Lawn Ground; 2006, The New Lawn (renamed The innocent New Lawn 2020; The Fully Charged New Lawn Stadium 2021).

First Football League Game: 5 August 2017, FL 2 v Barnet (h) D 2-2 – Collins B; Bennett, Collins L, Monthe, Evans (Bugiel), Laird, Traore (Mullings), Noble, Cooper, Brown (Marsh-Brown), Doidge (2).

Record Victory: 8–0 v Fareham T, Southern League Southern Division, 1996–97; 8–0 v Hyde U, Football Conference, 10 August 2013.

Record Defeat: 0–10 v Gloucester, Mid-Gloucestershire League, 13 January 1900.

Most League Points (3 for a win): 84, FL 2, 2021–22.

Most League Goals: 75, FL 2, 2021–22.

Highest League Scorer in Season: Christian Doidge, 20, FL 2, 2017–18.

Most League Goals in Total Aggregate: Jamille Matt, 35, 2020–22.

Most League Goals in One Match: 3, George Williams v Newport Co, FL 2, 26 December 2018; 3, Jamille Matt v Scunthorpe U, FL 2, 10 October 2020; 3, Nicky Cadden v Crawley T, FL 2, 21 August 2021.

Most Capped Player: Ebou Adams, 4 (11) Gambia.

Most League Appearances: Ebou Adams, 108, 2019–22.

Youngest League Player: Vaughan Covil, 16 years 159 days v Exeter C, 1 January 2020.

Record Transfer Fee Received: £500,000 from Barnsley for Ethan Pinnock, June 2017.

Record Transfer Fee Paid: £25,000 to Bury for Adrian Randall, August 1999.

Football League Record: 2017 Promoted from National League; 2017–22 FL 2; 2022– FL 1.

MANAGERS

Bill Thomas 1955–56
Eddie Cowley 1957–58
Don Cowley 1958–60
Jimmy Sewell 1966–67
Alan Morris 1967–68
Peter Goring 1968–79
Tony Morris 1979–80
Bob Mursell 1980–82
Roy Hillman 1982
Steve Millard 1983–87
John Evans 1987–90
Jeff Evans 1990
Bobby Jones 1990–91
Tim Harris 1991–92
Pat Casey 1992–94
Frank Gregan 1994–2000
Nigel Spink and David Norton 2000–01
Nigel Spink 2001–02
Colin Addison 2002–03
Tim Harris 2003–04
Alan Lewer 2004–05
Gary Owers 2005–06
Jim Harvey 2006–09
Dave Hockaday 2009–13
Adrian Pennock 2013–16
Mark Cooper 2016–21
Rob Edwards 2021–22
Ian Burchnall May 2022–

LATEST SEQUENCES

Longest Sequence of League Wins: 6, 1.5.2021 – 21.8.2021.

Longest Sequence of League Defeats: 5, 9.12.2017 – 1.1.2018.

Longest Sequence of League Draws: 4, 11.8.2018 – 25.8.2018.

Longest Sequence of Unbeaten League Matches: 19, 16.10.2021 – 12.2.2022.

Longest Sequence Without a League Win: 10, 26.8.2017 – 14.10.2017.

Successive Scoring Runs: 17 from 24.10.2020.

Successive Non-scoring Runs: 3 from 20.4.2021.

TEN YEAR LEAGUE RECORD

		P	W	D	L	F	A	Pts	Pos
2012-13	Conf	46	18	11	17	63	49	65	10
2013-14	Conf	46	19	10	17	80	66	67	10
2014-15	Conf	46	22	16	8	80	54	79*	5
2015-16	NL	46	26	11	9	69	42	89	2
2016-17	NL	46	25	11	10	88	56	86	3
2017-18	FL 2	46	13	8	25	54	77	47	21
2018-19	FL 2	46	20	14	12	68	47	74	5
2019-20	FL 2	36	13	10	13	43	40	49	10§
2020-21	FL 2	46	20	13	13	59	51	73	6
2021-22	FL 2	46	23	15	8	75	44	84	1

**3 pts deducted. §Decided on points-per-game (1.36)*

DID YOU KNOW ?

In July 1911 Rovers merged with local rivals Nailsworth and briefly played as Nailsworth and Forest Green United. In their first season under the new name the club won the first division of the Stroud and District League, losing just one game in the process.

FOREST GREEN ROVERS – SKY BET LEAGUE TWO 2021–22 LEAGUE RECORD

Match No.	*Date*	*Venue*	*Opponents*	*Result*		*H/T Score*	*Lg Pos.*	*Goalscorers*	*Attendance*
1	Aug 7	H	Sutton U	W	2-1	1-0	3	Stevens [30], Adams [90]	1883
2	14	A	Walsall	W	3-1	3-0	1	Stevens 2 (1 pen) [20, 45 (p)], Matt [43]	4310
3	17	A	Rochdale	W	2-1	1-0	1	Matt [33], Stevens [49]	2188
4	21	H	Crawley T	W	6-3	2-2	1	Cadden 3 [1, 67, 68], Stevens [24], Matt [48], Young [78]	1922
5	28	H	Port Vale	L	0-2	0-2	1		2402
6	Sept 4	A	Exeter C	D	0-0	0-0	2		4008
7	11	H	Northampton T	W	1-0	0-0	1	Matt [77]	2576
8	18	A	Stevenage	W	4-0	1-0	1	Wilson [2], Stevens [50], Matt [58], Young [81]	3111
9	25	H	Tranmere R	D	0-0	0-0	1		2356
10	Oct 2	A	Carlisle U	W	2-0	2-0	1	Matt [29], Cadden [32]	3963
11	9	H	Swindon T	L	0-2	0-0	1		3442
12	16	A	Scunthorpe U	W	2-0	0-0	1	Matt (pen) [60], Adams [65]	2140
13	19	A	Leyton Orient	D	1-1	0-0	1	Stevens [68]	4391
14	23	H	Salford C	W	3-1	1-1	1	Cadden [45], Wilson [71], Aitchison [90]	2245
15	30	A	Bradford C	D	1-1	0-1	1	Young [54]	14,873
16	Nov 20	A	Hartlepool U	W	3-1	3-0	1	Moore-Taylor [4], Matt [29], Stevens [45]	5612
17	23	H	Barrow	W	2-0	0-0	1	Stevens 2 [61, 83]	1842
18	27	H	Bristol R	W	2-0	1-0	1	Matt 2 (1 pen) [20, 77 (p)]	4128
19	Dec 7	A	Harrogate T	W	4-1	3-0	1	Aitchison [21], Cadden [26], Matt [45], Stevens [73]	1619
20	11	A	Oldham Ath	D	5-5	3-1	1	Aitchison [13], Matt 2 [27, 44], Stevens 2 [48, 63]	3621
21	Jan 1	H	Stevenage	W	2-0	0-0	1	March [57], Matt [64]	2454
22	4	H	Exeter C	D	0-0	0-0	1		2631
23	11	H	Colchester U	W	2-0	1-0	1	Matt [15], March [90]	1829
24	15	A	Northampton T	D	1-1	0-0	1	Stevens [69]	5415
25	22	H	Carlisle U	W	3-0	1-0	1	Feeney (og) [16], Stevens [52], Matt [77]	2864
26	29	A	Tranmere R	W	4-0	2-0	1	Stevens [6], Matt [42], Moore-Taylor [53], Hendry [70]	10,924
27	Feb 1	A	Port Vale	D	1-1	0-1	1	Stevens [80]	4508
28	5	H	Newport Co	W	2-0	1-0	1	Stevens 2 [33, 61]	3817
29	8	H	Rochdale	W	2-1	0-0	1	Aitchison [73], Stevens [86]	1923
30	12	A	Sutton U	D	1-1	0-1	1	Wilson [60]	3314
31	19	H	Walsall	L	0-1	0-1	1		3122
32	26	A	Crawley T	L	1-2	0-2	1	Bernard [80]	2086
33	Mar 1	A	Newport Co	D	1-1	0-1	1	Aitchison [55]	4448
34	5	A	Salford C	D	1-1	0-1	1	Stevens [53]	1987
35	12	H	Bradford C	L	0-2	0-0	1		3339
36	15	H	Leyton Orient	D	1-1	1-0	1	Stevens [10]	1891
37	21	A	Colchester U	W	1-0	1-0	1	Stevens [9]	6140
38	Apr 2	H	Scunthorpe U	W	1-0	0-0	1	Sweeney [75]	2484
39	5	H	Mansfield T	W	1-0	1-0	1	March [14]	2784
40	9	H	Hartlepool U	D	1-1	0-0	1	Hendry [53]	2484
41	15	A	Barrow	L	0-4	0-2	1		3098
42	18	H	Oldham Ath	W	2-0	2-0	1	Hendry [8], Matt [41]	3137
43	23	A	Bristol R	D	0-0	0-0	1		9690
44	26	A	Swindon T	L	1-2	0-2	1	March [69]	11,150
45	30	H	Harrogate T	L	1-3	1-1	2	Matt (pen) [45]	4040
46	May 7	A	Mansfield T	D	2-2	0-1	1	Adams [64], March [80]	7374

Final League Position: 1

GOALSCORERS

League (75): Stevens 23 (1 pen), Matt 19 (3 pens), Cadden 6, Aitchison 5, March 5, Adams 3, Hendry 3, Wilson 3, Young 3, Moore-Taylor 2, Bernard 1, Sweeney 1, own goal 1.
FA Cup (2): Aitchison 1, Stevens 1.
Carabao Cup (3): Aitchison 1, Hendry 1, Matt 1.
Papa John's Trophy (6): Stevens 3 (1 pen), March 1, Young 1, own goal 1.

McGee L 46	Godwin-Malife U 22 + 4	Moore-Taylor J 40	Bernard D 29 + 5	Wilson K 45	Hendry R 29 + 2	Stevenson B 39 + 2	Cadden N 44	Adams E 33 + 4	Stevens M 35 + 2	Matt J 46	Aitchison J 32 + 14	Sweeney D 20 + 16	Allen T 2 + 2	Young J 2 + 20	Cargill B 32 + 4	Diallo S 3 + 6	March J 7 + 28	McAteer K — + 9	*Match No.*
1	2	3	4	5	6	7	8^{2}	9	10^{1}	11	12	13							1
1	2		4	5	6	7	8^{2}	9	11^{1}	10^{3}	12	3	13	14					2
1	2^{3}		4	5	7	6	8^{2}	9	11^{1}	10	12	3	14		13				3
1			2	5	7^{2}	6	8	9	11^{1}	10^{3}	12	3		14	4	13			4
1			2	5	7	6^{2}			11	10	8	3	9^{1}	13	4		12		5
1		3		5	7	6	8		11^{1}	10^{2}	9	2		13	4		12		6
1		3	4	5	7	6	8		11^{1}	10	9	2					12		7
1		3	4	5	7^{3}	6	8	12	11^{2}	10	9^{1}	2		13		14			8
1		3	4	5	7	6^{3}	8	12	11^{2}	10	9^{1}	2		13			14		9
1		3	4	5	7^{3}	6	8	9	10^{2}	11	13	2^{1}			12		14		10
1		3	4	5	7	6	8		11^{3}	10	9^{1}	2^{2}		12	13		14		11
1		3	2	5	6^{2}	7	8	9	14	10^{3}	13			11^{1}	4		12		12
1		3	2	5	7^{2}	6	8	9	11^{1}	10	12			13	4				13
1	12	3^{1}	2	5	7^{2}	6	8	9	11^{3}	10	13				4		14		14
1	2		3	5	7^{1}	6	8	9	11^{2}	10	12			13	4				15
1		3	2	5		6	8	13	11^{1}	10^{2}	9			12	4	7^{3}	14		16
1	12	3	2	5^{1}	7^{2}	6	8	9	11^{3}	10	13	14			4				17
1	5■	3	2			6	8	7	11^{1}	10	9^{2}	12			4		13		18
1		3	2	5^{2}		6	8	7	11^{3}	10^{1}	9	13		14	4		12		19
1	12	3^{1}	2	5		7	8	6	11^{3}	10	9^{2}				4	13	14		20
1		3	2	5		12	8	6		11	9^{2}	14		13	4	7^{1}	10^{3}		21
1		3	2	5		6	8		12	10	9^{1}	13			4	7^{2}	11		22
1	2	3	4	5	7^{1}	6	8		11^{3}	10	9^{2}	12		13			14		23
1	2	3	4	5	13	6	8		11^{1}	10	9^{2}	7					12		24
1	2	3		5	7^{3}	6	8		11	10^{2}	12	13		9^{1}	4	14			25
1	2	3	12	5	7^{3}	6	8		11^{1}	10^{2}	9	13			4		14		26
1	2	3		5	7^{1}	6		12	11	10	9^{3}		8^{2}		4		14	13	27
1	2	3	14	5		6	8^{3}	7	11^{2}	10	9^{1}	13			4		12		28
1		3	2	5		6^{1}	8	7	11	10^{3}	9^{2}	14		13	4	12			29
1	2	3		5		6	8	7	11^{1}	10	9^{2}	13			4		12		30
1	2	3^{2}		5		7^{1}	8	6	11	10	9^{3}	13			4	12		14	31
1	2	3	4	5	7^{3}	6^{1}	8	9	11^{2}	10	12	14					13		32
1	2	3	4	5		12	8	6^{2}	11	10	9^{1}	7					13		33
1	2		4^{3}	5		6	8	7	11^{2}	10	9^{1}	3			14		13	12	34
1	2■	3		5			8	6	11^{3}	10	9^{1}	7^{2}		13	4		14	12	35
1		3		5	7^{1}	6	8	9	11^{2}	10	12	2			4		13		36
1		3		5		6	8	7	11^{1}	10	9	2			4		12		37
1		3		5		6^{3}	8	7	11^{1}	10	9^{2}	2		13	4		12	14	38
1		3	13	5	12	6^{1}	8	7		10	9^{2}	2			4		11		39
1		3		5	6		8	7		10^{1}	9^{2}	2		13	4		11	12	40
1	13	3	2^{3}	5	7		8	9		10	14	6^{2}		12	4^{1}		11		41
1	2	3	12	5	7		8^{2}	6		10	9^{1}	13			4		11		42
1	2	3	12	5	7	6	8^{2}	9		10^{1}	11^{3}				4		13	14	43
1	2	3		5	6	7^{2}	8	9		10^{1}	11			14	4^{3}		12	13	44
1	2	3^{1}		5	6^{2}		8	7		10	9	12		13	4^{3}		11	14	45
1	2	3	4	5	6^{1}	7	8	9		10	11						12		46

FA Cup

First Round	St Albans C	(a)	2-3

Carabao Cup

First Round	Bristol C	(h)	2-2
(Forest Green R won 6-5 on penalties)			
Second Round	Brentford	(a)	1-3

Papa John's Trophy

Group D (S)	Northampton T	(h)	1-1
(Northampton T won 4-2 on penalties)			
Group D (S)	Brighton & HA U21	(h)	2-2
(Forest Green R won 5-3 on penalties)			
Group D (S)	Walsall	(a)	2-0
Second Round	Chelsea U21	(h)	1-1
(Chelsea U21 won 4-1 on penalties)			

FULHAM

FOUNDATION

Churchgoers were responsible for the foundation of Fulham, which first saw the light of day as Fulham St Andrew's Church Sunday School FC in 1879. They won the West London Amateur Cup in 1887 and the championship of the West London League in its initial season of 1892–93. The name Fulham had been adopted in 1888.

Craven Cottage, Stevenage Road, London SW6 6HH.

Telephone: (0843) 208 1222.

Ticket Office: (0203) 871 0810.

Website: www.fulhamfc.com

Email: enquiries@fulhamfc.com

Ground Capacity: Temporarily 19,286.

Record Attendance: 49,335 v Millwall, Division 2, 8 October 1938.

Pitch Measurements: 100m × 65m (109.5yd × 71yd).

Chairman: Shahid Khan.

Chief Executive: Alistair Mackintosh.

Head Coach: Marco Silva.

Assistant Head Coach: Stuart Gray.

Colours: White shirts with thin black stripes, black shorts with white trim, white socks with black trim.

Year Formed: 1879.

Turned Professional: 1898.

Reformed: 1987.

Previous Name: 1879, Fulham St Andrew's; 1888, Fulham.

Club Nickname: 'The Cottagers'.

Grounds: 1879, Star Road, Fulham; c.1883, Eel Brook Common, 1884, Lillie Road; 1885, Putney Lower Common; 1886, Ranelagh House, Fulham; 1888, Barn Elms, Castelnau; 1889, Purser's Cross (Roskell's Field), Parsons Green Lane; 1891, Eel Brook Common; 1891, Half Moon, Putney; 1895, Captain James Field, West Brompton; 1896, Craven Cottage; 2002, Loftus Road (groundshare with QPR); 2004, Craven Cottage.

First Football League Game: 3 September 1907, Division 2, v Hull C (h) L 0–1 – Skene; Ross, Lindsay; Collins, Morrison, Goldie; Dalrymple, Freeman, Bevan, Hubbard, Threlfall.

Record League Victory: 10–1 v Ipswich T, Division 1, 26 December 1963 – Macedo; Cohen, Langley; Mullery (1), Keetch, Robson (1); Key, Cook (1), Leggat (4), Haynes, Howfield (3).

Record Cup Victory: 7–0 v Swansea C, FA Cup 1st rd, 11 November 1995 – Lange; Jupp (1), Herrera, Barkus (Brooker (1)), Moore, Angus, Thomas (1), Morgan, Brazil (Hamill), Conroy (3) (Bolt), Cusack (1).

Record Defeat: 0–10 v Liverpool, League Cup 2nd rd 1st leg, 23 September 1986.

HONOURS

League Champions: First Division – 2000–01; FL C – 2021–22; Division 2 – 1948–49; Second Division – 1998–99; Division 3S – 1931–32.
Runners-up: Division 2 – 1958–59; Division 3 – 1970–71; Third Division – 1996–97.

FA Cup: *Runners-up:* 1975.

League Cup: quarter-final – 1968, 1971, 2000, 2001, 2005.

European Competitions
UEFA Cup: 2002–03.
Europa League: 2009–10 *(runners-up)*, 2011–12.
Intertoto Cup: 2002 *(winners)*.

FOOTBALL YEARBOOK FACT FILE

Fulham mounted an effective campaign for promotion during 1921–22. However, in April 1922 record signing and leading scorer Barney Travers was alleged to have offered a South Shields defender a £20 bribe before a match. The Cottagers lost the game and an FA Commission banned Travers from the game for life shortly afterwards. Fulham went on to lose six of their last seven fixtures to finish in seventh position.

Most League Points (2 for a win): 60, Division 2, 1958–59 and Division 3, 1970–71.

Most League Points (3 for a win): 101, Division 2, 1998–99. 101, Division 1, 2000–01.

Most League Goals: 111, Division 3 (S), 1931–32.

Highest League Scorer in Season: Frank Newton, 43, Division 3 (S), 1931–32.

Most League Goals in Total Aggregate: Gordon Davies, 159, 1978–84, 1986–91.

Most League Goals in One Match: 5, Fred Harrison v Stockport Co, Division 2, 5 September 1908; 5, Bedford Jezzard v Hull C, Division 2, 8 October 1955; 5, Jimmy Hill v Doncaster R, Division 2, 15 March 1958; 5, Steve Earle v Halifax T, Division 3, 16 September 1969.

Most Capped Player: Johnny Haynes, 56, England.

Most League Appearances: Johnny Haynes, 594, 1952–70.

Youngest League Player: Harvey Elliott, 16 years 30 days v Wolverhampton W, 4 May 2019.

Record Transfer Fee Received: £25,000,000 from Tottenham H for Ryan Sessegnon, August 2019.

Record Transfer Fee Paid: £22,800,000 to Marseille for André-Frank Zambo Anguissa, August 2018.

Football League Record: 1907 Elected to Division 2; 1928–32 Division 3 (S); 1932–49 Division 2; 1949–52 Division 1; 1952–59 Division 2; 1959–68 Division 1; 1968–69 Division 2; 1969–71 Division 3; 1971–80 Division 2; 1980–82 Division 3; 1982–86 Division 2; 1986–92 Division 3; 1992–94 Division 2; 1994–97 Division 3; 1997–99 Division 2; 1999–2001 Division 1; 2001–14 Premier League; 2014–18 FL C; 2018–19 Premier League; 2019–20 FL C; 2020–21 Premier League; 2021–22 FL C; 2022– Premier League.

LATEST SEQUENCES

Longest Sequence of League Wins: 12, 7.5.2000 – 18.10.2000.

Longest Sequence of League Defeats: 11, 2.12.1961 – 24.2.1962.

Longest Sequence of League Draws: 6, 23.12.2006 – 20.1.2007.

Longest Sequence of Unbeaten League Matches: 23, 23.12.2017 – 27.4.2018.

Longest Sequence Without a League Win: 15, 25.2.1950 – 23.8.1950.

Successive Scoring Runs: 26 from 28.3.1931.

Successive Non-scoring Runs: 6 from 21.8.1971.

MANAGERS

Harry Bradshaw 1904–09
Phil Kelso 1909–24
Andy Ducat 1924–26
Joe Bradshaw 1926–29
Ned Liddell 1929–31
Jim McIntyre 1931–34
Jimmy Hogan 1934–35
Jack Peart 1935–48
Frank Osborne 1948–64
(was Secretary-Manager or General Manager for most of this period and Team Manager 1953–56)
Bill Dodgin Snr 1949–53
Duggie Livingstone 1956–58
Bedford Jezzard 1958–64
(General Manager for last two months)
Vic Buckingham 1965–68
Bobby Robson 1968
Bill Dodgin Jnr 1968–72
Alec Stock 1972–76
Bobby Campbell 1976–80
Malcolm Macdonald 1980–84
Ray Harford 1984–96
Ray Lewington 1986–90
Alan Dicks 1990–91
Don Mackay 1991–94
Ian Branfoot 1994–96
(continued as General Manager)
Micky Adams 1996–97
Ray Wilkins 1997–98
Kevin Keegan 1998–99
(Chief Operating Officer)
Paul Bracewell 1999–2000
Jean Tigana 2000–03
Chris Coleman 2003–07
Lawrie Sanchez 2007
Roy Hodgson 2007–10
Mark Hughes 2010–11
Martin Jol 2011–13
Rene Muelenstein 2013–14
Felix Magath 2014
Kit Symons 2014–15
Slavisa Jokanovic 2015–18
Claudio Ranieri 2018–19
Scott Parker 2019–21
Marco Silva July 2021–

TEN YEAR LEAGUE RECORD

		P	W	D	L	F	A	Pts	Pos
2012-13	PR Lge	38	11	10	17	50	60	43	12
2013-14	PR Lge	38	9	5	24	40	85	32	19
2014-15	FL C	46	14	10	22	62	83	52	17
2015-16	FL C	46	12	15	19	66	79	51	20
2016-17	FL C	46	22	14	10	85	57	80	6
2017-18	FL C	46	25	13	8	79	46	88	3
2018-19	PR Lge	38	7	5	26	34	81	26	19
2019-20	FL C	46	23	12	11	64	48	81	4
2020-21	PR Lge	38	5	13	20	27	53	28	18
2021-22	FL C	46	27	9	10	106	43	90	1

DID YOU KNOW ?

Fulham spent the period from July 2002 to the end of the 2003–04 season playing at Loftus Road, the home of near neighbours Queens Park Rangers, as their Craven Cottage ground was being refurbished. The move did not affect the club's form and in both seasons they finished in comfortable mid-table positions in the Premier League.

FULHAM – SKY BET CHAMPIONSHIP 2021–22 LEAGUE RECORD

Match No.	Date	Venue	Opponents	Result	H/T Score	Lg Pos.	Goalscorers	Attendance
1	Aug 8	H	Middlesbrough	D 1-1	1-0	9	Wilson [29]	16,058
2	14	A	Huddersfield T	W 5-1	3-1	1	Mitrovic [9], Onomah [37], Carvalho [42], Ivan Cavaleiro 2 [78, 90]	15,126
3	17	A	Millwall	W 2-1	2-0	1	Mitrovic [3], Carvalho [8]	12,700
4	21	H	Hull C	W 2-0	2-0	1	Mitrovic [22], Carvalho [34]	16,189
5	28	H	Stoke C	W 3-0	1-0	1	Wilson [5], Decordova-Reid [53], Mitrovic [72]	16,791
6	Sept 11	A	Blackpool	L 0-1	0-0	2		11,268
7	15	A	Birmingham C	W 4-1	2-0	1	Odoi [10], Mitrovic 2 (1 pen) [44 (p), 83], Wilson [54]	14,562
8	18	H	Reading	L 1-2	0-1	2	Rodrigo Muniz [86]	18,901
9	25	A	Bristol C	D 1-1	0-0	4	Mitrovic [50]	19,326
10	29	H	Swansea C	W 3-1	3-1	3	Mitrovic 3 [12, 32, 45]	16,113
11	Oct 2	A	Coventry C	L 1-4	1-0	5	McFadzean (og) [18]	18,497
12	16	H	QPR	W 4-1	1-0	3	Mitrovic 2 [10, 67], Decordova-Reid [71], Robinson [90]	18,371
13	20	H	Cardiff C	W 2-0	0-0	2	Cairney [57], Mitrovic [63]	15,789
14	24	A	Nottingham F	W 4-0	1-0	2	Spence (og) [7], Mitrovic 2 (1 pen) [58, 67 (p)], Kebano [61]	27,470
15	30	H	WBA	W 3-0	2-0	2	Mitrovic 3 (1 pen) [20 (p), 40, 82]	18,103
16	Nov 3	A	Blackburn R	W 7-0	2-0	2	Kebano 2 [6, 79], Mitrovic [19], Wilson 2 [54, 58], Rodrigo Muniz 2 [81, 90]	9326
17	6	A	Peterborough U	W 1-0	0-0	2	Mitrovic [74]	11,214
18	20	H	Barnsley	W 4-1	2-0	1	Mitrovic [24], Carvalho [34], Kebano [72], Wilson [81]	18,047
19	24	H	Derby Co	D 0-0	0-0	1		16,468
20	27	A	Preston NE	D 1-1	1-0	1	Ream [15]	9838
21	Dec 3	H	Bournemouth	D 1-1	0-0	1	Adarabioyo [84]	19,020
22	11	A	Luton T	D 1-1	1-0	1	Mitrovic [19]	9992
23	20	H	Sheffield U	L 0-1	0-1	1		17,308
24	Jan 11	A	Reading	W 7-0	2-0	2	Wilson 2 [13, 60], Mitrovic 2 (1 pen) [45 (p), 89], Tete [68], Kebano [70], Adarabioyo [75]	11,472
25	15	H	Bristol C	W 6-2	5-2	1	Mitrovic 3 [21, 41, 45], Kebano 2 [31, 57], Carvalho [36]	17,810
26	18	H	Birmingham C	W 6-2	4-1	1	Marc Roberts (og) [10], Kebano [35], Carvalho 2 [38, 75], Cairney [43], Robinson [90]	16,491
27	22	A	Stoke C	W 3-2	2-1	1	Rodrigo Muniz 2 [2, 33], Decordova-Reid [72]	21,749
28	29	H	Blackpool	D 1-1	1-0	1	Mitrovic [6]	19,092
29	Feb 8	H	Millwall	W 3-0	1-0	1	Mitrovic 2 [29, 50], Decordova-Reid [87]	16,606
30	12	A	Hull C	W 1-0	0-0	1	Mitrovic [57]	13,022
31	19	H	Huddersfield T	L 1-2	0-2	1	Decordova-Reid [82]	19,001
32	23	H	Peterborough U	W 2-1	1-0	1	Mitrovic 2 (1 pen) [28 (p), 62]	17,387
33	26	A	Cardiff C	W 1-0	1-0	1	Mitrovic [41]	18,928
34	Mar 5	H	Blackburn R	W 2-0	2-0	1	Kebano [25], Wilson [35]	19,343
35	8	A	Swansea C	W 5-1	0-0	1	Mitrovic [46], Cabango (og) [52], Decordova-Reid [73], Williams 2 [77, 85]	17,012
36	12	A	Barnsley	D 1-1	0-1	1	Wilson [86]	12,576
37	15	A	WBA	L 0-1	0-0	1		20,079
38	Apr 2	A	QPR	W 2-0	1-0	1	Mitrovic 2 (1 pen) [14, 78 (p)]	17,648
39	6	A	Middlesbrough	W 1-0	0-0	1	Mitrovic [73]	21,995
40	10	H	Coventry C	L 1-3	0-2	1	Decordova-Reid [82]	19,401
41	15	A	Derby Co	L 1-2	1-0	1	Carvalho [20]	23,773
42	19	H	Preston NE	W 3-0	3-0	1	Mitrovic 2 [9, 41], Carvalho [34]	17,760
43	23	A	Bournemouth	D 1-1	0-0	1	Mitrovic [56]	10,352
44	26	H	Nottingham F	L 0-1	0-1	1		19,218
45	May 2	H	Luton T	W 7-0	2-0	1	Cairney [29], Tete [39], Carvalho [54], Mitrovic 2 [62, 90], Decordova-Reid [65], Seri [79]	19,538
46	7	A	Sheffield U	L 0-4	0-3	1		30,813

Final League Position: 1

GOALSCORERS

League (106): Mitrovic 43 (6 pens), Carvalho 10, Wilson 10, Kebano 9, Decordova-Reid 8, Rodrigo Muniz 5, Cairney 3, Adarabioyo 2, Ivan Cavaleiro 2, Robinson 2, Tete 2, Williams 2, Odoi 1, Onomah 1, Ream 1, Seri 1, own goals 4.
FA Cup (2): Carvalho 1, Wilson 1.
Carabao Cup (2): Robinson 1, Stansfield 1.

Gazzaniga P 13	Tete K 15 + 5	Adarabioyo T 41	Ream T 46	Robinson A 33 + 3	Onomah J 8 + 12	Francois T 1 + 1	Wilson H 40 + 1	Carvalho F 33 + 3	Kebano N 31 + 9	Mitrovic A 44	Decordova-Reid B 26 + 15	Ivan Cavaleiro R 5 + 13	Kamara A — + 1	Seri J 26 + 7	Zambo A — + 3	Bryan J 13 + 2	Mawson A 1 + 5	Odoi D 17 + 1	Reed H 32 + 7	Quina D 1 + 1	Rodrigo Muniz C 2 + 23	Chalobah N 11 + 9	Rodak M 33	Cairney T 16 + 10	Stansfield J — + 1	Hector M 4	Knockaert A — + 4	Williams N 14	Match No.
1	2	3	4	5	6	7^{2}	8	9^{3}	10^{1}	11	12	13	14																1
1	2	3	4	5	6^{1}	14	8■	9^{2}		11	10	12		7^{3}	13														2
1	2	3	4	5	6^{1}			9	8^{3}	11		10^{2}		7	12	13	14												3
1	2^{2}	3	4^{1}	5	6			9^{3}	8	11	13	10		7	14		12												4
1		3	4	5	6		8^{3}	9^{2}	14	11	10^{1}	12		7				2	13										5
1		3	4	5	6^{2}				13	11	8	10		7				2^{3}	12	9^{1}	14								6
1		3	4				9^{3}			10	11^{2}	13		6		5	14	2	7^{1}	12		8							7
1		3	4	5	13		8		14	11	9^{1}	10		6^{2}				2^{3}			12	7							8
1		3	4	5	9^{2}		8		13	11	10^{3}	14		6				2	12			7^{1}							9
1		3	4				8^{3}		10	11^{2}	9	14		6		5^{1}	12	2	7		13								10
1			4	5	6^{1}		8		10^{3}	11	9^{2}	13		12			3	2	7		14								11
		3	4	13			9^{3}		8	11	12	10^{1}		6		5^{2}		2	7			14	1						12
		3	4	5			8^{3}		10	11^{2}	9			6				2	7^{1}		13		1	12	14				13
	13	3	4	5	12		8		10^{1}	11^{3}	9			6				2^{2}			14		1	7					14
		3■	4	5			8	12	10^{2}	11^{3}	9			6				2	7^{1}		14		1	13					15
			4	5			8	14	10	11^{2}	9^{3}			6^{1}				2	7		13		1	12		3			16
	12		4	5			8		10	11^{3}	9			6^{2}			14	2^{1}	7				1	13		3			17
	2		4	5^{3}	13		8	9	10	11				12		14			6^{2}				1	7^{1}		3			18
1	2	3	4	5	12		8^{2}	9	10					6					7^{1}		11						13		19
		3	4	5	12		8	9^{3}	10^{2}	11	13			6^{1}				2	7				1				14		20
		3	4				8	9^{2}	10	11	12			6^{1}		5		2	7				1	13					21
	2	3	4		13		9^{3}	12	11^{1}	10	6			7		5					14		1	8^{2}					22
	2	3	4	5^{3}			8	9^{2}	10	11	13			7^{1}					6		14		1	12					23
	2	3	4	5			8^{2}	9^{1}	10	11	12								7^{3}		13	14	1	6					24
	2	3	4	5			8	9	10^{1}	11^{3}	12								7		14	13	1	6^{2}					25
		3	4	5	14		8	9	10^{1}	11	12							2	7^{3}			13	1	6^{2}					26
	2^{1}	3	4	5				9	10^{2}		8^{3}							12	7		11	13	1	6			14		27
		3	4				8	9	10^{2}	11						5		2^{3}	7^{1}		12	13	1	6			14		28
		3	4	5			7	9	10^{2}	11^{3}	13								12		14	6	1	8^{1}				2	29
		3	4	5			8^{1}	9	10	11^{3}	13								12		14	7	1	6^{2}				2	30
		3	4	5			8^{3}	9	12	11	10	13							14			7^{2}	1	6^{1}				2	31
		3	4	5	14		12	9	10^{1}	11	8^{3}	13		7					6^{2}				1					2	32
	13	3	4		12		8	9		11	10^{3}	14				5			6^{1}			7	1					2^{2}	33
	13	3	4	5			8	9	10^{3}	11	14			7^{1}					6			12	1					2^{2}	34
		3	4	5			8	9^{1}	10^{2}	11	13	12		7^{3}					6				1	14				2	35
		3	4	5			8	9		11	10^{3}	13		7^{1}					6^{2}		14		1	12				2	36
		3	4	5			8	9		11	10^{2}	12							6^{1}		14	7	1	13				2^{3}	37
		3	4				8	9	13	11	10^{2}			14		5			6^{3}			12	1	7^{1}				2	38
	2	3	4	14	12		8	9	13	11	10^{1}					5^{3}			6			7^{2}	1						39
		3	4	5	14		8	9	10^{2}	11	12								6		13	7^{1}	1					2^{3}	40
		3	4				8^{1}	9	13	11	10			12		5			7		14		1	6^{2}				2^{3}	41
		3	4				8	9^{2}	10	11^{3}	13			12		5			7^{1}		14		1	6				2	42
	2	3	4	12			8	9	10	11				14		5^{1}			7^{2}			13	1	6^{3}					43
	13	3	4				8	9		11	10			7		5^{3}			6^{1}		14		1	12				2^{2}	44
	2	3	4	5			8	9^{2}	13	11	10			12					6^{1}		14		1	7^{3}					45
1	2		4	5	12			9	8	11^{2}	10			6^{3}					14		13	7^{1}				3			46

FA Cup

Third Round	Bristol C	(a)	1-0
(aet)			
Fourth Round	Manchester C	(a)	1-4

Carabao Cup

Second Round	Birmingham C	(a)	2-0
Third Round	Leeds U	(h)	0-0
(Leeds U won 6-5 on penalties)			

GILLINGHAM

FOUNDATION

The success of the pioneering Royal Engineers of Chatham excited the interest of the residents of the Medway Towns and led to the formation of many clubs including Excelsior. After winning the Kent Junior Cup and the Chatham District League in 1893, Excelsior decided to go for bigger things and it was at a meeting in the Napier Arms, Brompton, in 1893 that New Brompton FC came into being, buying and developing the ground which is now Priestfield Stadium. They changed their name to Gillingham in 1913, when they also changed their strip from black and white stripes to predominantly blue.

MEMS Priestfield Stadium, Redfern Avenue, Gillingham, Kent ME7 4DD.

Telephone: (01634) 300 000.

Ticket Office: (01634) 300 000 (option 1).

Website: www.gillinghamfootballclub.com

Email: enquries@priestfield.com

Ground Capacity: 11,582.

Record Attendance: 23,002 v QPR, FA Cup 3rd rd, 10 January 1948.

Pitch Measurements: 100.5m × 64m (110yd × 70yd).

Chairman: Paul Scally.

Manager: Neil Harris.

Assistant Manager: David Livermore.

Colours: Blue shirts with two thick black stripes and white trim, blue shorts with white and black trim, blue socks with white trim.

Year Formed: 1893.

Turned Professional: 1894.

Previous Name: 1893, New Brompton; 1913, Gillingham.

Club Nickname: 'The Gills'.

Ground: 1893, Priestfield Stadium (renamed KRBS Priestfield Stadium 2009; MEMS Priestfield Stadium 2011).

First Football League Game: 28 August 1920, Division 3, v Southampton (h) D 1–1 – Branfield; Robertson, Sissons; Battiste, Baxter, Wigmore; Holt, Hall, Gilbey (1), Roe, Gore.

Record League Victory: 10–0 v Chesterfield, Division 3, 5 September 1987 – Kite; Haylock, Pearce, Shipley (2) (Lillis), West, Greenall (1), Pritchard (2), Shearer (2), Lovell, Elsey (2), David Smith (1).

Record Cup Victory: 10–1 v Gorleston, FA Cup 1st rd, 16 November 1957 – Brodie; Parry, Hannaway; Riggs, Boswell, Laing; Payne, Fletcher (2), Saunders (5), Morgan (1), Clark (2).

Record Defeat: 2–9 v Nottingham F, Division 3 (S), 18 November 1950.

HONOURS

League Champions: FL 2 – 2012–13; Division 4 – 1963–64.
Runners-up: Third Division – 1995–96; Division 4 – 1973–74.

FA Cup: 6th rd – 2000.

League Cup: 4th rd – 1964, 1997.

FOOTBALL YEARBOOK FACT FILE

Gillingham began the 1987–88 season by failing to score in their opening two Football League games but then defeated Southend United 8-1 at the Priestfield Stadium. The following Saturday they faced a Chesterfield team which had not conceded a single goal in their first four League games. That run was shattered as the Gills set a new club record with a 10-0 victory.

Most League Points (2 for a win): 62, Division 4, 1973–74.

Most League Points (3 for a win): 85, Division 2, 1999–2000.

Most League Goals: 90, Division 4, 1973–74.

Highest League Scorer in Season: Ernie Morgan, 31, Division 3 (S), 1954–55; Brian Yeo, 31, Division 4, 1973–74.

Most League Goals in Total Aggregate: Brian Yeo, 135, 1963–75.

Most League Goals in One Match: 6, Fred Cheesmur v Merthyr T, Division 3 (S), 26 April 1930.

Most Capped Player: Andrew Crofts, 13 (includes 1 on loan from Brighton & HA) (29), Wales.

Most League Appearances: John Simpson, 571, 1957–72.

Youngest League Player: Luke Freeman, 15 years 247 days v Hartlepool U, 24 November 2007.

Record Transfer Fee Received: £1,500,000 from Manchester C for Robert Taylor, November 1999.

Record Transfer Fee Paid: £600,000 to Reading for Carl Asaba, August 1998.

Football League Record: 1920 Original Member of Division 3; 1921 Division 3 (S); 1938 Failed re-election; Southern League 1938–44; Kent League 1944–46; Southern League 1946–50; 1950 Re-elected to Division 3 (S); 1958–64 Division 4; 1964–71 Division 3; 1971–74 Division 4; 1974–89 Division 3; 1989–92 Division 4; 1992–96; Division 3; 1996–2000 Division 2; 2000–04 Division 1; 2004–05 FL C; 2005–08 FL 1; 2008–09 FL 2; 2009–10 FL 1; 2010–13 FL 2; 2013–22 FL 1; 2022– FL 2.

LATEST SEQUENCES

Longest Sequence of League Wins: 7, 18.12.1954 – 29.1.1955.

Longest Sequence of League Defeats: 10, 20.9.1988 – 5.11.1988.

Longest Sequence of League Draws: 5, 21.1.2017 – 14.2.2017.

Longest Sequence of Unbeaten League Matches: 20, 13.10.1973 – 10.2.1974.

Longest Sequence Without a League Win: 15, 1.4.1972 – 2.9.1972.

Successive Scoring Runs: 20 from 31.10.1959.

Successive Non-scoring Runs: 6 from 11.2.1961.

MANAGERS

W. Ironside Groombridge 1896–1906 *(Secretary-Manager) (previously Financial Secretary)*
Steve Smith 1906–08
W. I. Groombridge 1908–19 *(Secretary-Manager)*
George Collins 1919–20
John McMillan 1920–23
Harry Curtis 1923–26
Albert Hoskins 1926–29
Dick Hendrie 1929–31
Fred Mavin 1932–37
Alan Ure 1937–38
Bill Harvey 1938–39
Archie Clark 1939–58
Harry Barratt 1958–62
Freddie Cox 1962–65
Basil Hayward 1966–71
Andy Nelson 1971–74
Len Ashurst 1974–75
Gerry Summers 1975–81
Keith Peacock 1981–87
Paul Taylor 1988
Keith Burkinshaw 1988–89
Damien Richardson 1989–92
Glenn Roeder 1992–93
Mike Flanagan 1993–95
Neil Smillie 1995
Tony Pulis 1995–99
Peter Taylor 1999–2000
Andy Hessenthaler 2000–04
Stan Ternent 2004–05
Neale Cooper 2005
Ronnie Jepson 2005–07
Mark Stimson 2007–10
Andy Hessenthaler 2010–12
Martin Allen 2012–13
Peter Taylor 2013–14
Justin Edinburgh 2015–17
Adrian Pennock 2017
Steve Lovell 2017–19
Steve Evans 2019–22
Neil Harris January 2022–

TEN YEAR LEAGUE RECORD

		P	*W*	*D*	*L*	*F*	*A*	*Pts*	*Pos*
2012-13	FL 2	46	23	14	9	66	39	83	1
2013-14	FL 1	46	15	8	23	60	79	53	17
2014-15	FL 1	46	16	14	16	65	66	62	12
2015-16	FL 1	46	19	12	15	71	56	69	9
2016-17	FL 1	46	12	14	20	59	79	50	20
2017-18	FL 1	46	13	17	16	50	55	56	17
2018-19	FL 1	46	15	10	21	61	72	55	13
2019-20	FL 1	35	12	15	8	42	34	51	10§
2020-21	FL 1	46	19	10	17	63	60	67	10
2021-22	FL 1	46	8	16	22	35	69	40	21

§Decided on points-per-game (1.46)

DID YOU KNOW ?

Midfielder Paul Smith was voted Gillingham's Player of the Season on four occasions between 1998 and 2005, the only player to achieve this feat. Smith made almost 400 first-team appearances for the Gills during his time at Priestfield Stadium before leaving to play for Walsall.

GILLINGHAM – SKY BET LEAGUE ONE 2021–22 LEAGUE RECORD

Match No.	Date	Venue	Opponents	Result		H/T Score	Lg Pos.	Goalscorers	Attendance
1	Aug 7	H	Lincoln C	D	1-1	1-1	11	Lloyd 44	4837
2	14	A	Plymouth Arg	L	0-1	0-0	19		10,854
3	17	A	AFC Wimbledon	D	1-1	0-0	18	Kalambayi (og) 90	7027
4	21	H	Morecambe	W	2-1	1-1	15	Carayol 4, Oliver (pen) 79	3789
5	28	A	Shrewsbury T	L	1-2	1-0	16	Tucker 12	4625
6	Sept 11	A	Burton Alb	D	1-1	1-0	19	Oliver 18	2555
7	18	H	Milton Keynes D	L	1-4	1-2	20	Oliver 20	4119
8	21	H	Charlton Ath	D	1-1	0-1	19	Purrington (og) 56	7301
9	25	A	Oxford U	D	1-1	1-1	19	MacDonald 30	6664
10	28	A	Cambridge U	W	2-0	1-0	18	Oliver 26, Lloyd 60	4019
11	Oct 2	H	Wigan Ath	L	0-2	0-0	18		4503
12	9	A	Wycombe W	L	0-2	0-2	19		4992
13	16	H	Sunderland	L	1-2	1-1	20	Lloyd (pen) 24	6310
14	19	H	Doncaster R	W	1-0	0-0	19	Oliver 79	3713
15	23	A	Bolton W	D	2-2	2-0	19	Akinde 11, Dempsey 14	13,807
16	30	H	Accrington S	D	0-0	0-0	18		3609
17	Nov 13	A	Sheffield W	D	1-1	1-0	19	Oliver 22	20,593
18	20	A	Crewe Alex	L	0-2	0-1	20		4047
19	23	H	Cheltenham T	L	0-2	0-1	20		3115
20	27	H	Portsmouth	L	0-1	0-0	21		5637
21	Dec 7	A	Rotherham U	L	1-5	1-2	22	Lee 5	8008
22	11	A	Fleetwood T	L	1-2	0-1	22	McKenzie 74	2313
23	Jan 1	A	Milton Keynes D	D	0-0	0-0	22		7891
24	8	H	Ipswich T	L	0-4	0-3	22		6401
25	15	H	Burton Alb	L	1-3	1-0	23	McKenzie 3	4198
26	22	A	Wigan Ath	L	2-3	0-2	24	Reeves 53, O'Keefe 70	9359
27	25	H	Shrewsbury T	D	0-0	0-0	23		3213
28	29	H	Oxford U	L	2-7	0-3	23	Lloyd 62, McKenzie 85	4985
29	Feb 1	H	Crewe Alex	W	1-0	1-0	23	Lloyd (pen) 16	4917
30	5	A	Ipswich T	L	0-1	0-0	23		20,698
31	8	H	Cambridge U	W	1-0	0-0	22	Oliver 86	3824
32	12	A	Morecambe	D	1-1	0-0	22	Jackson 72	4499
33	19	H	Plymouth Arg	L	0-2	0-0	22		5197
34	22	H	AFC Wimbledon	D	0-0	0-0	23		4151
35	26	A	Lincoln C	W	2-0	0-0	22	Oliver 75, Thompson 90	8208
36	Mar 5	H	Bolton W	L	0-3	0-1	22		5109
37	12	A	Doncaster R	W	1-0	1-0	21	Kelman 1	6920
38	15	A	Charlton Ath	L	0-1	0-1	21		9728
39	19	H	Sheffield W	D	0-0	0-0	20		7433
40	26	A	Accrington S	W	2-1	0-0	19	Kelman 64, Oliver 73	2764
41	Apr 2	A	Sunderland	L	0-1	0-0	20		31,619
42	9	H	Wycombe W	D	1-1	0-1	21	Tucker 75	4858
43	15	A	Cheltenham T	D	2-2	1-1	20	Oliver 14, Reeves 59	4415
44	18	H	Fleetwood T	D	0-0	0-0	20		8436
45	23	A	Portsmouth	L	1-3	1-2	21	Jackson 29	15,540
46	30	H	Rotherham U	L	0-2	0-1	21		8542

Final League Position: 21

GOALSCORERS

League (35): Oliver 10 (1 pen), Lloyd 5 (2 pens), McKenzie 3, Jackson 2, Kelman 2, Reeves 2, Tucker 2, Akinde 1, Carayol 1, Dempsey 1, Lee 1, MacDonald 1, O'Keefe 1, Thompson 1, own goals 2.
FA Cup (1): Sithole 1.
Carabao Cup (3): Oliver 1, Phillips 1, Sithole 1.
Papa John's Trophy (1): McKenzie 1.

Cumming J 22	Bennett R 13 + 4	Ehmer M 45	Tucker J 44	Tutonda D 21 + 8	O'Keefe S 36 + 2	Philips D 13 + 11	Dempsey K 21	Lee O 29 + 3	Lloyd D 19 + 8	Oliver V 38 + 1	Carayol M 16 + 6	Reeves B 7 + 13	Sithole G 2 + 13	Jackson R 30 + 4	Akinde J 13 + 5	McKenzie R 37 + 1	Lintott H 2 + 4	Adshead D 11 + 4	MacDonald A 7	Kelman C 16 + 7	Akehurst B 2 + 3	Gbode J — + 2	Gale S — + 1	Chapman A 18	Dickson-Peters T 2 + 7	Dahlberg P 6	Masterson C 18	Thompson B 17	Chambers J 1 + 1	Match No.
1	2	3	4	5	6^{3}	7	8	9^{2}	10^{1}	11	12	13	14																	1
1	14	3	4	5	7^{2}	8	6	13	12	11	9			2^{3}	10^{1}															2
1	14	3	4	5■	6		9	10	7^{1}	11	13	8^{3}				2^{2}	12													3
1		3	4		7		9	13	12	11	10	8^{2}		2		5		6^{1}												4
1	3^{3}	4	5	12		7■	8		14	10	11	13		2^{1}		6		9^{2}												5
1		3	4	5	13		8		14	11^{3}	9				12	2		6^{2}	7	10^{1}										6
1	13	3	4	5^{2}	6■		7			11		12	14			2		9^{3}	8	10^{1}										7
1	2^{3}	3	4	14			7	9	13	10			12			5		6^{1}	8	11^{2}										8
1	2	3	4				7	8^{2}	11	10			9^{1}		12	5		13	6											9
1	4	3		5			8		9	11^{1}					10	2		6	7	12										10
1	4	3		5			9		8	11			12		10^{1}	2		6	7											11
1	13	3	4	5^{2}	12		7		9	10					11	2		6^{1}	8											12
1	6^{2}	4^{3}	3		9		8		7	11	10^{1}		14	2	12	5				13										13
1	3	4^{2}	6		9		8	14	7^{3}	11	10^{1}			2	12	5		13												14
1	4	3	6		8		7		9^{2}	11			13	2	10^{1}	5		12												15
1	3	4	6		7^{1}		9		8	11	12			2	10	5														16
1		4	3		7	6	9^{3}		8	10^{1}		14	12	2	11			13			5^{2}									17
1		4	3		6	7					13		10	2	11	9^{3}	12	8^{2}			5^{1}	14								18
1		4	3			7^{3}		9^{2}			10^{1}		12	2	11	5	8	6				13	14							19
1		4	3		6			9	8		10^{2}		13	2	11	5		7^{1}			12									20
		3^{1}	5		8	9^{3}		7	6		10		13	2■	11^{2}	4	12				14			1						21
	4		3	12	7	6^{1}		9	8^{2}		10		13		11	5	2							1						22
1	3	4	7	12	9	6			8^{2}	11^{1}	10	13		2		5														23
1	4	3	8	5^{1}	6	7■			13	11	9^{2}			2		10									12					24
		4	3	13	6^{1}		7	9	12	10	14	8^{3}		2		5^{2}				11						1				25
		4	3		8		9	6	7^{1}	11	10^{2}	13^{3}		2	14	5				12						1				26
		3	4		6	8^{2}	7	9	13					2	10^{1}	5				11					12	1				27
		3	4		8	12	7	6^{1}	9		11^{2}		13	2		5				10						1				28
		3	4	8	6	13		7	9^{3}	12	11^{1}			14		5				10^{2}				1			2			29
		3^{3}	4	8	6	14		7	11^{1}	10						5				12				1	13		2	9^{2}		30
		3	2	8^{2}	6	14		9		10^{3}				13		5				11^{1}				1	12		4	7		31
		3	4	8^{1}	7	13		6^{2}		11				12		5				14				1	10^{3}		2	9		32
		3	4	8^{1}	6			7^{2}		10		13		12		5								1	11		2	9		33
		3	4		6	13		9^{2}		11		10^{1}		5		8				12				1			2	7		34
		3	2		10	6		7^{1}		11		12		5		8								1			4	9		35
		3	2		6	7■				11^{2}	9^{1}	12		5		8				13				1			4	10		36
		3	2	12	6			7		11				5^{1}		8				10^{2}						1	4	9	13	37
		3	2	8^{2}	6			7		10						5^{1}	12			11					13	1	4	9		38
		3	2	9	6			7		10				5						11				1			4	8		39
		3	4	8	6^{1}	12		7		10		13		5						11^{2}				1			2	9		40
		3	2	9				7		11		12		5						10^{2}	13			1			4	8	6^{1}	41
		3	2	8^{1}	6^{3}			7		11		13		5		12				10				1	14		4^{2}	9		42
		4	3	13		12		9^{1}		10		8^{2}		2		6				11				1			5	7		43
		4	3	13	9^{1}	14		7		11		12		2		6^{2}				10■				1			5^{3}	8		44
		4	5	6^{2}	8^{1}	12		9		11		10		2										1	13		3	7		45
		4	3	6^{3}	8	13		9^{1}		11	12	7	14	2										1			5^{2}	10		46

FA Cup

First Round	Cheltenham T	(h)	1-1
Replay	Cheltenham T	(a)	0-1

Carabao Cup

First Round	Crawley T	(a)	2-2
(Gillingham won 10-9 on penalties)			
Second Round	Cheltenham T	(h)	1-1
(Cheltenham T won 5-4 on penalties)			

Papa John's Trophy

Group A (S)	Colchester U	(a)	1-0
Group A (S)	Ipswich T	(h)	0-2
Group A (S)	West Ham U U21	(h)	0-2

HARROGATE TOWN

FOUNDATION

An earlier club, Harrogate AFC, was formed in 1914, but did not start the 1914–15 season and was reformed in 1919. They competed in the Midland, Yorkshire and Northern Leagues before folding in 1932. The current club was established in the summer of 1935 as Harrogate Hotspurs, several of the players having previously played for Harrogate YMCA. Harry Lunn, the club's first secretary, had previously been secretary of the YMCA team. Hotspurs began life in the Harrogate & District League in 1935–36 when they finished in fourth position, gaining their first trophy when they won the Harrogate Charity Cup. By 1948 they had reached the West Yorkshire League and they changed their name to Harrogate Town to reflect their status as the town's leading club.

The EnviroVent Stadium, Wetherby Road, Harrogate HG2 7SA.

Telephone: (01423) 210 600.

Ticket Office: (01423) 210 600.

Website: harrogatetownafc.com

Email: enquiries@harrogatetownafc.com

Ground Capacity: 5,021.

Record Attendance: 4,280 v Harrogate Railway Ath, Whitworth Cup Final, May 1950.

Pitch Measurements: 100m × 66m (109.5yd × 72yd).

Chairman: Irving Weaver.

Vice-Chairman: Howard Matthews.

Chief Executive: Sarah Barry.

Manager: Simon Weaver.

Assistant Manager: Paul Thirlwell.

Colours: Yellow shirts with black trim, black shorts, black socks with yellow trim.

Year Formed: 1914. ***Turned Professional:*** 2017.

Previous Names: 1914, Harrogate AFC; 1935, Harrogate Hotspurs; 1948, Harrogate Town.

Club Nickname: 'Town', 'Sulphurites'.

Grounds: 1919, Starbeck Lane; 1920, Wetherby Lane; 1935, Christ Church Stray; 1937, Old Showground; 1946, Wetherby Road (renamed The EnviroVent Stadium 2020).

First League Game: (As Harrogate AFC) 30 August 1919, West Riding League v Horsforth (h) (at Starbeck Lane) W 1–0 – Middleton; Deans, Bell, Goodall, Carroll, Jenkinson, H (Capt), Day, O'Rourke, Priestley, Craven (1), Codd.

HONOURS

League: National League (2nd) promoted to FL 2 via play-offs – 2019–20.

FA Cup: 3rd rd – 2021–22.

League Cup: 2nd rd – 2021.

FA Trophy Winners: 2019–20 (final played in 2021).

FOOTBALL YEARBOOK FACT FILE

Harrogate Town made a tremendous start to the 2007–08 campaign, winning 11 and drawing two of their first 13 Conference North fixtures. They also reached the fourth qualifying round of the FA Cup where they were drawn away to local rivals Harrogate Railway Athletic. Town went down to a 2-1 defeat and thereafter their league form slumped, as they finished the season in sixth place, well short of promotion.

First Football League Game: 12 September 2020, FL 2 v Southend U (a) W 4–0 – Cracknell; Fallowfield, Falkingham, Smith, Burrell, Thomson, Beck (Stead 58), Martin (1) (Walker 75), Kerry (1), Muldoon (2), Hall.

Record League Victory: 6–1 v Scunthorpe U (h), FL 2, 9 October 2021 – Oxley; Fallowfield, Smith, Hall, Burrell, Thomson, Falkingham (Kerry), Pattison (2) (Power), Diamond (1), Muldoon (2) (Orsi-Dadomo (1 pen)), Armstrong.

Record Cup Victory: 11–2 v Yeadon Celtic, West Riding County Challenge Cup, 5 November 1938 – McLaren; Hebblethwaite, Keogan, Atha, Harker, Clelland, Annakin (4), Sibson, Stanley (7), Everitt C, Richardson.

Record Defeat: 1–10, v Methley U (h), West Yorkshire League Division One, 20 August 1956.

Most League Points in a Season (3 for a win): 57, FL 2, 2020–21.

Most League Goals in a Season: 64, FL 2, 2021–22.

Highest League Scorer in Season: Jack Muldoon, 15, FL 2, 2020–21.

Most League Goals in Total Aggregate: Jack Muldoon, 27, 2020–22.

Most League Goals in One Match: 3, Brendan Kiernan v Cambridge U, FL 2, 30 April 2021; 3, Jack Muldoon v Oldham Ath, FL 2, 22 January 2022.

Most League Appearances: George Thomson, 92, 2020–22.

Youngest League Player: Emmanuel Ilesanmi, 17 years 136 days v Colchester U, 2 April 2022.

Football League Record: 2020 Promoted from National League; 2020– FL 2.

LATEST SEQUENCES

Longest Sequence of League Wins: 3, 7.8.2021 – 24.8.2021.

Longest Sequence of League Defeats: 4, 2.4.2022 – 18.4.2022.

Longest Sequence of League Draws: 2, 26.2.2022 – 1.3.2022.

Longest Sequence of Unbeaten League Matches: 6, 7.8.2021 – 10.9.2021.

Longest Sequence Without a League Win: 7, 26.2.2022 – 22.3.2022.

Successive Scoring Runs: 9 from 24.4.2021.

Successive Non-scoring Runs: 4 from 20.3.2021.

MANAGERS

Tommy Codd 1919–20
J. C. Field 1920–21
Jimmy Dyer 1921–23
Mr Gill 1923–24
Mr Sixton 1924–29
C. Edwards 1929–30
Selection Committee 1930–31
Tom Bell 1931–32
Eddie Smith 1935–46
Selection Committee 1946–50
Walter Cook 1950–53
Bernard Cross 1953–55
Jack (Boss) Townrow 1955–67
Selection Committee 1967–69
Stan Hall 1969–70
Thomas (Chick) Farr 1970–71
Peter Gunby 1971–77
Alan Milburn 1977–78
Reg Taylor 1978–79
Alan Smith 1979–88
Denis Metcalf 1988–89
Alan Smith 1989–90
John Reed 1990–91
Alan Smith 1991–93
Mick Doig and John Deacey 1993
Frank Gray 1994
John Deacey then Alan Smith 1994–96
Mick Doig 1996–97
Paul Marshall 1997–98
Gavin Liddle 1998–99
Alan Smith (caretaker) 1999
Paul Ward 1999
Dave Fell 1999–2000
Mick Hennigan 2000–01
John Reed 2001–05
Neil Aspin 2005–09
Simon Weaver 2009–

TEN YEAR LEAGUE RECORD

		P	W	D	L	F	A	Pts	Pos
2012-13	NLN	42	20	9	13	72	50	69	6
2013-14	NLN	42	19	9	14	75	59	63*	9
2014-15	NLN	42	14	10	18	50	62	52	15
2015-16	NLN	42	21	9	12	73	46	72	4
2016-17	NLN	42	16	11	15	71	63	59	11
2017-18	NLN	42	26	7	9	100	49	85	2
2018-19	NL	46	21	11	14	78	57	74	6
2019-20	NL	37	19	9	9	61	44	66	2§
2020-21	FL 2	46	16	9	21	52	61	57	17
2021-22	FL 2	46	14	11	21	64	75	53	19

**3 pts deducted. §Decided on points-per-game (1.78).*

DID YOU KNOW ?

When Harrogate Town were promoted to the EFL for the 2020–21 season, they were required to remove the 3G playing surface that had been in place for the previous four seasons and install a turf pitch. As a result the club played their first three home games of the season at Doncaster Rovers' Keepmoat Stadium, finally making their EFL debut at Wetherby Road against Barrow on 17 October.

HARROGATE TOWN – SKY BET LEAGUE TWO 2021–22 LEAGUE RECORD

Match No.	*Date*	*Venue*	*Opponents*	*Result*		*H/T Score*	*Lg Pos.*	*Goalscorers*	*Attendance*
1	Aug 7	H	Rochdale	W	3-2	2-1	2	Armstrong [5], Pattison [10], Burrell [90]	1841
2	21	H	Barrow	W	2-1	0-1	6	Pattison 2 [60, 81]	1564
3	24	A	Leyton Orient	W	2-0	2-0	3	Armstrong 2 [8, 31]	3942
4	28	H	Exeter C	D	1-1	1-0	2	Muldoon (pen) [43]	1883
5	Sept 4	A	Mansfield T	W	3-1	2-1	1	Armstrong [5], Muldoon [45], Thomson [81]	4599
6	10	H	Newport Co	D	2-2	2-2	1	Muldoon [34], Armstrong [43]	2670
7	18	A	Port Vale	L	0-2	0-1	3		5435
8	21	A	Crawley T	D	2-2	1-2	3	Armstrong [2], Davies (og) [52]	1791
9	25	H	Stevenage	D	0-0	0-0	3		1667
10	Oct 2	A	Oldham Ath	W	2-1	1-0	2	Diamond [29], Armstrong [66]	3729
11	9	H	Scunthorpe U	W	6-1	5-0	2	Muldoon 2 [8, 45], Pattison 2 [14, 30], Diamond [16], Orsi-Dadomo (pen) [83]	3180
12	16	A	Colchester U	L	0-1	0-0	2		2439
13	19	H	Tranmere R	D	2-2	1-1	2	Muldoon (pen) [39], Armstrong [51]	2573
14	23	A	Hartlepool U	L	2-3	2-0	5	Thomson [28], Byrne (og) [35]	5807
15	30	H	Bristol R	L	0-1	0-0	7		2614
16	Nov 13	A	Walsall	W	3-1	1-0	5	Power [20], Diamond [61], Armstrong [82]	4651
17	20	H	Salford C	L	0-2	0-1	7		2814
18	23	A	Carlisle U	W	2-0	1-0	6	Thomson [45], Pattison [78]	3172
19	27	A	Swindon T	D	1-1	1-0	7	Diamond [24]	8199
20	Dec 7	H	Forest Green R	L	1-4	0-3	9	Kerry [57]	1619
21	11	H	Northampton T	L	1-2	1-1	10	Diamond [23]	2166
22	18	A	Sutton U	L	0-1	0-1	10		2720
23	Jan 15	A	Newport Co	L	0-4	0-2	14		0
24	22	H	Oldham Ath	W	3-0	1-0	11	Muldoon 3 [17, 73, 89]	2689
25	29	A	Stevenage	L	0-3	0-2	14		2935
26	Feb 1	H	Mansfield T	D	0-0	0-0	14		1800
27	5	H	Bradford C	W	2-0	0-0	11	Diamond 2 [62, 71]	2778
28	8	H	Crawley T	L	1-3	0-0	13	Diarra [61]	1785
29	12	A	Rochdale	D	3-3	2-1	13	Pattison 2 (1 pen) [3, 24 (p)], Diamond [47]	2264
30	15	A	Exeter C	L	3-4	2-1	15	Armstrong [4], Muldoon [19], Thomson [64]	3852
31	22	A	Bradford C	W	3-1	1-1	13	Burrell [45], Page [62], Diamond [90]	14,512
32	26	A	Barrow	D	0-0	0-0	14		2974
33	Mar 1	H	Port Vale	D	1-1	1-0	14	Pattison [23]	2257
34	5	H	Hartlepool U	L	1-2	1-1	14	Armstrong [21]	2638
35	12	A	Bristol R	L	0-3	0-2	14		7884
36	15	A	Tranmere R	L	0-2	0-0	16		5437
37	19	H	Walsall	D	1-1	0-0	16	Kavanagh [90]	2570
38	22	H	Leyton Orient	L	0-3	0-0	16		2339
39	26	A	Scunthorpe U	W	3-0	1-0	15	Thomson [22], Diamond [62], Smith [81]	2317
40	Apr 2	H	Colchester U	L	1-2	1-2	16	Muldoon [4]	1615
41	9	A	Salford C	L	0-2	0-0	17		1670
42	15	H	Swindon T	L	1-4	0-2	18	Armstrong [90]	2933
43	18	A	Northampton T	L	0-3	0-1	20		5168
44	23	H	Carlisle U	W	3-0	2-0	19	Diamond 2 [18, 90], McArdle [27]	2707
45	30	A	Forest Green R	W	3-1	1-1	17	Muldoon (pen) [40], Diamond [46], Kerry [72]	4040
46	May 7	H	Sutton U	L	0-2	0-1	19		2484

Final League Position: 19

GOALSCORERS

League (64): Diamond 13, Armstrong 12, Muldoon 12 (3 pens), Pattison 9 (1 pen), Thomson 5, Burrell 2, Kerry 2, Diarra 1, Kavanagh 1, McArdle 1, Orsi-Dadomo 1 (1 pen), Page 1, Power 1, Smith 1, own goals 2.
FA Cup (4): Armstrong 1, Diamond 1, Orsi-Dadomo 1, Power 1.
Papa John's Trophy (8): Orsi-Dadomo 4, Armstrong 1, Kerry 1, Muldoon 1, Pattison 1.

Oxley M 41	Fallowfield R 20 + 8	McArdle R 21 + 2	Hall C 20	Burrell W 44 + 1	Thomson G 44 + 2	Pattison A 38 + 3	Falkingham J 34	Power S 8 + 18	Muldoon J 33 + 9	Armstrong L 45	Kerry L 12 + 11	Page L 27 + 1	Orsi-Dadomo D 3 + 7	Martin A — + 8	Diamond J 39	Sheron N 22 + 6	Smith W 16 + 1	Legge L 5 + 3	Diarra B 7 + 3	Beck M 5 + 8	Austerfield J 5 + 4	Richards L 7 + 1	Kavanagh C 5 + 7	Ilesanmi E — + 1	Cracknell J 5 + 1	*Match No.*
1	2^2	3	4	5	6	7^1	8	9	10	11	12	13														1
1	12	3	4	2	6	7	8		9	11^3	13	5^1	10^2	14												2
1	12	3	4	2	9	6	7		11	10	8	5^1														3
1	13	3	4	2^2	9	6	7	12	11	10	8^1	5														4
1		3	4	2	6	8^2	7^1	13	11^3	10	12	5	14		9											5
1		3	4	2	6^1	8	7	12	11^2	10		5	13		9											6
1	13	3	4	2	6	8^1	7	12^3	11	10^4	14	5^2		15	9■											7
1	2	3	4	5	6		7	9	11	10	8															8
1	2	3^1	4	5	6^2	8	7	13	11^3	10			14		9	12										9
1	2		4	5	6	8^1	7	13	11	10	12				9^2		3									10
1	2		4	5	6	8^2	7^1	13	10^3	11	12		14		9		3									11
1	2		4	5	6^1	8	7^2		11	10^3	12		14	13	9		3									12
1	2			4	6	7	8		10	11		5^1			9	12	3									13
1	2			4	6		8	12	10^2	11	7^1	5	13		9		3									14
1			4	2	6^2	7	8	12	10^1	11^3		5	13	14	9		3									15
1			4	3	13	8	7	6^1	12	10^3		5	11^2	14	9	2										16
1	14		4	3	13	7	8	6^2	12	10		5^3	11^1		9	2										17
1			4	3	6	7	8^2	13	11^1	10	12	5			9	2										18
1			4	3	9	6	7	12	13	10	8^2	5^1			11	2										19
1			4	3	2	8	7	9		10	6				11	5										20
1	12		4	3	9	8	7		13	10	6^2	5			11	2^1										21
1	14		4	3	9^2	8	7	13	12	10	6^1	5			11	2^3										22
1	2^2	4			9	6	7		11^1	10		5				13		3	8^3	12	14					23
1		3		2	6		7		9	10	8^1	5				13			11		12	4^2				24
1		3		2	5	12	6		9^2	10	7^1	8			11	14						4^3	13			25
1		3^2		12	2	8	7		14	11		5			9			13	6			4^1	10^3			26
1				3	2	8	7		12	11^2		5			9			4	6	13			10^1			27
1				4	2	7	8		10	11^1		5			9			3	6	12						28
1				4	2	6^2	7		13	10	12	5			11			3	9		8^1					29
1				4^1	5	6	7		10	11		8^2			9	12	2	3			13					30
1	5^3			2	6		7		10^2	11^1		8			9	4	3	14	13	12						31
1	5			2	6	14	7^3		10^1	11^2		8			9	4	3		12	13						32
1	12			2	5	6	7^1		10^3	11^2		8			9	4	3		14	13						33
1	5^3			2	6	7		13	10^1	11		8			9		3			14		4^2	12			34
1	5	3^2		2	7	12	6			11^3					8	4			9^1	10		13	14			35
1	5	3		2^2	6	7			13	11■					9	4				10^1		8	12			36
1	5	3		2^2	6	7		13	11^1						9	4				10		8	12			37
1	5	3^3		2	6	7		12		10					9	4	14			11^2		8^1	13			38
1	5			4	6	7^1			9	10	12				8	3	2						11			39
1	2			5	7	8		12	6^2	11					9	4	3						10^1	13		40
1^3	2	13		5^2	6	7				11	8				9	4	3			12			10^1		14	41
	2^2	13		5	7	8^1		14	6	11					9	4	3			10^3	12				1	42
		3		5	6			8	10^2	11				13	9	2	4^1	12			7				1	43
		3		4	2	8		6	10	11^1				12	9	5					7				1	44
		3		5	2	7		8^1	10	11	12				9	4					6				1	45
		3		4	2	8		12^3	9^2	10	6^1			14	11	5					7		13		1	46

FA Cup

First Round	Wrexham	(h)	2-1
Second Round	Portsmouth	(a)	2-1
Third Round	Luton T	(a)	0-4

Carabao Cup

First Round	Rochdale	(h)	P-P

Rochdale received a bye to the second round due to positive COVID-19 tests in the Harrogate T squad.

Papa John's Trophy

Group H (N)	Mansfield T	(h)	3-1
Group H (N)	Newcastle U U21	(h)	2-0
Group H (N)	Sheffield W	(a)	0-4
Second Round	Tranmere R	(a)	2-1
Third Round	Carlisle U	(h)	1-0
Quarter-Final	Sutton U	(a)	0-1

HARTLEPOOL UNITED

FOUNDATION

The inspiration for the launching of Hartlepool United was the West Hartlepool club which won the FA Amateur Cup in 1904–05. They had been in existence since 1881 and their cup success led in 1908 to the formation of the new professional concern which first joined the North-Eastern League. In those days they were Hartlepools United and won the Durham Senior Cup in their first two seasons.

The Suit Direct Stadium, Clarence Road, Hartlepool TS24 8BZ.

Telephone: (01429) 272 584.

Ticket Office: (01429) 272 584 (option 2).

Website: www.hartlepoolunited.co.uk

Email: enquires@hartlepoolunited.co.uk

Ground Capacity: 7,833.

Record Attendance: 17,426 v Manchester U, FA Cup 3rd rd, 5 January 1957.

Pitch Measurements: 103m × 70m (112.5yd × 76.5yd).

Chairman: Raj Singh.

Honorary President: Jeff Stelling.

Manager: Paul Hartley.

Coach: Gordon Young.

Colours: Blue and white striped shirts with blue sleeves, white shorts, blue socks with white trim.

Year Formed: 1908.

Turned Professional: 1908.

Previous Names: 1908, Hartlepools United; 1968, Hartlepool; 1977, Hartlepool United.

Club Nickname: 'The Pool', 'Monkey Hangers'.

Ground: 1908, Victoria Park (renamed The Northern Gas & Power Stadium 2016; The Super Six Stadium 2018; Victoria Park 2019; The Suit Direct Stadium 2021).

First Football League Game: 27 August 1921, Division 3 (N), v Wrexham (a) W 2–0 – Gill; Thomas, Crilly; Dougherty, Hopkins, Short; Kessler, Mulholland (1), Lister (1), Robertson, Donald.

Record League Victory: 10–1 v Barrow, Division 4, 4 April 1959 – Oakley; Cameron, Waugh; Johnson, Moore, Anderson; Scott (1), Langland (1), Smith (3), Clark (2), Luke (2), (1 og).

Record Cup Victory: 6–0 v North Shields, FA Cup 1st rd, 30 November 1946 – Heywood; Brown, Gregory; Spelman, Lambert, Jones; Price, Scott (2), Sloan (4), Moses, McMahon; 6–0 v Gainsborough Trinity (a), FA Cup 1st rd, 10 November 2007 – Budtz; McCunnie, Humphreys, Liddle (1) (Antwi), Nelson, Clark, Moore (1), Sweeney, Barker (2) (Monkhouse), Mackay (Porter 1), Brown (1).

Record Defeat: 1–10 v Wrexham, Division 4, 3 March 1962.

HONOURS

League: *Runners-up:* Division 3N – 1956–57; FL 2 – 2006–07; Third Division – 2002–03.

FA Cup: 4th rd – 1955, 1978, 1989, 1993, 2005, 2009, 2022.

League Cup: 4th rd – 1975.

FOOTBALL YEARBOOK FACT FILE

When Hartlepools United lost their FA Cup fourth qualifying-round replay at Ashington in November 1924 they appeared to be out of the competition. However, club officials challenged the result on the grounds that their opponents had fielded an ineligible player. The move was successful, and after being reinstated Pools went on to defeat Bishop Auckland and St Albans to earn a money-spinning first-round tie away to Newcastle United.

Most League Points (2 for a win): 60, Division 4, 1967–68.

Most League Points (3 for a win): 88, FL 2, 2006–07.

Most League Goals: 90, Division 3 (N), 1956–57.

Highest League Scorer in Season: William Robinson, 28, Division 3 (N), 1927–28; Joe Allon, 28, Division 4, 1990–91.

Most League Goals in Total Aggregate: Ken Johnson, 98, 1949–64.

Most League Goals in One Match: 5, Harry Simmons v Wigan Borough, Division 3 (N), 1 January 1931; 5, Bobby Folland v Oldham Ath, Division 3 (N), 15 April 1961.

Most Capped Player: Zaine Francis-Angol 2 (includes 1 on loan at Stockport Co) (24), Antigua & Barbuda.

Most League Appearances: Richie Humphreys, 481, 2001–13.

Youngest League Player: David Foley, 16 years 105 days v Port Vale, 25 August 2003.

Record Transfer Fee Received: £750,000 from Ipswich T for Tommy Miller, July 2001.

Record Transfer Fee Paid: £80,000 to Mansfield T for Darrell Clarke, July 2001.

Football League Record: 1921 Original Member of Division 3 (N); 1958–68 Division 4; 1968–69 Division 3; 1969–91 Division 4; 1991–92 Division 3; 1992–94 Division 2; 1994–2003 Division 3; 2003–04 Division 2; 2004–06 FL 1; 2006–07 FL 2; 2007–13 FL 1; 2013–17 FL 2; 2017–21 National League; 2021– FL 2.

LATEST SEQUENCES

Longest Sequence of League Wins: 9, 18.11.2006 – 1.1.2007.

Longest Sequence of League Defeats: 8, 27.1.1993 – 27.2.1993.

Longest Sequence of League Draws: 6, 30.4.2011 – 20.8.2011.

Longest Sequence of Unbeaten League Matches: 23, 18.11.2006 – 30.3.2007.

Longest Sequence Without a League Win: 20, 8.9.2012 – 26.12.2012.

Successive Scoring Runs: 27 from 18.11.2006.

Successive Non-scoring Runs: 11 from 9.1.1993.

MANAGERS

Alfred Priest 1908–12
Percy Humphreys 1912–13
Jack Manners 1913–20
Cecil Potter 1920–22
David Gordon 1922–24
Jack Manners 1924–27
Bill Norman 1927–31
Jack Carr 1932–35
(had been Player-Coach from 1931)
Jimmy Hamilton 1935–43
Fred Westgarth 1943–57
Ray Middleton 1957–59
Bill Robinson 1959–62
Allenby Chilton 1962–63
Bob Gurney 1963–64
Alvan Williams 1964–65
Geoff Twentyman 1965
Brian Clough 1965–67
Angus McLean 1967–70
John Simpson 1970–71
Len Ashurst 1971–74
Ken Hale 1974–76
Billy Horner 1976–83
Johnny Duncan 1983
Mike Docherty 1983
Billy Horner 1984–86
John Bird 1986–88
Bobby Moncur 1988–89
Cyril Knowles 1989–91
Alan Murray 1991–93
Viv Busby 1993
John MacPhail 1993–94
David McCreery 1994–95
Keith Houchen 1995–96
Mick Tait 1996–99
Chris Turner 1999–2002
Mike Newell 2002–03
Neale Cooper 2003–05
Martin Scott 2005–06
Danny Wilson 2006–08
Chris Turner 2008–10
Mick Wadsworth 2010–11
Neale Cooper 2011–12
John Hughes 2012–13
Colin Cooper 2013–14
Paul Murray 2014
Ronnie Moore 2014–16
Craig Hignett 2016–17
Dave Jones 2017
Craig Harrison 2017–18
Matthew Bates 2018
Richard Money 2018–19
Craig Hignett 2019
Dave Challinor 2019–21
Graeme Lee 2021–22
Paul Hartley June 2022–

TEN YEAR LEAGUE RECORD

		P	W	D	L	F	A	Pts	Pos
2012-13	FL 1	46	9	14	23	39	67	41	23
2013-14	FL 2	46	14	11	21	50	56	53	19
2014-15	FL 2	46	12	9	25	39	70	45	22
2015-16	FL 2	46	15	6	25	49	72	51	16
2016-17	FL 2	46	11	13	22	54	75	46	23
2017-18	NL	46	14	14	18	53	63	56	15
2018-19	NL	46	15	14	17	56	62	59	16
2019-20	NL	39	14	13	12	56	50	55	12§
2020-21	NL	42	22	10	10	66	43	76	4
2021-22	FL 2	46	14	12	20	44	64	54	17

§Decided on points-per-game (1.41)

DID YOU KNOW ?

Hartlepool United have the distinction of possessing a 100 per cent record in competitive games played at Old Trafford. Their only visit to the home of Manchester United came on 27 November 1958 when they played against Rochdale in an FA Cup first-round second replay. Pools won 2-1 thanks to Ken Johnson's extra-time strike in front of a crowd of 6,126.

HARTLEPOOL UNITED – SKY BET LEAGUE TWO 2021–22 LEAGUE RECORD

Match No.	Date	Venue	Opponents	Result		H/T Score	Lg Pos.	Goalscorers	Attendance
1	Aug 7	H	Crawley T	W	1-0	0-0	5	Holohan [88]	5184
2	14	A	Barrow	L	2-3	1-1	11	Burey [17], Goodwin [61]	2846
3	21	H	Walsall	W	2-0	1-0	6	Burey [22], Featherstone (pen) [57]	4677
4	28	H	Carlisle U	W	2-1	1-1	5	Burey [12], Holohan [69]	6112
5	Sept 4	A	Tranmere R	L	0-1	0-0	7		6707
6	11	H	Bristol R	W	1-0	0-0	4	Sterry [69]	5193
7	14	A	Sutton U	L	0-1	0-1	5		2484
8	18	A	Oldham Ath	D	0-0	0-0	6		3934
9	25	H	Exeter C	D	1-1	1-1	7	Molyneux [25]	5194
10	Oct 2	A	Stevenage	L	0-2	0-1	13		2633
11	9	H	Northampton T	W	2-1	0-0	8	Ferguson [52], Molyneux [83]	5522
12	16	A	Salford C	L	0-2	0-1	11		2448
13	19	A	Bradford C	W	3-1	1-0	9	Cullen 2 [1, 59], Songo'o (og) [90]	14,344
14	23	H	Harrogate T	W	3-2	0-2	7	Ferguson [51], Cullen [53], Daly [59]	5807
15	30	A	Leyton Orient	L	0-5	0-2	10		6233
16	Nov 12	H	Newport Co	L	1-2	0-1	10	Ferguson [63]	5764
17	20	H	Forest Green R	L	1-3	0-3	12	Featherstone (pen) [80]	5612
18	23	A	Swindon T	L	1-3	0-0	15	Daly [61]	7714
19	27	A	Port Vale	L	0-2	0-1	17		4839
20	Dec 8	H	Rochdale	W	2-1	0-0	12	Cullen [64], Shelton [90]	4214
21	11	H	Scunthorpe U	D	0-0	0-0	13		4809
22	26	A	Mansfield T	L	2-3	1-0	15	Molyneux [25], Featherstone [51]	5558
23	Jan 1	H	Oldham Ath	D	0-0	0-0	15		5026
24	15	A	Bristol R	L	0-2	0-0	17		7004
25	18	A	Carlisle U	D	0-0	0-0	17		4570
26	22	H	Stevenage	D	1-1	0-0	16	Featherstone [77]	4841
27	29	A	Exeter C	D	0-0	0-0	16		5121
28	Feb 8	H	Barrow	W	3-1	3-1	15	Molyneux 2 [27, 39], Bogle [44]	4621
29	12	A	Crawley T	W	1-0	1-0	15	Bogle [40]	2228
30	15	H	Tranmere R	W	1-0	1-0	14	Clarke (og) [45]	5214
31	19	H	Sutton U	D	1-1	0-1	12	Crawford [51]	5487
32	22	A	Colchester U	W	2-1	0-1	12	Bogle [70], Fletcher [74]	2115
33	26	A	Walsall	L	1-3	0-2	12	Bogle [63]	4760
34	Mar 5	A	Harrogate T	W	2-1	1-1	12	Molyneux [25], Ferguson [62]	2638
35	12	H	Leyton Orient	D	0-0	0-0	12		5903
36	15	H	Bradford C	L	0-2	0-0	12		5106
37	18	A	Newport Co	W	3-2	2-1	11	Sterry [35], Molyneux [45], Byrne [73]	4768
38	26	A	Northampton T	L	0-2	0-1	13		5673
39	29	H	Mansfield T	D	2-2	2-2	12	Grey [41], Molyneux [43]	4577
40	Apr 2	H	Salford C	L	0-2	0-2	12		4949
41	9	A	Forest Green R	D	1-1	0-0	13	Bogle [69]	2484
42	15	H	Port Vale	L	0-1	0-0	13		5517
43	18	A	Rochdale	L	1-2	1-0	14	Morris [10]	2900
44	23	H	Swindon T	L	0-3	0-1	15		4786
45	30	A	Scunthorpe U	D	1-1	0-0	16	Featherstone (pen) [72]	4210
46	May 7	H	Colchester U	L	0-2	0-1	17		5375

Final League Position: 17

GOALSCORERS

League (44): Molyneux 8, Bogle 5, Featherstone 5 (3 pens), Cullen 4, Ferguson 4, Burey 3, Daly 2, Holohan 2, Sterry 2, Byrne 1, Crawford 1, Fletcher 1, Goodwin 1, Grey 1, Morris 1, Shelton 1, own goals 2.
FA Cup (6): Cullen 2, Ferguson 1, Grey 1, Molyneux 1, own goal 1.
Carabao Cup (0).
Papa John's Trophy (14): Daly 5, Molyneux 3, Grey 2, Goodwin 1, Olomola 1 (1 pen), Shelton 1, own goal 1.

Killip B 42	Sterry J 37	Byrne N 40	Liddle G 29 + 3	Odusina T 29 + 2	Ferguson D 41 + 1	Holohan G 12 + 6	Shelton M 27 + 6	Featherstone N 40	Olomola O 6 + 6	Molyneux L 35 + 8	Burey T 5 + 2	Daly M 15 + 4	Cullen M 11 + 6	Goodwin W 8 + 2	Lawlor J — + 1	Francis-Angol Z 16	Ogle R 8 + 10	Grey J 9 + 19	Smith M 4 + 3	Fondop-Talom M 3 + 5	Cook J 1 + 3	Hendrie L 7	Jones E 3	Mitchell J 2	Crawford T 22 + 6	Carver M 6 + 11	Hull J 5 + 2	Bogle O 19 + 1	Fletcher I 3 + 11	White J 9 + 6	Morris B 10	Bilokapic N 2	Match No.
1	2	3	4	5	6	7	8^{3}	9	10^{1}	11^{2}	12	13	14																				1
1	5	2	3^{1}	4	9	8	6^{2}	7		12	11^{3}	13		10	14																		2
1	5	2	3		9	8	6	7		12	10^{1}			11^{2}		4	13																3
1	2	3	4		6	9	7^{1}	8		13	10^{3}	12		11^{2}		5	14																4
1	2	3	4		6^{1}	9^{3}	7	8	14	12	11^{2}			10		5	13																5
1	2	3	4				7	9	11^{2}	6^{3}		8		10^{1}		5	12	13	14														6
1	2	3	4	5^{1}	12			8	13	7		10	14	11^{3}		6			9^{2}														7
1	2	3	4		6^{2}		7	8	11^{1}	9						5	13			10	12												8
1	2	4					7	8		10		9				5	12			11		3	6^{1}										9
1	2	4					7^{1}	8		10		9	12	13		5^{3}				11^{2}	14	3	6										10
1	2	4		14	6		7^{2}	8		10		9^{3}		11		5		13			12	3^{1}											11
1	5	3		2	8	14	12	7				6		10^{2}		4^{1}	9	11^{3}		13													12
1	2	4			5	8^{2}	6	7		10^{3}		9	11^{1}				14	12		13		3											13
	2^{1}	4	13		5	8	6^{2}	7		10		9	11^{3}				12	14				3		1									14
			3	13	8	7		6		10		9	11^{3}			4^{1}	5^{2}	14		12		2		1									15
1		3	4		6		9^{2}	7		11		8	10^{1}			5	2	12		13													16
1	2▪	3	4		6		7^{2}	8	13	10		9^{3}	11^{1}			5		14							12								17
1		3	4		6	14		7	12	10		9^{2}	11^{1}			5^{3}	2			13					8								18
1		3	4		10^{3}	13		9		6^{1}		8	11	14				12				2	5		7^{2}								19
1	2	5	4	3	6		7	8		10		9^{1}	11^{2}					13							12								20
1	2	5	4	3	6	13	7^{2}	8	14	10^{1}			11^{3}					12							9								21
1	2^{1}	5	4	3	6	14	8	7		10	13	9^{3}	11^{2}				12																22
1	2	5	4	3	6	9	7^{3}	8		12	10^{2}	13						14			11^{1}												23
1	2▪	3	4^{3}	5	6	9		8		10			12					13							7^{2}	11^{1}	14						24
1		3	4	5	6	9	13	8		10^{3}			12				2	14							7^{2}	11^{1}							25
1		3	4^{2}	5	6	8^{1}	7^{3}	9	13	11			10				2	12							14								26
1	2	3	4	5	6		7	8▪		10^{2}								13							9			11^{1}	12				27
1	2	3		4	5		13			9			12					11							8			10^{1}		6^{2}	7		28
1	2	3	13	4	5		12			9^{3}								11^{2}							8			10	14	6^{1}	7		29
1	2	3	13	4	5			7		9^{2}								11^{1}							8			10		12	6		30
1		3		4				7		9						5	2								8	12		10	13	11^{1}	6^{2}		31
1		3		4	5		6^{1}	7		9^{2}						2^{3}			14						8	13		10	12	11			32
1	2		3	4	5	13		7		9								12							8^{2}	14		10	6^{3}	11^{1}			33
1	2		3	4	5		6	7		9^{3}								11^{1}							8	13	14	10^{2}		12			34
1	2	3		4	5		6	7		13								11^{1}							8^{3}	12		10	14	9^{2}			35
1	2	3		4	5			7		9								11^{1}	8^{3}						14	10^{2}		13	12	6			36
1	5	2	3	4	8			6		9									7^{1}						11	13		10^{2}	12				37
	5	2	3^{1}	4	8			6		9								13							11^{3}	14		10	12		7^{2}	1	38
1	2	3		4	5		14	7		9^{1}								11							13			10	6^{3}	12	8^{2}		39
1	2	3		4	5		6^{2}	7										11^{1}							13	12		10	8	9			40
1	2	3	4	5	6		7^{1}											13							9	10^{2}		11^{3}	14	12	8		41
	2^{3}	5	4		6		8^{1}			13															9	10^{2}	3	11	14	12	7	1	42
1		5	4		6		14			12							2								9	10^{2}	3	11^{1}	13	8^{3}	7		43
1	2			4	5		6^{2}		11	9									7^{1}						8	13	3	10		12			44
1	2			4	5			7	11^{2}	9								12							8^{1}	13	3	10			6		45
1	5^{1}		3^{3}	4	8			6	11	9							12		14						7	13	2	10^{2}					46

FA Cup

First Round	Wycombe W	(h)	2-2
Replay	Wycombe W	(a)	1-0
Second Round	Lincoln C	(a)	1-0
Third Round	Blackpool	(h)	2-1
Fourth Round	Crystal Palace	(a)	0-2

Papa John's Trophy

Group A (N)	Carlisle U	(a)	3-3
(Carlisle U won 4-3 on penalties)			
Group A (N)	Morecambe	(h)	2-2
(Hartlepool won 4-2 on penalties)			
Group A (N)	Everton U21	(h)	1-0
Second Round	Sheffield W	(a)	3-0
Third Round	Bolton W	(h)	1-0
Quarter-Final	Charlton Ath	(h)	2-2
(Hartlepool U won 5-4 on penalties)			
Semi-Final	Rotherham U	(h)	2-2
(Rotherham U won 5-4 on penalties)			

Carabao Cup

First Round	Crewe Alex	(h)	0-1

HUDDERSFIELD TOWN

FOUNDATION

A meeting, attended largely by members of the Huddersfield & District FA, was held at the Imperial Hotel in 1906 to discuss the feasibility of establishing a football club in this rugby stronghold. However, it was not until a man with both the enthusiasm and the money to back the scheme came on the scene that real progress was made. This benefactor was Mr Hilton Crowther and it was at a meeting at the Albert Hotel in 1908 that the club formally came into existence with an investment of £2,000 and joined the North-Eastern League.

The John Smith's Stadium, Stadium Way, Leeds Road, Huddersfield, West Yorkshire HD1 6PX.

Telephone: (01484) 960 600.

Ticket Office: (01484) 960 606.

Website: www.htafc.com

Email: info@htafc.com

Ground Capacity: 24,436.

Record Attendance: 67,037 v Arsenal, FA Cup 6th rd, 27 February 1932 (at Leeds Road); 24,169 v Tottenham H, Premier League, 30 September 2017; 24,169 v Manchester U, Premier League, 21 October 2017; 24,169 v WBA, Premier League, 4 November 2017; 24,169 v Chelsea, Premier League, 12 December 2017 (at John Smith's Stadium).

Pitch Measurements: 106m × 68m (116yd × 74.5yd).

Chairman: Paul Hodgkinson.

Chief Executive: Mark Devlin.

Head Coach: Danny Schofield.

Assistant Head Coach: Narcís Pèlach.

Colours: Blue and white striped shirts, white shorts, black socks with white and blue trim.

Year Formed: 1908.

Turned Professional: 1908.

Club Nickname: 'The Terriers'.

Grounds: 1908, Leeds Road; 1994, The Alfred McAlpine Stadium (renamed The Galpharm Stadium 2004; The John Smith's Stadium 2012).

First Football League Game: 3 September 1910, Division 2, v Bradford PA (a) W 1–0 – Mutch; Taylor, Morris; Beaton, Hall, Bartlett; Blackburn, Wood, Hamilton (1), McCubbin, Jee.

Record League Victory: 10–1 v Blackpool, Division 1, 13 December 1930 – Turner; Goodall, Spencer; Redfern, Wilson, Campbell; Bob Kelly (1), McLean (4), Robson (3), Davies (1), Smailes (1).

Record Cup Victory: 7–0 v Lincoln U, FA Cup 1st rd, 16 November 1991 – Clarke; Trevitt, Charlton, Donovan (2), Mitchell, Doherty, O'Regan (1), Stapleton (1) (Wright), Roberts (2), Onuora (1), Barnett (Ireland). *N.B.* 11–0 v Heckmondwike (a), FA Cup pr rd, 18 September 1909 – Doggart; Roberts, Ewing; Hooton, Stevenson, Randall; Kenworthy (2), McCreadie (1), Foster (4), Stacey (4), Jee.

Record Defeat: 1–10 v Manchester C, Division 2, 7 November 1987.

HONOURS

League Champions: Division 1 – 1923–24, 1924–25, 1925–26; Division 2 – 1969–70; Division 4 – 1979–80.
Runners-up: Division 1 – 1926–27, 1927–28, 1933–34; Division 2 – 1919–20, 1952–53.

FA Cup Winners: 1922.
Runners-up: 1920, 1928, 1930, 1938.

League Cup: semi-final – 1968.

League Trophy: *Runners-up:* 1994.

FOOTBALL YEARBOOK FACT FILE

Huddersfield Town came close to folding in the spring of 1912 because of serious financial problems. The club entered voluntary liquidation on 24 April, and it was not until August that a rescue deal was agreed by the FA and the Football League, a new club of the same name taking over the assets of the original organisation.

Most League Points (2 for a win): 66, Division 4, 1979–80.

Most League Points (3 for a win): 87, FL 1, 2010–11.

Most League Goals: 101, Division 4, 1979–80.

Highest League Scorer in Season: Sam Taylor, 35, Division 2, 1919–20; George Brown, 35, Division 1, 1925–26; Jordan Rhodes, 35, 2011–12.

Most League Goals in Total Aggregate: George Brown, 142, 1921–29; Jimmy Glazzard, 142, 1946–56.

Most League Goals in One Match: 5, Dave Mangnall v Derby Co, Division 1, 21 November 1931; 5, Alf Lythgoe v Blackburn R, Division 1, 13 April 1935; 5, Jordan Rhodes v Wycombe W, FL 1, 6 January 2012.

Most Capped Player: Jimmy Nicholson, 31 (41), Northern Ireland.

Most League Appearances: Billy Smith, 521, 1914–34.

Youngest League Player: Denis Law, 16 years 303 days v Notts Co, 24 December 1956.

Record Transfer Fee Received: £15,000,000 from AFC Bournemouth for Philip Billing, July 2019; £15,000,000 from WBA for Karlan Grant, October 2020.

Record Transfer Fee Paid: £17,500,000 to Monaco for Terence Kongolo, June 2018.

Football League Record: 1910 Elected to Division 2; 1920–52 Division 1; 1952–53 Division 2; 1953–56 Division 1; 1956–70 Division 2; 1970–72 Division 1; 1972–73 Division 2; 1973–75 Division 3; 1975–80 Division 4; 1980–83 Division 3; 1983–88 Division 2; 1988–92 Division 3; 1992–95 Division 2; 1995–2001 Division 1; 2001–03 Division 2; 2003–04 Division 3; 2004–12 FL 1; 2012–17 FL C; 2017–19 Premier League; 2019– FL C.

LATEST SEQUENCES

Longest Sequence of League Wins: 11, 5.4.1920 – 4.9.1920.

Longest Sequence of League Defeats: 8, 2.3.2019 – 26.4.2019.

Longest Sequence of League Draws: 6, 3.3.1987 – 3.4.1987.

Longest Sequence of Unbeaten League Matches: 43, 1.1.2011 – 19.11.2011.

Longest Sequence Without a League Win: 22, 4.12.1971 – 29.4.1972.

Successive Scoring Runs: 27 from 12.3.2005.

Successive Non-scoring Runs: 7 from 14.10.2000.

MANAGERS

Fred Walker 1908–10
Richard Pudan 1910–12
Arthur Fairclough 1912–19
Ambrose Langley 1919–21
Herbert Chapman 1921–25
Cecil Potter 1925–26
Jack Chaplin 1926–29
Clem Stephenson 1929–42
Ted Magner 1942–43
David Steele 1943–47
George Stephenson 1947–52
Andy Beattie 1952–56
Bill Shankly 1956–59
Eddie Boot 1960–64
Tom Johnston 1964–68
Ian Greaves 1968–74
Bobby Collins 1974
Tom Johnston 1975–78
(had been General Manager since 1975)
Mike Buxton 1978–86
Steve Smith 1986–87
Malcolm Macdonald 1987–88
Eoin Hand 1988–92
Ian Ross 1992–93
Neil Warnock 1993–95
Brian Horton 1995–97
Peter Jackson 1997–99
Steve Bruce 1999–2000
Lou Macari 2000–02
Mick Wadsworth 2002–03
Peter Jackson 2003–07
Andy Ritchie 2007–08
Stan Ternent 2008
Lee Clark 2008–12
Simon Grayson 2012–13
Mark Robins 2013–14
Chris Powell 2014–15
David Wagner 2015–19
Jan Siewert 2019
Danny Cowley 2019–20
Carlos Corberán 2020–22
Danny Schofield July 2022–

TEN YEAR LEAGUE RECORD

		P	W	D	L	F	A	Pts	Pos
2012-13	FL C	46	15	13	18	53	73	58	19
2013-14	FL C	46	14	11	21	58	65	53	17
2014-15	FL C	46	13	16	17	58	75	55	16
2015-16	FL C	46	13	12	21	59	70	51	19
2016-17	FL C	46	25	6	15	56	58	81	5
2017-18	PR Lge	38	9	10	19	28	58	37	16
2018-19	PR Lge	38	3	7	28	22	76	16	20
2019-20	FL C	46	13	12	21	52	70	51	18
2020-21	FL C	46	12	13	21	50	71	49	20
2021-22	FL C	46	23	13	10	64	47	82	3

DID YOU KNOW ?

Steve Smith became the first substitute to be used by Huddersfield Town when he came on to replace John Coddington during the home game with Preston North End on 18 September 1965. The first substitute to score was Derek Parkin who netted in the 2-1 defeat at Carlisle United on 27 August 1966.

HUDDERSFIELD TOWN – SKY BET CHAMPIONSHIP 2021–22 LEAGUE RECORD

Match No.	Date	Venue	Opponents	Result	H/T Score	Lg Pos.	Goalscorers	Attendance
1	Aug 7	A	Derby Co	D 1-1	1-1	8	Sarr 45	16,249
2	14	H	Fulham	L 1-5	1-3	22	Pearson 41	15,126
3	17	H	Preston NE	W 1-0	0-0	15	van den Berg (og) 74	15,278
4	21	A	Sheffield U	W 2-1	0-0	10	Koroma 75, Colwill 90	28,036
5	28	H	Reading	W 4-0	1-0	4	O'Brien 39, Pearson 51, Thomas 66, Ward 68	14,613
6	Sept 11	A	Stoke C	L 1-2	0-0	8	Toffolo 47	20,447
7	14	A	Blackpool	W 3-0	0-0	4	Koroma 48, Pearson 54, Hogg 62	11,277
8	18	H	Nottingham F	L 0-2	0-1	7		17,462
9	25	A	Swansea C	L 0-1	0-1	7		17,091
10	28	H	Blackburn R	W 3-2	1-0	7	Vallejo 36, Ward 2 60, 84	15,283
11	Oct 2	A	Luton T	D 0-0	0-0	7		9977
12	16	H	Hull C	W 2-0	1-0	6	Lees 9, Holmes 73	17,510
13	20	H	Birmingham C	D 0-0	0-0	6		15,618
14	23	A	Bournemouth	L 0-3	0-2	8		9253
15	30	H	Millwall	W 1-0	0-0	5	Hogg 82	15,397
16	Nov 2	A	Peterborough U	D 1-1	0-0	5	Ward 74	7983
17	6	A	Cardiff C	L 1-2	1-0	8	Sinani 12	17,355
18	20	H	WBA	W 1-0	1-0	7	Sinani 6	17,297
19	24	A	QPR	L 0-1	0-0	8		11,591
20	27	H	Middlesbrough	L 1-2	0-2	8	Daniels (og) 90	19,192
21	Dec 4	A	Barnsley	D 1-1	1-1	11	O'Brien 33	15,190
22	11	H	Coventry C	D 1-1	1-0	10	Ward 18	16,493
23	18	A	Bristol C	W 3-2	1-1	10	Holmes 41, Sinani 46, Ward 55	18,169
24	26	H	Blackpool	W 3-2	1-2	6	Ward 3, Thomas 2 80, 84	18,968
25	30	A	Nottingham F	W 1-0	1-0	6	Holmes 30	27,159
26	Jan 2	A	Blackburn R	D 0-0	0-0	6		16,313
27	15	H	Swansea C	D 1-1	1-0	7	Sinani 15	20,535
28	22	A	Reading	W 4-3	3-3	6	Sinani 9, Ward 3 15, 25, 53	10,796
29	28	H	Stoke C	D 1-1	1-0	6	Koroma 27	16,342
30	Feb 2	H	Derby Co	W 2-0	0-0	5	Holmes 75, Rhodes 79	16,231
31	9	A	Preston NE	D 0-0	0-0	5		11,120
32	12	H	Sheffield U	D 0-0	0-0	5		17,523
33	19	A	Fulham	W 2-1	2-0	5	Ward 31, Holmes (pen) 43	19,001
34	23	H	Cardiff C	W 2-1	0-0	4	Koroma 88, Russell 90	20,167
35	26	A	Birmingham C	W 2-0	2-0	3	Colwill 27, O'Brien 44	17,318
36	Mar 4	H	Peterborough U	W 3-0	2-0	2	Sinani 3, Lees 2 7, 72	16,023
37	11	A	WBA	D 2-2	1-0	2	Ward 2 24, 74	20,846
38	16	A	Millwall	L 0-2	0-1	3		10,792
39	19	H	Bournemouth	L 0-3	0-2	4		20,336
40	Apr 1	A	Hull C	W 1-0	0-0	3	Toffolo 79	12,764
41	11	H	Luton T	W 2-0	0-0	3	Russell 59, Sarr 89	18,379
42	15	H	QPR	D 2-2	1-1	3	Barbet (og) 6, Toffolo 53	19,636
43	18	A	Middlesbrough	W 2-0	1-0	3	Sarr 41, Rhodes 60	24,230
44	22	H	Barnsley	W 2-1	2-0	3	Rhodes 4, Toffolo 45	17,258
45	30	A	Coventry C	W 2-1	1-0	4	Toffolo 45, Anjorin (pen) 79	23,828
46	May 7	H	Bristol C	W 2-0	2-0	3	Toffolo 33, Ward 44	17,797

Final League Position: 3

GOALSCORERS

League (64): Ward 14, Sinani 6, Toffolo 6, Holmes 5 (1 pen), Koroma 4, Lees 3, O'Brien 3, Pearson 3, Rhodes 3, Sarr 3, Thomas 3, Colwill 2, Hogg 2, Russell 2, Anjorin 1 (1 pen), Vallejo 1, own goals 3.
FA Cup (4): Holmes 1, Koroma 1, Lees 1, Pearson 1.
Carabao Cup (1): Lees 1.
Championship Play-offs (2): Rhodes 1, Sinani 1.

Schofield R 2	Pearson M 37	Sarr N 14 + 4	Colwill L 26 + 3	Turton O 25 + 15	Hogg J 31	High S 14 + 9	Thomas S 42 + 1	Ward D 37 + 3	Rhodes J 6 + 15	Holmes D 26 + 11	Campbell F 4 + 15	Koroma J 19 + 15	Sinani D 31 + 8	Vallejo A 2 + 3	Nicholls L 43	Lees T 39 + 1	O'Brien L 43	Toffolo H 40 + 2	Odubeko A — + 6	Ruffels J 2 + 6	Russell J 15 + 2	Aarons R — + 1	Rowe A — + 1	Pipa G 6 + 5	Eiting C 1 + 4	Anjorin F — + 7	Blackman J 1	Match No.
1	2	3	4	5	6	7	8	9[1]	10[2]	11[3]	12	13	14															1
1	3	4	5	2	6	12	10	11[1]	14	9[3]	13	8		7[2]														2
		3	4	5	7	6	9	11[1]		13	12	10		14	1	2[3]	8[2]											3
	2	3	4	5	7	6[2]	9	11[1]			13	10[3]		14	1		8	12										4
	2		4	12	6		5	10[2]		14	13	11[3]	9[1]		1	3	7	8										5
	2	4		12	6		5			9[2]	10[3]	11	13		1	3[1]	7	8	14									6
	2		4	12	6		5	10[1]				11[3]	9[2]	13	1	3	7	8	14									7
	2[1]		4	12	6		5	11[2]		14		10[3]	9		1	3	7	8	13									8
	2		4	5[1]	6[3]		10			13	11[2]	12	9		1	3	7	8	14									9
	2	4		13		12	5[2]	10		14		11[3]	9[4]	6[1]	1	3	7	8		15								10
	2	4				7	6	11[2]		12	13	9	10[1]		1	3	8	5										11
	2[2]	14	4	13	6	12	5[3]	10		11			9[1]		1	3	7	8										12
	2		4	14	6		5	10[2]		11[3]	13	12	9[1]		1	3	7	8										13
	2	4[1]		5	6		9[3]	14		13	10[2]	11	12		1	3	7	8										14
	2		4[2]	13	6		5	10		11[3]	14	12	9[1]		1	3	7	8										15
	2		4	14	6[1]	12	5	10		11[3]		13	9[2]		1	3	7	8										16
	2		4		6[1]	12	5	10[3]		11[2]	14	13	9		1	3	7	8										17
	2	3	4	5		6	9[2]	10[1]			12		11[3]		1		7	8		13	14							18
	2		4	5[3]		6	13	11[1]			12	10[2]	9		1	3	7	8	14									19
	2[1]	4		12		6	5	10		11[2]	13	14	9		1	3	7	8[3]										20
			4	2		8	6[2]	9			10[1]	11			1	3	7	5	12			13						21
	2		4	12		8	6	9[2]		11[3]	13	10[1]			1	3	7	5		14								22
	2		4	13		7	5[2]	11[1]	12	9[3]		14	10		1	3	6	8										23
	2	4[3]		12		6[2]	5	11	13	9[4]		15	10		1	3[1]	7	8					14					24
	3		4	2		6	5[2]	11[1]	12	10		13	9[3]		1		7	8						14				25
	2		4	13		6[2]	5		12	11		10[1]	9		1	3	7	8										26
	3			2[3]	6	12	5	11	14			10[2]	9[1]		1	4	7	8						13				27
	3				6		5	11[3]	14			10[1]	9[2]		1	4	7	8		13	12			2				28
	3			2	7	14	6	11[2]	12	13		9[1]	10[3]		1	4	8	5										29
	3[1]			2[2]	7[3]		6	11	14	9			10		1	4	8	5						13	12			30
	4			3	8		2	11[2]	13	10[3]		14	7[1]		1	5	9	6							12			31
	3				7		9	10[3]		12		11[1]	13		1	4	8	14		5[2]	6			2				32
	3	14		2	7		9[3]	10[2]	13	11[1]			12		1	4	8	5			6							33
	3			2			5	10	14	11[3]		13	9[1]		1	4	7			8[2]	6				12			34
	3		4	2	7		9[3]	13	10[2]	11[1]		14	12		1		8	5			6							35
	3			2			9	10	14	11[2]			6[1]		1	4	8[3]	5			7				12	13		36
	3		12	2	7		10[3]	11[2]	14				6[1]		1	4	9	5			8					13		37
	3[2]		5	13	9[1]		2[3]	11		7			12		1	4	10	6			8					14		38
	3		12	2			6	11		9[3]		13	10[2]		1	4[1]	8	5			7					14		39
			4	2[2]			9		10	6[1]	12	11[3]	14		1	3	8	5			7			13				40
		13	4		3		11[3]	10[2]	14	12			9[1]		1	2	7	8			6			5				41
			4	2[3]	6		10	11[1]		12			8[2]		1	3	9	5			7			14		13		42
		5		3	9	14	7[1]		11[3]			12			1	4	10	6[2]		13	8			2				43
		4		2	8	12			10	6[3]	14		9[1]		1	3	11	5[2]		13	7							44
		14	4		3[3]	6		12	10[1]	9[2]					1	2	11	8			7			5		13		45
		4	13	2	3[1]			11		6			10[3]			12		9[2]			7			5	8	14	1	46

FA Cup

Third Round	Burnley	(a)	2-1
Fourth Round	Barnsley	(h)	1-0
Fifth Round	Nottingham F	(a)	1-2

Carabao Cup

First Round	Sheffield W	(a)	0-0
(Huddersfield T won 4-2 on penalties)			
Second Round	Everton	(h)	1-2

Championship Play-offs

Semi-Final 1st leg	Luton T	(a)	1-1
Semi-Final 2nd leg	Luton T	(h)	1-0
Final	Nottingham F	(Wembley)	0-1

HULL CITY

FOUNDATION

The enthusiasts who formed Hull City in 1904 were brave men indeed. More than that, they were audacious for they immediately put the club on the map in this Rugby League fortress by obtaining a three-year agreement with the Hull Rugby League club to rent their ground! They had obtained quite a number of conversions to the dribbling code, before the Rugby League forbade the use of any of their club grounds by Association Football clubs. By that time, Hull City were well away, having entered the FA Cup in their initial season and the Football League, Second Division after only a year.

The MKM Stadium, West Park, Hull, East Yorkshire HU3 6HU.

Telephone: (01482) 504 600.

Ticket Office: (01482) 505 600.

Website: www.wearehullcity.co.uk

Email: info@wearehullcity.co.uk

Ground Capacity: 24,983.

Record Attendance: 55,019 v Manchester U, FA Cup 6th rd, 26 February 1949 (at Boothferry Park); 25,512 v Sunderland, FL C, 28 October 2007 (at KC Stadium).

Pitch Measurements: 104m × 74m (113.5yd × 81yd).

Chairman: Dr Assem Allam.

Vice-Chairman: Ehab Allam.

Manager: Shota Arveladze.

Assistant Manager: Peter van der Veen.

Colours: Amber shirts with black diagonal pattern, black shorts with amber trim, amber socks with black trim.

Year Formed: 1904.

Turned Professional: 1905.

Club Nickname: 'The Tigers'.

Grounds: 1904, Boulevard Ground (Hull RFC); 1905, Anlaby Road (Hull CC); 1944, Boulevard Ground; 1946, Boothferry Park; 2002, Kingston Communications Stadium (renamed The KCOM Stadium 2016; The MKM Stadium 2021).

First Football League Game: 2 September 1905, Division 2, v Barnsley (h) W 4–1 – Spendiff; Langley, Jones; Martin, Robinson, Gordon (2); Rushton, Spence (1), Wilson (1), Howe, Raisbeck.

Record League Victory: 11–1 v Carlisle U, Division 3 (N), 14 January 1939 – Ellis; Woodhead, Dowen; Robinson (1), Blyth, Hardy; Hubbard (2), Richardson (2), Dickinson (2), Davies (2), Cunliffe (2).

Record Cup Victory: 8–2 v Stalybridge Celtic (a), FA Cup 1st rd, 26 November 1932 – Maddison; Goldsmith, Woodhead; Gardner, Hill (1), Denby; Forward (1), Duncan, McNaughton (1), Wainscoat (4), Sargeant (1).

HONOURS

League Champions: FL 1 2020–21; Division 3 – 1965–66; Division 3N – 1932–33, 1948–49.

Runners-up: FL C – 2012–13; FL 1 – 2004–05; Division 3 – 1958–59; Third Division – 2003–04; Division 4 – 1982–83.

FA Cup: *Runners-up:* 2014.

League Cup: semi-final – 2017.

League Trophy: *Runners-up:* 1984.

European Competitions

Europa League: 2014–15.

FOOTBALL YEARBOOK FACT FILE

Hull City closed down activities between 1941–42 and 1943–44 but were then revived for the 1944–45 season, playing their home fixtures at The Boulevard, home of Hull rugby league club. However, the ground was unavailable for 1945–46 and with the Tigers' new Boothferry Park stadium not yet ready, they spent a further season without activity, missing out on taking part in the FA Cup for the only time in the club's history.

Record Defeat: 0–8 v Wolverhampton W, Division 2, 4 November 1911; 0–8 v Wigan Ath, FL C, 14 July 2020.

Most League Points (2 for a win): 69, Division 3, 1965–66.

Most League Points (3 for a win): 90, Division 4, 1982–83.

Most League Goals: 109, Division 3, 1965–66.

Highest League Scorer in Season: Bill McNaughton, 39, Division 3 (N), 1932–33.

Most League Goals in Total Aggregate: Chris Chilton, 193, 1960–71.

Most League Goals in One Match: 5, Ken McDonald v Bristol C, Division 2, 17 November 1928; 5, Simon 'Slim' Raleigh v Halifax T, Division 3 (N), 26 December 1930.

Most Capped Player: Theo Whitmore, 28 (119), Jamaica.

Most League Appearances: Andy Davidson, 520, 1952–67.

Youngest League Player: Matthew Edeson, 16 years 63 days v Fulham, 10 October 1992.

Record Transfer Fee Received: £17,000,000 (rising to £26,450,000) from Leicester C for Harry McGuire, June 2017.

Record Transfer Fee Paid: £13,000,000 to Tottenham H for Ryan Mason, August 2016.

Football League Record: 1905 Elected to Division 2; 1930–33 Division 3 (N); 1933–36 Division 2; 1936–49 Division 3 (N); 1949–56 Division 2; 1956–58 Division 3 (N); 1958–59 Division 3; 1959–60 Division 2; 1960–66 Division 3; 1966–78 Division 2; 1978–81 Division 3; 1981–83 Division 4; 1983–85 Division 3; 1985–91 Division 2; 1991–92 Division 3; 1992–96 Division 2; 1996–2004 Division 3; 2004–05 FL 1; 2005–08 FL C; 2008–10 Premier League; 2010–13 FL C; 2013–15 Premier League; 2015–16 FL C; 2016–17 Premier League; 2017–20 FL C; 2020–21 FL 1; 2021– FL C.

LATEST SEQUENCES

Longest Sequence of League Wins: 10, 23.2.1966 – 20.4.1966.

Longest Sequence of League Defeats: 8, 7.4.1934 – 8.9.1934.

Longest Sequence of League Draws: 5, 14.2.2012 – 10.3.2012.

Longest Sequence of Unbeaten League Matches: 19, 13.3.2001 – 22.9.2001.

Longest Sequence Without a League Win: 27, 27.3.1989 – 4.11.1989.

Successive Scoring Runs: 26 from 10.4.1990.

Successive Non-scoring Runs: 6 from 14.8.2021.

MANAGERS

James Ramster 1904–05 *(Secretary-Manager)*
Ambrose Langley 1905–13
Harry Chapman 1913–14
Fred Stringer 1914–16
David Menzies 1916–21
Percy Lewis 1921–23
Bill McCracken 1923–31
Haydn Green 1931–34
John Hill 1934–36
David Menzies 1936
Ernest Blackburn 1936–46
Major Frank Buckley 1946–48
Raich Carter 1948–51
Bob Jackson 1952–55
Bob Brocklebank 1955–61
Cliff Britton 1961–70 *(continued as General Manager to 1971)*
Terry Neill 1970–74
John Kaye 1974–77
Bobby Collins 1977–78
Ken Houghton 1978–79
Mike Smith 1979–82
Bobby Brown 1982
Colin Appleton 1982–84
Brian Horton 1984–88
Eddie Gray 1988–89
Colin Appleton 1989
Stan Ternent 1989–91
Terry Dolan 1991–97
Mark Hateley 1997–98
Warren Joyce 1998–2000
Brian Little 2000–02
Jan Molby 2002
Peter Taylor 2002–06
Phil Parkinson 2006
Phil Brown *(after caretaker role December 2006)* 2007–10
Ian Dowie *(consultant)* 2010
Nigel Pearson 2010–11
Nick Barmby 2011–12
Steve Bruce 2012–16
Mike Phelan 2016–17
Marco Silva 2017
Leonid Slutsky 2017
Nigel Adkins 2017–19
Grant McCann 2019–22
Shota Arveladze January 2022–

TEN YEAR LEAGUE RECORD

		P	*W*	*D*	*L*	*F*	*A*	*Pts*	*Pos*
2012-13	FL C	46	24	7	15	61	52	79	2
2013-14	PR Lge	38	10	7	21	38	53	37	16
2014-15	PR Lge	38	8	11	19	33	51	35	18
2015-16	FL C	46	24	11	11	69	35	83	4
2016-17	PR Lge	38	9	7	22	37	80	34	18
2017-18	FL C	46	11	16	19	70	70	49	18
2018-19	FL C	46	17	11	18	66	68	62	13
2019-20	FL C	46	12	9	25	57	87	45	24
2020-21	FL 1	46	27	8	11	80	38	89	1
2021-22	FL C	46	14	9	23	41	54	51	19

DID YOU KNOW ?

Hull City played at their Anlaby Road ground from 1906 until 1941. The ground attracted a record attendance for the visit of Newcastle United for the FA Cup sixth-round replay in March 1930. A crowd of 32,930 saw the Tigers win 1-0 to progress to the semi-finals.

HULL CITY – SKY BET CHAMPIONSHIP 2021–22 LEAGUE RECORD

Match No.	Date	Venue	Opponents	Result		H/T Score	Lg Pos.	Goalscorers	Attendance
1	Aug 7	A	Preston NE	W	4-1	1-1	1	Lewis-Potter [35], Smallwood [62], Magennis [85], Cannon [90]	12,452
2	14	H	QPR	L	0-3	0-1	12		10,728
3	18	H	Derby Co	L	0-1	0-0	18		10,451
4	21	A	Fulham	L	0-2	0-2	19		16,189
5	28	H	Bournemouth	D	0-0	0-0	18		10,199
6	Sept 11	A	Swansea C	D	0-0	0-0	20		16,317
7	14	A	Blackburn R	L	0-2	0-0	21		9140
8	18	H	Sheffield U	L	1-3	0-1	23	Lewis-Potter [74]	14,451
9	25	A	Stoke C	L	0-2	0-1	23		20,124
10	28	H	Blackpool	D	1-1	0-1	22	Eaves [84]	10,189
11	Oct 2	H	Middlesbrough	W	2-0	0-0	21	Lumley (og) [81], Wilks [90]	13,696
12	16	A	Huddersfield T	L	0-2	0-1	21		17,510
13	20	H	Peterborough U	L	1-2	1-1	22	Magennis [45]	10,245
14	23	A	Luton T	L	0-1	0-1	22		9999
15	30	H	Coventry C	L	0-1	0-1	22		11,901
16	Nov 3	A	WBA	L	0-1	0-0	23		19,659
17	6	A	Barnsley	W	2-0	1-0	22	Honeyman [33], Lewis-Potter [75]	13,003
18	20	H	Birmingham C	W	2-0	1-0	21	Honeyman [17], Wilks [57]	12,409
19	24	A	Cardiff C	W	1-0	1-0	19	Lewis-Potter [15]	17,180
20	27	H	Millwall	W	2-1	1-1	19	Honeyman [29], Longman [53]	10,613
21	Dec 4	A	Reading	D	1-1	0-1	19	Wilks [55]	11,827
22	11	H	Bristol C	D	2-2	1-0	19	Longman [3], Honeyman [79]	10,446
23	18	A	Nottingham F	L	1-2	1-0	19	Lewis-Potter [43]	26,513
24	Jan 1	A	Blackpool	L	0-1	0-1	19		11,300
25	16	H	Stoke C	L	0-2	0-1	19		11,067
26	19	H	Blackburn R	W	2-0	1-0	19	Honeyman [7], Eaves [67]	13,950
27	22	A	Bournemouth	W	1-0	0-0	19	Longman [77]	8823
28	29	H	Swansea C	W	2-0	2-0	18	Eaves [5], Lewis-Potter [17]	13,101
29	Feb 5	H	Preston NE	L	0-1	0-0	19		14,273
30	8	A	Derby Co	L	1-3	0-2	19	Forsyth (og) [65]	22,595
31	12	H	Fulham	L	0-1	0-0	19		13,022
32	15	A	Sheffield U	D	0-0	0-0	20		27,601
33	19	A	QPR	D	1-1	1-0	20	Forss [26]	14,945
34	22	H	Barnsley	L	0-2	0-2	20		16,421
35	26	A	Peterborough U	W	3-0	1-0	18	Smith, T [25], Lewis-Potter 2 [51, 70]	9463
36	Mar 5	H	WBA	L	0-2	0-1	20		13,643
37	12	A	Birmingham C	D	0-0	0-0	20		17,231
38	16	A	Coventry C	W	2-0	2-0	19	Smallwood [4], Longman [28]	15,587
39	19	H	Luton T	L	1-3	0-1	20	Eaves [90]	16,555
40	Apr 1	H	Huddersfield T	L	0-1	0-0	20		12,764
41	9	A	Middlesbrough	W	1-0	0-0	20	Lewis-Potter [74]	24,603
42	15	H	Cardiff C	W	2-1	2-0	19	Sayyadmanesh [8], Coyle [11]	15,685
43	18	A	Millwall	L	1-2	0-0	19	Eaves [87]	12,776
44	23	H	Reading	W	3-0	1-0	18	Lewis-Potter 2 [40, 90], Jones, A [53]	12,211
45	30	A	Bristol C	L	0-5	0-3	18		21,799
46	May 7	H	Nottingham F	D	1-1	0-0	19	Lewis-Potter [90]	18,399

Final League Position: 19

GOALSCORERS

League (41): Lewis-Potter 12, Eaves 5, Honeyman 5, Longman 4, Wilks 3, Magennis 2, Smallwood 2, Cannon 1, Coyle 1, Forss 1, Jones, A 1, Sayyadmanesh 1, Smith, T 1, own goals 2.
FA Cup (2): Longman 1, Smith T 1.
Carabao Cup (1): Lewis-Potter 1.

Ingram M 29	Coyle L 21 + 2	Jones A 21 + 2	Greaves J 46	Emmanuel J 3 + 3	Smallwood R 40 + 2	Docherty G 31 + 9	Wilks M 17 + 3	Moncur G 7 + 7	Lewis-Potter K 46	Magennis J 18 + 1	Smith M 6 + 3	Eaves T 12 + 19	Cannon A 4 + 6	Scott J — + 1	Elder C 21 + 7	Longman R 26 + 9	Williams R 4 + 9	Jarvis W — + 1	Huddlestone T 4 + 7	Bernard D 24 + 2	Smith T 7 + 16	Hinds J — + 1	Honeyman G 34 + 1	McLoughlin S 29 + 3	Baxter N 16	Mills J — + 1	Jones C — + 2	Fleming B 15 + 1	Slater R 12 + 4	Forss M 5 + 6	Sayyadmanesh A 6 + 6	Walsh L 1 + 2	Cartwright H 1 + 1	*Match No.*
1	2	3	4	5	6	7	8^{1}	9^{3}	10^{4}	11^{2}	12	13	14	15																				1
1	2^{3}	3	4	14	6^{2}	7		9▪	10	11	12				5	8^{1}	13																	2
1	2	3	4		6^{1}	7			10	11	9^{3}	14			5		8^{2}	12	13															3
1	2		4	12	7^{2}	9^{3}			10	11	6	13	14		5		8^{1}			3														4
1	2		4			9			10		6^{3}		14		5	8^{1}	12		7	3	11^{2}	13												5
1	2		4			7	10^{1}	9^{3}	8	11^{2}	12				5	14			6	3	13													6
1	2		4		6	9	8^{3}	12	10	11^{2}	7^{1}				5	13				3	14													7
1	2		4		7		8	9^{3}	10	11^{1}	6^{2}		12		5					3	14		13											8
1	2	3	4		6^{2}	7	8^{3}	13	10		9		12		5	14					11^{1}													9
1	2▪	3	4			6	11	9^{3}	10			13	7^{2}		5	8^{1}				14	12													10
1		3^{1}	4	5	7	13	14	9^{2}	8			11	6							2	10^{3}			12										11
1	2		4		7^{1}	12	8	14	10			13	6		5					3	11^{2}		9^{3}											12
1	2		4		12	7	10	14	8	11^{3}		13			5				6^{1}	3			9^{2}											13
1	2		4		6	7	8^{1}	12	10	11^{2}		13			5		14			3			9^{3}											14
1			4	2	6^{1}	9	14	8^{3}	10	13		11^{2}	7		5					3				12										15
1	2	3^{1}	4		6	7	8^{3}		10	11^{2}		14			5	13							9	12										16
	2^{1}		4	12	6	7	8^{3}		10	11^{2}					5	14				3	13		9		1									17
			4		6	7	11		5	10^{1}			14			8^{2}	12			2	13		9^{3}	3	1									18
			2		6	7	10^{2}		5	11^{3}		14			4^{1}	8	13		12				9^{4}	3	1	15								19
			4		6	7	10^{1}		5	11^{3}		14			12	8^{2}	13			2			9	3	1									20
			4		6	7	10		8	11^{2}					12	5^{1}				2	13		9	3	1									21
			4		6	7	11^{2}		5	10^{1}		12				8^{3}	14			2	13		9	3	1									22
			4		6	7	10^{1}		8	11^{3}		14			13	5^{2}				2	12		9	3	1									23
			4		6^{3}	7			11	10^{2}		13			8^{1}	5	14			2	12		9	3	1									24
			4		13	7^{1}		12	8			11				5	14		6^{3}	2	10^{2}		9	3	1									25
			4		6	7			11			10				8^{1}	5			2	12		9^{2}	3	1		13							26
			4		6	7			11			10				5^{1}	8^{2}			2	12		9	3	1			13						27
			4		6	7			11			10				5				2			9^{2}	3	1		13	8^{1}	12					28
1		13	4		6^{3}	7			11			10				5^{1}				2^{2}			9	3				8		12	14			29
1	5^{2}	2	4			7^{3}			11			13							14				9	3				8		10	12	6^{1}		30
1	2		4		7	13		14	9							6^{3}					12		10	3				5	8^{2}	11^{1}				31
1	2^{1}	14	4		7				9			13			12	6							10	3				5	8^{3}	11^{2}				32
1^{1}		7	4		6	14			10						5	8^{3}				2	13		9^{4}	3					15	11^{2}			12	33
			4		7^{1}	12			10							8^{3}				2	13		9	3				5	6	11^{2}		14	1	34
1		2	4		6	7^{2}	14		10										13		11^{3}		9^{1}	3				8	5			12		35
1		2	4		6	7^{1}			10			13				14					11^{2}		9	3				8	5^{3}		12			36
1		2	4		6	7^{3}			10			11^{1}				5^{2}			14				9	3				8	13	12				37
1		2	4		7	12			10			11^{3}			13	5^{2}							9	3				8	6^{1}		14			38
1		2	4		6^{1}	7^{2}			10			11			8	5^{3}			12				9	3						14	13			39
1		2	4		6	13			10			11▪			12	5^{1}							9	3				8^{3}	7^{2}		14			40
1		2	4		7^{2}	13			10						14	5^{3}					12		9	3				8	6		11^{1}			41
1	5^{3}	2	4		7^{2}				10							14				13			9	3				8	6	12	11^{1}			42
	14	2	4		7				10			12			8^{3}	5							9	3	1				6^{2}	13	11^{1}			43
	5^{2}	2	4		6	14			10			12				13							9^{3}	3	1			8	7		11^{1}			44
	5	2	4		6				10			11^{1}				14							7	3	1			8^{3}	12	13	9^{2}			45
	12	2	4		6^{3}				10			13			8	5^{1}			14				9	3	1				7		11^{2}			46

FA Cup
Third Round Everton (h) 2-3
(aet)

Carabao Cup
First Round Wigan Ath (h) 1-1
(Wigan Ath won 8-7 on penalties)

IPSWICH TOWN

FOUNDATION

Considering that Ipswich Town only reached the Football League in 1938, many people outside of East Anglia may be surprised to learn that this club was formed at a meeting held in the Town Hall as far back as 1878 when Mr T. C. Cobbold, MP, was voted president. Originally it was the Ipswich Association FC to distinguish it from the older Ipswich Football Club which played rugby. These two amalgamated in 1888 and the handling game was dropped in 1893.

Portman Road, Ipswich, Suffolk IP1 2DA.

Telephone: (01473) 400 500.

Ticket Office: (03330) 050 503.

Website: www.itfc.co.uk

Email: enquiries@itfc.co.uk

Ground Capacity: 30,311.

Record Attendance: 38,010 v Leeds U, FA Cup 6th rd, 8 March 1975.

Pitch Measurements: 102.5m × 66.1m (112yd × 72.5yd).

Chairman: Mike O'Leary.

Chief Executive: Mark Ashton.

Manager: Kieran McKenna.

Assistant Manager: Martyn Pert.

Colours: Blue shirts with thin black stripes and white trim, white shorts with blue trim, blue socks with blue and white trim.

Year Formed: 1878.

Turned Professional: 1936.

Previous Name: 1878, Ipswich Association FC; 1888, Ipswich Town.

Club Nicknames: 'The Blues', 'Town', 'The Tractor Boys'.

Grounds: 1878, Broom Hill and Brook's Hall; 1884, Portman Road.

First Football League Game: 27 August 1938, Division 3 (S), v Southend U (h) W 4–2 – Burns; Dale, Parry; Perrett, Fillingham, McLuckie; Williams, Davies (1), Jones (2), Alsop (1), Little.

Record League Victory: 7–0 v Portsmouth, Division 2, 7 November 1964 – Thorburn; Smith, McNeil; Baxter, Bolton, Thompson; Broadfoot (1), Hegan (2), Baker (1), Leadbetter, Brogan (3). 7–0 v Southampton, Division 1, 2 February 1974 – Sivell; Burley, Mills (1), Morris, Hunter, Beattie (1), Hamilton (2), Viljoen, Johnson, Whymark (2), Lambert (1) (Woods). 7–0 v WBA, Division 1, 6 November 1976 – Sivell; Burley, Mills, Talbot, Hunter, Beattie (1), Osborne, Wark (1), Mariner (1) (Bertschin), Whymark (4), Woods.

HONOURS

League Champions: Division 1 – 1961–62; Division 2 – 1960–61, 1967–68, 1991–92; Division 3S – 1953–54, 1956–57.
Runners-up: Division 1 – 1980–81, 1981–82.

FA Cup Winners: 1978.

League Cup: semi-final – 1982, 1985, 2001, 2011.

Texaco Cup Winners: 1973.

European Competitions
European Cup: 1962–63.
UEFA Cup: 1973–74 *(qf)*, 1974–75, 1975–76, 1977–78, 1979–80, 1980–81 *(winners)*, 1981–82, 1982–83, 2001–02, 2002–03.
European Cup-Winners' Cup: 1978–79 *(qf)*.

FOOTBALL YEARBOOK FACT FILE

In November 1911 the corrugated iron roof of the main grandstand at Ipswich Town's Portman Road ground was completely blown off in a gale. The roof landed on the adjoining road, damaging the tram line and trees. Just 24 hours earlier almost 700 people had been in the stand watching Town play local rivals Orwell Works in a friendly match.

Record Cup Victory: 10–0 v Floriana, European Cup prel. rd, 25 September 1962 – Bailey; Malcolm, Compton; Baxter, Laurel, Elsworthy (1); Stephenson, Moran (2), Crawford (5), Phillips (2), Blackwood.

Record Defeat: 1–10 v Fulham, Division 1, 26 December 1963.

Most League Points (2 for a win): 64, Division 3 (S), 1953–54 and 1955–56.

Most League Points (3 for a win): 87, Division 1, 1999–2000.

Most League Goals: 106, Division 3 (S), 1955–56.

Highest League Scorer in Season: Ted Phillips, 41, Division 3 (S), 1956–57.

Most League Goals in Total Aggregate: Ray Crawford, 204, 1958–63 and 1966–69.

Most League Goals in One Match: 5, Alan Brazil v Southampton, Division 1, 16 February 1981.

Most Capped Player: Allan Hunter, 47 (53), Northern Ireland.

Most League Appearances: Mick Mills, 591, 1966–82.

Youngest League Player: Connor Wickham, 16 years 11 days, v Doncaster R, 11 April 2009.

Record Transfer Fee Received: £8,000,000 (rising to £12,000,000) from Sunderland for Connor Wickham, June 2011.

Record Transfer Fee Paid: £4,800,000 to Sampdoria for Matteo Sereni, August 2001.

Football League Record: 1938 Elected to Division 3 (S); 1954–55 Division 2; 1955–57 Division 3 (S); 1957–61 Division 2; 1961–64 Division 1; 1964–68 Division 2; 1968–86 Division 1; 1986–92 Division 2; 1992–95 Premier League; 1995–2000 Division 1; 2000–02 Premier League; 2002–04 Division 1; 2004–19 FL C; 2019– FL 1.

MANAGERS

Mick O'Brien 1936–37
Scott Duncan 1937–55
(continued as Secretary)
Alf Ramsey 1955–63
Jackie Milburn 1963–64
Bill McGarry 1964–68
Bobby Robson 1969–82
Bobby Ferguson 1982–87
Johnny Duncan 1987–90
John Lyall 1990–94
George Burley 1994–2002
Joe Royle 2002–06
Jim Magilton 2006–09
Roy Keane 2009–11
Paul Jewell 2011–12
Mick McCarthy 2012–18
Paul Hurst 2018
Paul Lambert 2018–21
Paul Cook 2021
Kieran McKenna December 2021–

LATEST SEQUENCES

Longest Sequence of League Wins: 8, 23.9.1953 – 31.10.1953.

Longest Sequence of League Defeats: 10, 4.9.1954 – 16.10.1954.

Longest Sequence of League Draws: 7, 10.11.1990 – 21.12.1990.

Longest Sequence of Unbeaten League Matches: 23, 8.12.1979 – 26.4.1980.

Longest Sequence Without a League Win: 21, 28.8.1963 – 14.12.1963.

Successive Scoring Runs: 31 from 7.3.2004.

Successive Non-scoring Runs: 7 from 28.2.1995.

TEN YEAR LEAGUE RECORD

		P	*W*	*D*	*L*	*F*	*A*	*Pts*	*Pos*
2012-13	FL C	46	16	12	18	48	61	60	14
2013-14	FL C	46	18	14	14	60	54	68	9
2014-15	FL C	46	22	12	12	72	54	78	6
2015-16	FL C	46	18	15	13	53	51	69	7
2016-17	FL C	46	13	16	17	48	58	55	16
2017-18	FL C	46	17	9	20	57	60	60	12
2018-19	FL C	46	5	16	25	36	77	31	24
2019-20	FL 1	36	14	10	12	46	36	52	11§
2020-21	FL 1	46	19	12	15	46	46	69	9
2021-22	FL 1	46	18	16	12	67	46	70	11

§Decided on points-per-game (1.44)

DID YOU KNOW ?

Jason Dozzell became the youngest player to score in English top-flight football when he netted on his debut for Ipswich Town against Coventry City in February 1984. Dozzell, who was just 16 years and 57 days old, came on as a substitute in the game, scoring Town's final goal in their 3-1 win.

IPSWICH TOWN – SKY BET LEAGUE ONE 2021–22 LEAGUE RECORD

Match No.	Date		Venue	Opponents	Result		H/T Score	Lg Pos.	Goalscorers	Attendance
1	Aug	7	H	Morecambe	D	2-2	0-1	9	Fraser [61], Bonne [90]	21,037
2		14	A	Burton Alb	L	1-2	1-1	16	Pigott [22]	3766
3		17	A	Cheltenham T	L	1-2	1-0	19	Penney [9]	4746
4		21	H	Milton Keynes D	D	2-2	1-0	20	Bonne 2 [16, 71]	18,622
5		28	H	AFC Wimbledon	D	2-2	0-0	21	Pigott (pen) [52], Burns [54]	19,051
6	Sept	11	H	Bolton W	L	2-5	2-3	22	Bonne [5], Santos (og) [30]	19,267
7		18	A	Lincoln C	W	1-0	1-0	19	Bonne [30]	9874
8		25	H	Sheffield W	D	1-1	0-1	21	Chaplin [90]	21,338
9		28	H	Doncaster R	W	6-0	2-0	19	Bonne 2 [13, 73], Evans 3 [31, 70, 76], Edmundson [80]	18,111
10	Oct	2	A	Accrington S	L	1-2	1-0	19	Bonne [38]	2600
11		9	H	Shrewsbury T	W	2-1	1-1	14	Chaplin [23], Bonne [54]	19,256
12		16	A	Cambridge U	D	2-2	2-1	15	Aluko 2 [10, 36]	7944
13		19	A	Portsmouth	W	4-0	1-0	13	Bonne [41], Chaplin [54], Aluko [58], Burns [75]	16,301
14		23	H	Fleetwood T	W	2-1	0-0	10	Chaplin [49], Celina [90]	20,099
15		30	A	Plymouth Arg	L	1-2	1-1	11	Edmundson [14]	16,087
16	Nov	2	A	Wycombe W	W	4-1	1-1	9	Celina 2 [27, 90], Bonne [51], Burns [60]	6943
17		13	H	Oxford U	D	0-0	0-0	9		21,322
18		20	A	Sunderland	L	0-2	0-0	10		31,033
19		23	H	Rotherham U	L	0-2	0-1	13		18,221
20		28	H	Crewe Alex	W	2-1	2-0	11	Offord (og) [3], Celina [45]	18,883
21	Dec	7	A	Charlton Ath	L	0-2	0-1	11		26,376
22		11	A	Wigan Ath	D	1-1	0-1	12	Norwood [77]	10,296
23		18	H	Sunderland	D	1-1	1-0	11	Norwood [45]	29,005
24		29	H	Wycombe W	W	1-0	1-0	11	Norwood [44]	26,456
25	Jan	8	A	Gillingham	W	4-0	3-0	10	Norwood [9], Burns [13], Bonne [23], Chaplin (pen) [85]	6401
26		15	A	Bolton W	L	0-2	0-0	11		14,020
27		22	H	Accrington S	W	2-1	1-1	9	Burns [23], Chaplin [65]	20,126
28		25	A	AFC Wimbledon	W	2-0	0-0	8	Burns 2 [61, 86]	8117
29		29	A	Sheffield W	L	0-1	0-1	9		23,517
30	Feb	5	H	Gillingham	W	1-0	0-0	9	Chaplin [74]	20,698
31		8	A	Doncaster R	W	1-0	1-0	9	Bakinson [39]	6383
32		12	A	Milton Keynes D	D	0-0	0-0	9		15,311
33		19	H	Burton Alb	W	3-0	1-0	9	Jackson [1], Burns [62], Celina [78]	20,516
34		22	H	Cheltenham T	D	0-0	0-0	9		21,318
35		26	A	Morecambe	D	1-1	0-0	9	Burns [86]	4928
36	Mar	5	A	Fleetwood T	W	2-0	0-0	9	Morsy [72], Jackson [81]	4190
37		8	H	Lincoln C	W	2-0	2-0	9	Burns [22], Jackson [32]	24,989
38		12	H	Portsmouth	D	0-0	0-0	9		25,500
39		19	A	Oxford U	D	1-1	0-0	9	Celina [70]	11,029
40		26	H	Plymouth Arg	W	1-0	1-0	9	Morsy [37]	23,256
41	Apr	2	H	Cambridge U	L	0-1	0-0	9		26,515
42		9	A	Shrewsbury T	D	1-1	1-0	9	Norwood [6]	7682
43		16	A	Rotherham U	L	0-1	0-0	10		9394
44		19	H	Wigan Ath	D	2-2	0-1	11	Chaplin [61], Morsy [73]	21,329
45		23	A	Crewe Alex	D	1-1	1-0	11	Chaplin [45]	4986
46		30	H	Charlton Ath	W	4-0	2-0	11	Bakinson [7], Burns 2 [11, 50], Norwood [88]	26,002

Final League Position: 11

GOALSCORERS

League (67): Bonne 12, Burns 12, Chaplin 9 (1 pen), Celina 6, Norwood 6, Aluko 3, Evans 3, Jackson 3, Morsy 3, Bakinson 2, Edmundson 2, Pigott 2 (1 pen), Fraser 1, Penney 1, own goals 2.
FA Cup (3): Burns 1, Chaplin 1, El Mizouni 1.
Carabao Cup (0).
Papa John's Trophy (5): Jackson 2, Chaplin 1, Norwood 1, Pigott 1.

Hladky V 12	Vincent-Young K 11 + 4	Nsiala A 10 + 1	Woolfenden L 30 + 1	Penney M 18 + 4	Harper R 6 + 7	Evans L 26 + 1	Burns W 34 + 3	Chaplin C 24 + 15	Fraser S 14 + 1	Pigott J 10 + 12	Donacien J 40 + 3	Norwood J 12 + 11	Bonne M 29 + 14	Dobra A 1 + 1	Barry L 1 + 1	Edwards K 11 + 7	Burgess C 18 + 3	Jackson K 7 + 5	Carroll T 8 + 6	Coulson H 6	Aluko S 18 + 12	Walton C 34	Edmundson S 32	Celina B 23 + 9	El Mizouni I 3 + 2	Morsy S 33 + 1	Clements B 4	Humphreys C — + 2	Bakinson T 14 + 3	Thompson D 15 + 2	Baggott E 2	*Match No.*
1	2	3^{1}	4	5	6	7	8	9^{2}	10	11^{3}	12	13	14																			1
1	2		3	5	6	7			10	11	4		12	8^{2}	9^{1}	13																2
1			3	5	6^{3}	7			8	11^{1}	2		9^{2}		13	10	4	12	14													3
1	2		3	12	6	7	8^{2}		9^{3}				11	14		10	4		13	5^{1}												4
1	2^{1}		3	14	6	7	8^{2}		9	11	13					10	4			5^{3}	12											5
	2^{1}				6	7	8^{3}	9^{2}			12		11				4	14	13	5	10	1	3									6
1			12		13	6	8		10^{3}		2		11				4		7	5^{1}	14		3	9^{2}								7
1				5	12		8^{1}	13	10	14	2		11				4		7				3	9^{2}	6^{3}							8
1				5	14	6^{3}	8^{1}	13	10		2		11				4				12		3	9^{2}		7						9
1				5	12	6^{3}	8		10^{1}		2	14	11			13	4						3	9^{2}		7						10
1		13		5^{2}		7	8^{1}	9	10	14	2		11^{3}			12	4						3			6						11
1				5			12	9^{2}	10^{3}		2		11			14	4				8^{1}		3	13	7	6						12
		4		5	13	7	12	9^{2}			2		11			10^{1}					8^{3}	1	3	14		6						13
		4		5		7	12	9^{3}			2		11			10^{2}	14				8^{1}	1	3	13		6						14
		3	2	5	14	6^{3}		9^{2}		13			11			10				8^{1}		1	4	12		7						15
	2^{2}	3			13	7	8						11			10^{3}	12			5^{1}	14	1	4	9		6						16
		3				7	8^{1}	13		14	2		11			10^{2}					12	1	4	9^{3}		6	5					17
		3				6		13	12	14	2		11^{3}			10^{2}					8	1	4	9^{1}		7	5					18
		3		12		7^{2}		8^{3}	10	14	2		11			13						1	4	9		6	5^{1}					19
		3				13		9^{2}	7		2		11			12					8^{1}	1	4	10		6	5					20
	2	3				7		13	9^{1}	12	5		11			10^{3}					8^{2}	1	4			6		14				21
	2					7		6^{2}		11^{1}	5	12	10			9	4				13	1	3			8						22
	12		3	5^{1}		8	6	13			2	11^{2}	10								9	1	4			7						23
1			4	8		6	5	12		14	2	10^{2}	11^{3}						13		9^{1}		3			7						24
			3	8		6	5	14		12	2	11^{2}	10^{1}					13			9^{3}	1	4			7						25
	12		3	8^{1}		6	5	14			2	11^{2}	10								9^{3}	1	4	13		7						26
	8		3				5	10^{3}			2	13	11^{2}					14	7^{1}			1	4	9		6			12			27
	8▪		3				5	13			2	10^{3}	14					11^{2}	7		9^{1}	1	4	12					6			28
			3				5	9^{2}		14	2	12	11^{3}								13	1	4	10	6^{1}				7	8		29
			3			6	5^{1}	9^{3}		10^{2}	2	11	13			12			7			1	4						14	8		30
			3			6	5	10^{3}			2	13	11^{2}								14	1	4	9	12				7^{1}	8		31
			3				5	10^{2}			2	12	13					11^{1}			14	1	4	9		6			7^{3}	8		32
			3			6	5	13		10^{1}	2	14						11^{3}			9^{2}	1	4	12		7				8		33
	12		3				5	10		14	2		13					11^{2}	7^{3}			1	4	9		6				8^{1}		34
			3				5	14			2	11^{2}	10^{1}					13			9^{3}	1	4	12		6			7	8		35
			3				6	7		11^{1}	2	14	13					10^{2}				1	4	8^{3}		5			12	9		36
			3				5	14			2						12	11	13		9^{3}	1	4^{1}	10		6^{2}			7	8		37
			3				5^{3}	9			2		13				4	11^{2}	12		14	1		10		6^{1}			7	8		38
			3				5	9		11^{2}	2		12				4		7^{1}		14	1		10^{3}		13			6	8		39
			3				5	12			2	11^{2}	13				4				9^{1}	1		10		7			6	8		40
			3	14			5	9^{2}			2	11	12				4		7^{1}		13	1		10		6				8^{3}		41
			3	8			5	9			2	10^{2}	13				4▪				11^{1}	1				6			7	12		42
			3				5	13		14	2	11^{2}	12								9^{1}	1		10^{3}		7			6	8	4	43
			3	8^{1}			5	9			2	13	10^{2}				4					1		11		6			7	12		44
	5^{2}		3					9^{3}		10^{1}	2	11	14				4					1		13	12	7			6	8		45
	12		3	8			5	9^{2}			2^{1}	14	11^{3}									1		10		7		13	6		4	46

FA Cup

First Round	Oldham Ath	(h)	1-1
Replay	Oldham Ath	(a)	2-1
Second Round	Barrow	(h)	0-0
Replay	Barrow	(a)	0-2

Carabao Cup

First Round	Newport Co	(h)	0-1

Papa John's Trophy

Group A (S)	West Ham U U21	(h)	1-2
Group A (S)	Gillingham	(a)	2-0
Group A (S)	Colchester U	(h)	0-0
(Ipswich T won 4-3 on penalties)			
Second Round	Arsenal U21	(h)	2-2
(Arsenal U21 won 4-3 on penalties)			

LEEDS UNITED

FOUNDATION

Immediately the Leeds City club (founded in 1904) was wound up by the FA in October 1919, following allegations of illegal payments to players, a meeting was called by a Leeds solicitor, Mr Alf Masser, at which Leeds United was formed. They joined the Midland League, playing their first game in that competition in November 1919. It was in this same month that the new club had discussions with the directors of a virtually bankrupt Huddersfield Town who wanted to move to Leeds in an amalgamation. But Huddersfield survived even that crisis.

Elland Road Stadium, Elland Road, Leeds, West Yorkshire LS11 0ES.

Telephone: (0871) 334 1919.

Ticket Office: (0871) 334 1992.

Website: www.leedsunited.com

Email: reception@leedsunited.com

Ground Capacity: 37,678.

Record Attendance: 57,892 v Sunderland, FA Cup 5th rd (replay), 15 March 1967.

Pitch Measurements: 105m × 68m (115yd × 74.5yd).

Chairman: Andrea Radrizzani.

Chief Executive: Angus Kinnear.

Head Coach: Jesse Marsch.

Assistant Head Coaches: Franz Schiemer, Cameron Toshack, Mark Jackson.

Colours: White shirts with blue and limellow trim, white shorts with blue and limellow trim, white socks with blue and limellow trim.

Year Formed: 1919, as Leeds United after disbandment (by FA order) of Leeds City (formed in 1904).

Turned Professional: 1920.

Club Nickname: 'The Whites'.

Ground: 1919, Elland Road.

First Football League Game: 28 August 1920, Division 2, v Port Vale (a) L 0–2 – Down; Duffield, Tillotson; Musgrove, Baker, Walton; Mason, Goldthorpe, Thompson, Lyon, Best.

Record League Victory: 8–0 v Leicester C, Division 1, 7 April 1934 – Moore; George Milburn, Jack Milburn; Edwards, Hart, Copping; Mahon (2), Firth (2), Duggan (2), Furness (2), Cochrane.

HONOURS

League Champions: Division 1 – 1968–69, 1973–74, 1991–92; FL C – 2019–20. Division 2 – 1923–24, 1963–64, 1989–90.
Runners-up: Division 1 – 1964–65, 1965–66, 1969–70, 1970–71, 1971–72; Division 2 – 1927–28, 1931–32, 1955–56; FL 1 – 2009–10.

FA Cup Winners: 1972.
Runners-up: 1965, 1970, 1973.

League Cup Winners: 1968.
Runners-up: 1996.

European Competitions
European Cup: 1969–70 *(sf)*, 1974–75 *(runners-up)*.
Champions League: 1992–93, 2000–01 *(sf)*.
Fairs Cup: 1965–66 *(sf)*, 1966–67 *(runners-up)*, 1967–68 *(winners)*, 1968–69 *(qf)*, 1970–71 *(winners)*.
UEFA Cup: 1971–72, 1973–74, 1979–80, 1995–96, 1998–99, 1999–2000 *(sf)*, 2001–02, 2002–03.
European Cup-Winners' Cup: 1972–73 *(runners-up)*.

FOOTBALL YEARBOOK FACT FILE

Leeds United's Billy Poyntz was married at 1.30pm on 20 February 1922, then dashed off to Elland Road where he was playing in the Second Division fixture against Leicester City at 3.00. He went on to produce one of the best performances of his senior career, netting a hat-trick as United beat the Foxes 3-0. This was the only occasion that he scored three times in a Football League match.

Record Cup Victory: 10–0 v Lyn (Oslo), European Cup 1st rd 1st leg, 17 September 1969 – Sprake; Reaney, Cooper, Bremner (2), Charlton, Hunter, Madeley, Clarke (2), Jones (3), Giles (2) (Bates), O'Grady (1).

Record Defeat: 1–8 v Stoke C, Division 1, 27 August 1934.

Most League Points (2 for a win): 67, Division 1, 1968–69.

Most League Points (3 for a win): 93, FL C, 2019–20.

Most League Goals: 98, Division 2, 1927–28.

Highest League Scorer in Season: John Charles, 42, Division 2, 1953–54.

Most League Goals in Total Aggregate: Peter Lorimer, 168, 1965–79 and 1983–86.

Most League Goals in One Match: 5, Gordon Hodgson v Leicester C, Division 1, 1 October 1938.

Most Capped Player: Lucas Radebe, 58 (70), South Africa.

Most League Appearances: Jack Charlton, 629, 1953–73.

Youngest League Player: Peter Lorimer, 15 years 289 days v Southampton, 29 September 1962.

Record Transfer Fee Received: £42,000,000 (rising to £45,000,000) from Manchester C for Kalvin Phillips, July 2022.

Record Transfer Fee Paid: £30,000,000 to Valencia for Rodrigo, August 2020.

Football League Record: 1920 Elected to Division 2; 1924–27 Division 1; 1927–28 Division 2; 1928–31 Division 1; 1931–32 Division 2; 1932–47 Division 1; 1947–56 Division 2; 1956–60 Division 1; 1960–64 Division 2; 1964–82 Division 1; 1982–90 Division 2; 1990–92 Division 1; 1992–2004 Premier League; 2004–07 FL C; 2007–10 FL 1; 2010–20 FL C; 2020– Premier League.

MANAGERS

Dick Ray 1919–20
Arthur Fairclough 1920–27
Dick Ray 1927–35
Bill Hampson 1935–47
Willis Edwards 1947–48
Major Frank Buckley 1948–53
Raich Carter 1953–58
Bill Lambton 1958–59
Jack Taylor 1959–61
Don Revie OBE 1961–74
Brian Clough 1974
Jimmy Armfield 1974–78
Jock Stein CBE 1978
Jimmy Adamson 1978–80
Allan Clarke 1980–82
Eddie Gray MBE 1982–85
Billy Bremner 1985–88
Howard Wilkinson 1988–96
George Graham 1996–98
David O'Leary 1998–2002
Terry Venables 2002–03
Peter Reid 2003
Eddie Gray *(Caretaker)* 2003–04
Kevin Blackwell 2004–06
Dennis Wise 2006–08
Gary McAllister 2008
Simon Grayson 2008–12
Neil Warnock 2012–13
Brian McDermott 2013–14
Dave Hockaday 2014
Darko Milanic 2014
Neil Redfearn 2014–15
Uwe Rosler 2015
Steve Evans 2015–16
Garry Monk 2016–17
Thomas Christiansen 2017–18
Paul Heckingbottom 2018
Marcelo Bielsa 2018–22
Jesse Marsch February 2022–

LATEST SEQUENCES

Longest Sequence of League Wins: 9, 18.4.2009 – 5.9.2009.

Longest Sequence of League Defeats: 6, 12.2.2022 – 10.3.2022.

Longest Sequence of League Draws: 5, 2.5.2015 – 22.8.2015.

Longest Sequence of Unbeaten League Matches: 34, 26.10.1968 – 26.8.1969.

Longest Sequence Without a League Win: 17, 1.2.1947 – 26.5.1947.

Successive Scoring Runs: 30 from 27.8.1927.

Successive Non-scoring Runs: 6 from 30.1.1982.

TEN YEAR LEAGUE RECORD

		P	W	D	L	F	A	Pts	Pos
2012-13	FL C	46	17	10	19	57	66	61	13
2013-14	FL C	46	16	9	21	59	67	57	15
2014-15	FL C	46	15	11	20	50	61	56	15
2015-16	FL C	46	14	17	15	50	58	59	13
2016-17	FL C	46	22	9	15	61	47	75	7
2017-18	FL C	46	17	9	20	59	64	60	13
2018-19	FL C	46	25	8	13	73	50	83	3
2019-20	FL C	46	28	9	9	77	35	93	1
2020-21	PR Lge	38	18	5	15	62	54	59	9
2021-22	PR Lge	38	9	11	18	42	79	38	17

DID YOU KNOW ?

The legendary John Charles began his Leeds United career at centre-half but in October 1952 he was switched to playing at centre-forward with devastating effect. Between 25 October and 29 November, a run of five games, he scored every single one of United's 10 goals and went on to finish the season as the team's leading scorer.

LEEDS UNITED – PREMIER LEAGUE 2021–22 LEAGUE RECORD

Match No.	*Date*	*Venue*	*Opponents*	*Result*	*H/T Score*	*Lg Pos.*	*Goalscorers*	*Attendance*
1	Aug 14	A	Manchester U	L 1-5	0-1	20	Ayling [49]	72,732
2	21	H	Everton	D 2-2	1-1	14	Klich [41], Raphinha [72]	36,293
3	29	A	Burnley	D 1-1	0-0	15	Bamford [86]	18,665
4	Sept 12	H	Liverpool	L 0-3	0-1	17		36,507
5	17	A	Newcastle U	D 1-1	1-1	16	Raphinha [13]	50,407
6	25	H	West Ham U	L 1-2	1-0	18	Raphinha [19]	36,417
7	Oct 2	H	Watford	W 1-0	1-0	16	Llorente [18]	36,261
8	16	A	Southampton	L 0-1	0-0	17		30,506
9	23	H	Wolverhampton W	D 1-1	0-1	17	Rodrigo (pen) [90]	36,475
10	31	A	Norwich C	W 2-1	0-0	17	Raphinha [56], Rodrigo [60]	26,913
11	Nov 7	H	Leicester C	D 1-1	1-1	15	Raphinha [26]	36,478
12	21	A	Tottenham H	L 1-2	1-0	17	James [44]	58,989
13	27	A	Brighton & HA	D 0-0	0-0	17		31,166
14	30	H	Crystal Palace	W 1-0	0-0	15	Raphinha (pen) [90]	35,558
15	Dec 5	H	Brentford	D 2-2	1-0	14	Roberts [27], Bamford [90]	35,639
16	11	A	Chelsea	L 2-3	1-1	15	Raphinha (pen) [28], Gelhardt [83]	39,959
17	14	A	Manchester C	L 0-7	0-3	16		52,401
18	18	H	Arsenal	L 1-4	0-3	16	Raphinha (pen) [75]	36,166
19	Jan 2	H	Burnley	W 3-1	1-0	16	Harrison [39], Dallas [77], James [90]	36,083
20	16	A	West Ham U	W 3-2	2-1	15	Harrison 3 [10, 37, 60]	59,951
21	22	H	Newcastle U	L 0-1	0-0	15		36,405
22	Feb 9	A	Aston Villa	D 3-3	2-3	15	James 2 [9, 45], Llorente [63]	41,927
23	12	A	Everton	L 0-3	0-2	15		39,150
24	20	H	Manchester U	L 2-4	0-2	15	Rodrigo [53], Raphinha [54]	36,715
25	23	A	Liverpool	L 0-6	0-3	15		53,018
26	26	H	Tottenham H	L 0-4	0-3	16		36,599
27	Mar 5	A	Leicester C	L 0-1	0-0	16		32,236
28	10	H	Aston Villa	L 0-3	0-1	16		36,400
29	13	H	Norwich C	W 2-1	1-0	16	Rodrigo [14], Gelhardt [90]	36,321
30	18	A	Wolverhampton W	W 3-2	0-2	16	Harrison [63], Rodrigo [66], Ayling [90]	31,842
31	Apr 2	H	Southampton	D 1-1	1-0	16	Harrison [29]	36,580
32	9	A	Watford	W 3-0	1-0	16	Raphinha [21], Rodrigo [73], Harrison [85]	20,957
33	25	A	Crystal Palace	D 0-0	0-0	16		25,357
34	30	H	Manchester C	L 0-4	0-1	17		35,771
35	May 8	A	Arsenal	L 1-2	0-2	18	Llorente [66]	60,108
36	11	H	Chelsea	L 0-3	0-1	18		36,549
37	15	H	Brighton & HA	D 1-1	0-1	17	Struijk [90]	36,638
38	22	A	Brentford	W 2-1	0-0	17	Raphinha (pen) [56], Harrison [90]	16,957

Final League Position: 17

GOALSCORERS

League (42): Raphinha 11 (4 pens), Harrison 8, Rodrigo 6 (1 pen), James 4, Llorente 3, Ayling 2, Bamford 2, Gelhardt 2, Dallas 1, Klich 1, Roberts 1, Struijk 1.
FA Cup (0).
Carabao Cup (3): Harrison 2, Phillips 1.
Papa John's Trophy (7): Bate 1, Dean 1, Greenwood 1, Miller 1, Summerville 1 (1 pen), own goals 2.

Meslier I 38	Ayling L 26	Struijk P 22 + 7	Cooper L 21	Dallas S 34	Raphinha R 34 + 1	Koch R 17 + 3	Klich M 26 + 7	Harrison J 32 + 3	Rodrigo M 27 + 4	Bamford P 7 + 2	Firpo J 19 + 5	Helder Costa W — + 1	Roberts T 7 + 16	Phillips K 18 + 2	Shackleton J 7 + 7	Llorente D 28	James D 29 + 3	Summerville C — + 6	Cresswell C 1 + 4	Forshaw A 17 + 5	Gelhardt J 5 + 15	Drameh C 1 + 2	McKinstry S — + 1	Greenwood S 1 + 6	McCarron L — + 1	Bate L 1 + 2	Hjelde L — + 2	Klaesson K — + 1	*Match No.*
1	2	3	4	5	6	7	8	9^{2}	10^{1}	11^{3}	12	13	14																1
1	2	3	4	5	8		9^{2}	10		11	7^{1}		12	6	13														2
1	5	3	4	7	8			10	9^{2}	11			13	6	12	2^{1}													3
1	2	12■	4	8	7			10^{3}	9^{2}	11	5		13	6		3^{1}	14												4
1	3^{3}		4	2	7^{2}		9		8	11	5		12	6	14		10^{1}	13											5
1			4	9	7^{2}		8	12	11		5		13	6	2^{3}		10^{1}	14	3										6
1		13	4	8^{1}	7		9^{2}		11		5		12	6	2	3	10												7
1		3	4	8			6^{2}	9	10^{1}				7^{3}		5	2	11	14		12	13								8
1		7	4	5	6^{2}		8^{3}	9^{1}	11				12		2	3	10	13			14								9
1		4	3	7	8			11	9^{3}				14	6	5^{1}	2	10^{2}			13		12							10
1		5	4	2	7			10^{1}	9				12	6		3	11		13	8^{2}									11
1		5	4	7			9^{1}	10			12		13	3		2	8			6^{2}	11^{3}		14						12
1		12	4	5	8			10^{3}	9		7^{1}		14	3^{2}	13	2	11			6									13
1		5^{1}	4	2	7		9^{2}		13		12		11^{3}	6		3	10		14	8									14
1	2		4^{1}	5	9		13	12		14	8^{3}		10	6^{2}		3	11			7									15
1	3			2	10^{2}		12	8			5		9		6^{1}	4	11^{3}		14	7	13								16
1	3			6	8		12	10			5^{3}		9		2^{1}	4	11^{2}			7	13	14							17
1	4			5	8	3	6^{2}	10^{1}					9					12^{3}		7	11	2		13	14				18
1	2			5	9	3	6	11^{2}			8		10^{1}			4	13			7	12								19
1	3	4		2	8	7	9	10	14		5^{2}						11			6^{1}						12^{3}	13		20
1	2	4		5	8	6	7^{2}	10	9				12			3	11^{1}				13								21
1	2	4		5	8	6	7^{1}	10	9							3	11			12									22
1	2	4		5^{1}	7^{2}	6	9^{3}	10	8				14			3	11			13							12		23
1	2	4		5	13	7^{1}	9	10^{2}	11		12					3^{3}	8			6	14								24
1	3	4		2	7		8^{2}	10	9^{1}		5		12		13		11^{3}			6	14								25
1	2	4^{1}		8	7	6	12	10^{2}	13		5^{3}				14	3	11			9									26
1	3	4		2	8	7	6^{2}	10^{3}	9^{1}		5		14				11			13	12								27
1	3	4		2	8	7	14	10^{2}	9^{1}	13	5						11			6^{3}	12								28
1	2	4		5	10	13	6^{3}	12	9^{2}	11^{1}						3	8			7	14								29
1^{4}	2	4		5		13	6^{3}	10	9	11^{1}						3^{2}	8		14	7				12				15	30
1	2^{3}	14	4	5	8		6^{2}	10	9					13		3	11^{1}			7	12								31
1	2		4	5	8^{3}	6	7^{1}	10	9					12		3	11^{2}	14						13					32
1	2		4	5	8	12	6^{1}	10	9^{3}					7		3	11^{2}				14			13					33
1	3	5		2^{1}	7	4	8	10	11^{3}		6^{2}			9			12				13			14					34
1	2■	12			8^{3}	3	6^{2}	10	14		5			7		4	9				11^{1}					13			35
1		5	4		8^{3}	2	13	10^{1}	11		12			6		3	9■				14					7^{2}			36
1		14	4		9	2^{1}	6^{3}	8	11		5^{2}			7	12	3					10			13					37
1		12	4		6	2	13	9	10		5			8		3					11^{1}			7^{2}					38

FA Cup

Third Round	West Ham U	(a)	0-2

Carabao Cup

Second Round	Crewe Alex	(h)	3-0
Third Round	Fulham	(a)	0-0
(Leeds U won 6-5 on penalties)			
Fourth Round	Arsenal	(a)	0-2

Papa John's Trophy (Leeds U U21)

Group B (N)	Tranmere R	(a)	1-4
Group B (N)	Oldham Ath	(a)	3-2
Group B (N)	Salford C	(a)	3-5

LEICESTER CITY

FOUNDATION

In 1884 a number of young footballers, who were mostly old boys of Wyggeston School, held a meeting at a house on the Roman Fosse Way and formed Leicester Fosse FC. They collected 9d (less than 4p) towards the cost of a ball, plus the same amount for membership. Their first professional, Harry Webb from Stafford Rangers, was signed in 1888 for 2s 6d (12p) per week, plus travelling expenses.

King Power Stadium, Filbert Way, Leicester LE2 7FL.

Telephone: (0344) 815 5000.

Ticket Office: (0344) 815 5000 (option 1).

Website: www.lcfc.com

Email: lcfchelp@lcfc.co.uk

Ground Capacity: 32,261.

Record Attendance: 47,298 v Tottenham H, FA Cup 5th rd, 18 February 1928 (at Filbert Street); 32,242 v Sunderland, Premier League, 8 August 2015 (at King Power Stadium).

Pitch Measurements: 105m × 68m (115yd × 74.5yd).

Chairman: Aiyawatt 'Top' Srivaddhanaprabha.

Chief Executive: Susan Whelan.

Manager: Brendan Rodgers.

Assistant Manager: Chris Davies.

Colours: Blue shirts with white trim, white shorts with blue trim, blue socks with white trim.

Year Formed: 1884.

Turned Professional: 1888.

Previous Name: 1884, Leicester Fosse; 1919, Leicester City.

Club Nickname: 'The Foxes'.

Grounds: 1884, Victoria Park; 1887, Belgrave Road; 1888, Victoria Park; 1891, Filbert Street; 2002, Walkers Stadium (renamed King Power Stadium 2011).

First Football League Game: 1 September 1894, Division 2, v Grimsby T (a) L 3–4 – Thraves; Smith, Bailey; Seymour, Brown, Henrys; Hill, Hughes, McArthur (1), Skea (2), Priestman.

Record League Victory: 10–0 v Portsmouth, Division 1, 20 October 1928 – McLaren; Black, Brown; Findlay, Carr, Watson; Adcock, Hine (3), Chandler (6), Lochhead, Barry (1).

Record Cup Victory: 8–1 v Coventry C (a), League Cup 5th rd, 1 December 1964 – Banks; Sjoberg, Norman (2); Roberts, King, McDerment; Hodgson (2), Cross, Goodfellow, Gibson (1), Stringfellow (2), (1 og).

HONOURS

League Champions: Premier League – 2015–16; FL C – 2013–14; Division 2 – 1924–25, 1936–37, 1953–54, 1956–57, 1970–71, 1979–80; FL 1 – 2008–09.
Runners-up: Division 1 – 1928–29; First Division – 2002–03; Division 2 – 1907–08.

FA Cup Winners: 2021.
Runners-up: 1949, 1961, 1963, 1969.

League Cup Winners: 1964, 1997, 2000.
Runners-up: 1965, 1999.

European Competitions
UEFA Champions League: 2016–17 (*qf*).

UEFA Cup: 1997–98, 2000–01.
Europa League: 2020–21, 2021–22.
Europa Conference League: 2021–22 (*sf*).
European Cup-Winners' Cup: 1961–62.

FOOTBALL YEARBOOK FACT FILE

Leicester City used a hat-trick of goalkeepers in their FA Cup sixth-round tie with Shrewsbury Town on 6 March 1982. Regular keeper Mark Wallington started out between the sticks but left the field due to injury shortly before half-time. Alan Young took over, but he too was injured for a while, so Steve Lynex donned the gloves, before Young returned having recovered. Despite all the changes Leicester went on to win the tie 5-2.

Record Defeat: 0–12 (as Leicester Fosse) v Nottingham F, Division 1, 21 April 1909.

Most League Points (2 for a win): 61, Division 2, 1956–57.

Most League Points (3 for a win): 102, FL C, 2013–14.

Most League Goals: 109, Division 2, 1956–57.

Highest League Scorer in Season: Arthur Rowley, 44, Division 2, 1956–57.

Most League Goals in Total Aggregate: Arthur Chandler, 259, 1923–35.

Most League Goals in One Match: 6, John Duncan v Port Vale, Division 2, 25 December 1924; 6, Arthur Chandler v Portsmouth, Division 1, 20 October 1928.

Most Capped Player: Kasper Schmeichel, 84, Denmark.

Most League Appearances: Adam Black, 528, 1920–35.

Youngest League Player: Dave Buchanan, 16 years 192 days v Oldham Ath, 1 January 1979.

Record Transfer Fee Received: £80,000,000 from Manchester U for Harry Maguire, August 2019.

Record Transfer Fee Paid: £40,000,000 to Monaco for Youri Tielemans, July 2019.

Football League Record: 1894 Elected to Division 2; 1908–09 Division 1; 1909–25 Division 2; 1925–35 Division 1; 1935–37 Division 2; 1937–39 Division 1; 1946–54 Division 2; 1954–55 Division 1; 1955–57 Division 2; 1957–69 Division 1; 1969–71 Division 2; 1971–78 Division 1; 1978–80 Division 2; 1980–81 Division 1; 1981–83 Division 2; 1983–87 Division 1; 1987–92 Division 2; 1992–94 Division 1; 1994–95 Premier League; 1995–96 Division 1; 1996–2002 Premier League; 2002–03 Division 1; 2003–04 Premier League; 2004–08 FL C; 2008–09 FL 1; 2009–14 FL C; 2014– Premier League.

LATEST SEQUENCES

Longest Sequence of League Wins: 9, 21.12.2013 – 1.2.2014.

Longest Sequence of League Defeats: 8, 17.3.2001 – 28.4.2001.

Longest Sequence of League Draws: 6, 2.10.2004 – 2.11.2004.

Longest Sequence of Unbeaten League Matches: 23, 1.11.2008 – 7.3.2009.

Longest Sequence Without a League Win: 18, 12.4.1975 – 1.11.1975.

Successive Scoring Runs: 32 from 23.11.2013.

Successive Non-scoring Runs: 7 from 21.11.1987.

MANAGERS

Frank Gardner 1884–92
Ernest Marson 1892–94
J. Lee 1894–95
Henry Jackson 1895–97
William Clark 1897–98
George Johnson 1898–1912
Jack Bartlett 1912–14
Louis Ford 1914–15
Harry Linney 1915–19
Peter Hodge 1919–26
Willie Orr 1926–32
Peter Hodge 1932–34
Arthur Lochhead 1934–36
Frank Womack 1936–39
Tom Bromilow 1939–45
Tom Mather 1945–46
John Duncan 1946–49
Norman Bullock 1949–55
David Halliday 1955–58
Matt Gillies 1958–68
Frank O'Farrell 1968–71
Jimmy Bloomfield 1971–77
Frank McLintock 1977–78
Jock Wallace 1978–82
Gordon Milne 1982–86
Bryan Hamilton 1986–87
David Pleat 1987–91
Gordon Lee 1991
Brian Little 1991–94
Mark McGhee 1994–95
Martin O'Neill 1995–2000
Peter Taylor 2000–01
Dave Bassett 2001–02
Micky Adams 2002–04
Craig Levein 2004–06
Robert Kelly 2006–07
Martin Allen 2007
Gary Megson 2007
Ian Holloway 2007–08
Nigel Pearson 2008–10
Paulo Sousa 2010
Sven-Göran Eriksson 2010–11
Nigel Pearson 2011–15
Claudio Ranieri 2015–17
Craig Shakespeare 2017
Claude Puel 2017–19
Brendan Rodgers February 2019–

TEN YEAR LEAGUE RECORD

		P	W	D	L	F	A	Pts	Pos
2012-13	FL C	46	19	11	16	71	48	68	6
2013-14	FL C	46	31	9	6	83	43	102	1
2014-15	PR Lge	38	11	8	19	46	55	41	14
2015-16	PR Lge	38	23	12	3	68	36	81	1
2016-17	PR Lge	38	12	8	18	48	63	44	12
2017-18	PR Lge	38	12	11	15	56	60	47	9
2018-19	PR Lge	38	15	7	16	51	48	52	9
2019-20	PR Lge	38	18	8	12	67	41	62	5
2020-21	PR Lge	38	20	6	12	68	50	66	5
2021-22	PR Lge	38	14	10	14	62	59	52	8

DID YOU KNOW ?

When Leicester City visited Mansfield Town for a game in the wartime emergency competitions on 16 November 1940, they found themselves two men short and drafted in the Stags' second-choice keeper Dennis Wright to play outfield. Wright started the match at outside-right but quickly switched to centre-forward and went on to score both goals for the Foxes who went down to a 4-2 defeat.

LEICESTER CITY – PREMIER LEAGUE 2021–22 LEAGUE RECORD

Match No.	*Date*	*Venue*	*Opponents*	*Result*		*H/T Score*	*Lg Pos.*	*Goalscorers*	*Attendance*
1	Aug 14	H	Wolverhampton W	W	1-0	1-0	8	Vardy [41]	31,983
2	23	A	West Ham U	L	1-4	0-1	12	Tielemans [69]	59,901
3	28	A	Norwich C	W	2-1	1-1	8	Vardy [8], Albrighton [76]	26,765
4	Sept 11	H	Manchester C	L	0-1	0-0	9		32,087
5	19	A	Brighton & HA	L	1-2	0-1	12	Vardy [61]	31,078
6	25	H	Burnley	D	2-2	1-2	12	Vardy 2 [37, 85]	31,650
7	Oct 3	A	Crystal Palace	D	2-2	2-0	13	Iheanacho [31], Vardy [37]	22,445
8	16	H	Manchester U	W	4-2	1-1	11	Tielemans [31], Soyuncu [78], Vardy [83], Daka [90]	32,219
9	24	A	Brentford	W	2-1	1-0	9	Tielemans [14], Maddison [74]	16,814
10	30	H	Arsenal	L	0-2	0-2	10		32,209
11	Nov 7	A	Leeds U	D	1-1	1-1	12	Barnes [28]	36,478
12	20	H	Chelsea	L	0-3	0-2	12		32,192
13	28	H	Watford	W	4-2	3-1	10	Maddison [16], Vardy 2 [34, 42], Lookman [68]	32,020
14	Dec 1	A	Southampton	D	2-2	1-2	8	Evans [22], Maddison [49]	26,951
15	5	A	Aston Villa	L	1-2	1-1	11	Barnes [14]	41,572
16	12	H	Newcastle U	W	4-0	1-0	8	Tielemans 2 (1 pen) [38 (p), 81], Daka [57], Maddison [85]	31,959
17	26	A	Manchester C	L	3-6	0-4	10	Maddison [55], Lookman [59], Iheanacho [65]	53,226
18	28	H	Liverpool	W	1-0	0-0	9	Lookman [59]	32,230
19	Jan 19	H	Tottenham H	L	2-3	1-1	10	Daka [24], Maddison [76]	31,986
20	23	H	Brighton & HA	D	1-1	0-0	10	Daka [46]	31,231
21	Feb 10	A	Liverpool	L	0-2	0-1	12		53,050
22	13	H	West Ham U	D	2-2	1-1	11	Tielemans (pen) [45], Ricardo Pereira [57]	32,061
23	20	A	Wolverhampton W	L	1-2	1-1	11	Lookman [41]	31,497
24	Mar 1	A	Burnley	W	2-0	0-0	12	Maddison [82], Vardy [90]	17,825
25	5	H	Leeds U	W	1-0	0-0	12	Barnes [67]	32,236
26	13	A	Arsenal	L	0-2	0-1	12		60,111
27	20	H	Brentford	W	2-1	2-0	10	Castagne [20], Maddison [33]	31,830
28	Apr 2	A	Manchester U	D	1-1	0-0	9	Iheanacho [63]	73,444
29	10	H	Crystal Palace	W	2-1	2-0	9	Lookman [39], Dewsbury-Hall [45]	31,896
30	17	A	Newcastle U	L	1-2	1-1	9	Lookman [19]	52,104
31	20	A	Everton	D	1-1	1-0	9	Barnes [5]	39,153
32	23	H	Aston Villa	D	0-0	0-0	10		32,185
33	May 1	A	Tottenham H	L	1-3	0-1	11	Iheanacho [90]	59,482
34	8	H	Everton	L	1-2	1-2	14	Daka [11]	32,001
35	11	H	Norwich C	W	3-0	0-0	10	Vardy 2 [54, 62], Maddison [70]	30,892
36	15	A	Watford	W	5-1	2-1	9	Maddison [18], Vardy 2 [22, 70], Barnes 2 [46, 86]	20,257
37	19	A	Chelsea	D	1-1	1-1	9	Maddison [6]	31,478
38	22	H	Southampton	W	4-1	0-0	8	Maddison [49], Vardy [74], Perez 2 [81, 90]	32,003

Final League Position: 8

GOALSCORERS

League (62): Vardy 15, Maddison 12, Barnes 6, Lookman 6, Tielemans 6 (2 pens), Daka 5, Iheanacho 4, Perez 2, Albrighton 1, Castagne 1, Dewsbury-Hall 1, Evans 1, Ricardo Pereira 1, Soyuncu 1.
FA Cup (5): Albrighton 1, Barnes 1, Iheanacho 1, Maddison 1, Tielemans 1 (1 pen).
Carabao Cup (7): Lookman 2, Vardy 2, Barnes 1, Iheanacho 1, Maddison 1.
UEFA Europa League (12): Daka 5, Amartey 1, Barnes 1, Dewsbury-Hall 1, Evans 1, Maddison 1, Ndidi 1, Perez 1.
UEFA Europa Conference League (13): Maddison 3, Barnes 2, Albrighton 1, Daka 1, Dewsbury-Hall 1, Fofana 1, Iheanacho 1, Ndidi 1, Ricardo Pereira 1, own goal 1.
Papa John's Trophy (1): Wakeling 1.

Schmeichel K 37	Ricardo Pereira D 13 + 1	Amartey D 23 + 5	Soyuncu C 28	Thomas L 21 + 1	Tielemans Y 29 + 3	Ndidi O 18 + 1	Perez A 6 + 8	Maddison J 28 + 7	Barnes H 24 + 8	Vardy J 20 + 5	Vestergaard J 6 + 4	Soumare B 12 + 7	Iheanacho K 13 + 13	Daka P 13 + 10	Albrighton M 11 + 6	Castagne T 22 + 5	Dewsbury-Hall K 23 + 5	Bertrand R 4	Evans J 16 + 2	Lookman A 16 + 10	Choudhury H 4 + 2	McAteer K — + 1	Justin J 11 + 2	Mendy N 12 + 2	Fofana W 7	Brunt L — + 1	Ward D 1	*Match No.*
1	2	3	4	5	6	7	8^{2}	9^{1}	10^{3}	11	12	13	14															1
1	2	3	4	5	6	7	8■	9^{3}	10^{1}	11^{2}		14	13	12														2
1	2^{1}	3	4	5	8	7		11^{3}	9^{2}	10			13		6	12	14											3
1			3		7	8		11^{3}	9^{2}	10	4^{1}		14		6	2		5	12	13								4
1	2		3		6	7		9^{1}	11	10	4	8^{3}	14			13		5^{2}		12								5
1	2^{1}		3		6	7		14	11	10	4	8^{2}	13			12		5		9^{3}								6
1			3		8			13	9	11	4	12	10^{2}		14	2		5		6^{3}	7^{1}							7
1	5	2	4		6		12	9^{1}		11	14	7	10^{2}	13		8			3^{3}									8
1	5	2	4^{2}		6		14	9^{3}		11^{1}	13	7	10	12		8			3									9
1		2^{1}	4	8	6			9^{3}	13	11		7	10^{2}	14		5			3	12								10
1	2	12	3		8^{2}	6		14	11^{1}	10		7				5	13		4	9^{3}								11
1		2	4			7		13	11^{1}	10		6^{3}	12		5	8	14		3	9^{2}								12
1			4	5		7		9^{2}	10	11		6			12	2	13		3	8^{1}								13
1			4	5		7	13	9	10^{3}	11		6^{1}		14		2	12		3	8^{2}								14
1			4	5		7	13	9	10	12			14	11^{2}		2	6^{3}		3	8^{1}								15
1			4	5	6	7		8^{3}	10^{2}			12		11	13	2	9		3^{1}			14						16
1		3		5	7^{2}		6^{1}	10			4		11		2	12	8			9	13							17
1		3		5	13	4		9^{3}		10		7	11^{2}		14	2	8			12	6^{1}							18
1			3	9^{1}	7			6	13		4	14		10^{2}	5		8^{3}			11	2		12					19
1		3	4	5	6		14	9	10^{1}			13		11^{3}	12		7			8^{2}			2					20
1		3		5	13	4		9	14			6^{2}	12	11^{1}	8		7			10^{3}			2					21
1	2	3	4	12	6^{3}	7		9^{2}	11		14			10			8			13			5^{1}					22
1	2	3	4	5	6	7^{2}		13					12	10^{1}	9		8			11								23
1	2^{1}	3	4	5	6^{3}	7		13	11	14				10^{2}	9		8			12								24
1		3	4	5	6	7^{3}			11	10^{2}			13		9		8			12	2^{1}			14				25
1	2^{1}	3	4	5		12		9	10				11^{3}	14	8		7						13	6^{2}				26
1		3	4		6			8	10			13	11^{3}	14		5^{1}	9^{2}		12				2	7				27
1		12			6			8	10				11^{3}	13		5	9		4^{1}		14		2	7^{2}	3			28
1		3	4	5	6			9^{3}	13				12	10^{1}		14	8			11^{2}			2	7				29
1		3	4	5	8		7^{1}	12	13				14	11^{3}			9			10^{2}			2	6				30
1	2	14			7			8	10^{1}				11^{2}	13		5	9		4	12				6^{3}	3			31
1			4		8^{3}		14	7	13	12				11^{1}		5	9			10^{2}			2	6	3			32
1		3	4	9	14		8^{3}			12		6^{1}	10	11^{2}	5	2								7		13		33
1		2			7		8^{1}		12	13			10	11^{3}		6	9		4	14				5^{2}	3			34
1		3			6			9	10	11						2	7		4	8^{1}			5	12				35
		13			8			7	10	11^{3}				14	12	2	9		4^{2}				5	6^{1}	3		1	36
1		4		9			13	7	12	10^{2}			11^{1}			6	8		3					5	2			37
1	13	15			7		12	8^{4}	10^{3}	11						2^{2}	9^{1}		4	14			5	6	3			38

FA Cup

Third Round	Watford	(h)	4-1
Fourth Round	Nottingham F	(a)	1-4

Carabao Cup

Third Round	Millwall	(a)	2-0
Fourth Round	Brighton & HA	(h)	2-2
(Leicester C won 4-2 on penalties)			
Quarter-Final	Liverpool	(a)	3-3
(Liverpool won 5-4 on penalties)			

UEFA Europa League

Group C	Napoli	(h)	2-2
Group C	Legia Warsaw	(a)	0-1
Group C	Spartak Moscow	(a)	4-3
Group C	Spartak Moscow	(h)	1-1
Group C	Legia Warsaw	(h)	3-1
Group C	Napoli	(a)	2-3

UEFA Europa Conference League

Knockout Play-offs 1st leg	Randers	(h)	4-1
Knockout Play-offs 2nd leg	Randers	(a)	3-1
Round of 16 1st leg	Rennes	(h)	2-0
Round of 16 2nd leg	Rennes	(a)	1-2
Quarter-Final 1st leg	PSV Eindhoven	(h)	0-0
Quarter-Final 2nd leg	PSV Eindhoven	(a)	2-1
Semi-Final 1st leg	Roma	(h)	1-1
Semi-Final 2nd leg	Roma	(a)	0-1

Papa John's Trophy (Leicester C U21)

Group G (N)	Fleetwood T	(a)	1-4
Group G (N)	Accrington S	(a)	0-5
Group G (N)	Barrow	(a)	0-1

LEYTON ORIENT

FOUNDATION

There is some doubt about the foundation of Leyton Orient, and, indeed, some confusion with clubs like Leyton and Clapton over their early history. As regards the foundation, the most favoured version is that Leyton Orient was formed originally by members of Homerton Theological College who established Glyn Cricket Club in 1881 and then carried on through the following winter playing football. Eventually many employees of the Orient Shipping Line became involved and so the name Orient was chosen in 1888.

The Breyer Group Stadium, Brisbane Road, Leyton, London E10 5NF.

Telephone: (0208) 926 1111.

Ticket Office: (0208) 926 1010.

Website: www.leytonorient.com

Email: enquiries@leytonorient.net

Ground Capacity: 9,241.

Record Attendance: 34,345 v West Ham U, FA Cup 4th rd, 25 January 1964.

Pitch Measurements: 100m × 67m (109.5yd × 73.5yd).

Chairman: Nigel Travis.

Chief Executive: Danny Macklin.

Director of Football: Martin Ling.

Head Coach: Richie Wellens.

First-Team Coach: Matt Harrold.

Colours: Red shirts with white trim, red shorts, red socks with white trim.

Year Formed: 1881. ***Turned Professional:*** 1903.

Previous Names: 1881, Glyn Cricket and Football Club; 1886, Eagle Football Club; 1888, Orient Football Club; 1898, Clapton Orient; 1946, Leyton Orient; 1966, Orient; 1987, Leyton Orient.

Club Nickname: 'The O's'.

Grounds: 1884, Glyn Road; 1896, Whittles Athletic Ground; 1900, Millfields Road; 1930, Lea Bridge Road; 1937, Brisbane Road (renamed Matchroom Stadium 1995; The Breyer Group Stadium 2018).

First Football League Game: 2 September 1905, Division 2, v Leicester Fosse (a) L 1–2 – Butler; Holmes, Codling; Lamberton, Boden, Boyle; Kingaby (1), Wootten, Leigh, Evenson, Bourne.

Record League Victory: 8–0 v Crystal Palace, Division 3 (S), 12 November 1955 – Welton; Lee, Earl; Blizzard, Aldous, McKnight; White (1), Facey (3), Burgess (2), Heckman, Hartburn (2). 8–0 v Rochdale, Division 4, 20 October 1987 – Wells; Howard, Dickenson (1), Smalley (1), Day, Hull, Hales (2), Castle (Sussex), Shinners (2), Godfrey (Harvey), Comfort (2). 8–0 v Colchester U, Division 4, 15 October 1988 – Wells; Howard, Dickenson, Hales (1p), Day (1), Sitton (1), Baker (1), Ward, Hull (3), Juryeff, Comfort (1). 8–0 v Doncaster R, Division 3, 28 December 1997 – Hyde; Channing, Naylor, Smith (1p), Hicks, Clark, Ling, Roger Joseph, Griffiths (3) (Harris), Richards (2) (Baker (1)), Inglethorpe (1) (Simpson).

HONOURS

League Champions: Division 3 – 1969–70; Division 3S – 1955–56.
Runners-up: Division 2 – 1961–62; Division 3S – 1954–55.

FA Cup: semi-final – 1978.

League Cup: 5th rd – 1963.

FOOTBALL YEARBOOK FACT FILE

Clapton Orient, as the O's were then named, came close to folding in the summer of 1933. The club owed around £1,700 in wages to former players and staff and were suspended by the FA from 6 May. The fans rallied round, and Orient were able to show they had paid off their debts and also had around £1,000 in the bank by the deadline of 22 June that had been set, thus avoiding being thrown out of both the Football League and the FA.

Record Cup Victory: 9–2 v Chester, League Cup 3rd rd, 15 October 1962 – Robertson; Charlton, Taylor; Gibbs, Bishop, Lea; Deeley (1), Waites (3), Dunmore (2), Graham (3), Wedge.

Record Defeat: 0–8 v Aston Villa, FA Cup 4th rd, 30 January 1929.

Most League Points (2 for a win): 66, Division 3 (S), 1955–56.

Most League Points (3 for a win): 86, FL 1, 2013–14.

Most League Goals: 106, Division 3 (S), 1955–56.

Highest League Scorer in Season: Tom Johnston, 35, Division 2, 1957–58.

Most League Goals in Total Aggregate: Tom Johnston, 121, 1956–58, 1959–61.

Most League Goals in One Match: 4, Wally Leigh v Bradford C, Division 2, 13 April 1906; 4, Albert Pape v Oldham Ath, Division 2, 1 September 1924; 4, Peter Kitchen v Millwall, Division 3, 21 April 1984.

Most Capped Player: Jobi McAnuff, 22 (32), Jamaica.

Most League Appearances: Peter Allen, 432, 1965–78.

Youngest League Player: Paul Went, 15 years 327 days v Preston NE, 4 September 1965.

Record Transfer Fee Received: £1,000,000 (rising to £1,500,000) from Fulham for Gabriel Zakuani, July 2006.

Record Transfer Fee Paid: £200,000 to Oldham Ath for Liam Kelly, July 2016.

Football League Record: 1905 Elected to Division 2; 1929–56 Division 3 (S); 1956–62 Division 2; 1962–63 Division 1; 1963–66 Division 2; 1966–70 Division 3; 1970–82 Division 2; 1982–85 Division 3; 1985–89 Division 4; 1989–92 Division 3; 1992–95 Division 2; 1995–2004 Division 3; 2004–06 FL 2; 2006–15 FL 1; 2015–17 FL 2; 2017–19 National League; 2019– FL 2.

LATEST SEQUENCES

Longest Sequence of League Wins: 10, 21.1.1956 – 30.3.1956.

Longest Sequence of League Defeats: 9, 1.4.1995 – 6.5.1995.

Longest Sequence of League Draws: 6, 30.11.1974 – 28.12.1974.

Longest Sequence of Unbeaten League Matches: 15, 13.4.2013 – 19.10.2013.

Longest Sequence Without a League Win: 23, 6.10.1962 – 13.4.1963.

Successive Scoring Runs: 22 from 12.3.1927.

Successive Non-scoring Runs: 8 from 19.11.1994.

MANAGERS

Sam Omerod 1905–06
Ike Ivenson 1906
Billy Holmes 1907–22
Peter Proudfoot 1922–29
Arthur Grimsdell 1929–30
Peter Proudfoot 1930–31
Jimmy Seed 1931–33
David Pratt 1933–34
Peter Proudfoot 1935–39
Tom Halsey 1939
Bill Wright 1939–45
Willie Hall 1945
Bill Wright 1945–46
Charlie Hewitt 1946–48
Neil McBain 1948–49
Alec Stock 1949–59
Les Gore 1959–61
Johnny Carey 1961–63
Benny Fenton 1963–64
Dave Sexton 1965
Dick Graham 1966–68
Jimmy Bloomfield 1968–71
George Petchey 1971–77
Jimmy Bloomfield 1977–81
Paul Went 1981
Ken Knighton 1981–83
Frank Clark 1983–91 *(Managing Director)*
Peter Eustace 1991–94
Chris Turner and John Sitton 1994–95
Pat Holland 1995–96
Tommy Taylor 1996–2001
Paul Brush 2001–03
Martin Ling 2003–09
Geraint Williams 2009–10
Russell Slade 2010–14
Kevin Nugent 2014
Mauro Milanese 2014
Fabio Liverani 2014–15
Ian Hendon 2015–16
Kevin Nolan 2016
Andy Hessenthaler 2016
Alberto Cavasin 2016
Andy Edwards 2016–17
Danny Webb 2017
Martin Ling 2017
Omer Riza 2017
Steve Davis 2017
Justin Edinburgh 2017–19
Carl Fletcher 2019
Ross Embleton 2019–21
Kenny Jackett 2021–22
Richie Wellens March 2022–

TEN YEAR LEAGUE RECORD

		P	W	D	L	F	A	Pts	Pos
2012-13	FL 1	46	21	8	17	55	48	71	7
2013-14	FL 1	46	25	11	10	85	45	86	3
2014-15	FL 1	46	12	13	21	59	69	49	23
2015-16	FL 2	46	19	12	15	60	61	69	8
2016-17	FL 2	46	10	6	30	47	87	36	24
2017-18	NL	46	16	12	18	58	56	60	13
2018-19	NL	46	25	14	7	73	35	89	1
2019-20	FL 2	36	10	12	14	47	55	42	17§
2020-21	FL 2	46	17	10	19	53	55	61	11
2021-22	FL 2	46	14	16	16	62	47	58	13

§*Decided on points-per-game (1.17)*

DID YOU KNOW ?

Clapton Orient visited Paris in May 1921 to take part in a mini tournament which coincided with the Whitsun holidays. The O's lost both their games, going down 2-1 to Olympique and 1-0 to Huddersfield Town, with the fixtures being played at the Stade Bergeyre.

LEYTON ORIENT – SKY BET LEAGUE TWO 2021–22 LEAGUE RECORD

Match No.	Date	Venue	Opponents	Result		H/T Score	Lg Pos.	Goalscorers	Attendance
1	Aug 7	A	Salford C	D	1-1	1-1	10	Beckles[33]	1968
2	14	H	Exeter C	W	3-0	2-0	5	Drinan[7], Beckles[25], Archibald[76]	4860
3	21	A	Carlisle U	D	1-1	0-1	11	Smith[74]	4597
4	24	H	Harrogate T	L	0-2	0-2	11		3942
5	28	H	Bradford C	W	2-0	0-0	6	Sotiriou[66], Smith[82]	4901
6	Sept 4	A	Newport Co	D	2-2	1-1	6	Smith 2[34, 53]	3845
7	11	H	Oldham Ath	W	4-0	2-0	3	Drinan[16], James[26], Archibald[75], Smith[90]	5315
8	18	A	Bristol R	W	3-1	3-0	2	Smith[17], Archibald[33], Drinan[41]	6172
9	25	H	Mansfield T	D	0-0	0-0	2		5252
10	Oct 2	A	Port Vale	L	2-3	0-1	4	Jones, D (og)[60], James[86]	5667
11	9	A	Barrow	D	1-1	0-0	6	Beckles[69]	3374
12	16	H	Walsall	D	0-0	0-0	7		5826
13	19	H	Forest Green R	D	1-1	0-0	10	Sotiriou[76]	4391
14	23	A	Stevenage	D	0-0	0-0	9		3544
15	30	H	Hartlepool U	W	5-0	2-0	6	Drinan 3[20, 79, 90], Smith[35], James[51]	6233
16	Nov 13	A	Rochdale	D	2-2	1-1	9	Drinan[24], Clay[66]	2751
17	20	H	Sutton U	W	4-1	1-1	6	Archibald[30], Smith 2[46, 82], James[90]	5840
18	23	A	Scunthorpe U	D	1-1	1-0	8	Drinan[21]	2067
19	27	A	Northampton T	L	0-1	0-1	8		5769
20	Dec 7	H	Swindon T	W	4-1	1-1	7	Drinan 2[19, 59], Smith 2[64, 82]	4020
21	11	H	Crawley T	L	1-2	0-1	9	Morris (og)[62]	5142
22	18	A	Tranmere R	L	0-1	0-0	9		4000
23	Jan 22	H	Port Vale	D	0-0	0-0	13		5761
24	25	H	Newport Co	L	0-1	0-0	14		3413
25	29	A	Mansfield T	L	0-2	0-1	15		5851
26	Feb 1	A	Bradford C	D	1-1	0-0	15	Pratley[69]	13,646
27	5	H	Colchester U	L	0-1	0-1	15		5641
28	8	A	Exeter C	L	0-1	0-0	16		4111
29	12	H	Salford C	L	0-2	0-0	16		4427
30	22	H	Bristol R	L	0-2	0-2	18		3840
31	26	H	Carlisle U	L	0-1	0-1	18		5272
32	Mar 1	A	Colchester U	D	2-2	0-0	18	Sotiriou[66], Coleman[90]	3415
33	5	H	Stevenage	D	2-2	1-2	20	Sotiriou[30], Archibald[90]	4558
34	12	A	Hartlepool U	D	0-0	0-0	20		5903
35	15	A	Forest Green R	D	1-1	0-1	20	Sotiriou[67]	1891
36	19	H	Rochdale	W	3-1	1-1	18	Smyth[40], Sotiriou[58], Smith[80]	4791
37	22	A	Harrogate T	W	3-0	0-0	17	Drinan 2[51, 57], Sotiriou[73]	2339
38	26	H	Barrow	W	2-0	0-0	17	Smyth[52], Sotiriou[62]	6032
39	29	A	Oldham Ath	L	0-2	0-1	17		4619
40	Apr 2	A	Walsall	W	2-0	2-0	14	Smith[10], Khan[16]	4849
41	9	A	Sutton U	L	0-1	0-1	14		3152
42	15	H	Scunthorpe U	W	3-0	3-0	14	Smyth[15], Archibald[24], Sotiriou[30]	5342
43	18	A	Swindon T	W	2-1	1-0	13	Beckles 2[20, 54]	10,264
44	23	H	Northampton T	L	2-4	1-4	13	Archibald[45], Brown[50]	6237
45	30	A	Crawley T	W	2-0	1-0	13	Archibald[8], Drinan[90]	3372
46	May 7	H	Tranmere R	L	0-1	0-1	13		6623

Final League Position: 13

GOALSCORERS

League (62): Drinan 13, Smith 13, Sotiriou 9, Archibald 8, Beckles 5, James 4, Smyth 3, Brown 1, Clay 1, Coleman 1, Khan 1, Pratley 1, own goals 2.
FA Cup (5): Drinan 2 (1 pen), Smith 2, Beckles 1.
Carabao Cup (1): Drinan 1.
Papa John's Trophy (6): Sotiriou 2, Happe 1, Kemp 1, Papadopoulos 1, Smyth 1.

Vigouroux L 46	James T 21	Beckles O 44	Happe D 11 + 1	Wood C 29 + 3	Clay C 14 + 5	Pratley D 34 + 5	Kyprianou H 31 + 7	Kemp D 15 + 4	Drinan A 36 + 4	Smyth P 14 + 10	Archibald T 35 + 3	Sweeney J 3 + 2	Sotiriou R 19 + 15	Smith H 31 + 10	Ogie S 29 + 5	Omotoye T 1 + 3	Mitchell A 23 + 3	Reilly C — + 4	Thompson A 14	Young M 6 + 8	Moss D 3 + 1	Khan O 17 + 3	Brown J 6 + 5	Coleman E 12 + 3	Nouble F 3 + 5	Ray G 8 + 1	Tanga J — + 1	Nkrumah D — + 3	Obiero Z 1	*Match No.*
1	2	3	4	5^2	6^1	7	8	9	10	11^3	12	13	14																	1
1	2	3	4	5^2		7	6	8	10		11	13	9^1	12																2
1	2^3	3	4		14	7	6	8	10		11	5^2	9^1	12	13															3
1	2	3	4	12		7	6	9			10		13	11	5^1	8^2														4
1	2	3		5	6	7	8				11		9^1	10	4	12														5
1	5	3		8	7	6		12	9^1		11^2			10	4		2	13												6
1	5	3	4	8	6	7^1	12	14	9^2		11^3		13	10			2													7
1	5	3	4^1	8	7	6			11		9			10	12		2													8
1	5	3		8	7^1	6	12		11^2		9		13	10	4		2													9
1	5	3	4	8	13	7	6		11^2	12	9^1			10	2															10
1		3		8	5	7	6		9^1		11		12	10	4		2													11
1	5	3		8^1	13	7	6	14		12	9^3		11^2	10	4		2													12
1	5	3		8^2	14	7	6^3	11		9^1	12		13	10	4		2													13
1	5	3			13	6	7^1	11	12		8^2		9	10	4		2													14
1	5	3			7	6^1	12	9^2	10		8			11	4		2	13												15
1	5	3			7	12	6^1	9	10^2		8		13	11	4		2													16
1	5	3			7	12	6^1	9	10^2	13	8			11	4		2													17
1	5	3			7^2	13	6	9^1	10	12	8			11	4		2													18
1	5	3		12		7	6	9^3	11^2		8^1		13	10	4	14	2													19
1	5	3			7	6		9	10^1		8		12	11^2	4	13	2													20
1	5^1		12	13	6	7■		9	11		8			10	4^2		2^3		3	14										21
1			3	6	8			7^1	9	12		2		11	5				4	10										22
1		3		8		7	6^1	14	11	9^3				10	4		2			13	5^2	12								23
1		3		8^3			6	9^2	10^1	12			13	11	4		2				14	5	7							24
1		3	4				14		13	11^1	8		9^2	10			2			12		5	7^3	6						25
1		3	4			8	6		10		9			11			2					5	12	7^1						26
1		3				7	12		10				13	11^2	4		2			9	5	6	8^1							27
1		4	5^1			8	7		10				14		12		3	13	2	9^2		6			11^3					28
1		4				7	13		11		9			12	5				2^2			6		8	10^1	3				29
1		3				7			10^2		11		9^3	13	5			12		6^1		2		8	14	4				30
1		4		5		7	6^1		9^3		11■		12	10						14		2		8^2	13	3				31
1		4		5		7	12			13			11	10					2^3	8^2		9^1		6		3	14			32
1		4		5^2		7^3				12	9		6	10	13				2	11^1				8	14	3				33
1		4		5			7		12	11^1	9		6	10^2					2					8	13	3				34
1		4		5			8		9	14	13		11^3	10^2	12				2			6		7		3^1				35
1		4		5		12	7^2		10	11^3	9		6	14	3				2			13		8^1						36
1		4		5		6	7		10^2	12	9^3		11^1	13	3				2	14		8								37
1		3		5		6	7		10	11^2	9^1		8	12	4				2^3			13				14				38
1		4		5		13	7		12	9			8	11^3								2	14	6^2	10^1	3				39
1		3		5		7^3	8		9				6^2	10^1	2				4			11	14	13	12					40
1		4				7	6		9	10^1	11	5^3	12		3					13	2^2	8						14		41
1		3		5			7		10^2	11^3	9		8^1	12			4		2	14			6					13		42
1		3		5		8	7■		10	6^1	9^2		11^3		4		14					2	13	12						43
1		3		5		8			10	6	9		11^2	13	4■		14					2^3	12	7^1						44
1		3		5			7		10	11^3	9						4			14		8^2	2	12				13	6^1	45
1	2^1	3		5		8^3	7		10	11^2	9		14	12			13		4				6							46

FA Cup

First Round	Ebbsfleet U	(h)	1-0
Second Round	Tranmere R	(h)	4-0
Third Round	Stoke C	(a)	0-2

Carabao Cup

First Round	QPR	(h)	1-1

(QPR won 5-3 on penalties)

Papa John's Trophy

Group G (S)	Southampton U21	(h)	1-0
Group G (S)	Crawley T	(a)	4-0
Group G (S)	Charlton Ath	(h)	1-0
Second Round	Milton Keynes D	(h)	0-0

(Milton Keynes D won 5-4 on penalties)

LINCOLN CITY

FOUNDATION

The original Lincoln Football Club was established in the early 1860s and was one of the first provisional clubs to affiliate to the Football Association. In their early years, they regularly played matches against the famous Sheffield Football Club and later became known as Lincoln Lindum. The present organisation was formed at a public meeting held in the Monson Arms Hotel in June 1884 and won the Lincolnshire Cup in only their third season. They were founder members of the Midland League in 1889 and that competition's first champions.

LNER Stadium, Sincil Bank, Lincoln LN5 8LD.

Telephone: (01522) 880 011.

Ticket Office: (01522) 880 011.

Website: www.weareimps.com

Email: info@theredimps.com

Ground Capacity: 10,653.

Record Attendance: 23,196 v Derby Co, League Cup 4th rd, 15 November 1967.

Pitch Measurements: 100m × 65m (109.5yd × 71yd).

Chairman: Clive Nates.

Chief Executive Officer: Liam Scully.

Manager: Mark Kennedy.

Assistant Manager: David Kerslake.

Colours: Red and white striped shirts, black shorts with white trim, red socks with white trim.

Year Formed: 1884.

Turned Professional: 1885.

Ltd Co.: 1895.

Club Nickname: 'The Red Imps'.

Grounds: 1884, John O'Gaunt's; 1894, Sincil Bank (renamed LNER Stadium 2019).

First Football League Game: 3 September 1892, Division 2, v Sheffield U (a) L 2–4 – William Gresham; Coulton, Neill; Shaw, Mettam, Moore; Smallman, Irving (1), Cameron (1), Kelly, James Gresham.

Record League Victory: 11–1 v Crewe Alex, Division 3 (N), 29 September 1951 – Jones; Green (1p), Varney; Wright, Emery, Grummett (1); Troops (1), Garvey, Graver (6), Whittle (1), Johnson (1).

Record Cup Victory: 13-0 v Peterborough, FA Cup 1st qual rd, 12 October 1895 – Shaw, McFarlane, Eyre, Richardson, Neaves (1), Burke (2), Frettingham (2), Smith (1), Gillespie W (2), Gillespie M (3), Hulme (2).

Record Defeat: 3–11 v Manchester C, Division 2, 23 March 1895.

Most League Points (2 for a win): 74, Division 4, 1975–76.

Most League Points (3 for a win): 85, FL 2, 2018–19.

Most League Goals: 121, Division 3 (N), 1951–52.

HONOURS

League Champions: Division 3N – 1931–32, 1947–48, 1951–52; FL 2 – 2018–19; Division 4 – 1975–76; National League – 1987–88, 2016–17.
Runners-up: Division 3N – 1927–28, 1930–31, 1936–37; Division 4 – 1980–81.

FA Cup: quarter-final – 2017.

League Cup: 4th rd – 1968.

League Trophy Winners: 2018.

FOOTBALL YEARBOOK FACT FILE

In the period since squad numbers were introduced in 1993–94, Harry Anderson is the only player to have worn two different shirt numbers in the same season for Lincoln City. He did so during the club's successful National League campaign of 2016–17, when he had two spells at Sincil Bank on loan from Peterborough United. He wore the number 12 shirt between August and December, and number 26 between March and May.

Highest League Scorer in Season: Allan Hall, 41, Division 3 (N), 1931–32.

Most League Goals in Total Aggregate: Andy Graver, 143, 1950–55 and 1958–61.

Most League Goals in One Match: 6, Frank Keetley v Halifax T, Division 3 (N), 16 January 1932; 6, Andy Graver v Crewe Alex, Division 3 (N), 29 September 1951.

Most Capped Player: Delroy Facey, 8 (15) Grenada.

Most League Appearances: Grant Brown, 407, 1989–2002.

Youngest League Player: Jack Hobbs, 16 years 150 days v Bristol R, 15 January 2005.

Record Transfer Fee Received: £750,000 from Liverpool for Jack Hobbs, August 2005.

Record Transfer Fee Paid: £100,000 to Barnet for John Akinde, July 2018.

Football League Record: 1892 Founder member of Division 2. Remained in Division 2 until 1920 when they failed re-election but also missed seasons 1908–09 and 1911–12 when not re-elected. 1921–32 Division 3 (N); 1932–34 Division 2; 1934–48 Division 3 (N); 1948–49 Division 2; 1949–52 Division 3 (N); 1952–61 Division 2; 1961–62 Division 3; 1962–76 Division 4; 1976–79 Division 3; 1979–81 Division 4; 1981–86 Division 3; 1986–87 Division 4; 1987–88 GM Vauxhall Conference; 1988–92 Division 4; 1992–98 Division 3; 1998–99 Division 2; 1999–2004 Division 3; 2004–11 FL 2; 2011–17 Conference National League; 2017–19 FL 2; 2019– FL 1.

LATEST SEQUENCES

Longest Sequence of League Wins: 10, 1.9.1930 – 18.10.1930.

Longest Sequence of League Defeats: 12, 21.9.1896 – 9.1.1897.

Longest Sequence of League Draws: 5, 21.2.1981 – 7.3.1981.

Longest Sequence of Unbeaten League Matches: 19, 29.12.2018 – 13.4.2019.

Longest Sequence Without a League Win: 19, 22.8.1978 – 23.12.1978.

Successive Scoring Runs: 37 from 1.3.1930.

Successive Non-scoring Runs: 5 from 15.11.1913.

MANAGERS

Jack Strawson 1884–96 *(hon. secretary)*
Alf Martin 1896–97 *(sec.-manager)*
James West 1897–1900 *(hon. secretary)*
David Calderhead, snr 1900–07 *(sec.-manager)*
Jack Strawson 1907–08 *(managing director & secretary)*
Jack Strawson 1908–19 *(secretary)*
Clem Jackson 1919–20 *(player-manager)*
George Fraser 1919–21 *(sec.-manager)*
David Calderhead, jnr 1921–24 *(sec.-manager)*
Horace Henshall 1924–27 *(sec.-manager)*
Harry Parkes 1927–36 *(sec.-manager)*
Joe McClelland 1936–47 *(sec.-manager)*
Bill Anderson 1947–65
Con Moulson 1965–65
Roy Chapman 1965–66
Ron Gray 1966–70
Bert Loxley 1970–71
David Herd 1971–72
Graham Taylor 1972–77
George Kerr 1977
Willie Bell 1977–78
Colin Murphy 1978–85
John Pickering 1985
George Kerr 1985–87
Peter Daniel 1987 *(caretaker)*
Colin Murphy 1987–90
Allan Clarke 1990
Steve Thompson 1990–93
Keith Alexander 1993–94
Sam Ellis 1994–95
Steve Wicks 1995 *(head coach)*
John Beck 1995–98
Shane Westley 1998
John Reames 1998–2000 *(chairman-manager)*
Phil Stant 2000–01
Alan Buckley 2001–02
Keith Alexander 2002–06
John Schofield 2006–07
Peter Jackson 2007–09
Chris Sutton 2009–10
Steve Tilson 2010–11
David Holdsworth 2011–13
Gary Simpson 2013–14
Chris Moyses 2014–16
Danny Cowley 2016–19
Michael Appleton 2019–22
Mark Kennedy May 2022–

TEN YEAR LEAGUE RECORD

		P	W	D	L	F	A	Pts	Pos
2012-13	Conf	46	15	11	20	72	86	54	16
2013-14	Conf	46	17	14	15	60	59	65	14
2014-15	Conf	46	16	10	20	62	71	58	15
2015-16	NL	46	16	13	17	69	68	61	13
2016-17	NL	46	30	9	7	83	40	99	1
2017-18	FL 2	46	20	15	11	64	48	75	7
2018-19	FL 2	46	23	16	7	73	43	85	1
2019-20	FL 1	35	12	6	17	44	46	42	16§
2020-21	FL 1	46	22	11	13	69	50	77	5
2021-22	FL 1	46	14	10	22	55	63	52	17

§Decided on points-per-game (1.20)

DID YOU KNOW?

The two umpires for the Cricket World Cup fixture played between Pakistan and Sri Lanka at Trent Bridge on 14 June 1975 were both former Lincoln City players. Tom Spencer (1936–37) and Arthur Jepson (1948–50) both played League football for the Imps. This is believed to be the only occasion when two former footballers from the same club have umpired in the same international cricket match.

LINCOLN CITY – SKY BET LEAGUE ONE 2021–22 LEAGUE RECORD

Match No.	Date	Venue	Opponents	Result	H/T Score	Lg Pos.	Goalscorers	Attendance
1	Aug 7	A	Gillingham	D 1-1	1-1	11	Edun [4]	4837
2	14	H	Fleetwood T	W 2-1	0-1	8	Scully 2 (1 pen) [69, 87 (p)]	8241
3	17	H	Bolton W	L 0-1	0-0	13		9130
4	21	A	Wycombe W	L 0-1	0-1	17		5030
5	28	A	Oxford U	L 1-3	0-2	20	Scully (pen) [87]	7045
6	Sept 11	A	Cambridge U	W 5-1	3-0	16	Adelakun [1], McGrandles [16], Scully 2 [24, 72], Fiorini [57]	5833
7	14	H	Rotherham U	D 1-1	0-1	15	Fiorini [55]	8788
8	18	H	Ipswich T	L 0-1	0-1	17		9874
9	25	A	Burton Alb	W 2-1	1-0	17	Fiorini [10], Scully [50]	3359
10	28	A	Morecambe	L 0-2	0-0	17		3466
11	Oct 2	H	Plymouth Arg	D 2-2	0-1	16	Sorenson [66], Scully (pen) [90]	8375
12	16	H	Charlton Ath	W 2-1	0-0	13	Stockley (og) [58], Poole [90]	9169
13	19	H	AFC Wimbledon	L 0-1	0-1	15		7750
14	23	A	Sheffield W	D 1-1	0-0	15	Montsma [80]	23,521
15	26	A	Wigan Ath	W 2-1	1-0	12	N'Lundulu [14], Eyoma [57]	8707
16	30	H	Shrewsbury T	D 1-1	1-0	12	McGrandles [42]	8047
17	Nov 20	A	Doncaster R	D 0-0	0-0	16		8129
18	23	H	Portsmouth	L 0-3	0-1	16		8533
19	27	H	Accrington S	L 0-1	0-0	18		8547
20	Dec 7	A	Crewe Alex	L 0-2	0-0	18		3285
21	11	A	Cheltenham T	D 2-2	0-1	18	Bishop 2 [69, 90]	3512
22	26	H	Milton Keynes D	L 2-3	2-0	20	O'Hora (og) [4], Maguire (pen) [8]	8328
23	Jan 8	H	Oxford U	W 2-0	1-0	19	Scully [40], Whittaker [56]	8053
24	11	A	Sunderland	W 3-1	1-0	16	Maguire 3 (1 pen) [31, 57 (p), 75]	28,782
25	15	H	Cambridge U	L 0-1	0-0	18		8507
26	22	A	Plymouth Arg	W 2-1	0-1	16	Marquis [51], Melbourne [90]	12,269
27	29	H	Burton Alb	L 1-2	0-0	18	Marquis [49]	9159
28	Feb 5	A	Milton Keynes D	L 1-2	1-1	18	Marquis [8]	8723
29	8	H	Morecambe	W 2-1	2-0	17	Whittaker [10], Bramall [19]	7571
30	12	H	Wycombe W	D 1-1	1-0	17	Cullen [5]	8319
31	15	H	Doncaster R	L 0-1	0-0	17		9237
32	22	A	Bolton W	L 1-3	0-0	17	Bramall [65]	13,841
33	26	H	Gillingham	L 0-2	0-0	18		8208
34	Mar 5	H	Sheffield W	W 3-1	1-1	18	Marquis 2 [3, 76], Norton-Cuffy [62]	10,283
35	8	A	Ipswich T	L 0-2	0-2	18		24,989
36	12	A	AFC Wimbledon	W 2-0	1-0	16	Fiorini [38], Bishop [84]	8174
37	15	A	Rotherham U	L 1-2	0-2	18	Hopper [81]	9575
38	19	H	Sunderland	D 0-0	0-0	18		10,346
39	26	A	Shrewsbury T	L 0-1	0-0	18		6791
40	Apr 2	A	Charlton Ath	W 2-1	1-0	18	Whittaker [33], Scully [76]	10,091
41	5	A	Fleetwood T	D 1-1	0-1	18	Fiorini [64]	3341
42	9	H	Wigan Ath	L 1-3	1-2	18	Scully [14]	9498
43	15	A	Portsmouth	L 2-3	0-0	18	Bishop [70], House [78]	15,175
44	18	H	Cheltenham T	W 3-0	3-0	18	Whittaker 2 [4, 19], Scully [17]	8672
45	23	A	Accrington S	L 1-2	0-1	18	Fiorini [90]	3053
46	30	H	Crewe Alex	W 2-1	0-1	17	Hopper [79], Adelakun [90]	9147

Final League Position: 17

GOALSCORERS

League (55): Scully 11 (3 pens), Fiorini 6, Marquis 5, Whittaker 5, Bishop 4, Maguire 4 (2 pens), Adelakun 2, Bramall 2, Hopper 2, McGrandles 2, Cullen 1, Edun 1, Eyoma 1, House 1, Melbourne 1, Montsma 1, N'Lundulu 1, Norton-Cuffy 1, Poole 1, Sorenson 1, own goals 2.
FA Cup (1): Sanders 1.
Carabao Cup (2): Bishop 1, Hopper 1.
Papa John's Trophy (8): Scully 4, Adelakun 1, Hopper 1, Maguire 1, Montsma 1.

Griffiths J 33	Poole R 44	Jackson A 23 + 2	Melbourne M 5 + 2	Edun T 4	McGrandles C 39	Bridcutt L 14	Sorenson L 19 + 11	Scully A 31 + 4	Hopper T 14 + 6	Bramall C 22 + 7	Adelakun H 10 + 13	Bishop T 28 + 8	N'Lundulu D 6 + 10	Fiorini L 32 + 7	Montsma L 19	Howarth R — + 4	Eyoma T 20 + 3	Robson J 20 + 3	Maguire C 28 + 4	Sanders M 5 + 14	Walsh J 12	Draper F 3 + 5	Whittaker M 17 + 3	Cullen L 13 + 7	Long S 1	Marquis J 17 + 3	Norton-Cuffy B 13 + 4	House B 2 + 4	Wright J 12 + 1	Match No.
1	2	3	4	5	6	7	8^{2}	9	10	11^{1}	12	13																		1
1	2	3	4	5	6	7	8^{2}	9	10	11^{1}	12	13																		2
1	2	3	4	5	6^{3}	7	8^{2}	11^{1}	10	12	9		13	14																3
1	2	3	4	5	6^{2}	7	8^{3}	11	10^{1}		9	13	12	14																4
1	2	3			8^{1}	7	6	11		5	9^{2}	10		12	4	13														5
1	2				8	7^{3}	14	11	10^{2}		9	6^{1}		12	3		4	5	13											6
1	2	4			8^{1}	7	6	11	10	14	13			12	3			5^{3}	9^{2}											7
1	2					7^{3}	13	11	10	5	12	8^{2}	14	6	3		4		9^{1}											8
1	2						6	11		13	9^{2}	7^{1}	10^{3}	8	3	14	4	5		12										9
1	2					7	8^{2}	11		13	9^{1}	12	10^{3}	6	3	14	4	5												10
1	2^{2}					7^{1}	6	9		5^{3}		11	10	8	3		4	12	14	13										11
1	2				7		6^{1}	9			12	11	13	8	3			5	10^{2}		4									12
1		12			7^{3}		6^{2}	9			13	11	14	8	3		2	5	10		4^{1}									13
1	2	4			7^{2}		6	9^{1}				8	13	10	3			5	11			12								14
1	2				7		6					10^{2}	11^{3}	8^{1}	3	12	4	5	9	13		14								15
1	2	4^{1}			7		6^{5}			15	13	10^{2}	11	8^{3}	3		12	5^{4}	9	14		16								16
1	2	4			6		8	7^{1}			12		11^{2}	10	3			5	9			13								17
1	2				7		6^{2}				13	9^{1}	12	8	3		4	5	11	14		10^{3}								18
1	2	4			6		8^{1}				13	7^{3}	12	9^{2}	3			5	11	14		10								19
1	2	4^{1}			6	8^{3}	14			11	9^{4}	7	15	13	3		12■	5^{2}	10											20
1	2				7	8^{2}	13			4	9^{1}	6	12	11	3				10			5								21
1	3				8	7	13	12		5	9^{3}	6^{1}		11^{2}	4		2		10			14								22
1	4				7		12	11^{3}		5	14	8		6^{2}	3^{1}		2		10	13			9							23
1	4		12		7		13			5	11^{2}	2^{1}		6			3	14	10	8			9^{3}							24
1	4		14		7			9		5	13	2^{2}		8^{1}			3		10	12			6	11^{3}						25
	3		4		7			9		5		2^{1}		8									6	10	1	11	12			26
1	3	4^{2}			6			11		5		2^{1}		8			13						9	7^{3}		10	12	14		27
1	4				7^{3}			9		5		2^{1}		8			3		13	14			6	10^{2}		11	12			28
1	3				6			11^{3}		5							2^{2}		7	8	4		9^{1}	14		10	13	12		29
1	4				6			10^{1}		5							3		9	7			12	8^{2}		11	2	13		30
1	3				6			13	14	5		12							10^{3}	7^{1}	4■		8	9^{2}		11	2			31
1	4	3			6			10	12	5		7^{3}		13					9				8^{2}	14		11^{1}	2			32
1	3				8			9^{3}	10^{2}	5		7^{1}							6	12	4		13	14		11	2			33
1^{1}	3				8				11					6			2		7		4		9			10	5		12	34
	3	2			5		14	13		12				7^{3}			4		8^{2}				9	11^{1}		10	6		1	35
	3	14					7^{1}		10	13		12		6			4^{3}		8		2		9^{2}			11	5■		1	36
		3					13	8^{1}	11	9		6^{2}		7			2				4			12		10	5		1	37
	2	3			6				10	8				7					9		4^{1}		12	13		11^{2}	5		1	38
	2	3^{1}			7		12		10	8^{2}		6^{3}						13	9	14	4		5^{4}	15		11			1	39
	3	4			7	6^{1}		11^{2}	13					8				5	12				9■	10^{3}		14	2		1	40
	2	3			8			9	11^{1}			13		7				5	6		4			12		10^{2}			1	41
	2	3			7			11	13			6^{2}		8				5	9		4			10^{1}		12			1	42
	4	3			7			11				6^{2}		8				5		13				9		10^{1}	2	12	1	43
	4	3			7		14	11	12			2		8^{3}				5		13			9^{2}	10^{1}				6	1	44
	3	4			7^{1}			13				12^{3}		8				5		6			9	10		14	2	11^{2}	1	45
	4						6^{2}	11^{1}	13		14			8			3^{3}	5		12			9	7		10	2		1	46

FA Cup

First Round	Bowers & Pitsea	(h)	1-0
Second Round	Hartlepool U	(h)	0-1

Carabao Cup

First Round	Shrewsbury T	(a)	2-2

(Shrewsbury T won 4-2 on penalties)

Papa John's Trophy

Group F (N)	Manchester U U21	(h)	3-2
Group F (N)	Bradford C	(a)	3-0
Group F (N)	Sunderland	(h)	1-2
Second Round	Carlisle U	(a)	1-1

(Carlisle U won 4-3 on penalties)

LIVERPOOL

FOUNDATION

But for a dispute between Everton FC and their landlord at Anfield in 1892, there may never have been a Liverpool club. This dispute persuaded the majority of Evertonians to quit Anfield for Goodison Park, leaving the landlord, Mr John Houlding, to form a new club. He originally tried to retain the name 'Everton' but when this failed, he founded Liverpool Association FC on 15 March 1892.

Anfield Stadium, Anfield Road, Anfield, Liverpool L4 0TH.

Telephone: (0151) 263 2361.

Ticket Office: (0843) 170 5555.

Website: www.liverpoolfc.com

Email: customerservices@liverpoolfc.com

Ground Capacity: 53,394.

Record Attendance: 61,905 v Wolverhampton W, FA Cup 4th rd, 2 February 1952.

Pitch Measurements: 101m × 68m (110.5yd × 74.5yd).

Chairman: Tom Werner.

Chief Executive: Billy Hogan.

Manager: Jürgen Klopp.

Assistant Managers: Peter Krawietz, Pepijn Lijnders.

Colours: Red shirts, red shorts, red socks.

Year Formed: 1892.

Turned Professional: 1892.

Club Nicknames: 'The Reds', 'Pool'.

Ground: 1892, Anfield.

First Football League Game: 2 September 1893, Division 2, v Middlesbrough Ironopolis (a) W 2–0 – McOwen; Hannah, McLean; Henderson, McQue (1), McBride; Gordon, McVean (1), Matt McQueen, Stott, Hugh McQueen.

HONOURS

League Champions: Premier League – 2019–20; Division 1 – 1900–01, 1905–06, 1921–22, 1922–23, 1946–47, 1963–64, 1965–66, 1972–73, 1975–76, 1976–77, 1978–79, 1979–80, 1981–82, 1982–83, 1983–84, 1985–86, 1987–88, 1989–90; Division 2 – 1893–94, 1895–96, 1904–05, 1961–62.
Runners-up: Premier League – 2001–02, 2008–09, 2013–14, 2018–19, 2021–22; Division 1 – 1898–99, 1909–10, 1968–69, 1973–74, 1974–75, 1977–78, 1984–85, 1986–87, 1988–89, 1990–91.

FA Cup Winners: 1965, 1974, 1986, 1989, 1992, 2001, 2006, 2022.
Runners-up: 1914, 1950, 1971, 1977, 1988, 1996, 2012.

League Cup Winners: 1981, 1982, 1983, 1984, 1995, 2001, 2003, 2012, 2022.
Runners-up: 1978, 1987, 2005, 2016.

League Super Cup Winners: 1986.

European Competitions

European Cup: 1964–65 *(sf)*, 1966–67, 1973–74, 1976–77 *(winners)*, 1977–78 *(winners)*, 1978–79, 1979–80, 1980–81 *(winners)*, 1981–82 *(qf)*, 1982–83 *(qf)*, 1983–84 *(winners)*, 1984–85 *(runners-up)*.
Champions League: 2001–02 *(qf)*, 2002–03, 2004–05 *(winners)*, 2005–06, 2006–07 *(runners-up)*, 2007–08 *(sf)*, 2008–09 *(qf)*, 2009–10, 2014–15, 2017–18 *(runners-up)*, 2018–19 *(winners)*, 2019–20, 2020–21 *(qf)*, 2021–22 *(runners-up)*.
Fairs Cup: 1967–68, 1968–69, 1969–70, 1970–71 *(sf)*.
UEFA Cup: 1972–73 *(winners)*, 1975–76 *(winners)*, 1991–92 *(qf)*, 1995–96, 1997–98, 1998–99, 2000–01 *(winners)*, 2002–03 *(qf)*, 2003–04.
Europa League: 2009–10 *(sf)*, 2010–11, 2012–13, 2014–15, 2015–16 *(runners-up)*.
European Cup-Winners' Cup: 1965–66 *(runners-up)*, 1971–72, 1974–75, 1992–93, 1996–97 *(sf)*.
Super Cup: 1977 *(winners)*, 1978, 1984, 2001 *(winners)*, 2005 *(winners)*, 2019 *(winners)*.
World Club Championship: 1981, 1984.
FIFA Club World Cup: 2005, 2019 *(winners)*.

FOOTBALL YEARBOOK FACT FILE

Inside-forward Jack Balmer scored in seven consecutive games for Liverpool during the 1946–47 campaign. Included in this run was a sequence of three games in November 1946 when he scored a hat-trick on each occasion. He finished the season as joint-top scorer along with Albert Stubbins as the Reds won the first post-war Football League title.

Record League Victory: 10–1 v Rotherham T, Division 2, 18 February 1896 – Storer; Goldie, Wilkie; McCartney, McQue, Holmes; McVean (3), Ross (2), Allan (4), Becton (1), Bradshaw.

Record Cup Victory: 11–0 v Stromsgodset Drammen, ECWC 1st rd 1st leg, 17 September 1974 – Clemence; Smith (1), Lindsay (1p), Thompson (2), Cormack (1), Hughes (1), Boersma (2), Hall, Heighway (1), Kennedy (1), Callaghan (1).

Record Defeat: 1–9 v Birmingham C, Division 2, 11 December 1954.

Most League Points (2 for a win): 68, Division 1, 1978–79.

Most League Points (3 for a win): 99, Premier League, 2019–20.

Most League Goals: 106, Division 2, 1895–96.

Highest League Scorer in Season: Roger Hunt, 41, Division 2, 1961–62.

Most League Goals in Total Aggregate: Roger Hunt, 245, 1959–69.

Most League Goals in One Match: 5, Andy McGuigan v Stoke C, Division 1, 4 January 1902; 5, John Evans v Bristol R, Division 2, 15 September 1954; 5, Ian Rush v Luton T, Division 1, 29 October 1983.

MANAGERS

W. E. Barclay 1892–96
Tom Watson 1896–1915
David Ashworth 1920–23
Matt McQueen 1923–28
George Patterson 1928–36
(continued as Secretary)
George Kay 1936–51
Don Welsh 1951–56
Phil Taylor 1956–59
Bill Shankly 1959–74
Bob Paisley 1974–83
Joe Fagan 1983–85
Kenny Dalglish 1985–91
Graeme Souness 1991–94
Roy Evans 1994–98
(then Joint Manager)
Gerard Houllier 1998–2004
Rafael Benitez 2004–10
Roy Hodgson 2010–11
Kenny Dalglish 2011–12
Brendan Rodgers 2012–15
Jürgen Klopp October 2015–

Most Capped Player: Steven Gerrard, 114, England.

Most League Appearances: Ian Callaghan, 640, 1960–78.

Youngest League Player: Jack Robinson, 16 years 250 days v Hull C, 9 May 2010.

Record Transfer Fee Received: £142,000,000 from Barcelona for Philippe Coutinho, January 2018.

Record Transfer Fee Paid: £75,000,000 to Southampton for Virgil van Dijk, January 2018.

Football League Record: 1893 Elected to Division 2; 1894–95 Division 1; 1895–96 Division 2; 1896–1904 Division 1; 1904–05 Division 2; 1905–54 Division 1; 1954–62 Division 2; 1962–92 Division 1; 1992– Premier League.

LATEST SEQUENCES

Longest Sequence of League Wins: 18, 27.10.2019 – 24.2.2020.

Longest Sequence of League Defeats: 9, 29.4.1899 – 14.10.1899.

Longest Sequence of League Draws: 6, 19.2.1975 – 19.3.1975.

Longest Sequence of Unbeaten League Matches: 44, 12.1.2019 – 24.2.2020.

Longest Sequence Without a League Win: 14, 12.12.1953 – 20.3.1954.

Successive Scoring Runs: 36 from 10.3.2019.

Successive Non-scoring Runs: 5 from 21.4.2000.

TEN YEAR LEAGUE RECORD

		P	W	D	L	F	A	Pts	Pos
2012-13	PR Lge	38	16	13	9	71	43	61	7
2013-14	PR Lge	38	26	6	6	101	50	84	2
2014-15	PR Lge	38	18	8	12	52	48	62	6
2015-16	PR Lge	38	16	12	10	63	50	60	8
2016-17	PR Lge	38	22	10	6	78	42	76	4
2017-18	PR Lge	38	21	12	5	84	38	75	4
2018-19	PR Lge	38	30	7	1	89	22	97	2
2019-20	PR Lge	38	32	3	3	85	33	99	1
2020-21	PR Lge	38	20	9	9	68	42	69	3
2021-22	PR Lge	38	28	8	2	94	26	92	2

DID YOU KNOW ?

Christmas Day fixtures were a feature of the game until the late 1950s. Liverpool played their last-ever Christmas Day game at Grimsby Town's Blundell Park in 1957. It was not a particularly auspicious occasion as the home team finished 3-1 winners, with Tony Rowley netting a consolation goal.

LIVERPOOL – PREMIER LEAGUE 2021–22 LEAGUE RECORD

Match No.	*Date*	*Venue*	*Opponents*	*Result*	*H/T Score*	*Lg Pos.*	*Goalscorers*	*Attendance*
1	Aug 14	A	Norwich C	W 3-0	1-0	2	Jota [26], Firmino [65], Salah [74]	27,023
2	21	H	Burnley	W 2-0	1-0	1	Jota [18], Mane [69]	52,591
3	28	H	Chelsea	D 1-1	1-1	2	Salah (pen) [45]	52,550
4	Sept 12	A	Leeds U	W 3-0	1-0	2	Salah [20], Fabinho [50], Mane [90]	36,507
5	18	H	Crystal Palace	W 3-0	1-0	1	Mane [43], Salah [78], Keita [89]	52,985
6	25	A	Brentford	D 3-3	1-1	1	Jota [31], Salah [54], Jones [67]	16,876
7	Oct 3	H	Manchester C	D 2-2	0-0	2	Mane [59], Salah [76]	53,102
8	16	A	Watford	W 5-0	2-0	2	Mane [8], Firmino 3 [37, 52, 90], Salah [54]	21,085
9	24	A	Manchester U	W 5-0	4-0	2	Keita [5], Jota [13], Salah 3 [38, 45, 50]	73,088
10	30	H	Brighton & HA	D 2-2	2-1	2	Henderson [4], Mane [24]	53,197
11	Nov 7	A	West Ham U	L 2-3	1-1	4	Alexander-Arnold [41], Origi [83]	59,909
12	20	H	Arsenal	W 4-0	1-0	2	Mane [39], Jota [52], Salah [73], Minamino [77]	53,092
13	27	H	Southampton	W 4-0	3-0	2	Jota 2 [2, 32], Thiago [37], van Dijk [52]	53,040
14	Dec 1	A	Everton	W 4-1	2-1	3	Henderson [9], Salah 2 [19, 64], Jota [79]	39,641
15	4	A	Wolverhampton W	W 1-0	0-0	2	Origi [90]	30,729
16	11	H	Aston Villa	W 1-0	0-0	2	Salah (pen) [67]	53,093
17	16	H	Newcastle U	W 3-1	2-1	2	Jota [21], Salah [25], Alexander-Arnold [87]	52,951
18	19	A	Tottenham H	D 2-2	1-1	2	Jota [35], Robertson [69]	45,421
19	28	A	Leicester C	L 0-1	0-0	2		32,230
20	Jan 2	A	Chelsea	D 2-2	2-2	3	Mane [9], Salah [26]	40,072
21	16	H	Brentford	W 3-0	1-0	2	Fabinho [44], Oxlade-Chamberlain [69], Minamino [77]	52,824
22	23	A	Crystal Palace	W 3-1	2-0	2	van Dijk [8], Oxlade-Chamberlain [32], Fabinho (pen) [89]	25,002
23	Feb 10	H	Leicester C	W 2-0	1-0	2	Jota 2 [34, 87]	53,050
24	13	A	Burnley	W 1-0	1-0	2	Fabinho [40]	21,239
25	19	H	Norwich C	W 3-1	0-0	2	Mane [64], Salah [67], Diaz [81]	53,135
26	23	H	Leeds U	W 6-0	3-0	2	Salah 2 (2 pens) [15, 35], Matip [30], Mane 2 [80, 90], van Dijk [90]	53,018
27	Mar 5	H	West Ham U	W 1-0	1-0	2	Mane [27]	53,059
28	12	A	Brighton & HA	W 2-0	1-0	2	Diaz [19], Salah (pen) [61]	31,474
29	16	A	Arsenal	W 2-0	0-0	2	Jota [54], Firmino [62]	59,968
30	Apr 2	H	Watford	W 2-0	1-0	2	Jota [22], Fabinho (pen) [89]	53,104
31	10	A	Manchester C	D 2-2	1-2	2	Jota [13], Mane [46]	53,197
32	19	H	Manchester U	W 4-0	2-0	1	Diaz [5], Salah 2 [22, 85], Mane [68]	52,686
33	24	H	Everton	W 2-0	0-0	2	Robertson [62], Origi [85]	53,213
34	30	A	Newcastle U	W 1-0	1-0	2	Keita [19]	52,281
35	May 7	H	Tottenham H	D 1-1	0-0	1	Diaz [74]	53,177
36	10	A	Aston Villa	W 2-1	1-1	2	Matip [6], Mane [65]	41,919
37	17	A	Southampton	W 2-1	1-1	2	Minamino [27], Matip [67]	31,588
38	22	H	Wolverhampton W	W 3-1	1-1	2	Mane [24], Salah [84], Robertson [89]	53,097

Final League Position: 2

GOALSCORERS

League (94): Salah 23 (5 pens), Mane 16, Jota 15, Fabinho 5 (2 pens), Firmino 5, Diaz 4, Keita 3, Matip 3, Minamino 3, Origi 3, Robertson 3, van Dijk 3, Alexander-Arnold 2, Henderson 2, Oxlade-Chamberlain 2, Jones 1, Thiago 1.
FA Cup (13): Minamino 3, Fabinho 2 (1 pen), Jota 2, Mane 2, Elliott 1, Firmino 1, Gordon 1, Konate 1.
Carabao Cup (10): Minamino 4, Jota 3, Origi 2, Oxlade-Chamberlain 1.
UEFA Champions League (30): Salah 8 (1 pen), Firmino 5, Mane 5, Diaz 2, Konate 2, Fabinho 1, Henderson 1, Jota 1, Keita 1, Origi 1, Thiago 1, own goals 2.
Papa John's Trophy (1): Dixon-Bonner 1.

Alisson R 36	Alexander-Arnold T 32	Matip J 31	van Dijk V 34	Tsimikas K 9 + 4	Oxlade-Chamberlain A 9 + 8	Milner J 9 + 15	Keita N 14 + 9	Salah M 30 + 5	Jota D 27 + 8	Mane S 32 + 2	Firmino R 10 + 10	Fabinho H 26 + 3	Elliott H 4 + 2	Henderson J 29 + 6	Thiago A 17 + 8	Gomez J 4 + 4	Robertson A 29	Konate I 11	Jones C 10 + 5	Origi D — + 7	Kelleher C 2	Williams N — + 1	Minamino T 1 + 10	Morton T 1 + 1	Gordon K — + 1	Diaz L 11 + 2	*Match No.*
1	2	3	4	5	6^2	7	8^3	9	10^1	11	12	13	14														1
1	2	3	4	5^3			8^1	9	10^2	11	12		6	7	13	14											2
1	2	3	4	14				9	12	11	10^1	8	6	7^2	13		5^3										3
1	2	3	4		13		14	9	10^2	11		7	6^1	12	8^3		5										4
1			4	5		2	12	9	10^2	11		7		6^3	8^1			3	13	14							5
1	2	3	4					9	10	11	12	7		6			5		8^1								6
1		3	4			2^2		9	10^1	11	12	7		6		13	5		8								7
	2^2	3	4	12	13	6^3	8	9		11	10			7			5^1				1	14					8
1	2		4		13	8^1	6^2	9	11	14	10^3			7			5	3	12								9
1	2		4		12		6^1	9	13	11	10^2			7			5	3	8^3				14				10
1	2	3	4		8^1			9	10^2	11		7^3		6	12		5			13			14				11
1	2	3	4	5	8^2			9	10^1	11		7		12	6^3								13	14			12
1	2		4		12	13		9	10^3	11		7		6^2	8^1		5	3					14				13
1	2	3	4		13	12		9	10^3	11		7		6^2	8^1		5						14				14
1	2	3	4		13	14		9^3	10^2	11		7		6^1	8		5			12							15
1	2	3	4		10^1	13		9	12	11^3		7		6	8^2		5						14				16
1	2	3			6^1	14	13	9^2	10	11	12			7	8^3		5	4									17
1	2	3		13		8	6	9	10^3	11^2	12					14	5■	4						7^1			18
1	2	3	4	5	8^1	13	12	9	10	11	14	7^2		6^3													19
	2		4	5	13	8^2	12	9	10^1	11^3		7		6				3	14		1						20
1	2	3	4		9^1	13			11^3		10^2	7		6			5		8				12		14		21
1	2^2	3	4		9^1	14			11		10^3	7		6		13	5		8				12				22
1	2	3	4					12	9		10^2	7	13		6		5		8^1				14			11^3	23
1	2	3	4			14	8^3	9	13	11^2	10	7		6^1	12		5										24
1		3	4	5	6^1		8^2	9		10				7	13	2				12			14			11^3	25
1	2	3	4			13		9		10		7		12	8^1		5		6^2	14						11^3	26
1	2		4			14	8^3	9^1	12	10		7		6			5	3	13							11^2	27
1	2	3	4			14	8^2	9^1	13	10		7		6^3	12		5									11	28
1	2	3	4					12	10^2	9	13	7		6	8^3		5		14							11^1	29
1		3	4			14		9^2	11	13	10	12		7	8^3	2	5		6^1								30
1	2	3	4				13	9	10^1	11^3	14	7		6^2	8		5									12	31
1	2	3	4			14	13	9	12	10		7^3		6	8^2		5									11^1	32
1	2	3	4				6^1	9	11^3	10^2		7		14	8		5			12						13	33
1		3	4			8^3	6	12	10	11^1		13		7^2	14	2	5									9	34
1	2		4	12			14	9	13	10		7^3		6^2	8		5^1	3								11	35
1	2	3	4	5			6	14	11	10		7^1		12	13				8^2							9^3	36
1		3		5		7	14		11		10^3		6^2	12		2^1		4	8	13			9				37
1	2	3				12	6^3	13	9^2	10	14			7	8^1		5	4								11	38

FA Cup

Third Round	Shrewsbury T	(h)	4-1
Fourth Round	Cardiff C	(h)	3-1
Fifth Round	Norwich C	(h)	2-1
Sixth Round	Nottingham F	(a)	1-0
Semi-Final	Manchester C	(Wembley)	3-2
Final	Chelsea	(Wembley)	0-0

(Liverpool won 6-5 on penalties)

Carabao Cup

Third Round	Norwich C	(a)	3-0
Fourth Round	Preston NE	(a)	2-0
Quarter-Final	Leicester C	(h)	3-3

(Liverpool won 5-4 on penalties)

Semi-Final 1st leg	Arsenal	(h)	0-0
Semi-Final 2nd leg	Arsenal	(a)	2-0

(Liverpool won 2-0 on aggregate)

Final	Chelsea	(Wembley)	0-0

(Liverpool won 11-10 on penalties)

UEFA Champions League

Group B	AC Milan	(h)	3-2
Group B	Porto	(a)	5-1
Group B	Atletico Madrid	(a)	3-2
Group B	Atletico Madrid	(h)	2-0
Group B	Porto	(h)	2-0
Group B	AC Milan	(a)	2-1
Round of 16 1st leg	Inter Milan	(a)	2-0
Round of 16 2nd leg	Inter Milan	(h)	0-1
Quarter-Final 1st leg	Benfica	(a)	3-1
Quarter-Final 2nd leg	Benfica	(h)	3-3
Semi-Final 1st leg	Villarreal	(h)	2-0
Semi-Final 2nd leg	Villarreal	(a)	3-2
Final	Real Madrid	(Paris)	0-1

Papa John's Trophy (Liverpool U21)

Group D (N)	Rochdale	(a)	0-4
Group D (N)	Bolton W	(a)	1-4
Group D (N)	Port Vale	(a)	0-5

LUTON TOWN

FOUNDATION

Formed by an amalgamation of two leading local clubs, Wanderers and Excelsior a works team, at a meeting in Luton Town Hall in April 1885. The Wanderers had three months earlier changed their name to Luton Town Wanderers and did not take too kindly to the formation of another Town club but were talked around at this meeting. Wanderers had already appeared in the FA Cup and the new club entered in its inaugural season.

Kenilworth Road Stadium, 1 Maple Road, Luton, Bedfordshire LU4 8AW.

Telephone: (01582) 411 622.

Ticket Office: (01582) 416 976.

Website: www.lutontown.co.uk

Email: info@lutontown.co.uk

Ground Capacity: 10,265.

Record Attendance: 30,069 v Blackpool, FA Cup 6th rd replay, 4 March 1959.

Pitch Measurements: 100.6m × 65.8m (110yd × 72yd).

Chairman: David Wilkinson.

Chief Executive: Gary Sweet.

Manager: Nathan Jones.

Assistant Manager: Mick Harford.

Colours: Orange shirts with white trim, navy blue shorts with orange trim, orange socks with navy blue trim.

Year Formed: 1885.

Turned Professional: 1890.

Ltd Co.: 1897.

Club Nickname: 'The Hatters'.

Grounds: 1885, Excelsior, Dallow Lane; 1897, Dunstable Road; 1905, Kenilworth Road.

First Football League Game: 4 September 1897, Division 2, v Leicester Fosse (a) D 1–1 – Williams; McCartney, McEwen; Davies, Stewart, Docherty; Gallacher, Coupar, Birch, McInnes, Ekins (1).

Record League Victory: 12–0 v Bristol R, Division 3 (S), 13 April 1936 – Dolman; Mackey, Smith; Finlayson, Nelson, Godfrey; Rich, Martin (1), Payne (10), Roberts (1), Stephenson.

Record Cup Victory: 9–0 v Clapton, FA Cup 1st rd (replay after abandoned game), 30 November 1927 – Abbott; Kingham, Graham; Black, Rennie, Fraser; Pointon, Yardley (4), Reid (2), Woods (1), Dennis (2).

Record Defeat: 0–9 v Small Heath, Division 2, 12 November 1898.

HONOURS

League Champions: Division 2 – 1981–82; FL 1 – 2004–05, 2018–19; Division 3S – 1936–37; Division 4 – 1967–68; Conference – 2013–14.
Runners-up: FL 2 – 2017–18; Division 2 – 1954–55, 1973–74; Division 3 – 1969–70; Division 3S – 1935–36; Third Division – 2001–02.

FA Cup: *Runners-up:* 1959.

League Cup Winners: 1988.
Runners-up: 1989.

League Trophy Winners: 2009.

Full Members' Cup: *Runners-up:* 1988.

FOOTBALL YEARBOOK FACT FILE

Luton Town played two matches against Blackburn Rovers in Ireland at the end of the 1953–54 season, the two meeting at Dalymount Park in Dublin on 30 April and in Cork two days later. The Hatters won both games 4-2 with Gordon Turner scoring a hat-trick on each occasion. It is believed to be the first occasion that two English professional clubs had played each other in the Republic of Ireland.

Most League Points (2 for a win): 66, Division 4, 1967–68.

Most League Points (3 for a win): 98, FL 1 2004–05.

Most League Goals: 103, Division 3 (S), 1936–37.

Highest League Scorer in Season: Joe Payne, 55, Division 3 (S), 1936–37.

Most League Goals in Total Aggregate: Gordon Turner, 243, 1949–64.

Most League Goals in One Match: 10, Joe Payne v Bristol R, Division 3 (S), 13 April 1936.

Most Capped Player: Mal Donaghy, 58 (91), Northern Ireland.

Most League Appearances: Bob Morton, 495, 1948–64.

Youngest League Player: Mike O'Hara, 16 years 32 days v Stoke C, 1 October 1960.

Record Transfer Fee Received: £6,000,000 from Leicester C for James Justin, June 2019.

Record Transfer Fee Paid: £1,340,000 to HNK Rijeka for Simon Sluga, July 2019.

Football League Record: 1897 Elected to Division 2; 1900 Failed re-election; 1920 Division 3; 1921–37 Division 3 (S); 1937–55 Division 2; 1955–60 Division 1; 1960–63 Division 2; 1963–65 Division 3; 1965–68 Division 4; 1968–70 Division 3; 1970–74 Division 2; 1974–75 Division 1; 1975–82 Division 2; 1982–96 Division 1; 1996–2001 Division 2; 2001–02 Division 3; 2002–04 Division 2; 2004–05 FL 1; 2005–07 FL C; 2007–08 FL 1; 2008–09 FL 2; 2009–14 Conference Premier; 2014–18 FL 2; 2018–19 FL 1; 2019– FL C.

LATEST SEQUENCES

Longest Sequence of League Wins: 12, 19.2.2002 – 6.4.2002.

Longest Sequence of League Defeats: 8, 11.11.1899 – 6.1.1900.

Longest Sequence of League Draws: 5, 28.8.1971 – 18.9.1971.

Longest Sequence of Unbeaten League Matches: 28, 20.10.2018 – 6.4.2019.

Longest Sequence Without a League Win: 16, 9.9.1964 – 6.11.1964.

Successive Scoring Runs: 25 from 24.10.1931.

Successive Non-scoring Runs: 5 from 10.4.1973.

MANAGERS

Charlie Green 1901–28 *(Secretary-Manager)*
George Thomson 1925
John McCartney 1927–29
George Kay 1929–31
Harold Wightman 1931–35
Ted Liddell 1936–38
Neil McBain 1938–39
George Martin 1939–47
Dally Duncan 1947–58
Syd Owen 1959–60
Sam Bartram 1960–62
Bill Harvey 1962–64
George Martin 1965–66
Allan Brown 1966–68
Alec Stock 1968–72
Harry Haslam 1972–78
David Pleat 1978–86
John Moore 1986–87
Ray Harford 1987–89
Jim Ryan 1990–91
David Pleat 1991–95
Terry Westley 1995
Lennie Lawrence 1995–2000
Ricky Hill 2000
Lil Fuccillo 2000
Joe Kinnear 2001–03
Mike Newell 2003–07
Kevin Blackwell 2007–08
Mick Harford 2008–09
Richard Money 2009–11
Gary Brabin 2011–12
Paul Buckle 2012–13
John Still 2013–15
Nathan Jones 2016–19
Mick Harford 2019 *(caretaker)*
Graeme Jones 2019–20
Nathan Jones May 2020–

TEN YEAR LEAGUE RECORD

		P	*W*	*D*	*L*	*F*	*A*	*Pts*	*Pos*
2012-13	Conf P	46	18	13	15	70	62	67	7
2013-14	Conf P	46	30	11	5	102	35	101	1
2014-15	FL 2	46	19	11	16	54	44	68	8
2015-16	FL 2	46	19	9	18	63	61	66	11
2016-17	FL 2	46	20	17	9	70	43	77	4
2017-18	FL 2	46	25	13	8	94	46	88	2
2018-19	FL 1	46	27	13	6	90	42	94	1
2019-20	FL C	46	14	9	23	54	82	51	19
2020-21	FL C	46	17	11	18	41	52	62	12
2021-22	FL C	46	21	12	13	63	55	75	6

DID YOU KNOW ?

Luton Town had three regular first-team players absent on international duty when they entertained Portsmouth on 22 October 1921. The visitors were unbeaten in 10 matches, but the patched-up Hatters team won 1-0 thanks to a goal from centre-half Billy Walsh who had switched to playing at centre-forward due to the club's selection problems.

LUTON TOWN – SKY BET CHAMPIONSHIP 2021–22 LEAGUE RECORD

Match No.	*Date*	*Venue*	*Opponents*	*Result*		*H/T Score*	*Lg Pos.*	*Goalscorers*	*Attendance*
1	Aug 7	H	Peterborough U	W	3-0	1-0	2	Adebayo ^{30}, Cornick ^{68}, Onyedinma ^{71}	10,019
2	14	A	WBA	L	2-3	0-2	11	Cornick ^{70}, Ruddock ^{90}	23,283
3	17	A	Barnsley	W	1-0	1-0	3	Bell ^{4}	12,999
4	21	H	Birmingham C	L	0-5	0-2	11		10,014
5	28	H	Sheffield U	D	0-0	0-0	12		9774
6	Sept 11	A	Blackburn R	D	2-2	0-2	12	Berry 2 $^{73, 90}$	11,241
7	15	A	Bristol C	D	1-1	0-0	13	Hylton ^{90}	16,878
8	18	H	Swansea C	D	3-3	3-0	13	Berry ^{7}, Adebayo 2 (1 pen) $^{15 (p), 23}$	9721
9	25	A	Bournemouth	L	1-2	0-2	16	Kelly (og) ^{64}	9737
10	29	H	Coventry C	W	5-0	4-0	9	Adebayo 2 (1 pen) $^{3 (p), 45}$, Cornick 2 $^{18, 58}$, Berry ^{30}	9805
11	Oct 2	H	Huddersfield T	D	0-0	0-0	13		9977
12	16	A	Millwall	W	2-0	1-0	10	Cornick 2 $^{11, 53}$	14,227
13	19	A	Derby Co	D	2-2	0-1	9	Onyedinma ^{48}, Adebayo ^{83}	20,258
14	23	H	Hull C	W	1-0	1-0	5	Adebayo ^{17}	9999
15	30	A	Preston NE	L	0-2	0-2	10		11,059
16	Nov 2	H	Middlesbrough	W	3-1	0-1	6	Bradley ^{57}, Adebayo ^{60}, Cornick ^{62}	9790
17	6	H	Stoke C	L	0-1	0-1	11		10,068
18	19	A	QPR	L	0-2	0-1	11		15,062
19	23	A	Nottingham F	D	0-0	0-0	11		25,715
20	27	H	Cardiff C	L	1-2	0-1	14	Clark ^{64}	9987
21	Dec 4	A	Blackpool	W	3-0	1-0	12	Bradley ^{42}, Adebayo ^{54}, Clark ^{90}	11,366
22	11	H	Fulham	D	1-1	0-1	12	Adebayo ^{62}	9992
23	Jan 15	H	Bournemouth	W	3-2	2-0	13	Kelly (og) ^{30}, Campbell ^{42}, Naismith ^{90}	9649
24	19	A	Reading	W	2-0	1-0	11	Holmes (og) ^{33}, Campbell ^{58}	9611
25	22	A	Sheffield U	L	0-2	0-0	13		27,780
26	25	H	Bristol C	W	2-1	1-0	10	Lockyer ^{42}, Adebayo ^{68}	9202
27	29	H	Blackburn R	D	0-0	0-0	10		9987
28	Feb 1	A	Swansea C	W	1-0	0-0	9	Cornick ^{72}	16,598
29	8	H	Barnsley	W	2-1	1-1	7	Campbell ^{28}, Adebayo (pen) ^{59}	9101
30	12	A	Birmingham C	L	0-3	0-1	10		17,292
31	19	H	WBA	W	2-0	0-0	8	Jerome ^{55}, Campbell ^{82}	10,021
32	23	A	Stoke C	W	2-1	0-0	8	Hylton ^{56}, Jerome ^{81}	18,270
33	26	H	Derby Co	W	1-0	0-0	6	Hylton ^{67}	10,070
34	Mar 5	A	Middlesbrough	L	1-2	0-1	8	Cornick ^{90}	23,817
35	8	A	Coventry C	W	1-0	1-0	6	Adebayo ^{38}	16,996
36	13	H	QPR	L	1-2	1-0	7	Jerome ^{37}	10,073
37	16	H	Preston NE	W	4-0	3-0	5	Berry 2 $^{9, 42}$, Onyedinma ^{28}, Diaby (og) ^{59}	9408
38	19	A	Hull C	W	3-1	1-0	3	Adebayo ^{9}, Cornick ^{56}, Bree ^{72}	16,555
39	Apr 2	H	Millwall	D	2-2	1-1	4	Adebayo ^{33}, Cooper (og) ^{87}	10,069
40	5	A	Peterborough U	D	1-1	0-0	4	Hylton ^{49}	10,940
41	11	A	Huddersfield T	L	0-2	0-0	5		18,379
42	15	H	Nottingham F	W	1-0	1-0	4	Naismith (pen) ^{37}	10,070
43	18	A	Cardiff C	W	1-0	0-0	4	Cornick ^{71}	19,381
44	23	H	Blackpool	D	1-1	1-0	5	Adebayo ^{2}	9843
45	May 2	A	Fulham	L	0-7	0-2	6		19,538
46	7	H	Reading	W	1-0	1-0	6	Cornick ^{45}	10,070

Final League Position: 6

GOALSCORERS

League (63): Adebayo 16 (3 pens), Cornick 12, Berry 6, Campbell 4, Hylton 4, Jerome 3, Onyedinma 3, Bradley 2, Clark 2, Naismith 2 (1 pen), Bell 1, Bree 1, Lockyer 1, Ruddock 1, own goals 5.
FA Cup (9): Burke 2, Adebayo 1, Berry 1, Cornick 1, Jerome 1, Mendes Gomes 1, Muskwe 1, Naismith 1.
Carabao Cup (2): Jerome 1, Muskwe 1.
Championship Play-offs (1): Bradley 1.

Sluga S 19	Bree J 42	Osho G 16 + 7	Naismith K 42	Bell A 40 + 1	Campbell A 31 + 2	Ruddock P 31 + 3	Clark J 19 + 6	Cornick H 30 + 8	Adebayo E 38 + 2	Onyedinma F 14 + 15	Muskwe A 7 + 13	Mendes Gomes C 2 + 7	Lansbury H 18 + 16	Kioso P 8 + 8	Jerome C 14 + 17	Lockyer T 27 + 2	Rea G 8 + 4	Burke R 25 + 2	Potts D 9 + 1	Bradley S 20 + 2	Berry L 10 + 3	Hylton D 5 + 12	Shea J 19	Steer J 3	Palmer A 2	Snodgrass R 4 + 4	Isted H 1 + 1	Ingram M 2	Match No.
1	2	3	4	5	6	7^3	8	9^1	10	11^2	12	13	14																1
1	2	3	4	5	7^3	8	6^2	9	10^4	11^1	13		12	14	15														2
1	5	13	4	8		6		12	11		9^3		7	2	10^1	3^2	14												3
1	5		4	8	7^2	6		10^3	11	13	9			2^1	14	3	12												4
1	2	6	4	5	9^1	7		8	11	10^2	13						12	3											5
1	2	7	4		6^1	9		8				10^3	12		11			3	5^2	13	14								6
1	5		4	8		9		10^2	12			14	7		11^1	2		3			6^3	13							7
1	5	9	4			8	12	11^2	10^3				7		13	2	14	3			6^1								8
1	2	7^1	5	12			11	9^3	10			13	8		14	3		4			6^2								9
1	5	14	3	8			9	10^2	11^1			12			13	2	6^3			4	7								10
1	5		4	8			9^2	11^1	10			14	13		12	2	6			3	7^3								11
1	5		4	8		7	9^2	11^1	10^3		14		13		12	2^4	6	15		3									12
1	5		4^1	8		6	9^2	10	11	13	12		14			2	7^3			3									13
1	5			8		12	6	9	10^2	11^3					13	2	3	14		4	7^1								14
1	5		4	8		9	6	11^3		14	12		13		10	2	7^1			3^2									15
1	5	7	4			8		10^2	11^3	12			6		14			2	9^1	3		13							16
1	5	7^3	3	9	6	8	14	10^2	11	13	12							2^1		4									17
1	2		5		7^2	8		10^1	11	6	12		9		13	3				4									18
	2		5		7	8	13	12	11^3	6	10^2		9^1			3				4		14	1						19
1	2		5	6^1		9	8	10^2	11	12			14			3	7^3			4		13							20
	5		3	8	6	12	9		10^3		13	11^2	7^1					2		4		14	1						21
	5	13	3	8	7^2	6	9		10	12	11^1							2		4			1						22
	5	13	4	9	7^1	6	8		10	12			14		11^3			2^2		3			1						23
		14	4	9	7^3	6	8^1		11	13			12	5	10^2			2		3			1						24
		14	4	9^2	7	6	13		12		10^3		8	5	11^1			2■		3			1						25
	5	3	4	9	12	8			11	13	10^2			14		2^3	7				6^1		1						26
	5	3	4	9	6^3	8		13		10^2	12		7		11^1	2					14		1						27
	5	3	4	9	6	8		13		10^2			7^3		12			2			14	11^1	1						28
	5	3^1	4	9	6	8		10^2	11^3	12			7	13				2				14	1						29
	5	14	4	9	6	8		10^3	11	13		12	7^2			2^1		3					1						30
	5^3	3	4	8	6	7			11		9^1		12	14	10^2	2						13		1					31
	5	7	4	8	6^2			10^1	11					13	12	3		2				9		1					32
	6	5	4	9	7			10^2	11^3	14			8^1		13	3		2				12		1					33
	5	6^1	4^2	8	7^3		13	14	11				12		10	3		2				9			1				34
	5			8	13	6	7^3	10^1	11				14		12	3		2	4		9^2				1				35
	5		4	8	9	6^1	7^3	13	11				12		10^2	3		2					1			14			36
	5			8	6		7	10^2	11	12		14		2				3^1	4		9^3	13	1						37
	2			8	6	12	7	10^3	11	5				3^2	14	13			4		9^1		1						38
	5		3	8	9	6^3		10^1	11	12			7		14	2			4^2				1			13			39
	3		5	6	7	9		14	11	2^3			12	4	10^1					13		8^2	1						40
	2		4	8	9	6^1		10^3	11	5			7^2						13	3		14	1			12			41
	6		5	4	7			10^1	11^3	9				13		14		2		3■		12	1			8^2			42
	6^1		5	4	7			12	11	10^3				14		3		2	9				1^2			8	13		43
			5	9	7			11^3	10		12		13	6	14	2			4^2	3^1						8	1		44
			5	9			14			6^1	13		7	12	11^2	3		2	4			10				8^3		1	45
	6		4	9	7^2		8	11^1			12		5		10^3			2		3		14				13		1	46

FA Cup

Third Round	Harrogate T	(h)	4-0
Fourth Round	Cambridge U	(a)	3-0
Fifth Round	Chelsea	(h)	2-3

Carabao Cup

First Round	Stevenage	(a)	2-2

(Stevenage won 3-0 on penalties)

Championship Play-offs

Semi-Final 1st leg	Huddersfield T	(h)	1-1
Semi-Final 2nd leg	Huddersfield T	(a)	0-1

MANCHESTER CITY

FOUNDATION

Manchester City was formed as a limited company in 1894 after their predecessors Ardwick had been forced into bankruptcy. However, many historians like to trace the club's lineage as far back as 1880 when St Mark's Church, West Gorton added a football section to their cricket club. They amalgamated with Belle Vue for one season before splitting again under the name Gorton Association FC in 1884–85. In 1887 Gorton AFC turned professional and moved ground to Hyde Road under the new name Ardwick AFC.

Etihad Stadium, Etihad Campus, Manchester M11 3FF.

Telephone: (0161) 444 1894.

Ticket Office: (0161) 444 1894.

Website: www.mancity.com

Email: mancity@mancity.com

Ground Capacity: 55,017.

Record Attendance: 84,569 v Stoke C, FA Cup 6th rd, 3 March 1934 (at Maine Road; British record for any game outside London or Glasgow); 54,693 v Leicester C, Premier League, 6 February 2016 (at Etihad Stadium).

Pitch Measurements: 105m × 68m (115yd × 74.5yd).

Chairman: Khaldoon Al Mubarak.

Chief Executive: Ferran Soriano.

Manager: Pep Guardiola.

Assistant Managers: Juan Manuel Lillo, Rodolfo Borrell, Lorenzo Buenaventura, Manel Estiarte, Xabier Manisidor, Carles Planchart.

Colours: Light blue shirts with white trim, light blue shorts, light blue socks with white trim.

Year Formed: 1887 as Ardwick FC; 1894 as Manchester City.

Turned Professional: 1887 as Ardwick FC.

Previous Names: 1880, St Mark's Church, West Gorton; 1884, Gorton; 1887, Ardwick; 1894, Manchester City.

Club Nicknames: 'The Blues', 'The Citizens'.

Grounds: 1880, Clowes Street; 1881, Kirkmanshulme Cricket Ground; 1882, Queens Road; 1884, Pink Bank Lane; 1887, Hyde Road (1894–1923 as City); 1923, Maine Road; 2003, City of Manchester Stadium (renamed Etihad Stadium 2011).

First Football League Game: 3 September 1892, Division 2, v Bootle (h) W 7–0 – Douglas; McVickers, Robson; Middleton, Russell, Hopkins; Davies (3), Morris (2), Angus (1), Weir (1), Milarvie.

Record League Victory: 10–1 v Huddersfield T, Division 2, 7 November 1987 – Nixon; Gidman, Hinchcliffe, Clements, Lake, Redmond, White (3), Stewart (3), Adcock (3), McNab (1), Simpson.

Record Cup Victory: 10–1 v Swindon T, FA Cup 4th rd, 29 January 1930 – Barber; Felton, McCloy; Barrass, Cowan, Heinemann; Toseland, Marshall (5), Tait (3), Johnson (1), Brook (1).

HONOURS

League Champions: Premier League – 2011–12, 2013–14, 2017–18, 2018–19, 2020–21, 2021–22; Division 1 – 1936–37, 1967–68; First Division – 2001–02; Division 2 – 1898–99, 1902–03, 1909–10, 1927–28, 1946–47, 1965–66.
Runners-up: Premier League – 2012–13, 2014–15, 2019–20; Division 1 – 1903–04, 1920–21, 1976–77; First Division – 1999–2000; Division 2 – 1895–96, 1950–51, 1988–89.

FA Cup Winners: 1904, 1934, 1956, 1969, 2011, 2019.
Runners-up: 1926, 1933, 1955, 1981, 2013.

League Cup Winners: 1970, 1976, 2014, 2016, 2018, 2019, 2020, 2021.
Runners-up: 1974.

Full Members Cup: *Runners-up:* 1986.

European Competitions
European Cup: 1968–69.
Champions League: 2011–12, 2012–13, 2013–14, 2014–15, 2015–16 *(sf)*, 2016–17, 2017–18 *(qf)*, 2018–19 *(qf)*, 2019–20 *(qf)*, 2020–21 *(runners-up)*, 2021–22 *(sf)*.
UEFA Cup: 1972–73, 1976–77, 1977–78, 1978–79 *(qf)*, 2003–04, 2008–09 *(qf)*.
Europa League: 2010–11, 2011–12.
European Cup-Winners' Cup: 1969–70 *(winners)*, 1970–71 *(sf)*.

FOOTBALL YEARBOOK FACT FILE

Centre-forward Jack Milsom scored two hat-tricks in two days for Manchester City over the Christmas period in 1938, and both were against the same opponents. On Boxing Day he hit four as City won 9-3 away to Tranmere Rovers, and the following day he scored three as City again took both points with a 5-2 victory at Maine Road.

Record Defeat: 1–9 v Everton, Division 1, 3 September 1906.

Most League Points (2 for a win): 62, Division 2, 1946–47.

Most League Points (3 for a win): 100, Premier League, 2017–18.

Most League Goals: 108, Division 2, 1926–27, 108, Division 1, 2001–02.

Highest League Scorer in Season: Tommy Johnson, 38, Division 1, 1928–29.

Most League Goals in Total Aggregate: Sergio Aguero, 184, 2011–21.

Most League Goals in One Match: 5, Fred Williams v Darwen, Division 2, 18 February 1899; 5, Tom Browell v Burnley, Division 2, 24 October 1925; 5, Tom Johnson v Everton, Division 1, 15 September 1928; 5, George Smith v Newport Co, Division 2, 14 June 1947; 5, Sergio Aguero v Newcastle U, Premier League, 3 October 2015.

Most Capped Player: David Silva, 87 (125), Spain.

Most League Appearances: Alan Oakes, 564, 1959–76.

Youngest League Player: Glyn Pardoe, 15 years 314 days v Birmingham C, 11 April 1962.

Record Transfer Fee Received: £46,300,000 from Barcelona for Ferran Torres, December 2021.

Record Transfer Fee Paid: £100,000,000 to Aston Villa for Jack Grealish, August 2021.

Football League Record: 1892 Ardwick elected founder member of Division 2; 1894 Newly formed Manchester C elected to Division 2; Division 1 1899–1902, 1903–09, 1910–26, 1928–38, 1947–50, 1951–63, 1966–83, 1985–87, 1989–92; Division 2 1902–03, 1909–10, 1926–28, 1938–47, 1950–51, 1963–66, 1983–85, 1987–89; 1992–96 Premier League; 1996–98 Division 1; 1998–99 Division 2; 1999–2000 Division 1; 2000–01 Premier League; 2001–02 Division 1; 2002– Premier League.

LATEST SEQUENCES

Longest Sequence of League Wins: 18, 26.8.2017 – 27.12.2017.

Longest Sequence of League Defeats: 8, 23.8.1995 – 14.10.1995.

Longest Sequence of League Draws: 7, 5.10.2009 – 28.11.2009.

Longest Sequence of Unbeaten League Matches: 30, 8.4.2017 – 2.1.2018.

Longest Sequence Without a League Win: 17, 26.12.1979 – 7.4.1980.

Successive Scoring Runs: 44 from 3.10.1936.

Successive Non-scoring Runs: 6 from 30.1.1971.

MANAGERS

Joshua Parlby 1893–95 *(Secretary-Manager)*
Sam Omerod 1895–1902
Tom Maley 1902–06
Harry Newbould 1906–12
Ernest Magnall 1912–24
David Ashworth 1924–25
Peter Hodge 1926–32
Wilf Wild 1932–46 *(continued as Secretary to 1950)*
Sam Cowan 1946–47
John 'Jock' Thomson 1947–50
Leslie McDowall 1950–63
George Poyser 1963–65
Joe Mercer 1965–71 *(continued as General Manager to 1972)*
Malcolm Allison 1972–73
Johnny Hart 1973
Ron Saunders 1973–74
Tony Book 1974–79
Malcolm Allison 1979–80
John Bond 1980–83
John Benson 1983
Billy McNeill 1983–86
Jimmy Frizzell 1986–87 *(continued as General Manager)*
Mel Machin 1987–89
Howard Kendall 1989–90
Peter Reid 1990–93
Brian Horton 1993–95
Alan Ball 1995–96
Steve Coppell 1996
Frank Clark 1996–98
Joe Royle 1998–2001
Kevin Keegan 2001–05
Stuart Pearce 2005–07
Sven-Göran Eriksson 2007–08
Mark Hughes 2008–09
Roberto Mancini 2009–13
Manuel Pellegrini 2013–16
Pep Guardiola June 2016–

TEN YEAR LEAGUE RECORD

		P	W	D	L	F	A	Pts	Pos
2012-13	PR Lge	38	23	9	6	66	34	78	2
2013-14	PR Lge	38	27	5	6	102	37	86	1
2014-15	PR Lge	38	24	7	7	83	38	79	2
2015-16	PR Lge	38	19	9	10	71	41	66	4
2016-17	PR Lge	38	23	9	6	80	39	78	3
2017-18	PR Lge	38	32	4	2	106	27	100	1
2018-19	PR Lge	38	32	2	4	95	23	98	1
2019-20	PR Lge	38	26	3	9	102	35	81	2
2020-21	PR Lge	38	27	5	6	83	32	86	1
2021-22	PR Lge	38	29	6	3	99	26	93	1

DID YOU KNOW

Manchester City failed to score in either of their last two games at their former Maine Road ground, losing 1-0 to both West Ham United and Southampton. Their final goals at the ground came on 21 April 2003 when they beat Sunderland 3-0, with Marc Vivien Foé hitting the very last goal 10 minutes from time.

MANCHESTER CITY – PREMIER LEAGUE 2021–22 LEAGUE RECORD

Match No.	*Date*	*Venue*	*Opponents*	*Result*	*H/T Score*	*Lg Pos.*	*Goalscorers*	*Attendance*
1	Aug 15	A	Tottenham H	L 0-1	0-0	13		58,262
2	21	H	Norwich C	W 5-0	2-0	5	Krul (og) [7], Grealish [22], Laporte [64], Sterling [71], Mahrez [84]	51,437
3	28	H	Arsenal	W 5-0	3-0	5	Gundogan [7], Torres 2 [12, 84], Gabriel Jesus [43], Rodri [53]	52,276
4	Sept 11	A	Leicester C	W 1-0	0-0	3	Bernardo Silva [62]	32,087
5	18	H	Southampton	D 0-0	0-0	2		52,698
6	25	A	Chelsea	W 1-0	0-0	2	Gabriel Jesus [53]	40,036
7	Oct 3	A	Liverpool	D 2-2	0-0	3	Foden [69], De Bruyne [81]	53,102
8	16	H	Burnley	W 2-0	1-0	3	Bernardo Silva [12], De Bruyne [70]	52,711
9	23	A	Brighton & HA	W 4-1	3-0	2	Gundogan [13], Foden 2 [28, 31], Mahrez [90]	31,215
10	30	H	Crystal Palace	L 0-2	0-1	3		53,014
11	Nov 6	A	Manchester U	W 2-0	2-0	2	Bailly (og) [7], Bernardo Silva [45]	73,086
12	21	H	Everton	W 3-0	1-0	2	Sterling [44], Rodri [55], Bernardo Silva [86]	52,571
13	28	H	West Ham U	W 2-1	1-0	2	Gundogan [33], Fernandinho [90]	53,245
14	Dec 1	A	Aston Villa	W 2-1	2-0	2	Dias [27], Bernardo Silva [43]	41,400
15	4	A	Watford	W 3-1	2-0	1	Sterling [4], Bernardo Silva 2 [31, 63]	20,673
16	11	H	Wolverhampton W	W 1-0	0-0	1	Sterling (pen) [66]	52,613
17	14	H	Leeds U	W 7-0	3-0	1	Foden [8], Grealish [13], De Bruyne 2 [32, 62], Mahrez [49], Stones [74], Ake [78]	52,401
18	19	A	Newcastle U	W 4-0	2-0	1	Dias [5], Joao Cancelo [27], Mahrez [64], Sterling [86]	52,127
19	26	H	Leicester C	W 6-3	4-0	1	De Bruyne [5], Mahrez (pen) [14], Gundogan [21], Sterling 2 (1 pen) [25 (p), 87], Laporte [69]	53,226
20	29	A	Brentford	W 1-0	1-0	1	Foden [16]	17,009
21	Jan 1	A	Arsenal	W 2-1	0-1	1	Mahrez (pen) [57], Rodri [90]	59,757
22	15	H	Chelsea	W 1-0	0-0	1	De Bruyne [70]	53,319
23	22	A	Southampton	D 1-1	0-1	1	Laporte [65]	31,178
24	Feb 9	H	Brentford	W 2-0	1-0	1	Mahrez (pen) [40], De Bruyne [69]	51,658
25	12	A	Norwich C	W 4-0	1-0	1	Sterling 3 [31, 70, 90], Foden [48]	27,010
26	19	H	Tottenham H	L 2-3	1-1	1	Gundogan [33], Mahrez (pen) [90]	53,201
27	26	A	Everton	W 1-0	0-0	1	Foden [82]	39,105
28	Mar 6	H	Manchester U	W 4-1	2-1	1	De Bruyne 2 [5, 28], Mahrez 2 [68, 90]	53,165
29	14	A	Crystal Palace	D 0-0	0-0	1		25,309
30	Apr 2	A	Burnley	W 2-0	2-0	1	De Bruyne [5], Gundogan [25]	22,000
31	10	H	Liverpool	D 2-2	2-1	1	De Bruyne [5], Gabriel Jesus [37]	53,197
32	20	H	Brighton & HA	W 3-0	0-0	1	Mahrez [53], Foden [65], Bernardo Silva [82]	52,226
33	23	H	Watford	W 5-1	3-1	1	Gabriel Jesus 4 (1 pen) [4, 23, 49 (p), 53], Rodri [34]	53,013
34	30	A	Leeds U	W 4-0	1-0	1	Rodri [13], Ake [54], Gabriel Jesus [78], Fernandinho [90]	35,771
35	May 8	H	Newcastle U	W 5-0	2-0	1	Sterling 2 [19, 90], Laporte [38], Rodri [61], Foden [90]	53,336
36	11	A	Wolverhampton W	W 5-1	3-1	1	De Bruyne 4 [7, 16, 24, 60], Sterling [84]	30,914
37	15	A	West Ham U	D 2-2	0-2	1	Grealish [49], Coufal (og) [69]	59,972
38	22	H	Aston Villa	W 3-2	0-1	1	Gundogan 2 [76, 81], Rodri [78]	53,395

Final League Position: 1

GOALSCORERS

League (99): De Bruyne 15, Sterling 13 (2 pens), Mahrez 11 (4 pens), Foden 9, Bernardo Silva 8, Gabriel Jesus 8 (1 pen), Gundogan 8, Rodri 7, Laporte 4, Grealish 3, Ake 2, Dias 2, Fernandinho 2, Torres 2, Joao Cancelo 1, Stones 1, own goals 3.
FA Cup (16): Mahrez 4 (1 pen), Bernardo Silva 2, Grealish 2, Gundogan 2, De Bruyne 1 (1 pen), Foden 1, Gabriel Jesus 1, Palmer 1, Sterling 1, Stones 1.
Carabao Cup (6): Mahrez 2, De Bruyne 1, Foden 1, Palmer 1, Torres 1.
UEFA Champions League (29): Mahrez 7 (2 pens), Gabriel Jesus 4, Bernardo Silva 3, Foden 3, Sterling 3, De Bruyne 2, Joao Cancelo 2, Ake 1, Grealish 1, Palmer 1, Walker 1, own goal 1.
Papa John's Trophy (4): Bolton 1, Edozie 1, McAtee 1, Palmer 1.

Ederson d 37	Joao Cancelo C 36	Dias R 27 + 2	Ake N 10 + 4	Mendy B 1	Gundogan I 20 + 7	Fernandinho L 10 + 9	Grealish J 22 + 4	Mahrez R 15 + 13	Torres F 4	Sterling R 23 + 7	Gabriel Jesus F 21 + 7	De Bruyne K 25 + 5	Zinchenko A 10 + 5	Walker K 20	Laporte A 33	Bernardo Silva M 33 + 2	Rodri R 33	Palmer C 1 + 3	Foden P 24 + 4	Steffen Z 1	Stones J 12 + 2	McAtee J — + 2	Delap L — + 1	Kayky C — + 1	Egan-Riley C — + 1	*Match No.*
1	2	3	4	5[2]	6	7	8	9[3]	10	11[1]	12	13	14													1
1	5	3			8[2]		11[3]	14	10[1]	12	9			2	4	6	7	13								2
1	5	3			8		11	14	10	13	9[3]		12	2[1]	4	6[2]	7									3
1	5	3			6	13	11		10[1]	12	9[2]			2	4	8	7									4
1	5	3	4		6	7[1]	11	13		10	9[2]	12		2		8[3]			14							5
1	5	3				13	11[3]	12		14	9	8[1]		2	4	6	7		10[2]							6
1	5	3					10[1]			12	9	8		2	4	6	7		11							7
	2	12	5			13		9		10		8[2]			4[1]	6[3]	7	14	11	1	3					8
1	5	3			8[1]	12	11[2]	14			9[3]	13		2	4	6	7		10							9
1	5[2]	3					11[3]	14		13	9	6[1]		2	4■	8	7		10		12					10
1	5	4			8						9	6		2		10	7		11		3					11
1	5		13		8			12		9				2	4[2]	6	7	10[3]	11[1]		3	14				12
1	5	3			6	12		10		11[1]	9			2	4	8	7									13
1	2	3	4			7	12	9		11	10[1]		5			8	6									14
1	5	3			6[1]		10[2]	13		9	14	12		2	4	8	7		11[3]							15
1	2	3			8[1]		11[2]			9	10	13	5		4	6	7		12							16
1		3[3]	14		12	13	10	9				6	5		4	8[1]	7[2]		11		2					17
1	2	3[2]				12		8[3]		10	11	9	5		4	7	6[1]	14			13					18
1	2	3			8	7		9		11		6[1]	5		4	10			12							19
1	2	3	5			7	10				9	6			4	8			11							20
1	2	3	5		12			9		11	10[1]	8			4	6	7									21
1	5				12		11			9	13	8[1]		2	4	6	7		10[2]		3					22
1	5	3					10			9[1]	12	8		2	4	6	7		11							23
1	5	3			13		12	9[1]		11		6			4	8	7		10[2]		2					24
1		3	4		8	7		9[3]		11			5	2		6[1]			10[2]			12	13	14		25
1	5	3			8			12		9[1]		6		2	4	10	7		11							26
1	5	3			8[2]			12		11[1]	13	6			4	10	7		9		2					27
1	5				12		11	9				6[1]		2	4	8	7		10		3					28
1	5						11	9				6		2	4	8	7		10		3					29
1	5		4		8		11			9	12	6[2]		2	3	13	7		10[1]							30
1	5						13	12		10[1]	9[2]	8		2	4	6	7		11		3					31
1	2	12	5[1]		8			9			14	6[3]	13		4	10	7		11		3[2]					32
1	2	3	13		12	6	11	14		10	8	9[1]	5		4[2]		7[3]									33
1	2	3	5[1]		7	14	10			8	11		12		4	13	6[3]		9[2]							34
1	2	3[1]			7	12	10			8	11[2]	9	5		4[3]		6		13						14	35
1	2		12		7	3[2]	14	13		8		9	5		4[1]	11	6		10[3]							36
1	2					3	11	9			10	8	5		4	6	7									37
1	5				14	3[1]		9[2]		13	10	6	12		4	8[3]	7		11		2					38

FA Cup

Third Round	Swindon T	(a)	4-1
Fourth Round	Fulham	(h)	4-1
Fifth Round	Peterborough U	(a)	2-0
Sixth Round	Southampton	(a)	4-1
Semi-Final	Liverpool	(Wembley)	2-3

Carabao Cup

Third Round	Wycombe W	(h)	6-1
Fourth Round	West Ham U	(a)	0-0

(West Ham U won 5-3 on penalties)

Papa John's Trophy (Manchester C U21)

Group E (N)	Scunthorpe U	(a)	3-0
Group E (N)	Doncaster R	(a)	1-2
Group E (N)	Rotherham U	(a)	0-5

UEFA Champions League

Group A	RB Leipzig	(h)	6-3
Group A	Paris Saint-Germain	(a)	0-2
Group A	Club Brugge	(a)	5-1
Group A	Club Brugge	(h)	4-1
Group A	Paris Saint-Germain	(h)	2-1
Group A	RB Leipzig	(a)	1-2
Round of 16 1st leg	Sporting Lisbon	(a)	5-0
Round of 16 2nd leg	Sporting Lisbon	(h)	0-0
Quarter-Final 1st leg	Atletico Madrid	(h)	1-0
Quarter-Final 2nd leg	Atletico Madrid	(a)	0-0
Semi-Final 1st leg	Real Madrid	(h)	4-3
Semi-Final 2nd leg	Real Madrid	(a)	1-3

(aet)

MANCHESTER UNITED

FOUNDATION

Manchester United was formed as comparatively recently as 1902 after their predecessors, Newton Heath, went bankrupt. However, it is usual to give the date of the club's foundation as 1878 when the dining room committee of the carriage and waggon works of the Lancashire and Yorkshire Railway Company formed Newton Heath L and YR Cricket and Football Club. They won the Manchester Cup in 1886 and as Newton Heath FC were admitted to the Second Division in 1892.

Old Trafford, Sir Matt Busby Way, Manchester M16 0RA.

Telephone: (0161) 868 8000.

Ticket Office: (0161) 868 8000 (option 1).

Website: www.manutd.co.uk

Email: enquiries@manutd.co.uk

Ground Capacity: 74,140.

Record Attendance: 76,098 v Blackburn R, Premier League, 31 March 2007. 83,260 v Arsenal, First Division, 17 January 1948 (at Maine Road – United shared City's ground after Old Trafford suffered World War II bomb damage).

Ground Record Attendance: 76,962 Wolverhampton W v Grimsby T, FA Cup semi-final, 25 March 1939.

Pitch Measurements: 105m × 68m (115yd × 74.5yd).

Co-Chairmen: Joel Glazer, Avram Glazer.

Chief Executive: Edward Woodward.

Manager: Erik ten Hag.

Assistant Managers: Mitchell van der Gagg, Steve McLaren.

Colours: Red shirts with white trim, white shorts with red trim, black socks with red and white trim.

Year Formed: 1878 as Newton Heath LYR; 1902, Manchester United.

Turned Professional: 1885.

Previous Name: 1880, Newton Heath; 1902, Manchester United.

Club Nickname: 'Red Devils'.

Grounds: 1880, North Road, Monsall Road; 1893, Bank Street; 1910, Old Trafford (played at Maine Road 1941–49).

HONOURS

League Champions: Premier League – 1992–93, 1993–94, 1995–96, 1996–97, 1998–99, 1999–2000, 2000–01, 2002–03, 2006–07, 2007–08, 2008–09, 2010–11, 2012–13; Division 1 – 1907–08, 1910–11, 1951–52, 1955–56, 1956–57, 1964–65, 1966–67; Division 2 – 1935–36, 1974–75.
Runners-up: Premier League – 1994–95, 1997–98, 2005–06, 2009–10, 2011–12, 2017–18, 2020–21; Division 1 – 1946–47, 1947–48, 1948–49, 1950–51, 1958–59, 1963–64, 1967–68, 1979–80, 1987–88, 1991–92; Division 2 – 1896–97, 1905–06, 1924–25, 1937–38.

FA Cup Winners: 1909, 1948, 1963, 1977, 1983, 1985, 1990, 1994, 1996, 1999, 2004, 2016.
Runners-up: 1957, 1958, 1976, 1979, 1995, 2005, 2007, 2018.

League Cup Winners: 1992, 2006, 2009, 2010, 2017.
Runners-up: 1983, 1991, 1994, 2003.

European Competitions
European Cup: 1956–57 *(sf)*, 1957–58 *(sf)*, 1965–66 *(sf)*, 1967–68 *(winners)*, 1968–69 *(sf)*.
Champions League: 1993–94, 1994–95, 1996–97 *(sf)*, 1997–98 *(qf)*, 1998–99 *(winners)*, 1999–2000 *(qf)*, 2000–01 *(qf)*, 2001–02 *(sf)*, 2002–03 *(qf)*, 2003–04, 2004–05, 2005–06, 2006–07 *(sf)*, 2007–08 *(winners)*, 2008–09 *(runners-up)*, 2009–10 *(qf)*, 2010–11 *(runners-up)*, 2011–12, 2012–13, 2013–14 *(qf)*, 2015–16, 2017–18, 2018–19 *(qf)*, 2020–21, 2021–22.
Fairs Cup: 1964–65 *(sf)*.
UEFA Cup: 1976–77, 1980–81, 1982–83, 1984–85 *(qf)*, 1992–93, 1995–96.
Europa League: 2011–12, 2015–16, 2016–17 *(winners)*, 2019–20 *(sf)*, 2020–21 *(runners-up)*.
European Cup-Winners' Cup: 1963–64 *(qf)*, 1977–78, 1983–84 *(sf)*, 1990–91 *(winners)*. 1991–92.
Super Cup: 1991 *(winners)*, 1999, 2008.
World Club Championship: 1968, 1999 *(winners)*, 2000.
FIFA Club World Cup: 2008 *(winners)*.
NB: In 1958–59 FA refused permission to compete in European Cup.

FOOTBALL YEARBOOK FACT FILE

Manchester United did not fare well in the first-ever Football League Cup competition in 1960–61, only beating Fourth Division club Exeter City after a replay in the first round, and then losing to Bradford City from the Third Division in round two. Following this they entered the competition only once over the next eight seasons, before taking part regularly from 1969–70.

First Football League Game: 3 September 1892, Division 1, v Blackburn R (a) L 3–4 – Warner; Clements, Brown; Perrins, Stewart, Erentz; Farman (1), Coupar (1), Donaldson (1), Carson, Mathieson.
Record League Victory (as Newton Heath): 10–1 v Wolverhampton W, Division 1, 15 October 1892 – Warner; Mitchell, Clements; Perrins, Stewart (3), Erentz; Farman (1), Hood (1), Donaldson (3), Carson (1), Hendry (1).
Record League Victory (as Manchester U): 9–0 v Ipswich T, Premier League, 4 March 1995 – Schmeichel; Keane (1) (Sharpe), Irwin, Bruce (Butt), Kanchelskis, Pallister, Cole (5), Ince (1), McClair, Hughes (2), Giggs; 9–0 v Southampton, Premier League, 2 February 2021 – De Gea, Wan Bissaka (1), Lindelof, Maguire, Shaw (Martial (2)), McTominay (1), Fred, Rashford (1) (James (1)), Bruno Fernandes (1 pen), Greenwood, Cavani (1) (van der Beek), 1 own goal.
Record Cup Victory: 10–0 v RSC Anderlecht, European Cup prel. rd 2nd leg, 26 September 1956 – Wood; Foulkes, Byrne; Colman, Jones, Edwards; Berry (1), Whelan (2), Taylor (3), Viollet (4), Pegg.
Record Defeat: 0–7 v Blackburn R, Division 1, 10 April 1926; 0–7 v Aston Villa, Division 1, 27 December 1930; 0–7 v Wolverhampton W, Division 2, 26 December 1931.
Most League Points (2 for a win): 64, Division 1, 1956–57.
Most League Points (3 for a win): 92, Premier League, 1993–94.
Most League Goals: 103, Division 1, 1956–57 and 1958–59.
Highest League Scorer in Season: Dennis Viollet, 32, 1959–60.
Most League Goals in Total Aggregate: Bobby Charlton, 199, 1956–73.
Most League Goals in One Match: 5, Andrew Cole v Ipswich T, Premier League, 3 March 1995; 5, Dimitar Berbatov v Blackburn R, Premier League, 27 November 2010.
Most Capped Player: Bobby Charlton, 106, England.
Most League Appearances: Ryan Giggs, 672, 1991–2014.
Youngest League Player: Jeff Whitefoot, 16 years 105 days v Portsmouth, 15 April 1950.
Record Transfer Fee Received: £80,000,000 from Real Madrid for Cristiano Ronaldo, July 2009.
Record Transfer Fee Paid: £89,300,000 to Juventus for Paul Pogba, August 2016.
Football League Record: 1892 Newton Heath elected to Division 1; 1894–1906 Division 2; 1906–22 Division 1; 1922–25 Division 2; 1925–31 Division 1; 1931–36 Division 2; 1936–37 Division 1; 1937–38 Division 2; 1938–74 Division 1; 1974–75 Division 2; 1975–92 Division 1; 1992– Premier League.

MANAGERS

J. Ernest Mangnall 1903–12
John Bentley 1912–14
John Robson 1914–21 *(Secretary-Manager from 1916)*
John Chapman 1921–26
Clarence Hilditch 1926–27
Herbert Bamlett 1927–31
Walter Crickmer 1931–32
Scott Duncan 1932–37
Walter Crickmer 1937–45 *(Secretary-Manager)*
Matt Busby 1945–69 *(continued as General Manager then Director)*
Wilf McGuinness 1969–70
Sir Matt Busby 1970–71
Frank O'Farrell 1971–72
Tommy Docherty 1972–77
Dave Sexton 1977–81
Ron Atkinson 1981–86
Sir Alex Ferguson 1986–2013
David Moyes 2013–14
Louis van Gaal 2014–16
Jose Mourinho 2016–18
Ole Gunnar Solskjaer 2018–21
Ralf Rangnick 2021–22
Erik ten Hag June 2021–

LATEST SEQUENCES

Longest Sequence of League Wins: 14, 15.10.1904 – 3.1.1905.
Longest Sequence of League Defeats: 14, 26.4.1930 – 25.10.1930.
Longest Sequence of League Draws: 6, 30.10.1988 – 27.11.1988.
Longest Sequence of Unbeaten League Matches: 29, 11.4.2010 – 1.2.2011.
Longest Sequence Without a League Win: 16, 19.4.1930 – 25.10.1930.
Successive Scoring Runs: 36 from 3.12.2007.
Successive Non-scoring Runs: 5 from 7.2.1981.

TEN YEAR LEAGUE RECORD

		P	W	D	L	F	A	Pts	Pos
2012-13	PR Lge	38	28	5	5	86	43	89	1
2013-14	PR Lge	38	19	7	12	64	43	64	7
2014-15	PR Lge	38	20	10	8	62	37	70	4
2015-16	PR Lge	38	19	9	10	49	35	66	5
2016-17	PR Lge	38	18	15	5	54	29	69	6
2017-18	PR Lge	38	25	6	7	68	28	81	2
2018-19	PR Lge	38	19	9	10	65	54	66	6
2019-20	PR Lge	38	18	12	8	66	36	66	3
2020-21	PR Lge	38	21	11	6	73	44	74	2
2021-22	PR Lge	38	16	10	12	57	57	58	6

DID YOU KNOW ?

Charlie Mitten completed the rare feat of scoring a hat-trick of penalties playing for Manchester United against Aston Villa on 8 March 1950. He netted from the spot after 37, 47 and 88 minutes, and added a fourth goal with a 48th-minute header as United went on to record a 7-0 victory.

MANCHESTER UNITED – PREMIER LEAGUE 2021–22 LEAGUE RECORD

Match No.	*Date*	*Venue*	*Opponents*	*Result*		*H/T Score*	*Lg Pos.*	*Goalscorers*	*Attendance*
1	Aug 14	H	Leeds U	W	5-1	1-0	1	Bruno Fernandes 3 [30, 54, 60], Greenwood [52], Fred [68]	72,732
2	22	A	Southampton	D	1-1	0-1	5	Greenwood [55]	29,485
3	29	A	Wolverhampton W	W	1-0	0-0	3	Greenwood [80]	30,621
4	Sept 11	H	Newcastle U	W	4-1	1-0	1	Ronaldo 2 [45, 62], Bruno Fernandes [80], Lingard [90]	72,732
5	19	A	West Ham U	W	2-1	1-1	3	Ronaldo [35], Lingard [89]	59,958
6	25	H	Aston Villa	L	0-1	0-0	4		72,922
7	Oct 2	H	Everton	D	1-1	1-0	3	Martial [43]	73,128
8	16	A	Leicester C	L	2-4	1-1	5	Greenwood [19], Rashford [82]	32,219
9	24	H	Liverpool	L	0-5	0-4	7		73,088
10	30	A	Tottenham H	W	3-0	1-0	5	Ronaldo [39], Cavani [64], Rashford [86]	60,356
11	Nov 6	H	Manchester C	L	0-2	0-2	5		73,086
12	20	A	Watford	L	1-4	0-2	7	van de Beek [50]	21,087
13	28	A	Chelsea	D	1-1	0-0	8	Sancho [50]	40,041
14	Dec 2	H	Arsenal	W	3-2	1-1	7	Bruno Fernandes [44], Ronaldo 2 (1 pen) [52, 70 (p)]	73,123
15	5	H	Crystal Palace	W	1-0	0-0	6	Fred [77]	73,172
16	11	A	Norwich C	W	1-0	0-0	5	Ronaldo (pen) [75]	27,066
17	27	A	Newcastle U	D	1-1	0-1	7	Cavani [71]	52,178
18	30	H	Burnley	W	3-1	3-1	6	McTominay [8], Mee (og) [27], Ronaldo [35]	73,121
19	Jan 3	H	Wolverhampton W	L	0-1	0-0	7		73,045
20	15	A	Aston Villa	D	2-2	1-0	7	Bruno Fernandes 2 [6, 67]	41,968
21	19	A	Brentford	W	3-1	0-0	7	Elanga [55], Greenwood [62], Rashford [77]	17,094
22	22	H	West Ham U	W	1-0	0-0	4	Rashford [90]	73,130
23	Feb 8	A	Burnley	D	1-1	1-0	5	Pogba [18]	21,233
24	12	H	Southampton	D	1-1	1-0	5	Sancho [21]	73,084
25	15	H	Brighton & HA	W	2-0	0-0	4	Ronaldo [51], Bruno Fernandes [90]	73,012
26	20	A	Leeds U	W	4-2	2-0	4	Maguire [34], Bruno Fernandes [45], Fred [70], Elanga [88]	36,715
27	26	H	Watford	D	0-0	0-0	4		73,152
28	Mar 6	A	Manchester C	L	1-4	1-2	5	Sancho [22]	53,165
29	12	H	Tottenham H	W	3-2	2-1	4	Ronaldo 3 [12, 38, 81]	73,458
30	Apr 2	H	Leicester C	D	1-1	0-0	6	Fred [66]	73,444
31	9	A	Everton	L	0-1	0-1	7		39,080
32	16	H	Norwich C	W	3-2	2-1	5	Ronaldo 3 [7, 32, 76]	73,381
33	19	A	Liverpool	L	0-4	0-2	6		52,686
34	23	A	Arsenal	L	1-3	1-2	6	Ronaldo [34]	60,223
35	28	H	Chelsea	D	1-1	0-0	6	Ronaldo [62]	73,564
36	May 2	H	Brentford	W	3-0	1-0	6	Bruno Fernandes [9], Ronaldo (pen) [61], Varane [72]	73,482
37	7	A	Brighton & HA	L	0-4	0-1	6		31,637
38	22	A	Crystal Palace	L	0-1	0-1	6		25,434

Final League Position: 6

GOALSCORERS

League (57): Ronaldo 18 (3 pens), Bruno Fernandes 10, Greenwood 5, Fred 4, Rashford 4, Sancho 3, Cavani 2, Elanga 2, Lingard 2, Maguire 1, Martial 1, McTominay 1, Pogba 1, van de Beek 1, Varane 1, own goal 1.
FA Cup (2): McTominay 1, Sancho 1.
Carabao Cup (0).
UEFA Champions League (12): Ronaldo 6, Alex Telles 1, Elanga 1, Greenwood 1, Maguire 1, Rashford 1, Sancho 1.
Papa John's Trophy (6): Hardley 1, Hoogerwerf 1, Hugill 1, Iqbal 1, McNeill 1, own goal 1.

De Gea D 38	Wan Bissaka A 20	Lindelof V 26 + 2	Maguire H 28 + 2	Shaw L 19 + 1	McTominay S 28 + 2	Fred F 24 + 4	James D 2	Bruno Fernandes M 35 + 1	Pogba P 16 + 4	Greenwood M 16 + 2	Matic N 16 + 7	Sancho J 20 + 9	Martial A 2 + 6	Lingard J 2 + 14	Varane R 20 + 2	Cavani E 7 + 8	Dalot D 19 + 5	Ronaldo C 27 + 3	van de Beek D — + 8	Rashford M 13 + 12	Bailly E 3 + 1	Alex Telles N 18 + 3	Elanga A 14 + 7	Jones P 2 + 2	Mata J 2 + 5	Mejbri H 1 + 1	Garnacho A — + 2	Shoretire S — + 1	Match No.
1	2	3	4	5	6^{1}	7	8^{3}	9	10^{2}	11	12	13	14																1
1	2	3	4	5	13	6^{2}		9	10	8	7^{3}	12	11^{1}	14															2
1	2		4	5		7	8^{1}	9	6	11^{3}		10^{2}	13		3	12	14												3
1	2		4	5				9^{2}	6	8^{3}	7	10^{1}	14	12	3			11	13										4
1	2		4	5	6	7^{3}		9	10^{1}	8^{2}	14	12		13	3			11											5
1	2	13	4^{2}	5^{1}	6^{3}	7		9	10	8					3	14	12	11											6
1	2	3		5	6	7^{3}		9	14	8		12	10^{2}		4	11^{1}		13											7
1	2	3	4	5	13			9	6	8^{3}	7^{2}	10^{1}		14				11		12									8
1	2	3	4	5	6	7		9^{2}	12■	8^{1}						14	13	11		10^{3}									9
1	5	2	4	8	6	7		9^{2}			13			14	3	10^{3}		11^{1}		12									10
1	5	3	4	9^{3}	7	8^{4}		6		10^{2}		12						11	15	13	2^{1}	14							11
1	2	3	4■	5^{3}	6^{2}			9			7	8^{4}	13	15			14	11	12	10^{1}									12
1	2	3			6	8		9^{3}			7	10^{1}		13				12	14	11^{2}	4	5							13
1		3	4		6	7		9^{3}				10	13	12			2	11^{2}	14	8^{1}		5							14
1		3	4		6	7		9^{3}		12		8^{1}					2	11	14	10^{2}		5	13						15
1		3^{2}	4		6	7		9^{3}		12		8^{1}					2	10	14	11	13	5							16
1			4		6^{3}	7^{1}		9		10^{2}	14	12			3	13	2	11		8		5							17
1	2		4	5	6	14				8^{2}	7	9			12	10	13	11^{3}			3^{1}								18
1	2^{3}			5	6			12		8^{1}	7	9^{2}			4	10		11		13			14	3					19
1		3				6		9^{2}		8^{3}	7	12		14	4	11	2		13			5	10^{1}						20
1		3	13		7^{3}	6		9		8^{1}	14				4		2	11^{2}		12		5	10						21
1			4		6	7^{2}		9		8^{3}			14		3	13	2	11		12		5	10^{1}						22
1			4	5	7^{2}			9	6			10		13	3	11^{1}	2	12		8^{3}			14						23
1			4	5	6^{1}			9	7			10		13	3		2	11		8^{2}			12						24
1		3	4	5	6	7^{1}		9	12			10^{3}					2	11		13		14	8^{2}						25
1	2	3	4	5	7	12		9	6^{2}			10		8^{1}	14			11^{3}					13						26
1	2	3		14		6^{1}		10	9		7^{3}	12			4			11		13		5^{2}	8						27
1	2	3	4		6	7		11	9^{2}			10		13						12		5	8^{1}						28
1		14	4			7			9		6^{2}	10			3	13	2	11^{3}		8^{1}		5	12						29
1			3	5^{1}	6^{2}	7		11	9^{3}		14	10			4		2			13		12	8						30
1	2	3	4			6^{1}		9	12		7^{2}	8						11		10^{3}		5	14		13				31
1		4	3					6	7^{2}		12	11		8^{1}			2	10		13		5^{3}	9		14				32
1	5	2	4					9	6^{1}		7	13		12			8			11			10^{3}	3^{2}		14			33
1		3			6			9^{3}			7^{2}	10		13	4		2	11		12		5	8^{1}		14				34
1		3			6			9			7^{2}				4		2	11		10^{1}		5	8^{3}	12	13		14		35
1		3			6	12		10			7^{1}				4	14	2	11				5	8^{2}	13	9^{3}				36
1		3	14		6	13		10			7^{1}				4	12	2	11				5	8^{2}		9^{3}				37
1		3	4		6	7^{2}		9								11	2^{3}					5	8		12	10^{1}	14	13	38

FA Cup

Third Round	Aston Villa	(h)	1-0
Fourth Round	Middlesbrough	(h)	1-1

(aet; Middlesbrough won 8-7 on penalties)

Carabao Cup

Third Round	West Ham U	(h)	0-1

UEFA Champions League

Group F	Young Boys	(a)	1-2
Group F	Villarreal	(h)	2-1
Group F	Atalanta	(h)	3-2
Group F	Atalanta	(a)	2-2
Group F	Villarreal	(a)	2-0
Group F	Young Boys	(h)	1-1
Round of 16 1st leg	Atletico Madrid	(a)	1-1
Round of 16 2nd leg	Atletico Madrid	(h)	0-1

Papa John's Trophy (Manchester U U21)

Group F (N)	Lincoln C	(a)	2-3
Group F (N)	Bradford C	(a)	3-0
Group F (N)	Sunderland	(a)	1-2

MANSFIELD TOWN

FOUNDATION

The club was formed as Mansfield Wesleyans in 1897, and changed their name to Mansfield Wesley in 1906 and Mansfield Town in 1910. This was after the Mansfield Wesleyan Chapel trustees had requested that the club change its name as 'it has no longer had any connection with either the chapel or school'. The new club participated in the Notts and Derby District League, but in the following season 1911–12 joined the Central Alliance.

One Call Stadium, Quarry Lane, Mansfield, Nottinghamshire NG18 5DA.

Telephone: (01623) 482 482.

Ticket Office: (01623) 482 482 (option 1).

Website: www.mansfieldtown.net

Email: info@mansfieldtown.net

Ground Capacity: 9,376.

Record Attendance: 24,467 v Nottingham F, FA Cup 3rd rd, 10 January 1953.

Pitch Measurements: 100.5m × 64m (110yd × 70yd).

Chairman: John Radford.

Co-chairwoman: Carolyn Radford.

Chief Executive: David Sharpe.

Manager: Nigel Clough.

Assistant Manager: Gary Crosby.

Colours: Yellow shirts with blue sleeves, blue shorts with yellow trim, yellow socks with blue trim.

Year Formed: 1897.

Turned Professional: 1906.

Ltd Co.: 1922.

Previous Name: 1897, Mansfield Wesleyans; 1906, Mansfield Wesley; 1910, Mansfield Town.

Grounds: 1897–99, Westfield Lane; 1899–1901, Ratcliffe Gate; 1901–12, Newgate Lane; 1912–16, Ratcliffe Gate; 1916, Field Mill (renamed One Call Stadium 2012).

Club Nickname: 'The Stags'.

First Football League Game: 29 August 1931, Division 3 (S), v Swindon T (h) W 3–2 – Wilson; Clifford, England; Wake, Davis, Blackburn; Gilhespy, Readman (1), Johnson, Broom (2), Baxter.

Record League Victory: 9–2 v Rotherham U, Division 3 (N), 27 December 1932 – Wilson; Anthony, England; Davies, S. Robinson, Slack; Prior, Broom, Readman (3), Hoyland (3), Bowater (3).

Record Cup Victory: 8–0 v Scarborough (a), FA Cup 1st rd, 22 November 1952 – Bramley; Chessell, Bradley; Field, Plummer, Lewis; Scott, Fox (3), Marron (2), Sid Watson (1), Adam (2).

Record Defeat: 1–8 v Walsall, Division 3 (N), 19 January 1933.

Most League Points (2 for a win): 68, Division 4, 1974–75.

HONOURS

League Champions: Division 3 – 1976–77; Division 4 – 1974–75; Conference – 2012–13.
Runners-up: Division 3N – 1950–51, Third Division – (3rd) 2001–02 *(promoted to Second Division).*

FA Cup: 6th rd – 1969.

League Cup: 5th rd – 1976.

League Trophy Winners: 1987.

FOOTBALL YEARBOOK FACT FILE

Following Sam Clucas's penalty for Mansfield Town against Hartlepool United in October 2013, the Stags had to wait 85 League and Cup games before they were awarded another spot kick. Unfortunately, Matt Green's attempt against Oxford on 22 August 2015 was saved, but Craig Westcarr broke the run 10 days later with a successful penalty at Notts County in an EFL Trophy tie.

Most League Points (3 for a win): 81, Division 4, 1985–86.

Most League Goals: 108, Division 4, 1962–63.

Highest League Scorer in Season: Ted Harston, 55, Division 3 (N), 1936–37.

Most League Goals in Total Aggregate: Harry Johnson, 104, 1931–36.

Most League Goals in One Match: 7, Ted Harston v Hartlepools U, Division 3N, 23 January 1937.

Most Capped Player: John McClelland, 6 (53), Northern Ireland; Reggie Lambe, 6 (45), Bermuda; Omari Sterling-James, 6 (14), Saint Kitts & Nevis.

Most League Appearances: Rod Arnold, 440, 1970–83.

Youngest League Player: Cyril Poole, 15 years 351 days v New Brighton, 27 February 1937.

Record Transfer Fee Received: £30,000 (rising to £655,000) from Swindon T for Colin Calderwood, July 1985.

Record Transfer Fee Paid: £150,000 to Peterborough U for Lee Angol, May 2017.

Football League Record: 1931 Elected to Division 3 (S); 1932–37 Division 3 (N); 1937–47 Division 3 (S); 1947–58 Division 3 (N); 1958–60 Division 3; 1960–63 Division 4; 1963–72 Division 3; 1972–75 Division 4; 1975–77 Division 3; 1977–78 Division 2; 1978–80 Division 3; 1980–86 Division 4; 1986–91 Division 3; 1991–92 Division 4; 1992–93 Division 2; 1993–2002 Division 3; 2002–03 Division 2; 2003–04 Division 3; 2004–08 FL 2; 2008–13 Conference Premier; 2013– FL 2.

LATEST SEQUENCES

Longest Sequence of League Wins: 8, 27.11.2021 – 29.1.2022.

Longest Sequence of League Defeats: 7, 18.1.1947 – 15.3.1947.

Longest Sequence of League Draws: 5, 18.10.1986 – 22.11.1986.

Longest Sequence of Unbeaten League Matches: 20, 14.2.1976 – 21.8.1976.

Longest Sequence Without a League Win: 14, 25.3.2000 – 2.9.2000.

Successive Scoring Runs: 27 from 1.10.1962.

Successive Non-scoring Runs: 8 from 25.3.2000.

MANAGERS

John Baynes 1922–25
Ted Davison 1926–28
Jack Hickling 1928–33
Henry Martin 1933–35
Charlie Bell 1935
Harold Wightman 1936
Harold Parkes 1936–38
Jack Poole 1938–44
Lloyd Barke 1944–45
Roy Goodall 1945–49
Freddie Steele 1949–51
George Jobey 1952–53
Stan Mercer 1953–55
Charlie Mitten 1956–58
Sam Weaver 1958–60
Raich Carter 1960–63
Tommy Cummings 1963–67
Tommy Eggleston 1967–70
Jock Basford 1970–71
Danny Williams 1971–74
Dave Smith 1974–76
Peter Morris 1976–78
Billy Bingham 1978–79
Mick Jones 1979–81
Stuart Boam 1981–83
Ian Greaves 1983–89
George Foster 1989–93
Andy King 1993–96
Steve Parkin 1996–99
Billy Dearden 1999–2002
Stuart Watkiss 2002
Keith Curle 2002–04
Carlton Palmer 2004–05
Peter Shirtliff 2005–06
Billy Dearden 2006–08
Paul Holland 2008
Billy McEwan 2008
David Holdsworth 2008–10
Duncan Russell 2010–11
Paul Cox 2011–14
Adam Murray 2014–16
Steve Evans 2016–18
David Flitcroft 2018–19
John Dempster 2019
Graham Coughlan 2019–20
Nigel Clough November 2020–

TEN YEAR LEAGUE RECORD

		P	*W*	*D*	*L*	*F*	*A*	*Pts*	*Pos*
2012-13	Conf P	46	30	5	11	92	52	95	1
2013-14	FL 2	46	15	15	16	49	58	60	11
2014-15	FL 2	46	13	9	24	38	62	48	21
2015-16	FL 2	46	17	13	16	61	53	64	12
2016-17	FL 2	46	17	15	14	54	50	66	12
2017-18	FL 2	46	18	18	10	67	52	72	8
2018-19	FL 2	46	20	16	10	69	41	76	4
2019-20	FL 2	36	9	11	16	48	55	38	21§
2020-21	FL 2	46	13	19	14	57	55	58	16
2021-22	FL 2	46	22	11	13	67	52	77	7

§Decided on points-per-game (1.06)

DID YOU KNOW ?

Mansfield Town did not win a single game away from home in their first season as a Football League club in 1931–32. The winless run extended for a total of 37 games on opposition territory before being ended by a 3-1 success at Darlington on 18 March 1933 and remains a club record.

MANSFIELD TOWN – SKY BET LEAGUE TWO 2021–22 LEAGUE RECORD

Match No.	Date	Venue	Opponents	Result	H/T Score	Lg Pos.	Goalscorers	Attendance
1	Aug 7	H	Bristol R	W 2-1	1-0	3	Hawkins [42], Johnson (pen) [90]	6342
2	14	H	Newport Co	W 2-1	2-1	3	Maris [7], Clarke, O [43]	3793
3	17	A	Colchester U	D 1-1	0-0	3	Hewitt [72]	2354
4	21	H	Bradford C	L 2-3	1-1	4	Hawkins 2 [37, 52]	6058
5	28	A	Swindon T	L 0-1	0-0	7		8631
6	Sept 4	H	Harrogate T	L 1-3	1-2	14	Oates [3]	4599
7	11	A	Walsall	L 1-3	0-2	20	Johnson [84]	5203
8	18	H	Rochdale	D 1-1	0-0	20	Johnson [72]	4336
9	25	A	Leyton Orient	D 0-0	0-0	20		5252
10	Oct 2	H	Barrow	L 0-1	0-0	22		3951
11	9	H	Oldham Ath	D 0-0	0-0	21		4556
12	16	A	Northampton T	L 0-2	0-1	22		6034
13	19	H	Port Vale	D 1-1	0-1	21	Lapslie [64]	4202
14	23	A	Exeter C	L 1-2	0-0	23	Hawkins [50]	4329
15	30	H	Tranmere R	W 2-0	1-0	20	Oates [18], Johnson [67]	3831
16	Nov 13	A	Stevenage	W 2-1	1-0	18	O'Toole [19], Stirk [65]	2946
17	20	H	Scunthorpe U	W 3-1	2-1	17	Clarke, O 2 [28, 60], Bowery [45]	4904
18	23	A	Sutton U	L 0-2	0-1	18		2497
19	27	A	Crawley T	W 2-1	1-0	15	Hawkins [24], Oates [72]	1824
20	Dec 7	H	Carlisle U	W 1-0	1-0	11	McLaughlin [6]	3695
21	11	H	Salford C	W 2-1	2-1	11	Oates [36], McLaughlin [45]	4113
22	26	H	Hartlepool U	W 3-2	0-1	9	O'Toole [55], Bowery [62], Maris [66]	5558
23	Jan 11	H	Swindon T	W 3-2	3-1	8	Maris [4], McLaughlin (pen) [31], Bowery [43]	4129
24	15	H	Walsall	W 2-0	0-0	7	Charsley 2 [59, 90]	5728
25	22	A	Barrow	W 3-1	2-1	7	Oates [1], McLaughlin [25], Bowery [68]	3224
26	29	H	Leyton Orient	W 2-0	1-0	6	Bowery [44], Clarke, O [72]	5851
27	Feb 1	A	Harrogate T	D 0-0	0-0	6		1800
28	8	H	Colchester U	W 2-1	1-0	5	Oates [19], Bowery (pen) [90]	4815
29	12	A	Bristol R	D 0-0	0-0	6		7707
30	19	A	Newport Co	D 1-1	0-0	6	Pask (og) [68]	3956
31	26	A	Bradford C	W 2-0	1-0	6	Oates [44], Longstaff [48]	16,797
32	Mar 4	H	Exeter C	W 2-1	1-0	3	Rawson [34], Longstaff [67]	6702
33	11	A	Tranmere R	L 2-3	1-1	7	Longstaff [45], Hawkins [90]	7857
34	15	A	Port Vale	L 1-3	1-1	10	Oates [22]	5233
35	22	A	Rochdale	W 1-0	0-0	10	Bowery [86]	2088
36	26	A	Oldham Ath	W 2-1	0-1	8	Oates [53], Lapslie [90]	6045
37	29	A	Hartlepool U	D 2-2	2-2	8	Lapslie [21], Perch [25]	4577
38	Apr 2	H	Northampton T	W 1-0	1-0	6	Hawkins [21]	6678
39	5	A	Forest Green R	L 0-1	0-1	6		2784
40	9	A	Scunthorpe U	W 4-0	3-0	4	Grant (og) [16], McLaughlin [32], Stirk [38], Quinn [46]	4015
41	15	H	Sutton U	L 2-3	0-1	6	Goodliffe (og) [78], Longstaff [90]	6134
42	18	A	Carlisle U	L 0-1	0-0	8		5496
43	23	H	Crawley T	W 2-0	1-0	6	Murphy [26], Akins [72]	5022
44	26	H	Stevenage	W 2-0	0-0	5	Lapslie [51], Longstaff [90]	5086
45	May 2	A	Salford C	D 2-2	2-1	5	McLaughlin 2 (1 pen) [15, 45 (p)]	3765
46	7	H	Forest Green R	D 2-2	1-0	7	Longstaff [17], Bowery [78]	7374

Final League Position: 7

GOALSCORERS

League (67): Oates 9, Bowery 8 (1 pen), Hawkins 7, McLaughlin 7 (2 pens), Longstaff 6, Clarke, O 4, Johnson 4 (1 pen), Lapslie 4, Maris 3, Charsley 2, O'Toole 2, Stirk 2, Akins 1, Hewitt 1, Murphy 1, Perch 1, Quinn 1, Rawson 1, own goals 3.
FA Cup (6): Lapslie 2, Oates 2, Forrester 1, Hawkins 1.
Carabao Cup (0).
Papa John's Trophy (8): Johnson 3 (1 pen), Caine 1, Lapslie 1, O'Toole 1, Quinn 1, Sinclair 1 (1 pen).
League Two Play-offs (3): Bowery 1, McLaughlin 1, Oates 1.

Bishop N 46	Gordon K 6 + 1	Rawson F 23 + 7	Perch J 15 + 5	McLaughlin S 42 + 1	Maris G 30 + 7	Clarke O 24 + 2	Quinn S 36	Oates R 34 + 4	Hawkins O 39 + 2	Johnson D 9 + 13	Lapslie G 21 + 11	Stirk R 23 + 8	Hewitt E 40 + 3	Bowery J 25 + 15	Sinclair T 1 + 13	Nartey R 2 + 1	Charsley H 10 + 6	Burke R 1 + 3	Law J 1 + 4	Clarke J 3 + 1	Ward K — + 2	O'Toole J 25 + 2	Gale J — + 3	Forrester W 2 + 2	Akins L 15 + 4	Wallace K 3 + 14	Murphy J 14	Longstaff M 16	Match No.
1	2	3	4	5	6^{2}	7	8	9^{1}	10	11	12	13																	1
1	2^{2}	3	4	5	6	7	8^{3}	9^{1}	11	10	12		13	14															2
1		3	4	5	6	7	8	10^{3}	13	11^{2}	9^{1}	12	2	14															3
1		3	4	5	6^{1}	7^{3}	8	9^{2}	11	10	13	12	2		14														4
1	2	3		5	6	7^{2}	8	12	10	11^{1}	9^{3}		4	14	13														5
1	2	13		5	6	7■	8■	11^{2}	10^{3}	12	9^{1}		3	14		4													6
1	2	13		5	7^{3}			11^{1}	10	12	9	8	3^{2}	14	6	4													7
1	2	4		5	6^{2}	8		7^{1}	11	13	9^{3}	12	3	10			14												8
1		3		5	7^{1}	8		9^{3}	4	11^{2}	6		2	10	13■		12	14											9
1		3■		5	6^{2}	8		11^{1}	4	12	9		2	10			7		13										10
1				5	6^{1}	8^{3}		12	3^{2}	11	9		4	10			7	13		2	14								11
1		3		5^{2}		6		14	10	11^{3}	9		4	8			7^{1}	13		2	12								12
1		3		5		9	10^{3}	11^{2}	4	13	6		2^{1}	8	14		7			12									13
1		3			12	6	8	10^{3}	4	13	9^{2}			11^{1}	14		7	5		2									14
1	12	3		5^{1}	6	9	8	11^{3}	4	10^{2}			2		13		7					14							15
1		14		5	6^{3}	7	10	11^{2}	4		9^{1}	12	2		13		8					3							16
1				5	6	7	10^{1}		4			9^{3}	2	11^{2}	12		8					3	13	14					17
1				5	6^{2}	7	10^{1}		4^{3}		12	9	2	11	13		8					3		14					18
1		2		9	12	14	8^{1}	10^{2}	11		6^{3}	7	5		13							3		4					19
1		12		5	7^{2}		10				9	8	2	11	13		6					3		4^{1}					20
1		4		8	7		11^{2}	10^{1}	3		9	6	2	5	12		13												21
1		3		5	6^{1}			10^{2}	4			8	2	11	12				9			7	13						22
1				5	9^{2}	7^{1}	8	10^{3}	4			6	2	11		14	12		13			3							23
1		3		5	9	7^{1}	8	10^{3}	4^{2}	14			2	11			12					6	13						24
1		3■		5	7^{1}		8^{3}	9^{2}	10		12	6	2	11			14					4			13				25
1			14	5	9^{2}	7	8^{3}	10^{1}	4			6	2	11								3			12	13			26
1			14	5	9^{2}	7^{1}	8^{3}	10	4			6	2	11								3			13	12			27
1		15		5^{2}	7^{3}	12	8	10^{4}	4			6	2	14								3			11	13	9^{1}		28
1					12	7	8^{1}	11^{2}	4	13		14	2	10								3			5		9^{3}	6	29
1		12		5	9^{1}	7	8^{3}		4			11	2	13								3■			10	14		6^{2}	30
1		3		5	6^{1}		8^{2}	10^{3}			12	7	4	14											2	13	11	9	31
1		3	14	5			8^{2}	10^{3}			12	7	4	9											2	13	11	6^{1}	32
1		3^{3}	13	5	12		8^{2}	10	4		14	7	2												9^{1}		11	6	33
1		3	2	5^{3}		7^{1}		10^{2}	4	13	9	6		14								12				11	8		34
1			4	5			8^{1}	11	10		14	6^{3}	2	13								3				12	9^{2}	7	35
1			5	6			9	11	4		14	13	2^{1}	12								3				8^{2}	10	7^{3}	36
1			5	14			8^{2}	13	4		9	6	2	11^{3}					12			3			10		7^{1}		37
1		14		5			8^{2}	11^{1}	4		9	6	2	12								3			10	13		7^{3}	38
1			13	5			8^{3}		4^{1}	14	7■	12	2	10								3			11	6^{2}		9	39
1		3	5	9^{1}	13		10^{3}			12		6^{2}	2	7					14			4			11			8	40
1		3	5^{3}		13		9^{1}		10	12		8^{2}	2	11								4			6	14		7	41
1			4	5^{3}	14		8		3	13		6^{1}	2	10^{2}											11	12	9	7	42
1			4	5	6^{1}		8^{2}	10^{3}			13		2	14								3			11	12	9	7	43
1			4	5	6^{1}			11^{2}	13		7		2	14								3			10	12	9^{3}	8	44
1			2^{3}	5	6			10	4		7^{2}		14	12								3			11^{1}	13	8	9	45
1			2^{2}	5	6^{1}		8	10	4				13	11								3			14	12	9^{3}	7	46

FA Cup

First Round	Sunderland	(a)	1-0
Second Round	Doncaster R	(a)	3-2
Third Round	Middlesbrough	(h)	2-3

Carabao Cup

First Round	Preston NE	(h)	0-3

Papa John's Trophy

Group H (N)	Harrogate T	(a)	1-3
Group H (N)	Sheffield W	(h)	1-2
Group H (N)	Newcastle U U21	(h)	6-3

League Two Play-offs

Semi-Final 1st leg	Northampton T	(h)	2-1
Semi-Final 2nd leg	Northampton T	(a)	1-0
Final	Port Vale	(Wembley)	0-3

MIDDLESBROUGH

FOUNDATION

A previous belief that Middlesbrough Football Club was founded at a tripe supper at the Corporation Hotel has proved to be erroneous. In fact, members of Middlesbrough Cricket Club were responsible for forming it at a meeting in the gymnasium of the Albert Park Hotel in 1875.

Riverside Stadium, Middlehaven Way, Middlesbrough TS3 6RS.

Telephone: (01642) 929 420.

Ticket Office: (01642) 929 421.

Website: www.mfc.co.uk

Email: see website.

Ground Capacity: 34,742.

Record Attendance: 53,802 v Newcastle U, Division 1, 27 December 1949 (at Ayresome Park); 34,814 v Newcastle U, Premier League, 5 March 2003 (at Riverside Stadium); 35,000, England v Slovakia, Euro 2004 qualifier, 11 June 2003.

Pitch Measurements: 105m × 68m (115yd × 74.5yd).

Chairman: Steve Gibson.

Chief Executive: Neil Bausor.

Manager: Chris Wilder.

Assistant Manager: Alan Knill.

Colours: Red shirts with white trim, red shorts with white trim, red socks with white trim.

Year Formed: 1876; re-formed 1986.

Turned Professional: 1889; became amateur 1892, and professional again, 1899.

Club Nickname: 'Boro'.

Grounds: 1877, Old Archery Ground, Albert Park; 1879, Breckon Hill; 1882, Linthorpe Road Ground; 1903, Ayresome Park; 1995, Cellnet Riverside Stadium (renamed BT Cellnet Riverside Stadium 1995; Riverside Stadium 2002).

First Football League Game: 2 September 1899, Division 2, v Lincoln C (a) L 0–3 – Smith; Shaw, Ramsey; Allport, McNally, McCracken; Wanless, Longstaffe, Gettins, Page, Pugh.

Record League Victory: 9–0 v Brighton & HA, Division 2, 23 August 1958 – Taylor; Bilcliff, Robinson; Harris (2p), Phillips, Walley; Day, McLean, Clough (5), Peacock (2), Holliday.

Record Cup Victory: 7–0 v Hereford U, Coca-Cola Cup 2nd rd, 1st leg, 18 September 1996 – Miller; Fleming (1), Branco (1), Whyte, Vickers, Whelan, Emerson (1), Mustoe, Stamp, Juninho, Ravanelli (4).

HONOURS

League Champions: First Division – 1994–95; Division 2 – 1926–27, 1928–29, 1973–74.
Runners-up: FL C – 2015–16; First Division – 1997–98; Division 2 – 1901–02, 1991–92; Division 3 – 1966–67, 1986–87.

FA Cup: *Runners-up:* 1997.

League Cup Winners: 2004.
Runners-up: 1997, 1998.

Amateur Cup Winners: 1895, 1898.

Anglo-Scottish Cup Winners: 1976.

Full Members' Cup: *Runners-up:* 1990.

European Competitions
UEFA Cup: 2004–05, 2005–06 *(runners-up)*.

FOOTBALL YEARBOOK FACT FILE

Brian Clough scored 40 or more League and Cup goals for Middlesbrough in each of four consecutive seasons, between 1956–57 and 1959–60. His tally, which included five against Brighton & Hove Albion in the opening game of the 1958–59 season, left him with a career total of 205 goals from 222 competitive appearances, still well short of pre-war player George Camsell's club record.

Record Defeat: 0–9 v Blackburn R, Division 2, 6 November 1954.

Most League Points (2 for a win): 65, Division 2, 1973–74.

Most League Points (3 for a win): 94, Division 3, 1986–87.

Most League Goals: 122, Division 2, 1926–27.

Highest League Scorer in Season: George Camsell, 59, Division 2, 1926–27 (Second Division record).

Most League Goals in Total Aggregate: George Camsell, 325, 1925–39.

Most League Goals in One Match: 5, John Wilkie v Gainsborough T, Division 2, 2 March 1901; 5, Andy Wilson v Nottingham F, Division 1, 6 October 1923; 5, George Camsell v Manchester C, Division 2, 25 December 1926; 5, George Camsell v Aston Villa, Division 1, 9 September 1935; 5, Brian Clough v Brighton & HA, Division 2, 22 August 1958.

Most Capped Player: Mark Schwarzer, 52 (109), Australia.

Most League Appearances: Tim Williamson, 563, 1902–23.

Youngest League Player: Luke Williams, 16 years 200 days v Barnsley, 18 December 2009.

Record Transfer Fee Received: £18,000,000 from Wolverhampton W for Adama Traore, August 2019.

Record Transfer Fee Paid: £15,000,000 to Nottingham F for Britt Assombalonga, July 2017.

Football League Record: 1899 Elected to Division 2; 1902–24 Division 1; 1924–27 Division 2; 1927–28 Division 1; 1928–29 Division 2; 1929–54 Division 1; 1954–66 Division 2; 1966–67 Division 3; 1967–74 Division 2; 1974–82 Division 1; 1982–86 Division 2; 1986–87 Division 3; 1987–88 Division 2; 1988–89 Division 1; 1989–92 Division 2; 1992–93 Premier League; 1993–95 Division 1; 1995–97 Premier League; 1997–98 Division 1; 1998–2009 Premier League; 2009–16 FL C; 2016–17 Premier League; 2017– FL C.

MANAGERS

John Robson 1899–1905
Alex Mackie 1905–06
Andy Aitken 1906–09
J. Gunter 1908–10
(Secretary-Manager)
Andy Walker 1910–11
Tom McIntosh 1911–19
Jimmy Howie 1920–23
Herbert Bamlett 1923–26
Peter McWilliam 1927–34
Wilf Gillow 1934–44
David Jack 1944–52
Walter Rowley 1952–54
Bob Dennison 1954–63
Raich Carter 1963–66
Stan Anderson 1966–73
Jack Charlton 1973–77
John Neal 1977–81
Bobby Murdoch 1981–82
Malcolm Allison 1982–84
Willie Maddren 1984–86
Bruce Rioch 1986–90
Colin Todd 1990–91
Lennie Lawrence 1991–94
Bryan Robson 1994–2001
Steve McClaren 2001–06
Gareth Southgate 2006–09
Gordon Strachan 2009–10
Tony Mowbray 2010–13
Aitor Karanka 2013–17
Garry Monk 2017
Tony Pulis 2017–19
Jonathan Woodgate 2019–20
Neil Warnock 2020–21
Chris Wilder November 2021–

LATEST SEQUENCES

Longest Sequence of League Wins: 9, 16.2.1974 – 6.4.1974.

Longest Sequence of League Defeats: 8, 26.12.1995 – 17.2.1996.

Longest Sequence of League Draws: 8, 3.4.1971 – 1.5.1971.

Longest Sequence of Unbeaten League Matches: 24, 8.9.1973 – 19.1.1974.

Longest Sequence Without a League Win: 19, 3.10.1981 – 6.3.1982.

Successive Scoring Runs: 26 from 21.9.1946.

Successive Non-scoring Runs: 7, 25.1.2014 – 1.3.2014.

TEN YEAR LEAGUE RECORD

		P	*W*	*D*	*L*	*F*	*A*	*Pts*	*Pos*
2012-13	FL C	46	18	5	23	61	70	59	16
2013-14	FL C	46	16	16	14	62	50	64	12
2014-15	FL C	46	25	10	11	68	37	85	4
2015-16	FL C	46	26	11	9	63	31	89	2
2016-17	PR Lge	38	5	13	20	27	53	28	19
2017-18	FL C	46	22	10	14	67	45	76	5
2018-19	FL C	46	20	13	13	49	41	73	7
2019-20	FL C	46	13	14	19	48	61	53	17
2020-21	FL C	46	18	10	18	55	53	64	10
2021-22	FL C	46	20	10	16	59	50	70	7

DID YOU KNOW ?

Middlesbrough's EFL Cup third-round tie with Middlesbrough in September 2014 finished at 2-2 after extra time thanks to Patrick Bamford's penalty equaliser in the final minute of extra time. The penalty shootout that followed involved a competition record of 30 spot kicks before Boro eventually went down to a 14–13 defeat.

MIDDLESBROUGH – SKY BET CHAMPIONSHIP 2021–22 LEAGUE RECORD

Match No.	Date	Venue	Opponents	Result	H/T Score	Lg Pos.	Goalscorers	Attendance
1	Aug 8	A	Fulham	D 1-1	0-1	9	Bola [77]	16,058
2	14	H	Bristol C	W 2-1	1-0	6	Ikpeazu [38], Crooks [70]	22,004
3	18	H	QPR	L 2-3	1-0	10	Ikpeazu (pen) [7], Crooks [72]	22,436
4	21	A	Derby Co	D 0-0	0-0	12		16,123
5	28	H	Blackburn R	D 1-1	1-1	13	Howson [36]	20,542
6	Sept 11	A	Coventry C	L 0-2	0-0	15		18,515
7	15	A	Nottingham F	W 2-0	1-0	11	Sporar [24], Hernandez [72]	23,830
8	18	H	Blackpool	L 1-2	1-0	16	Tavernier [8]	21,022
9	25	A	Reading	L 0-1	0-0	18		12,469
10	28	H	Sheffield U	W 2-0	2-0	11	Watmore [9], McNair [37]	19,390
11	Oct 2	A	Hull C	L 0-2	0-0	15		13,696
12	16	H	Peterborough U	W 2-0	0-0	12	McNair (pen) [85], Coburn [90]	19,556
13	20	H	Barnsley	W 2-0	1-0	10	Sporar [20], Crooks [87]	17,931
14	23	A	Cardiff C	W 2-0	1-0	6	Sporar (pen) [35], Payero [74]	17,513
15	30	H	Birmingham C	L 0-2	0-0	11		21,582
16	Nov 2	A	Luton T	L 1-3	1-0	14	Coburn [15]	9790
17	6	A	WBA	D 1-1	1-0	14	Coburn [38]	22,596
18	20	H	Millwall	D 1-1	1-1	14	Crooks [15]	20,845
19	23	H	Preston NE	L 1-2	1-0	15	McNair [33]	18,013
20	27	A	Huddersfield T	W 2-1	2-0	12	Watmore 2 [16, 23]	19,192
21	Dec 4	H	Swansea C	W 1-0	1-0	9	Jones [26]	18,707
22	11	A	Stoke C	D 0-0	0-0	9		21,140
23	18	H	Bournemouth	W 1-0	0-0	9	Sporar (pen) [53]	18,323
24	26	H	Nottingham F	W 2-0	1-0	5	Yates (og) [17], Sporar [69]	29,832
25	29	A	Blackpool	W 2-1	0-0	5	Sporar [60], Watmore [90]	13,428
26	Jan 15	H	Reading	W 2-1	0-0	6	Crooks 2 [84, 90]	21,634
27	24	A	Blackburn R	L 0-1	0-0	7		14,670
28	29	H	Coventry C	W 1-0	0-0	6	Sporar [58]	22,940
29	Feb 9	A	QPR	D 2-2	1-1	7	Fry [45], Adomah (og) [60]	14,140
30	12	H	Derby Co	W 4-1	3-1	6	Buchanan (og) [15], Connolly [44], Crooks [45], Watmore [89]	26,266
31	19	A	Bristol C	L 1-2	0-1	7	Crooks [90]	20,148
32	22	H	WBA	W 2-1	0-1	6	McNair [60], Tavernier [69]	21,646
33	26	A	Barnsley	L 2-3	0-2	8	Sporar (pen) [61], Kitching (og) [90]	16,107
34	Mar 5	H	Luton T	W 2-1	1-0	6	McNair (pen) [17], Watmore [87]	23,817
35	8	A	Sheffield U	L 1-4	0-2	8	Balogun [62]	28,994
36	12	A	Millwall	D 0-0	0-0	8		16,734
37	15	A	Birmingham C	W 2-0	1-0	6	Connolly [23], Balogun [62]	15,852
38	Apr 2	A	Peterborough U	W 4-0	1-0	5	Tavernier [26], Balogun [49], Coburn [82], Watmore [90]	11,755
39	6	H	Fulham	L 0-1	0-0	7		21,995
40	9	H	Hull C	L 0-1	0-0	8		24,603
41	15	A	Bournemouth	D 0-0	0-0	7		9903
42	18	H	Huddersfield T	L 0-2	0-1	9		24,230
43	23	A	Swansea C	D 1-1	0-0	8	McGree [46]	18,246
44	27	H	Cardiff C	W 2-0	1-0	7	Tavernier [28], McGree [53]	19,727
45	30	H	Stoke C	W 3-1	2-0	7	Crooks 2 [21, 72], Baker (og) [25]	24,942
46	May 7	A	Preston NE	L 1-4	0-2	7	Tavernier [48]	17,691

Final League Position: 7

GOALSCORERS

League (59): Crooks 10, Sporar 8 (3 pens), Watmore 7, McNair 5 (2 pens), Tavernier 5, Coburn 4, Balogun 3, Connolly 2, Ikpeazu 2 (1 pen), McGree 2, Bola 1, Fry 1, Hernandez 1, Howson 1, Jones 1, Payero 1, own goals 5.
FA Cup (5): Boyd-Munce 1, Coburn 1, Crooks 1, Ikpeazu 1, own goal 1.
Carabao Cup (0).

Lumley J 34	Dijksteel A 34	Hall G 8	Fry D 32 + 1	Bola M 19 + 4	Howson J 44 + 1	Crooks M 40	Morsy S 3	McNair P 42	Ikpeazu U 8 + 12	Watmore D 22 + 19	Spence D 2 + 1	Tavernier M 43 + 1	Jones I 36 + 6	Payero M 6 + 7	Bamba S 18 + 6	Akpom C — + 1	Peltier L 17 + 4	Coburn J 3 + 15	Olusanya T — + 3	Hernandez O 9 + 8	Lea Siliki J 3 + 8	Sporar A 28 + 7	Daniels L 12	Kokolo W — + 1	Taylor N 14	Connolly A 13 + 6	Balogun F 9 + 9	McGree R 7 + 4	Boyd-Munce C — + 1	Match No.
1	2	3	4	5	6	7	8^{3}	9	10^{1}	11^{2}	12	13	14																	1
1	2	3	4	5	7	6		8	10^{1}		9		11^{2}	12	13															2
1	2	3	4	5	6	9		7	11^{1}		8^{2}		10	13		12														3
1	2		4	5	12	9	6	3	11^{2}			8	10				7^{1}	13												4
1	5	3	4	13	8	11	6■	2		10^{1}		7	9^{2}						12											5
1	5	3	2		7	6			10^{1}	14		8	9^{3}		4					11^{2}	12	13								6
1	2	3	4		6	9			13	14		8	12				5			10^{3}	7^{1}	11^{2}								7
1	2^{1}	3	4		6^{3}	9			14			8	12	13			5			10	7^{2}	11								8
1			4	5	6	7■		3		14		8	10^{2}	9^{1}			2		13		12	11^{3}								9
1			4	8	7	9		6	12	10^{2}		5			3		2		13			11^{1}								10
1			4^{1}	8^{2}	6	9		7	14	10^{3}		5	13		3		2				12	11								11
1					2	6		4	10^{1}	9^{3}		5	12	7	3			13		8	14	11^{2}								12
1					7	6^{3}		2	12	11^{2}		5	8	9	3		4			13	14	10^{1}								13
1					5	7		2	10^{3}	13		6	12	9	3		4	14		8^{1}		11^{2}								14
1					7	8^{3}		2	11^{1}	12		5		6	3		4	14		9^{2}	13	10								15
	2				7	8^{2}		4		12		6	5		3			11		9^{3}	13	10^{1}	1	14						16
		3			2			6		11^{2}		8	5	7^{1}	4		9	10^{3}		14	13	12	1							17
				9	7	6		2	14	10^{3}		8	5^{2}		3		4	12		13		11^{1}	1							18
				9	8	6		2	13	11^{1}		7	5		3		4^{2}			12		10	1							19
	2			9	7	6		4	13	11^{1}		8	5^{2}		3					12		10	1							20
	2^{3}		14	9	7	6		4	13	11^{2}		8	5		3					12		10^{1}	1							21
1	2		3	9	7	6^{1}		4	14	11^{2}		8	5		12					13		10^{3}								22
1	2		3		7	6		4	13	11^{1}		8	5^{3}		14					12		10^{2}			9					23
1	2		3		6	8		4		12		7	5^{2}	14			13			10^{1}		11^{3}			9					24
1	3		4			6		7	13	12		8	5		2		9			11^{1}		10^{2}								25
1	2^{2}		3		7^{3}	6		4		13		8	5					14				10			9	11^{1}	12			26
1	2^{2}		3		7^{1}	6		4		13		8	5					14				10			9^{3}	11	12			27
1	2		3		7^{2}	6		4				8	5	13								10			9	11^{1}	12			28
1	2		3		7	6^{3}		4		11^{1}		8	5	14								10^{2}			9	13	12			29
1	2		3		7	6^{1}		4		13		8	5									14			9	10^{2}	11^{3}	12		30
1	2^{2}		3		7	6		4		13		8	5												9^{1}	11	10	12		31
1	2		3		7			4		13		8	5				14					12			9^{2}	11^{3}	10^{1}	6		32
1	2		3		7			4		10^{2}		8	5								6^{1}	11			9^{3}	12	13		14	33
1	2		3		7	6		4		12		8	5^{3}		14			13							9	11^{2}	10^{1}			34
1			3	9^{1}	7	6		4		13		8	5				2^{3}	14				10^{2}				11	12			35
1			3		7	6		2		12		8	5				4								9	11^{1}	10			36
1	2		4	12	7	6		3		13		8	5^{3}				14								9^{1}	11	10^{2}			37
1	2		3	9	7	6		4		12		8	5^{3}				14	13								11^{2}	10^{1}			38
1	2		3	12	7	6^{3}		4		10		8					5^{2}	14				11			9^{1}			13		39
1	2		3^{1}	9	7	6^{2}		4		13		5			12			14								10	11^{3}	8		40
	2			9	7	6		4		11^{1}		8^{3}	5		3							12	1			10^{2}	13	14		41
	2			9	7			4		10^{3}		8	5		3^{1}			12				11^{2}	1			14	13	6		42
	2			9	7			4		10^{1}		8^{3}	5	14	3			11^{2}				13	1			12		6		43
	2			9	7			4		10^{2}		8	5		3							12	1			13	11^{1}	6		44
	2		3	12	7	6				11^{2}		9	5^{3}		14		4	13				10^{1}	1					8		45
	2^{3}		3		7	6		4■		10^{1}		9	5					12				11^{2}	1			14	13	8		46

FA Cup

Third Round	Mansfield T	(a)	3-2
Fourth Round	Manchester U	(a)	1-1
(aet; Middlesbrough won 8-7 on penalties)			
Fifth Round	Tottenham H	(h)	1-0
(aet)			
Sixth Round	Chelsea	(h)	0-2

Carabao Cup

First Round	Blackpool	(a)	0-3

MILLWALL

FOUNDATION

Formed in 1885 as Millwall Rovers by employees of Morton & Co, a jam and marmalade factory in West Ferry Road. The founders were predominantly Scotsmen. Their first headquarters was The Islanders pub in Tooke Street, Millwall. Their first trophy was the East End Cup in 1887.

The Den, Zampa Road, Bermondsey, London SE16 3LN.

Telephone: (020) 7232 1222.

Ticket Office: (0844) 826 2004.

Website: www.millwallfc.co.uk

Email: slo@millwallplc.com

Ground Capacity: 19,734.

Record Attendance: 48,672 v Derby Co, FA Cup 5th rd, 20 February 1937 (at The Den, Cold Blow Lane); 20,093 v Arsenal, FA Cup 3rd rd, 10 January 1994 (at The Den, Bermondsey).

Pitch Measurements: 106m × 68m (116yd × 74.5yd).

Chairman: John Berylson.

Chief Executive: Steve Kavanagh.

Manager: Gary Rowett.

Assistant Manager: Adam Barrett.

HONOURS

League Champions: Division 2 – 1987–88; Second Division – 2000–01; Division 3S – 1927–28, 1937–38; Division 4 – 1961–62.
Runners-up: Division 3 – 1965–66, 1984–85; Division 3S – 1952–53; Division 4 – 1964–65.

FA Cup: *Runners-up:* 2004.

League Cup: 5th rd – 1974, 1977, 1995.

League Trophy: *Runners-up:* 1999.

European Competitions
UEFA Cup: 2004–05.

Colours: Blue shirts with yellow trim, white shorts with blue trim, blue socks with yellow trim.

Year Formed: 1885.

Turned Professional: 1893.

Previous Names: 1885, Millwall Rovers; 1889, Millwall Athletic; 1899, Millwall; 1985, Millwall Football & Athletic Company.

Club Nickname: 'The Lions'.

Grounds: 1885, Glengall Road, Millwall; 1886, Back of 'Lord Nelson'; 1890, East Ferry Road; 1901, North Greenwich; 1910, The Den, Cold Blow Lane; 1993, The Den, Bermondsey.

First Football League Game: 28 August 1920, Division 3, v Bristol R (h) W 2–0 – Lansdale; Fort, Hodge; Voisey (1), Riddell, McAlpine; Waterall, Travers, Broad (1), Sutherland, Dempsey.

Record League Victory: 9–1 v Torquay U, Division 3 (S), 29 August 1927 – Lansdale, Tilling, Hill, Amos, Bryant (3), Graham, Chance, Hawkins (3), Landells (1), Phillips (2), Black. 9–1 v Coventry C, Division 3 (S), 19 November 1927 – Lansdale, Fort, Hill, Amos, Collins (1), Graham, Chance, Landells (4), Cock (2), Phillips (2), Black.

Record Cup Victory: 7–0 v Gateshead, FA Cup 2nd rd, 12 December 1936 – Yuill; Ted Smith, Inns; Brolly, Hancock, Forsyth; Thomas (1), Mangnall (1), Ken Burditt (2), McCartney (2), Thorogood (1).

Record Defeat: 1–9 v Aston Villa, FA Cup 4th rd, 28 January 1946.

Most League Points (2 for a win): 65, Division 3 (S), 1927–28 and Division 3, 1965–66.

FOOTBALL YEARBOOK FACT FILE

George Jacks became the first player to be used as a substitute by Millwall in a Football League game when he came on to replace wing-half Ken Jones 12 minutes from the end of the home fixture with Workington on the opening day of the 1965–66 campaign. At that time substitutions were only allowed for injured players and Jacks was refused permission to come on the field on three occasions before the referee eventually relented.

Most League Points (3 for a win): 93, Division 2, 2000–01.

Most League Goals: 127, Division 3 (S), 1927–28.

Highest League Scorer in Season: Richard Parker, 37, Division 3 (S), 1926–27.

Most League Goals in Total Aggregate: Neil Harris, 124, 1995–2004; 2006–11.

Most League Goals in One Match: 5, Richard Parker v Norwich C, Division 3 (S), 28 August 1926.

Most Capped Player: Shane Ferguson, 31 (including 4 whilst on loan from Newcastle U) (54), Northern Ireland.

Most League Appearances: Barry Kitchener, 523, 1967–82.

Youngest League Player: Moses Ashikodi, 15 years 240 days v Brighton & HA, 22 February 2003.

Record Transfer Fee Received: £8,000,000 from Middlesbrough for George Saville, January 2019.

Record Transfer Fee Paid: £1,700,000 to Fortuna Sittard for Zian Flemming, June 2022.

Football League Record: 1920 Original Members of Division 3; 1921 Division 3 (S); 1928–34 Division 2; 1934–38 Division 3 (S); 1938–48 Division 2; 1948–58 Division 3 (S); 1958–62 Division 4; 1962–64 Division 3; 1964–65 Division 4; 1965–66 Division 3; 1966–75 Division 2; 1975–76 Division 3; 1976–79 Division 2; 1979–85 Division 3; 1985–88 Division 2; 1988–90 Division 1; 1990–92 Division 2; 1992–96 Division 1; 1996–2001 Division 2; 2001–04 Division 1; 2004–06 FL C; 2006–10 FL 1; 2010–15 FL C; 2015–17 FL 1; 2017– FL C.

LATEST SEQUENCES

Longest Sequence of League Wins: 10, 10.3.1928 – 25.4.1928.

Longest Sequence of League Defeats: 11, 10.4.1929 – 16.9.1929.

Longest Sequence of League Draws: 5, 3.11.2020 – 28.11.2020.

Longest Sequence of Unbeaten League Matches: 19, 22.8.1959 – 31.10.1959.

Longest Sequence Without a League Win: 20, 26.12.1989 – 5.5.1990.

Successive Scoring Runs: 22 from 27.11.1954.

Successive Non-scoring Runs: 6 from 27.4.2013.

MANAGERS

F. B. Kidd 1894–99
(Hon. Treasurer/Manager)
E. R. Stopher 1899–1900
(Hon. Treasurer/Manager)
George Saunders 1900–11
(Hon. Treasurer/Manager)
Herbert Lipsham 1911–19
Robert Hunter 1919–33
Bill McCracken 1933–36
Charlie Hewitt 1936–40
Bill Voisey 1940–44
Jack Cock 1944–48
Charlie Hewitt 1948–56
Ron Gray 1956–57
Jimmy Seed 1958–59
Reg Smith 1959–61
Ron Gray 1961–63
Billy Gray 1963–66
Benny Fenton 1966–74
Gordon Jago 1974–77
George Petchey 1978–80
Peter Anderson 1980–82
George Graham 1982–86
John Docherty 1986–90
Bob Pearson 1990
Bruce Rioch 1990–92
Mick McCarthy 1992–96
Jimmy Nicholl 1996–97
John Docherty 1997
Billy Bonds 1997–98
Keith Stevens 1998–2000
(then Joint Manager)
(*plus* **Alan McLeary** 1999–2000)
Mark McGhee 2000–03
Dennis Wise 2003–05
Steve Claridge 2005
Colin Lee 2005
David Tuttle 2005–06
Nigel Spackman 2006
Willie Donachie 2006–07
Kenny Jackett 2007–13
Steve Lomas 2013
Ian Holloway 2014–15
Neil Harris 2015–19
Gary Rowett October 2019–

TEN YEAR LEAGUE RECORD

		P	*W*	*D*	*L*	*F*	*A*	*Pts*	*Pos*
2012-13	FL C	46	15	11	20	51	62	56	20
2013-14	FL C	46	11	15	20	46	74	48	19
2014-15	FL C	46	9	14	23	42	76	41	22
2015-16	FL 1	46	24	9	13	73	49	81	4
2016-17	FL 1	46	20	13	13	66	57	73	6
2017-18	FL C	46	19	15	12	56	45	72	8
2018-19	FL C	46	10	14	22	48	64	44	21
2019-20	FL C	46	17	17	12	57	51	68	8
2020-21	FL C	46	15	17	14	47	52	62	11
2021-22	FL C	46	18	15	13	53	45	69	9

DID YOU KNOW ?

George Robey, the well-known comedian and music hall artist, was also a talented footballer. In the early 1900s he turned out for Millwall in a handful of Western League games and also appeared for the Dockers, as they were then known, in both friendly and reserve-team fixtures.

MILLWALL – SKY BET CHAMPIONSHIP 2021–22 LEAGUE RECORD

Match No.	*Date*	*Venue*	*Opponents*	*Result*		*H/T Score*	*Lg Pos.*	*Goalscorers*	*Attendance*
1	Aug 7	A	QPR	D	1-1	1-1	8	Wallace, J 11	16,127
2	14	H	Blackburn R	D	1-1	0-0	16	Wallace, J 64	12,490
3	17	H	Fulham	L	1-2	0-2	18	Afobe 87	12,700
4	21	A	Cardiff C	L	1-3	0-0	21	Afobe 76	18,168
5	28	H	Blackpool	W	2-1	0-0	17	Wallace, J 63, Cooper 90	11,049
6	Sept 11	A	WBA	D	1-1	0-0	14	Ballard 55	23,142
7	15	A	Swansea C	D	0-0	0-0	15		16,007
8	18	H	Coventry C	D	1-1	1-1	18	Saville 21	12,516
9	25	A	Nottingham F	D	1-1	1-0	18	Smith 32	25,589
10	29	H	Bristol C	W	1-0	0-0	14	Wallace, J (pen) 64	11,389
11	Oct 2	A	Barnsley	W	1-0	0-0	11	Wallace, M 89	11,888
12	16	H	Luton T	L	0-2	0-1	14		14,227
13	19	A	Sheffield U	W	2-1	1-1	10	Wallace, J 11, Cooper 90	25,345
14	23	H	Stoke C	W	2-1	0-1	10	Bradshaw 2 51, 61	12,896
15	30	A	Huddersfield T	L	0-1	0-0	12		15,397
16	Nov 2	H	Reading	W	1-0	0-0	8	Afobe 71	11,004
17	6	H	Derby Co	D	1-1	1-1	9	Malone 45	14,372
18	20	A	Middlesbrough	D	1-1	1-1	9	Bamba (og) 27	20,845
19	24	H	Bournemouth	D	1-1	0-1	10	Afobe 67	12,237
20	27	A	Hull C	L	1-2	1-1	10	Bradshaw 45	10,613
21	Dec 4	H	Birmingham C	W	3-1	2-0	8	Wallace, M 10, Bradshaw 41, Evans 73	14,324
22	11	A	Peterborough U	L	1-2	1-0	11	Bradshaw 16	9140
23	29	A	Coventry C	W	1-0	0-0	11	Bradshaw 79	18,500
24	Jan 2	A	Bristol C	L	2-3	2-1	11	Bradshaw 23, Afobe (pen) 29	18,033
25	15	H	Nottingham F	L	0-1	0-0	11		13,297
26	22	A	Blackpool	L	0-1	0-0	14		10,696
27	29	H	WBA	W	2-0	0-0	15	Bennett 67, Afobe 76	12,855
28	Feb 1	H	Preston NE	D	0-0	0-0	14		10,183
29	8	A	Fulham	L	0-3	0-1	15		16,606
30	12	H	Cardiff C	W	2-1	0-0	15	Wallace, M 73, Bennett 82	12,710
31	15	H	QPR	W	2-0	0-0	14	Bennett 48, Burey 64	13,063
32	23	A	Derby Co	W	2-1	2-0	12	Wallace, J 2, Burey 30	23,943
33	26	H	Sheffield U	W	1-0	0-0	11	Cooper 61	14,638
34	Mar 5	A	Reading	W	1-0	1-0	10	Cooper 37	14,169
35	8	A	Blackburn R	D	0-0	0-0	9		12,874
36	12	H	Middlesbrough	D	0-0	0-0	11		16,734
37	16	H	Huddersfield T	W	2-0	1-0	10	Afobe 2 27, 57	10,792
38	19	A	Stoke C	L	0-2	0-1	10		20,526
39	Apr 2	A	Luton T	D	2-2	1-1	10	Bradshaw 25, Afobe 81	10,069
40	5	H	Swansea C	L	0-1	0-0	10		11,670
41	9	H	Barnsley	W	4-1	1-0	9	McNamara 2 31, 47, Burke 58, Afobe 72	13,231
42	15	A	Preston NE	D	1-1	1-1	10	Wallace, M 22	11,979
43	18	H	Hull C	W	2-1	0-0	7	Malone 51, Bradshaw 55	12,776
44	23	A	Birmingham C	D	2-2	0-0	7	Burke 68, Afobe (pen) 90	17,206
45	30	H	Peterborough U	W	3-0	0-0	8	Afobe 53, Knight (og) 73, Saville 76	16,705
46	May 7	A	Bournemouth	L	0-1	0-0	9		10,244

Final League Position: 9

GOALSCORERS

League (53): Afobe 12 (2 pens), Bradshaw 9, Wallace, J 6 (1 pen), Cooper 4, Wallace, M 4, Bennett 3, Burey 2, Burke 2, Malone 2, McNamara 2, Saville 2, Ballard 1, Evans 1, Smith 1, own goals 2.
FA Cup (1): Afobe 1.
Carabao Cup (5): Wallace M 2, Malone 1, Saville 1, Smith 1.

Bialkowski B 46	Ballard D 30 + 1	Hutchinson S 28 + 1	Wallace M 42	McNamara D 33 + 4	Evans G 12 + 11	Kieftenbeld M 19 + 8	Saville G 34 + 3	Malone S 36 + 3	Wallace J 33 + 5	Afobe B 34 + 4	Leonard R 11 + 8	Smith M 6 + 15	Mitchell B 35 + 7	Cooper J 41 + 1	Romeo M 2	Mahoney C 1 + 7	Thompson B — + 2	Ojo S 12 + 6	Bennett M 16 + 13	Bradshaw T 16 + 8	Pearce A 3 + 3	Lovelace Z — + 5	Burke O 10 + 4	Burey T 6 + 9	Freeman L — + 1	*Match No.*
1	2	3	4	5	6^3	7	8^1	9	10	11^2	12	13	14													1
1	2		3	5	6^3	7	8^1	9	11	10^2	12	13	14	4												2
1	2		3	14	13	7^2	9	8	10	11	6^3	12		4	5^1											3
1	2		3		6^1	7	9	8	10	11		12		4^2	5	13										4
1	2		3		13	8^2	6	9	10	7		11^3	5^1	4		12	14									5
1	2		3			6	7	8	9		13	11	5^2	4				10^1	12							6
1	2^2		3			6	7	8	9		13	14	5	4		12			10^1	11^3						7
1	2		3			6^2	7	8	9		5	10^1	12	4		14			13	11^3						8
1	2	3	4		14	6^2	7	8		12	5	10^4	13			9^1		11^3		15						9
1	2	3	4	5	6		7	8^3	12	11		10^1	13	14				9^2								10
1	2	3	8	5	6^1		7		9	11^3		14	12	4				10^2		13						11
1	2	3	8^2	5^1	6^4		7		9	11^3	13	12	15	4				10	14							12
1	2	3			6		7	8^3	9	13	5	12		4				11^2	14	10^1						13
1	2	3		14	6^1	13		8	9^3		5	12	7	4				10^2		11						14
1	2^3	3				12	6	8	9	13	5	14	7	4				10^1		11^2						15
1		3	5	14		7^2	8	13	9	11^3	2	10^1	6	4					12							16
1	2^1		4	13			7^3	8	9	11^4	5	14	6	3				15	10^2	12						17
1	2	3				13	6	8	9^3	11^2	5	14	7	4				12	10^1							18
1	2	3	4	5			6	8^2	9	11			7					13	10^1	12						19
1	2	3	4	5	14		7^3		10	11		12	6					8^2	13	9^1						20
1		2	4	5	6	12		8^2	9^1	10			7	3					14	11^3	13					21
1		2	4	5	6			8^2	9^3	10^1		14	7	3				13	12	11						22
1		2	8	5			7	13		12			6	4				9^2	11^1	10^3	3	14				23
1		2	8	5	12		7	14		11		13	6^2	4				9^1		10	3^3					24
1		2	4	5	7			8		11			6	3			13	9^2	12	10^1						25
1		2	4	5	6^2	7		9^3		11			8	3		14			10^1				12	13		26
1		2	4	5	13	6		8		11^2			7	3					10				9^1	12		27
1		2	4	5		6		8^2	12	10			7	3		13			11^3				9^1	14		28
1		2	8	5		6			12	11			7	4					9^3		3^1		10^2	14	13	29
1		2	4	5	14	6	13	8	9	11^3			7^2	3					12				10^1			30
1		2	4	5		6	14	8^2	9				7	3					11^3		13		10^1	12		31
1		2	4	5	12		7	8	9				6	3					11^2			13		10^1		32
1	13	2^2	4	5	12		7	8	9				6	3					11^1			14		10^3		33
1	2		4	5	12		7	8	9^2	11^3			6	3		13						14		10^1		34
1	2^1		4	5	12		7	8	9	10^3			6	3					14		13			11^2		35
1	2		4	5			7	8	9	11			6	3					10^1			12				36
1	2		4	5			7	8	9	11			6	3					10^1					12		37
1	2		4	5		12	7	8^1	9				6	3				14	10^3	13				11^2		38
1	2		4	5		13	7	8	9^2	11			6	3						10^1			12			39
1	2		4	5		12	7^2	8	9^3	11			6	3				14		10^1			13			40
1	2		4	5^3		7		8	9^2	11	13		6	3						14			10^1	12		41
1	2		4	5		7	13	8	9	11			6^2	3						12			10^1			42
1	2	12	4	5			7	8^1		10^3	14		6	3						11			13	9^2		43
1	2	3^1	8	5^3		6	7			10	14			4					12	11^2			9	13		44
1		3	8	5			7		12	10	2^1		6	4					13	11^2			9^3	14		45
1		3	8^1	5		12	7		13	11	2^3		6	4					10^2	14			9			46

FA Cup

Third Round	Crystal Palace	(h)	1-2

Carabao Cup

First Round	Portsmouth	(h)	2-1
Second Round	Cambridge U	(h)	3-1
Third Round	Leicester C	(h)	0-2

MILTON KEYNES DONS

FOUNDATION

In July 2004 Wimbledon became MK Dons and relocated to Milton Keynes. In 2007 it recognised itself as a new club with no connection to the old Wimbledon FC. In August of that year the replica trophies and other Wimbledon FC memorabilia were returned to the London Borough of Merton.

Stadium MK, Stadium Way West, Milton Keynes, Buckinghamshire MK1 1ST.

Telephone: (01908) 622 922.

Ticket Office: (01908) 622 933.

Website: www.mkdons.com

Email: info@mkdons.com

Ground Capacity: 30,303.

Record Attendance: 28,521 v Liverpool, EFL Cup 3rd rd, 25 September 2019.

Pitch Measurements: 105m × 68m (115yd × 74.5yd).

Chairman: Pete Winkelman.

Head Coach: Liam Manning.

Assistant Head Coach: Chris Hogg.

Colours: White shirts with black trim, white shorts with black trim, white socks.

Year Formed: 2004.

Turned Professional: 2004.

Club Nickname: 'The Dons'.

Grounds: 2004, The National Hockey Stadium; 2007, Stadium MK.

First Football League Game: 7 August 2004, FL 1, v Barnsley (h) D 1–1 – Rachubka; Palmer, Lewington, Harding, Williams, Oyedele, Kamara, Smith, Smart (Herve), McLeod (1) (Hornuss), Small.

Record League Victory: 7–0 v Oldham Ath, FL 1, 20 December 2014 – Martin; Spence, McFadzean, Kay (Baldock), Lewington; Potter (1), Alli (1); Baker C (1), Carruthers (Green), Bowditch (1) (Afobe (1)); Grigg (2).

HONOURS

League Champions: FL 2 – 2007–08.
Runners-up: FL 1 – 2014–15.

FA Cup: 5th rd – 2013.

League Cup: 4th rd – 2015.

League Trophy Winners: 2008.

FOOTBALL YEARBOOK FACT FILE

Scottish midfield player Alex Rae is the oldest player to appear for Milton Keynes Dons. He was 40 years and 229 days old when he appeared for the club in a League One game at home to Brighton on 1 May 2010. Alex, who was on the club's coaching staff, was called into action to cover for injuries. It was his last senior appearance in a career which spanned over 20 years.

Record Cup Victory: 6–0 v Nantwich T, FA Cup 1st rd, 12 November 2011 – Martin; Chicksen, Baldock G, Doumbe (1), Flanagan, Williams S, Powell (1) (O'Shea (1), Chadwick (Galloway), Bowditch (2), MacDonald (Williams G (1)), Balanta; 6–0 v Norwich C U21, EFL Trophy Southern Section 2nd rd, 8 December 2020 – Nicholls; Poole (2), Williams (Davies), Cargill, Harvie; Sorensen (1), Kasumu (Surman), Freeman (Johnson), Sorinola; Walker S (1), Agard (2).

Record Defeat: 0–6 v Southampton, Capital One Cup 3rd rd, 23 September 2015.

Most League Points (3 for a win): 97, FL 2, 2007–08.

Most League Goals: 101, FL 1, 2014–15.

Highest League Scorer in Season: Izale McLeod, 21, 2006–07.

MANAGERS

Stuart Murdock 2004
Danny Wilson 2004–06
Martin Allen 2006–07
Paul Ince 2007–08
Roberto Di Matteo 2008–09
Paul Ince 2009–10
Karl Robinson 2010–16
Robbie Neilson 2016–18
Dan Micciche 2018
Paul Tisdale 2018–19
Russell Martin 2019–21
Liam Manning August 2021–

Most League Goals in Total Aggregate: Izale McLeod, 62, 2004–07; 2012–14.

Most Capped Player: Lee Hodson, 7 (24), Northern Ireland; also Troy Parrott, 9 (15), Republic of Ireland (on loan from Tottenham H).

Most League Goals in One Match: 4, Will Grigg v Swindon T, FL 1, 24 April 2021; 4, Scott Twine v Plymouth Arg, FL 1, 30 April 2022.

Most League Appearances: Dean Lewington, 739, 2004–22.

Youngest League Player: Brendon Galloway, 16 years 42 days v Rochdale, 28 April 2012.

Record Transfer Fee Received: £5,000,000 from Tottenham H for Dele Alli, February 2015.

Record Transfer Fee Paid: £1,300,000 to Peterborough U for Mo Eisa, July 2021.

Football League Record: 2004–06 FL 1; 2006–08 FL 2; 2008–15 FL 1; 2015–16 FL C; 2016–18 FL 1; 2018–19 FL 2; 2019– FL 1.

LATEST SEQUENCES

Longest Sequence of League Wins: 8, 7.9.2007 – 20.10.2007.

Longest Sequence of League Defeats: 6, 2.4.2018 – 28.4.2018.

Longest Sequence of League Draws: 4, 12.2.2013 – 2.3.2013.

Longest Sequence of Unbeaten League Matches: 18, 29.1.2008 – 3.5.2008.

Longest Sequence Without a League Win: 12, 17.9.2019 – 7.12.2019.

Successive Scoring Runs: 18 from 21.8.2018.

Successive Non-scoring Runs: 5 from 5.10.2019.

TEN YEAR LEAGUE RECORD

		P	*W*	*D*	*L*	*F*	*A*	*Pts*	*Pos*
2012-13	FL 1	46	19	13	14	62	45	70	8
2013-14	FL 1	46	17	9	20	63	65	60	10
2014-15	FL 1	46	27	10	9	101	44	91	2
2015-16	FL C	46	9	12	25	39	69	39	23
2016-17	FL 1	46	16	13	17	60	58	61	12
2017-18	FL 1	46	11	12	23	43	69	45	23
2018-19	FL 2	46	23	10	13	71	49	79	3
2019-20	FL 1	35	10	7	18	36	47	37	19§
2020-21	FL 1	46	18	11	17	64	62	65	13
2021-22	FL 1	46	26	11	9	78	44	89	3

§Decided on points-per-game (1.06)

DID YOU KNOW ?

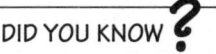

Milton Keynes Dons broke their record Football League win twice within three weeks during 2014–15. Their 6-0 home victory over Colchester United on 29 November was improved on when Oldham Athletic were defeated 7-0 on 20 December. During the season the Dons also equalled their best away score with a 5-0 win at Crewe in January.

MILTON KEYNES DONS – SKY BET LEAGUE ONE 2021–22 LEAGUE RECORD

Match No.	Date	Venue	Opponents	Result		H/T Score	Lg Pos.	Goalscorers	Attendance
1	Aug 7	A	Bolton W	D	3-3	1-1	7	Eisa 22, Twine 71, Boateng 83	16,087
2	14	H	Sunderland	L	1-2	0-1	15	Parrott 56	9830
3	17	H	Charlton Ath	W	2-1	1-1	12	Parrott 18, Eisa 64	7939
4	21	A	Ipswich T	D	2-2	0-1	13	Twine 58, O'Riley 75	18,622
5	28	H	Accrington S	W	2-0	1-0	11	Eisa 45, O'Riley 85	6816
6	Sept 4	A	Cheltenham T	D	1-1	0-1	10	Boateng 87	3704
7	11	H	Portsmouth	W	1-0	0-0	5	Robson 72	10,822
8	18	A	Gillingham	W	4-1	2-1	3	Twine 28, Kioso 39, Ehmer (og) 82, Watters 88	4119
9	25	H	Wycombe W	W	1-0	1-0	3	Parrott (pen) 40	9355
10	28	H	Fleetwood T	D	3-3	2-2	3	Twine 3 27, 39, 73	6564
11	Oct 2	A	Doncaster R	L	1-2	1-1	6	Kioso 24	5927
12	16	A	Shrewsbury T	L	0-1	0-0	6		5711
13	19	A	Wigan Ath	W	2-1	2-1	6	Kioso 30, Darikwa (og) 37	8351
14	23	H	Rotherham U	L	0-3	0-1	7		8448
15	30	A	Crewe Alex	W	4-1	1-0	7	Eisa 11, O'Riley 64, Kioso 82, Watters 90	4512
16	Nov 13	H	Cambridge U	W	4-1	3-0	5	Twine 2 13, 36, Watters 2 25, 76	9904
17	20	H	Burton Alb	W	1-0	0-0	5	Watters 65	9770
18	23	A	Sheffield W	L	1-2	0-0	8	Twine 47	18,581
19	27	A	Morecambe	W	4-0	2-0	6	Eisa 23, O'Riley 2 40, 82, Darling 64	3700
20	Dec 8	H	Plymouth Arg	D	1-1	1-0	7	Watson 21	7566
21	11	H	Oxford U	L	1-2	1-0	9	Boateng 11	9914
22	26	A	Lincoln C	W	3-2	0-2	7	Twine 2 59, 90, O'Riley 75	8328
23	Jan 1	H	Gillingham	D	0-0	0-0	7		7891
24	8	A	Accrington S	D	1-1	1-1	7	Eisa 25	1880
25	11	H	AFC Wimbledon	W	1-0	1-0	5	O'Riley 29	7663
26	15	A	Portsmouth	W	2-1	2-0	5	Eisa 20, Corbeanu 45	14,958
27	22	H	Doncaster R	L	0-1	0-1	5		7229
28	25	A	Burton Alb	W	1-0	0-0	5	Twine 90	2171
29	29	A	Wycombe W	W	1-0	1-0	4	Twine 13	7345
30	Feb 5	H	Lincoln C	W	2-1	1-1	3	Darling 39, O'Hora 47	8723
31	8	A	Fleetwood T	D	1-1	1-0	3	Darling 12	3227
32	12	H	Ipswich T	D	0-0	0-0	3		15,311
33	19	A	Sunderland	W	2-1	0-0	3	Eisa 48, Wickham 76	30,451
34	22	A	Charlton Ath	W	2-0	1-0	3	Watson 41, Hayden 59	8807
35	26	H	Bolton W	W	2-0	1-0	3	Eisa 17, Twine 74	10,388
36	Mar 5	A	Rotherham U	W	2-1	0-1	3	Darling 57, Eisa 59	9731
37	8	H	Cheltenham T	W	3-1	2-0	3	Parrott 2 25, 85, Eisa 28	6894
38	12	H	Wigan Ath	D	1-1	0-0	3	Darling 88	11,193
39	19	A	Cambridge U	W	1-0	0-0	3	O'Hora 60	6325
40	Apr 2	H	Shrewsbury T	W	2-0	1-0	3	Eisa 17, Twine 54	8984
41	5	H	Crewe Alex	W	2-1	2-0	2	Parrott 24, Coventry 40	7315
42	9	A	AFC Wimbledon	D	1-1	0-1	2	Parrott 80	7841
43	16	H	Sheffield W	L	2-3	1-3	3	Parrott 40, Twine 90	14,252
44	19	A	Oxford U	L	0-1	0-0	3		9685
45	23	H	Morecambe	W	2-0	1-0	3	Darling 20, Harvie 79	10,101
46	30	A	Plymouth Arg	W	5-0	3-0	3	Twine 4 17, 40, 60, 77, Darling 43	15,644

Final League Position: 3

GOALSCORERS

League (78): Twine 20, Eisa 12, Parrott 8 (1 pen), Darling 7, O'Riley 7, Watters 5, Kioso 4, Boateng 3, O'Hora 2, Watson 2, Corbeanu 1, Coventry 1, Harvie 1, Hayden 1, Robson 1, Wickham 1, own goals 2.
FA Cup (3): Darling 2, Watters 1.
Carabao Cup (0).
Papa John's Trophy (6): Bird 1, Boateng 1, Darling 1, Jules 1, Parrott 1, Watters 1.
League One Play-offs (1): Parrott 1.

Walker L 1	Darling H 40 + 1	O'Hora W 46	Jules Z 6 + 1	Watson T 20 + 8	O'Riley M 26	Twine S 44 + 1	Robson E 16 + 2	Harvie D 41	Parrott T 34 + 7	Eisa M 28 + 7	Baldwin A 4 + 5	Boateng H 9 + 20	Ilunga B — + 1	Fisher A 23	McEachran J 24 + 11	Martin J — + 5	Lewington D 42 + 2	Brown C 1 + 5	Kioso P 16 + 2	Watters M 5 + 6	Kasumu D 12 + 11	Ravizzoli F 1	Corbeanu T 9 + 7	Cumming J 21	Coventry C 20	Wickham C 2 + 11	Kemp D — + 5	Hayden K 13 + 2	Smith M 2 + 2	*Match No.*
1	2	3	4	5^1	6	7^3	8	9	10^2	11	12	13	14																	1
	2	3	4	5^3	6	9^2	7	8	10	11^1		13		1	12	14														2
	3	2	4	13	6	9^3	7	8^1	10	11	5^2	14		1			12													3
	3	2	8^3	5	6	9	7		11^1	10^2	14			1		12	4	13												4
	3	2		5	6	9^3	7^2	8	10	11^1		13		1	12	14	4													5
	3	2		14	6	10	8	9				13		1	7^1	12	4	11^2	5^3											6
	3	2		5^2	6	11	7	8	10^3			9^1		1	12		4		13	14										7
	3	2		13	7	10	8^3	9	11			6^1		1	14		4		5^2	12										8
	3	2		5	7	10^2	8	9	11			6^1		1	13		4			12										9
	3	2	4^3		6	9	7	8	10^2	12				1			14		5	11^1	13									10
	3	2			6	9^2	7	8	10	12		13		1			4		5	11^1										11
	3	2^3		14	6	9^1		8	10^2	11		12		1			4		5	13	7									12
	3	2			6	11		8	13	10^1		9		1			4		5	12	7^2									13
	3	2	8^1	12	6	11			13	10		9^2		1			4		5		7									14
	3	2	14		6	11		8^3		10^2		12		1	9^1		4		5	13	7									15
	3	2		13	9	11	12	8^2			14			1	7^1		4		5^3	10	6									16
		3			9	11		8		13	2	12		1	7^1		4		5	10^2	6									17
	13	3			6	11		8		12	2^2	9^3		1	14		4		5	10^1	7									18
	3	2			9^2	11	7^1	8	14	10^3		12		1	6		4	13	5											19
	3^1	2		5	9	11	6	8	13	10	12			1	7^2		4													20
		3		5	9		7	8	10^2		2	11^1		1	6	13	4	12												21
	3	2			6	11		8	12	10^3		9^1		1	7^2		4	14	5		13									22
	3	2			6	11	12	8	9^3	10^1				1	7^2		4	14	5		13									23
	3	2^2		13	6	11		8	9^3	10		14		1	12		4		5		7^1									24
	3	2		5^2	6^1	11	7	8	14	10					12		4		13			1	9^3							25
		3		5^2	6	11	7	8	14	10^1	13	12					4		2				9^3	1						26
		3		2		10		5	9^2	11		12			6		4						8	1	7^1	13				27
		3		2		9		5	10	11^1		13			6		4						8^2	1	7	12				28
	3	2		5		11		8	10			12			6^1		4						9^2	1	7	13				29
	3	2		5		11^2		8	10	12					6		4						9^1	1	7		13			30
	3	2		13		11		8	9	10^2							4							1	7	12		5^1	6	31
	3	2		5		9		8	10			13			6^2		4						11^1	1	7	12				32
	3	2		5^3		11		8	9	10^2					7^1		4				12			1	6	13		14		33
	3	2		8		11^2			9	12					7^3		4				14		13	1	6	10^1		5		34
	2	3		8		11			9	10^1					13		4				7^2			1	6	12		5		35
	3	2		5		11^3		8■	9^2	10		14			6^1		4				12			1	7			13		36
	3	2		5^1		14			11	10^3							4				13		9	1	7		12	8	6^2	37
	3	2				11		8	9	10^2		14			7^1		4^3				12		13	1	6			5		38
	3	2				11		8	9^2	10^3		13			12		4				6^1			1	7	14		5		39
	3	2				11		8	9	10^3					6^2		4				13		12	1	7	14		5^1		40
	3	2				11		8	9^2	10^1					6^3		4						12	1	7	13		5	14	41
	3	2				9		8	11	13					6^3		4						12	1	7	10^2	14	5^1		42
	3	2				11		8	9	10^1		12			7^2		4				13		14	1	6			5^3		43
	3	2				11		8	10^2			9^1			6		4				12		13	1	7			5		44
	3	2				11^2		8	10						12		4				6^1		9	1	7		13	5		45
	3	2				11^2		9	10						8^1		4				7^3			1	6	13	12	5	14	46

FA Cup

First Round	Stevenage	(h)	2-2
Replay	Stevenage	(a)	1-2
(aet)			

Carabao Cup

First Round	Bournemouth	(a)	0-5

League One Play-offs

Semi-Final 1st leg	Wycombe W	(a)	0-2
Semi-Final 2nd leg	Wycombe W	(h)	1-0

Papa John's Trophy

Group C (S)	Burton Alb	(a)	2-1
Group C (S)	Wycombe W	(h)	2-1
Group C (S)	Aston Villa U21	(h)	2-4
Second Round	Leyton Orient	(a)	0-0
(Milton Keynes D won 5-4 on penalties)			
Third Round	Charlton Ath	(a)	0-1

MORECAMBE

FOUNDATION

Several attempts to start a senior football club in a rugby stronghold finally succeeded on 7 May 1920 at the West View Hotel, Morecambe and a team competed in the Lancashire Combination for 1920–21. The club shared with a local cricket club at Woodhill Lane for the first season and a crowd of 3,000 watched the first game. The club moved to Roseberry Park, the name of which was changed to Christie Park after J.B. Christie who as President had purchased the ground.

Mazuma Stadium, Christie Way, Westgate, Morecambe, Lancashire LA4 4TB.

Telephone: (01524) 411 797.

Ticket Office: (01524) 411 797.

Website: www.morecambefc.com

Email: office@morecambefc.com

Ground Capacity: 6,241.

Record Attendance: 9,383 v Weymouth, FA Cup 3rd rd, 6 January 1962 (at Christie Park); 5,831 v Sunderland, FL 1, 30 April 2022 (at Mazuma Stadium).

Pitch Measurements: 103m × 71m (112.5yd × 77.5yd).

Co-Chairmen: Graham Howse, Rod Taylor.

Manager: Derek Adams.

Assistant Manager: John McMahon.

Colours: Red shirts with white diagonal stripe and white trim, white shorts with red trim, red socks.

Year Formed: 1920.

Turned Professional: 1920.

Club Nickname: 'The Shrimps'.

Grounds: 1920, Woodhill Lane; 1921, Christie Park; 2010, Globe Arena (renamed Mazuma Stadium 2020).

First Football League game: 11 August 2007, FL 2, v Barnet (h) D 0–0 – Lewis; Yates, Adams, Artell, Bentley, Stanley, Baker (Burns), Sorvel, Twiss (Newby), Curtis, Hunter (Thompson).

HONOURS

League: *Runners-up:* Conference – (3rd) 2006–07 *(promoted via play-offs)*.

FA Cup: 3rd rd – 1962, 2001, 2003, 2021, 2022.

League Cup: 3rd rd – 2008, 2021.

FOOTBALL YEARBOOK FACT FILE

Morecambe, then members of the Lancashire Combination, had their first set of floodlights installed in October 1960 at a cost of £5,000. The opening of the lights was celebrated by a game between the Shrimps and an All-Star XI which included former England internationals Tom Finney and Stan Mortensen. Morecambe won the game 4-3 and one of the highlights was a hat-trick for the losers by Mortensen.

Record League Victory: 6–0 v Crawley T, FL 2, 10 September 2011 – Roche; Reid, Wilson (pen), McCready, Haining (Parrish), Fenton (1), Drummond, McDonald, Price (Jevons), Carlton (3) (Alessandra), Ellison (1).

Record Cup Victory: 6–2 v Nelson (a), Lancashire Trophy, 27 January 2004.

Record Defeat: 0–7 v Cambridge U, FL 2, 19 April 2016; 0–7 v Newcastle U, League Cup 3rd rd, 23 September 2020.

Most League Points (3 for a win): 78, FL 2, 2020–21.

Most League Goals: 73, FL 2, 2009–10.

Highest League Scorer in Season: Phil Jevons, 18, 2009–10.

Most League Goals in Total Aggregate: Kevin Ellison, 81, 2011–20.

Most League Goals in One Match: 3, Jon Newby v Rotherham U, FL 2, 29 March 2008.

Most Capped Player: Greg Leigh 6 (8) Jamaica.

Most League Appearances: Barry Roche, 436, 2008–20.

Youngest League Player: Aaron McGowan, 16 years 263 days, 20 April 2013.

Record Transfer Fee Received: £225,000 from Stockport Co for Carl Baker, July 2008.

Record Transfer Fee Paid: £50,000 to Southport for Carl Baker, July 2007.

Football League Record: 2006–07 Promoted from Conference; 2007–21 FL 2; 2021– FL 1.

MANAGERS

Jimmy Milne 1947–48
Albert Dainty 1955–56
Ken Horton 1956–61
Joe Dunn 1961–64
Geoff Twentyman 1964–65
Ken Waterhouse 1965–69
Ronnie Clayton 1969–70
Gerry Irving and Ronnie Mitchell 1970
Ken Waterhouse 1970–72
Dave Roberts 1972–75
Alan Spavin 1975–76
Johnny Johnson 1976–77
Tommy Ferber 1977–78
Mick Hogarth 1978–79
Don Curbage 1979–81
Jim Thompson 1981
Les Rigby 1981–84
Sean Gallagher 1984–85
Joe Wojciechowicz 1985–88
Eric Whalley 1988
Billy Wright 1988–89
Lawrie Milligan 1989
Bryan Griffiths 1989–93
Leighton James 1994
Jim Harvey 1994–2006
Sammy McIlroy 2006–11
Jim Bentley 2011–19
Derek Adams 2019–21
Stephen Robinson 2021–22
Derek Adams February 2022–

LATEST SEQUENCES

Longest Sequence of League Wins: 7, 31.10.2009 – 12.12.2009.

Longest Sequence of League Defeats: 7, 4.3.2017 – 1.4.2017.

Longest Sequence of League Draws: 5, 3.1.2015 – 31.1.2015.

Longest Sequence of Unbeaten League Matches: 12, 31.1.2009 – 21.3.2009.

Longest Sequence Without a League Win: 13, 20.3.2018 – 18.8.2018.

Successive Scoring Runs: 17 from 13.8.2011.

Successive Non-scoring Runs: 7 from 21.4.2018.

TEN YEAR LEAGUE RECORD

		P	W	D	L	F	A	Pts	Pos
2012-13	FL 2	46	15	13	18	55	61	58	16
2013-14	FL 2	46	13	15	18	52	64	54	18
2014-15	FL 2	46	17	12	17	53	52	63	11
2015-16	FL 2	46	12	10	24	69	91	46	21
2016-17	FL 2	46	14	10	22	53	73	52	18
2017-18	FL 2	46	9	19	18	41	56	46	22
2018-19	FL 2	46	14	12	20	54	70	54	18
2019-20	FL 2	37	7	11	19	35	60	32	22§
2020-21	FL 2	46	23	9	14	69	58	78	4
2021-22	FL 1	46	10	12	24	57	88	42	19

§Decided on points-per-game (0.86)

DID YOU KNOW ?

Centre-forward Fred Bedford scored a hat-trick in each of his first three appearances for Morecambe after signing from neighbours Lancaster Town in the summer of 1928. By early October he had scored a fourth hat-trick and had 15 goals in seven Lancashire Combination appearances plus another two in FA Cup ties, performances which earned him a move into League football with Bradford City.

MORECAMBE – SKY BET LEAGUE ONE 2021–22 LEAGUE RECORD

Match No.	Date	Venue	Opponents	Result	H/T Score	Lg Pos.	Goalscorers	Attendance
1	Aug 7	A	Ipswich T	D 2-2	1-0	9	Stockton 2 [22, 72]	21,037
2	14	H	Shrewsbury T	W 2-0	2-0	5	Phillips (pen) [34], Stockton [44]	3772
3	17	H	Rotherham U	L 0-1	0-0	11		4004
4	21	A	Gillingham	L 1-2	1-1	16	Stockton [25]	3789
5	28	H	Sheffield W	W 1-0	0-0	14	Adeniran (og) [63]	5481
6	Sept 11	H	AFC Wimbledon	L 3-4	0-1	17	Stockton 2 [49, 66], McLoughlin [54]	3173
7	18	A	Doncaster R	L 0-1	0-0	18		5651
8	21	A	Crewe Alex	W 3-1	2-0	16	Phillips [8], Gnahoua 2 [27, 85]	3542
9	25	H	Accrington S	D 3-3	2-2	16	Stockton 2 [15, 81], Phillips [27]	4142
10	28	H	Lincoln C	W 2-0	0-0	11	Stockton [53], Wootton [79]	3466
11	Oct 2	A	Wycombe W	L 3-4	2-0	13	McCalmont [4], Phillips [26], Ayunga [80]	4161
12	15	A	Burton Alb	L 2-3	1-2	13	Gibson [3], Stockton [90]	2477
13	19	A	Cheltenham T	L 1-3	1-1	18	Phillips [38]	2909
14	23	H	Plymouth Arg	D 1-1	1-1	17	Ayunga [6]	4272
15	30	A	Oxford U	L 1-3	0-1	19	Stockton [64]	8766
16	Nov 2	H	Cambridge U	L 0-2	0-1	20		3414
17	20	A	Fleetwood T	W 2-1	1-0	18	Jones [11], Stockton [90]	3545
18	23	H	Charlton Ath	D 2-2	1-2	19	Stockton (pen) [29], O'Connor [72]	4009
19	27	H	Milton Keynes D	L 0-4	0-2	20		3700
20	Dec 7	A	Sunderland	L 0-5	0-2	20		26,516
21	11	A	Portsmouth	L 0-2	0-1	21		15,001
22	18	H	Fleetwood T	D 0-0	0-0	21		4018
23	29	H	Crewe Alex	L 1-2	1-0	21	Leigh [36]	3831
24	Jan 2	H	Doncaster R	W 4-3	0-3	19	Stockton 2 [52, 74], Obika [83], Diagouraga [85]	4001
25	15	A	AFC Wimbledon	D 0-0	0-0	21		7128
26	18	H	Wigan Ath	L 1-2	1-1	21	Stockton [7]	5359
27	22	H	Wycombe W	W 3-2	1-1	21	O'Connor [39], Ayunga [60], Stockton [67]	3865
28	29	A	Accrington S	D 2-2	2-2	21	Ayunga 2 [14, 26]	3527
29	Feb 1	A	Sheffield W	L 0-2	0-0	21		19,261
30	5	H	Bolton W	D 1-1	0-0	21	Stockton [73]	5617
31	8	A	Lincoln C	L 1-2	0-2	21	Diagouraga [56]	7571
32	12	H	Gillingham	D 1-1	0-0	21	Obika [84]	4499
33	22	A	Rotherham U	L 0-2	0-2	21		8376
34	26	H	Ipswich T	D 1-1	0-0	21	Wildig [59]	4928
35	Mar 5	A	Plymouth Arg	L 0-2	0-2	21		12,228
36	8	A	Bolton W	D 1-1	1-0	21	Stockton [41]	14,559
37	12	H	Cheltenham T	L 1-3	0-1	22	Leigh [52]	3733
38	15	A	Shrewsbury T	L 0-5	0-1	22		5804
39	19	A	Wigan Ath	L 1-4	0-2	22	Connolly (pen) [49]	10,072
40	Apr 2	H	Burton Alb	W 3-0	2-0	21	Gnahoua [41], Phillips [45], Stockton [46]	5238
41	5	H	Oxford U	W 2-1	2-1	20	Wildig [14], Stockton [25]	3882
42	9	A	Cambridge U	L 1-2	0-1	20	Stockton [68]	5813
43	15	A	Charlton Ath	W 3-2	2-0	19	Stockton [26], Gnahoua 2 [43, 59]	10,700
44	18	H	Portsmouth	D 1-1	0-1	19	Ayunga [90]	4893
45	23	A	Milton Keynes D	L 0-2	0-1	19		10,101
46	30	H	Sunderland	L 0-1	0-1	19		5831

Final League Position: 19

GOALSCORERS

League (57): Stockton 23 (1 pen), Ayunga 6, Phillips 6 (1 pen), Gnahoua 5, Diagouraga 2, Leigh 2, O'Connor 2, Obika 2, Wildig 2, Connolly 1 (1 pen), Gibson 1, Jones 1, McCalmont 1, McLoughlin 1, Wootton 1, own goal 1.
FA Cup (3): O'Connor 1, Stockton 1, Wildig 1.
Carabao Cup (4): Stockton 2, O'Connor 1, Phillips 1 (1 pen).
Papa John's Trophy (2): Jones 1 (1 pen), McLoughlin 1.

Letheren K 11 + 1	Cooney R 22 + 10	O'Connor A 39 + 1	Delaney R 10 + 3	Gibson L 23 + 6	McLoughlin S 31 + 5	Diagouraga T 32 + 8	McCalmont A 18 + 8	Gnahoua A 31 + 3	Stockton C 44	McDonald W 9 + 8	Lavelle S 4 + 1	Ayunga J 20 + 16	Leigh G 33 + 3	Andersson J 13	Phillips A 27 + 11	McPake J 3 + 2	Wootton S 9 + 1	Mellor K 1	Harrison S — + 3	Jones C 9 + 2	Duffus C 3 + 4	Wildig A 16 + 6	McLaughlin R 18 + 1	Price F — + 3	Obika J 3 + 9	Carson T 21	Bedeau J 22	Fane O 9 + 3	Bennett R 11 + 2	Connolly D 13 + 2	Smith A 1	Mensah J — + 1	*Match No.*
1	2	3	4^{1}	5	6	7	8	9^{3}	10	11^{2}	12	13	14																				1
	2	4			8^{3}	7	12	9	10	13	3		5	1	6^{1}	11^{2}	14																2
	5	4			6^{1}	7	8	9^{2}	10	13	3			1	12	11^{3}		2	14														3
	2	4			13	6		9	10	12	3		5	1	8^{3}	11^{1}				7^{2}	14												4
	2	4	13	14	6	7	8^{1}	11	10		3		5^{3}	1	12						9^{2}												5
	2	4	11	3^{1}	6	7	13	9	10	12			5	1								8^{2}											6
	2	4		13	8	7	6^{1}	9	10	11^{3}			5^{2}	1	12	14	3																7
1	2^{2}	4		12	8	7	14	9	10	11^{1}			5		6^{3}		3						13										8
1		3		5	8▮	7	12	11^{2}	10	9^{1}		13			6^{3}	14	4						2										9
1		3	13	5		7	8	11^{3}	10	9^{2}		14			6^{1}		4			12			2										10
1	12	3	5	6		8	7	10^{3}	11			14			9^{2}		4			13			2^{1}										11
1	2	3		5		7	6	11^{1}	10	9^{3}		12	14		8^{2}		4					13											12
	12	2	3	9^{1}	7	8^{2}		14	11	13		10	5	1	6		4^{3}																13
	2	3	4			7		9	10	12		11^{1}	5	1	6^{2}					8				13									14
	2	3	4			7	12		10	11		9^{3}	5	1	8^{1}				14	6^{2}				13									15
		4				7^{3}	8		10	11^{1}		9	5	1	12		3		14	6^{2}			2	13									16
		3	4		8^{1}	12	6	11	10			9^{2}	5	1	13					7			2										17
		3	4		8		6		10			9	5	1	12					7	11^{1}		2										18
		3	4	12	6		8	13		9		11	5	1						7	10^{2}		2^{1}										19
1		3	4			13	8	11^{2}	10			9	5		14					7^{1}	12	6^{3}	2										20
1		2	12	4	7		8		11			13	9		6		3^{1}						5		10^{2}								21
1	2	4		5	9	13	8^{2}		11			12	6		7^{3}							14	3		10^{1}								22
1		4		3	9	12		13		14		11	6		8^{1}					5		7^{3}	2		10^{2}								23
1	14	3		4	6	7	8^{1}	11^{2}	10			9^{3}	5									12	2		13								24
	13	3			6	7	14	11^{1}	10	12		9^{3}	5									8^{2}	2			1	4						25
	13	3		12	6^{3}	7		9	10			11^{2}	5^{1}		14							8	2			1	4						26
	2	3			6	7		11	10^{2}			9	5								13	8^{1}				1	4	12					27
	2	3		5^{1}	6	7		11	10			9			13							8^{2}				1	4		12				28
12	2^{3}	3			6	7		9^{2}	10			11^{4}			8								5		14	1^{1}	4		13	15			29
		3			6	7		11^{2}	10			9	5		8^{1}								2				4	12		13	1		30
	2	3			6	7	12		10			11^{2}	5		8										13	1	4			9^{1}			31
	2	3			8	7		9^{2}	10			11	5		6^{1}							12			13	1	4						32
	5	2			9	7^{3}			11			10^{1}	8								14	13			12	1	4	6^{2}	3				33
	5^{1}	2			9	7			11			10^{2}	8		12							13				1	4	6	3				34
	5	2		8	9		6		11^{1}			13			7										12	1	4		3	10^{2}			35
	14	3		6^{2}	2	9			10				13		7							8^{1}				1	5	12	4^{3}	11			36
		2		4^{2}	5	7	6^{1}		11			13	8		9										12	1	3			10			37
	12	2		4^{3}	5	7	8^{1}		11			13	9									6				1	3			10^{2}		14	38
	2	3		13	8^{1}	7		11^{3}	10			14	5		12							6				1	4^{2}			9			39
	13			5		12		11	10			14			6^{3}							8	2^{2}			1	4	7^{1}	3	9			40
	12			5	13	14		9^{2}	10						8^{3}							6	2^{1}			1	4	7	3	11			41
				5	14			11^{1}	10			12	2		8							6^{3}			13	1	4	7	3^{2}	9			42
	12	13		5^{1}	14			11	10				2		8							6^{3}				1	4	7	3	9^{2}			43
				5		13	14	11	10			12	2		6							8^{1}				1	4	7^{3}	3	9^{2}			44
				5	13	7		11^{1}	10			12	2		8											1	4	6^{2}	3	9			45
	2			5		13		11^{1}	10			12			6							8			14	1	4	7^{2}	3	9^{3}			46

FA Cup

First Round	Newport Co	(h)	1-0
Second Round	Buxton	(a)	1-0
Third Round	Tottenham H	(a)	1-3

Carabao Cup

First Round	Blackburn R	(a)	2-1
Second Round	Preston NE	(h)	2-4

Papa John's Trophy

Group A (N)	Everton U21	(h)	0-1
Group A (N)	Hartlepool U	(a)	2-2
(Hartlepool won 4-2 on penalties)			
Group A (N)	Carlisle U	(h)	0-2

NEWCASTLE UNITED

FOUNDATION

In October 1882 a club called Stanley, which had been formed in 1881, changed its name to Newcastle East End to avoid confusion with two other local clubs, Stanley Nops and Stanley Albion. Shortly afterwards another club, Rosewood, merged with them. Newcastle West End had been formed in August 1882 and they played on a pitch which was part of the Town Moor. They moved to Brandling Park in 1885 and St James' Park 1886 (home of Newcastle Rangers). West End went out of existence after a bad run and the remaining committee men invited East End to move to St James' Park. They accepted and, at a meeting in Bath Lane Hall in 1892, changed their name to Newcastle United.

St James' Park, Newcastle-upon-Tyne NE1 4ST.

Telephone: (0344) 372 1892.

Ticket Office: (0344) 372 1892 (option 1).

Website: www.nufc.co.uk

Email: admin@nufc.com

Ground Capacity: 52,305.

Record Attendance: 68,386 v Chelsea, Division 1, 3 September 1930.

Pitch Measurements: 105m × 68m (115yd × 74.5yd).

Managing Director: Lee Charnley.

Head Coach: Eddie Howe.

Assistant Head Coach: Jason Tindall.

Colours: Black and white striped shirts, black shorts with white trim, black socks with white and light blue trim.

Year Formed: 1881.

Turned Professional: 1889.

Previous Names: 1881, Stanley; 1882, Newcastle East End; 1892, Newcastle United.

Club Nickname: 'The Magpies', 'The Toon'.

Grounds: 1881, South Byker; 1886, Chillingham Road, Heaton; 1892, St James' Park.

First Football League Game: 2 September 1893, Division 2, v Royal Arsenal (a) D 2–2 – Ramsay; Jeffery, Miller; Crielly, Graham, McKane; Bowman, Crate (1), Thompson, Sorley (1), Wallace. Graham not Crate scored according to some reports.

Record League Victory: 13–0 v Newport Co, Division 2, 5 October 1946 – Garbutt; Cowell, Graham; Harvey, Brennan, Wright; Milburn (2), Bentley (1), Wayman (4), Shackleton (6), Pearson.

HONOURS

League Champions: Division 1 – 1904–05, 1906–07, 1908–09, 1926–27; FL C – 2009–10, 2016–17; First Division – 1992–93; Division 2 – 1964–65.
Runners-up: Premier League – 1995–96, 1996–97; Division 2 – 1897–98, 1947–48.

FA Cup Winners: 1910, 1924, 1932, 1951, 1952, 1955.
Runners-up: 1905, 1906, 1908, 1911, 1974, 1998, 1999.

League Cup: *Runners-up:* 1976.

Texaco Cup Winners: 1974, 1975.
Anglo-Italian Cup Winners: 1972–73.

European Competitions
Champions League: 1997–98, 2002–03, 2003–04.
Fairs Cup: 1968–69 *(winners)*, 1969–70 *(qf)*, 1970–71.
UEFA Cup: 1977–78, 1994–95, 1996–97 *(qf)*, 1999–2000, 2003–04 *(sf)*, 2004–05 *(qf)*, 2006–07.
Europa League: 2012–13 *(qf)*.
European Cup Winners' Cup: 1998–99.
Intertoto Cup: 2001 *(runners-up)*, 2005, 2006 *(winners)*.

FOOTBALL YEARBOOK FACT FILE

Newcastle United were tenants of St James' Park from their formation in 1892, the landlords being the local council. For many years they were in an insecure position, initially occupying the ground on seven-year leases and latterly 21 years, and as a result of this the directors were unwilling to make a substantial investment in ground development. This changed in 1971 when a 99-year lease was granted and since then the stadium has been completely modernised.

Record Cup Victory: 9–0 v Southport (at Hillsborough), FA Cup 4th rd, 1 February 1932 – McInroy; Nelson, Fairhurst; McKenzie, Davidson, Weaver (1); Boyd (1), Jimmy Richardson (3), Cape (2), McMenemy (1), Lang (1).

Record Defeat: 0–9 v Burton Wanderers, Division 2, 15 April 1895.

Most League Points (2 for a win): 57, Division 2, 1964–65.

Most League Points (3 for a win): 102, FL C, 2009–10.

Most League Goals: 98, Division 1, 1951–52.

Highest League Scorer in Season: Hughie Gallacher, 36, Division 1, 1926–27.

Most League Goals in Total Aggregate: Jackie Milburn, 177, 1946–57.

Most League Goals in One Match: 6, Len Shackleton v Newport Co, Division 2, 5 October 1946.

Most Capped Player: Shay Given, 82 (134), Republic of Ireland.

Most League Appearances: Jim Lawrence, 432, 1904–22.

Youngest League Player: Steve Watson, 16 years 223 days v Wolverhampton W, 10 November 1990.

Record Transfer Fee Received: £35,000,000 from Liverpool for Andy Carroll, January 2011.

Record Transfer Fee Paid: £40,000,000 to TSG 1899 Hoffenheim for Joelinton, July 2019.

Football League Record: 1893 Elected to Division 2; 1898–1934 Division 1; 1934–48 Division 2; 1948–61 Division 1; 1961–65 Division 2; 1965–78 Division 1; 1978–84 Division 2; 1984–89 Division 1; 1989–92 Division 2; 1992–93 Division 1; 1993–2009 Premier League; 2009–10 FL C; 2010–16 Premier League; 2016–17 FL C; 2017– Premier League.

MANAGERS

Frank Watt 1895–32
(Secretary-Manager)
Andy Cunningham 1930–35
Tom Mather 1935–39
Stan Seymour 1939–47
(Hon. Manager)
George Martin 1947–50
Stan Seymour 1950–54
(Hon. Manager)
Duggie Livingstone 1954–56
Stan Seymour 1956–58
(Hon. Manager)
Charlie Mitten 1958–61
Norman Smith 1961–62
Joe Harvey 1962–75
Gordon Lee 1975–77
Richard Dinnis 1977
Bill McGarry 1977–80
Arthur Cox 1980–84
Jack Charlton 1984
Willie McFaul 1985–88
Jim Smith 1988–91
Ossie Ardiles 1991–92
Kevin Keegan 1992–97
Kenny Dalglish 1997–98
Ruud Gullit 1998–99
Sir Bobby Robson 1999–2004
Graeme Souness 2004–06
Glenn Roeder 2006–07
Sam Allardyce 2007–08
Kevin Keegan 2008
Joe Kinnear 2008–09
Alan Shearer 2009
Chris Hughton 2009–10
Alan Pardew 2010–15
John Carver 2015
Steve McClaren 2015–16
Rafael Benitez 2016–19
Steve Bruce 2019–21
Eddie Howe November 2021–

LATEST SEQUENCES

Longest Sequence of League Wins: 13, 25.4.1992 – 18.10.1992.

Longest Sequence of League Defeats: 10, 23.8.1977 – 15.10.1977.

Longest Sequence of League Draws: 4, 15.11.2008 – 6.12.2008.

Longest Sequence of Unbeaten League Matches: 17, 13.2.2010 – 2.5.2010.

Longest Sequence Without a League Win: 21, 14.1.1978 – 23.8.1978.

Successive Scoring Runs: 25 from 15.4.1939.

Successive Non-scoring Runs: 6 from 29.10.1988.

TEN YEAR LEAGUE RECORD

		P	W	D	L	F	A	Pts	Pos
2012-13	PR Lge	38	11	8	19	45	68	41	16
2013-14	PR Lge	38	15	4	19	43	59	49	10
2014-15	PR Lge	38	10	9	19	40	63	39	15
2015-16	PR Lge	38	9	10	19	44	65	37	18
2016-17	FL C	46	29	7	10	85	40	94	1
2017-18	PR Lge	38	12	8	18	39	47	44	10
2018-19	PR Lge	38	12	9	17	42	48	45	13
2019-20	PR Lge	38	11	11	16	38	58	44	13
2020-21	PR Lge	38	12	9	17	46	62	45	12
2021-22	PR Lge	38	13	10	15	44	62	49	11

DID YOU KNOW ?

Legendary centre-forward Hughie Gallacher spent five seasons on the books of Newcastle United between 1925 and 1930 and finished as the team's top scorer on each occasion. Among his many feats for the Magpies were scoring a total of 14 hat-tricks and enjoying a run of six first-team appearances when he scored two or more goals on each occasion.

NEWCASTLE UNITED – PREMIER LEAGUE 2021–22 LEAGUE RECORD

Match No.	*Date*	*Venue*	*Opponents*	*Result*	*H/T Score*	*Lg Pos.*	*Goalscorers*	*Attendance*
1	Aug 15	H	West Ham U	L 2-4	2-1	15	Wilson ^{5}, Murphy ^{40}	50,673
2	21	A	Aston Villa	L 0-2	0-1	19		41,964
3	28	H	Southampton	D 2-2	0-0	15	Wilson ^{55}, Saint-Maximin ^{90}	44,017
4	Sept 11	A	Manchester U	L 1-4	0-1	19	Manquillo ^{56}	72,732
5	17	H	Leeds U	D 1-1	1-1	18	Saint-Maximin ^{44}	50,407
6	25	A	Watford	D 1-1	1-0	17	Longstaff, S ^{23}	20,650
7	Oct 2	A	Wolverhampton W	L 1-2	1-1	19	Hendrick ^{41}	30,483
8	17	H	Tottenham H	L 2-3	1-3	19	Wilson ^{2}, Dier (og) ^{89}	52,214
9	23	A	Crystal Palace	D 1-1	0-0	19	Wilson ^{65}	24,609
10	30	H	Chelsea	L 0-3	0-0	19		52,208
11	Nov 6	A	Brighton & HA	D 1-1	0-1	19	Hayden ^{66}	31,267
12	20	H	Brentford	D 3-3	2-2	20	Lascelles ^{10}, Joelinton ^{39}, Saint-Maximin ^{75}	52,131
13	27	A	Arsenal	L 0-2	0-0	20		59,886
14	30	H	Norwich C	D 1-1	0-0	20	Wilson (pen) ^{61}	50,757
15	Dec 4	H	Burnley	W 1-0	1-0	19	Wilson ^{40}	51,948
16	12	A	Leicester C	L 0-4	0-1	19		31,959
17	16	A	Liverpool	L 1-3	1-2	19	Shelvey ^{7}	52,951
18	19	H	Manchester C	L 0-4	0-2	19		52,127
19	27	H	Manchester U	D 1-1	1-0	19	Saint-Maximin ^{7}	52,178
20	Jan 15	H	Watford	D 1-1	0-0	19	Saint-Maximin ^{49}	52,223
21	22	A	Leeds U	W 1-0	0-0	18	Shelvey ^{75}	36,405
22	Feb 8	H	Everton	W 3-1	1-1	17	Holgate (og) ^{37}, Fraser ^{56}, Trippier ^{80}	52,186
23	13	H	Aston Villa	W 1-0	1-0	17	Trippier ^{35}	52,207
24	19	A	West Ham U	D 1-1	1-1	17	Willock ^{45}	59,949
25	26	A	Brentford	W 2-0	2-0	14	Joelinton ^{33}, Willock ^{44}	17,039
26	Mar 5	H	Brighton & HA	W 2-1	2-0	14	Fraser ^{12}, Schar ^{14}	52,214
27	10	A	Southampton	W 2-1	1-1	14	Wood ^{32}, Bruno Guimaraes ^{52}	31,016
28	13	A	Chelsea	L 0-1	0-0	14		40,026
29	17	A	Everton	L 0-1	0-0	14		39,068
30	Apr 3	A	Tottenham H	L 1-5	1-1	15	Schar ^{39}	57,553
31	8	H	Wolverhampton W	W 1-0	0-0	14	Wood (pen) ^{72}	52,164
32	17	H	Leicester C	W 2-1	1-1	14	Bruno Guimaraes 2 $^{30, 90}$	52,104
33	20	H	Crystal Palace	W 1-0	1-0	11	Almiron ^{32}	51,938
34	23	A	Norwich C	W 3-0	2-0	9	Joelinton 2 $^{35, 41}$, Bruno Guimaraes ^{49}	26,910
35	30	H	Liverpool	L 0-1	0-1	10		52,281
36	May 8	A	Manchester C	L 0-5	0-2	13		53,336
37	16	H	Arsenal	W 2-0	0-0	12	White (og) ^{55}, Bruno Guimaraes ^{85}	52,274
38	22	A	Burnley	W 2-1	1-0	11	Wilson 2 (1 pen) $^{20 (p), 60}$	21,361

Final League Position: 11

GOALSCORERS

League (44): Wilson 8 (2 pens), Bruno Guimaraes 5, Saint-Maximin 5, Joelinton 4, Fraser 2, Schar 2, Shelvey 2, Trippier 2, Willock 2, Wood 2 (1 pen), Almiron 1, Hayden 1, Hendrick 1, Lascelles 1, Longstaff, S 1, Manquillo 1, Murphy 1, own goals 3.
FA Cup (0).
Carabao Cup (0).
Papa John's Trophy (3): Ndiweni 1, Stephenson 1, White 1.

Woodman F 4	Murphy J 13 + 20	Krafth E 18 + 2	Fernandez F 5 + 2	Clark C 12 + 1	Ritchie M 14 + 4	Hayden I 12 + 2	Shelvey J 22 + 2	Almiron M 19 + 11	Wilson C 16 + 2	Saint-Maximin A 31 + 4	Fraser R 18 + 9	Longstaff S 15 + 9	Joelinton d 30 + 5	Schar F 25	Lascelles J 22 + 4	Willock J 24 + 5	Manquillo J 15 + 4	Lewis J 4 + 1	Hendrick J — + 3	Darlow K 8	Gayle D — + 8	Dubravka M 26	Trippier K 5 + 1	Dummett P 2 + 1	Wood C 15 + 2	Targett M 16	Bruno Guimaraes M 11 + 6	Burn D 16	*Match No.*
1	2	3^2	4	5	6	7	8^1	9	10^3	11	12	13	14																1
1	2		5^2		6	8^1		9	10	11	14	12	13	3	4	7^3													2
1	5		2		9			8	10^1	11	13	7	12	4	3	6^2													3
1	12			5^2	6	3		7		11		9	10		4	8^3	2^1	13	14										4
	14	13		5	6	3		7^1		11	12	9	10^3		4	8	2^2			1									5
	12		3	4	5	6		7^1		11		9	10			8^2	2			1	13								6
	13		3	4	5	9		7^3		11		6	10			8^1	2^2		12	1	14								7
	14			4	5	6	12■		11^2	7	13	9^1	10		3	8^3	2			1									8
		3		5	6	7		12	10	11^3	9^1	8^2	14		4	13	2			1									9
		3		5	6	8^2	14	13	10	11	9^1	7^3			4	12	2			1									10
	2	3^2		5	6	8	9	7^1	11	10			12		4					1	13								11
	5			4	8		7		10	11	12	13	9	2^1	3	6^2				1									12
	13	2			5^1	14	7^3	12	10	9	6		11^2	4	3	8						1							13
			12	4■		13	7	14	10	9^3	6^1		11	3		8^2	2	5				1							14
	13		12				7	6^1	10	9^2			11	3	4	8	2	5				1							15
	13				14		7^3	6^2	10	9	12		11	3	4	8	2	5^1				1							16
	6				12	7	8		13	11^2	10^3		9	3	4	14	2	5^1				1							17
	2			4	5	8^2		6^3	11	12	10	13	9		3	7^1			14			1							18
	12	2					8	13	11^1	10^3	6^2	7	9	3	4		5				14	1							19
	12						7	13		11^2	9^1	6	8	4	3							1	2	5	10				20
				14			7			11	9	12	8^1	4	3^3	6	13					1	2	5^2	10				21
	12						7			11	9^1		8	4	3	6^2	13					1	2^3		10	5	14		22
		13					7			11	9		8	3		6^3	5^1					1	2^2	12	10		14	4	23
	11	2					7	12			9^1		8	3		6^2						1			10	5	13	4	24
	9^1	2					7	14			11^3		8	3	13	6^2						1			10	5	12	4	25
	9^1	2					7			12	11^2	14	8	3		6^3						1			10	5	13	4	26
	9	2^3					7	13			11^2	12		3		6	14					1			10	5	8^1	4	27
	10^3							7^1		12	14	9		4	3		2^2				13	1			11	6	8	5	28
	13	2^3						9^1		12	11^2		8	3		6	14					1			10	5	7	4	29
	13						7			11	9		8^1	3	14	6	2^2					1			10^3	5	12	4	30
	14	2					7	12		11^3	9^1	13	8	3								1			10	5	6^2	4	31
	13	2					7	9^2		11^3			8	3		12					14	1			10^1	5	6	4	32
	12	2					7	9^2		11^1		14	8	3		13						1			10	5	6^3	4	33
	9^2	2			13			12		11		6	10^1		3	8					14	1				5	7^3	4	34
	14	2^3					7	9		10			11	3^1	12	8^2						1			13	5	6	4	35
	14	2^2						9^3	13	11		6	8		3							1	12		10^1	5	7	4	36
	13	2						9^2	10^4	11^3	14	6	8	3^1	12						15	1				5	7	4	37
	12				14			9^3	10	11^2		6	8^1		3							1	2		13	5	7	4	38

FA Cup
Third Round Cambridge U (h) 0-1

Carabao Cup
Second Round Burnley (h) 0-0
(Burnley won 4-3 on penalties)

Papa John's Trophy (Newcastle U U21)
Group H (N) Sheffield W (a) 0-3
Group H (N) Harrogate T (a) 0-2
Group H (N) Mansfield T (a) 3-6

NEWPORT COUNTY

FOUNDATION

In 1912 Newport County were formed following a meeting at The Tredegar Arms Hotel. A professional football club had existed in the town called Newport FC, but they ceased to exist in 1907. The first season as Newport County was in the second division of the Southern League. They started life playing at Somerton Park where they remained through their League years. They were elected to the Football League for the beginning of the 1920–21 season as founder members of Division 3. At the end of the 1987–88 season, they were relegated from the Football League and replaced by Lincoln City. On 27 February 1989, Newport County went out of business and from the ashes Newport AFC was born. Starting down the pyramid in the Hellenic League, they eventally gained promotion to the Conference in 2011 and were promoted to the Football League after a play-off with Wrexham in 2013.

Rodney Parade, Rodney Road, Newport, South Wales NP19 0UU.

Telephone: (01633) 302 012.

Ticket Office: (01633) 264 572.

Website: www.newport-county.co.uk

Email: office@newport-county.co.uk

Ground Capacity: 8,722.

Record Attendance: 24,268 v Cardiff C, Division 3 (S), 16 October 1937 (Somerton Park); 4,660 v Swansea C, FA Cup 1st rd, 11 November 2006 (Newport Stadium); 9,836 v Tottenham H, FA Cup 4th rd, 27 January 2018 (Rodney Parade).

Pitch Measurements: 100m × 68m (109.5yd × 74.5yd).

Chairman: Gavin Foxall.

Manager: James Rowberry.

Assistant Manager: Wayne Hatswell.

Colours: Amber shirts with black trim, black shorts with amber trim, amber socks with black trim.

Year Formed: 1912.

Turned Professional: 1912.

Previous Names: Newport County, 1912; Newport AFC, 1989; Newport County, 1999.

Club Nicknames: 'The Exiles', 'The Ironsides', 'The Port', 'The County'.

Grounds: 1912–89, 1990–92, Somerton Park; 1992–94, Meadow Park Stadium; 1994, Newport Stadium; 2012, Rodney Parade.

First Football League Game: 28 August 1920, Division 3, v Reading (h) L 0–1.

HONOURS

League Champions: Division 3S – 1938–39.
Runners-up: Conference – (3rd) 2012–13 *(promoted via play-offs)*.

FA Cup: 5th rd – 1949, 2019.

League Cup: 4th rd – 2021.

Welsh Cup Winners: 1980.
Runners-up: 1963, 1987.

European Competitions
European Cup Winners' Cup: 1980–81 *(qf)*.

FOOTBALL YEARBOOK FACT FILE

Frank Peed signed for Newport County, then members of the Southern League, in the summer of 1931 and proved to be a prolific goalscorer. He netted 65 goals in all competitions during the season including six in a Southern League game against Taunton Town. His former club Norwich City had retained his Football League registration, so when County returned to the League for 1932–33 County had to negotiate for his transfer.

Record League Victory: 10–0 v Merthyr T, Division 3(S), 10 April 1930 – Martin (5), Gittins (2), Thomas (1), Bagley (1), Lawson (1).

Record Cup Victory: 7–0 v Working, FA Cup 1st rd, 24 November 1928 – Young (3), Pugh (2) Gittins (1), Reid (1).

Record Defeat: 0–13 v Newcastle U, Division 2, 5 October 1946.

Most League Points (2 for a win): 61, Division 4, 1979–80.

Most League Points (3 for a win): 78, Division 3, 1982–83.

Most League Goals: 85, Division 4, 1964–65.

Highest League Scorer in Season: Tudor Martin, 34, Division 3 (S), 1929–30.

Most League Goals in Total Aggregate: Reg Parker, 99, 1948–54.

Most League Goals in One Match: 5, Tudor Martin v Merthyr T, Dvision 3 (S), 10 April 1930.

Most Capped Player: Keanu Marsh Brown, 10 (15), Guyana.

Most League Appearances: Len Weare, 527, 1955–70.

Youngest League Player: Regan Poole, 16 years 94 days v Shrewsbury T, 20 September 2014.

Record Transfer Fee Received: £500,000 (rising to £1,000,000) from Peterborough U for Conor Washington, January 2014.

Record Transfer Fee Paid: £80,000 to Swansea C for Alan Waddle, January 1981.

Football League Record: 1920 Original member of Division 3; 1921–31 Division 3 (S) – dropped out of Football League; 1932 Re-elected to Division 3 (S); 1932–39 Division 3 (S); 1946–47 Division 2; 1947–58 Division 3 (S); 1958–62 Division 3; 1962–80 Division 4; 1980–87 Division 3; 1987–88 Division 4 (relegated from Football League); 2011 Promoted to Conference; 2011–13 Conference Premier; 2013– FL 2.

LATEST SEQUENCES

Longest Sequence of League Wins: 5, 17.10.2020 – 31.10.2020.

Longest Sequence of League Defeats: 8, 22.11.2016 – 7.1.2017.

Longest Sequence of League Draws: 4, 31.10.2015 – 24.11.2015.

Longest Sequence of Unbeaten League Matches: 17, 15.3.2019 – 7.9.2019.

Longest Sequence Without a League Win: 12, 15.3.2016 – 6.8.2017.

Successive Scoring Runs: 20 from 12.9.2020.

Successive Non-scoring Runs: 4 from 1.2.2020.

MANAGERS

Davy McDougle 1912–13 *(Player-Manager)*
Sam Hollis 1913–17
Harry Parkes 1919–22
Jimmy Hindmarsh 1922–35
Louis Page 1935–36
Tom Bromilow 1936–37
Billy McCandless 1937–45
Tom Bromilow 1945–50
Fred Stansfield 1950–53
Billy Lucas 1953–61
Bobby Evans 1961–62
Billy Lucas 1962–67
Leslie Graham 1967–69
Bobby Ferguson 1969–70 *(Player-Manager)*
Billy Lucas 1970–74
Brian Harris 1974–75
Dave Elliott 1975–76 *(Player-Manager)*
Jimmy Scoular 1976–77
Colin Addison 1977–78
Len Ashurst 1978–82
Colin Addison 1982–85
Bobby Smith 1985–86
John Relish 1986
Jimmy Mullen 1986–87
John Lewis 1987
Brian Eastick 1987–88
David Williams 1988
Eddie May 1988
John Mahoney 1988–89
John Relish 1989–93
Graham Rogers 1993–96
Chris Price 1997
Tim Harris 1997–2002
Peter Nicholas 2002–04
John Cornforth 2004–05
Peter Beadle 2005–08
Dean Holdsworth 2008–11
Anthony Hudson 2011
Justin Edinburgh 2011–15
Jimmy Dack 2015
Terry Butcher 2015
John Sheridan 2015–16
Warren Feeney 2016
Graham Westley 2016–17
Michael Flynn 2017–21
James Rowberry October 2021–

TEN YEAR LEAGUE RECORD

		P	W	D	L	F	A	Pts	Pos
2012-13	Conf P	46	25	10	11	85	60	85	3
2013-14	FL 2	46	14	16	16	56	59	58	14
2014-15	FL 2	46	18	11	17	51	54	65	9
2015-16	FL 2	46	10	13	23	43	64	43	22
2016-17	FL 2	46	12	12	22	51	73	48	22
2017-18	FL 2	46	16	16	14	56	58	64	11
2018-19	FL 2	46	20	11	15	59	59	71	7
2019-20	FL 2	36	12	10	14	32	39	46	14§
2020-21	FL 2	46	20	13	13	57	42	73	5
2021-22	FL 2	46	19	12	15	67	58	69	11

§Decided on points-per-game (1.28)

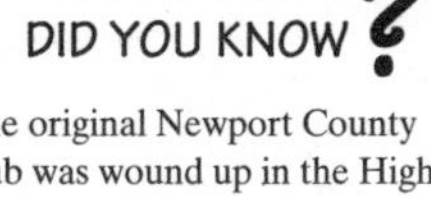

DID YOU KNOW ?

The original Newport County club was wound up in the High Court in February 1989 with debts of £16,145. Their final competitive game was in the third round of the Club Call Cup against Kidderminster Harriers. The match went into extra time before the visitors ran out 6-5 winners in front of a crowd of 895.

NEWPORT COUNTY – SKY BET LEAGUE TWO 2021–22 LEAGUE RECORD

Match No.	*Date*	*Venue*	*Opponents*	*Result*		*H/T Score*	*Lg Pos.*	*Goalscorers*	*Attendance*
1	Aug 7	A	Oldham Ath	W	1-0	0-0	5	Ellison [88]	4094
2	14	A	Mansfield T	L	1-2	1-2	13	Willmott [9]	3793
3	21	A	Tranmere R	W	1-0	0-0	8	Fisher [60]	6160
4	28	A	Salford C	L	0-3	0-3	15		1687
5	Sept 4	H	Leyton Orient	D	2-2	1-1	15	Dolan (pen) [45], Telford [80]	3845
6	10	A	Harrogate T	D	2-2	2-2	14	Bennett [3], Willmott [38]	2670
7	14	H	Northampton T	L	0-1	0-1	19		3168
8	18	H	Walsall	W	2-1	1-1	12	Demetriou [9], Clarke [87]	3825
9	24	A	Barrow	L	1-2	1-0	14	Azaz [10]	2427
10	Oct 2	H	Scunthorpe U	W	3-0	1-0	12	Cooper [6], Baker-Richardson [68], Telford [84]	3213
11	9	H	Bradford C	D	0-0	0-0	13		4089
12	16	A	Exeter C	D	2-2	2-1	14	Willmott [12], Baker-Richardson [28]	5078
13	19	H	Carlisle U	D	2-2	2-1	13	Telford 2 [27, 30]	2962
14	23	A	Bristol R	W	3-1	2-1	12	Baker-Richardson [27], Telford 2 [31, 61]	7500
15	30	H	Stevenage	W	5-0	3-0	8	Telford 3 [12, 27, 48], Baker-Richardson [34], Azaz [50]	3439
16	Nov 12	A	Hartlepool U	W	2-1	1-0	5	Baker-Richardson [32], Telford [90]	5764
17	20	H	Swindon T	L	1-2	0-0	8	Telford [74]	5141
18	23	A	Crawley T	D	1-1	0-0	9	Telford [84]	1483
19	26	A	Colchester U	D	1-1	1-0	9	Telford [36]	2401
20	Dec 7	H	Sutton U	W	3-2	0-2	8	Collins [53], Baker-Richardson [64], Dolan (pen) [90]	3368
21	11	H	Port Vale	W	2-1	0-1	4	Telford [69], Azaz [75]	4074
22	18	A	Rochdale	L	0-3	0-1	6		2232
23	Jan 1	A	Walsall	D	3-3	1-0	7	Telford 2 [4, 66], Wilkinson (og) [56]	4946
24	8	H	Salford C	L	0-2	0-1	7		1687
25	15	H	Harrogate T	W	4-0	2-0	6	Demetriou (pen) [8], Telford 2 [43, 49], Baker-Richardson [55]	0
26	22	A	Scunthorpe U	W	1-0	0-0	5	Baker-Richardson [56]	2604
27	25	A	Leyton Orient	W	1-0	0-0	3	Norman [85]	3413
28	29	H	Barrow	W	2-1	2-0	3	Telford 2 [2, 12]	4080
29	Feb 5	A	Forest Green R	L	0-2	0-1	5		3817
30	8	A	Northampton T	L	0-1	0-0	7		4255
31	12	H	Oldham Ath	D	3-3	2-1	7	Haynes [14], Telford [40], Demetriou [89]	3901
32	19	H	Mansfield T	D	1-1	0-0	8	Telford (pen) [82]	3956
33	26	H	Tranmere R	W	4-2	0-0	8	Lewis, A [49], Telford 2 (1 pen) [57 (p), 90], Azaz [88]	3924
34	Mar 1	H	Forest Green R	D	1-1	1-0	6	Azaz [3]	4448
35	5	H	Bristol R	W	1-0	1-0	4	Waite [33]	6237
36	12	A	Stevenage	W	2-0	0-0	3	Street [47], Haynes [70]	2733
37	15	A	Carlisle U	W	2-1	1-0	3	Demetriou [15], Azaz [65]	4445
38	18	H	Hartlepool U	L	2-3	1-2	3	Bogle (og) [16], Street [71]	4768
39	26	A	Bradford C	D	0-0	0-0	5		14,716
40	Apr 2	H	Exeter C	L	0-1	0-0	8		5697
41	9	A	Swindon T	W	1-0	0-0	7	Conroy (og) [90]	11,408
42	15	H	Crawley T	L	1-2	0-2	8	Waite [59]	5137
43	18	A	Sutton U	L	0-1	0-1	10		3447
44	22	H	Colchester U	L	1-2	1-0	10	Telford [40]	5989
45	May 2	A	Port Vale	W	2-1	1-0	11	Haynes [3], Azaz [72]	9048
46	7	H	Rochdale	L	0-2	0-1	11		5322

Final League Position: 11

GOALSCORERS

League (67): Telford 25 (2 pens), Baker-Richardson 8, Azaz 7, Demetriou 4 (1 pen), Haynes 3, Willmott 3, Dolan 2 (2 pens), Street 2, Waite 2, Bennett 1, Clarke 1, Collins 1, Cooper 1, Ellison 1, Fisher 1, Lewis, A 1, Norman 1, own goals 3.
FA Cup (0).
Carabao Cup (1): Abraham 1.
Papa John's Trophy (5): Abraham 2, Fisher 1, Greenidge 1, Telford 1.

Day J 27	Farquharson P 6 + 4	Dolan M 25 + 8	Demetriou M 39	Norman C 45 + 1	Willmott R 26 + 4	Upson E 15 + 1	Bennett S 31 + 2	Haynes R 29 + 5	Collins L 4 + 13	Hylton J 3 + 1	Clarke J 33 + 2	Abraham T 3 + 9	Ellison K 1 + 9	Azaz F 34 + 8	Missilou C 2 + 2	Fisher A 8 + 14	Greenidge J — + 1	Cooper O 28 + 5	Telford D 35 + 2	Livermore A 2 + 1	Lewis A 20 + 7	Cain J 16 + 9	Townsend N 19	Baker-Richardson C 25 + 6	Pask J 10	Waite J 9 + 7	Street R 11 + 7	Bright H — + 1	*Match No.*
1	2	3[1]	4	5	6	7	8	9	10[3]	11[2]	12	13	14																1
1	4			2	10	8	7	5	14		3[3]	11[2]		6	9[1]	12	13												2
1	4			2	8	6	7	5		10[2]	3	12	13	9[3]	14	11[1]													3
1	2[3]	12		5	10[2]	6	3	8	14	9	4	13			7[1]	11													4
1	13	3[2]	4	5	9	6	2[3]	8				11[1]				10		7	12	14									5
1	2	3[1]	4	5[2]	9	6	7	8				14		12		10[3]		11			13								6
1	2		4	5	9		3[3]	8	11[2]			10	13	14				12		7		6[1]							7
		3	4	5		6[3]					2			13	14	10[1]		11	9	7[2]	8		1	12					8
	13	3[2]		5	8	6		2		12	4	14		7[3]		10					9		1	11[1]					9
1		3	4	5	6	7		9			2	14		12		13		8[1]	10[3]					11[2]					10
1		3	4	5	6	7[1]		9			2			12		13		8	10[2]					11					11
1		3	4	5	6	7		9			2			12		13		8[3]	10[1]			14		11[2]					12
1		3	4	5	6	7■		9■			2			12		13		8[1]	10[2]		14			11[3]					13
1		3[1]	4	5	6						2	14	13	12				8	11[2]		9	7		10[3]					14
1			4	2	6[3]	14					3		12	7		13		9	10[2]		5	8		11[1]					15
1		3	4	5		7		9			2		13	6				8[1]	10			12		11[2]					16
1		3	4	5		7[3]		9			2	14	13	6				8[1]	10			12		11[2]					17
1		3[1]	4	5		7[3]					2		11[2]	6		14		8	10		9	12		13					18
1			4	5	7		3	9			2			6				8	10					11					19
1		3	4	5	7			9[1]	10		2[2]			8		14		6			12	13		11[3]					20
1		3	4	5	7		13		12		2		14	6[3]				8	10[2]		9			11[1]					21
1		7[1]	3	2	6						4	13		8				9	10		5[2]	12		11					22
	14	3		5[1]	7		4	12			2			6		13		8	11[3]		9		1	10[2]					23
			4	2	7		13	12	14		3			8[2]				6	11		5[1]	9[3]	1	10					24
			4	2			6[3]	5	13					8				7[1]	10[2]		14	9	1	11	3	12			25
		13	4	2			6	5			12			8				7[2]	10[3]			9	1	11	3[1]	14			26
	13	14	4	2	8[2]		6	5	12							10[1]		7				9[3]	1	11	3				27
		14	4	2	12		6	5			3			8				7	11[3]			9[1]	1	10[2]			13		28
			4	2			6	5						7				9[2]	11			8	1	10[1]	3	13	12		29
			4	2	7[2]		6	5						9				12	11			8[1]	1	10	3		13		30
		3	4	6[2]	12		5[1]	9						7				8	11				1	10[3]	2	13	14		31
		3[1]	4	13	12		5	9[2]						8					11		6	7[3]	1	10	2	14			32
		14	4	2	7[1]		6				3			8		13		9[3]	11		5	12	1				10[2]		33
			4	2			6	13			3■			9		14		7[1]	11[2]		5	8	1			12	10[3]		34
		14	4	3			6	5						9[3]		12		13	11		2	7	1			8[2]	10[1]		35
		12	3	2			6	13	14		4			9					11[3]		5[2]	7[1]	1			8	10		36
		7	4	2			6	5	12		3[2]			9		14			11[1]		13		1			8	10[3]		37
1		7[3]	3	2	14		6	5			4[2]			9				8[1]	11		13					12	10		38
1		14	4	2	6		7[3]	12			3[2]			8		13			10		5					9	11[1]		39
1			4	2	6		7[2]		13		3[3]			8		11[1]			10		5			12		9	14		40
1			4	2	8[3]		6		11[1]		3			7					12		5	14		13		9	10[2]		41
1			4	2			6		13		3			9					11		5	7[2]		10[1]		8	12		42
1		8	4	2			6[1]	5	13		3		14	7					10					12		9[2]	11[3]		43
1		8	4[3]	2			6[1]		14					9				13	11		5			12	3	7	10[2]		44
		4		2			7	6[3]			3			8				12	10		14	9[1]	1	11[2]	5		13		45
		6		2			7[2]		14		3			9				8[1]	10[3]		5	12	1		4		11	13	46

FA Cup

First Round	Morecambe	(a)	0-1

Carabao Cup

First Round	Ipswich T	(a)	1-0
Second Round	Southampton	(h)	0-8

Papa John's Trophy

Group F (S)	Plymouth Arg	(h)	2-0
Group F (S)	Arsenal U21	(h)	3-4
Group F (S)	Swindon T	(a)	0-1

NORTHAMPTON TOWN

FOUNDATION

Formed in 1897 by schoolteachers connected with the Northampton & District Elementary Schools' Association, they survived a financial crisis at the end of their first year when they were £675 in the red and became members of the Midland League – a fast move indeed for a new club. They achieved Southern League membership in 1901.

Sixfields Stadium, Upton Way, Northampton NN5 5QA.

Telephone: (01604) 683 700.

Ticket Office: (01604) 683 777.

Website: www.ntfc.co.uk

Email: wendy.lambell@ntfc.co.uk

Ground Capacity: 7,798.

Record Attendance: 24,523 v Fulham, Division 1, 23 April 1966 (at County Ground); 7,798 v Manchester U, EFL Cup 3rd rd, 21 September 2016; 7,798 v Derby Co, FA Cup 4th rd, 24 January 2019 (at Sixfields Stadium).

Pitch Measurements: 106m × 66m (116yd × 72yd).

Chairman: Kelvin Thomas.

Chief Executive: James Whiting.

Manager: Jon Brady.

Assistant Manager: Colin Calderwood.

Colours: Claret shirts with white trim, white shorts with claret trim, claret socks with white trim.

Year Formed: 1897.

Turned Professional: 1901.

Grounds: 1897, County Ground; 1994, Sixfields Stadium (renamed PTS Academy Stadium 2018; Sixfields Stadium 2021).

Club Nickname: 'The Cobblers'.

First Football League Game: 28 August 1920, Division 3, v Grimsby T (a) L 0–2 – Thorpe; Sproston, Hewison; Jobey, Tomkins, Pease; Whitworth, Lockett, Thomas, Freeman, MacKechnie.

Record League Victory: 10–0 v Walsall, Division 3 (S), 5 November 1927 – Hammond; Watson, Jeffs; Allen, Brett, Odell; Daley, Smith (3), Loasby (3), Hoten (1), Wells (3).

Record Cup Victory: 10–0 v Sutton T, FA Cup prel rd, 7 December 1907 – Cooch; Drennan, Lloyd Davies, Tirrell (1), McCartney, Hickleton, Badenock (3), Platt (3), Lowe (1), Chapman (2), McDiarmid.

Record Defeat: 0–11 v Southampton, Southern League, 28 December 1901.

Most League Points (2 for a win): 68, Division 4, 1975–76.

Most League Points (3 for a win): 99, Division 4, 1986–87; FL 2, 2015–16.

HONOURS

League Champions: Division 3 – 1962–63; FL 2 – 2015–16; Division 4 – 1986–87.
Runners-up: Division 2 – 1964–65; Division 3S – 1927–28, 1949–50; FL 2 – 2005–06; Division 4 – 1975–76.

FA Cup: 5th rd – 1934, 1950, 1970.

League Cup: 5th rd – 1965, 1967.

FOOTBALL YEARBOOK FACT FILE

Northampton Town first installed floodlights at their old County Ground at the beginning of the 1960–61 season. The lights were inaugurated with a friendly against Arsenal on 10 October 1960 when the Cobblers, wearing a specially commissioned set of white shirts with a claret band across the middle, went down to a 3-2 defeat.

Most League Goals: 109, Division 3, 1962–63 and Division 3 (S), 1952–53.

Highest League Scorer in Season: Cliff Holton, 36, Division 3, 1961–62.

Most League Goals in Total Aggregate: Jack English, 135, 1947–60.

Most League Goals in One Match: 5, Ralph Hoten v Crystal Palace, Division 3 (S), 27 October 1928.

Most Capped Player: Edwin Lloyd Davies, 12 (16), Wales.

Most League Appearances: Tommy Fowler, 521, 1946–61.

Youngest League Player: Adrian Mann, 16 years 297 days v Bury, 5 May 1984.

Record Transfer Fee Received: £1,000,000 (rising to £1,500,000) from Brentford for Charlie Goode, August 2020.

Record Transfer Fee Paid: £165,000 to Oldham Ath for Josh Low, July 2003.

Football League Record: 1920 Original Member of Division 3; 1921 Division 3 (S); 1958–61 Division 4; 1961–63 Division 3; 1963–65 Division 2; 1965–66 Division 1; 1966–67 Division 2; 1967–69 Division 3; 1969–76 Division 4; 1976–77 Division 3; 1977–87 Division 4; 1987–90 Division 3; 1990–92 Division 4; 1992–97 Division 3; 1997–99 Division 2; 1999–2000 Division 3; 2000–03 Division 2; 2003–04 Division 3; 2004–06 FL 2; 2006–09 FL 1; 2009–16 FL 2; 2016–18 FL 1; 2018–20 FL 2; 2020–21 FL 1; 2021– FL 2.

LATEST SEQUENCES

Longest Sequence of League Wins: 10, 28.12.2015 – 23.2.2016.

Longest Sequence of League Defeats: 8, 26.10.1935 – 21.12.1935.

Longest Sequence of League Draws: 6, 5.2.2011 – 26.2.2011.

Longest Sequence of Unbeaten League Matches: 31, 28.12.2015 – 10.9.2016.

Longest Sequence Without a League Win: 18, 5.2.2011 – 25.4.2011.

Successive Scoring Runs: 28 from 29.8.2015.

Successive Non-scoring Runs: 7 from 7.4.1939.

MANAGERS

Arthur Jones 1897–1907
(Secretary-Manager)
Herbert Chapman 1907–12
Walter Bull 1912–13
Fred Lessons 1913–19
Bob Hewison 1920–25
Jack Tresadern 1925–30
Jack English 1931–35
Syd Puddefoot 1935–37
Warney Cresswell 1937–39
Tom Smith 1939–49
Bob Dennison 1949–54
Dave Smith 1954–59
David Bowen 1959–67
Tony Marchi 1967–68
Ron Flowers 1968–69
Dave Bowen 1969–72
(continued as General Manager and Secretary 1972–85 when joined the board)
Billy Baxter 1972–73
Bill Dodgin Jnr 1973–76
Pat Crerand 1976–77
By committee 1977
Bill Dodgin Jnr 1977
John Petts 1977–78
Mike Keen 1978–79
Clive Walker 1979–80
Bill Dodgin Jnr 1980–82
Clive Walker 1982–84
Tony Barton 1984–85
Graham Carr 1985–90
Theo Foley 1990–92
Phil Chard 1992–93
John Barnwell 1993–94
Ian Atkins 1995–99
Kevin Wilson 1999–2001
Kevan Broadhurst 2001–03
Terry Fenwick 2003
Martin Wilkinson 2003
Colin Calderwood 2003–06
John Gorman 2006
Stuart Gray 2007–09
Ian Sampson 2009–11
Gary Johnson 2011
Aidy Boothroyd 2011–13
Chris Wilder 2014–16
Rob Page 2016–17
Justin Edinburgh 2017
Jimmy Floyd Hasselbaink 2017–18
Dean Austin 2018
Keith Curle 2018–21
Jon Brady February 2021–

TEN YEAR LEAGUE RECORD

		P	W	D	L	F	A	Pts	Pos
2012-13	FL 2	46	21	10	15	64	55	73	6
2013-14	FL 2	46	13	14	19	42	57	53	21
2014-15	FL 2	46	18	7	21	67	62	61	12
2015-16	FL 2	46	29	12	5	82	46	99	1
2016-17	FL 1	46	14	11	21	60	73	53	16
2017-18	FL 1	46	12	11	23	43	77	47	22
2018-19	FL 2	46	14	19	13	64	63	61	15
2019-20	FL 2	37	17	7	13	54	40	58	7§
2020-21	FL 1	46	11	12	23	41	67	45	22
2021-22	FL 2	46	23	11	12	60	38	80	4

§*Decided on points-per-game (1.57)*

DID YOU KNOW ?

Albert Dawes scored a total of six hat-tricks for Northampton Town in Football League matches, a club record. This tally included three in 1932–33 when he netted 22 goals in his first 15 League and Cup appearances for the club that season, including five in an FA Cup tie against Lloyd's of Sittingbourne.

NORTHAMPTON TOWN – SKY BET LEAGUE TWO 2021–22 LEAGUE RECORD

Match No.	Date	Venue	Opponents	Result		H/T Score	Lg Pos.	Goalscorers	Attendance
1	Aug 7	H	Port Vale	W	1-0	1-0	5	Ashley-Seal [23]	5804
2	14	A	Colchester U	W	1-0	1-0	4	Guthrie [22]	2772
3	21	H	Rochdale	L	1-3	1-1	10	Guthrie [20]	4870
4	28	A	Crawley T	D	0-0	0-0	8		2254
5	Sept 4	H	Scunthorpe U	W	2-0	0-0	5	Rose [63], Hoskins [90]	4870
6	11	A	Forest Green R	L	0-1	0-0	9		2576
7	14	A	Newport Co	W	1-0	1-0	3	Guthrie [43]	3168
8	18	H	Swindon T	D	1-1	0-0	4	Horsfall [83]	5863
9	25	A	Salford C	D	2-2	1-1	5	Lewis [16], Pinnock [77]	2037
10	Oct 2	H	Sutton U	L	0-2	0-1	10		4789
11	9	A	Hartlepool U	L	1-2	0-0	14	Hoskins [50]	5522
12	16	H	Mansfield T	W	2-0	1-0	8	McGowan [23], Horsfall [74]	6034
13	19	H	Stevenage	W	3-0	2-0	6	Etete [34], Hoskins [43], Horsfall [63]	4123
14	23	A	Tranmere R	W	2-0	0-0	3	Etete [52], Hoskins (pen) [68]	4025
15	30	H	Carlisle U	W	3-0	1-0	3	Lewis 3 (1 pen) [41, 57, 67 (p)]	4909
16	Nov 13	A	Bristol R	L	1-2	1-0	4	Hoskins (pen) [39]	6884
17	20	A	Bradford C	D	1-1	0-0	5	Pinnock [60]	15,372
18	23	H	Oldham Ath	W	2-1	2-0	4	Guthrie [14], Etete [38]	4059
19	27	H	Leyton Orient	W	1-0	1-0	2	Hoskins [41]	5769
20	Dec 7	A	Exeter C	W	2-1	1-0	2	Sowerby [33], Pinnock [74]	3823
21	11	A	Harrogate T	W	2-1	1-1	2	Horsfall [7], Guthrie [49]	2166
22	Jan 1	A	Swindon T	L	2-5	1-1	2	Hoskins [37], Guthrie [50]	9071
23	8	H	Crawley T	L	0-1	0-1	3		4714
24	15	H	Forest Green R	D	1-1	0-0	3	Pinnock [90]	5415
25	22	A	Sutton U	D	0-0	0-0	4		3588
26	29	H	Salford C	W	1-0	1-0	5	Lewis [12]	5237
27	Feb 1	H	Barrow	L	0-1	0-0	5		4604
28	5	A	Walsall	W	1-0	1-0	4	Appere [10]	5315
29	8	H	Newport Co	W	1-0	0-0	3	Horsfall [82]	4255
30	12	A	Port Vale	D	0-0	0-0	3		5979
31	19	H	Colchester U	W	3-0	1-0	3	Horsfall [16], Hoskins [49], Ashley-Seal [90]	5309
32	22	A	Scunthorpe U	D	0-0	0-0	2		2355
33	26	A	Rochdale	L	0-1	0-0	2		2643
34	Mar 1	H	Walsall	D	1-1	1-0	2	Pinnock [4]	4861
35	5	H	Tranmere R	W	3-2	2-0	2	Horsfall 2 [29, 37], Pinnock [66]	7379
36	12	A	Carlisle U	L	1-2	0-0	2	Lewis [79]	8514
37	15	A	Stevenage	W	2-1	1-0	2	McGowan [18], Pinnock [50]	2362
38	19	H	Bristol R	L	0-1	0-1	3		6405
39	26	H	Hartlepool U	W	2-0	1-0	3	Hoskins [6], Zimba [61]	5673
40	Apr 2	A	Mansfield T	L	0-1	0-1	4		6678
41	9	H	Bradford C	D	0-0	0-0	5		5548
42	15	A	Oldham Ath	W	2-0	1-0	4	Guthrie [44], Appere [66]	5789
43	18	H	Harrogate T	W	3-0	1-0	4	Hoskins 2 [28, 63], Appere [59]	5168
44	23	A	Leyton Orient	W	4-2	4-1	3	Pinnock [19], Guthrie [32], Eppiah 2 [38, 45]	6237
45	30	H	Exeter C	D	1-1	1-0	3	Pinnock [29]	7764
46	May 7	A	Barrow	W	3-1	3-1	4	Hoskins 2 [5, 21], Horsfall [14]	4603

Final League Position: 4

GOALSCORERS

League (60): Hoskins 13 (2 pens), Horsfall 9, Pinnock 9, Guthrie 8, Lewis 6 (1 pen), Appere 3, Etete 3, Ashley-Seal 2, Eppiah 2, McGowan 2, Rose 1, Sowerby 1, Zimba 1.
FA Cup (3): Etete 1, Lewis 1, Rose 1.
Carabao Cup (2): Etete 2.
Papa John's Trophy (3): Connolly 1 (1 pen), Kabamba 1, Pollock 1.
League Two Play-offs (1): Koiki 1.

Roberts L 46	McGowan A 42	Guthrie J 44	Horsfall F 45	Mills J 10 + 7	Connolly D 3 + 14	Lewis P 37 + 2	Flores J 6 + 5	Pinnock M 44 + 2	Kabamba N 6 + 15	Ashley-Seal B 1 + 8	Rose D 14 + 22	McWilliams S 34 + 2	Koiki A 37 + 5	Hoskins S 44	Etete K 15 + 3	Nelson S 1 + 1	Sowerby J 34	Harriman M — + 5	Revan D 1 + 2	Dyche M 1	Zimba C 2 + 10	Kanu I 1 + 5	Eppiah J 8 + 6	Magliore T 8 + 2	Lubula B 5 + 9	Appere L 16 + 2	Abimbola P — + 1	Pollock S 1 + 1	Match No.
1	2	3	4	5	6³	7	8²	9	10	11¹	12	13	14																1
1	2	3	4▮	5³		7		9²	11		12	8	13	6	10¹	14													2
1	2	4		5	14	7		9	11¹	12	13	8³		6	10²	3													3
1	2	4	3	5¹	13	7	8	9	14		11²		12	6	10³														4
1	2	3	4		12	8	7	9¹	13		11³	14	5	6	10²														5
1	2	4	3		13	6	8¹	12	14		11	7³	5	9	10²														6
1	2	4	3		14		12	9	10²		11¹	7	5	6	13		8³												7
1	2	4	3		12	13		9¹	14		10	8	5	6	11²		7³												8
1	2	4	3		9²	6		13	12		11³	8¹	5	10	14		7												9
1	4		3			7	13	9	11³		10	2¹	5	6	12		8²	14											10
1	3	4	5		12	9		10²	13	14		2	6	7	11³		8¹												11
1	2	4	3			9		10			12	7	5²	8	11¹		6	13											12
1	2	4	3		14	9		10³	12		13	7¹	5	8	11²		6												13
1	2	4	3			9		10			12	7	5²	8	11¹		6		13										14
1	2¹	4	3			9	8²	10	13		14	7³	5		11		6		12										15
1		4	3		12	10	8²	9¹	13			7	5	6	11			14	2³										16
1	2	4	3			10		9	13		12	7	5	6	11¹		8²												17
1	2	4	3		14	9		10	13		12	7	5	8³	11²		6¹												18
1	2		3			8		9	12	13	11		5	6²	10¹		7			4									19
1	2	4	3			9	12³	10	13	14	11²	6¹	5	8			7												20
1	2	4	3		12	7	13	9	11		10¹		5	6²			8												21
1	2	4	3		13	9	14	10	12		11²	6³	5	8			7¹												22
1	2	4	3		12	9¹		10	14		11³	7	5²	8			6				13								23
1	2	4	3		11²	9¹		10			13	7	5	8			6				12								24
1	2	4	3		13	9²		10			12	7	5	8			6				11¹								25
1	2	4	3			9²		10			14	7	5	8³			6					11¹	12	13					26
1	2	4	3			9³		10¹			13	6	5	8			7					14	11²		12				27
1	5¹	4	3			12		7				8	9³	10			6²					14		2	13	11			28
1		4	3	14		6		9				7	8³	5²								12	13	2	11¹	10			29
1		4	3	13		6		9			11³	7	8²	5				14						2	12	10¹			30
1	5²	4	3			7		11		14	13		8	9			6¹							2	12	10³			31
1	5	4	3			6		7		13	10²		8	9									12	2	11¹				32
1	5²	4	3	15		6		11		13		7	8⁴	9									10¹	2³	14	12			33
1	5	4	3	8¹		7²		11			14	6	12	9									13	2		10³			34
1	2	4	3			9		10³			12	7	5	8			6²							14	13	11¹			35
1	2	4	3			9		10		14	12	7¹	5	8³			6								13	11²			36
1	2	3	4	12		6		9			14		5¹	8			7				13				10³	11²			37
1	2	4	3	5		9		8						10³			7				13			6¹	14	11	12²		38
1	2	4	3	5		7		9						8²			6	14			12		13		10³	11¹			39
1	2	4	3	5³		8▮		7			14			9			6				11²		12		10¹	13			40
1	2	4	3	5²				9					13	7			6				12		10¹		14	11³		8	41
1	2	4	3					9			12	8	5	7³			6				13	14	10²			11¹			42
1	2	4	3	14				9				7	5³	6²			8				12		11¹			10		13	43
1	2	4	3	14				9			12	6	5³	10			7				13		8¹			11²			44
1	2¹	4	3	12				9				6	5	10			7						8			11			45
1▮		3	4	2³				9			12	7	8	11			6				14	13	5¹			10²			46

FA Cup

First Round	Cambridge U	(h)	2-2
Replay	Cambridge U	(a)	1-3

Carabao Cup

First Round	Coventry C	(a)	2-1
Second Round	AFC Wimbledon	(h)	0-1

League Two Play-offs

Semi-Final 1st leg	Mansfield T	(a)	1-2
Semi-Final 2nd leg	Mansfield T	(h)	0-1

Papa John's Trophy

Group D (S)	Forest Green R	(a)	1-1
(Northampton T won 4-2 on penalties)			
Group D (S)	Walsall	(h)	1-1
(Walsall won 4-2 on penalties)			
Group D (S)	Brighton & HA U21	(h)	1-2

NORWICH CITY

FOUNDATION

Formed in 1902, largely through the initiative of two local schoolmasters who called a meeting at the Criterion Cafe, they were shocked by an FA Commission which in 1904 declared the club professional and ejected them from the FA Amateur Cup. However, this only served to strengthen their determination. New officials were appointed and a professional club established at a meeting in the Agricultural Hall in March 1905.

Carrow Road, Norwich, Norfolk NR1 1JE.

Telephone: (01603) 721 902.

Ticket Office: (01603) 721 902 (option 1).

Website: www.canaries.co.uk

Email: reception@canaries.co.uk

Ground Capacity: 27,359.

Record Attendance: 25,037 v Sheffield W, FA Cup 5th rd, 16 February 1935 (at The Nest); 43,984 v Leicester C, FA Cup 6th rd, 30 March 1963 (at Carrow Road).

Pitch Measurements: 105m × 68m (115yd × 74.5yd).

Joint Majority Shareholders: Delia Smith, Michael Wynn-Jones.

Chief Operating Officer: Ben Kensell.

Head Coach: Dean Smith.

Assistant Head Coach: Craig Shakespeare.

Colours: Yellow shirts with green trim, green shorts with yellow trim, yellow socks with green trim.

Year Formed: 1902.

Turned Professional: 1905.

Club Nickname: 'The Canaries'.

Grounds: 1902, Newmarket Road; 1908, The Nest, Rosary Road; 1935, Carrow Road.

First Football League Game: 28 August 1920, Division 3, v Plymouth Arg (a) D 1–1 – Skermer; Gray, Gadsden; Wilkinson, Addy, Martin; Laxton, Kidger, Parker, Whitham (1), Dobson.

Record League Victory: 10–2 v Coventry C, Division 3 (S), 15 March 1930 – Jarvie; Hannah, Graham; Brown, O'Brien, Lochhead (1); Porter (1), Anderson, Hunt (5), Scott (2), Slicer (1).

Record Cup Victory: 8–0 v Sutton U, FA Cup 4th rd, 28 January 1989 – Gunn; Culverhouse, Bowen, Butterworth, Linighan, Townsend (Crook), Gordon, Fleck (3), Allen (4), Phelan, Putney (1).

Record Defeat: 2–10 v Swindon T, Southern League, 5 September 1908.

Most League Points (2 for a win): 64, Division 3 (S), 1950–51.

Most League Points (3 for a win): 97, FL C, 2020–21.

Most League Goals: 99, Division 3 (S), 1952–53.

Highest League Scorer in Season: Ralph Hunt, 31, Division 3 (S), 1955–56.

HONOURS

League Champions: FL C – 2018–19, 2020–21; First Division – 2003–04; Division 2 – 1971–72, 1985–86; FL 1 – 2009–10; Division 3S – 1933–34.
Runners-up: FL C – 2010–11; Division 3 – 1959–60; Division 3S – 1950–51.

FA Cup: semi-final – 1959, 1989, 1992.

League Cup Winners: 1962, 1985.
Runners-up: 1973, 1975.

European Competitions
UEFA Cup: 1993–94.

FOOTBALL YEARBOOK FACT FILE

When Norwich City moved to their new ground at The Nest in 1908, they found that although their pitch was adequate for Southern League games it did not meet the requirements for the FA Cup. As a result, their second-round tie at home to Fulham in 1907–08 was switched to Craven Cottage and the following season's home fixture against Reading was transferred to Stamford Bridge before the problem was resolved.

Most League Goals in Total Aggregate: Johnny Gavin, 122, 1945–54, 1955–58.

Most League Goals in One Match: 5, Tommy Hunt v Coventry C, Division 3 (S), 15 March 1930; 5, Roy Hollis v Walsall, Division 3 (S), 29 December 1951.

Most Capped Player: Wes Hoolahan, 42 (43), Republic of Ireland; Teemu Pukki 42 (106), Finland.

Most League Appearances: Ron Ashman, 592, 1947–64.

Youngest League Player: Ryan Jarvis, 16 years 282 days v Walsall, 19 April 2003.

Record Transfer Fee Received: £38,000,000 from Aston Villa for Emiliano Buendia, June 2021.

Record Transfer Fee Paid: £9,400,000 to Werden Bremen for Milot Rashica, June 2021; £9,400,000 to PAOK for Christos Tzolis, August 2021.

Football League Record: 1920 Original Member of Division 3; 1921 Division 3 (S); 1934–39 Division 2; 1946–58 Division 3 (S); 1958–60 Division 3; 1960–72 Division 2; 1972–74 Division 1; 1974–75 Division 2; 1975–81 Division 1; 1981–82 Division 2; 1982–85 Division 1; 1985–86 Division 2; 1986–92 Division 1; 1992–95 Premier League; 1995–2004 Division 1; 2004–05 Premier League; 2005–09 FL C; 2009–10 FL 1; 2010–11 FL C; 2011–14 Premier League; 2014–15 FL C; 2015–16 Premier League; 2016–19 FL C; 2019–20 Premier League; 2020–21 FL C; 2021–22 Premier League; 2022– FL C.

LATEST SEQUENCES

Longest Sequence of League Wins: 10, 23.11.1985 – 25.1.1986.

Longest Sequence of League Defeats: 10, 7.3.2020 – 26.7.2020.

Longest Sequence of League Draws: 7, 15.1.1994 – 26.2.1994.

Longest Sequence of Unbeaten League Matches: 20, 31.8.1950 – 30.12.1950.

Longest Sequence Without a League Win: 25, 22.9.1956 – 23.2.1957.

Successive Scoring Runs: 30 from 1.12.2018.

Successive Non-scoring Runs: 6 from 5.12.2021.

MANAGERS

John Bowman 1905–07
James McEwen 1907–08
Arthur Turner 1909–10
Bert Stansfield 1910–15
Major Frank Buckley 1919–20
Charles O'Hagan 1920–21
Albert Gosnell 1921–26
Bert Stansfield 1926
Cecil Potter 1926–29
James Kerr 1929–33
Tom Parker 1933–37
Bob Young 1937–39
Jimmy Jewell 1939
Bob Young 1939–45
Duggie Lochhead 1945–46
Cyril Spiers 1946–47
Duggie Lochhead 1947–50
Norman Low 1950–55
Tom Parker 1955–57
Archie Macaulay 1957–61
Willie Reid 1961–62
George Swindin 1962
Ron Ashman 1962–66
Lol Morgan 1966–69
Ron Saunders 1969–73
John Bond 1973–80
Ken Brown 1980–87
Dave Stringer 1987–92
Mike Walker 1992–94
John Deehan 1994–95
Martin O'Neill 1995
Gary Megson 1995–96
Mike Walker 1996–98
Bruce Rioch 1998–2000
Bryan Hamilton 2000
Nigel Worthington 2000–06
Peter Grant 2006–07
Glenn Roeder 2007–09
Bryan Gunn 2009
Paul Lambert 2009–12
Chris Hughton 2012–14
Neil Adams 2014–15
Alex Neil 2015–17
Daniel Farke 2017–21
Dean Smith November 2021–

TEN YEAR LEAGUE RECORD

		P	W	D	L	F	A	Pts	Pos
2012-13	PR Lge	38	10	14	14	41	58	44	11
2013-14	PR Lge	38	8	9	21	28	62	33	18
2014-15	FL C	46	25	11	10	88	48	86	3
2015-16	PR Lge	38	9	7	22	39	67	34	19
2016-17	FL C	46	20	10	16	85	69	70	8
2017-18	FL C	46	15	15	16	49	60	60	14
2018-19	FL C	46	27	13	6	93	57	94	1
2019-20	PR Lge	38	5	6	27	26	75	21	20
2020-21	FL C	46	29	10	7	75	36	97	1
2021-22	PR Lge	38	5	7	26	23	84	22	20

DID YOU KNOW ?

When Grant Holt scored a hat-trick for Norwich City against Ipswich Town in November 2010 he became the first Canaries player to achieve this feat against their East Anglian rivals in a Football League match. Back in September 1968 Hugh Curran had also netted a hat-trick against Ipswich, although that was in a Football League Cup tie.

NORWICH CITY – PREMIER LEAGUE 2021–22 LEAGUE RECORD

Match No.	Date	Venue	Opponents	Result		H/T Score	Lg Pos.	Goalscorers	Attendance
1	Aug 14	H	Liverpool	L	0-3	0-1	18		27,023
2	21	A	Manchester C	L	0-5	0-2	20		51,437
3	28	H	Leicester C	L	1-2	1-1	19	Pukki (pen) [44]	26,765
4	Sept 11	A	Arsenal	L	0-1	0-0	20		59,337
5	18	H	Watford	L	1-3	1-1	20	Pukki [35]	26,649
6	25	A	Everton	L	0-2	0-1	20		38,821
7	Oct 2	A	Burnley	D	0-0	0-0	20		17,427
8	16	H	Brighton & HA	D	0-0	0-0	20		26,777
9	23	A	Chelsea	L	0-7	0-3	20		40,113
10	31	H	Leeds U	L	1-2	0-0	20	Omobamidele [58]	26,913
11	Nov 6	A	Brentford	W	2-1	2-0	20	Normann [6], Pukki (pen) [29]	16,837
12	20	H	Southampton	W	2-1	1-1	19	Pukki [7], Hanley [79]	26,885
13	27	H	Wolverhampton W	D	0-0	0-0	19		26,911
14	30	A	Newcastle U	D	1-1	0-0	18	Pukki [79]	50,757
15	Dec 5	A	Tottenham H	L	0-3	0-1	20		57,088
16	11	H	Manchester U	L	0-1	0-0	20		27,066
17	14	H	Aston Villa	L	0-2	0-1	20		26,836
18	26	H	Arsenal	L	0-5	0-2	20		26,940
19	28	A	Crystal Palace	L	0-3	0-3	20		24,433
20	Jan 12	A	West Ham U	L	0-2	0-1	20		59,775
21	15	H	Everton	W	2-1	2-0	18	Keane (og) [16], Idah [18]	26,629
22	21	A	Watford	W	3-0	0-0	17	Sargent 2 [51, 74], Kucka (og) [90]	20,782
23	Feb 9	H	Crystal Palace	D	1-1	1-0	18	Pukki [1]	26,652
24	12	H	Manchester C	L	0-4	0-1	18		27,010
25	19	A	Liverpool	L	1-3	0-0	20	Rashica [48]	53,135
26	25	A	Southampton	L	0-2	0-1	20		31,182
27	Mar 5	H	Brentford	L	1-3	0-1	20	Pukki [90]	26,887
28	10	H	Chelsea	L	1-3	0-2	20	Pukki (pen) [69]	26,722
29	13	A	Leeds U	L	1-2	0-1	20	McLean [90]	36,321
30	Apr 2	A	Brighton & HA	D	0-0	0-0	20		31,245
31	10	H	Burnley	W	2-0	1-0	20	Lees-Melou [9], Pukki [86]	26,361
32	16	A	Manchester U	L	2-3	1-2	20	Dowell [45], Pukki [52]	73,381
33	23	H	Newcastle U	L	0-3	0-2	20		26,910
34	30	A	Aston Villa	L	0-2	0-1	20		40,290
35	May 8	H	West Ham U	L	0-4	0-3	20		26,428
36	11	A	Leicester C	L	0-3	0-0	20		30,892
37	15	A	Wolverhampton W	D	1-1	1-0	20	Pukki [37]	31,219
38	22	H	Tottenham H	L	0-5	0-2	20		27,022

Final League Position: 20

GOALSCORERS

League (23): Pukki 11 (3 pens), Sargent 2, Dowell 1, Hanley 1, Idah 1, Lees-Melou 1, McLean 1, Normann 1, Omobamidele 1, Rashica 1, own goals 2.
FA Cup (3): McLean 1, Rashica 1, Rupp 1.
Carabao Cup (6): Sargent 2, Tzolis 2, McLean 1, Rupp 1.

Krul T 29	Aarons M 32 + 2	Hanley G 33	Gibson B 28	Giannoulis D 14 + 4	Cantwell T 5 + 3	Lees-Melou P 27 + 6	Gilmour B 21 + 3	Rupp L 7 + 12	Rashica M 25 + 6	Pukki T 37	Idah A 6 + 11	Sargent J 18 + 8	Dowell K 11 + 8	McLean K 29 + 2	Mumba B — + 1	Williams B 23 + 3	Omobamidele A 4 + 1	Tzolis C 3 + 11	Kabak O 11	Normann M 20 + 3	Placheta P 6 + 6	Sorensen J 6 + 4	Byram S 11 + 4	Gunn A 9	Rowe J — + 13	Zimmermann C 2 + 1	Springett T 1 + 2	*Match No.*
1	2	3	4	5	6[3]	7	8	9	10[1]	11[2]	12	13	14															1
1	2	3	4	5[1]	9	6	7	8[2]	11	10[3]		14		12	13													2
1	2	3	4		9	6[1]	7[3]	12	11	10[2]	14	13		8		5												3
1	2	4			12	6		7[3]	13	10	14		9[1]	8		5	3	11[2]										4
1	2	4			13		6		11[3]	10	14	9[1]		8		5		12	3	7[2]								5
1	2	4	5	14		7			13	11		10		9		6[3]		12	3[1]	8[2]								6
1	2	4	5	6		7[1]		12	13	11[2]	14	10[3]		9					3	8								7
1	2	4	5	6		7		13	12	11[3]	14	10[1]		9					3	8[2]								8
1	5	3	4■	9[1]		6[2]			13	11		10[3]		8		12	14		2	7								9
1	5	3[3]							9	11	13	10[2]	6[1]	8			4	12	2	7	14							10
1	2		4	12		8			10[3]	11[2]	14	13	6[1]	9		5	3			7								11
1	2	3	4		11[1]		6[2]	13	9[3]	10		12		8		5		14		7								12
1	2	3	4				8	12	10[3]	11		7[2]	14	9		5		13		6[1]								13
1	2	3	4	14		12	8	6		11	13	7[2]		9		5[3]		10[1]										14
1	2	4	5			7[2]	8[3]			11	10[1]	12	13	9		6	3					14						15
1	2	3[1]		5	13	14	7	6[3]		10		11		8					4		9[2]	12						16
1	2		4		11[2]		6			10	13		14	8		5			3[1]		9[3]	7	12					17
	2		4			12	7			11	13	6[2]	10[1]	8		5		14	3		9[3]			1				18
			4	5[1]		9	6				11	14		7		12		10[2]			8[3]	3	2	1	13			19
1	2	3	4			6			10[2]	11	9[3]		12	7		5		13			8[1]				14			20
1	2[2]	3	4	13		6			10	11	9	8[3]				5[1]		14				7	12					21
	2	3	4			7			9[3]	11[2]	10	6		12		5					14	8[1]	13	1				22
	2	3	4			7[2]	12		9	11	10[3]			8		5				13	6[1]			1	14			23
	2[2]	3	4			7[1]	6		11	10		9[3]	14	8		5				13			12	1				24
	2	3	4			13	6		11[3]	10		9[1]		8		5				7[2]	12			1	14			25
	2	3	4			12	8[3]	13	10[1]	11		7	14	9		5				6[2]				1				26
1	14	3	4			13	6[1]		11	10		9		8		5[2]				7[3]			2		12			27
1	2	4				7		12	13	11		10[3]		9		6			5	8[2]					14	3[1]		28
1	2[3]		4			8	14	6[1]	11	10		9[2]		7		5			3	12					13			29
1		3	4	5		8[1]	7		11[2]	10			14	9[3]				13		6			2		12			30
1		3	4	5[2]		9[1]		12	10	11[3]			8	6		13		14		7			2					31
1		3	4	5		9[3]	12		10	11			8[2]	7[1]						6	13		2		14			32
1	13	3		5		9			10[3]	11			8	7				14		6[1]			2		12	4[2]		33
1	2	3				9[1]	6	14	10[2]	11		12[3]	8			5				7			4		13			34
1	2	3				9[1]	6	12	10[2]	11			8[3]			5					14	7	4				13	35
	2	3		5		6	9	8[1]	10[3]	11											14	12	4	1	13		7[2]	36
	5	3	4	8		10	6[1]	12		11			9[3]							7[2]		13	2	1	14			37
1	2	4		6		9[3]		14	10	11			7[2]							8		5	3[1]			12	13	38

FA Cup

Third Round	Charlton Ath	(a)	1-0
Fourth Round	Wolverhampton W	(a)	1-0
Fifth Round	Liverpool	(a)	1-2

Carabao Cup

Second Round	Bournemouth	(h)	6-0
Third Round	Liverpool	(h)	0-3

NOTTINGHAM FOREST

FOUNDATION

One of the oldest football clubs in the world, Nottingham Forest was formed at a meeting in the Clinton Arms in 1865. Known originally as the Forest Football Club, the game which first drew the founders together was 'shinney', a form of hockey. When they determined to change to football in 1865, one of their first moves was to buy a set of red caps to wear on the field.

The City Ground, Pavilion Road, Nottingham NG2 5FJ.
Telephone: (0115) 982 4444.
Ticket Office: (0115) 982 4388.
Website: www.nottinghamforest.co.uk
Email: enquiries@nottinghamforest.co.uk
Ground Capacity: 30,332.
Record Attendance: 49,946 v Manchester U, Division 1, 28 October 1967.
Pitch Measurements: 102.4m × 67.6m (112yd × 74yd).
Chairman: Nicholas Randall QC.
Chief Executive: Dane Murphy.
Manager: Steve Cooper.
Assistant Manager: Alan Tate.
Colours: Red shirts with white trim, white shorts with red trim, red socks.
Year Formed: 1865.
Turned Professional: 1889.
Previous Name: Forest Football Club.
Club Nickname: 'The Reds'.
Grounds: 1865, Forest Racecourse; 1879, The Meadows; 1880, Trent Bridge Cricket Ground; 1882, Parkside, Lenton; 1885, Gregory, Lenton; 1890, Town Ground; 1898, City Ground.
First Football League Game: 3 September 1892, Division 1, v Everton (a) D 2–2 – Brown; Earp, Scott; Hamilton, Albert Smith, McCracken; McCallum, 'Tich' Smith, Higgins (2), Pike, McInnes.
Record League Victory: 12–0 v Leicester Fosse, Division 1, 12 April 1909 – Iremonger; Dudley, Maltby; Hughes (1), Needham, Armstrong; Hooper (3), Marrison, West (3), Morris (2), Spouncer (3 incl. 1p).
Record Cup Victory: 14–0 v Clapton (away), FA Cup 1st rd, 17 January 1891 – Brown; Earp, Scott; Albert Smith, Russell, Jeacock; McCallum (2), 'Tich' Smith (1), Higgins (5), Lindley (4), Shaw (2).
Record Defeat: 1–9 v Blackburn R, Division 2, 10 April 1937.
Most League Points (2 for a win): 70, Division 3 (S), 1950–51.
Most League Points (3 for a win): 94, Division 1, 1997–98.
Most League Goals: 110, Division 3 (S), 1950–51.
Highest League Scorer in Season: Wally Ardron, 36, Division 3 (S), 1950–51.

HONOURS

League Champions: Division 1 – 1977–78; First Division – 1997–98; Division 2 – 1906–07, 1921–22; Division 3S – 1950–51.
Runners-up: Division 1 – 1966–67, 1978–79; First Division – 1993–94; Division 2 – 1956–57; FL 1 – 2007–08.
FA Cup Winners: 1898, 1959.
Runners-up: 1991.
League Cup Winners: 1978, 1979, 1989, 1990.
Runners-up: 1980, 1992.
Anglo-Scottish Cup Winners: 1977.
Full Members' Cup Winners: 1989, 1992.

European Competitions
European Cup: 1978–79 *(winners)*, 1979–80 *(winners)*, 1980–81.
Fairs Cup: 1961–62, 1967–68.
UEFA Cup: 1983–84 *(sf)*, 1984–85, 1995–96 *(qf)*.
Super Cup: 1979 *(winners)*, 1980.
World Club Championship: 1980.

FOOTBALL YEARBOOK FACT FILE

Ken Smales was club secretary of Nottingham Forest for over 25 years, serving from 1961 through to his retirement in the summer of 1987, when he became an honorary life member of the club. Prior to his arrival at the City Ground he had been a well-known cricketer with Yorkshire and then Nottinghamshire. In June 1956 he took all 10 Gloucestershire wickets in an innings, playing for Nottinghamshire at Stroud, but still ended up on the losing side.

Most League Goals in Total Aggregate: Grenville Morris, 199, 1898–1913.

Most League Goals in One Match: 4, Enoch West v Sunderland, Division 1, 9 November 1907; 4, Tommy Gibson v Burnley, Division 2, 25 January 1913; 4, Tom Peacock v Port Vale, Division 2, 23 December 1933; 4, Tom Peacock v Barnsley, Division 2, 9 November 1935; 4, Tom Peacock v Port Vale, Division 2, 23 November 1935; 4, Tom Peacock v Doncaster R, Division 2, 26 December 1935; 4, Tommy Capel v Gillingham, Division 3 (S), 18 November 1950; 4, Wally Ardron v Hull C, Division 2, 26 December 1952; 4, Tommy Wilson v Barnsley, Division 2, 9 February 1957; 4, Peter Withe v Ipswich T, Division 1, 4 October 1977; 4, Marlon Harewood v Stoke C, Division 1, 22 February 2003; Gareth McCleary v Leeds U, FL C, 20 March 2012.

Most Capped Player: Stuart Pearce, 76 (78), England.

Most League Appearances: Bob McKinlay, 614, 1951–70.

Youngest League Player: Craig Westcarr, 16 years 257 days v Burnley, 13 October 2001.

Record Transfer Fee Received: £15,000,000 from Middlesbrough for Britt Assombalonga, July 2017.

Record Transfer Fee Paid: £17,000,000 to Union Berlin for Taiwo Awoniyi, June 2022.

Football League Record: 1892 Elected to Division 1; 1906–07 Division 2; 1907–11 Division 1; 1911–22 Division 2; 1922–25 Division 1; 1925–49 Division 2; 1949–51 Division 3 (S); 1951–57 Division 2; 1957–72 Division 1; 1972–77 Division 2; 1977–92 Division 1; 1992–93 Premier League; 1993–94 Division 1; 1994–97 Premier League; 1997–98 Division 1; 1998–99 Premier League; 1999–2004 Division 1; 2004–05 FL C; 2005–08 FL 1; 2008– FL C.

LATEST SEQUENCES

Longest Sequence of League Wins: 7, 9.5.1979 – 1.9.1979.

Longest Sequence of League Defeats: 14, 21.3.1913 – 27.9.1913.

Longest Sequence of League Draws: 7, 29.4.1978 – 2.9.1978.

Longest Sequence of Unbeaten League Matches: 42, 26.11.1977 – 25.11.1978.

Longest Sequence Without a League Win: 19, 8.9.1998 – 16.1.1999.

Successive Scoring Runs: 22 from 28.3.1931.

Successive Non-scoring Runs: 7 from 26.11.2011.

MANAGERS

Harry Radford 1889–97
(Secretary-Manager)
Harry Haslam 1897–1909
(Secretary-Manager)
Fred Earp 1909–12
Bob Masters 1912–25
John Baynes 1925–29
Stan Hardy 1930–31
Noel Watson 1931–36
Harold Wightman 1936–39
Billy Walker 1939–60
Andy Beattie 1960–63
Johnny Carey 1963–68
Matt Gillies 1969–72
Dave Mackay 1972
Allan Brown 1973–75
Brian Clough 1975–93
Frank Clark 1993–96
Stuart Pearce 1996–97
Dave Bassett 1997–99
(previously General Manager)
Ron Atkinson 1999
David Platt 1999–2001
Paul Hart 2001–04
Joe Kinnear 2004
Gary Megson 2005–06
Colin Calderwood 2006–08
Billy Davies 2009–11
Steve McClaren 2011
Steve Cotterill 2011–12
Sean O'Driscoll 2012
Alex McLeish 2012–13
Billy Davies 2013–14
Stuart Pearce 2014–15
Dougie Freedman 2015–16
Philippe Montanier 2016–17
Mark Warburton 2017
Aitor Karanka 2018–19
Martin O'Neill 2019
Sabri Lamouchi 2019–20
Chris Hughton 2020–21
Steve Cooper September 2021–

TEN YEAR LEAGUE RECORD

		P	*W*	*D*	*L*	*F*	*A*	*Pts*	*Pos*
2012-13	FL C	46	17	16	13	63	59	67	8
2013-14	FL C	46	16	17	13	67	64	65	11
2014-15	FL C	46	15	14	17	71	69	59	14
2015-16	FL C	46	13	16	17	43	47	55	16
2016-17	FL C	46	14	9	23	62	72	51	21
2017-18	FL C	46	15	8	23	51	65	53	17
2018-19	FL C	46	17	15	14	61	54	66	9
2019-20	FL C	46	18	16	12	58	50	70	7
2020-21	FL C	46	12	16	18	37	45	52	17
2021-22	FL C	46	23	11	12	73	40	80	4

DID YOU KNOW ?

Nottingham Forest were one of the first clubs to take advantage of the FA's decision to allow Sunday football in January 1974. Their FA Cup third-round tie with Bristol Rovers on 6 January attracted an attendance of 23,456, over 8,000 up on their previous home fixture. Forest won an exciting game 4-3 with two goals from Neil Martin, one from Bob Chapman and a George Lyall penalty.

NOTTINGHAM FOREST – SKY BET CHAMPIONSHIP 2021–22 LEAGUE RECORD

Match No.	Date		Venue	Opponents	Result		H/T Score	Lg Pos.	Goalscorers	Attendance
1	Aug	8	A	Coventry C	L	1-2	1-0	20	Taylor, L [36]	20,843
2		14	H	Bournemouth	L	1-2	0-1	23	McKenna [48]	25,035
3		18	H	Blackburn R	L	1-2	0-0	23	Zinckernagel [69]	23,964
4		21	A	Stoke C	L	0-1	0-0	24		21,346
5		28	A	Derby Co	D	1-1	0-1	24	Johnson [82]	22,991
6	Sept	12	H	Cardiff C	L	1-2	1-0	24	Grabban [23]	24,153
7		15	H	Middlesbrough	L	0-2	0-1	24		23,830
8		18	A	Huddersfield T	W	2-0	1-0	24	Grabban [22], Nicholls (og) [48]	17,462
9		25	H	Millwall	D	1-1	0-1	22	Lowe [52]	25,589
10		29	A	Barnsley	W	3-1	0-1	20	Zinckernagel [61], Johnson [68], Grabban [81]	13,657
11	Oct	2	A	Birmingham C	W	3-0	2-0	17	Grabban [11], Yates [29], Spence [53]	15,148
12		16	H	Blackpool	W	2-1	1-0	16	Johnson [22], Grabban [61]	27,946
13		19	A	Bristol C	W	2-1	0-1	12	Taylor, L 2 (1 pen) [90, 90 (p)]	18,325
14		24	H	Fulham	L	0-4	0-1	15		27,470
15		29	A	QPR	D	1-1	0-1	15	Colback [90]	15,089
16	Nov	2	H	Sheffield U	D	1-1	0-0	16	Grabban [83]	25,238
17		6	H	Preston NE	W	3-0	2-0	13	Grabban 2 (1 pen) [32 (p), 70], Colback [41]	27,129
18		20	A	Reading	D	1-1	1-0	13	Zinckernagel [4]	14,907
19		23	H	Luton T	D	0-0	0-0	12		25,715
20		26	A	WBA	D	0-0	0-0	13		22,424
21	Dec	4	H	Peterborough U	W	2-0	0-0	13	Garner [72], Yates [84]	28,308
22		11	A	Swansea C	W	4-1	0-0	8	Zinckernagel [48], Grabban [50], Johnson [68], Cafu [90]	17,659
23		18	H	Hull C	W	2-1	0-1	7	Grabban (pen) [55], Johnson [72]	26,513
24		26	A	Middlesbrough	L	0-2	0-1	9		29,832
25		30	H	Huddersfield T	L	0-1	0-1	9		27,159
26	Jan	15	A	Millwall	W	1-0	0-0	9	Grabban [90]	13,297
27		22	H	Derby Co	W	2-1	0-0	8	Grabban [48], Johnson [82]	29,256
28		25	H	Barnsley	W	3-0	2-0	7	Davis [15], Yates [38], Johnson [75]	27,504
29		30	A	Cardiff C	L	1-2	0-1	8	Davis [90]	18,866
30	Feb	9	A	Blackburn R	W	2-0	1-0	6	Garner [22], Johnson (pen) [90]	13,869
31		12	H	Stoke C	D	2-2	0-0	7	Johnson [56], Yates [90]	28,990
32		22	A	Preston NE	D	0-0	0-0	9		12,598
33		26	H	Bristol C	W	2-0	1-0	9	Johnson [38], Garner [55]	28,506
34	Mar	4	A	Sheffield U	D	1-1	0-0	8	Yates [90]	28,841
35		12	H	Reading	W	4-0	1-0	9	Davis 2 [1, 62], Yates [75], Surridge [80]	28,128
36		16	H	QPR	W	3-1	0-1	8	Spence [55], Yates [83], Johnson [87]	27,872
37	Apr	2	A	Blackpool	W	4-1	3-0	7	Zinckernagel [11], Johnson 2 [30, 36], Surridge [82]	13,986
38		6	H	Coventry C	W	2-0	1-0	5	Johnson [25], Garner [61]	28,977
39		9	H	Birmingham C	W	2-0	1-0	3	Davis [5], McKenna [79]	29,293
40		15	A	Luton T	L	0-1	0-1	5		10,070
41		18	H	WBA	W	4-0	3-0	5	Johnson (pen) [19], Yates [23], Colback [45], Surridge [90]	28,926
42		23	A	Peterborough U	W	1-0	1-0	4	Surridge [45]	12,870
43		26	A	Fulham	W	1-0	1-0	3	Zinckernagel [15]	19,218
44		30	H	Swansea C	W	5-1	1-1	3	Christie (og) [22], Surridge 3 [48, 52, 69], Mighten [84]	28,659
45	May	3	A	Bournemouth	L	0-1	0-0	3		10,563
46		7	A	Hull C	D	1-1	0-0	4	Johnson (pen) [90]	18,399

Final League Position: 4

GOALSCORERS

League (73): Johnson 16 (3 pens), Grabban 12 (2 pens), Yates 8, Surridge 7, Zinckernagel 6, Davis 5, Garner 4, Colback 3, Taylor, L 3 (1 pen), McKenna 2, Spence 2, Cafu 1, Lowe 1, Mighten 1, own goals 2.
FA Cup (7): Grabban 1, Johnson 1, Spence 1, Surridge 1, Worrall 1, Yates 1, Zinckernagel 1.
Carabao Cup (2): Joao Carvalho 2.
Championship Play-offs (4): Johnson 2, Colback 1, own goal 1.

Samba B 40	Lawrence-Gabriel J 4	Mbe Soh L 2	McKenna S 45	Bong G 4 + 3	Yates R 41 + 2	Colback J 36 + 2	Lolley J 10 + 17	Johnson B 44 + 2	Mighten A 5 + 18	Taylor L 8 + 10	Tobias Figueiredo P 22 + 4	Zinckernagel P 35 + 7	Cafu D 2 + 12	Osei-Tutu J 4	Grabban L 23 + 9	Joao Carvalho A 2 + 5	Back F 2 + 1	Fornah T — + 1	Worrall J 39	Garner J 36 + 5	Spence D 38 + 1	Lowe M 19 + 1	Horvath E 6	Xande Silva N 2 + 6	Richardson J — + 2	Ojeda B 3	Cook S 13 + 1	Davis K 14 + 1	Konate A — + 1	Surridge S 5 + 12	Laryea R 1 + 4	Panzo J 1	Match No.
1	2	3^1	4	5	6	7	8	9	10^2	11^3	12	13	14																				1
1	2		4		6	7^3	8^1	9	12	11^2	3	10		5	13	14																	2
1	2■		4		7	8^3		10	9^2		3	6		5^1	11	13	12	14															3
1			4	5	6			13	10	11^1	3	8	7		12	9^2	2																4
1	2		4	5	7^2			10	12	11		8			13	9^1			3	6													5
1			4		7		12	9^2	13	11		6^1			10				3	8	2	5											6
		2^3	4		7		13	6		11^1		9			10				3	8^2		5	1	12	14								7
1			4		6	14	9^1	10^2	12		3				11				2	7	5^3	8			13								8
1			4		6		10^2	9^3	14	12	3	13			11^1				2	7	5	8											9
1			4		6	13	10^3	9	14		3^1	11			12				2	7^2	5	8											10
1			4		6	7		9^3	14	13	3	10^1			11^2				2	12	5	8											11
1			4		6	7^1	14	9^3	13		3	10^2			11				2	12	5	8											12
1			4		6		13	10	12	14	3^1	9^2			11^3				2	7	5	8											13
1			4		6	7^1	14	10	13		3^2	9^3			11				2	12	5	8											14
1			4		6	7	9^3	10	13	12	3^1	14			11^2				2		5	8											15
1			4		6	8	10^1	9	14	11^2	3^3	12			13				2	7	5												16
1			4		6	7	12	8	10^1	14		9^2			11^3				3	13	2	5											17
1			4	12	6	7	8^2	10			13	9^3			11				3	14	2	5^1											18
1			4	13		5■	8^2	10		11^1	12	9^3	14						3	7	2					6							19
1			4	8	6		12	9	13		3^2	10^1			11				2	7	5												20
1			4		7	5		8		13		10	12		11^2				3	9	2					6^1							21
1			4	14	3	7		9		13		10^1	12	8^3	11^2				2	6	5												22
1			4		3	7		9	12^2		14	10^3		8^1	11	13			2	6	5												23
1			4		6	8		10		14	3^1	9^2			11^3	12	5		2	7				13									24
1			4			5		8		13		9^3	12		11	14			3	6	2			10^2		7^1							25
1			4		6	8		10				12			9				2	7	5						3	11^1					26
1			4		2	7		9		13		12			10^2					6	5	8					3	11^1					27
1			4		6	5		8^3				9			10^2					7	2	12		13			3	11^1	14				28
1			4		6	7^2		8				10^1	14		11					9	2	5		13			3^3	12					29
1			4		6	7		10^2											2	8	5	9		13			3	11^1		12			30
1■			4		13	7		10	14			9^2							2	6	5	8					3^3	11^1		12			31
			4		6	7		10											2	9	5	8	1				3	11^1		12			32
			4		13	7		10				9^2	14						2	6^3	5	8	1				3	11^1		12			33
			4^1		6	8^3	14	10	13			9^2							2	7	5		1				3	11		12			34
			4		6	7		10^3					12						2	9	5	8^1	1	14			3	11^2		13			35
			4^1		6	8	12	10			3	9^3	14						2	7	5		1					11^2		13			36
1			4		6	8	14	10^1			3	9^3			12				2	7	5							11^2		13			37
1			4		6	8	12	10^2			3	9^1			13				2	7	5							11^3		14			38
1			4		6	8	13	10^2			3	9^3			12				2	7	5							11^1		14			39
1			4^1		6	8^3	14	9			3	12			10^2				2	7	5							11		13			40
1			4^1		6^2	8		10			3	9	13						2	7	5^3						12			11	14		41
1			4		6	8	12	10			3	9^1	14		13^3				2	7	5									11^2			42
1			4		6	8^3	12	10				9^1	13						2	7	5						3			11^2	14		43
1			4		6	8^3	12	10	13			9^1							2	7	5						3			11^2	14		44
1			4		6	8^3	12	10	13			9^1							2	7	5						3^2			11	14		45
1							8	13	10		3	9	6						2	7	14			11^2						12	5^3	4^1	46

FA Cup

Third Round	Arsenal	(h)	1-0
Fourth Round	Leicester C	(h)	4-1
Fifth Round	Huddersfield T	(h)	2-1
Sixth Round	Liverpool	(h)	0-1

Carabao Cup

First Round	Bradford C	(h)	2-1
Second Round	Wolverhampton W	(h)	0-4

Championship Play-offs

Semi-Final 1st leg	Sheffield U	(a)	2-1
Semi-Final 2nd leg	Sheffield U	(h)	1-2

(aet; Nottingham F won 3-2 on penalties)

Final	Huddersfield T	(Wembley)	1-0

OLDHAM ATHLETIC

FOUNDATION

It was in 1895 that John Garland, the landlord of the Featherstall and Junction Hotel, decided to form a football club. As Pine Villa they played in the Oldham Junior League. In 1899 the local professional club, Oldham County, went out of existence and one of the liquidators persuaded Pine Villa to take over their ground at Sheepfoot Lane and change their name to Oldham Athletic.

Boundary Park, Furtherwood Road, Oldham, Lancashire OL1 2PA.

Telephone: (0161) 624 4972.

Ticket Office: (0161) 785 5150.

Website: www.oldhamathletic.co.uk

Email: enquiries@oldhamathletic.co.uk

Ground Capacity: 13,513.

Record Attendance: 47,671 v Sheffield W, FA Cup 4th rd, 25 January 1930.

Pitch Measurements: 100m × 68m (109.5yd × 74.5yd).

Chairman: Abdallah Lemsagam.

Sporting Director: Mohamed Lemsagam.

Head Coach: John Sheridan.

First-Team Coach: Tommy Wright.

Colours: Blue shirts with thin red stripes and red and white trim, white shorts with blue trim, blue socks with white trim.

Year Formed: 1895.

Turned Professional: 1899.

Previous Name: 1895, Pine Villa; 1899, Oldham Athletic.

Club Nickname: 'The Latics'.

Grounds: 1895, Sheepfoot Lane; 1900, Hudson Field; 1906, Sheepfoot Lane; 1907, Boundary Park (renamed SportsDirect.com Park 2014; Boundary Park 2018).

First Football League Game: 9 September 1907, Division 2, v Stoke (a) W 3–1 – Hewitson; Hodson, Hamilton; Fay, Walders, Wilson; Ward, Billy Dodds (1), Newton (1), Hancock, Swarbrick (1).

Record League Victory: 11–0 v Southport, Division 4, 26 December 1962 – Bollands; Branagan, Marshall; McCall, Williams, Scott; Ledger (1), Johnstone, Lister (6), Colquhoun (1), Whitaker (3).

Record Cup Victory: 10–1 v Lytham, FA Cup 1st rd, 28 November 1925 – Gray; Wynne, Grundy; Adlam, Heaton, Naylor (1), Douglas, Pynegar (2), Ormston (2), Barnes (3), Watson (2).

Record Defeat: 4–13 v Tranmere R, Division 3 (N), 26 December 1935.

HONOURS

League Champions: Division 2 – 1990–91; Division 3 – 1973–74; Division 3N – 1952–53.
Runners-up: Division 1 – 1914–15; Division 2 – 1909–10; Division 4 – 1962–63.

FA Cup: semi-final – 1913, 1990, 1994.

League Cup: *Runners-up:* 1990.

FOOTBALL YEARBOOK FACT FILE

Oldham Athletic's floodlights were installed at the club's Boundary Park ground in 1961, the last Football League club in Lancashire to introduce lighting. They were first used for a friendly fixture with Burnley on 3 October of that year when a crowd of 15,520 turned out to watch a 3-3 draw. Latics' scorers were Bert Lister, Bobby Johnstone and John Colquhoun.

Most League Points (2 for a win): 62, Division 3, 1973–74.

Most League Points (3 for a win): 88, Division 2, 1990–91.

Most League Goals: 95, Division 4, 1962–63.

Highest League Scorer in Season: Tom Davis, 33, Division 3 (N), 1936–37.

Most League Goals in Total Aggregate: Roger Palmer, 141, 1980–94.

Most League Goals in One Match: 7, Eric Gemmell v Chester, Division 3 (N), 19 January 1952.

Most Capped Player: Gunnar Halle, 25 (64), Norway.

Most League Appearances: Ian Wood, 525, 1966–80.

Youngest League Player: Wayne Harrison, 16 years 347 days v Notts Co, 27 October 1984.

Record Transfer Fee Received: £1,700,000 from Aston Villa for Earl Barrett, February 1992.

Record Transfer Fee Paid: £750,000 to Aston Villa for Ian Olney, June 1992.

Football League Record: 1907 Elected to Division 2; 1910–23 Division 1; 1923–35 Division 2; 1935–53 Division 3 (N); 1953–54 Division 2; 1954–58 Division 3 (N); 1958–63 Division 4; 1963–69 Division 3; 1969–71 Division 4; 1971–74 Division 3; 1974–91 Division 2; 1991–92 Division 1; 1992–94 Premier League; 1994–97 Division 1; 1997–2004 Division 2; 2004–18 FL 1; 2018–22 FL 2; 2022– National League.

LATEST SEQUENCES

Longest Sequence of League Wins: 10, 12.1.1974 – 12.3.1974.

Longest Sequence of League Defeats: 8, 15.12.1934 – 2.2.1935.

Longest Sequence of League Draws: 5, 7.4.2018 – 21.4.2018.

Longest Sequence of Unbeaten League Matches: 20, 1.5.1990 – 10.11.1990.

Longest Sequence Without a League Win: 17, 4.9.1920 – 18.12.1920.

Successive Scoring Runs: 25 from 25.8.1962.

Successive Non-scoring Runs: 6 from 12.2.2011.

MANAGERS

David Ashworth 1906–14
Herbert Bamlett 1914–21
Charlie Roberts 1921–22
David Ashworth 1923–24
Bob Mellor 1924–27
Andy Wilson 1927–32
Bob Mellor 1932–33
Jimmy McMullan 1933–34
Bob Mellor 1934–45
(continued as Secretary to 1953)
Frank Womack 1945–47
Billy Wootton 1947–50
George Hardwick 1950–56
Ted Goodier 1956–58
Norman Dodgin 1958–60
Danny McLennan 1960
Jack Rowley 1960–63
Les McDowall 1963–65
Gordon Hurst 1965–66
Jimmy McIlroy 1966–68
Jack Rowley 1968–69
Jimmy Frizzell 1970–82
Joe Royle 1982–94
Graeme Sharp 1994–97
Neil Warnock 1997–98
Andy Ritchie 1998–2001
Mick Wadsworth 2001–02
Iain Dowie 2002–03
Brian Talbot 2004–05
Ronnie Moore 2005–06
John Sheridan 2006–09
Joe Royle 2009
Dave Penney 2009–10
Paul Dickov 2010–13
Lee Johnson 2013–15
Dean Holden 2015
Darren Kelly 2015
David Dunn 2015–16
John Sheridan 2016
Stephen Robinson 2016–17
John Sheridan 2017
Richie Wellens 2017–18
Frankie Bunn 2018
Paul Scholes 2019
Laurent Banide 2019
Dino Maamria 2019–20
Harry Kewell 2020–21
Keith Curle 2021
John Sheridan January 2022–

TEN YEAR LEAGUE RECORD

		P	W	D	L	F	A	Pts	Pos
2012-13	FL 1	46	14	9	23	46	59	51	19
2013-14	FL 1	46	14	14	18	50	59	56	15
2014-15	FL 1	46	14	15	17	54	67	57	15
2015-16	FL 1	46	12	18	16	44	58	54	17
2016-17	FL 1	46	12	17	17	31	44	53	17
2017-18	FL 1	46	11	17	18	58	75	50	21
2018-19	FL 2	46	16	14	16	67	60	62	14
2019-20	FL 2	37	9	14	14	44	57	41	19§
2020-21	FL 2	46	15	9	22	72	81	54	18
2021-22	FL 2	46	9	11	26	46	75	38	23

§Decided on points-per-game (1.11)

DID YOU KNOW ?

Joe Stafford is believed to be the only player to have appeared for Oldham Athletic in their junior club days as Pine Villa and for the Latics in a Football League match. After featuring for the club in the 1890s he returned in November 1903 but although he remained on the books until the 1912–13 season, he made just a single League appearance for them.

OLDHAM ATHLETIC – SKY BET LEAGUE TWO 2021–22 LEAGUE RECORD

Match No.	Date	Venue	Opponents	Result		H/T Score	Lg Pos.	Goalscorers	Attendance
1	Aug 7	H	Newport Co	L	0-1	0-0	19		4094
2	14	A	Bradford C	L	1-2	0-1	22	Bahamboula 90	17,624
3	17	A	Bristol R	L	0-1	0-1	24		6005
4	21	H	Colchester U	L	1-2	0-2	24	Bahamboula 73	3496
5	28	A	Sutton U	W	2-1	0-0	23	Piergianni 88, Luamba 90	3262
6	Sept 4	H	Barrow	L	0-3	0-1	23		4232
7	11	A	Leyton Orient	L	0-4	0-2	24		5315
8	18	H	Hartlepool U	D	0-0	0-0	24		3934
9	25	A	Rochdale	W	1-0	0-0	24	Keillor-Dunn 59	5234
10	Oct 2	H	Harrogate T	L	1-2	0-1	23	Vaughan 76	3729
11	9	A	Mansfield T	D	0-0	0-0	23		4556
12	16	H	Stevenage	W	3-0	2-0	21	Keillor-Dunn 2 5, 16, Bahamboula 58	3492
13	19	H	Walsall	L	1-3	0-2	22	Hope 67	3762
14	23	A	Carlisle U	D	0-0	0-0	21		4274
15	30	H	Swindon T	L	1-3	0-1	22	Piergianni 90	4085
16	Nov 13	A	Exeter C	L	1-2	0-1	23	Bowden 84	5103
17	20	H	Port Vale	W	3-2	1-1	22	Keillor-Dunn 31, Hart 81, Martin (og) 90	6080
18	23	A	Northampton T	L	1-2	0-2	22	Piergianni 54	4059
19	27	A	Salford C	L	0-2	0-1	23		3242
20	Dec 7	H	Tranmere R	L	0-1	0-0	23		4303
21	11	H	Forest Green R	D	5-5	1-3	23	Keillor-Dunn 2 11, 59, Hope 55, Stobbs 65, Wilson (og) 78	3621
22	26	H	Scunthorpe U	L	1-3	1-0	24	Couto 11	4693
23	29	A	Barrow	D	0-0	0-0	24		3495
24	Jan 1	A	Hartlepool U	D	0-0	0-0	24		5026
25	22	A	Harrogate T	L	0-3	0-1	24		2689
26	29	H	Rochdale	D	0-0	0-0	23		8199
27	Feb 5	A	Scunthorpe U	W	1-0	0-0	23	Luamba 83	5014
28	8	H	Bristol R	W	2-1	2-1	23	Keillor-Dunn 2 1, 31	5147
29	12	A	Newport Co	D	3-3	1-2	23	Keillor-Dunn 28, Fondop-Talom 2 49, 82	3901
30	19	H	Bradford C	W	2-0	2-0	22	Hope 19, Keillor-Dunn 24	7716
31	26	A	Colchester U	D	1-1	1-0	23	Keillor-Dunn 19	2983
32	Mar 1	A	Crawley T	D	2-2	0-0	23	Hope 56, Missilou 70	1927
33	5	H	Carlisle U	L	1-2	1-0	23	Hope 45	7327
34	12	A	Swindon T	L	0-1	0-0	23		11,390
35	15	A	Walsall	L	1-2	1-1	23	Sutton 21	4339
36	19	H	Exeter C	L	0-2	0-0	23		5111
37	22	H	Sutton U	L	1-3	0-1	23	Sutton 81	4624
38	26	H	Mansfield T	L	1-2	1-0	23	Keillor-Dunn 24	6045
39	29	H	Leyton Orient	W	2-0	1-0	22	Ray (og) 33, Whelan 90	4619
40	Apr 2	A	Stevenage	W	1-0	1-0	22	Hopcutt 16	4642
41	9	A	Port Vale	L	2-3	2-2	22	Missilou 16, Keillor-Dunn 45	8384
42	15	H	Northampton T	L	0-2	0-1	23		5789
43	18	A	Forest Green R	L	0-2	0-2	23		3137
44	23	H	Salford C	L	1-2	1-2	23	Keillor-Dunn (pen) 33	5752
45	30	A	Tranmere R	L	0-2	0-1	23		8008
46	May 7	H	Crawley T	D	3-3	2-2	23	Stobbs 26, Keillor-Dunn 28, Clarke 60	4591

Final League Position: 23

GOALSCORERS

League (46): Keillor-Dunn 15 (1 pen), Hope 5, Bahamboula 3, Piergianni 3, Fondop-Talom 2, Luamba 2, Missilou 2, Stobbs 2, Sutton 2, Bowden 1, Clarke 1, Couto 1, Hart 1, Hopcutt 1, Vaughan 1, Whelan 1, own goals 3.
FA Cup (2): Keillor-Dunn 1, McGahey 1.
Carabao Cup (2): Bahamboula 1, own goal 1.
Papa John's Trophy (6): Dearnley 3, Keillor-Dunn 1, Piergianni 1, Vaughan 1.

Rogers D 22	Clarke J 40	Sheehan A 5 + 1	Piergianni C 40	Adams N 31 + 5	Whelan C 39 + 4	Cisse O 8	Hart S 30 + 1	Bowden J 14 + 3	Keillor-Dunn D 43 + 3	Blyth J 1 + 2	Jameson K 6 + 5	Luamba J 9 + 6	Stobbs J 17 + 13	Bahamboula D 25 + 5	Hopcutt J 6 + 10	Hope H 29 + 10	Dearnley Z 7 + 5	Walker L 2	Fage D 10 + 4	Diarra R 9 + 3	Bettache F 5 + 5	Vaughan H 7 + 16	Leutwiler J 22	Da Silva V — + 3	McGahey H 25	Couto B 15 + 4	Modi I — + 2	Hunt A 7 + 6	Missilou C 18 + 2	Obadeyi T 4 + 4	Fondop-Talom M 1 + 1	Sutton W 9	*Match No.*
1	2^{3}	3^{1}	4	5	6	7	8	9	10	11^{2}	12	13	14																				1
1	2^{3}		3	5^{2}	7	6	4		10	14			8	9	11^{1}	12	13																2
	2		3	14	7	6	4		10^{3}	13			8^{2}	9		11		1	5^{1}	12													3
	2	3	4	5^{2}		6^{3}	8		10^{1}			13		9		11		1		14	7	12											4
	2	12	3		6		8^{1}		13			10		9		11			5^{3}	4	14	7^{2}	1										5
		4^{7}	3	6	7^{1}			8	12		5	11^{3}				10			2	13	9	14	1										6
	3		4	8^{1}				6	11		5					10	13		2^{3}	7	9^{2}	12	1	14									7
	2	4	3		7^{2}			13	9^{1}		5			10		11	14			6	8^{3}	12	1										8
	2		4		7				9^{1}		13			11		10^{3}			5	6	12		1	14	3	8^{2}							9
	2		4		7			12	9				5^{2}	11		10	13		8^{3}	6^{1}		14	1		3								10
	4		3		7			6	9				5	10^{2}		13	11^{1}				12		1		2	8							11
	4		3		7			6	9				5^{2}	10^{3}		14	11^{1}		12			13	1		2	8							12
	2	4^{1}			6			7	9				5^{3}	11		12	10^{2}				13	14	1		3	8							13
	4		3		6^{2}			7	10					11		5					13	9^{1}	1	12	2	8							14
	4		3		8^{1}			6^{2}	10					11		5					7	12	1		2	9	13						15
	2		3	5	7			6	9^{3}				12	11^{2}	14	10	13						1		4	8^{1}							16
	4^{3}		3	5^{2}	6	7^{1}	8		10						9	12	11		13				1		2	14							17
			3		8	7^{2}	4	6	11					12	13	14	10^{1}		5				1		2	9^{3}							18
			4	14	7		5	6	9				13	8	10^{1}	12	11^{2}		2^{3}				1		3								19
			3	2	12	6^{1}		7	10				14	13		11	8^{2}					9^{3}	1		4	5							20
	2		3	5	6		8	7	10			11^{2}	12	9^{3}		13						14	1			4^{1}							21
			4	2	6	7	13		12			14	10^{1}	8		11				3^{3}		9^{2}	1			5							22
	2		4	8	7		5	12	9^{2}				13		10^{1}	11				6^{3}			1		3	14							23
	2^{1}		4	9	6		5	8^{3}	10				12	14	13	11				7			1		3^{2}								24
	3		4	2	7^{3}		5		9				8	11	13	12							1			10^{2}		6^{1}	14				25
1	3		5	2	8		6		11^{2}				12	10	13										4			9^{1}	7				26
1	2		4	10	7		5		9^{2}			13		12											3				6	8	11^{1}		27
1	2		4	10	7		5		8			11^{1}		9											3			12	6				28
1	2		4	10^{2}	7		5		8			11^{1}	13	9■											3				6		12		29
1	2		4	8	7		5		9				10^{2}			11^{1}						[illegible]			3			14	6^{3}	12			30
1	2		4	6	8^{2}		5		11				9^{1}			10^{3}						4			3			13	7	12			31
1	2		4	10	12		5		9^{2}				14		13	11				6^{1}					3				7	8^{3}			32
1	2		4	10^{3}	7^{2}		5		8				14	9^{1}		11									3			13	6	12			33
1	2■		4	10	7		5		8				13	9		11^{2}			1[illegible]						3^{1}				6				34
1			4	6	14		5		11					12	13	10^{2}			[illegible]			7^{1}						9^{3}	8			3	35
1	2			8	7		4		10				13			11^{2}			5^{1}									6	12	9		3	36
1	4			2^{2}	7				8				10	9		11						12				5		6^{1}		13		3	37
1	2		4	8^{1}	6				10				7^{3}	9		11			13			14				5^{2}		12				3	38
1	2		4	10^{2}	7		5		9				8^{1}			11						12						13	6			3	39
1	2		4	6	7		5		11			12			8^{1}	10													9			3	40
1	2		4	8	7		5		9		13	11^{2}			12	10^{1}													6			3	41
1	2		4■	10			5		9		12	11^{2}			13										3	14		7^{1}	6	8^{3}			42
1	2			12	7		8		10		13		5	9^{3}	11^{1}							14			4				6			3^{2}	43
1	3			2	7^{2}		5		9		4	11	8^{1}		12	10^{3}						13				14			6				44
	2			14	12		5		8		4	11	10			13						9^{1}	1					7^{2}	6^{3}			3	45
1	2		3	14	7				11^{3}		4	12	8^{2}			10						9^{1}				5	13		6				46

FA Cup

First Round	Ipswich T	(a)	1-1
Replay	Ipswich T	(h)	1-2

Carabao Cup

First Round	Tranmere R	(h)	2-2
(Oldham Ath won 4-3 on penalties)			
Second Round	Accrington S	(h)	0-0
(Oldham Ath won 5-4 on penalties)			
Third Round	Brentford	(a)	0-7

Papa John's Trophy

Group B (N)	Salford C	(h)	1-0
Group B (N)	Leeds U U21	(h)	2-3
Group B (N)	Tranmere R	(a)	2-3
Second Round	Sunderland	(a)	1-0
Third Round	Wigan Ath	(h)	0-6

OXFORD UNITED

FOUNDATION

There had been an Oxford United club around the time of World War I but only in the Oxfordshire Thursday League and there is no connection with the modern club which began as Headington in 1893, adding 'United' a year later. Playing first on Quarry Fields and subsequently Wootten's Fields, they owe much to a Dr Hitchings for their early development.

The Kassam Stadium, Grenoble Road, Oxford OX4 4XP.

Telephone: (01865) 337 500.

Ticket Office: (01865) 337 533.

Website: www.oufc.co.uk

Email: feedback@oufc.co.uk

Ground Capacity: 12,537.

Record Attendance: 22,750 v Preston NE, FA Cup 6th rd, 29 February 1964 (at Manor Ground); 12,243 v Leyton Orient, FL 2, 6 May 2006 (at The Kassam Stadium).

Pitch Measurements: 101.2m × 67m (110.5yd × 73.5yd).

Chairman: Sumrith 'Tiger' Thanakarnjanasuth.

Managing Director: Niall McWilliams.

Head Coach: Karl Robinson.

Assistant Manager: Craig Short.

Colours: Yellow shirts with navy blue trim, navy blue shorts with yellow trim, yellow socks with navy blue trim.

Year Formed: 1893.

Turned Professional: 1949.

Previous Names: 1893, Headington; 1894, Headington United; 1960, Oxford United.

Club Nickname: 'The U's'.

Grounds: 1893, Headington Quarry; 1894, Wootten's Fields; 1898, Sandy Lane Ground; 1902, Britannia Field; 1909, Sandy Lane; 1910, Quarry Recreation Ground; 1914, Sandy Lane; 1922, The Paddock Manor Road; 1925, Manor Ground; 2001, The Kassam Stadium.

First Football League Game: 18 August 1962, Division 4, v Barrow (a) L 2–3 – Medlock; Beavon, Quartermain; Ron Atkinson, Kyle, Jones; Knight, Graham Atkinson (1), Houghton (1), Cornwell, Colfar.

Record League Victory: 7–0 v Barrow, Division 4, 19 December 1964 – Fearnley; Beavon, Quartermain; Ron Atkinson (1), Kyle, Jones; Morris, Booth (3), Willey (1), Graham Atkinson (1), Harrington (1).

Record Cup Victory: 9–1 v Dorchester T, FA Cup 1st rd, 11 November 1995 – Whitehead; Wood (2), Mike Ford (1), Smith, Elliott, Gilchrist, Rush (1), Massey (Murphy), Moody (3), Bobby Ford (1), Angel (Beauchamp (1)).

Record Defeat: 0–7 v Sunderland, Division 1, 19 September 1998; 0–7 v Wigan Ath, FL 1, 23 December 2017.

HONOURS

League Champions: Division 2 – 1984–85; Division 3 – 1967–68, 1983–84.
Runners-up: Second Division – 1995–96; FL 2 – 2015–16; Conference – (3rd) 2009–10 *(promoted via play-offs)*.

FA Cup: 6th rd – 1964.

League Cup Winners: 1986.

League Trophy: *Runners-up:* 2016, 2017.

FOOTBALL YEARBOOK FACT FILE

When Graham Atkinson left Oxford United in the summer of 1974, he was the last remaining player from the club's Southern League days. He made his first-team debut for the club as a 16-year-old in February 1960 and went on to become a prolific scorer for United. He netted twice in their final Southern League game at Yeovil in April 1962 and then scored the club's first Football League goal at Barrow on the opening day of 1962–63.

Most League Points (2 for a win): 61, Division 4, 1964–65.

Most League Points (3 for a win): 95, Division 3, 1983–84.

Most League Goals: 91, Division 3, 1983–84.

Highest League Scorer in Season: John Aldridge, 30, Division 2, 1984–85.

Most League Goals in Total Aggregate: Graham Atkinson, 77, 1962–73.

Most League Goals in One Match: 4, Tony Jones v Newport Co, Division 4, 22 September 1962; 4, Arthur Longbottom v Darlington, Division 4, 26 October 1963; 4, Richard Hill v Walsall, Division 2, 26 December 1988; 4, John Durnin v Luton T, 14 November 1992; 4, Tom Craddock v Accrington S, FL 2, 20 October 2011; 4, Cameron Brannagan v Gillingham, FL 1, 29 January 2022.

Most Capped Player: Jim Magilton, 18 (52), Northern Ireland.

Most League Appearances: John Shuker, 478, 1962–77.

Youngest League Player: Jason Seacole, 16 years 149 days v Mansfield T, 7 September 1976.

Record Transfer Fee Received: £3,000,000 from Leeds U for Kemar Roofe, July 2016.

Record Transfer Fee Paid: £470,000 to Aberdeen for Dean Windass, July 1998.

Football League Record: 1962 Elected to Division 4; 1965–68 Division 3; 1968–76 Division 2; 1976–84 Division 3; 1984–85 Division 2; 1985–88 Division 1; 1988–92 Division 2; 1992–94 Division 1; 1994–96 Division 2; 1996–99 Division 1; 1999–2001 Division 2; 2001–04 Division 3; 2004–06 FL 2; 2006–10 Conference; 2010–16 FL 2; 2016– FL 1.

MANAGERS

Harry Thompson 1949–58
(Player-Manager) 1949-51
Arthur Turner 1959–69
(continued as General Manager to 1972)
Ron Saunders 1969
Gerry Summers 1969–75
Mick Brown 1975–79
Bill Asprey 1979–80
Ian Greaves 1980–82
Jim Smith 1982–85
Maurice Evans 1985–88
Mark Lawrenson 1988
Brian Horton 1988–93
Denis Smith 1993–97
Malcolm Crosby 1997–98
Malcolm Shotton 1998–99
Micky Lewis 1999–2000
Denis Smith 2000
David Kemp 2000–01
Mark Wright 2001
Ian Atkins 2001–04
Graham Rix 2004
Ramon Diaz 2004–05
Brian Talbot 2005–06
Darren Patterson 2006
Jim Smith 2006–07
Darren Patterson 2007–08
Chris Wilder 2008–14
Gary Waddock 2014
Michael Appleton 2014–17
Pep Clotet 2017–18
Karl Robinson March 2018–

LATEST SEQUENCES

Longest Sequence of League Wins: 7, 15.12.2020 – 30.1.2021.

Longest Sequence of League Defeats: 8, 18.4.2014 – 23.8.2014.

Longest Sequence of League Draws: 5, 7.10.1978 – 28.10.1978.

Longest Sequence of Unbeaten League Matches: 20, 17.3.1984 – 29.9.1984.

Longest Sequence Without a League Win: 27, 14.11.1987 – 27.8.1988.

Successive Scoring Runs: 17 from 22.4.2006.

Successive Non-scoring Runs: 6 from 26.3.1988.

TEN YEAR LEAGUE RECORD

		P	W	D	L	F	A	Pts	Pos
2012-13	FL 2	46	19	8	19	60	61	65	9
2013-14	FL 2	46	16	14	16	53	50	62	8
2014-15	FL 2	46	15	16	15	50	49	61	13
2015-16	FL 2	46	24	14	8	84	41	86	2
2016-17	FL 1	46	20	9	17	65	52	69	8
2017-18	FL 1	46	15	11	20	61	66	56	16
2018-19	FL 1	46	15	15	16	58	64	60	12
2019-20	FL 1	35	17	9	9	61	37	60	4§
2020-21	FL 1	46	22	8	16	77	56	74	6
2021-22	FL 1	46	22	10	14	82	59	76	8

§*Decided on points-per-game (1.71)*

DID YOU KNOW ?

In 1984–85 six of the Oxford United team which won the old Division Two title were included in the PFA divisional team of the season. United, who were the first team to win the third tier and second tier titles in successive seasons, also won the FIAT Uno team of the year award and Jim Smith was Bell's Whisky Second Division manager of the season.

OXFORD UNITED – SKY BET LEAGUE ONE 2021–22 LEAGUE RECORD

Match No.	Date	Venue	Opponents	Result	H/T Score	Lg Pos.	Goalscorers	Attendance
1	Aug 7	A	Cambridge U	D 1-1	1-0	11	Seddon [42]	6444
2	14	H	Charlton Ath	W 2-1	2-1	8	Williams [23], Brannagan [31]	8440
3	17	H	Crewe Alex	W 1-0	1-0	5	Henry (pen) [33]	6757
4	21	A	Bolton W	L 1-2	1-1	10	Taylor [11]	15,073
5	28	H	Lincoln C	W 3-1	2-0	3	Henry 3 (1 pen) [12, 24, 73 (p)]	7045
6	Sept 4	A	AFC Wimbledon	L 1-3	1-0	7	Sykes [45]	7542
7	11	H	Wycombe W	D 0-0	0-0	10		9082
8	18	A	Cheltenham T	L 0-1	0-0	14		5004
9	25	H	Gillingham	D 1-1	1-1	13	Taylor [5]	6664
10	28	H	Accrington S	W 5-1	2-0	8	Holland 2 [18, 24], Taylor [50], Sykes [71], Nottingham (og) [90]	5654
11	Oct 2	A	Sheffield W	W 2-1	1-0	8	Brannagan [12], Henry [90]	22,060
12	16	H	Plymouth Arg	L 1-3	1-2	9	Taylor [5]	8877
13	19	H	Shrewsbury T	W 2-0	0-0	8	Sykes [46], Brannagan [87]	5763
14	23	A	Burton Alb	W 3-1	2-0	6	Taylor [1], Bostwick (og) [43], Henry (pen) [84]	3391
15	30	H	Morecambe	W 3-1	1-0	6	Seddon [29], Sykes [73], Taylor [87]	8766
16	Nov 13	A	Ipswich T	D 0-0	0-0	6		21,322
17	23	H	Fleetwood T	W 3-1	2-1	7	McNally [5], Brannagan [13], Holland [69]	5708
18	27	H	Rotherham U	D 0-0	0-0	8		7620
19	Dec 4	A	Sunderland	D 1-1	1-1	7	Taylor [36]	26,634
20	7	A	Doncaster R	W 2-1	1-0	5	Sykes [16], Henry [87]	5785
21	11	A	Milton Keynes D	W 2-1	0-1	5	Taylor [65], Sykes [79]	9914
22	18	H	Wigan Ath	L 2-3	1-2	6	Williams [33], Taylor [59]	8354
23	29	H	AFC Wimbledon	W 3-0	2-0	5	Sykes [27], Taylor [38], Long [60]	7915
24	Jan 1	H	Cheltenham T	D 1-1	0-0	5	Sykes [82]	8351
25	8	A	Lincoln C	L 0-2	0-1	5		8053
26	15	A	Wycombe W	L 0-2	0-1	7		8005
27	22	H	Sheffield W	W 3-2	1-1	6	Taylor 2 [45, 62], Winnall [84]	10,071
28	29	A	Gillingham	W 7-2	3-0	6	Bodin [8], Brannagan 4 (4 pens) [12, 48, 55, 83], Taylor [18], Forde [89]	4985
29	Feb 1	A	Wigan Ath	D 1-1	1-1	6	Taylor [23]	9958
30	5	H	Portsmouth	W 3-2	1-1	5	McNally [6], Brannagan [82], Holland [90]	10,373
31	8	A	Accrington S	L 0-2	0-1	5		1883
32	12	H	Bolton W	L 2-3	2-2	7	Bodin 2 [9, 32]	10,027
33	19	A	Charlton Ath	W 4-0	2-0	4	Taylor 2 [21, 28], Baldock [54], Brannagan [83]	14,029
34	22	A	Crewe Alex	W 1-0	0-0	4	Brown [64]	3968
35	26	H	Cambridge U	W 4-2	1-1	4	Taylor [35], Brannagan 2 [64, 90], Baldock [72]	10,004
36	Mar 1	A	Portsmouth	L 2-3	1-2	4	Browne [3], McNally [81]	15,113
37	5	H	Burton Alb	W 4-1	4-1	4	Baldock 2 [7, 40], Whyte [35], Taylor [45]	7631
38	12	A	Shrewsbury T	W 2-1	1-0	4	Taylor [11], Brannagan (pen) [83]	7302
39	19	H	Ipswich T	D 1-1	0-0	5	McNally [90]	11,029
40	Apr 2	A	Plymouth Arg	L 0-1	0-0	7		15,826
41	5	A	Morecambe	L 1-2	1-2	8	Taylor [3]	3882
42	9	H	Sunderland	L 1-2	1-1	8	Moore [35]	11,690
43	15	A	Fleetwood T	W 3-2	3-1	8	Holland [2], Brannagan [7], Bodin [16]	2589
44	19	H	Milton Keynes D	W 1-0	0-0	8	Bodin [86]	9685
45	23	A	Rotherham U	L 1-2	1-1	8	Barlaser (og) [10]	10,415
46	30	H	Doncaster R	D 1-1	1-0	8	Bodin [23]	9139

Final League Position: 8

GOALSCORERS

League (82): Taylor 20, Brannagan 14 (5 pens), Sykes 8, Henry 7 (3 pens), Bodin 6, Holland 5, Baldock 4, McNally 4, Seddon 2, Williams 2, Brown 1, Browne 1, Forde 1, Long 1, Moore 1, Whyte 1, Winnall 1, own goals 3.
FA Cup (5): Taylor 2 (1 pen), Bodin 1, McGuane 1, Seddon 1.
Carabao Cup (1): Holland 1.
Papa John's Trophy (5): Agyei 2, Cooper 2, Gorrin 1.

Stephens J 30	Forde A 10 + 3	Moore E 31	Thorniley J 21	Seddon S 35 + 1	Brannagan C 41	Henry J 17 + 9	Williams R 22 + 11	Sykes M 36 + 4	Whyte G 26 + 11	Taylor M 43 + 1	Bodin B 14 + 7	Winnall S 2 + 18	McGuane M 12 + 18	McNally L 28 + 2	Gorrin A 11 + 2	Holland N 21 + 14	Mousinho J 1 + 5	Agyei D — + 14	Kane H 34 + 1	Long S 35 + 1	Eastwood S 14	Trueman C 2	Hanson J 2	Cooper J — + 2	Brown C 11 + 2	Baldock S 4 + 3	Browne M 2 + 3	Golding J 1	O'Donkor G — + 1	Match No.
1	2	3	4	5	6	7	8^{1}	9^{3}	10	11^{2}	12	13	14																	1
1			4	5	8	6	2	9^{2}	11^{3}	12		10^{1}		3	7	13	14													2
1			4	5	8	6	2^{2}		14	10	9^{3}			3	7	11^{1}	13	12												3
1	2		4	5	8			6^{1}	11	10		9^{2}	12	3	7^{3}	13		14												4
1	2	3	4^{1}	5	8	6^{3}		9	11	10^{2}		13		12	7	14														5
1	2	3	4	5	8	6	11^{1}	9^{3}		10		14			7^{2}	12			13											6
1	2^{2}		4	5	8	6		9^{1}	11	10^{3}				3	7	13		14		12										7
1			4	5		6		9	11	10^{1}	14			3	7^{2}	13		12	8^{3}	2										8
1		3	4	5	8	9^{1}		12	11	10	13				7^{2}			14	6^{3}	2										9
1	2	4		5	8	6^{2}	12	9		10	13			3	14	11^{1}			7^{3}											10
1	9^{3}	3	4	5	8	12	14			10^{2}					7	11		13	6^{1}	2										11
1		3	4	5	7	8^{2}		12	9^{1}	11						10		13	6	2										12
1		3	4	5	8	13		9	11^{1}	10^{3}					7	12		14	6^{2}	2										13
		3	4	5	8	6^{2}	13	9^{1}	12	10					14	11^{3}			7	2	1									14
		3	4	5		6		9	12	10^{3}			13		7^{2}	11^{1}		14	8	2	1									15
		3	4	5	8	6^{1}	13	9		10^{3}			12			11^{2}		14	7	2	1									16
				5	8	6			10		9^{1}		12	3		11^{3}		13	7	4		1	2^{2}	14						17
				5	8	9			10				6^{1}	3		11^{2}		12	7	4		1	2	13						18
	2	4			8	6^{1}		14	9	10^{2}			13	3		11^{3}		12	7	5	1									19
		3	4	5	8^{1}	12	14	11	9^{2}	10			6^{3}			13			7	2	1									20
		3	4■	5	8	6^{1}	14	9	13	10^{3}			12			11^{2}			7	2	1									21
	2	3		5			11	8	9	10	6^{1}		7					12		4	1									22
	14	3	4	5	8		11	6^{3}	9^{1}	10^{2}		13	12						7	2	1									23
		3	4	5	8		11^{2}	9	12	10		13	6^{1}						7	2	1									24
		4		5	8^{1}	13	11^{3}	6	9^{2}	10			12	3		14			7■	2	1									25
		3	4	5	8	12	9^{2}	6	13	10		14	7^{1}			11^{3}				2	1									26
1		3^{1}	4^{3}	5	6			8		11	9	13	7	12		10^{2}	14			2										27
1	14	3		5	6		13	8		11^{1}	9^{3}	12	7	4		10^{2}				2										28
1		3		5	6		12	11^{3}		10^{2}	9^{1}	13	8	4			14		7	2										29
1		3		9^{4}	8		5^{2}	6		10	11^{3}	13	14	2		12	15		7						4^{1}					30
1	2	3		5	9		8	12		11		13	7^{2}			10^{1}			6						4^{3}	14				31
1		3		5^{3}	7		13	10	8^{2}	11	9^{1}		12	4					6	2						14				32
1		3			6		5	8	9	10^{3}		14	13	2^{1}					7	4					12	11^{2}				33
1		3^{1}		14	6		8	5	9	10^{3}			13	2					7	4					12	11^{2}				34
1				5	8	14	2	7^{3}	9^{1}	11^{2}				3		13			6	4						10	12			35
1	14			8^{2}	6		5		13	10				2		9^{3}			7	3					4	12	11^{1}			36
1					6		8	5	9	10^{2}		12	14	2		13			7^{3}	3					4	11^{1}				37
				2	7		8	5	11^{2}	10^{3}	12	14	13	4		9^{1}	3		6		1									38
					7		8	5	11^{3}	10	9^{1}	14	12	2		13			6	3	1				4^{2}					39
						12	8^{1}	5	9	10	11^{3}	13	7^{2}	2		14			6	3	1				4					40
1						12	5	6	11^{1}	10	13	14	8^{2}	2		9^{3}			7	3					4					41
1		4			8			9	12	10	6	13		3		11^{1}			7	2^{2}					5					42
1		4			8	13^{4}	14	9^{3}	12	10	6^{2}		15	3		11^{1}			7	2					5					43
1		4			8		14	9^{3}	11^{1}	10	12			3		6^{2}			7	2					5		13			44
1		4			8		6^{2}	11^{3}	14	10	9		12	3					7^{1}	2					5		13			45
1				8	7		5^{2}		12	10	9		6	2						3							11^{1}	4	13	46

FA Cup

First Round	Bristol R	(h)	2-2
Replay	Bristol R	(a)	3-4
(aet)			

Carabao Cup

First Round	Burton Alb	(a)	1-1
(Oxford U won 4-2 on penalties)			
Second Round	QPR	(a)	0-2

Papa John's Trophy

Group H (S)	Cambridge U	(a)	1-4
Group H (S)	Stevenage	(h)	1-2
Group H (S)	Tottenham H U21	(h)	3-2

PETERBOROUGH UNITED

FOUNDATION

The old Peterborough & Fletton club, founded in 1923, was suspended by the FA during season 1932–33 and disbanded. Local enthusiasts determined to carry on and in 1934 a new professional club, Peterborough United, was formed and entered the Midland League the following year. Peterborough's first success came in 1939–40, but from 1955–56 to 1959–60 they won five successive titles. During the 1958–59 season they were undefeated in the Midland League. They reached the third round of the FA Cup, won the Northamptonshire Senior Cup, the Maunsell Cup and were runners-up in the East Anglian Cup.

Weston Homes Stadium, London Road, Peterborough PE2 8AL.

Telephone: (01733) 563 947.

Ticket Office: (01733) 865 674.

Website: www.theposh.com

Email: info@theposh.com

Ground Capacity: 13,456.

Record Attendance: 30,096 v Swansea T, FA Cup 5th rd, 20 February 1965.

Pitch Measurements: 102m × 69m (111.5yd × 75.5yd).

Chairman: Darragh MacAnthony.

Chief Executive: Bob Symns.

Manager: Grant McCann.

Assistant Manager: Cliff Byrne.

Colours: Blue shirts with white diagonal patterned stripes and black trim, white shorts with black trim, blue socks with white trim.

Year Formed: 1934.

Turned Professional: 1934.

Club Nickname: 'The Posh'.

Ground: 1934, London Road Stadium (renamed ABAX Stadium 2014; Weston Homes Stadium 2019).

First Football League Game: 20 August 1960, Division 4, v Wrexham (h) W 3–0 – Walls; Stafford, Walker; Rayner, Rigby, Norris; Hails, Emery (1), Bly (1), Smith, McNamee (1).

Record League Victory: 9–1 v Barnet (a) Division 3, 5 September 1998 – Griemink; Hooper (1), Drury (Farell), Gill, Bodley, Edwards, Davies, Payne, Grazioli (5), Quinn (2) (Rowe), Houghton (Etherington) (1).

Record Cup Victory: 9–1 v Rushden T, FA Cup 1st qual rd, 6 October 1945 – Hilliard; Bryan, Parrott, Warner, Hobbs, Woods, Polhill (1), Fairchild, Laxton (6), Tasker (1), Rodgers (1); 9–1 v Kingstonian, FA Cup 1st rd, 25 November 1992. Match ordered to be replayed by FA. Peterborough won replay 1–0.

HONOURS

League Champions: Division 4 – 1960–61, 1973–74.
Runners-up: FL 1 – 2008–09, 2020–21; FL 2 – 2007–08.

FA Cup: 6th rd – 1965.

League Cup: semi-final – 1966.

League Trophy Winners: 2014.

FOOTBALL YEARBOOK FACT FILE

Peterborough United's first-ever victory over a top-flight club came in the fourth round of the FA Cup in 1964–65. Arsenal visited London Road and led 1-0 against the run of play at the half-time break. However, Posh came back with late goals from Derek Dougan and Peter McNamee and went on to win 2-1 in front of a crowd of 30,056.

Record Defeat: 1–8 v Northampton T, FA Cup 2nd rd (2nd replay), 18 December 1946.

Most League Points (2 for a win): 66, Division 4, 1960–61.

Most League Points (3 for a win): 92, FL 2, 2007–08.

Most League Goals: 134, Division 4, 1960–61.

Highest League Scorer in Season: Terry Bly, 52, Division 4, 1960–61.

Most League Goals in Total Aggregate: Jim Hall, 122, 1967–75.

Most League Goals in One Match: 5, Guiliano Grazioli v Barnet, Division 3, 5 September 1998.

Most Capped Player: Gabriel Zakuani, 17 (29), DR Congo.

Most League Appearances: Tommy Robson, 482, 1968–81.

Youngest League Player: Matthew Etherington, 15 years 262 days v Brentford, 3 May 1997.

Record Transfer Fee Received: £10,000,000 from Brentford for Ivan Toney, April 2020.

Record Transfer Fee Paid: £1,250,000 (in excess of) to Bristol C for Mo Eisa, June 2019.

Football League Record: 1960 Elected to Division 4; 1961–68 Division 3, when they were demoted for financial irregularities; 1968–74 Division 4; 1974–79 Division 3; 1979–91 Division 4; 1991–92 Division 3; 1992–94 Division 1; 1994–97 Division 2; 1997–2000 Division 3; 2000–04 Division 2; 2004–05 FL 1; 2005–08 FL 2; 2008–09 FL 1; 2009–10 FL C; 2010–11 FL 1; 2011–13 FL C; 2013–21 FL 1; 2021–22 FL C; 2022– FL 1.

LATEST SEQUENCES

Longest Sequence of League Wins: 9, 1.2.1992 – 14.3.1992.

Longest Sequence of League Defeats: 8, 16.12.2006 – 27.1.2007.

Longest Sequence of League Draws: 8, 18.12.1971 – 12.2.1972.

Longest Sequence of Unbeaten League Matches: 17, 15.1.2008 – 5.4.2008.

Longest Sequence Without a League Win: 17, 23.9.1978 – 30.12.1978.

Successive Scoring Runs: 33 from 20.9.1960.

Successive Non-scoring Runs: 6 from 13.8.2002.

MANAGERS

Jock Porter 1934–36
Fred Taylor 1936–37
Vic Poulter 1937–38
Sam Haden 1938–48
Jack Blood 1948–50
Bob Gurney 1950–52
Jack Fairbrother 1952–54
George Swindin 1954–58
Jimmy Hagan 1958–62
Jack Fairbrother 1962–64
Gordon Clark 1964–67
Norman Rigby 1967–69
Jim Iley 1969–72
Noel Cantwell 1972–77
John Barnwell 1977–78
Billy Hails 1978–79
Peter Morris 1979–82
Martin Wilkinson 1982–83
John Wile 1983–86
Noel Cantwell 1986–88 *(continued as General Manager)*
Mick Jones 1988–89
Mark Lawrenson 1989–90
Dave Booth 1990–91
Chris Turner 1991–92
Lil Fuccillo 1992–93
Chris Turner 1993–94
John Still 1994–95
Mick Halsall 1995–96
Barry Fry 1996–2005
Mark Wright 2005–06
Steve Bleasdale 2006
Keith Alexander 2006–07
Darren Ferguson 2007–09
Mark Cooper 2009–10
Jim Gannon 2010
Gary Johnson 2010–11
Darren Ferguson 2011–15
Dave Robertson 2015
Graham Westley 2015–16
Grant McCann 2016–18
Steve Evans 2018–19
Darren Ferguson 2019–22
Grant McCann February 2022–

TEN YEAR LEAGUE RECORD

		P	W	D	L	F	A	Pts	Pos
2012-13	FL C	46	15	9	22	66	75	54	22
2013-14	FL 1	46	23	5	18	72	58	74	6
2014-15	FL 1	46	18	9	19	53	56	63	9
2015-16	FL 1	46	19	6	21	82	73	63	13
2016-17	FL 1	46	17	11	18	62	62	62	11
2017-18	FL 1	46	17	13	16	68	60	64	9
2018-19	FL 1	46	20	12	14	71	62	72	7
2019-20	FL 1	35	17	8	10	68	40	59	7§
2020-21	FL 1	46	26	9	11	83	46	87	2
2021-22	FL C	46	9	10	27	43	87	37	22

§Decided on points-per-game (1.69)

DID YOU KNOW 

One of the lowest points in Peterborough United's history came on Boxing Day 1978. Posh, on a run of 15 games without a win, entertained Lincoln City, who had gone 19 games without a victory. The visitors won 1-0 and although Posh ended their winless streak soon afterwards, they were relegated at the end of the season.

PETERBOROUGH UNITED – SKY BET CHAMPIONSHIP 2021–22 LEAGUE RECORD

Match No.	Date	Venue	Opponents	Result		H/T Score	Lg Pos.	Goalscorers	Attendance
1	Aug 7	A	Luton T	L	0-3	0-1	24		10,019
2	14	H	Derby Co	W	2-1	0-0	15	Dembele 90, Burrows 90	10,477
3	17	H	Cardiff C	D	2-2	0-0	14	Burrows 49, Dembele 51	8534
4	21	A	Preston NE	L	0-1	0-1	17		9952
5	28	H	WBA	L	0-1	0-0	20		10,163
6	Sept 11	A	Sheffield U	L	2-6	1-1	23	Marriott 40, Clarke-Harris (pen) 79	27,359
7	14	A	Reading	L	1-3	0-0	23	Thompson 74	11,411
8	18	H	Birmingham C	W	3-0	2-0	22	Dean (og) 1, Clarke-Harris (pen) 35, Grant 50	12,199
9	24	A	Coventry C	L	0-3	0-0	21		20,652
10	29	H	Bournemouth	D	0-0	0-0	22		8971
11	Oct 2	H	Bristol C	L	2-3	2-2	23	Szmidics 2 22, 43	8560
12	16	A	Middlesbrough	L	0-2	0-0	23		19,556
13	20	A	Hull C	W	2-1	1-1	20	Jack Taylor 43, Dembele 72	10,245
14	23	H	QPR	W	2-1	0-0	20	Burrows 56, Dembele 90	12,035
15	30	A	Swansea C	L	0-3	0-3	20		16,639
16	Nov 2	H	Huddersfield T	D	1-1	0-0	20	Clarke-Harris 84	7983
17	6	H	Fulham	L	0-1	0-0	21		11,214
18	20	A	Stoke C	L	0-2	0-1	22		21,285
19	24	A	Blackburn R	L	0-4	0-3	22		9038
20	27	H	Barnsley	D	0-0	0-0	22		12,264
21	Dec 4	A	Nottingham F	L	0-2	0-0	22		28,308
22	11	H	Millwall	W	2-1	0-1	22	McNamara (og) 64, Clarke-Harris 67	9140
23	18	A	Blackpool	L	1-3	1-1	22	Dembele 11	9745
24	Jan 15	H	Coventry C	L	1-4	1-2	22	Grant 37	10,282
25	22	A	WBA	L	0-3	0-0	22		21,251
26	25	A	Birmingham C	D	2-2	1-0	22	Marriott 16, Clarke-Harris (pen) 67	16,380
27	29	H	Sheffield U	L	0-2	0-0	22		10,152
28	Feb 9	A	Cardiff C	L	0-4	0-2	22		17,297
29	12	H	Preston NE	L	0-1	0-0	22		9072
30	16	H	Reading	D	0-0	0-0	22		11,520
31	19	A	Derby Co	L	0-1	0-0	23		30,251
32	23	A	Fulham	L	1-2	0-1	23	Marriott 89	17,387
33	26	H	Hull C	L	0-3	0-1	24		9463
34	Mar 4	A	Huddersfield T	L	0-3	0-2	24		16,023
35	8	A	Bournemouth	D	1-1	1-0	24	Marriott 30	8293
36	12	H	Stoke C	D	2-2	1-1	24	Clarke-Harris 2 (1 pen) 33, 90 (p)	9060
37	16	H	Swansea C	L	2-3	0-1	24	Szmidics 51, Marriott 63	6832
38	20	A	QPR	W	3-1	1-1	23	Clarke-Harris 2 (1 pen) 39, 53 (p), Marriott 54	13,753
39	Apr 2	H	Middlesbrough	L	0-4	0-1	24		11,755
40	5	H	Luton T	D	1-1	0-0	24	Clarke-Harris 87	10,940
41	9	A	Bristol C	D	1-1	0-1	24	Clarke-Harris 65	19,052
42	15	H	Blackburn R	W	2-1	0-0	23	Szmidics 83, Marriott 87	9426
43	18	A	Barnsley	W	2-0	1-0	22	Marriott 25, Jack Taylor 75	12,197
44	23	H	Nottingham F	L	0-1	0-1	22		12,870
45	30	A	Millwall	L	0-3	0-0	23		16,705
46	May 7	H	Blackpool	W	5-0	1-0	22	Clarke-Harris 36, Szmidics 2 62, 70, Marriott 85, Jack Taylor 89	9118

Final League Position: 22

GOALSCORERS

League (43): Clarke-Harris 12 (5 pens), Marriott 9, Szmidics 6, Dembele 5, Burrows 3, Jack Taylor 3, Grant 2, Thompson 1, own goals 2.
FA Cup (4): Jade-Jones 1, Mumba 1, Szmodics 1, Ward 1.
Carabao Cup (0).

Pym C 7	Thompson N 27	Kent F 33 + 1	Beevers M 14	Butler D 19 + 3	Ward J 31 + 7	Knight J 31 + 5	Grant J 21 + 5	Tomlinson J 3 + 2	Szmidics S 26 + 10	Clarke-Harris J 32 + 9	Randall J 1 + 10	Hamilton E — + 2	Edwards R 31 + 3	Norburn O 34 + 2	Marriott J 16 + 12	Dembele S 22 + 2	Burrows H 29 + 8	Taylor Jack 29 + 5	Coventry C 4 + 8	Cornell D 30	Adubofour-Poku K 11 + 9	Kanu I 1 + 4	Corbett K 1	Mumba B 7 + 3	Jade-Jones R 6 + 12	Benda S 9	Morton C 3 + 4	Fuchs J 17 + 1	Coulson H 5 + 1	Brown R 5 + 3	Taylor Joseph — + 4	Fernandez E 1	Match No.
1	2	3^{3}	4	5	6	7^{2}	8	9^{1}	10	11	12	13	14																				1
1	3	2	4^{3}	8	5	13	7			10	9^{2}			6	11^{1}	12	14																2
1	3	2	4^{1}	8	5	6				10^{3}	14	12		7	13	11^{2}	9																3
1	3	2		8	5	4^{3}	9		13	11	14			6	12	10^{1}	7^{2}																4
1	2	3		4	5	14	7^{3}		9	10				6^{1}	11^{2}	13	8	12															5
1		3		4	5	2	14		9^{3}	13				6^{1}	10^{2}	11	8	12	7														6
1	2	4		5^{3}	6			14	13	11			3	8	10^{2}	9		12	7^{1}														7
	2	4		5	9		8^{3}		14	10			3	7		11^{2}	13	6^{1}	12	1													8
	2	4		5	9^{1}		8^{3}			10			3	7		11	14	6^{2}	13	1	12												9
	2	4		5	13		10^{3}		14	11			3	7		9^{1}	6	8^{2}	12	1													10
	2	4		5	6^{2}		14		10				3	7^{3}		11	9	12	8^{1}	1		13											11
	2^{3}		5	6	12	3	7^{2}		10				4	8		11^{1}	13	9		1		14											12
	5		4	8^{2}	12	2^{1}	9^{3}		11				3	7		10	13	6	14	1													13
	2		4	14	5^{1}		9^{2}		11				3	6		10	8	7^{3}	13	1		12											14
	2		4	12	14		9^{2}		11	13			3	6		10	8^{1}	7		1		5^{3}											15
	2		4^{3}	12	5^{1}		9^{2}		11	13			3	6		10	8	7		1	14												16
		3	4^{1}	5	2^{2}				10	11			12	8		9	6^{3}	7		1	14	13											17
	3	2	4^{3}	8^{2}	5	14	9		11	12				6^{1}		10	13	7		1													18
	3	2^{1}	4^{2}	8	5				10	11			12	6^{3}		9	13	7	14	1													19
	5			4		2			12	11	14		3	13		9	8^{3}	7	6^{2}	1			10^{1}										20
	5			4		2	6		13	11			3	7^{2}		10	8^{1}	9	12	1													21
	2			5^{1}		3	7	12	10^{2}	13			4	6		11	8	9^{3}	14	1													22
	2					3	6^{1}	5		11			4	7		10	8	9		1	12												23
	2					3	9		10^{3}	12			4	7		11^{1}	8	6^{2}		1	14			5	13								24
		2	4		15	12	9^{2}		13	10^{3}			3^{1}	7	14	11	8^{4}	6						5		1							25
	3	2	4			14			13	10^{3}				7	11^{1}		8	6			9^{2}			5		1	12						26
	3	2			13	4	7^{3}	8^{1}		10	14				11^{2}						9			5		1	12	6					27
		2			14	3^{1}				13			4	7	11^{3}						9			5		1	10	6	8^{2}	12			28
	2	4			9	3				10				8	13						11^{3}			12	14	1		7^{2}	5^{1}	6			29
	2	4			9	3				10^{3}				8	12						11^{2}				13	1	14	6	5	7^{1}			30
	2	4			9	3				13				8	10^{3}									12	14	1	11^{1}	6^{2}	5■	7			31
		4			7	2	8		10^{3}	11^{2}			3	9	12		5								14	1	13			6^{1}			32
		4			5	2	14		9				3	6	11^{1}		8^{2}								13	1	10		12	7^{3}			33
			4		5	2	7^{2}		10	14			3	12	13					1	9^{1}				11^{3}			6	8				34
		4			5	3			12	10^{3}			2	7	11^{2}		8	6^{1}		1					13			9			14		35
		4			5	3				10			2	7	11^{1}		8^{2}	6^{3}		1				13	12			9			14		36
		4			5	2			9^{2}	10^{3}			3	7	12			13		1				8	11^{1}			6			14		37
		4			5	3			9	11^{4}			2	7	10^{3}		12	6^{2}		1	14			8^{1}				13			15		38
		4			5	3	14		9	11^{1}					10		8	6^{3}		1	13				12			7				2^{2}	39
		4^{2}			5	2			13	11			3		10^{1}		8	6		1	9				12			7					40
		13			2■	3			9^{2}	11			4		12		5	6		1	8				10^{1}			7^{3}		14			41
		4				2			6	10	13		3		12		5	7		1	9^{3}				11^{1}			8^{2}		14			42
		4			5^{1}	2			9	10^{3}	14		3		11^{2}		8	6		1	12				13			7					43
		4				2			9	10	13		3		12		8	7		1	5				11^{1}			6^{2}					44
		4^{1}			5	2			9	10	14		3		11^{2}		8	7		1	12				13			6^{3}					45
					2	3	12		9	10^{2}	13		4		14		8	7		1	5				11^{3}			6^{1}					46

FA Cup

Third Round	Bristol R	(h)	2-1
Fourth Round	QPR	(h)	2-0
Fifth Round	Manchester C	(h)	0-2

Carabao Cup

First Round	Plymouth Arg	(h)	0-4

PLYMOUTH ARGYLE

FOUNDATION

The club was formed in September 1886 as the Argyle Athletic Club by former public and private school pupils who wanted to continue playing the game. The meeting was held in a room above the Borough Arms (a coffee house), Bedford Street, Plymouth. It was common then to choose a local street/terrace as a club name and Argyle or Argyll was a fashionable name throughout the land due to Queen Victoria's great interest in Scotland.

Home Park, Plymouth, Devon PL2 3DQ.

Telephone: (01752) 562 561.

Ticket Office: (01752) 907 700.

Website: www.pafc.co.uk

Email: argyle@pafc.co.uk

Ground Capacity: 18,050.

Record Attendance: 43,596 v Aston Villa, Division 2, 10 October 1936.

Pitch Measurements: 103m × 66m (112.5yd × 72yd).

Chairman: Simon Hallett.

Chief Executive: Andrew Parkinson.

Manager: Steven Schumacher.

First-Team Coach: Kevin Nancekivell.

Colours: Dark green shirts with thin black stripes and black trim, black shorts, dark green socks with black and white trim.

Year Formed: 1886.

Turned Professional: 1903.

Previous Name: 1886, Argyle Athletic Club; 1903, Plymouth Argyle.

Club Nickname: 'The Pilgrims'.

Ground: 1886, Home Park.

First Football League Game: 28 August 1920, Division 3, v Norwich C (h) D 1–1 – Craig; Russell, Atterbury; Logan, Dickinson, Forbes; Kirkpatrick, Jack, Bowler, Heeps (1), Dixon.

Record League Victory: 8–1 v Millwall, Division 2, 16 January 1932 – Harper; Roberts, Titmuss; Mackay, Pullan, Reed; Grozier, Bowden (2), Vidler (3), Leslie (1), Black (1), (1 og). 8–1 v Hartlepool U (a), Division 2, 7 May 1994 – Nicholls; Patterson (Naylor), Hill, Burrows, Comyn, McCall (1), Barlow, Castle (1), Landon (3), Marshall (1), Dalton (2).

Record Cup Victory: 6–0 v Corby T, FA Cup 3rd rd, 22 January 1966 – Leiper; Book, Baird; Williams, Nelson, Newman; Jones (1), Jackson (1), Bickle (3), Piper (1), Jennings.

Record Defeat: 0–9 v Stoke C, Division 2, 17 December 1960.

HONOURS

League Champions: Second Division – 2003–04; Division 3 – 1958–59; Division 3S – 1929–30, 1951–52; Third Division – 2001–02.
Runners-up: FL 2 – 2016–17; Division 3 – 1974–75, 1985–86; Division 3S – 1921–22, 1922–23, 1923–24, 1924–25, 1925–26, 1926–27.

FA Cup: semi-final – 1984.

League Cup: semi-final – 1965, 1974.

FOOTBALL YEARBOOK FACT FILE

Tommy Tynan finished as leading scorer for Plymouth Argyle in six out of seven seasons, missing out only in 1985–86 when he had switched to play for Rotherham United. Towards the end of that season he was loaned back to Argyle and scored nine goals in his nine appearances for the club, helping them win promotion from the old Division Three. Tynan was also the club's Player of the Year on a record three occasions.

Most League Points (2 for a win): 68, Division 3 (S), 1929–30.

Most League Points (3 for a win): 102, Division 3, 2001–02.

Most League Goals: 107, Division 3 (S), 1925–26 and 1951–52.

Highest League Scorer in Season: Jack Cock, 32, Division 3 (S), 1926–27.

Most League Goals in Total Aggregate: Sammy Black, 174, 1924–38.

Most League Goals in One Match: 5, Wilf Carter v Charlton Ath, Division 2, 27 December 1960.

Most Capped Player: Moses Russell, 20 (23), Wales.

Most League Appearances: Kevin Hodges, 530, 1978–92.

Youngest League Player: Lee Phillips, 16 years 43 days v Gillingham, 29 October 1996.

Record Transfer Fee Received: £2,000,000 from Hull C for Peter Halmosi, July 2008.

Record Transfer Fee Paid: £500,000 to Cardiff C for Steve MacLean, January 2008.

Football League Record: 1920 Original Member of Division 3; 1921–30 Division 3 (S); 1930–50 Division 2; 1950–52 Division 3 (S); 1952–56 Division 2; 1956–58 Division 3 (S); 1958–59 Division 3; 1959–68 Division 2; 1968–75 Division 3; 1975–77 Division 2; 1977–86 Division 3; 1986–95 Division 2; 1995–96 Division 3; 1996–98 Division 2; 1998–2002 Division 3; 2002–04 Division 2; 2004–10 FL C; 2010–11 FL 1; 2011–17 FL 2; 2017–19 FL 1; 2019–20 FL 2; 2020– FL 1.

LATEST SEQUENCES

Longest Sequence of League Wins: 9, 8.3.1986 – 12.4.1986.

Longest Sequence of League Defeats: 9, 12.10.1963 – 7.12.1963.

Longest Sequence of League Draws: 5, 26.2.2000 – 14.3.2000.

Longest Sequence of Unbeaten League Matches: 22, 20.4.1929 – 21.12.1929.

Longest Sequence Without a League Win: 13, 1.5.2018 – 2.10.2018.

Successive Scoring Runs: 39 from 15.4.1939.

Successive Non-scoring Runs: 5 from 21.11.2009.

MANAGERS

Frank Brettell 1903–05
Bob Jack 1905–06
Bill Fullerton 1906–07
Bob Jack 1910–38
Jack Tresadern 1938–47
Jimmy Rae 1948–55
Jack Rowley 1955–60
Neil Dougall 1961
Ellis Stuttard 1961–63
Andy Beattie 1963–64
Malcolm Allison 1964–65
Derek Ufton 1965–68
Billy Bingham 1968–70
Ellis Stuttard 1970–72
Tony Waiters 1972–77
Mike Kelly 1977–78
Malcolm Allison 1978–79
Bobby Saxton 1979–81
Bobby Moncur 1981–83
Johnny Hore 1983–84
Dave Smith 1984–88
Ken Brown 1988–90
David Kemp 1990–92
Peter Shilton 1992–95
Steve McCall 1995
Neil Warnock 1995–97
Mick Jones 1997–98
Kevin Hodges 1998–2000
Paul Sturrock 2000–04
Bobby Williamson 2004–05
Tony Pulis 2005–06
Ian Holloway 2006–07
Paul Sturrock 2007–09
Paul Mariner 2009–10
Peter Reid 2010–11
Carl Fletcher 2011–13
John Sheridan 2013–15
Derek Adams 2015–19
Ryan Lowe 2019–21
Steven Schumacher December 2021–

TEN YEAR LEAGUE RECORD

		P	W	D	L	F	A	Pts	Pos
2012-13	FL 2	46	13	13	20	46	55	52	21
2013-14	FL 2	46	16	12	18	51	58	60	10
2014-15	FL 2	46	20	11	15	55	37	71	7
2015-16	FL 2	46	24	9	13	72	46	81	5
2016-17	FL 2	46	26	9	11	71	46	87	2
2017-18	FL 1	46	19	11	16	58	59	68	7
2018-19	FL 1	46	13	11	22	56	80	50	21
2019-20	FL 2	37	20	8	9	61	39	68	3§
2020-21	FL 1	46	14	11	21	53	80	53	18
2021-22	FL 1	46	23	11	12	68	48	80	7

§Decided on points-per-game (1.84)

DID YOU KNOW ?

Richard Morris, who played for Plymouth Argyle in their Southern League days, became the first Argyle player to win an international cap when he appeared for Wales against Ireland in April 1908. Morris, an inside-left, played just one more game for the Greens before moving on to join Huddersfield Town.

PLYMOUTH ARGYLE – SKY BET LEAGUE ONE 2021–22 LEAGUE RECORD

Match No.	Date	Venue	Opponents	Result		H/T Score	Lg Pos.	Goalscorers	Attendance
1	Aug 7	A	Rotherham U	L	0-2	0-2	24		9417
2	14	H	Gillingham	W	1-0	0-0	13	Jephcott [88]	10,854
3	17	H	Cambridge U	D	1-1	0-0	16	Jephcott [68]	10,532
4	21	A	Shrewsbury T	W	3-0	1-0	8	Hardie 2 [24, 65], Jephcott [50]	5737
5	28	H	Fleetwood T	D	1-1	1-1	12	Hardie [20]	10,453
6	Sept 11	H	Sheffield W	W	3-0	2-0	8	Edwards [7], Scarr [40], Law [90]	13,448
7	18	A	AFC Wimbledon	W	1-0	0-0	4	Hardie [47]	7578
8	21	A	Portsmouth	D	2-2	0-1	4	Hardie 2 [48, 80]	13,375
9	25	H	Doncaster R	W	2-1	0-0	4	Jephcott (pen) [68], Grant (pen) [90]	11,003
10	28	H	Crewe Alex	D	1-1	0-1	4	Hardie [72]	11,138
11	Oct 2	A	Lincoln C	D	2-2	1-0	3	Hardie [25], Galloway [74]	8375
12	9	H	Burton Alb	W	2-1	2-0	1	Grant [15], Broom [43]	11,915
13	16	A	Oxford U	W	3-1	2-1	1	Garrick [11], Camara 2 [39, 84]	8877
14	19	H	Bolton W	W	3-0	2-0	1	Galloway [6], Grant [15], Broom [90]	12,813
15	23	A	Morecambe	D	1-1	1-1	1	Mayor [12]	4272
16	30	H	Ipswich T	W	2-1	1-1	1	Jephcott [44], Grant [50]	16,087
17	Nov 13	A	Accrington S	W	4-1	2-0	1	Hamilton (og) [23], Houghton [44], Broom [63], Hardie [76]	3130
18	20	A	Charlton Ath	L	0-2	0-0	1		26,090
19	23	H	Wycombe W	L	0-3	0-0	3		12,833
20	27	H	Wigan Ath	L	1-2	1-1	4	Mayor [43]	15,329
21	Dec 8	A	Milton Keynes D	D	1-1	0-1	5	Grant [66]	7566
22	11	A	Sunderland	L	1-2	0-2	6	Scarr [64]	28,987
23	18	H	Charlton Ath	W	1-0	1-0	5	Agard [45]	12,711
24	26	A	Cheltenham T	W	2-0	1-0	4	Camara [42], Garrick [75]	5703
25	Jan 15	A	Sheffield W	L	2-4	0-2	6	Randell [47], Johnson (og) [83]	20,872
26	22	H	Lincoln C	L	1-2	1-0	7	Jephcott [34]	12,269
27	25	A	Fleetwood T	D	3-3	1-1	7	Jephcott [20], Edwards [49], Ennis [75]	2584
28	29	A	Doncaster R	W	3-1	1-1	7	Jephcott [23], Edwards [63], Garrick [79]	6493
29	Feb 8	A	Crewe Alex	W	4-1	0-1	8	Hardie 3 [48, 56, 85], Ennis [55]	3874
30	12	H	Shrewsbury T	W	1-0	0-0	6	Grant [62]	14,714
31	19	A	Gillingham	W	2-0	0-0	5	Garrick [46], Jephcott (pen) [76]	5197
32	22	A	Cambridge U	L	0-2	0-2	5		5286
33	26	H	Rotherham U	L	0-1	0-0	7		14,193
34	Mar 5	H	Morecambe	W	2-0	2-0	8	Grant [14], Hardie [43]	12,228
35	8	H	AFC Wimbledon	W	2-0	1-0	6	Hardie [29], Broom [61]	11,247
36	12	A	Bolton W	W	1-0	1-0	6	Gillesphey [43]	16,078
37	15	H	Portsmouth	W	1-0	0-0	5	Hardie [65]	15,604
38	19	H	Accrington S	W	4-0	2-0	4	Camara [12], Edwards [37], Ennis [64], Hardie [79]	13,076
39	22	H	Cheltenham T	W	2-0	2-0	4	Ennis [14], Mayor [42]	12,274
40	26	A	Ipswich T	L	0-1	0-1	4		23,256
41	Apr 2	H	Oxford U	W	1-0	0-0	4	Edwards [56]	15,826
42	9	A	Burton Alb	D	0-0	0-0	4		3938
43	15	A	Wycombe W	L	0-2	0-2	4		8181
44	18	H	Sunderland	D	0-0	0-0	4		15,800
45	23	A	Wigan Ath	D	1-1	0-0	5	Jephcott [63]	14,130
46	30	H	Milton Keynes D	L	0-5	0-3	7		15,644

Final League Position: 7

GOALSCORERS

League (68): Hardie 16, Jephcott 10 (2 pens), Grant 7 (1 pen), Edwards 5, Broom 4, Camara 4, Ennis 4, Garrick 4, Mayor 3, Galloway 2, Scarr 2, Agard 1, Gillesphey 1, Houghton 1, Law 1, Randell 1, own goals 2.
FA Cup (7): Garrick 3, Gillesphey 1, Hardie 1, Jephcott 1, Law 1.
Carabao Cup (5): Hardie 2, Camara 1, Jephcott 1, Shirley 1.
Papa John's Trophy (2): Agard 2.

Cooper M 46	Wilson J 42	Scarr D 35	Gillesphey M 36 + 4	Edwards J 38 + 3	Camara P 36 + 4	Houghton J 42	Mayor D 26 + 7	Grant C 37 + 1	Jephcott L 27 + 13	Hardie R 34 + 3	Broom R 29 + 14	Randell A 8 + 16	Shirley R — + 3	Galloway B 12 + 2	Law R 4 + 10	Garrick J 19 + 23	Agard K 3 + 9	Davies W — + 1	Cooper G — + 1	Ennis N 13 + 12	Bolton J 12 + 1	Crichlow-Noble R 1 + 2	Lewis A — + 1	Sessegnon S 6 + 4	Match No.
1	2	3	4	5	6	7	8^{1}	9^{2}	10^{3}	11	12	13	14												1
1	2	3	13	5	6^{2}	7		9	10	11	8^{1}	12		4											2
1	2	3	4	5	6	7^{3}		9^{2}	10^{1}	11	8	12	14		13										3
1		3	2	5	6	7		9^{1}	10^{3}	11	8^{2}	13		4	12	14									4
1		3	2	5^{1}	6	7		9^{3}	10	11^{2}	8		13	4	14	12									5
1	2	3		5^{1}	6	7		9^{3}	10^{2}	11	8			4	14	12	13								6
1	2	3			6	7		9^{2}	10^{1}	11	8			4	13	5	12								7
1	2	3		5	6	7		9	10^{3}	11^{2}	8^{1}			4	12	13	14								8
1	2	3	12	5	6	7		9	10^{3}	11^{2}	8			4^{1}		13	14								9
1	2^{2}	3	4	5	6	7		9^{1}	10^{3}	11^{4}	8			13	14	12	15								10
1		3	2	5	6	7			10	11^{1}	8			4		9	12								11
1	2	3	4	12	6^{2}	7	13	9		11	8	14				5^{1}	10^{3}								12
1	3	4	5	2	7	8	12	6^{3}	10^{2}	13	9^{1}			14		11									13
1	2	3		5	6^{1}	7	12	9	13	10	8			4		11^{2}									14
1	2	3		5	6^{1}	7	8	9	11^{2}	10^{3}	12			4		14	13								15
1	2	3	14	5	6		13	9	11	10^{1}	8^{2}	7		4^{3}		12									16
1	2	3	4	5	6^{1}	7		9		11	8^{3}	12				10^{2}	13	14							17
1	2	3	4	5^{3}	6	7	13	9	12	11^{1}	8^{2}					10			14						18
1	2	3	12	5	6	7	8	9	10^{2}	11^{3}	13			4^{1}		14									19
1	2	3	4	5	6	7	8^{2}	9	10^{1}	11^{3}	13					12	14								20
1	2	3	4	5	6	7	12	9	10^{2}	11^{3}	8^{1}					13				14					21
1	2	3	4	5	6^{2}	7^{3}	8		14	11	9^{1}	13				10				12					22
1	2	3	4	5	6	7	8^{1}		14	11^{3}	12					9	10^{2}			13					23
1	2	3	4	5	6	7	8^{2}	9	14		13					10^{3}	11^{1}			12					24
1		3	4	5		7^{3}	8^{1}	9	13		12	6			14	10				11^{2}	2				25
1	2	3		5^{2}	12	7^{1}		9	11^{3}		8	6			14	13				10		4			26
1	2	3	4^{1}	5	6^{3}			9	11^{2}		8	7				10				13		12	14		27
1	3	4	5	2	13	8	12	6^{4}	10^{3}		9^{2}	7^{1}				14				11	15				28
1	2	3	4	12	6		8^{1}		14	11^{3}	5	7			9	13				10^{2}					29
1	4		5	2	7	8^{3}	9	6	10^{1}	11^{2}		14				13				12	3				30
1	3		5	2	7	8	9^{3}	6	12	13	14					11^{1}				10^{2}	4				31
1	3		5		7		9	6	11^{1}	12	2^{2}	8				14				10	4^{3}			13	32
1	2		4	5	6^{2}	7^{3}	8	9	14	10	13					11^{1}				12	3				33
1	2		4	5		7^{3}	8	9	10^{1}	11^{2}	6	14				13				12	3				34
1	2		4	5	12	7	8^{1}	9^{2}		11^{3}	6					14				10	3			13	35
1	2		4	5	12	7	8	9^{2}	14	11	6^{1}									10^{3}	3			13	36
1	2		4	5	6	7	8		10^{1}	11^{3}		14			13	12					3			9^{2}	37
1	2		4	5	8^{2}	7	6^{3}	9		10	14	13				11^{1}				12	3				38
1	2		4	5^{2}		7	8^{1}	9		11	6	12				14				10^{3}	3			13	39
1	2		4	5		7^{2}	8			11^{3}	13	6				14				10	3^{1}	12		9	40
1	2	3	4	5	6^{3}	7	8^{2}		12		14	13			9	11^{1}				10					41
1	2	3	4	5	6	7	8	12	13		14				9^{1}	11^{2}				10^{3}					42
1	2	3	4		6	7^{3}	8^{1}	9	10		13	14				11^{2}				12				5	43
1	2	3	4		6^{1}	7	8	9	13	11^{3}		12				14				10^{2}				5	44
1	2	3	4			7	8	9	10^{2}	11^{1}	6					12				13				5	45
1	2	3	4^{1}	14		7■	8		11^{2}		6	12			9	10^{3}				13				5	46

FA Cup

First Round	Sheffield W	(a)	0-0
Replay	Sheffield W	(h)	3-0
Second Round	Rochdale	(a)	2-1
Third Round	Birmingham C	(a)	1-0
(aet)			
Fourth Round	Chelsea	(a)	1-2
(aet)			

Carabao Cup

First Round	Peterborough U	(a)	4-0
Second Round	Swansea C	(a)	1-4

Papa John's Trophy

Group F (S)	Newport Co	(a)	0-2
Group F (S)	Swindon T	(h)	1-3
Group F (S)	Arsenal U21	(h)	1-1

(Plymouth Arg won 5-4 on penalties)

PORT VALE

FOUNDATION

Port Vale Football Club was formed in 1876 and took its name from the venue of the inaugural meeting at 'Port Vale House' situated in a suburb of Stoke-on-Trent. Upon moving to Burslem in 1884 the club changed its name to 'Burslem Port Vale' and after several seasons in the Midland League became founder members of the Football League Division Two in 1892. The prefix 'Burslem' was dropped from the name as a new ground several miles away was acquired.

Vale Park, Hamil Road, Burslem, Stoke-on-Trent, Staffordshire ST6 1AW.

Telephone: (01782) 655 800.

Ticket Office: (01782) 655 821.

Website: www.port-vale.co.uk

Email: enquiries@port-vale.co.uk

Ground Capacity: 14,406.

Record Attendance: 22,993 v Stoke C, Division 2, 6 March 1920 (at Recreation Ground); 49,768 v Aston Villa, FA Cup 5th rd, 20 February 1960 (at Vale Park).

Pitch Measurements: 105m × 70m (115yd × 76.5yd).

Co-Chair: Kevin Shanahan, Carol Shanahan.

Chief Executive: Colin Garlick.

Manager: Darrell Clarke.

Assistant Manager: Andy Crosby.

Colours: White shirts with gold trim, white shorts with gold trim, white socks with gold trim.

Year Formed: 1876.

Turned Professional: 1885.

Previous Names: 1876, Port Vale; 1884, Burslem Port Vale; 1909, Port Vale.

Club Nickname: 'Valiants'.

Grounds: 1876, Limekin Lane, Longport; 1881, Westport; 1884, Moorland Road, Burslem; 1886, Athletic Ground, Cobridge; 1913, Recreation Ground, Hanley; 1950, Vale Park.

First Football League Game: 3 September 1892, Division 2, v Small Heath (a) L 1–5 – Frail; Clutton, Elson; Farrington, McCrindle, Delves; Walker, Scarratt, Bliss (1), Jones. (Only 10 men).

Record League Victory: 9–1 v Chesterfield, Division 2, 24 September 1932 – Leckie; Shenton, Poyser; Sherlock, Round, Jones; McGrath, Mills, Littlewood (6), Kirkham (2), Morton (1).

Record Cup Victory: 7–1 v Irthlingborough, FA Cup 1st rd, 12 January 1907 – Matthews; Dunn, Hamilton; Eardley, Baddeley, Holyhead; Carter, Dodds (2), Beats, Mountford (2), Coxon (3).

Record Defeat: 0–10 v Sheffield U, Division 2, 10 December 1892. 0–10 v Notts Co, Division 2, 26 February 1895.

HONOURS

League Champions: Division 3N – 1929–30, 1953–54; Division 4 – 1958–59.

Runners-up: Second Division – 1993–94; Division 3N – 1952–53.

FA Cup: semi-final – 1954.

League Cup: 4th rd – 2007.

League Trophy Winners: 1993, 2001.

Anglo-Italian Cup: *Runners-up:* 1996.

FOOTBALL YEARBOOK FACT FILE

When Port Vale moved to their current ground on Hamil Road in Burslem a number of names were suggested for the title including Port Vale Stadium, The Vale, and Holdcroft Park (after club chairman Alderman W.A. Holdcroft) before the title Vale Park was selected. Although originally scheduled to open in April 1950 it was not until the start of the following season that Vale began playing there.

Most League Points (2 for a win): 69, Division 3 (N), 1953–54.

Most League Points (3 for a win): 89, Division 2, 1992–93.

Most League Goals: 110, Division 4, 1958–59.

Highest League Scorer in Season: Wilf Kirkham 38, Division 2, 1926–27.

Most League Goals in Total Aggregate: Wilf Kirkham, 153, 1923–29, 1931–33.

Most League Goals in One Match: 6, Stewart Littlewood v Chesterfield, Division 2, 24 September 1922.

Most Capped Player: Chris Birchall, 27 (44), Trinidad & Tobago.

Most League Appearances: Roy Sproson, 760, 1950–72.

Youngest League Player: Malcolm McKenzie, 15 years 347 days v Newport Co, 12 April 1966.

Record Transfer Fee Received: £2,000,000 from Wimbledon for Gareth Ainsworth, October 1998.

Record Transfer Fee Paid: £500,000 to Lincoln C for Gareth Ainsworth, September 1997.

Football League Record: 1892 Original Member of Division 2. Failed re-election in 1896; Re-elected 1898; Resigned 1907; Returned in Oct, 1919, when they took over the fixtures of Leeds City; 1929–30 Division 3 (N); 1930–36 Division 2; 1936–38 Division 3 (N); 1938–52 Division 3 (S); 1952–54 Division 3 (N); 1954–57 Division 2; 1957–58 Division 3 (S); 1958–59 Division 4; 1959–65 Division 3; 1965–70 Division 4; 1970–78 Division 3; 1978–83 Division 4; 1983–84 Division 3; 1984–86 Division 4; 1986–89 Division 3; 1989–94 Division 2; 1994–2000 Division 1; 2000–04 Division 2; 2004–08 FL 1; 2008–13 FL 2; 2013–17 FL 1; 2017– FL 2.

LATEST SEQUENCES

Longest Sequence of League Wins: 8, 8.4.1893 – 30.9.1893.

Longest Sequence of League Defeats: 9, 9.3.1957 – 20.4.1957.

Longest Sequence of League Draws: 6, 26.4.1981 – 12.9.1981.

Longest Sequence of Unbeaten League Matches: 19, 5.5.1969 – 8.11.1969.

Longest Sequence Without a League Win: 17, 7.12.1991 – 21.3.1992.

Successive Scoring Runs: 22 from 12.9.1992.

Successive Non-scoring Runs: 5 from 1.5.2021.

MANAGERS

Sam Gleaves 1896–1905
(Secretary-Manager)
Tom Clare 1905–11
A. S. Walker 1911–12
H. Myatt 1912–14
Tom Holford 1919–24
(continued as Trainer)
Joe Schofield 1924–30
Tom Morgan 1930–32
Tom Holford 1932–35
Warney Cresswell 1936–37
Tom Morgan 1937–38
Billy Frith 1945–46
Gordon Hodgson 1946–51
Ivor Powell 1951
Freddie Steele 1951–57
Norman Low 1957–62
Freddie Steele 1962–65
Jackie Mudie 1965–67
Sir Stanley Matthews
(General Manager) 1965–68
Gordon Lee 1968–74
Roy Sproson 1974–77
Colin Harper 1977
Bobby Smith 1977–78
Dennis Butler 1978–79
Alan Bloor 1979
John McGrath 1980–83
John Rudge 1983–99
Brian Horton 1999–2004
Martin Foyle 2004–07
Lee Sinnott 2007–08
Dean Glover 2008–09
Micky Adams 2009–10
Jim Gannon 2011
Micky Adams 2011–14
Robert Page 2014–16
Bruno Ribeiro 2016
Michael Brown 2017
Neil Aspin 2017–19
John Askey 2019–21
Darrell Clarke February 2021–

TEN YEAR LEAGUE RECORD

		P	W	D	L	F	A	Pts	Pos
2012-13	FL 2	46	21	15	10	87	52	78	3
2013-14	FL 1	46	18	7	21	59	73	61	9
2014-15	FL 1	46	15	9	22	55	65	54	18
2015-16	FL 1	46	18	11	17	56	58	65	12
2016-17	FL 1	46	12	13	21	45	70	49	21
2017-18	FL 2	46	11	14	21	49	67	47	20
2018-19	FL 2	46	12	13	21	39	55	49	20
2019-20	FL 2	37	14	15	8	50	44	57	8§
2020-21	FL 2	46	17	9	20	57	57	60	13
2021-22	FL 2	46	22	12	12	67	46	78	5

§Decided on points-per-game (1.54)

DID YOU KNOW 

Port Vale were expelled from the Football League for financial irregularities at the end of the 1967–68 season. However, they were allowed to submit their membership to a vote of confidence at the League's annual general meeting in June 1968 when they were successfully reinstated, winning the vote by 40 to 9.

PORT VALE – SKY BET LEAGUE TWO 2021–22 LEAGUE RECORD

Match No.	Date	Venue	Opponents	Result		H/T Score	Lg Pos.	Goalscorers	Attendance
1	Aug 7	A	Northampton T	L	0-1	0-1	19		5804
2	14	H	Tranmere R	D	0-0	0-0	17		6986
3	17	H	Carlisle U	D	0-0	0-0	18		4943
4	21	A	Stevenage	D	1-1	1-1	17	Rodney [20]	2727
5	28	A	Forest Green R	W	2-0	2-0	10	Proctor 2 [6, 9]	2402
6	Sept 4	H	Rochdale	L	2-3	1-1	17	Proctor 2 [8, 59]	6113
7	11	A	Swindon T	W	2-1	1-0	10	Garrity 2 [22, 81]	8734
8	18	H	Harrogate T	W	2-0	1-0	7	Worrall [27], Wilson [47]	5435
9	25	A	Scunthorpe U	W	1-0	1-0	4	Garrity [44]	2513
10	Oct 2	H	Leyton Orient	W	3-2	1-0	3	Wilson [6], Proctor [90], Politic [90]	5667
11	9	A	Sutton U	L	3-4	2-1	4	Smith [21], Proctor [28], Conlon [78]	3905
12	16	H	Barrow	W	3-1	0-1	3	Politic [51], Jones, J (og) [56], Benning [85]	5951
13	19	A	Mansfield T	D	1-1	1-0	4	Conlon [33]	4202
14	23	H	Colchester U	W	3-0	2-0	2	Gibbons [6], Wilson [16], Martin [61]	5423
15	30	A	Crawley T	W	4-1	0-1	2	Conlon [49], Pett [76], Francomb (og) [80], Amoo [90]	2234
16	Nov 13	H	Bradford C	D	1-1	0-0	2	Wilson [56]	7010
17	20	A	Oldham Ath	L	2-3	1-1	3	Worrall [20], Gibbons [52]	6080
18	23	H	Walsall	L	0-1	0-1	5		6248
19	27	H	Hartlepool U	W	2-0	1-0	5	Garrity [31], Pett [90]	4839
20	Dec 7	A	Bristol R	W	2-1	2-0	3	Garrity 2 [31, 33]	6071
21	11	A	Newport Co	L	1-2	1-0	3	Garrity [25]	4074
22	Jan 15	H	Swindon T	L	1-3	1-2	9	Harratt [26]	6064
23	18	H	Salford C	L	0-1	0-0	9		4311
24	22	A	Leyton Orient	D	0-0	0-0	9		5761
25	29	H	Scunthorpe U	W	1-0	0-0	9	Smith [72]	5467
26	Feb 1	H	Forest Green R	D	1-1	1-0	9	Edmondson [12]	4508
27	8	A	Carlisle U	W	3-1	2-1	8	Worrall [1], Wilson [43], Amoo [81]	3379
28	12	H	Northampton T	D	0-0	0-0	9		5979
29	19	A	Tranmere R	D	1-1	0-0	9	Proctor [90]	7456
30	22	A	Rochdale	D	1-1	1-0	10	Garrity [45]	2667
31	26	H	Stevenage	W	2-0	2-0	9	O'Neill (og) [6], Edmondson [12]	5157
32	Mar 1	A	Harrogate T	D	1-1	0-1	10	Edmondson [68]	2257
33	5	A	Colchester U	L	0-1	0-0	10		2772
34	12	H	Crawley T	W	4-1	2-1	10	Garrity 2 [26, 51], Worrall [37], Hall [61]	5131
35	15	H	Mansfield T	W	3-1	1-1	9	Wilson [33], Harratt 2 [76, 88]	5233
36	19	A	Bradford C	W	2-1	0-0	8	Garrity [50], Wilson [63]	16,046
37	22	H	Exeter C	D	0-0	0-0	9		5301
38	26	H	Sutton U	W	2-0	2-0	4	Wilson [7], Proctor [23]	6362
39	Apr 2	A	Barrow	W	2-1	0-1	3	Proctor [59], Martin [89]	3215
40	5	A	Salford C	W	1-0	0-0	3	Charsley [59]	2449
41	9	H	Oldham Ath	W	3-2	2-2	3	Proctor 2 [10, 34], Walker [54]	8384
42	15	A	Hartlepool U	W	1-0	0-0	3	Hall [67]	5517
43	18	H	Bristol R	L	1-3	1-2	3	Proctor [2]	10,840
44	23	A	Walsall	L	0-2	0-0	4		6840
45	May 2	H	Newport Co	L	1-2	0-1	6	Garrity [51]	9048
46	7	A	Exeter C	W	1-0	1-0	5	Wilson [36]	8147

Final League Position: 5

GOALSCORERS

League (67): Garrity 12, Proctor 12, Wilson 9, Worrall 4, Conlon 3, Edmondson 3, Harratt 3, Amoo 2, Gibbons 2, Hall 2, Martin 2, Pett 2, Politic 2, Smith 2, Benning 1, Charsley 1, Rodney 1, Walker 1, own goals 3.
FA Cup (8): Wilson 3, Politic 2, Cass 1, Harratt 1, Lloyd 1.
Carabao Cup (1): Proctor 1.
Papa John's Trophy (9): Amoo 2, Benning 1, Conlon 1, Lloyd 1, Martin 1, Politic 1, Taylor 1, own goal 1.
League Two Play-offs (5): Wilson 3, Benning 1, Harratt 1.

Lucas Covolan C 21	Smith N 44	Martin A 21 + 8	Johnson R 3 + 1	Worrall D 39 + 2	Pett T 39	Walker B 24 + 4	Conlon T 17 + 1	Jones D 20 + 2	Wilson J 38 + 3	Rodney D 9 + 5	Stone A 16 + 2	Hurst A — + 1	Proctor J 24 + 7	Legge L 4 + 1	Garrity B 42 + 1	Benning M 17 + 9	Cass L 16 + 3	Amoo D 7 + 19	Gibbons J 19 + 4	Lloyd G 1 + 6	Taylor J 1 + 10	Politic D 5 + 5	Burgess S — + 2	Bailey E — + 1	Hall C 24	Hussey C 15 + 4	Harratt K 5 + 14	Edmondson R 9 + 10	Holy T 9	Charsley H 13 + 7	Cooper J 4 + 2	Robinson S — + 1	*Match No.*
1■	2	3	4^{1}	5	6	7^{2}	8	9	10^{3}	11	12	13	14																				1
1	2			5	8	7^{2}		4	10^{3}	11			14	3	6	9^{1}	12	13															2
1	2			5	8	7		4	12	11			10^{1}	3	6	9^{2}		13															3
1	2	12	4^{2}	6	8	7		9	11^{3}	10			14	3^{1}	13		5																4
1	2	3		5	8	7^{2}	13	4	10^{1}	12			11^{3}		6	9		14															5
1	2	3		5	7	14	8	4^{2}	10^{3}	13			11		6^{1}	9	12																6
1	3			5	7		8	4	13	11^{2}			10^{3}		6	9^{1}	2		12	14													7
1	3	15		5^{4}	7		8	4	10^{2}				11		6^{3}	12	2		9^{1}	13	14												8
1	3			5	7		8	4	10^{2}				11		6^{3}	12	2		9^{1}	13	14												9
1	3			5	7		8	4	10^{2}				11		6^{1}		2	13	9^{3}		12	14											10
1	3		14	5	7		8	4	10^{2}				11^{1}		6		2	12	9^{3}	13													11
1	3	14		5	7		8	4	10				11^{1}		6	13	2^{2}		9^{3}			12											12
1	3	2		5	7		8	4	11^{1}	12					6	9^{3}			14	10^{2}		13											13
1	3	12		5^{1}	6		7	4	10	9^{3}							2	14	8		13	11^{2}											14
1	4				8		9	5	10						7^{2}	6	3^{1}	12	2	13	14	11^{3}											15
1	3			5	7		8	4	10^{3}	12					6^{2}		2	11^{1}	9	14	13												16
1		3		5^{1}	7		9	4		10				13	6^{2}		2	11^{3}	8		12	14											17
1	3			5^{1}	7^{3}		8■	4^{2}		12			14		6	13	2	11	9			10											18
1		3	4	5^{1}	8	7		12		10					6		2	11	9														19
	3	12		5^{1}	7	13	8	4		6^{2}	1				10		2		9			11^{3}	14										20
1	2				7	6^{1}	8	4■						3^{3}	10	14	5		9			11^{2}	12	13									21
1■	4			5	7^{2}		9		11^{1}		12				6		2					13			3	8	10^{3}	14					22
	3	12		5	6^{2}	7			14		1				9			13	2						4^{1}	8	10	11^{3}					23
	2	3			6	7			11^{3}		1				8		12	10^{2}	5^{1}						4	9	14	13					24
	2	3		5		7			9^{3}						6			11^{2}							4	8	10^{1}	12	1	13	14		25
	2	3		5	8^{3}	7			11^{2}						6			13							4	9	12	10^{1}	1	14			26
	2			5	6	3			9^{3}						7			12							4	8	10^{1}	11^{2}	1	14	13		27
	2	3		5	8	7^{2}			10^{3}				12		6										4	9	14	11^{1}	1	13			28
	2			5^{3}	6	3			9				12		7			13	14						4	8	10^{1}		1		11^{2}		29
	2			12	6	3			9				10^{2}		7			13	5^{1}						4	8			1	14	11^{3}		30
	2			5^{3}	7	3			9^{2}				10		6			14	8^{1}						4	12		11	1	13			31
	2	12		14	7^{3}	3^{1}			10						6				5						4	8^{2}		11	1	13	9		32
	2	3		5					10^{2}				12		6	14									4	8^{3}	13	11	1	7	9^{1}		33
	2	3		5	7	14			10^{1}		1		11^{2}		6^{3}	15									4	9^{4}	12	13		8			34
	2	3		5	7	13			10^{3}		1		11		6	12									4	9^{1}	14			8^{2}			35
	2			5	6	3			10^{1}		1		11^{2}		9	8		13							4		12	14		7^{3}			36
	2			5	6^{2}	3			10^{3}		1		11^{1}		9	8		13							4		12	14		7			37
	2	12		5^{3}	6^{1}	3			10^{2}		1		11		9	8		13							4					7		14	38
	2	3		5^{2}		7			9^{3}		1		11			8		10^{1}			14				4		12	13		6			39
	2	3		5		8			10^{1}		1		11		7	9		12							4					6			40
	2	3		5^{1}		7			10^{3}		1		11		9	8									4	13	14	12^{2}		6			41
	2	3				6^{1}			10^{3}		1		11		9	8					12				4	13	14	5^{2}		7			42
	2	3		5^{3}				12	10		1		11		9	8					7^{1}				4		13	14		6^{2}			43
	2	3		5^{2}	7^{1}				10		1		11		9	8^{3}		13							4	14		12		6			44
	2	3		5	6				11^{3}		1		10		9	8^{1}		14	12							4	13			7^{2}			45
	2	3			6				9^{3}		1		11		7	12			5		13				4	8^{1}	14	10^{2}					46

FA Cup

First Round	Accrington S	(h)	5-1
Second Round	Burton Alb	(a)	2-1
Third Round	Brentford	(h)	1-4

Carabao Cup

First Round	Sunderland	(h)	1-2

Papa John's Trophy

Group D (N)	Bolton W	(a)	2-3
Group D (N)	Rochdale	(h)	1-0
Group D (N)	Liverpool U21	(h)	5-0
Second Round	Rotherham U	(a)	1-1

(Rotherham U won 5-3 on penalties)

League Two Play-offs

Semi-Final 1st leg	Swindon T	(a)	1-2
Semi-Final 2nd leg	Swindon T	(h)	1-0

(aet; Port Vale won 6-5 on penalties)

Final	Mansfield T	(Wembley)	3-0

PORTSMOUTH

FOUNDATION

At a meeting held in his High Street, Portsmouth offices in 1898, solicitor Alderman J. E. Pink and five other business and professional men agreed to buy some ground close to Goldsmith Avenue for £4,950 which they developed into Fratton Park in record breaking time. A team of professionals was signed up by manager Frank Brettell and entry to the Southern League obtained for the new club's September 1899 kick-off.

Fratton Park, Frogmore Road, Portsmouth, Hampshire PO4 8RA.

Telephone: (0345) 646 1898.

Ticket Office: (0345) 646 1898.

Website: www.portsmouthfc.co.uk

Email: info@pompeyfc.co.uk

Ground Capacity: 16,708.

Record Attendance: 51,385 v Derby Co, FA Cup 6th rd, 26 February 1949.

Pitch Measurements: 100m × 66m (109.5yd × 72yd).

Chairman: Michael Eisner.

Chief Executive: Andrew Cullen.

Head Coach: Danny Cowley.

Assistant Head Coach: Nicky Cowley.

Colours: Blue shirts with white trim, white shorts with blue trim, red socks.

Year Formed: 1898.

Turned Professional: 1898.

Club Nickname: 'Pompey'.

Ground: 1898, Fratton Park.

First Football League Game: 28 August 1920, Division 3, v Swansea T (h) W 3–0 – Robson; Probert, Potts; Abbott, Harwood, Turner; Thompson, Stringfellow (1), Reid (1), James (1), Beedie.

Record League Victory: 9–1 v Notts Co, Division 2, 9 April 1927 – McPhail; Clifford, Ted Smith; Reg Davies (1), Foxall, Moffat; Forward (1), Mackie (2), Haines (3), Watson, Cook (2).

Record Cup Victory: 7–0 v Stockport Co, FA Cup 3rd rd, 8 January 1949 – Butler; Rookes, Ferrier; Scoular, Flewin, Dickinson; Harris (3), Barlow, Clarke (2), Phillips (2), Froggatt.

Record Defeat: 0–10 v Leicester C, Division 1, 20 October 1928.

Most League Points (2 for a win): 65, Division 3, 1961–62.

HONOURS

League Champions: Division 1 – 1948–49, 1949–50; First Division – 2002–03; Division 3 – 1961–62, 1982–83; Division 3S – 1923–24; FL 2 – 2016–17.
Runners-up: Division 2 – 1926–27, 1986–87.

FA Cup Winners: 1939, 2008.
Runners-up: 1929, 1934, 2010.

League Cup: 5th rd – 1961, 1986, 1994, 2005, 2010.

League Trophy Winners: 2019.
Runners-up: 2020.

European Competitions
UEFA Cup: 2008–09.

FOOTBALL YEARBOOK FACT FILE

When Portsmouth won promotion to top-flight football for the first time in 1926–27, they achieved the feat on goal average, bettering rivals Manchester City by 0.005 of a goal. On the final day City defeated Bradford City 8-0 but Pompey's 5-1 home win over Preston North End was just enough to see them into the second promotion place.

Most League Points (3 for a win): 98, Division 1, 2002–03.

Most League Goals: 97, Division 1, 2002–03.

Highest League Scorer in Season: Guy Whittingham, 42, Division 1, 1992–93.

Most League Goals in Total Aggregate: Peter Harris, 194, 1946–60.

Most League Goals in One Match: 5, Alf Strange v Gillingham, Division 3, 27 January 1923; 5, Peter Harris v Aston Villa, Division 1, 3 September 1958.

Most Capped Player: Jimmy Dickinson, 48, England.

Most League Appearances: Jimmy Dickinson, 764, 1946–65.

Youngest League Player: Clive Green, 16 years 259 days v Wrexham, 21 August 1976.

Record Transfer Fee Received: £18,800,000 from Real Madrid for Lassana Diarra, January 2009.

Record Transfer Fee Paid: £9,000,000 (rising to £11,000,000) to Liverpool for Peter Crouch, July 2008.

Football League Record: 1920 Original Member of Division 3; 1921 Division 3 (S); 1924–27 Division 2; 1927–59 Division 1; 1959–61 Division 2; 1961–62 Division 3; 1962–76 Division 2; 1976–78 Division 3; 1978–80 Division 4; 1980–83 Division 3; 1983–87 Division 2; 1987–88 Division 1; 1988–92 Division 2; 1992–2003 Division 1; 2003–10 Premier League; 2010–12 FL C; 2012–13 FL 1; 2013–17 FL 2; 2017– FL 1.

LATEST SEQUENCES

Longest Sequence of League Wins: 7, 12.3.2019 – 22.4.2019.

Longest Sequence of League Defeats: 9, 26.12.2012 – 9.2.2013.

Longest Sequence of League Draws: 5, 2.2.2019 – 23.2.2019.

Longest Sequence of Unbeaten League Matches: 15, 18.4.1924 – 18.10.1924.

Longest Sequence Without a League Win: 25, 29.11.1958 – 22.8.1959.

Successive Scoring Runs: 23 from 30.8.1930.

Successive Non-scoring Runs: 6 from 27.12.1993.

MANAGERS

Frank Brettell 1898–1901
Bob Blyth 1901–04
Richard Bonney 1905–08
Bob Brown 1911–20
John McCartney 1920–27
Jack Tinn 1927–47
Bob Jackson 1947–52
Eddie Lever 1952–58
Freddie Cox 1958–61
George Smith 1961–70
Ron Tindall 1970–73
(General Manager to 1974)
John Mortimore 1973–74
Ian St John 1974–77
Jimmy Dickinson 1977–79
Frank Burrows 1979–82
Bobby Campbell 1982–84
Alan Ball 1984–89
John Gregory 1989–90
Frank Burrows 1990–91
Jim Smith 1991–95
Terry Fenwick 1995–98
Alan Ball 1998–99
Tony Pulis 2000
Steve Claridge 2000–01
Graham Rix 2001–02
Harry Redknapp 2002–04
Velimir Zajec 2004–05
Alain Perrin 2005
Harry Redknapp 2005–08
Tony Adams 2008–09
Paul Hart 2009
Avram Grant 2009–10
Steve Cotterill 2010–11
Michael Appleton 2011–12
Guy Whittingham 2012–13
Richie Barker 2013–14
Andy Awford 2014–15
Paul Cook 2015–17
Kenny Jackett 2017–21
Danny Cowley March 2021–

TEN YEAR LEAGUE RECORD

		P	W	D	L	F	A	Pts	Pos
2012-13	FL 1	46	10	12	24	51	69	32*	24
2013-14	FL 2	46	14	17	15	56	66	59	13
2014-15	FL 2	46	14	15	17	52	54	57	16
2015-16	FL 2	46	21	15	10	75	44	78	6
2016-17	FL 2	46	26	9	11	79	40	87	1
2017-18	FL 1	46	20	6	20	57	56	66	8
2018-19	FL 1	46	25	13	8	83	51	88	4
2019-20	FL 1	35	17	9	9	53	36	60	5§
2020-21	FL 1	46	21	9	16	65	51	72	8
2021-22	FL 1	46	20	13	13	68	51	73	10

** 10 pts deducted. §Decided on points-per-game (1.71)*

DID YOU KNOW ?

The only full England international to be staged at Portsmouth's Fratton Park ground was on 2 March 1903. England defeated Wales 2-1 in 'terrible' weather conditions with heavy sleet and hail followed by torrential rain. As a result, the game attracted a much lower than anticipated attendance of just 5,000.

PORTSMOUTH – SKY BET LEAGUE ONE 2021–22 LEAGUE RECORD

Match No.	*Date*	*Venue*	*Opponents*	*Result*		*H/T Score*	*Lg Pos.*	*Goalscorers*	*Attendance*
1	Aug 7	A	Fleetwood T	W	1-0	0-0	5	Brown [60]	4562
2	14	H	Crewe Alex	W	2-0	0-0	2	Marquis [48], Harness [64]	11,470
3	17	H	Shrewsbury T	W	1-0	1-0	1	Tunnicliffe [2]	14,471
4	21	A	Doncaster R	D	0-0	0-0	3		6660
5	28	A	Wigan Ath	L	0-1	0-0	5		9571
6	Sept 11	A	Milton Keynes D	L	0-1	0-0	11		10,822
7	18	H	Cambridge U	L	1-2	0-1	15	Curtis [76]	15,330
8	21	H	Plymouth Arg	D	2-2	1-0	12	Brown [6], Raggett [90]	13,375
9	25	A	Charlton Ath	D	2-2	1-0	10	Curtis [6], Harness [72]	16,378
10	28	A	Burton Alb	L	1-2	0-1	13	Hackett-Fairchild [64]	2810
11	Oct 2	H	Sunderland	W	4-0	3-0	11	Harness [19], Brown [33], Marquis 2 [45, 61]	17,418
12	16	A	Rotherham U	L	1-4	0-1	12	Harness [49]	9684
13	19	H	Ipswich T	L	0-4	0-1	17		16,301
14	23	A	Accrington S	D	2-2	1-0	16	Curtis [18], Harness [86]	2889
15	30	H	Bolton W	W	1-0	0-0	13	Marquis [51]	16,231
16	Nov 2	H	Cheltenham T	D	1-1	1-1	14	Hackett-Fairchild [32]	14,322
17	13	A	Wycombe W	W	1-0	0-0	10	Harness [73]	6471
18	20	H	AFC Wimbledon	W	2-1	0-1	9	Jacobs [63], Harness [89]	16,234
19	23	A	Lincoln C	W	3-0	1-0	9	Harness [45], Hirst [66], Hackett-Fairchild [89]	8533
20	27	A	Gillingham	W	1-0	0-0	9	Jacobs [90]	5637
21	Dec 7	H	Sheffield W	D	0-0	0-0	9		16,472
22	11	H	Morecambe	W	2-0	1-0	8	Harness [11], Ogilvie [77]	15,001
23	Jan 3	A	Cambridge U	D	0-0	0-0	8		6832
24	15	H	Milton Keynes D	L	1-2	0-2	9	Hirst [60]	14,958
25	18	A	AFC Wimbledon	D	0-0	0-0	9		8086
26	22	A	Sunderland	L	0-1	0-1	10		32,220
27	31	H	Charlton Ath	L	1-2	0-1	11	Jacobs [79]	15,326
28	Feb 5	A	Oxford U	L	2-3	1-1	13	Jacobs [10], Curtis [51]	10,373
29	8	H	Burton Alb	W	2-1	2-0	11	Raggett [33], Jacobs [41]	13,407
30	12	H	Doncaster R	W	4-0	0-0	11	Hackett-Fairchild [56], Hirst [63], O'Brien [81], Raggett [90]	14,767
31	22	A	Shrewsbury T	W	2-1	1-1	11	O'Brien [29], Thompson [84]	5862
32	26	H	Fleetwood T	D	3-3	1-3	11	Curtis (pen) [45], Harness [80], O'Brien [90]	15,224
33	Mar 1	H	Oxford U	W	3-2	2-1	10	Raggett [42], Hirst [45], Carter [58]	15,113
34	5	H	Accrington S	W	4-0	2-0	10	Hirst 2 [16, 56], Raggett [28], Tunnicliffe [69]	15,051
35	8	A	Crewe Alex	W	3-1	2-0	10	Hirst 2 [3, 66], Walker [31]	4307
36	12	A	Ipswich T	D	0-0	0-0	10		25,500
37	15	A	Plymouth Arg	L	0-1	0-0	10		15,604
38	19	H	Wycombe W	D	0-0	0-0	10		15,092
39	Apr 5	A	Bolton W	D	1-1	0-0	10	O'Brien [50]	13,809
40	9	A	Cheltenham T	L	0-1	0-0	11		5117
41	12	H	Rotherham U	W	3-0	1-0	10	Robertson [35], Harness [59], Hirst [65]	14,154
42	15	H	Lincoln C	W	3-2	0-0	9	Hirst (pen) [50], Jacobs [68], Curtis [82]	15,175
43	18	A	Morecambe	D	1-1	1-0	9	Raggett [41]	4893
44	23	H	Gillingham	W	3-1	2-1	9	Curtis 2 [4, 45], Robertson [54]	15,540
45	26	H	Wigan Ath	W	3-2	0-2	9	Hirst 2 [62, 64], O'Brien [87]	14,637
46	30	A	Sheffield W	L	1-4	1-3	10	Hirst [4]	33,394

Final League Position: 10

GOALSCORERS

League (68): Hirst 13 (1 pen), Harness 11, Curtis 8 (1 pen), Jacobs 6, Raggett 6, O'Brien 5, Hackett-Fairchild 4, Marquis 4, Brown 3, Robertson 2, Tunnicliffe 2, Carter 1, Ogilvie 1, Thompson 1, Walker 1.
FA Cup (2): Harness 1, Harrison 1.
Carabao Cup (1): Hackett-Fairchild 1.
Papa John's Trophy (10): Harrison 3, Curtis 2, Hirst 2, Ahadme 1, Azeez 1, Jacobs 1.

Bass A 2	Freeman K 19	Raggett S 45	Robertson C 22 + 4	Brown L 18 + 1	Tunnicliffe R 21 + 9	Ogilvie C 31 + 3	Harness M 39 + 1	Ahadme G 2 + 3	Curtis R 37 + 6	Marquis J 15 + 4	Hackett-Fairchild R 16 + 11	Hirst G 27 + 13	Johnson C — + 1	Bazunu G 44	Williams S 24 + 7	Morrell J 29 + 7	Jacobs M 11 + 13	Harrison E 1 + 10	Romeo M 30 + 5	Downing P 1 + 1	Azeez M 4 + 2	Thompson L 22 + 10	Carter H 22	Walker T 9 + 6	Hume D 7 + 2	O'Brien A 8 + 9	Mingi J — + 3	*Match No.*
1	2	3	4	5	6	7	8[3]	9[1]	10	11[2]	12	13	14															1
	2	3	4	5	6		8		10	11[3]	9[2]	14		1	7[1]	12	13											2
	2	3	4[1]	5	6	12	8[2]	13	10	11[3]	9			1	7			14										3
	2	3	4		6	5		9	10	11[3]	8[2]	14		1	12	7[1]	13											4
	2	3	4	5	8[1]		9[3]	14	11	10[2]	12	13		1	7	6												5
	2[2]	3	4	5	9		8		12	11[3]	10[1]			1	7	6		14	13									6
		4		5	6		8		10	12		14		1	7			11[2]	2	3[3]	9[1]	13						7
	2[2]	3		8[1]	6		9		11	10	12			1	4	7		13	5									8
	2	3		8	6		9[1]		10	11[2]	12	13		1	4	7			5									9
	2[1]	3		8	6[2]		9		10	11[3]	13			1	4	7		12	5			14						10
	2	3		8	6		9[1]		10	11[2]				1	4	7		13	5			12						11
	2	3		9	7[2]	4	10			11[1]	13	12		1	5[3]	8			6			14						12
	2	3		8	6	14	9[2]		10	11[1]	13	12		1	4[3]	7			5									13
		3		5	13	4	9		10	11	8[3]			1	7[1]	6[2]	14		2			12						14
		3		5	6[1]	4	8		10	11[3]	9	14		1	7[2]	13			2			12						15
		3		5		4	8		10	11[3]	9[2]	14		1	12	7			2		13	6[1]						16
1		3		5		4	9[3]	13	11			10[2]			7		12		2	14	8[1]	6						17
		3		5		4	6		11		12	10[1]		1	8	13	9[3]	14	2			7[2]						18
	2	3				4	9[3]		11		8	10[1]		1	7	6[2]	12	14	5			13						19
	2					3	9		10		8[3]	11[2]		1	4	6	14	13	5		12	7[1]						20
	2	3				4	9		11		8	10[1]		1	7			12	5		6							21
	2	3				4	9[2]		10	12	8	11[1]		1	7			13	5		6							22
	2[1]	3		13		4	9		10	14	8[2]	11[3]		1	7	6	12		5									23
	2[3]	3				4	9		10	13	8	11[2]		1	7[1]	6	14		5			12						24
		3		8		4	9[3]		12			10[1]		1	13	6	14		5			7[2]	2	11				25
		3	4[3]				9		11[1]		8	12		1	13	6	14		5			7[2]	2	10				26
		3	4				9		13			11		1	7[1]	6	14		5			12	2[3]	10[2]	8			27
	5[1]	3	12		13	4			11		15	10[3]		1		7■	9					6[2]	2		8[4]	14		28
		3	14		12	4			9		13	10		1			7[3]		5			6[1]	2	11	8[2]			29
		3	4		12	14	5		9		8	11		1			7[2]					6[3]	2	10[1]		13		30
		3	4		7		12		9		14	11		1					5[3]			6	2[1]	13	8	10[2]		31
		3	4		6		5		10		9	13		1		7							2[2]	11	8[1]	12		32
		3	12		13	4	9[2]					10[3]		1		7			5			6	2	14	8[1]	11		33
		3	4		6	8	9■					10[2]		1		12			5			7[1]	2	13		11[3]	14	34
		3	4		12	8			9			11[2]		1		6			5			7[1]	2[3]	10	14	13		35
		3	4		7	8			9			10[3]		1		12			5			6[1]	2	14	13	11[2]		36
		3	12		13	4			9			10		1		7			5			6[2]	2	14	8[1]	11[3]		37
		3	4		7	8	9[3]		14			11		1		12	13		5			6[1]	2	10[2]				38
		3	4			8	5		13			11[3]		1	12	7	9[2]					6[1]	2	14		10		39
		4			7	5	6[2]		9			14		1	8[1]	12	13		2				3	11		10[3]		40
		3	4			5	6[2]		10			11		1	14	7	9[1]		13			8[3]	2			12		41
		3	4		12	5	6		14			10		1	13	7[1]	9					8[2]	2			11[3]		42
		3	4		7	5	6[3]		10			11		1	8[1]		9[2]		14			12	2			13		43
		3	4			5[2]	6[3]		10			11		1		7	9		13			8[1]	2			14	12	44
		3	4		13	5	8[3]		10			11		1		7	9[1]		14			6[2]	2			12		45
		3	4			5	6		9			10		1		7	11[1]					8[2]	2			12	13	46

FA Cup

First Round	Harrow Bor	(h)	1-0
Second Round	Harrogate T	(h)	1-2

Carabao Cup

First Round	Millwall	(a)	1-2

Papa John's Trophy

Group B (S)	AFC Wimbledon	(a)	3-5
Group B (S)	Sutton U	(h)	0-2
Group B (S)	Crystal Palace U21	(h)	3-0
Second Round	Exeter C	(a)	3-2
Third Round	Cambridge U	(a)	1-2

PRESTON NORTH END

FOUNDATION

North End Cricket and Rugby Club, which was formed in 1863, indulged in most sports before taking up soccer in about 1879. In 1881 they decided to stick to football to the exclusion of other sports and even a 16–0 drubbing by Blackburn Rovers in an invitation game at Deepdale, a few weeks after taking this decision, did not deter them for they immediately became affiliated to the Lancashire FA.

Deepdale Stadium, Sir Tom Finney Way, Deepdale, Preston, Lancashire PR1 6RU.

Telephone: (0344) 856 1964.

Ticket Office: (0344) 856 1966.

Website: www.pnefc.net

Email: enquiries@pne.co.uk

Ground Capacity: 23,404.

Record Attendance: 42,684 v Arsenal, Division 1, 23 April 1938.

Pitch Measurements: 100m × 68m (109.5yd × 74.5yd).

Chairman: Craig Hemmings.

Manager: Ryan Lowe.

First-Team Coaches: Steve Thompson, Paul Gallagher, Mike Marsh.

Colours: White shirts with blue patterned sleeves, blue shorts with white trim, white socks with blue trim.

Year Formed: 1880.

Turned Professional: 1885.

Club Nicknames: 'The Lilywhites', 'North End'.

Ground: 1881, Deepdale.

First Football League Game: 8 September 1888, Football League, v Burnley (h) W 5–2 – Trainer; Howarth, Holmes; Robertson, William Graham, Johnny Graham; Gordon (1), Jimmy Ross (2), Goodall, Dewhurst (2), Drummond.

Record League Victory: 10–0 v Stoke, Division 1, 14 September 1889 – Trainer; Howarth, Holmes; Kelso, Russell (1), Johnny Graham; Gordon, Jimmy Ross (2), Nick Ross (3), Thomson (2), Drummond (2).

Record Cup Victory: 26–0 v Hyde, FA Cup 1st rd, 15 October 1887 – Addision; Howarth, Nick Ross; Russell (1), Thomson (5), Johnny Graham (1); Gordon (5), Jimmy Ross (8), John Goodall (1), Dewhurst (3), Drummond (2).

Record Defeat: 0–7 v Nottingham F, Division 2, 9 April 1927; 0–7 v Blackpool, Division 1, 1 May 1948.

Most League Points (2 for a win): 61, Division 3, 1970–71.

Most League Points (3 for a win): 95, Division 2, 1999–2000.

Most League Goals: 100, Division 2, 1927–28 and Division 1, 1957–58.

HONOURS

League Champions: Football League 1888–89, 1889–90; Division 2 – 1903–04, 1912–13, 1950–51; Second Division – 1999–2000; Division 3 – 1970–71; Third Division – 1995–96.
Runners-up: Football League 1890–91, 1891–92; Division 1 – 1892–93, 1905–06, 1952–53, 1957–58; Division 2 – 1914–15, 1933–34; Division 4 – 1986–87.

FA Cup Winners: 1889, 1938.
Runners-up: 1888, 1922, 1937, 1954, 1964.

League Cup: 4th rd – 1963, 1966, 1972, 1981, 2003, 2017, 2021, 2022.

Double Performed: 1888–89.

FOOTBALL YEARBOOK FACT FILE

Preston North End won their FA Cup third-round tie away to Bolton Wanderers 3-2 on 12 December 1885. However, the Trotters objected to two of the North End players and Preston made similar allegations against one of their opponents, all on the grounds of a breach of residence rules and, implicitly, professionalism. The outcome was that the FA expelled both clubs from the competition.

Highest League Scorer in Season: Ted Harper, 37, Division 2, 1932–33.

Most League Goals in Total Aggregate: Tom Finney, 187, 1946–60.

Most League Goals in One Match: 4, Jimmy Ross v Stoke, Division 1, 6 October 1888; 4, Nick Ross v Derby Co, Division 1, 11 January 1890; 4, George Drummond v Notts Co, Division 1, 12 December 1891; 4, Frank Becton v Notts Co, Division 1, 31 March 1893; 4, George Harrison v Grimsby T, Division 2, 3 November 1928; 4, Alex Reid v Port Vale, Division 2, 23 February 1929; 4, James McClelland v Reading, Division 2, 6 September 1930; 4, Dick Rowley v Notts Co, Division 2, 16 April 1932; 4, Ted Harper v Burnley, Division 2, 29 August 1932; 4, Ted Harper v Lincoln C, Division 2, 11 March 1933; 4, Charlie Wayman v QPR, Division 2, 25 December 1950; 4, Alex Bruce v Colchester U, Division 3, 28 February 1978; 4, Joe Garner v Crewe Alex, FL 1, 14 March 2015.

Most Capped Player: Tom Finney, 76, England.

Most League Appearances: Alan Kelly, 447, 1961–75.

Youngest League Player: Ethan Walker, 16 years 154 days v Aston Villa, 29 December 2018.

Record Transfer Fee Received: £10,000,000 from West Ham U for Jordan Hugill, January 2018.

Record Transfer Fee Paid: £1,550,000 to Doncaster R for Ben Whiteman, January 2021.

Football League Record: 1888 Founder Member of League; 1901–04 Division 2; 1904–12 Division 1; 1912–13 Division 2; 1913–14 Division 1; 1914–15 Division 2; 1919–25 Division 1; 1925–34 Division 2; 1934–49 Division 1; 1949–51 Division 2; 1951–61 Division 1; 1961–70 Division 2; 1970–71 Division 3; 1971–74 Division 2; 1974–78 Division 3; 1978–81 Division 2; 1981–85 Division 3; 1985–87 Division 4; 1987–92 Division 3; 1992–93 Division 2; 1993–96 Division 3; 1996–2000 Division 2; 2000–04 Division 1; 2004–11 FL C; 2011–15 FL 1; 2015– FL C.

LATEST SEQUENCES

Longest Sequence of League Wins: 14, 25.12.1950 – 27.3.1951.

Longest Sequence of League Defeats: 8, 22.9.1984 – 27.10.1984.

Longest Sequence of League Draws: 6, 24.2.1979 – 20.3.1979.

Longest Sequence of Unbeaten League Matches: 23, 8.9.1888 – 14.9.1889.

Longest Sequence Without a League Win: 15, 14.4.1923 – 20.10.1923.

Successive Scoring Runs: 30 from 15.11.1952.

Successive Non-scoring Runs: 6 from 19.11.1960.

MANAGERS

Charlie Parker 1906–15
Vincent Hayes 1919–23
Jim Lawrence 1923–25
Frank Richards 1925–27
Alex Gibson 1927–31
Lincoln Hayes 1931–32
Run by committee 1932–36
Tommy Muirhead 1936–37
Run by committee 1937–49
Will Scott 1949–53
Scot Symon 1953–54
Frank Hill 1954–56
Cliff Britton 1956–61
Jimmy Milne 1961–68
Bobby Seith 1968–70
Alan Ball Snr 1970–73
Bobby Charlton 1973–75
Harry Catterick 1975–77
Nobby Stiles 1977–81
Tommy Docherty 1981
Gordon Lee 1981–83
Alan Kelly 1983–85
Tommy Booth 1985–86
Brian Kidd 1986
John McGrath 1986–90
Les Chapman 1990–92
Sam Allardyce 1992 (*Caretaker*)
John Beck 1992–94
Gary Peters 1994–98
David Moyes 1998–2002
Kelham O'Hanlon 2002 (*Caretaker*)
Craig Brown 2002–04
Billy Davies 2004–06
Paul Simpson 2006–07
Alan Irvine 2007–09
Darren Ferguson 2010
Phil Brown 2011
Graham Westley 2012–13
Simon Grayson 2013–17
Alex Neil 2017–21
Frankie McAvoy 2021
Ryan Lowe December 2021–

TEN YEAR LEAGUE RECORD

		P	W	D	L	F	A	Pts	Pos
2012-13	FL 1	46	14	17	15	54	49	59	14
2013-14	FL 1	46	23	16	7	72	46	85	5
2014-15	FL 1	46	25	14	7	79	40	89	3
2015-16	FL C	46	15	17	14	45	45	62	11
2016-17	FL C	46	16	14	16	64	63	62	11
2017-18	FL C	46	19	16	11	57	46	73	7
2018-19	FL C	46	16	13	17	67	67	61	14
2019-20	FL C	46	18	12	16	59	54	66	9
2020-21	FL C	46	18	7	21	49	56	61	13
2021-22	FL C	46	16	16	14	52	56	64	13

DID YOU KNOW ?

When Preston reached the FA Cup final in 1937 their centre-forward Frank O'Donnell had the distinction of scoring in every round. His tally included hat-tricks against Stoke City and Exeter City followed by two goals against West Bromwich Albion in the semi-final. O'Donnell opened the scoring in the final, but Sunderland fought back to win the game 3-1.

PRESTON NORTH END – SKY BET CHAMPIONSHIP 2021–22 LEAGUE RECORD

Match No.	Date	Venue	Opponents	Result		H/T Score	Lg Pos.	Goalscorers	Attendance
1	Aug 7	H	Hull C	L	1-4	1-1	23	Jakobsen [8]	12,452
2	14	A	Reading	L	1-2	0-1	24	Johnson (pen) [61]	12,156
3	17	A	Huddersfield T	L	0-1	0-0	24		15,278
4	21	H	Peterborough U	W	1-0	1-0	20	Bauer [14]	9952
5	28	H	Swansea C	W	3-1	2-1	16	van den Berg [21], Jakobsen [45], Whiteman [52]	10,180
6	Sept 11	A	Bristol C	D	0-0	0-0	13		17,967
7	14	A	Sheffield U	D	2-2	1-1	12	Johnson [19], Jakobsen [90]	25,463
8	18	H	WBA	D	1-1	1-1	17	Whiteman [26]	13,850
9	25	A	Birmingham C	D	0-0	0-0	15		14,925
10	28	H	Stoke C	D	1-1	1-1	15	Whiteman [38]	10,930
11	Oct 2	A	QPR	L	2-3	1-1	18	Jakobsen [27], Earl [46]	13,624
12	16	H	Derby Co	D	0-0	0-0	17		18,092
13	20	H	Coventry C	W	2-1	0-1	18	Bauer [61], Jakobsen [69]	10,837
14	23	A	Blackpool	L	0-2	0-1	19		13,946
15	30	H	Luton T	W	2-0	2-0	19	Jakobsen 2 (1 pen) [27, 45 (p)]	11,059
16	Nov 3	A	Bournemouth	W	2-1	0-0	15	Whiteman [52], McCann [78]	8578
17	6	A	Nottingham F	L	0-3	0-2	17		27,129
18	20	H	Cardiff C	L	1-2	1-0	16	Maguire [2]	10,749
19	23	A	Middlesbrough	W	2-1	0-1	14	Evans [77], Jakobsen [81]	18,013
20	27	H	Fulham	D	1-1	0-1	16	Evans [72]	9838
21	Dec 4	A	Blackburn R	L	0-1	0-0	18		18,487
22	11	H	Barnsley	W	2-1	0-0	14	Browne [57], Johnson [78]	11,106
23	Jan 3	A	Stoke C	W	2-1	0-0	14	Potts [59], Hughes [81]	20,002
24	15	H	Birmingham C	D	1-1	1-0	15	Bauer [31]	12,821
25	18	H	Sheffield U	D	2-2	0-2	13	Browne [71], Jakobsen [89]	12,954
26	22	A	Swansea C	L	0-1	0-0	15		16,842
27	26	A	WBA	W	2-0	1-0	13	Jakobsen [41], Archer [76]	20,776
28	29	H	Bristol C	D	2-2	0-1	13	Jakobsen 2 [52, 90]	11,936
29	Feb 1	A	Millwall	D	0-0	0-0	13		10,183
30	5	A	Hull C	W	1-0	0-0	11	Archer [51]	14,273
31	9	H	Huddersfield T	D	0-0	0-0	12		11,120
32	12	A	Peterborough U	W	1-0	0-0	11	Archer [80]	9072
33	19	H	Reading	L	2-3	0-2	12	Johnson [57], Archer [74]	12,817
34	22	H	Nottingham F	D	0-0	0-0	12		12,598
35	26	A	Coventry C	D	1-1	0-0	12	Johnson (pen) [89]	19,743
36	Mar 5	H	Bournemouth	W	2-1	0-0	12	Archer [54], Jakobsen [89]	12,173
37	12	A	Cardiff C	D	0-0	0-0	13		19,743
38	16	A	Luton T	L	0-4	0-3	14		9408
39	Apr 2	A	Derby Co	L	0-1	0-0	15		23,600
40	5	H	Blackpool	W	1-0	1-0	13	Archer [45]	18,740
41	9	H	QPR	W	2-1	1-0	12	Dunne (og) [42], Archer [50]	10,873
42	15	H	Millwall	D	1-1	1-1	13	Wallace, M (og) [6]	11,979
43	19	A	Fulham	L	0-3	0-3	15		17,760
44	25	H	Blackburn R	L	1-4	1-3	15	Browne [29]	15,229
45	30	A	Barnsley	W	3-1	1-1	14	Johnson 2 [23, 54], Jakobsen [74]	13,190
46	May 7	H	Middlesbrough	W	4-1	2-0	13	Browne [24], Fry (og) [35], Jakobsen 2 (1 pen) [53, 74 (p)]	17,691

Final League Position: 13

GOALSCORERS

League (52): Jakobsen 16 (2 pens), Archer 7, Johnson 7 (2 pens), Browne 4, Whiteman 4, Bauer 3, Evans 2, Earl 1, Hughes 1, Maguire 1, McCann 1, Potts 1, van den Berg 1, own goals 3.
FA Cup (1): Johnson 1 (1 pen).
Carabao Cup (11): Jakobsen 4, Sinclair 2, Hughes 1, Ledson 1, Maguire 1, Rafferty 1, van den Berg 1.

Rudd D 1	Storey J 15 + 2	Lindsay L 13 + 2	Hughes A 40	Barkhuizen T 10 + 3	Ledson R 15 + 10	Browne A 35 + 4	Whiteman B 42 + 2	Cunningham G 17 + 4	Evans C 14 + 9	Jakobsen E 38 + 6	Iversen D 45 + 1	van den Berg S 43 + 2	Potts B 23 + 12	Johnson D 35 + 6	Sinclair S 6 + 17	Maguire S 15 + 11	Earl J 24 + 5	Bauer P 34	Rodwell-Grant J — + 1	McCann A 16 + 12	Murphy J — + 12	Wickham C — + 1	Olosunde M 1 + 1	Rafferty J 2 + 3	Archer C 18 + 2	Diaby B 4 + 3	O'Neill M — + 3	Huntington P — + 1	Match No.
1^{1}	2	3	4	5	6	7	8^{4}	9^{3}	10	11^{2}	12	13	14	15															1
	2	3	4		8^{2}	7	13	9^{3}		11^{1}	1	5	12	6	10	14													2
	2	3	4			8	7		10^{2}	12	1	5	11^{1}	6	13	14	9^{3}												3
	2		4		8		7			12	1	5	13	6	10^{1}	11^{2}	9	3											4
	2		4		7^{3}		6			11^{1}	1	5	13	9	12	10^{2}	8	3	14										5
	2		4		7^{2}	12	6			11^{1}	1	5		9^{3}		10	8	3		13	14								6
	2		4		7		6			11	1	5	12	9^{2}		10^{1}	8	3^{3}		13	14								7
	2		4		6		7^{2}			11^{3}	1	5		9		10^{1}	8	3		13	14	12							8
	2		4		7		6^{1}			10	1	5	14	9^{3}		11^{2}	8	3		13	12								9
	2				7^{3}	12	6^{2}	4		10	1	5		9		11^{1}	8	3		13	14								10
	2	13			7	12		4		10	1	5	14	9		11^{3}	8	3^{2}		6^{1}									11
	2^{3}		4	10^{1}	6^{2}	7	13			11	1	5		9	12		8	3			14								12
	2		4	12		7	6			10^{3}	1	5	13	9^{2}	11^{1}		8	3			14								13
	2		4	12		7■	6^{3}			10	1	5	14	9^{1}	11	13	8^{2}	3											14
			4	5	13	9	7			10^{2}	1	2	14		12	11^{1}	8	3		6^{3}									15
			4	5		9	7	13		10	1	2	12	14		11^{1}	8^{2}	3		6^{3}									16
	12		4	5			7	13		10	1	2	9^{3}	11	14		8^{2}	3^{1}		6									17
			4	5	6^{2}	9		8^{1}		11	1	2		14	13	10^{3}	12	3		7									18
			4	5^{3}		9	7		12	11	1	2		13	14	10^{1}	8	3		6^{2}									19
	12	3	4^{3}	5^{1}		9	7	14	13	11	1	2				10^{2}	8			6									20
	2	3			14	9	7	4^{2}	10	11	1			12	13		8			6^{1}			5^{3}						21
			4		12	6	7			11	1	2	14	9^{3}	13	10^{2}	8	3		5^{1}									22
			4		13	6	7		10^{3}	11^{1}	1	2	5	9^{2}	12	14	8	3											23
			4	13		6	7	8	11^{3}	10^{1}	1	2	5^{2}	9	14	12		3											24
			4■	8^{3}		7	6	12	14	10	1	2	5^{2}	9	11^{1}			3						13					25
				5^{1}	14	7	6^{3}	4	11	10	1	2		9	13			3					12	8^{2}					26
			4		6^{3}	9	7	8	11^{2}	10^{1}	1	2	5			13		3		14					12				27
			4		6^{2}	9	7	8^{1}	14	10	1	2	5				12	3		13					11^{3}				28
		3	4^{1}		6^{3}	14	7	8	10^{2}	11	1	2	5				12			9					13				29
			4		14	6	7	9	12	11^{1}	1	2	5^{2}	13				3		8					10^{3}				30
			4			6	7	9^{1}	10^{2}	13	1	2	5	8	14		12	3							11^{3}				31
			4		14	9	6^{3}		12	11^{1}	1	2	5	7	13		8^{2}	3							10				32
		12	4		13	7	6^{2}		14	10^{3}	1	2	5^{1}	9	8			3							11				33
		4	8			7	6		10^{2}	13	1	2	5	9			12	3^{1}							11				34
		3■	4		14	6	7		10^{2}	12	1	2	5	9			8^{1}								11^{3}	13			35
			4			6	7		10^{3}	13	1	2	5^{2}	9			8^{1}			12	14				11	3			36
		4^{1}	9			6^{3}	7			11^{2}	1	2	5	8	13					12				14	10	3			37
			4			6	7		12	10^{1}	1	2	5^{3}	8	14					9^{2}	13				11	3			38
		3■	4			7	6		10^{2}	11^{1}	1	12		8		13		2			14			5	9^{3}				39
			4			7	5	9^{1}		10	1	2	6	8				3		12					11				40
			4			7	5	9^{2}		11^{1}	1	2		8		12		3		6	13				10^{3}		14		41
			4			7^{1}	5	9	13		1	2	6^{2}	8		10^{3}		3		12	14				11				42
		3	4				5		10^{1}		1	2	6^{3}	8	14	12	9^{2}			7					11	13			43
			4^{2}			7	5^{3}	9^{1}		10	1	2	6	8		12		3		14				13	11				44
		4				7	5			10^{3}	1	2	6	9		14		3^{1}		8					11^{2}	12	13		45
		4			14	7	5^{3}			10^{2}	1	2	6	9						8					11	3^{1}	13	12	46

FA Cup

Third Round	Cardiff C	(a)	1-2
(aet)			

Carabao Cup

First Round	Mansfield T	(a)	3-0
Second Round	Morecambe	(a)	4-2
Third Round	Cheltenham T	(h)	4-1
Fourth Round	Liverpool	(h)	0-2

QUEENS PARK RANGERS

FOUNDATION

There is an element of doubt about the date of the foundation of this club, but it is believed that in either 1885 or 1886 it was formed through the amalgamation of Christchurch Rangers and St Jude's Institute FC. The leading light was George Wodehouse, whose family maintained a connection with the club until comparatively recent times. Most of the players came from the Queen's Park district so this name was adopted after a year as St Jude's Institute.

The Kiyan Prince Foundation Stadium, South Africa Road, Shepherds Bush, London W12 7PJ.

Telephone: (020) 8743 0262.

Ticket Office: (08444) 777 007.

Website: www.qpr.co.uk

Email: boxoffice@qpr.co.uk

Ground Capacity: 18,193.

Record Attendance: 41,097 v Leeds U, FA Cup 3rd rd, 9 January 1932 (at White City); 35,353 v Leeds U, Division 1, 27 April 1974 (at Loftus Road).

Pitch Measurements: 100m × 66m (109.5yd × 72yd).

Chairman: Amit Bhatia.

Chief Executive: Lee Hoos.

Head Coach: Michael Beale.

Assistant Coaches: Neil Banfield, Damian Matthew.

Colours: Blue and white hooped shirts with blue and yellow trim, white shorts with blue and yellow trim, white socks with blue and yellow trim.

Year Formed: 1885* (*see Foundation*).

Turned Professional: 1898.

Previous Name: 1885, St Jude's; 1887, Queens Park Rangers. ***Club Nicknames:*** 'Rangers', 'The Hoops', 'R's'.

Grounds: 1885* (*see Foundation*), Welford's Fields; 1888–99, London Scottish Ground, Brondesbury, Home Farm, Kensal Rise Green, Gun Club Wormwood Scrubs, Kilburn Cricket Ground; 1899, Kensal Rise Athletic Ground; 1901, Latimer Road, Notting Hill; 1904, Agricultural Society, Park Royal; 1907, Park Royal Ground; 1917, Loftus Road; 1931, White City; 1933, Loftus Road; 1962, White City; 1963, Loftus Road (renamed The Kiyan Prince Foundation Stadium 2019).

First Football League Game: 28 August 1920, Division 3, v Watford (h) L 1–2 – Price; Blackman, Wingrove; McGovern, Grant, O'Brien; Faulkner, Birch (1), Smith, Gregory, Middlemiss.

Record League Victory: 9–2 v Tranmere R, Division 3, 3 December 1960 – Drinkwater; Woods, Ingham; Keen, Rutter, Angell; Lazarus (2), Bedford (2), Evans (2), Andrews (1), Clark (2).

Record Cup Victory: 8–1 v Bristol R (a), FA Cup 1st rd, 27 November 1937 – Gilfillan; Smith, Jefferson; Lowe, James, March; Cape, Mallett, Cheetham (3), Fitzgerald (3) Bott (2). 8–1 v Crewe Alex, Milk Cup 1st rd, 3 October 1983 – Hucker; Neill, Dawes, Waddock (1), McDonald (1), Fenwick, Micklewhite (1), Stewart (1), Allen (1), Stainrod (3), Gregory.

HONOURS

League Champions: FL C – 2010–11; Division 2 – 1982–83; Division 3 – 1966–67; Division 3S – 1947–48.
Runners-up: Division 1 – 1975–76; Division 2 – 1967–68, 1972–73; Second Division – 2003–04; Division 3S – 1946–47.

FA Cup: *Runners-up:* 1982.

League Cup Winners: 1967.
Runners-up: 1986.

European Competitions
UEFA Cup: 1976–77 (*qf*), 1984–85.

FOOTBALL YEARBOOK FACT FILE

After Clive Wilson scored with a penalty for Queens Park Rangers in their Premier League encounter with Manchester United on 5 February 1994, the R's had to wait over two years for their next success from the penalty spot in a Football League fixture. Simon Barker ended the sequence against Sheffield United on 30 November 1996 after 115 games, believed to be a Football/Premier League record.

Record Defeat: 1–8 v Mansfield T, Division 3, 15 March 1965. 1–8 v Manchester U, Division 1, 19 March 1969.

Most League Points (2 for a win): 67, Division 3, 1966–67.

Most League Points (3 for a win): 88, FL C, 2010–11.

Most League Goals: 111, Division 3, 1961–62.

Highest League Scorer in Season: George Goddard, 37, Division 3 (S), 1929–30.

Most League Goals in Total Aggregate: George Goddard, 174, 1926–34.

Most League Goals in One Match: 4, George Goddard v Merthyr T, Division 3 (S), 9 March 1929; 4, George Goddard v Swindon T, Division 3 (S), 12 April 1930; 4, George Goddard v Exeter C, Division 3 (S), 20 December 1930; 4, George Goddard v Watford, Division 3 (S), 19 September 1931; 4, Tom Cheetham v Aldershot, Division 3 (S), 14 September 1935; 4, Tom Cheetham v Aldershot, Division 3 (S), 12 November 1938.

Most Capped Player: Alan McDonald, 52, Northern Ireland.

Most League Appearances: Tony Ingham, 514, 1950–63.

Youngest League Player: Frank Sibley, 16 years 97 days v Bristol C, 10 March 1964.

Record Transfer Fee Received: £19,500,000 from Crystal Palace for Eberechi Eze, August 2020.

Record Transfer Fee Paid: £12,500,000 to Anzhi Makhachkala for Chris Samba, January 2013.

Football League Record: 1920 Original Members of Division 3; 1921–48 Division 3 (S); 1948–52 Division 2; 1952–58 Division 3 (S); 1958–67 Division 3; 1967–68 Division 2; 1968–69 Division 1; 1969–73 Division 2; 1973–79 Division 1; 1979–83 Division 2; 1983–92 Division 1; 1992–96 Premier League; 1996–2001 Division 1; 2001–04 Division 2; 2004–11 FL C; 2011–13 Premier League; 2013–14 FL C; 2014–15 Premier League; 2015– FL C.

LATEST SEQUENCES

Longest Sequence of League Wins: 8, 7.11.1931 – 28.12.1931.

Longest Sequence of League Defeats: 9, 25.2.1969 – 5.4.1969.

Longest Sequence of League Draws: 6, 29.1.2000 – 5.3.2000.

Longest Sequence of Unbeaten League Matches: 20, 11.3.1972 – 23.9.1972.

Longest Sequence Without a League Win: 20, 7.12.1968 – 7.4.1969.

Successive Scoring Runs: 33 from 9.12.1961.

Successive Non-scoring Runs: 6 from 18.3.1939.

MANAGERS

James Cowan 1906–13
Jimmy Howie 1913–20
Ned Liddell 1920–24
Will Wood 1924–25
(had been Secretary since 1903)
Bob Hewison 1925–31
John Bowman 1931
Archie Mitchell 1931–33
Mick O'Brien 1933–35
Billy Birrell 1935–39
Ted Vizard 1939–44
Dave Mangnall 1944–52
Jack Taylor 1952–59
Alec Stock 1959–65
(General Manager to 1968)
Bill Dodgin Jnr 1968
Tommy Docherty 1968
Les Allen 1968–71
Gordon Jago 1971–74
Dave Sexton 1974–77
Frank Sibley 1977–78
Steve Burtenshaw 1978–79
Tommy Docherty 1979–80
Terry Venables 1980–84
Gordon Jago 1984
Alan Mullery 1984
Frank Sibley 1984–85
Jim Smith 1985–88
Trevor Francis 1988–89
Don Howe 1989–91
Gerry Francis 1991–94
Ray Wilkins 1994–96
Stewart Houston 1996–97
Ray Harford 1997–98
Gerry Francis 1998–2001
Ian Holloway 2001–06
Gary Waddock 2006
John Gregory 2006–07
Luigi Di Canio 2007–08
Iain Dowie 2008
Paulo Sousa 2008–09
Jim Magilton 2009
Paul Hart 2009–10
Neil Warnock 2010–12
Mark Hughes 2012
Harry Redknapp 2012–15
Chris Ramsey 2015
Jimmy Floyd Hasselbaink 2015–16
Ian Holloway 2016–18
Steve McClaren 2018–19
Mark Warburton 2019–22
Michael Beale June 2022–

TEN YEAR LEAGUE RECORD

		P	W	D	L	F	A	Pts	Pos
2012-13	PR Lge	38	4	13	21	30	60	25	20
2013-14	FL C	46	23	11	12	60	44	80	4
2014-15	PR Lge	38	8	6	24	42	73	30	20
2015-16	FL C	46	14	18	14	54	54	60	12
2016-17	FL C	46	15	8	23	52	66	53	18
2017-18	FL C	46	15	11	20	58	70	56	16
2018-19	FL C	46	14	9	23	53	71	51	19
2019-20	FL C	46	16	10	20	67	76	58	13
2020-21	FL C	46	19	11	16	57	55	68	9
2021-22	FL C	46	19	9	18	60	59	66	11

DID YOU KNOW

Queens Park Rangers did not take part in the FA Cup in the 1926–27 season due to an administrative error. The club were required to submit their application for exemption from the qualifying rounds by 30 March of the previous season but failed to do so. Rather than play through a potential six rounds before reaching the competition proper they chose to withdraw.

QUEENS PARK RANGERS – SKY BET CHAMPIONSHIP 2021–22 LEAGUE RECORD

Match No.	Date	Venue	Opponents	Result		H/T Score	Lg Pos.	Goalscorers	Attendance
1	Aug 7	H	Millwall	D	1-1	1-1	8	Dickie 31	16,127
2	14	A	Hull C	W	3-0	1-0	2	Willock 16, Dykes 68, Dickie 74	10,728
3	18	A	Middlesbrough	W	3-2	0-1	3	Howson (og) 48, Dykes 56, Willock 76	22,436
4	21	H	Barnsley	D	2-2	0-2	5	Chair 76, Austin 90	11,882
5	28	H	Coventry C	W	2-0	0-0	3	Dykes 68, Barbet 76	14,774
6	Sept 11	A	Reading	D	3-3	1-1	4	Ball 11, Gray 79, Johansen 90	14,928
7	14	A	Bournemouth	L	1-2	0-2	6	McCallum 57	10,495
8	18	H	Bristol C	L	1-2	0-1	8	McCallum 54	14,922
9	24	A	WBA	L	1-2	1-0	8	Gray 1	21,825
10	28	H	Birmingham C	W	2-0	1-0	8	Chair 2 34, 64	12,257
11	Oct 2	H	Preston NE	W	3-2	1-1	6	Dykes 17, Dunne 71, Chair 74	13,624
12	16	A	Fulham	L	1-4	0-1	8	Dykes 55	18,371
13	19	H	Blackburn R	W	1-0	0-0	5	Chair 83	11,771
14	23	A	Peterborough U	L	1-2	0-0	7	Chair 50	12,035
15	29	H	Nottingham F	D	1-1	1-0	5	Dykes 45	15,089
16	Nov 3	A	Cardiff C	W	1-0	1-0	5	Gray 37	16,882
17	6	A	Blackpool	D	1-1	1-0	6	Willock 26	11,769
18	19	H	Luton T	W	2-0	1-0	5	Willock 10, Austin 55	15,062
19	24	H	Huddersfield T	W	1-0	0-0	4	Amos 81	11,591
20	29	A	Derby Co	W	2-1	0-1	3	Willock 50, Gray 90	20,003
21	Dec 5	H	Stoke C	L	0-2	0-1	5		13,968
22	27	H	Bournemouth	L	0-1	0-1	7		16,308
23	30	A	Bristol C	W	2-1	1-1	7	Austin (pen) 45, Barbet 90	19,543
24	Jan 2	A	Birmingham C	W	2-1	1-0	5	Adomah 14, Willock 71	18,279
25	15	H	WBA	W	1-0	0-0	4	Austin 89	16,018
26	22	A	Coventry C	W	2-1	1-0	4	Gray 6, Adomah 88	20,942
27	25	H	Swansea C	D	0-0	0-0	4		12,770
28	29	H	Reading	W	4-0	3-0	4	Dykes 2 13, 35, Amos 37, Dunne 51	16,057
29	Feb 9	H	Middlesbrough	D	2-2	1-1	4	Chair 29, Willock 46	14,140
30	12	A	Barnsley	L	0-1	0-0	4		12,476
31	15	A	Millwall	L	0-2	0-0	4		13,063
32	19	H	Hull C	D	1-1	0-1	4	Chair 75	14,945
33	23	H	Blackpool	W	2-1	1-0	3	Dunne 31, Amos 89	12,042
34	26	A	Blackburn R	L	0-1	0-0	5		14,293
35	Mar 5	H	Cardiff C	L	1-2	1-0	5	Gray 38	16,170
36	13	A	Luton T	W	2-1	0-1	4	Gray (pen) 55, Dickie 83	10,073
37	16	A	Nottingham F	L	1-3	1-0	6	Gray 40	27,872
38	20	H	Peterborough U	L	1-3	1-1	8	Amos 9	13,753
39	Apr 2	H	Fulham	L	0-2	0-1	9		17,648
40	5	A	Sheffield U	L	0-1	0-1	9		26,488
41	9	A	Preston NE	L	1-2	0-1	10	Gray (pen) 90	10,873
42	15	A	Huddersfield T	D	2-2	1-1	12	Amos 43, Chair 58	19,636
43	18	H	Derby Co	W	1-0	0-0	10	Amos 88	15,298
44	23	A	Stoke C	L	0-1	0-1	11		19,251
45	29	H	Sheffield U	L	1-3	1-0	11	Austin 31	15,824
46	May 7	A	Swansea C	W	1-0	0-0	11	Gray 80	18,608

Final League Position: 11

GOALSCORERS

League (60): Gray 10 (2 pens), Chair 9, Dykes 8, Willock 7, Amos 6, Austin 5 (1 pen), Dickie 3, Dunne 3, Adomah 2, Barbet 2, McCallum 2, Ball 1, Johansen 1, own goal 1.
FA Cup (1): Dykes 1.
Carabao Cup (5): Austin 2, Dickie 2, own goal 1.

Dieng T 28	Dickie R 38	De Wijs J 11 + 1	Barbet Y 41	Odubajo M 23 + 5	Johansen S 31 + 4	Ball D 13 + 7	Wallace L 21	Willock C 33 + 2	Austin C 15 + 19	Dykes L 27 + 6	Dozzell A 18 + 9	Thomas G 6 + 14	Chair I 37 + 2	Kelman C — + 1	Kakay O 4 + 9	Dunne J 34 + 4	Adomah A 22 + 11	McCallum S 15 + 2	Gray A 13 + 15	Amos L 15 + 14	Field S 26 + 3	Marshall D 10 + 1	Sanderson D 10 + 1	Hendrick J 7 + 3	Westwood K 6	Mahoney M 2	Match No.
1	2	3	4	5	6^{2}	7	8	9	10^{1}	11	12	13															1
1	2	3	4	5	7^{3}	6	8	11		10^{2}	12	14	9^{1}	13													2
1	2	3	4	5▮	6	7	8^{3}	11	13	10^{2}			9^{1}		12	14											3
1	2	3^{3}	4		6	12		9	11		7^{2}	5^{1}	10		8	14	13										4
1	2	3	4	5	6	7		9	11^{2}	12	13		10^{1}		14			8^{3}									5
1	2	3	4	5	7	6^{3}		11	10^{1}			14	9				13	8^{2}	12								6
1	2	3	4		7	6		11		10^{2}		14	9^{3}		5^{1}		13	8	12								7
1	2	3	4	6^{2}	5	14		8	12	11^{3}			7				13	9	10^{1}								8
1	2	3^{2}	8	5	7^{3}	6		10^{1}		12	14		9		13	4			11								9
1	2		4	5		6		8	11^{2}	10^{3}	7^{1}		9			3	14		13	12							10
1	2	14	4	5	7^{1}	6		8^{3}	12	10			9			3			11^{2}	13							11
1	2	3	4	5	7	6^{1}		10	11^{3}	12			9			13		8^{2}	14								12
1	2		4			6^{2}		9	13	11	7^{1}		10		14	3	5^{3}	8		12							13
1	2		4		7	6^{1}		14	11^{2}	10			9			3	5	8^{3}	13	12							14
1	2	3^{2}	4	12	6			10		11	7		9^{3}			13	5	8^{1}		14							15
1	2		4	8	7	13			12	10	6^{3}		9^{2}			3	5		11^{1}	14							16
1	2		4	8^{1}		13		10^{2}	14	11	7		9		12	3	5			6^{3}							17
1	2		4		7		8	9	10^{1}		6		11^{3}		13	3	5^{2}			14	12						18
1	2		4		7^{3}	14	8	11	10^{2}		6^{1}		9			3	5			12	13						19
1	2		4	12	6		8^{1}	11^{3}	10^{2}		7		9			3	5		13		14						20
1	2		4		6			10	11^{2}		7^{1}	14	9		5	3			13	12	8^{3}						21
1	2		4		7		8^{3}	10		11	12▮		9^{1}		5^{2}	3	14		13		6						22
1	2		4		7		8^{1}	11	10	12		13				3	5			9^{2}	6						23
1	2		4		12		9	7	13	11^{2}						3	5		10^{1}	8	6						24
	2		4		6	13	8	9^{2}	12	10						3	5		11^{1}		7	1					25
	2		4				8	9	14	10^{3}	6^{1}	13				3	5		11^{2}	12	7	1					26
	2		4	5	10		7^{1}	11^{3}	8	13		14				3	12			9^{2}	6	1					27
	2		4		7		8^{2}	10^{3}	14	11		12				3	5			9^{1}	6	1	13				28
	2		4	14	6^{2}		8^{3}	10		11			9^{1}			3	5		13		7	1		12			29
	2		4	5	13		8^{3}		12	11			9			3	14		10^{1}		7	1		6^{2}			30
	2		4	12	6^{3}		8^{1}	10	13	11			9			3	5^{2}			14	7	1					31
1			4	12				8	10^{2}				11			3	5		13	9^{1}	7		2	6			32
1			4	8	9^{2}	12		11^{1}				14	10^{3}			3	5			13	7		2▮	6			33
1^{1}	2		4	8	9			11^{2}					10			3	5^{3}	14	13		7	12		6			34
	2		4	5			8^{1}	9^{2}			14		10			3	12		11	13	6^{3}	1		7			35
	2		4	5	9		8	14	12				10^{1}			3			11^{3}	13	7	1		6^{2}			36
	3			5	14		9	10^{1}			8^{3}		12			2			11	6^{2}	7	1	4	13			37
	3								12		7^{1}	14	10			4	5	8	11^{3}	9^{2}	6		2	13	1		38
	3		4	5	7^{1}		8		13	11	14	10^{2}	12							9^{3}	6		2		1		39
	3		4				8^{3}			11	12	13	9			2	5	14	10^{1}		7			6^{2}	1		40
				2	8				13	10^{2}	9	12	11^{3}			4		5	14	6^{1}	7		3			1	41
			4	2					13	10^{2}	7	11^{1}	9			3	14	5	12	8^{3}	6				1		42
				2^{1}	14				13	11	6^{3}	10^{2}	9		12	4		5		8	7		3		1		43
			4						12	10^{1}	6	11^{3}	9			3	13	5	14	8^{2}	7		2		1		44
					7				10^{1}	12	8^{2}	14	11		13	3	5	9		6^{3}	4		2			1	45
1			4			3				10^{3}	14	8^{2}	11		12		5	9	13	6	7		2^{1}				46

FA Cup

Third Round	Rotherham U	(h)	1-1
(aet; QPR won 8-7 on penalties)			
Fourth Round	Peterborough U	(a)	0-2

Carabao Cup

First Round	Leyton Orient	(a)	1-1
(QPR won 5-3 on penalties)			
Second Round	Oxford U	(h)	2-0
Third Round	Everton	(h)	2-2
(QPR won 8-7 on penalties)			
Fourth Round	Sunderland	(h)	0-0
(Sunderland won 3-1 on penalties)			

READING

FOUNDATION

Reading was formed as far back as 1871 at a public meeting held at the Bridge Street Rooms. They first entered the FA Cup as early as 1877 when they amalgamated with the Reading Hornets. The club was further strengthened in 1889 when Earley FC joined them. They were the first winners of the Berks & Bucks Cup in 1878–79.

Select Car Leasing Stadium, Junction 11, M4, Reading, Berkshire RG2 0FL.

Telephone: (0118) 968 1100.

Ticket Office: (0118) 968 1313.

Website: www.readingfc.co.uk

Email: supporterservice@readingfc.co.uk

Ground Capacity: 24,162.

Record Attendance: 33,042 v Brentford, FA Cup 5th rd, 19 February 1927 (at Elm Park); 24,184 v Everton, Premier League, 17 November 2012 (at Madejski Stadium).

Pitch Measurements: 103m × 68m (112.5yd × 74.5yd).

Vice-Chairman: Sir John Madejski.

Chief Executive: Nigel Howe.

Manager: Paul Ince.

Assistant Manager: Alex Rae.

HONOURS

League Champions: FL C – 2005–06, 2011–12; Second Division – 1993–94; Division 3 – 1985–86; Division 3S – 1925–26; Division 4 – 1978–79.
Runners-up: First Division – 1994–95; Second Division – 2001–02; Division 3S – 1931–32, 1934–35, 1948–49, 1951–52.

FA Cup: semi-final – 1927, 2015.

League Cup: 5th rd – 1996, 1998.

Full Members' Cup Winners: 1988.

Colours: Blue and white hooped shirts with yellow trim, white shorts, white socks with blue hoops.

Year Formed: 1871.

Turned Professional: 1895.

Club Nickname: 'The Royals'.

Grounds: 1871, Reading Recreation; Reading Cricket Ground; 1882, Coley Park; 1889, Caversham Cricket Ground; 1896, Elm Park; 1998, Madejski Stadium (renamed Select Car Leasing Stadium 2021).

First Football League Game: 28 August 1920, Division 3, v Newport Co (a) W 1–0 – Crawford; Smith, Horler; Christie, Mavin, Getgood; Spence, Weston, Yarnell, Bailey (1), Andrews.

Record League Victory: 10–2 v Crystal Palace, Division 3 (S), 4 September 1946 – Groves; Glidden, Gulliver; McKenna, Ratcliffe, Young; Chitty, Maurice Edelston (3), McPhee (4), Barney (1), Deverell (2).

Record Cup Victory: 6–0 v Leyton, FA Cup 2nd rd, 12 December 1925 – Duckworth; Eggo, McConnell; Wilson, Messer, Evans; Smith (2), Braithwaite (1), Davey (1), Tinsley, Robson (2).

Record Defeat: 0–18 v Preston NE, FA Cup 1st rd, 1893–94.

Most League Points (2 for a win): 65, Division 4, 1978–79.

Most League Points (3 for a win): 106, Championship, 2005–06 (Football League Record).

FOOTBALL YEARBOOK FACT FILE

Reading changed their playing kit from blue and white striped shirts to blue and white hoops during the summer of 1938 and the new shirts were worn for the first time for the Football League Jubilee Fund fixture against Aldershot on 22 August. Although some fans thought they were more like rugby than soccer shirts, the Royals have, with just occasional exceptions, retained the hoops through to the present day.

Most League Goals: 112, Division 3 (S), 1951–52.

Highest League Scorer in Season: Ronnie Blackman, 39, Division 3 (S), 1951–52.

Most League Goals in Total Aggregate: Ronnie Blackman, 158, 1947–54.

Most League Goals in One Match: 6, Arthur Bacon v Stoke C, Division 2, 3 April 1931.

Most Capped Player: Chris Gunter, 59 (109), Wales.

Most League Appearances: Martin Hicks, 500, 1978–91.

Youngest League Player: Peter Castle, 16 years 49 days v Watford, 30 April 2003.

Record Transfer Fee Received: £8,000,000 from Crystal Palace for Michael Olise, July 2021.

Record Transfer Fee Paid: £7,500,000 to Internazionale for George Puscas, August 2019.

Football League Record: 1920 Original Member of Division 3; 1921–26 Division 3 (S); 1926–31 Division 2; 1931–58 Division 3 (S); 1958–71 Division 3; 1971–76 Division 4; 1976–77 Division 3; 1977–79 Division 4; 1979–83 Division 3; 1983–84 Division 4; 1984–86 Division 3; 1986–88 Division 2; 1988–92 Division 3; 1992–94 Division 2; 1994–98 Division 1; 1998–2002 Division 2; 2002–04 Division 1; 2004–06 FL C; 2006–08 Premier League; 2008–12 FL C; 2012–13 Premier League; 2013– FL C.

LATEST SEQUENCES

Longest Sequence of League Wins: 13, 17.8.1985 – 19.10.1985.

Longest Sequence of League Defeats: 8, 29.12.2007 – 24.2.2008.

Longest Sequence of League Draws: 6, 23.3.2002 – 20.4.2002.

Longest Sequence of Unbeaten League Matches: 33, 9.8.2005 – 14.2.2006.

Longest Sequence Without a League Win: 14, 30.4.1927 – 29.10.1927.

Successive Scoring Runs: 32 from 1.10.1932.

Successive Non-scoring Runs: 6 from 29.3.2008.

MANAGERS

Thomas Sefton 1897–1901 *(Secretary-Manager)*
James Sharp 1901–02
Harry Matthews 1902–20
Harry Marshall 1920–22
Arthur Chadwick 1923–25
H. S. Bray 1925–26 *(Secretary only since 1922 and 1926–35)*
Andrew Wylie 1926–31
Joe Smith 1931–35
Billy Butler 1935–39
John Cochrane 1939
Joe Edelston 1939–47
Ted Drake 1947–52
Jack Smith 1952–55
Harry Johnston 1955–63
Roy Bentley 1963–69
Jack Mansell 1969–71
Charlie Hurley 1972–77
Maurice Evans 1977–84
Ian Branfoot 1984–89
Ian Porterfield 1989–91
Mark McGhee 1991–94
Jimmy Quinn and Mick Gooding 1994–97
Terry Bullivant 1997–98
Tommy Burns 1998–99
Alan Pardew 1999–2003
Steve Coppell 2003–09
Brendan Rodgers 2009
Brian McDermott 2009–13
Nigel Adkins 2013–14
Steve Clarke 2014–15
Brian McDermott 2015–16
Jaap Stam 2016–18
Paul Clement 2018
José Gomes 2018–19
Mark Bowen 2019–20
Veljko Paunović 2020–22
Paul Ince February 2022–

TEN YEAR LEAGUE RECORD

		P	W	D	L	F	A	Pts	Pos
2012-13	PR Lge	38	6	10	22	43	73	28	19
2013-14	FL C	46	19	14	13	70	56	71	7
2014-15	FL C	46	13	11	22	48	69	50	19
2015-16	FL C	46	13	13	20	52	59	52	17
2016-17	FL C	46	26	7	13	68	64	85	3
2017-18	FL C	46	10	14	22	48	70	44	20
2018-19	FL C	46	10	17	19	49	66	47	20
2019-20	FL C	46	15	11	20	59	58	56	14
2020-21	FL C	46	19	13	14	62	54	70	7
2021-22	FL C	46	13	8	25	54	87	41*	21

**6 pts deducted.*

DID YOU KNOW ?

In April 1983 businessman Robert Maxwell announced plans to merge Reading with Oxford United to form a new club known as Thames Valley Royals to be based at a proposed stadium in Didcot. Reading fans, businesses and the local population were united in their opposition and on 13 May 1983, just 27 days after the initial announcement, the merger was dropped.

READING – SKY BET CHAMPIONSHIP 2021–22 LEAGUE RECORD

Match No.	Date	Venue	Opponents	Result		H/T Score	Lg Pos.	Goalscorers	Attendance
1	Aug 7	A	Stoke C	L	2-3	1-2	20	Swift [26], Moore [60]	19,068
2	14	H	Preston NE	W	2-1	1-0	12	Azeez [28], Swift [69]	12,156
3	17	H	Bristol C	L	2-3	1-2	17	Azeez [19], Moore [81]	14,207
4	21	A	Coventry C	L	1-2	1-0	18	Swift (pen) [40]	16,464
5	28	A	Huddersfield T	L	0-4	0-1	21		14,613
6	Sept 11	H	QPR	D	3-3	1-1	22	Swift 3 [35, 64, 77]	14,928
7	14	H	Peterborough U	W	3-1	0-0	15	Swift [64], Dele-Bashiru 2 [67, 88]	11,411
8	18	A	Fulham	W	2-1	1-0	14	Ejaria 2 [19, 53]	18,901
9	25	H	Middlesbrough	W	1-0	0-0	9	Halilovic [55]	12,469
10	29	A	Derby Co	L	0-1	0-1	11		18,769
11	Oct 2	A	Cardiff C	W	1-0	1-0	10	Hoilett [38]	18,400
12	16	H	Barnsley	W	1-0	0-0	7	Swift [77]	12,199
13	20	H	Blackpool	L	2-3	2-0	8	Dann [11], Dele-Bashiru [21]	10,587
14	23	A	Blackburn R	L	0-2	0-0	13		10,517
15	30	H	Bournemouth	L	0-2	0-1	16		13,551
16	Nov 2	A	Millwall	L	0-1	0-0	17		11,004
17	6	A	Birmingham C	W	2-1	0-1	16	Clarke 2 [70, 82]	17,535
18	20	H	Nottingham F	D	1-1	0-1	20	Dann [64]	14,907
19	23	H	Sheffield U	L	0-1	0-0	20		10,247
20	27	A	Swansea C	W	3-2	2-1	21	Dele-Bashiru [4], Carroll [30], Drinkwater [50]	16,980
21	Dec 4	H	Hull C	D	1-1	1-0	20	Holmes [45]	11,827
22	11	A	WBA	L	0-1	0-0	21		21,306
23	Jan 3	H	Derby Co	D	2-2	1-0	21	Hoilett 2 [37, 56]	12,512
24	11	H	Fulham	L	0-7	0-2	21		11,472
25	15	A	Middlesbrough	L	1-2	0-0	21	Carroll [68]	21,634
26	19	H	Luton T	L	0-2	0-1	21		9611
27	22	H	Huddersfield T	L	3-4	3-3	21	Lucas Joao [5], Puscas [22], Morrison [45]	10,796
28	29	A	QPR	L	0-4	0-3	21		16,057
29	Feb 9	A	Bristol C	L	1-2	0-1	21	Swift (pen) [74]	17,798
30	12	H	Coventry C	L	2-3	1-1	21	Lucas Joao [23], Yiadom [55]	22,692
31	16	A	Peterborough U	D	0-0	0-0	21		11,520
32	19	A	Preston NE	W	3-2	2-0	21	Lucas Joao 2 [2, 19], Swift [55]	12,817
33	22	H	Birmingham C	W	2-1	0-0	21	Lucas Joao [67], Swift (pen) [73]	12,073
34	26	A	Blackpool	L	1-4	1-1	21	Lucas Joao [17]	10,954
35	Mar 5	H	Millwall	L	0-1	0-1	21		14,169
36	12	A	Nottingham F	L	0-4	0-1	21		28,128
37	15	A	Bournemouth	D	1-1	0-1	21	Ince [83]	9085
38	19	H	Blackburn R	W	1-0	0-0	21	Laurent [78]	12,805
39	Apr 2	A	Barnsley	D	1-1	0-1	21	Laurent [82]	14,149
40	5	H	Stoke C	W	2-1	1-1	21	Morrison [13], Harwood-Bellis (og) [63]	9928
41	9	H	Cardiff C	L	1-2	1-0	21	Lucas Joao [7]	19,039
42	15	A	Sheffield U	W	2-1	1-0	21	Lucas Joao [17], McIntyre [90]	29,125
43	18	H	Swansea C	D	4-4	1-3	21	Lucas Joao 2 (1 pen) [3 (p), 71], Ince [61], McIntyre [90]	14,335
44	23	A	Hull C	L	0-3	0-1	21		12,211
45	30	H	WBA	L	0-1	0-0	21		15,509
46	May 7	A	Luton T	L	0-1	0-1	21		10,070

Final League Position: 21

GOALSCORERS

League (54): Swift 11 (3 pens), Lucas Joao 10 (1 pen), Dele-Bashiru 4, Hoilett 3, Azeez 2, Carroll 2, Clarke 2, Dann 2, Ejaria 2, Ince 2, Laurent 2, McIntyre 2, Moore 2, Morrison 2, Drinkwater 1, Halilovic 1, Holmes 1, Puscas 1, Yiadom 1, own goal 1.
FA Cup (1): Puscas 1.
Carabao Cup (0).

Rafael Cabral B 6	Yiadom A 38	Morrison M 29	Moore L 17	McIntyre T 18 + 1	Rinomhota A 19 + 1	Laurent J 41	Azeez F 5 + 8	Swift J 36 + 2	Bristow E 6	Lucas Joao E 21 + 3	Tetek D 5 + 5	Puscas G 17 + 8	Holmes T 27 + 5	Dele-Bashiru A 27 + 11	Clarke J — + 12	Hoilett J 20 + 7	Halilovic A 9 + 2	Baba A 29	Ejaria O 21 + 5	Southwood L 25	Drinkwater D 31 + 2	Stickland M — + 1	Dann S 14 + 4	Ashcroft T 4	Camara M — + 6	Carroll A 6 + 2	Felipe Araruna H — + 1	Hein K 5	Ince T 15	Meite Y 3 + 10	Abrefa K — + 3	Barker B — + 4	Nyland O 10	Thomas T 2	Scott R — + 1	*Match No.*
1	2	3	4	5	6	7	8^{3}	9^{2}	10	11^{1}	12	13	14																							1
1	2	3	4	5	6	7	8	9	10	11^{1}		12																								2
1	2	3	4	5	6	7	8	9	10^{1}			11^{2}		12	13																					3
1	2	3	4	5^{1}	6	7	8^{2}	9				11	12	10^{3}	14	13																				4
1	5	3	4		6	7		9^{2}			13	11^{3}	2	8^{1}	14	10	12																			5
1	2	3	4			7		9				11^{1}	12	6			8	5	10																	6
	2	4	3^{1}			6		7			14	11	12	9		13	8^{2}	5	10^{3}	1																7
	2	4				6		7			13	14	3^{1}	9		11^{3}	8^{2}	5	10	1	12															8
	3					4		9			2^{1}	13		7		11^{2}	8	5	10	1	6	12														9
	3					4		9			2^{3}	11^{1}		7	13	12	8^{2}	5	10	1	6		14													10
	2^{2}		3			4		9				11^{1}		6	13	8		5	10	1	7		12													11
	2		3			6	12	9				11^{1}		8				5	10	1	7		4													12
	2		3			7	12	9				11^{1}		8^{2}	13			5	10	1	6		4													13
	2		3			7	9^{1}	11				12		10	13			5	8^{2}	1	6		4													14
	2		3			7		9				11^{1}		8	12			5	10	1	6		4													15
			4			7		10				11^{1}	2	6	12			9	8^{2}	1			3	5	13											16
	5		4			7		10				11^{1}	2	6^{2}	12			9	8	1			3		13											17
	7		3^{1}			9		8				11	2	13				5	10	1	6^{2}		4			12										18
	2		3			10		9				11	14	7^{1}			13	5^{2}	8^{3}	1	6		4			12										19
	2					6	12	9				13	3	10			7^{1}	5		1	8		4			11^{2}										20
	2^{1}					6	13	9			12		3	10			7^{2}	5		1	8		4			11										21
			3^{2}			7					6^{1}	13	2	10		12	9	8		1			4	5		11										22
						7	13	9^{3}					3	6		10	8^{2}	5		1			4	2^{1}	14	11	12									23
					13	7		9	5		2^{2}	14	3	10		8				1	6^{3}		4^{1}		12	11										24
					7	4		9^{2}	5	13	2		3	10		8^{1}				1	6				12	11										25
		4			8	7		9	5	12		11^{1}	3	10^{2}	13					1	6			2^{3}	14											26
	2	4			8	7^{1}		9		11		10	3^{3}	13	14	12		5		1	6^{2}															27
	2	4			8	7^{2}		9		11		10^{1}	3	13				5	12	1	6															28
	2	3			6^{2}	7		12		11			4	10^{1}		9		5			13							1	8							29
	2	3			6^{1}	7		9		11			4^{2}			10■		5										1	8	12	13					30
	2	3			7			9		11			4	12				5			6							1	10	8^{1}						31
	2	3		12	7			9		11			4			10^{2}		5^{1}			6							1	8^{3}	13		14				32
	2	3		5	7			9		11			4	13		10^{1}					6							1	8^{2}	12						33
	5	3		4	2			9		11				7^{1}		10^{2}			13	1	6								8	12						34
	2	3		5	7^{2}			9		11			4			10^{1}			12	1	6		14						8^{3}	13						35
	2	3		5	6^{1}	9				13						10^{3}			12	1	7^{2}		4						8	11		14				36
	2	3		5	6	9				11^{1}			4			13			10^{2}		7								8	12			1			37
	2	3		5	6^{1}	9		12		11^{3}			4			13			10^{2}		7								8	14			1			38
	2	3		5		6		9		11			4	12					10^{1}		7								8				1			39
	2	3		5		6	13	9^{3}		11			4	12		8^{1}			10^{2}		7		14										1			40
	2	3		5		6	13	9^{2}		11			4	12		10^{1}					7								8^{3}			14	1			41
	2	3		8		10	12			11^{1}			4	13				5	9		7								6^{2}				1			42
	2	3		4		10				11				8		9^{1}		5			7								6	12			1			43
	2	3		4		10				11				8^{1}		9		5	12		7								6^{2}	13			1			44
		3		4		10				11				8^{3}		6		5	9^{2}		7									14	12	13	1	2^{1}		45
		3		7		6				11			4^{3}	13		10^{2}		5	9											8^{1}	14		1	2	12	46

FA Cup
Third Round Kidderminster H (a) 1-2

Carabao Cup
First Round Swansea C (h) 0-3

ROCHDALE

FOUNDATION

Considering the love of rugby in their area, it is not surprising that Rochdale had difficulty in establishing an Association Football club. The earlier Rochdale Town club formed in 1900 went out of existence in 1907 when the present club was immediately established and joined the Manchester League, before graduating to the Lancashire Combination in 1908.

Crown Oil Arena, Sandy Lane, Rochdale, Lancashire OL11 5DR.

Telephone: (01706) 644 648.

Ticket Office: (01706) 644 648 (option 8).

Website: www.rochdaleafc.co.uk

Email: office@rochdaleafc.co.uk

Ground Capacity: 9,507.

Record Attendance: 24,231 v Notts Co, FA Cup 2nd rd, 10 December 1949.

Pitch Measurements: 104m × 69.5m (114yd × 76yd).

Interim Chairman: Andrew Kelly.

Chief Executive: David Bottomley.

Manager: Robbie Stockdale.

Assistant Manager: Jimmy Shan.

Colours: Blue shirts with thin black stripes and white trim, white shorts with blue trim, white socks with blue trim.

Year Formed: 1907.

Turned Professional: 1907.

Club Nickname: 'The Dale'.

Ground: 1907, St Clements Playing Fields (renamed Spotland 1921; Crown Oil Arena 2016).

First Football League Game: 27 August 1921, Division 3 (N), v Accrington Stanley (h) W 6–3 – Crabtree; Nuttall, Sheehan; Hill, Farrer, Yarwood; Hoad, Sandiford, Dennison (2), Owens (3), Carney (1).

Record League Victory: 8–1 v Chesterfield, Division 3 (N), 18 December 1926 – Hill; Brown, Ward; Hillhouse, Parkes, Braidwood; Hughes, Bertram, Whitehurst (5), Schofield (2), Martin (1).

Record Cup Victory: 8–2 v Crook T, FA Cup 1st rd, 26 November 1927 – Moody; Hopkins, Ward; Braidwood, Parkes, Barker; Tompkinson, Clennell (3) Whitehurst (4), Hall, Martin (1).

Record Defeat: 1–9 v Tranmere R, Division 3 (N), 25 December 1931.

HONOURS

League: *Runners-up:* Division 3N – 1923–24, 1926–27.

FA Cup: 5th rd – 1990, 2003, 2018.

League Cup: *Runners-up:* 1962.

FOOTBALL YEARBOOK FACT FILE

Tony Collins, who was manager of Rochdale for seven years from September 1960, is recognised as being the first black manager of a Football League club. Although Dale were a Fourth Division club at the time his team reached the final of the League Cup in 1961–62, one of their greatest achievements.

Most League Points (2 for a win): 62, Division 3 (N), 1923–24.

Most League Points (3 for a win): 82, FL 2, 2009–10.

Most League Goals: 105, Division 3 (N), 1926–27.

Highest League Scorer in Season: Albert Whitehurst, 44, Division 3 (N), 1926–27.

Most League Goals in Total Aggregate: Reg Jenkins, 119, 1964–73.

Most League Goals in One Match: 6, Tommy Tippett v Hartlepools U, Division 3 (N), 21 April 1930.

Most Capped Player: Leo Bertos, 6 (56), New Zealand.

Most League Appearances: Gary Jones, 470, 1998–2001; 2003–12.

Youngest League Player: Zac Hughes, 16 years 105 days v Exeter C, 19 September 1987.

Record Transfer Fee Received: £1,000,000 from Wolverhampton W for Luke Matheson, January 2020.

Record Transfer Fee Paid: £150,000 to Stoke C for Paul Connor, March 2001.

Football League Record: 1921 Elected to Division 3 (N); 1958–59 Division 3; 1959–69 Division 4; 1969–74 Division 3; 1974–92 Division 4; 1992–2004 Division 3; 2004–10 FL 2; 2010–12 FL 1; 2012–14 FL 2; 2014–21 FL 1; 2021– FL 2.

LATEST SEQUENCES

Longest Sequence of League Wins: 8, 29.9.1969 – 3.11.1969.

Longest Sequence of League Defeats: 17, 14.11.1931 – 12.3.1932.

Longest Sequence of League Draws: 6, 17.8.1968 – 14.9.1968.

Longest Sequence of Unbeaten League Matches: 20, 15.9.1923 – 19.1.1924.

Longest Sequence Without a League Win: 28, 14.11.1931 – 29.8.1932.

Successive Scoring Runs: 29 from 10.10.2008.

Successive Non-scoring Runs: 9 from 14.3.1980.

MANAGERS

Billy Bradshaw 1920
Run by committee 1920–22
Tom Wilson 1922–23
Jack Peart 1923–30
Will Cameron 1930–31
Herbert Hopkinson 1932–34
Billy Smith 1934–35
Ernest Nixon 1935–37
Sam Jennings 1937–38
Ted Goodier 1938–52
Jack Warner 1952–53
Harry Catterick 1953–58
Jack Marshall 1958–60
Tony Collins 1960–68
Bob Stokoe 1967–68
Len Richley 1968–70
Dick Conner 1970–73
Walter Joyce 1973–76
Brian Green 1976–77
Mike Ferguson 1977–78
Doug Collins 1979
Bob Stokoe 1979–80
Peter Madden 1980–83
Jimmy Greenhoff 1983–84
Vic Halom 1984–86
Eddie Gray 1986–88
Danny Bergara 1988–89
Terry Dolan 1989–91
Dave Sutton 1991–94
Mick Docherty 1994–96
Graham Barrow 1996–99
Steve Parkin 1999–2001
John Hollins 2001–02
Paul Simpson 2002–03
Alan Buckley 2003
Steve Parkin 2003–06
Keith Hill 2007–11
(Caretaker from December 2006)
Steve Eyre 2011
John Coleman 2012–13
Keith Hill 2013–19
Brian Barry-Murphy 2019–21
Robbie Stockdale July 2021–

TEN YEAR LEAGUE RECORD

		P	*W*	*D*	*L*	*F*	*A*	*Pts*	*Pos*
2012-13	FL 2	46	16	13	17	68	70	61	12
2013-14	FL 2	46	24	9	13	69	48	81	3
2014-15	FL 1	46	19	6	21	72	66	63	8
2015-16	FL 1	46	19	12	15	68	61	69	10
2016-17	FL 1	46	19	12	15	71	62	69	9
2017-18	FL 1	46	11	18	17	49	57	51	20
2018-19	FL 1	46	15	9	22	54	87	54	16
2019-20	FL 1	34	10	6	18	39	57	36	18§
2020-21	FL 1	46	11	14	21	61	78	47	21
2021-22	FL 2	46	12	17	17	51	59	53	18

§*Decided on points-per-game (1.06)*

DID YOU KNOW ?

Rochdale were admitted to the Lancashire Section of the emergency Football League competition during the First World War. Dale played in all four seasons between 1915–16 and 1918–19, and in 1917–18 finished in fourth place, above both Manchester City and Manchester United.

ROCHDALE – SKY BET LEAGUE TWO 2021–22 LEAGUE RECORD

Match No.	Date	Venue	Opponents	Result		H/T Score	Lg Pos.	Goalscorers	Attendance
1	Aug 7	A	Harrogate T	L	2-3	1-2	16	Newby ^{15}, Grant ^{49}	1841
2	14	H	Scunthorpe U	D	0-0	0-0	15		2679
3	17	H	Forest Green R	L	1-2	0-1	22	Newby ^{48}	2188
4	21	A	Northampton T	W	3-1	1-1	15	Taylor ^{17}, Andrews ^{73}, Odoh ^{90}	4870
5	27	H	Colchester U	D	1-1	0-1	13	Keohane ^{61}	3054
6	Sept 4	A	Port Vale	W	3-2	1-1	10	Beesley 2 $^{24, 53}$, O'Keeffe ^{78}	6113
7	11	H	Tranmere R	W	1-0	0-0	5	Cashman ^{84}	4877
8	18	A	Mansfield T	D	1-1	0-0	8	Cashman ^{50}	4336
9	25	H	Oldham Ath	L	0-1	0-0	11		5234
10	Oct 2	A	Bradford C	L	0-2	0-1	16		15,809
11	9	H	Crawley T	L	0-1	0-1	18		2268
12	16	A	Swindon T	D	2-2	0-1	17	Broadbent ^{57}, Kelly, L ^{79}	9310
13	19	A	Salford C	D	0-0	0-0	18		2173
14	23	H	Sutton U	W	3-2	1-0	15	Newby ^{23}, Kelly, L ^{66}, Morley ^{90}	2248
15	30	A	Barrow	W	2-1	1-0	13	Beesley 2 $^{28, 72}$	3366
16	Nov 13	H	Leyton Orient	D	2-2	1-1	13	Newby 2 $^{1, 90}$	2751
17	20	A	Walsall	D	0-0	0-0	13		6144
18	23	H	Stevenage	D	2-2	2-1	13	Beesley ^{4}, Andrews ^{35}	3000
19	27	H	Exeter C	D	1-1	0-0	13	Taylor ^{69}	2102
20	Dec 8	A	Hartlepool U	L	1-2	0-0	16	Andrews ^{55}	4214
21	11	A	Bristol R	L	2-4	0-1	18	Beesley 2 (1 pen) $^{60, 66 (p)}$	6215
22	18	H	Newport Co	W	3-0	1-0	14	Beesley 2 (1 pen) $^{2, 72 (p)}$, Kelly, L ^{89}	2232
23	Jan 15	A	Tranmere R	L	0-2	0-2	18		7046
24	22	H	Bradford C	D	0-0	0-0	18		4941
25	29	A	Oldham Ath	D	0-0	0-0	18		8199
26	Feb 1	A	Colchester U	D	1-1	0-0	18	Grant ^{76}	2298
27	8	A	Forest Green R	L	1-2	0-0	18	Ball ^{47}	1923
28	12	H	Harrogate T	D	3-3	1-2	19	Clark ^{18}, Odoh ^{61}, Campbell ^{87}	2264
29	19	A	Scunthorpe U	W	2-1	0-1	17	Kelly, L ^{51}, Taylor ^{83}	2548
30	22	H	Port Vale	D	1-1	0-1	16	Ball ^{90}	2667
31	26	H	Northampton T	W	1-0	0-0	16	Campbell ^{53}	2643
32	Mar 1	A	Carlisle U	L	0-2	0-1	17		5360
33	5	A	Sutton U	L	0-3	0-2	17		2874
34	12	H	Barrow	D	0-0	0-0	18		2935
35	15	H	Salford C	D	1-1	1-0	17	Ball ^{27}	2041
36	19	A	Leyton Orient	L	1-3	1-1	19	Newby ^{5}	4791
37	22	H	Mansfield T	L	0-1	0-0	19		2088
38	26	A	Crawley T	L	0-1	0-1	20		2164
39	29	H	Carlisle U	W	2-0	1-0	19	Kelly, L (pen) ^{10}, Grant ^{81}	2160
40	Apr 2	H	Swindon T	D	0-0	0-0	20		2779
41	9	H	Walsall	W	1-0	0-0	16	Grant ^{55}	2437
42	15	A	Stevenage	L	0-1	0-0	17		3172
43	18	H	Hartlepool U	W	2-1	0-1	15	Keohane ^{61}, O'Connell ^{90}	2900
44	23	A	Exeter C	L	0-2	0-1	18		6935
45	30	H	Bristol R	L	3-4	2-0	20	Charman 2 $^{11, 17}$, O'Keeffe ^{60}	4628
46	May 7	A	Newport Co	W	2-0	1-0	18	Done ^{16}, Odoh ^{90}	5322

Final League Position: 18

GOALSCORERS

League (51): Beesley 9 (2 pens), Newby 6, Kelly, L 5 (1 pen), Grant 4, Andrews 3, Ball 3, Odoh 3, Taylor 3, Campbell 2, Cashman 2, Charman 2, Keohane 2, O'Keeffe 2, Broadbent 1, Clark 1, Done 1, Morley 1, O'Connell 1.
FA Cup (4): Andrews 1, Beesley 1, Morley 1, O'Keeffe 1.
Carabao Cup (3): Beesley 2 (1 pen), Cashman 1.
Papa John's Trophy (4): O'Keeffe 2 (1 pen), Andrews 1, Kelly L 1.

Lynch J 25	O'Keeffe C 39 + 4	Taylor M 19 + 3	McNulty J 9 + 3	White A 7 + 5	Dooley S 30 + 8	Grant C 21 + 12	Morley A 19 + 2	Odoh A 17 + 15	Newby A 27 + 9	Beesley J 21	Graham S 11 + 1	Cashman D 9 + 14	Broadbent G 13 + 8	O'Connell E 45	Done M 13 + 12	Andrews J 7 + 10	Dorsett J 36 + 1	Keohane J 25 + 1	Coleman J 19	Kelly L 24 + 6	Downing P 10	Clark M 22 + 1	Campbell T 13	Charman L 10 + 9	Ball J 11	Eastwood J 2	Brierley E 2	Match No.
1	2	3	4	5^{1}	6	7^{3}	8	9^{2}	10	11	12	13	14															1
1	5	3			13		7	12	6	10	2^{2}	11^{1}	8	4	9													2
1	5	4			7		6	9	11	10^{1}	2^{2}	13		3	8	12												3
1	5	4			7		6	9	11		2^{2}	14		3	8^{1}	10^{3}	12	13										4
	5	2			6	13	7	11^{1}	9^{2}	10		12		3			4	8	1									5
	5	2	3		6^{2}	14	7	11^{1}	9^{3}	10		12	13	4				8	1									6
	5	2			6	13	7	11^{2}	9^{1}	10^{3}		12		3		14	4	8	1									7
		2	12	14	7		6	13	9^{2}	10		11		3	8^{3}		4^{1}	5	1									8
	5						7	13	9^{3}	10	2	11^{2}	6^{1}	3		14	4	8	1	12								9
	5				6^{2}		7	9^{1}	12	10	2	11		3	14		4	8^{3}	1	13								10
	5			8^{3}		9^{2}	7	11^{1}	13	10	2	12		3	14		4		1	6								11
	5			14		9^{2}	7	13		10	2	11^{3}	6^{1}	3			4	8	1	12								12
	5			13			12	11^{3}	9	10	2	14	6^{1}	3			4	8	1	7^{2}								13
	5		4	13		14	7	11^{1}	9^{3}	10	2	12		3				8^{2}	1	6								14
	5				14	12	7	11^{2}	9^{1}	10	2		13	3			4	8	1	6^{3}								15
	5	14					7	11^{2}	9	10	2^{3}			3	13	12	4	8^{1}	1	6								16
1	5	2			12	14	7^{1}	13	11^{3}	9				3		10^{2}	4	8		6								17
1	5	2			6	12		13	11^{2}	9				3		10	4	8^{1}		7								18
1	5	2				11	6	8		9				3		10	4			7								19
1	5	2		8^{2}			7	11^{1}		9		12		3	13	10	4			6								20
1	5		3	8^{2}	13		7^{1}	11	9	10			14	2		12	4			6^{3}								21
	5	2	14	8^{3}	6^{1}	11^{2}	13		9	10			12	3			4		1	7								22
				8^{3}	6	11		12	9^{1}			14	5	3	13	10^{2}	4		1	7	2							23
				8^{1}	6	11		9	14				5	3	13	10^{2}	4		1	7^{3}	2	12						24
	5				7	11		12	9^{1}				6	3			4		1		2	8	10					25
	5				13	11			9^{1}				6^{2}	3	14		4		1	7	2	8	10^{3}	12				26
	5	14			12	9							6^{1}	3			4		1	7	2^{3}	8	10^{2}	13	11			27
	2				9	10^{2}		12	8					3			4		1	6^{1}		5	11	13	7			28
1	5	2			9^{2}	13			12				14	3			4			6		8	10	11^{1}	7^{3}			29
1	5	2			6	11^{2}		13	9^{1}					3			4^{3}			12		8	10	14	7			30
1	13	2			12	14			9^{3}					3	11^{2}		4	5		6		8	10^{4}	15	7^{1}			31
1	12				7	13			9^{3}					3	11^{1}		4	5		6		8^{2}	10	14	2			32
1	12		3		8	10^{3}			7^{1}					4			5	2^{2}		14		6	11	13	9			33
1	5				7^{2}				12			13	6	3	11^{1}		4	2				8	10		9			34
1	9^{1}		3		13	12							6^{2}	2	14		4	5		11^{3}		8	10		7			35
1	5				7^{2}				9					3	12		4	2^{1}		6		8	10	13	11			36
1	5				7	12			13				6	3	10^{3}		4				2	8	11^{2}	14	9^{1}			37
1	5				7				9^{2}			13	6^{1}	3	11^{3}	14	4			12	2	8		10				38
1	5		14		7	9		12				11^{1}	13	3^{3}			4	2		6^{2}		8		10				39
1	5				7	10						11^{1}	13	3	12		4	2		6^{2}		8		9				40
1	5				7	9^{2}		13	12			11^{1}		3	14		4			6	2	8		10^{3}				41
1	5^{2}				6	9		13				11^{1}		7	14	12	4	2			3	8^{3}		10				42
1	5^{1}	14	4^{3}		7	9		12	13					6	10^{2}			2			3	8		11				43
1	12	2	4^{1}		7	6		10	13					3	9^{3}	14		5				8		11^{2}				44
	5	4		13	7	10						12		3	9^{1}	14		2				8^{2}		11^{3}		1	6	45
	5	2	4		7	10		12						3	9^{2}	13						8		11^{1}		1	6	46

FA Cup

First Round	Notts Co	(h)	1-1
Replay	Notts Co	(a)	2-1
Second Round	Plymouth Arg	(h)	1-2

Papa John's Trophy

Group D (N)	Liverpool U21	(h)	4-0
Group D (N)	Port Vale	(a)	0-1
Group D (N)	Bolton W	(h)	0-3

Carabao Cup

First Round	Harrogate T	(a)	P-P

Rochdale received a bye to the second round due to positive COVID-19 tests in the Harrogate T squad.

Second Round	Shrewsbury T	(a)	2-0
Third Round	Burnley	(a)	1-4

ROTHERHAM UNITED

FOUNDATION

Rotherham were formed in 1870 before becoming Town in the late 1880s. Thornhill United were founded in 1877 and changed their name to Rotherham County in 1905. The Town amalgamated with Rotherham County to form Rotherham United in 1925.

The AESSEAL New York Stadium, New York Way, Rotherham, South Yorkshire S60 1AH.

Telephone: (0170) 9827 760.

Ticket Office: (0170) 9827 768.

Website: www.themillers.co.uk

Email: office@rotherhamunited.net

Ground Capacity: 12,088.

Record Attendance: 25,170 v Sheffield U, Division 2, 13 December 1952 (at Millmoor); 7,082 v Aldershot T, FL 2 Play-offs semi-final 2nd leg, 19 May 2010 (at Don Valley); 11,758 v Sheffield U, FL 1, 7 September 2013 (at New York Stadium).

Pitch Measurements: 102m × 64m (111.5yd × 70yd).

Chairman: Tony Stewart OBE.

Chief Operating Officer: Paul Douglas.

Manager: Paul Warne.

Assistant Manager: Richie Barker.

HONOURS

League Champions: Division 3 – 1980–81; Division 3N – 1950–51; Division 4 – 1988–89.

Runners-up: Second Division – 2000–01; FL 1 – 2019–20, 2021–22; Division 3N – 1946–47, 1947–48, 1948–49; FL 2 – 2012–13; Third Division – 1999–2000; Division 4 – 1991–92.

FA Cup: 5th rd – 1953, 1968.

League Cup: *Runners-up:* 1961.

League Trophy Winners: 1996, 2022.

Colours: Red shirts with white sleeves and black and white trim, white shorts, red socks with black and white trim.

Year Formed: 1870. ***Turned Professional:*** 1905. ***Club Nickname:*** 'The Millers'.

Previous Names: 1877, Thornhill United; 1905, Rotherham County; 1925, amalgamated with Rotherham Town under Rotherham United.

Grounds: 1870, Red House Ground; 1907, Millmoor; 2008, Don Valley Stadium; 2012, New York Stadium (renamed The AESSEAL New York Stadium 2014).

First Football League Game: 2 September 1893, Division 2, Rotherham T v Lincoln C (a) D 1–1 – McKay; Thickett, Watson; Barr, Brown, Broadhead; Longden, Cutts, Leatherbarrow, McCormick, Pickering, (1 og). 30 August 1919, Division 2, Rotherham Co v Nottingham F (h) W 2–0 – Branston; Alton, Baines; Bailey, Coe, Stanton; Lee (1), Cawley (1), Glennon, Lees, Lamb.

Record League Victory: 8–0 v Oldham Ath, Division 3 (N), 26 May 1947 – Warnes; Selkirk, Ibbotson; Edwards, Horace Williams, Danny Williams; Wilson (2), Shaw (1), Ardron (3), Guest (1), Hainsworth (1).

Record Cup Victory: 6–0 v Spennymoor U, FA Cup 2nd rd, 17 December 1977 – McAlister; Forrest, Breckin, Womble, Stancliffe, Green, Finney, Phillips (3), Gwyther (2) (Smith), Goodfellow, Crawford (1). 6–0 v Wolverhampton W, FA Cup 1st rd, 16 November 1985 – O'Hanlon; Forrest, Dungworth, Gooding (1), Smith (1), Pickering, Birch (2), Emerson, Tynan (1), Simmons (1), Pugh. 6–0 v King's Lynn, FA Cup 2nd rd, 6 December 1997 – Mimms; Clark, Hurst (Goodwin), Garner (1) (Hudson) (1), Warner (Bass), Richardson (1), Berry (1), Thompson, Druce (1), Glover (1), Roscoe; 6–0 v Doncaster R (a), Papa John's Trophy Northern Group E, 7 September 2021 – Vickers; Edmonds-Green, Hull (1), Mattock (1), Miller (1), Barlaser, Odofin, Bola, Sadlier (Rathbone 46), Grigg (1) (Gratton 65), Ladapo (1) (Smith 65), own goal 1.

Record Defeat: 1–11 v Bradford C, Division 3 (N), 25 August 1928.

FOOTBALL YEARBOOK FACT FILE

In 1954–55 Rotherham United were denied promotion to top-flight football on goal average. The Millers finished their season with a 6-1 home win over Liverpool, leaving them second in the Division Two table. However, Birmingham City had one game left to play, and their 5-1 win two nights later secured them the title ahead of both Luton Town and the Millers with all three teams finishing on 54 points.

Most League Points (2 for a win): 71, Division 3 (N), 1950–51.

Most League Points (3 for a win): 91, Division 2, 2000–01.

Most League Goals: 114, Division 3 (N), 1946–47.

Highest League Scorer in Season: Wally Ardron, 38, Division 3 (N), 1946–47.

Most League Goals in Total Aggregate: Gladstone Guest, 130, 1946–56.

Most League Goals in One Match: 4, Roland Bastow v York C, Division 3 (N), 9 November 1935; 4, Roland Bastow v Rochdale, Division 3 (N), 7 March 1936; 4, Wally Ardron v Crewe Alex, Division 3 (N), 5 October 1946; 4, Wally Ardron v Carlisle U, Division 3 (N), 13 September 1947; 4, Wally Ardron v Hartlepools U, Division 3 (N), 13 October 1948; 4, Ian Wilson v Liverpool, Division 2, 2 May 1955; 4, Carl Gilbert v Swansea C, Division 3, 28 September 1971; 4, Carl Airey v Chester, Division 3, 31 August 1987; 4, Shaun Goater v Hartlepool U, Division 3, 9 April 1994; 4, Lee Glover v Hull C, Division 3, 28 December 1997; 4, Darren Byfield v Millwall, Division 1, 10 August 2002; 4, Adam Le Fondre v Cheltenham T, FL 2, 21 August 2010.

Most Capped Player: Kari Arnason, 20 (90), Iceland.

Most League Appearances: Danny Williams, 461, 1946–62.

Youngest League Player: Kevin Eley, 16 years 72 days v Scunthorpe U, 15 May 1984.

Record Transfer Fee Received: £2,100,000 (rising to £3,500,000) from Cardiff C for Will Vaulks, June 2019.

Record Transfer Fee Paid: £500,000 (in excess of) to Plymouth Arg for Freddie Ladapo, June 2019.

Football League Record: 1893 Rotherham Town elected to Division 2; 1896 Failed re-election; 1919 Rotherham County elected to Division 2; 1923–51 Division 3 (N); 1951–68 Division 2; 1968–73 Division 3; 1973–75 Division 4; 1975–81 Division 3; 1981–83 Division 2; 1983–88 Division 3; 1988–89 Division 4; 1989–91 Division 3; 1991–92 Division 4; 1992–97 Division 2; 1997–2000 Division 3; 2000–01 Division 2; 2001–04 Division 1; 2004–05 FL C; 2005–07 FL 1; 2007–13 FL 2; 2013–14 FL 1; 2014–17 FL C; 2017–18 FL 1; 2018–19 FL C; 2019–20 FL 1; 2020–21 FL C; 2021–22 FL 1; 2022– FL C.

MANAGERS

Billy Heald 1925–29 *(Secretary only for several years)*
Stanley Davies 1929–30
Billy Heald 1930–33
Reg Freeman 1934–52
Andy Smailes 1952–58
Tom Johnston 1958–62
Danny Williams 1962–65
Jack Mansell 1965–67
Tommy Docherty 1967–68
Jimmy McAnearney 1968–73
Jimmy McGuigan 1973–79
Ian Porterfield 1979–81
Emlyn Hughes 1981–83
George Kerr 1983–85
Norman Hunter 1985–87
Dave Cusack 1987–88
Billy McEwan 1988–91
Phil Henson 1991–94
Archie Gemmill and John McGovern 1994–96
Danny Bergara 1996–97
Ronnie Moore 1997–2005
Mick Harford 2005
Alan Knill 2005–07
Mark Robins 2007–09
Ronnie Moore 2009–11
Andy Scott 2011–12
Steve Evans 2012–15
Neil Redfearn 2015–16
Neil Warnock 2016
Alan Stubbs 2016
Kenny Jackett 2016
Paul Warne November 2016–

LATEST SEQUENCES

Longest Sequence of League Wins: 9, 2.2.1982 – 6.3.1982.

Longest Sequence of League Defeats: 10, 14.2.2017 – 8.4.2017.

Longest Sequence of League Draws: 6, 13.10.1969 – 22.11.1969.

Longest Sequence of Unbeaten League Matches: 18, 13.10.1969 – 7.2.1970.

Longest Sequence Without a League Win: 21, 9.5.2004 – 20.11.2004.

Successive Scoring Runs: 30 from 3.4.1954.

Successive Non-scoring Runs: 6 from 21.8.2004.

TEN YEAR LEAGUE RECORD

		P	W	D	L	F	A	Pts	Pos
2012-13	FL 2	46	24	7	15	74	59	79	2
2013-14	FL 1	46	24	14	8	86	58	86	4
2014-15	FL C	46	11	16	19	46	67	46*	21
2015-16	FL C	46	13	10	23	53	71	49	21
2016-17	FL C	46	5	8	33	40	98	23	24
2017-18	FL 1	46	24	7	15	73	53	79	4
2018-19	FL C	46	8	16	22	52	83	40	22
2019-20	FL 1	35	18	8	9	61	38	62	2§
2020-21	FL C	46	11	9	26	44	60	42	23
2021-22	FL 1	46	27	9	10	70	33	90	2

**3 pts deducted. §Decided on points-per-game (1.77)*

DID YOU KNOW ?

Rotherham United played at home under floodlights for the first time on 23 November 1960 when they faced Bristol Rovers in a Football League Cup tie. The Millers won the game 2-0 with goals from Ken Houghton and Alan Kirkman in front of a crowd of 10,912.

ROTHERHAM UNITED – SKY BET LEAGUE ONE 2021–22 LEAGUE RECORD

Match No.	Date	Venue	Opponents	Result		H/T Score	Lg Pos.	Goalscorers	Attendance
1	Aug 7	H	Plymouth Arg	W	2-0	2-0	1	Ladapo [10], Wiles [38]	9417
2	14	A	Wigan Ath	L	0-1	0-0	10		10,217
3	17	A	Morecambe	W	1-0	0-0	6	Smith [60]	4004
4	21	H	Sheffield W	L	0-2	0-0	11		11,522
5	28	H	Doncaster R	W	2-0	2-0	8	Smith 2 [27, 45]	9748
6	Sept 11	H	Fleetwood T	L	2-4	2-1	13	Smith [38], Sadlier (pen) [45]	8463
7	14	A	Lincoln C	D	1-1	1-0	13	Smith [22]	8788
8	18	A	Bolton W	W	2-0	2-0	6	Wiles 2 [18, 21]	20,877
9	25	H	Crewe Alex	D	1-1	0-0	5	Rathbone [54]	8747
10	28	H	AFC Wimbledon	W	3-0	2-0	5	Grigg [36], Smith 2 [45, 89]	8004
11	Oct 2	A	Cheltenham T	W	2-0	0-0	4	Grigg [51], Edmonds-Green [75]	3748
12	16	H	Portsmouth	W	4-1	1-0	5	Smith 2 [29, 55], Wood [60], Wiles [62]	9684
13	19	H	Wycombe W	D	0-0	0-0	5		8104
14	23	A	Milton Keynes D	W	3-0	1-0	5	Ihiekwe [27], Smith [65], Ladapo [72]	8448
15	30	H	Sunderland	W	5-1	2-1	4	Smith 2 [10, 73], Ladapo 2 [41, 88], Ihiekwe [53]	10,573
16	Nov 2	A	Charlton Ath	D	1-1	1-0	3	Miller [45]	12,592
17	20	H	Cambridge U	W	3-1	2-0	2	Wiles [34], Barlaser (pen) [45], Ladapo [81]	9534
18	23	A	Ipswich T	W	2-0	1-0	1	Wiles [24], Ferguson [59]	18,221
19	27	A	Oxford U	D	0-0	0-0	1		7620
20	Dec 7	H	Gillingham	W	5-1	2-1	1	Ladapo [39], Miller [45], Barlaser 2 (1 pen) [59 (p), 81], Ogbene [89]	8008
21	11	H	Burton Alb	W	3-1	1-1	1	Ladapo 2 [23, 48], Barlaser [84]	9007
22	18	A	Cambridge U	W	1-0	0-0	1	Barlaser [66]	5323
23	26	A	Accrington S	L	0-1	0-0	1		4870
24	Jan 1	H	Bolton W	W	2-1	1-1	1	Smith 2 [40, 74]	9736
25	15	A	Fleetwood T	L	0-1	0-0	3		3385
26	22	H	Cheltenham T	W	1-0	1-0	3	Smith [24]	9187
27	29	A	Crewe Alex	W	2-0	1-0	1	Smith [7], Richards (og) [74]	5014
28	Feb 1	A	Doncaster R	W	5-0	2-0	1	Miller [8], Wiles [16], Ogbene [72], Barlaser (pen) [76], Lindsay [89]	9255
29	5	H	Accrington S	W	1-0	0-0	1	Barlaser [57]	8593
30	8	A	AFC Wimbledon	W	1-0	0-0	1	Kayode [60]	6387
31	13	A	Sheffield W	W	2-0	0-0	1	Ladapo [59], Smith [84]	26,418
32	18	H	Wigan Ath	D	1-1	0-1	1	Rathbone [75]	10,588
33	22	H	Morecambe	W	2-0	2-0	1	Ladapo 2 [4, 30]	8376
34	26	A	Plymouth Arg	W	1-0	0-0	1	Smith [63]	14,193
35	Mar 1	A	Shrewsbury T	D	0-0	0-0	1		5111
36	5	H	Milton Keynes D	L	1-2	1-0	1	Barlaser (pen) [25]	9731
37	12	A	Wycombe W	D	0-0	0-0	1		5742
38	15	H	Lincoln C	W	2-1	2-0	1	Wiles [11], Ogbene [13]	9575
39	19	H	Shrewsbury T	L	0-3	0-1	1		9253
40	Apr 9	H	Charlton Ath	L	0-1	0-0	3		9087
41	12	A	Portsmouth	L	0-3	0-1	3		14,154
42	16	H	Ipswich T	W	1-0	0-0	2	Smith [78]	9394
43	19	A	Burton Alb	L	0-2	0-1	2		3537
44	23	H	Oxford U	W	2-1	1-1	2	Barlaser (pen) [66], Edmonds-Green [45]	10,415
45	26	A	Sunderland	D	1-1	1-0	2	Ihiekwe [17]	33,119
46	30	A	Gillingham	W	2-0	1-0	2	Edmonds-Green [34], Kelly [89]	8542

Final League Position: 2

GOALSCORERS

League (70): Smith 19, Ladapo 11, Barlaser 9 (5 pens), Wiles 8, Edmonds-Green 3, Ihiekwe 3, Miller 3, Ogbene 3, Grigg 2, Rathbone 2, Ferguson 1, Kayode 1, Kelly 1, Lindsay 1, Sadlier 1 (1 pen), Wood 1, own goal 1.
FA Cup (5): Grigg 1, Ihiekwe 1, Ladapo 1, Smith 1, Wiles 1.
Carabao Cup (1): Sadlier 1.
Papa John's Trophy (27): Smith 5, Sadlier 4 (1 pen), Grigg 3, Ladapo 3, Hull 2, Harding 1, Ihiekwe 1, Kayode 1, Mattock 1, Miller 1, Odofin 1, Ogbene 1, Osei-Tutu 1, Wiles 1, own goal 1.

Johansson V 26	Ihiekwe M 42	Wood R 33 + 6	Harding W 32 + 6	Ogbene C 37 + 8	Lindsay J 15 + 13	Barlaser D 40 + 4	Wiles B 43 + 3	Miller M 11 + 12	Ladapo F 22 + 9	Smith M 45	Rathbone O 39 + 3	Odofin H 1 + 10	Ferguson S 25 + 7	Kayode J 6 + 14	Edmonds-Green R 26 + 2	Mattock J 10 + 10	Sadlier K 5 + 7	Grigg W 13 + 6	Bola T 3 + 1	Vickers J 20	MacDonald A 3 + 4	Osei-Tutu J 9 + 5	Kelly G — + 1	Match No.
1	2	3	4	5	6	7^{1}	8^{2}	9^{3}	10	11	12	13	14											1
1	2	3	4	5	6	7^{3}	8	9^{1}	13	10		14	12	11^{2}										2
1	2	12	4	6	7		8			10	5		9^{2}	11^{3}	3^{1}	13	14							3
1	2	3	4	6^{1}	5	14	8		13	10	7^{3}		9	11^{2}			12							4
1	2	3	4		5	13	7	9■	10^{1}	11	8^{3}				14	12	6^{2}							5
1	2	3^{1}	4	6	5^{3}	12	8		11	10	7^{2}				13		9	14						6
1	3			6	7^{3}	5	14		11^{1}	10	8				2	4	13	12	9^{2}					7
1		3	12	6^{1}	13	5^{2}	7			10	8				2	4	14	11^{3}	9					8
1		3	12■	6		5	8		14	10	7		13		2	4^{2}		11^{3}	9^{1}					9
1	4	3		6	7^{1}	5^{3}	12			10	8	14	9	13	2			11^{2}						10
1	4	3		13		5	8	12	14	10	7		9^{2}		2		6^{1}	11^{3}						11
1	4^{1}	3	6	12		5	8	9	13	10^{3}	7			14	2			11^{2}						12
		3	6	12		5	8	14	13	10	7		9^{3}		2	4^{1}		11^{2}		1				13
	3		4	6		5^{3}	8	13	12	10	7	14	9^{2}		2			11^{1}		1				14
	3		4	6^{1}		5	8	12	11	10^{2}	7		9^{3}	13	2		14			1				15
	4^{1}	3	6	12		5	8^{3}	9^{2}	11	10	7	14	13		2					1				16
		3	4	5	14	6	7	12	10				8^{1}	13	2		9^{3}	11^{2}		1				17
1	4	3	13	6^{2}	7	5	8	12	10^{3}	11			9^{1}		2		14							18
1	3	13	4	6^{2}	12	5	8	9	11^{3}	10	7^{1}			14	2									19
1	3		4	6		5	7	9^{1}	10^{3}	11^{2}	8		12	13	2			14						20
1	4	3		14	13	6	7		10	11	8^{3}		9^{1}		2	12	5^{2}							21
1	4	3	13	6	12	5	8		10^{3}	11	7^{1}		9		2^{2}			14						22
1	4	3	2	6	13	5	7	12	11^{3}	10	8^{2}		9^{1}					14						23
1	4	3		6	14	5	8^{1}		11^{2}	10	7^{3}		9	13	2		12							24
	4	3		5		6	7			11	8		9	12	2			10^{1}		1				25
	4	3	2	6	13	5	8	9^{1}	11^{3}	10	7^{2}		12					14		1				26
	4	3	13	6	14	5^{3}	8			10	7		9	12	2^{2}			11^{1}		1				27
	3	13	2	6^{2}	14	5	8^{3}	9		10	7			12		4		11^{1}		1				28
	4^{1}	3■	2	6		5	8	13		10	7		9^{2}	14		12		11^{3}		1				29
	3		2	6	7^{3}	5	8			10		14	9	12		4^{2}		11^{1}		1	13			30
	2	3	4	6	7^{1}	5	8		11^{3}	10	12		9^{2}			14				1		13		31
	2	3	4	5		7	8		11^{2}	10	6		9^{1}	13						1		12		32
	2	3	4	12		5^{2}	8		11	10	7	13	9^{3}							1	14	6^{1}		33
	3		2	6		5^{1}	8		11	10	7	12	9^{2}			4^{3}				1	14	13		34
	4	3	6^{1}	13	8		12		10	11	7^{2}	5				14				1	2^{3}	9		35
	3		2	6		5^{2}	8		11^{3}	10	7		9^{1}	13		4			14	1		12		36
	4	3	6^{2}	10		5	8	12		11	7		9^{1}			13				1	2			37
	2	3	12	6		5^{1}	8	9		10	7^{3}	14		11^{2}		4				1	13			38
	3	12		13		5^{2}	8	14		10	7		9	11^{1}	2					1	4■	6^{3}		39
1	4	3	2	6	13	5^{3}	8	12	10	11	7^{1}		9^{2}									14		40
1	2	3		6	7	5	8^{1}	14	13	10	12			11^{2}		4						9^{3}		41
1	3	13	4	10	6	12	8	9^{1}		11	7				2							5^{2}		42
1	3	14	4	5	6	7^{2}	10		13	11	8		12^{3}		2							9^{1}		43
1	4	3	5^{1}	9	13	7	10			11	6^{2}				2	12						8		44
1	4	3	5	9	13	7	10			11	6^{2}				2	12						8^{1}		45
1	4	3	5	9		7	10			11^{2}	6^{3}	14			2	12						8^{1}	13	46

FA Cup

First Round	Bromley	(h)	3-0
Second Round	Stockport Co	(h)	1-0
Third Round	QPR	(a)	1-1

(aet; QPR won 8-7 on penalties)

Papa John's Trophy

Group E (N)	Doncaster R	(a)	6-0
Group E (N)	Scunthorpe U	(h)	4-1
Group E (N)	Manchester C U21	(h)	5-0
Second Round	Port Vale	(h)	1-1

(Rotherham U won 5-3 on penalties)

Third Round	Crewe Alex	(a)	4-2
Quarter-Final	Cambridge U	(h)	1-1

(Rotherham U won 7-6 on penalties)

Semi-Final	Hartlepool U	(a)	2-2

(Rotherham U won 5-4 on penalties)

Final	Sutton U	(Wembley)	4-2

(aet)

Carabao Cup

First Round	Accrington S	(h)	1-2

SALFORD CITY

FOUNDATION

The club was formed as Salford Central Mission in 1940 and in 1947 changed its name to Salford Central. The club competed in local junior leagues including the Eccles and District League until 1963 when the name was changed to Salford Amateurs and they entered the Manchester League. In 1980 this club merged with another local club, Anson Villa, and adopted the name Salford. They were members of the Cheshire County League and then the North West Counties League. In 1990 Salford became Salford City and after gaining promotion to the Northern Premier League for 2008–09 they made rapid progress and went on to achieve Football League status.

The Peninsula Stadium, Moor Lane, Salford, Greater Manchester M7 3PZ.

Telephone: (0161) 241 9772.

Ticket Office: (0845) 847 2252.

Website: salfordcityfc.co.uk

Email: enquiries@salfordcityfc.co.uk

Ground Capacity: 5,032.

Record Attendance: 4,518 v Leeds U, EFL Cup 1st rd, 13 August 2019.

Pitch Measurements: 101m × 64m (110.5yd × 70yd).

Chairman: Karen Baird.

President: Dave Russell.

Manager: Neil Wood.

Colours: Red shirts with white trim, white shorts, white socks.

Year Formed: 1940.

Turned Professional: 2017.

Previous Names: 1940, Salford Central; 1963, Salford Amateurs; 1989, Salford City.

Club Nickname: 'The Ammies'.

Grounds: 1979, Moor Lane (renamed The Peninsula Stadium 2017).

First Football League Game: 3 August 2019, FL 2, v AFC Wimbledon (a) W 2–1 – Neal; Maynard, Pond, Piergianni, Wiseman, Towell (Armstrong), Smith, Shelton, Touray, Rooney (Beesley), Dieseruwe (2) (Threlkeld).

HONOURS

League: *Play-Off Winners:* National League – 2018–19 (*promoted to FL 2*).

FA Cup: 2nd rd – 2016, 2021, 2022.

League Cup: 2nd rd – 2021.

League Trophy: *Winners:* 2020 (final played in 2021).

FOOTBALL YEARBOOK FACT FILE

The involvement of former Manchester United stars in the ownership of Salford City dates from 2014, but two of the stars of United's FA Youth Cup winning team of 1992 had previously played for the Ammies. Defender George Switzer and winger Ben Thornley both played for the Moor Lane club after leaving Old Trafford.

Record League Victory: 5–1 v Scunthorpe U (h), FL 2, 19 March 2022 – King; Lowe, Vassell, Ndaba, Touray I, Kelly (1), Lund (Love), Watson, Thomas-Asante (3), Smith M (1) (Loughlin), Hunter (Bolton).

Record Cup Victory: 5–0 v Kennek Ryhope, FA Cup Preliminary rd, 2000–01; 5–0 v Atherton Laburnum R, FA Cup 1st Qualifying rd, 2008–09; 5–0 v Whitby T, FA Cup 1st Qualifying rd, 2015–16.

Record Cup Defeat: 1–7 v St Helen's T, FA Cup prel rd, 2001–02.

Most League Points (3 for a win): 71, FL 2, 2020–21.

Most League Goals: 60, FL 2, 2021–22.

Highest League Scorer in Season: Ian Henderson, 17, FL 2, 2020–21.

Most League Goals in Total Aggregate: Brandon Thomas-Asante, 22, 2019–22.

Most League Goals in One Match: 3, Ian Henderson v Grimsby T, FL 2, 19 September 2020; 3, Brandon Thomas-Asante v Scunthorpe U, FL 2, 19 March 2022.

Most Capped Player: Ibou Touray, 14 (16), Gambia.

Most League Appearances: Ibou Touray, 108, 2019–22.

Youngest League Player: Kelly N'Mai, 17 years 119 days v Newport Co, 28 August 2021.

Football League Record: 2019 Promoted from National League; 2019– FL 2.

MANAGERS

John Torkington 1983–84
David Entwhistle 1984–87
Alf Murphy 1987–89
Steve Canaghan 1989–92
Billy Garton 1992–93
Syd White 1993–96
Alan Lord 1996–99
Tom Foster and Matt Wardrop 1999–2001
Andy Brown 2001–03
Chris Willcock 2003–04
Mark Molyneaux 2004–05
Darren Lyons 2005
John Foster 2005
Gary Fellows 2005–08
Ashley Berry 2008
Paul Wright 2009–10
Rhodri Giggs 2010–12
Darren Sheridan 2012–13
Andy Heald 2013
Barry Massey and Phil Power 2013
Phil Power 2013–15
Anthony Johnson and Bernard Morley 2015–18
Graham Alexander 2018–20
Richie Wellens 2020–21
Gary Bowyer 2021–22
Neil Wood May 2022–

LATEST SEQUENCES

Longest Sequence of League Wins: 4, 19.3.2022 – 2.4.2022.

Longest Sequence of League Defeats: 3, 1.1.2020 – 11.1.2020.

Longest Sequence of League Draws: 5, 17.8.2019 – 7.9.2019.

Longest Sequence of Unbeaten League Matches: 11, 1.2.2022 – 2.4.2022.

Longest Sequence Without a League Win: 7, 10.8.2019 – 14.9.2019.

Successive Scoring Runs: 12 from 23.10.2021.

Successive Non-scoring Runs: 4 from 9.3.2021.

TEN YEAR LEAGUE RECORD

		P	*W*	*D*	*L*	*F*	*A*	*Pts*	*Pos*
2012–13	NPL1N	42	11	13	18	65	79	46	16
2013–14	NPL1N	42	15	7	20	68	80	52	12
2014–15	NPL1N	42	30	5	7	92	42	95	1
2015–16	NPLP	46	27	9	10	94	48	90	3
2016–17	NLN	42	22	11	9	79	44	77	4
2017–18	NLN	42	28	7	7	80	45	91	1
2018–19	NL	46	25	10	11	77	45	85	3
2019-20	FL 2	37	13	11	13	49	46	50	11§
2020-21	FL 2	46	19	14	13	54	34	71	8
2021-22	FL 2	46	19	13	14	60	46	70	10

§*Decided on points-per-game (1.35)*

DID YOU KNOW ?

Salford City were members of the North West Counties League throughout the 1990s but never finished higher than seventh position. They were more likely to be struggling towards the foot of the table, and in 1990–91 they finished in bottom position, 10 points adrift of their nearest rivals.

SALFORD CITY – SKY BET LEAGUE TWO 2021–22 LEAGUE RECORD

Match No.	Date	Venue	Opponents	Result	H/T Score	Lg Pos.	Goalscorers	Attendance
1	Aug 7	H	Leyton Orient	D 1-1	1-1	10	Willock [41]	1968
2	14	H	Sutton U	D 0-0	0-0	14		1460
3	17	A	Crawley T	L 1-2	1-1	16	Henderson [7]	2167
4	21	H	Swindon T	L 0-1	0-0	22		2229
5	28	H	Newport Co	W 3-0	3-0	16	Wright [1], McAleny [18], Henderson [30]	1687
6	Sept 4	A	Carlisle U	L 1-2	1-1	20	Morris [44]	4671
7	11	H	Bradford C	W 1-0	0-0	14	Lund [90]	2863
8	18	A	Tranmere R	L 0-2	0-1	17		5854
9	25	H	Northampton T	D 2-2	1-1	19	Lund [24], Eastham [90]	2037
10	Oct 2	A	Colchester U	W 2-0	2-0	15	Thomas-Asante [9], Elliott [25]	2566
11	9	A	Walsall	L 1-2	0-1	17	Eastham [78]	5005
12	16	H	Hartlepool U	W 2-0	1-0	15	Elliott [3], Willock [85]	2448
13	19	H	Rochdale	D 0-0	0-0	15		2173
14	23	A	Forest Green R	L 1-3	1-1	17	Thomas-Asante [17]	2245
15	30	H	Exeter C	L 1-2	0-0	19	Elliott [79]	1892
16	Nov 13	A	Scunthorpe U	D 1-1	0-1	17	McAleny [58]	2614
17	20	A	Harrogate T	W 2-0	1-0	16	Lund [37], Lowe [74]	2814
18	23	H	Bristol R	D 1-1	0-1	16	Thomas-Asante [90]	1740
19	27	H	Oldham Ath	W 2-0	1-0	11	Lund [45], Thomas-Asante [77]	3242
20	Dec 11	A	Mansfield T	L 1-2	1-2	17	Lund [9]	4113
21	18	H	Stevenage	W 1-0	1-0	13	Turnbull [34]	1375
22	Jan 8	A	Newport Co	W 2-0	1-0	12	Azaz (og) [44], Thomas-Asante [52]	1687
23	11	H	Tranmere R	D 1-1	1-0	11	Oteh [29]	2273
24	15	A	Bradford C	L 1-2	1-0	13	Thomas-Asante [35]	14,671
25	18	A	Port Vale	W 1-0	0-0	10	Elliott [50]	4311
26	22	H	Colchester U	L 0-3	0-2	10		1759
27	25	A	Barrow	W 2-0	0-0	9	Hunter [60], Hutton (og) [90]	3510
28	29	A	Northampton T	L 0-1	0-1	10		5237
29	Feb 1	H	Carlisle U	W 2-1	0-0	10	Watson (pen) [52], Smith, M [71]	2059
30	8	A	Sutton U	D 0-0	0-0	10		2491
31	12	A	Leyton Orient	W 2-0	0-0	10	Shephard [50], Vassell [60]	4427
32	26	A	Swindon T	W 2-1	0-0	11	Shephard [65], Watson [86]	10,153
33	Mar 5	H	Forest Green R	D 1-1	1-0	11	Smith, M [7]	1987
34	12	A	Exeter C	D 0-0	0-0	11		5775
35	15	A	Rochdale	D 1-1	0-1	11	Lund [66]	2041
36	19	H	Scunthorpe U	W 5-1	2-0	11	Smith, M [17], Thomas-Asante 3 [45, 67, 81], Kelly [77]	1972
37	26	H	Walsall	W 2-1	1-1	11	Smith, M [44], Watson (pen) [66]	2584
38	29	H	Crawley T	W 2-1	1-0	11	Thomas-Asante [18], Turnbull [77]	1290
39	Apr 2	A	Hartlepool U	W 2-0	2-0	9	Ndaba [19], Lowe [28]	4949
40	5	H	Port Vale	L 0-1	0-0	10		2449
41	9	H	Harrogate T	W 2-0	0-0	8	Smith, M 2 [70, 75]	1670
42	15	A	Bristol R	L 0-1	0-0	11		9590
43	18	H	Barrow	D 2-2	1-0	9	Watson [23], Henderson [89]	2575
44	23	A	Oldham Ath	W 2-1	2-1	8	Smith, M [8], Thomas-Asante [45]	5752
45	May 2	H	Mansfield T	D 2-2	1-2	10	Turnbull [2], Lund [52]	3765
46	7	A	Stevenage	L 2-4	1-2	10	Shephard [14], Ndaba [67]	3558

Final League Position: 10

GOALSCORERS

League (60): Thomas-Asante 11, Lund 7, Smith, M 7, Elliott 4, Watson 4 (2 pens), Henderson 3, Shephard 3, Turnbull 3, Eastham 2, Lowe 2, McAleny 2, Ndaba 2, Willock 2, Hunter 1, Kelly 1, Morris 1, Oteh 1, Vassell 1, Wright 1, own goals 2.
FA Cup (1): Turnbull 1.
Carabao Cup (3): Morris 2 (1 pen), Turnbull 1.
Papa John's Trophy (5): Thomas-Asante 2, Oteh 1, Touray I 1, Turnbull 1.

King T 36	Shephard L 30 + 5	Lowe J 45	Turnbull J 36 + 1	Touray I 25 + 2	Lund M 33 + 7	Willock M 6 + 6	Thomas-Asante B 34 + 5	Morris J 21	McAleny C 14 + 10	Henderson I 7 + 8	Eastham A 28	Hunter A 23 + 10	Elliott T 11 + 8	Wright T 7 + 9	Ndaba C 29	Burgess L — + 1	N'Mai K 1 + 6	Bughail-Mellor D — + 3	Jeacock Z 1	Oteh A 3 + 7	Love D 19 + 6	Ripley C 7	Golden T — + 2	Dackers M — + 1	Vassell T 24 + 3	Watson R 23	Kelly S 18 + 3	Smith M 21	Loughlin L — + 3	Bolton L 2 + 13	Fielding F 2	Match No.
1	2	3	4	5	6	7	8	9	10	11																						1
1	2	6	4	5	7		9^{1}	8	10^{2}	11	3	12	13																			2
1	2	7	4	5	8^{1}		13	6	9^{2}	10	3		11	12																		3
1	2^{2}	6		5	7		12	10	9	11^{3}	3		13	8^{1}	4	14																4
1	2	6		5	7		12	10	9^{2}	11^{3}	3			8^{1}	4		13	14														5
	2^{2}	6	3	5	7^{3}	14	10^{1}	8	9	11		12	13		4				1													6
1	2	6		5	7	14	12	10	9^{1}	11^{3}	3	13		8^{2}	4																	7
1	2	6	12	5■	9^{2}	7	11^{3}	10			3	14	13	8^{1}	4																	8
1	2	6	4		7^{3}		9^{2}	8^{1}			3	10	11	12	5		14			13												9
1	2	6	4		7^{3}	14	9■	8^{2}			3	10^{1}	11	13	5						12											10
1	2	6	4		7^{2}	13		8^{3}	9^{1}		3	10	11		5		12				14											11
	2^{1}	6	4	5	7	12	8		9^{2}		3	10	11^{3}	13			14					1										12
	2	6		5	7	9^{1}	11		8^{2}		3	10	13	12	4							1										13
	2		4	5	7	9	8				3	10^{1}	11^{3}	12	6^{2}					14		1	13									14
	2	6	4	5	7	9^{1}	8	10			3		11				12					1										15
	2	6	4		7		11	10	9^{2}		3						8^{1}			12	5	1		13								16
	2	6	4	5	7^{3}		11	9^{2}			3	12		10^{1}						13	8	1			14							17
	2	6	4	5		9■	11	10^{2}			3	13■	12	8^{1}							7	1										18
1	2	7	4	5	9		8	10	12		3		11^{1}								6											19
1	12	7	5	6	8			9^{2}	10^{1}		4		11	14						13	2				3^{3}							20
1	13	6	4	5	7			8	9^{1}		3	10^{2}	11^{3}	12						14					2							21
1	8^{1}	6	4		7		11	9			3			13						10^{2}	5		12		2							22
1		8	4		7		10^{2}	6	12		3			9				13		11^{1}	5				2							23
1		7	4		6^{1}		11■	8^{3}			3	10^{2}	12							14	5				2	9	13					24
1		7	4						12		3	13	11^{3}		5^{1}			14		10^{2}	8				2	9	6					25
1	12	7	4		6^{3}				13		3	10	14								5				2^{2}	9	8^{1}	11				26
1	2	7	4		6^{1}				13		3	10			5						8^{2}				14	9	12	11^{3}				27
1	8	6	4		13				9^{1}		3	10^{3}			5										2^{2}	7	12	11	14			28
1	6	2	4		13		11^{1}		12		3	9^{3}			5											8	7^{2}	10	14			29
1	6	2	4				11^{3}		14		3^{1}	9^{2}			5										12	8	7	10		13		30
1	6	2	4		12		11^{1}		14			9^{2}			5										3	7	8^{3}	10		13		31
1	6^{1}	2	4		12		10		14			9^{3}			5										3	8	7	11^{2}		13		32
1	6^{3}	2	4		14		10		12^{2}			9^{1}			5										3	8	7	11		13		33
1	9^{1}	2	4		7		11					13			5										3	8	6	10^{2}		12		34
1		2		5^{2}	7^{3}	14	11					9^{1}			4						13				3	8	6	10		12		35
1		2		5	7^{3}		9					11^{1}			4						14				3	8	6	10^{2}	13	12		36
		2	4		7		9					11^{1}			5						12				3	8	6^{2}	10		13	1	37
		2	4				9					11^{1}			5						7				3	8	6	10		12	1	38
1		2	4^{1}	12	13		9^{3}			14		11^{2}			5						7				3	8	6	10				39
1		2	4	13	6		9			14		11^{1}			5^{2}						7				3	8^{3}		10		12		40
1	12	2^{1}		5			9^{3}			14		13			4						7				3	8	6	10		11^{2}		41
1	12	2		5	13		11			14					4						7^{3}				3	8	6^{2}	10		9^{1}		42
1	9^{1}	2	4	11	6		12			13					5^{3}						7^{2}				3	8		10		14		43
1		2	4	5	7^{1}		9^{3}			14		11^{2}									12				3	8	6	10		13		44
1		2	4	5	9^{2}		10			12		13									7^{1}				3	8	6	11				45
1	7^{2}	2		5			11^{3}			13					4		12				8^{1}				3	9	6	10		14		46

FA Cup

First Round	Dagenham & R	(a)	1-0
Second Round	Chesterfield	(h)	0-2

Carabao Cup

First Round	Derby Co	(a)	3-3

(Derby Co won 5-3 on penalties)

Papa John's Trophy

Group B (N)	Oldham Ath	(a)	0-1
Group B (N)	Tranmere R	(h)	0-2
Group B (N)	Leeds U U21	(h)	5-3

SCUNTHORPE UNITED

FOUNDATION

The year of foundation for Scunthorpe United has often been quoted as 1910, but the club can trace its history back to 1899 when Brumby Hall FC, who played on the Old Showground, consolidated their position by amalgamating with some other clubs and changing their name to Scunthorpe United. The year 1910 was when that club amalgamated with North Lindsey United as Scunthorpe and Lindsey United. The link is Mr W. T. Lockwood whose chairmanship covers both years.

The Sands Venue Stadium, Glandford Park, Jack Brownsword Way, Scunthorpe, North Lincolnshire DN15 8TD.

Telephone: (01724) 840 139.

Ticket Office: (01724) 747 670.

Website: www.scunthorpe-united.co.uk

Email: admin@scunthorpe-united.co.uk

Ground Capacity: 9,187.

Record Attendance: 23,935 v Portsmouth, FA Cup 4th rd, 30 January 1954 (at Old Showground); 9,077 v Manchester U, League Cup 3rd rd, 22 September 2010 (at Glanford Park).

Pitch Measurements: 102.5m × 66m (112yd × 72yd).

Chairman: Peter Swann.

President: Sir Ian Botham.

Chief Executive: Leanne Mayo.

Manager: Keith Hill.

First-Team Coach: Tony McMahon.

Colours: Claret and light blue shirts with white and light blue trim, light blue shorts with claret trim, light blue socks with claret trim.

Year Formed: 1899.

Turned Professional: 1912.

Previous Names: Amalgamated first with Brumby Hall then North Lindsey United to become Scunthorpe and Lindsey United, 1910; 1958, Scunthorpe United.

Club Nickname: 'The Iron'.

Grounds: 1899, Old Showground; 1988, Glanford Park (renamed The Sands Venue Stadium 2019).

First Football League Game: 19 August 1950, Division 3 (N), v Shrewsbury T (h) D 0–0 – Thompson; Barker, Brownsword; Allen, Taylor, McCormick; Mosby, Payne, Gorin, Rees, Boyes.

Record League Victory: 8–1 v Luton T (h), Division 3, 24 April 1965 – Sidebottom; Horstead, Hemstead; Smith, Neale, Lindsey; Bramley (1), Scott, Thomas (5), Mahy (1), Wilson (1). 8–1 v Torquay U (a), Division 3, 28 October 1995 – Samways; Housham, Wilson, Ford (1), Knill (1), Hope (Nicholson), Thornber, Bullimore (Walsh), McFarlane (4) (Young), Eyre (2), Paterson.

HONOURS

League Champions: FL 1 – 2006–07; Division 3N – 1957–58.
Runners-up: FL 2 – 2004–05, 2013–14.

FA Cup: 5th rd – 1958, 1970.

League Cup: 4th rd – 2010.

League Trophy: *Runners-up:* 2009.

FOOTBALL YEARBOOK FACT FILE

Scunthorpe & Lindsey United, as the club was then known, were members of the North Lindsey League in 1911–12 when they recorded their first-ever FA Cup upset, beating Midland League club York City in a preliminary-round tie. They went out of the competition to Mexborough in the first qualifying round, but enjoyed a successful season overall, winning five local trophies.

Record Cup Victory: 9–0 v Boston U, FA Cup 1st rd, 21 November 1953 – Malan; Hubbard, Brownsword; Sharpe, White, Bushby; Mosby (1), Haigh (3), Whitfield (2), Gregory (1), Mervyn Jones (2).

Record Defeat: 0–8 v Carlisle U, Division 3 (N), 25 December 1952.

Most League Points (2 for a win): 66, Division 3 (N), 1956–57, 1957–58.

Most League Points (3 for a win): 91, FL 1, 2006–07.

Most League Goals: 88, Division 3 (N), 1957–58.

Highest League Scorer in Season: Barrie Thomas, 31, Division 2, 1961–62.

Most League Goals in Total Aggregate: Steve Cammack, 110, 1979–81, 1981–86.

Most League Goals in One Match: 5, Barrie Thomas v Luton T, Division 3, 24 April 1965.

Most Capped Player: Grant McCann, 12 (39), Northern Ireland.

Most League Appearances: Jack Brownsword, 597, 1950–65.

Youngest League Player: Harvey Cribb, 16 years 36 days v Sutton U, 26 February 2022.

Record Transfer Fee Received: £2,400,000 from Celtic for Gary Hooper, July 2010.

Record Transfer Fee Paid: £700,000 to Hibernian for Rob Jones, July 2009.

Football League Record: 1950 Elected to Division 3 (N); 1958–64 Division 2; 1964–68 Division 3; 1968–72 Division 4; 1972–73 Division 3; 1973–83 Division 4; 1983–84 Division 3; 1984–92 Division 4; 1992–99 Division 3; 1999–2000 Division 2; 2000–04 Division 3; 2004–05 FL 2; 2005–07 FL 1; 2007–08 FL C; 2008–09 FL 1; 2009–11 FL C; 2011–13 FL 1; 2013–14 FL 2; 2014–19 FL 1; 2019–22 FL 2; 2022– National League.

MANAGERS

Harry Allcock 1915–53
(Secretary-Manager)
Tom Crilly 1936–37
Bernard Harper 1946–48
Leslie Jones 1950–51
Bill Corkhill 1952–56
Ron Suart 1956–58
Tony McShane 1959
Bill Lambton 1959
Frank Soo 1959–60
Dick Duckworth 1960–64
Fred Goodwin 1964–66
Ron Ashman 1967–73
Ron Bradley 1973–74
Dick Rooks 1974–76
Ron Ashman 1976–81
John Duncan 1981–83
Allan Clarke 1983–84
Frank Barlow 1984–87
Mick Buxton 1987–91
Bill Green 1991–93
Richard Money 1993–94
David Moore 1994–96
Mick Buxton 1996–97
Brian Laws 1997–2004; 2004–06
Nigel Adkins 2006–10
Ian Baraclough 2010–11
Alan Knill 2011–12
Brian Laws 2012–13
Russ Wilcox 2013–14
Mark Robins 2014–16
Nick Daws 2016
Graham Alexander 2016–18
Nick Daws 2018
Stuart McCall 2018–19
Paul Hurst 2019–20
Neil Cox 2020–21
Keith Hill November 2021–

LATEST SEQUENCES

Longest Sequence of League Wins: 7, 9.4.2016 – 6.8.2017.

Longest Sequence of League Defeats: 8, 29.11.1997 – 20.1.1998.

Longest Sequence of League Draws: 6, 2.1.1984 – 25.2.1984.

Longest Sequence of Unbeaten League Matches: 28, 23.11.2013 – 21.4.2014.

Longest Sequence Without a League Win: 16, 12.2.2022 – 7.5.2022.

Successive Scoring Runs: 24 from 13.1.2007.

Successive Non-scoring Runs: 7 from 19.4.1975.

TEN YEAR LEAGUE RECORD

		P	W	D	L	F	A	Pts	Pos
2012-13	FL 1	46	13	9	24	49	73	48	21
2013-14	FL 2	46	20	21	5	68	44	81	2
2014-15	FL 1	46	14	14	18	62	75	56	16
2015-16	FL 1	46	21	11	14	60	47	74	7
2016-17	FL 1	46	24	10	12	80	54	82	3
2017-18	FL 1	46	19	17	10	65	50	74	5
2018-19	FL 1	46	12	10	24	53	83	46	23
2019-20	FL 2	37	10	10	17	44	56	40	20§
2020-21	FL 2	46	13	9	24	41	64	48	22
2021-22	FL 2	46	4	14	28	29	90	26	24

§Decided on points-per-game (1.08)

DID YOU KNOW ?

When Dudley Roberts scored a hat-trick for Scunthorpe United against Newport County at the Old Showground in January 1975 he became the first player for almost nine years to achieve this feat in a Football League game for the Iron. The previous occasion was back in April 1966 when Barry Thomas hit three in a 4-1 win over Workington.

SCUNTHORPE UNITED – SKY BET LEAGUE TWO 2021–22 LEAGUE RECORD

Match No.	*Date*	*Venue*	*Opponents*	*Result*		*H/T Score*	*Lg Pos.*	*Goalscorers*	*Attendance*
1	Aug 7	H	Swindon T	L	1-3	0-0	24	Loft (pen) [48]	3602
2	14	A	Rochdale	D	0-0	0-0	19		2679
3	17	A	Walsall	D	1-1	0-0	19	Beestin [90]	4009
4	21	H	Sutton U	D	1-1	0-0	18	Scrimshaw [51]	2429
5	28	H	Tranmere R	W	1-0	1-0	14	Hippolyte (pen) [4]	2737
6	Sept 4	A	Northampton T	L	0-2	0-0	19		4870
7	11	H	Exeter C	L	0-4	0-1	22		2443
8	18	A	Carlisle U	D	2-2	2-0	22	Jarvis [3], Onariase [44]	4499
9	25	H	Port Vale	L	0-1	0-1	23		2513
10	Oct 2	A	Newport Co	L	0-3	0-1	24		3213
11	9	A	Harrogate T	L	1-6	0-5	24	Davis [79]	3180
12	16	H	Forest Green R	L	0-2	0-0	24		2140
13	19	A	Barrow	D	1-1	1-0	24	Taft [42]	2739
14	23	H	Crawley T	W	2-1	1-0	24	Francomb (og) [32], Scrimshaw [55]	2112
15	30	A	Colchester U	L	1-2	0-2	24	Davis [82]	2433
16	Nov 13	H	Salford C	D	1-1	1-0	24	Loft [37]	2614
17	20	A	Mansfield T	L	1-3	1-2	24	Hippolyte (pen) [15]	4904
18	23	H	Leyton Orient	D	1-1	0-1	24	Scrimshaw [64]	2067
19	27	H	Bradford C	D	1-1	1-0	24	Jarvis [39]	3823
20	Dec 7	A	Stevenage	D	1-1	1-1	24	Hippolyte [14]	1808
21	11	A	Hartlepool U	D	0-0	0-0	24		4809
22	26	A	Oldham Ath	W	3-1	0-1	22	Loft 2 [51, 77], Hippolyte [74]	4693
23	Jan 1	H	Carlisle U	L	0-1	0-1	23		3020
24	8	A	Tranmere R	L	0-4	0-2	23		6056
25	15	A	Exeter C	L	0-2	0-0	23		4676
26	22	H	Newport Co	L	0-1	0-0	23		2604
27	25	H	Bristol R	L	2-3	0-1	23	Burns 2 [89, 90]	2403
28	29	A	Port Vale	L	0-1	0-0	24		5467
29	Feb 5	H	Oldham Ath	L	0-1	0-0	24		5014
30	8	H	Walsall	W	1-0	1-0	24	Rowe [34]	2123
31	12	A	Swindon T	L	0-3	0-0	24		9012
32	19	H	Rochdale	L	1-2	1-0	24	Onariase [13]	2548
33	22	H	Northampton T	D	0-0	0-0	24		2355
34	26	A	Sutton U	L	1-4	0-3	24	Beautyman (og) [79]	2870
35	Mar 5	A	Crawley T	D	0-0	0-0	24		2144
36	12	H	Colchester U	L	1-3	1-0	24	Nuttall [11]	2427
37	15	H	Barrow	L	0-1	0-1	24		2009
38	19	A	Salford C	L	1-5	0-2	24	Nuttall [61]	1972
39	26	H	Harrogate T	L	0-3	0-1	24		2317
40	Apr 2	A	Forest Green R	L	0-1	0-0	24		2484
41	9	H	Mansfield T	L	0-4	0-3	24		4015
42	15	A	Leyton Orient	L	0-3	0-3	24		5342
43	18	H	Stevenage	D	1-1	0-0	24	Bunn [75]	2439
44	23	A	Bradford C	L	1-2	1-2	24	Bass (og) [33]	15,248
45	30	H	Hartlepool U	D	1-1	0-0	24	Wilson [49]	4210
46	May 7	A	Bristol R	L	0-7	0-2	24		9790

Final League Position: 24

GOALSCORERS

League (29): Hippolyte 4 (2 pens), Loft 4 (1 pen), Scrimshaw 3, Burns 2, Davis 2, Jarvis 2, Nuttall 2, Onariase 2, Beestin 1, Bunn 1, Rowe 1, Taft 1, Wilson 1, own goals 3.
FA Cup (0).
Carabao Cup (0).
Papa John's Trophy (3): Loft 2, Scrimshaw 1.

Bilson T 1	Pugh T 18 + 6	Taft G 33 + 1	Davis H 14	Thompson L 13 + 1	Bunn H 10 + 10	Beestin A 24 + 14	Kenyon A 6 + 1	Green D 11 + 5	Moore-Billam J 3 + 3	Loft R 12 + 3	O'Neill T 1 + 3	Shrimpton F 3 + 1	Hallam J — + 8	Watson R 40 + 1	Wilson C 4 + 4	Onariase M 29 + 1	Young E 5 + 1	Perry A 12 + 2	Hippolyte M 19 + 3	Foster O 2	O'Malley M 20 + 5	Rowe J 34 + 4	Jessop H — + 2	Scrimshaw J 13 + 4	Lobley O 1	Jarvis A 11 + 8	Gallimore D 7 + 4	Wood H 7 + 3	Hackney H 20 + 8	Millen R 19 + 1	O'Hara K 3	Lewis H 6 + 5	Burns S 11 + 4	Matheson L 11 + 2	Dunnwald K — + 1	Sinclair T 10 + 4	Grant A 12 + 1	Feeney L 17 + 2	Delaney R 18	Nuttall J 13 + 3	Pyke R 6 + 4	Cribb H 7 + 1	Match No.
1^{2}	2	3	4	5	6	7	8	9^{3}		10	11^{1}		12	13	14																												1
	2	5	3	6^{3}	10	12	9^{2}	7		11^{1}				1		4		8	13		14																						2
	7	4^{2}	2	13	11	8		10						1	12	3		6			9^{3}	5^{1}	14																				3
	5	4	2	9^{2}		6		10^{1}						1		3		7	8^{3}		13	14	12	11																			4
	7	4	2	9		6		10^{3}			13			1	14	3			8^{1}			5				11^{2}	12																5
		4^{3}	2	9	14	6		10						1		3■		12				5		13		11^{2}		7	8^{1}														6
		5	4	6	10	13					12			1				7				3^{1}		11				8^{2}	9	2													7
	12	4				9					13			1		3		7	6		5	14		10		11^{2}		8^{1}		2^{3}													8
		4				9		13					14	1		3		7	6^{2}		5			10		11^{3}		8^{1}	12	2													9
		4	2		13	8				12				1		3		6^{3}	14		9			10		11^{1}			7^{2}	5													10
		3	4	5■		8		6^{3}		10^{1}			13	1					9					11^{2}		12		7	14	2													11
	6	4	2^{1}			13		12		10				1		3			8		9^{2}	5		11		14			7^{3}														12
	7	4		9		12				11				1		3			8^{1}			2		10^{2}		14		13	6^{3}	5													13
	8	5		6	13	12				10^{3}				1		4			9^{1}			3		11		14			7^{2}	2													14
	8^{1}	5	3	6		12		13		10^{3}				1		4			9^{2}					11		14			7	2													15
	14	4					6			10				1		3		8	7^{1}		5	2		11^{3}		13			9^{2}	12													16
	14	3				12	6^{1}			10^{2}						4		8^{3}	7		5	2		11		13			9		1												17
	6	4		5		8	7^{3}			11^{2}						3		12			9^{1}	14		13		10				2	1												18
		4		5		9	6^{1}	14								3		8	7			13		11^{2}		10			12^{3}	2	1												19
	8	4				7^{3}		10^{1}		12				1		3			9		5	6		13		11^{2}			14	2													20
	8	4^{1}			13	7				10^{2}				1		3			9		5	6				11	12			2													21
	8	4			10		13	2^{2}		12				1		3			7		5	6				11^{1}			9														22
	7^{3}	4	3		10			2		11^{1}			14	1					8		5	6^{2}		13					9			12											23
	9^{1}	4	3		11	14		2						1					7^{3}		5	6				12	8^{2}		10				13										24
	7	4				12								1		3			9^{4}		5	6^{2}				10		14	8^{3}			15	11^{1}	2	13								25
	6^{2}	4	3		11^{1}								14	1		2		8	12		9	7^{3}						13					10	5									26
	14	4				9^{3}								1		3		8^{2}	7		5^{1}	6						11				12	10	2		13							27
	13	4				15		14						1		3						8^{2}						11^{3}		2^{1}		5	10^{4}	12		9	6	7					28
	12				13	9							14	1		3														2		5^{3}				8^{1}	6	7	4	10^{2}	11		29
	5■	14												1		3						8					13			2			9^{3}			11^{1}	7	6	4	12	10^{2}		30
					14	9^{1}								1		4						8								5			10^{2}	2		12	7	6	3	11^{3}	13		31
						14								1		3					5	6							8	2			10^{1}			13	7	9^{3}	4	12	11^{2}		32
				5^{1}	10^{2}									1		3					12	8							13	2			14			9^{3}	7	6	4	11			33
					9^{2}									1		3					5	8							14	2						11	7^{3}	6	4	10^{1}	13	12	34
		4				13								1								3							7				11^{2}	2			8	10	5	12	9^{1}	6	35
		4				9^{2}								1		12						3							10^{1}					2■		13	6	7	5	11		8	36
		3												1							9^{1}	2							13			12	10^{2}			5	7■	6	4	11^{3}	14	8	37
		3				7^{2}								1								2							13			9^{1}	12	5		6		11	4	10		8	38
		3				12								1								2					14		9^{3}			5	10^{2}			6		7	4	11	13	8^{1}	39
					13	11^{1}			14					1								2					4		7^{2}			5	12			9		6^{3}	3	10		8	40
						14			12			6^{1}		1			13					2					3		7			9^{2}	11				8^{3}	5	4	10			41
						11			13					1	14		5					3					7		9^{1}					12		2^{3}	6^{2}	8	4		10		42
					13	10^{3}			8				12	1	9^{2}		5					3					7					14		2				6	4	11^{1}			43
					13	9^{3}			6			14		1	11^{1}		5				12	3					7							2				8	4		10^{2}		44
					13	9						7	14		10^{3}		4			1	5						6							2				12	3	11^{2}		8^{1}	45
						10			9^{2}			7^{3}			8		4			1	12	6			5^{1}									2			14	13	3	11			46

FA Cup

First Round	Doncaster R	(h)	0-1

Carabao Cup

First Round	Barrow	(a)	0-1

Papa John's Trophy

Group E (N)	Manchester C U21	(h)	0-3
Group E (N)	Rotherham U	(a)	1-4
Group E (N)	Doncaster R	(h)	2-3

SHEFFIELD UNITED

FOUNDATION

In March 1889, Yorkshire County Cricket Club formed Sheffield United six days after an FA Cup semi-final between Preston North End and West Bromwich Albion had finally convinced Charles Stokes, a member of the cricket club, that the formation of a professional football club would prove successful at Bramall Lane. The United's first secretary, Mr J. B. Wostinholm, was also secretary of the cricket club.

Bramall Lane Ground, Cherry Street, Bramall Lane, Sheffield, South Yorkshire S2 4SU.

Telephone: (01142) 537 200.

Ticket Office: (01142) 537 200 (option 1).

Website: www.sufc.co.uk

Email: info@sufc.co.uk

Ground Capacity: 31,884.

Record Attendance: 68,287 v Leeds U, FA Cup 5th rd, 15 February 1936.

Pitch Measurements: 101m × 68m (110.5yd × 74.5yd).

Chairman: H.H. Prince Musa'ad bin Khalid Al Saud.

Chief Executive Officer: Stephen Bettis.

Manager: Paul Heckingbottom.

Assistant Manager: Stuart McCall.

Colours: Red and white striped shirts with black trim, black shorts with white trim, red socks with white trim.

Year Formed: 1889.

Turned Professional: 1889.

Club Nickname: 'The Blades'.

Ground: 1889, Bramall Lane.

First Football League Game: 3 September 1892, Division 2, v Lincoln C (h) W 4–2 – Lilley; Witham, Cain; Howell, Hendry, Needham (1); Wallace, Dobson, Hammond (3), Davies, Drummond.

Record League Victory: 10–0 v Burslem Port Vale (a), Division 2, 10 December 1892 – Howlett; Witham, Lilley; Howell, Hendry, Needham; Drummond (1), Wallace (1), Hammond (4), Davies (2), Watson (2). 10–0 v Burnley, Division 1 (h), 19 January 1929.

Record Cup Victory: 6–0 v Leyton Orient (h), FA Cup 1st rd, 6 November 2016 – Ramsdale; Basham (1), O'Connell, Wright, Freeman (1), Coutts (Whiteman), Duffy (Brooks), Fleck, Lafferty, Scougall (1) (Lavery), Chapman (3).

Record Defeat: 0–13 v Bolton W, FA Cup 2nd rd, 1 February 1890.

Most League Points (2 for a win): 60, Division 2, 1952–53.

HONOURS

League Champions: Division 1 – 1897–98; Division 2 – 1952–53; FL 1 – 2016–17; Division 4 – 1981–82.
Runners-up: Division 1 – 1896–97, 1899–1900; FL C – 2005–06, 2018–19; Division 2 – 1892–93, 1938–39, 1960–61, 1970–71, 1989–90; Division 3 – 1988–89.

FA Cup Winners: 1899, 1902, 1915, 1925.
Runners-up: 1901, 1936.

League Cup: semi-final – 2003, 2015.

FOOTBALL YEARBOOK FACT FILE

Sheffield United played a total of 12 fixtures against Blackpool during the 1965 close season. The clubs met in an exhibition match held in Vancouver on 9 May on the way to New Zealand, where they faced each other in a marathon series of 11 games for the BOAC Trophy. United won six and drew one of the matches to gain the trophy and a cash prize of £1,000.

Most League Points (3 for a win): 100, FL 1, 2016–17.

Most League Goals: 102, Division 1, 1925–26.

Highest League Scorer in Season: Jimmy Dunne, 41, Division 1, 1930–31.

Most League Goals in Total Aggregate: Harry Johnson, 201, 1919–30.

Most League Goals in One Match: 5, Harry Hammond v Bootle, Division 2, 26 November 1892; 5, Harry Johnson v West Ham U, Division 1, 26 December 1927.

Most Capped Player: Billy Gillespie, 25, Northern Ireland; Enda Stevens, 25, Republic of Ireland.

Most League Appearances: Joe Shaw, 632, 1948–66.

Youngest League Player: Louis Reed, 16 years 257 days v Rotherham U, 8 April 2014.

Record Transfer Fee Received: £24,000,000 (rising to £30,000,000) from Arsenal for Aaron Ramsdale, August 2021.

Record Transfer Fee Paid: £23,500,000 to Liverpool for Rhian Brewster, October 2020.

Football League Record: 1892 Elected to Division 2; 1893–1934 Division 1; 1934–39 Division 2; 1946–49 Division 1; 1949–53 Division 2; 1953–56 Division 1; 1956–61 Division 2; 1961–68 Division 1; 1968–71 Division 2; 1971–76 Division 1; 1976–79 Division 2; 1979–81 Division 3; 1981–82 Division 4; 1982–84 Division 3; 1984–88 Division 2; 1988–89 Division 3; 1989–90 Division 2; 1990–92 Division 1; 1992–94 Premier League; 1994–2004 Division 1; 2004–06 FL C; 2006–07 Premier League; 2007–11 FL C; 2011–17 FL 1; 2017–19 FL C; 2019–21 Premier League; 2021– FL C.

LATEST SEQUENCES

Longest Sequence of League Wins: 8, 28.3.2017 – 5.8.2017.

Longest Sequence of League Defeats: 8, 24.10.2020 – 17.12.2020.

Longest Sequence of League Draws: 6, 6.5.2001 – 8.9.2001.

Longest Sequence of Unbeaten League Matches: 22, 2.9.1899 – 13.1.1900.

Longest Sequence Without a League Win: 20, 16.7.2020 – 2.1.2021.

Successive Scoring Runs: 34 from 30.3.1956.

Successive Non-scoring Runs: 6 from 4.12.1993.

MANAGERS

J. B. Wostinholm 1889–99 *(Secretary-Manager)*
John Nicholson 1899–1932
Ted Davison 1932–52
Reg Freeman 1952–55
Joe Mercer 1955–58
Johnny Harris 1959–68 *(continued as General Manager to 1970)*
Arthur Rowley 1968–69
Johnny Harris *(General Manager resumed Team Manager duties)* 1969–73
Ken Furphy 1973–75
Jimmy Sirrel 1975–77
Harry Haslam 1978–81
Martin Peters 1981
Ian Porterfield 1981–86
Billy McEwan 1986–88
Dave Bassett 1988–95
Howard Kendall 1995–97
Nigel Spackman 1997–98
Steve Bruce 1998–99
Adrian Heath 1999
Neil Warnock 1999–2007
Bryan Robson 2007–08
Kevin Blackwell 2008–10
Gary Speed 2010
Micky Adams 2010–11
Danny Wilson 2011–13
David Weir 2013
Nigel Clough 2013–15
Nigel Adkins 2015–16
Chris Wilder 2016–21
Paul Heckingbottom 2021
Slavisa Jokanovic 2021
Paul Heckingbottom November 2021–

TEN YEAR LEAGUE RECORD

		P	*W*	*D*	*L*	*F*	*A*	*Pts*	*Pos*
2012-13	FL 1	46	19	18	9	56	42	75	5
2013-14	FL 1	46	18	13	15	48	46	67	7
2014-15	FL 1	46	19	14	13	66	53	71	5
2015-16	FL 1	46	18	12	16	64	59	66	11
2016-17	FL 1	46	30	10	6	92	47	100	1
2017-18	FL C	46	20	9	17	62	55	69	10
2018-19	FL C	46	26	11	9	78	41	89	2
2019-20	PR Lge	38	14	12	12	39	39	54	9
2020-21	PR Lge	38	7	2	29	20	63	23	20
2021-22	FL C	46	21	12	13	63	45	75	5

DID YOU KNOW ?

Sheffield United's home game with Oldham Athletic, scheduled for 9 February 1985, was postponed following the discovery of an unexploded wartime bomb weighing around 2,200lb nearby. The whole area was evacuated, and the bomb made safe by Army experts. The fixture was switched to the following Tuesday with the Blades winning 2-0.

SHEFFIELD UNITED – SKY BET CHAMPIONSHIP 2021–22 LEAGUE RECORD

Match No.	Date	Venue	Opponents	Result	H/T Score	Lg Pos.	Goalscorers	Attendance
1	Aug 7	H	Birmingham C	L 0-1	0-1	22		29,043
2	14	A	Swansea C	D 0-0	0-0	20		15,946
3	18	A	WBA	L 0-4	0-1	22		23,113
4	21	H	Huddersfield T	L 1-2	0-0	23	Sharp [90]	28,036
5	28	A	Luton T	D 0-0	0-0	23		9774
6	Sept 11	H	Peterborough U	W 6-2	1-1	18	Ndiaye 2 [14, 70], Fleck [51], Osborn 2 [53, 90], Gibbs-White [68]	27,359
7	14	H	Preston NE	D 2-2	1-1	16	Gibbs-White [7], Berge [84]	25,463
8	18	A	Hull C	W 3-1	1-0	15	Sharp [17], Egan 2 [50, 61]	14,451
9	25	H	Derby Co	W 1-0	0-0	11	Sharp (pen) [89]	27,905
10	28	A	Middlesbrough	L 0-2	0-2	12		19,390
11	Oct 2	A	Bournemouth	L 1-2	0-0	14	Gibbs-White [56]	9349
12	16	H	Stoke C	W 2-1	0-0	13	Mousset [80], McGoldrick [83]	28,576
13	19	H	Millwall	L 1-2	1-1	15	Sharp (pen) [45]	25,345
14	24	A	Barnsley	W 3-2	0-0	14	Mousset 2 [51, 53], Osborn [72]	15,720
15	30	H	Blackpool	L 0-1	0-0	17		28,304
16	Nov 2	A	Nottingham F	D 1-1	0-0	15	Gibbs-White [78]	25,238
17	6	A	Blackburn R	L 1-3	1-1	18	Brewster [2]	17,291
18	20	H	Coventry C	D 0-0	0-0	17		28,075
19	23	A	Reading	W 1-0	0-0	16	Bogle [57]	10,247
20	28	H	Bristol C	W 2-0	1-0	13	Brewster [40], Sharp [89]	25,615
21	Dec 4	A	Cardiff C	W 3-2	0-1	10	Gibbs-White [61], Sharp [73], McGoldrick [75]	18,310
22	20	A	Fulham	W 1-0	1-0	11	Ndiaye [3]	17,308
23	Jan 15	A	Derby Co	L 0-2	0-0	14		24,597
24	18	A	Preston NE	D 2-2	2-0	11	Bogle [17], Sharp (pen) [39]	12,954
25	22	H	Luton T	W 2-0	0-0	11	Brewster [48], Robinson [51]	27,780
26	29	A	Peterborough U	W 2-0	0-0	11	Sharp [54], Morton (og) [81]	10,152
27	Feb 4	A	Birmingham C	W 2-1	0-0	10	Sharp [64], Bogle [74]	17,194
28	9	H	WBA	W 2-0	1-0	10	Sharp 2 [22, 80]	26,541
29	12	A	Huddersfield T	D 0-0	0-0	8		17,523
30	15	H	Hull C	D 0-0	0-0	8		27,601
31	19	H	Swansea C	W 4-0	3-0	6	Gibbs-White 2 [14, 78], Baldock [17], Sharp [38]	26,564
32	23	H	Blackburn R	W 1-0	0-0	6	Davies, B [90]	26,495
33	26	A	Millwall	L 0-1	0-0	7		14,638
34	Mar 4	H	Nottingham F	D 1-1	0-0	6	Sharp [69]	28,841
35	8	H	Middlesbrough	W 4-1	2-0	5	Berge [23], Sharp [25], Robinson [59], Gibbs-White [79]	28,994
36	12	A	Coventry C	L 1-4	1-1	5	Berge [16]	21,732
37	16	A	Blackpool	D 0-0	0-0	9		11,915
38	19	H	Barnsley	W 2-0	0-0	5	Berge [54], Gibbs-White [76]	28,515
39	Apr 2	A	Stoke C	L 0-1	0-0	8		22,631
40	5	H	QPR	W 1-0	1-0	5	Norwood [9]	26,488
41	9	H	Bournemouth	D 0-0	0-0	6		26,769
42	15	H	Reading	L 1-2	0-1	6	Ndiaye [90]	29,125
43	18	A	Bristol C	D 1-1	0-0	6	Gibbs-White [61]	18,934
44	23	H	Cardiff C	W 1-0	0-0	6	Ndiaye [47]	26,802
45	29	A	QPR	W 3-1	0-1	6	Ndiaye [54], Robinson [73], Hourihane [90]	15,824
46	May 7	H	Fulham	W 4-0	3-0	5	Gibbs-White [10], Ndiaye [21], Berge [25], Stevens [49]	30,813

Final League Position: 5

GOALSCORERS

League (63): Sharp 14 (3 pens), Gibbs-White 11, Ndiaye 7, Berge 5, Bogle 3, Brewster 3, Mousset 3, Osborn 3, Robinson 3, Egan 2, McGoldrick 2, Baldock 1, Davies, B 1, Fleck 1, Hourihane 1, Norwood 1, Stevens 1, own goal 1.
FA Cup (0).
Carabao Cup (5): Brewster 1, Freeman 1, McBurnie 1, Sharp 1, Stevens 1.
Championship Play-offs (3): Berge 1, Fleck 1, Gibbs-White 1.

Ramsdale A 2	Baldock G 24 + 1	Egan J 46	Robinson J 26 + 1	Osborn B 21 + 13	Fleck J 31 + 4	Berge S 22 + 9	Norwood O 42 + 2	McGoldrick D 9 + 10	Burke O 2 + 1	Mousset L 4 + 3	Brewster R 10 + 4	Sharp B 30 + 9	McBurnie O 9 + 19	Basham C 24 + 4	Bogle J 16 + 2	Verrips M 1	Freeman L 1 + 3	Foderingham W 32	Davies B 21 + 1	Norrington-Davies R 20 + 2	Ndiaye I 23 + 7	Gibbs-White M 33 + 2	Hourihane C 15 + 14	Olsen R 11	Guedioura A — + 1	Stevens E 21 + 1	Goode C 1 + 1	Jebbison D 1 + 7	Gordon K 4 + 1	Seriki F 1	Osula W — + 5	Uremovic F 3	Match No.
1	2	3	4	5	6^{2}	7	8	9	10^{3}	11^{1}	12	13	14																				1
1	2	4	5	12		6	7	9	8^{1}		10^{3}	11^{2}	13	3	14																		2
	2	4	5	11	8	6^{3}	7	9^{2}	12			10^{1}	13	3		1	14																3
	5	3		13	8^{3}	6	7	14			10^{1}	12	11	2				1	4	9^{2}													4
	5^{1}	3			8	6	7				14	10	11^{3}	2^{2}	12		13	1	4	9													5
	2	3	4	8	7		6^{1}					11	14				13	1		5	9^{2}	10^{3}	12										6
	2	3	4		7	12	6^{3}				13	11					10^{1}			5	9^{2}	8	14	1									7
	2	3		10	7						8	11^{2}	13	14					4^{3}	5		9	6^{1}	1	12								8
	2	3		10	7		6^{1}					11	12						4	5^{2}	9^{3}	8	14	1		13							9
	2	3		10	7		6^{1}	12				11							4	13	9^{3}	8	14	1		5^{2}							10
	2^{1}	3		10	7		6			13		11^{3}	14	12					4		9^{2}	8		1		5							11
		3		10^{1}	7		6^{2}	14		12		11			2				4		9^{3}	8	13	1		5							12
		3		10	7		14	9^{3}				11		13	2^{2}				4		12	8■	6^{1}	1		5							13
	2	3		10	7		6	13		11^{1}		12	9^{3}	14					4		8^{2}			1		5							14
	2	3		9^{1}	8^{3}		7	12		11^{2}		13	14						4		10	6		1		5							15
		4		10^{2}	7^{3}		6			11^{1}	8	13		3	2						12	9	14	1		5							16
	14	4		10	7^{2}		6			12	8^{1}	11		3	2^{3}						13	9		1		5							17
		3		13	7			12				10		2	5			1	4		11^{1}	9	6			8^{2}							18
		3		14	7^{1}		6	10^{3}			11^{2}	13		2	5			1	4			9	12			8							19
		3		13		14	6^{2}	10			11^{1}	12		2	5			1	4			9	7^{3}			8							20
		3		13			6	10				11^{1}	12	2	5			1	4			9^{2}	7			8							21
		3	4	14	13	12	6					11		2	5			1			10^{3}	9^{1}	7^{2}			8							22
		3	4^{3}	14		6^{2}	7	9^{1}			12	10		2	5			1		8	11		13										23
		3	4			13	6	12			10^{1}	11		2	5			1		14	9^{3}		7			8^{2}							24
		3	4			12	6	13			11^{1}	10^{3}	14	2	5			1		8	9^{2}		7										25
		3	4		13		6	12			10^{1}	11^{3}	14	2	5			1		8	9^{2}		7										26
		3			8	6	7	13				11^{2}	12	2	5			1	4	9	10^{1}												27
	8	3	4			14	6	10^{2}				11^{3}	13	2	5			1			9^{1}	12	7										28
	8	3	4		7	6	12					11	10^{2}	2	5			1			13	9^{1}											29
	5	3	4			13	6					12	11	2				1		8	10^{1}	9	7^{2}										30
	5^{1}	3	4		10	9	6					11^{2}	13	2				1		8		7^{3}					12	14					31
	5	3	4		10	9	6					11^{1}	12					1	13	8		7^{2}					2■						32
	5	3	4		14	13	6					11	10					1		8	9^{1}	12	7^{3}						2^{2}				33
		3	4	13	7	9	6^{1}					11^{3}	14					1	2	8		10						12		5^{2}			34
		3	4	5^{3}	7^{1}	9	6					11^{2}	13					1	2	8		10	12						14				35
		3	4	5^{2}		6	7^{1}					10	12^{3}					1		9	13	11	8					14	2				36
		3	4	5		7	6					11						1		8	10^{1}	9^{2}	12						2		13		37
		3	4	5	14	6^{2}	7					11^{1}	13					1		9		10^{3}	8					12	2				38
	5	3	4	14	8	6	7^{1}											1	2	9	12	10^{2}						11^{3}			13		39
	5	3	12	14	8	6^{3}	7						11^{2}					1	4			10				9		13				2^{1}	40
	5	3		12	8^{1}	6^{2}	7						11					1	4			10	13			9						2	41
	5	3		10		12	6						11^{2}					1	4		14	9	7^{3}			8		13				2^{1}	42
	5^{2}	3	4	13	8^{3}	6	7							2				1			11^{1}	10	14			9					12		43
		3	4	5	7	9	6					12		2				1			11^{1}	10				8							44
		3	4	5	7^{2}	9	6							2				1			11^{1}	10	13			8					12		45
		3	4	5	7^{2}	9	6							2				1			11^{1}	10^{3}	13			8		14			12		46

FA Cup

Third Round	Wolverhampton W	(a)	0-3

Carabao Cup

First Round	Carlisle U	(h)	1-0
Second Round	Derby Co	(h)	2-1
Third Round	Southampton	(h)	2-2

(Southampton won 4-2 on penalties)

Championship Play-offs

Semi-Final 1st leg	Nottingham F	(h)	1-2
Semi-Final 2nd leg	Nottingham F	(a)	2-1

(aet; Nottingham F won 3-2 on penalties)

SHEFFIELD WEDNESDAY

FOUNDATION

Sheffield being one of the principal centres of early Association Football, this club was formed as long ago as 1867 by the Sheffield Wednesday Cricket Club (formed 1825) and their colours from the start were blue and white. The inaugural meeting was held at the Adelphi Hotel and the original committee included Charles Stokes who was subsequently a founder member of Sheffield United.

Hillsborough Stadium, Hillsborough, Sheffield, South Yorkshire S6 1SW.

Telephone: (0370) 020 1867.

Ticket Office: (0370) 020 1867 (option 1).

Website: www.swfc.co.uk

Email: footballenquiries@swfc.co.uk

Ground Capacity: 34,945.

Record Attendance: 72,841 v Manchester C, FA Cup 5th rd, 17 February 1934.

Pitch Measurements: 105m × 64m (115yd × 70yd).

Chairman: Dejphon Chansiri.

Manager: Darren Moore.

Assistant Manager: Jamie Smith.

Colours: Blue and white striped shirts with blue sleeves and white trim, black shorts with blue and white trim, black socks with blue trim.

Year Formed: 1867 (fifth oldest League club).

Turned Professional: 1887.

Previous Name: The Wednesday until 1929.

Club Nickname: 'The Owls'.

Grounds: 1867, Highfield; 1869, Myrtle Road; 1877, Sheaf House; 1887, Olive Grove; 1899, Owlerton (since 1912 known as Hillsborough). Some games were played at Endcliffe in the 1880s. Until 1895 Bramall Lane was used for some games.

First Football League Game: 3 September 1892, Division 1, v Notts Co (a) W 1–0 – Allan; Tom Brandon (1), Mumford; Hall, Betts, Harry Brandon; Spiksley, Brady, Davis, Bob Brown, Dunlop.

Record League Victory: 9–1 v Birmingham, Division 1, 13 December 1930 – Brown; Walker, Blenkinsop; Strange, Leach, Wilson; Hooper (3), Seed (2), Ball (2), Burgess (1), Rimmer (1).

Record Cup Victory: 12–0 v Halliwell, FA Cup 1st rd, 17 January 1891 – Smith; Thompson, Brayshaw; Harry Brandon (1), Betts, Cawley (2); Winterbottom, Mumford (2), Bob Brandon (1), Woolhouse (5), Ingram (1).

Record Defeat: 0–10 v Aston Villa, Division 1, 5 October 1912.

Most League Points (2 for a win): 62, Division 2, 1958–59.

HONOURS

League Champions: Division 1 – 1902–03, 1903–04, 1928–29, 1929–30; Division 2 – 1899–1900, 1925–26, 1951–52, 1955–56, 1958–59.
Runners-up: Division 1 – 1960–61; Division 2 – 1949–50, 1983–84; FL 1 – 2011–12.

FA Cup Winners: 1896, 1907, 1935.
Runners-up: 1890, 1966, 1993.

League Cup Winners: 1991.
Runners-up: 1993.

European Competitions
Fairs Cup: 1961–62 *(qf)*, 1963–64.
UEFA Cup: 1992–93.
Intertoto Cup: 1995.

FOOTBALL YEARBOOK FACT FILE

Sheffield Wednesday's home FA Cup replay against Wolverhampton Wanderers in February 1914 was held up for 20 minutes after a wall collapsed at Hillsborough. Over 70 fans were injured but the game eventually resumed with the visitors reduced to 10 men after their goalkeeper fainted on seeing the injuries and was unable to continue. Wednesday won the second-round game 1-0 and a subsequent appeal by Wolves for the game to be replayed was rejected by the FA.

Most League Points (3 for a win): 93, FL 1, 2011–12.

Most League Goals: 106, Division 2, 1958–59.

Highest League Scorer in Season: Derek Dooley, 46, Division 2, 1951–52.

Most League Goals in Total Aggregate: Andrew Wilson, 199, 1900–20.

Most League Goals in One Match: 6, Doug Hunt v Norwich C, Division 2, 19 November 1938.

Most Capped Player: Nigel Worthington, 50 (66), Northern Ireland.

Most League Appearances: Andrew Wilson, 501, 1900–20.

Youngest League Player: Peter Fox, 15 years 269 days v Orient, 31 March 1973.

Record Transfer Fee Received: £5,000,000 from Reading for Lucas Joao, August 2019.

Record Transfer Fee Paid: £10,000,000 to Middlesbrough for Jordan Rhodes, July 2017.

Football League Record: 1892 Elected to Division 1; 1899–1900 Division 2; 1900–20 Division 1; 1920–26 Division 2; 1926–37 Division 1; 1937–50 Division 2; 1950–51 Division 1; 1951–52 Division 2; 1952–55 Division 1; 1955–56 Division 2; 1956–58 Division 1; 1958–59 Division 2; 1959–70 Division 1; 1970–75 Division 2; 1975–80 Division 3; 1980–84 Division 2; 1984–90 Division 1; 1990–91 Division 2; 1991–92 Division 1; 1992–2000 Premier League; 2000–03 Division 1; 2003–04 Division 2; 2004–05 FL 1; 2005–10 FL C; 2010–12 FL 1; 2012–21 FL C; 2021– FL 1.

LATEST SEQUENCES

Longest Sequence of League Wins: 9, 23.4.1904 – 15.10.1904.

Longest Sequence of League Defeats: 8, 9.9.2000 – 17.10.2000.

Longest Sequence of League Draws: 7, 15.3.2008 – 14.4.2008.

Longest Sequence of Unbeaten League Matches: 19, 10.12.1960 – 8.4.1961.

Longest Sequence Without a League Win: 20, 11.1.1975 – 30.8.1975.

Successive Scoring Runs: 40 from 14.11.1959.

Successive Non-scoring Runs: 8 from 8.3.1975.

MANAGERS

Arthur Dickinson 1891–1920 *(Secretary-Manager)*
Robert Brown 1920–33
Billy Walker 1933–37
Jimmy McMullan 1937–42
Eric Taylor 1942–58 *(continued as General Manager to 1974)*
Harry Catterick 1958–61
Vic Buckingham 1961–64
Alan Brown 1964–68
Jack Marshall 1968–69
Danny Williams 1969–71
Derek Dooley 1971–73
Steve Burtenshaw 1974–75
Len Ashurst 1975–77
Jackie Charlton 1977–83
Howard Wilkinson 1983–88
Peter Eustace 1988–89
Ron Atkinson 1989–91
Trevor Francis 1991–95
David Pleat 1995–97
Ron Atkinson 1997–98
Danny Wilson 1998–2000
Peter Shreeves *(Acting)* 2000
Paul Jewell 2000–01
Peter Shreeves 2001
Terry Yorath 2001–02
Chris Turner 2002–04
Paul Sturrock 2004–06
Brian Laws 2006–09
Alan Irvine 2010–11
Gary Megson 2011–12
Dave Jones 2012–13
Stuart Gray 2013–15
Carlos Carvalhal 2015–18
Jos Luhukay 2018
Steve Bruce 2019
Garry Monk 2019–20
Tony Pulis 2020
Darren Moore March 2021–

TEN YEAR LEAGUE RECORD

		P	*W*	*D*	*L*	*F*	*A*	*Pts*	*Pos*
2012-13	FL C	46	16	10	20	53	61	58	18
2013-14	FL C	46	13	14	19	63	65	53	16
2014-15	FL C	46	14	18	14	43	49	60	13
2015-16	FL C	46	19	17	10	66	45	74	6
2016-17	FL C	46	24	9	13	60	45	81	4
2017-18	FL C	46	14	15	17	59	60	57	15
2018-19	FL C	46	16	16	14	60	62	64	12
2019-20	FL C	46	15	11	20	58	66	56	16
2020-21	FL C	46	12	11	23	40	61	41*	24
2021-22	FL 1	46	24	13	9	78	50	85	4

**6 pts deducted.*

DID YOU KNOW ?

Sheffield Wednesday defeated Chesterfield in the opening game played on the new Hillsborough ground on 2 September 1899. The Lord Mayor William Clegg kicked off and Chesterfield centre-forward Herbert Munday netted after 10 minutes with what was not only the first goal at Hillsborough but also his club's first Football League goal. Wednesday, watched by a crowd estimated at 14,000, hit back and finished up 5-1 winners.

SHEFFIELD WEDNESDAY – SKY BET LEAGUE ONE 2021–22 LEAGUE RECORD

Match No.	Date	Venue	Opponents	Result		H/T Score	Lg Pos.	Goalscorers	Attendance
1	Aug 7	A	Charlton Ath	D	0-0	0-0	17		17,639
2	14	H	Doncaster R	W	2-0	0-0	6	Bannan 72, Adeniran 75	24,738
3	17	H	Fleetwood T	W	1-0	1-0	4	Gregory 15	21,130
4	21	A	Rotherham U	W	2-0	0-0	1	Kamberi 50, Gregory 77	11,522
5	28	A	Morecambe	L	0-1	0-0	2		5481
6	Sept 11	A	Plymouth Arg	L	0-3	0-2	12		13,448
7	18	H	Shrewsbury T	D	1-1	1-1	12	Berahino 6	21,976
8	25	A	Ipswich T	D	1-1	1-0	11	Adeniran 26	21,338
9	28	A	Wigan Ath	W	2-1	1-0	9	Power (og) 23, Paterson 60	11,884
10	Oct 2	H	Oxford U	L	1-2	0-1	12	Paterson 73	22,060
11	9	H	Bolton W	W	1-0	0-0	9	Gregory 66	23,692
12	16	A	AFC Wimbledon	D	2-2	1-0	7	Gregory 2 (1 pen) 13, 61 (p)	8224
13	19	A	Cambridge U	D	1-1	0-1	9	Dele-Bashiru 80	7342
14	23	H	Lincoln C	D	1-1	0-0	9	Adeniran 55	23,521
15	30	A	Cheltenham T	D	2-2	0-1	8	Dunkley 65, Blair (og) 82	5582
16	Nov 2	H	Sunderland	W	3-0	2-0	8	Corbeanu 11, Kamberi 39, Gregory 53	23,731
17	13	H	Gillingham	D	1-1	0-1	8	Kamberi 75	20,593
18	20	A	Accrington S	W	3-2	3-1	7	Dunkley 13, Corbeanu 20, Kamberi 22	4627
19	23	H	Milton Keynes D	W	2-1	0-0	5	Gregory 83, Windass 90	18,581
20	27	H	Wycombe W	D	2-2	1-1	7	Shodipo 45, Windass 50	20,761
21	Dec 7	A	Portsmouth	D	0-0	0-0	8		16,472
22	11	A	Crewe Alex	W	2-0	1-0	7	Bannan 27, Gregory 47	6325
23	30	A	Sunderland	L	0-5	0-3	8		34,652
24	Jan 2	A	Shrewsbury T	L	0-1	0-1	8		8270
25	15	H	Plymouth Arg	W	4-2	2-0	8	Sow 19, Mendez-Laing 40, Hutchinson 79, Windass 84	20,872
26	22	A	Oxford U	L	2-3	1-1	8	Bannan 7, Windass 61	10,071
27	29	H	Ipswich T	W	1-0	1-0	8	Johnson 6	23,517
28	Feb 1	H	Morecambe	W	2-0	0-0	8	Byers 55, Mendez-Laing 90	19,261
29	5	A	Burton Alb	W	2-0	1-0	7	Byers 32, Sow 81	4763
30	8	H	Wigan Ath	W	1-0	0-0	7	Bannan (pen) 53	20,210
31	13	H	Rotherham U	L	0-2	0-0	8		26,418
32	19	A	Doncaster R	W	3-1	0-1	8	Paterson 70, Berahino 80, Bannan 83	11,217
33	26	H	Charlton Ath	W	2-0	2-0	6	Byers 5, Paterson 45	21,845
34	Mar 1	H	Burton Alb	W	5-2	2-1	5	Palmer 13, Bannan 2 28, 87, Paterson 67, Johnson 75	20,309
35	5	A	Lincoln C	L	1-3	1-1	6	Berahino 33	10,283
36	12	H	Cambridge U	W	6-0	4-0	7	Jones (og) 6, Bannan 10, Berahino 3 37, 41, 54, Byers 48	22,646
37	15	H	Accrington S	D	1-1	0-0	7	Paterson 66	20,688
38	19	A	Gillingham	D	0-0	0-0	7		7433
39	26	H	Cheltenham T	W	4-1	1-1	6	Luongo 7, Gregory 58, Hunt, J 83, Byers 87	21,925
40	Apr 2	H	AFC Wimbledon	W	2-1	1-1	5	Hunt, J 11, Gregory 90	22,374
41	9	A	Bolton W	D	1-1	0-0	5	Storey 65	19,164
42	16	A	Milton Keynes D	W	3-2	3-1	5	Berahino 10, Gregory 20, Bannan 30	14,252
43	19	H	Crewe Alex	W	1-0	0-0	4	Gregory (pen) 54	22,566
44	23	A	Wycombe W	L	0-1	0-0	7		9005
45	26	A	Fleetwood T	W	3-2	1-2	4	Gregory 3 3, 73, 74	3901
46	30	H	Portsmouth	W	4-1	3-1	4	Gregory 17, Berahino 36, Storey 40, Byers 86	33,394

Final League Position: 4

GOALSCORERS

League (78): Gregory 16 (2 pens), Bannan 9 (1 pen), Berahino 8, Byers 6, Paterson 6, Kamberi 4, Windass 4, Adeniran 3, Corbeanu 2, Dunkley 2, Hunt, J 2, Johnson 2, Mendez-Laing 2, Sow 2, Storey 2, Dele-Bashiru 1, Hutchinson 1, Luongo 1, Palmer 1, Shodipo 1, own goals 3.
FA Cup (0).
Carabao Cup (0).
Papa John's Trophy (9): Sow 2, Adedoyin 1 (1 pen), Berahino 1, Byers 1, Johnson 1, Kamberi 1, Palmer 1, Wing 1.
League One Play-offs (1): Gregory 1.

Peacock-Farrell B 43	Hunt J 36 + 3	Iorfa D 16 + 3	Hutchinson S 28	Palmer L 37 + 2	Adeniran D 12 + 6	Wing L 15 + 3	Bannan B 45	Green A 2	Paterson C 27 + 13	Brown J 7 + 4	Kamberi F 12 + 11	Johnson M 38 + 1	Gregory L 31 + 5	Byers G 21 + 1	Dunkley C 15 + 6	Luongo M 23 + 2	Corbeanu T 6 + 7	Sow S 5 + 8	Shodipo O 7 + 8	Berahino S 13 + 16	Dele-Bashiru F 16 + 8	Wildsmith J 3	Gibson L 3 + 2	Brennan C 5 + 6	Windass J 3 + 6	Mendez-Laing N 12 + 6	Storey J 19	Dean H 6 + 1	John-Jules T — + 1	*Match No.*
1	2	3	4	5	6	7	8	9^2	10^1	11	12	13																		1
1	2	3	4	5	6	7	8	9^3		13	10^1	11^2	12	14																2
1	2	3	4^1	5	9	8	6		13		14	11	10^3	7^2	12															3
1	2	3		5	13	7^2	6		10	9	11^1		12		4	8														4
1	2	3		4	7^3	14	9		8^2	10^1	13	5	11	6			12													5
1	2^1	3	4	5		7	9					10	11	6^3			13	8^2	12	14										6
1	2	3	7	5	6^2	13	9				14		11		4		12		10^3	8^1										7
1		3	4	2	6	7	9^1		12			5	11		14				10^2	8^3	13									8
1	12	3	7^1	2	6	8			11	9^2		5	10		4				13											9
1		3		2	6	7^3	8		9			5	11^1		4			13	10^2	12	14									10
	5	3	6^1	2	12		7		9	8^3			11		13				14	10		1	4^2							11
	5	2		4		6	7		10	8			11		3					12	9^1	1								12
1	5^3	2		4	12	7^2	6		10^1			8	11		3				14	13	9									13
1	5	3		2	6		7		12	8^3		4	11^1				13		14	10^2	9									14
1	3^1			4	6		9		11		12	8	10		2		13		5^2	14	7^3									15
1				2	6	7	9^1		5	13	10	4	11^3		3		8^2			14	12									16
				2	14	7^1	9		10		11	4			3		5	13	8^2	12	6^3	1								17
1	5			4			9		10	12	11^2		13		3	7	8^1				6			2						18
1	5			4			7				11^1		10	6^2	3	13	9			14	8^3			2	12					19
1	5^1						7		4		10		11		3	6	13		9^2		14			2	8^3	12				20
1	5			3		12	7		2		10^1	4	11^2			8			9	13	6									21
1	6			3		5	8		10			4	11^2				9^3		14	13	7^1			2	12					22
1	6			2	14	5	7		11			4	10^3		3^1		13				8^2			12		9				23
1			3	2	8^2	5	7		6^1			4^3	10				9			11	13			12		14				24
1	5		3	2	13		8^3		14			4	10^2			7		11^1			6				12	9				25
1	5		3	2			8		14	13		4	10			7		11^1			6^3				12	9^2				26
1	14		4	12			8				11	9^3				7					6				10^2	5^1	2	3	13	27
1			4	12			8		13		11^3	9		7				14		15	6^2				10^4	5	2	3^1		28
1	5		3	4			7^3		10		12	9		6^1		8		13						14		11^2	2			29
1	5		3	4			8^2		10		11^1	9		6		7								13		12	2			30
1	5^1		3	4			8		10		13	9		6		7		12								11^2	2			31
1	5			4			8		12		11^1	9		6		7		10^2		13			14	2^3			3			32
1	5^2		3	4			8^4		10		12	9^3		6		7		15		11^1			13	14			2			33
1	6	13	3	5			8		10			9				7^3		11^1		12			4^2	14			2			34
1	5		3	4			8		10^1		13	9	12	6^3		7				11^2	14						2			35
1	5	13	3^1				8				12	9	11^2	6		7		14		10^3			4				2			36
1	12	2	3	5^1			8^3		10			9	13	6		7				11^2	14						4			37
1	5^1		4				8		10^2			9	11	6^3	3	7				12						13	2	14		38
1	5	13	4				8		14			9	11^3	6		7		12								10^1	2^2	3		39
1	5	2^1	4				8		14			9	11	6^3		7			13	12						10^2		3		40
1	5		4				7		12			9	11	6^1		8				13						10^2	2	3		41
1	5			4			7^2		13			9	11^3	6	12					10	8					14	2	3^1		42
1	5			2			7		6		13	4	11^1	8	14	12				10^3						9^2	3			43
1			4				7		13			9	11		3	6			12	10^1	8^2					5	2			44
1	5		3	4			7		11			9^1	10^3	6^2	14	8									13	12	2			45
1	5		3	4			7^2		13			9	11^3	6		8				10^1	14				12		2			46

FA Cup

First Round	Plymouth Arg	(h)	0-0
Replay	Plymouth Arg	(a)	0-3

Carabao Cup

First Round	Huddersfield T	(h)	0-0

(Huddersfield T won 4-2 on penalties)

Papa John's Trophy

Group H (N)	Newcastle U U21	(h)	3-0
Group H (N)	Mansfield T	(a)	2-1
Group H (N)	Harrogate T	(h)	4-0
Second Round	Hartlepool U	(h)	0-3

League One Play-offs

Semi-Final 1st leg	Sunderland	(a)	0-1
Semi-Final 2nd leg	Sunderland	(h)	1-1

SHREWSBURY TOWN

FOUNDATION

Shrewsbury School having provided a number of the early England and Wales international players it is not surprising that there was a Town club as early as 1876 which won the Birmingham Senior Cup in 1879. However, the present Shrewsbury Town club was formed in 1886 and won the Welsh FA Cup as early as 1891.

Montgomery Waters Meadow, Oteley Road, Shrewsbury, Shropshire SY2 6ST.

Telephone: (01743) 289 177.

Ticket Office: (01743) 273 943.

Website: www.shrewsburytown.com

Email: info@shrewsburytown.co.uk

Ground Capacity: 9,875.

Record Attendance: 18,917 v Walsall, Division 3, 26 April 1961 (at Gay Meadow); 10,210 v Chelsea, League Cup 4th rd, 28 October 2014 (at New Meadow).

Pitch Measurements: 105m × 68m (115yd × 74.5yd).

Chairman: Roland Wycherley.

Chief Executive: Brian Caldwell.

Manager: Steve Cotterill.

Assistant Manager: Aaron Wilbraham.

Colours: Blue and yellow striped shirts with yellow sleeves, blue shorts, blue socks with white trim.

Year Formed: 1886.

Turned Professional: 1896.

Club Nicknames: 'Town', 'Blues', 'Salop'. The name 'Salop' is a colloquialism for the county of Shropshire. Since Shrewsbury is the only club in Shropshire, cries of 'Come on Salop' are frequently used!

Grounds: 1886, Old Racecourse Ground; 1889, Ambler's Field; 1893, Sutton Lane; 1895, Barracks Ground; 1910, Gay Meadow; 2007, New Meadow (renamed ProStar Stadium 2008; Greenhous Meadow 2010; Montgomery Waters Meadow 2017).

First Football League Game: 19 August 1950, Division 3 (N), v Scunthorpe U (a) D 0–0 – Egglestone; Fisher, Lewis; Wheatley, Depear, Robinson; Griffin, Hope, Jackson, Brown, Barker.

Record League Victory: 7–0 v Swindon T, Division 3 (S), 6 May 1955 – McBride; Bannister, Skeech; Wallace, Maloney, Candlin; Price, O'Donnell (1), Weigh (4), Russell, McCue (2); 7–0 v Gillingham, FL 2, 13 September 2008 – Daniels; Herd, Tierney, Davies (2), Jackson (1) (Langmead), Coughlan (1), Cansdell-Sherriff (1), Thornton, Hibbert (1) (Hindmarch), Holt (pen), McIntyre (Ashton).

Record Cup Victory: 11–2 v Marine, FA Cup 1st rd, 11 November 1995 – Edwards; Seabury (Dempsey (1)), Withe (1), Evans (1), Whiston (2), Scott (1), Woods, Stevens (1), Spink (3) (Anthrobus), Walton, Berkley, (1 og).

HONOURS

League Champions: Division 3 – 1978–79; Third Division – 1993–94.
Runners-up: FL 2 – 2011–12, 2014–15; Division 4 – 1974–75; Conference – (3rd) 2003–04 *(promoted via play-offs)*.

FA Cup: 6th rd – 1979, 1982.

League Cup: semi-final – 1961.

League Trophy: *Runners-up:* 1996, 2018.

Welsh Cup Winners: 1891, 1938, 1977, 1979, 1984, 1985.
Runners-up: 1931, 1948, 1980.

FOOTBALL YEARBOOK FACT FILE

Shrewsbury Town's crucial end-of-season match at Watford in April 1959 was sabotaged when the fuses to the Vicarage Road floodlights were stolen before the game. The lights were unusable, and the game was abandoned in semi-darkness 12 minutes from time with Town leading 5-2. The Football League ordered the game to be replayed two weeks later with Town winning 4-1 to leapfrog Exeter City and earn promotion to Division Three.

Record Defeat: 1–8 v Norwich C, Division 3 (S), 13 September 1952; 1–8 v Coventry C, Division 3, 22 October 1963.

Most League Points (2 for a win): 62, Division 4, 1974–75.

Most League Points (3 for a win): 89, FL 2, 2014–15.

Most League Goals: 101, Division 4, 1958–59.

Highest League Scorer in Season: Arthur Rowley, 38, Division 4, 1958–59.

Most League Goals in Total Aggregate: Arthur Rowley, 152, 1958–65 (thus completing his League record of 434 goals).

Most League Goals in One Match: 5, Alf Wood v Blackburn R, Division 3, 2 October 1971.

Most Capped Player: Aaron Pierre, 11 (16), Grenada.

Most League Appearances: Mickey Brown, 418, 1986–91; 1992–94; 1996–2001.

Youngest League Player: Graham French, 16 years 177 days v Reading, 30 September 1961.

Record Transfer Fee Received: £600,000 (rising to £1,500,000) from Manchester C for Joe Hart, May 2006.

Record Transfer Fee Paid: £200,000 to Tranmere R for Oliver Norburn, August 2018.

Football League Record: 1950 Elected to Division 3 (N); 1951–58 Division 3 (S); 1958–59 Division 4; 1959–74 Division 3; 1974–75 Division 4; 1975–79 Division 3; 1979–89 Division 2; 1989–94 Division 3; 1994–97 Division 2; 1997–2003 Division 3; 2003–04 Conference; 2004–12 FL 2; 2012–14 FL 1; 2014–15 FL 2; 2015– FL 1.

MANAGERS

W. Adams 1905–12
(Secretary-Manager)
A. Weston 1912–34
(Secretary-Manager)
Jack Roscamp 1934–35
Sam Ramsey 1935–36
Ted Bousted 1936–40
Leslie Knighton 1945–49
Harry Chapman 1949–50
Sammy Crooks 1950–54
Walter Rowley 1955–57
Harry Potts 1957–58
Johnny Spuhler 1958
Arthur Rowley 1958–68
Harry Gregg 1968–72
Maurice Evans 1972–73
Alan Durban 1974–78
Richie Barker 1978
Graham Turner 1978–84
Chic Bates 1984–87
Ian McNeill 1987–90
Asa Hartford 1990–91
John Bond 1991–93
Fred Davies 1994–97
(previously Caretaker-Manager 1993–94)
Jake King 1997–99
Kevin Ratcliffe 1999–2003
Jimmy Quinn 2003–04
Gary Peters 2004–08
Paul Simpson 2008–10
Graham Turner 2010–14
Mike Jackson 2014
Micky Mellon 2014–16
Paul Hurst 2016–18
John Askey 2018
Sam Ricketts 2018–20
Steve Cotterill November 2020–

LATEST SEQUENCES

Longest Sequence of League Wins: 7, 28.10.1995 – 16.12.1995.

Longest Sequence of League Defeats: 11, 9.4.2003 – 14.8.2004. (Spread over 2 periods in Football League. 2003–04 season in Conference.)

Longest Sequence of League Draws: 6, 30.10.1963 – 14.12.1963.

Longest Sequence of Unbeaten League Matches: 16, 30.10.1993 – 26.2.1994.

Longest Sequence Without a League Win: 18, 8.3.2003 – 14.8.2004.

Successive Scoring Runs: 28 from 7.9.1960.

Successive Non-scoring Runs: 6 from 1.1.1991.

TEN YEAR LEAGUE RECORD

		P	W	D	L	F	A	Pts	Pos
2012-13	FL 1	46	13	16	17	54	60	55	16
2013-14	FL 1	46	9	15	22	44	65	42	23
2014-15	FL 2	46	27	8	11	67	31	89	2
2015-16	FL 1	46	13	11	22	58	79	50	20
2016-17	FL 1	46	13	12	21	46	63	51	18
2017-18	FL 1	46	25	12	9	60	39	87	3
2018-19	FL 1	46	12	16	18	51	59	52	18
2019-20	FL 1	34	10	11	13	31	42	41	15§
2020-21	FL 1	46	13	15	18	50	57	54	17
2021-22	FL 1	46	12	14	20	47	51	50	18

§Decided on points-per-game (1.21)

DID YOU KNOW ?

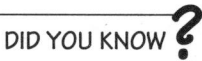

The biggest attendance that Shrewsbury Town have played in front of was when they faced Bristol Rovers in the League Two play-off final on 26 May 2007. A crowd of 61,589 saw Town lose 3-1 to Bristol Rovers at Wembley.

SHREWSBURY TOWN – SKY BET LEAGUE ONE 2021–22 LEAGUE RECORD

Match No.	*Date*	*Venue*	*Opponents*	*Result*	*H/T Score*	*Lg Pos.*	*Goalscorers*	*Atten-dance*
1	Aug 7	H	Burton Alb	L 0-1	0-1	22		5903
2	14	A	Morecambe	L 0-2	0-2	24		3772
3	17	A	Portsmouth	L 0-1	0-1	24		14,471
4	21	H	Plymouth Arg	L 0-3	0-1	24		5737
5	28	H	Gillingham	W 2-1	0-1	22	Bloxham [59], Cosgrove [68]	4625
6	Sept 4	A	Accrington S	L 0-1	0-1	22		2465
7	11	H	Crewe Alex	D 1-1	1-1	21	Cosgrove [19]	5867
8	18	A	Sheffield W	D 1-1	1-1	22	Bowman [37]	21,976
9	25	H	AFC Wimbledon	W 2-1	1-1	20	Leahy [41], Udoh [67]	5346
10	28	H	Wycombe W	L 1-2	0-0	21	Pennington [78]	4510
11	Oct 2	A	Bolton W	L 1-2	0-2	23	Leahy [89]	14,124
12	9	A	Ipswich T	L 1-2	1-1	23	Whalley [28]	19,256
13	16	H	Milton Keynes D	W 1-0	0-0	21	Whalley [56]	5711
14	19	A	Oxford U	L 0-2	0-0	21		5763
15	23	H	Cambridge U	W 4-1	1-0	20	Bowman 3 [6, 73, 83], Leahy [90]	5711
16	30	A	Lincoln C	D 1-1	0-1	21	Leahy [50]	8047
17	Nov 20	A	Cheltenham T	L 1-2	1-1	21	Udoh [4]	3914
18	23	H	Sunderland	D 1-1	0-1	21	Udoh [64]	6253
19	27	H	Charlton Ath	W 1-0	0-0	19	Udoh [90]	6158
20	Dec 8	A	Wigan Ath	L 1-2	1-1	19	Bowman [39]	8098
21	11	A	Doncaster R	L 0-1	0-0	20		5697
22	18	H	Cheltenham T	W 3-1	1-1	20	Udoh 2 [10, 48], Davis [78]	5741
23	26	A	Fleetwood T	W 3-0	0-0	18	Bowman [49], Vela [72], Udoh [80]	2878
24	29	H	Accrington S	D 0-0	0-0	16		5817
25	Jan 2	H	Sheffield W	W 1-0	1-0	14	Pennington [45]	8270
26	15	A	Crewe Alex	D 0-0	0-0	15		5587
27	22	H	Bolton W	L 0-1	0-0	18		8027
28	25	A	Gillingham	D 0-0	0-0	17		3213
29	29	A	AFC Wimbledon	D 1-1	0-1	16	Udoh [58]	7824
30	Feb 5	H	Fleetwood T	D 1-1	0-1	16	Leahy (pen) [48]	5808
31	8	A	Wycombe W	D 0-0	0-0	18		3871
32	12	A	Plymouth Arg	L 0-1	0-0	18		14,714
33	22	H	Portsmouth	L 1-2	1-1	18	Leahy [14]	5862
34	26	A	Burton Alb	W 2-0	1-0	17	Bloxham [35], Pennington [59]	3258
35	Mar 1	H	Rotherham U	D 0-0	0-0	17		5111
36	5	A	Cambridge U	D 0-0	0-0	17		5651
37	12	H	Oxford U	L 1-2	0-1	18	Bowman [60]	7302
38	15	H	Morecambe	W 5-0	1-0	17	Udoh 2 [44, 65], Leahy 2 (1 pen) [47 (p), 51], Bowman [70]	5804
39	19	A	Rotherham U	W 3-0	1-0	16	Udoh [36], Bennett [78], Bowman [90]	9253
40	26	H	Lincoln C	W 1-0	0-0	15	Udoh [84]	6791
41	Apr 2	A	Milton Keynes D	L 0-2	0-1	16		8984
42	9	H	Ipswich T	D 1-1	0-1	16	Whalley [84]	7682
43	15	A	Sunderland	L 2-3	0-2	17	Vela [50], Flanagan [58]	33,896
44	18	H	Doncaster R	D 3-3	3-0	16	Udoh [19], Bowman [34], Whalley [42]	6556
45	23	A	Charlton Ath	L 0-2	0-0	17		11,287
46	30	H	Wigan Ath	L 0-3	0-1	18		8369

Final League Position: 18

GOALSCORERS

League (47): Udoh 13, Bowman 10, Leahy 8 (2 pens), Whalley 4, Pennington 3, Bloxham 2, Cosgrove 2, Vela 2, Bennett 1, Davis 1, Flanagan 1.
FA Cup (8): Bowman 3, Bloxham 2, Bennett 1, Leahy 1, Udoh 1.
Carabao Cup (2): Udoh 2.
Papa John's Trophy (3): Bloxham 1, Lloyd 1, Pyke 1.

Marosi M 46	Pennington M 45	Ebanks-Landell E 33	Pierre A 15 + 10	Bennett E 42	Davis D 27	Vela J 36	Leahy L 42	Whalley S 14 + 7	Bowman R 35 + 7	Udoh D 42 + 4	Nurse G 41 + 4	Ogbeta N 19 + 7	Pyke R 4 + 12	Cosgrove S 8 + 9	Daniels J 9 + 12	Bloxham T 17 + 17	Leshabela T — + 3	Janneh S 1 + 11	Fornah T 17 + 2	Flanagan T 13 + 1	Match No.
1	2	3	4^1	5	6	7	8	9^2	10^3	11	12	13	14								1
1	2		3	5^3	6	9	8			10	4	7^1	11^2	12	13	14					2
1	3		4	7		8	9			10	5	13	12	11	2^2	6^1					3
1	3		4	2		7	8	12		11	5	9^1	13	10^2		6^3	14				4
1		4	3	2	8■	7	9		12	11	5^2	13	14	10^3		6^1					5
1	2	3	4	5		6	7	13	14	10^2	8^1	12		11		9^3					6
1	2	3	4^3	5	7	6	8	11	13	12	14			10^2		9^1					7
1	3	4	2	5	10	6	7	8^2	9	12	13			11^1							8
1	2	3	4	5^3	6	7^1	8	9	10	12	13			11^2	14						9
1	2	3	4	5	6		7	9^2	10	11^1	8	13				12					10
1	2	3	4	5	6		7	9^3	10^1	11^2	8	14		13		12					11
1	2	3	4^2	5	6		7	9	10^1	11^3	8	14		12		13					12
1	4	3		5	7		8	6	12	10^2	2^3	9	13	11^1		14					13
1	2	3	4	5	6			7	11^2	9^3		8	14	13	12	10^1					14
1	2	3	13	5^1	7		8	6^3	10	11	4	9^2	15		12^4	14					15
1	2	3		5	7		8	6	10^2	11^1	4	9	12			13					16
1	2	3	12	5■	7	6	8		11^3	10^2	4	9^1		14		13					17
1	2				6■	7	3		11	9	4	8	5	12		10^1					18
1	2			6		7	3		11	9	4	8	5^1	13		10^2	12				19
1	2			6		7	3		10^1	9	4	8	13	12	5	11^2					20
1	2			6		7	3			9	4	8	11^1		5	10	12				21
1	2		13	6	7	8	3		14	10^3	4	9^2	12		5^1	11■					22
1	2	3		5	7	6	8		10^2	11^1	4	9^3	13	12	14						23
1	2	3		5	7	6	8		10	11	4	9									24
1	2	3	13	5	7	6	8		10	11^1	4	9^2	12^3		14						25
1	2	3		5	7	6	8		10	11	4	9									26
1	2	3		5	7	6	8		10	11^1	4	9^2				13		12			27
1	2	3	12	5	7	6	8		10^2	11	4^3	9^1						13	14		28
1	2	3	13	5	7	8			10	11	4	9^2						12	6^1		29
1	2	3		5	7	8	9		10	11	4							12	6^1		30
1	2	3	4	5	7	6			12	13	9					10^2		11^1	8		31
1	2	3		5	7	6			10^2	11	4				9^3	14		13	8^1	12	32
1	2	3		5^3	7^1	6■	8		13	11	9					10^2		14	12	4	33
1	2	3	12	5^2			7		10	9^3	8				14	11^1		13	6	4	34
1	2	3		5			7		9	11^1	8					10		12	6	4	35
1	2	3		5			7		9	11	8					10			6	4	36
1	2	3		5^1		6^2	8	12	10	11^3	9					13		14	7	4	37
1	2	3		5^3		6^1	8	12	10	11^2	9				14	13			7	4	38
1	2	3	14	5^1		6	8		10	11^2	9^3				12	13			7	4	39
1	2	3	14	5^3		6	4	13	10	11^2	8				12	9^1			7		40
1	2	3^1		5		6	8		10	11^2	9				13			12	7	4	41
1	2			8		6	4	12	10	11^2	9				5^1	13			7	3	42
1	2		13	5^1		6	4	8^3	10	11^2	9				12	14			7	3	43
1	2					6	4	8	10	11	9				5				7	3	44
1	2					8	4	6	10	11^1	9				5	12			7	3	45
1	2		4			6	8	12	10^3	11^2	9^1				5	13		14	7	3	46

FA Cup

First Round	Stratford T	(a)	5-1
Second Round	Carlisle U	(a)	2-1
Third Round	Liverpool	(a)	1-4

Carabao Cup

First Round	Lincoln C	(h)	2-2
(Shrewsbury T won 4-2 on penalties)			
Second Round	Rochdale	(h)	0-2

Papa John's Trophy

Group C (N)	Crewe Alex	(h)	0-1
Group C (N)	Wolverhampton W U21	(h)	3-1
Group C (N)	Wigan Ath	(a)	0-2

SOUTHAMPTON

FOUNDATION

The club was formed by members of the St Mary's Church of England Young Men's Association at a meeting of the Y.M.A. in November 1885 and it was named as such. For the sake of brevity this was usually shortened to St Mary's Y.M.A. The rector Canon Albert Basil Orme Wilberforce was elected president. The name was changed to plain St Mary's during 1887–88 and did not become Southampton St Mary's until 1894, the inaugural season in the Southern League.

St Mary's Stadium, Britannia Road, Southampton, Hampshire SO14 5FP.

Telephone: (0845) 688 9448.

Ticket Office: (0845) 688 9288.

Website: www.southamptonfc.com

Email: sfc@southamptonfc.com

Ground Capacity: 32,384.

Record Attendance: 31,044 v Manchester U, Division 1, 8 October 1969 (at The Dell); 32,363 v Coventry C, FL C, 28 April 2012 (at St Mary's).

Pitch Measurements: 105m × 68m (115yd × 74.5yd).

Chairman: Gao Jisheng.

Managing Director: Toby Steele.

Manager: Ralph Hasenhüttl.

First-Team Assistant Coaches: Richard Kitzbichler, Dave Watson, Craig Fleming, Kelvin Davis.

Colours: Red and white striped shirts with black and red trim, black shorts with red and white trim, white socks with black and red trim.

Year Formed: 1885. ***Turned Professional:*** 1894.

Previous Names: 1885, St Mary's Young Men's Association; 1887–88, St Mary's; 1894–95, Southampton St Mary's; 1897, Southampton.

Club Nickname: 'Saints'.

Grounds: 1885, 'The Common' (from 1887 also used the County Cricket Ground and Antelope Cricket Ground); 1889, Antelope Cricket Ground; 1896, The County Cricket Ground; 1898, The Dell; 2001, St Mary's Stadium (renamed Provident St Mary's Stadium 2001; St Mary's Stadium 2006).

First Football League Game: 28 August 1920, Division 3, v Gillingham (a) D 1–1 – Allen; Parker, Titmuss; Shelley, Campbell, Turner; Barratt, Dominy (1), Rawlings, Moore, Foxall.

Record League Victory: 8–0 v Sunderland, Premier League, 18 October 2014 – Forster; Clyne, Fonte, Alderweireld, Bertrand; Davis S (Mané), Schneiderlin, Cork (1); Long (Wanyama (1)), Pelle (2) (Mayuka), Tadic (1) (plus 3 Sunderland own goals).

HONOURS

League Champions: Division 3 – 1959–60; Division 3S – 1921–22.
Runners-up: Division 1 – 1983–84; FL C – 2011–12; Division 2 – 1965–66, 1977–78; FL 1 – 2010–11; Division 3 – 1920–21.

FA Cup Winners: 1976.
Runners-up: 1900, 1902, 2003.

League Cup: *Runners-up:* 1979, 2017.

League Trophy Winners: 2010.

Full Members' Cup: *Runners-up:* 1992.

European Competitions
Fairs Cup: 1969–70.
UEFA Cup: 1971–72, 1981–82, 1982–83, 1984–85, 2003–04.
Europa League: 2015–16, 2016–17.
European Cup-Winners' Cup: 1976–77 *(qf)*.

FOOTBALL YEARBOOK FACT FILE

Southampton installed a form of modern floodlighting at The Dell in the early 1950s and an experimental game was played against Bournemouth on 31 October 1951. The match was not a great success, thick fog making it difficult for fans to see what was happening, despite the use of a white ball. The game was restricted to 35 minutes each way with neither side scoring.

Record Cup Victory: 8–0 v Newport Co, Carabao Cup 2nd rd, 25 August 2021 – Forster; Valery, Stephens, Bednarek, Walker-Peters (1), Elyounoussi (3), Diallo, Ward-Prowse (Walcott), Tella (1) (Obafemi), Redmond (1), Broja (2) (Long).

Record Defeat: 0–9 v Leicester C, Premier League, 25 October 2019; 0–9 v Manchester U, Premier League, 2 February 2021.

Most League Points (2 for a win): 61, Division 3 (S), 1921–22 and Division 3, 1959–60.

Most League Points (3 for a win): 92, FL 1, 2010–11.

Most League Goals: 112, Division 3 (S), 1957–58.

Highest League Scorer in Season: Derek Reeves, 39, Division 3, 1959–60.

Most League Goals in Total Aggregate: Mike Channon, 185, 1966–77, 1979–82.

Most League Goals in One Match: 5, Charlie Wayman v Leicester C, Division 2, 23 October 1948.

Most Capped Player: Maya Yoshida, 83 (117), Japan.

Most League Appearances: Terry Paine, 713, 1956–74.

Youngest League Player: Theo Walcott, 16 years 143 days v Wolverhampton W, 6 August 2005.

Record Transfer Fee Received: £75,000,000 from Liverpool for Virgil van Dijk, January 2018.

Record Transfer Fee Paid: £20,000,000 to Liverpool for Danny Ings, July 2019.

Football League Record: 1920 Original Member of Division 3; 1921–22 Division 3 (S); 1922–53 Division 2; 1953–58 Division 3 (S); 1958–60 Division 3; 1960–66 Division 2; 1966–74 Division 1; 1974–78 Division 2; 1978–92 Division 1; 1992–2005 Premier League; 2005–09 FL C; 2009–11 FL 1; 2011–12 FL C; 2012– Premier League.

LATEST SEQUENCES

Longest Sequence of League Wins: 10, 16.4.2011 – 20.8.2011.

Longest Sequence of League Defeats: 6, 16.1.2021 – 14.2.2021.

Longest Sequence of League Draws: 8, 29.8.2005 – 15.10.2005.

Longest Sequence of Unbeaten League Matches: 19, 5.9.1921 – 31.12.1921.

Longest Sequence Without a League Win: 20, 30.8.1969 – 27.12.1969.

Successive Scoring Runs: 28 from 10.2.2008.

Successive Non-scoring Runs: 5 from 22.9.2018.

MANAGERS

Cecil Knight 1894–95
(Secretary-Manager)
Charles Robson 1895–97
Ernest Arnfield 1897–1911
(Secretary-Manager)
(continued as Secretary)
George Swift 1911–12
Ernest Arnfield 1912–19
Jimmy McIntyre 1919–24
Arthur Chadwick 1925–31
George Kay 1931–36
George Gross 1936–37
Tom Parker 1937–43
J. R. Sarjantson stepped down from the board to act as Secretary-Manager 1943–47 with the next two listed being Team Managers during this period
Arthur Dominy 1943–46
Bill Dodgin Snr 1946–49
Sid Cann 1949–51
George Roughton 1952–55
Ted Bates 1955–73
Lawrie McMenemy 1973–85
Chris Nicholl 1985–91
Ian Branfoot 1991–94
Alan Ball 1994–95
Dave Merrington 1995–96
Graeme Souness 1996–97
Dave Jones 1997–2000
Glenn Hoddle 2000–01
Stuart Gray 2001
Gordon Strachan 2001–04
Paul Sturrock 2004
Steve Wigley 2004
Harry Redknapp 2004–05
George Burley 2005–08
Nigel Pearson 2008
Jan Poortvliet 2008–09
Mark Wotte 2009
Alan Pardew 2009–10
Nigel Adkins 2010–13
Mauricio Pochettino 2013–14
Ronald Koeman 2014–16
Claude Puel 2016–17
Mauricio Pellegrino 2017–18
Mark Hughes 2018
Ralph Hasenhüttl December 2018–

TEN YEAR LEAGUE RECORD

		P	W	D	L	F	A	Pts	Pos
2012-13	PR Lge	38	9	14	15	49	60	41	14
2013-14	PR Lge	38	15	11	12	54	46	56	8
2014-15	PR Lge	38	18	6	14	54	33	60	7
2015-16	PR Lge	38	18	9	11	59	41	63	6
2016-17	PR Lge	38	12	10	16	41	48	46	8
2017-18	PR Lge	38	7	15	16	37	56	36	17
2018-19	PR Lge	38	9	12	17	45	65	39	16
2019-20	PR Lge	38	15	7	16	51	60	52	11
2020-21	PR Lge	38	12	7	19	47	68	43	15
2021-22	PR Lge	38	9	13	16	43	67	40	15

DID YOU KNOW ?

The Football League Cup tie between Southampton and Leeds United played at The Dell on 5 December 1960 was a remarkable affair. Saints won 5-4 with a last-minute goal from Derek Reeves, his fifth of the game. The match was twice delayed when the floodlights failed and finished an hour late, while both teams finished with 10 men due to injuries.

SOUTHAMPTON – PREMIER LEAGUE 2021–22 LEAGUE RECORD

Match No.	*Date*	*Venue*	*Opponents*	*Result*	*H/T Score*	*Lg Pos.*	*Goalscorers*	*Attendance*
1	Aug 14	A	Everton	L 1-3	1-0	16	Armstrong, A [22]	38,487
2	22	H	Manchester U	D 1-1	1-0	13	Fred (og) [30]	29,485
3	28	A	Newcastle U	D 2-2	0-0	13	Elyounoussi [74], Ward-Prowse (pen) [90]	44,017
4	Sept 11	H	West Ham U	D 0-0	0-0	14		27,861
5	18	A	Manchester C	D 0-0	0-0	15		52,698
6	26	H	Wolverhampton W	L 0-1	0-0	16		28,002
7	Oct 2	A	Chelsea	L 1-3	0-1	17	Ward-Prowse (pen) [61]	40,109
8	16	H	Leeds U	W 1-0	0-0	15	Broja [53]	30,506
9	23	H	Burnley	D 2-2	1-1	16	Livramento [41], Broja [50]	29,145
10	30	A	Watford	W 1-0	1-0	14	Adams [20]	20,869
11	Nov 5	H	Aston Villa	W 1-0	1-0	12	Armstrong, A [3]	30,178
12	20	A	Norwich C	L 1-2	1-1	13	Adams [4]	26,885
13	27	A	Liverpool	L 0-4	0-3	14		53,040
14	Dec 1	H	Leicester C	D 2-2	2-1	15	Bednarek [3], Adams [34]	26,951
15	4	H	Brighton & HA	D 1-1	1-0	14	Broja [29]	28,706
16	11	A	Arsenal	L 0-3	0-2	16		59,653
17	15	A	Crystal Palace	D 2-2	2-1	15	Ward-Prowse [32], Broja [36]	22,861
18	26	A	West Ham U	W 3-2	1-0	14	Elyounoussi [8], Ward-Prowse (pen) [61], Bednarek [70]	41,027
19	28	H	Tottenham H	D 1-1	1-1	13	Ward-Prowse [25]	31,304
20	Jan 11	H	Brentford	W 4-1	2-1	11	Bednarek [5], Fernandez (og) [37], Broja [49], Adams [70]	27,383
21	15	A	Wolverhampton W	L 1-3	0-1	12	Ward-Prowse [84]	30,057
22	22	H	Manchester C	D 1-1	1-0	12	Walker-Peters [7]	31,178
23	Feb 9	A	Tottenham H	W 3-2	1-1	10	Broja [23], Elyounoussi [80], Adams [82]	54,012
24	12	A	Manchester U	D 1-1	0-1	10	Adams [48]	73,084
25	19	H	Everton	W 2-0	0-0	10	Armstrong, S [52], Long [84]	31,312
26	25	H	Norwich C	W 2-0	1-0	9	Adams [36], Romeu [88]	31,182
27	Mar 5	A	Aston Villa	L 0-4	0-2	9		41,855
28	10	H	Newcastle U	L 1-2	1-1	10	Armstrong, S [25]	31,016
29	13	H	Watford	L 1-2	1-2	10	Elyounoussi [45]	28,863
30	Apr 2	A	Leeds U	D 1-1	0-1	11	Ward-Prowse [49]	36,580
31	9	H	Chelsea	L 0-6	0-4	13		31,359
32	16	H	Arsenal	W 1-0	1-0	12	Bednarek [44]	31,465
33	21	A	Burnley	L 0-2	0-2	13		17,384
34	24	A	Brighton & HA	D 2-2	1-2	13	Ward-Prowse 2 [45, 54]	31,335
35	30	H	Crystal Palace	L 1-2	1-0	15	Romeu [9]	31,359
36	May 7	A	Brentford	L 0-3	0-2	15		17,051
37	17	H	Liverpool	L 1-2	1-1	15	Redmond [13]	31,588
38	22	A	Leicester C	L 1-4	0-0	15	Ward-Prowse (pen) [79]	32,003

Final League Position: 15

GOALSCORERS

League (43): Ward-Prowse 10 (4 pens), Adams 7, Broja 6, Bednarek 4, Elyounoussi 4, Armstrong, A 2, Armstrong, S 2, Romeu 2, Livramento 1, Long 1, Redmond 1, Walker-Peters 1, own goals 2.
FA Cup (9): Armstrong S 1, Broja 1, Elyounoussi 1, Long 1, Perraud 1, Redmond 1, Walker-Peters 1, Ward-Prowse 1 (1 pen), own goal 1.
Carabao Cup (11): Elyounoussi 3, Broja 2, Adams 1, Diallo 1, Redmond 1, Salisu 1, Tella 1, Walker-Peters 1.
Papa John's Trophy (5): Olaigbe 2, Lancashire 1, Mitchell 1, Small 1.

McCarthy A 17	Livramento V 25 + 3	Stephens J 9 + 2	Salisu M 33 + 1	Perraud R 18 + 2	Walcott T 5 + 4	Ward-Prowse J 36	Romeu O 34 + 2	Djenepo M 5 + 7	Adams C 23 + 7	Armstrong A 17 + 6	Diallo I 10 + 13	Tella N 10 + 4	Redmond N 20 + 7	Bednarek J 30 + 1	Walker-Peters K 29 + 3	Elyounoussi M 23 + 7	Broja A 21 + 11	Long S 3 + 10	Armstrong S 15 + 10	Lyanco V 9 + 6	Caballero W 2	Smallbone W 2 + 2	Forster F 19	Valery Y 3 + 2	*Match No.*
1	2	3	4	5^3	6^2	7	8^1	9	10	11	12	13	14												1
1	2	3	4	5^3	6^1	8	7	9^2	10	11	13			12	14										2
1	2	3	4			7	8^3	9^1	10^2	11	14		12		5	6	13								3
1	2	3	4	5		7	8^1	9		11^2	12		10			6	13								4
1	2^3	3^1	12	14		8	6		9^2	11			10	4	5	7	13								5
1	2		4			8	7	13	10^1	11			9^2	3	5^3	6	12	14							6
1	2		4		6^1	7■	8	13		10	12	9^2	11^3	3	5	14									7
1	2		4	5	13		8	9^1			7	14	11	3		6^3	10^2		12						8
1	2		4	5	6^1		7		13	14	8		11^3	3		9	10^2		12						9
1	2		4			7^2	8^3		11	10	13		9	3	5	6^1			12	14					10
1	2		4			7	8		11	10^3	13			3	5	9^2	14		6^1	12					11
1	2		4		13	7	8^3		11^2	10	6			3	5	9^1	12			14					12
1	5		4	8^3		6	7		10^1	11		12	13	2^2	14		9			3					13
1	2		4			7	8		10	11^2		9^1	6	3^3	5	13	12			14					14
1	2		4			7	8		10	12		9^2	6		5	13	11^1			3					15
	2	3				7				11^1	8	9	6	4	5	12	10^2			13	1				16
	2		4		14	7	8	13				10^3	9		5		11^1	12		3	1	6^2			17
	2		4		10^2	8	6^3		12		14		7	3	5	9	11^1		13				1		18
			5■	6		9				11^2	8		13	4	2		12	10^1	7				1	3	19
			4	9		6	7		12	14	8	5^2	10^1	2			11^3		13	3			1		20
			4	9		6	7		12	14	8^1	5^2	10	2			11^3		13	3			1		21
			4	5		7	8		11		14		6^1	3^2	2	12	10		9^3	13			1		22
			4	5	13	7	8		11^1		14			3	2	9^2	10^3	12	6				1		23
	13	12	4	5		7	8^3		11		14			3^1	2	9^2	10		6				1		24
	2		4			7	8	14	10^2	13				3	5	9	11^1	12	6^3				1		25
	2	12	4			7	8	14	10^2					3	5	9	11^1	13	6^3				1		26
	2	4		5^2		7	8^3		10		14			3	13	9^1	11		6				1	12	27
	2		4			7	8^2	14	11	12				3	5	9^3	10^1	13	6				1		28
			4	5		8	7^2		11				13	3	2	9	12^3	14	6			10^1	1		29
	2		4			6	7^1		11^2		8	13		3	5	9	10^3	14	12				1		30
	2^3		4			7	8^1		10	11^2	13			3	5	9			6			14	1	12	31
	14			8		6	7						13	4	5	11^3	10^1	12	9^2	3			1	2	32
	14			9		7	5		13				12	3	6^3	10^1	11		8^2	2			1	4	33
	2^1		4	12		7	8		10			9^2	6	3	5		14	11^3	13				1		34
			4	5		8	7		11^2			9^3	6	3	2	14	13	10^1	12				1		35
			4	5		7	13			10	8^1		9	3	2	12	11		6^2				1		36
1		4	5			8	13		14		9^1	10^2	6		2	7	11^3		12	3					37
1		3	5			6	7^4	13	12	11^1			10^3		2	8^2		14	9	4		15			38

FA Cup

Third Round	Swansea C	(a)	3-2
(aet)			
Fourth Round	Coventry C	(h)	2-1
(aet)			
Fifth Round	West Ham U	(h)	3-1
Sixth Round	Manchester C	(h)	1-4

Carabao Cup

Second Round	Newport Co	(a)	8-0
Third Round	Sheffield U	(a)	2-2
(Southampton won 4-2 on penalties)			
Fourth Round	Chelsea	(a)	1-1
(Chelsea won 4-3 on penalties)			

Papa John's Trophy (Southampton U21)

Group G (S)	Leyton Orient	(a)	0-1
Group G (S)	Charlton Ath	(a)	1-4
Group G (S)	Crawley T	(a)	4-0

STEVENAGE

FOUNDATION

There have been several clubs associated with the town of Stevenage. Stevenage Town was formed in 1884. They absorbed Stevenage Rangers in 1955 and later played at Broadhall Way. The club went into liquidation in 1968 and Stevenage Athletic was formed, but they, too, followed a similar path in 1976. Then Stevenage Borough was founded. The Broadhall Way pitch was dug up and remained unused for three years. Thus the new club started its life in the modest surrounds of the King George V playing fields with a roped-off ground in the Chiltern League. A change of competition followed to the Wallspan Southern Combination and by 1980 the club returned to the council-owned Broadhall Way when 'Borough' was added to the name. Entry into the United Counties League was so successful the league and cup were won in the first season. On to the Isthmian League Division Two and the climb up the pyramid continued. In 1995–96 Stevenage Borough won the Conference but was denied a place in the Football League as the ground did not measure up to the competition's standards. Subsequent improvements changed this and the 7,100 capacity venue became one of the best appointed grounds in non-league football. After winning elevation to the Football League the club dropped Borough from its title.

Lamex Stadium, Broadhall Way, Stevenage, Hertfordshire SG2 8RH.

Telephone: (01438) 223 223.

Ticket Office: (01438) 223 223.

Website: stevenagefc.com

Email: info@stevenagefc.com

Ground Capacity: 7,800.

Record Attendance: 8,040 v Newcastle U, FA Cup 4th rd, 25 January 1998.

Pitch Measurements: 104.2m × 64m (114yd × 70yd).

Chairman: Phil Wallace.

Chief Executive Officer: Alex Tunbridge.

Manager: Steve Evans.

Assistant Manager: Paul Raynor.

Colours: Red and white shirts, red shorts with white trim, red socks with white trim.

Year Formed: 1976.

Turned Professional: 1976.

Nickname: 'The Boro'.

Previous Name: 1976, Stevenage Borough; 2010, Stevenage.

HONOURS

League Champions: Conference – 1995–96, 2009–10.

FA Cup: 5th rd – 2012.

League Cup: 2nd rd – 2013, 2014, 2017, 2022.

FOOTBALL YEARBOOK FACT FILE

Despite enjoying a fine FA Cup run in 2010–11, their first season of League football, Stevenage struggled in their League Two fixtures and were in 17th position following their defeat at Gillingham on New Year's Day. Form improved in the second half of the campaign, with a run of six consecutive victories pushing them into the play-off positions, where they despatched both Accrington Stanley and Torquay United to gain promotion to League One at the first attempt.

Grounds: 1976, King George V playing fields; 1980, Broadhall Way (renamed Lamex Stadium 2009).

First Football League Game: 7 August 2010, FL 2, v Macclesfield T (h) D 2–2 – Day; Henry, Laird, Bostwick, Roberts, Foster, Wilson (Sinclair), Byrom, Griffin (1), Winn (Odubade), Vincenti (1) (Beardsley).

Record League Victory: 6–0 v Yeovil T, FL 2, 14 April 2012 – Day; Lascelles (1), Laird, Roberts (1), Ashton (1), Shroot (Mousinho), Wilson (Myrie-Williams), Long, Agyemang (1), Reid (Slew), Freeman (2).

Record Victory: 11–1 v British Timken Ath 1980–81.

Record Defeat: 0–8 v Charlton Ath, FL Trophy, 9 October 2018.

Most League Points (3 for a win): 73, FL 1, 2011–12.

Most League Goals: 69, FL 1, 2011–12.

Highest League Scorer in Season: Matthew Godden, 20, FL 2, 2016–17.

Most League Goals in Total Aggregate: Matthew Godden, 30, 2016–18.

Most League Goals in One Match: 3, Chris Holroyd v Hereford U, FL 2, 28 September 2010; 3, Dani Lopez v Sheffield U, FL 1, 16 March 2013; 3, Chris Whelpdale v Morecambe, FL 2, 28 November 2015; 3, Matthew Godden v Newport Co, FL 2, 7 January 2017; 3, Alex Revell v Exeter C, FL 2, 28 April 2018.

Most Capped Player: Terence Vancooten, 16, Guyana.

Most League Appearances: Ronnie Henry, 230, 2014–19.

Youngest League Player: Sam Tinubu, 17 years 18 days v Oldham Ath, 16 October 2021.

Record Transfer Fee Received: £1,500,000 from Watford for Ben Wilmot, May 2018.

Record Transfer Fee Paid: £125,000 to Exeter C for James Dunne, May 2012.

Football League Record: 2010 Promoted from Conference Premier; 2010–11 FL 2; 2011–14 FL 1; 2014– FL 2.

MANAGERS

Derek Montgomery 1976–83
Frank Cornwell 1983–87
John Bailey 1987–88
Brian Wilcox 1988–90
Paul Fairclough 1990–98
Richard Hill 1998–2000
Steve Wignall 2000
Paul Fairclough 2000–02
Wayne Turner 2002–03
Graham Westley 2003–06
Mark Stimson 2006–07
Peter Taylor 2007–08
Graham Westley 2008–12
Gary Smith 2012–13
Graham Westley 2013–15
Teddy Sheringham 2015–16
Darren Sarll 2016–18
Dino Maamria 2018–19
Graham Westley 2019–20
Alex Revell 2020–21
Paul Tisdale 2021–22
Steve Evans March 2022–

LATEST SEQUENCES

Longest Sequence of League Wins: 6, 12.3.2011 – 2.4.2011.

Longest Sequence of League Defeats: 8, 25.1.2020 – 7.3.2020.

Longest Sequence of League Draws: 5, 17.3.2012 – 31.3.2012.

Longest Sequence of Unbeaten League Matches: 17, 9.4.2012 – 5.10.2012.

Longest Sequence Without a League Win: 12, 3.8.2019 – 5.10.2019.

Successive Scoring Runs: 17 from 9.4.2012.

Successive Non-scoring Runs: 7 from 3.10.2020.

TEN YEAR LEAGUE RECORD

		P	*W*	*D*	*L*	*F*	*A*	*Pts*	*Pos*
2012-13	FL 1	46	15	9	22	47	64	54	18
2013-14	FL 1	46	11	9	26	46	72	42	24
2014-15	FL 2	46	20	12	14	62	54	72	6
2015-16	FL 2	46	11	15	20	52	67	48	18
2016-17	FL 2	46	20	7	19	67	63	67	10
2017-18	FL 2	46	14	13	19	60	65	55	16
2018-19	FL 2	46	20	10	16	59	55	70	10
2019-20	FL 2	36	3	13	20	24	50	22	23§
2020-21	FL 2	46	14	18	14	41	41	60	14
2021-22	FL 2	46	11	14	21	45	68	47	21

§*Decided on points-per-game (0.61)*

DID YOU KNOW ?

Stevenage Borough attracted an average attendance of 2,855 to their home games in the Vauxhall Conference in 1996–97, a figure that was not improved upon until the club were promoted to the Football League. Highest attendance that season was 6,489 for the visit of Kidderminster Harriers in January, more than all but two of the games played in the lower two divisions of the Football League on the same day.

STEVENAGE – SKY BET LEAGUE TWO 2021–22 LEAGUE RECORD

Match No.	Date	Venue	Opponents	Result	H/T Score	Lg Pos.	Goalscorers	Attendance
1	Aug 7	H	Barrow	W 1-0	0-0	5	Reeves 46	2536
2	14	A	Bristol R	W 2-0	0-0	2	Lines 88, Norris 90	7071
3	17	A	Bradford C	L 1-4	1-3	5	List 17	14,257
4	21	H	Port Vale	D 1-1	1-1	5	Norris 33	2727
5	28	A	Walsall	L 0-1	0-1	9		4257
6	Sept 4	H	Swindon T	D 1-1	0-0	12	Coker 53	3589
7	11	A	Sutton U	L 1-2	0-0	16	List 55	2427
8	18	H	Forest Green R	L 0-4	0-1	21		3111
9	25	A	Harrogate T	D 0-0	0-0	21		1667
10	Oct 2	H	Hartlepool U	W 2-0	1-0	17	Reid 21, List 46	2633
11	9	H	Exeter C	D 2-2	1-1	15	List 2 23, 59	3186
12	16	A	Oldham Ath	L 0-3	0-2	20		3492
13	19	A	Northampton T	L 0-3	0-2	20		4123
14	23	H	Leyton Orient	D 0-0	0-0	20		3544
15	30	A	Newport Co	L 0-5	0-3	21		3439
16	Nov 13	H	Mansfield T	L 1-2	0-1	21	Cuthbert 55	2946
17	20	H	Colchester U	W 1-0	1-0	21	List (pen) 45	2683
18	23	A	Rochdale	D 2-2	1-2	21	List 2 27, 47	3000
19	Dec 7	H	Scunthorpe U	D 1-1	1-1	21	Norris 6	1808
20	11	H	Carlisle U	L 0-2	0-1	22		2842
21	18	A	Salford C	L 0-1	0-1	22		1375
22	29	A	Swindon T	D 0-0	0-0	21		8131
23	Jan 1	A	Forest Green R	L 0-2	0-0	22		2454
24	8	H	Walsall	W 3-1	2-0	21	Menayese (og) 1, Lines 8, Taylor 90	2167
25	15	H	Sutton U	D 3-3	2-0	21	Norris 34, Reid 2 39, 64	2961
26	18	H	Crawley T	W 2-1	1-1	20	Taylor 28, Norris 72	1942
27	22	A	Hartlepool U	D 1-1	0-0	19	Norris (pen) 70	4841
28	29	H	Harrogate T	W 3-0	2-0	17	Reeves 9, Norris 21, Taylor 80	2935
29	Feb 1	A	Tranmere R	L 0-1	0-0	17		5723
30	5	A	Crawley T	D 2-2	0-1	16	Read 80, Cuthbert 90	2214
31	8	H	Bradford C	L 0-1	0-0	17		1953
32	12	A	Barrow	D 0-0	0-0	17		3001
33	19	H	Bristol R	L 0-4	0-1	19		3538
34	26	A	Port Vale	L 0-2	0-2	19		5157
35	Mar 5	A	Leyton Orient	D 2-2	2-1	21	Prosser 24, Norris 32	4558
36	12	H	Newport Co	L 0-2	0-0	22		2733
37	15	H	Northampton T	L 1-2	0-1	22	Lines 82	2362
38	26	A	Exeter C	L 1-2	1-2	22	Norris 38	5923
39	Apr 2	H	Oldham Ath	L 0-1	0-1	23		4642
40	9	A	Colchester U	W 2-0	1-0	23	Reid 45, Norris 49	3094
41	15	H	Rochdale	W 1-0	0-0	22	Cuthbert 48	3172
42	18	A	Scunthorpe U	D 1-1	0-0	22	Reid 53	2439
43	23	H	Tranmere R	W 2-0	1-0	22	Norris 2 (1 pen) 23 (p), 67	2969
44	26	A	Mansfield T	L 0-2	0-0	22		5086
45	30	A	Carlisle U	L 1-2	0-0	22	Norris (pen) 88	5701
46	May 7	H	Salford C	W 4-2	2-1	21	Reid 2 23, 43, Norris 48, List 80	3558

Final League Position: 21

GOALSCORERS

League (45): Norris 14 (3 pens), List 9 (1 pen), Reid 7, Cuthbert 3, Lines 3, Taylor 3, Reeves 2, Coker 1, Prosser 1, Read 1, own goal 1.
FA Cup (4): Barry 1, List 1, Norris 1 (1 pen), Reid 1.
Carabao Cup (4): List 2, Coker 1, Reid 1.
Papa John's Trophy (6): Daly 1, List 1, Marshall 1, Norris 1, Reid 1, own goal 1.

Anang J 13	Wildin L 38 + 2	Cuthbert S 39	Vancooten T 36 + 2	Coker B 36	Osborne E 10 + 4	Taylor J 42	Lines C 22 + 9	Reeves J 27	Reid J 26 + 12	Norris L 35 + 8	Carter C 4 + 16	List E 34 + 3	Marshall R 2 + 3	Daly J 2 + 13	Prosser L 23 + 4	Read A 9 + 10	Bastien S 1	Smith J 2 + 1	Andrade B 13 + 14	Barry B 6 + 6	Melbourne M 4 + 3	Tinubu S — + 1	Smith A 9	Cochrane O 1	Pym C 23	O'Neill L 10 + 2	Bostwick M 14	Upson E 10 + 5	Westbrooke Z 11 + 1	Clements B 4	Walker L — + 1	Match No.
1	2	3	4	5	6^1	7	8	9^3	10	11^2	12	13	14																			1
1	2	3	4	5	6^1	8	7	9	11^2	13	12	10^3		14																		2
1	2	4^1	3	5	13	7	9^2	8	14	11	6	10^3			12																	3
1	2		3	5	6^3	7		8	11^1	10^2		9	14	13	4	12																4
	2		3	5		6	12	7	10^3	11				14	4	8^2	1	9^1	13													5
1	2	4	3	5	6^2	7	8			11		10^1		9					12	13												6
1	2	4	3■	5		7^1	8	9	12	11		10^3		13					6^2	14												7
1	5	3^1		4		6		7	13	11		9^2	2	8^3	12				10	14												8
1	2	4	3	5	9	6		7	11^2	12		10^1							13	8												9
1	2	4	3	5	6	7		8	11^3	13		10^2			14			12	9^1													10
1	2	4	3	5	6^2	7		8	11^1	12		10							9		13											11
1	2	4	3	5	6			8	11^1	12		10						7^2	9^3		13	14										12
1	2		3	9	6^1	7		8	12	11^2		10			4				13		5											13
	2	4		5		7	8	9	12	11^2		10^1			3				13	6			1									14
	2	4	12	5^3		7	8^1	9		10		11			3^2				13	6	14		1									15
	2	4	3			8	12	9	11^2	13		10				7				6^1	5		1									16
	2	3		5	14	6	7^1	8	11^2	13		10^3	12						9		4		1									17
	2	4	3	9^1	6^3			8	10^2			11	7			12			13	14	5		1									18
	2		3	5		7	6	8	11^1	9		10			4				12				1									19
1	2		3	5	13	7	6^1	8	12	10		11			4	9^2																20
		3		5	13	8	7^1	6	12	10		9			4				11				1	2^2								21
	2	3		5		6^1	7	8		9^2	13	10^3		14	4	12			11				1									22
	2	4	3	6			7^2	8		10^3	13	11^1		14	5	12			9				1									23
		3	14	5		9	6	8		10^3	13				4				11^2						1	2	7^1	12				24
	2	3	7	5		9	6	8	11^1	10^2	12			13	4										1							25
	13	3	7	5		9^3	14		10	12					4^1				11						1	2^2		8	6			26
	2	4^2	3	6		11	7	8	12	10^3	14				5										1			13	9^1			27
		4	7	5		9		6	11^3	10^1	12				3^2				14						1	2		13	8			28
	2		3	5^1		9		6^2	11	10	13				14										1	12	4^3	7	8			29
		4				9			11^2	10	12			14	3	13									1	2^3	7^1	6	8	5		30
		4	3			9	13				10^3	12				14			11						1	2	7^2	6^1	8	5		31
	2	3				9^2	6		13	10	12	11^1			4■										1		7		8	5		32
	13	4	3			9	8		11^1	10	12								14						1	2^3	7^2	6		5		33
	6	3^1	4			9				11	12	10^3			5	14				13					1	2^2		8	7			34
	6	3	4			9			12	11		10^1			5										1	2		8	7			35
	5	4^3	7			9			11^1	10	12	13			3	14									1	2		8^2	6			36
	5		3			6	8			10^1	9	11			4	13									1	2		7^2	12			37
		3	7	5		6			14	11	9^1	10^3			4	12			13	2					1				8^2			38
	2	3	4	5		6	8^1		13	11		10				9^2			12						1		7^3	14				39
	2	3	4	5		6^1	12		11	10■	14	9^2				8^3			13						1		7					40
	2	4	3	5^3		7	12		11			10^2		13		8			9^1						1	14	6					41
	2	4	3	5		6	8		9	10		11^1		12											1		7					42
	2	3	4	5		6	12		9	10^2		11^3		13		8^1									1		7	14				43
	2	3	4	5		6	13		9	10^1		11^3		12		8^2			14						1		7					44
	2	3				6	13		9	10	12	11^1			4					5					1		7	8^2				45
	2	4	3	5			6		11	10^2		9		14		8^3				13					1^1		7				12	46

FA Cup

First Round	Milton Keynes D	(a)	2-2
Replay	Milton Keynes D	(h)	2-1
(aet)			
Second Round	Yeovil T	(a)	0-1

Carabao Cup

First Round	Luton T	(h)	2-2
(Stevenage won 3-0 on penalties)			
Second Round	Wycombe W	(h)	2-2
(Wycombe W won 5-3 on penalties)			

Papa John's Trophy

Group H (S)	Tottenham H U21	(h)	3-4
Group H (S)	Oxford U	(a)	2-1
Group H (S)	Cambridge U	(h)	1-0
Second Round	Sutton U	(a)	0-0
(Sutton U won 4-3 on penalties)			

STOKE CITY

FOUNDATION

The date of the formation of this club has long been in doubt. The year 1863 was claimed, but more recent research by local club historian Wade Martin has uncovered nothing earlier than 1868, when a couple of Old Carthusians, who were apprentices at the local works of the old North Staffordshire Railway Company, met with some others from that works, to form Stoke Ramblers. It should also be noted that the old Stoke club went bankrupt in 1908 when a new club was formed.

bet365 Stadium, Stanley Matthews Way, Stoke-on-Trent, Staffordshire ST4 4EG.

Telephone: (01782) 367 598 or (01782) 592 233.

Ticket Office: (01782) 367 599.

Website: www.stokecityfc.com

Email: info@stokecityfc.com

Ground Capacity: 30,089.

Record Attendance: 51,380 v Arsenal, Division 1, 29 March 1937 (at Victoria Ground); 30,022 v Everton, Premier League, 17 March 2018 (at bet365 Stadium).

Pitch Measurements: 105m × 68m (115yd × 74.5yd).

Joint Chairmen: John Coates, Peter Coates.

Chief Executive: Tony Scholes.

Manager: Michael O'Neill MBE.

Assistant Manager: Dean Holden.

Colours: Red and white striped shirts, white shorts with red trim, white socks with red trim.

Year Formed: 1863* (*see Foundation*).

Turned Professional: 1885.

Previous Names: 1868, Stoke Ramblers; 1870, Stoke; 1925, Stoke City.

Club Nickname: 'The Potters'.

Grounds: 1875, Sweeting's Field; 1878, Victoria Ground (previously known as the Athletic Club Ground); 1997, Britannia Stadium (renamed bet365 Stadium 2016).

First Football League Game: 8 September 1888, Football League, v WBA (h) L 0–2 – Rowley; Clare, Underwood; Ramsey, Shutt, Smith; Sayer, McSkimming, Staton, Edge, Tunnicliffe.

Record League Victory: 10–3 v WBA, Division 1, 4 February 1937 – Doug Westland; Brigham, Harbot; Tutin, Turner (1p), Kirton; Matthews, Antonio (2), Freddie Steele (5), Jimmy Westland, Johnson (2).

Record Cup Victory: 7–1 v Burnley, FA Cup 2nd rd (replay), 20 February 1896 – Clawley; Clare, Eccles; Turner, Grewe, Robertson; Willie Maxwell, Dickson, Alan Maxwell (3), Hyslop (4), Schofield.

Record Defeat: 0–10 v Preston NE, Division 1, 14 September 1889.

Most League Points (2 for a win): 63, Division 3 (N), 1926–27.

Most League Points (3 for a win): 93, Division 2, 1992–93.

HONOURS

League Champions: Division 2 – 1932–33, 1962–63; Second Division – 1992–93; Division 3N – 1926–27.
Runners-up: FL C – 2007–08; Division 2 – 1921–22.

FA Cup: *Runners-up:* 2011.

League Cup Winners: 1972.
Runners-up: 1964.

League Trophy Winners: 1992, 2000.

European Competitions
UEFA Cup: 1972–73, 1974–75.
Europa League: 2011–12.

FOOTBALL YEARBOOK FACT FILE

The first figures for official ground capacities were set by local police forces following the Burnden Park Disaster of 1946. Stoke City's Victoria Ground was deemed to hold 45,000 but the official attendance for the visit of Blackpool on 27 December 1947 was 47,725 and newspaper reports suggest another three or four thousand climbed over the gates to enter for free.

Most League Goals: 92, Division 3 (N), 1926–27.

Highest League Scorer in Season: Freddie Steele, 33, Division 1, 1936–37.

Most League Goals in Total Aggregate: Freddie Steele, 142, 1934–49.

Most League Goals in One Match: 7, Neville Coleman v Lincoln C, Division 2, 23 February 1957.

Most Capped Player: Glenn Whelan, 81 (91), Republic of Ireland.

Most League Appearances: Eric Skeels, 507, 1958–76.

Youngest League Player: Peter Bullock, 16 years 163 days v Swansea C, 19 April 1958.

Record Transfer Fee Received: £20,000,000 (rising to £25,000,000) from West Ham U for Marko Arnautovic, July 2017.

Record Transfer Fee Paid: £18,300,000 to Porto for Giannelli Imbula, February 2016.

Football League Record: 1888 Founder Member of Football League; 1890 Not re-elected; 1891 Re-elected; relegated in 1907, and after one year in Division 2, resigned for financial reasons; 1919 re-elected to Division 2; 1922–23 Division 1; 1923–26 Division 2; 1926–27 Division 3 (N); 1927–33 Division 2; 1933–53 Division 1; 1953–63 Division 2; 1963–77 Division 1; 1977–79 Division 2; 1979–85 Division 1; 1985–90 Division 2; 1990–92 Division 3; 1992–93 Division 2; 1993–98 Division 1; 1998–2002 Division 2; 2002–04 Division 1; 2004–08 FL C; 2008–18 Premier League; 2018– FL C.

LATEST SEQUENCES

Longest Sequence of League Wins: 8, 30.3.1895 – 21.9.1895.

Longest Sequence of League Defeats: 11, 6.4.1985 – 17.8.1985.

Longest Sequence of League Draws: 5, 13.5.2012 – 15.9.2012.

Longest Sequence of Unbeaten League Matches: 25, 5.9.1992 – 20.2.1993.

Longest Sequence Without a League Win: 17, 22.4.1989 – 14.10.1989.

Successive Scoring Runs: 21 from 24.12.1921.

Successive Non-scoring Runs: 8 from 29.12.1984.

MANAGERS

Tom Slaney 1874–83 *(Secretary-Manager)*
Walter Cox 1883–84 *(Secretary-Manager)*
Harry Lockett 1884–90
Joseph Bradshaw 1890–92
Arthur Reeves 1892–95
William Rowley 1895–97
H. D. Austerberry 1897–1908
A. J. Barker 1908–14
Peter Hodge 1914–15
Joe Schofield 1915–19
Arthur Shallcross 1919–23
John 'Jock' Rutherford 1923
Tom Mather 1923–35
Bob McGrory 1935–52
Frank Taylor 1952–60
Tony Waddington 1960–77
George Eastham 1977–78
Alan A'Court 1978
Alan Durban 1978–81
Richie Barker 1981–83
Bill Asprey 1984–85
Mick Mills 1985–89
Alan Ball 1989–91
Lou Macari 1991–93
Joe Jordan 1993–94
Lou Macari 1994–97
Chic Bates 1997–98
Chris Kamara 1998
Brian Little 1998–99
Gary Megson 1999
Gudjon Thordarson 1999–2002
Steve Cotterill 2002
Tony Pulis 2002–05
Johan Boskamp 2005–06
Tony Pulis 2006–13
Mark Hughes 2013–18
Paul Lambert 2018
Gary Rowett 2018–19
Nathan Jones 2019
Michael O'Neill November 2019–

TEN YEAR LEAGUE RECORD

		P	W	D	L	F	A	Pts	Pos
2012-13	PR Lge	38	9	15	14	34	45	42	13
2013-14	PR Lge	38	13	11	14	45	52	50	9
2014-15	PR Lge	38	15	9	14	48	45	54	9
2015-16	PR Lge	38	14	9	15	41	55	51	9
2016-17	PR Lge	38	11	11	16	41	56	44	13
2017-18	PR Lge	38	7	12	19	35	68	33	19
2018-19	FL C	46	11	22	13	45	52	55	16
2019-20	FL C	46	16	8	22	62	68	56	15
2020-21	FL C	46	15	15	16	50	52	60	14
2021-22	FL C	46	17	11	18	57	52	62	14

DID YOU KNOW ?

The first European team to play at Stoke City's Victoria Ground were FK Austria Wien who were touring England during their domestic season winter break in 1934. The teams met on 13 December, with the Potters winning 1-0 with a goal from Harry Davies in front of a crowd of 13,513.

STOKE CITY – SKY BET CHAMPIONSHIP 2021–22 LEAGUE RECORD

Match No.	Date	Venue	Opponents	Result	H/T Score	Lg Pos.	Goalscorers	Attendance
1	Aug 7	H	Reading	W 3-2	2-1	3	Powell[25], Brown[28], Surridge[85]	19,068
2	14	A	Birmingham C	D 0-0	0-0	6		10,189
3	17	A	Swansea C	W 3-1	1-0	2	Powell[15], Clucas[53], Ostigard[60]	15,927
4	21	H	Nottingham F	W 1-0	0-0	3	Tymon[66]	21,346
5	28	A	Fulham	L 0-3	0-1	5		16,791
6	Sept 11	H	Huddersfield T	W 2-1	0-0	3	Brown[50], Pearson (og)[63]	20,447
7	15	H	Barnsley	D 1-1	1-1	5	Surridge[17]	17,832
8	18	A	Derby Co	L 1-2	0-2	5	Ince[58]	20,545
9	25	H	Hull C	W 2-0	1-0	5	Vrancic[35], Powell[58]	20,124
10	28	A	Preston NE	D 1-1	1-1	4	Powell[6]	10,930
11	Oct 1	H	WBA	W 1-0	0-0	3	Powell[79]	22,703
12	16	A	Sheffield U	L 1-2	0-0	5	Brown[55]	28,576
13	19	H	Bournemouth	L 0-1	0-0	6		18,427
14	23	A	Millwall	L 1-2	1-0	9	Sawyers[20]	12,896
15	30	H	Cardiff C	D 3-3	2-0	9	Brown[9], Fletcher 2[16, 46]	21,413
16	Nov 3	A	Blackpool	W 1-0	0-0	6	Fletcher[79]	12,297
17	6	A	Luton T	W 1-0	1-0	5	Brown[34]	10,068
18	20	H	Peterborough U	W 2-0	1-0	4	Vrancic[3], Campbell[90]	21,285
19	24	A	Bristol C	L 0-1	0-1	6		16,949
20	27	H	Blackburn R	L 0-1	0-0	7		21,739
21	Dec 5	A	QPR	W 2-0	1-0	6	Campbell[14], Vrancic[78]	13,968
22	11	H	Middlesbrough	D 0-0	0-0	6		21,140
23	30	H	Derby Co	L 1-2	0-1	8	Ince[78]	22,235
24	Jan 3	H	Preston NE	L 1-2	0-0	8	Wilmot[46]	20,002
25	16	A	Hull C	W 2-0	1-0	8	Brown[22], Ince[50]	11,067
26	22	H	Fulham	L 2-3	1-2	9	Wright-Phillips[1], Baker[58]	21,749
27	25	A	Coventry C	L 0-1	0-0	11		16,860
28	28	A	Huddersfield T	D 1-1	0-1	10	Brown[78]	16,342
29	Feb 8	H	Swansea C	W 3-0	0-0	10	Philogene-Bidace[47], Baker (pen)[59], Brown[78]	17,720
30	12	A	Nottingham F	D 2-2	0-0	13	Maja[68], Baker (pen)[88]	28,990
31	19	H	Birmingham C	D 2-2	1-1	13	Campbell 2[25, 52]	23,502
32	23	H	Luton T	L 1-2	0-0	14	Baker[90]	18,270
33	26	A	Bournemouth	L 1-2	1-0	15	Smith[20]	9613
34	Mar 5	H	Blackpool	L 0-1	0-0	15		26,384
35	8	A	Barnsley	D 1-1	0-0	15	Baker[90]	12,512
36	12	A	Peterborough U	D 2-2	1-1	15	Brown[28], Baker (pen)[84]	9060
37	16	A	Cardiff C	L 1-2	1-2	16	Baker[23]	17,184
38	19	H	Millwall	W 2-0	1-0	15	Brown[19], Saville (og)[70]	20,526
39	Apr 2	H	Sheffield U	W 1-0	0-0	13	Egan (og)[77]	22,631
40	5	A	Reading	L 1-2	1-1	15	Sawyers[44]	9928
41	9	A	WBA	W 3-1	1-0	15	Livermore (og)[16], Brown[59], Baker[90]	22,761
42	15	H	Bristol C	L 0-1	0-0	15		20,298
43	18	A	Blackburn R	W 1-0	1-0	14	Brown[4]	30,428
44	23	H	QPR	W 1-0	1-0	12	Brown[45]	19,251
45	30	A	Middlesbrough	L 1-3	0-2	13	Powell[90]	24,942
46	May 7	H	Coventry C	D 1-1	1-1	14	Clucas[43]	23,086

Final League Position: 14

GOALSCORERS

League (57): Brown 13, Baker 8 (3 pens), Powell 6, Campbell 4, Fletcher 3, Ince 3, Vrancic 3, Clucas 2, Sawyers 2, Surridge 2, Maja 1, Ostigard 1, Philogene-Bidace 1, Smith 1, Tymon 1, Wilmot 1, Wright-Phillips 1, own goals 4.
FA Cup (5): Brown 1, Campbell 1, Ince 1, Maja 1, Tymon 1.
Carabao Cup (8): Surridge 2, Clucas 1, Ince 1, Powell 1, Sawyers 1, Souttar 1, Tymon 1.

Bursik J 19	Smith T 30 + 2	Wilmot B 31 + 4	Batth D 10 + 1	Fox M 9 + 1	Tymon J 44	Vrancic M 24 + 6	Allen J 38 + 3	Powell N 14 + 4	Brown J 38 + 7	Fletcher S 16 + 19	Clucas S 16 + 9	Surridge S 6 + 14	Doughty A — + 11	Thompson J 12 + 6	Ostigard L 12 + 1	Soutar H 16	Sawyers R 19 + 6	Sima A 1 + 1	Ince T 4 + 7	Davies A 12	Chester J 16 + 1	Duhaney D 3	Campbell T 10 + 16	Bonham J 15	Harwood-Bellis T 22	Jagielka P 20	Wright-Phillips D 6 + 4	Baker L 20 + 1	Philogene-Bidace J 6 + 5	Maja J 9 + 6	Moore L 4	Forrester W 3	Sparrow T 1	*Match No.*
1	2	3	4	5	6^{3}	7^{4}	8	9^{1}	10	11^{2}	12	13	14	15																				1
1	2	5			6		8	7	12	11^{2}	9	10^{1}		13	3	4																		2
1	5	4			9		7	6^{1}	10	13	8	11^{2}		12	2	3																		3
1	5	4			9	8^{2}	7		10	11^{1}	6^{3}	13		12	2	3	14																	4
1	5^{3}	4			9	8	7		10	11^{1}	6^{2}	12	14		2	3	13																	5
1	5	4			9	8^{3}	12		10	13	6	11^{2}	14		2	3	7^{1}																	6
1	5■	4			9	8	7^{1}		11^{2}		12	10^{3}	14		2	3	6	13																7
1		4			9	7		13	12		8	10^{2}	14		2	3	6^{3}	11^{1}	5															8
		2	14		9^{2}	8^{1}		10	11		6	12	13			3^{3}	7			1	4	5												9
	5	4			8	10^{1}		9	11^{2}		12	13		7	2	3	6			1														10
	5	2			8	10^{2}	6	9^{3}	11^{1}	13		12	14	7		3				1	4													11
	5	2			8	10^{1}	7	9^{3}	11^{2}	13	12	14				3	6			1	4													12
	5	2			9	12	7	10^{1}	11^{3}		6^{2}	13		8		3				1	4		14											13
1		5			9	8	7		10^{2}	12		11^{1}			2^{3}	3	6		14		4		13											14
1	5	2			9	14	6		11^{2}	10^{1}		12		8^{3}		3	7				4		13											15
1	5	4^{1}	3		9	14	7		11^{2}	10				8^{3}	12	2	6						13											16
1	5^{2}	13	4		9	12	7		11^{3}	10^{1}		14		8	2	3	6																	17
	5		3	12	9^{1}	8	7		11^{2}	10^{3}		14■			2		6			1	4		13											18
	5		3		9	8^{2}	7■		11^{1}	10			13		2^{3}		6		14	1	4		12											19
	5	2	3	8^{2}	7	9			10^{1}	12			14				6		13	1	4^{3}		11											20
	2	3	4	5	6	9	8		13	10^{3}	12						7^{1}		14	1			11^{2}											21
	5	2	3	4	9	8^{2}	7		12	10^{3}	6	14							13	1			11^{1}											22
	5	2	3	4^{2}	9	8	7		10^{1}	12	6^{3}	14							13	1			11											23
		2	3	9		8^{3}	7		14	10^{1}	6	12	13						5	1	4		11^{2}											24
	5				9^{1}		7		11^{3}		8		12						6		4		14	1	2	3	10^{2}	13						25
	5				9		7^{1}		11^{2}		8								12		4		13	1	2	3	10^{3}	6	14					26
	5				9		12	14	11		8^{1}								6		4^{3}			1	2	3	10^{2}	7	13					27
		2			5	9^{2}	12	13	14	11^{3}				7^{1}									8	1	4	3		6	10					28
1		2			5		7^{3}	8^{2}	10		13												9^{1}		4	3	14	6	11	12				29
1		2			5		7	8^{3}	9^{1}	13	12			14											4	3		6	11	10^{2}				30
1	14	2^{3}			5		7		10	13	8^{1}												9^{2}		4	3	12	6	11					31
1	13	2			5^{2}		7	8	12	14													9		4			6	11^{1}	10^{3}	3			32
	5^{3}			9■			6	10	11^{2}	14	12			8^{1}										1	4	3		7		13	2			33
	5^{4}	12			9	8^{3}		10^{2}		15							6						13	1	4	3		7	14	11	2^{1}			34
					9		6		10^{1}	14				8^{3}							3	5^{2}	13	1	4	2		7	12	11				35
		13			9		7		10	11				8^{3}							3	5^{1}	14	1	4	2^{2}		6		12				36
		2		5^{1}	11	13	7		10								8^{2}				3		9^{3}	1	4		14	6		12				37
					5	8^{1}	6		9	14				12									13	1	2	3	11^{2}	7		10^{3}	4			38
		2			5	9^{1}	6		8	14				7			12						13	1	4	3	10^{2}			11^{3}				39
		2			5		6		8	14				7^{1}			12						13	1	4	3	10^{2}	9		11^{3}				40
	5	13			9	7^{2}	8		10	11^{1}														1	4	3		6		12		2		41
	5				9	7^{2}	8		10	11^{1}							12						14	1	4	3		6		13		2^{3}		42
	6	2			9		5		11	13							8^{1}							1	4	3		7	12	10^{2}				43
1	6	2			9		5		10^{3}	12	13						8^{2}						14		4	3		7		11^{1}				44
1	6				9	14	5	13	10	12							8								4	3		7^{3}	11^{2}			2^{1}		45
1				4	9		5	11^{3}	10		8^{1}						14				13				2^{2}	3	12	7					6	46

FA Cup

Third Round	Leyton Orient	(h)	2-0
Fourth Round	Wigan Ath	(h)	2-0
Fifth Round	Crystal Palace	(a)	1-2

Carabao Cup

First Round	Fleetwood T	(h)	2-1
Second Round	Doncaster R	(h)	2-0
Third Round	Watford	(a)	3-1
Fourth Round	Brentford	(h)	1-2

SUNDERLAND

FOUNDATION

A Scottish schoolmaster named James Allan, working at Hendon Board School, took the initiative in the foundation of Sunderland in 1879 when they were formed as The Sunderland and District Teachers' Association FC at a meeting in the Adults School, Norfolk Street. Due to financial difficulties, they quickly allowed members from outside the teaching profession and so became Sunderland AFC in October 1880.

Stadium of Light, Sunderland, Tyne and Wear SR5 1SU.

Telephone: (0371) 911 1200.

Ticket Office: (0371) 911 1973.

Website: www.safc.com

Email: enquiries@safc.com

Ground Capacity: 48,095.

Record Attendance: 75,118 v Derby Co, FA Cup 6th rd replay, 8 March 1933 (at Roker Park); 48,335 v Liverpool, Premier League, 13 April 2002 (at Stadium of Light).

Pitch Measurements: 105m × 68m (115yd × 74.5yd).

Chairman: Kyril Louis-Dreyfus.

Sporting Director: Kristjaan Speakman.

Head Coach: Alex Neill.

Assistant Head Coach: Martin Canning.

Colours: Red and white striped shirts with white sleeves, black shorts with white trim, red socks.

Year Formed: 1879.

Turned Professional: 1886.

Previous Names: 1879, Sunderland and District Teachers AFC; 1880, Sunderland.

Club Nickname: 'The Black Cats'.

Grounds: 1879, Blue House Field, Hendon; 1882, Groves Field, Ashbrooke; 1883, Horatio Street; 1884, Abbs Field, Fulwell; 1886, Newcastle Road; 1898, Roker Park; 1997, Stadium of Light.

First Football League Game: 13 September 1890, Football League, v Burnley (h) L 2–3 – Kirtley; Porteous, Oliver; Wilson, Auld, Gibson; Spence (1), Miller, Campbell (1), Scott, Davy Hannah.

Record League Victory: 9–1 v Newcastle U (a), Division 1, 5 December 1908 – Roose; Forster, Melton; Daykin, Thomson, Low; Mordue (1), Hogg (3), Brown, Holley (3), Bridgett (2).

Record Cup Victory: 11–1 v Fairfield, FA Cup 1st rd, 2 February 1895 – Doig; McNeill, Johnston; Dunlop, McCreadie (1), Wilson; Gillespie (1), Millar (5), Campbell, Jimmy Hannah (3), Scott (1).

HONOURS

League Champions: Division 1 – 1892–93, 1894–95, 1901–02, 1912–13, 1935–36; Football League 1891–92; FL C – 2004–05, 2006–07; First Division – 1995–96, 1998–99; Division 2 – 1975–76; Division 3 – 1987–88.
Runners-up: Division 1 – 1893–94, 1897–98, 1900–01, 1922–23, 1934–35; Division 2 – 1963–64, 1979–80.

FA Cup Winners: 1937, 1973.
Runners-up: 1913, 1992.

League Cup: *Runners-up:* 1985, 2014.

League Trophy Winners: 2021.
Runners-up: 2019.

European Competitions
European Cup-Winners' Cup: 1973–74.

FOOTBALL YEARBOOK FACT FILE

In April 1903 Sunderland played their home Division One fixture against Middlesbrough at Newcastle United's St James' Park. Sunderland won 2-1 in front of a crowd of 22,000. The neutral venue was used because the FA ordered that Roker Park be closed for a week as punishment for a game against fellow title challengers Sheffield Wednesday, when missiles were thrown at the referee and the vehicle taking the visiting team and officials from the ground was stoned.

Record Defeat: 0–8 v Sheff Wed, Division 1, 26 December 1911; 0–8 v West Ham U, Division 1, 19 October 1968; 0–8 v Watford, Division 1, 25 September 1982; 0–8 v Southampton, Premier League, 18 October 2014.

Most League Points (2 for a win): 61, Division 2, 1963–64.

Most League Points (3 for a win): 105, Division 1, 1998–99.

Most League Goals: 109, Division 1, 1935–36.

Highest League Scorer in Season: Dave Halliday, 43, Division 1, 1928–29.

Most League Goals in Total Aggregate: Charlie Buchan, 209, 1911–25.

Most League Goals in One Match: 5, Charlie Buchan v Liverpool, Division 1, 7 December 1919; 5, Bobby Gurney v Bolton W, Division 1, 7 December 1935; 5, Dominic Sharkey v Norwich C, Division 2, 20 February 1962.

Most Capped Player: Seb Larsson, 59 (133), Sweden.

Most League Appearances: Jim Montgomery, 537, 1962–77.

Youngest League Player: Derek Forster, 15 years 184 days v Leicester C, 22 August 1964.

Record Transfer Fee Received: £25,000,000 (rising to £30,000,000) from Everton for Jordan Pickford, June 2017.

Record Transfer Fee Paid: £13,800,000 (rising to £17,100,000) to FC Lorient for Didier Ndong, August 2016.

Football League Record: 1890 Elected to Division 1; 1958–64 Division 2; 1964–70 Division 1; 1970–76 Division 2; 1976–77 Division 1; 1977–80 Division 2; 1980–85 Division 1; 1985–87 Division 2; 1987–88 Division 3; 1988–90 Division 2; 1990–91 Division 1; 1991–92 Division 2; 1992–96 Division 1; 1996–97 Premier League; 1997–99 Division 1; 1999–2003 Premier League; 2003–04 Division 1; 2004–05 FL C; 2005–06 Premier League; 2006–07 FL C; 2007–17 Premier League; 2017–18 FL C: 2018–22 FL 1; 2022– FL C.

LATEST SEQUENCES

Longest Sequence of League Wins: 13, 14.11.1891 – 2.4.1892.

Longest Sequence of League Defeats: 17, 18.1.2003 – 16.8.2003.

Longest Sequence of League Draws: 6, 26.3.1949 – 19.4.1949.

Longest Sequence of Unbeaten League Matches: 19, 26.12.2018 – 9.4.2019

Longest Sequence Without a League Win: 22, 21.12.2002 – 16.8.2003.

Successive Scoring Runs: 43 from 30.3.2018.

Successive Non-scoring Runs: 10 from 27.11.1976.

MANAGERS

Tom Watson 1888–96
Bob Campbell 1896–99
Alex Mackie 1899–1905
Bob Kyle 1905–28
Johnny Cochrane 1928–39
Bill Murray 1939–57
Alan Brown 1957–64
George Hardwick 1964–65
Ian McColl 1965–68
Alan Brown 1968–72
Bob Stokoe 1972–76
Jimmy Adamson 1976–78
Ken Knighton 1979–81
Alan Durban 1981–84
Len Ashurst 1984–85
Lawrie McMenemy 1985–87
Denis Smith 1987–91
Malcolm Crosby 1991–93
Terry Butcher 1993
Mick Buxton 1993–95
Peter Reid 1995–2002
Howard Wilkinson 2002–03
Mick McCarthy 2003–06
Niall Quinn 2006
Roy Keane 2006–08
Ricky Sbragia 2008–09
Steve Bruce 2009–11
Martin O'Neill 2011–13
Paolo Di Canio 2013
Gus Poyet 2013–15
Dick Advocaat 2015
Sam Allardyce 2015–16
David Moyes 2016–17
Simon Grayson 2017
Chris Coleman 2017–18
Jack Ross 2018–19
Phil Parkinson 2019–20
Lee Johnson 2020–22
Alex Neill February 2022–

TEN YEAR LEAGUE RECORD

		P	*W*	*D*	*L*	*F*	*A*	*Pts*	*Pos*
2012-13	PR Lge	38	9	12	17	41	54	39	17
2013-14	PR Lge	38	10	8	20	41	60	38	14
2014-15	PR Lge	38	7	17	14	31	53	38	16
2015-16	PR Lge	38	9	12	17	48	62	39	17
2016-17	PR Lge	38	6	6	26	29	69	24	20
2017-18	FL C	46	7	16	23	52	80	37	24
2018-19	FL 1	46	22	19	5	80	47	85	5
2019-20	FL 1	36	16	11	9	48	32	59	8§
2020-21	FL 1	46	20	17	9	70	42	77	4
2021-22	FL 1	46	24	12	10	79	53	84	5

§*Decided on points-per-game (1.64)*

DID YOU KNOW ?

Centre-forward Ronnie Turnbull marked his debut for Sunderland by scoring all four goals in their Division One victory over Portsmouth on 29 November 1947. Turnbull, who was signed earlier in the week from Dundee, took just 20 minutes to open his account for his new club who comfortably won the game 4-1.

SUNDERLAND – SKY BET LEAGUE ONE 2021–22 LEAGUE RECORD

Match No.	*Date*	*Venue*	*Opponents*	*Result*		*H/T Score*	*Lg Pos.*	*Goalscorers*	*Attendance*
1	Aug 7	H	Wigan Ath	W	2-1	1-1	2	McGeady (pen) [17], Stewart [53]	31,549
2	14	A	Milton Keynes D	W	2-1	1-0	3	Stewart [42], Embleton [52]	9830
3	17	A	Burton Alb	L	0-1	0-0	7		4239
4	21	H	AFC Wimbledon	W	1-0	0-0	4	Winchester [64]	29,093
5	28	H	Wycombe W	W	3-1	2-0	1	Stewart 2 [14, 83], Embleton [18]	29,344
6	Sept 11	H	Accrington S	W	2-1	1-1	1	Neill [15], Winchester [58]	29,830
7	18	A	Fleetwood T	D	2-2	1-0	2	Stewart [19], McGeady (pen) [76]	4250
8	25	H	Bolton W	W	1-0	1-0	2	Winchester [17]	32,368
9	28	H	Cheltenham T	W	5-0	3-0	1	Wright [11], Stewart 2 [28, 38], O'Nien [65], Dajaku [66]	28,313
10	Oct 2	A	Portsmouth	L	0-4	0-3	2		17,418
11	16	A	Gillingham	W	2-1	1-1	4	O'Brien [45], Flanagan [54]	6310
12	19	A	Crewe Alex	W	4-0	2-0	2	Thomas, T (og) [25], Stewart 2 [32, 55], Dajaku [73]	5618
13	23	H	Charlton Ath	L	0-1	0-0	4		31,883
14	30	A	Rotherham U	L	1-5	1-2	5	Stewart [24]	10,573
15	Nov 2	A	Sheffield W	L	0-3	0-2	5		23,731
16	20	H	Ipswich T	W	2-0	0-0	6	O'Nien [85], McGeady (pen) [90]	31,033
17	23	A	Shrewsbury T	D	1-1	1-0	6	Pritchard [16]	6253
18	27	A	Cambridge U	W	2-1	2-1	5	Mitov (og) [15], Broadhead [36]	7174
19	Dec 4	H	Oxford U	D	1-1	1-1	5	Dajaku [7]	26,634
20	7	H	Morecambe	W	5-0	2-0	3	Stewart [13], Broadhead 2 [17, 68], Pritchard [56], Dajaku [87]	26,516
21	11	H	Plymouth Arg	W	2-1	2-0	3	Neill [4], Broadhead [13]	28,987
22	18	A	Ipswich T	D	1-1	0-1	3	Broadhead [50]	29,005
23	27	A	Doncaster R	W	3-0	2-0	2	Stewart (pen) [7], Embleton [41], Blythe (og) [50]	10,751
24	30	H	Sheffield W	W	5-0	3-0	1	Stewart 3 [12, 36, 58], Doyle [40], Mgunga-Kimpioka [75]	34,652
25	Jan 8	A	Wycombe W	D	3-3	2-2	2	Stockdale (og) [3], Stewart 2 [39, 90]	7229
26	11	H	Lincoln C	L	1-3	0-1	2	Stewart [68]	28,782
27	15	A	Accrington S	D	1-1	0-0	2	O'Brien [48]	4498
28	22	H	Portsmouth	W	1-0	1-0	2	Embleton [40]	32,220
29	29	A	Bolton W	L	0-6	0-2	3		20,059
30	Feb 5	H	Doncaster R	L	1-2	0-2	4	Evans [89]	38,395
31	8	A	Cheltenham T	L	1-2	1-0	4	Pritchard [32]	5744
32	12	A	AFC Wimbledon	D	1-1	1-1	4	Pritchard [35]	8381
33	19	H	Milton Keynes D	L	1-2	0-0	7	Stewart [59]	30,451
34	22	H	Burton Alb	D	1-1	0-0	6	Stewart [90]	30,237
35	26	A	Wigan Ath	W	3-0	2-0	5	Wright [2], Stewart 2 (2 pens) [38, 87]	20,136
36	Mar 5	A	Charlton Ath	D	0-0	0-0	7		13,716
37	8	H	Fleetwood T	W	3-1	0-1	5	Embleton [55], O'Nien [82], Clarke [90]	28,017
38	12	H	Crewe Alex	W	2-0	0-0	5	Neill [84], Roberts [89]	30,036
39	19	A	Lincoln C	D	0-0	0-0	6		10,346
40	Apr 2	H	Gillingham	W	1-0	0-0	6	Broadhead [90]	31,619
41	9	A	Oxford U	W	2-1	1-1	7	Evans [15], Embleton [89]	11,690
42	15	H	Shrewsbury T	W	3-2	2-0	6	Embleton [4], Broadhead 2 [13, 90]	33,896
43	18	A	Plymouth Arg	D	0-0	0-0	6		15,800
44	23	H	Cambridge U	W	5-1	3-1	4	Stewart 2 (1 pen) [13 (p), 36], Embleton [29], Broadhead [53], Batth [71]	32,500
45	26	H	Rotherham U	D	1-1	0-1	5	Ihiekwe (og) [88]	33,119
46	30	A	Morecambe	W	1-0	1-0	5	Broadhead [10]	5831

Final League Position: 5

GOALSCORERS

League (79): Stewart 24 (4 pens), Broadhead 10, Embleton 8, Dajaku 4, Pritchard 4, McGeady 3 (3 pens), Neill 3, O'Nien 3, Winchester 3, Evans 2, O'Brien 2, Wright 2, Batth 1, Clarke 1, Doyle 1, Flanagan 1, Mgunga-Kimpioka 1, Roberts 1, own goals 5.
FA Cup (0).
Carabao Cup (8): O'Brien 4 (1 pen), Broadhead 2, Hawkes 1, O'Nien 1.
Papa John's Trophy (5): Wearne 2, Broadhead 1, Dyce 1, Neil 1.
League One Play-offs (4): Stewart 2, Embleton 1, Roberts 1.

Burge L 3	Winchester C 39 + 1	Flanagan T 25	Doyle C 33 + 3	Neill D 31 + 8	Evans C 26 + 7	O'Nien L 24 + 2	Gooch L 33 + 5	Embleton E 26 + 12	McGeady A 12 + 2	Stewart R 46	O'Brien A 7 + 10	Diamond J 1 + 2	Wright B 28 + 9	Cirkin D 31 + 3	Pritchard A 25 + 11	Broadhead N 15 + 5	Patterson A 20	Hoffmann R 23	Alves F — + 3	Dajaku L 14 + 8	Huggins N 1 + 1	Harris W — + 3	Hume D — + 4	Mgunga-Kimpioka B — + 2	Hawkes J — + 1	Batth D 8 + 1	Clarke J 9 + 8	Roberts P 6 + 8	Defoe J 2 + 5	Matete J 12 + 2	Hume T 3	Xhemajli A 3	Match No.
1	2²	3	4	5	6	7	8	9³	10¹	11	12	13	14																				1
1	2	3	4	7	6¹		8	9	10²	11	13		14	5³	12																		2
1	2	3	4	7		6	8	9²	10	11				5¹	12	13																	3
	2	3	4	5		7	8	6³	10¹	11			14	12	9²	13	1																4
	2	3	4	7		6	8	9²	10¹	11	13		14	5³	12		1																5
	2	3	4	7		6	10¹	9²	8	11			13	5	12			1															6
	2		4	7¹	12	6	8	9²	10³	11			3	5		13		1	14														7
	2	3	4⁴	7	14	6		10²	8	11			15	5³	9¹			1		12	13												8
	2	4¹			7	6			8²	11³	9		3		14	10		1	12	13	5												9
	2	3	12	14	6³	7		9¹		11	10		4	5	13			1		8²													10
	2	3	4	7		6		8■		11	10²		12	5	9¹			1				13											11
	2	3	4	7		6			10³	11	8		14	5²	9¹			1		12			13										12
	2	3	4	7³	14	6	12		10	11	8²			5	9¹			1		13													13
	2	3	4	7	14	6¹	12	9²	10■	11			13	5				1		8³													14
	2	3	4	8¹	7	6	9²	13		10	11³			5	12	14		1															15
	2		4	7	6²	5	8	9¹	12	11			3		13	10³		1		14													16
	6		3	7	12	5	2³		14	11	8¹		4		9²	10		1		13													17
	6	3	4	7			5			11			2		10¹	9		1		8		12											18
	8	3	4	6			5	12		10	13		2		7²	11		1		9¹													19
	7¹	3	4	6			5	12		10³	14		2		9	11²		1		8				13									20
	7	3	4	6			8¹	12		11	13		2		9²	10		1		5													21
	6	3	4	7			8	13		10	14		2		9²	11³		1		5¹			12										22
		3	4	6	7¹		8	10		11³			2	12	9²			1		5		14	13										23
		3	4	6²	7		5	10		11			2	12	9¹			1	14	8³				13									24
	2	3	4	7	6¹		8	10		11		12		5	9		1																25
	6■	3	4	7			2	8		11	13	10¹		5²	9³		1						12		14								26
		3	4	7			10	6		11	12		2	5	9¹			1		8													27
	12	2	4	7	6		5	9¹		10	13			8				1		11²						3							28
	2		4	7¹	6		10	9		11				5²	13			1		8³						3	12	14					29
	2¹		4	7²	6		8	9³		11				5	10			1								3	12		13	14			30
			4		6³			14		11				5	9		1			8¹						3	10²	12	13	7	2		31
	6²		4	7	13					10³			3	5	11		1										9¹	14	12	8	2		32
	2		4	8¹	7³			13		10			3	5	11		1			9²							12	14		6			33
	2		4	14	7¹		6³	12		11			3	5	9		1										13		10²	8			34
	2			13	7		8	10¹		11			3	5	9²		1										12			6		4	35
	2				7		8³	13		10			3	5	9²	11¹	1										12	14		6		4	36
	2				7¹	14	12	6		10			3	5			1										11	9³	13	8		4²	37
	2			12	7	6¹	5²			11			3	4			1			13							9	14	10³	8			38
	2		14	8¹	6	7	5³			11			3	4			1			13							9²	10	12				39
	2¹				6	7²	12	13		11			3	5	9³	14	1									4	10	8					40
	2				7	12	5	14		11			3	4		9²	1									13	8³	10¹		6			41
	2			14	12	8	5²	7¹		11			3	4		10	1										9	13		6³			42
	2			14	7	9¹	12	8²		11			3	4		10	1										5	13		6³			43
	4¹		12	14	7³	6	5	8		11			2		13	10²	1									3		9					44
			4		7	8	9	14		11			2		12	10¹	1									3	13			6³	5²		45
				14	6	4	5	7		11²			2		9³	10¹	1									3	12	8		13			46

FA Cup

First Round	Mansfield T	(h)	0-1

Carabao Cup

First Round	Port Vale	(a)	2-1
Second Round	Blackpool	(a)	3-2
Third Round	Wigan Ath	(a)	2-0
Fourth Round	QPR	(a)	0-0
(Sunderland won 3-1 on penalties)			
Quarter-Final	Arsenal	(a)	1-5

Papa John's Trophy

Group F (N)	Lincoln C	(a)	2-1
Group F (N)	Manchester U U21	(h)	2-1
Group F (N)	Bradford C	(h)	1-1
(Bradford C won 4-2 on penalties)			
Second Round	Oldham Ath	(h)	0-1

League One Play-offs

Semi-Final 1st leg	Sheffield W	(h)	1-0
Semi-Final 2nd leg	Sheffield W	(a)	1-1
Final	Wycombe W	(Wembley)	2-0

SUTTON UNITED

FOUNDATION

The club was formed at a meeting held on 5 March 1898, when two local clubs who were both members of the Surrey Herald League, Sutton Guild Rovers and Sutton Association, agreed on a merger. The amber and chocolate colours of Sutton Association were chosen for the new organisation. Sutton United were members of the Surrey Junior League (1898–1905), and then the Southern Suburban League (1905–1921) before joining the Athenian League. In 1909–10 they reached the final of the Surrey Junior Cup and the divisional final of the London Junior Cup, and the following season became a senior club. They remained an amateur organisation until 1974 when the FA abolished amateur status.

VBS Community Stadium, Gander Green Lane, Sutton, Surrey SM1 2EY.

Telephone: (0208) 644 4440.

Ticket Office: (0208) 644 4440.

Website: www.suttonunited.net

Email: info@suttonunited.net

Ground Capacity: 4,877.

Record Attendance: 14,000 v Leeds U, FA Cup 4th rd, 24 January 1970.

Pitch Measurements: 100m × 67m (109.5yd × 73.5yd).

Chairman: Bruce Elliott.

Commercial Manager: Graham Baker.

Manager: Matt Gray.

Assistant Managers: Micky Stephens, Jason Goodliffe.

Colours: Amber shirts with chocolate trim, amber sorts with chocolate trim, amber socks with chocolate trim.

Year Formed: 1898.

Previous Names: Sutton Guild Rovers, Sutton Association.

Club Nickname: 'The U's'.

Grounds: Western Road, Manor Lane, London Road, The Find, Gander Green Lane (renamed The Knights Community Stadium 2017; The Borough Sports Ground 2020; VBS Community Stadium 2021).

HONOURS

League Champions: National League – 2020–21.

FA Cup: 5th rd – 2017.

League Cup: 1st rd – 2022.

League Trophy: *Runners-up:* 2022.

FA Trophy: *Runners-up:* 1981.

FA Amateur Cup: *Runners-up:* 1963, 1969.

Anglo Italian Cup Winners: 1979. *Runners-up:* 1980, 1982.

FOOTBALL YEARBOOK FACT FILE

Sutton United joined the Isthmian League for the 1963–64 season and soon afterwards floodlights were installed at their Gander Green Lane ground. These were first used for a friendly fixture against an Arsenal team on 17 October 1963, with the teams drawing 1-1. Scorer for the U's was Keith Blunt who went on to give the club useful service both as a player and a manager.

First Football League Game: 7 August 2021, FL 2, v Forest Green R (a) L 1–2 – Bouzanis; Barden, Milsom, Eastmond, Goodliffe, John, Ajiboye, Wilson (Bennett 82), Bugiel (1), Beautyman, Boldewijn (Korboa 76).

Record League Victory: 4–0 v Carlisle U (h), FL 2, 25 September 2021 – Bouzanis; Kizzi, Goodliffe, John, Milsom, Ajiboye (1), Eastmond, Smith (2), Boldewijn, Wilson (1) (Olaofe 66), Bennett (Bugiel 80).

Record Cup Victory: 7–0 v Wimbledon (h), FA Cup 1st qual. rd, 22 September 1945.

Record Defeat: 0–13 v Barking, Athenian League, 1925–26.

Most League Points (3 for a win): 76, FL 2, 2021–22.

Most League Goals: 69, FL 2, 2021–22.

Highest League Scorer in Season: David Ajiboye, Isaac Olaofe, Alistair Smith, 8, FL 2, 2021–22.

Most League Goals in Total Aggregate: David Ajiboye, Isaac Olaofe, Alistair Smith, 8, FL 2, 2021–22.

MANAGERS

George Smith 1956–58
Don Stoker 1959
Peter Molloy
Sid Cann 1962–73
Ted Powell
Larry Pritchard
Dario Gradi 1976–77
Keith Blunt 1977–79
Barrie Williams 1979–89
Keith Blunt 1989–91
Alan Gane 1991–96
Larry Pritchard & Ted Shepherd
John Rains 1996–2006
Ian Hazel 2006
Ernie Howe 2007–08
Paul Doswell 2008–19
Ian Baird 2019
Matt Gray May 2019–

Most League Goals in One Match: No one with more than 2 goals.

Most Capped Player: Omar Bugiel, 5 (10), Lebanon.

Most League Appearances: Dean Bouzanis, 44, 2021–22.

Youngest League Player: Kylian Kouassi, 18 years 260 days v Rochdale, 5 March 2022.

Record Transfer Fee Received: £100,000 from Bournemouth for Efan Ekoku, May 1990.

Record Transfer Fee Paid: Undisclosed to Malmo for Paul McKinnon, 1983.

Football League Record: 2021 Promoted to FL 2.

LATEST SEQUENCES

Longest Sequence of League Wins: 4, 25.9.2021 – 16.10.2021.

Longest Sequence of League Defeats: 2, 12.3.2022 – 15.3.2022.

Longest Sequence of League Draws: 3, 5.2.2022 – 12.2.2022.

Longest Sequence of Unbeaten League Matches: 10, 11.12.2021 – 12.2.2022.

Longest Sequence Without a League Win: 5, 5.2.2022 – 19.2.2022.

Successive Scoring Runs: 10 from 13.11.2021.

Successive Non-scoring Runs: 1 from 23.4.2022.

TEN YEAR LEAGUE RECORD

		P	W	D	L	F	A	Pts	Pos
2012–13	ConfS	42	20	10	12	66	49	70	6
2013–14	ConfS	42	23	12	7	77	39	81	2
2014–15	ConfS	40	13	11	16	50	54	50	15
2015–16	NLS	42	26	12	4	83	32	90	1
2016–17	NL	46	15	13	18	61	63	58	12
2017–18	NL	46	23	10	13	67	53	79	3
2018–19	NL	46	17	14	15	55	60	65	10
2019–20	NL	38	12	14	12	47	42	50	15
2020–21	NL	42	25	9	8	72	36	84	1
2021-22	FL 2	46	22	10	14	69	53	76	8

DID YOU KNOW ?

Sutton United took part in the FA Amateur Cup every season from 1910–11 through to the final year of the competition in 1973–74, with the exception of 1914–15, when many clubs withdrew due to the First World War. The U's first-ever game in the competition was a second qualifying-round tie away to Redhill on 22 October 1910 when they went down to a 1-0 defeat.

SUTTON UNITED – SKY BET LEAGUE TWO 2021–22 LEAGUE RECORD

Match No.	*Date*	*Venue*	*Opponents*	*Result*		*H/T Score*	*Lg Pos.*	*Goalscorers*	*Attendance*
1	Aug 7	A	Forest Green R	L	1-2	0-1	17	Bugiel [69]	1883
2	14	A	Salford C	D	0-0	0-0	16		1460
3	21	A	Scunthorpe U	D	1-1	0-0	21	Wilson [84]	2429
4	28	H	Oldham Ath	L	1-2	0-0	24	Ajiboye [62]	3262
5	Sept 11	H	Stevenage	W	2-1	0-0	23	Bennett 2 (1 pen) [58, 63 (p)]	2427
6	14	H	Hartlepool U	W	1-0	1-0	15	Goodliffe [25]	2484
7	18	A	Exeter C	L	0-2	0-0	18		4511
8	25	H	Carlisle U	W	4-0	2-0	14	Wilson [3], Smith 2 [37, 70], Ajiboye [81]	2873
9	Oct 2	A	Northampton T	W	2-0	1-0	11	Kizzi [41], Wilson [46]	4789
10	9	H	Port Vale	W	4-3	1-2	7	Milsom [36], Garrity (og) [69], Randall [87], Rowe [90]	3905
11	16	A	Crawley T	W	1-0	0-0	5	Olaofe [84]	3572
12	19	H	Swindon T	L	1-2	1-2	8	Beautyman (pen) [39]	3443
13	23	A	Rochdale	L	2-3	0-1	10	Olaofe [82], Smith [90]	2248
14	26	A	Colchester U	W	3-1	2-1	6	Ajiboye [12], Milsom (pen) [28], Goodliffe [61]	3013
15	30	H	Walsall	L	0-1	0-0	9		3319
16	Nov 13	A	Tranmere R	W	1-0	0-0	8	Olaofe [71]	6452
17	20	A	Leyton Orient	L	1-4	1-1	9	Olaofe [18]	5840
18	23	H	Mansfield T	W	2-0	1-0	7	John [4], Bugiel [69]	2497
19	27	H	Barrow	W	1-0	1-0	6	Ajiboye [16]	2678
20	Dec 7	A	Newport Co	L	2-3	2-0	6	Ajiboye 2 [24, 42]	3368
21	11	A	Bradford C	D	2-2	1-1	6	Milsom (pen) [32], Smith [76]	14,658
22	18	H	Harrogate T	W	1-0	1-0	3	Wilson [30]	2720
23	Jan 1	H	Exeter C	W	2-1	1-1	3	Bugiel [8], Milsom (pen) [89]	3278
24	15	A	Stevenage	D	3-3	0-2	5	Smith [58], Milsom (pen) [66], Bennett [90]	2961
25	18	H	Colchester U	W	3-2	1-2	3	Olaofe 2 [9, 64], Randall [90]	2532
26	22	H	Northampton T	D	0-0	0-0	3		3588
27	29	A	Carlisle U	W	2-0	2-0	4	Olaofe [23], Ajiboye [31]	4399
28	Feb 5	H	Bristol R	D	1-1	1-0	3	Bennett [19]	3394
29	8	H	Salford C	D	0-0	0-0	4		2491
30	12	H	Forest Green R	D	1-1	1-0	5	Davis [37]	3314
31	15	A	Bristol R	L	0-2	0-1	5		6700
32	19	A	Hartlepool U	D	1-1	1-0	5	Kizzi [3]	5487
33	26	H	Scunthorpe U	W	4-1	3-0	5	Milsom (pen) [29], Randall 2 [30, 62], Kizzi [39]	2870
34	Mar 5	H	Rochdale	W	3-0	2-0	3	Boldewijn 2 [12, 45], Kizzi [57]	2874
35	12	A	Walsall	L	0-1	0-1	7		5801
36	15	A	Swindon T	L	1-2	1-1	8	Kizzi [28]	8243
37	19	H	Tranmere R	D	1-1	1-0	9	Goodliffe [15]	3366
38	22	A	Oldham Ath	W	3-1	1-0	8	Korboa 2 [20, 49], Beautyman (pen) [77]	4624
39	26	A	Port Vale	L	0-2	0-2	10		6362
40	Apr 9	H	Leyton Orient	W	1-0	1-0	10	Kizzi [20]	3152
41	15	A	Mansfield T	W	3-2	1-0	7	Bugiel [9], Ajiboye [49], Bennett [80]	6134
42	18	H	Newport Co	W	1-0	1-0	6	Milsom (pen) [45]	3447
43	23	A	Barrow	L	0-1	0-0	7		3019
44	26	H	Crawley T	W	3-0	2-0	7	Smith 2 [4, 85], Bennett [7]	3109
45	30	H	Bradford C	L	1-4	0-1	8	Smith [55]	4010
46	May 7	A	Harrogate T	W	2-0	1-0	8	Eastmond [8], Olaofe [78]	2484

Final League Position: 8

GOALSCORERS

League (69): Ajiboye 8, Olaofe 8, Smith 8, Milsom 7 (6 pens), Bennett 6 (1 pen), Kizzi 6, Bugiel 4, Randall 4, Wilson 4, Goodliffe 3, Beautyman 2 (2 pens), Boldewijn 2, Korboa 2, Davis 1, Eastmond 1, John 1, Rowe 1, own goal 1.
FA Cup (2): Randall 2.
Carabao Cup (2): Rowe 1, Wilson 1.
Papa John's Trophy (12): Wilson 3, Eastmond 2, John 1, Korboa 1, Olaofe 1, Randall 1, Sho-Silva 1, Smith 1, own goal 1.

Bouzanis D 44	Goodliffe B 43	John L 36	Milsom R 37 + 1	Barden J 18 + 3	Beautyman H 12 + 7	Eastmond C 31	Boldewijn E 27 + 12	Ajiboye D 42 + 1	Bugiel O 27 + 12	Wilson D 23 + 15	Korboa R 3 + 11	Bennett R 22 + 16	Davis K 12 + 8	Smith A 28 + 5	Rowe C 12 + 3	Wyatt B 13 + 3	Sho-Silva O 4 + 3	Kizzi J 31 + 1	Randall W 18 + 10	Dundas C — + 4	Olaofe I 18 + 9	Kouassi K — + 4	Nelson S 2	Lovatt A 3	*Match No.*
1	2	3	4	5	6	7	8^1	9	10	11^2	12	13													1
1	3	4	5	2	9	8	12	6	11^2	10^1		13	7^3	14											2
1	3			2	9	8	12	6^2	11^3	10	13		7^1	14	4	5									3
1	3	4	5^1	2	8	7	9^2	6	11	10^3	14			13		12									4
1	3	4	5	2^1		7	6	9				11^3		8			10^2	12	13	14					5
1	3	4	5			7	9	6	12	13		11^1		8			10^2	2							6
1	3	4	5		14	7	9^2	6		12		10		8^3			11^1	2	13						7
1	3^3	4	5			7	9	6	13	10^1		11^2		8	14			2			12				8
1	3	4	5		14	7	9	6^2	12	10^3		11^1		8				2	13						9
1		4	5			7	9^3	6^2		11^1	14	10		8	3			2	13		12				10
1		4	5		7		9	6^3	13	10^1		11^2		8	3			2	14		12				11
1	3	4		13	7^2			6	11^3	12		14		8		5		2	9		10^1				12
1	3	4^1	5	7			6^3		14	10^2		11▪		8	12			2	9		13				13
1	3		5	7^3			9	6	11^2	12			14	8	4		13	2			10^1				14
1	3		8				12	6	11^3	13				7	4	5	14	2	9^1		10^2				15
1	3		5			7^3		6		12		11^2	14	8	4			2	9	13	10^1				16
1	3	4	5	13		7		6^3	12	14		11^1		8				2^2	9		10				17
1	3	4	5	2		7		6	11^2	12	9^3	13		8					14		10^1				18
1	3	4	5	2		7		6	11^1	13		12	8						9		10^2				19
1	3		8	2		4▪	12	9	11	10^2		13	7^1			5			6						20
1	3	4	8	2			13	6^2	10^3	11	12	14		7		5			9^1						21
1	3	4	8	2			14	6^3	11^1	10^2		12		7		5			9		13				22
1	3	4	5	8^2			6		11^1	10		12	14	7		13		2			9^3				23
1	4	3	5	2		8^3		6		10^2		12	14	7			11^1		13		9				24
1	4	3	5			8	6^2		10^1	14	13	12		7				2	9		11^3				25
1	3	4	5			8▪	12	6^1	11^3			14	13	7				2	9		10^2				26
1	3	4	5			8	9^3	6		12	14	11^2		7			13	2			10^1				27
1	3	4	5			8	9	6	12	13		11^1	7					2			10^2				28
1	3	4	5	7		8^1	9	6	11^3	10^2		14				12		2			13				29
1	3	4		14			13	6	12	10		11^1	7	8^3		5		2	9^2						30
1	3				12		9	6	11	10^3	14		7^1	8	4^2	5		2	13						31
1	3	4	5		13	7^3	12	6^1	11	10^2			14	8				2	9						32
1	3	4^1	5		13	8^2		6^3	11	10	14		7		12			2	9						33
1	3	4	5		12	7	9^3	6	10^2		14	11	8^1					2				13			34
	3		13		8^2	7	6	14	12	10^1	9^3	11			4	5		2					1		35
	3^2						11	6	8			10^1			4	5		2	9	13		12	1	7	36
1	3					8^2	9	6	10		12	11^1	13		4	5		2						7	37
1	3				12		2	6	10^2		9	11^3	7^1		4	5				13		14		8	38
1	3	4			8	7	9	6^2	11^3	10^1		14				5		2	13		12				39
1		3	5		7^2	8	9	6	12			11^1		13	4			2			10				40
1	3	4	5		7^3	8	9	6	11^1	13		12	14					2			10^2				41
1	3	4	5	2		8^1	9	6	13			11^2	7	12							10				42
1	3	4	5				9^1	6	11	13		14	7^3	8				2	12		10^2				43
1	3	4	5	2^3	7		13	6		10^1		11		8					9^2		12	14			44
1	3	4	5	2^2	7		14	6	12	10^3		11^1		8					9		13				45
1	3	4	5			7	12	6^2	10	13				8				2	9^1		11				46

FA Cup

First Round	Hayes & Yeading U	(a)	1-0
Second Round	Bristol R	(a)	1-2

Carabao Cup

First Round	Cardiff C	(a)	2-3

Papa John's Trophy

Group B (S)	Crystal Palace U21	(h)	3-0
Group B (S)	Portsmouth	(a)	2-0
Group B (S)	AFC Wimbledon	(h)	1-0
Second Round	Stevenage	(h)	0-0
(Sutton U won 4-3 on penalties)			
Third Round	Colchester U	(h)	2-1
Quarter-Final	Harrogate T	(h)	1-0
Semi-Final	Wigan Ath	(a)	1-1
(Sutton U won 7-6 on penalties)			
Final	Rotherham U	(Wembley)	2-4
(aet)			

SWANSEA CITY

FOUNDATION

The earliest Association Football in Wales was played in the northern part of the country and no international took place in the south until 1894, when a local paper still thought it necessary to publish an outline of the rules and an illustration of the pitch markings. There had been an earlier Swansea club, but this has no connection with Swansea Town (now City) formed at a public meeting in June 1912.

Liberty Stadium, Morfa, Landore, Swansea SA1 2FA.

Telephone: (01792) 616 400.

Ticket Office: (01792) 616 400.

Website: www.swanseacity.com

Email: support@swanseacity.com

Ground Capacity: 20,996.

Record Attendance: 32,796 v Arsenal, FA Cup 4th rd, 17 February 1968 (at Vetch Field); 20,972 v Liverpool, Premier League, 1 May 2016 (at Liberty Stadium).

Pitch Measurements: 105m × 68m (115yd × 74.5yd).

Chief Executive: Julian Winter.

Head Coach: Russell Martin.

Assistant First-Team Coach: Luke Williams.

Colours: White shirts with black trim, white shorts with black trim, white socks with black trim.

Year Formed: 1912.

Turned Professional: 1912.

Previous Name: 1912, Swansea Town; 1970, Swansea City.

Club Nicknames: 'The Swans', 'The Jacks'.

Grounds: 1912, Vetch Field; 2005, Liberty Stadium.

First Football League Game: 28 August 1920, Division 3, v Portsmouth (a) L 0–3 – Crumley; Robson, Evans; Smith, Holdsworth, Williams; Hole, Ivor Jones, Edmundson, Rigsby, Spottiswood.

Record League Victory: 8–0 v Hartlepool U, Division 4, 1 April 1978 – Barber; Evans, Bartley, Lally (1) (Morris), May, Bruton, Kevin Moore, Robbie James (3 incl. 1p), Curtis (3), Toshack (1), Chappell.

Record Cup Victory: 12–0 v Sliema W (Malta), ECWC 1st rd 1st leg, 15 September 1982 – Davies; Marustik, Hadziabdic (1), Irwin (1), Kennedy, Rajkovic (1), Loveridge (2) (Leighton James), Robbie James, Charles (2), Stevenson (1), Latchford (1) (Walsh (3)).

Record Defeat: 0–8 v Liverpool, FA Cup 3rd rd, 9 January 1990; 0–8 v Monaco, ECWC, 1st rd 2nd leg, 1 October 1991.

Most League Points (2 for a win): 62, Division 3 (S), 1948–49.

Most League Points (3 for a win): 92, FL 1, 2007–08.

Most League Goals: 90, Division 2, 1956–57.

HONOURS

League Champions: FL 1 – 2007–08; Division 3S – 1924–25, 1948–49; Third Division – 1999–2000.

FA Cup: semi-final – 1926, 1964.

League Cup Winners: 2013.

League Trophy Winners: 1994, 2006.

Welsh Cup Winners: 10 times; *Runners-up:* 8 times.

European Competitions
Europa League: 2013–14.
European Cup-Winners' Cup: 1961–62, 1966–67, 1981–82, 1982–83, 1983–84, 1989–90, 1991–92.

FOOTBALL YEARBOOK FACT FILE

Swansea City fielded a full team of players born in Wales in a Football League game for the first time on 14 December 1957 in the home match with Bristol City. Eight of the players were born in Swansea and another in nearby Morriston, testament to the club's very successful youth development programme in the 1950s.

Highest League Scorer in Season: Cyril Pearce, 35, Division 2, 1931–32.

Most League Goals in Total Aggregate: Ivor Allchurch, 166, 1949–58, 1965–68.

Most League Goals in One Match: 5, Jack Fowler v Charlton Ath, Division 3S, 27 December 1924.

Most Capped Player: Ashley Williams, 64 (86), Wales.

Most League Appearances: Wilfred Milne, 587, 1919–37.

Youngest League Player: Nigel Dalling, 15 years 289 days v Southport, 6 December 1974.

Record Transfer Fee Received: £40,000,000 (rising to £45,000,000) from Everton for Gylfi Sigurdsson, August 2017.

Record Transfer Fee Paid: £18,000,000 to West Ham U for André Ayew, January 2018.

Football League Record: 1920 Original Member of Division 3; 1921–25 Division 3 (S); 1925–47 Division 2; 1947–49 Division 3 (S); 1949–65 Division 2; 1965–67 Division 3; 1967–70 Division 4; 1970–73 Division 3; 1973–78 Division 4; 1978–79 Division 3; 1979–81 Division 2; 1981–83 Division 1; 1983–84 Division 2; 1984–86 Division 3; 1986–88 Division 4; 1988–92 Division 3; 1992–96 Division 2; 1996–2000 Division 3; 2000–01 Division 2; 2001–04 Division 3; 2004–05 FL 2; 2005–08 FL 1; 2008–11 FL C; 2011–18 Premier League; 2018– FL C.

LATEST SEQUENCES

Longest Sequence of League Wins: 9, 27.11.1999 – 22.1.2000.

Longest Sequence of League Defeats: 9, 26.1.1991 – 19.3.1991.

Longest Sequence of League Draws: 8, 25.11.2008 – 28.12.2008.

Longest Sequence of Unbeaten League Matches: 19, 19.10.1970 – 9.3.1971.

Longest Sequence Without a League Win: 15, 25.3.1989 – 2.9.1989.

Successive Scoring Runs: 27 from 28.8.1947.

Successive Non-scoring Runs: 6 from 6.2.1996.

MANAGERS

Walter Whittaker 1912–14
William Bartlett 1914–15
Joe Bradshaw 1919–26
Jimmy Thomson 1927–31
Neil Harris 1934–39
Haydn Green 1939–47
Bill McCandless 1947–55
Ron Burgess 1955–58
Trevor Morris 1958–65
Glyn Davies 1965–66
Billy Lucas 1967–69
Roy Bentley 1969–72
Harry Gregg 1972–75
Harry Griffiths 1975–77
John Toshack 1978–83 *(resigned October re-appointed in December)* 1983–84
Colin Appleton 1984
John Bond 1984–85
Tommy Hutchison 1985–86
Terry Yorath 1986–89
Ian Evans 1989–90
Terry Yorath 1990–91
Frank Burrows 1991–95
Bobby Smith 1995
Kevin Cullis 1996
Jan Molby 1996–97
Micky Adams 1997
Alan Cork 1997–98
John Hollins 1998–2001
Colin Addison 2001–02
Nick Cusack 2002
Brian Flynn 2002–04
Kenny Jackett 2004–07
Roberto Martinez 2007–09
Paulo Sousa 2009–10
Brendan Rodgers 2010–12
Michael Laudrup 2012–14
Garry Monk 2014–15
Francesco Guidolin 2016
Bob Bradley 2016
Paul Clement 2017
Carlos Carvalhal 2017–18
Graham Potter 2018–19
Steve Cooper 2019–21
Russell Martin August 2021–

TEN YEAR LEAGUE RECORD

		P	*W*	*D*	*L*	*F*	*A*	*Pts*	*Pos*
2012-13	PR Lge	38	11	13	14	47	51	46	9
2013-14	PR Lge	38	11	9	18	54	54	42	12
2014-15	PR Lge	38	16	8	14	46	49	56	8
2015-16	PR Lge	38	12	11	15	42	52	47	12
2016-17	PR Lge	38	12	5	21	45	70	41	15
2017-18	PR Lge	38	8	9	21	28	56	33	18
2018-19	FL C	46	18	11	17	65	62	65	10
2019-20	FL C	46	18	16	12	62	53	70	6
2020-21	FL C	46	23	11	12	56	39	80	4
2021-22	FL C	46	16	13	17	58	68	61	15

DID YOU KNOW?

Swansea City made a sensational entry to top-flight football, defeating Leeds United 5-1 on 29 August 1981, with Bob Latchford netting a hat-trick. The Swans also won their second game, 2-1 away to Brighton, and briefly headed the Football League table before dropping back to finish in sixth position.

SWANSEA CITY – SKY BET CHAMPIONSHIP 2021–22 LEAGUE RECORD

Match No.	Date	Venue	Opponents	Result		H/T Score	Lg Pos.	Goalscorers	Attendance
1	Aug 7	A	Blackburn R	L	1-2	0-1	21	Paterson [52]	10,260
2	14	H	Sheffield U	D	0-0	0-0	19		15,946
3	17	H	Stoke C	L	1-3	0-1	21	Piroe [73]	15,927
4	20	A	Bristol C	W	1-0	1-0	16	Piroe [19]	20,139
5	28	A	Preston NE	L	1-3	1-2	19	Piroe [19]	10,180
6	Sept 11	H	Hull C	D	0-0	0-0	21		16,317
7	15	H	Millwall	D	0-0	0-0	20		16,007
8	18	A	Luton T	D	3-3	0-3	21	Paterson [63], Ntcham [86], Piroe [90]	9721
9	25	H	Huddersfield T	W	1-0	1-0	17	Piroe [17]	17,091
10	29	A	Fulham	L	1-3	1-3	19	Paterson [38]	16,113
11	Oct 2	A	Derby Co	D	0-0	0-0	19		21,640
12	17	H	Cardiff C	W	3-0	1-0	17	Paterson [29], Piroe [60], Bidwell [74]	19,288
13	20	H	WBA	W	2-1	0-1	15	Piroe [61], Paterson [83]	16,694
14	23	A	Birmingham C	L	1-2	0-0	15	Obafemi [77]	16,132
15	30	H	Peterborough U	W	3-0	3-0	13	Bidwell [2], Piroe [13], Ntcham [45]	16,639
16	Nov 2	A	Coventry C	W	2-1	2-1	10	Paterson [5], Piroe [12]	16,514
17	6	A	Bournemouth	L	0-4	0-1	12		9725
18	20	H	Blackpool	D	1-1	1-0	12	Piroe [35]	16,886
19	24	A	Barnsley	W	2-0	0-0	9	Ntcham [74], Paterson [79]	11,342
20	27	H	Reading	L	2-3	1-2	9	Paterson [3], Manning [49]	16,980
21	Dec 4	A	Middlesbrough	L	0-1	0-1	14		18,707
22	11	H	Nottingham F	L	1-4	0-0	16	Piroe [62]	17,659
23	Jan 15	A	Huddersfield T	D	1-1	0-1	17	Downes [78]	20,535
24	22	H	Preston NE	W	1-0	0-0	17	Manning [51]	16,842
25	25	A	QPR	D	0-0	0-0	17		12,770
26	29	A	Hull C	L	0-2	0-2	17		13,101
27	Feb 1	H	Luton T	L	0-1	0-0	19		16,598
28	5	H	Blackburn R	W	1-0	1-0	16	Obafemi [16]	16,933
29	8	A	Stoke C	L	0-3	0-0	16		17,720
30	13	H	Bristol C	W	3-1	0-1	16	Obafemi [54], Christie [79], Piroe [90]	19,162
31	19	A	Sheffield U	L	0-4	0-3	17		26,564
32	28	A	WBA	W	2-0	0-0	16	Piroe [79], Christie [84]	20,209
33	Mar 5	H	Coventry C	W	3-1	2-0	16	Paterson [12], Obafemi 2 [40, 48]	18,405
34	8	H	Fulham	L	1-5	0-0	16	Piroe [75]	17,012
35	12	A	Blackpool	L	0-1	0-1	16		12,344
36	16	A	Peterborough U	W	3-2	1-0	15	Obafemi 2 [44, 71], Piroe [90]	6832
37	19	H	Birmingham C	D	0-0	0-0	16		18,620
38	Apr 2	A	Cardiff C	W	4-0	1-0	16	Obafemi 2 [6, 82], Cabango [57], Wolf [78]	27,280
39	5	A	Millwall	W	1-0	0-0	14	Piroe [46]	11,670
40	9	H	Derby Co	W	2-1	2-1	13	Piroe 2 [8, 16]	18,374
41	15	H	Barnsley	D	1-1	0-0	14	Ntcham [64]	17,923
42	18	A	Reading	D	4-4	3-1	13	Wolf [6], Piroe 2 (1 pen) [12, 45 (p)], Obafemi [58]	14,335
43	23	H	Middlesbrough	D	1-1	0-0	14	Obafemi [48]	18,246
44	26	H	Bournemouth	D	3-3	2-0	14	Piroe 2 [5, 12], Christie [58]	17,780
45	30	A	Nottingham F	L	1-5	1-1	15	Obafemi [28]	28,659
46	May 7	H	QPR	L	0-1	0-0	15		18,608

Final League Position: 15

GOALSCORERS

League (58): Piroe 22 (1 pen), Obafemi 12, Paterson 9, Ntcham 4, Christie 3, Bidwell 2, Manning 2, Wolf 2, Cabango 1, Downes 1.
FA Cup (2): Piroe 1, own goal 1.
Carabao Cup (7): Whittaker 3, Cabango 1, Latibeaudiere 1, Lowe 1, Piroe 1.

Benda S 5	Cabango B 34+3	Bennett R 16+2	Latibeaudiere J 21+8	Naughton K 37+1	Paterson J 33+5	Grimes M 46	Bidwell J 16	Smith K 21+14	Cullen L 4+8	Lowe J 3+2	Dhanda Y 1+2	Whittaker M —+6	Cooper B 3+1	Manning R 34+4	Downes F 34+3	Piroe J 40+5	Fulton J 8+10	Laird E 18+2	Hamer B 21	Williams R 4+1	Ntcham J 20+17	Obafemi M 20+12	Walsh L 1+4	Christie C 23	Joseph K —+10	Wolf H 18+1	Fisher A 20	Burns F 3	Ogbeta N —+2	Congreve C 2+3	Match No.
1	2	3	4	5	6	7	8	9^1	10^2	11	12	13																			1
1	2		5		10^3	7	8		9^2	11^1	14	13	3	4	6	12															2
1	2		5^2		14	7	8			11	10^1		3	4	6	12	9^3	13													3
1			2		10	7	8		9^1	13		12	4	3		11^2	6	5													4
1		3^2	2^1	13	10	7	8		9	14			12	4		11	6^3	5													5
	14	2		3^3	11	7	8^2							12	6	10		5	1	4	9^1	13									6
	4	2		3	10^2	7			14					8	6	11^3		5	1		9^1	12	13								7
	12	2		3	10	7								8	6^1	13		5	1	4^2	14	11	9^3								8
	2			3	10^1	7	8	13	12					4	6	11^2	14	5	1		9^3										9
	2		14	3	10	7	8^3	12	13					4	6^2	11		5	1		9^1										10
	2		5^1	3	10	7	8	9^3	13			14		4	6	11^2		12	1												11
	13	2^2		3	10	7	8	9^1	14					4	6	11^3		5	1		12										12
	4^3	2	14	3	10	7	8^2	9							6^1	11		5	1	13	12										13
		2	8	3	10	6		7^1	14					4		11^3		5	1		9^2	12	13								14
		2		3	10	7	8	6				14		4	13	11^1		5^3	1		9^2	12									15
		2		3	10	7	8	6						4	13	11^2		5	1		9^1	12									16
		2		3	10	6	8^2	12				13		4	7^1	11		5	1		9^3		14								17
	2			3	10	6	8	13						4	7	11^1		5	1		9^2	12									18
	4	2		3	10	6	8^2	9	14					13	7^1	11^3		5	1		12										19
		2^2		3	10	6		9^1	13					8	12	11		5	1	4	7										20
	2		14	3	10	6		9^1						8	7	11		5^3	1	4^2	12	13									21
	4	2	12		10	6		7^2						8	3	11		5^1	1		9	13									22
	2		8	3		7		9						4	6	10			1		11^2	12		5^1	13						23
	2		8	3		7		9						4	6	11^2	14		1		10^1			5^3	13	12					24
	2		8	3		7		9						4	6■	11^1	13		1			12		5		10^2					25
	2		8	3		7		9^3						4		11	6^2		1		13	12	14	5		10^1					26
	4	3^3		2^1		7		12						8	6^2	13					9	11		5	14	10	1				27
	2	12	14		8	5		13						4■	3	11^3					7^2	10^1		6		9	1				28
	4	2■			14	6		7^1							3	12	8				10^3	11		5^2	13	9	1				29
	3		13		10^3	7		14						4	6	9					12	11^2		5		8	1	2^1			30
	3		8		10	7		13						4	6	11^2					9^1	12		5			1	2			31
	2			3	10^1	7		13						4	6	9^3					12	11^2		8	14	5	1				32
	2		13	3	10^1	7		8^3						4	6	9	14				12	11^2		5			1				33
	3	12		4	9	8		2						5■	7^2	10	13				6^1	11^3			14		1				34
	3			4	10	7		5^1							6	9					8^2	11		2			1		12	13	35
	4			3	8^3	5		7^1							2	11	14				12	10^2		6	13	9	1				36
	4		12	3		5		8^2								11					7	10		6	14	9^3	1	2^1	13		37
	2		4	3	10^1	6		13							7	9^3	12					11^2		5		8	1			14	38
	2		4	3	13	6		14						8		9^2	7^3				12	11		5		10^1	1				39
	2		4	3	10^1	7		13								9^2	6				12	11^3		5	14	8	1				40
	2		4^2	3	10^3	7								13		9	6^1				12	11		5		8	1			14	41
	2		4	3	10^2	6								14	7^1	9^3	12				13	11		5		8	1				42
	2		4	3		6								8^1	7	9					12	11		5		10	1				43
	3^1		2	4		7		12						5	6	9^3	13					11		8	14	10^2	1				44
			3	4	13	6								5^1	7	9^3	14				12	11		2		10	1			8^2	45
			3^3	4	13	6		14						5	7	9^2					12	11		2		10	1			8^1	46

FA Cup

Third Round *(aet)*	Southampton	(h)	2-3

Carabao Cup

First Round	Reading	(a)	3-0
Second Round	Plymouth Arg	(h)	4-1
Third Round	Brighton & HA	(a)	0-2

SWINDON TOWN

FOUNDATION

It is generally accepted that Swindon Town came into being in 1881, although there is no firm evidence that the club's founder, Rev. William Pitt, captain of the Spartans (an offshoot of a cricket club), changed his club's name to Swindon Town before 1883, when the Spartans amalgamated with St Mark's Young Men's Friendly Society.

The Energy Check County Ground, County Road, Swindon, Wiltshire SN1 2ED.

Telephone: (0330) 002 1879.

Ticket Office: (0330) 002 1879.

Website: www.swindontownfc.co.uk

Email: enquiries@swindontownfc.co.uk

Ground Capacity: 15,547.

Record Attendance: 32,000 v Arsenal, FA Cup 3rd rd, 15 January 1972.

Pitch Measurements: 100m × 66m (109.5yd × 72yd).

Chairman: Clem Morfuni.

Chief Executive: Robert Angus.

Head Coach: Scott Lindsey.

Assistant Coach: Jamie Day.

Colours: Red shirts with thin white stripes, white shorts, red socks.

Year Formed: 1881* (*see Foundation*).

Turned Professional: 1894.

Club Nickname: 'The Robins'.

Grounds: 1881, The Croft; 1896, County Ground (renamed The Energy Check County Ground 2017).

First Football League Game: 28 August 1920, Division 3, v Luton T (h) W 9–1 – Nash; Kay, Macconachie; Langford, Hawley, Wareing; Jefferson (1), Fleming (4), Rogers, Batty (2), Davies (1), (1 og).

Record League Victory: 9–1 v Luton T, Division 3 (S), 28 August 1920 – Nash; Kay, Macconachie; Langford, Hawley, Wareing; Jefferson (1), Fleming (4), Rogers, Batty (2), Davies (1), (1 og).

Record Cup Victory: 10–1 v Farnham U Breweries (a), FA Cup 1st rd (replay), 28 November 1925 – Nash; Dickenson, Weston, Archer, Bew, Adey; Denyer (2), Wall (1), Richardson (4), Johnson (3), Davies.

Record Defeat: 1–10 v Manchester C, FA Cup 4th rd (replay), 25 January 1930.

Most League Points (2 for a win): 64, Division 3, 1968–69.

Most League Points (3 for a win): 102, Division 4, 1985–86.

HONOURS

League Champions: Second Division – 1995–96; FL 2 – 2011–12, 2019–20; Division 4 – 1985–86.
Runners-up: Division 3 – 1962–63, 1968–69.

FA Cup: semi-final – 1910, 1912.

League Cup Winners: 1969.

League Trophy: *Runners-up:* 2012.

Anglo-Italian Cup Winners: 1970.

FOOTBALL YEARBOOK FACT FILE

A total of five Swindon Town players have scored hat-tricks on their Football League debut for the club including Harold Fleming who netted four in the club's first-ever fixture in the competition. The most recent to achieve this feat was Sam Parkin, who did so in the 3-1 home win over Barnsley in August 2002.

Most League Goals: 100, Division 3 (S), 1926–27.

Highest League Scorer in Season: Harry Morris, 47, Division 3 (S), 1926–27.

Most League Goals in Total Aggregate: Harry Morris, 216, 1926–33.

Most League Goals in One Match: 5, Harry Morris v QPR, Division 3 (S), 18 December 1926; 5, Harry Morris v Norwich C, Division 3 (S), 26 April 1930; 5, Keith East v Mansfield T, Division 3, 20 November 1965.

Most Capped Player: Rod Thomas, 30 (50), Wales.

Most League Appearances: John Trollope, 770, 1960–80.

Youngest League Player: Paul Rideout, 16 years 107 days v Hull C, 29 November 1980.

Record Transfer Fee Received: A combined £4,000,000 from QPR for Ben Gladwin and Massimo Luongo, May 2015.

Record Transfer Fee Paid: £800,000 to West Ham U for Joey Beauchamp, August 1994.

Football League Record: 1920 Original Member of Division 3; 1921–58 Division 3 (S); 1958–63 Division 3; 1963–65 Division 2; 1965–69 Division 3; 1969–74 Division 2; 1974–82 Division 3; 1982–86 Division 4; 1986–87 Division 3; 1987–92 Division 2; 1992–93 Division 1; 1993–94 Premier League; 1994–95 Division 1; 1995–96 Division 2; 1996–2000 Division 1; 2000–04 Division 2; 2004–06 FL 1; 2006–07 FL 2; 2007–11 FL 1; 2011–12 FL 2; 2012–17 FL 1; 2017–20 FL 2; 2020–21 FL 1; 2021– FL 2.

LATEST SEQUENCES

Longest Sequence of League Wins: 10, 31.12.2011 – 28.2.2012.

Longest Sequence of League Defeats: 8, 29.8.2005 – 8.10.2005.

Longest Sequence of League Draws: 6, 22.11.1991 – 28.12.1991.

Longest Sequence of Unbeaten League Matches: 22, 12.1.1986 – 23.8.1986.

Longest Sequence Without a League Win: 19, 30.10.1999 – 4.3.2000.

Successive Scoring Runs: 31 from 17.4.1926.

Successive Non-scoring Runs: 5 from 5.4.1997.

MANAGERS

Sam Allen 1902–33
Ted Vizard 1933–39
Neil Harris 1939–41
Louis Page 1945–53
Maurice Lindley 1953–55
Bert Head 1956–65
Danny Williams 1965–69
Fred Ford 1969–71
Dave Mackay 1971–72
Les Allen 1972–74
Danny Williams 1974–78
Bobby Smith 1978–80
John Trollope 1980–83
Ken Beamish 1983–84
Lou Macari 1984–89
Ossie Ardiles 1989–91
Glenn Hoddle 1991–93
John Gorman 1993–94
Steve McMahon 1994–98
Jimmy Quinn 1998–2000
Colin Todd 2000
Andy King 2000–01
Roy Evans 2001
Andy King 2001–05
Iffy Onuora 2005–06
Dennis Wise 2006
Paul Sturrock 2006–07
Maurice Malpas 2008
Danny Wilson 2008–11
Paul Hart 2011
Paolo Di Canio 2011–13
Kevin MacDonald 2013
Mark Cooper 2013–15
Martin Ling 2015
Luke Williams 2015–17
David Flitcroft 2017–18
Phil Brown 2018
Richie Wellens 2018–20
John Sheridan 2020–21
John McGreal 2021
Ben Garner 2021–22
Scott Lindsey June 2022–

TEN YEAR LEAGUE RECORD

		P	W	D	L	F	A	Pts	Pos
2012-13	FL 1	46	20	14	12	72	39	74	6
2013-14	FL 1	46	19	9	18	63	59	66	8
2014-15	FL 1	46	23	10	13	76	57	79	4
2015-16	FL 1	46	16	11	19	64	71	59	15
2016-17	FL 1	46	11	11	24	44	66	44	22
2017-18	FL 2	46	20	8	18	67	65	68	9
2018-19	FL 2	46	16	16	14	59	56	64	13
2019-20	FL 2	36	21	6	9	62	39	69	1§
2020-21	FL 1	46	13	4	29	55	89	43	23
2021-22	FL 2	46	22	11	13	77	54	77	6

§Decided on points-per-game (1.92)

DID YOU KNOW ?

Inside-left Archie Bown achieved the remarkable feat of scoring all six goals for Swindon Town in their 6-0 defeat of Watford in a Southern League match in April 1915. Bown was a prolific scorer for the Robins in their non-league days, netting a career total of 142 goals from 291 appearances.

SWINDON TOWN – SKY BET LEAGUE TWO 2021–22 LEAGUE RECORD

Match No.	Date	Venue	Opponents	Result		H/T Score	Lg Pos.	Goalscorers	Attendance
1	Aug 7	A	Scunthorpe U	W	3-1	0-0	1	Payne (pen) [57], Gladwin [68], McKirdy [88]	3602
2	14	H	Carlisle U	L	1-2	1-2	9	Crichlow-Noble [30]	9450
3	17	H	Tranmere R	D	0-0	0-0	9		8274
4	21	A	Salford C	W	1-0	0-0	3	Payne [49]	2229
5	28	H	Mansfield T	W	1-0	0-0	4	Simpson [59]	8631
6	Sept 4	A	Stevenage	D	1-1	0-0	4	Payne (pen) [90]	3589
7	11	H	Port Vale	L	1-2	0-1	7	Simpson [49]	8734
8	18	A	Northampton T	D	1-1	0-0	10	Simpson [57]	5863
9	25	H	Colchester U	D	0-0	0-0	9		8436
10	Oct 2	A	Bristol R	W	3-1	0-1	5	Payne [57], Gladwin (pen) [85], McKirdy [87]	7625
11	9	A	Forest Green R	W	2-0	0-0	3	McKirdy [54], Simpson [81]	3442
12	16	H	Rochdale	D	2-2	1-0	6	Gladwin [37], Williams [90]	9310
13	19	A	Sutton U	W	2-1	2-1	3	Reed [17], Williams [31]	3443
14	23	H	Bradford C	L	1-3	0-2	6	Payne (pen) [78]	9461
15	30	A	Oldham Ath	W	3-1	1-0	5	McKirdy [32], Simpson 2 [79, 90]	4085
16	Nov 20	A	Newport Co	W	2-1	0-0	4	Azaz (og) [72], Payne [88]	5141
17	23	H	Hartlepool U	W	3-1	0-0	3	Williams [52], Simpson [69], Payne [90]	7714
18	27	H	Harrogate T	D	1-1	0-1	4	Payne (pen) [83]	8199
19	Dec 7	A	Leyton Orient	L	1-4	1-1	5	McKirdy [42]	4020
20	11	A	Barrow	L	0-2	0-0	7		2863
21	29	H	Stevenage	D	0-0	0-0	7		8131
22	Jan 1	H	Northampton T	W	5-2	1-1	5	McKirdy 4 [28, 51, 55, 66], Simpson [60]	9071
23	11	A	Mansfield T	L	2-3	1-3	5	McKirdy [28], Iandolo [89]	4129
24	15	A	Port Vale	W	3-1	2-1	4	Williams [20], Gladwin (pen) [45], McKirdy [69]	6064
25	22	H	Bristol R	D	1-1	1-1	6	Simpson [16]	12,695
26	29	A	Colchester U	D	1-1	0-0	7	McKirdy [68]	3327
27	Feb 1	H	Crawley T	D	1-1	0-1	7	Gladwin [90]	7306
28	5	H	Exeter C	L	1-2	0-0	8	Tomlinson [58]	10,642
29	8	A	Tranmere R	L	0-3	0-1	9		5767
30	12	H	Scunthorpe U	W	3-0	0-0	8	McKirdy [58], Davison 2 (1 pen) [70, 85 (p)]	9012
31	19	A	Carlisle U	W	3-0	1-0	7	McKirdy [17], Davison [55], Barry [57]	4345
32	22	H	Walsall	W	5-0	2-0	5	Barry 2 [36, 63], Aguiar 2 [45, 56], Williams [71]	9840
33	26	H	Salford C	L	1-2	0-0	7	McKirdy [55]	10,153
34	Mar 5	A	Bradford C	W	2-1	1-1	7	McKirdy [21], Payne (pen) [90]	15,008
35	8	A	Exeter C	L	1-3	0-2	8	Payne [90]	5958
36	12	H	Oldham Ath	W	1-0	0-0	6	Conroy [90]	11,390
37	15	H	Sutton U	W	2-1	1-1	6	Davison [14], McKirdy [49]	8243
38	19	A	Crawley T	L	1-3	0-1	7	Davison [50]	2977
39	Apr 2	A	Rochdale	D	0-0	0-0	10		2779
40	9	H	Newport Co	L	0-1	0-0	11		11,408
41	15	A	Harrogate T	W	4-1	2-0	10	Barry 2 [24, 30], Davison 2 [51, 63]	2933
42	18	H	Leyton Orient	L	1-2	0-1	11	Davison [78]	10,264
43	23	A	Hartlepool U	W	3-0	1-0	10	McKirdy 2 [39, 55], Baudry [85]	4786
44	26	H	Forest Green R	W	2-1	2-0	8	Barry [15], Payne [40]	11,150
45	30	H	Barrow	W	2-1	1-0	7	Davison [22], Reed [85]	13,355
46	May 7	A	Walsall	W	3-0	3-0	6	McKirdy [3], Payne 2 (1 pen) [25, 45 (p)]	9089

Final League Position: 6

GOALSCORERS

League (77): McKirdy 20, Payne 13 (6 pens), Davison 9 (1 pen), Simpson 9, Barry 6, Gladwin 5 (2 pens), Williams 5, Aguiar 2, Reed 2, Baudry 1, Conroy 1, Crichlow-Noble 1, Iandolo 1, Tomlinson 1, own goal 1.
FA Cup (6): Reed 2, Simpson 2, Kesler 1, McKirdy 1.
Carabao Cup (0).
Papa John's Trophy (7): Crichlow-Noble 1, Dabre 1, Lyden 1, McKirdy 1, Mitchell-Lawson 1, own goals 2.
League Two Play-offs (2): McKirdy 2.

Wollacott J 37	Hayden K 16 + 2	Baudry M 13 + 2	Conroy D 35	Hunt R 35 + 2	Payne J 31 + 4	Grant A 5	Iandolo E 39 + 5	McKirdy H 32 + 3	Gladwin B 23 + 13	Simpson T 24 + 1	Crichlow-Noble R 15 + 3	Parsons H 1 + 14	East R 5 + 11	Reed L 39	Aguiar R 8 + 8	Odimayo A 30 + 5	Williams J 24 + 16	Mitchell-Lawson J 2 + 22	Gilbert A 5 + 3	Ward L 9	Lyden J 5 + 5	O'Brien J 16 + 3	Davison J 21	Cooper B 8	Barry L 12 + 2	Tomlinson J 10	Egbo M 6 + 3	*Match No.*
1	2^{1}	3	4	5	6	7	8	9^{3}	10^{2}	11	12	13	14															1
1	2■		4	5^{1}	10	7^{3}	12	8	9^{2}	11	3	13		6	14													2
1			3	5^{3}	10	6	14	8^{2}	12	11	4	9^{1}		7		2	13											3
1	5		3	13	9	6	8^{2}		10^{1}	11	4		14	7^{3}		2	12											4
1	5		3	8	9	6^{1}	13	14	10^{2}	11^{3}	4			7		2	12											5
1			3	5^{1}	10		7	8^{2}	9	11	4			6		2		12	13									6
1	2		3	5	8		13		9^{2}	11	4	14		7			6^{1}	12	10^{3}									7
1	8		3		9		5		12	11	4			6		2	7^{1}	13	10^{2}									8
1	6		3		8		5		9	11	4			7		2		12	10^{1}									9
1	2		4	15	9^{3}		6^{4}	12	7	11^{2}	5			8		3	14	13	10^{1}									10
		12	3	5	9^{2}		8	10^{1}	6^{3}	11	4		13	7		2				1	14							11
	12		4	2^{1}	9		6	10^{2}	7	11	5			8		3^{3}	14	13		1								12
1		4		2	9		6	10^{3}	13	11	5		12	8^{2}		3	7^{1}	14										13
1	12	3		5^{3}	9			11	6	10	4^{1}			8		2	7^{2}	14	13									14
1	2	3	4		13		6	11^{3}	7	10	5^{1}		14	8		12	9^{2}											15
1	2		4	3	9^{2}		6		7	11				8		5	12		10^{1}		13							16
1	2		4	3	7		6	10^{1}	12	11			14	8^{3}		5	9^{2}				13							17
1	2^{3}		4	3^{2}	9		6	12	7^{1}	11	14			8		5	10	13										18
1	5		3		6		9	11^{2}	8	10	4^{1}			7		2	12	13										19
1	2		4■	3^{3}	9		6	10^{2}	7	11			8^{1}			5	12	13	14									20
1	2			3	11		5	10^{2}	7	12			6^{3}	8		4	13	9^{1}			14							21
1	2			4	9^{1}		5	11	13	10	12		14	8^{3}		3	7^{2}				6							22
			3	6			9	10^{3}	12	11		14		5		4	8^{1}	13		1	7^{2}	2						23
			4	2			6	11	7	10^{3}			14	8^{2}		5	9^{1}	13		1	12	3						24
			3	6			9	11	7	10				5		4	8			1		2						25
1			3	6			9	10^{2}	12					5	14	4	7^{3}	13			8^{1}	2	11					26
1			3^{3}	5			9	10	6				7^{2}				13	14			8	2	11^{1}	4	12			27
1				5			12	11	6							4^{3}	8	14			7^{1}	2	10^{2}	3	13	9		28
1				2			7	11^{3}	6			13			14	5	8^{1}	12				3	10^{2}	4		9		29
1				2			8	9^{2}	6^{1}				14	7	12			13				3	10	4	11^{3}	5		30
1				2			8^{2}	9^{1}				14	13	7	6		12					3	10^{3}	4	11	5		31
1				2			8^{2}	9^{1}				14	13	7	6		12					3	10^{3}	4	11	5		32
1				2^{3}			8	9^{1}				14		7	6		12	13				3	10	4	11^{2}	5		33
1		12		5	13		8	9						7	6	2^{1}	11^{2}					3	10	4				34
1		3	4	5^{2}	12		9						8^{1}	7	6	14	10	13				2^{3}	11					35
1			4	2	9^{1}		8					14		7	6	5^{3}	12	11^{2}				3	10				13	36
1		3	4	2	12		8	9						7■	6^{1}	5	11^{2}						10				13	37
1			4	2	9		8	11				13	7^{3}		12	5^{1}	6^{2}	14				3	10					38
1		3	4	2	7		8					13			6^{1}		9						10		11^{2}	5	12	39
1		3	4	2	6^{1}		8		14					7	12		11	13					10		9^{2}	5^{3}		40
1		3	4	2	6		8		13			14		7			12						10		11^{3}	5^{2}	9^{1}	41
1			4		6		8					13		7	14	2^{2}	12					3	10		11	5^{1}	9^{3}	42
		3	4		6		5	9^{2}	14			13		7		12	8^{3}			1			10		11		2^{1}	43
		3	4		6		5■	9	13					7		12	8^{2}			1		14	10		11^{1}		2^{3}	44
		3	4		6^{1}			9	12					7	14	5^{2}	8^{3}			1		13	10		11		2	45
		3^{3}	4		6		5	9	12					7		13	8^{1}			1		14	10		11		2^{2}	46

FA Cup

First Round	Crewe Alex	(a)	3-0
Second Round	Walsall	(a)	2-1
Third Round	Manchester C	(h)	1-4

League Two Play-offs

Semi-Final 1st leg	Port Vale	(h)	2-1
Semi-Final 2nd leg	Port Vale	(a)	0-1

(aet; Port Vale won 6-5 on penalties)

Carabao Cup

First Round	Cambridge U	(a)	0-0

(Cambridge U won 3-1 on penalties)

Papa John's Trophy

Group F (S)	Arsenal U21	(h)	2-1
Group F (S)	Plymouth Arg	(a)	3-1
Group F (S)	Newport Co	(h)	1-0
Second Round	Colchester U	(h)	1-2

TOTTENHAM HOTSPUR

FOUNDATION

The Hotspur Football Club was formed from an older cricket club in 1882. Most of the founders were old boys of St John's Presbyterian School and Tottenham Grammar School. The Casey brothers were well to the fore as the family provided the club's first goalposts (painted blue and white) and their first ball. They soon adopted the local YMCA as their meeting place, but after a couple of moves settled at the Red House.

Tottenham Hotspur Stadium, Lilywhite House, 782 High Road, Tottenham, London N17 0BX.

Telephone: (0344) 499 5000.

Ticket Office: (0344) 844 0102.

Website: www.tottenhamhotspur.com

Email: supporterservices@tottenhamhotspur.com

Ground Capacity: 62,850.

Record Attendance: 75,038 v Sunderland, FA Cup 6th rd, 5 March 1938 (at White Hart Lane); 85,512 v Bayer Leverkusen, UEFA Champions League Group E, 2 November 2016 (at Wembley); 62,027 v Arsenal, Premier League, 12 May 2022 (at Tottenham Hotspur Stadium).

Pitch Measurements: 105m × 68m (115yd × 74.5yd).

Executive Chairman: Daniel Levy.

Head Coach: Antonio Conte.

Assistant Head Coach: Cristian Stellini.

Colours: White shirts with navy blue trim, navy blue shorts with white trim, navy blue socks.

Year Formed: 1882. ***Turned Professional:*** 1895.

Previous Names: 1882, Hotspur Football Club; 1884, Tottenham Hotspur.

Club Nickname: 'Spurs'.

Grounds: 1882, Tottenham Marshes; 1888, Northumberland Park; 1899, White Hart Lane; 2018, Tottenham Hotspur Stadium.

First Football League Game: 1 September 1908, Division 2, v Wolverhampton W (h) W 3–0 – Hewitson; Coquet, Burton; Morris (1), Danny Steel, Darnell; Walton, Woodward (2), Macfarlane, Bobby Steel, Middlemiss.

Record League Victory: 9–0 v Bristol R, Division 2, 22 October 1977 – Daines; Naylor, Holmes, Hoddle (1), McAllister, Perryman, Pratt, McNab, Moores (3), Lee (4), Taylor (1).

HONOURS

League Champions: Division 1 – 1950–51, 1960–61; Division 2 – 1919–20, 1949–50.
Runners-up: Premier League – 2016–17; Division 1 – 1921–22, 1951–52, 1956–57, 1962–63; Division 2 – 1908–09, 1932–33.

FA Cup Winners: 1901 (as non-league club), 1921, 1961, 1962, 1967, 1981, 1982, 1991.
Runners-up: 1987.

League Cup Winners: 1971, 1973, 1999, 2008.
Runners-up: 1982, 2002, 2009, 2015, 2021.

European Competitions
European Cup: 1961–62 *(sf)*.
Champions League: 2010–11 *(qf)*, 2016–17, 2017–18, 2018–19 *(runners-up)*, 2019–20.
UEFA Cup: 1971–72 *(winners)*, 1972–73 *(sf)*, 1973–74 *(runners-up)*, 1983–84 *(winners)*, 1984–85 *(qf)*, 1999–2000, 2006–07 *(qf)*, 2007–08, 2008–09.
Europa League: 2011–12, 2012–13 *(qf)*, 2013–14, 2014–15, 2015–16, 2016–17, 2020–21.
Europa Conference League: 2021–22.
European Cup-Winners' Cup: 1962–63 *(winners)*, 1963–64, 1967–68, 1981–82 *(sf)*, 1982–83, 1991–92 *(qf)*.
Intertoto Cup: 1995.

FOOTBALL YEARBOOK FACT FILE

Tottenham Hotspur formally became a professional club towards the end of 1895 and so were forced to withdraw from the FA Amateur, London Senior and Middlesex Cups. The first-ever player from the club to be registered as a professional with the FA was Reginald Clement on 18 December 1895 and he was soon followed by James Collins and Arch Cubberley.

Record Cup Victory: 13–2 v Crewe Alex, FA Cup 4th rd (replay), 3 February 1960 – Brown; Hills, Henry; Blanchflower, Norman, Mackay; White, Harmer (1), Smith (4), Allen (5), Jones (3 incl. 1p).

Record Defeat: 0–8 v Cologne, UEFA Intertoto Cup, 22 July 1995.

Most League Points (2 for a win): 70, Division 2, 1919–20.

Most League Points (3 for a win): 86, Premier League, 2016–17.

Most League Goals: 115, Division 1, 1960–61.

Highest League Scorer in Season: Jimmy Greaves, 37, Division 1, 1962–63.

Most League Goals in Total Aggregate: Jimmy Greaves, 220, 1961–70.

Most League Goals in One Match: 5, Ted Harper v Reading, Division 2, 30 August 1930; 5, Alf Stokes v Birmingham C, Division 1, 18 September 1957; 5, Bobby Smith v Aston Villa, Division 1, 29 March 1958; 5, Jermain Defoe v Wigan Ath, Premier League, 22 November 2009.

Most Capped Player: Hugo Lloris, 101 (139), France.

Most League Appearances: Steve Perryman, 655, 1969–86.

Youngest League Player: Ally Dick, 16 years 301 days v Manchester C, 20 February 1982.

Record Transfer Fee Received: £85,300,000 from Real Madrid for Gareth Bale, September 2013.

Record Transfer Fee Paid: £55,500,000 (rising to £63,000,000) to Lyon for Tanguy Ndombele, July 2019.

Football League Record: 1908 Elected to Division 2; 1909–15 Division 1; 1919–20 Division 2; 1920–28 Division 1; 1928–33 Division 2; 1933–35 Division 1; 1935–50 Division 2; 1950–77 Division 1; 1977–78 Division 2; 1978–92 Division 1; 1992– Premier League.

MANAGERS

Frank Brettell 1898–99
John Cameron 1899–1906
Fred Kirkham 1907–08
Peter McWilliam 1912–27
Billy Minter 1927–29
Percy Smith 1930–35
Jack Tresadern 1935–38
Peter McWilliam 1938–42
Arthur Turner 1942–46
Joe Hulme 1946–49
Arthur Rowe 1949–55
Jimmy Anderson 1955–58
Bill Nicholson 1958–74
Terry Neill 1974–76
Keith Burkinshaw 1976–84
Peter Shreeves 1984–86
David Pleat 1986–87
Terry Venables 1987–91
Peter Shreeves 1991–92
Doug Livermore 1992–93
Ossie Ardiles 1993–94
Gerry Francis 1994–97
Christian Gross *(Head Coach)* 1997–98
George Graham 1998–2001
Glenn Hoddle 2001–03
David Pleat (*Caretaker*) 2003–04
Jacques Santini 2004
Martin Jol 2004–07
Juande Ramos 2007–08
Harry Redknapp 2008–12
Andre Villas-Boas 2012–13
Tim Sherwood 2013–14
Mauricio Pochettino 2014–19
Jose Mourinho 2019–21
Nuno Espirito Santo 2021
Antonio Conte November 2021–

LATEST SEQUENCES

Longest Sequence of League Wins: 13, 23.4.1960 – 1.10.1960.

Longest Sequence of League Defeats: 7, 1.1.1994 – 27.2.1994.

Longest Sequence of League Draws: 6, 9.1.1999 – 27.2.1999.

Longest Sequence of Unbeaten League Matches: 22, 31.8.1949 – 31.12.1949.

Longest Sequence Without a League Win: 16, 29.12.1934 – 13.4.1935.

Successive Scoring Runs: 32 from 24.2.1962.

Successive Non-scoring Runs: 6 from 28.12.1985.

TEN YEAR LEAGUE RECORD

		P	*W*	*D*	*L*	*F*	*A*	*Pts*	*Pos*
2012-13	PR Lge	38	21	9	8	66	46	72	5
2013-14	PR Lge	38	21	6	11	55	51	69	6
2014-15	PR Lge	38	19	7	12	58	53	64	5
2015-16	PR Lge	38	19	13	6	69	35	70	3
2016-17	PR Lge	38	26	8	4	86	26	86	2
2017-18	PR Lge	38	23	8	7	74	36	77	3
2018-19	PR Lge	38	23	2	13	67	39	71	4
2019-20	PR Lg	38	16	11	11	61	47	59	6
2020-21	PR Lge	38	18	8	12	68	45	62	7
2021-22	PR Lge	38	22	5	11	69	40	71	4

DID YOU KNOW ?

Tottenham Hotspur did not enter the Football League Cup until the 1966–67 season, by which time the competition offered a Wembley final and a slot in the Inter-Cities Fairs Cup for the following campaign. Their first-ever League Cup match saw them lose 1-0 at West Ham United in a second-round tie on 14 September 1966.

TOTTENHAM HOTSPUR – PREMIER LEAGUE 2021–22 LEAGUE RECORD

Match No.	*Date*	*Venue*	*Opponents*	*Result*		*H/T Score*	*Lg Pos.*	*Goalscorers*	*Attendance*
1	Aug 15	H	Manchester C	W	1-0	0-0	9	Son [55]	58,262
2	22	A	Wolverhampton W	W	1-0	1-0	4	Alli (pen) [10]	30,368
3	29	H	Watford	W	1-0	1-0	1	Son [42]	57,672
4	Sept 11	A	Crystal Palace	L	0-3	0-0	5		22,740
5	19	H	Chelsea	L	0-3	0-0	7		60,059
6	26	A	Arsenal	L	1-3	0-3	11	Son [79]	59,919
7	Oct 3	H	Aston Villa	W	2-1	1-0	8	Hojbjerg [27], Targett (og) [71]	53,076
8	17	A	Newcastle U	W	3-2	3-1	5	Ndombele [17], Kane [22], Son [45]	52,214
9	24	A	West Ham U	L	0-1	0-0	6		59,924
10	30	H	Manchester U	L	0-3	0-1	8		60,356
11	Nov 7	A	Everton	D	0-0	0-0	9		39,059
12	21	H	Leeds U	W	2-1	0-1	7	Hojbjerg [58], Reguilon [69]	58,989
13	Dec 2	H	Brentford	W	2-0	1-0	6	Canos (og) [12], Son [65]	54,202
14	5	H	Norwich C	W	3-0	1-0	5	Lucas Moura [10], Sanchez [67], Son [77]	57,088
15	19	H	Liverpool	D	2-2	1-1	7	Kane [13], Son [74]	45,421
16	26	H	Crystal Palace	W	3-0	2-0	5	Kane [32], Lucas Moura [34], Son [74]	40,539
17	28	A	Southampton	D	1-1	1-1	6	Kane (pen) [41]	31,304
18	Jan 1	A	Watford	W	1-0	0-0	6	Sanchez [90]	20,391
19	19	A	Leicester C	W	3-2	1-1	5	Kane [38], Bergwijn 2 [90, 90]	31,986
20	23	A	Chelsea	L	0-2	0-0	7		40,020
21	Feb 9	H	Southampton	L	2-3	1-1	7	Bednarek (og) [18], Son [70]	54,012
22	13	H	Wolverhampton W	L	0-2	0-2	8		56,452
23	19	A	Manchester C	W	3-2	1-1	7	Kulusevski [4], Kane 2 [59, 90]	53,201
24	23	A	Burnley	L	0-1	0-0	8		19,488
25	26	A	Leeds U	W	4-0	3-0	7	Doherty [10], Kulusevski [15], Kane [27], Son [85]	36,599
26	Mar 7	H	Everton	W	5-0	3-0	7	Keane (og) [14], Son [17], Kane 2 [37, 55], Reguilon [46]	59,647
27	12	A	Manchester U	L	2-3	1-2	7	Kane (pen) [35], Maguire (og) [72]	73,458
28	16	A	Brighton & HA	W	2-0	1-0	7	Romero [37], Kane [57]	31,144
29	20	H	West Ham U	W	3-1	2-1	5	Zouma (og) [9], Son 2 [24, 88]	58,685
30	Apr 3	H	Newcastle U	W	5-1	1-1	4	Davies [43], Doherty [48], Son [54], Emerson [63], Bergwijn [83]	57,553
31	9	A	Aston Villa	W	4-0	1-0	4	Son 3 [3, 66, 71], Kulusevski [50]	41,949
32	16	H	Brighton & HA	L	0-1	0-0	4		58,685
33	23	A	Brentford	D	0-0	0-0	5		17,072
34	May 1	H	Leicester C	W	3-1	1-0	5	Kane [22], Son 2 [60, 79]	59,482
35	7	A	Liverpool	D	1-1	0-0	5	Son [56]	53,177
36	12	H	Arsenal	W	3-0	2-0	5	Kane 2 (1 pen) [22 (p), 37], Son [47]	62,027
37	15	H	Burnley	W	1-0	1-0	4	Kane (pen) [45]	61,729
38	22	A	Norwich C	W	5-0	2-0	4	Kulusevski 2 [16, 64], Kane [32], Son 2 [70, 75]	27,022

Final League Position: 4

GOALSCORERS

League (69): Son 23, Kane 17 (4 pens), Kulusevski 5, Bergwijn 3, Doherty 2, Hojbjerg 2, Lucas Moura 2, Reguilon 2, Sanchez 2, Alli 1 (1 pen), Davies 1, Emerson 1, Ndombele 1, Romero 1, own goals 6.
FA Cup (6): Kane 3, Lucas Moura 1, Winks 1, own goal 1.
Carabao Cup (5): Lucas Moura 2, Bergwijn 1, Kane 1, Ndombele 1.
UEFA Europa Conference League (14): Kane 6, Lo Celso 2, Alli 1 (1 pen), Hojbjerg 1, Lucas Moura 1, Son 1, own goals 2.
Papa John's Trophy (6): White 2, Alonso 1, Clarke 1, Lyons-Foster 1, Scarlett 1 (1 pen).

Lloris H 38	Tanganga J 10 + 1	Sanchez D 17 + 6	Dier E 35	Reguilon S 22 + 3	Hojbjerg P 36	Skipp O 14 + 4	Lucas Moura R 19 + 15	Alli B 8 + 2	Bergwijn S 4 + 21	Son H 35	Lo Celso G 2 + 7	Doherty M 9 + 6	Romero C 21 + 1	Kane H 36 + 1	Winks H 9 + 10	Gil Salvatierra B — + 9	Emerson J 26 + 5	Rodon J — + 3	Davies B 28 + 1	Ndombele T 6 + 3	Sessegnon R 13 + 2	Bentancur R 16 + 1	Kulusevski D 14 + 4	Scarlett D — + 1	Match No.
1	2^{2}	3	4	5	6^{3}	7	8	9	10^{1}	11	12	13	14												1
1	2	3	4	5	6	7	9^{1}	8	11^{3}	10^{2}	12			13	14										2
1	2	3	4	5	6	7	12	9	10^{1}	8^{2}				11		13									3
1	3■		4^{1}	5	6	7	9	10						11	8^{2}		2	12	13						4
1		14	4	5	7	13		8		11	9^{2}		3^{3}	10		12	2			6^{1}					5
1	2^{2}	3	4	5	7	12	9	6^{1}		11				10		14	13			8^{3}					6
1			4	5	6	7	8^{2}			10	12		3	11		13	2			9^{1}					7
1			4	5	6	7	8			10			3	11			2			9					8
1			4	5^{2}	6	7	8^{3}		14	10	13		3	11		12	2			9^{1}					9
1			4		6	7^{2}	8^{1}	14	12	10	9^{3}		3	11			2		5	13					10
1			3	8^{1}	6	7	9^{2}			10^{3}	13	12	2	11			5		4	14					11
1	2^{1}	12	3	8^{2}	6		9^{3}	14		10				11	7		5		4		13				12
1	13	2	3	8	7	6	9^{1}		14	10^{3}				11	12		5^{2}		4						13
1	5^{2}	2	3	8^{1}	7	6	9^{3}		14	10		13		11					4		12				14
1		3	4	14		12	13	9^{2}		11				10	8		2		5	7^{1}	6^{3}				15
1	4	2	3	8	7^{3}	6	9		12	10^{2}				11^{1}		13	5			14					16
1		2	3	8^{1}	7		13	9^{2}		10		12		11	6	14	5^{3}		4						17
1		2	3	8^{2}	7	6^{1}	9^{3}			11	13			10	12	14	5		4						18
1	3	4		6^{3}	9	7	11		14		13	12		10	8^{2}		2^{1}		5						19
1	2^{2}	4	3		8	12	13		11			6		10	7^{3}	14			5		9^{1}				20
1		2		8^{3}	7^{1}		9^{2}		14	10			3	11	6		5		4			12	13		21
1		2					9^{2}		13	10		5^{3}	3	11	6		14		4		8^{1}	7	12		22
1		14	3		7		12			10^{1}		13	2	11			5^{2}		4		8^{3}	6	9		23
1			3		7		13		14	10			2	11	12		5^{2}		4		8^{3}	6^{1}	9		24
1			3		6				12	10^{3}		5	2	11	7		13		4		8^{2}		9^{1}	14	25
1		13	3	12	7				14	10^{3}		5	2^{2}	11					4		8^{1}	6	9		26
1			3	8	7		12		13	10		5	2	11	14				4^{2}			6^{3}	9^{1}		27
1			3	8	7		12		14	10^{2}		5^{1}	2	11			13		4			6	9^{3}		28
1			3	8^{1}	7		14		13	10^{2}		5	2	11			12		4			6	9^{3}		29
1			3		7		13		14	10		8	2	11	12		5^{3}		4			6^{1}	9^{2}		30
1			3	12	7		13		14	11^{2}		8^{1}	2	10			5		4			6	9^{3}		31
1			3	8	7		12		14	11^{3}			2	10	13		5		4			6^{2}	9^{1}		32
1		12	3		7		13			11			2	10			5^{2}		4		8^{1}	6	9		33
1			3		7		9^{1}		14	11^{3}			2	10	13		5		4		8	6^{2}	12		34
1		12	3		7				14	11^{3}			2	10	13		5		4		8^{1}	6	9^{2}		35
1		2	3		7		13		12	10^{1}				11			5	14	4^{3}		8	6	9^{2}		36
1		2	3		7		9^{1}			10				11			5^{2}	13	4		8	6	12		37
1		2	3		6		12		14	10				11	13		5^{3}		4		8	7^{2}	9^{1}		38

FA Cup

Third Round	Morecambe	(h)	3-1
Fourth Round	Brighton & HA	(h)	3-1
Fifth Round	Middlesbrough	(a)	0-1

(aet)

Carabao Cup

Third Round	Wolverhampton W	(a)	2-2

(Tottenham H won 3-2 on penalties)

Fourth Round	Burnley	(a)	1-0
Quarter-Final	West Ham U	(h)	2-1
Semi-Final 1st leg	Chelsea	(a)	0-2
Semi-Final 2nd leg	Chelsea	(h)	0-1

(Chelsea won 3-0 on aggregate)

Papa John's Trophy (Tottenham H U21)

Group H (S)	Stevenage	(a)	4-3
Group H (S)	Cambridge U	(a)	0-1
Group H (S)	Oxford U	(a)	2-3

UEFA Europa Conference League

Play-off Round 1st leg	Pacos de Ferreira	(a)	0-1
Play-off Round 2nd leg	Pacos de Ferreira	(h)	3-0
Group G	Rennes	(a)	2-2
Group G	Mura	(h)	5-1
Group G	Vitesse	(a)	0-1
Group G	Vitesse	(h)	3-2
Group G	Mura	(a)	1-2
Group G	Rennes	(h)	0-3

Match awarded 0-3 win to Rennes, Tottenham H could not fulfill fixture due to positive COVID-19 tests.

TRANMERE ROVERS

FOUNDATION

Formed in 1884 as Belmont they adopted their present title the following year and eventually joined their first league, the West Lancashire League, in 1889–90, the same year as their first success in the Wirral Challenge Cup. The club almost folded in 1899–1900 when all the players left en bloc to join a rival club, but they survived the crisis and went from strength to strength, winning the 'Combination' title in 1907–08 and the Lancashire Combination in 1913–14. They joined the Football League in 1921 from the Central League.

Prenton Park, Prenton Road West, Birkenhead, Merseyside CH42 9PY.

Telephone: (0333) 014 4452.

Ticket Office: (0333) 014 4452 (Option 2).

Website: www.tranmererovers.co.uk

Email: via website.

Ground Capacity: 15,012.

Record Attendance: 24,424 v Stoke C, FA Cup 4th rd, 5 February 1972.

Pitch Measurements: 100m × 64m (109.5yd × 70yd).

Chairman: Mark Palios.

Vice-Chairman: Nicola Palios.

Manager: Micky Mellon.

Assistant Manager: Ian Dawes.

Colours: White shirts with blue and green trim, white shorts with blue and green trim, white socks with blue and green trim.

Year Formed: 1884.

Turned Professional: 1912.

Previous Name: 1884, Belmont AFC; 1885, Tranmere Rovers.

Club Nickname: 'Rovers'.

Grounds: 1884, Steeles Field; 1887, Ravenshaws Field/Old Prenton Park; 1912, Prenton Park.

First Football League Game: 27 August 1921, Division 3 (N), v Crewe Alex (h) W 4–1 – Bradshaw; Grainger, Stuart (1); Campbell, Milnes (1), Heslop; Moreton, Groves (1), Hyam, Ford (1), Hughes.

Record League Victory: 13–4 v Oldham Ath, Division 3 (N), 26 December 1935 – Gray; Platt, Fairhurst; McLaren, Newton, Spencer; Eden, MacDonald (1), Bell (9), Woodward (2), Urmson (1).

Record Cup Victory: 13–0 v Oswestry U, FA Cup 2nd prel. rd, 10 October 1914 – Ashcroft; Stevenson, Bullough, Hancock, Taylor, Holden (1), Moreton (1), Cunningham (2), Smith (5), Leck (3), Gould (1).

HONOURS

League Champions: Division 3N – 1937–38.
Runners-up: Division 4 – 1988–89.

FA Cup: quarter-final – 2000, 2001, 2004.

League Cup: *Runners-up:* 2000.

Welsh Cup Winners: 1935.
Runners-up: 1934.

League Trophy Winners: 1990.
Runners-up: 1991, 2021.

FOOTBALL YEARBOOK FACT FILE

Wing-half Tommy Neill, who spent three seasons on the books of Tranmere Rovers in the early 1960s, was also a talented golfer. He finished in the top 10 of the Professional Footballers' Golf Championship in each of his seasons at Prenton Park and won the tournament in 1963, becoming the first Merseyside-based player to win since the championship had become a national event.

Record Defeat: 1–9 v Tottenham H, FA Cup 3rd rd (replay), 14 January 1953.

Most League Points (2 for a win): 60, Division 4, 1964–65.

Most League Points (3 for a win): 80, Division 4, 1988–89; Division 3, 1989–90; Division 2, 2002–03.

Most League Goals: 111, Division 3 (N), 1930–31.

Highest League Scorer in Season: Bunny Bell, 35, Division 3 (N), 1933–34.

Most League Goals in Total Aggregate: Ian Muir, 142, 1985–95.

Most League Goals in One Match: 9, Bunny Bell v Oldham Ath, Division 3 (N), 26 December 1935.

Most Capped Player: John Aldridge, 30 (69), Republic of Ireland.

Most League Appearances: Harold Bell, 595, 1946–64 (incl. League record 401 consecutive appearances).

Youngest League Player: Iain Hume, 16 years 167 days v Swindon T, 15 April 2000.

Record Transfer Fee Received: £2,250,000 from WBA for Jason Koumas, August 2002.

Record Transfer Fee Paid: £450,000 to Aston Villa for Shaun Teale, August 1995.

Football League Record: 1921 Original Member of Division 3 (N): 1938–39 Division 2; 1946–58 Division 3 (N); 1958–61 Division 3; 1961–67 Division 4; 1967–75 Division 3; 1975–76 Division 4; 1976–79 Division 3; 1979–89 Division 4; 1989–91 Division 3; 1991–92 Division 2; 1992–2001 Division 1; 2001–04 Division 2; 2004–14 FL 1; 2014–15 FL 2; 2015–18 National League; 2018–19 FL 2; 2019–20 FL 1; 2020– FL 2.

MANAGERS

Bert Cooke 1912–35
Jackie Carr 1935–36
Jim Knowles 1936–39
Bill Ridding 1939–45
Ernie Blackburn 1946–55
Noel Kelly 1955–57
Peter Farrell 1957–60
Walter Galbraith 1961
Dave Russell 1961–69
Jackie Wright 1969–72
Ron Yeats 1972–75
John King 1975–80
Bryan Hamilton 1980–85
Frank Worthington 1985–87
Ronnie Moore 1987
John King 1987–96
John Aldridge 1996–2001
Dave Watson 2001–02
Ray Mathias 2002–03
Brian Little 2003–06
Ronnie Moore 2006–09
John Barnes 2009
Les Parry 2009–12
Ronnie Moore 2012–14
Robert Edwards 2014
Micky Adams 2014–15
Gary Brabin 2015–16
Paul Cardin 2016
Micky Mellon 2016–20
Mike Jackson 2020
Keith Hill 2020–21
Micky Mellon May 2021–

LATEST SEQUENCES

Longest Sequence of League Wins: 9, 9.2.1990 – 19.3.1990.

Longest Sequence of League Defeats: 8, 29.10.1938 – 17.12.1938.

Longest Sequence of League Draws: 5, 26.12.1997 – 31.1.1998.

Longest Sequence of Unbeaten League Matches: 18, 16.3.1970 – 4.9.1970.

Longest Sequence Without a League Win: 16, 8.11.1969 – 14.3.1970.

Successive Scoring Runs: 32 from 24.2.1934.

Successive Non-scoring Runs: 7 from 20.12.1997.

TEN YEAR LEAGUE RECORD

		P	*W*	*D*	*L*	*F*	*A*	*Pts*	*Pos*
2012-13	FL 1	46	19	10	17	58	48	67	11
2013-14	FL 1	46	12	11	23	52	79	47	21
2014-15	FL 2	46	9	12	25	45	67	39	24
2015-16	NL	46	22	12	12	61	44	78	6
2016-17	NL	46	29	8	9	79	39	95	2
2017-18	NL	46	24	10	12	78	46	82	2
2018-19	FL 2	46	20	13	13	63	50	73	6
2019-20	FL 1	34	8	8	18	36	60	32	21§
2020-21	FL 2	46	20	13	13	55	50	73	7
2021-22	FL 2	46	21	12	13	53	40	75	9

§Decided on points-per-game (0.94)

DID YOU KNOW ?

Charlie Cunningham became the first player to score a Football League hat-trick for Tranmere Rovers when he netted four times in a 7-0 win over Rochdale in what was the club's eighth match in the competition. Cunningham scored just two more goals for Rovers before moving into non-league football the following season.

TRANMERE ROVERS – SKY BET LEAGUE TWO 2021–22 LEAGUE RECORD

Match No.	Date		Venue	Opponents	Result		H/T Score	Lg Pos.	Goalscorers	Attendance
1	Aug	7	H	Walsall	W	1-0	0-0	5	McManaman 73	7728
2		14	A	Port Vale	D	0-0	0-0	8		6986
3		17	A	Swindon T	D	0-0	0-0	7		8274
4		21	H	Newport Co	L	0-1	0-0	14		6160
5		28	A	Scunthorpe U	L	0-1	0-1	19		2737
6	Sept	4	H	Hartlepool U	W	1-0	0-0	11	Davies 89	6707
7		11	A	Rochdale	L	0-1	0-0	15		4877
8		18	H	Salford C	W	2-0	1-0	11	Morris (pen) 13, Nevitt 48	5854
9		25	A	Forest Green R	D	0-0	0-0	13		2356
10	Oct	2	H	Crawley T	W	2-1	1-0	9	Clarke 2 28, 79	6046
11		8	H	Colchester U	W	2-0	0-0	4	Hawkes 54, Clarke 71	7324
12		16	A	Carlisle U	W	1-0	0-0	4	McDonald (og) 48	4831
13		19	A	Harrogate T	D	2-2	1-1	5	Spearing (pen) 32, Morris 55	2573
14		23	H	Northampton T	L	0-2	0-0	8		4025
15		30	A	Mansfield T	L	0-2	0-1	11		3831
16	Nov	13	H	Sutton U	L	0-1	0-0	12		6452
17		20	A	Bristol R	D	2-2	1-2	11	MacDonald 25, Glatzel 75	7165
18		23	H	Bradford C	W	2-1	0-1	10	Morris 50, Glatzel 56	5962
19	Dec	7	A	Oldham Ath	W	1-0	0-0	10	Jolley 90	4303
20		11	A	Exeter C	W	1-0	1-0	8	Nevitt 17	4850
21		18	H	Leyton Orient	W	1-0	0-0	5	Spearing 58	4000
22		26	H	Barrow	W	2-0	1-0	3	Maynard 7, Morris 87	3500
23	Jan	8	H	Scunthorpe U	W	4-0	2-0	2	Jolley 23, Nevitt 31, Foley 75, Watson 89	6056
24		11	A	Salford C	D	1-1	0-1	2	Glatzel 70	2273
25		15	H	Rochdale	W	2-0	2-0	2	Jolley 2 3, 16	7046
26		22	A	Crawley T	W	1-0	0-0	2	Spearing 65	2803
27		29	H	Forest Green R	L	0-4	0-2	2		10,924
28	Feb	1	H	Stevenage	W	1-0	0-0	2	Morris 48	5723
29		5	A	Barrow	D	1-1	1-0	2	Hawkes 16	3699
30		8	H	Swindon T	W	3-0	1-0	2	Hemmings 2 (1 pen) 6, 72 (p), Glatzel 58	5767
31		12	A	Walsall	L	0-1	0-0	2		5440
32		15	A	Hartlepool U	L	0-1	0-1	2		5214
33		19	H	Port Vale	D	1-1	0-0	2	Hawkes 50	7456
34		26	A	Newport Co	L	2-4	0-0	3	Dacres-Cogley 65, Demetriou (og) 84	3924
35	Mar	5	A	Northampton T	L	2-3	0-2	6	McPake 75, Hemmings (pen) 88	7379
36		11	H	Mansfield T	W	3-2	1-1	3	Clarke 5, Nevitt 2 76, 90	7857
37		15	H	Harrogate T	W	2-0	0-0	4	Warrington 49, Hemmings (pen) 65	5437
38		19	A	Sutton U	D	1-1	0-1	5	Hawkes 68	3366
39		26	A	Colchester U	L	0-1	0-0	7		2459
40	Apr	2	H	Carlisle U	D	2-2	1-0	7	Hemmings 15, Nevitt 76	6477
41		9	H	Bristol R	D	1-1	0-0	9	Hemmings 56	6637
42		15	A	Bradford C	D	1-1	0-1	9	McManaman 89	17,257
43		18	H	Exeter C	W	2-0	1-0	7	Hawkes 39, Nevitt 81	6666
44		23	A	Stevenage	L	0-2	0-1	9		2969
45		30	H	Oldham Ath	W	2-0	1-0	9	Hawkes 27, Hemmings 62	8008
46	May	7	A	Leyton Orient	W	1-0	1-0	9	Hemmings 37	6623

Final League Position: 9

GOALSCORERS

League (53): Hemmings 8 (3 pens), Nevitt 7, Hawkes 6, Morris 5 (1 pen), Clarke 4, Glatzel 4, Jolley 4, Spearing 3 (1 pen), McManaman 2, Dacres-Cogley 1, Davies 1, Foley 1, MacDonald 1, Maynard 1, McPake 1, Warrington 1, Watson 1, own goals 2.
FA Cup (1): McManaman 1.
Carabao Cup (2): Foley 1, Nevitt 1.
Papa John's Trophy (10): Maynard 4, Foley 2, Glatzel 2, Walker 1, Watson 1.

Murphy J 17	Dacres-Cogley J 45	Davies T 36	Clarke P 46	Merrie C 7 + 8	McManaman C 18 + 11	Spearing J 27 + 5	Watson R 6 + 10	Glatzel P 10 + 6	Feeney L 10 + 9	Dieseruvwe E 4 + 2	Morris K 34 + 3	Foley S 20 + 19	Maguire J — + 1	Knight-Percival N 14 + 2	Nevitt E 31 + 9	MacDonald C 34	Duffy M 1 + 2	Maynard N 3 + 7	Hawkes J 28 + 7	Doohan R 29 + 1	O'Connor L 26 + 5	Jolley C 10 + 2	McPake J 10 + 4	Hemmings K 22	Warrington L 17	Burton J 1	Match No.
1	2	3	4	5■	6²	7	8	9¹	10³	11	12	13	14														1
1	2	3	4		12	7	13	11¹	6²	10	9	8		5													2
1	5	2	3		9	6	7²	13	11¹	10³	8	12		4	14												3
1	5	2	3		12	6	14	10¹	9	13	8²	7³		4	11												4
1	2		3	12	8	7	6³	10¹	9	14	13			4	11	5²											5
1	2	3	4		12	7	6				9			5	10		8²	11¹	13								6
1²	2	3⁴	4		10¹	8	7³		12		6	14		5	11			15	9	13							7
	2	3	4		6¹	8■			12		7²	9		14	11	5			10³	1	13						8
	2	3	4		6	8	14		12		7³	9			11²	5■		13	10¹	1							9
	2	3	4	5	6	8			12		9²	7			11³			14	10¹	1	13						10
	2	3	4	14	6¹	8	13		12		7²	9			11	5			10³	1							11
	2	3	4		6³	8	14		12		7²	9			11	5			10¹	1	13						12
	2	3	4		6	8			12		7	9			11	5			10¹	1							13
	2	3	4		6	8	14		10²		7¹	9³			11	5	12	13		1							14
	2	3	4		6²	8		12	10¹	11³	7	9			14	5	13			1							15
	2		3		8	6	7	13	10¹		9²			4	11	5			12	1							16
	2	3²	4					10			7	13		5	11¹	6		12	9	1	8						17
	2		3		12	13	14	10			6	9		4		5¹		11²	8³	1	7						18
	2	3	4		6³	7²			12		14	8			11	5			9¹	1	13	10					19
	2	3	4	12	14■	7					6	8			10¹	5			9²	1	13	11³					20
	2	3	4	13		8	12				6				10	5			9²	1	7	11¹					21
		3	4	13		8³	14		12		6	7			11	5		10¹	9²	1	2						22
	2	3	4			7	14	13	6			12			11²	5				1	8	10³	9¹				23
	2	3	4			7		13	6			12			11¹	5				1	8	10	9²				24
	2	3	4			7					6	12			13	5				1	8	11¹	9	10²			25
	2		4	14	13	7³					6	3			12	5				1	8	10¹	9²	11			26
	2		3			7²					6			4	12	5			13	1	8	10¹	9	11			27
	2		3	14		8¹		10³			6	12		4		5			13	1	7		9²	11			28
	2		4					10¹			6	7		3	12	5			9	1	8			11			29
	2	3	4		14			10²			6				13	5			9³	1	8	12		11¹	7		30
	2	3	4								6	14			12	5			9²	1	7	11¹	13	10	8³		31
	2	3	4		12						6	7				5			9	1		10¹		11	8		32
	2	4	3								6	13			10	5			9¹	1	7		12	11²	8		33
	2	3	4								6	12			10	5			9¹	1	8			11	7		34
	2		3		5³			13			8	12		4					14	1	7		9	11	6²	10¹	35
1	2	3	4					10²			6¹	14			13	5			12		8		9³	11	7		36
1	2	3	4		12							13			11	5			9		8		6²	10¹	7		37
1	2	3	4									12			11	5			9		8		6¹	10	7		38
1	2	3	4	6								7			11	5			9¹			12		10	8		39
1	2	3	4	12		13					6■			14	10	5■			9¹		7			11³	8²		40
1	2		3	5	6¹	13						12		4	11				9²		7			10	8		41
1	2	3	4	5	12	7²						9			11³			14	13		6¹			10	8		42
1	2	3	4	5	6²							12			10				9¹		7		13	11	8		43
	2		4	5	6	12						3			10			13	9¹	1	7²			11	8		44
1	2	3	4								6¹	13			10²	5			9		7		12	11	8		45
1	2	3	4		12	13					6	14			10³	5			9¹		7²			11	8		46

FA Cup

First Round	Crawley T	(a)	1-0
Second Round	Leyton Orient	(a)	0-4

Carabao Cup

First Round	Oldham Ath	(a)	2-2

(Oldham Ath won 4-3 on penalties)

Papa John's Trophy

Group B (N)	Leeds U U21	(h)	4-1
Group B (N)	Salford C	(a)	2-0
Group B (N)	Oldham Ath	(h)	3-2
Second Round	Harrogate T	(h)	1-2

WALSALL

FOUNDATION

Two of the leading clubs around Walsall in the 1880s were Walsall Swifts (formed 1877) and Walsall Town (formed 1879). The Swifts were winners of the Birmingham Senior Cup in 1881, while the Town reached the 4th round (5th round modern equivalent) of the FA Cup in 1883. These clubs amalgamated as Walsall Town Swifts in 1888, becoming simply Walsall in 1895.

Banks's Stadium, Bescot Crescent, Walsall WS1 4SA.
Telephone: (01922) 622 791.
Ticket Office: (01922) 651 414/416.
Website: www.saddlers.co.uk
Email: info@walsallfc.co.uk
Ground Capacity: 10,862.
Record Attendance: 25,453 v Newcastle U, Division 2, 29 August 1961 (at Fellows Park); 11,049 v Rotherham U, Division 1, 9 May 2004 (at Bescot Stadium).
Pitch Measurements: 100.5m × 67m (110yd × 73.5yd).
Chairman: Lee Pomlett.
Chief Executive: Stefan Gamble.
Manager: Michael Flynn.
First-Team Coach: Wayne Hatswell.
Colours: Red shirts with white and green trim, white shorts with red and green trim, green socks with red and white trim.
Year Formed: 1888.
Turned Professional: 1888.
Previous Names: Walsall Swifts (founded 1877) and Walsall Town (founded 1879) amalgamated in 1888 as Walsall Town Swifts; 1895, Walsall.
Club Nickname: 'The Saddlers'.
Grounds: 1888, Hillary Street (renamed Fellows Park 1930); 1990, Bescot Stadium (renamed Banks's Stadium 2007).
First Football League Game: 3 September 1892, Division 2, v Darwen (h) L 1–2 – Hawkins; Withington, Pinches; Robinson, Whitrick, Forsyth; Marshall, Holmes, Turner, Gray (1), Pangbourn.
Record League Victory: 10–0 v Darwen, Division 2, 4 March 1899 – Tennent; Ted Peers (1), Davies; Hickinbotham, Jenkyns, Taggart; Dean (3), Vail (2), Aston (4), Martin, Griffin.
Record Cup Victory: 7–0 v Macclesfield T (a), FA Cup 2nd rd, 6 December 1997 – Walker; Evans, Marsh, Viveash (1), Ryder, Peron, Boli (2 incl. 1p) (Ricketts), Porter (2), Keates, Watson (Platt), Hodge (2 incl. 1p).
Record Defeat: 0–12 v Small Heath, 17 December 1892; 0–12 v Darwen, 26 December 1896, both Division 2.
Most League Points (2 for a win): 65, Division 4, 1959–60.
Most League Points (3 for a win): 89, FL 2, 2006–07.
Most League Goals: 102, Division 4, 1959–60.

HONOURS

League Champions: FL 2 – 2006–07; Division 4 – 1959–60.
Runners-up: Second Division – 1998–99; Division 3 – 1960–61; Third Division – 1994–95; Division 4 – 1979–80.

FA Cup: last 16 – 1889; 5th rd – 1939, 1975, 1978, 1987, 2002, 2003.

League Cup: semi-final – 1984.

League Trophy: *Runners-up:* 2015.

FOOTBALL YEARBOOK FACT FILE

Walsall's former ground was originally known as Hillary Street before being renamed Fellows Park in August 1930. The new title was in recognition of the financial assistance provided to the Saddlers by Howard Lawrence Fellows, who had been one of the first directors of the club when it was incorporated in 1921 and who served as chairman from 1926 until his death in October 1938.

Highest League Scorer in Season: Gilbert Alsop, 40, Division 3 (N), 1933–34 and 1934–35.

Most League Goals in Total Aggregate: Tony Richards, 184, 1954–63; Colin Taylor, 184, 1958–63, 1964–68, 1969–73.

Most League Goals in One Match: 5, Gilbert Alsop v Carlisle U, Division 3 (N), 2 February 1935; 5, Bill Evans v Mansfield T, Division 3 (N), 5 October 1935; 5, Johnny Devlin v Torquay U, Division 3 (S), 1 September 1949.

Most Capped Player: Mick Kearns, 14 (18), Republic of Ireland.

Most League Appearances: Colin Harrison, 473, 1964–82.

Youngest League Player: Geoff Morris, 16 years 218 days v Scunthorpe U, 14 September 1965.

Record Transfer Fee Received: £1,500,000 (rising to £5,000,000) from Brentford for Rico Henry, August 2016.

Record Transfer Fee Paid: £300,000 to Anorthosis Famagusta for Andreas Makris, August 2016.

Football League Record: 1892 Elected to Division 2; 1895 Failed re-election; 1896–1901 Division 2; 1901 Failed re-election; 1921 Original Member of Division 3 (N); 1927–31 Division 3 (S); 1931–36 Division 3 (N); 1936–58 Division 3 (S); 1958–60 Division 4; 1960–61 Division 3; 1961–63 Division 2; 1963–79 Division 3; 1979–80 Division 4; 1980–88 Division 3; 1988–89 Division 2; 1989–90 Division 3; 1990–92 Division 4; 1992–95 Division 3; 1995–99 Division 2; 1999–2000 Division 1; 2000–01 Division 2; 2001–04 Division 1; 2004–06 FL 1; 2006–07 FL 2; 2007–19 FL 1; 2019– FL 2.

LATEST SEQUENCES

Longest Sequence of League Wins: 7, 9.4.2005 – 9.8.2005.

Longest Sequence of League Defeats: 15, 29.10.1988 – 4.2.1989.

Longest Sequence of League Draws: 5, 7.5.1988 – 17.9.1988.

Longest Sequence of Unbeaten League Matches: 21, 6.11.1979 – 22.3.1980.

Longest Sequence Without a League Win: 18, 15.10.1988 – 4.2.1989.

Successive Scoring Runs: 27 from 6.11.1979.

Successive Non-scoring Runs: 5 from 10.4.2004.

MANAGERS

H. Smallwood 1888–91 *(Secretary-Manager)*
A. G. Burton 1891–93
J. H. Robinson 1893–95
C. H. Ailso 1895–96 *(Secretary-Manager)*
A. E. Parsloe 1896–97 *(Secretary-Manager)*
L. Ford 1897–98 *(Secretary-Manager)*
G. Hughes 1898–99 *(Secretary-Manager)*
L. Ford 1899–1901 *(Secretary-Manager)*
J. E. Shutt 1908–13 *(Secretary-Manager)*
Haydn Price 1914–20
Joe Burchell 1920–26
David Ashworth 1926–27
Jack Torrance 1927–28
James Kerr 1928–29
Sid Scholey 1929–30
Peter O'Rourke 1930–32
Bill Slade 1932–34
Andy Wilson 1934–37
Tommy Lowes 1937–44
Harry Hibbs 1944–51
Tony McPhee 1951
Brough Fletcher 1952–53
Major Frank Buckley 1953–55
John Love 1955–57
Billy Moore 1957–64
Alf Wood 1964
Reg Shaw 1964–68
Dick Graham 1968
Ron Lewin 1968–69
Billy Moore 1969–72
John Smith 1972–73
Ronnie Allen 1973
Doug Fraser 1973–77
Dave Mackay 1977–78
Alan Ashman 1978
Frank Sibley 1979
Alan Buckley 1979–86
Neil Martin *(Joint Manager with Buckley)* 1981–82
Tommy Coakley 1986–88
John Barnwell 1989–90
Kenny Hibbitt 1990–94
Chris Nicholl 1994–97
Jan Sorensen 1997–98
Ray Graydon 1998–2002
Colin Lee 2002–04
Paul Merson 2004–06
Kevin Broadhurst 2006
Richard Money 2006–08
Jimmy Mullen 2008–09
Chris Hutchings 2009–11
Dean Smith 2011–15
Sean O'Driscoll 2015–16
Jon Whitney 2016–18
Dean Keates 2018–19
Martin O'Connor 2019
Darrell Clarke 2019–21
Brian Dutton 2021
Matthew Taylor 2021–22
Michael Flynn February 2022–

TEN YEAR LEAGUE RECORD

		P	W	D	L	F	A	Pts	Pos
2012-13	FL 1	46	17	17	12	65	58	68	9
2013-14	FL 1	46	14	16	16	49	49	58	13
2014-15	FL 1	46	14	17	15	50	54	59	14
2015-16	FL 1	46	24	12	10	71	49	84	3
2016-17	FL 1	46	14	16	16	51	58	58	14
2017-18	FL 1	46	13	13	20	53	66	52	19
2018-19	FL 1	46	12	11	23	49	71	47	22
2019-20	FL 2	36	13	8	15	40	49	47	12§
2020-21	FL 2	46	11	20	15	45	53	53	19
2021-22	FL 2	46	14	12	20	47	60	54	16

§Decided on points-per-game (1.31)

DID YOU KNOW ?

Defender Andy Dornan made 149 first-team appearances for Walsall during a four-year stay with the Saddlers between 1986 and 1990. His only goal during this period came on 1 May 1990 when he netted from close range in the 1-1 draw with Rotherham United. The goal was of historic significance as it proved to be the club's final goal in a Football League game at Fellows Park.

WALSALL – SKY BET LEAGUE TWO 2021–22 LEAGUE RECORD

Match No.	Date		Venue	Opponents	Result		H/T Score	Lg Pos.	Goalscorers	Attendance
1	Aug	7	A	Tranmere R	L	0-1	0-0	19		7728
2		14	H	Forest Green R	L	1-3	0-3	23	Kiernan [90]	4310
3		17	H	Scunthorpe U	D	1-1	0-0	23	Phillips [47]	4009
4		21	A	Hartlepool U	L	0-2	0-1	23		4677
5		28	H	Stevenage	W	1-0	1-0	21	Wilkinson [5]	4257
6	Sept	4	A	Bradford C	D	1-1	1-1	21	Earing [42]	15,822
7		11	H	Mansfield T	W	3-1	2-0	18	Miller 2 [6, 48], Taylor [22]	5203
8		18	A	Newport Co	L	1-2	1-1	19	Shade [45]	3825
9		25	H	Bristol R	L	1-2	1-0	22	Phillips [32]	5434
10	Oct	2	A	Exeter C	D	2-2	1-1	21	Miller 2 (1 pen) [37 (p), 70]	4839
11		9	H	Salford C	W	2-1	1-0	19	Phillips [1], Wilkinson [90]	5005
12		16	A	Leyton Orient	D	0-0	0-0	18		5826
13		19	A	Oldham Ath	W	3-1	2-0	16	Earing [33], Miller [43], Osaoabe [85]	3762
14		23	H	Barrow	D	2-2	1-1	14	Miller 2 [4, 62]	4508
15		30	A	Sutton U	W	1-0	0-0	13	Shade [66]	3319
16	Nov	13	H	Harrogate T	L	1-3	0-1	15	Phillips [88]	4651
17		20	H	Rochdale	D	0-0	0-0	15		6144
18		23	A	Port Vale	W	1-0	1-0	11	Kiernan [29]	6248
19		27	A	Carlisle U	L	0-1	0-0	14		3795
20	Dec	7	H	Crawley T	D	1-1	1-1	12	Kiernan [41]	3609
21		11	H	Colchester U	W	3-0	2-0	12	Khan 2 [22, 32], Earing [66]	4065
22	Jan	1	H	Newport Co	D	3-3	0-1	13	Wilkinson 2 [53, 90], Dolan (og) [65]	4946
23		8	A	Stevenage	L	1-3	0-2	15	Kiernan [70]	2167
24		15	A	Mansfield T	L	0-2	0-0	15		5728
25		22	H	Exeter C	L	0-2	0-1	17		4750
26		25	H	Bradford C	L	1-2	0-1	17	Miller [57]	4097
27		29	A	Bristol R	L	0-1	0-0	19		8003
28	Feb	5	H	Northampton T	L	0-1	0-1	21		5315
29		8	A	Scunthorpe U	L	0-1	0-1	21		2123
30		12	H	Tranmere R	W	1-0	0-0	18	Wilkinson (pen) [85]	5440
31		19	A	Forest Green R	W	1-0	1-0	16	Miller [12]	3122
32		22	A	Swindon T	L	0-5	0-2	17		9840
33		26	H	Hartlepool U	W	3-1	2-0	17	Miller 2 [13, 67], Wilkinson [26]	4760
34	Mar	1	A	Northampton T	D	1-1	0-1	16	Wilkinson [50]	4861
35		5	A	Barrow	D	1-1	0-1	16	Daniels [67]	3439
36		12	H	Sutton U	W	1-0	1-0	16	Wilkinson (pen) [33]	5801
37		15	H	Oldham Ath	W	2-1	1-1	14	Osaoabe [32], Wilkinson [73]	4339
38		19	A	Harrogate T	D	1-1	0-0	14	Wilkinson (pen) [60]	2570
39		26	A	Salford C	L	1-2	1-1	16	Menayese [34]	2584
40	Apr	2	H	Leyton Orient	L	0-2	0-2	17		4849
41		9	A	Rochdale	L	0-1	0-0	18		2437
42		15	H	Carlisle U	W	1-0	1-0	15	Earing [45]	5114
43		18	A	Crawley T	L	0-1	0-0	16		2258
44		23	H	Port Vale	W	2-0	0-0	14	Perry [67], Osaoabe [90]	6840
45		30	A	Colchester U	D	2-2	1-1	15	Kiernan [39], Miller [48]	3520
46	May	7	H	Swindon T	L	0-3	0-3	16		9089

Final League Position: 16

GOALSCORERS

League (47): Miller 12 (1 pen), Wilkinson 10 (3 pens), Kiernan 5, Earing 4, Phillips 4, Osaoabe 3, Khan 2, Shade 2, Daniels 1, Menayese 1, Perry 1, Taylor 1, own goal 1.
FA Cup (2): Kiernan 1, Osadebe 1.
Carabao Cup (0).
Papa John's Trophy (2): Osadebe 1, Phillips 1.

Rushworth C 43	Mills Z 5 + 4	Taylor A 8 + 3	Monthe E 36 + 1	Ward S 26 + 1	Kinsella L 27 + 5	Labadie J 32 + 3	Shade T 26 + 13	Osaoabe E 35 + 8	Kiernan B 28 + 9	Wilkinson C 28 + 5	Phillips K 15 + 11	Earing J 42 + 3	White H 41 + 1	Menayese R 29 + 4	Perry S 7 + 13	Miller G 36 + 5	Rose J 3	Khan O 5 + 2	Willock S — + 2	Leak T 5 + 1	Daniels D 18	Devine R 8	Rodney D 2 + 12	Tomlin L 1 + 4	Shaw J — + 2	Sadler M — + 1	Match No.
1	2	3	4	5	6^{2}	7	8	9	10^{1}	11	12	13															1
1	2	3	4	5	13	8^{2}	6^{1}	7	9	10	11	12															2
1	13	3		5	8			12	9^{1}	11	6	10	2^{2}	4	7												3
1		3^{2}	13	5	8			12	9	11	6	10	2	4	7^{1}												4
1		13	4	5	6	7		12	10	8	11^{1}	9^{2}	2	3													5
1		13	4	5	6	7■	12		10^{2}		8	9^{3}	2	3	14	11^{1}											6
1		3	4	5	6		7^{1}	12	10		8^{2}	9	2		13	11											7
1			4	5	7^{2}		9^{1}	10	12		6	8	2	3	13	11											8
1	13	3	4	5			10	12^{3}	9^{1}		8^{2}	6	2	14	7	11											9
1			4	5		6	12	9	10^{1}		8	7	2	3		11											10
			4	5		6^{1}	13	9	10^{3}	14	11^{2}	7	2	3	12	8	1										11
1			4	5		8	12	9	10^{2}	13	7^{1}	6	2	3		11											12
1			4	5		6^{3}	10^{1}	9	12	8^{2}	13	7	2	3	14	11											13
1			4	5		6	12	9^{2}		8	10^{1}	7	2	3	13	11											14
1		14	4	5		6	12	9^{2}	10^{3}		8^{1}	7	2	3	13	11											15
1			4	5			8	9	10^{2}		13	6	2	3	7^{1}	11		12									16
1			4	5	14	6	10^{1}	9^{2}	13	8	12	7^{3}		3		11		2									17
1			4	5	13	6	12	9^{3}	10^{1}	8^{2}	14	7	2	3		11											18
1			4	5		6		9		8	12	7	2	3		11		10^{1}									19
1			4	5	12	6^{1}		8^{3}	11	10	9^{2}	7	2	3		13		14									20
1		3		5	7			9^{1}	10^{2}		12	6	2	4	13	11^{3}		8	14								21
1		3		5	7	13	14	9^{2}		12	10^{1}	6^{3}	2	4		11		8									22
1	2			5		6	13		10^{2}	9	12	7	3	4		11^{1}		8									23
1				5		6^{3}	8^{1}	9	10^{2}	13	12	7	2	4		11			14	3							24
1	12			5^{1}	7	6	8^{2}		10	11^{3}	14	9	2	3■		13				4							25
1	5				7	9^{1}	13	12	10^{2}	8	14	6	2			11				4^{3}	3						26
1					7	9^{1}	13	12	8^{2}	10		6	2	3		11					4	5					27
1					6	14	13	7^{1}	12	11		8^{3}	5	2		10				3	4	9^{2}					28
1			4		6	8	11	7^{2}	12	13			5	2^{1}		10					3	9					29
1			4		7		6^{3}	13	9	10		12	2	14	8^{1}	11^{2}					3	5					30
1			4		6		9	7		10^{2}		8	5	2	13	11^{1}					3		12				31
1			4		8	13	9	7	14	10		5^{3}	6	2		11^{1}					3^{2}		12				32
1			4		7	6	9	5^{3}	14	10^{1}		8	2			11^{2}					3		13	12			33
1			4		7	6	9	5		10^{2}		8	2			11^{1}					3		12	13			34
1			4		6	8	5	2	13	11		7				10^{1}					3		12	9^{2}			35
1			5		9	7	6	2		11^{1}		8	3			10					4		12				36
1			5		9	7^{2}	6	2	13	11		8^{3}	3		14	10^{1}					4		12				37
1			5		7	9	6	2		11		8	3			10^{1}					4		12				38
			5		8	7	6	2		11		9^{3}	3	12		13	1				4^{1}		10^{2}	14			39
1	13		4		6	9	5	10		11		7	2	3^{1}		14							8^{3}	12^{2}			40
			4	3^{2}	6^{1}	9		8	10^{3}	11		7	2		12	13	1					5	14				41
1			4	14		6	5	8	10^{1}			7	2^{2}			11				13	3	9^{3}	12				42
1	6^{2}		5			7	13	2	11			8	12	3	9^{1}	10^{3}				4			14				43
1			5			7^{1}	2	9	11			8	3	13	12	10					4	6^{2}					44
1			5		12		6	9^{2}	10^{3}			8	2	3	7^{1}	11					4		13		14		45
1			4^{3}		7		9	6	10			8^{2}	2		12	11					3	5^{1}			13	14	46

FA Cup
First Round King's Lynn T (a) 1-0
Second Round Swindon T (h) 1-2

Carabao Cup
First Round Doncaster R (h) 0-0
(Doncaster R won 4-3 on penalties)

Papa John's Trophy
Group D (S) Brighton & HA U21 (h) 1-0
Group D (S) Northampton T (a) 1-1
(Walsall won 4-2 on penalties)
Group D (S) Forest Green R (h) 0-2
Second Round Cambridge U (a) 0-2

WATFORD

FOUNDATION

The club was formed as Watford Rovers in 1881. The name was changed to West Herts in 1893 and then the name Watford was adopted after rival club Watford St Mary's was absorbed in 1898.

Vicarage Road Stadium, Vicarage Road, Watford, Hertfordshire WD18 0ER.

Telephone: (01923) 496 000.

Ticket Office: (01923) 223 023.

Website: www.watfordfc.com

Email: yourvoice@watfordfc.com

Ground Capacity: 22,200.

Record Attendance: 34,099 v Manchester U, FA Cup 4th rd (replay), 3 February 1969.

Pitch Measurements: 105m × 68m (115yd × 74.5yd).

Chairman and Chief Executive: Scott Duxbury.

Manager: Rob Edwards.

Assistant Manager: Richie Kyle.

Colours: Yellow and black hooped shirts, black shorts with yellow trim, yellow socks with black trim.

Year Formed: 1881.

Turned Professional: 1897.

Previous Names: 1881, Watford Rovers; 1893, West Herts; 1898, Watford.

Club Nickname: 'The Hornets'.

Grounds: 1883, Vicarage Meadow, Rose and Crown Meadow; 1889, Colney Butts; 1890, Cassio Road; 1922, Vicarage Road.

First Football League Game: 28 August 1920, Division 3, v QPR (a) W 2–1 – Williams; Horseman, Fred Gregory; Bacon, Toone, Wilkinson; Bassett, Ronald (1), Hoddinott, White (1), Waterall.

Record League Victory: 8–0 v Sunderland, Division 1, 25 September 1982 – Sherwood; Rice, Rostron, Taylor, Terry, Bolton, Callaghan (2), Blissett (4), Jenkins (2), Jackett, Barnes.

Record Cup Victory: 10–1 v Lowestoft T, FA Cup 1st rd, 27 November 1926 – Yates; Prior, Fletcher (1); Frank Smith, Bert Smith, Strain; Stephenson, Warner (3), Edmonds (3), Swan (1), Daniels (1), (1 og).

Record Defeat: 0–10 v Wolverhampton W, FA Cup 1st rd (replay), 24 January 1912.

Most League Points (2 for a win): 71, Division 4, 1977–78.

Most League Points (3 for a win): 91, FL C, 2020–21.

Most League Goals: 92, Division 4, 1959–60.

HONOURS

League Champions: Second Division – 1997–98; Division 3 – 1968–69; Division 4 – 1977–78.
Runners-up: Division 1 – 1982–83; FL C – 2014–15, 2020–21; Division 2 – 1981–82; Division 3 – 1978–79.

FA Cup: *Runners-up:* 1984, 2019.

League Cup: semi-final – 1979, 2005.

European Competitions
UEFA Cup: 1983–84.

FOOTBALL YEARBOOK FACT FILE

Centre-forward Bob White scored a hat-trick for Watford on his first-team debut against Newport County on 25 October 1930. Despite this he was back in the reserves the following week as George James was restored to the line-up. White was never able to establish himself in two seasons with the Hornets, although he scored 21 goals from 24 senior appearances.

Highest League Scorer in Season: Cliff Holton, 42, Division 4, 1959–60.

Most League Goals in Total Aggregate: Luther Blissett, 148, 1976–83, 1984–88, 1991–92.

Most League Goals in One Match: 5, Eddie Mummery v Newport Co, Division 3 (S), 5 January 1924.

Most Capped Player: Craig Cathcart, 51 (69), Northern Ireland.

Most League Appearances: Luther Blissett, 415, 1976–83, 1984–88, 1991–92.

Youngest League Player: Keith Mercer, 16 years 125 days v Tranmere R, 16 February 1973.

Record Transfer Fee Received: £35,000,000 from Everton for Richarlison, July 2018.

Record Transfer Fee Paid: £30,000,000 to Rennes for Ismaila Sarr, August 2019.

Football League Record: 1920 Original Member of Division 3; 1921–58 Division 3 (S); 1958–60 Division 4; 1960–69 Division 3; 1969–72 Division 2; 1972–75 Division 3; 1975–78 Division 4; 1978–79 Division 3; 1979–82 Division 2; 1982–88 Division 1; 1988–92 Division 2; 1992–96 Division 1; 1996–98 Division 2; 1998–99 Division 1; 1999–2000 Premier League; 2000–04 Division 1; 2004–06 FL C; 2006–07 Premier League; 2007–15 FL C; 2015–20 Premier League; 2020–21 FL C; 2021–22 Premier League; 2022– FL C.

LATEST SEQUENCES

Longest Sequence of League Wins: 7, 28.8.2000 – 14.10.2000.

Longest Sequence of League Defeats: 9, 26.12.1972 – 27.2.1973.

Longest Sequence of League Draws: 7, 16.2.2008 – 22.3.2008.

Longest Sequence of Unbeaten League Matches: 22, 1.10.1996 – 1.3.1997.

Longest Sequence Without a League Win: 19, 27.11.1971 – 8.4.1972.

Successive Scoring Runs: 22 from 20.8.1985.

Successive Non-scoring Runs: 7 from 18.12.1971.

MANAGERS

John Goodall 1903–10
Harry Kent 1910–26
Fred Pagnam 1926–29
Neil McBain 1929–37
Bill Findlay 1938–47
Jack Bray 1947–48
Eddie Hapgood 1948–50
Ron Gray 1950–51
Haydn Green 1951–52
Len Goulden 1952–55
(General Manager to 1956)
Johnny Paton 1955–56
Neil McBain 1956–59
Ron Burgess 1959–63
Bill McGarry 1963–64
Ken Furphy 1964–71
George Kirby 1971–73
Mike Keen 1973–77
Graham Taylor 1977–87
Dave Bassett 1987–88
Steve Harrison 1988–90
Colin Lee 1990
Steve Perryman 1990–93
Glenn Roeder 1993–96
Graham Taylor 1996
Kenny Jackett 1996–97
Graham Taylor 1997–2001
Gianluca Vialli 2001–02
Ray Lewington 2002–05
Adrian Boothroyd 2005–08
Brendan Rodgers 2008–09
Malky Mackay 2009–11
Sean Dyche 2011–12
Gianfranco Zola 2012–13
Beppe Sannino 2013–14
Oscar Garcia 2014
Billy McKinlay 2014
Slavisa Jokanovic 2014–15
Quique Sanchez Flores 2015–16
Walter Mazzarri 2016–17
Marco Silva 2017–18
Javi Gracia 2018–19
Quique Sanchez Flores 2019
Nigel Pearson 2019–20
Vladimir Ivić 2020
Xisco Muñoz 2020–21
Claudio Ranieri 2021–22
Roy Hodgson 2022
Rob Edwards June 2022–

TEN YEAR LEAGUE RECORD

		P	W	D	L	F	A	Pts	Pos
2012-13	FL C	46	23	8	15	85	58	77	3
2013-14	FL C	46	15	15	16	74	64	60	13
2014-15	FL C	46	27	8	11	91	50	89	2
2015-16	PR Lge	38	12	9	17	40	50	45	13
2016-17	PR Lge	38	11	7	20	40	68	40	17
2017-18	PR Lge	38	11	8	19	44	64	41	14
2018-19	PR Lge	38	14	8	16	52	59	50	11
2019-20	PR Lge	38	8	10	20	36	64	34	19
2020-21	FL C	46	27	10	9	63	30	91	2
2021-22	PR Lge	38	6	5	27	34	77	23	19

DID YOU KNOW ?

Len Dewick was an amateur goalkeeper who made seven first-team appearances for Watford between 1923 and 1925. Contemporary newspapers reported that he would take the field wearing a pair of spectacles, but that this did not appear to affect his performances.

WATFORD – PREMIER LEAGUE 2021–22 LEAGUE RECORD

Match No.	Date	Venue	Opponents	Result		H/T Score	Lg Pos.	Goalscorers	Attendance
1	Aug 14	H	Aston Villa	W	3-2	2-0	6	Bonaventure [10], Sarr [42], Hernandez [67]	20,051
2	21	A	Brighton & HA	L	0-2	0-2	12		29,485
3	29	A	Tottenham H	L	0-1	0-1	12		57,672
4	Sept 11	H	Wolverhampton W	L	0-2	0-0	15		20,019
5	18	A	Norwich C	W	3-1	1-1	11	Bonaventure [17], Sarr 2 [63, 80]	26,649
6	25	H	Newcastle U	D	1-1	0-1	11	Sarr [72]	20,650
7	Oct 2	A	Leeds U	L	0-1	0-1	14		36,261
8	16	H	Liverpool	L	0-5	0-2	16		21,085
9	23	A	Everton	W	5-2	1-1	14	King 3 [13, 80, 86], Kucka [78], Bonaventure [90]	38,834
10	30	H	Southampton	L	0-1	0-1	16		20,869
11	Nov 7	A	Arsenal	L	0-1	0-0	17		59,833
12	20	H	Manchester U	W	4-1	2-0	15	King [28], Sarr [44], Bonaventure [90], Joao Pedro [90]	21,087
13	28	A	Leicester C	L	2-4	1-3	16	King (pen) [30], Bonaventure [61]	32,020
14	Dec 1	H	Chelsea	L	1-2	1-1	17	Bonaventure [44]	20,388
15	4	H	Manchester C	L	1-3	0-2	17	Hernandez [74]	20,673
16	10	A	Brentford	L	1-2	1-0	17	Bonaventure [24]	16,861
17	28	H	West Ham U	L	1-4	1-2	17	Bonaventure [4]	20,073
18	Jan 1	H	Tottenham H	L	0-1	0-0	17		20,391
19	15	A	Newcastle U	D	1-1	0-0	17	Joao Pedro [87]	52,223
20	21	H	Norwich C	L	0-3	0-0	18		20,782
21	Feb 5	A	Burnley	D	0-0	0-0	18		19,527
22	8	A	West Ham U	L	0-1	0-0	19		59,581
23	12	H	Brighton & HA	L	0-2	0-1	19		20,795
24	19	A	Aston Villa	W	1-0	0-0	18	Bonaventure [78]	41,936
25	23	H	Crystal Palace	L	1-4	1-2	19	Sissoko [18]	20,012
26	26	A	Manchester U	D	0-0	0-0	19		73,152
27	Mar 6	H	Arsenal	L	2-3	1-2	19	Hernandez [11], Sissoko [87]	21,142
28	10	A	Wolverhampton W	L	0-4	0-3	19		29,658
29	13	A	Southampton	W	2-1	2-1	18	Hernandez 2 [14, 34]	28,863
30	Apr 2	A	Liverpool	L	0-2	0-1	18		53,104
31	9	H	Leeds U	L	0-3	0-1	19		20,957
32	16	H	Brentford	L	1-2	0-1	19	Bonaventure [55]	20,747
33	23	A	Manchester C	L	1-5	1-3	19	Kamara [28]	53,013
34	30	H	Burnley	L	1-2	1-0	19	Tarkowski (og) [8]	20,738
35	May 7	A	Crystal Palace	L	0-1	0-1	19		24,622
36	11	H	Everton	D	0-0	0-0	19		20,653
37	15	H	Leicester C	L	1-5	1-2	19	Joao Pedro [6]	20,257
38	22	A	Chelsea	L	1-2	0-1	19	Gosling [87]	32,089

Final League Position: 19

GOALSCORERS

League (34): Bonaventure 10, Hernandez 5, King 5 (1 pen), Sarr 5, Joao Pedro 3, Sissoko 2, Gosling 1, Kamara 1, Kucka 1, own goal 1.
FA Cup (1): Joao Pedro 1.
Carabao Cup (2): Fletcher 2.

Bachmann D 12	Cathcart C 27 + 4	Troost-Ekong W 15 + 2	Kabasele C 12 + 4	Masina A 13 + 2	Etebo P 4 + 5	Sarr I 21 + 1	Cleverley T 20 + 8	Kucka J 22 + 4	Sema K 7 + 11	Bonaventure E 30 + 3	Hernandez C 11 + 14	Gosling D 2 + 2	Deeney T — + 2	Louza I 17 + 3	King J 27 + 5	Sierralta F 5	Sissoko M 36	Ngakia J 9 + 7	Rose D 7 + 1	Foster B 26	Femenia K 26 + 1	Tufan O 4 + 3	Joao Pedro d 15 + 13	N'Koulou N 2 + 1	Fletcher A — + 3	Samir C 19	Kamara H 18 + 1	Kayembe E 9 + 4	Kalu S 2 + 2	*Match No.*
1	2	3	4	5	6	7	8[3]	9[2]	10	11[1]	12	13	14																	1
1	2[2]	3	4	5	6	7	8		10[3]	11	12		14	9[1]	13															2
1	2[1]	3		5	6	7	14	9		10	13				11[2]	4	8[3]	12												3
1		3			6[2]	7		9	13	10	12				11[1]	4	8	2	5											4
	4	3			14	8	9[3]	6	13	10[2]					11		7	12	5	1	2[1]									5
	4	3			15	8	9[1]	6[2]		10[4]					11		7	14	5	1	2[3]	12	13							6
		3	14			8		6	12	10					11[1]	4[3]	7		5	1	2	9[2]	13							7
	3	4		9[1]		10	12	7		6[3]	11						8	13	5	1	2[2]		14							8
	4	3		5		7[1]		9		13	10				11		6	2[3]		1		8[2]	12	14						9
	4	3		5		6	12	8	13		9[2]				11		7	2[3]		1			10[1]		14					10
	3[3]					7		8[▪]		10[2]	13				11		6		5	1	2	9[1]	12	4	14					11
	3	12		5		7[2]	9			10	13			8[3]	11		6			1	2		14	4[1]						12
1	3	4		5			8[1]			11[3]	7			6[2]	10		9				2	12	13		14					13
1	4	3		5[1]			8[3]	13		7				6[2]	11		9	14	12		2		10							14
1	4	3					8[2]	13		7	12			6[1]	11		9	14	5[3]		2		10							15
1	4	3					9[1]	6	13	11[3]	8[2]				10		7	5			2	14	12							16
1	4			5				6	14	11	7[2]			12	10	3	9				2[1]	8[3]	13							17
1	2	3		5			13	6	9[2]	11[1]	14			7[3]	10	4	8						12							18
	3						13	8[2]		9[3]	14				10		7	2[1]		1	12		11			4	5	6		19
1			3				6[1]	14	13	9[▪]	12				10		8				2[3]		11			4	5[2]	7		20
	3						12	6	9		13				11		7			1	2		10[2]			4	5	8[1]		21
	3						9[1]	6		11				13	10		7	14		1	2[3]		12			4	5	8[2]		22
	3					13	9[3]	6[2]		11				12	10		7			1	2		14			4	5	8[1]		23
	3		14			6[3]	9		12	11[1]	13			8	10		7			1	2					4[2]	5			24
	3					9	8[2]			11	12			7	10[1]		6			1	2					4	5	13		25
	3		13			9	8[3]	14	12	10				7	11[1]		6	2[2]		1						4	5			26
	3						8[2]			10	9			7[1]			6			1	2		11			4	5	12	13	27
	3		12		14		8[3]			10	9			7	11[2]		6			1	2[1]					4	5		13	28
	14		3					8	13	11[1]	9[2]			7	12		6			1	2[3]		10			4	5			29
			3			7	12	9		14	10[3]			6[2]	13		8			1	2		11[1]			4	5			30
			3			9		8[2]		12	11[1]			7	14		6			1	2		10[3]			4	5	13		31
	14		3			9	12	8[1]		11				7	13		6			1	2[3]		10[2]			4	5			32
	13		3			9[1]	8			11				7[3]	10		6	2		1			12			4[2]	5	14		33
			3			9		8		11				7			6			1	2		10			4	5			34
	3	14		13		9	8[1]		12	11[2]					10		6			1	2					4[3]	5[▪]	7		35
	12		3	5	13				11			8					6	2		1			10			4		7[2]	9[1]	36
	4		3	5	13				11[2]			8[1]					6	2		1			10				12	7	9	37
1			3	13			8		11		12	14			9[1]		6				2		10			4	5[2]	7[3]		38

FA Cup

Third Round	Leicester C	(a)	1-4

Carabao Cup

Second Round	Crystal Palace	(h)	1-0
Third Round	Stoke C	(h)	1-3

WEST BROMWICH ALBION

FOUNDATION

There is a well known story that when employees of Salter's Spring Works in West Bromwich decided to form a football club, they had to send someone to the nearby Association Football stronghold of Wednesbury to purchase a football. A weekly subscription of 2d (less than 1p) was imposed and the name of the new club was West Bromwich Strollers.

The Hawthorns, West Bromwich, West Midlands B71 4LF.

Telephone: (0871) 271 1100.

Ticket Office: (0121) 227 2227.

Website: www.wba.co.uk

Email: enquiries@wbafc.co.uk

Ground Capacity: 26,688.

Record Attendance: 64,815 v Arsenal, FA Cup 6th rd, 6 March 1937.

Pitch Measurements: 105m × 68m (115yd × 74.5yd).

Chairman: Li Piyue.

Chief Executive: Xu Ke.

Manager: Steve Bruce.

Assistant Managers: Stephen Clemence, Steve Agnew.

Colours: Navy blue and white striped shirts with red trim, white shorts with navy blue and red trim, navy blue socks with white and red trim.

Year Formed: 1878.

Turned Professional: 1885.

Previous Name: 1878, West Bromwich Strollers; 1881, West Bromwich Albion.

Club Nicknames: 'The Throstles', 'The Baggies', 'Albion'.

Grounds: 1878, Coopers Hill; 1879, Dartmouth Park; 1881, Bunns Field, Walsall Street; 1882, Four Acres (Dartmouth Cricket Club); 1885, Stoney Lane; 1900, The Hawthorns.

First Football League Game: 8 September 1888, Football League, v Stoke (a) W 2–0 – Roberts; Jack Horton, Green; Ezra Horton, Perry, Bayliss; Bassett, Woodhall (1), Hendry, Pearson, Wilson (1).

Record League Victory: 12–0 v Darwen, Division 1, 4 April 1892 – Reader; Jack Horton, McCulloch; Reynolds (2), Perry, Groves; Bassett (3), McLeod, Nicholls (1), Pearson (4), Geddes (1), (1 og).

Record Cup Victory: 10–1 v Chatham (away), FA Cup 3rd rd, 2 March 1889 – Roberts; Jack Horton, Green; Timmins (1), Charles Perry, Ezra Horton; Bassett (2), Walter Perry (1), Bayliss (2), Pearson, Wilson (3), (1 og).

Record Defeat: 3–10 v Stoke C, Division 1, 4 February 1937.

League Champions: Division 1 – 1919–20; FL C – 2007–08; Division 2 – 1901–02, 1910–11.
Runners-up: Division 1 – 1924–25, 1953–54; FL C – 2009–10, 2019–20; First Division – 2001–02, 2003–04; Division 2 – 1930–31, 1948–49.

FA Cup Winners: 1888, 1892, 1931, 1954, 1968.
Runners-up: 1886, 1887, 1895, 1912, 1935.

League Cup Winners: 1966.
Runners-up: 1967, 1970.

European Competitions
Fairs Cup: 1966–67.
UEFA Cup: 1978–79 *(qf)*, 1979–80, 1981–82.
European Cup-Winners' Cup: 1968–69 *(qf)*.

FOOTBALL YEARBOOK FACT FILE

West Bromwich Albion attracted an attendance of 22,372 for their reserve-team encounter with local rivals Aston Villa on 3 March 1934. The gate was bigger than several of the club's first-team fixtures at The Hawthorns that season and a club record for Central League games. The teams drew 2-2 and Albion went on to win the title for a second consecutive season.

Most League Points (2 for a win): 60, Division 1, 1919–20.

Most League Points (3 for a win): 91, FL C, 2009–10.

Most League Goals: 105, Division 2, 1929–30.

Highest League Scorer in Season: William 'Ginger' Richardson, 39, Division 1, 1935–36.

Most League Goals in Total Aggregate: Tony Brown, 218, 1963–79.

Most League Goals in One Match: 6, Jimmy Cookson v Blackpool, Division 2, 17 September 1927.

Most Capped Player: James Morrison, 46, Scotland.

Most League Appearances: Tony Brown, 574, 1963–80.

Youngest League Player: Charlie Wilson, 16 years 73 days v Oldham Ath, 1 October 1921.

Record Transfer Fee Received: £16,500,000 from Dalian Yifang for Salomon Rondon, July 2019.

Record Transfer Fee Paid: £18,000,000 to West Ham U for Grady Diangana, September 2020.

Football League Record: 1888 Founder Member of Football League; 1901–02 Division 2; 1902–04 Division 1; 1904–11 Division 2; 1911–27 Division 1; 1927–31 Division 2; 1931–38 Division 1; 1938–49 Division 2; 1949–73 Division 1; 1973–76 Division 2; 1976–86 Division 1; 1986–91 Division 2; 1991–92 Division 3; 1992–93 Division 2; 1993–2002 Division 1; 2002–03 Premier League; 2003–04 Division 1; 2004–06 Premier League; 2006–08 FL C; 2008–09 Premier League; 2009–10 FL C; 2010–18 Premier League; 2018–20 FL C; 2020–21 Premier League; 2021– FL C.

LATEST SEQUENCES

Longest Sequence of League Wins: 11, 5.4.1930 – 8.9.1930.

Longest Sequence of League Defeats: 11, 28.10.1995 – 26.12.1995.

Longest Sequence of League Draws: 5, 30.8.1999 – 3.10.1999.

Longest Sequence of Unbeaten League Matches: 17, 7.9.1957 – 7.12.1957.

Longest Sequence Without a League Win: 20, 27.8.2017 – 2.1.2018.

Successive Scoring Runs: 36 from 26.4.1958.

Successive Non-scoring Runs: 5 from 26.1.2022.

MANAGERS

Louis Ford 1890–92
(Secretary-Manager)
Henry Jackson 1892–94
(Secretary-Manager)
Edward Stephenson 1894–95
(Secretary-Manager)
Clement Keys 1895–96
(Secretary-Manager)
Frank Heaven 1896–1902
(Secretary-Manager)
Fred Everiss 1902–48
Jack Smith 1948–52
Jesse Carver 1952
Vic Buckingham 1953–59
Gordon Clark 1959–61
Archie Macaulay 1961–63
Jimmy Hagan 1963–67
Alan Ashman 1967–71
Don Howe 1971–75
Johnny Giles 1975–77
Ronnie Allen 1977
Ron Atkinson 1978–81
Ronnie Allen 1981–82
Ron Wylie 1982–84
Johnny Giles 1984–85
Nobby Stiles 1985–86
Ron Saunders 1986–87
Ron Atkinson 1987–88
Brian Talbot 1988–91
Bobby Gould 1991–92
Ossie Ardiles 1992–93
Keith Burkinshaw 1993–94
Alan Buckley 1994–97
Ray Harford 1997
Denis Smith 1997–1999
Brian Little 1999–2000
Gary Megson 2000–04
Bryan Robson 2004–06
Tony Mowbray 2006–09
Roberto Di Matteo 2009–11
Roy Hodgson 2011–12
Steve Clarke 2012–13
Pepe Mel 2014
Alan Irvine 2014
Tony Pulis 2015–17
Alan Pardew 2017–18
Darren Moore 2018–19
Slaven Bilic 2019–20
Sam Allardyce 2020–21
Valerien Ismael 2021–22
Steve Bruce February 2022–

TEN YEAR LEAGUE RECORD

		P	*W*	*D*	*L*	*F*	*A*	*Pts*	*Pos*
2012-13	PR Lge	38	14	7	17	53	57	49	8
2013-14	PR Lge	38	7	15	16	43	59	36	17
2014-15	PR Lge	38	11	11	16	38	51	44	13
2015-16	PR Lge	38	10	13	15	34	48	43	14
2016-17	PR Lge	38	12	9	17	43	51	45	10
2017-18	PR Lge	38	6	13	19	31	56	31	20
2018-19	FL C	46	23	11	12	87	62	80	4
2019-20	FL C	46	22	17	7	77	45	83	2
2020-21	PR Lge	38	5	11	22	35	76	26	19
2021-22	FL C	46	18	13	15	52	45	67	10

DID YOU KNOW ?

West Bromwich Albion's Tony Brown was the first player to score in every round of the Football League Cup. During the 1965–66 season he scored a total of 10 goals in the competition, including a hat-trick in the semi-final second leg against Peterborough United as the Baggies went on to win the trophy for the only time in their history.

WEST BROMWICH ALBION – SKY BET CHAMPIONSHIP 2021–22 LEAGUE RECORD

Match No.	Date	Venue	Opponents	Result		H/T Score	Lg Pos.	Goalscorers	Attendance
1	Aug 6	A	Bournemouth	D	2-2	1-1	1	O'Shea [33], Robinson [67]	9254
2	14	H	Luton T	W	3-2	2-0	4	Naismith (og) [5], Robinson [36], Ahearne-Grant [66]	23,283
3	18	H	Sheffield U	W	4-0	1-0	1	Robinson (og) [26], O'Shea [47], Mowatt [53], Robinson [59]	23,113
4	21	A	Blackburn R	W	2-1	2-0	2	Mowatt [1], Phillips [45]	11,926
5	28	A	Peterborough U	W	1-0	0-0	2	Ajayi [90]	10,163
6	Sept 11	H	Millwall	D	1-1	0-0	1	Bartley [49]	23,142
7	14	H	Derby Co	D	0-0	0-0	1		21,636
8	18	A	Preston NE	D	1-1	1-1	3	Phillips [45]	13,850
9	24	H	QPR	W	2-1	0-1	1	Ahearne-Grant 2 [75, 88]	21,825
10	28	A	Cardiff C	W	4-0	1-0	1	Ahearne-Grant [5], Nelson (og) [56], Mowatt [75], Phillips [82]	17,363
11	Oct 1	A	Stoke C	L	0-1	0-0	1		22,703
12	15	H	Birmingham C	W	1-0	0-0	1	Ahearne-Grant [75]	24,870
13	20	A	Swansea C	L	1-2	1-0	3	Ahearne-Grant [1]	16,694
14	23	H	Bristol C	W	3-0	2-0	2	Hugill [7], Bartley [42], Ahearne-Grant [52]	23,845
15	30	A	Fulham	L	0-3	0-2	3		18,103
16	Nov 3	H	Hull C	W	1-0	0-0	3	Ahearne-Grant [69]	19,659
17	6	H	Middlesbrough	D	1-1	0-1	3	Diangana [65]	22,596
18	20	A	Huddersfield T	L	0-1	0-1	3		17,297
19	23	A	Blackpool	D	0-0	0-0	3		11,517
20	26	H	Nottingham F	D	0-0	0-0	3		22,424
21	Dec 4	A	Coventry C	W	2-1	2-0	3	Ahearne-Grant [20], McFadzean (og) [43]	23,755
22	11	H	Reading	W	1-0	0-0	3	Robinson [62]	21,306
23	17	A	Barnsley	D	0-0	0-0	3		12,086
24	27	A	Derby Co	L	0-1	0-0	4		24,846
25	Jan 2	H	Cardiff C	D	1-1	0-1	4	Robinson [48]	22,925
26	15	A	QPR	L	0-1	0-0	5		16,018
27	22	H	Peterborough U	W	3-0	0-0	5	Kipre [78], Ahearne-Grant [85], Diangana [89]	21,251
28	26	H	Preston NE	L	0-2	0-1	5		20,776
29	29	A	Millwall	L	0-2	0-0	5		12,855
30	Feb 9	A	Sheffield U	L	0-2	0-1	9		26,541
31	14	H	Blackburn R	D	0-0	0-0	8		20,680
32	19	A	Luton T	L	0-2	0-0	11		10,021
33	22	A	Middlesbrough	L	1-2	1-0	11	Molumby [28]	21,646
34	28	H	Swansea C	L	0-2	0-0	13		20,209
35	Mar 5	A	Hull C	W	2-0	1-0	13	Ahearne-Grant 2 (1 pen) [17, 48 (p)]	13,643
36	11	H	Huddersfield T	D	2-2	0-1	12	Ahearne-Grant (pen) [84], Carroll [85]	20,846
37	15	H	Fulham	W	1-0	0-0	12	Robinson [64]	20,079
38	19	A	Bristol C	D	2-2	0-1	12	Ahearne-Grant (pen) [68], Reach [90]	20,586
39	Apr 3	A	Birmingham C	L	0-1	0-0	12		17,936
40	6	H	Bournemouth	W	2-0	2-0	11	Mowatt [8], Carroll [12]	20,501
41	9	H	Stoke C	L	1-3	0-1	11	Robinson [73]	22,761
42	15	H	Blackpool	W	2-1	1-0	11	Carroll [42], Ahearne-Grant [90]	21,717
43	18	A	Nottingham F	L	0-4	0-3	12		28,926
44	23	H	Coventry C	D	0-0	0-0	13		22,160
45	30	A	Reading	W	1-0	0-0	10	Ahearne-Grant [78]	15,509
46	May 7	H	Barnsley	W	4-0	2-0	10	Ahearne-Grant 2 (1 pen) [37 (p), 60], Reach [40], Clarke [52]	21,515

Final League Position: 10

GOALSCORERS

League (52): Ahearne-Grant 18 (4 pens), Robinson 7, Mowatt 4, Carroll 3, Phillips 3, Bartley 2, Diangana 2, O'Shea 2, Reach 2, Ajayi 1, Clarke 1, Hugill 1, Kipre 1, Molumby 1, own goals 4.
FA Cup (1): Robinson 1.
Carabao Cup (0).

Button D 10	Kipre C 14	Bartley K 38 + 1	O'Shea D 12 + 2	Furlong D 38 + 3	Livermore J 37	Mowatt A 34	Townsend C 43	Diangana G 22 + 19	Ahearne-Grant K 41 + 3	Robinson C 26 + 17	Phillips M 18 + 10	Zohore K — + 2	Johnstone S 36	Clarke M 33	Ajayi S 27 + 4	Reach A 21 + 13	Tulloch R — + 2	Hugill J 7 + 13	Snodgrass R 4 + 2	Bryan K 1 + 2	Molumby J 17 + 14	Gardner-Hickman T 14 + 5	Fellows T 1 + 3	Dike D 1 + 1	Carroll A 11 + 4	De Castro Q — + 2	Ashworth Z — + 2	Taylor C — + 1	Match No.
1	2	3	4	5	6	7	8	9¹	10²	11	12	13																	1
		3	2	5	6	7	8	9	11²	10¹	12	13	1	4³	14														2
		4	3	2	8²	9	6	7¹	11	10	12		1	5³	13	14													3
		3	2	5	6	7	8	13	11³	9	10²		1	4¹	12		14												4
		3¹	4	5	6	7	8	9²	10		11		1		2	12		13											5
	4	3		5	6	7	8	9¹	10²	13	11		1		2			12											6
		3		5	6³	7	4	10	9¹	11²	13		1		2	8		12	14										7
		3		5	6	7	4	10¹	12	13	9²		1		2	8		11											8
		3		5	6	7	4	9²	11³	12	10¹		1		2	8		13		14									9
		3		5	6³	7	4	13	11¹	9²	12		1		2	8		10			14								10
		3		5	6	7³	4	13	11²	9	12		1		2	8		10¹			14								11
		3		5	6	7²	8		11³	10¹	9		1	4	2	14		12			13								12
		3		5	6		8		11	10¹	9³		1	4	2	14		12	13		7²								13
		3		5			8⁴	13	11²	12	9¹		1	4³	2	15		10	6	14	7								14
		3		5■	6		8	12	10³	13	9²		1	4	2			11¹	7		14								15
	2				6		8	14	10	11³	9²		1	3		12		13	7	4¹		5							16
	2	12		5			4	9	10	11²			1	3¹		8		13	7		6								17
	2	3		14	6■	7²	8	9¹	10		11³		1	4				12			13	5							18
	2	3		5		7	8	9¹	10	13	11²		1	4				12			6								19
	2	3		5		7	8	9¹	10³	11²	12		1	4		13		14			6■								20
	2	3		5		7	8	9¹	10	11²			1	4	14	13		12				6³							21
		3		5	2	7			10	9¹			1			4		11			6	8	12						22
	2	3		5	6¹	7	8	13	10	9²			1	4		14		11³			12								23
	2	3		5³	6		8	9²		10			1	4		11¹		13			7	14	12						24
	2	3			6	7■	8	12	10	11³			1■	4²		13					14	5	9¹						25
1				2	6		4		11	9	10¹			3		8					7	5		12					26
1	2	3		5	6		8	12	10⁴	14	9²			4³		7					13		15	11¹					27
1	2¹	3		5	6³	7	4	9	10	13	11²					8					14	12							28
1	2	3		5	6	7	8	12	10²	13	9¹			4											11				29
			14	2³	6■	7²	5	8¹	10	13			1	4	3	9					12				11				30
				2		7	5	12	10¹	8			1	4	3	9					6²	13			11				31
		3		5		7²	8	12	9	13			1	4¹	2	10					6				11				32
		4	2	14		6	5³	8²	10	12			1		3	9¹	13				7				11				33
		4	2¹	12		7	5	9	14	10			1		3	8²					6³				11	13			34
		3		5	7	8	9	12	10³	11¹			1	4	2						13	6²			14				35
		3²		5¹	7	8	9	13	11	10			1	4	2							6			12				36
		3		5	7	8³	9	13	11²	10¹			1	4	2						14	6			12				37
		3²		5	7	8	9¹	12	11	10			1	4	2	13						6							38
		3		5	7	8	9³	12	11²	10			1	4	2	14						6¹			13				39
		3	14	5¹	7	8³	9	10²		13			1	4	2						12	6			11				40
		3			7	8²	9³	10¹	12	13			1	4	2	14					6	5			11				41
1			3	5³	6¹			14	10	9²	12			4	2	8					7	13			11				42
1		3	2	5■	7	8²	9		11¹		14			4		6					13	12			10³				43
1			3		6		8³	13	10	14	12			4	2	5					7²	9¹			11				44
1		4	2		7		5¹	10	11	13	6³				3	9²					8					14	12		45
1			4	2	7³			10	11	14	6			5²	3¹	9					8						13	12	46

FA Cup
Third Round Brighton & HA (h) 1-2
(aet)

Carabao Cup
Second Round Arsenal (h) 0-6

WEST HAM UNITED

FOUNDATION

Thames Ironworks FC was formed by employees of this famous shipbuilding company in 1895 and entered the FA Cup in their initial season at Chatham and the London League in their second. The committee wanted to introduce professional players, so Thames Ironworks was wound up in June 1900 and relaunched a month later as West Ham United.

London Stadium, Queen Elizabeth Olympic Park, London E20 2ST.

Telephone: (020) 8548 2748.

Ticket Office: (0333) 030 1966.

Website: www.whufc.com

Email: supporterservices@westhamunited.co.uk

Ground Capacity: 60,000.

Record Attendance: 42,322 v Tottenham H, Division 1, 17 October 1970 (at Boleyn Ground); 60,000 v Manchester C, Carabao Cup 4th rd, 27 October 2021; 60,000 v Eintracht Frankfurt, Europa League semi-final 1st leg, 28 April 2022 (at London Stadium).

Pitch Measurements: 105m × 68m (115yd × 74.5yd).

Joint Chairmen: David Sullivan and David Gold.

Vice-Chairman: Baroness Karren Brady CBE.

Manager: David Moyes.

First-Team Coaches: Stuart Pearce, Kevin Nolan.

Colours: Claret and sky blue shirts with white and sky blue trim, white shorts with claret and sky blue trim, claret socks with sky blue and white trim.

Year Formed: 1895.

Turned Professional: 1900.

Previous Name: 1895, Thames Ironworks FC; 1900, West Ham United.

Club Nicknames: 'The Hammers', 'The Irons'.

Grounds: 1895, Memorial Recreation Ground, Canning Town; 1904, Boleyn Ground, Upton Park; 2016, London Stadium.

First Football League Game: 30 August 1919, Division 2, v Lincoln C (h) D 1–1 – Hufton; Cope, Lee; Lane, Fenwick, McCrae; David Smith, Moyes (1), Puddefoot, Morris, Bradshaw.

Record League Victory: 8–0 v Rotherham U, Division 2, 8 March 1958 – Gregory; Bond, Wright; Malcolm, Brown, Lansdowne; Grice, Smith (2), Keeble (2), Dick (4), Musgrove. 8–0 v Sunderland, Division 1, 19 October 1968 – Ferguson; Bonds, Charles; Peters, Stephenson, Moore (1); Redknapp, Boyce, Brooking (1), Hurst (6), Sissons.

HONOURS

League Champions: Division 2 – 1957–58, 1980–81.
Runners-up: First Division – 1992–93; Division 2 – 1922–23, 1990–91.

FA Cup Winners: 1964, 1975, 1980.
Runners-up: 1923, 2006.

League Cup: *Runners-up:* 1966, 1981.

European Competitions
UEFA Cup: 1999–2000; 2006–07.
Europa League: 2015–16, 2016–17, 2021–22 *(sf)*.
European Cup-Winners' Cup: 1964–65 *(winners)*, 1965–66 *(sf)*, 1975–76 *(runners-up)*, 1980–81 *(qf)*.
Intertoto Cup: 1999 *(winners)*.

FOOTBALL YEARBOOK FACT FILE

West Ham United were one of the first English clubs to switch from the traditional 2-3-5 formation to a modern 4-2-4 set-up. Manager Ted Fenton made the change from the start of the 1960–61 campaign and, although they lost the opening game of the season 4-2 away to Wolverhampton Wanderers, the Hammers finished in 16th position in Division One.

Record Cup Victory: 10–0 v Bury, League Cup 2nd rd (2nd leg), 25 October 1983 – Parkes; Stewart (1), Walford, Bonds (Orr), Martin (1), Devonshire (2), Allen, Cottee (4), Swindlehurst, Brooking (2), Pike.

Record Defeat: 2–8 v Blackburn R, Division 1, 26 December 1963; 0–6 v Oldham Ath, League Cup semi-final (1st leg), 14 February 1990.

Most League Points (2 for a win): 66, Division 2, 1980–81.

Most League Points (3 for a win): 88, Division 1, 1992–93.

Most League Goals: 101, Division 2, 1957–58.

Highest League Scorer in Season: Vic Watson, 42, Division 1, 1929–30.

Most League Goals in Total Aggregate: Vic Watson, 298, 1920–35.

Most League Goals in One Match: 6, Vic Watson v Leeds U, Division 1, 9 February 1929; 6, Geoff Hurst v Sunderland, Division 1, 19 October 1968.

Most Capped Player: Bobby Moore, 108, England.

Most League Appearances: Billy Bonds, 663, 1967–88.

Youngest League Player: Billy Williams, 16 years 221 days v Blackpool, 6 May 1922.

Record Transfer Fee Received: £25,000,000 from Marseille for Dmitri Payet, January 2017.

Record Transfer Fee Paid: £45,000,000 to Eintracht Frankfurt for Sebastien Haller, July 2019.

Football League Record: 1919 Elected to Division 2; 1923–32 Division 1; 1932–58 Division 2; 1958–78 Division 1; 1978–81 Division 2; 1981–89 Division 1; 1989–91 Division 2; 1991–93 Division 1; 1993–2003 Premier League; 2003–04 Division 1; 2004–05 FL C; 2005–11 Premier League; 2011–12 FL C; 2012– Premier League.

MANAGERS

Syd King 1902–32
Charlie Paynter 1932–50
Ted Fenton 1950–61
Ron Greenwood 1961–74
(continued as General Manager to 1977)
John Lyall 1974–89
Lou Macari 1989–90
Billy Bonds 1990–94
Harry Redknapp 1994–2001
Glenn Roeder 2001–03
Alan Pardew 2003–06
Alan Curbishley 2006–08
Gianfranco Zola 2008–10
Avram Grant 2010–11
Sam Allardyce 2011–15
Slaven Bilic 2015–17
David Moyes 2017–18
Manuel Pellegrini 2018–19
David Moyes December 2019–

LATEST SEQUENCES

Longest Sequence of League Wins: 9, 19.10.1985 – 14.12.1985.

Longest Sequence of League Defeats: 9, 28.3.1932 – 29.8.1932.

Longest Sequence of League Draws: 5, 29.11.2015 – 26.12.2015.

Longest Sequence of Unbeaten League Matches: 27, 27.12.1980 – 10.10.1981.

Longest Sequence Without a League Win: 17, 31.1.1976 – 21.8.1976.

Successive Scoring Runs: 27 from 5.10.1957.

Successive Non-scoring Runs: 5 from 17.9.2006.

TEN YEAR LEAGUE RECORD

		P	W	D	L	F	A	Pts	Pos
2012-13	PR Lge	38	12	10	16	45	53	46	10
2013-14	PR Lge	38	11	7	20	40	51	40	13
2014-15	PR Lge	38	12	11	15	44	47	47	12
2015-16	PR Lge	38	16	14	8	65	51	62	7
2016-17	PR Lge	38	12	9	17	47	64	45	11
2017-18	PR Lge	38	10	12	16	48	68	42	13
2018-19	PR Lge	38	15	7	16	52	55	52	10
2019-20	PR Lge	38	10	9	19	49	62	39	16
2020-21	PR Lge	38	19	8	11	62	47	65	6
2021-22	PR Lge	38	16	8	14	60	51	56	7

DID YOU KNOW ?

When the Football Association relaxed its opposition to clubs touring Germany in 1924 (a legacy of the First World War) West Ham United were one of a group of English teams to travel there in the close season. The Hammers played six games, losing just once when they went down 5-2 to Freiburger FC.

WEST HAM UNITED – PREMIER LEAGUE 2021–22 LEAGUE RECORD

Match No.	*Date*	*Venue*	*Opponents*	*Result*		*H/T Score*	*Lg Pos.*	*Goalscorers*	*Attendance*
1	Aug 15	A	Newcastle U	W	4-2	1-2	4	Cresswell 18, Benrahma 53, Soucek 63, Antonio 86	50,673
2	23	H	Leicester C	W	4-1	1-0	1	Fornals 26, Benrahma 56, Antonio 2 80, 84	59,901
3	28	H	Crystal Palace	D	2-2	1-0	1	Fornals 39, Antonio 68	59,751
4	Sept 11	A	Southampton	D	0-0	0-0	6		27,861
5	19	H	Manchester U	L	1-2	1-1	8	Benrahma 30	59,958
6	25	A	Leeds U	W	2-1	0-1	7	Firpo (og) 67, Antonio 90	36,417
7	Oct 3	H	Brentford	L	1-2	0-1	9	Bowen 80	49,940
8	17	A	Everton	W	1-0	0-0	7	Ogbonna 74	39,132
9	24	H	Tottenham H	W	1-0	0-0	4	Antonio 72	59,924
10	31	A	Aston Villa	W	4-1	2-1	4	Johnson 7, Rice 38, Fornals 80, Bowen 84	41,874
11	Nov 7	H	Liverpool	W	3-2	1-1	3	Alisson (og) 4, Fornals 67, Zouma 74	59,909
12	20	A	Wolverhampton W	L	0-1	0-0	4		30,667
13	28	A	Manchester C	L	1-2	0-1	4	Lanzini 90	53,245
14	Dec 1	H	Brighton & HA	D	1-1	1-0	4	Soucek 5	59,626
15	4	H	Chelsea	W	3-2	1-2	4	Lanzini (pen) 40, Bowen 56, Masuaku 87	59,942
16	12	A	Burnley	D	0-0	0-0	4		18,065
17	15	A	Arsenal	L	0-2	0-0	5		59,777
18	26	H	Southampton	L	2-3	0-1	6	Antonio 49, Benrahma 64	41,027
19	28	A	Watford	W	4-1	2-1	5	Soucek 27, Benrahma 29, Noble (pen) 58, Vlasic 90	20,073
20	Jan 1	A	Crystal Palace	W	3-2	3-0	5	Antonio 22, Lanzini 2 (1 pen) 25, 45 (p)	24,351
21	12	H	Norwich C	W	2-0	1-0	4	Bowen 2 42, 83	59,775
22	16	H	Leeds U	L	2-3	1-2	4	Bowen 33, Fornals 52	59,951
23	22	A	Manchester U	L	0-1	0-0	5		73,130
24	Feb 8	H	Watford	W	1-0	0-0	4	Bowen 68	59,581
25	13	A	Leicester C	D	2-2	1-1	4	Bowen 10, Dawson 90	32,061
26	19	H	Newcastle U	D	1-1	1-1	5	Dawson 32	59,949
27	27	H	Wolverhampton W	W	1-0	0-0	5	Soucek 59	59,946
28	Mar 5	A	Liverpool	L	0-1	0-1	5		53,059
29	13	H	Aston Villa	W	2-1	0-0	6	Yarmolenko 70, Fornals 82	59,957
30	20	A	Tottenham H	L	1-3	1-2	7	Benrahma 35	58,685
31	Apr 3	H	Everton	W	2-1	1-0	6	Cresswell 32, Bowen 58	59,953
32	10	A	Brentford	L	0-2	0-0	6		17,032
33	17	H	Burnley	D	1-1	0-1	7	Soucek 74	59,958
34	24	A	Chelsea	L	0-1	0-0	7		32,231
35	May 1	H	Arsenal	L	1-2	1-1	7	Bowen 45	59,959
36	8	A	Norwich C	W	4-0	3-0	7	Benrahma 2 12, 45, Antonio 30, Lanzini (pen) 65	26,428
37	15	H	Manchester C	D	2-2	2-0	7	Bowen 2 24, 45	59,972
38	22	A	Brighton & HA	L	1-3	1-0	7	Antonio 40	31,604

Final League Position: 7

GOALSCORERS

League (60): Bowen 12, Antonio 10, Benrahma 8, Fornals 6, Lanzini 5 (3 pens), Soucek 5, Cresswell 2, Dawson 2, Johnson 1, Masuaku 1, Noble 1 (1 pen), Ogbonna 1, Rice 1, Vlasic 1, Yarmolenko 1, Zouma 1, own goals 2.
FA Cup (5): Bowen 2, Antonio 1, Lanzini 1, Rice 1.
Carabao Cup (2): Bowen 1, Lanzini 1.
UEFA Europa League (18): Benrahma 3, Bowen 3, Rice 3, Antonio 2, Dawson 2, Yarmolenko 2, Diop 1, Noble 1 (1 pen), Soucek 1.
Papa John's Trophy (4): Appiah-Forson 1, Ashby 1, Nevers 1, Okoflex 1 (1 pen).

Fabianski L 37	Coufal V 25 + 3	Dawson C 30 + 4	Ogbonna A 11	Cresswell A 31	Rice D 35 + 1	Soucek T 34 + 1	Bowen J 34 + 2	Benrahma S 26 + 6	Fornals P 32 + 4	Antonio M 34 + 2	Fredericks R 3 + 4	Yarmolenko A 1 + 18	Johnson B 16 + 4	Noble M 3 + 8	Lanzini M 19 + 11	Vlasic N 6 + 13	Zouma K 24	Masuaku A 6 + 7	Diop I 10 + 3	Ashby H — + 1	Kral A — + 1	Perkins S — + 1	Areola A 1	Chesters D — + 1	Match No.
1	2	3	4	5	6	7	8^{3}	9^{1}	10	11^{2}	12	13	14												1
1	2	3	4	5	7	6	8	10^{1}	9	11^{2}		13		12											2
1	2	3	4	5	7	6	8^{1}	10	9^{2}	11		13			12										3
1	2	3	4	5	7	6	8^{2}	9^{1}	10	11■		13				12									4
1	2		4	5	8	7	10^{3}	11^{2}	6			12		14	13	9^{1}	3								5
1	2	14	4	5	7	6	8^{3}	10	9^{1}	11^{2}		13				12	3								6
1	2		4	5	7	6	8	9	10	11							3								7
1		12	4	5	7	6^{1}	8^{3}	9^{2}	10	11		14	2		13		3								8
1		13	4	5	7	6	8^{2}	9^{1}	10	11			2		12		3								9
1	14		4	5	7	6	8^{2}	10^{1}	9^{3}	11			2		12	13	3								10
1	13	12	4^{1}	5	7	6	8^{2}	10^{3}	9	11			2				3	14							11
1		3		5	7	6	8^{3}	9^{2}	10^{1}	11		14	2		12	13	4								12
1	13	3		5^{2}	7	6	14	9^{1}	8	11			2		12		4	10^{3}							13
1	2	3			7	6	8	10^{1}	9^{2}	11			5		12		4	13							14
1	5	2			7	6	9	14	13	11			8^{1}		10^{3}		3^{2}	12	4						15
1	2	3			7	6	8	10^{1}	13	11					9^{2}	12		5	4						16
1	2■	3			7	6	8	12	9^{2}	11					10^{1}			5	4	13					17
1	2	3			7	6	11	10^{3}	9^{2}	12		14			13	8^{1}		5	4						18
1	2	3				7	8	10^{2}		11			5^{1}	6	9^{3}	13		12	4		14				19
1	2	3			6	7	8	10^{2}		11			5^{1}	14	9^{3}	13		12	4						20
1	2	3		5	7		8		9	11^{2}		13			6	10^{1}		12	4						21
1	2	3		5	7		8		9^{2}	11		13			6	10^{1}		12	4^{3}			14			22
	2^{1}	3		5	7	6	8		10	11	12				9		4						1		23
1	2	3		5	7	6	8	10^{1}	9	11					12		4								24
1	2^{1}	3		5	7	6	8	13	10^{2}	11	12				9^{3}	14			4						25
1		3		5	7	6	8	9^{2}	10	11	2^{1}		12			13	4								26
1		2		4	7	6	9		8^{2}	11^{1}			5		10	12	3		13						27
1		3		5		7	6^{1}	12	10^{3}	11			2	13	8	9^{2}	4							14	28
1		3		5^{2}	7	6		11^{3}	9	10^{1}	13	12	2		8		4		14						29
1		3		4	7	6		9	12	11^{2}		13	5		10^{3}	14	2	8^{1}							30
1		3		5	7	6	8^{1}	9^{2}	10	11	2	13		12			4								31
1	2	3		5	7	6	8	13	10	11^{3}					9^{2}	14	4^{1}		12						32
1		3		5	7	6	8	12	13	11			2		9^{2}	10^{1}			4						33
1	5	3■		4	12	6	13	11^{3}	10			9^{2}	2	7^{1}	14			8							34
1	2			4	7	13	11	10^{3}	8	12	5	14		6^{2}	9^{1}		3								35
1	2	3^{2}		5	7		8	10^{3}	9	11^{1}		12		13	6	14	4								36
1	2	3		5	7	6	8		10^{2}	11^{3}		13	14	12	9^{1}		4								37
1	2^{1}	3		5	7	6	8		9^{3}	11		12	14	13	10^{2}		4								38

FA Cup

Third Round	Leeds U	(h)	2-0
Fourth Round	Kidderminster H	(a)	2-1
(aet)			
Fifth Round	Southampton	(a)	1-3

Carabao Cup

Third Round	Manchester U	(a)	1-0
Fourth Round	Manchester C	(h)	0-0
(West Ham U won 5-3 on penalties)			
Quarter-Final	Tottenham H	(a)	1-2

Papa John's Trophy (West Ham U U21)

Group A (S)	Ipswich T	(a)	2-1
Group A (S)	Colchester U	(a)	0-1
Group A (S)	Gillingham	(a)	2-0

UEFA Europa League

Group H	Dinamo Zagreb	(a)	2-0
Group H	Rapid Vienna	(h)	2-0
Group H	Genk	(h)	3-0
Group H	Genk	(a)	2-2
Group H	Rapid Vienna	(a)	2-0
Group H	Dinamo Zagreb	(h)	0-1
Round of 16 1st leg	Sevilla	(a)	0-1
Round of 16 2nd leg	Sevilla	(h)	2-0
(aet)			
Quarter-Final 1st leg	Lyon	(h)	1-1
Quarter-Final 2nd leg	Lyon	(a)	3-0
Semi-Final 1st leg	Eintracht Frankfurt	(h)	1-2
Semi-Final 2nd leg	Eintracht Frankfurt	(a)	0-1

WIGAN ATHLETIC

FOUNDATION

Following the demise of Wigan Borough and their resignation from the Football League in 1931, a public meeting was called in Wigan at the Queen's Hall in May 1932 at which a new club, Wigan Athletic, was founded in the hope of carrying on in the Football League. With this in mind, they bought Springfield Park for £2,250, but failed to gain admission to the Football League until 46 years later.

DW Stadium, Loire Drive, Newtown, Wigan, Lancashire WN5 0UZ.

Telephone: (01942) 774 000.

Ticket Office: (01942) 311 111.

Website: www.wiganathletic.com

Email: feedback@wiganathletic.com

Ground Capacity: 25,133.

Record Attendance: 27,526 v Hereford U, 12 December 1953 (at Springfield Park); 25,133 v Manchester U, Premier League, 11 May 2008 (at DW Stadium).

Pitch Measurements: 105m × 68m (115yd × 74.5yd).

Chairman: Talal Al-Hammad.

Chief Executive: Mal Brannigan.

Manager: Leam Richardson.

Assistant Manager: Gregor Rioch.

Colours: Blue and white striped shirts with blue sleeves, blue shorts with white trim, blue socks with white trim.

Year Formed: 1932.

Turned Professional: 1932.

Club Nickname: 'The Latics'.

Grounds: 1932, Springfield Park; 1999, JJB Stadium (renamed DW Stadium 2009).

First Football League Game: 19 August 1978, Division 4, v Hereford U (a) D 0–0 – Brown; Hinnigan, Gore, Gillibrand, Ward, Davids, Corrigan, Purdie, Houghton, Wilkie, Wright.

Record League Victory: 8–0 v Hull C, FL C, 14 July 2020 – Marshall; Byrne, Kipre, Balogun (Dobre), Robinson (Evans), Williams (1) (Massey), Morsy, Naismith (1), Dowell (3) (Roberts), Lowe (1), Moore (2) (Pearce).

Record Cup Victory: 6–0 v Carlisle U (a), FA Cup 1st rd, 24 November 1934 – Caunce; Robinson, Talbot; Paterson, Watson, Tufnell; Armes (2), Robson (1), Roberts (2), Felton, Scott (1); 6–0 v Oldham Ath (a), Papa John's Trophy 3rd rd, 4 January 2022 – Amos; Darikwa, Whatmough (Kerr), Tilt, Pearce (Robinson), Power (1), Naylor (1), Massey (1) (Aasgaard), Lang (Jordan Jones), Edwards (2), Keane (1) (Humphrys).

HONOURS

League Champions: FL 1 – 2015–16, 2017–18, 2021–22; Second Division – 2002–03; Third Division – 1996–97.
Runners-up: FL C – 2004–05.

FA Cup Winners: 2013.

League Cup: *Runners-up:* 2006.

League Trophy Winners: 1985, 1999.

European Competitions
Europa League: 2013–14.

FOOTBALL YEARBOOK FACT FILE

The main stand at Wigan Athletic's Springfield Park ground was gutted by fire just hours after their final home game of the 1952–53 season when the team was presented with the trophy for winning the Lancashire Combination. The dressing rooms and the supporters' club canteen were also destroyed and the Latics had to borrow kit for their remaining fixture at Marine.

Record Defeat: 1–9 v Tottenham H, Premier League, 22 November 2009; 0–8 v Chelsea, Premier League, 9 May 2010.

Most League Points (2 for a win): 55, Division 4, 1978–79 and 1979–80.

Most League Points (3 for a win): 100, Division 2, 2002–03.

Most League Goals: 89, FL 1, 2017–18.

Highest League Scorer in Season: Graeme Jones, 31, Division 3, 1996–97.

Most League Goals in Total Aggregate: Andy Liddell, 70, 1998–2004.

Most League Goals in One Match: Not more than three goals by one player.

Most Capped Players: James McLean, 29 (94), Republic of Ireland.

Most League Appearances: Kevin Langley, 317, 1981–86, 1990–94.

Youngest League Player: Steve Nugent, 16 years 132 days v Leyton Orient, 16 September 1989.

Record Transfer Fee Received: £15,250,000 from Manchester U for Antonio Valencia, June 2009.

Record Transfer Fee Paid: £7,000,000 to Newcastle U for Charles N'Zogbia, January 2009.

Football League Record: 1978 Elected to Division 4; 1982–92 Division 3; 1992–93 Division 2; 1993–97 Division 3; 1997–2003 Division 2; 2003–04 Division 1; 2004–05 FL C; 2005–13 Premier League; 2013–15 FL C; 2015–16 FL 1; 2016–17 FL C; 2017–18 FL 1; 2018–20 FL C; 2020–22 FL 1; 2022– FL C.

LATEST SEQUENCES

Longest Sequence of League Wins: 11, 2.11.2002 – 18.1.2003.

Longest Sequence of League Defeats: 8, 10.9.2011 – 6.11.2011.

Longest Sequence of League Draws: 6, 11.12.2001 – 5.1.2002.

Longest Sequence of Unbeaten League Matches: 25, 8.5.1999 – 3.1.2000.

Longest Sequence Without a League Win: 14, 9.5.1989 – 17.10.1989.

Successive Scoring Runs: 31 from 10.4.2021.

Successive Non-scoring Runs: 4 from 8.12.2018.

MANAGERS

Charlie Spencer 1932–37
Jimmy Milne 1946–47
Bob Pryde 1949–52
Ted Goodier 1952–54
Walter Crook 1954–55
Ron Suart 1955–56
Billy Cooke 1956
Sam Barkas 1957
Trevor Hitchen 1957–58
Malcolm Barrass 1958–59
Jimmy Shirley 1959
Pat Murphy 1959–60
Allenby Chilton 1960
Johnny Ball 1961–63
Allan Brown 1963–66
Alf Craig 1966–67
Harry Leyland 1967–68
Alan Saunders 1968
Ian McNeill 1968–70
Gordon Milne 1970–72
Les Rigby 1972–74
Brian Tiler 1974–76
Ian McNeill 1976–81
Larry Lloyd 1981–83
Harry McNally 1983–85
Bryan Hamilton 1985–86
Ray Mathias 1986–89
Bryan Hamilton 1989–93
Dave Philpotts 1993
Kenny Swain 1993–94
Graham Barrow 1994–95
John Deehan 1995–98
Ray Mathias 1998–99
John Benson 1999–2000
Bruce Rioch 2000–01
Steve Bruce 2001
Paul Jewell 2001–07
Chris Hutchings 2007
Steve Bruce 2007–09
Roberto Martinez 2009–13
Owen Coyle 2013
Uwe Rosler 2013–14
Malky Mackay 2014–15
Gary Caldwell 2015–16
Warren Joyce 2016–17
Paul Cook 2017–20
John Sheridan 2020
Leam Richardson November 2020–

TEN YEAR LEAGUE RECORD

		P	W	D	L	F	A	Pts	Pos
2012-13	PR Lge	38	9	9	20	47	73	36	18
2013-14	FL C	46	21	10	15	61	48	73	5
2014-15	FL C	46	9	12	25	39	64	39	23
2015-16	FL 1	46	24	15	7	82	45	87	1
2016-17	FL C	46	10	12	24	40	57	42	23
2017-18	FL 1	46	29	11	6	89	29	98	1
2018-19	FL C	46	13	13	20	51	64	52	18
2019-20	FL C	46	15	14	17	57	56	47*	23
2020-21	FL 1	46	13	9	24	54	77	48	20
2021-22	FL 1	46	27	11	8	82	44	92	1

** 12 pts deducted.*

DID YOU KNOW ?

Ted Robinson, an experienced full-back who saw Football League action with Southampton and Southport, signed for Wigan Athletic in the summer of 1933 and went on to make 185 consecutive appearances. His club record was later broken in 1950 by Harry Parkinson, who was also a full-back.

WIGAN ATHLETIC – SKY BET LEAGUE ONE 2021–22 LEAGUE RECORD

Match No.	*Date*	*Venue*	*Opponents*	*Result*		*H/T Score*	*Lg Pos.*	*Goalscorers*	*Attendance*
1	Aug 7	A	Sunderland	L	1-2	1-1	19	Edwards [15]	31,549
2	14	H	Rotherham U	W	1-0	0-0	12	Keane [90]	10,217
3	17	H	Wycombe W	D	1-1	0-0	13	Lang [47]	8671
4	21	A	Charlton Ath	W	2-0	0-0	9	Darikwa [88], McClean [90]	13,839
5	28	H	Portsmouth	W	1-0	0-0	4	Lang [78]	9571
6	Sept 11	H	Doncaster R	W	2-1	1-1	2	Keane 2 [24, 52]	8975
7	18	A	Accrington S	W	4-1	2-0	1	Whatmough [6], Keane [18], Wyke 2 [58, 90]	4517
8	25	H	Cheltenham T	W	2-0	1-0	1	Lang [8], Wyke [46]	8867
9	28	H	Sheffield W	L	1-2	0-1	2	Wyke (pen) [81]	11,884
10	Oct 2	A	Gillingham	W	2-0	0-0	1	Power [64], Keane [82]	4503
11	16	A	Bolton W	W	4-0	1-0	3	Keane [6], McClean 2 [50, 81], Lang [65]	20,892
12	19	H	Milton Keynes D	L	1-2	1-2	4	Wyke [20]	8351
13	23	A	AFC Wimbledon	W	2-0	0-0	3	Kalambayi (og) [50], McClean [54]	7979
14	26	H	Lincoln C	L	1-2	0-1	3	Massey [90]	8707
15	30	H	Burton Alb	W	2-0	1-0	2	McClean [9], Tilt [51]	9020
16	Nov 2	A	Fleetwood T	W	3-2	0-1	1	Lang [62], Keane [68], Tilt [72]	3246
17	23	A	Cambridge U	D	2-2	0-1	4	Keane [84], Lang [87]	4101
18	27	A	Plymouth Arg	W	2-1	1-1	2	Keane [35], Lang [90]	15,329
19	Dec 8	H	Shrewsbury T	W	2-1	1-1	2	Darikwa [2], Aasgaard [90]	8098
20	11	H	Ipswich T	D	1-1	1-0	2	Lang [22]	10,296
21	18	A	Oxford U	W	3-2	2-1	2	Keane [8], Power [32], McClean [86]	8354
22	Jan 15	A	Doncaster R	W	2-1	1-0	4	Power [10], Keane [54]	7169
23	18	A	Morecambe	W	2-1	1-1	2	Keane [45], Humphrys [73]	5359
24	22	H	Gillingham	W	3-2	2-0	1	Keane 2 [8, 77], Humphrys [21]	9359
25	29	A	Cheltenham T	D	0-0	0-0	2		4405
26	Feb 1	H	Oxford U	D	1-1	1-1	2	Lang [36]	9958
27	8	A	Sheffield W	L	0-1	0-0	2		20,210
28	12	H	Charlton Ath	W	2-1	1-1	2	Keane (pen) [26], Humphrys [74]	9657
29	15	H	Crewe Alex	W	2-0	0-0	2	Lang [57], McClean [82]	8509
30	18	A	Rotherham U	D	1-1	1-0	2	Humphrys [28]	10,588
31	22	A	Wycombe W	W	3-1	0-1	2	Naylor [70], Lang 2 [78, 82]	4826
32	26	H	Sunderland	L	0-3	0-2	2		20,136
33	Mar 1	H	Fleetwood T	W	2-0	2-0	2	Keane (pen) [37], McClean [42]	8627
34	5	H	AFC Wimbledon	W	1-0	1-0	2	Keane [21]	9780
35	12	A	Milton Keynes D	D	1-1	0-0	2	Naylor [58]	11,193
36	15	A	Crewe Alex	W	2-0	1-0	2	Magennis [43], Keane [53]	5310
37	19	H	Morecambe	W	4-1	2-0	2	Magennis [19], Kerr [44], Keane [67], Humphrys [68]	10,072
38	Apr 2	H	Bolton W	D	1-1	1-0	2	McClean [7]	15,279
39	5	H	Accrington S	W	3-0	2-0	1	Bennett [37], Magennis [42], Keane [57]	9139
40	9	A	Lincoln C	W	3-1	2-1	1	Lang 2 [8, 72], Keane [21]	9498
41	12	A	Burton Alb	D	0-0	0-0	1		3589
42	16	H	Cambridge U	L	1-2	0-2	1	Naylor [77]	10,576
43	19	A	Ipswich T	D	2-2	1-0	1	Keane 2 [45, 86]	21,329
44	23	H	Plymouth Arg	D	1-1	0-0	1	Whatmough [74]	14,130
45	26	A	Portsmouth	L	2-3	2-0	1	Lang [38], Keane [45]	14,637
46	30	A	Shrewsbury T	W	3-0	1-0	1	Vela (og) [43], Keane 2 (1 pen) [50 (p), 65]	8369

Final League Position: 1

GOALSCORERS

League (82): Keane 26 (3 pens), Lang 15, McClean 9, Humphrys 5, Wyke 5 (1 pen), Magennis 3, Naylor 3, Power 3, Darikwa 2, Tilt 2, Whatmough 2, Aasgaard 1, Bennett 1, Edwards 1, Kerr 1, Massey 1, own goals 2.
FA Cup (7): Lang 3, Aasgaard 1, Kerr 1, Power 1, own goal 1.
Carabao Cup (1): Humphrys 1.
Papa John's Trophy (11): Edwards 2, Baningime 1, Humphrys 1, Keane 1, Long 1, Massey 1, McClean 1, Naylor 1, Power 1, Sze 1.

Amos B 46	Darikwa T 42 + 1	Whatmough J 46	Long A 1	Pearce T 9 + 7	Naylor T 43	Power M 44	Lang C 41 + 1	Keane W 43 + 1	Edwards G 9 + 21	Wyke C 15	Jones Jordan 3 + 6	Humphrys S 12 + 26	Cousins J 13 + 3	Watts K 25 + 1	Robinson L 1	Massey G 9 + 24	Aasgaard T 1 + 4	McClean J 31 + 2	Tilt C 18 + 2	Bayliss T 6 + 2	Kerr J 16 + 8	Bennett J 10 + 1	Shinnie G 6 + 4	Magennis J 14 + 3	McGrath J 1 + 1	Rea G 1 + 2	Match No.
1	2	3	4	5	6^3	7	8	9^1	10^2	11	12	13	14														1
1	2	3			7	6	10	9		11		8^2	12	4	5^1	13											2
1	5	3			6	2	8^2	9		11^3	10^1	14	7	4		12	13										3
1	5	3			6	2	8^1	9^3		11	10^2	14	7	4		13		12									4
1	2	3		5^2	6		8^3	9	14	11	10^1		7	4		13		12									5
1	5	3			6	2	8^2	9	13	11^3	12	14	7	4				10^1									6
1	5	3			6	2	8^2	9^1	12	11	14	13	7	4				10^3									7
1	5	3^1			6	2	8^3	9	14	11			7	4		13		10^2	12								8
1	5	3			6	2	8	9^2		11	12	13	7	4				10^1									9
1	5	3			6	2	8^2	9	13	11			7	4		12		10^1									10
1	5	3		12	6	2	8	9		11^3		14	7^1	4		13		10^2									11
1	5	3			6	2	8^1	9		11	13	14		4		12		10^2		7^3							12
1	5	3			6	2	8^1	9^3	12	11		14		4		13		10^2		7							13
1	5	3		12	6	2	8	9	14			11^2		4		13		10^3		7^1							14
1	5^1	3		14		8		6		11		10				12	13	9^3	4	7^2	2						15
1	5	3				8	10	6	12	11								9	4	7	2^1						16
1		3		5^3		7	10	8	9^1		12					2	13	11	4	6^2	14						17
1	5	3			7	6	11	10				12				13	9^1	8^2	4		2						18
1	2	3			6		11	9	13			14	7^1			8^3	12	10	4			5^2					19
1	2	3		5^2	6	7	9	11	8^1			13				12		10	4								20
1	2	3			7	6	9^2	11	13			12				8		10	4			5^1					21
1	2	3		5^2	7	6	9^3	11	13			14		4		8^1		10			12						22
1	2	3		5^1	7	6	9^3	11	13			12		4		8^2		10			14						23
1	5	3			6	2		9	8^1			11^2		4		13		10			12		7				24
1	5^3	3			6	2	12	9^1	8^2					4		13		10			14		7	11			25
1	5	3			6	2	9		13			11^1				8^2		10	4				7	12			26
1	5^3	3			6	2	8					12				14		10	4		13		7^1	11	9^2		27
1	5	3			7	6	9^2	10^1	13			12						8	4		2			11			28
1	2	3			7	6	8	9^1	10^3			12		4				5			14		13	11^2			29
1	13	3			7	6	9	12				11^1				5		8^2	4		2			10^3		14	30
1	2	3			7	6	8	9^3	13			12				10^2		5	4					11^1		14	31
1	2	3			7^3	6	8	9	10^2			12				14		5	4				13	11^1			32
1	5^3	3			6	2	8^2	9				11^1		4		13		10■	14				7	12			33
1		3		13	7	2	8^3	9	10			11				14			4	12		5^2				6^1	34
1		3		8^3	7	6	9	10	12			11^2				5^1			4	14	2			13			35
1	5	3		12	7^3	6		10	13			9^2							4		2	8^1	14	11			36
1	5	3			7	6^1		9	13			11^2						8	4		2		12	10			37
1	5	3			7	6	9^2	10	13			12		14				8	4^3		2			11^1			38
1	5	3			7	6	9^1	10^3				12		4		13					2	8^2		11	14		39
1	5	3			7	6	10	9^1				12		4		13					2	8^2		11			40
1	5	3			7	6	11	9^2				12		4		13					2	8^1		10			41
1	5^3	3		12	6	2	8	9	10^2			14		4							13		7^1	11			42
1	5	3		13	7	6	9	10	14			11^1	12	4^2							2^3	8					43
1	5	3		8^1	7	9	11	10					6			12					2	4					44
1	5	3		8^1	6	9	10	11	13			14	7^3			12					2	4^2					45
1	6	3			5	7	10	11					8	4				9^1			2	12					46

FA Cup First Round	Solihull Moors	(h)	0-0
Replay (aet)	Solihull Moors	(a)	2-1
Second Round	Colchester U	(a)	2-1
Third Round	Blackburn R	(h)	3-2
Fourth Round	Stoke C	(a)	0-2
Carabao Cup First Round	Hull C	(a)	1-1
(won 8-7 on penalties)			
Second Round	Bolton W	(h)	0-0
(Wigan Ath won 5-4 on penalties)			
Third Round	Sunderland	(h)	0-2

Papa John's Trophy

Group C (N)	Wolverhampton W U21	(h)	0-0
(Wolverhampton W U21 won 4-2 on penalties)			
Group C (N)	Crewe Alex	(a)	0-2
Group C (N)	Shrewsbury T	(h)	2-0
Second Round	Accrington S	(a)	1-1
(Wigan Ath won 5-4 on penalties)			
Third Round	Oldham Ath	(a)	6-0
Quarter-Final	Arsenal U21	(h)	1-0
Semi-Final	Sutton U	(h)	1-1
(Sutton U won 7-6 on penalties)			

WOLVERHAMPTON WANDERERS

FOUNDATION

Enthusiasts of the game at St Luke's School, Blakenhall formed a club in 1877. In the same neighbourhood a cricket club called Blakenhall Wanderers had a football section. Several St Luke's footballers played cricket for them and shortly before the start of the 1879–80 season the two amalgamated and Wolverhampton Wanderers FC was brought into being.

Molineux Stadium, Waterloo Road, Wolverhampton, West Midlands WV1 4QR.

Telephone: (0371) 222 2220.

Ticket Office: (0371) 222 1877.

Website: wolves.co.uk

Email: info@wolves.co.uk

Ground Capacity: 32,050.

Record Attendance: 61,315 v Liverpool, FA Cup 5th rd, 11 February 1939.

Pitch Measurements: 105m × 68m (115yd × 74.5yd).

Executive Chairman: Jeff Shi.

Head Coach: Bruno Lage.

Assistant Head Coach: Alex Silva.

Colours: Gold shirts with black trim, black shorts with gold trim, gold socks with black trim.

Year Formed: 1877* (*see Foundation*).

Turned Professional: 1888.

Previous Names: 1879, St Luke's combined with Wanderers Cricket Club to become Wolverhampton Wanderers (1923) Ltd. New limited companies followed in 1982 and 1986 (current).

Club Nickname: 'Wolves'.

Grounds: 1877, Windmill Field; 1879, John Harper's Field; 1881, Dudley Road; 1889, Molineux.

First Football League Game: 8 September 1888, Football League, v Aston Villa (h) D 1–1 – Baynton; Baugh, Mason; Fletcher, Allen, Lowder; Hunter, Cooper, Anderson, White, Cannon, (1 og).

Record League Victory: 10–1 v Leicester C, Division 1, 15 April 1938 – Sidlow; Morris, Dowen; Galley, Cullis, Gardiner; Maguire (1), Horace Wright, Westcott (4), Jones (1), Dorsett (4).

Record Cup Victory: 14–0 v Crosswell's Brewery, FA Cup 2nd rd, 13 November 1886 – Ike Griffiths; Baugh, Mason; Pearson, Allen (1), Lowder; Hunter (4), Knight (2), Brodie (4), Bernie Griffiths (2), Wood. Plus one goal 'scrambled through'.

Record Defeat: 1–10 v Newton Heath, Division 1, 15 October 1892.

Most League Points (2 for a win): 64, Division 1, 1957–58.

HONOURS

League Champions: Division 1 – 1953–54, 1957–58, 1958–59; FL C – 2008–09, 2017–18; Division 2 – 1931–32, 1976–77; FL 1 – 2013–14; Division 3 – 1988–89; Division 3N – 1923–24; Division 4 – 1987–88.
Runners-up: Division 1 – 1937–38, 1938–39, 1949–50, 1954–55, 1959–60; Division 2 – 1966–67, 1982–83.

FA Cup Winners: 1893, 1908, 1949, 1960.
Runners-up: 1889, 1896, 1921, 1939.

League Cup Winners: 1974, 1980.

League Trophy Winners: 1988.

Texaco Cup Winners: 1971.

European Competitions
European Cup: 1958–59, 1959–60 *(qf)*.
UEFA Cup: 1971–72 (*runners-up*), 1973–74, 1974–75, 1980–81.
Europa League: 2019–20 *(qf)*.
European Cup-Winners' Cup: 1960–61 *(sf)*.

FOOTBALL YEARBOOK FACT FILE

Wolverhampton Wanderers' Molineux ground hosted a title fight for the British and Empire heavyweight boxing championship between Henry Cooper and Jack Bodell in June 1967. Cooper, the reigning champion, comfortably retained his titles when the referee stopped the fight after two minutes and 15 seconds of the second round. Around 8,000 fans were in attendance.

Most League Points (3 for a win): 103, FL 1, 2013–14.

Most League Goals: 115, Division 2, 1931–32.

Highest League Scorer in Season: Dennis Westcott, 38, Division 1, 1946–47.

Most League Goals in Total Aggregate: Steve Bull, 250, 1986–99.

Most League Goals in One Match: 5, Joe Butcher v Accrington, Division 1, 19 November 1892; 5, Tom Phillipson v Barnsley, Division 2, 26 April 1926; 5, Tom Phillipson v Bradford C, Division 2, 25 December 1926; 5, Billy Hartill v Notts Co, Division 2, 12 October 1929; 5, Billy Hartill v Aston Villa, Division 1, 3 September 1934.

Most Capped Player: Billy Wright, 105, England (70 consecutive).

Most League Appearances: Derek Parkin, 501, 1967–82.

Youngest League Player: Jimmy Mullen, 16 years 43 days v Leeds U, 18 February 1939.

Record Transfer Fee Received: £41,000,000 from Liverpool for Diogo Jota, September 2020.

Record Transfer Fee Paid: £35,600,000 to Porto for Fabio Silva, September 2020.

Football League Record: 1888 Founder Member of Football League: 1906–23 Division 2; 1923–24 Division 3 (N); 1924–32 Division 2; 1932–65 Division 1; 1965–67 Division 2; 1967–76 Division 1; 1976–77 Division 2; 1977–82 Division 1; 1982–83 Division 2; 1983–84 Division 1; 1984–85 Division 2; 1985–86 Division 3; 1986–88 Division 4; 1988–89 Division 3; 1989–92 Division 2; 1992–2003 Division 1; 2003–04 Premier League; 2004–09 FL C; 2009–12 Premier League; 2012–13 FL C; 2013–14 FL 1; 2014–18 FL C; 2018– Premier League.

MANAGERS

George Worrall 1877–85
(Secretary-Manager)
John Addenbrooke 1885–1922
George Jobey 1922–24
Albert Hoskins 1924–26
(had been Secretary since 1922)
Fred Scotchbrook 1926–27
Major Frank Buckley 1927–44
Ted Vizard 1944–48
Stan Cullis 1948–64
Andy Beattie 1964–65
Ronnie Allen 1966–68
Bill McGarry 1968–76
Sammy Chung 1976–78
John Barnwell 1978–81
Ian Greaves 1982
Graham Hawkins 1982–84
Tommy Docherty 1984–85
Bill McGarry 1985
Sammy Chapman 1985–86
Brian Little 1986
Graham Turner 1986–94
Graham Taylor 1994–95
Mark McGhee 1995–98
Colin Lee 1998–2000
Dave Jones 2001–04
Glenn Hoddle 2004–06
Mick McCarthy 2006–12
Stale Solbakken 2012–13
Dean Saunders 2013
Kenny Jackett 2013–16
Walter Zenga 2016
Paul Lambert 2016–17
Nuno Espirito Santo 2017–21
Bruno Lage June 2021–

LATEST SEQUENCES

Longest Sequence of League Wins: 9, 11.1.2014 – 11.3.2014.

Longest Sequence of League Defeats: 8, 5.12.1981 – 13.2.1982.

Longest Sequence of League Draws: 6, 22.4.1995 – 20.8.1995.

Longest Sequence of Unbeaten League Matches: 21, 15.1.2005 – 13.8.2005.

Longest Sequence Without a League Win: 19, 1.12.1984 – 6.4.1985.

Successive Scoring Runs: 41 from 20.12.1958.

Successive Non-scoring Runs: 7 from 2.2.1985.

TEN YEAR LEAGUE RECORD

		P	W	D	L	F	A	Pts	Pos
2012-13	FL C	46	14	9	23	55	69	51	23
2013-14	FL 1	46	31	10	5	89	31	103	1
2014-15	FL C	46	22	12	12	70	56	78	7
2015-16	FL C	46	14	16	16	53	58	58	14
2016-17	FL C	46	16	10	20	54	58	58	15
2017-18	FL C	46	30	9	7	82	39	99	1
2018-19	PR Lge	38	16	9	13	47	46	57	7
2019-20	PR Lge	38	15	14	9	51	40	59	7
2020-21	PR Lge	38	12	9	17	36	52	45	13
2021-22	PR Lge	38	15	6	17	38	43	51	10

DID YOU KNOW ?

Wolverhampton Wanderers have only once gone unbeaten at home in a Football League season. That was in 1923–24 when they won 18 and drew 3 of their Division Three North games at Molineux on the way to securing the divisional title. Their only loss at home that season was in an FA Cup third-round tie against West Bromwich Albion.

WOLVERHAMPTON WANDERERS – PREMIER LEAGUE 2021–22 LEAGUE RECORD

Match No.	*Date*	*Venue*	*Opponents*	*Result*	*H/T Score*	*Lg Pos.*	*Goalscorers*	*Attendance*
1	Aug 14	A	Leicester C	L 0-1	0-1	15		31,983
2	22	H	Tottenham H	L 0-1	0-1	16		30,368
3	29	H	Manchester U	L 0-1	0-0	18		30,621
4	Sept 11	A	Watford	W 2-0	0-0	13	Sierralta (og) [74], Hwang [83]	20,019
5	18	H	Brentford	L 0-2	0-2	16		29,724
6	26	A	Southampton	W 1-0	0-0	14	Jimenez [61]	28,002
7	Oct 2	H	Newcastle U	W 2-1	1-1	11	Hwang 2 [20, 58]	30,483
8	16	A	Aston Villa	W 3-2	0-0	8	Saiss [80], Coady [85], Neves [90]	41,951
9	23	A	Leeds U	D 1-1	1-0	10	Hwang [10]	36,475
10	Nov 1	H	Everton	W 2-1	2-0	7	Kilman [28], Jimenez [32]	30,617
11	6	A	Crystal Palace	L 0-2	0-0	8		24,390
12	20	H	West Ham U	W 1-0	0-0	6	Jimenez [58]	30,667
13	27	A	Norwich C	D 0-0	0-0	6		26,911
14	Dec 1	H	Burnley	D 0-0	0-0	6		30,328
15	4	H	Liverpool	L 0-1	0-0	8		30,729
16	11	A	Manchester C	L 0-1	0-0	8		52,613
17	15	A	Brighton & HA	W 1-0	1-0	8	Saiss [45]	30,362
18	19	H	Chelsea	D 0-0	0-0	8		30,631
19	Jan 3	A	Manchester U	W 1-0	0-0	8	Joao Moutinho [82]	73,045
20	15	H	Southampton	W 3-1	1-0	8	Jimenez (pen) [37], Coady [59], Traore [90]	30,057
21	22	A	Brentford	W 2-1	0-0	8	Joao Moutinho [48], Neves [78]	16,982
22	Feb 10	H	Arsenal	L 0-1	0-1	8		31,523
23	13	A	Tottenham H	W 2-0	2-0	7	Jimenez [6], Dendoncker [18]	56,452
24	20	H	Leicester C	W 2-1	1-1	7	Neves [9], Daniel Podence [66]	31,497
25	24	A	Arsenal	L 1-2	1-0	7	Hwang [10]	59,888
26	27	A	West Ham U	L 0-1	0-0	8		59,946
27	Mar 5	H	Crystal Palace	L 0-2	0-2	8		31,395
28	10	H	Watford	W 4-0	3-0	8	Jimenez [13], Hernandez (og) [18], Daniel Podence [21], Neves [85]	29,658
29	13	A	Everton	W 1-0	0-0	7	Coady [49]	39,112
30	18	H	Leeds U	L 2-3	2-0	8	Jonny [26], Trincao [45]	31,842
31	Apr 2	H	Aston Villa	W 2-1	2-0	7	Jonny [7], Young (og) [36]	31,012
32	8	A	Newcastle U	L 0-1	0-0	8		52,164
33	24	A	Burnley	L 0-1	0-0	8		19,246
34	30	H	Brighton & HA	L 0-3	0-1	8		31,243
35	May 7	A	Chelsea	D 2-2	0-0	8	Trincao [79], Coady [90]	32,190
36	11	H	Manchester C	L 1-5	1-3	8	Dendoncker [11]	30,914
37	15	H	Norwich C	D 1-1	0-1	8	Ait Nouri [55]	31,219
38	22	A	Liverpool	L 1-3	1-1	10	Pedro Neto [3]	53,097

Final League Position: 10

GOALSCORERS

League (38): Jimenez 6 (1 pen), Hwang 5, Coady 4, Neves 4, Daniel Podence 2, Dendoncker 2, Joao Moutinho 2, Jonny 2, Saiss 2, Trincao 2, Ait Nouri 1, Kilman 1, Pedro Neto 1, Traore 1, own goals 3.
FA Cup (3): Daniel Podence 2, Nelson Semedo 1.
Carabao Cup (6): Daniel Podence 2, Dendoncker 1, Gibbs-White 1, Saiss 1, Trincao 1.
Papa John's Trophy (1): Hasketh 1.

Jose Sa P 37	Kilman M 30	Coady C 38	Saiss R 31	Hoever K 4+4	Neves R 31+2	Joao Moutinho F 34+1	Marcal F 17+1	Trincao F 16+12	Jimenez R 30+4	Traore A 10+10	Dendoncker L 21+9	Gibbs-White M —+2	Silva F 6+16	Nelson Semedo C 25	Ait Nouri R 20+3	Daniel Podence C 15+11	Hwang H 20+10	Gomes T 4	Cundle L 2+2	Chiquinho O 1+7	Pedro Neto L 5+8	Jonny C 10+3	Boly W 10	Campbell C —+1	Ruddy J 1+1	*Match No.*
1	2[3]	3	4	5	6	7[1]	8	9[2]	10	11	12	13	14													1
1	2	3	4[3]		6	7[1]	8	9[2]	10	11	12		13	5	14											2
1	2	3[2]	4		6	7	8	9[1]	10	11[3]		13	14	5		12										3
1	2	3	4		6	7	8	9[1]	10	11[2]				5		13	12									4
1	2	3	4[1]		6	7	8[2]	9	10	11			14	5[3]		13	12									5
1	2	3	4	13	14	6	8		10	12	7			5[2]		9[1]	11[3]									6
1	2	3	4		6	7	8	9[1]	10	13	12			5			11[2]									7
1	2	3	4		6	7[1]	8[2]		14	10	9		12	5		13	11[3]									8
1	2	3	4	13	14	7[3]			11	9[1]	6			5	8[2]	12	10									9
1	2	3	4		6	7		9[1]	11[3]		13		14	5	8	12	10[2]									10
1	2	3	4		6	7		9[2]	11	12			14	5[1]	8	13	10[3]									11
1	2	3	4		6	7			11	12	13			5	8	9[1]	10[2]									12
1	2	3	4	14	6	7		9[1]	10	12	13			5[2]	8		11[3]									13
1	2	3	4			7		12	10	9	6			5	8		11[1]									14
1	2	3	4	14	6	12		13	10	9[2]	7			5	8[3]		11[1]									15
1	2	3	4		7[2]	8		13	10■	11[1]	6[3]			5	9	14	12									16
1	2	3	4		6	7	8	9[3]		12[2]	13		14	5		10	11[1]									17
1	2	3	4	5	7	8	9	13	10[2]	12	6					11[1]										18
1	2	3	4		6	7	8	9[1]	10[2]	12	14		13	5		11[3]										19
1	2	3				7		9[1]	10[2]	12	6		13	5	8	11[3]		4	14							20
1	2	3			7	8		13		12	6		11[1]	5	9	10[2]		4								21
1	2	3[3]	4		6		8[2]	9[1]	10		7		14	5	13	11				12						22
1	2	3	4		7			13	10[3]		6		14	5	9	11[1]	12		8[2]							23
1	2	3	4		7	8[1]	14		10		6			5	9[3]	11[2]	12				13					24
1	2	3	4		6	7			10		14			5[1]	8	9[3]	11[2]				13	12				25
1	2	3	4	5	6		8[2]	9[1]	14		7		11			12	10[3]				13					26
1	2[3]	3	4	5[1]	6	7	8		13							11	10			14	9[2]	12				27
1		3	4		6	7			11[2]				13		8	9	10[1]			14	12	5[3]	2			28
1	2	3	4		6	8	9	13	11[3]		7[2]		14			12	10[1]					5				29
1		3	4		6[1]	7		12	11■		9[3]		14		8	10[2]	13			15		5[4]	2			30
1	4	3				7	8	9[2]			6		11[3]			10[1]	12			14	13	5	2			31
1	4	3				7	8[3]	9[1]					11		14		10[2]		6		13	5	2	12		32
1		3	4[2]			7		13	9		6		11[1]	5			10				12	8	2			33
1		3	4		6[1]	8			12		7		10[2]	5[3]	9		11				13	14	2			34
1		3	4[1]		7[3]	8		14	10		6				9		12			13	11[2]	5	2			35
1		3			7	8[3]		12	11[1]		6				9		13		14	5	10[2]	2	4			36
		3[1]			6	7			9				13		8	14	11[2]	4		12	10[3]	5	2		1	37
1[2]		3			7	8		14	10		6[3]				9		12	4			11[1]	5	2		13	38

FA Cup

Third Round	Sheffield U	(h)	3-0
Fourth Round	Norwich C	(h)	0-1

Carabao Cup

Second Round	Nottingham F	(a)	4-0
Third Round	Tottenham H	(h)	2-2

(Tottenham H won 3-2 on penalties)

Papa John's Trophy (Wolverhampton W U21)

Group C (N)	Wigan Ath	(a)	0-0
(Wolverhampton W U21 won 4-2 on penalties)			
Group C (N)	Shrewsbury T	(a)	1-3
Group C (N)	Crewe Alex	(a)	0-3

WYCOMBE WANDERERS

FOUNDATION

In 1887 a group of young furniture trade workers called a meeting at the Steam Engine public house with the aim of forming a football club and entering junior football. It is thought that they were named after the famous FA Cup winners, The Wanderers, who had visited the town in 1877 for a tie with the original High Wycombe club. It is also possible that they played informally before their formation, although there is no proof of this.

Adams Park, Hillbottom Road, High Wycombe, Buckinghamshire HP12 4HJ.

Telephone: (01494) 472 100.

Ticket Office: (01494) 441 118.

Website: www.wycombewanderers.co.uk

Email: wwfc@wwfc.com

Ground Capacity: 9,558.

Record Attendance: 15,850 v St Albans C, FA Amateur Cup 4th rd, 25 February 1950 (at Loakes Park); 9,921 v Fulham, FA Cup 3rd rd, 9 January 2002 (at Adams Park).

Pitch Measurements: 100m × 64m (109.5yd × 70yd).

Chairman: Rob Couhig.

Manager: Gareth Ainsworth.

Assistant Manager: Richard Dobson.

Colours: Light blue and dark blue quartered shirts, dark blue shorts with light blue trim, dark blue socks.

Year Formed: 1887. ***Turned Professional:*** 1974.

Club Nicknames: 'The Chairboys' (after High Wycombe's tradition of furniture making), 'The Blues'.

Grounds: 1887, The Rye; 1893, Spring Meadow; 1895, Loakes Park; 1899, Daws Hill Park; 1901, Loakes Park; 1990, Adams Park.

First Football League Game: 14 August 1993, Division 3 v Carlisle U (a) D 2–2: Hyde; Cousins, Horton (Langford), Kerr, Crossley, Ryan, Carroll, Stapleton, Thompson, Scott, Guppy (1) (Hutchinson), (1 og).

Record League Victory: 5–0 v Burnley, Division 2, 15 April 1997 – Parkin; Cousins, Bell, Kavanagh, McCarthy, Forsyth, Carroll (2p) (Simpson), Scott (Farrell), Stallard (1), McGavin (1) (Read (1)), Brown.
5–0 v Northampton T, Division 2, 4 January 2003 – Talia; Senda, Ryan, Thomson, McCarthy, Johnson, Bulman, Simpson (1), Faulconbridge (Harris), Dixon (1) (Roberts 3), Brown (Currie).
5–0 v Hartlepool U, FL 1, 25 February 2012 – Bull; McCoy, Basey, Eastmond (Bloomfield), Laing, Doherty (1), Hackett, Lewis, Bevon (2) (Strevons), Hayes (2) (McClure), McNamee.

Record Cup Victory: 5–0 v Hitchin T (a), FA Cup 2nd rd, 3 December 1994 – Hyde; Cousins, Brown, Crossley, Evans, Ryan (1), Carroll, Bell (1), Thompson, Garner (3) (Hemmings), Stapleton (Langford).
5–0 v Chesterfield (a), FA Cup 2nd rd, 3 December 2017 – Blackman; Harriman, Stewart (1), Pierre, Jacobson, Bloomfield (Wood), O'Nien, Gape (Bean), Kashket (3) (Cowan-Hall), Hayes (1), Akinfenwa.

Record Defeat: 0–7 v Shrewsbury T, Johnstone's Paint Trophy, 7 October 2008.

HONOURS

League Champions: Conference – 1992–93.
Runners-up: Conference – 1991–92.

FA Cup: semi-final – 2001.

League Cup: semi-final – 2007.

FA Amateur Cup Winners: 1931.

FOOTBALL YEARBOOK FACT FILE

Centre-forward Reg Boreham was the first Wycombe Wanderers player to win an England amateur cap when he appeared against Ireland in November 1921. He was part of the Chairboys team which won the Spartan League championship in successive seasons, and he went on to sign amateur forms with Arsenal, making over 50 first-team appearances for the Gunners. He later returned to Wycombe initially as a player and later as club secretary.

Most League Points (3 for a win): 84, FL 2, 2014–15; 84, FL 2, 2017–18.

Most League Goals: 79, FL 2, 2017–18.

Highest League Scorer in Season: Scott McGleish, 25, 2007–08.

Most League Goals in Total Aggregate: Adebayo Akinfenwa, 52, 2016–22.

Most League Goals in One Match: 3, Miquel Desouza v Bradford C, Division 2, 2 September 1995; 3, John Williams v Stockport Co, Division 2, 24 February 1996; 3, Mark Stallard v Walsall, Division 2, 21 October 1997; 3, Sean Devine v Reading, Division 2, 2 October 1999; 3, Sean Divine v Bury, Division 2, 26 February 2000; 3, Stuart Roberts v Northampton T, Division 2, 4 January 2003; 3, Nathan Tyson v Lincoln C, FL 2, 5 March 2005; 3, Nathan Tyson v Kidderminster H, FL 2, 2 April 2005; 3, Nathan Tyson v Stockport Co, FL 2, 10 September 2005; 3, Kevin Betsy v Mansfield T, FL 2, 24 September 2005; 3, Scott McGleish v Mansfield T, FL 2, 8 January 2008; 3, Stuart Beavon v Bury, FL 1, 17 March 2012; 3, Craig Mackail-Smith v Crawley T, FL 2, 18 November 2017; 3, Joe Jacobson v Lincoln C, FL 1, 7 September 2019.

Most Capped Player: Daryl Horgan, 11 (17), Republic of Ireland.

Most League Appearances: Matt Bloomfield, 486, 2003–21.

Youngest League Player: Jordon Ibe, 15 years 311 days v Hartlepool U, 15 October 2011.

Record Transfer Fee Received: £750,000 (rising to £1,000,000) from Middlesbrough for Uche Ikpeazu, July 2021.

Record Transfer Fee Paid: £200,000 to Barnet for Sean Devine, April 1999; £200,000 to Barnet for Darren Currie, July 2001.

Football League Record: 1993 Promoted to Division 3 from Conference; 1993–94 Division 3; 1994–2004 Division 2; 2004–09 FL 2; 2009–10 FL 1; 2010–11 FL 2; 2011–12 FL 1; 2012–18 FL 2; 2018–20 FL 1; 2020–21 FL C; 2021– FL 1.

MANAGERS

First coach appointed 1951.
Prior to Brian Lee's appointment in 1969 the team was selected by a Match Committee which met every Monday evening.

James McCormack 1951–52
Sid Cann 1952–61
Graham Adams 1961–62
Don Welsh 1962–64
Barry Darvill 1964–68
Brian Lee 1969–76
Ted Powell 1976–77
John Reardon 1977–78
Andy Williams 1978–80
Mike Keen 1980–84
Paul Bence 1984–86
Alan Gane 1986–87
Peter Suddaby 1987–88
Jim Kelman 1988–90
Martin O'Neill 1990–95
Alan Smith 1995–96
John Gregory 1996–98
Neil Smillie 1998–99
Lawrie Sanchez 1999–2003
Tony Adams 2003–04
John Gorman 2004–06
Paul Lambert 2006–08
Peter Taylor 2008–09
Gary Waddock 2009–12
Gareth Ainsworth November 2012–

LATEST SEQUENCES

Longest Sequence of League Wins: 6, 12.11.2016 – 17.12.2016.

Longest Sequence of League Defeats: 8, 29.2.2020 – 24.10.2020.

Longest Sequence of League Draws: 5, 24.1.2004 – 21.2.2004.

Longest Sequence of Unbeaten League Matches: 21, 6.8.2005 – 10.12.2005.

Longest Sequence Without a League Win: 13, 10.1.2004 – 20.3.2004.

Successive Scoring Runs: 16 from 13.9.2014.

Successive Non-scoring Runs: 5 from 15.10.1996.

TEN YEAR LEAGUE RECORD

		P	W	D	L	F	A	Pts	Pos
2012-13	FL 2	46	17	9	20	50	60	60	15
2013-14	FL 2	46	12	14	20	46	54	50	22
2014-15	FL 2	46	23	15	8	67	45	84	4
2015-16	FL 2	46	17	13	16	45	44	64	13
2016-17	FL 2	46	19	12	15	58	53	69	9
2017-18	FL 2	46	24	12	10	79	60	84	3
2018-19	FL 1	46	14	11	21	55	67	53	17
2019-20	FL 1	34	17	8	9	45	40	59	3§
2020-21	FL C	46	11	10	25	39	69	43	22
2021-22	FL 1	46	23	14	9	75	51	83	6

§Decided on points-per-game (1.74)

DID YOU KNOW ?

Wycombe Wanderers, the reigning Isthmian League champions, were selected to represent England in the inaugural Anglo Italian Semi-Professional Cup. They lost 1-0 at AC Monza in September 1975 but a fortnight later secured the trophy by winning the second leg at Loakes Park 2-0.

WYCOMBE WANDERERS – SKY BET LEAGUE ONE 2021–22 LEAGUE RECORD

Match No.	Date	Venue	Opponents	Result		H/T Score	Lg Pos.	Goalscorers	Attendance
1	Aug 7	H	Accrington S	W	2-1	2-0	2	McCleary 2 [9, 15]	4551
2	14	A	Cheltenham T	W	3-1	1-1	1	Vokes [14], Pendlebury 2 [74, 79]	3860
3	17	A	Wigan Ath	D	1-1	0-0	3	Stewart [90]	8671
4	21	H	Lincoln C	W	1-0	1-0	2	Vokes [3]	5030
5	28	A	Sunderland	L	1-3	0-2	6	Wheeler [90]	29,344
6	Sept 11	A	Oxford U	D	0-0	0-0	9		9082
7	18	H	Charlton Ath	W	2-1	1-0	5	McCleary 2 [43, 71]	5832
8	25	A	Milton Keynes D	L	0-1	0-1	6		9355
9	28	A	Shrewsbury T	W	2-1	0-0	6	Jacobson [52], Tafazolli [66]	4510
10	Oct 2	H	Morecambe	W	4-3	0-2	5	Horgan [50], Vokes [53], Tafazolli [73], Thompson [90]	4161
11	9	H	Gillingham	W	2-0	2-0	2	McCleary [2], Hanlan [7]	4992
12	16	A	Doncaster R	W	2-0	2-0	2	Stewart [2], Akinfenwa [17]	6134
13	19	A	Rotherham U	D	0-0	0-0	3		8104
14	23	H	Crewe Alex	W	2-1	1-0	2	Tafazolli 2 [45, 90]	4813
15	30	A	Fleetwood T	D	3-3	2-1	3	Hanlan [24], Akinfenwa [30], Vokes [50]	2657
16	Nov 2	H	Ipswich T	L	1-4	1-1	4	Wheeler [17]	6943
17	13	H	Portsmouth	L	0-1	0-0	4		6471
18	20	H	Bolton W	W	1-0	0-0	4	Vokes [72]	5710
19	23	A	Plymouth Arg	W	3-0	0-0	2	Vokes [62], Mehmeti 2 [84, 90]	12,833
20	27	A	Sheffield W	D	2-2	1-1	3	Mehmeti [23], Obita [65]	20,761
21	Dec 7	H	Burton Alb	W	2-1	2-0	2	Hanlan [16], McCleary [45]	3602
22	11	H	AFC Wimbledon	D	2-2	0-1	4	Akinfenwa [74], Jacobson (pen) [90]	4915
23	29	A	Ipswich T	L	0-1	0-1	6		26,456
24	Jan 1	A	Charlton Ath	W	1-0	1-0	4	Vokes [35]	18,895
25	8	H	Sunderland	D	3-3	2-2	3	Mehmeti [13], Vokes [36], Jacobson [90]	7229
26	11	A	Bolton W	W	2-0	1-0	3	Hanlan [35], Grimmer [52]	12,584
27	15	H	Oxford U	W	2-0	1-0	1	Thompson [33], Hanlan [60]	8005
28	22	A	Morecambe	L	2-3	1-1	4	Akinfenwa [2], Grimmer [54]	3865
29	29	H	Milton Keynes D	L	0-1	0-1	5		7345
30	Feb 8	H	Shrewsbury T	D	0-0	0-0	6		3871
31	12	A	Lincoln C	D	1-1	0-1	5	Joseph [85]	8319
32	19	H	Cheltenham T	D	5-5	3-1	6	Obita 2 [26, 31], Hanlan [33], Vokes 2 [68, 69]	5574
33	22	H	Wigan Ath	L	1-3	1-0	7	KaiKai [22]	4826
34	26	A	Accrington S	L	2-3	2-1	8	Vokes [13], KaiKai [22]	2242
35	Mar 1	H	Cambridge U	W	3-0	2-0	7	Mehmeti 2 [11, 85], McCleary [15]	4083
36	5	A	Crewe Alex	W	3-1	1-0	5	Vokes [14], Wing 2 [55, 90]	4031
37	12	H	Rotherham U	D	0-0	0-0	8		5742
38	15	H	Fleetwood T	W	1-0	0-0	8	McCarthy [90]	3391
39	19	A	Portsmouth	D	0-0	0-0	8		15,092
40	Apr 2	H	Doncaster R	W	2-0	1-0	8	McCleary [18], Mehmeti [75]	5943
41	5	A	Cambridge U	W	4-1	1-0	6	Vokes 2 [7, 54], Scowen [56], McCleary [89]	4751
42	9	A	Gillingham	D	1-1	1-0	6	Vokes [20]	4858
43	15	H	Plymouth Arg	W	2-0	2-0	5	McCleary 2 [14, 31]	8181
44	18	A	AFC Wimbledon	D	1-1	0-1	5	Akinfenwa [80]	8502
45	23	H	Sheffield W	W	1-0	0-0	6	Obita [62]	9005
46	30	A	Burton Alb	W	2-1	1-0	6	Vokes [43], Obita [85]	4440

Final League Position: 6

GOALSCORERS

League (75): Vokes 16, McCleary 11, Mehmeti 7, Hanlan 6, Akinfenwa 5, Obita 5, Tafazolli 4, Jacobson 3 (1 pen), Grimmer 2, KaiKai 2, Pendlebury 2, Stewart 2, Thompson 2, Wheeler 2, Wing 2, Horgan 1, Joseph 1, McCarthy 1, Scowen 1.
FA Cup (2): Jacobson 1 (1 pen), Joseph 1.
Carabao Cup (3): Akinfenwa 1, De Barr 1, Hanlan 1.
Papa John's Trophy (2): Hanlan 1, Parsons 1.
League One Play-offs (2): Tafazolli 1, Vokes 1.

Stockdale D 46	McCarthy J 31	Grimmer J 23 + 3	Stewart A 34 + 2	Jacobson J 40	Obita J 37 + 4	Pendlebury O 3 + 1	Horgan D 21 + 13	Scowen J 36 + 1	McCleary G 37 + 5	Vokes S 42 + 1	Akinfenwa A 3 + 31	Mehmeti A 23 + 9	Freeman N 1 + 2	KaiKai S 8 + 9	Thompson C 24 + 4	Tafazolli R 33	Wheeler D 8 + 22	De Barr T — + 5	Hanlan B 25 + 11	Gape D 7 + 3	Joseph C 13 + 2	Wing L 11 + 2	Young J — + 2	Match No.
1	2^{3}	3	4	5	6	7	8	9	10^{2}	11^{1}	12	13	14											1
1		3	4	5	6	7		9	11^{1}	10^{2}	13	8^{3}	12	2	14									2
1		3	4	5	6	7^{2}	13	8	10	11^{3}	14	9^{1}		2	12									3
1		3	4	5	6		8^{2}	9	11	10		13	2^{1}	12	7									4
1		2		4	8		10	7		11^{3}	13	9^{1}		5^{2}	6	3	12	14						5
1		5	2	4	8^{3}		12	6	9	10^{2}	13				7	3	14		11^{1}					6
1		2	3	5	9		11^{3}	8	7^{2}	10^{1}	12			13	6	4			14					7
1		2	3■	5	9		11^{3}	8	7^{2}	10^{1}	12				6	4	14		13					8
1	6	2	3	5				7	13	10^{3}	14			9^{1}	8	4	12		11^{2}					9
1	2		3	5	9^{1}		11^{2}	8	7^{3}	10		13			6	4	14		12					10
1	2		3	5	9			8	7	11^{1}	12	13			6^{3}	4	14		10^{2}					11
1	2		3	5	9		13	8	7		11^{1}				6^{3}	4	12		10^{2}	14				12
1	5		2	4	8		9^{1}	7	10^{2}	11				12	14	3			13	6^{3}				13
1	5		2	4	8			7	9^{2}	10^{3}	14			13	6^{1}	3			11	12				14
1		2	3	5	12		6^{3}	8		9	10^{1}	14			7^{2}	4	13		11					15
1	5		2	4^{2}	8		14	6		11	12			13		3	9^{3}		10	7^{1}				16
1	5		2	4^{2}	8			7		10	12	9^{1}			6	3	13		11					17
1	5		2		4				12	11		9		8^{1}	7	3	6		10					18
1	5		2	4^{2}	8	12			13	11^{3}	14	9			7^{1}	3	6		10					19
1	5		2		4		12		8^{3}	11^{2}	13	9^{1}		14	7	3	6		10					20
1	5	2		4	8		14		10^{3}	11^{2}	13	6^{1}			7		12		9		3			21
1	5	2^{2}		4	8		12		6	11^{3}	13	9^{1}		14	7	3			10					22
1	6		2	4	9			13	8	11	14	12			5^{2}		7^{1}		10		3^{3}			23
1	5	2	13	4	8			6	9	11^{2}		7^{1}					12		10		3			24
1		5	2^{3}	4	8		14	7	9	10^{1}	12	6^{2}						13	11		3			25
1		5	2	4^{1}	8		13	7	9	10		6^{2}			12	3		14	11^{3}					26
1		5	2	4	8		13	7	9			10^{2}			6^{1}	3	12	14	11^{3}					27
1		5	2	4^{3}	8		13		9		11	7^{1}			6^{2}	3	12	14	10					28
1		5	2	4^{1}	8		13		9	12	14	10^{2}			7	3	6		11^{3}					29
1	5	2		4	8				9	11^{2}	13	14		12	7				10^{1}		3	6^{3}		30
1	5^{3}	2		4	8		14	6■	11^{1}	10					7		13		12		3	9^{2}		31
1		2		4^{1}	8		6		12	11		13		9^{2}	7^{3}		5		10		3	14		32
1		2	3		5			7	12	11	13			9^{2}			6		10^{1}	14	4	8^{3}		33
1	5	2	3	4^{2}	8			7	9^{3}	11		12		10^{1}					14	6	13			34
1	2^{2}	13	3		5		7^{1}	8	9	11^{3}	14	10				4	12					6		35
1	2		3		5		9^{3}	7	8^{2}	11		10^{4}				4^{1}	13		14		12	6	15	36
1	2		3	5			9	7	8	11^{2}	13	10^{1}				4			12			6		37
1	2		3	5			9^{1}	7	8	11	14	10^{3}				4			12			6^{2}	13	38
1	2		3	5			9	6	8	11^{2}	13	10^{1}				4			12			7		39
1	2		3	5^{2}	13		9	7	8^{1}	11^{3}	14	10				4	12					6		40
1	2			5^{2}	13		9^{1}	7	8	11^{3}	14	10				3	12				4	6		41
1	2			5			9^{2}	7	8	11^{3}	14	10^{1}				3	13		12		4	6■		42
1	2	13		5	14		9^{1}	7	8^{3}	11						3	12		10	6^{2}	4			43
1	2^{3}		13		5		9^{1}	7	8	11	12			14		4			10^{2}	6	3			44
1	2	14		5^{1}	10		9	7	8	11^{2}	13					4	12			6^{3}	3			45
1	2		3	5	10		9^{1}	7	8	11^{3}	14					4	12			6^{2}		13		46

FA Cup

First Round	Hartlepool U	(a)	2-2
Replay	Hartlepool U	(h)	0-1

Papa John's Trophy

Group C (S)	Aston Villa U21	(h)	1-3
Group C (S)	Milton Keynes D	(a)	1-2
Group C (S)	Burton Alb	(h)	0-5

Carabao Cup

First Round	Exeter C	(a)	0-0
(Wycombe W won 4-3 on penalties)			
Second Round	Stevenage	(a)	2-2
(Wycombe W won 5-3 on penalties)			
Third Round	Manchester C	(a)	1-6

League One Play-offs

Semi-Final 1st leg	Milton Keynes D	(h)	2-0
Semi-Final 2nd leg	Milton Keynes D	(a)	0-1
Final	Sunderland	(Wembley)	0-2

ENGLISH LEAGUE PLAYERS DIRECTORY

Players listed represent those with their clubs during the 2021–22 season.

Club names in *italic* indicate loans.

Players are listed alphabetically on pages 530–537 where the number alongside each player corresponds to the team number heading. (Aarons, Maximillian 59 = team 59 (Norwich C)).

ACCRINGTON S (1)

ADEDOYIN, Korede (F) 12 1
H: 6 0 W: 11 11 b.Lagos 14-11-00

2018–19	Everton	0	0		
2019–20	Everton	0	0		
2019–20	*Hamilton A*	0	0		
2020–21	Sheffield W	0	0		
2021–22	Sheffield W	0	0		
2021–22	Accrington S	12	1	12	1

BISHOP, Colby (M) 113 32
H: 5 11 W: 11 05 b.Nottingham 14-11-94

2013–14	Notts Co	0	0		
2014–15	Notts Co	3	0		
2015–16	Notts Co	1	0	4	0
From Worcester C, Boston U, Leamington.					
2019–20	Accrington S	27	10		
2020–21	Accrington S	41	10		
2021–22	Accrington S	41	12	109	32

BUTCHER, Matt (M) 115 8
H: 6 2 W: 12 13 b.Portsmouth 14-5-97
From Poole T.

2015–16	Bournemouth	0	0		
2016–17	Bournemouth	0	0		
2016–17	*Yeovil T*	34	2	34	2
2017–18	Bournemouth	0	0		
2018–19	Bournemouth	0	0		
2019–20	Bournemouth	0	0		
2019–20	*St Johnstone*	6	0	6	0
2020–21	Accrington S	42	2		
2021–22	Accrington S	33	4	75	6

CLARK, Mitchell (D) 80 2
H: 5 8 W: 10 10 b.Nuneaton 13-3-99
Internationals: Wales U17, U19.

2017–18	Aston Villa	0	0		
2018–19	Aston Villa	0	0		
2018–19	*Port Vale*	40	0		
2019–20	Leicester C	0	0		
2019–20	*Port Vale*	4	0		
2020–21	Leicester C	0	0		
2020–21	*Port Vale*	11	1	55	1
2021–22	Accrington S	25	1	25	1

CONNEELY, Seamus (D) 396 17
H: 5 9 W: 10 10 b.Galway 9-7-88
Internationals: Republic of Ireland U21, U23.

2008	Galway U	20	0		
2009	Galway U	34	2		
2010	Galway U	32	0	86	2
2010–11	Sheffield U	0	0		
2011–12	Sheffield U	0	0		
2012	Sligo R	13	1		
2013	Sligo R	21	1		
2014	Sligo R	25	1	59	3
2014–15	Accrington S	16	3		
2015–16	Accrington S	46	3		
2016–17	Accrington S	38	1		
2017–18	Accrington S	33	2		
2018–19	Accrington S	27	1		
2019–20	Accrington S	31	1		
2020–21	Accrington S	38	1		
2021–22	Accrington S	22	0	251	12

COYLE, Liam (M) 19 1
b.Liverpool 6-12-99

2016–17	Liverpool	0	0		
2017–18	Liverpool	0	0		
2018–19	Liverpool	0	0		
2019–20	Liverpool	0	0		
2020–21	Liverpool	0	0		
2021–22	Accrington S	19	1	19	1

FENLON, Rhys-James (M) 2 0
b. 2-11-01
From Mancheste C, Burnley.

2020–21	Accrington S	2	0		
2021–22	Accrington S	0	0	2	0

HAMILTON, Ethan (M) 117 11
H: 6 2 W: 11 11 b.Edinburgh 18-10-98
Internationals: Scotland U16, U19.

2017–18	Manchester U	0	0		
2018–19	Manchester U	0	0		
2018–19	*Rochdale*	14	4	14	4
2019–20	Manchester U	0	0		
2019–20	*Southend U*	14	0	14	0
2019–20	*Bolton W*	12	1	12	1
2020–21	Peterborough U	34	0		
2021–22	Peterborough U	2	0	36	0
2021–22	Accrington S	41	6	41	6

HARDY, Joe (F) 12 1
b.Wirral 26-9-98
From Manchester C, Brentford.

2019–20	Liverpool	0	0		
2020–21	Liverpool	0	0		
2021–22	Accrington S	0	0		
2021–22	*Inverness CT*	12	1	12	1

ISHERWOOD, Liam (G) 4 0
H: 6 4 b.Clitheroe 13-7-02
From Portsmouth, Baffins Milton R, Bognor Regis T.

2020–21	Accrington S	0	0		
2021–22	Accrington S	4	0	4	0

LEIGH, Tommy (M) 24 6
b.Portsmouth 13-4-00
From Baffins Milton R, Bognor Regis T.

2021–22	Accrington S	24	6	24	6

LEWIS, Marcel (M) 3 0
b.Cambridge 30-9-01

2019–20	Chelsea	0	0		
2020–21	Chelsea	0	0		
2021–22	Union SG	0	0		
2021–22	Accrington S	3	0	3	0

LONGELO, Rosaire (M) 12 1
b.Kinshasa 20-10-99
From West Ham U.

2020–21	Newcastle U	0	0		
2021–22	Accrington S	12	1	12	1

MANSELL, Lewis (F) 29 3
H: 6 2 W: 11 11 b.Burnley 20-9-97

2017–18	Blackburn R	0	0		
2018–19	Blackburn R	0	0		
2018–19	*Partick Thistle*	8	1		
2019–20	Partick Thistle	13	1	21	2
2020–21	Accrington S	2	0		
2021–22	Accrington S	6	1	8	1

MARTIN, Dan (M) 0 0

2019–20	Accrington S	0	0		
2020–21	Accrington S	0	0		
2021–22	Accrington S	0	0		

McCONVILLE, Sean (M) 346 61
H: 5 11 W: 11 07 b.Liverpool 6-3-89

2008–09	Accrington S	5	0		
2009–10	Accrington S	28	1		
2010–11	Accrington S	43	13		
2011–12	Rochdale	4	0	4	0
From Barrow, Stalybridge Celtic, Chester.					
2015–16	Accrington S	42	5		
2016–17	Accrington S	41	5		
2017–18	Accrington S	43	12		
2018–19	Accrington S	45	15		
2019–20	Accrington S	18	5		
2020–21	Accrington S	31	1		
2021–22	Accrington S	46	4	342	61

MORGAN, David (M) 31 0
H: 5 8 W: 10 10 b.Belfast 4-7-94
Internationals: Northern Ireland U17, U19, U21.

2011–12	Nottingham F	0	0		
2012–13	Nottingham F	0	0		
2012–13	*Dundee*	1	0	1	0
2013–14	Nottingham F	0	0		
From Ilkeston, Nuneaton T, AFC Fylde, Harrogate T, Southport.					
2020–21	Accrington S	16	0		
2021–22	Accrington S	14	0	30	0

NOLAN, Jack (M) 18 0
H: 5 11 W: 11 05 b.Portsmouth 25-5-01
Internationals: England U17.

2018–19	Reading	0	0		
2019–20	Walsall	4	0		
2020–21	Walsall	9	0	13	0
2021–22	Accrington S	5	0	5	0

NOTTINGHAM, Michael (D) 135 13
H: 6 4 W: 13 12 b.Birmingham 14-4-89
Internationals: Saint Kitts and Nevis Full caps.
From Gresley, Solihull Moors, Salford C.

2018–19	Blackpool	29	2		
2019–20	Blackpool	3	0		
2019–20	*Crewe Alex*	12	1	12	1
2020–21	Blackpool	3	0	35	2
2020–21	Accrington S	42	4		
2021–22	Accrington S	46	6	88	10

O'SULLIVAN, John (M) 222 16
H: 5 11 W: 13 01 b.Dublin 18-9-93
Internationals: Republic of Ireland U19, U21.

2011–12	Blackburn R	0	0		
2012–13	Blackburn R	1	0		
2013–14	Blackburn R	0	0		
2014–15	Blackburn R	2	0		
2014–15	*Accrington S*	13	4		
2014–15	*Barnsley*	8	0	8	0
2015–16	Blackburn R	2	0		
2015–16	*Rochdale*	2	0	2	0
2015–16	*Bury*	19	0	19	0
2016–17	Blackburn R	0	0	5	0
2016–17	*Accrington S*	19	1		
2016–17	Carlisle U	17	1		
2017–18	Carlisle U	18	1	35	2
2018–19	Blackpool	13	0	13	0
2018–19	*Dundee*	11	0	11	0
2019–20	Morecambe	34	3		
2020–21	Morecambe	38	4		
2021–22	Morecambe	0	0	72	7
2021–22	Accrington S	25	2	57	7

PELL, Harry (M) 300 38
H: 6 4 W: 13 05 b.Tilbury 21-10-91

2009–10	Charlton Ath	0	0		
2010–11	Bristol R	10	0	10	0
2010–11	*Hereford U*	7	0		
2011–12	Hereford U	30	3	37	3
2012–13	AFC Wimbledon	17	2		
2013–14	AFC Wimbledon	33	4		
2014–15	AFC Wimbledon	9	0	59	6
From Eastleigh.					
2016–17	Cheltenham T	42	7		
2017–18	Cheltenham T	37	5	79	12
2018–19	Colchester U	31	6		
2019–20	Colchester U	22	3		
2020–21	Colchester U	25	2	78	11
2021–22	Accrington S	37	6	37	6

PERRITT, Harry (M) 4 0
H: 6 1 W: 10 06 b.Knowsley 16-2-01

2018–19	Accrington S	0	0		
2019–20	Accrington S	0	0		
2020–21	Accrington S	2	0		
2021–22	Accrington S	2	0	4	0

PRITCHARD, Joe (M) 72 9
H: 5 8 W: 10 06 b.Watford 10-9-96
From Tottenham H.

2018–19	Bolton W	4	0	4	0
2019–20	Accrington S	30	2		
2020–21	Accrington S	28	7		
2021–22	Accrington S	10	0	68	9

PROCTER, Archie (D) 0 0
H: 6 1 W: 11 07 b.Blackburn 13-11-01

2019–20	AFC Wimbledon	0	0		
2020–21	AFC Wimbledon	0	0		
2021–22	AFC Wimbledon	0	0		
2021–22	Accrington S	0	0		

RICH-BAGHUELOU, Jay (D) 13 2
H: 6 5 b.Sydney 22-10-99
Internationals: Australia U23.
From Crystal Palace.

2021–22	Accrington S	13	2	13	2

RODGERS, Harvey (D) 86 1
H: 6 2 W: 12 06 b.York 20-10-96

2016–17	Hull C	0	0		
2016–17	*Accrington S*	19	1		
2017–18	Fleetwood T	0	0		
2017–18	Accrington S	5	0		
2018–19	Accrington S	6	0		
2019–20	Accrington S	6	0		
2020–21	Accrington S	28	0		
2021–22	Accrington S	22	0	86	1

SAMA, Stephen (D) 29 0
H: 6 2 W: 13 01 b.Cameroon 5-3-93
Internationals: Germany U17, U18, U19, U20.

2009–10	Liverpool	0	0		
2010–11	Liverpool	0	0		
2011–12	Liverpool	0	0		
2012–13	Liverpool	0	0		
2013–14	Liverpool	0	0		
2014–15	Liverpool	0	0		
2015–16	Stuttgart	0	0		
2016–17	Greuther Furth	4	0		
2017–18	Greuther Furth	0	0	4	0
2017–18	*Osnabruck*	13	0	13	0
2018–19	Heracles	8	0		
2019–20	Heracles	0	0	8	0

2020–21 Accrington S 4 0
2021–22 Accrington S 0 0 **4 0**

SAVIN, Toby (G) 64 0
H: 6 4 W: 12 08 b.Ormskirk 4-5-01
2017–18 Accrington S 0 0
2018–19 Accrington S 0 0
2019–20 Accrington S 0 0
2020–21 Accrington S 31 0
2021–22 Accrington S 33 0 **64 0**

SCULLY, Thomas (M) 3 0
H: 6 0 W: 10 08 b.Liverpool 1-10-99
2019–20 Norwich C 0 0
2020–21 Accrington S 3 0
2021–22 Accrington S 0 0 **3 0**

SPINELLI, Kevin (F) 0 0
2020–21 Accrington S 0 0
2021–22 Accrington S 0 0

STOWE, Luke (M) 0 0
b. 15-9-02
2020–21 Accrington S 0 0
2021–22 Accrington S 0 0

SYKES, Ross (D) 101 8
H: 6 5 W: 11 07 b.Burnley 26-3-99
2016–17 Accrington S 0 0
2017–18 Accrington S 2 0
2018–19 Accrington S 20 3
2019–20 Accrington S 31 1
2020–21 Accrington S 9 1
2021–22 Accrington S 39 3 **101 8**

WOODS, Josh (F) 3 0
b. 5-7-00
From Clay Brow.
2021–22 Accrington S 3 0 **3 0**

Players retained or with offer of contract
Adekoya, Leslie; Carson, Matty; Hood, Louis; Moonan, Dylan; Patrick, Oliver; Poilly, Emerich.

Scholars
Adekoya, Leslie Toluwani Adetokunbo; Akukwe, Vandis Chima; Clayton, Max Alexander; Devonport, Owen Nicholas; Doherty, Jack Edward; Eze, George Emenaike; Gough, Brandon Jay Sydney; Harper, Calvin Robert; Henderson, Alex William; Hood, Louis Owen; Kardacz, Mateusz; Monk, Harvey Dylan; Newton, Jasper William; O'Brien, Connor David; Pickles, Aaron Thomas; Trickett, Lewis James.

AFC WIMBLEDON (2)

ADJEI-HERSEY, Dylan (F) 2 0
b. 6-9-02
2021–22 AFC Wimbledon 2 0 **2 0**

ALEXANDER, Cheye (D) 50 0
H: 5 8 W: 10 10 b.Newham 6-1-95
Internationals: England C.
2013–14 Port Vale 0 0
From Concorde Rangers, Bishop's Stortford, Aldershot T, Barnet.
2020–21 AFC Wimbledon 29 0
2021–22 AFC Wimbledon 21 0 **50 0**

ANDREWS, Corie (F) 11 1
b.Lambeth 20-9-97
From Kingstonian.
2020–21 AFC Wimbledon 0 0
2021–22 AFC Wimbledon 0 0
2021–22 *Colchester U* 11 1 **11 1**

ASSAL, Ayoub (M) 56 12
H: 5 7 W: 10 03 b.Maidstone 21-1-02
2019–20 AFC Wimbledon 0 0
2020–21 AFC Wimbledon 14 4
2021–22 AFC Wimbledon 42 8 **56 12**

BENDLE, Alfie (M) 1 0
2021–22 AFC Wimbledon 1 0 **1 0**

BILER, Huseyin (D) 0 0
b.Enfield 26-2-02
2019–20 AFC Wimbledon 0 0
2020–21 AFC Wimbledon 0 0
2021–22 AFC Wimbledon 0 0

BOLTON, Elliott (M) 0 0
b.Kingston upon Thames 18-10-01
2020–21 AFC Wimbledon 0 0
2021–22 AFC Wimbledon 0 0

BROWN, Lee (M) 369 25
H: 6 0 W: 12 06 b.Bromley 10-8-90
Internationals: England C.
2008–09 QPR 0 0
2009–10 QPR 1 0
2010–11 QPR 0 0 **1 0**
2011–12 Bristol R 42 7
2012–13 Bristol R 39 3
2013–14 Bristol R 41 2
From Bristol R.
2015–16 Bristol R 46 6
2016–17 Bristol R 41 0
2017–18 Bristol R 33 1 **242 19**
2018–19 Portsmouth 44 0
2019–20 Portsmouth 16 1
2020–21 Portsmouth 32 2
2021–22 Portsmouth 19 3 **111 6**
2021–22 AFC Wimbledon 15 0 **15 0**

CHARLES, Darius (D) 290 18
H: 6 1 W: 13 05 b.Ealing 10-12-87
Internationals: England C.
2004–05 Brentford 1 0
2005–06 Brentford 2 0
2006–07 Brentford 17 1
2007–08 Brentford 17 0 **37 1**
From Ebbsfleet U.
2010–11 Stevenage 28 2
2011–12 Stevenage 28 4
2012–13 Stevenage 37 1
2013–14 Stevenage 22 4
2014–15 Stevenage 29 2 **144 13**
2015–16 Burton Alb 0 0
2015–16 *AFC Wimbledon* 9 0
2016–17 AFC Wimbledon 34 2
2017–18 AFC Wimbledon 31 0
2018–19 Wycombe W 5 0
2019–20 Wycombe W 25 2
2020–21 Wycombe W 5 0 **35 2**
2021–22 AFC Wimbledon 0 0 **74 2**

CHISLETT, Ethan (M) 56 4
H: 5 10 W: 10 10 b.Durban 11-8-98
From Metropolitan Police, Aldershot T.
2020–21 AFC Wimbledon 27 2
2021–22 AFC Wimbledon 29 2 **56 4**

COSGRAVE, Aaron (F) 9 1
b.Shenfield 17-7-99
From Coggeshall T, Havant & Waterlooville, Chelmsford C, Welling U, Lewes.
2021–22 AFC Wimbledon 9 1 **9 1**

CSOKA, Daniel (D) 38 1
H: 6 2 W: 12 04 b.Zalaegerszeg 4-4-00
Internationals: Hungary U16, U17, U18, U19.
2017–18 Wolverhampton W 0 0
2018–19 Wolverhampton W 0 0
2018–19 *DAC* 0 0
2019–20 Wolverhampton W 0 0
2019–20 *Samorin* 1 0 **1 0**
2020–21 AFC Wimbledon 20 1
2021–22 AFC Wimbledon 17 0 **37 1**

CURRIE, Jack (D) 0 0
b.Kingston upon Thames 16-12-01
2020–21 AFC Wimbledon 0 0
2021–22 AFC Wimbledon 0 0

FISHER, David (F) 0 0
2019–20 AFC Wimbledon 0 0
2020–21 AFC Wimbledon 0 0
2021–22 AFC Wimbledon 0 0

GUINNESS-WALKER, Nesta (D) 82 3
H: 5 9 W: 11 00 b.Hounslow 30-11-99
From Metropolitan Police.
2019–20 AFC Wimbledon 23 1
2020–21 AFC Wimbledon 31 1
2021–22 AFC Wimbledon 28 1 **82 3**

HARTIGAN, Anthony (M) 129 1
H: 5 11 W: 10 10 b.Kingston upon Thames 27-1-00
2017–18 AFC Wimbledon 11 0
2018–19 AFC Wimbledon 31 0
2019–20 AFC Wimbledon 27 0
2020–21 AFC Wimbledon 15 0
2020–21 *Newport Co* 11 0 **11 0**
2021–22 AFC Wimbledon 34 1 **118 1**

HENEGHAN, Ben (D) 173 8
H: 6 3 W: 12 06 b.Manchester 19-9-93
Internationals: England C.
From Everton, Stoke C, Chester.
2016–17 Motherwell 37 0
2017–18 Motherwell 4 1 **41 1**
2017–18 Sheffield U 0 0
2018–19 Sheffield U 0 0
2018–19 *Blackpool* 42 1
2019–20 Sheffield U 0 0
2019–20 *Blackpool* 26 2 **68 3**
2020–21 AFC Wimbledon 23 2
2021–22 AFC Wimbledon 41 2 **64 4**

KAJA, Egli (M) 37 0
H: 5 10 W: 12 04 b.Prelezi I Jerlive 26-7-97
Internationals: Albania U21.
2015–16 AFC Wimbledon 2 0
2016–17 AFC Wimbledon 1 0
2017–18 AFC Wimbledon 19 0
2018–19 AFC Wimbledon 0 0
2018–19 *Livingston* 6 0 **6 0**
2019–20 Northampton T 4 0 **4 0**
2021–22 AFC Wimbledon 5 0 **27 0**

KALAMBAYI, Paul (D) 60 0
H: 6 0 W: 11 00 b.Dulwich 28-7-99
2015–16 AFC Wimbledon 0 0
2016–17 AFC Wimbledon 0 0
2017–18 AFC Wimbledon 0 0
2018–19 AFC Wimbledon 17 0
2019–20 AFC Wimbledon 16 0
2020–21 AFC Wimbledon 14 0
2021–22 AFC Wimbledon 13 0 **60 0**

MADELIN, Jack (D) 1 0
b. 19-4-02
Internationals: Wales U16, U17.
2019–20 AFC Wimbledon 1 0
2020–21 AFC Wimbledon 0 0
2021–22 AFC Wimbledon 0 0 **1 0**

MARSH, George (M) 53 0
H: 5 10 W: 10 10 b.Pembury 5-11-98
2018–19 Tottenham H 0 0
2019–20 Tottenham H 0 0
2019–20 *Leyton Orient* 26 0 **26 0**
2020–21 Tottenham H 0 0
2021–22 AFC Wimbledon 27 0 **27 0**

McCORMICK, Luke (M) 84 13
H: 5 11 W: 11 09 b.Bury St Edmunds 21-1-99
2019–20 Chelsea 0 0
2019–20 *Shrewsbury T* 5 0 **5 0**
2020–21 Chelsea 0 0
2020–21 *Bristol R* 39 6 **39 6**
2021–22 AFC Wimbledon 40 7 **40 7**

NIGHTINGALE, Will (M) 153 6
H: 6 1 W: 13 03 b.Wandsworth 2-8-95
2013–14 AFC Wimbledon 0 0
2014–15 AFC Wimbledon 4 0
2015–16 AFC Wimbledon 4 0
2016–17 AFC Wimbledon 12 0
2017–18 AFC Wimbledon 18 1
2018–19 AFC Wimbledon 39 0
2019–20 AFC Wimbledon 9 0
2020–21 AFC Wimbledon 32 2
2021–22 AFC Wimbledon 35 3 **153 6**

OSEI YAW, Derick (F) 30 1
b.Toulouse 10-9-98
Internationals: France U19, U20.
2016–17 Toulouse 0 0
2017–18 Toulouse 0 0
2018–19 Brest 3 0
2019–20 Brest 0 0 **3 0**
2019–20 *Beziers* 7 1 **7 1**
2020–21 Oxford U 3 0
2020–21 *Walsall* 11 0
2021–22 *Walsall* 0 0 **11 0**
2021–22 Oxford U 0 0 **3 0**
2021–22 AFC Wimbledon 6 0 **6 0**

OSEW, Paul (D) 55 1
H: 5 4 W: 8 11 b.Wandsworth 25-11-00
From Brentford.
2019–20 AFC Wimbledon 18 1
2020–21 AFC Wimbledon 10 0
2021–22 AFC Wimbledon 27 0 **55 1**

PALMER, Oliver (F) 290 65
H: 6 5 W: 12 02 b.Epsom 21-1-92
From Woking, Havant & Waterlooville.
2013–14 Mansfield T 38 4
2014–15 Mansfield T 16 1 **54 5**
2015–16 Leyton Orient 45 7
2016–17 Leyton Orient 20 5 **65 12**
2016–17 *Luton T* 17 3 **17 3**
2017–18 Lincoln C 45 8 **45 8**
2018–19 Crawley T 40 14
2019–20 Crawley T 28 13
2020–21 Crawley T 0 0 **68 27**
2020–21 AFC Wimbledon 23 5
2021–22 AFC Wimbledon 18 5 **41 10**
Transferred to Wrexham, January 2022.

ROBINSON, Zach (F) 11 1
H: 6 2 W: 12 04 b.Lambeth 11-6-02
2019–20 AFC Wimbledon 0 0
2020–21 AFC Wimbledon 5 0
2021–22 AFC Wimbledon 6 1 **11 1**

RUDONI, Jack (M) 91 16
H: 6 1 W: 11 03 b.Wandsworth 26-5-01
2018–19 AFC Wimbledon 0 0
2019–20 AFC Wimbledon 11 0
2020–21 AFC Wimbledon 39 4
2021–22 AFC Wimbledon 41 12 **91 16**

SUTCLIFFE, Ethan (D) 0 0
b.Lambeth 20-2-04
2020–21 AFC Wimbledon 0 0
2021–22 AFC Wimbledon 0 0

TZANEV, Nikola (G) 63 0
H: 6 5 W: 14 02 b.Wellington 23-12-96
Internationals: New Zealand U20, Full caps.
From Brentford.
2016–17 AFC Wimbledon 0 0
2017–18 AFC Wimbledon 0 0
2018–19 AFC Wimbledon 0 0
2019–20 AFC Wimbledon 2 0
2020–21 AFC Wimbledon 15 0
2021–22 AFC Wimbledon 46 0 **63 0**

WOODYARD, Alex (M) 198 5
H: 5 9 W: 9 02 b.Gravesend 3-5-93
Internationals: England C.
From Charlton Ath.
2010–11 Southend U 3 0

2011–12 Southend U 0 0
2012–13 Southend U 5 0
2013–14 Southend U 0 0 **8 0**
From Dartford, Concord Rangers, Braintree T.
2017–18 Lincoln C 46 2 **46 2**
2018–19 Peterborough U 43 0
2019–20 Peterborough U 14 0 **57 0**
2019–20 *Tranmere R* 11 1 **11 1**
2020–21 AFC Wimbledon 40 1
2021–22 AFC Wimbledon 36 1 **76 2**

Players retained or with offer of contract
Ali, Abdi; Bartley, Quaine; Broome, Nathan; Campbell, Marcel; Frimpong, Kwaku; Hallard, Josh; Jenkins, Luke; Jones, Aaron; Mason, Reuben; Ogundere, Issac; Olaniyan, Isaac; Oualah, Zaki; Sasu, Aron; Williams, Morgan.

Scholars
Bangura, Ibrahim Rasheed; Bartley, Quaine Asani; Campbell, Marcel Simon; Griffiths, Harry Neil; Hallard, Josh Robert; Jones, Aaron Michael; Lahan, Adejola; Lock, Paris Alexander; Mason, Benjamin Nicholas; Onabanjo, Oluremi Chanda Yaw; Sasu, Aron Kwame Jolle; Shiekh Ali, Abdkariim Abdulkadir; Sutcliffe, Ethan Jack; Williams, Morgan Charles; Yeboah, Obed Kwabena; Ziger, Luka.

ARSENAL (3)

AKINOLA, Tim (M) 1 0
H: 5 11 b. 8-5-01
From Lincoln C, Huddersfield T.
2020–21 Arsenal 0 0
2021–22 Arsenal 0 0
2021–22 *Dundee U* 1 0 **1 0**

ALEBIOSU, Ryan (D) 6 0
b.Islington 17-12-01
From Fulham.
2021–22 Arsenal 0 0
2021–22 *Crewe Alex* 6 0 **6 0**

AUBAMEYANG, Pierre-Emerick (F) 426 215
H: 6 2 W: 11 09 b.Laval 18-6-89
Internationals: France U21. Gabon U23, Full caps.
2008–09 AC Milan 0 0
2008–09 *Dijon* 34 8 **34 8**
2009–10 AC Milan 0 0
2009–10 *Lille* 14 2 **14 2**
2010–11 AC Milan 0 0
2010–11 *Monaco* 19 2 **19 2**
2010–11 *Saint-Etienne* 14 2
2011–12 Saint-Etienne 36 16
2012–13 Saint-Etienne 37 19 **87 37**
2013–14 Borussia Dortmund 32 13
2014–15 Borussia Dortmund 33 16
2015–16 Borussia Dortmund 31 25
2016–17 Borussia Dortmund 32 31
2017–18 Borussia Dortmund 16 13 **144 98**
2017–18 Arsenal 13 10
2018–19 Arsenal 36 22
2019–20 Arsenal 36 22
2020–21 Arsenal 29 10
2021–22 Arsenal 14 4 **128 68**
Transferred to Barcelona, February 2022.

AZEEZ, Miguel (M) 6 0
H: 5 11 W: 10 03 b.Camden 20-9-02
Internationals: England U16, U17, U18, U19, U20.
2019–20 Arsenal 0 0
2020–21 Arsenal 0 0
2021–22 Arsenal 0 0
2021–22 *Portsmouth* 6 0 **6 0**

BALLARD, Daniel (D) 57 3
H: 6 2 W: 13 05 b.Stevenage 22-9-99
Internationals: Northern Ireland U18, U21, Full caps.
2019–20 Arsenal 0 0
2019–20 *Swindon T* 1 0 **1 0**
2020–21 Arsenal 0 0
2020–21 *Blackpool* 25 2 **25 2**
2021–22 Arsenal 0 0
2021–22 *Millwall* 31 1 **31 1**

BALOGUN, Folarin (F) 20 3
H: 5 10 W: 10 06 b.New York 3-7-01
Internationals: England U17, U18, U20, U21. USA U18.
2019–20 Arsenal 0 0
2020–21 Arsenal 0 0
2021–22 Arsenal 2 0 **2 0**
2021–22 *Middlesbrough* 18 3 **18 3**

BELLERIN, Hector (D) 214 8
H: 5 10 W: 11 09 b.Barcelona 19-3-95
Internationals: Spain U16, U17, U19, U21, Full caps.
From Barcelona.
2012–13 Arsenal 0 0
2013–14 Arsenal 0 0
2013–14 *Watford* 8 0 **8 0**
2014–15 Arsenal 20 2
2015–16 Arsenal 36 1
2016–17 Arsenal 33 1
2017–18 Arsenal 35 2
2018–19 Arsenal 19 0
2019–20 Arsenal 15 1
2020–21 Arsenal 25 1
2021–22 Arsenal 0 0 **183 8**
2021–22 *Real Betis* 23 0 **23 0**

CEDRIC SOARES, Ricardo (D) 251 5
H: 5 7 W: 10 08 b.Gelsenkirchen 31-8-91
Internationals: Portugal U16, U17, U18, U19, U20, U21, Full caps.
2010–11 Sporting Lisbon 2 0
2011–12 Sporting Lisbon 0 0
2011–12 *Academica* 24 0 **24 0**
2012–13 Sporting Lisbon 13 1
2013–14 Sporting Lisbon 28 1
2014–15 Sporting Lisbon 24 0 **67 2**
2015–16 Southampton 24 0
2016–17 Southampton 30 0
2017–18 Southampton 32 0
2018–19 Southampton 18 1
2018–19 *Inter Milan* 4 0 **4 0**
2019–20 Southampton 16 0 **120 1**
2019–20 Arsenal 5 1
2020–21 Arsenal 10 0
2021–22 Arsenal 21 1 **36 2**

CIRJAN, Catalin (M) 0 0
b. 1-12-02
Internationals: Romania U16, U19.
From Viitorul Domnesti.
2020–21 Arsenal 0 0
2021–22 Arsenal 0 0

CLARKE, Harrison (D) 56 5
b.Ipswich 2-3-01
Internationals: England U17.
2019–20 Arsenal 0 0
2020–21 Arsenal 0 0
2020–21 *Oldham Ath* 32 1 **32 1**
2021–22 Arsenal 0 0
2021–22 *Ross Co* 17 3 **17 3**
2021–22 *Hibernian* 7 1 **7 1**

COTTRELL, Ben (M) 0 0
b. 31-10-01
Internationals: England U18.
2020–21 Arsenal 0 0
2021–22 Arsenal 0 0

DINZEYI, Jonathan (D) 1 0
H: 6 0 W: 13 01 b.Islington 13-10-99
2016–17 Tottenham H 0 0
2017–18 Tottenham H 0 0
2018–19 Tottenham H 0 0
2019–20 Tottenham H 0 0
2020–21 Arsenal 0 0
2021–22 Arsenal 0 0
2021–22 *Carlisle U* 1 0 **1 0**

ELNENY, Mohamed (M) 236 9
H: 5 11 W: 11 00 b.Al-Mahalla Al-Kubra 11-7-92
Internationals: Egypt U20, U23, Full caps.
2010–11 Al Mokawloon 21 2
2011–12 Al Mokawloon 14 0 **35 2**
2012–13 Basel 15 0
2013–14 Basel 32 1
2014–15 Basel 28 2 **75 3**
2015–16 Basle 16 2 **16 2**
2015–16 Arsenal 11 0
2016–17 Arsenal 14 0
2017–18 Arsenal 13 0
2018–19 Arsenal 8 0
2019–20 Arsenal 0 0
2019–20 *Besiktas* 27 1 **27 1**
2020–21 Arsenal 23 1
2021–22 Arsenal 14 0 **83 1**

GABRIEL, Magalhaes (D) 120 10
H: 6 3 W: 12 04 b.Sao Paulo 19-12-97
Internationals: Brazil U20, U23.
2016 Avai 21 1 **21 1**
2016–17 Lille 1 0
2017–18 Lille 0 0
2017–18 *Troyes* 1 0 **1 0**
2017–18 *Dinamo Zagreb* 1 0 **1 0**
2018–19 Lille 14 1
2019–20 Lille 24 1
2020–21 Lille 0 0 **39 2**
2020–21 Arsenal 23 2
2021–22 Arsenal 35 5 **58 7**

GRACZYK, Hubert (G) 0 0
H: 6 4 b.Skwierzyna 28-2-03
Internationals: England U16, U18.
2020–21 Arsenal 0 0
2021–22 Arsenal 0 0

GUENDOUZI, Matteo (M) 145 6
H: 5 11 W: 10 10 b.Poissy 14-4-99
Internationals: France U18, U19, U20, U21, Full caps.
2015–16 Lorient 0 0
2016–17 Lorient 8 0
2017–18 Lorient 18 0 **26 0**
2018–19 Arsenal 33 0
2019–20 Arsenal 24 0
2020–21 Arsenal 0 0
2020–21 *Hertha Berlin* 24 2 **24 2**
2021–22 Arsenal 0 0 **57 0**
2021–22 *Marseille* 38 4 **38 4**

HEIN, Karl Jakob (G) 5 0
H: 6 4 W: 12 02 b.Polva 13-4-02
Internationals: Estonia U16, U17, U19, U21, Full caps.
From Nomme U.
2019–20 Arsenal 0 0
2020–21 Arsenal 0 0
2021–22 Arsenal 0 0
2021–22 *Reading* 5 0 **5 0**

HILLSON, James (G) 0 0
b. 14-1-01
From Reading.
2019–20 Arsenal 0 0
2020–21 Arsenal 0 0
2021–22 Arsenal 0 0

HOLDING, Rob (D) 111 2
H: 6 2 W: 11 11 b.Stalybridge 20-9-95
Internationals: England U21.
2014–15 Bolton W 0 0
2014–15 *Bury* 1 0 **1 0**
2015–16 Bolton W 26 1 **26 1**
2016–17 Arsenal 9 0
2017–18 Arsenal 12 0
2018–19 Arsenal 10 0
2019–20 Arsenal 8 0
2020–21 Arsenal 30 0
2021–22 Arsenal 15 1 **84 1**

IDEHO, Joel (F) 0 0
b. 17-7-03
From Willem II.
2020–21 Arsenal 0 0
2021–22 Arsenal 0 0

JOHN-JULES, Tyreece (F) 37 6
H: 6 0 W: 11 11 b.Westminster 14-2-01
Internationals: England U16, U17, U18, U19, U21.
2018–19 Arsenal 0 0
2019–20 Arsenal 0 0
2019–20 *Lincoln C* 7 1 **7 1**
2020–21 Arsenal 0 0
2020–21 *Doncaster R* 18 5 **18 5**
2021–22 Arsenal 0 0
2021–22 *Blackpool* 11 0 **11 0**
2021–22 *Sheffield W* 1 0 **1 0**

KIRK, Alex (D) 0 0
b. 27-10-02
2020–21 Arsenal 0 0
2021–22 Arsenal 0 0

KOLASINAC, Sead (D) 191 7
H: 6 0 W: 12 13 b.Karlsruhe 20-6-93
Internationals: Germany U18, U19, U20. Bosnia and Herzegovina Full caps.
2012–13 Schalke 04 16 0
2013–14 Schalke 04 24 0
2014–15 Schalke 04 6 0
2015–16 Schalke 04 23 1
2016–17 Schalke 04 25 3
2017–18 Arsenal 27 2
2018–19 Arsenal 24 0
2019–20 Arsenal 26 0
2020–21 Arsenal 1 0
2020–21 *Schalke 04* 17 1 **111 5**
2021–22 Arsenal 2 0 **80 2**
Transferred to Marseille, January 2022.

LACAZETTE, Alexandre (F) 361 154
H: 5 9 W: 10 12 b.Lyon 28-5-91
Internationals: France U16, U17, U18, U19, U20, U21, Full caps.
2009–10 Lyon 1 0
2010–11 Lyon 9 1
2011–12 Lyon 29 5
2012–13 Lyon 31 3
2013–14 Lyon 36 15
2014–15 Lyon 33 27
2015–16 Lyon 34 21
2016–17 Lyon 30 28 **203 100**
2017–18 Arsenal 32 14
2018–19 Arsenal 35 13
2019–20 Arsenal 30 10
2020–21 Arsenal 31 13
2021–22 Arsenal 30 4 **158 54**

LENO, Bernd (G) 334 0
H: 6 3 W: 12 06 b.Bietigheim-Bissingen 4-3-92
Internationals: Germany, U17, U18, U19, U21, Full caps.
From Stuttgart.
2011–12 Bayer Leverkusen 33 0
2012–13 Bayer Leverkusen 32 0
2013–14 Bayer Leverkusen 34 0
2014–15 Bayer Leverkusen 34 0
2015–16 Bayer Leverkusen 33 0
2016–17 Bayer Leverkusen 34 0
2017–18 Bayer Leverkusen 33 0 **233 0**

2018–19 Arsenal 32 0
2019–20 Arsenal 30 0
2020–21 Arsenal 35 0
2021–22 Arsenal 4 0 **101 0**

LEWIS, George (F) 0 0
H: 5 7 b.Kigali 16-6-00
From Fram Larvik.
2020–21 Arsenal 0 0
2021–22 Arsenal 0 0

LOPEZ SALGUERO, Joel (D) 0 0
b.Barcelona 31-3-02
Internationals: Spain U17.
From Barcelona.
2019–20 Arsenal 0 0
2020–21 Arsenal 0 0
2021–22 Arsenal 0 0

MAITLAND-NILES, Ainsley (F) 125 2
H: 5 10 W: 11 05 b.Goodmayes 29-8-97
Internationals: England U17, U18, U19, U20, U21, Full caps.
2014–15 Arsenal 1 0
2015–16 Arsenal 0 0
2015–16 *Ipswich T* 30 1 **30 1**
2016–17 Arsenal 1 0
2017–18 Arsenal 15 0
2018–19 Arsenal 16 1
2019–20 Arsenal 20 0
2020–21 Arsenal 11 0
2020–21 *WBA* 15 0 **15 0**
2021–22 Arsenal 8 0 **72 1**
2021–22 *Roma* 8 0 **8 0**

MARTINELLI, Gabriel (F) 57 11
H: 5 11 W: 11 11 b.Guarulhos 18-6-01
Internationals: Brazil U23, Full caps.
From Ituano.
2019–20 Arsenal 14 3
2020–21 Arsenal 14 2
2021–22 Arsenal 29 6 **57 11**

MAVROPANOS, Konstantinos (D) 86 7
H: 6 4 W: 12 08 b.Athens 11-12-97
Internationals: Greece U21, Full caps.
2016–17 PAS Giannina 2 0
2017–18 PAS Giannina 14 3 **16 3**
2017–18 Arsenal 3 0
2018–19 Arsenal 4 0
2019–20 Arsenal 0 0
2019–20 *Nurnberg* 11 0 **11 0**
2019–20 *Stuttgart* 0 0
2020–21 Arsenal 0 0
2020–21 *Stuttgart* 21 0
2021–22 Arsenal 0 0 **7 0**
2021–22 *Stuttgart* 31 4 **52 4**

McENEFF, Jordan John (F) 13 0
b.Londonderry 8-1-01
Internationals: Republic of Ireland U17.
2019–20 Arsenal 0 0
2020–21 Arsenal 0 0
2021–22 Arsenal 0 0
2022 *Shelbourne* 13 0 **13 0**

MOLLER, Nikolaj (F) 21 2
H: 6 3 W: 11 05 b.Helsingborg 20-7-02
Internationals: Sweden U18.
From Bologna, Malmo.
2020–21 Arsenal 0 0
2021–22 Arsenal 0 0
2021–22 *Viktoria Koln* 10 0 **10 0**
2021–22 *Den Bosch* 11 2 **11 2**

MONLOUIS, Zane (D) 0 0
b.Lewisham 16-10-03
Internationals: England U17.
2020–21 Arsenal 0 0
2021–22 Arsenal 0 0

NELSON, Reiss (F) 67 10
H: 5 9 W: 11 00 b.Lambeth 10-12-99
Internationals: England U16, U17, U18, U19, U20, U21.
From Lewisham Bor.
2017–18 Arsenal 3 0
2018–19 Arsenal 0 0
2018–19 *Hoffenheim* 23 7 **23 7**
2019–20 Arsenal 17 1
2020–21 Arsenal 2 0
2021–22 Arsenal 1 0 **23 1**
2021–22 *Feyenoord* 21 2 **21 2**

NKETIAH, Eddie (F) 76 13
H: 5 9 W: 11 00 b.Lewisham 30-5-99
Internationals: England U18, U19, U20, U21.
From Chelsea.
2017–18 Arsenal 3 0
2018–19 Arsenal 5 1
2019–20 Arsenal 13 2
2019–20 *Leeds U* 17 3 **17 3**
2020–21 Arsenal 17 2
2021–22 Arsenal 21 5 **59 10**

NORTON-CUFFY, Brooke (D) 17 1
b.Hammersmith 12-1-04
Internationals: England U16, U18, U19.
From Chelsea.
2020–21 Arsenal 0 0
2021–22 Arsenal 0 0
2021–22 *Lincoln C* 17 1 **17 1**

ODEGAARD, Martin (M) 181 28
H: 5 7 W: 9 06 b.Drammen 17-12-98
Internationals: Norway U16, U17, U21, Full caps.
2014 Stromsgodset 23 5 **23 5**
2014–15 Real Madrid 1 0
2015–16 Real Madrid 0 0
2016–17 Real Madrid 0 0
2016–17 *Heerenveen* 14 1
2017–18 Real Madrid 0 0
2017–18 *Heerenveen* 24 2 **38 3**
2018–19 Real Madrid 0 0
2018–19 Vitesse 31 8 **31 8**
2019–20 Real Madrid 0 0
2019–20 *Real Sociedad* 31 4 **31 4**
2020–21 Real Madrid 7 0
2020–21 *Arsenal* 14 1
2021–22 Real Madrid 0 0 **8 0**
2021–22 Arsenal 36 7 **50 8**

OKONKWO, Arthur (G) 0 0
H: 6 5 W: 13 05 b.Camden 9-9-01
Internationals: England U16, U17, U18.
2019–20 Arsenal 0 0
2020–21 Arsenal 0 0
2021–22 Arsenal 0 0

OLAYINKA, James (M) 21 2
b. 5-10-00
2019–20 Arsenal 0 0
2019–20 *Northampton T* 1 0 **1 0**
2020–21 Arsenal 0 0
2020–21 *Southend U* 20 2 **20 2**
2021–22 Arsenal 0 0

OSEI-TUTU, Jordi (D) 47 5
H: 5 9 W: 11 00 b.Slough 2-10-98
2017–18 Arsenal 0 0
2018–19 Arsenal 0 0
2019–20 Arsenal 0 0
2019–20 *Bochum* 21 5 **21 5**
2020–21 Arsenal 0 0
2020–21 *Cardiff C* 8 0
2021–22 Cardiff C 0 0 **8 0**
2021–22 *Nottingham F* 4 0 **4 0**
2021–22 Arsenal 0 0
2021–22 *Rotherham U* 14 0 **14 0**

OULAD M'HAND, Salah (M) 0 0
H: 5 10 b.Den Haag 20-8-03
Internationals: Netherlands U17.
From Feyenoord.
2020–21 Arsenal 0 0
2021–22 Arsenal 0 0

PABLO MARI, Villar (M) 210 13
H: 6 4 W: 13 10 b.Almussafes 31-8-93
2011–12 Real Mallorca 2 0
2012–13 Real Mallorca 0 0 **2 0**
2013–14 Gimnastic 29 2
2014–15 Gimnastic 37 3
2015–16 Gimnastic 25 1 **91 6**
2016–17 Manchester C 0 0
2016–17 *Girona* 8 0 **8 0**
2017–18 Manchester C 0 0
2017–18 NAC Breda 20 1 **20 1**
2018–19 Manchester C 0 0
2018–19 *Deportivo la Coruna* 38 2 **38 2**
2019 Flamengo 22 2 **22 2**
2019–20 *Arsenal* 2 0
2020–21 Arsenal 10 0
2021–22 Arsenal 2 0 **14 0**
2021–22 *Udinese* 15 2 **15 2**

PATINO, Charlie (M) 0 0
H: 6 0 b.Watford 17-10-03
Internationals: England U16, U17, U19.
2020–21 Arsenal 0 0
2021–22 Arsenal 0 0

PEPE, Nicolas (F) 223 61
H: 6 0 W: 10 10 b.Mantes la Jolie 29-5-95
Internationals: Ivory Coast Full caps.
From Poitiers.
2014–15 Angers 7 0
2015–16 Angers 0 0
2015–16 *Orleans* 29 7 **29 7**
2016–17 Angers 33 3 **40 3**
2017–18 Lille 36 13
2018–19 Lille 38 22 **74 35**
2019–20 Arsenal 31 5
2020–21 Arsenal 29 10
2021–22 Arsenal 20 1 **80 16**

RAMSDALE, Aaron (G) 150 0
H: 6 2 W: 12 02 b.Stoke-on-Trent 14-5-98
Internationals: England U18, U19, U20, U21, Full caps.
2015–16 Sheffield U 0 0
2016–17 Sheffield U 0 0
2016–17 Bournemouth 0 0
2017–18 Bournemouth 0 0
2017–18 *Chesterfield* 19 0 **19 0**
2018–19 Bournemouth 0 0
2018–19 *AFC Wimbledon* 20 0 **20 0**
2019–20 Bournemouth 37 0 **37 0**
2020–21 Sheffield U 38 0
2021–22 Sheffield U 2 0 **40 0**
2021–22 Arsenal 34 0 **34 0**

REKIK, Omar (D) 0 0
H: 6 1 W: 12 08 b.Den Haag 20-12-01
Internationals: Netherlands U18. Tunisia U21, Full caps.
From Hertha Berlin.
2020–21 Arsenal 0 0
2021–22 Arsenal 0 0

RUNARSSON, Runar (G) 118 0
b.Reykjavík 18-2-95
Internationals: Iceland U16, U17, U18, U19, U21, Full caps.
2013 Reykjavik 3 0 **3 0**
2013–14 Nordsjaelland 0 0
2014–15 Nordsjaelland 1 0
2015–16 Nordsjaelland 3 0
2016–17 Nordsjaelland 20 0
2017–18 Nordsjaelland 36 0 **60 0**
2018–19 Dijon 25 0
2019–20 Dijon 11 0
2020–21 Dijon 0 0 **36 0**
2020–21 Arsenal 1 0
2021–22 Arsenal 0 0 **1 0**
2021–22 *OH Leuven* 18 0 **18 0**

SAKA, Bukayo (M) 97 17
H: 5 10 W: 10 03 b.Ealing 5-9-01
Internationals: England U16, U17, U18, U19, U21, Full caps.
2018–19 Arsenal 1 0
2019–20 Arsenal 26 1
2020–21 Arsenal 32 5
2021–22 Arsenal 38 11 **97 17**

SALIBA, William Alain Andre Gabriel (D) 84 1
b.Bondy 24-3-01
Internationals: France U16, U17, U18, U19, U20, U21, Full caps.
2018–19 Saint Etienne 16 0
2019–20 Arsenal 0 0
2019–20 *Saint Etienne* 12 0 **28 0**
2020–21 Arsenal 0 0
2020–21 *Nice* 20 1 **20 1**
2021–22 Arsenal 0 0
2021–22 *Marseille* 36 0 **36 0**

SAMBI LOKONGA, Albert-Mboyo (M) 88 3
H: 5 11 W: 11 03 b.Verviers 22-10-99
Internationals: Belgium U17, U19, U21, Full caps.
2017–18 Anderlecht 7 0
2018–19 Anderlecht 6 0
2019–20 Anderlecht 23 0
2020–21 Anderlecht 33 3
2021–22 Anderlecht 0 0 **69 3**
2021–22 Arsenal 19 0 **19 0**

SMITH, Matthew (M) 75 2
H: 5 9 b.Harlow 5-10-00
2019–20 Arsenal 0 0
2020–21 Swindon T 24 2 **24 2**
2020–21 Arsenal 0 0
2020–21 *Charlton Ath* 8 0 **8 0**
2021–22 Arsenal 0 0
2021–22 *Doncaster R* 43 0 **43 0**

SMITH, Tom (G) 0 0
b. 30-1-02
Internationals: England U16.
2019–20 Arsenal 0 0
2020–21 Arsenal 0 0
2021–22 Arsenal 0 0

SMITH ROWE, Emile (M) 77 14
H: 6 0 W: 11 07 b.Croydon 28-7-00
Internationals: England U16, U17, U18, U19, U20, U21, Full caps.
2017–18 Arsenal 0 0
2018–19 Arsenal 0 0
2018–19 *RB Leipzig* 3 0 **3 0**
2019–20 Arsenal 2 0
2019–20 *Huddersfield T* 19 2 **19 2**
2020–21 Arsenal 20 2
2021–22 Arsenal 33 10 **55 12**

SWANSON, Zak (D) 0 0
b. 28-9-00
2019–20 Arsenal 0 0
2020–21 Arsenal 0 0
2021–22 Arsenal 0 0

TAVARES, Nuno (D) 47 2
H: 6 0 W: 11 11 b.Lisbon 26-1-00
Internationals: Portugal U18, U19, U21.
2018–19 Benfica 0 0
2019–20 Benfica 11 1
2020–21 Benfica 14 0
2021–22 Benfica 0 0 **25 1**
2021–22 Arsenal 22 1 **22 1**

THOMAS, Partey (M) 245 23
H: 6 1 W: 11 07 b.Odumase Krobo 13-6-93
Internationals: Ghana Full caps.
2011–12 Atletico Madrid 0 0
2012–13 Atletico Madrid 0 0
2013–14 Atletico Madrid 0 0

2013–14 *Mallorca* 37 5 **37 5**
2014–15 Atletico Madrid 0 0
2014–15 *Almeria* 31 4 **31 4**
2015–16 Atletico Madrid 13 2
2016–17 Atletico Madrid 16 1
2017–18 Atletico Madrid 33 3
2018–19 Atletico Madrid 32 3
2019–20 Atletico Madrid 35 3
2020–21 Atletico Madrid 0 0 **129 12**
2020–21 Arsenal 24 0
2021–22 Arsenal 24 2 **48 2**

TIERNEY, Kieran (D) 166 8
H: 5 10 W: 11 00 b.Douglas 5-6-97
Internationals: Scotland U18, U19, Full caps.
2014–15 Celtic 2 0
2015–16 Celtic 23 1
2016–17 Celtic 24 1
2017–18 Celtic 32 3
2018–19 Celtic 21 0 **102 5**
2019–20 Arsenal 15 1
2020–21 Arsenal 27 1
2021–22 Arsenal 22 1 **64 3**

TOMIYASU, Takehiro (D) 165 5
H: 6 2 W: 11 00 b.Fukuoka 5-11-98
Internationals: Japan U16, U20, U23, Full caps.
2015 Avispa Fukuoka 0 0
2016 Avispa Fukuoka 10 0
2017 Avispa Fukuoka 35 1 **45 1**
2017–18 Sint-Truiden 1 0
2018–19 Sint-Truiden 37 1 **38 1**
2019–20 Bologna 29 1
2020–21 Bologna 31 2
2021–22 Bologna 1 0 **61 3**
2021–22 Arsenal 21 0 **21 0**

TORREIRA, Lucas (M) 218 17
H: 5 5 W: 9 06 b.Fray Bentos 11-2-96
Internationals: Uruguay Full caps.
2014–15 Pescara 5 0
2015–16 Sampdoria 0 0
2015–16 *Pescara* 29 4 **34 4**
2016–17 Sampdoria 35 0
2017–18 Sampdoria 36 4 **71 4**
2018–19 Arsenal 34 2
2019–20 Arsenal 29 1
2020–21 Arsenal 0 0
2020–21 *Atletico Madrid* 19 1 **19 1**
2021–22 Arsenal 0 0 **63 3**
2021–22 *Fiorentina* 31 5 **31 5**

WHITE, Ben (D) 171 3
H: 6 0 W: 12 04 b.Poole 8-11-97
Internationals: England Full caps.
2016–17 Brighton & HA 0 0
2017–18 Brighton & HA 0 0
2017–18 *Newport Co* 42 1 **42 1**
2018–19 Brighton & HA 0 0
2018–19 *Peterborough U* 15 1 **15 1**
2019–20 Brighton & HA 0 0
2019–20 *Leeds U* 46 1 **46 1**
2020–21 Brighton & HA 36 0 **36 0**
2021–22 Arsenal 32 0 **32 0**

XHAKA, Granit (M) 338 17
H: 6 0 W: 11 00 b.Gnjilane 27-9-92
Internationals: Switzerland U17, U18, U19, U21, Full caps.
2010–11 Basel 19 1
2011–12 Basel 23 0 **42 1**
2012–13 Borussia M'gladbach 22 1
2013–14 Borussia M'gladbach 28 0
2014–15 Borussia M'gladbach 30 2
2015–16 Borussia M'gladbach 28 3 **108 6**
2016–17 Arsenal 32 2
2017–18 Arsenal 38 1
2018–19 Arsenal 29 4
2019–20 Arsenal 31 1
2020–21 Arsenal 31 1
2021–22 Arsenal 27 1 **188 10**

Players retained or with offer of contract
Awe, Zach; Biereth, Mika; Butler-Oyedeji, Nathan; Da Cruz Sousa, Lino; Davies, Henry Timi; Edwards, Khayon; Ejeheri, Ovie; Flores, Marcelo; Henry-Francis, Jack; Hutchinson, Omari; Ibrahim, Bradley; Ogungbo, Mazeed; Taylor-Hart, Kido; Trusty, Auston; Walters, Reuell.

Scholars
Cozier-Duberry, Amario Oswald Gerardo; Foran, Taylor; Gomes, Bandeira Mauro; Gower, Jimi Mark; Green, Kaleel Shai; Jeffcott, Henry; Kovacevic, Alexandar; Lannin-Sweet, James; Oulad M'Hand, Ismail; Quamina, Tinochika Chukwu; Quesada Thorn, Kristopher Elian; Roberts, Mathaeus Andrew; Robinson, Joshua Noah Lynnford; Sagoe Jr, Charles Kwame; Vigar, Billy Joseph.

ASTON VILLA (4)

ABLDEEN-GOODRIDGE, Tristan (F) 0 0
H: 5 5 b. 28-11-02
From AFC Wimbledon.
2020–21 Aston Villa 0 0
2021–22 Aston Villa 0 0

APPIAH, Paul (D) 0 0
H: 6 0 W: 11 00 b.Enfield 13-10-02
From Chelsea.
2020–21 Aston Villa 0 0
2021–22 Aston Villa 0 0

ARCHER, Cameron (F) 23 7
H: 6 1 W: 11 03 b.Walsall 21-7-01
Internationals: England U20, U21.
2019–20 Aston Villa 0 0
2020–21 Aston Villa 0 0
2021–22 Aston Villa 3 0 **3 0**
2021–22 *Preston NE* 20 7 **20 7**

AZAZ, Finn (M) 79 8
H: 6 1 W: 11 00 b.Westminster 7-9-00
2020–21 WBA 0 0
2020–21 *Cheltenham T* 37 1 **37 1**
2021–22 Aston Villa 0 0
2021–22 *Newport Co* 42 7 **42 7**

BAILEY, Leon (F) 193 37
H: 5 11 W: 11 00 b.Kingston 9-8-97
Internationals: Jamaica U23, Full caps.
From Trencin.
2015–16 Genk 37 6
2016–17 Genk 19 2 **56 8**
2016–17 Bayer Leverkusen 8 0
2017–18 Bayer Leverkusen 30 9
2018–19 Bayer Leverkusen 29 5
2019–20 Bayer Leverkusen 22 5
2020–21 Bayer Leverkusen 30 9
2021–22 Bayer Leverkusen 0 0 **119 28**
2021–22 Aston Villa 18 1 **18 1**

BARRY, Louie (F) 16 6
H: 5 7 W: 10 03 b.Aston 21-6-03
Internationals: England U16, U17, U18.
From WBA, Barcelona.
2020–21 Aston Villa 0 0
2021–22 Aston Villa 0 0
2021–22 *Ipswich T* 2 0 **2 0**
2021–22 *Swindon T* 14 6 **14 6**

BOGARDE, Lamar (M) 0 0
H: 6 0 W: 11 14 b.Rotterdam 5-1-04
Internationals: Netherlands U16, U18.
From Feyenoord.
2020–21 Aston Villa 0 0
2021–22 Aston Villa 0 0

BRIDGE, Mungo (D) 2 0
2020–21 Aston Villa 0 0
2021–22 Aston Villa 0 0
2021–22 *Annecy* 2 0 **2 0**

BURCHALL, Ajani (M) 1 0
b. 5-11-04
2020–21 Bournemouth 1 0 **1 0**
2021–22 Aston Villa 0 0

CAMPTON-STURRIDGE, DJ (F) 0 0
H: 5 9 b. 17-10-02
2020–21 Aston Villa 0 0
2021–22 Aston Villa 0 0

CASH, Matty (M) 207 18
H: 6 2 W: 10 01 b.Slough 7-8-97
Internationals: Poland Full caps.
2015–16 Nottingham F 0 0
2015–16 *Dagenham & R* 12 3 **12 3**
2016–17 Nottingham F 28 0
2017–18 Nottingham F 23 2
2018–19 Nottingham F 36 6
2019–20 Nottingham F 42 3
2020–21 Nottingham F 0 0 **129 11**
2020–21 Aston Villa 28 0
2021–22 Aston Villa 38 4 **66 4**

CHAMBERS, Calum (D) 162 7
H: 6 0 W: 10 05 b.Petersfield 20-1-95
Internationals: England U17, U19, U21, Full caps.
2011–12 Southampton 0 0
2012–13 Southampton 0 0
2013–14 Southampton 22 0 **22 0**
2014–15 Arsenal 23 1
2015–16 Arsenal 12 0
2016–17 Arsenal 1 1
2016–17 *Middlesbrough* 24 1 **24 1**
2017–18 Arsenal 12 0
2018–19 Arsenal 0 0
2018–19 *Fulham* 31 2 **31 2**
2019–20 Arsenal 14 1
2020–21 Arsenal 10 0
2021–22 Arsenal 2 0 **74 3**
2021–22 Aston Villa 11 1 **11 1**

CHRISENE, Benjamin (M) 1 0
b. 12-1-04
Internationals: England U16, U17.
2019–20 Exeter C 1 0 **1 0**
2020–21 Aston Villa 0 0
2021–22 Aston Villa 0 0

CHUKWUEMEKA, Caleb (F) 30 1
H: 6 0 W: 11 11 b.Eisenstadt 25-1-02
2019–20 Northampton T 0 0
2020–21 Northampton T 22 1 **22 1**
2021–22 Aston Villa 0 0
2021–22 *Livingston* 8 0 **8 0**

CHUKWUEMEKA, Carney (M) 14 0
H: 6 0 b.Eisenstadt 20-10-03
Internationals: England U17, U18, U19.
2020–21 Aston Villa 2 0
2021–22 Aston Villa 12 0 **14 0**

COUTINHO, Phillippe (M) 302 72
H: 5 7 W: 10 10 b.Rio de Janeiro 12-6-92
Internationals: Brazil U17, U20, Full caps.
2009–10 Vasco da Gama 7 1 **7 1**
2010–11 Inter Milan 12 1
2011–12 Inter Milan 5 1
2011–12 *Espanyol* 16 5 **16 5**
2012–13 Inter Milan 10 1 **27 3**
2012–13 Liverpool 13 3
2013–14 Liverpool 33 5
2014–15 Liverpool 35 5
2015–16 Liverpool 26 8
2016–17 Liverpool 31 13
2017–18 Liverpool 14 7 **152 41**
2018–19 Barcelona 34 5
2019–20 Barcelona 0 0
2019–20 *Bayern Munich* 23 8 **23 8**
2020–21 Barcelona 12 2
2021–22 Barcelona 12 2 **58 9**
2021–22 *Aston Villa* 19 5 **19 5**

DAVIS, Keinan (M) 88 8
H: 5 6 W: 10 10 b.Stevenage 13-2-98
Internationals: England U20.
From Stevenage, Biggleswade T.
2015–16 Aston Villa 0 0
2016–17 Aston Villa 6 0
2017–18 Aston Villa 28 2
2018–19 Aston Villa 5 0
2019–20 Aston Villa 18 0
2020–21 Aston Villa 15 1
2021–22 Aston Villa 1 0 **73 3**
2021–22 *Nottingham F* 15 5 **15 5**

DIGNE, Lucas (D) 270 9
H: 5 10 W: 11 11 b.Meaux 20-7-93
Internationals: France U16, U17, U18, U19, U21, Full caps.
2011–12 Lille 16 0
2012–13 Lille 33 2 **49 2**
2013–14 Paris Saint-Germain 15 0
2014–15 Paris Saint-Germain 15 0
2014–15 Paris Saint-Germain 0 0
2015–16 Paris Saint-Germain 0 0 **30 0**
2015–16 *Roma* 33 3 **33 3**
2016–17 Barcelona 17 0
2017–18 Barcelona 12 0 **29 0**
2018–19 Everton 35 4
2019–20 Everton 35 0
2020–21 Everton 30 0
2021–22 Everton 13 0 **113 4**
2021–22 Aston Villa 16 0 **16 0**

DOUGLAS LUIZ, de Paulo (M) 166 8
H: 5 10 W: 10 03 b.Rio 9-5-98
Internationals: Brazil U20, U23, Full caps.
2016 Vasco da Gama 14 2
2017 Vasco da Gama 11 1 **25 3**
2017–18 Manchester C 0 0
2017–18 *Girona* 15 0
2018–19 Manchester C 0 0
2018–19 *Girona* 23 0 **38 0**
2019–20 Aston Villa 36 3
2020–21 Aston Villa 33 0
2021–22 Aston Villa 34 2 **103 5**

EL GHAZI, Anwar (F) 213 45
H: 6 2 W: 12 00 b.Barendrecht 3-5-95
Internationals: Netherlands U17, U18, U21, Full caps.
2014–15 Ajax 31 9
2015–16 Ajax 27 11
2016–17 Ajax 12 0 **70 20**
2016–17 Lille 12 1
2017–18 Lille 27 4 **39 5**
2018–19 *Aston Villa* 31 5
2019–20 Aston Villa 34 4
2020–21 Aston Villa 28 10
2021–22 Aston Villa 9 1 **102 20**
2021–22 *Everton* 2 0 **2 0**

EMI, Buendia (M) 223 37
H: 5 7 W: 11 05 b.Mar del Plata 25-12-96
Internationals: Spain U19. Argentina U20, Full caps.
2013–14 Getafe 0 0
2014–15 Getafe 6 0
2015–16 Getafe 17 1

2016–17	Getafe	12	2		
2017–18	Getafe	0	0	**35**	**3**
2017–18	*Cultural Leonesa*	40	6	**40**	**6**
2018–19	Norwich C	38	8		
2019–20	Norwich C	36	1		
2020–21	Norwich C	39	15		
2021–22	Norwich C	0	0	**113**	**24**
2021–22	Aston Villa	35	4	**35**	**4**

FEENEY, Josh (D) 0 0
H: 6 4 b. 6-5-05
Internationals: England U16, U17.

2020–21	Fleetwood T	0	0		
2021–22	Aston Villa	0	0		

GUILBERT, Frederic (D) 228 3
H: 5 10 W: 11 00 b.Valognes 24-12-94
Internationals: France U21.

2011–12	Caen	0	0		
2012–13	Caen	0	0		
2013–14	Cherbourg	28	0	**28**	**0**
2014–15	Bordeaux	3	0		
2015–16	Bordeaux	30	0		
2016–17	Bordeaux	3	0	**36**	**0**
2016–17	*Caen*	23	0		
2017–18	Caen	36	1		
2018–19	Caen	34	1	**93**	**2**
2019–20	Aston Villa	25	0		
2020–21	Aston Villa	0	0		
2020–21	*Strasbourg*	13	1		
2021–22	Aston Villa	0	0	**25**	**0**
2021–22	*Strasbourg*	33	0	**46**	**1**

HAUSE, Kortney (D) 147 9
H: 6 2 W: 13 03 b.Goodmayes 16-7-95
Internationals: England U20, U21.

2012–13	Wycombe W	9	1		
2013–14	Wycombe W	14	1	**23**	**2**
2013–14	Wolverhampton W	0	0		
2014–15	Wolverhampton W	17	0		
2014–15	*Gillingham*	14	1	**14**	**1**
2015–16	Wolverhampton W	25	0		
2016–17	Wolverhampton W	24	2		
2017–18	Wolverhampton W	1	0		
2018–19	Wolverhampton W	0	0	**67**	**2**
2018–19	*Aston Villa*	11	1		
2019–20	Aston Villa	18	1		
2020–21	Aston Villa	7	1		
2021–22	Aston Villa	7	1	**43**	**4**

HAYDEN, Kaine (D) 33 1
H: 5 9 W: 9 11 b.Birmingham 23-10-02
Internationals: England U20.

2019–20	Aston Villa	0	0		
2020–21	Aston Villa	0	0		
2021–22	Aston Villa	0	0		
2021–22	*Swindon T*	18	0	**18**	**0**
2021–22	*Milton Keynes D*	15	1	**15**	**1**

HOURIHANE, Conor (M) 417 73
H: 5 11 W: 9 11 b.Cork 2-2-91
Internationals: Republic of Ireland U19, U21, Full caps.

2008–09	Sunderland	0	0		
2009–10	Sunderland	0	0		
2010–11	Ipswich T	0	0		
2011–12	Plymouth Arg	38	2		
2012–13	Plymouth Arg	42	5		
2013–14	Plymouth Arg	45	8	**125**	**15**
2014–15	Barnsley	46	13		
2015–16	Barnsley	41	10		
2016–17	Barnsley	25	6	**112**	**29**
2016–17	Aston Villa	17	1		
2017–18	Aston Villa	41	11		
2018–19	Aston Villa	43	7		
2019–20	Aston Villa	27	3		
2020–21	Aston Villa	4	1		
2020–21	*Swansea C*	19	5		
2021–22	Swansea C	0	0	**19**	**5**
2021–22	Aston Villa	0	0	**132**	**23**
2021–22	*Sheffield U*	29	1	**29**	**1**

INGS, Danny (F) 284 96
H: 5 10 W: 11 07 b.Winchester 16-3-92
Internationals: England U21, Full caps.

2009–10	Bournemouth	0	0		
2010–11	Bournemouth	26	7		
2011–12	Bournemouth	1	0	**27**	**7**
2011–12	Burnley	15	3		
2012–13	Burnley	32	3		
2013–14	Burnley	40	21		
2014–15	Burnley	35	11	**122**	**38**
2015–16	Liverpool	6	2		
2016–17	Liverpool	0	0		
2017–18	Liverpool	8	1		
2018–19	Liverpool	0	0	**14**	**3**
2018–19	*Southampton*	24	7		
2019–20	Southampton	38	22		
2020–21	Southampton	29	12		
2021–22	Southampton	0	0	**91**	**41**
2021–22	Aston Villa	30	7	**30**	**7**

IROEGBUNAM, Tim (M) 3 0
b.West Bromwich 30-6-03
Internationals: England U19.

2020–21	WBA	0	0		
2021–22	Aston Villa	3	0	**3**	**0**

KALINIC, Lovre (G) 269 0
H: 6 7 W: 12 06 b.Split 3-4-90
Internationals: Croatia U16, U17, U21, Full caps.

2008–09	Hadjuk Split	0	0		
2008–09	*Junak Sinj*	4	0	**4**	**0**
2009–10	Hadjuk Split	0	0		
2009–10	*Novalja*	23	0	**23**	**0**
2010–11	Hadjuk Split	1	0		
2011–12	Hadjuk Split	1	0		
2011–12	*Karlovac*	11	0	**11**	**0**
2012–13	Hadjuk Split	4	0		
2013–14	Hadjuk Split	24	0		
2014–15	Hadjuk Split	28	0		
2015–16	Hadjuk Split	31	0		
2016–17	Hadjuk Split	13	0	**102**	**0**
2016–17	Gent	19	0		
2017–18	Gent	35	0		
2018–19	Gent	14	0	**68**	**0**
2018–19	Aston Villa	7	0		
2019–20	Aston Villa	0	0		
2019–20	*Toulouse*	4	0	**4**	**0**
2020–21	Aston Villa	0	0		
2020–21	*Hajduk Split*	21	0		
2021–22	Aston Villa	0	0	**7**	**0**
2021–22	*Hajduk Split*	29	0	**50**	**0**

KONSA, Ezri (D) 203 6
H: 6 0 W: 12 02 b.Newham 23-10-97
Internationals: England U20, U21.

2015–16	Charlton Ath	0	0		
2016–17	Charlton Ath	32	0		
2017–18	Charlton Ath	39	0	**71**	**0**
2018–19	Brentford	42	1	**42**	**1**
2019–20	Aston Villa	25	1		
2020–21	Aston Villa	36	2		
2021–22	Aston Villa	29	2	**90**	**5**

LINDLEY, Hayden (M) 0 0
H: 6 0 W: 11 00 b.Huddersfield 2-9-02
From Manchester C.

2020–21	Aston Villa	0	0		
2021–22	Aston Villa	0	0		

MARTINEZ, Damian (G) 145 0
H: 6 4 W: 13 05 b.Mar del Plata 2-9-92
Internationals: Argentina U17, U20, Full caps.
From Independiente.

2010–11	Arsenal	0	0		
2011–12	Arsenal	0	0		
2011–12	*Oxford U*	1	0	**1**	**0**
2012–13	Arsenal	0	0		
2013–14	Arsenal	0	0		
2013–14	*Sheffield W*	11	0	**11**	**0**
2014–15	Arsenal	4	0		
2014–15	*Rotherham U*	8	0	**8**	**0**
2015–16	Arsenal	0	0		
2015–16	*Wolverhampton W*	13	0	**13**	**0**
2016–17	Arsenal	2	0		
2017–18	Arsenal	0	0		
2017–18	*Getafe*	5	0	**5**	**0**
2018–19	Arsenal	0	0		
2018–19	*Reading*	18	0		
2019–20	Arsenal	9	0		
2019–20	*Reading*	0	0	**18**	**0**
2020–21	Arsenal	0	0	**15**	**0**
2020–21	Aston Villa	38	0		
2021–22	Aston Villa	36	0	**74**	**0**

McGINN, John (M) 328 31
H: 5 8 W: 10 08 b.Glasgow 18-10-94
Internationals: Scotland U19, U21, Full caps.

2012–13	St Mirren	22	1		
2013–14	St Mirren	35	3		
2014–15	St Mirren	30	0	**87**	**4**
2015–16	Hibernian	36	3		
2016–17	Hibernian	29	4		
2017–18	Hibernian	35	5		
2018–19	Hibernian	1	0	**101**	**12**
2018–19	Aston Villa	40	6		
2019–20	Aston Villa	28	3		
2020–21	Aston Villa	37	3		
2021–22	Aston Villa	35	3	**140**	**15**

MINGS, Tyrone (D) 194 8
H: 6 3 W: 12 02 b.Bath 13-3-93
Internationals: England Full caps.
From Southampton.

2012–13	Ipswich T	1	0		
2013–14	Ipswich T	16	0		
2014–15	Ipswich T	40	1	**57**	**1**
2015–16	Bournemouth	1	0		
2016–17	Bournemouth	7	0		
2017–18	Bournemouth	4	0		
2018–19	Bournemouth	5	0	**17**	**0**
2018–19	*Aston Villa*	15	2		
2019–20	Aston Villa	33	2		
2020–21	Aston Villa	36	2		
2021–22	Aston Villa	36	1	**120**	**7**

NAKAMBA, Marvelous (M) 180 2
H: 5 10 W: 11 03 b.Hwange 19-1-94
Internationals: Zimbabwe U20, Full caps.

2012–13	Nancy	0	0		
2013–14	Nancy	2	0	**2**	**0**
2014–15	Vitesse	6	0		
2015–16	Vitesse	30	1		
2016–17	Vitesse	31	1	**67**	**2**
2017–18	Club Brugge	35	0		
2018–19	Club Brugge	18	0	**53**	**0**
2019–20	Aston Villa	29	0		
2020–21	Aston Villa	13	0		
2021–22	Aston Villa	16	0	**58**	**0**

OLSEN, Robin (G) 243 0
H: 6 5 W: 14 00 b.Malmo 8-1-90
Internationals: Sweden Full caps.

2007	Limhamn Bunkeflo	0	0		
2008	Limhamn Bunkeflo	0	0		
2009	Limhamn Bunkeflo	8	0	**8**	**0**
2010	Bunkeflo	18	0	**18**	**0**
2011	Klagshamn	19	0	**19**	**0**
2012	Malmo	1	0		
2013	Malmo	10	0		
2014	Malmo	29	0		
2015	Malmo	13	0	**53**	**0**
2015–16	PAOK	11	0	**11**	**0**
2015–16	*Copenhagen*	14	0		
2016–17	Copenhagen	33	0		
2017–18	Copenhagen	24	0	**71**	**0**
2018–19	Roma	27	0		
2019–20	Roma	0	0		
2019–20	*Cagliari*	17	0	**17**	**0**
2020–21	Roma	0	0		
2020–21	*Everton*	7	0	**7**	**0**
2021–22	Roma	0	0	**27**	**0**
2021–22	*Sheffield U*	11	0	**11**	**0**
2021–22	*Aston Villa*	1	0	**1**	**0**

ONODI, Akos (G) 0 0
Internationals: Hungary U16, U19.
From Gyor.

2020–21	Aston Villa	0	0		
2021–22	Aston Villa	0	0		

PHILOGENE-BIDACE, Jayden (M) 13 1
H: 5 9 W: 10 01 b.Hammersmith 18-5-02
Internationals: England U19, U20.

2020–21	Aston Villa	1	0		
2021–22	Aston Villa	1	0	**2**	**0**
2021–22	*Stoke C*	11	1	**11**	**1**

RAIKHY, Arjan (M) 0 0

2020–21	Aston Villa	0	0		
2021–22	Aston Villa	0	0		

RAMSEY, Aaron (M) 15 1
H: 5 10 b.Birmingham 21-1-03
Internationals: England U16, U17, U18, U19.

2020–21	Aston Villa	0	0		
2021–22	Aston Villa	0	0		
2021–22	*Cheltenham T*	15	1	**15**	**1**

RAMSEY, Jacob (M) 64 9
H: 5 11 W: 11 05 b.Birmingham 28-5-01
Internationals: England U18, U19, U20, U21.

2018–19	Aston Villa	1	0		
2019–20	Aston Villa	0	0		
2019–20	*Doncaster R*	7	3	**7**	**3**
2020–21	Aston Villa	22	0		
2021–22	Aston Villa	34	6	**57**	**6**

REVAN, Dominic (D) 3 0
H: 6 4 W: 12 11 b.West Bromwich 19-9-00

2018–19	Aston Villa	0	0		
2019–20	Aston Villa	0	0		
2020–21	Aston Villa	0	0		
2021–22	Aston Villa	0	0		
2021–22	*Northampton T*	3	0	**3**	**0**

SANSON, Morgan (M) 254 36
H: 6 0 W: 11 00 b.Saint-Doulchard 18-8-94
Internationals: France U19, U21.

2012–13	Le Mans	27	3	**27**	**3**
2013–14	Montpellier	32	1		
2014–15	Montpellier	32	6		
2015–16	Montpellier	14	3		
2016–17	Montpellier	20	3	**98**	**13**
2016–17	Marseille	17	1		
2017–18	Marseille	33	9		
2018–19	Marseille	33	5		
2019–20	Marseille	27	5		
2020–21	Marseille	0	0	**110**	**20**
2020–21	Aston Villa	9	0		
2021–22	Aston Villa	10	0	**19**	**0**

SHAKPOKE, Ruben (F) 0 0
b. 23-4-04
From Norwich C.

2020–21	Aston Villa	0	0		
2021–22	Aston Villa	0	0		

SINISALO, Viljami (G) 22 0
H: 6 3 W: 12 04 b.Espoo 11-10-01
Internationals: Finland U17, U19, U21.
From Espoo.

2020–21	Aston Villa	0	0		
2020–21	*Ayr U*	22	0	**22**	**0**
2021–22	Aston Villa	0	0		

SMITH, Kerr (D) 10 0
b.Montrose 12-12-04
Internationals: Scotland U19.

2020–21	Dundee U	5	0		
2021–22	Dundee U	5	0	**10**	**0**
2021–22	Aston Villa	0	0		

STEER, Jed (G) **116** **0**
H: 6 2 W: 12 08 b.Norwich 23-9-92
Internationals: England U16, U17, U19.

2009–10	Norwich C	0	0		
2010–11	Norwich C	0	0		
2011–12	Norwich C	0	0		
2011–12	*Yeovil T*	12	0		
2012–13	Cambridge U	0	0		
2012–13	Norwich C	0	0		
2013–14	Aston Villa	0	0		
2014–15	Aston Villa	1	0		
2014–15	*Doncaster R*	13	0	**13**	**0**
2014–15	*Yeovil T*	12	0	**24**	**0**
2015–16	Aston Villa	0	0		
2015–16	*Huddersfield T*	38	0	**38**	**0**
2016–17	Aston Villa	0	0		
2017–18	Aston Villa	0	0		
2018–19	Aston Villa	16	0		
2018–19	*Charlton Ath*	19	0	**19**	**0**
2019–20	Aston Villa	1	0		
2020–21	Aston Villa	0	0		
2021–22	Aston Villa	1	0	**19**	**0**
2021–22	*Luton T*	3	0	**3**	**0**

SWINKELS, Sil (D) **0** **0**
H: 6 3 W: 12 04 b.Sint-Oedenrode 6-1-04
Internationals: Netherlands U18.
From Vitesse.

2020–21	Aston Villa	0	0
2021–22	Aston Villa	0	0

TARGETT, Matt (D) **160** **4**
H: 6 0 W: 11 00 b.Eastleigh 18-9-95
Internationals: Scotland U19, England U19, U20, U21.

2013–14	Southampton	0	0		
2014–15	Southampton	6	0		
2015–16	Southampton	14	0		
2016–17	Southampton	5	0		
2017–18	Southampton	2	0		
2017–18	*Fulham*	18	1	**18**	**1**
2018–19	Southampton	16	1	**43**	**1**
2019–20	Aston Villa	28	1		
2020–21	Aston Villa	38	0		
2021–22	Aston Villa	17	1	**83**	**2**
2021–22	*Newcastle U*	16	0	**16**	**0**

TRAORE, Bertrand (M) **208** **55**
H: 5 11 W: 11 05 b.Bob-Dioulasso 6-9-95
Internationals: Burkina Faso U17, Full caps
From Auxerre.

2013–14	Chelsea	0	0		
2013–14	*Vitesse*	13	3		
2014–15	Chelsea	0	0		
2014–15	*Vitesse*	29	13	**42**	**16**
2015–16	Chelsea	10	2		
2016–17	Chelsea	0	0	**10**	**2**
2016–17	*Ajax*	24	9	**24**	**9**
2017–18	Lyon	31	13		
2018–19	Lyon	33	7		
2019–20	Lyon	23	1	**87**	**21**
2020–21	Aston Villa	36	7		
2021–22	Aston Villa	9	0	**45**	**7**

TREZEGUET, Mahmoud (M) **220** **47**
H: 5 10 W: 10 03 b.Kafr el-Sheikh 1-10-94
Internationals: Egypt U20, U23, Full caps.

2012–13	Al Ahly	7	0		
2013–14	Al Ahly	20	2		
2014–15	Al Ahly	31	5		
2015–16	Al Ahly	0	0	**58**	**7**
2015–16	*Anderlecht*	7	0		
2016–17	Anderlecht	1	0		
2016–17	*Royal Excel Mouscron*	20	4	**20**	**4**
2017–18	Anderlecht	0	0	**8**	**0**
2017–18	*Kasimpasa*	31	13		
2018–19	Kasimpasa	34	9	**65**	**22**
2019–20	Aston Villa	34	6		
2020–21	Aston Villa	21	2		
2021–22	Aston Villa	1	0	**56**	**8**
2021–22	*Istanbul Basaksehir*	13	6	**13**	**6**

VASSILEV, Indiana (M) **56** **5**
b.Georgia 16-2-01
Internationals: USA U17, U18, U20.

2019–20	Aston Villa	4	0		
2020–21	Aston Villa	0	0		
2020–21	*Burton Alb*	12	0	**12**	**0**
2020–21	*Cheltenham T*	12	0	**12**	**0**
2021–22	Aston Villa	0	0	**4**	**0**
2021–22	*Inter Miami*	28	5	**28**	**5**

WATKINS, Ollie (F) **272** **91**
H: 5 10 W: 11 00 b.Torbay 30-12-95
Internationals: England Full caps.

2013–14	Exeter C	1	0		
2014–15	Exeter C	2	0		
2015–16	Exeter C	20	8		
2016–17	Exeter C	45	13	**68**	**21**
2017–18	Brentford	45	10		
2018–19	Brentford	41	10		
2019–20	Brentford	46	25		
2020–21	Brentford	0	0	**132**	**45**
2020–21	Aston Villa	37	14		
2021–22	Aston Villa	35	11	**72**	**25**

WESLEY, Moraes (F) **168** **44**
H: 6 3 W: 14 09 b.Juiz de Fora 26-11-96
Internationals: Brazil Full caps.

2015–16	Trencin	18	6	**18**	**6**
2015–16	Club Brugge	6	2		
2016–17	Club Brugge	25	6		
2017–18	Club Brugge	38	11		
2018–19	Club Brugge	38	13		
2019–20	Aston Villa	21	5		
2020–21	Aston Villa	3	0		
2021–22	Aston Villa	1	0	**25**	**5**
2021–22	*Club Brugge*	3	0	**110**	**32**
2022	*Internacional*	15	1	**15**	**1**

WRIGHT, Tyreik (M) **44** **2**
H: 5 10 b.Cork 22-9-01
Internationals: Republic of Ireland U17, U18, U19, U21.

2020–21	Aston Villa	0	0		
2020–21	*Walsall*	16	0		
2021–22	*Walsall*	0	0	**16**	**0**
2021–22	Aston Villa	0	0		
2021–22	*Salford C*	16	1	**16**	**1**
2021–22	*Colchester U*	12	1	**12**	**1**

YOUNG, Ashley (M) **515** **69**
H: 5 9 W: 10 03 b.Stevenage 9-7-85
Internationals: England U21, Full caps.

2002–03	Watford	0	0		
2003–04	Watford	5	3		
2004–05	Watford	34	0		
2005–06	Watford	39	13		
2006–07	Watford	20	3	**98**	**19**
2006–07	Aston Villa	13	2		
2007–08	Aston Villa	37	9		
2008–09	Aston Villa	36	7		
2009–10	Aston Villa	37	5		
2010–11	Aston Villa	34	7		
2011–12	Manchester U	25	6		
2012–13	Manchester U	19	0		
2013–14	Manchester U	20	2		
2014–15	Manchester U	26	2		
2015–16	Manchester U	18	1		
2016–17	Manchester U	12	0		
2017–18	Manchester U	30	2		
2018–19	Manchester U	30	2		
2019–20	Manchester U	12	0	**192**	**15**
2019–20	Inter Milan	18	4		
2020–21	Inter Milan	26	1	**44**	**5**
2021–22	Aston Villa	24	0	**181**	**30**

Transferred to Inter Milan, January 2020.

YOUNG, Brad (F) **14** **0**
H: 5 9 b.Birmingham 4-8-02

2020–21	Aston Villa	0	0		
2021–22	Aston Villa	0	0		
2021–22	*Carlisle U*	14	0	**14**	**0**

ZYCH, Oliwier (G) **0** **0**
b. 28-6-04
Internationals: Poland U18.
From Lubin.

2020–21	Aston Villa	0	0
2021–22	Aston Villa	0	0

Players retained or with offer of contract
Afoka, Chisom; Frith, Declan; Marshall, Filip; O'Reilly, Aaron; O'Reilly, Tommi; Revan, Sebastian; Sohna, Myles.

Scholars
Alcock, Todd Rees; Barber, Jayden Christopher; Barnes, Mikell; Ealing, Frankie; Feeney, Joshua Philip; Hart, Taylor-Jay Phillip; Lane, Joshua Thomas; Lutz, Charlie Ethan; Moore, Kobei; Munroe, Finley Christopher Ryan; Pierre, Kyrie Jay Victor; Rhoades, Harvey Jack Owen; Rowe, Edward James; Softley, Luke Paul; Wright, James Thomas.

BARNSLEY (5)

ADEBOYEJO, Victor (F) **124** **9**
H: 5 10 W: 9 13 b.Ibadan 12-1-98
From Arsenal, AFC Wimbledon, Charlton Ath.

2014–15	Leyton Orient	1	0		
2015–16	Leyton Orient	1	0		
2016–17	Leyton Orient	13	1	**15**	**1**
2017–18	Barnsley	0	0		
2018–19	Barnsley	25	2		
2019–20	*Bristol R*	18	1	**18**	**1**
2019–20	*Cambridge U*	8	0	**8**	**0**
2020–21	Barnsley	32	2		
2021–22	Barnsley	26	3	**83**	**7**

AITCHISON, Jack (F) **117** **13**
H: 5 11 W: 11 00 b.Fauldhouse 5-3-00
Internationals: Scotland U16, U17, U19.

2015–16	Celtic	1	1		
2016–17	Celtic	2	0		
2017–18	Celtic	0	0		
2018–19	Celtic	0	0		
2018–19	*Dumbarton*	4	0	**4**	**0**
2018–19	*Alloa Ath*	10	1	**10**	**1**
2019–20	Celtic	0	0	**3**	**1**
2019–20	*Forest Green R*	28	5		
2020–21	Barnsley	0	0		
2020–21	*Stevenage*	26	1	**26**	**1**
2021–22	Barnsley	0	0		
2021–22	*Forest Green R*	46	5	**74**	**10**

ANDERSEN, Mads (D) **165** **8**
H: 6 5 W: 12 11 b.Albertslund 27-12-97
Internationals: Denmark U19.

2016–17	Brondy	0	0		
2016–17	*Koge*	25	2	**25**	**2**
2017–18	Horsens	8	1		
2018–19	Horsens	20	3	**28**	**4**
2019–20	Barnsley	38	0		
2020–21	Barnsley	46	1		
2021–22	Barnsley	28	1	**112**	**2**

BASSI, Amine (M) **126** **26**
H: 5 8 W: 11 04 b.Bezons 27-11-97
Internationals: Morocco U21.

2016–17	Nancy	1	0		
2017–18	Nancy	33	7		
2018–19	Nancy	31	6		
2019–20	Nancy	22	4		
2020–21	Nancy	19	7	**106**	**24**
2021–22	Metz	5	0	**5**	**0**
2021–22	*Barnsley*	15	2	**15**	**2**

BENSON, Josh (M) **42** **2**
H: 5 9 W: 11 03 b.Thurrock 5-12-99
From Arsenal.

2018–19	Burnley	0	0		
2019–20	Burnley	0	0		
2019–20	*Grimsby T*	11	2	**11**	**2**
2020–21	Burnley	6	0		
2021–22	Burnley	0	0	**6**	**0**
2021–22	Barnsley	25	0	**25**	**0**

BREMANG, David (F) **2** **0**
H: 5 11 W: 11 00 b.Hammersmith 21-3-00

2018–19	Coventry C	0	0		
2019–20	Coventry C	0	0		
2020–21	Coventry C	0	0		
2021–22	Barnsley	2	0	**2**	**0**

BRITTAIN, Callum (D) **183** **4**
H: 5 10 W: 10 10 b.Bedford 12-3-98
Internationals: England U20.

2015–16	Milton Keynes D	0	0		
2016	*Prottur Reykjavik*	6	0	**6**	**0**
2016–17	Milton Keynes D	6	0		
2017–18	Milton Keynes D	29	2		
2018–19	Milton Keynes D	31	1		
2019–20	Milton Keynes D	31	1		
2020–21	Milton Keynes D	4	0	**101**	**4**
2020–21	Barnsley	40	0		
2021–22	Barnsley	36	0	**76**	**0**

CHRISTIE-DAVIES, Isaac (M) **2** **0**
b.Brighton 18-9-97
Internationals: England U16, U17. Wales U21.
From Chelsea.

2018–19	Liverpool	0	0		
2019–20	Liverpool	0	0		
2019–20	*Cercle Brugge*	0	0		
2020–21	Barnsley	0	0		
2021–22	Barnsley	2	0	**2**	**0**

COLE, Devante (F) **209** **44**
H: 6 1 W: 11 07 b.Alderley Edge 10-5-95
Internationals: England U16, U17, U18, U19.

2013–14	Manchester C	0	0		
2014–15	Manchester C	0	0		
2014–15	*Barnsley*	19	5		
2014–15	*Milton Keynes D*	15	3	**15**	**3**
2015–16	Bradford C	19	5	**19**	**5**
2015–16	Fleetwood T	14	2		
2016–17	Fleetwood T	35	5		
2017–18	Fleetwood T	28	10	**77**	**17**
2017–18	Wigan Ath	6	0		
2018–19	Wigan Ath	0	0	**6**	**0**
2018–19	*Burton Alb*	13	2	**13**	**2**
2019–20	*Motherwell*	0	0		
2019–20	Doncaster R	9	0	**9**	**0**
2020–21	Motherwell	27	11	**27**	**11**
2021–22	Barnsley	24	1	**43**	**6**

COLLINS, Bradley (G) **151** **0**
H: 6 0 W: 10 12 b.Southampton 18-2-97

2017–18	Chelsea	0	0		
2017–18	*Forest Green R*	39	0	**39**	**0**
2018–19	Chelsea	0	0		
2018–19	*Burton Alb*	31	0	**31**	**0**
2019–20	Barnsley	19	0		
2020–21	Barnsley	22	0		
2021–22	Barnsley	40	0	**81**	**0**

FRIESER, Dominik (F) **259** **32**
H: 5 9 W: 12 00 b.Graz 9-9-93

2013–14	Hartberg	7	0		
2013–14	*Kalsdorf*	14	1	**14**	**1**
2014–15	Hartberg	30	1	**37**	**1**
2015–16	Kapfenberger	35	5		
2016–17	Kapfenberger	34	2	**69**	**7**
2017–18	Wolfsberger	22	4	**22**	**4**
2018–19	LASK Linz	31	6		
2019–20	LASK Linz	30	8	**61**	**14**
2020–21	LASK	0	0		

2020–21 Barnsley 42 3
2021–22 Barnsley 14 2 **56** **5**

HALME, Aapo (D) **104** **5**
H: 6 5 W: 12 04 b.Helsinki 22-5-98
Internationals: Finland U16, U17, U18, U19, U21.
2014 Honka 1 0 **1** **0**
2015 Klubi 04 15 1 **15** **1**
2015 HJK Helsinki 2 0
2016 HJK Helsinki 14 0
2017 HJK Helsinki 13 0 **29** **0**
2018–19 Leeds U 4 0 **4** **0**
2019–20 Barnsley 32 4
2020–21 Barnsley 18 0
2021–22 Barnsley 5 0 **55** **4**

HELIK, Michal (D) **214** **16**
H: 6 3 W: 12 08 b.Chorzow 9-9-95
Internationals: Poland Full caps.
2013–14 Ruch Chorzow 8 0
2014–15 Ruch Chorzow 18 1
2015–16 Ruch Chorzow 0 0
2016–17 Ruch Chorzow 20 0 **46** **1**
2017–18 Cracovia 32 8
2018–19 Cracovia 32 0
2019–20 Cracovia 23 1
2020–21 Cracovia 0 0 **87** **9**
2020–21 Barnsley 43 5
2021–22 Barnsley 38 1 **81** **6**

HELLIWELL, Jordan (D) **2** **0**
H: 5 7 b.Wakefield 23-9-01
2018–19 Barnsley 0 0
2019–20 Barnsley 0 0
2020–21 Barnsley 0 0
2021–22 Barnsley 2 0 **2** **0**

HONDERMARCK, William (M) **12** **0**
H: 6 1 W: 11 09 b.Orleans 21-11-00
From Drogheda U.
2020–21 Norwich C 0 0
2020–21 *Harrogate T* 3 0 **3** **0**
2021–22 Barnsley 9 0 **9** **0**

ISEKA, Aaron (F) **141** **19**
H: 5 11 W: 12 04 b.Brussels 15-11-97
Internationals: Belgium U21.
2014–15 Anderlecht 9 0
2015–16 Anderlecht 3 0
2016–17 Anderlecht 0 0
2016–17 *Marseille* 8 0 **8** **0**
2017–18 Anderlecht 0 0 **12** **0**
2017–18 *Zulte Waregem* 23 6 **23** **6**
2018–19 Toulouse 28 4
2019–20 Toulouse 22 2
2020–21 Toulouse 2 0 **52** **6**
2020–21 *Metz* 21 4 **21** **4**
2021–22 Barnsley 25 3 **25** **3**

KALINAUSKAS, Tomas (F) **2** **0**
H: 5 10 b.Lithuania 27-4-00
Internationals: Lithuania U19, U21.
From Windsor, Hayes & Yeading U, Farnborough.
2021–22 Barnsley 0 0
2021–22 *AFC Wimbledon* 2 0 **2** **0**

KANE, Herbie (M) **104** **6**
H: 5 9 W: 10 08 b.Bristol 23-11-98
Internationals: England U16, U17, U18.
From Bristol C.
2018–19 Liverpool 0 0
2018–19 *Doncaster R* 38 4 **38** **4**
2019–20 Liverpool 0 0
2019–20 *Hull C* 7 2 **7** **2**
2020–21 Barnsley 24 0
2021–22 Barnsley 0 0 **24** **0**
2021–22 *Oxford U* 35 0 **35** **0**

KITCHING, Liam (D) **77** **0**
H: 6 3 W: 12 08 b.Harrogate 1-10-99
2017–18 Leeds U 0 0
2018–19 Leeds U 0 0
2019–20 Forest Green R 29 0
2020–21 Forest Green R 15 0 **44** **0**
2020–21 Barnsley 1 0
2021–22 Barnsley 32 0 **33** **0**

LANCASTER, Will (M) **0** **0**
H: 6 0 W: 10 12 b.Sheffield 3-8-02
2020–21 Barnsley 0 0
2021–22 Barnsley 0 0

MARSH, Aiden (F) **4** **1**
H: 5 8 W: 9 06 b.Barnsley 5-5-03
2019–20 Barnsley 0 0
2020–21 Barnsley 0 0
2021–22 Barnsley 4 1 **4** **1**

MILLER, George (F) **149** **31**
H: 5 10 W: 10 01 b.Bolton 11-8-98
2015–16 Bury 1 0
2016–17 Bury 28 7
2017–18 Middlesbrough 0 0
2017–18 *Bury* 19 8 **48** **15**
2018–19 Middlesbrough 0 0
2018–19 *Bradford C* 39 3 **39** **3**
2018–19 Barnsley 0 0
2019–20 Barnsley 1 0
2019–20 *Scunthorpe U* 15 1 **15** **1**
2020–21 Barnsley 5 0
2021–22 Barnsley 0 0 **6** **0**
2021–22 *Walsall* 41 12 **41** **12**

MOON, Jasper (M) **28** **0**
H: 6 1 W: 12 02 b.Coventry 24-11-00
From Leicester C.
2018–19 Barnsley 0 0
2019–20 Barnsley 0 0
2020–21 Barnsley 3 0
2021–22 Barnsley 25 0 **28** **0**

MORRIS, Carlton (F) **198** **36**
H: 6 1 W: 13 05 b.Cambridge 16-12-95
Internationals: England U19.
2014–15 Norwich C 1 0
2014–15 *Oxford U* 7 0 **7** **0**
2014–15 *York C* 8 0 **8** **0**
2015–16 Norwich C 0 0
2015–16 *Hamilton A* 32 8 **32** **8**
2016–17 Norwich C 0 0
2016–17 *Rotherham U* 8 0
2017–18 Norwich C 0 0
2017–18 *Shrewsbury T* 42 6 **42** **6**
2018–19 Norwich C 0 0
2019–20 Norwich C 0 0
2019–20 *Rotherham U* 21 3 **29** **3**
2019–20 *Milton Keynes D* 10 2
2020–21 Norwich C 0 0 **1** **0**
2020–21 *Milton Keynes D* 18 3 **28** **5**
2020–21 Barnsley 23 7
2021–22 Barnsley 28 7 **51** **14**

ODOUR, Clarke (F) **47** **1**
H: 5 10 W: 11 05 b.Siaya 25-6-99
Internationals: Kenya Full caps.
2018–19 Leeds U 0 0
2019–20 Leeds U 0 0
2019–20 Barnsley 16 1
2020–21 Barnsley 11 0
2021–22 Barnsley 20 0 **47** **1**

OULARE, Obbi (F) **95** **15**
H: 6 5 W: 15 02 b.Waregem 8-1-96
Internationals: Belgium U18, U19, U21.
2014–15 Club Brugge 19 3
2015–16 Club Brugge 6 1 **25** **4**
2015–16 Watford 2 0
2016–17 Watford 0 0
2016–17 *Zulte Waregem* 10 1 **10** **1**
2016–17 *Willem II* 11 3 **11** **3**
2017–18 Watford 0 0
2017–18 *Antwerp* 10 2 **10** **2**
2018–19 Watford 0 0 **2** **0**
2018–19 *Standard Liege* 6 1
2019–20 Standard Liege 14 2
2020–21 Standard Liege 12 2 **32** **5**
2021–22 Barnsley 2 0 **2** **0**
2021–22 *RWD Molenbeek* 3 0 **3** **0**

PALMER, Romal (M) **70** **2**
H: 5 11 W: 11 00 b.Wigan 30-9-99
From Manchester C.
2019–20 Barnsley 3 0
2020–21 Barnsley 34 1
2021–22 Barnsley 33 1 **70** **2**

SCHMIDT, Patrick (F) **132** **21**
b.Eisenstadt 22-7-98
Internationals: Austria U16, U17, U18, U19, U21.
2016–17 Admira Wacker 15 1
2017–18 Admira Wacker 20 6
2018–19 Admira Wacker 27 8
2019–20 Admira Wacker 2 0 **64** **15**
2019–20 Barnsley 29 3
2020–21 Barnsley 8 0
2020–21 *SV Ried* 10 1 **10** **1**
2021–22 Barnsley 0 0 **37** **3**
2021–22 *Esbjerg* 21 2 **21** **2**

SIBBICK, Toby (D) **79** **1**
H: 6 0 W: 10 12 b.Isleworth 23-5-99
2016–17 AFC Wimbledon 2 0
2017–18 AFC Wimbledon 1 0
2018–19 AFC Wimbledon 23 0 **26** **0**
2019–20 Barnsley 18 0
2019–20 *Hearts* 2 0 **2** **0**
2020–21 Barnsley 21 0
2020–21 *KV Oostende* 0 0
2021–22 Barnsley 12 1 **51** **1**

SRAHA, Jason (D) **2** **0**
H: 6 2 b. 19-11-02
From Chelsea, Arsenal.
2021–22 Barnsley 2 0 **2** **0**
Transferred to Hearts, January 2022.

STYLES, Callum (M) **150** **8**
H: 5 6 W: 9 06 b.Bury 28-3-00
Internationals: Hungary Full caps.
From Burnley.
2015–16 Bury 1 0
2016–17 Bury 13 0
2017–18 Bury 11 0
2018–19 Bury 16 0 **41** **0**
2018–19 Barnsley 7 0
2019–20 Barnsley 17 1
2020–21 Barnsley 42 4
2021–22 Barnsley 43 3 **109** **8**

THOMAS, Luke (F) **136** **5**
H: 5 7 W: 10 08 b.Gloucester 19-2-99
Internationals: England U20.
From Cheltenham T.
2015–16 Derby Co 0 0
2016–17 Derby Co 0 0
2017–18 Derby Co 2 0
2018–19 Derby Co 0 0 **2** **0**
2018–19 *Coventry C* 43 4 **43** **4**
2019–20 Barnsley 39 1
2020–21 Barnsley 19 0
2020–21 *Ipswich T* 5 0 **5** **0**
2021–22 Barnsley 0 0 **58** **1**
2021–22 *Bristol R* 28 0 **28** **0**

THOMPSON, Cameron (F) **1** **0**
H: 5 7 W: 11 11 b.London 21-2-00
From Fulham.
2020–21 Barnsley 0 0
2021–22 Barnsley 1 0 **1** **0**

VITA, Remy (D) **24** **0**
H: 5 7 W: 10 06 b.Alencon 1-4-01
From Alencon.
2018–19 Troyes 0 0
2019–20 Troyes 0 0
2020–21 Troyes 5 0 **5** **0**
2020–21 Bayern Munich 0 0
2021–22 Bayern Munich 0 0
2021–22 *Barnsley* 19 0 **19** **0**

WALTON, Jack (G) **46** **0**
H: 6 0 W: 12 02 b.Bury 23-4-98
From Bolton W.
2014–15 Barnsley 0 0
2015–16 Barnsley 0 0
2016–17 Barnsley 0 0
2017–18 Barnsley 3 0
2018–19 Barnsley 3 0
2019–20 Barnsley 9 0
2020–21 Barnsley 24 0
2021–22 Barnsley 7 0 **46** **0**

WILLIAMS, Jordan (D) **92** **0**
H: 5 10 W: 11 11 b.Huddersfield 22-10-99
Internationals: England U17, U18.
2017–18 Huddersfield T 0 0
2017–18 *Bury* 9 0 **9** **0**
2018–19 Barnsley 11 0
2019–20 Barnsley 30 0
2020–21 Barnsley 21 0
2021–22 Barnsley 21 0 **83** **0**

WINFIELD, Charlie (D) **14** **1**
H: 5 7 W: 9 02 b.Barnsley 8-5-02
2020–21 Barnsley 0 0
2021–22 Barnsley 0 0
2021–22 *Esbjerg* 14 1 **14** **1**

WOLFE, Matthew (M) **17** **0**
H: 6 1 W: 11 09 b.Wakefield 12-6-00
2017–18 Barnsley 0 0
2018–19 Barnsley 0 0
2019–20 Barnsley 1 0
2020–21 Barnsley 0 0
2021–22 Barnsley 16 0 **17** **0**
2021–22 *Esbjerg* 0 0

WOODROW, Cauley (F) **242** **63**
H: 6 0 W: 12 04 b.Hemel Hempstead 2-12-94
Internationals: England U17, U20, U21.
From Luton T.
2011–12 Fulham 0 0
2012–13 Fulham 0 0
2013–14 Fulham 6 1
2013–14 *Southend U* 19 2 **19** **2**
2014–15 Fulham 29 3
2015–16 Fulham 14 4
2016–17 Fulham 5 0
2016–17 *Burton Alb* 14 5 **14** **5**
2017–18 Fulham 0 0 **54** **8**
2017–18 *Bristol C* 14 2 **14** **2**
2018–19 Barnsley 31 16
2019–20 Barnsley 40 14
2020–21 Barnsley 42 12
2021–22 Barnsley 28 4 **141** **46**

Players retained or with offer of contract
Ackroyd, Joe; Arielly, Amir; Benson, Danny; Flavell, Kieran; Hassan-Smith, Kareem; Jinadu, Daniel.

Scholars
Anaman, Alex Kofi; Benjamin, Mylan Eric; Benson, Daniel Richard; Brown, Archie Myles; Chapman, Angus Charles; Chapman, Theo Caleb; Doyle, Matthew James Henry; Dyer, Josiah Jude Emmanuel; Flavell, Kieren James; Goucher, Blake Callum; Hall, Ben Lawson; Hartley, Keegan James; Hickingbottom, Charlie Ellis Andrew; Joof, Alex John; Lacey, Luis Frances John; Makiessi Tsibi, Jean Claude; McKay, Joshua Samuel; Murchison, Kynan Javon; Nejman, Harrison Luke; Pickard, Hayden; Sherlock, Jack Edward; Smith, Lloyd Dion.

BARROW (6)

BANKS, Oliver (M) **257 30**
H: 6 3 W: 11 11 b.Rotherham 21-9-92

Season	Club	Apps	Gls	Total Apps	Total Gls
2010–11	Rotherham U	1	1		
2011–12	Rotherham U	0	0	**1**	**1**

From FC United of Manchester.

Season	Club	Apps	Gls	Total Apps	Total Gls
2013–14	Chesterfield	25	7		
2014–15	Chesterfield	24	0		
2014–15	*Northampton T*	3	0	**3**	**0**
2015–16	Chesterfield	32	2	**81**	**9**
2016–17	Oldham Ath	33	2		
2017–18	Oldham Ath	7	0	**40**	**2**
2017–18	*Swindon T*	17	3	**17**	**3**
2018–19	Tranmere R	33	3		
2019–20	Tranmere R	11	3		
2020–21	Tranmere R	12	0	**56**	**6**
2020–21	Barrow	20	0		
2021–22	Barrow	39	9	**59**	**9**

BEADLING, Tom (M) **94 6**
H: 6 1 W: 12 08 b.Barrow-in-Furness 16-1-96

Season	Club	Apps	Gls	Total Apps	Total Gls
2014–15	Sunderland	0	0		
2015–16	Sunderland	0	0		
2016–17	Sunderland	0	0		
2016–17	*Bury*	2	0	**2**	**0**
2017–18	Sunderland	0	0		
2017–18	*Dunfermline Ath*	11	1		
2018–19	Dunfermline Ath	19	3		
2019–20	Dunfermline Ath	21	0	**51**	**4**
2020–21	Barrow	29	2		
2021–22	Barrow	12	0	**41**	**2**

BROUGH, Patrick (D) **160 6**
H: 6 3 W: 11 09 b.Carlisle 20-2-96

Season	Club	Apps	Gls	Total Apps	Total Gls
2013–14	Carlisle U	3	0		
2014–15	Carlisle U	29	0		
2015–16	Carlisle U	7	0		
2016–17	Carlisle U	1	0	**40**	**0**
2017–18	Morecambe	20	0	**20**	**0**
2018–19	Falkirk	16	0	**16**	**0**

From Barrow.

Season	Club	Apps	Gls	Total Apps	Total Gls
2020–21	Barrow	43	6		
2021–22	Barrow	41	0	**84**	**6**

BROWN, Connor (D) **137 2**
H: 5 8 W: 10 12 b.Sheffield 2-10-91

Season	Club	Apps	Gls	Total Apps	Total Gls
2010–11	Sheffield U	0	0		
2011–12	Sheffield U	0	0		
2012–13	Oldham Ath	25	0		
2013–14	Oldham Ath	27	1		
2014–15	Oldham Ath	24	0		
2014–15	*Carlisle U*	8	0	**8**	**0**
2015–16	Oldham Ath	13	0	**89**	**1**

From Guiseley, York C.

Season	Club	Apps	Gls	Total Apps	Total Gls
2020–21	Barrow	19	1		
2021–22	Barrow	21	0	**40**	**1**

CANAVAN, Niall (D) **325 24**
H: 6 3 W: 12 00 b.Guiseley 11-4-91
Internationals: Republic of Ireland U21.

Season	Club	Apps	Gls	Total Apps	Total Gls
2009–10	Scunthorpe U	7	1		
2010–11	Scunthorpe U	8	0		
2010–11	*Shrewsbury T*	3	0	**3**	**0**
2011–12	Scunthorpe U	12	1		
2012–13	Scunthorpe U	40	6		
2013–14	Scunthorpe U	45	4		
2014–15	Scunthorpe U	32	3		
2015–16	Scunthorpe U	10	0	**154**	**15**
2015–16	*Rochdale*	11	1		
2016–17	Rochdale	25	2		
2017–18	Rochdale	3	0	**39**	**3**
2018–19	Plymouth Arg	33	2		
2019–20	Plymouth Arg	33	2		
2020–21	Plymouth Arg	12	1	**78**	**5**
2020–21	Bradford C	16	0		
2021–22	Bradford C	17	1	**33**	**1**
2021–22	Barrow	18	0	**18**	**0**

ELLIS, Mark (D) **321 21**
H: 6 2 W: 12 04 b.Kingsbridge 30-9-88

Season	Club	Apps	Gls	Total Apps	Total Gls
2007–08	Bolton W	0	0		

From Torquay U.

Season	Club	Apps	Gls	Total Apps	Total Gls
2009–10	Torquay U	27	3		
2010–11	Torquay U	27	2		
2011–12	Torquay U	35	3	**89**	**8**
2012–13	Crewe Alex	44	5		
2013–14	Crewe Alex	37	1	**81**	**6**
2014–15	Shrewsbury T	32	2		
2015–16	Shrewsbury T	9	1	**41**	**3**
2015–16	Carlisle U	30	0		
2016–17	Carlisle U	7	0		
2017–18	Carlisle U	23	2	**60**	**2**
2018–19	Tranmere R	25	0		
2019–20	Tranmere R	3	2		
2020–21	Tranmere R	6	0	**34**	**2**
2021–22	Barrow	16	0	**16**	**0**

FARMAN, Paul (G) **169 0**
H: 6 5 W: 14 07 b.North Shields 2-11-89
From Blyth Spartans, Gateshead.

Season	Club	Apps	Gls	Total Apps	Total Gls
2017–18	Lincoln C	13	0	**13**	**0**
2018–19	Stevenage	33	0		
2019–20	Stevenage	35	0	**68**	**0**
2020–21	Carlisle U	42	0		
2021–22	Carlisle U	0	0	**42**	**0**
2021–22	Barrow	46	0	**46**	**0**

GORDON, Josh (F) **143 27**
H: 5 10 W: 11 00 b.Stoke-on-Trent 19-1-95
From Stafford Rangers.

Season	Club	Apps	Gls	Total Apps	Total Gls
2017–18	Leicester C	0	0		
2018–19	Walsall	37	7		
2019–20	Walsall	34	9		
2020–21	Walsall	36	5	**107**	**21**
2021–22	Barrow	36	6	**36**	**6**

GOTTS, Robbie (M) **66 5**
H: 5 10 W: 11 03 b.Harrogate 9-11-99

Season	Club	Apps	Gls	Total Apps	Total Gls
2018–19	Leeds U	0	0		
2019–20	Leeds U	1	0		
2020–21	Leeds U	0	0		
2020–21	*Lincoln C*	7	0	**7**	**0**
2020–21	*Salford C*	23	3		
2021–22	*Salford C*	0	0	**23**	**3**
2021–22	Leeds U	0	0	**1**	**0**
2021–22	Barrow	35	2	**35**	**2**

GRAYSON, Joe (M) **38 4**
H: 5 10 W: 11 09 b.Leicester 26-3-99

Season	Club	Apps	Gls	Total Apps	Total Gls
2018–19	Blackburn R	0	0		
2018–19	*Grimsby T*	8	2	**8**	**2**
2019–20	Blackburn R	0	0		
2020–21	Blackburn R	0	0		
2020–21	*Oxford U*	4	0	**4**	**0**
2021–22	Barrow	26	2	**26**	**2**

HUTTON, Remeao (D) **70 0**
H: 5 9 W: 11 05 b.Walsall 28-9-98
From Hednesford T.

Season	Club	Apps	Gls	Total Apps	Total Gls
2017–18	Birmingham C	0	0		
2018–19	Birmingham C	0	0		
2019–20	Birmingham C	0	0		
2020–21	Birmingham C	0	0		
2020–21	*Stevenage*	26	0	**26**	**0**
2021–22	Barrow	44	0	**44**	**0**

JAMES, Luke (F) **253 24**
H: 6 0 W: 12 08 b.Amble 4-11-94
Internationals: England C.

Season	Club	Apps	Gls	Total Apps	Total Gls
2011–12	Hartlepool U	19	3		
2012–13	Hartlepool U	26	3		
2013–14	Hartlepool U	42	13		
2014–15	Hartlepool U	4	0		
2014–15	Peterborough U	32	1		
2015–16	Peterborough U	0	0		
2015–16	*Bradford C*	9	0	**9**	**0**
2015–16	*Hartlepool U*	20	1	**111**	**20**
2016–17	Peterborough U	0	0	**32**	**1**
2016–17	*Bristol R*	24	0	**24**	**0**
2017–18	Forest Green R	14	0	**14**	**0**

From Hartlepool U.

Season	Club	Apps	Gls	Total Apps	Total Gls
2020–21	Barrow	44	3		
2021–22	Barrow	19	0	**63**	**3**

JONES, James (D) **46 2**
H: 6 4 W: 12 06 b.Wrexham 13-3-97
From The New Saints, Altrincham.

Season	Club	Apps	Gls	Total Apps	Total Gls
2020–21	Barrow	21	1		
2021–22	Barrow	25	1	**46**	**2**

JONES, Mike (M) **496 38**
H: 6 0 W: 12 04 b.Birkenhead 15-8-87

Season	Club	Apps	Gls	Total Apps	Total Gls
2005–06	Tranmere R	1	0		
2006–07	Tranmere R	0	0		
2006–07	*Shrewsbury T*	13	1	**13**	**1**
2007–08	Tranmere R	9	1	**10**	**1**
2008–09	Bury	46	4		
2009–10	Bury	41	5		
2010–11	Bury	42	8		
2011–12	Bury	24	3	**153**	**20**
2011–12	Sheffield W	10	0		
2012–13	Sheffield W	0	0	**10**	**0**
2012–13	Crawley T	40	1		
2013–14	Crawley T	42	3	**82**	**4**
2014–15	Oldham Ath	45	6		
2015–16	Oldham Ath	35	3	**80**	**9**
2016–17	Carlisle U	28	0		
2017–18	Carlisle U	43	0		
2018–19	Carlisle U	24	1		
2019–20	Carlisle U	37	0	**132**	**1**
2020–21	Barrow	13	2		
2021–22	Barrow	3	0	**16**	**2**

KAY, Josh (M) **75 10**
H: 5 5 W: 10 01 b.Blackpool 28-10-96
From AFC Fylde.

Season	Club	Apps	Gls	Total Apps	Total Gls
2015–16	Barnsley	0	0		
2016–17	Barnsley	1	0		
2017–18	Barnsley	0	0	**1**	**0**
2017–18	*Chesterfield*	11	0	**11**	**0**

From Barrow.

Season	Club	Apps	Gls	Total Apps	Total Gls
2020–21	Barrow	29	5		
2021–22	Barrow	34	5	**63**	**10**

LILLIS, Josh (G) **299 0**
H: 6 0 W: 12 08 b.Derby 24-6-87

Season	Club	Apps	Gls	Total Apps	Total Gls
2006–07	Scunthorpe U	1	0		
2007–08	Scunthorpe U	3	0		
2008–09	Scunthorpe U	5	0		
2008–09	*Notts Co*	5	0	**5**	**0**
2009–10	Scunthorpe U	8	0		
2009–10	*Grimsby T*	4	0	**4**	**0**
2009–10	*Rochdale*	1	0		
2010–11	Scunthorpe U	15	0		
2010–11	*Rochdale*	23	0		
2011–12	Scunthorpe U	6	0	**38**	**0**
2012–13	Rochdale	46	0		
2013–14	Rochdale	45	0		
2014–15	Rochdale	16	0		
2015–16	Rochdale	40	0		
2016–17	Rochdale	14	0		
2017–18	Rochdale	40	0		
2018–19	Rochdale	27	0		
2019–20	Rochdale	0	0	**252**	**0**
2020–21	Barrow	0	0		
2021–22	Barrow	0	0		

MALONEY, Scott (G) **0 0**
H: 6 3 W: 11 00 b.Ashton-under-Lyne 15-4-00

Season	Club	Apps	Gls	Total Apps	Total Gls
2017–18	Bury	0	0		
2018–19	Bury	0	0		
2020–21	Barrow	0	0		
2021–22	Barrow	0	0		

NTLHE, Kgosietsile (D) **182 8**
H: 5 9 W: 10 06 b.Pretoria 21-2-94
Internationals: South Africa U20, Full caps.

Season	Club	Apps	Gls	Total Apps	Total Gls
2010–11	Peterborough U	0	0		
2011–12	Peterborough U	2	0		
2012–13	Peterborough U	12	1		
2013–14	Peterborough U	27	2		
2014–15	Peterborough U	28	1		
2015–16	Peterborough U	7	0		
2016–17	Peterborough U	0	0	**76**	**4**
2016–17	Stevenage	22	0	**22**	**0**
2017–18	Rochdale	20	0		
2018–19	Rochdale	19	3	**39**	**3**
2019–20	Scunthorpe U	18	1	**18**	**1**
2020–21	Barrow	22	0		
2021–22	Barrow	5	0	**27**	**0**

PLATT, Matt (D) **52 4**
H: 6 0 W: 10 08 b.Knowsley 3-10-97

Season	Club	Apps	Gls	Total Apps	Total Gls
2016–17	Blackburn R	0	0		
2017–18	Blackburn R	0	0		
2018–19	Blackburn R	0	0		
2018–19	*Accrington S*	0	0		
2019–20	Blackburn R	0	0		
2020–21	Barrow	24	2		
2021–22	Barrow	28	2	**52**	**4**

ROONEY, John (M) **68 8**
H: 5 11 W: 12 02 b.Liverpool 17-12-90

Season	Club	Apps	Gls	Total Apps	Total Gls
2007–08	Macclesfield T	2	0		
2008–09	Macclesfield T	14	2		
2009–10	Macclesfield T	25	1	**41**	**3**
2010–11	New York RB	2	0		
2011–12	New York RB	3	0	**5**	**0**
2012–13	Barnsley	0	0		
2013–14	Bury	3	0	**3**	**0**

From Chester, Wrexham, Guiseley, Barrow, Stockport Co.

Season	Club	Apps	Gls	Total Apps	Total Gls
2021–22	Barrow	19	5	**19**	**5**

SEA, Dimitri (F) **18 1**
H: 5 11 W: 12 02 b.Paris 2-5-01

Season	Club	Apps	Gls	Total Apps	Total Gls
2019–20	Aston Villa	0	0		
2020–21	Barrow	8	0		
2021–22	Barrow	10	1	**18**	**1**

STEVENS, Jordan (M) **62 2**
H: 5 8 W: 10 03 b.Gloucester 25-3-00

Season	Club	Apps	Gls	Total Apps	Total Gls
2017–18	Forest Green R	9	0	**9**	**0**
2017–18	Leeds U	0	0		
2018–19	Leeds U	1	0		
2019–20	Leeds U	4	0		
2020–21	Leeds U	0	0		
2020–21	*Swindon T*	13	1	**13**	**1**
2020–21	*Bradford C*	16	0		
2021–22	Bradford C	0	0	**16**	**0**
2021–22	Leeds U	0	0	**5**	**0**
2021–22	Barrow	19	1	**19**	**1**

TAYLOR, Jason (M) **407 20**
H: 6 1 W: 11 03 b.Ashton-under-Lyne 28-1-87

Season	Club	Apps	Gls	Total Apps	Total Gls
2005–06	Oldham Ath	0	0		
2005–06	*Stockport Co*	9	0		
2006–07	Stockport Co	45	1		
2007–08	Stockport Co	42	4		
2008–09	Stockport Co	8	1	**104**	**6**
2008–09	Rotherham U	15	1		
2009–10	Rotherham U	2	0		
2009–10	*Rochdale*	23	1	**23**	**1**
2010–11	Rotherham U	42	5		
2011–12	Rotherham U	39	2		
2012–13	Rotherham U	20	2	**118**	**10**
2012–13	Cheltenham T	16	0		
2013–14	Cheltenham T	33	2		
2014–15	Cheltenham T	16	0	**65**	**2**
2014–15	Northampton T	21	0		
2015–16	Northampton T	30	1	**51**	**1**

From Eastleigh, AFC Fylde.

Season	Club	Apps	Gls	Total Apps	Total Gls
2020–21	Barrow	34	0		
2021–22	Barrow	12	0	**46**	**0**

WHITE, Tom (M) **36 0**
H: 5 11 W: 10 06 b.Newcastle upon Tyne 9-5-97
Internationals: England C.
From Gateshead.
2020–21 Blackburn R 0 0
2020–21 *Bolton W* 9 0 **9 0**
2021–22 Hartlepool U 0 0
2021–22 Barrow 27 0 **27 0**

WILLIAMS, George C (F) **132 11**
H: 5 8 W: 11 07 b.Milton Keynes 7-9-95
Internationals: Wales U17, U19, U21, Full caps.
2011–12 Milton Keynes D 2 0
2012–13 Fulham 0 0
2013–14 Fulham 0 0
2014–15 Fulham 14 0
2014–15 *Milton Keynes D* 4 0
2015–16 Fulham 1 0
2015–16 *Gillingham* 10 0 **10 0**
2016–17 Fulham 0 0
2016–17 *Milton Keynes D* 11 0 **17 0**
2017–18 Fulham 0 0 **15 0**
2017–18 *St Johnstone* 11 0 **11 0**
2018–19 Forest Green R 38 7
2019–20 Forest Green R 4 1 **42 8**
2020–21 Grimsby T 19 2 **19 2**
2021–22 Barrow 18 1 **18 1**

ZANZALA, Offrande (F) **120 21**
H: 6 1 W: 11 05 b.Brazzaville 13-12-97
2015–16 Derby Co 0 0
2015–16 *Stevenage* 2 0 **2 0**
2016–17 Derby Co 0 0
2017–18 Derby Co 0 0
2017–18 *Accrington S* 6 1
2018–19 Accrington S 27 4
2019–20 Accrington S 24 6 **57 11**
2020–21 Crewe Alex 5 0 **5 0**
2020–21 Carlisle U 22 5 **22 5**
2021–22 Barrow 19 3 **19 3**
2021–22 *Exeter C* 15 2 **15 2**

BIRMINGHAM C (7)

ANDREWS, Josh (F) **20 3**
b.Solihull 16-10-01
2020–21 Birmingham C 0 0
2020–21 *Harrogate T* 3 0 **3 0**
2021–22 Birmingham C 0 0
2021–22 *Rochdale* 17 3 **17 3**

ANNESLEY, Louie (D) **0 0**
b.St Helier 3-5-00
Internationals: Gibraltar U16, U17, U19, U21, Full caps.
From Lincoln Red Imps.
2020–21 Blackburn R 0 0
2021–22 Birmingham C 0 0

BACUNA, Juninho (F) **207 17**
H: 6 1 W: 12 04 b.Groningen 7-8-97
Internationals: Netherlands U18, U20, U21. Curacao Full caps.
2014–15 Groningen 11 0
2015–16 Groningen 14 0
2016–17 Groningen 24 1
2017–18 Groningen 33 1 **82 2**
2018–19 Huddersfield T 21 1
2019–20 Huddersfield T 38 6
2020–21 Huddersfield T 43 5
2021–22 Huddersfield T 0 0 **102 12**
2021–22 Rangers 6 1 **6 1**
2021–22 Birmingham C 17 2 **17 2**

BAILEY, Odin (M) **76 9**
b. 8-12-99
Internationals: England U16.
2017–18 Birmingham C 0 0
2018–19 Birmingham C 0 0
2019–20 Birmingham C 6 1
2019–20 *Forest Green R* 5 1
2020–21 Birmingham C 0 0
2020–21 *Forest Green R* 34 4 **39 5**
2021–22 Birmingham C 0 0 **6 1**
2021–22 *Livingston* 31 3 **31 3**

BELA, Jeremie (M) **254 34**
H: 5 8 W: 10 12 b.Melun 8-4-93
Internationals: France U16. Angola Full aps.
2010–11 Lens 0 0
2011–12 Lens 0 0
2012–13 Lens 16 1
2013–14 Lens 1 0 **17 1**
2013–14 Dijon 4 0
2014–15 Dijon 33 6
2015–16 Dijon 23 4
2016–17 Dijon 14 0 **74 10**
2017–18 Albacete 33 5
2018–19 Albacete 34 11
2019–20 Albacete 0 0 **67 16**
2019–20 Birmingham C 30 2
2020–21 Birmingham C 35 3
2021–22 Birmingham C 31 2 **96 7**

BELLINGHAM, Jobe (M) **2 0**
b.Stourbridge 23-9-05
Internationals: England U16, U17.
2021–22 Birmingham C 2 0 **2 0**

CAMPBELL, Tate (M) **0 0**
b.Birmingham 27-6-02
2020–21 Birmingham C 0 0
2021–22 Birmingham C 0 0

COLIN, Maxime (D) **385 10**
H: 5 11 W: 12 00 b.Arras 15-11-91
Internationals: France U20.
2010–11 Boulogne 26 0
2011–12 Boulogne 23 0
2012–13 Boulogne 4 0 **53 0**
2012–13 Troyes 18 0
2013–14 Troyes 35 0
2014–15 Troyes 2 0 **55 0**
2014–15 Anderlecht 17 1
2015–16 Anderlecht 1 0 **18 1**
2015–16 Brentford 21 0
2016–17 Brentford 38 4
2017–18 Brentford 3 0 **62 4**
2017–18 Birmingham C 35 2
2018–19 Birmingham C 43 0
2019–20 Birmingham C 44 1
2020–21 Birmingham C 42 1
2021–22 Birmingham C 33 1 **197 5**

COSGROVE, Sam (F) **131 35**
H: 6 2 W: 10 08 b.Beverley 2-12-96
2014–15 Wigan Ath 0 0
2015–16 Wigan Ath 0 0
2016–17 Wigan Ath 0 0
2017–18 Carlisle U 8 1 **8 1**
2017–18 Aberdeen 5 0
2018–19 Aberdeen 35 17
2019–20 Aberdeen 25 11
2020–21 Aberdeen 14 3 **79 31**
2020–21 Birmingham C 12 0
2021–22 Birmingham C 0 0 **12 0**
2021–22 *Shrewsbury T* 17 2 **17 2**
2021–22 *AFC Wimbledon* 15 1 **15 1**

DEAN, Harlee (D) **407 15**
H: 6 3 W: 11 11 b.Basingstoke 26-7-91
2008–09 Dagenham & R 0 0
2009–10 Dagenham & R 1 0 **1 0**
2010–11 Southampton 0 0
2011–12 Southampton 0 0
2011–12 *Brentford* 26 1
2012–13 Brentford 44 3
2013–14 Brentford 32 0
2014–15 Brentford 35 1
2015–16 Brentford 42 0
2016–17 Brentford 42 3
2017–18 Brentford 3 0 **224 8**
2017–18 Birmingham C 34 1
2018–19 Birmingham C 44 1
2019–20 Birmingham C 39 1
2020–21 Birmingham C 43 4
2021–22 Birmingham C 15 0 **175 7**
2021–22 *Sheffield W* 7 0 **7 0**

DEENEY, Troy (F) **533 163**
H: 6 0 W: 14 02 b.Solihull 29-6-88
From Chelmsley T.
2006–07 Walsall 1 0
2007–08 Walsall 35 1
2008–09 Walsall 45 12
2009–10 Walsall 42 14 **123 27**
2010–11 Watford 36 3
2011–12 Watford 43 11
2012–13 Watford 40 19
2013–14 Watford 44 24
2014–15 Watford 42 21
2015–16 Watford 38 13
2016–17 Watford 37 10
2017–18 Watford 29 5
2018–19 Watford 32 9
2019–20 Watford 27 10
2020–21 Watford 19 7
2021–22 Watford 2 0 **389 132**
2021–22 Birmingham C 21 4 **21 4**

ETHERIDGE, Neil (G) **264 0**
H: 6 2 W: 14 00 b.Enfield 7-2-90
Internationals: England U16. Philippines Full caps.
From Chelsea.
2008–09 Fulham 0 0
2009–10 Fulham 0 0
2010–11 Fulham 0 0
2011–12 Fulham 0 0
2012–13 Fulham 0 0
2012–13 *Bristol R* 12 0 **12 0**
2013–14 Fulham 0 0
2013–14 *Crewe Alex* 4 0 **4 0**
2014–15 Oldham Ath 0 0
2014–15 Charlton Ath 4 0 **4 0**
2015–16 Walsall 40 0
2016–17 Walsall 41 0 **81 0**
2017–18 Cardiff C 45 0
2018–19 Cardiff C 38 0
2019–20 Cardiff C 16 0
2020–21 Cardiff C 0 0 **99 0**
2020–21 Birmingham C 43 0
2021–22 Birmingham C 21 0 **64 0**

FRIEND, George (D) **405 12**
H: 6 2 W: 13 01 b.Barnstaple 19-10-87
2008–09 Exeter C 4 0
2008–09 Wolverhampton W 6 0
2009–10 Wolverhampton W 1 0 **7 0**
2009–10 *Millwall* 6 0 **6 0**
2009–10 *Southend U* 6 1 **6 1**
2009–10 *Scunthorpe U* 4 0 **4 0**
2009–10 *Exeter C* 13 1 **17 1**
2010–11 Doncaster R 32 1
2011–12 Doncaster R 27 0
2012–13 Doncaster R 0 0 **59 1**
2012–13 Middlesbrough 34 0
2013–14 Middlesbrough 41 3
2014–15 Middlesbrough 42 1
2015–16 Middlesbrough 40 1
2016–17 Middlesbrough 24 0
2017–18 Middlesbrough 33 2
2018–19 Middlesbrough 38 2
2019–20 Middlesbrough 14 0
2020–21 Middlesbrough 0 0 **266 9**
2020–21 Birmingham C 26 0
2021–22 Birmingham C 14 0 **40 0**

GARDNER, Gary (M) **280 26**
H: 6 1 W: 12 13 b.Solihull 29-6-92
Internationals: England U17, U19, U20, U21.
2009–10 Aston Villa 0 0
2010–11 Aston Villa 0 0
2011–12 Aston Villa 14 0
2011–12 *Coventry C* 4 1 **4 1**
2012–13 Aston Villa 2 0
2013–14 Aston Villa 0 0
2013–14 *Sheffield W* 3 0 **3 0**
2014–15 Aston Villa 0 0
2014–15 *Brighton & HA* 17 2 **17 2**
2014–15 Nottingham F 18 4
2015–16 Aston Villa 0 0
2015–16 *Nottingham F* 20 2 **38 6**
2016–17 Aston Villa 26 1
2017–18 Aston Villa 0 0
2017–18 *Barnsley* 29 2 **29 2**
2018–19 Aston Villa 0 0 **42 1**
2018–19 *Birmingham C* 40 2
2019–20 Birmingham C 35 4
2020–21 Birmingham C 37 2
2021–22 Birmingham C 35 6 **147 14**

GEORGE, Adan (F) **1 0**
b. 30-7-02
From WBA.
2020–21 Birmingham C 1 0
2020–21 *Walsall* 0 0
2021–22 Birmingham C 0 0 **1 0**

GORDON, Nico (D) **15 1**
b.Birmingham 28-4-02
2019–20 Birmingham C 2 0
2020–21 Birmingham C 2 0
2021–22 Birmingham C 11 1 **15 1**

GRAHAM, Jordan (M) **115 14**
H: 6 0 W: 10 10 b.Coventry 5-3-95
Internationals: England U16, U17.
2011–12 Aston Villa 0 0
2012–13 Aston Villa 0 0
2013–14 Aston Villa 0 0
2013–14 *Ipswich T* 2 0
2013–14 *Bradford C* 1 0 **1 0**
2014–15 Wolverhampton W 0 0
2015–16 Wolverhampton W 11 1
2015–16 *Oxford U* 5 0
2016–17 Wolverhampton W 2 0
2017–18 Wolverhampton W 1 0
2017–18 *Fulham* 3 0 **3 0**
2018–19 Wolverhampton W 0 0
2018–19 *Ipswich T* 4 0 **6 0**
2018–19 *Oxford U* 16 1 **21 1**
2019–20 Wolverhampton W 0 0 **14 1**
2019–20 *Gillingham* 7 0
2020–21 Gillingham 39 12 **46 12**
2021–22 Birmingham C 24 0 **24 0**

HALL, George (M) **2 0**
b.Redditch 15-7-04
Internationals: England U18.
2021–22 Birmingham C 2 0 **2 0**

HOGAN, Scott (F) **229 74**
H: 5 11 W: 10 01 b.Salford 13-4-92
Internationals: Republic of Ireland Full caps.
2009–10 Rochdale 0 0
From FC Halifax T, Stocksbridge PS, Ashton U, Hyde U.
2013–14 Rochdale 33 17 **33 17**
2014–15 Brentford 1 0
2015–16 Brentford 7 7
2016–17 Brentford 25 14 **33 21**
2016–17 Aston Villa 13 1
2017–18 Aston Villa 37 6
2018–19 Aston Villa 6 0
2018–19 *Sheffield U* 8 2 **8 2**
2019–20 Aston Villa 0 0
2019–20 *Stoke C* 13 3 **13 3**
2019–20 *Birmingham C* 17 7

2020–21	Aston Villa	0	0	**56**	**7**
2020–21	Birmingham C	33	7		
2021–22	Birmingham C	36	10	**86**	**24**

HURST, Kyle (M) 0 0

b.Milton Keynes 20-1-02

2020–21	Birmingham C	0	0		
2021–22	Birmingham C	0	0		

IVAN SANCHEZ, Aguayo (M) 203 14

H: 5 7 W: 10 06 b.Campillo de Arenas 23-9-92

2014–15	Almeria	0	0		
2015–16	Almeria	24	0		
2016–17	Almeria	9	0	**33**	**0**
2016–17	*Albacete*	14	1		
2017–18	Albacete	0	0	**14**	**1**
2017–18	*Elche*	29	1		
2018–19	Elche	36	7		
2019–20	Elche	37	1		
2020–21	Elche	0	0	**102**	**9**
2020–21	Birmingham C	40	2		
2021–22	Birmingham C	2	0	**42**	**2**
2021–22	*Valladolid*	12	2	**12**	**2**

JAMES, Jordan (M) 20 1

b.Hereford 2-7-04

Internationals: Wales U18. England U20.

2021–22	Birmingham C	20	1	**20**	**1**

JEACOCK, Zach (G) 5 0

H: 6 2 W: 12 02 b.Birmingham 8-5-01

Internationals: England U19.

2020–21	Birmingham C	2	0		
2021–22	Birmingham C	2	0	**4**	**0**
2021–22	*Salford C*	1	0	**1**	**0**

JUTKIEWICZ, Lucas (F) 509 108

H: 6 1 W: 11 08 b.Southampton 28-3-89

2005–06	Swindon T	5	0		
2006–07	Swindon T	33	5	**38**	**5**
2006–07	Everton	0	0		
2007–08	Everton	0	0		
2007–08	*Plymouth Arg*	3	0	**3**	**0**
2008–09	Everton	1	0		
2008–09	*Huddersfield T*	7	0	**7**	**0**
2009–10	Everton	0	0	**1**	**0**
2009–10	*Motherwell*	33	12	**33**	**12**
2010–11	Coventry C	42	9		
2011–12	Coventry C	25	9	**67**	**18**
2011–12	Middlesbrough	19	2		
2012–13	Middlesbrough	24	8		
2013–14	Middlesbrough	22	1	**65**	**11**
2013–14	*Bolton W*	20	7	**20**	**7**
2014–15	Burnley	25	0		
2015–16	Burnley	5	0		
2016–17	Burnley	2	0	**32**	**0**
2016–17	Birmingham C	38	11		
2017–18	Birmingham C	35	5		
2018–19	Birmingham C	46	14		
2019–20	Birmingham C	46	15		
2020–21	Birmingham C	42	8		
2021–22	Birmingham C	36	2	**243**	**55**

LEKO, Jonathan (F) 111 7

H: 6 0 W: 11 11 b.Kinshasa 24-4-99

Internationals: England U16, U17, U18, U19, U20.

2015–16	WBA	5	0		
2016–17	WBA	9	0		
2017–18	Bristol C	11	0	**11**	**0**
2017–18	WBA	0	0		
2018–19	WBA	2	0		
2019–20	WBA	0	0	**16**	**0**
2019–20	*Charlton Ath*	21	5		
2020–21	Birmingham C	34	0		
2021–22	Birmingham C	4	0	**38**	**0**
2021–22	*Charlton Ath*	25	2	**46**	**7**

MASAMPU, Renedi (D) 0 0

b.Lambeth 17-9-99

From Metropolitan Police, Chelsea, Whyteleafe, Dulwich Hamlet.

2021–22	Birmingham C	0	0		

MATTHEWS, Archie (G) 1 0

b. 2-8-01

2018–19	Swindon T	0	0		
2019–20	Swindon T	0	0		
2020–21	Swindon T	1	0	**1**	**0**
2021–22	Birmingham C	0	0		

OAKLEY, Marcel (D) 2 0

b.Birmingham 30-10-02

2021–22	Birmingham C	2	0	**2**	**0**

PEDERSEN, Kristian (D) 274 12

H: 6 2 W: 13 01 b.Ringsted 4-8-94

Internationals: Denmark U21, Full caps.

2014–15	HB Koge	28	1		
2015–16	HB Koge	30	1	**58**	**2**
2016–17	Union Berlin	29	0		
2017–18	Union Berlin	32	1	**61**	**1**
2018–19	Birmingham C	39	1		
2019–20	Birmingham C	44	4		
2020–21	Birmingham C	35	2		
2021–22	Birmingham C	37	2	**155**	**9**

ROBERTS, Marc (D) 219 12

H: 6 0 W: 12 11 b.Wakefield 26-7-90

Internationals: England C.

From FC Halifax T.

2014–15	Barnsley	0	0		
2015–16	Barnsley	32	1		
2016–17	Barnsley	40	4	**72**	**5**
2017–18	Birmingham C	30	1		
2018–19	Birmingham C	8	0		
2019–20	Birmingham C	34	0		
2020–21	Birmingham C	36	4		
2021–22	Birmingham C	39	2	**147**	**7**

ROBERTS, Mitchell (D) 11 0

H: 6 0 W: 11 07 b.Stourbridge 16-9-00

2020–21	Birmingham C	0	0		
2020–21	*Harrogate T*	4	0	**4**	**0**
2021–22	Birmingham C	1	0	**1**	**0**
2021–22	*Carlisle U*	6	0	**6**	**0**

SIMMONDS, Keyendrah (F) 1 0

b.Manchester 31-5-01

Internationals: England U18.

2020–21	Birmingham C	1	0		
2021–22	Birmingham C	0	0	**1**	**0**

SOLDEVILA, Oriol (M) 0 0

H: 6 1 b.Barcelona 26-3-01

Internationals: Spain U16, U18.

From Barcelona.

2020–21	Birmingham C	0	0		
2021–22	Birmingham C	0	0		

STIRK, Ryan (M) 33 2

H: 5 10 W: 11 11 b.Birmingham 25-9-00

Internationals: Wales U17, U19, U21.

2019–20	Birmingham C	0	0		
2020–21	Birmingham C	2	0		
2021–22	Birmingham C	0	0	**2**	**0**
2021–22	*Mansfield T*	31	2	**31**	**2**

SUNJIC, Ivan (M) 211 13

H: 6 0 W: 11 11 b.Zenica 9-10-96

Internationals: Croatia U16, U17, U18, U19, U21, Full caps.

2013–14	Dinamo Zagreb	1	0		
2014–15	Dinamo Zagreb	0	0		
2015–16	Dinamo Zagreb	0	0		
2015–16	Lokomativa	10	0		
2016–17	Lokomativa	23	1		
2017–18	Lokomativa	29	6	**62**	**7**
2018–19	Dinamo Zagreb	24	0	**25**	**0**
2019–20	Birmingham C	40	3		
2020–21	Birmingham C	43	0		
2021–22	Birmingham C	41	3	**124**	**6**

TRUEMAN, Connal (G) 39 0

H: 6 1 W: 11 10 b.Birmingham 26-3-96

2014–15	Birmingham C	0	0		
2014–15	*Oldham Ath*	0	0		
2015–16	Birmingham C	0	0		
2016–17	Birmingham C	0	0		
2017–18	Birmingham C	0	0		
2018–19	Birmingham C	2	0		
2019–20	Birmingham C	10	0		
2020–21	Birmingham C	1	0		
2020–21	*AFC Wimbledon*	19	0	**19**	**0**
2020–21	*Swindon T*	4	0	**4**	**0**
2021–22	Oxford U	2	0	**2**	**0**
2021–22	Birmingham C	1	0	**14**	**0**

WOODS, Ryan (M) 337 4

H: 5 8 W: 13 01 b.Norton Canes 13-12-93

2012–13	Shrewsbury T	2	0		
2013–14	Shrewsbury T	41	1		
2014–15	Shrewsbury T	43	0		
2015–16	Shrewsbury T	5	0	**91**	**1**
2015–16	Brentford	41	2		
2016–17	Brentford	42	0		
2017–18	Brentford	39	1		
2018–19	Brentford	0	0	**122**	**3**
2018–19	Stoke C	27	0		
2019–20	Stoke C	8	0		
2019–20	*Millwall*	18	0		
2020–21	Stoke C	0	0	**35**	**0**
2020–21	*Millwall*	41	0	**59**	**0**
2021–22	Birmingham C	30	0	**30**	**0**

Players retained or with offer of contract

Basey, Oliver; Chang, Alfie; Khela, Brandon; Walker, Remi; Williams, Josh.

Scholars

Beresford, Benjamin Peter; Brooks, Alfie Joe; Brooks, Kobi Alexander Stewart; Browne, Rico Franklin; Carsley, Luke James; Dance, Morgan John; Fogarty, Tommy Patrick; Hamilton, Harley Farrell; Home, Josh William; Khela, Brandon; Manton, Harry James; Mayo, Bradley Paul; Oduka, Engwau Charles Jacob; Ogor, Chris; Oni, Ifeoluwa Oluseyi Daniel; Patterson, Rico Amani; Rushton, Niall George; Sullivan, Callum John; Wakefield, Kieran Lee; Williams, Pharrell Benjamin Curtis; Zohore, Yoane.

BLACKBURN R (8)

AYALA, Daniel (M) 273 25

H: 6 3 W: 13 03 b.Sevilla 7-11-90

Internationals: Spain U21.

From Sevilla.

2007–08	Liverpool	0	0		
2008–09	Liverpool	0	0		
2009–10	Liverpool	5	0		
2010–11	Liverpool	0	0	**5**	**0**
2010–11	*Hull C*	12	1	**12**	**1**
2010–11	*Derby Co*	17	0	**17**	**0**
2011–12	Norwich C	7	0		
2012–13	Norwich C	0	0		
2012–13	*Nottingham F*	12	1	**12**	**1**
2013–14	Norwich C	0	0	**7**	**0**
2013–14	Middlesbrough	19	3		
2014–15	Middlesbrough	30	4		
2015–16	Middlesbrough	35	3		
2016–17	Middlesbrough	14	1		
2017–18	Middlesbrough	33	7		
2018–19	Middlesbrough	33	1		
2019–20	Middlesbrough	25	2	**189**	**21**
2020–21	Blackburn R	10	0		
2021–22	Blackburn R	21	2	**31**	**2**

BARNES, Samuel (D) 0 0

b.Blackburn 10-3-01

2020–21	Blackburn R	0	0		
2021–22	Blackburn R	0	0		

BRENNAN, Luke (M) 1 0

b. 19-10-01

2020–21	Blackburn R	1	0		
2021–22	Blackburn R	0	0	**1**	**0**

BRERETON, Ben (F) 170 39

H: 6 1 W: 11 11 b.Stoke-on-Trent 18-4-99

Internationals: England U19, U20. Chile Full caps.

From Stoke C.

2016–17	Nottingham F	18	3		
2017–18	Nottingham F	35	5	**53**	**8**
2018–19	Blackburn R	25	1		
2019–20	Blackburn R	15	1		
2020–21	Blackburn R	40	7		
2021–22	Blackburn R	37	22	**117**	**31**

BROWN, James (D) 1 0

b.Ireland 4-6-98

From Shelbourne, Drogheda U.

2021–22	Blackburn R	1	0	**1**	**0**

BUCKLEY, John (M) 92 6

H: 5 8 W: 9 13 b.Manchester 13-10-99

2018–19	Blackburn R	2	0		
2019–20	Blackburn R	20	2		
2020–21	Blackburn R	28	1		
2021–22	Blackburn R	42	3	**92**	**6**

BURNS, Sam (F) 15 2

b. 9-8-02

2021–22	Blackburn R	0	0		
2021–22	*Scunthorpe U*	15	2	**15**	**2**

BURNS, Samuel (F) 15 12

b. 9-8-02

2020–21	Blackburn R	0	0		
2021–22	Blackburn R	0	0		
2021–22	*Scunthorpe U*	15	12	**15**	**12**

BUTTERWORTH, Daniel (F) 25 1

H: 5 11 W: 10 12 b.Manchester 14-9-94

From Manchester U.

2017–18	Blackburn R	0	0		
2018–19	Blackburn R	1	0		
2019–20	Blackburn R	0	0		
2020–21	Blackburn R	1	0		
2021–22	Blackburn R	11	0	**13**	**0**
2021–22	*Fleetwood T*	12	1	**12**	**1**

CARTER, Hayden (D) 58 5

H: 6 2 W: 10 08 b.Stockport 17-12-99

From Manchester C.

2019–20	Blackburn R	2	0		
2020–21	Blackburn R	1	0		
2020–21	*Burton Alb*	24	4	**24**	**4**
2021–22	Blackburn R	9	0	**12**	**0**
2021–22	*Portsmouth*	22	1	**22**	**1**

CHAPMAN, Harry (M) 101 11

H: 5 10 W: 11 00 b.Hartlepool 5-11-97

Internationals: England U18, U20.

2015–16	Middlesbrough	0	0		
2015–16	*Barnsley*	11	1	**11**	**1**
2016–17	Middlesbrough	0	0		
2016–17	*Sheffield U*	12	1	**12**	**1**
2017–18	Middlesbrough	0	0		
2017–18	*Blackburn R*	12	1		
2018–19	Middlesbrough	0	0		
2018–19	*Blackburn R*	2	0		
2019–20	Blackburn R	5	0		
2020–21	Blackburn R	5	0		
2020–21	*Shrewsbury T*	23	7	**23**	**7**
2021–22	Blackburn R	3	0	**27**	**1**
2021–22	*Burton Alb*	28	1	**28**	**1**

DACK, Bradley (M) **291** **77**
H: 5 9 b.Greenwich 31-12-93

2012–13	Gillingham	16	1		
2013–14	Gillingham	28	3		
2014–15	Gillingham	42	9		
2015–16	Gillingham	40	13		
2016–17	Gillingham	34	5	**160**	**31**
2017–18	Blackburn R	42	18		
2018–19	Blackburn R	42	15		
2019–20	Blackburn R	22	9		
2020–21	Blackburn R	16	3		
2021–22	Blackburn R	9	1	**131**	**46**

DAVENPORT, Jacob (M) **51** **2**
H: 5 10 W: 10 12 b.Manchester 28-12-98

2017–18	Manchester C	0	0		
2017–18	*Burton Alb*	17	1	**17**	**1**
2018–19	Blackburn R	1	0		
2019–20	Blackburn R	9	0		
2020–21	Blackburn R	15	1		
2021–22	Blackburn R	9	0	**34**	**1**

DOLAN, Tyrhys (M) **71** **7**
H: 5 7 W: 8 09 b.Manchester 28-12-98
Internationals: England U20.

2020–21	Blackburn R	37	3		
2021–22	Blackburn R	34	4	**71**	**7**

EASTHAM, Jordan (G) **0** **0**
H: 5 11 W: 10 08 b.Preston 8-9-01

2019–20	Blackburn R	0	0		
2020–21	Blackburn R	0	0		
2021–22	Blackburn R	0	0		

EDUN, Tayo (M) **79** **3**
H: 5 9 W: 9 13 b.Islington 14-5-98
Internationals: England U17, U18, U19, U20.

2016–17	Fulham	0	0		
2017–18	Fulham	2	0		
2018–19	Fulham	0	0		
2018–19	*Ipswich T*	6	1	**6**	**1**
2019–20	Fulham	0	0	**2**	**0**
2019–20	Lincoln C	6	0		
2020–21	Lincoln C	41	1		
2021–22	Lincoln C	4	1	**51**	**2**
2021–22	Blackburn R	20	0	**20**	**0**

GALLAGHER, Sam (F) **229** **41**
H: 6 4 W: 11 11 b.Crediton 15-9-95
Internationals: Scotland U19, England U19, U20.
From Plymouth Arg.

2013–14	Southampton	18	1		
2014–15	Southampton	0	0		
2015–16	Southampton	0	0		
2015–16	*Milton Keynes D*	13	0	**13**	**0**
2016–17	Southampton	0	0		
2016–17	*Blackburn R*	43	11		
2017–18	Southampton	0	0		
2017–18	*Birmingham C*	33	6	**33**	**6**
2018–19	Southampton	4	0	**22**	**1**
2019–20	Blackburn R	42	6		
2020–21	Blackburn R	39	8		
2021–22	Blackburn R	37	9	**161**	**34**

GARRETT, Jake (D) **0** **0**
b. 10-3-03
Internationals: England U16.

2020–21	Blackburn R	0	0		
2021–22	Blackburn R	0	0		

HEDGES, Ryan (M) **173** **19**
H: 6 1 W: 10 03 b.Swansea 7-9-95
Internationals: Wales U19, U21, Full caps.

2013–14	Swansea C	0	0		
2014–15	Swansea C	0	0		
2014–15	*Leyton Orient*	17	2	**17**	**2**
2015–16	Swansea C	0	0		
2015–16	*Stevenage*	6	0	**6**	**0**
2016–17	Swansea C	0	0		
2016–17	*Yeovil T*	21	4	**21**	**4**
2016–17	Barnsley	8	0		
2017–18	Barnsley	23	2		
2018–19	Barnsley	21	0	**52**	**2**
2019–20	Aberdeen	22	4		
2020–21	Aberdeen	28	5		
2021–22	Aberdeen	16	2	**66**	**11**
2021–22	Blackburn R	11	0	**11**	**0**

HILTON, Joe (G) **18** **0**
b. 11-10-99
From Manchester C.

2018–19	Everton	0	0		
2019–20	Blackburn R	0	0		
2020–21	Blackburn R	0	0		
2020–21	*Fleetwood T*	2	0	**2**	**0**
2020–21	*Ross Co*	0	0		
2021–22	Blackburn R	0	0		
2021–22	*Hamilton A*	16	0	**16**	**0**

JOHNSON, Bradley (M) **530** **68**
H: 5 10 W: 10 10 b.Hackney 28-4-87

2004–05	Cambridge U	1	0	**1**	**0**
2005–06	Northampton T	3	0		
2006–07	Northampton T	27	5		
2007–08	Northampton T	23	2	**53**	**7**
2007–08	Leeds U	21	3		
2008–09	Leeds U	15	1		
2008–09	*Brighton & HA*	10	4	**10**	**4**
2009–10	Leeds U	36	7		
2010–11	Leeds U	45	5	**117**	**16**
2011–12	Norwich C	28	2		
2012–13	Norwich C	37	1		
2013–14	Norwich C	32	3		
2014–15	Norwich C	41	15		
2015–16	Norwich C	4	0	**142**	**21**
2015–16	Derby Co	31	5		
2016–17	Derby Co	33	3		
2017–18	Derby Co	33	4		
2018–19	Derby Co	28	2	**125**	**14**
2019–20	Blackburn R	34	3		
2020–21	Blackburn R	30	3		
2021–22	Blackburn R	18	0	**82**	**6**

KAMINSKI, Thomas (G) **327** **0**
H: 6 2 W: 11 00 b.Dendermonde 23-10-92
Internationals: Belgium U16, U17, U19, U21.

2008–09	Beerschot	2	0		
2009–10	Beerschot	4	0		
2010–11	Beerschot	30	0		
2011–12	Beerschot	2	0	**38**	**0**
2011–12	OH Leuven	25	0	**25**	**0**
2012–13	Anderlecht	1	0		
2013–14	Anderlecht	10	0		
2014–15	Anderlecht	2	0		
2014–15	*Anorthosis Famagusta*	30	0	**30**	**0**
2015–16	Anderlecht	0	0	**13**	**0**
2015–16	*FC Copenhagen*	2	0	**2**	**0**
2016–17	Kortrijk	32	0		
2017–18	Kortrijk	34	0		
2018–19	Kortrijk	18	0	**84**	**0**
2018–19	Gent	19	0		
2019–20	Gent	29	0		
2020–21	Gent	0	0	**48**	**0**
2020–21	Blackburn R	43	0		
2021–22	Blackburn R	44	0	**87**	**0**

LENIHAN, Darragh (M) **250** **10**
H: 5 10 W: 12 00 b.Dublin 16-3-94
Internationals: Republic of Ireland U17, U19, U21, Full caps.

2011–12	Blackburn R	0	0		
2012–13	Blackburn R	0	0		
2013–14	Blackburn R	0	0		
2014–15	Blackburn R	3	0		
2014–15	*Burton Alb*	17	1	**17**	**1**
2015–16	Blackburn R	23	0		
2016–17	Blackburn R	40	0		
2017–18	Blackburn R	14	1		
2018–19	Blackburn R	34	2		
2019–20	Blackburn R	37	3		
2020–21	Blackburn R	41	0		
2021–22	Blackburn R	41	3	**233**	**9**

MAGLIORE, Tyler (D) **28** **0**
H: 6 1 W: 11 07 b.Bradford 21-12-98

2018–19	Blackburn R	2	0		
2019–20	Blackburn R	0	0		
2019–20	*Rochdale*	2	0	**2**	**0**
2020–21	Blackburn R	0	0		
2020–21	*Motherwell*	10	0	**10**	**0**
2021–22	Blackburn R	4	0	**6**	**0**
2021–22	*Northampton T*	10	0	**10**	**0**

MARKANDAY, Dilan (M) **2** **0**
H: 5 10 W: 10 01 b.Barnet 20-8-01

2020–21	Tottenham H	0	0		
2021–22	Tottenham H	0	0		
2021–22	Blackburn R	2	0	**2**	**0**

McBRIDE, Connor (F) **0** **0**
H: 6 2 b.Falkirk 20-3-01
Internationals: Scotland U17.
From Falkirk, Celtic.

2020–21	Blackburn R	0	0		
2021–22	Blackburn R	0	0		
2021–22	*Queen's Park*	0	0		

NOLAN, Joseph (M) **0** **0**
b. 25-3-02

2020–21	Blackburn R	0	0		
2021–22	Blackburn R	0	0		

NYAMBE, Ryan (D) **183** **0**
H: 6 0 W: 12 00 b.Katima Mulilo 4-12-97
Internationals: Namibia Full caps.

2014–15	Blackburn R	0	0		
2015–16	Blackburn R	0	0		
2016–17	Blackburn R	25	0		
2017–18	Blackburn R	29	0		
2018–19	Blackburn R	29	0		
2019–20	Blackburn R	31	0		
2020–21	Blackburn R	38	0		
2021–22	Blackburn R	31	0	**183**	**0**

PEARS, Aynsley (G) **30** **0**
H: 6 1 W: 12 08 b.Durham 23-4-98
Internationals: England U19.

2017–18	Middlesbrough	0	0		
2018–19	Middlesbrough	0	0		
2019–20	Middlesbrough	24	0	**24**	**0**
2020–21	Blackburn R	3	0		
2021–22	Blackburn R	3	0	**6**	**0**

PICKERING, Harry (D) **178** **11**
H: 6 1 W: 12 04 b.Chester 29-12-98

2017–18	Crewe Alex	35	3		
2018–19	Crewe Alex	32	0		
2019–20	Crewe Alex	35	3		
2020–21	Blackburn R	0	0		
2020–21	*Crewe Alex*	44	3	**146**	**9**
2021–22	Blackburn R	32	2	**32**	**2**

PIKE, Dan (D) **0** **0**
b.Liverpool 9-1-02

2020–21	Blackburn R	0	0		
2021–22	Blackburn R	0	0		

RANKIN-COSTELLO, Joe (M) **35** **0**
H: 5 10 W: 11 00 b.Stockport 26-7-99
From Manchester U.

2017–18	Blackburn R	0	0		
2018–19	Blackburn R	0	0		
2019–20	Blackburn R	11	0		
2020–21	Blackburn R	14	0		
2021–22	Blackburn R	10	0	**35**	**0**

ROTHWELL, Joe (M) **225** **16**
H: 6 1 W: 12 02 b.Manchester 11-1-95
Internationals: England U16, U17, U19, U20.

2014–15	Manchester U	0	0		
2014–15	*Blackpool*	3	0	**3**	**0**
2015–16	Manchester U	0	0		
2015–16	*Barnsley*	4	0	**4**	**0**
2016–17	Oxford U	33	1		
2017–18	Oxford U	36	5	**69**	**6**
2018–19	Blackburn R	33	2		
2019–20	Blackburn R	36	2		
2020–21	Blackburn R	39	3		
2021–22	Blackburn R	41	3	**149**	**10**

SAADI, Jalil (M) **0** **0**
H: 6 3 b. 3-11-01
From Toulouse.

2020–21	Blackburn R	0	0		
2021–22	Blackburn R	0	0		

STERGIAKIS, Antonios (G) **61** **0**
H: 6 5 W: 12 12 b.Thessaloniki 16-3-99
Internationals: Greece U17, U19, U21.
From Thyella Filota.

2015–16	Slavia Sofia	0	0		
2016–17	Slavia Sofia	8	0		
2017–18	Slavia Sofia	22	0		
2018–19	Slavia Sofia	17	0		
2019–20	Slavia Sofia	14	0		
2020–21	Slavia Sofia	0	0	**61**	**0**
2020–21	Blackburn R	0	0		
2021–22	Blackburn R	0	0		

TRAVIS, Lewis (D) **138** **4**
H: 6 0 W: 13 01 b.Whiston 16-10-97

2016–17	Blackburn R	0	0		
2017–18	Blackburn R	5	0		
2018–19	Blackburn R	26	1		
2019–20	Blackburn R	43	2		
2020–21	Blackburn R	19	0		
2021–22	Blackburn R	45	1	**138**	**4**

VALE, Jack (F) **6** **0**
b. 3-3-01
Internationals: Wales U17, U19, U21.
From The New Saints.

2019–20	Blackburn R	1	0		
2020–21	Blackburn R	0	0		
2020–21	*Rochdale*	3	0	**3**	**0**
2021–22	Blackburn R	2	0	**3**	**0**

WHARTON, Scott (D) **120** **11**
H: 6 0 W: 11 11 b.Blackburn 3-10-97

2015–16	Blackburn R	0	0		
2016–17	Blackburn R	2	0		
2016–17	*Cambridge U*	9	1	**9**	**1**
2017–18	Blackburn R	0	0		
2017–18	*Lincoln C*	14	2		
2018–19	Blackburn R	0	0		
2018–19	*Lincoln C*	11	1	**25**	**3**
2018–19	*Bury*	15	2	**15**	**2**
2019–20	Blackburn R	0	0		
2019–20	*Northampton T*	32	3	**32**	**3**
2020–21	Blackburn R	7	0		
2021–22	Blackburn R	30	2	**39**	**2**

WHITEHALL, Isaac (M) **0** **0**
b. 29-3-02

2020–21	Blackburn R	0	0		
2021–22	Blackburn R	0	0		

ZEEFUIK, Deyovaisio (D) **116** **2**
H: 6 1 W: 13 05 b.Amsterdam 11-3-98
Internationals: Netherlands U17, U18, U19.

2016–17	Ajax	1	0		
2017–18	Ajax	5	0	**6**	**0**
2017–18	Groningen	13	0		
2018–19	Groningen	32	1		
2019–20	Groningen	26	0	**71**	**1**
2020–21	Hertha Berlin	22	1		
2021–22	Hertha Berlin	11	0	**33**	**1**
2021–22	*Blackburn R*	6	0	**6**	**0**

Players retained or with offer of contract
Baker, Alexander; Cirino, Lenni Rae; Dowling, Aidan; Gent, Georgie; Gilsenan, Zak; Harlock, Jared; Leonard, Harry; Phillips, Ashley; Wharton, Adam.

Scholars
Batty, Jake Thomas; Biniek, Dominik Andrzej; Blease, William Edward; Caddick, Adam Graham; Chmiel, George Samuel; Cunningham, Evan William; Duru, Leonard Chibueze; Ferguson, Joseph Martua; Fyles, Ben William; Gamble, Patrick; Goddard, Felix Benjamin; Haddow, Jay; Lonsdale, Brandon Lee James; Montgomery, Kristi Julian; O'Grady Macken, Harley Paul; Olson, Charles Kamel; Phillips, Ashley; Pratt, George Christopher John; Weston, Charlie Daniel; Wilson, Ryan David; Wood, Harrison Jack.

BLACKPOOL (9)

ANDERSON, Keshi (F) 178 28
H: 5 9 W: 10 10 b.Luton 15-11-95
2014–15 Crystal Palace 0 0
2015–16 Crystal Palace 0 0
2015–16 *Doncaster R* 7 3 7 3
2016–17 Crystal Palace 0 0
2016–17 *Bolton W* 8 1 8 1
2016–17 *Northampton T* 14 3 14 3
2017–18 Swindon T 37 5
2018–19 Swindon T 43 4
2019–20 Swindon T 20 6 100 15
2020–21 Blackpool 17 2
2021–22 Blackpool 32 4 49 6

ANTWI, Cameron (M) 0 0
H: 5 10 W: 9 13 b.Sutton 7-10-01
From Fulham.
2020–21 Blackpool 0 0
2021–22 Blackpool 0 0

APTER, Robert (M) 1 0
b. 16-1-03
Internationals: Scotland U19.
2020–21 Blackpool 1 0
2021–22 Blackpool 0 0 1 0

BANGE, Ewan (M) 0 0
2019–20 Blackpool 0 0
2020–21 Blackpool 0 0
2021–22 Blackpool 0 0

BEESLEY, Jake (F) 68 19
H: 6 1 W: 10 08 b.Sheffield 2-12-96
2013–14 Chesterfield 0 0
2014–15 Chesterfield 0 0
2015–16 Chesterfield 0 0
2016–17 Chesterfield 7 0 7 0
From Chesterfield.
2019–20 Salford C 7 2 7 2
2020–21 Solihull Moors 0 0
2020–21 Rochdale 27 6
2021–22 Rochdale 21 9 48 15
2021–22 Blackpool 6 2 6 2

BOWLER, Josh (M) 71 8
H: 5 9 b.Chertsey 5-3-99
2016–17 QPR 1 0 1 0
2017–18 Everton 0 0
2018–19 Everton 0 0
2019–20 Everton 0 0
2019–20 *Hull C* 28 1 28 1
2021–22 Blackpool 42 7 42 7

CAREY, Sonny (M) 11 1
H: 6 0 W: 11 07 b.Norwich 20-1-01
From King's Lynn T.
2021–22 Blackpool 11 1 11 1

CASEY, Oliver (D) 7 1
H: 6 2 W: 12 06 b.Leeds 14-10-00
2019–20 Leeds U 1 0
2020–21 Leeds U 0 0
2021–22 Leeds U 0 0 1 0
2021–22 Blackpool 6 1 6 1

CONNOLLY, Callum (D) 183 15
H: 6 1 W: 11 00 b.Liverpool 23-9-97
Internationals: England U17, U18, U19, U20, U21.
2015–16 Everton 1 0
2015–16 *Barnsley* 3 0 3 0
2016–17 Everton 0 0
2016–17 *Wigan Ath* 17 2
2017–18 Everton 0 0
2017–18 *Ipswich T* 34 4 34 4
2018–19 Everton 0 0
2018–19 *Wigan Ath* 17 1 34 3
2018–19 *Bolton W* 16 2 16 2
2019–20 Everton 0 0
2019–20 *Lincoln C* 11 0 11 0
2019–20 *Fleetwood T* 13 2
2020–21 Everton 0 0 1 0
2020–21 *Fleetwood T* 40 2 53 4
2021–22 Blackpool 31 2 31 2

DALE, Owen (F) 107 14
H: 5 9 W: 10 03 b.Warrington 1-11-98
2016–17 Crewe Alex 0 0
2017–18 Crewe Alex 4 0
2018–19 Crewe Alex 16 1
2019–20 Crewe Alex 27 0
2020–21 Crewe Alex 43 11
2021–22 Crewe Alex 2 0 92 12
2021–22 Blackpool 15 2 15 2

DANIELS, Jake (F) 1 0
b.Blackpool 8-1-05
2021–22 Blackpool 1 0 1 0

DOUGALL, Kenneth (M) 257 15
H: 6 0 W: 12 06 b.Brisbane 7-5-93
Internationals: Australia U23, Full caps.
2013–14 Brisbane C 34 10 34 10
2014–15 Telstar 29 1 29 1
2015–16 Sparta Rotterdam 32 0
2016–17 Sparta Rotterdam 20 1
2017–18 Sparta Rotterdam 29 1 81 2
2018–19 Barnsley 27 0
2019–20 Barnsley 12 0 39 0
2020–21 Blackpool 34 1
2021–22 Blackpool 40 1 74 2

EKPITETA, Marvin (D) 95 7
H: 6 4 W: 13 05 b.Enfield 26-8-95
Internationals: Nigeria U20. England C.
From Chelmsford C, Concord Rangers, East Thurrock U.
2019–20 Leyton Orient 27 0 27 0
2020–21 Blackpool 28 2
2021–22 Blackpool 40 5 68 7

GARBUTT, Luke (D) 192 18
H: 5 10 W: 11 07 b.Harrogate 21-5-93
Internationals: England U16, U17, U18, U19, U20, U21.
From Leeds U.
2010–11 Everton 0 0
2011–12 Everton 0 0
2011–12 *Cheltenham T* 34 2 34 2
2012–13 Everton 0 0
2013–14 Everton 1 0
2013–14 *Colchester U* 19 2 19 2
2014–15 Everton 4 0
2015–16 Everton 0 0
2015–16 *Fulham* 25 1 25 1
2016–17 Everton 0 0
2016–17 *Wigan Ath* 8 0 8 0
2017–18 Everton 0 0
2018–19 Everton 0 0
2018–19 *Oxford U* 25 4 25 4
2019–20 Everton 0 0 5 0
2019–20 *Ipswich T* 28 5 28 5
2020–21 Blackpool 31 4
2021–22 Blackpool 17 0 48 4

GRETARSSON, Daniel (D) 169 10
H: 6 1 W: 12 00 b.Keflavik 2-10-95
Internationals: Iceland U19, U21, Full caps.
2012 Grindavik 6 1
2013 Grindavik 21 3
2014 Grindavik 22 1 49 5
2015 Aalesund 8 0
2016 Aalesund 12 0
2017 Aalesund 27 1
2018 Aalesund 15 1
2019 Aalesund 29 3
2020 Aalesund 14 0
2020–21 Aalesund 0 0 105 5
2020–21 Blackpool 12 0
2021–22 Blackpool 3 0 15 0
Transferred to Slask Wroclaw, January 2022.

GRIMSHAW, Daniel (G) 36 0
H: 6 1 W: 12 02 b.Manchester 16-1-98
2018–19 Manchester C 0 0
2019–20 Manchester C 0 0
2020–21 Manchester C 0 0
2020–21 *Lommel* 10 0 10 0
2021–22 Blackpool 26 0 26 0

HAMILTON, CJ (M) 188 22
H: 5 7 W: 11 09 b.Harrow 23-3-95
Internationals: Republic of Ireland Full caps.
2015–16 Sheffield U 0 0
2016–17 Mansfield T 29 0
2017–18 Mansfield T 33 2
2018–19 Mansfield T 46 11
2019–20 Mansfield T 34 2 142 15
2019–20 Blackpool 0 0
2020–21 Blackpool 22 5
2021–22 Blackpool 24 2 46 7

HOLMES, Bradley (F) 5 0
b.Blackpool 16-12-02
From Bolton W.
2020–21 Blackpool 5 0
2021–22 Blackpool 0 0 5 0

HUSBAND, James (D) 234 6
H: 5 11 W: 10 02 b.Leeds 3-1-94
2011–12 Doncaster R 3 0
2012–13 Doncaster R 33 3
2013–14 Doncaster R 28 1 64 4
2014–15 Middlesbrough 3 0
2014–15 *Fulham* 5 0
2015–16 Middlesbrough 0 0
2015–16 *Fulham* 12 0 17 0
2015–16 *Huddersfield T* 11 0 11 0
2016–17 Middlesbrough 1 0 4 0
2017–18 Norwich C 18 0
2018–19 Norwich C 1 0 19 0
2018–19 *Fleetwood T* 33 1 33 1
2019–20 Blackpool 28 0
2020–21 Blackpool 27 0
2021–22 Blackpool 31 1 86 1

JAMES, Reece (D) 176 11
H: 5 6 W: 11 03 b.Bacup 7-11-93
2012–13 Manchester U 0 0
2013–14 Manchester U 0 0
2013–14 *Carlisle U* 1 0 1 0
2014–15 Manchester U 0 0
2014–15 *Rotherham U* 7 0 7 0
2014–15 *Huddersfield T* 6 1 6 1
2015–16 Wigan Ath 26 1
2016–17 Wigan Ath 0 0
2017–18 Wigan Ath 22 0 48 1
2018–19 Sunderland 27 0 27 0
2019–20 Doncaster R 27 2
2020–21 Doncaster R 43 7
2021–22 Doncaster R 0 0 70 9
2021–22 Blackpool 17 0 17 0

KEOGH, Richard (D) 617 19
H: 6 2 W: 13 10 b.Harlow 11-8-86
Internationals: Republic of Ireland U21, Full caps.
2004–05 Stoke C 0 0
2005–06 Bristol C 9 1
2005–06 *Wycombe W* 3 0 3 0
2006–07 Bristol C 31 2
2007–08 Bristol C 0 0 40 3
2007–08 *Huddersfield T* 9 1
2007–08 *Carlisle U* 7 0
2007–08 *Cheltenham T* 10 0 10 0
2008–09 Carlisle U 32 1
2009–10 Carlisle U 41 3 80 4
2010–11 Coventry C 46 1
2011–12 Coventry C 45 0 91 1
2012–13 Derby Co 46 4
2013–14 Derby Co 41 1
2014–15 Derby Co 45 0
2015–16 Derby Co 46 1
2016–17 Derby Co 42 0
2017–18 Derby Co 42 1
2018–19 Derby Co 46 3
2019–20 Derby Co 8 0 316 10
2020–21 Milton Keynes D 18 0 18 0
2020–21 Huddersfield T 21 0
2021–22 Huddersfield T 0 0 30 1
2021–22 Blackpool 29 0 29 0

LAVERY, Shayne (F) 99 41
H: 6 0 W: 11 07 b.Aghagallon 8-12-98
Internationals: Northern Ireland U17, U19, U21, Full caps.
From Glenavon.
2017–18 Everton 0 0
2018–19 Everton 0 0
2018–19 *Falkirk* 6 0 6 0
2019–20 Linfield 25 10
2020–21 Linfield 31 23 56 33
2021–22 Blackpool 37 8 37 8

LAWRENCE-GABRIEL, Jordan (D) 62 0
H: 5 10 W: 10 12 b.London 25-9-98
From Southend U.
2019–20 Nottingham F 0 0
2019–20 *Scunthorpe U* 9 0 9 0
2020–21 Nottingham F 1 0
2020–21 *Blackpool* 27 0
2021–22 Nottingham F 4 0 5 0
2021–22 Blackpool 21 0 48 0

LUBULA, Beryly (F) 64 12
H: 5 10 W: 12 00 b.DR Congo 8-1-98
2017–18 Birmingham C 1 0
2018–19 Birmingham C 3 0 4 0
2019–20 Crawley T 34 12 34 12
2020–21 Blackpool 12 0
2021–22 Blackpool 0 0 12 0
2021–22 *Northampton T* 14 0 14 0

MADINE, Gary (F) 417 89
H: 6 3 W: 11 11 b.Gateshead 24-8-90
2007–08 Carlisle U 11 0
2008–09 Carlisle U 14 1
2008–09 *Rochdale* 3 0 3 0
2009–10 Carlisle U 20 4
2009–10 *Coventry C* 9 0
2009–10 *Chesterfield* 4 0 4 0
2010–11 Carlisle U 21 8
2010–11 Sheffield W 22 5
2011–12 Sheffield W 38 18
2012–13 Sheffield W 30 3
2013–14 Sheffield W 1 0
2013–14 *Carlisle U* 5 2 71 15
2014–15 Sheffield W 10 0 101 26
2014–15 *Coventry C* 11 3 20 3
2014–15 *Blackpool* 15 3
2015–16 Bolton W 32 5
2016–17 Bolton W 36 9
2017–18 Bolton W 28 10 96 24
2017–18 Cardiff C 13 0
2018–19 Cardiff C 5 0
2018–19 *Sheffield U* 16 3 16 3
2019–20 Cardiff C 8 0 26 0

2019–20	Blackpool	10	2		
2020–21	Blackpool	21	4		
2021–22	Blackpool	34	9	**80**	**18**

MARIETTE, Luke (M) **1** **0**
b.Denbigh 8-10-03
Internationals: Wales U18.

2020–21	Blackpool	0	0		
2021–22	Blackpool	1	0	**1**	**0**

MAXWELL, Chris (G) **271** **0**
H: 6 1 W: 11 07 b.St Asaph 30-7-90
Internationals: Wales U17, U19, U21, U23.
From Wrexham.

2012–13	Fleetwood T	0	0		
2013–14	Fleetwood T	18	0		
2014–15	Fleetwood T	46	0		
2015–16	Fleetwood T	46	0	**110**	**0**
2016–17	Preston NE	38	0		
2017–18	Preston NE	30	0		
2018–19	Preston NE	8	0		
2018–19	*Charlton Ath*	0	0		
2019–20	Preston NE	0	0	**76**	**0**
2019–20	*Hibernian*	12	0	**12**	**0**
2019–20	Blackpool	9	0		
2020–21	Blackpool	43	0		
2021–22	Blackpool	21	0	**73**	**0**

MITCHELL, Demetri (M) **75** **1**
H: 5 9 W: 11 11 b.Manchester 11-1-97
Internationals: England U16, U17, U18, U20.

2016–17	Manchester U	1	0		
2017–18	Manchester U	0	0		
2017–18	*Hearts*	9	0		
2018–19	Manchester U	0	0		
2018–19	*Hearts*	20	0	**29**	**0**
2019–20	Manchester U	0	0	**1**	**0**
2020–21	Blackpool	32	1		
2021–22	Blackpool	13	0	**45**	**1**

Transferred to Hearts, January 2022.

MONKS, Charles (G) **0** **0**
b.Preston 10-1-03

2020–21	Blackpool	0	0		
2021–22	Blackpool	0	0		

MOORE, Stuart (G) **30** **0**
H: 6 2 W: 11 05 b.Sandown 8-9-94

2013–14	Reading	0	0		
2014–15	Reading	0	0		
2015–16	Reading	0	0		
2015–16	*Peterborough U*	4	0	**4**	**0**
2016–17	Reading	0	0		
2016–17	*Luton T*	8	0	**8**	**0**
2017–18	Swindon T	10	0	**10**	**0**
2018–19	Milton Keynes D	6	0		
2019–20	Milton Keynes D	0	0	**6**	**0**
2020–21	Blackpool	1	0		
2021–22	Blackpool	1	0	**2**	**0**

ROBSON, Ethan (M) **86** **6**
H: 5 11 W: 10 10 b.Durham 25-10-96

2016–17	Sunderland	0	0		
2017–18	Sunderland	9	0		
2018–19	Sunderland	0	0		
2018–19	*Dundee*	13	2	**13**	**2**
2019–20	Sunderland	0	0	**9**	**0**
2019–20	*Grimsby T*	16	3	**16**	**3**
2020–21	Blackpool	28	0		
2021–22	Blackpool	2	0	**30**	**0**
2021–22	*Milton Keynes D*	18	1	**18**	**1**

STEWART, Kevin (M) **127** **6**
H: 5 11 W: 11 07 b.Enfield 7-9-93
Internationals: Jamaica Full caps.

2012–13	Tottenham H	0	0		
2012–13	*Crewe Alex*	4	0		
2013–14	Crewe Alex	0	0	**4**	**0**
2014–15	Liverpool	0	0		
2014–15	*Cheltenham T*	4	1	**4**	**1**
2014–15	*Burton Alb*	7	2	**7**	**2**
2015–16	Liverpool	7	0		
2015–16	*Swindon T*	5	0	**5**	**0**
2016–17	Liverpool	4	0	**11**	**0**
2017–18	Hull C	17	0		
2018–19	Hull C	27	0		
2019–20	Hull C	27	3	**71**	**3**
2020–21	Blackpool	13	0		
2021–22	Blackpool	12	0	**25**	**0**

STRAWN, Joe (M) **0** **0**
b.Blackpool 25-9-03

2021–22	Blackpool	0	0		

THORNILEY, Jordan (D) **101** **0**
H: 5 11 W: 10 01 b.Warrington 24-11-96
From Everton.

2016–17	Sheffield W	0	0		
2017–18	Sheffield W	11	0		
2017–18	*Accrington S*	14	0	**14**	**0**
2018–19	Sheffield W	20	0		
2019–20	Sheffield W	0	0	**31**	**0**
2019–20	Blackpool	2	0		
2020–21	Blackpool	19	0		
2021–22	Oxford U	21	0	**21**	**0**
2021–22	Blackpool	14	0	**35**	**0**

VIRTUE, Matthew (M) **69** **7**
b.Epsom 2-5-97

2017–18	Liverpool	0	0		
2017–18	*Notts Co*	13	0	**13**	**0**
2018–19	Blackpool	13	3		
2019–20	Blackpool	24	2		
2020–21	Blackpool	16	2		
2021–22	Blackpool	3	0	**56**	**7**

WARD, Grant (M) **213** **12**
H: 5 10 W: 11 07 b.Lewisham 5-12-94

2013–14	Tottenham H	0	0		
2014	*Chicago Fire*	23	1	**23**	**1**
2014–15	Tottenham H	0	0		
2014–15	*Coventry C*	11	0	**11**	**0**
2015–16	Tottenham H	0	0		
2015–16	*Rotherham U*	40	2	**40**	**2**
2016–17	Ipswich T	43	6		
2017–18	Ipswich T	37	2		
2018–19	Ipswich T	14	0	**94**	**8**
2019–20	Blackpool	5	0		
2020–21	Blackpool	36	1		
2021–22	Blackpool	4	0	**45**	**1**

YATES, Jerry (F) **184** **49**
H: 5 9 W: 10 10 b.Doncaster 10-11-96

2014–15	Rotherham U	1	0		
2015–16	Rotherham U	0	0		
2016–17	Rotherham U	21	1		
2017–18	Rotherham U	17	1		
2018–19	Carlisle U	23	6	**23**	**6**
2018–19	Rotherham U	7	0		
2019–20	Rotherham U	1	0	**47**	**2**
2019–20	*Swindon T*	31	13	**31**	**13**
2020–21	Blackpool	44	20		
2021–22	Blackpool	39	8	**83**	**28**

Players retained or with offer of contract
Moore, Jack; Tharme, Douglas; Trusty, Tayt-Lemar.

Scholars
Abdiu, Kron; Bjork, Bobby; Byron, Luke Francis; Cunningham, Archie Gary; Donkor, Kwaku Poku Agyeman; Fitzgerald, Michael Stephen; Francis, Dannen Letaj; Harrison, James; Littler, Zack; Matshazi, Arnold Tawanda; McLachlan, Alexander James Chree; Nyame, Joshua Nathaniel Kwaku; Sinclair, Kobe; Squires, William Joseph; Strawn, Joseph Michael; Yelegon, Prince Junior.

BOLTON W (10)

AFOLAYAN, Oladapo (F) **81** **14**
H: 5 11 W: 11 07 b.Westminster 11-9-97
Internationals: England C.
From Solihull Moors.

2018–19	West Ham U	0	0		
2018–19	*Oldham Ath*	10	0	**10**	**0**
2019–20	West Ham U	0	0		
2019–20	*Mansfield T*	6	1	**6**	**1**
2020–21	West Ham U	0	0		
2020–21	Bolton W	21	1		
2021–22	Bolton W	44	12	**65**	**13**

AIMSON, Will (D) **159** **7**
H: 5 10 W: 11 00 b.Christchurch 1-1-94
From Eastleigh.

2013–14	Hull C	0	0		
2014–15	Hull C	0	0		
2014–15	*Tranmere R*	2	0	**2**	**0**
2015–16	Hull C	0	0		
2015–16	Blackpool	15	0		
2016–17	Blackpool	18	0		
2017–18	Blackpool	17	0	**50**	**0**
2018–19	Bury	37	4	**37**	**4**
2019–20	Plymouth Arg	5	2		
2020–21	Plymouth Arg	40	0	**45**	**2**
2021–22	Bolton W	25	1	**25**	**1**

ALEXANDER, Matthew (G) **1** **0**

2019–20	Bolton W	1	0		
2020–21	Bolton W	0	0		
2021–22	Bolton W	0	0	**1**	**0**

AMAECHI, Xavier (M) **20** **1**
H: 5 10 W: 11 11 b.Bath 5-1-01
Internationals: England U16, U17, U19, U20.
From Arsenal.

2019–20	Hamburger	2	0		
2020–21	Hamburger	1	0		
2020–21	*Karlsruher*	7	0	**7**	**0**
2021–22	Hamburger	0	0	**3**	**0**
2021–22	*Bolton W*	10	1	**10**	**1**

BAKAYOKO, Amadou (F) **193** **30**
H: 6 4 W: 13 05 b.Kenema 1-1-96
Internationals: Sierra Leone Full caps.

2013–14	Walsall	6	0		
2014–15	Walsall	7	0		
2015–16	Walsall	0	0		
2016–17	Walsall	39	4		
2017–18	Walsall	41	5	**93**	**9**
2018–19	Coventry C	31	7		
2019–20	Coventry C	23	4		
2020–21	Coventry C	14	0	**68**	**11**
2021–22	Bolton W	32	10	**32**	**10**

BAPTISTE, Alex (D) **536** **25**
H: 5 11 W: 11 09 b.Sutton-in-Ashfield 31-1-86

2002–03	Mansfield T	4	0		
2003–04	Mansfield T	17	0		
2004–05	Mansfield T	41	1		
2005–06	Mansfield T	41	1		
2006–07	Mansfield T	46	3		
2007–08	Mansfield T	25	0	**174**	**5**
2008–09	Blackpool	21	1		
2009–10	Blackpool	42	3		
2010–11	Blackpool	21	2		
2011–12	Blackpool	43	1		
2012–13	Blackpool	43	1	**170**	**8**
2013–14	Bolton W	39	4		
2014–15	Bolton W	0	0		
2014–15	*Blackburn R*	32	3	**32**	**3**
2015–16	Middlesbrough	0	0		
2015–16	*Sheffield U*	11	1	**11**	**1**
2016–17	Middlesbrough	0	0		
2016–17	*Preston NE*	24	3	**24**	**3**
2017–18	QPR	26	0		
2018–19	QPR	4	0	**30**	**0**
2018–19	*Luton T*	2	0	**2**	**0**
2019–20	Doncaster R	2	0	**2**	**0**
2020–21	Bolton W	40	0		
2021–22	Bolton W	12	1	**91**	**5**

BODVARSSON, Jon Dadi (F) **361** **64**
H: 6 3 W: 13 05 b.Selfoss 25-5-92
Internationals: Iceland U19, U21, Full caps.

2008	Selfoss	0	0		
2009	Selfoss	16	1		
2010	Selfoss	21	3		
2011	Selfoss	21	7		
2012	Selfoss	22	7	**80**	**18**
2013	Viking	23	1		
2014	Viking	29	5		
2015	Viking	29	9	**81**	**15**
2015–16	Kaiserslautern	15	2	**15**	**2**
2016–17	Wolverhampton W	42	3	**42**	**3**
2017–18	Reading	33	7		
2018–19	Reading	20	7	**53**	**14**
2019–20	Millwall	31	4		
2020–21	Millwall	38	1		
2021–22	Millwall	0	0	**69**	**5**
2021–22	Bolton W	21	7	**21**	**7**

BROCKBANK, Harry (D) **31** **0**
H: 5 11 W: 12 08 b.Bolton 26-9-98

2017–18	Bolton W	0	0		
2018–19	Bolton W	3	0		
2019–20	Bolton W	6	0		
2020–21	Bolton W	18	0		
2021–22	Bolton W	4	0	**31**	**0**

Transferred to El Paso Locomotive, January 2022.

CHARLES, Dion (F) **104** **35**
H: 5 10 W: 10 08 b.Preston 7-10-95
Internationals: Northern Ireland U21, Full caps.

2013–14	Blackpool	0	0		

From AFC Fylde.

2016–17	Fleetwood T	0	0		

From Southport.

2019–20	Accrington S	33	8		
2020–21	Accrington S	42	19		
2021–22	Accrington S	6	0	**81**	**27**
2021–22	Bolton W	23	8	**23**	**8**

COMLEY, Brandon (M) **132** **2**
H: 5 11 W: 11 05 b.Islington 18-11-95
Internationals: Montserrat Full caps.

2014–15	QPR	1	0		
2015–16	QPR	0	0		
2015–16	*Carlisle U*	12	0	**12**	**0**
2016–17	QPR	1	0	**2**	**0**
2016–17	*Grimsby T*	33	0		
2017–18	Grimsby T	0	0	**33**	**0**
2017–18	Colchester U	38	1		
2018–19	Colchester U	13	0		
2019–20	Colchester U	24	1	**75**	**2**
2020–21	Bolton W	10	0		
2021–22	Bolton W	0	0	**10**	**0**

Transferred to Prescott Cables, December 2021.

CONWAY, Max (M) **0** **0**
b.Manchester 5-9-03

2020–21	Bolton W	0	0		
2021–22	Bolton W	0	0		

DARCY, Ronan (F) **29** **1**
H: 5 9 W: 9 06 b.Ormskirk 4-11-00

2018–19	Bolton W	1	0		
2019–20	Bolton W	19	1		
2020–21	Bolton W	8	0		
2021–22	Bolton W	1	0	**29**	**1**
2021–22	*Sogndal*	0	0		
2021–22	*Queen's Park*	0	0		

DEMPSEY, Kyle (M) **269** **25**
H: 5 10 W: 11 11 b.Whitehaven 17-9-95

2013–14	Carlisle U	4	0		
2014–15	Carlisle U	43	10	**47**	**10**
2015–16	Huddersfield T	21	1		
2016–17	Huddersfield T	0	0	**21**	**1**

2016–17 *Fleetwood T* 38 2
2017–18 Fleetwood T 45 1
2018–19 Fleetwood T 14 0
2018–19 *Peterborough U* 11 0 **11 0**
2019–20 Fleetwood T 21 2 **118 5**
2020–21 Gillingham 40 8
2021–22 Gillingham 21 1 **61 9**
2021–22 Bolton W 11 0 **11 0**

DIXON, Joel (G) 69 0
H: 6 4 W: 12 00 b.Middlesbrough 9-12-93
2012–13 Sunderland 0 0
2013–14 Sunderland 0 0
From Barrow.
2020–21 Barrow 46 0 **46 0**
2021–22 Bolton W 23 0 **23 0**

DOYLE, Eoin (F) 473 163
H: 6 0 W: 11 07 b.Tallaght 12-3-88
2008 Shamrock R 30 5
2009 Shamrock R 2 0 **32 5**
2009 Sligo 15 3
2010 Sligo 35 6
2011 Sligo 34 20 **84 29**
2011–12 Hibernian 13 1
2012–13 Hibernian 36 10 **49 11**
2013–14 Chesterfield 43 11
2014–15 Chesterfield 26 21 **69 32**
2014–15 Cardiff C 16 5
2015–16 Cardiff C 0 0 **16 5**
2015–16 *Preston NE* 28 4
2016–17 Preston NE 11 1
2016–17 *Portsmouth* 12 2 **12 2**
2017–18 Preston NE 0 0 **39 5**
2017–18 *Oldham Ath* 30 14 **30 14**
2018–19 Bradford C 44 11
2019–20 Bradford C 6 0 **50 11**
2019–20 Swindon T 28 25 **28 25**
2020–21 Bolton W 43 19
2021–22 Bolton W 21 5 **64 24**
Transferred to St Patricks Ath, January 2022.

EDWARDS, Liam (D) 6 0
H: 6 3 W: 12 08 b.Crewe 2-10-96
From Stoke C.
2018–19 Birmingham C 0 0
2019–20 Bolton W 6 0
2020–21 Bolton W 0 0
2021–22 Bolton W 0 0 **6 0**

FITZMARTIN, Jay (M) 0 0
2019–20 Bolton W 0 0
2020–21 Bolton W 0 0
2021–22 Bolton W 0 0

GILKS, Matthew (G) 471 0
H: 6 1 W: 12 10 b.Rochdale 4-6-82
Internationals: Scotland Full caps.
2000–01 Rochdale 3 0
2001–02 Rochdale 19 0
2002–03 Rochdale 20 0
2003–04 Rochdale 12 0
2004–05 Rochdale 30 0
2005–06 Rochdale 46 0
2006–07 Rochdale 46 0 **176 0**
2007–08 Norwich C 0 0
2008–09 Blackpool 5 0
2008–09 *Shrewsbury T* 4 0 **4 0**
2009–10 Blackpool 26 0
2010–11 Blackpool 18 0
2011–12 Blackpool 42 0
2012–13 Blackpool 45 0
2013–14 Blackpool 46 0 **182 0**
2014–15 Burnley 0 0
2015–16 Burnley 0 0
2016–17 Rangers 0 0
2016–17 Wigan Ath 14 0 **14 0**
2017–18 Scunthorpe U 42 0
2018–19 Scunthorpe U 0 0 **42 0**
2018–19 Lincoln C 12 0 **12 0**
2019–20 Fleetwood T 5 0 **5 0**
2020–21 Bolton W 35 0
2021–22 Bolton W 1 0 **36 0**

GORDON, Liam (D) 23 0
H: 6 0 W: 12 00 b.Croyden 15-5-99
Internationals: Guyana Full caps.
From Dagenham & R.
2020–21 Bolton W 10 0
2021–22 Bolton W 13 0 **23 0**

GREENIDGE, Reiss (D) 43 2
b. 10-8-96
Internationals: Guyana Full caps.
2014–15 WBA 0 0
2014–15 *Port Vale* 0 0
From Ebbsfleet U.
2017 Sogndal 10 1
2018 Sogndal 9 0
2019 Sogndal 0 0
2019 *Arendal* 19 1 **19 1**
2020 Sogndal 0 0 **19 1**
2020 *Arandal* 0 0
2020–21 Bolton W 5 0
2021–22 Bolton W 0 0 **5 0**

HENRY, Mitchell (M) 0 0
b.Salford 2-9-03
2020–21 Bolton W 0 0
2021–22 Bolton W 0 0

HURFORD-LOCKETT, Finlay (M) 3 0
b. 10-4-03
2019–20 Bolton W 2 0
2020–21 Bolton W 1 0
2021–22 Bolton W 0 0 **3 0**

HUTCHINSON, Luke (G) 0 0
H: 6 1 b.Bury 1-9-02
2019–20 Bolton W 0 0
2020–21 Bolton W 0 0
2021–22 Bolton W 0 0

ISGROVE, Lloyd (M) 141 5
H: 5 10 W: 11 05 b.Yeovil 12-1-93
Internationals: Wales U21, Full caps.
2011–12 Southampton 0 0
2012–13 Southampton 0 0
2013–14 Southampton 0 0
2013–14 *Peterborough U* 8 1 **8 1**
2014–15 Southampton 1 0
2014–15 *Sheffield W* 8 0 **8 0**
2015–16 Southampton 0 0
2015–16 *Barnsley* 27 0
2016–17 Southampton 0 0 **1 0**
2017–18 Barnsley 16 1
2018–19 Barnsley 2 0 **45 1**
2018–19 *Portsmouth* 0 0
2019–20 Swindon T 29 0
2020–21 Swindon T 0 0 **29 0**
2020–21 Bolton W 32 3
2021–22 Bolton W 18 0 **50 3**

JOHN, Declan (D) 160 9
H: 5 10 W: 11 11 b.Merthyr Tydfil 30-6-95
Internationals: Wales U17, U19, Full caps.
2010–11 Llanelli 1 0 **1 0**
2011–12 Afan Lido 5 0 **5 0**
2012–13 Cardiff C 0 0
2013–14 Cardiff C 20 0
2014–15 Cardiff C 6 0
2014–15 *Barnsley* 9 0 **9 0**
2015–16 Cardiff C 1 0
2015–16 *Chesterfield* 6 0 **6 0**
2016–17 Cardiff C 15 0
2017–18 Cardiff C 0 0 **42 0**
2017–18 Rangers 26 3 **26 3**
2018–19 Swansea C 10 0
2019–20 Swansea C 1 0
2019–20 *Sunderland* 0 0
2020–21 Swansea C 0 0 **11 0**
2020–21 *Bolton W* 21 2
2021–22 Bolton W 39 4 **60 6**

JOHNSTON, George (D) 69 3
H: 5 11 W: 11 05 b.Manchester 1-9-98
Internationals: Scotland U20, U21.
2019–20 Feyenoord 0 0
2020–21 Feyenoord 4 0 **4 0**
2020–21 Liverpool 0 0
2020–21 *Wigan Ath* 22 1 **22 1**
2021–22 Bolton W 43 2 **43 2**

JONES, Gethin (D) 148 3
H: 5 10 W: 11 09 b.Perth, Australia 13-10-95
Internationals: Wales U17, U19, U21.
2014–15 Everton 0 0
2014–15 *Plymouth Arg* 6 0 **6 0**
2015–16 Everton 0 0
2016–17 Everton 0 0
2016–17 *Barnsley* 17 0 **17 0**
2017–18 Fleetwood T 10 0
2018–19 Fleetwood T 3 0 **13 0**
2018–19 *Mansfield T* 15 0 **15 0**
2019–20 Carlisle U 30 0
2020–21 Carlisle U 0 0 **30 0**
2020–21 Bolton W 38 3
2021–22 Bolton W 29 0 **67 3**

KACHUNGA, Elias (F) 285 43
H: 5 9 W: 10 01 b.Cologne 22-4-92
Internationals: Germany U19, U21, DR Congo Full caps.
2009–10 Borussia M'gladbach 0 0
2010–11 Borussia M'gladbach 2 0
2011–12 Borussia M'gladbach 0 0
2011–12 *Osnabruck* 17 10 **17 10**
2012–13 Borussia M'gladbach 0 0 **2 0**
2012–13 *Hertha Berlin* 2 0 **2 0**
2012–13 *Paderborn* 13 3
2013–14 Paderborn 33 6
2014–15 Paderborn 32 6 **78 15**
2015–16 Ingolstadt 10 0
2016–17 Ingolstadt 0 0 **10 0**
2016–17 *Huddersfield T* 42 12
2017–18 Huddersfield T 19 1
2018–19 Huddersfield T 20 0
2019–20 Huddersfield T 36 3 **117 16**
2020–21 Sheffield W 27 0 **27 0**
2021–22 Bolton W 32 2 **32 2**

LEE, Kieran (M) 366 32
H: 6 1 W: 12 00 b.Stalybridge 22-6-88
2006–07 Manchester U 1 0
2007–08 Manchester U 0 0 **1 0**
2007–08 *QPR* 7 0 **7 0**
2008–09 Oldham Ath 7 0
2009–10 Oldham Ath 24 1
2010–11 Oldham Ath 43 2
2011–12 Oldham Ath 43 2 **117 5**
2012–13 Sheffield W 23 0
2013–14 Sheffield W 26 1
2014–15 Sheffield W 33 6
2015–16 Sheffield W 43 5
2016–17 Sheffield W 26 5
2017–18 Sheffield W 15 3
2018–19 Sheffield W 2 0
2019–20 Sheffield W 28 0
2020–21 Sheffield W 0 0 **196 20**
2020–21 Bolton W 20 2
2021–22 Bolton W 25 5 **45 7**

MORLEY, Aaron (M) 114 7
H: 5 9 W: 10 08 b.Bury 27-2-00
2016–17 Rochdale 2 0
2017–18 Rochdale 0 0
2018–19 Rochdale 3 0
2019–20 Rochdale 23 3
2020–21 Rochdale 44 2
2021–22 Rochdale 21 1 **93 6**
2021–22 Bolton W 21 1 **21 1**

POLITIC, Dennis (M) 34 5
H: 6 1 W: 12 04 b.Brasov 5-3-00
Internationals: Romania U17.
2019–20 Bolton W 24 3
2020–21 Bolton W 0 0
2021–22 Bolton W 0 0 **24 3**
2021–22 *Port Vale* 10 2 **10 2**
Transferred to Cremonese, January 2022.

SADLIER, Kieran (M) 200 54
H: 5 10 W: 10 06 b.Haywards Heath 14-9-94
Internationals: Republic of Ireland U17, U19, U21.
2013–14 West Ham U 0 0
2014–15 St Mirren 11 1 **11 1**
2015–16 Peterborough U 0 0
2015–16 *FC Halifax T* 0 0
2016 Sligo R 29 8
2017 Sligo R 20 7 **49 15**
2017 Cork C 13 2
2018 Cork C 35 16 **48 18**
2018–19 Doncaster R 14 3
2019–20 Doncaster R 33 11 **47 14**
2020–21 Rotherham U 15 1
2021–22 Rotherham U 12 1 **27 2**
2021–22 Bolton W 18 4 **18 4**

SANTOS, Ricardo (D) 203 6
H: 6 5 W: 12 02 b.Almada 18-6-95
2012–13 Dagenham & R 0 0
2013–14 Dagenham & R 0 0
2013–14 Peterborough U 1 0
2014–15 Peterborough U 24 0
2015–16 Peterborough U 37 1
2016–17 Peterborough U 1 0 **63 1**
2016–17 Barnet 15 2
2017–18 Barnet 42 3 **57 5**
From Barnet.
2020–21 Bolton W 46 0
2021–22 Bolton W 37 0 **83 0**

SARCEVIC, Antoni (M) 304 47
H: 6 1 W: 13 05 b.Manchester 13-3-92
Internationals: England C.
2009–10 Crewe Alex 0 0
2010–11 Crewe Alex 6 1
2011–12 Crewe Alex 6 0 **12 1**
From Chester.
2013–14 Fleetwood T 42 13
2014–15 Fleetwood T 37 2
2015–16 Fleetwood T 39 3 **118 18**
2016–17 Shrewsbury T 12 0 **12 0**
2016–17 Plymouth Arg 17 2
2017–18 Plymouth Arg 30 3
2018–19 Plymouth Arg 37 3
2019–20 Plymouth Arg 32 10 **116 18**
2020–21 Bolton W 32 7
2021–22 Bolton W 14 3 **46 10**

SENIOR, Adam (D) 4 0
H: 6 0 W: 10 10 b.Bolton 20-2-02
2019–20 Bolton W 2 0
2020–21 Bolton W 0 0
2021–22 Bolton W 2 0 **4 0**

SHEEHAN, Josh (M) 183 19
H: 6 0 W: 11 11 b.Pembrey 30-3-95
Internationals: Wales U19, U21, Full caps.
2013–14 Swansea C 0 0
2014–15 Swansea C 0 0
2014–15 *Yeovil T* 13 0
2015–16 Swansea C 0 0
2015–16 *Yeovil T* 13 2 **26 2**
2016–17 Swansea C 0 0
2016–17 *Newport Co* 20 5
2017–18 Newport Co 13 2

2018–19 Newport Co 33 1
2019–20 Newport Co 33 2
2020–21 Newport Co 43 3
2021–22 Newport Co 0 0 **142 13**
2021–22 Bolton W 15 4 **15 4**

THOMASON, George (M) 37 2
b.Barrow-in-Furness 12-1-01
From Longridge T.
2019–20 Bolton W 0 0
2020–21 Bolton W 24 1
2021–22 Bolton W 13 1 **37 2**

TUTTE, Andrew (M) 277 23
H: 5 9 W: 11 11 b.Huyton 21-9-90
Internationals: England U19, U20.
2007–08 Manchester C 0 0
2008–09 Manchester C 0 0
2009–10 Manchester C 0 0
2010–11 Manchester C 0 0
2010–11 *Rochdale* 7 0
2010–11 *Shrewsbury T* 2 0 **2 0**
2010–11 *Yeovil T* 15 2 **15 2**
2011–12 Rochdale 40 1
2012–13 Rochdale 37 7
2013–14 Rochdale 11 2 **95 10**
2013–14 Bury 19 1
2014–15 Bury 42 3
2015–16 Bury 22 4
2016–17 Bury 17 1
2017–18 Bury 16 0 **116 9**
2018–19 Morecambe 18 2
2019–20 Morecambe 12 0 **30 2**
2020–21 Bolton W 19 0
2021–22 Bolton W 0 0 **19 0**

TWEEDLEY, Matthew (M) 0 0
b.Rochdale 16-4-04
2020–21 Bolton W 0 0
2021–22 Bolton W 0 0

WILLIAMS, M Jordan (M) 156 1
H: 6 0 W: 12 02 b.Bangor 6-11-95
Internationals: Wales U17, U21.
2014–15 Liverpool 0 0
2014–15 *Notts Co* 8 0 **8 0**
2015–16 Liverpool 0 0
2015–16 *Swindon T* 9 0
2016–17 Liverpool 0 0
2016–17 *Swindon T* 0 0 **9 0**
2017–18 Liverpool 0 0
2017–18 *Rochdale* 12 0
2018–19 Rochdale 28 0
2019–20 Rochdale 28 0 **68 0**
2020–21 Blackpool 10 0 **10 0**
2020–21 Bolton W 21 0
2021–22 Bolton W 40 1 **61 1**

Players retained or with offer of contract
Pettifer, Arran.

Scholars
Amoateng, Bright; Beardsworth, Adam Mathew; Brown, Joseph Christopher; Burgess, Joel Thomas Ronald; Conway, Maxwell John; Frimpong, Wesley Danso Agyekum; Halford, Noah Marco; Henry, Mitchell Devon; Jones, Danny Rhys; Kamara, Abdul Salam; Litherland-Riding, Ellis James; Pettifer, Arran James; Sharples-Ahmed, Sonny; Thompson, Jack William Nicholas; Toure, Lamine Cheriff; Tweedley, Matthew James; Wilcox, Max Keith.

BOURNEMOUTH (11)

ANTHONY, Jaidon (F) 50 8
H: 5 9 W: 9 11 b.Hackney 1-12-99
From Arsenal.
2019–20 Bournemouth 0 0
2020–21 Bournemouth 5 0
2021–22 Bournemouth 45 8 **50 8**

BILLING, Phillip (M) 189 24
H: 6 4 W: 12 08 b.Copenhagen 11-6-96
Internationals: Denmark U19, U21, Full caps.
From Esbjerg.
2013–14 Huddersfield T 1 0
2014–15 Huddersfield T 0 0
2015–16 Huddersfield T 13 1
2016–17 Huddersfield T 24 2
2017–18 Huddersfield T 16 0
2018–19 Huddersfield T 27 2 **81 5**
2019–20 Bournemouth 34 1
2020–21 Bournemouth 34 8
2021–22 Bournemouth 40 10 **108 19**

BRADY, Robert (F) 260 21
H: 5 9 W: 10 12 b.Dublin 14-1-92
Internationals: Republic of Ireland Youth, U21, Full caps.
2008–09 Manchester U 0 0
2009–10 Manchester U 0 0
2010–11 Manchester U 0 0
2011–12 Manchester U 0 0
2011–12 *Hull C* 39 3
2012–13 Manchester U 0 0
2012–13 Hull C 32 4
2013–14 Hull C 16 3
2014–15 Hull C 27 0 **114 10**
2015–16 Norwich C 36 3
2016–17 Norwich C 23 4 **59 7**
2016–17 Burnley 14 1
2017–18 Burnley 15 1
2018–19 Burnley 16 0
2019–20 Burnley 17 1
2020–21 Burnley 19 1 **81 4**
2021–22 Bournemouth 6 0 **6 0**

BROOKS, David (M) 108 17
H: 5 10 W: 11 09 b.Warrington 8-7-97
Internationals: England U20. Wales U21, Full caps.
From Manchester C.
2015–16 Sheffield U 0 0
2016–17 Sheffield U 0 0
2017–18 Sheffield U 30 3 **30 3**
2018–19 Bournemouth 30 7
2019–20 Bournemouth 9 1
2020–21 Bournemouth 32 5
2021–22 Bournemouth 7 1 **78 14**

CAHILL, Gary (D) 459 31
H: 6 3 W: 13 08 b.Dronfield 19-12-85
Internationals: England U20, U21, Full caps.
2003–04 Aston Villa 0 0
2004–05 Aston Villa 0 0
2004–05 *Burnley* 27 1 **27 1**
2005–06 Aston Villa 7 1
2006–07 Aston Villa 20 0
2007–08 Aston Villa 1 0 **28 1**
2007–08 *Sheffield U* 16 2 **16 2**
2007–08 Bolton W 13 0
2008–09 Bolton W 33 3
2009–10 Bolton W 29 5
2010–11 Bolton W 36 3
2011–12 Bolton W 19 2 **130 13**
2011–12 Chelsea 10 1
2012–13 Chelsea 26 2
2013–14 Chelsea 30 1
2014–15 Chelsea 36 1
2015–16 Chelsea 23 2
2016–17 Chelsea 37 6
2017–18 Chelsea 27 0
2018–19 Chelsea 2 0
2019–20 Chelsea 0 0 **191 13**
2019–20 Crystal Palace 25 0
2020–21 Crystal Palace 20 1
2021–22 Crystal Palace 0 0 **45 1**
2021–22 Bournemouth 22 0 **22 0**

CAMP, Brennan (D) 0 0
H: 6 0 W: 11 05 b.Dorchester 12-10-00
Internationals: Scotland U19.
2019–20 Bournemouth 0 0
2020–21 Bournemouth 0 0
2021–22 Bournemouth 0 0

CHRISTIE, Ryan (M) 241 50
H: 5 10 W: 11 00 b.Inverness 22-2-95
Internationals: Scotland U21, Full caps.
2013–14 Inverness CT 15 3
2014–15 Inverness CT 35 4
2015–16 Inverness CT 13 3 **63 10**
2015–16 Celtic 5 1
2016–17 Celtic 5 1
2016–17 *Aberdeen* 13 6
2017–18 Celtic 0 0
2017–18 *Aberdeen* 32 4 **45 10**
2018–19 Celtic 23 9
2019–20 Celtic 24 11
2020–21 Celtic 34 5
2021–22 Celtic 4 0 **95 27**
2021–22 Bournemouth 38 3 **38 3**

COOK, Lewis (M) 214 3
H: 5 9 W: 11 03 b.York 3-2-97
Internationals: England U16, U17, U18, U19, U20, U21, Full caps.
2014–15 Leeds U 37 0
2015–16 Leeds U 43 1 **80 1**
2016–17 Bournemouth 6 0
2017–18 Bournemouth 29 0
2018–19 Bournemouth 13 0
2019–20 Bournemouth 27 0
2020–21 Bournemouth 31 1
2021–22 Bournemouth 28 1 **134 2**

DEMBELE, Siriki (M) 178 32
H: 5 7 W: 10 08 b.Ivory Coast 7-9-96
From Dundee U, Ayr U.
2017–18 Grimsby T 36 4 **36 4**
2018–19 Peterborough U 38 5
2019–20 Peterborough U 25 5
2020–21 Peterborough U 42 11
2021–22 Peterborough U 24 5 **129 26**
2021–22 Bournemouth 13 2 **13 2**

DENNIS, William (G) 0 0
H: 6 4 b.Watford 10-7-00
From Watford.
2019–20 Bournemouth 0 0
2020–21 Bournemouth 0 0
2021–22 Bournemouth 0 0

GENESINI, Brooklyn (D) 0 0
b. 12-12-01
2019–20 Bournemouth 0 0
2020–21 Bournemouth 0 0
2021–22 Bournemouth 0 0

GLOVER, Ryan (M) 0 0
H: 5 10 b.Yeovil 9-11-00
2020–21 Bournemouth 0 0
2021–22 Bournemouth 0 0

HILL, James (D) 44 1
H: 6 0 W: 11 07 b.Bristol 10-1-02
Internationals: England U20, U21.
2018–19 Fleetwood T 2 0
2019–20 Fleetwood T 0 0
2020–21 Fleetwood T 28 0
2021–22 Fleetwood T 13 1 **43 1**
2021–22 Bournemouth 1 0 **1 0**

KELLY, Lloyd (D) 128 4
H: 5 10 W: 11 00 b.Bristol 1-10-98
Internationals: England U20, U21.
2016–17 Bristol C 0 0
2017–18 Bristol C 11 1
2018–19 Bristol C 32 1 **43 2**
2019–20 Bournemouth 8 0
2020–21 Bournemouth 36 1
2021–22 Bournemouth 41 1 **85 2**

KILKENNY, Gavin (M) 15 0
H: 5 8 W: 10 01 b.Dublin 1-2-00
Internationals: Republic of Ireland U18, U21.
2019–20 Bournemouth 0 0
2020–21 Bournemouth 1 0
2021–22 Bournemouth 14 0 **15 0**

LERMA, Jefferson (M) 312 16
H: 5 10 W: 11 00 b.El Cerrito 25-10-94
Internationals: Colombia Full caps.
2013 Atletico Huila 24 0
2014 Atletico Huila 37 4
2015 Atletico Huila 23 2 **84 6**
2015–16 *Levante* 33 1
2016–17 Levante 30 2
2017–18 Levante 26 0 **89 3**
2018–19 Bournemouth 30 2
2019–20 Bournemouth 33 1
2020–21 Bournemouth 42 3
2021–22 Bournemouth 34 1 **139 7**

LOWE, Jamal (F) 242 52
H: 6 0 W: 12 06 b.Harrow 21-7-94
Internationals: England C. Jamaica Full caps.
2012–13 Barnet 8 0 **8 0**
From St Albans C, Hemel Hempstead T, Hampton & Richmond.
2016–17 Portsmouth 14 4
2017–18 Portsmouth 44 6
2018–19 Portsmouth 45 15
2019–20 Portsmouth 0 0 **103 25**
2019–20 Wigan Ath 46 6 **46 6**
2020–21 Swansea C 46 14
2021–22 Swansea C 5 0 **51 14**
2021–22 Bournemouth 34 7 **34 7**

MARCONDES, Emiliano (M) 222 44
H: 6 0 W: 11 11 b.Hvidovre 9-3-95
Internationals: Denmark U17, U18, U19, U20, U21.
2012–13 Nordsjaelland 3 0
2013–14 Nordsjaelland 11 1
2014–15 Nordsjaelland 24 5
2015–16 Nordsjaelland 30 2
2016–17 Nordsjaelland 25 12
2017–18 Nordsjaelland 19 17 **112 37**
2017–18 Brentford 12 0
2018–19 Brentford 13 0
2019–20 Brentford 25 2
2019–20 *Midtjylland* 12 2 **12 2**
2020–21 Brentford 31 1
2021–22 Brentford 0 0 **81 3**
2021–22 Bournemouth 17 2 **17 2**

MEPHAM, Chris (D) 114 3
H: 6 3 W: 11 11 b.Hammersmith 5-11-97
Internationals: Wales U20, U21, Full caps.
2016–17 Brentford 0 0
2017–18 Brentford 21 1
2018–19 Brentford 22 0 **43 1**
2018–19 Bournemouth 13 0
2019–20 Bournemouth 12 1
2020–21 Bournemouth 24 1
2021–22 Bournemouth 22 0 **71 2**

MOORE, Kieffer (F) 247 80
H: 6 5 W: 13 01 b.Torquay 8-8-92
Internationals: England C. Wales Full caps.
From Truro C, Dorchester T.
2013–14 Yeovil T 20 4
2014–15 Yeovil T 30 3 **50 7**
2015 Viking 9 0 **9 0**
From Forest Green R.
2016–17 Ipswich T 11 0
2017–18 Ipswich T 0 0 **11 0**
2017–18 *Rotherham U* 22 13 **22 13**
2017–18 Barnsley 20 4
2018–19 Barnsley 31 17
2019–20 Barnsley 0 0 **51 21**

2019–20	Wigan Ath	36	10	**36**	**10**
2020–21	Cardiff C	42	20		
2021–22	Cardiff C	22	5	**64**	**25**
2021–22	Bournemouth	4	4	**4**	**4**

MORIAH-WELSH, Nathan (M) 0 0
H: 5 8 b.Chelsea 18-3-02
Internationals: Guyana Full caps.
From Reading.

2020–21	Bournemouth	0	0		
2021–22	Bournemouth	0	0		

NIPPARD, Luke (M) 0 0
b. 29-12-00

2020–21	Bournemouth	0	0		
2021–22	Bournemouth	0	0		

PEARSON, Ben (M) 242 4
H: 5 9 W: 11 03 b.Oldham 4-1-95
Internationals: England U16, U17, U18, U19, U21, Full caps.

2013–14	Manchester U	0	0		
2014–15	Manchester U	0	0		
2014–15	*Barnsley*	22	1		
2015–16	Manchester U	0	0		
2015–16	*Barnsley*	23	1	**45**	**2**
2015–16	Preston NE	15	0		
2016–17	Preston NE	31	1		
2017–18	Preston NE	35	0		
2018–19	Preston NE	30	0		
2019–20	Preston NE	38	1		
2020–21	Preston NE	9	0	**158**	**2**
2020–21	Bournemouth	16	0		
2021–22	Bournemouth	23	0	**39**	**0**

ROSSI, Zeno (D) 21 0
H: 6 4 W: 12 04 b.Streatham 28-10-00
From Brentford, Southampton.

2020–21	Bournemouth	0	0		
2020–21	*Kilmarnock*	14	0	**14**	**0**
2021–22	Bournemouth	4	0	**4**	**0**
2021–22	*Dundee*	3	0	**3**	**0**

SAYDEE, Christian (F) 20 0
H: 5 11 W: 11 03 b.Hillingdon 10-5-02

2019–20	Bournemouth	0	0		
2020–21	Bournemouth	0	0		
2021–22	Bournemouth	2	0	**2**	**0**
2021–22	*Burton Alb*	18	0	**18**	**0**

SCRIMSHAW, Jake (F) 47 8
H: 5 9 W: 11 03 b.Ryde 13-9-00

2018–19	Bournemouth	0	0		
2019–20	Bournemouth	0	0		
2020–21	Bournemouth	0	0		
2020–21	*Walsall*	14	2	**14**	**2**
2020–21	*Newport Co*	16	3	**16**	**3**
2021–22	Bournemouth	0	0		
2021–22	*Scunthorpe U*	17	3	**17**	**3**

SHERRING, Sam (D) 24 0
H: 6 2 W: 12 04 b.Dorchester 8-5-00

2020–21	Bournemouth	0	0		
2021–22	Bournemouth	0	0		
2021–22	*Accrington S*	10	0	**10**	**0**
2021–22	*Cambridge U*	14	0	**14**	**0**

SMITH, Adam (D) 349 9
H: 5 11 W: 12 04 b.Leytonstone 29-4-91
Internationals: England U16, U17, U19, U20, U21.

2007–08	Tottenham H	0	0		
2008–09	Tottenham H	0	0		
2009–10	Tottenham H	0	0		
2009–10	*Wycombe W*	3	0	**3**	**0**
2009–10	*Torquay U*	16	0	**16**	**0**
2010–11	Tottenham H	0	0		
2010–11	*Bournemouth*	38	1		
2011–12	Tottenham H	1	0		
2011–12	*Milton Keynes D*	17	2	**17**	**2**
2011–12	*Leeds U*	3	0	**3**	**0**
2012–13	Tottenham H	0	0		
2012–13	*Millwall*	25	1	**25**	**1**
2013–14	Tottenham H	0	0	**1**	**0**
2013–14	*Derby Co*	8	0	**8**	**0**
2013–14	Bournemouth	5	0		
2014–15	Bournemouth	29	0		
2015–16	Bournemouth	31	2		
2016–17	Bournemouth	36	1		
2017–18	Bournemouth	27	1		
2018–19	Bournemouth	25	1		
2019–20	Bournemouth	24	0		
2020–21	Bournemouth	41	0		
2021–22	Bournemouth	20	0	**276**	**6**

SOLANKE, Dominic (F) 174 55
H: 6 1 W: 11 11 b.Reading 14-9-97
Internationals: England U16, U17, U18, U19, U20, U21, Full caps.

2014–15	Chelsea	0	0		
2015–16	Chelsea	0	0		
2015–16	*Vitesse*	25	7	**25**	**7**
2016–17	Chelsea	0	0		
2017–18	Liverpool	21	1		
2018–19	Liverpool	0	0	**21**	**1**
2018–19	Bournemouth	10	0		
2019–20	Bournemouth	32	3		
2020–21	Bournemouth	40	15		
2021–22	Bournemouth	46	29	**128**	**47**

STACEY, Jack (M) 211 8
H: 6 4 W: 13 05 b.Bracknell 6-4-96

2014–15	Reading	6	0		
2015–16	Reading	0	0		
2015–16	*Barnet*	2	0	**2**	**0**
2015–16	*Carlisle U*	9	2	**9**	**2**
2016–17	Reading	0	0	**6**	**0**
2016–17	*Exeter C*	34	0	**34**	**0**
2017–18	Luton T	41	1		
2018–19	Luton T	45	4	**86**	**5**
2019–20	Bournemouth	19	0		
2020–21	Bournemouth	30	1		
2021–22	Bournemouth	25	0	**74**	**1**

STANISLAS, Junior (M) 295 45
H: 6 0 W: 12 00 b.Kidbrooke 26-11-89
Internationals: England U20, U21.

2007–08	West Ham U	0	0		
2008–09	West Ham U	9	2		
2008–09	*Southend U*	6	1	**6**	**1**
2009–10	West Ham U	26	3		
2010–11	West Ham U	6	1		
2011–12	West Ham U	1	0	**42**	**6**
2011–12	Burnley	31	0		
2012–13	Burnley	35	5		
2013–14	Burnley	27	2	**93**	**7**
2014–15	Bournemouth	13	1		
2015–16	Bournemouth	21	3		
2016–17	Bournemouth	21	7		
2017–18	Bournemouth	19	5		
2018–19	Bournemouth	23	2		
2019–20	Bournemouth	15	3		
2020–21	Bournemouth	35	10		
2021–22	Bournemouth	7	0	**154**	**31**

TRAVERS, Mark (G) 57 0
H: 6 3 W: 12 13 b.Maynooth 18-5-99
Internationals: Republic of Ireland U16, U17, U18, U19, U21, Full caps.
From Shamrock R.

2018–19	Bournemouth	2	0		
2019–20	Bournemouth	1	0		
2020–21	Bournemouth	1	0		
2020–21	*Swindon T*	8	0	**8**	**0**
2021–22	Bournemouth	45	0	**49**	**0**

ZEMURA, Jordan (D) 35 3
H: 5 8 b.Lambeth 14-11-99
Internationals: Zimbabwe Full caps.

2018–19	Charlton Ath	0	0		
2019–20	Bournemouth	0	0		
2020–21	Bournemouth	2	0		
2021–22	Bournemouth	33	3	**35**	**3**

Players retained or with offer of contract
Gidaree, Tarik; Greenwood, Benjamin; Plain, Cameron.

Scholars
Adu-Adjei, Daniel William Kwabena; Bevan, Owen Lucas; Boutin, Noa; Brown, Lewis Phillip; Burgess, Matthew Richard; Camis, Oliver James; Dacosta Gonzalez, Michael; Daws, Marcus James; Ferguson, Joshua; Gidaree, Tarik Andre Calvin; Harris, Archie Andrew Philip; Johnson, Baylin Tyrell; Kinsey, Maxwell Benjamin; Okoh, Osanebi Ferdinand; Palmer, Owen; Pollock, Euan George; Roberts, Aaron Joseph; Seddon, Jack; Terrell, Billy Edwards James; Tonks, Finn Robert John; Tydeman, Kian Bruce; Wadham, Jack; Williams, Toure Shakur; Winterburn, Benjamin George.

BRADFORD C (12)

ANGOL, Lee (F) 153 35
H: 5 10 W: 11 05 b.Carshalton 4-8-94

2012–13	Wycombe W	3	0		
2013–14	Wycombe W	0	0	**3**	**0**
2014–15	Luton T	0	0		
2015–16	Peterborough U	33	11		
2016–17	Peterborough U	13	1	**46**	**12**
2017–18	Mansfield T	29	9	**29**	**9**
2018–19	*Lincoln C*	2	0	**2**	**0**
2018–19	Shrewsbury T	17	3	**17**	**3**
2019–20	Leyton Orient	26	4		
2020–21	Leyton Orient	12	1	**38**	**5**
2021–22	Bradford C	18	6	**18**	**6**

COOK, Andy (F) 151 43
H: 6 0 W: 11 03 b.Bishop Auckland 18-10-90
Internationals: England C.
From Carlisle U, Barrow, Grimsby T, Barrow, Tranmere R.

2018–19	Walsall	43	13	**43**	**13**
2019–20	Mansfield T	23	7		
2019–20	*Tranmere R*	5	0	**5**	**0**
2020–21	Mansfield T	20	3	**43**	**10**
2020–21	*Bradford C*	21	8		
2021–22	Bradford C	39	12	**60**	**20**

COOKE, Callum (F) 162 12
H: 5 8 W: 11 05 b.Peterlee 21-2-97
Internationals: England U16, U17, U18.

2016–17	Middlesbrough	0	0		
2016–17	*Crewe Alex*	18	4	**18**	**4**
2017–18	Middlesbrough	0	0		
2017–18	*Blackpool*	30	2	**30**	**2**
2018–19	Peterborough U	13	1		
2019–20	Peterborough U	0	0	**13**	**1**
2019–20	*Bradford C*	25	0		
2020–21	Bradford C	34	3		
2021–22	Bradford C	42	2	**101**	**5**

COUSIN-DAWSON, Finn (D) 34 0
H: 6 0 W: 11 03 b.Stockton 10-5-01
Internationals: Northern Ireland U21.

2019–20	Bradford C	0	0		
2020–21	Bradford C	23	0		
2021–22	Bradford C	11	0	**34**	**0**

CRANKSHAW, Oliver (F) 44 2
H: 6 0 W: 11 11 b.Preston 12-8-98

2020–21	Wigan Ath	19	1	**19**	**1**
2020–21	Bradford C	19	1		
2021–22	Bradford C	6	0	**25**	**1**

Transferred to Stockport Co, September 2021.

DELFOUNESO, Nathan (F) 372 47
H: 6 1 W: 12 04 b.Birmingham 2-2-91
Internationals: England U16, U17, U19, U21.

2007–08	Aston Villa	0	0		
2008–09	Aston Villa	4	0		
2009–10	Aston Villa	9	1		
2010–11	Aston Villa	11	1		
2010–11	*Burnley*	11	1	**11**	**1**
2011–12	Aston Villa	6	0		
2011–12	*Leicester C*	4	0	**4**	**0**
2012–13	Aston Villa	1	0		
2012–13	*Blackpool*	40	6		
2013–14	Aston Villa	0	0	**31**	**2**
2013–14	*Blackpool*	11	0		
2013–14	*Coventry C*	14	3	**14**	**3**
2014–15	Blackpool	38	3		
2015–16	Blackburn R	15	1	**15**	**1**
2015–16	*Bury*	4	0	**4**	**0**
2016–17	Swindon T	18	1	**18**	**1**
2016–17	Blackpool	18	5		
2017–18	Blackpool	40	9		
2018–19	Blackpool	39	7		
2019–20	Blackpool	28	3		
2020–21	Blackpool	0	0	**214**	**33**
2020–21	Bolton W	44	6		
2021–22	Bolton W	11	0	**55**	**6**
2021–22	Bradford C	6	0	**6**	**0**

EISA, Abobaker (M) 95 17
H: 5 11 W: 11 11 b.Khartoum 5-1-96
From Uxbridge, Wealdstone.

2017–18	Shrewsbury T	5	1		
2018–19	Shrewsbury T	4	0		
2018–19	*Colchester U*	14	2	**14**	**2**
2019–20	Shrewsbury T	1	0	**10**	**1**
2019–20	Scunthorpe U	28	5		
2020–21	Scunthorpe U	39	9	**67**	**14**
2021–22	Bradford C	4	0	**4**	**0**

EVANS, Gary (F) 519 87
H: 5 10 W: 12 08 b.Macclesfield 26-4-88

2006–07	Crewe Alex	0	0		
2007–08	Macclesfield T	42	7		
2008–09	Macclesfield T	40	12	**82**	**19**
2009–10	Bradford C	43	11		
2010–11	Bradford C	36	3		
2011–12	Rotherham U	32	7		
2012–13	Rotherham U	13	2	**45**	**9**
2012–13	Fleetwood T	16	1		
2013–14	Fleetwood T	34	6		
2014–15	Fleetwood T	43	3	**93**	**10**
2015–16	Portsmouth	40	10		
2016–17	Portsmouth	41	5		
2017–18	Portsmouth	32	2		
2018–19	Portsmouth	42	10		
2019–20	Portsmouth	17	5		
2020–21	Portsmouth	1	0	**173**	**32**
2020–21	Bradford C	27	2		
2021–22	Bradford C	20	1	**126**	**17**

FOULDS, Matthew (D) 29 2
H: 6 0 W: 11 09 b.Bradford 1-2-98

2015–16	Bury	0	0		
2015–16	Everton	0	0		
2016–17	Everton	0	0		
2017–18	Everon	0	0		
2018–19	Everton	0	0		
2019–20	Everton	0	0		
2020–21	Como	3	0	**3**	**0**
2020–21	Bradford C	3	0		
2021–22	Bradford C	23	2	**26**	**2**

GILLIEAD, Alex (F) 253 16
H: 6 0 W: 11 00 b.Shotley Bridge 11-2-96
Internationals: England U16, U17, U18, U20.

2014–15	Newcastle U	0	0		
2015–16	Newcastle U	0	0		
2015–16	*Carlisle U*	35	5	**35**	**5**
2016–17	Newcastle U	0	0		
2016–17	*Luton T*	18	1	**18**	**1**
2016–17	*Bradford C*	9	0		
2017–18	Newcastle U	0	0		
2017–18	*Bradford C*	42	1		
2018–19	Shrewsbury T	27	1	**27**	**1**

2019–20 Scunthorpe U 35 6
2020–21 Scunthorpe U 44 1 **79 7**
2021–22 Bradford C 43 1 **94 2**

HENDRIE, Luke (D) 210 5
H: 6 2 W: 12 13 b.Leeds 27-8-94
Internationals: England U16, U17.
2012–13 Manchester U 0 0
2013–14 Derby Co 0 0
2014–15 Derby Co 0 0
2015–16 Burnley 0 0
2015–16 *Hartlepool U* 3 0
2015–16 *York C* 18 0 **18 0**
2016–17 Burnley 0 0
2016–17 *Kilmarnock* 32 0 **32 0**
2017–18 Burnley 0 0
2017–18 *Bradford C* 13 0
2017–18 Shrewsbury T 10 0 **10 0**
2018–19 Grimsby T 41 2
2019–20 Grimsby T 32 1
2020–21 Grimsby T 38 2 **111 5**
2021–22 Hartlepool U 7 0 **10 0**
2021–22 Bradford C 16 0 **29 0**

HORNBY, Sam (G) 43 0
H: 6 2 W: 12 08 b.Sutton Coldfield 14-2-95
From Hednesford T, Redditch U.
2015–16 Burton Alb 0 0
2016–17 Burton Alb 0 0
2017–18 Port Vale 11 0
2018–19 Port Vale 0 0 **11 0**
2019–20 Bradford C 0 0
2020–21 Bradford C 18 0
2021–22 Bradford C 6 0 **24 0**
2021–22 *Colchester U* 8 0 **8 0**

KELLEHER, Fiacre (D) 88 2
H: 6 3 W: 12 08 b.Cork 10-3-96
2016–17 Celtic 0 0
2016–17 Peterhead 0 0
2017–18 Oxford U 0 0
2018–19 Oxford U 0 0
2018–19 *Macclesfield T* 42 1
2019–20 Macclesfield T 37 1 **79 2**
From Wrexham.
2021–22 Bradford C 9 0 **9 0**

LAVERY, Caolan (F) 220 38
H: 5 11 W: 12 00 b.Red Deer 22-10-92
Internationals: Canada U17. Northern Ireland U19, U21.
2012–13 Sheffield W 0 0
2012–13 *Southend U* 3 0 **3 0**
2013–14 Sheffield W 21 4
2013–14 *Plymouth Arg* 8 3 **8 3**
2014–15 Sheffield W 13 2
2014–15 *Chesterfield* 8 3 **8 3**
2015–16 Sheffield W 0 0 **34 6**
2015–16 *Portsmouth* 13 4 **13 4**
2016–17 Sheffield U 27 4
2017–18 Sheffield U 3 0
2017–18 *Rotherham U* 14 2 **14 2**
2018–19 Sheffield U 0 0 **30 4**
2018–19 *Bury* 23 5 **23 5**
2019–20 Walsall 27 4
2020–21 Walsall 41 6 **68 10**
2021–22 Bradford C 19 1 **19 1**

O'CONNOR, Paudie (D) 129 7
H: 6 3 W: 12 02 b.Limerick 14-7-97
From Limerick.
2017–18 Leeds U 4 0
2018–19 Leeds U 0 0 **4 0**
2018–19 *Blackpool* 10 0 **10 0**
2018–19 *Bradford C* 9 0
2019–20 Bradford C 19 2
2020–21 Bradford C 42 2
2021–22 Bradford C 45 3 **115 7**

O'DONNELL, Richard (G) 336 0
H: 6 2 W: 13 05 b.Sheffield 12-9-88
2007–08 Sheffield W 0 0
2007–08 *Rotherham U* 0 0
2007–08 *Oldham Ath* 4 0 **4 0**
2008–09 Sheffield W 0 0
2009–10 Sheffield W 0 0
2010–11 Sheffield W 9 0
2011–12 Sheffield W 6 0 **15 0**
2011–12 *Macclesfield T* 11 0 **11 0**
2012–13 Chesterfield 14 0 **14 0**
2013–14 Walsall 46 0
2014–15 Walsall 44 0 **90 0**
2015–16 Wigan Ath 10 0 **10 0**
2015–16 Bristol C 21 0
2016–17 Bristol C 8 0 **29 0**
2016–17 Rotherham U 12 0
2017–18 Rotherham U 10 0 **22 0**
2017–18 Northampton T 19 0 **19 0**
2018–19 Bradford C 42 0
2019–20 Bradford C 33 0
2020–21 Bradford C 28 0
2021–22 Bradford C 19 0 **122 0**

RIDEHALGH, Liam (D) 239 3
H: 5 10 W: 11 05 b.Halifax 20-4-91
2009–10 Huddersfield T 0 0
2010–11 Huddersfield T 20 0
2011–12 Huddersfield T 0 0
2011–12 *Swindon T* 11 0 **11 0**
2011–12 *Chesterfield* 20 1
2012–13 Huddersfield T 0 0
2012–13 *Chesterfield* 14 0 **34 1**
2012–13 *Rotherham U* 20 0 **20 0**
2013–14 Huddersfield T 0 0 **20 0**
2013–14 *Tranmere R* 36 1
2014–15 Tranmere R 18 0
2018–19 Tranmere R 18 0
2019–20 Tranmere R 29 1
2020–21 Tranmere R 24 0
2021–22 Tranmere R 0 0 **125 2**
2021–22 Bradford C 29 0 **29 0**

ROBINSON, Theo (F) 465 104
H: 5 9 W: 10 03 b.Birmingham 22-1-89
Internationals: Jamaica Full caps.
2005–06 Watford 1 0
2006–07 Watford 1 0
2007–08 Watford 0 0
2007–08 *Hereford U* 43 13 **43 13**
2008–09 Watford 3 0 **5 0**
2008–09 *Southend U* 21 7
2009–10 Huddersfield T 37 13
2010–11 Huddersfield T 1 0
2010–11 Millwall 11 3
2010–11 *Derby Co* 13 2
2011–12 Derby Co 39 10
2012–13 Derby Co 28 8
2012–13 *Huddersfield T* 6 0 **44 13**
2013–14 Millwall 0 0 **11 3**
2013–14 Derby Co 0 0 **80 20**
2013–14 Doncaster R 31 5
2014–15 Doncaster R 32 4 **63 9**
2014–15 *Scunthorpe U* 8 3 **8 3**
2015–16 Motherwell 10 0 **10 0**
2015–16 Port Vale 14 2
2016–17 Southend U 18 2
2017–18 Southend U 25 5
2018–19 Southend U 24 4
2018–19 *Swindon T* 16 7 **16 7**
2019–20 Southend U 3 0 **91 18**
2019–20 *Colchester U* 28 11 **28 11**
2020–21 Port Vale 29 3
2021–22 Port Vale 0 0 **43 5**
2021–22 Bradford C 23 2 **23 2**

SCALES, Kian (M) 22 1
H: 5 11 W: 10 06 b.Leeds 9-11-01
2020–21 Bradford C 20 1
2021–22 Bradford C 2 0 **22 1**

SIKORA, Jorge (D) 1 0
H: 5 10 W: 10 03 b.Bradford 29-3-02
2019–20 Bradford C 0 0
2020–21 Bradford C 1 0
2021–22 Bradford C 0 0 **1 0**

SONGO'O, Yann (D) 251 15
H: 6 0 W: 12 02 b.Yaounde 17-11-91
Internationals: France U16. Cameroon U20.
From Real Zaragoza.
2011–12 Sabadell 6 0 **6 0**
2013 Sporting Kansas C 0 0
2013 *Orlando C* 12 1 **12 1**
2013–14 Blackburn R 0 0
2013–14 *Ross Co* 17 3 **17 3**
2014–15 Blackburn R 0 0
2016–17 Plymouth Arg 46 2
2017–18 Plymouth Arg 33 0
2018–19 Plymouth Arg 42 0 **121 2**
2019–20 Scunthorpe U 16 0 **16 0**
2020–21 Morecambe 38 6
2021–22 Morecambe 0 0 **38 6**
2021–22 Bradford C 41 3 **41 3**

STAUNTON, Reece (D) 10 1
H: 6 0 W: 12 00 b.Bradford 10-12-01
Internationals: Republic of Ireland U18.
2017–18 Bradford C 1 0
2018–19 Bradford C 0 0
2019–20 Bradford C 0 0
2020–21 Bradford C 8 1
2021–22 Bradford C 1 0 **10 1**

SUTTON, Levi (M) 124 5
H: 5 11 W: 11 09 b.Scunthorpe 24-3-96
2014–15 Scunthorpe U 0 0
2015–16 Scunthorpe U 1 0
2016–17 Scunthorpe U 8 0
2017–18 Scunthorpe U 15 0
2018–19 Scunthorpe U 18 1
2019–20 Scunthorpe U 16 0 **58 1**
2019–20 Bradford C 0 0
2020–21 Bradford C 34 2
2021–22 Bradford C 32 2 **66 4**

THRELKELD, Oscar (D) 183 4
H: 6 0 W: 12 04 b.Bolton 15-2-94
2013–14 Bolton W 2 0
2014–15 Bolton W 4 0
2015–16 Bolton W 3 0 **9 0**
2015–16 *Plymouth Arg* 25 1
2016–17 Plymouth Arg 36 2
2017–18 Plymouth Arg 24 0
2018–19 Waasland-Beveren 2 0 **2 0**
2018–19 *Plymouth Arg* 12 1 **97 4**
2019–20 Salford C 18 0
2020–21 Salford C 35 0
2021–22 Salford C 0 0 **53 0**
2021–22 Bradford C 22 0 **22 0**

VERNAM, Charles (F) 147 24
H: 5 7 W: 11 09 b.Lincoln 8-10-96
From Scunthorpe U.
2013–14 Derby Co 0 0
2014–15 Derby Co 0 0
2015–16 Derby Co 0 0
2016 *Vestmannaeyjar* 9 1 **9 1**
2016–17 Derby Co 0 0
2016–17 *Coventry C* 4 0 **4 0**
2017–18 Derby Co 0 0
2017–18 *Grimsby T* 9 1
2018–19 Grimsby T 35 3
2019–20 Grimsby T 27 7 **71 11**
2020–21 Burton Alb 14 2 **14 2**
2020–21 Bradford C 21 2
2021–22 Bradford C 28 8 **49 10**

WALKER, Jamie (M) 258 55
H: 5 9 W: 11 00 b.Edinburgh 25-6-93
Internationals: Scotland U16, U17, U19, U21.
2011–12 Hearts 0 0
2011–12 *Raith R* 23 3 **23 3**
2012–13 Hearts 24 2
2013–14 Hearts 26 3
2014–15 Hearts 33 11
2015–16 Hearts 23 7
2016–17 Hearts 34 12
2017–18 Hearts 16 2
2017–18 Wigan Ath 8 0
2018–19 Wigan Ath 0 0 **8 0**
2018–19 *Peterborough U* 12 1 **12 1**
2019–20 Hearts 15 3
2020–21 Hearts 21 7
2021–22 Hearts 4 0 **196 47**
2021–22 Bradford C 19 4 **19 4**

WATT, Elliot (M) 99 6
H: 5 9 W: 12 04 b.Preston 11-3-00
Internationals: Scotland U17, U19, U21.
From Preston NE.
2018–19 Wolverhampton W 0 0
2019–20 Wolverhampton W 0 0
2019–20 *Carlisle U* 12 1 **12 1**
2020–21 Bradford C 46 3
2021–22 Bradford C 41 2 **87 5**

WOOD, Charlie (F) 0 0
2020–21 Bradford C 0 0
2021–22 Bradford C 0 0

YOUNG , Jake (F) 51 9
H: 6 1 W: 12 02 b.Huddersfield 22-7-01
2020–21 Forest Green R 29 6
2021–22 Forest Green R 22 3 **51 9**
2021–22 Bradford C 0 0

Scholars
Ajibode, Oluwagbemileke Immanuel; Bentley, Samuel James; Breaks, Casey James; Dalghous, Ali Abdulbaset; Gellan, Munro Charles; Harrop, Luke; Jeffers, Rakealan Rommel; Jeffreys, Freddy; Kamga, Ian Gaston; Maumbe, Tanaka Christian; Monthe Youmbi, Rooney Dylan; Pointon, Bobby; Roberts, Cole; Rowe, Harvey Oliver; Thewlis, George Gary; Tinsdale, Jay Dillan; Tinsdale, Nathan Scott; Tunkara Saho, Yahaya; Wadsworth, Noah John Michael; Wilson, Jack Lewis.

BRENTFORD (13)

AJER, Kristoffer (D) 209 15
H: 6 5 W: 13 03 b.RÊlingen 17-4-98
Internationals: Norway U16, U17, U18, U19, U21, Full caps.
2013 Lillestrom 0 0
2014 Lillestrom 0 0
2014 Start 13 1
2015 Start 30 8
2016 Start 11 0 **54 9**
2016–17 Celtic 0 0
2016–17 *Kilmarnock* 16 0 **16 0**
2017–18 Celtic 24 0
2018–19 Celtic 28 0
2019–20 Celtic 28 3
2020–21 Celtic 35 2
2021–22 Celtic 0 0 **115 5**
2021–22 Brentford 24 1 **24 1**

BALCOMBE, Ellery (G) 23 0
H: 6 0 W: 12 00 b.Watford 15-10-99
Internationals: England U18, U19, U20.
2016–17 Brentford 0 0
2017–18 Brentford 0 0
2018–19 Brentford 0 0
2019–20 Brentford 0 0
2019–20 *Viborg* 8 0 **8 0**
2020–21 Brentford 0 0
2020–21 *Doncaster R* 15 0 **15 0**
2021–22 Brentford 0 0
2021–22 *Burton Alb* 0 0

BAPTISTE, Shandon (M) 61 2
H: 5 11 W: 10 08 b.Grenada 8-4-98
Internationals: Grenada Full caps.
2017–18 Oxford U 0 0
2018–19 Oxford U 9 0
2019–20 Oxford U 17 1 **26 1**
2019–20 Brentford 12 0
2020–21 Brentford 1 0
2021–22 Brentford 22 1 **35 1**

BIDSTRUP, Mads (M) 21 0
H: 5 9 b.K˜ge 25-2-01
Internationals: Denmark U16, U17, U18, U19, U21.
From RB Leipzig.
2020–21 Brentford 4 0
2021–22 Brentford 4 0 **8 0**
2021–22 *Nordsjaelland* 13 0 **13 0**

BROOK, Lachlan (F) 27 1
H: 5 10 b.Gawler 8-2-01
Internationals: Australia U17, U20, U23.
2016–17 Adelaide U 0 0
2017–18 Adelaide U 1 0
2018–19 Adelaide U 0 0
2019–20 Adelaide U 7 1
2020–21 Brentford 0 0
2021–22 Brentford 0 0
2021–22 *Adelaide U* 19 0 **27 1**

CANOS, Sergi (F) 224 33
H: 5 8 W: 11 11 b.Nules 2-2-97
Internationals: Spain U16, U17, U19, U20.
From Barcelona.
2015–16 Liverpool 1 0 **1 0**
2015–16 *Brentford* 38 7
2016–17 Norwich C 3 0 **3 0**
2016–17 Brentford 18 4
2017–18 Brentford 30 3
2018–19 Brentford 44 7
2019–20 Brentford 13 0
2020–21 Brentford 46 9
2021–22 Brentford 31 3 **220 33**

COX, Matthew (G) 0 0
H: 6 0 W: 10 01 b.London Borough of Sutton 2-5-03
Internationals: England U19, U20
2020–21 AFC Wimbledon 0 0
2021–22 AFC Wimbledon 0 0
2021–22 Brentford 0 0

CRAMA, Tristan (D) 0 0
H: 6 4 b.Beziers 8-11-01
From Beziers.
2020–21 Brentford 0 0
2021–22 Brentford 0 0

DA SILVA, Josh (M) 98 16
H: 5 11 W: 11 11 b.London Borough of Redbridge 23-10-98
Internationals: England U19, U20, U21.
2016–17 Arsenal 0 0
2017–18 Arsenal 0 0
2018–19 Brentford 17 1
2019–20 Brentford 42 10
2020–21 Brentford 30 5
2021–22 Brentford 9 0 **98 16**

DERVISOGLU, Halil (F) 104 22
H: 6 0 W: 12 00 b.Rotterdam 8-12-99
Internationals: Turkey U19, U21, Full caps.
2017–18 Sparta Rotterdam 0 0
2018–19 Sparta Rotterdam 34 10
2019–20 Sparta Rotterdam 17 5 **51 15**
2019–20 Brentford 4 0
2020–21 Brentford 0 0
2020–21 *FC Twente* 9 0 **9 0**
2020–21 *Galatasaray* 12 3
2021–22 Brentford 0 0 **4 0**
2021–22 *Galatasaray* 28 4 **40 7**

ERIKSEN, Christian (M) 393 81
H: 5 9 W: 10 02 b.Middelfart 14-2-92
Internationals: Denmark U17, U18, U19, U21, Full caps.
2009–10 Ajax 15 0
2010–11 Ajax 28 6
2011–12 Ajax 33 7
2012–13 Ajax 33 10
2013–14 Ajax 4 2 **113 25**
2013–14 Tottenham H 25 7
2014–15 Tottenham H 38 10
2015–16 Tottenham H 35 6
2016–17 Tottenham H 36 8
2017–18 Tottenham H 37 10
2018–19 Tottenham H 35 8
2019–20 Tottenham H 20 2 **226 51**
2019–20 Inter Milan 17 1
2020–21 Inter Milan 26 3 **43 4**
2021–22 Brentford 11 1 **11 1**
Transferred to Inter Milan, January 2020.

FERNANDEZ, Alvaro (G) 88 0
H: 6 1 W: 11 11 b.Arnedo 13-4-98
Internationals: Spain U18, U19, U20, U21, U23, Full caps.
2014–15 Osasuna 0 0
2015–16 Osasuna 0 0
2016–17 Osasuna 1 0 **1 0**
2017–18 Monaco 0 0
2018–19 Monaco 0 0
2018–19 *Extremadura* 17 0 **17 0**
2019–20 Huesca 36 0
2020–21 Huesca 22 0
2021–22 Huesca 0 0 **58 0**
2021–22 *Brentford* 12 0 **12 0**

FORSS, Marcus (F) 83 20
H: 6 0 W: 11 07 b.Turku 18-6-99
Internationals: Finland U17, U18, U19, U21, Full caps.
From WBA.
2018–19 Brentford 6 1
2019–20 Brentford 2 0
2019–20 *AFC Wimbledon* 18 11 **18 11**
2020–21 Brentford 39 7
2021–22 Brentford 7 0 **54 8**
2021–22 *Hull C* 11 1 **11 1**

FOSU, Tarique (M) 180 33
H: 5 11 W: 11 11 b.Wandsworth 5-11-95
Internationals: England U18. Ghana Full caps.
2013–14 Reading 0 0
2014–15 Reading 1 0
2015–16 Reading 0 0
2015–16 *Fleetwood T* 6 1 **6 1**
2015–16 *Accrington S* 8 3 **8 3**
2016–17 Reading 0 0 **1 0**
2016–17 *Colchester U* 33 5 **33 5**
2017–18 Charlton Ath 30 9
2018–19 Charlton Ath 27 2 **57 11**
2019–20 Oxford U 25 8 **25 8**
2019–20 Brentford 10 1
2020–21 Brentford 39 4
2021–22 Brentford 1 0 **50 5**

GHODDOS, Saman (F) 269 55
H: 5 9 W: 11 11 b.Malm^ 6-9-93
Internationals: Sweden Full caps. Iran Full caps.
2011 Limhamn Bunkeflo 17 0
2012 Limhamn Bunkeflo 24 4 **41 4**
2013 Trelleborg 18 1 **18 1**
2014 Syrianska 29 6
2015 Syrianska 25 8 **54 14**
2016 Ostersund 27 10
2017 Ostersund 23 8
2018 Ostersund 15 9 **65 27**
2018–19 Amiens 27 4
2019–20 Amiens 5 1
2020–21 Amiens 2 0 **34 5**
2020–21 Brentford 40 3
2021–22 Brentford 17 1 **57 4**

GILBERT, Alex (F) 8 0
H: 6 0 b.Birmingham 28-12-01
Internationals: Republic of Ireland U19, U21.
From WBA.
2020–21 Brentford 0 0
2021–22 Brentford 0 0
2021–22 *Swindon T* 8 0 **8 0**

GOODE, Charlie (D) 133 8
H: 6 5 W: 11 11 b.Watford 3-8-95
Internationals: England C.
From Hadley, AFC Hayes, Hendon.
2015–16 Scunthorpe U 10 1
2016–17 Scunthorpe U 20 0
2017–18 Scunthorpe U 13 1
2018–19 Scunthorpe U 21 3 **64 5**
2018–19 *Northampton T* 17 0
2019–20 Northampton T 36 3 **53 3**
2020–21 Brentford 8 0
2021–22 Brentford 6 0 **14 0**
2021–22 *Sheffield U* 2 0 **2 0**

GORDON, Lewis (D) 0 0
b. 12-2-01
Internationals: Scotland U17, U19.
2018–19 Watford 0 0
2019–20 Watford 0 0
2020–21 Brentford 0 0
2021–22 Brentford 0 0

GUNNARSSON, Patrik (G) 35 0
H: 6 3 W: 13 03 b.KÛpavogur 15-11-00
Internationals: Iceland U16, U17, U18, U19, U21, Full caps.
From Breidablik.
2018–19 Brentford 1 0
2018–19 *IR* 5 0 **5 0**
2019–20 Brentford 0 0
2019–20 *Southend U* 3 0 **3 0**
2020–21 Brentford 0 0
2020–21 *Viborg* 12 0 **12 0**
2020–21 *Silkeborg* 14 0 **14 0**
2021–22 Brentford 0 0 **1 0**
2021–22 *Viking FK* 0 0
Transferred to Viking, August 2021.

HAYGARTH, Max (M) 1 0
H: 5 9 b.Manchester 21-1-02
2019–20 Manchester U 0 0
2020–21 Manchester U 0 0
2020–21 Brentford 1 0
2021–22 Brentford 0 0 **1 0**

HENRY, Rico (D) 190 7
H: 5 7 W: 10 06 b.Birmingham 8-7-97
Internationals: England U19, U20.
2014–15 Walsall 9 0
2015–16 Walsall 35 2
2016–17 Walsall 2 0 **46 2**
2016–17 Brentford 12 0
2017–18 Brentford 8 0
2018–19 Brentford 14 1
2019–20 Brentford 46 0
2020–21 Brentford 30 1
2021–22 Brentford 34 3 **144 5**

HERCULES, Wraynel (F) 0 0
b. 19-1-02
From Barnet.
2020–21 Brentford 0 0
2021–22 Brentford 0 0

HOCKENHULL, Ben (D) 0 0
H: 6 1 b. 3-9-01
From Manchester U.
2020–21 Brentford 0 0
2021–22 Brentford 0 0

JANELT, Vitaly (M) 125 9
H: 6 0 W: 12 06 b.Hamburg 10-5-98
Internationals: Germany U17, U19, U20, U21.
2016–17 RB Leipzig 0 0
2016–17 *VfL Bochum* 7 0
2017–18 RB Leipzig 0 0
2017–18 *VfL Bochum* 13 0
2018–19 VfL Bochum 9 1
2019–20 VfL Bochum 24 1
2020–21 VfL Bochum 0 0 **53 2**
2020–21 Brentford 41 3
2021–22 Brentford 31 4 **72 7**

JANSSON, Pontus (D) 333 23
H: 6 4 W: 13 08 b.Arl'v 13-2-91
Internationals: Sweden U17, U19, U21, Full caps.
2009 Malmo 2 0
2009 *IFK Malmo* 9 4 **9 4**
2010 Malmo 18 1
2011 Malmo 15 2
2012 Malmo 30 1
2013 Malmo 24 1
2014 Malmo 9 1 **98 6**
2014–15 Torino 9 0
2015–16 Torino 7 1
2015–16 Torino 0 0 **16 1**
2016–17 *Leeds U* 34 3
2017–18 Leeds U 42 3
2018–19 Leeds U 39 3 **115 9**
2019–20 Brentford 34 0
2020–21 Brentford 24 0
2021–22 Brentford 37 3 **95 3**

JEANVIER, Julian (D) 163 10
H: 6 0 W: 12 04 b.Clichy 31-3-92
Internationals: Guinea Full caps.
2012–13 Nancy 6 0 **6 0**
2013–14 Lille 0 0
2014–15 Lille 0 0
2014–15 *Mouscron-Peruwelz* 17 0 **17 0**
2015–16 Lille 0 0
2015–16 *Red Star* 24 2 **24 2**
2016–17 Reims 29 3
2017–18 Reims 33 2 **62 5**
2018–19 Brentford 24 2
2019–20 Brentford 26 1
2020–21 Brentford 0 0
2020–21 *Kasimpasa* 4 0 **4 0**
2021–22 Brentford 0 0 **50 3**

JEFFERIES, Dom (M) 0 0
2019–20 Newport Co 0 0
From Salisbury.
2021–22 Brentford 0 0

JENSEN, Mathias (M) 184 18
H: 5 8 W: 10 10 b.Horsens 1-1-96
Internationals: Denmark U18, U19, U20, U21, Full caps.
2015–16 Nordsjaelland 5 1
2016–17 Nordsjaelland 22 2
2017–18 Nordsjaelland 35 12
2018–19 Nordsjaelland 1 0 **63 15**
2018–19 Celta Vigo 6 0 **6 0**
2019–20 Brentford 39 1
2020–21 Brentford 45 2
2021–22 Brentford 31 0 **115 3**

JONES, Nico (D) 34 0
b. 3-2-02
Internationals: Republic of Ireland U18.
From Fulham.
2018–19 Oxford U 3 0
2019–20 Oxford U 31 0
2020–21 Oxford U 0 0 **34 0**
2021–22 Brentford 0 0

JORGENSEN, Mathias Zanka (D) 322 19
H: 6 3 W: 12 06 b.Copenhagen 23-4-90
Internationals: Denmark U16, U17, U18, U21, Full caps.
2007–08 Copenhagen 12 1
2008–09 Copenhagen 20 0
2009–10 Copenhagen 24 4
2010–11 Copenhagen 25 1
2011–12 Copenhagen 11 0
2012–13 PSV Eindhoven 5 2
2013–14 PSV Eindhoven 9 0 **14 2**
2014–15 Copenhagen 29 1
2015–16 Copenhagen 31 3
2016–17 Copenhagen 33 0 **185 10**
2017–18 Huddersfield T 38 0
2018–19 Huddersfield T 24 3 **62 3**
2019–20 Fenerbahce 16 2
2019–20 *Fortuna Dusseldorf* 9 0 **9 0**
2020–21 Fenerbahce 2 0 **18 2**
2020–21 *FC Copenhagen* 26 1 **26 1**
2021–22 Brentford 8 1 **8 1**

LOSSL, Jonas (G) 307 0
H: 6 5 W: 14 00 b.Kolding 1-2-89
Internationals: Denmark U17, U18, U19, U20, U21, Full caps.
2009–10 Midtjylland 12 0
2010–11 Midtjylland 30 0
2011–12 Midtjylland 25 0
2012–13 Midtjylland 27 0
2013–14 Midtjylland 33 0
2014–15 Guingamp 30 0
2015–16 Guingamp 37 0 **67 0**
2016–17 Mainz 27 0
2017–18 Mainz 0 0 **27 0**
2017–18 *Huddersfield T* 38 0
2018–19 Huddersfield T 31 0
2019–20 Everton 0 0
2019–20 *Huddersfield T* 15 0 **84 0**
2020–21 Everton 0 0
2021–22 Midtjylland 0 0 **127 0**
2021–22 *Brentford* 2 0 **2 0**

MAGHOMA, Edmond-Paris (M) 0 0
H: 5 11 W: 11 00 b.Enfield 8-5-01
Internationals: England U18, U19, U20.
From Tottenham H.
2020–21 Brentford 0 0
2021–22 Brentford 0 0

MBEUMO, Bryan (M) 162 38
H: 5 7 W: 11 11 b.Avallon 7-8-99
Internationals: France U17, U20, U21.
2016–17 Troyes 0 0
2017–18 Troyes 4 0
2018–19 Troyes 35 10
2019–20 Troyes 2 1 **41 11**
2019–20 Brentford 42 15
2020–21 Brentford 44 8
2021–22 Brentford 35 4 **121 27**

MOGENSEN, Gustav (F) 0 0
b. 19-4-01
Internationals: Denmark U16, U17, U18, U19.
From Aarhus.
2019–20 Brentford 0 0
2020–21 Brentford 0 0
2021–22 Brentford 0 0

NORGAARD, Christian (M) 217 11
H: 6 1 W: 11 11 b.Copenhagen 10-3-94
Internationals: Denmark U16, U17, U19, U20, U21, Full caps.
2011–12 Lyngby 1 0 **1 0**
2012–13 Hamburger 0 0
2013–14 Brondby 13 0
2014–15 Brondby 21 3
2015–16 Brondby 16 0
2016–17 Brondby 31 4
2017–18 Brondby 34 1
2018–19 Brondby 1 0 **116 8**
2018–19 Fiorentina 6 0 **6 0**
2019–20 Brentford 42 0
2020–21 Brentford 17 0
2021–22 Brentford 35 3 **94 3**

OKSANEN, Jaako (D) 66 2
H: 6 0 W: 11 05 b.Helsinki 7-11-00
Internationals: Finland U16, U17, U18, U19, U21.
From HJK Helsinki.
2016 Klubi 04 1 0
2017 Klubi 04 22 2 **23 2**
2017 HJK Helsinki 1 0 **1 0**
2018–19 Brentford 1 0
2019–20 Brentford 1 0
2020–21 Brentford 0 0
2020–21 *AFC Wimbledon* 27 0 **27 0**
2021–22 Brentford 0 0 **2 0**
2021–22 *Greenock Morton* 13 0 **13 0**

ONYEKA, Frank (M) 115 15
H: 6 0 W: 11 00 b.Abuja 1-1-98
Internationals: Nigeria Full caps.
From Ebedei.
2017–18 Midtjylland 15 4
2018–19 Midtjylland 21 4
2019–20 Midtjylland 32 4
2020–21 Midtjylland 27 3 **95 15**
2021–22 FC Midtjylland 0 0
2021–22 Brentford 20 0 **20 0**

PINNOCK, Ethan (D) 165 7
H: 6 2 W: 12 06 b.Lambeth 29-5-93
Internationals: England C. Jamaica Full caps.
From Dulwich Hamlet.
2017–18 Barnsley 12 2
2018–19 Barnsley 46 1 **58 3**
2019–20 Brentford 36 2
2020–21 Brentford 39 1
2021–22 Brentford 32 1 **107 4**

PRESSLEY, Aaron (F) 23 2
H: 6 2 W: 11 11 b.Edinburgh 7-11-01
Internationals: Scotland U17.
From Hearts.
2019–20 Aston Villa 0 0
2020–21 Aston Villa 0 0
2020–21 Brentford 2 0
2021–22 Brentford 0 0 **2 0**
2021–22 *AFC Wimbledon* 21 2 **21 2**

RACIC, Luka (D) 26 3
b.Greve 8-5-99
Internationals: Denmark U16, U17, U18, U19, U20, U21.
From Copenhagen.
2018–19 Brentford 2 0
2019–20 Brentford 4 1
2020–21 Brentford 0 0
2020–21 *Northampton T* 6 0 **6 0**
2021–22 Brentford 0 0 **6 1**
2021–22 *HB Koge* 14 2 **14 2**

RAYA, David (G) 210 0
H: 6 0 W: 12 08 b.Barcelona 15-9-95
Internationals: Spain Full caps.
2013–14 Blackburn R 0 0
2014–15 Blackburn R 2 0
2015–16 Blackburn R 5 0
2016–17 Blackburn R 5 0
2017–18 Blackburn R 45 0
2018–19 Blackburn R 41 0 **98 0**
2019–20 Brentford 46 0
2020–21 Brentford 42 0
2021–22 Brentford 24 0 **112 0**

ROERSLEV RASMUSSEN, Mads (D) 59 1
H: 5 11 W: 10 08 b.Copenhagen 24-6-99
Internationals: Denmark U17, U18, U19, U20, U21.
2016–17 FC Copenhagen 3 0
2016–17 *Halmstads* 1 0 **1 0**
2017–18 FC Copenhagen 2 0
2018–19 FC Copenhagen 0 0 **5 0**
2018–19 *Vendsyssel* 4 0 **4 0**
2019–20 Brentford 11 0
2020–21 Brentford 17 0
2021–22 Brentford 21 1 **49 1**

SORENSEN, Mads (D) 81 3
H: 6 1 W: 11 07 b.Horsens 7-1-99
Internationals: Denmark U18, U19, U21.
2014–15 Horsens 6 0
2015–16 Horsens 5 0
2016–17 Horsens 6 0
2017–18 Horsens 3 1 **20 1**
2017–18 Brentford 0 0
2018–19 Brentford 8 0
2019–20 Brentford 1 0
2019–20 *AFC Wimbledon* 9 0 **9 0**
2020–21 Brentford 32 2
2021–22 Brentford 11 0 **52 2**

STEVENS, Fin (D) 3 0
H: 5 10 b.Brighton 10-4-01
Internationals: Wales U21.
From Arsenal, Worthing.
2020–21 Brentford 2 0
2021–22 Brentford 1 0 **3 0**

THOMPSON, Dominic (M) 50 0
H: 6 0 W: 11 11 b.London Borough of Brent 26-7-00
2018–19 Arsenal 0 0
2019–20 Brentford 2 0
2020–21 Brentford 4 0
2020–21 *Swindon T* 25 0 **25 0**
2021–22 Brentford 2 0 **8 0**
2021–22 *Ipswich T* 17 0 **17 0**

TONEY, Ivan (F) 298 119
H: 5 10 W: 12 00 b.Northampton 16-3-96
2012–13 Northampton T 0 0
2013–14 Northampton T 13 3
2014–15 Northampton T 40 8 **53 11**
2015–16 Newcastle U 2 0
2015–16 *Barnsley* 15 1 **15 1**
2016–17 Newcastle U 0 0
2016–17 *Shrewsbury T* 19 6 **19 6**
2016–17 *Scunthorpe U* 15 6
2017–18 Newcastle U 0 0 **2 0**
2017–18 *Wigan Ath* 24 4 **24 4**
2017–18 *Scunthorpe U* 16 8 **31 14**
2018–19 Peterborough U 44 16
2019–20 Peterborough U 32 24 **76 40**
2020–21 Brentford 45 31
2021–22 Brentford 33 12 **78 43**

TREVITT, Ryan (M) 0 0
b. 12-3-03
2020–21 Brentford 0 0
2021–22 Brentford 0 0

VALENCIA, Joel (F) 181 12
b.Esmeraldas 16-11-94
Internationals: Spain U17. Ecuador U17.
2011–12 Zaragoza 1 0
2012–13 Zaragoza 0 0
2013–14 Zaragoza 0 0 **1 0**
2014–15 Logrones 33 1
2015–16 Logrones 17 0 **50 1**
2015–16 Koper 13 1
2016–17 Koper 13 0 **26 1**
2017–18 Piast Gliwice 25 3
2018–19 Piast Gliwice 33 6
2019–20 Piast Gliwice 1 0 **59 9**
2019–20 Brentford 19 1
2020–21 Brentford 0 0
2020–21 *Legia Warsaw* 8 0 **8 0**
2021–22 Brentford 0 0 **19 1**
2021–22 *Alcorcon* 18 0 **18 0**

WINTERBOTTOM, Ben (G) 0 0
b.Preston 16-7-01
From Blackburn R.
2019–20 Liverpool 0 0
2020–21 Brentford 0 0
2021–22 Brentford 0 0

WISSA, Yoane (F) 207 59
H: 5 11 W: 11 11 b.Epinay-sous-Senart 3-9-96
Internationals: DR Congo Full caps.
2013–14 Chateauroux 0 0
2014–15 Chateauroux 0 0
2015–16 Chateauroux 23 7 **23 7**
2016–17 Angers 2 0
2016–17 *Stade Laval* 15 2 **15 2**
2017–18 Angers 0 0 **2 0**
2017–18 *Ajaccio* 20 8 **20 8**
2017–18 Lorient 15 4
2018–19 Lorient 36 6
2019–20 Lorient 28 15
2020–21 Lorient 38 10
2021–22 Lorient 0 0 **117 35**
2021–22 Brentford 30 7 **30 7**

YOUNG-COOMBES, Nathan (F) 1 0
b.Sutton 15-1-03
Internationals: England U17.
From Crystal Palace, Chelsea, Rangers.
2021–22 Brentford 1 0 **1 0**

Players retained or with offer of contract
Adedokun, Valentino; Oyegoke, Daniel; Peart-Harris, Myles; Rees, Roco.

BRIGHTON & HA (14)

ALZATE, Steve (M) 77 4
H: 5 10 W: 10 03 b.Camden Town 1-9-98
Internationals: Colombia Full caps.
2016–17 Leyton Orient 12 1 **12 1**
2017–18 Brighton & HA 0 0
2018–18 Brighton & HA 0 0
2018–19 *Swindon T* 22 2 **22 2**
2019–20 Brighton & HA 19 0
2020–21 Brighton & HA 15 1
2021–22 Brighton & HA 9 0 **43 1**

ANDONE, Florin (F) 196 63
H: 6 0 W: 11 07 b.Botosani 5-1-94
Internationals: Romania U19, Full caps.
2012–13 Villarreal 0 0
2013–14 Villarreal 0 0
2013–14 *Atletico Baleares* 34 12 **34 12**
2014–15 Cordoba 20 5
2015–16 Cordoba 36 21 **56 26**
2016–17 Deportivo la Coruna 37 12
2017–18 Deportivo la Coruna 29 7 **66 19**
2018–19 Brighton & HA 23 3
2019–20 Brighton & HA 3 1
2019–20 *Galatasaray* 9 2 **9 2**
2020–21 Brighton & HA 0 0
2021–22 Brighton & HA 0 0 **26 4**
2021–22 *Cadiz* 5 0 **5 0**

BALUTA, Tudor (M) 58 2
b.Craiova 27-3-99
Internationals: Romania U19, U21, Full caps.
2015–16 Viitorul Constanta 2 0
2016–17 Viitorul Constanta 0 0
2017–18 Viitorul Constanta 24 0
2018–19 Viitorul Constanta 27 2 **53 2**
2019–20 Brighton & HA 0 0
2019–20 *Den Haag* 4 0 **4 0**
2020–21 Brighton & HA 0 0
2020–21 *Dynamo Kyiv* 1 0 **1 0**
2021–22 Brighton & HA 0 0

BEADLE, James (G) **0 0**
b. 16-7-04
Internationals: England U18.
2021–22 Charlton Ath 0 0
2021–22 Brighton & HA 0 0

BISSOUMA, Yves (M) **159 6**
H: 5 9 W: 12 04 b.Issia 30-8-96
Internationals: Mali Full caps.
From Real Bamako.
2016–17 Lille 23 1
2017–18 Lille 24 2 **47 3**
2018–19 Brighton & HA 28 0
2019–20 Brighton & HA 22 1
2020–21 Brighton & HA 36 1
2021–22 Brighton & HA 26 1 **112 3**

CAICEDO, Moises (M) **33 5**
H: 5 9 W: 11 07 b.Santo Domingo 2-11-01
Internationals: Ecuador Full caps.
2019 Independiente del Valle 3 0
2020 Independiente del Valle 22 4
2020–21 Independiente del Valle0 0 **25**
4
2020–21 Brighton & HA 0 0
2021–22 Brighton & HA 8 1 **8 1**
2021–22 *Beerschot VA* 0 0

CLARKE, Matthew (M) **264 9**
H: 5 11 W: 11 00 b.Ipswich 22-9-96
2013–14 Ipswich T 0 0
2014–15 Ipswich T 4 0
2015–16 Ipswich T 0 0 **4 0**
2015–16 *Portsmouth* 29 1
2016–17 Portsmouth 33 1
2017–18 Portsmouth 42 2
2018–19 Portsmouth 46 3 **150 7**
2019–20 Brighton & HA 0 0
2019–20 *Derby Co* 35 1
2020–21 Brighton & HA 0 0
2020–21 *Derby Co* 42 0 **77 1**
2021–22 Brighton & HA 0 0
2021–22 *WBA* 33 1 **33 1**

CONNOLLY, Aaron (F) **66 7**
H: 5 8 W: 12 02 b.Galway 28-1-00
Internationals: Republic of Ireland U17, U19, U21, Full caps.
2017–18 Brighton & HA 0 0
2018–19 Brighton & HA 0 0
2018–19 *Luton T* 2 0 **2 0**
2019–20 Brighton & HA 24 3
2020–21 Brighton & HA 17 2
2021–22 Brighton & HA 4 0 **45 5**
2021–22 *Middlesbrough* 19 2 **19 2**

CUCURELLA, Marc (D) **141 6**
H: 5 8 W: 10 10 b.Alella 22-7-98
Internationals: Spain U16, U17, U18, U19, U20, U21, U23, Full caps.
From Espanyol.
2016–17 Barcelona 0 0
2017–18 Barcelona 0 0
2018–19 Barcelona 0 0
2018–19 *Eibar* 31 1 **31 1**
2019–20 Barcelona 0 0
2019–20 *Getafe* 37 1
2020–21 Getafe 37 3
2021–22 Getafe 1 0 **75 4**
2021–22 Brighton & HA 35 1 **35 1**

DENDONCKER, Lars (D) **6 0**
b.Passandale 3-4-01
From Club Brugge.
2020–21 Brighton & HA 0 0
2021–22 Brighton & HA 0 0
2021–22 *St Johnstone* 6 0 **6 0**

DESBOIS, Adam (G) **0 0**
b.Reading 5-1-01
2020–21 Brighton & HA 0 0
2021–22 Brighton & HA 0 0

DUFFY, Shane (D) **282 20**
H: 6 4 W: 12 00 b.Derry 1-1-92
Internationals: Northern Ireland U16, U17, U19, U21, B. Republic of Ireland U19, U21, Full caps.
2008–09 Everton 0 0
2009–10 Everton 0 0
2010–11 Everton 0 0
2010–11 *Burnley* 1 0 **1 0**
2011–12 Everton 4 0
2011–12 *Scunthorpe U* 18 2 **18 2**
2012–13 Everton 1 0
2013–14 Everton 0 0
2013–14 *Yeovil T* 37 1 **37 1**
2014–15 Everton 0 0 **5 0**
2014–15 Blackburn R 19 1
2015–16 Blackburn R 41 4
2016–17 Blackburn R 3 0 **63 5**
2016–17 Brighton & HA 31 2
2017–18 Brighton & HA 37 0
2018–19 Brighton & HA 35 5
2019–20 Brighton & HA 19 1
2020–21 Brighton & HA 0 0
2020–21 *Celtic* 18 3 **18 3**
2021–22 Brighton & HA 18 1 **140 9**

DUNK, Lewis (D) **344 22**
H: 6 4 W: 13 11 b.Brighton 1-12-91
Internationals: England Full caps.
2009–10 Brighton & HA 1 0
2010–11 Brighton & HA 5 0
2011–12 Brighton & HA 31 0
2012–13 Brighton & HA 8 0
2013–14 Brighton & HA 6 0
2013–14 *Bristol C* 2 0 **2 0**
2014–15 Brighton & HA 38 5
2015–16 Brighton & HA 38 3
2016–17 Brighton & HA 43 2
2017–18 Brighton & HA 38 1
2018–19 Brighton & HA 36 2
2019–20 Brighton & HA 36 3
2020–21 Brighton & HA 33 5
2021–22 Brighton & HA 29 1 **342 22**

ENEME ELLA, Ulrick (F) **0 0**
H: 6 0 W: 11 11 b.Sens 22-5-01
Internationals: France U16, U17, U18, U19. Gabon Full caps.
From Amiens.
2020–21 Brighton & HA 0 0
2021–22 Brighton & HA 0 0

FERGUSON, Evan (F) **4 0**
H: 6 0 b.Bettystown 19-10-04
Internationals: Republic of Ireland U17, U21.
From St Kevin's Boys.
2019 Bohemians 1 0
2020 Bohemians 2 0 **3 0**
2021–22 Brighton & HA 1 0 **1 0**

FURLONG, James (D) **0 0**
H: 5 10 W: 11 03 b.Dublin 7-6-02
2020–21 Brighton & HA 0 0
2021–22 Brighton & HA 0 0

GROSS, Pascal (M) **343 37**
H: 5 7 W: 10 06 b.Bad Salzungen 15-6-91
Internationals: Germany U18, U19.
2008–09 1899 Hoffenheim 4 0
2009–10 1899 Hoffenheim 1 0
2010–11 1899 Hoffenheim 0 0 **5 0**
2010–11 Karlsruher 3 1
2011–12 Karlsruher 22 2 **25 3**
2012–13 Ingolstadt 04 30 2
2013–14 Ingolstadt 04 29 2
2014–15 Ingolstadt 04 34 7
2015–16 Ingolstadt 04 32 1
2016–17 Ingolstadt 04 33 5 **158 17**
2017–18 Brighton & HA 38 7
2018–19 Brighton & HA 25 3
2019–20 Brighton & HA 29 2
2020–21 Brighton & HA 34 3
2021–22 Brighton & HA 29 2 **155 17**

IFILL, Markus (M) **0 0**
b. 2-11-03
2019–20 Brighton & HA 0 0
2020–21 Brighton & HA 0 0
2021–22 Brighton & HA 0 0

JENKS, Teddy (M) **18 2**
b. 12-3-02
Internationals: England U16, U17.
2019–20 Brighton & HA 0 0
2020–21 Brighton & HA 0 0
2021–22 Brighton & HA 0 0
2021–22 *Aberdeen* 18 2 **18 2**

KARBOWNIK, Michal (D) **48 0**
H: 5 9 W: 11 00 b.Radom 13-3-01
Internationals: Poland U16, U17, U18, U19, U21, Full caps.
2017–18 Legia Warsaw 0 0
2018–19 Legia Warsaw 0 0
2019–20 Legia Warzaw 28 0 **28 0**
2020–21 Brighton & HA 0 0
2020–21 *Legia Warsaw* 8 0 **8 0**
2021–22 Brighton & HA 0 0
2021–22 *Olympiacos* 12 0 **12 0**

KHADRA, Reda (F) **28 4**
H: 5 9 b.Berlin 4-7-01
Internationals: Germany U18.
From Borussia Dortmund.
2020–21 Brighton & HA 1 0
2021–22 Brighton & HA 0 0 **1 0**
2021–22 *Blackburn R* 27 4 **27 4**

KOZLOWSKI, Kacper (M) **49 4**
b.Koszalin 16-10-03
Internationals: Poland U17, U19, U21, Full caps.
2018–19 Pogon Szczecin 1 0
2019–20 Pogon Szczecin 3 0
2020–21 Pogon Szczecin 20 1
2021–22 Pogon Szczecin 16 3 **40 4**
2021–22 Brighton & HA 0 0
2021–22 *Union SG* 9 0 **9 0**

LALLANA, Adam (M) **420 67**
H: 5 10 W: 11 06 b.St Albans 10-5-88
Internationals: England U18, U19, U21, Full caps.
2005–06 Southampton 0 0
2006–07 Southampton 1 0
2007–08 Southampton 5 1
2007–08 *Bournemouth* 3 0 **3 0**
2008–09 Southampton 40 1
2009–10 Southampton 44 15
2010–11 Southampton 36 8
2011–12 Southampton 41 11
2012–13 Southampton 30 3
2013–14 Southampton 38 9 **235 48**
2014–15 Liverpool 27 5
2015–16 Liverpool 30 4
2016–17 Liverpool 31 8
2017–18 Liverpool 12 0
2018–19 Liverpool 13 0
2019–20 Liverpool 15 1 **128 18**
2020–21 Brighton & HA 30 1
2021–22 Brighton & HA 24 0 **54 1**

LAMPTEY, Tariq (D) **50 1**
H: 5 9 W: 10 12 b.Hillingdon 30-9-00
Internationals: England U18, U19, U20, Full caps.
2019–20 Chelsea 1 0 **1 0**
2019–20 Brighton & HA 8 0
2020–21 Brighton & HA 11 1
2021–22 Brighton & HA 30 0 **49 1**

LEONARD, Marc (M) **0 0**
H: 5 11 b.Glasgow 19-12-01
Internationals: Scotland U17, U18, U19, U21.
From Hearts.
2020–21 Brighton & HA 0 0
2021–22 Brighton & HA 0 0

LOCADIA, Jurgen (F) **200 55**
H: 6 2 W: 12 04 b.Emmen 7-11-93
Internationals: Netherlands U17, U18, U19, U20, U21.
2011–12 PSV Eindhoven 0 0
2012–13 PSV Eindhoven 15 6
2013–14 PSV Eindhoven 31 13
2014–15 PSV Eindhoven 23 6
2015–16 PSV Eindhoven 29 8
2016–17 PSV Eindhoven 14 3
2017–18 PSV Eindhoven 15 9 **127 45**
2017–18 Brighton & HA 6 1
2018–19 Brighton & HA 26 2
2019–20 Brighton & HA 2 0
2019–20 *Hoffenheim* 11 4 **11 4**
2020 *Cincinnati* 18 2
2020–21 Brighton & HA 0 0
2021 *Cincinnati* 9 1 **27 3**
2021–22 Brighton & HA 1 0 **35 3**
Transferred to Bochum, January 2022.

MAC ALLISTER, Alexis (M) **142 17**
H: 5 9 W: 11 05 b.La Pampa 24-12-98
Internationals: Argentina U23, Full caps.
2016–17 Argentinos Juniors 23 3
2017–18 Argentinos Juniors 24 2
2018–19 Argentinos Juniors 19 5 **66 10**
2019–20 Brighton & HA 9 0
2019–20 *Boca Juniors* 13 1 **13 1**
2020–21 Brighton & HA 21 1
2021–22 Brighton & HA 33 5 **63 6**

MARCH, Solly (M) **217 11**
H: 5 11 W: 12 02 b.Lewes 26-7-94
Internationals: England U20, U21.
From Lewes.
2012–13 Brighton & HA 0 0
2013–14 Brighton & HA 23 0
2014–15 Brighton & HA 11 1
2015–16 Brighton & HA 16 3
2016–17 Brighton & HA 25 3
2017–18 Brighton & HA 36 1
2018–19 Brighton & HA 35 1
2019–20 Brighton & HA 19 0
2020–21 Brighton & HA 21 2
2021–22 Brighton & HA 31 0 **217 11**

MAUPAY, Neal (F) **274 81**
H: 5 7 W: 10 12 b.Versailles 14-8-96
Internationals: France U16, U17, U19, U21.
2012–13 Nice 15 3
2013–14 Nice 16 2
2014–15 Nice 13 1 **44 6**
2015–16 Saint-Etienne 15 1
2016–17 Saint-Etienne 0 0 **15 1**
2016–17 *Brest* 28 11 **28 11**
2017–18 Brentford 42 12
2018–19 Brentford 43 25 **85 37**
2019–20 Brighton & HA 37 10
2020–21 Brighton & HA 33 8
2021–22 Brighton & HA 32 8 **102 26**

McGILL, Thomas (G) **1 0**
H: 6 1 W: 12 08 b.Haywards Heath 25-3-00
Internationals: England U16, U17, U19, U20.
2019–20 Brighton & HA 0 0
2019–20 *Crawley T* 0 0
2020–21 Brighton & HA 0 0
2020–21 *Crawley T* 1 0 **1 0**
2021–22 Brighton & HA 0 0

MILLER, Todd (M) **1 0**
b. 1-10-02
2018–19 Colchester U 1 0 **1 0**
2019–20 Brighton & HA 0 0

2020–21 Brighton & HA 0 0
2021–22 Brighton & HA 0 0

MITOMA, Kaoru (F) 77 28
H: 5 10 b.Kanagawa 20-5-97
Internationals: Japan U21, U23, Full caps.
2018 Kawasaki Frontale 0 0
2019 Kawasaki Frontale 0 0
2020 Kawasaki Frontale 30 13 **30 13**
2021–22 Kawasaki Frontale 20 8 **20 8**
2021–22 Brighton & HA 0 0
2021–22 *Union SG* 27 7 **27 7**

MODER, Jakub (M) 98 9
H: 6 3 W: 12 04 b.Szczecinek 7-4-99
Internationals: Poland U17, U18, U19, U20, Full caps.
2016–17 Lech Poznan 0 0
2017–18 Lech Poznan 1 0
2018–19 Lech Poznan 0 0
2018–19 *Odra Opole* 31 4 **31 4**
2019–20 Lech Poznan 26 5
2020–21 Lech Poznan 0 0 **27 5**
2020–21 Brighton & HA 12 0
2021–22 Brighton & HA 28 0 **40 0**

MOLUMBY, Jayson (M) 83 2
H: 5 10 W: 11 07 b.Waterford 6-8-99
Internationals: Republic of Ireland U16, U17, U19, U21, Full caps.
2017–18 Brighton & HA 0 0
2018–19 Brighton & HA 0 0
2019–20 Brighton & HA 0 0
2019–20 *Millwall* 36 1 **36 1**
2020–21 Brighton & HA 1 0
2020–21 *Preston NE* 15 0 **15 0**
2021–22 Brighton & HA 0 0 **1 0**
2021–22 *WBA* 31 1 **31 1**

MORAN, Andrew (M) 3 1
b.Dublin 15-10-03
Internationals: Germany U17, U19, U20, U21.
From St Joseph's Boys.
2019 Bray W 2 0
2020 Bray W 1 1 **3 1**
2021–22 Brighton & HA 0 0

MWEPU, Enock (M) 122 19
H: 6 0 W: 12 02 b.Lusaka 1-1-98
Internationals: Zambia U20, Full caps.
From Napsa Stars Lusaka, Kafue Celtic.
2017–18 Red Bull Salzburg 8 1
2017–18 *Liefering* 23 6 **23 6**
2018–19 Red Bull Salzburg 19 1
2019–20 Red Bull Salzburg 25 4
2020–21 Red Bull Salzburg 29 5
2021–22 Red Bull Salzburg 0 0 **81 11**
2021–22 Brighton & HA 18 2 **18 2**

OFFIAH, Odel (D) 0 0
H: 6 2 b.Camden 26-10-02
2020–21 Brighton & HA 0 0
2021–22 Brighton & HA 0 0

OSTIGARD, Leo (D) 113 4
H: 6 0 W: 12 08 b.Molde 28-11-99
Internationals: Norway U16, U17, U18, U19, U20, U21, U23, Full caps.
2017 Molde 7 0
2018 Molde 0 0 **7 0**
2018 *Viking* 11 0 **11 0**
2018–19 Brighton & HA 0 0
2019–20 Brighton & HA 0 0
2019–20 *St Pauli* 28 1 **28 1**
2020–21 Brighton & HA 0 0
2020–21 *Coventry C* 39 2 **39 2**
2021–22 Brighton & HA 0 0
2021–22 *Stoke C* 13 1 **13 1**
2021–22 *Genoa* 15 0 **15 0**

PACKHAM, Sam (M) 6 0
b.Redhill 8-11-01
2020–21 Brighton & HA 0 0
2021–22 Brighton & HA 0 0
2022 *Bohemians* 6 0 **6 0**

PEUPION, Cameron (M) 0 0
H: 5 9 b.Sydney 23-9-02
From Sydney FC.
2020–21 Brighton & HA 0 0
2021–22 Brighton & HA 0 0

RICHARDS, Taylor (M) 49 10
H: 5 11 W: 12 08 b.Hammersmith 4-12-00
Internationals: England U17.
2018–19 Manchester C 0 0
2019–20 Brighton & HA 0 0
2020–21 Brighton & HA 0 0
2020–21 *Doncaster R* 41 10 **41 10**
2021–22 Brighton & HA 2 0 **2 0**
2021–22 *Birmingham C* 6 0 **6 0**

ROBERTS, Haydon (D) 26 0
H: 5 11 W: 10 12 b.Brighton 10-5-02
Internationals: England U17, U18.
2019–20 Brighton & HA 0 0
2020–21 Brighton & HA 0 0
2020–21 *Rochdale* 26 0 **26 0**
2021–22 Brighton & HA 0 0

RUSHWORTH, Carl (G) 43 0
b.Halifax 2-7-01
From Halifax T.
2021–22 Brighton & HA 0 0
2021–22 *Walsall* 43 0 **43 0**

SANCHEZ, Robert (G) 107 0
H: 6 6 W: 14 02 b.Cartagena 18-11-97
Internationals: Spain Full caps.
From Levante.
2018–19 Brighton & HA 0 0
2018–19 *Forest Green R* 17 0 **17 0**
2019–20 Brighton & HA 0 0
2019–20 *Rochdale* 26 0 **26 0**
2020–21 Brighton & HA 27 0
2021–22 Brighton & HA 37 0 **64 0**

SARMIENTO, Jeremy (F) 5 0
H: 6 0 b.Madrid 16-6-02
Internationals: England U16, U17, U18. Ecuador Full caps.
From Charlton Ath, Benfica.
2021–22 Brighton & HA 5 0 **5 0**

SCHERPEN, Kjell (G) 44 0
H: 6 8 W: 13 05 b.Emmen 23-1-00
Internationals: Netherlands U19, U21.
2017–18 Emmen 1 0
2018–19 Emmen 34 0 **35 0**
2019–20 Ajax 0 0
2020–21 Ajax 2 0 **2 0**
2021–22 Brighton & HA 0 0
2021–22 *Oostende* 7 0 **7 0**

SIMA, Abdallah (F) 26 11
H: 6 2 W: 11 09 b.Dakar 17-6-01
Internationals: Senegal Full caps.
2020–21 Slavia Prague 21 11
2021–22 Slavia Prague 3 0 **24 11**
2021–22 Brighton & HA 0 0
2021–22 *Stoke C* 2 0 **2 0**

SPONG, Jack (M) 0 0
b. 4-2-02
2019–20 Brighton & HA 0 0
2020–21 Brighton & HA 0 0
2021–22 Brighton & HA 0 0

STEELE, Jason (G) 273 0
H: 6 2 W: 12 06 b.Newton Aycliffe 18-8-90
Internationals: England U16, U17, U19, U21. Great Britain.
2007–08 Middlesbrough 0 0
2008–09 Middlesbrough 0 0
2009–10 Middlesbrough 0 0
2009–10 *Northampton T* 13 0 **13 0**
2010–11 Middlesbrough 35 0
2011–12 Middlesbrough 34 0
2012–13 Middlesbrough 46 0
2013–14 Middlesbrough 16 0
2014–15 Middlesbrough 0 0 **131 0**
2014–15 *Blackburn R* 31 0
2015–16 Blackburn R 41 0
2016–17 Blackburn R 41 0 **113 0**
2017–18 Sunderland 15 0 **15 0**
2018–19 Brighton & HA 0 0
2019–20 Brighton & HA 0 0
2020–21 Brighton & HA 0 0
2021–22 Brighton & HA 1 0 **1 0**

TALLEY, Fynn (G) 0 0
b.Bexley 14-9-02
From Arsenal.
2020–21 Brighton & HA 0 0
2021–22 Brighton & HA 0 0

TANIMOWO, Ayo (D) 0 0
b.Redbridge 9-11-01
From Norwich C.
2020–21 Brighton & HA 0 0
2021–22 Brighton & HA 0 0

TOLAJ, Lorent (F) 4 0
H: 5 9 b.Aigle 23-10-01
Internationals: Switzerland U17, U18, U19.
From Sion.
2020–21 Brighton & HA 0 0
2021–22 Brighton & HA 0 0
2021–22 *Cambridge U* 4 0 **4 0**

TROSSARD, Leandro (M) 272 79
H: 5 8 W: 9 08 b.Waterschei 4-12-94
Internationals: Belgium U16, U17, U18, U19, U21, Full caps.
2011–12 Genk 1 0
2012–13 Genk 0 0
2012–13 *Lommel U* 12 7
2013–14 Genk 0 0
2013–14 *Westerlo* 17 3 **17 3**
2014–15 Genk 0 0
2014–15 *Lommel U* 30 16 **42 23**
2015–16 Genk 0 0
2015–16 *OH Leuven* 30 8 **30 8**
2016–17 Genk 31 6
2017–18 Genk 17 7
2018–19 Genk 34 14 **83 27**
2019–20 Brighton & HA 31 5
2020–21 Brighton & HA 35 5
2021–22 Brighton & HA 34 8 **100 18**

TSOUNGUI, Antef (D) 0 0
H: 6 1 b.Brussels 30-12-02
Internationals: Belgium U17, U18.
From Chelsea.
2020–21 Brighton & HA 0 0
2021–22 Brighton & HA 0 0

UNDAV, Deniz (F) 201 98
H: 5 10 b.Achim 19-7-96
2014–15 Havelse 3 0
2015–16 Havelse 32 16
2016–17 Havelse 32 16 **67 32**
2017–18 Eintracht Brauschweig 0 0
2018–19 Meppen 35 6
2019–20 Meppen 34 17 **69 23**
2020–21 Union SG 26 17
2021–22 Union SG 25 18
2021–22 Brighton & HA 0 0
2021–22 *Union SG* 14 8 **65 43**

VAN HECKE, Jan (D) 42 4
H: 6 2 W: 12 04 b.Amemuiden 8-6-00
Internationals: Netherlands U21.
2019–20 NAC Breda 11 3 **11 3**
2020–21 Brighton & HA 0 0
2021–22 Heerenveen 0 0
2021–22 Brighton & HA 0 0
2021–22 *Blackburn R* 31 1 **31 1**

VELTMAN, Joel (D) 241 12
H: 6 0 W: 11 07 b.Velsen 15-1-92
Internationals: Netherlands U17, U19, U20, Full caps.
2011–12 Ajax 0 0
2012–13 Ajax 7 0
2013–14 Ajax 25 2
2014–15 Ajax 25 4
2015–16 Ajax 34 2
2016–17 Ajax 30 0
2017–18 Ajax 30 1
2018–19 Ajax 9 1
2019–20 Ajax 19 0 **179 10**
2020–21 Brighton & HA 28 1
2021–22 Brighton & HA 34 1 **62 2**

WEBSTER, Adam (D) 244 15
H: 6 1 W: 11 11 b.West Wittering 4-1-95
Internationals: England U18, U19.
2011–12 Portsmouth 3 0
2012–13 Portsmouth 18 0
2013–14 Portsmouth 4 2
2014–15 Portsmouth 15 1
2015–16 Portsmouth 27 2 **67 5**
2016–17 Ipswich T 23 1
2017–18 Ipswich T 28 0 **51 1**
2018–19 Bristol C 44 3
2019–20 Bristol C 0 0 **44 3**
2019–20 Brighton & HA 31 3
2020–21 Brighton & HA 29 1
2021–22 Brighton & HA 22 2 **82 6**

WEIR, Jensen (M) 16 1
H: 6 0 W: 11 09 b.Warrington 31-1-02
Internationals: Scotland U16, U17. England U17, U18, U20.
2017–18 Wigan Ath 0 0
2018–19 Wigan Ath 1 0
2019–20 Wigan Ath 0 0 **1 0**
2020–21 Brighton & HA 0 0
2021–22 Brighton & HA 0 0
2021–22 *Cambridge U* 15 1 **15 1**

WELBECK, Danny (F) 281 58
H: 6 0 W: 11 07 b.Manchester 26-11-90
Internationals: England U17, U18, U19, U21, Full caps.
2007–08 Manchester U 0 0
2008–09 Manchester U 3 1
2009–10 Manchester U 5 0
2009–10 *Preston NE* 8 2 **8 2**
2010–11 Manchester U 0 0
2010–11 *Sunderland* 26 6 **26 6**
2011–12 Manchester U 30 9
2012–13 Manchester U 27 1
2013–14 Manchester U 25 9
2014–15 Manchester U 2 0 **92 20**
2014–15 Arsenal 25 4
2015–16 Arsenal 11 4
2016–17 Arsenal 16 2
2017–18 Arsenal 28 5
2018–19 Arsenal 8 1 **88 16**
2019–20 Watford 18 2
2020–21 Watford 0 0 **18 2**
2020–21 Brighton & HA 24 6
2021–22 Brighton & HA 25 6 **49 12**

ZEQIRI, Andi (F) 124 30
H: 6 1 W: 11 05 b.Lausanne 22-6-99
Internationals: Switzerland U16, U17, U18, U19, U20, U21, Full caps.
2014–15 Lausanne 3 0
2015–16 Lausanne 14 2
2016–17 Lausanne 0 0
2017–18 Lausanne 19 2
2018–19 Lausanne 24 7
2019–20 Lausanne 33 17 **93 28**
2020–21 Lahti 0 0
2020–21 Lausanne Sports 0 0

2020–21 Brighton & HA 9 0
2021–22 Brighton & HA 0 0 **9 0**
2021–22 *Augsburg* 22 2 **22 2**

Players retained or with offer of contract
Bull, Toby; Cahill, Killian; Chouchane, Samy; Clark, Billie; Emmerson, Zak; Everitt, Matthew; Hinchy, Jack; Jackson, Benjamin; Kavanagh, Leigh; Nilsson, Casper; Shann, Casey; Turns, Ed; Wilson, Benjamin.

Scholars
Bull, Toby Graham; Duffus, Joshua James Leslie; Fisher, Hugo Dov; Gee, Jake Ian; Hinshelwood, Jack Luca; Jenks, Eliot Steven; McConville, Ruairi Conor; Reid, Tommy; Ryan, Kain Sharif; Smith, Bailey Leo; Sturge, Zak Norton; Winstanley, Joseph Louie.

BRISTOL C (15)

ATKINSON, Robert (D) **73 3**
H: 6 4 W: 13 05 b.Chesterfield 13-7-98
From Basingstoke T.
2017–18 Fulham 0 0
2018–19 Fulham 0 0
From Eastleigh.
2019–20 Oxford U 0 0
2020–21 Oxford U 39 1 **39 1**
2021–22 Bristol C 34 2 **34 2**

BAKER, Nathan (D) **273 4**
H: 6 2 W: 12 13 b.Worcester 23-4-91
Internationals: England U19, U20, U21.
2008–09 Aston Villa 0 0
2009–10 Aston Villa 0 0
2009–10 *Lincoln C* 18 0 **18 0**
2010–11 Aston Villa 4 0
2011–12 Aston Villa 8 0
2011–12 *Millwall* 6 0 **6 0**
2012–13 Aston Villa 26 0
2013–14 Aston Villa 30 0
2014–15 Aston Villa 11 0
2015–16 Aston Villa 0 0
2015–16 *Bristol C* 36 1
2016–17 Aston Villa 32 1 **111 1**
2017–18 Bristol C 34 0
2018–19 Bristol C 16 0
2019–20 Bristol C 34 1
2020–21 Bristol C 3 0
2021–22 Bristol C 15 1 **138 3**

BAKINSON, Tyreeq (M) **109 10**
H: 6 1 W: 11 00 b.Camden 8-1-98
2015–16 Luton T 1 0
2016–17 Luton T 0 0
2017–18 Luton T 0 0 **1 0**
2017–18 Bristol C 0 0
2018–19 Bristol C 0 0
2018–19 *Newport Co* 30 1 **30 1**
2019–20 Bristol C 0 0
2019–20 *Plymouth Arg* 14 2 **14 2**
2020–21 Bristol C 34 4
2021–22 Bristol C 13 1 **47 5**
2021–22 *Ipswich T* 17 2 **17 2**

BELL, Sam (F) **9 0**
b.Bristol 23-5-02
2018–19 Bristol C 0 0
2019–20 Bristol C 0 0
2020–21 Bristol C 4 0
2021–22 Bristol C 5 0 **9 0**

BENAROUS, Ayman (M) **11 0**
H: 5 11 b.Bristol 27-7-03
Internationals: England U17.
2021–22 Bristol C 11 0 **11 0**

BENTLEY, Daniel (G) **388 0**
H: 6 2 W: 11 05 b.Basildon 13-7-93
2011–12 Southend U 1 0
2012–13 Southend U 9 0
2013–14 Southend U 46 0
2014–15 Southend U 42 0
2015–16 Southend U 43 0 **141 0**
2016–17 Brentford 45 0
2017–18 Brentford 45 0
2018–19 Brentford 33 0 **123 0**
2019–20 Bristol C 43 0
2020–21 Bristol C 43 0
2021–22 Bristol C 38 0 **124 0**

BRITTON, Louis (F) **19 11**
b. 17-3-01
2020–21 Bristol C 1 1
2021–22 Bristol C 0 0 **1 1**
2022 *Waterford* 18 10 **18 10**

BUSE, William (G) **0 0**
2020–21 Bristol C 0 0
2021–22 Bristol C 0 0

CONWAY, Tommy (F) **9 1**
b.Taunton 6-8-02
2020–21 Bristol C 5 1
2021–22 Bristol C 4 0 **9 1**

CUNDY, Robbie (D) **49 1**
H: 6 2 W: 12 13 b.Oxford 30-5-97
2014–15 Oxford U 0 0
2015–16 Oxford U 0 0
2016–17 Oxford U 0 0
From Gloucester C.
2019–20 Bristol C 0 0
2020–21 Bristol C 0 0
2020–21 *Cambridge U* 17 0 **17 0**
2020–21 *Gillingham* 18 1 **18 1**
2021–22 Bristol C 14 0 **14 0**

DASILVA, Jay (D) **147 2**
H: 5 7 W: 10 01 b.Luton 22-4-98
Internationals: England U16, U17, U18, U19, U20, U21.
2016–17 Chelsea 0 0
2016–17 *Charlton Ath* 10 0
2017–18 Chelsea 0 0
2017–18 *Charlton Ath* 38 0 **48 0**
2018–19 Chelsea 0 0
2018–19 *Bristol C* 28 0
2019–20 Bristol C 24 0
2020–21 Bristol C 11 1
2021–22 Bristol C 36 1 **99 2**

EDWARDS, Owura (F) **43 4**
H: 5 8 b. 10-4-01
2020–21 Grimsby T 17 1 **17 1**
2020–21 Bristol C 3 0
2021–22 Bristol C 0 0 **3 0**
2021–22 *Exeter C* 10 0 **10 0**
2021–22 *Colchester U* 13 3 **13 3**

FRANCOIS, Marlee (F) **0 0**
H: 5 11 b.Sydney 29-12-02
From Fulham.
2020–21 Bristol C 0 0
2021–22 Bristol C 0 0

IDEHEN, Duncan (M) **8 0**
b. 3-7-02
2018–19 Lincoln C 0 0
2019–20 Grimsby T 0 0
2020–21 Grimsby T 6 0 **6 0**
2021–22 Bristol C 2 0 **2 0**

JAMES, Matthew (M) **218 11**
H: 5 10 W: 11 08 b.Bacup 22-7-91
Internationals: England U16, U17, U19, U20.
2007–08 Manchester U 0 0
2008–09 Manchester U 0 0
2009–10 Manchester U 0 0
2009–10 *Preston NE* 18 2
2010–11 Manchester U 0 0
2010–11 *Preston NE* 10 0 **28 2**
2011–12 Manchester U 0 0
2012–13 Leicester C 24 3
2013–14 Leicester C 35 1
2014–15 Leicester C 27 0
2015–16 Leicester C 0 0
2016–17 Leicester C 1 0
2016–17 *Barnsley* 18 1
2017–18 Leicester C 13 0
2018–19 Leicester C 0 0
2019–20 Leicester C 1 0
2020–21 Leicester C 0 0 **101 4**
2020–21 *Barnsley* 15 0 **33 1**
2020–21 *Coventry C* 23 3 **23 3**
2021–22 Bristol C 33 1 **33 1**

JANNEH, Saikou (F) **25 1**
H: 5 11 W: 10 12 b.Gunjur 11-1-00
From Bath C, Clevedon T.
2018–19 Bristol C 0 0
2019–20 Bristol C 0 0
2020–21 Bristol C 4 0
2020–21 *Newport Co* 8 1 **8 1**
2021–22 Bristol C 1 0 **5 0**
2021–22 *Shrewsbury T* 12 0 **12 0**

KALAS, Tomas (D) **289 3**
H: 6 0 W: 12 00 b.Olomouc 15-5-93
Internationals: Czech Republic U17, U18, U19, U21, Full caps.
2009–10 Sigma Olomouc 1 0
2010–11 Chelsea 0 0
2010–11 *Sigma Olomouc* 4 0 **5 0**
2011–12 Chelsea 0 0
2012–13 Chelsea 0 0
2012–13 *Vitesse* 34 1 **34 1**
2013–14 Chelsea 2 0
2014–15 Chelsea 0 0
2014–15 *Cologne* 0 0
2014–15 *Middlesbrough* 17 0
2015–16 Chelsea 0 0
2015–16 *Middlesbrough* 26 0 **43 0**
2016–17 Chelsea 0 0
2016–17 *Fulham* 36 1
2017–18 Chelsea 0 0
2017–18 *Fulham* 33 0 **69 1**
2018–19 Chelsea 0 0 **2 0**
2018–19 *Bristol C* 38 0
2019–20 Bristol C 23 0
2020–21 Bristol C 40 1
2021–22 Bristol C 35 0 **136 1**

KING, Andy (M) **375 58**
H: 6 0 W: 11 09 b.Barnstaple 29-10-88
Internationals: Wales U19, U21, Full caps.
2007–08 Leicester C 11 1
2008–09 Leicester C 45 9
2009–10 Leicester C 43 9
2010–11 Leicester C 45 15
2011–12 Leicester C 30 4
2012–13 Leicester C 42 7
2013–14 Leicester C 30 4
2014–15 Leicester C 24 2
2015–16 Leicester C 25 2
2016–17 Leicester C 23 1
2017–18 Leicester C 11 1
2017–18 *Swansea C* 11 2 **11 2**
2018–19 Leicester C 0 0
2018–19 *Derby Co* 4 0 **4 0**
2019–20 Leicester C 0 0 **329 55**
2019–20 *Rangers* 2 0 **2 0**
2019–20 *Huddersfield T* 14 0 **14 0**
2020–21 OH Leuven 1 0 **1 0**
2021–22 Bristol C 14 1 **14 1**

KLOSE, Timm (D) **297 22**
H: 6 5 W: 13 10 b.Frankfurt am Main 9-5-88
Internationals: Switzerland U21, U23, Full caps.
2009–10 Thun 29 2
2010–11 Thun 30 3 **59 5**
2011–12 Nuremburg 13 0
2012–13 Nuremburg 32 2 **45 2**
2013–14 VfL Wolfsburg 10 0
2014–15 VfL Wolfsburg 12 1
2015–16 VfL Wolfsburg 8 1 **30 2**
2015–16 Norwich C 10 1
2016–17 Norwich C 32 1
2017–18 Norwich C 37 4
2018–19 Norwich C 31 4
2019–20 Norwich C 7 0
2020–21 Norwich C 0 0
2020–21 *FC Basel* 28 2
2021–22 *FC Basel* 0 0 **28 2**
2021–22 Norwich C 0 0 **117 10**
2021–22 Bristol C 18 1 **18 1**

LOW, Joseph (D) **0 0**
b. 20-2-02
Internationals: Wales U17.
2020–21 Bristol C 0 0
2021–22 Bristol C 0 0

MARTIN, Chris (F) **522 138**
H: 5 10 W: 11 07 b.Beccles 4-11-88
Internationals: England U19. Scotland Full caps.
2006–07 Norwich C 18 4
2007–08 Norwich C 7 0
2008–09 Norwich C 0 0
2008–09 *Luton T* 40 11 **40 11**
2009–10 Norwich C 42 17
2010–11 Norwich C 30 4
2011–12 Norwich C 4 0
2011–12 *Crystal Palace* 26 7 **26 7**
2012–13 Norwich C 1 0 **102 25**
2012–13 *Swindon T* 12 1 **12 1**
2012–13 *Derby Co* 13 2
2013–14 Derby Co 44 20
2014–15 Derby Co 35 18
2015–16 Derby Co 45 15
2016–17 Derby Co 5 0
2016–17 *Fulham* 31 10 **31 10**
2017–18 Derby Co 23 1
2017–18 *Reading* 10 1 **10 1**
2018–19 Derby Co 0 0
2018–19 *Hull C* 30 2 **30 2**
2019–20 Derby Co 35 11 **200 67**
2020–21 Bristol C 26 2
2021–22 Bristol C 45 12 **71 14**

MASSENGO, Han-Noah (M) **92 0**
H: 5 9 W: 10 06 b.Villepinte 7-7-01
Internationals: France U17, U18.
2018–19 Monaco 3 0 **3 0**
2019–20 Bristol C 25 0
2020–21 Bristol C 27 0
2021–22 Bristol C 37 0 **89 0**

MOORE, Taylor (D) **170 2**
H: 6 0 W: 12 08 b.Walthamstow 12-5-97
Internationals: England U17, U18, U19, U20.
From West Ham U.
2014–15 Lens 4 0
2015–16 Lens 5 0 **9 0**
2016–17 Bristol C 5 0
2016–17 *Bury* 19 0 **19 0**
2017–18 Bristol C 0 0
2017–18 *Cheltenham T* 36 0 **36 0**
2018–19 Bristol C 0 0
2018–19 *Southend U* 34 1 **34 1**
2019–20 Bristol C 21 1
2019–20 *Blackpool* 8 0 **8 0**
2020–21 Bristol C 22 0
2021–22 Bristol C 0 0 **48 1**
2021–22 *Hearts* 16 0 **16 0**

MORTON, James (M) **20 0**
b. 22-4-99
2017–18 Bristol C 0 0
2018–19 Bristol C 0 0
2019–20 Bristol C 0 0
2019–20 *Forest Green R* 12 0 **12 0**
2020–21 Bristol C 0 0
2020–21 *Grimsby T* 7 0 **7 0**
2020–21 *Gillingham* 1 0 **1 0**
2021–22 Bristol C 0 0

NAGY, Adam (M) **131 4**
H: 5 10 W: 12 00 b.Budapest 17-6-95
Internationals: Hungary U20, U21, Full caps.
2013–14 Ferencvaros 0 0
2014–15 Ferencvaros 1 0
2015–16 Ferencvaros 25 0 **26 0**
2016–17 Bologna 25 0
2017–18 Bologna 12 1
2018–19 Bologna 14 0 **51 1**
2019–20 Bristol C 23 1
2020–21 Bristol C 31 2
2021–22 Bristol C 0 0 **54 3**
Transferred to Pisa, August 2021.

O'DOWDA, Callum (M) **247 20**
H: 5 11 W: 11 11 b.Oxford 23-4-95
Internationals: Republic of Ireland U21, Full caps.
2012–13 Oxford U 0 0
2013–14 Oxford U 10 0
2014–15 Oxford U 39 4
2015–16 Oxford U 38 8 **87 12**
2016–17 Bristol C 34 0
2017–18 Bristol C 24 1
2018–19 Bristol C 31 4
2019–20 Bristol C 32 1
2020–21 Bristol C 19 1
2021–22 Bristol C 20 1 **160 8**

O'LEARY, Max (G) **57 0**
H: 6 1 W: 12 04 b.Bath 10-10-96
2013–14 Bristol C 0 0
2014–15 Bristol C 0 0
2015–16 Bristol C 0 0
2016–17 Bristol C 0 0
2017–18 Bristol C 0 0
2018–19 Bristol C 15 0
2019–20 Bristol C 0 0
2019–20 *Shrewsbury T* 30 0 **30 0**
2020–21 Bristol C 3 0
2021–22 Bristol C 9 0 **27 0**

PALMER, Kasey (M) **138 14**
H: 5 9 W: 10 10 b.Lewisham 9-11-96
Internationals: England U17, U18, U20, U21. Jamaica Full caps.
From Charlton Ath.
2015–16 Chelsea 0 0
2016–17 Chelsea 0 0
2016–17 *Huddersfield T* 24 4
2017–18 Chelsea 0 0
2017–18 *Huddersfield T* 4 0 **28 4**
2017–18 *Derby Co* 15 2 **15 2**
2018–19 Chelsea 0 0
2018–19 *Blackburn R* 14 1 **14 1**
2018–19 *Bristol C* 15 2
2019–20 Bristol C 25 1
2020–21 Bristol C 23 2
2020–21 *Swansea C* 12 1 **12 1**
2021–22 Bristol C 6 1 **69 6**

PEARSON, Sam (M) **13 1**
b. 26-10-01
Internationals: Wales U19, U21.
2018–19 Bristol C 0 0
2019–20 Bristol C 0 0
2020–21 Bristol C 5 0
2021–22 Bristol C 0 0 **5 0**
2021–22 *Inverness CT* 8 1 **8 1**

PRING, Cameron (D) **77 1**
H: 6 1 W: 11 03 b.Bristol 22-1-98
2018–19 Bristol C 0 0
2018–19 *Newport Co* 7 1 **7 1**
2018–19 *Cheltenham T* 8 0 **8 0**
2019–20 Bristol C 0 0
2019–20 *Walsall* 21 0 **21 0**
2020–21 Bristol C 0 0
2020–21 *Portsmouth* 9 0 **9 0**
2021–22 Bristol C 32 0 **32 0**

SCOTT, Alex (M) **41 4**
b.Guernsey 21-8-03
Internationals: England U18, U19.
From Guernsey.
2020–21 Bristol C 3 0
2021–22 Bristol C 38 4 **41 4**

SEMENYO, Antoine (F) **117 13**
H: 5 10 W: 9 13 b.Chelsea 7-1-00
Internationals: Ghana Full caps.
2017–18 Bristol C 1 0
2018–19 Bristol C 4 0
2018–19 *Newport Co* 21 3 **21 3**
2019–20 Bristol C 9 0
2019–20 *Sunderland* 7 0 **7 0**
2020–21 Bristol C 44 2
2021–22 Bristol C 31 8 **89 10**

SIMPSON, Danny (D) **338 1**
H: 5 10 W: 12 04 b.Eccles 4-1-87
2005–06 Manchester U 0 0
2006–07 Manchester U 0 0
2006–07 *Sunderland* 14 0 **14 0**
2007–08 Manchester U 3 0
2007–08 *Ipswich T* 8 0 **8 0**
2008–09 Manchester U 0 0
2008–09 *Blackburn R* 12 0 **12 0**
2009–10 Manchester U 0 0 **3 0**
2009–10 Newcastle U 39 1
2010–11 Newcastle U 30 0
2011–12 Newcastle U 35 0
2012–13 Newcastle U 19 0 **123 1**
2013–14 QPR 33 0
2014–15 QPR 1 0 **34 0**
2014–15 Leicester C 14 0
2015–16 Leicester C 30 0
2016–17 Leicester C 35 0
2017–18 Leicester C 28 0
2018–19 Leicester C 6 0 **113 0**
2019–20 Huddersfield T 24 0 **24 0**
2020–21 Bristol C 4 0
2021–22 Bristol C 3 0 **7 0**

TANNER, George (D) **78 4**
H: 5 11 W: 11 03 b.Blackpool 16-11-99
2019–20 Manchester U 0 0
2019–20 *Morecambe* 23 0 **23 0**
2019–20 *Salford C* 0 0
2020–21 Carlisle U 37 3
2021–22 Carlisle U 5 0 **42 3**
2021–22 Bristol C 13 1 **13 1**

TOWLER, Ryley (M) **4 0**
H: 6 1 W: 11 03 b.Bristol 6-5-01
2020–21 Bristol C 3 0
2021–22 Bristol C 1 0 **4 0**

VYNER, Zak (D) **161 4**
H: 5 10 W: 10 10 b.Bath 14-5-97
2015–16 Bristol C 4 0
2016–17 Bristol C 3 0
2016–17 *Accrington S* 16 0 **16 0**
2017–18 Bristol C 1 0
2017–18 *Plymouth Arg* 17 1 **17 1**
2018–19 Bristol C 0 0
2018–19 *Rotherham U* 31 0 **31 0**
2019–20 Bristol C 8 0
2019–20 *Aberdeen* 16 1 **16 1**
2020–21 Bristol C 43 2
2021–22 Bristol C 22 0 **81 2**

WEIMANN, Andreas (F) **376 75**
H: 6 2 W: 12 00 b.Vienna 5-8-91
Internationals: Austria U17, U19, U20, U21, Full caps.
From Rapid Vienna.
2008–09 Aston Villa 0 0
2009–10 Aston Villa 0 0
2010–11 Aston Villa 1 0
2010–11 *Watford* 18 4
2011–12 Aston Villa 14 2
2011–12 *Watford* 3 0 **21 4**
2012–13 Aston Villa 30 7
2013–14 Aston Villa 37 5
2014–15 Aston Villa 31 3 **113 17**
2015–16 Derby Co 30 4
2016–17 Derby Co 11 0
2016–17 *Wolverhampton W* 19 2 **19 2**
2017–18 Derby Co 40 5 **81 9**
2018–19 Bristol C 44 10
2019–20 Bristol C 45 9
2020–21 Bristol C 7 2
2021–22 Bristol C 46 22 **142 43**

WELLS, Nahki (F) **408 125**
H: 5 7 W: 10 12 b.Bermuda 1-6-90
Internationals: Bermuda Full caps.
2010–11 Carlisle U 3 0 **3 0**
2011–12 Bradford C 33 10
2012–13 Bradford C 39 18
2013–14 Bradford C 19 14 **91 42**
2013–14 Huddersfield T 22 7
2014–15 Huddersfield T 35 11
2015–16 Huddersfield T 44 17
2016–17 Huddersfield T 43 10
2017–18 Huddersfield T 0 0 **144 45**
2017–18 Burnley 9 0
2018–19 Burnley 0 0
2018–19 *QPR* 40 7
2019–20 Burnley 0 0 **9 0**
2019–20 *QPR* 26 13 **66 20**
2019–20 Bristol C 17 5
2020–21 Bristol C 46 10
2021–22 Bristol C 32 3 **95 18**

WILES-RICHARDS, Harvey (G) **0 0**
b.Bath 27-5-02
2020–21 Bristol C 0 0
2021–22 Bristol C 0 0

WILLIAMS, Joe (M) **125 2**
H: 5 10 W: 10 06 b.Liverpool 8-12-96
Internationals: England U20.
2014–15 Everton 0 0
2015–16 Everton 0 0
2016–17 Everton 0 0
2017–18 Everton 0 0
2017–18 *Barnsley* 34 1 **34 1**
2018–19 Everton 0 0
2018–19 *Bolton W* 30 0 **30 0**
2019–20 Wigan Ath 38 1 **38 1**
2020–21 Bristol C 1 0
2021–22 Bristol C 22 0 **23 0**

Players retained or with offer of contract
Backwell, Tommy; Bell, Zachary; Henry, Prince; Kadji, Dylan; Leeson, Harry; Owers, Josh; Taylor, James; Williams, Nathaniel; Wood, Callum.

Scholars
Araoye, Raphael Damilola; Boyd, McIntosh Grant; Brown, Jaden Aaron; Casa-Grande, Josey Brian; Churchley, Kai David; Hutton, Callum James; Knight-Lebel, Jamie Mathieu; Lewis, Dylan Maxwell; Morris, Matthew Thomas; Nelson, Rohan Eugene; Oputeri, Brandon Tadiwanashe; Owusu-Antwi, Filbert; Palmer Houlden, Sebastian Alexander; Richards, Isaac Bruce Tilston; Rose, Marley Venton; Sage, William Mark; Smith, Luca Alexander Mark; South Thomas, Jemar D'Andre; Taylor-Clarke, Omar Rivaldo; Thomas, Oliver Charlie; Walker, James Dylan; White, Thomas Ray.

BRISTOL R (16)

ANDERSON, Harry (F) **202 25**
H: 5 6 W: 9 11 b.Slouth 9-1-97
From Crawley T.
2014–15 Peterborough U 10 0
2015–16 Peterborough U 5 0
2016–17 Peterborough U 1 0 **16 0**
2017–18 Lincoln C 40 6
2018–19 Lincoln C 43 5
2019–20 Lincoln C 30 5
2020–21 Lincoln C 29 3
2021–22 Lincoln C 0 0 **142 19**
2021–22 Bristol R 44 6 **44 6**

ANDERTON, Nick (D) **122 5**
H: 6 2 W: 12 06 b.Preston 22-4-96
2014–15 Preston NE 0 0
2015–16 Preston NE 0 0
From Barrow.
2017–18 Blackpool 4 0
2018–19 Accrington S 22 0 **22 0**
2018–19 Blackpool 10 0
2019–20 Blackpool 2 0 **16 0**
2019–20 Carlisle U 10 2
2020–21 Carlisle U 40 2 **50 4**
2021–22 Bristol R 34 1 **34 1**

BALDWIN, Jack (D) **265 13**
H: 6 1 W: 11 00 b.Barking 30-6-93
2011–12 Hartlepool U 17 0
2012–13 Hartlepool U 32 2
2013–14 Hartlepool U 28 2 **77 4**
2013–14 Peterborough U 11 0
2014–15 Peterborough U 11 0
2015–16 Peterborough U 18 1
2016–17 Peterborough U 27 1
2017–18 Peterborough U 33 2 **100 4**
2018–19 Sunderland 34 3
2019–20 Sunderland 0 0 **34 3**
2019–20 *Salford C* 13 1 **13 1**
2020–21 Bristol R 38 1
2021–22 Bristol R 3 0 **41 1**
Transferred to Ross Co, August 2021.

BELSHAW, James (G) **80 0**
H: 6 3 W: 13 01 b.Nottingham 12-10-90
2020–21 Harrogate T 38 0
2021–22 Harrogate T 0 0 **38 0**
2021–22 Bristol R 42 0 **42 0**

BRAIN, Owen (M) **0 0**
2021–22 Bristol R 0 0

BROWN, Junior (D) **260 21**
H: 5 9 W: 10 10 b.Crewe 7-5-89
2006–07 Crewe Alex 0 0
2007–08 Crewe Alex 1 0 **1 0**
From Halifax T, Northwich Vic.
2012–13 Fleetwood T 43 11
2013–14 Fleetwood T 21 1 **64 12**
2013–14 *Tranmere R* 9 1 **9 1**
2014–15 Oxford U 11 0 **11 0**
2014–15 Mansfield T 24 2 **24 2**
2015–16 Shrewsbury T 31 0
2016–17 Shrewsbury T 43 5
2017–18 Shrewsbury T 15 1 **89 6**
2018–19 Coventry C 22 0
2019–20 Coventry C 0 0 **22 0**
2019–20 *Scunthorpe U* 20 0

2020–21 Scunthorpe U 14 0 **34 0**
2021–22 Bristol R 6 0 **6 0**

CLARKE, Leon (F) **479 141**
H: 6 2 W: 14 02 b.Birmingham 10-2-85
2003–04 Wolverhampton W 0 0
2003–04 *Kidderminster H* 4 0 **4 0**
2004–05 Wolverhampton W 28 7
2005–06 Wolverhampton W 24 1
2005–06 *QPR* 1 0
2005–06 *Plymouth Arg* 5 0 **5 0**
2006–07 Wolverhampton W 22 5
2006–07 Sheffield W 10 1
2006–07 *Oldham Ath* 5 3 **5 3**
2007–08 Sheffield W 8 3
2007–08 *Southend U* 16 8 **16 8**
2008–09 Sheffield W 29 8
2009–10 Sheffield W 36 6 **83 18**
2010–11 QPR 13 0 **14 0**
2010–11 *Preston NE* 6 1 **6 1**
2011–12 Swindon T 2 0 **2 0**
2011–12 *Chesterfield* 14 9 **14 9**
2011–12 Charlton Ath 7 0
2011–12 *Crawley T* 4 1 **4 1**
2012–13 Charlton Ath 0 0 **7 0**
2012–13 *Scunthorpe U* 15 11 **15 11**
2012–13 Coventry C 12 8
2013–14 Coventry C 23 15 **35 23**
2013–14 Wolverhampton W 13 1
2014–15 Wolverhampton W 16 2 **103 16**
2014–15 *Wigan Ath* 10 1
2015–16 Bury 32 15 **32 15**
2016–17 Sheffield U 23 7
2017–18 Sheffield U 39 19
2018–19 Sheffield U 24 3
2018–19 *Wigan Ath* 15 3 **25 4**
2019–20 Sheffield U 2 0 **88 29**
2020–21 Shrewsbury T 10 1 **10 1**
2021–22 Bristol R 11 2 **11 2**

CLARKE, Trevor (D) **104 5**
H: 5 5 W: 10 03 b.Dublin 26-3-98
Internationals: Republic of Ireland U17, U19, U21.
2016 Shamrock R 26 1
2017 Shamrock R 27 3
2018 Shamrock R 6 0
2019 Shamrock R 21 1 **80 5**
2019–20 Rotherham U 8 0
2020–21 Rotherham U 9 0
2021–22 Rotherham U 0 0 **17 0**
2021–22 Bristol R 7 0 **7 0**

COLLINS, Aaron (F) **187 42**
H: 6 1 W: 11 09 b.Newport 27-5-97
Internationals: Wales U19.
2014–15 Newport Co 2 0
2015–16 Newport Co 18 2
2015–16 Wolverhampton W 0 0
2016–17 Wolverhampton W 0 0
2016–17 *Notts Co* 18 2 **18 2**
2017–18 Wolverhampton W 0 0
2017–18 *Newport Co* 10 0 **30 2**
2018–19 Wolverhampton W 0 0
2018–19 *Colchester U* 7 0 **7 0**
2018–19 Morecambe 15 8 **15 8**
2019–20 Forest Green R 28 4
2020–21 Forest Green R 44 10
2021–22 Forest Green R 0 0 **72 14**
2021–22 Bristol R 45 16 **45 16**

COUTTS, Paul (M) **423 10**
H: 6 0 W: 11 11 b.Aberdeen 22-7-88
Internationals: Scotland U21.
From Aberdeen.
2008–09 Peterborough U 37 0
2009–10 Peterborough U 16 0 **53 0**
2009–10 Preston NE 13 1
2010–11 Preston NE 23 1
2011–12 Preston NE 41 2 **77 4**
2012–13 Derby Co 44 3
2013–14 Derby Co 8 0
2014–15 Derby Co 7 0 **59 3**
2014–15 Sheffield U 20 0
2015–16 Sheffield U 32 0
2016–17 Sheffield U 43 2
2017–18 Sheffield U 16 1
2018–19 Sheffield U 13 0 **124 3**
2019–20 Fleetwood T 32 0
2020–21 Fleetwood T 20 0 **52 0**
2020–21 *Salford C* 19 0 **19 0**
2021–22 Bristol R 39 0 **39 0**

EVANS, Antony (M) **81 12**
H: 6 1 W: 10 10 b.Fazakerley 23-9-98
Internationals: England U19.
2016–17 Everton 0 0
2016–17 *Morecambe* 14 2 **14 2**
2017–18 Everton 0 0
2018–19 Everton 0 0
2018–19 *Blackpool* 12 0 **12 0**
2019–20 Paderborn 6 0
2020–21 Paderborn 0 0
2020–21 *Crewe Alex* 14 0 **14 0**
2021–22 Paderborn 0 0 **6 0**
2021–22 Bristol R 35 10 **35 10**

FINLEY, Sam (M) **133 11**
H: 5 7 W: 10 10 b.Liverpool 4-8-92
From Southport, Warrington T, The New Saints, AFC Fylde.
2018–19 Accrington S 37 1
2019–20 Accrington S 31 2 **68 3**
2020–21 Fleetwood T 29 3 **29 3**
2021–22 Bristol R 36 5 **36 5**

GRANT, Josh (D) **84 4**
H: 6 0 W: 12 04 b.Lambeth 11-10-98
Internationals: England U18, U20.
2018–19 Chelsea 0 0
2018–19 *Yeovil T* 8 0 **8 0**
2019–20 Chelsea 0 0
2019–20 *Plymouth Arg* 22 0 **22 0**
2020–21 Bristol R 32 1
2021–22 Bristol R 22 3 **54 4**

HARGREAVES, Cameron (M) **20 0**
H: 5 10 W: 11 00 b.Plymouth 1-12-98
From Exeter C.
2017–18 Bristol R 0 0
2018–19 Bristol R 0 0
2019–20 Bristol R 6 0
2020–21 Bristol R 13 0
2021–22 Bristol R 1 0 **20 0**

HARRIES, Cian (D) **66 2**
H: 6 1 W: 12 02 b.Birmingham 1-4-97
Internationals: Wales U17, U19, U20, U21.
2015–16 Coventry C 1 0
2016–17 Coventry C 8 0 **9 0**
2017–18 Swansea C 0 0
2018–19 Swansea C 2 0
2019–20 Swansea C 0 0 **2 0**
2019–20 *Fortuna Sittard* 8 1 **8 1**
2019–20 Bristol R 3 0
2020–21 Bristol R 28 0
2021–22 Bristol R 16 1 **47 1**

HEAL, Sam (D) **0 0**
2020–21 Bristol R 0 0
2021–22 Bristol R 0 0

HOOLE, Luca (D) **29 1**
H: 5 10 W: 10 01 b.Newport 2-6-02
Internationals: Wales U19, U21.
2019–20 Bristol R 0 0
2020–21 Bristol R 0 0
2021–22 Bristol R 29 1 **29 1**

HUGHES, Mark (D) **530 27**
H: 6 4 W: 13 03 b.Liverpool 9-12-86
2004–05 Everton 0 0
2005–06 Everton 0 0
2005–06 *Stockport Co* 3 0 **3 0**
2006–07 Everton 1 0 **1 0**
2006–07 Northampton T 17 2
2007–08 Northampton T 35 1
2008–09 Northampton T 41 1 **93 4**
2009–10 Walsall 26 1 **26 1**
2010–11 N Queensland Fury 30 4 **30 4**
2011–12 Bury 25 0
2012–13 Bury 27 0 **52 0**
2012–13 *Accrington S* 5 0
2013–14 Morecambe 44 5
2014–15 Morecambe 40 3 **84 8**
2015–16 Stevenage 20 1 **20 1**
2015–16 Accrington S 15 1
2016–17 Accrington S 36 2
2017–18 Accrington S 46 4
2018–19 Accrington S 46 1
2019–20 Accrington S 31 1
2020–21 Accrington S 36 0 **215 9**
2021–22 Bristol R 6 0 **6 0**

HULBERT, Ollie (F) **0 0**
H: 5 11 b.Bristol 25-2-03
2020–21 Bristol R 0 0
2021–22 Bristol R 0 0

JAAKKOLA, Anssi (G) **184 0**
H: 6 4 W: 13 12 b.Kemi 13-3-87
Internationals: Finland U21, Full caps.
2005 TP-47 3 0
2006 TP-47 14 0 **17 0**
2006–07 Siena 0 0
2007–08 Siena 1 0
2008–09 Siena 0 0
2008–09 *Colligiana* 7 0 **7 0**
2009–10 Siena 0 0 **1 0**
2010–11 Slavia Prague 2 0 **2 0**
2010–11 Kilmarnock 8 0
2011–12 Kilmarnock 5 0
2012–13 Kilmarnock 0 0 **13 0**
2013–14 Ajax Cape Town 24 0
2014–15 Ajax Cape Town 28 0
2015–16 Ajax Cape Town 26 0 **78 0**
2016–17 Reading 0 0
2017–18 Reading 5 0
2018–19 Reading 15 0 **20 0**
2019–20 Bristol R 21 0
2020–21 Bristol R 21 0
2021–22 Bristol R 4 0 **46 0**

JONES, Ryan (M) **0 0**
b. 23-5-02
From Weston-super-Mare.
2020–21 Bristol R 0 0
2021–22 Bristol R 0 0

KILGOUR, Alfie (D) **83 4**
H: 5 10 W: 11 11 b.Bath 18-5-98
2015–16 Bristol R 0 0
2016–17 Bristol R 0 0
2017–18 Bristol R 0 0
2018–19 Bristol R 4 0
2019–20 Bristol R 33 2
2020–21 Bristol R 35 1
2021–22 Bristol R 11 1 **83 4**

LIDDLE, Ben (M) **27 1**
H: 5 7 W: 11 11 b.Durham 21-9-98
2018–19 Middlesbrough 0 0
2018–19 *Forest Green R* 2 0 **2 0**
2019–20 Middlesbrough 1 0 **1 0**
2019–20 *Scunthorpe U* 4 0 **4 0**
2020–21 Bristol R 3 0
2021–22 Bristol R 0 0 **3 0**
2021–22 *Queen of the South* 17 1 **17 1**

LOFT, Ryan (F) **105 17**
H: 6 3 W: 11 07 b.Gravesend 14-9-97
2016–17 Tottenham H 0 0
2016–17 *Stevenage* 9 0 **9 0**
2017–18 Tottenham H 0 0
2017–18 *Exeter C* 1 0 **1 0**
2018–19 Leicester C 0 0
2019–20 Leicester C 0 0
2019–20 *Carlisle U* 26 4 **26 4**
2020–21 Scunthorpe U 41 8
2021–22 Scunthorpe U 15 4 **56 12**
2021–22 Bristol R 13 1 **13 1**

MARTINEZ, Pablo (D) **9 0**
H: 6 1 W: 11 11 b.Oxford 11-10-00
Internationals: Wales U17, U19.
From Reading, WBA.
2020–21 Bristol R 8 0
2021–22 Bristol R 1 0 **9 0**

MEHEW, Tom (M) **1 0**
H: 5 11 W: 10 03 b.Bristol 26-5-01
2020–21 Bristol R 1 0
2021–22 Bristol R 0 0 **1 0**

NICHOLSON, Sam (M) **241 30**
H: 5 9 W: 11 03 b.Edinburgh 20-1-95
Internationals: Scotland U18, U19, U21.
2013–14 Hearts 25 2
2014–15 Hearts 29 5
2015–16 Hearts 36 3
2016–17 Hearts 19 3 **109 13**
2017 Minnesota U 12 1
2018 Minnesota U 8 1 **20 2**
2018 Colorado Rapids 19 2
2019 Colorado Rapids 27 2
2020 Colorado Rapids 2 0 **48 4**
2020–21 Bristol R 30 6
2021–22 Bristol R 34 5 **64 11**

NOLAN, Jon (M) **135 18**
H: 5 11 W: 11 05 b.Huyton 22-4-92
Internationals: England C.
From Everton, Stockport Co, Lindoln C, Grimsby T.
2016–17 Chesterfield 30 1 **30 1**
2017–18 Shrewsbury T 43 9 **43 9**
2018–19 Ipswich T 26 3
2019–20 Ipswich T 22 2
2020–21 Ipswich T 13 3
2021–22 Ipswich T 0 0 **61 8**
2021–22 Bristol R 1 0 **1 0**

PHILLIPS, Kieran (F) **0 0**
H: 5 11 W: 11 09 b.Bristol 13-8-02
2019–20 Bristol R 0 0
2020–21 Bristol R 0 0
2021–22 Bristol R 0 0

PITMAN, Brett (F) **544 181**
H: 6 0 W: 11 00 b.Jersey 31-1-88
From St Paul's.
2005–06 Bournemouth 19 1
2006–07 Bournemouth 29 5
2007–08 Bournemouth 39 6
2008–09 Bournemouth 39 17
2009–10 Bournemouth 46 26
2010–11 Bournemouth 2 3
2010–11 Bristol C 39 13
2011–12 Bristol C 35 7
2012–13 Bristol C 3 0 **77 20**
2012–13 Bournemouth 26 19
2013–14 Bournemouth 34 5
2014–15 Bournemouth 34 13 **268 95**
2015–16 Ipswich T 42 10
2016–17 Ipswich T 22 4 **64 14**
2017–18 Portsmouth 38 24
2018–19 Portsmouth 32 11
2019–20 Portsmouth 11 2 **81 37**
2020–21 Swindon T 38 11 **38 11**
2021–22 Bristol R 16 4 **16 4**

RODMAN, Alex (M) 243 27
H: 6 2 W: 12 08 b.Sutton Coldfield 15-2-87
Internationals: England C.

2010–11	Aldershot T	14	5		
2011–12	Aldershot T	18	1		
2012–13	Aldershot T	11	1	**43**	**7**
2012–13	*York C*	18	1	**18**	**1**

From Grimsby T, Gateshead.

2015–16	Newport Co	29	4	**29**	**4**
2016–17	Notts Co	16	1	**16**	**1**
2016–17	Shrewsbury T	20	1		
2017–18	Shrewsbury T	41	5	**61**	**6**
2018–19	Bristol R	27	5		
2019–20	Bristol R	29	2		
2020–21	Bristol R	16	1		
2021–22	Bristol R	4	0	**76**	**8**

SAUNDERS, Harvey (F) 48 5
H: 5 11 W: 11 05 b.Wolverhampton 20-7-97
From Darlington Railway Ath, Bishop Auckland, Durham C, Darlington.

2018–19	Fleetwood T	0	0		
2019–20	Fleetwood T	6	0		
2020–21	Fleetwood T	21	3	**27**	**3**
2021–22	Bristol R	21	2	**21**	**2**

TOMLINSON, Lucas (M) 1 0

2019–20	Bristol R	1	0		
2020–21	Bristol R	0	0		
2021–22	Bristol R	0	0	**1**	**0**

WALKER, Zain (M) 11 0
H: 5 8 W: 9 02 b.Wandsworth 8-1-02
From Fulham.

2018–19	Bristol R	0	0		
2019–20	Bristol R	0	0		
2020–21	Bristol R	11	0		
2021–22	Bristol R	0	0	**11**	**0**

Transferred to King's Lynn T, November 2021.

WARD, Jed (G) 1 0
b. 20-5-03

2020–21	Bristol R	1	0		
2021–22	Bristol R	0	0	**1**	**0**

WESTBROOKE, Zain (M) 90 6
H: 5 11 W: 10 03 b.Chertsey 28-10-96
From Chelsea.

2016–17	Brentford	1	0		
2017–18	Brentford	0	0	**1**	**0**
2017–18	Coventry C	0	0		
2018–19	Coventry C	7	0		
2019–20	Coventry C	25	4	**32**	**4**
2020–21	Bristol R	42	2		
2021–22	Bristol R	3	0	**45**	**2**
2021–22	*Stevenage*	12	0	**12**	**0**

WHELAN, Glenn (M) 594 19
H: 5 11 W: 12 07 b.Dublin 13-1-84
Internationals: Republic of Ireland U16, U21, B, Full caps.

2000–01	Manchester C	0	0		
2001–02	Manchester C	0	0		
2002–03	Manchester C	0	0		
2003–04	Manchester C	0	0		
2003–04	*Bury*	13	0	**13**	**0**
2004–05	Sheffield W	36	2		
2005–06	Sheffield W	43	1		
2006–07	Sheffield W	38	7		
2007–08	Sheffield W	25	2	**142**	**12**
2007–08	Stoke C	14	1		
2008–09	Stoke C	26	1		
2009–10	Stoke C	33	2		
2010–11	Stoke C	29	0		
2011–12	Stoke C	30	1		
2012–13	Stoke C	32	0		
2013–14	Stoke C	32	0		
2014–15	Stoke C	28	0		
2015–16	Stoke C	37	0		
2016–17	Stoke C	30	0	**291**	**5**
2017–18	Aston Villa	33	1		
2018–19	Aston Villa	35	1	**68**	**2**
2019–20	Hearts	15	0	**15**	**0**
2019–20	Fleetwood T	11	0		
2020–21	Fleetwood T	23	0	**34**	**0**
2021–22	Bristol R	31	0	**31**	**0**

Players retained or with offer of contract
Budd, Joseph; Edwards, Max; Greenslade, Harvey; Langlais, Jarmani; Lawrence, Jerry; Lovelock, Niall; Mbuenimo, Tyron; Sesay, Malik; Vaughan, Lucas; Vilinauskas, Airidas.

Scholars
Allen, Jahiem Malachi Marlon; Brain, Owen Barry James; Burden, Lene William; Egan, Jamie; Ford, Zak Terence Samuel; Greenslade, Harvey Thomas; Jenkins, Joshua Robert; Langlais, Jamarni Patrick; Lawrence, Jerry Karl Sonzahi; Lovelock, Niall Christopher; Mbuenimo, Tyron Thomson; McKayle, Josiah Daniel; Reed, Matthew James; Sesay, Malik John; Smolka, Andreas Jonas; Vaughan, Lucas Robert; Vilinauskas, Airidas.

BURNLEY (17)

BARDSLEY, Phillip (D) 336 8
H: 5 11 W: 12 04 b.Salford 28-6-85
Internationals: Scotland Full caps.

2003–04	Manchester U	0	0		
2003–04	*Royal Antwerp*	6	0	**6**	**0**
2004–05	Manchester U	0	0		
2005–06	Manchester U	8	0		
2005–06	*Burnley*	6	0		
2006–07	Manchester U	0	0		
2006–07	*Rangers*	5	1	**5**	**1**
2006–07	*Aston Villa*	13	0	**13**	**0**
2007–08	Manchester U	0	0	**8**	**0**
2007–08	*Sheffield U*	16	0	**16**	**0**
2007–08	Sunderland	11	0		
2008–09	Sunderland	28	0		
2009–10	Sunderland	26	0		
2010–11	Sunderland	34	3		
2011–12	Sunderland	31	1		
2012–13	Sunderland	18	1		
2013–14	Sunderland	26	2	**174**	**7**
2014–15	Stoke C	25	0		
2015–16	Stoke C	11	0		
2016–17	Stoke C	15	0	**51**	**0**
2017–18	Burnley	13	0		
2018–19	Burnley	19	0		
2019–20	Burnley	21	0		
2020–21	Burnley	4	0		
2021–22	Burnley	0	0	**63**	**0**

BARNES, Ashley (F) 406 93
H: 6 1 W: 12 02 b.Bath 30-10-89
Internationals: Austria U20.
From Paulton R.

2006–07	Plymouth Arg	0	0		
2007–08	Plymouth Arg	0	0		
2008–09	Plymouth Arg	15	1		
2009–10	Plymouth Arg	7	1	**22**	**2**
2009–10	*Torquay U*	6	0	**6**	**0**
2009–10	*Brighton & HA*	8	4		
2010–11	Brighton & HA	42	18		
2011–12	Brighton & HA	43	11		
2012–13	Brighton & HA	34	8		
2013–14	Brighton & HA	22	5	**149**	**46**
2013–14	Burnley	21	3		
2014–15	Burnley	35	5		
2015–16	Burnley	8	0		
2016–17	Burnley	28	6		
2017–18	Burnley	36	9		
2018–19	Burnley	37	12		
2019–20	Burnley	19	6		
2020–21	Burnley	22	3		
2021–22	Burnley	23	1	**229**	**45**

BEDEAU, Jacob (D) 74 2
H: 6 0 W: 12 04 b.Waltham Forest 24-12-99

2016–17	Bury	7	0	**7**	**0**
2017–18	Aston Villa	0	0		
2018–19	Aston Villa	0	0		
2019–20	Scunthorpe U	11	1		
2020–21	Scunthorpe U	34	1	**45**	**2**
2021–22	Burnley	0	0		
2021–22	*Morecambe*	22	0	**22**	**0**

BROWNHILL, Josh (M) 290 25
H: 5 10 W: 10 12 b.Warrington 19-12-95

2013–14	Preston NE	24	3		
2014–15	Preston NE	18	2		
2015–16	Preston NE	3	0	**45**	**5**
2015–16	*Barnsley*	22	2	**22**	**2**
2016–17	Bristol C	27	1		
2017–18	Bristol C	45	5		
2018–19	Bristol C	45	5		
2019–20	Bristol C	28	5	**145**	**16**
2019–20	Burnley	10	0		
2020–21	Burnley	33	0		
2021–22	Burnley	35	2	**78**	**2**

COLLINS, Nathan (D) 58 4
H: 6 4 W: 11 05 b.Leixlip 30-4-01
Internationals: Republic of Ireland U17, U19, U21, Full caps.

2018–19	Stoke C	3	0		
2019–20	Stoke C	14	0		
2020–21	Stoke C	22	2		
2021–22	Stoke C	0	0	**39**	**2**
2021–22	Burnley	19	2	**19**	**2**

CORK, Jack (M) 490 14
H: 6 1 W: 10 12 b.Carshalton 25-6-89
Internationals: England U16, U17, U18, U19, U20, U21, Full caps. Great Britain.

2006–07	Chelsea	0	0		
2006–07	*Bournemouth*	7	0	**7**	**0**
2007–08	Chelsea	0	0		
2007–08	*Scunthorpe U*	34	2	**34**	**2**
2008–09	Chelsea	0	0		
2008–09	*Southampton*	23	0		
2008–09	*Watford*	19	0	**19**	**0**
2009–10	Chelsea	0	0		
2009–10	*Coventry C*	21	0	**21**	**0**
2009–10	*Burnley*	11	1		
2010–11	Chelsea	0	0		
2010–11	*Burnley*	40	3		
2011–12	Southampton	46	0		
2012–13	Southampton	28	0		
2013–14	Southampton	28	0		
2014–15	Southampton	12	2	**137**	**2**
2014–15	Swansea C	15	1		
2015–16	Swansea C	35	1		
2016–17	Swansea C	30	0	**80**	**2**
2017–18	Burnley	38	2		
2018–19	Burnley	37	1		
2019–20	Burnley	30	0		
2020–21	Burnley	16	0		
2021–22	Burnley	20	1	**192**	**8**

CORNET, Maxwel (F) 233 41
H: 5 10 W: 10 12 b.Bregbo 27-9-96
Internationals: France U16, U17, U18, U19, U20, U21. Ivory Coast Full caps.

2012–13	Metz	9	1		
2013–14	Metz	14	0		
2014–15	Metz	0	0	**23**	**1**
2014–15	Lyon	4	0		
2015–16	Lyon	31	8		
2016–17	Lyon	33	6		
2017–18	Lyon	30	4		
2018–19	Lyon	27	7		
2019–20	Lyon	22	4		
2020–21	Lyon	36	2		
2021–22	Lyon	1	0	**184**	**31**
2021–22	Burnley	26	9	**26**	**9**

DRISCOLL-GLENNON, Anthony (D) 27 1
H: 5 11 W: 11 05 b.Bootle 26-11-99
From Liverpool.

2018–19	Burnley	0	0		
2019–20	Burnley	0	0		
2019–20	*Grimsby T*	12	1	**12**	**1**
2020–21	Burnley	0	0		
2021–22	Burnley	0	0		
2021–22	*Barrow*	15	0	**15**	**0**

GUDMUNDSSON, Johann Berg (M) 336 34
H: 6 1 W: 12 06 b.Reykjavik 27-10-90
Internationals: Iceland U19, U21, Full caps.

2009–10	AZ Alkmaar	0	0		
2010–11	AZ Alkmaar	23	1		
2011–12	AZ Alkmaar	30	3		
2012–13	AZ Alkmaar	31	2		
2013–14	AZ Alkmaar	35	3	**119**	**9**
2014–15	Charlton Ath	41	10		
2015–16	Charlton Ath	40	6	**81**	**16**
2016–17	Burnley	20	1		
2017–18	Burnley	35	2		
2018–19	Burnley	29	3		
2019–20	Burnley	12	1		
2020–21	Burnley	22	2		
2021–22	Burnley	18	0	**136**	**9**

HARKER, Rob (F) 0 0
H: 6 2 b.Gargrave 6-3-00

2015–16	Bury	0	0		
2016–17	Bury	0	0		
2017–18	Bury	0	0		
2018–19	Burnley	0	0		
2019–20	Burnley	0	0		
2020–21	Burnley	0	0		
2021–22	Burnley	0	0		

HELM, Mark (M) 0 0
H: 5 8 W: 9 08 b.Warrington 21-10-01
From Manchester U.

2021–22	Burnley	0	0		

HENNESSEY, Wayne (G) 291 0
H: 6 6 W: 14 02 b.Bangor 24-1-87
Internationals: Wales U17, U19, U21, Full caps.

2004–05	Wolverhampton W	0	0		
2005–06	Wolverhampton W	0	0		
2006–07	Wolverhampton W	0	0		
2006–07	*Bristol C*	0	0		
2006–07	*Stockport Co*	15	0	**15**	**0**
2007–08	Wolverhampton W	46	0		
2008–09	Wolverhampton W	35	0		
2009–10	Wolverhampton W	13	0		
2010–11	Wolverhampton W	24	0		
2011–12	Wolverhampton W	34	0		
2012–13	Wolverhampton W	0	0		
2013–14	Wolverhampton W	0	0	**152**	**0**
2013–14	*Yeovil T*	12	0	**12**	**0**
2013–14	Crystal Palace	1	0		
2014–15	Crystal Palace	3	0		
2015–16	Crystal Palace	29	0		
2016–17	Crystal Palace	29	0		
2017–18	Crystal Palace	27	0		
2018–19	Crystal Palace	18	0		
2019–20	Crystal Palace	3	0		
2020–21	Crystal Palace	0	0		
2021–22	Crystal Palace	0	0	**110**	**0**
2021–22	Burnley	2	0	**2**	**0**

JENSEN, Lukas (G) 13 0
H: 6 0 W: 11 11 b.Helsingor 18-3-99

2017–18	Helsingor	1	0		
2018–19	Helsingor	0	0	**1**	**0**
2018–19	HIK	6	0	**6**	**0**
2019–20	Burnley	0	0		
2020–21	Burnley	0	0		

2020–21	*Bolton W*	0	0		
2020–21	*Kordrengir*	5	0		
2021–22	*Kordrengir*	0	0	**5**	**0**
2021–22	Burnley	0	0		
2021–22	*Carlisle U*	1	0	**1**	**0**

LENNON, Aaron (M) **479 37**
H: 5 5 W: 9 12 b.Leeds 16-4-87
Internationals: England U17, U19, U21, B, Full caps.

2003–04	Leeds U	11	0		
2004–05	Leeds U	27	1	**38**	**1**
2005–06	Tottenham H	27	2		
2006–07	Tottenham H	26	3		
2007–08	Tottenham H	29	2		
2008–09	Tottenham H	35	5		
2009–10	Tottenham H	22	3		
2010–11	Tottenham H	34	3		
2011–12	Tottenham H	23	3		
2012–13	Tottenham H	34	4		
2013–14	Tottenham H	27	1		
2014–15	Tottenham H	9	0		
2014–15	*Everton*	14	2		
2015–16	Tottenham H	0	0	**266**	**26**
2015–16	Everton	25	5		
2016–17	Everton	11	0		
2017–18	Everton	15	0	**65**	**7**
2017–18	Burnley	14	0		
2018–19	Burnley	16	1		
2019–20	Burnley	16	0		
2020–21	Kayserispor	36	0	**36**	**0**
2021–22	Burnley	28	2	**74**	**3**

LONG, Kevin (D) **158 8**
H: 6 2 W: 13 01 b.Cork 18-8-90
Internationals: Republic of Ireland Full caps.

2009	Cork C	16	1	**16**	**1**
2009–10	Burnley	0	0		
2010–11	Burnley	0	0		
2010–11	*Accrington S*	15	0		
2011–12	Burnley	0	0		
2011–12	*Accrington S*	24	4	**39**	**4**
2011–12	*Rochdale*	16	0	**16**	**0**
2012–13	Burnley	14	0		
2012–13	*Portsmouth*	5	0	**5**	**0**
2013–14	Burnley	7	0		
2014–15	Burnley	1	0		
2015–16	Burnley	0	0		
2015–16	*Barnsley*	11	2	**11**	**2**
2015–16	*Milton Keynes D*	2	0	**2**	**0**
2016–17	Burnley	3	0		
2017–18	Burnley	16	1		
2018–19	Burnley	6	0		
2019–20	Burnley	8	0		
2020–21	Burnley	8	0		
2021–22	Burnley	6	0	**69**	**1**

LOWTON, Matt (M) **341 15**
H: 5 11 W: 12 04 b.Chesterfield 9-6-89

2008–09	Sheffield U	0	0		
2009–10	Sheffield U	2	0		
2009–10	*Ferencvaros*	5	0	**5**	**0**
2010–11	Sheffield U	32	4		
2011–12	Sheffield U	44	6	**78**	**10**
2012–13	Aston Villa	37	2		
2013–14	Aston Villa	23	0		
2014–15	Aston Villa	12	0	**72**	**2**
2015–16	Burnley	27	1		
2016–17	Burnley	36	0		
2017–18	Burnley	26	0		
2018–19	Burnley	21	0		
2019–20	Burnley	17	0		
2020–21	Burnley	34	1		
2021–22	Burnley	25	1	**186**	**3**

MANCINI, Anthony (M) **0 0**
b.Saint Priest 6-4-01
Internationals: France U18.
From Tours.

2018–19	Angers	0	0		
2019–20	Angers	0	0		
2020–21	Angers	0	0		
2020–21	*Burnley*	0	0		
2021–22	Burnley	0	0		

McNEIL, Dwight (M) **134 7**
H: 6 0 W: 11 00 b.Rochdale 22-11-99
Internationals: England U20, U21.
From Manchester U.

2017–18	Burnley	1	0		
2018–19	Burnley	21	3		
2019–20	Burnley	38	2		
2020–21	Burnley	36	2		
2021–22	Burnley	38	0	**134**	**7**

MEE, Ben (D) **366 12**
H: 5 11 W: 11 09 b.Sale 21-9-89
Internationals: England U19, U20, U21.

2007–08	Manchester C	0	0		
2008–09	Manchester C	0	0		
2009–10	Manchester C	0	0		
2010–11	Manchester C	0	0		
2010–11	*Leicester C*	15	0	**15**	**0**
2011–12	Manchester C	0	0		
2011–12	Burnley	31	0		
2012–13	Burnley	19	1		
2013–14	Burnley	38	0		
2014–15	Burnley	33	2		
2015–16	Burnley	46	2		
2016–17	Burnley	34	1		
2017–18	Burnley	29	0		
2018–19	Burnley	38	0		
2019–20	Burnley	32	1		
2020–21	Burnley	30	2		
2021–22	Burnley	21	3	**351**	**12**

MUMBONGO, Joel (F) **29 9**
H: 6 2 W: 13 12 b.Gothenburg 9-1-99
Internationals: Sweden U17, U18, U19.

2017	Hacken	0	0		
2018	Utsiktens	15	7	**15**	**7**
2018–19	Verona	0	0		
2019–20	Burnley	0	0		
2020–21	Burnley	4	0		
2021–22	Burnley	0	0	**4**	**0**
2021–22	*Accrington S*	10	2	**10**	**2**

NARTEY, Richard (D) **28 0**
H: 6 0 W: 12 04 b.Hammersmith 6-9-98

2019–20	Chelsea	0	0		
2019–20	*Burton Alb*	25	0	**25**	**0**
2020–21	Burnley	0	0		
2021–22	Burnley	0	0		
2021–22	*Mansfield T*	3	0	**3**	**0**

NORRIS, Will (G) **88 0**
H: 6 5 W: 11 09 b.Watford 12-8-93
From Hatfield T, Royston T.

2014–15	Cambridge U	3	0		
2015–16	Cambridge U	21	0		
2016–17	Cambridge U	45	0	**69**	**0**
2017–18	Wolverhampton W	1	0		
2018–19	Wolverhampton W	1	0		
2019–20	Wolverhampton W	0	0	**2**	**0**
2019–20	*Ipswich T*	15	0	**15**	**0**
2020–21	Burnley	2	0		
2021–22	Burnley	0	0	**2**	**0**

PEACOCK-FARRELL, Bailey (G) **87 0**
H: 6 4 W: 11 07 b.Darlington 29-10-96
Internationals: Northern Ireland U21, Full caps.
From Middlesbrough.

2015–16	Leeds U	1	0		
2016–17	Leeds U	0	0		
2017–18	Leeds U	11	0		
2018–19	Leeds U	28	0		
2019–20	Leeds U	0	0	**40**	**0**
2019–20	Burnley	0	0		
2020–21	Burnley	4	0		
2021–22	Burnley	0	0	**4**	**0**
2021–22	*Sheffield W*	43	0	**43**	**0**

PHILLIPS, Adam (M) **100 20**
H: 5 11 W: 12 00 b.Garstang 15-1-98
Internationals: England U16, U17.

2014–15	Liverpool	0	0		
2015–16	Liverpool	0	0		
2016–17	Liverpool	0	0		
2017–18	Norwich C	0	0		
2017–18	*Cambridge U*	4	0	**4**	**0**
2018–19	Norwich C	0	0		
2018–19	*Hamilton A*	0	0		
2019–20	Burnley	0	0		
2019–20	*Morecambe*	11	4		
2020–21	Burnley	0	0		
2020–21	*Morecambe*	25	8		
2020–21	*Accrington S*	22	2	**22**	**2**
2021–22	Burnley	0	0		
2021–22	*Morecambe*	38	6	**74**	**18**

PIETERS, Erik (D) **405 6**
H: 6 0 W: 13 01 b.Tiel 7-8-88
Internationals: Netherlands U17, U19, U21, Full caps.

2006–07	Utrecht	20	0		
2007–08	Utrecht	31	2	**51**	**2**
2008–09	PSV Eindhoven	17	0		
2009–10	PSV Eindhoven	27	0		
2010–11	PSV Eindhoven	31	0		
2011–12	PSV Eindhoven	16	0		
2012–13	PSV Eindhoven	2	0	**93**	**0**
2013–14	Stoke C	36	1		
2014–15	Stoke C	31	0		
2015–16	Stoke C	35	0		
2016–17	Stoke C	36	0		
2017–18	Stoke C	31	0		
2018–19	Stoke C	21	2	**190**	**3**
2018–19	*Amiens*	15	1	**15**	**1**
2019–20	Burnley	24	0		
2020–21	Burnley	20	0		
2021–22	Burnley	12	0	**56**	**0**

POPE, Nick (G) **218 0**
H: 6 6 W: 12 00 b.Cambridge 19-4-92
Internationals: England Full caps.
From Bury T.

2011–12	Charlton Ath	0	0		
2012–13	Charlton Ath	1	0		
2013–14	Charlton Ath	0	0		
2013–14	*York C*	22	0	**22**	**0**
2014–15	Charlton Ath	8	0		
2014–15	*Bury*	22	0	**22**	**0**
2015–16	Charlton Ath	24	0	**33**	**0**
2016–17	Burnley	0	0		
2017–18	Burnley	35	0		
2018–19	Burnley	0	0		
2019–20	Burnley	38	0		
2020–21	Burnley	32	0		
2021–22	Burnley	36	0	**141**	**0**

RICHARDSON, Lewis (F) **2 0**
H: 5 10 W: 10 03 b.Manchester 7-2-03
Internationals: England U16, U17.

2019–20	Burnley	0	0		
2020–21	Burnley	2	0		
2021–22	Burnley	0	0	**2**	**0**

ROBERTS, Connor (D) **202 12**
H: 5 9 W: 11 03 b.Neath 23-9-95
Internationals: Wales U19, U21, Full caps.

2014–15	Swansea C	0	0		
2015–16	Swansea C	0	0		
2015–16	*Yeovil T*	45	0	**45**	**0**
2016–17	Swansea C	0	0		
2016–17	*Bristol R*	2	0	**2**	**0**
2017–18	Swansea C	4	0		
2017–18	*Middlesbrough*	1	0	**1**	**0**
2018–19	Swansea C	45	5		
2019–20	Swansea C	38	1		
2020–21	Swansea C	46	5		
2021–22	Swansea C	0	0	**133**	**11**
2021–22	Burnley	21	1	**21**	**1**

RODRIGUEZ, Jay (F) **404 101**
H: 6 1 W: 13 03 b.Burnley 29-7-89
Internationals: England U21, Full caps.

2007–08	Burnley	1	0		
2007–08	*Stirling Alb*	11	3	**11**	**3**
2008–09	Burnley	25	2		
2009–10	Burnley	0	0		
2009–10	*Barnsley*	6	1	**6**	**1**
2010–11	Burnley	42	14		
2011–12	Burnley	37	15		
2012–13	Southampton	35	6		
2013–14	Southampton	33	15		
2014–15	Southampton	0	0		
2015–16	Southampton	12	0		
2016–17	Southampton	24	5	**104**	**26**
2017–18	WBA	37	7		
2018–19	WBA	45	22	**82**	**29**
2019–20	Burnley	36	8		
2020–21	Burnley	31	1		
2021–22	Burnley	29	2	**201**	**42**

STEPHENS, Dale (M) **388 37**
H: 6 1 W: 12 04 b.Bolton 12-6-89

2006–07	Bury	3	0		
2007–08	Bury	6	1	**9**	**1**
2008–09	Oldham Ath	0	0		
2009–10	Oldham Ath	26	2		
2009–10	*Rochdale*	6	1	**6**	**1**
2010–11	Oldham Ath	34	9	**60**	**11**
2010–11	*Southampton*	6	0	**6**	**0**
2011–12	Charlton Ath	30	5		
2012–13	Charlton Ath	28	2		
2013–14	Charlton Ath	26	3	**84**	**10**
2013–14	Brighton & HA	14	2		
2014–15	Brighton & HA	16	2		
2015–16	Brighton & HA	45	7		
2016–17	Brighton & HA	39	2		
2017–18	Brighton & HA	36	0		
2018–19	Brighton & HA	30	1		
2019–20	Brighton & HA	33	0		
2020–21	Brighton & HA	0	0	**213**	**14**
2020–21	Burnley	7	0		
2021–22	Burnley	3	0	**10**	**0**

TARKOWSKI, James (D) **340 16**
H: 6 2 W: 12 11 b.Manchester 19-11-92
Internationals: England Full caps.

2010–11	Oldham Ath	9	0		
2011–12	Oldham Ath	16	1		
2012–13	Oldham Ath	21	2		
2013–14	Oldham Ath	26	2	**72**	**5**
2013–14	Brentford	13	2		
2014–15	Brentford	34	1		
2015–16	Brentford	23	1	**70**	**4**
2015–16	Burnley	4	0		
2016–17	Burnley	19	0		
2017–18	Burnley	31	0		
2018–19	Burnley	35	3		
2019–20	Burnley	38	2		
2020–21	Burnley	36	1		
2021–22	Burnley	35	1	**198**	**7**

TAYLOR, Charlie (D) **272 3**
H: 6 1 W: 11 00 b.York 18-9-93
Internationals: England U19.

2011–12	Leeds U	2	0		
2011–12	*Bradford C*	3	0	**3**	**0**
2012–13	Leeds U	0	0		
2012–13	*York C*	4	0	**4**	**0**
2012–13	*Inverness CT*	7	0	**7**	**0**
2013–14	Leeds U	0	0		
2013–14	*Fleetwood T*	32	0	**32**	**0**
2014–15	Leeds U	23	2		
2015–16	Leeds U	39	1		
2016–17	Leeds U	29	0	**93**	**3**
2017–18	Burnley	11	0		
2018–19	Burnley	38	0		
2019–20	Burnley	24	0		

2020–21	Burnley	29	0		
2021–22	Burnley	31	0	**133**	**0**

THOMAS, Bobby (D)				**21**	**1**
H: 6 1 W: 12 02 b.Chester 30-1-01					
2019–20	Burnley	0	0		
2020–21	Burnley	0	0		
2020–21	*Barrow*	21	1	**21**	**1**
2021–22	Burnley	0	0		

THOMPSON, Max (F)				**1**	**0**
b. 9-2-02					
From Everton.					
2019–20	Burnley	1	0		
2020–21	Burnley	0	0		
2021–22	Burnley	0	0	**1**	**0**

VYDRA, Matej (F)				**337**	**85**
H: 5 10 W: 11 10 b.Chotebor 1-5-92					
Internationals: Czech Republic U16, U17, U18, U19, U21, Full caps.					
2008–09	Vysocina Jihlava	12	2		
2009–10	Vysocina Jihlava	15	3	**27**	**5**
2009–10	Banik Ostrava	14	4	**14**	**4**
2010–11	Udinese	2	0		
2011–12	Udinese	0	0		
2011–12	*Club Brugge*	1	0	**1**	**0**
2012–13	Udinese	0	0		
2012–13	*Watford*	41	20		
2013–14	Udinese	0	0		
2013–14	*WBA*	23	3	**23**	**3**
2014–15	Udinese	0	0	**2**	**0**
2014–15	*Watford*	42	16		
2015–16	Watford	0	0		
2015–16	*Reading*	31	3	**31**	**3**
2016–17	Watford	1	0	**84**	**36**
2016–17	Derby Co	33	5		
2017–18	Derby Co	40	21	**73**	**26**
2018–19	Burnley	13	1		
2019–20	Burnley	19	2		
2020–21	Burnley	28	3		
2021–22	Burnley	22	2	**82**	**8**

WEGHORST, Wouter (F)				**324**	**131**
H: 6 6 W: 13 03 b.Borne 8-7-92					
Internationals: Netherlands U21, Full caps.					
From Willem II.					
2012–13	Emmen	28	8		
2013–14	Emmen	34	11	**62**	**19**
2014–15	Heracles	31	8		
2015–16	Heracles	33	12	**64**	**20**
2016–17	AZ Alkmaar	29	13		
2017–18	AZ Alkmaar	31	18	**60**	**31**
2018–19	VfL Wolfsburg	34	17		
2019–20	VfL Wolfsburg	32	16		
2020–21	VfL Wolfsburg	34	20		
2021–22	VfL Wolfsburg	18	6	**118**	**59**
2021–22	Burnley	20	2	**20**	**2**

WESTWOOD, Ashley (M)				**437**	**26**
H: 5 7 W: 12 09 b.Nantwich 1-4-90					
2008–09	Crewe Alex	2	0		
2009–10	Crewe Alex	36	6		
2010–11	Crewe Alex	46	5		
2011–12	Crewe Alex	41	3		
2012–13	Crewe Alex	3	0	**128**	**14**
2012–13	Aston Villa	30	0		
2013–14	Aston Villa	35	3		
2014–15	Aston Villa	27	0		
2015–16	Aston Villa	32	2		
2016–17	Aston Villa	23	0	**147**	**5**
2016–17	Burnley	9	0		
2017–18	Burnley	19	0		
2018–19	Burnley	34	2		
2019–20	Burnley	35	2		
2020–21	Burnley	38	3		
2021–22	Burnley	27	0	**162**	**7**

Players retained or with offer of contract

Costelloe, Dara; Dodgson, Owen; McGlynn, Joe; Mellon, Michael; Rooney, Jake; Thomas, Lewis; Tucker, Ne'Jai; Waller, Sam; Woods, Benjamin.

Scholars

Armstrong, Finlay Patric; Bryan, Trevon Nataniel; Casper, Charlie; Coppack, Jacson David; Grant, Bradley George; Gromek, Wiktor Adam; Hamilton, Jacob Luke; Hugill, William James; James, Nathan; Le Fondre, Kian Asa Gene; McCullough, Dane Neil; McGlynn, Joseph Peter; Moss, Harry Robert; Olopade, Oluwatosin Fiyinfoluwa; Ratchford, Kade; Sassi, Daniel; Waller, Sam William John; Ward, Benn David; Westley, Joseph Anthony; Williams, Keelan Ellis.

BURTON ALB (18)

AHADME, Gassan (F)				**19**	**3**
b.Vic 17-11-00					
2020–21	Norwich C	0	0		
2021–22	*Portsmouth*	5	0	**5**	**0**
2021–22	Burton Alb	14	3	**14**	**3**

AMADI-HOLLOWAY, Aaron (F)				**209**	**18**
H: 6 2 W: 13 01 b.Cardiff 21-2-93					
Internationals: Wales U17, U19.					
2012–13	Bristol C	0	0		
2013–14	Bristol C	0	0		
2013–14	Newport Co	4	0	**4**	**0**
2014–15	Wycombe W	29	3		
2015–16	Wycombe W	23	3	**52**	**6**
2015–16	*Oldham Ath*	10	2		
2016–17	Fleetwood T	6	0	**6**	**0**
2016–17	Oldham Ath	15	0		
2017–18	Oldham Ath	36	2	**61**	**4**
2018–19	Shrewsbury T	30	2	**30**	**2**
2019–20	Brisbane Roar	23	1	**23**	**1**
2020–21	East Bengal	13	2	**13**	**2**
2021–22	Burton Alb	6	0	**6**	**0**
2021–22	*Barrow*	14	3	**14**	**3**

BLAKE-TRACY, Frazer (D)				**30**	**0**
H: 6 0 W: 10 01 b.Dereham 10-9-95					
From Dereham T, Lowestoft, King's Lynn T.					
2019–20	Peterborough U	14	0		
2020–21	Peterborough U	9	0	**23**	**0**
2021–22	Burton Alb	7	0	**7**	**0**

BORTHWICK-JACKSON, Cameron (D)				**123**	**6**
H: 6 3 W: 13 10 b.Manchester 2-2-97					
Internationals: England U16, U17, U19, U20.					
2015–16	Manchester U	10	0		
2016–17	Manchester U	0	0		
2016–17	*Wolverhampton W*	6	0	**6**	**0**
2017–18	Manchester U	0	0		
2017–18	*Leeds U*	1	0	**1**	**0**
2018–19	Manchester U	0	0		
2018–19	*Scunthorpe U*	29	2	**29**	**2**
2019–20	Manchester U	0	0	**10**	**0**
2019–20	*Tranmere R*	3	0	**3**	**0**
2019–20	*Oldham Ath*	6	0		
2020–21	Oldham Ath	31	2	**37**	**2**
2021–22	Burton Alb	37	2	**37**	**2**

BOSTWICK, Michael (D)				**437**	**43**
H: 6 4 W: 14 00 b.Eltham 17-5-88					
Internationals: England C.					
2006–07	Millwall	0	0		
From Rushden & D, Ebbsfleet U					
2010–11	Stevenage	41	2		
2011–12	Stevenage	43	7		
2012–13	Peterborough U	39	5		
2013–14	Peterborough U	42	4		
2014–15	Peterborough U	38	7		
2015–16	Peterborough U	36	4		
2016–17	Peterborough U	39	3	**194**	**23**
2017–18	Lincoln C	44	6		
2018–19	Lincoln C	45	2		
2019–20	Lincoln C	18	1	**107**	**9**
2020–21	Burton Alb	28	2		
2021–22	Burton Alb	10	0	**38**	**2**
2021–22	*Stevenage*	14	0	**98**	**9**

BRAYFORD, John (D)				**483**	**22**
H: 5 8 W: 11 03 b.Stoke 29-12-87					
Internationals: England C.					
From Burton Alb.					
2008–09	Crewe Alex	36	2		
2009–10	Crewe Alex	45	0	**81**	**2**
2010–11	Derby Co	46	1		
2011–12	Derby Co	23	0		
2012–13	Derby Co	40	1	**109**	**2**
2013–14	Cardiff C	0	0		
2013–14	*Sheffield U*	15	1		
2014–15	Cardiff C	26	0	**26**	**0**
2014–15	Sheffield U	22	1		
2015–16	Sheffield U	19	1		
2016–17	Sheffield U	3	0		
2016–17	*Burton Alb*	33	0		
2017–18	Sheffield U	0	0	**59**	**3**
2017–18	Burton Alb	28	0		
2018–19	Burton Alb	41	3		
2019–20	Burton Alb	32	2		
2020–21	Burton Alb	41	4		
2021–22	Burton Alb	33	6	**208**	**15**

GARRATT, Ben (G)				**294**	**0**
H: 6 1 W: 10 06 b.Market Drayton 25-4-94					
Internationals: England U17, U18, U19.					
2011–12	Crewe Alex	0	0		
2012–13	Crewe Alex	1	0		
2013–14	Crewe Alex	26	0		
2014–15	Crewe Alex	30	0		
2015–16	Crewe Alex	46	0		
2016–17	Crewe Alex	46	0		
2017–18	Crewe Alex	36	0		
2018–19	Crewe Alex	38	0	**223**	**0**
2019–20	Burton Alb	3	0		
2020–21	Burton Alb	28	0		
2021–22	Burton Alb	40	0	**71**	**0**

GILLIGAN, Ciaran (M)				**26**	**0**
b. 5-2-02					
2020–21	Burton Alb	18	0		
2021–22	Burton Alb	8	0	**26**	**0**

GUEDIOURA, Adiene (M)				**334**	**26**
H: 5 10 W: 12 11 b.La Roche-sur-Yon 12-11-85					
Internationals: Algeria Full caps.					
2004–05	Sedan	0	0		
2005–06	Noisy-Le-Sec	15	1	**15**	**1**
2006–07	L'Entente	21	3	**21**	**3**
2007–08	Creteil	24	6	**24**	**6**
2008–09	Kortrijk	10	0	**10**	**0**
2008–09	Charleroi	12	0		
2009–10	Charleroi	13	1	**25**	**1**
2009–10	Wolverhampton W	14	1		
2010–11	Wolverhampton W	10	1		
2011–12	Wolverhampton W	10	0	**34**	**2**
2011–12	*Nottingham F*	19	1		
2012–13	Nottingham F	35	3		
2013–14	Nottingham F	5	0		
2013–14	Crystal Palace	8	0		
2014–15	Crystal Palace	7	0		
2014–15	*Watford*	17	3		
2015–16	Crystal Palace	0	0	**15**	**0**
2015–16	Watford	18	0		
2016–17	Watford	12	0	**47**	**3**
2016–17	Middlesbrough	5	0		
2017–18	Middlesbrough	1	0	**6**	**0**
2017–18	Nottingham F	11	0		
2018–19	Nottingham F	27	2	**97**	**6**
2019–20	Al Gharafa	15	1		
2020–21	Al Gharafa	20	1	**35**	**2**
2021–22	Sheffield U	1	0	**1**	**0**
2021–22	Burton Alb	4	2	**4**	**2**

HAWKINS, Callum (G)				**0**	**0**
H: 6 2 W: 12 02 b.Rotherham 12-12-99					
2018–19	Burton Alb	0	0		
2019–20	Burton Alb	0	0		
2020–21	Burton Alb	0	0		
2021–22	Burton Alb	0	0		

HAYMER, Tom (D)				**150**	**10**
H: 6 2 W: 12 08 b.Bolton 16-11-99					
2017–18	Oldham Ath	7	1		
2018–19	Oldham Ath	28	2		
2019–20	Oldham Ath	37	3		
2020–21	Oldham Ath	12	0	**84**	**6**
2020–21	Burton Alb	21	3		
2021–22	Burton Alb	45	1	**66**	**4**

HEWLETT, Tom (F)				**1**	**0**
	Burton Alb	0	0		
2020–21	Rushall Olympic	0	0		
2021–22	Burton Alb	1	0	**1**	**0**

HUGHES, Sam (D)				**43**	**3**
H: 5 10 W: 11 00 b.West Kirby 15-4-97					
From Chester.					
2017–18	Leicester C	0	0		
2018–19	Leicester C	0	0		
2019–20	Leicester C	0	0		
2019–20	*Salford C*	8	0	**8**	**0**
2020–21	Leicester C	0	0		
2020–21	*Burton Alb*	14	2		
2021–22	Leicester C	0	0		
2021–22	Burton Alb	21	1	**35**	**3**

KOKOLO, Williams (D)				**16**	**1**
H: 5 11 b.France 9-6-00					
From Monaco.					
2018–19	Sunderland	0	0		
2019–20	Middlesbrough	0	0		
2020–21	Middlesbrough	0	0		
2021–22	Middlesbrough	1	0	**1**	**0**
2021–22	Burton Alb	15	1	**15**	**1**

LAKIN, Charlie (M)				**76**	**6**
H: 5 11 W: 12 00 b.Solihull 8-5-99					
2017–18	Birmingham C	0	0		
2018–19	Birmingham C	10	0		
2019–20	Birmingham C	0	0		
2019–20	*Stevenage*	20	2	**20**	**2**
2020–21	Birmingham C	0	0		
2020–21	*Ross Co*	19	3	**19**	**3**
2021–22	Birmingham C	0	0	**10**	**0**
2021–22	Burton Alb	27	1	**27**	**1**

LATTY-FAIRWEATHER, Thierry (D)				**0**	**0**
b.Birmingham 5-12-02					
2020–21	Burton Alb	0	0		
2021–22	Burton Alb	0	0		

LEAK, Ryan (D)				**85**	**1**
H: 6 3 b.Burton 28-2-98					
Internationals: Wales U17.					
2016–17	Wolverhampton W	0	0		
2017–18	Wolverhampton W	0	0		
2017–18	*The New Saints*	12	1	**12**	**1**
2018–19	Wolverhampton W	0	0		
2018–19	*Jumilla*	32	0	**32**	**0**
2019–20	Burgos	14	0		
2020–21	Burgos	11	0	**25**	**0**
2021–22	Burton Alb	16	0	**16**	**0**

MADDOX, Jacob (M)				**57**	**1**
H: 5 10 W: 11 05 b.Bristol 3-11-98					
Internationals: England U16, U17, U19, U20.					
2018–19	Chelsea	0	0		
2018–19	*Cheltenham T*	38	1	**38**	**1**
2019–20	Chelsea	0	0		
2019–20	*Tranmere R*	0	0		
2019–20	*Southampton*	0	0		
2020–21	Vitoria Guimaraes	3	0	**3**	**0**
2021–22	Vitoria Guimaraes	0	00		
2021–22	*Burton Alb*	16	0	**16**	**0**

MANCIENNE, Michael (D) **363 1**
H: 6 0 W: 11 09 b.Isleworth 8-1-88
Internationals: England U16, U17, U18, U19, U21. Seychelles Full caps.

2005–06	Chelsea	0	0		
2006–07	Chelsea	0	0		
2006–07	*QPR*	28	0		
2007–08	Chelsea	0	0		
2007–08	*QPR*	30	0	**58**	**0**
2008–09	Chelsea	4	0		
2008–09	*Wolverhampton W*	10	0		
2009–10	Chelsea	0	0		
2009–10	*Wolverhampton W*	30	0		
2010–11	Chelsea	0	0	**4**	**0**
2010–11	*Wolverhampton W*	16	0	**56**	**0**
2011–12	Hamburger SV	16	0		
2012–13	Hamburger SV	21	0		
2013–14	Hamburger SV	12	0	**49**	**0**
2014–15	Nottingham F	36	0		
2015–16	Nottingham F	31	0		
2016–17	Nottingham F	28	0		
2017–18	Nottingham F	29	0	**124**	**0**
2018	New England Revolution	10	0		
2019	New England Revolution	16	1		
2020	New England Revolution	7	0	**33**	**1**
2020–21	Burton Alb	17	0		
2021–22	Burton Alb	22	0	**39**	**0**

MORRIS, Bryn (M) **122 5**
H: 6 0 W: 11 03 b.Hartlepool 25-4-96
Internationals: England U16, U17, U18, U19, U20.

2012–13	Middlesbrough	1	0		
2013–14	Middlesbrough	1	0		
2014–15	Middlesbrough	0	0		
2014–15	*Burton Alb*	5	0		
2015–16	Middlesbrough	0	0		
2015–16	*Coventry C*	6	0	**6**	**0**
2015–16	*York C*	3	0	**3**	**0**
2015–16	*Walsall*	1	0	**1**	**0**
2016–17	Middlesbrough	0	0	**2**	**0**
2016–17	*Shrewsbury T*	13	0		
2017–18	Shrewsbury T	18	0		
2018–19	Shrewsbury T	0	0	**31**	**0**
2018–19	*Wycombe W*	19	3	**19**	**3**
2018–19	Portsmouth	7	1		
2019–20	Portsmouth	0	0		
2020–21	Portsmouth	9	0	**16**	**1**
2020–21	*Northampton T*	22	0	**22**	**0**
2021–22	Burton Alb	7	0	**12**	**0**
2021–22	*Hartlepool U*	10	1	**10**	**1**

MOULT, Louis (F) **159 48**
H: 6 0 W: 13 05 b.Stoke 14-5-92

2009–10	Stoke C	1	0		
2010–11	Stoke C	0	0		
2010–11	*Bradford C*	11	1	**11**	**1**
2011–12	Stoke C	0	0		
2011–12	*Accrington S*	4	0	**4**	**0**
2012–13	Stoke C	0	0	**1**	**0**
2012–13	Northampton T	13	1	**13**	**1**

From Nuneaton T, Wrexham.

2015–16	Motherwell	38	15		
2016–17	Motherwell	31	15		
2017–18	Motherwell	15	8	**84**	**38**
2017–18	Preston NE	10	2		
2018–19	Preston NE	24	4		
2019–20	Preston NE	2	1		
2020–21	Preston NE	0	0	**36**	**7**
2021–22	Burton Alb	10	1	**10**	**1**

NIASSE, Oumar (F) **139 39**
H: 6 0 b.Ouakam 18-4-90
Internationals: Senegal U23, Full caps.

2013–14	Akhisar Belediyespor	34	12	**34**	**12**
2014–15	Lokomotiv Moscow	13	4		
2015–16	Lokomotiv Moscow	15	8	**28**	**12**
2015–16	Everton	5	0		
2016–17	Everton	0	0		
2016–17	*Hull C*	17	4	**17**	**4**
2017–18	Everton	22	8		
2018–19	Everton	5	0		
2018–19	*Cardiff C*	13	0	**13**	**0**
2019–20	Everton	3	0	**35**	**8**
2020–21	Huddersfield T	0	0		
2021–22	Burton Alb	12	3	**12**	**3**

O'CONNOR, Thomas (M) **80 6**
H: 5 11 W: 11 00 b.Kilkenny 21-4-99
Internationals: Republic of Ireland U19, U21.

2019–20	Southampton	0	0		
2019–20	*Gillingham*	28	1		
2020–21	Southampton	0	0		
2020–21	*Gillingham*	34	0	**62**	**1**
2021–22	Burton Alb	18	5	**18**	**5**

Transferred to Wrexham, January 2022.

OSHILAJA, Adedeji (D) **227 10**
H: 5 11 W: 11 11 b.Bermondsey 16-7-93

2012–13	Cardiff C	0	0		
2013–14	Cardiff C	0	0		
2013–14	*Newport Co*	8	0	**8**	**0**
2013–14	*Sheffield W*	2	0	**2**	**0**
2014–15	Cardiff C	0	0		
2014–15	*AFC Wimbledon*	23	1		
2015–16	Cardiff C	0	0		
2015–16	*Gillingham*	22	3		
2016–17	Cardiff C	0	0		
2016–17	*Gillingham*	33	2	**55**	**5**
2017–18	AFC Wimbledon	42	2		
2018–19	AFC Wimbledon	25	1	**90**	**4**
2019–20	Charlton Ath	25	0		
2020–21	Charlton Ath	17	1	**42**	**1**
2021–22	Burton Alb	30	0	**30**	**0**

POWELL, Joe (M) **93 14**
H: 5 10 W: 10 10 b.Newham 30-10-98

2018–19	West Ham U	0	0		
2018–19	*Northampton T*	10	2	**10**	**2**
2019–20	West Ham U	0	0		
2019–20	Burton Alb	10	3		
2020–21	Burton Alb	39	6		
2021–22	Burton Alb	34	3	**83**	**12**

ROWE, Danny (M) **93 7**
H: 6 0 W: 11 11 b.Wythenshawe 9-3-92

2008–09	Stockport Co	3	0		
2009–10	Stockport Co	4	0		
2010–11	Stockport Co	17	1	**24**	**1**

From Stockport Co, Barrow, Macclesfield T.

2016–17	Ipswich T	4	0		
2017–18	Ipswich T	2	0		
2017–18	*Lincoln C*	12	1		
2018–19	Ipswich T	3	0		
2018–19	*Lincoln C*	17	4	**29**	**5**
2019–20	Ipswich T	14	1	**23**	**1**
2020–21	Burton Alb	15	0		
2021–22	Burton Alb	2	0	**17**	**0**

SHAUGHNESSY, Conor (D) **98 4**
H: 6 3 W: 11 09 b.Galway 30-6-96
Internationals: Republic of Ireland U16, U17, U18, U21, Full caps.
From Reading.

2017–18	Leeds U	9	0		
2018–19	Leeds U	0	0		
2018–19	*Hearts*	10	0	**10**	**0**
2019–20	Leeds U	0	0		
2019–20	*Mansfield T*	15	0	**15**	**0**
2019–20	*Burton Alb*	8	0		
2020–21	Leeds U	0	0	**9**	**0**
2020–21	Rochdale	18	1	**18**	**1**
2021–22	Burton Alb	38	3	**46**	**3**

SMITH, Jonny (M) **89 16**
H: 5 10 W: 10 01 b.Liverpool 28-7-97
From Wrexham.

2019–20	Bristol C	0	0		
2019–20	*Oldham Ath*	28	9	**28**	**9**
2020–21	Burton Alb	16	2		
2020–21	*Swindon T*	16	1	**16**	**1**
2021–22	Burton Alb	29	4	**45**	**6**

TAYLOR, Terry (M) **45 0**
H: 6 1 W: 11 00 b.Aberdeen 29-6-01
Internationals: Scotland U17, U18. Wales U21.
From Aberdeen.

2019–20	Wolverhampton W	0	0		
2020–21	Wolverhampton W	0	0		
2020–21	*Grimsby T*	13	0	**13**	**0**
2020–21	Burton Alb	16	0		
2021–22	Burton Alb	16	0	**32**	**0**

WILLIAMS, Charlie (M) **0 0**

2020–21	Burton Alb	0	0		
2021–22	Burton Alb	0	0		

Players retained or with offer of contract
Moore, Daniel; Nyahwema, Joe; Radcliffe, Ben.

Scholars
Bennett, Tristan Tyreese; Delap, Finn Anthony; Emery, Huw Alexander; Hazell, Oakley Milton; Hill, Tommy; Lewis, Gregory Alexander Leslie; Maginness, Ben Joseph; Matthews, James Keith; Niemczyk, Jakub Michal; Niven, Callum Marcus; Noon-Brandy, Braeden Harold; Nyahwema, Joseph Michael; Power, John Joseph; Radcliffe, William Benjamin Callister; Raine, Max Robert; Robinson, Drew William.

CAMBRIDGE U (19)

BENNETT, Liam (D) **5 0**
b. 30-11-01

2021–22	Cambridge U	5	0	**5**	**0**

BROPHY, James (M) **185 5**
H: 5 10 W: 10 10 b.Brent 25-7-94
From Harrow Bor, Woodlands U, Broadfields U.

2015–16	Swindon T	28	0		
2016–17	Swindon T	30	0		
2017–18	Swindon T	6	0	**64**	**0**
2018–19	Leyton Orient	0	0		
2019–20	Leyton Orient	34	2		
2020–21	Leyton Orient	44	2		
2021–22	Leyton Orient	0	0	**78**	**4**
2021–22	Cambridge U	43	1	**43**	**1**

DAVIES, Leon (D) **44 0**
H: 5 11 W: 11 00 b. 21-11-99

2015–16	Cambridge U	0	0		
2016–17	Cambridge U	5	0		
2017–18	Cambridge U	4	0		
2018–19	Cambridge U	6	0		
2019–20	Cambridge U	16	0		
2020–21	Cambridge U	13	0		
2021–22	Cambridge U	0	0	**44**	**0**

DICKENS, Tom (D) **0 0**
H: 6 4 b.Cambridge 10-12-02

2019–20	Cambridge U	0	0		
2020–21	Cambridge U	0	0		
2021–22	Cambridge U	0	0		

DIGBY, Paul (M) **177 2**
H: 5 9 W: 10 01 b.Sheffield 2-2-95
Internationals: England U19, U20.

2011–12	Barnsley	4	0		
2012–13	Barnsley	0	0		
2013–14	Barnsley	5	0		
2014–15	Barnsley	11	0		
2015–16	Barnsley	1	0	**21**	**0**
2015–16	*Ipswich T*	4	0		
2016–17	Ipswich T	4	0	**8**	**0**
2016–17	Mansfield T	0	0		
2017–18	Mansfield T	15	0	**15**	**0**
2018–19	Forest Green R	37	1	**37**	**1**
2019–20	Stevenage	17	0	**17**	**0**
2020–21	Cambridge U	35	0		
2021–22	Cambridge U	44	1	**79**	**1**

DUNK, Harrison (M) **282 11**
H: 6 0 W: 11 07 b.Hammersmith 25-10-90
From Bromley.

2014–15	Cambridge U	32	2		
2015–16	Cambridge U	45	4		
2016–17	Cambridge U	38	2		
2017–18	Cambridge U	37	2		
2018–19	Cambridge U	26	0		
2019–20	Cambridge U	29	0		
2020–21	Cambridge U	41	0		
2021–22	Cambridge U	34	1	**282**	**11**

HOOLAHAN, Wes (M) **597 77**
H: 5 6 W: 11 03 b.Dublin 20-5-82
Internationals: Republic of Ireland U21, B, Full caps.

2001–02	Shelbourne	20	3		
2002–03	Shelbourne	23	0		
2004	Shelbourne	31	2		
2005	Shelbourne	29	4	**103**	**9**
2005–06	Livingston	16	0	**16**	**0**
2006–07	Blackpool	42	8		
2007–08	Blackpool	45	5	**87**	**13**
2008–09	Norwich C	32	2		
2009–10	Norwich C	37	11		
2010–11	Norwich C	41	10		
2011–12	Norwich C	33	4		
2012–13	Norwich C	33	3		
2013–14	Norwich C	16	1		
2014–15	Norwich C	36	4		
2015–16	Norwich C	30	4		
2016–17	Norwich C	33	7		
2017–18	Norwich C	29	1	**320**	**47**
2018–19	WBA	6	0	**6**	**0**
2019–20	Newcastle Jets	5	0	**5**	**0**
2020–21	Cambridge U	34	7		
2021–22	Cambridge U	26	1	**60**	**8**

IREDALE, Jack (D) **168 14**
H: 6 0 W: 9 13 b.Greenock 2-5-96
Internationals: Australia U17.

2016–17	Perth Glory	23	2	**23**	**2**
2017	ECU Joondalup	4	1	**4**	**1**
2017–18	Greenock Morton	9	2		
2017–18	*Queen's Park*	14	1	**14**	**1**
2018–19	Greenock Morton	23	1	**32**	**3**
2019–20	Carlisle U	22	2	**22**	**2**
2020–21	Cambridge U	38	4		
2021–22	Cambridge U	35	1	**73**	**5**

IRONSIDE, Joe (F) **135 35**
H: 5 11 W: 11 11 b.Middlesbrough 16-10-93
Internationals: England C.

2012–13	Sheffield U	12	0		
2013–14	Sheffield U	4	0		
2014–15	Sheffield U	0	0	**16**	**0**
2014–15	*Hartlepool U*	4	1	**4**	**1**

From Alfreton T, Nuneaton T, Kidderminster H.

2019–20	Macclesfield T	33	6	**33**	**6**
2020–21	Cambridge U	44	14		
2021–22	Cambridge U	38	14	**82**	**28**

JONES, Lloyd (D) **125 4**
H: 6 3 W: 11 11 b.Plymouth 7-10-95
Internationals: Wales U17, U19. England U19, U20.

2012–13	Liverpool	0	0		
2013–14	Liverpool	0	0		
2014–15	Liverpool	0	0		
2014–15	*Cheltenham T*	6	0	**6**	**0**
2014–15	*Accrington S*	11	1	**11**	**1**
2015–16	Liverpool	0	0		
2015–16	*Blackpool*	10	0	**10**	**0**

2016–17 Liverpool 0 0
2016–17 *Swindon T* 24 2 **24 2**
2017–18 Liverpool 0 0
2017–18 Luton T 1 0
2018–19 Luton T 1 0
2018–19 *Plymouth Arg* 9 1 **9 1**
2019–20 Luton T 4 0 **6 0**
2019–20 *Northampton T* 7 0
2020–21 Northampton T 27 0 **34 0**
2021–22 Cambridge U 25 0 **25 0**

KNIBBS, Harvey (F) 81 13
H: 5 9 W: 11 03 b.Bristol 26-4-99
2017–18 Aston Villa 0 0
2018–19 Aston Villa 0 0
2019–20 Cambridge U 24 7
2020–21 Cambridge U 23 2
2021–22 Cambridge U 34 4 **81 13**

LANKESTER, Jack (F) 46 4
H: 5 10 W: 9 06 b.Bury St Edmunds 19-1-00
2018–19 Ipswich T 11 1
2019–20 Ipswich T 0 0
2020–21 Ipswich T 17 2
2021–22 Ipswich T 0 0 **28 3**
2021–22 Cambridge U 18 1 **18 1**

MANNION, Will (G) 2 0
H: 6 1 W: 11 09 b.Hillingdon 5-5-98
Internationals: England U19.
From AFC Wimbledon.
2016–17 Hull C 0 0
2017–18 Hull C 0 0
2017–18 *Plymouth Arg* 0 0
2018–19 Hull C 0 0
2019–20 Hull C 0 0
2020–21 Pafos 0 0
2021–22 Cambridge U 2 0 **2 0**

MAY, Adam (M) 100 8
H: 6 0 W: 11 07 b.Southampton 6-12-97
2014–15 Portsmouth 1 0
2015–16 Portsmouth 1 0
2016–17 Portsmouth 0 0
2017–18 Portsmouth 13 0
2018–19 Portsmouth 0 0
2019–20 Portsmouth 0 0 **15 0**
2019–20 *Swindon T* 9 0 **9 0**
2020–21 Cambridge U 38 3
2021–22 Cambridge U 38 5 **76 8**

McKENZIE-LYLE, Kai (G) 2 0
H: 6 5 W: 13 08 b.Haringey 30-11-97
Internationals: Guyana Full caps.
2015–16 Barnet 1 0
2016–17 Barnet 0 0
2017–18 Barnet 0 0 **1 0**
2018–19 Liverpool 0 0
2019–20 Liverpool 0 0
2020–21 Cambridge U 0 0
2021–22 Cambridge U 1 0 **1 0**

MITOV, Dimitar (G) 113 0
H: 6 2 W: 12 00 b.Kozloduy 22-1-97
Internationals: Bulgaria U16, U17, U19, U21.
2014–15 Charlton Ath 0 0
2015–16 Charlton Ath 0 0
2016–17 Charlton Ath 0 0
2017–18 Cambridge U 3 0
2018–19 Cambridge U 21 0
2019–20 Cambridge U 27 0
2020–21 Cambridge U 20 0
2021–22 Cambridge U 42 0 **113 0**

O'NEIL, Liam (M) 214 10
H: 5 11 W: 12 06 b.Cambridge 31-7-93
2011–12 WBA 0 0
2011–12 *VPS* 18 1 **18 1**
2012–13 WBA 0 0
2013–14 WBA 3 0
2014–15 WBA 0 0 **3 0**
2014–15 *Scunthorpe U* 22 2 **22 2**
2015–16 Chesterfield 26 0
2016–17 Chesterfield 17 2 **43 2**
2016–17 Cambridge U 13 1
2017–18 Cambridge U 26 0
2018–19 Cambridge U 19 0
2019–20 Cambridge U 28 1
2020–21 Cambridge U 21 2
2021–22 Cambridge U 21 1 **128 5**

OKEDINA, Jubril (D) 44 0
H: 6 0 W: 11 00 b.Woolwich 26-10-00
2020–21 Tottenham H 0 0
2020–21 *Cambridge U* 14 0
2021–22 Cambridge U 30 0 **44 0**

SIMPER, Lewis (D) 2 0
H: 5 11 W: 10 10 b.Cambridge 7-4-01
2019–20 Cambridge U 0 0
2020–21 Cambridge U 0 0
2021–22 Cambridge U 2 0 **2 0**

SMITH, Sam (F) 126 27
H: 5 11 W: 11 07 b.Manchester 8-3-98
2017–18 Reading 8 1
2018–19 Reading 0 0
2018–19 *Oxford U* 15 0 **15 0**
2018–19 *Shrewsbury T* 3 0 **3 0**
2019–20 Reading 0 0
2019–20 *Cambridge U* 28 7
2020–21 Reading 0 0 **8 1**
2020–21 *Tranmere R* 5 0 **5 0**
2020–21 *Cheltenham T* 21 4 **21 4**
2021–22 Cambridge U 46 15 **74 22**

TAYLOR, Greg (D) 256 6
H: 6 1 W: 12 04 b.Bedford 15-1-90
Internationals: England C.
2008–09 Northampton T 0 0
From Kettering T, Darlington, Luton T.
2014–15 Cambridge U 43 0
2015–16 Cambridge U 16 0
2016–17 Cambridge U 36 2
2017–18 Cambridge U 43 1
2018–19 Cambridge U 39 2
2019–20 Cambridge U 30 1
2020–21 Cambridge U 46 0
2021–22 Cambridge U 3 0 **256 6**

TRACEY, Shilow (M) 58 4
H: 5 10 W: 12 00 b.Newham 29-4-98
From Ebbsfleet U.
2016–17 Tottenham H 0 0
2017–18 Tottenham H 0 0
2018–19 Tottenham H 0 0
2019–20 Tottenham H 0 0
2019–20 *Macclesfield T* 7 1 **7 1**
2020–21 Tottenham H 0 0
2020–21 Shrewsbury T 8 0 **8 0**
2020–21 *Cambridge U* 17 1
2021–22 Cambridge U 26 2 **43 3**

WILLIAMS, George B (D) 233 6
H: 5 9 W: 11 00 b.Hillingdon 14-4-93
2011–12 Milton Keynes D 2 0
From Worcester C.
2014–15 Barnsley 4 0
2015–16 Barnsley 19 1 **23 1**
2016–17 Milton Keynes D 33 2
2017–18 Milton Keynes D 43 1
2018–19 Milton Keynes D 30 0
2019–20 Milton Keynes D 28 1
2020–21 Milton Keynes D 8 0 **144 4**
2020–21 Bristol R 26 0
2021–22 Bristol R 0 0 **26 0**
2021–22 Cambridge U 40 1 **40 1**

WORMAN, Ben (M) 14 1
H: 5 8 W: 10 08 b.Cambridge 30-8-01
2017–18 Cambridge U 0 0
2018–19 Cambridge U 1 0
2019–20 Cambridge U 0 0
2020–21 Cambridge U 0 0
2021–22 Cambridge U 13 1 **14 1**

YEARN, Kai (M) 1 0
H: 5 11 b.Cambridge 21-5-05
2020–21 Cambridge U 0 0
2021–22 Cambridge U 1 0 **1 0**

Players retained or with offer of contract
Akanbi, Saleem; Beckett, Harvey; Gill, Jonah; Jobe, Mamadou; McConnell, Glenn.

Scholars
Barton, Daniel Thomas; Brathwaite, Nathan; Brumby, Adam William; Chipps, Jordan; Finch, Thomas Frederick Albert; Gill, Jonah James; Lott, Jaydyn Daniel; Njoku, Brandon Chimere; Nzeh, Chibuikem; Sandiford, Gregory; Tarpey, Joe Robert; Usman, Faruq John; Winterbone, Oscar Ace.

CARDIFF C (20)

BACUNA, Leandro (M) 393 29
H: 6 2 W: 12 02 b.Groningen 21-8-91
Internationals: Netherlands U19, U21. Curacao Full caps.
2009–10 Groningen 20 2
2010–11 Groningen 24 0
2011–12 Groningen 32 7
2012–13 Groningen 33 5 **109 14**
2013–14 Aston Villa 35 5
2014–15 Aston Villa 19 0
2015–16 Aston Villa 31 1
2016–17 Aston Villa 30 1
2017–18 Aston Villa 1 0 **116 7**
2017–18 Reading 33 1
2018–19 Reading 26 3 **59 4**
2018–19 Cardiff C 11 0
2019–20 Cardiff C 41 1
2020–21 Cardiff C 42 2
2021–22 Cardiff C 15 1 **109 4**

BAGAN, Joel (D) 33 3
H: 6 4 W: 12 00 b.Basingstoke 3-9-01
Internationals: Republic of Ireland U21.
From Southampton.
2019–20 Cardiff C 0 0
2020–21 Cardiff C 7 0
2021–22 Cardiff C 26 3 **33 3**

BAKARE, Ibrahim (D) 0 0
2019–20 Morecambe 0 0
2020–21 Cardiff C 0 0
2021–22 Cardiff C 0 0

BOWEN, Sam (M) 4 0
H: 5 11 b.Wales 14-1-01
Internationals: Wales U17, U19, U21.
2019–20 Cardiff C 0 0
2020–21 Cardiff C 0 0
2021–22 Cardiff C 4 0 **4 0**

BROWN, Ciaron (D) 61 2
H: 6 1 W: 12 00 b.Hillingdon 14-1-98
Internationals: Northern Ireland U21, Full caps.
From Bedfont Sports, Wealdstone.
2018–19 Cardiff C 0 0
2018–19 *Livingston* 6 0
2019–20 Cardiff C 0 0
2019–20 *Livingston* 9 0
2020–21 Cardiff C 12 0
2020–21 *Livingston* 16 1 **31 1**
2021–22 Cardiff C 5 0 **17 0**
2021–22 *Oxford U* 13 1 **13 1**

COLLINS, James S (F) 498 168
H: 6 2 W: 13 08 b.Coventry 1-12-90
Internationals: Republic of Ireland U19, U21, Full caps.
2008–09 Aston Villa 0 0
2009–10 Aston Villa 0 0
2009–10 *Darlington* 7 2 **7 2**
2010–11 Aston Villa 0 0
2010–11 *Burton Alb* 10 4 **10 4**
2010–11 Shrewsbury T 24 8
2011–12 Shrewsbury T 42 14
2012–13 Swindon T 45 15 **45 15**
2013–14 Hibernian 36 6 **36 6**
2014–15 Shrewsbury T 45 15
2015–16 Shrewsbury T 23 5 **134 42**
2015–16 *Northampton T* 21 8 **21 8**
2016–17 Crawley T 45 20 **45 20**
2017–18 Luton T 42 19
2018–19 Luton T 44 25
2019–20 Luton T 46 14
2020–21 Luton T 42 10 **174 68**
2021–22 Cardiff C 26 3 **26 3**

COLWILL, Rubin (M) 40 5
H: 6 0 W: 11 11 b.Neath 27-4-02
Internationals: Wales U17, U21, Full caps.
2020–21 Cardiff C 6 0
2021–22 Cardiff C 34 5 **40 5**

CONNOLLY, James (D) 24 1
b. 2-11-01
Internationals: Wales U21.
From Blackburn R.
2020–21 Cardiff C 0 0
2021–22 Cardiff C 0 0
2021–22 *Bristol R* 24 1 **24 1**

D'ALMEIDA, Tavio (D) 0 0
H: 5 10 W: 11 03 b. 11-12-00
From Auxerre.
2019–20 Cardiff C 0 0
2020–21 Cardiff C 0 0
2021–22 Cardiff C 0 0

DAVIES, Isaak (F) 28 2
b. 25-9-01
Internationals: Wales U19, U21.
2020–21 Cardiff C 0 0
2021–22 Cardiff C 28 2 **28 2**

DENHAM, Oliver (D) 5 0
H: 6 0 W: 10 06 b.Blackpool 4-5-02
From Manchester U.
2021–22 Cardiff C 5 0 **5 0**

EVANS, Kieron (M) 5 0
H: 5 10 W: 10 10 b.Caerphilly 19-12-01
2020–21 Cardiff C 0 0
2021–22 Cardiff C 5 0 **5 0**
2021–22 *Linfield* 0 0

FLINT, Aiden (D) 402 51
H: 6 6 W: 12 00 b.Pinxton 11-7-89
Internationals: England C.
From Alfreton T.
2010–11 Swindon T 3 0
2011–12 Swindon T 32 2
2012–13 Swindon T 29 2 **64 4**
2013–14 Bristol C 34 3
2014–15 Bristol C 46 14
2015–16 Bristol C 44 6
2016–17 Bristol C 46 5
2017–18 Bristol C 39 8 **209 36**
2018–19 Middlesbrough 39 1 **39 1**
2019–20 Cardiff C 26 3
2020–21 Cardiff C 22 1
2020–21 *Sheffield W* 4 0 **4 0**
2021–22 Cardiff C 38 6 **86 10**

HARRIS, Mark (F) 74 8
H: 6 0 W: 11 11 b.Swansea 29-12-98
Internationals: Wales U17, U19, U20, U21, Wales Full caps.
2016–17 Cardiff C 2 0

2017–18 Cardiff C 0 0
2018–19 Cardiff C 0 0
2018–19 *Newport Co* 16 2 **16 2**
2018–19 *Port Vale* 6 0 **6 0**
2019–20 Cardiff C 0 0
2020–21 Cardiff C 16 3
2021–22 Cardiff C 34 3 **52 6**

HUGHES, Caleb (M) 0 0
2020–21 Cardiff C 0 0
2021–22 Cardiff C 0 0

KING, Eli (M) 4 0
b. 23-12-02
2021–22 Cardiff C 4 0 **4 0**

MAYEMBE, Ntazana (M) 0 0
Internationals: Zambia Full caps.
2019–20 Cardiff C 0 0
2020–21 Cardiff C 0 0
2021–22 Cardiff C 0 0

McGUINNESS, Mark (D) 58 4
H: 6 4 W: 11 00 b.Slough 5-1-01
Internationals: Republic of Ireland U19, U21.
2019–20 Arsenal 0 0
2020–21 Arsenal 0 0
2020–21 *Ipswich T* 24 1 **24 1**
2021–22 Cardiff C 34 3 **34 3**

MORRISON, Sean (D) 393 44
H: 6 4 W: 12 03 b.Plymouth 8-1-91
2007–08 Swindon T 2 0
2008–09 Swindon T 20 1
2009–10 Swindon T 9 1
2009–10 *Southend U* 8 0 **8 0**
2010–11 Swindon T 19 4 **50 6**
2010–11 Reading 0 0
2010–11 *Huddersfield T* 0 0
2011–12 Reading 0 0
2011–12 *Huddersfield T* 19 1 **19 1**
2012–13 Reading 16 2
2013–14 Reading 21 1
2014–15 Reading 1 1 **38 4**
2014–15 Cardiff C 41 6
2015–16 Cardiff C 30 3
2016–17 Cardiff C 44 4
2017–18 Cardiff C 39 7
2018–19 Cardiff C 34 1
2019–20 Cardiff C 36 4
2020–21 Cardiff C 38 5
2021–22 Cardiff C 16 3 **278 33**

MURPHY, Josh (F) 237 27
H: 5 8 W: 10 08 b.Wembley 24-2-95
Internationals: England U18, U19, U20.
2012–13 Norwich C 0 0
2013–14 Norwich C 9 0
2014–15 Norwich C 13 1
2014–15 *Wigan Ath* 5 0 **5 0**
2015–16 Norwich C 0 0
2015–16 *Milton Keynes D* 42 5 **42 5**
2016–17 Norwich C 27 4
2017–18 Norwich C 41 7 **90 12**
2018–19 Cardiff C 29 3
2019–20 Cardiff C 27 5
2020–21 Cardiff C 32 2
2021–22 Cardiff C 0 0 **88 10**
2021–22 *Preston NE* 12 0 **12 0**

NELSON, Curtis (D) 417 17
H: 6 0 W: 11 09 b.Newcastle-under-Lyme 21-5-93
Internationals: England U18.
From Stoke C.
2010–11 Plymouth Arg 35 0
2011–12 Plymouth Arg 17 0
2012–13 Plymouth Arg 27 3
2013–14 Plymouth Arg 44 1
2014–15 Plymouth Arg 42 1
2015–16 Plymouth Arg 46 3 **211 8**
2016–17 Oxford U 33 2
2017–18 Oxford U 20 1
2018–19 Oxford U 46 4 **99 7**
2019–20 Cardiff C 33 1
2020–21 Cardiff C 44 1
2021–22 Cardiff C 30 0 **107 2**

NG, Perry (D) 213 7
H: 5 11 W: 12 02 b.Liverpool 24-6-94
2014–15 Crewe Alex 0 0
2015–16 Crewe Alex 6 0
2016–17 Crewe Alex 16 0
2017–18 Crewe Alex 38 4
2018–19 Crewe Alex 44 0
2019–20 Crewe Alex 36 2
2020–21 Crewe Alex 15 1 **155 7**
2020–21 Cardiff C 19 0
2021–22 Cardiff C 39 0 **58 0**

PACK, Marlon (M) 494 31
H: 6 0 W: 11 09 b.Portsmouth 25-3-91
2008–09 Portsmouth 0 0
2009–10 Portsmouth 0 0
2009–10 *Wycombe W* 8 0 **8 0**
2009–10 *Dagenham & R* 17 1 **17 1**
2010–11 Portsmouth 1 0 **1 0**
2010–11 *Cheltenham T* 38 2
2011–12 Cheltenham T 43 5
2012–13 Cheltenham T 43 7
2013–14 Cheltenham T 0 0 **124 14**
2013–14 Bristol C 43 0
2014–15 Bristol C 34 3
2015–16 Bristol C 45 1
2016–17 Bristol C 33 2
2017–18 Bristol C 42 3
2018–19 Bristol C 46 2
2019–20 Bristol C 1 0 **244 11**
2019–20 Cardiff C 37 2
2020–21 Cardiff C 39 2
2021–22 Cardiff C 24 1 **100 5**

PATTEN, Keenan (M) 0 0
b.Cardiff 7-4-01
Internationals: Wales U19.
2020–21 Penybont 0 0
2020–21 Cardiff C 0 0
2021–22 Cardiff C 0 0

PHILLIPS, Dillon (M) 114 0
H: 6 2 W: 11 11 b.Hornchurch 11-6-95
2012–13 Charlton Ath 0 0
2013–14 Charlton Ath 0 0
2014–15 Charlton Ath 0 0
2015–16 Charlton Ath 0 0
2016–17 Charlton Ath 8 0
2017–18 Charlton Ath 0 0
2018–19 Charlton Ath 27 0
2019–20 Charlton Ath 46 0 **81 0**
2020–21 Cardiff C 16 0
2021–22 Cardiff C 17 0 **33 0**

RALLS, Joe (M) 324 33
H: 5 10 W: 11 00 b.Aldershot 12-10-93
Internationals: England U19.
From Aldershot T, Farnborough.
2011–12 Cardiff C 10 1
2012–13 Cardiff C 4 0
2013–14 Cardiff C 0 0
2013–14 *Yeovil T* 37 3 **37 3**
2014–15 Cardiff C 28 2
2015–16 Cardiff C 43 1
2016–17 Cardiff C 42 6
2017–18 Cardiff C 37 7
2018–19 Cardiff C 28 0
2019–20 Cardiff C 27 7
2020–21 Cardiff C 39 5
2021–22 Cardiff C 29 1 **287 30**

RATCLIFFE, George (G) 0 0
H: 6 2 W: 11 09 b.Newport 12-9-00
Internationals: Wales U17, U19, U21.
2020–21 Cardiff C 0 0
2021–22 Cardiff C 0 0

SANG, Tom (M) 31 0
H: 6 2 W: 12 06 b.Liverpool 29-6-99
From Bolton W, Manchester U.
2019–20 Cardiff C 0 0
2020–21 Cardiff C 9 0
2020–21 *Cheltenham T* 10 0 **10 0**
2021–22 Cardiff C 3 0 **12 0**
2021–22 *St Johnstone* 9 0 **9 0**

SMITHIES, Alex (G) 444 0
H: 6 3 W: 13 03 b.Huddersfield 5-3-90
Internationals: England U16, U17, U18, U19.
2006–07 Huddersfield T 0 0
2007–08 Huddersfield T 2 0
2008–09 Huddersfield T 27 0
2009–10 Huddersfield T 46 0
2010–11 Huddersfield T 22 0
2011–12 Huddersfield T 13 0
2012–13 Huddersfield T 46 0
2013–14 Huddersfield T 46 0
2014–15 Huddersfield T 44 0
2015–16 Huddersfield T 1 0 **247 0**
2015–16 QPR 18 0
2016–17 QPR 46 0
2017–18 QPR 43 0 **107 0**
2018–19 Cardiff C 0 0
2019–20 Cardiff C 30 0
2020–21 Cardiff C 31 0
2021–22 Cardiff C 29 0 **90 0**

VASSELL, Isaac (F) 73 12
H: 5 7 W: 11 02 b.Newquay 9-9-93
2011–12 Plymouth Arg 6 0
2012–13 Plymouth Arg 0 0
2013–14 Plymouth Arg 0 0 **6 0**
From Truro C.
2016–17 Luton T 40 8
2017–18 Luton T 2 2 **42 10**
2017–18 Birmingham C 9 1
2018–19 Birmingham C 14 0
2019–20 Birmingham C 0 0 **23 1**
2019–20 Cardiff C 2 1
2020–21 Cardiff C 0 0
2021–22 Cardiff C 0 0 **2 1**

VAULKS, Will (D) 338 34
H: 5 11 W: 11 11 b.Birkenhead 13-9-93
Internationals: Wales Full caps.
2012–13 Tranmere R 0 0
2012–13 Falkirk 6 0
2013–14 Falkirk 33 1
2014–15 Falkirk 34 3
2015–16 Falkirk 35 6 **108 10**
2016–17 Rotherham U 40 1
2017–18 Rotherham U 44 5
2018–19 Rotherham U 41 7 **125 13**
2019–20 Cardiff C 27 4
2020–21 Cardiff C 42 5
2021–22 Cardiff C 36 2 **105 11**

WATKINS, Marley (M) 221 29
H: 5 10 W: 10 03 b.Lewisham 17-10-90
Internationals: Wales Full caps.
From Swansea C.
2008–09 Cheltenham T 12 0
2009–10 Cheltenham T 13 1
2010–11 Cheltenham T 1 0 **26 1**
From Bath C, Hereford U
2013–14 Inverness CT 26 1
2014–15 Inverness CT 33 7 **59 8**
2015–16 Barnsley 34 5
2016–17 Barnsley 42 10 **76 15**
2017–18 Norwich C 24 0 **24 0**
2018–19 Bristol C 16 2
2019–20 Bristol C 9 1
2020–21 Bristol C 2 0 **27 3**
2020–21 *Aberdeen* 9 2 **9 2**
2021–22 Cardiff C 0 0
Transferred to Aberdeen, August 2021.

WATTERS, Max (F) 42 19
H: 6 2 W: 12 08 b.Camden 23-3-99
From Thurrock, Barking, Ashford U.
2019–20 Doncaster R 5 0 **5 0**
2020–21 Crawley T 15 13 **15 13**
2020–21 Cardiff C 3 0
2021–22 Cardiff C 8 1 **11 1**
2021–22 *Milton Keynes D* 11 5 **11 5**

WHYTE, Gavin (F) 256 55
H: 5 7 W: 10 08 b.Belfast 31-1-96
Internationals: Northern Ireland U21, Full caps.
2013–14 Crusaders 1 0
2014–15 Crusaders 34 9
2015–16 Crusaders 27 3
2016–17 Crusaders 34 10
2017–18 Crusaders 36 21 **132 43**
2018–19 Oxford U 36 7
2019–20 Cardiff C 24 0
2020–21 Cardiff C 7 0
2020–21 *Hull C* 20 4 **20 4**
2021–22 Cardiff C 0 0 **31 0**
2021–22 *Oxford U* 37 1 **73 8**

WINTLE, Ryan (M) 205 9
H: 5 5 W: 10 01 b.Newcastle-under-Lyme 13-6-97
2015–16 Crewe Alex 3 0
2016–17 Crewe Alex 17 1
2017–18 Crewe Alex 18 2
2018–19 Crewe Alex 46 1
2019–20 Crewe Alex 37 3
2020–21 Crewe Alex 43 2
2021–22 Crewe Alex 0 0 **164 9**
2021–22 *Blackpool* 18 0 **18 0**
2021–22 Cardiff C 23 0 **23 0**

ZIMBA, Chanka (F) 13 1
b.Zambia 29-12-01
From Blackburn R.
2020–21 Cardiff C 0 0
2021–22 Cardiff C 1 0 **1 0**
2021–22 *Northampton T* 12 1 **12 1**

Players retained or with offer of contract
Ashford, Cian; Davies, Thomas; Jones, Taylor; Kavanagh, Ryan; Leahy, Jack; Luthra, Rohan; Pritchard, Owen; Semenyo, Jai; Turner, Matthew.

Scholars
Clay, Jac Rhys; Coley, Benjamin William; Colwill, Joel William; Coomer, Adam Thomas; Crole, James William Thomas; Dennis, Jacob Rees; Jefferies, Isaac James; Jones, Callum Jacob; Jones, Tana Huish; Keeping, Joseph James; Kenniford, Kyle Edward; Lewis, Morgan James; MacNamara, Aidan; Rippon, Joshua Marshall; Schwank, Rhys Morgan; Ware, Lewys Morgan; Wigley, Morgan.

CARLISLE U (21)

ABRAHAMS, Tristan (F) 130 17
H: 5 9 W: 11 00 b.Lewisham 29-12-98
2016–17 Leyton Orient 9 2
2017–18 Norwich C 0 0
2018–19 Norwich C 0 0
2018–19 *Exeter C* 16 1 **16 1**
2018–19 *Yeovil T* 15 3 **15 3**
2019–20 Newport Co 33 4
2020–21 Newport Co 23 4 **56 8**
2020–21 *Leyton Orient* 14 0 **23 2**
2021–22 Carlisle U 20 3 **20 3**

ALESSANDRA, Lewis (F) 466 70
H: 5 9 W: 11 07 b.Heywood 8-2-89
2007–08 Oldham Ath 15 2

2008–09	Oldham Ath	32	5		
2009–10	Oldham Ath	1	0		
2010–11	Oldham Ath	19	1	**67**	**8**
2011–12	Morecambe	42	4		
2012–13	Morecambe	40	3		
2013–14	Plymouth Arg	42	7		
2014–15	Plymouth Arg	44	11	**86**	**18**
2015–16	Rochdale	8	1	**8**	**1**
2015–16	*York C*	11	2	**11**	**2**
2016–17	Hartlepool U	46	9	**46**	**9**
2017–18	Notts Co	39	7		
2018–19	Notts Co	26	2	**65**	**9**
2019–20	Morecambe	22	5	**104**	**12**
2019–20	Carlisle U	10	1		
2020–21	Carlisle U	45	8		
2021–22	Carlisle U	24	2	**79**	**11**

ARMER, Jack (D)				**65**	**1**
H: 6 1 W: 12 04 b.Preston 16-4-01					
Internationals: Scotland U17, U18, U19.					
2019–20	Preston NE	0	0		
2020–21	Carlisle U	24	1		
2021–22	Carlisle U	41	0	**65**	**1**

BELL, Lewis (M)				**2**	**0**
b.Carlisle 29-9-02					
2020–21	Carlisle U	1	0		
2021–22	Carlisle U	1	0	**2**	**0**

BREEZE, Gabriel (G)				**0**	**0**
b.Carlisle 30-12-03					
2020–21	Carlisle U	0	0		
2021–22	Carlisle U	0	0		

CHARTERS, Taylor (M)				**25**	**0**
H: 6 1 W: 11 11 b.Whitehaven 2-10-01					
2019–20	Carlisle U	7	0		
2020–21	Carlisle U	9	0		
2021–22	Carlisle U	9	0	**25**	**0**

CLOUGH, Zach (F)				**134**	**29**
H: 5 7 W: 10 01 b.Manchester 8-3-95					
2013–14	Bolton W	0	0		
2014–15	Bolton W	8	5		
2015–16	Bolton W	28	7		
2016–17	Bolton W	23	9		
2016–17	Nottingham F	14	4		
2017–18	Nottingham F	13	0		
2017–18	*Bolton W*	9	1	**68**	**22**
2018–19	Nottingham F	0	0		
2018–19	*Rochdale*	9	0	**9**	**0**
2019–20	Nottingham F	0	0		
2020–21	Nottingham F	0	0	**27**	**4**
2020–21	Wigan Ath	13	1	**13**	**1**
2021–22	Carlisle U	17	2	**17**	**2**
Transferred to Adelaide U, February 2022.					

DENNIS, Kristian (F)				**153**	**37**
H: 5 11 W: 11 00 b.Macclesfield 12-3-90					
2007–08	Macclesfield T	1	0		
2008–09	Macclesfield T	3	1		
2009–10	Macclesfield T	0	0	**4**	**1**
From Woodley Sports, Mossley, Curzon Ashton, Stockport Co.					
2015–16	Chesterfield	0	0		
2016–17	Chesterfield	35	8		
2017–18	Chesterfield	43	19	**78**	**27**
2018–19	Notts Co	24	3	**24**	**3**
2018–19	*Grimsby T*	13	1	**13**	**1**
From Notts Co.					
2020–21	St Mirren	17	3	**17**	**3**
2021–22	Carlisle U	17	2	**17**	**2**

DEVINE, Daniel (M)				**58**	**1**
H: 5 11 W: 12 00 b.Bradford 4-9-97					
2015–16	Bradford C	0	0		
2016–17	Bradford C	11	0		
2017–18	Bradford C	3	0		
2018–19	Bradford C	3	0		
2019–20	Bradford C	13	1	**30**	**1**
2020–21	Carlisle U	11	0		
2021–22	Carlisle U	17	0	**28**	**0**

DEVITT, Jamie (M)				**317**	**45**
H: 5 10 W: 10 06 b.Dublin 6-7-90					
Internationals: Republic of Ireland U21.					
2007–08	Hull C	0	0		
2008–09	Hull C	0	0		
2009–10	Hull C	0	0		
2009–10	*Darlington*	6	1	**6**	**1**
2009–10	*Shrewsbury T*	9	2	**9**	**2**
2009–10	*Grimsby T*	15	5	**15**	**5**
2010–11	Hull C	16	0		
2011–12	Hull C	0	0		
2011–12	*Bradford C*	7	1		
2011–12	*Accrington S*	16	2	**16**	**2**
2012–13	Hull C	0	0	**16**	**0**
2012–13	*Rotherham U*	1	0	**1**	**0**
2013–14	Chesterfield	7	0	**7**	**0**
2013–14	*Morecambe*	14	2		
2014–15	Morecambe	36	3		
2015–16	Morecambe	39	6	**89**	**11**
2016–17	Carlisle U	35	0		
2017–18	Carlisle U	40	10		
2018–19	Carlisle U	35	11		
2019–20	Blackpool	0	0		
2019–20	*Bradford C*	5	0	**12**	**1**
2020–21	Blackpool	0	0		
2020–21	Newport Co	8	1	**8**	**1**
2020–21	Barrow	17	1		
2021–22	Barrow	4	0	**21**	**1**
2021–22	Carlisle U	7	0	**117**	**21**

DICKENSON, Brennan (F)				**251**	**26**
H: 6 0 W: 12 08 b.Ferndown 26-2-93					
From Dorchester T.					
2012–13	Brighton & HA	0	0		
2012–13	*Chesterfield*	11	1	**11**	**1**
2012–13	*AFC Wimbledon*	7	2	**7**	**2**
2013–14	Brighton & HA	0	0		
2013–14	*Northampton T*	13	1	**13**	**1**
2014–15	Gillingham	34	1		
2015–16	Gillingham	33	1	**67**	**2**
2016–17	Colchester U	36	12		
2017–18	Colchester U	7	0		
2018–19	Colchester U	42	3	**85**	**15**
2019–20	Milton Keynes D	7	0	**7**	**0**
2019–20	Exeter C	10	2	**10**	**2**
2020–21	Carlisle U	12	1		
2021–22	Carlisle U	39	2	**51**	**3**

DIXON, Josh (M)				**2**	**0**
H: 5 11 W: 9 11 b.Carlisle 7-2-01					
2020–21	Carlisle U	2	0		
2021–22	Carlisle U	0	0	**2**	**0**

ELLIS, Jack (D)				**2**	**0**
b. 24-10-03					
2021–22	Carlisle U	2	0	**2**	**0**

FEENEY, Morgan (D)				**36**	**1**
H: 6 3 W: 12 02 b.Bootle 8-2-98					
Internationals: England U17, U18, U19.					
2017–18	Everton	0	0		
2018–19	Everton	0	0		
2019–20	Everton	0	0		
2019–20	*Tranmere R*	1	0	**1**	**0**
2020–21	Sunderland	0	0		
2020–21	Carlisle U	0	0		
2021–22	Carlisle U	35	1	**35**	**1**

FISHBURN, Sam (F)				**9**	**0**
b.Gateshead 26-11-03					
2020–21	Carlisle U	0	0		
2021–22	Carlisle U	9	0	**9**	**0**

GIBSON, Jordan (F)				**103**	**17**
H: 5 10 W: 12 08 b.Birmingham 26-2-98					
From Rangers.					
2017–18	Bradford C	5	1		
2018–19	Bradford C	11	0		
2018–19	*Stevenage*	6	1	**6**	**1**
2019–20	Bradford C	6	0	**22**	**1**
2020	St Patricks Ath	14	2	**14**	**2**
2021	Sligo R	22	7	**22**	**7**
2021–22	Carlisle U	39	6	**39**	**6**

GUY, Callum (M)				**138**	**0**
H: 5 10 W: 10 01 b.Nottingham 25-11-96					
2015–16	Derby Co	0	0		
2016–17	Derby Co	0	0		
2016–17	*Port Vale*	11	0	**11**	**0**
2017–18	Derby Co	0	0		
2017–18	*Bradford C*	17	0	**17**	**0**
2018–19	Blackpool	15	0		
2019–20	Blackpool	15	0	**30**	**0**
2019–20	Carlisle U	3	0		
2020–21	Carlisle U	43	0		
2021–22	Carlisle U	34	0	**80**	**0**

HOWARD, Mark (G)				**289**	**0**
H: 6 0 W: 12 00 b.Southwark 21-9-86					
2005–06	Arsenal	0	0		
2005–06	*Falkirk*	8	0	**8**	**0**
2006–07	Cardiff C	0	0		
2006–07	*Swansea C*	0	0		
2007–08	St Mirren	10	0		
2008–09	St Mirren	33	0		
2009–10	St Mirren	2	0	**45**	**0**
2010–11	Aberdeen	9	0	**9**	**0**
2011–12	Blackpool	4	0		
2011–12	Sheffield U	0	0		
2012–13	Sheffield U	11	0		
2013–14	Sheffield U	19	0		
2014–15	Sheffield U	35	0		
2015–16	Sheffield U	15	0	**80**	**0**
2016–17	Bolton W	27	0		
2017–18	Bolton W	8	0	**35**	**0**
2018–19	Blackpool	32	0		
2019–20	*Salford C*	3	0	**3**	**0**
2019–20	Blackpool	4	0	**40**	**0**
2020–21	Scunthorpe U	34	0	**34**	**0**
2021–22	Carlisle U	35	0	**35**	**0**

KILSBY, Max (D)				**0**	**0**
b.North Shields 4-10-03					
2020–21	Carlisle U	0	0		
2021–22	Carlisle U	0	0		

MAMPALA, Manasse (D)				**8**	**0**
H: 6 2 b.Kinshasa 18-7-00					
2018–19	Everton	0	0		
2019–20	Everton	0	0		
2020–21	QPR	0	0		
2021–22	Carlisle U	8	0	**8**	**0**

McDONALD, Rod (D)				**165**	**4**
H: 6 3 W: 12 13 b.Liverpool 11-4-92					
2009–10	Stoke C	0	0		
2010–11	Oldham Ath	0	0		
From Colwyn Bay, Hereford U, AFC Telford U.					
2015–16	Northampton T	23	3		
2016–17	Northampton T	7	0	**30**	**3**
2016–17	Coventry C	0	0		
2017–18	Coventry C	37	0	**37**	**0**
2018–19	AFC Wimbledon	23	0		
2019–20	AFC Wimbledon	15	0	**38**	**0**
2020–21	Carlisle U	29	0		
2021–22	Carlisle U	31	1	**60**	**1**

MELLISH, Jon (D)				**101**	**14**
H: 6 2 W: 11 07 b.South Shields 19-9-97					
Internationals: England C.					
From Gateshead.					
2019–20	Carlisle U	15	0		
2020–21	Carlisle U	44	11		
2021–22	Carlisle U	42	3	**101**	**14**

MELLOR, Kelvin (D)				**336**	**19**
H: 6 2 W: 11 11 b.Crewe 25-1-91					
From Nantwich T.					
2007–08	Crewe Alex	0	0		
2008–09	Crewe Alex	0	0		
2009–10	Crewe Alex	0	0		
2010–11	Crewe Alex	1	0		
2011	*IBV*	10	2	**10**	**2**
2011–12	Crewe Alex	12	1		
2012–13	Crewe Alex	35	0		
2013–14	Crewe Alex	28	1	**76**	**2**
2014–15	Plymouth Arg	37	1		
2015–16	Plymouth Arg	41	1	**78**	**2**
2016–17	Blackpool	44	4		
2017–18	Blackpool	29	6	**73**	**10**
2018–19	Bradford C	20	1		
2019–20	Bradford C	25	1	**45**	**2**
2020–21	Morecambe	32	1		
2021–22	Morecambe	1	0	**33**	**1**
2021–22	Carlisle U	21	0	**21**	**0**

NORMAN, Magnus (G)				**21**	**0**
H: 6 3 W: 12 13 b.Kingston Upon Thames 19-1-97					
Internationals: England U16, U18.					
2017–18	Fulham	0	0		
2018–19	Fulham	0	0		
2018–19	*Rochdale*	7	0	**7**	**0**
2019–20	Fulham	0	0		
2020–21	Carlisle U	4	0		
2021–22	Carlisle U	10	0	**14**	**0**

PATRICK, Omari (F)				**87**	**17**
H: 6 1 W: 12 08 b.Slough 24-5-96					
From Kidderminster H.					
2018–19	Bradford C	1	0		
2018–19	*Yeovil T*	9	1	**9**	**1**
2019–20	Bradford C	2	0	**3**	**0**
2019–20	Carlisle U	7	2		
2020–21	Carlisle U	37	5		
2021–22	Burton Alb	7	0	**7**	**0**
2021–22	Carlisle U	24	9	**68**	**16**

RILEY, Joe (D)				**81**	**5**
H: 6 0 W: 11 03 b.Blackpool 6-12-96					
2016–17	Manchester U	0	0		
2016–17	*Sheffield U*	2	0	**2**	**0**
2017–18	Manchester u	0	0		
2018–19	Bradford C	6	0		
2019–20	Bradford C	0	0	**6**	**0**
2020–21	Carlisle U	42	2		
2021–22	Carlisle U	31	3	**73**	**5**

SENIOR, Joel (D)				**4**	**0**
H: 5 11 W: 11 00 b.Manchester 24-6-99					
From FC United of Manchester, Curzon Ath, Burnley, Altrincham.					
2021–22	Carlisle U	4	0	**4**	**0**

SHO-SILVA, Oluwatobi (F)				**25**	**4**
H: 6 0 W: 11 11 b.Thamesmead 27-3-95					
Internationals: England U18.					
2012–13	Charlton Ath	0	0		
2013–14	Charlton Ath	0	0		
2014–15	Charlton Ath	0	0		
2015–16	Charlton Ath	0	0		
2015–16	*Inverness CT*	5	0	**5**	**0**
From Bromley, Dover Ath, FC Halifax T.					
2021–22	Sutton U	7	0	**7**	**0**
2021–22	Carlisle U	13	4	**13**	**4**

TOURE, Gime (F)				**39**	**2**
H: 6 3 W: 13 05 b. 7-5-94					
2020–21	Carlisle U	34	2		
2021–22	Carlisle U	5	0	**39**	**2**

WHELAN, Corey (D)				**89**	**1**
H: 5 11 W: 11 07 b.Chester 12-12-97					
Internationals: Republic of Ireland U17, U21.					
2017–18	Liverpool	0	0		
2017–18	*Yeovil T*	7	0	**7**	**0**
2018–19	Liverpool	0	0		
2018–19	*Crewe Alex*	16	1	**16**	**1**
2019	Phoenix Rising	7	0		
2019	*Tucson*	1	0	**1**	**0**
2020	Phoenix Rising	15	0	**22**	**0**

2020–21 Wigan Ath 8 0
2021–22 Wigan Ath 0 0 **8 0**
2021–22 Carlisle U 35 0 **35 0**

Players retained or with offer of contract
Carr, Ryan; Simons, Scott.

Scholars
Barnett, Joshua Kenneth; Bell, Matthew Christopher; Bollado, Nicolas Valentin Etxeberria; Boyd, Lewis Paul; Carr, Ryan George; Ellis, Jack Ethan James; Garvey, Dylan Paul; Gordon, Harvey William; Hardy, Mason Lewis; Hill, Daniel James; Kilsby, Max Robert; Nugent, Kai David; Potts, Alex George; Taylor, Dj; Watt, Charles Neal.

CHARLTON ATH (22)

ANEKE, Chuks (M) 293 78
H: 6 3 W: 13 01 b.Newham 3-7-93
Internationals: England U16, U17, U18, U19.
2010–11 Arsenal 0 0
2011–12 Arsenal 0 0
2011–12 *Stevenage* 6 0 **6 0**
2011–12 *Preston NE* 7 1 **7 1**
2012–13 Arsenal 0 0
2012–13 *Crewe Alex* 30 6
2013–14 Arsenal 0 0
2013–14 *Crewe Alex* 40 15 **70 21**
2014–15 Arsenal 0 0
2014–15 Zulte-Waregem 30 2
2015–16 Zulte-Waregem 11 2 **41 4**
2016–17 Milton Keynes D 15 4
2017–18 Milton Keynes D 31 9
2018–19 Milton Keynes D 38 17 **84 30**
2019–20 Charlton Ath 20 1
2020–21 Charlton Ath 38 15
2021–22 Birmingham C 18 2 **18 2**
2021–22 Charlton Ath 9 4 **67 20**

AOUACHIRA, Wassim (M) 0 0
H: 6 2 b.Roubaix 12-3-00
Internationals: Algeria U18.
From Marseille.
2020–21 Charlton Ath 0 0
2021–22 Charlton Ath 0 0

BARKER, Charlie (D) 3 0
b. 12-2-03
2020–21 Charlton Ath 3 0
2021–22 Charlton Ath 0 0 **3 0**

CAMPBELL, Tyreece (M) 2 0
2021–22 Charlton Ath 2 0 **2 0**

CLARE, Sean (M) 165 12
H: 6 3 W: 12 06 b.Sheffield 18-9-96
2015–16 Sheffield W 0 0
2015–16 *Bury* 4 0 **4 0**
2016–17 Sheffield W 0 0
2016–17 *Accrington S* 8 1 **8 1**
2017–18 Sheffield W 5 1 **5 1**
2017–18 *Gillingham* 21 1 **21 1**
2018–19 Hearts 28 3
2019–20 Hearts 26 4 **54 7**
2020–21 Oxford U 17 0 **17 0**
2020–21 *Burton Alb* 20 1 **20 1**
2021–22 Charlton Ath 36 1 **36 1**

CLAYDEN, Charles (F) 2 0
b. 16-11-00
From Leyton Orient.
2019–20 Charlton Ath 0 0
2020–21 Charlton Ath 0 0
2021–22 Charlton Ath 2 0 **2 0**

DAVISON, Joshua (F) 65 15
H: 5 11 W: 12 06 b.Enfield 16-9-99
From Peterborough U, Enfield T.
2019–20 Charlton Ath 9 1
2020–21 Charlton Ath 0 0
2020–21 *Forest Green R* 20 3 **20 3**
2021–22 Charlton Ath 15 2 **24 3**
2021–22 *Swindon T* 21 9 **21 9**

DEMPSEY, Ben (M) 11 0
H: 5 10 W: 11 05 b.Tooting 25-11-99
2018–19 Charlton Ath 0 0
2019–20 Charlton Ath 4 0
2020–21 Charlton Ath 0 0
2021–22 Charlton Ath 0 0 **4 0**
2021–22 *Ayr U* 7 0 **7 0**

DOBSON, George (M) 182 4
H: 6 1 W: 11 07 b.Harold Wood 15-11-97
From Arsenal.
2015–16 West Ham U 0 0
2016–17 West Ham U 0 0
2016–17 *Walsall* 21 1
2017–18 Sparta Rotterdam 5 0 **5 0**
2017–18 Walsall 21 1
2018–19 Walsall 39 0 **81 2**
2019–20 Sunderland 29 0
2020–21 Sunderland 5 0 **34 0**
2020–21 *AFC Wimbledon* 24 1 **24 1**
2021–22 Charlton Ath 38 1 **38 1**

ELEREWE, Ayodeji (D) 3 0
H: 6 3 b. 14-9-03
2021–22 Charlton Ath 3 0 **3 0**

FORSTER-CASKEY, Jake (M) 215 22
H: 5 10 W: 10 00 b.Southend 25-4-94
Internationals: England U16, U17, U18, U20, U21.
2009–10 Brighton & HA 1 0
2010–11 Brighton & HA 0 0
2011–12 Brighton & HA 4 1
2012–13 Brighton & HA 3 0
2012–13 *Oxford U* 16 3 **16 3**
2013–14 Brighton & HA 28 3
2014–15 Brighton & HA 29 1
2015–16 Brighton & HA 2 0 **67 5**
2015–16 *Milton Keynes D* 20 1 **20 1**
2016–17 Charlton Ath 15 2
2016–17 *Rotherham U* 6 0 **6 0**
2017–18 Charlton Ath 41 5
2018–19 Charlton Ath 1 0
2019–20 Charlton Ath 11 0
2020–21 Charlton Ath 34 6
2021–22 Charlton Ath 4 0 **106 13**

FRASER, Scott (M) 249 40
H: 6 0 W: 10 12 b.Dundee 30-3-95
2013–14 Dundee U 1 0
2014–15 Dundee U 0 0
2014–15 *Airdrieonians* 28 5 **28 5**
2015–16 Dundee U 32 1
2016–17 Dundee U 25 4
2017–18 Dundee U 23 4 **81 9**
2018–19 Burton Alb 42 6
2019–20 Burton Alb 30 5 **72 11**
2020–21 Milton Keynes D 44 14
2021–22 Milton Keynes D 0 0 **44 14**
2021–22 Ipswich T 15 1 **15 1**
2021–22 Charlton Ath 9 0 **9 0**

FRENCH, Billy (D) 0 0
b. 27-11-02
2020–21 Charlton Ath 0 0
2021–22 Charlton Ath 0 0

GAVIN, Dylan (F) 0 0
b.Athlone 16-1-03
2020–21 Charlton Ath 0 0
2021–22 Charlton Ath 0 0

GHANDOUR, Hady (F) 0 0
H: 6 2 b.Westminster 27-1-00
Internationals: Lebanon U16, U19, Full caps.
From Tooting & Mitcham U.
2020–21 Charlton Ath 0 0
2021–22 Charlton Ath 0 0

GILBEY, Alex (M) 279 25
H: 6 0 W: 11 07 b.Dagenham 9-12-94
2011–12 Colchester U 0 0
2012–13 Colchester U 3 0
2013–14 Colchester U 36 1
2014–15 Colchester U 34 1
2015–16 Colchester U 37 5 **110 7**
2016–17 Wigan Ath 15 2
2017–18 Wigan Ath 2 0 **17 2**
2017–18 Milton Keynes D 23 3
2018–19 Milton Keynes D 39 3
2019–20 Milton Keynes D 30 5 **92 11**
2020–21 Charlton Ath 23 3
2021–22 Charlton Ath 37 2 **60 5**

GUNTER, Chris (D) 508 5
H: 5 11 W: 11 02 b.Newport 21-7-89
Internationals: Wales U17, U19, U21, Full caps.
2006–07 Cardiff C 15 0
2007–08 Cardiff C 13 0 **28 0**
2007–08 Tottenham H 2 0
2008–09 Tottenham H 3 0 **5 0**
2008–09 *Nottingham F* 8 0
2009–10 Nottingham F 44 1
2010–11 Nottingham F 43 0
2011–12 Nottingham F 46 1 **141 2**
2012–13 Reading 20 0
2013–14 Reading 44 0
2014–15 Reading 38 0
2015–16 Reading 44 0
2016–17 Reading 46 1
2017–18 Reading 46 1
2018–19 Reading 22 0
2019–20 Reading 20 0 **280 2**
2020–21 Charlton Ath 36 1
2021–22 Charlton Ath 18 0 **54 1**

HARNESS, Nathan (G) 1 0
H: 6 1 b. 19-1-00
From Stevenage, Dunstable.
2019–20 Charlton Ath 0 0
2020–21 Charlton Ath 0 0
2021–22 Charlton Ath 1 0 **1 0**

HENDERSON, Stephen (G) 168 0
H: 6 4 W: 13 10 b.Dublin 2-5-88
Internationals: Republic of Ireland U16, U17, U19, U21.
2005–06 Aston Villa 0 0
2006–07 Aston Villa 0 0
2007–08 Bristol C 1 0
2008–09 Bristol C 1 0
2009–10 Bristol C 3 0
2009–10 *Aldershot T* 8 0 **8 0**
2010–11 Bristol C 0 0 **5 0**
2010–11 *Yeovil T* 33 0 **33 0**
2011–12 Portsmouth 25 0
2011–12 *West Ham U* 0 0
2012–13 West Ham U 0 0
2012–13 *Ipswich T* 24 0 **24 0**
2013–14 West Ham U 0 0
2013–14 *Bournemouth* 2 0 **2 0**
2014–15 Charlton Ath 31 0
2015–16 Charlton Ath 22 0
2016–17 Nottingham F 12 0
2017–18 Nottingham F 0 0
2017–18 *Portsmouth* 1 0 **26 0**
2018–19 Nottingham F 0 0 **12 0**
2018–19 *Wycombe W* 3 0 **3 0**
2019–20 Crystal Palace 0 0
2020–21 Crystal Palace 0 0
2021–22 Charlton Ath 2 0 **55 0**

HENRY, Aaron (M) 0 0
b. 31-8-03
Internationals: England U16.
2019–20 Charlton Ath 0 0
2020–21 Charlton Ath 0 0
2021–22 Charlton Ath 0 0

INNISS, Ryan (D) 120 3
H: 6 5 W: 13 03 b.Farnborough 5-6-95
Internationals: England U16, U17.
2012–13 Crystal Palace 0 0
2013–14 Crystal Palace 0 0
2013–14 *Cheltenham T* 2 0 **2 0**
2013–14 *Gillingham* 3 0 **3 0**
2014–15 Crystal Palace 0 0
2014–15 *Yeovil T* 6 0 **6 0**
2014–15 *Port Vale* 5 0
2015–16 Crystal Palace 0 0
2015–16 *Port Vale* 15 0 **20 0**
2016–17 Crystal Palace 0 0
2016–17 *Southend U* 10 0 **10 0**
2017–18 Crystal Palace 0 0
2017–18 *Colchester U* 18 0 **18 0**
2018–19 Crystal Palace 0 0
2018–19 *Dundee* 11 0 **11 0**
2019–20 Crystal Palace 0 0
2019–20 *Newport Co* 22 1 **22 1**
2020–21 Charlton Ath 13 1
2021–22 Charlton Ath 15 1 **28 2**

JAIYESIMI, Diallang (M) 125 14
H: 5 11 W: 11 05 b.Southwark 18-3-99
From Dulwich Hamlet.
2017–18 Norwich C 0 0
2017–18 *Grimsby T* 30 0 **30 0**
2018–19 Norwich C 0 0
2018–19 *Yeovil T* 9 2 **9 2**
2019–20 Norwich C 0 0
2019–20 *Swindon T* 21 5
2020–21 Swindon T 18 4 **39 9**
2020–21 Charlton Ath 14 1
2021–22 Charlton Ath 33 2 **47 3**

KANU, Daniel (M) 2 0
b. 14-11-04
2021–22 Charlton Ath 2 0 **2 0**

KIRK, Charlie (M) 198 29
H: 5 7 W: 11 00 b.Winsford 24-12-97
2015–16 Crewe Alex 14 0
2016–17 Crewe Alex 22 0
2017–18 Crewe Alex 25 5
2018–19 Crewe Alex 42 11
2019–20 Crewe Alex 36 7
2020–21 Crewe Alex 42 6 **181 29**
2021–22 Charlton Ath 8 0 **8 0**
2021–22 *Blackpool* 9 0 **9 0**

LAVELLE, Sam (D) 158 6
H: 6 2 W: 12 00 b.Blackpool 3-10-96
Internationals: Scotland U18, U19.
2015–16 Blackburn R 0 0
2016–17 Bolton W 0 0
2017–18 Morecambe 27 1
2018–19 Morecambe 31 1
2019–20 Morecambe 31 1
2020–21 Morecambe 45 1
2021–22 Morecambe 5 0 **139 4**
2021–22 Charlton Ath 19 2 **19 2**

MACGILLIVRAY, Craig (G) 175 0
H: 6 2 W: 12 04 b.Harrogate 12-1-93
From Stalybridge Celtic, Harrogate T.
2014–15 Walsall 2 0
2015–16 Walsall 5 0
2016–17 Walsall 5 0 **12 0**
2017–18 Shrewsbury T 8 0 **8 0**
2018–19 Portsmouth 46 0
2019–20 Portsmouth 20 0
2020–21 Portsmouth 46 0
2021–22 Portsmouth 0 0 **112 0**
2021–22 Charlton Ath 43 0 **43 0**

MATTHEWS, Adam (D) **304** **7**
H: 5 10 W: 11 02 b.Swansea 13-1-92
Internationals: Wales U17, U19, U21, Full caps.
From Kilmarnock, Rangers.

2008–09	Cardiff C	0	0		
2009–10	Cardiff C	32	1		
2010–11	Cardiff C	8	0	**40**	**1**
2011–12	Celtic	27	0		
2012–13	Celtic	22	2		
2013–14	Celtic	23	1		
2014–15	Celtic	29	1	**101**	**4**
2015–16	Sunderland	1	0		
2015–16	*Bristol C*	9	0		
2016–17	Sunderland	0	0		
2016–17	*Bristol C*	12	0	**21**	**0**
2017–18	Sunderland	34	1		
2018–19	Sunderland	23	1	**58**	**2**
2019–20	Charlton Ath	29	0		
2020–21	Charlton Ath	27	0		
2021–22	Charlton Ath	28	0	**84**	**0**

MAYNARD-BREWER, Ashley (G) **17** **0**
b. 25-6-99
Internationals: Australia U23.

2017–18	Charlton Ath	0	0		
2018–19	Charlton Ath	0	0		
2019–20	Charlton Ath	0	0		
2020–21	Charlton Ath	0	0		
2021–22	Charlton Ath	0	0		
2021–22	*Ross Co*	17	0	**17**	**0**

MORGAN, Albie (M) **79** **2**
H: 5 11 b.Portsmouth 2-2-00

2018–19	Charlton Ath	8	0		
2019–20	Charlton Ath	21	0		
2020–21	Charlton Ath	28	1		
2021–22	Charlton Ath	22	1	**79**	**2**

O'CONNOR, Harris (D) **0** **0**
b. 28-5-02
Internationals: Scotland U16, U17.

2021–22	Brechin C	0	0		
2021–22	Charlton Ath	0	0		

PEARCE, Jason (D) **513** **21**
H: 6 1 W: 11 03 b.Hillingdon 6-12-87

2006–07	Portsmouth	0	0		
2007–08	Bournemouth	33	1		
2008–09	Bournemouth	44	2		
2009–10	Bournemouth	39	1		
2010–11	Bournemouth	46	3	**162**	**7**
2011–12	Portsmouth	43	2	**43**	**2**
2011–12	Leeds U	0	0		
2012–13	Leeds U	33	0		
2013–14	Leeds U	45	2		
2014–15	Leeds U	21	0	**99**	**2**
2014–15	Wigan Ath	16	2		
2015–16	Wigan Ath	31	2	**47**	**4**
2016–17	Charlton Ath	23	1		
2017–18	Charlton Ath	25	2		
2018–19	Charlton Ath	26	2		
2019–20	Charlton Ath	39	1		
2020–21	Charlton Ath	26	0		
2021–22	Charlton Ath	23	0	**162**	**6**

POWELL, Johl (M) **0** **0**
H: 5 9 b. 6-6-01

2019–20	Charlton Ath	0	0		
2020–21	Charlton Ath	0	0		
2021–22	Charlton Ath	0	0		

PURRINGTON, Ben (D) **202** **7**
H: 6 0 W: 11 07 b.Exeter 5-5-96

2013–14	Plymouth Arg	12	0		
2014–15	Plymouth Arg	8	0		
2015–16	Plymouth Arg	13	0		
2016–17	Plymouth Arg	19	0	**52**	**0**
2016–17	Rotherham U	10	0		
2017–18	Rotherham U	10	0		
2018–19	Rotherham U	0	0	**20**	**0**
2018–19	*AFC Wimbledon*	26	0	**26**	**0**
2018–19	*Charlton Ath*	18	0		
2019–20	Charlton Ath	31	2		
2020–21	Charlton Ath	28	2		
2021–22	Charlton Ath	27	3	**104**	**7**

SOUARE, Pape (D) **153** **3**
H: 5 10 W: 10 10 b.Mbao 6-6-90
Internationals: Senegal U23, Full caps.

2010–11	Lille	4	0		
2011–12	Lille	7	0		
2012–13	Lille	0	0		
2012–13	*Reims*	23	0	**23**	**0**
2013–14	Lille	33	3		
2014–15	Lille	12	0	**56**	**3**
2014–15	Crystal Palace	9	0		
2015–16	Crystal Palace	34	0		
2016–17	Crystal Palace	3	0		
2017–18	Crystal Palace	1	0		
2018–19	Crystal Palace	1	0	**48**	**0**
2019–20	Troyes	17	0		
2020–21	Troyes	0	0	**17**	**0**
2021–22	Charlton Ath	9	0	**9**	**0**

STOCKLEY, Jayden (F) **312** **92**
H: 6 2 W: 12 06 b.Poole 10-10-93

2009–10	Bournemouth	2	0		
2010–11	Bournemouth	4	0		
2011–12	Bournemouth	10	0		
2011–12	*Accrington S*	9	3	**9**	**3**
2012–13	Bournemouth	0	0		
2013–14	Bournemouth	0	0		
2013–14	*Leyton Orient*	8	1	**8**	**1**
2013–14	*Torquay U*	19	1	**19**	**1**
2014–15	Bournemouth	0	0		
2014–15	*Cambridge U*	3	2	**3**	**2**
2014–15	*Luton T*	13	3	**13**	**3**
2015–16	Bournemouth	0	0	**16**	**0**
2015–16	*Portsmouth*	9	2	**9**	**2**
2015–16	*Exeter C*	22	10		
2016–17	Aberdeen	27	5	**27**	**5**
2017–18	Exeter C	41	19		
2018–19	Exeter C	25	16	**88**	**45**
2018–19	Preston NE	17	4		
2019–20	Preston NE	32	4		
2020–21	Preston NE	16	1	**65**	**9**
2020–21	*Charlton Ath*	22	8		
2021–22	Charlton Ath	33	13	**55**	**21**

TAYLOR, Corey (F) **82** **5**
H: 5 7 W: 10 08 b.Erdington 23-9-97
Internationals: England U17, U19.

2015–16	Aston Villa	0	0		
2016–17	Aston Villa	1	0		
2017–18	Aston Villa	0	0		
2018–19	Aston Villa	0	0	**1**	**0**
2018–19	*Walsall*	10	0	**10**	**0**
2019–20	Tranmere R	24	2		
2020–21	Tranmere R	20	1		
2021–22	Tranmere R	0	0	**44**	**3**
2021–22	Charlton Ath	27	2	**27**	**2**

VENNINGS, James (M) **4** **0**
H: 5 8 b. 20-11-00

2019–20	Charlton Ath	3	0		
2020–21	Charlton Ath	1	0		
2021–22	Charlton Ath	0	0	**4**	**0**

WASHINGTON, Conor (F) **299** **69**
H: 5 10 W: 11 09 b.Chatham 18-5-92
Internationals: Northern Ireland Full caps.
From St Ives T.

2013–14	Newport Co	24	4	**24**	**4**
2013–14	Peterborough U	17	4		
2014–15	Peterborough U	40	13		
2015–16	Peterborough U	25	10	**82**	**27**
2015–16	QPR	15	0		
2016–17	QPR	40	7		
2017–18	QPR	33	6		
2018–19	QPR	4	0	**92**	**13**
2018–19	Sheffield U	15	0	**15**	**0**
2019–20	Hearts	15	3	**15**	**3**
2020–21	Charlton Ath	36	11		
2021–22	Charlton Ath	35	11	**71**	**22**

WATSON, Ben (M) **484** **40**
H: 5 10 W: 10 11 b.Camberwell 9-7-85
Internationals: England U21.

2002–03	Crystal Palace	5	0		
2003–04	Crystal Palace	16	1		
2004–05	Crystal Palace	21	0		
2005–06	Crystal Palace	42	4		
2006–07	Crystal Palace	25	3		
2007–08	Crystal Palace	42	5		
2008–09	Crystal Palace	18	5	**169**	**18**
2008–09	Wigan Ath	10	2		
2009–10	Wigan Ath	5	1		
2009–10	*QPR*	16	2	**16**	**2**
2009–10	*WBA*	7	1	**7**	**1**
2010–11	Wigan Ath	29	3		
2011–12	Wigan Ath	21	3		
2012–13	Wigan Ath	12	1		
2013–14	Wigan Ath	25	2		
2014–15	Wigan Ath	9	1	**111**	**13**
2014–15	Watford	20	0		
2015–16	Watford	35	2		
2016–17	Watford	4	0		
2017–18	Watford	8	0	**67**	**2**
2017–18	Nottingham F	14	0		
2018–19	Nottingham F	17	0		
2019–20	Nottingham F	45	3	**76**	**3**
2020–21	Charlton Ath	29	1		
2021–22	Charlton Ath	9	0	**38**	**1**

Players retained or with offer of contract
Anderson, Karoy; Bakrin, Nazir; Chin, Richard; French, Billy; Harvey, Nathan; Huke, Ryan; Ness, Lucas; Oguntayo, Samuel; Roddy, Jacob; Santos Hurtado, Jeremy; Viggars, Ryan; Williams, Euan.

Scholars
Adigun, Jason David Abiodun Dayo; Asiimwe, Nathan George; Bower, Toby William; Dench, Matthew Robert; Hand, Ralfi William George; Hobden, Oliver Henry; Kamara, Sahid Muktarr; Kedwell, Harvey Daniel; Kone, Ahmed Bassir; Ladapo, Joseph Toluwadara; Leaburn, Miles Lester; Mitchell, Zach Joseph; Molyneux, Henry Edward Arthur; Okechukwu, Chibike C Samuel; Reilly, Mack Kevin David; Toure, Seydil Moukhtar; Whitling, Harry James.

CHELSEA (23)

ABRAHAM, Tammy (F) **167** **74**
H: 6 3 W: 12 13 b.Camberwell 2-10-97
Internationals: England U18, U19, U21, Full caps.

2015–16	Chelsea	2	0		
2016–17	Chelsea	0	0		
2016–17	*Bristol C*	41	23	**41**	**23**
2017–18	Chelsea	0	0		
2017–18	*Swansea C*	31	5	**31**	**5**
2018–19	Chelsea	0	0		
2018–19	*Aston Villa*	37	25	**37**	**25**
2019–20	Chelsea	34	15		
2020–21	Chelsea	22	6		
2021–22	Chelsea	0	0	**58**	**21**

ABU, Derrick (D) **0** **0**
b.Regensburg 18-12-03

2020–21	Chelsea	0	0		
2021–22	Chelsea	0	0		

ADEGOKE, Prince (G) **0** **0**
b.Farnborough 3-11-03

2020–21	Chelsea	0	0		
2021–22	Chelsea	0	0		

ALONSO, Marcus (D) **264** **34**
H: 6 2 W: 13 05 b.Madrid 28-12-90
Internationals: Spain U19, Full caps.

2008–09	Real Madrid	0	0		
2009–10	Real Madrid	0	0		
2009–10	Real Madrid	1	0	**1**	**0**
2010–11	Bolton W	4	0		
2011–12	Bolton W	5	1		
2012–13	Bolton W	26	4	**35**	**5**
2013–14	Fiorentina	3	0		
2013–14	*Sunderland*	16	0	**16**	**0**
2014–15	Fiorentina	22	1		
2015–16	Fiorentina	31	3		
2016–17	Fiorentina	2	0	**58**	**4**
2016–17	Chelsea	31	6		
2017–18	Chelsea	33	7		
2018–19	Chelsea	31	2		
2019–20	Chelsea	18	4		
2020–21	Chelsea	13	2		
2021–22	Chelsea	28	4	**154**	**25**

AMPADU, Ethan (M) **66** **0**
b.Exeter 14-9-00
Internationals: England U16, Wales U17, U19, Full caps.

2016–17	Exeter C	8	0	**8**	**0**
2017–18	Chelsea	1	0		
2018–19	Chelsea	0	0		
2019–20	Chelsea	0	0		
2019–20	*RB Leipzig*	3	0	**3**	**0**
2020–21	Chelsea	0	0		
2020–21	*Sheffield U*	25	0	**25**	**0**
2021–22	Chelsea	0	0	**1**	**0**
2021–22	*Venezia*	29	0	**29**	**0**

ANDERSSON, Edwin (F) **0** **0**
b.Domkyrko 7-11-03
Internationals: Sweden U16, U17, U18, U19.
From Gothenburg.

2020–21	Chelsea	0	0		
2021–22	Chelsea	0	0		

ANJORIN, Faustino (M) **8** **1**
b.Poole 23-11-01
Internationals: England U17, U18, U19, U20.

2019–20	Chelsea	1	0		
2020–21	Chelsea	0	0		
2021–22	Chelsea	0	0	**1**	**0**
2021–22	*Lokomotiv Moscow*	0	0		
2021–22	*Huddersfield T*	7	1	**7**	**1**

ARRIZABALAGA, Kepa (G) **273** **0**
H: 6 1 W: 12 11 b.Ondorroa 3-10-94
Internationals: Spain U18, U19, U21, Full caps.

2011–12	Basconia	12	0		
2012–13	Basconia	19	0	**31**	**0**
2012–13	Athletic Bilbao	7	0		
2013–14	Athletic Bilbao	26	0		
2014–15	Athletic Bilbao	17	0		
2014–15	*Ponferradina*	20	0	**20**	**0**
2015–16	Athletic Bilbao	0	0		
2015–16	*Vallodolid*	39	0	**39**	**0**
2016–17	Athletic Bilbao	23	0		
2017–18	Athletic Bilbao	30	0	**103**	**0**
2018–19	Chelsea	36	0		
2019–20	Chelsea	33	0		
2020–21	Chelsea	7	0		
2021–22	Chelsea	4	0	**80**	**0**

Transferred to Roma, August 2021.

AZPILICUETA, Cesar (D) **470** **11**
H: 5 10 W: 12 00 b.Pamplona 28-8-89
Internationals: Spain U16, U17, U19, U20, U21, U23, Full caps.

2006–07	Osasuna	1	0		
2007–08	Osasuna	29	0		
2008–09	Osasuna	36	0		
2009–10	Osasuna	33	0	**99**	**0**
2010–11	Marseille	15	0		

2011–12	Marseille	30	1		
2012–13	Marseille	2	0	**47**	**1**
2012–13	Chelsea	27	0		
2013–14	Chelsea	29	0		
2014–15	Chelsea	29	0		
2015–16	Chelsea	37	2		
2016–17	Chelsea	38	1		
2017–18	Chelsea	37	2		
2018–19	Chelsea	38	1		
2019–20	Chelsea	36	2		
2020–21	Chelsea	26	1		
2021–22	Chelsea	27	1	**324**	**10**

BABA, Abdul Rahman (D) 186 4

H: 5 10 W: 12 00 b.Tamale 2-7-94

Internationals: Ghana U20, Full caps.

2011–12	Asante Kotoko	25	0	**25**	**0**
2012–13	Greuther Furth	20	0		
2013–14	Greuther Furth	22	0		
2014–15	Greuther Furth	2	2	**44**	**2**
2014–15	Augsburg	31	0	**31**	**0**
2015–16	Chelsea	15	0		
2016–17	Chelsea	0	0		
2016–17	*Schalke 04*	13	0		
2017–18	Chelsea	0	0		
2017–18	*Schalke 04*	1	0		
2018–19	Chelsea	0	0		
2018–19	*Schalke 04*	2	0	**16**	**0**
2018–19	*Reims*	11	1	**11**	**1**
2019–20	Chelsea	0	0		
2019–20	*Mallorca*	2	0	**2**	**0**
2020–21	Chelsea	0	0		
2020–21	*PAOK*	13	1	**13**	**1**
2021–22	Chelsea	0	0	**15**	**0**
2021–22	*Reading*	29	0	**29**	**0**

BADLEY-MORGAN, Luke (D) 0 0

b.London 22-10-03

Internationals: England U17. Jamaica U20.

2020–21	Chelsea	0	0		
2021–22	Chelsea	0	0		

BAKAYOKO, Tiemoue (M) 213 10

H: 6 1 W: 12 02 b.Paris 17-8-94

Internationals: France U16, U17, U18, U20, U21, Full caps.

2013–14	Rennes	24	1	**24**	**1**
2014–15	Monaco	12	0		
2015–16	Monaco	19	1		
2016–17	Monaco	32	2		
2017–18	Chelsea	29	2		
2018–19	Chelsea	0	0		
2018–19	*AC Milan*	31	1		
2019–20	Chelsea	0	0		
2019–20	*Monaco*	20	1	**83**	**4**
2020–21	Chelsea	0	0		
2020–21	*Napoli*	32	2	**32**	**2**
2021–22	Chelsea	0	0	**29**	**2**
2021–22	*AC Milan*	14	0	**45**	**1**

BALLO, Thierno (M) 8 0

H: 5 8 W: 9 06 b.Abidjan 2-1-02

Internationals: Austria U16, U17, U18, U19, U21.

2020–21	Chelsea	0	0		
2021–22	Chelsea	0	0		
2021–22	*Rapid Vienna*	8	0	**8**	**0**

BARKLEY, Ross (M) 249 33

H: 6 1 W: 12 00 b.Liverpool 5-12-93

Internationals: England U16, U17, U19, U20, U21, Full caps.

2010–11	Everton	0	0		
2011–12	Everton	6	0		
2012–13	Everton	7	0		
2012–13	*Sheffield W*	13	4	**13**	**4**
2012–13	*Leeds U*	4	0	**4**	**0**
2013–14	Everton	34	6		
2014–15	Everton	29	2		
2015–16	Everton	38	8		
2016–17	Everton	36	5		
2017–18	Everton	0	0	**150**	**21**
2017–18	Chelsea	2	0		
2018–19	Chelsea	27	3		
2019–20	Chelsea	21	1		
2020–21	Chelsea	2	0		
2020–21	*Aston Villa*	24	3	**24**	**3**
2021–22	Chelsea	6	1	**58**	**5**

BATSHUAYI, Michy (F) 294 102

H: 5 11 W: 12 04 b.Brussels 2-10-93

Internationals: Belgium U21, Full caps.

2010–11	Standard Liege	2	0		
2011–12	Standard Liege	23	6		
2012–13	Standard Liege	34	12		
2013–14	Standard Liege	38	21	**97**	**39**
2014–15	Marseille	26	9		
2015–16	Marseille	36	17	**62**	**26**
2016–17	Chelsea	20	5		
2017–18	Chelsea	12	2		
2017–18	*Borussia Dortmund*	10	7	**10**	**7**
2018–19	Chelsea	0	0		
2018–19	*Valencia*	15	1	**15**	**1**
2018–19	*Crystal Palace*	11	5		
2019–20	Chelsea	16	1		
2020–21	Chelsea	0	0		
2020–21	*Crystal Palace*	18	2	**29**	**7**
2021–22	Chelsea	0	0	**48**	**8**
2021–22	*Besiktas*	33	14	**33**	**14**

BAXTER, Nathan (G) 79 0

H: 6 3 W: 12 00 b.Westminster 8-11-98

2018–19	Chelsea	0	0		
2018–19	*Yeovil T*	34	0	**34**	**0**
2019–20	Chelsea	0	0		
2019–20	*Ross Co*	13	0	**13**	**0**
2020–21	Chelsea	0	0		
2020–21	*Accrington S*	16	0	**16**	**0**
2021–22	Chelsea	0	0		
2021–22	*Hull C*	16	0	**16**	**0**

BERGSTROM, Lucas (G) 0 0

H: 6 9 W: 12 13 b.Paragas 5-9-02

Internationals: Finland U16, U17.

2020–21	Chelsea	0	0		
2021–22	Chelsea	0	0		

BETTINELLI, Marcus (G) 183 0

H: 6 4 W: 12 13 b.Camberwell 24-5-92

Internationals: England U21.

2010–11	Fulham	0	0		
2011–12	Fulham	0	0		
2012–13	Fulham	0	0		
2013–14	Fulham	0	0		
2013–14	*Accrington S*	39	0	**39**	**0**
2014–15	Fulham	39	0		
2015–16	Fulham	11	0		
2016–17	Fulham	6	0		
2017–18	Fulham	26	0		
2018–19	Fulham	7	0		
2019–20	Fulham	14	0		
2020–21	Fulham	0	0	**103**	**0**
2020–21	*Middlesbrough*	41	0	**41**	**0**
2021–22	Chelsea	0	0		

BROJA, Armando (F) 63 16

H: 6 0 W: 11 00 b.Slough 10-9-01

Internationals: Albania U19, U21, Full caps.

2019–20	Chelsea	1	0		
2020–21	Chelsea	0	0		
2020–21	*Vitesse*	30	10	**30**	**10**
2021–22	Chelsea	0	0	**1**	**0**
2021–22	*Southampton*	32	6	**32**	**6**

BROOKING, Josh (D) 0 0

b.Reading 1-9-02

Internationals: England U16.

From Reading.

2020–21	Chelsea	0	0		
2021–22	Chelsea	0	0		

BURSTOW, Mason (F) 16 2

H: 6 2 b.Plumstead 4-8-03

2021–22	Charlton Ath	16	2	**16**	**2**
2021–22	Chelsea	0	0		

CASTILLO, Juan (M) 22 0

H: 5 11 W: 12 00 b.Amsterdam 13-1-96

Internationals: Netherlands U16, U17, U18, U19, U20.

From Ajax.

2019–20	Chelsea	0	0		
2019–20	*Ajax*	0	0		
2020–21	Chelsea	0	0		
2020–21	*AZ Alkmaar*	1	0	**1**	**0**
2020–21	*ADO Den Haag*	16	0	**16**	**0**
2021–22	Chelsea	0	0		
2021–22	*Birmingham C*	3	0	**3**	**0**
2021–22	*Charlton Ath*	2	0	**2**	**0**

CHALOBAH, Trevor (D) 128 8

H: 6 3 W: 11 11 b.Freetown 5-7-99

Internationals: England U16, U17, U19, U20, U21.

2017–18	Chelsea	0	0		
2018–19	Chelsea	0	0		
2018–19	*Ipswich T*	43	2	**43**	**2**
2019–20	Chelsea	0	0		
2019–20	*Huddersfield T*	36	1	**36**	**1**
2020–21	Chelsea	0	0		
2020–21	*Lorient*	29	2		
2021–22	Chelsea	20	3	**20**	**3**
2021–22	*Lorient*	0	0	**29**	**2**

CHILWELL, Ben (D) 141 10

H: 5 10 W: 11 03 b.Milton Keynes 21-12-96

Internationals: England U18, U19, U20, U21, Full caps.

2015–16	Leicester C	0	0		
2015–16	*Huddersfield T*	8	0	**8**	**0**
2016–17	Leicester C	12	1		
2017–18	Leicester C	24	0		
2018–19	Leicester C	36	0		
2019–20	Leicester C	27	3	**99**	**4**
2020–21	Chelsea	27	3		
2021–22	Chelsea	7	3	**34**	**6**

CHRISTENSEN, Andreas (D) 155 5

H: 6 2 W: 12 04 b.Allerod 10-4-96

Internationals: Denmark U16, U17, U19, U21, Full caps.

From Bondby.

2012–13	Chelsea	0	0		
2013–14	Chelsea	0	0		
2014–15	Chelsea	1	0		
2015–16	Chelsea	0	0		
2015–16	*Borussia M'gladbach*	31	3		
2016–17	Chelsea	0	0		
2016–17	*Borussia M'gladbach*	31	2	**62**	**5**
2017–18	Chelsea	27	0		
2018–19	Chelsea	8	0		
2019–20	Chelsea	21	0		
2020–21	Chelsea	17	0		
2021–22	Chelsea	19	0	**93**	**0**

CLARKE-SALTER, Jake (D) 110 3

H: 6 2 W: 11 00 b.Carshalton 22-9-97

Internationals: England U18, U19, U20, U21.

2015–16	Chelsea	1	0		
2016–17	Chelsea	0	0		
2016–17	*Bristol R*	12	1	**12**	**1**
2017–18	Chelsea	0	0		
2017–18	*Sunderland*	11	0	**11**	**0**
2018–19	Chelsea	0	0		
2018–19	*Vitesse*	28	1	**28**	**1**
2019–20	Chelsea	0	0		
2019–20	*Birmingham C*	19	1		
2020–21	Chelsea	0	0		
2020–21	*Birmingham C*	10	0	**29**	**1**
2021–22	Chelsea	0	0	**1**	**0**
2021–22	*Coventry C*	29	0	**29**	**0**

COLWILL, Levi (D) 29 2

H: 6 2 W: 11 11 b.Southampton 26-2-99

Internationals: England U16, U17, U19, U21.

2021–22	Chelsea	0	0		
2021–22	*Huddersfield T*	29	2	**29**	**2**

CUMMING, Jamie (G) 84 0

H: 6 1 W: 12 06 b.Winchester 4-9-99

Internationals: England U17, U19.

2018–19	Chelsea	0	0		
2019–20	Chelsea	0	0		
2020–21	Chelsea	0	0		
2020–21	*Stevenage*	41	0	**41**	**0**
2021–22	Chelsea	0	0		
2021–22	*Gillingham*	22	0	**22**	**0**
2021–22	*Milton Keynes D*	21	0	**21**	**0**

DRINKWATER, Daniel (M) 325 18

H: 5 10 W: 11 00 b.Manchester 5-3-90

Internationals: England U18, U19, Full caps.

2008–09	Manchester U	0	0		
2009–10	Manchester U	0	0		
2009–10	*Huddersfield T*	33	2	**33**	**2**
2010–11	Manchester U	0	0		
2010–11	*Cardiff C*	9	0	**9**	**0**
2010–11	*Watford*	12	0	**12**	**0**
2011–12	Manchester U	0	0		
2011–12	*Barnsley*	17	1	**17**	**1**
2011–12	Leicester C	19	2		
2012–13	Leicester C	42	1		
2013–14	Leicester C	45	7		
2014–15	Leicester C	23	0		
2015–16	Leicester C	35	2		
2016–17	Leicester C	29	1		
2017–18	Leicester C	0	0	**193**	**13**
2017–18	Chelsea	12	1		
2018–19	Chelsea	0	0		
2019–20	Chelsea	0	0		
2019–20	*Burnley*	1	0	**1**	**0**
2019–20	*Aston Villa*	4	0	**4**	**0**
2020–21	Chelsea	0	0		
2020–21	*Kasimpasa*	11	0	**11**	**0**
2021–22	Chelsea	0	0	**12**	**1**
2021–22	*Reading*	33	1	**33**	**1**

EMERSON, dos Santos (D) 123 3

H: 5 9 W: 9 13 b.Santos 13-3-94

Internationals: Brazil U17. Italy Full caps.

2011	Santos	0	0		
2012	Santos	1	0		
2013	Santos	14	1		
2014	Santos	3	0	**18**	**1**
2014–15	*Palermo*	9	0	**9**	**0**
2015–16	Roma	8	1		
2016–17	Roma	25	0		
2017–18	Roma	1	0	**34**	**1**
2017–18	Chelsea	5	0		
2018–19	Chelsea	10	0		
2019–20	Chelsea	15	0		
2020–21	Chelsea	2	0		
2021–22	Chelsea	1	0	**33**	**0**
2021–22	*Lyon*	29	1	**29**	**1**

FIABEMA, Bryan (F) 6 0

H: 6 0 b.Tromso 16-2-03

Internationals: Norway U16, 17, U18.

2019	Tromso	1	0	**1**	**0**
2020–21	Chelsea	0	0		
2021–22	Chelsea	0	0		
2022	*Rosenborg*	5	0	**5**	**0**

GALLAGHER, Conor (M) 109 16

H: 6 0 W: 11 09 b.Epsom 6-2-00

Internationals: England U17, U18, U19, U20, U21, Full caps.

2019–20	Chelsea	0	0		
2019–20	*Charlton Ath*	26	6	**26**	**6**
2019–20	*Swansea C*	19	0	**19**	**0**
2020–21	Chelsea	0	0		
2020–21	*WBA*	30	2	**30**	**2**
2021–22	Chelsea	0	0		
2021–22	*Crystal Palace*	34	8	**34**	**8**

GILMOUR, Billy (M) **35 0**
H: 5 6 W: 9 06 b.Glasgow 11-6-01
Internationals: Scotland U16, U17, U19, U21, Full caps.
From Rangers.
2019–20 Chelsea 6 0
2020–21 Chelsea 5 0
2021–22 Chelsea 0 0 **11 0**
2021–22 *Norwich C* 24 0 **24 0**

HAIGH, Joe (M) **0 0**
b.Tooting 16-3-03
2020–21 Chelsea 0 0
2021–22 Chelsea 0 0

HAVERTZ, Kai (M) **174 48**
H: 6 2 W: 11 11 b.Aachen 11-6-99
Internationals: Germany U16, U17, U19, Full caps.
2016–17 Bayer Leverkusen 24 4
2017–18 Bayer Leverkusen 30 3
2018–19 Bayer Leverkusen 34 17
2019–20 Bayer Leverkusen 30 12
2020–21 Bayer Leverkusen 0 0 **118 36**
2020–21 Chelsea 27 4
2021–22 Chelsea 29 8 **56 12**

HUDSON-ODOI, Callum (M) **72 4**
H: 6 0 W: 11 11 b.Wandsworth 7-11-00
Internationals: England U16, U17, U18, U19, Full caps.
2017–18 Chelsea 2 0
2018–19 Chelsea 10 0
2019–20 Chelsea 22 1
2020–21 Chelsea 23 2
2021–22 Chelsea 15 1 **72 4**

HUMPHREYS, Bashir (D) **0 0**
b.Exeter 15-3-03
Internationals: England U16, U19.
2020–21 Chelsea 0 0
2021–22 Chelsea 0 0

JAMES, Reece (D) **127 9**
H: 5 11 W: 12 13 b.Redbridge 8-12-99
Internationals: England U18, U19, U20, U21, Full caps.
2018–19 Chelsea 0 0
2018–19 *Wigan Ath* 45 3 **45 3**
2019–20 Chelsea 24 0
2020–21 Chelsea 32 1
2021–22 Chelsea 26 5 **82 6**

JORGINHO, Filho Jorge (M) **378 33**
H: 5 11 W: 11 03 b.Imbituba 20-12-91
Internationals: Italy Full caps.
2010–11 Verona 0 0
2010–11 *Sambonifacese* 31 1 **31 1**
2011–12 Verona 30 2
2012–13 Verona 41 2
2013–14 Verona 18 7 **89 11**
2013–14 Napoli 15 0
2014–15 Napoli 23 0
2015–16 Napoli 35 0
2016–17 Napoli 27 0
2017–18 Napoli 33 2 **133 2**
2018–19 Chelsea 37 2
2019–20 Chelsea 31 4
2020–21 Chelsea 28 7
2021–22 Chelsea 29 6 **125 19**

KANTE, Ngolo (M) **333 19**
H: 5 7 W: 10 10 b.Paris 29-3-91
Internationals: France Full caps.
2011–12 Boulogne 1 0
2012–13 Boulogne 37 3 **38 3**
2013–14 Caen 38 2
2014–15 Caen 37 2 **75 4**
2015–16 Leicester C 37 1 **37 1**
2016–17 Chelsea 35 1
2017–18 Chelsea 34 1
2018–19 Chelsea 36 4
2019–20 Chelsea 22 3
2020–21 Chelsea 30 0
2021–22 Chelsea 26 2 **183 11**

KENEDY, Robert (F) **132 11**
H: 6 0 W: 12 08 b.Santa Rita do Sapucai 8-2-96
Internationals: Brazil U17, U20, U23.
2013 Fluminense 9 0
2014 Fluminense 20 2
2015 Fluminense 1 0 **30 2**
2015–16 Chelsea 14 1
2016–17 Chelsea 1 0
2016–17 *Watford* 1 0 **1 0**
2017–18 Chelsea 0 0
2017–18 *Newcastle U* 13 2
2018–19 Chelsea 0 0
2018–19 *Newcastle U* 25 1 **38 3**
2019–20 Chelsea 0 0
2019–20 *Getafe* 19 1 **19 1**
2020–21 Chelsea 0 0
2020–21 *Granada* 28 4 **28 4**
2021–22 Chelsea 1 0 **16 1**
2021–22 *Flamengo* 0 0

KOVACIC, Mateo (M) **311 15**
H: 5 11 W: 11 07 b.Linz 6-5-94
Internationals: Croatia U17, U19, U21, Full caps.
2010–11 Dinamo Zagreb 7 1
2011–12 Dinamo Zagreb 25 4
2012–13 Dinamo Zagreb 11 1 **43 6**
2012–13 InterMilan 13 0
2013–14 InterMilan 32 0
2014–15 InterMilan 35 5 **80 5**
2015–16 Real Madrid 25 0
2016–17 Real Madrid 27 1
2017–18 Real Madrid 21 0
2018–19 Real Madrid 0 0 **73 1**
2018–19 *Chelsea* 32 0
2019–20 Chelsea 31 1
2020–21 Chelsea 27 0
2021–22 Chelsea 25 2 **115 3**

LAWRENCE, Henry (D) **24 0**
H: 5 7 b.Southwark 21-9-01
Internationals: England U19, U20.
2020–21 Chelsea 0 0
2021–22 Chelsea 0 0
2021–22 *AFC Wimbledon* 24 0 **24 0**

LOFTUS-CHEEK, Ruben (M) **132 10**
H: 6 4 W: 11 03 b.Lewisham 23-1-96
Internationals: England U16, U17, U19, U21, Full caps.
2012–13 Chelsea 0 0
2013–14 Chelsea 0 0
2014–15 Chelsea 3 0
2015–16 Chelsea 13 1
2016–17 Chelsea 6 0
2017–18 Chelsea 0 0
2017–18 *Crystal Palace* 24 2 **24 2**
2018–19 Chelsea 24 6
2019–20 Chelsea 7 0
2020–21 Chelsea 1 0
2020–21 *Fulham* 30 1 **30 1**
2021–22 Chelsea 24 0 **78 7**

LUKAKU, Romelu (F) **423 201**
H: 6 3 W: 15 11 b.Antwerp 13-5-93
Internationals: Belgium U15, U18, U21, Full caps.
2008–09 Anderlecht 1 0
2009–10 Anderlecht 33 15
2010–11 Anderlecht 37 16
2011–12 Anderlecht 2 2 **73 33**
2011–12 Chelsea 8 0
2012–13 Chelsea 0 0
2012–13 *WBA* 35 17 **35 17**
2013–14 Chelsea 2 0
2013–14 *Everton* 31 15
2014–15 Everton 36 10
2015–16 Everton 37 18
2016–17 Everton 37 25 **141 68**
2017–18 Manchester U 34 16
2018–19 Manchester U 32 12 **66 28**
2019–20 Inter Milan 36 23
2020–21 Inter Milan 36 24 **72 47**
2021–22 Chelsea 26 8 **36 8**

MAATSEN, Ian (D) **74 4**
H: 5 6 W: 9 11 b.Vlaardingen 10-3-02
Internationals: Netherlands U16, U17, U18, U21.
From PSV Eindhoven.
2019–20 Chelsea 0 0
2020–21 Chelsea 0 0
2020–21 *Charlton Ath* 34 1 **34 1**
2021–22 Chelsea 0 0
2021–22 *Coventry C* 40 3 **40 3**

MBUYAMBA, Xavier (D) **11 0**
H: 6 5 W: 12 08 b.Maastricht 31-12-01
Internationals: Netherlands U19.
2018–19 Maastricht 11 0 **11 0**
2019–20 Barcelona 0 0
2020–21 Chelsea 0 0
2021–22 Chelsea 0 0

McCLELLAND, Sam (D) **0 0**
H: 6 3 b.Coleraine 4-1-02
Internationals: Northern Ireland U17, U19, Full caps.
From Coleraine.
2020–21 Chelsea 0 0
2021–22 Chelsea 0 0

McEACHRAN, George (M) **5 0**
H: 5 8 b.Oxford 30-8-00
Internationals: England U16, U17, U18, U19.
2018–19 Chelsea 0 0
2019–20 Chelsea 0 0
2019–20 *Cambuur* 2 0 **2 0**
2020–21 Chelsea 0 0
2020–21 *Maastricht* 3 0 **3 0**
2021–22 Chelsea 0 0

MENDY, Edouard (G) **195 0**
H: 6 6 W: 13 08 b.Montivilliers 1-3-92
Internationals: Senegal Full caps.
2011–12 Cherbourg 5 0
2012–13 Cherbourg 3 0
2013–14 Cherbourg 18 0 **26 0**
2014–15 Marseille 0 0
2015–16 Marseille 0 0
2016–17 Reims 8 0
2017–18 Reims 34 0
2018–19 Reims 38 0 **80 0**
2019–20 Rennes 24 0
2020–21 Rennes 0 0 **24 0**
2020–21 Chelsea 31 0
2021–22 Chelsea 34 0 **65 0**

MIAZGA, Matt (D) **182 8**
H: 6 4 W: 12 08 b.Clifton, NJ 19-7-95
Internationals: Poland U18. USA U18, U20, U23, Full caps.
2013 New York Red Bulls 1 0
2014 New York Red Bulls 7 0
2015 New York Red Bulls 26 1 **34 1**
2015–16 Chelsea 2 0
2016–17 Chelsea 0 0
2016–17 *Vitesse* 23 0
2017–18 Chelsea 0 0
2017–18 *Vitesse* 36 4 **59 4**
2018–19 Chelsea 0 0
2018–19 *Nantes* 8 0 **8 0**
2018–19 *Reading* 18 0
2019–20 Chelsea 0 0
2019–20 *Reading* 20 2 **38 2**
2020–21 Chelsea 0 0
2020–21 *Anderlecht* 30 1 **30 1**
2021–22 Chelsea 0 0 **2 0**
2021–22 *Alaves* 11 0 **11 0**

MOTHERSILLE, Malik (F) **0 0**
b.London 23-10-03
From Leyton Orient.
2020–21 Chelsea 0 0
2021–22 Chelsea 0 0

MOUNT, Mason (M) **169 41**
H: 5 10 W: 11 00 b.Portsmouth 10-1-99
Internationals: England U16, U17, U18, U19, U21, Full caps.
2017–18 Chelsea 0 0
2017–18 *Vitesse* 29 9 **29 9**
2018–19 Chelsea 0 0
2018–19 *Derby Co* 35 8 **35 8**
2019–20 Chelsea 37 7
2020–21 Chelsea 36 6
2021–22 Chelsea 32 11 **105 24**

MUSONDA, Charly (M) **59 2**
H: 5 8 W: 10 10 b.Brussels 15-10-96
Internationals: Belgium U16, U17, U19, U21.
2015–16 Chelsea 0 0
2015–16 *Real Betis* 16 1
2016–17 Chelsea 0 0
2016–17 Real Betis 8 0
2016–17 Chelsea 0 0
2016–17 *Real Betis* 24 1 **48 2**
2017–18 Chelsea 3 0
2017–18 *Celtic* 4 0 **4 0**
2018–19 Chelsea 0 0
2018–19 *Vitesse* 1 0
2019–20 Chelsea 0 0
2019–20 *Vitesse* 3 0 **4 0**
2020–21 Chelsea 0 0
2021–22 Chelsea 0 0 **3 0**

NUNN, George (F) **0 0**
b.Crewe 23-11-01
Internationals: Republic of Ireland U18.
From Crewe Alex.
2020–21 Chelsea 0 0
2021–22 Chelsea 0 0

PULISIC, Christian (F) **164 32**
H: 5 8 W: 9 13 b.Hershey 18-9-98
Internationals: USA U17, Full caps.
2015–16 Borussia Dortmund 9 2
2016–17 Borussia Dortmund 29 3
2017–18 Borussia Dortmund 32 4
2018–19 Borussia Dortmund 20 4 **90 13**
2019–20 Chelsea 25 9
2020–21 Chelsea 27 4
2021–22 Chelsea 22 6 **74 19**

RANKINE, Dion (M) **0 0**
b.Barnet 15-10-02
2020–21 Chelsea 0 0
2021–22 Chelsea 0 0

RUDIGER, Antonio (D) **255 13**
H: 6 3 W: 13 05 b.Berlin 3-3-93
Internationals: Germany U18, U19, U20, U21, Full caps.
2011–12 Stuttgart 1 0
2012–13 Stuttgart 16 0
2013–14 Stuttgart 30 2
2014–15 Stuttgart 19 0 **66 2**
2015–16 *Roma* 30 2
2016–17 Roma 26 0 **56 2**
2017–18 Chelsea 27 2
2018–19 Chelsea 33 1
2019–20 Chelsea 20 2
2020–21 Chelsea 19 1
2021–22 Chelsea 34 3 **133 9**

SARR, Malang (D) 118 3
H: 6 0 W: 11 07 b.Nice 23-1-99
Internationals: France U16, U17, U18, U19, U20, U21.
2016–17 Nice 27 1
2017–18 Nice 21 0
2018–19 Nice 35 1
2019–20 Nice 19 1 **102 3**
2020–21 Chelsea 0 0
2020–21 *Porto* 8 0 **8 0**
2021–22 Chelsea 8 0 **8 0**

SAUL, Niguez (M) 274 28
H: 5 11 W: 11 00 b.Elche 21-11-94
Internationals: Spain U16, U17, U18, U19, U20, U21, Full caps.
2010–11 Atletico Madrid 0 0
2011–12 Atletico Madrid 0 0
2012–13 Atletico Madrid 2 0
2013–14 Atletico Madrid 0 0
2013–14 *Rayo Vallecano* 34 2 **34 2**
2014–15 Atletico Madrid 24 4
2015–16 Atletico Madrid 31 4
2016–17 Atletico Madrid 33 4
2017–18 Atletico Madrid 36 2
2018–19 Atletico Madrid 33 4
2019–20 Atletico Madrid 35 6
2020–21 Atletico Madrid 33 2
2021–22 Atletico Madrid 3 0 **230 26**
2021–22 *Chelsea* 10 0 **10 0**

SHARMAN-LOWE, Teddy (G) 0 0
H: 6 2 W: 11 07 b.Leicester 3-3-03
Internationals: England U17, U19.
2019–20 Burton Alb 0 0
2020–21 Chelsea 0 0
2020–21 *Burton Alb* 0 0
2021–22 Chelsea 0 0

SIMONS, Xavier (M) 0 0
H: 6 0 b.Hammersmith 20-2-03
Internationals: England U16, U17, U19.
2020–21 Chelsea 0 0
2021–22 Chelsea 0 0

SOONSUP-BELL, Jude (F) 0 0
H: 6 0 b.Chippenham 10-1-04
Internationals: England U16, U18, U19.
2020–21 Chelsea 0 0
2021–22 Chelsea 0 0

STERLING, Dujon (D) 70 0
H: 5 11 W: 11 05 b.Islington 24-10-99
Internationals: England U16, U17, U19, U20.
2017–18 Chelsea 0 0
2018–19 Chelsea 0 0
2018–19 *Coventry C* 38 0 **38 0**
2019–20 Chelsea 0 0
2019–20 *Wigan Ath* 8 0 **8 0**
2020–21 Chelsea 0 0
2021–22 Chelsea 0 0
2021–22 *Blackpool* 24 0 **24 0**

TAURIAINEN, Jimi (F) 0 0
b.Helsinki 8-3-04
Internationals: Finland U16, U18.
From Helsinki.
2020–21 Chelsea 0 0
2021–22 Chelsea 0 0

THIAGO SILVA, Emiliano (D) 461 28
H: 6 0 W: 12 06 b.Rio De Janeiro 22-9-84
Internationals: Brazil U23, Full caps.
2002 RS Futebol 0 0
2003 RS Futebol 0 0
2004 Juventude 28 3 **28 3**
2004–05 Porto 0 0
2005 Dynamo Moscow 0 0
2006 Fluminense 31 0
2007 Fluminense 30 5
2008 Fluminense 20 1 **81 6**
2009–10 AC Milan 33 2
2010–11 AC Milan 33 1
2011–12 AC Milan 27 2 **93 5**
2012–13 Paris Saint-Germain 22 0
2013–14 Paris Saint-Germain 28 3
2014–15 Paris Saint-Germain 26 1
2015–16 Paris Saint-Germain 30 1
2016–17 Paris Saint-Germain 27 3
2017–18 Paris Saint-Germain 25 1
2018–19 Paris Saint-Germain 25 0
2019–20 Paris Saint-Germain 21 0 **204 9**
2020–21 Chelsea 23 2
2021–22 Chelsea 32 3 **55 5**

VALE, Harvey (M) 0 0
H: 5 11 b.Hawyards Heath 11-9-03
Internationals: England U16, U17, U19.
2020–21 Chelsea 0 0
2021–22 Chelsea 0 0

WADY, Ethan (G) 0 0
b.San Jose 25-1-02
2020–21 Chelsea 0 0
2021–22 Chelsea 0 0

WAREHAM, Jayden (F) 0 0
b.Windsor 30-5-03
From QPR.
2020–21 Chelsea 0 0
2021–22 Chelsea 0 0

WERNER, Timo (F) 278 101
H: 5 11 W: 11 11 b.Stuttgart 6-3-96
Internationals: Germany U16, U17, U18, U19, U21, Full caps.
2013–14 VfB Stuttgart 30 4
2014–15 VfB Stuttgart 32 3
2015–16 VfB Stuttgart 33 6
2016–17 VfB Stuttgart 31 21
2017–18 VfB Stuttgart 32 13
2018–19 VfB Stuttgart 30 16
2019–20 VfB Stuttgart 34 28 **222 91**
2020–21 Chelsea 35 6
2021–22 Chelsea 21 4 **56 10**

WILLIAMS, Dylan (D) 6 0
b. 3-12-03
2020–21 Derby Co 0 0
2021–22 Derby Co 6 0 **6 0**
2021–22 Chelsea 0 0

ZIGER, Karlo (G) 16 0
b.Zagreb 11-5-01
Internationals: Croatia U17, U18, U19.
From NK Zegreb.
2020–21 Chelsea 0 0
2021–22 Chelsea 0 0
2021–22 *Rudar Velenje* 16 0 **16 0**

ZIYECH, Hakim (M) 262 85
H: 5 11 W: 10 03 b.Dronten 19-3-93
Internationals: Netherlands U20, U21. Morocco Full caps.
2012–13 Heerenveen 3 0
2013–14 Heerenveen 31 9
2014–15 Heerenveen 2 2 **36 11**
2014–15 FC Twente 31 11
2015–16 FC Twente 33 17
2016–17 FC Twente 4 2 **68 30**
2016–17 Ajax 28 7
2017–18 Ajax 34 9
2018–19 Ajax 29 16
2019–20 Ajax 21 6 **112 38**
2020–21 Chelsea 23 2
2021–22 Chelsea 23 4 **46 6**

Players retained or with offer of contract
Elliott, Benjamin; Flower, Louis; Gilchrist, Alfie; Hall, Lewis; Hughes, Brodi; Kpakpe, Alex; Olise, Richard; Stutter, Ronnie; Thomas, Silko; Tlemcani, Sami; Tobin, Joshua; Webster, Charlie.

Scholars
Castledine, Leo Alexander Francis; Gee, William Peter; Mendel-Idowu, Tudor Oldrunninbe; Rak Sakyi, Samuel; Silcott-Duberry, Zain Rio; Smith, James Dean.

CHELTENHAM T (24)

BARKERS, Dylan (M) 5 0
H: 6 4 W: 12 13 b.Rotterdam 4-6-00
2021–22 Cheltenham T 5 0 **5 0**

BLAIR, Matty (M) 338 25
H: 5 10 W: 11 09 b.Coventry 30-11-87
Internationals: England C.
From Stratford T, Bedworth U, Redditch U, AFC Telford U, Kidderminster Harriers.
2012–13 York C 44 6 **44 6**
2013–14 Fleetwood T 24 3
2013–14 *Northampton T* 3 1 **3 1**
2014–15 Fleetwood T 8 0 **32 3**
2014–15 *Cambridge U* 2 0 **2 0**
2014–15 Mansfield T 3 0
2015–16 Mansfield T 32 2 **35 2**
2016–17 Doncaster R 45 3
2017–18 Doncaster R 40 2
2018–19 Doncaster R 42 3
2019–20 Doncaster R 12 0 **139 8**
2020–21 Cheltenham T 44 2
2021–22 Cheltenham T 39 3 **83 5**

BONDS, Elliott (M) 28 1
H: 5 10 W: 10 06 b.Brent 23-3-00
Internationals: Guyana Full caps.
From Dagenham & R.
2019–20 Hull C 0 0
2020–21 Hull C 0 0
2020–21 *Cheltenham T* 5 0
2021–22 Cheltenham T 23 1 **28 1**

BOYLE, William (D) 191 23
H: 6 2 W: 11 00 b.Garforth 1-9-95
2014–15 Huddersfield T 1 0
2015–16 Huddersfield T 1 0
2015–16 *York C* 12 0 **12 0**
2016–17 Huddersfield T 0 0 **2 0**
2016–17 *Kilmarnock* 11 0 **11 0**
2016–17 Cheltenham T 21 2
2017–18 Cheltenham T 34 5
2018–19 Cheltenham T 38 4
2019–20 Cheltenham T 13 2
2020–21 Cheltenham T 29 6
2021–22 Cheltenham T 31 4 **166 23**

BROWN, Charlie (F) 32 3
b.Ipswich 23-9-99
2018–19 Chelsea 0 0
2019–20 Chelsea 0 0
2019–20 *Union SG* 3 0 **3 0**
2020–21 Milton Keynes D 20 3
2021–22 Milton Keynes D 6 0 **26 3**
2021–22 Cheltenham T 3 0 **3 0**

CHAPMAN, Ellis (M) 62 0
H: 6 3 W: 12 00 b.Lincoln 8-1-01
From Leicester C.
2017–18 Lincoln C 0 0
2018–19 Lincoln C 5 0
2019–20 Lincoln C 11 0 **16 0**
2020–21 Cheltenham T 21 0
2021–22 Cheltenham T 25 0 **46 0**

COLKETT, Charlie (M) 108 5
H: 5 9 W: 10 03 b.Newham 4-9-96
Internationals: England U16, U17, U18, U19, U20.
2015–16 Chelsea 0 0
2016–17 Chelsea 0 0
2016–17 *Bristol R* 15 3 **15 3**
2016–17 *Swindon T* 19 1 **19 1**
2017–18 Chelsea 0 0
2018–19 Chelsea 0 0
2018–19 *Shrewsbury T* 1 0 **1 0**
2019 Ostersunds 25 1
2020 Ostersunds 24 0
2021 Ostersunds 15 0 **64 1**
2021–22 Cheltenham T 9 0 **9 0**
Transferred to Ostersunds FK January 2019.

CROWLEY, Daniel (M) 152 10
H: 5 9 W: 10 10 b.Coventry 3-8-97
Internationals: Republic of Ireland U16, U17. England U16, U17, U19.
From Aston Villa.
2015–16 Arsenal 0 0
2015–16 *Barnsley* 11 0 **11 0**
2016–17 Arsenal 0 0
2016–17 *Oxford U* 6 2 **6 2**
2016–17 *Go Ahead Eagles* 16 2 **16 2**
2017–18 Willem II 10 0
2018–19 Willem II 34 5 **44 5**
2019–20 Birmingham C 38 1
2020–21 Birmingham C 3 0 **41 1**
2020–21 *Hull C* 22 0 **22 0**
2021–22 Cheltenham T 12 0 **12 0**
Transferred to Willem II, February 2022.

EBANKS, Callum (F) 0 0
b.Birmingham 8-10-02
2019–20 Cheltenham T 0 0
2020–21 Cheltenham T 0 0
2021–22 Cheltenham T 0 0

EVANS, Owen (G) 63 0
H: 6 0 W: 11 00 b.Newport 28-11-96
Internationals: Wales U19, U21.
From Hereford U.
2016–17 Wigan Ath 0 0
2017–18 Wigan Ath 0 0
2018–19 Wigan Ath 0 0
2019–20 Wigan Ath 0 0
2019–20 *Macclesfield T* 24 0 **24 0**
2019–20 *Cheltenham T* 11 0
2020–21 Wigan Ath 1 0
2021–22 Wigan Ath 0 0 **1 0**
2021–22 Cheltenham T 27 0 **38 0**

FLINDERS, Scott (G) 480 1
H: 6 4 W: 13 10 b.Rotherham 12-6-86
Internationals: England U20.
2004–05 Barnsley 11 0
2005–06 Barnsley 3 0 **14 0**
2006–07 Crystal Palace 8 0
2006–07 *Gillingham* 9 0 **9 0**
2006–07 *Brighton & HA* 12 0 **12 0**
2007–08 Crystal Palace 0 0
2007–08 *Yeovil T* 9 0 **9 0**
2008–09 Crystal Palace 0 0 **8 0**
2009–10 Hartlepool U 46 0
2010–11 Hartlepool U 26 1
2011–12 Hartlepool U 45 0
2012–13 Hartlepool U 46 0
2013–14 Hartlepool U 43 0
2014–15 Hartlepool U 46 0 **252 1**
2015–16 York C 43 0 **43 0**
From Macclesfield T.
2017–18 Cheltenham T 41 0
2018–19 Cheltenham T 46 0
2019–20 Cheltenham T 25 0
2020–21 Cheltenham T 2 0
2021–22 Cheltenham T 19 0 **133 0**

FREESTONE, Lewis (D) 50 1
H: 5 9 W: 10 01 b.King's Lynn 26-10-99
2016–17 Peterborough U 4 0
2017–18 Peterborough U 4 0
2018–19 Peterborough U 0 0 **8 0**
2019–20 Brighton & HA 0 0

2020–21 Cheltenham T 14 0
2021–22 Cheltenham T 28 1 **42 1**

HARRIS, Max (G) 0 0
b.Gloucester 14-9-99
2018–19 Oxford U 0 0
2019–20 Oxford U 0 0
2020–21 Cheltenham T 0 0
2021–22 Cheltenham T 0 0

HORTON, Grant (D) 15 1
H: 6 1 W: 12 06 b.Colchester 13-9-01
2019–20 Cheltenham T 1 0
2020–21 Cheltenham T 1 0
2021–22 Cheltenham T 2 0 **4 0**
2021–22 *Bohemians* 11 1 **11 1**

HUTCHINSON, Reece (D) 49 0
H: 5 10 W: 11 00 b.Birmingham 14-4-00
2017–18 Burton Alb 0 0
2018–19 Burton Alb 25 0
2019–20 Burton Alb 17 0
2020–21 Burton Alb 1 0 **43 0**
2021–22 Cheltenham T 6 0 **6 0**

JAKEWAYS, Connor (D) 0 0
2020–21 Cheltenham T 0 0
2021–22 Cheltenham T 0 0

LLOYD, George (F) 78 6
H: 5 8 W: 9 13 b.Gloucester 11-2-00
2017–18 Cheltenham T 7 2
2018–19 Cheltenham T 7 1
2019–20 Cheltenham T 13 0
2020–21 Cheltenham T 32 2
2021–22 Port Vale 7 0 **7 0**
2021–22 Cheltenham T 12 1 **71 6**

LONG, Sean (D) 133 4
H: 5 10 W: 11 00 b.Dublin 2-5-95
Internationals: Republic of Ireland U16, U17, U18, U19, U21.
2013–14 Reading 0 0
2014–15 Reading 0 0
2015–16 Reading 0 0
2015–16 *Luton T* 9 0 **9 0**
2016–17 Reading 0 0
2016–17 *Cambridge U* 7 0 **7 0**
2017–18 Lincoln C 17 0 **17 0**
2018–19 Cheltenham T 5 0
2019–20 Cheltenham T 34 1
2020–21 Cheltenham T 22 2
2021–22 Cheltenham T 39 1 **100 4**

MAY, Alfie (F) 194 48
H: 5 9 W: 11 05 b.Gravesend 2-7-93
From Billericay T, Chatham T, VCD Ath, Erith & Belvedere, Farnborough, Hythe T.
2016–17 Doncaster R 16 3
2017–18 Doncaster R 27 4
2018–19 Doncaster R 34 2
2019–20 Doncaster R 15 1 **92 10**
2019–20 Cheltenham T 12 6
2020–21 Cheltenham T 44 9
2021–22 Cheltenham T 46 23 **102 38**

MILES, Felix (M) 0 0
H: 5 8 b.Bisley 26-3-03
2020–21 Cheltenham T 0 0
2021–22 Cheltenham T 0 0

RAGLAN, Charlie (D) 195 6
H: 6 0 W: 12 00 b.Wythenshawe 28-4-93
2011–12 Port Vale 0 0
2012–13 Port Vale 0 0
2013–14 Port Vale 0 0
2014–15 Chesterfield 18 1
2015–16 Chesterfield 27 0
2016–17 Chesterfield 1 0 **46 1**
2016–17 *Oxford U* 16 0
2017–18 Oxford U 0 0
2017–18 *Port Vale* 10 0 **10 0**
2018–19 Oxford U 1 0 **17 0**
2018–19 *Cheltenham T* 19 2
2019–20 Cheltenham T 35 1
2020–21 Cheltenham T 40 1
2021–22 Cheltenham T 28 1 **122 5**

SERCOMBE, Liam (M) 493 63
H: 5 10 W: 10 12 b.Exeter 25-4-90
2008–09 Exeter C 29 2
2009–10 Exeter C 28 1
2010–11 Exeter C 42 3
2011–12 Exeter C 33 7
2012–13 Exeter C 20 1
2013–14 Exeter C 44 5
2014–15 Exeter C 40 4 **236 23**
2015–16 Oxford U 45 14
2016–17 Oxford U 30 3 **75 17**
2017–18 Bristol R 42 8
2018–19 Bristol R 39 4
2019–20 Bristol R 22 1 **103 13**
2020–21 Cheltenham T 38 7
2021–22 Cheltenham T 41 3 **79 10**

SKUREK, Harvey (D) 0 0
b.Bristol
2020–21 Cheltenham T 0 0
2021–22 Cheltenham T 0 0

THOMAS, Conor (M) 255 20
H: 6 1 W: 11 05 b.Coventry 29-10-93
Internationals: England U17, U18.
2010–11 Coventry C 0 0
2010–11 *Liverpool* 0 0
2011–12 Coventry C 27 1
2012–13 Coventry C 11 0
2013–14 Coventry C 43 0
2014–15 Coventry C 16 0
2015–16 Coventry C 3 0 **100 1**
2016–17 Swindon T 33 1
2017–18 Swindon T 2 0 **35 1**
2018–19 Cheltenham T 32 6
2019–20 Cheltenham T 26 6
2020–21 Cheltenham T 38 5
2021–22 Cheltenham T 24 1 **120 18**

TOZER, Ben (M) 384 16
H: 6 1 W: 12 11 b.Plymouth 1-3-90
From Plymouth Arg.
2007–08 Swindon T 2 0 **2 0**
2007–08 Newcastle U 0 0
2008–09 Newcastle U 0 0
2009–10 Newcastle U 1 0
2010–11 Newcastle U 0 0 **1 0**
2010–11 *Northampton T* 31 3
2011–12 Northampton T 45 3
2012–13 Northampton T 46 0
2013–14 Northampton T 29 0
2013–14 *Colchester U* 1 0 **1 0**
2014–15 Northampton T 22 0 **173 6**
2015–16 Yeovil T 26 0 **26 0**
2016–17 Newport Co 23 1
2017–18 Newport Co 39 3 **62 4**
2017–18 Cheltenham T 0 0
2018–19 Cheltenham T 37 1
2019–20 Cheltenham T 34 3
2020–21 Cheltenham T 46 2
2021–22 Cheltenham T 2 0 **119 6**
Transferred to Wrexham, August 2021.

VASSELL, Kyle (F) 215 38
H: 6 0 W: 12 04 b.Milton Keynes 7-2-93
Internationals: Northern Ireland Full caps.
2013–14 Peterborough U 6 0
2014–15 Peterborough U 17 5
2014–15 *Oxford U* 6 1 **6 1**
2015–16 Peterborough U 5 0 **28 5**
2015–16 *Dagenham & R* 8 0 **8 0**
2015–16 *Shrewsbury T* 13 0 **13 0**
2016–17 Blackpool 34 11
2017–18 Blackpool 29 11 **63 22**
2018–19 Rotherham U 23 0
2019–20 Rotherham U 20 4
2020–21 Rotherham U 12 0 **55 4**
2020–21 *Fleetwood T* 26 4 **26 4**
2021–22 Cheltenham T 16 2 **16 2**
Transferred to San Diego Loyal, January 2022.

WILLIAMS, Andy (F) 556 127
H: 6 2 W: 10 10 b.Hereford 14-8-86
2006–07 Hereford U 41 8
2007–08 Bristol R 41 4
2008–09 Bristol R 4 1
2008–09 *Hereford U* 26 2 **67 10**
2009–10 Bristol R 43 3 **88 8**
2010–11 Yeovil T 37 6
2011–12 Yeovil T 35 16
2012–13 Swindon T 40 11
2013–14 Swindon T 3 0
2013–14 *Yeovil T* 9 0 **81 22**
2014–15 Swindon T 46 21 **89 32**
2015–16 Doncaster R 46 12
2016–17 Doncaster R 37 11
2017–18 Doncaster R 9 0 **92 23**
2018–19 Northampton T 39 12
2019–20 Northampton T 32 8 **71 20**
2020–21 Cheltenham T 45 8
2021–22 Cheltenham T 23 4 **68 12**

WILLIAMS, Ben (D) 47 1
H: 5 10 W: 11 00 b.Preston 31-3-99
Internationals: Wales U17, U19, U21.
From Blackburn R.
2017–18 Barnsley 0 0
2018–19 Barnsley 11 0
2019–20 Barnsley 20 0
2020–21 Barnsley 0 0
2021–22 Barnsley 5 0 **36 0**
2021–22 Cheltenham T 11 1 **11 1**

Players retained or with offer of contract
Clark, George; Denness-Barrett, Brennan; Guinan, Zachary; Hunt, Joe; Taylor, William.

Scholars
Aldridge, Joshua Francis; Dashfield, Charlie Thomas; Denness-Barrett, Brennan H'Onre; Guinan, Zachary Josiah; Hoy, Benjamin James; Hunt, Joseph Daniel; Jakeways, Connor John; Miles, Felix William; Parsisson, Jake William; Pledger, Alfie Douglas Keith; Sambu, Adulai; Simpson, Jay Ord Keith; Skurek, Harvey Scott; Spencer, Rio James; Spencer, Thomas Jonathan; Taylor, William Alexander; Woodall, Archie Joe.

COLCHESTER U (25)

AKINDE, John (F) 380 99
H: 6 2 W: 13 10 b.Camberwell 8-7-89
2008–09 Bristol C 7 1
2008–09 *Wycombe W* 11 7
2009–10 Bristol C 7 0
2009–10 *Wycombe W* 6 1 **17 8**
2009–10 *Brentford* 2 0 **2 0**
2010–11 Bristol C 2 0 **16 1**
2010–11 *Bristol R* 14 0 **14 0**
2010–11 *Dagenham & R* 9 2
2011–12 Crawley T 25 1
2011–12 *Dagenham & R* 5 0 **14 2**
2012–13 Crawley T 6 0 **31 1**
2012–13 Portsmouth 11 0
2013–14 Portsmouth 0 0 **11 0**
From Alfreton T.
2015–16 Barnet 43 23
2016–17 Barnet 46 26
2017–18 Barnet 32 7 **121 56**
2018–19 Lincoln C 45 15
2019–20 Lincoln C 23 5 **68 20**
2019–20 Gillingham 9 1
2020–21 Gillingham 44 7
2021–22 Gillingham 18 1 **71 9**
2021–22 Colchester U 15 2 **15 2**

BENNET, Kaan (F) 1 0
b. 31-8-04
2021–22 Colchester U 1 0 **1 0**

CHAMBERS, Luke (D) 748 37
H: 6 1 W: 13 10 b.Kettering 29-8-85
2002–03 Northampton T 1 0
2003–04 Northampton T 24 0
2004–05 Northampton T 27 0
2005–06 Northampton T 43 0
2006–07 Northampton T 29 1 **124 1**
2006–07 Nottingham F 14 0
2007–08 Nottingham F 42 6
2008–09 Nottingham F 39 2
2009–10 Nottingham F 23 3
2010–11 Nottingham F 44 6
2011–12 Nottingham F 43 0 **205 17**
2012–13 Ipswich T 44 3
2013–14 Ipswich T 46 3
2014–15 Ipswich T 45 1
2015–16 Ipswich T 45 3
2016–17 Ipswich T 46 4
2017–18 Ipswich T 37 1
2018–19 Ipswich T 43 0
2019–20 Ipswich T 31 1
2020–21 Ipswich T 39 2 **376 18**
2021–22 Colchester U 43 1 **43 1**

CHILVERS, Noah (M) 84 10
H: 5 8 W: 10 01 b.Chelmsford 22-2-01
2018–19 Colchester U 2 0
2019–20 Colchester U 0 0
2020–21 Colchester U 44 2
2021–22 Colchester U 38 8 **84 10**

CLAMPIN, Ryan (D) 39 1
H: 5 11 W: 11 00 b.Colchester 29-1-99
2018–19 Colchester U 0 0
2019–20 Colchester U 13 0
2020–21 Colchester U 21 1
2021–22 Colchester U 5 0 **39 1**

COLLINS, Ted (G) 1 0
b.Colchester 28-1-03
2021–22 Colchester U 1 0 **1 0**

COOPER, Chay (M) 1 1
H: 5 6 W: 8 07 b.Harlow 17-11-01
2021–22 Colchester U 1 1 **1 1**

CORNISH, Sam (M) 0 0
2020–21 Colchester U 0 0
2021–22 Colchester U 0 0

COXE, Cameron (D) 31 0
H: 5 9 W: 11 00 b.Merthyr Tydfil 18-12-98
Internationals: Wales U17, U19, U20, U21.
2017–18 Cardiff C 0 0
2018–19 Cardiff C 0 0
2019–20 Cardiff C 0 0
From Solihull Moors.
2021–22 Colchester U 31 0 **31 0**

CRACKNELL, Billy (D) 1 0
b.Brentwood 19-1-02
2020–21 Colchester U 1 0
2021–22 Colchester U 0 0 **1 0**

DALLISON, Tom (M) 95 3
H: 5 10 W: 14 02 b.Dagenham 2-2-96
2012–13 Arsenal 0 0
2013–14 Brighton & HA 0 0
2014–15 Brighton & HA 0 0
2015–16 Brighton & HA 0 0
2015–16 *Crawley T* 1 0
2016–17 Brighton & HA 0 0
2016–17 *Cambridge U* 5 0 **5 0**
2017–18 Brighton & HA 0 0
2017–18 *Accrington S* 2 0 **2 0**
2018–19 Falkirk 12 0 **12 0**

2018–19 Crawley T 19 0
2019–20 Crawley T 21 0
2020–21 Crawley T 14 2
2021–22 Crawley T 12 0 **67 2**
2021–22 Colchester U 9 1 **9 1**

DANIELS, Charlie (M) 453 23
H: 5 10 W: 11 11 b.Harlow 7-9-86
2005–06 Tottenham H 0 0
2006–07 Tottenham H 0 0
2006–07 *Chesterfield* 2 0 **2 0**
2007–08 Tottenham H 0 0
2007–08 *Leyton Orient* 31 2
2008–09 Tottenham H 0 0
2008–09 *Gillingham* 5 1 **5 1**
2008–09 Leyton Orient 21 2
2009–10 Leyton Orient 41 0
2010–11 Leyton Orient 42 0
2011–12 Leyton Orient 13 0 **148 4**
2011–12 Bournemouth 21 2
2012–13 Bournemouth 34 4
2013–14 Bournemouth 23 0
2014–15 Bournemouth 42 1
2015–16 Bournemouth 37 3
2016–17 Bournemouth 34 4
2017–18 Bournemouth 35 1
2018–19 Bournemouth 21 1
2019–20 Bournemouth 2 0
2020–21 Bournemouth 0 0 **249 16**
2020–21 Shrewsbury T 14 1 **14 1**
2020–21 Portsmouth 17 1 **17 1**
2021–22 Colchester U 18 0 **18 0**

EASTMAN, Tom (D) 412 22
H: 6 3 W: 13 12 b.Colchester 21-10-91
2009–10 Ipswich T 1 0
2010–11 Ipswich T 9 0 **10 0**
2011–12 Colchester U 25 3
2011–12 *Crawley T* 6 0 **6 0**
2012–13 Colchester U 29 2
2013–14 Colchester U 36 0
2014–15 Colchester U 46 1
2015–16 Colchester U 43 2
2016–17 Colchester U 35 3
2017–18 Colchester U 42 3
2018–19 Colchester U 31 3
2019–20 Colchester U 36 2
2020–21 Colchester U 45 2
2021–22 Colchester U 28 1 **396 22**

FREITAS GOUVEIA, Diogo (M) 0 0
b. 16-6-01
2020–21 Colchester U 0 0
2021–22 Colchester U 0 0

GBADEBO, Camron (D) 0 0
b.Lambeth 1-7-02
From Leicester C.
2020–21 Manchester C 0 0
2021–22 Colchester U 0 0

GEORGE, Shamal (G) 49 0
H: 6 3 W: 11 11 b.Birkenhead 6-1-98
2017–18 Liverpool 0 0
2017–18 *Carlisle U* 4 0 **4 0**
2018–19 Liverpool 0 0
2018–19 *Tranmere R* 0 0
2019–20 Liverpool 0 0
2020–21 Colchester U 15 0
2021–22 Colchester U 30 0 **45 0**

GERKEN, Dean (G) 342 0
H: 6 0 W: 12 02 b.Southend 22-5-85
2003–04 Colchester U 1 0
2004–05 Colchester U 13 0
2005–06 Colchester U 7 0
2006–07 Colchester U 27 0
2007–08 Colchester U 40 0
2008–09 Colchester U 21 0
2008–09 *Darlington* 7 0 **7 0**
2009–10 Bristol C 39 0
2010–11 Bristol C 1 0
2011–12 Bristol C 10 0
2012–13 Bristol C 3 0 **53 0**
2013–14 Ipswich T 41 0
2014–15 Ipswich T 16 0
2015–16 Ipswich T 26 0
2016–17 Ipswich T 2 0
2017–18 Ipswich T 1 0
2018–19 Ipswich T 18 0 **104 0**
2019–20 Colchester U 36 0
2020–21 Colchester U 33 0
2021–22 Colchester U 0 0 **178 0**

HANNANT, Luke (M) 170 9
H: 5 11 W: 10 08 b.Great Yarmouth 4-11-93
From Dereham T, Team Northumbria, Gateshead.
2017–18 Port Vale 18 1
2018–19 Port Vale 45 3 **63 4**
2019–20 Cambridge U 27 1
2020–21 Cambridge U 43 4
2021–22 Cambridge U 0 0 **70 5**
2021–22 Colchester U 37 0 **37 0**

HUTCHINSON, Jake (F) 0 0
H: 6 1 W: 11 09 b.Colchester 8-4-02
2020–21 Colchester U 0 0
2021–22 Colchester U 0 0

HUWS, Emyr (M) 132 12
H: 5 10 W: 11 07 b.Llanelli 30-9-93
Internationals: Wales U17, U19, U21, Full caps.
2010–11 Manchester C 0 0
2011–12 Manchester C 0 0
2012–13 Manchester C 0 0
2012–13 *Northampton T* 10 0 **10 0**
2013–14 Manchester C 0 0
2013–14 *Birmingham C* 17 2 **17 2**
2014–15 Wigan Ath 16 0
2015–16 Wigan Ath 0 0 **16 0**
2015–16 *Huddersfield T* 30 5 **30 5**
2016–17 Cardiff C 3 0
2016–17 *Ipswich T* 13 3
2017–18 Cardiff C 0 0 **3 0**
2017–18 Ipswich T 5 0
2018–19 Ipswich T 0 0
2019–20 Ipswich T 17 0
2020–21 Ipswich T 9 1 **44 4**
2021–22 Colchester U 12 1 **12 1**

IHIONVIEN, Brad (F) 1 0
b. 1-1-04
2021–22 Colchester U 1 0 **1 0**

JUDGE, Alan (F) 411 58
H: 5 7 W: 10 13 b.Dublin 11-11-88
Internationals: Republic of Ireland U17, U8, U19, U21, U23, Full caps.
2006–07 Blackburn R 0 0
2007–08 Blackburn R 0 0
2008–09 Blackburn R 0 0
2008–09 *Plymouth Arg* 17 2
2009–10 Blackburn R 0 0
2009–10 *Plymouth Arg* 37 5 **54 7**
2010–11 Blackburn R 0 0
2010–11 Notts Co 19 1
2011–12 Notts Co 43 7
2012–13 Notts Co 39 8 **101 16**
2013–14 Blackburn R 11 0 **11 0**
2013–14 Brentford 22 7
2014–15 Brentford 37 3
2015–16 Brentford 38 14
2016–17 Brentford 0 0
2017–18 Brentford 13 0
2018–19 Brentford 20 1 **130 25**
2018–19 Ipswich T 19 0
2019–20 Ipswich T 30 3
2020–21 Ipswich T 34 4 **83 7**
2021–22 Colchester U 32 3 **32 3**

KAZEEM, Al-Amin (D) 0 0
H: 5 9 W: 10 06 b. 6-4-02
2021–22 Concord Rangers 0 0
2021–22 Colchester U 0 0

KENNEDY, Gene (M) 6 0
b.Harlow 18-4-03
2021–22 Colchester U 6 0 **6 0**

MARSHALL, Marley (M) 1 0
H: 5 9 W: 9 08 b.Madrid 22-10-02
2020–21 Colchester U 1 0
2021–22 Colchester U 0 0 **1 0**

McCOULSKY, Shawn (F) 67 6
H: 6 0 W: 11 00 b.Lewisham 6-1-97
From Dulwich Hamlet.
2017–18 Bristol C 0 0
2017–18 *Newport Co* 27 6 **27 6**
2018–19 Bristol C 0 0
2018–19 *Southend U* 15 0 **15 0**
2018–19 Forest Green R 13 0
2019–20 Forest Green R 6 0
2020–21 Forest Green R 2 0 **21 0**
2021–22 Colchester U 4 0 **4 0**
Transferred to Maidenhead U, January 2022.

NOUBLE, Frank (F) 378 49
H: 6 3 W: 12 13 b.Lewisham 24-9-91
Internationals: England U17, U19.
From Chelsea.
2009–10 West Ham U 8 0
2009–10 *WBA* 3 0 **3 0**
2009–10 *Swindon T* 8 0 **8 0**
2010–11 West Ham U 2 0
2010–11 *Swansea C* 6 1 **6 1**
2010–11 *Barnsley* 4 0
2010–11 *Charlton Ath* 9 1 **9 1**
2011–12 West Ham U 3 1 **13 1**
2011–12 *Gillingham* 13 5
2011–12 *Barnsley* 6 0 **10 0**
2012–13 Wolverhampton W 2 0 **2 0**
2012–13 Ipswich T 17 2
2013–14 Ipswich T 38 2
2014–15 Ipswich T 1 0 **56 4**
2014–15 Coventry C 31 6 **31 6**
2015 Tianjin Songjiang 15 3 **15 3**
2016–17 Gillingham 12 1 **25 6**
2016–17 Southend U 5 0 **5 0**
2017–18 Newport Co 45 9 **45 9**
2018–19 Colchester U 43 9

2019–20 Colchester U 36 5
2020–21 Plymouth Arg 24 1 **24 1**
2020–21 *Colchester U* 20 3
2021–22 Colchester U 19 0 **118 17**
2021–22 *Leyton Orient* 8 0 **8 0**

SARPENG-WIREDU, Brendan (M) 65 2
b.London 7-11-99
2018–19 Charlton Ath 0 0
2019–20 Charlton Ath 0 0
2019–20 *Colchester U* 7 0
2020–21 Charlton Ath 0 0
2020–21 Colchester U 20 1
2021–22 Colchester U 38 1 **65 2**

SAYER, Harvey (D) 4 0
b.Great Yarmouth 6-1-03
2020–21 Colchester U 4 0
2021–22 Colchester U 0 0 **4 0**

SEARS, Freddie (F) 433 79
H: 5 7 W: 11 11 b.Hornchurch 27-11-89
Internationals: England U19, U20, U21.
2007–08 West Ham U 7 1
2008–09 West Ham U 17 0
2009–10 West Ham U 1 0
2009–10 *Crystal Palace* 18 0 **18 0**
2009–10 *Coventry C* 10 0 **10 0**
2010–11 West Ham U 11 1
2010–11 *Scunthorpe U* 9 0 **9 0**
2011–12 West Ham U 10 0 **46 2**
2011–12 *Colchester U* 11 2
2012–13 Colchester U 35 7
2013–14 Colchester U 32 12
2014–15 Colchester U 24 10
2014–15 Ipswich T 21 9
2015–16 Ipswich T 45 6
2016–17 Ipswich T 40 7
2017–18 Ipswich T 36 2
2018–19 Ipswich T 24 6
2019–20 Ipswich T 11 1
2020–21 Ipswich T 26 1 **203 32**
2021–22 Colchester U 45 14 **147 45**

SKUSE, Cole (M) 588 11
H: 6 1 W: 11 05 b.Bristol 29-3-86
2004–05 Bristol C 7 0
2005–06 Bristol C 38 2
2006–07 Bristol C 42 0
2007–08 Bristol C 25 0
2008–09 Bristol C 33 2
2009–10 Bristol C 43 2
2010–11 Bristol C 30 1
2011–12 Bristol C 36 2
2012–13 Bristol C 25 0 **279 9**
2013–14 Ipswich T 43 0
2014–15 Ipswich T 40 1
2015–16 Ipswich T 39 0
2016–17 Ipswich T 40 0
2017–18 Ipswich T 39 1
2018–19 Ipswich T 34 0
2019–20 Ipswich T 29 0
2020–21 Ipswich T 4 0 **268 2**
2021–22 Colchester U 41 0 **41 0**

SMITH, Tommy (D) 398 31
H: 6 2 W: 12 13 b.Macclesfield 31-3-90
Internationals: England U17, U18. New Zealand Full caps.
2007–08 Ipswich T 0 0
2008–09 Ipswich T 2 0
2009–10 Ipswich T 14 0
2009–10 *Brentford* 8 0 **8 0**
2010–11 Ipswich T 22 3
2010–11 *Colchester U* 6 0
2011–12 Ipswich T 26 3
2012–13 Ipswich T 38 3
2013–14 Ipswich T 45 6
2014–15 Ipswich T 42 4
2015–16 Ipswich T 45 2
2016–17 Ipswich T 10 0
2017–18 Ipswich T 3 0 **247 21**
2018 Colorado Rapids 33 4
2019 Colorado Rapids 27 3 **60 7**
2019–20 Sunderland 0 0
2020–21 Colchester U 45 2
2021–22 Colchester U 32 1 **83 3**

TCHAMADEU, Junior (D) 37 1
b.Redbridge 22-12-03
2020–21 Colchester U 11 0
2021–22 Colchester U 26 1 **37 1**

THOMAS, Donnell (M) 1 0
b. 4-8-03
2021–22 Colchester U 1 0 **1 0**

TOVIDE, Samson (F) 6 0
b.Hackney 4-1-04
2020–21 Colchester U 0 0
2021–22 Colchester U 6 0 **6 0**

WELCH-HAYES, Miles (D) 98 2
H: 5 11 W: 12 02 b.Oxford 25-10-96
2016–17 Oxford U 1 0 **1 0**
From Bath C.
2018–19 Macclesfield T 23 0
2019–20 Macclesfield T 24 1 **47 1**
2019–20 Colchester U 0 0

2020–21 Colchester U 38 1
2021–22 Colchester U 12 0 **50 1**

Players retained or with offer of contract
Beadle, Harry; Lowe, Ryan; Terry, Frankie.

Scholars
Akolbire, Lordon; Aman, Bayan Mohammed; Asare-Williams, Darnell Nana Kwame; Brown, Sean Tyler; Chakawa, Bradley Kudakwashe; Drakes-Thomas, Jaiden Daniel; Johnson, Endurance Izogie Isokpan; Kane, Namory Olorunleke Ahmed; Marcel Dilaver, Taizo Tevfik; Parish, Kacy Ray; Price, Freddie John; Redgrave, Kai Christopher Ray; Stagg, Thomas Jack; Sullivan, Ellis Daniel; Tedaldi, Jaime David; Thomas, Donell Tyrell Arnold; Tovide, Samson Jolaoluwa Gbolahan; Yates, Matthew Alfie.

COVENTRY C (26)

ALLEN, Jamie (M) 275 22
H: 5 11 W: 11 05 b.Rochdale 29-1-95
2012–13 Rochdale 0 0
2013–14 Rochdale 25 6
2014–15 Rochdale 35 0
2015–16 Rochdale 38 3
2016–17 Rochdale 31 2
2017–18 Rochdale 4 0 **133 11**
2017–18 Burton Alb 29 1
2018–19 Burton Alb 42 7 **71 8**
2019–20 Coventry C 11 1
2020–21 Coventry C 22 1
2021–22 Coventry C 38 1 **71 3**

BAPAGA, Will (F) 3 0
b. 11-2-03
2019–20 Coventry C 1 0
2020–21 Coventry C 2 0
2021–22 Coventry C 0 0 **3 0**

BIDWELL, Jake (D) 420 8
H: 6 0 W: 11 00 b.Southport 21-3-93
Internationals: England U16, U17, U18, U19.
2009–10 Everton 0 0
2010–11 Everton 0 0
2011–12 Everton 0 0
2011–12 *Brentford* 24 0
2012–13 Everton 0 0
2012–13 *Brentford* 40 0
2013–14 Brentford 38 0
2014–15 Brentford 43 0
2015–16 Brentford 45 3 **190 3**
2016–17 QPR 36 0
2017–18 QPR 46 2
2018–19 QPR 40 0 **122 2**
2019–20 Swansea C 37 0
2020–21 Swansea C 39 1
2021–22 Swansea C 16 2 **92 3**
2021–22 Coventry C 16 0 **16 0**

BILSON, Tom (G) 1 0
H: 6 2 W: 11 07 b.Shrewsbury 18-10-00
2017–18 Coventry C 0 0
2018–19 Coventry C 0 0
2019–20 Coventry C 0 0
2020–21 Coventry C 0 0
2021–22 Coventry C 0 0
2021–22 *Scunthorpe U* 1 0 **1 0**

BURROUGHS, Jack (M) 19 0
b. 21-3-01
Internationals: Scotland U19, U21.
2018–19 Coventry C 0 0
2019–20 Coventry C 0 0
2020–21 Coventry C 2 0
2021–22 Coventry C 0 0 **2 0**
2021–22 *Ross Co* 17 0 **17 0**

CASHMAN, Danny (F) 23 2
b.Crawley 8-1-01
2017–18 Brighton & HA 0 0
2018–19 Brighton & HA 0 0
2019–20 Brighton & HA 0 0
2020–21 Brighton & HA 0 0
2021–22 Coventry C 0 0
2021–22 *Rochdale* 23 2 **23 2**

DA COSTA, Julien (D) 108 0
H: 6 0 W: 12 02 b.Marseille 29-5-96
2015–16 Marseille 0 0
2016–17 Marseille 0 0
2017–18 Chamois Niortas 26 0
2018–19 Chamois Niortas 27 0
2019–20 Chamois Niortas 22 0 **75 0**
2020–21 Coventry C 18 0
2021–22 Coventry C 4 0 **22 0**
2021–22 *Portimonense* 11 0 **11 0**

DABO, Fankaty (D) 151 1
H: 5 11 W: 12 00 b.Southwark 11-10-95
Internationals: England U16, U17, U20.
2016–17 Chelsea 0 0
2016–17 *Swindon T* 15 1 **15 1**
2017–18 Chelsea 0 0
2017–18 *Vitesse* 26 0 **26 0**
2018–19 Chelsea 0 0
2018–19 *Sparta Rotterdam* 21 0 **21 0**
2019–20 Coventry C 32 0
2020–21 Coventry C 28 0
2021–22 Coventry C 29 0 **89 0**

DINANGA, Ricardo (F) 0 0
b.Cork 6-12-01
2021–22 Cork City 0 0
2021–22 Coventry C 0 0

DRYSDALE, Declan (D) 29 1
H: 6 1 W: 10 12 b.Birkenhead 14-11-99
2018–19 Tranmere R 0 0
2018–19 Coventry C 0 0
2019–20 Coventry C 1 0
2020–21 Coventry C 0 0
2020–21 *Gillingham* 10 0 **10 0**
2020–21 *Cambridge U* 13 1 **13 1**
2021–22 Coventry C 0 0 **1 0**
2021–22 *Ross Co* 5 0 **5 0**

ECCLES, Josh (D) 27 0
H: 5 11 W: 10 06 b.Coventry 6-4-00
2018–19 Coventry C 0 0
2019–20 Coventry C 3 0
2020–21 Coventry C 7 0
2020–21 *Gillingham* 12 0 **12 0**
2021–22 Coventry C 5 0 **15 0**

ENOBAKHARE, Bright (F) 80 11
H: 6 0 W: 12 06 b.Benin City 8-2-98
Internationals: Nigeria U23.
2015–16 Wolverhampton W 7 0
2016–17 Wolverhampton W 13 0
2017–18 Wolverhampton W 21 1
2018–19 Wolverhampton W 0 0
2018–19 *Kilmarnock* 6 0 **6 0**
2018–19 *Coventry C* 18 6
2019–20 Wolverhampton W 0 0 **41 1**
2019–20 *Wigan Ath* 2 0 **2 0**
2020–21 AEK Athens 1 1 **1 1**
2020–21 East Bengal 12 3 **12 3**
2021–22 Coventry C 0 0 **18 6**
Transferred to Hapoel Jerusalem, January 2022.

EVANS-HARRIOT, Aaron (M) 0 0
From Cheltenham T.
2019–20 Coventry C 0 0
2020–21 Coventry C 0 0
2021–22 Coventry C 0 0

FINNEGAN, Aidan (M) 0 0
b.Solihull 18-2-03
From Birmingham C.
2020–21 Coventry C 0 0
2021–22 Coventry C 0 0

GODDEN, Matthew (F) 205 76
H: 6 1 W: 12 04 b.Canterbury 29-7-91
2009–10 Scunthorpe U 0 0
2010–11 Scunthorpe U 5 0
2011–12 Scunthorpe U 1 0
2012–13 Scunthorpe U 8 0
2013–14 Scunthorpe U 4 0
2014–15 Scunthorpe U 0 0 **18 0**
From Ebbsfleet U.
2016–17 Stevenage 38 20
2017–18 Stevenage 38 10 **76 30**
2018–19 Peterborough U 38 14
2019–20 Peterborough U 0 0 **38 14**
2019–20 Coventry C 26 14
2020–21 Coventry C 23 6
2021–22 Coventry C 24 12 **73 32**

GYOKERES, Viktor (F) 157 47
H: 6 2 W: 13 08 b.Stockholm 4-6-98
Internationals: Sweden U19, U21, Full caps.
2015 Brommapojkarna 8 0
2016 Brommapojkarna 19 7
2017 Brommapojkarna 29 13 **56 20**
2017–18 Brighton & HA 0 0
2018–19 Brighton & HA 0 0
2019–20 Brighton & HA 0 0
2019–20 *St Pauli* 26 7 **26 7**
2020–21 Brighton & HA 0 0
2020–21 *Swansea C* 11 0 **11 0**
2020–21 *Coventry C* 19 3
2021–22 Coventry C 45 17 **64 20**

HAMER, Gustavo (M) 165 15
H: 5 7 W: 9 08 b.Itajai 24-6-97
Internationals: Netherlands U18, U20.
2016–17 Feyenoord 2 0
2017–18 Feyenoord 0 0 **2 0**
2017–18 *Dordrecht* 34 3 **34 3**
2018–19 PEC Zwolle 23 0
2019–20 PEC Zwolle 25 4 **48 4**
2020–21 Coventry C 42 5
2021–22 Coventry C 39 3 **81 8**

HILSSNER, Marcel (M) 90 9
b. 30-1-95
Internationals: Germany U16, U17, U18, U19.
2013–14 Werder Bremen 0 0
2014–15 Werder Bremen 0 0
2015–16 Werder Bremen 1 0 **1 0**
2016–17 Dynamo Dresden 8 0
2017–18 Dynamo Dresden 0 0 **8 0**
2017–18 Hansa Rostock 18 4
2018–19 Hansa Rostock 21 2 **39 6**
2019–20 Paderborn 07 0 0
2019–20 *Hallescher* 14 2 **14 2**
2020–21 Coventry C 0 0
2020–21 *Oldham Ath* 20 1 **20 1**
2021–22 Coventry C 0 0
2021–22 *Zwickau* 8 0 **8 0**

HOWLEY, Ryan (M) 1 0
b.Nuneaton 23-11-03
Internationals: Wales U19.
2021–22 Coventry C 1 0 **1 0**

HYAM, Dominic (D) 183 8
H: 6 2 W: 11 00 b.Leuchars 20-12-95
Internationals: Scotland U19, U21.
2014–15 Reading 0 0
2015–16 Reading 0 0
2015–16 *Dagenham & R* 16 0 **16 0**
2016–17 Reading 0 0
2016–17 *Portsmouth* 0 0
2017–18 Coventry C 14 0
2018–19 Coventry C 38 1
2019–20 Coventry C 29 2
2020–21 Coventry C 43 3
2021–22 Coventry C 43 2 **167 8**

JONES, Jodi (M) 111 11
H: 5 10 W: 11 07 b.Bow 22-10-97
2014–15 Dagenham & R 8 1
2015–16 Dagenham & R 27 3 **35 4**
2015–16 Coventry C 6 0
2016–17 Coventry C 34 1
2017–18 Coventry C 19 5
2018–19 Coventry C 8 1
2019–20 Coventry C 0 0
2020–21 Coventry C 0 0
2021–22 Coventry C 9 0 **76 7**

KANE, Todd (D) 244 14
H: 5 11 W: 11 00 b.Huntingdon 17-9-93
Internationals: England U19.
2011–12 Chelsea 0 0
2012–13 Chelsea 0 0
2012–13 *Preston NE* 3 0 **3 0**
2012–13 *Blackburn R* 14 0
2013–14 Chelsea 0 0
2013–14 *Blackburn R* 27 2 **41 2**
2014–15 Chelsea 0 0
2014–15 *Bristol C* 5 0 **5 0**
2014–15 *Nottingham F* 8 1 **8 1**
2015–16 Chelsea 0 0
2015–16 *NEC* 31 1 **31 1**
2016–17 Chelsea 0 0
2017–18 Chelsea 0 0
2017–18 *FC Groningen* 11 0 **11 0**
2017–18 *Oxford U* 17 3 **17 3**
2018–19 Chelsea 0 0
2018–19 *Hull C* 39 3 **39 3**
2019–20 QPR 32 1
2020–21 QPR 28 2
2021–22 QPR 0 0 **60 3**
2021–22 Coventry C 29 1 **29 1**

KELLY, Liam (M) 349 29
H: 6 2 W: 13 12 b.Milton Keynes 10-2-90
Internationals: Scotland U18, U21, Full caps.
2009–10 Kilmarnock 15 1
2010–11 Kilmarnock 32 7
2011–12 Kilmarnock 34 1
2012–13 Kilmarnock 19 6 **100 15**
2012–13 Bristol C 19 0
2013–14 Bristol C 2 0 **21 0**
2014–15 Oldham Ath 37 1
2015–16 Oldham Ath 41 6 **78 7**
2016–17 Leyton Orient 21 4 **21 4**
2017–18 Coventry C 33 1
2018–19 Coventry C 30 0
2019–20 Coventry C 27 0
2020–21 Coventry C 23 2
2021–22 Coventry C 16 0 **129 3**

McFADZEAN, Kyle (D) 389 19
H: 6 1 W: 13 05 b.Sheffield 20-2-87
Internationals: England C.
2004–05 Sheffield U 0 0
2005–06 Sheffield U 0 0
2006–07 Sheffield U 0 0
From Alfreton T.
2011–12 Crawley T 37 2
2012–13 Crawley T 17 3
2013–14 Crawley T 42 1 **96 6**
2014–15 Milton Keynes D 41 3
2015–16 Milton Keynes D 39 0 **80 3**
2016–17 Burton Alb 31 1
2017–18 Burton Alb 42 0
2018–19 Burton Alb 35 4 **108 5**
2018–19 Coventry C 0 0
2019–20 Coventry C 30 0
2020–21 Coventry C 38 2
2021–22 Coventry C 37 3 **105 5**

McGRATH, Jay (D) 0 0
2020–21 Coventry C 0 0
2021–22 Coventry C 0 0

MOORE, Simon (G) **196 0**
H: 6 3 W: 13 01 b.Sandown 19-5-90
Internationals: Isle of Wight Full caps.

Season	Club	Apps	Gls	Total	
2009–10	Brentford	1	0		
2010–11	Brentford	10	0		
2011–12	Brentford	10	0		
2012–13	Brentford	43	0	**64**	**0**
2013–14	Cardiff C	0	0		
2013–14	*Bristol C*	11	0	**11**	**0**
2014–15	Cardiff C	10	0		
2015–16	Cardiff C	7	0	**17**	**0**
2016–17	Sheffield U	43	0		
2017–18	Sheffield U	18	0		
2018–19	Sheffield U	0	0		
2019–20	Sheffield U	2	0		
2020–21	Sheffield U	0	0	**63**	**0**
2021–22	Coventry C	41	0	**41**	**0**

NGANDU, Jonny (M) **4 0**
H: 5 9 W: 11 03 b.Redbridge 25-10-01

Season	Club	Apps	Gls	Total	
2018–19	Coventry C	0	0		
2019–20	Coventry C	0	0		
2020–21	Coventry C	0	0		
2020–21	*Keflavik*	4	0	**4**	**0**
2021–22	Coventry C	0	0		

O'HARE, Callum (M) **140 14**
H: 5 8 W: 10 03 b.Solihull 1-5-98
Internationals: England U20.

Season	Club	Apps	Gls	Total	
2016–17	Aston Villa	0	0		
2017–18	Aston Villa	4	0		
2018–19	Aston Villa	0	0		
2018–19	*Carlisle U*	16	3	**16**	**3**
2019–20	Aston Villa	0	0	**4**	**0**
2019–20	*Coventry C*	29	3		
2020–21	Coventry C	46	3		
2021–22	Coventry C	45	5	**120**	**11**

PASK, Josh (D) **44 0**
H: 6 2 W: 12 00 b.Waltham Forest 1-11-97

Season	Club	Apps	Gls	Total	
2015–16	West Ham U	0	0		
2015–16	*Dagenham & R*	5	0	**5**	**0**
2016–17	West Ham U	0	0		
2016–17	*Gillingham*	10	0	**10**	**0**
2017–18	West Ham U	0	0		
2018–19	West Ham U	0	0		
2019–20	Coventry C	2	0		
2020–21	Coventry C	17	0		
2021–22	Coventry C	0	0	**19**	**0**
2021–22	*Newport Co*	10	0	**10**	**0**

REID, Josh (D) **20 0**
H: 5 11 W: 10 08 b.Dingwall 3-5-02

Season	Club	Apps	Gls	Total	
2019–20	Ross Co	0	0		
2020–21	Ross Co	20	0	**20**	**0**
2020–21	Coventry C	0	0		
2021–22	Coventry C	0	0		

ROSE, Michael (D) **173 9**
H: 5 11 W: 11 00 b.Aberdeen 11-10-95

Season	Club	Apps	Gls	Total	
2015–16	Aberdeen	1	0	**1**	**0**
2015–16	*Forfar Ath*	7	0	**7**	**0**
2016–17	Ayr U	20	1		
2017–18	Ayr U	34	2		
2018–19	Ayr U	34	2	**88**	**5**
2019–20	Coventry C	31	2		
2020–21	Coventry C	17	0		
2021–22	Coventry C	29	2	**77**	**4**

ROWE, Blaine (D) **3 0**

Season	Club	Apps	Gls	Total	
2019–20	Coventry C	0	0		
2020–21	Coventry C	0	0		
2021–22	Coventry C	0	0		
2021–22	*Ayr U*	3	0	**3**	**0**

SHEAF, Ben (M) **107 3**
H: 5 10 W: 10 01 b.Dartford 5-2-98
Internationals: England U16, U18.

Season	Club	Apps	Gls	Total	
2015–16	Arsenal	0	0		
2016–17	Arsenal	0	0		
2017–18	Arsenal	0	0		
2017–18	*Stevenage*	10	0	**10**	**0**
2018–19	Arsenal	0	0		
2019–20	Arsenal	0	0		
2019–20	*Doncaster R*	32	1	**32**	**1**
2020–21	Arsenal	0	0		
2020–21	*Coventry C*	30	0		
2021–22	Coventry C	35	2	**65**	**2**

SHIPLEY, Jordan (M) **133 16**
H: 6 0 W: 11 07 b.Leamington Spa 26-9-97
Internationals: Republic of Ireland U21.

Season	Club	Apps	Gls	Total	
2016–17	Coventry C	1	0		
2017–18	Coventry C	30	4		
2018–19	Coventry C	33	3		
2019–20	Coventry C	31	5		
2020–21	Coventry C	27	3		
2021–22	Coventry C	11	1	**133**	**16**

TAVARES, Fabio (F) **33 3**
H: 5 11 W: 11 00 b.Matosinhos 22-1-01

Season	Club	Apps	Gls	Total	
2018–19	Rochdale	0	0		
2019–20	Rochdale	14	1		
2020–21	Rochdale	12	1	**26**	**2**
2020–21	Coventry C	0	0		
2021–22	Coventry C	7	1	**7**	**1**

TYLER, Cian (G) **0 0**
H: 6 2 W: 12 06 b.Leamington Spa 22-3-02
Internationals: Wales U17.

Season	Club	Apps	Gls	Total	
2019–20	Coventry C	0	0		
2020–21	Coventry C	0	0		
2021–22	Coventry C	0	0		

WAGHORN, Martyn (F) **412 103**
H: 5 10 W: 13 01 b.South Shields 23-1-90
Internationals: England U19, U21.

Season	Club	Apps	Gls	Total	
2007–08	Sunderland	3	0		
2008–09	Sunderland	1	0		
2008–09	*Charlton Ath*	7	1	**7**	**1**
2009–10	Sunderland	0	0		
2009–10	*Leicester C*	43	12		
2010–11	Sunderland	2	0	**6**	**0**
2010–11	Leicester C	30	4		
2011–12	Leicester C	4	1		
2011–12	*Hull C*	5	1	**5**	**1**
2012–13	Leicester C	24	3		
2013–14	Leicester C	2	0	**103**	**20**
2013–14	*Millwall*	14	3	**14**	**3**
2013–14	Wigan Ath	15	5		
2014–15	Wigan Ath	23	3	**38**	**8**
2015–16	Rangers	25	20		
2016–17	Rangers	32	7	**57**	**27**
2017–18	Ipswich T	44	16	**44**	**16**
2018–19	Derby Co	36	9		
2019–20	Derby Co	43	12		
2020–21	Derby Co	32	5		
2021–22	Derby Co	0	0	**111**	**26**
2021–22	Coventry C	27	1	**27**	**1**

WALKER, Tyler (F) **203 57**
H: 5 10 W: 9 13 b.Nottingham 17-10-96
Internationals: England U20.

Season	Club	Apps	Gls	Total	
2013–14	Nottingham F	0	0		
2014–15	Nottingham F	7	1		
2015–16	Nottingham F	14	0		
2015–16	*Burton Alb*	6	1	**6**	**1**
2016–17	Nottingham F	0	0		
2016–17	*Stevenage*	8	3	**8**	**3**
2016–17	*Port Vale*	6	2	**6**	**2**
2017–18	Nottingham F	12	3		
2017–18	*Bolton W*	5	0	**5**	**0**
2018–19	Nottingham F	0	0		
2018–19	*Mansfield T*	44	22	**44**	**22**
2019–20	*Lincoln C*	29	14	**29**	**14**
2019–20	Nottingham F	7	1	**40**	**5**
2020–21	Coventry C	31	7		
2021–22	Coventry C	19	2	**50**	**9**
2021–22	*Portsmouth*	15	1	**15**	**1**

WILSON, Ben (G) **60 0**
H: 6 1 W: 11 09 b.Stanley 9-8-92

Season	Club	Apps	Gls	Total	
2010–11	Sunderland	0	0		
2011–12	Sunderland	0	0		
2012–13	Sunderland	0	0		
2013–14	Accrington S	0	0		
2013–14	Cardiff C	0	0		
2014–15	Cardiff C	0	0		
2015–16	Cardiff C	0	0		
2015–16	*AFC Wimbledon*	8	0	**8**	**0**
2016–17	Cardiff C	3	0		
2016–17	*Rochdale*	8	0	**8**	**0**
2017–18	Cardiff C	0	0	**3**	**0**
2017–18	*Oldham Ath*	5	0	**5**	**0**
2018–19	Bradford C	4	0	**4**	**0**
2019–20	Coventry C	0	0		
2020–21	Coventry C	27	0		
2021–22	Coventry C	5	0	**32**	**0**

Players retained or with offer of contract
Alabi, Abel; Burroughs, George; Nee, Harrison; Rus, Marco; Stretton, Bradley; Crawley T; Kevser-Junior, Kaan; Ransom, Harry.

Scholars
Aisowieren, Evan Eghosa; Bell, Luke Stephen; Berry, Oliver Steven; Callaghan, Charlie Harry; Grant, Rio Christopher Clinton; Hewitt, Craig; Manners, Charlie George; Massey, Reece Peter; McCafferty, Lewys John; O'Brien, Fionn Eamonn; Obikwu, Justin Patrick Nnamdi; Reeve, Malakai Sean Alexander; Rodber, Samuel Leslie; Shepherd, Talon Lorenzo; Wynne, Joseph Charles; Young, Shay Joseph.

CRAWLEY T (27)

ADEBOWALE, Emmanuel (D) **2 0**
b. 19-9-97
From Sheffield U, Hayes & Yeading U, Bishop's Stortford, Dover Ath, Eastbourne Bor.

Season	Club	Apps	Gls	Total	
2019–20	Crawley T	1	0		
2020–21	Crawley T	1	0		
2021–22	Crawley T	0	0	**2**	**0**

AL-HUSSAINI, Zaid (M) **0 0**
H: 5 9 W: 10 03 b.Chelsea 7-6-00
Internationals: Iraq U19.

Season	Club	Apps	Gls	Total	
2020–21	Crawley T	0	0		
2021–22	Crawley T	0	0		

APPIAH, Kwesi (F) **157 38**
H: 5 11 W: 12 08 b.Camberwell 12-8-90
Internationals: Ghana Full caps.

Season	Club	Apps	Gls	Total	
2008–09	Peterborough U	0	0		

From Brackley T, Thurrock, Margate.

Season	Club	Apps	Gls	Total	
2011–12	Crystal Palace	4	0		
2012–13	Crystal Palace	2	0		
2012–13	*Aldershot T*	2	0	**2**	**0**
2012–13	*Yeovil T*	5	0	**5**	**0**
2013–14	Crystal Palace	0	0		
2013–14	*Notts Co*	7	0	**7**	**0**
2013–14	*AFC Wimbledon*	7	3		
2014–15	Crystal Palace	0	0		
2014–15	*Cambridge U*	19	6	**19**	**6**
2014–15	*Reading*	6	1	**6**	**1**
2015–16	Crystal Palace	0	0		
2016–17	Crystal Palace	0	0		
2017–18	Crystal Palace	0	0	**6**	**0**
2017–18	*Viking FK*	12	3	**12**	**3**
2017–18	AFC Wimbledon	14	3		
2018–19	AFC Wimbledon	26	4		
2019–20	AFC Wimbledon	19	4	**66**	**14**
2020–21	NorthEast U	8	3	**8**	**3**
2021–22	Crawley T	26	11	**26**	**11**

ASHFORD, Sam (F) **20 1**
H: 6 0 W: 11 07 b.Chelmsford 21-12-95
Internationals: England C.
From Maldon & Tiptree, Heybridge Swifts, Stansted, Witham T, Brightlingsea Regent, East Thurrock U, Concorde R, Hemel Hempstead T.

Season	Club	Apps	Gls	Total	
2020–21	Crawley T	8	0		
2021–22	Crawley T	12	1	**20**	**1**

Transferred to Ayr U, January 2022.

BATTLE, Alex (F) **2 0**
H: 5 10 b.Plymouth 23-1-99

Season	Club	Apps	Gls	Total	
2017–18	Plymouth Arg	1	0		
2018–19	Plymouth Arg	0	0	**1**	**0**

From Truro C.

Season	Club	Apps	Gls	Total	
2021–22	Crawley T	1	0	**1**	**0**

BURNETT, Henry (M) **0 0**
From Dagenham & R.

Season	Club	Apps	Gls	Total	
2019–20	Southend U	0	0		
2020–21	Crawley T	0	0		
2021–22	Crawley T	0	0		

CRAIG, Tony (D) **582 15**
H: 6 1 W: 12 06 b.Greenwich 20-4-85

Season	Club	Apps	Gls	Total	
2002–03	Millwall	2	1		
2003–04	Millwall	9	0		
2004–05	Millwall	10	0		
2004–05	*Wycombe W*	14	0	**14**	**0**
2005–06	Millwall	28	0		
2006–07	Millwall	30	1		
2007–08	Crystal Palace	13	0	**13**	**0**
2007–08	*Millwall*	5	1		
2008–09	Millwall	44	2		
2009–10	Millwall	30	2		
2010–11	Millwall	24	0		
2011–12	Millwall	23	0		
2011–12	*Leyton Orient*	4	0	**4**	**0**
2012–13	Brentford	44	0		
2013–14	Brentford	44	0		
2014–15	Brentford	23	0	**111**	**0**
2015–16	Millwall	18	1		
2016–17	Millwall	43	1		
2017–18	Millwall	4	0	**270**	**9**
2017–18	Bristol R	17	1		
2018–19	Bristol R	46	2		
2019–20	Bristol R	34	2	**97**	**5**
2020–21	Crawley T	38	0		
2021–22	Crawley T	35	1	**73**	**1**

DAVIES, Archie (M) **67 0**
H: 6 1 W: 12 06 b.Hastings 7-10-98

Season	Club	Apps	Gls	Total	
2019–20	Brighton & HA	0	0		
2020–21	Brighton & HA	0	0		
2020–21	Crawley T	34	0		
2021–22	Crawley T	33	0	**67**	**0**

FRANCILLETTE, Ludwig (D) **26 1**
H: 6 4 b.Basse-Terre 1-5-99
From Dijon.

Season	Club	Apps	Gls	Total	
2019–20	Newcastle U	0	0		
2020–21	Newcastle U	0	0		
2021–22	Crawley T	26	1	**26**	**1**

FRANCOMB, George (M) **352 19**
H: 5 11 W: 11 07 b.Hackney 8-9-91

Season	Club	Apps	Gls	Total	
2009–10	Norwich C	2	0		
2010–11	Norwich C	0	0		
2010–11	*Barnet*	13	0	**13**	**0**
2011–12	Norwich C	0	0		
2011–12	*Hibernian*	14	0	**14**	**0**
2012–13	Norwich C	0	0	**2**	**0**
2012–13	*AFC Wimbledon*	15	0		
2013–14	AFC Wimbledon	33	3		
2014–15	AFC Wimbledon	37	3		
2015–16	AFC Wimbledon	40	3		
2016–17	AFC Wimbledon	34	2		
2017–18	AFC Wimbledon	37	0	**196**	**11**
2018–19	Crawley T	41	0		
2019–20	Crawley T	15	0		
2020–21	Crawley T	33	6		
2021–22	Crawley T	38	2	**127**	**8**

FROST, Tyler (M) **37 2**
H: 5 9 W: 11 00 b.Reading 7-7-99
2017–18 Reading 0 0
2018–19 Reading 0 0
2019–20 Reading 0 0
2020–21 Crawley T 23 2
2021–22 Crawley T 14 0 **37 2**

GALLACHER, Owen (D) **12 0**
b.Newcastle upon Tyne 6-4-99
Internationals: Scotland U16, U19.
From Newcastle U, Nottingham F.
2020–21 Burton Alb 9 0 **9 0**
2021–22 Crawley T 3 0 **3 0**

GREGO-COX, Reece (F) **78 6**
H: 5 7 W: 10 03 b.Hammersmith 12-11-96
Internationals: Republic of Ireland U17, U19, U21.
2014–15 QPR 4 0
2015–16 QPR 0 0
2016–17 Newport Co 7 0 **7 0**
2016–17 QPR 1 0
2017–18 QPR 0 0 **5 0**
2018–19 Crawley T 28 2
2019–20 Crawley T 28 4
2020–21 Crawley T 0 0
2021–22 Crawley T 10 0 **66 6**

HENRY, Dion (G) **1 0**
H: 5 11 W: 10 03 b.Ipswich 12-9-97
2014–15 Peterborough U 0 0
2015–16 Peterborough U 1 0
2016–17 Peterborough U 0 0 **1 0**
2017–18 Crystal Palace 0 0
2018–19 Crystal Palace 0 0
2019–20 Crystal Palace 0 0
From Billericay T.
2021–22 Crawley T 0 0
Transferred to AFC Sudbury, January 2022.

HESSENTHALER, Jake (M) **309 13**
H: 5 9 W: 10 01 b.Gravesend 20-4-94
2012–13 Gillingham 0 0
2013–14 Gillingham 19 1
2014–15 Gillingham 37 1
2015–16 Gillingham 38 4
2016–17 Gillingham 28 1
2017–18 Gillingham 37 0 **159 7**
2018–19 Grimsby T 44 0
2019–20 Grimsby T 28 1 **72 1**
2020–21 Crawley T 46 1
2021–22 Crawley T 32 4 **78 5**

HUSSEIN, Mustafa (F) **0 0**
b. 8-6-99
From Tampere U.
2020–21 Crawley T 0 0
2021–22 Crawley T 0 0

JONES, Alfie (G) **0 0**
H: 6 1 W: 11 09 b.Watford 2-10-00
2017–18 Milton Keynes D 0 0
2018–19 Crawley T 0 0
2019–20 Crawley T 0 0
2020–21 Crawley T 0 0
2021–22 Crawley T 0 0

KASTRATI, Florian (M) **1 0**
b. 7-7-02
2021–22 Crawley T 1 0 **1 0**

KHALEEL, Rafiq (M) **0 0**
H: 5 10 W: 10 01 b.Camden 24-2-03
2020–21 Crawley T 0 0
2021–22 Crawley T 0 0

KOWALCZYK, Szymon (M) **0 0**
H: 5 8 b. 20-8-03
2020–21 Crawley T 0 0
2021–22 Crawley T 0 0

LYNCH, Joel (D) **411 22**
H: 6 1 W: 12 11 b.Eastbourne 3-10-87
Internationals: England Youth. Wales Full caps.
2005–06 Brighton & HA 16 1
2006–07 Brighton & HA 39 0
2007–08 Brighton & HA 22 1
2008–09 Brighton & HA 2 0 **79 2**
2008–09 *Nottingham F* 23 0
2009–10 Nottingham F 10 0
2010–11 Nottingham F 12 0
2011–12 Nottingham F 35 3 **80 3**
2012–13 Huddersfield T 22 1
2013–14 Huddersfield T 29 2
2014–15 Huddersfield T 34 3
2015–16 Huddersfield T 37 2 **122 8**
2016–17 QPR 30 3
2017–18 QPR 25 1
2018–19 QPR 35 3 **90 7**
2019–20 Sunderland 16 0 **16 0**
2021–22 Crawley T 24 2 **24 2**

MARSHALL, Mark (M) **353 23**
H: 5 7 W: 12 00 b.Jamaica 5-5-87
From Grays Ath, Eastleigh.
2008–09 Swindon T 12 0
2009–10 Swindon T 7 0 **19 0**
2009–10 *Hereford U* 8 0 **8 0**
2010–11 Barnet 46 6
2011–12 Barnet 25 1 **71 7**
2013–14 Coventry C 14 0 **14 0**
2014–15 Port Vale 46 7 **46 7**
2015–16 Bradford C 31 0
2016–17 Bradford C 42 6 **73 6**
2017–18 Charlton Ath 27 1
2018–19 Charlton Ath 22 1 **49 2**
2019–20 Gillingham 18 0 **18 0**
2019–20 Northampton T 7 0
2020–21 Northampton T 29 1 **36 1**
2021–22 Crawley T 19 0 **19 0**

MATTHEWS, Sam (M) **54 1**
H: 5 9 W: 11 05 b.Poole 1-3-97
2013–14 Bournemouth 0 0
2014–15 Bournemouth 0 0
2015–16 Bournemouth 0 0
2016–17 Bournemouth 0 0
2017–18 Bournemouth 0 0
From Braintree T, Eastleigh.
2018–19 Bristol R 16 0
2019–20 Bristol R 0 0 **16 0**
2020–21 Crawley T 30 1
2021–22 Crawley T 8 0 **38 1**

MORRIS, Glenn (G) **450 0**
H: 6 0 W: 11 00 b.Woolwich 20-12-83
2001–02 Leyton Orient 2 0
2002–03 Leyton Orient 23 0
2003–04 Leyton Orient 27 0
2004–05 Leyton Orient 12 0
2005–06 Leyton Orient 4 0
2006–07 Leyton Orient 3 0
2007–08 Leyton Orient 16 0
2008–09 Leyton Orient 26 0
2009–10 Leyton Orient 11 0 **124 0**
2010–11 Southend U 33 0
2011–12 Southend U 24 0
2012–13 Southend U 0 0 **57 0**
2012–13 Aldershot T 2 0 **2 0**
From Woking, Eastleigh.
2014–15 Gillingham 10 0
2015–16 Gillingham 0 0 **10 0**
2016–17 Crawley T 39 0
2017–18 Crawley T 44 0
2018–19 Crawley T 46 0
2019–20 Crawley T 37 0
2020–21 Crawley T 45 0
2021–22 Crawley T 46 0 **257 0**

NADESAN, Ashley (F) **165 32**
H: 6 2 W: 11 11 b.Redhill 9-9-94
2015–16 Fleetwood T 0 0
2016–17 Fleetwood T 0 0
2017–18 Fleetwood T 1 0
2017–18 *Carlisle U* 15 4
2018–19 Fleetwood T 20 1 **21 1**
2018–19 *Carlisle U* 25 8 **40 12**
2019–20 Crawley T 25 5
2020–21 Crawley T 40 5
2021–22 Crawley T 39 9 **104 19**

NICHOLS, Tom (F) **329 68**
H: 5 10 W: 10 10 b.Wellington 1-9-93
2010–11 Exeter C 1 0
2011–12 Exeter C 7 1
2012–13 Exeter C 3 0
2013–14 Exeter C 28 6
2014–15 Exeter C 36 15
2015–16 Exeter C 23 10 **98 32**
2015–16 Peterborough U 7 1
2016–17 Peterborough U 43 10 **50 11**
2017–18 Bristol R 39 1
2018–19 Bristol R 36 1
2019–20 Bristol R 19 2 **94 4**
2019–20 *Cheltenham T* 5 0 **5 0**
2020–21 Crawley T 43 11
2021–22 Crawley T 39 10 **82 21**

OTEH, Aramide (F) **92 13**
H: 5 9 W: 11 07 b.Lewisham 10-9-98
From Tottenham H.
2017–18 QPR 6 1
2018–19 QPR 2 0
2018–19 *Walsall* 13 1 **13 1**
2019–20 *Bradford C* 18 3 **18 3**
2019–20 QPR 9 0
2020–21 QPR 0 0 **17 1**
2020–21 *Stevenage* 13 4 **13 4**
2020–21 *Colchester U* 13 1 **13 1**
2021–22 Salford C 10 1 **10 1**
2021–22 Crawley T 8 2 **8 2**

PAYNE, Jack (M) **289 13**
H: 5 9 W: 9 02 b.Gravesend 5-12-91
2008–09 Gillingham 2 0
2009–10 Gillingham 19 0
2010–11 Gillingham 31 1
2011–12 Gillingham 30 2
2012–13 Gillingham 19 2 **101 5**
2012–13 *Peterborough U* 14 0
2013–14 Peterborough U 32 2
2014–15 Peterborough U 41 3
2015–16 Peterborough U 2 0 **89 5**
2015–16 *Leyton Orient* 29 1 **29 1**
2016–17 Blackpool 35 1 **35 1**
From Ebbsfleet U, Eastleigh.
2021–22 Crawley T 35 1 **35 1**

POWELL, Jack (M) **93 4**
H: 5 10 W: 9 11 b.Canning Town 29-1-94
Internationals: England C.
2013–14 Millwall 0 0
2014–15 Millwall 5 0
2015–16 Millwall 1 0 **6 0**
From Ebbsfleet U, Maidstone U.
2019–20 Crawley T 6 0
2020–21 Crawley T 44 3
2021–22 Crawley T 37 1 **87 4**

RODARI, Davide (F) **13 1**
b.Switzerland 23-6-99
2020–21 Crawley T 12 1
2021–22 Crawley T 1 0 **13 1**

SEYMOUR, Taylor (G) **0 0**
H: 6 3 W: 12 08 b.Worthing 17-9-01
2020–21 Portsmouth 0 0
2021–22 Portsmouth 0 0
2021–22 Crawley T 0 0

TILLEY, James (F) **92 8**
H: 5 6 W: 9 04 b.Billingshurt 13-6-98
2014–15 Brighton & HA 1 0
2015–16 Brighton & HA 0 0
2016–17 Brighton & HA 0 0
2017–18 Brighton & HA 0 0
2018–19 Brighton & HA 0 0
2019 *Cork C* 19 0 **19 0**
2019–20 Brighton & HA 0 0 **1 0**
2019–20 Grimsby T 10 0
2020–21 Grimsby T 14 2 **24 2**
2020–21 Crawley T 18 3
2021–22 Crawley T 30 3 **48 6**

TSAROULLA, Nicholas (D) **44 3**
H: 5 10 W: 11 00 b.Bristol 29-3-99
Internationals: Cyprus U21.
2020–21 Crawley T 17 0
2021–22 Crawley T 27 3 **44 3**

TUNNICLIFFE, Jordan (D) **94 5**
H: 6 1 W: 12 13 b.Nuneaton 13-10-93
Internationals: England C.
From WBA.
2013–14 Barnsley 0 0
2014–15 Barnsley 0 0
2014–15 Kidderminster H 0 0
From Kidderminster H, AFC Fylde.
2019–20 Crawley T 37 1
2020–21 Crawley T 39 3
2021–22 Crawley T 18 1 **94 5**

Players retained or with offer of contract
Silva, Ronan.

CREWE ALEX (28)

ADEBISI, Rio (D) **39 0**
H: 5 9 W: 11 07 b.Croydon 27-9-00
2019–20 Crewe Alex 2 0
2020–21 Crewe Alex 15 0
2021–22 Crewe Alex 22 0 **39 0**

AGYEI, Daniel (F) **121 17**
H: 6 0 W: 12 02 b.Dansoman 1-6-97
2014–15 AFC Wimbledon 0 0
2015–16 Burnley 0 0
2016–17 Burnley 3 0
2016–17 *Coventry C* 16 4 **16 4**
2017–18 Burnley 0 0
2017–18 *Walsall* 18 4 **18 4**
2017–18 *Blackpool* 9 0 **9 0**
2018–19 Burnley 0 0
2019–20 Burnley 0 0 **3 0**
2019–20 Oxford U 13 3
2020–21 Oxford U 39 5
2021–22 Oxford U 14 0 **66 8**
2021–22 Crewe Alex 9 1 **9 1**

AINLEY, Callum (M) **209 15**
H: 5 8 W: 10 01 b.Swindon 2-11-97
2015–16 Crewe Alex 16 1
2016–17 Crewe Alex 27 1
2017–18 Crewe Alex 45 4
2018–19 Crewe Alex 43 6
2019–20 Crewe Alex 25 2
2020–21 Crewe Alex 22 1
2021–22 Crewe Alex 31 0 **209 15**

BILLINGTON, Lewis (D) **1 0**
b. 17-2-04
2021–22 Crewe Alex 1 0 **1 0**

BOOTH, Sam (G) **0 0**
H: 6 5 b.Liverpool 6-12-00
2019–20 Crewe Alex 0 0
2020–21 Crewe Alex 0 0
2021–22 Crewe Alex 0 0

FINNEY, Oliver (M) **91 14**
H: 5 7 W: 11 00 b.Stoke-on-Trent 15-12-97
2015–16 Crewe Alex 0 0
2016–17 Crewe Alex 1 0
2017–18 Crewe Alex 1 0
2018–19 Crewe Alex 17 0

2019–20 Crewe Alex 18 5
2020–21 Crewe Alex 26 7
2021–22 Crewe Alex 28 2 **91 14**

GOMES, Madger (M) 58 3
H: 5 10 W: 11 09 b.Alicante 1-2-97
Internationals: Spain U17, U18.
From Villareal, Liverpool.
2017–18 Leeds U 0 0
2018–19 Istra 1961 5 0 **5 0**
2019–20 Doncaster R 23 0
2020–21 Doncaster R 22 3 **45 3**
2021–22 Crewe Alex 8 0 **8 0**

GRIFFITHS, Regan (M) 23 0
H: 5 11 W: 11 03 b.Liverpool 1-5-00
2019–20 Crewe Alex 0 0
2020–21 Crewe Alex 2 0
2021–22 Crewe Alex 21 0 **23 0**

JAASKELAINEN, William (G) 84 0
H: 6 0 W: 11 07 b.Bolton 25-7-98
Internationals: Finland U17, U18, U19, U21.
2015–16 Bolton W 0 0
2016–17 Bolton W 0 0
2017–18 Bolton W 0 0
2017–18 Crewe Alex 0 0
2018–19 Crewe Alex 4 0
2019–20 Crewe Alex 35 0
2020–21 Crewe Alex 31 0
2021–22 Crewe Alex 14 0 **84 0**

JOHNSON, Travis (D) 28 0
H: 5 11 W: 10 01 b.Stoke-on-Trent 28-8-00
2018–19 Crewe Alex 0 0
2019–20 Crewe Alex 1 0
2020–21 Crewe Alex 7 0
2021–22 Crewe Alex 20 0 **28 0**

KASHKET, Scott (M) 139 24
H: 5 9 W: 10 06 b.Chigwell 29-2-96
2014–15 Leyton Orient 1 0
2015–16 Leyton Orient 15 1
2016–17 Leyton Orient 0 0 **16 1**
2016–17 Wycombe W 21 10
2017–18 Wycombe W 9 1
2018–19 Wycombe W 27 3
2019–20 Wycombe W 19 4
2020–21 Wycombe W 29 4
2021–22 Wycombe W 0 0 **105 22**
2021–22 Crewe Alex 18 1 **18 1**

LAWTON, Sean (D) 2 0
b. 12-9-03
2021–22 Crewe Alex 2 0 **2 0**

LONG, Chris (F) 201 42
H: 5 7 W: 12 02 b.Huyton 25-2-95
Internationals: England U16, U17, U18, U19, U20.
2013–14 Everton 0 0
2013–14 *Milton Keynes D* 4 1 **4 1**
2014–15 Everton 0 0
2014–15 *Brentford* 10 4 **10 4**
2015–16 Burnley 10 0
2016–17 Burnley 0 0
2016–17 *Fleetwood T* 18 4
2016–17 *Bolton W* 10 1 **10 1**
2017–18 Burnley 0 0 **10 0**
2017–18 *Northampton T* 38 9 **38 9**
2018–19 Fleetwood T 8 0 **26 4**
2018–19 Blackpool 17 2 **17 2**
2019–20 Motherwell 25 7
2020–21 Motherwell 29 4 **54 11**
2021–22 Crewe Alex 32 10 **32 10**

LOWERY, Tom (M) 151 13
H: 5 6 W: 11 11 b.Holmes Chapel 31-12-97
2016–17 Crewe Alex 7 0
2017–18 Crewe Alex 31 0
2018–19 Crewe Alex 15 1
2019–20 Crewe Alex 29 5
2020–21 Crewe Alex 37 3
2021–22 Crewe Alex 32 4 **151 13**

LUNDSTRAM, Josh (M) 26 0
H: 5 9 W: 9 08 b.Stoke-on-Trent 19-2-99
2017–18 Crewe Alex 0 0
2018–19 Crewe Alex 0 0
2019–20 Crewe Alex 0 0
2020–21 Crewe Alex 4 0
2021–22 Crewe Alex 22 0 **26 0**

MACDONALD, Shaun (M) 243 11
H: 6 1 W: 11 05 b.Swansea 17-6-88
Internationals: Wales U19, U21, Full caps.
2005–06 Swansea C 7 0
2006–07 Swansea C 8 0
2007–08 Swansea C 1 0
2008–09 Swansea C 5 0
2008–09 *Yeovil T* 4 2
2009–10 Swansea C 3 0
2009–10 *Yeovil T* 31 3
2010–11 Swansea C 0 0
2010–11 *Yeovil T* 26 4 **61 9**
2011–12 Swansea C 0 0 **24 0**
2011–12 Bournemouth 25 1
2012–13 Bournemouth 28 0
2013–14 Bournemouth 23 0
2014–15 Bournemouth 5 0
2015–16 Bournemouth 3 0 **84 1**
2016–17 Wigan Ath 39 1
2017–18 Wigan Ath 0 0
2018–19 Wigan Ath 0 0 **39 1**
2019–20 Rotherham U 13 0
2020–21 Rotherham U 19 0 **32 0**
2021–22 Crewe Alex 3 0 **3 0**
Transferred to Penybont, December 2021.

MANDRON, Mikael (F) 208 36
H: 6 3 W: 12 13 b.Boulogne 11-10-94
2011–12 Sunderland 0 0
2012–13 Sunderland 2 0
2013–14 Sunderland 0 0
2013–14 *Fleetwood T* 11 1 **11 1**
2014–15 Sunderland 1 0
2014–15 *Shrewsbury T* 3 0 **3 0**
2015–16 Sunderland 0 0 **3 0**
2015–16 *Hartlepool U* 5 0 **5 0**
2016–17 Wigan Ath 3 0 **3 0**
2017–18 Colchester U 44 10
2018–19 Colchester U 41 2 **85 12**
2019–20 Gillingham 23 5 **23 5**
2020–21 Crewe Alex 42 11
2021–22 Crewe Alex 33 7 **75 18**

McFADZEAN, Callum (D) 146 6
H: 5 11 W: 11 11 b.Sheffield 16-1-94
Internationals: England U16. Scotland U21.
2010–11 Sheffield U 0 0
2011–12 Sheffield U 0 0
2012–13 Sheffield U 8 0
2013–14 Sheffield U 7 0
2013–14 *Chesterfield* 4 0 **4 0**
2013–14 *Burton Alb* 7 1
2014–15 Sheffield U 0 0
2014–15 *Burton Alb* 9 1 **16 2**
2015–16 Sheffield U 1 0 **16 0**
2015–16 *Stevenage* 6 0 **6 0**
2016–17 Kilmarnock 4 0 **4 0**
From Alfreton T, Guiseley.
2018–19 Bury 40 0 **40 0**
2019–20 Plymouth Arg 25 3 **25 3**
2020–21 Sunderland 25 1 **25 1**
2021–22 Crewe Alex 10 0 **10 0**
Transferred to Wrexham, January 2022.

MURPHY, Luke (M) 439 33
H: 6 1 W: 12 09 b.Macclesfield 21-10-89
2008–09 Crewe Alex 9 1
2009–10 Crewe Alex 32 3
2010–11 Crewe Alex 39 3
2011–12 Crewe Alex 42 8
2012–13 Crewe Alex 39 6
2013–14 Leeds U 37 3
2014–15 Leeds U 30 3
2015–16 Leeds U 36 1
2016–17 Leeds U 0 0
2016–17 *Burton Alb* 19 1
2017–18 Leeds U 0 0
2017–18 *Burton Alb* 38 1 **57 2**
2018–19 Leeds U 0 0 **103 7**
2018–19 Bolton W 11 0
2019–20 Bolton W 29 2 **40 2**
2020–21 Crewe Alex 40 0
2021–22 Crewe Alex 38 1 **239 22**

O'RIORDAN, Connor (D) 11 0
H: 6 4 b.Crewe 19-10-03
2021–22 Crewe Alex 11 0 **11 0**

OFFORD, Luke (D) 81 1
H: 5 7 W: 10 06 b.Chichester 19-11-99
2017–18 Crewe Alex 0 0
2018–19 Crewe Alex 0 0
2019–20 Crewe Alex 9 0
2020–21 Crewe Alex 28 1
2021–22 Crewe Alex 44 0 **81 1**

ONYEKA, Tyreece (F) 1 0
H: 6 1 b.Stoke-on-Trent 1-8-01
2020–21 Crewe Alex 0 0
2021–22 Crewe Alex 1 0 **1 0**

PORTER, Chris (F) 595 170
H: 6 1 W: 13 01 b.Wigan 12-12-83
2002–03 Bury 2 0
2003–04 Bury 37 9
2004–05 Bury 32 9 **71 18**
2005–06 Oldham Ath 31 7
2006–07 Oldham Ath 35 21 **66 28**
2007–08 Motherwell 37 14
2008–09 Motherwell 22 9 **59 23**
2008–09 Derby Co 5 3
2009–10 Derby Co 21 4
2010–11 Derby Co 18 2 **44 9**
2011–12 Sheffield U 34 5
2012–13 Sheffield U 21 3
2012–13 *Shrewsbury T* 5 1 **5 1**
2013–14 Sheffield U 32 7
2013–14 *Chesterfield* 3 0 **3 0**
2014–15 Sheffield U 1 0 **88 15**
2014–15 Colchester U 21 7
2015–16 Colchester U 32 7
2016–17 Colchester U 38 16 **91 30**
2017–18 Crewe Alex 31 9
2018–19 Crewe Alex 40 13
2019–20 Crewe Alex 26 12
2020–21 Crewe Alex 35 6
2021–22 Crewe Alex 36 6 **168 46**

RICHARDS, Dave (G) 64 0
H: 5 11 W: 12 13 b.Abergavenny 31-12-93
2013–14 Cardiff C 0 0
2013–14 Bristol C 0 0
2014–15 Bristol C 0 0
2015–16 Crewe Alex 0 0
2016–17 Crewe Alex 0 0
2017–18 Crewe Alex 11 0
2018–19 Crewe Alex 4 0
2019–20 Crewe Alex 2 0
2020–21 Crewe Alex 15 0
2021–22 Crewe Alex 32 0 **64 0**

ROBBINS, Joe (M) 0 0
H: 5 9 W: 10 06 b.Manchester 20-2-02
2020–21 Crewe Alex 0 0
2021–22 Crewe Alex 0 0

ROBERTSON, Scott (M) 50 1
H: 5 8 b.Dundee 27-7-01
2019–20 Celtic 0 0
2019–20 Celtic 0 0
2020–21 Celtic 0 0
2020–21 *Gillingham* 15 0 **15 0**
2020–21 *Doncaster R* 15 0
2021–22 Doncaster R 0 0 **15 0**
2021–22 Celtic 0 0
2021–22 *Crewe Alex* 20 1 **20 1**

SALISBURY, Connor (F) 4 0
H: 6 0 b. 27-9-03
Internationals: Wales U18.
2021–22 Crewe Alex 4 0 **4 0**

SAMBOU, Bassala (F) 72 5
H: 6 1 W: 11 11 b.Hannover 15-10-97
2015–16 Coventry C 0 0
2016–17 Everton 0 0
2017–18 Everton 0 0
2018–19 Everton 0 0
2019–20 Fortuna Sittard 22 2
2020–21 Fortuna Sittard 3 0
2020–21 *Randers* 23 1 **23 1**
2021–22 Fortuna Sittard 8 0 **33 2**
2021–22 Crewe Alex 16 2 **16 2**

SASS-DAVIES, Billy (D) 24 0
H: 6 1 W: 12 06 b.Manchester 17-2-00
Internationals: Wales U19, U21.
2017–18 Crewe Alex 0 0
2018–19 Crewe Alex 2 0
2019–20 Crewe Alex 0 0
2020–21 Crewe Alex 0 0
2021–22 Crewe Alex 22 0 **24 0**

TABINER, Joel (F) 1 0
H: 6 0 b.Liverpool 30-11-03
2021–22 Crewe Alex 1 0 **1 0**

UWAKWE , Tariq (M) 23 1
H: 5 10 W: 10 01 b.Islington 19-11-99
Internationals: England U19, U20.
2020–21 Chelsea 0 0
2020–21 *Accrington S* 15 1 **15 1**
2021–22 Crewe Alex 8 0 **8 0**

WILLIAMS, Michael (D) 19 0
b. 27-3-05
Internationals: Wales U18, U19.
2021–22 Crewe Alex 19 0 **19 0**

WOODTHORPE, Nathan (D) 0 0
H: 6 0 b.Northwich 6-12-01
2020–21 Crewe Alex 0 0
2021–22 Crewe Alex 0 0

Players retained or with offer of contract
Finney, Charlie; Holicek, Matus.

Scholars
Bebbington, Harrison Thomas; Bhatti, Samuel Adam; Crolla, Samuel Steven; Flint, Jack Spencer; Higgins, Alex Kieran; Kempster-Down, Zak Lewis George; Lunt, Owen Alan; Martins, Marquise Kayode; Salisbury, Connor Paul; Washington, Harvey Thomas; Webster, Ty Gary; Williams, Michael Isaac; Wood, Ben Christopher; Woodcock, Max Elliot.

CRYSTAL PALACE (29)

AKROBAR-BOATENG, David (D) 0 0
H: 5 9 b. 8-5-01
2020–21 Crystal Palace 0 0
2021–22 Crystal Palace 0 0

ANDERSEN, Joachim (D) 174 6
H: 6 2 W: 14 02 b.Frederiksberg 31-5-96
Internationals: Denmark U16, U17, U19, U20, U21, Full caps.
2014–15 FC Twente 7 1
2015–16 FC Twente 18 1
2016–17 FC Twente 22 2
2017–18 FC Twente 2 0 **49 4**
2017–18 Sampdoria 7 0
2018–19 Sampdoria 32 0 **39 0**

2019–20	Lyon	18	1		
2020–21	Lyon	3	0		
2020–21	*Fulham*	31	1	**31**	**1**
2021–22	Lyon	0	0	**21**	**1**
2021–22	Crystal Palace	34	0	**34**	**0**

AYEW, Jordan (F) **381 62**
H: 6 0 W: 12 11 b.Marseille 11-9-91
Internationals: Ghana U20, Full caps.

2009–10	Marseille	4	1		
2010–11	Marseille	22	2		
2011–12	Marseille	34	3		
2012–13	Marseille	35	7		
2013–14	Marseille	16	1	**111**	**14**
2013–14	*Sochaux*	17	5	**17**	**5**
2014–15	Lorient	31	12	**31**	**12**
2015–16	Aston Villa	30	7		
2016–17	Aston Villa	21	2	**51**	**9**
2016–17	Swansea C	14	1		
2017–18	Swansea C	36	7		
2018–19	Swansea C	0	0	**50**	**8**
2018–19	*Crystal Palace*	20	1		
2019–20	Crystal Palace	37	9		
2020–21	Crystal Palace	33	1		
2021–22	Crystal Palace	31	3	**121**	**14**

BANKS, Scott (M) **28 1**
H: 6 0 W: 11 09 b.Linlithgow 26-9-01
Internationals: Scotland U19, U21.

2018–19	Dundee U	0	0		
2018–19	*Clyde*	12	1	**12**	**1**
2019–20	Dundee U	1	0	**1**	**0**
2019–20	Crystal Palace	0	0		
2019–20	*Alloa Ath*	4	0	**4**	**0**
2020–21	Crystal Palace	0	0		
2020–21	*Dunfermline Ath*	11	0	**11**	**0**
2021–22	Crystal Palace	0	0		

BENTEKE, Christian (F) **397 129**
H: 6 3 W: 13 01 b.Kinshasa 3-12-90
Internationals: Belgium U17, U18, U19, U21, Full caps.

2007–08	Genk	7	1		
2008–09	Genk	3	0		
2008–09	Standard Liege	9	3		
2009–10	*KV Kortrijk*	34	14	**34**	**14**
2010–11	Standard Liege	5	0		
2010–11	*KV Mechelen*	18	6	**18**	**6**
2011–12	Standard Liege	4	0	**18**	**3**
2011–12	Genk	32	16		
2012–13	Genk	5	3	**47**	**20**
2012–13	Aston Villa	34	19		
2013–14	Aston Villa	26	10		
2014–15	Aston Villa	29	13	**89**	**42**
2015–16	Liverpool	29	9	**29**	**9**
2016–17	Crystal Palace	36	15		
2017–18	Crystal Palace	31	3		
2018–19	Crystal Palace	16	1		
2019–20	Crystal Palace	24	2		
2020–21	Crystal Palace	30	10		
2021–22	Crystal Palace	25	4	**162**	**35**

BOATENG, Malachi (M) **0 0**
H: 6 0 b. 5-7-02

2020–21	Crystal Palace	0	0
2021–22	Crystal Palace	0	0

BUTLAND, Jack (G) **272 0**
H: 6 5 W: 14 12 b.Bristol 10-3-93
Internationals: England U16, U17, U19, U20, U21, Full caps.

2009–10	Birmingham C	0	0		
2010–11	Birmingham C	0	0		
2011–12	Birmingham C	0	0		
2011–12	*Cheltenham T*	24	0	**24**	**0**
2012–13	Birmingham C	46	0	**46**	**0**
2012–13	Stoke C	0	0		
2013–14	Stoke C	3	0		
2013–14	*Barnsley*	13	0	**13**	**0**
2013–14	*Leeds U*	16	0	**16**	**0**
2014–15	Stoke C	3	0		
2014–15	*Derby Co*	6	0	**6**	**0**
2015–16	Stoke C	31	0		
2016–17	Stoke C	5	0		
2017–18	Stoke C	35	0		
2018–19	Stoke C	45	0		
2019–20	Stoke C	35	0		
2020–21	Stoke C	0	0	**157**	**0**
2020–21	Crystal Palace	1	0		
2021–22	Crystal Palace	9	0	**10**	**0**

CLYNE, Nathaniel (D) **336 5**
H: 5 9 W: 10 08 b.Stockwell 5-4-91
Internationals: England U19, U21, Full caps.

2008–09	Crystal Palace	26	0		
2009–10	Crystal Palace	22	1		
2010–11	Crystal Palace	46	0		
2011–12	Crystal Palace	28	0		
2012–13	Southampton	34	1		
2013–14	Southampton	25	0		
2014–15	Southampton	35	2	**94**	**3**
2015–16	Liverpool	33	1		
2016–17	Liverpool	37	0		
2017–18	Liverpool	3	0		
2018–19	Liverpool	4	0		
2018–19	*Bournemouth*	14	0	**14**	**0**
2019–20	Liverpool	0	0	**77**	**1**
2020–21	Crystal Palace	13	0		
2021–22	Crystal Palace	16	0	**151**	**1**

DREHER, Luke (M) **1 0**
H: 6 1 W: 12 00 b.Epsom 27-11-98

2015–16	Crystal Palace	0	0		
2016–17	Crystal Palace	0	0		
2017–18	Crystal Palace	0	0		
2018–19	Crystal Palace	1	0		
2019–20	Crystal Palace	0	0		
2020–21	Crystal Palace	0	0		
2021–22	Crystal Palace	0	0	**1**	**0**

EDOUARD, Odsonne (F) **160 73**
H: 6 0 W: 11 09 b.Kourou 16-1-98
Internationals: France U17, U18, U19, U21.
From AF Bobigny.

2015–16	Paris Saint-Germain	0	0		
2016–17	Paris Saint-Germain	0	0		
2016–17	*Toulouse*	16	1	**16**	**1**
2017–18	Paris Saint-Germain	0	0		
2017–18	*Celtic*	22	9		
2018–19	Celtic	32	15		
2019–20	Celtic	27	22		
2020–21	Celtic	31	18		
2021–22	Celtic	4	2	**116**	**66**
2021–22	Crystal Palace	28	6	**28**	**6**

EZE, Eberechi (M) **171 30**
H: 5 8 W: 10 08 b.Greenwich 29-6-98
Internationals: England U20, U21.
From Millwall.

2016–17	QPR	0	0		
2017–18	*Wycombe W*	20	5	**20**	**5**
2017–18	QPR	16	2		
2018–19	QPR	42	4		
2019–20	QPR	46	14	**104**	**20**
2020–21	Crystal Palace	34	4		
2021–22	Crystal Palace	13	1	**47**	**5**

FERGUSON, Nathan (D) **22 1**
H: 5 10 W: 12 00 b.Birmingham 6-10-00
Internationals: England U18, U19, U20.

2017–18	WBA	0	0		
2018–19	WBA	0	0		
2019–20	WBA	21	1	**21**	**1**
2020–21	Crystal Palace	0	0		
2021–22	Crystal Palace	1	0	**1**	**0**

GORDON, John-Kymani (F) **0 0**
b.London 13-2-03
Internationals: England U16.

2019–20	Crystal Palace	0	0
2020–21	Crystal Palace	0	0
2021–22	Crystal Palace	0	0

GREGORY, David (G) **1 0**
H: 6 1 W: 11 00 b.Croydon 1-10-94

2016–17	Cambridge U	1	0	**1**	**0**

From Bromley, Boreham Wood.

2021–22	Crystal Palace	0	0

GUAITA, Vicente (G) **336 0**
H: 6 3 W: 12 08 b.Torrent 10-1-87

2006–07	Valencia	0	0		
2007–08	Valencia	0	0		
2008–09	Valencia	2	0		
2009–10	Valencia	0	0		
2009–10	*Recreativo*	30	0	**30**	**0**
2010–11	Valencia	21	0		
2011–12	Valencia	26	0		
2012–13	Valencia	14	0		
2013–14	Valencia	13	0	**76**	**0**
2014–15	Getafe	29	0		
2015–16	Getafe	38	0		
2016–17	Getafe	8	0		
2017–18	Getafe	33	0	**108**	**0**
2018–19	Crystal Palace	20	0		
2019–20	Crystal Palace	35	0		
2020–21	Crystal Palace	37	0		
2021–22	Crystal Palace	30	0	**122**	**0**

GUEHI, Marc (D) **88 2**
H: 6 0 W: 12 13 b.Abidjan 13-7-00
Internationals: England U16, U17, U18, U19, U20, U21, Full caps.

2018–19	Chelsea	0	0		
2019–20	Chelsea	0	0		
2019–20	*Swansea C*	12	0		
2020–21	Chelsea	0	0		
2020–21	*Swansea C*	40	0		
2021–22	Chelsea	0	0		
2021–22	*Swansea C*	0	0	**52**	**0**
2021–22	Crystal Palace	36	2	**36**	**2**

HANNAM, Reece (D) **0 0**
H: 5 7 W: 11 09 b.Enfield 19-9-00
From West Ham U.

2020–21	Crystal Palace	0	0
2021–22	Crystal Palace	0	0

HUGHES, Will (M) **288 16**
H: 6 1 W: 11 09 b.Weybridge 7-4-95
Internationals: England U17, U21.

2011–12	Derby Co	3	0		
2012–13	Derby Co	35	2		
2013–14	Derby Co	41	3		
2014–15	Derby Co	42	2		
2015–16	Derby Co	6	0		
2016–17	Derby Co	38	2	**165**	**9**
2017–18	Watford	15	2		
2018–19	Watford	32	2		
2019–20	Watford	30	1		
2020–21	Watford	30	2		
2021–22	Watford	0	0	**107**	**7**
2021–22	Crystal Palace	16	0	**16**	**0**

IMRAY, Daniel (D) **0 0**
H: 5 10 b.Harold Wood 27-7-03
From Chelmsford.

2020–21	Crystal Palace	0	0
2021–22	Crystal Palace	0	0

JACH, Jaroslaw (D) **112 4**
H: 6 3 W: 12 11 b.Bielawa 17-2-94
Internationals: Poland U21, Full caps.

2013–14	Zagkebie Lubin	2	0		
2014–15	Zagkebie Lubin	13	0		
2015–16	Zagkebie Lubin	13	2		
2016–17	Zagkebie Lubin	23	1		
2017–18	Zagkebie Lubin	17	1	**68**	**4**
2017–18	Crystal Palace	0	0		
2018–19	Crystal Palace	0	0		
2018–19	*Caykur Rizesport*	5	0	**5**	**0**
2018–19	*Sheriff Tiraspol*	14	0	**14**	**0**
2019–20	Crystal Palace	0	0		
2019–20	*Rakow Czestochowa*	12	0		
2020–21	Crystal Palace	0	0		
2020–21	*Fortuna Sittard*	3	0	**3**	**0**
2020–21	*Rakow Czestochowa*	10	0	**22**	**0**
2021–22	Crystal Palace	0	0		

KELLY, Martin (D) **161 1**
H: 6 3 W: 12 02 b.Bolton 27-4-90
Internationals: England U19, U20, U21, Full caps.

2007–08	Liverpool	0	0		
2008–09	Liverpool	0	0		
2008–09	*Huddersfield T*	7	1	**7**	**1**
2009–10	Liverpool	1	0		
2010–11	Liverpool	11	0		
2011–12	Liverpool	12	0		
2012–13	Liverpool	4	0		
2013–14	Liverpool	5	0	**33**	**0**
2014–15	Crystal Palace	31	0		
2015–16	Crystal Palace	13	0		
2016–17	Crystal Palace	29	0		
2017–18	Crystal Palace	15	0		
2018–19	Crystal Palace	13	0		
2019–20	Crystal Palace	19	0		
2020–21	Crystal Palace	1	0		
2021–22	Crystal Palace	0	0	**121**	**0**

KIRBY, Nya (M) **17 1**
H: 5 9 W: 10 06 b.Islington 31-1-00
Internationals: England U16, U17, U18, U19.
From Tottenham H.

2017–18	Crystal Palace	0	0		
2018–19	Crystal Palace	0	0		
2018–19	*Blackpool*	11	1	**11**	**1**
2019–20	Crystal Palace	0	0		
2020–21	Crystal Palace	0	0		
2020–21	*Tranmere R*	6	0	**6**	**0**
2021–22	Crystal Palace	0	0		

KOUYATE, Cheikhou (M) **447 21**
H: 6 4 W: 11 11 b.Dakar 21-12-89
Internationals: Senegal U20, Full caps.

2007–08	Brussels	10	0	**10**	**0**
2008–09	Anderlecht	0	0		
2008–09	*Kortrijk*	26	3	**26**	**3**
2009–10	Anderlecht	21	1		
2010–11	Anderlecht	23	1		
2011–12	Anderlecht	38	0		
2012–13	Anderlecht	33	1		
2013–14	Anderlecht	38	1	**153**	**4**
2014–15	West Ham U	31	4		
2015–16	West Ham U	34	5		
2016–17	West Ham U	31	1		
2017–18	West Ham U	33	2	**129**	**12**
2018–19	Crystal Palace	31	0		
2019–20	Crystal Palace	35	1		
2020–21	Crystal Palace	36	1		
2021–22	Crystal Palace	27	0	**129**	**2**

MATETA, Jean-Philippe (F) **161 62**
H: 6 4 W: 13 03 b.Clamart 28-6-97
Internationals: France U19, U21.

2015–16	Chateauroux	22	11		
2016–17	Chateauroux	4	2	**26**	**13**
2016–17	Lyon	2	0		
2017–18	Lyon	0	0	**2**	**0**
2017–18	*Le Havre*	37	19	**37**	**19**
2018–19	Mainz 05	34	14		
2019–20	Mainz 05	18	3		
2020–21	Mainz 05	15	7	**67**	**24**
2020–21	*Crystal Palace*	7	1		
2021–22	Mainz	0	0		
2021–22	Crystal Palace	22	5	**29**	**6**

MATTHEWS, Remi (G) **111 0**
H: 6 4 W: 12 04 b.Gorleston 10-2-94

2014–15	Norwich C	0	0		
2014–15	*Burton Alb*	0	0		
2015–16	Norwich C	0	0		
2015–16	*Burton Alb*	2	0	**2**	**0**
2015–16	*Doncaster R*	9	0	**9**	**0**
2016–17	Norwich C	0	0		

2016–17 *Hamilton A* 17 0 **17 0**
2017–18 Norwich C 0 0
2017–18 *Plymouth Arg* 26 0 **26 0**
2018–19 Bolton W 18 0
2019–20 Bolton W 33 0 **51 0**
2020–21 Sunderland 6 0 **6 0**
2021–22 Crystal Palace 0 0

McARTHUR, James (M) 533 37
H: 5 10 W: 10 00 b.Glasgow 7-10-87
Internationals: Scotland U21, Full caps.
2004–05 Hamilton A 6 0
2005–06 Hamilton A 20 1
2006–07 Hamilton A 36 1
2007–08 Hamilton A 34 4
2008–09 Hamilton A 37 2
2009–10 Hamilton A 35 1 **168 9**
2010–11 Wigan Ath 18 0
2011–12 Wigan Ath 31 3
2012–13 Wigan Ath 34 3
2013–14 Wigan Ath 41 4
2014–15 Wigan Ath 5 1 **129 11**
2014–15 Crystal Palace 32 2
2015–16 Crystal Palace 28 2
2016–17 Crystal Palace 29 5
2017–18 Crystal Palace 33 5
2018–19 Crystal Palace 38 3
2019–20 Crystal Palace 37 0
2020–21 Crystal Palace 18 0
2021–22 Crystal Palace 21 0 **236 17**

MILIVOJEVIC, Luka (M) 336 50
H: 6 0 W: 11 11 b.Kragujevac 7-4-91
Internationals: Serbia U21, Full caps.
2007–08 Radnicki Kraguejevac 5 1 **5 1**
2008–09 Rad Belgrade 1 0
2009–10 Rad Belgrade 9 0
2010–11 Rad Belgrade 26 0
2011–12 Rad Belgrade 13 3 **49 3**
2011–12 Red Star Belgrade 11 1
2012–13 Red Star Belgrade 25 6 **36 7**
2013–14 Anderlecht 16 0
2014–15 Anderlecht 3 0 **19 0**
2014–15 Olympiacos 23 2
2015–16 Olympiacos 22 3
2016–17 Olympiacos 17 6 **62 11**
2016–17 Crystal Palace 14 2
2017–18 Crystal Palace 36 10
2018–19 Crystal Palace 38 12
2019–20 Crystal Palace 31 3
2020–21 Crystal Palace 31 1
2021–22 Crystal Palace 15 0 **165 28**

MITCHELL, Tyrick (D) 59 1
H: 5 9 W: 10 03 b.Brent 1-9-99
Internationals: England Full caps.
From Brentford.
2019–20 Crystal Palace 4 0
2020–21 Crystal Palace 19 1
2021–22 Crystal Palace 36 0 **59 1**

MOONEY, Fionn (M) 0 0
b. 12-10-03
2020–21 Crystal Palace 0 0
2021–22 Crystal Palace 0 0

NASCIMENTO, Adler (F) 1 0
2020–21 Peterborough U 1 0 **1 0**
2021–22 Crystal Palace 0 0

O'BRIEN, Jake (D) 28 0
b.Cork 15-5-01
Internationals: Republic of Ireland U21.
2019 Cork C 1 0
2020 Cork C 8 0
2021 Cork C 0 0 **9 0**
2021–22 Crystal Palace 0 0
2021–22 *Swindon T* 19 0 **19 0**

OLISE, Michael (M) 93 9
H: 6 2 W: 11 07 b. 12-12-01
Internationals: France U18, U21.
2018–19 Reading 4 0
2019–20 Reading 19 0
2020–21 Reading 44 7
2021–22 Reading 0 0 **67 7**
2021–22 Crystal Palace 26 2 **26 2**

OMILABU, David (F) 0 0
b. 27-9-02
2020–21 Crystal Palace 0 0
2021–22 Crystal Palace 0 0

PLANGE, Luke (F) 26 4
b.Kingston upon Thames 4-11-02
Internationals: England U20.
From Arsenal.
2021–22 Crystal Palace 0 0
2021–22 *Derby Co* 26 4 **26 4**

RAK-SAKYI, Jesurun (M) 2 0
H: 5 10 W: 10 03 b.Southwark 5-10-02
Internationals: England U20.
2020–21 Crystal Palace 0 0
2021–22 Crystal Palace 2 0 **2 0**

RAYMOND, Jadan (M) 0 0
b.London 15-10-03
Internationals: England U16, U17. Wales U19.
2020–21 Crystal Palace 0 0
2021–22 Crystal Palace 0 0

RIEDEWALD, Jairo (D) 128 4
H: 6 0 W: 12 06 b.Amsterdam 9-9-96
Internationals: Netherlands U16, U17, U19, U21, Full caps.
2013–14 Ajax 5 2
2014–15 Ajax 19 0
2015–16 Ajax 23 0
2016–17 Ajax 16 0 **63 2**
2017–18 Crystal Palace 12 0
2018–19 Crystal Palace 0 0
2019–20 Crystal Palace 17 0
2020–21 Crystal Palace 33 2
2021–22 Crystal Palace 3 0 **65 2**

SCHLUPP, Jeffrey (F) 280 29
H: 5 10 W: 11 05 b.Hamburg 23-12-92
Internationals: Ghana Full caps.
2010–11 Leicester C 0 0
2010–11 *Brentford* 9 6 **9 6**
2011–12 Leicester C 21 2
2012–13 Leicester C 19 3
2013–14 Leicester C 26 1
2014–15 Leicester C 32 3
2015–16 Leicester C 24 1
2016–17 Leicester C 4 0 **126 10**
2016–17 Crystal Palace 15 0
2017–18 Crystal Palace 24 0
2018–19 Crystal Palace 30 4
2019–20 Crystal Palace 17 3
2020–21 Crystal Palace 27 2
2021–22 Crystal Palace 32 4 **145 13**

SPENCE, Sion (M) 6 1
b. 2-10-00
Internationals: Wales U19, U21.
From Cardiff C.
2021–22 Crystal Palace 0 0
2021–22 *Bristol R* 6 1 **6 1**

STREET, Rob (F) 18 2
H: 6 2 b.Oxford 26-9-01
2020–21 Crystal Palace 0 0
2021–22 Crystal Palace 0 0
2021–22 *Newport Co* 18 2 **18 2**

TAYLOR, James (M) 0 0
b.Hereford 20-1-02
From Bristol C.
2020–21 Crystal Palace 0 0
2021–22 Crystal Palace 0 0

TOMKINS, James (D) 330 17
H: 6 4 W: 11 09 b.Basildon 29-3-89
Internationals: England U16, U17, U18, U19, U20, U21. Great Britain.
2005–06 West Ham U 0 0
2006–07 West Ham U 0 0
2007–08 West Ham U 6 0
2008–09 West Ham U 12 1
2008–09 *Derby Co* 7 0 **7 0**
2009–10 West Ham U 23 0
2010–11 West Ham U 19 1
2011–12 West Ham U 44 4
2012–13 West Ham U 26 1
2013–14 West Ham U 31 0
2014–15 West Ham U 22 1
2015–16 West Ham U 25 0 **208 8**
2016–17 Crystal Palace 24 3
2017–18 Crystal Palace 28 3
2018–19 Crystal Palace 29 1
2019–20 Crystal Palace 18 1
2020–21 Crystal Palace 8 0
2021–22 Crystal Palace 8 1 **115 9**

WARD, Joel (D) 385 11
H: 6 2 W: 13 00 b.Emsworth 29-10-89
2008–09 Portsmouth 0 0
2008–09 *Bournemouth* 21 1 **21 1**
2009–10 Portsmouth 3 0
2010–11 Portsmouth 42 3
2011–12 Portsmouth 44 3 **89 6**
2012–13 Crystal Palace 25 0
2013–14 Crystal Palace 36 0
2014–15 Crystal Palace 37 1
2015–16 Crystal Palace 30 2
2016–17 Crystal Palace 38 0
2017–18 Crystal Palace 19 0
2018–19 Crystal Palace 7 1
2019–20 Crystal Palace 29 0
2020–21 Crystal Palace 26 0
2021–22 Crystal Palace 28 0 **275 4**

ZAHA, Wilfried (F) 404 74
H: 5 11 W: 10 06 b.Abidjan 10-11-92
Internationals: England U19, U21, Full caps. Ivory Coast Full caps.
2009–10 Crystal Palace 1 0
2010–11 Crystal Palace 41 1
2011–12 Crystal Palace 41 6
2012–13 Crystal Palace 43 6
2012–13 Manchester U 0 0
2013–14 Manchester U 2 0 **2 0**
2013–14 *Cardiff C* 12 0 **12 0**
2014–15 Crystal Palace 31 4
2015–16 Crystal Palace 34 2
2016–17 Crystal Palace 35 7
2017–18 Crystal Palace 29 9
2018–19 Crystal Palace 34 10
2019–20 Crystal Palace 38 4
2020–21 Crystal Palace 30 11
2021–22 Crystal Palace 33 14 **390 74**

Players retained or with offer of contract
Adaramola, Tayo; Addae, Joshua; Akinwale, Victor; Goodman, Owen; Ola-Adebomi, Ademola; Phillips, Killian; Quick, Daniel; Raymond, Jadan; Rodney, Kaden; Siddik, Cardo; Watson, Noah; Wells-Morrison, Jack; Whitworth, Joseph.

Scholars
Bartley, Ryan Christopher; Barton, Kalani Josiah Adrian Patrick; Bell, Frederick Joseph; Cadogan, Maliq Anthony; Dixon, Junior Anthony; Izquierdo, Jackson; Leonard, James Nicholas; Lewis-Brown, Cameron Jorrell Locksley; Ozoh, David Ikechukwu; Rieno Socoliche, Basilio; Shala, Laurence; Sheridan, Joe; Vigor, Matthew; Williams, Vonnte.

DERBY CO (30)

AGHATISE, Osazee (M) 3 0
H: 5 11 W: 9 13 b.Germany 12-11-02
From Manchester C.
2020–21 Derby Co 0 0
2021–22 Derby Co 3 0 **3 0**

ALLSOP, Ryan (G) 261 2
H: 6 2 W: 12 08 b.Birmingham 17-6-92
Internationals: England U17.
2009–10 WBA 0 0
2010–11 WBA 0 0
2011–12 Millwall 0 0
2012 Hottur 8 2 **8 2**
2012–13 Leyton Orient 20 0 **20 0**
2012–13 Bournemouth 10 0
2013–14 Bournemouth 12 0
2014–15 Bournemouth 0 0
2014–15 *Coventry C* 24 0 **24 0**
2015–16 Bournemouth 1 0
2015–16 *Wycombe W* 18 0
2015–16 *Portsmouth* 0 0
2016–17 Bournemouth 1 0
2017–18 Bournemouth 0 0 **24 0**
2017–18 *Blackpool* 22 0 **22 0**
2017–18 *Lincoln C* 16 0 **16 0**
2018–19 Wycombe W 38 0
2019–20 Wycombe W 32 0
2020–21 Wycombe W 29 0 **117 0**
2021–22 Derby Co 30 0 **30 0**

BARDWELL, Max (D) 0 0
H: 5 11 b.Huddersfield 14-11-02
From Manchester C.
2020–21 Derby Co 0 0
2021–22 Derby Co 0 0

BIELIK, Krystian (M) 94 6
H: 5 10 W: 11 00 b.Vrinnevi 4-1-98
Internationals: Poland U16, U17, U18, U19, U21, Full caps.
2014–15 Legia Warsaw 5 0 **5 0**
2014–15 Arsenal 0 0
2015–16 Arsenal 0 0
2016–17 Arsenal 0 0
2016–17 *Birmingham C* 10 0 **10 0**
2017–18 Arsenal 0 0
2017–18 *Walsall* 0 0
2018–19 Arsenal 0 0
2018–19 *Charlton Ath* 31 3 **31 3**
2019–20 Derby Co 20 0
2020–21 Derby Co 13 2
2021–22 Derby Co 15 1 **48 3**

BIRD, Max (M) 101 2
H: 6 0 W: 10 10 b.Burton 18-9-00
2017–18 Derby Co 0 0
2018–19 Derby Co 4 0
2019–20 Derby Co 22 0
2020–21 Derby Co 33 0
2021–22 Derby Co 42 2 **101 2**

BUCHANAN, Lee (D) 70 0
H: 5 9 W: 10 08 b.Mansfield 7-3-01
Internationals: England U19, U20, U21.
2018–19 Derby Co 0 0
2019–20 Derby Co 5 0
2020–21 Derby Co 35 0
2021–22 Derby Co 30 0 **70 0**

BYRNE, Nathan (D) 372 16
H: 5 11 W: 13 04 b.St Albans 5-6-92
2010–11 Tottenham H 0 0
2010–11 *Brentford* 11 0 **11 0**
2011–12 Tottenham H 0 0
2011–12 *Bournemouth* 9 0 **9 0**
2012–13 Tottenham H 0 0
2012–13 *Crawley T* 12 1 **12 1**

2012–13	*Swindon T*	7	0		
2013–14	Swindon T	36	4		
2014–15	Swindon T	42	3		
2015–16	Swindon T	5	3	**90**	**10**
2015–16	Wolverhampton W	24	2		
2016–17	Wolverhampton W	0	0	**24**	**2**
2016–17	Wigan Ath	14	0		
2016–17	*Charlton Ath*	17	1	**17**	**1**
2017–18	Wigan Ath	44	0		
2018–19	Wigan Ath	30	1		
2019–20	Wigan Ath	39	1	**127**	**2**
2020–21	Derby Co	41	0		
2021–22	Derby Co	41	0	**82**	**0**

CASHIN, Eiran (D) **18** **1**
H: 6 0 b.Mansfield 9-11-01
Internationals: Republic of Ireland U18, U21.

2020–21	Derby Co	0	0		
2021–22	Derby Co	18	1	**18**	**1**

CLARKE, Courtney (M) **0** **0**
From Whytleafe

2020–21	Derby Co	0	0		
2021–22	Derby Co	0	0		

CYBULSKI, Bartosz (F) **4** **0**
b.Poland 15-10-02

2020–21	Derby Co	0	0		
2021–22	Derby Co	4	0	**4**	**0**

DAVIES, Curtis (D) **536** **27**
H: 6 2 W: 12 00 b.Waltham Forest 15-3-85
Internationals: England U21.

2003–04	Luton T	6	0		
2004–05	Luton T	44	1		
2005–06	Luton T	6	1	**56**	**2**
2005–06	WBA	33	2		
2006–07	WBA	32	0		
2007–08	WBA	0	0	**65**	**2**
2007–08	*Aston Villa*	12	1		
2008–09	Aston Villa	35	1		
2009–10	Aston Villa	2	1		
2010–11	Aston Villa	0	0	**49**	**3**
2010–11	*Leicester C*	12	0	**12**	**0**
2010–11	Birmingham C	6	0		
2011–12	Birmingham C	42	5		
2012–13	Birmingham C	41	6	**89**	**11**
2013–14	Hull C	37	2		
2014–15	Hull C	21	0		
2015–16	Hull C	39	2		
2016–17	Hull C	26	0	**123**	**4**
2017–18	Derby Co	46	1		
2018–19	Derby Co	5	0		
2019–20	Derby Co	32	0		
2020–21	Derby Co	13	0		
2021–22	Derby Co	46	4	**142**	**5**

DIXON, Connor (M) **0** **0**
b. 20-9-00

2020–21	Derby Co	0	0		
2021–22	Derby Co	0	0		

DUNCAN, Bobby (F) **0** **0**
b. 26-1-01
Internationals: England U16, U17, U18, U19, U20.
From Wigan Ath, Manchester C, Liverpool.

2020–21	Fiorentina	0	0		
2020–21	Derby Co	0	0		
2021–22	Derby Co	0	0		

EBIOWEI, Malcolm (F) **16** **1**
H: 6 1 b.Lambeth 4-9-03
Internationals: England U16.
From Arsenal.

2019–20	Rangers	0	0		
2020–21	Rangers	0	0		
2021–22	Derby Co	16	1	**16**	**1**

EBOSELE , Festy (D) **38** **2**
H: 5 11 W: 10 01 b.Wexford 2-8-02
Internationals: Republic of Ireland U16, U17, U19, U21.
From Bray W.

2020–21	Derby Co	3	0		
2021–22	Derby Co	35	2	**38**	**2**

FORSYTH, Craig (D) **350** **22**
H: 6 2 W: 13 01 b.Carnoustie 24-2-89
Internationals: Scotland Full caps.

2006–07	Dundee	1	0		
2007–08	Dundee	0	0		
2007–08	*Montrose*	9	0	**9**	**0**
2008–09	Dundee	1	0		
2008–09	*Arbroath*	26	2	**26**	**2**
2009–10	Dundee	24	2		
2010–11	Dundee	33	8	**59**	**10**
2011–12	Watford	20	3		
2012–13	Watford	2	0	**22**	**3**
2012–13	*Bradford C*	7	0	**7**	**0**
2012–13	*Derby Co*	10	0		
2013–14	Derby Co	46	2		
2014–15	Derby Co	44	1		
2015–16	Derby Co	12	0		
2016–17	Derby Co	3	1		
2017–18	Derby Co	31	0		
2018–19	Derby Co	13	0		
2019–20	Derby Co	22	0		
2020–21	Derby Co	20	0		
2021–22	Derby Co	26	3	**227**	**7**

HUTCHINSON, Isaac (M) **62** **3**
H: 5 10 W: 11 00 b.Eastbourne 10-4-00
From Brighton & HA.

2018–19	Southend U	8	0		
2019–20	Southend U	22	1		
2020–21	Southend U	2	0	**32**	**1**
2020–21	Derby Co	0	0		
2020–21	*Forest Green R*	10	0	**10**	**0**
2021–22	Derby Co	1	0	**1**	**0**
2021–22	*Crawley T*	19	2	**19**	**2**

IBRAHIM, Ola (M) **0** **0**
b. 23-9-03
From Manchester U.

2020–21	Derby Co	0	0		
2021–22	Derby Co	0	0		

JOZWIAK, Kamil (F) **160** **16**
H: 5 9 W: 11 00 b.Miedzyrzecz 22-4-98
Internationals: Poland U16, U17, U18, U19, U21, Full caps.

2015–16	Lech Poznan	10	1		
2016–17	Lech Poznan	6	0		
2017–18	Lech Poznan	20	3		
2018–19	Lech Poznan	31	3		
2019–20	Lech Poznan	35	8		
2020–21	Lech Poznan	0	0	**102**	**15**
2020–21	Derby Co	41	1		
2021–22	Derby Co	17	0	**58**	**1**

KAZIM-RICHARDS, Colin (F) **457** **68**
H: 6 1 W: 10 10 b.Leyton 26-8-86
Internationals: Turkey U21, Full caps.

2004–05	Bury	30	3	**30**	**3**
2005–06	Brighton & HA	42	6		
2006–07	Brighton & HA	1	0	**43**	**6**
2006–07	Sheffield U	27	1	**27**	**1**
2007–08	Fenerbahce	28	0		
2008–09	Fenerbahce	22	2		
2009–10	Fenerbahce	11	3		
2009–10	*Toulouse*	15	2	**15**	**2**
2010–11	Fenerbahce	5	0	**66**	**5**
2010–11	Galatasaray	13	3		
2011–12	Galatasaray	18	2	**31**	**5**
2011–12	*Olympiacos*	9	1	**9**	**1**
2012–13	*Blackburn R*	28	3	**28**	**3**
2013–14	Bursaspor	16	0		
2014–15	Bursaspor	0	0	**16**	**0**
2014–15	*Feyenoord*	27	11		
2015–16	Feyenoord	11	1	**38**	**12**
2015–16	Celtic	11	1	**11**	**1**
2016	Coritiba	21	3	**21**	**3**
2017	Corinthians	14	1		
2018	Corinthians	1	0	**15**	**1**
2018–19	*Lobos BUAP*	10	3	**10**	**3**
2018–19	Veracruz	15	4		
2019–20	Veracruz	8	4	**23**	**8**
2019–20	Pachuca	9	2		
2020–21	Pachuca	4	1	**13**	**3**
2020–21	Derby Co	38	8		
2021–22	Derby Co	23	3	**61**	**11**

KNIGHT, Jason (M) **112** **10**
H: 5 8 W: 9 13 b.Dublin 13-2-01
Internationals: Republic of Ireland U17, U18, U19, U21, Full caps.

2018–19	Derby Co	0	0		
2019–20	Derby Co	31	6		
2020–21	Derby Co	43	2		
2021–22	Derby Co	38	2	**112**	**10**

LAWRENCE, Tom (F) **277** **53**
H: 5 9 W: 11 11 b.Wrexham 13-1-94
Internationals: Wales U17, U19, U21, Full caps.

2012–13	Manchester U	0	0		
2013–14	Manchester U	1	0	**1**	**0**
2013–14	*Carlisle U*	9	3	**9**	**3**
2013–14	*Yeovil T*	19	2	**19**	**2**
2014–15	Leicester C	3	0		
2014–15	*Rotherham U*	6	1	**6**	**1**
2015–16	Leicester C	0	0		
2015–16	*Blackburn R*	21	2	**21**	**2**
2015–16	*Cardiff C*	14	0	**14**	**0**
2016–17	Leicester C	0	0	**3**	**0**
2016–17	*Ipswich T*	34	9	**34**	**9**
2017–18	Derby Co	39	6		
2018–19	Derby Co	33	6		
2019–20	Derby Co	37	10		
2020–21	Derby Co	23	3		
2021–22	Derby Co	38	11	**170**	**36**

McDONALD, Kornell (D) **7** **0**
b.Nottingham 1-10-01

2020–21	Derby Co	7	0		
2021–22	Derby Co	0	0	**7**	**0**

MORRISON, Ravel (M) **144** **19**
H: 5 9 W: 11 03 b.Wythenshawe 2-2-93
Internationals: England U16, U17, U18, U21.

2009–10	Manchester U	0	0		
2010–11	Manchester U	0	0		
2011–12	Manchester U	0	0		
2011–12	West Ham U	1	0		
2012–13	West Ham U	0	0		
2012–13	*Birmingham C*	27	3	**27**	**3**
2013–14	West Ham U	16	3		
2013–14	*QPR*	15	6		
2014–15	West Ham U	1	0	**18**	**3**
2014–15	*Cardiff C*	7	0	**7**	**0**
2015–16	Lazio	4	0		
2016–17	Lazio	0	0		
2016–17	*QPR*	5	0	**20**	**6**
2017–18	Lazio	0	0	**4**	**0**
2017–18	*Atlas*	18	3	**18**	**3**
2018–19	Ostersund	6	0	**6**	**0**
2019–20	Sheffield U	1	0	**1**	**0**
2019–20	*Middlesbrough*	3	0	**3**	**0**
2020–21	ADO Den Haag	4	0	**4**	**0**
2021–22	Derby Co	36	4	**36**	**4**

RICHARDS, Carlos Peliza (F) **1** **0**
b. 30-8-05
Internationals: Gibraltar U17.

2021–22	Derby Co	1	0	**1**	**0**

ROBINSON, Darren (M) **1** **0**
H: 5 11 b. 29-12-04
Internationals: Northern Ireland U19.
From Dungannon Swifts.

2021–22	Derby Co	1	0	**1**	**0**

ROOS, Kelle (G) **119** **0**
H: 6 5 W: 14 02 b.Rijkevoort 31-5-92
From PSV Eindhoven, Willem II, NEC Nijmegen, Nuneaton T.

2013–14	Derby Co	0	0		
2014–15	Derby Co	0	0		
2015–16	Derby Co	0	0		
2015–16	*Rotherham U*	4	0	**4**	**0**
2015–16	*AFC Wimbledon*	17	0	**17**	**0**
2016–17	Derby Co	0	0		
2016–17	*Bristol R*	16	0	**16**	**0**
2017–18	Derby Co	0	0		
2017–18	*Port Vale*	8	0	**8**	**0**
2017–18	*Plymouth Arg*	4	0	**4**	**0**
2018–19	Derby Co	16	0		
2019–20	Derby Co	22	0		
2020–21	Derby Co	14	0		
2021–22	Derby Co	18	0	**70**	**0**

SIBLEY, Louie (M) **67** **7**
H: 5 11 W: 11 09 b.Birmingham 1-9-01
Internationals: England U17, U18, U19, U20.

2019–20	Derby Co	11	5		
2020–21	Derby Co	30	1		
2021–22	Derby Co	26	1	**67**	**7**

SOLOMON, Harrison (D) **0** **0**
b.Burton 1-11-02

2020–21	Derby Co	0	0		
2021–22	Derby Co	0	0		

STEARMAN, Richard (D) **486** **15**
H: 6 3 W: 12 00 b.Wolverhampton 19-8-87
Internationals: England U16, U17, U19, U21.

2004–05	Leicester C	8	1		
2005–06	Leicester C	34	3		
2006–07	Leicester C	35	1		
2007–08	Leicester C	39	2	**116**	**7**
2008–09	Wolverhampton W	37	1		
2009–10	Wolverhampton W	16	1		
2010–11	Wolverhampton W	31	0		
2011–12	Wolverhampton W	30	0		
2012–13	Wolverhampton W	12	1		
2012–13	*Ipswich T*	15	0	**15**	**0**
2013–14	Wolverhampton W	40	2		
2014–15	Wolverhampton W	42	0		
2015–16	Wolverhampton W	4	0		
2015–16	Fulham	29	0		
2016–17	Fulham	0	0	**29**	**0**
2016–17	*Wolverhampton W*	18	0	**230**	**5**
2017–18	Sheffield U	28	2		
2018–19	Sheffield U	16	1		
2019–20	Sheffield U	0	0	**44**	**3**
2019–20	Huddersfield T	17	0		
2020–21	Huddersfield T	21	0	**38**	**0**
2021–22	Derby Co	14	0	**14**	**0**

STRETTON, Jack (F) **13** **1**
b.Newell 6-9-01
Internationals: Scotland U19.
From Nottingham F.

2020–21	Derby Co	4	0		
2021–22	Derby Co	9	1	**13**	**1**

THOMPSON, Liam (M) **23** **0**
b.Nottingham 29-4-02

2020–21	Derby Co	0	0		
2021–22	Derby Co	23	0	**23**	**0**

WATSON, Louis (M) **13** **0**
H: 5 9 W: 9 06 b.Croydon 7-6-01
Internationals: Republic of Ireland U18, U21.
From West Ham U.

2020–21	Derby Co	9	0		
2021–22	Derby Co	4	0	**13**	**0**

WILSON, Tyree (M) **0** **0**

2018–19	Derby Co	0	0		
2019–20	Derby Co	0	0		
2020–21	Derby Co	0	0		
2021–22	Derby Co	0	0		

Players retained or with offer of contract
Borkovic, Marko; Foulkes, Harrison; Grewal-Pollard, William; Kellyman, Omari; Roberts, Alfie.

Scholars
Aideyan, Nelson Nosa; Borkovic, Marko; Brailsford, Rhys Ellis; Christie, Eli James; Dixon, Zion Isaiah; Evans, Harry Jack; Fapetu, Adebayo Joseph Ifeoluwa; Kelly Caprani, Cian Mark; Moloney, Riley Christopher Owen; Moore, Callum Stephen; Nicholas-Davies, Reece James; Richards, Carlos Peliza; Robinson, Darren Robert Russell; Rutt, Charlie Owen; Sebagabo, Samuel Niyigena.

DONCASTER R (31)

AGARD, Kieran (F) **345** **90**
H: 5 8 W: 10 08 b.Newham 10-10-89

2006–07	Everton	0	0		
2007–08	Everton	0	0		
2008–09	Everton	0	0		
2009–10	Everton	1	0		
2010–11	Everton	0	0	**1**	**0**
2010–11	*Kilmarnock*	8	1	**8**	**1**
2010–11	*Peterborough U*	0	0		
2011–12	Yeovil T	29	6	**29**	**6**
2012–13	Rotherham U	30	6		
2013–14	Rotherham U	46	21		
2014–15	Rotherham U	2	0	**78**	**27**
2014–15	Bristol C	39	13		
2015–16	Bristol C	25	2	**64**	**15**
2016–17	Milton Keynes D	42	12		
2017–18	Milton Keynes D	41	6		
2018–19	Milton Keynes D	43	20		
2019–20	Milton Keynes D	19	2		
2020–21	Milton Keynes D	0	0		
2021–22	Milton Keynes D	0	0	**145**	**40**
2021–22	Plymouth Arg	12	1	**12**	**1**
2021–22	Doncaster R	8	0	**8**	**0**

ANDERSON, Thomas (D) **206** **9**
H: 6 4 W: 13 01 b.Burnley 2-9-93

2012–13	Burnley	0	0		
2013–14	Burnley	0	0		
2014–15	Burnley	0	0		
2014–15	*Carlisle U*	8	0	**8**	**0**
2015–16	Burnley	0	0		
2015–16	*Chesterfield*	18	0		
2016–17	Burnley	0	0		
2016–17	*Chesterfield*	35	2	**53**	**2**
2017–18	Burnley	0	0		
2017–18	*Port Vale*	20	0	**20**	**0**
2017–18	*Doncaster R*	7	2		
2018–19	Doncaster R	23	1		
2019–20	Doncaster R	32	1		
2020–21	Doncaster R	44	2		
2021–22	Doncaster R	19	1	**125**	**7**

BARLOW, Aidan (M) **35** **3**
H: 5 9 W: 11 11 b.Salford 10-1-00
Internationals: England U17, U18.

2019–20	Manchester U	0	0		
2019–20	*Tromso*	7	2	**7**	**2**
2021–22	Doncaster R	28	1	**28**	**1**

BLYTHE, Ben (D) **3** **0**
b.Leeds 13-1-02

2020–21	Doncaster R	1	0		
2021–22	Doncaster R	2	0	**3**	**0**

BOSTOCK, John (M) **240** **28**
H: 5 10 W: 11 11 b.Lambeth 15-1-92
Internationals: England U16, U17, U19.

2007–08	Crystal Palace	4	0	**4**	**0**
2008–09	Tottenham H	0	0		
2009–10	Tottenham H	0	0		
2009–10	*Brentford*	9	2	**9**	**2**
2010–11	Tottenham H	0	0		
2010–11	*Hull C*	11	2	**11**	**2**
2011–12	Tottenham H	0	0		
2011–12	*Sheffield W*	4	0	**4**	**0**
2011–12	*Swindon T*	3	0		
2012–13	Tottenham H	0	0		
2012–13	*Swindon T*	8	0	**11**	**0**
2013	*Toronto*	7	0	**7**	**0**
2013–14	Royal Antwerp	29	1		
2014–15	Royal Antwerp	2	0	**31**	**1**
2014–15	OH Leuven	26	11		
2015–16	OH Leuven	25	7	**51**	**18**
2016–17	Lens	31	5		
2017–18	Lens	11	0	**42**	**5**
2017–18	Bursaspor	8	0	**8**	**0**
2018–19	Toulouse	16	0		
2019–20	Toulouse	0	0	**16**	**0**
2019–20	*Nottingham F*	7	0	**7**	**0**
2020–21	Doncaster R	18	0		
2021–22	Doncaster R	21	0	**39**	**0**

BOTTOMLEY, Ben (G) **0** **0**
b.Pontefract 22-10-02

2020–21	Doncaster R	0	0		
2021–22	Doncaster R	0	0		

CLAYTON, Adam (M) **412** **20**
H: 5 9 W: 11 11 b.Manchester 14-1-89
Internationals: England U20.

2007–08	Manchester C	0	0		
2008–09	Manchester C	0	0		
2009–10	Manchester C	0	0		
2009–10	*Carlisle U*	28	1	**28**	**1**
2010–11	Leeds U	4	0		
2010–11	*Peterborough U*	7	0	**7**	**0**
2010–11	*Milton Keynes D*	6	1	**6**	**1**
2011–12	Leeds U	43	6	**47**	**6**
2012–13	Huddersfield T	43	4		
2013–14	Huddersfield T	42	7	**85**	**11**
2014–15	Middlesbrough	41	0		
2015–16	Middlesbrough	43	1		
2016–17	Middlesbrough	34	0		
2017–18	Middlesbrough	32	0		
2018–19	Middlesbrough	36	0		
2019–20	Middlesbrough	27	0		
2020–21	Middlesbrough	0	0	**213**	**1**
2020–21	Birmingham C	14	0		
2021–22	Birmingham C	0	0	**14**	**0**
2021–22	Doncaster R	12	0	**12**	**0**

CLOSE, Ben (M) **152** **14**
H: 5 9 W: 11 11 b.Portsmouth 8-8-96

2013–14	Portsmouth	0	0		
2014–15	Portsmouth	6	0		
2015–16	Portsmouth	7	0		
2016–17	Portsmouth	0	0		
2017–18	Portsmouth	40	2		
2018–19	Portsmouth	34	8		
2019–20	Portsmouth	29	3		
2020–21	Portsmouth	22	1		
2021–22	Portsmouth	0	0	**138**	**14**
2021–22	Doncaster R	14	0	**14**	**0**

DODOO, Joseph (F) **125** **19**
H: 6 0 W: 12 08 b.Nottingham 6-1-95
Internationals: England U18.

2013–14	Leicester C	0	0		
2014–15	Leicester C	0	0		
2015–16	Leicester C	1	0	**1**	**0**
2015–16	*Bury*	4	1	**4**	**1**
2016–17	Rangers	20	3		
2017–18	Rangers	0	0		
2017–18	*Charlton Ath*	5	1	**5**	**1**
2018–19	Rangers	0	0	**20**	**3**
2018–19	*Blackpool*	18	2	**18**	**2**
2019–20	Bolton W	24	4	**24**	**4**
2020–21	Wigan Ath	20	4		
2021–22	Wigan Ath	0	0	**20**	**4**
2021–22	Doncaster R	33	4	**33**	**4**

GARDNER, Dan (M) **232** **19**
H: 6 1 W: 12 06 b.Manchester 5-4-90

2008–09	Celtic	4	0	**4**	**0**
2009–10	Crewe Alex	2	0	**2**	**0**
From Droylsden, FC Halifax T					
2013–14	Chesterfield	16	3		
2014–15	Chesterfield	17	1		
2014–15	*Tranmere R*	4	2	**4**	**2**
2015–16	Chesterfield	30	4		
2015–16	*Bury*	6	0	**6**	**0**
2016–17	Chesterfield	34	2	**97**	**10**
2017–18	Oldham Ath	43	1		
2018–19	Oldham Ath	20	2		
2019–20	Oldham Ath	0	0	**63**	**3**
2019–20	Salford C	0	0		
2020–21	Wigan Ath	36	1		
2021–22	Wigan Ath	0	0	**36**	**1**
2021–22	Doncaster R	20	3	**20**	**3**

GREAVES, Anthony (M) **11** **0**
H: 5 10 W: 11 03 b.Sheffield 17-11-00

2018–19	Doncaster R	0	0		
2019–20	Doncaster R	0	0		
2020–21	Doncaster R	10	0		
2021–22	Doncaster R	1	0	**11**	**0**

GRIFFITHS, Reo (F) **49** **15**
H: 5 11 b.Islington 27-6-00
Internationals: England U17.

2016–17	Tottenham H	0	0		
2017–18	Tottenham H	0	0		
2018–19	Lyon	8	1		
2019–20	Lyon	16	6		
2020–21	Lyon	9	6	**33**	**13**
2021–22	Doncaster R	16	2	**16**	**2**

HASANI, Lirak (M) **11** **0**
H: 6 0 b.Doncaster 25-6-02

2018–19	Doncaster R	2	0		
2019–20	Doncaster R	0	0		
2020–21	Doncaster R	2	0		
2021–22	Doncaster R	7	0	**11**	**0**

HIWULA, Jordy (F) **221** **46**
H: 5 10 W: 12 00 b.Manchester 24-9-94
Internationals: England U18, U19.

2013–14	Manchester C	0	0		
2014–15	Manchester C	0	0		
2014–15	*Yeovil T*	8	0	**8**	**0**
2014–15	*Walsall*	19	9		
2015–16	Huddersfield T	0	0		
2015–16	*Wigan Ath*	14	2	**14**	**2**
2015–16	*Walsall*	13	3	**32**	**12**
2016–17	Huddersfield T	0	0		
2016–17	*Bradford C*	41	9	**41**	**9**
2017–18	Huddersfield T	0	0		
2017–18	*Fleetwood T*	43	8	**43**	**8**
2018–19	Coventry C	39	12		
2019–20	Coventry C	15	2	**54**	**14**
2020–21	Portsmouth	9	0	**9**	**0**
2021–22	Doncaster R	20	1	**20**	**1**

HORTON, Branden (D) **31** **2**
H: 5 10 W: 11 11 b.Doncaster 9-9-00

2017–18	Doncaster R	0	0		
2018–19	Doncaster R	0	0		
2019–20	Doncaster R	0	0		
2020–21	Doncaster R	11	0		
2021–22	Doncaster R	20	2	**31**	**2**

JOHN, Cameron (D) **54** **4**
H: 5 11 W: 12 04 b.Romford 24-8-99
From Southend U.

2018–19	Wolverhampton W	0	0		
2019–20	Wolverhampton W	0	0		
2019–20	*Doncaster R*	18	2		
2020–21	Doncaster R	31	2		
2021–22	Doncaster R	5	0	**54**	**4**

JONES, Louis (G) **23** **0**
H: 6 1 W: 11 09 b.Doncaster 12-10-98

2015–16	Doncaster R	0	0		
2016–17	Doncaster R	0	0		
2017–18	Doncaster R	0	0		
2018–19	Doncaster R	0	0		
2019–20	Doncaster R	0	0		
2020–21	Doncaster R	13	0		
2021–22	Doncaster R	10	0	**23**	**0**

KNOYLE, Kyle (D) **187** **4**
H: 5 10 W: 9 13 b.Newham 24-9-96
Internationals: England U18.

2015–16	West Ham U	0	0		
2015–16	*Dundee U*	9	0	**9**	**0**
2016–17	West Ham U	0	0		
2016–17	*Wigan Ath*	1	0	**1**	**0**
2017–18	Swindon T	18	0		
2018–19	Swindon T	42	0	**60**	**0**
2019–20	Cambridge U	26	1		
2020–21	Cambridge U	46	2		
2021–22	Cambridge U	0	0	**72**	**3**
2021–22	Doncaster R	45	1	**45**	**1**

MITCHELL, Jonathan (G) **90** **0**
H: 5 11 W: 13 08 b.Hartlepool 24-11-94
Internationals: England U21.

2012–13	Newcastle U	0	0		
2013–14	Newcastle U	0	0		
2014–15	Derby Co	0	0		
2015–16	Derby Co	0	0		
2015–16	*Luton T*	5	0	**5**	**0**
2016–17	Derby Co	0	0		
2017–18	Derby Co	0	0		
2018–19	Derby Co	0	0		
2018–19	*Oxford U*	10	0	**10**	**0**
2018–19	*Shrewsbury T*	9	0	**9**	**0**
2019–20	Derby Co	0	0		
2019–20	*Macclesfield T*	11	0	**11**	**0**
2020–21	Derby Co	0	0		
2020–21	*Northampton T*	35	0	**35**	**0**
2021–22	Hartlepool U	2	0	**2**	**0**
2021–22	Doncaster R	18	0	**18**	**0**

OKENABIRHIE, Fejiri (F) **102** **25**
H: 5 10 W: 11 09 b. 25-2-96
Internationals: England C.

2013–14	Stevenage	3	0		
2014–15	Stevenage	0	0		
2015–16	Stevenage	0	0	**3**	**0**
From Harrow Bor, Dagenham & R.					
2018–19	Shrewsbury T	38	10		
2019–20	Shrewsbury T	17	2	**55**	**12**
2019–20	Doncaster R	5	2		
2020–21	Doncaster R	39	11		
2021–22	Doncaster R	0	0	**44**	**13**

OLOWU, Joseph Olugbenga (D) **35** **4**
H: 6 0 b.Ibadan 27-11-99

2018–19	Arsenal	0	0		
2019–20	Arsenal	0	0		
2020–21	Arsenal	0	0		
2021–22	Doncaster R	35	4	**35**	**4**

RAVENHILL, Liam (M) **3** **0**
b.Doncaster 28-11-02

2020–21	Doncaster R	0	0		
2021–22	Doncaster R	3	0	**3**	**0**

ROWE, Tommy (M) **509** **72**
H: 5 11 W: 12 11 b.Manchester 24-9-88

2006–07	Stockport Co	4	0		
2007–08	Stockport Co	24	6		
2008–09	Stockport Co	44	7	**72**	**13**
2008–09	Peterborough U	0	0		
2009–10	Peterborough U	32	2		
2010–11	Peterborough U	35	5		
2011–12	Peterborough U	43	4		
2012–13	Peterborough U	31	5		
2013–14	Peterborough U	34	7	**175**	**23**
2014–15	Wolverhampton W	14	0		
2015–16	Wolverhampton W	3	0	**17**	**0**
2015–16	*Scunthorpe U*	14	1	**14**	**1**
2015–16	*Doncaster R*	10	3		

2016–17 Doncaster R 46 13
2017–18 Doncaster R 40 4
2018–19 Doncaster R 32 5
2019–20 Bristol C 29 2
2020–21 Bristol C 31 1 **60 3**
2021–22 Doncaster R 43 7 **171 32**

SEAMAN, Charlie (D) 24 1
H: 5 8 b. 30-9-99
From West Ham U.
2018–19 Bournemouth 0 0
2018–19 *Dundee U* 10 0 **10 0**
2019–20 Bournemouth 0 0
2020–21 Doncaster R 0 0
2021–22 Doncaster R 14 1 **14 1**

TAYLOR, Jon (M) 365 58
H: 5 6 W: 12 02 b.Liverpool 23-12-89
2009–10 Shrewsbury T 2 0
2010–11 Shrewsbury T 20 6
2011–12 Shrewsbury T 33 0
2012–13 Shrewsbury T 37 7
2013–14 Shrewsbury T 41 9 **133 22**
2014–15 Peterborough U 24 3
2015–16 Peterborough U 44 11 **68 14**
2016–17 Rotherham U 42 4
2017–18 Rotherham U 25 4
2018–19 Rotherham U 41 4
2019–20 Rotherham U 0 0 **108 12**
2019–20 Doncaster R 28 6
2020–21 Doncaster R 25 4
2021–22 Doncaster R 3 0 **56 10**

WILLIAMS, Ed (M) 12 0
H: 5 7 W: 10 06 b.Cheltenham 20-7-95
Internationals: England C.
2012–13 Cheltenham T 0 0
2013–14 Cheltenham T 0 0
From Kidderminster H.
2020–21 Doncaster R 11 0
2021–22 Doncaster R 1 0 **12 0**

WILLIAMS, Ro-Shaun (M) 113 0
H: 6 0 W: 13 05 b.Manchester 3-9-98
Internationals: England U17, U18, U19.
2015–16 Manchester U 0 0
2016–17 Manchester U 0 0
2017–18 Manchester U 0 0
2018–19 Manchester U 0 0
2018–19 Shrewsbury T 16 0
2019–20 Shrewsbury T 25 0
2020–21 Shrewsbury T 40 0 **81 0**
2021–22 Doncaster R 32 0 **32 0**

YOUNGER, Ollie (D) 17 0
H: 6 0 W: 11 00 b.Skipton 14-11-99
2017–18 Burnley 0 0
2018–19 Burnley 0 0
2019–20 Burnley 0 0
2020–21 Sunderland 1 0
2021–22 Sunderland 0 0 **1 0**
2021–22 Doncaster R 16 0 **16 0**

Players retained or with offer of contract
Cole, Corie; Faulkner, Bobby; Fletcher, Alexander; Goodman, Jack; Harrison, Ethan; Henson, Thomas; Hollings, William; Kuleya, Tavonga; Raper, Jack; Wilds, Daniel; Wolny, Aleksander.

Scholars
Chadwick, Luke William; Chambers, Thomas Michael; Cole, Corie Matthew; Fletcher, Alexander Jack; Goodman, Jack Connor; Harrison, Ethan James; Henson, Thomas Owen; Hollings, William John Wing Houng; Khan, Faris Mujahid; Kuleya, Tavonga Daniel; Lindley, Joshua Owen; Nesbitt, Michael Robert; Parkinson, Thomas Michael Fred; Petch, Charlie James Robert; Raper, Jack William; Whiting, Jak Alfie; Wilds, Daniel Peter; Wolny, Aleksander Jan.

EVERTON (32)

ALLAN, Marques (M) 365 12
H: 5 8 W: 11 07 b.Rio de Janeiro 8-1-91
Internationals: Brazil U20, Full caps.
2009 Vasco da Gama 13 0
2010 Vasco da Gama 15 0
2011 Vasco da Gama 19 0
2012 Vasco da Gama 4 0 **51 0**
2012–13 Udinese 36 0
2013–14 Udinese 33 0
2014–15 Udinese 35 1 **104 1**
2015–16 Napoli 35 3
2016–17 Napoli 29 1
2017–18 Napoli 38 4
2018–19 Napoli 33 1
2019–20 Napoli 23 2
2020–21 Napoli 0 0 **158 11**
2020–21 Everton 24 0
2021–22 Everton 28 0 **52 0**

ALLI, Bamidele (M) 264 73
H: 6 1 W: 12 00 b.Milton Keynes 11-4-96
Internationals: England U17, U18, U19, U21, Full caps.
2012–13 Milton Keynes D 0 0
2013–14 Milton Keynes D 33 6
2014–15 Milton Keynes D 39 16 **72 22**
2015–16 Tottenham H 33 10
2016–17 Tottenham H 37 18
2017–18 Tottenham H 36 9
2018–19 Tottenham H 25 5
2019–20 Tottenham H 25 8
2020–21 Tottenham H 15 0
2021–22 Tottenham H 10 1 **181 51**
2021–22 Everton 11 0 **11 0**

ANDRE GOMES, Filipe (M) 211 13
H: 6 2 W: 13 01 b.Grijo 30-7-93
Internationals: Portugal U17, U28, U19, U20, U21, Full caps.
2012–13 Benfica 7 1
2013–14 Benfica 7 1
2014–15 Benfica 0 0 **14 2**
2014–15 *Valencia* 33 4
2015–16 Valencia 30 3 **63 7**
2016–17 Barcelona 30 3
2017–18 Barcelona 16 0
2018–19 Barcelona 0 0 **46 3**
2018–19 *Everton* 27 1
2019–20 Everton 19 0
2020–21 Everton 28 0
2021–22 Everton 14 0 **88 1**

ASTLEY, Ryan (D) 0 0
b. 4-10-01
Internationals: Wales U17, U19, U21.
2020–21 Everton 0 0
2021–22 Everton 0 0

BARRETT, Jack (G) 0 0
b. 4-6-02
2020–21 Everton 0 0
2021–22 Everton 0 0

BEGOVIC, Asmir (G) 347 1
H: 6 6 W: 13 01 b.Trebinje 20-6-87
Internationals: Canada U20. Bosnia & Herzogovina Full caps.
2005–06 Portsmouth 0 0
2005–06 *La Louviere* 2 0 **2 0**
2006–07 Portsmouth 0 0
2006–07 *Macclesfield T* 3 0 **3 0**
2007–08 Portsmouth 0 0
2007–08 *Bournemouth* 8 0
2007–08 *Yeovil T* 2 0
2008–09 Portsmouth 2 0
2008–09 *Yeovil T* 14 0 **16 0**
2009–10 Portsmouth 9 0 **11 0**
2009–10 *Ipswich T* 6 0 **6 0**
2009–10 Stoke C 4 0
2010–11 Stoke C 28 0
2011–12 Stoke C 23 0
2012–13 Stoke C 38 0
2013–14 Stoke C 32 1
2014–15 Stoke C 35 0 **160 1**
2015–16 Chelsea 17 0
2016–17 Chelsea 2 0 **19 0**
2017–18 Bournemouth 38 0
2018–19 Bournemouth 24 0
2019–20 Bournemouth 0 0
2019–20 *Qarabag* 10 0 **10 0**
2019–20 *AC Milan* 2 0 **2 0**
2020–21 Bournemouth 45 0
2021–22 Bournemouth 0 0 **115 0**
2021–22 Everton 3 0 **3 0**

BRANTHWAITE, Jarrad (D) 29 1
H: 6 5 W: 10 08 b.Carlisle 27-6-02
Internationals: England U20.
2018–19 Carlisle U 0 0
2019–20 Carlisle U 9 0 **9 0**
2019–20 Everton 4 0
2020–21 Everton 0 0
2020–21 *Blackburn R* 10 0 **10 0**
2021–22 Everton 6 1 **10 1**

BROADHEAD, Nathan (F) 40 12
H: 5 10 W: 11 07 b.Bangor 5-4-98
Internationals: Wales U17, U19, U20, U21.
2017–18 Everton 0 0
2018–19 Everton 0 0
2019–20 Everton 0 0
2019–20 *Burton Alb* 19 2 **19 2**
2020–21 Everton 1 0
2021–22 Everton 0 0 **1 0**
2021–22 *Sunderland* 20 10 **20 10**

BUTTERFIELD, Luke (M) 0 0
H: 5 9 b. 29-9-03
Internationals: Scotland U16, U19.
2020–21 Everton 0 0
2021–22 Everton 0 0

CALVERT-LEWIN, Dominic (F) 195 50
H: 5 9 W: 10 01 b.Sheffield 16-3-97
Internationals: England U20, U21, Full caps.
2013–14 Sheffield U 0 0
2014–15 Sheffield U 2 0
2015–16 Sheffield U 9 0
2015–16 *Northampton T* 20 5 **20 5**
2016–17 Sheffield U 0 0 **11 0**
2016–17 Everton 11 1
2017–18 Everton 32 4
2018–19 Everton 35 6
2019–20 Everton 36 13
2020–21 Everton 33 16
2021–22 Everton 17 5 **164 45**

CANNON, Thomas (F) 0 0
b.Aintree 28-11-02
Internationals: Republic of Ireland U19.
2020–21 Everton 0 0
2021–22 Everton 0 0

COLEMAN, Seamus (D) 394 23
H: 6 4 W: 10 08 b.Donegal 11-10-88
Internationals: Republic of Ireland U21, U23, Full caps.
2006 Sligo R 4 0
2007 Sligo R 26 0
2008 Sligo R 26 1 **56 1**
2008–09 Everton 0 0
2009–10 Everton 3 0
2009–10 *Blackpool* 9 1 **9 1**
2010–11 Everton 34 4
2011–12 Everton 18 0
2012–13 Everton 26 0
2013–14 Everton 36 6
2014–15 Everton 35 3
2015–16 Everton 28 1
2016–17 Everton 26 4
2017–18 Everton 12 0
2018–19 Everton 29 2
2019–20 Everton 27 0
2020–21 Everton 25 0
2021–22 Everton 30 1 **329 21**

CRELLIN, Billy (G) 16 0
H: 6 1 W: 9 06 b.Blackpool 30-1-00
Internationals: England U17, U18, U19, U20.
2017–18 Fleetwood T 0 0
2018–19 Fleetwood T 0 0
2019–20 Fleetwood T 5 0
2020–21 Fleetwood T 0 0
2020–21 *Bolton W* 11 0 **11 0**
2021–22 Fleetwood T 0 0 **5 0**
2021–22 Everton 0 0

DAVIES, Tom (M) 136 6
H: 5 11 W: 11 00 b.Liverpool 30-6-98
Internationals: England U16, U17, U18, U19, U21.
2015–16 Everton 2 0
2016–17 Everton 24 2
2017–18 Everton 33 2
2018–19 Everton 16 0
2019–20 Everton 30 1
2020–21 Everton 25 0
2021–22 Everton 6 1 **136 6**

DELPH, Fabian (M) 253 13
H: 5 9 W: 9 06 b.Bradford 21-11-89
Internationals: England U19, U21, Full caps.
2006–07 Leeds U 1 0
2007–08 Leeds U 1 0
2008–09 Leeds U 42 6
2009–10 Aston Villa 8 0
2010–11 Aston Villa 7 0
2011–12 Aston Villa 11 0
2011–12 *Leeds U* 5 0 **49 6**
2012–13 Aston Villa 24 0
2013–14 Aston Villa 34 3
2014–15 Aston Villa 28 0 **112 3**
2015–16 Manchester C 17 2
2016–17 Manchester C 7 1
2017–18 Manchester C 22 1
2018–19 Manchester C 11 0 **57 4**
2019–20 Everton 16 0
2020–21 Everton 8 0
2021–22 Everton 11 0 **35 0**

DOBBIN, Lewis (F) 3 0
H: 5 9 b.Stoke-on-Trent 3-1-03
Internationals: England U16, U17, U19.
2021–22 Everton 3 0 **3 0**

DOUCOURE, Abdoulaye (M) 278 33
H: 6 0 W: 12 00 b.Meulan-en-Yvelines 1-1-93
Internationals: France U17, U18, U19, U20, U21. Mali Full caps.
2012–13 Rennes 4 1
2013–14 Rennes 20 6
2014–15 Rennes 35 3
2015–16 Rennes 16 2 **75 12**
2015–16 Watford 0 0
2015–16 *Granada* 15 0 **15 0**
2016–17 Watford 20 1
2017–18 Watford 37 7
2018–19 Watford 35 5
2019–20 Watford 37 4 **129 17**
2020–21 Everton 29 2
2021–22 Everton 30 2 **59 4**

GARCIA FERREIRA, Rafael (F) **0** **0**
H: 5 9 b.London 7-10-02
Internationals: England U16.
From Fulham.

2020–21	Everton	0	0		
2021–22	Everton	0	0		

GBAMIN, Jean-Philippe (M) **194** **6**
H: 6 1 W: 13 01 b.San Pedro 25-5-95
Internationals: France U18, U19, U20, U21. Ivory Coast Full caps.

2012–13	Lens	2	0		
2013–14	Lens	30	2		
2014–15	Lens	33	0		
2015–16	Lens	26	1	**91**	**3**
2016–17	Mainz 05	25	0		
2017–18	Mainz 05	30	1		
2018–19	Mainz 05	31	1	**86**	**2**
2019–20	Everton	2	0		
2020–21	Everton	1	0		
2021–22	Everton	3	0	**6**	**0**
2021–22	*CSKA Moscow*	11	1	**11**	**1**

GIBSON, Lewis (D) **27** **0**
H: 6 1 W: 11 07 b.Durham 19-7-00
Internationals: England U17, U18, U20.
From Newcastle U.

2019–20	Everton	0	0		
2019–20	*Fleetwood T*	9	0	**9**	**0**
2020–21	Everton	0	0		
2020–21	*Reading*	13	0	**13**	**0**
2021–22	Everton	0	0		
2021–22	*Sheffield W*	5	0	**5**	**0**

GODFREY, Ben (D) **172** **6**
H: 6 0 W: 11 09 b.York 15-1-98
Internationals: England U20, U21, Full caps.

2014–15	York C	0	0		
2015–16	York C	12	1	**12**	**1**
2015–16	Norwich C	0	0		
2016–17	Norwich C	2	0		
2017–18	Norwich C	0	0		
2017–18	*Shrewsbury T*	40	1		
2018–19	Norwich C	31	4		
2019–20	Norwich C	30	0		
2019–20	*Shrewsbury T*	0	0	**40**	**1**
2020–21	Norwich C	3	0	**66**	**4**
2020–21	Everton	31	0		
2021–22	Everton	23	0	**54**	**0**

GORDON, Anthony (M) **60** **4**
H: 5 9 W: 11 00 b.Liverpool 24-2-01
Internationals: England U18, U19, U20, U21.

2017–18	Everton	0	0		
2018–19	Everton	0	0		
2019–20	Everton	11	0		
2020–21	Everton	3	0		
2020–21	*Preston NE*	11	0	**11**	**0**
2021–22	Swindon T	0	0		
2021–22	Everton	35	4	**49**	**4**

GRAY, Demarai (M) **239** **23**
H: 5 10 W: 10 05 b.Birmingham 28-6-96
Internationals: England U18, U19, U20, U21.

2013–14	Birmingham C	7	1		
2014–15	Birmingham C	41	6		
2015–16	Birmingham C	24	1	**72**	**8**
2015–16	Leicester C	12	0		
2016–17	Leicester C	30	1		
2017–18	Leicester C	35	3		
2018–19	Leicester C	34	4		
2019–20	Leicester C	21	2		
2020–21	Leicester C	1	0	**133**	**10**
2021–22	Bayer Leverkusen	0	0		
2021–22	Everton	34	5	**34**	**5**

Transferred to Bayer Leverkusen January 2021.

HAGAN, Harry (D) **0** **0**
b.Liverpool 24-4-03
Internationals: England U16.

2020–21	Everton	0	0		
2021–22	Everton	0	0		

HOLGATE, Mason (D) **157** **5**
H: 5 11 W: 11 11 b.Doncaster 22-10-96
Internationals: England U20, U21.

2014–15	Barnsley	20	1	**20**	**1**
2015–16	Everton	0	0		
2016–17	Everton	18	0		
2017–18	Everton	15	0		
2018–19	Everton	5	0		
2018–19	*WBA*	19	1	**19**	**1**
2019–20	Everton	27	0		
2020–21	Everton	28	1		
2021–22	Everton	25	2	**118**	**3**

HUGHES, Rhys (M) **0** **0**
b.Wrexham 21-9-01
Internationals: Wales U17, U19, U21.

2020–21	Everton	0	0		
2021–22	Everton	0	0		

HUNT, MacKenzie (M) **0** **0**
b. 14-11-01

2020–21	Everton	0	0		
2021–22	Everton	0	0		

IVERSEN, Einar (M) **0** **0**
b.Stord 6-6-01
Internationals: Norway U17, U18, U21.

2020–21	Everton	0	0		
2021–22	Everton	0	0		

IWOBI, Alex (M) **183** **15**
H: 5 11 W: 11 12 b.Lagos 3-5-96
Internationals: England U16, U17, U18. Nigeria Full caps.

2012–13	Arsenal	0	0		
2013–14	Arsenal	0	0		
2014–15	Arsenal	0	0		
2015–16	Arsenal	13	2		
2016–17	Arsenal	26	3		
2017–18	Arsenal	26	3		
2018–19	Arsenal	35	3		
2019–20	Arsenal	0	0	**100**	**11**
2019–20	Everton	25	1		
2020–21	Everton	30	1		
2021–22	Everton	28	2	**83**	**4**

JAGNE, Seedy (M) **1** **0**
H: 6 0 b.Gambia 1-10-03
Internationals: Sweden U17, U19.

2019	Hacken	0	0		
2020	Hacken	1	0	**1**	**0**

From Hacken.

2020–21	Everton	0	0		
2021–22	Everton	0	0		

KEAN, Moise (F) **125** **31**
H: 6 0 W: 11 05 b.Vercelli 28-2-00
Internationals: Italy U16, U17, U19, U20, U21, Full caps.

2016–17	Juventus	3	1		
2017–18	Juventus	0	0		
2017–18	*Verona*	19	4	**19**	**4**
2018–19	Juventus	13	6		
2019–20	Everton	29	2		
2020–21	Everton	2	0		
2020–21	*Paris Saint-Germain*	26	13	**26**	**13**
2021–22	Everton	1	0	**32**	**2**
2021–22	*Juventus*	32	5	**48**	**12**

KEANE, Michael (D) **304** **21**
H: 6 3 W: 12 13 b.Stockport 11-1-93
Internationals: Republic of Ireland U17, U19. England U19, U20, U21, Full caps.

2011–12	Manchester U	0	0		
2012–13	Manchester U	0	0		
2012–13	*Leicester C*	22	2	**22**	**2**
2013–14	Manchester U	0	0		
2013–14	*Derby Co*	7	0	**7**	**0**
2013–14	*Blackburn R*	13	3	**13**	**3**
2014–15	Manchester U	1	0	**1**	**0**
2014–15	Burnley	21	0		
2015–16	Burnley	44	5		
2016–17	Burnley	35	2	**100**	**7**
2017–18	Everton	30	0		
2018–19	Everton	33	1		
2019–20	Everton	31	2		
2020–21	Everton	35	3		
2021–22	Everton	32	3	**161**	**9**

KENNY, Jonjoe (D) **119** **2**
H: 5 9 W: 10 08 b.Kirkdale 15-3-97
Internationals: England U16, U17, U18, U19, U20, U21.

2014–15	Everton	0	0		
2015–16	Everton	1	0		
2015–16	*Wigan Ath*	7	0	**7**	**0**
2015–16	*Oxford U*	17	0	**17**	**0**
2016–17	Everton	1	0		
2017–18	Everton	19	0		
2018–19	Everton	10	0		
2019–20	Everton	0	0		
2019–20	*Schalke 04*	31	2	**31**	**2**
2020–21	Everton	4	0		
2020–21	*Celtic*	14	0	**14**	**0**
2021–22	Everton	15	0	**50**	**0**

KRISTENSEN, Sebastian (D) **0** **0**
b. 4-2-03
From Lyngby.

2020–21	Everton	0	0		
2021–22	Everton	0	0		

LEBAN, Zan-Luk (G) **0** **0**
b. 15-12-02
Internationals: Slovenia U16, U17.
From Escola.

2020–21	Everton	0	0		
2021–22	Everton	0	0		

LONERGAN, Andrew (G) **353** **1**
H: 6 4 W: 13 10 b.Preston 19-10-83
Internationals: Republic of Ireland U16. England U20.

2000–01	Preston NE	1	0		
2001–02	Preston NE	0	0		
2002–03	Preston NE	0	0		
2002–03	*Darlington*	2	0	**2**	**0**
2003–04	Preston NE	8	0		
2004–05	Preston NE	23	1		
2005–06	Preston NE	0	0		
2005–06	*Wycombe W*	2	0	**2**	**0**
2006–07	Preston NE	13	0		
2006–07	*Swindon T*	1	0	**1**	**0**
2007–08	Preston NE	43	0		
2008–09	Preston NE	46	0		
2009–10	Preston NE	45	0		
2010–11	Preston NE	29	0	**208**	**1**
2011–12	Leeds U	35	0		
2012–13	Bolton W	5	0		
2013–14	Bolton W	17	0		
2014–15	Bolton W	29	0	**51**	**0**
2015–16	Fulham	29	0	**29**	**0**
2016–17	Wolverhampton W	11	0		
2017–18	Wolverhampton W	0	0	**11**	**0**
2017–18	Leeds U	7	0	**42**	**0**
2018–19	Middlesbrough	0	0		
2018–19	*Rochdale*	7	0	**7**	**0**
2019–20	Liverpool	0	0		
2020–21	Stoke C	0	0		
2020–21	WBA	0	0		
2021–22	Everton	0	0		

McALLISTER, Sean (M) **0** **0**
H: 5 10 b.Randalstown 1-1-03
From Dungannon.

2020–21	Everton	0	0		
2021–22	Everton	0	0		

MINA, Yerry (D) **193** **19**
H: 6 5 W: 11 11 b.Guachene 23-9-94
Internationals: Colombia U23, Full caps.

2013	Deportivo Pasto	14	1	**14**	**1**
2014	Santa Fe	34	3		
2015	Santa Fe	23	2		
2016	Santa Fe	10	2	**67**	**7**
2016	Palmeiras	13	4		
2017	Palmeiras	15	2	**28**	**6**
2017–18	Barcelona	5	0	**5**	**0**
2018–19	Everton	13	1		
2019–20	Everton	29	2		
2020–21	Everton	24	2		
2021–22	Everton	13	0	**79**	**5**

MYKOLENKO, Vitaliy (D) **101** **6**
H: 5 10 W: 11 03 b.Cherkasy 29-5-99
Internationals: Ukraine U17, U18, U19, U21, Full caps.

2017–18	Dynamo Kyiv	5	0		
2018–19	Dynamo Kyiv	23	0		
2019–20	Dynamo Kyiv	23	3		
2020–21	Dynamo Kyiv	22	2	**73**	**5**
2021–22	Dynamo Kiev	15	0	**15**	**0**
2021–22	Everton	13	1	**13**	**1**

NKOUNKOU, Niels (D) **25** **0**
H: 6 0 W: 11 00 b.Pontoise 1-11-00
Internationals: France U17, U19, U23.

2017–18	Marseille	0	0		
2018–19	Marseille	0	0		
2019–20	Marseille	0	0		
2020–21	Everton	2	0		
2021–22	Everton	0	0	**2**	**0**
2021–22	*Standard Liege*	23	0	**23**	**0**

ONYANGO, Tyler (M) **3** **0**
H: 6 3 b.Luton 4-3-03
Internationals: England U17.

2019–20	Everton	0	0		
2020–21	Everton	0	0		
2021–22	Everton	3	0	**3**	**0**

PATTERSON, Nathan (D) **7** **0**
H: 6 0 W: 11 05 b.Glasgow 16-10-01
Internationals: Scotland U17, U18, U19, U21, Full caps.

2019–20	Rangers	0	0		
2020–21	Rangers	7	0		
2021–22	Rangers	0	0	**7**	**0**
2021–22	Everton	0	0		

PICKFORD, Jordan (G) **298** **0**
H: 6 1 W: 12 02 b.Washington 7-3-94
Internationals: England U16, U17, U18, U19, U20, U21, Full caps.

2010–11	Sunderland	0	0		
2011–12	Sunderland	0	0		
2012–13	Sunderland	0	0		
2013–14	Sunderland	0	0		
2013–14	*Burton Alb*	12	0	**12**	**0**
2013–14	*Carlisle U*	18	0	**18**	**0**
2014–15	Sunderland	0	0		
2014–15	*Bradford C*	33	0	**33**	**0**
2015–16	Sunderland	2	0		
2015–16	*Preston NE*	24	0	**24**	**0**
2016–17	Sunderland	29	0	**31**	**0**
2017–18	Everton	38	0		
2018–19	Everton	38	0		
2019–20	Everton	38	0		
2020–21	Everton	31	0		
2021–22	Everton	35	0	**180**	**0**

PRICE, Isaac (M) **1** **0**
b. 26-9-03
Internationals: Northern Ireland U16, U17, U19, U21.

2020–21	Everton	0	0		
2021–22	Everton	1	0	**1**	**0**

QUIRK, Sebastian (M) **0 0**
b.Liverpool 5-12-01
2020–21 Everton 0 0
2021–22 Everton 0 0

RICHARLISON, de Andrade (F) **239 66**
H: 5 10 W: 11 03 b.Nova Venecia 10-5-97
Internationals: Brazil U20, Full caps.
2015 America Mineiro 24 9 **24 9**
2016 Fluminense 28 4
2017 Fluminense 14 5 **42 9**
2017–18 Watford 38 5 **38 5**
2018–19 Everton 35 13
2019–20 Everton 36 13
2020–21 Everton 34 7
2021–22 Everton 30 10 **135 43**

RONDON, Jose Salomon (F) **432 139**
H: 6 1 W: 13 08 b.Caracas 16-9-89
Internationals: Venezuela U20, Full caps.
2006–07 Aragua 21 7
2007–08 Aragua 28 8 **49 15**
2008–09 Las Palmas 10 0
2009–10 Las Palmas 36 12 **46 12**
2010–11 Malaga 30 14
2011–12 Malaga 37 11 **67 25**
2012–13 Rubin Kazan 25 7
2013–14 Rubin Kazan 11 6 **36 13**
2013–14 Zenit St Petersburg 10 7
2014–15 Zenit St Petersburg 26 13
2015–16 Zenit St Petersburg 1 0 **37 20**
2015–16 WBA 34 9
2016–17 WBA 38 8
2017–18 WBA 36 7
2018–19 WBA 0 0 **108 24**
2018–19 *Newcastle U* 32 11 **32 11**
2019 Dalian Professional 11 5
2020 Dalian Professional 16 9 **27 14**
2021–22 *CSKA Moscow* 10 4 **10 4**
2021–22 Everton 20 1 **20 1**

SIMMS, Ellis (F) **39 13**
H: 6 0 W: 11 07 b.Oldham 5-1-01
Internationals: England U20.
From Manchester C.
2019–20 Everton 0 0
2020–21 Everton 0 0
2020–21 *Blackpool* 21 8 **21 8**
2021–22 Everton 1 0 **1 0**
2021–22 *Hearts* 17 5 **17 5**

TOSUN, Cenk (F) **264 93**
H: 6 0 W: 12 04 b.Wetzlar 7-6-91
Internationals: Germany U16, U18, U19, U21. Turkey U21, Full caps.
2009–10 Eintracht Frankfurt 1 0 **1 0**
2010–11 Gaziantepspor 14 10
2011–12 Gaziantepspor 32 6
2012–13 Gaziantepspor 32 10
2013–14 Gaziantepspor 31 13 **109 39**
2014–15 Besiktas 18 5
2015–16 Besiktas 29 8
2016–17 Besiktas 33 20
2017–18 Besiktas 16 8
2017–18 Everton 14 5
2018–19 Everton 25 3
2019–20 Everton 5 1
2019–20 *Crystal Palace* 5 1 **5 1**
2020–21 Everton 5 0
2020–21 *Besiktas* 3 3
2021–22 Everton 1 0 **50 9**
2021–22 *Besiktas* 0 0 **99 44**

TOWNSEND, Andros (M) **353 34**
H: 5 11 W: 12 02 b.Chingford 16-7-91
Internationals: England U16, U17, U19, U21, Full caps.
2008–09 Tottenham H 0 0
2008–09 *Yeovil T* 10 1 **10 1**
2009–10 Tottenham H 0 0
2009–10 *Leyton Orient* 22 2 **22 2**
2009–10 *Milton Keynes D* 9 2 **9 2**
2010–11 Tottenham H 0 0
2010–11 *Ipswich T* 13 1 **13 1**
2010–11 *Watford* 3 0 **3 0**
2010–11 *Millwall* 11 2 **11 2**
2011–12 Tottenham H 0 0
2011–12 *Leeds U* 6 1 **6 1**
2011–12 *Birmingham C* 15 0 **15 0**
2012–13 Tottenham H 5 0
2012–13 *QPR* 12 2 **12 2**
2013–14 Tottenham H 25 1
2014–15 Tottenham H 17 2
2015–16 Tottenham H 3 0 **50 3**
2015–16 Newcastle U 13 4 **13 4**
2016–17 Crystal Palace 36 3
2017–18 Crystal Palace 36 2
2018–19 Crystal Palace 38 6
2019–20 Crystal Palace 24 1
2020–21 Crystal Palace 34 1
2021–22 Crystal Palace 0 0 **168 13**
2021–22 Everton 21 3 **21 3**

TYRER, Harry (G) **0 0**
H: 6 4 b.Crosby 6-12-01
2020–21 Everton 0 0
2021–22 Everton 0 0

VIRGINIA, Joao (G) **3 0**
H: 6 3 W: 13 01 b.Faro 10-10-99
Internationals: Portugal U16, U17, U18, U19, U20, U21.
From Benfica, Arsenal.
2018–19 Everton 0 0
2019–20 *Reading* 2 0 **2 0**
2019–20 Everton 0 0
2020–21 Everton 1 0
2021–22 Everton 0 0 **1 0**
2021–22 *Sporting Lisbon* 0 0

WARRINGTON, Lewis (M) **17 1**
b.Birkenhead 10-10-02
2021–22 Everton 0 0
2021–22 *Tranmere R* 17 1 **17 1**

WELCH, Reece (D) **0 0**
b.Huddersfield 19-9-03
Internationals: England U16, U17, U19, U20.
2020–21 Everton 0 0
2021–22 Everton 0 0

WHITAKER, Charlie (M) **0 0**
b. 16-9-03
2020–21 Everton 0 0
2021–22 Everton 0 0

Players retained or with offer of contract
Anderson, Joseph; Dixon, Roman; John, Kyle; Kouyate, Mohamed; Metcalfe, Jenson; Mills, Stanley; Nash, Patrick; Okoronkwo, Francis.

Scholars
Barker, Owen William; Cahill, Shae Lou Tim; Campbell, Elijah Xavier; Coughlan, Sam Frederick; Djankpata, Halid; Graham, Dylan Paul; Heath, Isaac Theodor Lambie; Higgins, Liam Thomas; Jones, Edward Michael; Mallon, Mathew John; Manafa, Saja; Smikle-James, Troy; Tierney, Jack; Wilson, Charles Robert; Wright, Harry Bernard.

EXETER C (33)

ARTHUR, Jack (G) **0 0**
2019–20 Exeter C 0 0
2020–21 Exeter C 0 0
2021–22 Exeter C 0 0

ATANGANA, Nigel (M) **212 6**
H: 6 2 W: 11 05 b.Corbeil-Essonnes 9-9-89
From Havant & Waterlooville.
2014–15 Portsmouth 30 1
2015–16 Portsmouth 13 0 **43 1**
2015–16 Leyton Orient 16 0
2016–17 Leyton Orient 29 0 **45 0**
2017–18 Cheltenham T 32 1
2018–19 Cheltenham T 26 2 **58 3**
2019–20 Exeter C 22 1
2020–21 Exeter C 28 0
2021–22 Exeter C 16 1 **66 2**

BROWN, Jevani (F) **183 27**
H: 5 9 W: 11 11 b.Letchworth 16-10-94
Internationals: Jamaica U17.
2013–14 Peterborough U 0 0
2014–15 Peterborough U 0 0
From Barton R, Arlesey T, Kettering T, Stamford, St Neots T.
2017–18 Cambridge U 41 6
2018–19 Cambridge U 43 7 **84 13**
2019–20 Colchester U 11 0
2019–20 *Forest Green R* 5 0 **5 0**
2020–21 Colchester U 40 7 **51 7**
2021–22 Exeter C 43 7 **43 7**

BROWN, Scott (G) **490 0**
H: 6 2 W: 13 10 b.Wolverhampton 26-4-85
From Birmingham C, Welshpool T.
2003–04 Bristol C 0 0
2004–05 Cheltenham T 0 0
2005–06 Cheltenham T 1 0
2006–07 Cheltenham T 11 0
2007–08 Cheltenham T 0 0
2008–09 Cheltenham T 35 0
2009–10 Cheltenham T 46 0
2010–11 Cheltenham T 46 0
2011–12 Cheltenham T 22 0
2012–13 Cheltenham T 46 0
2013–14 Cheltenham T 45 0
2014–15 Aberdeen 25 0
2015–16 Aberdeen 13 0 **38 0**
2016–17 Wycombe W 3 0
2016–17 *Cheltenham T* 21 0 **273 0**
2017–18 Wycombe W 46 0 **49 0**
2018–19 Port Vale 46 0
2019–20 Port Vale 37 0
2020–21 Port Vale 46 0 **129 0**
2021–22 Exeter C 1 0 **1 0**

CAPRICE, Jake (D) **143 1**
H: 5 10 W: 11 07 b.Lambeth 11-11-92
2011–12 Crystal Palace 0 0
2012–13 Blackpool 0 0
2012–13 *Dagenham & R* 8 0 **8 0**
2013–14 Blackpool 0 0
2013–14 *St Mirren* 6 0 **6 0**
From Lincoln C, Woking, Leyton Orient.
2018–19 Tranmere R 41 0
2019–20 Tranmere R 20 0 **61 0**
2020–21 Exeter C 34 0
2021–22 Exeter C 34 1 **68 1**

COLEY, Josh (M) **25 0**
H: 5 10 W: 11 00 b.Stevenage 24-7-98
From Ardley T, Letchworth GCE, Hitchin T.
2018–19 Norwich C 0 0
2019–20 Norwich C 0 0
2019–20 *Dunfermline Ath* 7 0 **7 0**
From Stotfold, Maidenhead U.
2021–22 Exeter C 18 0 **18 0**

COLLINS, Archie (M) **146 6**
H: 5 9 W: 9 13 b.Taunton 31-8-99
2016–17 Exeter C 0 0
2017–18 Exeter C 0 0
2018–19 Exeter C 26 1
2019–20 Exeter C 36 1
2020–21 Exeter C 46 4
2021–22 Exeter C 38 0 **146 6**

COX, Sonny (F) **0 0**
H: 5 10 b. 11-10-04
2020–21 Exeter C 0 0
2021–22 Exeter C 0 0

DANIEL, Colin (F) **386 33**
H: 5 11 W: 11 07 b.Eastwood 15-2-88
From Eastwood T.
2006–07 Crewe Alex 0 0
2007–08 Crewe Alex 1 0
2008–09 Crewe Alex 13 1 **14 1**
2008–09 *Macclesfield T* 8 0
2009–10 Macclesfield T 38 3
2010–11 Macclesfield T 43 8
2011–12 Macclesfield T 36 2 **125 13**
From Mansfield T.
2013–14 Mansfield T 28 2
2014–15 Port Vale 28 4
2015–16 Port Vale 20 2 **48 6**
2015–16 *Mansfield T* 9 2 **37 4**
2016–17 Blackpool 34 4
2017–18 Blackpool 44 4 **78 8**
2018–19 Peterborough U 20 0 **20 0**
2018–19 Burton Alb 17 0
2019–20 Burton Alb 24 0
2020–21 Burton Alb 19 1 **60 1**
2021–22 Exeter C 4 0 **4 0**

DIABATE, Cheick (D) **18 2**
H: 6 4 W: 13 10 b.Southwark 19-6-01
2019–20 Exeter C 0 0
2020–21 Exeter C 0 0
2021–22 Exeter C 18 2 **18 2**

DIENG, Timothee (M) **273 26**
H: 5 11 W: 12 00 b.Grenoble 9-4-92
2011–12 Brest 0 0
2012–13 Brest 2 0
2013–14 Brest 4 0 **6 0**
2014–15 Oldham Ath 22 0
2015–16 Oldham Ath 38 1 **60 1**
2016–17 Bradford C 39 3
2017–18 Bradford C 26 2 **65 5**
2018–19 Southend U 43 3
2019–20 Southend U 21 2
2020–21 Southend U 36 3 **100 8**
2021–22 Exeter C 42 12 **42 12**

DODD, James (M) **0 0**
H: 5 4 W: 8 11 b.Exeter 27-10-00
2018–19 Exeter C 0 0
2019–20 Exeter C 0 0
2020–21 Exeter C 0 0
2021–22 Exeter C 0 0

DYER, Jordan (D) **2 0**
H: 6 0 W: 12 04 b.Exeter 29-5-00
2018–19 Exeter C 0 0
2019–20 Exeter C 0 0
2020–21 Exeter C 1 0
2021–22 Exeter C 1 0 **2 0**

GROUNDS, Jonathan (D) **395 13**
H: 6 1 W: 12 08 b.Thornaby 2-2-88
2007–08 Middlesbrough 5 0
2008–09 Middlesbrough 2 0
2008–09 *Norwich C* 16 3 **16 3**
2009–10 Middlesbrough 20 0
2010–11 Middlesbrough 6 1
2010–11 *Hibernian* 13 0 **13 0**
2011–12 Middlesbrough 0 0 **33 1**
2011–12 *Chesterfield* 13 0 **13 0**
2011–12 *Yeovil T* 14 0 **14 0**
2012–13 Oldham Ath 44 1
2013–14 Oldham Ath 45 2 **89 3**
2014–15 Birmingham C 45 1
2015–16 Birmingham C 45 1
2016–17 Birmingham C 42 2
2017–18 Birmingham C 26 0
2018–19 Birmingham C 0 0
2018–19 *Bolton W* 13 0 **13 0**
2019–20 Birmingham C 0 0 **158 4**
2020–21 Swindon T 31 0

2021–22 Swindon T 0 0 **31 0**
2021–22 Exeter C 15 2 **15 2**

HARTRIDGE, Alex (D) 60 0
H: 6 1 W: 13 03 b.Torquay 9-3-99
2017–18 Exeter C 0 0
2018–19 Exeter C 3 0
2019–20 Exeter C 0 0
2020–21 Exeter C 29 0
2021–22 Exeter C 28 0 **60 0**

ISEGUAN, Nelson (M) 0 0
b. 11-12-02
2020–21 Exeter C 0 0
2021–22 Exeter C 0 0

JAY, Matt (F) 145 41
H: 5 10 W: 10 12 b.Torbay 27-2-96
2013–14 Exeter C 2 0
2014–15 Exeter C 3 0
2015–16 Exeter C 0 0
2016–17 Exeter C 2 0
2017–18 Exeter C 17 1
2018–19 Exeter C 18 4
2019–20 Exeter C 14 4
2020–21 Exeter C 44 18
2021–22 Exeter C 45 14 **145 41**

KEY, Josh (M) 87 3
H: 5 10 W: 10 12 b.Torquay 19-11-99
2017–18 Exeter C 0 0
2018–19 Exeter C 0 0
2019–20 Exeter C 0 0
2020–21 Exeter C 43 1
2021–22 Exeter C 44 2 **87 3**

KITE, Harry (M) 18 1
H: 5 9 W: 10 12 b.Exeter 29-6-00
2017–18 Exeter C 0 0
2018–19 Exeter C 0 0
2019–20 Exeter C 0 0
2020–21 Exeter C 4 0
2021–22 Exeter C 14 1 **18 1**

LEE, Harry (G) 0 0
b. 20-12-05
2020–21 Exeter C 0 0
2021–22 Exeter C 0 0

NOMBE, Sam (F) 70 10
H: 5 11 W: 11 00 b.Croydon 22-10-98
2016–17 Milton Keynes D 0 0
2017–18 Milton Keynes D 6 0
2018–19 Milton Keynes D 0 0
2019–20 Milton Keynes D 21 2
2020–21 Milton Keynes D 4 0 **31 2**
2020–21 *Luton T* 11 0 **11 0**
2021–22 Exeter C 28 8 **28 8**

POND, Alfie (D) 0 0
H: 6 3 b.Exeter 17-2-04
2020–21 Exeter C 0 0
2021–22 Exeter C 0 0

RAY, George (D) 191 7
H: 5 10 W: 11 03 b.Warrington 13-10-93
Internationals: Wales U21.
2011–12 Crewe Alex 0 0
2012–13 Crewe Alex 4 0
2013–14 Crewe Alex 9 0
2014–15 Crewe Alex 35 2
2015–16 Crewe Alex 22 0
2016–17 Crewe Alex 23 1
2017–18 Crewe Alex 12 0
2018–19 Crewe Alex 32 2 **137 5**
2019–20 Tranmere R 15 0
2020–21 Tranmere R 11 1 **26 1**
2021–22 Exeter C 19 1 **19 1**
2021–22 *Leyton Orient* 9 0 **9 0**

ROWE, Callum (D) 8 0
b.Leicester 2-9-99
2020–21 Aston Villa 0 0
2021–22 Exeter C 8 0 **8 0**

SEYMOUR, Ben (F) 50 1
H: 5 8 W: 9 13 b.Watford 16-4-99
2019–20 Exeter C 11 0
2020–21 Exeter C 33 1
2021–22 Exeter C 6 0 **50 1**

SPARKES, Jack (M) 83 5
H: 5 9 W: 9 13 b.Exeter 29-9-00
2017–18 Exeter C 3 0
2018–19 Exeter C 0 0
2019–20 Exeter C 17 0
2020–21 Exeter C 42 3
2021–22 Exeter C 21 2 **83 5**

STUBBS, Sam (D) 71 3
H: 6 0 W: 10 01 b.Liverpool 20-11-98
From Everton.
2016–17 Wigan Ath 0 0
2017–18 Wigan Ath 0 0
2017–18 *Crewe Alex* 5 0 **5 0**
2018–19 Middlesbrough 0 0
2018–19 *Notts Co* 17 0 **17 0**
2019–20 Middlesbrough 0 0
2019–20 *Hamilton A* 19 0
2019–20 *ADO Den Haag* 3 0 **3 0**
2020–21 Hamilton A 0 0 **19 0**
2020–21 Middlesbrough 0 0
2020–21 Fleetwood T 5 1 **5 1**
2020–21 Exeter C 0 0
2021–22 Exeter C 22 2 **22 2**

SWEENEY, Pierce (D) 241 17
H: 5 10 W: 12 08 b.Dublin 11-9-94
Internationals: Republic of Ireland U17, U19, U21.
2012 Bray W 12 0 **12 0**
2012–13 Reading 0 0
2013–14 Reading 0 0
2014–15 Reading 0 0
2015–16 Reading 0 0
2016–17 Exeter C 29 0
2017–18 Exeter C 40 8
2018–19 Exeter C 43 4
2019–20 Exeter C 36 2
2020–21 Exeter C 38 3
2021–22 Exeter C 43 0 **229 17**

TAYLOR, Kyle (M) 50 2
H: 5 10 W: 11 00 b.Poole 26-5-99
2017–18 Bournemouth 0 0
2018–19 Bournemouth 0 0
2019–20 Bournemouth 0 0
2019–20 *Forest Green R* 5 0 **5 0**
2020–21 Bournemouth 0 0
2020–21 *Southend U* 31 1 **31 1**
2021–22 Bournemouth 0 0
2021–22 Exeter C 14 1 **14 1**

VEALE, Jack (M) 0 0
2020–21 Exeter C 0 0
2021–22 Exeter C 0 0

Players retained or with offer of contract
Hanson, Charlie; Lilley, Michael.

Non-contract
Brown, Scott Peter Andrew.

Scholars
Beardmore, Mitchel Reuben; Billington, Gabriel James; Clark, Alfie George; Collins, Eli; Collins, Zeph; Hanson, Charles Harry; James, Edward George Martin; King, Harrison John; Lilley, Michael; Nevile, Toby John Sandford; Nicholson, Jamie Keletea; O'Connor, Joseph Edward; Sowden, Andrew James; Spencer, George Edward; Stanford Neubronner, Aamir Malichi Ivelaw Deon; Wragg, Joseph.

FLEETWOOD T (34)

ANDREW, Danny (D) 297 18
H: 5 11 W: 11 07 b.Holbeach 23-12-90
2009–10 Peterborough U 2 0 **2 0**
2009–10 *Cheltenham T* 10 0
2010–11 Cheltenham T 43 4
2011–12 Cheltenham T 10 0
2012–13 Cheltenham T 1 0 **64 4**
From Gloucester C, Macclesfield T.
2014–15 Fleetwood T 7 0
2015–16 Fleetwood T 9 0
2016–17 Grimsby T 46 0 **46 0**
2017–18 Doncaster R 4 0
2018–19 Doncaster R 46 4 **50 4**
2019–20 Fleetwood T 35 2
2020–21 Fleetwood T 45 2
2021–22 Fleetwood T 39 6 **135 10**

BAGGLEY, Barry (M) 12 1
H: 5 9 W: 10 01 b.Belfast 11-2-02
Internationals: Northern Ireland U17, U19, U21.
2018–19 Fleetwood T 3 0
2019–20 Fleetwood T 0 0
2020–21 Fleetwood T 2 0
2021–22 Fleetwood T 7 1 **12 1**

BATCH, Billy (D) 0 0
2020–21 Fleetwood T 0 0
2021–22 Fleetwood T 0 0

BATTY, Daniel (M) 111 3
H: 5 10 W: 11 11 b.Featherstone 10-12-97
2016–17 Hull C 0 0
2017–18 Hull C 1 0
2018–19 Hull C 27 0
2019–20 Hull C 30 1
2020–21 Hull C 6 0 **64 1**
2020–21 Fleetwood T 17 0
2021–22 Fleetwood T 30 2 **47 2**

BIGGINS, Harrison (M) 104 8
H: 5 9 W: 12 06 b.Sheffield 15-3-96
From Stocksbridge Park Steels.
2017–18 Fleetwood T 7 0
2018–19 Fleetwood T 23 1
2019–20 Fleetwood T 10 0
2020–21 Fleetwood T 10 0
2020–21 *Barrow* 22 2 **22 2**
2021–22 Fleetwood T 32 5 **82 6**

BIRD, Samuel (D) 0 0
b. 12-3-03
2020–21 Fleetwood T 0 0
2021–22 Fleetwood T 0 0

BOYLE, Dylan (M) 10 0
H: 5 8 W: 9 06 b.Belfast 15-1-02
Internationals: Northern Ireland U17.
2018–19 Fleetwood T 0 0
2019–20 Fleetwood T 0 0
2020–21 Fleetwood T 0 0
2021–22 Fleetwood T 10 0 **10 0**

CAIRNS, Alex (G) 210 0
H: 6 0 W: 11 05 b.Doncaster 4-1-93
2011–12 Leeds U 1 0
2012–13 Leeds U 0 0
2013–14 Leeds U 0 0
2014–15 Leeds U 0 0 **1 0**
2015–16 Chesterfield 0 0
2015–16 Rotherham U 0 0
2016–17 Fleetwood T 30 0
2017–18 Fleetwood T 38 0
2018–19 Fleetwood T 46 0
2019–20 Fleetwood T 25 0
2020–21 Fleetwood T 28 0
2021–22 Fleetwood T 42 0 **209 0**

CAMPS, Callum (M) 274 37
H: 5 11 W: 11 11 b.Stockport 30-11-95
Internationals: Northern Ireland U18, U21.
2012–13 Rochdale 2 0
2013–14 Rochdale 0 0
2014–15 Rochdale 12 1
2015–16 Rochdale 32 5
2016–17 Rochdale 44 8
2017–18 Rochdale 42 2
2018–19 Rochdale 41 3
2019–20 Rochdale 28 6 **201 25**
2020–21 Fleetwood T 42 9
2021–22 Fleetwood T 31 3 **73 12**

CLARKE, Tom (D) 390 19
H: 5 11 W: 12 02 b.Sowerby Bridge 21-12-87
Internationals: England U18, U19.
2004–05 Huddersfield T 12 0
2005–06 Huddersfield T 17 1
2006–07 Huddersfield T 9 0
2007–08 Huddersfield T 3 0
2008–09 Huddersfield T 15 1
2008–09 *Bradford C* 6 0 **6 0**
2009–10 Huddersfield T 21 0
2010–11 Huddersfield T 5 1
2011–12 Huddersfield T 14 0
2011–12 *Leyton Orient* 10 0 **10 0**
2012–13 Huddersfield T 0 0 **96 3**
2013–14 Preston NE 42 4
2014–15 Preston NE 43 1
2015–16 Preston NE 35 0
2016–17 Preston NE 42 4
2017–18 Preston NE 18 2
2018–19 Preston NE 21 1
2019–20 Preston NE 10 0 **211 12**
2020–21 Salford C 32 2
2021–22 Salford C 0 0 **32 2**
2021–22 Fleetwood T 35 2 **35 2**

CONN-CLARKE, Chris (F) 5 0
b. 22-11-01
Internationals: Northern Ireland U17, U19, U21.
2017–18 Glentoran 1 0 **1 0**
2018–19 Burnley 0 0
2019–20 Burnley 0 0
2020–21 Burnley 0 0
2021–22 Fleetwood T 4 0 **4 0**

EDWARDS, Danny (M) 0 0
2020–21 Fleetwood T 0 0
2021–22 Fleetwood T 0 0

GARNER, Gerard (F) 46 10
H: 6 2 W: 11 07 b.Liverpool 2-11-98
2017–18 Fleetwood 0 0
2018–19 Fleetwood T 1 0
2019–20 Fleetwood T 0 0
2020–21 Fleetwood T 17 3
2021–22 Fleetwood T 28 7 **46 10**

GARNER, Joe (F) 453 125
H: 5 10 W: 11 07 b.Blackburn 12-4-88
Internationals: England U16, U17, U19.
2004–05 Blackburn R 0 0
2005–06 Blackburn R 0 0
2006–07 Blackburn R 0 0
2006–07 *Carlisle U* 18 5
2007–08 Carlisle U 31 14
2008–09 Nottingham F 28 7
2009–10 Nottingham F 18 2
2010–11 Nottingham F 0 0
2010–11 *Huddersfield T* 16 0 **16 0**
2010–11 *Scunthorpe U* 18 6 **18 6**
2011–12 Nottingham F 2 0 **48 9**
2011–12 Watford 22 1
2012–13 Watford 2 0 **24 1**
2012–13 *Carlisle U* 16 7 **65 26**
2012–13 Preston NE 14 0

2013–14 Preston NE 35 18
2014–15 Preston NE 37 25
2015–16 Preston NE 41 6
2016–17 Preston NE 2 0 **129 49**
2016–17 Rangers 31 7 **31 7**
2017–18 Ipswich T 32 10 **32 10**
2018–19 Wigan Ath 33 8
2019–20 Wigan Ath 28 2
2020–21 Wigan Ath 11 3 **72 13**
2021–22 Apoel Nicosia 0 0
2021–22 Fleetwood T 18 4 **18 4**
Transferred to APOEL January 2021.

HALLIDAY, Bradley (D) 247 4
H: 5 11 W: 10 10 b.Redcar 10-7-95
2013–14 Middlesbrough 0 0
2014–15 Middlesbrough 0 0
2014–15 *York C* 24 1 **24 1**
2015–16 Middlesbrough 0 0
2015–16 *Hartlepool U* 6 0 **6 0**
2015–16 *Accrington S* 32 0 **32 0**
2016–17 Middlesbrough 0 0
2016–17 Cambridge U 30 1
2017–18 Cambridge U 43 1
2018–19 Cambridge U 38 0 **111 2**
2019–20 Doncaster R 34 0
2020–21 Doncaster R 37 1
2021–22 Doncaster R 0 0 **71 1**
2021–22 Fleetwood T 3 0 **3 0**

HARRISON, Ellis (F) 250 47
H: 5 11 W: 12 06 b.Newport 1-2-94
Internationals: Wales U21.
2010–11 Bristol R 1 0
2011–12 Bristol R 0 0
2012–13 Bristol R 13 3
2013–14 Bristol R 25 1
2014–15 Bristol R 0 0
2015–16 Bristol R 30 7
2015–16 *Hartlepool U* 2 0 **2 0**
2016–17 Bristol R 37 8
2017–18 Bristol R 44 12 **150 31**
2018–19 Ipswich T 16 1 **16 1**
2019–20 Portsmouth 28 5
2020–21 Portsmouth 25 4
2021–22 Portsmouth 11 0 **64 9**
2021–22 Fleetwood T 18 6 **18 6**

HAYES, Cian (F) 24 1
b.Preston 29-6-03
Internationals: Republic of Ireland U19.
2019–20 Fleetwood T 0 0
2020–21 Fleetwood T 0 0
2021–22 Fleetwood T 24 1 **24 1**

HOLGATE, Harrison (D) 24 0
H: 6 1 W: 11 00 b.Leeds 5-10-00
2018–19 Fleetwood T 0 0
2019–20 Fleetwood T 0 0
2020–21 Fleetwood T 18 0
2021–22 Fleetwood T 6 0 **24 0**

JOHNSON, Darnell (D) 25 1
H: 6 1 W: 13 01 b.Leicester 3-9-98
Internationals: England U16, U17, U18, U19, U20.
2019–20 Leicester C 0 0
2019–20 *Hibernian* 1 0 **1 0**
2020–21 Leicester C 0 0
2020–21 *Wigan Ath* 10 0 **10 0**
2020–21 *AFC Wimbledon* 11 0 **11 0**
2021–22 Fleetwood T 3 1 **3 1**

JOHNSTON, Carl (M) 17 0
H: 5 9 W: 10 01 b.Belfast 29-5-02
Internationals: Northern Ireland U17, U19, U21.
From Linfield.
2019–20 Fleetwood T 0 0
2020–21 Fleetwood T 0 0
2021–22 Fleetwood T 17 0 **17 0**

LANE, Paddy (F) 37 5
b.Halifax 18-2-01
Internationals: Northern Ireland U21, Full caps.
From Hyde U.
2021–22 Fleetwood T 37 5 **37 5**

MACADAM, Harvey (M) 10 1
H: 6 4 b.Burnley 9-1-02
From Ashton U.
2021–22 Fleetwood T 10 1 **10 1**

McLAUGHLIN, Conor (D) 281 8
H: 6 0 W: 11 03 b.Belfast 26-7-91
Internationals: Northern Ireland U21, Full caps.
2009–10 Preston NE 0 0
2010–11 Preston NE 7 0
2011–12 Preston NE 17 0 **24 0**
2011–12 *Shrewsbury T* 4 0 **4 0**
2012–13 Fleetwood T 19 0
2013–14 Fleetwood T 35 0
2014–15 Fleetwood T 39 1
2015–16 Fleetwood T 37 2
2016–17 Fleetwood T 42 4
2017–18 Millwall 24 1
2018–19 Millwall 8 0 **32 1**
2019–20 Sunderland 15 0
2020–21 Sunderland 25 0 **40 0**
2021–22 Fleetwood T 9 0 **181 7**

McMILLAN, Max (F) 0 0
H: 6 0 b.York 3-10-02
From Leeds U.
2020–21 Fleetwood T 0 0
2021–22 Fleetwood T 0 0

MORRIS, Shayden (F) 31 2
H: 6 0 W: 10 10 b.Newham 30-3-02
From Southend U.
2019–20 Fleetwood T 0 0
2020–21 Fleetwood T 5 0
2021–22 Fleetwood T 26 2 **31 2**

NSIALA, Aristote (D) 227 6
H: 6 4 W: 13 01 b.Kinshasa 25-3-92
Internationals: DR Congo Full caps.
2009–10 Everton 0 0
2010–11 Everton 0 0
2010–11 *Macclesfield T* 10 0 **10 0**
2011–12 Everton 0 0
2011–12 *Accrington S* 19 0
2012–13 Accrington S 17 0
2013–14 Accrington S 0 0 **36 0**
From Southport, Grimsby T.
2016–17 Hartlepool U 21 1 **21 1**
2016–17 Shrewsbury T 21 1
2017–18 Shrewsbury T 44 3 **65 4**
2018–19 Ipswich T 22 1
2019–20 Ipswich T 3 0
2019–20 *Bolton W* 12 0 **12 0**
2020–21 Ipswich T 27 0
2021–22 Ipswich T 11 0 **63 1**
2021–22 Fleetwood T 20 0 **20 0**

O'HARA, Kieran (G) 99 0
H: 6 3 W: 12 04 b.Manchester 22-4-96
Internationals: Republic of Ireland U21, Full caps.
2015–16 Manchester U 0 0
2015–16 *Morecambe* 5 0
2016–17 Morecambe 0 0 **5 0**
2016–17 Manchester U 0 0
2017–18 Manchester U 0 0
2018–19 Manchester U 0 0
2018–19 *Macclesfield T* 37 0 **37 0**
2019–20 Manchester U 0 0
2019–20 *Burton Alb* 33 0
2020–21 Burton Alb 17 0
2021–22 Burton Alb 0 0 **50 0**
2021–22 Scunthorpe U 3 0 **3 0**
2021–22 Fleetwood T 4 0 **4 0**

PILKINGTON, Anthony (M) 414 79
H: 5 11 W: 12 11 b.Blackburn 6-6-88
Internationals: Republic of Ireland U21, Full caps.
2006–07 Stockport Co 24 5
2007–08 Stockport Co 29 6
2008–09 Stockport Co 24 5 **77 16**
2008–09 Huddersfield T 16 2
2009–10 Huddersfield T 43 7
2010–11 Huddersfield T 31 10 **90 19**
2011–12 Norwich C 30 8
2012–13 Norwich C 30 5
2013–14 Norwich C 15 1 **75 14**
2014–15 Cardiff C 20 1
2015–16 Cardiff C 41 9
2016–17 Cardiff C 34 7
2017–18 Cardiff C 8 3
2018–19 Cardiff C 0 0 **103 20**
2018–19 Wigan Ath 10 0
2019–20 Wigan Ath 16 3 **26 3**
2020–21 East Bengal 17 3 **17 3**
2021–22 Fleetwood T 26 4 **26 4**

RAFFIE, Akiel (M) 0 0
b.Australia 15-2-03
2020–21 Fleetwood T 0 0
2021–22 Fleetwood T 0 0

ROSSITER, Jordan (M) 87 3
H: 5 10 W: 10 10 b.Liverpool 24-3-97
Internationals: England U16, U17, U18, U19.
2013–14 Liverpool 0 0
2014–15 Liverpool 0 0
2015–16 Liverpool 1 0 **1 0**
2016–17 Rangers 4 0
2017–18 Rangers 2 1
2018–19 Rangers 4 0
2018–19 *Bury* 16 1 **16 1**
2019–20 Rangers 0 0 **10 1**
2019–20 *Fleetwood T* 15 0
2020–21 Fleetwood T 35 1
2021–22 Fleetwood T 10 0 **60 1**

TEALE, Connor (D) 0 0
b.Harlow 8-10-02
From Leeds U.
2020–21 Fleetwood T 0 0
2021–22 Fleetwood T 0 0

THIAM, Chiekh (D) 3 0
H: 6 4 b. 27-9-03
From Stockport T.
2021–22 Fleetwood T 3 0 **3 0**

WRIGHT, Harry (G) 0 0
H: 5 11 W: 11 07 b.Ipswich 3-11-98
2018–19 Ipswich T 0 0
2019–20 Ipswich T 0 0
2020 *GAIS* 0 0
2020–21 Ipswich T 0 0
2021–22 Fleetwood T 0 0

Players retained or with offer of contract
Baker, Andrew; Donaghy, Tom; Hoyle, Thomas; Leggett, Oliver; Rees, Luc; Thompson, Ben; White, Kyle; Wilson, Harry.

Scholars
Arthur, Bradley Philip; Brown, Pharrell Dior; Clarke, Harry James; Cragg, Rio Jaden; Eastham, Connor Jake; Fenton, Matthew James; Hand, Ryan David; Johnson, William Jack; Jones, William Thorber; Kearns, Joshua James; Khela, Roman Paul Singh; King, Kyle Harrison; Marsh, Zane Marcel; Smith, Covy-Leigh Mark; Thompson-Prempeh, Donte; Wallace, Jake David.

FOREST GREEN R (35)

ADAMS, Ebou (M) 113 9
H: 5 11 W: 12 00 b.Greenwich 15-1-96
Internationals: Gambia Full caps.
From Dartford.
2017–18 Norwich C 0 0
2017–18 *Shrewsbury T* 5 0 **5 0**
From Ebbsfleet U.
2019–20 Forest Green R 34 4
2020–21 Forest Green R 37 2
2021–22 Forest Green R 37 3 **108 9**

ALLEN, Taylor (M) 14 1
H: 5 10 W: 11 05 b.Walsall 16-6-00
From Romulus, Nuneaton Bor.
2019–20 Forest Green R 5 1
2020–21 Forest Green R 5 0
2021–22 Leamington 0 0
2021–22 Forest Green R 4 0 **14 1**

BELL, Finn (M) 0 0
2020–21 Forest Green R 0 0
2021–22 Forest Green R 0 0

BERNARD, Dominic (D) 87 1
H: 5 11 W: 11 07 b.Gloucester 29-3-97
Internationals: Republic of Ireland U17, U18.
2018–19 Birmingham C 0 0
2019–20 Forest Green R 28 0
2020–21 Forest Green R 25 0
2021–22 Forest Green R 34 1 **87 1**

BUNKER, Harvey (M) 0 0
H: 6 3 b.Portsmouth 15-4-03
2019–20 Forest Green R 0 0
2020–21 Forest Green R 0 0
2021–22 Forest Green R 0 0

CADDEN, Nicky (M) 221 24
H: 5 10 W: 11 00 b.Bellshill 19-9-96
2013–14 Airdrieonians 12 0
2014–15 Airdrieonians 4 0
2015–16 Airdrieonians 24 3 **40 3**
2016–17 Livingston 34 6
2017–18 Livingston 26 1
2018–19 Livingston 12 0 **72 7**
2018–19 *Ayr U* 10 0 **10 0**
2019–20 Greenock Morton 22 5 **22 5**
2020–21 Forest Green R 33 3
2021–22 Forest Green R 44 6 **77 9**

CARGILL, Baily (D) 158 5
H: 6 2 W: 13 10 b.Winchester 5-7-95
Internationals: England U20.
2012–13 Bournemouth 0 0
2013–14 Bournemouth 0 0
2013–14 *Torquay U* 5 0 **5 0**
2014–15 Bournemouth 0 0
2015–16 Bournemouth 0 0
2015–16 *Coventry C* 5 1 **5 1**
2016–17 Bournemouth 1 0
2016–17 *Gillingham* 9 1 **9 1**
2017–18 Bournemouth 0 0 **1 0**
2017–18 *Fleetwood T* 11 0 **11 0**
2017–18 *Partick Thistle* 16 0 **16 0**
2018–19 Milton Keynes D 29 0
2019–20 Milton Keynes D 12 0
2020–21 Milton Keynes D 11 1 **52 1**
2020–21 Forest Green R 23 2
2021–22 Forest Green R 36 0 **59 2**

CARTER, Jack (M) 0 0
2020–21 Forest Green R 0 0
2021–22 Forest Green R 0 0

COVIL, Vaughn (M) 2 0
b. 26-7-03
Internationals: USA U16.
From Southampton.
2019–20 Forest Green R 2 0
2020–21 Forest Green R 0 0
2021–22 Forest Green R 0 0 **2 0**

DIALLO, Sadou (M) **18 0**
H: 5 11 W: 11 05 b.Guinea 10-6-99
Internationals: England U19.
From Manchester C.

2018–19	Wolverhampton W	0	0		
2019–20	Wolverhampton W	0	0		
2019–20	*Accrington S*	9	0	**9**	**0**
2020–21	Wolverhampton W	0	0		
2021–22	Forest Green R	9	0	**9**	**0**

EDWARDS, Opi (M) **4 0**
H: 5 7 W: 10 03 b.Bristol 30-4-99

2017–18	Bristol C	0	0		
2018–19	Bristol C	0	0		
2019–20	Bristol C	0	0		
2020–21	Bristol C	4	0	**4**	**0**
2021–22	Forest Green R	0	0		

EVANS, Jack (D) **2 0**
H: 5 8 W: 10 01 b.Warrington 10-8-00

2019–20	Blackburn R	0	0		
2020–21	Forest Green R	2	0		
2021–22	Forest Green R	0	0	**2**	**0**

GODWIN-MALIFE, Udoka (D) **87 0**
H: 5 11 W: 12 06 b. 9-5-00
From Oxford C.

2018–19	Forest Green R	5	0		
2019–20	Forest Green R	12	0		
2020–21	Forest Green R	44	0		
2021–22	Forest Green R	26	0	**87**	**0**

HENDRY, Regan (M) **93 7**
H: 5 10 W: 11 07 b.Edinburgh 21-1-98
Internationals: Scotland U16, U17.

2017–18	Celtic	0	0		
2017–18	*Raith R*	11	0		
2018–19	Celtic	0	0		
2018–19	*Raith R*	4	0		
2019–20	Raith R	22	1		
2020–21	Raith R	25	3		
2021–22	Raith R	0	0	**62**	**4**
2021–22	Forest Green R	31	3	**31**	**3**

MARCH, Josh (F) **63 12**
H: 5 9 W: 13 03 b.Stourbridge 18-3-97

2019–20	Forest Green R	10	2		
2020–21	Forest Green R	4	0		
2020–21	*Harrogate T*	14	5	**14**	**5**
2021–22	Forest Green R	35	5	**49**	**7**

MATT, Jamille (F) **299 82**
H: 6 1 W: 11 11 b.Walsall 20-10-89
From Sutton Coldfield T, Kidderminster H.

2012–13	Fleetwood T	14	3		
2013–14	Fleetwood T	25	8		
2014–15	Fleetwood T	0	0		
2015–16	Fleetwood T	17	3	**56**	**14**
2015–16	*Stevenage*	8	1	**8**	**1**
2015–16	*Plymouth Arg*	11	5	**11**	**5**
2016–17	Blackpool	32	3		
2017–18	Blackpool	0	0	**32**	**3**
2017–18	*Grimsby T*	34	4	**34**	**4**
2018–19	Newport Co	43	14		
2019–20	Newport Co	33	6	**76**	**20**
2020–21	Forest Green R	36	16		
2021–22	Forest Green R	46	19	**82**	**35**

McGEE, Luke (G) **166 0**
H: 6 2 W: 12 08 b.Edgware 2-9-95
Internationals: England U17.

2014–15	Tottenham H	0	0		
2015–16	Tottenham H	0	0		
2016–17	Tottenham H	0	0		
2016–17	*Peterborough U*	39	0	**39**	**0**
2017–18	Portsmouth	44	0		
2018–19	Portsmouth	0	0		
2019–20	Portsmouth	0	0	**44**	**0**
2019–20	*Bradford C*	4	0	**4**	**0**
2020–21	Forest Green R	33	0		
2021–22	Forest Green R	46	0	**79**	**0**

MOORE-TAYLOR, Jordan (D) **266 15**
H: 5 10 W: 13 01 b.Exeter 21-1-94

2012–13	Exeter C	7	0		
2013–14	Exeter C	29	1		
2014–15	Exeter C	26	2		
2015–16	Exeter C	32	0		
2016–17	Exeter C	42	5		
2017–18	Exeter C	24	2	**160**	**10**
2018–19	Milton Keynes D	23	1		
2019–20	Milton Keynes D	14	0	**37**	**1**
2020–21	Forest Green R	29	2		
2021–22	Forest Green R	40	2	**69**	**4**

STEVENS, Mathew (F) **108 31**
H: 5 11 W: 11 09 b.Frimley 12-2-98

2015–16	Barnet	10	1	**10**	**1**
2016–17	Peterborough U	1	0		
2017–18	Peterborough U	0	0		
2018–19	Peterborough U	3	0	**4**	**0**
2019–20	Forest Green R	29	4		
2020–21	Forest Green R	10	2		
2020–21	*Stevenage*	18	1	**18**	**1**
2021–22	Forest Green R	37	23	**76**	**29**

STEVENSON, Ben (M) **161 8**
H: 6 0 W: 10 08 b.Leicester 23-3-97

2015–16	Coventry C	0	0		
2016–17	Coventry C	28	2		
2017–18	Coventry C	5	0	**33**	**2**
2017–18	Wolverhampton W	0	0		
2017–18	*Colchester U*	13	2		
2018–19	Wolverhampton W	0	0		
2018–19	Colchester U	14	0		
2019–20	Colchester U	28	2		
2020–21	Colchester U	32	2		
2021–22	Colchester U	0	0	**87**	**6**
2021–22	Forest Green R	41	0	**41**	**0**

SWEENEY, Dan (M) **82 1**
H: 6 3 W: 12 04 b.Kingston upon Thames 25-4-94
Internationals: England C.
From AFC Wimbledon, Kingstonian, Dulwich Hamlet, Maidstone U.

2016–17	Barnet	4	0		
2017–18	Barnet	21	0	**25**	**0**

From Barnet.

2020–21	Forest Green R	21	0		
2021–22	Forest Green R	36	1	**57**	**1**

THOMAS, Lewis (G) **28 0**
H: 6 0 W: 11 00 b.Mancelton 20-9-97
Internationals: Wales U17.
From Swansea C.

2018–19	Forest Green R	0	0		
2019–20	Forest Green R	15	0		
2020–21	Forest Green R	13	0		
2021–22	Forest Green R	0	0	**28**	**0**

WHITEHOUSE, Elliott (M) **117 8**
H: 5 11 W: 12 08 b.Worksop 27-10-93
Internationals: England C.

2012–13	Sheffield U	3	0		
2013–14	Sheffield U	0	0	**3**	**0**
2013–14	*York C*	15	0	**15**	**0**
2014–15	Notts Co	7	1	**7**	**1**

From Nuneaton Bor, Lincoln C.

2017–18	Lincoln C	32	2	**32**	**2**

From FC Halifax T, Nuneaton Bor.

2019–20	Grimsby T	33	3	**33**	**3**
2020–21	Forest Green R	27	2		
2021–22	Forest Green R	0	0	**27**	**2**

WILSON, Kane (D) **133 5**
H: 5 10 W: 11 03 b.Birmingham 11-3-00
Internationals: England U16, U17.

2016–17	WBA	0	0		
2017–18	WBA	0	0		
2017–18	*Exeter C*	19	1		
2018–19	WBA	0	0		
2018–19	*Walsall*	14	0	**14**	**0**
2018–19	*Exeter C*	17	0	**36**	**1**
2019–20	WBA	0	0		
2019–20	*Tranmere R*	13	0	**13**	**0**
2020–21	Forest Green R	25	1		
2021–22	Forest Green R	45	3	**70**	**4**

Players retained or with offer of contract
Bennett, Murphy; McIntosh, Marcel; Young, Jake.

Scholars
Baxter, Benjamin David; Bennett, Murphy John; Clapp, Thomas Patrick; Dunn, Curtis Morgan; John, Dylan Ryan; Mason, Joshua Lewis; McIntosh, Marcel Philip; McLaughlin, Jotham Edward; Olawale Oyebamiji, Jireh Joshua; Thompson-Roberts, Jago; Woodhouse, Owen.

FULHAM (36)

ABLADE, Terry (F) **32 4**
b.Accra 12-10-01
Internationals: Finland U16, U17, U18, U19, U21.

2017	Jazz	14	2		
2018	Jazz	6	2	**20**	**4**
2018–19	Fulham	0	0		
2019–20	Fulham	0	0		
2020–21	Fulham	0	0		
2021–22	Fulham	0	0		
2021–22	*AFC Wimbledon*	12	0	**12**	**0**

ABRAHAM, Timmy (F) **26 0**
H: 6 1 W: 12 02 b.Lambeth 28-12-00
From Charlton Ath.

2019–20	Fulham	0	0		
2019–20	*Bristol R*	4	0	**4**	**0**
2020–21	Fulham	0	0		
2020–21	*Plymouth Arg*	3	0	**3**	**0**
2020–21	*Raith R*	7	0		
2021–22	Raith R	0	0	**7**	**0**
2021–22	Fulham	0	0		
2021–22	*Newport Co*	12	0	**12**	**0**

ADARABIOYO, Tosin (D) **137 5**
H: 6 3 W: 12 08 b.Manchester 24-9-97
Internationals: England U16, U17, U18, U19.

2014–15	Manchester C	0	0		
2015–16	Manchester C	0	0		
2016–17	Manchester C	0	0		
2017–18	Manchester C	0	0		
2018–19	Manchester C	0	0		
2018–19	*WBA*	29	0	**29**	**0**
2019–20	Manchester C	0	0		
2019–20	*Blackburn R*	34	3	**34**	**3**
2020–21	Fulham	33	0		
2021–22	Fulham	41	2	**74**	**2**

AMEYAW, Eric (D) **0 0**
b. 17-6-02

2020–21	Fulham	0	0		
2021–22	Fulham	0	0		

ASHBY-HAMMOND, Luca (G) **0 0**
b.Kingston upon Thames 25-3-01
Internationals: England U16, U17, U18, U19, U20.

2018–19	Fulham	0	0		
2019–20	Fulham	0	0		
2020–21	Fulham	0	0		
2021–22	Fulham	0	0		

BRYAN, Joe (D) **315 19**
H: 5 7 W: 11 05 b.Bristol 17-9-93

2011–12	Bristol C	1	0		
2012–13	Bristol C	13	0		
2012–13	*Plymouth Arg*	10	1	**10**	**1**
2013–14	Bristol C	21	2		
2014–15	Bristol C	41	6		
2015–16	Bristol C	39	2		
2016–17	Bristol C	44	1		
2017–18	Bristol C	43	5		
2018–19	Bristol C	1	0	**203**	**16**
2018–19	Fulham	28	0		
2019–20	Fulham	43	1		
2020–21	Fulham	16	1		
2021–22	Fulham	15	0	**102**	**2**

CAIRNEY, Tom (M) **370 48**
H: 6 0 W: 11 05 b.Nottingham 20-1-91
Internationals: Scotland U19, U21, Full caps.
From Leeds U.

2009–10	Hull C	11	1		
2010–11	Hull C	22	1		
2011–12	Hull C	27	0		
2012–13	Hull C	10	0		
2013–14	Hull C	0	0	**70**	**2**
2013–14	Blackburn R	37	5		
2014–15	Blackburn R	39	3	**76**	**8**
2015–16	Fulham	39	8		
2016–17	Fulham	45	12		
2017–18	Fulham	34	5		
2018–19	Fulham	31	1		
2019–20	Fulham	39	8		
2020–21	Fulham	10	1		
2021–22	Fulham	26	3	**224**	**38**

CARVALHO, Fabio (M) **40 11**
H: 5 7 W: 9 13 b.Lisbon 30-8-02
Internationals: England U16, U17, U18. Portugal U21.

2020–21	Oliveirense	0	0		
2020–21	Fulham	4	1		
2021–22	Fulham	36	10	**40**	**11**

CHALOBAH, Nathaniel (D) **198 12**
H: 6 1 W: 11 11 b.Sierra Leone 12-12-94
Internationals: England U16, U17, U19, U20, U21, Full caps.

2010–11	Chelsea	0	0		
2011–12	Chelsea	0	0		
2012–13	Chelsea	0	0		
2012–13	*Watford*	38	5		
2013–14	Chelsea	0	0		
2013–14	*Nottingham F*	12	2	**12**	**2**
2013–14	*Middlesbrough*	19	1	**19**	**1**
2014–15	Chelsea	0	0		
2014–15	*Burnley*	4	0	**4**	**0**
2014–15	*Reading*	15	1	**15**	**1**
2015–16	Chelsea	0	0		
2015–16	*Napoli*	5	0	**5**	**0**
2016–17	Chelsea	10	0	**10**	**0**
2017–18	Watford	6	0		
2018–19	Watford	9	0		
2019–20	Watford	22	0		
2020–21	Watford	38	3		
2021–22	Watford	0	0	**113**	**8**
2021–22	Fulham	20	0	**20**	**0**

CHRISTIE, Cyrus (D) **358 9**
H: 6 2 W: 12 04 b.Coventry 30-9-92
Internationals: Republic of Ireland Full caps.

2011–12	Coventry C	37	0		
2012–13	Coventry C	31	2		
2013–14	Coventry C	34	0	**102**	**2**
2014–15	Derby Co	38	0		
2015–16	Derby Co	42	1		
2016–17	Derby Co	27	1		
2017–18	Derby Co	0	0	**107**	**2**
2017–18	Middlesbrough	25	1	**25**	**1**
2017–18	Fulham	5	0		
2018–19	Fulham	28	0		
2019–20	Fulham	24	1		
2020–21	Fulham	0	0		
2020–21	*Nottingham F*	44	0	**44**	**0**
2021–22	Fulham	0	0	**57**	**1**
2021–22	*Swansea C*	23	3	**23**	**3**

DECORDOVA-REID, Bobby (M) 319 53
H: 5 7 W: 10 10 b.Bristol 2-2-93
Internationals: Jamaica Full caps.

2010–11	Bristol C	1	0		
2011–12	Bristol C	0	0		
2011–12	*Cheltenham T*	1	0	**1**	**0**
2012–13	Bristol C	4	1		
2012–13	*Oldham Ath*	7	0	**7**	**0**
2013–14	Bristol C	24	1		
2014–15	Bristol C	2	0		
2014–15	*Plymouth Arg*	33	3	**33**	**3**
2015–16	Bristol C	28	2		
2016–17	Bristol C	30	3		
2017–18	Bristol C	46	19	**135**	**26**
2018–19	Cardiff C	27	5		
2019–20	Cardiff C	1	0	**28**	**5**
2019–20	Fulham	41	6		
2020–21	Fulham	33	5		
2021–22	Fulham	41	8	**115**	**19**

FOSSEY, Marlon (D) 22 1
H: 5 10 W: 12 00 b.Los Angeles 9-9-98
Internationals: USA U20.

2019–20	Fulham	0	0		
2020–21	Fulham	0	0		
2020–21	*Shrewsbury T*	7	0		
2021–22	Shrewsbury T	0	0	**7**	**0**
2021–22	Fulham	0	0		
2021–22	*Bolton W*	15	1	**15**	**1**

FRANCOIS, Tyrese (M) 3 0
H: 5 6 W: 8 11 b.Campbelltown 16-7-00
Internationals: Australia U23.

2019–20	Fulham	0	0		
2020–21	Fulham	1	0		
2021–22	Fulham	2	0	**3**	**0**

GAZZANIGA, Paulo (G) 116 0
H: 6 5 W: 14 02 b.Santa Fe, Argentina 2-1-92
Internationals: Argentina Full caps.

2011–12	Gillingham	20	0	**20**	**0**
2012–13	Southampton	9	0		
2013–14	Southampton	8	0		
2014–15	Southampton	2	0		
2015–16	Southampton	2	0		
2016–17	Southampton	0	0	**21**	**0**
2016–17	*Rayo Vallecano*	32	0	**32**	**0**
2017–18	Tottenham H	1	0		
2018–19	Tottenham H	3	0		
2019–20	Tottenham H	18	0		
2020–21	Tottenham H	0	0	**22**	**0**
2020–21	*Elche*	8	0	**8**	**0**
2021–22	Fulham	13	0	**13**	**0**

HECTOR, Michael (D) 295 15
H: 6 4 W: 12 13 b.Newham 19-7-92
Internationals: Jamaica Full caps.

2009–10	Reading	0	0		
2010–11	Reading	0	0		
2011	*Dundalk*	11	2	**11**	**2**
2011–12	Reading	0	0		
2011–12	*Barnet*	27	2	**27**	**2**
2012–13	Reading	0	0		
2012–13	*Shrewsbury T*	8	0	**8**	**0**
2012–13	*Aldershot T*	8	1	**8**	**1**
2012–13	*Cheltenham T*	18	1	**18**	**1**
2013–14	Reading	9	0		
2013–14	*Aberdeen*	20	1	**20**	**1**
2014–15	Reading	41	3		
2015–16	Chelsea	0	0		
2015–16	*Reading*	30	1	**80**	**4**
2016–17	Chelsea	0	0		
2016–17	*Eintracht Frankfurt*	22	1	**22**	**1**
2017–18	Chelsea	0	0		
2017–18	*Hull C*	36	1	**36**	**1**
2018–19	Chelsea	0	0		
2018–19	*Sheffield W*	37	2	**37**	**2**
2019–20	Fulham	20	0		
2020–21	Fulham	4	0		
2021–22	Fulham	4	0	**28**	**0**

HILTON, Sonny (M) 0 0
H: 5 5 W: 9 00 b.Liverpool 30-1-01
Internationals: England U16, U17, U19.

2020–21	Fulham	0	0		
2021–22	Fulham	0	0		

IVAN CAVALEIRO, Ricardo (M) 249 32
H: 5 9 W: 11 07 b.Vialonga 18-10-93
Internationals: Portugal U17, U18, U19, U20, U21, Full caps.

2012–13	Benfica	0	0		
2013–14	Benfica	8	0		
2014–15	Benfica	0	0	**8**	**0**
2014–15	*Deportivo la Coruna*	34	3	**34**	**3**
2015–16	Monaco	12	1		
2016–17	Monaco	2	0	**14**	**1**
2016–17	Wolverhampton W	31	5		
2017–18	Wolverhampton W	42	9		
2018–19	Wolverhampton W	23	3	**96**	**17**
2019–20	Fulham	43	6		
2020–21	Fulham	36	3		
2021–22	Fulham	18	2	**97**	**11**

JASPER, Sylvester (F) 33 2
H: 5 11 W: 10 03 b.Southwark 13-9-01
Internationals: Bulgaria U21.

2019–20	Fulham	2	0		
2020–21	Fulham	0	0		
2021–22	Fulham	0	0	**2**	**0**
2021–22	*Colchester U*	18	2	**18**	**2**
2021–22	*Hibernian*	13	0	**13**	**0**

KAMARA, Aboubakar (F) 159 31
H: 5 10 W: 12 08 b.Gonesse 7-3-95
Internationals: Mauritania Full caps.

2013–14	Monaco	0	0		
2014–15	Monaco	2	0	**2**	**0**
2015–16	Kortrijk	12	0	**12**	**0**
2015–16	Amiens	16	5		
2016–17	Amiens	29	10	**45**	**15**
2017–18	Fulham	30	7		
2018–19	Fulham	13	3		
2018–19	*Yeni Malatyaspor*	10	1	**10**	**1**
2019–20	Fulham	25	4		
2020–21	Fulham	11	0		
2020–21	*Dijon*	10	1		
2021–22	Fulham	1	0	**80**	**14**
2021–22	*Dijon*	0	0	**10**	**1**

Transferred to Aris Thessaloniki, August 2021.

KEBANO, Neeskens (M) 256 47
H: 5 11 W: 11 11 b.Montereau 10-3-92
Internationals: France U17, U18, U19, U20. DR Congo Full caps.

2010–11	Paris Saint-Germain	3	0		
2011–12	Paris Saint-Germain	0	0		
2012–13	Paris Saint-Germain	0	0	**3**	**0**
2012–13	*Caen*	12	1	**12**	**1**
2013–14	Charleroi	26	5		
2014–15	Charleroi	33	12		
2015–16	Charleroi	5	1	**64**	**18**
2015–16	Genk	34	6		
2016–17	Genk	3	0	**37**	**6**
2016–17	Fulham	28	6		
2017–18	Fulham	26	3		
2018–19	Fulham	7	0		
2019–20	Fulham	16	3		
2020–21	Fulham	5	0		
2020–21	*Middlesbrough*	18	1	**18**	**1**
2021–22	Fulham	40	9	**122**	**21**

KNOCKAERT, Anthony (M) 354 58
H: 5 8 W: 10 12 b.Lille 20-11-91
Internationals: France U20, U21.

2011–12	Guingamp	34	10	**34**	**10**
2012–13	Leicester C	42	8		
2013–14	Leicester C	42	5		
2014–15	Leicester C	9	0	**93**	**13**
2015–16	Standard Liege	20	5	**20**	**5**
2015–16	Brighton & HA	19	5		
2016–17	Brighton & HA	45	15		
2017–18	Brighton & HA	33	3		
2018–19	Brighton & HA	30	2	**127**	**25**
2019–20	Fulham	42	3		
2020–21	Fulham	0	0		
2020–21	*Nottingham F*	34	2	**34**	**2**
2021–22	Fulham	4	0	**46**	**3**

KONGOLO, Terence (D) 167 2
H: 6 0 W: 11 00 b.Rotterdam 14-2-94
Internationals: Netherlands U16, U17, U18, U19, U20, U21, Full caps.

2011–12	Feyenoord	1	0		
2012–13	Feyenoord	5	0		
2013–14	Feyenoord	17	0		
2014–15	Feyenoord	31	0		
2015–16	Feyenoord	29	0		
2016–17	Feyenoord	23	1	**106**	**1**
2017–18	Monaco	3	0	**3**	**0**
2017–18	*Huddersfield T*	13	0		
2018–19	Huddersfield T	32	1		
2019–20	Huddersfield T	11	0	**56**	**1**
2019–20	*Fulham*	1	0		
2020–21	Fulham	1	0		
2021–22	Fulham	0	0	**2**	**0**

LARKECHE, Ziyad (D) 0 0
H: 6 0 W: 10 08 b.Paris 19-9-02
Internationals: France U20.
From Paris Saint-Germain.

2020–21	Fulham	0	0		
2021–22	Fulham	0	0		

LAS, Damian (G) 0 0
H: 6 1 W: 11 05 b.Des Plaines 11-4-02
Internationals: USA U17.
From North Carolina.

2020–21	Fulham	0	0		
2021–22	Fulham	0	0		

Transferred to Austin FC, January 2022.

MAWSON, Alfie (D) 218 20
H: 6 2 W: 14 02 b.Hillingdon 19-1-94
Internationals: England U21.

2012–13	Brentford	0	0		
2013–14	Brentford	0	0		
2014–15	Brentford	0	0		
2014–15	*Wycombe W*	45	6	**45**	**6**
2015–16	Barnsley	45	6		
2016–17	Barnsley	4	2	**49**	**8**
2016–17	Swansea C	27	4		
2017–18	Swansea C	38	2	**65**	**6**
2018–19	Fulham	15	0		
2019–20	Fulham	27	0		
2020–21	Fulham	0	0		
2020–21	*Bristol C*	11	0	**11**	**0**
2021–22	Fulham	6	0	**48**	**0**

McAVOY, Connor (D) 0 0
b.Chertsey 16-2-02
Internationals: Scotland U17, U19.

2020–21	Fulham	0	0		
2021–22	Fulham	0	0		

MITROVIC, Aleksandar (F) 352 165
H: 6 2 W: 13 10 b.Smederevo 16-9-94
Internationals: Serbia U19, U21, Full caps.

2011–12	Teleoptik	25	7	**25**	**7**
2012–13	Partizan Belgrade	25	10		
2013–14	Partizan Belgrade	3	3	**28**	**13**
2013–14	Anderlecht	32	16		
2014–15	Anderlecht	37	20	**69**	**36**
2015–16	Newcastle U	34	9		
2016–17	Newcastle U	25	4		
2017–18	Newcastle U	6	1	**65**	**14**
2017–18	*Fulham*	17	12		
2018–19	Fulham	37	11		
2019–20	Fulham	40	26		
2020–21	Fulham	27	3		
2021–22	Fulham	44	43	**165**	**95**

ODOI, Denis (D) 410 12
H: 5 10 W: 11 09 b.Leuven 27-5-88
Internationals: Belgium U20, U21, Full caps.

2006–07	Oud-Heverlee Leuven	3	0		
2007–08	Oud-Heverlee Leuven	21	0		
2008–09	Oud-Heverlee Leuven	33	3	**57**	**3**
2009–10	Sint-Truiden	26	1		
2010–11	Sint-Truiden	33	2	**59**	**3**
2011–12	Anderlecht	19	0		
2012–13	Anderlecht	14	0	**33**	**0**
2013–14	Lokeren	37	1		
2014–15	Lokeren	35	0		
2015–16	Lokeren	35	1	**107**	**2**
2016–17	Fulham	30	2		
2017–18	Fulham	38	1		
2018–19	Fulham	31	0		
2019–20	Fulham	34	0		
2020–21	Fulham	3	0		
2021–22	Fulham	18	1	**154**	**4**

Transferred to Club Brugge, February 2022.

ONOMAH, Joshua (M) 123 8
H: 5 11 W: 10 01 b.Enfield 27-4-97
Internationals: England U16, U17, U18, U19, U20, U21.

2013–14	Tottenham H	0	0		
2014–15	Tottenham H	0	0		
2015–16	Tottenham H	8	0		
2016–17	Tottenham H	5	0		
2017–18	Tottenham H	0	0		
2017–18	*Aston Villa*	33	4	**33**	**4**
2018–19	Tottenham H	0	0	**13**	**0**
2018–19	*Sheffield W*	15	0	**15**	**0**
2019–20	Fulham	31	3		
2020–21	Fulham	11	0		
2021–22	Fulham	20	1	**62**	**4**

OPOKU, Jerome (D) 74 1
b.London 14-10-98

2019–20	Fulham	0	0		
2019–20	*Accrington S*	21	0	**21**	**0**
2020–21	Fulham	0	0		
2020–21	*Plymouth Arg*	33	1	**33**	**1**
2021–22	Fulham	0	0		
2021–22	*Velje*	20	0	**20**	**0**

PAGE, Jonathon (M) 0 0
b.Chertsey 6-9-01

2020–21	Fulham	0	0		
2021–22	Fulham	0	0		

PAJAZITI, Adrion (M) 0 0
H: 5 11 b.Camden 16-11-02
Internationals: Albania U19. Kosovo U21.

2020–21	Fulham	0	0		
2021–22	Fulham	0	0		

RAMIREZ, Fabricio (G) 170 0
H: 6 1 W: 12 02 b.Las Palmas 31-12-87
Internationals: Spain U20.

2006–07	Deportivo la Coruna	0	0		
2007–08	Deportivo la Coruna	6	0		
2008–09	Deportivo la Coruna	0	0		
2009–10	Valladolid	1	0		
2010–11	Valladolid	0	0	**1**	**0**
2010–11	*Recreativo*	40	0	**40**	**0**
2011–12	Real Betis	15	0		
2012–13	Real Betis	2	0	**17**	**0**
2013–14	Deportivo la Coruna	6	0		
2014–15	Deportivo la Coruna	31	0		
2015–16	Deportivo la Coruna	0	0	**43**	**0**
2016–17	Besiktas	32	0		
2017–18	Besiktas	34	0	**66**	**0**
2018–19	Fulham	2	0		
2019–20	Fulham	0	0		
2019–20	*Mallorca*	1	0	**1**	**0**

2020–21 Fulham 0 0
2021–22 Fulham 0 0 **2 0**

REAM, Tim (D) 503 10
H: 6 1 W: 11 05 b.St Louis 5-10-87
Internationals: USA Full caps.
2006 St Louis Billikens 19 0
2007 St Louis Billikens 19 0
2008 St Louis Billikens 22 0
2008 Chicago Fire 12 0
2009 Chicago Fire 7 0 **19 0**
2009 St Louis Billikens 22 6 **82 6**
2010 New York RB 30 1
2011 New York RB 28 0 **58 1**
2011–12 Bolton W 13 0
2012–13 Bolton W 15 0
2013–14 Bolton W 42 0
2014–15 Bolton W 44 0 **114 0**
2015–16 Fulham 29 0
2016–17 Fulham 34 1
2017–18 Fulham 44 1
2018–19 Fulham 26 0
2019–20 Fulham 44 0
2020–21 Fulham 7 0
2021–22 Fulham 46 1 **230 3**

REED, Harrison (M) 184 4
H: 5 11 W: 11 09 b.Worthing 27-1-95
Internationals: England U19, U20.
2011–12 Southampton 0 0
2012–13 Southampton 0 0
2013–14 Southampton 4 0
2014–15 Southampton 9 0
2015–16 Southampton 1 0
2016–17 Southampton 3 0
2017–18 Southampton 0 0
2017–18 *Norwich C* 39 1 **39 1**
2018–19 Southampton 0 0
2018–19 *Blackburn R* 33 3 **33 3**
2019–20 Southampton 0 0 **17 0**
2019–20 *Fulham* 25 0
2020–21 Fulham 31 0
2021–22 Fulham 39 0 **95 0**

ROBINSON, Antonee (D) 158 3
H: 6 0 W: 11 07 b.Milton Keynes 8-8-97
Internationals: USA U18, Full caps.
2015–16 Everton 0 0
2016–17 Everton 0 0
2017–18 Everton 0 0
2017–18 *Bolton W* 30 0 **30 0**
2018–19 Everton 0 0
2018–19 *Wigan Ath* 26 0
2019–20 Wigan Ath 38 1 **64 1**
2020–21 Fulham 28 0
2021–22 Fulham 36 2 **64 2**

RODAK, Marek (G) 168 0
H: 6 4 W: 10 12 b.Kosice 13-12-96
Internationals: Slovakia U17, U19, U21, Full caps.
2014–15 Fulham 0 0
2015–16 Fulham 0 0
2016–17 Fulham 0 0
2016–17 *Accrington S* 20 0 **20 0**
2017–18 Fulham 0 0
2017–18 *Rotherham U* 35 0
2018–19 Fulham 0 0
2018–19 *Rotherham U* 45 0 **80 0**
2019–20 Fulham 33 0
2020–21 Fulham 2 0
2021–22 Fulham 33 0 **68 0**

RODRIGO MUNIZ, Carvalho (F) 44 9
H: 6 0 W: 12 06 b.Sao Domingos de Prata 4-5-01
2020 Flamengo 4 0
2020 *Coritiba* 6 1 **6 1**
2021 Flamengo 9 3
2021–22 Flamengo 0 0 **13 3**
2021–22 Fulham 25 5 **25 5**

SERI, Jean (M) 261 18
H: 5 5 W: 10 08 b.Grand-Bereby 19-7-91
Internationals: Ivory Coast U23, Full caps.
2013–14 Pacos de Ferreira 21 1
2014–15 Pacos de Ferreira 33 1 **54 2**
2015–16 Nice 38 3
2016–17 Nice 34 7
2017–18 Nice 31 2 **103 12**
2018–19 Fulham 32 1
2019–20 Fulham 0 0
2019–20 *Galatasaray* 27 2 **27 2**
2020–21 Fulham 0 0
2020–21 *Bordeaux* 12 0
2021–22 Fulham 33 1 **65 2**
2021–22 *Bordeaux* 0 0 **12 0**

SESSEGNON, Steven (D) 40 0
H: 5 8 W: 10 06 b.Roehampton 18-5-00
Internationals: England U16, U17, U18, U19, U20, U21.
2017–18 Fulham 0 0
2018–19 Fulham 0 0
2019–20 Fulham 14 0
2020–21 Fulham 0 0
2020–21 *Bristol C* 16 0 **16 0**
2021–22 Fulham 0 0 **14 0**
2021–22 *Plymouth Arg* 10 0 **10 0**

STANSFIELD, Jay (F) 2 0
H: 5 11 W: 10 12 b.Exeter 24-11-02
Internationals: England U18, U20.
From Exeter C.
2019–20 Fulham 1 0
2020–21 Fulham 0 0
2021–22 Fulham 1 0 **2 0**

TETE, Kenny (D) 126 3
H: 5 9 W: 11 00 b.Amsterdam 9-10-95
Internationals: Netherlands U17, U19, U20, U21, Full caps.
2013–14 Ajax 0 0
2014–15 Ajax 5 0
2015–16 Ajax 21 0
2016–17 Ajax 5 0 **31 0**
2017–18 Lyon 22 1
2018–19 Lyon 13 0
2019–20 Lyon 18 0
2020–21 Lyon 0 0 **53 1**
2020–21 Fulham 22 0
2021–22 Fulham 20 2 **42 2**

TIEHI, Jean-Pierre (F) 0 0
b.Paris 24-1-02
From Le Havre.
2020–21 Fulham 0 0
2021–22 Fulham 0 0

WICKENS, George (G) 0 0
b.Petersfield 8-11-01
Internationals: England U18.
2020–21 Fulham 0 0
2021–22 Fulham 0 0

WILSON, Harry (M) 169 46
H: 5 8 W: 11 00 b.Wrexham 22-3-97
Internationals: Wales U17, U19, U21, Full caps.
2015–16 Liverpool 0 0
2015–16 *Crewe Alex* 7 0 **7 0**
2016–17 Liverpool 0 0
2017–18 Liverpool 0 0
2017–18 *Hull C* 13 7 **13 7**
2018–19 Liverpool 0 0
2018–19 *Derby Co* 40 15 **40 15**
2019–20 Liverpool 0 0
2019–20 *Bournemouth* 31 7 **31 7**
2020–21 Liverpool 0 0
2020–21 *Cardiff C* 37 7 **37 7**
2021–22 Fulham 41 10 **41 10**

ZAMBO, Andre-Franck (M) 197 2
H: 6 0 W: 11 09 b.Yaounde 16-11-95
Internationals: Cameroon Full caps.
From Reims.
2015–16 Marseille 9 0
2016–17 Marseille 33 0
2017–18 Marseille 37 0 **79 0**
2018–19 Fulham 22 0
2019–20 Fulham 0 0
2019–20 *Villarreal* 36 2 **36 2**
2020–21 Fulham 36 0
2021–22 Fulham 3 0 **61 0**
2021–22 *Napoli* 21 0 **21 0**

Players retained or with offer of contract
Antonsson, Thorsteinn; Araujo, Harvey; Ashby-Hammond, Taye; Borto, Alexander; Bowat, Ibane; Bowie, Kieron; D'Auria-Henry, Luciano; Dibley-Dias, Matthew; Odutayo, Idris; O'Neill, Oliver; Parkes, Stefan; Tanton Pedraza, Devan; Williams, Jay.

Scholars
Allen, Michael Thomas; Avenell, Caelan Brandon; Benjamin, Xavier Deandrae; Caton, Tyler Lewis; Harris, Luke Bernard; Lanquedoc, Imani Jamal; McNally, Alfie Shane; Okkas, Georgios; Olakigbe, Michael Oluwakorede; Parker, Murphy; Robinson, Charlie James; Sanderson, Oliver; Splatt, Delano M'Coy; Wildbore, Jaylan Sebastian; Works, Terrell Lawreece Isaiah.

GILLINGHAM (37)

AKEHURST, Bailey (D) 5 0
H: 5 10 b. 8-9-03
2021–22 Gillingham 5 0 **5 0**

CARAYOL, Mustapha (M) 247 35
H: 5 10 W: 11 09 b.Gambia 10-6-89
Internationals: Gambia Full caps.
2007–08 Milton Keynes D 0 0
From Torquay U.
2009–10 Torquay U 20 6 **20 6**
2010–11 Lincoln C 33 3 **33 3**
2011–12 Bristol R 30 4
2012–13 Bristol R 0 0 **30 4**
2012–13 Middlesbrough 18 3
2013–14 Middlesbrough 32 8
2014–15 Middlesbrough 0 0
2014–15 *Brighton & HA* 5 0 **5 0**
2015–16 Middlesbrough 0 0 **50 11**
2015–16 *Huddersfield T* 15 3 **15 3**
2015–16 *Leeds U* 12 1 **12 1**
2016–17 Nottingham F 19 1
2017–18 Nottingham F 15 1 **34 2**
2017–18 Ipswich T 8 1 **8 1**
2018–19 Apollon Limassol 10 2 **10 2**
2019–20 Adana Demirspor 8 1 **8 1**
2021–22 Gillingham 22 1 **22 1**

CHAMBERS, Josh (M) 2 0
b. 13-11-03
2021–22 Gillingham 2 0 **2 0**

CHAPMAN, Aaron (G) 130 0
H: 6 8 W: 14 07 b.Rotherham 29-5-90
2013–14 Chesterfield 0 0
2014–15 Chesterfield 0 0
2014–15 *Accrington S* 3 0
2015–16 Chesterfield 0 0
2015–16 *Bristol R* 5 0 **5 0**
2016–17 Accrington S 15 0
2017–18 Accrington S 45 0 **63 0**
2018–19 Peterborough U 32 0
2019–20 *Tranmere R* 6 0 **6 0**
2019–20 Peterborough U 0 0 **32 0**
2020–21 Motherwell 6 0 **6 0**
2021–22 Gillingham 18 0 **18 0**

EHMER, Max (D) 371 14
H: 6 2 W: 11 00 b.Frankfurt 3-2-92
2009–10 QPR 0 0
2010–11 QPR 0 0
2010–11 *Yeovil T* 27 0
2011–12 QPR 0 0
2011–12 *Yeovil T* 24 0 **51 0**
2011–12 *Preston NE* 9 0 **9 0**
2012–13 QPR 0 0
2012–13 *Stevenage* 6 1 **6 1**
2013–14 QPR 1 0
2013–14 *Carlisle U* 12 1 **12 1**
2014–15 QPR 0 0 **1 0**
2014–15 *Gillingham* 27 1
2015–16 Gillingham 30 0
2016–17 Gillingham 45 6
2017–18 Gillingham 42 2
2018–19 Gillingham 40 1
2019–20 Gillingham 35 1
2020–21 Bristol R 28 1
2021–22 Bristol R 0 0 **28 1**
2021–22 Gillingham 45 0 **264 11**

GALE, Sam (M) 1 0
b. 1-10-04
2021–22 Gillingham 1 0 **1 0**

GBODE, Joseph (M) 2 0
b. 8-4-05
2021–22 Gillingham 2 0 **2 0**

JACKSON, Ryan (D) 340 11
H: 5 9 W: 10 03 b.Streatham 31-7-90
Internationals: England C.
2011–12 AFC Wimbledon 7 0 **7 0**
From Macclesfield T.
2013–14 Newport Co 29 0
2014–15 Newport Co 34 0 **63 0**
2015–16 Gillingham 37 2
2016–17 Gillingham 34 1
2017–18 Colchester U 42 2
2018–19 Colchester U 46 2
2019–20 Colchester U 34 2 **122 6**
2020–21 Gillingham 43 0
2021–22 Gillingham 34 2 **148 5**

LEE, Oliver (M) 302 30
H: 5 11 W: 12 08 b.Hornchurch 11-7-91
2009–10 West Ham U 0 0
2010–11 West Ham U 0 0
2010–11 *Dagenham & R* 5 0
2011–12 West Ham U 0 0
2011–12 *Dagenham & R* 16 3 **21 3**
2011–12 *Gillingham* 8 0
2012–13 Barnet 11 0 **11 0**
2012–13 Birmingham C 0 0
2013–14 Birmingham C 16 1
2014–15 Birmingham C 0 0 **16 1**
2014–15 *Plymouth Arg* 15 2 **15 2**
2015–16 Luton T 34 3
2016–17 Luton T 33 1
2017–18 Luton T 38 6 **105 10**
2018–19 Hearts 31 3
2019–20 *Gillingham* 28 4
2020–21 Hearts 10 1 **41 4**
2020–21 *Gillingham* 25 5
2021–22 Gillingham 32 1 **93 10**

LINTOTT, Harvey (D) 6 0
H: 6 2 b. 20-2-03
2020–21 Gillingham 0 0
2021–22 Gillingham 6 0 **6 0**

LLOYD, Danny (F) 98 18
H: 5 8 W: 9 13 b.Liverpool 3-12-91
From Stockport Co, Colwyn Bay, Lincoln C, Tamworth, AFC Fylde, Stockport Co.
2017–18 Peterborough U 31 8 **31 8**
From Salford C.
2019–20 Salford C 9 2 **9 2**

2020–21 Tranmere R 31 3 **31 3**
2021–22 Gillingham 27 5 **27 5**

MACDONALD, Alex (F) 367 30
H: 5 7 W: 11 05 b.Warrington 14-4-90
Internationals: Scotland U19, U21.
2007–08 Burnley 2 0
2008–09 Burnley 3 0
2009–10 Burnley 0 0
2009–10 *Falkirk* 11 0 **11 0**
2010–11 Burnley 0 0
2010–11 *Inverness CT* 10 1 **10 1**
2011–12 Burnley 5 0
2011–12 *Plymouth Arg* 18 4
2012–13 Burnley 1 0 **11 0**
2012–13 *Plymouth Arg* 16 1 **34 5**
2012–13 *Burton Alb* 15 1
2013–14 Burton Alb 35 0
2014–15 Burton Alb 21 6 **71 7**
2014–15 Oxford U 15 3
2015–16 Oxford U 40 5
2016–17 Oxford U 22 1 **77 9**
2016–17 Mansfield T 18 1
2017–18 Mansfield T 41 3
2018–19 Mansfield T 21 1
2019–20 Mansfield T 29 1 **109 6**
2020–21 Gillingham 37 1
2021–22 Gillingham 7 1 **44 2**

MAGHOMA, Christian (D) 39 0
H: 6 1 W: 14 02 b.Lubumbashi 8-11-97
Internationals: England U16, DR Congo Full caps.
2015–16 Tottenham H 0 0
2015–16 *Yeovil T* 0 0
2016–17 Tottenham H 0 0
2017–18 Tottenham H 0 0
2018–19 Arka Gdynia 15 0
2019–20 Arka Gdynia 20 0 **35 0**
2020–21 Gillingham 4 0
2021–22 Gillingham 0 0 **4 0**

McKENZIE, Robbie (D) 97 4
H: 6 0 W: 11 09 b.Kingston upon Hull 25-9-98
2017–18 Hull C 0 0
2018–19 Hull C 18 0
2019–20 Hull C 8 0 **26 0**
2020–21 Gillingham 33 1
2021–22 Gillingham 38 3 **71 4**

O'KEEFE, Stuart (M) 230 11
H: 5 8 W: 10 01 b.Eye 4-3-91
2008–09 Southend U 3 0
2009–10 Southend U 7 0
2010–11 Southend U 0 0 **10 0**
2010–11 Crystal Palace 4 0
2011–12 Crystal Palace 13 0
2012–13 Crystal Palace 5 0
2013–14 Crystal Palace 12 1
2014–15 Crystal Palace 2 0 **36 1**
2014–15 *Blackpool* 4 0 **4 0**
2014–15 Cardiff C 6 0
2015–16 Cardiff C 24 2
2016–17 Cardiff C 8 0
2016–17 *Milton Keynes D* 18 4 **18 4**
2017–18 Cardiff C 0 0
2017–18 *Portsmouth* 21 0 **21 0**
2018–19 Cardiff C 0 0 **38 2**
2018–19 *Plymouth Arg* 11 0 **11 0**
2019–20 Gillingham 30 3
2020–21 Gillingham 24 0
2021–22 Gillingham 38 1 **92 4**

OLIVER, Vadaine (F) 296 56
H: 6 2 W: 12 04 b.Sheffield 21-10-91
2010–11 Sheffield W 0 0
2011–12 Sheffield W 0 0
From Lincoln C.
2013–14 Crewe Alex 25 2
2014–15 Crewe Alex 9 1 **34 3**
2014–15 *Mansfield T* 30 7 **30 7**
2015–16 York C 37 7 **37 7**
2016–17 Notts Co 19 1 **19 1**
2017–18 Morecambe 34 3
2018–19 Morecambe 30 4 **64 7**
2019–20 Northampton T 30 4 **30 4**
2020–21 Gillingham 43 17
2021–22 Gillingham 39 10 **82 27**

REEVES, Ben (M) 253 35
H: 5 7 W: 10 08 b.Verwood 19-11-91
Internationals: Northern Ireland Full caps.
2008–09 Southampton 0 0
2009–10 Southampton 0 0
2010–11 Southampton 0 0
2011–12 Southampton 2 0
2011–12 *Dagenham & R* 5 0 **5 0**
2012–13 Southampton 3 0 **5 0**
2012–13 *Southend U* 10 1 **10 1**
2013–14 Milton Keynes D 28 7
2014–15 Milton Keynes D 30 7
2015–16 Milton Keynes D 18 3
2016–17 Milton Keynes D 34 7
2017–18 Charlton Ath 29 3
2018–19 Charlton Ath 29 4 **58 7**
2019–20 Milton Keynes D 17 1 **127 25**
2020–21 Plymouth Arg 28 0 **28 0**
2021–22 Gillingham 20 2 **20 2**

SITHOLE, Gerald (F) 16 0
H: 5 11 b. 28-12-02
2020–21 Gillingham 1 0
2021–22 Gillingham 15 0 **16 0**

THOMPSON, Ben (M) 182 12
H: 5 11 W: 12 04 b.Sidcup 3-10-95
2014–15 Millwall 0 0
2015–16 Millwall 28 1
2016–17 Millwall 38 0
2017–18 Millwall 3 0
2018–19 Millwall 0 0
2018–19 *Portsmouth* 23 2 **23 2**
2018–19 Millwall 13 4
2019–20 Millwall 28 1
2020–21 Millwall 30 3
2021–22 Millwall 2 0 **142 9**
2021–22 Gillingham 17 1 **17 1**

TUCKER, Jack (D) 116 3
H: 6 4 W: 13 05 b.Canterbury 13-11-99
2017–18 Gillingham 1 0
2018–19 Gillingham 0 0
2019–20 Gillingham 28 0
2020–21 Gillingham 43 1
2021–22 Gillingham 44 2 **116 3**

TUTONDA, David (D) 121 3
H: 5 11 W: 11 00 b.Kinshasa 11-10-95
2014–15 Cardiff C 0 0
2014–15 *Newport Co* 12 2 **12 2**
2015–16 Cardiff C 0 0
2015–16 *York C* 12 0 **12 0**
2016–17 Cardiff C 0 0
2016–17 Barnet 7 1
2017–18 Barnet 41 0 **48 1**
From Barnet.
2020–21 Bristol R 20 0
2021–22 Bristol R 0 0 **20 0**
2021–22 Gillingham 29 0 **29 0**

WOODS, Henry (M) 4 0
b. 7-9-99
2018–19 Gillingham 0 0
2019–20 Gillingham 0 0
2020–21 Gillingham 4 0
2021–22 Gillingham 0 0 **4 0**

Players retained or with offer of contract
Crump, Tommy.

Scholars
Akehurst, Bailey Roy; Britton, Oliver Joseph; Carter, Freddie Thomas Allan; Chambers, Joshua James; Crump, Thomas James Frederick; Dempsey, Will Frederick; Gale, Sam Rodin; Gbode, Joseph Paul Caleb; Giles, Alexander; Kuhr, Julian Thomas; Leach, Joshua Leslie; MacArthur, Matthew Jason; Moore, Elliott Paul; Sithole, Ronald Sibusiso; Smith, Ethan Michael.

HARROGATE T (38)

ARMSTRONG, Luke (F) 92 16
H: 6 1 W: 11 00 b.Durham 2-7-96
2015–16 Cowdenbeath 6 0 **6 0**
From Blyth Spartans
2017–18 Middlesbrough 0 0
2018–19 Middlesbrough 0 0
2018–19 *Accrington S* 16 3 **16 3**
2019–20 Salford C 21 1
2020–21 Salford C 4 0 **25 1**
2021–22 Hartlepool U 0 0
2021–22 Bristol R 0 0
2021–22 Harrogate T 45 12 **45 12**

BECK, Mark (F) 128 16
H: 6 5 W: 12 08 b.Sunderland 2-2-94
Internationals: Scotland U19.
2011–12 Carlisle U 2 0
2012–13 Carlisle U 27 4
2013–14 Carlisle U 10 0
2013–14 *Falkirk* 15 5 **15 5**
2014–15 Carlisle U 27 3 **66 7**
2015–16 Yeovil T 8 0 **8 0**
From Darlington, Harrogate T.
2020–21 Harrogate T 26 4
2021–22 Harrogate T 13 0 **39 4**

BURRELL, Warren (D) 88 2
H: 5 10 W: 12 00 b.Sheffield 3-6-90
2020–21 Harrogate T 43 0
2021–22 Harrogate T 45 2 **88 2**

CRACKNELL, Joe (G) 14 0
H: 6 0 W: 11 03 b.Kingston upon Hull 5-6-94
2012–13 Hull C 0 0
2013–14 Hull C 0 0
From Bradford Park Avenue.
2015–16 Bradford C 0 0
2016–17 Bradford C 0 0
From Bradford Park Avenue, Harrogate T.
2020–21 Harrogate T 8 0
2021–22 Harrogate T 6 0 **14 0**

FALKINGHAM, Joshua (M) 268 31
H: 5 6 W: 10 06 b.Leeds 25-8-90
2009–10 St Johnstone 1 0 **1 0**
2010–11 Arbroath 35 9
2011–12 Arbroath 35 8 **70 17**
2012–13 Dunfermline Ath 30 3
2013–14 Dunfermline Ath 30 5
2014–15 Dunfermline Ath 32 3
2015–16 Dunfermline Ath 28 3 **120 14**
From Darlington.
2020–21 Harrogate T 43 0
2021–22 Harrogate T 34 0 **77 0**

FALLOWFIELD, Ryan (D) 59 0
H: 5 9 W: 10 03 b.Kingston upon Hull 3-1-96
2020–21 Harrogate T 31 0
2021–22 Harrogate T 28 0 **59 0**

ILESANMI, Emmanuel (F) 1 0
b. 17-11-04
2021–22 Harrogate T 1 0 **1 0**

KERRY, Lloyd (M) 54 4
H: 5 5 W: 12 04 b.Chesterfield 22-7-88
2020–21 Harrogate T 31 2
2021–22 Harrogate T 23 2 **54 4**

KIRBY, Connor (M) 52 1
b. 10-9-98
2017–18 Sheffield W 1 0
2018–19 Sheffield W 1 0
2019–20 Sheffield W 0 0 **2 0**
2019–20 *Macclesfield T* 34 1 **34 1**
2020–21 Harrogate T 16 0
2021–22 Harrogate T 0 0 **16 0**

LEESLEY, Joe (F) 8 0
b. 29-4-94
Internationals: England C.
2019–20 *Stevenage* 8 0 **8 0**
2020–21 Harrogate T 0 0
2021–22 Harrogate T 0 0

LEGGE, Leon (D) 407 36
H: 6 4 W: 12 08 b.Bexhill 1-7-85
From Hailsham T, Lewes, Tonbridge Angels.
2009–10 Brentford 29 2
2010–11 Brentford 30 3
2011–12 Brentford 28 4
2012–13 Brentford 7 0 **94 9**
2012–13 Gillingham 22 2
2013–14 Gillingham 37 2
2014–15 Gillingham 22 4 **81 8**
2015–16 Cambridge U 39 3
2016–17 Cambridge U 44 6
2017–18 Cambridge U 27 2 **110 11**
2018–19 Port Vale 35 1
2019–20 Port Vale 37 4
2020–21 Port Vale 37 3
2021–22 Port Vale 5 0 **114 8**
2021–22 Harrogate T 8 0 **8 0**

MARTIN, Aaron (F) 44 5
H: 6 0 W: 12 00 b.Sheffield 5-7-91
2020–21 Harrogate T 36 5
2021–22 Harrogate T 8 0 **44 5**

McARDLE, Rory (D) 529 26
H: 6 1 W: 11 05 b.Doncaster 1-5-87
Internationals: Northern Ireland U21, Full caps.
2005–06 Sheffield W 0 0
2005–06 *Rochdale* 19 1
2006–07 Sheffield W 1 0 **1 0**
2006–07 Rochdale 25 0
2007–08 Rochdale 43 3
2008–09 Rochdale 41 2
2009–10 Rochdale 20 0 **148 6**
2010–11 Aberdeen 28 2
2011–12 Aberdeen 25 0 **53 2**
2012–13 Bradford C 40 2
2013–14 Bradford C 41 3
2014–15 Bradford C 43 3
2015–16 Bradford C 35 3
2016–17 Bradford C 24 1 **183 12**
2017–18 Scunthorpe U 36 1
2018–19 Scunthorpe U 38 0
2019–20 Scunthorpe U 26 3 **100 4**
2020–21 Exeter C 21 1
2021–22 Exeter C 0 0 **21 1**
2021–22 Harrogate T 23 1 **23 1**

MULDOON, Jack (F) 87 27
H: 5 10 W: 10 12 b.Scunthorpe 19-5-89
2014–15 Rochdale 3 0 **3 0**
From Brigg T, Sheffield, Glapwell, Alfreton T, Stocksbridge Park Steels, Brigg T, North Ferriby U, Worksop T.
2020–21 Harrogate T 42 15
2021–22 Harrogate T 42 12 **84 27**

ORSI-DADOMO, Danilo (F) 10 1
H: 6 2 W: 11 07 b.Camden 19-4-96
From Cockfosters, East Thurrock U, Hungerford T, Hampton & Richmond Bor, Maidenhead U.
2021–22 Harrogate T 10 1 **10 1**

OXLEY, Mark (G) 304 1
H: 6 3 W: 11 07 b.Sheffield 2-6-90
Internationals: England U18.
2007–08 Rotherham U 0 0
2008–09 Hull C 0 0
2009–10 Hull C 0 0
2009–10 *Grimsby T* 3 0 3 0
2010–11 Hull C 0 0
2011–12 Hull C 0 0
2012–13 Hull C 1 0
2012–13 *Burton Alb* 3 0 3 0
2013–14 Hull C 0 0
2013–14 *Oldham Ath* 36 0 36 0
2014–15 Hull C 0 0 1 0
2014–15 *Hibernian* 35 1
2015–16 Hibernian 34 0 69 1
2016–17 Southend U 20 0
2017–18 Southend U 46 0
2018–19 Southend U 25 0
2019–20 Southend U 19 0
2020–21 Southend U 41 0 151 0
2021–22 Harrogate T 41 0 41 0

PAGE, Lewis (D) 115 2
H: 5 10 W: 11 05 b.Enfield 20-5-96
2014–15 West Ham U 0 0
2015–16 West Ham U 0 0
2015–16 *Cambridge U* 6 0 6 0
2016–17 West Ham U 0 0
2016–17 *Coventry C* 22 0 22 0
2016–17 Charlton Ath 8 0
2017–18 Charlton Ath 8 1
2018–19 Charlton Ath 11 0
2019–20 Charlton Ath 0 0 27 1
2020–21 Exeter C 32 0
2021–22 Exeter C 0 0 32 0
2021–22 Harrogate T 28 1 28 1

PATTISON, Alex (F) 93 9
H: 5 8 W: 11 00 b.Darlington 6-9-97
2016–17 Middlesbrough 0 0
2017–18 Middlesbrough 0 0
2018–19 Middlesbrough 0 0
2018–19 *Yeovil T* 29 0 29 0
2019–20 Wycombe W 17 0
2020–21 Wycombe W 6 0 23 0
2021–22 Harrogate T 41 9 41 9

POWER, Simon (M) 50 3
H: 5 10 W: 11 03 b.Greystones 13-5-98
Internationals: Republic of Ireland U18, U19, U21.
2018–19 Norwich C 0 0
2018–19 *Dordrecht* 10 1 10 1
2019–20 Norwich C 0 0
2019–20 *Ross Co* 1 0 1 0
2020–21 Harrogate T 13 1
2021–22 Harrogate T 26 1 39 2

SHERON, Nathan (D) 69 0
H: 6 0 W: 10 01 b.Whiston 4-10-97
2017–18 Fleetwood T 0 0
2018–19 Fleetwood T 26 0
2019–20 Fleetwood T 0 0
2019–20 *Walsall* 7 0 7 0
2020–21 Fleetwood T 1 0 27 0
2020–21 *St Mirren* 7 0 7 0
2021–22 Harrogate T 28 0 28 0

SMITH, Will (D) 49 3
H: 6 1 W: 11 07 b.Leeds 4-11-98
2016–17 Barnsley 0 0
2017–18 Barnsley 0 0
2018–19 Barnsley 0 0
From Lincoln C, AFC Fylde, Harrogate T.
2020–21 Harrogate T 32 2
2021–22 Harrogate T 17 1 49 3

THOMSON, George (M) 92 8
H: 5 9 W: 11 00 b.Melton Mowbray 19-5-92
2020–21 Harrogate T 46 3
2021–22 Harrogate T 46 5 92 8

Players retained or with offer of contract
Attree, Bobby; Giles, Harvey; O'Boyle, Finn; Tweed, Benjamin; Williams, Bradley; Wilson, Mason.

Scholars
Attree, Bobby Daniel Kenneth; Birmingham, James Michael; Giles, Harvey Lee; Ilesanmi, Emmanuel tobiloba; Kerr, Alasdair miles James; Liddle, Tom; O'Boyle, Finn James Joseph; Tweed, Benjamin Charles; Williams, Bradley ryan; Wilson, Mason James.

HARTLEPOOL U (39)

BOGLE, Omar (F) 167 43
H: 6 3 W: 12 08 b.Birmingham 26-7-92
Internationals: England C.
From Celtic, Hinckley U, Solihull Moors.
2016–17 Grimsby T 27 19 27 19
2016–17 Wigan Ath 14 3 14 3
2017–18 Cardiff C 10 3
2017–18 *Peterborough U* 9 1 9 1
2018–19 Cardiff C 0 0
2018–19 *Birmingham C* 15 1 15 1
2018–19 *Portsmouth* 12 4 12 4
2019–20 Cardiff C 11 1 21 4
2019–20 *ADO Den Haag* 5 1 5 1
2020–21 Charlton Ath 17 2 17 2
2020–21 Doncaster R 17 2
2021–22 Doncaster R 10 1 27 3
2021–22 Hartlepool U 20 5 20 5

BYRNE, Neil (D) 43 1
H: 5 7 W: 8 09 b.Dublin 2-2-93
Internationals: Republic of Ireland U19.
2010–11 Nottingham F 0 0
2011–12 Nottingham F 0 0
2011–12 Rochdale 3 0
2012–13 Rochdale 0 0 3 0
From AFC Telford U, Macclesfield T, Gateshead, AFC Fylde, FC Halifax T.
2021–22 Hartlepool U 40 1 40 1

CARVER, Marcus (F) 55 1
H: 5 11 W: 11 11 b.Blackburn 22-10-93
2011–12 Accrington S 2 0
2012–13 Accrington S 11 0
2013–14 Accrington S 6 0
2014–15 Accrington S 17 1
2015–16 Accrington S 2 0 38 1
From Chorley, Southport.
2021–22 Hartlepool U 17 0 17 0

COOK, Jordan (F) 194 22
H: 5 9 W: 12 08 b.Hetton-le-Hole 20-3-90
2007–08 Sunderland 0 0
2008–09 Sunderland 0 0
2009–10 Sunderland 0 0
2009–10 *Darlington* 5 0 5 0
2010–11 Sunderland 3 0
2010–11 *Walsall* 8 1
2011–12 Sunderland 0 0 3 0
2011–12 *Carlisle U* 14 4 14 4
2012–13 Charlton Ath 7 0
2012–13 *Yeovil T* 1 0 1 0
2013–14 Charlton Ath 3 0 10 0
2014–15 Walsall 32 5
2015–16 Walsall 34 3 74 9
2016–17 Luton T 35 3
2017–18 Luton T 10 0 45 3
2018–19 Grimsby T 24 4
2019–20 Grimsby T 14 2 38 6
2021–22 Hartlepool U 4 0 4 0

CRAWFORD, Tom (M) 32 1
H: 6 1 W: 11 05 b.Chester 30-5-99
Internationals: England C.
2018–19 Notts Co 4 0 4 0
From Notts Co.
2021–22 Hartlepool U 28 1 28 1

CULLEN, Mark (F) 235 47
H: 5 9 W: 11 11 b.Ashington 21-4-92
2009–10 Hull C 3 1
2010–11 Hull C 17 0
2010–11 *Bradford C* 4 0 4 0
2011–12 Hull C 4 0
2011–12 *Bury* 4 0
2012–13 Hull C 0 0
2012–13 Hull C 0 0 24 1
2012–13 *Bury* 10 1 14 1
From Luton T.
2014–15 Luton T 42 13 42 13
2015–16 Blackpool 41 9
2016–17 Blackpool 27 9
2017–18 Blackpool 9 0
2018–19 Blackpool 12 3 89 21
2018–19 *Carlisle U* 9 0 9 0
2019–20 Port Vale 18 5
2020–21 Port Vale 18 2 36 7
2021–22 Hartlepool U 17 4 17 4
Transferred to AFC Fylde, February 2022.

FEATHERSTONE, Nicky (M) 289 9
H: 5 9 W: 11 03 b.Ferriby 22-9-88
2006–07 Hull C 2 0
2007–08 Hull C 6 0
2008–09 Hull C 0 0
2009–10 Hull C 0 0 8 0
2009–10 *Grimsby T* 8 0 8 0
2010–11 Hereford U 27 1
2011–12 Hereford U 38 0 65 1
2012–13 Walsall 31 0
2013–14 Walsall 25 0 56 0
2014–15 Scunthorpe U 0 0
2014–15 Hartlepool U 25 0
2015–16 Hartlepool U 44 0
2016–17 Hartlepool U 43 3
From Hartlepool U.
2021–22 Hartlepool U 40 5 152 8

FERGUSON, David (D) 82 5
H: 5 10 W: 12 00 b.Sunderland 7-6-94
Internationals: England C.
2012–13 Sunderland 0 0
2013–14 Sunderland 0 0
2014–15 Sunderland 0 0
2014–15 Blackpool 10 1
2015–16 Blackpool 30 0 40 1
From Darlington, York C, Hartlepool U.
2021–22 Hartlepool U 42 4 42 4

FRANCIS-ANGOL, Zaine (D) 87 3
H: 5 8 W: 12 04 b.Walthamstow 30-6-93
Internationals: Antiqua and Barbuda Full caps.
2012–13 Motherwell 22 0
2013–14 Motherwell 33 3
2014–15 Motherwell 11 0 66 3
From Kidderminster H, AFC Fylde.
2019–20 Accrington S 5 0 5 0
From Boreham Wood, Hartlepool U.
2021–22 Hartlepool U 16 0 16 0

GREY, Joe (F) 28 1
H: 5 9 W: 11 00 b.Newcastle upon Tyne 4-5-03
2021–22 Hartlepool U 28 1 28 1

HOLOHAN, Gavan (M) 144 21
H: 5 11 W: 11 11 b.Dublin 15-12-91
2010–11 Hull C 0 0
2011–12 Hull C 0 0
From Alfreton T.
2013 Drogheda U 4 0
2014 Drogheda U 27 5 31 5
2015 Cork C 18 1
2016 Cork C 20 2 38 3
2017 Galway U 27 6 27 6
2018 Waterford 30 5 30 5
From Hartlepool U.
2021–22 Hartlepool U 18 2 18 2

KILLIP, Ben (G) 49 0
H: 6 2 W: 11 09 b.Isleworth 24-11-95
Internationals: England C.
From Norwich C.
2017–18 Grimsby T 7 0 7 0
From Braintree T, Hartlepool U.
2021–22 Hartlepool U 42 0 42 0

LAWLOR, Jake (M) 18 0
H: 5 10 W: 11 09 b.Halifax 8-4-91
2020–21 Harrogate T 17 0 17 0
2021–22 Hartlepool U 1 0 1 0
Transferred to Darlington, November 2021.

LIDDLE, Gary (D) 572 28
H: 6 1 W: 11 11 b.Middlesbrough 15-6-86
2003–04 Middlesbrough 0 0
2004–05 Middlesbrough 0 0
2005–06 Middlesbrough 0 0
2006–07 Hartlepool U 42 3
2007–08 Hartlepool U 41 2
2008–09 Hartlepool U 43 0
2009–10 Hartlepool U 40 3
2010–11 Hartlepool U 42 6
2011–12 Hartlepool U 39 4
2012–13 Notts Co 46 0
2013–14 Notts Co 32 4 78 4
2014–15 Bradford C 41 1
2015–16 Bradford C 20 2 61 3
2015–16 Chesterfield 15 0
2016–17 Chesterfield 26 1 41 1
2016–17 Carlisle U 21 1
2017–18 Carlisle U 41 0
2018–19 Carlisle U 39 1 101 2
2019–20 Walsall 12 0 12 0
From Hartlepool U.
2021–22 Hartlepool U 32 0 279 18

MOLYNEUX, Luke (M) 46 8
H: 5 11 W: 11 09 b.Bishop Auckland 29-3-98
2017–18 Sunderland 1 0
2018–19 Sunderland 2 0 3 0
From Hartlepool U.
2021–22 Hartlepool U 43 8 43 8

ODUSINA, Timi (D) 31 0
H: 6 1 W: 11 09 b.Croydon 28-10-99
2018–19 Norwich C 0 0
2019–20 Norwich C 0 0
From Hartlepool U.
2021–22 Hartlepool U 31 0 31 0

OGLE, Reagan (D) 22 0
H: 5 8 W: 10 06 b.Woolongong 29-3-99
2016–17 Accrington S 1 0
2017–18 Accrington S 3 0
2018–19 Accrington S 0 0
2019–20 Accrington S 0 0
2020–21 Accrington S 0 0 4 0
2021–22 Hartlepool U 18 0 18 0

OLOMOLA, Olufela (F) 88 15
H: 5 7 W: 10 08 b.Harrow 5-9-97
From Huddersfield T.
2015–16 Southampton 0 0
2016–17 Southampton 0 0
2017–18 Southampton 0 0
2017–18 *Yeovil T* 21 7
2018–19 Scunthorpe U 6 0
2018–19 *Yeovil T* 17 3 38 10
2019–20 Scunthorpe U 0 0
2019–20 *Carlisle U* 27 5 27 5
2020–21 Scunthorpe U 5 0 11 0
2021–22 Hartlepool U 12 0 12 0

SHELTON, Mark (M) **38 2**
H: 6 0 W: 11 00 b.Nottingham 12-9-96

Season	Club				
2014–15	Burton Alb	0	0		
2015–16	Burton Alb	0	0		

From Ilkeston, Alfreton T.

Season	Club				
2019–20	Salford C	5	1	**5**	**1**

From Hartlepool U.

Season	Club				
2021–22	Hartlepool U	33	1	**33**	**1**

SMITH, Martin (M) **38 1**
H: 5 10 W: 11 00 b.Sunderland 25-1-96

Season	Club				
2014–15	Sunderland	0	0		
2015–16	Sunderland	0	0		
2015–16	*Carlisle U*	2	0	**2**	**0**
2016–17	Kilmarnock	10	1	**10**	**1**

From Coleraine.

Season	Club				
2018–19	Swindon T	11	0	**11**	**0**
2019–20	Salford C	4	0		
2020–21	Salford C	4	0	**8**	**0**
2021–22	Hartlepool U	7	0	**7**	**0**

Transferred to Chesterfield January 2021.

STERRY, Jamie (D) **66 2**
H: 5 11 W: 11 00 b.Newcastle upon Tyne 21-11-95

Season	Club				
2014–15	Newcastle U	0	0		
2015–16	Newcastle U	1	0		
2016–17	Newcastle U	2	0		
2016–17	*Coventry C*	16	0	**16**	**0**
2017–18	Newcastle U	0	0		
2017–18	*Crewe Alex*	9	0		
2018–19	Newcastle U	0	0		
2018–19	*Crewe Alex*	1	0	**10**	**0**
2019–20	Newcastle U	0	0	**3**	**0**

From South Shields, Hartlepool U.

Season	Club				
2021–22	Hartlepool U	37	2	**37**	**2**

Players retained or with offer of contract
Boyes, Patrick.

HUDDERSFIELD T (40)

AARONS, Rolando (M) **81 4**
H: 5 9 W: 10 08 b.Kingston 16-11-95
Internationals: England U20. Jamaica Full caps.
From Bristol C.

Season	Club				
2014–15	Newcastle U	4	1		
2015–16	Newcastle U	10	1		
2016–17	Newcastle U	4	0		
2017–18	Newcastle U	4	0		
2017–18	*Verona*	11	0	**11**	**0**
2018–19	Newcastle U	0	0		
2018–19	*Liberec*	12	0	**12**	**0**
2018–19	*Sheffield W*	9	1	**9**	**1**
2019–20	Newcastle U	0	0		
2019–20	*Wycombe W*	10	1	**10**	**1**
2019–20	*Motherwell*	6	0	**6**	**0**
2020–21	Newcastle U	0	0	**22**	**2**
2020–21	Huddersfield T	10	0		
2021–22	Huddersfield T	1	0	**11**	**0**

AUSTERFIELD, Joshua (M) **9 0**
H: 5 10 W: 9 00 b.Leeds 2-11-01

Season	Club				
2019–20	Huddersfield T	0	0		
2020–21	Huddersfield T	0	0		
2021–22	Huddersfield T	0	0		
2021–22	*Harrogate T*	9	0	**9**	**0**

AYINA, Loick (D) **0 0**
b.Brazzaville 20-4-03
From Sarcelles.

Season	Club				
2020–21	Huddersfield T	0	0		
2021–22	Huddersfield T	0	0		

BILOKAPIC, Nicholas (G) **2 0**
H: 6 5 b.Australia 8-9-02
Internationals: Australia U17, U23.
From Sydney U.

Season	Club				
2020–21	Huddersfield T	0	0		
2021–22	Huddersfield T	0	0		
2021–22	*Hartlepool U*	2	0	**2**	**0**

BLACKMAN, Jamal (G) **122 0**
H: 6 6 W: 14 09 b.Croydon 27-10-93
Internationals: England U16, U17, U18, U19.

Season	Club				
2011–12	Chelsea	0	0		
2012–13	Chelsea	0	0		
2013–14	Chelsea	0	0		
2014–15	Chelsea	0	0		
2014–15	*Middlesbrough*	0	0		
2015–16	Chelsea	0	0		
2015–16	*Ostersunds FK*	12	0	**12**	**0**
2016–17	Chelsea	0	0		
2016–17	*Wycombe W*	42	0	**42**	**0**
2017–18	Chelsea	0	0		
2017–18	*Sheffield U*	31	0	**31**	**0**
2018–19	Chelsea	0	0		
2018–19	*Leeds U*	0	0		
2019–20	Chelsea	0	0		
2019–20	*Vitesse*	0	0		
2019–20	*Bristol R*	10	0	**10**	**0**
2020–21	Chelsea	0	0		
2020–21	*Rotherham U*	26	0	**26**	**0**
2021–22	Los Angeles FC	0	0		
2021–22	Huddersfield T	1	0	**1**	**0**

BRIGHT, Myles (M) **0 0**
b.London 18-10-02

Season	Club				
2020–21	Huddersfield T	0	0		
2021–22	Huddersfield T	0	0		

BROWN, Reece (M) **155 15**
H: 5 9 W: 12 04 b.Dudley 3-3-96
Internationals: England U16, U17, U18, U20.

Season	Club				
2013–14	Birmingham C	6	0		
2014–15	Birmingham C	1	0		
2014–15	*Notts Co*	3	0	**3**	**0**
2015–16	Birmingham C	1	0		
2016–17	Birmingham C	8	0	**16**	**0**
2016–17	*Chesterfield*	2	0	**2**	**0**
2017–18	Forest Green R	33	2		
2018–19	Forest Green R	45	11	**78**	**13**
2019–20	Huddersfield T	0	0		
2019–20	*Peterborough U*	10	0		
2020–21	Huddersfield T	0	0		
2020–21	*Peterborough U*	38	2		
2021–22	Huddersfield T	0	0		
2021–22	*Peterborough U*	8	0	**56**	**2**

CAMARA, Etienne (D) **0 0**
b. 30-3-03
From Angers.

Season	Club				
2020–21	Huddersfield T	0	0		
2021–22	Huddersfield T	0	0		

CAMPBELL, Frazier (F) **394 88**
H: 5 8 W: 13 00 b.Huddersfield 13-9-87
Internationals: England U16, U17, U18, U21, Full caps.

Season	Club				
2005–06	Manchester U	0	0		
2006–07	Manchester U	0	0		
2006–07	*Antwerp*	31	20	**31**	**20**
2007–08	Manchester U	1	0		
2007–08	*Hull C*	34	15		
2008–09	Manchester U	1	0		
2008–09	*Tottenham H*	10	1	**10**	**1**
2009–10	Manchester U	0	0	**2**	**0**
2009–10	Sunderland	31	4		
2010–11	Sunderland	3	0		
2011–12	Sunderland	12	1		
2012–13	Sunderland	12	1	**58**	**6**
2012–13	Cardiff C	12	7		
2013–14	Cardiff C	37	6	**49**	**13**
2014–15	Crystal Palace	20	4		
2015–16	Crystal Palace	11	0		
2016–17	Crystal Palace	12	1	**43**	**5**
2017–18	Hull C	36	6		
2018–19	Hull C	39	12	**109**	**33**
2019–20	Huddersfield T	33	3		
2020–21	Huddersfield T	40	7		
2021–22	Huddersfield T	19	0	**92**	**10**

CHAPMAN, Jacob (G) **0 0**
b. 22-10-00
Internationals: Australia U23.

Season	Club				
2019–20	Huddersfield T	0	0		
2020–21	Huddersfield T	0	0		
2021–22	Huddersfield T	0	0		

CRICHLOW-NOBLE, Romoney (D) **25 1**
H: 6 0 W: 11 09 b.Luton 3-6-99
From Enfield Bor.

Season	Club				
2017–18	Huddersfield T	0	0		
2018–19	Huddersfield T	0	0		
2019–20	Huddersfield T	0	0		
2020–21	Huddersfield T	4	0		
2021–22	Huddersfield T	0	0	**4**	**0**
2021–22	*Swindon T*	18	1	**18**	**1**
2021–22	*Plymouth Arg*	3	0	**3**	**0**

DALEY, Luke (D) **0 0**
b. 30-1-03
From Port Vale.

Season	Club				
2020–21	Huddersfield T	0	0		
2021–22	Huddersfield T	0	0		

DALY, Matty (M) **39 4**
H: 5 9 W: 11 11 b.Stockport 10-3-01
Internationals: England U17, U18.

Season	Club				
2018–19	Huddersfield T	2	0		
2019–20	Huddersfield T	4	1		
2020–21	Huddersfield T	5	0		
2021–22	Huddersfield T	0	0	**11**	**1**
2021–22	*Hartlepool U*	19	2	**19**	**2**
2021–22	*Bradford C*	9	1	**9**	**1**

DIARRA, Brahima (M) **11 1**
H: 5 9 W: 10 10 b.Paris 5-7-03

Season	Club				
2020–21	Huddersfield T	1	0		
2021–22	Huddersfield T	0	0	**1**	**0**
2021–22	*Harrogate T*	10	1	**10**	**1**

EDMONDS-GREEN, Rarmani (D) **63 6**
H: 5 11 W: 11 07 b.Peckham 14-1-99

Season	Club				
2019–20	Huddersfield T	2	0		
2019–20	*Swindon T*	9	1	**9**	**1**
2020–21	Huddersfield T	24	2		
2021–22	Huddersfield T	0	0	**26**	**2**
2021–22	*Rotherham U*	28	3	**28**	**3**

EITING, Carel (M) **45 3**
H: 5 11 W: 11 09 b.Amsterdam 11-2-98
Internationals: Netherlands U16, U17, U18, U19, U20, U21.

Season	Club				
2016–17	Ajax	0	0		
2017–18	Ajax	4	0		
2018–19	Ajax	7	0		
2019–20	Ajax	6	0		
2020–21	Ajax	0	0	**17**	**0**
2020–21	*Huddersfield T*	23	3		
2021–22	Genk	0	0		
2021–22	Huddersfield T	5	0	**28**	**3**

GRANT, Daniel (F) **60 14**
H: 5 8 W: 11 00 b.Dublin 23-10-00
Internationals: Republic of Ireland U21.

Season	Club				
2018	Bohemians	20	3		
2019	Bohemians	24	4		
2020	Bohemians	16	7	**60**	**14**
2020–21	Huddersfield T	0	0		
2021–22	Huddersfield T	0	0		

HARRATT, Kian (F) **20 3**
H: 5 10 W: 10 02 b.Pontefract 21-6-02
From Barnsley, Leeds U.

Season	Club				
2019–20	Huddersfield T	1	0		
2020–21	Huddersfield T	0	0		
2021–22	Huddersfield T	0	0	**1**	**0**
2021–22	*Port Vale*	19	3	**19**	**3**

HEADLEY, Jaheim (D) **0 0**
b.London 24-9-01

Season	Club				
2020–21	Huddersfield T	0	0		
2021–22	Huddersfield T	0	0		

HIGH, Scott (M) **50 0**
H: 5 10 W: 10 03 b.Dewsbury 15-2-01
Internationals: Scotland U21.

Season	Club				
2019–20	Huddersfield T	1	0		
2020–21	Huddersfield T	14	0		
2020–21	*Shrewsbury T*	12	0	**12**	**0**
2021–22	Huddersfield T	23	0	**38**	**0**

HOGG, Jonathan (M) **390 5**
H: 5 10 W: 11 08 b.Middlesbrough 6-12-88

Season	Club				
2007–08	Aston Villa	0	0		
2008–09	Aston Villa	0	0		
2009–10	Aston Villa	0	0		
2009–10	*Darlington*	5	1	**5**	**1**
2010–11	Aston Villa	5	0		
2010–11	*Portsmouth*	19	0	**19**	**0**
2011–12	Aston Villa	0	0	**5**	**0**
2011–12	Watford	40	0		
2012–13	Watford	38	0	**78**	**0**
2013–14	Huddersfield T	34	0		
2014–15	Huddersfield T	26	0		
2015–16	Huddersfield T	22	0		
2016–17	Huddersfield T	37	1		
2017–18	Huddersfield T	30	0		
2018–19	Huddersfield T	29	0		
2019–20	Huddersfield T	37	0		
2020–21	Huddersfield T	37	1		
2021–22	Huddersfield T	31	2	**283**	**4**

HOLMES, Duane (M) **239 23**
H: 5 8 W: 10 03 b.Wakefield 6-11-94
Internationals: USA Full caps.

Season	Club				
2012–13	Huddersfield T	0	0		
2013–14	Huddersfield T	16	0		
2013–14	*Yeovil T*	5	0	**5**	**0**
2014–15	Huddersfield T	0	0		
2014–15	*Bury*	6	0	**6**	**0**
2015–16	Huddersfield T	6	1		
2016–17	Scunthorpe U	32	3		
2017–18	Scunthorpe U	45	7		
2018–19	Scunthorpe U	1	0	**78**	**10**
2018–19	Derby Co	25	2		
2019–20	Derby Co	33	2		
2020–21	Derby Co	14	1	**72**	**5**
2020–21	Huddersfield T	19	2		
2021–22	Huddersfield T	37	5	**78**	**8**

JACKSON, Ben (M) **21 1**
H: 5 10 W: 11 00 b.Stockport 22-2-01

Season	Club				
2019–20	Huddersfield T	0	0		
2020–21	Huddersfield T	1	0		
2020–21	*Bolton W*	5	1	**5**	**1**
2021–22	Huddersfield T	0	0	**1**	**0**
2021–22	*Doncaster R*	15	0	**15**	**0**

JONES, Patrick (F) **2 0**
b. 9-6-03
Internationals: Wales U17, U21.
From Wrexham.

Season	Club				
2020–21	Huddersfield T	2	0		
2021–22	Huddersfield T	0	0	**2**	**0**

KHERBOUCHE, Nasim (D) **0 0**
H: 6 4 b.London 9-1-02

Season	Club				
2020–21	Huddersfield T	0	0		
2021–22	Huddersfield T	0	0		

KOROMA, Josh (F) **91 15**
H: 5 10 W: 10 06 b.Southwark 8-11-98
Internationals: England C.

Season	Club				
2015–16	Leyton Orient	3	0		
2016–17	Leyton Orient	22	3	**25**	**3**

From Leyton Orient.

Season	Club				
2019–20	Huddersfield T	7	0		
2019–20	*Rotherham U*	5	0	**5**	**0**
2020–21	Huddersfield T	20	8		
2021–22	Huddersfield T	34	4	**61**	**12**

KRASNIQI, Ernaldo (M) **5** **0**
b.London 25-2-03
Internationals: Albania U19.

2021–22	Huddersfield T	0	0		
2021–22	*Falkirk*	5	0	**5**	**0**

LEES, Tom (D) **496** **20**
H: 6 0 W: 11 07 b.Warwick 28-11-90
Internationals: England U21.

2008–09	Leeds U	0	0		
2009–10	Leeds U	0	0		
2009–10	*Accrington S*	39	0	**39**	**0**
2010–11	Leeds U	0	0		
2010–11	*Bury*	45	4	**45**	**4**
2011–12	Leeds U	42	2		
2012–13	Leeds U	40	1		
2013–14	Leeds U	41	0	**123**	**3**
2014–15	Sheffield W	44	0		
2015–16	Sheffield W	34	3		
2016–17	Sheffield W	35	1		
2017–18	Sheffield W	29	1		
2018–19	Sheffield W	42	2		
2019–20	Sheffield W	27	2		
2020–21	Sheffield W	38	1	**249**	**10**
2021–22	Huddersfield T	40	3	**40**	**3**

NICHOLLS, Lee (G) **253** **0**
H: 6 3 W: 13 05 b.Huyton 5-10-92
Internationals: England U19.

2009–10	Wigan Ath	0	0		
2010–11	Wigan Ath	0	0		
2010–11	*Hartlepool U*	0	0		
2010–11	*Shrewsbury T*	0	0		
2010–11	*Sheffield W*	0	0		
2011–12	Wigan Ath	0	0		
2011–12	*Accrington S*	9	0	**9**	**0**
2012–13	Wigan Ath	0	0		
2012–13	*Northampton T*	46	0	**46**	**0**
2013–14	Wigan Ath	6	0		
2014–15	Wigan Ath	1	0		
2015–16	Wigan Ath	2	0	**9**	**0**
2015–16	*Bristol R*	15	0	**15**	**0**
2016–17	Milton Keynes D	8	0		
2017–18	Milton Keynes D	41	0		
2018–19	Milton Keynes D	40	0		
2019–20	Milton Keynes D	35	0		
2020–21	Milton Keynes D	7	0	**131**	**0**
2021–22	Huddersfield T	43	0	**43**	**0**

O'BRIEN, Lewis (M) **163** **12**
H: 5 8 W: 9 13 b.Colchester 14-10-98

2017–18	Huddersfield T	0	0		
2018–19	Huddersfield T	0	0		
2018–19	*Bradford C*	40	4	**40**	**4**
2019–20	Huddersfield T	38	2		
2020–21	Huddersfield T	42	3		
2021–22	Huddersfield T	43	3	**123**	**8**

OBIERO, Micah (F) **4** **0**
b. 22-2-01

2018–19	Huddersfield T	0	0		
2019–20	Huddersfield T	0	0		
2020–21	Huddersfield T	0	0		
2020–21	*Carlisle U*	4	0	**4**	**0**
2021–22	Huddersfield T	0	0		

OLAGUNJU, Mustapha (D) **6** **0**
b. 1-1-02

2020–21	Huddersfield T	0	0		
2020–21	*Port Vale*	6	0	**6**	**0**
2021–22	Huddersfield T	0	0		

PEARSON, Matthew (D) **280** **24**
H: 6 3 W: 11 05 b.Keighley 3-8-93
Internationals: England U18, C.

2011–12	Blackburn R	0	0		
2012–13	Rochdale	9	0		
2013–14	Rochdale	0	0	**9**	**0**
From FC Halifax T.					
2015–16	Accrington S	46	3		
2016–17	Accrington S	43	8	**89**	**11**
2017–18	Barnsley	17	0	**17**	**0**
2018–19	Luton T	46	6		
2019–20	Luton T	42	2		
2020–21	Luton T	40	2	**128**	**10**
2021–22	Huddersfield T	37	3	**37**	**3**

PHILLIPS, Kieran (F) **47** **6**
H: 6 1 b.Huddersfield 18-2-00
From Everton.

2020–21	Huddersfield T	10	0		
2021–22	Huddersfield T	0	0	**10**	**0**
2021–22	*Walsall*	26	4	**26**	**4**
2021–22	*Exeter C*	11	2	**11**	**2**

PIPA, Gonzalo (D) **73** **2**
H: 5 9 W: 10 10 b.Esparraguera 26-1-98
Internationals: Spain U19, U20, U21.

2015–16	Espanyol	0	0		
2016–17	Espanyol	0	0		
2017–18	Espanyol	0	0		
2018–19	Espanyol	0	0		
2019–20	Espanyol	7	0		
2019–20	*Gimnastic*	18	0	**18**	**0**
2020–21	Espanyol	0	0	**7**	**0**
2020–21	Huddersfield T	37	2		
2021–22	Huddersfield T	11	0	**48**	**2**

RHODES, Jordan (F) **494** **198**
H: 6 1 W: 11 03 b.Oldham 5-2-90
Internationals: Scotland U21, Full caps.

2007–08	Ipswich T	8	1		
2008–09	Ipswich T	2	0	**10**	**1**
2008–09	*Rochdale*	5	2	**5**	**2**
2008–09	*Brentford*	14	7	**14**	**7**
2009–10	Huddersfield T	45	19		
2010–11	Huddersfield T	37	16		
2011–12	Huddersfield T	40	35		
2012–13	Huddersfield T	2	2		
2012–13	Blackburn R	43	27		
2013–14	Blackburn R	46	25		
2014–15	Blackburn R	45	21		
2015–16	Blackburn R	25	10	**159**	**83**
2015–16	Middlesbrough	18	6		
2016–17	Middlesbrough	6	0	**24**	**6**
2016–17	*Sheffield W*	18	3		
2017–18	Sheffield W	31	5		
2018–19	Sheffield W	0	0		
2018–19	*Norwich C*	36	6	**36**	**6**
2019–20	Sheffield W	16	3		
2020–21	Sheffield W	36	7	**101**	**18**
2021–22	Huddersfield T	21	3	**145**	**75**

ROWE, Aaron (M) **24** **1**
H: 5 10 W: 10 12 b.Hackney 7-9-00
From Leyton Orient.

2018–19	Huddersfield T	2	0		
2019–20	Huddersfield T	1	0		
2020–21	Huddersfield T	20	1		
2021–22	Huddersfield T	1	0	**24**	**1**

RUFFELS, Joshua (D) **266** **21**
H: 5 10 W: 11 11 b.Oxford 23-10-93

2011–12	Coventry C	1	0		
2012–13	Coventry C	0	0	**1**	**0**
2013–14	Oxford U	29	1		
2014–15	Oxford U	33	0		
2015–16	Oxford U	16	0		
2016–17	Oxford U	20	2		
2017–18	Oxford U	38	5		
2018–19	Oxford U	44	4		
2019–20	Oxford U	35	3		
2020–21	Oxford U	42	6		
2021–22	Oxford U	0	0	**257**	**21**
2021–22	Huddersfield T	8	0	**8**	**0**

RUSSELL, Jonathan (M) **42** **4**
H: 6 4 W: 12 11 b.Hounslow 9-10-00

2020–21	Chelsea	0	0		
2020–21	*Accrington S*	25	2	**25**	**2**
2021–22	Huddersfield T	17	2	**17**	**2**

SARR, Naby (D) **186** **15**
H: 6 5 W: 14 00 b.Marseille 13-8-93
Internationals: France U20, U21.

2012–13	Lyon	0	0		
2013–14	Lyon	2	0	**2**	**0**
2014–15	Sporting Lisbon	8	0	**8**	**0**
2015–16	Charlton Ath	12	1		
2016–17	Charlton Ath	0	0		
2016–17	*Red Star*	22	2	**22**	**2**
2017–18	Charlton Ath	18	0		
2018–19	Charlton Ath	36	2		
2019–20	Charlton Ath	29	3	**95**	**6**
2020–21	Huddersfield T	41	4		
2021–22	Huddersfield T	18	3	**59**	**7**

SCHOFIELD, Ryan (G) **51** **0**
H: 6 3 W: 11 00 b.Huddersfield 11-12-99
Internationals: England U18, U19, U20.

2018–19	Huddersfield T	0	0		
2018–19	*Notts Co*	17	0	**17**	**0**
2019–20	Huddersfield T	1	0		
2019–20	*Livingston*	1	0	**1**	**0**
2020–21	Huddersfield T	30	0		
2021–22	Huddersfield T	2	0	**33**	**0**

SHANKS, Connor (M) **0** **0**
b.Halifax 11-4-02

2020–21	Bradford C	0	0		
2021–22	Huddersfield T	0	0		

SHARROCK-PEPLOW, Sam (D) **0** **0**
b.Leigh 14-7-02

2020–21	Huddersfield T	0	0		
2021–22	Huddersfield T	0	0		

THOMAS, Sorba (F) **50** **3**
H: 6 1 W: 11 09 b.Newham 22-8-99
Internationals: Wales Full caps.
From Boreham Wood.

2020–21	Huddersfield T	7	0		
2021–22	Huddersfield T	43	3	**50**	**3**

TOFFOLO, Harry (D) **241** **16**
H: 6 0 W: 11 03 b.Welwyn Garden City 19-8-95
Internationals: England U18, U19, U20.

2014–15	Norwich C	0	0		
2014–15	*Swindon T*	28	1	**28**	**1**
2015–16	Norwich C	0	0		
2015–16	*Rotherham U*	7	0	**7**	**0**
2015–16	*Peterborough U*	7	0	**7**	**0**
2016–17	Norwich C	0	0		
2016–17	*Scunthorpe U*	22	2	**22**	**2**
2017–18	Norwich C	0	0		
2017–18	*Doncaster R*	13	0	**13**	**0**
2017–18	Millwall	0	0		
2018–19	Lincoln C	46	3		
2019–20	Lincoln C	26	1	**72**	**4**
2019–20	Huddersfield T	19	1		
2020–21	Huddersfield T	31	2		
2021–22	Huddersfield T	42	6	**92**	**9**

TURTON, Oliver (D) **350** **6**
H: 5 11 W: 11 11 b.Manchester 6-12-92

2010–11	Crewe Alex	1	0		
2011–12	Crewe Alex	2	0		
2012–13	Crewe Alex	20	0		
2013–14	Crewe Alex	12	1		
2014–15	Crewe Alex	44	1		
2015–16	Crewe Alex	46	1		
2016–17	Crewe Alex	45	1	**170**	**4**
2017–18	Blackpool	41	1		
2018–19	Blackpool	32	1		
2019–20	Blackpool	30	0		
2020–21	Blackpool	37	0		
2021–22	Blackpool	0	0	**140**	**2**
2021–22	Huddersfield T	40	0	**40**	**0**

VALLEJO, Alex (M) **108** **2**
H: 6 2 W: 11 06 b.Vitoria-Gasteiz 16-1-92

2011–12	Alaves	1	0	**1**	**0**
2011–12	*Sestao*	7	0	**7**	**0**
2012–13	Mallorca	0	0		
2013–14	Mallorca	6	0		
2014–15	Mallorca	4	1		
2015–16	Mallorca	0	0		
2016–17	Mallorca	13	0	**23**	**1**
2017–18	Cordoba	18	0		
2018–19	Cordoba	28	0	**46**	**0**
2019–20	Fuenlabrada	10	0		
2020–21	Fuenlabrada	0	0	**10**	**0**
2020–21	Huddersfield T	16	0		
2021–22	Huddersfield T	5	1	**21**	**1**

WARD, Danny (F) **369** **70**
H: 5 11 W: 13 11 b.Bradford 9-12-90
From Leeds U.

2008–09	Bolton W	0	0		
2009–10	Bolton W	2	0		
2009–10	*Swindon T*	28	7	**28**	**7**
2010–11	Bolton W	0	0	**2**	**0**
2010–11	*Coventry C*	5	0	**5**	**0**
2010–11	*Huddersfield T*	7	3		
2011–12	Huddersfield T	39	4		
2012–13	Huddersfield T	28	2		
2013–14	Huddersfield T	38	10		
2014–15	Huddersfield T	12	0		
2014–15	*Rotherham U*	16	3		
2015–16	Rotherham U	34	4		
2016–17	Rotherham U	41	10	**91**	**17**
2017–18	Cardiff C	18	4		
2018–19	Cardiff C	14	1		
2019–20	Cardiff C	28	7	**60**	**12**
2020–21	Huddersfield T	19	1		
2021–22	Huddersfield T	40	14	**183**	**34**

Players retained or with offer of contract
Adewoju, David; Bellagambi, Giosue; Eccleston, Neo; Falls, Conor; Gilmore, Brodie; Maroodza, Shane; Midgley, Benjamin; Nduwuisi Ondo, Charles; Roxburgh, Michael; Stone, Michael.

Scholars
Acquah, Michael Earl Jesse; Ailemen, Michael Akpoyibo; Deru, Fopefoluwa Oluwanifemi; Grubb, Evander Marvin; Helliwell, Dylan Robert; Iorpenda, Thomas Achi; Johnson, Joseph Omokayode; O'Brien-Brady, Donay Kaylin; Parker, Michael Ato Kwamena; Philpott, Cian James; Roxburgh, Michael David; Sandah, Hakeem Kwabena Owusu; Sanusi, Tyree Ridwan Teniola; Sheppard, Archie Arthur James; Stewart, Jeremy Robert; Taylor, Samuel Edward; Weston, Ajay Thomas; Whittingham, Sonny.

HULL C (41)

ARTHUR, Festus (D) **9** **0**
H: 6 3 W: 13 01 b.Hamburg 27-2-00
From Stockport Co.

2020–21	Hull C	0	0		
2021–22	Hull C	0	0		
2021–22	*Barrow*	9	0	**9**	**0**

BECKETT, Louis (M) **0** **0**
b.Scarborough 8-10-02

2020–21	Hull C	0	0		
2021–22	Hull C	0	0		

CANNON, Andy (M) **174** **8**
H: 5 9 W: 11 09 b.Ashton-under-Lyne 14-3-96

2014–15	Rochdale	18	0		
2015–16	Rochdale	25	0		
2016–17	Rochdale	25	2		
2017–18	Rochdale	21	2		
2018–19	Rochdale	12	0	**101**	**4**
2018–19	Portsmouth	2	0		
2019–20	Portsmouth	18	1		

2020–21 Portsmouth 43 2 63 3
2021–22 Hull C 10 1 10 1

CARTWRIGHT, Harvey (G) 2 0
H: 6 4 b.Grimsby 9-5-02
Internationals: England U18, U20.
2020–21 Hull C 0 0
2021–22 Hull C 2 0 2 0

CHADWICK, Billy (M) 15 0
b.Hull 19-1-00
2020–21 Hull C 3 0
2021–22 Hull C 0 0 3 0
2021–22 *Linfield* 12 0 12 0

COYLE, Lewie (D) 183 2
H: 5 8 W: 10 08 b.Hull 15-10-95
2015–16 Leeds U 11 0
2016–17 Leeds U 4 0
2017–18 Leeds U 0 0
2017–18 *Fleetwood T* 42 0
2018–19 Leeds U 0 0 15 0
2018–19 *Fleetwood T* 41 0
2019–20 Fleetwood T 34 1
2020–21 Fleetwood T 0 0 117 1
2020–21 Hull C 28 0
2021–22 Hull C 23 1 51 1

DOCHERTY, Greg (M) 236 18
H: 5 10 W: 11 05 b.Glasgow 10-9-96
Internationals: Scotland U17, U21.
2013–14 Hamilton A 3 0
2014–15 Hamilton A 7 1
2015–16 Hamilton A 34 1
2016–17 Hamilton A 29 1
2017–18 Hamilton A 21 3 94 6
2017–18 Rangers 11 0
2018–19 Rangers 0 0
2018–19 *Shrewsbury T* 41 7 41 7
2019–20 Rangers 0 0 11 0
2019–20 *Hibernian* 6 0 6 0
2020–21 Hull C 44 5
2021–22 Hull C 40 0 84 5

EAVES, Tom (F) 313 72
H: 6 3 W: 13 08 b.Liverpool 14-1-92
2009–10 Oldham Ath 15 0
2010–11 Bolton W 0 0
2010–11 *Oldham Ath* 0 0 15 0
2011–12 Bolton W 0 0
2012–13 Bolton W 3 0
2012–13 *Bristol R* 16 7 16 7
2012–13 *Shrewsbury T* 10 6
2013–14 Bolton W 0 0
2013–14 *Rotherham U* 8 0 8 0
2013–14 *Shrewsbury T* 25 2 35 8
2014–15 Bolton W 1 0
2014–15 *Yeovil T* 5 0
2014–15 *Bury* 9 1 9 1
2015–16 Bolton W 0 0 4 0
2016–17 Yeovil T 40 4 45 4
2017–18 Gillingham 41 17
2018–19 Gillingham 43 21 84 38
2019–20 Hull C 40 5
2020–21 Hull C 26 4
2021–22 Hull C 31 5 97 14

ELDER, Callum (D) 183 2
H: 5 11 W: 10 08 b.Sydney 27-1-95
Internationals: Australia U20, Full caps.
2013–14 Leicester C 0 0
2014–15 Leicester C 0 0
2014–15 *Mansfield T* 21 0 21 0
2015–16 Leicester C 0 0
2015–16 *Peterborough U* 18 1 18 1
2016–17 Leicester C 0 0
2016–17 *Brentford* 6 0 6 0
2016–17 *Barnsley* 5 0 5 0
2017–18 Leicester C 0 0
2017–18 *Wigan Ath* 27 0 27 0
2018–19 Leicester C 0 0
2018–19 *Ipswich T* 4 0
2019–20 Ipswich T 0 0 4 0
2019–20 Hull C 30 0
2020–21 Hull C 44 1
2021–22 Hull C 28 0 102 1

EMMANUEL, Josh (D) 131 0
H: 5 11 W: 11 00 b.London 18-8-97
From West Ham U.
2015–16 Ipswich T 4 0
2015–16 *Crawley T* 2 0 2 0
2016–17 Ipswich T 15 0
2017–18 Ipswich T 0 0
2017–18 *Rotherham U* 31 0 31 0
2018–19 Ipswich T 4 0
2018–19 *Shrewsbury T* 14 0 14 0
2019–20 Ipswich T 0 0 23 0
2019–20 Bolton W 27 0 27 0
2020–21 Hull C 28 0
2021–22 Hull C 6 0 34 0

FLEMING, Brandon (D) 37 0
H: 5 9 W: 10 03 b.Dewsbury 3-12-99
2017–18 Hull C 0 0
2018–19 Hull C 4 0
2019–20 Hull C 4 0
2019–20 *Bolton W* 10 0 10 0
2020–21 Hull C 3 0
2021–22 Hull C 16 0 27 0

GREAVES, Jacob (D) 114 0
H: 6 1 W: 11 00 b.Cottingham 12-9-00
2019–20 Hull C 0 0
2019–20 *Cheltenham T* 29 0 29 0
2020–21 Hull C 39 0
2021–22 Hull C 46 0 85 0

HINDS, Josh (F) 1 0
b.Essex 29-3-03
From West Ham U.
2021–22 Hull C 1 0 1 0

HONEYMAN, George (M) 202 22
H: 5 8 W: 11 05 b.Prudhoe 8-9-94
2014–15 Sunderland 0 0
2015–16 Sunderland 1 0
2016–17 Sunderland 5 0
2017–18 Sunderland 42 6
2018–19 Sunderland 35 6
2019–20 Sunderland 0 0 83 12
2019–20 Hull C 42 1
2020–21 Hull C 42 4
2021–22 Hull C 35 5 119 10

HUDDLESTONE, Tom (M) 470 18
H: 6 2 W: 11 02 b.Nottingham 28-12-86
Internationals: England U16, U17, U19, U20, U21, Full caps.
2003–04 Derby Co 43 0
2004–05 Derby Co 45 0
2005–06 Tottenham H 4 0
2005–06 *Wolverhampton W* 13 1 13 1
2006–07 Tottenham H 21 1
2007–08 Tottenham H 28 3
2008–09 Tottenham H 22 0
2009–10 Tottenham H 33 2
2010–11 Tottenham H 14 2
2011–12 Tottenham H 2 0
2012–13 Tottenham H 20 0
2013–14 Tottenham H 0 0 144 8
2013–14 Hull C 36 3
2014–15 Hull C 31 0
2015–16 Hull C 37 2
2016–17 Hull C 31 1
2017–18 Derby Co 44 2
2018–19 Derby Co 24 0
2019–20 Derby Co 11 1 167 3
2021–22 Hull C 11 0 146 6

INGRAM, Matt (G) 225 0
H: 6 3 W: 12 13 b.Croydon 18-12-93
2011–12 Wycombe W 0 0
2012–13 Wycombe W 8 0
2013–14 Wycombe W 46 0
2014–15 Wycombe W 46 0
2015–16 Wycombe W 24 0
2015–16 QPR 4 0
2016–17 QPR 0 0
2017–18 Northampton T 20 0 20 0
2017–18 QPR 2 0
2018–19 Wycombe W 1 0 125 0
2018–19 QPR 4 0 10 0
2019–20 Hull C 1 0
2020–21 Hull C 38 0
2021–22 Hull C 29 0 68 0
2021–22 *Luton T* 2 0 2 0

JACOB, Matty (D) 0 0
b.Barnsley 3-6-01
2020–21 Hull C 0 0
2021–22 Hull C 0 0

JARVIS, William (F) 1 0
b.York 17-12-02
2021–22 Hull C 1 0 1 0

JONES, Alfie (D) 98 4
H: 6 0 W: 11 00 b.Bristol 7-10-97
2018–19 Southampton 0 0
2018–19 *St Mirren* 14 1 14 1
2019–20 Southampton 0 0
2019–20 *Gillingham* 30 2 30 2
2020–21 Hull C 31 0
2021–22 Hull C 23 1 54 1

JONES, Callum (M) 14 1
H: 5 9 b.Birkenhead 5-4-01
Internationals: Wales U18.
From The New Saints, Owestry T, Bury.
2019–20 Hull C 0 0
2020–21 Hull C 1 0
2021–22 Hull C 2 0 3 0
2021–22 *Morecambe* 11 1 11 1

LEAKE, Jake (D) 0 0
b.Hull 20-2-03
2020–21 Hull C 0 0
2021–22 Hull C 0 0

LEWIS-POTTER, Keane (F) 110 27
H: 5 7 W: 10 08 b.Kingston upon Hull 22-2-01
Internationals: England U21.
2018–19 Hull C 0 0
2019–20 Hull C 21 2
2020–21 Hull C 43 13
2021–22 Hull C 46 12 110 27

LONGMAN, Ryan (M) 79 12
H: 5 11 W: 11 07 b.Redhill 6-11-00
2019–20 Brighton & HA 0 0
2020–21 Brighton & HA 0 0
2020–21 *AFC Wimbledon* 44 8
2021–22 AFC Wimbledon 0 0 44 8
2021–22 Hull C 35 4 35 4

LOVICK, Harry (M) 0 0
b.Cottingham 20-12-02
2020–21 Hull C 0 0
2021–22 Hull C 0 0

McLOUGHLIN, Sean (D) 111 6
H: 6 3 W: 12 04 b.Cork 13-11-96
Internationals: Republic of Ireland U21.
2017 Cork C 1 0
2018 Cork C 27 3
2019 Cork C 20 2 48 5
2019–20 Hull C 7 0
2019–20 *St Mirren* 21 1 21 1
2020–21 Hull C 3 0
2021–22 Hull C 32 0 42 0

MILLS, Jevon (D) 7 0
b.Nottingham 27-9-03
Internationals: Republic of Ireland U19.
2021–22 Hull C 1 0 1 0
2021–22 *Falkirk* 6 0 6 0

MONCUR, George (M) 254 40
H: 5 9 W: 9 13 b.Swindon 18-8-93
Internationals: England U18.
2010–11 West Ham U 0 0
2011–12 West Ham U 0 0
2011–12 *AFC Wimbledon* 20 2 20 2
2012–13 West Ham U 0 0
2013–14 West Ham U 0 0
2013–14 *Partick Thistle* 2 1 2 1
2014–15 Colchester U 41 8
2015–16 Colchester U 45 12 86 20
2016–17 Peterborough U 13 2 13 2
2016–17 Barnsley 12 2
2017–18 Barnsley 34 2
2018–19 Barnsley 21 1 67 5
2018–19 Luton T 14 6
2019–20 Luton T 17 1
2020–21 Luton T 21 3
2021–22 Luton T 0 0 52 10
2021–22 Hull C 14 0 14 0

ROBSON, David (G) 0 0
b.North Allerton 22-1-02
2020–21 Hull C 0 0
2021–22 Hull C 0 0

SALAM, Ahmed (M) 27 2
b.Hull 30-12-00
2020–21 Hull C 0 0
2021–22 Hull C 0 0
2021–22 *Linfield* 27 2 27 2

SAYYADMANESH, Allahyar (F) 71 15
H: 6 0 W: 11 09 b.Amol 29-6-01
Internationals: Iran U17, U23, Full caps.
2018–19 Esteghlal 15 2 15 2
2019–20 Fenerbahce 2 0
2019–20 *Istanbulspor* 7 0 7 0
2020–21 Fenerbahce 0 0
2020–21 *Zorya Luhansk* 19 5
2021–22 Fenerbahce 0 0 2 0
2021–22 *Zorya Luhansk* 16 7 35 12
2021–22 *Hull C* 12 1 12 1

SCOTT, James (F) 78 10
H: 6 2 W: 13 10 b.Glasgow 30-8-00
Internationals: Scotland U21.
2016–17 Motherwell 0 0
2017–18 Motherwell 2 0
2018–19 Motherwell 12 1
2019–20 Motherwell 22 3 36 4
2019–20 Hull C 7 1
2020–21 Hull C 18 1
2021–22 Hull C 1 0 26 2
2021–22 *Hibernian* 16 4 16 4

SLATER, Regan (M) 91 3
H: 5 8 W: 10 03 b.Sheffield 11-9-99
2016–17 Sheffield U 0 0
2017–18 Sheffield U 1 0
2018–19 Sheffield U 0 0
2018–19 *Carlisle U* 35 2 35 2
2019–20 Sheffield U 0 0
2019–20 *Scunthorpe U* 12 0 12 0
2020–21 Sheffield U 0 0
2020–21 *Hull C* 27 1
2021–22 Sheffield U 0 0 1 0
2021–22 Hull C 16 0 43 1

SMALLWOOD, Richard (M) 351 11
H: 5 11 W: 11 05 b.Redcar 29-12-90
Internationals: England U18.
2008–09 Middlesbrough 0 0
2009–10 Middlesbrough 0 0
2010–11 Middlesbrough 13 1
2011–12 Middlesbrough 13 0
2012–13 Middlesbrough 22 2
2013–14 Middlesbrough 13 0
2013–14 *Rotherham U* 18 0

2014–15	Middlesbrough	0	0	**61**	**3**
2014–15	*Rotherham U*	41	1		
2015–16	Rotherham U	43	1		
2016–17	Scunthorpe U	16	1	**16**	**1**
2016–17	Rotherham U	25	1	**127**	**3**
2017–18	Blackburn R	46	2		
2018–19	Blackburn R	32	0		
2019–20	Blackburn R	0	0	**78**	**2**
2020–21	Hull C	27	0		
2021–22	Hull C	42	2	**69**	**2**

SMITH, Andy (D) **0 0**
b.Banbury 11-9-01

2019–20	Hull C	0	0		
2020–21	Hull C	0	0		
2021–22	Hull C	0	0		
2021–22	*Salford C*	0	0		

SMITH, Tyler (F) **84 14**
H: 5 10 W: 10 08 b.Sheffield 4-12-98

2018–19	Sheffield U	0	0		
2018–19	*Doncaster R*	14	2	**14**	**2**
2019–20	Sheffield U	0	0		
2019–20	*Bristol R*	20	3	**20**	**3**
2019–20	*Rochdale*	4	1	**4**	**1**
2020–21	Sheffield U	0	0		
2020–21	*Swindon T*	23	7	**23**	**7**
2021–22	Hull C	23	1	**23**	**1**

SNELGROVE, McCauley (M) **0 0**
b. 9-9-02

2020–21	Hull C	0	0		
2021–22	Hull C	0	0		

WILKS, Mallik (F) **168 45**
H: 5 11 W: 11 03 b.Leeds 15-12-98

2016–17	Leeds U	0	0		
2017–18	Leeds U	0	0		
2017–18	*Accrington S*	19	3	**19**	**3**
2017–18	*Grimsby T*	6	0	**6**	**0**
2018–19	Leeds U	0	0		
2018–19	*Doncaster R*	46	14	**46**	**14**
2019–20	Barnsley	15	1	**15**	**1**
2019–20	*Hull C*	18	5		
2020–21	Hull C	44	19		
2021–22	Hull C	20	3	**82**	**27**

WILLIAMS, Randell (M) **115 12**
H: 6 3 W: 12 00 b.Lambeth 30-12-96
From Tower Hamlets.

2016–17	Crystal Palace	0	0		
2017–18	Watford	0	0		
2017–18	*Wycombe W*	6	1		
2018–19	Watford	0	0		
2018–19	*Wycombe W*	20	2	**26**	**3**
2018–19	Exeter C	10	0		
2019–20	Exeter C	37	5		
2020–21	Exeter C	29	4		
2021–22	Exeter C	0	0	**76**	**9**
2021–22	Hull C	13	0	**13**	**0**

WOOD, Harry (M) **11 0**
b.Leeds 2-8-02

2020–21	Hull C	1	0		
2021–22	Scunthorpe U	10	0	**10**	**0**
2021–22	Hull C	0	0	**1**	**0**

Players retained or with offer of contract
Fisk, Harry; Green, Oliver; Hall, Sincere; MacAuley, Thomas; Nixon, Thomas; Taylor, Alfie; Wallis, Harry.

Scholars
Brown, Jake; Carr, James David; Curtis, Henry James Martland; Deacon, Samuel Joseph; Dyer, Rio Laurence; Fanning, Kyle Lewis; Green, Keegan Lee; Leach, Billy Ben; Panesar, Aman Singh; Sani Vernyuy, Verla Glen; Voase, Benjamin Lewis.

IPSWICH T (42)

ALUKO, Sone (F) **402 55**
H: 5 8 W: 9 11 b.Hounslow 19-2-89
Internationals: England U16, U17, U18, U19. Nigeria U20, Full caps.

2005–06	Birmingham C	0	0		
2006–07	Birmingham C	0	0		
2007–08	Birmingham C	0	0		
2007–08	*Aberdeen*	20	3		
2008–09	Birmingham C	0	0		
2008–09	*Blackpool*	1	0	**1**	**0**
2008–09	Aberdeen	32	2		
2009–10	Aberdeen	22	3		
2010–11	Aberdeen	28	2	**102**	**10**
2011–12	Rangers	21	12	**21**	**12**
2012–13	Hull C	23	8		
2013–14	Hull C	17	1		
2014–15	Hull C	25	1		
2015–16	Hull C	25	3	**90**	**13**
2016–17	Fulham	45	8		
2017–18	Fulham	4	0	**49**	**8**
2017–18	Reading	39	3		
2018–19	Reading	19	1		
2019	*Beijing Renhe*	16	3	**16**	**3**
2019–20	Reading	2	0		
2020–21	Reading	33	2	**93**	**6**
2021–22	Ipswich T	30	3	**30**	**3**

ANDOH, Levi (D) **0 0**
b.Amsterdam 12-3-00
From Worcester C, Solihull U.

2020–21	Ipswich T	0	0		
2021–22	Ipswich T	0	0		

ARMIN, Albie (D) **0 0**
b.Colchester 12-4-04

2020–21	Ipswich T	0	0		
2021–22	Ipswich T	0	0		

BAGGOTT, Elkan (D) **2 0**
H: 6 4 W: 13 08 b.Bangkok 23-10-02
Internationals: Indonesia U19, Full caps.

2020–21	Ipswich T	0	0		
2021–22	Ipswich T	2	0	**2**	**0**

BURGESS, Cameron (D) **201 9**
H: 6 4 W: 12 11 b.Aberdeen 21-10-95
Internationals: Scotland U18, U19. Australia U20, U23.

2014–15	Fulham	4	0		
2014–15	*Ross Co*	0	0		
2015–16	Fulham	0	0		
2016–17	Fulham	0	0	**4**	**0**
2016–17	*Oldham Ath*	23	1	**23**	**1**
2016–17	*Bury*	18	0	**18**	**0**
2017–18	Scunthorpe U	25	2		
2018–19	Scunthorpe U	36	1		
2019–20	Scunthorpe U	0	0	**61**	**3**
2019–20	*Salford C*	29	2	**29**	**2**
2020–21	Accrington S	44	3		
2021–22	Accrington S	1	0	**45**	**3**
2021–22	Ipswich T	21	0	**21**	**0**

BURNS, Wes (F) **274 41**
H: 5 8 W: 10 10 b.Cardiff 23-11-94
Internationals: Wales U21, Full caps.

2012–13	Bristol C	6	0		
2013–14	Bristol C	20	1		
2014–15	Bristol C	3	1		
2014–15	*Oxford U*	9	1	**9**	**1**
2014–15	*Cheltenham T*	14	4	**14**	**4**
2015–16	Bristol C	14	1	**43**	**3**
2015–16	*Fleetwood T*	14	5		
2016–17	Fleetwood T	10	0		
2016–17	*Aberdeen*	13	0	**13**	**0**
2017–18	Fleetwood T	28	2		
2018–19	Fleetwood T	39	7		
2019–20	Fleetwood T	34	2		
2020–21	Fleetwood T	33	5		
2021–22	Fleetwood T	0	0	**158**	**21**
2021–22	Ipswich T	37	12	**37**	**12**

CARROLL, Tommy (M) **202 3**
H: 5 10 W: 10 00 b.Watford 28-5-92
Internationals: England U19, U21.

2010–11	Tottenham H	0	0		
2010–11	*Leyton Orient*	12	0	**12**	**0**
2011–12	Tottenham H	0	0		
2011–12	*Derby Co*	12	1	**12**	**1**
2012–13	Tottenham H	7	0		
2013–14	Tottenham H	0	0		
2013–14	*QPR*	26	0		
2014–15	Tottenham H	0	0		
2014–15	*Swansea C*	13	0		
2015–16	Tottenham H	19	1		
2016–17	Tottenham H	1	0	**27**	**1**
2016–17	Swansea C	17	1		
2017–18	Swansea C	37	0		
2018–19	Swansea C	12	0		
2018–19	*Aston Villa*	2	0	**2**	**0**
2019–20	Swansea C	8	0	**87**	**1**
2020–21	QPR	22	0		
2021–22	QPR	0	0	**48**	**0**
2021–22	Ipswich T	14	0	**14**	**0**

CELINA, Bersant (M) **200 25**
H: 5 4 W: 9 06 b.Prizren 9-9-96
Internationals: Norway U16, U17. Kosovo Full caps.

2014–15	Manchester C	0	0		
2015–16	Manchester C	1	0		
2016–17	Manchester C	0	0		
2016–17	*FC Twente*	27	5	**27**	**5**
2017–18	Manchester C	0	0	**1**	**0**
2017–18	*Ipswich T*	35	7		
2018–19	Swansea C	38	5		
2019–20	Swansea C	35	2	**73**	**7**
2020–21	Dijon	32	0	**32**	**0**
2021–22	Dijon	0	0		
2021–22	*Ipswich T*	32	6	**67**	**13**

CHAPLIN, Conor (M) **252 54**
H: 5 10 W: 10 12 b.Worthing 16-2-97

2014–15	Portsmouth	9	1		
2015–16	Portsmouth	30	8		
2016–17	Portsmouth	39	8		
2017–18	Portsmouth	26	5	**104**	**22**
2018–19	Coventry C	31	8	**31**	**8**
2019–20	Barnsley	44	11		
2020–21	Barnsley	34	4		
2021–22	Barnsley	0	0	**78**	**15**
2021–22	Ipswich T	39	9	**39**	**9**

CHIREWA, Tawanda (M) **0 0**

2019–20	Ipswich T	0	0		
2020–21	Ipswich T	0	0		
2021–22	Ipswich T	0	0		

CLEMENTS, Bailey (D) **8 0**
H: 6 1 W: 10 03 b.Ipswich 15-11-00

2019–20	Ipswich T	0	0		
2020–21	Ipswich T	0	0		
2021–22	Ipswich T	4	0	**4**	**0**
2021–22	*Stevenage*	4	0	**4**	**0**

CROWE, Dylan (M) **0 0**
b. 13-4-01
Internationals: England U16, U17, U18.

2020–21	Ipswich T	0	0		
2021–22	Ipswich T	0	0		

DOBRA, Armando (M) **33 1**
H: 5 9 W: 11 00 b.Redbridge 14-4-01
Internationals: Albania U19, U21.

2019–20	Ipswich T	3	0		
2020–21	Ipswich T	17	0		
2021–22	Ipswich T	2	0	**22**	**0**
2021–22	*Colchester U*	11	1	**11**	**1**

DONACIEN, Janoi (D) **246 1**
H: 6 0 W: 11 11 b.St Lucia 3-11-93
Internationals: St Lucia Full caps.

2011–12	Aston Villa	0	0		
2012–13	Aston Villa	0	0		
2013–14	Aston Villa	0	0		
2014–15	Aston Villa	0	0		
2014–15	*Tranmere R*	31	0	**31**	**0**
2015–16	Aston Villa	0	0		
2015–16	*Wycombe W*	2	0	**2**	**0**
2015–16	*Newport Co*	29	0	**29**	**0**
2016–17	Accrington S	35	1		
2017–18	Accrington S	45	0		
2018–19	Ipswich T	10	0		
2018–19	*Accrington S*	19	0	**99**	**1**
2019–20	Ipswich T	13	0		
2020–21	Ipswich T	0	0		
2020–21	*Fleetwood T*	19	0	**19**	**0**
2021–22	Ipswich T	43	0	**66**	**0**

EDMUNDSON, Sam (D) **115 7**
H: 6 3 W: 11 11 b.Timperley 15-8-97

2015–16	Oldham Ath	2	0		
2016–17	Oldham Ath	3	0		
2017–18	Oldham Ath	15	1		
2018–19	Oldham Ath	45	2	**65**	**3**
2019–20	Rangers	7	1		
2020–21	Rangers	1	0		
2020–21	*Derby Co*	10	1	**10**	**1**
2021–22	Rangers	0	0	**8**	**1**
2021–22	Ipswich T	32	2	**32**	**2**

EDWARDS, Kyle (M) **78 3**
H: 5 8 W: 10 01 b.Dudley 17-2-98
Internationals: England U16, U17, U20.

2015–16	WBA	0	0		
2016–17	WBA	0	0		
2017–18	WBA	0	0		
2017–18	*Exeter C*	23	0	**23**	**0**
2018–19	WBA	6	1		
2019–20	WBA	26	2		
2020–21	WBA	5	0	**37**	**3**
2021–22	Ipswich T	18	0	**18**	**0**

EL MIZOUNI, Idris (M) **36 1**
H: 6 1 W: 11 09 b.Paris 26-9-00
Internationals: Tunisia U23, Tunisia Full caps.

2018–19	Ipswich T	4	0		
2019–20	Ipswich T	3	0		
2019–20	*Cambridge U*	7	1		
2020–21	Ipswich T	0	0		
2020–21	*Cambridge U*	11	0	**18**	**1**
2020–21	*Grimsby T*	6	0	**6**	**0**
2021–22	Ipswich T	5	0	**12**	**0**

EVANS, Lee (M) **249 18**
H: 6 1 W: 13 12 b.Newport 24-7-94
Internationals: Wales U21, Full caps.
From Newport Co.

2012–13	Wolverhampton W	0	0		
2013–14	Wolverhampton W	26	2		
2014–15	Wolverhampton W	18	1		
2015–16	Wolverhampton W	0	0		
2015–16	*Bradford C*	35	4	**35**	**4**
2016–17	Wolverhampton W	15	0		
2017–18	Wolverhampton W	0	0	**59**	**3**
2017–18	*Wigan Ath*	20	1		
2017–18	Sheffield U	19	2		
2018–19	Sheffield U	2	0	**21**	**2**
2018–19	*Wigan Ath*	34	1		
2019–20	Wigan Ath	32	2		
2020–21	Wigan Ath	21	2		
2021–22	Wigan Ath	0	0	**107**	**6**
2021–22	Ipswich T	27	3	**27**	**3**

HARPER, Rekeem (M) **79 1**
H: 6 0 W: 10 01 b.Birmingham 8-3-00
Internationals: England U17, U19.

2016–17	WBA	0	0		
2017–18	WBA	1	0		
2017–18	*Blackburn R*	4	0	**4**	**0**
2018–19	WBA	16	1		
2019–20	WBA	10	0		

2020–21 WBA 2 0
2020–21 *Birmingham C* 18 0 18 0
2021–22 WBA 0 0 29 1
2021–22 Ipswich T 13 0 13 0
2021–22 *Crewe Alex* 15 0 15 0

HAYES, Nick (G) 0 0
Internationals: England U17.
From Ipswich T, Woking, Dunstable, Norwich C.
2020–21 Salford C 0 0
2021–22 Ipswich T 0 0

HEALY, Matthew (M) 14 4
b. 12-4-02
From Corinthians.
2020–21 Ipswich T 0 0
2021–22 Ipswich T 0 0
2022 *Cork C* 14 4 14 4

HLADKY, Vaclav (G) 178 0
H: 6 2 W: 12 08 b.Brno 14-11-90
Internationals: Czech Republic U16, U17, U18, U19, U20.
2010–11 Zbrojovka Brno 0 0
2011–12 Zbrojovka Brno 0 0
2012–13 Zbrojovka Brno 1 0
2013–14 Zbrojovka Brno 25 0
2014–15 Zbrojovka Brno 16 0 42 0
2015–16 Slovan Liberec 5 0
2016–17 Slovan Liberec 2 0
2017–18 Slovan Liberec 15 0
2018–19 Slovan Liberec 9 0 31 0
2018–19 St Mirren 17 0
2019–20 St Mirren 30 0 47 0
2020–21 Salford C 46 0
2021–22 Salford C 0 0 46 0
2021–22 Ipswich T 12 0 12 0

HOLY, Tomas (G) 235 0
H: 6 9 W: 16 05 b.Rychnov nad Kneznou 10-12-91
Internationals: Czech Republic U16, U17, U18.
2010–11 Sparta Prague 0 0
2011–12 Sparta Prague 0 0
2012–13 Sparta Prague 0 0
2013–14 Sparta Prague 0 0
2013–14 *Vlasim* 9 0 9 0
2013–14 *Viktoria Zizkov* 14 0
2014–15 Sparta Prague 0 0
2014–15 *Viktoria Zizkov* 27 0 41 0
2015–16 Sparta Prague 0 0
2015–16 *Fastav Zlin* 20 0 20 0
2016–17 Sparta Prague 0 0
2016–17 *Fastav Zlin* 0 0
2016–17 Gillingham 6 0
2017–18 Gillingham 45 0
2018–19 Gillingham 46 0 97 0
2019–20 Ipswich T 21 0
2020–21 Ipswich T 36 0
2021–22 Ipswich T 0 0 57 0
2021–22 *Cambridge U* 2 0 2 0
2021–22 *Port Vale* 9 0 9 0

HUGHES, Thomas (F) 0 0
b. 21-10-00
2019–20 Ipswich T 0 0
2020–21 Ipswich T 0 0
2021–22 Ipswich T 0 0

HUMPHREYS, Cameron (M) 2 0
b. 30-10-03
2021–22 Ipswich T 2 0 2 0

JACKSON, Kayden (F) 170 35
H: 5 11 W: 11 07 b.Bradford 22-2-94
Internationals: England C.
2013–14 Swindon T 0 0
2014–15 Swindon T 0 0
From Oxford C, Tamworth, Wrexham.
2016–17 Barnsley 0 0
2016–17 *Grimsby T* 20 1 20 1
2017–18 Accrington S 44 16
2018–19 Accrington S 1 0 45 16
2018–19 Ipswich T 36 3
2019–20 Ipswich T 32 11
2020–21 Ipswich T 25 1
2021–22 Ipswich T 12 3 105 18

KENLOCK, Myles (D) 105 3
H: 6 1 W: 10 08 b.Croydon 29-11-96
2015–16 Ipswich T 2 0
2016–17 Ipswich T 18 0
2017–18 Ipswich T 16 0
2018–19 Ipswich T 19 0
2019–20 Ipswich T 9 0
2020–21 Ipswich T 21 0
2021–22 Ipswich T 0 0 85 0
2021–22 *Colchester U* 20 3 20 3

MANLY, Jack (M) 0 0
b. 19-10-04
2020–21 Ipswich T 0 0
2021–22 Ipswich T 0 0

McGAVIN, Brett (M) 7 0
b.Bury St Edmunds 21-12-99
2019–20 Ipswich T 1 0
2020–21 Ipswich T 5 0
2020–21 *Ayr U* 1 0 1 0
2021–22 Ipswich T 0 0 6 0

MORRIS, Ben (F) 8 1
H: 5 9 W: 9 06 b.Colchester 6-7-99
Internationals: England U17, U18, U19.
2016–17 Ipswich T 0 0
2017–18 Ipswich T 3 0
2018–19 Ipswich T 1 0
2018–19 *Forest Green R* 4 1 4 1
2019–20 Ipswich T 0 0
2020–21 Ipswich T 0 0
2021–22 Ipswich T 0 0 4 0
2021–22 *GAIS* 0 0

MORSY, Sam (M) 407 23
H: 5 9 W: 12 06 b.Wolverhampton 10-9-91
Internationals: Egypt Full caps.
2009–10 Port Vale 1 0
2010–11 Port Vale 16 1
2011–12 Port Vale 26 1
2012–13 Port Vale 28 2 71 4
2013–14 Chesterfield 34 1
2014–15 Chesterfield 39 2
2015–16 Chesterfield 26 4 99 7
2015–16 Wigan Ath 16 1
2016–17 Wigan Ath 15 1
2016–17 *Barnsley* 14 0 14 0
2017–18 Wigan Ath 41 2
2018–19 Wigan Ath 40 1
2019–20 Wigan Ath 43 3 155 8
2020–21 Middlesbrough 31 1
2021–22 Middlesbrough 3 0 34 1
2021–22 Ipswich T 34 3 34 3

NDABA, Corrie (D) 42 2
H: 6 2 W: 12 13 b.Dublin 25-12-99
Internationals: Republic of Ireland U18.
2018–19 Ipswich T 0 0
2019–20 Ipswich T 0 0
2020–21 Ipswich T 0 0
2020–21 *Ayr U* 13 0 13 0
2021–22 Ipswich T 0 0
2021–22 *Salford C* 29 2 29 2

NORWOOD, James (F) 126 55
H: 6 0 W: 12 13 b.Eastbourne 5-9-90
Internationals: England U18, C.
From Eastbourne T.
2009–10 Exeter C 3 0
2010–11 Exeter C 1 0 4 0
From Forest Green R.
2018–19 Tranmere R 45 29 45 29
2019–20 Ipswich T 28 11
2020–21 Ipswich T 26 9
2021–22 Ipswich T 23 6 77 26

PENNEY, Matt (D) 70 2
H: 5 8 W: 10 01 b.Chesterfield 11-2-98
2016–17 Sheffield W 0 0
2016–17 *Bradford C* 1 0 1 0
2017–18 Sheffield W 0 0
2017–18 *Mansfield T* 2 0 2 0
2018–19 Sheffield W 16 0
2019–20 Sheffield W 0 0
2019–20 *St Pauli* 17 1 17 1
2020–21 Sheffield W 12 0 28 0
2021–22 Ipswich T 22 1 22 1

PIGOTT, Joe (F) 256 66
H: 6 2 W: 9 06 b.London 24-11-93
2012–13 Charlton Ath 0 0
2013–14 Charlton Ath 11 0
2013–14 *Gillingham* 7 1 7 1
2014–15 Charlton Ath 1 0
2014–15 *Newport Co* 10 3 10 3
2014–15 *Southend U* 20 6
2015–16 Charlton Ath 0 0 12 0
2015–16 *Southend U* 23 3 43 9
2015–16 *Luton T* 15 4 15 4
2016–17 Cambridge U 10 0 10 0
From Maidstone U.
2017–18 AFC Wimbledon 18 5
2018–19 AFC Wimbledon 40 15
2019–20 AFC Wimbledon 34 7
2020–21 AFC Wimbledon 45 20
2021–22 AFC Wimbledon 0 0 137 47
2021–22 Ipswich T 22 2 22 2

SIMPSON, Tyreece (F) 29 9
b.Ipswich 7-2-02
2019–20 Ipswich T 3 0
2020–21 Ipswich T 1 0
2021–22 Ipswich T 0 0 4 0
2021–22 *Swindon T* 25 9 25 9

SIZIBA, Zanda (M) 0 0
H: 5 9 b. 19-7-03
From Dagenham & R, Tottenham H.
2020–21 Ipswich T 0 0
2021–22 Ipswich T 0 0

SMITH, Tom (D) 0 0
b. 18-11-01
2019–20 Ipswich T 0 0
2020–21 Ipswich T 0 0
2021–22 Ipswich T 0 0

VINCENT-YOUNG, Kane (D) 143 6
H: 5 11 W: 11 00 b.Camden Town 15-3-96
From Tottenham H, Banbury U.
2014–15 Colchester U 0 0
2015–16 Colchester U 14 0
2016–17 Colchester U 18 0
2017–18 Colchester U 38 1
2018–19 Colchester U 40 3
2019–20 Colchester U 2 0 112 4
2019–20 Ipswich T 9 2
2020–21 Ipswich T 7 0
2021–22 Ipswich T 15 0 31 2

WALTON, Christian (G) 190 0
H: 6 0 W: 11 11 b.Wadebridge 9-11-95
Internationals: England U19, U20, U21.
2011–12 Plymouth Arg 0 0
2012–13 Plymouth Arg 0 0
2013–14 Brighton & HA 0 0
2014–15 Brighton & HA 3 0
2015–16 Brighton & HA 0 0
2015–16 *Bury* 4 0 4 0
2015–16 *Plymouth Arg* 4 0 4 0
2016–17 Brighton & HA 0 0
2016–17 *Luton T* 27 0 27 0
2016–17 *Southend U* 7 0 7 0
2017–18 Brighton & HA 0 0
2017–18 *Wigan Ath* 31 0
2018–19 Brighton & HA 0 0
2018–19 *Wigan Ath* 34 0 65 0
2019–20 Brighton & HA 0 0
2019–20 *Blackburn R* 46 0 46 0
2020–21 Brighton & HA 0 0 3 0
2021–22 Ipswich T 34 0 34 0

WHITE, Albert (G) 0 0
b. 29-10-01
From AFC Wimbledon.
2020–21 Ipswich T 0 0
2021–22 Ipswich T 0 0

WOOLFENDEN, Luke (D) 122 4
H: 6 4 W: 11 00 b.Ipswich 21-10-98
2017–18 Ipswich T 2 0
2018–19 Ipswich T 1 0
2018–19 *Swindon T* 32 2 32 2
2019–20 Ipswich T 31 1
2020–21 Ipswich T 25 1
2021–22 Ipswich T 31 0 90 2

YENGI, Tete (M) 20 5
H: 6 5 W: 13 01 b.Adelaide 15-1-99
2020–21 Newcastle Jets 9 0 9 0
2021–22 Ipswich T 0 0
2021–22 *VPS* 11 5 11 5

Players retained or with offer of contract
Alexander, Fraser; Bort, Antoni; Curtis, Harley; Cutbush, Alfie; Kabongolo, Brooklyn; Page, Callum; Stewart, Cameron; Ward, Matt.

Scholars
Agbaje, Edwin Olamide; Barbrook, Finley Frank; Barbrook, Harry Thomas; Boatswain, Ashley Frank; Bradshaw, Zak Dominic; Buabo, Gerrard Bantu; Catley, Jack Samuel; Corrigan, Finlay Joseph; Cousens, Daniel Thomas; Hoque, Yousuf Zulqumain; Kieran, Archie William; Knock, Harry John; Moodie, Paul Stewart; Nwabueze, Jesse Chizoba; O'Neill, Seth Taylor-Lee; Osbourne, Tyrese Lamar; Ridd, Lewis Paul Joseph; Steele, Finn Franco; Stephenson, Sean; Valentine, Nico Andre.

LEEDS U (43)

ALLEN, Charlie (F) 4 0
b.Belfast 22-11-03
Internationals: Northern Ireland U17.
2018–19 Linfield 1 0
2019–20 Linfield 3 0 4 0
2020–21 Leeds U 0 0
2021–22 Leeds U 0 0

AYLING, Luke (D) 454 14
H: 6 0 W: 11 05 b.Lambeth 25-8-91
2009–10 Arsenal 0 0
2009–10 *Yeovil T* 4 0
2010–11 Yeovil T 37 0
2011–12 Yeovil T 44 0
2012–13 Yeovil T 39 0
2013–14 Yeovil T 42 2 166 2
2014–15 Bristol C 46 4
2015–16 Bristol C 33 0
2016–17 Bristol C 1 0 80 4
2016–17 Leeds U 42 0
2017–18 Leeds U 27 0
2018–19 Leeds U 38 2
2019–20 Leeds U 37 4
2020–21 Leeds U 38 0
2021–22 Leeds U 26 2 208 8

BAMFORD, Patrick (F) **278** **99**
H: 6 1 W: 11 03 b.Newark 5-9-93
Internationals: Republic of Ireland U18. England U18, U19, U21, Full caps.

2010–11	Nottingham F	0	0		
2011–12	Nottingham F	2	0	**2**	**0**
2011–12	Chelsea	0	0		
2012–13	Chelsea	0	0		
2012–13	*Milton Keynes D*	14	4		
2013–14	Chelsea	0	0		
2013–14	*Milton Keynes D*	23	14	**37**	**18**
2013–14	*Derby Co*	21	8	**21**	**8**
2014–15	Chelsea	0	0		
2014–15	*Middlesbrough*	38	17		
2015–16	Chelsea	0	0		
2015–16	*Crystal Palace*	6	0	**6**	**0**
2015–16	*Norwich C*	7	0	**7**	**0**
2016–17	Chelsea	0	0		
2016–17	*Burnley*	6	0	**6**	**0**
2016–17	*Middlesbrough*	8	1		
2017–18	Middlesbrough	39	11	**85**	**29**
2018–19	Leeds U	22	9		
2019–20	Leeds U	45	16		
2020–21	Leeds U	38	17		
2021–22	Leeds U	9	2	**114**	**44**

BATE, Lewis (M) **3** **0**
H: 5 7 b.Sidcup 29-10-02
Internationals: England U17, U18, U20.

2019–20	Chelsea	0	0		
2020–21	Chelsea	0	0		
2021–22	Leeds U	3	0	**3**	**0**

BOGUSZ, Mateusz (M) **44** **5**
H: 5 9 b.Ruda Slalka 22-8-01
Internationals: Poland U16, U17, U19, U20, U21.

2018–19	Leeds U	0	0		
2019–20	Leeds U	1	0		
2020–21	Leeds U	0	0		
2020–21	*Logrones*	23	1	**23**	**1**
2021–22	Leeds U	0	0	**1**	**0**
2021–22	*Ibiza*	20	4	**20**	**4**

CAPRILE, Elia (G) **38** **0**
b.Verona 25-8-01
Internationals: Italy U18.
From Verona.

2019–20	Leeds U	0	0		
2020–21	Leeds U	0	0		
2021–22	Leeds U	0	0		
2021–22	*Pro Patria*	38	0	**38**	**0**

CASILLA, Francisco (G) **311** **0**
H: 6 4 W: 13 01 b.Alcocer 2-10-86
Internationals: Spain U19, U21, Full caps.

2004–05	Real Madrid	0	0		
2005–06	Real Madrid	0	0		
2006–07	Real Madrid	0	0		
2007–08	Espanyol	4	0		
2008–09	Espanyol	0	0		
2008–09	*Cadiz*	35	0		
2009–10	Espanyol	0	0		
2009–10	*Cadiz*	31	0	**66**	**0**
2010–11	Espanyol	0	0		
2010–11	*Cartagena*	35	0	**35**	**0**
2011–12	Espanyol	16	0		
2012–13	Espanyol	21	0		
2013–14	Espanyol	37	0		
2014–15	Espanyol	37	0	**115**	**0**
2015–16	Real Madrid	4	0		
2016–17	Real Madrid	11	0		
2017–18	Real Madrid	10	0	**25**	**0**
2018–19	Leeds U	17	0		
2019–20	Leeds U	36	0		
2020–21	Leeds U	3	0		
2021–22	Leeds U	0	0	**56**	**0**
2021–22	*Elche*	14	0	**14**	**0**

COOPER, Liam (D) **321** **15**
H: 5 11 W: 11 07 b.Hull 30-8-91
Internationals: Scotland U17, U19, Full caps.

2008–09	Hull C	0	0		
2009–10	Hull C	2	0		
2010–11	Hull C	2	0		
2010–11	*Carlisle U*	6	1	**6**	**1**
2011–12	Hull C	7	0		
2011–12	*Huddersfield T*	4	0	**4**	**0**
2012–13	Hull C	0	0	**11**	**0**
2012–13	Chesterfield	29	2		
2013–14	Chesterfield	41	3		
2014–15	Chesterfield	1	0	**71**	**5**
2014–15	Leeds U	29	1		
2015–16	Leeds U	39	1		
2016–17	Leeds U	11	0		
2017–18	Leeds U	30	1		
2018–19	Leeds U	36	3		
2019–20	Leeds U	38	2		
2020–21	Leeds U	25	1		
2021–22	Leeds U	21	0	**229**	**9**

CRESSWELL, Charlie (D) **5** **0**
H: 6 0 W: 10 06 b.Preston 7-12-00
Internationals: England U21.

2020–21	Leeds U	0	0		
2021–22	Leeds U	5	0	**5**	**0**

DALLAS, Stuart (M) **344** **60**
H: 6 0 W: 12 11 b.Cookstown 19-4-91
Internationals: Northern Ireland U21, U23, Full caps.

2010–11	Crusaders	13	16		
2011–12	Crusaders	8	8	**21**	**24**
2012–13	Brentford	7	0		
2013–14	Brentford	18	2		
2013–14	*Northampton T*	12	3	**12**	**3**
2014–15	Brentford	38	6	**63**	**8**
2015–16	Leeds U	45	5		
2016–17	Leeds U	31	2		
2017–18	Leeds U	29	2		
2018–19	Leeds U	26	2		
2019–20	Leeds U	45	5		
2020–21	Leeds U	38	8		
2021–22	Leeds U	34	1	**248**	**25**

DAVIS, Leif (D) **21** **0**
H: 5 5 W: 10 08 b.Newcastle upon Tyne 12-1-00
From Morecambe.

2018–19	Leeds U	4	0		
2019–20	Leeds U	3	0		
2020–21	Leeds U	2	0		
2021–22	Leeds U	0	0	**9**	**0**
2021–22	*Bournemouth*	12	0	**12**	**0**

DE BOCK, Laurens (D) **307** **5**
b. 7-11-92
Internationals: Belgium U16, U17, U18, U19, U21.

2009–10	Lokeren	5	0		
2010–11	Lokeren	25	0		
2011–12	Lokeren	29	1		
2012–13	Lokeren	21	0	**80**	**1**
2012–13	Club Brugge	11	0		
2013–14	Club Brugge	33	0		
2014–15	Club Brugge	36	0		
2015–16	Club Brugge	31	1		
2016–17	Club Brugge	18	0		
2017–18	Club Brugge	6	0	**135**	**1**
2017–18	Leeds U	7	0		
2018–19	Leeds U	0	0		
2018–19	*Oostende*	13	1	**13**	**1**
2019–20	Leeds U	0	0		
2019–20	*Sunderland*	5	0	**5**	**0**
2019–20	*Den Haag*	8	0	**8**	**0**
2020–21	Leeds U	0	0		
2020–21	*Zulte Waregem*	31	2		
2021–22	Leeds U	0	0	**7**	**0**
2021–22	*Zulte Waregem*	28	0	**59**	**2**

DEAN, Max (F) **0** **0**
H: 5 10 b.Ormskirk 21-2-04

2020–21	Leeds U	0	0		
2021–22	Leeds U	0	0		

DRAMEH, Cody (D) **25** **0**
H: 5 9 W: 10 12 b.Lambeth 8-12-01
Internationals: England U18, U20, U21.
From Fulham.

2020–21	Leeds U	0	0		
2021–22	Leeds U	3	0	**3**	**0**
2021–22	*Cardiff C*	22	0	**22**	**0**

EDMONDSON, Ryan (F) **67** **7**
H: 6 2 W: 12 06 b.York 20-5-01
Internationals: England U19.
From York C.

2017–18	Leeds U	1	0		
2018–19	Leeds U	1	0		
2019–20	Leeds U	0	0		
2020–21	Leeds U	0	0		
2020–21	*Aberdeen*	14	2	**14**	**2**
2020–21	*Northampton T*	21	2	**21**	**2**
2021–22	Leeds U	0	0	**2**	**0**
2021–22	*Fleetwood T*	11	0	**11**	**0**
2021–22	*Port Vale*	19	3	**19**	**3**

FIRPO, Junior (D) **86** **7**
H: 6 0 W: 12 04 b.Santo Domingo 22-8-96
Internationals: Dominican Republic Full caps. Spain U21.

2014–15	Real Betis	0	0		
2015–16	Real Betis	0	0		
2016–17	Real Betis	0	0		
2017–18	Real Betis	14	2		
2018–19	Real Betis	24	3	**38**	**5**
2019–20	Barcelona	17	1		
2020–21	Barcelona	7	1		
2021–22	Barcelona	0	0	**24**	**2**
2021–22	Leeds U	24	0	**24**	**0**

FORSHAW, Adam (M) **269** **14**
H: 5 9 W: 11 03 b.Liverpool 8-10-91

2009–10	Everton	0	0		
2010–11	Everton	1	0		
2011–12	Everton	0	0	**1**	**0**
2011–12	*Brentford*	7	0		
2012–13	Brentford	43	3		
2013–14	Brentford	39	8	**89**	**11**
2014–15	Wigan Ath	16	1	**16**	**1**
2014–15	Middlesbrough	18	0		
2015–16	Middlesbrough	29	2		
2016–17	Middlesbrough	34	0		
2017–18	Middlesbrough	11	0	**92**	**2**
2017–18	Leeds U	12	0		
2018–19	Leeds U	30	0		
2019–20	Leeds U	7	0		
2020–21	Leeds U	0	0		
2021–22	Leeds U	22	0	**71**	**0**

GALLOWAY, Josh (M) **0** **0**
b.Glasgow 21-1-02
From Carlisle U.

2019–20	Leeds U	0	0		
2020–21	Leeds U	0	0		
2021–22	Leeds U	0	0		

GELHARDT, Joe (F) **39** **3**
H: 5 10 W: 11 03 b.Liverpool 4-5-02
Internationals: England U16, U17, U18, U20.

2018–19	Wigan Ath	1	0		
2019–20	Wigan Ath	18	1	**19**	**1**
2020–21	Leeds U	0	0		
2021–22	Leeds U	20	2	**20**	**2**

GRAY, Archie (F) **0** **0**
b.Durham 12-3-06

2021–22	Leeds U	0	0		

GREENWOOD, Sam (F) **7** **0**
H: 5 11 W: 10 01 b.Sunderland 26-1-02
Internationals: England U16, U17, U18, U19, U20, U21.

2019–20	Arsenal	0	0		
2020–21	Leeds U	0	0		
2021–22	Leeds U	7	0	**7**	**0**

HARRISON, Jack (M) **213** **40**
H: 5 9 W: 11 03 b.Stoke-on-Trent 20-11-96
Internationals: England U21.

2016	New York C	21	4		
2017	New York C	34	10	**55**	**14**
2017–18	Manchester C	0	0		
2017–18	*Middlesbrough*	4	0	**4**	**0**
2018–19	Manchester C	0	0		
2018–19	*Leeds U*	37	4		
2019–20	Manchester C	0	0		
2019–20	*Leeds U*	46	6		
2020–21	Manchester C	0	0		
2020–21	*Leeds U*	36	8		
2021–22	Manchester C	0	0		
2021–22	Leeds U	35	8	**154**	**26**

HELDER COSTA, Wander (M) **215** **26**
H: 5 10 W: 11 07 b.Luanda 12-1-94
Internationals: Portugal U16, U17, U18, U19, U20, U21, U23, Full caps.

2013–14	Benfica	0	0		
2014–15	Benfica	0	0		
2014–15	*Deportivo la Coruna*	6	0	**6**	**0**
2015–16	Benfica	0	0		
2015–16	*Monaco*	25	3	**25**	**3**
2016–17	Benfica	0	0		
2016–17	*Wolverhampton W*	35	10		
2017–18	Wolverhampton W	36	5		
2018–19	Wolverhampton W	25	1		
2019–20	Wolverhampton W	0	0	**96**	**16**
2019–20	*Leeds U*	43	4		
2020–21	Leeds U	22	3		
2021–22	Leeds U	1	0	**66**	**7**
2021–22	*Valencia*	22	0	**22**	**0**

HJELDE, Leo (D) **13** **1**
H: 6 2 b.Nottingham 26-8-03
Internationals: Norway U16, U17, U18, U19, U21.
From Rosenborg.

2020–21	Celtic	0	0		
2020–21	*Ross Co*	11	1	**11**	**1**
2021–22	Leeds U	2	0	**2**	**0**

JAMES, Daniel (M) **115** **14**
H: 5 11 W: 12 00 b.Kingston upon Hull 10-11-97
Internationals: Wales U17, U19, U20, U21, Full caps.
Full Hull C.

2015–16	Swansea C	0	0		
2016–17	Swansea C	0	0		
2017–18	Swansea C	0	0		
2017–18	*Shrewsbury T*	0	0		
2018–19	Swansea C	33	4	**33**	**4**
2019–20	Manchester U	33	3		
2020–21	Manchester U	15	3		
2021–22	Manchester U	2	0	**50**	**6**
2021–22	Leeds U	32	4	**32**	**4**

JENKINS, Jack (M) **0** **0**
H: 5 10 W: 11 00 b.Leeds 23-3-02

2020–21	Leeds U	0	0		
2021–22	Leeds U	0	0		

KAMWA, Bobby (M) **7** **0**
H: 6 0 W: 12 02 b.Yaounde 18-3-00

2020–21	Leeds U	0	0		
2021–22	Leeds U	0	0		
2021–22	*Dunfermline Ath*	7	0	**7**	**0**

KLAESSON, Kristoffer (G) **56** **0**
H: 6 2 W: 12 00 b.Oslo 27-11-00
Internationals: Norway U16, U17, U18, U19, U21.

2019	Valerenga	12	0		
2020	Valerenga	29	0		

2021	Valerenga	14	0	**55**	**0**
2021–22	Leeds U	1	0	**1**	**0**

KLICH, Mateusz (M) 323 43
H: 6 0 W: 10 10 b.Tarnow 13-6-90
Internationals: Poland U18, U19, U20, U21, Full caps.

2008–09	Cracovia	5	0		
2009–10	Cracovia	21	1		
2010–11	Cracovia	27	4	**53**	**5**
2011–12	VfL Wolfsburg	0	0		
2012–13	VfL Wolfsburg	0	0		
2012–13	*Zwolle*	13	2		
2013–14	Zwolle	30	4	**43**	**6**
2014–15	VfL Wolfsburg	0	0		
2014–15	Kaiserslautern	5	1		
2015–16	Kaiserslautern	16	3	**21**	**4**
2016–17	FC Twente	29	6	**29**	**6**
2017–18	Leeds U	4	0		
2017–18	*Utrecht*	14	1	**14**	**1**
2018–19	Leeds U	46	10		
2019–20	Leeds U	45	6		
2020–21	Leeds U	35	4		
2021–22	Leeds U	33	1	**163**	**21**

KOCH, Robin (D) 146 4
H: 6 3 W: 13 05 b.Kaiserslaurten 17-7-96
Internationals: Germany U21, Full caps.

2015–16	Kaiserslautern	0	0		
2016–17	Kaiserslautern	24	0		
2017–18	Kaiserslautern	3	0	**27**	**0**
2017–18	Freiburg	26	2		
2018–19	Freiburg	24	1		
2019–20	Freiburg	32	1		
2020–21	Freiburg	0	0	**82**	**4**
2020–21	Leeds U	17	0		
2021–22	Leeds U	20	0	**37**	**0**

LLORENTE, Diego (D) 180 12
H: 6 1 W: 11 09 b.Madrid 16-8-93
Internationals: Spain U20, Full caps.

2012–13	Real Madrid	1	0		
2013–14	Real Madrid	1	0		
2014–15	Real Madrid	0	0		
2015–16	Real Madrid	0	0		
2015–16	*Vallecano*	33	2	**33**	**2**
2016–17	Real Madrid	0	0	**2**	**0**
2016–17	*Malaga*	25	2	**25**	**2**
2017–18	Real Sociedad	27	3		
2018–19	Real Sociedad	21	0		
2019–20	Real Sociedad	29	1		
2020–21	Real Sociedad	0	0	**77**	**4**
2020–21	Leeds U	15	1		
2021–22	Leeds U	28	3	**43**	**4**

McCALMONT, Alfie (M) 61 9
H: 5 8 W: 11 11 b.Thirsk 25-3-00
Internationals: Northern Ireland U17, U19, U21, Full caps.

2019–20	Leeds U	0	0		
2020–21	Leeds U	0	0		
2020–21	*Oldham Ath*	35	8	**35**	**8**
2021–22	Leeds U	0	0		
2021–22	*Morecambe*	26	1	**26**	**1**

McCARRON, Liam (M) 17 0
H: 5 9 W: 9 08 b.Preston 7-3-01
Internationals: Scotland U19.

2018–19	Carlisle U	16	0	**16**	**0**
2019–20	Leeds U	0	0		
2020–21	Leeds U	0	0		
2021–22	Leeds U	1	0	**1**	**0**

McKINSTRY, Stuart (M) 1 0
H: 5 10 W: 10 10 b.Wishaw 18-9-02
Internationals: Scotland U17.
From Motherwell.

2021–22	Leeds U	1	0	**1**	**0**

MESLIER, Illan (G) 111 0
H: 6 6 W: 11 09 b.Lorient 2-3-00
Internationals: France U18, U19, U20, U21.

2016–17	Lorient	0	0		
2017–18	Lorient	0	0		
2018–19	Lorient	28	0		
2019–20	Lorient	0	0	**28**	**0**
2019–20	*Leeds U*	10	0		
2020–21	Leeds U	35	0		
2021–22	Leeds U	38	0	**83**	**0**

MIHAYLOV, Dzhoshkun (F) 46 6
H: 5 10 b.Haskovo 1-2-00
Internationals: Bulgaria U16, U17, U18, U19, U21.

2019–20	Leeds U	0	0		
2019–20	*La Nucia*	2	0	**2**	**0**
2020–21	Leeds U	0	0		
2020–21	*Real Union*	19	3		
2021–22	Leeds U	0	0		
2021–22	*Real Union*	25	3	**44**	**6**

MILLER, Amari (M) 5 0
b. 4-11-02

2020–21	Birmingham C	5	0	**5**	**0**
2021–22	Leeds U	0	0		

MOORE, Kris (D) 0 0
b.Leeds 13-11-03

2021–22	Leeds U	0	0		

PHILLIPS, Kalvin (M) 214 13
H: 5 10 W: 11 05 b.Leeds 2-12-95
Internationals: England Full caps.

2014–15	Leeds U	2	1		
2015–16	Leeds U	10	0		
2016–17	Leeds U	33	1		
2017–18	Leeds U	41	7		
2018–19	Leeds U	42	1		
2019–20	Leeds U	37	2		
2020–21	Leeds U	29	1		
2021–22	Leeds U	20	0	**214**	**13**

POVEDA-OCAMPO, Ian (M) 28 1
H: 5 6 W: 9 08 b.Southwark 9-2-00
Internationals: England U16, U17, U18, U19, U20.
From Chelsea, Arsenal, Barcelona, Brentford.

2018–19	Manchester C	0	0		
2019–20	Manchester C	0	0		
2019–20	Leeds U	4	0		
2020–21	Leeds U	14	0		
2021–22	Leeds U	0	0	**18**	**0**
2021–22	*Blackburn R*	10	1	**10**	**1**

RAPHINHA, Raphael (F) 180 47
H: 5 9 W: 10 10 b.Porto Alegre 14-2-96
Internationals: Brazil Full caps.

2014–15	Avai	0	0		
2015–16	Vitoria Guimaraes	1	0		
2016–17	Vitoria Guimaraes	32	4		
2017–18	Vitoria Guimaraes	32	15	**65**	**19**
2018–19	Sporting Lisbon	24	4		
2019–20	Sporting Lisbon	4	2	**28**	**6**
2019–20	Rennes	22	5		
2020–21	Rennes	0	0	**22**	**5**
2020–21	Leeds U	30	6		
2021–22	Leeds U	35	11	**65**	**17**

ROBERTS, Tyler (F) 146 18
H: 5 11 W: 11 11 b.Gloucester 12-1-98
Internationals: Wales U16, U17, U19, U20, U21, Full caps.

2014–15	WBA	0	0		
2015–16	WBA	1	0		
2016–17	WBA	0	0	**1**	**0**
2016–17	*Oxford U*	14	0	**14**	**0**
2016–17	*Shrewsbury T*	13	4	**13**	**4**
2017–18	Leeds U	0	0		
2017–18	*Walsall*	17	5	**17**	**5**
2018–19	Leeds U	28	3		
2019–20	Leeds U	23	4		
2020–21	Leeds U	27	1		
2021–22	Leeds U	23	1	**101**	**9**

RODRIGO, Moreno (F) 314 79
H: 5 10 W: 11 09 b.Rio de Janeiro 6-3-91
Internationals: Spain U19, U20, U21, U23, Full caps.

2009–10	Real Madrid	0	0		
2010–11	Real Madrid	0	0		
2010–11	*Bolton W*	17	1	**17**	**1**
2011–12	Benfica	22	9		
2012–13	Benfica	20	7		
2013–14	Benfica	26	11	**68**	**27**
2014–15	Valencia	31	3		
2015–16	Valencia	25	2		
2016–17	Valencia	19	5		
2017–18	Valencia	37	16		
2018–19	Valencia	33	8		
2019–20	Valencia	27	4		
2020–21	Valencia	0	0	**172**	**38**
2020–21	Leeds U	26	7		
2021–22	Leeds U	31	6	**57**	**13**

SHACKLETON, Jamie (M) 68 2
H: 5 6 W: 10 01 b.Leeds 8-10-99
Internationals: England U20.

2018–19	Leeds U	19	0		
2019–20	Leeds U	22	2		
2020–21	Leeds U	13	0		
2021–22	Leeds U	14	0	**68**	**2**

SPENCER, Morten (M) 0 0
b.Darlington 14-3-04
Internationals: Norway U18.
From Sunderland.

2020–21	Leeds U	0	0		
2021–22	Leeds U	0	0		

STRUIJK, Pascal (D) 61 2
H: 6 3 W: 12 06 b.Deurne 11-8-99
Internationals: Netherlands U17.
From Ajax.

2017–18	Leeds U	0	0		
2018–19	Leeds U	0	0		
2019–20	Leeds U	5	0		
2020–21	Leeds U	27	1		
2021–22	Leeds U	29	1	**61**	**2**

SUMMERVILLE, Crysencio (M) 45 7
H: 5 9 W: 10 10 b.Rotterdam 30-10-01
Internationals: Netherlands U16, U17, U18, U19, U21.

2018–19	Feyenoord	0	0		
2018–19	*Dordrecht*	18	5	**18**	**5**
2019–20	Feyenoord	0	0		
2019–20	*ADO Den Haag*	21	2	**21**	**2**
2020–21	Leeds U	0	0		
2021–22	Leeds U	6	0	**6**	**0**

VAN DEN HEUVEL, Dani (G) 0 0
H: 6 0 W: 11 07 b.Delft 28-5-03
Internationals: Netherlands U16, U17, U19.
From Ajax.

2020–21	Leeds U	0	0		
2021–22	Leeds U	0	0		

Players retained or with offer of contract
Chilokoa Mullen, Jeremiah; Christy, Harry; Joseph Fernandez-Regatillo, Mateo; Kenneh, Nohan; McGurk, Sean; Snowdon, Joseph; Spencer, Morten.

Scholars
Andreucci, Benjamin; Brook, William Michael; Buchan, Jay; Carole, Keenan Nino; Coleman, Cian Eric; Debayo, James Boluwatife; Diboe, Cuba Peter Jayden; Ferguson, Connor Gary Ian; Godden, Scott Mackenzie; McGrath, Ronnie Eric; Ombang, Daryl Merveil; Sutcliffe, Harvey Frederick; Thomas, Luca Ty.

LEICESTER C (44)

ALBRIGHTON, Marc (M) 308 19
H: 5 9 W: 10 08 b.Tamworth 18-11-89
Internationals: England U20, U21.

2008–09	Aston Villa	0	0		
2009–10	Aston Villa	3	0		
2010–11	Aston Villa	29	5		
2011–12	Aston Villa	26	2		
2012–13	Aston Villa	9	0		
2013–14	Aston Villa	19	0	**86**	**7**
2013–14	*Wigan Ath*	4	0	**4**	**0**
2014–15	Leicester C	18	2		
2015–16	Leicester C	38	2		
2016–17	Leicester C	33	2		
2017–18	Leicester C	34	2		
2018–19	Leicester C	27	2		
2019–20	Leicester C	20	0		
2020–21	Leicester C	31	1		
2021–22	Leicester C	17	1	**218**	**12**

AMARTEY, Daniel (M) 164 5
H: 6 0 W: 12 04 b.Accra 1-12-94
Internationals: Ghana U20, Full caps.

2013	Djurgardens	23	0		
2014	Djurgardens	11	0	**34**	**0**
2014–15	Copenhagen	29	3		
2015–16	Copenhagen	15	0	**44**	**3**
2015–16	Leicester C	5	0		
2016–17	Leicester C	24	1		
2017–18	Leicester C	8	0		
2018–19	Leicester C	9	0		
2019–20	Leicester C	0	0		
2020–21	Leicester C	12	1		
2021–22	Leicester C	28	0	**86**	**2**

BARNES, Harvey (M) 182 42
H: 5 9 W: 10 06 b.Burnley 8-12-97
Internationals: England U18, U20, U21, Full caps.

2016–17	Leicester C	0	0		
2016–17	*Milton Keynes D*	21	6	**21**	**6**
2017–18	Leicester C	3	0		
2017–18	*Barnsley*	23	5	**23**	**5**
2018–19	Leicester C	16	1		
2018–19	*WBA*	26	9	**26**	**9**
2019–20	Leicester C	36	6		
2020–21	Leicester C	25	9		
2021–22	Leicester C	32	6	**112**	**22**

BENKOVIC, Filip (D) 88 10
H: 6 4 W: 14 05 b.Zagreb 13-7-97
Internationals: Croatia U17, U19, U21, Full caps.

2015–16	Dinamo Zagreb	13	0		
2016–17	Dinamo Zagreb	18	2		
2017–18	Dinamo Zagreb	25	4	**56**	**6**
2018–19	Leicester C	0	0		
2018–19	*Celtic*	20	2	**20**	**2**
2019–20	Leicester C	0	0		
2019–20	*Bristol C*	10	2	**10**	**2**
2020–21	Leicester C	0	0		
2020–21	*Cardiff C*	1	0	**1**	**0**
2020–21	*OH Leuven*	1	0	**1**	**0**
2021–22	Leicester C	0	0		

Transferred to Udinese, January 2022.

BERTRAND, Ryan (D) 407 8
H: 5 10 W: 13 05 b.Southwark 5-8-89
Internationals: England U17, U18, U19, U20, U21, Full caps. Great Britain.

2006–07	Chelsea	0	0		
2006–07	*Bournemouth*	5	0	**5**	**0**
2007–08	Chelsea	0	0		
2007–08	*Oldham Ath*	21	0	**21**	**0**
2007–08	*Norwich C*	18	0		
2008–09	Chelsea	0	0		
2008–09	*Norwich C*	38	0	**56**	**0**
2009–10	Chelsea	0	0		
2009–10	*Reading*	44	1	**44**	**1**
2010–11	Chelsea	1	0		

2010–11 *Nottingham F* 19 0 **19 0**
2011–12 Chelsea 7 0
2012–13 Chelsea 19 0
2013–14 Chelsea 1 0 **28 0**
2013–14 *Aston Villa* 16 0 **16 0**
2014–15 Southampton 34 2
2015–16 Southampton 32 1
2016–17 Southampton 28 2
2017–18 Southampton 35 0
2018–19 Southampton 24 1
2019–20 Southampton 32 1
2020–21 Southampton 29 0 **214 7**
2021–22 Leicester C 4 0 **4 0**

BRUNT, Lewis (M) 1 0
H: 6 2 W: 11 03 b.Burton-upon-Trent 6-11-00
2019–20 Aston Villa 0 0
2020–21 Aston Villa 0 0
2021–22 Leicester C 1 0 **1 0**

CASTAGNE, Timothy (D) 209 9
H: 6 1 W: 12 08 b.Arlon 5-12-95
Internationals: Belgium U18, U19, U21, Full caps.
2013–14 Genk 0 0
2014–15 Genk 27 1
2015–16 Genk 21 0
2016–17 Genk 32 0 **80 1**
2017–18 Atalanta 20 0
2018–19 Atalanta 28 4
2019–20 Atalanta 27 1
2020–21 Atalanta 0 0 **75 5**
2020–21 Leicester C 27 2
2021–22 Leicester C 27 1 **54 3**

CHOUDHURY, Hamza (M) 79 1
H: 5 10 W: 10 01 b.Loughborough 1-10-97
Internationals: England U21.
2015–16 Leicester C 0 0
2015–16 *Burton Alb* 13 0
2016–17 Leicester C 0 0
2016–17 *Burton Alb* 13 0 **26 0**
2017–18 Leicester C 8 0
2018–19 Leicester C 9 0
2019–20 Leicester C 20 1
2020–21 Leicester C 10 0
2021–22 Leicester C 6 0 **53 1**

DAKA, Patson (F) 132 65
H: 6 0 W: 11 03 b.Kafue 9-10-98
Internationals: Zambia U17, U20, Full caps.
2016–17 Kafue Celtic 0 0
2016–17 *Liefering* 9 2
2017–18 Red Bull Salzburg 8 0
2017–18 *Liefering* 18 4 **27 6**
2018–19 Red Bull Salzburg 15 3
2019–20 Red Bull Salzburg 31 24
2020–21 Red Bull Salzburg 28 27
2021–22 Red Bull Salzburg 0 0 **82 54**
2021–22 Leicester C 23 5 **23 5**

DALEY-CAMPBELL, Vontae (D) 9 0
H: 5 9 W: 11 00 b.Lambeth 2-4-01
Internationals: England U16, U17, U18, U19.
From Arsenal.
2020–21 Leicester C 0 0
2021–22 Leicester C 0 0
2021–22 *Dundee* 9 0 **9 0**

DEWSBURY-HALL, Kiernan (M) 77 8
H: 5 10 W: 11 00 b.Nottingham 6-9-98
2019–20 Leicester C 0 0
2019–20 *Blackpool* 10 4 **10 4**
2020–21 Leicester C 0 0
2020–21 *Luton T* 39 3 **39 3**
2021–22 Leicester C 28 1 **28 1**

EPPIAH, Josh (G) 25 2
b.Belgium 11-10-98
Internationals: Belgium U21.
2016–17 Leicester C 0 0
2017–18 Leicester C 0 0
2018–19 Leicester C 0 0
2019–20 Leicester C 0 0
2020–21 Leicester C 0 0
2020–21 *Leuven* 11 0 **11 0**
2021–22 Leicester C 0 0
2021–22 *Northampton T* 14 2 **14 2**

EVANS, Jonny (D) 372 17
H: 6 2 W: 12 02 b.Belfast 3-1-88
Internationals: Northern Ireland U16, U17, U21, Full caps.
2004–05 Manchester U 0 0
2005–06 Manchester U 0 0
2006–07 Manchester U 0 0
2006–07 *Antwerp* 11 2 **11 2**
2006–07 *Sunderland* 18 1
2007–08 Manchester U 0 0
2007–08 *Sunderland* 15 0 **33 1**
2008–09 Manchester U 17 0
2009–10 Manchester U 18 0
2010–11 Manchester U 13 0
2011–12 Manchester U 29 1
2012–13 Manchester U 23 3
2013–14 Manchester U 17 0
2014–15 Manchester U 14 0
2015–16 Manchester U 0 0 **131 4**
2015–16 WBA 30 1
2016–17 WBA 31 2
2017–18 WBA 28 2 **89 5**
2018–19 Leicester C 24 1
2019–20 Leicester C 38 1
2020–21 Leicester C 28 2
2021–22 Leicester C 18 1 **108 5**

FITZHUGH, Ethan (M) 0 0
b. 27-11-02
2020–21 Leicester C 0 0
2021–22 Leicester C 0 0

FLYNN, Shane (M) 0 0
b.Dublin 14-10-01
Internationals: Republic of Ireland U21.
From St Joseph's, Bray W.
2020–21 Leicester C 0 0
2021–22 Leicester C 0 0

FOFANA, Wesley (D) 51 1
H: 6 3 b.Marseille 17-12-00
Internationals: France U21.
2018–19 Saint-Etienne 2 0
2019–20 Saint-Etienne 14 1 **16 1**
2020–21 St Etienne 0 0
2020–21 Leicester C 28 0
2021–22 Leicester C 7 0 **35 0**

GRIST, Ben (D) 0 0
2020–21 Grimsby T 0 0
2021–22 Leicester C 0 0

HIRST, George (F) 96 16
H: 6 3 W: 11 00 b.Sheffield 15-2-99
Internationals: England U17, U18, U19, U20.
2016–17 Sheffield W 1 0
2017–18 Sheffield W 0 0 **1 0**
2018–19 Oh Leuven 22 3 **22 3**
2019–20 Leicester C 2 0
2020–21 Leicester C 0 0
2020–21 *Rotherham U* 31 0 **31 0**
2021–22 Leicester C 0 0 **2 0**
2021–22 *Portsmouth* 40 13 **40 13**

HULME, Callum (M) 1 0
b. 10-11-00
From Manchester C.
2016–17 Bury 0 0
2017–18 Bury 0 0
2018–19 Bury 1 0 **1 0**
2019–20 Leicester C 0 0
2020–21 Leicester C 0 0
2021–22 Leicester C 0 0

IHEANACHO, Kelechi (F) 168 37
H: 6 2 W: 13 08 b.Imo 3-10-96
Internationals: Nigeria U17, U20, Full caps.
2014–15 Manchester C 0 0
2015–16 Manchester C 26 8
2016–17 Manchester C 20 4 **46 12**
2017–18 Leicester C 21 3
2018–19 Leicester C 30 1
2019–20 Leicester C 20 5
2020–21 Leicester C 25 12
2021–22 Leicester C 26 4 **122 25**

IVERSEN, Daniel (G) 150 0
H: 6 5 W: 12 08 b.Gording 19-7-97
Internationals: Denmark U16, U17, U18, U19, U20, U21.
2014–15 Esbjerg 0 0
2015–16 Esbjerg 0 0
2015–16 Leicester C 0 0
2016–17 Leicester C 0 0
2017–18 Leicester C 0 0
2018–19 Leicester C 0 0
2018–19 *Oldham Ath* 42 0 **42 0**
2019–20 Leicester C 0 0
2019–20 *Rotherham U* 34 0 **34 0**
2020–21 Leicester C 0 0
2020–21 *OH Leuven* 5 0 **5 0**
2020–21 *Preston NE* 23 0
2021–22 Leicester C 0 0
2021–22 *Preston NE* 46 0 **69 0**

JAKUPOVIC, Eldin (G) 189 1
H: 6 3 W: 13 01 b.Kozarac 2-10-84
Internationals: Bosnia & Herzegovina U21, Switzerland U21, Full caps.
2004–05 Grasshoppers 8 0
2005–06 FC Thun 22 0 **22 0**
2006–07 Lokomotiv Moscow 20 0
2007–08 Lokomotiv Moscow 0 0
2007–08 *Grasshoppers* 23 1
2008–09 Lokomotiv Moscow 0 0 **20 0**
2008–09 *Grasshoppers* 34 0 **65 1**
2010–11 Olympiacos Volou 33 0 **33 0**
2011–12 Aris Salonika 1 0 **1 0**
2012–13 Hull C 5 0
2013–14 Hull C 1 0
2013–14 *Leyton Orient* 13 0 **13 0**
2014–15 Hull C 3 0
2015–16 Hull C 2 0
2016–17 Hull C 22 0 **33 0**
2017–18 Leicester C 2 0
2018–19 Leicester C 0 0
2019–20 Leicester C 0 0
2020–21 Leicester C 0 0
2021–22 Leicester C 0 0 **2 0**

JUSTIN, James (D) 139 8
H: 6 0 W: 11 03 b.Luton 23-2-98
Internationals: England U20, U21, Full caps.
2015–16 Luton T 1 0
2016–17 Luton T 29 1
2017–18 Luton T 17 2
2018–19 Luton T 43 3 **90 6**
2019–20 Leicester C 13 0
2020–21 Leicester C 23 2
2021–22 Leicester C 13 0 **49 2**

LESHABELA, Thakgalo (M) 4 0
H: 5 9 W: 11 05 b.Pretoria 18-9-99
Internationals: South Africa U20.
2018–19 Leicester C 0 0
2019–20 Leicester C 0 0
2020–21 Leicester C 1 0
2021–22 Leicester C 0 0 **1 0**
2021–22 *Shrewsbury T* 3 0 **3 0**

LOOKMAN, Ademola (F) 163 26
H: 5 9 W: 12 04 b.Wandsworth 20-10-97
Internationals: England U19, U20, U21. Nigeria Full caps.
2015–16 Charlton Ath 24 5
2016–17 Charlton Ath 21 5 **45 10**
2016–17 Everton 8 1
2017–18 Everton 7 0
2017–18 *RB Leipzig* 11 5
2018–19 Everton 21 0 **36 1**
2019–20 RB Leipzig 11 0
2020–21 RB Leipzig 0 0
2020–21 *Fulham* 34 4 **34 4**
2021–22 RB Leipzig 0 0 **22 5**
2021–22 *Leicester C* 26 6 **26 6**

MADDISON, James (M) 229 55
H: 5 9 W: 11 07 b.Coventry 23-11-96
Internationals: England U21, Full caps.
2013–14 Coventry C 0 0
2014–15 Coventry C 12 2
2015–16 Norwich C 0 0
2015–16 *Coventry C* 23 3 **35 5**
2016–17 Norwich C 3 1
2016–17 *Aberdeen* 14 2 **14 2**
2017–18 Norwich C 44 14 **47 15**
2018–19 Leicester C 36 7
2019–20 Leicester C 31 6
2020–21 Leicester C 31 8
2021–22 Leicester C 35 12 **133 33**

MASWANHISE, Tawanda (M) 0 0
2020–21 Leicester C 0 0
2021–22 Leicester C 0 0

McATEER, Kasey (M) 10 0
H: 5 10 b.Northampton 22-11-01
2021–22 Leicester C 1 0 **1 0**
2021–22 *Forest Green R* 9 0 **9 0**

MENDY, Nampalys (D) 277 1
H: 5 6 W: 10 10 b.La Seyne-sur-Mer 23-6-92
Internationals: France U18, U19, U20, U21. Senegal Full caps.
2010–11 Monaco 14 0
2011–12 Monaco 28 0
2012–13 Monaco 32 0 **74 0**
2013–14 Nice 36 0
2014–15 Nice 36 0
2015–16 Nice 38 1
2016–17 Leicester C 4 0
2017–18 Leicester C 0 0
2017–18 *Nice* 14 0 **124 1**
2018–19 Leicester C 31 0
2019–20 Leicester C 7 0
2020–21 Leicester C 23 0
2021–22 Leicester C 14 0 **79 0**

NDIDI, Onyinye (M) 228 11
H: 6 2 W: 12 08 b.Lagos 16-12-96
Internationals: Nigeria U20, Full caps.
2014–15 Genk 6 0
2015–16 Genk 38 4
2016–17 Genk 19 0 **63 4**
2016–17 Leicester C 17 2
2017–18 Leicester C 33 0
2018–19 Leicester C 38 2
2019–20 Leicester C 32 2
2020–21 Leicester C 26 1
2021–22 Leicester C 19 0 **165 7**

NELSON, Ben (D) 0 0
H: 5 11 b.Northampton 18-3-04
Internationals: England U18.
2020–21 Leicester C 0 0
2021–22 Leicester C 0 0

ODUNZE, Chituru (G) 0 0
H: 6 7 W: 12 06 b.Raleigh 14-10-02
Internationals: USA U17, U20.
From Vancouver Whitecaps.
2020–21 Leicester C 0 0
2021–22 Leicester C 0 0

PENNANT, Terell (F) 0 0
b.Leicester 14-9-02
Internationals: England U16.
2020–21 Leicester C 0 0
2021–22 Leicester C 0 0

PEREZ, Ayoze (F) 301 71
H: 5 10 W: 10 06 b.Santa Cruz de Tenerife 23-7-93
Internationals: Spain U21.
2012–13 Tenerife 16 1
2013–14 Tenerife 34 16 **50 17**
2014–15 Newcastle U 36 7
2015–16 Newcastle U 34 6
2016–17 Newcastle U 36 9
2017–18 Newcastle U 36 8
2018–19 Newcastle U 37 12 **179 42**
2019–20 Leicester C 33 8
2020–21 Leicester C 25 2
2021–22 Leicester C 14 2 **72 12**

PRAET, Dennis (M) 302 28
H: 5 11 W: 10 03 b.Leuven 14-5-94
Internationals: Belgium U16, U17, U18, U19, U21, Full caps.
2011–12 Anderlecht 7 0
2012–13 Anderlecht 27 2
2013–14 Anderlecht 37 5
2014–15 Anderlecht 30 7
2015–16 Anderlecht 37 6
2016–17 Anderlecht 1 0 **139 20**
2016–17 Sampdoria 32 1
2017–18 Sampdoria 32 1
2018–19 Sampdoria 34 2 **98 4**
2019–20 Leicester C 27 1
2020–21 Leicester C 15 1
2021–22 Leicester C 0 0 **42 2**
2021–22 *Torino* 23 2 **23 2**
Transferred to Lyon January 2021.

RICARDO PEREIRA, Domingos (D) 218 12
H: 5 9 W: 11 00 b.Lisbon 6-10-93
Internationals: Portugal U19, U20, U21, Full caps.
2011–12 Vitoria Guimaraes 3 0
2012–13 Vitoria Guimaraes 27 0 **30 0**
2013–14 Porto 14 2
2014–15 Porto 5 0
2015–16 Porto 0 0
2015–16 *Nice* 26 0
2016–17 Porto 0 0
2016–17 *Nice* 24 2 **50 2**
2017–18 Porto 27 2 **46 4**
2018–19 Leicester C 35 2
2019–20 Leicester C 28 3
2020–21 Leicester C 15 0
2021–22 Leicester C 14 1 **92 6**

SCHMEICHEL, Kasper (G) 573 0
H: 6 2 W: 14 00 b.Copenhagen 5-11-86
Internationals: Denmark U19, U20, U21, Full caps.
2003–04 Manchester C 0 0
2004–05 Manchester C 0 0
2005–06 Manchester C 0 0
2005–06 *Darlington* 4 0 **4 0**
2005–06 *Bury* 15 0
2006–07 Manchester C 0 0
2006–07 *Falkirk* 15 0 **15 0**
2006–07 *Bury* 14 0 **29 0**
2007–08 Manchester C 7 0
2007–08 *Cardiff C* 14 0 **14 0**
2007–08 *Coventry C* 9 0 **9 0**
2008–09 Manchester C 1 0
2009–10 Manchester C 0 0 **8 0**
2009–10 Notts Co 43 0 **43 0**
2010–11 Leeds U 37 0 **37 0**
2011–12 Leicester C 46 0
2012–13 Leicester C 46 0
2013–14 Leicester C 46 0
2014–15 Leicester C 24 0
2015–16 Leicester C 38 0
2016–17 Leicester C 30 0
2017–18 Leicester C 33 0
2018–19 Leicester C 38 0
2019–20 Leicester C 38 0
2020–21 Leicester C 38 0
2021–22 Leicester C 37 0 **414 0**

SHADE, Tyrese (M) 39 2
H: 6 0 W: 12 04 b.Birmingham 9-6-00
Internationals: Saint Kitts and Nevis U20.
From Solihull Moors.
2021–22 Leicester C 0 0
2021–22 *Walsall* 39 2 **39 2**

SOUMARE, Boubakary (M) 103 1
H: 6 2 W: 11 00 b.Noisy-le-Sec 27-2-99
Internationals: France U16, U17, U18, U19, U20, U21.
2016–17 Paris Saint-Germain 0 0
2017–18 Lille 14 0
2018–19 Lille 18 1
2019–20 Lille 20 0
2020–21 Lille 32 0
2021–22 Lille 0 0 **84 1**
2021–22 Leicester C 19 0 **19 0**

SOYUNCU, Caglar (D) 175 6
H: 6 2 W: 12 08 b.Izmir 23-5-96
Internationals: Turkey U18, U19, U20, U21, Full caps.
2014–15 Altinordu 4 0
2015–16 Altinordu 30 2 **34 2**
2016–17 Freiburg 24 0
2017–18 Freiburg 26 1 **50 1**
2018–19 Leicester C 6 0
2019–20 Leicester C 34 1
2020–21 Leicester C 23 1
2021–22 Leicester C 28 1 **91 3**

SPENCER-ADAMS, Bayli (D) 0 0
b. 26-6-01
Internationals: Guyana Full caps.
From Arsenal.
2019–20 Watford 0 0
2020–21 Watford 0 0
2021–22 Leicester C 0 0

STOLARCZYK, Jakub (G) 11 0
H: 6 4 W: 12 11 b.Checiny 19-12-00
Internationals: Poland U18, U19, U21.
2020–21 Leicester C 0 0
2021–22 Leicester C 0 0
2021–22 *Dunfermline Ath* 11 0 **11 0**

SUENGCHITTHAWON, Thanawat (M) 0 0
b. 8-1-00
Internationals: France U16, U17. Thailand U23, Full caps.
From Nancy.
2020–21 Leicester C 0 0
2021–22 Leicester C 0 0

THOMAS, Luke (D) 39 1
H: 5 11 W: 11 00 b.Leicester 10-6-01
Internationals: England U18, U19, U20, U21.
2019–20 Leicester C 3 0
2020–21 Leicester C 14 1
2021–22 Leicester C 22 0 **39 1**

TIELEMANS, Youri (M) 306 49
H: 5 9 W: 10 08 b.Sint-Pieters-Leeuw 7-5-97
Internationals: Belgium U16, U21, Full caps.
2013–14 Anderlecht 29 1
2014–15 Anderlecht 39 6
2015–16 Anderlecht 34 6
2016–17 Anderlecht 37 13 **139 26**
2017–18 Monaco 27 0
2018–19 Monaco 20 5 **47 5**
2018–19 *Leicester C* 13 3
2019–20 Leicester C 37 3
2020–21 Leicester C 38 6
2021–22 Leicester C 32 6 **120 18**

VARDY, Jamie (F) 333 153
H: 5 10 W: 12 00 b.Sheffield 11-1-87
Internationals: England Full caps.
From Stocksbridge Park Steels, FC Halifax T, Fleetwood T.
2012–13 Leicester C 26 4
2013–14 Leicester C 37 16
2014–15 Leicester C 34 5
2015–16 Leicester C 36 24
2016–17 Leicester C 35 13
2017–18 Leicester C 37 20
2018–19 Leicester C 34 18
2019–20 Leicester C 35 23
2020–21 Leicester C 34 15
2021–22 Leicester C 25 15 **333 153**

VESTERGAARD, Jannik (D) 267 18
H: 6 6 W: 15 02 b.Copenhagen 3-8-92
Internationals: Denmark U18, U19, U20, U21, Full caps.
2010–11 Hoffenheim 1 0
2011–12 Hoffenheim 23 2
2012–13 Hoffenheim 16 0
2013–14 Hoffenheim 25 1
2014–15 Hoffenheim 6 1 **71 4**
2014–15 Werder Bremen 15 1
2015–16 Werder Bremen 33 2 **48 3**
2016–17 Borussia M'gladbach 34 4
2017–18 Borussia M'gladbach 32 3 **66 7**
2018–19 Southampton 23 0
2019–20 Southampton 19 1
2020–21 Southampton 30 3
2021–22 Southampton 0 0 **72 4**
2021–22 Leicester C 10 0 **10 0**

WAKELING, Jacob (F) 4 0
b.Redditch 15-9-01
2021–22 Leicester C 0 0
2021–22 *Barrow* 4 0 **4 0**

WARD, Danny (G) 72 0
H: 5 11 W: 13 12 b.Wrexham 22-6-93
Internationals: Wales U17, U19, U21, Full caps.
From Wrexham.
2011–12 Liverpool 0 0
2012–13 Liverpool 0 0
2013–14 Liverpool 0 0
2014–15 Liverpool 0 0
2014–15 *Morecambe* 5 0 **5 0**
2015–16 Liverpool 2 0
2015–16 *Aberdeen* 21 0 **21 0**
2016–17 Liverpool 0 0
2016–17 *Huddersfield T* 43 0 **43 0**
2017–18 Liverpool 0 0 **2 0**
2018–19 Leicester C 0 0
2019–20 Leicester C 0 0
2020–21 Leicester C 0 0
2021–22 Leicester C 1 0 **1 0**

WRIGHT, Callum (M) 50 13
b.Liverpool 2-5-00
2020–21 Leicester C 0 0
2020–21 *Cheltenham T* 16 4
2021–22 Leicester C 0 0
2021–22 *Cheltenham T* 34 9 **50 13**

Players retained or with offer of contract
Alves, Will; Booth, Chadwick; Braybrooke, Sammy; Chibueze, Kelechi; Ewing, Oliver; Hughes, Iestyn; Louis-Marie Richards, Amani; Marcal-Madivadua, Wanya; Nelson, Ronny; Pennant, Kian; Popov, Christopher; Young, Bradley.

Scholars
Addai, Dillon Charles Kojo; Alves, William Thomas; Cartwright, Henry; Cook, Freddie Robert Joseph; Cover, Brandon Ashley; Doherty, Arlo Ricky Hugh; Godsmark-Ford, Harvey George; Javaid, Abdullah; Lewis, Jack Robert; Lindsay, Jahmari Samuel; Weeks, Tyler-Jack; Wilson-Brown, Thomas; Wormleighton, Joseph Oliver.

LEYTON ORIENT (45)

BECKLES, Omar (D) 225 16
H: 6 3 W: 12 04 b.Kettering 25-10-91
Internationals: Grenada Full caps.
From Jerez Industrial, Boreham Wood, Kettering T, Billericay T, Histon, St Albans C, Aldershot T.
2016–17 Accrington S 41 2
2017–18 Accrington S 2 1 **43 3**
2017–18 Shrewsbury T 33 3
2018–19 Shrewsbury T 36 1
2019–20 Shrewsbury T 28 3 **97 7**
2020–21 Crewe Alex 41 1
2021–22 Crewe Alex 0 0 **41 1**
2021–22 Leyton Orient 44 5 **44 5**

BROWN, Jordan (D) 12 1
H: 5 11 W: 11 00 b.Stoke-on-Trent 21-6-01
2019–20 Derby Co 1 0
2020–21 Derby Co 0 0
2021–22 Derby Co 0 0 **1 0**
2021–22 Leyton Orient 11 1 **11 1**

CLAY, Craig (M) 163 4
H: 5 11 W: 11 07 b.Nottingham 5-5-92
Internationals: England C.
2010–11 Chesterfield 3 1
2011–12 Chesterfield 5 0
2012–13 Chesterfield 19 0 **27 1**
2013–14 York C 8 0 **8 0**
From Grimsby T.
2016–17 Motherwell 35 1
2017–18 Motherwell 0 0 **35 1**
From Leyton Orient.
2019–20 Leyton Orient 35 0
2020–21 Leyton Orient 39 1
2021–22 Leyton Orient 19 1 **93 2**

COLEMAN, Ethan (M) 15 1
H: 6 0 W: 12 06 b.Reading 28-1-00
2019–20 Reading 0 0
From Brackley T, King's Lynn T.
2021–22 Leyton Orient 15 1 **15 1**

DRINAN, Aaron (F) 67 15
H: 6 0 W: 11 07 b.Cork 6-5-98
Internationals: Republic of Ireland U21.
From Cork C.
2017 Waterford 5 1 **5 1**
2017–18 Ipswich T 0 0
2018–19 Ipswich T 0 0
2019–20 Ipswich T 0 0
2020–21 Ipswich T 22 1
2021–22 Ipswich T 0 0 **22 1**
2021–22 Leyton Orient 40 13 **40 13**

HAPPE, Daniel (D) 86 4
H: 6 6 W: 14 00 b.Tower Hamlets 28-9-98
Internationals: England C.
2016–17 Leyton Orient 2 0
From Leyton Orient.
2019–20 Leyton Orient 32 1
2020–21 Leyton Orient 40 3
2021–22 Leyton Orient 12 0 **86 4**

JAMES, Tom (D) 130 13
H: 5 11 W: 11 00 b.Cardiff 15-4-96
Internationals: Wales U19.
2013–14 Cardiff C 1 0
2014–15 Cardiff C 0 0
2015–16 Cardiff C 0 0
2016–17 Cardiff C 0 0 **1 0**
2016–17 Yeovil T 2 0

2017–18 Yeovil T 38 0
2018–19 Yeovil T 38 6 **78 6**
2019–20 Hibernian 6 0
2020–21 Hibernian 0 0 **6 0**
2020–21 *Wigan Ath* 20 3 **20 3**
2020–21 *Salford C* 4 0 **4 0**
2021–22 Leyton Orient 21 4 **21 4**

KHAN, Otis (M) 182 20
H: 5 9 W: 11 03 b.Ashton-under-Lyme 5-9-95
2013–14 Sheffield U 2 0
2014–15 Sheffield U 0 0
2015–16 Sheffield U 0 0 **2 0**
2015–16 Barnsley 3 0 **3 0**
2016–17 Yeovil T 29 6
2017–18 Yeovil T 38 6 **67 12**
2018–19 Mansfield T 22 2
2019–20 Mansfield T 21 1 **43 3**
2019–20 *Newport Co* 5 0 **5 0**
2020–21 Tranmere R 35 2
2021–22 Tranmere R 0 0 **35 2**
2021–22 Walsall 7 2 **7 2**
2021–22 Leyton Orient 20 1 **20 1**

KYPRIANOU, Hector (M) 66 0
H: 6 2 W: 12 04 b.Enfield 27-5-01
Internationals: Cyprus U19, U21.
2019–20 Leyton Orient 6 0
2020–21 Leyton Orient 22 0
2021–22 Leyton Orient 38 0 **66 0**

NKRUMAH, Daniel (M) 3 0
b.Redbridge 5-11-03
2021–22 Leyton Orient 3 0 **3 0**

OBIERO, Zech (M) 1 0
b. 18-1-05
2021–22 Leyton Orient 1 0 **1 0**

OGIE, Shadrach (D) 34 0
H: 6 1 W: 11 07 b.Limerick 26-8-01
Internationals: Republic of Ireland U18, U19.
From Hornchurch.
2019–20 Leyton Orient 0 0
2020–21 Leyton Orient 0 0
2021–22 Leyton Orient 34 0 **34 0**

PRATLEY, Darren (M) 544 49
H: 6 1 W: 11 00 b.Barking 22-4-85
2001–02 Fulham 0 0
2002–03 Fulham 0 0
2003–04 Fulham 1 0
2004–05 Fulham 0 0
2004–05 *Brentford* 14 1
2005–06 Fulham 0 0 **1 0**
2005–06 *Brentford* 32 4 **46 5**
2006–07 Swansea C 28 1
2007–08 Swansea C 42 5
2008–09 Swansea C 37 4
2009–10 Swansea C 36 7
2010–11 Swansea C 34 9 **177 26**
2011–12 Bolton W 25 1
2012–13 Bolton W 31 2
2013–14 Bolton W 20 2
2014–15 Bolton W 22 4
2015–16 Bolton W 36 1
2016–17 Bolton W 12 0
2017–18 Bolton W 32 2 **178 12**
2018–19 Charlton Ath 28 2
2019–20 Charlton Ath 36 2
2020–21 Charlton Ath 39 1 **103 5**
2021–22 Leyton Orient 39 1 **39 1**

REILLY, Callum (M) 214 12
H: 6 1 W: 12 04 b.Warrington 3-10-93
Internationals: Republic of Ireland U21.
2012–13 Birmingham C 18 1
2013–14 Birmingham C 25 0
2014–15 Birmingham C 17 1 **60 2**
2014–15 *Burton Alb* 2 0
2015–16 Burton Alb 14 0
2016–17 Burton Alb 0 0 **16 0**
2016–17 *Coventry C* 18 0 **18 0**
2017–18 Bury 18 0 **18 0**
2017–18 *Gillingham* 15 0
2018–19 Gillingham 25 5 **40 5**
2019–20 AFC Wimbledon 30 4
2020–21 AFC Wimbledon 28 1 **58 5**
2021–22 Leyton Orient 4 0 **4 0**

SARGEANT, Sam (G) 28 0
H: 6 2 W: 10 08 b.Greenwich 23-9-97
2014–15 Leyton Orient 0 0
2015–16 Leyton Orient 1 0
2016–17 Leyton Orient 15 0
From Leyton Orient.
2019–20 Leyton Orient 12 0
2020–21 Leyton Orient 0 0
2021–22 Leyton Orient 0 0 **28 0**

SMITH, Harry (F) 138 31
H: 6 5 W: 13 01 b.Chatham 18-5-95
From Sittingbourne, Folkestone Invicta.
2016–17 Millwall 9 1
2017–18 Millwall 0 0 **9 1**
2017–18 *Swindon T* 14 2 **14 2**
2018–19 Macclesfield T 39 8 **39 8**
2019–20 Northampton T 19 4
2020–21 Motherwell 0 0
2020–21 Northampton T 16 3
2021–22 Northampton T 0 0 **35 7**
2021–22 Leyton Orient 41 13 **41 13**

SMYTH, Paul (F) 112 13
H: 5 10 W: 11 07 b.Belfast 10-9-97
Internationals: Northern Ireland U19, U21, Full caps.
2017–18 Linfield 0 0
2017–18 QPR 13 2
2018–19 QPR 3 0
2018–19 *Accrington S* 15 3
2019–20 QPR 0 0
2019–20 *Wycombe W* 19 1 **19 1**
2020–21 QPR 3 0 **19 2**
2020–21 *Charlton Ath* 14 1 **14 1**
2020–21 *Accrington S* 21 3 **36 6**
2021–22 Leyton Orient 24 3 **24 3**

SOTIRIOU, Ruel (F) 66 15
H: 5 11 W: 11 03 b.Edmonton 24-8-00
Internationals: Cyprus U19, U21.
2019–20 Leyton Orient 10 5
2020–21 Leyton Orient 22 1
2021–22 Leyton Orient 34 9 **66 15**

SWEENEY, Jayden (D) 6 0
H: 5 10 W: 10 10 b.Camden 4-12-01
2019–20 Leyton Orient 0 0
2020–21 Leyton Orient 1 0
2021–22 Leyton Orient 5 0 **6 0**

TANGA, Jephte (M) 1 0
b.Lambeth 16-6-04
2021–22 Leyton Orient 1 0 **1 0**

THOMPSON, Adam (D) 244 5
H: 6 1 W: 12 05 b.Harlow 28-9-92
Internationals: Northern Ireland U17, U19, U21, Full caps.
2010–11 Watford 10 1
2011–12 Watford 0 0
2011–12 *Brentford* 20 0 **20 0**
2012–13 Watford 4 0
2012–13 *Wycombe W* 2 0 **2 0**
2012–13 *Barnet* 1 0 **1 0**
2013–14 Watford 0 0 **14 1**
2013–14 Southend U 16 0
2014–15 Southend U 28 0
2015–16 Southend U 25 2
2016–17 Southend U 40 1 **109 3**
2017–18 Bury 15 0
2017–18 *Bradford C* 9 0 **9 0**
2018–19 Bury 44 1 **59 1**
2019–20 Rotherham U 10 0
2020–21 Rotherham U 0 0 **10 0**
2020–21 Leyton Orient 6 0
2021–22 Leyton Orient 14 0 **20 0**

VIGOUROUX, Lawrence (G) 217 0
H: 6 4 W: 12 00 b.Camden 19-11-93
Internationals: Chile U20.
2012–13 Tottenham H 0 0
2013–14 Tottenham H 0 0
2014–15 Liverpool 0 0
2015–16 Liverpool 0 0
2015–16 *Swindon T* 33 0
2016–17 Swindon T 43 0
2017–18 Swindon T 14 0
2018–19 Swindon T 29 0 **119 0**
2019–20 Leyton Orient 6 0
2020–21 Leyton Orient 46 0
2021–22 Leyton Orient 46 0 **98 0**

WOOD, Connor (D) 135 2
H: 5 10 W: 12 04 b.Harlow 17-7-96
From Soham Town Rangers, Chesham U.
2016–17 Leicester C 0 0
2017–18 Leicester C 0 0
2018–19 Bradford C 22 1
2019–20 Bradford C 35 0
2020–21 Bradford C 46 1 **103 2**
2021–22 Leyton Orient 32 0 **32 0**

YOUNG, Matt (M) 15 0
b. 6-2-03
2020–21 Leyton Orient 1 0
2021–22 Leyton Orient 14 0 **15 0**

Players retained or with offer of contract
Byrne, Rhys; Fish, Sonny; Papadopoulos, Antony; Phillips, Noah; Smith-Kouassi, Reon.

Scholars
Apat, Mert; Campbell, Sean Kehinde Temitope; Clements, Antonio Edward; Davies, Ebraima John Colbert; Eaton, Shimron Clan; Kwatchey, Emmanuel Nana Yao Anpim; Nallo, Sahid; Ojo, Ayodele Olalekan Charles; Pegrum, Charlie Joe; Pegrum, Reggie John; Phillips, Noah; Saponara, Lorenzo Matteo; Sodje, Harrison Okiemute; Staerck, Benjamin Laurie; Sworder, Henry Thomas; Tanga, Jephte Matuba.

LINCOLN C (46)

ADELAKUN, Hakeeb (F) 192 21
H: 6 3 W: 11 11 b.Hackney 11-6-96
2012–13 Scunthorpe U 2 0
2013–14 Scunthorpe U 28 2
2014–15 Scunthorpe U 32 6
2015–16 Scunthorpe U 21 2
2016–17 Scunthorpe U 17 2
2017–18 Scunthorpe U 39 4 **139 16**
2018–19 Bristol C 5 0
2019–20 Bristol C 0 0
2019–20 *Rotherham U* 9 0 **9 0**
2020–21 Bristol C 2 0 **7 0**
2020–21 *Hull C* 14 3 **14 3**
2021–22 Lincoln C 23 2 **23 2**

ARCHIBALD, Theo (M) 103 13
H: 5 11 W: 9 06 b.Glasgow 5-3-98
Internationals: Scotland U16, U19, U21.
2016–17 Celtic 0 0
2016–17 *Albion R* 14 0 **14 0**
2017–18 Brentford 2 0
2018–19 Brentford 0 0 **2 0**
2018–19 *Forest Green R* 14 1 **14 1**
2018–19 Brentford 0 0
2019–20 Macclesfield T 28 4 **28 4**
2020–21 Lincoln C 7 0
2021–22 Lincoln C 0 0 **7 0**
2021–22 *Leyton Orient* 38 8 **38 8**

BISHOP, Teddy (M) 159 9
H: 5 11 W: 10 03 b.Cambridge 15-7-96
2013–14 Ipswich T 0 0
2014–15 Ipswich T 33 1
2015–16 Ipswich T 4 0
2016–17 Ipswich T 19 0
2017–18 Ipswich T 4 0
2018–19 Ipswich T 18 0
2019–20 Ipswich T 9 0
2020–21 Ipswich T 36 4
2021–22 Ipswich T 0 0 **123 5**
2021–22 Lincoln C 36 4 **36 4**

BRAMALL, Cohen (D) 98 3
H: 5 9 W: 11 00 b.Crewe 2-4-96
From Hednesford T.
2017–18 Arsenal 0 0
2017–18 *Birmingham C* 5 0 **5 0**
2018–19 Arsenal 0 0
2019–20 Colchester U 24 1
2020–21 Colchester U 23 0 **47 1**
2020–21 Lincoln C 17 0
2021–22 Lincoln C 29 2 **46 2**

BRIDCUTT, Liam (M) 322 4
H: 5 9 W: 11 11 b.Reading 8-5-89
Internationals: Scotland Full caps.
2007–08 Chelsea 0 0
2007–08 *Yeovil T* 9 0 **9 0**
2008–09 Chelsea 0 0
2008–09 *Watford* 6 0 **6 0**
2009–10 Chelsea 0 0
2009–10 *Stockport Co* 15 0 **15 0**
2010–11 Chelsea 0 0
2010–11 Brighton & HA 37 2
2011–12 Brighton & HA 43 0
2012–13 Brighton & HA 41 0
2013–14 Brighton & HA 11 0 **132 2**
2013–14 Sunderland 12 0
2014–15 Sunderland 18 0
2015–16 Sunderland 0 0 **30 0**
2015–16 *Leeds U* 24 0
2016–17 Leeds U 25 0 **49 0**
2017–18 Nottingham F 27 1
2018–19 Nottingham F 1 0
2019–20 Nottingham F 0 0
2019–20 *Bolton W* 11 0 **11 0**
2019–20 *Lincoln C* 5 1
2020–21 Nottingham F 0 0 **28 1**
2020–21 Lincoln C 23 0
2021–22 Lincoln C 14 0 **42 1**

CANN, Hayden (D) 0 0
2020–21 Lincoln C 0 0
2021–22 Lincoln C 0 0

DRAPER, Freddie (F) 8 0
H: 5 10 b. 28-7-04
2020–21 Lincoln C 0 0
2021–22 Lincoln C 8 0 **8 0**

EYOMA, Timothy (D) 62 2
H: 6 0 W: 11 11 b.Hackney 29-1-00
Internationals: England U16, U17, U18, U19.
2018–19 Tottenham H 0 0
2019–20 Tottenham H 0 0
2019–20 *Lincoln C* 0 0
2020–21 Tottenham H 0 0
2020–21 *Lincoln C* 39 1
2021–22 Lincoln C 23 1 **62 2**

HOPPER, Tom (F) 232 48
H: 6 1 W: 12 00 b.Boston 14-12-93
Internationals: England U18.
From Boston U.

2011–12	Leicester C	0	0		
2012–13	Leicester C	0	0		
2012–13	*Bury*	22	3	**22**	**3**
2013–14	Leicester C	0	0		
2014–15	Leicester C	0	0		
2014–15	*Scunthorpe U*	12	4		
2015–16	Scunthorpe U	34	8		
2016–17	Scunthorpe U	31	5		
2017–18	Scunthorpe U	38	7	**115**	**24**
2018–19	Southend U	14	7		
2019–20	Southend U	14	2	**28**	**9**
2019–20	Lincoln C	8	2		
2020–21	Lincoln C	39	8		
2021–22	Lincoln C	20	2	**67**	**12**

HOUSE, Ben (F) 12 1
H: 5 9 W: 11 00 b.Guildford 5-7-99
Internationals: Scotland U20, U21.

2018–19	Reading	0	0		
2018–19	*Swindon T*	6	0	**6**	**0**
2019–20	Reading	0	0		

From Eastleigh.

2021–22	Lincoln C	6	1	**6**	**1**

HOWARTH, Ramirez (F) 15 1
b. 14-9-97
From Ashton U, West Didsbury & Chorlton, Cefn Druids.

2020–21	Lincoln C	11	1		
2021–22	Lincoln C	4	0	**15**	**1**

JACKSON, Adam (D) 134 8
H: 6 2 W: 12 04 b.Darlington 18-5-94
Internationals: England U16, U17, U18, U19.

2011–12	Middlesbrough	0	0		
2012–13	Middlesbrough	0	0		
2013–14	Middlesbrough	0	0		
2014–15	Middlesbrough	0	0		
2015–16	Middlesbrough	0	0		
2015–16	*Coventry C*	0	0		
2015–16	*Hartlepool U*	29	3	**29**	**3**
2016–17	Barnsley	10	0		
2017–18	Barnsley	22	1		
2018–19	Barnsley	6	0	**38**	**1**
2019–20	Hibernian	14	3	**14**	**3**
2020–21	Lincoln C	28	1		
2021–22	Lincoln C	25	0	**53**	**1**

JONES, James (M) 203 20
H: 5 9 W: 10 10 b.Winsford 1-2-96
Internationals: Scotland U19, U21.

2014–15	Crewe Alex	24	1		
2015–16	Crewe Alex	31	0		
2016–17	Crewe Alex	45	10		
2017–18	Crewe Alex	6	1		
2018–19	Crewe Alex	38	5		
2019–20	Crewe Alex	23	2	**167**	**19**
2019–20	Lincoln C	0	0		
2020–21	Lincoln C	36	1		
2021–22	Lincoln C	0	0	**36**	**1**

Transferred to Wrexham, August 2021.

KENDALL, Charley (F) 0 0
b. 15-12-00

2020–21	QPR	0	0		
2021–22	Lincoln C	0	0		

LONG, Sam (G) 16 0
b.Redbridge 12-11-02

2020–21	Lincoln C	0	0		
2021–22	Lincoln C	1	0	**1**	**0**
2022	*Drogheda U*	15	0	**15**	**0**

MAGUIRE, Chris (F) 479 89
H: 5 7 W: 10 08 b.Bellshill 16-1-89
Internationals: Scotland U16, U19, U21, Full caps.

2005–06	Aberdeen	1	0		
2006–07	Aberdeen	19	1		
2007–08	Aberdeen	28	4		
2008–09	Aberdeen	31	3		
2009–10	Aberdeen	17	1		
2009–10	*Kilmarnock*	14	4	**14**	**4**
2010–11	Aberdeen	35	7	**131**	**16**
2011–12	Derby Co	7	1	**7**	**1**
2011–12	*Portsmouth*	11	3	**11**	**3**
2012–13	Sheffield W	10	1		
2013–14	Sheffield W	27	9		
2013–14	*Coventry C*	3	2	**3**	**2**
2014–15	Sheffield W	42	8	**79**	**18**
2015–16	Rotherham U	14	0	**14**	**0**
2015–16	Oxford U	21	4		
2016–17	Oxford U	42	13	**63**	**17**
2017–18	Bury	24	2	**24**	**2**
2018–19	Sunderland	33	7		
2019–20	Sunderland	35	10		
2020–21	Sunderland	33	5	**101**	**22**
2021–22	Lincoln C	32	4	**32**	**4**

MARQUIS, John (F) 385 120
H: 6 1 W: 11 03 b.Lewisham 16-5-92

2009–10	Millwall	1	0		
2010–11	Millwall	11	4		
2011–12	Millwall	17	1		
2012–13	Millwall	10	0		
2013–14	Millwall	2	0		
2013–14	*Portsmouth*	5	1		
2013–14	*Torquay U*	5	3	**5**	**3**
2013–14	*Northampton T*	14	2		
2014–15	Millwall	1	0		
2014–15	*Cheltenham T*	13	1	**13**	**1**
2014–15	*Gillingham*	21	8	**21**	**8**
2015–16	Millwall	10	0	**52**	**5**
2015–16	*Leyton Orient*	13	0	**13**	**0**
2015–16	*Northampton T*	15	6	**29**	**8**
2016–17	Doncaster R	45	26		
2017–18	Doncaster R	45	14		
2018–19	Doncaster R	44	21	**134**	**61**
2019–20	Portsmouth	33	8		
2020–21	Portsmouth	41	16		
2021–22	Portsmouth	19	4	**98**	**29**
2021–22	Lincoln C	20	5	**20**	**5**

McGRANDLES, Conor (M) 224 15
H: 6 0 W: 10 00 b.Falkirk 24-9-95

2012–13	Falkirk	26	2		
2013–14	Falkirk	36	5		
2014–15	Falkirk	3	0		
2014–15	Norwich C	1	0		
2015–16	Norwich C	0	0		
2015–16	*Falkirk*	5	0	**70**	**7**
2016–17	Norwich C	0	0	**1**	**0**
2017–18	Milton Keynes D	19	0		
2018–19	Milton Keynes D	25	1		
2019–20	Milton Keynes D	31	1	**75**	**2**
2020–21	Lincoln C	39	4		
2021–22	Lincoln C	39	2	**78**	**6**

MELBOURNE, Max (D) 56 2
H: 5 10 W: 10 03 b.Solihull 24-10-98

2017–18	WBA	0	0		
2017–18	*Ross Co*	3	0	**3**	**0**
2018–19	WBA	0	0		
2018–19	*Partick Thistle*	3	0	**3**	**0**
2019–20	Lincoln C	8	0		
2020–21	Lincoln C	8	0		
2020–21	*Walsall*	20	1	**20**	**1**
2021–22	Lincoln C	7	1	**23**	**1**
2021–22	*Stevenage*	7	0	**7**	**0**

MONTSMA, Lewis (D) 105 8
H: 6 3 W: 12 13 b.Amsterdam 25-4-98

2018–19	Dordrecht	23	1		
2019–20	Dordrecht	23	0	**46**	**1**
2020–21	Lincoln C	40	6		
2021–22	Lincoln C	19	1	**59**	**7**

POOLE, Regan (D) 162 2
H: 5 11 W: 11 00 b.Cardiff 18-6-98
Internationals: Wales U17, U19, U20, U21.

2014–15	Newport Co	11	0		
2015–16	Newport Co	4	0		
2015–16	Manchester U	0	0		
2016–17	Manchester U	0	0		
2017–18	Manchester U	0	0		
2017–18	*Northampton T*	22	0	**22**	**0**
2018–19	Manchester U	0	0		
2018–19	*Newport Co*	20	0	**35**	**0**
2019–20	Milton Keynes D	19	0		
2020–21	Milton Keynes D	20	1	**39**	**1**
2020–21	Lincoln C	22	0		
2021–22	Lincoln C	44	1	**66**	**1**

ROBSON, Jamie (D) 162 5
H: 5 8 W: 10 10 b.Perth 19-12-97

2014–15	Dundee U	0	0		
2015–16	Dundee U	0	0		
2015–16	*Brechin C*	6	2	**6**	**2**
2016–17	Dundee U	21	1		
2017–18	Dundee U	30	1		
2018–19	Dundee U	19	0		
2019–20	Dundee U	23	0		
2020–21	Dundee U	36	0		
2021–22	Dundee U	4	1	**133**	**3**
2021–22	Lincoln C	23	0	**23**	**0**

ROUGHAN, Sean (D) 21 0
b.Dublin 14-3-03
Internationals: Republic of Ireland U17, U19.

2020–21	Lincoln C	6	0		
2021–22	Lincoln C	0	0	**6**	**0**
2021–22	*Drogheda U*	15	0	**15**	**0**

SANDERS, Max (M) 44 1
H: 5 9 W: 12 08 b.Horsham 4-1-99
Internationals: England U19.

2017–18	Brighton & HA	0	0		
2018–19	Brighton & HA	0	0		
2019–20	Brighton & HA	0	0		
2019–20	*AFC Wimbledon*	20	1	**20**	**1**
2020–21	Brighton & HA	0	0		
2020–21	Lincoln C	5	0		
2021–22	Lincoln C	19	0	**24**	**0**

SCULLY, Anthony (M) 80 24
H: 5 7 W: 10 06 b.Watford 19-4-99
Internationals: Republic of Ireland U17, U19, U21.

2018–19	West Ham U	0	0		
2019–20	Lincoln C	5	2		
2020–21	Lincoln C	40	11		
2021–22	Lincoln C	35	11	**80**	**24**

SORENSON, Lasse (M) 62 1
H: 6 1 W: 12 04 b.Vejen 21-10-99
Internationals: Denmark U16, U17, U18, U19, U20.
From Esbjerg.

2017–18	Stoke C	1	0		
2018–19	Stoke C	1	0		
2019–20	Stoke C	6	0		
2020–21	Stoke C	0	0	**8**	**0**
2020–21	*Milton Keynes D*	24	0	**24**	**0**
2021–22	Lincoln C	30	1	**30**	**1**

WALSH, Joe (D) 253 12
H: 5 11 W: 11 00 b.Cardiff 13-5-92
Internationals: Wales U17, U19, U21.

2010–11	Swansea C	0	0		
2011–12	Swansea C	0	0		
2012–13	Crawley T	30	2		
2013–14	Crawley T	39	5		
2014–15	Crawley T	28	1	**97**	**8**
2014–15	*Milton Keynes D*	2	0		
2015–16	Milton Keynes D	18	1		
2016–17	Milton Keynes D	39	1		
2017–18	Milton Keynes D	10	0		
2018–19	Milton Keynes D	30	2		
2019–20	Milton Keynes D	24	0	**123**	**4**
2020–21	Lincoln C	21	0		
2021–22	Lincoln C	12	0	**33**	**0**

WRIGHT, Jordan (G) 13 0
H: 6 3 W: 11 11 b.Stoke-on-Trent 27-2-99

2015–16	Nottingham F	0	0		
2016–17	Nottingham F	0	0		
2017–18	Nottingham F	0	0		
2018–19	Nottingham F	0	0		
2019–20	Nottingham F	0	0		
2020–21	Nottingham F	0	0		
2021–22	*Alloa Ath*	0	0		
2021–22	Lincoln C	13	0	**13**	**0**

Players retained or with offer of contract
Boylan, Matt; Brooks, Billy; Gallagher, Oisin; Makama, Jovon.

Scholars
Alexander-Tucker, Tayo-Sharn Costin Lloyd; Angol, Mekhi Hayden; Boffah, Osei Kofi; Boylan, Matthew Edward; Brooks, Billy; Dale, Harry Jay; Deane, Robert Louis; Donnery, Julian Edward; Green, Sam Edward; Hilton, Ethan James; Kabeya, Nathan Sebastien; Mussell, Theo Adam Peter; Powell, Darryl Joseph; Simpson, Joshua Luke; Wheatley, Kyrell Thomas.

LIVERPOOL (47)

ADRIAN (G) 171 0
H: 6 2 W: 12 02 b.Seville 3-1-87

2008–09	Real Betis	0	0		
2009–10	Real Betis	0	0		
2010–11	Real Betis	0	0		
2011–12	Real Betis	0	0		
2012–13	Real Betis	32	0	**32**	**0**
2013–14	West Ham U	20	0		
2014–15	West Ham U	38	0		
2015–16	West Ham U	32	0		
2016–17	West Ham U	16	0		
2017–18	West Ham U	19	0		
2018–19	West Ham U	0	0	**125**	**0**
2019–20	Liverpool	11	0		
2020–21	Liverpool	3	0		
2021–22	Liverpool	0	0	**14**	**0**

ALEXANDER-ARNOLD, Trent (D) 161 10
H: 5 9 W: 10 12 b.Liverpool 7-10-98
Internationals: England U16, U17, U18, U19, U21, Full caps.

2016–17	Liverpool	7	0		
2017–18	Liverpool	19	1		
2018–19	Liverpool	29	1		
2019–20	Liverpool	38	4		
2020–21	Liverpool	36	2		
2021–22	Liverpool	32	2	**161**	**10**

ALISSON, Ramses (G) 217 1
H: 6 4 W: 14 05 b.Novo Hamburgo 2-10-92
Internationals: Brazil U17, U21, Full caps.

2013	Internacional	6	0		
2014	Internacional	11	0		
2015	Internacional	26	0		
2016	Internacional	1	0	**44**	**0**
2016–17	Roma	0	0		
2017–18	Roma	37	0	**37**	**0**
2018–19	Liverpool	38	0		
2019–20	Liverpool	29	0		
2020–21	Liverpool	33	1		
2021–22	Liverpool	36	0	**136**	**1**

ARROYO, Anderson (D) 79 0
H: 5 9 b.Quibdo 27-9-99
Internationals: Colombia U17, U20, U23.

2015	Fortaleza	2	0		
2016	Fortaleza	8	0		
2017	Fortaleza	4	0	**14**	**0**
2018–19	Liverpool	0	0		
2018–19	*Mallorca*	0	0		

2018–19	*Gent*	0	0		
2019–20	Liverpool	0	0		
2019–20	*Mlada Boleslav*	5	0	**5**	**0**
2020–21	Liverpool	0	0		
2020–21	*Salamanca*	21	0	**21**	**0**
2021–22	Liverpool	0	0		
2021–22	*Mirandes*	39	0	**39**	**0**

BALAGIZI, James (M) **0 0**
H: 6 2 b.Manchester 20-9-03
Internationals: England U16, U17, U18, U19.

2021–22	Liverpool	0	0

BEARNE, Jack (F) **0 0**
b.Nottingham 15-9-01

2019–20	Liverpool	0	0
2020–21	Liverpool	0	0
2021–22	Liverpool	0	0

BECK, Owen (D) **0 0**
b.Wrexham 9-8-02
Internationals: Wales U17, U21.

2020–21	Liverpool	0	0
2021–22	Liverpool	0	0

BLAIR, Harvey (F) **0 0**
b.Huddersfield 14-9-03

2020–21	Liverpool	0	0
2021–22	Liverpool	0	0

BRADLEY, Conor (M) **0 0**
H: 5 11 b.Tyrone 9-7-03
Internationals: Northern Ireland U16, U17, Full caps.
From Dungannon Swifts.

2020–21	Liverpool	0	0
2021–22	Liverpool	0	0

CAIN, Jake (M) **25 0**
H: 5 9 W: 9 04 b.Wigan 2-9-01

2019–20	Liverpool	0	0		
2020–21	Liverpool	0	0		
2021–22	Liverpool	0	0		
2021–22	*Newport Co*	25	0	**25**	**0**

CLARKSON, Leighton (M) **7 0**
H: 5 9 W: 9 11 b.Blackburn 19-10-01
Internationals: England U20.

2019–20	Liverpool	0	0		
2020–21	Liverpool	0	0		
2021–22	Liverpool	0	0		
2021–22	*Blackburn R*	7	0	**7**	**0**

CLAYTON, Tom (D) **0 0**
b.Rainford 16-11-00
Internationals: Scotland U19, U21.

2019–20	Liverpool	0	0
2020–21	Liverpool	0	0
2021–22	Liverpool	0	0

CORNESS, Dominic (M) **0 0**
b.Liverpool 5-5-03

2020–21	Liverpool	0	0
2021–22	Liverpool	0	0

DAVIES, Ben (D) **246 4**
H: 6 1 W: 11 09 b.Barrow 11-8-95

2012–13	Preston NE	3	0		
2013–14	Preston NE	0	0		
2013–14	*York C*	44	0	**44**	**0**
2014–15	Preston NE	4	0		
2014–15	*Tranmere R*	3	0	**3**	**0**
2015–16	Preston NE	0	0		
2015–16	*Newport Co*	19	0	**19**	**0**
2016–17	Preston NE	0	0		
2016–17	*Fleetwood T*	22	1	**22**	**1**
2017–18	Preston NE	34	1		
2018–19	Preston NE	40	1		
2019–20	Preston NE	36	0		
2020–21	Preston NE	19	0	**136**	**2**
2020–21	Liverpool	0	0		
2021–22	Liverpool	0	0		
2021–22	*Sheffield U*	22	1	**22**	**1**

DAVIES, Harvey (G) **0 0**
H: 6 3 b.Liverpool 3-9-03
Internationals: England U19.

2020–21	Liverpool	0	0
2021–22	Liverpool	0	0

DIAZ, Luis (F) **191 38**
H: 5 11 W: 11 07 b.Barrancas 13-1-97
Internationals: Colombia U20, Full caps.

2016	Barranquilla	19	2		
2017	Barranquilla	15	1	**34**	**3**
2017	Junior	12	0		
2018	Junior	38	13		
2019	Junior	17	2	**67**	**15**
2019–20	Porto	29	6		
2020–21	Porto	30	6		
2021–22	Porto	18	4	**77**	**16**
2021–22	Liverpool	13	4	**13**	**4**

DIXON-BONNER, Elijah (M) **0 0**
H: 5 8 W: 9 11 b.Harlow 1-1-01
Internationals: England U16, U17.

2019–20	Liverpool	0	0
2020–21	Liverpool	0	0
2021–22	Liverpool	0	0

ELLIOTT, Harvey (M) **51 7**
H: 5 7 W: 10 08 b.Chertsey 4-4-03
Internationals: England U16, U17, U21.

2018–19	Fulham	2	0	**2**	**0**
2019–20	Liverpool	2	0		
2020–21	Liverpool	0	0		
2020–21	*Blackburn R*	41	7	**41**	**7**
2021–22	Liverpool	6	0	**8**	**0**

FABINHO, Henrique (M) **283 31**
H: 6 2 W: 12 04 b.Campinas 23-10-93
Internationals: Brazil Full caps.
From Fluminese.

2012–13	Rio Ave	0	0		
2012–13	*Real Madrid*	1	0	**1**	**0**
2013–14	Rio Ave	0	0		
2013–14	*Monaco*	26	0		
2014–15	Rio Ave	0	0		
2014–15	*Monaco*	36	1		
2015–16	Monaco	34	6		
2016–17	Monaco	37	9		
2017–18	Monaco	34	7	**167**	**23**
2018–19	Liverpool	28	1		
2019–20	Liverpool	28	2		
2020–21	Liverpool	30	0		
2021–22	Liverpool	29	5	**115**	**8**

FIRMINO, Roberto (F) **409 117**
H: 5 11 W: 12 00 b.Maceio 2-10-91
Internationals: Brazil Full caps.

2009	Figueirense	2	0		
2010	Figueirense	36	8	**38**	**8**
2010–11	Hoffenheim	11	3		
2011–12	Hoffenheim	30	7		
2012–13	Hoffenheim	33	5		
2013–14	Hoffenheim	33	16		
2014–15	Hoffenheim	33	7	**140**	**38**
2015–16	Liverpool	31	10		
2016–17	Liverpool	35	11		
2017–18	Liverpool	37	15		
2018–19	Liverpool	34	12		
2019–20	Liverpool	38	9		
2020–21	Liverpool	36	9		
2021–22	Liverpool	20	5	**231**	**71**

FRAUENDORF, Melkamu (M) **0 0**
b.Kembata 12-1-04
Internationals: Germany U16, U18.
From Hoffenheim.

2021–22	Liverpool	0	0

GLATZEL, Paul (F) **16 4**
b.Liverpool 20-2-01
Internationals: England U16. Germany U18.

2021–22	Liverpool	0	0		
2021–22	*Tranmere R*	16	4	**16**	**4**

GOMEZ, Joseph (D) **108 0**
H: 6 2 W: 14 00 b.Catford 23-5-97
Internationals: England U16, U17, U19, U21, Full caps.

2014–15	Charlton Ath	21	0	**21**	**0**
2015–16	Liverpool	5	0		
2016–17	Liverpool	0	0		
2017–18	Liverpool	23	0		
2018–19	Liverpool	16	0		
2019–20	Liverpool	28	0		
2020–21	Liverpool	7	0		
2021–22	Liverpool	8	0	**87**	**0**

GORDON, Kaide (F) **2 0**
H: 5 8 b.Burton-upon-Trent 5-10-04
Internationals: England U16, U18.

2020–21	Derby Co	1	0	**1**	**0**
2020–21	Liverpool	0	0		
2021–22	Liverpool	1	0	**1**	**0**

HENDERSON, Jordan (M) **406 34**
H: 6 2 W: 10 08 b.Sunderland 17-6-90
Internationals: England U19, U20, U21, Full caps.

2008–09	Sunderland	1	0		
2008–09	*Coventry C*	10	1	**10**	**1**
2009–10	Sunderland	33	1		
2010–11	Sunderland	37	3	**71**	**4**
2011–12	Liverpool	37	2		
2012–13	Liverpool	30	5		
2013–14	Liverpool	35	4		
2014–15	Liverpool	37	6		
2015–16	Liverpool	17	2		
2016–17	Liverpool	24	1		
2017–18	Liverpool	27	1		
2018–19	Liverpool	32	1		
2019–20	Liverpool	30	4		
2020–21	Liverpool	21	1		
2021–22	Liverpool	35	2	**325**	**29**

HILL, Thomas (M) **0 0**
b.Formby 13-10-02

2019–20	Liverpool	0	0
2020–21	Liverpool	0	0
2021–22	Liverpool	0	0

HUGHES, Liam (G) **0 0**
H: 6 4 b.Craigavon 19-8-01
Internationals: Northern Ireland U21.
From Portadown, Dungannon Swifts, Celtic.

2020–21	Liverpool	0	0
2021–22	Liverpool	0	0

JAROS, Vitezslav (G) **0 0**
b.Pribram 23-7-01
Internationals: Czech Republic U16, U18, U21.
From Slavia Prague.

2020–21	Liverpool	0	0
2021–22	Liverpool	0	0

JONES, Curtis (M) **45 3**
H: 6 1 W: 11 11 b.Liverpool 30-1-01
Internationals: England U16, U17, U18, U19, U21.

2017–18	Liverpool	0	0		
2018–19	Liverpool	0	0		
2019–20	Liverpool	6	1		
2020–21	Liverpool	24	1		
2021–22	Liverpool	15	1	**45**	**3**

JOTA, Diogo (F) **233 79**
H: 5 10 W: 11 00 b.Massarelos 4-12-96
Internationals: Portugal U19, U21, U23, Full caps.

2014–15	Pacos Ferreira	10	2		
2015–16	Pacos Ferreira	31	12	**41**	**14**
2016–17	Atletico Madrid	0	0		
2016–17	*Porto*	27	8	**27**	**8**
2017–18	Atletico Madrid	0	0		
2017–18	*Wolverhampton W*	44	17		
2018–19	Wolverhampton W	33	9		
2019–20	Wolverhampton W	34	7	**111**	**33**
2020–21	Liverpool	19	9		
2021–22	Liverpool	35	15	**54**	**24**

KARIUS, Loris (G) **179 0**
H: 6 2 W: 11 11 b.Biberach 22-6-93
Internationals: Germany U16, U17, U18, U19, U20, U21.

2009–10	Manchester C	0	0		
2010–11	Manchester C	0	0		
2011–12	Manchester C	0	0		
2012–13	Manchester C	0	0		
2012–13	Mainz 05	1	0		
2013–14	Mainz 05	23	0		
2014–15	Mainz 05	33	0		
2015–16	Mainz 05	34	0	**91**	**0**
2016–17	Liverpool	10	0		
2017–18	Liverpool	19	0		
2018–19	Liverpool	0	0		
2018–19	*Besiktas*	30	0		
2019–20	Liverpool	0	0		
2019–20	*Besiktas*	25	0	**55**	**0**
2020–21	Liverpool	0	0		
2020–21	*Union Berlin*	4	0	**4**	**0**
2021–22	Liverpool	0	0	**29**	**0**

KEITA, Naby (M) **216 42**
H: 5 8 W: 10 01 b.Conakry 10-2-95
Internationals: Guinea Full caps.

2013–14	Istres	23	4	**23**	**4**
2014–15	Red Bull Salzburg	30	5		
2015–16	Red Bull Salzburg	29	12	**59**	**17**
2016–17	RB Leipzig	31	8		
2017–18	RB Leipzig	27	6	**58**	**14**
2018–19	Liverpool	25	2		
2019–20	Liverpool	18	2		
2020–21	Liverpool	10	0		
2021–22	Liverpool	23	3	**76**	**7**

KELLEHER, Caoimhin (G) **4 0**
H: 5 11 W: 11 03 b.Cork 23-11-98
Internationals: Republic of Ireland U17, U19, U21, Full caps.

2018–19	Liverpool	0	0		
2019–20	Liverpool	0	0		
2020–21	Liverpool	2	0		
2021–22	Liverpool	2	0	**4**	**0**

KONATE, Ibrahima (D) **89 3**
H: 6 4 W: 13 03 b.Paris 25-5-99
Internationals: France U16, U17, U19, U20, U21, Full caps.

2016–17	Sochaux	12	1	**12**	**1**
2017–18	RB Leipzig	16	0		
2018–19	RB Leipzig	28	1		
2019–20	RB Leipzig	8	0		
2020–21	RB Leipzig	14	1	**66**	**2**
2021–22	Liverpool	11	0	**11**	**0**

KOURMETIO, Billy (D) **0 0**
H: 6 5 W: 12 06 b.Lyon 14-11-02
Internationals: France U18.
From Lyon, Orleans.

2019–20	Liverpool	0	0
2020–21	Liverpool	0	0
2021–22	Liverpool	0	0

LEWIS, Adam (D) **38 1**
b.Liverpool 8-11-99
Internationals: England U16, U17, U19, U20.

2019–20	Liverpool	0	0		
2020–21	Liverpool	0	0		
2020–21	*Amiens*	9	0	**9**	**0**
2020–21	*Plymouth Arg*	20	1	**20**	**1**
2021–22	Liverpool	0	0		
2021–22	*Livingston*	9	0	**9**	**0**

LONGSTAFF, Luis (M) **28 4**
b.Darlington 24-2-00
Internationals: England U16, U17.

2019–20	Liverpool	0	0		
2020–21	Liverpool	0	0		
2021–22	Liverpool	0	0		
2021–22	*Queen's Park*	28	4	**28**	**4**

MABAYA, Isaac (M) **0 0**
b.Preston 22-9-04
Internationals: England U16, U18.

2021–22	Liverpool	0	0		

MANE, Sadio (F) **348 144**
H: 5 9 W: 12 00 b.Sedhiou 10-4-92
Internationals: Senegal U23, Full caps.

2011–12	Metz	19	1		
2012–13	Metz	3	1	**22**	**2**
2012–13	Red Bull Salzburg	26	16		
2013–14	Red Bull Salzburg	33	13		
2014–15	Red Bull Salzburg	4	2	**63**	**31**
2014–15	Southampton	30	10		
2015–16	Southampton	37	11	**67**	**21**
2016–17	Liverpool	27	13		
2017–18	Liverpool	29	10		
2018–19	Liverpool	36	22		
2019–20	Liverpool	35	18		
2020–21	Liverpool	35	11		
2021–22	Liverpool	34	16	**196**	**90**

MARCELO (G) **0 0**
H: 6 3 W: 12 04 b.Niteroi 20-12-02
Internationals: Brazil U17.
From Fluminese.

2020–21	Liverpool	0	0		
2021–22	Liverpool	0	0		

MATIP, Joel (D) **320 22**
H: 6 4 W: 13 01 b.Bochum 8-8-91
Internationals: Cameroon Full caps.

2009–10	Schalke 04	20	3		
2010–11	Schalke 04	26	0		
2011–12	Schalke 04	30	3		
2012–13	Schalke 04	32	0		
2013–14	Schalke 04	31	3		
2014–15	Schalke 04	21	2		
2015–16	Schalke 04	34	3	**194**	**14**
2016–17	Liverpool	29	1		
2017–18	Liverpool	25	1		
2018–19	Liverpool	22	1		
2019–20	Liverpool	9	1		
2020–21	Liverpool	10	1		
2021–22	Liverpool	31	3	**126**	**8**

MILNER, James (M) **594 57**
H: 5 9 W: 11 00 b.Leeds 4-1-86
Internationals: England U16, U17, U19, U20, U21, Full caps.

2002–03	Leeds U	18	2		
2003–04	Leeds U	30	3	**48**	**5**
2003–04	*Swindon T*	6	2	**6**	**2**
2004–05	Newcastle U	25	1		
2005–06	Newcastle U	3	0		
2005–06	*Aston Villa*	27	1		
2006–07	Newcastle U	35	3		
2007–08	Newcastle U	29	2		
2008–09	Newcastle U	2	0	**94**	**6**
2008–09	Aston Villa	36	3		
2009–10	Aston Villa	36	7		
2010–11	Aston Villa	1	1	**100**	**12**
2010–11	Manchester C	32	0		
2011–12	Manchester C	26	3		
2012–13	Manchester C	26	4		
2013–14	Manchester C	31	1		
2014–15	Manchester C	32	5	**147**	**13**
2015–16	Liverpool	28	5		
2016–17	Liverpool	36	7		
2017–18	Liverpool	32	0		
2018–19	Liverpool	31	5		
2019–20	Liverpool	22	2		
2020–21	Liverpool	26	0		
2021–22	Liverpool	24	0	**199**	**19**

MINAMINO, Takumi (F) **238 55**
H: 5 9 W: 10 08 b.Osaka 16-1-95
Internationals: Japan U17, U20, U23, Full caps.

2012	Cerezo Osaka	3	0		
2013	Cerezo Osaka	29	5		
2014	Cerezo Osaka	30	2	**62**	**7**
2014–15	Red Bull Salzburg	14	3		
2015–16	Red Bull Salzburg	32	10		
2016–17	Red Bull Salzburg	21	11		
2017–18	Red Bull Salzburg	28	7		
2018–19	Red Bull Salzburg	27	6		
2019–20	Red Bull Salzburg	14	5	**136**	**42**
2019–20	Liverpool	10	0		
2020–21	Liverpool	9	1		
2020–21	*Southampton*	10	2	**10**	**2**
2021–22	Liverpool	11	3	**30**	**4**

MORTON, Tyler (M) **2 0**
H: 5 10 b.Wirral 31-10-02
Internationals: England U20.

2020–21	Liverpool	0	0		
2021–22	Liverpool	2	0	**2**	**0**

NORRIS, James (D) **0 0**
H: 5 8 W: 9 06 b.Liverpool 4-4-03
Internationals: England U16, U17, U18, U19.

2019–20	Liverpool	0	0		
2020–21	Liverpool	0	0		
2021–22	Liverpool	0	0		

O'ROURKE, Fidel (F) **0 0**
b.Liverpool 5-2-02
Internationals: England U16.

2020–21	Liverpool	0	0		
2021–22	Liverpool	0	0		

OJO, Sheyi (F) **151 12**
H: 5 10 W: 10 01 b.Hemel Hempstead 19-6-97
Internationals: England U16, U17, U18, U19, U20, U21.

2014–15	Liverpool	0	0		
2014–15	*Wigan Ath*	11	0	**11**	**0**
2015–16	Liverpool	8	0		
2015–16	*Wolverhampton W*	17	2	**17**	**2**
2016–17	Liverpool	0	0		
2017–18	Liverpool	0	0		
2017–18	*Fulham*	22	4	**22**	**4**
2018–19	Liverpool	0	0		
2018–19	*Reims*	15	0	**15**	**0**
2019–20	Liverpool	0	0		
2019–20	*Rangers*	19	1	**19**	**1**
2020–21	Liverpool	0	0		
2020–21	*Cardiff C*	41	5	**41**	**5**
2021–22	Liverpool	0	0	**8**	**0**
2021–22	*Millwall*	18	0	**18**	**0**

OJRZYNSKI, Jakub (G) **0 0**
b. 19-2-03
Internationals: Poland U16, U17, U19.
From Korona, Legia Warsaw.

2020–21	Liverpool	0	0		
2021–22	Liverpool	0	0		

ORIGI, Divock (F) **211 42**
H: 6 1 W: 11 11 b.Oostende 18-4-95
Internationals: Belgium U16, U17, U19, U21, Full caps.
From Genk.

2012–13	Lille	10	1		
2013–14	Lille	30	5		
2014–15	Lille	33	8	**73**	**14**
2015–16	Liverpool	16	5		
2016–17	Liverpool	34	7		
2017–18	Liverpool	1	0		
2017–18	*VfL Wolfsburg*	31	6	**31**	**6**
2018–19	Liverpool	12	3		
2019–20	Liverpool	28	4		
2020–21	Liverpool	9	0		
2021–22	Liverpool	7	3	**107**	**22**

OXLADE-CHAMBERLAIN, Alex (M) **262 28**
H: 5 9 W: 11 00 b.Portsmouth 15-8-93
Internationals: England U18, U19, U21, Full caps.

2009–10	Southampton	2	0		
2010–11	Southampton	34	9	**36**	**9**
2011–12	Arsenal	16	2		
2012–13	Arsenal	25	1		
2013–14	Arsenal	14	2		
2014–15	Arsenal	23	1		
2015–16	Arsenal	22	1		
2016–17	Arsenal	29	2		
2017–18	Arsenal	3	0	**132**	**9**
2017–18	Liverpool	32	3		
2018–19	Liverpool	2	0		
2019–20	Liverpool	30	4		
2020–21	Liverpool	13	1		
2021–22	Liverpool	17	2	**94**	**10**

PHILLIPS, Nathaniel (D) **53 1**
H: 6 3 W: 11 07 b.Bolton 21-3-97

2019–20	Liverpool	0	0		
2019–20	*Stuttgart*	19	0	**19**	**0**
2020–21	Liverpool	17	1		
2021–22	Liverpool	0	0	**17**	**1**
2021–22	*Bournemouth*	17	0	**17**	**0**

QUANSAH, Jarell (D) **0 0**
b.Warrington 29-1-03
Internationals: England U16, U17, U18, U19.

2020–21	Liverpool	0	0		
2021–22	Liverpool	0	0		

RITACCIO, Matteo (M) **0 0**
b.Westbury, New York 4-10-01
Internationals: USA U20.

2020–21	Liverpool	0	0		
2021–22	Liverpool	0	0		
2022	*Charleston*	0	0		

ROBERTSON, Andrew (D) **330 15**
H: 5 10 W: 10 00 b.Glasgow 11-3-94
Internationals: Scotland U21, Full caps.

2012–13	Queen's Park	34	2	**34**	**2**
2013–14	Dundee U	36	3	**36**	**3**
2014–15	Hull C	24	0		
2015–16	Hull C	42	2		
2016–17	Hull C	33	1	**99**	**3**
2017–18	Liverpool	22	1		
2018–19	Liverpool	36	0		
2019–20	Liverpool	36	2		
2020–21	Liverpool	38	1		
2021–22	Liverpool	29	3	**161**	**7**

SALAH, Mohamed (F) **359 175**
H: 5 9 W: 11 05 b.Basion 15-6-92
Internationals: Egypt U20, U23, Full caps.

2009–10	Al-Mokawloon	3	0		
2010–11	Al-Mokawloon	20	4		
2011–12	Al-Mokawloon	15	7	**38**	**11**
2012–13	Basle	29	5		
2013–14	Basle	18	4	**47**	**9**
2013–14	Chelsea	10	2		
2014–15	Chelsea	3	0		
2014–15	*Fiorentina*	16	6	**16**	**6**
2015–16	Chelsea	0	0	**13**	**2**
2015–16	*Roma*	34	14		
2016–17	Roma	31	15	**65**	**29**
2017–18	Liverpool	36	32		
2018–19	Liverpool	38	22		
2019–20	Liverpool	34	19		
2020–21	Liverpool	37	22		
2021–22	Liverpool	35	23	**180**	**118**

STEWART, Layton (F) **0 0**
b.Liverpool 2-9-02
Internationals: England U18.

2019–20	Liverpool	0	0		
2020–21	Liverpool	0	0		
2021–22	Liverpool	0	0		

THIAGO, Alcantara (M) **267 26**
H: 5 9 W: 10 03 b.San Pietro Vernotico, Italy 11-4-91
Internationals: Spain U16, U17, U18, U19, U21, Full caps.

2007–08	Barcelona	0	0		
2008–09	Barcelona	1	0		
2009–10	Barcelona	1	1		
2010–11	Barcelona	12	2		
2011–12	Barcelona	27	2		
2012–13	Barcelona	27	2	**68**	**7**
2013–14	Bayern Munich	16	2		
2014–15	Bayern Munich	7	0		
2015–16	Bayern Munich	27	2		
2016–17	Bayern Munich	27	6		
2017–18	Bayern Munich	19	2		
2018–19	Bayern Munich	30	2		
2019–20	Bayern Munich	24	3		
2020–21	Bayern Munich	0	0	**150**	**17**
2020–21	Liverpool	24	1		
2021–22	Liverpool	25	1	**49**	**2**

TSIMIKAS, Konstantinos (D) **70 2**
H: 5 10 W: 11 00 b.Thessaloniki 12-5-96
Internationals: Greece U19, U21, Full caps.

2015–16	Olympiacos	3	0		
2016–17	Olympiacos	1	0		
2016–17	*Esbjerg*	9	2	**9**	**2**
2017–18	Olympiacos	0	0		
2017–18	*Willem*	0	0		
2018–19	Olympiacos	15	0		
2019–20	Olympiacos	27	0		
2020–21	Olympiacos	0	0	**46**	**0**
2020–21	Liverpool	2	0		
2021–22	Liverpool	13	0	**15**	**0**

VAN DEN BERG, Sepp (D) **83 1**
H: 6 2 W: 12 04 b.Zwolle 20-12-01
Internationals: Netherlands U19, U21.

2017–18	PEC Zwolle	7	0		
2018–19	PEC Zwolle	15	0	**22**	**0**
2019–20	Liverpool	0	0		
2020–21	Liverpool	0	0		
2020–21	*Preston NE*	16	0		
2021–22	Liverpool	0	0		
2021–22	*Preston NE*	45	1	**61**	**1**

VAN DIJK, Virgil (D) **334 33**
H: 6 4 W: 14 07 b.Breda 8-7-91
Internationals: Netherlands U19, U21, Full caps.
From Willem II.

2010–11	Groningen	5	2		
2011–12	Groningen	23	3		
2012–13	Groningen	34	2	**62**	**7**
2013–14	Celtic	36	5		
2014–15	Celtic	35	4		
2015–16	Celtic	5	0	**76**	**9**
2015–16	Southampton	34	3		
2016–17	Southampton	21	1		
2017–18	Southampton	12	0	**67**	**4**
2017–18	Liverpool	14	0		
2018–19	Liverpool	38	4		
2019–20	Liverpool	38	5		
2020–21	Liverpool	5	1		
2021–22	Liverpool	34	3	**129**	**13**

WILLIAMS, Neco (D) **27 2**
H: 5 10 W: 9 06 b.Wrexham 13-4-01
Internationals: Wales U19, Full caps.

2019–20	Liverpool	6	0		
2020–21	Liverpool	6	0		
2021–22	Liverpool	1	0	**13**	**0**
2021–22	*Fulham*	14	2	**14**	**2**

WILLIAMS, Rhys (D) **14** **0**
H: 6 5 W: 11 05 b.Preston 3-2-01
Internationals: England U18, U19, U21.
2019–20 Liverpool 0 0
2020–21 Liverpool 9 0
2021–22 Liverpool 0 0 **9** **0**
2021–22 *Swansea C* 5 0 **5** **0**

WOLTMAN, Max (F) **0** **0**
H: 5 11 b.Wirral 20-8-03
2020–21 Liverpool 0 0
2021–22 Liverpool 0 0

WOODBURN, Ben (F) **62** **4**
H: 5 9 W: 11 05 b.Nottingham 16-11-99
Internationals: Wales U16, U17, U19, Full caps.
2016–17 Liverpool 5 0
2017–18 Liverpool 1 0
2018–19 Liverpool 0 0
2018–19 *Sheffield U* 7 0 **7** **0**
2019–20 Liverpool 0 0
2019–20 *Oxford U* 11 1 **11** **1**
2020–21 Liverpool 0 0
2020–21 *Blackpool* 10 0 **10** **0**
2021–22 Liverpool 0 0 **6** **0**
2021–22 *Hearts* 28 3 **28** **3**

Players retained or with offer of contract
Bajcetic Maquieira, Stefan; Cannonier, Oakley; Chambers, Luke; Clark, Bobby; Hewitson, Luke; Jonas, Lee; Kelly, Oscar; McConnell, James; McLoughlin Miles, Terence; Mrozek, Fabian; Musialowski, Mateusz; Scanlon, Calum; Stephenson, Luca.

Scholars
Hayes-Green, Charles Frederick Jack; Osborne, Niall Declan; Pilling, Tommy James; Roberts, Iwan.

LUTON T (48)

ADDY, TQ (F) **0** **0**
b.London 1-2-02
2020–21 Luton T 0 0
2021–22 Luton T 0 0

ADEBAYO, Elijah (F) **147** **46**
H: 6 4 W: 14 00 b.Brent 7-1-98
2017–18 Fulham 0 0
2017–18 *Cheltenham T* 7 2 **7** **2**
2018–19 Fulham 0 0
2018–19 *Swindon T* 25 5 **25** **5**
2018–19 *Stevenage* 2 0 **2** **0**
2019–20 Walsall 30 8
2020–21 Walsall 25 10 **55** **18**
2020–21 Luton T 18 5
2021–22 Luton T 40 16 **58** **21**

BECKWITH, Sam (M) **0** **0**
H: 5 10 W: 10 01 b.Bedford 11-12-01
2020–21 Luton T 0 0
2021–22 Luton T 0 0

BELL, Amari (D) **264** **10**
H: 5 11 W: 12 00 b.Burton-upon-Trent 5-5-94
Internationals: Jamaica Full caps.
2012–13 Birmingham C 0 0
2013–14 Birmingham C 1 0
2014–15 Birmingham C 0 0 **1** **0**
2014–15 *Swindon T* 10 0 **10** **0**
2014–15 *Gillingham* 7 0 **7** **0**
2015–16 Fleetwood T 44 0
2016–17 Fleetwood T 44 2
2017–18 Fleetwood T 27 4 **115** **6**
2017–18 Blackburn R 12 0
2018–19 Blackburn R 38 3
2019–20 Blackburn R 21 0
2020–21 Blackburn R 19 0 **90** **3**
2021–22 Luton T 41 1 **41** **1**

BERRY, Luke (M) **245** **49**
H: 5 10 W: 11 05 b.Bassingbourn 12-7-92
From Cambridge U.
2014–15 Barnsley 31 1 **31** **1**
2015–16 Cambridge U 46 12
2016–17 Cambridge U 45 17
2017–18 Cambridge U 3 0 **94** **29**
2017–18 Luton T 34 7
2018–19 Luton T 21 3
2019–20 Luton T 21 1
2020–21 Luton T 31 2
2021–22 Luton T 13 6 **120** **19**

BRADLEY, Sonny (D) **391** **21**
H: 6 0 W: 11 05 b.Kingston upon Hull 13-9-91
2011–12 Hull C 2 0
2011–12 *Aldershot T* 14 0
2012–13 Hull C 0 0 **2** **0**
2012–13 *Aldershot T* 42 1 **56** **1**
2013–14 Portsmouth 33 2 **33** **2**
2014–15 Crawley T 26 1
2015–16 Crawley T 46 1 **72** **2**
2016–17 Plymouth Arg 44 7
2017–18 Plymouth Arg 40 4 **84** **11**
2018–19 Luton T 45 0
2019–20 Luton T 40 3
2020–21 Luton T 37 0
2021–22 Luton T 22 2 **144** **5**

BREE, James (D) **190** **2**
H: 5 10 W: 11 09 b.Wakefield 11-12-97
2013–14 Barnsley 1 0
2014–15 Barnsley 11 0
2015–16 Barnsley 19 0
2016–17 Barnsley 19 0 **50** **0**
2016–17 Aston Villa 7 0
2017–18 Aston Villa 6 0
2018–19 Aston Villa 8 0
2018–19 *Ipswich T* 14 0 **14** **0**
2019–20 Aston Villa 0 0 **21** **0**
2019–20 *Luton T* 39 0
2020–21 Luton T 24 1
2021–22 Luton T 42 1 **105** **2**

BURKE, Reece (D) **205** **8**
H: 6 2 W: 12 11 b.Newham 2-9-96
Internationals: England U18, U19, U20.
2013–14 West Ham U 0 0
2014–15 West Ham U 5 0
2015–16 West Ham U 0 0
2015–16 *Bradford C* 34 2 **34** **2**
2016–17 West Ham U 0 0
2016–17 *Wigan Ath* 10 1 **10** **1**
2017–18 West Ham U 0 0 **5** **0**
2017–18 *Bolton W* 25 1 **25** **1**
2018–19 Hull C 34 0
2019–20 Hull C 36 0
2020–21 Hull C 34 4
2021–22 Hull C 0 0 **104** **4**
2021–22 Luton T 27 0 **27** **0**

CAMPBELL, Allan (M) **168** **18**
H: 5 8 W: 10 08 b.Glasgow 4-7-98
Internationals: Scotland U21, Full caps.
2015–16 Motherwell 0 0
2016–17 Motherwell 7 1
2017–18 Motherwell 29 2
2018–19 Motherwell 35 2
2019–20 Motherwell 30 5
2020–21 Motherwell 34 4 **135** **14**
2021–22 Luton T 33 4 **33** **4**

CLARK, Jordan (M) **277** **28**
H: 6 0 W: 11 07 b.Barnsley 22-9-93
2010–11 Barnsley 4 0
2011–12 Barnsley 2 0
2012–13 Barnsley 0 0
2012–13 *Chesterfield* 2 0 **2** **0**
2013–14 Barnsley 0 0 **6** **0**
2013–14 *Scunthorpe U* 1 0 **1** **0**
2014–15 Shrewsbury T 27 3
2015–16 Shrewsbury T 20 2 **47** **5**
2016–17 Accrington S 42 1
2017–18 Accrington S 43 8
2018–19 Accrington S 43 5
2019–20 Accrington S 34 6 **162** **20**
2020–21 Luton T 34 1
2021–22 Luton T 25 2 **59** **3**

CORNICK, Harry (F) **245** **41**
H: 5 11 W: 13 03 b.Poole 6-3-95
From Christchurch.
2013–14 Bournemouth 0 0
2014–15 Bournemouth 0 0
2015–16 Bournemouth 0 0
2015–16 *Yeovil T* 36 7 **36** **7**
2016–17 Bournemouth 0 0
2016–17 *Leyton Orient* 11 1 **11** **1**
2016–17 *Gillingham* 6 0 **6** **0**
2017–18 Luton T 37 5
2018–19 Luton T 32 6
2019–20 Luton T 45 9
2020–21 Luton T 40 1
2021–22 Luton T 38 12 **192** **33**

HYLTON, Danny (F) **411** **115**
H: 6 0 W: 11 03 b.Camden 25-2-89
2008–09 Aldershot T 29 5
2009–10 Aldershot T 21 3
2010–11 Aldershot T 33 5
2011–12 Aldershot T 44 13
2012–13 Aldershot T 27 4 **154** **30**
2013–14 Rotherham U 1 0 **1** **0**
2013–14 *Bury* 7 2 **7** **2**
2013–14 *AFC Wimbledon* 17 3 **17** **3**
2014–15 Oxford U 44 14
2015–16 Oxford U 41 12 **85** **26**
2016–17 Luton T 39 21
2017–18 Luton T 39 21
2018–19 Luton T 25 8
2019–20 Luton T 11 0
2020–21 Luton T 16 0
2021–22 Luton T 17 4 **147** **54**

ISTED, Harry (G) **2** **0**
H: 6 1 W: 11 00 b.Chichester 5-3-97
From Southampton, Stoke C.
2017–18 Luton T 0 0
2018–19 Luton T 0 0
2019–20 Luton T 0 0
2020–21 Luton T 0 0
2021–22 Luton T 2 0 **2** **0**

JEROME, Cameron (F) **595** **137**
H: 6 1 W: 13 06 b.Huddersfield 14-8-86
Internationals: England U21.
From Huddersfield T, Grimsby T, Sheffield W, Middlesbrough.
2004–05 Cardiff C 29 6
2005–06 Cardiff C 44 18 **73** **24**
2005–06 Birmingham C 0 0
2006–07 Birmingham C 38 7
2007–08 Birmingham C 33 7
2008–09 Birmingham C 43 9
2009–10 Birmingham C 32 11
2010–11 Birmingham C 34 3
2011–12 Birmingham C 1 0 **181** **37**
2011–12 Stoke C 23 4
2012–13 Stoke C 26 3
2013–14 Stoke C 1 0 **50** **7**
2013–14 *Crystal Palace* 28 2 **28** **2**
2014–15 Norwich C 41 18
2015–16 Norwich C 34 3
2016–17 Norwich C 40 16
2017–18 Norwich C 15 1 **130** **38**
2017–18 Derby Co 18 5 **18** **5**
2018–19 Goztepe 28 5
2019–20 Goztepe 22 3 **50** **8**
2020–21 Milton Keynes D 34 13
2021–22 Milton Keynes D 0 0 **34** **13**
2021–22 Luton T 31 3 **31** **3**

KIOSO, Peter (D) **69** **10**
H: 6 0 W: 11 00 b.Swords 15-8-99
From Milton Keynes D, Dunstable T, Hartlepool U.
2019–20 Luton T 1 0
2020–21 Bolton W 13 3 **13** **3**
2020–21 Luton T 0 0
2020–21 *Northampton T* 21 3 **21** **3**
2021–22 Luton T 16 0 **17** **0**
2021–22 *Milton Keynes D* 18 4 **18** **4**

LANSBURY, Henri (M) **337** **48**
H: 6 0 W: 13 05 b.Enfield 12-10-90
Internationals: England U16, U17, U19, U21.
2007–08 Arsenal 0 0
2008–09 Arsenal 0 0
2008–09 *Scunthorpe U* 16 4 **16** **4**
2009–10 Arsenal 1 0
2009–10 *Watford* 37 5 **37** **5**
2010–11 Arsenal 0 0
2010–11 *Norwich C* 23 4 **23** **4**
2011–12 Arsenal 2 0
2011–12 *West Ham U* 22 1 **22** **1**
2012–13 Arsenal 0 0 **3** **0**
2012–13 Nottingham F 32 5
2013–14 Nottingham F 29 7
2014–15 Nottingham F 39 10
2015–16 Nottingham F 28 4
2016–17 Nottingham F 17 6 **145** **32**
2016–17 Aston Villa 18 0
2017–18 Aston Villa 10 2
2018–19 Aston Villa 3 0
2019–20 Aston Villa 10 0
2020–21 Aston Villa 0 0 **41** **2**
2020–21 Bristol C 16 0 **16** **0**
2021–22 Luton T 34 0 **34** **0**

LAWLESS, Conor (M) **0** **0**
2020–21 Reading 0 0
2021–22 Luton T 0 0

LEE, Elliot (F) **187** **39**
H: 5 11 W: 11 05 b.Durham 16-12-94
2011–12 West Ham U 0 0
2012–13 West Ham U 0 0
2013–14 West Ham U 1 0
2013–14 *Colchester U* 4 1
2014–15 West Ham U 1 0
2014–15 *Southend U* 0 0
2014–15 *Luton T* 11 3
2015–16 West Ham U 0 0 **2** **0**
2015–16 *Blackpool* 4 0 **4** **0**
2015–16 *Colchester U* 15 2 **19** **3**
2016–17 Barnsley 6 0 **6** **0**
2017–18 Luton T 32 10
2018–19 Luton T 38 12
2019–20 Luton T 11 1
2020–21 Luton T 12 1
2020–21 *Oxford U* 18 6 **18** **6**
2021–22 Luton T 0 0 **104** **27**
2021–22 *Charlton Ath* 34 3 **34** **3**

LOCKYER, Tom (D) **303** **7**
H: 6 0 W: 11 05 b.Bristol 30-12-94
Internationals: Wales U21, Full caps.
2012–13 Bristol R 4 0
2013–14 Bristol R 41 1
From Bristol R.
2015–16 Bristol R 43 0
2016–17 Bristol R 46 0
2017–18 Bristol R 37 1
2018–19 Bristol R 40 3 **211** **5**
2019–20 Charlton Ath 43 1 **43** **1**
2020–21 Luton T 20 0
2021–22 Luton T 29 1 **49** **1**

MENDES GOMES, Carlos (F) **83** **17**
H: 5 10 W: 10 06 b.Yeumbeul 14-11-98
From Atletico Madrid, West Didsbury & Chorlton.

2018–19	Morecambe	15	0		
2019–20	Morecambe	16	2		
2020–21	Morecambe	43	15		
2021–22	Morecambe	0	0	**74**	**17**
2021–22	Luton T	9	0	**9**	**0**

MUSKWE, Admiral (F) **42** **3**
H: 6 0 W: 11 03 b.Harare 21-8-98
Internationals: England U17. Zimbabwe Full caps.

2019–20	Leicester C	0	0		
2019–20	*Swindon T*	5	0	**5**	**0**
2020–21	Leicester C	0	0		
2020–21	*Wycombe W*	17	3		
2021–22	Leicester C	0	0		
2021–22	*Wycombe W*	0	0	**17**	**3**
2021–22	Luton T	20	0	**20**	**0**

NAISMITH, Kal (F) **336** **44**
H: 5 7 W: 13 03 b.Glasgow 18-2-92
Internationals: Scotland U16, U17.

2011–12	Rangers	0	0		
2011–12	*Cowdenbeath*	9	2	**9**	**2**
2011–12	*Partick Thistle*	8	0	**8**	**0**
2012–13	Rangers	17	1	**17**	**1**
2013–14	Accrington S	38	10		
2014–15	Accrington S	35	4	**73**	**14**
2015–16	Portsmouth	19	3		
2015–16	*Hartlepool U*	4	0	**4**	**0**
2016–17	Portsmouth	37	13		
2017–18	Portsmouth	26	2	**82**	**18**
2018–19	Wigan Ath	30	1		
2019–20	Wigan Ath	37	3		
2020–21	Wigan Ath	12	2	**79**	**6**
2020–21	Luton T	22	1		
2021–22	Luton T	42	2	**64**	**3**

NEUFVILLE, Josh (F) **0** **0**
H: 6 0 W: 11 09 b.Luton 22-3-01

2017–18	Luton T	0	0		
2018–19	Luton T	0	0		
2019–20	Luton T	0	0		
2020–21	Luton T	0	0		
2021–22	Luton T	0	0		

ONYEDINMA, Fred (M) **251** **30**
H: 6 1 W: 11 00 b.Lagos 24-11-96

2013–14	Millwall	4	0		
2014–15	Millwall	2	0		
2014–15	*Wycombe W*	25	8		
2015–16	Millwall	34	4		
2016–17	Millwall	42	3		
2017–18	Millwall	37	1		
2018–19	Millwall	1	0	**120**	**8**
2018–19	*Wycombe W*	21	4		
2019–20	Wycombe W	13	4		
2020–21	Wycombe W	43	3		
2021–22	Wycombe W	0	0	**102**	**19**
2021–22	Luton T	29	3	**29**	**3**

OSHO, Gabriel (D) **52** **1**
H: 6 0 b.Reading 14-8-98

2018–19	Reading	2	0		
2019–20	Reading	5	0	**7**	**0**
2020–21	Luton T	0	0		
2020–21	*Rochdale*	22	1	**22**	**1**
2021–22	Luton T	23	0	**23**	**0**

PANTER, Corey (D) **1** **0**

2018–19	Luton T	0	0		
2019–20	Luton T	0	0		
2020–21	Luton T	0	0		
2021–22	Luton T	0	0		
2021–22	*Dundee*	1	0	**1**	**0**

PECK, Jake (M) **0** **0**

2017–18	Luton T	0	0		
2018–19	Luton T	0	0		
2019–20	Luton T	0	0		
2020–21	Luton T	0	0		
2021–22	Luton T	0	0		

PEREIRA, Dion (M) **31** **1**
H: 5 9 W: 11 00 b.Watford 25-3-99

2016–17	Watford	2	0		
2017–18	Watford	0	0		
2018–19	Watford	0	0	**2**	**0**
2019	Atalanta U	18	0	**18**	**0**
2020–21	Luton T	1	0		
2021–22	Luton T	0	0	**1**	**0**
2021–22	*Bradford C*	10	1	**10**	**1**

POTTS, Danny (D) **185** **9**
H: 5 8 W: 11 00 b.Barking 13-4-94
Internationals: USA U20. England U18, U19, U20.

2011–12	West Ham U	3	0		
2012–13	West Ham U	2	0		
2012–13	*Colchester U*	5	0	**5**	**0**
2013–14	West Ham U	0	0		
2013–14	*Portsmouth*	5	0	**5**	**0**
2014–15	West Ham U	0	0	**5**	**0**
2015–16	Luton T	14	0		
2016–17	Luton T	23	0		
2017–18	Luton T	42	6		
2018–19	Luton T	24	1		
2019–20	Luton T	33	1		
2020–21	Luton T	24	1		
2021–22	Luton T	10	0	**170**	**9**

REA, Glen (D) **201** **7**
H: 6 0 W: 11 07 b.Brighton 3-9-94
Internationals: Republic of Ireland U21.

2013–14	Brighton & HA	0	0		
2014–15	Brighton & HA	0	0		
2015–16	Brighton & HA	0	0		
2015–16	*Southend U*	14	0	**14**	**0**
2015–16	*Luton T*	10	0		
2016–17	Luton T	39	2		
2017–18	Luton T	46	1		
2018–19	Luton T	22	1		
2019–20	Luton T	15	0		
2020–21	Luton T	40	3		
2021–22	Luton T	12	0	**184**	**7**
2021–22	*Wigan Ath*	3	0	**3**	**0**

RUDDOCK, Pelly (M) **275** **18**
H: 5 9 W: 9 13 b.Hendon 17-7-93
Internationals: DR Congo Full caps.

2011–12	West Ham U	0	0		
2012–13	West Ham U	0	0		
2013–14	West Ham U	0	0		
2014–15	Luton T	16	1		
2015–16	Luton T	21	2		
2016–17	Luton T	42	2		
2017–18	Luton T	28	2		
2018–19	Luton T	46	5		
2019–20	Luton T	44	3		
2020–21	Luton T	44	2		
2021–22	Luton T	34	1	**275**	**18**

SHEA, James (G) **184** **0**
H: 5 11 W: 12 00 b.Islington 16-6-91

2009–10	Arsenal	0	0		
2010–11	Arsenal	0	0		
2011–12	Arsenal	0	0		
2011–12	*Dagenham & R*	1	0	**1**	**0**
2012–13	Arsenal	0	0		
2013–14	Arsenal	0	0		
2014–15	AFC Wimbledon	38	0		
2015–16	AFC Wimbledon	21	0		
2016–17	AFC Wimbledon	36	0	**95**	**0**
2017–18	Luton T	8	0		
2018–19	Luton T	41	0		
2019–20	Luton T	13	0		
2020–21	Luton T	7	0		
2021–22	Luton T	19	0	**88**	**0**

SLUGA, Simon (G) **212** **0**
H: 6 3 W: 12 11 b.Porec 17-3-93
Internationals: Croatia U17, U18, U19, U20, U21, Full caps.

2013–14	Rijeka	0	0		
2013–14	*Pomorac*	31	0	**31**	**0**
2014–15	Rijeka	0	0		
2014–15	*Lokomotiva*	26	0	**26**	**0**
2015–16	Rijeka	2	0		
2015–16	*Spezia*	0	0		
2016–17	Rijeka	0	0		
2017–18	Rijeka	27	0		
2018–19	Rijeka	35	0	**64**	**0**
2019–20	Luton T	33	0		
2020–21	Luton T	39	0		
2021–22	Luton T	19	0	**91**	**0**

Transferred to Ludogorets Razgrad, January 2022.

SNODGRASS, Robert (M) **508** **92**
H: 6 0 W: 12 02 b.Glasgow 7-9-87
Internationals: Scotland U20, U21, Full caps.

2003–04	Livingston	0	0		
2004–05	Livingston	17	2		
2005–06	Livingston	27	4		
2006–07	Livingston	6	0		
2006–07	*Stirling Alb*	12	5	**12**	**5**
2007–08	Livingston	31	9	**81**	**15**
2008–09	Leeds U	42	9		
2009–10	Leeds U	44	7		
2010–11	Leeds U	37	6		
2011–12	Leeds U	43	13	**166**	**35**
2012–13	Norwich C	37	6		
2013–14	Norwich C	30	6	**67**	**12**
2014–15	Hull C	1	0		
2015–16	Hull C	24	4		
2016–17	Hull C	20	7	**45**	**11**
2016–17	West Ham U	15	0		
2017–18	West Ham U	0	0		
2017–18	*Aston Villa*	40	7	**40**	**7**
2018–19	West Ham U	33	2		
2019–20	West Ham U	24	5		
2020–21	West Ham U	3	0	**75**	**7**
2020–21	WBA	8	0		
2021–22	WBA	6	0	**14**	**0**
2021–22	Luton T	8	0	**8**	**0**

Players retained or with offer of contract
Francis-Clarke, Aidan; Horlick, Jameson; Jones, Avan; Lucas, Tra; McJannet, Ed; Nicolson, Callum; Pettit, Casey; Thorpe, Elliot; Williams, Joshua.

Scholars
Allen, Joshua Richard Charles; Bateson, Jack Cameron; Bentley, Samuel David; Burger, Jake John Philip; Corbit, Edward Leigh; Cowler, Jacob Mackenzie; Hemlin, Oliver John; Heron, Archie Michael; Lynch, Oliver David James; Martucci Bedingfield, Rio Adam; Matthews Lewis, Millar Lee; Moffat, Darcy Simon; Moloney, Matthew Thomas; Nelson, Zack Mark Anthony Emeka; Newton, Tyrelle Benjamin; Odell Bature, Joshua Ryan; Pinnington, Jacob George; Stevens, Ben Charles; Swan, Joshua Leigh; Tompkins, Ben Joseph; Wedd, Adam John.

MANCHESTER C (49)

AGUILAR, Kluiverth (D) **36** **2**
H: 5 10 b.Lima 5-5-03
Internationals: Peru U17, U20, U23.

2019	Alianza Lima	7	0		
2020	Alianza Lima	18	2		
2021	Alianza Lima	8	0	**33**	**2**
2021–22	Manchester C	0	0		
2021–22	*Lommel*	3	0	**3**	**0**

AKE, Nathan (M) **175** **15**
H: 5 11 W: 11 11 b.Den Haag 18-2-95
Internationals: Netherlands U15, U16, U17, U19, U21, Full caps.
From Feyenoord.

2012–13	Chelsea	3	0		
2013–14	Chelsea	1	0		
2014–15	Chelsea	1	0		
2014–15	*Reading*	5	0	**5**	**0**
2015–16	Chelsea	0	0		
2015–16	*Watford*	24	1	**24**	**1**
2016–17	Chelsea	2	0	**7**	**0**
2016–17	*Bournemouth*	10	3		
2017–18	Bournemouth	38	2		
2018–19	Bournemouth	38	4		
2019–20	Bournemouth	29	2	**115**	**11**
2020–21	Manchester C	10	1		
2021–22	Manchester C	14	2	**24**	**3**

ALVAREZ, Julian (F) **38** **13**
H: 5 7 b.Cordoba 21-1-00
Internationals: Argentina U20, U23, Full caps.

2018–19	River Plate	5	1		
2019–20	River Plate	7	0		
2020–21	River Plate	10	2		
2021	River Plate	0	0		
2021–22	Manchester C	0	0		
2022	*River Plate*	16	10	**38**	**13**

AMANKWAH, Yeboah (D) **24** **0**
H: 6 3 W: 11 09 b.Lewisham 19-10-00

2019–20	Manchester C	0	0		
2020–21	Manchester C	0	0		
2020–21	*Rochdale*	0	0		
2021–22	Manchester C	0	0		
2021–22	*Accrington S*	24	0	**24**	**0**

AMINU, Mohammed (F) **0** **0**
H: 5 9 b. 10-8-00
Internationals: Ghana U17.

2019–20	Manchester C	0	0		
2019–20	*Dordrecht*	0	0		
2020–21	Manchester C	0	0		
2020–21	*Lommel*	0	0		
2021–22	Manchester C	0	0		
2021–22	*Lommel*	0	0		

ARZANI, Daniel (M) **44** **3**
H: 5 7 W: 11 07 b.Khorramabad 4-1-99
Internationals: Australia U17, U20, U23, Full caps.

2016–17	Melbourne C	6	0		
2017–18	Melbourne C	16	2	**22**	**2**
2018–19	Manchester C	0	0		
2018–19	*Celtic*	1	0		
2019–20	Manchester C	0	0		
2019–20	*Celtic*	0	0	**1**	**0**
2020–21	Manchester C	0	0		
2020–21	*Utrecht*	4	0	**4**	**0**
2020–21	*AGF Aarhus*	4	0	**4**	**0**
2021–22	Manchester C	0	0		
2021–22	*Lommel*	13	1	**13**	**1**

BAZUNU, Gavin (G) **73** **0**
H: 6 0 W: 12 06 b.Dublin 20-2-02
Internationals: Republic of Ireland U17, U21, Full caps.
From Shamrock R.

2019–20	Manchester C	0	0		
2020–21	Manchester C	0	0		
2020–21	*Rochdale*	29	0	**29**	**0**
2021–22	Manchester C	0	0		
2021–22	*Portsmouth*	44	0	**44**	**0**

BERNARDO SILVA, Mota (M) **268** **53**
H: 5 8 W: 9 11 b.Lisbon 10-8-94
Internationals: Portugal U19, U21, Full caps.

2013–14	Benfica	1	0	**1**	**0**
2014–15	Monaco	32	9		
2015–16	Monaco	32	7		
2016–17	Monaco	37	8	**101**	**24**

2017–18	Manchester C	35	6		
2018–19	Manchester C	36	7		
2019–20	Manchester C	34	6		
2020–21	Manchester C	26	2		
2021–22	Manchester C	35	8	**166**	**29**

BOBB, Oscar (M) **0 0**

H: 5 9 b.Oslo 12-7-03

Internationals: Norway U16, U17, U18.

From Valerenga.

2020–21	Manchester C	0	0		
2021–22	Manchester C	0	0		

BRAAF, Jayden (F) **4 1**

H: 5 10 W: 10 03 b.Amsterdam 31-8-02

Internationals: Netherlands U17, U18.

2020–21	Manchester C	0	0		
2020–21	*Udinese*	4	1	**4**	**1**
2021–22	Manchester C	0	0		

BURNS, Finley (D) **3 0**

H: 6 1 b.Southwark 17-6-03

Internationals: England U16, U17.

2020–21	Manchester C	0	0		
2021–22	Manchester C	0	0		
2021–22	*Swansea C*	3	0	**3**	**0**

BUSTOS, Nahuel (F) **114 27**

H: 5 9 b.Cordoba 4-7-98

Internationals: Argentina U23.

2016–17	Talleres	4	0		
2017–18	Talleres	0	0		
2018–19	Talleres	11	5		
2018–19	*Pachuna*	4	0	**4**	**0**
2019–20	Talleres	20	9	**35**	**14**
2020–21	Manchester C	0	0		
2020–21	*Girona*	33	2		
2021–22	Manchester C	0	0		
2021–22	*Girona*	42	11	**75**	**13**

CARSON, Scott (G) **469 0**

H: 6 0 W: 13 07 b.Whitehaven 3-9-85

Internationals: England U18, U21, B, Full caps.

2002–03	Leeds U	0	0		
2003–04	Leeds U	3	0		
2004–05	Leeds U	0	0	**3**	**0**
2004–05	Liverpool	4	0		
2005–06	Liverpool	0	0		
2005–06	*Sheffield W*	9	0	**9**	**0**
2006–07	Liverpool	0	0		
2006–07	*Charlton Ath*	36	0	**36**	**0**
2007–08	Liverpool	0	0	**4**	**0**
2007–08	*Aston Villa*	35	0	**35**	**0**
2008–09	WBA	35	0		
2009–10	WBA	43	0		
2010–11	WBA	32	0	**110**	**0**
2011–12	Bursaspor	34	0		
2012–13	Bursaspor	29	0	**63**	**0**
2013–14	Wigan Ath	16	0		
2014–15	Wigan Ath	34	0	**50**	**0**
2015–16	Derby Co	36	0		
2016–17	Derby Co	46	0		
2017–18	Derby Co	46	0		
2018–19	Derby Co	30	0		
2019–20	Derby Co	0	0		
2019–20	*Manchester C*	0	0		
2020–21	Derby Co	0	0		
2020–21	*Manchester C*	1	0		
2021–22	Derby Co	0	0	**158**	**0**
2021–22	Manchester C	0	0	**1**	**0**

COUTO, Yan (D) **53 3**

H: 5 6 b.Curitiba 3-6-02

Internationals: Brazil U17.

2020	Coritiba	2	0	**2**	**0**
2020–21	Manchester C	0	0		
2020–21	*Girona*	23	2	**23**	**2**
2021–22	Manchester C	0	0		
2021–22	*Braga*	28	1	**28**	**1**

DE BRUYNE, Kevin (M) **392 96**

H: 5 11 W: 10 10 b.Ghent 28-6-91

Internationals: Belgium U18, U19, U21, Full caps.

2008–09	Genk	2	0		
2009–10	Genk	35	3		
2010–11	Genk	32	5		
2011–12	Genk	28	8	**97**	**16**
2011–12	Chelsea	0	0		
2012–13	Chelsea	0	0		
2012–13	*Werder Bremen*	33	10	**33**	**10**
2013–14	Chelsea	3	0	**3**	**0**
2013–14	VfL Wolfsburg	16	3		
2014–15	VfL Wolfsburg	34	10		
2015–16	VfL Wolfsburg	2	0	**52**	**13**
2015–16	Manchester C	25	7		
2016–17	Manchester C	36	6		
2017–18	Manchester C	37	8		
2018–19	Manchester C	19	2		
2019–20	Manchester C	35	13		
2020–21	Manchester C	25	6		
2021–22	Manchester C	30	15	**207**	**57**

DELAP, Liam (F) **2 0**

H: 6 1 W: 11 05 b.Winchester 8-2-03

Internationals: England U16, U17, U18, U19.

From Derby Co.

2020–21	Manchester C	1	0		
2021–22	Manchester C	1	0	**2**	**0**

DIAS, Ruben (D) **150 11**

H: 6 1 W: 11 00 b.Amadora 14-5-97

Internationals: Portugal U16, U17, U19, U20, U21, Full caps.

2015–16	Benfica	0	0		
2016–17	Benfica	0	0		
2017–18	Benfica	24	3		
2018–19	Benfica	32	3		
2019–20	Benfica	33	2		
2020–21	Benfica	0	0	**89**	**8**
2020–21	Manchester C	32	1		
2021–22	Manchester C	29	2	**61**	**3**

DOYLE, Callum (D) **36 1**

H: 6 1 b.Manchester 3-10-03

Internationals: England U18, U19.

2021–22	Manchester C	0	0		
2021–22	*Sunderland*	36	1	**36**	**1**

DOYLE, Tommy (M) **20 2**

H: 5 10 W: 11 05 b.Manchester 17-10-01

Internationals: England U16, U17, U18, U19, U20, U21.

2019–20	Manchester C	1	0		
2020–21	Manchester C	0	0		
2021–22	Manchester C	0	0	**1**	**0**
2021–22	*Hamburger SV*	0	0		
2021–22	*Cardiff C*	19	2	**19**	**2**

EDERSON, de Moraes (G) **285 0**

H: 6 2 W: 13 08 b.Osasco 17-8-93

Internationals: Brazil U23, Full caps.

2011–12	Ribeirao	29	0	**29**	**0**
2012–13	Rio Ave	2	0		
2013–14	Rio Ave	18	0		
2014–15	Rio Ave	17	0	**37**	**0**
2015–16	Benfica	10	0		
2016–17	Benfica	27	0	**37**	**0**
2017–18	Manchester C	36	0		
2018–19	Manchester C	38	0		
2019–20	Manchester C	35	0		
2020–21	Manchester C	36	0		
2021–22	Manchester C	37	0	**182**	**0**

EDOZIE, Samuel (F) **0 0**

H: 5 11 b.Lewisham 28-1-03

Internationals: England U18, U19.

From Millwall.

2020–21	Manchester C	0	0		
2021–22	Manchester C	0	0		

EGAN-RILEY, CJ (D) **1 0**

H: 6 0 W: 11 00 b.Manchester 2-1-03

Internationals: England U16, U17, U18, U19.

2021–22	Manchester C	1	0	**1**	**0**

FERNANDINHO, Luis (M) **519 65**

H: 5 10 W: 10 10 b.Londrina 4-5-85

Internationals: Brazil Full caps.

2003	Paranaense	29	5		
2004	Paranaense	41	9		
2005	Paranaense	2	0	**72**	**14**
2005–06	Shakhtar Donetsk	22	1		
2006–07	Shakhtar Donetsk	25	1		
2007–08	Shakhtar Donetsk	29	11		
2008–09	Shakhtar Donetsk	21	5		
2009–10	Shakhtar Donetsk	24	4		
2010–11	Shakhtar Donetsk	15	3		
2011–12	Shakhtar Donetsk	24	4		
2012–13	Shakhtar Donetsk	23	2	**183**	**31**
2013–14	Manchester C	33	5		
2014–15	Manchester C	33	3		
2015–16	Manchester C	33	2		
2016–17	Manchester C	32	2		
2017–18	Manchester C	34	5		
2018–19	Manchester C	29	1		
2019–20	Manchester C	30	0		
2020–21	Manchester C	21	0		
2021–22	Manchester C	19	2	**264**	**20**

FIORINI, Lewis (M) **71 11**

H: 5 10 b.Manchester 17-5-02

Internationals: Scotland U16, U17, U19, U21.

2020–21	Manchester C	0	0		
2020–21	*NAC Breda*	32	5	**32**	**5**
2021–22	Manchester C	0	0		
2021–22	*Lincoln C*	39	6	**39**	**6**

FODEN, Phil (M) **97 24**

H: 5 7 W: 11 00 b.Stockport 28-5-00

Internationals: England U16, U17, U18, U19, U21, Full caps.

2016–17	Manchester C	0	0		
2017–18	Manchester C	5	0		
2018–19	Manchester C	13	1		
2019–20	Manchester C	23	5		
2020–21	Manchester C	28	9		
2021–22	Manchester C	28	9	**97**	**24**

GABRIEL JESUS, Fernando (F) **206 74**

H: 5 9 W: 11 07 b.Sao Paulo 3-4-97

Internationals: Brazil U20, U23, Full caps.

2015	Palmeiras	20	4		
2016	Palmeiras	27	12	**47**	**16**
2016–17	Manchester C	10	7		
2017–18	Manchester C	29	13		
2018–19	Manchester C	29	7		
2019–20	Manchester C	34	14		
2020–21	Manchester C	29	9		
2021–22	Manchester C	28	8	**159**	**58**

GOMES, Claudio (M) **31 1**

H: 5 11 W: 11 00 b.Argenteuil 23-7-00

Internationals: France U16, U17, U18, U19, U20.

2017–18	Paris Saint-Germain	0	0		
2018–19	Manchester C	0	0		
2019–20	Manchester C	0	0		
2019–20	*PSV Eindhoven*	0	0		
2020–21	Manchester C	0	0		
2021–22	Manchester C	0	0		
2021–22	*Barnsley*	31	1	**31**	**1**

GREALISH, Jack (M) **248 37**

H: 5 9 W: 10 10 b.Birmingham 10-9-95

Internationals: Republic of Ireland U17, U18, U21. England U21, Full caps.

2012–13	Aston Villa	0	0		
2013–14	Aston Villa	1	0		
2013–14	*Notts Co*	37	5	**37**	**5**
2014–15	Aston Villa	17	0		
2015–16	Aston Villa	16	1		
2016–17	Aston Villa	31	5		
2017–18	Aston Villa	27	3		
2018–19	Aston Villa	31	6		
2019–20	Aston Villa	36	8		
2020–21	Aston Villa	26	6		
2021–22	Aston Villa	0	0	**185**	**29**
2021–22	Manchester C	26	3	**26**	**3**

GUNDOGAN, Ilkay (M) **310 52**

H: 5 11 W: 11 00 b.Gelsenkirchen 24-10-90

Internationals: Germany U18, U19, U20, U21, Full caps.

2008–09	Bochum	0	0		
2008–09	Nuremburg	1	0		
2009–10	Nuremburg	22	1		
2010–11	Nuremburg	25	5	**48**	**6**
2011–12	Borussia Dortmund	28	3		
2012–13	Borussia Dortmund	28	3		
2013–14	Borussia Dortmund	1	0		
2014–15	Borussia Dortmund	23	3		
2015–16	Borussia Dortmund	25	1	**105**	**10**
2016–17	Manchester C	10	3		
2017–18	Manchester C	30	4		
2018–19	Manchester C	31	6		
2019–20	Manchester C	31	2		
2020–21	Manchester C	28	13		
2021–22	Manchester C	27	8	**157**	**36**

HARWOOD-BELLIS, Taylor (D) **57 0**

H: 6 1 W: 11 05 b.Stockport 30-1-02

Internationals: England U16, U17, U19, U20, U21.

2019–20	Manchester C	0	0		
2020–21	Manchester C	0	0		
2020–21	*Blackburn R*	19	0	**19**	**0**
2021–22	Manchester C	0	0		
2021–22	*Anderlecht*	16	0	**16**	**0**
2021–22	*Stoke C*	22	0	**22**	**0**

HERRERA, Yangel (M) **206 19**

H: 6 0 b.La Guaira 7-1-98

Internationals: Venezuela U17, U20, Full caps.

2014	Monagas	19	4		
2015	Monagas	16	5	**35**	**9**
2016	Atletico Venezuela	32	3	**32**	**3**
2017	*New York C*	20	1		
2017–18	Manchester C	0	0		
2018	*New York C*	18	0	**38**	**1**
2018–19	Manchester C	0	0		
2018–19	*Huesca*	16	0	**16**	**0**
2019–20	Manchester C	0	0		
2019–20	*Granada*	30	2		
2020–21	Manchester C	0	0		
2020–21	*Granada*	32	3	**62**	**5**
2021–22	Manchester C	0	0		
2021–22	*Espanyol*	23	1	**23**	**1**

ITAKURA, Ko (D) **119 8**

H: 6 1 b.Yokohama 27-1-97

Internationals: Japan U16, U18, U19, U20, U21, U23, Full caps.

2015	Kawasaki Frontale	0	0		
2016	Kawasaki Frontale	2	0		
2017	Kawasaki Frontale	5	0		
2018	Kawasaki Frontale	0	0	**7**	**0**
2018	*Vegallta Sendai*	24	3	**24**	**3**
2018–19	Manchester C	0	0		
2018–19	*Groningen*	0	0		
2019–20	Manchester C	0	0		
2019–20	*Groningen*	22	0		
2020–21	Manchester C	0	0		
2020–21	*Groningen*	35	1	**57**	**1**
2021–22	Manchester C	0	0		
2021–22	*Schalke 04*	31	4	**31**	**4**

JOAO CANCELO, Cavaco (D) 207 7

H: 5 11 W: 10 06 b.Barreiro 27-5-94

Internationals: Portugal U16, U17, U18, U19, U20, U21, Full caps.

2012–13	Benfica	0	0		
2013–14	Benfica	1	0		
2014–15	Benfica	0	0	**1**	**0**
2014–15	*Valencia*	10	0		
2015–16	Valencia	28	1		
2016–17	Valencia	35	1		
2017–18	Valencia	1	0	**74**	**2**
2017–18	*Inter Milan*	26	1	**26**	**1**
2018–19	Juventus	25	1		
2019–20	Juventus	0	0	**25**	**1**
2019–20	Manchester C	17	0		
2020–21	Manchester C	28	2		
2021–22	Manchester C	36	1	**81**	**3**

KABORE, Issa (D) 63 0

b.Ouagadougou 12-5-01

Internationals: Burkina Faso U20, Full caps.

2019–20	Mechelen	5	0		
2019–20	Manchester C	0	0		
2020–21	Manchester C	0	0		
2020–21	*Mechelen*	27	0	**32**	**0**
2021–22	Manchester C	0	0		
2021–22	*Troyes*	31	0	**31**	**0**

KAYKY, Chagas (F) 1 0

H: 5 9 W: 10 10 b.Rio de Janeiro 11-6-03

Internationals: Brazil U16.

2021–22	Manchester C	1	0	**1**	**0**

KNIGHT, Ben (M) 6 0

H: 5 3 W: 8 05 b.Cambridge 14-6-02

Internationals: England U16, U17, U18.

From Ipswich T.

2020–21	Manchester C	0	0		
2021–22	Manchester C	0	0		
2021–22	*Crewe Alex*	6	0	**6**	**0**

LAPORTE, Aymeric (D) 302 17

H: 6 2 W: 13 05 b.Agen 27-5-94

Internationals: France U17, U18, U19, U21. Spain full caps.

2011–12	Basconia	33	2	**33**	**2**
2012–13	Athletic Bilbao	15	0		
2013–14	Athletic Bilbao	35	2		
2014–15	Athletic Bilbao	33	0		
2015–16	Athletic Bilbao	26	3		
2016–17	Athletic Bilbao	33	2		
2017–18	Athletic Bilbao	19	0	**161**	**7**
2017–18	Manchester C	9	0		
2018–19	Manchester C	35	3		
2019–20	Manchester C	15	1		
2020–21	Manchester C	16	0		
2021–22	Manchester C	33	4	**108**	**8**

MAHREZ, Riyad (F) 333 86

H: 5 10 W: 9 11 b.Sarcelles 21-2-91

Internationals: Algeria Full caps.

From Quimper.

2011–12	Le Havre	9	0		
2012–13	Le Havre	34	4		
2013–14	Le Havre	17	2	**60**	**6**
2013–14	Leicester C	19	3		
2014–15	Leicester C	30	4		
2015–16	Leicester C	37	17		
2016–17	Leicester C	36	6		
2017–18	Leicester C	36	12	**158**	**42**
2018–19	Manchester C	27	7		
2019–20	Manchester C	33	11		
2020–21	Manchester C	27	9		
2021–22	Manchester C	28	11	**115**	**38**

MBETE-TABU, Luke (D) 0 0

H: 6 1 b.Westminster 18-9-03

Internationals: England U16, U19.

2020–21	Manchester C	0	0		
2021–22	Manchester C	0	0		

McATEE, James (M) 2 0

H: 5 11 b.Salford 18-10-02

Internationals: England U18, U20, U21.

2020–21	Manchester C	0	0		
2021–22	Manchester C	2	0	**2**	**0**

McDONALD, Rowan (D) 0 0

H: 5 11 b.Oldham 20-10-01

Internationals: England U18.

2020–21	Manchester C	0	0		
2021–22	Manchester C	0	0		

MENDY, Benjamin (D) 213 4

H: 6 1 W: 13 05 b.Longjumeau 17-7-94

Internationals: France U16, U17, U18, U19, U21, Full caps.

2011–12	Le Havre	29	0		
2012–13	Le Havre	28	0	**57**	**0**
2013–14	Marseille	24	1		
2014–15	Marseille	33	0		
2015–16	Marseille	24	1	**81**	**2**
2016–17	Monaco	25	0	**25**	**0**
2017–18	Manchester C	7	0		
2018–19	Manchester C	10	0		
2019–20	Manchester C	19	0		
2020–21	Manchester C	13	2		
2021–22	Manchester C	1	0	**50**	**2**

MESHINO, Ryotaro (F) 65 10

H: 5 7 b.Osaka 18-6-98

Internationals: Japan U23.

2017	Gamba Osaka	0	0		
2018	Gamba Osaka	11	0		
2019	Gamba Osaka	12	3	**23**	**3**
2019–20	Manchester C	0	0		
2019–20	*Hearts*	20	3	**20**	**3**
2020–21	Manchester C	0	0		
2020–21	*Rio Ave*	13	3	**13**	**3**
2021–22	Manchester C	0	0		
2021–22	*Estoril*	9	1	**9**	**1**

MORENO, Marlos (F) 151 14

H: 5 7 b.Medellin 20-9-96

Internationals: Colombia U17, Full caps.

2014	Atletico Nacional	1	0		
2015	Atletico Nacional	17	5		
2016	Atletico Nacional	9	0	**27**	**5**
2016–17	Manchester C	0	0		
2016–17	*Deportivo la Coruna*	19	0	**19**	**0**
2017–18	Manchester C	0	0		
2017–18	*Girona*	2	0	**2**	**0**
2018–19	Manchester C	0	0		
2018–19	*Flamengo*	21	1	**21**	**1**
2018–19	*Santa Laguna*	11	1	**11**	**1**
2019–20	Manchester C	0	0		
2019–20	*Portimonense*	16	0	**16**	**0**
2020–21	Manchester C	0	0		
2020–21	*Lommel*	23	5	**23**	**5**
2021–22	Manchester C	0	0		
2021–22	*Kortrijk*	32	2	**32**	**2**

MORENO , Pablo (F) 44 3

H: 5 11 b.Granada 3-5-02

Internationals: Spain U16, U17, U18.

From Juventus.

2020–21	Manchester C	0	0		
2020–21	*Girona*	27	2		
2021–22	Manchester C	0	0		
2021–22	*Girona*	17	1	**44**	**3**

MURIC, Arijanet (G) 52 0

H: 6 6 W: 12 11 b.Zurich 7-11-98

Internationals: Montenegro U21. Kosovo Full caps.

2017–18	Manchester C	0	0		
2018–19	Manchester C	0	0		
2018–19	*NAC Breda*	1	0	**1**	**0**
2019–20	Manchester C	0	0		
2019–20	*Nottingham F*	4	0	**4**	**0**
2020–21	Manchester C	0	0		
2020–21	*Girona*	2	0	**2**	**0**
2020–21	*Willem II*	14	0	**14**	**0**
2021–22	Manchester C	0	0		
2021–22	*Adana Demirspor*	31	0	**31**	**0**

PALAVERSA, Ante (M) 73 5

H: 6 2 b.Split 6-4-00

Internationals: Croatia U16, U17, U18, U19, U20.

2017–18	Hajduk Split	0	0		
2018–19	Hajduk Split	14	2	**14**	**2**
2019–20	Manchester C	0	0		
2019–20	*Oostende*	19	0	**19**	**0**
2020–21	Manchester C	0	0		
2020–21	*Getafe*	2	0	**2**	**0**
2020–21	*Kortrijk*	9	2		
2021–22	Manchester C	0	0		
2021–22	*Kortrijk*	29	1	**38**	**3**

PALMER, Cole (M) 4 0

H: 6 2 W: 11 05 b.Wythenshawe 6-5-02

Internationals: England U16, U17, U18, U21.

2019–20	Manchester C	0	0		
2020–21	Manchester C	0	0		
2021–22	Manchester C	4	0	**4**	**0**

PORRO, Pedro (D) 108 13

H: 5 9 b.Don Benito 13-9-99

Internationals: Spain U21, Full caps.

2017–18	Peralada	5	3	**5**	**3**
2017–18	Girona	5	3		
2018–19	Girona	32	0	**37**	**3**
2019–20	Manchester C	0	0		
2019–20	*Real Valladolid*	13	0	**13**	**0**
2020–21	Manchester C	0	0		
2020–21	*Sporting Lisbon*	30	3		
2021–22	Manchester C	0	0		
2021–22	*Sporting Lisbon*	23	4	**53**	**7**

POZO, Iker (M) 28 3

H: 5 8 b.Fuengirola 6-8-00

2020–21	Manchester C	0	0		
2020–21	*PSV Eindhoven*	28	3	**28**	**3**
2021–22	Manchester C	0	0		

ROBERTSON, Alexander (M) 3 0

b.Dundee 17-4-03

Internationals: England U16, U17, U18.

2020–21	Manchester C	0	0		
2021–22	Manchester C	0	0		
2021–22	*Ross Co*	3	0	**3**	**0**

RODRI, Rodrigo Hernandez (M) 199 16

H: 6 3 W: 12 13 b.Madrid 22-6-96

Internationals: Spain U16, U19, U21, Full caps.

2014–15	Villareal	0	0		
2015–16	Villareal	3	0		
2016–17	Villareal	23	0		
2017–18	Villareal	37	1	**63**	**1**
2018–19	Atletico Madrid	34	3	**34**	**3**
2019–20	Manchester C	35	3		
2020–21	Manchester C	34	2		
2021–22	Manchester C	33	7	**102**	**12**

ROGERS, Morgan (M) 40 7

H: 6 2 b.Halesowen 26-7-02

Internationals: England U16, U17, U18, U20.

2018–19	WBA	0	0		
2019–20	Manchester C	0	0		
2020–21	Manchester C	0	0		
2020–21	*Lincoln C*	25	6	**25**	**6**
2021–22	Manchester C	0	0		
2021–22	*Bournemouth*	15	1	**15**	**1**

ROSA, Diego (M) 26 2

H: 5 10 b.Salvador 12-10-02

Internationals: Brazil U16, U17.

2020–21	Manchester C	0	0		
2020–21	*Lommel*	7	0		
2021–22	Manchester C	0	0		
2021–22	*Lommel*	19	2	**26**	**2**

SARMIENTO, Dario (F) 23 0

H: 5 6 b.Florencio Varela 29-3-03

Internationals: Argentina U16.

2019–20	Estudiantes	5	0		
2020–21	Estudiantes	9	0	**14**	**0**
2021–22	Manchester C	0	0		
2021–22	*Girona*	9	0	**9**	**0**

SLICKER, Cieran (G) 0 0

b.Oldham 15-9-02

Internationals: Scotland U17, U18, U21.

2020–21	Manchester C	0	0		
2021–22	Manchester C	0	0		

STEFFEN, Zackary (G) 104 0

H: 6 3 W: 13 08 b.Coatesville 2-4-95

Internationals: USA U18, U20, U23, Full caps.

2014–15	Frieburg	0	0		
2015–16	Frieburg	0	0		
2016	Columbus Crew	0	0		
2016	*Pittsburg Riverhounds*	9	0	**9**	**0**
2017	Columbus Crew	34	0		
2018	Columbus Crew	29	0		
2019	Columbus Crew	13	0	**76**	**0**
2019–20	Manchester C	0	0		
2019–20	*Fortuna Dusseldorf*	17	0	**17**	**0**
2020–21	Manchester C	1	0		
2021–22	Manchester C	1	0	**2**	**0**

STERLING, Raheem (F) 320 109

H: 5 7 W: 10 12 b.Kingston 8-12-94

Internationals: England U16, U17, U19, U21, Full caps.

From QPR.

2011–12	Liverpool	3	0		
2012–13	Liverpool	24	2		
2013–14	Liverpool	33	9		
2014–15	Liverpool	35	7	**95**	**18**
2015–16	Manchester C	31	6		
2016–17	Manchester C	33	7		
2017–18	Manchester C	33	18		
2018–19	Manchester C	34	17		
2019–20	Manchester C	33	20		
2020–21	Manchester C	31	10		
2021–22	Manchester C	30	13	**225**	**91**

STEVANOVIC, Filip (F) 77 12

H: 5 9 b.Arilje 25-9-02

Internationals: Serbia U16, U19, U21.

2018–19	Partizan Belgrade	4	0		
2019–20	Partizan Belgrade	25	7		
2020–21	Partizan Belgrade	27	4	**56**	**11**
2020–21	Manchester C	0	0		
2021–22	Manchester C	0	0		
2021–22	*Heerenveen*	21	1	**21**	**1**

STONES, John (D) 222 6

H: 6 2 W: 11 00 b.Barnsley 28-5-94

Internationals: England U19, U20, U21, Full caps.

2010–11	Barnsley	0	0		
2011–12	Barnsley	2	0		
2012–13	Barnsley	22	0	**24**	**0**
2012–13	Everton	0	0		
2013–14	Everton	21	0		
2014–15	Everton	23	1		
2015–16	Everton	33	0	**77**	**1**
2016–17	Manchester C	27	0		
2017–18	Manchester C	18	0		
2018–19	Manchester C	24	0		
2019–20	Manchester C	16	0		
2020–21	Manchester C	22	4		
2021–22	Manchester C	14	1	**121**	**5**

TARENSI, Oscar (D) 0 0

b. 10-1-03

From Espanyol.

2020–21	Manchester C	0	0		
2021–22	Manchester C	0	0		
2021–22	*Girona*	0	0		

TEDIC, Slobodan (F) **104 16**
H: 6 3 b.Podorica 13-4-00
Internationals: Serbia, U16, U17, U18, U19, U21.

2017–18	Cukaricki	8	1		
2017–18	*Vojvodina*	0	0		
2018–19	Cukaricki	31	4		
2019–20	Cukaricki	27	9	**66**	**14**
2019–20	Manchester C	0	0		

From Cukaricki.

2020–21	Manchester C	0	0		
2020–21	*PEC Zwolle*	15	2		
2021–22	Manchester C	0	0		
2021–22	*PEC Zwolle*	23	0	**38**	**2**

TORRES, Ferran (F) **99 15**
H: 6 0 W: 12 02 b.Foios 29-2-00
Internationals: Spain U17, U19, U21, Full caps.

2016–17	Valencia	0	0		
2017–18	Valencia	13	0		
2018–19	Valencia	24	2		
2019–20	Valencia	34	4		
2020–21	Valencia	0	0	**71**	**6**
2020–21	Manchester C	24	7		
2021–22	Manchester C	4	2	**28**	**9**

Transferred to Barcelona, December 2021.

TRAFFORD, James (G) **33 0**
H: 6 6 W: 13 01 b.Cockermouth 10-10-02
Internationals: England U17, U18, U18, U20, U21.

2020–21	Manchester C	0	0		
2021–22	Manchester C	0	0		
2021–22	*Accrington S*	11	0	**11**	**0**
2021–22	*Bolton W*	22	0	**22**	**0**

WALKER, Kyle (D) **393 8**
H: 5 10 W: 11 07 b.Sheffield 28-5-90
Internationals: England U19, U21, Full caps.

2008–09	Sheffield U	2	0		
2008–09	*Northampton T*	9	0	**9**	**0**
2009–10	Tottenham H	2	0		
2009–10	*Sheffield U*	26	0	**28**	**0**
2010–11	Tottenham H	1	0		
2010–11	*QPR*	20	0	**20**	**0**
2010–11	*Aston Villa*	15	1	**15**	**1**
2011–12	Tottenham H	37	2		
2012–13	Tottenham H	36	0		
2013–14	Tottenham H	26	1		
2014–15	Tottenham H	15	0		
2015–16	Tottenham H	33	1		
2016–17	Tottenham H	33	0	**183**	**4**
2017–18	Manchester C	32	0		
2018–19	Manchester C	33	1		
2019–20	Manchester C	29	1		
2020–21	Manchester C	24	1		
2021–22	Manchester C	20	0	**138**	**3**

WILSON-ESBRAND, Josh (D) **0 0**
H: 5 9 b.Hackney 26-12-02
Internationals: England U18, U20.
From West Ham U.

2020–21	Manchester C	0	0		
2021–22	Manchester C	0	0		

ZINCHENKO, Alexander (D) **119 2**
H: 5 9 W: 9 08 b.Radomyshi 15-12-96
Internationals: Ukraine U16, U17, U18, U19, U21, Full caps.

2014–15	Ufa	7	0		
2015–16	Ufa	24	2	**31**	**2**
2016–17	Manchester C	0	0		
2016–17	*PSV Eindhoven*	12	0	**12**	**0**
2017–18	Manchester C	8	0		
2018–19	Manchester C	14	0		
2019–20	Manchester C	19	0		
2020–21	Manchester C	20	0		
2021–22	Manchester C	15	0	**76**	**0**

Players retained or with offer of contract
Adam, Josh; Awokoya-Mebude, Adedire; Breckin, Kian; Charles, Shea; Forbs Borges, Carlos; Gyabi, Darko; Hamilton, Micah; Larios Lopez, Juan; Lavia, Romeo; McNamara, Joshua; Smith, Liam; Sodje, Taione; Van Sas, Mikki.

Scholars
Alleyne, Max Lewis Rowe; Barrington, Luca; Dickson, William Steven; Galvez, Tomas Kristian; Katongo, Jadel Chanda; Lewis, Rico Mark; Madubugwu Ogwuru, Daniel Odinakachi Chisomu; Murray-Jones, George David; O'Reilly, Nico; Smith, Isaac James; Susoho Sissoho, Mahamadou; Taylor, Kane Ellis; Whittingham, Matthew Joseph.

MANCHESTER U (50)

ALEX TELLES, Nicolao (D) **265 24**
H: 5 11 W: 11 03 b.Caxias do Sul 15-12-92
Internationals: Brazil Full caps.

2011	Juventide	4	1		
2012	Juventide	9	1	**13**	**2**
2013	Gremio	36	1	**36**	**1**
2013–14	Galatasaray	15	1		
2014–15	Galatasaray	22	1		
2015–16	Galatasaray	2	0	**39**	**2**
2015–16	*Inter Milan*	21	0	**21**	**0**
2016–17	Porto	32	1		
2017–18	Porto	30	3		
2018–19	Porto	33	4		
2019–20	Porto	31	11	**126**	**19**
2020–21	FC Porto	0	0		
2020–21	Manchester U	9	0		
2021–22	Manchester U	21	0	**30**	**0**

BAILLY, Eric (D) **110 1**
H: 6 2 W: 12 02 b.Bingerville 12-4-94
Internationals: Ivory Coast Full caps.

2014–15	Espanyol	5	0	**5**	**0**
2014–15	Villareal	10	0		
2015–16	Villareal	25	0	**35**	**0**
2016–17	Manchester U	25	0		
2017–18	Manchester U	13	1		
2018–19	Manchester U	12	0		
2019–20	Manchester U	4	0		
2020–21	Manchester U	12	0		
2021–22	Manchester U	4	0	**70**	**1**

BERNARD, Di'shon (D) **56 2**
H: 6 2 W: 12 11 b.London 14-10-00
From Chelsea.

2019–20	Manchester U	0	0		
2020–21	Manchester U	0	0		
2020–21	*Salford C*	30	2	**30**	**2**
2021–22	Manchester U	0	0		
2021–22	*Hull C*	26	0	**26**	**0**

BISHOP, Nathan (G) **77 0**
H: 6 1 W: 11 05 b.Hillingdon 15-10-99
Internationals: England U20.

2016–17	Southend U	0	0		
2017–18	Southend U	1	0		
2018–19	Southend U	18	0		
2019–20	Southend U	12	0	**31**	**0**
2019–20	Manchester U	0	0		
2020–21	Manchester U	0	0		
2021–22	Manchester U	0	0		
2021–22	*Mansfield T*	46	0	**46**	**0**

BRUNO FERNANDES, Miguel (M) **312 94**
H: 5 8 W: 9 08 b.Maia 8-9-94
Internationals: Portugal U19, U20, U21, U23, Full caps.

2012–13	Novara	23	4	**23**	**4**
2013–14	Udinese	24	4		
2014–15	Udinese	31	3		
2015–16	Udinese	31	3	**86**	**10**
2016–17	Sampdoria	33	5	**33**	**5**
2017–18	Sporting Lisbon	33	11		
2018–19	Sporting Lisbon	33	20		
2019–20	Sporting Lisbon	17	8	**83**	**39**
2019–20	Manchester U	14	8		
2020–21	Manchester U	37	18		
2021–22	Manchester U	36	10	**87**	**36**

BUGHAIL-MELLOR, D'Mani (F) **3 0**
H: 6 1 W: 11 09 b.Manchester 20-9-00

2019–20	Manchester U	0	0		
2020–21	Manchester U	0	0		
2021–22	Manchester U	0	0		
2021–22	*Salford C*	3	0	**3**	**0**

CAVANI, Edinson (F) **479 271**
H: 6 2 W: 11 03 b.Salto 14-2-87
Internationals: Uruguay U20, U23, Full caps.

2005–06	Danubio	10	4		
2006–07	Danubio	15	5	**25**	**9**
2006–07	Palermo	7	2		
2007–08	Palermo	33	5		
2008–09	Palermo	35	14		
2009–10	Palermo	34	13	**109**	**34**
2010–11	Napoli	35	26		
2011–12	Napoli	35	23		
2012–13	Napoli	34	29	**104**	**78**
2013–14	Paris Saint-Germain	30	16		
2014–15	Paris Saint-Germain	35	18		
2015–16	Paris Saint-Germain	32	19		
2016–17	Paris Saint-Germain	36	35		
2017–18	Paris Saint-Germain	32	28		
2018–19	Paris Saint-Germain	21	18		
2019–20	Paris Saint-Germain	14	4	**200**	**138**
2020–21	Manchester U	26	10		
2021–22	Manchester U	15	2	**41**	**12**

CHONG, Tahith (F) **48 1**
H: 6 1 W: 11 00 b.Willemstad 4-12-99
Internationals: Netherlands U16, U17, U19, U20, U21.
From Feyenoord.

2018–19	Manchester U	2	0		
2019–20	Manchester U	3	0		
2020–21	Manchester U	0	0		
2020–21	*Werder Bremen*	13	0	**13**	**0**
2020–21	*Club Brugge*	10	0	**10**	**0**
2021–22	Manchester U	0	0	**5**	**0**
2021–22	*Birmingham C*	20	1	**20**	**1**

COLLYER, Toby (M) **0 0**
b.Worthing 3-1-04
Internationals: England U16.

2020–21	Brighton & HA	0	0		
2021–22	Manchester U	0	0		

DALOT, Diogo (D) **71 1**
H: 6 0 W: 11 11 b.Braga 18-3-99
Internationals: Portugal U16, U17, U19, U20, U21, Full caps.

2016–17	Porto	0	0		
2017–18	Porto	6	0	**6**	**0**
2018–19	Manchester U	16	0		
2019–20	Manchester U	4	0		
2020–21	Manchester U	0	0		
2020–21	*AC Milan*	21	1	**21**	**1**
2021–22	Manchester U	24	0	**44**	**0**

DE GEA, David (G) **434 0**
H: 6 3 W: 12 13 b.Madrid 7-11-90
Internationals: Spain U15, U17, U19, U20, U21, U23, Full caps.

2009–10	Atletico Madrid	19	0		
2010–11	Atletico Madrid	38	0	**57**	**0**
2011–12	Manchester U	29	0		
2012–13	Manchester U	28	0		
2013–14	Manchester U	37	0		
2014–15	Manchester U	37	0		
2015–16	Manchester U	34	0		
2016–17	Manchester U	35	0		
2017–18	Manchester U	37	0		
2018–19	Manchester U	38	0		
2019–20	Manchester U	38	0		
2020–21	Manchester U	26	0		
2021–22	Manchester U	38	0	**377**	**0**

DEVINE, Reece (D) **8 0**
H: 6 0 b.Stourbridge 18-12-01

2020–21	Manchester U	0	0		
2021–22	Manchester U	0	0		
2021–22	*St Johnstone*	0	0		
2021–22	*Walsall*	8	0	**8**	**0**

DIALLO, Amad (F) **16 4**
H: 5 9 W: 11 00 b.Abidjan 11-7-02
Internationals: Ivory Coast U23, Full caps.

2019–20	Atalanta	3	1		
2020–21	Atalanta	0	0	**3**	**1**
2020–21	Manchester U	3	0		
2021–22	Manchester U	0	0	**3**	**0**
2021–22	*Rangers*	10	3	**10**	**3**

ELANGA, Anthony (F) **23 3**
H: 5 10 W: 10 03 b.Malmo 27-4-02
Internationals: Sweden U17, U19, U21, Full caps.

2020–21	Manchester U	2	1		
2021–22	Manchester U	21	2	**23**	**3**

EMERAN, Noam (F) **0 0**
H: 5 10 W: 11 00 b.Paray-le-Monial 24-9-02
Internationals: France U16.
From Amiens.

2020–21	Manchester U	0	0		
2021–22	Manchester U	0	0		

FERNANDEZ, Alvaro (D) **0 0**
b.El Ferrol 23-3-03
Internationals: Spain U19.
From Real Madrid.

2020–21	Manchester U	0	0		
2021–22	Manchester U	0	0		

FISH, William (D) **1 0**
b. 17-2-03
Internationals: England U17, U18, U19.

2020–21	Manchester U	1	0		
2021–22	Manchester U	0	0	**1**	**0**

FRED, Frederico (M) **238 23**
H: 5 7 W: 10 10 b.Belo Horizonte 5-3-93
Internationals: Brazil U20, Full caps.

2012	Internacional	28	6		
2013	Internacional	5	1	**33**	**7**
2013–14	Shakhtar Donetsk	23	2		
2014–15	Shakhtar Donetsk	22	1		
2015–16	Shakhtar Donetsk	12	2		
2016–17	Shakhtar Donetsk	18	2		
2017–18	Shakhtar Donetsk	26	3	**101**	**10**
2018–19	Manchester U	17	1		
2019–20	Manchester U	29	0		
2020–21	Manchester U	30	1		
2021–22	Manchester U	28	4	**104**	**6**

GALBRAITH, Ethan (M) **33 1**
H: 5 9 W: 10 08 b.Belfast 11-5-01
Internationals: Northern Ireland U17, U19, U21, Full caps.
From Linfield.

2019–20	Manchester U	0	0		
2020–21	Manchester U	0	0		
2021–22	Manchester U	0	0		
2021–22	*Doncaster R*	33	1	**33**	**1**

GARNACHO, Alejandro (F) **2 0**
b. 1-7-04
Internationals: Argentina U20.

2021–22	Manchester U	2	0	**2**	**0**

GARNER, James (M) **83 8**
H: 5 10 W: 11 11 b.Birkenhead 13-3-01
Internationals: England U17, U18, U19, U20, U21.

2018–19	Manchester U	1	0		
2019–20	Manchester U	1	0		

2020–21 Manchester U 0 0
2020–21 *Watford* 20 0 **20 0**
2020–21 *Nottingham F* 20 4
2021–22 Manchester U 0 0 **2 0**
2021–22 *Nottingham F* 41 4 **61 8**

GRANT, Lee (G) 468 0
H: 6 4 W: 13 01 b.Hemel Hempstead 27-1-83
Internationals: England U16, U17, U18, U19, U21.
2000–01 Derby Co 0 0
2001–02 Derby Co 0 0
2002–03 Derby Co 29 0
2003–04 Derby Co 36 0
2004–05 Derby Co 2 0
2005–06 Derby Co 0 0
2005–06 *Burnley* 1 0
2005–06 *Oldham Ath* 16 0 **16 0**
2006–07 Derby Co 7 0
2007–08 Sheffield W 44 0
2008–09 Sheffield W 46 0
2009–10 Sheffield W 46 0 **136 0**
2010–11 Burnley 25 0
2011–12 Burnley 43 0
2012–13 Burnley 46 0 **115 0**
2013–14 Derby Co 46 0
2014–15 Derby Co 40 0
2015–16 Derby Co 10 0
2016–17 Derby Co 0 0 **170 0**
2016–17 *Stoke C* 28 0
2017–18 Stoke C 3 0 **31 0**
2018–19 Manchester U 0 0
2019–20 Manchester U 0 0
2020–21 Manchester U 0 0
2021–22 Manchester U 0 0

GREENWOOD, Mason (F) 83 22
H: 5 11 W: 11 00 b.Bradford 1-10-01
Internationals: England U17, U18, U21, Full caps.
2018–19 Manchester U 3 0
2019–20 Manchester U 31 10
2020–21 Manchester U 31 7
2021–22 Manchester U 18 5 **83 22**

HARDLEY, Bjorn (D) 0 0
H: 6 2 W: 11 11 b.Tilburg 19-12-02
From NAC Breda.
2020–21 Manchester U 0 0
2021–22 Manchester U 0 0

HEATON, Tom (G) 343 0
H: 6 2 W: 13 06 b.Chester 15-4-86
Internationals: England U16, U17, U18, U19, U21, Full caps.
2003–04 Manchester U 0 0
2004–05 Manchester U 0 0
2005–06 Manchester U 0 0
2005–06 *Swindon T* 14 0 **14 0**
2006–07 Manchester U 0 0
2007–08 Manchester U 0 0
2008–09 Manchester U 0 0
2008–09 *Cardiff C* 21 0
2009–10 Manchester U 0 0
2009–10 *Rochdale* 12 0 **12 0**
2009–10 *Wycombe W* 16 0 **16 0**
2010–11 Cardiff C 27 0
2011–12 Cardiff C 2 0 **50 0**
2012–13 Bristol C 43 0 **43 0**
2013–14 Burnley 46 0
2014–15 Burnley 38 0
2015–16 Burnley 46 0
2016–17 Burnley 35 0
2017–18 Burnley 4 0
2018–19 Burnley 19 0 **188 0**
2019–20 Aston Villa 20 0
2020–21 Aston Villa 0 0 **20 0**
2021–22 Manchester U 0 0

HENDERSON, Dean (G) 140 0
H: 6 3 W: 12 13 b.Whitehaven 12-3-97
Internationals: England U16, U17, U20, U21, Full caps.
2015–16 Manchester U 0 0
2016–17 Manchester U 0 0
2016–17 *Grimsby T* 7 0 **7 0**
2017–18 Manchester U 0 0
2017–18 *Shrewsbury T* 38 0 **38 0**
2018–19 Manchester U 0 0
2018–19 *Sheffield U* 46 0
2019–20 Manchester U 0 0
2019–20 *Sheffield U* 36 0 **82 0**
2020–21 Manchester U 13 0
2021–22 Manchester U 0 0 **13 0**

HUGILL, Joe (F) 0 0
b.Durham 19-10-03
From Sunderland.
2020–21 Manchester U 0 0
2021–22 Manchester U 0 0

IQBAL, Zidane (M) 0 0
H: 5 11 b.Manchester 27-4-03
Internationals: Iraq U23, Full caps.
2020–21 Manchester U 0 0
2021–22 Manchester U 0 0

JONES, Phil (D) 204 2
H: 6 1 W: 11 02 b.Preston 21-2-92
Internationals: England U19, U21, Full caps.
2009–10 Blackburn R 9 0
2010–11 Blackburn R 26 0 **35 0**
2011–12 Manchester U 29 1
2012–13 Manchester U 17 0
2013–14 Manchester U 26 1
2014–15 Manchester U 22 0
2015–16 Manchester U 10 0
2016–17 Manchester U 18 0
2017–18 Manchester U 23 0
2018–19 Manchester U 18 0
2019–20 Manchester U 2 0
2020–21 Manchester U 0 0
2021–22 Manchester U 4 0 **169 2**

JURADO, Marc (D) 0 0
H: 5 10 b.Sabadell 13-4-04
From Barcelona.
2020–21 Manchester U 0 0
2021–22 Manchester U 0 0

KOVAR, Matej (G) 24 0
H: 6 4 W: 13 01 b.Uherske Hradiste 17-5-00
Internationals: Czech Republic U18, U19, U20, U21.
From Slovacko.
2019–20 Manchester U 0 0
2020–21 Manchester U 0 0
2020–21 *Swindon T* 18 0 **18 0**
2021–22 Manchester U 0 0
2021–22 *Burton Alb* 6 0 **6 0**

LAIRD, Ethan (D) 50 0
H: 5 10 W: 10 06 b.Basingstoke 5-8-01
Internationals: England U17, U18, U19.
2019–20 Manchester U 0 0
2020–21 Manchester U 0 0
2020–21 *Milton Keynes D* 24 0 **24 0**
2021–22 Manchester U 0 0
2021–22 *Swansea C* 20 0 **20 0**
2021–22 *Bournemouth* 6 0 **6 0**

LEVITT, Dylan (M) 35 5
b. 17-11-00
Internationals: Wales U17, U19, U21, Full caps.
2019–20 Manchester U 0 0
2020–21 Manchester U 0 0
2020–21 *Charlton Ath* 3 0 **3 0**
2020–21 *Istra 1961* 7 0 **7 0**
2021–22 Manchester U 0 0
2021–22 Dundee U 25 5 **25 5**

LINDELOF, Victor (D) 237 5
H: 6 2 W: 12 11 b.Vasteras 17-7-94
Internationals: Sweden U17, U19, U21, Full caps.
2009 Vasteras 1 0
2010 Vasteras 9 0
2011 Vasteras 27 0
2012 Vasteras 13 0 **50 0**
2012–13 Benfica 0 0
2013–14 Benfica 1 0
2014–15 Benfica 0 0
2015–16 Benfica 15 1
2016–17 Benfica 32 1 **48 2**
2017–18 Manchester U 17 0
2018–19 Manchester U 30 1
2019–20 Manchester U 35 1
2020–21 Manchester U 29 1
2021–22 Manchester U 28 0 **139 3**

LINGARD, Jesse (M) 212 40
H: 5 9 W: 9 02 b.Warrington 15-12-92
Internationals: England U17, U21, Full caps.
2011–12 Manchester U 0 0
2012–13 Manchester U 0 0
2012–13 *Leicester C* 5 0 **5 0**
2013–14 Manchester U 0 0
2013–14 *Birmingham C* 13 6 **13 6**
2013–14 *Brighton & HA* 15 3 **15 3**
2014–15 Manchester U 1 0
2014–15 *Derby Co* 14 2 **14 2**
2015–16 Manchester U 25 4
2016–17 Manchester U 25 1
2017–18 Manchester U 33 8
2018–19 Manchester U 27 4
2019–20 Manchester U 22 1
2020–21 Manchester U 0 0
2020–21 *West Ham U* 16 9 **16 9**
2021–22 Manchester U 16 2 **149 20**

MAGUIRE, Harry (D) 375 21
H: 6 4 W: 15 10 b.Sheffield 5-3-93
Internationals: England U21, Full caps.
2010–11 Sheffield U 5 0
2011–12 Sheffield U 44 1
2012–13 Sheffield U 44 3
2013–14 Sheffield U 41 5 **134 9**
2014–15 Hull C 3 0
2014–15 *Wigan Ath* 16 1 **16 1**
2015–16 Hull C 22 0
2016–17 Hull C 29 2 **54 2**
2017–18 Leicester C 38 2
2018–19 Leicester C 31 3
2019–20 Leicester C 0 0 **69 5**
2019–20 Manchester U 38 1
2020–21 Manchester U 34 2
2021–22 Manchester U 30 1 **102 4**

MARTIAL, Anthony (F) 236 67
H: 5 11 W: 12 08 b.Massy 5-12-95
Internationals: France U16, U17, U18, U19, U21, Full caps.
2012–13 Lyon 3 0 **3 0**
2013–14 Monaco 11 2
2014–15 Monaco 35 9
2015–16 Monaco 3 0 **49 11**
2015–16 Manchester U 31 11
2016–17 Manchester U 25 4
2017–18 Manchester U 30 9
2018–19 Manchester U 27 10
2019–20 Manchester U 32 17
2020–21 Manchester U 22 4
2021–22 Manchester U 8 1 **175 56**
2021–22 *Sevilla* 9 0 **9 0**

MASTNY, Ondrej (G) 0 0
H: 6 0 W: 11 00 b.Trebic 8-3-02
Internationals: Czech Republic U16, U18.
From Vysocina.
2020–21 Manchester U 0 0
2021–22 Manchester U 0 0

MATA, Juan (M) 407 85
H: 5 7 W: 9 08 b.Burgos 28-4-88
Internationals: Spain U16, U17, U19, U20, U21, U23, Full caps.
From Real Oviedo.
2006–07 Real Madrid 0 0
2007–08 Valencia 24 5
2008–09 Valencia 37 11
2009–10 Valencia 35 9
2010–11 Valencia 33 8 **129 33**
2011–12 Chelsea 34 6
2012–13 Chelsea 35 12
2013–14 Chelsea 13 0 **82 18**
2013–14 Manchester U 15 6
2014–15 Manchester U 33 9
2015–16 Manchester U 38 6
2016–17 Manchester U 25 6
2017–18 Manchester U 28 3
2018–19 Manchester U 22 3
2019–20 Manchester U 19 0
2020–21 Manchester U 9 1
2021–22 Manchester U 7 0 **196 34**

MATIC, Nemanja (M) 417 18
H: 6 4 W: 13 03 b.Sabac 1-8-88
Internationals: Serbia U21, Full caps.
2005–06 Jedinstvo 7 0
2006–07 Jedinstvo 9 0 **16 0**
2006–07 Kosice 13 1
2007–08 Kosice 25 1
2008–09 Kosice 29 2 **67 4**
2009–10 Chelsea 2 0
2010–11 Chelsea 0 0
2010–11 *Vitesse* 27 2 **27 2**
2011–12 Benfica 16 1
2012–13 Benfica 26 3
2013–14 Benfica 14 2 **56 6**
2013–14 Chelsea 17 0
2014–15 Chelsea 36 1
2015–16 Chelsea 33 2
2016–17 Chelsea 35 1 **123 4**
2017–18 Manchester U 36 1
2018–19 Manchester U 28 1
2019–20 Manchester U 21 0
2020–21 Manchester U 20 0
2021–22 Manchester U 23 0 **128 2**

McNEILL, Charlie (F) 0 0
H: 6 0 b. 9-9-03
Internationals: England U16.
2020–21 Manchester U 0 0
2021–22 Manchester U 0 0

McSHANE, Paul (D) 369 14
H: 6 0 W: 11 05 b.Wicklow 6-1-86
Internationals: Republic of Ireland U21, Full caps.
2002–03 Manchester U 0 0
2003–04 Manchester U 0 0
2004–05 Manchester U 0 0
2004–05 *Walsall* 4 1 **4 1**
2005–06 Manchester U 0 0
2005–06 *Brighton & HA* 38 3 **38 3**
2006–07 WBA 32 2 **32 2**
2007–08 Sunderland 21 0
2008–09 Sunderland 3 0
2008–09 *Hull C* 17 1
2009–10 Sunderland 0 0 **24 0**
2009–10 Hull C 27 0
2010–11 Hull C 19 0
2010–11 *Barnsley* 10 1 **10 1**
2011–12 Hull C 1 0
2011–12 *Crystal Palace* 11 0 **11 0**
2012–13 Hull C 25 2
2013–14 Hull C 10 0
2014–15 Hull C 20 1 **119 4**
2015–16 Reading 35 0
2016–17 Reading 30 3

2017–18 Reading 26 0
2018–19 Reading 5 0 **96 3**
2019–20 Rochdale 16 0
2020–21 Rochdale 19 0 **35 0**
2021–22 Manchester U 0 0

McTOMINAY, Scott (M) 120 11
H: 6 4 W: 10 08 b.Lancaster 8-12-96
Internationals: Scotland Full caps.
2016–17 Manchester U 2 0
2017–18 Manchester U 13 0
2018–19 Manchester U 16 2
2019–20 Manchester U 27 4
2020–21 Manchester U 32 4
2021–22 Manchester U 30 1 **120 11**

MEJBRI, Hannibal (M) 3 0
H: 6 0 W: 11 00 b.Ivry-sur-Seine 21-1-03
Internationals: France U16, U17. Tunisia Full caps.
2020–21 Manchester U 1 0
2021–22 Manchester U 2 0 **3 0**

MEJIA, Mateo (F) 0 0
H: 6 2 b.Zaragoza 31-3-03
From Real Zaragoza.
2020–21 Manchester U 0 0
2021–22 Manchester U 0 0

MENGI, Teden (D) 18 0
H: 6 0 W: 12 04 b.Manchester 30-4-02
Internationals: England U16, U17, U18, U20.
2019–20 Manchester U 0 0
2020–21 Manchester U 0 0
2020–21 *Derby Co* 9 0
2021–22 *Derby Co* 0 0 **9 0**
2021–22 Manchester U 0 0
2021–22 *Birmingham C* 9 0 **9 0**

PELLISTRI , Facundo (M) 63 1
b.Montevideo 20-12-01
Internationals: Uruguay U16, Full caps.
2019 Penarol 18 1
2020 Penarol 12 0
2020–21 Penarol 0 0 **30 1**
2020–21 Manchester U 0 0
2020–21 *Alaves* 12 0
2021–22 Manchester U 0 0
2021–22 *Alaves* 21 0 **33 0**

PEREIRA, Andreas (M) 150 11
H: 5 10 W: 10 06 b.Duffel 1-1-96
Internationals: Belgium U16, U17. Brazil U20, U23, Full caps.
From PSV Eindhoven.
2014–15 Manchester U 1 0
2015–16 Manchester U 4 0
2016–17 Manchester U 0 0
2016–17 *Granada* 35 5 **35 5**
2017–18 Manchester U 0 0
2017–18 *Valencia* 23 1 **23 1**
2018–19 Manchester U 15 1
2019–20 Manchester U 25 1
2020–21 Manchester U 0 0
2020–21 *Lazio* 26 1 **26 1**
2021–22 Manchester U 0 0 **45 2**
2022 *Flamengo* 21 2 **21 2**

POGBA, Paul (M) 281 57
H: 6 3 W: 13 03 b.Lagny-sur-Marne 15-3-93
Internationals: France U16, U17, U18, U19, U20, Full caps.
From Le Havre.
2009–10 Manchester U 0 0
2010–11 Manchester U 0 0
2011–12 Manchester U 3 0
2012–13 Juventus 27 5
2013–14 Juventus 36 7
2014–15 Juventus 26 8
2015–16 Juventus 35 8 **124 28**
2016–17 Manchester U 30 5
2017–18 Manchester U 27 6
2018–19 Manchester U 35 13
2019–20 Manchester U 16 1
2020–21 Manchester U 26 3
2021–22 Manchester U 20 1 **157 29**

PYE, Logan (D) 0 0
H: 5 10 b.Sunderland 26-10-03
Internationals: England U16.
From Sunderland.
2020–21 Manchester U 0 0
2021–22 Manchester U 0 0

RASHFORD, Marcus (F) 204 59
H: 6 1 W: 11 00 b.Manchester 31-10-97
Internationals: England U16, U18, U20, U21, Full caps.
2015–16 Manchester U 11 5
2016–17 Manchester U 32 5
2017–18 Manchester U 35 7
2018–19 Manchester U 33 10
2019–20 Manchester U 31 17
2020–21 Manchester U 37 11
2021–22 Manchester U 25 4 **204 59**

RONALDO, Cristiano (F) 641 497
H: 6 1 W: 11 11 b.Funchal, Madeira 5-2-85
Internationals: Portugal U17, U20, U21, U23, Full caps.
2002–03 Sporting Lisbon 25 3 **25 3**
2003–04 Manchester U 29 4
2004–05 Manchester U 33 5
2005–06 Manchester U 33 9
2006–07 Manchester U 34 17
2007–08 Manchester U 34 31
2008–09 Manchester U 33 18
2009–10 Real Madrid 29 26
2010–11 Real Madrid 34 40
2011–12 Real Madrid 38 46
2012–13 Real Madrid 34 34
2013–14 Real Madrid 30 31
2014–15 Real Madrid 35 48
2015–16 Real Madrid 36 35
2016–17 Real Madrid 29 25
2017–18 Real Madrid 27 26 **292 311**
2018–19 Juventus 31 21
2019–20 Juventus 33 31
2020–21 Juventus 33 29
2021–22 Juventus 1 0 **98 81**
2021–22 Manchester U 30 18 **226 102**

SANCHO, Jadon (M) 133 41
H: 5 10 W: 11 07 b.Camberwell 25-3-00
Internationals: England U16, U17, U19, Full caps.
2016–17 Manchester C 0 0
2017–18 Borussia Dortmund 12 1
2018–19 Borussia Dortmund 34 12
2019–20 Borussia Dortmund 32 17
2020–21 Borussia Dortmund 26 8
2021–22 Borussia Dortmund 0 0 **104 38**
2021–22 Manchester U 29 3 **29 3**

SAVAGE, Charlie (M) 0 0
H: 6 0 b.Leicester 2-5-03
Internationals: Wales U17, U18, U19.
2020–21 Manchester U 0 0
2021–22 Manchester U 0 0

SHAW, Luke (D) 208 2
H: 6 1 W: 11 11 b.Kingston 12-7-95
Internationals: England U16, U17, U21, Full caps.
2011–12 Southampton 0 0
2012–13 Southampton 25 0
2013–14 Southampton 35 0 **60 0**
2014–15 Manchester U 16 0
2015–16 Manchester U 5 0
2016–17 Manchester U 11 0
2017–18 Manchester U 11 0
2018–19 Manchester U 29 1
2019–20 Manchester U 24 0
2020–21 Manchester U 32 1
2021–22 Manchester U 20 0 **148 2**

SHORETIRE, Shola (F) 3 0
H: 5 7 b.Newcastle upon Tyne 2-2-04
Internationals: England U16, U18, U19.
From Newcastle U.
2020–21 Manchester U 2 0
2021–22 Manchester U 1 0 **3 0**

STANLEY, Connor (M) 0 0
H: 5 9 b.Redditch 30-12-01
From Birmingham C.
2020–21 Manchester U 0 0
2021–22 Manchester U 0 0

SVIDERSKY, Martin (D) 0 0
H: 5 11 W: 10 01 b.Presov 4-10-02
Internationals: Slovakia U17, U21.
2020–21 Manchester U 0 0
2021–22 Manchester U 0 0

TUANZEBE, Axel (D) 58 0
H: 6 0 W: 11 11 b.Bunia 14-11-97
Internationals: England U19, U20, U21.
2015–16 Manchester U 0 0
2016–17 Manchester U 4 0
2017–18 Manchester U 1 0
2017–18 *Aston Villa* 5 0
2018–19 Manchester U 0 0
2018–19 *Aston Villa* 25 0
2019–20 Manchester U 5 0
2020–21 Manchester U 9 0
2021–22 Manchester U 0 0 **19 0**
2021–22 *Aston Villa* 9 0 **39 0**
2021–22 *Napoli* 0 0

VAN DE BEEK, Donny (M) 152 31
H: 6 2 W: 11 07 b.Nijkerkerveen 18-4-97
Internationals: Netherlands U7, U19, U20, U21, Full caps.
2015–16 Ajax 8 0
2016–17 Ajax 19 0
2017–18 Ajax 34 11
2018–19 Ajax 34 9
2019–20 Ajax 23 8
2020–21 Ajax 0 0 **118 28**
2020–21 Manchester U 19 1
2021–22 Manchester U 8 1 **27 2**
2021–22 *Everton* 7 1 **7 1**

VARANE, Raphael (D) 281 11
H: 6 3 W: 12 11 b.Lille 25-4-93
Internationals: France U18, U20, U21, Full caps.
2010–11 Lens 23 2 **23 2**
2011–12 Real Madrid 9 1
2012–13 Real Madrid 15 0
2013–14 Real Madrid 14 0
2014–15 Real Madrid 27 0
2015–16 Real Madrid 26 0
2016–17 Real Madrid 23 1
2017–18 Real Madrid 27 0
2018–19 Real Madrid 32 2
2019–20 Real Madrid 32 2
2020–21 Real Madrid 31 2
2021–22 Real Madrid 0 0 **236 8**
2021–22 Manchester U 22 1 **22 1**

VITEK, Radek (G) 0 0
H: 6 6 b.Vsetin 24-10-03
Internationals: Czech Republic U17.
From Olomouc.
2020–21 Manchester U 0 0
2021–22 Manchester U 0 0

WAN BISSAKA, Aaron (D) 131 2
H: 6 0 W: 11 05 b.Croyden 26-11-97
Internationals: DR Congo U20. England U20, U21.
2016–17 Crystal Palace 0 0
2017–18 Crystal Palace 7 0
2018–19 Crystal Palace 35 0 **42 0**
2019–20 Manchester U 35 0
2020–21 Manchester U 34 2
2021–22 Manchester U 20 0 **89 2**

WILLIAMS, Brandon (D) 47 1
H: 6 0 W: 9 13 b.Manchester 3-9-00
Internationals: England U20, U21.
2018–19 Manchester U 0 0
2019–20 Manchester U 17 1
2020–21 Manchester U 4 0
2021–22 Manchester U 0 0 **21 1**
2021–22 *Norwich C* 26 0 **26 0**

WOOLSTON, Paul (G) 0 0
H: 5 11 W: 13 05 b.North Shields 14-8-98
Internationals: England U17, U18.
2020–21 Manchester U 0 0
2021–22 Manchester U 0 0

Players retained or with offer of contract
Bennett, Rhys; Ennis, Ethan; Forson, Omari; Fredricson, Tyler; Gore, Daniel; Hansen-Aaroen, Isak; Kambwala Ndengushi, Willy; Mainoo, Kobbie; Mather, Samuel; Mee, Dermot; Oyedele, Maximillian; Wellens, Charlie; Wooster, Thomas.

Scholars
Aljofree, Sonny; Hanbury, Eric Nicolas; Lawrence, Marcus Levi; Murray, Samuel Alexander; Norkett, Manni Sam Retained.

MANSFIELD T (51)

AKINS, Lucas (F) 505 87
H: 5 11 W: 12 06 b.Huddersfield 25-2-89
2006–07 Huddersfield T 2 0
2007–08 Huddersfield T 3 0 **5 0**
2008–09 Hamilton A 11 0
2008–09 *Partick Thistle* 9 1 **9 1**
2009–10 Hamilton A 0 0 **11 0**
2010–11 Tranmere R 33 2
2011–12 Tranmere R 44 5 **77 7**
2012–13 Stevenage 46 10
2013–14 Stevenage 31 3 **77 13**
2014–15 Burton Alb 35 9
2015–16 Burton Alb 44 12
2016–17 Burton Alb 38 5
2017–18 Burton Alb 42 5
2018–19 Burton Alb 46 13
2019–20 Burton Alb 35 9
2020–21 Burton Alb 45 9
2021–22 Burton Alb 22 3 **307 65**
2021–22 Mansfield T 19 1 **19 1**

BOWERY, Jordan (F) 389 65
H: 6 1 W: 12 00 b.Nottingham 2-7-91
2008–09 Chesterfield 3 0
2009–10 Chesterfield 10 0
2010–11 Chesterfield 27 1
2011–12 Chesterfield 40 8
2012–13 Chesterfield 3 1 **83 10**
2012–13 Aston Villa 10 0
2013–14 Aston Villa 9 0 **19 0**
2013–14 *Doncaster R* 3 0 **3 0**
2014–15 Rotherham U 33 5
2015–16 Rotherham U 7 0 **40 5**
2015–16 *Bradford C* 3 0 **3 0**
2015–16 Oxford U 17 7 **17 7**
2016–17 Leyton Orient 17 1 **17 1**
2016–17 *Crewe Alex* 19 2
2017–18 Crewe Alex 45 12
2018–19 Crewe Alex 44 8 **108 22**
2019–20 Milton Keynes D 16 2 **16 2**

2020–21 Mansfield T 43 10
2021–22 Mansfield T 40 8 **83 18**

BURKE, Ryan (D) 5 0
b.Dublin 23-11-00
Internationals: Republic of Ireland U16.
From St Patrick's.
2019–20 Birmingham C 1 0
2020–21 Birmingham C 0 0 **1 0**
2021–22 Mansfield T 4 0 **4 0**

CAINE, Nathan (F) 0 0
H: 6 0 W: 12 02 b.Stockport 20-11-02
2020–21 Mansfield T 0 0
2021–22 Mansfield T 0 0

CHARLES, Jaden (M) 2 0
H: 5 11 W: 11 11 b.Bristol 25-1-02
Internationals: Republic of Ireland U18.
2020–21 Mansfield T 2 0
2021–22 Mansfield T 0 0 **2 0**

CLARKE, James (D) 18 0
H: 6 0 W: 11 00 b.Birkenhead 2-4-00
Internationals: Republic of Ireland U18.
2018–19 Burnley 0 0
2019–20 Mansfield T 12 0
2020–21 Mansfield T 2 0
2021–22 Mansfield T 4 0 **18 0**

CLARKE, Ollie (M) 267 23
H: 5 11 W: 11 11 b.Bristol 29-6-92
2009–10 Bristol R 0 0
2010–11 Bristol R 1 0
2011–12 Bristol R 0 0
2012–13 Bristol R 5 0
2013–14 Bristol R 32 2
From Bristol R.
2015–16 Bristol R 33 2
2016–17 Bristol R 30 4
2017–18 Bristol R 40 1
2018–19 Bristol R 40 6
2019–20 Bristol R 27 1 **208 16**
2019–20 Mansfield T 0 0
2020–21 Mansfield T 33 3
2021–22 Mansfield T 26 4 **59 7**

GALE, James (F) 3 0
b. 20-12-01
From Long Eaton U.
2021–22 Mansfield T 3 0 **3 0**

GORDON, Kellan (D) 89 6
H: 5 10 W: 12 00 b.Burton 25-12-97
From Stoke C.
2017–18 Derby Co 0 0
2017–18 *Swindon T* 26 3 **26 3**
2018–19 Derby Co 0 0
2018–19 *Lincoln C* 6 2
2019–20 *Lincoln C* 0 0 **6 2**
2019–20 Mansfield T 18 1
2020–21 Mansfield T 32 0
2021–22 Mansfield T 7 0 **57 1**

HAWKINS, Oliver (F) 156 23
H: 6 2 W: 11 00 b.Ealing 8-4-92
From North Greenford U, Hillingdon Bor, Northwood, Hemel Hempstead T.
2015–16 Dagenham & R 18 1 **18 1**
From Dagenham & R.
2017–18 Portsmouth 31 7
2018–19 Portsmouth 39 7
2019–20 Portsmouth 7 0 **77 14**
2020–21 Ipswich T 20 1
2021–22 Ipswich T 0 0 **20 1**
2021–22 Mansfield T 41 7 **41 7**

HEWITT, Elliott (D) 312 11
H: 5 11 W: 11 11 b.Rhyl 30-5-94
Internationals: Wales U17, U21.
2010–11 Macclesfield T 1 0
2011–12 Macclesfield T 21 0 **22 0**
2012–13 Ipswich T 7 0
2013–14 Ipswich T 4 0
2013–14 *Gillingham* 20 0 **20 0**
2014–15 Ipswich T 3 0 **14 0**
2014–15 *Colchester U* 21 1 **21 1**
2015–16 Notts Co 38 0
2016–17 Notts Co 29 2
2017–18 Notts Co 43 4
2018–19 Notts Co 25 2 **135 8**
2019–20 Grimsby T 20 0
2020–21 Grimsby T 37 1 **57 1**
2020–21 Mansfield T 0 0
2021–22 Mansfield T 43 1 **43 1**

JOHNSON, Danny (F) 119 34
H: 5 10 W: 12 13 b.Middlesbrough 28-2-93
From Harrogate T, Billingham Synthonia, Guisborough T.
2014–15 Cardiff C 0 0
2014–15 *Tranmere R* 4 0 **4 0**
2014–15 *Stevenage* 4 0 **4 0**
From Gateshead.
2018–19 Motherwell 22 6 **22 6**
2019–20 Dundee 19 5 **19 5**
2019–20 Leyton Orient 6 2
2020–21 Leyton Orient 42 17
2021–22 Leyton Orient 0 0 **48 19**
2021–22 Mansfield T 22 4 **22 4**

KNOWLES, Jimmy (F) 16 1
2018–19 Mansfield T 0 0
2019–20 Mansfield T 5 1
2020–21 Mansfield T 0 0
2021–22 Mansfield T 0 0 **5 1**
2021–22 *Greenock Morton* 11 0 **11 0**

LAPSLIE, George (M) 101 13
H: 5 11 W: 11 09 b.Waltham Forest 5-9-97
2016–17 Charlton Ath 0 0
2017–18 Charlton Ath 1 0
2018–19 Charlton Ath 27 0
2019–20 Charlton Ath 10 1
2020–21 Charlton Ath 2 0 **40 1**
2020–21 Mansfield T 29 8
2021–22 Mansfield T 32 4 **61 12**

LAW, Jason (F) 22 1
H: 5 10 W: 11 03 b.Nottingham 26-4-99
From Burton Alb, Derby Co, Carlton T.
2015–16 Mansfield T 0 0
2016–17 Mansfield T 0 0
2017–18 Mansfield T 0 0
2018–19 Mansfield T 0 0
2019–20 Mansfield T 0 0
2020–21 Mansfield T 17 1
2021–22 Mansfield T 5 0 **22 1**

MARIS, George (F) 212 24
H: 5 11 W: 11 11 b.Sheffield 6-3-96
2014–15 Barnsley 2 0
2015–16 Barnsley 1 0 **3 0**
2016–17 Cambridge U 23 4
2017–18 Cambridge U 40 10
2018–19 Cambridge U 39 5
2019–20 Cambridge U 30 1 **132 20**
2020–21 Mansfield T 40 1
2021–22 Mansfield T 37 3 **77 4**

McLAUGHLIN, Stephen (M) 370 46
H: 5 9 W: 12 02 b.Donegal 14-6-90
2009 Finn Harps 16 1
2010 Finn Harps 32 1 **48 2**
2011 Derry C 33 3
2012 Derry C 24 10 **57 13**
2012–13 Nottingham F 0 0
2013–14 Nottingham F 3 0
2013–14 *Bristol C* 5 0 **5 0**
2014–15 Nottingham F 6 0 **9 0**
2014–15 *Notts Co* 13 0 **13 0**
2014–15 *Southend U* 6 1
2015–16 Southend U 17 1
2016–17 Southend U 34 7
2017–18 Southend U 45 6
2018–19 Southend U 30 1
2019–20 Southend U 27 4
2020–21 Southend U 0 0 **159 20**
2020–21 Mansfield T 36 4
2021–22 Mansfield T 43 7 **79 11**

MURPHY, Jamie (F) 428 74
H: 6 0 W: 12 00 b.Glasgow 28-8-89
Internationals: Scotland U19, U21, Full caps.
2006–07 Motherwell 2 0
2007–08 Motherwell 16 1
2008–09 Motherwell 30 2
2009–10 Motherwell 35 6
2010–11 Motherwell 35 6
2011–12 Motherwell 36 9
2012–13 Motherwell 22 10 **176 34**
2012–13 Sheffield U 17 2
2013–14 Sheffield U 34 4
2014–15 Sheffield U 43 11
2015–16 Sheffield U 1 0 **95 17**
2015–16 Brighton & HA 37 6
2016–17 Brighton & HA 35 2
2017–18 Brighton & HA 4 0 **76 8**
2017–18 *Rangers* 16 4
2018–19 Rangers 2 0
2019–20 Rangers 2 0
2019–20 *Burton Alb* 10 7 **10 7**
2020–21 Rangers 0 0 **20 4**
2020–21 *Hibernian* 19 1
2021–22 Hibernian 18 2 **37 3**
2021–22 *Mansfield T* 14 1 **14 1**

O'TOOLE, John (M) 440 65
H: 6 2 W: 12 13 b.Harrow 30-9-88
Internationals: Republic of Ireland U21.
2007–08 Watford 35 3
2008–09 Watford 22 7
2008–09 *Sheffield U* 9 1 **9 1**
2009–10 Watford 0 0 **57 10**
2009–10 Colchester U 31 2
2010–11 Colchester U 11 0
2011–12 Colchester U 15 0
2012–13 Colchester U 15 0 **72 2**
2012–13 *Bristol R* 18 3
2013–14 Bristol R 41 13 **59 16**
2014–15 Northampton T 35 2
2014–15 *Southend U* 2 0 **2 0**
2015–16 Northampton T 38 12
2016–17 Northampton T 40 10
2017–18 Northampton T 29 6
2018–19 Northampton T 31 3 **173 33**
2019–20 Burton Alb 25 0
2020–21 Burton Alb 16 1 **41 1**
2021–22 Mansfield T 27 2 **27 2**

OATES, Rhys (F) 147 20
H: 6 0 W: 11 09 b.Pontefract 4-12-94
2012–13 Barnsley 0 0
2013–14 Barnsley 0 0
2014–15 Barnsley 9 0 **9 0**
2015–16 Hartlepool U 38 2
2016–17 Hartlepool U 26 3 **64 5**
From Hartlepool U.
2018–19 Morecambe 31 6
2019–20 Morecambe 5 0 **36 6**
From Hartlepool U.
2021–22 Mansfield T 38 9 **38 9**

PERCH, James (D) 533 23
H: 5 11 W: 12 11 b.Mansfield 28-9-85
2002–03 Nottingham F 0 0
2003–04 Nottingham F 0 0
2004–05 Nottingham F 22 0
2005–06 Nottingham F 38 3
2006–07 Nottingham F 46 5
2007–08 Nottingham F 30 0
2008–09 Nottingham F 37 3
2009–10 Nottingham F 17 1 **190 12**
2010–11 Newcastle U 13 0
2011–12 Newcastle U 25 0
2012–13 Newcastle U 27 1 **65 1**
2013–14 Wigan Ath 40 0
2014–15 Wigan Ath 41 3 **81 3**
2015–16 QPR 35 0
2016–17 QPR 32 0
2017–18 QPR 7 0 **74 0**
2018–19 Scunthorpe U 41 2
2019–20 Scunthorpe U 30 1 **71 3**
2020–21 Mansfield T 32 3
2021–22 Mansfield T 20 1 **52 4**

QUINN, Stephen (M) 509 30
H: 5 6 W: 9 06 b.Dublin 4-4-86
Internationals: Republic of Ireland U21, Full caps.
2004 St Patricks Ath 1 0
2005 St Patricks Ath 0 0 **1 0**
2005–06 Sheffield U 0 0
2005–06 *Milton Keynes D* 15 0 **15 0**
2005–06 *Rotherham U* 16 0 **16 0**
2006–07 Sheffield U 15 2
2007–08 Sheffield U 19 2
2008–09 Sheffield U 43 7
2009–10 Sheffield U 44 4
2010–11 Sheffield U 37 1
2011–12 Sheffield U 45 4
2012–13 Sheffield U 3 0 **206 20**
2012–13 Hull C 42 3
2013–14 Hull C 15 0
2014–15 Hull C 28 1 **85 4**
2015–16 Reading 27 1
2016–17 Reading 7 0
2017–18 Reading 0 0 **34 1**
2018–19 Burton Alb 42 1
2019–20 Burton Alb 29 0
2020–21 Burton Alb 22 1
2020–21 *Mansfield T* 23 2
2021–22 Burton Alb 0 0 **93 2**
2021–22 Mansfield T 36 1 **59 3**

RAWSON, Farrend (D) 205 7
H: 6 1 W: 11 07 b.Nottingham 11-7-96
2014–15 Derby Co 0 0
2014–15 *Rotherham U* 4 0
2015–16 Derby Co 0 0
2015–16 *Rotherham U* 16 2 **20 2**
2016–17 Derby Co 0 0
2016–17 *Coventry C* 14 0 **14 0**
2017–18 Derby Co 0 0
2017–18 *Accrington S* 12 0 **12 0**
2017–18 Forest Green R 18 1
2018–19 Forest Green R 38 0
2019–20 Forest Green R 30 3 **86 4**
2020–21 Mansfield T 43 0
2021–22 Mansfield T 30 1 **73 1**

SCOTT, Josh (F) 0 0
b. 20-9-01
2020–21 Mansfield T 0 0
2021–22 Mansfield T 0 0

SINCLAIR, Tyrese (F) 47 3
H: 5 9 W: 11 00 b.Kingston upon Thames 4-2-01
2018–19 Mansfield T 0 0
2019–20 Radcliffe 0 0
2019–20 Mansfield T 0 0
2020–21 Mansfield T 19 3
2021–22 Mansfield T 14 0 **33 3**
2021–22 *Scunthorpe U* 14 0 **14 0**

STECH, Marek (G) 168 0
H: 6 3 W: 14 00 b.Prague 28-1-90
Internationals: Czech Republic U17 U21, Full caps.
From Sparta Prague.
2008–09 West Ham U 0 0
2008–09 *Wycombe W* 2 0 **2 0**
2009–10 West Ham U 0 0
2009–10 *Bournemouth* 1 0 **1 0**

2010–11 West Ham U 0 0
2011–12 West Ham U 0 0
2011–12 *Yeovil T* 5 0
2011–12 *Leyton Orient* 2 0 **2 0**
2012–13 Yeovil T 46 0
2013–14 Yeovil T 26 0 **77 0**
2014–15 Sparta Prague 17 0
2015–16 Sparta Prague 2 0
2016–17 Sparta Prague 0 0 **19 0**
2017–18 Luton T 38 0
2018–19 Luton T 5 0
2019–20 Luton T 0 0 **43 0**
2020–21 Mansfield T 24 0
2021–22 Mansfield T 0 0 **24 0**

WALLACE, Kieran (D) 92 2
H: 6 1 W: 11 11 b.Nottingham 26-1-95
Internationals: England U16, U17.
2013–14 Nottingham F 0 0
From Ilkeston.
2014–15 Sheffield U 4 0
2015–16 Sheffield U 11 0
2016–17 Sheffield U 0 0 **15 0**
2016–17 *Fleetwood T* 0 0
From Matlock T.
2018–19 Burton Alb 22 1
2019–20 Burton Alb 26 1
2020–21 Burton Alb 12 0
2021–22 Burton Alb 0 0 **60 2**
2021–22 Mansfield T 17 0 **17 0**

WARD, Keaton (M) 9 0
H: 6 0 W: 10 12 b.Mansfield 4-5-00
2020–21 Mansfield T 7 0
2021–22 Mansfield T 2 0 **9 0**

Players retained or with offer of contract
Anderson, Taylor; Cooper, George; Hill, Ethan; Mason, Owen; Turner, Louie.

Scholars
Abdullah, McKeal Aroon; Bouch, Jonty Charles; Carter, Charlie Thomas; Collins, Cody Sam; Davies, Curtis James Patrick; Deakin, Jack Mark; Edwards, Diego Antonio; Flanagan, Finn Frank; Hill-Smith, Lewis; Hurdis, Max; Kruszynski, Jakub Aleksander; Pitts, Freddie Lewis; Reynolds, Colt Mikey; Turner, Louie Jack; Wauchope, Darien Ruel Benjamin; Whelan, Ben Alexander; Wilson, Oliver Luke.

MIDDLESBROUGH (52)

AKPOM, Chuba (F) 209 35
H: 6 0 W: 12 02 b.Newham 9-10-95
Internationals: England U16, U17, U19, U20, U21.
2012–13 Arsenal 0 0
2013–14 Arsenal 1 0
2013–14 *Brentford* 4 0 **4 0**
2013–14 *Coventry C* 6 0 **6 0**
2014–15 Arsenal 3 0
2014–15 *Nottingham F* 7 0 **7 0**
2015–16 Arsenal 0 0
2015–16 *Hull C* 35 3 **35 3**
2016–17 Arsenal 0 0
2016–17 *Brighton & HA* 10 0 **10 0**
2017–18 Arsenal 0 0 **4 0**
2017–18 *Sint Truidense* 16 6 **16 6**
2018–19 PAOK 20 6
2019–20 PAOK 33 8
2020–21 PAOK 1 0
2020–21 Middlesbrough 38 5
2021–22 Middlesbrough 1 0 **39 5**
2021–22 *PAOK* 34 7 **88 21**

AMEOBI, Sammy (F) 265 22
H: 6 3 W: 10 04 b.Newcastle upon Tyne 1-5-92
Internationals: Nigeria U20. England U21.
2010–11 Newcastle U 1 0
2011–12 Newcastle U 10 0
2012–13 Newcastle U 8 0
2012–13 *Middlesbrough* 9 1
2013–14 Newcastle U 10 0
2014–15 Newcastle U 25 2
2015–16 Newcastle U 0 0
2015–16 *Cardiff C* 36 1 **36 1**
2016–17 Newcastle U 4 0 **58 2**
2016–17 *Bolton W* 20 2
2017–18 Bolton W 35 4
2018–19 Bolton W 30 4 **85 10**
2019–20 Nottingham F 45 5
2020–21 Nottingham F 32 3 **77 8**
2021–22 Middlesbrough 0 0 **9 1**

BALDE, Alberto (F) 0 0
H: 5 10 b.Madrid 21-3-02
Internationals: Northern Ireland U16. Dominican Republic Full caps.
From Portadown.
2020–21 Middlesbrough 0 0
2021–22 Middlesbrough 0 0

BAMBA, Souleymane (D) 382 22
H: 6 3 W: 14 02 b.Ivry-sur-Seine 13-1-85
Internationals: Ivory Coast Full caps.
2004–05 Paris Saint-Germain 1 0
2005–06 Paris Saint-Germain 0 0 **1 0**
2006–07 Dunfermline Ath 23 0
2007–08 Dunfermline Ath 15 0
2008–09 Dunfermline Ath 1 0 **39 0**
2008–09 Hibernian 29 0
2009–10 Hibernian 30 2
2010–11 Hibernian 16 2 **75 4**
2010–11 Leicester C 16 2
2011–12 Leicester C 36 1 **52 3**
2012–13 Trabzonspor 18 0
2013–14 Trabzonspor 9 0 **27 0**
2014–15 Palermo 1 0 **1 0**
2014–15 *Leeds U* 19 1
2015–16 Leeds U 30 4
2016–17 Leeds U 2 0 **51 5**
2016–17 Cardiff C 26 2
2017–18 Cardiff C 46 4
2018–19 Cardiff C 28 4
2019–20 Cardiff C 6 0
2020–21 Cardiff C 6 0 **112 10**
2021–22 Middlesbrough 24 0 **24 0**

BOLA, Marc (D) 142 4
H: 6 1 W: 12 04 b.Greenwich 9-12-97
2016–17 Arsenal 0 0
2016–17 *Notts Co* 13 0 **13 0**
2017–18 Arsenal 0 0
2017–18 *Bristol R* 18 0 **18 0**
2018–19 Blackpool 35 2
2019–20 Middlesbrough 7 0
2019–20 *Blackpool* 5 0 **40 2**
2020–21 Middlesbrough 41 1
2021–22 Middlesbrough 23 1 **71 2**

BOYD-MUNCE, Caolan (M) 8 0
b.Belfast 26-1-00
Internationals: Northern Ireland U16, U17, U19, U21.
From Glentoran.
2018–19 Birmingham C 0 0
2019–20 Birmingham C 6 0
2020–21 Birmingham C 1 0
2021–22 Birmingham C 0 0 **7 0**
2021–22 Middlesbrough 1 0 **1 0**

BRYNN, Solomon (G) 16 0
2019–20 Middlesbrough 0 0
2020–21 Middlesbrough 0 0
2021–22 Middlesbrough 0 0
2021–22 *Queen of the South* 16 0 **16 0**

BURRELL, Rumarn (F) 25 0
b.Birmingham 16-12-00
2018–19 Grimsby T 4 0 **4 0**
2019–20 Middlesbrough 0 0
2020–21 Middlesbrough 0 0
2020–21 *Bradford C* 2 0 **2 0**
2021–22 Middlesbrough 0 0
2021–22 *Kilmarnock* 19 0 **19 0**

COBURN, Josh (F) 22 5
H: 6 3 b.Bedale 6-12-02
2020–21 Middlesbrough 4 1
2021–22 Middlesbrough 18 4 **22 5**

COULSON, Hayden (D) 78 1
H: 5 8 W: 11 00 b.Gateshead 17-6-98
Internationals: England U16, U17, U18, U19.
2018–19 Middlesbrough 0 0
2018–19 *St Mirren* 6 0 **6 0**
2018–19 *Cambridge U* 14 0 **14 0**
2019–20 Middlesbrough 29 1
2020–21 Middlesbrough 17 0
2021–22 Middlesbrough 0 0 **46 1**
2021–22 *Ipswich T* 6 0 **6 0**
2021–22 *Peterborough U* 6 0 **6 0**

CROOKS, Matt (M) 246 46
H: 6 0 W: 11 05 b.Leeds 20-1-94
2011–12 Huddersfield T 0 0
2012–13 Huddersfield T 0 0
2013–14 Huddersfield T 0 0
2014–15 Huddersfield T 1 0 **1 0**
2014–15 *Hartlepool U* 3 0 **3 0**
2014–15 Accrington S 16 0
2015–16 Accrington S 32 6 **48 6**
2016–17 Rangers 2 0 **2 0**
2016–17 *Scunthorpe U* 12 3 **12 3**
2017–18 Northampton T 30 4
2018–19 Northampton T 21 5 **51 9**
2018–19 Rotherham U 16 3
2019–20 Rotherham U 33 9
2020–21 Rotherham U 40 6
2021–22 Rotherham U 0 0 **89 18**
2021–22 Middlesbrough 40 10 **40 10**

DANIELS, Luke (G) 227 0
H: 6 5 W: 14 02 b.Bolton 5-1-88
Internationals: England U18, U19.
2006–07 WBA 0 0
2007–08 *Motherwell* 2 0 **2 0**
2007–08 WBA 0 0
2008–09 WBA 0 0
2008–09 *Shrewsbury T* 38 0 **38 0**
2009–10 WBA 0 0
2009–10 *Tranmere R* 37 0 **37 0**
2010–11 WBA 0 0
2010–11 *Charlton Ath* 0 0
2010–11 *Rochdale* 1 0 **1 0**
2010–11 *Bristol R* 9 0 **9 0**
2011–12 WBA 0 0
2011–12 *Southend U* 9 0 **9 0**
2012–13 WBA 0 0
2013–14 WBA 1 0
2014–15 WBA 0 0 **1 0**
2014–15 Scunthorpe U 23 0
2015–16 Scunthorpe U 39 0
2016–17 Scunthorpe U 39 0 **101 0**
2016–17 Brentford 0 0
2017–18 Brentford 1 0
2018–19 Brentford 12 0
2019–20 Brentford 0 0
2020–21 Brentford 4 0
2021–22 Brentford 0 0 **17 0**
2021–22 Middlesbrough 12 0 **12 0**

DIJKSTEEL, Anfernee (D) 120 1
H: 6 0 W: 11 05 b.Amsterdam 27-10-96
Internationals: Netherlands U20.
2016–17 Charlton Ath 0 0
2017–18 Charlton Ath 10 0
2018–19 Charlton Ath 30 1
2019–20 Charlton Ath 1 0 **41 1**
2019–20 Middlesbrough 16 0
2020–21 Middlesbrough 29 0
2021–22 Middlesbrough 34 0 **79 0**

DODDS, Daniel (D) 0 0
b. 17-1-01
2020–21 Middlesbrough 0 0
2021–22 Middlesbrough 0 0

FISHER, Darnell (M) 197 2
H: 5 9 W: 11 00 b.Reading 1-5-94
2012–13 Celtic 0 0
2013–14 Celtic 12 0
2014–15 Celtic 5 0
2015–16 Celtic 0 0 **17 0**
2015–16 *St Johnstone* 23 1 **23 1**
2016–17 Rotherham U 34 0 **34 0**
2017–18 Preston NE 34 0
2018–19 Preston NE 35 0
2019–20 Preston NE 28 0
2020–21 Preston NE 14 1 **111 1**
2020–21 Middlesbrough 12 0
2021–22 Middlesbrough 0 0 **12 0**

FLETCHER, Isaac (M) 14 1
H: 6 4 b. 1-6-02
2020–21 Middlesbrough 0 0
2021–22 Middlesbrough 0 0
2021–22 *Hartlepool U* 14 1 **14 1**

FOLARIN, Sam (M) 9 0
b. 23-9-00
From Tooting & Mitcham U.
2020–21 Middlesbrough 2 0
2021–22 Middlesbrough 0 0 **2 0**
2021–22 *Queen of the South* 7 0 **7 0**

FRY, Dael (D) 165 2
H: 6 4 W: 11 05 b.Middlesbrough 30-8-97
Internationals: England U17, U18, U19, U20, U21.
2015–16 Middlesbrough 7 0
2016–17 Middlesbrough 0 0
2016–17 *Rotherham U* 10 0 **10 0**
2017–18 Middlesbrough 13 0
2018–19 Middlesbrough 34 0
2019–20 Middlesbrough 36 0
2020–21 Middlesbrough 32 1
2021–22 Middlesbrough 33 1 **155 2**

GIBSON, Joseph (M) 0 0
b.Bishop Auckland 6-9-01
2020–21 Middlesbrough 0 0
2021–22 Middlesbrough 0 0

GREEN, Harry (F) 0 0
b.Stockton-on-Tees 24-9-01
2020–21 Middlesbrough 0 0
2021–22 Middlesbrough 0 0

HACKNEY, Hayden (M) 29 0
H: 5 10 W: 11 00 b.Redcar 26-6-02
2019–20 Middlesbrough 0 0
2020–21 Middlesbrough 1 0
2021–22 Middlesbrough 0 0 **1 0**
2021–22 *Scunthorpe U* 28 0 **28 0**

HALL, Grant (D) 193 9
H: 5 9 W: 11 03 b.Brighton 29-10-91
From Lewes.
2009–10 Brighton & HA 0 0
2010–11 Brighton & HA 0 0
2011–12 Brighton & HA 1 0 **1 0**
2012–13 Tottenham H 0 0
2013–14 Tottenham H 0 0
2013–14 *Swindon T* 27 0 **27 0**
2014–15 Tottenham H 0 0
2014–15 *Birmingham C* 7 0 **7 0**
2014–15 *Blackpool* 12 1 **12 1**
2015–16 QPR 39 1
2016–17 QPR 34 0

2017–18	QPR	4	0		
2018–19	QPR	12	0		
2019–20	QPR	30	5	**119**	**6**
2020–21	Middlesbrough	19	2		
2021–22	Middlesbrough	8	0	**27**	**2**

HANNAH, Jack (D) 0 0
H: 6 2 b.Stockton-on-Tees 25-12-02

2020–21	Middlesbrough	0	0		
2021–22	Middlesbrough	0	0		

HEMMING, Zachary (G) 36 0
b.Bishop Auckland 7-3-00

2020–21	Middlesbrough	0	0		
2021–22	Middlesbrough	0	0		
2021–22	*Kilmarnock*	36	0	**36**	**0**

HOWSON, Jonathan (M) 577 51
H: 5 11 W: 12 01 b.Morley 21-5-88
Internationals: England U21.

2006–07	Leeds U	9	1		
2007–08	Leeds U	26	3		
2008–09	Leeds U	40	4		
2009–10	Leeds U	45	4		
2010–11	Leeds U	46	10		
2011–12	Leeds U	19	1	**185**	**23**
2011–12	Norwich C	11	1		
2012–13	Norwich C	30	2		
2013–14	Norwich C	27	2		
2014–15	Norwich C	34	8		
2015–16	Norwich C	36	3		
2016–17	Norwich C	38	6	**176**	**22**
2017–18	Middlesbrough	43	3		
2018–19	Middlesbrough	46	1		
2019–20	Middlesbrough	41	0		
2020–21	Middlesbrough	41	1		
2021–22	Middlesbrough	45	1	**216**	**6**

IKPEAZU, Uche (F) 245 46
H: 6 3 W: 12 04 b.Harrow 28-2-95

2011–12	Reading	0	0		
2012–13	Reading	0	0		
2013–14	Watford	0	0		
2013–14	*Crewe Alex*	15	4		
2014–15	Watford	0	0		
2014–15	*Crewe Alex*	17	2	**32**	**6**
2014–15	*Doncaster R*	7	0	**7**	**0**
2015–16	Watford	0	0		
2015–16	*Port Vale*	21	5	**21**	**5**
2015–16	*Blackpool*	12	0	**12**	**0**
2016–17	Cambridge U	29	6		
2017–18	Cambridge U	40	13	**69**	**19**
2018–19	Hearts	17	3		
2019–20	Hearts	23	2	**40**	**5**
2020–21	Wycombe W	31	6		
2021–22	Wycombe W	0	0	**31**	**6**
2021–22	Middlesbrough	20	2	**20**	**2**
2021–22	*Cardiff C*	13	3	**13**	**3**

JAMES, Bradley (G) 0 0
b. 5-7-99

2020–21	Middlesbrough	0	0		
2021–22	Middlesbrough	0	0		

JONES, Isaiah (M) 53 2
H: 5 11 W: 10 10 b.Lambeth 26-6-99
From Tooting & Mitcham U.

2019–20	Middlesbrough	0	0		
2019–20	*St Johnstone*	0	0		
2020–21	Middlesbrough	0	0		
2020–21	*Queen of the South*	11	1	**11**	**1**
2021–22	Middlesbrough	42	1	**42**	**1**

KAVANAGH, Calum (F) 12 1
H: 6 0 b.Cardiff 5-9-03
Internationals: Republic of Ireland U17.

2020–21	Middlesbrough	0	0		
2021–22	Middlesbrough	0	0		
2021–22	*Harrogate T*	12	1	**12**	**1**

LEA SILIKI, James (M) 95 3
H: 6 0 W: 11 00 b.Sarcelles 12-6-96
Internationals: France U19. Cameroon Full caps.
From Paris Saint-Germain.

2013–14	Guingamp	0	0		
2014–15	Rennes	0	0		
2015–16	Rennes	0	0		
2016–17	Rennes	1	0		
2017–18	Rennes	32	3		
2018–19	Rennes	24	0		
2019–20	Rennes	20	0		
2020–21	Rennes	7	0		
2021–22	Rennes	0	0	**84**	**3**
2021–22	*Middlesbrough*	11	0	**11**	**0**

LUMLEY, Joe (G) 162 0
H: 6 3 W: 11 07 b.Harlow 15-2-95

2013–14	QPR	0	0		
2014–15	QPR	0	0		
2014–15	*Accrington S*	5	0	**5**	**0**
2014–15	*Morecambe*	0	0		
2015–16	QPR	1	0		
2015–16	*Stevenage*	0	0		
2016–17	QPR	0	0		
2016–17	*Bristol R*	19	0	**19**	**0**
2017–18	QPR	2	0		
2017–18	*Blackpool*	17	0	**17**	**0**
2018–19	QPR	42	0		
2019–20	QPR	27	0		
2020–21	QPR	5	0	**77**	**0**
2020–21	*Gillingham*	2	0	**2**	**0**
2020–21	*Doncaster R*	8	0	**8**	**0**
2021–22	Middlesbrough	34	0	**34**	**0**

MALLEY, Connor (M) 11 1
H: 6 1 W: 10 03 b.Newcastle upon Tyne 20-3-00

2018–19	Middlesbrough	0	0		
2019–20	Middlesbrough	0	0		
2019–20	*Ayr U*	5	1	**5**	**1**
2020–21	Middlesbrough	3	0		
2020–21	*Carlisle U*	3	0	**3**	**0**
2021–22	Middlesbrough	0	0	**3**	**0**

McGREE, Riley (M) 118 28
H: 5 10 W: 11 05 b.Gawler 2-11-98
Internationals: Australia U17, U23, Full caps.

2015–16	Adelaide U	1	0		
2016–17	Adelaide U	16	1		
2017–18	Club Brugge	0	0		
2017–18	*Newcastle Jets*	12	5	**12**	**5**
2018–19	Club Brugge	0	0		
2018–19	*Melbourne C*	27	7	**27**	**7**
2019–20	Adelaide U	23	10	**40**	**11**
2020–21	Charlotte	0	0		
2020–21	*Birmingham C*	15	1		
2021–22	Charlotte	0	0		
2021–22	*Birmingham C*	13	2	**28**	**3**
2021–22	Middlesbrough	11	2	**11**	**2**

McNAIR, Paddy (D) 194 18
H: 6 0 W: 11 05 b.Ballyclare 27-4-95
Internationals: Northern Ireland U16, U17, U19, U21, Full caps.

2011–12	Manchester U	0	0		
2012–13	Manchester U	0	0		
2013–14	Manchester U	0	0		
2014–15	Manchester U	16	0		
2015–16	Manchester U	8	0	**24**	**0**
2016–17	Sunderland	9	0		
2017–18	Sunderland	16	5	**25**	**5**
2018–19	Middlesbrough	16	0		
2019–20	Middlesbrough	41	6		
2020–21	Middlesbrough	46	2		
2021–22	Middlesbrough	42	5	**145**	**13**

OLUSANYA, Toyosi (F) 4 1
H: 5 9 W: 10 10 b.Lambeth 1-2-98

2015–16	AFC Wimbledon	1	1		
2016–17	AFC Wimbledon	0	0	**1**	**1**

From Walton Casuals, Fleet T, Gosport Bor, Cheshunt, Billericay T.

2021–22	Middlesbrough	3	0	**3**	**0**

PAYERO, Martin (M) 66 3
H: 6 2 W: 12 11 b.Pascanas 11-9-98
Internationals: Argentina U23.

2017–18	Banfield	4	0		
2018–19	Banfield	10	0		
2019–20	Banfield	1	0		
2019–20	*Talleres*	16	1	**16**	**1**
2020–21	Banfield	12	1		
2021–22	Banfield	10	0	**37**	**1**
2021–22	Middlesbrough	13	1	**13**	**1**

PELTIER, Lee (D) 464 5
H: 5 10 W: 11 07 b.Liverpool 11-12-86
Internationals: England U18.

2004–05	Liverpool	0	0		
2005–06	Liverpool	0	0		
2006–07	Liverpool	0	0		
2006–07	*Hull C*	7	0	**7**	**0**
2007–08	Liverpool	0	0		
2007–08	Yeovil T	34	0		
2008–09	Yeovil T	35	1	**69**	**1**
2009–10	Huddersfield T	42	0		
2010–11	Huddersfield T	38	1		
2011–12	Leicester C	40	2		
2012–13	Leicester C	0	0	**40**	**2**
2012–13	Leeds U	41	0		
2013–14	Leeds U	25	1	**66**	**1**
2013–14	*Nottingham F*	7	0	**7**	**0**
2014–15	Huddersfield T	11	0	**91**	**1**
2014–15	Cardiff C	15	0		
2015–16	Cardiff C	41	0		
2016–17	Cardiff C	28	0		
2017–18	Cardiff C	30	0		
2018–19	Cardiff C	20	0		
2019–20	Cardiff C	25	0	**159**	**0**
2019–20	WBA	0	0		
2020–21	WBA	4	0	**4**	**0**
2021–22	Middlesbrough	21	0	**21**	**0**

RIDLEY, Joseph (F) 0 0
b. 12-3-03
Internationals: England U16.

2020–21	Middlesbrough	0	0		
2021–22	Middlesbrough	0	0		

ROBINSON, Jack (D) 1 0
b. 21-6-01

2020–21	Middlesbrough	1	0		
2021–22	Middlesbrough	0	0	**1**	**0**

SPENCE, Djed (D) 102 4
H: 6 0 W: 11 03 b.London 9-8-00
Internationals: England U21.
From Fulham.

2018–19	Middlesbrough	0	0		
2019–20	Middlesbrough	22	1		
2020–21	Middlesbrough	38	1		
2021–22	Middlesbrough	3	0	**63**	**2**
2021–22	*Nottingham F*	39	2	**39**	**2**

SPORAR, Andraz (F) 277 123
H: 5 11 W: 11 09 b.Ljubljana 27-2-94
Internationals: Slovenia U19, U20, U21, Full caps.

2011–12	Interblock	21	10	**21**	**10**
2012–13	Olimpija Ljubljana	28	11		
2013–14	Olimpija Ljubljana	17	5		
2014–15	Olimpija Ljubljana	32	13		
2015–16	Olimpija Ljubljana	18	17	**95**	**46**
2015–16	Basel	1	0		
2016–17	Basel	18	1		
2017–18	Basel	0	0	**19**	**1**
2017–18	*Arminia Bielefeld*	9	2	**9**	**2**
2017–18	Slovan Bratislava	12	3		
2018–19	Slovan Bratislava	30	29		
2019–20	Slovan Bratislava	11	12	**53**	**44**
2019–20	Sporting Lisbon	16	6		
2020–21	Sporting Lisbon	13	3		
2020–21	*Braga*	16	3	**16**	**3**
2021–22	Sporting Lisbon	0	0	**29**	**9**
2021–22	*Middlesbrough*	35	8	**35**	**8**

STOJANOVIC, Dejan (G) 141 0
H: 6 5 W: 14 00 b.Feldkirch 19-7-93
Internationals: Macedonia U21.

2009–10	Lustenau	1	0		
2010–11	Lustenau	23	0	**24**	**0**
2011–12	Bologna	0	0		
2012–13	Bologna	4	0		
2013–14	Bologna	1	0		
2014–15	Bologna	5	0		
2014–15	*Crotone*	2	0	**2**	**0**
2015–16	Bologna	0	0	**10**	**0**
2016–17	St Gallen	4	0		
2017–18	St Gallen	13	0		
2018–19	St Gallen	34	0		
2019–20	St Gallen	18	0	**69**	**0**
2019–20	Middlesbrough	8	0		
2020–21	Middlesbrough	0	0		
2020–21	*St Pauli*	19	0	**19**	**0**
2021–22	Middlesbrough	0	0	**8**	**0**
2021–22	*Ingolstadt*	9	0	**9**	**0**

SYKES, Cain (D) 0 0
b.Sunderland 14-8-02

2020–21	Middlesbrough	0	0		
2021–22	Middlesbrough	0	0		

TAVERNIER, Marcus (M) 142 15
H: 5 10 W: 11 00 b.Leeds 22-3-99
Internationals: England U19, U20.

2017–18	Middlesbrough	5	1		
2017–18	*Milton Keynes D*	7	0	**7**	**0**
2018–19	Middlesbrough	20	3		
2019–20	Middlesbrough	37	3		
2020–21	Middlesbrough	29	3		
2021–22	Middlesbrough	44	5	**135**	**15**

TAYLOR, Neil (D) 289 0
H: 5 9 W: 11 11 b.St Asaph 7-2-89
Internationals: Wales U17, U19, U21, C, Full caps. Great Britain.

2007–08	Wrexham	26	0	**26**	**0**

From Wrexham.

2010–11	Swansea C	29	0		
2011–12	Swansea C	36	0		
2012–13	Swansea C	6	0		
2013–14	Swansea C	10	0		
2014–15	Swansea C	34	0		
2015–16	Swansea C	34	0		
2016–17	Swansea C	11	0	**160**	**0**
2016–17	Aston Villa	14	0		
2017–18	Aston Villa	29	0		
2018–19	Aston Villa	31	0		
2019–20	Aston Villa	14	0		
2020–21	Aston Villa	1	0	**89**	**0**
2021–22	Middlesbrough	14	0	**14**	**0**

WALKER, Stephen (F) 43 4
H: 5 11 b.Middlesbrough 11-10-00
Internationals: England U17, U18, U19.

2018–19	Middlesbrough	0	0		
2018–19	*Milton Keynes D*	7	0		
2019–20	Middlesbrough	7	0		
2019–20	*Crewe Alex*	6	1		
2020–21	Middlesbrough	0	0		
2020–21	*Milton Keynes D*	12	2	**19**	**2**
2020–21	*Crewe Alex*	11	1	**17**	**2**
2021–22	Middlesbrough	0	0	**7**	**0**
2021–22	*Tranmere R*	0	0		

WATMORE, Duncan (F) 151 22
H: 5 9 W: 11 05 b.Cheadle Hulme 8-3-94
Internationals: England U20, U21.
From Altrincham.

2013–14	Sunderland	0	0		
2013–14	*Hibernian*	9	1	**9**	**1**
2014–15	Sunderland	0	0		

2015–16 Sunderland 23 3
2016–17 Sunderland 14 0
2017–18 Sunderland 6 0
2018–19 Sunderland 11 1
2019–20 Sunderland 17 1 **71 5**
2020–21 Middlesbrough 30 9
2021–22 Middlesbrough 41 7 **71 16**

WOOD-GORDON, Nathan (D) 17 0
H: 6 2 W: 11 05 b.Middlesbrough 31-5-02
Internationals: England U16, U17, U18, U20.
From Stockton T.
2018–19 Middlesbrough 0 0
2019–20 Middlesbrough 1 0
2020–21 Middlesbrough 4 0
2020–21 *Crewe Alex* 12 0 **12 0**
2021–22 Middlesbrough 0 0 **5 0**
2021–22 *Hibernian* 0 0

Players retained or with offer of contract
Akono Bilongo, Bryant; Cornet, Isiah; Dijksteel, Malik; Gitau, George; Metcalfe, Max; Sivi, Jeremy; Stott, Jack; Wells, Joshua.

Scholars
Beals, Ben Alan; Bridge, Aidan James; Bulmer, Jacob Martin; Collins, Sam Robert; Costello, James Dean; Doherty, Alfie John; Evans, Louie James; Finch, Sonny; Fisher, Nathan Joseph; Howe, Lucas Oliver; Howells, Max Isaak; Hutchinson, Alex Lee; John, Fenton Lorimer; MacCarthy, Bandile Ashley James; Makiesse Lindo, Afonso Mozinho; Marshall, Joshua Rae; McCormick, George Mark; Popple, Henry James; Simpson, Nathan Taylor; Swan, Oliver Jay; Traore, Yacou Jack; Wallace-Ming, Tylah Sanchez; Whelan, Frankie Kevin; Willis, Pharrell Jeremiah Kieran; Woolston, Luke James.

MILLWALL (53)

BENNETT, Mason (F) 181 18
H: 5 10 W: 10 01 b.Shirebrook 15-7-96
Internationals: England U16, U17, U19.
2011–12 Derby Co 9 0
2012–13 Derby Co 6 0
2013–14 Derby Co 13 1
2013–14 *Chesterfield* 5 0 **5 0**
2014–15 Derby Co 2 0
2014–15 *Bradford C* 11 1 **11 1**
2015–16 Derby Co 0 0
2015–16 *Burton Alb* 16 1 **16 1**
2016–17 Derby Co 2 0
2017–18 Derby Co 3 0
2017–18 *Notts Co* 2 1 **2 1**
2018–19 Derby Co 30 3
2019–20 Derby Co 7 0 **72 4**
2019–20 *Millwall* 9 2
2020–21 Millwall 37 6
2021–22 Millwall 29 3 **75 11**

BIALKOWSKI, Bartosz (G) 421 0
H: 6 3 W: 13 08 b.Braniewo 6-7-87
Internationals: Poland U20, U21, Full caps.
2004–05 Gornik Zabrze 7 0 **7 0**
2005–06 Southampton 5 0
2006–07 Southampton 8 0
2007–08 Southampton 1 0
2008–09 Southampton 0 0
2009–10 Southampton 7 0
2009–10 *Barnsley* 2 0 **2 0**
2010–11 Southampton 0 0
2011–12 Southampton 1 0 **22 0**
2012–13 Notts Co 40 0
2013–14 Notts Co 44 0 **84 0**
2014–15 Ipswich T 31 0
2015–16 Ipswich T 20 0
2016–17 Ipswich T 44 0
2017–18 Ipswich T 45 0
2018–19 Ipswich T 28 0 **168 0**
2019–20 Millwall 46 0
2020–21 Millwall 46 0
2021–22 Millwall 46 0 **138 0**

BRADSHAW, Tom (F) 352 90
H: 5 10 W: 11 03 b.Shrewsbury 27-7-92
Internationals: Wales U19, U21, Full caps.
From Aberystwyth T.
2009–10 Shrewsbury T 6 3
2010–11 Shrewsbury T 26 6
2011–12 Shrewsbury T 8 1
2012–13 Shrewsbury T 21 0
2013–14 Shrewsbury T 28 7 **89 17**
2014–15 Walsall 29 17
2015–16 Walsall 41 17 **70 34**
2016–17 Barnsley 42 8
2017–18 Barnsley 39 9
2018–19 Barnsley 4 1 **85 18**
2018–19 *Millwall* 10 0
2019–20 Millwall 45 8
2020–21 Millwall 29 4
2021–22 Millwall 24 9 **108 21**

BUREY, Tyler (M) 39 5
b.Hillingdon 9-1-01
2018–19 AFC Wimbledon 3 0 **3 0**
2019–20 Millwall 1 0
2020–21 Millwall 13 0
2021–22 Millwall 15 2 **29 2**
2021–22 *Hartlepool U* 7 3 **7 3**

COOPER, Jake (D) 271 24
H: 6 4 W: 13 05 b.Bracknell 3-2-95
Internationals: England U18, U19, U20.
2013–14 Reading 0 0
2014–15 Reading 15 2
2015–16 Reading 24 2
2016–17 Reading 3 0 **42 4**
2016–17 *Millwall* 15 2
2017–18 Millwall 38 4
2018–19 Millwall 46 6
2019–20 Millwall 46 3
2020–21 Millwall 42 1
2021–22 Millwall 42 4 **229 20**

DAVIS, Jayden (M) 0 0
b. 19-11-01
2020–21 Millwall 0 0
2021–22 Millwall 0 0

EVANS, George (M) 186 10
H: 6 0 W: 12 00 b.Cheadle 13-12-94
Internationals: England U16, U17, U19.
2012–13 Manchester C 0 0
2013–14 Manchester C 0 0
2013–14 *Crewe Alex* 23 1 **23 1**
2014–15 Manchester C 0 0
2014–15 *Scunthorpe U* 16 1 **16 1**
2015–16 Manchester C 0 0
2015–16 *Walsall* 12 3 **12 3**
2015–16 Reading 6 0
2016–17 Reading 35 2
2017–18 Reading 18 1 **59 3**
2018–19 Derby Co 11 0
2019–20 Derby Co 17 0
2020–21 Derby Co 6 0 **34 0**
2020–21 Millwall 19 1
2021–22 Millwall 23 1 **42 2**

HUTCHINSON, Shaun (D) 347 21
H: 6 1 W: 12 04 b.Newcastle upon Tyne 23-11-90
2008–09 Motherwell 1 0
2009–10 Motherwell 5 3
2010–11 Motherwell 19 1
2011–12 Motherwell 30 1
2012–13 Motherwell 31 1
2013–14 Motherwell 35 1 **121 7**
2014–15 Fulham 25 2
2015–16 Fulham 9 0 **34 2**
2016–17 Millwall 16 2
2017–18 Millwall 46 2
2018–19 Millwall 26 1
2019–20 Millwall 36 6
2020–21 Millwall 39 1
2021–22 Millwall 29 0 **192 12**

KIEFTENBELD, Maikel (M) 423 10
H: 5 10 W: 11 11 b.Lemelerveld 26-6-90
Internationals: Netherlands U21.
2008–09 Go Ahead Eagles 30 1
2009–10 Go Ahead Eagles 33 2 **63 3**
2010–11 Groningen 33 0
2011–12 Groningen 26 1
2012–13 Groningen 29 1
2013–14 Groningen 31 0
2014–15 Groningen 33 0 **152 2**
2015–16 Birmingham C 42 3
2016–17 Birmingham C 39 1
2017–18 Birmingham C 35 0
2018–19 Birmingham C 36 1
2019–20 Birmingham C 8 0
2020–21 Birmingham C 10 0 **170 5**
2020–21 Millwall 11 0
2021–22 Millwall 27 0 **38 0**

LEONARD, Ryan (D) 344 24
H: 5 9 W: 12 13 b.Plympton 24-5-92
2009–10 Plymouth Arg 1 0
2010–11 Plymouth Arg 0 0 **1 0**
2011–12 Southend U 17 1
2012–13 Southend U 22 2
2013–14 Southend U 43 5
2014–15 Southend U 41 3
2015–16 Southend U 37 2
2016–17 Southend U 43 3
2017–18 Southend U 25 4 **228 20**
2017–18 Sheffield U 13 0
2018–19 Sheffield U 3 0 **16 0**
2018–19 Millwall 37 2
2019–20 Millwall 17 1
2020–21 Millwall 26 1
2021–22 Millwall 19 0 **99 4**

LONG, George (G) 225 0
H: 6 4 W: 14 11 b.Sheffield 5-11-93
Internationals: England U18, U20.
2010–11 Sheffield U 1 0
2011–12 Sheffield U 2 0
2012–13 Sheffield U 36 0
2013–14 Sheffield U 27 0
2014–15 Sheffield U 0 0
2014–15 *Oxford U* 10 0 **10 0**
2014–15 *Motherwell* 13 0 **13 0**
2015–16 Sheffield U 31 0
2016–17 Sheffield U 3 0
2017–18 Sheffield U 0 0 **100 0**
2017–18 *AFC Wimbledon* 45 0 **45 0**
2018–19 Hull C 4 0
2019–20 Hull C 45 0
2020–21 Hull C 8 0 **57 0**
2021–22 Millwall 0 0

LOVELACE, Zak (F) 5 0
b.Wandsworth 23-1-06
2021–22 Millwall 5 0 **5 0**

MAHONEY, Connor (M) 118 5
H: 5 9 W: 10 08 b.Blackburn 12-2-97
Internationals: England U17, U18, U20.
2013–14 Accrington S 4 0 **4 0**
2013–14 Blackburn R 0 0
2014–15 Blackburn R 0 0
2015–16 Blackburn R 2 0
2016–17 Blackburn R 14 0 **16 0**
2017–18 Bournemouth 0 0
2017–18 *Barnsley* 8 0 **8 0**
2018–19 Bournemouth 0 0
2018–19 *Birmingham C* 30 2 **30 2**
2019–20 Millwall 38 2
2020–21 Millwall 14 1
2021–22 Millwall 8 0 **60 3**

MALONE, Scott (D) 383 30
H: 6 2 W: 11 11 b.Rowley Regis 25-3-91
Internationals: England U19.
2008–09 Wolverhampton W 0 0
2008–09 *Ujpest* 7 1 **7 1**
2009–10 Wolverhampton W 0 0
2009–10 *Southend U* 17 0 **17 0**
2010–11 Wolverhampton W 0 0
2010–11 *Burton Alb* 22 1 **22 1**
2011–12 Wolverhampton W 0 0
2011–12 Bournemouth 32 5 **32 5**
2012–13 Millwall 15 1
2013–14 Millwall 33 3
2014–15 Millwall 20 1
2014–15 Cardiff C 13 0
2015–16 Cardiff C 41 2 **54 2**
2016–17 Fulham 36 6 **36 6**
2017–18 Huddersfield T 22 0 **22 0**
2018–19 Derby Co 27 2
2019–20 Derby Co 18 1
2020–21 Derby Co 0 0 **45 3**
2020–21 *Millwall* 41 5
2021–22 Millwall 39 2 **148 12**

McNAMARA, Danny (D) 96 3
H: 5 9 W: 11 05 b.Sidcup 27-12-98
Internationals: Republic of Ireland U21.
2018–19 Millwall 0 0
2019–20 Millwall 0 0
2019–20 Millwall 0 0
2019–20 *Newport Co* 21 0 **21 0**
2020–21 Millwall 16 0
2020–21 *St Johnstone* 22 1 **22 1**
2021–22 Millwall 37 2 **53 2**

MITCHELL, Alex (D) 26 0
H: 6 3 b. 7-10-01
2020–21 Millwall 0 0
2021–22 Millwall 0 0
2021–22 *Leyton Orient* 26 0 **26 0**

MITCHELL, Billy (M) 66 1
H: 5 10 W: 11 11 b.Orpington 7-4-01
2018–19 Millwall 1 0
2019–20 Millwall 7 0
2020–21 Millwall 16 1
2021–22 Millwall 42 0 **66 1**

MOSS, Dan (D) 4 0
b. 4-11-00
2020–21 Millwall 0 0
2021–22 Millwall 0 0
2021–22 *Leyton Orient* 4 0 **4 0**

MULLER, Hayden (D) 3 0
H: 6 4 b.Croydon 7-2-02
2019–20 Millwall 1 0
2020–21 Millwall 2 0
2021–22 Millwall 0 0 **3 0**
2021–22 *St Johnstone* 0 0

O'BRIEN, Sean (F) 0 0
H: 5 11 b. 13-10-01
From QPR.
2020–21 Millwall 0 0
2021–22 Millwall 0 0

OLAOFE, Isaac (F) 29 8
H: 5 10 W: 12 13 b.Lewisham 21-11-99
2019–20 Millwall 0 0
2020–21 Millwall 0 0
2020–21 *St Johnstone* 2 0 **2 0**
2021–22 Millwall 0 0
2021–22 *Sutton U* 27 8 **27 8**

PEARCE, Alex (D) 383 20
H: 6 2 W: 13 05 b.Wallingford 9-11-88
Internationals: Scotland U19, U21, Full caps.
2006–07 Reading 0 0
2006–07 *Northampton T* 15 1 **15 1**
2007–08 Reading 0 0
2007–08 *Bournemouth* 11 0 **11 0**
2007–08 *Norwich C* 11 0 **11 0**
2008–09 Reading 16 1
2008–09 *Southampton* 9 2 **9 2**
2009–10 Reading 25 4
2010–11 Reading 21 1
2011–12 Reading 46 5
2012–13 Reading 19 0
2013–14 Reading 45 3
2014–15 Reading 40 0 **212 14**
2015–16 Derby Co 0 0
2015–16 *Bristol C* 7 0 **7 0**
2016–17 Derby Co 40 2
2017–18 Derby Co 7 1
2018–19 Derby Co 1 0 **48 3**
2018–19 *Millwall* 11 0
2019–20 Millwall 29 0
2020–21 Millwall 24 0
2021–22 Millwall 6 0 **70 0**

ROMEO, Mahlon (M) 234 3
H: 5 10 W: 11 07 b.Westminster 19-9-95
Internationals: Antigua and Barbuda Full caps.
2012–13 Gillingham 1 0
2013–14 Gillingham 0 0
2014–15 Gillingham 0 0 **1 0**
2015–16 Millwall 18 1
2016–17 Millwall 32 0
2017–18 Millwall 27 1
2018–19 Millwall 41 0
2019–20 Millwall 43 0
2020–21 Millwall 35 1
2021–22 Millwall 2 0 **198 3**
2021–22 *Portsmouth* 35 0 **35 0**

SANDFORD, Ryan (G) 0 0
b. 21-2-99
Internationals: England U16, U17, U18.
2019–20 Millwall 0 0
2020–21 Millwall 0 0
2021–22 Millwall 0 0

SAVILLE, George (M) 310 33
H: 5 9 W: 11 07 b.Camberley 1-6-93
Internationals: Northern Ireland Full caps.
2010–11 Chelsea 0 0
2011–12 Chelsea 0 0
2012–13 Chelsea 0 0
2012–13 *Millwall* 3 0
2013–14 Chelsea 0 0
2013–14 *Brentford* 40 3 **40 3**
2014–15 Wolverhampton W 7 0
2014–15 *Bristol C* 7 1 **7 1**
2015–16 Wolverhampton W 19 5
2015–16 *Millwall* 12 0
2016–17 Wolverhampton W 24 1 **50 6**
2017–18 Millwall 44 10
2018–19 Millwall 4 0
2018–19 *Middlesbrough* 34 4
2019–20 Middlesbrough 37 1
2020–21 Middlesbrough 42 6
2021–22 Middlesbrough 0 0 **113 11**
2021–22 Millwall 37 2 **100 12**

TIENSIA, Junior (D) 0 0
2019–20 Millwall 0 0
2020–21 Millwall 0 0
2021–22 Millwall 0 0

WALLACE, Jed (M) 367 69
H: 5 10 W: 10 12 b.Reading 15-12-93
Internationals: England U19.
2011–12 Portsmouth 0 0
2012–13 Portsmouth 22 6
2013–14 Portsmouth 44 7
2014–15 Portsmouth 44 14 **110 27**
2015–16 Wolverhampton W 9 0
2015–16 *Millwall* 12 1
2016–17 Wolverhampton W 9 0 **18 0**
2016–17 *Millwall* 16 3
2017–18 Millwall 43 6
2018–19 Millwall 42 5
2019–20 Millwall 43 10
2020–21 Millwall 45 11
2021–22 Millwall 38 6 **239 42**

WALLACE, Murray (D) 338 19
H: 6 2 W: 11 11 b.Glasgow 10-1-93
Internationals: Scotland U20, U21.
2010–11 Falkirk 0 0
2011–12 Falkirk 19 2
2011–12 Huddersfield T 0 0
2011–12 *Falkirk* 15 2 **34 4**
2012–13 Huddersfield T 6 1
2013–14 Huddersfield T 17 0
2014–15 Huddersfield T 26 2
2015–16 Huddersfield T 2 0 **51 3**
2015–16 *Scunthorpe U* 33 2
2016–17 Scunthorpe U 46 2
2017–18 Scunthorpe U 45 1 **124 5**
2018–19 Millwall 21 2
2019–20 Millwall 43 0
2020–21 Millwall 23 1
2021–22 Millwall 42 4 **129 7**

WRIGHT, Joe (G) 0 0
b. 10-4-01
2020–21 Millwall 0 0
2021–22 Millwall 0 0

Players retained or with offer of contract
Abdulmalik, Abdulsabur; Allen, Alfie-John; Boateng, Nana; Briscoe, Tyrese; Drozd, Sebastian; Gillmore, Jordan; Penney, Arthur; Topalloj, Besart.

Scholars
Adom-Malaki, Sashiel Nino Junior; Cheeseman, Ernie Dean; Clark Evans, George David; Coleman, Laquay Thierry; Cotton, Finley George; Dailly, Bobby Alistair Neil; Donaldson, Kallen Omar; Esse, Romain Joy Kouakou; Evans, Oliver Joseph; Hammond, Ryan Thomas; Hamouchene, Arezki; Hearn, Henry Roy; Hefzalla, Ramez Alaa Morsi Mohamed; Leahy, Tomas Raymond; Okoli, Chinwike Ebubechukwu; Smith, Kyle Ray; Walker, George Julian Robinson.

MILTON KEYNES D (54)

BALDWIN, Aden (D) 13 0
H: 6 0 W: 11 00 b.Gloucester 10-6-97
2018–19 Bristol C 0 0
2018–19 *Cheltenham T* 4 0 **4 0**
2019–20 Bristol C 0 0
2020–21 Bristol C 0 0
2021–22 Milton Keynes D 9 0 **9 0**

BIRD, Jay (F) 2 0
H: 6 1 W: 11 00 b.Hartlepool 13-9-00
2017–18 Milton Keynes D 0 0
2018–19 Milton Keynes D 0 0
2019–20 Milton Keynes D 0 0
2020–21 Milton Keynes D 2 0
2021–22 Milton Keynes D 0 0 **2 0**

BOATENG, Hiram (M) 190 6
H: 5 7 W: 11 00 b.Wandsworth 8-1-96
2012–13 Crystal Palace 0 0
2013–14 Crystal Palace 0 0
2013–14 *Crawley T* 1 0 **1 0**
2014–15 Crystal Palace 0 0
2015–16 Crystal Palace 1 0
2015–16 *Plymouth Arg* 24 1 **24 1**
2016–17 Crystal Palace 0 0 **1 0**
2016–17 *Bristol R* 9 0 **9 0**
2016–17 *Northampton T* 16 0 **16 0**
2017–18 Exeter C 38 1
2018–19 Exeter C 27 1 **65 2**
2019–20 Milton Keynes D 20 0
2020–21 Milton Keynes D 0 0
2020–21 *Cambridge U* 25 0 **25 0**
2021–22 Milton Keynes D 29 3 **49 3**

DARLING, Harry (D) 119 9
H: 5 11 W: 11 11 b.Cambridge 8-8-99
2016–17 Cambridge U 0 0
2017–18 Cambridge U 3 0
2018–19 Cambridge U 12 0
2019–20 Cambridge U 24 2
2020–21 Cambridge U 16 0 **55 2**
2020–21 Milton Keynes D 23 0
2021–22 Milton Keynes D 41 7 **64 7**

DAVIES, Jack (M) 1 0
b.Milton Keynes 3-12-02
2020–21 Milton Keynes D 1 0
2021–22 Milton Keynes D 0 0 **1 0**

EISA, Mohamed (F) 141 51
H: 6 0 W: 11 00 b.Khartoum 12-7-94
From Dartford, VCD Ath, Corinthian, Greenwich Bor.
2017–18 Cheltenham T 45 23 **45 23**
2018–19 Bristol C 5 0 **5 0**
2019–20 Peterborough U 29 14
2020–21 Peterborough U 27 2
2021–22 Peterborough U 0 0 **56 16**
2021–22 Milton Keynes D 35 12 **35 12**

FREEMAN, John (M) 4 0
H: 5 11 W: 10 08 b.Stevenage 4-11-01
2019–20 Milton Keynes D 0 0
2020–21 Milton Keynes D 4 0
2021–22 Milton Keynes D 0 0 **4 0**

HARVIE, Daniel (D) 170 8
H: 5 7 W: 9 11 b.Drumchapel 14-7-98
Internationals: Scotland U16, U17, U19, U21.
2015–16 Aberdeen 2 0
2016–17 Aberdeen 0 0
2016–17 *Dumbarton* 34 3 **34 3**
2017–18 Aberdeen 2 0 **4 0**
2018–19 Ayr U 33 0
2019–20 Ayr U 27 1 **60 1**
2020–21 Milton Keynes D 31 3
2021–22 Milton Keynes D 41 1 **72 4**

ILUNGA, Brooklyn (F) 2 0
b. 21-11-03
2020–21 Milton Keynes D 1 0
2021–22 Milton Keynes D 1 0 **2 0**

JOHNSON, Lewis (F) 4 0
b. 9-1-04
From Aston Villa.
2020–21 Milton Keynes D 4 0
2021–22 Milton Keynes D 0 0 **4 0**

JULES, Zak (D) 113 3
H: 6 3 W: 11 05 b.Islington 2-7-97
Internationals: Scotland U17, U18, U19, U20, U21.
2016–17 Reading 0 0
2016–17 *Motherwell* 10 1 **10 1**
2017–18 Shrewsbury T 0 0
2017–18 *Chesterfield* 6 0 **6 0**
2017–18 *Port Vale* 2 0 **2 0**
2018–19 Macclesfield T 14 0 **14 0**
2019–20 Walsall 17 0
2020–21 Walsall 17 1 **34 1**
2020–21 Milton Keynes D 20 1
2021–22 Milton Keynes D 7 0 **27 1**
2021–22 *Fleetwood T* 20 0 **20 0**

KASUMU, David (M) 69 1
H: 5 11 W: 11 00 b.Lambeth 5-10-99
2015–16 Milton Keynes D 0 0
2016–17 Milton Keynes D 0 0
2017–18 Milton Keynes D 1 0
2018–19 Milton Keynes D 0 0
2019–20 Milton Keynes D 21 1
2020–21 Milton Keynes D 24 0
2021–22 Milton Keynes D 23 0 **69 1**

KEMP, Daniel (M) 62 6
H: 5 3 W: 9 13 b.Sidcup 11-1-99
Internationals: England U19, U20.
From Chelsea.
2016–17 West Ham U 0 0
2017–18 West Ham U 0 0
2018–19 West Ham U 0 0
2019–20 West Ham U 0 0
2019–20 *Stevenage* 6 1 **6 1**
2020–21 West Ham U 0 0
2020–21 *Blackpool* 8 0 **8 0**
2020–21 Leyton Orient 24 5
2021–22 Leyton Orient 19 0 **43 5**
2021–22 Milton Keynes D 5 0 **5 0**

LEWINGTON, Dean (D) 768 22
H: 5 11 W: 11 00 b.Kingston 18-5-84
2002–03 Wimbledon 1 0
2003–04 Wimbledon 28 1 **29 1**
2004–05 Milton Keynes D 43 2
2005–06 Milton Keynes D 44 1
2006–07 Milton Keynes D 45 1
2007–08 Milton Keynes D 45 0
2008–09 Milton Keynes D 40 2
2009–10 Milton Keynes D 42 1
2010–11 Milton Keynes D 42 3
2011–12 Milton Keynes D 46 3
2012–13 Milton Keynes D 38 1
2013–14 Milton Keynes D 43 1
2014–15 Milton Keynes D 41 3
2015–16 Milton Keynes D 46 1
2016–17 Milton Keynes D 36 1
2017–18 Milton Keynes D 22 0
2018–19 Milton Keynes D 46 1
2019–20 Milton Keynes D 33 0
2020–21 Milton Keynes D 43 0
2021–22 Milton Keynes D 44 0 **739 21**

MASON, Brandon (M) 46 0
H: 5 9 W: 11 00 b.Westminster 30-9-97
2016–17 Watford 2 0
2017–18 Watford 0 0 **2 0**
2017–18 *Dundee U* 1 0 **1 0**
2018–19 Coventry C 25 0
2019–20 Coventry C 11 0
2020–21 Coventry C 0 0
2020–21 *St Mirren* 7 0 **7 0**
2021–22 Coventry C 0 0 **36 0**
2021–22 Milton Keynes D 0 0

McEACHRAN, Josh (D) 234 1
H: 5 10 W: 10 03 b.Oxford 1-3-93
Internationals: England U16, U17, U19, U20, U21.
2010–11 Chelsea 9 0
2011–12 Chelsea 2 0
2011–12 *Swansea C* 4 0 **4 0**
2012–13 Chelsea 0 0
2012–13 *Middlesbrough* 38 0 **38 0**
2013–14 Chelsea 0 0
2013–14 *Watford* 7 0 **7 0**
2013–14 *Wigan Ath* 8 0 **8 0**
2014–15 Chelsea 0 0 **11 0**
2014–15 *Vitesse* 19 0 **19 0**
2015–16 Brentford 14 0
2016–17 Brentford 27 0
2017–18 Brentford 25 0
2018–19 Brentford 24 1 **90 1**
2019–20 Birmingham C 8 0
2020–21 Birmingham C 0 0 **8 0**

2020–21 Milton Keynes D 14 0
2021–22 Milton Keynes D 35 0 **49 0**

O'HORA, Warren (D) 88 4
H: 6 2 W: 11 11 b.Dublin 19-4-99
Internationals: Republic of Ireland U18, U19.
2016 Bohemians 0 0
2017 Bohemians 11 0 **11 0**
2018–19 Brighton & HA 0 0
2019–20 Brighton & HA 0 0
2020–21 Brighton & HA 0 0
2020–21 Milton Keynes D 31 2
2021–22 Milton Keynes D 46 2 **77 4**

O'RILEY, Matt (M) 50 10
H: 6 2 W: 12 02 b.Hounslow 21-11-00
Internationals: England U16, U18.
2017–18 Fulham 0 0
2018–19 Fulham 0 0
2019–20 Fulham 1 0 **1 0**
2020–21 Milton Keynes D 23 3
2021–22 Milton Keynes D 26 7 **49 10**
Transferred to Celtic, January 2022.

RAVIZZOLI, Franco (G) 1 0
b.Mar el Plata 9-7-97
From Eastbourne Bor.
2021–22 Milton Keynes D 1 0 **1 0**

SMITH, Matthew (M) 97 3
H: 5 10 W: 10 10 b.Redditch 22-11-99
Internationals: Wales U17, U19, U21, Full caps.
2018–19 Manchester C 0 0
2018–19 *FC Twente* 34 2 **34 2**
2019–20 Manchester C 0 0
2019–20 *QPR* 8 0 **8 0**
2019–20 *Charlton Ath* 2 0 **2 0**
2020–21 Manchester C 0 0
2020–21 *Doncaster R* 40 1
2021–22 Doncaster R 0 0 **40 1**
2021–22 Hull C 9 0 **9 0**
2021–22 Milton Keynes D 4 0 **4 0**

TWINE, Scott (F) 114 34
H: 5 9 W: 10 12 b.Swindon 14-7-99
2015–16 Swindon T 0 0
2016–17 Swindon T 1 0
2017–18 Swindon T 4 0
2018–19 Swindon T 14 1
2019–20 Swindon T 6 0
2020–21 Swindon T 25 7
2020–21 *Newport Co* 19 6 **19 6**
2021–22 Swindon T 0 0 **50 8**
2021–22 Milton Keynes D 45 20 **45 20**

WATSON, Tennai (D) 59 2
H: 6 0 W: 11 07 b.Hillingdon 4-3-97
2015–16 Reading 0 0
2016–17 Reading 3 0
2017–18 Reading 0 0
2018–19 Reading 0 0
2018–19 *AFC Wimbledon* 24 0 **24 0**
2019–20 Reading 0 0
2019–20 *Coventry C* 3 0 **3 0**
2020–21 Reading 1 0 **4 0**
2021–22 Milton Keynes D 28 2 **28 2**

WICKHAM, Connor (F) 234 44
H: 6 2 W: 14 02 b.Hereford 31-3-93
Internationals: England U16, U17, U19, U21.
2008–09 Ipswich T 2 0
2009–10 Ipswich T 26 4
2010–11 Ipswich T 37 9 **65 13**
2011–12 Sunderland 16 1
2012–13 Sunderland 12 0
2012–13 *Sheffield W* 6 1
2013–14 Sunderland 15 5
2013–14 *Sheffield W* 11 8
2013–14 *Leeds U* 5 0 **5 0**
2014–15 Sunderland 36 5 **79 11**
2015–16 Crystal Palace 21 5
2016–17 Crystal Palace 8 2
2017–18 Crystal Palace 0 0
2018–19 Crystal Palace 6 0
2019–20 Crystal Palace 6 1
2019–20 *Sheffield W* 13 2 **30 11**
2020–21 Crystal Palace 0 0
2021–22 Crystal Palace 0 0 **41 8**
2021–22 Preston NE 1 0 **1 0**
2021–22 Milton Keynes D 13 1 **13 1**

Players retained or with offer of contract
Gyamfi, Junior; Sandford, Ronnie; Tripp, Callum.

Scholars
Anderson, Jacob Lindel; Anker, Joel Donald Unashe; Blennerhassett, Thomas; Bombo, Jediah Amour Bolingo; Holmes, Ryan John; Mann, Liam Anthony; Ogundega, Olutobi Jason Taufiq; Sandford, Ronnie Wiliam; Smith, Charlie Alex; Waller, Charlie James O'Meara.

MORECAMBE (55)

ANDRE MENDES, Filipe Silva (G) 0 0
b.Portugal 15-5-03
2019–20 Morecambe 0 0
2020–21 Morecambe 0 0
2021–22 Morecambe 0 0

AYUNGA, Jonah (F) 66 8
H: 6 1 W: 12 08 b.Beauminster 24-5-97
From Sutton U, Havant & Waterlooville.
2020–21 Bristol R 30 2
2021–22 Bristol R 0 0 **30 2**
2021–22 Morecambe 36 6 **36 6**

BENNETT, Rhys (D) 317 19
H: 6 3 W: 12 00 b.Bolton 1-9-91
2011–12 Bolton W 0 0
2011–12 *Falkirk* 19 0 **19 0**
2012–13 Rochdale 33 2
2013–14 Rochdale 22 0
2014–15 Rochdale 39 2
2015–16 Rochdale 16 2 **110 6**
2016–17 Mansfield T 46 2
2017–18 Mansfield T 38 2 **84 4**
2018–19 Peterborough U 37 4
2019–20 Peterborough U 13 0 **50 4**
2020–21 Carlisle U 24 5
2021–22 Carlisle U 0 0 **24 5**
2021–22 Gillingham 17 0 **17 0**
2021–22 Morecambe 13 0 **13 0**

CARSON, Trevor (G) 317 0
H: 6 0 W: 12 08 b.Downpatrick 5-3-88
Internationals: Northern Ireland U17, U18, U19, U20, U21, B, Full caps.
2004–05 Sunderland 0 0
2005–06 Sunderland 0 0
2006–07 Sunderland 0 0
2007–08 Sunderland 0 0
2008–09 Sunderland 0 0
2008–09 *Chesterfield* 18 0 **18 0**
2009–10 Sunderland 0 0
2010–11 Sunderland 0 0
2010–11 *Lincoln C* 16 0 **16 0**
2010–11 *Brentford* 1 0 **1 0**
2011–12 Sunderland 0 0
2011–12 *Hull C* 0 0
2011–12 Bury 17 0
2012–13 Bury 39 0
2013–14 Bury 5 0 **61 0**
2013–14 *Portsmouth* 36 0 **36 0**
2014–15 Cheltenham T 46 0 **46 0**
2015–16 Hartlepool U 34 0
2016–17 Hartlepool U 23 0 **57 0**
2017–18 Motherwell 33 0
2018–19 Motherwell 12 0
2019–20 Motherwell 0 0
2020–21 Motherwell 12 0 **57 0**
2021–22 Dundee U 4 0 **4 0**
2021–22 *Morecambe* 21 0 **21 0**

CONNOLLY, Dylan (F) 102 4
H: 5 9 W: 10 12 b.Dublin 2-5-95
Internationals: Republic of Ireland U17, U21.
2014–15 Ipswich T 0 0
2015–16 Ipswich T 0 0
From Bray W, Dundalk.
2018–19 AFC Wimbledon 12 0
2019–20 AFC Wimbledon 3 0 **15 0**
2019–20 *Bradford C* 27 1 **27 1**
2020–21 St Mirren 28 2 **28 2**
2021–22 Northampton T 17 0 **17 0**
2021–22 Morecambe 15 1 **15 1**

COONEY, Ryan (D) 100 0
H: 5 10 W: 12 02 b.Manchester 26-2-00
2016–17 Bury 0 0
2017–18 Bury 12 0
2018–19 Bury 9 0 **21 0**
2019–20 Burnley 0 0
2019–20 *Morecambe* 11 0
2020–21 Burnley 0 0
2020–21 *Morecambe* 36 0
2021–22 Morecambe 32 0 **79 0**

DELANEY, Ryan (D) 147 12
H: 6 0 W: 11 05 b.Wexford 6-9-96
Internationals: Republic of Ireland U21.
From Wexford.
2016–17 Burton Alb 0 0
2017 *Cork C* 30 6 **30 6**
2017–18 Rochdale 18 2
2018–19 Rochdale 30 1
2019–20 *AFC Wimbledon* 14 1 **14 1**
2019–20 Rochdale 0 0 **48 3**
2019–20 Bolton W 4 1
2020–21 Bolton W 20 1 **24 2**
2021–22 Morecambe 13 0 **13 0**
2021–22 *Scunthorpe U* 18 0 **18 0**

DIAGOURAGA, Toumani (M) 501 22
H: 6 2 W: 11 05 b.Paris 10-6-87
2004–05 Watford 0 0
2005–06 Watford 1 0
2005–06 *Swindon T* 8 0
2006–07 Watford 0 0
2006–07 *Rotherham U* 7 0 **7 0**
2007–08 Watford 0 0 **1 0**
2007–08 *Hereford U* 41 2
2008–09 Hereford U 45 2 **86 4**
2009–10 Peterborough U 19 0 **19 0**
2009–10 *Brentford* 20 0
2010–11 Brentford 32 1
2011–12 Brentford 35 4
2012–13 Brentford 39 1
2013–14 Brentford 19 0
2013–14 *Portsmouth* 8 0 **8 0**
2014–15 Brentford 38 0
2015–16 Brentford 27 0 **210 6**
2015–16 Leeds U 17 2
2016–17 Leeds U 1 0
2016–17 *Ipswich T* 12 0 **12 0**
2017–18 Leeds U 0 0 **18 2**
2017–18 Plymouth Arg 15 3 **15 3**
2017–18 Fleetwood T 17 1 **17 1**
2018–19 Swindon T 12 0
2019–20 Swindon T 0 0 **20 0**
2019–20 Morecambe 12 1
2020–21 Morecambe 36 3
2021–22 Morecambe 40 2 **88 6**

DUFFUS, Courtney (F) 32 1
H: 5 7 W: 12 00 b.Cheltenham 24-10-95
Internationals: Republic of Ireland U21.
2013–14 Everton 0 0
2014–15 Everton 0 0
2014–15 *Bury* 3 0 **3 0**
2015–16 Everton 0 0
2016–17 Everton 0 0
2017–18 Oldham Ath 6 0
2018–19 Oldham Ath 0 0 **6 0**
2018–19 Yeovil T 16 1 **16 1**
From Yeovil T, Bromley.
2021–22 Morecambe 7 0 **7 0**

FANE, Ousmane (M) 112 0
H: 6 4 W: 12 08 b.Paris 13-12-93
From Kidderminster H.
2016–17 Oldham Ath 39 0
2017–18 Oldham Ath 41 0
2018–19 Oldham Ath 0 0 **80 0**
2019–20 Shrewsbury T 0 0
2020 UiTM 9 0
2021 UiTM 11 0 **20 0**
2021–22 Morecambe 12 0 **12 0**
Transferred to UiTM, February 2020.

GIBSON, Liam (D) 74 1
H: 6 1 W: 12 08 b.Stanley 25-4-97
2015–16 Newcastle U 0 0
2016–17 Newcastle U 0 0
2017–18 Newcastle U 0 0
2018–19 Newcastle U 0 0
2018–19 *Accrington S* 5 0 **5 0**
2019–20 Newcastle U 0 0
2019–20 *Grimsby T* 17 0 **17 0**
2020–21 Morecambe 23 0
2021–22 Morecambe 29 1 **52 1**

GNAHOUA, Arthur (F) 104 12
H: 6 2 W: 12 08 b.Saint-Denis 5-4-92
From Stalybridge Celtic, Macclesfield T, Kidderminster H.
2017–18 Shrewsbury T 11 1
2018–19 Shrewsbury T 1 0 **12 1**
2018–19 Carlisle U 1 0 **1 0**
2019–20 Macclesfield T 29 4 **29 4**
2020–21 Bolton W 28 2 **28 2**
2021–22 Morecambe 34 5 **34 5**

HARRISON, Shayon (F) 73 13
H: 6 0 W: 10 10 b.Hornsey 13-7-97
2016–17 Tottenham H 0 0
2016–17 *Yeovil T* 14 1 **14 1**
2017–18 Tottenham H 0 0
2017–18 *Southend U* 13 0 **13 0**
2018–19 Tottenham H 0 0
2018–19 *Melbourne C* 10 4 **10 4**
2019–20 Almere C 21 7
2020–21 Almere C 11 1 **32 8**
2020–21 AFC Wimbledon 1 0 **1 0**
2021–22 Morecambe 3 0 **3 0**
Transferred to Hayes & Yeading U, March 2022.

LEIGH, Greg (D) 208 8
H: 5 11 W: 11 07 b.Manchester 30-9-94
Internationals: England U19. Jamaica Full caps.
2013–14 Manchester C 0 0
2014–15 Manchester C 0 0
2014–15 *Crewe Alex* 38 1 **38 1**
2015–16 Bradford C 6 1 **6 1**
2016–17 Bury 45 1
2017–18 Bury 41 1 **86 2**
2018–19 NAC Breda 16 1
2019–20 NAC Breda 0 0 **16 1**
2019–20 *Aberdeen* 18 1
2020–21 Aberdeen 8 0 **26 1**
2021–22 Morecambe 36 2 **36 2**

LETHEREN, Kyle (G) 138 0
H: 6 2 W: 13 00 b.Swansea 26-12-87
Internationals: Wales U21.

2005–06	Swansea C	0	0		
2006–07	Barnsley	0	0		
2007–08	Barnsley	0	0		
2008–09	Barnsley	0	0		
2008–09	*Doncaster R*	0	0		
2009–10	Plymouth Arg	0	0		
2010–11	Kilmarnock	0	0		
2011–12	Kilmarnock	2	0		
2012–13	Kilmarnock	9	0	**11**	**0**
2013–14	Dundee	35	0		
2014–15	Dundee	15	0	**50**	**0**
2015–16	Blackpool	5	0		
2016–17	Blackpool	0	0	**5**	**0**

From York C.

2017–18	Plymouth Arg	7	0		
2018–19	Plymouth Arg	13	0	**20**	**0**
2019–20	Salford C	19	0	**19**	**0**
2020–21	Morecambe	21	0		
2021–22	Morecambe	12	0	**33**	**0**

McDONALD, Wesley (F) 95 7
H: 5 9 W: 12 02 b.Lambeth 4-5-97

2015–16	Birmingham C	0	0		
2016–17	Birmingham C	0	0		
2017–18	Birmingham C	0	0		
2018–19	Yeovil T	9	0	**9**	**0**
2019–20	Walsall	28	5		
2020–21	Walsall	41	2	**69**	**7**
2021–22	Morecambe	17	0	**17**	**0**

McLAUGHLIN, Ryan (D) 140 3
H: 5 9 W: 10 12 b.Belfast 30-9-94
Internationals: Northern Ireland U16, U17, U19, U21, Full caps.
From Glenavon.

2011–12	Liverpool	0	0		
2012–13	Liverpool	0	0		
2013–14	Liverpool	0	0		
2013–14	*Barnsley*	9	0	**9**	**0**
2014–15	Liverpool	0	0		
2015–16	Liverpool	0	0		
2015–16	*Aberdeen*	4	0	**4**	**0**
2016–17	Oldham Ath	36	2		
2017–18	Oldham Ath	16	1	**52**	**3**
2018–19	Blackpool	6	0	**6**	**0**
2018–19	Rochdale	13	0		
2019–20	Rochdale	3	0		
2020–21	Rochdale	34	0	**50**	**0**
2021–22	Morecambe	19	0	**19**	**0**

McLOUGHLIN, Shane (D) 108 4
H: 5 9 W: 11 00 b.Castleisland 1-3-97
Internationals: Republic of Ireland U16, U18.

2014–15	Ipswich T	0	0		
2015–16	Ipswich T	0	0		
2016–17	Ipswich T	0	0		
2017–18	Ipswich T	1	0		
2018–19	Ipswich T	0	0	**1**	**0**
2018–19	AFC Wimbledon	10	1		
2019–20	AFC Wimbledon	23	1		
2020–21	AFC Wimbledon	38	1		
2021–22	AFC Wimbledon	0	0	**71**	**3**
2021–22	Morecambe	36	1	**36**	**1**

MENSAH, Jacob (D) 1 0
b.Lambeth 18-7-00
From Crystal Palace, Weymouth.

2021–22	Morecambe	1	0	**1**	**0**

O'CONNOR, Anthony (D) 371 19
H: 6 2 W: 11 11 b.Cork 25-10-92
Internationals: Republic of Ireland U17, U19, U21.

2010–11	Blackburn R	0	0		
2011–12	Blackburn R	0	0		
2012–13	Blackburn R	0	0		
2012–13	*Burton Alb*	46	0		
2013–14	Blackburn R	0	0		
2013–14	*Torquay U*	31	0	**31**	**0**
2014–15	Plymouth Arg	40	3	**40**	**3**
2015–16	Burton Alb	21	1	**67**	**1**
2016–17	Aberdeen	32	3		
2017–18	Aberdeen	38	2	**70**	**5**
2018–19	Bradford C	42	6		
2019–20	Bradford C	36	0		
2020–21	Bradford C	45	2	**123**	**8**
2021–22	Morecambe	40	2	**40**	**2**

OBIKA, Jonathan (F) 338 69
H: 5 11 W: 12 02 b.Enfield 12-9-90
Internationals: England U19, U20.

2008–09	Tottenham H	0	0		
2008–09	*Yeovil T*	10	4		
2009–10	Tottenham H	0	0		
2009–10	*Yeovil T*	22	6		
2009–10	*Millwall*	12	2	**12**	**2**
2010–11	Tottenham H	0	0		
2010–11	*Crystal Palace*	7	0	**7**	**0**
2010–11	*Peterborough U*	1	1	**1**	**1**
2010–11	*Swindon T*	5	0		
2010–11	*Yeovil T*	11	3		
2011–12	Tottenham H	0	0		
2011–12	*Yeovil T*	27	4	**70**	**17**
2012–13	Tottenham H	0	0		
2012–13	*Charlton Ath*	10	3		
2013–14	Tottenham H	0	0		
2013–14	*Brighton & HA*	5	0	**5**	**0**
2013–14	*Charlton Ath*	12	0	**22**	**3**
2014–15	Tottenham H	0	0		
2014–15	Swindon T	32	8		
2015–16	Swindon T	32	11		
2016–17	Swindon T	30	6	**99**	**25**
2017–18	Oxford U	35	5		
2018–19	Oxford U	11	1	**46**	**6**
2019–20	St Mirren	30	8		
2020–21	St Mirren	34	5	**64**	**13**
2021–22	Morecambe	12	2	**12**	**2**

PRICE, Freddie (M) 14 1
H: 5 11 W: 10 12 b.Stafford 12-5-02

2018–19	Morecambe	0	0		
2019–20	Morecambe	0	0		
2020–21	Morecambe	11	1		
2021–22	Morecambe	3	0	**14**	**1**

ROCHE, Barry (G) 575 1
H: 6 4 W: 14 02 b.Dublin 6-4-82
Internationals: Republic of Ireland U21.

1999–2000	Nottingham F	0	0		
2000–01	Nottingham F	2	0		
2001–02	Nottingham F	0	0		
2002–03	Nottingham F	1	0		
2003–04	Nottingham F	8	0		
2004–05	Nottingham F	2	0	**13**	**0**
2005–06	Chesterfield	41	0		
2006–07	Chesterfield	40	0		
2007–08	Chesterfield	45	0	**126**	**0**
2008–09	Morecambe	46	0		
2009–10	Morecambe	42	0		
2010–11	Morecambe	42	0		
2011–12	Morecambe	44	0		
2012–13	Morecambe	42	0		
2013–14	Morecambe	45	0		
2014–15	Morecambe	14	0		
2015–16	Morecambe	42	1		
2016–17	Morecambe	41	0		
2017–18	Morecambe	42	0		
2018–19	Morecambe	20	0		
2019–20	Morecambe	16	0		
2021–22	Morecambe	0	0	**436**	**1**

SMITH, Adam (G) 136 0
H: 5 11 W: 11 00 b.Sunderland 23-11-92

2010–11	Leicester C	0	0		
2011–12	Leicester C	0	0		
2011–12	*Chesterfield*	0	0		
2011–12	*Bristol R*	0	0		
2012–13	Leicester C	0	0		
2013–14	Leicester C	0	0		
2013–14	*Stevenage*	0	0		
2014–15	Leicester C	0	0		
2014–15	*Mansfield T*	4	0	**4**	**0**
2015–16	Northampton T	46	0		
2016–17	Northampton T	40	0	**86**	**0**
2017–18	Bristol R	23	0		
2018–19	Bristol R	5	0	**28**	**0**
2019–20	Forest Green R	8	0		
2020–21	Forest Green R	0	0	**8**	**0**
2021–22	Stevenage	9	0	**9**	**0**
2021–22	Morecambe	1	0	**1**	**0**

STOCKTON, Cole (F) 255 59
H: 6 1 W: 11 11 b.Huyton 13-3-94

2011–12	Tranmere R	1	0		
2012–13	Tranmere R	31	3		
2013–14	Tranmere R	21	2		
2014–15	Tranmere R	22	4		
2015–16	Tranmere R	0	0		
2015–16	*Morecambe*	7	2		
2016–17	Tranmere R	0	0		
2016–17	*Morecambe*	19	5		
2017–18	Hearts	12	0	**12**	**0**
2017–18	Carlisle U	12	1	**12**	**1**
2018–19	Tranmere R	16	1	**91**	**10**
2019–20	Morecambe	30	5		
2020–21	Morecambe	40	13		
2021–22	Morecambe	44	23	**140**	**48**

WILDIG, Aaron (M) 293 26
H: 5 9 W: 11 07 b.Hereford 15-4-92
Internationals: Wales U16.

2009–10	Cardiff C	11	1		
2010–11	Cardiff C	2	0		
2010–11	*Hamilton A*	3	0	**3**	**0**
2011–12	Cardiff C	0	0	**13**	**1**
2011–12	*Shrewsbury T*	12	2		
2012–13	Shrewsbury T	21	1		
2013–14	Shrewsbury T	30	2		
2014–15	Shrewsbury T	1	0	**64**	**5**
2014–15	*Morecambe*	9	1		
2015–16	Morecambe	32	2		
2016–17	Morecambe	28	2		
2017–18	Morecambe	31	1		
2018–19	Morecambe	26	1		
2019–20	Morecambe	28	3		
2020–21	Morecambe	37	8		
2021–22	Morecambe	22	2	**213**	**20**

WOOTTON, Scott (D) 222 6
H: 6 2 W: 12 04 b.Birkenhead 12-9-91
Internationals: England U17.
From Liverpool.

2009–10	Manchester U	0	0		
2010–11	Manchester U	0	0		
2010–11	*Tranmere R*	7	1	**7**	**1**
2011–12	Manchester U	0	0		
2011–12	*Peterborough U*	11	0		
2011–12	*Nottingham F*	13	0	**13**	**0**
2012–13	Manchester U	0	0		
2012–13	*Peterborough U*	2	1	**13**	**1**
2013–14	Manchester U	0	0		
2013–14	Leeds U	20	0		
2014–15	Leeds U	23	0		
2014–15	*Rotherham U*	7	0	**7**	**0**
2015–16	Leeds U	23	0	**66**	**0**
2016–17	Milton Keynes D	1	1		
2017–18	Milton Keynes D	38	0	**39**	**1**
2018–19	Plymouth Arg	9	0		
2019–20	Plymouth Arg	35	1		
2020–21	Plymouth Arg	10	0	**54**	**1**
2020–21	*Wigan Ath*	13	1	**13**	**1**
2021–22	Morecambe	10	1	**10**	**1**

Transferred to Wellington Phoenix, January 2022.

Players retained or with offer of contract
Nicholson, Jamie; Pye, Connor; Rooney, Cameron.

Scholars
Connolly, Lewis Michael; Cooper, Oliver Claude; Davidson, Mani; Flitcroft, Bobby Jon; Foden, Daniel Anthony; Huddleston, Keallen Daniel; Jarvis, Ben Patrick; Jones, Benjamin Michael Francis; Koleni, Koko Wiliam Ali Seima; Lancaster, Louie Carl; Lawton, Joseph Lee; Mayor, Adam Matthew; Nicholson, Jamie Gerard; Pedley, George Sydney; Rooney, Cameron John; Sandle, Callum Anthony.

NEWCASTLE U (56)

ALLAN, Thomas (F) 12 0
H: 5 8 W: 12 04 b.Newcastle upon Tyne 23-9-99

2019–20	Newcastle U	0	0		
2020–21	Newcastle U	0	0		
2020–21	*Accrington S*	4	0	**4**	**0**
2021–22	Newcastle U	0	0		
2021–22	*Greenock Morton*	8	0	**8**	**0**

ALMIRON, Miguel (M) 246 39
H: 5 10 W: 11 00 b.Asuncion 10-2-94
Internationals: Paraguay U17, U20, Full caps.

2013	Cerro Porteno	6	1		
2014	Cerro Porteno	14	0		
2015	Cerro Porteno	19	5	**39**	**6**
2015	Lanus	10	0		
2016	Lanus	25	3	**35**	**3**
2017	Atalanta	30	9		
2018	Atalanta	32	12	**62**	**21**
2018–19	Newcastle U	10	0		
2019–20	Newcastle U	36	4		
2020–21	Newcastle U	34	4		
2021–22	Newcastle U	30	1	**110**	**9**

ANDERSON, Elliot (M) 22 7
H: 5 9 W: 9 13 b.Whitley Bay 6-11-02
Internationals: Scotland U16, U17, U18, U21. England U19.

2020–21	Newcastle U	1	0		
2021–22	Newcastle U	0	0	**1**	**0**
2021–22	*Bristol R*	21	7	**21**	**7**

BARRETT, Ryan (D) 0 0
b.Wrexham 5-6-01
Internationals: Wales U17.

2020–21	Newcastle U	0	0		
2021–22	Newcastle U	0	0		

BONDSWELL, Matthew (D) 6 0
b.Nottingham 18-4-02
Internationals: England U16, U17, U18.
From Nottingham F.

2018–19	RB Leipzig	0	0		
2019–20	RB Leipzig	0	0		
2020–21	RB Leipzig	0	0		
2020–21	*Dordrecht*	6	0	**6**	**0**
2021–22	Newcastle U	0	0		
2021–22	*Shrewsbury T*	0	0		

BROOKWELL, Niall (M) 0 0
b.Wigan 22-3-02
From Liverpool.

2020–21	Newcastle U	0	0		
2021–22	Newcastle U	0	0		

BROWN, Will (G) 0 0
b.Newcastle upon Tyne 10-1-02

2020–21	Newcastle U	0	0		
2021–22	Newcastle U	0	0		

BRUNO GUIMARAES, Moura (M) 134 11
b. 16-11-97
Internationals: Brazil U23, Full caps.
From Audax.

2017	Athletico Paranaense	4	0		
2018	Athletico Paranaense	32	1		
2019	Athletico Paranaense	25	2	**61**	**3**
2019–20	Lyon	3	0		
2020–21	Lyon	33	3		
2021–22	Lyon	20	0	**56**	**3**
2021–22	Newcastle U	17	5	**17**	**5**

BURN, Dan (D) 314 11
H: 6 6 W: 13 10 b.Blyth 1-5-92

2009–10	Darlington	4	0	**4**	**0**
2010–11	Fulham	0	0		
2011–12	Fulham	0	0		
2012–13	Fulham	0	0		
2012–13	*Yeovil T*	34	2	**34**	**2**
2013–14	Fulham	9	0		
2013–14	*Birmingham C*	24	0	**24**	**0**
2014–15	Fulham	20	1		
2015–16	Fulham	32	0	**61**	**1**
2016–17	Wigan Ath	42	1		
2017–18	Wigan Ath	45	5		
2018–19	Brighton & HA	0	0		
2018–19	*Wigan Ath*	14	0	**101**	**6**
2019–20	Brighton & HA	34	0		
2020–21	Brighton & HA	27	1		
2021–22	Brighton & HA	13	1	**74**	**2**
2021–22	Newcastle U	16	0	**16**	**0**

CASS, Lewis (D) 19 0
H: 6 1 W: 11 09 b.North Shields 27-2-00

2018–19	Newcastle U	0	0		
2019–20	Newcastle U	0	0		
2020–21	Newcastle U	0	0		
2021–22	Newcastle U	0	0		
2021–22	*Port Vale*	19	0	**19**	**0**

CLARK, Ciaran (D) 248 18
H: 6 2 W: 12 00 b.Harrow 26-9-89
Internationals: England U17, U18, U19, U20. Republic of Ireland Full caps.

2008–09	Aston Villa	0	0		
2009–10	Aston Villa	1	0		
2010–11	Aston Villa	19	3		
2011–12	Aston Villa	15	1		
2012–13	Aston Villa	29	1		
2013–14	Aston Villa	27	0		
2014–15	Aston Villa	25	1		
2015–16	Aston Villa	18	1	**134**	**7**
2016–17	Newcastle U	34	3		
2017–18	Newcastle U	20	2		
2018–19	Newcastle U	11	3		
2019–20	Newcastle U	14	2		
2020–21	Newcastle U	22	1		
2021–22	Newcastle U	13	0	**114**	**11**

CROSS, Bradley (D) 0 0
H: 6 0 W: 12 02 b.Gauteng 30-1-01
From Schalke 04.

2020–21	Newcastle U	0	0		
2021–22	Newcastle U	0	0		

DARLOW, Karl (G) 201 0
H: 6 1 W: 12 06 b.Northampton 8-10-90

2009–10	Nottingham F	0	0		
2010–11	Nottingham F	1	0		
2011–12	Nottingham F	0	0		
2012–13	Nottingham F	20	0		
2012–13	*Walsall*	9	0	**9**	**0**
2013–14	Nottingham F	43	0		
2014–15	Newcastle U	0	0		
2014–15	*Nottingham F*	42	0	**106**	**0**
2015–16	Newcastle U	9	0		
2016–17	Newcastle U	34	0		
2017–18	Newcastle U	10	0		
2018–19	Newcastle U	0	0		
2019–20	Newcastle U	0	0		
2020–21	Newcastle U	25	0		
2021–22	Newcastle U	8	0	**86**	**0**

DUBRAVKA, Martin (G) 330 0
H: 6 3 W: 13 01 b.Zilina 15-1-89
Internationals: Slovakia U19, U21, Full caps.

2008–09	Zilina	1	0		
2009–10	Zilina	26	0		
2010–11	Zilina	24	0		
2011–12	Zilina	8	0		
2012–13	Zilina	26	0		
2013–14	Zilina	13	0	**98**	**0**
2013–14	Esbjerg	15	0		
2014–15	Esbjerg	33	0		
2015–16	Esbjerg	18	0	**66**	**0**
2016–17	Slovan Liberec	28	0	**28**	**0**
2017–18	Sparta Prague	11	0	**11**	**0**
2017–18	*Newcastle U*	12	0		
2018–19	Newcastle U	38	0		
2019–20	Newcastle U	38	0		
2020–21	Newcastle U	13	0		
2021–22	Newcastle U	26	0	**127**	**0**

DUMMETT, Paul (D) 221 5
H: 5 10 W: 10 03 b.Newcastle upon Tyne 26-9-91
Internationals: Wales U21, Full caps.

2010–11	Newcastle U	0	0		
2011–12	Newcastle U	0	0		
2012–13	Newcastle U	0	0		
2012–13	*St Mirren*	30	2	**30**	**2**
2013–14	Newcastle U	18	1		
2014–15	Newcastle U	25	0		
2015–16	Newcastle U	23	1		
2016–17	Newcastle U	45	0		
2017–18	Newcastle U	20	0		
2018–19	Newcastle U	26	0		
2019–20	Newcastle U	16	0		
2020–21	Newcastle U	15	1		
2021–22	Newcastle U	3	0	**191**	**3**

FERNANDEZ, Federico (D) 317 9
H: 6 3 W: 13 01 b.Tres Algarrobos 21-2-89
Internationals: Argentina U20, Full caps.

2008–09	Estudiantes	14	2		
2009–10	Estudiantes	12	1		
2010–11	Estudiantes	33	1	**59**	**4**
2011–12	Napoli	16	0		
2012–13	Napoli	2	0		
2012–13	*Getafe*	14	1	**14**	**1**
2013–14	Napoli	26	0	**44**	**0**
2014–15	Swansea C	28	0		
2015–16	Swansea C	32	1		
2016–17	Swansea C	27	0		
2017–18	Swansea C	30	1		
2018–19	Swansea C	1	0	**118**	**2**
2018–19	Newcastle U	19	0		
2019–20	Newcastle U	32	2		
2020–21	Newcastle U	24	0		
2021–22	Newcastle U	7	0	**82**	**2**

FRASER, Ryan (M) 267 26
H: 5 4 W: 11 00 b.Aberdeen 24-2-94
Internationals: Scotland U19, U21, Full caps.

2010–11	Aberdeen	2	0		
2011–12	Aberdeen	3	0		
2012–13	Aberdeen	16	0	**21**	**0**
2012–13	Bournemouth	5	0		
2013–14	Bournemouth	37	3		
2014–15	Bournemouth	21	1		
2015–16	Bournemouth	0	0		
2015–16	*Ipswich T*	18	4	**18**	**4**
2016–17	Bournemouth	28	3		
2017–18	Bournemouth	26	5		
2018–19	Bournemouth	38	7		
2019–20	Bournemouth	28	1	**183**	**20**
2020–21	Newcastle U	18	0		
2021–22	Newcastle U	27	2	**45**	**2**

GAYLE, Dwight (F) 263 92
H: 5 10 W: 11 07 b.Walthamstow 20-10-89

2011–12	Dagenham & R	0	0		
2012–13	Dagenham & R	18	7	**18**	**7**
2012–13	Peterborough U	29	13	**29**	**13**
2013–14	Crystal Palace	23	7		
2014–15	Crystal Palace	25	5		
2015–16	Crystal Palace	16	3	**64**	**15**
2016–17	Newcastle U	32	23		
2017–18	Newcastle U	35	6		
2018–19	Newcastle U	0	0		
2018–19	*WBA*	39	23	**39**	**23**
2019–20	Newcastle U	20	4		
2020–21	Newcastle U	18	1		
2021–22	Newcastle U	8	0	**113**	**34**

GILLESPIE, Mark (G) 241 0
H: 6 1 W: 13 08 b.Newcastle upon Tyne 27-3-92
From Newcastle U.

2009–10	Carlisle U	1	0		
2010–11	Carlisle U	0	0		
2011–12	Carlisle U	0	0		
2012–13	Carlisle U	35	0		
2013–14	Carlisle U	15	0		
2014–15	Carlisle U	19	0		
2015–16	Carlisle U	45	0		
2016–17	Carlisle U	46	0	**161**	**0**
2017–18	Walsall	23	0	**23**	**0**
2018–19	Motherwell	27	0		
2019–20	Motherwell	30	0	**57**	**0**
2020–21	Newcastle U	0	0		
2021–22	Newcastle U	0	0		

HAYDEN, Isaac (D) 169 7
H: 6 2 W: 12 06 b.Chelmsford 22-3-95
Internationals: England U16, U17, U18, U19, U20, U21.

2011–12	Arsenal	0	0		
2012–13	Arsenal	0	0		
2013–14	Arsenal	0	0		
2014–15	Arsenal	0	0		
2015–16	Arsenal	0	0		
2015–16	*Hull C*	18	1	**18**	**1**
2016–17	Newcastle U	33	2		
2017–18	Newcastle U	26	1		
2018–19	Newcastle U	25	1		
2019–20	Newcastle U	29	1		
2020–21	Newcastle U	24	0		
2021–22	Newcastle U	14	1	**151**	**6**

HENDRICK, Jeff (M) 353 34
H: 6 1 W: 12 06 b.Dublin 31-1-92
Internationals: Republic of Ireland U17, U19, U21, Full caps.

2010–11	Derby Co	4	0		
2011–12	Derby Co	42	3		
2012–13	Derby Co	45	6		
2013–14	Derby Co	30	4		
2014–15	Derby Co	41	7		
2015–16	Derby Co	32	2		
2016–17	Derby Co	2	0	**196**	**22**
2016–17	Burnley	32	2		
2017–18	Burnley	34	2		
2018–19	Burnley	32	3		
2019–20	Burnley	24	2		
2020–21	Burnley	0	0	**122**	**9**
2020–21	Newcastle U	22	2		
2021–22	Newcastle U	3	1	**25**	**3**
2021–22	*QPR*	10	0	**10**	**0**

JOELINTON, de Lira (F) 205 35
H: 6 1 W: 12 11 b.Alianca 14-8-96
Internationals: Brazil U17.

2014	Sport Recife	7	2		
2015	Sport Recife	5	1	**12**	**3**
2015–16	Hoffenheim	1	0		
2016–17	Hoffenheim	0	0		
2016–17	*Rapid Vienna*	33	8		
2017–18	Hoffenheim	0	0		
2017–18	*Rapid Vienna*	27	7	**60**	**15**
2018–19	Hoffenheim	28	7	**29**	**7**
2019–20	Newcastle U	38	2		
2020–21	Newcastle U	31	4		
2021–22	Newcastle U	35	4	**104**	**10**

KRAFTH, Emil (D) 230 5
H: 6 0 W: 12 02 b.Ljungby 2-8-94
Internationals: Sweden U17, U19, U21, Full caps.
From Lagans.

2011	Osters	24	0	**24**	**0**
2012	Helsingborgs	9	0		
2013	Helsingborgs	27	1		
2014	Helsingborgs	28	1		
2015	Helsingborgs	12	1	**76**	**3**
2015–16	Bologna	4	0		
2016–17	Bologna	26	0		
2017–18	Bologna	12	0	**42**	**0**
2018–19	Amiens	35	1	**35**	**1**
2019–20	Newcastle U	17	0		
2020–21	Newcastle U	16	1		
2021–22	Newcastle U	20	0	**53**	**1**

LANGLEY, Dan (G) 0 0
b.Newcastle upon Tyne 28-12-00

2020–21	Newcastle U	0	0		
2021–22	Newcastle U	0	0		

LASCELLES, Jamaal (D) 260 16
H: 6 2 W: 13 01 b.Derby 11-11-93
Internationals: England U18, U19, U20, U21.

2010–11	Nottingham F	0	0		
2011–12	Nottingham F	1	0		
2011–12	*Stevenage*	7	1	**7**	**1**
2012–13	Nottingham F	2	0		
2013–14	Nottingham F	29	2		
2014–15	Newcastle U	0	0		
2014–15	*Nottingham F*	26	1	**58**	**3**
2015–16	Newcastle U	18	2		
2016–17	Newcastle U	43	3		
2017–18	Newcastle U	33	3		
2018–19	Newcastle U	32	0		
2019–20	Newcastle U	24	1		
2020–21	Newcastle U	19	2		
2021–22	Newcastle U	26	1	**195**	**12**

LEWIS, Jamal (D) 121 1
H: 5 10 W: 11 00 b.Luton 25-1-98
Internationals: Northern Ireland U19, U21, Full caps.

2017–18	Norwich C	22	0		
2018–19	Norwich C	42	0		
2019–20	Norwich C	28	1		
2020–21	Norwich C	0	0	**92**	**1**
2020–21	Newcastle U	24	0		
2021–22	Newcastle U	5	0	**29**	**0**

LONGSTAFF, Matthew (M) 30 8
H: 5 7 W: 9 06 b.Rotherham 21-3-00
Internationals: England U20.

2019–20	Newcastle U	9	2		
2020–21	Newcastle U	5	0		
2021–22	Aberdeen	0	0		
2021–22	Newcastle U	0	0	**14**	**2**
2021–22	*Mansfield T*	16	6	**16**	**6**

LONGSTAFF, Sean (M) 152 17
H: 5 11 W: 10 03 b.North Shields 30-10-97

2016–17	Newcastle U	0	0		
2016–17	*Kilmarnock*	16	3		
2016–17	Newcastle U	0	0		
2016–17	*Kilmarnock*	16	3	**32**	**6**
2017–18	Newcastle U	0	0		
2017–18	*Blackpool*	42	8	**42**	**8**
2018–19	Newcastle U	9	1		
2019–20	Newcastle U	23	1		
2020–21	Newcastle U	22	0		
2021–22	Newcastle U	24	1	**78**	**3**

MANQUILLO, Javier (D) 159 2
H: 5 11 W: 12 04 b.Madrid 5-5-94
Internationals: Spain U16, U17, U18, U19, U20, U21.

2012–13	Atletico Madrid	3	0		
2013–14	Atletico Madrid	3	0		
2014–15	Atletico Madrid	0	0		
2014–15	*Liverpool*	10	0	**10**	**0**
2015–16	Atletico Madrid	0	0		
2015–16	*Marseille*	31	0	**31**	**0**
2016–17	Atletico Madrid	0	0	**6**	**0**
2016–17	*Sunderland*	20	1	**20**	**1**
2017–18	Newcastle U	21	0		
2018–19	Newcastle U	18	0		
2019–20	Newcastle U	21	0		
2020–21	Newcastle U	13	0		
2021–22	Newcastle U	19	1	**92**	**1**

McENTEE, Oisin (D) 25 1
H: 6 4 W: 12 04 b.New York 5-1-01
Internationals: Republic of Ireland U17, U18, U19, U21.

2020–21	Newcastle U	0	0		
2021–22	Newcastle U	0	0		
2021–22	*Greenock Morton*	25	1	**25**	**1**

MURPHY, Jacob (M) 258 40
H: 5 9 W: 11 03 b.Wembley 24-2-95
Internationals: England U18, U19, U20, U21.

2013–14	Norwich C	0	0		
2013–14	*Swindon T*	6	0	**6**	**0**
2013–14	*Southend U*	7	1	**7**	**1**
2014–15	Norwich C	0	0		
2014–15	*Blackpool*	9	2	**9**	**2**
2014–15	*Scunthorpe U*	3	0	**3**	**0**
2014–15	*Colchester U*	11	4	**11**	**4**
2015–16	Norwich C	0	0		
2015–16	*Coventry C*	40	9	**40**	**9**
2016–17	Norwich C	37	9	**37**	**9**
2017–18	Newcastle U	25	1		
2018–19	Newcastle U	9	0		
2018–19	*WBA*	13	2	**13**	**2**
2019–20	Newcastle U	0	0		
2019–20	*Sheffield W*	39	9	**39**	**9**
2020–21	Newcastle U	26	2		
2021–22	Newcastle U	33	1	**93**	**4**

RITCHIE, Matt (M) 464 90
H: 5 8 W: 11 02 b.Gosport 10-9-89
Internationals: Scotland Full caps.

2008–09	Portsmouth	0	0		
2008–09	*Dagenham & R*	37	11	**37**	**11**
2009–10	Portsmouth	2	0		
2009–10	*Notts Co*	16	3	**16**	**3**
2009–10	*Swindon T*	4	0		
2010–11	Portsmouth	5	0	**7**	**0**
2010–11	Swindon T	36	7		
2011–12	Swindon T	40	10		
2012–13	Swindon T	27	9	**107**	**26**
2012–13	Bournemouth	17	3		
2013–14	Bournemouth	30	9		
2014–15	Bournemouth	46	15		
2015–16	Bournemouth	37	4	**130**	**31**
2016–17	Newcastle U	42	12		
2017–18	Newcastle U	35	3		
2018–19	Newcastle U	36	2		
2019–20	Newcastle U	18	2		
2020–21	Newcastle U	18	0		
2021–22	Newcastle U	18	0	**167**	**19**

SAINT-MAXIMIN, Allan (F) 213 24
H: 5 8 W: 10 08 b.Chatenay-Malabry 12-3-97
Internationals: France U16, U17, U20, U21.

2013–14	Saint-Etienne	3	0		
2014–15	Saint-Etienne	9	0		
2015–16	Saint-Etienne	0	0		
2015–16	*Hannover 96*	16	1	**16**	**1**
2016–17	Saint-Etienne	0	0	**12**	**0**
2016–17	*Bastia*	34	3	**34**	**3**
2017–18	Monaco	1	0	**1**	**0**
2017–18	Nice	30	3		
2018–19	Nice	34	6	**64**	**9**
2019–20	Newcastle U	26	3		
2020–21	Newcastle U	25	3		
2021–22	Newcastle U	35	5	**86**	**11**

SANGARE, Mohammed (M) 2 0
b. 28-12-98
Internationals: Liberia Full caps.

2019–20	Newcastle U	0	0		
2020–21	Newcastle U	0	0		
2020–21	*Accrington S*	2	0	**2**	**0**
2021–22	Newcastle U	0	0		

SAVAGE, Remi (D) 0 0
b.Liverpool 26-10-01

2020–21	Liverpool	0	0		
2021–22	Newcastle U	0	0		

SCHAR, Fabian (D) 273 26
H: 6 2 W: 13 05 b.Wil 20-12-91
Internationals: Switzerland U20, U21, U23, Full caps.

2009–10	FC Wil	2	0		
2010–11	FC Wil	24	4		
2011–12	FC Wil	30	1	**56**	**5**
2012–13	FC Basel	21	4		
2013–14	FC Basel	22	4		
2014–15	FC Basel	30	1	**73**	**9**
2015–16	1899 Hoffenheim	24	1		
2016–17	1899 Hoffenheim	6	0	**30**	**1**
2017–18	Deportivo la Coruna	25	2	**25**	**2**
2018–19	Newcastle U	24	4		
2019–20	Newcastle U	22	2		
2020–21	Newcastle U	18	1		
2021–22	Newcastle U	25	2	**89**	**9**

SHELVEY, Jonjo (M) 361 41
H: 5 9 W: 12 04 b.Romford 27-2-92
Internationals: England U16, U17, U19, U21, Full caps.

2007–08	Charlton Ath	2	0		
2008–09	Charlton Ath	16	3		
2009–10	Charlton Ath	24	4	**42**	**7**
2010–11	Liverpool	15	0		
2011–12	Liverpool	13	1		
2011–12	*Blackpool*	10	6	**10**	**6**
2012–13	Liverpool	19	1	**47**	**2**
2013–14	Swansea C	32	6		
2014–15	Swansea C	31	3		
2015–16	Swansea C	16	1	**79**	**10**
2015–16	Newcastle U	15	0		
2016–17	Newcastle U	42	5		
2017–18	Newcastle U	30	1		
2018–19	Newcastle U	16	1		
2019–20	Newcastle U	26	6		
2020–21	Newcastle U	30	1		
2021–22	Newcastle U	24	2	**183**	**16**

THOMSON, Reagan (M) 0 0
H: 5 8 W: 9 00 b.Glasgow 5-8-03
Internationals: Scotland U17.
From Queen's Park.

2020–21	Newcastle U	0	0		
2021–22	Newcastle U	0	0		

TRIPPIER, Keiran (D) 355 10
H: 5 10 W: 11 02 b.Bury 19-9-90
Internationals: England U18, U19, U20, U21, Full caps.

2007–08	Manchester C	0	0		
2008–09	Manchester C	0	0		
2009–10	Manchester C	0	0		
2009–10	*Barnsley*	3	0		
2010–11	Manchester C	0	0		
2010–11	*Barnsley*	39	2	**42**	**2**
2011–12	Manchester C	0	0		
2011–12	Burnley	46	3		
2012–13	Burnley	45	0		
2013–14	Burnley	41	1		
2014–15	Burnley	38	0	**170**	**4**
2015–16	Tottenham H	6	1		
2016–17	Tottenham H	12	0		
2017–18	Tottenham H	24	0		
2018–19	Tottenham H	27	1	**69**	**2**
2019–20	Atletico Madrid	25	0		
2020–21	Atletico Madrid	28	0		
2021–22	Atletico Madrid	15	0	**68**	**0**
2021–22	Newcastle U	6	2	**6**	**2**

TURNER, Jake (G) 23 0
H: 6 0 W: 12 13 b.Wilmslow 25-2-99
Internationals: England U18, U19.

2016–17	Bolton W	0	0		
2017–18	Bolton W	0	0		
2018–19	Bolton W	0	0		
2019–20	Newcastle U	0	0		
2020–21	Newcastle U	0	0		
2020–21	*Morecambe*	14	0	**14**	**0**
2021–22	Newcastle U	0	0		
2021–22	*Colchester U*	9	0	**9**	**0**

TURNER-COOKE, Jay (M) 0 0
b. 31-12-02
From Sunderland.

2020–21	Newcastle U	0	0		
2021–22	Newcastle U	0	0		

VILCA, Rodrigo (M) 34 5
H: 5 9 W: 11 00 b.Lima 12-3-99

2018	Deportivo Municipal	1	0		
2019	Deportivo Municipal	13	1		
2020	Deportivo Municipal	10	3	**24**	**4**
2020–21	Newcastle U	0	0		
2021–22	Newcastle U	0	0		
2021–22	*Doncaster R*	10	1	**10**	**1**

WATTS, Kelland (D) 94 3
H: 6 4 W: 11 11 b.Alnwick 3-11-99
Internationals: England U19.

2018–19	Newcastle U	0	0		
2019–20	*Stevenage*	16	0	**16**	**0**
2019–20	Newcastle U	1	0		
2019–20	*Mansfield T*	7	1	**7**	**1**
2020–21	Newcastle U	0	0		
2020–21	*Plymouth Arg*	44	2	**44**	**2**
2021–22	Newcastle U	0	0	**1**	**0**
2021–22	*Wigan Ath*	26	0	**26**	**0**

WHITE, Joe (M) 15 0
H: 6 1 W: 11 00 b.Carlisle 1-10-02
Internationals: England U18.

2020–21	Newcastle U	0	0		
2021–22	Newcastle U	0	0		
2021–22	*Hartlepool U*	15	0	**15**	**0**

WIGGETT, Charlie (D) 0 0
b.Reading 2-11-02

2020–21	Chelsea	0	0		
2021–22	Newcastle U	0	0		

WILLOCK, Joe (M) 83 11
H: 5 10 W: 11 09 b.Waltham Forest 20-8-99
Internationals: England U16, U19, U20, U21.

2017–18	Arsenal	2	0		
2018–19	Arsenal	2	0		
2019–20	Arsenal	29	1		
2020–21	Arsenal	7	0		
2020–21	*Newcastle U*	14	8		
2021–22	Arsenal	0	0	**40**	**1**
2021–22	Newcastle U	29	2	**43**	**10**

WILSON, Adam (F) 0 0
b.Ashington 10-4-00
Internationals: England U18.

2020–21	Newcastle U	0	0		
2021–22	Newcastle U	0	0		

WILSON, Callum (F) 264 103
H: 5 11 W: 10 06 b.Coventry 27-2-92
Internationals: England U21, Full caps.

2009–10	Coventry C	0	0		
2010–11	Coventry C	1	0		
2011–12	Coventry C	0	0		
2012–13	Coventry C	11	1		
2013–14	Coventry C	37	21	**49**	**22**
2014–15	Bournemouth	45	20		
2015–16	Bournemouth	13	5		
2016–17	Bournemouth	20	6		
2017–18	Bournemouth	28	8		
2018–19	Bournemouth	30	14		
2019–20	Bournemouth	35	8		
2020–21	Bournemouth	0	0	**171**	**61**
2020–21	Newcastle U	26	12		
2021–22	Newcastle U	18	8	**44**	**20**

WOOD, Chris (F) 423 138
H: 6 3 W: 14 12 b.Auckland 7-12-91
Internationals: New Zealand U17, U23, Full caps.
From Waikato.

2008–09	WBA	2	0		
2009–10	WBA	18	1		
2010–11	WBA	1	0		
2010–11	*Barnsley*	7	0	**7**	**0**
2010–11	*Brighton & HA*	29	8	**29**	**8**
2011–12	WBA	0	0		
2011–12	*Birmingham C*	23	9	**23**	**9**
2011–12	*Bristol C*	19	3	**19**	**3**
2012–13	WBA	0	0	**21**	**1**
2012–13	*Millwall*	19	11	**19**	**11**
2012–13	Leicester C	20	9		
2013–14	Leicester C	26	4		
2014–15	Leicester C	7	1	**53**	**14**
2014–15	*Ipswich T*	8	0	**8**	**0**
2015–16	Leeds U	36	13		
2016–17	Leeds U	44	27		
2017–18	Leeds U	3	1	**83**	**41**
2017–18	Burnley	24	10		
2018–19	Burnley	38	10		
2019–20	Burnley	32	14		
2020–21	Burnley	33	12		
2021–22	Burnley	17	3	**144**	**49**
2021–22	Newcastle U	17	2	**17**	**2**

WOODMAN, Freddie (G) 122 0
H: 6 1 W: 10 12 b.Croydon 4-3-97
Internationals: England U16, U17, U18, U19, U20, U21.
From Crystal Palace.

2014–15	Newcastle U	0	0		
2014–15	*Hartlepool U*	0	0		
2015–16	Newcastle U	0	0		
2015–16	*Crawley T*	11	0	**11**	**0**
2016–17	Newcastle U	0	0		
2016–17	*Kilmarnock*	14	0	**14**	**0**
2017–18	Newcastle U	0	0		
2017–18	*Aberdeen*	5	0	**5**	**0**
2018–19	Newcastle U	0	0		
2019–20	Newcastle U	0	0		
2019–20	*Swansea C*	43	0		
2020–21	Newcastle U	0	0		
2020–21	*Swansea C*	45	0	**88**	**0**
2021–22	Newcastle U	4	0	**4**	**0**
2021–22	*Bournemouth*	0	0		

Players retained or with offer of contract
Carlyon, Nathan; De Bolle, Lucas; Ferguson, Cameron; Oliver, Joe; Scott, Joshua; Stephenson, Dylan; Thompson, Max; Westendorf, Isaac.

Scholars
Barclay, Harry; Beresford, Beau Bewley; Bessent, Steven Andrew; Cooper, Lucas James; Crossley, Kyle; Huntley, James Alan; Mavididi, Shaun Antonio; McNally, Callum Jamie; Miley, Jamie; Ndiweni, Michael Nqobile; Nkunku, Nathan; Page, Eden; Parkinson, Ben; Stanton, Ellis Christopher; Stewart, Joshua Thomas; Thompson, Ciaran James.

NEWPORT CO (57)

AMOND, Padraig (F) **513 130**
H: 5 11 W: 11 11 b.Carlow 15-4-88
Internationals: Republic of Ireland U21.
2006 Shamrock R 9 1
2007 Shamrock R 6 1
2007 *Kildare Co* 13 5 **13 5**
2008 Shamrock R 27 9
2009 Shamrock R 20 4 **62 15**
2010 Sligo R 27 17 **27 17**
2010–11 Pacos 17 0 **17 0**
2011–12 Accrington S 42 7
2012–13 Accrington S 36 9
2013–14 Accrington S 0 0 **78 16**
2013–14 Morecambe 45 11
2014–15 Morecambe 37 8 **82 19**
From Grimsby T.
2016–17 Hartlepool U 46 14 **46 14**
2017–18 Newport Co 43 13
2018–19 Newport Co 45 14
2019–20 Newport Co 33 8
2020–21 Newport Co 41 6
2021–22 Newport Co 0 0 **162 41**
2021–22 *Exeter C* 26 3 **26 3**

BAKER-RICHARDSON, Courtney (F) **50 11**
H: 6 1 W: 11 07 b.Coventry 5-12-95
2013–14 Coventry C 0 0
2014–15 Coventry C 0 0
From Tamworth, Nuneaton T, Redditch U, Kettering T, Leamington.
2017–18 Swansea C 0 0
2018–19 Swansea C 17 3
2019–20 Swansea C 0 0 **17 3**
2019–20 *Accrington S* 2 0 **2 0**
2020–21 Barrow 0 0
2021–22 Newport Co 31 8 **31 8**

BENNETT, Scott (D) **365 26**
H: 5 10 W: 12 11 b.Newquay 30-11-90
2008–09 Exeter C 0 0
2009–10 Exeter C 0 0
2010–11 Exeter C 1 0
2011–12 Exeter C 15 3
2012–13 Exeter C 43 6
2013–14 Exeter C 45 6
2014–15 Exeter C 28 3 **132 18**
2015–16 Notts Co 6 0 **6 0**
2015–16 *Newport Co* 12 0
2015–16 *York C* 11 0 **11 0**
2016–17 Newport Co 39 0
2017–18 Newport Co 28 2
2018–19 Newport Co 38 2
2019–20 Newport Co 28 1
2020–21 Newport Co 38 2
2021–22 Newport Co 33 1 **216 8**

BRIGHT, Harrison (D) **1 0**
b.Monmouth 1-1-04
2020–21 Newport Co 0 0
2021–22 Newport Co 1 0 **1 0**

CLARKE, James (D) **205 8**
H: 6 0 W: 13 03 b.Aylesbury 17-11-89
From Watford, Oxford U, Oxford C, Salisbury C, Woking.
2015–16 Bristol R 37 0
2016–17 Bristol R 22 0
2017–18 Bristol R 11 0
2018–19 Bristol R 42 2 **112 2**
2019–20 Walsall 27 3
2020–21 Walsall 31 2 **58 5**
2021–22 Newport Co 35 1 **35 1**

COLLINS, Lewis (M) **39 2**
H: 5 10 W: 10 08 b.Newport 9-5-01
Internationals: Wales U17, U19, U21.
2017–18 Newport Co 0 0
2018–19 Newport Co 0 0
2019–20 Newport Co 6 0
2020–21 Newport Co 16 1
2021–22 Newport Co 17 1 **39 2**

DAY, Joe (G) **270 0**
H: 6 1 W: 12 00 b.Brighton 13-8-90
From Rushden & D.
2011–12 Peterborough U 0 0
2012–13 Peterborough U 0 0
2013–14 Peterborough U 4 0
2014–15 Peterborough U 0 0 **4 0**
2014–15 *Newport Co* 36 0
2015–16 Newport Co 41 0
2016–17 Newport Co 45 0
2017–18 Newport Co 46 0
2018–19 Newport Co 43 0
2019–20 Cardiff C 1 0
2019–20 *AFC Wimbledon* 9 0 **9 0**
2020–21 Cardiff C 0 0 **1 0**
2020–21 *Bristol R* 18 0 **18 0**
2021–22 Newport Co 27 0 **238 0**

DEMETRIOU, Mickey (D) **271 26**
H: 6 2 W: 12 06 b.Durrington 12-3-90
Internationals: England C.
From Bognor Regis T, Eastbourne Bor, Kidderminster H.
2014–15 Shrewsbury T 42 3
2015–16 Shrewsbury T 1 0
2015–16 *Cambridge U* 15 0 **15 0**
2016–17 Shrewsbury T 0 0 **43 3**
2016–17 Newport Co 17 4
2017–18 Newport Co 46 7
2018–19 Newport Co 45 4
2019–20 Newport Co 21 0
2020–21 Newport Co 45 4
2021–22 Newport Co 39 4 **213 23**

DOLAN, Matthew (M) **296 23**
H: 5 9 W: 11 00 b.Hartlepool 11-2-93
2010–11 Middlesbrough 0 0
2011–12 Middlesbrough 0 0
2012–13 Middlesbrough 0 0
2012–13 *Yeovil T* 8 1
2013–14 Middlesbrough 0 0
2013–14 *Hartlepool U* 20 2
2013–14 *Bradford C* 11 0
2014–15 Bradford C 13 0 **24 0**
2014–15 *Hartlepool U* 2 0 **22 2**
2015–16 Yeovil T 39 3
2016–17 Yeovil T 38 4 **85 8**
2017–18 Newport Co 40 3
2018–19 Newport Co 32 2
2019–20 Newport Co 22 0
2020–21 Newport Co 38 6
2021–22 Newport Co 33 2 **165 13**

ELLISON, Kevin (M) **686 132**
H: 6 0 W: 12 00 b.Liverpool 23-2-79
From Southport, Chorley, Conwy U, Altrincham.
2000–01 Leicester C 1 0
2001–02 Leicester C 0 0 **1 0**
2001–02 Stockport Co 11 0
2002–03 Stockport Co 23 1
2003–04 Stockport Co 14 1 **48 2**
2003–04 *Lincoln C* 11 0 **11 0**
2004–05 Chester C 24 9
2004–05 Hull C 16 1
2005–06 Hull C 23 1 **39 2**
2006–07 Tranmere R 34 4 **34 4**
2007–08 Chester C 36 11
2008–09 Chester C 39 8 **99 28**
2008–09 Rotherham U 0 0
2009–10 Rotherham U 39 8
2010–11 Rotherham U 23 3 **62 11**
2010–11 *Bradford C* 7 1 **7 1**
2011–12 Morecambe 34 15
2012–13 Morecambe 40 11
2013–14 Morecambe 42 10
2014–15 Morecambe 43 11
2015–16 Morecambe 44 9
2016–17 Morecambe 45 8
2017–18 Morecambe 40 9
2018–19 Morecambe 43 7
2019–20 Morecambe 21 1 **352 81**
2020–21 Newport Co 23 2
2021–22 Newport Co 10 1 **33 3**

FARQUHARSON, Priestley (D) **23 0**
H: 6 3 W: 13 00 b.Halifax 15-3-97
2020–21 Connah's Quay Nomads0 0
2020–21 Newport Co 13 0
2021–22 Newport Co 10 0 **23 0**

FISHER, Alex (F) **244 49**
H: 6 3 W: 12 08 b.Westminster 30-6-90
2006–07 Oxford U 0 0
2007–08 Oxford U 10 1
2008–09 Oxford U 3 1 **13 2**
2009–10 Jerez Industrial 0 0
2010–11 Jerez Industrial 21 11 **21 11**
2011–12 Tienen 7 1 **7 1**
2012–13 Racing Mechelen 27 7 **27 7**
2013–14 Heist 2 0 **2 0**
2013–14 Monza 14 2 **14 2**
2014–15 Mansfield T 14 1 **14 1**
From Torquay U.
2015–16 Inverness CT 1 0
2016–17 Inverness CT 21 8 **22 8**
2017–18 Motherwell 11 0 **11 0**
2017–18 Yeovil T 17 6
2018–19 Yeovil T 40 7 **57 13**
2019–20 Exeter C 16 1
2020–21 Exeter C 18 2 **34 3**
2021–22 Newport Co 22 1 **22 1**

GREENIDGE, Jordan (F) **3 0**
b.Enfield 5-1-00
From Stoke C.
2018–19 Omonia 1 0 **1 0**
2018–19 Badajoz 1 0 **1 0**
2021–22 Newport Co 1 0 **1 0**
Transferred to Weymouth, January 2022.

HALL, Louis (D) **0 0**
b.West Bromwich 23-5-99
From Oxford C.
2021–22 Newport Co 0 0
Transferred to Weymouth, January 2022.

HAYNES, Ryan (D) **207 6**
H: 5 7 W: 10 10 b.Northampton 27-9-95
2012–13 Coventry C 1 0
2013–14 Coventry C 2 0
2014–15 Coventry C 26 1
2015–16 Coventry C 9 0
2015–16 *Cambridge U* 10 0 **10 0**
2016–17 Coventry C 19 0
2017–18 Coventry C 21 0 **78 1**
2018–19 Shrewsbury T 16 0 **16 0**
2019–20 Newport Co 32 1
2020–21 Newport Co 37 1
2021–22 Newport Co 34 3 **103 5**

HILLIER, Ryan (F) **0 0**
b.Newport 18-1-03
2019–20 Newport Co 0 0
2020–21 Newport Co 0 0
2021–22 Newport Co 0 0
2021–22 *Cardiff Met Uni* 0 0

HYLTON, Jermaine (F) **94 4**
H: 5 10 W: 11 00 b.Birmingham 28-6-93
2014–15 Swindon T 11 1
2015–16 Swindon T 16 0
2016–17 Swindon T 12 0 **39 1**
From Solihull Moors.
2019–20 Motherwell 28 2
2020–21 Motherwell 5 0 **33 2**
2020–21 Ross Co 18 1 **18 1**
2021–22 Newport Co 4 0 **4 0**

LEWIS, Aaron (D) **56 3**
H: 6 0 W: 13 05 b.Swansea 26-6-98
Internationals: Wales U20, U21.
2018–19 Swansea C 0 0
2018–19 *Doncaster R* 7 0 **7 0**
2019–20 Lincoln C 2 1
2020–21 Lincoln C 0 0 **2 1**
2020–21 Newport Co 20 1
2021–22 Newport Co 27 1 **47 2**

LEWIS, Sonny (M) **0 0**
H: 5 9 b.Newport 2-1-05
2020–21 Newport Co 0 0
2021–22 Newport Co 0 0

LIVERMORE, Aneurin (M) **3 0**
b.Newport 18-1-03
2020–21 Newport Co 0 0
2021–22 Newport Co 3 0 **3 0**

MAHER, Zack (M) **0 0**
b.Newport 5-12-02
2020–21 Newport Co 0 0
2021–22 Newport Co 0 0

NORMAN, Cameron (D) **115 1**
H: 6 2 W: 11 09 b.Norwich 12-10-95
From Norwich C, Concord Rangers, Needham Market, King's Lynn T.
2018–19 Oxford U 7 0 **7 0**
2018–19 Walsall 9 0
2019–20 Walsall 18 0
2020–21 Walsall 35 0 **62 0**
2021–22 Newport Co 46 1 **46 1**

OVENDALE, Evan (G) **0 0**
b. 21-2-05
2020–21 Newport Co 0 0
2021–22 Newport Co 0 0

RYAN-PHILLIP, Callum (M) **0 0**
b.Monmouth 14-5-04
2020–21 Newport Co 0 0
2021–22 Newport Co 0 0

SENIOR, Courtney (F) **125 12**
b. 30-6-97
2014–15 Brentford 0 0
2014–15 *Wycombe W* 1 0 **1 0**
2015–16 Brentford 0 0
2016–17 Colchester U 0 0
2017–18 Colchester U 18 4
2018–19 Colchester U 42 6
2019–20 Colchester U 29 2
2020–21 Colchester U 35 0 **124 12**
2021–22 Newport Co 0 0

TELFORD, Dominic (F) **158 39**
H: 5 9 W: 11 05 b.Burnley 5-12-96
2014–15 Blackpool 14 1
2015–16 Blackpool 0 0 **14 1**
2016–17 Stoke C 0 0
2017–18 Stoke C 0 0
2017–18 *Bristol R* 19 3 **19 3**
2018–19 Bury 38 6 **38 6**
2019–20 Plymouth Arg 19 2
2020–21 Plymouth Arg 16 1 **35 3**
2020–21 Newport Co 15 1
2021–22 Newport Co 37 25 **52 26**

TOWNSEND, Nick (G) **81 0**
H: 5 11 W: 14 05 b.Solihull 1-11-94
Internationals: Antigua and Barbuda Full caps.
2012–13 Birmingham C 0 0
2013–14 Birmingham C 0 0
2014–15 Birmingham C 0 0
2015–16 Barnsley 8 0
2016–17 Barnsley 0 0

2017–18 Barnsley 8 0 **16 0**
2018–19 Newport Co 3 0
2019–20 Newport Co 5 0
2020–21 Newport Co 38 0
2021–22 Newport Co 19 0 **65 0**

TWAMLEY, Lewys (F) 0 0
b.Cardiff 26-5-03. *Internationals:* Wales U18.
2020–21 Newport Co 0 0
2021–22 Newport Co 0 0

WAITE, James (M) 33 9
H: 6 5 W: 12 11 b.Monmouth 11-5-91
Internationals: Wales U19, U21.
2019–20 Cardiff C 0 0
2020–21 Cardiff C 0 0
2021–22 Penybont 17 7 **17 7**
2021–22 Newport Co 16 2 **16 2**

WILLMOTT, Robbie (M) 225 12
H: 5 9 W: 12 02 b.Harlow 16-5-90
Internationals: England C.
From Cambridge U, Luton T, Cambridge U.
2013–14 Newport Co 46 3
2014–15 Newport Co 16 1
From Ebbsfleet U, Chelmsford C.
2017–18 Newport Co 39 2
2018–19 Newport Co 31 2
2019–20 Newport Co 27 0
2020–21 Newport Co 19 0
2020–21 *Exeter C* 17 1 **17 1**
2021–22 Newport Co 30 3 **208 11**

WOODIWISS, Joe (D) 0 0
H: 5 10 b.Cardiff 10-11-02
2019–20 Newport Co 0 0
2020–21 Newport Co 0 0
2021–22 Newport Co 0 0

Players retained or with offer of contract
Bullock, Charlie; Evans, Lestyn; Hall, Louis; Karadogan, Jack; Stokes, Tom; Williams, Jonah.

Scholars
Bullock, Charles; Cadwallader, Evan Lewis; Evans, Caleb Jacob; Evans, Iestyn James; Graham, Mallachi Isaac; Haines, Ben Owen; Hancock, Kyle Luis Gerard; Kabongo, Dixon Diyoka; Lewis, Sonny Jay; Livermore, Aneurin Riley; Maher, Zachary Jamie; Morgan, Ethan Thomas Stephen; Pritchard, Kian Troy Wayne; Rai, Kiban Hang; Ryan-Phillips, Callum Rhys; Stokes, Thomas Martin; Williams, Jonah.

NORTHAMPTON T (58)

ABIMBOLA, Peter (M) 1 0
b.Northampton 22-2-04
2021–22 Northampton T 1 0 **1 0**

APPERE, Louis (F) 79 9
H: 6 1 W: 12 13 b.Perth 26-3-99
2017–18 Dundee U 0 0
2018–19 Dundee U 0 0
2019–20 Dundee U 26 4
2020–21 Dundee U 22 1
2021–22 Dundee U 13 1 **61 6**
2021–22 Northampton T 18 3 **18 3**

ASHLEY-SEAL, Benny (F) 37 2
H: 6 1 W: 12 08 b.Southwark 21-11-98
From Norwich C.
2018–19 Wolverhampton W 0 0
2019–20 Wolverhampton W 0 0
2019–20 *Accrington S* 5 0 **5 0**
2019–20 *Famalicao* 0 0
2020–21 Northampton T 23 0
2021–22 Northampton T 9 2 **32 2**

CROSS, Liam (M) 1 0
b. 8-4-03
2020–21 Northampton T 1 0
2021–22 Northampton T 0 0 **1 0**

DYCHE, Max (D) 3 0
b.Northampton 22-2-03
2020–21 Northampton T 2 0
2021–22 Northampton T 1 0 **3 0**

FLANAGAN, Josh (D) 0 0
b.Milton Keynes 30-6-03
2020–21 Northampton T 0 0
2021–22 Northampton T 0 0

FLORES, Jordan (M) 81 9
H: 5 9 W: 10 08 b.Wigan 4-10-95
2014–15 Wigan Ath 1 0
2015–16 Wigan Ath 3 1
2016–17 Wigan Ath 2 0
2016–17 *Blackpool* 19 3 **19 3**
2017–18 Wigan Ath 0 0
2017–18 *Chesterfield* 13 1 **13 1**
2018–19 Wigan Ath 0 0 **6 1**
2018–19 *Ostersund* 0 0
2019 Dundalk 16 1
2020 Dundalk 13 3 **29 4**
2020–21 Hull C 3 0 **3 0**
2021–22 Northampton T 11 0 **11 0**
Transferred to Bohemians, January 2022.

GUTHRIE, Jon (D) 318 23
H: 5 10 W: 11 00 b.Devizes 1-2-93
2011–12 Crewe Alex 0 0
2012–13 Crewe Alex 2 0
2013–14 Crewe Alex 23 0
2014–15 Crewe Alex 25 0
2015–16 Crewe Alex 39 1
2016–17 Crewe Alex 33 0 **122 1**
2017–18 Walsall 46 1
2018–19 Walsall 42 2 **88 3**
2019–20 Livingston 28 6
2020–21 Livingston 36 5 **64 11**
2021–22 Northampton T 44 8 **44 8**

HARRIMAN, Michael (D) 272 10
H: 5 6 W: 11 10 b.Chichester 23-10-92
Internationals: Republic of Ireland U18, U19, U21.
2010–11 QPR 0 0
2011–12 QPR 1 0
2012–13 QPR 1 0
2012–13 *Wycombe W* 20 0
2013–14 QPR 0 0
2013–14 *Gillingham* 34 1 **34 1**
2014–15 QPR 0 0 **2 0**
2014–15 *Luton T* 35 1 **35 1**
2015–16 Wycombe W 45 7
2016–17 Wycombe W 38 0
2017–18 Wycombe W 18 1
2018–19 Wycombe W 24 0 **145 8**
2019–20 Northampton T 21 0
2020–21 Northampton T 30 0
2021–22 Northampton T 5 0 **56 0**

HORSFALL, Fraser (D) 111 12
H: 6 3 W: 12 13 b.Huddersfield 12-11-96
Internationals: England C.
2015–16 Huddersfield T 0 0
2016–17 Huddersfield T 0 0
2017–18 Huddersfield T 0 0
From Kidderminster H.
2019–20 Macclesfield T 26 0 **26 0**
2020–21 Northampton T 40 3
2021–22 Northampton T 45 9 **85 12**

HOSKINS, Sam (F) 308 48
H: 5 8 W: 10 07 b.Dorchester 4-2-93
2011–12 Southampton 0 0
2011–12 *Preston NE* 0 0
2011–12 *Rotherham U* 8 2 **8 2**
2012–13 Southampton 0 0
2012–13 *Stevenage* 14 1 **14 1**
2013–14 Yeovil T 19 0
2014–15 Yeovil T 12 1 **31 1**
2015–16 Northampton T 34 6
2016–17 Northampton T 25 3
2017–18 Northampton T 27 2
2018–19 Northampton T 42 5
2019–20 Northampton T 37 8
2020–21 Northampton T 46 7
2021–22 Northampton T 44 13 **255 44**

KABAMBA, Nicke (F) 76 7
H: 6 3 W: 11 11 b.Brent 1-2-93
From Uxbridge, Hayes, Burnham, Hampton & Richmond.
2016–17 Portsmouth 4 0
2017–18 Portsmouth 1 0 **5 0**
2017–18 *Colchester U* 8 0 **8 0**
From Havant & Waterlooville, Hartlepool U.
2019–20 Kilmarnock 9 2
2020–21 Kilmarnock 33 5 **42 7**
2021–22 Northampton T 21 0 **21 0**

KOIKI, Ali (D) 67 0
H: 6 2 W: 12 11 b.Chelsea 22-8-99
2018–19 Burnley 0 0
2018–19 *Swindon T* 15 0 **15 0**
2019–20 Burnley 0 0
2020–21 Burnley 0 0
2020–21 Bristol R 10 0 **10 0**
2021–22 Northampton T 42 0 **42 0**

LEWIS, Paul (M) 163 21
H: 6 1 W: 11 00 b.Liverpool 17-12-94
Internationals: England C.
From Macclesfield T.
2016–17 Cambridge U 13 0
2017–18 Cambridge U 12 1
2018–19 Cambridge U 23 4
2019–20 Cambridge U 36 4 **84 9**
2020–21 Tranmere R 40 6
2021–22 Tranmere R 0 0 **40 6**
2021–22 Northampton T 39 6 **39 6**

MAXTED, Jonathan (G) 46 0
H: 6 0 W: 11 03 b.Tadcaster 26-10-93
2012–13 Doncaster R 0 0
2013–14 Doncaster R 0 0
2014–15 Hartlepool U 0 0
From Forest Green R, Guiseley.
2017–18 Accrington S 1 0
2018–19 Accrington S 19 0 **20 0**
2019–20 Exeter C 17 0
2020–21 Exeter C 9 0 **26 0**
2021–22 Northampton T 0 0

McGOWAN, Aaron (D) 219 6
H: 5 9 W: 11 07 b.Liverpool 24-7-97
2012–13 Morecambe 1 0
2013–14 Morecambe 2 0
2014–15 Morecambe 8 1
2015–16 Morecambe 21 0
2016–17 Morecambe 30 0
2017–18 Morecambe 40 0 **102 1**
2018–19 Hamilton A 35 2
2019–20 Hamilton A 22 1 **57 3**
2020–21 Kilmarnock 18 0 **18 0**
2021–22 Northampton T 42 2 **42 2**

McWILLIAMS, Shaun (M) 134 1
H: 5 11 W: 10 12 b.Northampton 14-8-98
2014–15 Northampton T 0 0
2015–16 Northampton T 0 0
2016–17 Northampton T 5 0
2017–18 Northampton T 19 0
2018–19 Northampton T 25 0
2019–20 Northampton T 17 1
2020–21 Northampton T 32 0
2021–22 Northampton T 36 0 **134 1**

MILLS, Joseph (D) 308 15
H: 5 9 W: 11 00 b.Swindon 30-10-89
Internationals: England U17, U18.
2006–07 Southampton 0 0
2007–08 Southampton 0 0
2008–09 Southampton 8 0
2008–09 *Scunthorpe U* 14 0 **14 0**
2009–10 Southampton 16 0
2010–11 Southampton 2 0
2010–11 *Doncaster R* 18 2 **18 2**
2011–12 Southampton 0 0 **26 0**
2011–12 Reading 15 0
2012–13 Reading 0 0 **15 0**
2012–13 *Burnley* 10 0
2013–14 Burnley 0 0 **10 0**
2013–14 *Oldham Ath* 11 0
2013–14 *Shrewsbury T* 13 0 **13 0**
2014–15 Oldham Ath 30 0
2015–16 Oldham Ath 15 1 **56 1**
2016–17 Perth Glory 22 1
2017–18 Perth Glory 22 0 **44 1**
2018–19 Forest Green R 44 4
2019–20 Forest Green R 24 7 **68 11**
2020–21 Northampton T 27 0
2021–22 Northampton T 17 0 **44 0**

NELSON, Sid (D) 124 1
H: 6 1 W: 11 11 b.Lewisham 1-1-96
2013–14 Millwall 0 0
2014–15 Millwall 14 0
2015–16 Millwall 9 0
2016–17 Millwall 3 0
2016–17 *Newport Co* 14 0 **14 0**
2017–18 Millwall 0 0
2017–18 *Yeovil T* 12 0 **12 0**
2017–18 *Chesterfield* 15 1 **15 1**
2018–19 Millwall 0 0 **26 0**
2018–19 *Swindon T* 20 0 **20 0**
2018–19 *Tranmere R* 7 0
2019–20 Tranmere R 19 0
2020–21 Tranmere R 9 0
2021–22 Tranmere R 0 0 **35 0**
2021–22 Northampton T 2 0 **2 0**

PINNOCK, Mitch (M) 137 19
H: 5 10 W: 10 12 b.Gravesend 12-12-94
Internationals: England C.
2012–13 Southend U 2 0
2013–14 Southend U 0 0 **2 0**
From Bromley, Maidstone U, Dover Ath, Kingstonian, Dover Ath.
2018–19 AFC Wimbledon 34 3
2019–20 AFC Wimbledon 25 3 **59 6**
2020–21 Kilmarnock 30 4 **30 4**
2021–22 Northampton T 46 9 **46 9**

POLLOCK, Scott (M) 18 1
H: 5 10 W: 10 06 b.Northampton 12-3-01
2018–19 Northampton T 5 0
2019–20 Northampton T 11 1
2020–21 Northampton T 0 0
2021–22 Northampton T 2 0 **18 1**

ROBERTS, Liam (G) 177 0
H: 6 0 W: 12 13 b.Walsall 24-11-94
2012–13 Walsall 0 0
2013–14 Walsall 0 0
2014–15 Walsall 0 0
2015–16 Walsall 1 0
2016–17 Walsall 0 0
2017–18 Walsall 24 0
2018–19 Walsall 42 0
2019–20 Walsall 32 0
2020–21 Walsall 32 0
2021–22 Walsall 0 0 **131 0**
2021–22 Northampton T 46 0 **46 0**

ROSE, Danny (F) 302 62
H: 5 8 W: 8 05 b.Barnsley 10-12-93
2010–11 Barnsley 1 0
2011–12 Barnsley 4 0
2012–13 Barnsley 8 1
2013–14 Barnsley 3 0
2013–14 *Bury* 6 3

2014–15	Barnsley	1	0	**17**	**1**
2014–15	*Bury*	35	10		
2015–16	Bury	28	5	**69**	**18**
2016–17	Mansfield T	37	9		
2017–18	Mansfield T	39	14		
2018–19	Mansfield T	34	4		
2019–20	Mansfield T	31	11		
2020–21	Mansfield T	0	0	**141**	**38**
2020–21	Northampton T	39	4		
2021–22	Northampton T	36	1	**75**	**5**

SOWERBY, Jack (M) 164 8
H: 5 9 W: 12 04 b.Preston 23-3-95

2014–15	Fleetwood T	0	0		
2015–16	Fleetwood T	8	0		
2016–17	Fleetwood T	8	1		
2017–18	Fleetwood T	22	2		
2018–19	Fleetwood T	15	0		
2018–19	*Carlisle U*	25	4	**25**	**4**
2019–20	Fleetwood T	24	0		
2020–21	Fleetwood T	0	0	**77**	**3**
2020–21	Northampton T	28	0		
2021–22	Northampton T	34	1	**62**	**1**

WOODS, Charlie (G) 0 0
b.Coventry 24-5-04

2020–21	Northampton T	0	0		
2021–22	Northampton T	0	0		

Players retained or with offer of contract
Connor, Jack; Curry, Tommy; Hill, Dylan; Lashley, Courtney; Ndefo, Kenny; Ngwa, Miguel; Nolan, Ryan; Tomlinson, Joshua.

Scholars
Abimbola, Peter Olanrewaju Enibola; Brown, Joshua Ruelle Kieran; Connor, Jack Joseph; Cook, Callum David; Curry, Thomas James; Dadge, James Michael; Duggan, Rico Lee; Hill, Dylan John; Irwin, Reece Ellis; Lack, Ethan Thomas; Lashley, Courtney John; Lekuti, Ayomide Abdul-Awaal; Ndefo, Kenechukwu Izunna; Ngwa, Miguel Suh Tunfong; O'Keeffe, Kai Decious; Smith-Howes, Bradleigh; Thomas, Conor William; Woods, Charlie Elliot.

NORWICH C (59)

AARONS, Maximillian (D) 156 4
H: 5 10 W: 11 07 b.Hammersmith 4-1-00
Internationals: England U19, U21.
From Luton T.

2018–19	Norwich C	41	2		
2019–20	Norwich C	36	0		
2020–21	Norwich C	45	2		
2021–22	Norwich C	34	0	**156**	**4**

ADSHEAD, Daniel (M) 54 0
H: 5 6 W: 10 03 b.Manchester 2-9-01
Internationals: England U18, U19.

2017–18	Rochdale	1	0		
2018–19	Rochdale	10	0	**11**	**0**
2019–20	Norwich C	0	0		
2020–21	Norwich C	0	0		
2020–21	*Telstar*	28	0	**28**	**0**
2021–22	Norwich C	0	0		
2021–22	*Gillingham*	15	0	**15**	**0**

BARDEN, Daniel (G) 2 0
b. 2-1-01
Internationals: Wales U21.
From Arsenal.

2020–21	Norwich C	2	0		
2021–22	Norwich C	0	0	**2**	**0**
2021–22	*Livingston*	0	0		

BERRY, Dylan (G) 0 0

2020–21	Northampton T	0	0		
2021–22	Norwich C	0	0		

BLAIR, Sam (G) 0 0
b. 27-12-02

2020–21	Norwich C	0	0		
2021–22	Norwich C	0	0		

BROOKE, Harry (M) 0 0
From Millwall.

2020–21	Norwich C	0	0		
2021–22	Norwich C	0	0		

BUSHIRI, Rocky (D) 71 0
b. 30-11-99
Internationals: Belgium U19, U21.

2017–18	Oostende	8	0		
2018–19	Oostende	0	0	**8**	**0**
2018–19	*Eupen*	31	0		
2019–20	Norwich C	0	0		
2019–20	*Blackpool*	4	0	**4**	**0**
2019–20	*Sint-Truiden*	7	0	**7**	**0**
2020–21	Norwich C	0	0		
2020–21	*Mechelen*	6	0	**6**	**0**
2020–21	*Eupen*	1	0	**32**	**0**
2021–22	Norwich C	0	0		
2021–22	*Hibernian*	14	0	**14**	**0**

BYRAM, Samuel (D) 195 9
H: 5 11 W: 11 05 b.Thurrock 16-9-93

2012–13	Leeds U	44	3		
2013–14	Leeds U	25	0		
2014–15	Leeds U	39	3		
2015–16	Leeds U	22	3	**130**	**9**
2015–16	West Ham U	4	0		
2016–17	West Ham U	18	0		
2017–18	West Ham U	5	0		
2018–19	West Ham U	0	0	**27**	**0**
2018–19	*Nottingham F*	6	0	**6**	**0**
2019–20	Norwich C	17	0		
2020–21	Norwich C	0	0		
2021–22	Norwich C	15	0	**32**	**0**

CANTWELL, Todd (M) 123 15
H: 5 10 W: 10 06 b.Norwich 27-2-98
Internationals: England U17, U21.

2017–18	Norwich C	0	0		
2017–18	*Fortuna Sittard*	10	2	**10**	**2**
2018–19	Norwich C	24	1		
2019–20	Norwich C	37	6		
2020–21	Norwich C	33	6		
2021–22	Norwich C	8	0	**102**	**13**
2021–22	*Bournemouth*	11	0	**11**	**0**

CLARKE, Flynn (M) 4 0
b. 19-12-02
Internationals: Scotland U19.

2019–20	Peterborough U	0	0		
2020–21	Peterborough U	4	0	**4**	**0**
2021–22	Norwich C	0	0		

COKER, Kenny (F) 4 0
b. 10-11-03

2019–20	Southend U	2	0		
2020–21	Southend U	2	0	**4**	**0**
2020–21	Norwich C	0	0		
2021–22	Norwich C	0	0		

DENNIS, Matthew (M) 0 0
b. 15-4-02
From Arsenal.

2020–21	Norwich C	0	0		
2021–22	Norwich C	0	0		

DICKSON-PETERS, Thomas (F) 9 0
H: 5 8 b.Slough 16-9-02
Internationals: Scotland U17, U18.

2020–21	Norwich C	0	0		
2021–22	Norwich C	0	0		
2021–22	*Gillingham*	9	0	**9**	**0**

DOWELL, Kieran (F) 121 22
H: 5 9 W: 9 04 b.Ormskirk 10-10-97
Internationals: England U16, U17, U18, U20, U21.

2014–15	Everton	0	0		
2015–16	Everton	2	0		
2016–17	Everton	0	0		
2017–18	Everton	0	0		
2017–18	*Nottingham F*	38	9	**38**	**9**
2018–19	Everton	0	0		
2018–19	*Sheffield U*	16	2	**16**	**2**
2019–20	Everton	0	0	**2**	**0**
2019–20	*Derby Co*	10	0	**10**	**0**
2019–20	*Wigan Ath*	12	5	**12**	**5**
2020–21	Norwich C	24	5		
2021–22	Norwich C	19	1	**43**	**6**

DRMIC, Josip (F) 236 77
b.Lachen 8-8-92
Internationals: Switzerland U19, U21, U23, Full caps.

2009–10	FC Zurich	4	0		
2010–11	FC Zurich	7	0		
2011–12	FC Zurich	20	5		
2012–13	FC Zurich	31	13	**62**	**18**
2013–14	Nurenberg	33	17	**33**	**17**
2014–15	Bayer Leverkusen	25	6	**25**	**6**
2015–16	Borussia M'gladbach	13	1		
2015–16	*Hamburg*	6	1	**6**	**1**
2016–17	Borussia M'gladbach	12	0		
2017–18	Borussia M'gladbach	13	4		
2018–19	Borussia M'gladbach	5	2	**43**	**7**
2019–20	Norwich C	21	1		
2020–21	Norwich C	0	0		
2020–21	*Rijeka*	16	6		
2021–22	Norwich C	0	0	**21**	**1**
2021–22	*Rijeka*	30	21	**46**	**27**

FAMEWO, Akin (D) 85 1
H: 6 2 W: 10 06 b.Lewisham 9-11-98

2016–17	Luton T	3	0		
2017–18	Luton T	3	0		
2018–19	Luton T	0	0	**6**	**0**
2018–19	*Grimsby T*	10	0	**10**	**0**
2018–19	Norwich C	0	0		
2019–20	Norwich C	1	0		
2019–20	*St Mirren*	9	0	**9**	**0**
2020–21	Norwich C	0	0		
2020–21	*Charlton Ath*	22	0		
2021–22	Norwich C	0	0	**1**	**0**
2021–22	*Charlton Ath*	37	1	**59**	**1**

GIANNOULIS, Dimitrios (D) 221 3
H: 5 10 W: 11 00 b.Katerini 17-10-95
Internationals: Greece U21, Greece.

2012–13	Vataniakos	14	1		
2013–14	Vataniakos	19	2	**33**	**3**
2014–15	PAOK	0	0		
2014–15	*Pierikos*	26	0	**26**	**0**
2015–16	PAOK	0	0		
2015–16	*Veria*	24	0	**24**	**0**
2016–17	PAOK	0	0		
2016–17	*Anorthosis Famagusta*	8	0	**8**	**0**
2017–18	PAOK	0	0		
2017–18	*Atromitos*	27	0		
2018–19	PAOK	8	0		
2018–19	*Atromitos*	15	0	**42**	**0**
2019–20	PAOK	34	0		
2020–21	PAOK	12	0	**54**	**0**
2020–21	Norwich C	16	0		
2021–22	Norwich C	18	0	**34**	**0**

GIBBS, Liam (M) 1 0
b.Bury St Edmunds 16-12-02

2019–20	Ipswich T	0	0		
2020–21	Ipswich T	1	0	**1**	**0**
2021–22	Norwich C	0	0		

GIBSON, Ben (D) 282 6
H: 6 1 W: 12 04 b.Nunthorpe 15-1-93
Internationals: England U17, U18, U20, U21.

2010–11	Middlesbrough	1	0		
2011–12	Middlesbrough	0	0		
2011–12	*Plymouth Arg*	13	0	**13**	**0**
2012–13	Middlesbrough	1	0		
2012–13	*Tranmere R*	28	1	**28**	**1**
2013–14	Middlesbrough	31	1		
2014–15	Middlesbrough	36	0		
2015–16	Middlesbrough	33	1		
2016–17	Middlesbrough	38	1		
2017–18	Middlesbrough	45	1	**185**	**4**
2018–19	Burnley	1	1		
2019–20	Burnley	0	0		
2020–21	Burnley	0	0	**1**	**1**
2020–21	*Norwich C*	27	0		
2021–22	Norwich C	28	0	**55**	**0**

GUNN, Angus (G) 92 0
H: 6 5 W: 12 02 b.Norwich 22-1-96
Internationals: England U16, U17, U18, U19, U20, U21.

2013–14	Manchester C	0	0		
2014–15	Manchester C	0	0		
2015–16	Manchester C	0	0		
2016–17	Manchester C	0	0		
2017–18	Manchester C	0	0		
2017–18	*Norwich C*	46	0		
2018–19	Southampton	12	0		
2019–20	Southampton	10	0		
2020–21	Southampton	0	0		
2020–21	*Stoke C*	15	0	**15**	**0**
2021–22	Southampton	0	0	**22**	**0**
2021–22	Norwich C	9	0	**55**	**0**

HANLEY, Grant (D) 324 12
H: 6 3 W: 12 00 b.Dumfries 20-11-91
Internationals: Scotland U19, U21, Full caps.
From Rangers.

2008–09	Blackburn R	0	0		
2009–10	Blackburn R	1	0		
2010–11	Blackburn R	7	0		
2011–12	Blackburn R	23	1		
2012–13	Blackburn R	39	2		
2013–14	Blackburn R	38	1		
2014–15	Blackburn R	31	1		
2015–16	Blackburn R	44	2	**183**	**7**
2016–17	Newcastle U	10	1		
2017–18	Newcastle U	0	0	**10**	**1**
2017–18	Norwich C	32	1		
2018–19	Norwich C	9	1		
2019–20	Norwich C	15	0		
2020–21	Norwich C	42	1		
2021–22	Norwich C	33	1	**131**	**4**

HERNANDEZ, Onel (M) 217 19
H: 5 8 W: 10 12 b.Moron 1-2-93
Internationals: Germany U18. Cuba Full caps.

2010–11	Arminia Bielefeld	10	0		
2011–12	Arminia Bielefeld	18	0	**28**	**0**
2012–13	Werder Bremen	0	0		
2013–14	Werder Bremen	0	0		
2013–14	VfL Wolfsburg	0	0		
2014–15	VfL Wolfsburg	0	0		
2015–16	VfL Wolfsburg	0	0		
2016–17	Eintracht Brauschweig	34	5		
2017–18	Eintracht Brauschweig	17	1	**51**	**6**
2017–18	Norwich C	12	0		
2018–19	Norwich C	40	8		
2019–20	Norwich C	26	1		
2020–21	Norwich C	21	0		
2021–22	Norwich C	0	0	**99**	**9**
2021–22	*Middlesbrough*	17	1	**17**	**1**
2021–22	*Birmingham C*	22	3	**22**	**3**

HUGILL, Jordan (F) 285 60
H: 6 0 W: 10 01 b.Middlesbrough 4-6-92
From Seaham Red Star, Consett, Whitby T.

2013–14	Port Vale	20	4	**20**	**4**
2014–15	Preston NE	3	0		
2014–15	*Tranmere R*	6	1	**6**	**1**
2014–15	*Hartlepool U*	8	4	**8**	**4**
2015–16	Preston NE	29	3		
2016–17	Preston NE	44	12		
2017–18	Preston NE	27	8	**103**	**23**
2017–18	West Ham U	3	0		
2018–19	West Ham U	0	0		

2018–19	*Middlesbrough*	37	6	**37**	**6**
2019–20	West Ham U	0	0	**3**	**0**
2019–20	*QPR*	39	13		
2020–21	QPR	0	0	**39**	**13**
2020–21	Norwich C	31	4		
2021–22	Norwich C	0	0	**31**	**4**
2021–22	*WBA*	20	1	**20**	**1**
2021–22	*Cardiff C*	18	4	**18**	**4**

IDAH, Adam (F) **46** **4**
H: 6 3 W: 13 01 b.Cork 11-2-01
Internationals: Republic of Ireland U16, U17, U18, U19, U21, Full caps.

2019–20	Norwich C	12	0		
2020–21	Norwich C	17	3		
2021–22	Norwich C	17	1	**46**	**4**

KABAK, Ozan (D) **89** **6**
H: 6 1 W: 13 08 b.Ankara 25-3-00
Internationals: Turkey U16, U17, U18, Full caps.

2017–18	Galatasaray	1	0		
2018–19	Galatasaray	13	0	**14**	**0**
2018–19	VfB Stuttgart	15	3	**15**	**3**
2019–20	Schalke 04	26	3		
2020–21	Schalke 04	14	0		
2020–21	*Liverpool*	9	0	**9**	**0**
2021–22	Schalke 04	0	0	**40**	**3**
2021–22	*Norwich C*	11	0	**11**	**0**

KAMARA, Abu (D) **0** **0**

2021–22	Norwich C	0	0		

KRUL, Tim (G) **356** **0**
H: 6 4 W: 13 00 b.Den Haag 3-4-88
Internationals: Netherlands U16, U17, U19, U20, U21, Full caps.
From ADO Den Haag.

2005–06	Newcastle U	0	0		
2006–07	Newcastle U	0	0		
2007–08	*Falkirk*	22	0	**22**	**0**
2007–08	Newcastle U	0	0		
2008–09	Newcastle U	0	0		
2008–09	*Carlisle U*	9	0	**9**	**0**
2009–10	Newcastle U	3	0		
2010–11	Newcastle U	21	0		
2011–12	Newcastle U	38	0		
2012–13	Newcastle U	24	0		
2013–14	Newcastle U	36	0		
2014–15	Newcastle U	30	0		
2015–16	Newcastle U	8	0		
2016–17	Newcastle U	0	0		
2016–17	*Ajax*	0	0		
2016–17	*AZ Alkmaar*	18	0	**18**	**0**
2017–18	Newcastle U	0	0	**160**	**0**
2017–18	*Brighton & HA*	0	0		
2018–19	Norwich C	46	0		
2019–20	Norwich C	36	0		
2020–21	Norwich C	36	0		
2021–22	Norwich C	29	0	**147**	**0**

LEES-MELOU, Pierre (M) **200** **26**
H: 6 1 W: 12 00 b.Langon 25-5-93
From US Lege Cap Ferret.

2015–16	Dijon	16	2		
2016–17	Dijon	32	7	**48**	**9**
2017–18	Nice	34	5		
2018–19	Nice	30	2		
2019–20	Nice	26	5		
2020–21	Nice	29	4		
2021–22	Nice	0	0	**119**	**16**
2021–22	Norwich C	33	1	**33**	**1**

MAIR, Archie (G) **0** **0**
H: 6 6 W: 12 08 b.Turriff 10-2-01
Internationals: Scotland U17, U19, U21.
From Aberdeen.

2019–20	Norwich C	0	0		
2020–21	Norwich C	0	0		
2021–22	Norwich C	0	0		
2021–22	*Lincoln C*	0	0		

MARTIN, Josh (M) **39** **5**
H: 5 9 W: 11 00 b.Luton 9-9-01
From Arsenal.

2019–20	Norwich C	5	0		
2020–21	Norwich C	9	1		
2021–22	Norwich C	0	0	**14**	**1**
2021–22	*Milton Keynes D*	5	0	**5**	**0**
2021–22	*Doncaster R*	20	4	**20**	**4**

McALEAR, Reece (M) **29** **4**
b.Glasgow 12-2-02
Internationals: Scotland U16, U17, U18.
From Motherwell.

2020–21	Norwich C	1	0		
2021–22	Norwich C	0	0	**1**	**0**
2021–22	*Inverness CT*	28	4	**28**	**4**

McCALLUM, Sam (D) **91** **5**
H: 5 10 W: 10 10 b.Canterbury 2-9-00
From Herne Bay.

2018–19	Coventry C	7	0		
2019–20	Norwich C	0	0		
2019–20	*Coventry C*	26	2		
2020–21	Norwich C	0	0		
2020–21	*Coventry C*	41	1	**74**	**3**
2021–22	Norwich C	0	0		
2021–22	*QPR*	17	2	**17**	**2**

McCRACKEN, Jon (G) **0** **0**
H: 6 1 W: 12 02 b.Wishaw 24-5-00
Internationals: Scotland U16, U17.
From Hamilton A.

2020–21	Norwich C	0	0		
2021–22	Norwich C	0	0		

McGOVERN, Michael (G) **302** **0**
H: 6 2 W: 13 07 b.Enniskillen 12-7-84
Internationals: Northern Ireland U19, U21, Full caps.

2004–05	Celtic	0	0		
2004–05	*Stranraer*	19	0	**19**	**0**
2005–06	Celtic	0	0		
2006–07	Celtic	0	0		
2006–07	*St Johnstone*	1	0	**1**	**0**
2007–08	Celtic	0	0		
2008–09	Dundee U	0	0		
2009–10	Ross Co	35	0		
2010–11	Ross Co	36	0	**71**	**0**
2011–12	Falkirk	35	0		
2012–13	Falkirk	35	0		
2013–14	Falkirk	34	0	**104**	**0**
2014–15	Hamilton A	38	0		
2015–16	Hamilton A	37	0	**75**	**0**
2016–17	Norwich C	20	0		
2017–18	Norwich C	0	0		
2018–19	Norwich C	0	0		
2019–20	Norwich C	2	0		
2020–21	Norwich C	10	0		
2021–22	Norwich C	0	0	**32**	**0**

McLEAN, Kenny (M) **403** **46**
H: 6 0 W: 11 00 b.Rutherglen 8-1-92
Internationals: Scotland U19, U21, Full caps.

2009–10	St Mirren	0	0		
2009–10	*Arbroath*	20	1	**20**	**1**
2010–11	St Mirren	19	0		
2011–12	St Mirren	28	4		
2012–13	St Mirren	29	3		
2013–14	St Mirren	30	6		
2014–15	St Mirren	25	7	**131**	**20**
2014–15	Aberdeen	13	0		
2015–16	Aberdeen	38	6		
2016–17	Aberdeen	38	4		
2017–18	Aberdeen	22	3		
2017–18	Norwich C	0	0		
2017–18	*Aberdeen*	15	5	**126**	**18**
2018–19	Norwich C	20	3		
2019–20	Norwich C	37	1		
2020–21	Norwich C	38	2		
2021–22	Norwich C	31	1	**126**	**7**

MUMBA, Bali (D) **20** **0**
H: 5 6 W: 9 11 b.South Shields 8-10-01
Internationals: England U16, U17, U18, U19.

2017–18	Sunderland	1	0		
2018–19	Sunderland	4	0		
2019–20	Sunderland	0	0	**5**	**0**
2020–21	Norwich C	4	0		
2021–22	Norwich C	1	0	**5**	**0**
2021–22	*Peterborough U*	10	0	**10**	**0**

NORMANN, Mathias (M) **144** **7**
H: 5 10 W: 11 11 b.Svolvaer 28-5-96
Internationals: Norway U17, U18, U21, Full caps.

2012	Lofoten	5	1	**5**	**1**
2013	Bodo/Glimt	0	0		
2014	Bodo/Glimt	0	0		
2015	Bodo/Glimt	0	0		
2015	*Alta*	16	2	**16**	**2**
2016	Bodo/Glimt	27	0		
2017	Bodo/Glimt	7	0		
2017	*Molde*	5	0		
2018	Bodo/Glimt	0	0	**34**	**0**
2018	*Molde*	10	1	**15**	**1**
2018–19	Rostov	9	0		
2019–20	Rostov	23	1		
2020–21	Rostov	15	1		
2021–22	Rostov	4	0	**51**	**2**
2021–22	*Norwich C*	23	1	**23**	**1**

OMOBAMIDELE, Andrew (D) **14** **1**
H: 6 2 W: 11 11 b.Dublin 23-6-02
Internationals: Republic of Ireland U17, U19, U21, Full caps.

2019–20	Norwich C	0	0		
2020–21	Norwich C	9	0		
2021–22	Norwich C	5	1	**14**	**1**

OMOTOYE, Tyrese (F) **27** **0**
b.Hassell 23-9-02
Internationals: Belgium U16.
From Cray W.

2020–21	Norwich C	3	0		
2020–21	*Swindon T*	7	0	**7**	**0**
2021–22	Norwich C	0	0	**3**	**0**
2021–22	*Leyton Orient*	4	0	**4**	**0**
2021–22	*Carlisle U*	13	0	**13**	**0**

OXBOROUGH, Aston (G) **0** **0**
H: 6 5 b.Great Yarmouth 9-5-98
Internationals: England U16, U17.

2018–19	Norwich C	0	0		
2019–20	Norwich C	0	0		
2020–21	Norwich C	0	0		
2021–22	Norwich C	0	0		

PLACHETA, Przemyslaw (M) **109** **17**
H: 5 10 W: 11 05 b.Lowicz 23-9-98
Internationals: Poland U18, U19, U20, U21, Full caps.

2017–18	Sonnenhof Grossaspach	2	0	**2**	**0**
2017–18	Pogon Siedice	11	2	**11**	**2**
2018–19	Podbeskidzie	23	6	**23**	**6**
2019–20	Slask Wroclaw	35	8	**35**	**8**
2020–21	Norwich C	26	1		
2021–22	Norwich C	12	0	**38**	**1**

PUKKI, Teemu (F) **404** **163**
H: 5 11 W: 10 06 b.Kotka 29-3-90
Internationals: Finland U17, U19, U21, Full caps.

2006	KooTeePee	5	0		
2007	KooTeePee	24	3	**29**	**3**
2008–09	Sevilla	0	0		
2010	HJK Helsinki	7	2		
2011	HJK Helsinki	18	11	**25**	**13**
2011–12	Schalke 04	19	5		
2012–13	Schalke 04	17	3		
2013–14	Schalke 04	1	0	**37**	**8**
2013–14	Celtic	25	7		
2014–15	Celtic	1	0	**26**	**7**
2014–15	*Brondby*	27	9		
2015–16	Brondby	33	9		
2016–17	Brondby	34	20		
2017–18	Brondby	36	17	**130**	**55**
2018–19	Norwich C	43	29		
2019–20	Norwich C	36	11		
2020–21	Norwich C	41	26		
2021–22	Norwich C	37	11	**157**	**77**

RASHICA, Milot (M) **222** **44**
H: 5 10 W: 11 11 b.Vushtrri, Kosovo 28-6-96
Internationals: Albania U17, U19, U21, Full caps. Kosovo Full caps.

2013–14	Vushtrria	5	2		
2014–15	Vushtrria	16	7	**21**	**9**
2015–16	Vitesse	31	8		
2016–17	Vitesse	33	2		
2017–18	Vitesse	19	3	**83**	**13**
2017–18	Werder Bremen	9	1		
2018–19	Werder Bremen	26	9		
2019–20	Werder Bremen	28	8		
2020–21	Werder Bremen	24	3		
2021–22	Werder Bremen	0	0	**87**	**21**
2021–22	Norwich C	31	1	**31**	**1**

RILEY, Regan (M) **1** **0**

2019–20	Bolton W	1	0		
2020–21	Bolton W	0	0	**1**	**0**
2020–21	Norwich C	0	0		
2021–22	Norwich C	0	0		

ROSE, Joseph (G) **0** **0**
H: 6 1 b. 5-11-01
Internationals: England U16.

2020–21	Norwich C	0	0		
2021–22	Norwich C	0	0		

ROWE, Jonathan (F) **13** **0**
H: 5 8 b.Westminster 30-4-03

2020–21	Norwich C	0	0		
2021–22	Norwich C	13	0	**13**	**0**

RUPP, Lukas (M) **232** **19**
H: 5 10 W: 11 07 b.Heidelberg 8-1-91

2009–10	Karlsruher	2	0		
2010–11	Karlsruher	24	3	**26**	**3**
2011–12	Borussia M'gladbach	3	0		
2011–12	*Paderborn*	15	2		
2012–13	Borussia M'gladbach	21	0		
2013–14	Borussia M'gladbach	10	0	**34**	**0**
2014–15	Paderborn	31	4	**46**	**6**
2015–16	Stuttgart	29	5	**29**	**5**
2016–17	Hoffenheim	14	2		
2017–18	Hoffenheim	21	3		
2018–19	Hoffenheim	1	0		
2019–20	Hoffenheim	7	0	**43**	**5**
2019–20	Norwich C	12	0		
2020–21	Norwich C	23	0		
2021–22	Norwich C	19	0	**54**	**0**

SARGENT, Josh (F) **98** **15**
H: 6 1 W: 12 06 b.Missouri 20-2-00
Internationals: USA U17, U20, U23, Full caps.
From Saint Louis.

2018–19	Werder Bremen	10	2		
2019–20	Werder Bremen	28	4		
2020–21	Werder Bremen	32	5		
2021–22	Werder Bremen	2	2	**72**	**13**
2021–22	Norwich C	26	2	**26**	**2**

SHIPLEY, Lewis (D) **0** **0**
b.Cambridge 29-11-03

2020–21	Norwich C	0	0		
2021–22	Norwich C	0	0		

SINANI, Danel (M) **183** **51**
H: 6 1 b.Belgrade 5-4-97
Internationals: Luxembourg U19, U21, Full caps.

2014–15	Racing	15	3		
2015–16	Racing	23	3		
2016–17	Racing	24	6	**62**	**12**

2017–18 Dudelange 22 9
2018–19 Dudelange 25 7
2019–20 Dudelange 17 14 **64 30**
2020–21 Norwich C 0 0
2020–21 *Waasland-Beveren* 18 3 **18 3**
2021–22 Norwich C 0 0
2021–22 *Huddersfield T* 39 6 **39 6**

SORENSEN, Jacob (M) 144 6
H: 5 9 W: 11 07 b.Esbjerg 3-3-98
Internationals: Denmark U18, U20, U21.
2016–17 Esbjerg 8 0
2017–18 Esbjerg 29 1
2018–19 Esbjerg 36 3
2019–20 Esbjerg 29 1 **102 5**
2020–21 Norwich C 32 1
2021–22 Norwich C 10 0 **42 1**

SOTO, Sebastian (F) 29 7
H: 6 0 W:] b.California 28-7-00
Internationals: USA U19, U20, U23, Full caps.
2018–19 Hannover 96 3 0
2019–20 Hannover 96 2 0 **5 0**
2020–21 Norwich C 0 0
2020–21 *Telstar* 12 7 **12 7**
2021–22 Norwich C 0 0
2021–22 *Porto* 0 0
2021–22 *Livingston* 12 0 **12 0**

SPRINGETT, Tony (F) 3 0
b. 22-9-02
Internationals: Republic of Ireland U18.
2021–22 Norwich C 3 0 **3 0**

STEWART, Sean (D) 0 0
H: 5 11 b. 21-1-03
Internationals: Northern Ireland U17, U21.
2020–21 Norwich C 0 0
2021–22 Norwich C 0 0

TOMKINSON, Jonathan (D) 0 0
H: 6 3 W: 11 00 b.Plano 11-4-02
Internationals: USA U17.
2020–21 Norwich C 0 0
2021–22 Norwich C 0 0

TZOLIS, Christos (F) 56 7
H: 5 10 W: 11 07 b.Thessaloniki 30-1-02
Internationals: Greece U17, U19, U21, Full caps.
2019–20 PAOK 9 1
2020–21 PAOK 33 6 **42 7**
2021–22 Norwich C 14 0 **14 0**

WARNER, Jaden (D) 0 0
b.Hillingdon 28-10-02
2020–21 Norwich C 0 0
2021–22 Norwich C 0 0

ZIMMERMANN, Christoph (D) 121 3
H: 6 4 W: 14 07 b.Dusseldorf 12-1-93
2011–12 Borussia M'gladbach 0 0
2012–13 Borussia M'gladbach 0 0
2013–14 Borussia M'gladbach 0 0
2014–15 Borussia Dortmund 0 0
2015–16 Borussia Dortmund 0 0
2016–17 Borussia Dortmund 0 0
2017–18 Norwich C 39 1
2018–19 Norwich C 40 2
2019–20 Norwich C 17 0
2020–21 Norwich C 22 0
2021–22 Norwich C 3 0 **121 3**

Players retained or with offer of contract
Aboh, Kenneth; Campbell, Charles; Duffy, Joseph; Earley, Saxon; Hills, Bradley; Matos, Alex; St Paul, Jayden; Thorn, Oscar.

Scholars
Aziaya, David Chukwuemeka; Eze, Chukwu-Dubem Darren; Foyo, Osman Sidibay; Jambang, Ayyuba; Reindorf Junior, Michael Douglas Kwabena; Trueman, Reece; Welch, Finley Paul.

NOTTINGHAM F (60)

ARTER, Harry (M) 307 31
H: 5 9 W: 11 00 b.Sidcup 28-12-89
Internationals: Republic of Ireland U17, U19, Full caps.
2007–08 Charlton Ath 0 0
2008–09 Charlton Ath 0 0
From Woking.
2010–11 Bournemouth 18 0
2010–11 *Carlisle U* 5 1 **5 1**
2011–12 Bournemouth 34 5
2012–13 Bournemouth 37 8
2013–14 Bournemouth 31 3
2014–15 Bournemouth 43 9
2015–16 Bournemouth 21 1
2016–17 Bournemouth 35 1
2017–18 Bournemouth 13 1
2018–19 Bournemouth 0 0
2018–19 *Cardiff C* 25 0 **25 0**
2019–20 Bournemouth 0 0 **232 28**
2019–20 *Fulham* 28 2 **28 2**
2020–21 Nottingham F 13 0
2021–22 Nottingham F 0 0 **13 0**
2021–22 *Charlton Ath* 4 0 **4 0**

BACK, Finley (D) 3 0
b. 25-9-02
2021–22 Nottingham F 3 0 **3 0**

BARNES, Joshua (M) 0 0
b. 1-11-00
2020–21 Nottingham F 0 0
2021–22 Nottingham F 0 0

BONG, Gaetan (D) 301 3
H: 6 0 W: 11 09 b.Sakbayeme 25-4-88
Internationals: France U21. Cameroon Full caps.
2005–06 Metz 3 0
2006–07 Metz 2 0
2007–08 Metz 11 0
2008–09 Metz 0 0 **16 0**
2008–09 *Tours* 34 0 **34 0**
2009–10 Valenciennes 29 2
2010–11 Valenciennes 22 1
2011–12 Valenciennes 28 0
2012–13 Valenciennes 29 0
2013–14 Valenciennes 1 0 **109 3**
2013–14 Olympiacos 19 0 **19 0**
2014–15 Wigan Ath 14 0 **14 0**
2015–16 Brighton & HA 16 0
2016–17 Brighton & HA 24 0
2017–18 Brighton & HA 25 0
2018–19 Brighton & HA 22 0
2019–20 Brighton & HA 4 0 **91 0**
2019–20 Nottingham F 1 0
2020–21 Nottingham F 10 0
2021–22 Nottingham F 7 0 **18 0**

CAFU, Dias (M) 187 12
H: 6 1 W: 12 13 b.Guimaraes 26-2-93
Internationals: Portugal U16, U17, U18, U19, U20.
2012–13 Benfica 0 0
2013–14 Vitoria Guimaraes 0 0
2014–15 Vitoria Guimaraes 29 0
2015–16 Vitoria Guimaraes 32 3 **61 3**
2016–17 Lorient 18 0 **18 0**
2017–18 Metz 10 0
2017–18 *Legia Warzaw* 7 2
2018–19 Metz 0 0 **10 0**
2018–19 *Legia Warzaw* 31 4
2019–20 Legia Warzaw 6 0 **44 6**
2019–20 Olympiacos 7 1
2020–21 Olympiacos 2 1
2020–21 Nottingham F 31 0
2021–22 Olympiacos 0 0 **9 2**
2021–22 Nottingham F 14 1 **45 1**

COLBACK, Jack (M) 367 20
H: 5 10 W: 11 13 b.Killingworth 24-10-89
Internationals: England U20.
2007–08 Sunderland 0 0
2008–09 Sunderland 0 0
2009–10 Sunderland 1 0
2009–10 *Ipswich T* 37 4
2010–11 Sunderland 11 0
2010–11 *Ipswich T* 13 0 **50 4**
2011–12 Sunderland 35 1
2012–13 Sunderland 35 0
2013–14 Sunderland 33 3 **115 4**
2014–15 Newcastle U 35 4
2015–16 Newcastle U 29 1
2016–17 Newcastle U 29 0
2017–18 Newcastle U 0 0
2017–18 *Nottingham F* 16 1
2018–19 Newcastle U 0 0
2018–19 *Nottingham F* 38 3
2019–20 Newcastle U 0 0 **93 5**
2020–21 Nottingham F 17 0
2021–22 Nottingham F 38 3 **109 7**

COOK, Steve (D) 373 19
H: 6 1 W: 12 13 b.Hastings 19-4-91
2008–09 Brighton & HA 2 0
2009–10 Brighton & HA 0 0
2010–11 Brighton & HA 0 0
2011–12 Brighton & HA 1 0 **3 0**
2011–12 Bournemouth 26 0
2012–13 Bournemouth 33 1
2013–14 Bournemouth 38 3
2014–15 Bournemouth 46 5
2015–16 Bournemouth 36 4
2016–17 Bournemouth 38 2
2017–18 Bournemouth 34 2
2018–19 Bournemouth 31 1
2019–20 Bournemouth 29 1
2020–21 Bournemouth 42 0
2021–22 Bournemouth 3 0 **356 19**
2021–22 Nottingham F 14 0 **14 0**

DRAGER, Mohamed (D) 77 4
H: 5 11 W: 11 09 b.Freiburg 25-6-96
Internationals: Tunisia U17, Full caps.
2017–18 Freiburg 2 0
2018–19 Freiburg 0 0
2018–19 *Paderborn* 32 0
2019–20 Freiburg 0 0 **2 0**
2019–20 *Paderborn* 18 1 **50 1**
2020–21 Olympiacos 8 0 **8 0**
2021–22 Nottingham F 0 0
2021–22 *Lucerne* 17 3 **17 3**

FERNANDES, Baba (D) 0 0
H: 6 2 W: 11 00 b.Bissau 7-3-00
Internationals: Portugal U17.
2018–19 Vitoria Setubal 0 0
2019–20 Vitoria Setubal 0 0
2020–21 Vitoria Setubal 0 0
2021–22 Nottingham F 0 0
2021–22 Nottingham F 0 0

FORNAH, Tyrese (M) 64 0
H: 5 11 W: 12 04 b.Camden 11-9-99
From Brighton & HA.
2019–20 Nottingham F 0 0
2019–20 *Casa Pia* 5 0 **5 0**
2020–21 Nottingham F 0 0
2020–21 *Plymouth Arg* 39 0 **39 0**
2021–22 Nottingham F 1 0 **1 0**
2021–22 *Shrewsbury T* 19 0 **19 0**

GIBSON-HAMMOND, Alexander (M)0 0
b. 10-11-02
2020–21 Nottingham F 0 0
2021–22 Nottingham F 0 0

GRABBAN, Lewis (F) 492 160
H: 6 0 W: 12 04 b.Croydon 12-1-88
2005–06 Crystal Palace 0 0
2006–07 Crystal Palace 8 1
2006–07 *Oldham Ath* 9 0 **9 0**
2007–08 Crystal Palace 2 0 **10 1**
2007–08 *Motherwell* 6 0 **6 0**
2007–08 Millwall 13 3
2008–09 Millwall 31 6
2009–10 Millwall 11 0
2009–10 *Brentford* 7 2
2010–11 Millwall 1 0 **56 9**
2010–11 Brentford 22 5 **29 7**
2011–12 Rotherham U 43 18 **43 18**
2012–13 Bournemouth 42 13
2013–14 Bournemouth 44 22
2014–15 Norwich C 35 12
2015–16 Norwich C 6 1 **41 13**
2015–16 Bournemouth 15 0
2016–17 Bournemouth 3 0
2016–17 *Reading* 16 3 **16 3**
2017–18 Bournemouth 0 0 **104 35**
2017–18 *Sunderland* 19 12 **19 12**
2017–18 *Aston Villa* 15 8 **15 8**
2018–19 Nottingham F 39 16
2019–20 Nottingham F 45 20
2020–21 Nottingham F 28 6
2021–22 Nottingham F 32 12 **144 54**

HAMMOND, Oliver (M) 0 0
b. 13-11-02
Internationals: Wales U21.
2020–21 Nottingham F 0 0
2021–22 Nottingham F 0 0

HORVATH, Ethan (G) 96 0
H: 6 4 W: 12 06 b.Highlands Ranch, Colorado 9-6-95
Internationals: USA U18, U20, U23, Full caps.
From Real Colorado.
2013 Molde 0 0
2014 Molde 0 0
2015 Molde 17 0
2016 Molde 22 0 **39 0**
2016–17 Club Brugge 4 0
2017–18 Club Brugge 15 0
2018–19 Club Brugge 28 0
2019–20 Club Brugge 2 0
2020–21 Club Brugge 2 0
2021–22 Club Brugge 0 0 **51 0**
2021–22 Nottingham F 6 0 **6 0**

IOANNOU, Nicholas (D) 125 7
b.Limassol 10-11-95
Internationals: Cyprus U19, U21, Full caps.
From Manchester U.
2014–15 APOEL 3 0
2015–16 APOEL 5 0
2016–17 APOEL 17 0
2017–18 APOEL 10 1
2018–19 APOEL 25 4
2019–20 APOEL 19 0
2020–21 APOEL 2 0 **81 5**
2020–21 Nottingham F 5 0
2020–21 *Aris* 9 1 **9 1**
2021–22 Nottingham F 0 0 **5 0**
2021–22 *Como* 30 1 **30 1**

JENKINSON, Carl (D) 141 5
H: 6 1 W: 12 02 b.Harlow 8-2-92
Internationals: Finland U19, U21. England U17, U21, Full caps.
2010–11 Charlton Ath 8 0 **8 0**
2010–11 Arsenal 0 0
2011–12 Arsenal 9 0
2012–13 Arsenal 14 0
2013–14 Arsenal 14 1
2014–15 Arsenal 0 0
2014–15 *West Ham U* 32 0 **32 0**
2015–16 Arsenal 0 0

2015–16 *West Ham U* 20 2 **52 2**
2016–17 Arsenal 1 0
2017–18 Arsenal 0 0
2017–18 *Birmingham C* 7 0 **7 0**
2018–19 Arsenal 3 0
2019–20 Arsenal 0 0 **41 1**
2019–20 Nottingham F 8 0
2020–21 Nottingham F 3 0
2021–22 Nottingham F 0 0 **11 0**
2022 *Melbourne C* 22 2 **22 2**

JOAO CARVALHO, Antonio (M) 123 6
H: 5 8 W: 10 06 b.Castanheira de Pera 9-3-97
Internationals: Portugal U16, U17, U18, U19, U20, U21.
2014–15 Benfica 0 0
2015–16 Benfica 0 0
2016–17 Benfica 0 0
2016–17 *Vitoria Setubal* 15 1 **15 1**
2017–18 Benfica 7 0 **7 0**
2018–19 Nottingham F 38 4
2019–20 Nottingham F 23 1
2020–21 Nottingham F 0 0
2020–21 *Almeria* 33 0 **33 0**
2021–22 Nottingham F 7 0 **68 5**
Transferred to Olympiacos, January 2022.

JOHNSON, Brennan (M) 90 26
H: 5 10 W: 11 07 b.Nottingham 23-5-01
Internationals: England U16, U17. Wales U19, U21, Full caps.
2019–20 Nottingham F 4 0
2020–21 Nottingham F 0 0
2020–21 *Lincoln C* 40 10 **40 10**
2021–22 Nottingham F 46 16 **50 16**

KONATE, Ateef (M) 1 0
H: 5 10 W: 10 06 b.Aubervilliers 4-4-01
From Le Havre.
2020–21 Nottingham F 0 0
2021–22 Le Havre 0 0
2021–22 Nottingham F 1 0 **1 0**

LARSSON, Julian (F) 0 0
b. 21-4-01
Internationals: Sweden U16, U17, U19, U20.
From AIK Solna.
2020–21 Nottingham F 0 0
2021–22 Nottingham F 0 0

LARYEA, Richie (M) 102 13
H: 5 9 W: 10 10 b.Toronto 7-1-95
Internationals: Canada U23, Full caps.
2015 Sigma 9 5 **9 5**
2016 Orlando C 0 0
2017 Orlando C 12 0
2018 Orlando C 9 0 **21 0**
2019 Toronto 20 1
2020 Toronto 20 4
2021 Toronto 27 3 **67 8**
2021–22 Nottingham F 5 0 **5 0**

LOLLEY, Joe (F) 245 33
H: 5 10 W: 11 05 b.Redditch 25-8-92
Internationals: England C.
2013–14 Huddersfield T 6 1
2014–15 Huddersfield T 17 2
2015–16 Huddersfield T 32 4
2015–16 *Scunthorpe U* 6 0 **6 0**
2016–17 Huddersfield T 19 1
2017–18 Huddersfield T 6 1 **80 9**
2017–18 Nottingham F 16 3
2018–19 Nottingham F 46 11
2019–20 Nottingham F 42 9
2020–21 Nottingham F 28 1
2021–22 Nottingham F 27 0 **159 24**

MBE SOH, Loic (D) 12 1
H: 6 2 W: 13 08 b.Souza Gare 13-6-01
Internationals: France U16, U17, U18, U19.
2017–18 Paris Saint-Germain 0 0
2018–19 Paris Saint-Germain 2 0
2019–20 Paris Saint-Germain 1 0 **3 0**
2020–21 Nottingham F 7 1
2021–22 Nottingham F 2 0 **9 1**

McDONNELL, Jamie (M) 0 0
b. 16-2-04
Internationals: Northern Ireland U17.
From Glentoran.
2020–21 Nottingham F 0 0
2021–22 Nottingham F 0 0

McKENNA, Scott (D) 183 9
H: 6 2 W: 11 07 b.Kirriemuir 12-11-96
Internationals: Scotland U19, U21, Full caps.
2014–15 Aberdeen 0 0
2014–15 *Ayr U* 12 0
2015–16 Aberdeen 3 0
2015–16 *Alloa Ath* 4 0 **4 0**
2016–17 Aberdeen 0 0
2016–17 *Ayr U* 11 1 **23 1**
2017–18 Aberdeen 30 2
2018–19 Aberdeen 30 2
2019–20 Aberdeen 24 1 **87 5**
2020–21 Nottingham F 24 1
2021–22 Nottingham F 45 2 **69 3**

MIGHTEN, Alex (F) 55 4
H: 5 7 W: 11 03 b.Nottingham 11-4-02
Internationals: England U16, U17, U18, U20.
2019–20 Nottingham F 8 0
2020–21 Nottingham F 24 3
2021–22 Nottingham F 23 1 **55 4**

NUNO DA COSTA, Joia (F) 180 47
H: 6 0 W: 11 00 b.Praia 10-2-91
Internationals: Cape Verde Full caps.
From Aubagne.
2015–16 Valenciennes 23 10
2016–17 Valenciennes 22 9 **45 19**
2017–18 Strasbourg 26 5
2018–19 Strasbourg 34 8
2019–20 Strasbourg 14 1 **74 14**
2019–20 Nottingham F 10 0
2020–21 Nottingham F 2 0
2020–21 *Royal Excel Mouscron* 25 6 **25 6**
2021–22 Nottingham F 0 0 **12 0**
2021–22 *Caen* 24 8 **24 8**

OJEDA, Braian (M) 41 1
H: 5 8 W: 10 10 b.Itaugua 27-6-00
Internationals: Paraguay U17, U20, U23, Full caps.
2018 Olimpia 2 0
2019 Olimpia 0 0
2019–20 *Defensa y Justicia* 10 0 **10 0**
2020 Olimpia 13 0
2021 Olimpia 13 1
2021–22 Olimpia 0 0 **28 1**
2021–22 Nottingham F 3 0 **3 0**

PANZO, Jonathan (D) 42 0
b.London 25-10-00
Internationals: England U16, U17, U18, U19, U21.
2019–20 Monaco 2 0 **2 0**
2019–20 *Cercle Brugge* 17 0 **17 0**
2020–21 Dijon 22 0 **22 0**
2021–22 Nottingham F 1 0 **1 0**

RICHARDSON, Jayden (D) 52 1
H: 6 0 W: 12 00 b.Nottingham 4-9-00
2019–20 Nottingham F 0 0
2019–20 *Exeter C* 18 1 **18 1**
2020–21 Nottingham F 0 0
2020–21 *Forest Green R* 32 0 **32 0**
2021–22 Nottingham F 2 0 **2 0**

SAMBA, Brice (G) 171 0
H: 6 1 W: 12 06 b.Linzolo 25-4-94
2010–11 Le Havre 0 0
2011–12 Le Havre 0 0
2012–13 Le Havre 0 0
2012–13 Marseille 0 0
2013–14 Marseille 1 0
2014–15 Marseille 0 0
2015–16 Marseille 0 0
2015–16 *Nancy* 2 0 **2 0**
2016–17 Marseille 0 0 **1 0**
2017–18 Caen 4 0
2018–19 Caen 38 0
2019–20 Caen 1 0 **43 0**
2019–20 Nottingham F 40 0
2020–21 Nottingham F 45 0
2021–22 Nottingham F 40 0 **125 0**

SANDERS, Samuel (F) 0 0
2020–21 Nottingham F 0 0
2021–22 Nottingham F 0 0

SHELVEY, George (G) 0 0
H: 6 2 W: 13 01 b.Nottingham 22-4-01
2019–20 Nottingham F 0 0
2020–21 Nottingham F 0 0
2021–22 Nottingham F 0 0
2021–22 *Mansfield T* 0 0

SMITH, Jordan (G) 60 0
H: 6 1 W: 11 11 b.South Normanton 8-12-94
Internationals: Costa Rica U17, U20, Full caps.
2013–14 Nottingham F 0 0
2014–15 Nottingham F 0 0
2015–16 Nottingham F 0 0
2016–17 Nottingham F 15 0
2017–18 Nottingham F 29 0
2018–19 Nottingham F 0 0
2018–19 *Barnsley* 1 0 **1 0**
2018–19 *Mansfield T* 12 0 **12 0**
2019–20 Nottingham F 2 0
2020–21 Nottingham F 1 0
2021–22 Nottingham F 0 0 **47 0**

SURRIDGE, Sam (F) 148 33
H: 6 3 W: 12 02 b.Slough 28-7-98
Internationals: England U21.
2015–16 Bournemouth 0 0
2016–17 Bournemouth 0 0
2017–18 Bournemouth 0 0
2017–18 *Yeovil T* 41 8 **41 8**
2018–19 Bournemouth 2 0
2018–19 *Oldham Ath* 15 8 **15 8**
2019–20 Bournemouth 4 0
2019–20 *Swansea C* 20 4 **20 4**
2020–21 Bournemouth 29 4 **35 4**
2021–22 Stoke C 20 2 **20 2**
2021–22 Nottingham F 17 7 **17 7**

SWAN, Will (F) 12 1
b.Mansfield 26-10-00
2020–21 Nottingham F 2 0
2020–21 *Port Vale* 10 1 **10 1**
2021–22 Nottingham F 0 0 **2 0**

TAYLOR, Dale (F) 0 0
Internationals: Northern Ireland U17, U21, Full caps.
2021–22 Linfield 0 0
2021–22 Nottingham F 0 0

TAYLOR, Lyle (F) 409 129
H: 6 2 W: 12 06 b.Greenwich 29-3-90
Internationals: Montserrat Full caps.
2007–08 Millwall 0 0
2008–09 Millwall 0 0
From Concord R
2010–11 Bournemouth 11 0
2011–12 Bournemouth 18 0 **29 0**
2011–12 *Hereford U* 8 2 **8 2**
2012–13 Falkirk 34 24 **34 24**
2013–14 Sheffield U 20 2 **20 2**
2013–14 *Partick Thistle* 20 7
2014–15 Scunthorpe U 18 3 **18 3**
2014–15 *Partick Thistle* 15 3 **35 10**
2015–16 AFC Wimbledon 42 20
2016–17 AFC Wimbledon 43 10
2017–18 AFC Wimbledon 46 14 **131 44**
2018–19 Charlton Ath 41 21
2019–20 Charlton Ath 22 11 **63 32**
2020–21 Nottingham F 39 4
2021–22 Nottingham F 18 3 **57 7**
2021–22 *Birmingham C* 14 5 **14 5**

TOBIAS FIGUEIREDO, Pereira (D) 163 7
H: 6 2 W: 13 03 b.Satao 2-2-94
Internationals: Portugal U17, U18, U19, U20, U21, U23.
2012–13 Sporting Lisbon 0 0
2013–14 Sporting Lisbon 0 0
2013–14 *Reus* 13 1 **13 1**
2014–15 Sporting Lisbon 14 2
2015–16 Sporting Lisbon 1 0
2016–17 Sporting Lisbon 0 0
2016–17 *Nacional* 22 1 **22 1**
2017–18 Sporting Lisbon 0 0
2017–18 *Nottingham F* 12 0
2018–19 Sporting Lisbon 0 0 **15 2**
2018–19 *Nottingham F* 13 0
2019–20 Nottingham F 30 3
2020–21 Nottingham F 32 0
2021–22 Nottingham F 26 0 **113 3**

WORRALL, Joe (D) 204 4
H: 6 3 W: 10 01 b.Hucknall 10-1-97
Internationals: England U20, U21.
2015–16 Nottingham F 0 0
2015–16 *Dagenham & R* 14 1 **14 1**
2016–17 Nottingham F 21 0
2017–18 Nottingham F 31 1
2018–19 Nottingham F 0 0
2018–19 *Rangers* 22 0 **22 0**
2019–20 Nottingham F 46 1
2020–21 Nottingham F 31 1
2021–22 Nottingham F 39 0 **168 3**

XANDE SILVA, Nascimento (F) 64 5
H: 5 10 W: 9 06 b.Lisbon 16-3-97
Internationals: Portugal U16, U17, U18, U19, U20.
2014–15 Vitoria Guimaraes 1 0
2015–16 Vitoria Guimaraes 20 1
2016–17 Vitoria Guimaraes 4 0
2017–18 Vitoria Guimaraes 1 0 **26 1**
2018–19 West Ham U 1 0
2019–20 West Ham U 0 0
2020–21 West Ham U 0 0
2020–21 *Aris* 29 4
2021–22 *Aris* 0 0 **29 4**
2021–22 West Ham U 0 0 **1 0**
2021–22 Nottingham F 8 0 **8 0**

YATES, Ryan (M) 173 19
H: 6 3 W: 12 02 b.Nottingham 21-11-97
2016–17 Nottingham F 0 0
2016–17 *Shrewsbury T* 12 0 **12 0**
2017–18 Nottingham F 0 0
2017–18 *Notts Co* 25 3 **25 3**
2017–18 *Scunthorpe U* 16 2 **16 2**
2018–19 Nottingham F 16 1
2019–20 Nottingham F 27 3
2020–21 Nottingham F 34 2
2021–22 Nottingham F 43 8 **120 14**

Players retained or with offer of contract
Clarridge, James; Donnelly, Aaron; Fewster, William; Hammond, Benjamin; Harbottle, Riley; Hogarth, Nicky; Osong, Detlef; Salmon, Lewis.

Scholars
Akers, Alexander Matthew; Barker, Lewis Ryan; Bott, Aaron Charlie; Collins, Samuel Haig; Draper, Kane Ace; Gardner, Joseph Charles; Hanks, Justin Thomas; Hull, Ethan

J-Kwon Dermecoe; Johnson, Pharrell Junior; Korpal, Aaron Jay; McAdam, Kyle James; McAleese, Bobby Jack; Nadin, Jack Richard; Perkins, Jack William; Perry, Benjamin Marshall; Powell, Joshua Alan; Solomon, Osakpolor Clearance; Thompson, Jack Ethan.

OLDHAM ATH (61)

ADAMS, Nicky (F) **582 39**
H: 5 9 W: 11 00 b.Bolton 16-10-86
Internationals: Wales U21.

2005–06	Bury	15	1		
2006–07	Bury	19	1		
2007–08	Bury	43	12		
2008–09	Leicester C	12	0		
2008–09	*Rochdale*	14	1		
2009–10	Leicester C	18	0	**30**	**0**
2009–10	*Leyton Orient*	6	0	**6**	**0**
2010–11	Brentford	7	0	**7**	**0**
2010–11	Rochdale	30	0		
2011–12	Rochdale	41	4	**85**	**5**
2012–13	Crawley T	46	8		
2013–14	Crawley T	24	1	**70**	**9**
2013–14	Rotherham U	15	1	**15**	**1**
2013–14	Bury	0	0		
2014–15	Bury	38	1		
2015–16	Northampton T	39	3		
2016–17	Carlisle U	42	3		
2017–18	Carlisle U	17	0	**59**	**3**
2018–19	Bury	46	2	**161**	**17**
2019–20	Northampton T	37	1		
2020–21	Northampton T	14	0	**90**	**4**
2020–21	Oldham Ath	23	0		
2021–22	Oldham Ath	36	0	**59**	**0**

BADAN, Andrea (D) **66 0**
H: 5 9 W: 11 00 b.Monselice 21-3-98

2015–16	Verona	0	0		
2016–17	Verona	0	0		
2017–18	Verona	0	0		
2017–18	*Prato*	20	0	**20**	**0**
2017–18	*Albino Leffe*	1	0	**1**	**0**
2018–19	Verona	0	0		
2018–19	*Alessandria*	25	0	**25**	**0**
2019–20	Verona	0	0		
2019–20	*Carrarese*	1	0	**1**	**0**
2019–20	*Cavese*	1	0	**1**	**0**
2020–21	Oldham Ath	18	0		
2021–22	Oldham Ath	0	0	**18**	**0**

BAHAMBOULA, Dylan (M) **160 20**
H: 6 1 W: 10 01 b.Corbeil Essonnes 22-5-95
Internationals: France U20. DR Congo Full caps.

2012–13	Monaco	0	0		
2013–14	Monaco	0	0		
2014–15	Monaco	0	0		
2015–16	Monaco	0	0		
2015–16	*Paris FC*	29	4	**29**	**4**
2016–17	Dijon	11	1		
2017–18	Dijon	4	0	**15**	**1**
2017–18	*Gazelec Ajaccio*	13	1	**13**	**1**
2018–19	Astra Giurgiu	5	1	**5**	**1**
2018–19	CS Constantine	12	2		
2019–20	CS Constantine	1	0	**13**	**2**
2019–20	Tsarsko Selo	17	2	**17**	**2**
2020–21	Oldham Ath	38	6		
2021–22	Oldham Ath	30	3	**68**	**9**

BLYTH, Jacob (F) **82 12**
H: 6 3 W: 12 02 b.Nuneaton 14-8-92

2012–13	Leicester C	0	0		
2012–13	*Burton Alb*	2	0		
2012–13	*Notts Co*	4	0	**4**	**0**
2013–14	Leicester C	0	0		
2013–14	*Northampton T*	11	3	**11**	**3**
2014–15	Leicester C	0	0		
2014–15	*Burton Alb*	22	5	**24**	**5**
2015–16	Leicester C	0	0		
2015–16	*Cambridge U*	5	1	**5**	**1**
2015–16	*Blackpool*	8	2	**8**	**2**
2016–17	Motherwell	8	0	**8**	**0**

From Barrow.

2019–20	Macclesfield T	19	1	**19**	**1**

From Altrincham, Gateshead.

2021–22	Oldham Ath	3	0	**3**	**0**

Transferred to Chorley, September 2021.

CISSE, Ousseynou (D) **288 12**
H: 6 5 W: 13 05 b.Suresnes 7-4-91
Internationals: Mali Full caps.

2009–10	Amiens	9	0		
2010–11	Amiens	8	0		
2011–12	Amiens	19	0	**36**	**0**
2012–13	Dijon	24	0		
2013–14	Dijon	36	4		
2014–15	Dijon	35	1	**95**	**5**
2015–16	Rayo Vallecano	0	0		
2015–16	*Waasland-Beveren*	12	1	**12**	**1**
2016–17	Tours	25	1	**25**	**1**
2017–18	Milton Keynes D	32	0		
2018–19	Milton Keynes D	26	2	**58**	**2**
2019–20	Gillingham	2	1	**2**	**1**
2019–20	*Leyton Orient*	10	1		
2020–21	Leyton Orient	42	1		
2021–22	Leyton Orient	0	0	**52**	**2**
2021–22	Oldham Ath	8	0	**8**	**0**

CLARKE, Jordan (D) **323 12**
H: 6 0 W: 11 03 b.Coventry 19-11-91
Internationals: England U19, U20.

2009–10	Coventry C	12	0		
2010–11	Coventry C	21	1		
2011–12	Coventry C	19	1		
2012–13	Coventry C	20	0		
2013–14	Coventry C	41	1		
2014–15	Coventry C	11	1	**124**	**4**
2014–15	*Yeovil T*	5	2	**5**	**2**
2014–15	Scunthorpe U	24	0		
2015–16	Scunthorpe U	33	2		
2016–17	Scunthorpe U	23	1		
2017–18	Scunthorpe U	23	0		
2018–19	Scunthorpe U	15	1		
2019–20	Scunthorpe U	12	0		
2020–21	Scunthorpe U	24	1	**154**	**5**
2021–22	Oldham Ath	40	1	**40**	**1**

COUTO, Benny (D) **19 1**
b.Porto 27-9-03

2021–22	Oldham Ath	19	1	**19**	**1**

DA SILVA, Vani (F) **3 0**
H: 6 0 b. 27-11-02

2020–21	Curzon Ashton	0	0		
2020–21	Oldham Ath	0	0		
2021–22	Oldham Ath	3	0	**3**	**0**

DEARNLEY, Zachary (M) **44 11**
H: 5 9 W: 10 06 b.Sheffield 28-9-98
Internationals: England U16, U18.

2016–17	Manchester U	0	0		
2017–18	Manchester U	0	0		
2018–19	Manchester U	0	0		
2018–19	*Oldham Ath*	9	1		
2019–20	Oldham Ath	8	4		
2020–21	Oldham Ath	15	6		
2021–22	Oldham Ath	12	0	**44**	**11**

Transferred to FC Halifax T, January 2022.

DIARRA, Raphael (D) **74 1**
H: 5 8 W: 10 00 b.Paris 27-5-95
Internationals: France U19, U20.

2013–14	Monaco	0	0		
2014–15	Monaco	0	0		
2015–16	Monaco	0	0		
2016–17	Monaco	0	0		
2016–17	*Cercle Brugge*	15	1	**15**	**1**
2017–18	Monaco	0	0		
2018–19	Quevilly-Rouuen	14	0		
2019–20	Quevilly-Rouuen	17	0	**31**	**0**
2020–21	Oldham Ath	16	0		
2021–22	Oldham Ath	12	0	**28**	**0**

FAGE, Dylan (M) **60 1**
H: 5 10 W: 11 00 b. 18-3-99

2016–17	Auxerre	0	0		
2017–18	Auxerre	0	0		
2018–19	Auxerre	0	0		
2019–20	Oldham Ath	12	0		
2020–21	Oldham Ath	34	1		
2021–22	Oldham Ath	14	0	**60**	**1**

FONDOP-TALOM, Mike (F) **27 4**
H: 6 3 W: 13 08 b.Yaounde 27-11-93

2020–21	Burton Alb	17	2	**17**	**2**
2021–22	Hartlepool U	8	0	**8**	**0**
2021–22	Oldham Ath	2	2	**2**	**2**

HART, Sam (D) **102 2**
H: 5 11 W: 11 05 b.Bolton 10-9-96

2016–17	Liverpool	0	0		
2016–17	*Port Vale*	11	1		
2017–18	Port Vale	0	0	**11**	**1**
2017–18	Blackburn R	3	0		
2017–18	*Rochdale*	3	0		
2018–19	Blackburn R	0	0		
2018–19	*Rochdale*	11	0	**14**	**0**
2018–19	*Southend U*	18	0		
2019–20	Blackburn R	0	0	**3**	**0**
2019–20	*Shrewsbury T*	4	0	**4**	**0**
2020–21	Southend U	21	0	**39**	**0**
2021–22	Oldham Ath	31	1	**31**	**1**

HOPCUTT, Jamie (F) **207 48**
H: 5 11 W: 11 09 b.York 23-6-92
From York C, Ossett T, Tadcaster Alb.

2012	Ostersund	24	3		
2013	Ostersund	30	6		
2014	Ostersund	24	9		
2015	Ostersund	24	15		
2016	Ostersund	1	0		
2017	Ostersund	22	5		
2018	Ostersund	23	5		
2019	Ostersund	19	1	**167**	**44**
2020	Sundsvall	14	3	**14**	**3**
2020–21	Hapoel Kfar Saba	10	0	**10**	**0**
2021–22	Oldham Ath	16	1	**16**	**1**

HOPE, Hallam (F) **274 50**
H: 5 10 W: 12 00 b.Manchester 17-3-94
Internationals: England U16, U17, U18, U19. Barbados Full caps.

2010–11	Everton	0	0		
2011–12	Everton	0	0		
2012–13	Everton	0	0		
2013–14	Everton	0	0		
2013–14	*Northampton T*	3	1	**3**	**1**
2013–14	*Bury*	8	5		
2014–15	Everton	0	0		
2014–15	*Sheffield W*	4	0	**4**	**0**
2014–15	Bury	19	0		
2015–16	Bury	6	0		
2015–16	*Carlisle U*	21	4		
2016–17	Bury	33	3	**66**	**8**
2017–18	Carlisle U	41	9		
2018–19	Carlisle U	40	14		
2019–20	Carlisle U	23	2	**125**	**29**
2019–20	Swindon T	5	2		
2020–21	Swindon T	32	5	**37**	**7**
2021–22	Oldham Ath	39	5	**39**	**5**

JAMESON, Kyle (D) **36 2**
H: 6 0 W: 12 06 b.Urmston 11-9-98
From Chelsea.

2017–18	WBA	0	0		

From AFC Fylde.

2020–21	Oldham Ath	25	2		
2021–22	Oldham Ath	11	0	**36**	**2**

KEILLOR-DUNN, Davis (M) **138 32**
H: 5 11 W: 10 10 b.Sunderland 2-11-97

2016–17	Ross Co	0	0		
2017–18	Ross Co	29	3		
2018–19	Ross Co	11	1	**40**	**4**
2018–19	*Falkirk*	11	3	**11**	**3**

From Wrexham.

2020–21	Oldham Ath	41	10		
2021–22	Oldham Ath	46	15	**87**	**25**

KILNER, Oliver (D) **0 0**
b.Stockport 27-3-04
Transferred to Olympiacos, January 2022.

2021–22	Oldham Ath	0	0		

LEUTWILER, Jayson (G) **165 0**
H: 6 4 W: 12 08 b.Basel 25-4-89
Internationals: Switzerland U16, U17, U18, U19, U20, U21. Canada Full caps.
From Basel.

2012–13	Middlesbrough	0	0		
2013–14	Middlesbrough	3	0	**3**	**0**
2014–15	Shrewsbury T	46	0		
2015–16	Shrewsbury T	29	0		
2016–17	Shrewsbury T	43	0	**118**	**0**
2017–18	Blackburn R	1	0		
2018–19	Blackburn R	5	0		
2019–20	Blackburn R	0	0	**6**	**0**
2020–21	Fleetwood T	16	0	**16**	**0**
2020–21	Huddersfield T	0	0		
2021–22	Oldham Ath	22	0	**22**	**0**

LUAMBA, Junior (F) **17 2**
b. 27-4-03

2020–21	Oldham Ath	2	0		
2021–22	Oldham Ath	15	2	**17**	**2**

McGAHEY, Harrison (D) **212 1**
H: 6 2 W: 13 05 b.Preston 26-9-95

2013–14	Blackpool	4	0	**4**	**0**
2014–15	Sheffield U	15	0		
2014–15	*Tranmere R*	4	0	**4**	**0**
2015–16	Sheffield U	7	0	**22**	**0**
2016–17	Rochdale	36	0		
2017–18	Rochdale	42	0		
2018–19	Rochdale	21	0	**99**	**0**
2018–19	Scunthorpe U	10	0		
2019–20	Scunthorpe U	32	0		
2020–21	Scunthorpe U	16	1		
2021–22	Scunthorpe U	0	0	**58**	**1**
2021–22	Oldham Ath	25	0	**25**	**0**

MISSILOU, Christopher (M) **192 18**
H: 5 11 W: 11 00 b.Auxerre 18-7-92
Internationals: France U18. Congo Full caps.

2009–10	Auxerre	0	0		
2010–11	Auxerre	0	0		
2011–12	Auxerre	1	0		
2012–13	Auxerre	0	0	**1**	**0**
2013–14	Evry	11	1	**11**	**1**
2014–15	Stade Brestpos 29	1	0	**1**	**0**
2015–16	Montceau	12	0		
2016–17	Montceau	24	7	**36**	**7**
2017–18	Entente Sannois	6	0	**6**	**0**
2017–18	Le Puy Foot 43	15	3	**15**	**3**
2018–19	Oldham Ath	42	1		
2019–20	Oldham Ath	30	3		
2020–21	Northampton T	15	1	**15**	**1**
2020–21	Swindon T	11	0	**11**	**0**
2021–22	Newport Co	4	0	**4**	**0**
2021–22	Oldham Ath	20	2	**92**	**6**

MODI, Isaac (M) **2 0**
b. 26-1-04

2021–22	Oldham Ath	2	0	**2**	**0**

OBADEYI, Temitope (F) 211 22
H: 6 3 W: 13 10 b.Birmingham 29-10-89
Internationals: England U19, U20.
2006–07 Bolton W 0 0
2007–08 Bolton W 0 0
2008–09 Bolton W 3 0
2009–10 Bolton W 0 0
2009–10 *Swindon T* 12 2 **12 2**
2009–10 *Rochdale* 11 1
2010–11 Bolton W 0 0
2010–11 *Shrewsbury T* 9 0 **9 0**
2011–12 Bolton W 0 0 **3 0**
2011–12 *Chesterfield* 5 0 **5 0**
2011–12 *Rochdale* 6 1 **17 2**
2012–13 Rio Ave 11 0 **11 0**
2013–14 Bury 7 0 **7 0**
2013–14 *Plymouth Arg* 14 1 **14 1**
2014–15 Kilmarnock 29 9
2015–16 Kilmarnock 30 3 **59 12**
2016–17 Dundee U 18 2 **18 2**
2016–17 Oldham Ath 15 2
2017–18 Oldham Ath 22 1
2018–19 Sochaux 11 0
2019–20 Sochaux 0 0 **11 0**
2021–22 Oldham Ath 8 0 **45 3**

PIERGIANNI, Carl (D) 103 8
H: 6 1 W: 13 05 b.Peterborough 3-5-92
2010–11 Peterborough U 1 0 **1 0**
From Stockport Co, Corby T, Boston U, South Melbourne.
2019–20 Salford C 13 0 **13 0**
2019–20 *Oldham Ath* 11 0
2020–21 Oldham Ath 38 5
2021–22 Oldham Ath 40 3 **89 8**

ROGERS, Danny (G) 179 0
H: 6 1 W: 12 02 b.Dublin 23-3-94
Internationals: Republic of Ireland U21.
2011–12 Aberdeen 0 0
2012–13 Aberdeen 0 0
2013–14 Aberdeen 0 0
2013–14 *Airdrieonians* 6 0 **6 0**
2014–15 Aberdeen 0 0
2014–15 *Dumbarton* 34 0 **34 0**
2015–16 Aberdeen 0 0
2015–16 *Falkirk* 35 0
2016–17 Aberdeen 0 0
2016–17 *Falkirk* 28 0 **63 0**
2017–18 Aberdeen 3 0
2018–19 Aberdeen 0 0
2018–19 *St Mirren* 4 0 **4 0**
2019–20 Aberdeen 0 0 **3 0**
2019–20 *Greenock Morton* 20 0 **20 0**
2020–21 Kilmarnock 27 0
2021–22 Kilmarnock 0 0 **27 0**
2021–22 Oldham Ath 22 0 **22 0**

SHEEHAN, Alan (D) 401 25
H: 5 11 W: 12 11 b.Athlone 14-9-86
Internationals: Republic of Ireland U21.
From Belvedere.
2004–05 Leicester C 1 0
2005–06 Leicester C 2 0
2006–07 Leicester C 0 0
2006–07 *Mansfield T* 10 0 **10 0**
2007–08 Leicester C 20 1 **23 1**
2007–08 *Leeds U* 10 1
2008–09 Leeds U 11 1
2008–09 *Crewe Alex* 3 0 **3 0**
2009–10 Leeds U 0 0 **21 2**
2009–10 *Oldham Ath* 8 1
2009–10 *Swindon T* 22 1
2010–11 Swindon T 21 1 **43 2**
2011–12 Notts Co 39 2
2012–13 Notts Co 33 0
2013–14 Notts Co 42 7
2014–15 Bradford C 23 1
2014–15 *Peterborough U* 2 0 **2 0**
2015–16 Bradford C 2 0 **25 1**
2015–16 *Notts Co* 14 2 **128 11**
2015–16 *Luton T* 20 1
2016–17 Luton T 34 2
2017–18 Luton T 42 3
2018–19 Luton T 17 0
2019–20 Luton T 4 0 **117 6**
2019–20 Lincoln C 1 0 **1 0**
2020–21 Northampton T 14 1 **14 1**
2021–22 Oldham Ath 6 0 **14 1**

STOBBS, Jack (M) 44 2
H: 5 11 W: 13 05 b.Leeds 27-2-97
2013–14 Sheffield W 1 0
2014–15 Sheffield W 0 0
2015–16 Sheffield W 1 0
2016–17 Sheffield W 0 0
2017–18 Sheffield W 3 0
2017–18 *Port Vale* 5 0 **5 0**
2018–19 Sheffield W 0 0
2019–20 Sheffield W 0 0 **5 0**
2019–20 *Livingston* 4 0 **4 0**
From Grantham T.
2021–22 Oldham Ath 30 2 **30 2**

SUTTON, Will (D) 10 2
b. 30-10-02
2020–21 Oldham Ath 1 0
2021–22 Oldham Ath 9 2 **10 2**

VAUGHAN, Harry (M) 29 1
b. 6-4-04
Internationals: Republic of Ireland U19.
2020–21 Oldham Ath 6 0
2021–22 Oldham Ath 23 1 **29 1**

WHELAN, Callum (M) 74 1
H: 5 9 W: 11 03 b.Barnsley 24-9-98
2018–19 Manchester U 0 0
2018–19 *Port Vale* 0 0
2019–20 Watford 0 0
2020–21 Oldham Ath 31 0
2021–22 Oldham Ath 43 1 **74 1**

Players retained or with offer of contract
Atkinson, Aaron; Danielewicz, Kacper; Edwards, Joseph; Simms, James; Southerington, Luke; Turner, Trey.

Scholars
Atkinson, Aaron John; Chapman, Llyton Levi; Cookson, Frazer; Edwards, Joseph Dean; Forshaw, Jake Andrew; Green, Harvey Leon; Hemmingsen, Gustav Winkler Elmerdahl; Hughes, Asa William; Kilner, Oliver Joseph; Modi, Isaac Tombe Wani; Moore, Kofi Rio; Okeke, Favour Jidechi; Simms, James George William; Southerington, Luke Tomos; Turner, Trey Donnelly; Williams, Jack Bobby Owen.

OXFORD U (62)

ANIFOWOSE, Joshua (M) 0 0
b. 2-2-04
2020–21 Oxford U 0 0
2021–22 Oxford U 0 0

BALDOCK, Sam (F) 372 106
H: 5 7 W: 10 08 b.Buckingham 15-3-89
Internationals: England U20.
2005–06 Milton Keynes D 0 0
2006–07 Milton Keynes D 1 0
2007–08 Milton Keynes D 5 0
2008–09 Milton Keynes D 40 12
2009–10 Milton Keynes D 20 5
2010–11 Milton Keynes D 30 12
2011–12 Milton Keynes D 4 4 **100 33**
2011–12 West Ham U 23 5
2012–13 West Ham U 0 0 **23 5**
2012–13 Bristol C 34 10
2013–14 Bristol C 45 24
2014–15 Bristol C 4 0 **83 34**
2014–15 Brighton & HA 20 3
2015–16 Brighton & HA 28 4
2016–17 Brighton & HA 31 11
2017–18 Brighton & HA 2 0 **81 18**
2018–19 Reading 21 5
2019–20 Reading 24 5
2020–21 Reading 20 0 **65 10**
2021–22 Derby Co 13 2 **13 2**
2021–22 Oxford U 7 4 **7 4**

BODIN, Billy (M) 270 58
H: 5 11 W: 11 00 b.Swindon 24-3-92
Internationals: Wales U17, U19, U21, Full caps.
2009–10 Swindon T 0 0
2010–11 Swindon T 5 0
2011–12 Swindon T 11 3 **16 3**
2011–12 *Torquay U* 17 5
2011–12 *Crewe Alex* 8 0 **8 0**
2012–13 Torquay U 43 5
2013–14 Torquay U 27 1 **87 11**
2014–15 Northampton T 4 0 **4 0**
2015–16 Bristol R 38 13
2016–17 Bristol R 36 13
2017–18 Bristol R 21 9 **95 35**
2017–18 Preston NE 17 1
2018–19 Preston NE 0 0
2019–20 Preston NE 18 2
2020–21 Preston NE 4 0 **39 3**
2021–22 Oxford U 21 6 **21 6**

BRANNAGAN, Cameron (M) 171 23
H: 5 11 W: 11 03 b.Manchester 9-5-96
Internationals: England U18, U20.
2013–14 Liverpool 0 0
2014–15 Liverpool 0 0
2015–16 Liverpool 3 0
2016–17 Liverpool 0 0
2016–17 *Fleetwood T* 13 0 **13 0**
2017–18 Liverpool 0 0 **3 0**
2017–18 Oxford U 12 0
2018–19 Oxford U 41 3
2019–20 Oxford U 30 5
2020–21 Oxford U 31 1
2021–22 Oxford U 41 14 **155 23**

BREAREY, Eddie (G) 0 0
b.Oxford 9-6-04
2020–21 Oxford U 0 0
2021–22 Oxford U 0 0

BROWNE, Marcus (M) 68 13
b. 18-12-97
2015–16 West Ham U 0 0
2016–17 West Ham U 0 0
2016–17 *Wigan Ath* 0 0
2017–18 West Ham U 0 0
2018–19 West Ham U 0 0
2018–19 *Oxford U* 34 6
2019–20 Middlesbrough 13 0
2019–20 *Oxford U* 11 4
2020–21 Middlesbrough 5 2
2021–22 Middlesbrough 0 0 **18 2**
2021–22 Oxford U 5 1 **50 11**

CHAMBERS, Leon (M) 3 0
b.Luton 5-11-01
From Luton T, Aston Villa.
2020–21 Oxford U 3 0
2021–22 Oxford U 0 0 **3 0**

CHAPMAN, Mackenzie (G) 1 0
2020–21 Oldham Ath 1 0 **1 0**
2021–22 Oxford U 0 0

COOPER, Joel (M) 32 3
H: 6 2 W: 11 00 b.Ballyclare 29-2-96
Internationals: Northern Ireland U21.
From Glenavon.
2020–21 Oxford U 4 0
2020–21 *Linfield* 20 3 **20 3**
2021–22 Oxford U 2 0 **6 0**
2021–22 *Port Vale* 6 0 **6 0**

DAVIS, Benjamin (M) 0 0
H: 6 1 W: 10 06 b.Phuket 24-11-00
Internationals: Singapore U16, U19. Thailand U23.
2019–20 Fulham 0 0
2020–21 Fulham 0 0
2021–22 Fulham 0 0
2021–22 Oxford U 0 0

EASTWOOD, Simon (G) 245 0
H: 6 2 W: 14 02 b.Luton 26-6-89
Internationals: England U18, U19.
2005–06 Huddersfield T 0 0
2006–07 Huddersfield T 0 0
2007–08 Huddersfield T 0 0
2008–09 Huddersfield T 1 0
2009–10 Huddersfield T 0 0 **1 0**
2009–10 *Bradford C* 22 0 **22 0**
2010–11 Oxford U 0 0
From FC Halifax T.
2012–13 Portsmouth 27 0 **27 0**
2013–14 Blackburn R 7 0
2014–15 Blackburn R 6 0
2015–16 Blackburn R 0 0 **13 0**
2016–17 Oxford U 46 0
2017–18 Oxford U 46 0
2018–19 Oxford U 34 0
2019–20 Oxford U 29 0
2020–21 Oxford U 13 0
2021–22 Oxford U 14 0 **182 0**

ELECHI, Michael (D) 0 0
H: 6 1 W: 10 10 b.Westminster 10-10-01
From Manchester U.
2020–21 Oxford U 0 0
2021–22 Oxford U 0 0

FORDE, Anthony (M) 274 15
H: 5 9 W: 10 10 b.Limerick 16-11-93
Internationals: Republic of Ireland U19, U21.
2011–12 Wolverhampton W 6 0
2012–13 Wolverhampton W 12 0
2012–13 *Scunthorpe U* 8 0 **8 0**
2013–14 Wolverhampton W 3 0 **21 0**
2014–15 Walsall 37 3
2015–16 Walsall 41 4 **78 7**
2016–17 Rotherham U 32 2
2017–18 Rotherham U 41 2
2018–19 Rotherham U 28 1 **101 5**
2019–20 Oxford U 18 1
2020–21 Oxford U 35 1
2021–22 Oxford U 13 1 **66 3**

GOLDING, James (D) 1 0
b. 10-8-04
Internationals: Republic of Ireland U19.
2021–22 Oxford U 1 0 **1 0**

GOODRHAM, Tyler (M) 0 0
b.High Wycombe 7-8-03
2019–20 Oxford U 0 0
2020–21 Oxford U 0 0
2021–22 Oxford U 0 0

GORRIN, Alejandro (M) 183 2
H: 6 1 W: 11 00 b.Santa Cruz, Tenerife 1-8-93
2011–12 Sunderland 0 0
2012–13 Sunderland 0 0
2013–14 Sunderland 0 0
2014–15 Wellington Phoenix 25 0
2015–16 Wellington Phoenix 24 0
2016–17 Wellington Phoenix 23 1 **72 1**
2017–18 Boavista 0 0
2017–18 Sepsi 12 0 **12 0**
2018–19 Motherwell 20 0 **20 0**

2019–20 Oxford U 31 0
2020–21 Oxford U 35 1
2021–22 Oxford U 13 0 **79 1**

HANSON, Jamie (F) 109 1
H: 6 3 W: 12 06 b.Burton-upon-Trent 10-11-95
Internationals: England U20.
2012–13 Derby Co 0 0
2013–14 Derby Co 0 0
2014–15 Derby Co 2 1
2015–16 Derby Co 18 0
2016–17 Derby Co 5 0
2016–17 *Wigan Ath* 17 0 **17 0**
2017–18 Derby Co 6 0 **31 1**
2018–19 Oxford U 30 0
2019–20 Oxford U 5 0
2020–21 Oxford U 24 0
2021–22 Oxford U 2 0 **61 0**

HENRY, James (F) 490 92
H: 6 0 W: 12 02 b.Reading 10-6-89
Internationals: Scotland U16, U19. England U18, U19.
2006–07 Reading 0 0
2006–07 *Nottingham F* 1 0 **1 0**
2007–08 Reading 0 0
2007–08 *Bournemouth* 11 4 **11 4**
2007–08 *Norwich C* 3 0 **3 0**
2008–09 Reading 7 0
2008–09 *Millwall* 16 3
2009–10 Reading 3 0 **10 0**
2009–10 *Millwall* 9 5
2010–11 Millwall 42 5
2011–12 Millwall 39 0
2012–13 Millwall 35 5
2013–14 Millwall 5 0 **146 18**
2013–14 Wolverhampton W 32 10
2014–15 Wolverhampton W 37 5
2015–16 Wolverhampton W 39 7
2016–17 Wolverhampton W 2 0 **110 22**
2016–17 *Bolton W* 30 1 **30 1**
2017–18 Oxford U 42 10
2018–19 Oxford U 44 11
2019–20 Oxford U 30 12
2020–21 Oxford U 37 7
2021–22 Oxford U 26 7 **179 47**

LONG, Sam (D) 124 9
H: 5 10 W: 11 11 b.Oxford 16-1-95
2012–13 Oxford U 1 0
2013–14 Oxford U 3 0
2014–15 Oxford U 10 1
2015–16 Oxford U 1 0
2016–17 Oxford U 3 0
2017–18 Oxford U 0 0
2018–19 Oxford U 18 0
2019–20 Oxford U 16 1
2020–21 Oxford U 36 6
2021–22 Oxford U 36 1 **124 9**

McGUANE, Marcus (M) 59 1
H: 5 10 W: 11 07 b.Greenwich 2-2-99
Internationals: Republic of Ireland U17. England U17, U18, U19.
2017–18 Arsenal 0 0
2018–19 Barcelona 0 0
2019–20 Barcelona 0 0
2019–20 *Telstar* 14 1 **14 1**
2019–20 Nottingham F 0 0
2020–21 Nottingham F 0 0
2020–21 *Oxford U* 15 0
2021–22 Oxford U 30 0 **45 0**

McNALLY, Luke (D) 30 4
H: 6 0 b.County Meath 20-9-99
Internationals: Republic of Ireland U19.
From Drogheda U, St Patricks Ath.
2020–21 Oxford U 0 0
2021–22 Oxford U 30 4 **30 4**

MOORE, Elliott (D) 149 14
H: 6 5 W: 12 04 b.Leicester 16-3-97
Internationals: England U18, U20.
2016–17 Leicester C 0 0
2017–18 Leicester C 0 0
2017–18 *OH Leuven* 24 2
2018–19 Leicester C 0 0
2018–19 *OH Leuven* 28 5 **52 7**
2019–20 Oxford U 20 1
2020–21 Oxford U 46 5
2021–22 Oxford U 31 1 **97 7**

MOUSINHO, John (D) 475 23
H: 6 1 W: 12 06 b.Isleworth 30-4-86
2005–06 Brentford 7 0
2006–07 Brentford 34 0
2007–08 Brentford 23 2 **64 2**
2008–09 Wycombe W 34 2
2009–10 Wycombe W 39 1 **73 3**
2010–11 Stevenage 38 7
2011–12 Stevenage 19 3
2012–13 Preston NE 24 1
2013–14 Preston NE 2 0 **26 1**
2013–14 *Gillingham* 4 1 **4 1**
2013–14 *Stevenage* 16 1 **73 11**
2014–15 Burton Alb 42 2
2015–16 Burton Alb 46 0
2016–17 Burton Alb 32 0
2017–18 Burton Alb 1 0 **121 2**
2017–18 Oxford U 40 1
2018–19 Oxford U 35 2
2019–20 Oxford U 26 0
2020–21 Oxford U 7 0
2021–22 Oxford U 6 0 **114 3**

O'DONKOR, Gatlin (F) 1 0
b. 14-10-04
2020–21 Oxford U 0 0
2021–22 Oxford U 1 0 **1 0**

SADE LICHTENFELD, Yoav (D) 0 0
2020–21 Oxford U 0 0
2021–22 Oxford U 0 0

SEDDON, Steve (D) 116 10
H: 5 10 W: 10 10 b.Reading 25-12-97
2017–18 Birmingham C 0 0
2018–19 Birmingham C 0 0
2018–19 *Stevenage* 23 3 **23 3**
2018–19 *AFC Wimbledon* 18 3
2019–20 Birmingham C 4 0
2019–20 *Portsmouth* 12 1 **12 1**
2020–21 Birmingham C 7 0
2020–21 *AFC Wimbledon* 16 1 **34 4**
2021–22 Birmingham C 0 0 **11 0**
2021–22 Oxford U 36 2 **36 2**

SMYTH, Oisin (M) 98 9
b.Derrytrasna 5-5-00
Internationals: Northern Ireland U21.
2018–19 Dungannon Swifts 15 2
2019–20 Dungannon Swifts 27 4
2020–21 Dungannon Swifts 33 2
2021–22 Dungannon Swifts 23 1 **98 9**
2021–22 Oxford U 0 0

SPASOV, Slavi (F) 1 0
b. 31-12-01
2018–19 Oxford U 1 0
2019–20 Oxford U 0 0
2020–21 Oxford U 0 0
2021–22 Oxford U 0 0 **1 0**

STEPHENS, Jack (G) 65 0
H: 6 2 W: 12 02 b.Ealing 2-8-97
2014–15 Oxford U 0 0
2015–16 Oxford U 0 0
2016–17 Oxford U 0 0
2017–18 Oxford U 0 0
2018–19 Oxford U 2 0
2019–20 Oxford U 0 0
2020–21 Oxford U 33 0
2021–22 Oxford U 30 0 **65 0**

SYKES, Mark (M) 104 9
H: 6 0 W: 12 04 b.Belfast 4-8-97
Internationals: Northern Ireland U19, U21.
From Glenavon.
2018–19 Oxford U 9 0
2019–20 Oxford U 23 1
2020–21 Oxford U 32 0
2021–22 Oxford U 40 8 **104 9**

TAYLOR, Matty (F) 256 101
H: 5 9 W: 11 05 b.Oxford 30-3-90
Internationals: England C.
From Oxford U, North Leigh, Forest Green R.
2015–16 Bristol R 46 27
2016–17 Bristol R 27 16 **73 43**
2016–17 Bristol C 15 2
2017–18 Bristol C 18 1
2018–19 Bristol C 33 4
2019–20 Bristol C 1 0 **67 7**
2019–20 *Oxford U* 26 13
2020–21 Oxford U 46 18
2021–22 Oxford U 44 20 **116 51**

WILLIAMS, Ryan (M) 249 23
H: 5 8 W: 10 07 b.Perth, Australia 28-10-93
Internationals: Australia U20, U23, Full caps.
2011–12 Portsmouth 4 0
2011–12 Fulham 0 0
2012–13 Fulham 0 0
2012–13 *Gillingham* 0 0
2013–14 Fulham 0 0
2013–14 *Oxford U* 36 7
2014–15 Fulham 2 0 **2 0**
2014–15 *Barnsley* 5 0
2015–16 Barnsley 5 0
2016–17 Barnsley 16 1 **26 1**
2017–18 Rotherham U 42 4
2018–19 Rotherham U 39 1 **81 5**
2019–20 Portsmouth 26 3
2020–21 Portsmouth 41 5
2021–22 Portsmouth 0 0 **71 8**
2021–22 Oxford U 33 2 **69 9**

WINNALL, Sam (F) 272 89
H: 5 9 W: 11 03 b.Wolverhampton 19-1-91
2009–10 Wolverhampton W 0 0
2010–11 Wolverhampton W 0 0
2010–11 *Burton Alb* 19 7 **19 7**
2011–12 Wolverhampton W 0 0
2011–12 *Hereford U* 8 2 **8 2**
2011–12 *Inverness CT* 2 0 **2 0**
2012–13 Wolverhampton W 0 0
2012–13 *Shrewsbury T* 4 0 **4 0**
2013–14 Scunthorpe U 45 23 **45 23**
2014–15 Barnsley 32 9
2015–16 Barnsley 43 21
2016–17 Barnsley 22 11 **97 41**
2016–17 Sheffield W 14 3
2017–18 Sheffield W 2 1
2017–18 *Derby Co* 17 6 **17 6**
2018–19 Sheffield W 7 0
2019–20 Sheffield W 13 1 **36 5**
2020–21 Oxford U 24 4
2021–22 Oxford U 20 1 **44 5**

Players retained or with offer of contract
Johnson, Joshua; Nosakhare, Clinton; Plumley, Kie; Smith, Adam; Watt, Benjamin.

Scholars
Anifowose, Joshua Ayodele Temitayo; Barnsley, Fraser Paul; Brearey, Edward Charles; Coe, Elijah Luke; Davis-Stephenson, Amari Jermaine Jevonte'; Franklin, George Samuel; Giles, Owen Christopher; Johnson, Joshua Emmanuel; Masters-Spence, Mac; Nosakhare, Clinton; O'Donkor, Gatlin Teye; Owens, William Robert; Sankoh, Ibrahim Gbanabom; Smith, Adam Peter; Tiamuna, Enrique Ngizafumu; Watt, Benjamin Alexander; Zabeli, Erion.

PETERBOROUGH U (63)

ADUBOFOUR-POKU, Kwame (M) 82 5
H: 5 10 W: 10 08 b.Croydon 11-8-01
Internationals: Ghana Full caps.
From Cray W, Worthing.
2019–20 Colchester U 29 5
2020–21 Colchester U 33 0
2021–22 Colchester U 0 0 **62 5**
2021–22 Peterborough U 20 0 **20 0**

BARKER, Kyle (M) 1 0
H: 5 9 W: 11 03 b.King's Lynn 16-12-00
2019–20 Peterborough U 0 0
2020–21 Peterborough U 1 0
2021–22 Peterborough U 0 0 **1 0**

BEEVERS, Mark (D) 496 21
H: 6 4 W: 12 08 b.Barnsley 21-11-89
Internationals: England U19.
2006–07 Sheffield W 2 0
2007–08 Sheffield W 28 0
2008–09 Sheffield W 34 0
2009–10 Sheffield W 35 0
2010–11 Sheffield W 28 2
2011–12 Sheffield W 7 0
2011–12 *Milton Keynes D* 14 1 **14 1**
2012–13 Sheffield W 6 0 **140 2**
2012–13 Millwall 35 1
2013–14 Millwall 28 0
2014–15 Millwall 25 2
2015–16 Millwall 42 4 **130 7**
2016–17 Bolton W 45 7
2017–18 Bolton W 44 1
2018–19 Bolton W 32 3 **121 11**
2019–20 Peterborough U 32 0
2020–21 Peterborough U 45 0
2021–22 Peterborough U 14 0 **91 0**

BLACKMORE, Will (G) 1 0
H: 6 1 b.Worthing 1-10-01
2020–21 Peterborough U 1 0
2021–22 Peterborough U 0 0 **1 0**

BODIE, Dave (D) 0 0
2020–21 Peterborough U 0 0
2021–22 Peterborough U 0 0

BROOM, Ryan (M) 151 17
H: 5 10 W: 12 08 b.Newport 4-9-96
2015–16 Bristol R 1 0
2016–17 Bristol R 5 0
2017–18 Bristol R 3 0 **9 0**
2018–19 Cheltenham T 39 2
2019–20 Cheltenham T 34 8 **73 10**
2020–21 Peterborough U 15 1
2020–21 *Burton Alb* 11 2 **11 2**
2021–22 Peterborough U 0 0 **15 1**
2021–22 *Plymouth Arg* 43 4 **43 4**

BURROWS, Harrison (M) 62 4
H: 5 11 W: 10 10 b.Peterborough 12-1-02
2017–18 Peterborough U 0 0
2018–19 Peterborough U 0 0
2019–20 Peterborough U 4 0
2020–21 Peterborough U 21 1
2021–22 Peterborough U 37 3 **62 4**

BUTLER, Dan (D) 270 10
H: 5 9 W: 11 11 b.Cowes 26-8-94
2012–13 Portsmouth 17 0
2013–14 Portsmouth 1 0
2014–15 Portsmouth 30 0
2015–16 Portsmouth 0 0 **48 0**
2016–17 Newport Co 40 3
2017–18 Newport Co 44 1
2018–19 Newport Co 45 3 **129 7**

2019–20 Peterborough U 29 2
2020–21 Peterborough U 42 1
2021–22 Peterborough U 22 0 **93 3**

CLARKE-HARRIS, Jonson (F) 317 96
H: 6 0 W: 11 03 b.Leicester 21-7-94
Internationals: Jamaica Full caps.
2010–11 Coventry C 0 0
2011–12 Coventry C 0 0
2012–13 Peterborough U 0 0
2012–13 *Southend U* 3 0 **3 0**
2012–13 *Bury* 12 4 **12 4**
2013–14 Oldham Ath 40 6
2014–15 Oldham Ath 5 1 **45 7**
2014–15 Rotherham U 15 3
2014–15 *Milton Keynes D* 5 0 **5 0**
2014–15 *Doncaster R* 9 1 **9 1**
2015–16 Rotherham U 35 6
2016–17 Rotherham U 7 0
2017–18 Rotherham U 14 0 **71 9**
2017–18 *Coventry C* 17 3
2018–19 Coventry C 27 5 **44 8**
2018–19 Bristol R 16 11
2019–20 Bristol R 26 13 **42 24**
2020–21 Peterborough U 45 31
2021–22 Peterborough U 41 12 **86 43**

CORBETT, Kai (F) 1 0
H: 6 0 b.Barcelona 8-10-02
From West Ham U.
2021–22 Peterborough U 1 0 **1 0**

CORNELL, David (G) 176 0
H: 6 2 W: 12 07 b.Waunarlwydd 28-3-91
Internationals: Wales U17, U19, U21.
2009–10 Swansea C 0 0
2010–11 Swansea C 0 0
2011–12 Swansea C 0 0
2011–12 *Hereford U* 25 0 **25 0**
2012–13 Swansea C 0 0
2013–14 Swansea C 0 0
2013–14 *St Mirren* 5 0 **5 0**
2014–15 Swansea C 0 0
2014–15 *Portsmouth* 0 0
2015–16 Oldham Ath 14 0 **14 0**
2016–17 Northampton T 6 0
2017–18 Northampton T 6 0
2018–19 Northampton T 46 0
2019–20 Northampton T 34 0 **92 0**
2020–21 Ipswich T 10 0
2021–22 Ipswich T 0 0 **10 0**
2021–22 Peterborough U 30 0 **30 0**

EDWARDS, Ronnie (D) 36 0
H: 5 11 b.Harlow 28-3-03
Internationals: England U19.
From Barnet.
2020–21 Peterborough U 2 0
2021–22 Peterborough U 34 0 **36 0**

FERNANDEZ, Emmanuel (D) 1 0
H: 6 4 W: 12 08 b. 20-11-01
From Gillingham, Ramsgate.
2021–22 Peterborough U 1 0 **1 0**

FUCHS, Jeando (M) 167 5
H: 5 9 W: 11 00 b.Yaounde 11-10-97
Internationals: France U19, U20. Cameroon Full caps.
2014–15 Sochaux 1 0
2015–16 Sochaux 24 0
2016–17 Sochaux 27 2
2017–18 Sochaux 31 1
2018–19 Sochaux 22 2 **105 5**
2019–20 Alaves 0 0
2019–20 *Maccabi Haifa* 6 0 **6 0**
2020–21 Dundee U 20 0
2021–22 Dundee U 18 0 **38 0**
2021–22 Peterborough U 18 0 **18 0**

GRANT, Jorge (M) 207 44
H: 5 9 W: 11 07 b.Oxford 26-9-94
2013–14 Nottingham F 0 0
2014–15 Nottingham F 1 0
2015–16 Nottingham F 10 0
2016–17 Nottingham F 6 0
2016–17 *Notts Co* 17 6
2017–18 Nottingham F 0 0
2017–18 *Notts Co* 45 15 **62 21**
2018–19 Nottingham F 0 0 **17 0**
2018–19 *Luton T* 17 2 **17 2**
2018–19 *Mansfield T* 17 4 **17 4**
2019–20 Lincoln C 32 2
2020–21 Lincoln C 36 13 **68 15**
2021–22 Peterborough U 26 2 **26 2**

HARRIS, Luke (M) 0 0
b. 25-4-03
2019–20 Peterborough U 0 0
2020–21 Peterborough U 0 0
2021–22 Peterborough U 0 0

JADE-JONES, Ricky (M) 44 1
H: 6 0 W: 10 12 b.Peterborough 24-6-01
2019–20 Peterborough U 11 0
2020–21 Peterborough U 15 1
2021–22 Peterborough U 18 0 **44 1**

KANU, Idris (F) 55 3
H: 6 0 W: 11 11 b.London 5-12-99
Internationals: Sierra Leone Full caps.
From West Ham U, Aldershot T.
2017–18 Peterborough U 18 0
2018–19 Peterborough U 0 0
2018–19 *Port Vale* 3 1 **3 1**
2019–20 Peterborough U 6 0
2020–21 Peterborough U 17 2
2021–22 Peterborough U 5 0 **46 2**
2021–22 *Northampton T* 6 0 **6 0**

KENT, Frankie (D) 234 8
H: 6 2 W: 12 00 b.Romford 21-11-95
2013–14 Colchester U 1 0
2014–15 Colchester U 10 0
2015–16 Colchester U 26 0
2016–17 Colchester U 13 0
2017–18 Colchester U 37 2
2018–19 Colchester U 40 4 **127 6**
2019–20 Peterborough U 28 1
2020–21 Peterborough U 45 1
2021–22 Peterborough U 34 0 **107 2**

KNIGHT, Josh (D) 105 4
H: 6 0 W: 11 11 b.Leicester 7-9-97
2017–18 Leicester C 0 0
2018–19 Leicester C 0 0
2018–19 *Peterborough U* 8 0
2019–20 Leicester C 0 0
2019–20 *Peterborough U* 24 3
2020–21 Leicester C 0 0
2020–21 *Wycombe W* 37 1 **37 1**
2021–22 Peterborough U 36 0 **68 3**

MARRIOTT, Jack (F) 244 69
H: 5 8 W: 11 03 b.Beverley 9-9-94
2012–13 Ipswich T 1 0
2013–14 Ipswich T 1 0
2013–14 *Gillingham* 1 0 **1 0**
2014–15 Ipswich T 0 0 **2 0**
2014–15 *Carlisle U* 4 0 **4 0**
2014–15 *Colchester U* 5 1 **5 1**
2015–16 Luton T 40 14
2016–17 Luton T 39 8 **79 22**
2017–18 Peterborough U 44 27
2018–19 Derby Co 33 7
2019–20 Derby Co 32 2
2020–21 Derby Co 4 1 **69 10**
2020–21 *Sheffield W* 12 0 **12 0**
2021–22 Peterborough U 28 9 **72 36**

MENSAH, Benjamin (M) 0 0
2019–20 Peterborough U 0 0
2020–21 Peterborough U 0 0
2021–22 Peterborough U 0 0

NORBURN, Oliver (M) 203 19
H: 6 1 W: 12 13 b.Leicester 26-10-92
Internationals: Grenada Full caps.
2011–12 Leicester C 0 0
2011–12 *Bristol R* 5 0
2012–13 Bristol R 35 3
2013–14 Bristol R 16 0 **56 3**
2014–15 Plymouth Arg 14 0 **14 0**
From Guiseley, Macclesfield T, Tranmere R.
2018–19 Shrewsbury T 41 9
2019–20 Shrewsbury T 17 3
2020–21 Shrewsbury T 39 4
2021–22 Shrewsbury T 0 0 **97 16**
2021–22 Peterborough U 36 0 **36 0**

O'CONNELL, Charlie (D) 1 0
b.Chelsea 19-12-02. From West Ham U.
2020–21 Peterborough U 1 0
2021–22 Peterborough U 0 0 **1 0**

OLUWABORI, Andrew (F) 0 0
b. 30-9-01
2021–22 Peterborough U 0 0

POWELL, Aaron (D) 0 0
b. 14-11-02
2020–21 Peterborough U 0 0
2021–22 Peterborough U 0 0

PYM, Christy (G) 256 0
H: 6 0 W: 11 09 b.Exeter 24-4-95
Internationals: England U20.
2012–13 Exeter C 0 0
2013–14 Exeter C 9 0
2014–15 Exeter C 25 0
2015–16 Exeter C 0 0
2016–17 Exeter C 28 0
2017–18 Exeter C 46 0
2018–19 Exeter C 43 0 **151 0**
2019–20 Peterborough U 35 0
2020–21 Peterborough U 40 0
2021–22 Peterborough U 7 0 **82 0**
2021–22 *Stevenage* 23 0 **23 0**

RANDALL, Joel (M) 43 8
H: 5 10 W: 10 06 b.Salisbury 29-10-99
2017–18 Exeter C 0 0
2018–19 Exeter C 0 0
2019–20 Exeter C 2 0
2020–21 Exeter C 30 8
2021–22 Exeter C 0 0 **32 8**
2021–22 Peterborough U 11 0 **11 0**

SZMIDICS, Sammie (M) 233 60
H: 5 6 W: 10 01 b.Colchester 24-9-95
2013–14 Colchester U 7 0
2014–15 Colchester U 31 4
2015–16 Colchester U 5 0
2016–17 Colchester U 19 5
2017–18 Colchester U 37 12
2018–19 Colchester U 43 14 **142 35**
2019–20 Bristol C 3 0 **3 0**
2019–20 *Peterborough U* 10 4
2020–21 Peterborough U 42 15
2021–22 Peterborough U 36 6 **88 25**

TASDEMIR, Serhat (M) 17 0
b. 21-7-00
Internationals: Azerbaijan U19.
From AFC Fylde.
2019–20 Peterborough U 10 0
2020–21 Peterborough U 0 0
2020–21 *Oldham Ath* 7 0 **7 0**
2021–22 Peterborough U 0 0 **10 0**

TAYLOR, Jack (D) 133 11
H: 6 1 W: 11 00 b.Hammersmith 23-6-98
Internationals: Republic of Ireland U21.
2016–17 Barnet 14 0
2017–18 Barnet 38 2 **52 2**
From Barnet.
2019–20 Peterborough U 11 2
2020–21 Peterborough U 36 4
2021–22 Peterborough U 34 3 **81 9**

TAYLOR, Joseph (F) 4 0
b. 18-11-02
From King's Lynn T.
2021–22 Peterborough U 4 0 **4 0**

THOMPSON, Nathan (D) 315 7
H: 5 7 W: 11 03 b.Chester 9-11-90
2009–10 Swindon T 0 0
2010–11 Swindon T 3 0
2011–12 Swindon T 5 0
2012–13 Swindon T 26 0
2013–14 Swindon T 41 1
2014–15 Swindon T 35 0
2015–16 Swindon T 23 1
2016–17 Swindon T 34 2 **167 4**
2017–18 Portsmouth 36 0
2018–19 Portsmouth 31 0 **67 0**
2019–20 Peterborough U 15 0
2020–21 Peterborough U 39 2
2021–22 Peterborough U 27 1 **81 3**

TOMLINSON, Joseph (D) 15 1
H: 5 9 W: 11 00 b. 9-6-00
From Brighton & HA, Hungerford T, Eastleigh.
2021–22 Peterborough U 5 0 **5 0**
2021–22 *Swindon T* 10 1 **10 1**

WARD, Joe (M) 163 12
H: 5 6 W: 10 10 b.Chelmsford 9-4-95
Internationals: England C.
From Chelmsford C.
2015–16 Brighton & HA 0 0
2016–17 Brighton & HA 0 0
2017–18 Peterborough U 17 0
2018–19 Peterborough U 43 4
2019–20 Peterborough U 28 3
2020–21 Peterborough U 37 5
2021–22 Peterborough U 38 0 **163 12**

Players retained or with offer of contract
Bodnar, Janos; Gyamfi, Johnson; Hickinson, Kellan; Ishola, Harmeed; Lakin, William.

Scholars
Bodnar, Gergo Janos; Challinor, Ben Spencer; Chiha, Hisham; Darlington, Lewis Charlie; Dornelly, James Daniel; Goodley, Jacob Kenny; Lakin, William John Geoffrey; Laycock, Matthew James; Lukyamuzi, Theophilus Luke Bamutenda; Marshall, Reuben Peter; Mason, McKenzie Matthew; McGlinchey, Roddy; Overton, Gabriel Drew; Peters, Connor Troy; Thomas, Harry James Alan; Titchmarsh, Harry Anthony; Tonge, Oscar Joseph; Van Lier, William Lewis.

PLYMOUTH ARG (64)

BOLTON, James (D) 113 4
H: 5 11 W: 11 11 b.Stone 13-8-94
Internationals: England C.
From Macclesfield T, Halifax T, Gateshead.
2017–18 Shrewsbury T 33 1
2018–19 Shrewsbury T 31 1 **64 2**
2019–20 Portsmouth 23 1
2020–21 Portsmouth 13 1
2021–22 Portsmouth 0 0 **36 2**
2021–22 Plymouth Arg 13 0 **13 0**

BURTON, Callum (G) 38 0
H: 6 2 W: 12 00 b.Newport, Shropshire 15-8-96
Internationals: England U16, U17, U18.
2013–14 Shrewsbury T 0 0
2014–15 Shrewsbury T 0 0

2015–16 Shrewsbury T 1 0
2016–17 Shrewsbury T 0 0 **1 0**
2017–18 Hull C 0 0
2018–19 Cambridge U 0 0
2019–20 Cambridge U 10 0
2020–21 Cambridge U 27 0 **37 0**
2021–22 Plymouth Arg 0 0

CAMARA, Panutche (F) 185 12
H: 6 1 W: 9 13 b.Canchungo 28-2-97
Internationals: Guinea-Bissau Full caps.
From Dulwich Hamlet.
2017–18 Crawley T 30 2
2018–19 Crawley T 45 3
2019–20 Crawley T 29 1 **104 6**
2020–21 Plymouth Arg 41 2
2021–22 Plymouth Arg 40 4 **81 6**

COOPER, George (M) 196 22
H: 5 9 W: 11 05 b.Warrington 2-11-96
2014–15 Crewe Alex 22 3
2015–16 Crewe Alex 27 1
2016–17 Crewe Alex 46 9
2017–18 Crewe Alex 27 1 **122 14**
2017–18 Peterborough U 13 2
2018–19 Peterborough U 21 2
2019–20 Peterborough U 0 0 **34 4**
2019–20 *Plymouth Arg* 27 3
2020–21 Plymouth Arg 12 1
2021–22 Plymouth Arg 1 0 **40 4**

COOPER, Michael (G) 94 0
H: 6 1 W: 26 00 b.Exeter 8-10-99
2017–18 Plymouth Arg 1 0
2018–19 Plymouth Arg 1 0
2019–20 Plymouth Arg 0 0
2020–21 Plymouth Arg 46 0
2021–22 Plymouth Arg 46 0 **94 0**

CRASKE, Finley (D) 1 0
b.Plymouth 27-1-03
2020–21 Plymouth Arg 1 0
2021–22 Plymouth Arg 0 0 **1 0**

DAVIES, William (M) 1 0
b. 22-10-04.
Internationals: Wales U16, U17, U18.
2021–22 Plymouth Arg 1 0 **1 0**

EDWARDS, Joe (D) 373 33
H: 5 8 W: 11 07 b.Gloucester 31-10-90
2009–10 Bristol C 0 0
2010–11 Bristol C 2 0
2011–12 Bristol C 2 0
2011–12 *Yeovil T* 4 1
2012–13 Bristol C 0 0 **4 0**
2012–13 Yeovil T 35 2
2013–14 Yeovil T 46 1
2014–15 Yeovil T 34 0 **119 4**
2015–16 Colchester U 42 2 **42 2**
2016–17 Walsall 43 3
2017–18 Walsall 30 7
2018–19 Walsall 20 2 **93 12**
2019–20 Plymouth Arg 34 3
2020–21 Plymouth Arg 40 7
2021–22 Plymouth Arg 41 5 **115 15**

ENNIS, Niall (F) 88 16
H: 5 11 W: 12 00 b.Wolverhampton 20-5-99
Internationals: England U17, U18, U19.
2017–18 Wolverhampton W 0 0
2017–18 *Shrewsbury T* 1 0 **1 0**
2018–19 Wolverhampton W 0 0
2019–20 Wolverhampton W 0 0
2019–20 *Doncaster R* 29 6 **29 6**
2020–21 Wolverhampton W 0 0
2020–21 *Burton Alb* 9 0 **9 0**
2020–21 Plymouth Arg 24 6
2021–22 Plymouth Arg 25 4 **49 10**

GALLOWAY, Brendon (D) 54 2
H: 6 2 W: 13 10 b.Harare, Zimbabwe 17-3-96
Internationals: England U17, U18, U19, U21. Zimbabwe Full caps.
2011–12 Milton Keynes D 1 0
2012–13 Milton Keynes D 1 0
2013–14 Milton Keynes D 8 0 **10 0**
2014–15 Everton 2 0
2015–16 Everton 15 0
2016–17 Everton 0 0
2016–17 *WBA* 3 0 **3 0**
2017–18 Everton 0 0
2017–18 *Sunderland* 7 0 **7 0**
2018–19 Everton 0 0 **17 0**
2019–20 Luton T 3 0
2020–21 Shrewsbury T 0 0
2020–21 Luton T 0 0
2021–22 Luton T 0 0 **3 0**
2021–22 Plymouth Arg 14 2 **14 2**

GILLESPHEY, Macaulay (D) 169 7
H: 5 11 W: 11 00 b.Ashington 24-11-95
2015–16 Newcastle U 0 0
2015–16 *Carlisle U* 23 2
2016–17 Newcastle U 0 0
2016–17 *Carlisle U* 32 0
2017–18 Newcastle U 0 0
2018–19 Carlisle U 24 0 **79 2**
2019–20 Brisbane Roar 27 1
2020–21 Brisbane Roar 23 3 **50 4**
2021–22 Plymouth Arg 40 1 **40 1**

GRANT, Conor (M) 177 17
H: 5 9 W: 12 08 b.Fazakerley 18-4-95
Internationals: England U18.
2013–14 Everton 0 0
2014–15 Everton 0 0
2014–15 *Motherwell* 11 1 **11 1**
2015–16 Everton 0 0
2015–16 *Doncaster R* 19 2
2016–17 Everton 0 0
2016–17 *Ipswich T* 6 0 **6 0**
2016–17 *Doncaster R* 21 1 **40 3**
2017–18 Everton 0 0
2017–18 *Crewe Alex* 17 0 **17 0**
2018–19 Plymouth Arg 10 0
2019–20 Plymouth Arg 17 2
2020–21 Plymouth Arg 38 4
2021–22 Plymouth Arg 38 7 **103 13**

HARDIE, Ryan (F) 194 60
H: 5 10 W: 9 11 b.Stranraer 17-3-97
Internationals: Scotland U16, U17, U19, U20, U21.
2014–15 Rangers 5 2
2015–16 Rangers 1 0
2015–16 *Raith R* 10 6
2016–17 Rangers 0 0
2016–17 *St Mirren* 16 3 **16 3**
2016–17 *Raith R* 18 6 **28 12**
2017–18 Rangers 7 0
2017–18 *Livingston* 16 8
2018–19 Rangers 0 0 **13 2**
2018–19 Livingston 21 7 **37 15**
2019–20 Blackpool 7 0 **7 0**
2019–20 *Plymouth Arg* 13 7
2020–21 Plymouth Arg 43 5
2021–22 Plymouth Arg 37 16 **93 28**

HOUGHTON, Jordan (M) 225 8
H: 6 2 W: 12 13 b.Chertsey 9-11-95
Internationals: England U16, U17, U20.
2015–16 Chelsea 0 0
2015–16 *Gillingham* 11 1 **11 1**
2015–16 *Plymouth Arg* 10 1
2016–17 Chelsea 0 0
2016–17 *Doncaster R* 32 1
2017–18 Chelsea 0 0
2017–18 *Doncaster R* 37 0 **69 1**
2018–19 Milton Keynes D 44 2
2019–20 Milton Keynes D 30 2
2020–21 Milton Keynes D 19 0 **93 4**
2021–22 Plymouth Arg 42 1 **52 2**

JEPHCOTT, Luke (F) 104 33
H: 5 10 W: 11 11 b.Truro 26-1-00
Internationals: Wales U19, U21.
2018–19 Plymouth Arg 9 0
2019–20 Plymouth Arg 14 7
2020–21 Plymouth Arg 41 16
2021–22 Plymouth Arg 40 10 **104 33**

LAW, Ryan (D) 18 1
H: 5 10 W: 10 10 b.Torquay 8-9-99
2017–18 Plymouth Arg 0 0
2018–19 Plymouth Arg 0 0
2019–20 Plymouth Arg 0 0
2020–21 Plymouth Arg 4 0
2021–22 Plymouth Arg 14 1 **18 1**

LEWIS, Alfie (M) 32 3
H: 5 7 W: 10 01 b.Leigh-on-Sea 28-9-99
2019–20 West Ham U 0 0
2020–21 St Patricks Ath 31 3 **31 3**
2021–22 Plymouth Arg 1 0 **1 0**

MAYOR, Danny (M) 398 37
H: 6 0 W: 12 00 b.Leyland 18-10-90
2008–09 Preston NE 0 0
2008–09 *Tranmere R* 3 0 **3 0**
2009–10 Preston NE 7 0
2010–11 Preston NE 21 0
2011–12 Preston NE 36 2
2012–13 Preston NE 0 0 **64 2**
2012–13 Sheffield W 8 0
2012–13 *Southend U* 5 0 **5 0**
2013–14 Sheffield W 0 0 **8 0**
2013–14 *Bury* 39 5
2014–15 Bury 44 8
2015–16 Bury 44 5
2016–17 Bury 21 3
2017–18 Bury 20 1
2018–19 Bury 39 8 **207 30**
2019–20 Plymouth Arg 34 1
2020–21 Plymouth Arg 44 1
2021–22 Plymouth Arg 33 3 **111 5**

McCORMICK, Luke (G) 352 0
H: 6 0 W: 13 12 b.Coventry 15-8-83
2000–01 Plymouth Arg 1 0
2001–02 Plymouth Arg 0 0
2002–03 Plymouth Arg 3 0
2003–04 Plymouth Arg 40 0
2004–05 Plymouth Arg 23 0
2005–06 Plymouth Arg 1 0
2006–07 Plymouth Arg 40 0
2007–08 Plymouth Arg 30 0
From Truro C.
2012–13 Oxford U 15 0 **15 0**
2013–14 Plymouth Arg 27 0
2014–15 Plymouth Arg 46 0
2015–16 Plymouth Arg 40 0
2016–17 Plymouth Arg 46 0
2017–18 Plymouth Arg 9 0
2018–19 Swindon T 17 0
2019–20 Swindon T 12 0 **29 0**
2020–21 Plymouth Arg 2 0
2021–22 Plymouth Arg 0 0 **308 0**

MITCHELL, Ethan (M) 0 0
H: 6 3 b.Liverpool 13-2-03
2020–21 Plymouth Arg 0 0
2021–22 Plymouth Arg 0 0

PURSALL, Brandon (D) 0 0
b.Cornwall 16-3-04
2020–21 Plymouth Arg 0 0
2021–22 Plymouth Arg 0 0

RANDELL, Adam (M) 28 1
H: 5 9 W: 10 12 b.Plymouth 1-10-00
2018–19 Plymouth Arg 0 0
2019–20 Plymouth Arg 4 0
2020–21 Plymouth Arg 0 0
2021–22 Plymouth Arg 24 1 **28 1**

SCARR, Dan (D) 142 8
H: 6 2 W: 12 08 b.Bromsgrove 24-12-94
From Reddich U, Stourbridge.
2017–18 Birmingham C 0 0
2017–18 *Wycombe W* 22 1 **22 1**
2018–19 Birmingham C 0 0
2018–19 Walsall 17 1
2019–20 Walsall 33 0
2020–21 Walsall 35 4
2021–22 Walsall 0 0 **85 5**
2021–22 Plymouth Arg 35 2 **35 2**

SHIRLEY, Rhys (F) 3 0
b.Callington 18-1-03
2021–22 Plymouth Arg 3 0 **3 0**

TOMLINSON, Ollie (D) 2 0
H: 6 1 b.Ivybridge 19-5-02
2020–21 Plymouth Arg 2 0
2021–22 Plymouth Arg 0 0 **2 0**

WILSON, James (D) 289 8
H: 6 2 W: 12 13 b.Chepstow 26-2-89
Internationals: Wales U19. U21, Full caps.
2005–06 Bristol C 0 0
2006–07 Bristol C 0 0
2007–08 Bristol C 0 0
2008–09 Bristol C 2 0
2008–09 *Brentford* 14 0
2009–10 Bristol C 0 0
2009–10 *Brentford* 13 0 **27 0**
2010–11 Bristol C 2 0
2011–12 Bristol C 21 0
2012–13 Bristol C 6 0
2013–14 Bristol C 0 0 **31 0**
2013–14 *Cheltenham T* 4 0 **4 0**
2013–14 Oldham Ath 16 1
2014–15 Oldham Ath 41 1
2015–16 Oldham Ath 43 0 **100 2**
2016–17 Sheffield U 7 1
2017–18 Sheffield U 0 0 **7 1**
2017–18 *Walsall* 19 1 **19 1**
2017–18 Lincoln C 8 1
2018–19 Lincoln C 11 1
2019–20 Lincoln C 0 0 **19 2**
2019–20 Ipswich T 23 0
2020–21 Ipswich T 17 2 **40 2**
2020–21 Plymouth Arg 0 0
2021–22 Plymouth Arg 42 0 **42 0**

Players retained or with offer of contract
Baker, Zak; Garside, Carlo; Halls, Oscar; Issaka, Frederick; Massey, Oscar; Roberts, Caleb; Rutherford, Oscar; Wariuh, Angel.

Scholars
Baker, Zak Andrew; Craske, Finley Thomas; Endacott, Jack Joseph David; Forkuo, Jeffrey Pascal; Garside, Carlo Marcel; Massey, Oscar; Mitchell, Ethan Francis; Morley, James Matthew; Moyle, Lewis William; N'Sapu Jr, Samuel-Serge Muteba; Rutherford, Oscar Thor; Salawu, Jamal Rasaq Michael; Shirley, Rhys Bowles; Waruih, Angel Michael Mathaiya; Wotton, Alfie Samuel.

PORT VALE (65)

AMOO, David (F) 348 39
H: 5 10 W: 12 02 b.Southwark 23-4-91
From Millwall.
2007–08 Liverpool 0 0
2008–09 Liverpool 0 0
2009–10 Liverpool 0 0
2010–11 Liverpool 0 0
2010–11 *Milton Keynes D* 3 0 **3 0**
2010–11 *Hull C* 7 1 **7 1**
2011–12 Liverpool 0 0

2011–12 *Bury* 27 4 **27 4**
2012–13 Preston NE 17 0 **17 0**
2012–13 Tranmere R 11 1
2013–14 Tranmere R 0 0 **11 1**
2013–14 Carlisle U 43 8
2014–15 Carlisle U 27 5 **70 13**
2015–16 Partick Thistle 37 5
2016–17 Partick Thistle 25 1 **62 6**
2017–18 Cambridge U 24 2
2018–19 Cambridge U 43 5 **67 7**
2019–20 Port Vale 32 4
2020–21 Port Vale 26 1
2021–22 Port Vale 26 2 **84 7**

AMOS, Danny (D) 14 0
H: 5 11 W: 10 10 b.Sheffield 22-12-99
Internationals: Northern Ireland U19, U21.
2016–17 Doncaster R 0 0
2017–18 Doncaster R 3 0
2018–19 Doncaster R 1 0
2019–20 Doncaster R 2 0
2020–21 Doncaster R 8 0 **14 0**
2021–22 Port Vale 0 0

BAILEY, Eden (F) 1 0
H: 5 10 b.Stoke-on-Trent 4-2-04
2020–21 Port Vale 0 0
2021–22 Port Vale 1 0 **1 0**

BENNING, Malvind (D) 295 12
H: 5 10 W: 12 02 b.Sandwell 2-11-93
2012–13 Walsall 10 0
2013–14 Walsall 16 2
2014–15 Walsall 20 0 **46 2**
2014–15 *York C* 9 0 **9 0**
2015–16 Mansfield T 31 4
2016–17 Mansfield T 45 1
2017–18 Mansfield T 28 1
2018–19 Mansfield T 45 3
2019–20 Mansfield T 33 0
2020–21 Mansfield T 32 0
2021–22 Mansfield T 0 0 **214 9**
2021–22 Port Vale 26 1 **26 1**

BURGESS, Scott (M) 70 5
H: 5 10 W: 11 00 b.Warrington 27-6-96
2013–14 Bury 1 0
2014–15 Bury 0 0
2015–16 Bury 3 0
2016–17 Bury 16 2
2017–18 Bury 0 0
2018–19 Bury 0 0 **20 2**
2019–20 Port Vale 24 3
2020–21 Port Vale 24 0
2021–22 Port Vale 2 0 **50 3**

CHARSLEY, Harry (M) 89 7
H: 5 10 W: 10 01 b.Wirral 1-11-96
Internationals: Republic of Ireland U17, U19, U21.
2017–18 Everton 0 0
2017–18 *Bolton W* 1 0 **1 0**
2018–19 Everton 0 0
2019–20 Mansfield T 9 0
2020–21 Mansfield T 43 4
2021–22 Mansfield T 16 2 **68 6**
2021–22 Port Vale 20 1 **20 1**

CONLON, Tom (M) 178 19
H: 5 8 W: 9 11 b.Stoke-on-Trent 3-2-96
2013–14 Peterborough U 1 0 **1 0**
2014–15 Stevenage 13 0
2015–16 Stevenage 32 2
2016–17 Stevenage 4 0
2017–18 Stevenage 12 0 **61 2**
2018–19 Port Vale 34 3
2019–20 Port Vale 22 1
2020–21 Port Vale 42 10
2021–22 Port Vale 18 3 **116 17**

GARRITY, Ben (M) 72 14
H: 6 0 W: 11 09 b.Liverpool 21-2-97
From Warrington T.
2019–20 Blackpool 0 0
2020–21 Blackpool 0 0
2020–21 *Oldham Ath* 29 2 **29 2**
2021–22 Port Vale 43 12 **43 12**

GIBBONS, James (D) 111 3
H: 5 9 W: 9 11 b.Stoke-on-Trent 16-3-98
2016–17 Port Vale 0 0
2017–18 Port Vale 30 0
2018–19 Port Vale 15 0
2019–20 Port Vale 32 1
2020–21 Port Vale 11 0
2021–22 Port Vale 23 2 **111 3**

HALL, Connor (D) 85 3
H: 6 4 W: 14 07 b.Huntingdon 23-5-93
2020–21 Harrogate T 41 1
2021–22 Harrogate T 20 0 **61 1**
2021–22 Port Vale 24 2 **24 2**

HURST, Alex (M) 21 1
H: 5 8 W: 11 00 b.Stoke-on-Trent 6-10-99
From Matlock T, Bradford PA.
2019–20 Port Vale 0 0
2020–21 Port Vale 20 1
2021–22 Port Vale 1 0 **21 1**

HUSSEY, Chris (D) 371 9
H: 5 10 W: 10 03 b.Hammersmith 2-1-89
From AFC Wimbledon.
2009–10 Coventry C 8 0
2010–11 Coventry C 11 0
2010–11 *Crewe Alex* 0 0
2011–12 Coventry C 29 0
2012–13 Coventry C 10 0 **58 0**
2012–13 AFC Wimbledon 19 0
2013–14 AFC Wimbledon 0 0 **19 0**
2013–14 Burton Alb 27 1 **27 1**
2013–14 *Bury* 11 2
2014–15 Bury 38 0
2015–16 Bury 41 1 **90 3**
2016–17 Sheffield U 7 0
2017–18 Sheffield U 0 0 **7 0**
2017–18 *Swindon T* 18 1 **18 1**
2018–19 Cheltenham T 34 1
2019–20 Cheltenham T 33 2
2020–21 Cheltenham T 43 1
2021–22 Cheltenham T 23 0 **133 4**
2021–22 Port Vale 19 0 **19 0**

JOHNSON, Ryan (D) 17 0
H: 6 2 W: 13 05 b.Birmingham 2-10-96
Internationals: Northern Ireland U21.
2013–14 Stevenage 1 0
2014–15 Stevenage 4 0
2015–16 Stevenage 7 0
2016–17 Stevenage 0 0
2017–18 Stevenage 1 0 **13 0**
From Kidderminster H, Rushall Olympic, Hartlepool U.
2021–22 Port Vale 4 0 **4 0**
Transferred to Stockport Co, January 2022.

JONES, Dan (D) 86 1
H: 6 0 W: 12 06 b.Bishop Auckland 14-12-94
Internationals: England C.
2013–14 Hartlepool U 1 0
2014–15 Hartlepool U 25 0
2015–16 Hartlepool U 11 0 **37 0**
2016–17 Grimsby T 3 0 **3 0**
From Barrow.
2019–20 Salford C 3 0
2020–21 Salford C 0 0 **3 0**
2020–21 *Harrogate T* 21 1 **21 1**
2021–22 Port Vale 22 0 **22 0**

LUCAS COVOLAN, Cavagnari (G) 21 0
H: 6 4 W: 13 05 b.Curitiba 6-6-91
Internationals: Brazil U20.
From Esportivo, Whitehawk, Torquay U.
2021–22 Port Vale 21 0 **21 0**

MARTIN, Aaron (D) 239 13
H: 6 3 W: 12 00 b.Newport (IW) 29-9-89
Internationals: England U18.
2009–10 Southampton 2 0
2010–11 Southampton 8 0
2011–12 Southampton 10 1
2012–13 Southampton 0 0
2012–13 *Crystal Palace* 4 0 **4 0**
2012–13 *Coventry C* 12 0
2013–14 Southampton 0 0 **20 1**
2013–14 Birmingham C 8 0 **8 0**
2014–15 Yeovil T 12 3 **12 3**
2014–15 Coventry C 27 0
2015–16 Coventry C 29 2 **68 2**
2016–17 Oxford U 4 0
2017–18 Oxford U 12 0 **16 0**
2018–19 Exeter C 23 3
2019–20 Exeter C 35 2 **58 5**
2020–21 Hamilton A 24 0 **24 0**
2021–22 Port Vale 29 2 **29 2**

PETT, Tom (M) 266 28
H: 5 8 W: 11 00 b.Potters Bar 3-12-91
Internationals: England C.
From Potters Bar T, Wealdstone.
2014–15 Stevenage 34 7
2015–16 Stevenage 40 1
2016–17 Stevenage 40 6
2017–18 Stevenage 27 6
2017–18 Lincoln C 9 1
2018–19 Lincoln C 44 3
2019–20 Lincoln C 2 0 **55 4**
2020–21 Stevenage 31 2
2021–22 Stevenage 0 0 **172 22**
2021–22 Port Vale 39 2 **39 2**

PROCTOR, Jamie (F) 320 56
H: 6 2 W: 12 04 b.Preston 25-3-92
2009–10 Preston NE 1 0
2010–11 Preston NE 5 1
2010–11 *Stockport Co* 7 0 **7 0**
2011–12 Preston NE 31 3 **37 4**
2012–13 Swansea C 0 0
2012–13 *Shrewsbury T* 2 0 **2 0**
2012–13 Crawley T 18 7
2013–14 Crawley T 44 6 **62 13**
2014–15 Fleetwood T 41 8
2015–16 Fleetwood T 23 4 **64 12**
2015–16 Bradford C 18 5 **18 5**
2016–17 Bolton W 21 0 **21 0**
2016–17 *Carlisle U* 17 4 **17 4**
2017–18 Rotherham U 4 0
2018–19 Rotherham U 16 2
2019–20 Rotherham U 3 0
2019–20 *Scunthorpe U* 13 1 **13 1**
2020–21 Rotherham U 0 0 **23 2**
2020–21 *Newport Co* 10 1 **10 1**
2020–21 *Wigan Ath* 15 2 **15 2**
2021–22 Port Vale 31 12 **31 12**

ROBINSON, Sammy (D) 1 0
b.Cheltenham 9-1-02
Internationals: England U16, U17.
2020–21 Manchester C 0 0
2021–22 Port Vale 1 0 **1 0**

SMITH, Nathan (D) 258 16
H: 6 0 W: 11 05 b.Madeley 3-4-96
2013–14 Port Vale 0 0
2014–15 Port Vale 0 0
2015–16 Port Vale 0 0
2016–17 Port Vale 46 4
2017–18 Port Vale 46 1
2018–19 Port Vale 44 0
2019–20 Port Vale 34 5
2020–21 Port Vale 44 4
2021–22 Port Vale 44 2 **258 16**

STONE, Aiden (G) 43 0
H: 6 1 W: 11 11 b.Stafford 20-7-99
Internationals: England U18.
2018–19 Burnley 0 0
2019–20 Mansfield T 3 0
2020–21 Mansfield T 22 0 **25 0**
2021–22 Port Vale 18 0 **18 0**

TAYLOR, Jake (M) 54 6
H: 5 10 W: 12 02 b.Manchester 8-9-98
2019–20 Nottingham F 0 0
2019–20 *Port Vale* 18 5
2020–21 Nottingham F 0 0
2020–21 *Scunthorpe U* 13 0 **13 0**
2020–21 Port Vale 12 1
2021–22 Port Vale 11 0 **41 6**

WALKER, Brad (M) 201 13
H: 6 1 W: 12 08 b.Billingham 25-4-95
2012–13 Hartlepool U 0 0
2013–14 Hartlepool U 36 3
2014–15 Hartlepool U 28 5
2015–16 Hartlepool U 23 1
2016–17 Hartlepool U 20 1 **107 10**
2017–18 Crewe Alex 27 1
2018–19 Crewe Alex 1 0 **28 1**
2019–20 Shrewsbury T 15 0
2020–21 Shrewsbury T 23 1 **38 1**
2021–22 Port Vale 28 1 **28 1**

WILSON, James (F) 157 31
H: 6 0 W: 12 04 b.Biddulph 1-12-95
Internationals: England U16, U19, U20, U21.
2013–14 Manchester U 1 2
2014–15 Manchester U 13 1
2015–16 Manchester U 1 0
2015–16 *Brighton & HA* 25 5 **25 5**
2016–17 Manchester U 0 0
2016–17 *Derby Co* 4 0 **4 0**
2017–18 Manchester U 0 0
2017–18 *Sheffield U* 8 1 **8 1**
2018–19 Manchester U 0 0 **15 3**
2018–19 *Aberdeen* 24 4
2019–20 Aberdeen 11 0 **35 4**
2019–20 Salford C 5 2
2020–21 Salford C 24 7
2021–22 Salford C 0 0 **29 9**
2021–22 Port Vale 41 9 **41 9**

WORRALL, David (M) 480 41
H: 6 0 W: 11 02 b.Manchester 12-6-90
2006–07 Bury 1 0
2007–08 Bury 0 0
2007–08 WBA 0 0
2008–09 *Accrington S* 4 0 **4 0**
2008–09 *Shrewsbury T* 9 0 **9 0**
2009–10 WBA 0 0
2009–10 Bury 40 4
2010–11 Bury 40 2
2011–12 Bury 41 3
2012–13 Bury 41 2 **163 11**
2013–14 Rotherham U 3 1 **3 1**
2013–14 *Oldham Ath* 18 1 **18 1**
2014–15 Southend U 38 6
2015–16 Southend U 35 3 **73 9**
2016–17 Millwall 33 1 **33 1**
2017–18 Port Vale 40 4
2018–19 Port Vale 25 1
2019–20 Port Vale 34 4
2020–21 Port Vale 37 5
2021–22 Port Vale 41 4 **177 18**

Players retained or with offer of contract
Jones, Ellis; McDermott, Tommy; McFarlane, Kamani.

Scholars
Bailey, Eden Mark; Chibaya, Tazivaishe Sean; Collinge, Joseph Oliver; Ilori, Dayo Harrison; Jones, Ellis Raymond; Manhertz, Durell Rudi Isaiah; McDermott, Thomas Vincent; McFarlane, Kamani Lloyd; Okenla, Henry Samuel Kolade; Osman, Abdimajid;

Perry, Reuben Philip Samson; Plant, James John; Sangare, Siaka Ben Ardjoum; Stinton, Logan Thomas; Uchechukwu Chale, Festus; Uva Filho, Celeany France.

PORTSMOUTH (66)

BASS, Alex (G) **40 0**
H: 6 2 W: 11 00 b.Southampton 1-4-98

2014–15	Portsmouth	0	0		
2015–16	Portsmouth	0	0		
2016–17	Portsmouth	0	0		
2017–18	Portsmouth	1	0		
2018–19	Portsmouth	0	0		
2019–20	Portsmouth	15	0		
2020–21	Portsmouth	0	0		
2020–21	*Southend U*	1	0	**1**	**0**
2021–22	Portsmouth	2	0	**18**	**0**
2021–22	*Bradford C*	21	0	**21**	**0**

BRIDGMAN, Alfie (M) **0 0**
b.Portsmouth 11-4-04
Internationals: Malta U19.

2020–21	Portsmouth	0	0		
2021–22	Portsmouth	0	0		

CURTIS, Ronan (F) **250 58**
H: 6 0 W: 12 02 b.Derry 29-3-96
Internationals: Republic of Ireland U21, Full caps.

2015	Derry C	13	1		
2016	Derry C	24	4		
2017	Derry C	32	8		
2018	Derry C	22	5	**91**	**18**
2018–19	Portsmouth	41	11		
2019–20	Portsmouth	33	11		
2020–21	Portsmouth	42	10		
2021–22	Portsmouth	43	8	**159**	**40**

DOWNING, Paul (D) **295 7**
H: 6 1 W: 12 06 b.Taunton 26-10-91

2009–10	WBA	0	0		
2009–10	*Hereford U*	6	0		
2010–11	WBA	0	0		
2010–11	*Hereford U*	0	0	**6**	**0**
2010–11	*Shrewsbury T*	0	0		
2011–12	WBA	0	0		
2011–12	*Barnet*	26	0	**26**	**0**
2012–13	Walsall	31	1		
2013–14	Walsall	44	1		
2014–15	Walsall	35	1		
2015–16	Walsall	46	3	**156**	**6**
2016–17	Milton Keynes D	37	0		
2017–18	Milton Keynes D	0	0	**37**	**0**
2017–18	Blackburn R	28	1		
2018–19	Blackburn R	3	0	**31**	**1**
2018–19	*Doncaster R*	18	0	**18**	**0**
2019–20	Portsmouth	6	0		
2020–21	Portsmouth	3	0		
2021–22	Portsmouth	2	0	**11**	**0**
2021–22	*Rochdale*	10	0	**10**	**0**

FREEMAN, Kieron (D) **222 15**
H: 5 10 W: 12 06 b.Nottingham 21-3-92
Internationals: Wales U17, U19, U21, Full caps.

2010–11	Nottingham F	0	0		
2011–12	Nottingham F	0	0		
2011–12	*Notts Co*	19	1		
2012–13	Derby Co	19	0		
2013–14	Derby Co	6	0		
2013–14	*Notts Co*	16	0	**35**	**1**
2013–14	*Sheffield U*	12	0		
2014–15	Derby Co	0	0	**25**	**0**
2014–15	*Mansfield T*	11	0	**11**	**0**
2014–15	Sheffield U	19	1		
2015–16	Sheffield U	19	0		
2015–16	*Portsmouth*	7	0		
2016–17	Sheffield U	41	10		
2017–18	Sheffield U	10	1		
2018–19	Sheffield U	20	2		
2019–20	Sheffield U	2	0		
2020–21	Sheffield U	0	0	**123**	**14**
2020–21	Swindon T	2	0	**2**	**0**
2020–21	Swansea C	0	0		
2021–22	Swansea C	0	0		
2021–22	Portsmouth	19	0	**26**	**0**

HACKETT-FAIRCHILD, Recco (F) **64 5**
H: 6 3 W: 11 00 b.Redbridge 30-6-98
From Norwich C.

2017–18	Charlton Ath	5	0		
2018–19	Charlton Ath	7	0	**12**	**0**
2019–20	Portsmouth	0	0		
2020–21	Portsmouth	0	0		
2020–21	*Southend U*	25	1	**25**	**1**
2021–22	Portsmouth	27	4	**27**	**4**

HARNESS, Marcus (M) **214 29**
H: 6 0 W: 11 00 b.Coventry 1-8-94

2013–14	Burton Alb	3	0		
2014–15	Burton Alb	18	0		
2015–16	Burton Alb	5	0		
2016–17	Burton Alb	10	0		
2017–18	Burton Alb	0	0		
2017–18	*Port Vale*	35	1	**35**	**1**
2018–19	Burton Alb	32	5	**68**	**5**
2019–20	Portsmouth	25	5		
2020–21	Portsmouth	46	7		
2021–22	Portsmouth	40	11	**111**	**23**

HUGHES, Harvey (D) **0 0**
b.Lyndhurst 20-12-03

2020–21	Portsmouth	0	0		
2021–22	Portsmouth	0	0		

HUME, Denver (D) **77 2**
H: 5 10 W: 11 05 b.Ashington 11-8-98

2017–18	Sunderland	1	0		
2018–19	Sunderland	8	0		
2019–20	Sunderland	32	1		
2020–21	Sunderland	23	1		
2021–22	Sunderland	4	0	**68**	**2**
2021–22	Portsmouth	9	0	**9**	**0**

JACOBS, Michael (M) **395 62**
H: 5 9 W: 11 09 b.Rothwell 4-11-91

2009–10	Northampton T	0	0		
2010–11	Northampton T	41	5		
2011–12	Northampton T	46	6	**87**	**11**
2012–13	Derby Co	38	2		
2013–14	Derby Co	3	0	**41**	**2**
2013–14	Wolverhampton W	30	8		
2014–15	Wolverhampton W	12	0	**42**	**8**
2014–15	*Blackpool*	5	1	**5**	**1**
2015–16	Wigan Ath	35	10		
2016–17	Wigan Ath	43	3		
2017–18	Wigan Ath	44	12		
2018–19	Wigan Ath	22	4		
2019–20	Wigan Ath	32	3	**176**	**32**
2020–21	Portsmouth	20	2		
2021–22	Portsmouth	24	6	**44**	**8**

JEWITT-WHITE, Harry (M) **0 0**
b.Portsmouth 26-3-04
Internationals: Wales U16, U18.

2020–21	Portsmouth	0	0		
2021–22	Portsmouth	0	0		

JOHNSON, Callum (M) **181 5**
H: 6 2 W: 11 03 b.Yarm 23-10-96
From Middlesbrough.

2017–18	Accrington S	31	1		
2018–19	Accrington S	41	0		
2019–20	Accrington S	33	0	**105**	**1**
2020–21	Portsmouth	40	0		
2021–22	Portsmouth	1	0	**41**	**0**
2021–22	*Fleetwood T*	35	4	**35**	**4**

MINGI, Jade (M) **3 0**
b. 22-10-00
From West Ham U.

2020–21	Charlton Ath	0	0		
2021–22	Portsmouth	3	0	**3**	**0**

MNOGA, Haji (D) **5 0**
H: 6 1 W: 12 04 b.Portsmouth 16-4-02
Internationals: England U17. Tanzania Full caps.

2018–19	Portsmouth	0	0		
2019–20	Portsmouth	0	0		
2020–21	Portsmouth	5	0		
2021–22	Portsmouth	0	0	**5**	**0**

MORRELL, Joe (M) **114 3**
H: 5 3 W: 11 05 b.Ipswich 3-1-97
Internationals: Wales U17, U19, U21, Full caps.

2013–14	Bristol C	0	0		
2014–15	Bristol C	0	0		
2015–16	Bristol C	0	0		
2016–17	Bristol C	0	0		
2017–18	Bristol C	0	0		
2017–18	*Cheltenham T*	38	3	**38**	**3**
2018–19	Bristol C	1	0		
2019–20	Bristol C	0	0	**1**	**0**
2019–20	*Lincoln C*	29	0	**29**	**0**
2020–21	Luton T	10	0		
2021–22	Luton T	0	0	**10**	**0**
2021–22	Portsmouth	36	0	**36**	**0**

O'BRIEN, Aiden (F) **266 45**
H: 5 8 W: 10 12 b.Islington 4-10-93
Internationals: Republic of Ireland U17, U19, U21, Full caps.

2010–11	Millwall	0	0		
2011–12	Millwall	0	0		
2012–13	Millwall	0	0		
2012–13	*Crawley T*	9	0	**9**	**0**
2013–14	Millwall	0	0		
2013–14	*Torquay U*	3	0	**3**	**0**
2014–15	Millwall	19	2		
2015–16	Millwall	43	10		
2016–17	Millwall	43	13		
2017–18	Millwall	30	4		
2018–19	Millwall	35	2		
2019–20	Millwall	18	3	**188**	**34**
2020–21	Sunderland	32	4		
2021–22	Sunderland	17	2	**49**	**6**
2021–22	Portsmouth	17	5	**17**	**5**

OGILVIE, Connor (D) **219 11**
H: 6 0 W: 12 08 b.Harlow 14-2-96
Internationals: England U16, U17.

2013–14	Tottenham H	0	0		
2014–15	Tottenham H	0	0		
2015–16	Tottenham H	0	0		
2015–16	*Stevenage*	21	1		
2016–17	Tottenham H	0	0		
2016–17	*Stevenage*	18	0	**39**	**1**
2017–18	Tottenham H	0	0		
2017–18	*Gillingham*	37	1		
2018–19	Tottenham H	0	0		
2018–19	*Gillingham*	31	0		
2019–20	Gillingham	33	4		
2020–21	Gillingham	45	4	**146**	**9**
2021–22	Portsmouth	34	1	**34**	**1**

RAGGETT, Sean (D) **150 14**
H: 6 5 W: 12 04 b.Gillingham 17-4-93
Internationals: England C.
From Dover Ath.

2017–18	Lincoln C	25	2	**25**	**2**
2017–18	Norwich C	2	0		
2018–19	Norwich C	0	0		
2018–19	*Rotherham U*	7	1	**7**	**1**
2019–20	Norwich C	0	0	**2**	**0**
2019–20	*Portsmouth*	26	2		
2020–21	Portsmouth	45	3		
2021–22	Portsmouth	45	6	**116**	**11**

REID, Jayden (F) **15 0**
b. 22-4-01
From Swansea C.

2019–20	Birmingham C	4	0		
2020–21	Birmingham C	0	0	**4**	**0**
2020–21	*Barrow*	10	0	**10**	**0**
2020–21	*Walsall*	1	0	**1**	**0**
2021–22	Portsmouth	0	0		

ROBERTSON, Clark (D) **265 11**
H: 6 2 W: 12 00 b.Aberdeen 5-9-93
Internationals: Scotland U19, U21.

2009–10	Aberdeen	3	0		
2010–11	Aberdeen	13	0		
2011–12	Aberdeen	9	0		
2012–13	Aberdeen	23	0		
2013–14	Aberdeen	8	0		
2014–15	Aberdeen	1	0	**57**	**0**
2015–16	Blackpool	38	1		
2016–17	Blackpool	44	0		
2017–18	Blackpool	39	3	**121**	**4**
2018–19	Rotherham U	28	3		
2019–20	Rotherham U	17	2		
2020–21	Rotherham U	16	0	**61**	**5**
2021–22	Portsmouth	26	2	**26**	**2**

SETTERS, David (D) **0 0**
b.Makati City 19-5-04

2020–21	Portsmouth	0	0		
2021–22	Portsmouth	0	0		

THOMPSON, Louis (M) **169 7**
H: 5 11 W: 11 11 b.Bristol 19-12-94
Internationals: Wales U19, U21.

2012–13	Swindon T	4	0		
2013–14	Swindon T	28	2		
2014–15	Norwich C	0	0		
2014–15	*Swindon T*	32	2		
2015–16	Norwich C	0	0		
2015–16	*Swindon T*	28	2	**92**	**6**
2016–17	Norwich C	3	0		
2017–18	Norwich C	0	0		
2018–19	Norwich C	6	0		
2019–20	Norwich C	0	0		
2019–20	*Shrewsbury T*	10	0	**10**	**0**
2019–20	*Milton Keynes D*	9	0		
2020–21	Norwich C	0	0	**9**	**0**
2020–21	*Milton Keynes D*	17	0	**26**	**0**
2021–22	Portsmouth	32	1	**32**	**1**

TUNNICLIFFE, Ryan (M) **290 13**
H: 6 0 W: 14 02 b.Bury 30-12-92
Internationals: England U16, U17.

2009–10	Manchester U	0	0		
2010–11	Manchester U	0	0		
2011–12	Manchester U	0	0		
2011–12	*Peterborough U*	27	0	**27**	**0**
2012–13	Manchester U	0	0		
2012–13	*Barnsley*	2	0	**2**	**0**
2013–14	Manchester U	0	0		
2013–14	*Ipswich T*	27	0	**27**	**0**
2013–14	Fulham	3	0		
2013–14	*Wigan Ath*	5	0		
2014–15	Fulham	22	0		
2014–15	*Blackburn R*	17	1	**17**	**1**
2015–16	Fulham	27	2		
2016–17	Fulham	7	0	**59**	**2**
2016–17	*Wigan Ath*	9	1	**14**	**1**
2017–18	Millwall	24	1		
2018–19	Millwall	26	3	**50**	**4**
2019–20	Luton T	40	1		
2020–21	Luton T	24	2		
2021–22	Luton T	0	0	**64**	**3**
2021–22	Derby Co	0	0		
2021–22	Portsmouth	30	2	**30**	**2**

VINCENT, Liam (M) **0 0**
H: 5 6 b.Bromley 11-2-03
From Bromley.

2021–22	Portsmouth	0	0		

WEBBER, Oliver (G) **0 0**
b.Portsmouth 26-6-00
Internationals: Northern Ireland U19, U21.
From Glelntoran.

2020–21	Crystal Palace	0	0		
2021–22	Portsmouth	0	0		

WILLIAMS, Shaun (M) **479 60**
H: 6 0 W: 12 08 b.Dublin 19-10-86
Internationals: Republic of Ireland U21, U23, Full caps.

2007	Drogheda U	0	0		
2007	*Dundalk*	19	9	**19**	**9**
2008	Drogheda U	4	0		
2008	*Finn Harps*	14	2	**14**	**2**
2009	Drogheda U	1	0	**5**	**0**
2009	Sporting Fingal	13	7		
2010	Sporting Fingal	32	5	**45**	**12**
2011–12	Milton Keynes D	39	8		
2012–13	Milton Keynes D	44	3		
2013–14	Milton Keynes D	25	8	**108**	**19**
2013–14	Millwall	17	1		
2014–15	Millwall	38	2		
2015–16	Millwall	33	2		
2016–17	Millwall	44	4		
2017–18	Millwall	35	2		
2018–19	Millwall	31	5		
2019–20	Millwall	32	2		
2020–21	Millwall	27	0	**257**	**18**
2021–22	Portsmouth	31	0	**31**	**0**

Players retained or with offer of contract
Gifford, Dan; Howell, Jamie; Kaba, Issiaga; Payce, Adam; Simpson, Elliott; Steward, Toby.

Scholars
Bridgman, Alfie Jack; Dockerill, Joshua Robert; Gifford, Daniel Thomas; Howell, James Christopher Edward; Hughes, Harvey Russell; Jewitt-White, Harry George; Kaba, Issiaga; Kamavuako, Gabriel; Manderson, Conor Stephen; Payce, Adam Stuart; Setters, David Kevin; Simpson, Elliott Lee; Spurway, Spencer Nicholas Daniel.

PRESTON NE (67)

BARKHUIZEN, Tom (F) **330 61**
H: 5 9 W: 11 00 b.Blackpool 4-7-93

2011–12	Blackpool	0	0		
2011–12	*Hereford U*	38	11	**38**	**11**
2012–13	Blackpool	0	0		
2012–13	*Fleetwood T*	13	1	**13**	**1**
2013–14	Blackpool	14	1		
2014–15	Blackpool	7	0	**21**	**1**
2014–15	*Morecambe*	5	0		
2015–16	Morecambe	40	10		
2016–17	Morecambe	14	5	**59**	**15**
2016–17	Preston NE	17	6		
2017–18	Preston NE	46	8		
2018–19	Preston NE	34	6		
2019–20	Preston NE	44	9		
2020–21	Preston NE	45	4		
2021–22	Preston NE	13	0	**199**	**33**

BAUER, Patrick (D) **256 17**
H: 6 4 W: 13 08 b.Backnang 28-10-92
Internationals: Germany U17, U18, U20.

2010–11	Stuttgart	0	0		
2011–12	Stuttgart	0	0		
2012–13	Stuttgart	0	0		
2013–14	Maritimo	16	0		
2014–15	Maritimo	29	2	**45**	**2**
2015–16	Charlton Ath	19	1		
2016–17	Charlton Ath	36	4		
2017–18	Charlton Ath	34	3		
2018–19	Charlton Ath	35	0	**124**	**8**
2019–20	Preston NE	41	3		
2020–21	Preston NE	12	1		
2021–22	Preston NE	34	3	**87**	**7**

BAXTER, Jack (M) **9 2**
b.Chorley 27-10-00

2018–19	Preston NE	0	0		
2019–20	Preston NE	0	0		
2020–21	Preston NE	0	0		
2020–21	*Cork C*	9	2	**9**	**2**
2021–22	Preston NE	0	0		

BAYLISS, Tom (M) **82 9**
H: 6 0 W: 12 04 b.Leicester 6-4-99
Internationals: England U19.

2017–18	Coventry C	24	5		
2018–19	Coventry C	38	3		
2019–20	Coventry C	0	0	**62**	**8**
2019–20	Preston NE	1	0		
2020–21	Preston NE	11	1		
2021–22	Preston NE	0	0	**12**	**1**
2021–22	*Wigan Ath*	8	0	**8**	**0**

BROWN, Isaiah (M) **117 9**
H: 6 0 W: 10 13 b.Peterborough 7-1-97
Internationals: England U16, U17, U19, U20.

2012–13	WBA	1	0	**1**	**0**
2013–14	Chelsea	0	0		
2014–15	Chelsea	1	0		
2015–16	Chelsea	0	0		
2015–16	*Vitesse*	22	1	**22**	**1**
2016–17	Chelsea	0	0		
2016–17	*Rotherham U*	20	3	**20**	**3**
2016–17	*Huddersfield T*	15	4	**15**	**4**
2017–18	Chelsea	0	0		
2017–18	*Brighton & HA*	13	0	**13**	**0**
2018–19	Chelsea	0	0		
2018–19	*Leeds U*	1	0	**1**	**0**
2019–20	Chelsea	0	0		
2019–20	*Luton T*	25	1	**25**	**1**
2020–21	Chelsea	0	0	**1**	**0**
2020–21	*Sheffield W*	19	0	**19**	**0**
2021–22	Preston NE	0	0		

BROWNE, Alan (M) **297 38**
H: 5 8 W: 11 03 b.Cork 15-4-95
Internationals: Republic of Ireland U19, U21, Full caps.

2013	Cork C	0	0		
2013–14	Preston NE	8	1		
2014–15	Preston NE	20	3		
2015–16	Preston NE	36	3		
2016–17	Preston NE	31	0		
2017–18	Preston NE	44	7		
2018–19	Preston NE	38	12		
2019–20	Preston NE	43	4		
2020–21	Preston NE	38	4		
2021–22	Preston NE	39	4	**297**	**38**

COULTON, Lewis (D) **0 0**
b. 3-3-03
Internationals: Scotland U16, U17, U19.

2020–21	Preston NE	0	0		
2021–22	Preston NE	0	0		

CUNNINGHAM, Greg (D) **288 9**
H: 6 0 W: 11 00 b.Galway 31-1-91
Internationals: Republic of Ireland U17, U21, Full caps.

2008–09	Manchester C	0	0		
2009–10	Manchester C	2	0		
2010–11	Manchester C	0	0		
2010–11	*Leicester C*	13	0	**13**	**0**
2011–12	Manchester C	0	0		
2011–12	*Nottingham F*	27	0	**27**	**0**
2012–13	Manchester C	0	0	**2**	**0**
2012–13	Bristol C	30	1		
2013–14	Bristol C	37	1		
2014–15	Bristol C	24	2	**91**	**4**
2015–16	Preston NE	43	2		
2016–17	Preston NE	40	1		
2017–18	Preston NE	20	1		
2018–19	Cardiff C	7	0		
2019–20	Cardiff C	0	0		
2019–20	*Blackburn R*	8	0	**8**	**0**
2020–21	Cardiff C	5	0	**12**	**0**
2020–21	Preston NE	11	1		
2021–22	Preston NE	21	0	**135**	**5**

DIABY, Bambo (D) **88 6**
H: 6 2 W: 12 11 b.Mataro 17-12-97

2015–16	Cornelia	1	0	**1**	**0**
2016–17	Sampdoria	0	0		
2016–17	*Mantova*	7	0	**7**	**0**
2017–18	Sampdoria	0	0		
2017–18	*Peralada*	34	4	**34**	**4**
2017–18	*Girona*	0	0		
2018–19	Lokeren	18	1	**18**	**1**
2019–20	Barnsley	21	1	**21**	**1**
2021–22	Preston NE	7	0	**7**	**0**

EARL, Joshua (D) **91 1**
H: 6 4 W: 12 04 b.Southport 24-10-98

2017–18	Preston NE	19	0		
2018–19	Preston NE	14	0		
2019–20	Preston NE	0	0		
2019–20	*Bolton W*	9	0	**9**	**0**
2019–20	*Ipswich T*	7	0	**7**	**0**
2020–21	Preston NE	5	0		
2020–21	*Burton Alb*	8	0	**8**	**0**
2021–22	Preston NE	29	1	**67**	**1**

EVANS, Ched (F) **309 96**
H: 6 0 W: 12 00 b.Rhyl 28-12-88
Internationals: Wales U21, Full caps.
From Chester.

2006–07	Manchester C	0	0		
2007–08	Manchester C	0	0		
2007–08	*Norwich C*	28	10	**28**	**10**
2008–09	Manchester C	16	1	**16**	**1**
2009–10	Sheffield U	33	4		
2010–11	Sheffield U	34	9		
2011–12	Sheffield U	36	29		
2016–17	Chesterfield	25	5	**25**	**5**
2017–18	Sheffield U	9	0		
2018–19	Sheffield U	0	0	**112**	**42**
2018–19	*Fleetwood T*	39	17		
2019–20	Fleetwood T	28	9		
2020–21	Fleetwood T	17	5	**84**	**31**
2020–21	Preston NE	21	5		
2021–22	Preston NE	23	2	**44**	**7**

HARROP, Josh (M) **104 8**
H: 5 9 W: 11 00 b.Stockport 15-12-95
Internationals: England U20.

2016–17	Manchester U	1	1	**1**	**1**
2017–18	Preston NE	38	2		
2018–19	Preston NE	8	0		
2019–20	Preston NE	32	5		
2020–21	Preston NE	5	0		
2020–21	*Ipswich T*	15	0	**15**	**0**
2021–22	Preston NE	0	0	**83**	**7**
2021–22	*Fleetwood T*	5	0	**5**	**0**

HOLLAND-WILKINSON, Jacob (F) **0 0**
b.Bury 30-10-02

2020–21	Preston NE	0	0		
2021–22	Preston NE	0	0		

HUDSON, Matthew (G) **1 0**
H: 6 4 W: 11 00 b.Southport 29-7-98

2014–15	Preston NE	0	0		
2015–16	Preston NE	1	0		
2016–17	Preston NE	0	0		
2017–18	Preston NE	0	0		
2018–19	Preston NE	0	0		
2018–19	*Bury*	0	0		
2019–20	Preston NE	0	0		
2020–21	Preston NE	0	0		
2021–22	Preston NE	0	0	**1**	**0**

HUGHES, Andrew (D) **283 10**
H: 6 0 W: 11 11 b.Cardiff 5-6-92
Internationals: Wales U18, U23.

2013–14	Newport Co	26	2		
2014–15	Newport Co	16	1		
2015–16	Newport Co	25	0	**67**	**3**
2016–17	Peterborough U	39	1		
2017–18	Peterborough U	43	2	**82**	**3**
2018–19	Preston NE	32	3		
2019–20	Preston NE	28	0		
2020–21	Preston NE	34	0		
2021–22	Preston NE	40	1	**134**	**4**

HUNTINGTON, Paul (D) **395 22**
H: 6 3 W: 12 08 b.Carlisle 17-9-87
Internationals: England U18.

2005–06	Newcastle U	0	0		
2006–07	Newcastle U	11	1		
2007–08	Newcastle U	0	0	**11**	**1**
2007–08	Leeds U	17	2		
2008–09	Leeds U	4	0		
2009–10	Leeds U	0	0	**21**	**2**
2009–10	Stockport Co	26	0	**26**	**0**
2010–11	Yeovil T	40	5		
2011–12	Yeovil T	37	2	**77**	**7**
2012–13	Preston NE	37	3		
2013–14	Preston NE	23	2		
2014–15	Preston NE	32	5		
2015–16	Preston NE	38	0		
2016–17	Preston NE	33	1		
2017–18	Preston NE	44	1		
2018–19	Preston NE	22	0		
2019–20	Preston NE	9	0		
2020–21	Preston NE	21	0		
2021–22	Preston NE	1	0	**260**	**12**

JAKOBSEN, Emil (F) **148 31**
H: 6 3 W: 13 01 b.Hobro 24-6-98
Internationals: Denmark U16, U17, U19, U20, U21.

2017–18	Derby Co	0	0		
2017–18	*VVV-Venlo*	3	0	**3**	**0**
2018–19	Randers	30	4		
2019–20	Randers	33	9	**63**	**13**
2020–21	Randers FC	0	0		
2020–21	Preston NE	38	2		
2021–22	Preston NE	44	16	**82**	**18**

JOHNSON, Daniel (M) **300 55**
H: 5 9 W: 10 08 b.Kingston, Jamaica 8-10-92
Internationals: Jamaica Full caps.

2010–11	Aston Villa	0	0		
2011–12	Aston Villa	0	0		
2012–13	Aston Villa	0	0		
2012–13	*Yeovil T*	5	0	**5**	**0**
2013–14	Aston Villa	0	0		
2014–15	Aston Villa	0	0		
2014–15	*Chesterfield*	11	0	**11**	**0**
2014–15	*Oldham Ath*	6	3	**6**	**3**
2014–15	Preston NE	20	8		
2015–16	Preston NE	43	8		
2016–17	Preston NE	40	4		
2017–18	Preston NE	33	3		
2018–19	Preston NE	35	6		
2019–20	Preston NE	33	12		
2020–21	Preston NE	33	4		
2021–22	Preston NE	41	7	**278**	**52**

LEDSON, Ryan (M) **191 6**
H: 5 9 W: 10 12 b.Liverpool 19-8-97
Internationals: England U16, U17, U18, U19, U20.

2013–14	Everton	0	0		
2014–15	Everton	0	0		
2015–16	Everton	0	0		
2015–16	*Cambridge U*	27	0	**27**	**0**
2016–17	Oxford U	22	1		
2017–18	Oxford U	44	3	**66**	**4**
2018–19	Preston NE	24	0		
2019–20	Preston NE	13	0		
2020–21	Preston NE	36	2		
2021–22	Preston NE	25	0	**98**	**2**

LEIGH, Lewis (M) **0 0**
b. 5-12-03

2020–21	Preston NE	0	0		
2021–22	Preston NE	0	0		

LINDSAY, Liam (D) **218 13**
H: 6 4 W: 12 06 b.Paisley 12-10-95

2012–13	Partick Thistle	1	0		
2013–14	*Alloa Ath*	10	0	**10**	**0**
2013–14	Partick Thistle	1	0		
2014–15	Partick Thistle	1	0		
2014–15	*Airdrieonians*	13	1	**13**	**1**
2015–16	Partick Thistle	25	1		
2016–17	Partick Thistle	36	6	**64**	**7**
2017–18	Barnsley	42	1		
2018–19	Barnsley	41	1	**83**	**2**
2019–20	Stoke C	20	1		
2020–21	Stoke C	0	0		
2020–21	*Preston NE*	13	2		
2021–22	Stoke C	0	0	**20**	**1**
2021–22	Preston NE	15	0	**28**	**2**

MAGUIRE, Sean (F) **291 82**
H: 5 9 W: 11 11 b.Luton 1-5-94
Internationals: Republic of Ireland U19, U21, Full caps.

2010–11	West Ham U	0	0		
2011	*Waterford U*	8	1		
2011–12	West Ham U	0	0		
2012	*Waterford U*	26	13	**34**	**14**
2012–13	West Ham U	0	0		
2013–14	West Ham U	0	0		
2014	*Sligo R*	18	1	**18**	**1**
2014–15	West Ham U	0	0		
2014–15	*Accrington S*	33	7	**33**	**7**
2015	Dundalk	6	0	**6**	**0**
2016	Cork C	30	18		
2017	Cork C	21	20	**51**	**38**
2017–18	Preston NE	24	10		
2018–19	Preston NE	26	3		
2019–20	Preston NE	44	5		
2020–21	Preston NE	29	3		
2021–22	Preston NE	26	1	**149**	**22**

McCANN, Alistair (M) **112 8**
H: 5 9 W: 10 01 b.Edinburgh 4-12-99
Internationals: Northern Ireland U21, Full caps.

2016–17	St Johnstone	0	0		
2017–18	St Johnstone	3	0		
2018–19	St Johnstone	1	0		
2018–19	*Stranraer*	13	1	**13**	**1**
2019–20	St Johnstone	29	4		
2020–21	St Johnstone	34	2		
2021–22	St Johnstone	4	0	**71**	**6**
2021–22	Preston NE	28	1	**28**	**1**

O'NEILL, Mikey (M) **3 0**
b.Liverpool 8-6-04

2021–22	Preston NE	3	0	**3**	**0**

O'REILLY, Adam (M) **37 0**
H: 5 6 W: 9 06 b.Cork 11-5-01
Internationals: Republic of Ireland U17, U19.

2017–18	Preston NE	0	0		
2018–19	Preston NE	1	0		
2019–20	Preston NE	0	0		
2020–21	Preston NE	0	0		
2020–21	*Waterford*	14	0	**14**	**0**
2021–22	Preston NE	0	0	**1**	**0**
2022	*St Patricks Ath*	22	0	**22**	**0**

OLOSUNDE, Matthew (D) **66 0**
H: 6 1 W: 11 05 b.Philadelphia 7-3-98
Internationals: USA U17, U20, U23, Full caps.
From Manchester U.

2019–20	Rotherham U	32	0		
2020–21	Rotherham U	32	0		
2021–22	Rotherham U	0	0	**64**	**0**
2021–22	Preston NE	2	0	**2**	**0**

POTTS, Brad (M) **368 44**
H: 6 2 W: 12 11 b.Hexham 3-7-94
Internationals: England U19.

2012–13	Carlisle U	27	0		
2013–14	Carlisle U	37	2		
2014–15	Carlisle U	39	7	**103**	**9**
2015–16	Blackpool	45	6		
2016–17	Blackpool	42	10	**87**	**16**
2017–18	Barnsley	37	3		
2018–19	Barnsley	22	6	**59**	**9**
2018–19	Preston NE	10	2		
2019–20	Preston NE	32	2		
2020–21	Preston NE	42	5		
2021–22	Preston NE	35	1	**119**	**10**

RAFFERTY, Joe (D) **276 4**
H: 5 11 W: 11 11 b.Liverpool 6-10-93
Internationals: Republic of Ireland U18, U19.
From Liverpool.

2012–13	Rochdale	21	0		
2013–14	Rochdale	31	0		
2014–15	Rochdale	31	1		
2015–16	Rochdale	31	1		
2016–17	Rochdale	40	0		
2017–18	Rochdale	33	1		
2018–19	Rochdale	27	0	**214**	**3**
2018–19	Preston NE	6	0		
2019–20	Preston NE	29	1		
2020–21	Preston NE	22	0		
2021–22	Preston NE	5	0	**62**	**1**

RIPLEY, Connor (G) **147 0**
H: 6 3 W: 15 02 b.Middlesbrough 13-2-93
Internationals: England U19, U20.

2010–11	Middlesbrough	1	0		
2011–12	Middlesbrough	1	0		
2011–12	*Oxford U*	1	0	**1**	**0**
2012–13	Middlesbrough	0	0		
2013–14	Middlesbrough	0	0		
2013–14	*Bradford C*	0	0		
2014	*Ostersunds*	14	0	**14**	**0**
2014–15	Middlesbrough	0	0		
2015–16	Middlesbrough	0	0		
2015–16	*Motherwell*	36	0	**36**	**0**
2016–17	Middlesbrough	0	0		
2016–17	*Oldham Ath*	46	0	**46**	**0**
2017–18	Middlesbrough	0	0		
2017–18	*Burton Alb*	2	0	**2**	**0**
2017–18	*Bury*	15	0	**15**	**0**
2018–19	Middlesbrough	0	0	**2**	**0**
2018–19	*Accrington S*	21	0	**21**	**0**
2018–19	Preston NE	2	0		
2019–20	Preston NE	0	0		
2020–21	Preston NE	1	0		
2021–22	Salford C	7	0	**7**	**0**
2021–22	Preston NE	0	0	**3**	**0**

RODWELL-GRANT, Joe (F) **1 0**
H: 6 2 b.Haslingden 18-10-02

2020–21	Preston NE	0	0		
2021–22	Preston NE	1	0	**1**	**0**

RUDD, Declan (G) **240 0**
H: 6 3 W: 13 05 b.Diss 16-1-91
Internationals: England U16, U17, U19, U20, U21, Full caps.

2008–09	Norwich C	0	0		
2009–10	Norwich C	7	0		
2010–11	Norwich C	1	0		
2011–12	Norwich C	2	0		
2012–13	Norwich C	0	0		
2012–13	*Preston NE*	14	0		
2013–14	Norwich C	0	0		
2013–14	*Preston NE*	46	0		
2014–15	Norwich C	0	0		
2015–16	Norwich C	11	0		
2016–17	Norwich C	0	0	**21**	**0**
2016–17	*Charlton Ath*	38	0	**38**	**0**
2017–18	Preston NE	16	0		
2018–19	Preston NE	36	0		
2019–20	Preston NE	46	0		
2020–21	Preston NE	22	0		
2021–22	Preston NE	1	0	**181**	**0**

SINCLAIR, Scott (F) **394 89**
H: 5 10 W: 10 12 b.Bath 26-3-89
Internationals: England U17, U18, U19, U20, U21. Great Britain.

2004–05	Bristol R	2	0	**2**	**0**
2005–06	Chelsea	0	0		
2006–07	Chelsea	2	0		
2006–07	*Plymouth Arg*	15	2	**15**	**2**
2007–08	Chelsea	1	0		
2007–08	*QPR*	9	1	**9**	**1**
2007–08	*Charlton Ath*	3	0	**3**	**0**
2007–08	*Crystal Palace*	6	2	**6**	**2**
2008–09	Chelsea	2	0		
2008–09	*Birmingham C*	14	0	**14**	**0**
2009–10	Chelsea	0	0	**5**	**0**
2009–10	*Wigan Ath*	18	1	**18**	**1**
2010–11	Swansea C	43	19		
2011–12	Swansea C	38	8		
2012–13	Swansea C	1	1	**82**	**28**
2012–13	Manchester C	11	0		
2013–14	Manchester C	0	0		
2013–14	*WBA*	8	0	**8**	**0**
2014–15	Manchester C	2	0	**13**	**0**
2014–15	*Aston Villa*	9	1		
2015–16	Aston Villa	27	2	**36**	**3**
2016–17	Celtic	35	21		
2017–18	Celtic	35	10		
2018–19	Celtic	33	9		
2019–20	Celtic	2	0	**105**	**40**
2019–20	Preston NE	18	3		
2020–21	Preston NE	37	9		
2021–22	Preston NE	23	0	**78**	**12**

STOREY, Jordan (D) **117 6**
H: 6 2 W: 11 11 b.Yeovil 2-9-97

2016–17	Exeter C	0	0		
2017–18	Exeter C	13	2	**13**	**2**
2018–19	Preston NE	28	1		
2019–20	Preston NE	10	0		
2020–21	Preston NE	30	1		
2021–22	Preston NE	17	0	**85**	**2**
2021–22	*Sheffield W*	19	2	**19**	**2**

THOMAS, Jamie (F) **3 0**
H: 5 10 W: 11 00 b.Blackpool 10-1-97
Internationals: Wales U19.

2015–16	Bolton W	0	0		
2016–17	Burnley	0	0		
2016–17	*Ayr U*	3	0	**3**	**0**
2017–18	Burnley	0	0		

From Squires Gate, AFC Blackpool, Bamber Bridge.

2021–22	Preston NE	0	0		

WALKER, Ethan (F) **17 0**
b. 28-7-02

2018–19	Preston NE	1	0		
2019–20	Preston NE	0	0		
2020–21	Preston NE	0	0		
2020–21	*Carlisle U*	16	0	**16**	**0**
2021–22	Preston NE	0	0	**1**	**0**

WHITEMAN, Ben (M) **231 31**
H: 6 1 W: 10 10 b.Rochdale 17-6-96

2014–15	Sheffield U	0	0		
2015–16	Sheffield U	6	0		
2016–17	Sheffield U	2	0	**8**	**0**
2016–17	*Mansfield T*	23	7	**23**	**7**
2017–18	Doncaster R	42	6		
2018–19	Doncaster R	40	3		
2019–20	Doncaster R	33	5		
2020–21	Doncaster R	18	5	**133**	**19**
2020–21	Preston NE	23	1		
2021–22	Preston NE	44	4	**67**	**5**

Players retained or with offer of contract
Mawene, Noah; Seary, Joshua.

Scholars
Bennett, Aaron James Anthony; Best, Kian Andrew; Blanchard, Joseph Kirkcaldy; Cross-Adair, Finlay Douglas; De Oliveira Amaral, Dana; Duggan, Declyn; Green, Vaughn Killian; Lewis, Levi Aaron; Mfuni, Teddy Mbiya; Nelson, Kitt Edward; Nevin, Harry; O'Neill, Michael; Pemberton, Rio-Karlos Isaac; Pradic, James Charles; Slater, Jacob Vaughan; Taylor, Kian Derrick; Wallbank, Finlay Jacob.

QPR (68)

ADOMAH, Albert (F) **586 86**
H: 6 0 W: 11 09 b.Lambeth 13-12-87
Internationals: Ghana Full caps.
From Harrow Bor.

2007–08	Barnet	22	5		
2008–09	Barnet	45	9		
2009–10	Barnet	45	5	**112**	**19**
2010–11	Bristol C	46	5		
2011–12	Bristol C	45	5		
2012–13	Bristol C	40	7	**131**	**17**
2013–14	Middlesbrough	42	12		
2014–15	Middlesbrough	43	5		
2015–16	Middlesbrough	43	6		
2016–17	Middlesbrough	2	0	**130**	**23**
2016–17	Aston Villa	38	3		
2017–18	Aston Villa	39	14		
2018–19	Aston Villa	36	4	**113**	**21**
2019–20	Nottingham F	24	2	**24**	**2**
2019–20	*Cardiff C*	9	0	**9**	**0**
2020–21	QPR	34	2		
2021–22	QPR	33	2	**67**	**4**

AJOSE, Joseph (M) **0 0**
b.London 21-1-01
From Newcastle U, Port Vale.

2020–21	Reading	0	0		
2021–22	QPR	0	0		

ALFA, Ody (F) **0 0**
H: 5 9 W: 10 12 b.Kaduna 9-3-99

2019–20	QPR	0	0		
2020–21	QPR	0	0		
2021–22	QPR	0	0		

AMOS, Luke (M) **88 10**
H: 5 10 W: 11 00 b.Hatfield 23-2-97
Internationals: England U18.

2016–17	Tottenham H	0	0		
2016–17	*Southend U*	3	0	**3**	**0**
2017–18	Tottenham H	0	0		
2017–18	*Stevenage*	16	2	**16**	**2**
2018–19	Tottenham H	1	0	**1**	**0**
2019–20	*QPR*	34	2		
2020–21	QPR	5	0		
2021–22	QPR	29	6	**68**	**8**

ARCHER, Jordan (G) **199 0**
H: 6 1 W: 12 08 b.Walthamstow 12-4-93
Internationals: Scotland U19, U20, U21, Full caps.

2011–12	Tottenham H	0	0		
2012–13	Tottenham H	0	0		
2012–13	*Wycombe W*	27	0	**27**	**0**
2013–14	Tottenham H	0	0		
2014–15	Tottenham H	0	0		
2014–15	*Northampton T*	13	0	**13**	**0**
2014–15	*Millwall*	0	0		
2015–16	Millwall	39	0		
2016–17	Millwall	36	0		
2017–18	Millwall	45	0		
2018–19	Millwall	24	0	**144**	**0**
2019–20	Oxford U	6	0	**6**	**0**
2019–20	Fulham	0	0		
2020–21	Fulham	0	0		
2020–21	Motherwell	4	0	**4**	**0**

2020–21 Middlesbrough 5 0
2021–22 Middlesbrough 0 0 **5 0**
2021–22 QPR 0 0

AUSTIN, Charlie (F) 383 156
H: 6 2 W: 13 03 b.Hungerford 5-7-89
From Kintbury Rangers, Hungerford T, Thatcham T, Poole T.
2009–10 Swindon T 33 19
2010–11 Swindon T 21 12 **54 31**
2010–11 Burnley 4 0
2011–12 Burnley 41 16
2012–13 Burnley 37 25 **82 41**
2013–14 QPR 31 17
2014–15 QPR 35 18
2015–16 QPR 16 10
2015–16 Southampton 7 1
2016–17 Southampton 15 6
2017–18 Southampton 24 7
2018–19 Southampton 25 2
2019–20 Southampton 0 0 **71 16**
2019–20 WBA 34 10
2020–21 WBA 5 0 **39 10**
2020–21 *QPR* 21 8
2021–22 QPR 34 5 **137 58**

BALL, Dominic (D) 188 4
H: 6 0 W: 12 06 b.Welwyn Garden City 2-8-95
Internationals: Northern Ireland U16, U17, U19, U21. England U19, U20.
2013–14 Tottenham H 0 0
2014–15 Tottenham H 0 0
2014–15 *Cambridge U* 11 0 **11 0**
2015–16 Tottenham H 0 0
2015–16 *Rangers* 21 0 **21 0**
2016–17 Rotherham U 13 0
2016–17 *Peterborough U* 6 1 **6 1**
2017–18 Rotherham U 0 0
2017–18 *Aberdeen* 16 0
2018–19 Rotherham U 0 0 **13 0**
2018–19 *Aberdeen* 31 0 **47 0**
2019–20 QPR 31 1
2020–21 QPR 39 1
2021–22 QPR 20 1 **90 3**

BANSAL-McNULTY, Amrit (M) 7 0
H: 5 9 W: 10 06 b.Hackney 16-3-00
Internationals: Northern Ireland U21.
2018–19 QPR 0 0
2019–20 QPR 0 0
2020–21 QPR 0 0
2020–21 *Como* 3 0 **3 0**
2021–22 QPR 0 0
2021–22 *Crawley T* 4 0 **4 0**

BARBET, Yoann (D) 254 12
H: 6 2 W: 12 11 b.Libourne 10-5-93
Internationals: France U18.
2013–14 Bordeaux 0 0
2014–15 Chamois Niortais 33 2 **33 2**
2015–16 Brentford 18 1
2016–17 Brentford 23 1
2017–18 Brentford 34 3
2018–19 Brentford 32 1 **107 6**
2019–20 QPR 27 0
2020–21 QPR 46 2
2021–22 QPR 41 2 **114 4**

BARNES, Dillon (G) 29 0
H: 6 4 W: 11 11 b. 8-4-96
Internationals: Jamaica Full caps.
2014–15 Fulham 0 0
2015–16 Colchester U 0 0
2016–17 Colchester U 0 0
2017–18 Colchester U 2 0
2018–19 Colchester U 22 0 **24 0**
2019–20 QPR 0 0
2020–21 QPR 0 0
2020–21 *Hibernian* 4 0 **4 0**
2020–21 *Burton Alb* 1 0 **1 0**
2021–22 QPR 0 0

BETTACHE, Faysal (M) 19 0
H: 6 2 W: 11 02 b.Westminster 7-7-00
2018–19 QPR 0 0
2019–20 QPR 3 0
2020–21 QPR 6 0
2021–22 QPR 0 0 **9 0**
2021–22 *Oldham Ath* 10 0 **10 0**

BONNE, Macauley (F) 188 33
H: 5 11 W: 12 00 b.Ipswich 26-10-95
Internationals: Zimbabwe U23, Full caps.
2013–14 Colchester U 14 2
2014–15 Colchester U 10 1
2015–16 Colchester U 33 3
2016–17 Colchester U 18 1 **75 7**
From Leyton Orient.
2019–20 Charlton Ath 33 11
2020–21 Charlton Ath 3 0 **36 11**
2020–21 QPR 34 3
2021–22 QPR 0 0 **34 3**
2021–22 *Ipswich T* 43 12 **43 12**

CARLYLE, Nathan (D) 0 0
2018–19 QPR 0 0
2019–20 QPR 0 0
2020–21 QPR 0 0
2021–22 QPR 0 0

CHAIR, Ilias (M) 151 28
H: 5 2 W: 8 09 b.Antwerp 30-10-97
Internationals: Morocco U20, U23, Full caps.
2015–16 Lierse 2 0
2016–17 Lierse 0 0 **2 0**
2017–18 QPR 4 1
2018–19 QPR 4 0
2018–19 *Stevenage* 16 6 **16 6**
2019–20 QPR 41 4
2020–21 QPR 45 8
2021–22 QPR 39 9 **133 22**

DE SILVA, Dillon (M) 0 0
b. 18-4-02
Internationals: Sri Lanka Full caps.
2020–21 QPR 0 0
2021–22 QPR 0 0

DE WIJS, Jordy (D) 141 5
H: 6 2 W: 13 03 b.Vlijmen 8-1-95
Internationals: Netherlands U17, U18, U20, U21.
2014–15 PSV Eindhoven 0 0
2015–16 PSV Eindhoven 1 0
2016–17 PSV Eindhoven 0 0
2016–17 *Excelsior* 15 0
2017–18 PSV Eindhoven 1 0 **2 0**
2017–18 *Excelsior* 19 0 **34 0**
2018–19 Hull C 32 1
2019–20 Hull C 35 2
2020–21 Hull C 7 0 **74 3**
2020–21 QPR 9 1
2021–22 QPR 12 0 **21 1**
2021–22 *Fortuna Dusseldorf* 10 1 **10 1**

DICKIE, Rob (D) 206 10
H: 6 0 W: 11 09 b.Wokingham 3-3-96
Internationals: England U18, U19.
2015–16 Reading 1 0
2016–17 Reading 0 0
2016–17 *Cheltenham T* 20 2 **20 2**
2017–18 Reading 0 0 **1 0**
2017–18 *Lincoln C* 18 0 **18 0**
2017–18 Oxford U 15 1
2018–19 Oxford U 37 1
2019–20 Oxford U 34 0 **86 2**
2020–21 QPR 43 3
2021–22 QPR 38 3 **81 6**

DIENG, Timothy (G) 129 0
H: 6 4 W: 14 02 b.Zurich 23-11-94
Internationals: Senegal Full caps.
2010–11 Red Star Zurich 0 0
2011–12 Grasshoppers 0 0
2012–13 Grasshoppers 0 0
2012–13 *Grenchen* 3 0 **3 0**
2013–14 Grasshoppers 0 0
2014–15 Grasshoppers 0 0
2015–16 MSV Duisburg 0 0
2016–17 QPR 0 0
2017–18 QPR 0 0
2018–19 QPR 0 0
2018–19 *Stevenage* 13 0 **13 0**
2018–19 *Dundee* 16 0 **16 0**
2019–20 QPR 0 0
2019–20 *Doncaster R* 27 0 **27 0**
2020–21 QPR 42 0
2021–22 QPR 28 0 **70 0**

DOMI, Franklin (D) 0 0
H: 6 0 b.London 19-9-00
Internationals: Albania U21.
2020–21 QPR 0 0
2021–22 QPR 0 0

DOZZELL, Andre (M) 108 2
H: 5 10 W: 10 01 b.Ipswich 2-5-99
Internationals: England U16, U17, U18, U19, U20.
2015–16 Ipswich T 2 1
2016–17 Ipswich T 6 0
2017–18 Ipswich T 1 0
2018–19 Ipswich T 19 1
2019–20 Ipswich T 10 0
2020–21 Ipswich T 43 0
2021–22 Ipswich T 0 0 **81 2**
2021–22 QPR 27 0 **27 0**

DREWE, Aaron (D) 0 0
b. 8-2-01
2020–21 QPR 0 0
2021–22 QPR 0 0

DUKE-McKENNA, Stephen (M) 1 0
H: 5 9 W: 11 00 b.Liverpool 17-8-00
Internationals: Guyana Full caps.
2017–18 Everton 0 0
2018–19 Bolton W 0 0
2019–20 QPR 0 0
2020–21 QPR 1 0
2021–22 QPR 0 0 **1 0**

DUNNE, Jimmy (D) 94 8
H: 6 1 W: 11 05 b.Drogheda 19-10-97
Internationals: Republic of Ireland U21.
From Manchester U.
2017–18 Burnley 0 0
2017–18 *Accrington S* 20 0 **20 0**
2018–19 Burnley 0 0
2018–19 *Hearts* 12 2 **12 2**
2018–19 *Sunderland* 12 1 **12 1**
2019–20 Burnley 0 0
2019–20 *Fleetwood T* 9 1 **9 1**
2020–21 Burnley 3 1
2021–22 Burnley 0 0 **3 1**
2021–22 QPR 38 3 **38 3**

DYKES, Lyndon (F) 200 40
H: 6 2 W: 13 03 b.Queensland, Australia 7-10-95
Internationals: Scotland Full caps.
From Mudgeeraba, Merrimac, Redlands U, Gold Cost C, Surfers Paradise Apollo.
2016–17 Queen of the South 30 2
2017–18 Queen of the South 34 7
2018–19 Queen of the South 36 2 **100 11**
2019–20 Livingston 25 9
2020–21 Livingston 0 0 **25 9**
2020–21 QPR 42 12
2021–22 QPR 33 8 **75 20**

FIELD, Sam (M) 99 3
H: 5 10 W: 11 07 b.Stourbridge 8-5-98
Internationals: England U18, U19, U20.
2015–16 WBA 1 0
2016–17 WBA 8 0
2017–18 WBA 10 1
2018–19 WBA 12 1
2019–20 WBA 0 0
2019–20 *Charlton Ath* 17 0
2020–21 Charlton Ath 0 0 **17 0**
2020–21 WBA 3 0 **34 2**
2020–21 *QPR* 19 1
2021–22 QPR 29 0 **48 1**

FLAHERTY, Stan (M) 0 0
b.Hillingdon 5-12-01
From Arsenal.
2020–21 Newcastle U 0 0
2021–22 QPR 0 0

FRAILING, Jake (M) 0 0
b. 17-8-01
2020–21 QPR 0 0
2021–22 QPR 0 0

GUBBINS, Joseph (D) 1 0
H: 6 0 W: 11 11 b.Oxford 3-8-01
2019–20 QPR 1 0
2020–21 QPR 0 0
2021–22 QPR 0 0 **1 0**

HALWAX, Harry (G) 0 0
Internationals: Republic of Ireland U16, U17, U18.
2021–22 QPR 0 0

HAMALAINEN, Niko (M) 71 0
b.Florida 3-5-97
Internationals: Finland U18, U19, U21, Full caps.
2014–15 QPR 0 0
2015–16 QPR 0 0
2015–16 *Dagenham & R* 1 0 **1 0**
2016–17 QPR 3 0
2017–18 QPR 0 0
2018–19 QPR 0 0
2018–19 *Los Angeles FC* 3 0 **3 0**
2019–20 QPR 0 0
2019–20 *Kilmarnock* 28 0 **28 0**
2020–21 QPR 22 0
2021–22 QPR 0 0 **25 0**
2021–22 *LA Galaxy* 14 0 **14 0**

JOHANSEN, Stefan (M) 363 46
H: 6 0 W: 12 04 b.Vardo 8-1-91
Internationals: Norway U16, U17, U18, U19, U21, U23, Full caps.
2007 Bodo/Glimt 4 0
2008 Bodo/Glimt 1 0
2009 Bodo/Glimt 4 0
2010 Bodo/Glimt 20 0 **29 0**
2011 Stromsgodset 13 1
2012 Stromsgodset 27 3
2013 Stromsgodset 27 4 **67 8**
2013–14 Celtic 16 2
2014–15 Celtic 34 9
2015–16 Celtic 23 1 **73 12**
2016–17 Fulham 36 11
2017–18 Fulham 45 8
2018–19 Fulham 12 0
2018–19 *WBA* 12 2 **12 2**
2019–20 Fulham 33 0
2020–21 Fulham 0 0 **126 19**
2020–21 *QPR* 21 4
2021–22 QPR 35 1 **56 5**

KAKAY, Osman (D) 72 1
H: 5 11 W: 11 05 b.Westminster 25-8-97
Internationals: Sierra Leone Full caps.
2015–16 QPR 0 0
2015–16 *Livingston* 10 0 **10 0**
2016–17 QPR 1 0
2016–17 Chesterfield 8 0
2017–18 Chesterfield 0 0 **8 0**
2017–18 QPR 2 0

2018–19 QPR 3 0
2019–20 *Partick Thistle* 0 0
2019–20 QPR 7 0
2020–21 QPR 28 1
2021–22 QPR 13 0 **54 1**

KARGBO, Hamzad (F) 0 0
H: 6 6 b. 20-1-02
2020–21 QPR 0 0
2021–22 QPR 0 0

KELMAN, Charlie (F) 66 8
H: 5 11 W: 11 00 b.Basildon 2-11-01
Internationals: USA U18, U20.
2018–19 Southend U 10 1
2019–20 Southend U 18 5
2020–21 Southend U 3 0 **31 6**
2020–21 QPR 11 0
2021–22 QPR 1 0 **12 0**
2021–22 *Gillingham* 23 2 **23 2**

LITTLE, Max (G) 0 0
2020–21 QPR 0 0
2021–22 QPR 0 0

LLOYD, Alfie (F) 0 0
b. 30-4-03
2020–21 QPR 0 0
2021–22 QPR 0 0

MAHONEY, Murphy (G) 2 0
b.Reading 27-12-01
2021–22 QPR 2 0 **2 0**

MAHORN, Trent (D) 0 0
b. 8-9-01
2020–21 QPR 0 0
2021–22 QPR 0 0

MARSHALL, David (G) 537 0
H: 6 3 W: 13 00 b.Glasgow 5-3-85
Internationals: Scotland Youth, U21, B, Full caps.
2003–04 Celtic 11 0
2004–05 Celtic 18 0
2005–06 Celtic 4 0
2006–07 Celtic 2 0 **35 0**
2006–07 Norwich C 2 0
2007–08 Norwich C 46 0
2008–09 Norwich C 46 0 **94 0**
2008–09 Cardiff C 0 0
2009–10 Cardiff C 43 0
2010–11 Cardiff C 11 0
2011–12 Cardiff C 45 0
2012–13 Cardiff C 46 0
2013–14 Cardiff C 37 0
2014–15 Cardiff C 38 0
2015–16 Cardiff C 40 0
2016–17 Cardiff C 4 0 **264 0**
2016–17 Hull C 16 0
2017–18 Hull C 2 0
2018–19 Hull C 43 0 **61 0**
2019–20 Wigan Ath 39 0 **39 0**
2020–21 Derby Co 33 0
2021–22 Derby Co 0 0 **33 0**
2021–22 QPR 11 0 **11 0**

MASTERSON, Conor (D) 55 1
H: 6 1 W: 11 11 b.Dublin 8-9-98
Internationals: Republic of Ireland U16, U17, U18, U19, U21.
2015–16 Liverpool 0 0
2016–17 Liverpool 0 0
2017–18 Liverpool 0 0
2018–19 Liverpool 0 0
2019–20 QPR 12 1
2020–21 QPR 4 0
2020–21 *Swindon T* 5 0 **5 0**
2021–22 QPR 0 0 **16 1**
2021–22 *Cambridge U* 16 0 **16 0**
2021–22 *Gillingham* 18 0 **18 0**

MEMA, Armelindo (F) 0 0
b. 23-5-02
Internationals: Albania U21.
2020–21 QPR 0 0
2021–22 QPR 0 0

MIDDLEHURST, Thomas (G) 0 0
2020–21 QPR 0 0
2021–22 QPR 0 0

ODUBAJO, Moses (M) 278 16
H: 5 10 W: 11 05 b.Greenwich 28-7-93
Internationals: England U20.
2011–12 Leyton Orient 3 1
2012–13 Leyton Orient 44 2
2013–14 Leyton Orient 46 10 **93 13**
2014–15 Brentford 45 3
2015–16 Hull C 42 0
2016–17 Hull C 0 0
2017–18 Hull C 0 0 **42 0**
2018–19 Brentford 30 0 **75 3**
2019–20 Sheffield W 22 0
2020–21 Sheffield W 18 0 **40 0**
2021–22 QPR 28 0 **28 0**

OWENS, Charlie (M) 2 0
b. 7-12-97
Internationals: Northern Ireland U19, U21.
2017–18 QPR 0 0
2018–19 QPR 0 0
2018–19 *Wycombe W* 2 0 **2 0**
2019–20 QPR 0 0
2020–21 QPR 0 0
2021–22 QPR 0 0

RAMKILDE, Marco (F) 5 0
b.Aalborg 9-5-98
Internationals: Denmark U16, U17, U18, U19.
2015–16 AaB 1 0
2016–17 AaB 3 0
2017–18 AaB 0 0
2018–19 AaB 0 0 **4 0**
2019–20 QPR 1 0
2020–21 QPR 0 0
2021–22 QPR 0 0 **1 0**

REMY, Shiloh (M) 0 0
b. 28-12-00
2020–21 QPR 0 0
2021–22 QPR 0 0

SHODIPO, Olamide (M) 93 11
H: 5 9 W: 11 00 b.Dublin 5-7-97
Internationals: Republic of Ireland U19, U21.
2016–17 QPR 11 0
2016–17 *Port Vale* 6 0 **6 0**
2017–18 QPR 0 0
2017–18 *Colchester U* 6 0 **6 0**
2018–19 QPR 4 0
2019–20 QPR 12 0
2020–21 QPR 0 0
2020–21 *Oxford U* 39 10 **39 10**
2021–22 QPR 0 0 **27 0**
2021–22 *Sheffield W* 15 1 **15 1**

THOMAS, George (M) 123 8
H: 5 8 W: 12 00 b.Leicester 24-3-97
Internationals: Wales U17, U19, U20, U21, Full caps.
2013–14 Coventry C 1 0
2014–15 Coventry C 6 0
2015–16 Coventry C 7 0
2015–16 *Yeovil T* 5 0 **5 0**
2016–17 Coventry C 28 5 **42 5**
2017–18 Leicester C 0 0
2018–19 Leicester C 0 0
2018–19 *Scunthorpe U* 37 3 **37 3**
2019–20 Leicester C 0 0
2019–20 *ADO Den Haag* 2 0 **2 0**
2020–21 QPR 17 0
2021–22 QPR 20 0 **37 0**

WALLACE, Lee (D) 388 25
H: 6 1 W: 12 00 b.Edinburgh 1-8-87
Internationals: Scotland U19, U20, U21, Full caps.
2004–05 Hearts 13 0
2005–06 Hearts 13 0
2006–07 Hearts 17 0
2007–08 Hearts 21 0
2008–09 Hearts 34 2
2009–10 Hearts 32 1
2010–11 Hearts 9 0 **139 3**
2011–12 Rangers 28 2
2012–13 Rangers 33 3
2013–14 Rangers 28 3
2014–15 Rangers 31 3
2015–16 Rangers 36 7
2016–17 Rangers 27 3
2017–18 Rangers 5 0
2018–19 Rangers 2 0 **190 21**
2019–20 QPR 11 0
2020–21 QPR 27 1
2021–22 QPR 21 0 **59 1**

WALSH, Joe (G) 1 0
H: 6 4 W: 11 11 b.Gillingham 1-4-02
2019–20 Gillingham 0 0
2020–21 Gillingham 1 0 **1 0**
2020–21 QPR 0 0
2021–22 QPR 0 0

WESTWOOD, Keiren (G) 475 0
H: 6 1 W: 13 10 b.Manchester 23-10-84
Internationals: Republic of Ireland Full caps.
2001–02 Manchester C 0 0
2002–03 Manchester C 0 0
2003–04 Manchester C 0 0
2003–04 *Oldham Ath* 0 0
2004–05 Manchester C 0 0
2005–06 Manchester C 0 0
2005–06 Carlisle U 35 0
2006–07 Carlisle U 46 0
2007–08 Carlisle U 46 0 **127 0**
2008–09 Coventry C 46 0
2009–10 Coventry C 44 0
2010–11 Coventry C 41 0 **131 0**
2011–12 Sunderland 9 0
2012–13 Sunderland 0 0
2013–14 Sunderland 10 0 **19 0**
2014–15 Sheffield W 43 0
2015–16 Sheffield W 34 0
2016–17 Sheffield W 43 0
2017–18 Sheffield W 18 0
2018–19 Sheffield W 20 0
2019–20 Sheffield W 14 0
2020–21 Sheffield W 20 0 **192 0**
2021–22 QPR 6 0 **6 0**

WILLIAMS-LOWE, Kayden (D) 0 0
b. 4-12-00
2020–21 QPR 0 0
2021–22 QPR 0 0

WILLOCK, Chris (M) 87 12
H: 5 10 W: 10 08 b.Waltham Forest 31-1-98
Internationals: England U16, U17, U18, U19, U20.
2015–16 Arsenal 0 0
2016–17 Arsenal 0 0
2017–18 Arsenal 0 0
2018–19 Arsenal 0 0
2019–20 Arsenal 0 0
2019–20 *WBA* 0 0
2019–20 *Huddersfield T* 14 2 **14 2**
2020–21 QPR 38 3
2021–22 QPR 35 7 **73 10**

WOOLLARD-INNOCENT, Kai (D) 0 0
b. 28-9-00
2020–21 QPR 0 0
2021–22 QPR 0 0

Players retained or with offer of contract
Adarkwa, Sean; Aoraha, Alexander; Armstrong, Sinclair; Bala, Steven; Evangelista Conte, Raheem; Pedder, Rafferty; Pitblado, Isaac; Woodman, Deonysus.

Scholars
Anthony, Elijah Oluwaseyi; Anthony, Micah Oluwapelumi; Bagan, Samuel William; Brown, Shannon; Cant, Harry Peter; Castillo-Anderson, Matthew William; Cotter, Riley Haslett; Danso, Ferrell Michael Kofi Abiam; Dougui, Adam; Eisa, Omar Mamoun Elaisir Kafi; Hamid, Harun Ar-Rashid Faheem; Harrack, Kayden Michael; Hawkins, Henry; Jude-Boyd, Arkell Nicholas Cecil; Kolli, Rayan Jawad; Leal Siqueira, Guilherme; Luzinda, Moses Derek Kitaka; Marino, Salvatore Federico; McDonald, Charles Anthony Dawkins; McLean, Mason Ashley Francis; Murphy, Harrison Thomas; Obeng, Mason Charlie Yaw; Rossi, Ivo Matas; Sackey, Samuel Ebenezer; Sacopon, Jaime Alcantara; Talla, Lorent; Zapieraczynski, Kacper.

READING (69)

ABBEY, Nelson (D) 0 0
H: 6 2 b. 28-8-03
Internationals: England U17.
2020–21 Reading 0 0
2021–22 Reading 0 0

ABREFA, Kelvin (D) 3 0
H: 6 2 b. 9-12-03
Internationals: Ghana U20.
2021–22 Reading 3 0 **3 0**

ANDRESSON, Jokull (G) 44 0
H: 6 4 W: 12 13 b.Mosfellsbaer 25-8-01
Internationals: Iceland U17, U19, U21, Full caps.
From Afturelding.
2019–20 Reading 0 0
2020–21 Reading 0 0
2020–21 *Morecambe* 2 0
2020–21 *Exeter C* 29 0 **29 0**
2021–22 Reading 0 0
2021–22 *Morecambe* 13 0 **15 0**

ASHCROFT, Tyrell (D) 4 0
b. 7-7-04
2021–22 Reading 4 0 **4 0**

AZEEZ, Femi (F) 14 2
H: 5 11 b. 5-6-01
From Wealdstone.
2020–21 Reading 1 0
2021–22 Reading 13 2 **14 2**

BARKER, Brandon (M) 98 9
H: 5 9 W: 10 10 b.Manchester 4-10-96
Internationals: England U18, U19, U20.
2014–15 Manchester C 0 0
2015–16 Manchester C 0 0
2015–16 *Rotherham U* 4 1 **4 1**
2016–17 Manchester C 0 0
2016–17 *NAC Breda* 22 2 **22 2**
2017–18 Manchester C 0 0
2017–18 *Hibernian* 27 2 **27 2**
2018–19 Manchester C 0 0
2018–19 *Preston NE* 16 0 **16 0**
2019–20 Rangers 6 1
2020–21 Rangers 0 0
2020–21 *Oxford U* 19 3
2021–22 *Oxford U* 0 0 **19 3**

2021–22 Rangers 0 0 **6 1**
2021–22 Reading 4 0 **4 0**

BOYCE-CLARKE, Coniah (G) 0 0
H: 6 2 b.Reading 1-3-03
Internationals: England U16, U17. Jamaica U20.
2019–20 Reading 0 0
2020–21 Reading 0 0
2021–22 Reading 0 0

BRISTOW, Ethan (D) 6 0
H: 6 2 W: 11 03 b.Maidenhead 27-11-01
2020–21 Reading 0 0
2021–22 Reading 6 0 **6 0**

CAMARA, Mamadi (F) 7 0
H: 5 9 b.Guinea-Bissau 31-12-03
Internationals: Guinea-Bissau Full caps.
2020–21 Reading 1 0
2021–22 Reading 6 0 **7 0**

CLARKE, Jahmari (F) 12 2
H: 6 3 b. 2-10-03
Internationals: Jamaica U20.
2021–22 Reading 12 2 **12 2**

DANN, Scott (D) 436 32
H: 6 5 W: 12 05 b.Liverpool 14-2-87
Internationals: England U21.
2004–05 Walsall 1 0
2005–06 Walsall 0 0
2006–07 Walsall 30 4
2007–08 Walsall 28 3 **59 7**
2007–08 Coventry C 16 0
2008–09 Coventry C 31 3 **47 3**
2009–10 Birmingham C 30 0
2010–11 Birmingham C 20 2
2011–12 Birmingham C 0 0 **50 2**
2011–12 Blackburn R 27 1
2012–13 Blackburn R 46 4
2013–14 Blackburn R 25 0 **98 5**
2013–14 Crystal Palace 14 1
2014–15 Crystal Palace 34 2
2015–16 Crystal Palace 35 5
2016–17 Crystal Palace 23 3
2017–18 Crystal Palace 17 1
2018–19 Crystal Palace 10 0
2019–20 Crystal Palace 16 0
2020–21 Crystal Palace 15 1
2021–22 Crystal Palace 0 0 **164 13**
2021–22 Reading 18 2 **18 2**

DORSETT, Jeriel (D) 37 0
H: 5 10 W: 10 01 b.Enfield 4-5-02
Internationals: England U17, U18.
2019–20 Reading 0 0
2020–21 Reading 0 0
2021–22 Reading 0 0
2021–22 *Rochdale* 37 0 **37 0**

EJARIA, Oviemuno (M) 143 11
H: 6 0 W: 11 11 b.Southwark 18-11-97
Internationals: England U20, U21.
From Arsenal.
2016–17 Liverpool 2 0
2017–18 Liverpool 0 0
2017–18 *Sunderland* 11 1 **11 1**
2018–19 Liverpool 0 0
2018–19 *Rangers* 14 1 **14 1**
2018–19 *Reading* 16 1
2019–20 Liverpool 0 0 **2 0**
2019–20 *Reading* 36 3
2020–21 Reading 38 3
2021–22 Reading 26 2 **116 9**

FELIPE ARARUNA, Hoffmann (M) 34 0
H: 5 9 W: 10 12 b.Porto Alegre 12-3-96
2016 Sao Paulo 0 0
2017 Sao Paulo 8 0
2018 Sao Paulo 11 0
2019 Sao Paulo 0 0 **19 0**
2019 *Fortaleza* 9 0 **9 0**
2019–20 Reading 3 0
2020–21 Reading 2 0
2021–22 Reading 1 0 **6 0**

HALILOVIC, Alen (M) 183 15
H: 5 7 W: 8 09 b.Dubrovnik 18-6-96
Internationals: Croatia U16, U17, U21, Full caps.
2012–13 Dinamo Zagreb 18 2
2013–14 Dinamo Zagreb 26 5 **44 7**
2014–15 Barcelona 0 0
2015–16 Barcelona 0 0
2015–16 *Sporting Gijon* 36 3 **36 3**
2016–17 Hamburger SV 6 0
2016–17 *Las Palmas* 18 0
2017–18 Hamburger SV 0 0 **6 0**
2017–18 *Las Palmas* 20 2 **38 2**
2018–19 AC Milan 0 0
2018–19 *Standard Liege* 14 0 **14 0**
2019–20 AC Milan 0 0
2019–20 *Heerenveen* 17 1 **17 1**
2020–21 AC Milan 0 0
2020–21 Birmingham C 17 1
2021–22 Birmingham C 0 0 **17 1**
2021–22 Reading 11 1 **11 1**

HOILETT, Junior (M) 426 56
H: 5 8 W: 11 00 b.Ontario, Canada 5-6-90
Internationals: Canada Full caps.
2007–08 Blackburn R 0 0
2007–08 *Paderborn* 12 1 **12 1**
2008–09 Blackburn R 0 0
2008–09 *St Pauli* 21 6 **21 6**
2009–10 Blackburn R 23 0
2010–11 Blackburn R 24 5
2011–12 Blackburn R 34 7 **81 12**
2012–13 QPR 26 1
2013–14 QPR 35 4
2014–15 QPR 22 0
2015–16 QPR 29 6
2016–17 QPR 0 0 **112 11**
2016–17 Cardiff C 33 2
2017–18 Cardiff C 46 9
2018–19 Cardiff C 32 3
2019–20 Cardiff C 41 7
2020–21 Cardiff C 21 2 **173 23**
2021–22 Reading 27 3 **27 3**

HOLDEN, James (G) 0 0
b.Milton Keynes 4-9-01
From Bury.
2020–21 Reading 0 0
2021–22 Reading 0 0

HOLMES, Thomas (D) 83 1
H: 6 1 W: 12 13 b.Ealing 12-3-00
2017–18 Reading 1 0
2018–19 Reading 0 0
2019–20 Reading 0 0
2019–20 *KSV Roeselare* 11 0 **11 0**
2020–21 Reading 39 0
2021–22 Reading 32 1 **72 1**

LAURENT, Josh (M) 213 11
H: 6 0 W: 11 00 b.Leytonstone 6-5-95
From Wycombe W.
2013–14 QPR 0 0
2014–15 QPR 0 0
2015–16 Brentford 0 0
2015–16 *Newport Co* 3 0 **3 0**
2015–16 Hartlepool U 3 0
2016–17 Hartlepool U 25 1 **28 1**
2016–17 Wigan Ath 1 0
2017–18 Wigan Ath 0 0 **1 0**
2017–18 *Bury* 22 1 **22 1**
2018–19 Shrewsbury T 42 2
2019–20 Shrewsbury T 31 2 **73 4**
2020–21 Reading 45 3
2021–22 Reading 41 2 **86 5**

LUCAS JOAO, Eduardo (F) 281 82
H: 6 4 W: 12 08 b.Lisbon 4-9-93
Internationals: Portugal U20, U21, U23, Full caps.
2012–13 Nacional 0 0
2012–13 *Mirandela* 27 12 **27 12**
2013–14 Nacional 16 0
2014–15 Nacional 30 6 **46 6**
2015–16 Sheffield W 40 6
2016–17 Sheffield W 10 0
2016–17 *Blackburn R* 13 3 **13 3**
2017–18 Sheffield W 31 9
2018–19 Sheffield W 31 10
2019–20 Sheffield W 1 1 **113 26**
2019–20 Reading 19 6
2020–21 Reading 39 19
2021–22 Reading 24 10 **82 35**

McINTYRE, Tom (D) 57 4
H: 6 1 W: 11 07 b.Reading 6-11-98
Internationals: Scotland U17, U20, U21.
2018–19 Reading 2 0
2019–20 Reading 10 0
2020–21 Reading 26 2
2021–22 Reading 19 2 **57 4**

McNULTY, Marc (M) 322 97
H: 5 10 W: 11 00 b.Edinburgh 14-9-92
Internationals: Scotland Full caps.
2009–10 Livingston 9 1
2010–11 Livingston 5 1
2011–12 Livingston 30 11
2012–13 Livingston 26 7
2013–14 Livingston 35 17 **105 37**
2014–15 Sheffield U 31 9
2015–16 Sheffield U 5 1
2015–16 *Portsmouth* 27 10 **27 10**
2016–17 Sheffield U 4 0 **40 10**
2016–17 *Bradford C* 15 1 **15 1**
2016–17 Coventry C 0 0
2017–18 Coventry C 42 23 **42 23**
2018–19 Reading 13 1
2018–19 *Hibernian* 15 7
2019–20 Reading 0 0
2019–20 *Sunderland* 15 2 **15 2**
2019–20 *Hibernian* 6 1 **21 8**
2020–21 Reading 0 0
2020–21 *Dundee U* 25 3
2021–22 Reading 0 0 **13 1**
2021–22 *Dundee U* 19 2 **44 5**

MEITE, Yakou (M) 161 41
H: 6 0 W: 11 05 b.Paris 11-2-96
Internationals: Ivory Coast U17, U20, U23, Full caps.
2013–14 Paris Saint-Germain 0 0
2014–15 Paris Saint-Germain 0 0
2015–16 Paris Saint-Germain 1 0 **1 0**
2016–17 Reading 14 1
2017–18 Reading 0 0
2017–18 *Sochaux* 31 3 **31 3**
2018–19 Reading 37 12
2019–20 Reading 40 13
2020–21 Reading 25 12
2021–22 Reading 13 0 **129 38**

MELVIN-LAMBERT, Nahum (F) 16 3
2020–21 Reading 0 0
2020–21 *St Patricks Ath* 16 3 **16 3**
2021–22 Reading 0 0

MOORE, Liam (D) 316 9
H: 6 1 W: 13 08 b.Loughborough 31-1-93
Internationals: England U17, U20, U21. Jamaica Full caps.
2011–12 Leicester C 2 0
2011–12 *Bradford C* 17 0 **17 0**
2012–13 Leicester C 16 0
2012–13 *Brentford* 7 0
2013–14 Leicester C 30 1
2014–15 Leicester C 11 0
2014–15 *Brentford* 3 0 **10 0**
2015–16 Leicester C 0 0 **59 1**
2015–16 *Bristol C* 10 0 **10 0**
2016–17 Reading 40 1
2017–18 Reading 46 3
2018–19 Reading 38 1
2019–20 Reading 43 1
2020–21 Reading 32 0
2021–22 Reading 17 2 **216 8**
2021–22 *Stoke C* 4 0 **4 0**

MORRISON, Michael (D) 507 33
H: 6 0 W: 12 00 b.Bury St Edmunds 3-3-88
Internationals: England C.
From Cambridge U.
2008–09 Leicester C 35 3
2009–10 Leicester C 31 2
2010–11 Leicester C 11 0 **77 5**
2010–11 Sheffield W 12 0 **12 0**
2011–12 Charlton Ath 45 4
2012–13 Charlton Ath 44 1
2013–14 Charlton Ath 45 1
2014–15 Charlton Ath 2 0 **136 6**
2014–15 Birmingham C 21 0
2015–16 Birmingham C 46 3
2016–17 Birmingham C 31 3
2017–18 Birmingham C 33 1
2018–19 Birmingham C 43 7 **174 14**
2019–20 Reading 44 2
2020–21 Reading 35 4
2021–22 Reading 29 2 **108 8**

NYLAND, Orjan (G) 206 0
H: 6 4 W: 12 04 b.Volda 10-9-90
Internationals: Norway U18, U21, Full caps.
2011 Hodd 28 0
2012 Hodd 28 0 **56 0**
2013 Molde 20 0
2014 Molde 28 0
2015 Molde 13 0 **61 0**
2015–16 Ingolstadt 6 0
2016–17 Ingolstadt 12 0
2017–18 Ingolstadt 30 0 **48 0**
2018–19 Aston Villa 23 0
2019–20 Aston Villa 7 0
2020–21 Aston Villa 0 0 **30 0**
2020–21 Norwich C 0 0
2021–22 Bournemouth 1 0 **1 0**
2021–22 Reading 10 0 **10 0**

PUSCAS, George (F) 224 58
H: 6 2 W: 10 08 b.Marghita 8-4-96
Internationals: Romania U17, U19, U21, Full caps.
2012–13 Bihor Oradea 13 2 **13 2**
2013–14 Inter Milan 0 0
2014–15 Inter Milan 4 0
2015–16 Inter Milan 0 0
2015–16 *Bari* 17 5 **17 5**
2016–17 Inter Milan 0 0
2016–17 *Benevento* 21 7
2017–18 Inter Milan 0 0 **4 0**
2017–18 *Benevento* 11 1 **32 8**
2017–18 *Novara* 19 9 **19 9**
2018–19 Palermo 33 9 **33 9**
2019–20 Reading 38 12
2020–21 Reading 21 4
2021–22 Reading 25 1 **84 17**
2021–22 *Pisa* 22 8 **22 8**

RAFAEL CABRAL, Barbosa (G) 223 0
H: 6 1 W: 13 01 b.Sorocaba 20-5-90
Internationals: Brazil U23, Full caps.
2010 Santos 32 0
2011 Santos 32 0
2012 Santos 25 0
2013 Santos 5 0 **94 0**

2013–14 Napoli 8 0
2014–15 Napoli 23 0
2015–16 Napoli 0 0
2016–17 Napoli 1 0
2017–18 Napoli 0 0 **32 0**
2018–19 Sampdoria 2 0
2019–20 Sampdoria 0 0 **2 0**
2019–20 Reading 44 0
2020–21 Reading 45 0
2021–22 Reading 6 0 **95 0**
Transferred to Cruzeiro, January 2022.

RINOMHOTA, Andy (M) 125 3
H: 5 9 W: 10 01 b.Leeds 21-4-97
From AFC Portchester.
2017–18 Reading 0 0
2018–19 Reading 26 1
2019–20 Reading 37 1
2020–21 Reading 42 1
2021–22 Reading 20 0 **125 3**

SACKEY, Lynford (M) 0 0
H: 5 11 b. 18-2-03
2020–21 Reading 0 0
2021–22 Reading 0 0

SAMUELS, Imari (D) 0 0
H: 6 2 b. 5-2-03
Internationals: England U16, U17.
2020–21 Reading 0 0
2021–22 Reading 0 0

SCOTT, Rashawn (F) 1 0
b. 22-3-04
2021–22 Reading 1 0 **1 0**

SENGA-NGOYI, Jack (G) 0 0
b. 27-1-04
2021–22 Reading 0 0

SOUTHERN-COOPER, Jake (M) 0 0
b. 1-1-00
2018–19 Rotherham U 0 0
2019–20 Rotherham U 0 0
2020–21 Rotherham U 0 0
2021–22 Reading 0 0

SOUTHWOOD, Luke (G) 41 0
H: 6 1 W: 11 05 b.Oxford 6-12-97
Internationals: England U19, U20. Northern Ireland Full caps.
2019–20 Reading 0 0
2019–20 *Hamilton A* 15 0 **15 0**
2020–21 Reading 1 0
2021–22 Reading 25 0 **26 0**

STICKLAND, Michael (D) 1 0
H: 6 3 b. 9-11-03
2021–22 Reading 1 0 **1 0**

SWIFT, John (M) 236 40
H: 6 0 W: 11 07 b.Portsmouth 23-6-95
Internationals: England U16, U17, U18, U19, U20, U21.
2013–14 Chelsea 1 0
2014–15 Chelsea 0 0
2014–15 *Rotherham U* 3 0 **3 0**
2014–15 *Swindon T* 18 2 **18 2**
2015–16 Chelsea 0 0 **1 0**
2015–16 *Brentford* 27 7 **27 7**
2016–17 Reading 36 8
2017–18 Reading 24 2
2018–19 Reading 34 3
2019–20 Reading 41 6
2020–21 Reading 14 1
2021–22 Reading 38 11 **187 31**

TETEK, Dejan (M) 17 0
H: 5 11 W: 10 03 b.Oxford 24-9-02
Internationals: England U18. Serbia U19, U21.
2020–21 Reading 7 0
2021–22 Reading 10 0 **17 0**

THOMAS, Terell (D) 91 1
H: 6 0 W: 11 03 b.Rainham 18-10-97
Internationals: Saint Lucia Full caps.
From Arsenal.
2014–15 Charlton Ath 0 0
2015–16 Charlton Ath 0 0
2016–17 Charlton Ath 0 0
2017–18 Wigan Ath 3 0 **3 0**
2018–19 AFC Wimbledon 23 0
2019–20 AFC Wimbledon 31 1
2020–21 AFC Wimbledon 19 0
2021–22 AFC Wimbledon 0 0 **73 1**
2021–22 Crewe Alex 13 0 **13 0**
2021–22 Reading 2 0 **2 0**

YIADOM, Andy (M) 278 14
H: 5 11 W: 11 11 b.Camden 9-12-91
Internationals: England C. Ghana Full caps.
From Hayes & Yeading U, Braintree T.
2011–12 Barnet 7 1
2012–13 Barnet 39 3
From Barnet.
2015–16 Barnet 40 6 **86 10**
2016–17 Barnsley 32 0
2017–18 Barnsley 32 0 **64 0**
2018–19 Reading 45 1
2019–20 Reading 24 1
2020–21 Reading 21 1
2021–22 Reading 38 1 **128 4**

Players retained or with offer of contract
Collins, Harvey; Ehibhationham, Kelvin; Giscombe, Ajani; Holzman, Louie; Leavy, Kian; Osorio, Claudio; Purcell, Ben.

Scholars
Abdel Salam, Hamid Awad; Addo-Antoine, Jordan Kwesi; Ashcroft, Tyrell Dean; Campbell, Ryley Oscar Glenn; Clarke, Jahmari Oshown; Daniel-Spray, Kyle Ashley; Furlong, Harrison James; Greaver, Aston Lindon; Hammond-Chambers-, Jacob; Holzman, Louie James; Hutchings, Louis Glen Ian; Maudner, Harvey James Troy; Murray, Troy Alexander; Nditi, Zion Chebe Alban; Norcott, Thomas Christopher; Nyarko, David; Okine-Peters, Jeremiah Nii-Ayikwoa; Paul, Samuel Benjamin; Purcell, Benjamin David; Rowley, Matthew Christopher; Stickland, Michael George; Tuma, Basil Tenywa; Vickers, Caylan David.

ROCHDALE (70)

BALL, James (M) 29 6
b. 1-12-95
From Bolton W, Northwich Vic, Staybridge Celtic, Stockport Co.
2018–19 Stevenage 18 3 **18 3**
From Ebbsfleet U, Solihull Moors.
2021–22 Rochdale 11 3 **11 3**

BRIERLEY, Ethan (M) 7 0
H: 5 6 b.Rochdale 23-11-03
2019–20 Rochdale 0 0
2020–21 Rochdale 5 0
2021–22 Rochdale 2 0 **7 0**

CAMPBELL, Tahvon (F) 108 9
H: 5 7 W: 10 10 b.Birmingham 10-1-97
2015–16 WBA 0 0
2015–16 *Yeovil T* 17 1
2016–17 WBA 0 0
2016–17 *Yeovil T* 19 1 **36 2**
2016–17 *Notts Co* 11 0 **11 0**
2017–18 WBA 0 0
2017–18 *Forest Green R* 14 2
2018–19 Forest Green R 18 3 **32 5**
2018–19 *Gillingham* 5 0 **5 0**
2019–20 Cheltenham T 11 0
2020–21 Cheltenham T 0 0 **11 0**
2021–22 Rochdale 13 2 **13 2**

CHARMAN, Luke (F) 19 2
H: 6 1 b.Durham 9-12-97
2018–19 Newcastle U 0 0
2018–19 *Accrington S* 0 0
2019–20 Newcastle U 0 0
From Darlington.
2021–22 Rochdale 19 2 **19 2**

CLARK, Max (D) 142 4
H: 5 11 W: 11 07 b.Kingston-upon-Hull 19-1-96
Internationals: England U16, U17.
2015–16 Hull C 0 0
2015–16 *Cambridge U* 9 0
2016–17 Hull C 0 0
2016–17 *Cambridge U* 27 1 **36 1**
2017–18 Hull C 27 0
2018–19 Vitesse 23 1
2019–20 Vitesse 23 1
2020–21 Vitesse 0 0 **46 2**
2020–21 Hull C 0 0 **27 0**
2021–22 Fleetwood T 10 0 **10 0**
2021–22 Rochdale 23 1 **23 1**

COLEMAN, Joel (G) 87 0
H: 6 6 W: 12 13 b.Bolton 26-9-95
2013–14 Oldham Ath 0 0
2014–15 Oldham Ath 11 0
2015–16 Oldham Ath 32 0 **43 0**
2016–17 Huddersfield T 5 0
2017–18 Huddersfield T 0 0
2018–19 Huddersfield T 1 0
2018–19 *Shrewsbury T* 16 0 **16 0**
2019–20 Huddersfield T 3 0 **9 0**
2020–21 Fleetwood T 0 0
2021–22 Fleetwood T 0 0
2021–22 Rochdale 19 0 **19 0**

DONE, Matt (M) 512 46
H: 5 10 W: 10 03 b.Oswestry 22-6-88
2005–06 Wrexham 6 0
2006–07 Wrexham 34 1
2007–08 Wrexham 26 0 **66 1**
2008–09 Hereford U 36 0
2009–10 Hereford U 20 0 **56 0**
2010–11 Rochdale 33 5
2011–12 Barnsley 31 4
2012–13 Barnsley 13 0 **44 4**
2012–13 *Hibernian* 7 0 **7 0**
2013–14 Rochdale 38 0
2014–15 Rochdale 23 10
2014–15 Sheffield U 15 7
2015–16 Sheffield U 31 4
2016–17 Sheffield U 31 3 **77 14**
2017–18 Rochdale 46 6
2018–19 Rochdale 36 2
2019–20 Rochdale 24 0
2020–21 Rochdale 37 3
2021–22 Rochdale 25 1 **262 27**

DOOLEY, Stephen (M) 195 16
H: 5 11 W: 12 08 b.Portstewart 19-10-91
Internationals: Northern Ireland U17, U19.
2014 Derry C 14 1
2015 Derry C 15 2 **29 3**
2016 Cork C 26 5
2017 Cork C 27 4 **53 9**
2018–19 Rochdale 22 0
2019–20 Rochdale 22 3
2020–21 Rochdale 31 1
2021–22 Rochdale 38 0 **113 4**

DUNNE, Joe (D) 0 0
H: 6 0 W: 11 07 b.Stafford 25-10-01
2018–19 Rochdale 0 0
2019–20 Rochdale 0 0
2020–21 Rochdale 0 0
2021–22 Rochdale 0 0

GRAHAM, Sam (D) 27 0
b.Sheffield 13-8-00
2018–19 Sheffield U 0 0
2018–19 *Oldham Ath* 7 0 **7 0**
2018–19 *Central Coast Mariners* 8 0 **8 0**
2019–20 Sheffield U 0 0
2020–21 Sheffield U 0 0
2021–22 Rochdale 12 0 **12 0**

GRANT, Conor (M) 53 5
H: 6 1 W: 11 00 b.Dublin 23-7-01
Internationals: Republic of Ireland U17, U19, U21.
From Shamrock R.
2019–20 Sheffield W 0 0
2020–21 Sheffield W 0 0
2020–21 Rochdale 20 1
2021–22 Sheffield W 0 0
2021–22 Rochdale 33 4 **53 5**

KELLY, Liam (M) 142 12
H: 5 10 W: 11 09 b.Basingstoke 22-11-95
Internationals: Republic of Ireland U19, U21.
2014–15 Reading 0 0
2015–16 Reading 0 0
2016–17 Reading 28 1
2017–18 Reading 34 5
2018–19 Reading 20 1 **82 7**
2019–20 Feyenoord 1 0
2019–20 *Oxford U* 3 0
2020–21 Feyenoord 0 0 **1 0**
2020–21 *Oxford U* 26 0 **29 0**
2021–22 Rochdale 30 5 **30 5**

KEOHANE, Jimmy (M) 261 28
H: 5 11 W: 11 05 b.Kilkenny 22-1-91
Internationals: Republic of Ireland U19.
2009 Wexford Youths 16 2
2010 Wexford Youths 18 4 **34 6**
2010–11 Bristol C 0 0
2011–12 Bristol C 0 0
2011–12 Exeter C 4 0
2012–13 Exeter C 33 3
2013–14 Exeter C 20 3
2014–15 Exeter C 23 3 **80 9**
From Woking.
2016 Sligo R 31 1 **31 1**
2017 Cork C 10 0 **10 0**
2018–19 Rochdale 8 0
2019–20 Rochdale 28 0
2020–21 Rochdale 44 10
2021–22 Rochdale 26 2 **106 12**

LYNCH, Jay (G) 52 0
H: 6 0 W: 12 13 b.Salford 31-3-93
2012–13 Bolton W 0 0
2013–14 Bolton W 0 0
2014–15 Accrington S 2 0 **2 0**
From Salford C, AFC Fylde.
2019–20 Rochdale 8 0
2020–21 Rochdale 17 0
2021–22 Rochdale 25 0 **50 0**

McNULTY, Jim (D) 396 7
H: 6 0 W: 12 02 b.Runcorn 13-2-85
Internationals: Scotland U17, U19.
From Everton, Wrexham.
2006–07 Macclesfield T 15 0
2007–08 Macclesfield T 19 1 **34 1**
2007–08 Stockport Co 11 0
2008–09 Stockport Co 26 1 **37 1**
2008–09 Brighton & HA 5 1
2009–10 Brighton & HA 8 0
2009–10 *Scunthorpe U* 3 0
2010–11 Brighton & HA 0 0 **13 1**
2010–11 *Scunthorpe U* 6 0 **9 0**
2011–12 Barnsley 44 2
2012–13 Barnsley 12 0
2013–14 Barnsley 0 0 **56 2**
2013–14 *Tranmere R* 12 0 **12 0**
2013–14 Bury 21 0

2014–15 Bury 25 0 **46 0**
2015–16 Rochdale 46 0
2016–17 Rochdale 35 0
2017–18 Rochdale 40 1
2018–19 Rochdale 25 1
2019–20 Rochdale 14 0
2020–21 Rochdale 17 0
2021–22 Rochdale 12 0 **189 2**

NEWBY, Alex (M) 74 12
H: 5 8 W: 11 00 b.Barrow-in-Furness 21-11-95
From Barrow, Clitheroe, Chorley.
2020–21 Rochdale 38 6
2021–22 Rochdale 36 6 **74 12**

O'CONNELL, Eoghan (D) 191 6
H: 6 2 W: 12 08 b.Cork 13-8-95
Internationals: Republic of Ireland U19, U21.
2013–14 Celtic 1 0
2014–15 Celtic 3 0
2015–16 Celtic 1 0
2015–16 *Oldham Ath* 2 0 **2 0**
2016 *Cork C* 7 1 **7 1**
2016–17 Celtic 2 0 **7 0**
2016–17 *Walsall* 17 1 **17 1**
2017–18 Bury 12 0
2018–19 Bury 31 2 **43 2**
2019–20 Rochdale 31 0
2020–21 Rochdale 39 1
2021–22 Rochdale 45 1 **115 2**

O'KEEFFE, Corey (M) 88 2
H: 6 1 W: 11 00 b.Birmingham 5-6-98
Internationals: Republic of Ireland U17, U18, U19.
2016–17 Birmingham C 1 0
2017–18 Birmingham C 0 0
2018–19 Birmingham C 0 0
2019–20 Birmingham C 0 0 **1 0**
2019–20 *Macclesfield T* 31 0 **31 0**
2020–21 Mansfield T 13 0
2021–22 Mansfield T 0 0 **13 0**
2021–22 Rochdale 43 2 **43 2**

ODOH, Abraham (M) 34 3
H: 5 6 b.Lambeth 25-6-00
From Tooting & Mitcham U.
2019–20 Charlton Ath 0 0
2020–21 Rochdale 2 0
2021–22 Rochdale 32 3 **34 3**

TAYLOR, Max (D) 22 3
H: 6 4 W: 12 02 b.Manchester 10-1-00
2019–20 Manchester U 0 0
2020–21 Manchester U 0 0
2021–22 Rochdale 22 3 **22 3**

THOMAS, Peter (F) 0 0
2019–20 Rochdale 0 0
2020–21 Rochdale 0 0
2021–22 Rochdale 0 0

WADE, Bradley (G) 0 0
H: 6 2 W: 12 13 b.Gloucester 3-7-00
2018–19 Rochdale 0 0
2019–20 Rochdale 0 0
2020–21 Rochdale 0 0
2021–22 Rochdale 0 0

WHITE, Aidan (D) 185 5
H: 5 9 W: 9 08 b.Otley 10-10-91
Internationals: England U19. Republic of Ireland U21.
2008–09 Leeds U 5 0
2009–10 Leeds U 8 0
2010–11 Leeds U 2 0
2010–11 *Oldham Ath* 24 4 **24 4**
2011–12 Leeds U 36 0
2012–13 Leeds U 24 1
2013–14 Leeds U 9 0
2013–14 *Sheffield U* 8 0 **8 0**
2014–15 Leeds U 1 0 **85 1**
2015–16 Rotherham U 8 0 **8 0**
2015–16 Barnsley 14 0
2016–17 Barnsley 10 0 **24 0**
2019–20 Hearts 14 0
2020–21 Hearts 10 0 **24 0**
2021–22 Rochdale 12 0 **12 0**

Players retained or with offer of contract
Kelly, Bradley; Kershaw, Ben; Scanlon, Jordan.

Scholars
Anderson, Liam Mark; Caldwell, Mikey Lee Ryan; Craven, Ellis Anthony; Cunningham, Joseph David; Greenwell, Zak Edwin Eric; Kershaw, Benjamin Joshua; Kyffin, Paul Michael; Kyle, Cameron James Shaun; Lawless, Tom; Mandey, Bassit; Mialkowski, Kacper; Scanlon, Jordan Michael; Sousa De Bom Jesus, Anisio; Sutton, Max; Thomas, Peter Anthony; Watts, Patrick Joseph; Yaduat, Jadel.

ROTHERHAM U (71)

BARLASER, Daniel (M) 147 15
H: 6 0 W: 9 11 b.Gateshead 18-1-97
Internationals: Turkey U16, U17. England U18.
2015–16 Newcastle U 0 0
2016–17 Newcastle U 0 0
2017–18 Newcastle U 0 0
2017–18 *Crewe Alex* 4 0 **4 0**
2018–19 Newcastle U 0 0
2018–19 *Accrington S* 39 1 **39 1**
2019–20 Newcastle U 0 0
2019–20 *Rotherham U* 27 2
2020–21 Rotherham U 33 3
2021–22 Rotherham U 44 9 **104 14**

BOLA, Tolaji (D) 15 0
H: 5 11 W: 12 08 b.Camden 4-1-99
Internationals: England U16, U17, U18.
2019–20 Arsenal 0 0
2020–21 Arsenal 0 0
2020–21 *Rochdale* 11 0 **11 0**
2021–22 Rotherham U 4 0 **4 0**

FERGUSON, Shane (D) 264 9
H: 5 9 W: 10 03 b.Limavady 12-7-91
Internationals: Northern Ireland U17, U19, U21, B, Full caps.
2008–09 Newcastle U 0 0
2009–10 Newcastle U 0 0
2010–11 Newcastle U 7 0
2011–12 Newcastle U 7 0
2012–13 Newcastle U 9 0
2012–13 *Birmingham C* 11 1
2013–14 Newcastle U 0 0
2013–14 *Birmingham C* 18 0 **29 1**
2014–15 Newcastle U 0 0
2014–15 *Rangers* 0 0
2015–16 Newcastle U 0 0 **23 0**
2015–16 Millwall 39 3
2016–17 Millwall 40 2
2017–18 Millwall 24 0
2018–19 Millwall 35 2
2019–20 Millwall 29 0
2020–21 Millwall 13 0 **180 7**
2021–22 Rotherham U 32 1 **32 1**

GRATTON, Jacob (F) 0 0
H: 6 0 W: 10 08 b.Rotherham 5-1-02
2019–20 Rotherham U 0 0
2020–21 Rotherham U 0 0
2021–22 Rotherham U 0 0

GREAVES, Jerome (F) 0 0
b.Pontefract 22-3-03
2020–21 Rotherham U 0 0
2021–22 Rotherham U 0 0

HARDING, Wes (D) 135 0
H: 5 11 W: 12 06 b.Leicester 20-10-96
Internationals: Jamaica Full caps.
2017–18 Birmingham C 9 0
2018–19 Birmingham C 27 0
2019–20 Birmingham C 15 0 **51 0**
2020–21 Rotherham U 46 0
2021–22 Rotherham U 38 0 **84 0**

HULL, Jake (D) 7 0
H: 6 6 b.Sheffield 22-10-01
2020–21 Rotherham U 0 0
2021–22 Rotherham U 0 0
2021–22 *Hartlepool U* 7 0 **7 0**

IHIEKWE, Michael (D) 234 12
H: 6 1 W: 12 09 b.Liverpool 20-11-92
Internationals: England C.
2011–12 Wolverhampton W 0 0
2012–13 Wolverhampton W 0 0
2013–14 Wolverhampton W 0 0
2013–14 *Cheltenham T* 13 0 **13 0**
2014–15 Tranmere R 38 1 **38 1**
From Tranmere R.
2017–18 Rotherham U 31 1
2018–19 Rotherham U 15 2
2018–19 *Accrington S* 20 1 **20 1**
2019–20 Rotherham U 33 2
2020–21 Rotherham U 42 2
2021–22 Rotherham U 42 3 **163 10**

JOHANSSON, Viktor (G) 47 0
H: 6 1 W: 11 05 b.Stockholm 14-9-98
Internationals: Sweden U17, U19, U21.
From Hammarby.
2017–18 Aston Villa 0 0
2018–19 Leicester C 0 0
2019–20 Leicester C 0 0
2020–21 Rotherham U 21 0
2021–22 Rotherham U 26 0 **47 0**

KAYODE, Joshua (F) 59 12
H: 6 3 W: 11 11 b.Lagos 4-5-00
Internationals: Republic of Ireland U21.
2017–18 Rotherham U 0 0
2018–19 Rotherham U 0 0
2019–20 Rotherham U 0 0
2019–20 *Carlisle U* 5 3
2020–21 Rotherham U 0 0
2020–21 *Carlisle U* 34 8
2021–22 Rotherham U 20 1 **20 1**
2021–22 *Carlisle U* 0 0 **39 11**

KELLY, Georgie (F) 83 33
b.Donegal 12-11-96
2015 Derry C 3 0 **3 0**
From University College Dublin.
2018 Dundalk 7 0
2019 Dundalk 27 8
2020 Dundalk 2 0 **36 8**
2020 *St Patrick's Ath* 12 3 **12 3**
2021 Bohemians 31 21 **31 21**
2021–22 Rotherham U 1 1 **1 1**

LADAPO, Freddie (F) 198 58
H: 6 0 W: 12 06 b.Romford 1-2-93
2011–12 Colchester U 0 0
2012–13 Colchester U 4 0
2013–14 Colchester U 2 0 **6 0**
From Margate.
2015–16 Crystal Palace 0 0
2016–17 Crystal Palace 0 0
2016–17 *Oldham Ath* 17 2 **17 2**
2016–17 *Shrewsbury T* 15 4 **15 4**
2017–18 Crystal Palace 1 0 **1 0**
2017–18 Southend U 10 0 **10 0**
2018–19 Plymouth Arg 45 18 **45 18**
2019–20 Rotherham U 31 14
2020–21 Rotherham U 42 9
2021–22 Rotherham U 31 11 **104 34**

LINDSAY, Jamie (M) 200 13
H: 5 10 W: 10 08 b.Rutherglen 11-10-95
Internationals: Scotland U16, U17, U19.
2015–16 Celtic 0 0
2015–16 *Dumbarton* 23 0 **23 0**
2016–17 Celtic 0 0
2016–17 *Greenock Morton* 31 0 **31 0**
2017–18 Celtic 0 0
2017–18 *Ross County* 26 2
2018–19 Ross County 35 6 **61 8**
2019–20 Rotherham U 22 1
2020–21 Rotherham U 35 3
2021–22 Rotherham U 28 1 **85 5**

MACDONALD, Angus (D) 134 2
H: 6 0 W: 11 00 b.Winchester 15-10-92
Internationals: England U16, U19, C.
2011–12 Reading 0 0
2011–12 *Torquay U* 2 0
2012–13 Reading 0 0
2012–13 *AFC Wimbledon* 4 0 **4 0**
2012–13 *Torquay U* 14 0 **16 0**
From Salisbury C, Torquay U.
2016–17 Barnsley 39 1
2017–18 Barnsley 11 0 **50 1**
2017–18 Hull C 12 0
2018–19 Hull C 1 0
2019–20 Hull C 5 0 **18 0**
2020–21 Rotherham U 39 1
2021–22 Rotherham U 7 0 **46 1**

MATTOCK, Joe (D) 395 8
H: 5 11 W: 12 04 b.Leicester 15-5-90
Internationals: England U17, U19, U21.
2006–07 Leicester C 4 0
2007–08 Leicester C 31 0
2008–09 Leicester C 31 1
2009–10 Leicester C 0 0 **66 1**
2009–10 WBA 29 0
2010–11 WBA 0 0
2010–11 *Sheffield U* 13 0 **13 0**
2011–12 WBA 0 0 **29 0**
2011–12 *Portsmouth* 7 0 **7 0**
2011–12 *Brighton & HA* 15 1 **15 1**
2012–13 Sheffield W 7 0
2013–14 Sheffield W 23 2
2014–15 Sheffield W 27 0 **57 2**
2015–16 Rotherham U 35 1
2016–17 Rotherham U 36 0
2017–18 Rotherham U 35 1
2018–19 Rotherham U 44 1
2019–20 Rotherham U 24 1
2020–21 Rotherham U 14 0
2021–22 Rotherham U 20 0 **208 4**

MILLER, Mickel (F) 102 11
H: 5 8 W: 10 03 b.Croydon 2-12-95
From Carshalton Ath.
2017–18 Hamilton A 6 0
2018–19 Hamilton A 31 5
2019–20 Hamilton A 21 3 **58 8**
2020–21 Rotherham U 9 0
2020–21 *Northampton T* 12 0 **12 0**
2021–22 Rotherham U 23 3 **32 3**

ODOFIN, Hakeem (D) 81 3
H: 6 3 W: 12 11 b.Barnet 13-4-98
2015–16 Barnet 1 0 **1 0**
2016–17 Wolverhampton W 0 0
2017–18 Wolverhampton W 0 0
2018–19 Northampton T 12 0 **12 0**
2018–19 Livingston 13 0
2019–20 Livingston 7 0 **20 0**
2020–21 Hamilton A 37 3 **37 3**
2021–22 Rotherham U 11 0 **11 0**
Transferred to Livingston January 2019.

OGBENE, Chiedozie (M) **142 15**

H: 5 11 W: 11 11 b.Lagos 1-5-97

Internationals: Republic of Ireland Full caps.

2015	Cork C	1	0		
2016	Cork C	8	3	**9**	**3**
2017	Limerick	32	8	**32**	**8**
2017–18	Brentford	2	0		
2018–19	Brentford	4	0	**6**	**0**
2018–19	*Exeter C*	14	0	**14**	**0**
2019–20	Rotherham U	25	1		
2020–21	Rotherham U	11	0		
2021–22	Rotherham U	45	3	**81**	**4**

RATHBONE, Oliver (M) **194 14**

H: 5 7 W: 10 06 b.Blackburn 10-10-96

From Manchester U.

2016–17	Rochdale	27	2		
2017–18	Rochdale	33	1		
2018–19	Rochdale	28	4		
2019–20	Rochdale	24	2		
2020–21	Rochdale	40	3		
2021–22	Rochdale	0	0	**152**	**12**
2021–22	Rotherham U	42	2	**42**	**2**

SMITH, Michael (F) **406 102**

H: 6 4 W: 11 03 b.Wallsend 17-10-91

2009–10	Darlington	7	1		
2010–11	Darlington	29	5	**36**	**6**
2011–12	Charlton Ath	0	0		
2011–12	*Accrington S*	6	3	**6**	**3**
2012–13	Charlton Ath	0	0		
2012–13	*Colchester U*	8	1	**8**	**1**
2013–14	Charlton Ath	0	0		
2013–14	*AFC Wimbledon*	23	9	**23**	**9**
2013–14	Swindon T	20	8		
2014–15	Swindon T	40	13		
2015–16	Swindon T	5	0	**65**	**21**
2015–16	*Barnsley*	13	0	**13**	**0**
2015–16	*Portsmouth*	16	4		
2016–17	Portsmouth	18	3	**34**	**7**
2016–17	*Northampton T*	14	2		
2017–18	Northampton T	0	0	**14**	**2**
2017–18	Bury	19	1	**19**	**1**
2017–18	Rotherham U	20	6		
2018–19	Rotherham U	45	8		
2019–20	Rotherham U	34	9		
2020–21	Rotherham U	44	10		
2021–22	Rotherham U	45	19	**188**	**52**

VICKERS, Josh (G) **113 0**

H: 6 0 W: 11 05 b.Billericay 1-12-95

From Arsenal.

2015–16	Swansea C	0	0		
2016–17	Swansea C	0	0		
2016–17	*Barnet*	23	0	**23**	**0**
2017–18	Lincoln C	17	0		
2018–19	Lincoln C	18	0		
2019–20	Lincoln C	35	0	**70**	**0**
2020–21	Rotherham U	0	0		
2021–22	Rotherham U	20	0	**20**	**0**

WILES, Ben (M) **143 13**

H: 5 9 W: 10 06 b.Rotherham 17-4-99

2017–18	Rotherham U	0	0		
2018–19	Rotherham U	20	0		
2019–20	Rotherham U	33	3		
2020–21	Rotherham U	44	2		
2021–22	Rotherham U	46	8	**143**	**13**

WOOD, Richard (D) **532 33**

H: 6 3 W: 12 13 b.Ossett 5-7-85

2002–03	Sheffield W	3	1		
2003–04	Sheffield W	12	0		
2004–05	Sheffield W	34	1		
2005–06	Sheffield W	30	1		
2006–07	Sheffield W	12	0		
2007–08	Sheffield W	27	2		
2008–09	Sheffield W	42	0		
2009–10	Sheffield W	11	2	**171**	**7**
2009–10	Coventry C	24	3		
2010–11	Coventry C	40	1		
2011–12	Coventry C	17	1		
2012–13	Coventry C	36	3	**117**	**8**
2013–14	Charlton Ath	21	0	**21**	**0**
2014–15	Rotherham U	6	0		
2014–15	*Crawley T*	10	3	**10**	**3**
2015–16	Rotherham U	13	0		
2015–16	*Fleetwood T*	6	0	**6**	**0**
2015–16	*Chesterfield*	5	0	**5**	**0**
2016–17	Rotherham U	29	3		
2017–18	Rotherham U	36	4		
2018–19	Rotherham U	26	2		
2019–20	Rotherham U	23	3		
2020–21	Rotherham U	30	2		
2021–22	Rotherham U	39	1	**202**	**15**

Players retained or with offer of contract

Chapman, Josh; Durose, Curtis; Exton, Nathan; Greenhouse, Sam; McGuckin, Ciaran; Warne, MacKenzie.

Scholars

Bond, Zack; Booth, Mason Jay; Burnett, Alfie George; Carroll, Billy Fredrick; Champion, Jake Lewis; Clark, Adam Rhys; Day, Archie William; Douglas, Hamish Hubertus; Exton, Nathan John; Ford, Nathaniel Cade; Greenhouse, Samuel Lewis; Holvey, Joel James Hunter; Jenkinson, William Mathew Ian; Nisbett, Kanye Rico; Watson, Nathan Christopher.

SALFORD C (72)

ANDO, Cerny (D) **0 0**

b. 24-11-03

2020–21	Salford C	0	0		
2021–22	Salford C	0	0		

BERKOE, Kevin (D) **0 0**

H: 5 10 W: 10 03 b.Redbridge 5-7-01

From Wolverhampton W.

2019–20	Oxford U	0	0		
2020–21	Salford C	0	0		
2021–22	Salford C	0	0		

BOLTON, Luke (F) **73 1**

b.Manchester 7-10-99

Internationals: England U20.

2018–19	Manchester C	0	0		
2018–19	*Wycombe W*	10	0	**10**	**0**
2019–20	Manchester C	0	0		
2019–20	*Luton T*	24	0	**24**	**0**
2020–21	Manchester C	0	0		
2020–21	*Dundee U*	24	1		
2021–22	Dundee U	0	0	**24**	**1**
2021–22	Salford C	15	0	**15**	**0**

BURGESS, Luke (M) **18 3**

H: 5 9 W: 10 06 b.Liverpool 3-3-99

2017–18	Wigan Ath	0	0		
2018–19	Wigan Ath	0	0		
2019–20	Wigan Ath	0	0		
2019–20	Salford C	0	0		
2020–21	Salford C	17	3		
2021–22	Salford C	1	0	**18**	**3**

CAMPBELL, Hayden (M) **0 0**

H: 5 10 W: 10 10 b.Stafford 24-2-02

2020–21	Salford C	0	0		
2021–22	Salford C	0	0		

DACKERS, Marcus (M) **1 0**

H: 6 7 b. 9-1-03

Internationals: Wales U16, U17.

From Manchester C.

2018–19	Brighton & HA	0	0		
2019–20	Brighton & HA	0	0		
2020–21	Brighton & HA	0	0		
2021–22	Salford C	1	0	**1**	**0**

DENNY, Alex (M) **15 0**

H: 6 1 W: 12 11 b.Chester 12-4-00

Internationals: England U17, U18.

2017–18	Everton	0	0		
2018–19	Everton	0	0		
2019–20	Everton	0	0		
2020–21	Salford C	9	0		
2020–21	*Morecambe*	6	0	**6**	**0**
2021–22	Salford C	0	0	**9**	**0**

Transferred to The New Saints, January 2022.

EASTHAM, Ashley (D) **360 16**

H: 6 3 W: 12 07 b.Preston 22-3-91

2009–10	Blackpool	1	0		
2009–10	*Cheltenham T*	20	0		
2010–11	Blackpool	0	0		
2010–11	*Cheltenham T*	9	0	**29**	**0**
2010–11	*Carlisle U*	0	0		
2011–12	Blackpool	0	0		
2011–12	*Bury*	25	2		
2012–13	Blackpool	0	0	**1**	**0**
2012–13	*Fleetwood T*	1	0		
2012–13	*Notts Co*	4	0	**4**	**0**
2012–13	*Bury*	19	0	**44**	**2**
2013–14	Rochdale	15	0		
2014–15	Rochdale	41	2		
2015–16	Rochdale	20	2	**76**	**4**
2016–17	Fleetwood T	35	2		
2017–18	Fleetwood T	45	3		
2018–19	Fleetwood T	45	2		
2019–20	Fleetwood T	9	0	**135**	**7**
2019–20	Salford C	4	0		
2020–21	Salford C	39	1		
2021–22	Salford C	28	2	**71**	**3**

ELLIOTT, Tom (F) **293 43**

H: 6 3 W: 12 00 b.Leeds 9-11-90

Internationals: England U16, U18.

2006–07	Leeds U	3	0		
2007–08	Leeds U	0	0		
2008–09	Leeds U	0	0		
2008–09	*Macclesfield T*	6	0	**6**	**0**
2009–10	Leeds U	0	0		
2009–10	*Bury*	16	1	**16**	**1**
2010–11	Leeds U	0	0	**3**	**0**
2010–11	*Rotherham U*	6	0	**6**	**0**
2011–12	Hamilton A	7	0	**7**	**0**
2011–12	Stockport Co	42	7	**42**	**7**

From Cambridge U.

2014–15	Cambridge U	30	8	**30**	**8**
2015–16	AFC Wimbledon	39	6		
2016–17	AFC Wimbledon	39	9	**78**	**15**
2017–18	Millwall	24	4		
2018–19	Millwall	33	3		
2019–20	Millwall	0	0	**57**	**7**
2019–20	Salford C	8	1		
2020–21	Salford C	14	0		
2021–22	Salford C	19	4	**41**	**5**
2021–22	*Bradford C*	7	0	**7**	**0**

GOLDEN, Tylor (D) **9 0**

H: 5 7 b.South Carolina 8-11-99

2017–18	Wigan Ath	0	0		
2018–19	Wigan Ath	0	0		
2019–20	Wigan Ath	0	0		
2020–21	Salford C	7	0		
2021–22	Salford C	2	0	**9**	**0**

HENDERSON, Ian (F) **608 164**

H: 5 10 W: 10 08 b.Thetford 25-1-85

Internationals: England U18, U20.

2002–03	Norwich C	20	1		
2003–04	Norwich C	19	4		
2004–05	Norwich C	3	0		
2005–06	Norwich C	24	1		
2006–07	Norwich C	2	0	**68**	**6**
2006–07	*Rotherham U*	18	1	**18**	**1**
2007–08	Northampton T	23	0		
2008–09	Northampton T	3	0	**26**	**0**
2008–09	Luton T	19	1	**19**	**1**
2009–10	Colchester U	13	2		
2009–10	*Ankaragucu*	2	0	**2**	**0**
2010–11	Colchester U	36	10		
2011–12	Colchester U	46	9		
2012–13	Colchester U	22	3	**117**	**24**
2012–13	Rochdale	12	3		
2013–14	Rochdale	45	11		
2014–15	Rochdale	44	22		
2015–16	Rochdale	39	13		
2016–17	Rochdale	42	15		
2017–18	Rochdale	39	13		
2018–19	Rochdale	45	20		
2019–20	Rochdale	31	15	**297**	**112**
2020–21	Salford C	46	17		
2021–22	Salford C	15	3	**61**	**20**

HUNTER, Ashley (F) **266 44**

H: 5 10 W: 10 08 b.Derby 29-9-93

From Ilkeston.

2014–15	Fleetwood T	12	1		
2015–16	Fleetwood T	24	5		
2016–17	Fleetwood T	44	8		
2017–18	Fleetwood T	44	9		
2018–19	Fleetwood T	43	8		
2019–20	Fleetwood T	14	0	**181**	**31**
2019–20	*Salford C*	11	5		
2020–21	Salford C	41	7		
2021–22	Salford C	33	1	**85**	**13**

KELLY, Stephen (M) **73 6**

H: 5 9 W: 10 10 b.Port Glasgow 13-4-00

Internationals: Scotland U16, U17, U19, U21.

2018–19	Rangers	0	0		
2019–20	Rangers	0	0		
2019–20	*Ayr U*	27	5	**27**	**5**
2020–21	Rangers	0	0		
2020–21	*Ross Co*	25	0	**25**	**0**
2021–22	Rangers	0	0		
2021–22	*Salford C*	21	1	**21**	**1**

KING, Tom (G) **117 1**

H: 6 1 W: 12 08 b.Plymouth 9-3-95

Internationals: England U17.

2011–12	Crystal Palace	0	0		
2012–13	Crystal Palace	0	0		
2013–14	Crystal Palace	0	0		
2014–15	Millwall	0	0		
2015–16	Millwall	0	0		
2016–17	Millwall	11	0		
2017–18	Millwall	0	0		
2017–18	*Stevenage*	18	0	**18**	**0**
2018–19	Millwall	0	0	**11**	**0**
2018–19	*AFC Wimbledon*	12	0	**12**	**0**
2019–20	Newport Co	31	0		
2020–21	Newport Co	9	1		
2021–22	Newport Co	0	0	**40**	**1**
2021–22	Salford C	36	0	**36**	**0**

LOUGHLIN, Liam (M) **3 0**

b.Leicester 24-4-02

2020–21	Salford C	0	0		
2021–22	Salford C	3	0	**3**	**0**

LOVE, Donald (D) **102 0**

H: 5 10 W: 11 05 b.Rochdale 2-12-94

Internationals: Scotland U17, U19, U21.

2015–16	Manchester U	1	0	**1**	**0**
2015–16	*Wigan Ath*	7	0	**7**	**0**
2016–17	Sunderland	12	0		
2017–18	Sunderland	11	0		
2018–19	Sunderland	4	0	**27**	**0**
2019–20	Shrewsbury T	28	0		
2020–21	Shrewsbury T	14	0	**42**	**0**
2021–22	Salford C	25	0	**25**	**0**

LOWE, Jason (M) **343 5**

H: 5 10 W: 12 08 b.Wigan 2-9-91

Internationals: England U20, U21.

2009–10	Blackburn R	0	0		
2010–11	Blackburn R	1	0		
2010–11	*Oldham Ath*	7	2	**7**	**2**
2011–12	Blackburn R	32	0		
2012–13	Blackburn R	36	0		

2013–14 Blackburn R 39 1
2014–15 Blackburn R 12 0
2015–16 Blackburn R 10 0
2016–17 Blackburn R 43 0 **173 1**
2017–18 WBA 0 0
2017–18 Birmingham C 9 0 **9 0**
2018–19 Bolton W 35 0
2019–20 Bolton W 29 0 **64 0**
2019–20 Salford C 0 0
2020–21 Salford C 45 0
2021–22 Salford C 45 2 **90 2**

LUND, Matthew (M) **303 53**
H: 6 0 W: 12 00 b.Manchester 21-11-90
Internationals: Northern Ireland U21, Full caps.
From Crewe Alex.
2009–10 Stoke C 0 0
2010–11 Stoke C 0 0
2010–11 *Hereford U* 2 0 **2 0**
2011–12 Stoke C 0 0
2011–12 *Oldham Ath* 3 0 **3 0**
2011–12 *Bristol R* 13 2
2012–13 Stoke C 0 0
2012–13 *Bristol R* 18 2 **31 4**
2012–13 Southend U 12 1 **12 1**
2013–14 Rochdale 40 8
2014–15 Rochdale 14 2
2015–16 Rochdale 29 1
2016–17 Rochdale 29 9
2017–18 Burton Alb 12 1 **12 1**
2017–18 *Bradford C* 10 2 **10 2**
2018–19 Scunthorpe U 22 2
2019–20 Scunthorpe U 22 4 **44 6**
2019–20 Rochdale 5 1
2020–21 Rochdale 32 11
2021–22 Rochdale 0 0 **149 32**
2021–22 Salford C 40 7 **40 7**

McALENY, Conor (F) **191 45**
H: 5 10 W: 12 05 b.Liverpool 12-8-92
2009–10 Everton 0 0
2010–11 Everton 0 0
2011–12 Everton 2 0
2011–12 *Scunthorpe U* 3 0 **3 0**
2012–13 Everton 0 0
2013–14 Everton 0 0
2013–14 *Brentford* 4 0 **4 0**
2014–15 Everton 0 0
2014–15 *Cardiff C* 8 2 **8 2**
2015–16 Everton 0 0
2015–16 *Charlton Ath* 8 0 **8 0**
2015–16 *Wigan Ath* 13 4 **13 4**
2016–17 Everton 0 0 **2 0**
2016–17 *Oxford U* 18 10 **18 10**
2017–18 Fleetwood T 29 5
2018–19 Fleetwood T 14 0
2018–19 *Kilmarnock* 11 3 **11 3**
2019–20 Fleetwood T 12 2 **55 7**
2019–20 *Shrewsbury T* 5 0 **5 0**
2020–21 Oldham Ath 40 17
2021–22 Oldham Ath 0 0 **40 17**
2021–22 Salford C 24 2 **24 2**

MORRIS, Josh (M) **293 54**
H: 6 0 W: 11 06 b.Preston 30-9-91
Internationals: England U20.
2010–11 Blackburn R 4 0
2011–12 Blackburn R 2 0
2011–12 *Yeovil T* 5 0 **5 0**
2012–13 Blackburn R 10 0
2012–13 *Rotherham U* 5 0 **5 0**
2013–14 Blackburn R 4 0
2013–14 *Carlisle U* 6 0 **6 0**
2013–14 *Fleetwood T* 14 2
2014–15 Blackburn R 0 0 **20 0**
2014–15 *Fleetwood T* 45 8
2015–16 Bradford C 13 1 **13 1**
2016–17 Scunthorpe U 44 19
2017–18 Scunthorpe U 44 11
2018–19 Scunthorpe U 19 5 **107 35**
2019–20 Fleetwood T 33 7
2020–21 Fleetwood T 24 0 **116 17**
2021–22 Salford C 21 1 **21 1**

N'MAI, Kelly (M) **7 0**
b.Netherlands 1-5-04
2021–22 Salford C 7 0 **7 0**

SARGENT, Matthew (M) **0 0**
H: 6 0 W: 10 10 b.Bodelwyddan 24-7-01
Internationals: Wales U16, U17.
From Wrexham.
2020–21 Salford C 0 0
2021–22 Salford C 0 0

SHEPHARD, Liam (D) **223 12**
H: 5 10 W: 10 08 b.Rhondda 22-11-94
Internationals: Wales U21.
2013–14 Swansea C 0 0
2014–15 Swansea C 0 0
2014–15 *Yeovil T* 20 0
2015–16 Swansea C 0 0
2015–16 *Yeovil T* 6 0
2016–17 Swansea C 0 0
2016–17 *Yeovil T* 38 1 **64 1**
2017–18 Peterborough U 24 0 **24 0**

2018–19 Forest Green R 39 5
2019–20 Forest Green R 19 1 **58 6**
2020–21 Newport Co 42 2
2021–22 Newport Co 0 0 **42 2**
2021–22 Salford C 35 3 **35 3**

SMITH, Matt (F) **381 83**
H: 6 6 W: 11 11 b.Birmingham 7-6-89
From New Mills, Redditch U, Droylsden, Solihull Moors.
2011–12 Oldham Ath 28 3
2011–12 *Macclesfield T* 8 1 **8 1**
2012–13 Oldham Ath 34 6 **62 9**
2013–14 Leeds U 39 12
2014–15 Leeds U 3 0 **42 12**
2014–15 Fulham 15 5
2014–15 *Bristol C* 14 7 **14 7**
2015–16 Fulham 20 2
2016–17 Fulham 16 2 **51 9**
2016–17 QPR 16 4
2017–18 QPR 41 11
2018–19 QPR 35 6 **92 21**
2019–20 Millwall 41 13
2020–21 Millwall 29 3
2021–22 Millwall 21 1 **91 17**
2021–22 Salford C 21 7 **21 7**

THOMAS-ASANTE, Brandon (F) **123 22**
H: 5 11 W: 13 01 b.Milton Keynes 29-12-98
2016–17 Milton Keynes D 6 0
2017–18 Milton Keynes D 15 0
2018–19 Milton Keynes D 1 0 **22 0**
2019–20 Salford C 20 6
2020–21 Salford C 42 5
2021–22 Salford C 39 11 **101 22**

TORRANCE, Joel (G) **0 0**
b.Bolton 2-4-02
From Altrincham.
2021–22 Salford C 0 0

TOURAY, Ibou (D) **108 5**
H: 5 10 W: 10 10 b.Liverpool 24-12-94
Internationals: Gambia Full caps.
2013–14 Everton 0 0
2014–15 Everton 0 0
From Rhyl, Chester.
2019–20 Salford C 35 4
2020–21 Salford C 46 1
2021–22 Salford C 27 0 **108 5**

TOURAY, Momodou (F) **1 0**
H: 5 11 W: 10 06 b. 30-7-99
Internationals: Wales U18, U19, U21.
2016–17 Newport Co 0 0
2017–18 Newport Co 1 0
2018–19 Newport Co 0 0
2019–20 Newport Co 0 0 **1 0**
2020–21 Salford C 0 0
2021–22 Salford C 0 0

TURNBULL, Jordan (D) **277 10**
H: 6 1 W: 11 05 b.Trowbridge 30-10-94
Internationals: England U19, U20.
2014–15 Southampton 0 0
2014–15 *Swindon T* 44 1
2015–16 Southampton 0 0
2015–16 *Swindon T* 42 0 **86 1**
2016–17 Coventry C 36 0
2017–18 Coventry C 0 0 **36 0**
2017–18 *Partick Thistle* 0 0
2017–18 Northampton T 14 0
2018–19 Northampton T 31 0
2019–20 Northampton T 31 5 **76 5**
2020–21 Salford C 42 1
2021–22 Salford C 37 3 **79 4**

VASSELL, Theo (D) **59 3**
H: 6 0 W: 10 10 b.Stoke 2-1-97
2014–15 Stoke C 0 0
2015–16 Oldham Ath 0 0
2016–17 Walsall 0 0
From Gateshead.
2018–19 Port Vale 15 0 **15 0**
2019–20 Macclesfield T 17 2 **17 2**
From Wrexham.
2021–22 Salford C 27 1 **27 1**

WATSON, Ryan (M) **188 20**
H: 6 1 W: 11 07 b.Crewe 7-7-93
2011–12 Wigan Ath 0 0
2012–13 Wigan Ath 0 0
2012–13 *Accrington S* 0 0
2013–14 Leicester C 0 0
2014–15 Leicester C 0 0
2014–15 *Northampton T* 5 0
2015–16 Leicester C 0 0
2015–16 *Northampton T* 11 0
2016–17 Barnet 19 1
2017–18 Barnet 28 1 **47 2**
2018–19 Milton Keynes D 22 0 **22 0**
2019–20 Northampton T 25 5
2020–21 Northampton T 39 8
2021–22 Northampton T 0 0 **80 13**
2021–22 Tranmere R 16 1 **16 1**
2021–22 Salford C 23 4 **23 4**

WILLOCK, Matthew (M) **67 3**
H: 5 8 W: 10 03 b.Waltham Forest 20-8-96
Internationals: Montserrat Full caps.
2016–17 Manchester U 0 0
2017–18 Manchester U 0 0
2017–18 *Utrecht* 3 0 **3 0**
2017–18 *St Johnstone* 11 1 **11 1**
2018–19 Manchester U 0 0
2018–19 *St Mirren* 12 0 **12 0**
2018–19 *Crawley T* 11 0 **11 0**
2019–20 Gillingham 7 0
2020–21 Gillingham 11 0 **18 0**
2021–22 Salford C 12 2 **12 2**

Players retained or with offer of contract
Kirnon, Lucas; Melhado, James; Rydel, Ben; Smith, Anton.

Scholars
Bartram, Finlay; Berry, Lucas James; Collins, Benjamin Murat; Cooper, Kyle John; Finley, Ben David; Freckleton, Nathan Antony; Henderson, Alfie Darren; Humbles, Liam Andres; Kirnon, Lucas William; Lara, Jacob Winston Orin Patrick; Lescott, Donovan Joleon; McEvoy, Rio James; Padrao, Stephen De Abreu; Pedro, Djavan Michael; Roberts, Charlie Paul; Rose, Bradley Daniel.

SCUNTHORPE U (73)

BAKER, Harry (D) **0 0**
b. 11-1-03
2020–21 Scunthorpe U 0 0
2021–22 Scunthorpe U 0 0

BEESTIN, Alfie (F) **115 8**
H: 5 10 W: 11 11 b.Leeds 1-10-97
2016–17 Doncaster R 3 0
2017–18 Doncaster R 26 2
2018–19 Doncaster R 5 0 **34 2**
2019–20 Scunthorpe U 3 0
2020–21 Scunthorpe U 40 5
2021–22 Scunthorpe U 38 1 **81 6**

BUNN, Harry (F) **200 24**
H: 5 9 W: 11 10 b.Oldham 21-11-92
2010–11 Manchester C 0 0
2011–12 Manchester C 0 0
2011–12 *Rochdale* 6 0 **6 0**
2011–12 *Preston NE* 1 1 **1 1**
2011–12 *Oldham Ath* 11 0 **11 0**
2012–13 Manchester C 0 0
2012–13 *Crewe Alex* 4 0 **4 0**
2013–14 Manchester C 0 0
2013–14 *Sheffield U* 2 0 **2 0**
2013–14 *Huddersfield T* 3 0
2014–15 Manchester C 0 0
2014–15 *Huddersfield T* 30 9
2015–16 Huddersfield T 42 6
2016–17 Huddersfield T 16 0 **91 15**
2017–18 Bury 37 3
2018–19 Bury 1 0 **38 3**
2018–19 *Southend U* 24 4 **24 4**
2019–20 Kilmarnock 3 0 **3 0**
From York C.
2021–22 Scunthorpe U 20 1 **20 1**

COLLINS, Tom (G) **0 0**
H: 6 4 W: 12 06 b.Scunthorpe 4-8-02
2019–20 Scunthorpe U 0 0
2020–21 Scunthorpe U 0 0
2021–22 Scunthorpe U 0 0

CRIBB, Harvey (M) **8 0**
b. 21-1-06
2021–22 Scunthorpe U 8 0 **8 0**

DAVIS, Harry (D) **307 23**
H: 6 1 W: 13 01 b.Burnley 24-9-91
2009–10 Crewe Alex 1 0
2010–11 Crewe Alex 1 0
2011–12 Crewe Alex 41 5
2012–13 Crewe Alex 42 1
2013–14 Crewe Alex 32 3
2014–15 Crewe Alex 31 1
2015–16 Crewe Alex 11 1
2016–17 Crewe Alex 25 1 **184 12**
2016–17 *St Mirren* 6 2
2017–18 St Mirren 20 3 **26 5**
2018–19 Grimsby T 35 4
2019–20 Grimsby T 21 0 **56 4**
2020–21 Morecambe 27 0 **27 0**
2021–22 Scunthorpe U 14 2 **14 2**
Transferred to AFC Fylde, January 2022.

DUNNWALD, Kenan (F) **35 5**
H: 6 2 W: 12 08 b.Dusseldorf 14-11-95
From TSG Sprockhovel.
2017–18 Bristol R 1 0 **1 0**
2018–19 Kaan-Marienborn 10 3 **10 3**
2018–19 Wuppertaler 9 2 **9 2**
2019–20 Fortuna 3 0 **3 0**
2019–20 Bonner 6 0 **6 0**
2020–21 Scunthorpe U 5 0
2021–22 Scunthorpe U 1 0 **6 0**

FEENEY, Liam (M) **478** **30**
H: 6 0 W: 12 00 b.Hammersmith 28-4-86
From Hayes, Salisbury C.

2008–09	Southend U	1	0	**1**	**0**
2008–09	Bournemouth	14	3		
2009–10	Bournemouth	44	5		
2010–11	Bournemouth	46	4		
2011–12	Bournemouth	5	0	**109**	**12**
2011–12	Millwall	34	4		
2012–13	Millwall	22	1		
2013–14	Millwall	17	0	**73**	**5**
2013–14	*Bolton W*	4	0		
2013–14	*Blackburn R*	6	0		
2014–15	Bolton W	41	3		
2015–16	Bolton W	37	5	**82**	**8**
2015–16	*Ipswich T*	9	1	**9**	**1**
2016–17	Blackburn R	34	0		
2017–18	Blackburn R	1	0	**41**	**0**
2017–18	*Cardiff C*	15	0	**15**	**0**
2018–19	Blackpool	34	0		
2019–20	Blackpool	35	1		
2020–21	Blackpool	0	0	**69**	**1**
2020–21	*Tranmere R*	41	3		
2021–22	Tranmere R	19	0	**60**	**3**
2021–22	Scunthorpe U	19	0	**19**	**0**

FOSTER, Owen (G) **2** **0**
b. 7-1-05

2021–22	Scunthorpe U	2	0	**2**	**0**

GALLIMORE, Dan (M) **11** **0**
b.Grimsby 21-3-03

2021–22	Scunthorpe U	11	0	**11**	**0**

GRANT, Anthony (M) **558** **18**
H: 5 10 W: 11 03 b.Lambeth 4-6-87
Internationals: England U16, U17, U19. Jamaica Full caps.

2004–05	Chelsea	1	0		
2005–06	Chelsea	0	0		
2005–06	*Oldham Ath*	2	0	**2**	**0**
2006–07	Chelsea	0	0		
2006–07	*Wycombe W*	40	0	**40**	**0**
2007–08	Chelsea	0	0	**1**	**0**
2007–08	*Luton T*	4	0	**4**	**0**
2007–08	*Southend U*	10	0		
2008–09	Southend U	35	1		
2009–10	Southend U	38	0		
2010–11	Southend U	43	8		
2011–12	Southend U	33	1	**159**	**10**
2012–13	Stevenage	41	0	**41**	**0**
2013–14	Crewe Alex	38	2		
2014–15	Crewe Alex	43	2	**81**	**4**
2015–16	Port Vale	38	1		
2016–17	Port Vale	20	0	**58**	**1**
2016–17	Peterborough U	11	0		
2017–18	Peterborough U	38	0	**49**	**0**
2018–19	Shrewsbury T	42	0		
2019–20	*Shrewsbury T*	0	0	**42**	**0**
2019–20	Swindon T	30	0		
2020–21	Swindon T	33	3		
2021–22	Swindon T	5	0	**68**	**3**
2021–22	Scunthorpe U	13	0	**13**	**0**

GREEN, Devarn (F) **54** **3**
H: 5 11 W: 10 01 b.Sandwell 26-8-96

2014–15	Blackburn R	0	0		
2015–16	Blackburn R	0	0		

From Tranmere R, Southport.

2019–20	Scunthorpe U	2	0		
2020–21	Scunthorpe U	36	3		
2021–22	Scunthorpe U	16	0	**54**	**3**

Transferred to Telford U, March 2022.

HALLAM, Jordan (M) **33** **3**
H: 5 8 W: 9 13 b.Sheffield 6-10-98

2016–17	Sheffield U	0	0		
2017–18	Sheffield U	0	0		
2018	*Viking*	5	0	**5**	**0**
2018–19	Scunthorpe U	7	1		
2019–20	Scunthorpe U	0	0		
2020–21	Scunthorpe U	13	2		
2021–22	Scunthorpe U	8	0	**28**	**3**

HIPPOLYTE, Myles (M) **189** **21**
H: 6 0 W: 11 09 b.Harrow 9-11-94

2012–13	Brentford	0	0		

From Southall, Tamworth, Hayes & Yeading U, Burnham.

2014–15	Livingston	33	2		
2015–16	Livingston	17	1	**50**	**3**
2015–16	Falkirk	12	1		
2016–17	Falkirk	30	7		
2017–18	Falkirk	10	2	**52**	**10**
2017–18	St Mirren	8	1	**8**	**1**
2018–19	Dunfermline Ath	31	2	**31**	**2**

From Yeovil T.

2020–21	Scunthorpe U	26	1		
2021–22	Scunthorpe U	22	4	**48**	**5**

Transferred to Stockport Co, January 2022.

JARVIS, Aaron (F) **49** **4**
H: 6 2 W: 12 08 b.Basingstoke 24-1-98
From Basingstoke T.

2017–18	Luton T	1	0		
2018–19	Luton T	4	0	**5**	**0**
2018–19	*Falkirk*	12	0	**12**	**0**

From Sutton U.

2020–21	Scunthorpe U	13	2		
2021–22	Scunthorpe U	19	2	**32**	**4**

JESSOP, Harry (F) **5** **0**
H: 5 11 b.Chesterfield 1-8-02

2020–21	Scunthorpe U	3	0		
2021–22	Scunthorpe U	2	0	**5**	**0**

KENYON, Alex (M) **246** **9**
H: 5 11 W: 12 00 b.Preston 17-7-92
From Everton, Chorley, Lancaster C, Stockport Co.

2013–14	Morecambe	39	0		
2014–15	Morecambe	37	3		
2015–16	Morecambe	29	3		
2016–17	Morecambe	19	0		
2017–18	Morecambe	38	0		
2018–19	Morecambe	32	1		
2019–20	Morecambe	27	1		
2020–21	Morecambe	18	1		
2021–22	Morecambe	0	0	**239**	**9**
2021–22	Scunthorpe U	7	0	**7**	**0**

Transferred to Ayr U, March 2022.

LEWIS, Harry (M) **11** **0**
b.Scunthorpe 9-1-04

2021–22	Scunthorpe U	11	0	**11**	**0**

LOBLEY, Oliver (D) **1** **0**
b. 23-3-04

2021–22	Scunthorpe U	1	0	**1**	**0**

MILLEN, Ross (D) **183** **12**
H: 5 8 W: 10 00 b.Glasgow 28-9-94

2012–13	Dunfermline Ath	11	0		
2013–14	Dunfermline Ath	22	1		
2014–15	Dunfermline Ath	27	2	**60**	**3**
2015–16	Livingston	9	0	**9**	**0**
2015–16	Clyde	15	0	**15**	**0**
2016–17	Queen's Park	27	7		
2017–18	Queen's Park	25	1	**52**	**8**
2018–19	Kilmarnock	4	1		
2019–20	Kilmarnock	4	0		
2020–21	Kilmarnock	19	0		
2021–22	Kilmarnock	0	0	**27**	**1**
2021–22	Scunthorpe U	20	0	**20**	**0**

MOORE-BILLAM, Jack (F) **6** **0**
b. 5-3-04

2021–22	Scunthorpe U	6	0	**6**	**0**

NUTTALL, Joe (F) **85** **10**
H: 6 0 W: 11 05 b.Bury 27-1-97
From Manchester C.

2015–16	Aberdeen	2	0		
2016–17	Aberdeen	0	0	**2**	**0**
2016–17	*Stranraer*	9	2	**9**	**2**
2016–17	*Dumbarton*	2	0	**2**	**0**
2017–18	Blackburn R	13	2		
2018–19	Blackburn R	15	2	**28**	**4**
2019–20	Blackpool	27	2		
2020–21	Blackpool	0	0		
2020–21	*Northampton T*	1	0	**1**	**0**
2021–22	Blackpool	0	0	**27**	**2**
2021–22	Scunthorpe U	16	2	**16**	**2**

O'MALLEY, Mason (D) **54** **0**
H: 5 7 b.Leeds 8-6-01
Internationals: Republic of Ireland U21.
From Huddersfield T.

2019–20	Scunthorpe U	0	0		
2020–21	Scunthorpe U	29	0		
2021–22	Scunthorpe U	25	0	**54**	**0**

O'NEILL, Tyrone (F) **5** **0**
H: 6 1 W: 11 11 b.Middlesbrough 12-10-99

2018–19	Middlesbrough	0	0		
2019–20	Middlesbrough	1	0		
2020–21	Middlesbrough	0	0	**1**	**0**
2021–22	Scunthorpe U	4	0	**4**	**0**

ONARIASE, Manny (D) **83** **5**
H: 6 1 W: 12 13 b.Croydon 21-10-96

2014–15	West Ham U	0	0		
2015–16	West Ham U	0	0		
2016–17	Brentford	0	0		
2016–17	*Cheltenham T*	22	1		
2017–18	Rotherham U	0	0		
2017–18	*Cheltenham T*	5	0	**27**	**1**
2018–19	Rotherham U	0	0		

From Dagenham & R.

2020–21	Scunthorpe U	26	2		
2021–22	Scunthorpe U	30	2	**56**	**4**

Transferred to Dagenham & R, March 2022.

PERRY, Alex (M) **35** **0**
H: 5 9 W: 11 11 b.Liverpool 4-3-98

2016–17	Bolton W	0	0		
2017–18	Bolton W	0	0		
2018–19	Wigan Ath	0	0		
2019–20	Wigan Ath	0	0		
2020–21	Wigan Ath	21	0		
2021–22	Wigan Ath	0	0	**21**	**0**
2021–22	Scunthorpe U	14	0	**14**	**0**

PUGH, Tom (M) **26** **0**
H: 5 7 W: 9 08 b.Doncaster 27-9-00
Internationals: Wales U21.

2018–19	Scunthorpe U	0	0		
2019–20	Scunthorpe U	1	0		
2020–21	Scunthorpe U	1	0		
2021–22	Scunthorpe U	24	0	**26**	**0**

ROWE, Jai (D) **64** **2**
H: 5 11 W: 10 08 b.Nuneaton 8-8-01
From Nuneaton, Barwell.

2019–20	Scunthorpe U	1	0		
2020–21	Scunthorpe U	25	1		
2021–22	Scunthorpe U	38	1	**64**	**2**

SHRIMPTON, Finley (M) **4** **0**
b.Scunthorpe 24-8-02

2020–21	Scunthorpe U	0	0		
2021–22	Scunthorpe U	4	0	**4**	**0**

TAFT, George (D) **200** **7**
H: 6 3 W: 11 09 b.Leicester 29-7-93
Internationals: England U18, U19.

2010–11	Leicester C	0	0		
2011–12	Leicester C	0	0		
2012–13	Leicester C	0	0		
2013–14	Leicester C	0	0		
2013–14	*York C*	3	0	**3**	**0**
2014–15	Burton Alb	30	1		
2015–16	Burton Alb	0	0	**30**	**1**
2015–16	*Cambridge U*	11	1		
2016–17	Mansfield T	13	0		
2017–18	Mansfield T	0	0	**13**	**0**
2017–18	*Cambridge U*	28	1		
2018–19	Cambridge U	37	2		
2019–20	Cambridge U	27	1	**103**	**5**
2019–20	Bolton W	0	0		
2020–21	Bolton W	1	0	**1**	**0**
2020–21	Scunthorpe U	16	0		
2021–22	Scunthorpe U	34	1	**50**	**1**

THOMPSON, Lewis (D) **14** **0**
H: 6 1 b.Ashton-under-Lyme 10-10-99
Internationals: Northern Ireland U21.
From Blackburn R.

2021–22	Scunthorpe U	14	0	**14**	**0**

WATSON, Rory (G) **85** **0**
H: 6 3 W: 14 02 b.York 5-2-96

2014–15	Hull C	0	0		
2015–16	Hull C	0	0		
2015–16	*Scunthorpe U*	0	0		
2016–17	Scunthorpe U	0	0		
2017–18	Scunthorpe U	4	0		
2018–19	Scunthorpe U	5	0		
2019–20	Scunthorpe U	23	0		
2020–21	Scunthorpe U	12	0		
2021–22	Scunthorpe U	41	0	**85**	**0**

WILSON, Cameron (M) **8** **1**
b.Scunthorpe 1-12-02

2021–22	Scunthorpe U	8	1	**8**	**1**

YOUNG, Ethan (D) **6** **0**
H: 6 2 b.Peterborough 13-1-04

2021–22	Scunthorpe U	6	0	**6**	**0**

Players retained or with offer of contract
Balme, Jake; Poulter, Harrison; Sellars-Fleming, Tyrell.

Scholars
Balme, Jake Paul; Elliott-Bell, Harry; Foster, Owen Jacob Anthony; Franklin, Benjamin James; Lewis, Harry James; Lobley, Oliver Shay Sherratt; Moore, Jamie Matthew; Moore-Billam, Jack Billy James; Pike, Benjamin James; Poulter, Harrison; Robertson, Josh Michael; Sellars-Fleming, Tyrell; Strouther, Charley Joseph Neil; Wallace, Nathaniel Patrick Barrie; Young, Ethan Kai.

SHEFFIELD U (74)

AMISSAH, Jordan (G) **0** **0**
H: 6 6 b. 2-8-01
From Borussia Dortmund.

2020–21	Sheffield U	0	0		
2021–22	Sheffield U	0	0		

ARBLASTER, Oliver (M) **0** **0**
H: 5 8 b. 5-5-04 *Internationals:* England U18.

2020–21	Sheffield U	0	0		
2021–22	Sheffield U	0	0		

BALDOCK, George (M) **304** **10**
H: 5 9 W: 10 08 b.Buckingham 26-1-93
Internationals: Greece Full caps.

2009–10	Milton Keynes D	1	0		
2010–11	Milton Keynes D	2	0		
2011–12	Milton Keynes D	0	0		
2011–12	*Northampton T*	5	0	**5**	**0**
2012–13	Milton Keynes D	2	0		
2013–14	Milton Keynes D	38	2		
2014–15	Milton Keynes D	9	0		
2014–15	*Oxford U*	12	1		
2015–16	Milton Keynes D	15	0		
2015–16	*Oxford U*	27	2	**39**	**3**
2016–17	Milton Keynes D	37	0	**104**	**2**
2017–18	Sheffield U	34	1		
2018–19	Sheffield U	27	1		
2019–20	Sheffield U	38	2		
2020–21	Sheffield U	32	0		
2021–22	Sheffield U	25	1	**156**	**5**

BASHAM, Chris (M) **424** **17**
H: 5 11 W: 12 08 b.Hebburn 20-7-88
From Newcastle U.

2007–08	Bolton W	0	0		
2007–08	*Rochdale*	13	0	**13**	**0**
2008–09	Bolton W	11	1		
2009–10	Bolton W	8	0	**19**	**1**
2010–11	Blackpool	2	0		
2011–12	Blackpool	17	2		
2012–13	Blackpool	26	1		
2013–14	Blackpool	40	2	**85**	**5**
2014–15	Sheffield U	37	0		
2015–16	Sheffield U	44	3		
2016–17	Sheffield U	43	2		
2017–18	Sheffield U	45	2		
2018–19	Sheffield U	41	4		
2019–20	Sheffield U	38	0		
2020–21	Sheffield U	31	0		
2021–22	Sheffield U	28	0	**307**	**11**

BELEHOUAN, Jean (D) **0** **0**
b. 1-9-00

2020–21	Sheffield U	0	0		
2021–22	Sheffield U	0	0		

BERGE, Sander (M) **177** **11**
H: 6 5 W: 15 02 b.Baerum 14-2-98
Internationals: Norway U16, U17, U18, U19, U21, Full caps.

2013	Asker	1	0		
2014	Asker	7	0	**8**	**0**
2015	Valerenga	11	0		
2016	Valerenga	25	0	**36**	**0**
2016–17	Genk	9	0		
2017–18	Genk	13	0		
2018–19	Genk	28	0		
2019–20	Genk	23	4	**73**	**4**
2019–20	Sheffield U	14	1		
2020–21	Sheffield U	15	1		
2021–22	Sheffield U	31	5	**60**	**7**

BOGLE, Jayden (D) **111** **8**
H: 5 10 W: 10 12 b.Reading 27-7-00
Internationals: England U20.

2017–18	Derby Co	0	0		
2018–19	Derby Co	40	2		
2019–20	Derby Co	37	1	**77**	**3**
2020–21	Sheffield U	16	2		
2021–22	Sheffield U	18	3	**34**	**5**

BOYES, Harry (M) **0** **0**
b. 2-11-01
From Manchester C.

2020–21	Sheffield U	0	0		
2021–22	Sheffield U	0	0		

BREWSTER, Rhian (F) **61** **13**
H: 5 9 W: 11 11 b.Chadwell Heath 1-4-00
Internationals: England U16, U17, U18, U21
From Chelsea.

2016–17	Liverpool	0	0		
2017–18	Liverpool	0	0		
2018–19	Liverpool	0	0		
2019–20	Liverpool	0	0		
2019–20	*Swansea C*	20	10	**20**	**10**
2020–21	Sheffield U	27	0		
2021–22	Sheffield U	14	3	**41**	**3**

BROADBENT, George (M) **23** **1**
H: 5 10 W: 12 06 b. 30-9-00

2020–21	Sheffield U	0	0		
2020–21	*Beerschot*	2	0	**2**	**0**
2021–22	Sheffield U	0	0		
2021–22	*Rochdale*	21	1	**21**	**1**

BROOKS, Andre (M) **0** **0**
H: 5 11 b. 20-8-03

2020–21	Sheffield U	0	0		
2021–22	Sheffield U	0	0		

BRUNT, Zak (M) **0** **0**
H: 5 9 W: 10 08 b.Chesterfield 17-11-01
From Matlock.

2020–21	Sheffield U	0	0		
2021–22	Sheffield U	0	0		

BURKE, Oliver (M) **159** **15**
H: 5 9 W: 11 11 b.Kirkcaldy 7-4-97
Internationals: Scotland U19, U20, Full caps.

2014–15	Nottingham F	2	0		
2014–15	*Bradford C*	2	0	**2**	**0**
2015–16	Nottingham F	18	2		
2016–17	Nottingham F	5	4	**25**	**6**
2016–17	RB Leipzig	25	1	**25**	**1**
2017–18	WBA	15	0		
2018–19	WBA	3	0		
2018–19	*Celtic*	14	4	**14**	**4**
2019–20	WBA	2	0	**20**	**0**
2019–20	*Alaves*	31	1	**31**	**1**
2020–21	Sheffield U	25	1		
2021–22	Sheffield U	3	0	**28**	**1**
2021–22	*Millwall*	14	2	**14**	**2**

CAPELLO, Angelo (F) **0** **0**
b. 27-1-02
Internationals: Belize Full caps.

2020–21	Sheffield U	0	0		
2021–22	Sheffield U	0	0		

COULIBALY, Ismaila (M) **69** **9**
H: 6 0 b.Mali 25-12-00
Internationals: Mali U20.

2019	Sarpsborg 08	13	0		
2020	Sarpsborg 08	14	4	**27**	**4**
2020–21	Sheffield U	0	0		
2020–21	*Beerschot*	22	5		
2021–22	Sheffield U	0	0		
2021–22	*Beerschot*	20	0	**42**	**5**

DAVIES, Adam (G) **217** **0**
H: 6 1 W: 11 11 b.Rinteln 17-7-92
Internationals: Wales Full caps.

2009–10	Everton	0	0		
2010–11	Everton	0	0		
2011–12	Everton	0	0		
2012–13	Sheffield W	0	0		
2013–14	Sheffield W	0	0		
2014–15	Barnsley	23	0		
2015–16	Barnsley	38	0		
2016–17	Barnsley	46	0		
2017–18	Barnsley	35	0		
2018–19	Barnsley	42	0	**184**	**0**
2019–20	Stoke C	4	0		
2020–21	Stoke C	17	0		
2021–22	Stoke C	12	0	**33**	**0**
2021–22	Sheffield U	0	0		

DEWHURST, Marcus (G) **0** **0**
b.Kingston upon Hull
Internationals: England U17, U18, U19, U20.

2019–20	Sheffield U	0	0		
2019–20	*Carlisle U*	0	0		
2020–21	Sheffield U	0	0		
2020–21	*Carlisle U*	0	0		
2021–22	Sheffield U	0	0		

EASTWOOD, Jake (G) **26** **0**
H: 6 3 W: 11 00 b.Sheffield 3-10-96

2017–18	Chesterfield	4	0	**4**	**0**
2017–18	Sheffield U	1	0		
2018–19	Sheffield U	0	0		
2019–20	Sheffield U	0	0		
2019–20	*Scunthorpe U*	11	0	**11**	**0**
2020–21	Sheffield U	0	0		
2020–21	*Kilmarnock*	1	0	**1**	**0**
2020–21	*Grimsby T*	7	0	**7**	**0**
2021–22	Sheffield U	0	0	**1**	**0**
2021–22	*Portsmouth*	0	0		
2021–22	*Rochdale*	2	0	**2**	**0**

EGAN, John (D) **324** **22**
H: 6 1 W: 11 05 b.Cork 20-10-92
Internationals: Republic of Ireland U17, U19, U21, Full caps.

2009–10	Sunderland	0	0		
2010–11	Sunderland	0	0		
2011–12	Sunderland	0	0		
2011–12	*Crystal Palace*	1	0	**1**	**0**
2011–12	*Sheffield U*	1	0		
2012–13	Sunderland	0	0		
2012–13	*Bradford C*	4	0	**4**	**0**
2013–14	Sunderland	0	0		
2013–14	*Southend U*	13	1	**13**	**1**
2014–15	Gillingham	45	4		
2015–16	Gillingham	36	6	**81**	**10**
2016–17	Brentford	34	4		
2017–18	Brentford	33	2	**67**	**6**
2018–19	Sheffield U	44	1		
2019–20	Sheffield U	36	2		
2020–21	Sheffield U	31	0		
2021–22	Sheffield U	46	2	**158**	**5**

FLECK, John (M) **436** **24**
H: 5 7 W: 11 05 b.Glasgow 24-8-91
Internationals: Scotland U17, U19, U21, Full caps.

2007–08	Rangers	1	0		
2008–09	Rangers	8	1		
2009–10	Rangers	15	1		
2010–11	Rangers	13	0		
2011–12	Rangers	4	0	**41**	**2**
2011–12	*Blackpool*	7	0	**7**	**0**
2012–13	Coventry C	35	3		
2013–14	Coventry C	43	1		
2014–15	Coventry C	44	0		
2015–16	Coventry C	40	4	**162**	**8**
2016–17	Sheffield U	44	4		
2017–18	Sheffield U	41	2		
2018–19	Sheffield U	45	2		
2019–20	Sheffield U	30	5		
2020–21	Sheffield U	31	0		
2021–22	Sheffield U	35	1	**226**	**14**

FODERINGHAM, Wesley (G) **308** **0**
H: 6 1 W: 11 11 b.Hammersmith 14-1-91
Internationals: England U16, U17, U19.

2009–10	Fulham	0	0		
2010–11	Crystal Palace	0	0		
2011–12	Crystal Palace	0	0		
2011–12	Swindon T	33	0		
2012–13	Swindon T	46	0		
2013–14	Swindon T	41	0		
2014–15	Swindon T	44	0	**164**	**0**
2015–16	Rangers	36	0		
2016–17	Rangers	37	0		
2017–18	Rangers	33	0		
2018–19	Rangers	4	0		
2019–20	Rangers	2	0	**112**	**0**
2020–21	Sheffield U	0	0		
2021–22	Sheffield U	32	0	**32**	**0**

FREEMAN, Luke (F) **372** **42**
H: 5 11 W: 10 01 b.Dartford 22-3-92
Internationals: England U16, U17.

2007–08	Gillingham	1	0	**1**	**0**
2008–09	Arsenal	0	0		
2009–10	Arsenal	0	0		
2010–11	Arsenal	0	0		
2010–11	*Yeovil T*	13	2	**13**	**2**
2011–12	Arsenal	0	0		
2011–12	Stevenage	26	7		
2012–13	Stevenage	39	2		
2013–14	Stevenage	45	6	**110**	**15**
2014–15	Bristol C	46	7		
2015–16	Bristol C	41	1		
2016–17	Bristol C	18	2	**105**	**10**
2016–17	QPR	16	2		
2017–18	QPR	45	5		
2018–19	QPR	43	7	**104**	**14**
2019–20	Sheffield U	11	0		
2020–21	Sheffield U	0	0		
2020–21	*Nottingham F*	23	1	**23**	**1**
2021–22	Sheffield U	4	0	**15**	**0**
2021–22	*Millwall*	1	0	**1**	**0**

GAXHA, Leonardo (F) **0** **0**
b. 2-3-02
Internationals: Republic of Ireland U16, U17. Albania U18.

2020–21	Sheffield U	0	0		
2021–22	Sheffield U	0	0		

GOMIS, Nicksoen (D) **0** **0**
b. 15-3-02
Internationals: France U18.

2020–21	Sheffield U	0	0		
2021–22	Sheffield U	0	0		

GORDON, Kyron (D) **5** **0**
H: 6 0 W: 11 00 b.Sheffield 24-5-02

2020–21	Sheffield U	0	0		
2021–22	Sheffield U	5	0	**5**	**0**

HACKFORD, Antwoine (F) **1** **0**
b.Sheffield 20-3-04
Internationals: England U16.

2020–21	Sheffield U	1	0		
2021–22	Sheffield U	0	0	**1**	**0**

JEBBISON, Daniel (F) **32** **8**
H: 6 3 W: 10 12 b.Oakville, Canada 11-7-03
Internationals: England U18, U19.

2020–21	Sheffield U	4	1		
2021–22	Sheffield U	8	0	**12**	**1**
2021–22	*Burton Alb*	20	7	**20**	**7**

LOPATA, Kacper (D) **7** **0**
H: 6 2 W: 12 08 b.Krakow 27-8-01
Internationals: Poland U18, U19, U20, U21.
From Bristol C.

2019–20	Brighton & HA	0	0		
2019–20	*Zaglebie Sosnowiec*	7	0	**7**	**0**
2020–21	Sheffield U	0	0		
2021–22	Sheffield U	0	0		

LOWE, Max (D) **114** **3**
H: 5 9 W: 11 09 b.Birmingham 11-5-97
Internationals: England U16, U17, U18, U20.

2013–14	Derby Co	0	0		
2014–15	Derby Co	0	0		
2015–16	Derby Co	0	0		
2016–17	Derby Co	9	0		
2017–18	Derby Co	0	0		
2017–18	*Shrewsbury T*	12	0	**12**	**0**
2018–19	Derby Co	3	0		
2018–19	*Aberdeen*	33	2	**33**	**2**
2019–20	Derby Co	29	0	**41**	**0**
2020–21	Sheffield U	8	0		
2021–22	Sheffield U	0	0	**8**	**0**
2021–22	*Nottingham F*	20	1	**20**	**1**

MAGUIRE, Frankie (M) **0** **0**
b. 29-7-03

2020–21	Sheffield U	0	0		
2021–22	Sheffield U	0	0		

McBURNIE, Oliver (F) **185** **41**
H: 6 2 W: 10 06 b.Leeds 4-6-96
Internationals: Scotland U19, U21, Full caps.

2013–14	Bradford C	8	0		
2014–15	Bradford C	7	0	**15**	**0**
2015–16	Swansea C	0	0		
2015–16	*Newport Co*	3	3	**3**	**3**
2015–16	*Bristol R*	5	0	**5**	**0**
2016–17	Swansea C	5	0		
2017–18	Swansea C	11	0		
2017–18	*Barnsley*	17	9	**17**	**9**
2018–19	Swansea C	42	22		
2019–20	Swansea C	0	0	**58**	**22**
2019–20	Sheffield U	36	6		
2020–21	Sheffield U	23	1		
2021–22	Sheffield U	28	0	**87**	**7**

McGOLDRICK, David (F) 465 112
H: 6 0 W: 11 09 b.Nottingham 29-11-87
Internationals: Republic of Ireland Full caps.
2003–04 Notts Co 4 0
2004–05 Notts Co 0 0
2005–06 Southampton 1 0
2005–06 *Notts Co* 6 0 **10 0**
2006–07 Southampton 9 0
2006–07 *Bournemouth* 12 6 **12 6**
2007–08 Southampton 8 0
2007–08 *Port Vale* 17 2 **17 2**
2008–09 Southampton 46 12 **64 12**
2009–10 Nottingham F 33 3
2010–11 Nottingham F 21 5
2011–12 Nottingham F 9 0
2011–12 *Sheffield W* 4 1 **4 1**
2012–13 Nottingham F 0 0 **63 8**
2012–13 *Coventry C* 22 16 **22 16**
2012–13 *Ipswich T* 13 4
2013–14 Ipswich T 31 14
2014–15 Ipswich T 26 7
2015–16 Ipswich T 24 4
2016–17 Ipswich T 30 5
2017–18 Ipswich T 22 6 **146 40**
2018–19 Sheffield U 45 15
2019–20 Sheffield U 28 2
2020–21 Sheffield U 35 8
2021–22 Sheffield U 19 2 **127 27**

MOUSSET, Lys (M) 146 26
H: 6 0 W: 12 08 b.Montvilliers 8-2-96
Internationals: France U20, U21.
2013–14 Le Havre 5 0
2014–15 Le Havre 1 0
2015–16 Le Havre 28 14 **34 14**
2016–17 Bournemouth 11 0
2017–18 Bournemouth 23 2
2018–19 Bournemouth 24 1 **58 3**
2019–20 Sheffield U 30 6
2020–21 Sheffield U 11 0
2021–22 Sheffield U 7 3 **48 9**
2021–22 *Salernitana* 6 0 **6 0**

NDIAYE, Iliman-Cheikh (M) 31 7
H: 5 11 W: 9 08 b.Rouen 6-3-00
Internationals: Senegal Full caps.
From Boreham Wood.
2019–20 Sheffield U 0 0
2020–21 Sheffield U 1 0
2021–22 Sheffield U 30 7 **31 7**

NEAL, Harrison (M) 0 0
b. 12-5-01
2020–21 Sheffield U 0 0
2021–22 Sheffield U 0 0

NORRINGTON-DAVIES, Rhys (D) 87 2
H: 5 11 W: 10 10 b.Riyadh 22-4-99
Internationals: Wales U19, U21, Full caps.
2017–18 Sheffield U 0 0
2018–19 Sheffield U 0 0
2019–20 Sheffield U 0 0
2019–20 *Rochdale* 27 1 **27 1**
2020–21 Sheffield U 0 0
2020–21 *Luton T* 18 0 **18 0**
2020–21 *Stoke C* 20 1 **20 1**
2021–22 Sheffield U 22 0 **22 0**

NORWOOD, Oliver (M) 426 25
H: 5 11 W: 12 00 b.Burnley 12-4-91
Internationals: England U16, U17. Northern Ireland U19, U21, B, Full caps.
2009–10 Manchester U 0 0
2010–11 Manchester U 0 0
2010–11 *Carlisle U* 6 0 **6 0**
2011–12 Manchester U 0 0
2011–12 *Scunthorpe U* 15 1 **15 1**
2011–12 *Coventry C* 18 2 **18 2**
2012–13 Huddersfield T 39 3
2013–14 Huddersfield T 40 5
2014–15 Huddersfield T 1 0 **80 8**
2014–15 Reading 38 1
2015–16 Reading 43 3 **81 4**
2016–17 Brighton & HA 33 0
2017–18 Brighton & HA 0 0 **33 0**
2017–18 *Fulham* 36 5 **36 5**
2018–19 Sheffield U 43 3
2019–20 Sheffield U 38 1
2020–21 Sheffield U 32 0
2021–22 Sheffield U 44 1 **157 5**

O'CONNELL, Jack (D) 270 13
H: 6 3 W: 13 05 b.Liverpool 29-3-94
Internationals: England U18, U19.
2012–13 Blackburn R 0 0
2012–13 *Rotherham U* 3 0 **3 0**
2012–13 *York C* 18 0 **18 0**
2013–14 Blackburn R 0 0
2013–14 *Rochdale* 38 0
2014–15 Blackburn R 0 0
2014–15 *Rochdale* 29 5 **67 5**
2014–15 Brentford 0 0
2015–16 Brentford 16 1 **16 1**
2016–17 Sheffield U 44 4
2017–18 Sheffield U 46 0
2018–19 Sheffield U 41 3
2019–20 Sheffield U 33 0
2020–21 Sheffield U 2 0
2021–22 Sheffield U 0 0 **166 7**

OSBORN, Ben (M) 283 19
H: 5 9 W: 11 11 b.Derby 5-8-94
Internationals: England U18, U19, U20.
2011–12 Nottingham F 0 0
2012–13 Nottingham F 0 0
2013–14 Nottingham F 8 0
2014–15 Nottingham F 37 3
2015–16 Nottingham F 36 3
2016–17 Nottingham F 46 4
2017–18 Nottingham F 46 4
2018–19 Nottingham F 39 1 **212 15**
2019–20 Sheffield U 13 0
2020–21 Sheffield U 24 1
2021–22 Sheffield U 34 3 **71 4**

OSULA, William (F) 5 0
H: 5 11 b.Denmark 4-8-03
Internationals: Denmark U19.
2020–21 Sheffield U 0 0
2021–22 Sheffield U 5 0 **5 0**

ROBINSON, Jack (D) 217 7
H: 5 11 W: 10 08 b.Warrington 1-9-93
Internationals: England U16, U17, U18, U19, U21.
2009–10 Liverpool 1 0
2010–11 Liverpool 2 0
2011–12 Liverpool 0 0
2012–13 Liverpool 0 0
2012–13 *Wolverhampton W* 11 0 **11 0**
2013–14 Liverpool 0 0 **3 0**
2013–14 *Blackpool* 34 0 **34 0**
2014–15 QPR 0 0
2014–15 *Huddersfield T* 30 0 **30 0**
2015–16 QPR 1 0
2016–17 QPR 7 0
2017–18 QPR 31 2 **39 2**
2018–19 Nottingham F 38 2
2019–20 Nottingham F 18 0 **56 2**
2019–20 Sheffield U 6 0
2020–21 Sheffield U 11 0
2021–22 Sheffield U 27 3 **44 3**

SERIKI, Femi (F) 3 0
b. 28-4-02
2018–19 Bury 0 0
2019–20 Sheffield U 0 0
2020–21 Sheffield U 1 0
2021–22 Sheffield U 1 0 **2 0**
2021–22 *Beerschot VA* 1 0 **1 0**

SHARP, Billy (F) 592 247
H: 5 9 W: 11 00 b.Sheffield 5-2-86
2004–05 Sheffield U 2 0
2004–05 *Rushden & D* 16 9 **16 9**
2005–06 Scunthorpe U 37 23
2006–07 Scunthorpe U 45 30 **82 53**
2007–08 Sheffield U 29 4
2008–09 Sheffield U 22 4
2009–10 Sheffield U 0 0
2009–10 *Doncaster R* 33 15
2010–11 Doncaster R 29 15
2011–12 Doncaster R 20 10
2011–12 Southampton 15 9
2012–13 Southampton 2 0
2012–13 *Nottingham F* 39 10 **39 10**
2013–14 Southampton 0 0 **17 9**
2013–14 *Reading* 10 2 **10 2**
2013–14 *Doncaster R* 16 4 **98 44**
2014–15 Leeds U 33 5 **33 5**
2015–16 Sheffield U 44 21
2016–17 Sheffield U 46 30
2017–18 Sheffield U 34 13
2018–19 Sheffield U 40 23
2019–20 Sheffield U 25 3
2020–21 Sheffield U 16 3
2021–22 Sheffield U 39 14 **297 115**

STARBUCK, Joseph (D) 6 0
H: 5 8 W: 10 10 b. 3-8-02
2019–20 Grimsby T 0 0
2020–21 Grimsby T 6 0 **6 0**
2021–22 Sheffield U 0 0

STEVENS, Enda (D) 402 11
H: 6 0 W: 12 04 b.Dublin 9-7-90
Internationals: Republic of Ireland U21, Full caps.
2008 UCD 2 0 **2 0**
2009 St Patricks Ath 30 0 **30 0**
2010 Shamrock R 18 0
2011 Shamrock R 28 0 **46 0**
2011–12 Aston Villa 0 0
2012–13 Aston Villa 7 0
2013–14 Aston Villa 0 0
2013–14 *Notts Co* 2 0 **2 0**
2013–14 *Doncaster R* 13 0
2014–15 Aston Villa 0 0 **7 0**
2014–15 *Northampton T* 4 1 **4 1**
2014–15 *Doncaster R* 28 1 **41 1**
2015–16 Portsmouth 45 0
2016–17 Portsmouth 45 1 **90 1**
2016–17 Sheffield U 0 0
2017–18 Sheffield U 45 1
2018–19 Sheffield U 45 4
2019–20 Sheffield U 38 2
2020–21 Sheffield U 30 0
2021–22 Sheffield U 22 1 **180 8**

UREMOVIC, Filip (D) 123 2
b. 11-2-97
Internationals: Croatia U19, U21, Full caps.
2013–14 Cibalia 0 0
2014–15 Cibalia 6 0
2015–16 Cibalia 3 0
2016–17 Cibalia 3 0 **12 0**
2016–17 Dinamo Zagreb 0 0
2017–18 Dinamo Zagreb 0 0
2017–18 Olimpija Ljubljana 18 1 **18 1**
2018–19 Rubin Kazan 23 1
2019–20 Rubin Kazan 25 0
2020–21 Rubin Kazan 24 0
2021–22 Rubin Kazan 18 0 **90 1**
2021–22 *Sheffield U* 3 0 **3 0**

VERRIPS, Michael (G) 83 0
H: 6 5 W: 13 05 b.Velp 3-12-96
Internationals: Netherlands U19, U21.
2014–15 FC Twente 0 0
2015–16 FC Twente 0 0
2016–17 Sparta Rotterdam 1 0
2017–18 Sparta Rotterdam 0 0 **1 0**
2017–18 *MVV Maastricht* 38 0 **38 0**
2018–19 Mechelen 27 0
2019–20 Mechelen 0 0 **27 0**
2019–20 Sheffield U 0 0
2020–21 Sheffield U 0 0
2020–21 *Emmen* 14 0 **14 0**
2021–22 Sheffield U 1 0 **1 0**
2021–22 *Fortuna Sittard* 2 0 **2 0**

Players retained or with offer of contract
Ayari, Hassan; Barratt, Connor; Buyabu, Jili; Freckleton, Miguel; Williams, Theo.

Scholars
Anderson, Beau James; Angell, Thomas Harry; Bailey-Green, Tyrese; De Macedo Geremias, Fernando; Dickinson, George Simon; Drake, Benjamin Daniel; Faxon, Luke John; Hampshaw, Henry Kit; Hampson, Owen Matthew; Hiddleston, Callum; Lankshear, William Terence; Marsh, Louie; Oluleye, John Ayomipo Iyanuoluwa; Peck, Sydie Frederick; Pitan, Levis Omodele; Potter, Finley John; Sachdev, Sai Sachin Rony; Slater, Ethan; Smith, Joshua James; Staniland, Charlie; Williams, Luther Cornelius Mclachlan.

SHEFFIELD W (75)

ADENIRAN, Dennis (M) 40 3
H: 5 11 W: 11 09 b.Southwark 2-1-99
Internationals: England U17, U18, U19.
2016–17 Fulham 1 0 **1 0**
2017–18 Everton 0 0
2018–19 Everton 0 0
2019–20 Everton 0 0
2020–21 Everton 0 0
2020–21 *Wycombe W* 21 0 **21 0**
2021–22 Sheffield W 18 3 **18 3**

BANNAN, Barry (M) 422 25
H: 5 7 W: 9 08 b.Glasgow 1-12-89
Internationals: Scotland U21, Full caps.
2008–09 Aston Villa 0 0
2008–09 *Derby Co* 10 1 **10 1**
2009–10 Aston Villa 0 0
2009–10 *Blackpool* 20 1 **20 1**
2010–11 Aston Villa 12 0
2010–11 *Leeds U* 7 0 **7 0**
2011–12 Aston Villa 28 1
2012–13 Aston Villa 24 0
2013–14 Aston Villa 0 0 **64 1**
2013–14 Crystal Palace 15 1
2014–15 Crystal Palace 7 0
2014–15 *Bolton W* 16 0 **16 0**
2015–16 Crystal Palace 0 0 **22 1**
2015–16 Sheffield W 35 2
2016–17 Sheffield W 43 1
2017–18 Sheffield W 29 0
2018–19 Sheffield W 41 5
2019–20 Sheffield W 44 2
2020–21 Sheffield W 46 2
2021–22 Sheffield W 45 9 **283 21**

BERAHINO, Saido (F) 217 46
H: 5 11 W: 12 13 b.Bujumbura, Burundi 4-8-93
Internationals: England U16, U17, U18, U19, U20, U21.
2010–11 WBA 0 0
2011–12 WBA 0 0
2011–12 *Northampton T* 14 6 **14 6**
2011–12 *Brentford* 8 4 **8 4**
2012–13 WBA 0 0
2012–13 *Peterborough U* 10 2 **10 2**
2013–14 WBA 32 5
2014–15 WBA 38 14

2015–16 WBA 31 4
2016–17 WBA 4 0 **105 23**
2016–17 Stoke C 13 0
2017–18 Stoke C 15 0
2018–19 Stoke C 23 3 **51 3**
2021–22 *Charleroi* 0 0
2021–22 Zulte-Waregem 0 0
2021–22 Sheffield W 29 8 **29 8**

BOATENG, Kwame (D) 10 1
H: 5 10 W: 10 08 b.London 1-8-99
2016–17 Bradford C 0 0
2017–18 Bradford C 0 0
2020–21 The New Saints 10 1 **10 1**
From Guiseley, Farsley Celtic.
2021–22 Sheffield W 0 0

BRENNAN, Ciaran (D) 11 0
H: 6 2 W: 12 04 b.Kilkenny 5-5-00
Internationals: Republic of Ireland U18, U19.
From Waterford.
2019–20 Sheffield W 0 0
2020–21 Sheffield W 0 0
2021–22 Sheffield W 11 0 **11 0**

BROWN, Jaden (D) 39 0
H: 5 9 W: 11 05 b.Lewisham 24-1-99
Internationals: England U16, U17, U18, U19.
From Tottenham H.
2018–19 Huddersfield T 0 0
2018–19 *Exeter C* 0 0
2019–20 Huddersfield T 15 0
2020–21 Huddersfield T 13 0 **28 0**
2021–22 Sheffield W 11 0 **11 0**

BYERS, George (M) 93 10
H: 5 11 W: 11 07 b.Ilford 29-5-96
Internationals: Scotland U16, U17.
2014–15 Watford 1 0
2015–16 Watford 0 0 **1 0**
2016–17 Swansea C 0 0
2017–18 Swansea C 0 0
2018–19 Swansea C 21 2
2019–20 Swansea C 35 2
2020–21 Swansea C 0 0 **56 4**
2020–21 *Portsmouth* 14 0 **14 0**
2021–22 Sheffield W 22 6 **22 6**

DAWODU, Joshua (D) 0 0
b. 10-10-00
2020–21 Sheffield W 0 0
2021–22 Sheffield W 0 0

DAWSON, Cameron (G) 113 0
H: 6 0 W: 10 12 b.Sheffield 7-7-95
Internationals: England U18, U19.
2013–14 Sheffield W 0 0
2013–14 *Plymouth Arg* 0 0
2014–15 Sheffield W 0 0
2015–16 Sheffield W 0 0
2016–17 Sheffield W 4 0
2016–17 *Wycombe W* 1 0 **1 0**
2017–18 Sheffield W 3 0
2017–18 *Chesterfield* 2 0 **2 0**
2018–19 Sheffield W 26 0
2019–20 Sheffield W 24 0
2020–21 Sheffield W 8 0
2021–22 Sheffield W 0 0 **65 0**
2021–22 *Exeter C* 45 0 **45 0**

DELE-BASHIRU, Fisayo (M) 32 1
H: 5 9 W: 11 00 b.Hamburg 6-2-01
From Manchester C.
2020–21 Sheffield W 8 0
2021–22 Sheffield W 24 1 **32 1**

DUNKLEY, Cheyenne (D) 218 22
H: 6 2 W: 13 05 b.Wolverhampton 13-2-92
Internationals: England C.
From Crewe Alex, Hednesford T, Kidderminster H.
2014–15 Oxford U 9 0
2015–16 Oxford U 29 4
2016–17 Oxford U 40 3 **78 7**
2017–18 Wigan Ath 43 7
2018–19 Wigan Ath 38 0
2019–20 Wigan Ath 26 6 **107 13**
2020–21 Sheffield W 12 0
2021–22 Sheffield W 21 2 **33 2**

ERATT-THOMPSON, Declan (D) 0 0
From Stocksbridge Park Steels.
2020–21 Sheffield W 0 0
2021–22 Sheffield W 0 0

FARMER, Lewis (M) 0 0
b. 17-5-02
2020–21 Sheffield W 0 0
2021–22 Sheffield W 0 0

GALVIN, Ryan (D) 0 0
From Wigan Ath.
2020–21 Sheffield W 0 0
2021–22 Sheffield W 0 0

GREEN, Andre (F) 76 5
H: 5 11 W: 11 03 b.Solihull 2-5-98
Internationals: England U16, U17, U18, U19, U20.
2014–15 Aston Villa 0 0
2015–16 Aston Villa 2 0
2016–17 Aston Villa 15 0
2017–18 Aston Villa 5 1
2018–19 Aston Villa 18 1
2018–19 *Portsmouth* 6 1 **6 1**
2019–20 Aston Villa 0 0 **40 2**
2019–20 *Preston NE* 4 0 **4 0**
2019–20 *Charlton Ath* 13 2 **13 2**
2020–21 Sheffield W 11 0
2021–22 Sheffield W 2 0 **13 0**
Transferred to Slovan Bratislava, August 2021.

GREGORY, Lee (F) 297 90
H: 6 2 W: 12 08 b.Sheffield 26-8-88
2014–15 Millwall 39 9
2015–16 Millwall 41 18
2016–17 Millwall 37 17
2017–18 Millwall 43 10
2018–19 Millwall 44 10 **204 64**
2019–20 Stoke C 40 6
2020–21 Stoke C 6 1
2020–21 *Derby Co* 11 3 **11 3**
2021–22 Stoke C 0 0 **46 7**
2021–22 Sheffield W 36 16 **36 16**

HAGAN, Charles (F) 0 0
b. 6-9-01
From Chelsea.
2020–21 Sheffield W 0 0
2021–22 Sheffield W 0 0

HUNT, Alex (M) 22 0
H: 5 8 W: 10 08 b.Sheffield 29-5-00
2018–19 Sheffield W 0 0
2019–20 Sheffield W 6 0
2020–21 Sheffield W 3 0
2021–22 Sheffield W 0 0 **9 0**
2021–22 *Oldham Ath* 13 0 **13 0**

HUNT, Jack (D) 411 7
H: 5 9 W: 11 02 b.Rothwell 6-12-90
2009–10 Huddersfield T 0 0
2010–11 Huddersfield T 19 1
2010–11 *Chesterfield* 20 0 **20 0**
2011–12 Huddersfield T 43 1
2012–13 Huddersfield T 40 0
2013–14 Huddersfield T 2 0 **104 2**
2013–14 Crystal Palace 0 0
2013–14 *Barnsley* 11 0 **11 0**
2014–15 Crystal Palace 0 0
2014–15 *Nottingham F* 17 0 **17 0**
2014–15 *Rotherham U* 16 0 **16 0**
2015–16 Sheffield W 34 0
2016–17 Sheffield W 32 0
2017–18 Sheffield W 29 0
2018–19 Bristol C 33 1
2019–20 Bristol C 35 0
2020–21 Bristol C 41 2 **109 3**
2021–22 Sheffield W 39 2 **134 2**

HUTCHINSON, Sam (M) 213 7
H: 6 0 W: 11 07 b.Windsor 3-8-89
Internationals: England U18, U19.
2006–07 Chelsea 1 0
2007–08 Chelsea 0 0
2008–09 Chelsea 0 0
2009–10 Chelsea 2 0
2010–11 Chelsea 0 0
2011–12 Chelsea 2 0
2012–13 Chelsea 0 0
2012–13 *Nottingham F* 9 1 **9 1**
2013–14 Chelsea 0 0 **5 0**
2013–14 *Vitesse* 1 0 **1 0**
2013–14 *Sheffield W* 10 1
2014–15 Sheffield W 20 0
2015–16 Sheffield W 25 0
2016–17 Sheffield W 33 2
2017–18 Sheffield W 8 0
2018–19 Sheffield W 24 0
2019–20 Sheffield W 23 1
2020–21 Pafos 5 0 **5 0**
2020–21 Sheffield W 22 1
2021–22 Sheffield W 28 1 **193 6**

IORFA, Dominic (D) 196 6
H: 6 2 W: 12 04 b.Southend-on-Sea 24-6-95
Internationals: England U18, U20, U21.
2013–14 Wolverhampton W 0 0
2013–14 *Shrewsbury T* 7 0 **7 0**
2014–15 Wolverhampton W 20 0
2015–16 Wolverhampton W 42 0
2016–17 Wolverhampton W 22 0
2017–18 Wolverhampton W 0 0
2017–18 *Ipswich T* 23 1 **23 1**
2018–19 Wolverhampton W 0 0 **84 0**
2018–19 Sheffield W 12 3
2019–20 Sheffield W 41 2
2020–21 Sheffield W 10 0
2021–22 Sheffield W 19 0 **82 5**

JACKSON, Luke (G) 0 0
b. 18-3-02
2020–21 Sheffield W 0 0
2021–22 Sheffield W 0 0

JOHNSON, Marvin (F) 241 16
H: 5 10 W: 11 09 b.Birmingham 1-12-90
From Solihull Moors, Kidderminster H.
2014–15 Motherwell 11 0
2015–16 Motherwell 38 5
2016–17 Motherwell 4 1 **53 6**
2016–17 Oxford U 39 3
2017–18 Oxford U 2 0 **41 3**
2017–18 Middlesbrough 17 1
2018–19 Middlesbrough 0 0
2018–19 *Sheffield U* 11 0 **11 0**
2019–20 Middlesbrough 38 1
2020–21 Middlesbrough 42 3 **97 5**
2021–22 Sheffield W 39 2 **39 2**

KAMBERI, Florian (F) 162 29
H: 6 2 W: 13 03 b.Zurich 8-3-91
Internationals: Switzerland U20, U21.
From Rapperswil-Jona.
2015–16 Grasshopper 28 3
2016–17 Grasshopper 4 0
2016–17 *Karlsruher* 15 1 **15 1**
2017–18 Grasshopper 0 0 **32 3**
2017–18 *Hibernian* 14 9
2018–19 Hibernian 33 8
2019–20 Hibernian 20 3 **67 20**
2019–20 *Rangers* 6 1 **6 1**
2020–21 St Gallen 8 0
2020–21 *Aberdeen* 11 0 **11 0**
2021–22 St Gallen 0 0 **8 0**
2021–22 *Sheffield W* 23 4 **23 4**

LUONGO, Massimo (F) 303 27
H: 5 9 W: 12 00 b.Sydney 25-9-92
Internationals: Australia U20, Full caps.
2010–11 Tottenham H 0 0
2011–12 Tottenham H 0 0
2012–13 Tottenham H 0 0
2012–13 *Ipswich T* 9 0 **9 0**
2012–13 *Swindon T* 7 1
2013–14 Swindon T 44 6
2014–15 Swindon T 34 6 **85 13**
2015–16 QPR 30 0
2016–17 QPR 35 1
2017–18 QPR 39 6
2018–19 QPR 41 3 **145 10**
2019–20 Sheffield W 27 3
2020–21 Sheffield W 12 0
2021–22 Sheffield W 25 1 **64 4**

MENDEZ-LAING, Nathaniel (M) 301 42
H: 5 10 W: 11 12 b.Birmingham 15-4-92
Internationals: England U16, U17.
2009–10 Wolverhampton W 0 0
2010–11 Wolverhampton W 0 0
2010–11 *Peterborough U* 33 5
2011–12 Wolverhampton W 0 0
2011–12 *Sheffield U* 8 1 **8 1**
2012–13 Peterborough U 21 3
2012–13 *Portsmouth* 8 0 **8 0**
2013–14 Peterborough U 16 1
2013–14 *Shrewsbury T* 6 0 **6 0**
2014–15 Peterborough U 14 0 **84 9**
2014–15 *Cambridge U* 11 1 **11 1**
2015–16 Rochdale 33 7
2016–17 Rochdale 39 8 **72 15**
2017–18 Cardiff C 38 6
2018–19 Cardiff C 20 4
2019–20 Cardiff C 27 3
2020–21 Cardiff C 0 0 **85 13**
2020–21 Middlesbrough 9 1 **9 1**
2021–22 Sheffield W 18 2 **18 2**

ONEN, Jayden (M) 1 0
b. 17-2-01
From Arsenal, Crystal Palace, Brighton & HA, Brentford.
2020–21 Reading 1 0 **1 0**
2021–22 Sheffield W 0 0

PALMER, Liam (M) 347 3
H: 6 2 W: 12 11 b.Worksop 19-9-91
Internationals: Scotland U19, U21, Full caps.
2010–11 Sheffield W 9 0
2011–12 Sheffield W 14 1
2012–13 Sheffield W 0 0
2012–13 *Tranmere R* 43 0 **43 0**
2013–14 Sheffield W 39 0
2014–15 Sheffield W 35 0
2015–16 Sheffield W 15 0
2016–17 Sheffield W 21 0
2017–18 Sheffield W 25 0
2018–19 Sheffield W 35 0
2019–20 Sheffield W 33 0

2020–21 Sheffield W 39 1
2021–22 Sheffield W 39 1 **304 3**

PATERSON, Callum (D) 315 66
H: 6 2 W: 12 00 b.London 13-10-94
Internationals: Scotland U18, U19, U21, Full caps.
2012–13 Hearts 22 3
2013–14 Hearts 37 11
2014–15 Hearts 29 6
2015–16 Hearts 29 5
2016–17 Hearts 20 8 **137 33**
2017–18 Cardiff C 32 10
2018–19 Cardiff C 27 4
2019–20 Cardiff C 36 5 **95 19**
2020–21 Sheffield W 43 8
2021–22 Sheffield W 40 6 **83 14**

RENDER, Joshua (G) 0 0
H: 6 0 W: 11 07 b.Kingston-upon-Hull 25-9-00
2020–21 Sheffield W 0 0
2021–22 Sheffield W 0 0

SOW, Sylla (F) 62 9
H: 6 0 W: 11 09 b.Nijmegen 8-8-96
2017–18 Utrecht 1 0
2018–19 Utrecht 0 0 **1 0**
2019–20 Waalwijk 20 4
2020–21 Waalwijk 28 3 **48 7**
2021–22 RKC 0 0
2021–22 Sheffield W 13 2 **13 2**

WALDOCK, Liam (M) 0 0
H: 5 10 W: 11 03 b.Sheffield 25-9-00
2019–20 Sheffield W 0 0
2020–21 Sheffield W 0 0
2021–22 Sheffield W 0 0

WILDSMITH, Joe (G) 69 0
H: 6 0 W: 10 03 b.Sheffield 28-12-95
Internationals: England U20.
2013–14 Sheffield W 0 0
2014–15 Sheffield W 0 0
2014–15 *Barnsley* 2 0 **2 0**
2015–16 Sheffield W 9 0
2016–17 Sheffield W 1 0
2017–18 Sheffield W 26 0
2018–19 Sheffield W 0 0
2019–20 Sheffield W 9 0
2020–21 Sheffield W 19 0
2021–22 Sheffield W 3 0 **67 0**

WINDASS, Josh (M) 243 59
H: 5 9 W: 10 10 b.Hull 9-1-94
From Huddersfield T, Harrogate Railway Ath.
2013–14 Accrington S 10 0
2014–15 Accrington S 35 6
2015–16 Accrington S 30 15 **75 21**
2016–17 Rangers 21 0
2017–18 Rangers 33 13
2018–19 Rangers 1 0 **55 13**
2018–19 Wigan Ath 39 5
2019–20 Wigan Ath 15 4 **54 9**
2019–20 *Sheffield W* 9 3
2020–21 Sheffield W 41 9
2021–22 Sheffield W 9 4 **59 16**

Players retained or with offer of contract
Agbontohoma, David; Davidson, Leojo; Dutra Aguas, Paulo; Glover, Jay; Hall, Jack; Trueman, William.

Scholars
Al-Jahadhmy, Murtadha Fuad; Asfha, Filimon Drar; Ashman, Joshua David; Bradford, Jake Melvyn John; Cadamarteri, Bailey-Tye; Chapman, Joshua Owen; Charles, Pierce Joseph; Flannery, Cian Michael; Fusire, Sean Sheunesu; Kilheeney, Caelan Michael Carl; MacIag, Kamil; Maltby, MacKenzie James; Phuthi, Joey; Rhule, Danai Sterling; Sesay, Fuad; Shipston, Rio Joel; Tapudzai, Tafadzwa Brendon; Wassell, Daniel Lewis; Whitham, Jenson.

SHREWSBURY T (76)

BENNETT, Elliott (M) 472 29
H: 5 10 W: 11 07 b.Telford 18-12-88
2006–07 Wolverhampton W 0 0
2007–08 Wolverhampton W 0 0
2007–08 *Crewe Alex* 9 1 **9 1**
2007–08 *Bury* 19 1
2008–09 Wolverhampton W 0 0
2008–09 *Bury* 46 3 **65 4**
2009–10 Wolverhampton W 0 0
2009–10 *Brighton & HA* 43 7
2010–11 Brighton & HA 46 6
2011–12 Norwich C 33 1
2012–13 Norwich C 24 1
2013–14 Norwich C 2 0
2014–15 Norwich C 9 0
2014–15 *Brighton & HA* 7 0 **96 13**
2015–16 Norwich C 0 0 **68 2**
2015–16 *Bristol C* 15 0 **15 0**
2015–16 Blackburn R 21 2
2016–17 Blackburn R 25 3
2017–18 Blackburn R 41 2
2018–19 Blackburn R 40 1
2019–20 Blackburn R 41 0
2020–21 Blackburn R 9 0
2021–22 Blackburn R 0 0 **177 8**
2021–22 Shrewsbury T 42 1 **42 1**

BEVAN, Jaden (G) 0 0
H: 6 2 b.Shrewsbury 20-12-02
2020–21 Shrewsbury T 0 0
2021–22 Shrewsbury T 0 0

BLOXHAM, Tom (F) 38 2
H: 6 5 b.Leicester 1-11-03
2020–21 Shrewsbury T 4 0
2021–22 Shrewsbury T 34 2 **38 2**

BOWMAN, Ryan (F) 257 60
H: 6 2 W: 12 00 b.Carlisle 30-11-91
2009–10 Carlisle U 6 0
2010–11 Carlisle U 3 0 **9 0**
From Darlington, Hereford U
2013–14 York C 37 8 **37 8**
From York C, Gateshead.
2016–17 Motherwell 24 2
2017–18 Motherwell 32 7
2018–19 Motherwell 16 1 **72 10**
2018–19 Exeter C 18 5
2019–20 Exeter C 37 13
2020–21 Exeter C 42 14
2021–22 Exeter C 0 0 **97 32**
2021–22 Shrewsbury T 42 10 **42 10**

BURGOYNE, Harry (G) 42 0
H: 6 4 W: 13 05 b.Ludlow 28-12-96
2015–16 Wolverhampton W 0 0
2016–17 Barnet 2 0 **2 0**
2016–17 Wolverhampton W 6 0
2017–18 Wolverhampton W 1 0
2018–19 Wolverhampton W 0 0
2018–19 *Falkirk* 15 0 **15 0**
2019–20 Wolverhampton W 0 0 **7 0**
2019–20 Shrewsbury T 0 0
2020–21 Shrewsbury T 18 0
2021–22 Shrewsbury T 0 0 **18 0**

CATON, Charlie (F) 3 0
b.Bodelwyddan 25-11-02
2019–20 Shrewsbury T 0 0
2020–21 Shrewsbury T 3 0
2021–22 Shrewsbury T 0 0 **3 0**

DANIELS, Josh (F) 40 2
H: 5 9 W: 11 07 b.Derry 22-2-96
Internationals: Northern Ireland U17, U19. Republic of Ireland U21.
From Derry C, Glenavon.
2020–21 Shrewsbury T 19 2
2021–22 Shrewsbury T 21 0 **40 2**

DAVIS, David (M) 328 13
H: 5 9 W: 12 12 b.Smethwick 20-2-91
2009–10 Wolverhampton W 0 0
2009–10 *Darlington* 5 0 **5 0**
2010–11 Wolverhampton W 0 0
2010–11 *Walsall* 7 0 **7 0**
2010–11 *Shrewsbury T* 19 2
2011–12 Wolverhampton W 7 0
2011–12 *Chesterfield* 9 0 **9 0**
2012–13 Wolverhampton W 28 0
2013–14 Wolverhampton W 18 0 **53 0**
2014–15 Birmingham C 42 3
2015–16 Birmingham C 35 1
2016–17 Birmingham C 41 4
2017–18 Birmingham C 38 2
2018–19 Birmingham C 11 0
2019–20 Birmingham C 15 0
2019–20 *Charlton Ath* 5 0 **5 0**
2020–21 Birmingham C 0 0 **182 10**
2020–21 Shrewsbury T 21 0
2021–22 Shrewsbury T 27 1 **67 3**

EBANKS-LANDELL, Ethan (D) 247 16
H: 6 2 W: 13 12 b.Oldbury 16-12-92
2009–10 Wolverhampton W 0 0
2010–11 Wolverhampton W 0 0
2011–12 Wolverhampton W 0 0
2012–13 Wolverhampton W 0 0
2012–13 *Bury* 24 0 **24 0**
2013–14 Wolverhampton W 7 2
2014–15 Wolverhampton W 14 2
2015–16 Wolverhampton W 21 1
2016–17 Wolverhampton W 0 0
2016–17 *Sheffield U* 34 5 **34 5**
2017–18 Wolverhampton W 0 0
2017–18 *Milton Keynes D* 29 2 **29 2**
2018–19 Wolverhampton W 0 0 **42 5**
2018–19 *Rochdale* 16 2 **16 2**
2019–20 Shrewsbury T 28 1
2020–21 Shrewsbury T 41 1
2021–22 Shrewsbury T 33 0 **102 2**

FLANAGAN, Tom (D) 245 11
H: 6 2 W: 11 05 b.Hammersmith 21-10-91
Internationals: Northern Ireland U21, Full caps.
2009–10 Milton Keynes D 1 0
2010–11 Milton Keynes D 2 0
2011–12 Milton Keynes D 21 3
2012–13 Milton Keynes D 0 0
2012–13 *Gillingham* 13 1 **13 1**
2012–13 *Barnet* 9 0 **9 0**
2013–14 Milton Keynes D 7 0
2013–14 *Stevenage* 2 0 **2 0**
2014–15 Milton Keynes D 6 0 **37 3**
2014–15 *Plymouth Arg* 4 0 **4 0**
2015–16 Burton Alb 18 0
2016–17 Burton Alb 30 0
2017–18 Burton Alb 27 2 **75 2**
2018–19 Sunderland 32 2
2019–20 Sunderland 18 1
2020–21 Sunderland 16 0
2021–22 Sunderland 25 1 **91 4**
2021–22 Shrewsbury T 14 1 **14 1**

GREGORY, Cameron (G) 0 0
H: 6 4 W: 11 11 b.Sutton Coldfield 20-1-00
2017–18 Shrewsbury T 0 0
2018–19 Shrewsbury T 0 0
2019–20 Shrewsbury T 0 0
2020–21 Shrewsbury T 0 0
2021–22 Shrewsbury T 0 0

LEAHY, Luke (M) 329 32
H: 5 10 W: 11 07 b.Coventry 19-11-92
From Rugby T.
2012–13 Falkirk 8 1
2013–14 Falkirk 19 1
2014–15 Falkirk 33 3
2015–16 Falkirk 36 3
2016–17 Falkirk 31 3 **127 11**
2017–18 Walsall 46 2
2018–19 Walsall 44 3 **90 5**
2019–20 Bristol R 32 0
2020–21 Bristol R 38 8 **70 8**
2021–22 Shrewsbury T 42 8 **42 8**

LLOYD, Louis (F) 0 0
H: 6 0 b. 15-10-03
From Connah's Quay Nomads.
2020–21 Shrewsbury T 0 0
2021–22 Shrewsbury T 0 0

MAROSI, Marko (G) 178 0
H: 6 3 W: 12 08 b.Michalovce 23-10-93
Internationals: Slovakia U21.
From Barnoldswick T.
2013–14 Wigan Ath 0 0
2014–15 Doncaster R 3 0
2015–16 Doncaster R 1 0
2016–17 Doncaster R 25 0
2017–18 Doncaster R 13 0
2018–19 Doncaster R 36 0 **78 0**
2019–20 Coventry C 34 0
2020–21 Coventry C 20 0
2021–22 Coventry C 0 0 **54 0**
2021–22 Shrewsbury T 46 0 **46 0**

NURSE, George (D) 72 2
H: 5 11 W: 12 04 b.Bristol 30-4-99
2019–20 Bristol C 0 0
2019–20 *Newport Co* 17 1 **17 1**
2020–21 Bristol C 0 0
2020–21 *Walsall* 10 1
2021–22 Walsall 0 0 **10 1**
2021–22 Bristol C 0 0
2021–22 Shrewsbury T 45 0 **45 0**

PENNINGTON, Matthew (D) 185 9
H: 6 1 W: 12 02 b.Warrington 6-10-94
Internationals: England U19.
2013–14 Everton 0 0
2013–14 *Tranmere R* 17 2 **17 2**
2014–15 Everton 0 0
2014–15 *Coventry C* 24 0 **24 0**
2015–16 Everton 4 0
2015–16 *Walsall* 5 0 **5 0**
2016–17 Everton 3 1
2017–18 Everton 0 0
2017–18 *Leeds U* 24 0 **24 0**
2018–19 Everton 0 0
2018–19 *Ipswich T* 30 1 **30 1**
2019–20 Everton 0 0
2019–20 *Hull C* 14 0 **14 0**
2020–21 Everton 0 0
2020–21 *Shrewsbury T* 19 2
2021–22 Everton 0 0 **7 1**
2021–22 Shrewsbury T 45 3 **64 5**

PIERRE, Aaron (D) 270 22
H: 6 1 W: 13 12 b.Southall 17-2-93
Internationals: Grenada Full caps.
2011–12 Brentford 0 0
2012–13 Brentford 0 0
2013–14 Brentford 0 0

2013–14 *Wycombe W* 8 1
2014–15 Wycombe W 42 4
2015–16 Wycombe W 40 2
2016–17 Wycombe W 39 2 **129 9**
2017–18 Northampton T 19 0
2018–19 Northampton T 41 6 **60 6**
2019–20 Shrewsbury T 30 3
2020–21 Shrewsbury T 26 4
2021–22 Shrewsbury T 25 0 **81 7**

PYKE, Rekeil (F) 77 1
H: 6 2 W: 10 03 b.Leeds 1-9-97
2016–17 Huddersfield T 0 0
2016–17 *Colchester U* 12 0 **12 0**
2017–18 Huddersfield T 0 0
2017–18 *Port Vale* 7 0 **7 0**
2018–19 Huddersfield T 0 0
2018–19 *Rochdale* 6 0
2019–20 Huddersfield T 1 0 **1 0**
2019–20 *Rochdale* 13 1 **19 1**
2020–21 Shrewsbury T 12 0
2021–22 Shrewsbury T 16 0 **28 0**
2021–22 *Scunthorpe U* 10 0 **10 0**

UDOH, Daniel (F) 125 21
H: 6 0 W: 13 01 b.Lagos 30-8-96
Internationals: Nigeria U17.
From Worcester C, North Greenwood U, Grays Ath, Hoddesdon T, Ilkeston.
2015–16 Crewe Alex 6 0
2016–17 Crewe Alex 9 0 **15 0**
From AFC Telford U.
2019–20 Shrewsbury T 25 4
2020–21 Shrewsbury T 39 4
2021–22 Shrewsbury T 46 13 **110 21**

VELA, Joshua (M) 260 17
H: 5 11 W: 11 07 b.Salford 14-12-93
2010–11 Bolton W 0 0
2011–12 Bolton W 3 0
2012–13 Bolton W 4 0
2013–14 Bolton W 0 0
2013–14 *Notts Co* 7 0 **7 0**
2014–15 Bolton W 29 0
2015–16 Bolton W 31 2
2016–17 Bolton W 46 9
2017–18 Bolton W 30 1
2018–19 Bolton W 17 0 **160 12**
2019–20 Hibernian 9 0 **9 0**
2019–20 Shrewsbury T 4 0
2020–21 Shrewsbury T 44 3
2021–22 Shrewsbury T 36 2 **84 5**

WHALLEY, Shaun (M) 286 42
H: 5 9 W: 10 08 b.Whiston 7-8-87
2004–05 Chester C 3 0 **3 0**
From Runcorn, Witton Alb.
2006–07 Accrington S 20 2
2007–08 Accrington S 31 3 **51 5**
From Wrexham, Droylsden, Hyde U, Southport.
2014–15 Luton T 18 3 **18 3**
2015–16 Shrewsbury T 24 6
2016–17 Shrewsbury T 32 3
2017–18 Shrewsbury T 44 8
2018–19 Shrewsbury T 32 2
2019–20 Shrewsbury T 23 2
2020–21 Shrewsbury T 38 9
2021–22 Shrewsbury T 21 4 **214 34**

Players retained or with offer of contract
Barlow, Josh; Craig, Kade; Kaninda, Ben; Wilson, Callum.

Scholars
Antal, Dennis-Zsombor; Bailey, Joshua Roy; Barlow, Joshua Daniel; Brown, Amarie Solomon; Cooper, Jenson George; Etienne, Kelechi Mijah Methuselah; Harper, Remmiko Jasiah; Hutchings, Declan Roy; Kaninda, Ben Benedict Tshiba; Knight, Theo Martin Robert; Lloyd, Louis Charles; Owusu-Gyimah, Nana Jr; Thompson, Reece John; Vicente, Savy Samuel Mulato.

SOUTHAMPTON (77)

ADAMS, Che (F) 259 65
H: 5 10 W: 10 06 b.Leicester 13-7-96
Internationals: England C, U20. Scotland Full caps.
From Ilkeston.
2014–15 Sheffield U 10 0
2015–16 Sheffield U 36 11
2016–17 Sheffield U 1 0 **47 11**
2016–17 Birmingham C 40 7
2017–18 Birmingham C 30 5
2018–19 Birmingham C 46 22 **116 34**
2019–20 Southampton 30 4
2020–21 Southampton 36 9
2021–22 Southampton 30 7 **96 20**

ARMITAGE, Will (D) 0 0
b. 7-3-05
2021–22 Cheltenham T 0 0
2021–22 Southampton 0 0

ARMSTRONG, Adam (F) 285 87
H: 5 8 W: 10 12 b.Newcastle upon Tyne 10-2-97
Internationals: England U16, U17, U18, U19, U20, U21.
2013–14 Newcastle U 4 0
2014–15 Newcastle U 11 0
2015–16 Newcastle U 0 0
2015–16 *Coventry C* 40 20 **40 20**
2016–17 Newcastle U 2 0
2016–17 *Barnsley* 34 6 **34 6**
2017–18 Newcastle U 0 0 **17 0**
2017–18 *Bolton W* 20 1 **20 1**
2017–18 *Blackburn R* 21 9
2018–19 Blackburn R 44 5
2019–20 Blackburn R 46 16
2020–21 Blackburn R 40 28
2021–22 Blackburn R 0 0 **151 58**
2021–22 Southampton 23 2 **23 2**

ARMSTRONG, Stuart (M) 342 55
H: 6 0 W: 10 10 b.Inverness 30-3-92
Internationals: Scotland U19, U21, Full caps.
2010–11 Dundee U 12 0
2011–12 Dundee U 23 1
2012–13 Dundee U 36 3
2013–14 Dundee U 36 8
2014–15 Dundee U 20 6 **127 18**
2014–15 Celtic 15 1
2015–16 Celtic 25 4
2016–17 Celtic 31 15
2017–18 Celtic 27 3 **98 23**
2018–19 Southampton 29 3
2019–20 Southampton 30 5
2020–21 Southampton 33 4
2021–22 Southampton 25 2 **117 14**

BEDNAREK, Jan (D) 179 8
H: 6 2 W: 12 02 b.Slupca 12-4-96
Internationals: Poland U16, U17, U18, U19, U20, U21, Full caps.
2013–14 Lech Poznan 2 0
2014–15 Lech Poznan 2 0
2015–16 Lech Poznan 0 0
2015–16 *Gornik Leczna* 17 0 **17 0**
2016–17 Lech Poznan 27 1 **31 1**
2017–18 Southampton 5 1
2018–19 Southampton 25 0
2019–20 Southampton 34 1
2020–21 Southampton 36 1
2021–22 Southampton 31 4 **131 7**

BELLIS, Sam (M) 0 0
b.Manchester 30-12-02
From Manchester C.
2020–21 Southampton 0 0
2021–22 Southampton 0 0

BYCROFT, Jack (G) 0 0
H: 6 0 W: 11 03 b.Salisbury 21-9-01
Internationals: England U19.
2020–21 Southampton 0 0
2021–22 Southampton 0 0

CABALLERO, Willy (G) 367 0
H: 6 1 W: 12 08 b.Santa Elena de UairÈn 28-9-81
Internationals: Argentina U21, Full caps.
2001–02 Boca Juniors 4 0
2002–03 Boca Juniors 4 0
2003–04 Boca Juniors 1 0
2004–05 Boca Juniors 6 0 **15 0**
2005–06 Elche 10 0
2006–07 Elche 39 0
2006–07 *Arsenal Sarandi* 13 0 **13 0**
2007–08 Elche 38 0
2008–09 Elche 38 0
2009–10 Elche 39 0
2010–11 Elche 22 0 **186 0**
2010–11 Malaga 15 0
2011–12 Malaga 28 0
2012–13 Malaga 36 0
2013–14 Malaga 38 0 **117 0**
2014–15 Manchester C 2 0
2015–16 Manchester C 4 0
2016–17 Manchester C 17 0 **23 0**
2017–18 Chelsea 3 0
2018–19 Chelsea 2 0
2019–20 Chelsea 5 0
2020–21 Chelsea 1 0
2021–22 Chelsea 0 0 **11 0**
2021–22 Southampton 2 0 **2 0**

CHAUKE, Kgaogelo (M) 0 0
H: 5 10 b.Pretoria 8-1-03
From Thatcham T.
2020–21 Southampton 0 0
2021–22 Southampton 0 0

DIALLO, Ibrahima (M) 87 0
H: 5 10 W: 10 10 b.Tours 8-3-99
Internationals: France U18, U19, U20, U21.
2017–18 Monaco 0 0
2018–19 Monaco 0 0
2018–19 *Brest* 23 0
2019–20 Brest 19 0
2020–21 Brest 0 0 **42 0**
2020–21 Southampton 22 0
2021–22 Southampton 23 0 **45 0**

DJENEPO, Moussa (F) 106 12
H: 5 10 W: 10 03 b.Bamako 15-6-98
Internationals: Mali U20, Full caps.
2017–18 Standard Liege 17 1
2018–19 Standard Liege 32 8 **49 9**
2019–20 Southampton 18 2
2020–21 Southampton 27 1
2021–22 Southampton 12 0 **57 3**

ELYOUNOUSSI, Mohamed (M) 289 84
H: 5 10 W: 11 00 b.Al Hoceima 4-8-94
Internationals: Norway U17, U18, U19, U21, Full caps.
2011 Sarpsborg 08 9 0
2012 Sarpsborg 08 26 9
2013 Sarpsborg 08 29 6 **64 15**
2014 Molde 30 13
2015 Molde 28 12
2016 Molde 12 5 **70 30**
2016–17 FC Basel 32 10
2017–18 FC Basel 33 11 **65 21**
2018–19 Southampton 16 0
2019–20 Southampton 0 0
2019–20 *Celtic* 10 4
2020–21 Southampton 0 0
2020–21 *Celtic* 34 10 **44 14**
2021–22 Southampton 30 4 **46 4**

FERRY, Will (M) 36 1
H: 5 9 b. 7-12-01
Internationals: Republic of Ireland U18, U19, U21.
2016–17 Bury 0 0
2017–18 Southampton 0 0
2018–19 Southampton 0 0
2019–20 Southampton 0 0
2020–21 Southampton 0 0
2021–22 Southampton 0 0
2021–22 *Crawley T* 36 1 **36 1**

FINNIGAN, Ryan (M) 0 0
b. 23-9-03
2020–21 Southampton 0 0
2021–22 Southampton 0 0

FORSTER, Fraser (G) 350 0
H: 6 7 W: 14 09 b.Hexham 17-3-88
Internationals: England Full caps.
2007–08 Newcastle U 0 0
2008–09 Newcastle U 0 0
2008–09 *Stockport Co* 6 0 **6 0**
2009–10 Newcastle U 0 0
2009–10 *Bristol R* 4 0 **4 0**
2009–10 *Norwich C* 38 0 **38 0**
2010–11 Newcastle U 0 0
2010–11 *Celtic* 36 0
2011–12 Newcastle U 0 0
2011–12 *Celtic* 33 0
2012–13 Celtic 34 0
2013–14 Celtic 37 0
2014–15 Southampton 30 0
2015–16 Southampton 18 0
2016–17 Southampton 38 0
2017–18 Southampton 20 0
2018–19 Southampton 1 0
2019–20 Southampton 0 0
2019–20 *Celtic* 28 0 **168 0**
2020–21 Southampton 8 0
2021–22 Southampton 19 0 **134 0**

LANCASHIRE, Oliver (D) 294 7
H: 6 1 W: 11 10 b.Basingstoke 13-12-88
2006–07 Southampton 0 0
2007–08 Southampton 0 0
2008–09 Southampton 11 0
2009–10 Southampton 2 0
2009–10 *Grimsby T* 25 1 **25 1**
2010–11 Walsall 29 0
2011–12 Walsall 20 1 **49 1**
2012–13 Aldershot T 12 0 **12 0**
2013–14 Rochdale 38 0
2014–15 Rochdale 21 0
2015–16 Rochdale 34 2 **93 2**
2016–17 Shrewsbury T 16 1 **16 1**
2017–18 Swindon T 35 1
2018–19 Swindon T 20 0 **55 1**
2019–20 Crewe Alex 9 0
2020–21 Crewe Alex 22 1 **31 1**
2021–22 Southampton 0 0 **13 0**

LEWIS, Harry (G) 30 0
H: 6 3 W: 12 02 b.Shrewsbury 20-12-97
Internationals: England U18.

2015–16	Shrewsbury T	0	0		
2016–17	Shrewsbury T	0	0		
2016–17	Southampton	0	0		
2017–18	Southampton	0	0		
2017–18	*Dundee U*	30	0	**30**	**0**
2018–19	Southampton	0	0		
2019–20	Southampton	0	0		
2020–21	Southampton	0	0		
2021–22	Southampton	0	0		

LIVRAMENTO, Valentino (D) 28 1
H: 5 8 W: 9 13 b.Croydon 12-11-02
Internationals: England U16, U17, U18, U19, U21.

2020–21	Chelsea	0	0		
2021–22	Chelsea	0	0		
2021–22	*Scunthorpe U*	0	0		
2021–22	Southampton	28	1	**28**	**1**

LONG, Shane (F) 480 97
H: 5 11 W: 12 11 b.Gortnahoe 22-1-87
Internationals: Republic of Ireland B, U21, Full caps.

2005	Cork C	1	0	**1**	**0**
2005–06	Reading	11	3		
2006–07	Reading	21	2		
2007–08	Reading	29	3		
2008–09	Reading	37	9		
2009–10	Reading	31	6		
2010–11	Reading	44	21		
2011–12	Reading	1	0	**174**	**44**
2011–12	WBA	32	8		
2012–13	WBA	34	8		
2013–14	WBA	15	3	**81**	**19**
2013–14	Hull C	15	4	**15**	**4**
2014–15	Southampton	32	5		
2015–16	Southampton	28	10		
2016–17	Southampton	32	3		
2017–18	Southampton	30	2		
2018–19	Southampton	26	5		
2019–20	Southampton	26	2		
2020–21	Southampton	11	0		
2020–21	*Bournemouth*	11	2	**11**	**2**
2021–22	Southampton	13	1	**198**	**28**

LYANCO, Vojnovic (D) 95 2
H: 6 2 W: 13 01 b.Vitoria-Gasteiz 1-2-97
Internationals: Serbia U19. Brazil U20, U23.
From Botafogo.

2015	Sao Paulo	9	0		
2016	Sao Paulo	12	1		
2017	Sao Paulo	0	0	**21**	**1**
2017–18	Torino	4	0		
2018–19	Torino	2	0		
2018–19	*Bologna*	13	1	**13**	**1**
2019–20	Torino	17	0		
2020–21	Torino	23	0		
2021–22	Torino	0	0	**46**	**0**
2021–22	Southampton	15	0	**15**	**0**

McCARTHY, Alex (G) 265 0
H: 6 4 W: 12 07 b.Guildford 3-12-89
Internationals: England U21, Full caps.

2008–09	Reading	0	0		
2008–09	*Aldershot T*	4	0	**4**	**0**
2009–10	Reading	0	0		
2009–10	*Yeovil T*	44	0	**44**	**0**
2010–11	Reading	13	0		
2010–11	*Brentford*	3	0	**3**	**0**
2011–12	Reading	0	0		
2011–12	*Leeds U*	6	0	**6**	**0**
2011–12	*Ipswich T*	10	0	**10**	**0**
2012–13	Reading	13	0		
2013–14	Reading	44	0	**70**	**0**
2014–15	QPR	3	0	**3**	**0**
2015–16	Crystal Palace	7	0	**7**	**0**
2016–17	Southampton	0	0		
2017–18	Southampton	18	0		
2018–19	Southampton	25	0		
2019–20	Southampton	28	0		
2020–21	Southampton	30	0		
2021–22	Southampton	17	0	**118**	**0**

MITCHELL, Ramello (M) 0 0
b.Birmingham 1-1-03
From Birmingham C.

2020–21	Southampton	0	0		
2021–22	Southampton	0	0		

N'LUNDULU, Daniel (F) 33 2
H: 6 1 b.France 5-2-99
Internationals: England U16.

2016–17	Southampton	0	0		
2017–18	Southampton	0	0		
2018–19	Southampton	0	0		
2019–20	Southampton	0	0		
2020–21	Southampton	13	0		
2021–22	Southampton	0	0	**13**	**0**
2021–22	*Lincoln C*	16	1	**16**	**1**
2021–22	*Cheltenham T*	4	1	**4**	**1**

OLAIGBE, Kazeem (F) 0 0
b. 2-1-03
Internationals: Belgium U16, U17, U19.
From Anderlecht.

2020–21	Southampton	0	0		
2021–22	Southampton	0	0		

PAMBOU, Leon (D) 0 0
b. 25-1-04
From Metz.

2020–21	Southampton	0	0		
2021–22	Southampton	0	0		

PEARCE, Luke (F) 0 0
Internationals: Republic of Ireland U18, U19.

2019–20	Walsall	0	0		
2020–21	Southampton	0	0		
2021–22	Southampton	0	0		

PERRAUD, Romain (D) 110 8
H: 5 8 W: 10 10 b.Toulouse 22-9-97
Internationals: France U17, U18, U19, U21.

2016–17	Nice	0	0		
2017–18	Nice	1	0		
2018–19	Nice	0	0	**1**	**0**
2018–19	*Paris FC*	33	5	**33**	**5**
2019–20	Brest	20	0		
2020–21	Brest	36	3		
2021–22	Brest	0	0	**56**	**3**
2021–22	Southampton	20	0	**20**	**0**

RAMSAY, Kayne (D) 30 1
H: 5 10 W: 12 13 b.Hackney 10-10-00
From Chelsea.

2018–19	Southampton	1	0		
2019–20	Southampton	0	0		
2019–20	*Shrewsbury T*	5	0	**5**	**0**
2020–21	Southampton	1	0		
2021–22	Southampton	0	0	**2**	**0**
2021–22	*Crewe Alex*	15	0	**15**	**0**
2021–22	*Ross Co*	8	1	**8**	**1**

REDMOND, Nathan (M) 368 39
H: 5 8 W: 11 11 b.Birmingham 6-3-94
Internationals: England U16, U17, U18, U19, U20, U21, Full caps.

2011–12	Birmingham C	24	5		
2012–13	Birmingham C	38	2	**62**	**7**
2013–14	Norwich C	34	1		
2014–15	Norwich C	43	4		
2015–16	Norwich C	35	6	**112**	**11**
2016–17	Southampton	37	7		
2017–18	Southampton	31	1		
2018–19	Southampton	38	6		
2019–20	Southampton	32	4		
2020–21	Southampton	29	2		
2021–22	Southampton	27	1	**194**	**21**

RODRIGUEZ, Jeremi (D) 0 0
From Las Palmas.

2020–21	Southampton	0	0		
2021–22	Southampton	0	0		
2021–22	*Burgos*	0	0		

ROMEU, Oriol (M) 328 8
H: 6 0 W: 13 01 b.Ulldecona 24-9-91
Internationals: Spain U17, U19, U20, U21, U23.

2008–09	Barcelona B	5	0		
2009–10	Barcelona B	26	0		
2010–11	Barcelona B	18	1	**49**	**1**
2010–11	Barcelona	1	0	**1**	**0**
2011–12	Chelsea	16	0		
2012–13	Chelsea	6	0		
2013–14	Chelsea	0	0		
2013–14	*Valencia*	13	0	**13**	**0**
2014–15	Chelsea	0	0	**22**	**0**
2014–15	*Stuttgart*	27	0	**27**	**0**
2015–16	Southampton	29	1		
2016–17	Southampton	35	1		
2017–18	Southampton	34	1		
2018–19	Southampton	31	1		
2019–20	Southampton	30	0		
2020–21	Southampton	21	1		
2021–22	Southampton	36	2	**216**	**7**

ROSS-LANG, Fedel (F) 0 0
Internationals: England U17.
From Manchester C.

2020–21	Southampton	0	0		
2021–22	Southampton	0	0		

SALISU, Mohammed (D) 77 1
H: 6 3 W: 12 13 b.Kumasi, Ghana 17-4-99

2017–18	Real Valladolid	0	0		
2018–19	Real Valladolid	0	0		
2019–20	Real Valladolid	31	1	**31**	**1**
2020–21	Valladolid	0	0		
2020–21	Southampton	12	0		
2021–22	Southampton	34	0	**46**	**0**

SIMEU, Dynel (D) 18 0
b.Yaounde, Cameroon 13-3-02
Internationals: England U17, U18.

2020–21	Chelsea	0	0		
2021–22	Chelsea	0	0		
2021–22	Southampton	0	0		
2021–22	*Carlisle U*	18	0	**18**	**0**

SMALES-BRAITHWAITE, Benni (F) 0 0
b.Leeds 29-4-02
Internationals: England U16.
From Manchester C.

2020–21	Southampton	0	0		
2021–22	Southampton	0	0		

SMALL, Thierry (D) 0 0
H: 5 9 b.Solihull 1-8-04
Internationals: England U18.
From WBA.

2020–21	Everton	0	0		
2021–22	Southampton	0	0		

SMALLBONE, William (M) 16 0
H: 5 8 W: 9 08 b.Basingstoke 21-2-00
Internationals: Republic of Ireland U18, U19, U21.

2016–17	Southampton	0	0		
2017–18	Southampton	0	0		
2018–19	Southampton	0	0		
2019–20	Southampton	9	0		
2020–21	Southampton	3	0		
2021–22	Southampton	4	0	**16**	**0**

STEPHENS, Jack (D) 189 5
H: 6 1 W: 11 11 b.Torpoint 27-1-94
Internationals: England U18, U19, U20, U21.

2010–11	Plymouth Arg	5	0	**5**	**0**
2010–11	Southampton	0	0		
2011–12	Southampton	0	0		
2012–13	Southampton	0	0		
2013–14	Southampton	0	0		
2013–14	*Swindon T*	10	0		
2014–15	Southampton	0	0		
2014–15	*Swindon T*	37	1	**47**	**1**
2015–16	Southampton	0	0		
2015–16	*Middlesbrough*	1	0	**1**	**0**
2015–16	*Coventry C*	16	0	**16**	**0**
2016–17	Southampton	17	0		
2017–18	Southampton	22	2		
2018–19	Southampton	24	1		
2019–20	Southampton	28	1		
2020–21	Southampton	18	0		
2021–22	Southampton	11	0	**120**	**4**

TELLA, Nathan (M) 33 1
H: 5 8 W: 11 00 b.Lambeth 5-7-99
From Arsenal.

2017–18	Southampton	0	0		
2018–19	Southampton	0	0		
2019–20	Southampton	1	0		
2020–21	Southampton	18	1		
2021–22	Southampton	14	0	**33**	**1**

VALERY, Yann (D) 49 2
H: 5 11 W: 11 00 b.Champigny-sur-Marne 22-2-99
Internationals: France U17, U18.
From Rennes.

2018–19	Southampton	23	2		
2019–20	Southampton	11	0		
2020–21	Southampton	3	0		
2020–21	*Birmingham C*	7	0	**7**	**0**
2021–22	Southampton	5	0	**42**	**2**

VOKINS, Jake (D) 26 0
b.Oxford 17-3-00
Internationals: England U17, U18, U19.

2019–20	Southampton	1	0		
2020–21	Southampton	1	0		
2020–21	*Sunderland*	4	0	**4**	**0**
2021–22	Southampton	0	0	**2**	**0**
2021–22	*Ross Co*	20	0	**20**	**0**

WALCOTT, Theo (F) 398 82
H: 5 9 W: 10 10 b.Stanmore 16-3-89
Internationals: England U16, U17, U19, U21, Full caps.

2005–06	Southampton	21	4		
2005–06	Arsenal	0	0		
2006–07	Arsenal	16	0		
2007–08	Arsenal	25	4		
2008–09	Arsenal	22	2		
2009–10	Arsenal	23	3		
2010–11	Arsenal	28	9		
2011–12	Arsenal	35	8		
2012–13	Arsenal	32	14		
2013–14	Arsenal	13	5		
2014–15	Arsenal	14	5		
2015–16	Arsenal	28	5		
2016–17	Arsenal	28	10		
2017–18	Arsenal	6	0	**270**	**65**
2017–18	Everton	14	3		
2018–19	Everton	37	5		
2019–20	Everton	25	2		
2020–21	Everton	1	0		
2020–21	*Southampton*	21	3		
2021–22	Everton	0	0	**77**	**10**
2021–22	Southampton	9	0	**51**	**7**

WALKER-PETERS, Kyle (F) 84 1
H: 5 8 W: 9 13 b.Edmonton 13-4-97
Internationals: England U18, U19, U20, U21, Full caps.

2015–16	Tottenham H	0	0		
2016–17	Tottenham H	0	0		
2017–18	Tottenham H	3	0		
2018–19	Tottenham H	6	0		
2019–20	Tottenham H	3	0	**12**	**0**
2019–20	*Southampton*	10	0		
2020–21	Southampton	30	0		
2021–22	Southampton	32	1	**72**	**1**

WARD-PROWSE, James (M) 305 40
H: 5 8 W: 10 06 b.Portsmouth 1-11-94
Internationals: England U17, U19, U20, U21, Full caps.

2011–12	Southampton	0	0		
2012–13	Southampton	15	0		
2013–14	Southampton	34	0		
2014–15	Southampton	25	1		
2015–16	Southampton	33	2		
2016–17	Southampton	30	4		
2017–18	Southampton	30	3		
2018–19	Southampton	26	7		
2019–20	Southampton	38	5		
2020–21	Southampton	38	8		
2021–22	Southampton	36	10	**305**	**40**

WATTS, Caleb (M) 4 0
H: 5 7 b. 16-1-02
Internationals: Australia U17, U23.
From QPR.

2020–21	Southampton	3	0		
2021–22	Southampton	0	0	**3**	**0**
2021–22	*Crawley T*	1	0	**1**	**0**

Players retained or with offer of contract
Babic, Goran; Ballard, Dominic; Dibling, Tyler; Edwards, Milan; Hall, Matthew; Lawrence, Nico; Otseh-Taiwo, Zuriel; Payne, Lewis; Tizzard, William; Turner, Jack; Wright, Oliver.

Scholars
Bailey, Samuel James; Beach, Edward James; Bragg, Cameron Roger; Carson, Matthew; Chavez-Munoz, Ryan Jorge; Davis, Sonnie; Doyle, Kamari Olivier; Hewlett, Jeremiah James; Higgs, Tommy Lee; Jeffries, Josh David; Lett, Joshua Matthew; Mohamed, Adli Hatim Othman Husain; Squires, Joshua David; Woods, Harvey James; Wright, Rylee Retained.

STEVENAGE (78)

ANDRADE, Bruno (M) 167 14
H: 5 9 W: 11 09 b.Viseu 2-10-93

2010–11	QPR	1	0		
2011–12	QPR	1	0		
2011–12	*Aldershot T*	1	0	**1**	**0**
2012–13	QPR	0	0		
2012–13	*Wycombe W*	23	2	**23**	**2**
2013–14	QPR	0	0		
2013–14	*Stevenage*	13	0		
2014–15	QPR	0	0	**2**	**0**
2014–15	*Stevenage*	16	1		

From Woking, Boreham Wood.

2018–19	Lincoln C	42	10		
2019–20	Lincoln C	17	1	**59**	**11**
2019–20	Salford C	7	0		
2020–21	Salford C	19	0		
2021–22	Salford C	0	0	**26**	**0**
2021–22	Stevenage	27	0	**56**	**1**

BARRY, Bradley (D) 132 2
H: 6 0 W: 12 00 b.Hastings 13-12-95

2013–14	Brighton & HA	0	0		
2014–15	Brighton & HA	0	0		
2015–16	Swindon T	35	0		
2016–17	Swindon T	23	1	**58**	**1**
2016–17	Chesterfield	0	0		
2017–18	Chesterfield	29	0	**29**	**0**

From Chesterfield.

2020–21	Barrow	33	1	**33**	**1**
2021–22	Stevenage	12	0	**12**	**0**

BASTIEN, Sacha (G) 16 0
H: 6 5 W: 14 05 b.Metz 22-1-95

2013–14	Reims	0	0		
2014–15	Reims	1	0	**1**	**0**
2017–18	Bastia-Borgo	3	0	**3**	**0**
2018–19	US Granville	10	0	**10**	**0**
2019–20	Stevenage	1	0		
2020–21	Gillingham	0	0		
2021–22	Stevenage	1	0	**2**	**0**

CARTER, Charlie (M) 67 8
H: 6 1 W: 11 11 b.London 25-10-96
From Woking.

2019–20	Stevenage	29	5		
2020–21	Stevenage	18	3		
2021–22	Stevenage	20	0	**67**	**8**

COCHRANE, Owen (D) 1 0
b.Huntingdon 3-9-04

2021–22	Stevenage	1	0	**1**	**0**

COKER, Ben (D) 301 5
H: 5 11 W: 11 09 b.Hatfield 17-6-89
From Histon.

2010–11	Colchester U	20	0		
2011–12	Colchester U	20	0		
2012–13	Colchester U	1	0	**41**	**0**
2013–14	Southend U	45	2		
2014–15	Southend U	32	1		
2015–16	Southend U	40	1		
2016–17	Southend U	31	0		
2017–18	Southend U	22	0		
2018–19	Southend U	16	0	**186**	**4**
2019–20	Lincoln C	0	0		
2019–20	*Cambridge U*	0	0		
2020–21	Stevenage	38	0		
2021–22	Stevenage	36	1	**74**	**1**

CUTHBERT, Scott (D) 482 24
H: 6 2 W: 14 01 b.Alexandria 15-6-87
Internationals: Scotland U19, U20, U21, B.

2004–05	Celtic	0	0		
2005–06	Celtic	0	0		
2006–07	Celtic	0	0		
2006–07	*Livingston*	4	1	**4**	**1**
2007–08	Celtic	0	0		
2008–09	Celtic	0	0		
2008–09	*St Mirren*	29	0	**29**	**0**
2009–10	Swindon T	39	3		
2010–11	Swindon T	41	2	**80**	**5**
2011–12	Leyton Orient	33	1		
2012–13	Leyton Orient	18	0		
2013–14	Leyton Orient	44	4		
2014–15	Leyton Orient	38	2	**133**	**7**
2015–16	Luton T	36	0		
2016–17	Luton T	38	1		
2017–18	Luton T	23	2	**97**	**3**
2018–19	Stevenage	46	2		
2019–20	Stevenage	21	2		
2020–21	Stevenage	33	1		
2021–22	Stevenage	39	3	**139**	**8**

DALY, James (F) 46 3
H: 5 10 W: 11 05 b.Brighton 12-1-00

2017–18	Crystal Palace	0	0		
2018–19	Crystal Palace	0	0		
2019–20	Crystal Palace	0	0		
2019–20	Bristol R	3	0		
2020–21	Bristol R	28	3		
2021–22	Bristol R	0	0	**31**	**3**
2021–22	Stevenage	15	0	**15**	**0**

DREYER, Sam (D) 0 0
b. 3-1-04

2020–21	Stevenage	0	0		
2021–22	Stevenage	0	0		

FERNANDEZ, Luis (D) 5 0
b. 28-9-01

2019–20	Stevenage	4	0		
2020–21	Stevenage	1	0		
2021–22	Stevenage	0	0	**5**	**0**

JOHNSON, Finlay (M) 0 0
b. 7-7-04

2020–21	Stevenage	0	0		
2021–22	Stevenage	0	0		

LINES, Chris (M) 516 41
H: 6 2 W: 12 00 b.Bristol 30-11-85

2005–06	Bristol R	4	0		
2006–07	Bristol R	7	0		
2007–08	Bristol R	27	3		
2008–09	Bristol R	45	4		
2009–10	Bristol R	42	10		
2010–11	Bristol R	42	3		
2011–12	Bristol R	1	0		
2011–12	Sheffield W	41	3		
2012–13	Sheffield W	6	0	**47**	**3**
2012–13	*Milton Keynes D*	16	0	**16**	**0**
2013–14	Port Vale	34	1		
2014–15	Port Vale	27	2	**61**	**3**
2015–16	Bristol R	33	0		
2016–17	Bristol R	44	3		
2017–18	Bristol R	42	5		
2018–19	Bristol R	19	1	**306**	**29**
2019–20	Northampton T	31	2		
2020–21	Northampton T	4	1	**35**	**3**
2020–21	Stevenage	20	0		
2021–22	Stevenage	31	3	**51**	**3**

LIST, Elliott (M) 187 27
H: 5 10 W: 11 05 b.Camberwell 12-5-97
From Crystal Palace.

2015–16	Gillingham	6	0		
2016–17	Gillingham	15	0		
2017–18	Gillingham	23	2		
2018–19	Gillingham	37	5		
2019–20	Gillingham	4	0	**85**	**7**
2019–20	Stevenage	21	2		
2020–21	Stevenage	44	9		
2021–22	Stevenage	37	9	**102**	**20**

MARSHALL, Ross (D) 20 0
H: 6 3 W: 12 08 b.Norwich 9-10-99
From Ipswich T, Maidstone U.

2020–21	Stevenage	15	0		
2021–22	Stevenage	5	0	**20**	**0**

NORRIS, Luke (F) 324 80
H: 6 0 W: 13 03 b.Stevenage 3-6-93

2011–12	Brentford	1	0		
2012–13	Brentford	0	0		
2013–14	Brentford	1	0	**2**	**0**
2013–14	*Northampton T*	10	4	**10**	**4**
2013–14	*Dagenham & R*	19	4	**19**	**4**
2014–15	Gillingham	37	6		
2015–16	Gillingham	33	8	**70**	**14**
2016–17	Swindon T	39	4		
2017–18	Swindon T	35	13	**74**	**17**
2018–19	Colchester U	34	7		
2019–20	Colchester U	32	9		
2020–21	Colchester U	17	4	**83**	**20**
2020–21	Stevenage	23	7		
2021–22	Stevenage	43	14	**66**	**21**

O'NEILL, Luke (D) 221 7
H: 6 0 W: 11 05 b.Slough 20-8-91
Internationals: England U17.

2009–10	Leicester C	1	0	**1**	**0**
2009–10	*Tranmere R*	4	0	**4**	**0**

From Kettering T, Mansfield T

2012–13	Burnley	1	0		
2013–14	Burnley	0	0		
2013–14	*York C*	15	1	**15**	**1**
2013–14	*Southend U*	1	0		
2014–15	Burnley	0	0	**1**	**0**
2014–15	*Scunthorpe U*	13	0	**13**	**0**
2014–15	*Leyton Orient*	8	0	**8**	**0**
2015–16	Southend U	14	0		
2016–17	Southend U	17	1	**32**	**1**
2017–18	Gillingham	38	1		
2018–19	Gillingham	38	3	**76**	**4**
2019–20	AFC Wimbledon	31	1		
2020–21	AFC Wimbledon	28	0		
2021–22	AFC Wimbledon	0	0	**59**	**1**
2021–22	Stevenage	12	0	**12**	**0**

O'REILLY, Luke (G) 0 0
H: 6 0 W: 11 09 b.Hackney 27-5-96
From Cardiff C, Tottenham H.

2018–19	Carlisle U	0	0		
2021–22	Stevenage	0	0		

OSBORNE, Elliot (M) 51 2
H: 6 0 W: 11 11 b.Stoke-on-Trent 12-5-96

2016–17	Fleetwood T	0	0		
2017–18	Fleetwood T	0	0		
2017–18	*Morecambe*	11	0	**11**	**0**

From Southport, Stockport Co.

2020–21	Stevenage	26	2		
2021–22	Stevenage	14	0	**40**	**2**

Transferred to Altrincham, January 2022.

PROSSER, Luke (D) 332 17
H: 6 3 W: 12 06 b.Enfield 28-5-88
From Tottenham H.

2005–06	Port Vale	0	0		
2006–07	Port Vale	0	0		
2007–08	Port Vale	5	0		
2008–09	Port Vale	26	1		
2009–10	Port Vale	2	1	**33**	**2**
2010–11	Southend U	17	1		
2011–12	Southend U	21	1		
2012–13	Southend U	25	0		
2013–14	Southend U	25	3		
2014–15	Southend U	30	0		
2015–16	Southend U	13	2	**131**	**7**
2015–16	*Northampton T*	8	0	**8**	**0**
2016–17	Colchester U	14	0		
2017–18	Colchester U	16	1		
2018–19	Colchester U	38	2		
2019–20	Colchester U	35	3	**103**	**6**
2020–21	Stevenage	30	1		
2021–22	Stevenage	27	1	**57**	**2**

READ, Arthur (M) 51 3
H: 5 10 W: 10 01 b.Leighton Buzzard 3-11-99

2018–19	Luton T	0	0		
2019–20	Brentford	0	0		
2020–21	Brentford	0	0		
2020–21	*Stevenage*	32	2		
2021–22	Stevenage	19	1	**51**	**3**

REEVES, Jake (M) 229 8
H: 5 8 W: 11 00 b.Lewisham 30-6-93

2010–11	Brentford	1	0		
2011–12	Brentford	8	0		
2012–13	Brentford	6	0		
2012–13	*AFC Wimbledon*	5	0		
2013–14	Brentford	20	0	**35**	**0**
2014–15	Swindon T	10	1	**10**	**1**
2014–15	AFC Wimbledon	23	2		
2015–16	AFC Wimbledon	40	1		
2016–17	AFC Wimbledon	46	1	**114**	**4**
2017–18	Bradford C	25	0		

2018–19 Bradford C 0 0
2019–20 Bradford C 18 1 **43 1**
From Notts Co.
2021–22 Stevenage 27 2 **27 2**

REID, Jamie (F) 100 16
H: 5 11 W: 11 09 b.Torquay 15-7-94
Internationals: Northern Ireland U21.
2012–13 Exeter C 4 2
2013–14 Exeter C 6 0
2014–15 Exeter C 0 0
2015–16 Exeter C 13 1
2016–17 Exeter C 0 0 **23 3**
From Torquay U.
2020–21 Mansfield T 39 6
2021–22 Mansfield T 0 0 **39 6**
2021–22 Stevenage 38 7 **38 7**

SMITH, Jack (M) 29 0
H: 6 1 W: 13 05 b.Hatfield 15-9-01
2019–20 Stevenage 1 0
2020–21 Stevenage 25 0
2021–22 Stevenage 3 0 **29 0**

SMITH, Timmy (G) 0 0
b. 29-11-03
2020–21 Stevenage 0 0
2021–22 Stevenage 0 0

TAYLOR, Jake (M) 354 36
H: 5 10 W: 12 02 b.Ascot 1-12-91
Internationals: Wales U17, U19, U21, Full caps.
2010–11 Reading 1 0
2011–12 Reading 0 0
2011–12 *Aldershot T* 3 0 **3 0**
2011–12 *Exeter C* 30 3
2012–13 Reading 0 0
2012–13 *Cheltenham T* 8 1 **8 1**
2012–13 *Crawley T* 4 0 **4 0**
2013–14 Reading 8 0
2014–15 Reading 22 2
2014–15 *Leyton Orient* 3 0 **3 0**
2015–16 Reading 0 0 **31 2**
2015–16 *Motherwell* 7 0 **7 0**
2015–16 Exeter C 16 4
2016–17 Exeter C 43 4
2017–18 Exeter C 44 8
2018–19 Exeter C 46 3
2019–20 Exeter C 33 2
2020–21 Exeter C 44 6
2021–22 Exeter C 0 0 **256 30**
2021–22 Stevenage 42 3 **42 3**

TINUBU, Sam (M) 1 0
b.Enfield 28-9-04
2020–21 Stevenage 0 0
2021–22 Stevenage 1 0 **1 0**

TOWNSEND-WEST, Mackye (D) 0 0
b.Camden 1-8-03
2019–20 Stevenage 0 0
2020–21 Stevenage 0 0
2021–22 Stevenage 0 0

UPSON, Edward (M) 410 22
H: 5 10 W: 11 07 b.Bury St Edmunds 21-11-89
Internationals: England U17, U19.
2006–07 Ipswich T 0 0
2007–08 Ipswich T 0 0
2008–09 Ipswich T 0 0
2009–10 Ipswich T 0 0
2009–10 *Barnet* 9 1 **9 1**
2010–11 Yeovil T 23 0
2011–12 Yeovil T 41 3
2012–13 Yeovil T 41 2
2013–14 Yeovil T 24 4 **129 9**
2013–14 Millwall 10 0
2014–15 Millwall 26 2
2015–16 Millwall 32 0 **68 2**
2016–17 Milton Keynes D 42 3
2017–18 Milton Keynes D 37 3 **79 6**
2018–19 Bristol R 35 1
2019–20 Bristol R 33 2
2020–21 Bristol R 26 1 **94 4**
2021–22 Newport Co 16 0 **16 0**
2021–22 Stevenage 15 0 **15 0**

VANCOOTEN, Terence (D) 117 0
H: 6 1 W: 12 04 b.Kingston upon Thames 29-12-97
Internationals: Guyana Full caps.
From Staines T.
2016–17 Reading 0 0
2017–18 Stevenage 22 0
2018–19 Stevenage 12 0
2019–20 Stevenage 16 0
2020–21 Stevenage 29 0
2021–22 Stevenage 38 0 **117 0**

WALKER, Laurie (G) 17 0
H: 6 5 W: 11 09 b.Bedford 14-10-89
From Oxford C, Brackley T, Hemel Hempstead T.
2020–21 Milton Keynes D 0 0
2020–21 *Oldham Ath* 13 0
2021–22 Oldham Ath 2 0 **15 0**
2021–22 Milton Keynes D 1 0 **1 0**
2021–22 Stevenage 1 0 **1 0**

WILDIN, Luther (D) 139 4
H: 5 10 W: 11 11 b.Leicester 3-12-97
Internationals: Antigua and Barbuda U20, Full caps.
2015–16 Notts Co 0 0
2016–17 Notts Co 0 0
From Nuneaton T.
2018–19 Stevenage 39 1
2019–20 Stevenage 21 1
2020–21 Stevenage 39 2
2021–22 Stevenage 40 0 **139 4**

WILLIAMS, Alfie (M) 1 0
b.Hemel Hempstead 20-4-03
2020–21 Stevenage 1 0
2021–22 Stevenage 0 0 **1 0**

Scholars
Aitken, Alexander James; Alexandrou, Theo Andreas; Bugyei-Kyei, Kwadwo Ankapong; Cochrane, Owen Jamie; Edgeworth, George David; Giroud, Harry Marcel; Granville, Max Reece Kai; Halpin, Cian James; Johnson, Finlay Joseph; Lynn, Lewis Stephen; Mahoney, Morgan James; Ogwuazor, Jaden Ogochukwu; Onyeagwara, Obidinma Chigozie Chibuzo; Siggers, Ben Kenneth; Smith, Harrison James; Stanley, Freddie Marc; Stevenson, Teddy Dean; Watkiss, Jake Philip Keith; Wilson, Jack Robert Michael.

STOKE C (79)

ADEBAMBO, Gabriel (M) 0 0
b. 27-2-02
Internationals: Republic of Ireland U18.
From Dundalk.
2020–21 Stoke C 0 0
2021–22 Stoke C 0 0

AFOBE, Benik (F) 339 85
H: 6 0 W: 12 04 b.Leyton 12-2-93
Internationals: England U16, U17, U19, U21. DR Congo Full caps.
2009–10 Arsenal 0 0
2010–11 Arsenal 0 0
2010–11 *Huddersfield T* 28 5 **28 5**
2011–12 Arsenal 0 0
2011–12 *Reading* 3 0 **3 0**
2012–13 Arsenal 0 0
2012–13 *Bolton W* 20 2 **20 2**
2012–13 *Millwall* 5 0
2013–14 Arsenal 0 0
2013–14 *Sheffield W* 12 2 **12 2**
2014–15 Arsenal 0 0
2014–15 *Milton Keynes D* 22 10 **22 10**
2014–15 Wolverhampton W 21 13
2015–16 Wolverhampton W 25 9
2015–16 Bournemouth 15 4
2016–17 Bournemouth 31 6
2017–18 Bournemouth 17 0 **63 10**
2017–18 *Wolverhampton W* 16 6
2018–19 Wolverhampton W 0 0 **62 28**
2018–19 *Stoke C* 45 8
2019–20 Stoke C 1 0
2019–20 *Bristol C* 12 3 **12 3**
2020–21 Stoke C 0 0
2020–21 *Trabzonspor* 28 5 **28 5**
2021–22 Stoke C 0 0 **46 8**
2021–22 *Millwall* 38 12 **43 12**

ALLEN, Joe (M) 430 29
H: 5 7 W: 9 11 b.Carmarthen 14-3-90
Internationals: Wales U17, U19, U21, Full caps. Great Britain.
2006–07 Swansea C 1 0
2007–08 Swansea C 6 0
2008–09 Swansea C 23 1
2009–10 Swansea C 21 0
2010–11 Swansea C 40 2
2011–12 Swansea C 36 4
2012–13 Swansea C 0 0 **127 7**
2012–13 Liverpool 27 0
2013–14 Liverpool 24 1
2014–15 Liverpool 21 1
2015–16 Liverpool 19 2 **91 4**
2016–17 Stoke C 36 6
2017–18 Stoke C 36 2
2018–19 Stoke C 46 6
2019–20 Stoke C 35 4
2020–21 Stoke C 18 0
2021–22 Stoke C 41 0 **212 18**

BAKER, Lewis (M) 185 30
H: 6 1 W: 11 00 b.Luton 25-4-95
Internationals: England U17, U19, U20, U21.
2012–13 Chelsea 0 0
2013–14 Chelsea 0 0
2014–15 Chelsea 0 0
2014–15 *Sheffield W* 4 0 **4 0**
2014–15 *Milton Keynes D* 12 3 **12 3**
2015–16 Chelsea 0 0
2015–16 *Vitesse* 31 5
2016–17 Chelsea 0 0
2016–17 *Vitesse* 33 10 **64 15**
2017–18 Chelsea 0 0
2017–18 *Middlesbrough* 12 1 **12 1**
2018–19 Chelsea 0 0
2018–19 *Leeds U* 11 0 **11 0**
2018–19 *Reading* 19 1 **19 1**
2019–20 Chelsea 0 0
2019–20 *Fortuna Dusseldorf* 8 0 **8 0**
2020–21 Chelsea 0 0
2020–21 *Trabzonspor* 34 2 **34 2**
2021–22 Chelsea 0 0
2021–22 Stoke C 21 8 **21 8**

BONHAM, Jack (G) 179 0
H: 6 4 W: 14 13 b.Stevenage 14-9-93
Internationals: Republic of Ireland U17.
2010–11 Watford 0 0
2011–12 Watford 0 0
2012–13 Watford 1 0 **1 0**
2013–14 Brentford 1 0
2014–15 Brentford 0 0
2015–16 Brentford 0 0
2016–17 Brentford 1 0
2017–18 Brentford 0 0
2017–18 *Carlisle U* 42 0 **42 0**
2018–19 Brentford 0 0 **2 0**
2018–19 *Bristol R* 40 0 **40 0**
2019–20 Gillingham 35 0
2020–21 Gillingham 44 0 **79 0**
2021–22 Stoke C 15 0 **15 0**

BROWN, Jacob (F) 173 29
H: 5 10 W: 9 11 b.Halifax 10-4-98
Internationals: Scotland Full caps.
From Guiseley.
2014–15 Barnsley 0 0
2015–16 Barnsley 0 0
2016–17 Barnsley 2 0
2017–18 Barnsley 0 0
2017–18 *Chesterfield* 13 0 **13 0**
2018–19 Barnsley 32 8
2019–20 Barnsley 40 3 **74 11**
2020–21 Stoke C 41 5
2021–22 Stoke C 45 13 **86 18**

BURSIK, Josef (G) 66 0
H: 6 2 W: 11 00 b.Lambeth 12-7-00
Internationals: England U17, U18, U19, U20, U21.
From AFC Wimbledon.
2019–20 Stoke C 0 0
2019–20 *Accrington S* 16 0 **16 0**
2020–21 Stoke C 15 0
2020–21 *Doncaster R* 10 0 **10 0**
2020–21 *Peterborough U* 6 0 **6 0**
2020–21 *Lincoln C* 0 0
2021–22 Stoke C 19 0 **34 0**

CAMPBELL, Tyrese (F) 97 24
H: 6 0 W: 11 11 b.Cheadle Hulme 28-12-99
Internationals: England U17, U20.
From Manchester C.
2017–18 Stoke C 4 0
2018–19 Stoke C 3 0
2018–19 *Shrewsbury T* 15 5 **15 5**
2019–20 Stoke C 33 9
2020–21 Stoke C 16 6
2021–22 Stoke C 26 4 **82 19**

CHESTER, James (D) 379 21
H: 5 10 W: 11 11 b.Warrington 23-1-89
Internationals: Wales Full caps.
2007–08 Manchester U 0 0
2008–09 Manchester U 0 0
2008–09 *Peterborough U* 5 0 **5 0**
2009–10 Manchester U 0 0
2009–10 *Plymouth Arg* 3 0 **3 0**
2010–11 Manchester U 0 0
2010–11 *Carlisle U* 18 2 **18 2**
2010–11 Hull C 21 1
2011–12 Hull C 44 2
2012–13 Hull C 44 1
2013–14 Hull C 24 1
2014–15 Hull C 23 2 **156 7**
2015–16 WBA 13 0 **13 0**
2016–17 Aston Villa 45 3
2017–18 Aston Villa 46 4
2018–19 Aston Villa 28 5
2019–20 Aston Villa 0 0 **119 12**
2019–20 *Stoke C* 16 0
2020–21 Stoke C 32 0
2021–22 Stoke C 17 0 **65 0**

CLUCAS, Sam (M) 353 47
H: 5 10 W: 11 09 b.Lincoln 25-9-90
Internationals: England C.
2009–10 Lincoln C 0 0

2010–11 Jerez Industrial 20 0 **20 0**
2011–12 Hereford U 17 0 **17 0**
From Hereford U.
2013–14 Mansfield T 38 8
2014–15 Mansfield T 5 0 **43 8**
2014–15 Chesterfield 41 9 **41 9**
2015–16 Hull C 44 6
2016–17 Hull C 37 3
2017–18 Hull C 3 0 **84 9**
2017–18 Swansea C 29 3 **29 3**
2018–19 Stoke C 26 3
2019–20 Stoke C 44 11
2020–21 Stoke C 24 2
2021–22 Stoke C 25 2 **119 18**

COATES, Kieran (D) 8 0
b.Smallthorne 9-12-00
2020–21 Stoke C 0 0
2021–22 Stoke C 0 0
2022 *Cork C* 8 0 **8 0**

DOUGHTY, Alfie (M) 56 4
H: 6 0 W: 10 10 b.Poplar 21-12-99
2018–19 Charlton Ath 0 0
2019–20 Charlton Ath 29 2
2020–21 Charlton Ath 7 1 **36 3**
2020–21 Stoke C 0 0
2021–22 Stoke C 11 0 **11 0**
2021–22 *Cardiff C* 9 1 **9 1**

DUHANEY, Demeaco (D) 23 0
H: 5 11 W: 11 00 b.Manchester 13-10-98
Internationals: England U18, U20.
2017–18 Manchester C 0 0
2018–19 Huddersfield T 1 0
2019–20 Huddersfield T 6 0
2020–21 Huddersfield T 13 0 **20 0**
2021–22 Stoke C 3 0 **3 0**

EDWARDS, Thomas (D) 102 1
b. 22-1-99
Internationals: England U20.
2016–17 Stoke C 0 0
2017–18 Stoke C 6 0
2018–19 Stoke C 27 1
2019–20 Stoke C 13 0
2020–21 Stoke C 0 0
2020–21 *Fleetwood T* 11 0 **11 0**
2021 *New York Red Bulls* 28 0
2021–22 Stoke C 0 0 **46 1**
2022 *New York Red Bulls* 17 0 **45 0**

ETEBO, Peter (M) 147 10
H: 5 8 W: 11 00 b.Warri, Nigeria 9-11-95
Internationals: Nigeria U23, Full caps.
From Warri Wolves.
2015–16 Feirense 4 1
2016–17 Feirense 23 2
2017–18 Feirense 18 4 **45 7**
2017–18 *Las Palmas* 14 0 **14 0**
2018–19 Stoke C 34 2
2019–20 Stoke C 11 0
2019–20 *Getafe* 10 1 **10 1**
2020–21 Stoke C 0 0
2020–21 *Galatasaray* 24 0 **24 0**
2021–22 Stoke C 0 0 **45 2**
2021–22 *Watford* 9 0 **9 0**

FIELDING, Frank (G) 326 0
H: 6 1 W: 12 00 b.Blackburn 4-4-88
Internationals: England U19, U21.
2006–07 Blackburn R 0 0
2007–08 Blackburn R 0 0
2007–08 *Wycombe W* 36 0 **36 0**
2008–09 Blackburn R 0 0
2008–09 *Northampton T* 12 0 **12 0**
2008–09 *Rochdale* 23 0
2009–10 Blackburn R 0 0
2009–10 *Rochdale* 18 0 **41 0**
2009–10 *Leeds U* 0 0
2010–11 Blackburn R 0 0
2010–11 *Derby Co* 16 0
2011–12 Derby Co 44 0
2012–13 Derby Co 16 0 **76 0**
2013–14 Bristol C 16 0
2014–15 Bristol C 46 0
2015–16 Bristol C 21 0
2016–17 Bristol C 27 0
2017–18 Bristol C 43 0
2018–19 Bristol C 5 0 **158 0**
2019–20 Millwall 1 0
2020–21 Millwall 0 0 **1 0**
2021–22 Stoke C 0 0
2021–22 *Salford C* 2 0 **2 0**

FLETCHER, Steven (F) 554 146
H: 6 1 W: 12 00 b.Shrewsbury 26-3-87
Internationals: Scotland U20, U21, B, Full caps.
2003–04 Hibernian 5 0
2004–05 Hibernian 20 5
2005–06 Hibernian 34 8
2006–07 Hibernian 31 6
2007–08 Hibernian 32 13
2008–09 Hibernian 34 11 **156 43**
2009–10 Burnley 35 8 **35 8**
2010–11 Wolverhampton W 29 10
2011–12 Wolverhampton W 32 12 **61 22**
2012–13 Sunderland 28 11
2013–14 Sunderland 20 3
2014–15 Sunderland 30 5
2015–16 Sunderland 16 4 **94 23**
2015–16 *Marseille* 12 2 **12 2**
2016–17 Sheffield W 38 10
2017–18 Sheffield W 19 2
2018–19 Sheffield W 40 11
2019–20 Sheffield W 27 13 **124 36**
2020–21 Stoke C 37 9
2021–22 Stoke C 35 3 **72 12**

FORRESTER, William (D) 8 1
H: 6 0 W: 11 09 b.Stoke-on-Trent 29-6-01
2020–21 Stoke C 1 1
2021–22 Stoke C 3 0 **4 1**
2021–22 *Mansfield T* 4 0 **4 0**

FOX, Morgan (D) 230 5
H: 6 1 W: 12 04 b.Chelmsford 21-9-93
Internationals: Wales U21.
2012–13 Charlton Ath 0 0
2013–14 Charlton Ath 6 0
2013–14 *Notts Co* 7 1 **7 1**
2014–15 Charlton Ath 31 0
2015–16 Charlton Ath 42 1
2016–17 Charlton Ath 24 0 **103 1**
2016–17 Sheffield W 10 1
2017–18 Sheffield W 28 0
2018–19 Sheffield W 25 0
2019–20 Sheffield W 27 2 **90 3**
2020–21 Stoke C 20 0
2021–22 Stoke C 10 0 **30 0**

GOODWIN, William (F) 10 1
H: 6 1 b.Tarporley 7-5-02
From FC Chester.
2020–21 Stoke C 0 0
2021–22 Stoke C 0 0
2021–22 *Hartlepool U* 10 1 **10 1**

HEMFREY, Robbie (G) 0 0
H: 6 4 W: 13 05 b.Wishaw 21-2-02
Internationals: Scotland U16, U17.
From Motherwell.
2020–21 Stoke C 0 0
2021–22 Stoke C 0 0

INCE, Tom (M) 381 87
H: 5 10 W: 10 06 b.Stockport 30-1-92
Internationals: England U17, U19, U21.
2009–10 Liverpool 0 0
2010–11 Liverpool 0 0
2010–11 *Notts Co* 6 2 **6 2**
2011–12 Blackpool 33 6
2012–13 Blackpool 44 18
2013–14 Blackpool 23 7 **100 31**
2013–14 *Crystal Palace* 8 1 **8 1**
2014–15 Hull C 7 0 **7 0**
2014–15 *Nottingham F* 6 0 **6 0**
2014–15 *Derby Co* 18 11
2015–16 Derby Co 42 12
2016–17 Derby Co 45 14 **105 37**
2017–18 Huddersfield T 33 2 **33 2**
2018–19 Stoke C 38 6
2019–20 Stoke C 38 3
2020–21 Stoke C 7 0
2020–21 *Luton T* 7 0 **7 0**
2021–22 Stoke C 11 3 **94 12**
2021–22 *Reading* 15 2 **15 2**

JAGIELKA, Phil (D) 632 32
H: 6 0 W: 13 01 b.Sale 17-8-82
Internationals: England U20, U21, B, Full caps.
1999–2000 Sheffield U 1 0
2000–01 Sheffield U 15 0
2001–02 Sheffield U 23 3
2002–03 Sheffield U 42 0
2003–04 Sheffield U 43 3
2004–05 Sheffield U 46 0
2005–06 Sheffield U 46 8
2006–07 Sheffield U 38 4
2007–08 Everton 34 1
2008–09 Everton 34 0
2009–10 Everton 12 0
2010–11 Everton 33 1
2011–12 Everton 30 2
2012–13 Everton 36 2
2013–14 Everton 26 0
2014–15 Everton 37 4
2015–16 Everton 21 0
2016–17 Everton 27 3
2017–18 Everton 25 0
2018–19 Everton 7 1 **322 14**
2019–20 Sheffield U 6 0
2020–21 Sheffield U 10 0
2021–22 Sheffield U 0 0 **270 18**
2021–22 Derby Co 20 0 **20 0**
2021–22 Stoke C 20 0 **20 0**

JARRETT, Patrick (M) 0 0
H: 5 10 b.Nantwich 23-11-01
2020–21 Stoke C 0 0
2021–22 Stoke C 0 0

JONES, Edward (D) 3 0
b.Chester 25-10-01
Internationals: Wales U17, U21.
From Bury.
2020–21 Stoke C 0 0
2021–22 Stoke C 0 0
2021–22 *Hartlepool U* 3 0 **3 0**

MACARI, Lewis (D) 21 0
Internationals: Scotland U18, U19.
2020–21 Stoke C 0 0
2021–22 Stoke C 0 0
2022 *Dundalk* 21 0 **21 0**

MAJA, Josh (F) 118 29
H: 5 11 W: 11 09 b.Lewisham 27-12-98
Internationals: Nigeria Full caps.
From Fulham.
2016–17 Sunderland 0 0
2017–18 Sunderland 17 1
2018–19 Sunderland 24 15 **41 16**
2018–19 Bordeaux 7 1
2019–20 Bordeaux 21 6
2020–21 Bordeaux 17 2
2020–21 *Fulham* 15 3 **15 3**
2021–22 Bordeaux 2 0 **47 9**
2021–22 *Stoke C* 15 1 **15 1**

MALONE, Dan (M) 0 0
b. 9-5-02
Internationals: Wales U17.
2020–21 Stoke C 0 0
2021–22 Stoke C 0 0

NNA NOUKEU, Blondy (G) 0 0
H: 6 0 W: 11 00 b.Douala, Cameroon 17-9-01
2019–20 Stoke C 0 0
2020–21 Stoke C 0 0
2021–22 Stoke C 0 0
2021–22 *Crawley T* 0 0

NORTON, Christian (F) 15 0
b.Westminster 21-5-01
Internationals: Wales U19, U21.
2020–21 Southampton 0 0
2020–21 Stoke C 6 0
2021–22 Stoke C 0 0 **6 0**
2021–22 *Cheltenham T* 9 0 **9 0**

O'DRISCOLL VARIAN, Ethon (F) 32 2
b. 11-8-02
Internationals: Republic of Ireland U21.
2020–21 Stoke C 0 0
2021–22 Stoke C 0 0
2021–22 *Raith R* 32 2 **32 2**

OAKLEY-BOOTHE, Tashan (M) 18 0
H: 6 0 W: 11 00 b.Lambeth 14-2-00
Internationals: England U16, U17, U18.
2017–18 Tottenham H 0 0
2018–19 Tottenham H 0 0
2019–20 Tottenham H 0 0
2019–20 Stoke C 2 0
2020–21 Stoke C 16 0
2021–22 Stoke C 0 0 **18 0**

PORTER, Adam (M) 0 0
H: 6 2 W: 12 02 b.Stoke-on-Trent 8-4-02
2019–20 Stoke C 0 0
2020–21 Stoke C 0 0
2021–22 Stoke C 0 0

POWELL, Nick (F) 273 74
H: 6 0 W: 10 06 b.Crewe 23-3-94
Internationals: England U16, U17, U18, U19, U21.
2010–11 Crewe Alex 17 0
2011–12 Crewe Alex 38 14 **55 14**
2012–13 Manchester U 2 1
2013–14 Manchester U 0 0
2013–14 *Wigan Ath* 31 7
2014–15 Manchester U 0 0
2014–15 *Leicester C* 3 0 **3 0**
2015–16 Manchester U 1 0 **3 1**
2015–16 *Hull C* 3 0 **3 0**
2016–17 Wigan Ath 21 6
2017–18 Wigan Ath 39 15
2018–19 Wigan Ath 32 8 **123 36**
2019–20 Stoke C 29 5
2020–21 Stoke C 39 12
2021–22 Stoke C 18 6 **86 23**

SMITH, Tommy (D) 279 7
H: 6 1 W: 13 02 b.Warrington 14-4-92
2012–13 Huddersfield T 0 0
2013–14 Huddersfield T 24 0
2014–15 Huddersfield T 41 0
2015–16 Huddersfield T 36 0
2016–17 Huddersfield T 42 4
2017–18 Huddersfield T 24 0

2018–19 Huddersfield T 15 0 **182 4**
2019–20 Stoke C 30 0
2020–21 Stoke C 35 2
2021–22 Stoke C 32 1 **97 3**

SOUTAR, Harry (D) 114 6
H: 6 6 W: 12 08 b.Aberdeen 22-10-98
Internationals: Scotland U17, U19. Australia U23, Full caps.
2015–16 Dundee U 2 1
2016–17 Dundee U 0 0 **2 1**
2016–17 Stoke C 0 0
2017–18 Stoke C 0 0
2017–18 *Ross Co* 13 0 **13 0**
2018–19 Stoke C 0 0
2018–19 *Fleetwood T* 11 1
2019–20 Stoke C 0 0
2019–20 *Fleetwood T* 34 3 **45 4**
2020–21 Stoke C 38 1
2021–22 Stoke C 16 0 **54 1**

SPARROW, Tom (M) 1 0
b. 3-2-03
Internationals: Wales U21.
2020–21 Stoke C 0 0
2021–22 Stoke C 1 0 **1 0**

SY, Ibrahima (M) 0 0
b. 16-12-02
Internationals: Senegal U17.
From Reims.
2020–21 Stoke C 0 0
2021–22 Stoke C 0 0

TAYLOR, Connor (D) 43 3
H: 6 0 b.Stoke-on-Trent 25-10-01
From Stafford R.
2020–21 Stoke C 1 0
2021–22 Stoke C 0 0 **1 0**
2021–22 *Bristol R* 42 3 **42 3**

THOMPSON, Jordan (M) 172 7
H: 5 9 W: 10 03 b.Belfast 3-1-97
Internationals: Northern Ireland U17, U19, U21, Full caps.
From Manchester U.
2015–16 Rangers 2 0
2015–16 *Airdrieonians* 7 1 **7 1**
2016–17 Rangers 0 0
2016–17 *Raith R* 29 1 **29 1**
2017–18 Rangers 0 0 **2 0**
2017–18 *Livingston* 11 0 **11 0**
2018–19 Blackpool 38 3
2019–20 Blackpool 18 1 **56 4**
2019–20 Stoke C 15 0
2020–21 Stoke C 34 1
2021–22 Stoke C 18 0 **67 1**

TYMON, Josh (D) 95 1
H: 5 10 W: 11 09 b.Kingston-upon-Hull 22-5-99
Internationals: England U17, U18, U19, U20.
2015–16 Hull C 0 0
2016–17 Hull C 5 0 **5 0**
2017–18 Stoke C 3 0
2017–18 *Milton Keynes D* 9 0 **9 0**
2018–19 Stoke C 1 0
2019–20 Stoke C 2 0
2019–20 *Famalicao* 5 0 **5 0**
2020–21 Stoke C 26 0
2021–22 Stoke C 44 1 **76 1**

VRANCIC, Mario (M) 312 36
H: 6 1 W: 12 02 b.Slavonski Brod 23-5-89
Internationals: Germany U17, U19, U20. Bosnia-Herzegovina Full caps.
From VfR Kesselstadt.
2006–07 Mainz 05 1 0
2007–08 Mainz 05 5 0
2008–09 Mainz 05 3 0
2009–10 Mainz 05 0 0 **9 0**
2009–10 *Rot Weiss Ahlen* 12 0 **12 0**
2010–11 Borussia Dortmund 0 0
2011–12 Borussia Dortmund 0 0
2012–13 Paderborn 33 5
2013–14 Paderborn 30 5
2014–15 Paderborn 30 2 **93 12**
2015–16 Darmstadt 22 2
2016–17 Darmstadt 23 4 **45 6**
2017–18 Norwich C 35 1
2018–19 Norwich C 36 10
2019–20 Norwich C 20 1
2020–21 Norwich C 32 3 **123 15**
2021–22 Stoke C 30 3 **30 3**

WILMOT, Ben (D) 98 4
H: 6 2 W: 12 08 b.Stevenage 4-11-99
Internationals: England U19, U20, U21.
2016–17 Stevenage 0 0
2017–18 Stevenage 10 0 **10 0**
2018–19 Watford 2 0
2018–19 *Udinese* 5 0 **5 0**
2019–20 Watford 0 0
2019–20 *Swansea C* 21 2 **21 2**
2020–21 Watford 25 1
2021–22 Watford 0 0 **27 1**
2021–22 Stoke C 35 1 **35 1**

WRIGHT-PHILLIPS, D'Margio (M) 10 1
b.Manchester 24-9-01
From Manchester C.
2021–22 Stoke C 10 1 **10 1**

Players retained or with offer of contract
Baker, Matthew; Roney, Joshua; Simkin, Tommy; Taylor, Douglas; Tezgel, Emre.

Scholars
Asplin-Rowley, Max; Cargill, Ted Makinson; Cartwright, Jake Owen; Curl, Thomas Daniel Andrew; Griffiths, Jack Joseph Alan; Ireland, Joshua Stephen; Iwobi, Justin Ifechukwude; Knowles, Samuel James; Laird, Logan William; Lewis, George Samuel; Leybourn, Charles Stanley Francis; Lusakueno, Matthew Henry; Malbon, Ryanjay Simon; McMahon, Taylor Matthew; Okagbue, David Chukwudubem; Parke, Xander; Robson, Conor Jon; Udanoh, Ifeanyi Dunhill; Waite, Joshua Morgan; Waldo, Shilo Daniel O'Neil; Wilson, Luke James.

SUNDERLAND (80)

ALMOND, Patrick (D) 0 0
H: 6 1 b.Northumberland 13-12-02
2020–21 Sunderland 0 0
2021–22 Sunderland 0 0

BATTH, Danny (D) 386 23
H: 6 3 W: 14 02 b.Brierley Hill 21-9-90
2009–10 Wolverhampton W 0 0
2009–10 *Colchester U* 17 1 **17 1**
2010–11 Wolverhampton W 0 0
2010–11 *Sheffield U* 1 0 **1 0**
2010–11 *Sheffield W* 10 0
2011–12 Wolverhampton W 0 0
2011–12 *Sheffield W* 44 2 **54 2**
2012–13 Wolverhampton W 12 1
2013–14 Wolverhampton W 46 2
2014–15 Wolverhampton W 44 4
2015–16 Wolverhampton W 38 2
2016–17 Wolverhampton W 39 4
2017–18 Wolverhampton W 16 1
2018–19 Wolverhampton W 0 0 **195 14**
2018–19 *Middlesbrough* 10 0 **10 0**
2018–19 Stoke C 17 0
2019–20 Stoke C 43 4
2020–21 Stoke C 29 1
2021–22 Stoke C 11 0 **100 5**
2021–22 Sunderland 9 1 **9 1**

BURGE, Lee (G) 189 0
H: 5 11 W: 11 00 b.Hereford 9-1-93
2011–12 Coventry C 0 0
2012–13 Coventry C 0 0
2013–14 Coventry C 0 0
2014–15 Coventry C 18 0
2015–16 Coventry C 9 0
2016–17 Coventry C 33 0
2017–18 Coventry C 40 0
2018–19 Coventry C 40 0 **140 0**
2019–20 Sunderland 5 0
2020–21 Sunderland 41 0
2021–22 Sunderland 3 0 **49 0**

CARNEY, Jacob (G) 26 0
H: 6 2 b.Rotherham 21-4-01
2016–17 Manchester U 0 0
2017–18 Manchester U 0 0
2018–19 Manchester U 0 0
2019–20 Manchester U 0 0
2020–21 Manchester U 0 0
2020–21 *Portadown* 26 0 **26 0**
2021–22 Sunderland 0 0

CIRKIN, Dennis (D) 34 0
H: 5 11 W: 22 07 b.Dublin 6-4-02
Internationals: England U16, U17, U18, U20.
2019–20 Tottenham H 0 0
2020–21 Tottenham H 0 0
2021–22 Tottenham H 0 0
2021–22 Sunderland 34 0 **34 0**

DAJAKU, Leon (M) 28 4
H: 5 11 W: 11 11 b.Waiblingen 12-4-01
Internationals: Germany U17, U18, U19.
2018–19 VfB Stuttgart 2 0 **2 0**
2019–20 Bayern Munich 2 0
2020–21 Bayern Munich 0 0 **2 0**
2020–21 *Union Berlin* 2 0
2021–22 Union Berlin 0 0 **2 0**
2021–22 *Sunderland* 22 4 **22 4**

DEFOE, Jermain (F) 646 240
H: 5 7 W: 10 03 b.Beckton 7-10-82
Internationals: England U16, U18, U21, B, Full caps.
1999–2000 West Ham U 0 0
2000–01 West Ham U 1 0
2000–01 *Bournemouth* 29 18
2001–02 West Ham U 35 10
2002–03 West Ham U 38 8
2003–04 West Ham U 19 11 **93 29**
2003–04 Tottenham H 15 7
2004–05 Tottenham H 35 13
2005–06 Tottenham H 36 9
2006–07 Tottenham H 34 10
2007–08 Tottenham H 19 4
2007–08 Portsmouth 12 8
2008–09 Portsmouth 19 7 **31 15**
2008–09 Tottenham H 8 3
2009–10 Tottenham H 34 18
2010–11 Tottenham H 22 4
2011–12 Tottenham H 25 11
2012–13 Tottenham H 34 11
2013–14 Tottenham H 14 1 **276 91**
2014 Toronto 19 11 **19 11**
2014–15 Sunderland 17 4
2015–16 Sunderland 33 15
2016–17 Sunderland 37 15
2017–18 Bournemouth 24 4
2018–19 Bournemouth 4 0
2018–19 *Rangers* 17 8
2019–20 Bournemouth 0 0 **57 22**
2019–20 *Rangers* 20 13
2019–20 Rangers 20 13
2020–21 Rangers 15 4
2021–22 Rangers 4 0 **76 38**
2021–22 Sunderland 7 0 **94 34**

DIAMOND, Jack (F) 66 14
H: 5 9 W: 9 08 b.Gateshead 12-1-00
2018–19 Sunderland 0 0
2019–20 Sunderland 0 0
2020–21 Sunderland 24 1
2021–22 Sunderland 3 0 **27 1**
2021–22 *Harrogate T* 39 13 **39 13**

DUNNE, Cieran (M) 0 0
H: 5 10 W: 10 10 b.Falkirk 8-2-00
From Falkirk.
2020–21 Sunderland 0 0
2021–22 Sunderland 0 0

EMBLETON, Elliot (M) 97 12
H: 5 8 W: 10 01 b.Durham 2-4-99
Internationals: England U17, U18, U19, U20.
2016–17 Sunderland 0 0
2017–18 Sunderland 2 0
2018–19 Sunderland 0 0
2018–19 *Grimsby T* 27 3 **27 3**
2019–20 Sunderland 3 0
2020–21 Sunderland 9 0
2020–21 *Blackpool* 18 1
2021–22 Sunderland 38 8 **52 8**
2021–22 *Blackpool* 0 0 **18 1**

EVANS, Corry (M) 333 12
H: 5 8 W: 11 00 b.Belfast 30-7-90
Internationals: Northern Ireland U16, U17, U19, U21, B, Full caps.
2007–08 Manchester U 0 0
2008–09 Manchester U 0 0
2009–10 Manchester U 0 0
2010–11 Manchester U 0 0
2010–11 *Carlisle U* 1 0 **1 0**
2010–11 *Hull C* 18 3
2011–12 Hull C 43 2
2012–13 Hull C 32 1
2013–14 Hull C 0 0 **93 6**
2013–14 Blackburn R 21 1
2014–15 Blackburn R 38 1
2015–16 Blackburn R 30 1
2016–17 Blackburn R 19 0
2017–18 Blackburn R 32 0
2018–19 Blackburn R 35 0
2019–20 Blackburn R 13 1
2020–21 Blackburn R 18 0 **206 4**
2021–22 Sunderland 33 2 **33 2**

GOOCH, Lynden (M) 190 20
H: 5 8 W: 10 12 b.Santa Cruz, California 24-12-95
Internationals: Republic of Ireland U18. USA U20, Full caps.
2015–16 Sunderland 0 0
2015–16 *Doncaster R* 10 0 **10 0**
2016–17 Sunderland 11 0
2017–18 Sunderland 24 1
2018–19 Sunderland 39 5
2019–20 Sunderland 30 10
2020–21 Sunderland 38 4
2021–22 Sunderland 38 0 **180 20**

GRIGG, Will (M) 396 120
H: 5 11 W: 11 00 b.Solihull 3-7-91
Internationals: Northern Ireland U19, U21, Full caps.
From Stratford T.
2008–09 Walsall 1 0
2009–10 Walsall 0 0
2010–11 Walsall 28 4

2011–12	Walsall	29	4		
2012–13	Walsall	41	19	**99**	**27**
2013–14	Brentford	34	5		
2014–15	Brentford	0	0	**34**	**5**
2014–15	*Milton Keynes D*	44	20		
2015–16	Wigan Ath	40	25		
2016–17	Wigan Ath	33	5		
2017–18	Wigan Ath	43	19		
2018–19	Wigan Ath	17	4	**133**	**53**
2018–19	Sunderland	18	4		
2019–20	Sunderland	20	1		
2020–21	Sunderland	9	0		
2020–21	*Milton Keynes D*	20	8	**64**	**28**
2021–22	Sunderland	0	0	**47**	**5**
2021–22	*Rotherham U*	19	2	**19**	**2**

GYIMAH, Nicky (M) **0 0**

2020–21	Peterborough U	0	0		
2021–22	Sunderland	0	0		

HARRIS, Will (F) **12 0**
b.South Shields 1-10-00
From Burnley.

2020–21	Sunderland	0	0		
2021–22	Sunderland	3	0	**3**	**0**
2021–22	*Barrow*	9	0	**9**	**0**

HOFFMANN, Ron-Thorben (G) **23 0**
H: 6 4 W: 13 03 b.Rostock 4-4-99
Internationals: Germany U18.
From RB Leipzig.

2017–18	Bayern Munich	0	0		
2018–19	Bayern Munich	0	0		
2019–20	Bayern Munich	0	0		
2020–21	Bayern Munich	0	0		
2021–22	Bayern Munich	0	0		
2021–22	*Sunderland*	23	0	**23**	**0**

HUGGINS, Niall (D) **3 0**
H: 5 8 W: 11 00 b.York 18-12-00
Internationals: Wales U21.

2020–21	Leeds U	1	0	**1**	**0**
2021–22	Sunderland	2	0	**2**	**0**

HUME, Trai (D) **58 8**
b.Ballymena 18-3-02
Internationals: Northern Ireland U17, U19, U21, Full caps.

2018–19	Linfield	2	0		
2019–20	Linfield	2	0		
2020–21	Linfield	0	0		
2020–21	*Ballymena U*	34	5	**34**	**5**
2021–22	Linfield	17	3	**21**	**3**
2021–22	Sunderland	3	0	**3**	**0**

KACHOSA, Ethan (D) **0 0**
b.Leeds 23-1-03
From Leeds U.

2021–22	Sunderland	0	0		

MATETE, Jay (M) **61 4**
H: 5 8 W: 9 08 b.Lambeth 11-2-01
From Reading.

2019–20	Fleetwood T	0	0		
2020–21	Fleetwood T	7	0		
2020–21	*Grimsby T*	20	3	**20**	**3**
2021–22	Fleetwood T	20	1	**27**	**1**
2021–22	Sunderland	14	0	**14**	**0**

McGEADY, Aiden (M) **473 81**
H: 5 10 W: 11 04 b.Glasgow 4-4-86
Internationals: Republic of Ireland Full caps.

2003–04	Celtic	4	1		
2004–05	Celtic	27	4		
2005–06	Celtic	20	4		
2006–07	Celtic	34	5		
2007–08	Celtic	36	7		
2008–09	Celtic	29	3		
2009–10	Celtic	35	7	**185**	**31**
2010–11	Spartak Moscow	11	2		
2011–12	Spartak Moscow	31	3		
2012–13	Spartak Moscow	17	5		
2013–14	Spartak Moscow	13	1	**72**	**11**
2013–14	Everton	16	0		
2014–15	Everton	16	1		
2015–16	Everton	0	0		
2015–16	*Sheffield W*	13	1	**13**	**1**
2016–17	Everton	0	0	**32**	**1**
2016–17	*Preston NE*	34	8	**34**	**8**
2017–18	Sunderland	35	7		
2018–19	Sunderland	34	11		
2019–20	Sunderland	15	4		
2019–20	*Charlton Ath*	10	0	**10**	**0**
2020–21	Sunderland	29	4		
2021–22	Sunderland	14	3	**127**	**29**

MGUNGA-KIMPIOKA, Benjamin (M) **10 2**
H: 6 0 W: 10 08 b.Knivsta, Sweden 21-2-00
Internationals: Sweden U19, U21.
From IK Sirius.

2018–19	Sunderland	4	0		
2019–20	Sunderland	4	1		
2020–21	Sunderland	0	0		
2021–22	Sunderland	2	1	**10**	**2**

Transferred to AIK, March 2022.

NEIL, Daniel (M) **41 3**
H: 5 10 W: 9 11 b.South Shields 30-11-01
Internationals: England U20.

2018–19	Sunderland	0	0		
2019–20	Sunderland	0	0		
2020–21	Sunderland	2	0		
2021–22	Sunderland	39	3	**41**	**3**

O'NIEN, Luke (M) **238 29**
H: 5 9 W: 11 09 b.Hemel Hempstead 21-11-94

2013–14	Watford	1	0		
2014–15	Watford	0	0	**1**	**0**
2015–16	Wycombe W	35	5		
2016–17	Wycombe W	31	3		
2017–18	Wycombe W	35	7	**101**	**15**
2018–19	Sunderland	37	5		
2019–20	Sunderland	35	4		
2020–21	Sunderland	38	2		
2021–22	Sunderland	26	3	**136**	**14**

PATTERSON, Anthony (G) **20 0**
H: 6 2 W: 12 02 b.North Shields 10-5-00

2018–19	Sunderland	0	0		
2019–20	Sunderland	0	0		
2020–21	Sunderland	0	0		
2021–22	Sunderland	20	0	**20**	**0**

PRITCHARD, Alex (M) **245 32**
H: 5 6 W: 9 11 b.Grays 3-5-93
Internationals: England U20, U21.

2011–12	Tottenham H	0	0		
2012–13	Tottenham H	0	0		
2012–13	*Peterborough U*	6	0	**6**	**0**
2013–14	Tottenham H	1	0		
2013–14	*Swindon T*	36	6	**36**	**6**
2014–15	Tottenham H	0	0		
2014–15	*Brentford*	45	12	**45**	**12**
2015–16	Tottenham H	1	0	**2**	**0**
2015–16	*WBA*	2	0	**2**	**0**
2016–17	Norwich C	30	6		
2017–18	Norwich C	8	1	**38**	**7**
2017–18	Huddersfield T	14	1		
2018–19	Huddersfield T	30	2		
2019–20	Huddersfield T	18	0		
2020–21	Huddersfield T	18	0	**80**	**3**
2021–22	Sunderland	36	4	**36**	**4**

RICHARDSON, Adam (G) **0 0**
Internationals: England U17, U18.

2020–21	Sunderland	0	0		
2021–22	Sunderland	0	0		

RICHARDSON, Kenton (D) **11 0**
H: 6 1 W: 11 00 b.Durham 26-6-99

2016–17	Hartlepool U	11	0	**11**	**0**

From Hartlepool U.

2020–21	Sunderland	0	0		
2021–22	Sunderland	0	0		

ROBERTS, Patrick (M) **145 18**
H: 5 6 W: 10 06 b.Kingston upon Thames 5-2-97
Internationals: England U16, U17, U18, U19, U20.

2013–14	Fulham	2	0		
2014–15	Fulham	17	0	**19**	**0**
2015–16	Manchester C	1	0		
2015–16	*Celtic*	11	6		
2016–17	Manchester C	0	0		
2016–17	*Celtic*	32	9		
2017–18	Manchester C	0	0		
2017–18	*Celtic*	12	0	**55**	**15**
2018–19	Manchester C	0	0		
2018–19	*Girona*	19	0	**19**	**0**
2019–20	Manchester C	0	0		
2019–20	*Norwich C*	3	0	**3**	**0**
2019–20	*Middlesbrough*	10	1		
2020–21	Manchester C	0	0		
2020–21	*Middlesbrough*	9	0	**19**	**1**
2020–21	*Derby Co*	15	1	**15**	**1**
2021–22	Manchester C	0	0	**1**	**0**
2021–22	Troyes	0	0		
2021–22	Sunderland	14	1	**14**	**1**

SOHNA, Harrison (M) **0 0**
H: 5 10 W: 9 08 b.Gloucester 1-7-02

2020–21	Aston Villa	0	0		
2021–22	Sunderland	0	0		

STEELS, Vinny (M) **0 0**
b. 9-8-01
From Darlington, York C, Burnley.

2020–21	Sunderland	0	0		
2021–22	Sunderland	0	0		

STEWART, Ross C (F) **155 58**
H: 6 2 W: 13 05 b.Irvine 1-9-96
Internationals: Scotland Full caps.

2016–17	Albion R	25	12	**25**	**12**
2017–18	St Mirren	9	0		
2017–18	*Alloa Ath*	19	7	**19**	**7**
2018–19	St Mirren	1	0	**10**	**0**
2018–19	Ross Co	23	6		
2019–20	Ross Co	21	7		
2020–21	Ross Co	0	0	**44**	**13**
2020–21	Sunderland	11	2		
2021–22	Sunderland	46	24	**57**	**26**

WEARNE, Stephen (M) **0 0**
H: 5 11 W: 12 00 b.Stockton-on-Tees 16-12-00
From Newcastle U.

2020–21	Middlesbrough	0	0		
2020–21	Sunderland	0	0		
2021–22	Sunderland	0	0		

WILDING, Samuel (M) **0 0**
b.Walsall 31-1-00
From WBA.

2020–21	Sunderland	0	0		
2021–22	Sunderland	0	0		

WILLIS, Jordan (D) **229 6**
H: 5 11 W: 11 00 b.Coventry 24-8-94
Internationals: England U18, U19.

2011–12	Coventry C	3	0		
2012–13	Coventry C	1	0		
2013–14	Coventry C	28	0		
2014–15	Coventry C	34	0		
2015–16	Coventry C	4	0		
2016–17	Coventry C	36	3		
2017–18	Coventry C	35	0		
2018–19	Coventry C	38	1	**179**	**4**
2019–20	Sunderland	35	2		
2020–21	Sunderland	15	0		
2021–22	Sunderland	0	0	**50**	**2**

WINCHESTER, Carl (M) **342 28**
H: 5 10 W: 11 09 b.Belfast 12-4-93
Internationals: Northern Ireland U16, U17, U18, U19, U21, Full caps.
From Linfield.

2010–11	Oldham Ath	6	1		
2011–12	Oldham Ath	12	0		
2012–13	Oldham Ath	9	0		
2013–14	Oldham Ath	12	1		
2014–15	Oldham Ath	41	4		
2015–16	Oldham Ath	31	1		
2016–17	Oldham Ath	9	1	**120**	**8**
2016–17	Cheltenham T	20	1		
2017–18	Cheltenham T	44	5	**64**	**6**
2018–19	Forest Green R	45	3		
2019–20	Forest Green R	35	5		
2020–21	Forest Green R	18	2	**98**	**10**
2020–21	Sunderland	20	1		
2021–22	Sunderland	40	3	**60**	**4**

WRIGHT, Bailey (D) **326 13**
H: 6 0 W: 13 05 b.Melbourne, Australia 28-7-92
Internationals: Australia U17, Full caps.

2010–11	Preston NE	2	0		
2011–12	Preston NE	13	1		
2012–13	Preston NE	38	2		
2013–14	Preston NE	43	4		
2014–15	Preston NE	27	1		
2015–16	Preston NE	38	0		
2016–17	Preston NE	18	0	**179**	**8**
2016–17	Bristol C	21	1		
2017–18	Bristol C	36	0		
2018–19	Bristol C	12	0		
2019–20	Bristol C	3	0	**72**	**1**
2019–20	*Sunderland*	5	0		
2020–21	Sunderland	33	2		
2021–22	Sunderland	37	2	**75**	**4**

XHEMAJLI, Arbenit (D) **49 2**
H: 6 3 W: 12 11 b.Brugg, Switzerland 23-4-98
Internationals: Kosovo U21, Full caps.

2017–18	Neuchatel Xamax	6	0		
2018–19	Neuchatel Xamax	17	0		
2019–20	Neuchatel Xamax	23	2		
2020–21	Neuchatel Xamax	0	0	**46**	**2**
2020–21	Sunderland	0	0		
2021–22	Sunderland	3	0	**3**	**0**

Players retained or with offer of contract
Bond, Harrison; Dyce, Tyrese; Jessup, Cameron; Johnson, Zak; Kelly, Caden; McIntyre, Jack; Middlemas, Ben; Newall, Nathan; Ryder, Joseph; Scott, Tom; Taylor, Ellis.

Scholars
Bainbridge, Oliver James; Bond, Harrison; Burke, Marshall Aaron; Cain, Will Thomas; Chapman, Luke; Dowling, William Michael; Fieldson, Henry Boyd; Gardiner, Harry Jay; Irons, Samuel Alan; Johnson, Zak Robert; Jones, Harrison Martin; Kelly, Caden Christopher; Lohia, Lakhraj Singh; Middlemas, Ben; Moore, Ethan Anthony; Ryder, Joseph Philip; Salkeld, Louie Robert; Williams, Ben Tyler.

SUTTON U (81)

AJIBOYE, David (F) 43 8
H: 5 8 b.Bromley 28-9-98
2021–22 Sutton U 43 8 43 8

BARDEN, Jonathan (M) 93 1
H: 6 0 W: 12 04 b.Harrow 9-11-92
2015 IBV 16 0
2016 IBV 17 0 33 0
2017 Ottawa Fury 27 1 27 1
2018 Saint Louis 12 0 12 0
From Sutton U.
2021–22 Sutton U 21 0 21 0

BEAUTYMAN, Harry (M) 90 10
H: 5 10 W: 11 09 b.Newham 1-4-92
Internationals: England C.
2010–11 Leyton Orient 0 0
From Sutton U, Welling U.
2014–15 Peterborough U 18 2
2015–16 Peterborough U 22 3 40 5
2016–17 Northampton T 21 3 21 3
2017–18 Stevenage 10 0 10 0
From Sutton U.
2021–22 Sutton U 19 2 19 2

BENNETT, Richie (F) 139 27
H: 6 4 W: 14 02 b.Oldham 3-3-91
From Ashton U, Northwich Vic, Barrow.
2017–18 Carlisle U 38 6
2018–19 Carlisle U 21 4 59 10
2018–19 *Morecambe* 16 5 16 5
2019–20 Port Vale 26 6 26 6
From Stockport Co.
2021–22 Sutton U 38 6 38 6

BOLDEWIJN, Enzio (F) 301 39
H: 6 1 W: 12 06 b.Almere 17-11-92
2010–11 Utrecht 0 0
2011–12 Utrecht 11 0 11 0
2012–13 Den Bosch 31 1 31 1
2013–14 Almere City 27 2
2014–15 Almere City 31 7
2015–16 Almere City 35 7 93 16
2015–16 Crawley T 0 0
2016–17 Crawley T 46 5
2017–18 Crawley T 45 10 91 15
2018–19 Notts Co 36 5 36 5
From Notts Co.
2021–22 Sutton U 39 2 39 2

BOUZANIS, Dean (G) 153 0
H: 6 0 W: 12 08 b.Sydney 2-10-90
Internationals: Greece U19. Australia U17, U20, U23.
2007–08 Liverpool 0 0
2008–09 Liverpool 0 0
2009–10 Liverpool 0 0
2009–10 *Accrington S* 14 0 14 0
2010–11 Liverpool 0 0
2011–12 Oldham Ath 9 0
2012–13 Oldham Ath 36 0 45 0
2013–14 Aris Thessaloniki 0 0
2013–14 Carlisle U 0 0
2014–15 Western Sydney W 6 0
2015–16 Western Sydney W 0 0 6 0
2015–16 Melbourne C 1 0
2016–17 Melbourne C 22 0
2017–18 Melbourne C 21 0
2018–19 Melbourne C 0 0 44 0
2018–19 *PEC Zwolle* 0 0
From Sutton U.
2021–22 Sutton U 44 0 44 0

BUGIEL, Omar (F) 58 7
H: 6 1 W: 12 02 b.Berlin 3-1-94
Internationals: Lebanon Full caps.
From Worthing.
2017–18 Forest Green R 19 3 19 3
From Bromley, Sutton U.
2021–22 Sutton U 39 4 39 4

DAVIS, Kenny (M) 20 1
H: 5 8 W: 11 03 b.Camden 17-4-88
From Chelsea, Dagenham & R, Harlow, Grays Ath, Braintree, Boreham Wood, Sutton U.
2021–22 Sutton U 20 1 20 1

DUNDAS, Craig (F) 4 0
H: 6 2 b.Lambeth 16-2-81
From Hampton & Richmond Bor, Sutton U.
2021–22 Sutton U 4 0 4 0

EASTMOND, Craig (D) 117 8
H: 5 8 W: 11 11 b.Wandsworth 9-12-90
2009–10 Arsenal 4 0
2010–11 Arsenal 0 0
2010–11 *Millwall* 6 0 6 0
2011–12 Arsenal 0 0
2011–12 *Wycombe W* 14 0 14 0
2012–13 Arsenal 0 0 4 0
2012–13 *Colchester U* 12 2
2013–14 Colchester U 39 4
2014–15 Colchester U 10 1 61 7
2014–15 Yeovil T 1 0 1 0
From Sutton U.
2021–22 Sutton U 31 1 31 1

GOODLIFFE, Ben (D) 43 3
H: 6 2 W: 12 08 b.Watford 19-6-99
From Boreham Wood, Wolverhampton W, Sutton U.
2021–22 Sutton U 43 3 43 3

JOHN, Louis (D) 58 1
H: 6 3 W: 13 05 b.Croydon 19-4-94
Internationals: England C.
2013–14 Crawley T 0 0
From Sutton U.
2018–19 Cambridge U 22 0
2019–20 Cambridge U 0 0 22 0
2021–22 Sutton U 36 1 36 1

KIZZI, Joe (D) 32 6
H: 6 2 W: 13 12 b.Enfield 24-6-93
From Waltham Abbey, Cheshunt, Wingate & Finchley, Billericay T, Bromley.
2021–22 Sutton U 32 6 32 6

KORBOA, Ricky (F) 30 4
b.Liverpool 2-8-96
From Carshalton Ath.
2020–21 Northampton T 16 2 16 2
2021–22 Sutton U 14 2 14 2

KOUASSI, Kylian (F) 4 0
H: 5 9 b. 18-6-03
2021–22 Sutton U 4 0 4 0

LOVATT, Adam (M) 3 0
H: 5 11 b. 11-5-99
From Hastings U.
2021–22 Sutton U 3 0 3 0

MILSOM, Robert (M) 265 12
H: 5 10 W: 11 05 b.Redhill 2-1-87
2005–06 Fulham 0 0
2006–07 Fulham 0 0
2007–08 Fulham 0 0
2007–08 *Brentford* 6 0 6 0
2008–09 Fulham 1 0
2008–09 *Southend U* 6 0 6 0
2009–10 Fulham 0 0
2010 *TPS Turku* 14 0 14 0
2010–11 Fulham 0 0 1 0
2010–11 Aberdeen 18 1
2011–12 Aberdeen 22 1
2012–13 Aberdeen 13 0 53 2
2013–14 Rotherham U 27 1
2014–15 Rotherham U 8 0 35 1
2014–15 *Bury* 2 0 2 0
2015–16 Notts Co 14 0
2016–17 Notts Co 38 0
2017–18 Notts Co 17 1
2018–19 Crawley T 3 0 3 0
2018–19 *Notts Co* 38 1 107 2
From Sutton U.
2021–22 Sutton U 38 7 38 7

NELSON, Stuart (G) 443 0
H: 6 2 W: 13 03 b.Stroud 17-9-81
From Doncaster R, Hucknall T.
2003–04 Brentford 9 0
2004–05 Brentford 43 0
2005–06 Brentford 45 0
2006–07 Brentford 19 0 116 0
2007–08 Leyton Orient 30 0 30 0
2008–09 Norwich C 0 0
2009–10 Aberdeen 3 0 3 0
2010–11 Notts Co 33 0
2011–12 Notts Co 46 0 79 0
2012–13 Gillingham 45 0
2013–14 Gillingham 46 0
2014–15 Gillingham 24 0
2015–16 Gillingham 46 0
2016–17 Gillingham 34 0
2017–18 Gillingham 0 0 195 0
2017–18 Yeovil T 5 0
2018–19 Yeovil T 12 0 17 0
From Yeovil T.
2020–21 Crawley T 1 0 1 0
2021–22 Sutton U 2 0 2 0

PALMER, Harry (G) 0 0
H: 6 0 b.Chelmsford 20-6-95
From Heybridge Swift, Braintree, Haringey, Dorking, Canvey Island, Ebbsfleet, Yeovil T, Billericay T.
2021–22 Sutton U 0 0
Transferred to Maidenhead U, January 2022.

RANDALL, Will (M) 47 4
H: 5 11 W: 10 03 b.Swindon 2-5-97
2013–14 Swindon T 1 0
2014–15 Swindon T 4 0
2015–16 Swindon T 4 0 9 0
2015–16 Wolverhampton W 0 0
2016–17 Wolverhampton W 0 0
2016–17 *Walsall* 2 0 2 0
2017–18 Wolverhampton W 0 0
2017–18 *Forest Green R* 7 0 7 0
2018–19 Newport Co 1 0 1 0
From Sutton U.
2021–22 Sutton U 28 4 28 4

ROWE, Coby (D) 15 1
H: 6 4 W: 13 05 b.Waltham Forest 2-10-95
From Hillingdon Bor, Wingate & Finchley, Haringey Bor, Sutton U.
2021–22 Sutton U 15 1 15 1

SMITH, Alistair (M) 39 8
H: 5 10 W: 10 08 b.Beverley 19-5-99
2018–19 Mansfield T 0 0
2019–20 Mansfield T 5 0
2020–21 Mansfield T 1 0 6 0
2021–22 Sutton U 33 8 33 8

WILSON, Donovan (F) 62 5
H: 5 11 W: 11 00 b.Yate 14-3-97
2014–15 Wolverhampton W 0 0
2015–16 Wolverhampton W 0 0
2016–17 Wolverhampton W 1 0
2017–18 Wolverhampton W 0 0
2017–18 *Port Vale* 8 1 8 1
2018–19 Wolverhampton W 0 0 1 0
2018–19 *Exeter C* 10 0 10 0
2019–20 Macclesfield T 5 0 5 0
From Bath C.
2021–22 Sutton U 38 4 38 4

WYATT, Ben (D) 16 0
H: 5 8 W: 10 01 b.Norwich 4-2-96
2014–15 Ipswich T 0 0
From Maldon & Tiptree, Colchester U, Braintree T, St Albans C.
2021–22 Sutton U 16 0 16 0

Players retained or with offer of contract
Chalupniczak, Filip; House, Brad; Palmer, Harry.

Scholars
Charles-Cook, Roman Omar; Khinda, Oliver Sonny; McNally, Jordan Armani; Nunes, Joshua Samuel Lucas; Olabiyi, Daniel Oladipupo; Soulya-Osekanongo, Gucci; Tanner, Kai Finley; Throp, Joseph William.

SWANSEA C (82)

BENDA, Steven (G) 39 0
H: 6 4 W: 13 01 b.Stuttgart 1-1-98
From Aalen, Heidenheim, TSV 1860.
2018–19 Swansea C 0 0
2019–20 Swansea C 0 0
2019–20 *Swindon T* 24 0 24 0
2020–21 Swansea C 1 0
2021–22 Swansea C 5 0 6 0
2021–22 *Peterborough U* 9 0 9 0

BENNETT, Ryan (D) 417 16
H: 5 11 W: 12 04 b.Orsett 6-3-90
Internationals: England U18, U21.
2006–07 Grimsby T 5 0
2007–08 Grimsby T 40 1
2008–09 Grimsby T 45 5
2009–10 Grimsby T 13 0 103 6
2009–10 Peterborough U 22 1
2010–11 Peterborough U 34 4
2011–12 Peterborough U 32 1 88 6
2011–12 Norwich C 8 0
2012–13 Norwich C 15 1
2013–14 Norwich C 16 1
2014–15 Norwich C 7 0
2015–16 Norwich C 22 0
2016–17 Norwich C 33 0 101 2
2017–18 Wolverhampton W 29 1
2018–19 Wolverhampton W 34 1
2019–20 Wolverhampton W 11 0 74 2
2019–20 *Leicester C* 5 0 5 0
2020–21 Swansea C 28 0
2021–22 Swansea C 18 0 46 0

CABANGO, Ben (D) 88 6
H: 6 3 W: 11 11 b.Cardiff 30-5-00
Internationals: Wales U17, U19, U21, Full caps.
2018–19 Swansea C 0 0
2019–20 Swansea C 21 1
2020–21 Swansea C 30 4
2021–22 Swansea C 37 1 **88** **6**

CAMPBELL, Rio (F) 0 0
b. 6-10-02
2020–21 Swansea C 0 0
2021–22 Swansea C 0 0

CONGREVE, Cameron (M) 5 0
b. 24-1-04
Internationals: Wales U18.
2021–22 Swansea C 5 0 **5** **0**

COOPER, Brandon (D) 32 1
H: 6 1 W: 11 09 b.Bridgend 14-1-00
Internationals: Wales U21.
2018–19 Swansea C 0 0
2019–20 Swansea C 0 0
2020–21 Swansea C 1 0
2020–21 *Newport Co* 19 1 **19** **1**
2021–22 Swansea C 4 0 **5** **0**
2021–22 *Swindon T* 8 0 **8** **0**

COOPER, Oliver (M) 36 1
H: 5 9 W: 10 10 b.Derby 14-12-99
Internationals: Wales U19, U21.
2020–21 Swansea C 3 0
2021–22 Swansea C 0 0 **3** **0**
2021–22 *Newport Co* 33 1 **33** **1**

CULLEN, Liam (F) 51 3
H: 5 8 W: 10 06 b.Kilgetty 23-4-99
Internationals: Wales U16, U17, U19, U20, U21.
2018–19 Swansea C 0 0
2019–20 Swansea C 6 1
2020–21 Swansea C 13 1
2021–22 Swansea C 12 0 **31** **2**
2021–22 *Lincoln C* 20 1 **20** **1**

DHANDA, Yan (M) 50 5
H: 5 8 W: 10 03 b.Birmingham 14-12-98
Internationals: England U16, U17.
From Liverpool.
2018–19 Swansea C 5 1
2019–20 Swansea C 16 3
2020–21 Swansea C 26 1
2021–22 Swansea C 3 0 **50** **5**

DOWNES, Flynn (M) 139 4
H: 5 8 W: 11 00 b.Brentwood 20-1-99
Internationals: England U19, U20.
2016–17 Ipswich T 0 0
2017–18 Ipswich T 10 0
2017–18 *Luton T* 10 0 **10** **0**
2018–19 Ipswich T 29 1
2019–20 Ipswich T 29 2
2020–21 Ipswich T 24 0
2021–22 Ipswich T 0 0 **92** **3**
2021–22 Swansea C 37 1 **37** **1**

FISHER, Andy (G) 82 0
H: 6 0 W: 13 01 b.Wigan 12-2-98
2016–17 Blackburn R 0 0
2017–18 Blackburn R 0 0
2018–19 Blackburn R 0 0
2019–20 Blackburn R 0 0
2019–20 *Northampton T* 0 0
2019–20 *Milton Keynes D* 0 0
2020–21 Blackburn R 0 0
2020–21 Milton Keynes D 39 0
2021–22 Milton Keynes D 23 0 **62** **0**
2021–22 Swansea C 20 0 **20** **0**

FULTON, Jay (M) 162 9
H: 5 10 W: 10 10 b.Bolton 4-4-94
Internationals: Scotland U18, U19, U21.
From Falkirk.
2013–14 Swansea C 2 0
2014–15 Swansea C 2 0
2015–16 Swansea C 2 0
2015–16 *Oldham Ath* 11 0 **11** **0**
2016–17 Swansea C 11 0
2017–18 Swansea C 2 0
2017–18 *Wigan Ath* 5 1 **5** **1**
2018–19 Swansea C 33 2
2019–20 Swansea C 36 3
2020–21 Swansea C 40 3
2021–22 Swansea C 18 0 **146** **8**

GARRICK, Jordan (F) 75 8
H: 5 11 b.Jamaica 15-7-98
From Ossett T.
2019–20 Swansea C 11 2
2020–21 Swansea C 3 0
2020–21 *Swindon T* 19 2 **19** **2**
2021–22 Swansea C 0 0 **14** **2**
2021–22 *Plymouth Arg* 42 4 **42** **4**

GOULD, Joshua (G) 0 0
2019–20 Swansea C 0 0
2020–21 Swansea C 0 0
2021–22 Swansea C 0 0

GRIMES, Matt (M) 308 12
H: 5 10 W: 11 00 b.Exeter 15-7-95
Internationals: England U20, U21.
2013–14 Exeter C 35 1
2014–15 Exeter C 23 4 **58** **5**
2014–15 Swansea C 3 0
2015–16 Swansea C 1 0
2015–16 *Blackburn R* 13 0 **13** **0**
2016–17 Swansea C 0 0
2016–17 *Leeds U* 7 0 **7** **0**
2017–18 Swansea C 0 0
2017–18 *Northampton T* 44 4 **44** **4**
2018–19 Swansea C 45 1
2019–20 Swansea C 46 0
2020–21 Swansea C 45 2
2021–22 Swansea C 46 0 **186** **3**

HAMER, Ben (G) 291 0
H: 6 4 W: 12 04 b.Chard 20-11-87
2006–07 Reading 0 0
2007–08 Reading 0 0
2007–08 *Brentford* 20 0
2008–09 Reading 0 0
2008–09 *Brentford* 45 0
2009–10 Reading 0 0
2010–11 Reading 0 0
2010–11 *Brentford* 10 0 **75** **0**
2010–11 *Exeter C* 18 0 **18** **0**
2011–12 Charlton Ath 41 0
2012–13 Charlton Ath 41 0
2013–14 Charlton Ath 32 0 **114** **0**
2014–15 Leicester C 8 0
2015–16 Leicester C 0 0
2015–16 *Bristol C* 4 0 **4** **0**
2016–17 Leicester C 0 0
2017–18 Leicester C 4 0 **12** **0**
2018–19 Huddersfield T 7 0
2019–20 *Derby Co* 25 0 **25** **0**
2020–21 Huddersfield T 15 0 **22** **0**
2020–21 Swansea C 0 0
2021–22 Swansea C 21 0 **21** **0**

JONES, Harry (D) 11 0
b. 8-10-02
Internationals: Wales U16, U17, U18, U19.
From Arsenal.
2020–21 Swansea C 0 0
2021–22 Swansea C 0 0
2021–22 *Barry T* 11 0 **11** **0**

JONES, Jacob (D) 0 0
b. 5-9-01
Internationals: Wales U19.
2020–21 Swansea C 0 0
2021–22 Swansea C 0 0

JOSEPH, Kyle (F) 47 9
H: 6 1 W: 11 11 b.Barnet 10-9-01
Internationals: Scotland U18, U19, U21.
2020–21 Wigan Ath 18 5
2021–22 Wigan Ath 0 0 **18** **5**
2021–22 *Cheltenham T* 19 4 **19** **4**
2021–22 Swansea C 10 0 **10** **0**

LATIBEAUDIERE, Joel (D) 42 1
H: 6 3 W: 11 03 b.Doncaster 6-1-00
Internationals: England U16, U17, U18, U20. Jamaica Full caps.
2017–18 Manchester C 0 0
2018–19 Manchester C 0 0
2019–20 Manchester C 0 0
2019–20 *FC Twente* 5 1 **5** **1**
2020–21 Swansea C 8 0
2021–22 Swansea C 29 0 **37** **0**

MANNING, Ryan (M) 207 26
H: 5 8 W: 10 06 b.Galway 14-6-96
Internationals: Republic of Ireland U17, U19, U21, Full caps.
2013 Mervue U 26 9 **26** **9**
2014 Galway U 21 4 **21** **4**
2014–15 QPR 0 0
2015–16 QPR 0 0
2016–17 QPR 18 1
2017–18 QPR 19 2
2018–19 QPR 9 0
2018–19 *Rotherham U* 18 4 **18** **4**
2019–20 QPR 41 4
2020–21 QPR 0 0 **87** **7**
2020–21 Swansea C 17 0
2021–22 Swansea C 38 2 **55** **2**

NAUGHTON, Kyle (D) 418 11
H: 5 11 W: 11 07 b.Sheffield 11-11-88
Internationals: England U21.
2006–07 Sheffield U 0 0
2007–08 *Gretna* 18 0 **18** **0**
2007–08 Sheffield U 0 0
2008–09 Sheffield U 40 1
2009–10 Sheffield U 0 0 **40** **1**
2009–10 Tottenham H 1 0
2009–10 *Middlesbrough* 15 0 **15** **0**
2010–11 Tottenham H 0 0
2010–11 *Leicester C* 34 5 **34** **5**
2011–12 Tottenham H 0 0
2011–12 *Norwich C* 32 0 **32** **0**
2012–13 Tottenham H 14 0
2013–14 Tottenham H 22 0
2014–15 Tottenham H 5 0 **42** **0**
2014–15 Swansea C 10 0
2015–16 Swansea C 27 0
2016–17 Swansea C 31 1
2017–18 Swansea C 34 0
2018–19 Swansea C 35 1
2019–20 Swansea C 32 3
2020–21 Swansea C 30 0
2021–22 Swansea C 38 0 **237** **5**

NTCHAM, Jules Olivier (M) 165 20
H: 5 11 W: 12 08 b.Longjumeau 9-2-96
Internationals: France U16, U17, U18, U19, U20, U21.
2013–14 Manchester C 0 0
2014–15 Manchester C 0 0
2015–16 Manchester C 0 0
2015–16 *Genoa* 17 0
2016–17 Manchester C 0 0
2016–17 *Genoa* 20 3 **37** **3**
2017–18 Celtic 30 5
2018–19 Celtic 20 3
2019–20 Celtic 23 4
2020–21 Celtic 14 1 **87** **13**
2020–21 *Marseille* 4 0 **4** **0**
2021–22 Swansea C 37 4 **37** **4**

OBAFEMI, Michael (F) 64 16
H: 5 7 W: 11 03 b.Dublin 6-7-00
Internationals: Republic of Ireland U19, Full caps.
From Leyton Orient.
2017–18 Southampton 1 0
2018–19 Southampton 6 1
2019–20 Southampton 21 3
2020–21 Southampton 4 0
2021–22 Southampton 0 0 **32** **4**
2021–22 Swansea C 32 12 **32** **12**

OGBETA, Nathaniel (D) 53 2
b.Salford 28-4-01
Internationals: England U17, U18, U20.
2018–19 Manchester C 0 0
2019–20 Manchester C 0 0
2020–21 Shrewsbury T 25 2
2021–22 Shrewsbury T 26 0 **51** **2**
2021–22 Swansea C 2 0 **2** **0**

PATERSON, Jamie (F) 374 63
H: 5 9 W: 10 08 b.Coventry 20-12-91
2010–11 Walsall 14 0
2011–12 Walsall 34 3
2012–13 Walsall 46 12 **94** **15**
2013–14 Nottingham F 32 8
2014–15 Nottingham F 21 1
2015–16 Nottingham F 1 0 **54** **9**
2015–16 *Huddersfield T* 34 6 **34** **6**
2016–17 Bristol C 22 4
2017–18 Bristol C 41 5
2018–19 Bristol C 40 5
2019–20 Bristol C 21 6
2019–20 *Derby Co* 10 1 **10** **1**
2020–21 Bristol C 20 3 **144** **23**
2021–22 Swansea C 38 9 **38** **9**

PIROE, Joel (F) 74 25
H: 5 11 W: 11 09 b.Wijchen, Netherlands 2-8-99
Internationals: Netherlands U16, U18, U19, U20.
2016–17 PSV Eindhoven 0 0
2017–18 PSV Eindhoven 0 0
2018–19 PSV Eindhoven 0 0
2019–20 PSV Eindhoven 0 0
2019–20 *Sparta Rotterdam* 18 2 **18** **2**
2020–21 PSV Eindhoven 11 1
2021–22 PSV Eindhoven 0 0 **11** **1**
2021–22 Swansea C 45 22 **45** **22**

RUSHESHA, Tivonge (D) 0 0
H: 5 11 W: 11 11 b.Zimbabwe 24-7-02
Internationals: Wales U17.
2019–20 Swansea C 0 0
2020–21 Swansea C 0 0
2021–22 Swansea C 0 0

SEARLE, Jamie (G) 0 0
b. 25-11-00
Internationals: New Zealand U23, Full caps.
From Aston Villa.
2020–21 Swansea C 0 0
2021–22 Swansea C 0 0

SMITH, Korey (M) 395 6
H: 6 0 W: 12 04 b.Hatfield 31-1-91
2008–09 Norwich C 2 0

2009–10	Norwich C	37	4		
2010–11	Norwich C	28	0		
2011–12	Norwich C	0	0		
2011–12	*Barnsley*	12	0	**12**	**0**
2012–13	Norwich C	0	0	**67**	**4**
2012–13	*Yeovil T*	17	0	**17**	**0**
2012–13	*Oldham Ath*	10	0		
2013–14	Oldham Ath	42	1	**52**	**1**
2014–15	Bristol C	44	0		
2015–16	Bristol C	36	0		
2016–17	Bristol C	23	0		
2017–18	Bristol C	45	1		
2018–19	Bristol C	5	0		
2019–20	Bristol C	22	0		
2020–21	Bristol C	0	0	**175**	**1**
2020–21	Swansea C	37	0		
2021–22	Swansea C	35	0	**72**	**0**

THOMAS, Joshua (F) **0 0**
H: 5 8 b. 24-9-02
Internationals: Wales U17, U19.

2020–21	Swansea C	0	0		
2021–22	Swansea C	0	0		

WALSH, Liam (M) **70 4**
H: 5 10 W: 10 06 b.Huyton 15-9-97
Internationals: England U16, U18.

2015–16	Everton	0	0		
2015–16	*Yeovil T*	15	1	**15**	**1**
2016–17	Everton	0	0		
2017–18	Everton	0	0		
2017–18	*Birmingham C*	3	0	**3**	**0**
2017–18	Bristol C	6	0		
2018–19	Bristol C	9	0		
2019–20	Bristol C	0	0		
2019–20	*Coventry C*	26	3	**26**	**3**
2020–21	Bristol C	3	0	**18**	**0**
2021–22	Swansea C	5	0	**5**	**0**
2021–22	*Hull C*	3	0	**3**	**0**

WEBB, Lewis (G) **7 0**
H: 6 1 W: 11 05 b.Newport 12-9-01
Internationals: Wales U19, U21.

2020–21	Swansea C	0	0		
2021–22	Swansea C	0	0		
2022	*Shelbourne*	7	0	**7**	**0**

WHITTAKER, Morgan (F) **63 7**
H: 6 0 W: 10 12 b.Derby 7-1-01
Internationals: England U16, U17, U18, U19, U20.

2019–20	Derby Co	16	1		
2020–21	Derby Co	9	0	**25**	**1**
2020–21	Swansea C	12	1		
2021–22	Swansea C	6	0	**18**	**1**
2021–22	*Lincoln C*	20	5	**20**	**5**

WILLIAMS, Daniel (M) **10 0**
H: 5 8 W: 10 03 b.Swansea 19-4-01
Internationals: Wales U21.

2020–21	Swansea C	0	0		
2021–22	Swansea C	0	0		
2022	*Dundalk*	10	0	**10**	**0**

WOLF, Hannes (M) **143 28**
H: 5 10 W: 10 06 b.Graz 16-4-99
Internationals: Austria U16, U21.

2015–16	Liefering	10	1		
2016–17	Liefering	25	6	**35**	**7**
2016–17	Red Bull Salzburg	3	0		
2017–18	Red Bull Salzburg	27	8		
2018–19	Red Bull Salzburg	22	8	**52**	**16**
2019–20	RB Leipzig	5	0		
2020–21	RB Leipzig	0	0		
2020–21	*Borussia M'gladbach*	32	3	**32**	**3**
2021–22	RB Leipzig	0	0	**5**	**0**
2021–22	*Swansea C*	19	2	**19**	**2**

Players retained or with offer of contract
Abdulai, Azeem; Cotterill, Joel; Defreitas-Hansen, Nicolas; Hurford, Corey; Leverett, Samuel; Lloyd, Ben; McFayden, Lincoln; Stafford, Jack; Thomas, Joe; Whittaker, Tarrelle.

Scholars
Bassett, Ryan David Harry; Bony, Nandi Geoffroy Israel; Carey, Joshua John; Cotterill, Joel Leigh; Davies, Ruben James; Edwards, Joshua; Evans, Andrew Tyler Jay; Faakye, Richard Somuah; Hillier, Aaron Jac; Hughes, Benjamin Rhys; Jenkins, Kian John; Lissah, Filip Augustus; Lloyd, Ben Nicholas; Ludvigsen, Kai; Mawongo, Jada Arsen Nylopuke; Myers, Zane Harley; Perkins, Dylan Anthony; Roberts, David Antuomwin; Veevers, Charlie Gary; Watts, Evan Thomas; Wilson, Kyrell Jeremiah.

SWINDON T (83)

AGUIAR, Ricky (M) **16 2**
b. 17-3-01
From Worthing.

2021–22	Swindon T	16	2	**16**	**2**

BAUDRY, Mathieu (D) **288 18**
H: 6 2 W: 12 08 b.Le Havre 24-2-88
From Le Havre.

2007–08	Troyes	2	1		
2008–09	Troyes	17	0		
2009–10	Troyes	7	0	**26**	**1**
2010–11	Bournemouth	3	1		
2011–12	Bournemouth	7	0	**10**	**1**
2011–12	*Dagenham & R*	11	0	**11**	**0**
2012–13	Leyton Orient	24	3		
2013–14	Leyton Orient	39	2		
2014–15	Leyton Orient	31	1		
2015–16	Leyton Orient	34	2	**128**	**8**
2016–17	Doncaster R	31	5		
2017–18	Doncaster R	22	1	**53**	**6**
2018–19	Milton Keynes D	5	0	**5**	**0**
2019–20	Swindon T	24	0		
2020–21	Swindon T	16	1		
2021–22	Swindon T	15	1	**55**	**2**

CONROY, Dion (D) **113 2**
H: 6 2 W: 11 07 b.Redhill 11-12-95
From Chelsea.

2016–17	Swindon T	14	0		
2017–18	Swindon T	7	0		
2018–19	Swindon T	27	1		
2019–20	Swindon T	11	0		
2020–21	Swindon T	19	0		
2021–22	Swindon T	35	1	**113**	**2**

EAST, Ryan (M) **17 0**
H: 5 9 W: 11 00 b. 7-8-98

2017–18	Reading	0	0		
2018–19	Reading	1	0		
2019–20	Reading	0	0		
2020–21	Reading	0	0		
2021–22	Reading	0	0	**1**	**0**
2021–22	Swindon T	16	0	**16**	**0**

EGBO, Mandela (D) **53 3**
b. 17-8-97
Internationals: England U16, U17, U18.

2018–19	Borussia M'gladbach	1	0	**1**	**0**
2019–20	Darmstadt	5	0	**5**	**0**
2020	New York Red Bulls	9	1		
2021	New York Red Bulls	29	2	**43**	**3**
2021–22	Swindon T	9	0	**9**	**0**

GLADWIN, Ben (M) **169 20**
H: 6 3 W: 13 08 b.Reading 8-6-92
From Hayes & Yeading U, Marlow.

2013–14	Swindon T	13	0		
2014–15	Swindon T	34	8		
2015–16	QPR	7	0		
2015–16	*Swindon T*	13	2		
2015–16	*Bristol C*	1	0	**1**	**0**
2016–17	QPR	7	0	**14**	**0**
2016–17	*Swindon T*	18	2		
2017–18	Blackburn R	5	0		
2018–19	Blackburn R	0	0	**5**	**0**
2019–20	Milton Keynes D	9	1		
2020–21	Milton Keynes D	26	2		
2021–22	Milton Keynes D	0	0	**35**	**3**
2021–22	Swindon T	36	5	**114**	**17**

HUNT, Robert (D) **172 2**
H: 5 7 W: 10 08 b.Dagenham 7-7-95

2013–14	Brighton & HA	0	0		
2014–15	Brighton & HA	0	0		
2015–16	Brighton & HA	0	0		
2016–17	Brighton & HA	1	0	**1**	**0**
2016–17	*Oldham Ath*	10	0		
2017–18	Oldham Ath	33	0		
2018–19	Oldham Ath	38	1	**81**	**1**
2019–20	Swindon T	34	1		
2020–21	Swindon T	19	0		
2021–22	Swindon T	37	0	**90**	**1**

IANDOLO, Ellis (D) **114 2**
H: 6 4 W: 14 00 b.Chatham 22-8-97
From Maidstone U.

2015–16	Swindon T	12	0		
2016–17	Swindon T	10	0		
2017–18	Swindon T	12	1		
2018–19	Swindon T	15	0		
2019–20	Swindon T	13	0		
2020–21	Swindon T	8	0		
2021–22	Swindon T	44	1	**114**	**2**

IDEM, Manny (G) **0 0**
H: 6 2 W: 10 06 b.Lambeth 6-12-98

2018–19	Aston Villa	0	0		
2018–19	Macclesfield T	0	0		
From Canvey Island.					
2020–21	Derby Co	0	0		
2021–22	Derby Co	0	0		
2021–22	Swindon T	0	0		

LYDEN, Jordan (M) **59 2**
H: 5 10 W: 11 00 b.Perth, Australia 30-1-96
Internationals: Australia U20.

2015–16	Aston Villa	4	0		
2016–17	Aston Villa	0	0		
2017–18	Aston Villa	0	0		
2018–19	Aston Villa	0	0	**4**	**0**
2018–19	*Oldham Ath*	10	1	**10**	**1**
2019–20	Swindon T	21	1		
2020–21	Swindon T	14	0		
2021–22	Swindon T	10	0	**45**	**1**

McKIRDY, Harry (M) **110 30**
H: 5 9 W: 11 00 b.Stoke-on-Trent 29-3-97
From Stoke C.

2016–17	Aston Villa	0	0		
2016–17	*Stevenage*	11	1	**11**	**1**
2017–18	Aston Villa	0	0		
2017–18	*Crewe Alex*	16	3	**16**	**3**
2018–19	Aston Villa	0	0		
2018–19	*Newport Co*	12	1	**12**	**1**
2019–20	Carlisle U	28	5	**28**	**5**
2020–21	Port Vale	8	0	**8**	**0**
2021–22	Swindon T	35	20	**35**	**20**

MILDENHALL, Steve (G) **431 1**
H: 6 4 W: 14 00 b.Swindon 13-5-78

1996–97	Swindon T	1	0		
1997–98	Swindon T	4	0		
1998–99	Swindon T	0	0		
1999–2000	Swindon T	5	0		
2000–01	Swindon T	23	0		
2001–02	Notts Co	26	0		
2002–03	Notts Co	21	0		
2003–04	Notts Co	28	0		
2004–05	Notts Co	1	0	**76**	**0**
2004–05	Oldham Ath	6	0	**6**	**0**
2005–06	Grimsby T	46	1	**46**	**1**
2006–07	Yeovil T	46	0		
2007–08	Yeovil T	29	0	**75**	**0**
2008–09	Southend U	34	0		
2009–10	Southend U	44	0		
2010–11	Southend U	0	0	**78**	**0**
2010–11	Millwall	0	0		
2011–12	Millwall	10	0		
2012–13	Millwall	0	0	**10**	**0**
2012–13	*Scunthorpe U*	9	0	**9**	**0**
2012–13	Bristol R	22	0		
2013–14	Bristol R	46	0		
From Bristol R.					
2015–16	Bristol R	26	0		
2016–17	Bristol R	4	0	**98**	**0**
2021–22	Swindon T	0	0	**33**	**0**

MINTURN, Harrison (M) **0 0**
b. 26-12-03

2021–22	Swindon T	0	0		

MITCHELL-LAWSON, Jayden (M) **41 2**
H: 5 6 W: 9 06 b.Basingstoke 17-9-99
From Swindon T.

2018–19	Derby Co	1	0		
2019–20	Derby Co	0	0		
2019–20	*Bristol R*	10	2		
2020–21	Derby Co	1	0		
2020–21	*Bristol R*	5	0	**15**	**2**
2021–22	Derby Co	0	0	**2**	**0**
2021–22	Swindon T	24	0	**24**	**0**

ODIMAYO, Akinwale (D) **69 0**
H: 6 0 W: 11 11 b.Camden 28-11-99

2019–20	Reading	0	0		
2020	*Waterford*	4	0	**4**	**0**
2020–21	Swindon T	30	0		
2021–22	Swindon T	35	0	**65**	**0**

PARSONS, Harry (F) **17 0**
b.Swindon 9-10-02

2019–20	Swindon T	0	0		
2020–21	Swindon T	2	0		
2021–22	Swindon T	15	0	**17**	**0**

PAYNE, Jack (M) **286 49**
H: 5 5 W: 9 06 b.Tower Hamlets 25-10-94

2013–14	Southend U	11	0		
2014–15	Southend U	34	6		
2015–16	Southend U	32	9	**77**	**15**
2016–17	Huddersfield T	23	2		
2017–18	Huddersfield T	0	0		
2017–18	*Oxford U*	28	3	**28**	**3**
2017–18	*Blackburn R*	18	1	**18**	**1**
2018–19	Huddersfield T	0	0	**23**	**2**
2018–19	*Bradford C*	39	9	**39**	**9**
2019–20	Lincoln C	23	2	**23**	**2**
2020–21	Swindon T	43	4		
2021–22	Swindon T	35	13	**78**	**17**

REED, Louis (M) **189 8**
H: 5 8 W: 9 06 b.Sheffield 25-7-97
Internationals: England U18, U19, U20.

2013–14	Sheffield U	1	0		
2014–15	Sheffield U	19	0		

2015–16	Sheffield U	19	0		
2016–17	Sheffield U	0	0		
2017–18	Sheffield U	0	0	**39**	**0**
2017–18	*Chesterfield*	42	4	**42**	**4**
2018–19	Peterborough U	28	1		
2019–20	Peterborough U	24	1		
2020–21	Peterborough U	17	0	**69**	**2**
2021–22	Swindon T	39	2	**39**	**2**

WARD, Lewis (G) 49 0
H: 6 5 W: 12 11 b. 5-3-97
Internationals: England U16.

2014–15	Reading	0	0		
2015–16	Reading	0	0		
2016–17	Reading	0	0		
2017–18	Reading	0	0		
2018–19	Reading	0	0		
2018–19	*Northampton T*	0	0		
2018–19	*Forest Green R*	12	0	**12**	**0**
2019–20	Exeter C	20	0		
2020–21	Exeter C	8	0	**28**	**0**
2020–21	*Portsmouth*	0	0		
2021–22	Swindon T	9	0	**9**	**0**

WILLIAMS, Jon (M) 227 10
H: 5 6 W: 9 06 b.Tunbridge Wells 9-10-93
Internationals: Wales U17, U19, U21, Full caps.

2010–11	Crystal Palace	0	0		
2011–12	Crystal Palace	14	0		
2012–13	Crystal Palace	29	0		
2013–14	Crystal Palace	9	0		
2013–14	*Ipswich T*	13	1		
2014–15	Crystal Palace	2	0		
2014–15	*Ipswich T*	7	1		
2015–16	Crystal Palace	1	0		
2015–16	*Nottingham F*	10	0	**10**	**0**
2015–16	*Milton Keynes D*	13	0	**13**	**0**
2016–17	Crystal Palace	0	0		
2016–17	*Ipswich T*	8	0	**28**	**2**
2017–18	Crystal Palace	0	0		
2017–18	*Sunderland*	12	1	**12**	**1**
2018–19	Crystal Palace	0	0	**55**	**0**
2018–19	Charlton Ath	16	0		
2019–20	Charlton Ath	26	0		
2020–21	Charlton Ath	18	2	**60**	**2**
2020–21	Cardiff C	9	0	**9**	**0**
2021–22	Swindon T	40	5	**40**	**5**

WOLLACOTT, Jojo (G) 49 0
H: 6 3 W: 12 08 b.Bristol 8-9-96
Internationals: Ghana Full caps.

2015–16	Bristol C	0	0		
2016–17	Bristol C	0	0		
2017–18	Bristol C	0	0		
2018–19	Bristol C	0	0		
2019–20	Bristol C	0	0		
2019–20	*Forest Green R*	10	0	**10**	**0**
2020–21	Bristol C	0	0		
2020–21	*Swindon T*	2	0		
2021–22	Bristol C	0	0		
2021–22	Swindon T	37	0	**39**	**0**

Players retained or with offer of contract
Afenyo, Jedidiah; Bunch, Jacob; Cowmeadow, George; Dabre, Mohammad; Dworzak, Anton; Fox, Harvey; Francis, Levi; Gordon, Donell; Winchcombe, Callum; Wynn-Davis, Tom.

Scholars
Afenyo, Jedidiah Kafui Nutefeworla; Bell, Alexander Ethan; Boulden, Benjamin Steven; Bryan, Joshua Bartholomew; Bunch, Jacob Daniel; Cowmeadow, George Ross; Dworzak, Anton Gabriel Ryan; Fox, Harvey James; Francis, Levi Lloyd; Gordon, Donell David; Kern, Sami Seng; Lawrence, Charlie Robert; Minturn, Harrison James; Taank, Shyam Anand; Weir, Taye Isaac Mark; Winchcombe, Callum George; Wynn-Davis, Thomas Albert Max.

TOTTENHAM H (84)

AUSTIN, Brandon (G) 15 0
H: 6 2 W: 12 13 b.Hemel Hempstead 8-1-99
Internationals: USA U18. England U20, U21.

2019–20	Tottenham H	0	0		
2019–20	*Viborg*	14	0	**14**	**0**
2020–21	Tottenham H	0	0		
2021	*Orlando C*	1	0	**1**	**0**
2021–22	Tottenham H	0	0		

BENNETT, J'Neil (F) 9 1
H: 5 9 W: 9 13 b.Camden 7-12-01
Internationals: England U18.
From QPR.

2021–22	Tottenham H	0	0		
2021–22	*Crewe Alex*	9	1	**9**	**1**

BENTANCUR, Rodrigo (M) 201 3
H: 6 2 W: 11 07 b.Nueva Helvecia 25-6-97
Internationals: Uruguay U20, Full caps.

2015	Boca Juniors	18	0		
2016	Boca Juniors	11	1		
2016–17	Boca Juniors	22	0	**51**	**1**
2017–18	Juventus	20	0		
2018–19	Juventus	31	2		
2019–20	Juventus	30	0		
2020–21	Juventus	33	0		
2021–22	Juventus	19	0	**133**	**2**
2021–22	Tottenham H	17	0	**17**	**0**

BERGWIJN, Steven (M) 172 36
H: 5 10 W: 11 09 b.Amsterdam 8-10-97
Internationals: Netherlands U17, U18, U19, U20, U21, Full caps.

2014–15	PSV Eindhoven	1	0		
2015–16	PSV Eindhoven	5	0		
2016–17	PSV Eindhoven	25	2		
2017–18	PSV Eindhoven	32	8		
2018–19	PSV Eindhoven	33	14		
2019–20	PSV Eindhoven	16	5	**112**	**29**
2019–20	Tottenham H	14	3		
2020–21	Tottenham H	21	1		
2021–22	Tottenham H	25	3	**60**	**7**

BOWDEN, Jamie (M) 17 1
H: 5 9 W: 10 01 b.Edmonton 9-7-01
Internationals: Republic of Ireland U19.

2020–21	Tottenham H	0	0		
2021–22	Tottenham H	0	0		
2021–22	*Oldham Ath*	17	1	**17**	**1**

CARTER-VICKERS, Cameron (D) 146 6
H: 6 1 W: 13 08 b.Westcliff on Sea 31-12-97
Internationals: USA U18, U20, U23, Full caps.

2015–16	Tottenham H	0	0		
2016–17	Tottenham H	0	0		
2017–18	Tottenham H	0	0		
2017–18	*Sheffield U*	17	1	**17**	**1**
2017–18	*Ipswich T*	17	0	**17**	**0**
2018–19	Tottenham H	0	0		
2018–19	*Swansea C*	30	0	**30**	**0**
2019–20	Tottenham H	0	0		
2019–20	*Stoke C*	12	0	**12**	**0**
2019–20	*Luton T*	16	0	**16**	**0**
2020–21	Tottenham H	0	0		
2020–21	*Bournemouth*	21	1	**21**	**1**
2021–22	Tottenham H	0	0		
2021–22	*Celtic*	33	4	**33**	**4**

CLARKE, Jack (F) 60 3
H: 5 11 W: 11 00 b.York 23-11-00
Internationals: England U20.

2017–18	Leeds U	0	0		
2018–19	Leeds U	22	2		
2019–20	Tottenham H	0	0		
2019–20	*Leeds U*	1	0	**23**	**2**
2019–20	*QPR*	6	0	**6**	**0**
2020–21	Tottenham H	0	0		
2020–21	*Stoke C*	14	0	**14**	**0**
2021–22	Tottenham H	0	0		
2021–22	*Sunderland*	17	1	**17**	**1**

DAVIES, Ben (D) 248 7
H: 5 7 W: 12 00 b.Neath 24-4-93
Internationals: Wales U19, Full caps.

2011–12	Swansea C	0	0		
2012–13	Swansea C	37	1		
2013–14	Swansea C	34	2	**71**	**3**
2014–15	Tottenham H	14	0		
2015–16	Tottenham H	17	0		
2016–17	Tottenham H	23	1		
2017–18	Tottenham H	29	2		
2018–19	Tottenham H	27	0		
2019–20	Tottenham H	18	0		
2020–21	Tottenham H	20	0		
2021–22	Tottenham H	29	1	**177**	**4**

DEVINE, Alfie (M) 0 0
b.Warrington 1-8-04
Internationals: England U16, U19.
From Wigan Ath.

2020–21	Tottenham H	0	0		
2021–22	Tottenham H	0	0		

DIER, Eric (D) 264 11
H: 6 3 W: 13 08 b.Cheltenham 15-1-94
Internationals: England U18, U19, U20, U21, Full caps.

2012–13	Sporting Lisbon	14	1		
2013–14	Sporting Lisbon	13	0	**27**	**1**
2014–15	Tottenham H	28	2		
2015–16	Tottenham H	37	3		
2016–17	Tottenham H	36	2		
2017–18	Tottenham H	34	0		
2018–19	Tottenham H	20	3		
2019–20	Tottenham H	19	0		
2020–21	Tottenham H	28	0		
2021–22	Tottenham H	35	0	**237**	**10**

DOHERTY, Matthew (D) 322 25
H: 6 0 W: 14 01 b.Dublin 16-1-92
Internationals: Republic of Ireland U19, U21, Full caps.

2010–11	Wolverhampton W	0	0		
2011–12	Wolverhampton W	1	0		
2011–12	*Hibernian*	13	2	**13**	**2**
2012–13	Wolverhampton W	13	1		
2012–13	*Bury*	17	1	**17**	**1**
2013–14	Wolverhampton W	18	1		
2014–15	Wolverhampton W	33	0		
2015–16	Wolverhampton W	34	2		
2016–17	Wolverhampton W	42	4		
2017–18	Wolverhampton W	45	4		
2018–19	Wolverhampton W	38	4		
2019–20	Wolverhampton W	36	4	**260**	**20**
2020–21	Tottenham H	17	0		
2021–22	Tottenham H	15	2	**32**	**2**

EMERSON, Junior (D) 133 6
H: 6 0 W: 11 00 b.Sao Paulo 14-1-99
Internationals: Brazil U20, U23, Full caps.

2016	Ponte Preta	0	0		
2017	Ponte Preta	3	0		
2018	Ponte Preta	0	0	**3**	**0**
2018	Atletico Mineiro	23	1	**23**	**1**
2018–19	Barcelona	0	0		
2018–19	*Real Betis*	6	0		
2019–20	Barcelona	0	0		
2019–20	*Real Betis*	33	3		
2020–21	Barcelona	0	0		
2020–21	*Real Betis*	34	1	**73**	**4**
2021–22	Barcelona	3	0	**3**	**0**
2021–22	Tottenham H	31	1	**31**	**1**

ETETE, Kion (F) 35 6
H: 6 1 W: 11 00 b.Derby 28-11-01

2018–19	Notts Co	4	0	**4**	**0**
2019–20	Tottenham H	0	0		
2020–21	Tottenham H	0	0		
2021–22	Tottenham H	0	0		
2021–22	*Northampton T*	18	3	**18**	**3**
2021–22	*Cheltenham T*	13	3	**13**	**3**

GIL SALVATIERRA, Bryan (M) 74 6
H: 5 9 W: 9 06 b.Barbate 11-2-01
Internationals: Spain U16, U17, U18, U19, U21, U23, Full caps.

2018–19	Sevilla	11	1		
2019–20	Sevilla	2	0		
2019–20	*Leganes*	12	1	**12**	**1**
2020–21	Sevilla	1	0	**14**	**1**
2020–21	*Eibar*	28	4	**28**	**4**
2021–22	Tottenham H	9	0	**9**	**0**
2021–22	*Valencia*	11	0	**11**	**0**

GOLLINI, Pierluigi (G) 138 0
H: 6 2 W: 12 13 b.Bologna 18-3-95
Internationals: Italy U18, U19, U20, U21, Full caps.

2013–14	Manchester U	0	0		
2014–15	Verona	3	0		
2015–16	Verona	26	0	**29**	**0**
2016–17	Aston Villa	20	0		
2016–17	*Atalanta*	4	0		
2017–18	Aston Villa	0	0	**20**	**0**
2017–18	*Atalanta*	7	0		
2018–19	Atalanta	20	0		
2019–20	Atalanta	33	0		
2020–21	Atalanta	25	0		
2021–22	Atalanta	0	0	**89**	**0**
2021–22	*Tottenham H*	0	0		

HOJBJERG, Pierre (M) 239 10
H: 6 1 W: 12 11 b.Copenhagen 5-8-95
Internationals: Denmark U16, U17, U19, U21, Full caps.
From Brondby.

2012–13	Bayern Munich	2	0		
2013–14	Bayern Munich	7	0		
2014–15	Bayern Munich	8	0		
2014–15	*Augsburg*	16	2	**16**	**2**
2015–16	Bayern Munich	0	0	**17**	**0**
2015–16	*Schalke*	23	0	**23**	**0**
2016–17	Southampton	22	0		
2017–18	Southampton	23	0		
2018–19	Southampton	31	4		
2019–20	Southampton	33	0	**109**	**4**
2020–21	Tottenham H	38	2		
2021–22	Tottenham H	36	2	**74**	**4**

JOHN, Nile (M) 0 0
Internationals: England U16, U17, U19.

2020–21	Tottenham H	0	0		
2021–22	Tottenham H	0	0		
2021–22	*Charlton Ath*	0	0		

KANE, Harry (F) 335 197
H: 6 0 W: 14 02 b.Walthamstow 28-7-93
Internationals: England U17, U19, U20, U21, Full caps.

2010–11	Tottenham H	0	0		
2010–11	*Leyton Orient*	18	5	**18**	**5**
2011–12	Tottenham H	0	0		

2011–12	*Millwall*	22	7	**22**	**7**
2012–13	Tottenham H	1	0		
2012–13	*Norwich C*	3	0	**3**	**0**
2012–13	*Leicester C*	13	2	**13**	**2**
2013–14	Tottenham H	10	3		
2014–15	Tottenham H	34	21		
2015–16	Tottenham H	38	25		
2016–17	Tottenham H	30	29		
2017–18	Tottenham H	37	30		
2018–19	Tottenham H	28	17		
2019–20	Tottenham H	29	18		
2020–21	Tottenham H	35	23		
2021–22	Tottenham H	37	17	**279**	**183**

KULUSEVSKI, Dejan (F) **112 20**
H: 6 1 W: 11 11 b.Stockholm 25-4-00
Internationals: Macedonia U17. Sweden U17, U19, U21, Full caps.

2018–19	Atalanta	3	0		
2019–20	Atalanta	0	0	**3**	**0**
2019–20	*Parma*	17	4		
2019–20	Juventus	0	0		
2019–20	*Parma*	19	6	**36**	**10**
2020–21	Juventus	35	4		
2021–22	Juventus	20	1	**55**	**5**
2021–22	*Tottenham H*	18	5	**18**	**5**

LAVINIER, Marcel (D) **0 0**
b. 16-12-00
Internationals: England U16, U17.
From Chelsea.

2020–21	Tottenham H	0	0		
2021–22	Tottenham H	0	0		

LLORIS, Hugo (G) **554 0**
H: 6 2 W: 12 04 b.Nice 26-12-86
Internationals: France U18, U19, U20, U21, Full caps.

2005–06	Nice	5	0		
2006–07	Nice	37	0		
2007–08	Nice	30	0	**72**	**0**
2008–09	Lyon	35	0		
2009–10	Lyon	36	0		
2010–11	Lyon	37	0		
2011–12	Lyon	36	0		
2012–13	Lyon	2	0	**146**	**0**
2012–13	Tottenham H	27	0		
2013–14	Tottenham H	37	0		
2014–15	Tottenham H	35	0		
2015–16	Tottenham H	37	0		
2016–17	Tottenham H	34	0		
2017–18	Tottenham H	36	0		
2018–19	Tottenham H	33	0		
2019–20	Tottenham H	21	0		
2020–21	Tottenham H	38	0		
2021–22	Tottenham H	38	0	**336**	**0**

LO CELSO, Giovani (M) **177 18**
H: 5 10 W: 10 10 b.Rosario 9-4-96
Internationals: Argentina U23, Full caps.

2014	Rosario Central	0	0		
2015	Rosario Central	13	0		
2016	Rosario Central	14	2		
2016–17	Paris Saint-Germain	4	0		
2016–17	*Rosario Central*	9	1	**36**	**3**
2017–18	Paris Saint-Germain	33	4		
2018–19	Paris Saint-Germain	1	0	**38**	**4**
2018–19	Real Betis	32	9		
2019–20	Real Betis	0	0	**32**	**9**
2019–20	Tottenham H	28	0		
2020–21	Tottenham H	18	1		
2021–22	Tottenham H	9	0	**55**	**1**
2021–22	*Villarreal*	16	1	**16**	**1**

LUCAS MOURA, Rodrigues (M) **364 72**
H: 5 9 W: 11 00 b.Sao Paulo 13-8-92
Internationals: Brazil U20, U23, Full caps.

2010	Sao Paulo	25	4		
2011	Sao Paulo	28	9		
2012	Sao Paulo	21	6	**74**	**19**
2012–13	Paris Saint-Germain	10	0		
2013–14	Paris Saint-Germain	36	5		
2014–15	Paris Saint-Germain	29	7		
2015–16	Paris Saint-Germain	36	9		
2016–17	Paris Saint-Germain	37	12		
2017–18	Paris Saint-Germain	5	1	**153**	**34**
2017–18	Tottenham H	6	0		
2018–19	Tottenham H	32	10		
2019–20	Tottenham H	35	4		
2020–21	Tottenham H	30	3		
2021–22	Tottenham H	34	2	**137**	**19**

LUSALA, Dermi (D) **0 0**
b.London 16-1-03
Internationals: England U16.

2020–21	Tottenham H	0	0		
2021–22	Tottenham H	0	0		

LYONS-FOSTER, Brooklyn (D) **0 0**
b.London 1-12-00
Internationals: England U17, U18.

2020–21	Tottenham H	0	0		
2021–22	Tottenham H	0	0		

MUIR, Marques (D) **0 0**
b.London 21-9-02

2020–21	Tottenham H	0	0		
2021–22	Tottenham H	0	0		

MUKENDI, Jeremie (F) **0 0**
b.London 12-9-00

2020–21	Tottenham H	0	0		
2021–22	Tottenham H	0	0		

MUNDLE, Romaine (M) **0 0**
b.London 24-4-03

2020–21	Tottenham H	0	0		
2021–22	Tottenham H	0	0		

NDOMBELE, Tanguy (M) **173 9**
H: 5 9 W: 10 10 b.Longjumeau 28-12-96
Internationals: France U21, Full caps.

2016–17	Amiens	30	2		
2017–18	Amiens	3	0	**33**	**2**
2017–18	*Lyon*	32	0		
2018–19	Lyon	34	1		
2019–20	Tottenham H	21	2		
2020–21	Tottenham H	33	3		
2021–22	Tottenham H	9	1	**63**	**6**
2021–22	*Lyon*	11	0	**77**	**1**

OMOLE, Tobi (D) **0 0**
H: 6 2 b.Brockley 17-12-99
From Arsenal.

2020–21	Tottenham H	0	0		
2021–22	Tottenham H	0	0		

PARROTT, Troy (F) **72 10**
H: 6 1 b.Dublin 4-2-02
Internationals: Republic of Ireland U17, U19, U21, Full caps.
From Belvedere.

2019–20	Tottenham H	2	0		
2020–21	Tottenham H	0	0		
2020–21	*Millwall*	11	0	**11**	**0**
2020–21	*Ipswich T*	18	2	**18**	**2**
2021–22	Tottenham H	0	0	**2**	**0**
2021–22	*Milton Keynes D*	41	8	**41**	**8**

PASKOTSI, Maksim (D) **0 0**
b.Tallinn 19-1-03
Internationals: Estonia U16, U17, Full caps.
From Flora.

2020–21	Tottenham H	0	0		
2021–22	Tottenham H	0	0		

REGUILON, Sergio (D) **136 12**
H: 5 11 W: 10 08 b.Madrid 16-12-96
Internationals: Spain U21, Full caps.

2015–16	Real Madrid	0	0		
2015–16	*Logrones*	9	0		
2016–17	Real Madrid	0	0		
2016–17	*Logrones*	30	8	**39**	**8**
2017–18	Real Madrid	0	0		
2018–19	Real Madrid	14	0		
2019–20	Real Madrid	0	0	**14**	**0**
2019–20	*Sevilla*	31	2		
2020–21	Sevilla	0	0	**31**	**2**
2020–21	Tottenham H	27	0		
2021–22	Tottenham H	25	2	**52**	**2**

ROBSON, Max (M) **0 0**
b. 17-10-02

2020–21	Tottenham H	0	0		
2021–22	Tottenham H	0	0		

RODON, Joe (D) **79 0**
H: 6 4 W: 12 08 b.Swansea 22-10-97
Internationals: Wales U20, U21, Full caps.

2015–16	Swansea C	0	0		
2016–17	Swansea C	0	0		
2017–18	Swansea C	0	0		
2017–18	*Cheltenham T*	12	0	**12**	**0**
2018–19	Swansea C	27	0		
2019–20	Swansea C	21	0		
2020–21	Swansea C	4	0	**52**	**0**
2020–21	Tottenham H	12	0		
2021–22	Tottenham H	3	0	**15**	**0**

ROMERO, Cristian (D) **126 6**
H: 6 1 W: 12 06 b.Cordoba 27-4-98
Internationals: Argentina U20, Full caps.

2016–17	Belgrano	13	0		
2017–18	Belgrano	3	0	**16**	**0**
2018–19	Genoa	27	2		
2019–20	Juventus	0	0		
2019–20	*Genoa*	30	1	**57**	**3**
2020–21	Juventus	0	0		
2020–21	*Atalanta*	31	2		
2021–22	Atalanta	0	0	**31**	**2**
2021–22	Tottenham H	22	1	**22**	**1**

SANCHEZ, Davinson (D) **182 9**
H: 6 2 W: 13 01 b.Caloto 12-6-96
Internationals: Columbia U17, U20, U23, Full caps.

2013	Atletico Nacional	3	0		
2014	Atletico Nacional	2	0		
2015	Atletico Nacional	7	0		
2016	Atletico Nacional	14	0	**26**	**0**
2016–17	Ajax	32	6		
2017–18	Ajax	0	0	**32**	**6**
2017–18	Tottenham H	31	0		
2018–19	Tottenham H	23	1		
2019–20	Tottenham H	29	0		
2020–21	Tottenham H	18	0		
2021–22	Tottenham H	23	2	**124**	**3**

SANTIAGO, Yago (M) **0 0**
H: 5 10 b.Vigo 15-4-03
From Celta Vigo.

2020–21	Tottenham H	0	0		
2021–22	Tottenham H	0	0		

SARR, Pape (M) **55 4**
b.Thiaroye 14-9-02
Internationals: Senegal U17, Full caps.

2020–21	Metz	22	3		
2021–22	Metz	3	0		
2021–22	Tottenham H	0	0		
2021–22	*Metz*	30	1	**55**	**4**

SCARLETT, Dane (F) **2 0**
H: 6 1 W: 12 00 b.Hillingdon 24-3-04
Internationals: England U16, U19.

2020–21	Tottenham H	1	0		
2021–22	Tottenham H	1	0	**2**	**0**

SESSEGNON, Ryan (M) **150 24**
H: 5 10 W: 11 02 b.Roehampton 18-5-00
Internationals: England U16, U17, U19, U21.

2016–17	Fulham	25	5		
2017–18	Fulham	46	15		
2018–19	Fulham	35	2		
2019–20	Fulham	0	0	**106**	**22**
2019–20	Tottenham H	6	0		
2020–21	Tottenham H	0	0		
2020–21	*Hoffenheim*	23	2	**23**	**2**
2021–22	Tottenham H	15	0	**21**	**0**

SKIPP, Oliver (M) **78 1**
H: 5 9 W: 11 00 b.Hatfield 16-9-00
Internationals: England U16, U17, U18, U21.

2018–19	Tottenham H	8	0		
2019–20	Tottenham H	7	0		
2020–21	Tottenham H	0	0		
2020–21	*Norwich C*	45	1	**45**	**1**
2021–22	Tottenham H	18	0	**33**	**0**

SOLBERG, Isak (G) **0 0**
b.Voss 28-6-03
Internationals: Norway U16, U18, U19.
From Bryne.

2020–21	Tottenham H	0	0		
2021–22	Tottenham H	0	0		

SON, Heung-Min (F) **367 134**
H: 6 0 W: 12 00 b.Chuncheon 8-7-92
Internationals: South Korea U17, U23, Full caps.

2010–11	Hamburg SV	13	3		
2011–12	Hamburg SV	27	5		
2012–13	Hamburg SV	33	12	**73**	**20**
2013–14	Bayer Leverkusen	31	10		
2014–15	Bayer Leverkusen	30	11		
2015–16	Bayer Leverkusen	1	0	**62**	**21**
2015–16	Tottenham H	28	4		
2016–17	Tottenham H	34	14		
2017–18	Tottenham H	37	12		
2018–19	Tottenham H	31	12		
2019–20	Tottenham H	30	11		
2020–21	Tottenham H	37	17		
2021–22	Tottenham H	35	23	**232**	**93**

TANGANGA, Japhet (D) **23 0**
H: 6 0 W: 11 07 b.Hackney 31-3-99
Internationals: England U16, U17, U18, U19, U20, U21.

2019–20	Tottenham H	6	0		
2020–21	Tottenham H	6	0		
2021–22	Tottenham H	11	0	**23**	**0**

WALCOTT, Malachi (D) **2 0**
Internationals: England U16, U17.

2019–20	Tottenham H	0	0		
2020–21	Tottenham H	0	0		
2020–21	*Dundee*	2	0	**2**	**0**
2021–22	Tottenham H	0	0		

WHITE, Harvey (M) **21 1**
H: 5 7 W: 9 06 b.Maidstone 19-9-01
Internationals: England U18.

2019–20	Tottenham H	0	0		
2020–21	Tottenham H	0	0		
2020–21	*Portsmouth*	21	1	**21**	**1**
2021–22	Tottenham H	0	0		

WHITEMAN, Alfie (G) **24 0**
b. 2-10-98
Internationals: England U16, U17, U18, U19.

2016–17	Tottenham H	0	0		
2017–18	Tottenham H	0	0		
2018–19	Tottenham H	0	0		
2019–20	Tottenham H	0	0		
2020–21	Tottenham H	0	0		
2021	*Degerfors*	13	0		

2021–22	Tottenham H	0	0		
2021–22	*Degerfors*	11	0	**24**	**0**

WINKS, Harry (M) **128** **2**
H: 5 10 W: 10 03 b.Hemel Hempstead 2-2-96
Internationals: England U17, U18, U19, U20, U21, Full caps.

2013–14	Tottenham H	0	0		
2014–15	Tottenham H	0	0		
2015–16	Tottenham H	0	0		
2016–17	Tottenham H	21	1		
2017–18	Tottenham H	16	0		
2018–19	Tottenham H	26	1		
2019–20	Tottenham H	31	0		
2020–21	Tottenham H	15	0		
2021–22	Tottenham H	19	0	**128**	**2**

Players retained or with offer of contract
Cesay, Kallum; Craig, Matthew; Donley, Jamie; Dorrington, Alfie; Gunter, Luca; Oluwayemi, Oluwaferanmi; Sayers, Charlie.

Scholars
Abbott, George Benedict; Andiyapan, William; Bloxham, Thomas Joel; Bryan-Waugh, Brandon; Cassanova, Dante Jamel; Hayton, Adam Paul; Heaps, Billy; Kyerematen, Rio; Linton, Jahziah; Lo-Tutala, Thimothee Jacques Orcel; Maguire, Aaron Joseph; Mathurin, Roshaun Andre; McKnight, Maxwell; Owen, Riley Jay; Williams, Jaden Pharell Earl.

TRANMERE R (85)

BURTON, Jake (F) **3** **0**
b.Liverpool 15-11-01

2019–20	Tranmere R	0	0		
2020–21	Tranmere R	2	0		
2021–22	Tranmere R	1	0	**3**	**0**

CLARKE, Peter (D) **764** **56**
H: 6 2 W: 13 02 b.Southport 3-1-82
Internationals: England U21.

1998–99	Everton	0	0		
1999–2000	Everton	0	0		
2000–01	Everton	1	0		
2001–02	Everton	7	0		
2002–03	Everton	0	0		
2002–03	*Blackpool*	16	3		
2002–03	*Port Vale*	13	1	**13**	**1**
2003–04	Everton	1	0		
2003–04	*Coventry C*	5	0	**5**	**0**
2004–05	Everton	0	0	**9**	**0**
2004–05	Blackpool	38	5		
2005–06	Blackpool	46	6		
2006–07	Southend U	38	2		
2007–08	Southend U	45	4		
2008–09	Southend U	43	4	**126**	**10**
2009–10	Huddersfield T	46	5		
2010–11	Huddersfield T	46	4		
2011–12	Huddersfield T	31	0		
2012–13	Huddersfield T	43	0		
2013–14	Huddersfield T	26	0	**192**	**9**
2014–15	Blackpool	39	2	**139**	**16**
2015–16	Bury	45	1		
2016–17	Oldham Ath	46	5		
2017–18	Oldham Ath	19	2		
2017–18	*Bury*	18	1	**63**	**2**
2018–19	Oldham Ath	42	3	**107**	**10**
2019–20	Fleetwood T	12	1	**12**	**1**
2019–20	Tranmere R	6	0		
2020–21	Tranmere R	46	3		
2021–22	Tranmere R	46	4	**98**	**7**

DACRES-COGLEY, Josh (D) **84** **1**
H: 5 9 W: 10 10 b.Coventry 12-3-96

2016–17	Birmingham C	14	0		
2017–18	Birmingham C	3	0		
2018–19	Birmingham C	1	0		
2019–20	Birmingham C	0	0		
2019–20	*Crawley T*	16	0	**16**	**0**
2020–21	Birmingham C	5	0	**23**	**0**
2021–22	Tranmere R	45	1	**45**	**1**

DAVIES, Scott (G) **221** **0**
H: 6 0 W: 10 13 b.Blackpool 27-2-87

2007–08	Morecambe	10	0		
2008–09	Morecambe	0	0		
2009–10	Morecambe	1	0		
2012–13	Fleetwood T	45	0		
2013–14	Fleetwood T	28	0		
2014–15	Fleetwood T	0	0	**73**	**0**
2014–15	*Morecambe*	10	0	**21**	**0**
2014–15	*Accrington S*	19	0	**19**	**0**

From Tranmere R.

2018–19	Tranmere R	46	0		
2019–20	Tranmere R	28	0		
2020–21	Tranmere R	34	0		
2021–22	Tranmere R	0	0	**108**	**0**

DAVIES, Tom (D) **155** **4**
H: 5 11 W: 11 00 b.Warrington 18-4-92
From FC United of Manchester.

2014–15	Fleetwood T	0	0		
2015–16	Accrington S	32	1	**32**	**1**
2016–17	Portsmouth	12	0		
2017–18	Portsmouth	0	0	**12**	**0**
2017–18	Coventry C	21	0		
2018–19	Coventry C	23	0	**44**	**0**
2019–20	Bristol R	19	1		
2020–21	Bristol R	0	0	**19**	**1**
2020–21	*Barrow*	12	1	**12**	**1**
2021–22	Tranmere R	36	1	**36**	**1**

DIESERUVWE, Emmanuel (F) **83** **4**
H: 6 5 W: 11 05 b.Leeds 5-1-94

2013–14	Sheffield W	0	0		
2013–14	*Fleetwood T*	4	0	**4**	**0**
2014–15	Sheffield W	0	0		
2014–15	*Chesterfield*	9	0		
2015–16	Chesterfield	16	0	**25**	**0**
2015–16	*Mansfield T*	10	1	**10**	**1**

From Kidderminster H, Salford C.

2019–20	Salford C	20	3		
2019–20	*Oldham Ath*	4	0	**4**	**0**
2020–21	Salford C	14	0	**34**	**3**
2021–22	Tranmere R	6	0	**6**	**0**

DOOHAN, Ross (G) **100** **0**
H: 6 1 W: 11 07 b.Clydebank 29-3-98
Internationals: Scotland U16, U17, U19, U20, U21.

2015–16	Celtic	0	0		
2016–17	Celtic	0	0		
2017–18	Celtic	0	0		
2017–18	*Greenock Morton*	0	0		
2018–19	Celtic	0	0		
2018–19	*Ayr U*	36	0		
2019–20	Celtic	0	0		
2019–20	*Ayr U*	27	0	**63**	**0**
2020–21	Celtic	0	0		
2020–21	*Ross Co*	5	0	**5**	**0**
2020–21	*Dundee U*	2	0	**2**	**0**
2021–22	Celtic	0	0		
2021–22	*Tranmere R*	30	0	**30**	**0**

DUFFY, Mark (M) **405** **38**
H: 5 9 W: 11 05 b.Liverpool 7-10-85
From Vauxhall Motor, Prescott Cables, Southport.

2008–09	Morecambe	9	1		
2009–10	Morecambe	35	4		
2010–11	Morecambe	22	0	**66**	**5**
2010–11	Scunthorpe U	22	1		
2011–12	Scunthorpe U	37	2		
2012–13	Scunthorpe U	43	5	**102**	**8**
2013–14	Doncaster R	36	2	**36**	**2**
2014–15	Birmingham C	4	0		
2014–15	*Chesterfield*	3	0	**3**	**0**
2015–16	Birmingham C	0	0	**4**	**0**
2015–16	*Burton Alb*	45	8	**45**	**8**
2016–17	Sheffield U	39	6		
2017–18	Sheffield U	36	3		
2018–19	Sheffield U	36	6		
2019–20	Sheffield U	0	0	**111**	**15**
2019–20	*Stoke C*	6	0	**6**	**0**
2019–20	*ADO Den Haag*	5	0	**5**	**0**
2020–21	Fleetwood T	24	0	**24**	**0**
2021–22	Tranmere R	3	0	**3**	**0**

Transferred to Macclesfield, January 2022.

FOLEY, Sam (M) **315** **20**
H: 6 0 W: 11 09 b.St Albans 17-10-86
Internationals: Republic of Ireland U18.

2012–13	Yeovil T	41	5		
2013–14	Yeovil T	7	0		
2013–14	*Shrewsbury T*	9	0	**9**	**0**
2014–15	Yeovil T	40	2	**88**	**7**
2015–16	Port Vale	45	6		
2016–17	Port Vale	32	1	**77**	**7**
2016–17	Northampton T	0	0		
2017–18	Northampton T	24	2		
2018–19	Northampton T	36	2	**60**	**4**
2019–20	St Mirren	27	1		
2020–21	St Mirren	11	0	**38**	**1**
2020–21	Motherwell	4	0	**4**	**0**
2021–22	Tranmere R	39	1	**39**	**1**

HAWKES, Josh (M) **38** **6**
H: 6 0 W: 12 08 b.Stockton-on-Tees 28-1-99

2016–17	Hartlepool U	2	0	**2**	**0**

From Hartlepool U.

2020–21	Sunderland	0	0		
2021–22	Sunderland	1	0	**1**	**0**
2021–22	Tranmere R	35	6	**35**	**6**

HAYDE, Kyle (D) **0** **0**
b.Liverpool 25-9-21

2019–20	Tranmere R	0	0		
2020–21	Tranmere R	0	0		
2021–22	Marine	0	0		
2021–22	Tranmere R	0	0		

HEMMINGS, Kane (F) **321** **119**
H: 6 1 W: 12 04 b.Burton-upon-Trent 8-4-92
From Tamworth.

2010–11	Rangers	0	0		
2011–12	Rangers	4	0		
2012–13	Rangers	5	1	**9**	**1**
2012–13	*Cowdenbeath*	7	4		
2013–14	Cowdenbeath	31	18	**38**	**22**
2014–15	Barnsley	23	3	**23**	**3**
2015–16	Dundee	37	21		
2016–17	Oxford U	40	6		
2017–18	Oxford U	0	0	**40**	**6**
2017–18	*Mansfield T*	37	15	**37**	**15**
2018–19	Notts Co	36	14	**36**	**14**
2019–20	Dundee	25	10	**62**	**31**
2020–21	Burton Alb	36	15		
2021–22	Burton Alb	18	4	**54**	**19**
2021–22	Tranmere R	22	8	**22**	**8**

HEWELT, Mateusz (G) **11** **1**
b. 23-9-96

2016–17	Everton	0	0		
2017–18	Everton	0	0		
2018–19	Everton	0	0		
2019–20	Miedz Legnica	1	0		
2020–21	Miedz Legnica	10	1	**11**	**1**
2021–22	Tranmere R	0	0		

JOLLEY, Charlie (F) **17** **4**
H: 5 11 W: 11 05 b.Liverpool 13-1-01

2018–19	Wigan Ath	1	0		
2019–20	Wigan Ath	0	0		
2020–21	Wigan Ath	2	0	**3**	**0**
2020–21	Tranmere R	2	0		
2021–22	Tranmere R	12	4	**14**	**4**

JONES, Ben (G) **0** **0**
b. 29-11-00

2019–20	Tranmere R	0	0		
2020–21	Tranmere R	0	0		
2021–22	Tranmere R	0	0		

KNIGHT-PERCIVAL, Nathaniel (D) **289** **13**
H: 6 0 W: 11 07 b.Cambridge 31-3-87
Internationals: England C.
From Histon, Wrexham.

2012–13	Peterborough U	31	0		
2013–14	Peterborough U	15	1	**46**	**1**
2014–15	Shrewsbury T	28	1		
2015–16	Shrewsbury T	35	5	**63**	**6**
2016–17	Bradford C	42	0		
2017–18	Bradford C	41	4		
2018–19	Bradford C	35	2	**118**	**6**
2019–20	Carlisle U	15	0	**15**	**0**
2020–21	Morecambe	31	0		
2021–22	Morecambe	0	0	**31**	**0**
2021–22	Tranmere R	16	0	**16**	**0**

MACDONALD, Calum (D) **85** **2**
H: 5 11 W: 9 06 b.Nottingham 18-12-97
Internationals: Scotland U21.

2016–17	Derby Co	0	0		
2017–18	Derby Co	0	0		
2018–19	Derby Co	0	0		
2019–20	Derby Co	0	0		
2019–20	Blackpool	12	0		
2020–21	Blackpool	0	0	**12**	**0**
2020–21	Tranmere R	39	1		
2021–22	Tranmere R	34	1	**73**	**2**

MAGUIRE, Joe (D) **49** **1**
H: 5 10 W: 11 00 b.Manchester 18-1-96

2015–16	Liverpool	0	0		
2015–16	*Leyton Orient*	0	0		
2016–17	Liverpool	0	0		
2016–17	Fleetwood T	3	0		
2017–18	Fleetwood T	2	0		
2018–19	Fleetwood T	0	0	**5**	**0**
2018–19	*Crawley T*	27	1	**27**	**1**
2019–20	Accrington S	11	0		
2020–21	Accrington S	5	0	**16**	**0**
2021–22	Tranmere R	1	0	**1**	**0**

MAYNARD, Nicky (F) **436** **134**
H: 5 11 W: 11 00 b.Winsford 11-12-86

2005–06	Crewe Alex	1	1		
2006–07	Crewe Alex	31	16		
2007–08	Crewe Alex	27	14	**59**	**31**
2008–09	Bristol C	43	11		
2009–10	Bristol C	42	20		
2010–11	Bristol C	13	6		
2011–12	Bristol C	27	8	**125**	**45**
2011–12	West Ham U	14	2		
2012–13	West Ham U	0	0	**14**	**2**
2012–13	Cardiff C	4	1		
2013–14	Cardiff C	8	0		
2013–14	*Wigan Ath*	16	4	**16**	**4**
2014–15	Cardiff C	10	1	**22**	**2**
2015–16	Milton Keynes D	35	7		
2016–17	Milton Keynes D	31	2	**66**	**9**
2017–18	Aberdeen	18	0	**18**	**0**
2018–19	Bury	37	21	**37**	**21**
2019–20	Mansfield T	33	14		

2020–21 Mansfield T 17 3 **50 17**
2020–21 *Newport Co* 19 2 **19 2**
2021–22 Tranmere R 10 1 **10 1**

McMANAMAN, Callum (F) 240 24
H: 5 9 W: 11 07 b.Huyton 25-4-91
Internationals: England U20.
2008–09 Wigan Ath 1 0
2009–10 Wigan Ath 0 0
2010–11 Wigan Ath 3 0
2011–12 Wigan Ath 2 0
2011–12 *Blackpool* 14 2 **14 2**
2012–13 Wigan Ath 20 2
2013–14 Wigan Ath 30 3
2014–15 Wigan Ath 23 5
2014–15 WBA 8 0
2015–16 WBA 12 0
2016–17 WBA 0 0 **20 0**
2016–17 *Sheffield W* 11 0 **11 0**
2017–18 Sunderland 24 1 **24 1**
2018–19 Wigan Ath 22 1 **101 11**
2019–20 Luton T 23 4 **23 4**
2020–21 Melbourne Victory 18 4 **18 4**
2021–22 Tranmere R 29 2 **29 2**

McPAKE, Joshua (M) 55 5
H: 6 0 W: 11 00 b.Coatbridge 31-8-01
Internationals: Scotland U18, U21.
2018–19 Rangers 0 0
2019–20 Rangers 0 0
2019–20 *Dundee* 7 0 **7 0**
2020–21 Rangers 0 0
2020–21 *Greenock Morton* 6 0 **6 0**
2020–21 *Harrogate T* 23 4 **23 4**
2021–22 Rangers 0 0
2021–22 *Morecambe* 5 0 **5 0**
2021–22 *Tranmere R* 14 1 **14 1**

MERRIE, Christopher (M) 41 0
H: 5 11 W: 11 05 b.Liverpool 2-11-98
From Everton.
2017–18 Wigan Ath 0 0
2018–19 Wigan Ath 0 0
2019–20 Wigan Ath 0 0
2020–21 Wigan Ath 26 0
2021–22 Wigan Ath 0 0 **26 0**
2021–22 Tranmere R 15 0 **15 0**

MORRIS, Kieron (M) 270 28
H: 5 10 W: 11 03 b.Hereford 3-6-94
2012–13 Walsall 0 0
2013–14 Walsall 2 0
2014–15 Walsall 14 2
2015–16 Walsall 33 3
2016–17 Walsall 35 5
2017–18 Walsall 42 3
2018–19 Walsall 17 2 **143 15**
2018–19 *Tranmere R* 14 1
2019–20 Tranmere R 34 2
2020–21 Tranmere R 42 5
2021–22 Tranmere R 37 5 **127 13**

MURPHY, Joe (G) 567 0
H: 6 2 W: 12 08 b.Dublin 21-8-81
Internationals: Republic of Ireland U21, Full caps.
1999–2000 Tranmere R 21 0
2000–01 Tranmere R 20 0
2001–02 Tranmere R 22 0
2002–03 WBA 2 0
2003–04 WBA 3 0
2004–05 WBA 0 0 **5 0**
2004–05 *Walsall* 25 0
2005–06 Sunderland 0 0
2005–06 *Walsall* 14 0 **39 0**
2006–07 Scunthorpe U 45 0
2007–08 Scunthorpe U 45 0
2008–09 Scunthorpe U 42 0
2009–10 Scunthorpe U 40 0
2010–11 Scunthorpe U 29 0 **201 0**
2011–12 Coventry C 46 0
2012–13 Coventry C 45 0
2013–14 Coventry C 46 0 **137 0**
2014–15 Huddersfield T 2 0
2014–15 *Chesterfield* 0 0
2015–16 Huddersfield T 7 0
2016–17 Huddersfield T 0 0 **9 0**
2016–17 *Bury* 16 0
2017–18 Bury 17 0
2018–19 Bury 46 0 **79 0**
2019–20 Shrewsbury T 4 0 **4 0**
2020–21 Tranmere R 13 0
2021–22 Tranmere R 17 0 **93 0**

NEVITT, Elliott (F) 40 7
b. 30-10-96
2021–22 Tranmere R 40 7 **40 7**

O'CONNOR, Lee (D) 68 0
H: 6 1 W: 11 11 b.Waterford 28-7-00
Internationals: Republic of Ireland U17, U19, U21, Full caps.
From Waterford.
2019–20 Manchester U 0 0
2019–20 Celtic 0 0
2019–20 *Partick Thistle* 4 0 **4 0**
2020–21 Celtic 0 0
2020–21 *Tranmere R* 33 0
2021–22 Celtic 0 0
2021–22 *Tranmere R* 31 0 **64 0**

SPEARING, Jay (M) 394 22
H: 5 6 W: 11 00 b.Wallasey 25-11-88
2006–07 Liverpool 0 0
2007–08 Liverpool 0 0
2008–09 Liverpool 0 0
2009–10 Liverpool 3 0
2009–10 *Leicester C* 7 1 **7 1**
2010–11 Liverpool 11 0
2011–12 Liverpool 16 0
2012–13 Liverpool 0 0
2012–13 *Bolton W* 37 2
2013–14 Liverpool 0 0 **30 0**
2013–14 Bolton W 45 2
2014–15 Bolton W 21 1
2014–15 *Blackburn R* 15 1 **15 1**
2015–16 Bolton W 22 2
2016–17 Bolton W 37 3
2017–18 Bolton W 0 0 **162 10**
2017–18 Blackpool 33 0
2018–19 Blackpool 42 4
2019–20 Blackpool 30 2 **105 6**
2020–21 Tranmere R 43 1
2021–22 Tranmere R 32 3 **75 4**

Players retained or with offer of contract
Dwyer, Dylan; Jones, Ethan; Stratulis, Ryan; Taylor, Samuel.

Scholars
Capps, Robbie Jason; Duncan, Oliver Joseph; Fisher, Max Steven; Haley, Joe Peter; Jones, Ethan Robert; Timlin, Jamie Benjamin.

WALSALL (86)

BATES, Alfie (M) 49 1
H: 5 7 W: 10 01 b.Coventry 3-5-01
2018–19 Walsall 0 0
2019–20 Walsall 13 1
2020–21 Walsall 36 0
2021–22 Walsall 0 0 **49 1**

DANIELS, Donervon (D) 184 8
H: 6 1 W: 14 05 b.Montserrat 24-11-93
Internationals: Montserrat Full caps.
2011–12 WBA 0 0
2012–13 WBA 0 0
2012–13 *Tranmere R* 13 1 **13 1**
2013–14 WBA 0 0
2013–14 *Gillingham* 3 1 **3 1**
2014–15 WBA 0 0
2014–15 *Blackpool* 19 1
2014–15 *Aberdeen* 9 0 **9 0**
2015–16 Wigan Ath 42 3
2016–17 Wigan Ath 1 0
2017–18 Wigan Ath 1 0 **44 3**
2017–18 *Rochdale* 15 0 **15 0**
2018–19 Blackpool 24 0 **43 1**
2019–20 Luton T 3 1 **3 1**
2019–20 *Doncaster R* 10 0 **10 0**
2020–21 Crewe Alex 15 0
2021–22 Crewe Alex 11 0 **26 0**
2021–22 Walsall 18 1 **18 1**

EARING, Jack (M) 46 4
H: 6 0 W: 12 08 b.Bury 21-1-99
2016–17 Bolton W 0 0
2017–18 Bolton W 0 0
2018–19 Bolton W 1 0 **1 0**
From FC Halifax T.
2021–22 Walsall 45 4 **45 4**

HOLDEN, Rory (F) 69 7
H: 5 7 W: 10 10 b.Derry 23-8-97
Internationals: Northern Ireland U21.
2016 Derry C 4 0
2017 Derry C 9 1 **13 1**
2017–18 Bristol C 0 0
2018–19 Bristol C 0 0
2018–19 *Rochdale* 6 0 **6 0**
2019–20 Bristol C 0 0
2019–20 *Walsall* 29 2
2020–21 Walsall 21 4
2021–22 Walsall 0 0 **50 6**

KIERNAN, Brendan (M) 82 9
H: 5 9 W: 11 11 b.Lambeth 10-11-92
2011–12 AFC Wimbledon 9 0
2012–13 AFC Wimbledon 6 0
2013–14 AFC Wimbledon 0 0 **15 0**
From Bromley, Staines T, Ebbsfleet U, Lingfield, Hayes & Yeading U, Bromley, Hampton & Richmond Bor, Welling U.
2020–21 Harrogate T 30 4
2021–22 Harrogate T 0 0 **30 4**
2021–22 Walsall 37 5 **37 5**

KINSELLA, Liam (M) 175 1
H: 5 9 W: 11 11 b.Colchester 23-2-96
Internationals: Republic of Ireland U19, U21.
2013–14 Walsall 0 0
2014–15 Walsall 4 0
2015–16 Walsall 7 1
2016–17 Walsall 8 0
2017–18 Walsall 19 0
2018–19 Walsall 31 0
2019–20 Walsall 31 0
2020–21 Walsall 43 0
2021–22 Walsall 32 0 **175 1**

LABADIE, Joss (M) 360 42
H: 6 2 W: 14 00 b.Croydon 31-8-90
2008–09 WBA 0 0
2008–09 *Shrewsbury T* 1 0
2009–10 WBA 0 0
2009–10 *Shrewsbury T* 13 5 **14 5**
2009–10 *Cheltenham T* 11 0 **11 0**
2009–10 *Tranmere R* 9 3
2010–11 Tranmere R 34 2
2011–12 Tranmere R 27 5 **70 10**
2012–13 Notts Co 24 2
2012–13 *Torquay U* 7 4
2013–14 Notts Co 15 1 **39 3**
2013–14 *Torquay U* 10 1 **17 5**
2014–15 Dagenham & R 24 2
2015–16 Dagenham & R 28 4 **52 6**
2016–17 Newport Co 19 3
2017–18 Newport Co 25 3
2018–19 Newport Co 13 0
2019–20 Newport Co 27 3
2020–21 Newport Co 38 4
2021–22 Newport Co 0 0 **122 13**
2021–22 Walsall 35 0 **35 0**

LEAK, Tom (D) 12 0
H: 6 2 W: 12 08 b.Burton-upon-Trent 31-10-00
2019–20 Walsall 0 0
2020–21 Walsall 6 0
2021–22 Walsall 6 0 **12 0**

MENAYESE, Rollin (D) 94 2
H: 6 3 W: 12 08 b.Kinshasa 4-12-97
Internationals: Wales U17.
From Weston-super-Mare.
2017–18 Bristol R 3 0
2017–18 *Swindon T* 14 0 **14 0**
2018–19 Bristol R 0 0
2019–20 Bristol R 13 0 **16 0**
2020–21 Mansfield T 10 1
2020–21 *Grimsby T* 21 0 **21 0**
2021–22 Mansfield T 0 0 **10 1**
2021–22 Walsall 33 1 **33 1**

MILLS, Zak (D) 151 2
H: 6 0 W: 13 01 b.Peterborough 28-5-92
From Histon, Boston U.
2016–17 Grimsby T 30 0
2017–18 Grimsby T 28 0 **58 0**
2018–19 Morecambe 38 1 **38 1**
2019–20 Oldham Ath 25 1 **25 1**
2020–21 Port Vale 21 0 **21 0**
2021–22 Walsall 9 0 **9 0**

MONTHE, Emmanuel (D) 158 3
H: 6 4 W: 12 08 b.Douala, Cameroon 26-1-95
2013–14 QPR 0 0
From Southport, Whitehawk, Hayes & Yeading, Havant & Waterford, Bath C.
2017–18 Forest Green R 13 0 **13 0**
2018–19 Tranmere R 43 2
2019–20 Tranmere R 31 1
2020–21 Tranmere R 34 0
2021–22 Tranmere R 0 0 **108 3**
2021–22 Walsall 37 0 **37 0**

OSAOABE, Emmanuel (M) 167 13
H: 6 2 W: 11 03 b.Dundalk 1-10-96
2015–16 Gillingham 18 2
2016–17 Gillingham 24 1 **42 3**
2017–18 Cambridge U 4 0
2017–18 *Newport Co* 3 0 **3 0**
2018–19 Cambridge U 12 0 **16 0**
2019–20 Macclesfield T 25 4 **25 4**
2019–20 Southend U 0 0
2020–21 Walsall 38 3
2021–22 Walsall 43 3 **81 6**

PERRY, Sam (M) 36 2
H: 6 0 W: 11 00 b.Walsall 29-12-01
From Aston Villa.
2019–20 Walsall 0 0
2020–21 Walsall 16 1
2021–22 Walsall 20 1 **36 2**

RODNEY, Devante (F) 75 14
H: 5 10 W: 10 12 b.Manchester 19-5-98
From Sheffield W.
2016–17 Hartlepool U 4 2 **4 2**

From Hartlepool U.
2019–20 Salford C 3 0 **3 0**
2020–21 Port Vale 40 11
2021–22 Port Vale 14 1 **54 12**
2021–22 Walsall 14 0 **14 0**

ROSE, Jack (G) 31 0
H: 6 3 W: 11 11 b.Solihull 31-1-95
2014–15 WBA 0 0
2014–15 *Accrington S* 4 0 **4 0**
2015–16 WBA 0 0
2015–16 *Crawley T* 5 0 **5 0**
2016–17 WBA 0 0
2017–18 Southampton 0 0
2018–19 Southampton 0 0
2019–20 Southampton 0 0
2019–20 *Walsall* 4 0
2020–21 Walsall 15 0
2021–22 Walsall 3 0 **22 0**

SADLER, Matthew (D) 493 11
H: 5 11 W: 11 09 b.Birmingham 26-2-85
Internationals: England U17, U18, U19.
2001–02 Birmingham C 0 0
2002–03 Birmingham C 2 0
2003–04 Birmingham C 0 0
2003–04 *Northampton T* 7 0 **7 0**
2004–05 Birmingham C 0 0
2005–06 Birmingham C 8 0
2006–07 Birmingham C 36 0
2007–08 Birmingham C 5 0 **51 0**
2007–08 Watford 15 0
2008–09 Watford 15 0
2009–10 Watford 0 0
2009–10 *Stockport Co* 20 0 **20 0**
2010–11 Watford 0 0 **30 0**
2010–11 *Shrewsbury T* 46 0
2011–12 Walsall 46 1
2012–13 Crawley T 46 1
2013–14 Crawley T 46 1
2014–15 Rotherham U 0 0
2014–15 *Crawley T* 10 0 **102 2**
2014–15 *Oldham Ath* 8 0 **8 0**
2014–15 Shrewsbury T 0 0
2015–16 Shrewsbury T 24 2
2016–17 Shrewsbury T 34 2
2017–18 Shrewsbury T 42 1
2018–19 Shrewsbury T 29 0 **175 5**
2019–20 Walsall 27 2
2020–21 Walsall 26 1
2021–22 Walsall 1 0 **100 4**

SHAW, Jack (M) 2 0
b. 21-1-05
2021–22 Walsall 2 0 **2 0**

TAYLOR, Ash (M) 417 26
H: 6 0 W: 12 00 b.Bromborough 2-9-90
Internationals: Wales U19, U21.
2008–09 Tranmere R 1 0
2009–10 Tranmere R 33 1
2010–11 Tranmere R 26 0
2011–12 Tranmere R 37 2
2012–13 Tranmere R 44 2
2013–14 Tranmere R 42 3 **183 8**
2014–15 Aberdeen 32 3
2015–16 Aberdeen 37 4
2016–17 Aberdeen 31 2
2017–18 Northampton T 45 6
2018–19 Northampton T 33 0 **78 6**
2019–20 Aberdeen 14 1
2020–21 Aberdeen 31 1 **145 11**
2021–22 Walsall 11 1 **11 1**
Transferred to Kilmarnock, January 2022.

TOMLIN, Lee (F) 343 71
H: 5 11 W: 11 09 b.Leicester 12-1-89
Internationals: England C.
From Rushden & D.
2010–11 Peterborough U 37 8
2011–12 Peterborough U 37 8
2012–13 Peterborough U 42 11
2013–14 Peterborough U 19 5
2013–14 Middlesbrough 14 4
2014–15 Middlesbrough 42 7 **56 11**
2015–16 Bournemouth 6 0 **6 0**
2015–16 *Bristol C* 18 6
2016–17 Bristol C 38 6 **56 12**
2017–18 Cardiff C 13 1
2017–18 *Nottingham F* 15 4 **15 4**
2018–19 Cardiff C 0 0
2018–19 *Peterborough U* 19 2 **154 34**
2019–20 Cardiff C 33 8
2020–21 Cardiff C 5 1
2021–22 Cardiff C 0 0 **51 10**
2021–22 Walsall 5 0 **5 0**

WARD, Stephen (D) 513 27
H: 6 0 W: 12 13 b.Dublin 20-8-85
Internationals: Republic of Ireland U20, U21, B, Full caps.
2003 Bohemians 6 0
2004 Bohemians 16 2
2005 Bohemians 29 7
2006 Bohemians 23 2 **74 11**
2006–07 Wolverhampton W 18 3
2007–08 Wolverhampton W 29 0
2008–09 Wolverhampton W 42 0
2009–10 Wolverhampton W 22 0
2010–11 Wolverhampton W 34 1
2011–12 Wolverhampton W 38 3
2012–13 Wolverhampton W 39 2
2013–14 Wolverhampton W 0 0 **222 9**
2013–14 *Brighton & HA* 44 4 **44 4**
2014–15 Burnley 9 0
2015–16 Burnley 24 1
2016–17 Burnley 37 1
2017–18 Burnley 28 1
2018–19 Burnley 3 0 **101 3**
2019–20 Stoke C 15 0 **15 0**
2020–21 Ipswich T 30 0 **30 0**
2021–22 Walsall 27 0 **27 0**

WHITE, Hayden (D) 198 3
H: 6 1 W: 10 10 b.Greenwich 15-4-95
From Sheffield W.
2013–14 Bolton W 2 0
2014–15 Bolton W 3 0
2014–15 *Carlisle U* 8 0 **8 0**
2014–15 *Bury* 2 0 **2 0**
2014–15 *Notts Co* 3 0 **3 0**
2015–16 Bolton W 0 0 **5 0**
2015–16 *Blackpool* 29 1 **29 1**
2016–17 Peterborough U 6 0 **6 0**
2016–17 *Mansfield T* 18 1
2017–18 Mansfield T 28 1
2018–19 Mansfield T 19 0
2019–20 Mansfield T 10 0 **75 2**
2020–21 Walsall 28 0
2021–22 Walsall 42 0 **70 0**

WILKINSON, Conor (F) 208 39
H: 6 1 W: 12 02 b.Croydon 23-1-95
Internationals: Republic of Ireland U17, U19, U21.
2012–13 Millwall 0 0
2013–14 Bolton W 0 0
2013–14 *Torquay U* 3 0 **3 0**
2014–15 Bolton W 4 0
2014–15 *Oldham Ath* 17 3 **17 3**
2015–16 Bolton W 0 0
2015–16 *Barnsley* 8 1 **8 1**
2015–16 *Newport Co* 12 1 **12 1**
2015–16 *Portsmouth* 1 0 **1 0**
2016–17 Bolton W 9 0 **13 0**
2016–17 *Chesterfield* 12 4 **12 4**
2017–18 Gillingham 34 3
2018–19 Gillingham 7 0 **41 3**
2019–20 Leyton Orient 26 5
2020–21 Leyton Orient 42 12
2021–22 Leyton Orient 0 0 **68 17**
2021–22 Crawley T 0 0
2021–22 Walsall 33 10 **33 10**

WILLIS, Joe (M) 2 0
H: 5 11 W: 11 00 b.Walsall 3-10-01
2019–20 Walsall 0 0
2020–21 Walsall 2 0
2021–22 Walsall 0 0 **2 0**

WILLOCK, Shay (M) 2 0
H: 6 3 b.Birmingham 15-9-03
2021–22 Walsall 2 0 **2 0**

Players retained or with offer of contract
Foulkes, Joseph; Jackson, Tommy; Sawyers, Rio.

Scholars
Angafor, Noel; Baldwin, Daniel Christopher; Cristofaro, Antonio Michael; Derry, Callum Anthony; Hedge, Zach Reuben; Hunter, Ky-Mani Ter; Jackson, Tommy; Maher, Ronan Arjun; Onabirekhanlen, Marvellous; Perry, Joseph; Robinson, Tayshen Teniyah Mickel; Sarvari, Samim; Sawyers, Rio Jayden; Shaw, Jack James; Simcox, Joshua James; Taylor, Bradley Michael; Toor, Arjun Singh; Willock, Shay Carter.

WATFORD (87)

AGYAKWA, Derek (D) 0 0
H: 6 0 b.Amsterdam 19-12-91
2020–21 Watford 0 0
2020–21 *Como* 0 0
2021–22 Watford 0 0

ALVARADO, Jamie (M) 34 0
H: 5 11 W: 12 00 b.Santa Marta 26-7-99
Internationals: Colombia U20, U23.
2017–18 Watford 0 0
2017–18 *Valladolid* 0 0
2018–19 Watford 0 0
2018–19 *Hercules* 11 0
2019–20 Watford 0 0
2019–20 *Hercules* 6 0 **17 0**
2019–20 *Badalona* 3 0 **3 0**
2020–21 Watford 0 0
2020–21 *Athletico Paranaense* 14 0 **14 0**
2021–22 Watford 0 0
2021–22 *Racing Ferrol* 0 0

ASPRILLA, Yaser (M) 40 6
H: 6 1 b.Bajo Baudo 19-11-03
Internationals: Colombia Full caps.
2020 Envigado 2 0
2021 Envigado 20 5
2021–22 Watford 0 0
2022 *Envigado* 18 1 **40 6**

BAAH, Kwadwo (F) 37 3
H: 6 0 W: 11 11 b.Horb am Neckar 27-1-03
Internationals: England U18. Germany U19.
2019–20 Rochdale 7 0
2020–21 Rochdale 30 3
2021–22 Rochdale 0 0 **37 3**
2021–22 Watford 0 0

BACHMANN, Daniel (G) 69 0
H: 6 3 W: 12 11 b.Vienna 9-7-94
Internationals: Austria U16, U17, U18, U19, U21, Full caps.
2011–12 Stoke C 0 0
2012–13 Stoke C 0 0
2013–14 Stoke C 0 0
2014–15 Stoke C 0 0
2015–16 Stoke C 0 0
2015–16 *Ross Co* 1 0 **1 0**
2015–16 *Bury* 8 0 **8 0**
2016–17 Stoke C 0 0
2017–18 Watford 0 0
2018–19 Watford 0 0
2018–19 *Kilmarnock* 25 0 **25 0**
2019–20 Watford 0 0
2020–21 Watford 23 0
2021–22 Watford 12 0 **35 0**

BONAVENTURE, Emmanuel (F) 149 35
H: 5 9 W: 10 08 b.Yola, Nigeria 15-11-97
Internationals: Nigeria U23, Full caps.
2016–17 Zorya Luhansk 22 6 **22 6**
2017–18 Club Brugge 30 7
2018–19 Club Brugge 26 7
2019–20 Club Brugge 20 5
2020–21 Club Brugge 9 0 **85 19**
2020–21 *Cologne* 9 0 **9 0**
2021–22 Watford 33 10 **33 10**

CASSIDY, Ryan (M) 11 2
b. 2-3-01
Internationals: Republic of Ireland U17, U18, U19.
2020–21 Watford 0 0
2020–21 *Accrington S* 11 2 **11 2**
2021–22 Watford 0 0

CATHCART, Craig (D) 375 14
H: 6 2 W: 11 06 b.Belfast 6-2-89
Internationals: Northern Ireland U16, U17, U20, U21, Full caps.
2005–06 Manchester U 0 0
2006–07 Manchester U 0 0
2007–08 Manchester U 0 0
2007–08 *Antwerp* 13 2 **13 2**
2008–09 Manchester U 0 0
2008–09 *Plymouth Arg* 31 1 **31 1**
2009–10 Manchester U 0 0
2009–10 *Watford* 12 0
2010–11 Blackpool 30 1
2011–12 Blackpool 27 0
2012–13 Blackpool 25 1
2013–14 Blackpool 30 1 **112 3**
2014–15 Watford 29 3
2015–16 Watford 35 1
2016–17 Watford 15 0
2017–18 Watford 7 0
2018–19 Watford 36 3
2019–20 Watford 29 0
2020–21 Watford 25 1
2021–22 Watford 31 0 **219 8**

CLEVERLEY, Tom (M) 324 31
H: 5 9 W: 10 08 b.Basingstoke 12-8-89
Internationals: England U20, U21, Full caps. Great Britain.
2007–08 Manchester U 0 0
2008–09 Manchester U 0 0
2008–09 *Leicester C* 15 2 **15 2**
2009–10 Manchester U 0 0
2009–10 *Watford* 33 11
2010–11 Manchester U 0 0
2010–11 *Wigan Ath* 25 3 **25 3**
2011–12 Manchester U 10 0
2012–13 Manchester U 22 2
2013–14 Manchester U 22 1
2014–15 Manchester U 1 0 **55 3**
2014–15 *Aston Villa* 31 3 **31 3**
2015–16 Everton 22 2
2016–17 Everton 10 0 **32 2**

2016–17 Watford 17 0
2017–18 Watford 23 1
2018–19 Watford 13 1
2019–20 Watford 18 1
2020–21 Watford 34 4
2021–22 Watford 28 0 **166 18**

CRICHLOW, Kane (M) 0 0
Internationals: Bermuda Full caps.
From AFC Wimbledon.
2020–21 Watford 0 0
2021–22 Watford 0 0

CUKUR, Tiago (F) 21 1
H: 6 3 b.Amsterdam 29-11-98
Internationals: Turkey U17, U21, Full caps.
From Feyenoord, AZ Alkmaar.
2021–22 Watford 0 0
2021–22 *Doncaster R* 21 1 **21 1**

DAHLBERG, Pontus (G) 85 0
H: 6 4 W: 13 03 b.Alvangen 21-1-99
Internationals: Sweden U17, U19, U21, Full caps.
2015 Gothenburg 0 0
2016 Gothenburg 0 0
2017 Gothenburg 29 0
2018 Gothenburg 10 0 **39 0**
2018–19 Watford 0 0
2019–20 Watford 0 0
2019–20 *Emmen* 0 0
2020 *BK Hacken* 14 0
2020–21 Watford 0 0
2021 *BK Hacken* 8 0 **22 0**
2021–22 Watford 0 0
2021–22 *Doncaster R* 18 0 **18 0**
2021–22 *Gillingham* 6 0 **6 0**

DELE-BASHIRU, Ayotomiwa (M) 40 4
H: 6 0 W: 10 10 b.Manchester 17-9-99
Internationals: England U16. Nigeria U20, U23.
2017–18 Manchester C 0 0
2018–19 Manchester C 0 0
2019–20 Watford 0 0
2020–21 Watford 2 0
2021–22 Watford 0 0 **2 0**
2021–22 *Reading* 38 4 **38 4**

ELITIM, Juergen (M) 131 4
H: 5 8 b.Cartagena de Indias 13-7-99
2018–19 Watford 0 0
2018–19 *Marbella* 32 2
2019–20 Watford 0 0
2019–20 *Marbella* 22 1 **54 3**
From Grenada.
2020–21 Watford 0 0
2020–21 *Ponferradina* 41 0 **41 0**
2021–22 Watford 0 0
2021–22 *Deportivo la Coruna* 36 1 **36 1**

ELLIOT, Rob (G) 162 0
H: 6 2 W: 14 11 b.Chatham 30-4-86
Internationals: Republic of Ireland U19, Full caps.
2004–05 Charlton Ath 0 0
2004–05 *Notts Co* 4 0 **4 0**
2005–06 Charlton Ath 0 0
2006–07 Charlton Ath 0 0
2006–07 *Accrington S* 7 0 **7 0**
2007–08 Charlton Ath 1 0
2008–09 Charlton Ath 23 0
2009–10 Charlton Ath 33 0
2010–11 Charlton Ath 35 0
2011–12 Charlton Ath 4 0 **96 0**
2011–12 Newcastle U 0 0
2012–13 Newcastle U 10 0
2013–14 Newcastle U 2 0
2014–15 Newcastle U 3 0
2015–16 Newcastle U 21 0
2016–17 Newcastle U 3 0
2017–18 Newcastle U 16 0
2018–19 Newcastle U 0 0
2019–20 Newcastle U 0 0
2020–21 Newcastle U 0 0 **55 0**
2020–21 Watford 0 0
2021–22 Watford 0 0

FEMENIA, Kiko (M) 301 11
H: 5 9 W: 9 11 b.Sanet i Negrals 2-2-91
Internationals: Spain U18, U19, U20.
2007–08 Hercules 1 0
2008–09 Hercules 1 0
2009–10 Hercules 35 3
2010–11 Hercules 34 1 **71 4**
2011–12 Barcelona 0 0
2012–13 Barcelona 0 0
2013–14 Real Madrid 0 0
2014–15 Alcorcon 17 0 **17 0**
2015–16 Alaves 38 5
2016–17 Alaves 31 0 **69 5**
2017–18 Watford 23 1
2018–19 Watford 29 1
2019–20 Watford 28 0
2020–21 Watford 37 0
2021–22 Watford 27 0 **144 2**

FLETCHER, Ashley (F) 155 26
H: 6 1 W: 12 04 b.Keighley 2-10-95
Internationals: England U20.
2015–16 Manchester U 0 0
2015–16 *Barnsley* 21 5 **21 5**
2016–17 West Ham U 16 0 **16 0**
2017–18 Middlesbrough 16 1
2017–18 *Sunderland* 16 2 **16 2**
2018–19 Middlesbrough 21 5
2019–20 Middlesbrough 43 11
2020–21 Middlesbrough 12 2 **92 19**
2021–22 Watford 3 0 **3 0**
2022 *New York Red Bulls* 7 0 **7 0**

FORDE, Shaqai (F) 0 0
b.Watford 5-5-04
2021–22 Watford 0 0

FOSTER, Ben (G) 476 0
H: 6 4 W: 14 02 b.Leamington Spa 3-4-83
Internationals: England Full caps.
2000–01 Stoke C 0 0
2001–02 Stoke C 0 0
2002–03 Stoke C 0 0
2003–04 Stoke C 0 0
2004–05 Stoke C 0 0
2004–05 *Kidderminster H* 2 0 **2 0**
2004–05 *Wrexham* 17 0 **17 0**
2005–06 Manchester U 0 0
2005–06 *Watford* 44 0
2006–07 Manchester U 0 0
2006–07 *Watford* 29 0
2007–08 Manchester U 1 0
2008–09 Manchester U 2 0
2009–10 Manchester U 9 0 **12 0**
2010–11 Birmingham C 38 0
2011–12 Birmingham C 0 0 **38 0**
2011–12 *WBA* 37 0
2012–13 WBA 30 0
2013–14 WBA 24 0
2014–15 WBA 28 0
2015–16 WBA 15 0
2016–17 WBA 38 0
2017–18 WBA 37 0 **209 0**
2018–19 Watford 38 0
2019–20 Watford 38 0
2020–21 Watford 23 0
2021–22 Watford 26 0 **198 0**

GOSLING, Dan (M) 270 26
H: 6 0 W: 12 07 b.Brixham 2-2-90
Internationals: England U17, U18, U19, U21.
2006–07 Plymouth Arg 12 2
2007–08 Plymouth Arg 10 0 **22 2**
2007–08 Everton 0 0
2008–09 Everton 11 2
2009–10 Everton 11 2 **22 4**
2010–11 Newcastle U 1 0
2011–12 Newcastle U 12 1
2012–13 Newcastle U 3 0
2013–14 Newcastle U 8 0 **24 1**
2013–14 *Blackpool* 14 2 **14 2**
2014–15 Bournemouth 18 0
2015–16 Bournemouth 34 3
2016–17 Bournemouth 27 2
2017–18 Bournemouth 28 2
2018–19 Bournemouth 25 2
2019–20 Bournemouth 24 3
2020–21 Bournemouth 15 2 **171 14**
2020–21 Watford 13 2
2021–22 Watford 4 1 **17 3**

GRAY, Andre (F) 265 79
H: 5 10 W: 13 01 b.Wolverhampton 26-6-91
Internationals: England C. Jamaica Full caps.
2009–10 Shrewsbury T 4 0 **4 0**
From Hinckley U, Luton T.
2014–15 Brentford 45 16
2015–16 Brentford 2 2 **47 18**
2015–16 Burnley 41 23
2016–17 Burnley 32 9 **73 32**
2017–18 Watford 31 5
2018–19 Watford 29 7
2019–20 Watford 23 2
2020–21 Watford 30 5
2021–22 Watford 0 0 **113 19**
2021–22 *QPR* 28 10 **28 10**

HERNANDEZ, Cucho (F) 211 56
H: 5 9 W: 11 07 b.Pereira 22-4-99
Internationals: Colombia U20, Full caps.
2015 Deportivo Pereira 22 3
2016 Deportivo Pereira 33 20 **55 23**
2017 Granada 0 0
2017 *America de Cali* 17 1 **17 1**
2017–18 Watford 0 0
2017–18 *Huesca* 35 16
2018–19 Watford 0 0
2018–19 *Huesca* 34 4 **69 20**
2019–20 Watford 0 0
2019–20 *Mallorca* 22 5 **22 5**
2020–21 Watford 0 0
2020–21 *Getafe* 23 2 **23 2**
2021–22 Watford 25 5 **25 5**

HUNGBO, Joseph (M) 38 7
b. 15-1-00
2018–19 Crystal Palace 0 0
2019–20 Watford 0 0
2020–21 Watford 5 0
2021–22 Watford 0 0 **5 0**
2021–22 *Ross Co* 33 7 **33 7**

JOAO PEDRO, de Jesus (F) 94 16
H: 6 0 W: 11 00 b.Ribeirao Preto 26-9-01
2019 Fluminense 25 4 **25 4**
2019–20 Watford 3 0
2020–21 Watford 38 9
2021–22 Watford 28 3 **69 12**

KABASELE, Christian (D) 278 21
H: 6 2 W: 13 08 b.Lubumbashi 24-2-91
Internationals: Belgium U19, U20, Full caps.
2008–09 Eupen 3 0
2009–10 Eupen 1 0
2010–11 Eupen 3 0
2010–11 *Mechelen* 4 1 **4 1**
2011–12 Ludogorets 11 3 **11 3**
2012–13 Eupen 26 4
2013–14 Eupen 26 2 **59 6**
2014–15 Genk 34 2
2015–16 Genk 42 4 **76 6**
2016–17 Watford 16 2
2017–18 Watford 28 2
2018–19 Watford 21 0
2019–20 Watford 27 0
2020–21 Watford 20 1
2021–22 Watford 16 0 **128 5**

KALU, Samuel (F) 156 23
b.Aba 26-8-97
Internationals: Nigeria Full caps.
2015–16 Trencin 13 3
2016–17 Trencin 19 1 **32 4**
2016–17 Gent 16 3
2017–18 Gent 32 7 **48 10**
2018–19 Bordeaux 21 3
2019–20 Bordeaux 20 1
2020–21 Bordeaux 20 4
2021–22 Bordeaux 11 1 **72 9**
2021–22 Watford 4 0 **4 0**

KAMARA, Hassane (D) 172 13
H: 5 6 W: 10 08 b.Saint-Denis 5-3-94
Internationals: Ivory Coast Full caps.
2013–14 Chateauroux 5 1
2014–15 Chateauroux 21 4
2015–16 Chateauroux 1 0 **27 5**
2015–16 Reims 2 0
2016–17 Reims 1 0
2016–17 *Creteil* 15 2 **15 2**
2017–18 Reims 22 1
2018–19 Reims 16 0
2019–20 Reims 23 2 **64 3**
2020–21 Nice 36 2
2021–22 Nice 11 0 **47 2**
2021–22 Watford 19 1 **19 1**

KAYEMBE, Edo (M) 86 4
H: 6 0 W: 12 02 b.Kananga 3-6-98
Internationals: DR Congo U23, Full caps.
2017–18 Anderlecht 1 0
2018–19 Anderlecht 12 0
2019–20 Anderlecht 18 0
2020–21 Anderlecht 2 0 **33 0**
2020–21 Eupen 23 0
2021–22 Eupen 17 4 **40 4**
2021–22 Watford 13 0 **13 0**

KING, Josh (F) 308 59
H: 5 11 W: 11 09 b.Oslo 15-1-92
Internationals: Norway U15, U16, U18, U19, U21, Full caps.
2008–09 Manchester U 0 0
2009–10 Manchester U 0 0
2010–11 Manchester U 0 0
2010–11 *Preston NE* 8 0 **8 0**
2011–12 Manchester U 0 0
2011–12 *Borussia M'gladbach* 2 0 **2 0**
2011–12 *Hull C* 18 1 **18 1**
2012–13 Manchester U 0 0
2012–13 Blackburn R 16 2
2013–14 Blackburn R 32 2
2014–15 Blackburn R 16 1 **64 5**
2015–16 Bournemouth 31 6
2016–17 Bournemouth 36 16
2017–18 Bournemouth 33 8
2018–19 Bournemouth 35 12
2019–20 Bournemouth 26 6
2020–21 Bournemouth 12 0 **173 48**
2020–21 Everton 11 0
2021–22 Everton 0 0 **11 0**
2021–22 Watford 32 5 **32 5**

KUCKA, Juraj (M) **426 54**
H: 6 1 W: 13 01 b.Bojnice 26-2-87
Internationals: Slovakia U21, Full caps.

2005–06	Podbrezova	0	0		
2006–07	Podbrezova	21	1	**21**	**1**
2006–07	Ruzomberok	6	0		
2007–08	Ruzomberok	24	5		
2008–09	Ruzomberok	18	3	**48**	**8**
2008–09	Sparta Prague	12	3		
2009–10	Sparta Prague	20	5		
2010–11	Sparta Prague	13	3	**45**	**11**
2010–11	Genoa	17	0		
2011–12	Genoa	26	2		
2012–13	Genoa	33	3		
2013–14	Genoa	11	2		
2014–15	Genoa	34	2		
2015–16	Genoa	1	0	**122**	**9**
2015–16	AC Milan	29	1		
2016–17	AC Milan	30	3	**59**	**4**
2017–18	Trabzonspor	25	3		
2018–19	Trabzonspor	8	0	**33**	**3**
2018–19	Parma	18	4		
2019–20	Parma	26	6		
2020–21	Parma	28	7		
2021–22	Parma	0	0	**72**	**17**
2021–22	*Watford*	26	1	**26**	**1**

LO-EVERTON, Sonny (F) **0 0**
H: 5 7 b.London 15-9-02
Internationals: Scotland U17, U18, U19.

2020–21	Watford	0	0		
2021–22	Watford	0	0		

LOUZA, Imran (M) **78 9**
H: 5 10 W: 10 03 b.Nantes 1-5-99
Internationals: France U20, U21. Morocco U20, Full caps.

2017–18	Nantes	0	0		
2018–19	Nantes	1	0		
2019–20	Nantes	24	2		
2020–21	Nantes	33	7	**58**	**9**
2021–22	Watford	20	0	**20**	**0**

MASINA, Adam (D) **207 7**
H: 6 3 W: 10 12 b.Khouribga 2-1-94
Internationals: Italy U21. Morocco Full caps.

2013–14	Bologna	0	0		
2014–15	Bologna	28	1		
2015–16	Bologna	33	2		
2016–17	Bologna	32	1		
2017–18	Bologna	34	0	**127**	**4**
2018–19	Watford	14	0		
2019–20	Watford	26	1		
2020–21	Watford	25	2		
2021–22	Watford	15	0	**80**	**3**

MEBUDE, Dapo (F) **37 4**
H: 5 9 b.London 29-7-01
Internationals: Scotland U16, U17, U18, U19, U21.

2018–19	Rangers	1	0		
2019–20	Rangers	0	0		
2020–21	Rangers	0	0	**1**	**0**
2020–21	*Queen of the South*	11	2	**11**	**2**
2021–22	Watford	0	0		
2021–22	*AFC Wimbledon*	25	2	**25**	**2**

N'KOULOU, Nicolas (D) **378 11**
H: 6 1 W: 12 02 b.Yaounde 27-3-90
Internationals: Cameroon U23, Full caps.

2008–09	Monaco	24	0		
2009–10	Monaco	24	0		
2010–11	Monaco	30	0	**78**	**0**
2011–12	Marseille	30	0		
2012–13	Marseille	38	1		
2013–14	Marseille	37	2		
2014–15	Marseille	24	2		
2015–16	Marseille	33	0	**162**	**5**
2016–17	Lyon	13	0	**13**	**0**
2017–18	Torino	37	2		
2018–19	Torino	36	2		
2019–20	Torino	31	1		
2020–21	Torino	18	1		
2021–22	Torino	0	0	**122**	**6**
2021–22	Watford	3	0	**3**	**0**

NGAKIA, Jeremy (D) **46 0**
H: 6 0 W: 11 03 b.Deptford 7-9-00

2019–20	West Ham U	5	0	**5**	**0**
2020–21	Watford	25	0		
2021–22	Watford	16	0	**41**	**0**

OKOYE, Maduka (G) **73 0**
H: 6 6 b.Dusseldorf 28-8-99
Internationals: Nigeria Full caps.

2016–17	Bayer Leverkusen	0	0		
2017–18	Fortuna Dusseldorf	0	0		
2018–19	Fortuna Dusseldorf	0	0		
2019–20	Fortuna Dusseldorf	14	0	**14**	**0**
2020–21	Sparta Rotterdam	29	0		
2021–22	Sparta Rotterdam	14	0	**59**	**0**
2021–22	Watford	0	0		
2021–22	*Sparta Rotterdam*	16	0		

PARKES, Adam (G) **0 0**
b. 30-11-99
Internationals: England U17.
From Southampton.

2019–20	Watford	0	0		
2020–21	Watford	0	0		
2021–22	Watford	0	0		

PENARANDA, Adalberto (F) **99 11**
b.El Vigia 31-5-97
Internationals: Venezuela U17, U20, Full caps.

2013–14	Dep La Guaira	18	1		
2014–15	Dep La Guaira	19	3	**37**	**4**
2015–16	Udinese	0	0		
2015–16	Watford	0	0		
2015–16	*Granada*	23	5	**23**	**5**
2016–17	Watford	0	0		
2016–17	*Malaga*	3	0		
2017–18	Watford	0	0		
2017–18	*Malaga*	13	0	**16**	**0**
2018–19	Watford	0	0		
2019–20	Watford	0	0		
2019–20	*Eupen*	5	0	**5**	**0**
2020–21	Watford	0	0		
2020–21	*CSKA Sofia*	0	0		
2021–22	Watford	0	0		
2021–22	*Las Palmas*	18	2	**18**	**2**

PHILIPS, Daniel (M) **26 0**
H: 5 9 W: 11 00 b.Enfield 18-1-01
Internationals: Trinidad and Tobago Full caps.
From Chelsea.

2020–21	Watford	2	0		
2021–22	Watford	0	0	**2**	**0**
2021–22	*Gillingham*	24	0	**24**	**0**

POCHETTINO, Maurizio (M) **1 0**
b. 30-3-01
From Southampton, Tottenham H.

2020–21	Watford	1	0		
2021–22	Watford	0	0	**1**	**0**

POLLOCK, Matthew (D) **80 4**
H: 6 3 W: 12 08 b.Redhill 28-9-01

2018–19	Grimsby T	2	0		
2019–20	Grimsby T	19	0		
2020–21	Grimsby T	25	3	**46**	**3**
2021–22	Watford	0	0		
2021–22	*Cheltenham T*	34	1	**34**	**1**

PUSSETTO , Ignacio (M) **180 27**
b.Canada Rosquin 21-12-95

2012–13	Atletico de Rafaela	0	0		
2013–14	Atletico de Rafaela	11	0		
2014	Atletico de Rafaela	3	0		
2015	Atletico de Rafaela	19	2		
2016	Atletico de Rafaela	11	2	**44**	**4**
2016–17	Huracan	15	2		
2017–18	Huracan	27	9	**42**	**11**
2018–19	Udinese	35	4		
2019–20	Udinese	12	1		
2019–20	Watford	7	0		
2020–21	Watford	1	0		
2020–21	*Udinese*	11	3		
2021–22	Watford	0	0	**8**	**0**
2021–22	*Udinese*	28	4	**86**	**12**

QUINA, Domingos (M) **52 6**
H: 5 8 W: 10 03 b.Bissau 18-11-99
Internationals: Portugal U17, U18, U19, U20, U21.

2016–17	West Ham U	0	0		
2017–18	West Ham U	0	0		
2018–19	Watford	8	1		
2019–20	Watford	4	0		
2020–21	Watford	14	1		
2020–21	*Granada*	8	2	**8**	**2**
2021–22	Watford	0	0	**26**	**2**
2021–22	*Fulham*	2	0	**2**	**0**
2021–22	*Barnsley*	16	2	**16**	**2**

ROBERTS, Myles (G) **0 0**
b. 9-12-01
From Reading.

2020–21	Watford	0	0		
2021–22	Watford	0	0		

ROSE, Danny (D) **226 9**
H: 5 8 W: 11 11 b.Doncaster 2-6-90
Internationals: England U17, U19, U21, Full caps. Great Britain.

2007–08	Tottenham H	0	0		
2008–09	Tottenham H	0	0		
2008–09	*Watford*	7	0		
2009–10	Tottenham H	1	1		
2010–11	Tottenham H	4	0		
2010–11	*Bristol C*	17	0	**17**	**0**
2011–12	Tottenham H	11	0		
2012–13	Tottenham H	0	0		
2012–13	*Sunderland*	27	1	**27**	**1**
2013–14	Tottenham H	22	1		
2014–15	Tottenham H	28	3		
2015–16	Tottenham H	24	1		
2016–17	Tottenham H	18	2		
2017–18	Tottenham H	10	0		
2018–19	Tottenham H	26	0		
2019–20	Tottenham H	12	0		
2019–20	*Newcastle U*	11	0	**11**	**0**
2020–21	Tottenham H	0	0	**156**	**8**
2021–22	Watford	8	0	**15**	**0**

SAMIR, Caetano (D) **213 8**
H: 6 2 W: 12 08 b.Rio de Janeiro 5-12-94
Internationals: Brazil U21.

2013	Flamengo	13	0		
2014	Flamengo	17	1		
2015	Flamengo	20	0	**50**	**1**
2015–16	Udinese	0	0		
2015–16	*Verona*	3	1	**3**	**1**
2016–17	Udinese	21	0		
2017–18	Udinese	31	2		
2018–19	Udinese	21	2		
2019–20	Udinese	21	1		
2020–21	Udinese	30	1		
2021–22	Udinese	17	0	**141**	**6**
2021–22	Watford	19	0	**19**	**0**

SARR, Ismaila (F) **179 41**
H: 6 1 W: 12 00 b.Saint-Louis 25-2-98
Internationals: Senegal U23, Full caps.

2016–17	Metz	31	5	**31**	**5**
2017–18	Rennes	24	5		
2018–19	Rennes	35	8	**59**	**13**
2019–20	Watford	28	5		
2020–21	Watford	39	13		
2021–22	Watford	22	5	**89**	**23**

SEGURA, Jorge (D) **109 3**
H: 6 4 b.Zarzal 18-1-97
Internationals: Colombia U20.

2015	Envigado	0	0		
2016	Envigado	23	2		
2017	Envigado	8	0	**31**	**2**
2017–18	Watford	0	0		
2017–18	*Vallodolid*	0	0		
2018–19	Watford	0	0		
2018–19	*Independiente Medellin*	26	0	**26**	**0**
2019–20	Watford	0	0		
2019–20	*Atlas*	18	1	**18**	**1**
2020–21	Watford	0	0		
2020–21	*Atletico Nacional*	8	0	**8**	**0**
2021–22	Watford	0	0		
2022	*America de Cali*	26	0	**26**	**0**

SEMA, Ken (M) **248 31**
H: 5 11 W: 11 03 b.Norrkoping 30-9-93
Internationals: Sweden U23, Full caps.

2013	IFK Norrkoping	0	0		
2013	*IF Sylvia*	22	4	**22**	**4**
2014	Ljungskile	30	7		
2015	Ljungskile	30	4	**60**	**11**
2016	Ostersunds	23	4		
2017	Ostersunds	24	4		
2018	Ostersunds	11	0	**58**	**8**
2018–19	Watford	17	1		
2019–20	Watford	0	0		
2019–20	*Udinese*	32	2	**32**	**2**
2020–21	Watford	41	5		
2021–22	Watford	18	0	**76**	**6**

SIERRALTA, Francisco (D) **77 4**
H: 6 4 W: 13 01 b.Las Condes 6-5-97
Internationals: Chile U20, Full caps.

2015–16	Universidad Catolica	2	1		
2016–17	Universidad Catolica	0	0	**2**	**1**
2016–17	Palestino	17	1	**17**	**1**
2017–18	Udinese	0	0		
2017–18	*Parma*	10	0		
2018–19	Udinese	0	0		
2018–19	*Parma*	6	0	**16**	**0**
2019–20	Udinese	0	0		
2019–20	*Empoli*	11	1		
2020–21	Empoli	0	0	**11**	**1**
2020–21	Udinese	0	0		
2020–21	Watford	26	1		
2021–22	Watford	5	0	**31**	**1**

SISSOKO, Moussa (M) **487 36**
H: 6 2 W: 13 01 b.Le Blanc Mesnil 16-8-89
Internationals: France U16, U17, U18, U19, U21, Full caps.

2007–08	Toulouse	30	1		
2008–09	Toulouse	35	4		
2009–10	Toulouse	37	7		
2010–11	Toulouse	36	5		
2011–12	Toulouse	35	2		
2012–13	Toulouse	19	1	**192**	**20**
2012–13	Newcastle U	12	3		
2013–14	Newcastle U	35	3		
2014–15	Newcastle U	34	4		
2015–16	Newcastle U	37	1	**118**	**11**
2016–17	Tottenham H	25	0		
2017–18	Tottenham H	33	1		
2018–19	Tottenham H	29	0		

2019–20	Tottenham H	29	2		
2020–21	Tottenham H	25	0		
2021–22	Tottenham H	0	0	**141**	**3**
2021–22	Watford	36	2	**36**	**2**

TOURE, Fandje (F) 8 0
H: 5 9 b.Conakry 1-11-02
Internationals: Guinea U17.

2020–21	Watford	0	0		
2020–21	*Chaleroi*	0	0		
2021–22	Watford	0	0		
2021–22	*Horn*	8	0	**8**	**0**

TROOST-EKONG, William (D) 216 7
H: 6 3 W: 11 09 b.Haarlem 1-9-93
Internationals: Netherlands U18, U20. Nigeria U23, Full caps.

2013–14	Groningen	2	0	**2**	**0**
2013–14	Dordrecht	10	0		
2014–15	Dordrecht	22	0	**32**	**0**
2015	Haugesund	13	0		
2016	Haugesund	24	3	**37**	**3**
2016–17	Gent	3	0	**3**	**0**
2017–18	Bursaspor	27	2	**27**	**2**
2018–19	Busaspor	1	1	**1**	**1**
2018–19	Udinese	35	0		
2019–20	Udinese	30	0		
2020–21	Udinese	0	0	**65**	**0**
2020–21	Watford	32	1		
2021–22	Watford	17	0	**49**	**1**

TUFAN, Ozan (M) 197 21
H: 5 10 W: 11 00 b.Bursa 23-3-95
Internationals: Turkey U17, U18, U19 Full caps.

2012–13	Bursaspor	1	0		
2013–14	Bursaspor	8	0		
2014–15	Bursaspor	32	3		
2015–16	Bursaspor	0	0	**41**	**3**
2015–16	Fenerbachce	26	0		
2016–17	Fenerbachce	22	3		
2017–18	Fenerbachce	9	3		
2018–19	Fenerbachce	0	0		
2018–19	*Alanyaspor*	17	0	**17**	**0**
2019–20	Fenerbachce	33	6		
2020–21	Fenerbachce	37	6	**127**	**18**
2021–22	Fenerbahce	5	0	**5**	**0**
2021–22	*Watford*	7	0	**7**	**0**

ZINCKERNAGEL, Philip (F) 273 52
H: 5 9 W: 11 00 b.Copenhagen 16-12-94
Internationals: Denmark U18, U20.

2012–13	Nordsjaelland	0	0		
2013–14	HB Koge	29	3		
2014–15	HB Koge	27	2	**56**	**5**
2015–16	Helsingor	23	3		
2016–17	Helsingor	6	2	**29**	**5**
2016–17	SonderjyskE	24	1		
2017–18	SonderjyskE	20	3	**44**	**4**
2018	Bodo/Glimt	24	6		
2019	Bodo/Glimt	30	6		
2020	Bodo/Glimt	28	19		
2020–21	Bodo/Glimt	0	0	**82**	**31**
2020–21	Watford	20	1		
2021–22	Watford	0	0	**20**	**1**
2021–22	*Nottingham F*	42	6	**42**	**6**

Players retained or with offer of contract
Abbott, George; Angelini, Vincent; Blake, Adrian; Conteh, Kamil; Grieves, Jack; McKiernan, John; Morris, James; O'Brien, Joshua.

Scholars
Adeyemo, Emmanuel Oluwatobi; Aguilar, Andres Albert Edwin; Andrews, Ryan Tyler Wayne; Balogun, Hamzat Alamu; Batzelis, Christos; Benn, Aaron Samuel; Blake, Adrian Miles Heris F S; Davis, Charlie Russell; Enahoro-Marcus, Darrin; Forde, Shaqai Tyreece Steven; Goulding, Ethan John Lindsay; Grieves, Jack Alexander; MacAulay, Jonathan Ludvig; Manning, Adian Antoine; Marian, Bogdan Nicolae; Marriott, Alfie Simon Rodney; Osborn, Billy James; Peters, Harvey William.

WBA (88)

AHEARNE-GRANT, Karlan (F) 219 67
H: 6 0 W: 11 00 b.Greenwich 19-12-97
Internationals: England U17, U18, U19.

2014–15	Charlton Ath	5	0		
2015–16	Charlton Ath	17	1		
2015–16	*Cambridge U*	3	0	**3**	**0**
2016–17	Charlton Ath	8	0		
2017–18	Charlton Ath	22	1		
2017–18	*Crawley T*	15	9	**15**	**9**
2018–19	Charlton Ath	28	14	**80**	**16**
2018–19	Huddersfield T	13	4		
2019–20	Huddersfield T	43	19	**56**	**23**
2020–21	WBA	21	1		
2021–22	WBA	44	18	**65**	**19**

AJAYI, Semi (D) 223 20
H: 6 4 W: 13 01 b.Crayford 9-11-93
Internationals: Nigeria U20, Full caps.

2012–13	Charlton Ath	0	0		
2013–14	Charlton Ath	0	0		
2014–15	Arsenal	0	0		
2014–15	*Cardiff C*	0	0		
2015–16	Cardiff C	0	0		
2015–16	*AFC Wimbledon*	5	0	**5**	**0**
2015–16	*Crewe Alex*	13	0	**13**	**0**
2016–17	Cardiff C	0	0		
2016–17	*Rotherham U*	17	1		
2017–18	Rotherham U	35	4		
2018–19	Rotherham U	46	7	**98**	**12**
2019–20	WBA	43	5		
2020–21	WBA	33	2		
2021–22	WBA	31	1	**107**	**8**

ASHWORTH, Zachary (D) 2 0
H: 5 9 b. 6-9-02
Internationals: Wales U21.

2021–22	WBA	2	0	**2**	**0**

BARTLEY, Kyle (D) 277 18
H: 6 4 W: 14 11 b.Stockport 22-5-91
Internationals: England U16, U17.

2008–09	Arsenal	0	0		
2009–10	Arsenal	0	0		
2009–10	*Sheffield U*	14	0		
2010–11	Arsenal	0	0		
2010–11	*Sheffield U*	21	0	**35**	**0**
2010–11	*Rangers*	5	1		
2011–12	Arsenal	0	0		
2011–12	*Rangers*	19	0	**24**	**1**
2012–13	Arsenal	0	0		
2012–13	Swansea C	2	0		
2013–14	Swansea C	2	0		
2013–14	*Birmingham C*	17	3	**17**	**3**
2014–15	Swansea C	7	0		
2015–16	Swansea C	5	0		
2016–17	Swansea C	0	0		
2016–17	*Leeds U*	45	6	**45**	**6**
2017–18	Swansea C	5	0	**21**	**0**
2018–19	WBA	28	1		
2019–20	WBA	38	2		
2020–21	WBA	30	3		
2021–22	WBA	39	2	**135**	**8**

BRYAN, Kean (M) 66 4
H: 6 1 W: 11 05 b.Manchester 1-11-96
Internationals: England U16, U17, U19, U20.

2016–17	Manchester C	0	0		
2016–17	*Bury*	12	0	**12**	**0**
2017–18	Manchester C	0	0		
2017–18	*Oldham Ath*	32	2	**32**	**2**
2018–19	Sheffield U	0	0		
2019–20	Sheffield U	0	0		
2019–20	*Bolton W*	6	1	**6**	**1**
2020–21	Sheffield U	13	1		
2021–22	Sheffield U	0	0	**13**	**1**
2021–22	WBA	3	0	**3**	**0**

BUTTON, David (G) 304 0
H: 6 3 W: 11 00 b.Stevenage 27-2-89
Internationals: England U16, U17, U19, U20.

2005–06	Tottenham H	0	0		
2006–07	Tottenham H	0	0		
2007–08	*Rochdale*	0	0		
2007–08	Tottenham H	0	0		
2008–09	Tottenham H	0	0		
2008–09	*Bournemouth*	4	0	**4**	**0**
2008–09	*Luton T*	0	0		
2008–09	*Dagenham & R*	3	0	**3**	**0**
2009–10	Tottenham H	0	0		
2009–10	*Crewe Alex*	10	0	**10**	**0**
2009–10	*Shrewsbury T*	26	0	**26**	**0**
2010–11	Tottenham H	0	0		
2010–11	*Plymouth Arg*	30	0	**30**	**0**
2011–12	Tottenham H	0	0		
2011–12	*Leyton Orient*	1	0	**1**	**0**
2011–12	*Doncaster R*	7	0	**7**	**0**
2011–12	*Barnsley*	9	0	**9**	**0**
2012–13	Tottenham H	0	0		
2012–13	Charlton Ath	5	0	**5**	**0**
2013–14	Brentford	42	0		
2014–15	Brentford	46	0		
2015–16	Brentford	46	0	**134**	**0**
2016–17	Fulham	40	0		
2017–18	Fulham	20	0	**60**	**0**
2018–19	Brighton & HA	4	0		
2019–20	Brighton & HA	0	0		
2020–21	Brighton & HA	0	0	**4**	**0**
2020–21	WBA	1	0		
2021–22	WBA	10	0	**11**	**0**

CARROLL, Andy (F) 321 77
H: 6 3 W: 12 00 b.Gateshead 6-1-89
Internationals: England U19, U21, Full caps.

2006–07	Newcastle U	4	0		
2007–08	Newcastle U	4	0		
2007–08	*Preston NE*	11	1	**11**	**1**
2008–09	Newcastle U	14	3		
2009–10	Newcastle U	39	17		
2010–11	Newcastle U	19	11		
2010–11	Liverpool	7	2		
2011–12	Liverpool	35	4		
2012–13	Liverpool	2	0	**44**	**6**
2012–13	*West Ham U*	24	7		
2013–14	West Ham U	15	2		
2014–15	West Ham U	14	5		
2015–16	West Ham U	27	9		
2016–17	West Ham U	18	7		
2017–18	West Ham U	16	3		
2018–19	West Ham U	12	0	**126**	**33**
2019–20	Newcastle U	19	0		
2020–21	Newcastle U	18	1		
2021–22	Newcastle U	0	0	**117**	**32**
2021–22	Reading	8	2	**8**	**2**
2021–22	WBA	15	3	**15**	**3**

DE CASTRO, Quevin (F) 2 0
H: 6 4 b.Portugal 16-8-01
From Leiston, Bury T.

2021–22	WBA	2	0	**2**	**0**

DIANGANA, Grady (F) 108 11
H: 5 11 W: 11 07 b.Lubumbashi 19-4-98
Internationals: England U20, U21.

2016–17	West Ham U	0	0		
2017–18	West Ham U	0	0		
2018–19	West Ham U	17	0		
2019–20	West Ham U	0	0	**17**	**0**
2019–20	*WBA*	30	8		
2020–21	WBA	20	1		
2021–22	WBA	41	2	**91**	**11**

DIKE, Daryl (F) 38 17
H: 6 2 b.Edmond 3-6-00
Internationals: United States Full caps.
From OKC Energy.

2020	Orlando C	17	8	**17**	**8**
2020–21	*Barnsley*	19	9		
2021–22	*Barnsley*	0	0	**19**	**9**
2021–22	Orlando C	0	0		
2021–22	WBA	2	0	**2**	**0**

FELLOWS, Tom (F) 4 0
H: 6 0 b. 25-7-03

2021–22	WBA	4	0	**4**	**0**

FURLONG, Darnell (D) 226 6
H: 5 11 W: 12 00 b.Luton 31-10-95

2014–15	QPR	3	0		
2015–16	QPR	0	0		
2015–16	*Northampton T*	10	0	**10**	**0**
2015–16	*Cambridge U*	21	0	**21**	**0**
2016–17	QPR	14	0		
2016–17	*Swindon T*	24	2	**24**	**2**
2017–18	QPR	22	0		
2018–19	QPR	25	1	**64**	**1**
2019–20	WBA	31	2		
2020–21	WBA	35	1		
2021–22	WBA	41	0	**107**	**3**

GARDNER-HICKMAN, Taylor (D) 19 0
H: 6 2 b.Telford 30-12-01
Internationals: England U20.

2020–21	WBA	0	0		
2021–22	WBA	19	0	**19**	**0**

GRIFFITHS, Joshua (G) 77 0
H: 6 1 W: 11 03 b.Hereford 5-9-01
Internationals: England U18.

2020–21	WBA	0	0		
2020–21	*Cheltenham T*	44	0	**44**	**0**
2021–22	WBA	0	0		
2021–22	*Lincoln C*	33	0	**33**	**0**

JOHNSTONE, Samuel (G) 305 0
H: 6 3 W: 13 05 b.Preston 25-3-93
Internationals: England U16, U17, U19, U20, Full caps.

2009–10	Manchester U	0	0		
2010–11	Manchester U	0	0		
2011–12	Manchester U	0	0		
2011–12	*Oldham Ath*	0	0		
2011–12	*Scunthorpe U*	12	0	**12**	**0**
2012–13	Manchester U	0	0		
2012–13	*Walsall*	7	0	**7**	**0**
2013–14	Manchester U	0	0		
2013–14	*Yeovil T*	1	0	**1**	**0**
2013–14	*Doncaster R*	18	0		
2014–15	Manchester U	0	0		
2014–15	*Doncaster R*	10	0	**28**	**0**
2014–15	*Preston NE*	22	0		
2015–16	Manchester U	0	0		
2015–16	*Preston NE*	4	0	**26**	**0**
2016–17	Manchester U	0	0		
2016–17	*Aston Villa*	21	0		
2017–18	Manchester U	0	0		
2017–18	*Aston Villa*	45	0	**66**	**0**
2018–19	WBA	46	0		
2019–20	WBA	46	0		
2020–21	WBA	37	0		
2021–22	WBA	36	0	**165**	**0**

JOSHUA, Kevin (D) **8 0**
b. 30-11-01
From Solihull Moors.

2020–21	WBA	0	0		
2021–22	WBA	0	0		
2021–22	*Waterford*	8	0	**8**	**0**

KING, Toby (M) **0 0**
b. 4-1-02

2020–21	WBA	0	0		
2021–22	WBA	0	0		

KIPRE, Cedric (D) **129 4**
H: 6 3 W: 12 02 b.Paris 9-12-96
Internationals: Ivory Coast U23.
From Paris Saint-Germain.

2014–15	Leicester C	0	0		
2015–16	Leicester C	0	0		
2016–17	Leicester C	0	0		
2017–18	Motherwell	36	1	**36**	**1**
2018–19	Wigan Ath	38	0		
2019–20	Wigan Ath	36	2		
2020–21	Wigan Ath	0	0	**74**	**2**
2020–21	WBA	0	0		
2020–21	*Charleroi*	5	0		
2021–22	WBA	14	1	**14**	**1**
2021–22	*Charleroi*	0	0	**5**	**0**

LIVERMORE, Jake (M) **398 18**
H: 5 11 W: 12 00 b.Enfield 14-11-89
Internationals: England Full caps.

2006–07	Tottenham H	0	0		
2007–08	Tottenham H	0	0		
2007–08	*Milton Keynes D*	5	0	**5**	**0**
2008–09	Tottenham H	0	0		
2008–09	*Crewe Alex*	0	0		
2009–10	Tottenham H	1	0		
2009–10	*Derby Co*	16	1	**16**	**1**
2009–10	*Peterborough U*	9	1	**9**	**1**
2010–11	Tottenham H	0	0		
2010–11	*Ipswich T*	12	0	**12**	**0**
2010–11	*Leeds U*	5	0	**5**	**0**
2011–12	Tottenham H	24	0		
2012–13	Tottenham H	11	0		
2013–14	Tottenham H	0	0	**36**	**0**
2013–14	*Hull C*	36	3		
2014–15	Hull C	35	1		
2015–16	Hull C	34	4		
2016–17	Hull C	21	1	**126**	**9**
2016–17	WBA	16	0		
2017–18	WBA	34	2		
2018–19	WBA	39	2		
2019–20	WBA	45	3		
2020–21	WBA	18	0		
2021–22	WBA	37	0	**189**	**7**

MALCOLM, Jovan (F) **10 0**
b. 10-12-02

2021–22	WBA	0	0		
2021–22	*Accrington S*	10	0	**10**	**0**

MORTON, Callum (F) **51 11**
H: 5 10 b.Torquay 19-1-00
From Yeovil T.

2019–20	WBA	0	0		
2019–20	*Northampton T*	9	5	**9**	**5**
2020–21	WBA	0	0		
2020–21	*Lincoln C*	17	2	**17**	**2**
2021–22	WBA	0	0		
2021–22	*Fleetwood T*	18	4	**18**	**4**
2021–22	*Peterborough U*	7	0	**7**	**0**

MOWATT, Alex (D) **326 38**
H: 5 10 W: 11 03 b.Doncaster 13-2-95
Internationals: England U19, U20.

2013–14	Leeds U	29	1		
2014–15	Leeds U	38	9		
2015–16	Leeds U	34	2		
2016–17	Leeds U	15	0	**116**	**12**
2016–17	Barnsley	11	1		
2017–18	Barnsley	1	0		
2017–18	*Oxford U*	30	2	**30**	**2**
2018–19	Barnsley	46	8		
2019–20	Barnsley	44	3		
2020–21	Barnsley	44	8		
2021–22	Barnsley	0	0	**146**	**20**
2021–22	WBA	34	4	**34**	**4**

O'SHEA, Dara (D) **86 5**
H: 6 2 W: 10 03 b.Dublin 4-3-99
Internationals: Republic of Ireland U18, U19, U21, Full caps.

2018–19	WBA	0	0		
2018–19	*Exeter C*	27	0	**27**	**0**
2019–20	WBA	17	3		
2020–21	WBA	28	0		
2021–22	WBA	14	2	**59**	**5**

PALMER, Alex (G) **87 0**
H: 6 3 W: 11 05 b.Kidderminster 10-8-96
Internationals: England U16.

2014–15	WBA	0	0		
2015–16	WBA	0	0		
2016–17	WBA	0	0		
2017–18	WBA	0	0		
2018–19	WBA	0	0		
2018–19	*Oldham Ath*	1	0	**1**	**0**
2018–19	*Notts Co*	1	0	**1**	**0**
2019–20	WBA	0	0		
2019–20	*Plymouth Arg*	37	0	**37**	**0**
2020–21	WBA	0	0		
2020–21	*Lincoln C*	46	0	**46**	**0**
2021–22	WBA	0	0		
2021–22	*Luton T*	2	0	**2**	**0**

PHILLIPS, Matthew (M) **455 62**
H: 6 0 W: 11 11 b.Aylesbury 13-3-91
Internationals: England U19, U20. Scotland Full caps.

2007–08	Wycombe W	2	0		
2008–09	Wycombe W	37	3		
2009–10	Wycombe W	36	5		
2010–11	Wycombe W	3	0	**78**	**8**
2010–11	Blackpool	27	1		
2011–12	Blackpool	33	7		
2011–12	*Sheffield U*	6	5	**6**	**5**
2012–13	Blackpool	34	4		
2013–14	Blackpool	0	0	**94**	**12**
2013–14	QPR	21	3		
2014–15	QPR	25	3		
2015–16	QPR	44	8	**90**	**14**
2016–17	WBA	27	4		
2017–18	WBA	30	2		
2018–19	WBA	30	5		
2019–20	WBA	39	7		
2020–21	WBA	33	2		
2021–22	WBA	28	3	**187**	**23**

REACH, Adam (M) **380 39**
H: 6 1 W: 11 07 b.Gateshead 3-2-93
Internationals: England U19, U20.

2010–11	Middlesbrough	1	1		
2011–12	Middlesbrough	1	0		
2012–13	Middlesbrough	16	2		
2013–14	Middlesbrough	2	0		
2013–14	*Shrewsbury T*	22	3	**22**	**3**
2013–14	*Bradford C*	18	3	**18**	**3**
2014–15	Middlesbrough	39	2		
2015–16	Middlesbrough	4	1		
2015–16	*Preston NE*	35	4	**35**	**4**
2016–17	Middlesbrough	0	0	**63**	**6**
2016–17	Sheffield W	39	3		
2017–18	Sheffield W	46	4		
2018–19	Sheffield W	42	8		
2019–20	Sheffield W	37	1		
2020–21	Sheffield W	44	5	**208**	**21**
2021–22	WBA	34	2	**34**	**2**

RICHARDS, Rico (M) **0 0**
H: 5 9 W: 10 10 b.Birmingham 27-9-03
Internationals: England U16, U17.

2019–20	WBA	0	0		
2020–21	WBA	0	0		
2021–22	WBA	0	0		

ROBINSON, Callum (F) **262 51**
H: 5 10 W: 11 11 b.Northampton 2-2-95
Internationals: England U16, U17, U19, U20. Republic of Ireland Full caps.

2013–14	Aston Villa	4	0		
2014–15	Aston Villa	0	0		
2014–15	*Preston NE*	25	4		
2015–16	Aston Villa	0	0	**4**	**0**
2015–16	*Bristol C*	6	0	**6**	**0**
2015–16	*Preston NE*	14	2		
2016–17	Preston NE	42	10		
2017–18	Preston NE	41	7		
2018–19	Preston NE	27	12	**149**	**35**
2019–20	Sheffield U	16	1	**16**	**1**
2019–20	*WBA*	16	3		
2020–21	WBA	28	5		
2021–22	WBA	43	7	**87**	**15**

SAWYERS, Romaine (M) **357 25**
H: 5 9 W: 10 08 b.Birmingham 2-11-91
Internationals: St Kitts and Nevis U23, Full caps.

2009–10	WBA	0	0		
2010–11	WBA	0	0		
2010–11	*Port Vale*	1	0	**1**	**0**
2011–12	WBA	0	0		
2011–12	*Shrewsbury T*	7	0	**7**	**0**
2012–13	WBA	0	0		
2012–13	Walsall	4	0		
2013–14	Walsall	44	6		
2014–15	Walsall	42	4		
2015–16	Walsall	46	6	**136**	**16**
2016–17	Brentford	43	2		
2017–18	Brentford	42	4		
2018–19	Brentford	42	0	**127**	**6**
2019–20	WBA	42	1		
2020–21	WBA	19	0		
2021–22	WBA	0	0	**61**	**1**
2021–22	*Stoke C*	25	2	**25**	**2**

SHOTTON, Saul (D) **4 0**
H: 6 0 W: 11 11 b.Stoke-on-Trent 10-11-00

2017–18	Bury	4	0		
2018–19	Bury	0	0	**4**	**0**
2019–20	WBA	0	0		
2020–21	WBA	0	0		
2021–22	WBA	0	0		

SOULE, Jamie (F) **1 0**
b. 26-11-00
Internationals: England U17.

2019–20	WBA	0	0		
2020–21	WBA	0	0		
2020–21	*Lincoln C*	1	0		
2021–22	WBA	0	0		
2021–22	*Lincoln C*	0	0	**1**	**0**
2021–22	*Cheltenham T*	0	0		

TAYLOR, Caleb (D) **1 0**
H: 5 6 W: 8 09 b.Burnley 14-1-03

2020–21	WBA	0	0		
2021–22	WBA	1	0	**1**	**0**

TOWNSEND, Conor (D) **236 6**
H: 5 4 W: 9 11 b.Hessle 4-3-93

2011–12	Hull C	0	0		
2012–13	Hull C	0	0		
2012–13	*Chesterfield*	20	1	**20**	**1**
2013–14	Hull C	0	0		
2013–14	*Carlisle U*	12	0	**12**	**0**
2014–15	Hull C	0	0		
2014–15	*Dundee U*	17	0	**17**	**0**
2014–15	*Scunthorpe U*	6	0		
2015–16	Hull C	0	0		
2015–16	Scunthorpe U	20	1		
2016–17	Scunthorpe U	24	0		
2017–18	Scunthorpe U	30	4	**80**	**5**
2018–19	WBA	12	0		
2019–20	WBA	27	0		
2020–21	WBA	25	0		
2021–22	WBA	43	0	**107**	**0**

TULLOCH, Rayhaan (F) **4 0**
H: 5 9 W: 10 03 b.Birmingham 20-1-01
Internationals: England U16, U17, U18.

2017–18	WBA	0	0		
2018–19	WBA	0	0		
2019–20	WBA	0	0		
2020–21	*Doncaster R*	2	0		
2021–22	Doncaster R	0	0	**2**	**0**
2021–22	WBA	2	0	**2**	**0**

WINDSOR, Owen (F) **16 2**
b. 17-9-01
From Cirencester T.

2020–21	WBA	0	0		
2020–21	*Grimsby T*	12	1	**12**	**1**
2020–21	*Newport Co*	1	0	**1**	**0**
2021–22	WBA	0	0		
2021–22	*Carlisle U*	3	1	**3**	**1**

ZOHORE, Kenneth (F) **205 46**
H: 6 4 W: 15 06 b.Copenhagen 31-1-94
Internationals: Denmark U17, U18, U19, U21.

2009–10	Copenhagen	1	0		
2010–11	Copenhagen	15	1		
2011–12	Copenhagen	0	0	**16**	**1**
2011–12	Fiorentina	0	0		
2012–13	Fiorentina	0	0		
2013–14	Fiorentina	0	0		
2013–14	*Brondby*	25	5	**25**	**5**
2014	*Gothenburg*	5	2	**5**	**2**
2014–15	Fiorentina	0	0		
2014–15	Odense BK	11	2		
2015–16	Odense BK	16	7	**27**	**9**
2015–16	KV Kortrijk	0	0		
2015–16	*Cardiff C*	12	2		
2016–17	Cardiff C	29	12		
2017–18	Cardiff C	36	9		
2018–19	Cardiff C	19	1	**96**	**24**
2019–20	WBA	17	3		
2020–21	WBA	0	0		
2020–21	*Millwall*	17	2	**17**	**2**
2021–22	WBA	2	0	**19**	**3**

Players retained or with offer of contract
Andrews, Jamie; Cann, Ted; Cleary, Reyes; Delaney, Zak; Faal, Mo; Ingram, Ethan; Nguepissi, Cianole.

Scholars
Ayomide Oluwatobi, Samuel; Chidi, Mark Onyemaechi; Cleary, Reyes Demar Uriah; Hall, Reece Daniel; Heard, Fenton William James; Higgins, Akeel Adriano Billy; Hollingshead, Ronnie; Hudd, Beau; Hurlock, Tobias Christopher; Jakobsen-Olofinjana, Oluwafemi Emanuel; Lamb, MacKenzie Craig; Love, Layton; MacHisa, Leon Tafara; Ngoma Muanda, Daniel; Okoka, Samuel; Oliver, Archie; Phillips, Narel Aston; Richards, Matthew William; Shaw, Joshua Aaron; Wangusi, Jesse; Williams, Alexander David.

WEST HAM U (89)

ALESE, Ajibola (D) **12 0**
H: 6 4 W: 12 04 b.Islington 17-1-01
Internationals: England U16, U17, U18, U19, U20.
2019–20 West Ham U 0 0
2019–20 *Accrington S* 10 0 **10 0**
2020–21 West Ham U 0 0
2020–21 *Cambridge U* 2 0 **2 0**
2021–22 West Ham U 0 0

ALVES, Frederik (D) **36 0**
H: 6 2 W: 13 03 b.Hvidovre 8-11-99
Internationals: Denmark U20, U21.
2018–19 Silkeborg 17 0
2019–20 Silkeborg 16 0
2020–21 Silkeborg 0 0 **33 0**
2020–21 West Ham U 0 0
2021–22 West Ham U 0 0
2021–22 *Sunderland* 3 0 **3 0**
Transferred to Brondby, January 2022.

ANANG, Joseph (G) **36 0**
H: 6 0 W: 11 05 b.Ghana 8-6-00
Internationals: England U20.
2019–20 West Ham U 0 0
2020–21 West Ham U 0 0
2021–22 West Ham U 0 0
2021–22 *Stevenage* 13 0 **13 0**
2021–22 *St Patricks Ath* 23 0 **23 0**

ANTONIO, Michael (F) **403 97**
H: 5 11 W: 12 11 b.Wandsworth 28-3-90
Internationals: Jamaica Full caps.
From Tooting & Mitcham U.
2008–09 Reading 0 0
2008–09 *Cheltenham T* 9 0 **9 0**
2009–10 Reading 1 0
2009–10 *Southampton* 28 3 **28 3**
2010–11 Reading 21 1
2011–12 Reading 6 0
2011–12 *Colchester U* 15 4 **15 4**
2011–12 *Sheffield W* 14 5
2012–13 Reading 0 0 **28 1**
2012–13 Sheffield W 37 8
2013–14 Sheffield W 27 4 **78 17**
2014–15 Nottingham F 46 14
2015–16 Nottingham F 4 2 **50 16**
2015–16 West Ham U 26 8
2016–17 West Ham U 29 9
2017–18 West Ham U 21 3
2018–19 West Ham U 33 6
2019–20 West Ham U 24 10
2020–21 West Ham U 26 10
2021–22 West Ham U 36 10 **195 56**

APPIAH-FORSON, Keenan (M) **0 0**
H: 5 9 b.Greenwich 16-10-01
2020–21 West Ham U 0 0
2021–22 West Ham U 0 0

AREOLA, Alphonse (G) **218 0**
H: 6 5 W: 13 05 b.Paris 27-2-93
Internationals: France U16, U17, U18, U19, U20, U21, Full caps.
2012–13 Paris Saint-Germain 2 0
2013–14 Paris Saint-Germain 0 0
2013–14 *Lens* 35 0 **35 0**
2014–15 Paris Saint-Germain 0 0
2014–15 *Bastia* 35 0 **35 0**
2015–16 Paris Saint-Germain 0 0
2015–16 *Villarreal* 32 0 **32 0**
2016–17 Paris Saint-Germain 15 0
2017–18 Paris Saint-Germain 34 0
2018–19 Paris Saint-Germain 21 0
2019–20 Paris Saint-Germain 3 0
2019–20 *Real Madrid* 4 0 **4 0**
2020–21 Paris Saint-Germain 0 0
2020–21 *Fulham* 36 0 **36 0**
2021–22 Paris Saint-Germain 0 0 **75 0**
2021–22 *West Ham U* 1 0 **1 0**

ASHBY, Harrison (D) **1 0**
H: 5 10 W: 11 05 b.Milton Keynes 14-11-01
Internationals: Scotland U17, U19, U21.
2020–21 West Ham U 0 0
2021–22 West Ham U 1 0 **1 0**

ASHLEY, Ossama (M) **0 0**
2017–18 AFC Wimbledon 0 0
2018–19 AFC Wimbledon 0 0
2019–20 AFC Wimbledon 0 0
2020–21 West Ham U 0 0
2021–22 West Ham U 0 0

BAPTISTE, Jamal (M) **0 0**
H: 6 0 b.Redbridge 11-11-03
Internationals: England U16, U17, U19.
2020–21 West Ham U 0 0
2021–22 West Ham U 0 0

BENRAHMA, Said (F) **220 52**
H: 5 8 W: 10 08 b.Ain Temouchent 10-8-95
Internationals: Algeria Full caps.
2013–14 Nice 5 0
2014–15 Nice 3 1
2015–16 Nice 9 2
2015–16 *Angers* 12 1 **12 1**
2016–17 Nice 0 0
2016–17 *Gazelec Ajaccio* 15 3 **15 3**
2017–18 Nice 0 0 **17 3**
2017–18 *Chateauroux* 31 9 **31 9**
2018–19 Brentford 38 10
2019–20 Brentford 43 17
2020–21 Brentford 2 0 **83 27**
2020–21 West Ham U 30 1
2021–22 West Ham U 32 8 **62 9**

BOWEN, Jarrod (F) **211 73**
H: 5 9 W: 11 00 b.Leominster 20-12-96
Internationals: England Full caps.
2014–15 Hull C 0 0
2015–16 Hull C 0 0
2016–17 Hull C 7 0
2017–18 Hull C 42 14
2018–19 Hull C 46 22
2019–20 Hull C 29 16 **124 52**
2019–20 West Ham U 13 1
2020–21 West Ham U 38 8
2021–22 West Ham U 36 12 **87 21**

CARDOSO, Goncalo (D) **20 0**
H: 6 2 W: 12 08 b.Marco de Canaveses 21-10-00
Internationals: Portugal U19, U20.
2018–19 Boavista 15 0 **15 0**
2019–20 West Ham U 0 0
2020–21 West Ham U 0 0
2020–21 *FC Basel* 5 0 **5 0**
2021–22 West Ham U 0 0
2021–22 *Real Betis* 0 0

CHESTERS, Daniel (F) **1 0**
H: 5 10 W: 10 03 b.Hitchin 4-4-02
2020–21 West Ham U 0 0
2021–22 West Ham U 1 0 **1 0**

COSTA DA ROSA, Bernardo (M) **0 0**
2019–20 West Ham U 0 0
2020–21 West Ham U 0 0
2021–22 West Ham U 0 0

COUFAL, Vladimir (D) **267 10**
H: 5 9 W: 11 00 b.Ludgerovice 22-8-92
Internationals: Czech Republic U21, Full caps.
2010–11 Hlucin 14 0
2011–12 Hlucin 0 0 **14 0**
2011–12 *Opava* 13 1 **13 1**
2012–13 Slovan Liberec 10 0
2013–14 Slovan Liberec 21 0
2014–15 Slovan Liberec 13 0
2015–16 Slovan Liberec 27 1
2016–17 Slovan Liberec 17 0
2017–18 Slovan Liberec 30 2 **118 3**
2018–19 Slavia Prague 28 3
2019–20 Slavia Prague 32 3
2020–21 Slavia Prague 0 0 **60 6**
2020–21 West Ham U 34 0
2021–22 West Ham U 28 0 **62 0**

COVENTRY, Conor (M) **39 1**
H: 5 9 W: 10 03 b.Waltham Forest 25-3-00
Internationals: Republic of Ireland U17, U19, U21.
2018–19 West Ham U 0 0
2019–20 West Ham U 0 0
2019–20 *Lincoln C* 7 0 **7 0**
2020–21 West Ham U 0 0
2021–22 West Ham U 0 0
2021–22 *Peterborough U* 12 0 **12 0**
2021–22 *Milton Keynes D* 20 1 **20 1**

CRESSWELL, Aaron (D) **457 21**
H: 5 7 W: 10 06 b.Liverpool 15-12-89
Internationals: England Full caps.
2008–09 Tranmere R 13 1
2009–10 Tranmere R 14 0
2010–11 Tranmere R 43 4 **70 5**
2011–12 Ipswich T 44 1
2012–13 Ipswich T 46 3
2013–14 Ipswich T 42 2 **132 6**
2014–15 West Ham U 38 2
2015–16 West Ham U 37 2
2016–17 West Ham U 26 0
2017–18 West Ham U 36 1
2018–19 West Ham U 20 0
2019–20 West Ham U 31 3
2020–21 West Ham U 36 0
2021–22 West Ham U 31 2 **255 10**

DAWSON, Craig (D) **382 44**
H: 6 2 W: 13 05 b.Rochdale 6-5-90
Internationals: England U21. Great Britain.
2008–09 Rochdale 0 0
2009–10 Rochdale 42 9
2010–11 WBA 0 0
2010–11 *Rochdale* 45 10 **87 19**
2011–12 WBA 8 0
2012–13 WBA 1 0
2012–13 *Bolton W* 16 4 **16 4**
2013–14 WBA 12 0
2014–15 WBA 29 2
2015–16 WBA 38 4
2016–17 WBA 37 4
2017–18 WBA 28 2
2018–19 WBA 41 2 **194 14**
2019–20 Watford 29 2
2020–21 Watford 0 0 **29 2**
2020–21 *West Ham U* 22 3
2021–22 West Ham U 34 2 **56 5**

DIALLO, Amadou (F) **0 0**
b. 15-2-03
Internationals: England U16, U17.
2020–21 West Ham U 0 0
2021–22 West Ham U 0 0

DIOP, Issa (D) **173 11**
H: 6 4 W: 13 03 b.Toulouse 9-1-97
Internationals: France U16, U17, U18, U19, U20, U21.
2015–16 Toulouse 21 1
2016–17 Toulouse 30 2
2017–18 Toulouse 26 2 **77 5**
2018–19 West Ham U 33 1
2019–20 West Ham U 32 3
2020–21 West Ham U 18 2
2021–22 West Ham U 13 0 **96 6**

EKWAH, Pierre (D) **0 0**
H: 6 2 b.Massy 15-1-02
Internationals: France U16, U20.
From Nantes.
2020–21 Chelsea 0 0
2021–22 West Ham U 0 0

EMMANUEL, Mbule (D) **0 0**
H: 6 0 W: 11 00 b.Barking 27-12-00
2020–21 West Ham U 0 0
2021–22 West Ham U 0 0

FABIANSKI, Lukasz (G) **369 0**
H: 6 3 W: 13 01 b.Costrzyn nad Odra 18-4-85
Internationals: Poland U21, Full caps.
2004–05 Lech Poznan 0 0
2005–06 Legia Warsaw 30 0
2006–07 Legia Warsaw 23 0 **53 0**
2007–08 Arsenal 3 0
2008–09 Arsenal 6 0
2009–10 Arsenal 4 0
2010–11 Arsenal 14 0
2011–12 Arsenal 0 0
2012–13 Arsenal 4 0
2013–14 Arsenal 1 0 **32 0**
2014–15 Swansea C 37 0
2015–16 Swansea C 37 0
2016–17 Swansea C 37 0
2017–18 Swansea C 38 0 **149 0**
2018–19 West Ham U 38 0
2019–20 West Ham U 25 0
2020–21 West Ham U 35 0
2021–22 West Ham U 37 0 **135 0**

FORNALS, Pablo (M) **234 25**
H: 5 10 W: 10 08 b.Castellon de la Plana 22-2-96
Internationals: Spain U21, Full caps.
2015–16 Malaga 27 1
2016–17 Malaga 32 6 **59 7**
2017–18 Villareal 35 3
2018–19 Villareal 35 2 **70 5**
2019–20 West Ham U 36 2
2020–21 West Ham U 33 5
2021–22 West Ham U 36 6 **105 13**

FREDERICKS, Ryan (D) **208 3**
H: 5 8 W: 11 04 b.Hammersmith 10-10-92
Internationals: England U19.
2010–11 Tottenham H 0 0
2011–12 Tottenham H 0 0
2012–13 Tottenham H 0 0
2012–13 *Brentford* 4 0 **4 0**
2013–14 Tottenham H 0 0
2013–14 *Millwall* 14 1 **14 1**
2014–15 Tottenham H 0 0
2014–15 *Middlesbrough* 17 0 **17 0**
2015–16 Bristol C 4 0 **4 0**
2015–16 Fulham 32 0
2016–17 Fulham 30 0
2017–18 Fulham 44 0 **106 0**
2018–19 West Ham U 15 1
2019–20 West Ham U 27 0

2020–21	West Ham U	14	1		
2021–22	West Ham U	7	0	**63**	**2**

HEGYI, Krisztian (G) 0 0
H: 6 4 W: 13 05 b.Budapest 24-9-02
Internationals: Hungary U16, U17, U18, U21.

2020–21	West Ham U	0	0		
2021–22	West Ham U	0	0		

HOLLAND, Nathan (M) 47 7
H: 5 10 W: 11 00 b.Wythenshawe 19-6-98
Internationals: England U16, U17, U18, U19.
From Everton.

2016–17	West Ham U	0	0		
2017–18	West Ham U	0	0		
2018–19	West Ham U	0	0		
2019–20	West Ham U	2	0		
2019–20	*Oxford U*	10	2		
2020–21	West Ham U	0	0		
2021–22	West Ham U	0	0	**2**	**0**
2021–22	*Oxford U*	35	5	**45**	**7**

JOHNSON, Ben (D) 38 2
H: 5 9 W: 10 08 b.Waltham Forest 24-1-00
Internationals: England U21.

2017–18	West Ham U	0	0		
2018–19	West Ham U	1	0		
2019–20	West Ham U	3	0		
2020–21	West Ham U	14	1		
2021–22	West Ham U	20	1	**38**	**2**

KRAL, Alex (M) 115 1
H: 6 1 W: 11 05 b.Kosice 19-5-98
Internationals: Czech Republic U17, U18, U19, U20, U21, Full caps.

2016–17	Teplice	3	0		
2017–18	Teplice	23	1		
2018–19	Teplice	17	0	**43**	**1**
2018–19	Slavia Prague	12	0		
2019–20	Slavia Prague	6	0	**18**	**0**
2019–20	Spartak Moscow	19	0		
2020–21	Spartak Moscow	29	0		
2021–22	Spartak Moscow	5	0	**53**	**0**
2021–22	*West Ham U*	1	0	**1**	**0**

LANZINI, Manuel (M) 305 49
H: 5 7 W: 11 00 b.Ituzaingo 15-2-93
Internationals: Argentina U20, Full caps.

2010–11	River Plate	22	0		
2010–11	*Fluminense*	22	2		
2011–12	River Plate	0	0		
2011–12	*Fluminense*	6	1	**28**	**3**
2012–13	River Plate	26	8	**26**	**8**
2013–14	River Plate	36	4	**58**	**4**
2014–15	Al-Jazira	24	8		
2015–16	Al-Jazira	0	0	**24**	**8**
2015–16	*West Ham U*	26	6		
2016–17	West Ham U	35	8		
2017–18	West Ham U	27	5		
2018–19	West Ham U	10	1		
2019–20	West Ham U	24	0		
2020–21	West Ham U	17	1		
2021–22	West Ham U	30	5	**169**	**26**

MARTIN, David E (G) 347 0
H: 6 2 W: 13 07 b.Romford 22-1-86
Internationals: England U16, U17, U18, U19.

2003–04	Wimbledon	2	0	**2**	**0**
2004–05	Milton Keynes D	15	0		
2005–06	Milton Keynes D	0	0		
2005–06	Liverpool	0	0		
2006–07	Liverpool	0	0		
2006–07	*Accrington S*	10	0	**10**	**0**
2007–08	Liverpool	0	0		
2008–09	Liverpool	0	0		
2008–09	*Leicester C*	25	0	**25**	**0**
2009–10	Liverpool	0	0		
2009–10	*Tranmere R*	3	0	**3**	**0**
2009–10	*Leeds U*	0	0		
2009–10	*Derby Co*	2	0	**2**	**0**
2010–11	Milton Keynes D	43	0		
2011–12	Milton Keynes D	46	0		
2012–13	Milton Keynes D	31	0		
2013–14	Milton Keynes D	40	0		
2014–15	Milton Keynes D	39	0		
2015–16	Milton Keynes D	35	0		
2016–17	Milton Keynes D	40	0	**289**	**0**
2017–18	Millwall	1	0		
2018–19	Millwall	10	0	**11**	**0**
2019–20	West Ham U	5	0		
2020–21	West Ham U	0	0		
2021–22	West Ham U	0	0	**5**	**0**

MASUAKU, Arthur (D) 183 3
H: 5 10 W: 11 00 b.Lille 7-11-93
Internationals: France U18, U19. DR Congo Full caps.

2012–13	Valenciennes	0	0		
2013–14	Valenciennes	27	1	**27**	**1**
2014–15	Olympiacos	27	0		
2015–16	Olympiacos	24	1	**51**	**1**
2016–17	West Ham U	13	0		
2017–18	West Ham U	27	0		
2018–19	West Ham U	23	0		
2019–20	West Ham U	17	0		
2020–21	West Ham U	12	0		
2021–22	West Ham U	13	1	**105**	**1**

NEVERS, Thierry (M) 0 0
b. 26-3-02

2019–20	Reading	0	0		
2020–21	Reading	0	0		
2021–22	West Ham U	0	0		

NOBLE, Mark (M) 490 56
H: 5 11 W: 12 00 b.Canning Town 8-5-87
Internationals: England U16, U17, U18, U19, U21.

2004–05	West Ham U	13	0		
2005–06	West Ham U	5	0		
2005–06	*Hull C*	5	0	**5**	**0**
2006–07	West Ham U	10	2		
2006–07	*Ipswich T*	13	1	**13**	**1**
2007–08	West Ham U	31	3		
2008–09	West Ham U	29	3		
2009–10	West Ham U	27	2		
2010–11	West Ham U	26	4		
2011–12	West Ham U	45	8		
2012–13	West Ham U	28	4		
2013–14	West Ham U	38	3		
2014–15	West Ham U	28	2		
2015–16	West Ham U	37	7		
2016–17	West Ham U	30	3		
2017–18	West Ham U	29	4		
2018–19	West Ham U	31	5		
2019–20	West Ham U	33	4		
2020–21	West Ham U	21	0		
2021–22	West Ham U	11	1	**472**	**55**

ODUBEKO, Ademipo (F) 22 2
H: 5 11 b.Tallaght 21-10-02
Internationals: Republic of Ireland U16, U17, U21.
From Manchester U.

2020–21	West Ham U	0	0		
2021–22	West Ham U	0	0		
2021–22	*Huddersfield T*	6	0	**6**	**0**
2021–22	*Doncaster R*	16	2	**16**	**2**

OGBONNA, Angelo (D) 387 9
H: 6 3 W: 13 08 b.Cassino 23-5-88
Internationals: Italy U21, Full caps.

2006–07	Torino	4	0		
2007–08	Torino	0	0		
2007–08	*Crotone*	22	0	**22**	**0**
2008–09	Torino	19	0		
2009–10	Torino	31	1		
2010–11	Torino	35	0		
2011–12	Torino	39	0		
2012–13	Torino	22	0	**150**	**1**
2013–14	Juventus	16	0		
2014–15	Juventus	25	0	**41**	**0**
2015–16	West Ham U	28	0		
2016–17	West Ham U	20	0		
2017–18	West Ham U	32	1		
2018–19	West Ham U	24	1		
2019–20	West Ham U	31	2		
2020–21	West Ham U	28	3		
2021–22	West Ham U	11	1	**174**	**8**

OKOFLEX, Armstrong (F) 0 0
b.Dublin 2-3-02
Internationals: England U16. Republic of Ireland U16, U19.
From Arsenal, Celtic.

2021–22	West Ham U	0	0		

PERKINS, Sonny (M) 1 0
H: 5 10 b.Waltham Forest 10-2-04
Internationals: England U16, U18.

2021–22	West Ham U	1	0	**1**	**0**

RANDOLPH, Darren (G) 385 0
H: 6 2 W: 12 04 b.Dublin 12-5-87
Internationals: Republic of Ireland U21, B, Full caps.

2004–05	Charlton Ath	0	0		
2005–06	Charlton Ath	0	0		
2006–07	Charlton Ath	1	0		
2006–07	*Gillingham*	3	0	**3**	**0**
2007–08	Charlton Ath	1	0		
2007–08	*Bury*	14	0	**14**	**0**
2008–09	Charlton Ath	1	0		
2008–09	*Hereford U*	13	0	**13**	**0**
2009–10	Charlton Ath	11	0	**14**	**0**
2010–11	Motherwell	37	0		
2011–12	Motherwell	38	0		
2012–13	Motherwell	36	0	**111**	**0**
2013–14	Birmingham C	46	0		
2014–15	Birmingham C	45	0	**91**	**0**
2015–16	West Ham U	6	0		
2016–17	West Ham U	22	0		
2017–18	Middlesbrough	46	0		
2018–19	Middlesbrough	46	0		
2019–20	Middlesbrough	14	0	**106**	**0**
2019–20	West Ham U	2	0		
2020–21	West Ham U	3	0		
2021–22	West Ham U	0	0	**33**	**0**

RICE, Declan (M) 167 6
H: 6 1 W: 12 00 b.Kingston-upon-Thames 14-1-99
Internationals: Republic of Ireland U16, U17, U19, U21, Full caps.
From Chelsea.

2016–17	West Ham U	1	0		
2017–18	West Ham U	26	0		
2018–19	West Ham U	34	2		
2019–20	West Ham U	38	1		
2020–21	West Ham U	32	2		
2021–22	West Ham U	36	1	**167**	**6**

SOUCEK, Tomas (M) 226 49
H: 6 4 W: 13 08 b.Havlickuv Brod 27-2-95
Internationals: Czech Republic U19, U20, U21, Full caps.

2014–15	Slavia Prague	0	0		
2014–15	*Viktoria Zizkov*	14	0	**14**	**0**
2015–16	Slavia Prague	29	7		
2016–17	Slavia Prague	7	0		
2016–17	*Slovan Liberec*	12	0	**12**	**0**
2017–18	Slavia Prague	27	3		
2018–19	Slavia Prague	34	13		
2019–20	Slavia Prague	17	8	**114**	**31**
2019–20	*West Ham U*	13	3		
2020–21	West Ham U	38	10		
2021–22	West Ham U	35	5	**86**	**18**

SWYER, Kamarai (M) 0 0
b.Redbridge 4-12-02

2020–21	West Ham U	0	0		
2021–22	West Ham U	0	0		

TROTT, Nathan (G) 45 0
H: 6 0 W: 11 00 b. 21-11-98
Internationals: Bermuda U17. England U18, U20.

2017–18	West Ham U	0	0		
2018–19	West Ham U	0	0		
2019–20	West Ham U	0	0		
2019–20	*AFC Wimbledon*	23	0	**23**	**0**
2020–21	West Ham U	0	0		
2021–22	West Ham U	0	0		
2021–22	*Nancy*	22	0	**22**	**0**

VLASIC, Nikola (M) 203 40
H: 5 10 W: 12 08 b.Split 4-10-97
Internationals: Croatia U16, U17, U18, U19, U21, Full caps.

2014–15	Hajduk Split	27	3		
2015–16	Hajduk Split	23	1		
2016–17	Hajduk Split	30	4		
2017–18	Hajduk Split	6	3	**86**	**11**
2017–18	Everton	12	0		
2018–19	Everton	0	0	**12**	**0**
2018–19	*CSKA Moscow*	25	5		
2019–20	CSKA Moscow	30	12		
2020–21	CSKA Moscow	26	11		
2021–22	CSKA Moscow	5	0	**86**	**28**
2021–22	West Ham U	19	1	**19**	**1**

YARMOLENKO, Andriy (F) 321 114
H: 6 2 W: 12 00 b.Saint Petersburg 23-10-89
Internationals: Ukraine U19, U21, Full caps.

2006–07	Desna Chernihiv	9	4	**9**	**4**
2007–08	Dynamo Kyiv	1	1		
2008–09	Dynamo Kyiv	10	0		
2009–10	Dynamo Kyiv	28	7		
2010–11	Dynamo Kyiv	26	11		
2011–12	Dynamo Kyiv	28	12		
2012–13	Dynamo Kyiv	27	11		
2013–14	Dynamo Kyiv	26	12		
2014–15	Dynamo Kyiv	26	14		
2015–16	Dynamo Kyiv	23	13		
2016–17	Dynamo Kyiv	28	15		
2017–18	Dynamo Kyiv	5	3	**228**	**99**
2017–18	Borussia Dortmund	18	3	**18**	**3**
2018–19	West Ham U	9	2		
2019–20	West Ham U	23	5		
2020–21	West Ham U	15	0		
2021–22	West Ham U	19	1	**66**	**8**

ZOUMA, Kurt (D) 251 13
H: 6 2 W: 13 05 b.Lyon 27-10-94
Internationals: France U16, U17, U19, U20, U21, Full caps.

2010–11	Saint-Etienne	0	0		
2011–12	Saint-Etienne	20	1		
2012–13	Saint-Etienne	18	2		
2013–14	Chelsea	0	0		
2013–14	*Saint-Etienne*	24	0	**62**	**3**
2014–15	Chelsea	15	0		
2015–16	Chelsea	23	1		
2016–17	Chelsea	9	0		
2017–18	Chelsea	0	0		
2017–18	*Stoke C*	34	1	**34**	**1**
2018–19	Chelsea	0	0		
2018–19	*Everton*	32	2	**32**	**2**
2019–20	Chelsea	28	0		
2020–21	Chelsea	24	5		

2021–22	Chelsea	0	0	**99**	**6**
2021–22	West Ham U	24	1	**24**	**1**

Players retained or with offer of contract
Greenidge, William; Kinnear, Brian; Laing, Levi; Longelo Mbule, Emmanuel; Mubama, Divin; Potts, Freddie.

Scholars
Bates, Billy Alfred; Casey, Kaelan Michael; Clayton, Regan Kent; Coddington, Remy Taye Stephon; Earthy, George Robert; Falase, Asher Tayo; Forbes, Michael; Knightbridge, Jacob Christopher; Kodua, Gideon Nana Kwame Fosu; Marshall, Callum; Perkins, Sonny Tufail Retained; Robinson, Carl Junior; Tarima, Sean Tapuwa; Terry, Mason James; Woods, Archie James.

WIGAN ATH (90)

AASGAARD, Thelo (M) 38 4
H: 5 7 b.Liverpool 2-5-02
Internationals: Norway U16, U20.

2020–21	Wigan Ath	33	3		
2021–22	Wigan Ath	5	1	**38**	**4**

AMOS, Ben (G) 267 0
H: 6 1 W: 14 02 b.Macclesfield 10-4-90
Internationals: England U16, U17, U18, U19, U20, U21.

2007–08	Manchester U	0	0		
2008–09	Manchester U	0	0		
2009–10	Manchester U	0	0		
2009–10	*Peterborough U*	1	0	**1**	**0**
2010	*Molde*	8	0	**8**	**0**
2010–11	Manchester U	0	0		
2010–11	*Oldham Ath*	16	0	**16**	**0**
2011–12	Manchester U	1	0		
2012–13	Manchester U	0	0		
2012–13	*Hull C*	17	0	**17**	**0**
2013–14	Manchester U	0	0		
2013–14	*Carlisle U*	9	0	**9**	**0**
2014–15	Manchester U	0	0	**1**	**0**
2014–15	*Bolton W*	9	0		
2015–16	Bolton W	40	0		
2016–17	Bolton W	0	0		
2016–17	*Cardiff C*	16	0	**16**	**0**
2017–18	Bolton W	0	0		
2017–18	*Charlton Ath*	46	0		
2018–19	Bolton W	0	0	**49**	**0**
2018–19	*Millwall*	12	0	**12**	**0**
2019–20	Charlton Ath	0	0		
2020–21	Charlton Ath	46	0		
2021–22	Charlton Ath	0	0	**92**	**0**
2021–22	Wigan Ath	46	0	**46**	**0**

BANINGIME, Divin (F) 0 0
H: 5 9 W: 10 08 b.Kinshasa 13-10-00

2017–18	Wigan Ath	0	0		
2018–19	Wigan Ath	0	0		
2019–20	Wigan Ath	0	0		
2020–21	Wigan Ath	0	0		
2021–22	Wigan Ath	0	0		

BENNETT, Joe (D) 334 8
H: 5 10 W: 11 09 b.Rochdale 28-3-90
Internationals: England U19, U20, U21.

2008–09	Middlesbrough	1	0		
2009–10	Middlesbrough	12	0		
2010–11	Middlesbrough	31	0		
2011–12	Middlesbrough	41	1		
2012–13	Middlesbrough	0	0	**85**	**1**
2012–13	Aston Villa	25	0		
2013–14	Aston Villa	5	0		
2014–15	Aston Villa	0	0		
2014–15	*Brighton & HA*	41	1	**41**	**1**
2015–16	Aston Villa	0	0		
2015–16	*Bournemouth*	0	0		
2015–16	*Sheffield W*	3	0	**3**	**0**
2016–17	Aston Villa	0	0	**30**	**0**
2016–17	Cardiff C	24	3		
2017–18	Cardiff C	38	1		
2018–19	Cardiff C	30	0		
2019–20	Cardiff C	44	0		
2020–21	Cardiff C	28	1	**164**	**5**
2021–22	Wigan Ath	11	1	**11**	**1**

COUSINS, Jordan (D) 241 8
H: 5 10 W: 11 05 b.Greenwich 6-3-94
Internationals: England U16, U17, U18, U20. Jamaica Full caps.

2011–12	Charlton Ath	0	0		
2012–13	Charlton Ath	0	0		
2013–14	Charlton Ath	42	2		
2014–15	Charlton Ath	44	3		
2015–16	Charlton Ath	39	2	**125**	**7**
2016–17	QPR	18	0		
2017–18	QPR	15	0		
2018–19	QPR	28	1	**61**	**1**
2019–20	Stoke C	20	0		
2020–21	Stoke C	19	0		
2021–22	Stoke C	0	0	**39**	**0**
2021–22	Wigan Ath	16	0	**16**	**0**

DARIKWA, Tendayi (D) 273 12
H: 6 2 W: 12 02 b.Nottingham 13-12-91
Internationals: Zimbabwe Full caps.

2010–11	Chesterfield	0	0		
2011–12	Chesterfield	2	0		
2012–13	Chesterfield	36	5		
2013–14	Chesterfield	41	3		
2014–15	Chesterfield	46	1	**125**	**9**
2015–16	Burnley	21	1		
2016–17	Burnley	0	0	**21**	**1**
2017–18	Nottingham F	30	0		
2018–19	Nottingham F	28	0		
2019–20	Nottingham F	0	0		
2020–21	Nottingham F	0	0	**58**	**0**
2020–21	Wigan Ath	26	0		
2021–22	Wigan Ath	43	2	**69**	**2**

EDWARDS, Gwion (M) 289 40
H: 5 9 W: 12 00 b.Carmarthen 1-3-93
Internationals: Wales U19, U21.

2011–12	Swansea C	0	0		
2012–13	Swansea C	0	0		
2012–13	*St Johnstone*	6	0		
2013–14	Swansea C	0	0		
2013–14	*St Johnstone*	13	0	**19**	**0**
2013–14	*Crawley T*	6	2		
2014–15	Crawley T	37	4		
2015–16	Crawley T	42	8	**85**	**14**
2016–17	Peterborough U	33	7		
2017–18	Peterborough U	26	4	**59**	**11**
2018–19	Ipswich T	33	6		
2019–20	Ipswich T	27	2		
2020–21	Ipswich T	36	6		
2021–22	Ipswich T	0	0	**96**	**14**
2021–22	Wigan Ath	30	1	**30**	**1**

HUMPHRYS, Stephen (F) 146 34
H: 6 1 W: 10 12 b.Oldham 15-9-97

2016–17	Fulham	2	0		
2016–17	*Shrewsbury T*	14	2	**14**	**2**
2017–18	Fulham	0	0		
2017–18	*Rochdale*	16	2		
2018–19	Fulham	0	0	**2**	**0**
2018–19	*Scunthorpe U*	16	4	**16**	**4**
2018–19	Southend U	10	5		
2019–20	Southend U	21	5		
2020–21	Southend U	0	0	**31**	**10**
2020–21	Rochdale	29	11		
2021–22	Rochdale	0	0	**45**	**13**
2021–22	Wigan Ath	38	5	**38**	**5**

JONES, Jamie (G) 334 0
H: 6 3 W: 14 05 b.Kirkby 18-2-89

2007–08	Everton	0	0		
2008–09	Leyton Orient	20	0		
2009–10	Leyton Orient	36	0		
2010–11	Leyton Orient	35	0		
2011–12	Leyton Orient	6	0		
2012–13	Leyton Orient	26	0		
2013–14	Leyton Orient	28	0	**151**	**0**
2014–15	Preston NE	17	0		
2014–15	*Coventry C*	4	0	**4**	**0**
2014–15	*Rochdale*	13	0	**13**	**0**
2015–16	Preston NE	0	0	**17**	**0**
2015–16	*Colchester U*	17	0	**17**	**0**
2015–16	*Stevenage*	17	0		
2016–17	Stevenage	36	0	**53**	**0**
2017–18	Wigan Ath	15	0		
2018–19	Wigan Ath	12	0		
2019–20	Wigan Ath	7	0		
2020–21	Wigan Ath	45	0		
2021–22	Wigan Ath	0	0	**79**	**0**

JONES, Jordan (M) 158 15
H: 5 9 W: 9 08 b.Redcar 24-10-94
Internationals: Northern Ireland U19, Full caps.

2012–13	Middlesbrough	0	0		
2013–14	Middlesbrough	0	0		
2014–15	Middlesbrough	0	0		
2014–15	*Hartlepool U*	11	0	**11**	**0**
2015–16	Middlesbrough	0	0		
2015–16	*Cambridge U*	1	0	**1**	**0**
2016–17	Kilmarnock	37	3		
2017–18	Kilmarnock	32	4		
2018–19	Kilmarnock	28	4	**97**	**11**
2019–20	Rangers	7	0		
2020–21	Rangers	3	1	**10**	**1**
2020–21	*Sunderland*	19	3	**19**	**3**
2021–22	Wigan Ath	9	0	**9**	**0**
2021–22	*St Mirren*	11	0	**11**	**0**

KEANE, Will (F) 181 47
H: 6 2 W: 11 05 b.Stockport 11-1-93
Internationals: England U16, U17, U19, U20, U21. Republic of Ireland Full caps.

2009–10	Manchester U	0	0		
2010–11	Manchester U	0	0		
2011–12	Manchester U	1	0		
2012–13	Manchester U	0	0		
2013–14	Manchester U	0	0		
2013–14	*Wigan Ath*	4	0		
2013–14	*QPR*	10	0	**10**	**0**
2014–15	Manchester U	0	0		
2014–15	*Sheffield W*	13	3	**13**	**3**
2015–16	Manchester U	1	0		
2015–16	*Preston NE*	20	1	**20**	**1**
2016–17	Manchester U	0	0	**2**	**0**
2016–17	Hull C	5	0		
2017–18	Hull C	9	1		
2018–19	Hull C	8	0	**22**	**1**
2018–19	*Ipswich T*	11	3		
2019–20	Ipswich T	23	3	**34**	**6**
2020–21	Wigan Ath	32	10		
2021–22	Wigan Ath	44	26	**80**	**36**

KERR, Jason (D) 224 21
H: 5 11 W: 11 00 b.Edinburgh 6-2-97
Internationals: Scotland U21.

2015–16	St Johnstone	0	0		
2015–16	*East Fife*	34	3		
2016–17	St Johnstone	0	0		
2016–17	*East Fife*	33	8	**67**	**11**
2017–18	St Johnstone	15	1		
2017–18	*Queen of the South*	18	4	**18**	**4**
2018–19	St Johnstone	37	2		
2019–20	St Johnstone	29	1		
2020–21	St Johnstone	31	1		
2021–22	St Johnstone	3	0	**115**	**5**
2021–22	Wigan Ath	24	1	**24**	**1**

LANG, Callum (F) 171 53
H: 5 11 W: 11 00 b.Liverpool 8-9-98

2016–17	Wigan Ath	0	0		
2017–18	Wigan Ath	0	0		
2017–18	*Morecambe*	30	10	**30**	**10**
2018–19	Wigan Ath	0	0		
2018–19	*Oldham Ath*	42	13	**42**	**13**
2019–20	Wigan Ath	1	0		
2019–20	*Shrewsbury T*	16	3	**16**	**3**
2020–21	Wigan Ath	23	9		
2020–21	*Motherwell*	17	3	**17**	**3**
2021–22	Wigan Ath	42	15	**66**	**24**

LLOYD, Kieran (D) 0 0
b. 13-10-02
From Liverpool.

2021–22	Wigan Ath	0	0		

LONG, Adam (D) 14 0
H: 6 0 W: 12 00 b.Douglas 11-11-00

2017–18	Wigan Ath	0	0		
2018–19	Wigan Ath	0	0		
2019–20	Wigan Ath	0	0		
2020–21	Wigan Ath	13	0		
2021–22	Wigan Ath	1	0	**14**	**0**

MAGENNIS, Josh (F) 429 79
H: 6 2 W: 14 07 b.Bangor 15-8-90
Internationals: Northern Ireland U17, U19, U21, Full caps.

2009–10	Cardiff C	9	0	**9**	**0**
2009–10	*Grimsby T*	2	0	**2**	**0**
2010–11	Aberdeen	29	3		
2011–12	Aberdeen	23	1		
2012–13	Aberdeen	35	5		
2013–14	Aberdeen	18	1	**105**	**10**
2013–14	*St Mirren*	13	0	**13**	**0**
2014–15	Kilmarnock	38	8		
2015–16	Kilmarnock	34	10	**72**	**18**
2016–17	Charlton Ath	39	10		
2017–18	Charlton Ath	42	10	**81**	**20**
2018–19	Bolton W	42	4		
2019–20	Bolton W	0	0	**42**	**4**
2019–20	Hull C	29	4		
2020–21	Hull C	40	18		
2021–22	Hull C	19	2	**88**	**24**
2021–22	Wigan Ath	17	3	**17**	**3**

MASSEY, Gavin (F) 367 43
H: 5 11 W: 11 12 b.Watford 14-10-92

2009–10	Watford	1	0		
2010–11	Watford	3	0		
2011–12	Watford	3	0		
2011–12	*Yeovil T*	16	3	**16**	**3**
2011–12	*Colchester U*	8	0		
2012–13	Watford	0	0	**7**	**0**
2012–13	Colchester U	40	6		
2013–14	Colchester U	30	3		
2014–15	Colchester U	46	7		
2015–16	Colchester U	42	4	**166**	**20**
2016–17	Leyton Orient	36	8	**36**	**8**
2017–18	Wigan Ath	42	6		
2018–19	Wigan Ath	20	5		
2019–20	Wigan Ath	31	0		
2020–21	Wigan Ath	16	0		
2021–22	Wigan Ath	33	1	**142**	**12**

McCLEAN, James (M) 444 57
H: 5 11 W: 11 00 b.Derry 22-4-89
Internationals: Northern Ireland U21. Republic of Ireland Full caps.

2008	Derry C	1	0		
2009	Derry C	26	1		

2010 Derry C 30 8
2011 Derry C 21 7 **78 16**
2011–12 Sunderland 23 5
2012–13 Sunderland 36 2
2013–14 Sunderland 0 0 **59 7**
2013–14 Wigan Ath 37 3
2014–15 Wigan Ath 36 6
2015–16 WBA 35 2
2016–17 WBA 34 1
2017–18 WBA 30 1 **99 4**
2018–19 Stoke C 42 3
2019–20 Stoke C 36 7
2020–21 Stoke C 24 2
2021–22 Stoke C 0 0 **102 12**
2021–22 Wigan Ath 33 9 **106 18**

McGRATH, Jamie (M) 193 26
H: 5 9 W: 11 00 b.Athboy 30-9-96
Internationals: Republic of Ireland U19, U21, Full caps.
2014 St Patricks Ath 1 0
2015 St Patricks Ath 23 2
2016 St Patricks Ath 23 2 **47 4**
2017 Dundalk 28 6
2018 Dundalk 30 2
2019 Dundalk 26 2 **84 10**
2019–20 St Mirren 7 0
2020–21 St Mirren 35 10
2021–22 St Mirren 18 2 **60 12**
2021–22 Wigan Ath 2 0 **2 0**

McHUGH, Harry (F) 1 0
b.Liverpool 14-10-02
From Everton.
2020–21 Wigan Ath 1 0
2021–22 Wigan Ath 0 0 **1 0**

NAYLOR, Tom (D) 343 27
H: 5 11 W: 11 05 b.Kirkby-in-Ashfield 28-6-91
From Mansfield T.
2011–12 Derby Co 8 0
2012–13 Derby Co 0 0
2012–13 *Bradford C* 5 0 **5 0**
2013–14 Derby Co 0 0
2013–14 *Newport Co* 33 1 **33 1**
2014–15 Derby Co 0 0 **8 0**
2014–15 *Cambridge U* 8 0 **8 0**
2014–15 *Burton Alb* 17 0
2015–16 Burton Alb 41 6
2016–17 Burton Alb 33 3
2017–18 Burton Alb 33 3 **124 12**
2018–19 Portsmouth 43 4
2019–20 Portsmouth 33 1
2020–21 Portsmouth 46 6
2021–22 Portsmouth 0 0 **122 11**
2021–22 Wigan Ath 43 3 **43 3**

PEARCE, Tom (D) 62 2
H: 6 1 W: 12 06 b.Ormskirk 12-4-98
Internationals: England U20, U21.
From Everton.
2017–18 Leeds U 5 1
2018–19 Leeds U 2 0 **7 1**
2018–19 *Scunthorpe U* 9 1 **9 1**
2019–20 Wigan Ath 7 0
2020–21 Wigan Ath 23 0
2021–22 Wigan Ath 16 0 **46 0**

POWER, Max (M) 388 37
H: 5 11 W: 12 04 b.Berkinhead 27-7-93
2010–11 Tranmere R 0 0
2011–12 Tranmere R 4 0
2012–13 Tranmere R 27 3
2013–14 Tranmere R 33 2
2014–15 Tranmere R 45 7 **109 12**
2015–16 Wigan Ath 44 6
2016–17 Wigan Ath 42 0
2017–18 Wigan Ath 40 5
2018–19 Wigan Ath 1 0
2018–19 Sunderland 35 4
2019–20 Sunderland 31 2
2020–21 Sunderland 42 5 **108 11**
2021–22 Wigan Ath 44 3 **171 14**

ROBINSON, Luke (D) 26 0
H: 5 9 b.Berkinhead 19-11-01
Internationals: Scotland U18, U19.
From Wrexham.
2020–21 Wigan Ath 25 0
2021–22 Wigan Ath 1 0 **26 0**

SHINNIE, Graeme (D) 395 20
H: 5 9 W: 11 05 b.Aberdeen 4-8-91
Internationals: Scotland U21, Full caps.
2009–10 Inverness CT 1 0
2010–11 Inverness CT 19 0
2011–12 Inverness CT 26 1
2012–13 Inverness CT 37 0
2013–14 Inverness CT 36 3
2014–15 Inverness CT 37 2 **156 6**
2015–16 Aberdeen 37 1
2016–17 Aberdeen 36 2
2017–18 Aberdeen 35 2
2018–19 Aberdeen 36 3 **144 8**
2019–20 Derby Co 23 2
2020–21 Derby Co 41 3
2021–22 Derby Co 21 1 **85 6**
2021–22 Wigan Ath 10 0 **10 0**

SMITH, Scott (M) 0 0
H: 5 8 b.Wigan 7-2-01
Internationals: Wales U19.
2020–21 Wigan Ath 0 0
2021–22 Wigan Ath 0 0

TICKLE, Sam (G) 0 0
H: 6 2 b.Warrington 31-3-02
2020–21 Wigan Ath 0 0
2021–22 Wigan Ath 0 0

TILT, Curtis (D) 156 10
H: 6 4 W: 11 11 b.Walsall 4-8-91
Internationals: Jamaica Full caps.
From Halesowen T, Hednesford T, AFC Telford U, Wrexham.
2017–18 Blackpool 42 1
2018–19 Blackpool 37 4
2019–20 Blackpool 20 0 **99 5**
2019–20 Rotherham U 1 0
2020–21 Rotherham U 0 0 **1 0**
2020–21 *Wigan Ath* 36 3
2021–22 Wigan Ath 20 2 **56 5**

WHATMOUGH, Jack (D) 167 5
H: 6 0 W: 10 06 b.Gosport 19-8-96
Internationals: England U18, U19.
2012–13 Portsmouth 0 0
2013–14 Portsmouth 12 0
2014–15 Portsmouth 22 0
2015–16 Portsmouth 2 0
2016–17 Portsmouth 10 1
2017–18 Portsmouth 14 0
2018–19 Portsmouth 26 0
2019–20 Portsmouth 1 0
2020–21 Portsmouth 34 2
2021–22 Portsmouth 0 0 **121 3**
2021–22 Wigan Ath 46 2 **46 2**

WYKE, Charlie (F) 297 101
H: 5 11 W: 11 09 b.Middlesbrough 6-12-92
2011–12 Middlesbrough 0 0
2012–13 Middlesbrough 0 0
2012–13 *Hartlepool U* 25 2
2013–14 Middlesbrough 0 0
2013–14 *AFC Wimbledon* 17 2 **17 2**
2014–15 Middlesbrough 0 0
2014–15 *Hartlepool U* 13 4 **38 6**
2014–15 Carlisle U 17 6
2015–16 Carlisle U 34 12
2016–17 Carlisle U 26 14 **77 32**
2016–17 Bradford C 16 7
2017–18 Bradford C 40 15 **56 22**
2018–19 Sunderland 24 4
2019–20 Sunderland 27 5
2020–21 Sunderland 43 25
2021–22 Sunderland 0 0 **94 34**
2021–22 Wigan Ath 15 5 **15 5**

Players retained or with offer of contract
Adams, Joseph; Adeeko, Badajide; Carragher, James ; Costello, Tom; Hughes, Charlie; McGee, Harry; Mooney, Owen; Pinnington, Dean; Sze, Chris; Watson, Thomas.

Scholars
Brooks, Adam James; Campbell, Sam Kevin; Corran, Matthew Nicholas; Gill, Samuel Lucas; Grewal, Ruben Singh; Knowles, Kristian William John; Latona, Luca; Lomax-Jones, Arthur Michael; Payne, Kai Anthony; Reilly, Jack Edward; Smith, Daniel Alexander; Sumner, Steven; Welsby, Danny Jay; Welsh, Levi Jordan Joshua; Worsley, Kyle Leigh.

WOLVERHAMPTON W (91)

AGBOOLA, Michael (D) 0 0
H: 6 3 W: 11 11 b.Newham 12-8-01
From Dagenham & R.
2020–21 Wolverhampton W 0 0
2021–22 Wolverhampton W 0 0

AIT NOURI, Rayan (D) 67 2
H: 5 10 W: 11 00 b.Montreuil 6-6-01
Internationals: France U18, U21.
2018–19 Angers 3 0
2019–20 Angers 17 0
2020–21 Angers 3 0
2020–21 *Wolverhampton W* 21 1
2021–22 Angers 0 0 **23 0**
2021–22 Wolverhampton W 23 1 **44 2**

ARINBJORNSSON, Palmi (G) 0 0
H: 6 3 b.Reykjanesbaer 29-11-03
Internationals: Iceland U16, U17, U19.
From Njardvik.
2020–21 Wolverhampton W 0 0
2021–22 Wolverhampton W 0 0

BOLLA, Bendeguz (D) 93 8
H: 5 10 b.Szekesfehervar 22-11-99
Internationals: Hungary U18, U19, U21, Full caps.
2017–18 Fehervar 1 0
2018–19 Fehervar 0 0
2018–19 *Siofok* 18 3 **18 3**
2019–20 Fehervar 0 0
2019–20 *Zalaegerszeg* 17 0 **17 0**
2020–21 Fehervar 27 1 **28 1**
2021–22 Wolverhampton W 0 0
2021–22 *Grasshopper* 30 4 **30 4**

BOLY, Willy (D) 251 13
H: 6 1 W: 12 11 b.Melun 3-2-91
Internationals: France U16, U17, U19. Ivory Coast Full caps.
2010–11 Auxerre 8 1
2011–12 Auxerre 33 1
2012–13 Auxerre 25 1
2013–14 Auxerre 30 0
2014–15 Auxerre 1 0 **97 3**
2014–15 Braga 0 0
2015–16 Braga 22 2
2016–17 Braga 3 0 **25 2**
2016–17 Porto 4 0
2017–18 Porto 0 0 **4 0**
2017–18 *Wolverhampton W* 36 3
2018–19 Wolverhampton W 36 4
2019–20 Wolverhampton W 22 0
2020–21 Wolverhampton W 21 1
2021–22 Wolverhampton W 10 0 **125 8**

BRUNO JORDAO, Andre (M) 48 5
H: 5 11 W: 11 07 b.Marinha Grande 12-10-98
Internationals: Portugal U18, U19, U20, U21.
2015–16 Uniao de Leiria 23 4 **23 4**
2016–17 Braga 0 0
2017–18 Braga 0 0
2017–18 *Lazio* 0 0
2018–19 Braga 0 0
2018–19 *Lazio* 3 0
2019–20 Lazio 0 0 **3 0**
2019–20 Wolverhampton W 1 0
2020–21 Wolverhampton W 0 0
2020–21 *Famalicao* 9 1 **9 1**
2021–22 Wolverhampton W 0 0 **1 0**
2021–22 *Grasshoppers* 12 0 **12 0**

BUENO, Hugo (D) 0 0
H: 5 11 W: 11 07 b.Vigo 18-9-02
Internationals: Spain U18.
2020–21 Wolverhampton W 0 0
2021–22 Wolverhampton W 0 0

CAMPANA, Leonardo (F) 35 12
b.Guayaquil 24-7-00
Internationals: Ecuador U20, Full caps.
2016–17 Barcelona 0 0
2017–18 Barcelona 0 0
2018–19 Barcelona 0 0
2019–20 Barcelona 0 0
2019–20 Wolverhampton W 0 0
2020–21 Wolverhampton W 0 0
2020–21 *Famalicao* 9 2 **9 2**
2021–22 Wolverhampton W 0 0
2021–22 *Grasshopper* 10 3 **10 3**
2022 *Inter Miami* 16 7 **16 7**

CAMPBELL, Chem (M) 1 0
H: 5 11 W: 11 05 b.Birmingham 30-12-02
Internationals: Wales U17.
2019–20 Wolverhampton W 0 0
2020–21 Wolverhampton W 0 0
2021–22 Wolverhampton W 1 0 **1 0**

CARTY, Conor (F) 0 0
H: 6 0 W: 11 07 b. 25-5-02
Internationals: Republic of Ireland U16, U17, U18.
2020–21 Wolverhampton W 0 0
2021–22 Wolverhampton W 0 0

CHIQUINHO, Oliveira (F) 44 4
H: 5 10 W: 11 05 b.Cascais 5-2-00
Internationals: Portugal U20, U21.
From Sporting Lisbon.
2019–20 Estoril 8 1
2020–21 Estoril 13 0
2021–22 Estoril 15 3 **36 4**
2021–22 Wolverhampton W 8 0 **8 0**

COADY, Conor (D) 358 14
H: 6 1 W: 11 11 b.Liverpool 25-2-93
Internationals: England U16, U17, U18, U19, U20, Full caps.
2010–11 Liverpool 0 0

2011–12 Liverpool 0 0
2012–13 Liverpool 1 0
2013–14 Liverpool 0 0 **1 0**
2013–14 *Sheffield U* 39 5 **39 5**
2014–15 Huddersfield T 45 3 **45 3**
2015–16 Wolverhampton W 37 0
2016–17 Wolverhampton W 40 0
2017–18 Wolverhampton W 45 1
2018–19 Wolverhampton W 38 0
2019–20 Wolverhampton W 38 0
2020–21 Wolverhampton W 37 1
2021–22 Wolverhampton W 38 4 **273 6**

CORBEANU, Theo (M) 30 3
H: 6 3 W: 12 00 b.Burlington 17-5-02
Internationals: Romania U16, U17. Canada Full caps.
From Toronto.
2020–21 Wolverhampton W 1 0
2021–22 Wolverhampton W 0 0 **1 0**
2021–22 *Sheffield W* 13 2 **13 2**
2021–22 *Milton Keynes D* 16 1 **16 1**

CUNDLE, Luke (M) 4 0
H: 5 7 W: 10 08 b.Warrington 26-4-02
2019–20 Wolverhampton W 0 0
2020–21 Wolverhampton W 0 0
2021–22 Wolverhampton W 4 0 **4 0**

CUTRONE, Patrick (F) 142 22
b.Como 3-1-98
Internationals: Italy U16, U17, U18, U19, U21, Full caps.
2016–17 AC Milan 1 0
2017–18 AC Milan 28 10
2018–19 AC Milan 34 3 **63 13**
2019–20 Wolverhampton W 12 2
2019–20 *Fiorentina* 19 4
2020–21 Wolverhampton W 2 0
2020–21 *Fiorentina* 11 0 **30 4**
2020–21 *Valencia* 7 0 **7 0**
2021–22 Wolverhampton W 0 0 **14 2**
2021–22 *Empoli* 28 3 **28 3**

DADASHOV, Renat (F) 59 6
H: 6 1 b.Rudesheim 17-5-99
Internationals: Germany U16, U17. Azerbaijan U16, U21, Full caps.
2017–18 Eintracht Frankfurt 0 0
2018–19 Estoril 22 4 **22 4**
2019–20 Wolverhampton W 0 0
2019–20 *Pacos de Ferreira* 7 0 **7 0**
2020–21 Wolverhampton W 0 0
2020–21 *Grasshopper* 0 0
2021–22 Wolverhampton W 0 0
2021–22 *Tondela* 30 2 **30 2**

DANIEL PODENCE, Castelo (F) 140 18
H: 5 5 W: 9 02 b.Oeiras 21-10-95
Internationals: Portugal U16, U18, U19, U20, U21, Full caps
2012–13 Sporting Lisbon 0 0
2013–14 Sporting Lisbon 0 0
2014–15 Sporting Lisbon 0 0
2015–16 Sporting Lisbon 0 0
2016–17 Sporting Lisbon 13 0
2016–17 *Moreirense* 14 4 **14 4**
2017–18 Sporting Lisbon 12 0 **25 0**
2018–19 Olympiacos 27 5
2019–20 Olympiacos 15 3 **42 8**
2019–20 Wolverhampton W 9 1
2020–21 Wolverhampton W 24 3
2021–22 Wolverhampton W 26 2 **59 6**

DENDONCKER, Leander (M) 245 18
H: 6 2 W: 12 02 b.Passendale 15-4-95
Internationals: Belgium U16, U17, U19, U21, Full caps.
2013–14 Anderlecht 0 0
2014–15 Anderlecht 26 2
2015–16 Anderlecht 23 1
2016–17 Anderlecht 40 5
2017–18 Anderlecht 36 1 **125 9**
2018–19 *Wolverhampton W* 19 2
2019–20 Wolverhampton W 38 4
2020–21 Wolverhampton W 33 1
2021–22 Wolverhampton W 30 2 **120 9**

ESTRADA, Pascal (D) 0 0
H: 6 1 W: 10 10 b.Leonding 12-3-02
Internationals: Austria U18.
From Lask.
2020–21 Wolverhampton W 0 0
2021–22 Wolverhampton W 0 0

GIBBS-WHITE, Morgan (M) 106 13
H: 5 10 W: 11 07 b.Stafford 27-1-00
Internationals: England U16, U17, U18, U19, U21.
2016–17 Wolverhampton W 7 0
2017–18 Wolverhampton W 13 0
2018–19 Wolverhampton W 26 0
2019–20 Wolverhampton W 7 0
2020–21 Wolverhampton W 11 1
2020–21 *Swansea C* 5 1 **5 1**
2021–22 Wolverhampton W 2 0 **66 1**
2021–22 *Sheffield U* 35 11 **35 11**

GILES, Ryan (M) 94 3
H: 5 10 W: 11 00 b.Telford 26-1-00
Internationals: England U20.
2018–19 Wolverhampton W 0 0
2019–20 Wolverhampton W 0 0
2019–20 *Shrewsbury T* 19 1 **19 1**
2019–20 *Coventry C* 1 0
2020–21 Wolverhampton W 0 0
2020–21 *Coventry C* 19 0 **20 0**
2020–21 *Rotherham U* 23 2 **23 2**
2021–22 Wolverhampton W 0 0
2021–22 *Cardiff C* 21 0 **21 0**
2021–22 *Blackburn R* 11 0 **11 0**

GOMES, Tote (D) 40 2
H: 6 2 W: 13 01 b.Bissau 16-1-99
Internationals: Portugal U20.
2018–19 Estoril 3 0
2019–20 Estoril 0 0 **3 0**
2020–21 Wolverhampton W 0 0
2020–21 *Grosshopper* 33 2 **33 2**
2021–22 Wolverhampton W 4 0 **4 0**
2021–22 *Grasshoppers* 0 0

HE, Zhenyu (F) 10 0
H: 5 11 b.Shenyang 28-6-01
2019–20 Wolverhampton W 0 0
2020–21 Wolverhampton W 0 0
2021 *Beijing Guoan* 10 0 **10 0**
2021–22 Wolverhampton W 0 0

HESKETH, Owen (M) 0 0
H: 5 11 W: 10 08 b.Manchester 10-10-02
Internationals: Wales U17.
From Manchester C.
2020–21 Wolverhampton W 0 0
2021–22 Wolverhampton W 0 0

HODGE, Joseph (M) 0 0
b. 14-9-02
Internationals: Republic of Ireland U16, U17, U19. England U16, U17.
2020–21 Manchester C 0 0
2021–22 Wolverhampton W 0 0

HODNETT, Jack (M) 0 0
H: 5 6 W: 9 11 b.Telford 17-1-03
Internationals: England U16.
2020–21 Wolverhampton W 0 0
2021–22 Wolverhampton W 0 0

HOEVER, Ki-Jana (D) 20 0
H: 5 11 W: 10 03 b.Amsterdam 18-1-02
Internationals: Netherlands U16, U17, U18, U21.
From Ajax.
2018–19 Liverpool 0 0
2019–20 Liverpool 0 0
2020–21 Wolverhampton W 12 0
2021–22 Wolverhampton W 8 0 **20 0**

HWANG, Hee-Chan (F) 187 48
H: 5 10 W: 12 02 b.Chuncheon 26-1-96
Internationals: South Korea U17, U20, U23, Full caps.
2014–15 Red Bull Salzburg 0 0
2014–15 *Liefering* 13 2
2015–16 Red Bull Salzburg 13 0
2015–16 *Liefering* 18 11 **31 13**
2016–17 Red Bull Salzburg 26 12
2017–18 Red Bull Salzburg 20 5
2018–19 Red Bull Salzburg 0 0
2018–19 *Hamburger SV* 20 2 **20 2**
2019–20 Red Bull Salzburg 27 11 **86 28**
2020–21 RB Leipzig 18 0
2021–22 RB Leipzig 2 0 **20 0**
2021–22 *Wolverhampton W* 30 5 **30 5**

JIMENEZ, Raul (F) 296 88
H: 6 2 W: 12 04 b.Tepeji 5-5-91
Internationals: Mexico U23, Full caps.
2011–12 America 15 2
2012–13 America 29 11
2013–14 America 27 12
2014–15 America 4 4 **75 29**
2014–15 Atletico Madrid 21 1 **21 1**
2015–16 Benfica 28 5
2016–17 Benfica 19 7
2017–18 Benfica 33 6
2018–19 Benfica 0 0 **80 18**
2018–19 *Wolverhampton W* 38 13
2019–20 Wolverhampton W 38 17
2020–21 Wolverhampton W 10 4
2021–22 Wolverhampton W 34 6 **120 40**

JOAO MOUTINHO, Felipe (M) 548 39
H: 5 7 W: 9 08 b.Portimao 8-9-86
Internationals: Portugal U17, U18, U19, U21, B, Full caps.
2004–05 Sporting Lisbon 15 0
2005–06 Sporting Lisbon 34 4
2006–07 Sporting Lisbon 29 4
2007–08 Sporting Lisbon 30 5
2008–09 Sporting Lisbon 27 3
2009–10 Sporting Lisbon 28 5 **163 21**
2010–11 Porto 27 0
2011–12 Porto 29 3
2012–13 Porto 27 1 **83 4**
2013–14 Monaco 31 1
2014–15 Monaco 37 4
2015–16 Monaco 26 1
2016–17 Monaco 31 2
2017–18 Monaco 33 1 **158 9**
2018–19 Wolverhampton W 38 1
2019–20 Wolverhampton W 38 1
2020–21 Wolverhampton W 33 1
2021–22 Wolverhampton W 35 2 **144 5**

JONNY, Castro (D) 271 8
H: 5 9 W: 11 00 b.Vigo 3-3-94
Internationals: Spain U18, U19, U20, U21, Full caps.
2011–12 Celta Vigo 0 0
2012–13 Celta Vigo 19 0
2013–14 Celta Vigo 26 0
2014–15 Celta Vigo 36 0
2015–16 Celta Vigo 36 1
2016–17 Celta Vigo 30 0
2017–18 Celta Vigo 36 2 **183 3**
2018–19 Atletico Madrid 0 0
2018–19 *Wolverhampton W* 33 1
2019–20 Wolverhampton W 35 2
2020–21 Wolverhampton W 7 0
2021–22 Wolverhampton W 13 2 **88 5**

JOSE SA, Pedro (G) 151 0
H: 6 4 W: 13 03 b.Braga 17-1-93
Internationals: Portugal U20, U21, U23.
2012–13 Maritimo 0 0
2013–14 Maritimo 8 0
2014–15 Maritimo 3 0
2015–16 Maritimo 5 0 **16 0**
2015–16 Porto 0 0
2016–17 Porto 1 0
2017–18 Porto 14 0 **15 0**
2018–19 Olympiacos 21 0
2019–20 Olympiacos 33 0
2020–21 Olympiacos 29 0
2021–22 Olympiacos 0 0 **83 0**
2021–22 Wolverhampton W 37 0 **37 0**

KAWABE, Hayao (M) 249 25
H: 5 10 b.Hiroshima 8-9-95
Internationals: Japan U17, Full caps.
2013 Sanfrecce Hiroshima 3 0
2014 Sanfrecce Hiroshima 1 0
2015 Sanfrecce Hiroshima 0 0
2015 *Jubilo Iwata* 33 3 **33 3**
2016 Sanfrecce Hiroshima 0 0
2016 *Jubilow Iwata* 26 2
2017 Sanfreece Hiroshima 0 0
2017 *Jubilow Iwata* 32 4 **58 6**
2018 Sanfrecce Hiroshima 33 0 **33 0**
2019 Sanfrecce Hiroshima 34 3
2020 Sanfrecce Hiroshima 34 3
2021 Sanfrecce Hiroshima 19 3 **91 9**
2021–22 Wolverhampton W 0 0
2021–22 *Grasshopper* 34 7 **34 7**

KILMAN, Max (D) 52 1
H: 6 4 W: 12 06 b.Chelsea 23-5-97
From Welling U, Maidenhead U.
2018–19 Wolverhampton W 1 0
2019–20 Wolverhampton W 3 0
2020–21 Wolverhampton W 18 0
2021–22 Wolverhampton W 30 1 **52 1**

LEMBIKISA, Dexter (D) 0 0
b.Lambeth 4-11-03
2021–22 Wolverhampton W 0 0

LEO BONATINI, Lohner (F) 206 66
b. 28-3-94
Internationals: Brazil U17.
2013 Cruzeiro 0 0
2013 *Goias* 5 0
2014 Cruzeiro 0 0
2014 Goias 1 0 **6 0**
2014–15 Estoril 15 4
2015 Cruzeiro 0 0
2015–16 Estoril 33 17 **48 21**
2016–17 Al Hilal 25 12
2017–18 Al Hilal 0 0 **25 12**
2017–18 *Wolverhampton W* 43 12
2018–19 Wolverhampton W 7 0
2018–19 *Nottingham F* 5 0 **5 0**
2019–20 Wolverhampton W 0 0
2019–20 *Vitoria Guimaraes* 15 3 **15 3**
2020–21 Wolverhampton W 0 0
2020–21 *Grasshopper* 31 11
2021–22 Wolverhampton W 0 0 **50 12**
2021–22 *Grasshopper* 26 7 **57 18**

LONWIJK, Nigel (D) **22** **1**

b.Goirle 27-10-02

Internationals: Netherlands U16.

From PSV Eindhoven.

2020–21	Wolverhampton W	0	0		
2021–22	Wolverhampton W	0	0		
2021–22	*Fortuna Sittard*	22	1	**22**	**1**

MARCAL, Fernando (D) **265** **5**

H: 5 10 W: 11 05 b.Sao Paulo 19-2-89

2010	Guaratingueta	3	0	**3**	**0**
2010–11	Torreense	28	2		
2011–12	Torreense	12	1	**40**	**3**
2011–12	Nacional	14	0		
2012–13	Nacional	27	0		
2013–14	Nacional	27	2		
2014–15	Nacional	29	0	**97**	**2**
2015–16	Benfica	0	0		
2015–16	*Gaziantepspor*	21	0	**21**	**0**
2016–17	Benfica	0	0		
2016–17	*Guingamp*	31	0	**31**	**0**
2017–18	Lyon	18	0		
2018–19	Lyon	12	0		
2019–20	Lyon	11	0		
2020–21	Lyon	1	0	**42**	**0**
2020–21	Wolverhampton W	13	0		
2021–22	Wolverhampton W	18	0	**31**	**0**

MARQUES, Christian (D) **0** **0**

H: 6 2 W: 11 07 b.Uster 15-1-03

Internationals: Switzerland U17.

From Grasshopper.

2020–21	Wolverhampton W	0	0		
2021–22	Wolverhampton W	0	0		
2021–22	*Belenenses*	0	0		

MATHESON, Luke (D) **38** **1**

H: 5 5 W: 11 00 b.Manchester 3-10-02

Internationals: England U17, U18.

2018–19	Rochdale	3	0		
2019–20	Wolverhampton W	0	0		
2019–20	*Rochdale*	20	1	**23**	**1**
2020–21	Wolverhampton W	0	0		
2020–21	*Ipswich T*	2	0	**2**	**0**
2021–22	Wolverhampton W	0	0		
2021–22	*Hamilton A*	0	0		
2021–22	*Scunthorpe U*	13	0	**13**	**0**

MOSQUERA, Yerson (D) **16** **1**

H: 6 2 W: 13 03 b.Apartado 2-5-01

Internationals: Colombia U18, U20.

2020	Atletico Nacional	4	1		
2021	Atletico Nacional	12	0		
2021–22	Atletico Nacional	0	0	**16**	**1**
2021–22	Wolverhampton W	0	0		

NELSON SEMEDO, Cabral (D) **239** **10**

H: 5 10 W: 10 08 b.Lisbon 16-11-93

Internationals: Portugal U23, Full caps.

2011–12	Sintrense	26	5	**26**	**5**
2012–13	Benfica	0	0		
2012–13	*Fatima*	29	0	**29**	**0**
2013–14	Benfica	0	0		
2014–15	Benfica	0	0		
2015–16	Benfica	12	1		
2016–17	Benfica	31	1	**43**	**2**
2017–18	Barcelona	24	0		
2018–19	Barcelona	26	1		
2019–20	Barcelona	32	1		
2020–21	Barcelona	0	0	**82**	**2**
2020–21	Wolverhampton W	34	1		
2021–22	Wolverhampton W	25	0	**59**	**1**

NEVES, Ruben (M) **243** **24**

H: 5 11 W: 12 08 b.Mozelos 13-3-97

Internationals: Portugal U16, U17, U18, U21, U23, Full caps.

2014–15	Porto	24	1		
2015–16	Porto	22	1		
2016–17	Porto	13	1	**59**	**3**
2017–18	Wolverhampton W	42	6		
2018–19	Wolverhampton W	35	4		
2019–20	Wolverhampton W	38	2		
2020–21	Wolverhampton W	36	5		
2021–22	Wolverhampton W	33	4	**184**	**21**

NYA, Raphael (D) **0** **0**

H: 6 0 W: 10 10 b. 16-6-00

From Paris Saint-Germain.

2020–21	Wolverhampton W	0	0		
2021–22	Wolverhampton W	0	0		

O'SHAUGHNESSY, Joseph (G) **0** **0**

H: 6 6 b.Warrington 5-1-03

From Burnley.

2020–21	Wolverhampton W	0	0		
2021–22	Wolverhampton W	0	0		

PARDINGTON, James (G) **2** **0**

b. 20-7-00

From Rushall.

2018–19	Wolverhampton W	0	0		
2019–20	Wolverhampton W	0	0		
2020–21	Wolverhampton W	0	0		
2020–21	*Mansfield T*	2	0	**2**	**0**
2021–22	Wolverhampton W	0	0		

PEDRO NETO, Lomba (M) **80** **10**

b.Viana do Castelo 9-3-00

Internationals: Portugal U17, U18, U19, U20, U21, Full caps.

2016–17	Braga	2	1		
2017–18	Braga	1	0		
2018–19	Braga	0	0	**3**	**1**
2018–19	*Lazio*	4	0	**4**	**0**
2019–20	Wolverhampton W	29	3		
2020–21	Wolverhampton W	31	5		
2021–22	Wolverhampton W	13	1	**73**	**9**

PERRY, Taylor (M) **10** **1**

H: 5 11 W: 12 06 b.Stourbridge 15-8-01

2019–20	Wolverhampton W	0	0		
2020–21	Wolverhampton W	0	0		
2021–22	Wolverhampton W	0	0		
2021–22	*Cheltenham T*	10	1	**10**	**1**

RICHARDS, Lewis (D) **8** **0**

H: 6 0 W: 10 08 b.Liverpool 15-10-01

Internationals: Republic of Ireland U19.

2019–20	Wolverhampton W	0	0		
2020–21	Wolverhampton W	0	0		
2021–22	Wolverhampton W	0	0		
2021–22	*Harrogate T*	8	0	**8**	**0**

RONAN, Connor (M) **129** **10**

H: 5 8 W: 11 00 b.Rochdale 6-3-98

Internationals: England U17. Republic of Ireland U17, U19, U21.

2015–16	Wolverhampton W	0	0		
2016–17	Wolverhampton W	4	0		
2017–18	Wolverhampton W	3	0		
2017–18	*Portsmouth*	16	0	**16**	**0**
2018–19	Wolverhampton W	0	0		
2018–19	*Walsall*	11	0	**11**	**0**
2019–20	Wolverhampton W	0	0		
2019–20	*Dunajska Streda*	28	1	**28**	**1**
2019–20	*Blackpool*	10	1	**10**	**1**
2020–21	Wolverhampton W	0	0		
2020–21	*Grasshopper*	30	1	**30**	**1**
2021–22	Wolverhampton W	0	0	**7**	**0**
2021–22	*St Mirren*	27	7	**27**	**7**

RUBEN VINAGRE, Goncalo (D) **78** **1**

b. 9-4-99

Internationals: Portugal U16, U17, U18, U19, U20, U21.

2016–17	Monaco	0	0		
2017–18	Monaco	0	0		
2017–18	*Wolverhampton W*	9	1		
2018–19	Wolverhampton W	17	0		
2019–20	Wolverhampton W	16	0		
2020–21	Wolverhampton W	2	0		
2020–21	*Olympiacos*	2	0	**2**	**0**
2020–21	*Famalicao*	20	0	**20**	**0**
2021–22	Wolverhampton W	0	0	**44**	**1**
2021–22	*Sporting Lisbon*	12	0	**12**	**0**

RUDDY, John (G) **419** **0**

H: 6 4 W: 15 04 b.St Ives 24-10-86

Internationals: England Full caps.

2003–04	Cambridge U	1	0		
2004–05	Cambridge U	38	0	**39**	**0**
2005–06	Everton	1	0		
2005–06	*Walsall*	5	0	**5**	**0**
2005–06	*Rushden & D*	3	0	**3**	**0**
2005–06	*Chester C*	4	0	**4**	**0**
2006–07	Everton	0	0		
2006–07	*Stockport Co*	11	0		
2006–07	*Wrexham*	5	0	**5**	**0**
2006–07	*Bristol C*	1	0	**1**	**0**
2007–08	Everton	0	0		
2007–08	*Stockport Co*	12	0	**23**	**0**
2008–09	Everton	0	0		
2008–09	*Crewe Alex*	19	0	**19**	**0**
2009–10	Everton	0	0	**1**	**0**
2009–10	*Motherwell*	34	0	**34**	**0**
2010–11	Norwich C	45	0		
2011–12	Norwich C	37	0		
2012–13	Norwich C	15	0		
2013–14	Norwich C	38	0		
2014–15	Norwich C	46	0		
2015–16	Norwich C	27	0		
2016–17	Norwich C	27	0	**235**	**0**
2017–18	Wolverhampton W	45	0		
2018–19	Wolverhampton W	1	0		
2019–20	Wolverhampton W	0	0		
2020–21	Wolverhampton W	2	0		
2021–22	Wolverhampton W	2	0	**50**	**0**

SAISS, Romain (D) **333** **23**

H: 6 3 W: 12 08 b.Bourg-de-Peage 26-3-90

Internationals: Morocco Full caps.

2010–11	Valence	13	4	**13**	**4**
2011–12	Clermont	17	1		
2012–13	Clermont	31	0	**48**	**1**
2013–14	Le Havre	27	1		
2014–15	Le Havre	34	2	**61**	**3**
2015–16	Angers	35	2	**35**	**2**
2016–17	Wolverhampton W	24	0		
2017–18	Wolverhampton W	42	4		
2018–19	Wolverhampton W	19	2		
2019–20	Wolverhampton W	33	2		
2020–21	Wolverhampton W	27	3		
2021–22	Wolverhampton W	31	2	**176**	**13**

SANDERSON, Dion (D) **62** **1**

H: 6 2 W: 12 04 b.Wolverhampton 15-12-99

2019–20	Wolverhampton W	0	0		
2019–20	*Cardiff C*	10	0	**10**	**0**
2020–21	Wolverhampton W	0	0		
2020–21	*Sunderland*	26	1	**26**	**1**
2021–22	Wolverhampton W	0	0		
2021–22	*Birmingham C*	15	0	**15**	**0**
2021–22	*QPR*	11	0	**11**	**0**

SANG-BIN, Jeong (F) **34** **6**

b.Cheonan 1-4-02

Internationals: South Korea U17, U23, Full caps.

2019	Suwon Samsung Bluewings	0	0		
2020	Suwon Samsung Bluewings	28	6	**28**	**6**
2021–22	Wolverhampton W	0	0		
2021–22	*Grasshopper*	6	0	**6**	**0**

SARKIC, Matija (G) **63** **0**

H: 6 4 W: 11 07 b.Grimsby 23-7-97

Internationals: Montenegro U17, U19, U21, Full caps.

2014–15	Anderlecht	0	0		
2015–16	Aston Villa	0	0		
2016–17	Aston Villa	0	0		
2017–18	Aston Villa	0	0		
2017–18	*Wigan Ath*	0	0		
2018–19	Aston Villa	0	0		
2019–20	Aston Villa	0	0		
2019–20	*Livingston*	14	0	**14**	**0**
2020–21	Wolverhampton W	0	0		
2020–21	*Shrewsbury T*	26	0	**26**	**0**
2021–22	Wolverhampton W	0	0		
2021–22	*Birmingham C*	23	0	**23**	**0**

SCOTT, Jack (D) **16** **1**

H: 6 0 W: 11 11 b. 22-9-02

Internationals: Northern Ireland U17, U21.

From Linfield.

2020–21	Wolverhampton W	0	0		
2021–22	Wolverhampton W	0	0		
2022	*St Patricks Ath*	16	1	**16**	**1**

SHABANI, Meritan (M) **7** **0**

b.Munich 15-3-99

Internationals: Germany U20.

2017–18	Bayern Munich	1	0		
2018–19	Bayern Munich	1	0	**2**	**0**
2019–20	Wolverhampton W	0	0		
2020–21	Wolverhampton W	0	0		
2020–21	*VVV Venlo*	5	0	**5**	**0**
2021–22	Wolverhampton W	0	0		

SILVA, Fabio (F) **66** **5**

H: 6 1 W: 11 11 b.Porto 19-7-02

Internationals: Portugal U16, U17, U19, U21.

2019–20	Porto	12	1	**12**	**1**
2020–21	Wolverhampton W	32	4		
2021–22	Wolverhampton W	22	0	**54**	**4**

SONDERGAARD, Andreas (G) **0** **0**

H: 6 2 W: 11 11 b.Nyborg 17-1-01

Internationals: Denmark U16, U17, U18, U19.

From Odense.

2019–20	Wolverhampton W	0	0		
2020–21	Wolverhampton W	0	0		
2021–22	Wolverhampton W	0	0		

TIPTON, Ollie (D) **0** **0**

b.Wolverhampton 22-9-03

2020–21	Wolverhampton W	0	0		
2021–22	Wolverhampton W	0	0		

TRAORE, Adama (F) **207** **13**

H: 5 10 W: 12 00 b.L'Hospitalet de Llobregat 25-1-96

Internationals: Spain U16, U17, U19, U21, Full caps.

2013–14	Barcelona	1	0		
2014–15	Barcelona	0	0		
2015–16	Aston Villa	10	0		
2016–17	Aston Villa	1	0	**11**	**0**
2016–17	Middlesbrough	27	0		
2017–18	Middlesbrough	34	5	**61**	**5**
2018–19	Wolverhampton W	29	1		
2019–20	Wolverhampton W	37	4		
2020–21	Wolverhampton W	37	2		
2021–22	Wolverhampton W	20	1	**123**	**8**
2021–22	*Barcelona*	11	0	**12**	**0**

TRINCAO, Francisco (F) **89** **13**

H: 6 0 W: 12 02 b.Viana do Castelo 29-12-95

Internationals: Portugal U17, U18, U19, U20, U21, Full caps.

2015–16	Braga	0	0		
2016–17	Braga	0	0		

2017–18 Braga 0 0
2018–19 Braga 6 0
2019–20 Braga 27 8 **33 8**
2020–21 Barcelona 28 3
2021–22 Barcelona 0 0 **28 3**
2021–22 *Wolverhampton W* 28 2 **28 2**

YOUNG, Joe (G) 0 0
H: 5 10 W: 11 11 b.Telford 22-9-02
Internationals: England U17.
2020–21 Wolverhampton W 0 0
2021–22 Wolverhampton W 0 0

Players retained or with offer of contract
Birtwistle, Ryan; Diyawa, Aaron; Fraser, Nathan; Griffiths, Harvey; Hubner, Justin; Kandola, Kamran; McLaughlin, Lee; Moulden, Louie; Roberts, Tyler; Smith, Jackson; Storer, James.

Scholars
Barnett, Ty Kimoni; Esen, Halis Joshua; Farmer, Owen John-Paul; Francis-Burrell, Ackeme Cameron; Kaleta, Marvin Marvellous; Mabete, Filozofe; McLeod, Ethan Lucius; Ojinnaka, Temple Uchenna; Storer, James Lee.

WYCOMBE W (92)

AKINFENWA, Adebayo (F) 686 200
H: 6 1 W: 16 01 b.Islington 10-5-82
2001 Atlantas 18 4
2002 Atlantas 4 1 **22 5**
From Barry T.
2003–04 Boston U 3 0 **3 0**
2003–04 Leyton Orient 1 0 **1 0**
2003–04 Rushden & D 0 0
2003–04 Doncaster R 9 4 **9 4**
2004–05 Torquay U 37 14 **37 14**
2005–06 Swansea C 34 9
2006–07 Swansea C 25 5
2007–08 Swansea C 0 0 **59 14**
2007–08 Millwall 7 0 **7 0**
2007–08 Northampton T 15 7
2008–09 Northampton T 33 13
2009–10 Northampton T 40 17
2010–11 Gillingham 44 11
2011–12 Northampton T 39 18
2012–13 Northampton T 41 16 **168 71**
2013–14 Gillingham 34 10 **78 21**
2014–15 AFC Wimbledon 45 13
2015–16 AFC Wimbledon 38 6 **83 19**
2016–17 Wycombe W 42 12
2017–18 Wycombe W 42 17
2018–19 Wycombe W 36 7
2019–20 Wycombe W 32 10
2020–21 Wycombe W 33 1
2021–22 Wycombe W 34 5 **219 52**

AL-HAMADI, Ali (F) 0 0
H: 6 2 b.Maysan Governorate 1-3-02
Internationals: Iraq U23, Full caps.
From Tranmere R.
2020–21 Swansea C 0 0
2021–22 Wycombe W 0 0

ANDERSON, Curtis (G) 0 0
H: 6 0 W: 12 13 b.Barrow 27-9-00
Internationals: England U16, U17, U18, U19.
From Manchester C, Charlotte Independence.
2020–21 Wycombe W 0 0
2021–22 Wycombe W 0 0
Transferred to Lancaster C, January 2022.

BLOOMFIELD, Matt (M) 486 39
H: 5 8 W: 11 07 b.Felixstowe 8-2-84
Internationals: England U19.
2001–02 Ipswich T 0 0
2002–03 Ipswich T 0 0
2003–04 Ipswich T 0 0
2003–04 Wycombe W 12 1
2004–05 Wycombe W 26 2
2005–06 Wycombe W 39 5
2006–07 Wycombe W 41 4
2007–08 Wycombe W 35 4
2008–09 Wycombe W 20 0
2009–10 Wycombe W 14 2
2010–11 Wycombe W 34 3
2011–12 Wycombe W 31 2
2012–13 Wycombe W 2 1
2013–14 Wycombe W 32 0
2014–15 Wycombe W 33 1
2015–16 Wycombe W 27 1
2016–17 Wycombe W 33 5
2017–18 Wycombe W 37 3
2018–19 Wycombe W 28 2
2019–20 Wycombe W 26 2
2020–21 Wycombe W 16 1
2021–22 Wycombe W 0 0 **486 39**

BURLEY, Andre (D) 3 0
H: 5 11 W: 11 05 b.Slough 10-9-99
Internationals: Saint Kitts and Nevis Full caps.
2019–20 Reading 0 0
2020 *Waterford* 3 0 **3 0**
2020–21 Wycombe W 0 0
2021–22 Wycombe W 0 0

CLARK, James (D) 0 0
b.Ealing 5-9-01
From Chelsea.
2020–21 Wycombe W 0 0
2021–22 Wycombe W 0 0

DE BARR, Tjay (F) 75 17
H: 5 9 b.Gibraltar 13-3-00
Internationals: Gibraltar U16, U17, U19, U21, Full caps.
2016–17 Lincoln Red Imps 1 0
2016–17 *Europa Point* 11 0 **11 0**
2017–18 Lincoln Red Imps 13 0
2018–19 Europa 25 14
2019–20 Europa 0 0 **25 14**
2019–20 Oviedo 0 0
2020–21 Lincoln Red Imps 20 3 **34 3**
2021–22 Wycombe W 5 0 **5 0**

DICKINSON, Tyla (G) 0 0
b. 3-4-01
From QPR.
2021–22 Wycombe W 0 0

FREEMAN, Nick (M) 119 5
H: 5 11 W: 12 04 b.Stevenage 7-11-95
From Histon, Hemel Hempstead T, Biggleswade T.
2016–17 Wycombe W 14 0
2017–18 Wycombe W 27 3
2018–19 Wycombe W 27 0
2019–20 Wycombe W 26 2
2020–21 Wycombe W 7 0
2020–21 *Leyton Orient* 15 0
2021–22 Wycombe W 3 0 **104 5**
2021–22 *Leyton Orient* 0 0 **15 0**

GAPE, Dominic (M) 163 3
H: 5 11 W: 11 00 b.Southampton 9-9-94
2012–13 Southampton 0 0
2013–14 Southampton 0 0
2014–15 Southampton 1 0
2015–16 Southampton 0 0
2016–17 Southampton 0 0 **1 0**
2016–17 Wycombe W 32 1
2017–18 Wycombe W 35 1
2018–19 Wycombe W 43 1
2019–20 Wycombe W 28 0
2020–21 Wycombe W 14 0
2021–22 Wycombe W 10 0 **162 3**

GRIMMER, Jack (D) 218 5
H: 6 0 W: 12 13 b.Aberdeen 25-1-94
Internationals: Scotland U16, U17, U18, U19, U21.
2009–10 Aberdeen 2 0
2010–11 Aberdeen 2 0
2011–12 Aberdeen 0 0 **4 0**
2011–12 Fulham 0 0
2012–13 Fulham 0 0
2013–14 Fulham 0 0
2013–14 *Port Vale* 13 1 **13 1**
2014–15 Fulham 13 0
2014–15 *Shrewsbury T* 6 0
2015–16 Fulham 0 0
2015–16 *Shrewsbury T* 21 1
2016–17 Fulham 0 0 **13 0**
2016–17 *Shrewsbury T* 24 0 **51 1**
2017–18 Coventry C 42 1
2018–19 Coventry C 11 0 **53 1**
2019–20 Wycombe W 18 0
2020–21 Wycombe W 40 0
2021–22 Wycombe W 26 2 **84 2**

HANLAN, Brandon (F) 182 28
H: 6 0 W: 11 07 b.Chelsea 31-5-97
2016–17 Charlton Ath 9 0
2017–18 *Colchester U* 18 2 **18 2**
2017–18 Charlton Ath 0 0 **9 0**
2018–19 Gillingham 39 9
2019–20 Gillingham 35 4 **74 13**
2020–21 Bristol R 44 7
2021–22 Bristol R 1 0 **45 7**
2021–22 Wycombe W 36 6 **36 6**

HORGAN, Daryl (M) 176 10
H: 5 7 W: 10 10 b.Galway 10-8-92
Internationals: Republic of Ireland U19, U21, Full caps.
From Dundalk.
2016–17 Preston NE 19 2
2017–18 Preston NE 20 1
2018–19 Preston NE 1 0 **40 3**
2018–19 Hibernian 34 3
2019–20 Hibernian 28 3 **62 6**
2020–21 Wycombe W 40 0
2021–22 Wycombe W 34 1 **74 1**

JACOBSON, Joe (D) 536 47
H: 5 11 W: 12 06 b.Cardiff 17-11-86
Internationals: Wales U21.
2005–06 Cardiff C 1 0
2006–07 Cardiff C 0 0 **1 0**
2006–07 *Accrington S* 6 1
2006–07 *Bristol R* 11 0
2007–08 Bristol R 40 1
2008–09 Bristol R 22 0 **73 1**
2009–10 Oldham Ath 15 0
2010–11 Oldham Ath 1 0 **16 0**
2010–11 Accrington S 26 2 **32 3**
2011–12 Shrewsbury T 39 1
2012–13 Shrewsbury T 30 2
2013–14 Shrewsbury T 41 4 **110 7**
2014–15 Wycombe W 42 3
2015–16 Wycombe W 34 1
2016–17 Wycombe W 39 3
2017–18 Wycombe W 46 6
2018–19 Wycombe W 36 7
2019–20 Wycombe W 30 9
2020–21 Wycombe W 37 4
2021–22 Wycombe W 40 3 **304 36**

JOSEPH, Christian (D) 15 1
H: 6 3 W: 13 01 b.Islington 26-4-00
From Colchester U, Wingate, Loughborough.
2021–22 Wycombe W 15 1 **15 1**

KAIKAI, Sullay (F) 172 33
H: 6 0 W: 11 07 b.Southwark 26-8-95
Internationals: Sierra Leone Full caps.
2013–14 Crystal Palace 0 0
2013–14 *Crawley T* 5 0 **5 0**
2014–15 Crystal Palace 0 0
2014–15 *Cambridge U* 25 5 **25 5**
2015–16 Crystal Palace 1 0
2015–16 *Shrewsbury T* 26 12 **26 12**
2016–17 Brentford 18 3 **18 3**
2016–17 Crystal Palace 1 0
2017–18 Crystal Palace 1 0
2017–18 *Charlton Ath* 14 0 **14 0**
2018–19 Crystal Palace 0 0 **3 0**
2018–19 NAC Breda 6 0 **6 0**
2019–20 Blackpool 22 4
2020–21 Blackpool 36 7
2021–22 Blackpool 0 0 **58 11**
2021–22 Wycombe W 17 2 **17 2**

LINTON, Malachi (F) 0 0
H: 6 0 W: 10 03 b.Ipswich 22-12-00
From Ipswich T, Crewe Alex, Lowestoft.
2020–21 Wycombe W 0 0
2021–22 Wycombe W 0 0

McCARTHY, Jason (D) 213 13
H: 6 1 W: 12 08 b.Southampton 7-11-95
2013–14 Southampton 0 0
2014–15 Southampton 1 0
2015–16 Southampton 0 0
2015–16 *Wycombe W* 35 2
2016–17 Southampton 0 0 **1 0**
2016–17 *Walsall* 46 5 **46 5**
2017–18 Barnsley 21 0 **21 0**
2018–19 Wycombe W 44 2
2019–20 Millwall 2 0 **2 0**
2019–20 *Wycombe W* 9 1
2020–21 Wycombe W 24 2
2021–22 Wycombe W 31 1 **143 8**

McCLEARY, Garath (M) 427 51
H: 6 2 W: 12 00 b.Oxford 15-5-87
Internationals: Jamaica Full caps.
From Oxford C, Slough T, Bromley.
2007–08 Nottingham F 8 1
2008–09 Nottingham F 39 1
2009–10 Nottingham F 24 0
2010–11 Nottingham F 18 2
2011–12 Nottingham F 22 9 **111 13**
2011–12 Reading 0 0
2012–13 Reading 31 3
2013–14 Reading 42 5
2014–15 Reading 26 1
2015–16 Reading 34 4
2016–17 Reading 41 9
2017–18 Reading 18 0
2018–19 Reading 31 0
2019–20 Reading 19 1 **242 23**
2020–21 Wycombe W 32 4
2021–22 Wycombe W 42 11 **74 15**

MEHMETI, Anis (M) 61 10
H: 5 11 W: 9 13 b.Islington 9-1-01
Internationals: Albania U19, U21.
2019–20 Norwich C 0 0
2020–21 Wycombe W 29 3
2021–22 Wycombe W 32 7 **61 10**

OBITA, Jordan (M) 252 15
H: 5 11 W: 11 08 b.Oxford 8-12-93
Internationals: England U18, U19, U20.
2010–11 Reading 0 0

Season	Club	Apps	Gls	Total Apps	Total Gls
2011–12	Reading	0	0		
2011–12	*Barnet*	5	0	**5**	**0**
2011–12	*Gillingham*	6	3	**6**	**3**
2012–13	Reading	0	0		
2012–13	*Portsmouth*	8	1	**8**	**1**
2012–13	*Oldham Ath*	8	0	**8**	**0**
2013–14	Reading	34	1		
2014–15	Reading	43	0		
2015–16	Reading	26	0		
2016–17	Reading	37	2		
2017–18	Reading	2	0		
2018–19	Reading	0	0		
2019–20	Reading	21	2		
2020–21	Reading	0	0	**163**	**5**
2020–21	Oxford U	12	1	**12**	**1**
2020–21	Wycombe W	9	0		
2021–22	Wycombe W	41	5	**50**	**5**

PENDLEBURY, Oliver (M) **4** **2**
H: 5 11 b. 19-1-02
Internationals: England U16.

Season	Club	Apps	Gls	Total Apps	Total Gls
2020–21	Reading	0	0		
2021–22	Reading	0	0		
2021–22	Wycombe W	4	2	**4**	**2**

PRZYBEK, Adam (G) **0** **0**
H: 6 3 b.Nuneaton 2-4-00
Internationals: England U16. Wales U16, U17, U19, U21.

Season	Club	Apps	Gls	Total Apps	Total Gls
2018–19	WBA	0	0		
2019–20	Ipswich T	0	0		
2020–21	Ipswich T	0	0		
2021–22	Wycombe W	0	0		

SAMUEL, Alex (F) **138** **10**
H: 6 0 W: 11 11 b.Neath 20-9-95
Internationals: Wales U18.
From Aberystwyth T.

Season	Club	Apps	Gls	Total Apps	Total Gls
2014–15	Swansea C	0	0		
2015–16	Swansea C	0	0		
2015–16	*Greenock Morton*	26	2	**26**	**2**
2016–17	Swansea C	0	0		
2016–17	*Newport Co*	18	2	**18**	**2**
2017–18	Stevenage	22	0	**22**	**0**
2018–19	Wycombe W	30	5		
2019–20	Wycombe W	21	1		
2020–21	Wycombe W	21	0		
2021–22	Wycombe W	0	0	**72**	**6**

SCOWEN, Josh (M) **366** **18**
H: 5 10 W: 11 09 b.Cheshunt 28-3-93

Season	Club	Apps	Gls	Total Apps	Total Gls
2010–11	Wycombe W	2	0		
2011–12	Wycombe W	0	0		
2012–13	Wycombe W	34	1		
2013–14	Wycombe W	37	1		
2014–15	Wycombe W	18	1		
2014–15	Barnsley	21	4		
2015–16	Barnsley	34	4		
2016–17	Barnsley	41	2	**96**	**10**
2017–18	QPR	42	1		
2018–19	QPR	35	2		
2019–20	QPR	18	0	**95**	**3**
2019–20	Sunderland	4	0		
2020–21	Sunderland	43	1	**47**	**1**
2021–22	Wycombe W	37	1	**128**	**4**

STEWART, Anthony (D) **260** **12**
H: 6 0 W: 12 00 b.Brixton 18-9-92

Season	Club	Apps	Gls	Total Apps	Total Gls
2011–12	Wycombe W	4	0		
2012–13	Wycombe W	19	1		
2013–14	Wycombe W	33	3		
2014–15	Crewe Alex	10	0	**10**	**0**
2015–16	Wycombe W	27	1		
2016–17	Wycombe W	31	1		
2017–18	Wycombe W	17	1		
2018–19	Wycombe W	17	0		
2019–20	Wycombe W	34	2		
2020–21	Wycombe W	32	1		
2021–22	Wycombe W	36	2	**250**	**12**

STOCKDALE, David (G) **412** **0**
H: 6 3 W: 13 03 b.Leeds 20-9-85
Internationals: England C.

Season	Club	Apps	Gls	Total Apps	Total Gls
2002–03	York C	1	0		
2003–04	York C	0	0		
2004–05	York C	0	0		
2005–06	York C	0	0	**1**	**0**
2006–07	Darlington	6	0		
2007–08	Darlington	41	0	**47**	**0**
2008–09	Fulham	0	0		
2008–09	*Rotherham U*	8	0	**8**	**0**
2008–09	*Leicester C*	8	0	**8**	**0**
2009–10	Fulham	1	0		
2009–10	*Plymouth Arg*	21	0	**21**	**0**
2010–11	Fulham	7	0		
2011–12	Fulham	8	0		
2011–12	*Ipswich T*	18	0	**18**	**0**
2012–13	Fulham	2	0		
2012–13	*Hull C*	24	0	**24**	**0**
2013–14	Fulham	21	0	**39**	**0**
2014–15	Brighton & HA	42	0		
2015–16	Brighton & HA	46	0		
2016–17	Brighton & HA	45	0	**133**	**0**
2017–18	Birmingham C	36	0		
2018–19	Birmingham C	0	0	**36**	**0**
2018–19	*Southend U*	3	0	**3**	**0**
2018–19	*Wycombe W*	2	0		
2018–19	*Coventry C*	2	0	**2**	**0**
2019–20	Wycombe W	2	0		
2020–21	Wycombe W	17	0		
2020–21	*Stevenage*	5	0	**5**	**0**
2021–22	Wycombe W	46	0	**67**	**0**

TAFAZOLLI, Ryan (D) **273** **21**
H: 6 5 W: 14 09 b.Sutton Bonington 28-9-91

Season	Club	Apps	Gls	Total Apps	Total Gls
2010–11	Southampton	0	0		

From Concorde Rangers, Cambridge C.

Season	Club	Apps	Gls	Total Apps	Total Gls
2013–14	Mansfield T	24	2		
2014–15	Mansfield T	36	1		
2015–16	Mansfield T	44	5	**104**	**8**
2016–17	Peterborough U	31	3		
2017–18	Peterborough U	33	1		
2018–19	Peterborough U	37	1	**101**	**5**
2019–20	Hull C	15	2	**15**	**2**
2020–21	Wycombe W	20	2		
2021–22	Wycombe W	33	4	**53**	**6**

THOMPSON, Curtis (M) **211** **5**
H: 5 10 W: 12 01 b.Nottingham 2-9-93
From Lincoln C.

Season	Club	Apps	Gls	Total Apps	Total Gls
2011–12	Notts Co	0	0		
2012–13	Notts Co	2	0		
2013–14	Notts Co	11	0		
2014–15	Notts Co	31	0		
2015–16	Notts Co	26	2		
2016–17	Notts Co	13	0		
2017–18	Notts Co	0	0	**83**	**2**
2017–18	*Wycombe W*	7	0		
2018–19	Wycombe W	39	1		
2019–20	Wycombe W	21	0		
2020–21	Wycombe W	33	0		
2021–22	Wycombe W	28	2	**128**	**3**

VOKES, Sam (F) **494** **110**
H: 6 1 W: 14 02 b.Lymington 21-10-89
Internationals: Wales U21, Full caps.

Season	Club	Apps	Gls	Total Apps	Total Gls
2006–07	Bournemouth	13	4		
2007–08	Bournemouth	41	12	**54**	**16**
2008–09	Wolverhampton W	36	6		
2009–10	Wolverhampton W	5	0		
2009–10	*Leeds U*	8	1	**8**	**1**
2010–11	Wolverhampton W	2	0		
2010–11	*Bristol C*	1	0	**1**	**0**
2010–11	*Sheffield U*	6	1	**6**	**1**
2010–11	*Norwich C*	4	1	**4**	**1**
2011–12	Wolverhampton W	4	0		
2011–12	*Burnley*	9	2		
2011–12	*Brighton & HA*	14	3	**14**	**3**
2012–13	Wolverhampton W	0	0	**47**	**6**
2012–13	Burnley	46	4		
2013–14	Burnley	39	20		
2014–15	Burnley	15	0		
2015–16	Burnley	43	15		
2016–17	Burnley	37	10		
2017–18	Burnley	30	4		
2018–19	Burnley	20	3	**239**	**58**
2018–19	Stoke C	12	3		
2019–20	Stoke C	36	5		
2020–21	Stoke C	30	0		
2021–22	Stoke C	0	0	**78**	**8**
2021–22	Wycombe W	43	16	**43**	**16**

WHEELER, David (M) **289** **46**
H: 5 11 W: 12 00 b.Brighton 4-10-90
From Brighton & HA.

Season	Club	Apps	Gls	Total Apps	Total Gls
2013–14	Exeter C	35	3		
2014–15	Exeter C	45	7		
2015–16	Exeter C	31	6		
2016–17	Exeter C	38	17		
2017–18	Exeter C	2	0	**151**	**33**
2017–18	QPR	9	1		
2018–19	QPR	0	0	**9**	**1**
2018–19	*Portsmouth*	11	0	**11**	**0**
2018–19	*Milton Keynes D*	19	4	**19**	**4**
2019–20	Wycombe W	31	3		
2020–21	Wycombe W	38	3		
2021–22	Wycombe W	30	2	**99**	**8**

WING, Lewis (M) **151** **19**
H: 5 9 W: 11 00 b.Newton Aycliffe 23-5-95
From Tow Law T, Seaham Red Star, Darlington 1883, Newton Aycliffe, Seaham Red Star, Shildon.

Season	Club	Apps	Gls	Total Apps	Total Gls
2017–18	Middlesbrough	0	0		
2017–18	*Yeovil T*	20	3	**20**	**3**
2018–19	Middlesbrough	28	3		
2019–20	Middlesbrough	40	7		
2020–21	Middlesbrough	12	2		
2020–21	*Rotherham U*	20	2	**20**	**2**
2021–22	Middlesbrough	0	0	**80**	**12**
2021–22	*Sheffield W*	18	0	**18**	**0**
2021–22	Wycombe W	13	2	**13**	**2**

YOUNG, Jack (M) **7** **0**
b. 21-10-00

Season	Club	Apps	Gls	Total Apps	Total Gls
2019–20	Newcastle U	0	0		
2020–21	Newcastle U	0	0		
2020–21	*Tranmere R*	5	0	**5**	**0**
2021–22	Wycombe W	2	0	**2**	**0**

Players retained or with offer of contract
Fischer, Jean-Baptiste; Leathers, Adam; Parsons, Connor; Ram, Max; Wakely, Jack.

ENGLISH LEAGUE PLAYERS – INDEX

Aarons, Maximillian 59
Aarons, Rolando 40
Aasgaard, Thelo 90
Abbey, Nelson 69
Abimbola, Peter 58
Ablade, Terry 36
Abldeen-Goodridge, Tristan 4
Abraham, Tammy 23
Abraham, Timmy 36
Abrahams, Tristan 21
Abrefa, Kelvin 69
Abu, Derrick 23
Adams, Che 77
Adams, Ebou 35
Adams, Nicky 61
Adarabioyo, Tosin 36
Addy, TQ 48
Adebambo, Gabriel 79
Adebayo, Elijah 48
Adebisi, Rio 28
Adebowale, Emmanuel 27
Adeboyejo, Victor 5
Adedoyin, Korede 1
Adegoke, Prince 23
Adelakun, Hakeeb 46
Adeniran, Dennis 75
Adjei-Hersey, Dylan 2
Adomah, Albert 68
Adrian 47
Adshead, Daniel 59
Adubofour-Poku, Kwame 63
Afobe, Benik 79
Afolayan, Oladapo 10
Agard, Kieran 31
Agboola, Michael 91
Aghatise, Osazee 30
Aguiar, Ricky 83
Aguilar, Kluiverth 49
Agyakwa, Derek 87
Agyei, Daniel 28
Ahadme, Gassan 18
Ahearne-Grant, Karlan 88
Aimson, Will 10
Ainley, Callum 28
Ait Nouri, Rayan 91
Aitchison, Jack 5
Ajayi, Semi 88
Ajer, Kristoffer 13
Ajiboye, David 81
Ajose, Joseph 68
Ake, Nathan 49
Akehurst, Bailey 37
Akinde, John 25
Akinfenwa, Adebayo 92
Akinola, Tim 3
Akins, Lucas 51
Akpom, Chuba 52
Akrobar-Boateng, David 29
Al-Hamadi, Ali 92
Al-Hussaini, Zaid 27
Albrighton, Marc 44
Alebiosu, Ryan 3
Alese, Ajibola 89
Alessandra, Lewis 21
Alex Telles, Nicolao 50
Alexander, Cheye 2
Alexander, Matthew 10
Alexander-Arnold, Trent 47
Alfa, Ody 68
Alisson, Ramses 47
Allan, Marques 32
Allan, Thomas 56
Allen, Charlie 43
Allen, Jamie 26
Allen, Joe 79
Allen, Taylor 35
Alli, Bamidele 32
Allsop, Ryan 30
Almiron, Miguel 56
Almond, Patrick 80
Alonso, Marcus 23
Aluko, Sone 42
Alvarado, Jamie 87
Alvarez, Julian 49
Alves, Frederik 89
Alzate, Steve 14
Amadi-Holloway, Aaron 18
Amaechi, Xavier 10
Amankwah, Yeboah 49
Amartey, Daniel 44
Ameobi, Sammy 52
Ameyaw, Eric 36
Aminu, Mohammed 49
Amissah, Jordan 74
Amond, Padraig 57
Amoo, David 65
Amos, Ben 90
Amos, Danny 65
Amos, Luke 68
Ampadu, Ethan 23
Anang, Joseph 89
Andersen, Joachim 29
Andersen, Mads 5
Anderson, Curtis 92
Anderson, Elliot 56
Anderson, Harry 16
Anderson, Keshi 9
Anderson, Thomas 31
Andersson, Edwin 23
Anderton, Nick 16
Ando, Cerny 72
Andoh, Levi 42
Andone, Florin 14
Andrade, Bruno 78
Andre Gomes, Filipe 32
Andre Mendes, Filipe Silva 55
Andresson, Jokull 69
Andrew, Danny 34
Andrews, Corie 2
Andrews, Josh 7
Aneke, Chuks 22
Angol, Lee 12
Anifowose, Joshua 62
Anjorin, Faustino 23
Annesley, Louie 7
Anthony, Jaidon 11
Antonio, Michael 89
Antwi, Cameron 9
Aouachira, Wassim 22
Appere, Louis 58
Appiah, Kwesi 27
Appiah, Paul 4
Appiah-Forson, Keenan 89
Apter, Robert 9
Arblaster, Oliver 74
Archer, Cameron 4
Archer, Jordan 68
Archibald, Theo 46
Areola, Alphonse 89
Arinbjornsson, Palmi 91
Armer, Jack 21
Armin, Albie 42
Armitage, Will 77
Armstrong, Adam 77
Armstrong, Luke 38
Armstrong, Stuart 77
Arrizabalaga, Kepa 23
Arroyo, Anderson 47
Arter, Harry 60
Arthur, Festus 41
Arthur, Jack 33
Arzani, Daniel 49
Ashby, Harrison 89
Ashby-Hammond, Luca 36
Ashcroft, Tyrell 69
Ashford, Sam 27
Ashley, Ossama 89
Ashley-Seal, Benny 58
Ashworth, Zachary 88
Asprilla, Yaser 87
Assal, Ayoub 2
Astley, Ryan 32
Atangana, Nigel 33
Atkinson, Robert 15
Aubameyang, Pierre-Emerick 3
Austerfield, Joshua 40
Austin, Brandon 84
Austin, Charlie 68
Ayala, Daniel 8
Ayew, Jordan 29
Ayina, Loick 40
Ayling, Luke 43
Ayunga, Jonah 55
Azaz, Finn 4
Azeez, Femi 69
Azeez, Miguel 3
Azpilicueta, Cesar 23
Baah, Kwadwo 87
Baba, Abdul Rahman 23
Bachmann, Daniel 87
Back, Finley 60
Bacuna, Juninho 7
Bacuna, Leandro 20
Badan, Andrea 61
Badley-Morgan, Luke 23
Bagan, Joel 20
Baggley, Barry 34
Baggott, Elkan 42
Bahamboula, Dylan 61
Bailey, Eden 65
Bailey, Leon 4
Bailey, Odin 7
Bailly, Eric 50
Bakare, Ibrahim 20
Bakayoko, Amadou 10
Bakayoko, Tiemoue 23
Baker, Harry 73
Baker, Lewis 79
Baker, Nathan 15
Baker-Richardson, Courtney 57
Bakinson, Tyreeq 15
Balagizi, James 47
Balcombe, Ellery 13
Balde, Alberto 52
Baldock, George 74
Baldock, Sam 62
Baldwin, Aden 54
Baldwin, Jack 16
Ball, Dominic 68
Ball, James 70
Ballard, Daniel 3
Ballo, Thierno 23
Balogun, Folarin 3
Baluta, Tudor 14
Bamba, Souleymane 52
Bamford, Patrick 43
Bange, Ewan 9
Baningime, Divin 90
Banks, Oliver 6
Banks, Scott 29
Bannan, Barry 75
Bansal-McNulty, Amrit 68
Bapaga, Will 26
Baptiste, Alex 10
Baptiste, Jamal 89
Baptiste, Shandon 13
Barbet, Yoann 68
Barden, Daniel 59
Barden, Jonathan 81
Bardsley, Phillip 17
Bardwell, Max 30
Barker, Brandon 69
Barker, Charlie 22
Barker, Kyle 63
Barkers, Dylan 24
Barkhuizen, Tom 67
Barkley, Ross 23
Barlaser, Daniel 71
Barlow, Aidan 31
Barnes, Ashley 17
Barnes, Dillon 68
Barnes, Harvey 44
Barnes, Joshua 60
Barnes, Samuel 8
Barrett, Jack 32
Barrett, Ryan 56
Barry, Bradley 78
Barry, Louie 4
Bartley, Kyle 88
Basham, Chris 74
Bass, Alex 66
Bassi, Amine 5
Bastien, Sacha 78
Batch, Billy 34
Bate, Lewis 43
Bates, Alfie 86
Batshuayi, Michy 23
Batth, Danny 80
Battle, Alex 27
Batty, Daniel 34
Baudry, Mathieu 83
Bauer, Patrick 67
Baxter, Jack 67
Baxter, Nathan 23
Bayliss, Tom 67
Bazunu, Gavin 49
Beadle, James 14
Beadling, Tom 6
Bearne, Jack 47
Beautyman, Harry 81
Beck, Mark 38
Beck, Owen 47
Beckett, Louis 41
Beckles, Omar 45
Beckwith, Sam 48
Bedeau, Jacob 17
Bednarek, Jan 77
Beesley, Jake 9
Beestin, Alfie 73
Beevers, Mark 63
Begovic, Asmir 32
Bela, Jeremie 7
Belehouan, Jean 74
Bell, Amari 48
Bell, Finn 35
Bell, Lewis 21
Bell, Sam 15
Bellerin, Hector 3
Bellingham, Jobe 7
Bellis, Sam 77
Belshaw, James 16
Benarous, Ayman 15
Benda, Steven 82
Bendle, Alfie 2
Benkovic, Filip 44
Bennet, Kaan 25
Bennett, Elliott 76
Bennett, J'Neil 84
Bennett, Joe 90
Bennett, Liam 19
Bennett, Mason 53
Bennett, Rhys 55
Bennett, Richie 81
Bennett, Ryan 82
Bennett, Scott 57
Benning, Malvind 65
Benrahma, Said 89
Benson, Josh 5
Bentancur, Rodrigo 84
Benteke, Christian 29
Bentley, Daniel 15
Berahino, Saido 75
Berge, Sander 74
Bergstrom, Lucas 23
Bergwijn, Steven 84
Berkoe, Kevin 72
Bernard, Di'shon 50
Bernard, Dominic 35
Bernardo Silva, Mota 49
Berry, Dylan 59
Berry, Luke 48
Bertrand, Ryan 44
Bettache, Faysal 68
Bettinelli, Marcus 23
Bevan, Jaden 76
Bialkowski, Bartosz 53
Bidstrup, Mads 13
Bidwell, Jake 26
Bielik, Krystian 30
Biggins, Harrison 34
Biler, Huseyin 2
Billing, Phillip 11
Billington, Lewis 28
Bilokapic, Nicholas 40
Bilson, Tom 26
Bird, Jay 54
Bird, Max 30
Bird, Samuel 34
Bishop, Colby 1
Bishop, Nathan 50
Bishop, Teddy 46
Bissouma, Yves 14
Blackman, Jamal 40
Blackmore, Will 63
Blair, Harvey 47
Blair, Matty 24
Blair, Sam 59
Blake-Tracy, Frazer 18
Bloomfield, Matt 92
Bloxham, Tom 76
Blyth, Jacob 61
Blythe, Ben 31
Boateng, Hiram 54
Boateng, Kwame 75
Boateng, Malachi 29
Bobb, Oscar 49
Bodie, Dave 63
Bodin, Billy 62
Bodvarsson, Jon Dadi 10
Bogarde, Lamar 4
Bogle, Jayden 74
Bogle, Omar 39
Bogusz, Mateusz 43
Bola, Marc 52
Bola, Tolaji 71
Boldewijn, Enzio 81
Bolla, Bendeguz 91
Bolton, Elliott 2
Bolton, James 64
Bolton, Luke 72
Boly, Willy 91
Bonaventure, Emmanuel 87
Bonds, Elliott 24
Bondswell, Matthew 56
Bong, Gaetan 60
Bonham, Jack 79
Bonne, Macauley 68
Booth, Sam 28
Borthwick-Jackson, Cameron 18
Bostock, John 31
Bostwick, Michael 18
Bottomley, Ben 31
Bouzanis, Dean 81
Bowden, Jamie 84
Bowen, Jarrod 89
Bowen, Sam 20
Bowery, Jordan 51
Bowler, Josh 9
Bowman, Ryan 76
Boyce-Clarke, Coniah 69
Boyd-Munce, Caolan 52
Boyes, Harry 74
Boyle, Dylan 34
Boyle, William 24
Braaf, Jayden 49
Bradley, Conor 47
Bradley, Sonny 48
Bradshaw, Tom 53
Brady, Robert 11
Brain, Owen 16
Bramall, Cohen 46
Brannagan, Cameron 62
Branthwaite, Jarrad 32
Brayford, John 18
Brearey, Eddie 62
Bree, James 48
Breeze, Gabriel 21
Bremang, David 5
Brennan, Ciaran 75
Brennan, Luke 8
Brereton, Ben 8
Brewster, Rhian 74
Bridcutt, Liam 46
Bridge, Mungo 4
Bridgman, Alfie 66
Brierley, Ethan 70
Bright, Harrison 57
Bright, Myles 40
Bristow, Ethan 69
Brittain, Callum 5
Britton, Louis 15
Broadbent, George 74
Broadhead, Nathan 32
Brockbank, Harry 10
Broja, Armando 23
Brook, Lachlan 13
Brooke, Harry 59
Brooking, Josh 23
Brooks, Andre 74
Brooks, David 11
Brookwell, Niall 56
Broom, Ryan 63
Brophy, James 19
Brough, Patrick 6
Brown, Charlie 24
Brown, Ciaron 20
Brown, Connor 6
Brown, Isaiah 67
Brown, Jacob 79
Brown, Jaden 75
Brown, James 8
Brown, Jevani 33
Brown, Jordan 45
Brown, Junior 16
Brown, Lee 2
Brown, Reece 40
Brown, Scott 33
Brown, Will 56
Browne, Alan 67
Browne, Marcus 62
Brownhill, Josh 17
Bruno Fernandes, Miguel 50
Bruno Guimaraes, Moura 56
Bruno Jordao, Andre 91
Brunt, Lewis 44
Brunt, Zak 74
Bryan, Joe 36
Bryan, Kean 88
Brynn, Solomon 52
Buchanan, Lee 30
Buckley, John 8
Bueno, Hugo 91
Bughail-Mellor, D'Mani 50
Bugiel, Omar 81
Bunker, Harvey 35
Bunn, Harry 73
Burchall, Ajani 4
Burey, Tyler 53
Burge, Lee 80
Burgess, Cameron 42
Burgess, Luke 72
Burgess, Scott 65
Burgoyne, Harry 76
Burke, Oliver 74
Burke, Reece 48

Burke, Ryan 51
Burley, Andre 92
Burn, Dan 56
Burnett, Henry 27
Burns, Finley 49
Burns, Sam 8
Burns, Samuel 8
Burns, Wes 42
Burrell, Rumarn 52
Burrell, Warren 38
Burroughs, Jack 26
Burrows, Harrison 63
Bursik, Josef 79
Burstow, Mason 23
Burton, Callum 64
Burton, Jake 85
Buse, William 15
Bushiri, Rocky 59
Bustos, Nahuel 49
Butcher, Matt 1
Butland, Jack 29
Butler, Dan 63
Butterfield, Luke 32
Butterworth, Daniel 8
Button, David 88
Bycroft, Jack 77
Byers, George 75
Byram, Samuel 59
Byrne, Nathan 30
Byrne, Neil 39
Caballero, Willy 77
Cabango, Ben 82
Cadden, Nicky 35
Cafu, Dias 60
Cahill, Gary 11
Caicedo, Moises 14
Cain, Jake 47
Caine, Nathan 51
Cairney, Tom 36
Cairns, Alex 34
Calvert-Lewin, Dominic 32
Camara, Etienne 40
Camara, Mamadi 69
Camara, Panutche 64
Camp, Brennan 11
Campana, Leonardo 91
Campbell, Allan 48
Campbell, Chem 91
Campbell, Frazier 40
Campbell, Hayden 72
Campbell, Rio 82
Campbell, Tahvon 70
Campbell, Tate 7
Campbell, Tyreece 22
Campbell, Tyrese 79
Camps, Callum 34
Campton-Sturridge, DJ 4
Canavan, Niall 6
Cann, Hayden 46
Cannon, Andy 41
Cannon, Thomas 32
Canos, Sergi 13
Cantwell, Todd 59
Capello, Angelo 74
Caprice, Jake 33
Caprile, Elia 43
Carayol, Mustapha 37
Cardoso, Goncalo 89
Carey, Sonny 9
Cargill, Baily 35
Carlyle, Nathan 68
Carney, Jacob 80
Carroll, Andy 88
Carroll, Tommy 42
Carson, Scott 49
Carson, Trevor 55
Carter, Charlie 78
Carter, Hayden 8
Carter, Jack 35
Carter-Vickers, Cameron 84
Cartwright, Harvey 41
Carty, Conor 91
Carvalho, Fabio 36
Carver, Marcus 39
Casey, Oliver 9
Cash, Matty 4
Cashin, Eiran 30
Cashman, Danny 26
Casilla, Francisco 43
Cass, Lewis 56
Cassidy, Ryan 87
Castagne, Timothy 44
Castillo, Juan 23
Cathcart, Craig 87
Caton, Charlie 76
Cavani, Edinson 50
Cedric Soares, Ricardo 3
Celina, Bersant 42
Chadwick, Billy 41
Chair, Ilias 68
Chalobah, Nathaniel 36
Chalobah, Trevor 23
Chambers, Calum 4
Chambers, Josh 37
Chambers, Leon 62
Chambers, Luke 25
Chaplin, Conor 42
Chapman, Aaron 37
Chapman, Ellis 24
Chapman, Harry 8
Chapman, Jacob 40
Chapman, Mackenzie 62
Charles, Darius 2
Charles, Dion 10
Charles, Jaden 51
Charman, Luke 70
Charsley, Harry 65
Charters, Taylor 21
Chauke, Kgaogelo 77
Chester, James 79
Chesters, Daniel 89
Chilvers, Noah 25
Chilwell, Ben 23
Chiquinho, Oliveira 91
Chirewa, Tawanda 42
Chislett, Ethan 2
Chong, Tahith 50
Choudhury, Hamza 44
Chrisene, Benjamin 4
Christensen, Andreas 23
Christie, Cyrus 36
Christie, Ryan 11
Christie-Davies, Isaac 5
Chukwuemeka, Caleb 4
Chukwuemeka, Carney 4
Cirjan, Catalin 3
Cirkin, Dennis 80
Cisse, Ousseynou 61
Clampin, Ryan 25
Clare, Sean 22
Clark, Ciaran 56
Clark, James 92
Clark, Jordan 48
Clark, Max 70
Clark, Mitchell 1
Clarke, Courtney 30
Clarke, Flynn 59
Clarke, Harrison 3
Clarke, Jack 84
Clarke, Jahmari 69
Clarke, James 57
Clarke, James 51
Clarke, Jordan 61
Clarke, Leon 16
Clarke, Matthew 14
Clarke, Ollie 51
Clarke, Peter 85
Clarke, Tom 34
Clarke, Trevor 16
Clarke-Harris, Jonson 63
Clarke-Salter, Jake 23
Clarkson, Leighton 47
Clay, Craig 45
Clayden, Charles 22
Clayton, Adam 31
Clayton, Tom 47
Clements, Bailey 42
Cleverley, Tom 87
Close, Ben 31
Clough, Zach 21
Clucas, Sam 79
Clyne, Nathaniel 29
Coady, Conor 91
Coates, Kieran 79
Coburn, Josh 52
Cochrane, Owen 78
Coker, Ben 78
Coker, Kenny 59
Colback, Jack 60
Cole, Devante 5
Coleman, Ethan 45
Coleman, Joel 70
Coleman, Seamus 32
Coley, Josh 33
Colin, Maxime 7
Colkett, Charlie 24
Collins, Aaron 16
Collins, Archie 33
Collins, Bradley 5
Collins, James S 20
Collins, Lewis 57
Collins, Nathan 17
Collins, Ted 25
Collins, Tom 73
Collyer, Toby 50
Colwill, Levi 23
Colwill, Rubin 20
Comley, Brandon 10
Congreve, Cameron 82
Conlon, Tom 65
Conn-Clarke, Chris 34
Conneely, Seamus 1
Connolly, Aaron 14
Connolly, Callum 9
Connolly, Dylan 55
Connolly, James 20
Conroy, Dion 83
Conway, Max 10
Conway, Tommy 15
Cook, Andy 12
Cook, Jordan 39
Cook, Lewis 11
Cook, Steve 60
Cooke, Callum 12
Cooney, Ryan 55
Cooper, Brandon 82
Cooper, Chay 25
Cooper, George 64
Cooper, Jake 53
Cooper, Joel 62
Cooper, Liam 43
Cooper, Michael 64
Cooper, Oliver 82
Corbeanu, Theo 91
Corbett, Kai 63
Cork, Jack 17
Cornell, David 63
Corness, Dominic 47
Cornet, Maxwel 17
Cornick, Harry 48
Cornish, Sam 25
Cosgrave, Aaron 2
Cosgrove, Sam 7
Costa Da Rosa, Bernardo 89
Cottrell, Ben 3
Coufal, Vladimir 89
Coulibaly, Ismaila 74
Coulson, Hayden 52
Coulton, Lewis 67
Cousin-Dawson, Finn 12
Cousins, Jordan 90
Coutinho, Phillippe 4
Couto, Benny 61
Couto, Yan 49
Coutts, Paul 16
Coventry, Conor 89
Covil, Vaughn 35
Cox, Matthew 13
Cox, Sonny 33
Coxe, Cameron 25
Coyle, Lewie 41
Coyle, Liam 1
Cracknell, Billy 25
Cracknell, Joe 38
Craig, Tony 27
Crama, Tristan 13
Crane, Ross 42
Crankshaw, Oliver 12
Craske, Finley 64
Crawford, Tom 39
Crellin, Billy 32
Cresswell, Aaron 89
Cresswell, Charlie 43
Cribb, Harvey 73
Crichlow, Kane 87
Crichlow-Noble, Romoney 40
Crooks, Matt 52
Cross, Bradley 56
Cross, Liam 58
Crowe, Dylan 42
Crowley, Daniel 24
Csoka, Daniel 2
Cucurella, Marc 14
Cukur, Tiago 87
Cullen, Liam 82
Cullen, Mark 39
Cumming, Jamie 23
Cundle, Luke 91
Cundy, Robbie 15
Cunningham, Greg 67
Currie, Jack 2
Curtis, Ronan 66
Cuthbert, Scott 78
Cutrone, Patrick 91
Cybulski, Bartosz 30
d'Almeida, Tavio 20
Da Costa, Julien 26
Da Silva, Josh 13
Da Silva, Vani 61
Dabo, Fankaty 26
Dack, Bradley 8
Dackers, Marcus 72
Dacres-Cogley, Josh 85
Dadashov, Renat 91
Dahlberg, Pontus 87
Dajaku, Leon 80
Daka, Patson 44
Dale, Owen 9
Daley, Luke 40
Daley-Campbell, Vontae 44
Dallas, Stuart 43
Dallison, Tom 25
Dalot, Diogo 50
Daly, James 78
Daly, Matty 40
Daniel, Colin 33
Daniel Podence, Castelo 91
Daniels, Charlie 25
Daniels, Donervon 86
Daniels, Jake 9
Daniels, Josh 76
Daniels, Luke 52
Dann, Scott 69
Darcy, Ronan 10
Darikwa, Tendayi 90
Darling, Harry 54
Darlow, Karl 56
Dasilva, Jay 15
Davenport, Jacob 8
Davies, Adam 74
Davies, Archie 27
Davies, Ben 84
Davies, Ben 47
Davies, Curtis 30
Davies, Harvey 47
Davies, Isaak 20
Davies, Jack 54
Davies, Leon 19
Davies, Scott 85
Davies, Tom 85
Davies, Tom 32
Davies, William 64
Davis, Benjamin 62
Davis, David 76
Davis, Harry 73
Davis, Jayden 53
Davis, Keinan 4
Davis, Kenny 81
Davis, Leif 43
Davison, Joshua 22
Dawodu, Joshua 75
Dawson, Cameron 75
Dawson, Craig 89
Day, Joe 57
De Barr, Tjay 92
De Bock, Laurens 43
De Bruyne, Kevin 49
De Castro, Quevin 88
De Gea, David 50
De Silva, Dillon 68
De Wijs, Jordy 68
Dean, Harlee 7
Dean, Max 43
Dearnley, Zachary 61
Decordova-Reid, Bobby 36
Deeney, Troy 7
Defoe, Jermain 80
Delaney, Ryan 55
Delap, Liam 49
Dele-Bashiru, Ayotomiwa 87
Dele-Bashiru, Fisayo 75
Delfouneso, Nathan 12
Delph, Fabian 32
Dembele, Siriki 11
Demetriou, Mickey 57
Dempsey, Ben 22
Dempsey, Kyle 10
Dendoncker, Lars 14
Dendoncker, Leander 91
Denham, Oliver 20
Dennis, Kristian 21
Dennis, Matthew 59
Dennis, William 11
Denny, Alex 72
Dervisoglu, Halil 13
Desbois, Adam 14
Devine, Alfie 84
Devine, Daniel 21
Devine, Reece 50
Devitt, Jamie 21
Dewhurst, Marcus 74
Dewsbury-Hall, Kiernan 44
Dhanda, Yan 82
Diabate, Cheick 33
Diaby, Bambo 67
Diagouraga, Toumani 55
Diallo, Amad 50
Diallo, Amadou 89
Diallo, Ibrahima 77
Diallo, Sadou 35
Diamond, Jack 80
Diangana, Grady 88
Diarra, Brahima 40
Diarra, Raphael 61
Dias, Ruben 49
Diaz, Luis 47
Dickens, Tom 19
Dickenson, Brennan 21
Dickie, Rob 68
Dickinson, Tyla 92
Dickson-Peters, Thomas 59
Dieng, Timothee 33
Dieng, Timothy 68
Dier, Eric 84
Dieseruvwe, Emmanuel 85
Digby, Paul 19
Digne, Lucas 4
Dijksteel, Anfernee 52
Dike, Daryl 88
Dinanga, Ricardo 26
Dinzeyi, Jonathan 3
Diop, Issa 89
Dixon, Connor 30
Dixon, Joel 10
Dixon, Josh 21
Dixon-Bonner, Elijah 47
Djenepo, Moussa 77
Dobbin, Lewis 32
Dobra, Armando 42
Dobson, George 22
Docherty, Greg 41
Dodd, James 33
Dodds, Daniel 52
Dodoo, Joseph 31
Doherty, Matthew 84
Dolan, Matthew 57
Dolan, Tyrhys 8
Domi, Franklin 68
Donacien, Janoi 42
Done, Matt 70
Doohan, Ross 85
Dooley, Stephen 70
Dorsett, Jeriel 69
Doucoure, Abdoulaye 32
Dougall, Kenneth 9
Doughty, Alfie 79
Douglas Luiz, de Paulo 4
Dowell, Kieran 59
Downes, Flynn 82
Downing, Paul 66
Doyle, Callum 49
Doyle, Eoin 10
Doyle, Tommy 49
Dozzell, Andre 68
Drager, Mohamed 60
Drameh, Cody 43
Draper, Freddie 46
Dreher, Luke 29
Drewe, Aaron 68
Dreyer, Sam 78
Drinan, Aaron 45
Drinkwater, Daniel 23
Driscoll-Glennon, Anthony 17
Drmic, Josip 59
Drysdale, Declan 26
Dubravka, Martin 56
Duffus, Courtney 55
Duffy, Mark 85
Duffy, Shane 14
Duhaney, Demeaco 79
Duke-Mckenna, Stephen 68
Dummett, Paul 56
Duncan, Bobby 30
Dundas, Craig 81
Dunk, Harrison 19
Dunk, Lewis 14
Dunkley, Cheyenne 75
Dunne, Cieran 80
Dunne, Jimmy 68
Dunne, Joe 70
Dunnwald, Kenan 73
Dyche, Max 58
Dyer, Jordan 33
Dykes, Lyndon 68
Earing, Jack 86
Earl, Joshua 67
East, Ryan 83
Eastham, Ashley 72
Eastham, Jordan 8
Eastman, Tom 25
Eastmond, Craig 81
Eastwood, Jake 74
Eastwood, Simon 62
Eaves, Tom 41
Ebanks, Callum 24
Ebanks-Landell, Ethan 76
Ebiowei, Malcolm 30
Ebosele , Festy 30
Eccles, Josh 26
Ederson, de Moraes 49
Edmonds-Green, Rarmani 40
Edmondson, Ryan 43
Edmundson, Sam 42
Edouard, Odsonne 29
Edozie, Samuel 49
Edun, Tayo 8
Edwards, Danny 34
Edwards, Gwion 90
Edwards, Joe 64
Edwards, Kyle 42

Edwards, Liam 10
Edwards, Opi 35
Edwards, Owura 15
Edwards, Ronnie 63
Edwards, Thomas 79
Egan, John 74
Egan-Riley, CJ 49
Egbo, Mandela 83
Ehmer, Max 37
Eisa, Abobaker 12
Eisa, Mohamed 54
Eiting, Carel 40
Ejaria, Oviemuno 69
Ekpiteta, Marvin 9
Ekwah, Pierre 89
El Ghazi, Anwar 4
El Mizouni, Idris 42
Elanga, Anthony 50
Elder, Callum 41
Elechi, Michael 62
Elerewe, Ayodeji 22
Elitim, Juergen 87
Elliot, Rob 87
Elliott, Harvey 47
Elliott, Tom 72
Ellis, Jack 21
Ellis, Mark 6
Ellison, Kevin 57
Elneny, Mohamed 3
Elyounoussi, Mohamed 77
Embleton, Elliot 80
Emeran, Noam 50
Emerson, dos Santos 23
Emerson, Junior 84
Emi, Buendia 4
Emmanuel, Josh 41
Emmanuel, Mbule 89
Eneme Ella, Ulrick 14
Ennis, Niall 64
Enobakhare, Bright 26
Eppiah, Josh 44
Eratt-Thompson, Declan 75
Eriksen, Christian 13
Estrada, Pascal 91
Etebo, Peter 79
Etete, Kion 84
Etheridge, Neil 7
Evans, Antony 16
Evans, Cameron James 82
Evans, Ched 67
Evans, Corry 80
Evans, Gary 12
Evans, George 53
Evans, Jack 35
Evans, Jonny 44
Evans, Kieron 20
Evans, Lee 42
Evans, Owen 24
Evans-Harriott, Aaron 26
Eyoma, Timothy 46
Eze, Eberechi 29
Fabianski, Lukasz 89
Fabinho, Henrique 47
Fage, Dylan 61
Falkingham, Joshua 38
Fallowfield, Ryan 38
Famewo, Akin 59
Fane, Ousmane 55
Farman, Paul 6
Farmer, Lewis 75
Farquharson, Priestley 57
Featherstone, Nicky 39
Feeney, Josh 4
Feeney, Liam 73
Feeney, Morgan 21
Felipe Araruna, Hoffmann 69
Fellows, Tom 88
Femenia, Kiko 87
Fenlon, Rhys-James 1
Ferguson, David 39
Ferguson, Evan 14
Ferguson, Nathan 29
Ferguson, Shane 71
Fernandes, Baba 60
Fernandez, Alvaro 50
Fernandez, Alvaro 13
Fernandez, Emmanuel 63
Fernandez, Federico 56
Fernandez, Luis 78
Fernandinho, Luis 49
Ferry, Will 77
Fiabema, Bryan 23
Field, Sam 68
Fielding, Frank 79
Finley, Sam 16
Finnegan, Aidan 26
Finney, Oliver 28
Finnigan, Ryan 77
Fiorini, Lewis 49
Firmino, Roberto 47
Firpo, Junior 43
Fish, William 50
Fishburn, Sam 21
Fisher, Alex 57
Fisher, Andy 82
Fisher, Darnell 52
Fisher, David 2
Fitzhugh, Ethan 44
Fitzmartin, Jay 10
Flaherty, Stan 68
Flanagan, Josh 58
Flanagan, Tom 76
Fleck, John 74
Fleming, Brandon 41
Fletcher, Ashley 87
Fletcher, Isaac 52
Fletcher, Steven 79
Flinders, Scott 24
Flint, Aiden 20
Flores, Jordan 58
Flynn, Shane 44
Foden, Phil 49
Foderingham, Wesley 74
Fofana, Wesley 44
Folarin, Sam 52
Foley, Sam 85
Fondop-Talom, Mike 61
Forde, Anthony 62
Forde, Shaqai 87
Fornah, Tyrese 60
Fornals, Pablo 89
Forrester, William 79
Forshaw, Adam 43
Forss, Marcus 13
Forster, Fraser 77
Forster-Caskey, Jake 22
Forsyth, Craig 30
Fossey, Marlon 36
Foster, Ben 87
Foster, Owen 73
Fosu, Tarique 13
Foulds, Matthew 12
Fox, Morgan 79
Frailing, Jake 68
Francillette, Ludwig 27
Francis-Angol, Zaine 39
Francois, Marlee 15
Francois, Tyrese 36
Francomb, George 27
Fraser, Ryan 56
Fraser, Scott 22
Frauendorf, Melkamu 47
Fred, Frederico 50
Fredericks, Ryan 89
Freeman, John 54
Freeman, Kieron 66
Freeman, Luke 74
Freeman, Nick 92
Freestone, Lewis 24
Freitas Gouveia, Diogo 25
French, Billy 22
Friend, George 7
Frieser, Dominik 5
Frost, Tyler 27
Fry, Dael 52
Fuchs, Jeando 63
Fulton, Jay 82
Furlong, Darnell 88
Furlong, James 14
Gabriel, Magalhaes 3
Gabriel Jesus, Fernando 49
Galbraith, Ethan 50
Gale, James 51
Gale, Sam 37
Gallacher, Owen 27
Gallagher, Conor 23
Gallagher, Sam 8
Gallimore, Dan 73
Galloway, Brendon 64
Galloway, Josh 43
Galvin, Ryan 75
Gape, Dominic 92
Garbutt, Luke 9
Garcia Ferreira, Rafael 32
Gardner, Dan 31
Gardner, Gary 7
Gardner-Hickman, Taylor 88
Garnacho, Alejandro 50
Garner, Gerard 34
Garner, James 50
Garner, Joe 34
Garratt, Ben 18
Garrett, Jake 8
Garrick, Jordan 82
Garrity, Ben 65
Gavin, Dylan 22
Gaxha, Leonardo 74
Gayle, Dwight 56
Gazzaniga, Paulo 36
Gbadebo, Camron 25
Gbamin, Jean-Philippe 32
Gbode, Joseph 37
Gelhardt, Joe 43
Genesini, Brooklyn 11
George, Adan 7
George, Shamal 25
Gerken, Dean 25
Ghandour, Hady 22
Ghoddos, Saman 13
Giannoulis, Dimitrios 59
Gibbons, James 65
Gibbs, Liam 59
Gibbs-White, Morgan 91
Gibson, Ben 59
Gibson, Jordan 21
Gibson, Joseph 52
Gibson, Lewis 32
Gibson, Liam 55
Gibson-Hammond, Alexander 60
Gil Salvatierra, Bryan 84
Gilbert, Alex 13
Gilbey, Alex 22
Giles, Ryan 91
Gilks, Matthew 10
Gillesphey, Macaulay 64
Gillespie, Mark 56
Gilliead, Alex 12
Gilligan, Ciaran 18
Gilmour, Billy 23
Gladwin, Ben 83
Glatzel, Paul 47
Glover, Ryan 11
Gnahoua, Arthur 55
Godden, Matthew 26
Godfrey, Ben 32
Godwin-Malife, Udoka 35
Golden, Tylor 72
Golding, James 62
Gollini, Pierluigi 84
Gomes, Claudio 49
Gomes, Madger 28
Gomes, Tote 91
Gomez, Joseph 47
Gomis, Nicksoen 74
Gooch, Lynden 80
Goode, Charlie 13
Goodliffe, Ben 81
Goodrham, Tyler 62
Goodwin, William 79
Gordon, Anthony 32
Gordon, John-Kymani 29
Gordon, Josh 6
Gordon, Kaide 47
Gordon, Kellan 51
Gordon, Kyron 74
Gordon, Lewis 13
Gordon, Liam 10
Gordon, Nico 7
Gorrin, Alejandro 62
Gosling, Dan 87
Gotts, Robbie 6
Gould, Joshua 82
Grabban, Lewis 60
Graczyk, Hubert 3
Graham, Jordan 7
Graham, Sam 70
Grant, Anthony 73
Grant, Conor 64
Grant, Conor 70
Grant, Daniel 40
Grant, Jorge 63
Grant, Josh 16
Grant, Lee 50
Gratton, Jacob 71
Gray, Andre 87
Gray, Archie 43
Gray, Demarai 32
Grayson, Joe 6
Grealish, Jack 49
Greaves, Anthony 31
Greaves, Jacob 41
Greaves, Jerome 71
Green, Andre 75
Green, Devarn 73
Green, Harry 52
Greenidge, Jordan 57
Greenidge, Reiss 10
Greenwood, Mason 50
Greenwood, Sam 43
Grego-Cox, Reece 27
Gregory, Cameron 76
Gregory, David 29
Gregory, Lee 75
Gretarsson, Daniel 9
Grey, Joe 39
Griffiths, Joshua 88
Griffiths, Regan 28
Griffiths, Reo 31
Grigg, Will 80
Grimes, Matt 82
Grimmer, Jack 92
Grimshaw, Daniel 9
Grist, Ben 44
Gross, Pascal 14
Grounds, Jonathan 33
Guaita, Vicente 29
Gubbins, Joseph 68
Gudmundsson, Johann Berg 17
Guedioura, Adiene 18
Guehi, Marc 29
Guendouzi, Matteo 3
Guilbert, Frederic 4
Guinness-Walker, Nesta 2
Gundogan, Ilkay 49
Gunn, Angus 59
Gunnarsson, Patrik 13
Gunter, Chris 22
Guthrie, Jon 58
Guy, Callum 21
Gyimah, Nicky 80
Gyokeres, Viktor 26
Hackett-Fairchild, Recco 66
Hackford, Antwoine 74
Hackney, Hayden 52
Hagan, Charles 75
Hagan, Harry 32
Haigh, Joe 23
Halilovic, Alen 69
Hall, Connor 65
Hall, George 7
Hall, Grant 52
Hall, Louis 57
Hallam, Jordan 73
Halliday, Bradley 34
Halme, Aapo 5
Halwax, Harry 68
Hamalainen, Niko 68
Hamer, Ben 82
Hamer, Gustavo 26
Hamilton, CJ 9
Hamilton, Ethan 1
Hammond, Oliver 60
Hanlan, Brandon 92
Hanley, Grant 59
Hannah, Jack 52
Hannam, Reece 29
Hannant, Luke 25
Hanson, Jamie 62
Happe, Daniel 45
Hardie, Ryan 64
Harding, Wes 71
Hardley, Bjorn 50
Hardy, Joe 1
Hargreaves, Cameron 16
Harker, Rob 17
Harness, Marcus 66
Harness, Nathan 22
Harper, Rekeem 42
Harratt, Kian 40
Harries, Cian 16
Harriman, Michael 58
Harris, Luke 63
Harris, Mark 20
Harris, Max 24
Harris, Will 80
Harrison, Ellis 34
Harrison, Jack 43
Harrison, Shayon 55
Harrop, Josh 67
Hart, Sam 61
Hartigan, Anthony 2
Hartridge, Alex 33
Harvie, Daniel 54
Harwood-Bellis, Taylor 49
Hasani, Lirak 31
Hause, Kortney 4
Havertz, Kai 23
Hawkes, Josh 85
Hawkins, Callum 18
Hawkins, Oliver 51
Hawley, Kyle 55
Hayde, Kyle 85
Hayden, Isaac 56
Hayden, Kaine 4
Hayes, Cian 34
Hayes, Nick 42
Haygarth, Max 13
Haymer, Tom 18
Haynes, Ryan 57
He, Zhenyu 91
Headley, Jaheim 40
Heal, Sam 16
Healy, Matthew 42
Heaton, Tom 50
Hector, Michael 36
Hedges, Ryan 8
Hegyi, Krisztian 89
Hein, Karl Jakob 3
Helder Costa, Wander 43
Helik, Michal 5
Helliwell, Jordan 5
Helm, Mark 17
Hemfrey, Robbie 79
Hemming, Zachary 52
Hemmings, Kane 85
Henderson, Dean 50
Henderson, Ian 72
Henderson, Jordan 47
Henderson, Stephen 22
Hendrick, Jeff 56
Hendrie, Luke 12
Hendry, Regan 35
Heneghan, Ben 2
Hennessey, Wayne 17
Henry, Aaron 22
Henry, Dion 27
Henry, James 62
Henry, Mitchell 10
Henry, Rico 13
Hercules, Wraynel 13
Hernandez, Cucho 87
Hernandez, Onel 59
Herrera, Yangel 49
Hesketh, Owen 91
Hessenthaler, Jake 27
Hewelt, Mateusz 85
Hewitt, Elliott 51
Hewlett, Tom 18
High, Scott 40
Hill, James 11
Hill, Thomas 47
Hillier, Ryan 57
Hillson, James 3
Hilssner, Marcel 26
Hilton, Joe 8
Hilton, Sonny 36
Hinds, Josh 41
Hippolyte, Myles 73
Hirst, George 44
Hiwula, Jordy 31
Hjelde, Leo 43
Hladky, Vaclav 42
Hockenhull, Ben 13
Hodge, Joseph 91
Hodnett, Jack 91
Hoever, Ki-Jana 91
Hoffmann, Ron-Thorben 80
Hogan, Scott 7
Hogg, Jonathan 40
Hoilett, Junior 69
Hojbjerg, Pierre 84
Holden, James 69
Holden, Rory 86
Holding, Rob 3
Holgate, Harrison 34
Holgate, Mason 32
Holland, Nathan 89
Holland-Wilkinson, Jacob 67
Holmes, Bradley 9
Holmes, Duane 40
Holmes, Thomas 69
Holohan, Gavan 39
Holy, Tomas 42
Hondermarck, William 5
Honeyman, George 41
Hoolahan, Wes 19
Hoole, Luca 16
Hopcutt, Jamie 61
Hope, Hallam 61
Hopper, Tom 46
Horgan, Daryl 92
Hornby, Fraser 32
Hornby, Sam 12
Horsfall, Fraser 58
Horton, Branden 31
Horton, Grant 24
Horvath, Ethan 60
Hoskins, Sam 58
Houghton, Jordan 64
Hourihane, Conor 4
House, Ben 46
Howard, Mark 21
Howarth, Ramirez 46
Howley, Ryan 26
Howson, Jonathan 52
Huddlestone, Tom 41
Hudson, Matthew 67
Hudson-Odoi, Callum 23
Huggins, Niall 80
Hughes, Andrew 67
Hughes, Caleb 20
Hughes, Harvey 66
Hughes, Liam 47
Hughes, Mark 16
Hughes, Rhys 32
Hughes, Sam 18
Hughes, Thomas 42
Hughes, Will 29
Hugill, Joe 50
Hugill, Jordan 59

Hulbert, Ollie 16
Hull, Jake 71
Hulme, Callum 44
Hume, Denver 66
Hume, Trai 80
Humphreys, Bashir 23
Humphreys, Cameron 42
Humphrys, Stephen 90
Hungbo, Joseph 87
Hunt, Alex 75
Hunt, Jack 75
Hunt, MacKenzie 32
Hunt, Robert 83
Hunter, Ashley 72
Huntington, Paul 67
Hurford-Lockett, Finlay 10
Hurst, Alex 65
Hurst, Kyle 7
Husband, James 9
Hussein, Mustafa 27
Hussey, Chris 65
Hutchinson, Isaac 30
Hutchinson, Jake 25
Hutchinson, Luke 10
Hutchinson, Reece 24
Hutchinson, Sam 75
Hutchinson, Shaun 53
Hutton, Remeao 6
Huws, Emyr 25
Hwang, Hee-Chan 91
Hyam, Dominic 26
Hylton, Danny 48
Hylton, Jermaine 57
Iandolo, Ellis 83
Ibrahim, Ola 30
Idah, Adam 59
Idehen, Duncan 15
Ideho, Joel 3
Idem, Manny 83
Ifill, Markus 14
Iheanacho, Kelechi 44
Ihiekwe, Michael 71
Ihionvien, Brad 25
Ikpeazu, Uche 52
Ilesanmi, Emmanuel 38
Ilunga, Brooklyn 54
Imray, Daniel 29
Ince, Tom 79
Ingram, Matt 41
Ings, Danny 4
Inniss, Ryan 22
Ioannou, Nicholas 60
Iorfa, Dominic 75
Iqbal, Zidane 50
Iredale, Jack 19
Iroegbunam, Tim 4
Ironside, Joe 19
Iseguan, Nelson 33
Iseka, Aaron 5
Isgrove, Lloyd 10
Isherwood, Liam 1
Isted, Harry 48
Itakura, Ko 49
Ivan Cavaleiro, Ricardo 36
Ivan Sanchez, Aguayo 7
Iversen, Daniel 44
Iversen, Einar 32
Iwobi, Alex 32
Jaakkola, Anssi 16
Jaaskelainen, William 28
Jach, Jaroslaw 29
Jackson, Adam 46
Jackson, Ben 40
Jackson, Kayden 42
Jackson, Luke 75
Jackson, Ryan 37
Jacob, Matty 41
Jacobs, Michael 66
Jacobson, Joe 92
Jade-Jones, Ricky 63
Jagielka, Phil 79
Jagne, Seedy 32
Jaiyesimi, Diallang 22
Jakeways, Connor 24
Jakobsen, Emil 67
Jakupovic, Eldin 44
James, Bradley 52
James, Daniel 43
James, Jordan 7
James, Luke 6
James, Matthew 15
James, Reece 9
James, Reece 23
James, Tom 45
Jameson, Kyle 61
Janelt, Vitaly 13
Janneh, Saikou 15
Jansson, Pontus 13
Jaros, Vitezslav 47
Jarrett, Patrick 79
Jarvis, Aaron 73
Jarvis, William 41
Jasper, Sylvester 36
Jay, Matt 33
Jeacock, Zach 7
Jeanvier, Julian 13
Jebbison, Daniel 74
Jefferies, Dom 13
Jenkins, Jack 43
Jenkinson, Carl 60
Jenks, Teddy 14
Jensen, Lukas 17
Jensen, Mathias 13
Jephcott, Luke 64
Jerome, Cameron 48
Jessop, Harry 73
Jewitt-White, Harry 66
Jimenez, Raul 91
Joao Cancelo, Cavaco 49
Joao Carvalho, Antonio 60
Joao Moutinho, Felipe 91
Joao Pedro, de Jesus 87
Joelinton, de Lira 56
Johansen, Stefan 68
Johansson, Viktor 71
John, Cameron 31
John, Declan 10
John, Louis 81
John, Nile 84
John-Jules, Tyreece 3
Johnson, Ben 89
Johnson, Bradley 8
Johnson, Brennan 60
Johnson, Callum 66
Johnson, Daniel 67
Johnson, Danny 51
Johnson, Darnell 34
Johnson, Finlay 78
Johnson, Lewis 54
Johnson, Marvin 75
Johnson, Ryan 65
Johnson, Travis 28
Johnston, Carl 34
Johnston, George 10
Johnstone, Samuel 88
Jolley, Charlie 85
Jones, Alfie 27
Jones, Alfie 41
Jones, Ben 85
Jones, Callum 41
Jones, Curtis 47
Jones, Dan 65
Jones, Edward 79
Jones, Gethin 10
Jones, Harry 82
Jones, Isaiah 52
Jones, Jacob 82
Jones, James 46
Jones, James 6
Jones, Jamie 90
Jones, Jodi 26
Jones, Jordan 90
Jones, Lloyd 19
Jones, Louis 31
Jones, Mike 6
Jones, Nico 13
Jones, Patrick 40
Jones, Phil 50
Jones, Ryan 16
Jonny, Castro 91
Jorgensen, Mathias Zanka 13
Jorginho, Filho Jorge 23
Jose Sa, Pedro 91
Joseph, Christian 92
Joseph, Kyle 82
Joshua, Kevin 88
Jota, Diogo 47
Jozwiak, Kamil 30
Judge, Alan 25
Jules, Zak 54
Jurado, Marc 50
Justin, James 44
Jutkiewicz, Lucas 7
Kabak, Ozan 59
Kabamba, Nicke 58
Kabasele, Christian 87
Kabore, Issa 49
Kachosa, Ethan 80
Kachunga, Elias 10
KaiKai, Sullay 92
Kaja, Egli 2
Kakay, Osman 68
Kalambayi, Paul 2
Kalas, Tomas 15
Kalinauskas, Tomas 5
Kalinic, Lovre 4
Kalu, Samuel 87
Kamara, Aboubakar 36
Kamara, Abu 59
Kamara, Hassane 87
Kamberi, Florian 75
Kaminski, Thomas 8
Kamwa, Bobby 43
Kane, Harry 84
Kane, Herbie 5
Kane, Todd 26
Kante, Ngolo 23
Kanu, Daniel 22
Kanu, Idris 63
Karbownik, Michal 14
Kargbo, Hamzad 68
Karius, Loris 47
Kashket, Scott 28
Kastrati, Florian 27
Kasumu, David 54
Kavanagh, Calum 52
Kawabe, Hayao 91
Kay, Josh 6
Kayembe, Edo 87
Kayky, Chagas 49
Kayode, Joshua 71
Kazeem, Al-Amin 25
Kazim-Richards, Colin 30
Kean, Moise 32
Keane, Michael 32
Keane, Will 90
Kebano, Neeskens 36
Keillor-Dunn, Davis 61
Keita, Naby 47
Kelleher, Caoimhin 47
Kelleher, Fiacre 12
Kelly, Georgie 71
Kelly, Liam 26
Kelly, Liam 70
Kelly, Lloyd 11
Kelly, Martin 29
Kelly, Stephen 72
Kelman, Charlie 68
Kemp, Daniel 54
Kendall, Charley 46
Kenedy, Robert 23
Kenlock, Myles 42
Kennedy, Gene 25
Kenny, Jonjoe 32
Kent, Frankie 63
Kenyon, Alex 73
Keogh, Richard 9
Keohane, Jimmy 70
Kerr, Jason 90
Kerry, Lloyd 38
Key, Josh 33
Khadra, Reda 14
Khaleel, Rafiq 27
Khan, Otis 45
Kherbouche, Nasim 40
Kieftenbeld, Maikel 53
Kiernan, Brendan 86
Kilgour, Alfie 16
Kilkenny, Gavin 11
Killip, Ben 39
Kilman, Max 91
Kilner, Oliver 61
Kilsby, Max 21
King, Andy 15
King, Eli 20
King, Josh 87
King, Toby 88
King, Tom 72
Kinsella, Liam 86
Kioso, Peter 48
Kipre, Cedric 88
Kirby, Connor 38
Kirby, Nya 29
Kirk, Alex 3
Kirk, Charlie 22
Kitching, Liam 5
Kite, Harry 33
Kizzi, Joe 81
Klaesson, Kristoffer 43
Klich, Mateusz 43
Klose, Timm 15
Knibbs, Harvey 19
Knight, Ben 49
Knight, Jason 30
Knight, Josh 63
Knight-Percival, Nathaniel 85
Knockaert, Anthony 36
Knowles, Jimmy 51
Knoyle, Kyle 31
Koch, Robin 43
Koiki, Ali 58
Kokolo, Williams 18
Kolasinac, Sead 3
Konate, Ateef 60
Konate, Ibrahima 47
Kongolo, Terence 36
Konsa, Ezri 4
Korboa, Ricky 81
Koroma, Josh 40
Kouassi, Kylian 81
Kourmetio, Billy 47
Kouyate, Cheikhou 29
Kovacic, Mateo 23
Kovar, Matej 50
Kowalczyk, Szymon 27
Kozlowski, Kacper 14
Krafth, Emil 56
Kral, Alex 89
Krasniqi, Ernaldo 40
Kristensen, Sebastian 32
Krul, Tim 59
Kucka, Juraj 87
Kulusevski, Dejan 84
Kyprianou, Hector 45
Labadie, Joss 86
Lacazette, Alexandre 3
Ladapo, Freddie 71
Laird, Ethan 50
Lakin, Charlie 18
Lallana, Adam 14
Lamptey, Tariq 14
Lancashire, Oliver 77
Lancaster, Will 5
Lane, Paddy 34
Lang, Callum 90
Langley, Dan 56
Lankester, Jack 19
Lansbury, Henri 48
Lanzini, Manuel 89
Laporte, Aymeric 49
Lapslie, George 51
Larkeche, Ziyad 36
Larsson, Julian 60
Laryea, Richie 60
Las, Damian 36
Lascelles, Jamaal 56
Latibeaudiere, Joel 82
Latty-Fairweather, Thierry 18
Laurent, Josh 69
Lavelle, Sam 22
Lavery, Caolan 12
Lavery, Shayne 9
Lavinier, Marcel 84
Law, Jason 51
Law, Ryan 64
Lawless, Conor 48
Lawlor, Jake 39
Lawrence, Henry 23
Lawrence, Tom 30
Lawrence-Gabriel, Jordan 9
Lawton, Sean 28
Lea Siliki, James 52
Leahy, Luke 76
Leak, Ryan 18
Leak, Tom 86
Leake, Jake 41
Leban, Zan-Luk 32
Ledson, Ryan 67
Lee, Elliot 48
Lee, Harry 33
Lee, Kieran 10
Lee, Oliver 37
Lees, Tom 40
Lees-Melou, Pierre 59
Leesley, Joe 38
Legge, Leon 38
Leigh, Greg 55
Leigh, Lewis 67
Leigh, Tommy 1
Leko, Jonathan 7
Lembikisa, Dexter 91
Lenihan, Darragh 8
Lennon, Aaron 17
Leno, Bernd 3
Leo Bonatini, Lohner 91
Leonard, Marc 14
Leonard, Ryan 53
Lerma, Jefferson 11
Leshabela, Thakgalo 44
Letheren, Kyle 55
Leutwiler, Jayson 61
Levitt, Dylan 50
Lewington, Dean 54
Lewis, Aaron 57
Lewis, Adam 47
Lewis, Alfie 64
Lewis, George 3
Lewis, Harry 77
Lewis, Harry 73
Lewis, Jamal 56
Lewis, Marcel 1
Lewis, Paul 58
Lewis, Sonny 57
Lewis-Potter, Keane 41
Liddle, Ben 16
Liddle, Gary 39
Lillis, Josh 6
Lindelof, Victor 50
Lindley, Hayden 4
Lindsay, Jamie 71
Lindsay, Liam 67
Lines, Chris 78
Lingard, Jesse 50
Linton, Malachi 92
Lintott, Harvey 37
List, Elliott 78
Little, Max 68
Livermore, Aneurin 57
Livermore, Jake 88
Livramento, Valentino 77
Llorente, Diego 43
Lloris, Hugo 84
Lloyd, Alfie 68
Lloyd, Danny 37
Lloyd, George 24
Lloyd, Kieran 90
Lloyd, Louis 76
Lo Celso, Giovani 84
Lo-Everton, Sonny 87
Lobley, Oliver 73
Locadia, Jurgen 14
Lockyer, Tom 48
Loft, Ryan 16
Loftus-Cheek, Ruben 23
Lolley, Joe 60
Lonergan, Andrew 32
Long, Adam 90
Long, Chris 28
Long, George 53
Long, Kevin 17
Long, Sam 62
Long, Sam 46
Long, Sean 24
Long, Shane 77
Longelo, Rosaire 1
Longman, Ryan 41
Longstaff, Luis 47
Longstaff, Matthew 56
Longstaff, Sean 56
Lonwijk, Nigel 91
Lookman, Ademola 44
Lopata, Kacper 74
Lopez Salguero, Joel 3
Lossl, Jonas 13
Loughlin, Liam 72
Louza, Imran 87
Lovatt, Adam 81
Love, Donald 72
Lovelace, Zak 53
Lovick, Harry 41
Low, Joseph 15
Lowe, Jamal 11
Lowe, Jason 72
Lowe, Max 74
Lowery, Tom 28
Lowton, Matt 17
Luamba, Junior 61
Lubula, Beryly 9
Lucas Covolan, Cavagnari 65
Lucas Joao, Eduardo 69
Lucas Moura, Rodrigues 84
Lukaku, Romelu 23
Lumley, Joe 52
Lund, Matthew 72
Lundstram, Josh 28
Luongo, Massimo 75
Lusala, Dermi 84
Lyanco, Vojnovic 77
Lyden, Jordan 83
Lynch, Jay 70
Lynch, Joel 27
Lyons-Foster, Brooklyn 84
Maatsen, Ian 23
Mabaya, Isaac 47
Mac Allister, Alexis 14
Macadam, Harvey 34
Macari, Lewis 79
MacDonald, Alex 37
MacDonald, Angus 71
MacDonald, Calum 85
MacDonald, Shaun 28
MacGillivray, Craig 22
Maddison, James 44
Maddox, Jacob 18
Madelin, Jack 2
Madine, Gary 9
Magennis, Josh 90
Maghoma, Christian 37
Maghoma, Edmond-Paris 13
Magliore, Tyler 8
Maguire, Chris 46
Maguire, Frankie 74
Maguire, Harry 50
Maguire, Joe 85
Maguire, Sean 67
Maher, Zack 57
Mahoney, Connor 53
Mahoney, Murphy 68
Mahorn, Trent 68
Mahrez, Riyad 49

Mair, Archie 59
Maitland-Niles, Ainsley 3
Maja, Josh 79
Malcolm, Jovan 88
Malley, Connor 52
Malone, Dan 79
Malone, Scott 53
Maloney, Scott 6
Mampala, Manasse 21
Mancienne, Michael 18
Mancini, Anthony 17
Mandron, Mikael 28
Mane, Sadio 47
Manly, Jack 42
Manning, Ryan 82
Mannion, Will 19
Manquillo, Javier 56
Mansell, Lewis 1
Marcal, Fernando 91
Marcelo 47
March, Josh 35
March, Solly 14
Marcondes, Emiliano 11
Mariette, Luke 9
Maris, George 51
Markanday, Dilan 8
Marosi, Marko 76
Marques, Christian 91
Marquis, John 46
Marriott, Jack 63
Marsh, Aiden 5
Marsh, George 2
Marshall, David 68
Marshall, Mark 27
Marshall, Marley 25
Marshall, Ross 78
Martial, Anthony 50
Martin, Aaron 65
Martin, Aaron 38
Martin, Chris 15
Martin, Dan 1
Martin, David E 89
Martin, Josh 59
Martinelli, Gabriel 3
Martinez, Damian 4
Martinez, Pablo 16
Masampu, Renedi 7
Masina, Adam 87
Mason, Brandon 54
Massengo, Han-Noah 15
Massey, Gavin 90
Masterson, Conor 68
Mastny, Ondrej 50
Masuaku, Arthur 89
Maswanhise, Tawanda 44
Mata, Juan 50
Mateta, Jean-Philippe 29
Matete, Jay 80
Matheson, Luke 91
Matic, Nemanja 50
Matip, Joel 47
Matt, Jamille 35
Matthews, Adam 22
Matthews, Archie 7
Matthews, Remi 29
Matthews, Sam 27
Mattock, Joe 71
Maupay, Neal 14
Mavropanos, Konstantinos 3
Mawson, Alfie 36
Maxted, Jonathan 58
Maxwell, Chris 9
May, Adam 19
May, Alfie 24
Mayembe, Ntazana 20
Maynard, Nicky 85
Maynard-Brewer, Ashley 22
Mayor, Danny 64
Mbe Soh, Loic 60
Mbete-Tabu, Luke 49
Mbeumo, Bryan 13
Mbuyamba, Xavier 23
McAlear, Reece 59
McAleny, Conor 72
McAllister, Sean 32
McArdle, Rory 38
McArthur, James 29
McAtee, James 49
McAteer, Kasey 44
McAvoy, Connor 36
McBride, Connor 8
McBurnie, Oliver 74
McCallum, Sam 59
McCalmont, Alfie 43
McCann, Alistair 67
McCarron, Liam 43
McCarthy, Alex 77
McCarthy, Jason 92
McClean, James 90
McCleary, Garath 92
McClelland, Sam 23
McConville, Sean 1
McCormick, Luke 2
McCormick, Luke 64
McCoulsky, Shawn 25
McCracken, Jon 59
McDonald, Kornell 30
McDonald, Rod 21
McDonald, Rowan 49
McDonald, Wesley 55
McDonnell, Jamie 60
McEachran, George 23
McEachran, Josh 54
McEneff, Jordan John 3
McEntee, Oisin 56
McFadzean, Callum 28
McFadzean, Kyle 26
McGahey, Harrison 61
McGavin, Brett 42
McGeady, Aiden 80
McGee, Luke 35
McGill, Thomas 14
McGinn, John 4
McGoldrick, David 74
McGovern, Michael 59
McGowan, Aaron 58
McGrandles, Conor 46
McGrath, Jamie 90
McGrath, Jay 26
McGree, Riley 52
McGuane, Marcus 62
McGuinness, Mark 20
Mchugh, Harry 90
McIntyre, Tom 69
McKenna, Scott 60
McKenzie, Robbie 37
McKenzie-Lyle, Kai 19
McKinstry, Stuart 43
McKirdy, Harry 83
McLaughlin, Conor 34
McLaughlin, Ryan 55
McLaughlin, Stephen 51
McLean, Kenny 59
McLoughlin, Sean 41
McLoughlin, Shane 55
McManaman, Callum 85
McMillan, Max 34
McNair, Paddy 52
McNally, Luke 62
McNamara, Danny 53
McNeil, Dwight 17
McNeill, Charlie 50
McNulty, Jim 70
McNulty, Marc 69
McPake, Joshua 85
McShane, Paul 50
McTominay, Scott 50
McWilliams, Shaun 58
Mebude, Dapo 87
Mee, Ben 17
Mehew, Tom 16
Mehmeti, Anis 92
Meite, Yakou 69
Mejbri, Hannibal 50
Mejia, Mateo 50
Melbourne, Max 46
Mellish, Jon 21
Mellor, Kelvin 21
Melvin-Lambert, Nahum 69
Mema, Armelindo 68
Menayese, Rollin 86
Mendes Gomes, Carlos 48
Mendez-Laing, Nathaniel 75
Mendy, Benjamin 49
Mendy, Edouard 23
Mendy, Nampalys 44
Mengi, Teden 50
Mensah, Benjamin 63
Mensah, Jacob 55
Mepham, Chris 11
Merrie, Christopher 85
Meshino, Ryotaro 49
Meslier, Illan 43
Mgunga-Kimpioka, Benjamin 80
Miazga, Matt 23
Middlehurst, Thomas 68
Mighten, Alex 60
Mihaylov, Dzhoshkun 43
Mildenhall, Steve 83
Miles, Felix 24
Milivojevic, Luka 29
Millen, Ross 73
Miller, Amari 43
Miller, George 5
Miller, Mickel 71
Miller, Todd 14
Mills, Jevon 41
Mills, Joseph 58
Mills, Zak 86
Milner, James 47
Milsom, Robert 81
Mina, Yerry 32
Minamino, Takumi 47
Mingi, Jade 66
Mings, Tyrone 4
Minturn, Harrison 83
Missilou, Christopher 61
Mitchell, Alex 53
Mitchell, Billy 53
Mitchell, Demetri 9
Mitchell, Ethan 64
Mitchell, Jonathan 31
Mitchell, Ramello 77
Mitchell, Tyrick 29
Mitchell-Lawson, Jayden 83
Mitoma, Kaoru 14
Mitov, Dimitar 19
Mitrovic, Aleksandar 36
Mnoga, Haji 66
Moder, Jakub 14
Modi, Isaac 61
Mogensen, Gustav 13
Moller, Nikolaj 3
Molumby, Jayson 14
Molyneux, Luke 39
Moncur, George 41
Monks, Charles 9
Monlouis, Zane 3
Monthe, Emmanuel 86
Montsma, Lewis 46
Moon, Jasper 5
Mooney, Fionn 29
Moore, Elliott 62
Moore, Kieffer 11
Moore, Kris 43
Moore, Liam 69
Moore, Simon 26
Moore, Stuart 9
Moore, Taylor 15
Moore-Billam, Jack 73
Moore-Taylor, Jordan 35
Moran, Andrew 14
Moreno, Marlos 49
Moreno , Pablo 49
Morgan, Albie 22
Morgan, David 1
Moriah-Welsh, Nathan 11
Morley, Aaron 10
Morrell, Joe 66
Morris, Ben 42
Morris, Bryn 18
Morris, Carlton 5
Morris, Glenn 27
Morris, Josh 72
Morris, Kieron 85
Morris, Shayden 34
Morrison, Michael 69
Morrison, Ravel 30
Morrison, Sean 20
Morsy, Sam 42
Morton, Callum 88
Morton, James 15
Morton, Tyler 47
Mosquera, Yerson 91
Moss, Dan 53
Mothersille, Malik 23
Moult, Louis 18
Mount, Mason 23
Mousinho, John 62
Mousset, Lys 74
Mowatt, Alex 88
Muir, Marques 84
Mukendi, Jeremie 84
Muldoon, Jack 38
Muller, Hayden 53
Mumba, Bali 59
Mumbongo, Joel 17
Mundle, Romaine 84
Muric, Arijanet 49
Murphy, Jacob 56
Murphy, Jamie 51
Murphy, Joe 85
Murphy, Josh 20
Murphy, Luke 28
Muskwe, Admiral 48
Musonda, Charly 23
Mwepu, Enock 14
Mykolenko, Vitaliy 32
N'Koulou, Nicolas 87
N'Lundulu, Daniel 77
N'Mai, Kelly 72
Nadesan, Ashley 27
Nagy, Adam 15
Naismith, Kal 48
Nakamba, Marvelous 4
Nartey, Richard 17
Nascimento, Adler 29
Naughton, Kyle 82
Naylor, Tom 90
Ndaba, Corrie 42
Ndiaye, Iliman-Cheikh 74
Ndidi, Onyinye 44
Ndombele, Tanguy 84
Neal, Harrison 74
Neil, Daniel 80
Nelson, Ben 44
Nelson, Curtis 20
Nelson, Reiss 3
Nelson, Sid 58
Nelson, Stuart 81
Nelson Semedo, Cabral 91
Neufville, Josh 48
Nevers, Thierry 89
Neves, Ruben 91
Nevitt, Elliott 85
Newby, Alex 70
Ng, Perry 20
Ngakia, Jeremy 87
Ngandu, Jonny 26
Niasse, Oumar 18
Nicholls, Lee 40
Nichols, Tom 27
Nicholson, Sam 16
Nightingale, Will 2
Nippard, Luke 11
Nketiah, Eddie 3
Nkounkou, Niels 32
Nkrumah, Daniel 45
Nna Noukeu, Blondy 79
Noble, Mark 89
Nolan, Jack 1
Nolan, Jon 16
Nolan, Joseph 8
Nombe, Sam 33
Norburn, Oliver 63
Norgaard, Christian 13
Norman, Cameron 57
Norman, Magnus 21
Normann, Mathias 59
Norrington-Davies, Rhys 74
Norris, James 47
Norris, Luke 78
Norris, Will 17
Norton, Christian 79
Norton-Cuffy, Brooke 3
Norwood, James 42
Norwood, Oliver 74
Nottingham, Michael 1
Nouble, Frank 25
Nsiala, Aristote 34
Ntcham, Jules Olivier 82
Ntlhe, Kgosietsile 6
Nunn, George 23
Nuno Da Costa, Joia 60
Nurse, George 76
Nuttall, Joe 73
Nya, Raphael 91
Nyambe, Ryan 8
Nyland, Orjan 69
O'Brien, Aiden 66
O'Brien, Jake 29
O'Brien, Lewis 40
O'Brien, Sean 53
O'Connell, Charlie 63
O'Connell, Eoghan 70
O'Connell, Jack 74
O'Connor, Anthony 55
O'Connor, Harris 22
O'Connor, Lee 85
O'Connor, Paudie 12
O'Connor, Thomas 18
O'Donkor, Gatlin 62
O'Donnell, Richard 12
O'Dowda, Callum 15
O'Driscoll Varian, Ethon 79
O'Hara, Kieran 34
O'Hare, Callum 26
O'Hora, Warren 54
O'Keefe, Stuart 37
O'Keeffe, Corey 70
O'Leary, Max 15
O'Malley, Mason 73
O'Neil, Liam 19
O'Neill, Luke 78
O'Neill, Mikey 67
O'Neill, Tyrone 73
O'Nien, Luke 80
O'Reilly, Adam 67
O'Reilly, Luke 78
O'Riley, Matt 54
O'Riordan, Connor 28
O'Rourke, Fidel 47
O'Shaughnessy, Joseph 91
O'Shea, Dara 88
O'Sullivan, John 1
O'Toole, John 51
Oakley, Marcel 7
Oakley-Boothe, Tashan 79
Oates, Rhys 51
Obadeyi, Temitope 61
Obafemi, Michael 82
Obiero, Micah 40
Obiero, Zech 45
Obika, Jonathan 55
Obita, Jordan 92
Odegaard, Martin 3
Odimayo, Akinwale 83
Odofin, Hakeem 71
Odoh, Abraham 70
Odoi, Denis 36
Odour, Clarke 5
Odubajo, Moses 68
Odubeko, Ademipo 89
Odunze, Chituru 44
Odusina, Timi 39
Offiah, Odel 14
Offord, Luke 28
Ogbene, Chiedozie 71
Ogbeta, Nathaniel 82
Ogbonna, Angelo 89
Ogie, Shadrach 45
Ogilvie, Connor 66
Ogle, Reagan 39
Ojeda, Braian 60
Ojo, Sheyi 47
Ojrzynski, Jakub 47
Okedina, Jubril 19
Okenabirhie, Fejiri 31
Okoflex, Armstrong 89
Okonkwo, Arthur 3
Okoye, Maduka 87
Oksanen, Jaako 13
Olagunju, Mustapha 40
Olaigbe, Kazeem 77
Olaofe, Isaac 53
Olayinka, James 3
Olise, Michael 29
Oliver, Vadaine 37
Olomola, Olufela 39
Olosunde, Matthew 67
Olowu, Joseph Olugbenga 31
Olsen, Robin 4
Olufunwa, Dare 77
Olusanya, Toyosi 52
Oluwabori, Andrew 63
Omilabu, David 29
Omobamidele, Andrew 59
Omole, Tobi 84
Omotoye, Tyrese 59
Onariase, Manny 73
Onen, Jayden 75
Onodi, Akos 4
Onomah, Joshua 36
Onyango, Tyler 32
Onyedinma, Fred 48
Onyeka, Frank 13
Onyeka, Tyreece 28
Opoku, Jerome 36
Origi, Divock 47
Orsi-Dadomo, Danilo 38
Osaoabe, Emmanuel 86
Osborn, Ben 74
Osborne, Elliot 78
Osei Yaw, Derick 2
Osei-Tutu, Jordi 3
Osew, Paul 2
Oshilaja, Adedeji 18
Osho, Gabriel 48
Ostigard, Leo 14
Osula, William 74
Oteh, Aramide 27
Oulad M'Hand, Salah 3
Oulare, Obbi 5
Ovendale, Evan 57
Owens, Charlie 68
Oxborough, Aston 59
Oxlade-Chamberlain, Alex 47
Oxley, Mark 38
Pablo Mari, Villar 3
Pack, Marlon 20
Packham, Sam 14
Page, Jonathon 36
Page, Lewis 38
Pajaziti, Adrion 36
Palaversa, Ante 49
Palmer, Alex 88
Palmer, Cole 49
Palmer, Harry 81
Palmer, Kasey 15
Palmer, Liam 75
Palmer, Oliver 2
Palmer, Romal 5
Pambou, Leon 77
Panter, Corey 48
Panzo, Jonathan 60
Pardington, James 91
Parkes, Adam 87
Parrott, Troy 84
Parsons, Harry 83
Pask, Josh 26

Paskotsi, Maksim 84
Paterson, Callum 75
Paterson, Jamie 82
Patino, Charlie 3
Patrick, Omari 21
Patten, Keenan 20
Patterson, Anthony 80
Patterson, Nathan 32
Pattison, Alex 38
Payero, Martin 52
Payne, Jack 27
Payne, Jack 83
Peacock-Farrell, Bailey 17
Pearce, Alex 53
Pearce, Jason 22
Pearce, Luke 77
Pearce, Tom 90
Pears, Aynsley 8
Pearson, Ben 11
Pearson, Matthew 40
Pearson, Sam 15
Peck, Jake 48
Pedersen, Kristian 7
Pedro Neto, Lomba 91
Pell, Harry 1
Pellistri , Facundo 50
Peltier, Lee 52
Penaranda, Adalberto 87
Pendlebury, Oliver 92
Pennant, Terell 44
Penney, Matt 42
Pennington, Matthew 76
Pepe, Nicolas 3
Perch, James 51
Pereira, Andreas 50
Pereira, Dion 48
Perez, Ayoze 44
Perkins, Sonny 89
Perraud, Romain 77
Perritt, Harry 1
Perry, Alex 73
Perry, Sam 86
Perry, Taylor 91
Pett, Tom 65
Peupion, Cameron 14
Philips, Daniel 87
Phillips, Adam 17
Phillips, Dillon 20
Phillips, Kalvin 43
Phillips, Kieran 16
Phillips, Kieran 40
Phillips, Matthew 88
Phillips, Nathaniel 47
Philogene-Bidace, Jayden 4
Pickering, Harry 8
Pickford, Jordan 32
Piergianni, Carl 61
Pierre, Aaron 76
Pieters, Erik 17
Pigott, Joe 42
Pike, Dan 8
Pilkington, Anthony 34
Pinnock, Ethan 13
Pinnock, Mitch 58
Pipa, Gonzalo 40
Piroe, Joel 82
Pitman, Brett 16
Placheta, Przemyslaw 59
Plange, Luke 29
Platt, Matt 6
Pochettino, Maurizio 87
Pogba, Paul 50
Politic, Dennis 10
Pollock, Matthew 87
Pollock, Scott 58
Pond, Alfie 33
Poole, Regan 46
Pope, Nick 17
Porro, Pedro 49
Porter, Adam 79
Porter, Chris 28
Potts, Brad 67
Potts, Danny 48
Poveda-Ocampo, Ian 43
Powell, Aaron 63
Powell, Jack 27
Powell, Joe 18
Powell, Johl 22
Powell, Nick 79
Power, Max 90
Power, Simon 38
Pozo, Iker 49
Praet, Dennis 44
Pratley, Darren 45
Pressley, Aaron 13
Price, Freddie 55
Price, Isaac 32
Pring, Cameron 15
Pritchard, Alex 80
Pritchard, Joe 1
Procter, Archie 1
Proctor, Jamie 65
Prosser, Luke 78
Przybek, Adam 92
Pugh, Tom 73
Pukki, Teemu 59
Pulisic, Christian 23
Purrington, Ben 22
Pursall, Brandon 64
Puscas, George 69
Pussetto , Ignacio 87
Pye, Logan 50
Pyke, Rekeil 76
Pym, Christy 63
Quansah, Jarell 47
Quina, Domingos 87
Quinn, Stephen 51
Quirk, Sebastian 32
Racic, Luka 13
Rafael Cabral, Barbosa 69
Rafferty, Joe 67
Raffie, Akiel 34
Raggett, Sean 66
Raglan, Charlie 24
Raikhy, Arjan 4
Rak-Sakyi, Jesurun 29
Ralls, Joe 20
Ramirez, Fabricio 36
Ramkilde, Marco 68
Ramsay, Kayne 77
Ramsdale, Aaron 3
Ramsey, Aaron 4
Ramsey, Jacob 4
Randall, Joel 63
Randall, Will 81
Randell, Adam 64
Randolph, Darren 89
Rankin-Costello, Joe 8
Rankine, Dion 23
Raphinha, Raphael 43
Rashford, Marcus 50
Rashica, Milot 59
Ratcliffe, George 20
Rathbone, Oliver 71
Ravenhill, Liam 31
Ravizzoli, Franco 54
Rawson, Farrend 51
Ray, George 33
Raya, David 13
Raymond, Jadan 29
Rea, Glen 48
Reach, Adam 88
Read, Arthur 78
Ream, Tim 36
Redmond, Nathan 77
Reed, Harrison 36
Reed, Louis 83
Reeves, Ben 37
Reeves, Jake 78
Reguilon, Sergio 84
Reid, Jamie 78
Reid, Jayden 66
Reid, Josh 26
Reilly, Callum 45
Rekik, Omar 3
Remy, Shiloh 68
Render, Joshua 75
Revan, Dominic 4
Rhodes, Jordan 40
Ricardo Pereira, Domingos 44
Rice, Declan 89
Rich-Baghuelou, Jay 1
Richards, Carlos Peliza 30
Richards, Dave 28
Richards, Lewis 91
Richards, Rico 88
Richards, Taylor 14
Richardson, Adam 80
Richardson, Jayden 60
Richardson, Kenton 80
Richardson, Lewis 17
Richarlison, de Andrade 32
Ridehalgh, Liam 12
Ridley, Joseph 52
Riedewald, Jairo 29
Riley, Joe 21
Riley, Regan 59
Rinomhota, Andy 69
Ripley, Connor 67
Ritaccio, Matteo 47
Ritchie, Matt 56
Robbins, Joe 28
Roberts, Connor 17
Roberts, Haydon 14
Roberts, Liam 58
Roberts, Marc 7
Roberts, Mitchell 7
Roberts, Myles 87
Roberts, Patrick 80
Roberts, Tyler 43
Robertson, Alexander 49
Robertson, Andrew 47
Robertson, Clark 66
Robertson, Scott 28
Robinson, Antonee 36
Robinson, Callum 88
Robinson, Darren 30
Robinson, Jack 74
Robinson, Jack 52
Robinson, Luke 90
Robinson, Sammy 65
Robinson, Theo 12
Robinson, Zach 2
Robson, David 41
Robson, Ethan 9
Robson, Jamie 46
Robson, Max 84
Roche, Barry 55
Rodak, Marek 36
Rodari, Davide 27
Rodgers, Harvey 1
Rodman, Alex 16
Rodney, Devante 86
Rodon, Joe 84
Rodri, Rodrigo Hernandez 49
Rodrigo, Moreno 43
Rodrigo Muniz, Carvalho 36
Rodriguez, Jay 17
Rodriguez, Jeremi 77
Rodwell-Grant, Joe 67
Roerslev Rasmussen, Mads 13
Rogers, Danny 61
Rogers, Morgan 49
Romeo, Mahlon 53
Romero, Cristian 84
Romeu, Oriol 77
Ronaldo, Cristiano 50
Ronan, Connor 91
Rondon, Jose Salomon 32
Rooney, John 6
Roos, Kelle 30
Rosa, Diego 49
Rose, Danny 87
Rose, Danny 58
Rose, Jack 86
Rose, Joseph 59
Rose, Michael 26
Ross-Lang, Fedel 77
Rossi, Zeno 11
Rossiter, Jordan 34
Rothwell, Joe 8
Roughan, Sean 46
Rowe, Aaron 40
Rowe, Blaine 26
Rowe, Callum 33
Rowe, Coby 81
Rowe, Danny 18
Rowe, Jai 73
Rowe, Jonathan 59
Rowe, Tommy 31
Ruben Vinagre, Goncalo 91
Rudd, Declan 67
Ruddock, Pelly 48
Ruddy, John 91
Rudiger, Antonio 23
Rudoni, Jack 2
Ruffels, Joshua 40
Runarsson, Runar 3
Rupp, Lukas 59
Rushesha, Tivonge 82
Rushworth, Carl 14
Russell, Jonathan 40
Ryan-Phillip, Callum 57
Saadi, Jalil 8
Sackey, Lynford 69
Sade Lichtenfeld, Yoav 62
Sadler, Matthew 86
Sadlier, Kieran 10
Saint-Maximin, Allan 56
Saiss, Romain 91
Saka, Bukayo 3
Salah, Mohamed 47
Salam, Ahmed 41
Saliba, William Alain Andre Gabriel 3
Salisbury, Connor 28
Salisu, Mohammed 77
Sama, Stephen 1
Samba, Brice 60
Sambi Lokonga, Albert-Mboyo 3
Sambou, Bassala 28
Samir, Caetano 87
Samuel, Alex 92
Samuels, Imari 69
Sanchez, Davinson 84
Sanchez, Robert 14
Sancho, Jadon 50
Sanders, Max 46
Sanders, Samuel 60
Sanderson, Dion 91
Sandford, Ryan 53
Sang, Tom 20
Sang-bin, Jeong 91
Sangare, Mohammed 56
Sanson, Morgan 4
Santiago, Yago 84
Santos, Ricardo 10
Sarcevic, Antoni 10
Sargeant, Sam 45
Sargent, Josh 59
Sargent, Matthew 72
Sarkic, Matija 91
Sarmiento, Dario 49
Sarmiento, Jeremy 14
Sarpeng-Wiredu, Brendan 25
Sarr, Ismaila 87
Sarr, Malang 23
Sarr, Naby 40
Sarr, Pape 84
Sass-Davies, Billy 28
Saul, Niguez 23
Saunders, Harvey 16
Savage, Charlie 50
Savage, Remi 56
Saville, George 53
Savin, Toby 1
Sawyers, Romaine 88
Saydee, Christian 11
Sayer, Harvey 25
Sayyadmanesh, Allahyar 41
Scales, Kian 12
Scarlett, Dane 84
Scarr, Dan 64
Schar, Fabian 56
Scherpen, Kjell 14
Schlupp, Jeffrey 29
Schmeichel, Kasper 44
Schmidt, Patrick 5
Schofield, Ryan 40
Scott, Alex 15
Scott, Jack 91
Scott, James 41
Scott, Josh 51
Scott, Rashawn 69
Scowen, Josh 92
Scrimshaw, Jake 11
Scully, Anthony 46
Scully, Thomas 1
Sea, Dimitri 6
Seaman, Charlie 31
Searle, Jamie 82
Sears, Freddie 25
Seddon, Steve 62
Segura, Jorge 87
Sema, Ken 87
Semenyo, Antoine 15
Senga-Ngoyi, Jack 69
Senior, Adam 10
Senior, Courtney 57
Senior, Joel 21
Sercombe, Liam 24
Seri, Jean 36
Seriki, Femi 74
Sessegnon, Ryan 84
Sessegnon, Steven 36
Setters, David 66
Seymour, Ben 33
Seymour, Taylor 27
Shabani, Meritan 91
Shackleton, Jamie 43
Shade, Tyrese 44
Shakpoke, Ruben 4
Shanks, Connor 40
Sharman-Lowe, Teddy 23
Sharp, Billy 74
Sharrock-Peplow, Sam 40
Shaughnessy, Conor 18
Shaw, Jack 86
Shaw, Luke 50
Shea, James 48
Sheaf, Ben 26
Sheehan, Alan 61
Sheehan, Josh 10
Shelton, Mark 39
Shelvey, George 60
Shelvey, Jonjo 56
Shephard, Liam 72
Sheron, Nathan 38
Sherring, Sam 11
Shinnie, Graeme 90
Shipley, Jordan 26
Shipley, Lewis 59
Shirley, Rhys 64
Sho-Silva, Oluwatobi 21
Shodipo, Olamide 68
Shoretire, Shola 50
Shotton, Saul 88
Shrimpton, Finley 73
Sibbick, Toby 5
Sibley, Louie 30
Sierralta, Francisco 87
Sikora, Jorge 12
Silva, Fabio 91
Sima, Abdallah 14
Simeu, Dynel 77
Simmonds, Keyendrah 7
Simms, Ellis 32
Simons, Xavier 23
Simper, Lewis 19
Simpson, Danny 15
Simpson, Tyreece 42
Sinani, Danel 59
Sinclair, Scott 67
Sinclair, Tyrese 51
Sinisalo, Viljami 4
Sissoko, Moussa 87
Sithole, Gerald 37
Siziba, Zanda 42
Skipp, Oliver 84
Skurek, Harvey 24
Skuse, Cole 25
Slater, Regan 41
Slicker, Cieran 49
Sluga, Simon 48
Smales-Braithwaite, Benni 77
Small, Thierry 77
Smallbone, William 77
Smallwood, Richard 41
Smith, Adam 11
Smith, Adam 55
Smith, Alistair 81
Smith, Andy 41
Smith, Harry 45
Smith, Jack 78
Smith, Jonny 18
Smith, Jordan 60
Smith, Kerr 4
Smith, Korey 82
Smith, Martin 39
Smith, Matt 72
Smith, Matthew 54
Smith, Matthew 3
Smith, Michael 71
Smith, Nathan 65
Smith, Sam 19
Smith, Scott 90
Smith, Timmy 78
Smith, Tom 42
Smith, Tom 3
Smith, Tommy 25
Smith, Tommy 79
Smith, Tyler 41
Smith, Will 38
Smith Rowe, Emile 3
Smithies, Alex 20
Smyth, Oisin 62
Smyth, Paul 45
Snelgrove, McCauley 41
Snodgrass, Robert 48
Sohna, Harrison 80
Solanke, Dominic 11
Solberg, Isak 84
Soldevila, Oriol 7
Solomon, Harrison 30
Son, Heung-Min 84
Sondergaard, Andreas 91
Songo'o, Yann 12
Soonsup-Bell, Jude 23
Sorensen, Jacob 59
Sorensen, Mads 13
Sorenson, Lasse 46
Sotiriou, Ruel 45
Soto, Sebastian 59
Souare, Pape 22
Soucek, Tomas 89
Soule, Jamie 88
Soumare, Boubakary 44
Soutar, Harry 79
Southern-Cooper, Jake 69
Southwood, Luke 69
Sow, Sylla 75
Sowerby, Jack 58
Soyuncu, Caglar 44
Sparkes, Jack 33
Sparrow, Tom 79
Spasov, Slavi 62
Spearing, Jay 85
Spence, Djed 52
Spence, Sion 29
Spencer, Morten 43
Spencer-Adams, Bayli 44
Spinelli, Kevin 1
Spong, Jack 14
Sporar, Andraz 52
Springett, Tony 59
Sraha, Jason 5
Stacey, Jack 11
Stanislas, Junior 11
Stanley, Connor 50
Stansfield, Jay 36

Starbuck, Joseph 74
Staunton, Reece 12
Stearman, Richard 30
Stech, Marek 51
Steele, Jason 14
Steels, Vinny 80
Steer, Jed 4
Steffen, Zackary 49
Stephens, Dale 17
Stephens, Jack 77
Stephens, Jack 62
Stergiakis, Antonios 8
Sterling, Dujon 23
Sterling, Raheem 49
Sterry, Jamie 39
Stevanovic, Filip 49
Stevens, Enda 74
Stevens, Fin 13
Stevens, Jordan 6
Stevens, Mathew 35
Stevenson, Ben 35
Stewart, Anthony 92
Stewart, Kevin 9
Stewart, Layton 47
Stewart, Ross C 80
Stewart, Sean 59
Stickland, Michael 69
Stirk, Ryan 7
Stobbs, Jack 61
Stockdale, David 92
Stockley, Jayden 22
Stockton, Cole 55
Stojanovic, Dejan 52
Stolarczyk, Jakub 44
Stone, Aiden 65
Stones, John 49
Storey, Jordan 67
Stowe, Luke 1
Strawn, Joe 9
Street, Rob 29
Stretton, Jack 30
Struijk, Pascal 43
Stubbs, Sam 33
Styles, Callum 5
Suengchitthawon, Thanawat 44
Summerville, Crysencio 43
Sunjic, Ivan 7
Surridge, Sam 60
Sutcliffe, Ethan 2
Sutton, Levi 12
Sutton, Will 61
Svidersky, Martin 50
Swan, Will 60
Swanson, Zak 3
Sweeney, Dan 35
Sweeney, Jayden 45
Sweeney, Pierce 33
Swift, John 69
Swinkels, Sil 4
Swyer, Kamarai 89
Sy, Ibrahima 79
Sykes, Cain 52
Sykes, Mark 62
Sykes, Ross 1
Szmidics, Sammie 63
Tabiner, Joel 28
Tafazolli, Ryan 92
Taft, George 73
Talley, Fynn 14
Tanga, Jephte 45
Tanganga, Japhet 84
Tanimowo, Ayo 14
Tanner, George 15
Tarensi, Oscar 49
Targett, Matt 4
Tarkowski, James 17
Tasdemir, Serhat 63
Tauriainen, Jimi 23
Tavares, Fabio 26
Tavares, Nuno 3
Tavernier, Marcus 52
Taylor, Ash 86
Taylor, Caleb 88
Taylor, Charlie 17
Taylor, Connor 79
Taylor, Corey 22
Taylor, Dale 60
Taylor, Greg 19
Taylor, Jack 63
Taylor, Jake 78
Taylor, Jake 65
Taylor, James 29
Taylor, Jason 6
Taylor, Jon 31
Taylor, Joseph 63
Taylor, Kyle 33
Taylor, Lyle 60
Taylor, Matty 62
Taylor, Max 70
Taylor, Neil 52
Taylor, Terry 18
Tchamadeu, Junior 25
Teale, Connor 34
Tedic, Slobodan 49
Telford, Dominic 57
Tella, Nathan 77
Tete, Kenny 36
Tetek, Dejan 69
Thiago, Alcantara 47
Thiago Silva, Emiliano 23
Thiam, Chiekh 34
Thomas, Bobby 17
Thomas, Conor 24
Thomas, Donnell 25
Thomas, George 68
Thomas, Jamie 67
Thomas, Joshua 82
Thomas, Lewis 35
Thomas, Luke 5
Thomas, Luke 44
Thomas, Partey 3
Thomas, Peter 70
Thomas, Sorba 40
Thomas, Terell 69
Thomas-Asante, Brandon 72
Thomason, George 10
Thompson, Adam 45
Thompson, Ben 37
Thompson, Cameron 5
Thompson, Curtis 92
Thompson, Dominic 13
Thompson, Jordan 79
Thompson, Lewis 73
Thompson, Liam 30
Thompson, Louis 66
Thompson, Max 17
Thompson, Nathan 63
Thomson, George 38
Thomson, Reagan 56
Thorniley, Jordan 9
Threlkeld, Oscar 12
Tickle, Sam 90
Tiehi, Jean-Pierre 36
Tielemans, Youri 44
Tiensia, Junior 53
Tierney, Kieran 3
Tilley, James 27
Tilt, Curtis 90
Tinubu, Sam 78
Tipton, Ollie 91
Tobias Figueiredo, Pereira 60
Toffolo, Harry 40
Tolaj, Lorent 14
Tomiyasu, Takehiro 3
Tomkins, James 29
Tomkinson, Jonathan 59
Tomlin, Lee 86
Tomlinson, Joseph 63
Tomlinson, Lucas 16
Tomlinson, Ollie 64
Toney, Ivan 13
Torrance, Joel 72
Torreira, Lucas 3
Torres, Ferran 49
Tosun, Cenk 32
Touray, Ibou 72
Touray, Momodou 72
Toure, Fandje 87
Toure, Gime 21
Tovide, Samson 25
Towler, Ryley 15
Townsend, Andros 32
Townsend, Conor 88
Townsend, Nick 57
Townsend-West, Mackye 78
Tozer, Ben 24
Tracey, Shilow 19
Trafford, James 49
Traore, Adama 91
Traore, Bertrand 4
Travers, Mark 11
Travis, Lewis 8
Trevitt, Ryan 13
Trezeguet, Mahmoud 4
Trincao, Francisco 91
Trippier, Keiran 56
Troost-Ekong, William 87
Trossard, Leandro 14
Trott, Nathan 89
Trueman, Connal 7
Tsaroulla, Nicholas 27
Tsimikas, Konstantinos 47
Tsoungui, Antef 14
Tuanzebe, Axel 50
Tucker, Jack 37
Tufan, Ozan 87
Tulloch, Rayhaan 88
Tunnicliffe, Jordan 27
Tunnicliffe, Ryan 66
Turnbull, Jordan 72
Turner, Jake 56
Turner-Cooke, Jay 56
Turton, Oliver 40
Tutonda, David 37
Tutte, Andrew 10
Twamley, Lewys 57
Tweedley, Matthew 10
Twine, Scott 54
Tyler, Cian 26
Tymon, Josh 79
Tyrer, Harry 32
Tzanev, Nikola 2
Tzolis, Christos 59
Udoh, Daniel 76
Undav, Deniz 14
Upson, Edward 78
Uremovic, Filip 74
Uwakwe , Tariq 28
Vale, Harvey 23
Vale, Jack 8
Valencia, Joel 13
Valery, Yann 77
Vallejo, Alex 40
van de Beek, Donny 50
van den Berg, Sepp 47
Van den Heuvel, Dani 43
van Dijk, Virgil 47
Van Hecke, Jan 14
Vancooten, Terence 78
Varane, Raphael 50
Vardy, Jamie 44
Vassell, Isaac 20
Vassell, Kyle 24
Vassell, Theo 72
Vassilev, Indiana 4
Vaughan, Harry 61
Vaulks, Will 20
Veale, Jack 33
Vela, Joshua 76
Veltman, Joel 14
Vennings, James 22
Vernam, Charles 12
Verrips, Michael 74
Vestergaard, Jannik 44
Vickers, Josh 71
Vigouroux, Lawrence 45
Vilca, Rodrigo 56
Vincent, Liam 66
Vincent-Young, Kane 42
Virginia, Joao 32
Virtue, Matthew 9
Vita, Remy 5
Vitek, Radek 50
Vlasic, Nikola 89
Vokes, Sam 92
Vokins, Jake 77
Vrancic, Mario 79
Vydra, Matej 17
Vyner, Zak 15
Wade, Bradley 70
Wady, Ethan 23
Waghorn, Martyn 26
Waite, James 57
Wakefield, Charlie 26
Wakeling, Jacob 44
Walcott, Malachi 84
Walcott, Theo 77
Waldock, Liam 75
Walker, Brad 65
Walker, Ethan 67
Walker, Jamie 12
Walker, Kyle 49
Walker, Laurie 78
Walker, Stephen 52
Walker, Tyler 26
Walker, Zain 16
Walker-Peters, Kyle 77
Wallace, Jed 53
Wallace, Kieran 51
Wallace, Lee 68
Wallace, Murray 53
Walsh, Joe 46
Walsh, Joe 68
Walsh, Liam 82
Walton, Christian 42
Walton, Jack 5
Wan Bissaka, Aaron 50
Ward, Danny 40
Ward, Danny 44
Ward, Grant 9
Ward, Jed 16
Ward, Joe 63
Ward, Joel 29
Ward, Keaton 51
Ward, Lewis 83
Ward, Stephen 86
Ward-Prowse, James 77
Wareham, Jayden 23
Warner, Jaden 59
Warrington, Lewis 32
Washington, Conor 22
Watkins, Marley 20
Watkins, Ollie 4
Watmore, Duncan 52
Watson, Ben 22
Watson, Louis 30
Watson, Rory 73
Watson, Ryan 72
Watson, Tennai 54
Watt, Elliot 12
Watters, Max 20
Watts, Caleb 77
Watts, Kelland 56
Wearne, Stephen 80
Webb, Lewis 82
Webber, Oliver 66
Webster, Adam 14
Weghorst, Wouter 17
Weimann, Andreas 15
Weir, Jensen 14
Welbeck, Danny 14
Welch, Reece 32
Welch-Hayes, Miles 25
Wells, Nahki 15
Werner, Timo 23
Wesley, Moraes 4
Westbrooke, Zain 16
Westwood, Ashley 17
Westwood, Keiren 68
Whalley, Shaun 76
Wharton, Scott 8
Whatmough, Jack 90
Wheeler, David 92
Whelan, Callum 61
Whelan, Corey 21
Whelan, Glenn 16
Whitaker, Charlie 32
White, Aidan 70
White, Albert 42
White, Ben 3
White, Harvey 84
White, Hayden 86
White, Joe 56
White, Tom 6
Whitehall, Isaac 8
Whitehouse, Elliott 35
Whiteman, Alfie 84
Whiteman, Ben 67
Whittaker, Morgan 82
Whyte, Gavin 20
Wickens, George 36
Wickham, Connor 54
Wiggett, Charlie 56
Wildig, Aaron 55
Wildin, Luther 78
Wilding, Samuel 80
Wildsmith, Joe 75
Wiles, Ben 71
Wiles-Richards, Harvey 15
Wilkinson, Conor 86
Wilks, Mallik 41
Williams, Alfie 78
Williams, Andy 24
Williams, Ben 24
Williams, Brandon 50
Williams, Charlie 18
Williams, Daniel 82
Williams, Dylan 23
Williams, Ed 31
Williams, George B 19
Williams, George C 6
Williams, Joe 15
Williams, Jon 83
Williams, Jordan 5
Williams, M Jordan 10
Williams, Michael 28
Williams, Neco 47
Williams, Randell 41
Williams, Rhys 47
Williams, Ro-Shaun 31
Williams, Ryan 62
Williams, Shaun 66
Williams-Lowe, Kayden 68
Willis, Joe 86
Willis, Jordan 80
Willmott, Robbie 57
Willock, Chris 68
Willock, Joe 56
Willock, Matthew 72
Willock, Shay 86
Wilmot, Ben 79
Wilson, Adam 56
Wilson, Ben 26
Wilson, Callum 56
Wilson, Cameron 73
Wilson, Donovan 81
Wilson, Harry 36
Wilson, James 64
Wilson, James 65
Wilson, Kane 35
Wilson, Tyree 30
Wilson-Esbrand, Josh 49
Winchester, Carl 80
Windass, Josh 75
Windsor, Owen 88
Winfield, Charlie 5
Wing, Lewis 92
Winks, Harry 84
Winnall, Sam 62
Winterbottom, Ben 13
Wintle, Ryan 20
Wissa, Yoane 13
Wolf, Hannes 82
Wolfe, Matthew 5
Wollacott, Jojo 83
Woltman, Max 47
Wood, Charlie 12
Wood, Chris 56
Wood, Connor 45
Wood, Harry 41
Wood, Richard 71
Wood-Gordon, Nathan 52
Woodburn, Ben 47
Woodiwiss, Joe 57
Woodman, Freddie 56
Woodrow, Cauley 5
Woods, Charlie 58
Woods, Henry 37
Woods, Josh 1
Woods, Ryan 7
Woodthorpe, Nathan 28
Woodyard, Alex 2
Woolfenden, Luke 42
Woollard-Innocent, Kai 68
Woolston, Paul 50
Wootton, Scott 55
Worman, Ben 19
Worrall, David 65
Worrall, Joe 60
Wright, Bailey 80
Wright, Callum 44
Wright, Harry 34
Wright, Joe 53
Wright, Jordan 46
Wright, Tyreik 4
Wright-Phillips, D'Margio 79
Wyatt, Ben 81
Wyke, Charlie 90
Xande Silva, Nascimento 60
Xhaka, Granit 3
Xhemajli, Arbenit 80
Yarmolenko, Andriy 89
Yates, Jerry 9
Yates, Ryan 60
Yearn, Kai 19
Yengi, Tete 42
Yiadom, Andy 69
Young, Ashley 4
Young, Brad 4
Young, Ethan 73
Young, Jack 92
Young, Joe 91
Young, Matt 45
Young , Jake 12
Young-Coombes, Nathan 13
Younger, Ollie 31
Zaha, Wilfried 29
Zambo, Andre-Franck 36
Zanzala, Offrande 6
Zeefuik, Deyovaisio 8
Zemura, Jordan 11
Zeqiri, Andi 14
Ziger, Karlo 23
Zimba, Chanka 20
Zimmermann, Christoph 59
Zinchenko, Alexander 49
Zinckernagel, Philip 87
Ziyech, Hakim 23
Zohore, Kenneth 88
Zouma, Kurt 89
Zych, Oliwier 4

CUPS AND UPS AND DOWNS DIARY 2021–22

AUGUST 2021

6 Women's Olympic Gold Medal match: Sweden 1 Canada 1 *(aet; Canada won 3-2 on penalties).*
7 FA Community Shield: Leicester C 1 Manchester C 0; Men's Olympic Gold Medal match: Brazil 2 Spain 1 *(aet).*
11 European Super Cup 2021: Chelsea 1 Villareal 1 *(aet; Chelsea won 6-5 on penalties).*

OCTOBER 2021

10 Nations League Final: Spain 1 France 2.

DECEMBER 2021

5 The Vitality Women's FA Cup Final 2020–21: Chelsea 3 Arsenal 0.
11 MLS Cup Final 2021: Portland Timbers 1 New York City 1 *(aet; New York C won 4-2 on penalties).*
19 Premier Sports Scottish League Cup Final 2021–22: Celtic 2 Hibernian 1.

FEBRUARY 2022

6 Nathaniel MG Welsh League Cup Final: Connah's Quay Nomads 0 Cardiff Metropolitan University 0 *(Connah's Quay Nomads won 10-9 on penalties)*; African Cup of Nations Final: Senegal 0 Egypt 0 *(aet; Senegal won 4-2 on penalties).*
12 FIFA Club World Cup Final: Chelsea 2 Palmeiras 1 *(aet).*
26 Kelty Hearts champions of Scottish League Two and promoted to Scottish League One.
27 Carabao Cup Final: Liverpool 0 Chelsea 0 *(aet; Liverpool won 11-10 on penalties).*

MARCH 2022

5 Women's Continental Tyres Cup Final: Manchester C 3 Chelsea 1.
13 BetMcLean Northern Irish League Cup Final: Cliftonville 4 Coleraine 3 *(aet).*
21 Boodles Independent Schools FA Cup Final: Bradfield 4 Rossall 0.

APRIL 2022

3 Papa John's EFL Trophy Final: Rotherham U 4 Sutton U 2 *(aet)*; SPFL Trust Trophy Final: Raith R 3 Queen of the South 1.
9 Crewe Alex relegated from EFL League One to EFL League Two.
15 Scunthorpe U relegated from EFL League Two to National League.
16 East Fife relegated from Scottish League One to Scottish League Two.
18 Derby Co relegated from EFL Championship to EFL League One.
22 Barnsley relegated from EFL Championship to EFL League One; Kilmarnock champions of Scottish Championship and promoted to Scottish Premiership.
23 Peterborough U relegated from EFL Championship to EFL League One; Oldham Ath relegated from EFL League Two to National League; Queen of the South relegated from Scottish Championship to Scottish League One; Cove Rangers champions of Scottish League One and promoted to Scottish Championship.
24 Welsh FAW Trophy Final: Mold Alexandra 1 Baglan Dragons 0.
25 UEFA Youth League Final: Benfica 6 Red Bull Salzburg 0.
26 Exeter C promoted from EFL League Two to EFL League One.
30 Norwich C relegated from Premier League to EFL Championship; Wigan Ath champions of EFL League One and promoted to EFL Championship; Rotherham U promoted from EFL League One to EFL Championship; Gillingham relegated from EFL League One to EFL League Two; AFC Wimbledon relegated from EFL League One to EFL League Two; Doncaster R relegated from EFL League One to EFL League Two; Maidstone U champions of National League South and promoted to National League.

MAY 2022

1 Welsh FA Cup Final: The New Saints 3 Penybont 2. FA Sunday Cup Final: Baiteze 2 Highgate Alb 0.
2 Fulham champions of EFL Championship and promoted to Premier League *(promotion won 19 April)*; Gateshead champions of National League North and promoted to National League.
3 Bournemouth promoted from EFL Championship to Premier League.
7 Watford relegated from Premier League to EFL Championship; Forest Green R champions of EFL League Two and promoted to EFL League One *(promotion won 23 April)*; Bristol R promoted from EFL League Two to EFL League One; Scottish League One Play-Off Final First Leg: Edinburgh C 2 Annan Ath 0; Scottish League Two Play-Off Final First Leg: Bonnyrigg Rose 3 Cowdenbeath 0; Sadler's Peaky Blinder Irish FA Cup Final: Crusaders 2 Ballymena U 1 *(aet).*
11 Celtic champions of Scottish Premiership and qualify for Champions League Group Stage; Dundee relegated from Scottish Premiership to Scottish Championship; FA Youth Cup Final: Manchester U 3 Nottingham F 1.
12 Scottish Championship Play-Off Final First Leg: Queen's Park 1 Airdrieonians 1.
14 The Emirates FA Cup Final: Liverpool 0 Chelsea 0 *(aet; Liverpool won 6-5 on penalties)*; Scottish League One Play-Off Final First Leg: Annan Ath 2 Edinburgh C 1 *(Edinburgh C won 3-2 on aggregate and promoted from Scottish League Two to Scottish League One)*; Scottish League Two Play-Off Final Second Leg: Cowdenbeath 0 Bonnyrigg Rose Ath 1 *(Bonnyrigg Ross Ath won 4-0 on aggregate and promoted to Scottish League Two; Cowdenbeath relegated from Scottish League Two to Lowland League).*
15 Scottish Championship Play-Off Final Second Leg: Airdrieonians 1 Queen's Park 2 *(aet; Queen's Park won 3-2 on aggregate and promoted from Scottish League One to Scottish Championship)*; Vitality Women's FA Cup Final: Chelsea 3 Manchester C 2 *(aet)*; Stockport Co champions of National League and promoted to EFL League Two.
18 UEFA Europa League Final: Eintracht Frankfurt 1 Rangers 1 *(aet; Eintracht Frankfurt won 5-4 on penalties).*
20 Scottish Premiership Play-Off Final First Leg: Inverness CT 2 St Johnstone 2.
21 William Hill Scottish FA Cup Final: Rangers 2 Hearts 0 *(aet)*; EFL League One Play-Off Final: Sunderland 2 Wycombe W 0 *(Sunderland promoted to EFL Championship).*
22 Manchester C champions of Premier League; Burnley relegated from Premier League to EFL Championship; UEFA Women's Champions League Final: Lyon 3 Barcelona 1; The Buildbase FA Trophy Final: Bromley 1 Wrexham 0; The Buildbase FA Vase Final: Newport Pagnell T 3 Littlehampton T 0.
23 Scottish Premiership Play-Off Final Second Leg: St Johnstone 4 Inverness CT 0 *(St Johnstone won 6-2 on aggregate and remain in the Scottish Premiership).*
25 UEFA Europa Conference League Final: Roma 1 Feyenoord 0.
28 UEFA Champions League Final: Real Madrid 1 Liverpool 0; EFL League Two Play-Off Final: Port Vale 3 Mansfield T 0 *(Port Vale promoted to EFL League One).*
29 EFL Championship Play-Off Final: Nottingham F 1 Huddersfield 0 *(Nottingham F promoted to Premier League).*

JUNE 2022

5 National League Play-Off Final: Grimsby T 2 Solihull Moors 1 *(aet; Grimsby T promoted to EFL League Two).*

MANAGERS – IN AND OUT 2021–22

JULY 2021

21 Steve Cooper leaves as manager of Swansea C.
21 Ben Garner appointed manager of Swindon T.

AUGUST 2021

1 Russell Martin leaves as manager of Milton Keynes D and is appointed manager of Swansea C.
13 Liam Manning appointed manager of Milton Keynes D.

SEPTEMBER 2021

16 Chris Hughton sacked as manager of Nottingham F. First-team coach Steven Reid takes temporary charge.
21 Steve Cooper appointed manager of Nottingham F.

OCTOBER 2021

1 Mike Flynn leaves as manager of Newport Co. Assistant Wayne Hatswell takes temporary charge.
3 Xisco Munoz sacked as manager of Watford.
4 Claudio Ranieri appointed manager of Watford.
10 Chris Beech sacked as manager of Carlisle U. Assistant manager Gavin Skelton and Academy Coach Eric Kinder take temporary charge.
19 James Rowberry appointed manager of Newport Co.
20 Steve Bruce leaves as manager of Newcastle U by mutual consent. First-team coach Graeme Jones takes temporary charge.
21 Nigel Adkins sacked as manager of Charlton Ath. Assistant manager Johnnie Jackson takes temporary charge.
23 Mick McCarthy leaves as manager of Cardiff C by mutual consent. Under-23 coach Steve Morison takes temporary charge.
26 Keith Millen appointed manager of Carlisle U.

NOVEMBER 2021

1 Nuno Espirito Santo sacked as manager of Tottenham H.
1 Markus Schopp sacked as manager of Barnsley. Assistant manager Joseph Laumann takes temporary charge.
1 Neil Cox sacked as manager of Scunthorpe U. Coach Tony McMahon and goalkeeping coach Paul Musselwhite take temporary charge.
1 Dave Challinor leaves as manager of Hartlepool U to become manager of Stockport Co.
2 Antonio Conte appointed manager of Tottenham H.
5 Keith Hill appointed manager of Scunthorpe U.
6 Daniel Farke sacked as manager of Norwich C.
6 Neil Warnock sacked as manager of Middlesbrough.
7 Dean Smith sacked as manager of Aston Villa.
7 Chris Wilder appointed manager of Middlesbrough.
8 Eddie Howe appointed manager of Newcastle U.
11 Steven Gerrard leaves Rangers and is appointed manager of Aston Villa.
12 Steve Morison appointed manager of Cardiff C after being in temporary charge.
14 Alex Revell sacked as manager of Stevenage.
15 Dean Smith appointed manager of Norwich C.
17 Poya Asbaghi appointed manager of Barnsley.
18 Giovanni van Bronckhorst appointed manager of Rangers
21 Ole Gunnar Solskjaer sacked as manager of Manchester U. Assistant Michael Carrick takes temporary charge.
24 Simon Grayson sacked as manager of Fleetwood T. Under-23 coach Stephen Crainey takes temporary charge.
24 Keith Curle leaves as manager of Oldham Ath by mutual consent. Academy coach Selim Benachour takes temporary charge.
25 Slavisa Jokanovic sacked as manager of Sheffield U. Paul Heckingbottom appointed manager.
28 Paul Tisdale appointed manager of Stevenage.

DECEMBER 2021

1 Graeme Lee appointed manager of Hartlepool U.
2 Richie Wellens sacked as manager of Doncaster R. Under-18 manager Gary McSheffrey takes temporary charge.
4 Paul Cook sacked as manager of Ipswich T. John McGreal takes temporary charge.
6 Frankie McAvoy sacked as manager of Preston NE.
7 Ryan Lowe leaves as manager of Plymouth Arg to take charge at Preston NE.
7 Steven Schumacher appointed manager of Plymouth Arg.
16 Kieran McKenna appointed manager of Ipswich T.
17 Johnnie Jackson appointed manager of Charlton Ath after being in temporary charge.
21 Stephen Crainey appointed manager of Fleetwood T after being in temporary charge.
29 Gary McSheffrey appointed manager of Doncaster R after being in temporary charge.

JANUARY 2022

9 Steve Evans leaves as manager of Gillingham by mutual consent. Steve Lovell takes temporary charge.
16 Rafael Benitez sacked as manager of Everton. Assistant Duncan Ferguson takes temporary charge.
19 Hayden Mullins sacked as manager of Colchester U. Wayne Brown takes temporary charge.
22 John Sheridan appointed manager of Oldham Ath.
24 Claudio Ranieri sacked as manager of Watford.
25 Roy Hodgson appointed manager of Watford.
25 Grant McCann sacked as manager of Hull C.

27 Shota Arveladze appointed manager of Hull C.
30 Lee Johnson sacked as manager of Sunderland. Mike Dodds takes temporary charge.
31 Frank Lampard appointed manager of Everton.
31 Neil Harris appointed manager of Gillingham.

FEBRUARY 2022

2 Valerien Ismael sacked as manager of WBA.
3 Steve Bruce appointed manager of WBA.
9 Matt Taylor sacked as manager of Walsall. First-team coach Neil McDonald takes temporary charge.
11 Alex Neill appointed manager of Sunderland.
15 Derek Adams sacked as manager of Bradford C. Assistant manager Mark Trueman takes temporary charge.
15 Michael Flynn appointed manager of Walsall.
19 Veljko Paunovic sacked as manager of Reading.
19 Paul Ince appointed interim manager of Reading.
20 Darren Ferguson resigns as manager of Peterborough U.
22 Stephen Robinson resigns as manager of Morecambe to become manager of St Mirren.
23 Kenny Jackett sacked as manager of Leyton Orient. Coach Matt Harrold takes temporary charge.
23 Keith Millen sacked as manager of Carlisle U.
23 Paul Simpson appointed manager of Carlisle U until the end of the season.
24 Derek Adams appointed manager of Morecambe.
24 Mark Hughes appointed manager of Bradford C.
24 Grant McCann appointed manager of Peterborough U.

MARCH 2022

9 Richie Wellens appointed manager of Leyton Orient.
16 Paul Tisdale sacked as manager of Stevenage.
16 Steve Evans appointed manager of Stevenage.
20 Mark Cooper sacked as manager of Barrow.
21 Phil Brown appointed manager of Barrow.
29 Mark Robinson leaves as manager of AFC Wimbledon by mutual consent. Darius Charles takes temporary charge.
30 Mark Bowen appointed manager of AFC Wimbledon.

APRIL 2022

11 David Artell sacked as manager of Crewe Alex. Assistant manager Alex Morris takes temporary charge.
15 Sean Dyche sacked as manager of Burnley. Under-23s coach Mike Jackson takes temporary charge.
24 Poya Asbaghi leaves as manager of Barnsley by mutual consent. Under-23s manager Martin Devaney takes temporary charge.
28 Alex Morris appointed Crewe Alex manager having been in temporary charge.
30 Michael Appleton leaves as manager of Lincoln C by mutual consent.

MAY 2022

3 Johnnie Jackson sacked as manager of Charlton Ath.
4 Stephen Crainey moves as manager of Fleetwood to take up his former role of Under-23 manager at the club.
5 Graham Lee sacked as manager of Hartlepool U. Assistant manager Michael Nelson and first-team coach Anthony Sweeney take temporary charge.
8 Mark Bowen leaves as manager of AFC Wimbledon.
11 Tony Mowbray leaves as manager of Blackburn R.
11 Rob Edwards leaves as manager of Forest Green R and becomes manager of Watford.
12 Mark Kennedy appointed manager of Lincoln C.
12 Scott Brown appointed manager of Fleetwood T.
12 Phil Brown leaves as manager of Barrow.
16 Johnnie Jackson appointed manager of AFC Wimbledon.
16 Paul Ince appointed manager of Reading having been in interim charge.
17 Wayne Brown appointed manager of Colchester U having been in temporary charge.
17 Gary Bowyer sacked as manager of Salford C.
20 Neil Wood appointed manager of Salford C.
27 Pete Wild appointed manager of Barrow.
27 Ian Burchnall appointed manager of Forest Green R.

JUNE 2022

1 Michael Beale appointed manager of QPR.
2 Neil Critchley leaves as manager of Blackpool to become assistant manager at Aston Villa.
3 Paul Hartley appointed manager of Hartlepool U.
6 Kevin Betsy appointed manager of Crawley T.
8 Ben Garner leaves as manager of Swindon T to become manager of Charlton Ath.
14 Vincent Kompany appointed manager of Burnley.
14 Jon Dahl Tomasson appointed as manager of Blackburn R.
15 Michael Duff leaves as manager of Cheltenham T to become manager of Barnsley.
17 Michael Appleton appointed manager of Blackpool.
20 Scott Lindsey appointed manager of Swindon T.
27 Wade Elliott appointed manager of Cheltenham T.

JULY 2022

2 Lee Bowyer sacked as manager of Birmingham C.
3 John Eustace appointed manager of Birmingham C.

ENGLISH LEAGUE HONOURS 1888–2022

**Won or placed on goal average (ratio), goal difference or most goals scored. ‡Not promoted after play-offs. No official competition during 1915–19 and 1939–46, regional leagues operated.*

FOOTBALL LEAGUE (1888–89 to 1891–92) – TIER 1

MAXIMUM POINTS: ***a*** **44;** ***b*** **52.**

1	1888–89*a*	Preston NE	40	Aston Villa	29	Wolverhampton W	28
1	1889–90*a*	Preston NE	33	Everton	31	Blackburn R	27
1	1890–91*a*	Everton	29	Preston NE	27	Notts Co	26
1	1891–92*b*	Sunderland	42	Preston NE	37	Bolton W	36

DIVISION 1 (1892–93 to 1991–92)

MAXIMUM POINTS: ***c*** **60;** ***d*** **68;** ***e*** **76;** ***f*** **84;** ***g*** **126;** ***h*** **120;** ***k*** **114.**

1	1892–93*c*	Sunderland	48	Preston NE	37	Everton	36
1	1893–94*c*	Aston Villa	44	Sunderland	38	Derby Co	36
1	1894–95*c*	Sunderland	47	Everton	42	Aston Villa	39
1	1895–96*c*	Aston Villa	45	Derby Co	41	Everton	39
1	1896–97*c*	Aston Villa	47	Sheffield U*	36	Derby Co	36
1	1897–98*c*	Sheffield U	42	Sunderland	37	Wolverhampton W*	35
1	1898–99*d*	Aston Villa	45	Liverpool	43	Burnley	39
1	1899–1900*d*	Aston Villa	50	Sheffield U	48	Sunderland	41
1	1900–01*d*	Liverpool	45	Sunderland	43	Notts Co	40
1	1901–02*d*	Sunderland	44	Everton	41	Newcastle U	37
1	1902–03*d*	The Wednesday	42	Aston Villa*	41	Sunderland	41
1	1903–04*d*	The Wednesday	47	Manchester C	44	Everton	43
1	1904–05*d*	Newcastle U	48	Everton	47	Manchester C	46
1	1905–06*e*	Liverpool	51	Preston NE	47	The Wednesday	44
1	1906–07*e*	Newcastle U	51	Bristol C	48	Everton*	45
1	1907–08*e*	Manchester U	52	Aston Villa*	43	Manchester C	43
1	1908–09*e*	Newcastle U	53	Everton	46	Sunderland	44
1	1909–10*e*	Aston Villa	53	Liverpool	48	Blackburn R*	45
1	1910–11*e*	Manchester U	52	Aston Villa	51	Sunderland*	45
1	1911–12*e*	Blackburn R	49	Everton	46	Newcastle U	44
1	1912–13*e*	Sunderland	54	Aston Villa	50	The Wednesday	49
1	1913–14*e*	Blackburn R	51	Aston Villa	44	Middlesbrough*	43
1	1914–15*e*	Everton	46	Oldham Ath	45	Blackburn R*	43
1	1919–20*f*	WBA	60	Burnley	51	Chelsea	49
1	1920–21*f*	Burnley	59	Manchester C	54	Bolton W	52
1	1921–22*f*	Liverpool	57	Tottenham H	51	Burnley	49
1	1922–23*f*	Liverpool	60	Sunderland	54	Huddersfield T	53
1	1923–24*f*	Huddersfield T*	57	Cardiff C	57	Sunderland	53
1	1924–25*f*	Huddersfield T	58	WBA	56	Bolton W	55
1	1925–26*f*	Huddersfield T	57	Arsenal	52	Sunderland	48
1	1926–27*f*	Newcastle U	56	Huddersfield T	51	Sunderland	49
1	1927–28*f*	Everton	53	Huddersfield T	51	Leicester C	48
1	1928–29*f*	The Wednesday	52	Leicester C	51	Aston Villa	50
1	1929–30*f*	Sheffield W	60	Derby Co	50	Manchester C*	47
1	1930–31*f*	Arsenal	66	Aston Villa	59	Sheffield W	52
1	1931–32*f*	Everton	56	Arsenal	54	Sheffield W	50
1	1932–33*f*	Arsenal	58	Aston Villa	54	Sheffield W	51
1	1933–34*f*	Arsenal	59	Huddersfield T	56	Tottenham H	49
1	1934–35*f*	Arsenal	58	Sunderland	54	Sheffield W	49
1	1935–36*f*	Sunderland	56	Derby Co*	48	Huddersfield T	48
1	1936–37*f*	Manchester C	57	Charlton Ath	54	Arsenal	52
1	1937–38*f*	Arsenal	52	Wolverhampton W	51	Preston NE	49
1	1938–39*f*	Everton	59	Wolverhampton W	55	Charlton Ath	50
1	1946–47*f*	Liverpool	57	Manchester U*	56	Wolverhampton W	56
1	1947–48*f*	Arsenal	59	Manchester U*	52	Burnley	52
1	1948–49*f*	Portsmouth	58	Manchester U*	53	Derby Co	53
1	1949–50*f*	Portsmouth*	53	Wolverhampton W	53	Sunderland	52
1	1950–51*f*	Tottenham H	60	Manchester U	56	Blackpool	50
1	1951–52*f*	Manchester U	57	Tottenham H*	53	Arsenal	53
1	1952–53*f*	Arsenal*	54	Preston NE	54	Wolverhampton W	51
1	1953–54*f*	Wolverhampton W	57	WBA	53	Huddersfield T	51
1	1954–55*f*	Chelsea	52	Wolverhampton W*	48	Portsmouth*	48
1	1955–56*f*	Manchester U	60	Blackpool*	49	Wolverhampton W	49
1	1956–57*f*	Manchester U	64	Tottenham H*	56	Preston NE	56
1	1957–58*f*	Wolverhampton W	64	Preston NE	59	Tottenham H	51
1	1958–59*f*	Wolverhampton W	61	Manchester U	55	Arsenal*	50
1	1959–60*f*	Burnley	55	Wolverhampton W	54	Tottenham H	53
1	1960–61*f*	Tottenham H	66	Sheffield W	58	Wolverhampton W	57
1	1961–62*f*	Ipswich T	56	Burnley	53	Tottenham H	52
1	1962–63*f*	Everton	61	Tottenham H	55	Burnley	54
1	1963–64*f*	Liverpool	57	Manchester U	53	Everton	52
1	1964–65*f*	Manchester U*	61	Leeds U	61	Chelsea	56

1	1965–66*f*	Liverpool	61	Leeds U*	55	Burnley	55
1	1966–67*f*	Manchester U	60	Nottingham F*	56	Tottenham H	56
1	1967–68*f*	Manchester C	58	Manchester U	56	Liverpool	55
1	1968–69*f*	Leeds U	67	Liverpool	61	Everton	57
1	1969–70*f*	Everton	66	Leeds U	57	Chelsea	55
1	1970–71*f*	Arsenal	65	Leeds U	64	Tottenham H*	52
1	1971–72*f*	Derby Co	58	Leeds U*	57	Liverpool*	57
1	1972–73*f*	Liverpool	60	Arsenal	57	Leeds U	53
1	1973–74*f*	Leeds U	62	Liverpool	57	Derby Co	48
1	1974–75*f*	Derby Co	53	Liverpool*	51	Ipswich T	51
1	1975–76*f*	Liverpool	60	QPR	59	Manchester U	56
1	1976–77*f*	Liverpool	57	Manchester C	56	Ipswich T	52
1	1977–78*f*	Nottingham F	64	Liverpool	57	Everton	55
1	1978–79*f*	Liverpool	68	Nottingham F	60	WBA	59
1	1979–80*f*	Liverpool	60	Manchester U	58	Ipswich T	53
1	1980–81*f*	Aston Villa	60	Ipswich T	56	Arsenal	53
1	1981–82*g*	Liverpool	87	Ipswich T	83	Manchester U	78
1	1982–83*g*	Liverpool	82	Watford	71	Manchester U	70
1	1983–84*g*	Liverpool	80	Southampton	77	Nottingham F*	74
1	1984–85*g*	Everton	90	Liverpool*	77	Tottenham H	77
1	1985–86*g*	Liverpool	88	Everton	86	West Ham U	84
1	1986–87*g*	Everton	86	Liverpool	77	Tottenham H	71
1	1987–88*h*	Liverpool	90	Manchester U	81	Nottingham F	73
1	1988–89*k*	Arsenal*	76	Liverpool	76	Nottingham F	64
1	1989–90*k*	Liverpool	79	Aston Villa	70	Tottenham H	63
1	1990–91*k*	Arsenal[1]	83	Liverpool	76	Crystal Palace	69
1	1991–92*g*	Leeds U	82	Manchester U	78	Sheffield W	75

[1] *Arsenal deducted 2pts due to player misconduct in match on 20/10/1990 v Manchester U at Old Trafford.*

PREMIER LEAGUE (1992–93 to 2021–22)

MAXIMUM POINTS: *a* 126; *b* 114.

1	1992–93*a*	Manchester U	84	Aston Villa	74	Norwich C	72
1	1993–94*a*	Manchester U	92	Blackburn R	84	Newcastle U	77
1	1994–95*a*	Blackburn R	89	Manchester U	88	Nottingham F	77
1	1995–96*b*	Manchester U	82	Newcastle U	78	Liverpool	71
1	1996–97*b*	Manchester U	75	Newcastle U*	68	Arsenal*	68
1	1997–98*b*	Arsenal	78	Manchester U	77	Liverpool	65
1	1998–99*b*	Manchester U	79	Arsenal	78	Chelsea	75
1	1999–2000*b*	Manchester U	91	Arsenal	73	Leeds U	69
1	2000–01*b*	Manchester U	80	Arsenal	70	Liverpool	69
1	2001–02*b*	Arsenal	87	Liverpool	80	Manchester U	77
1	2002–03*b*	Manchester U	83	Arsenal	78	Newcastle U	69
1	2003–04*b*	Arsenal	90	Chelsea	79	Manchester U	75
1	2004–05*b*	Chelsea	95	Arsenal	83	Manchester U	77
1	2005–06*b*	Chelsea	91	Manchester U	83	Liverpool	82
1	2006–07*b*	Manchester U	89	Chelsea	83	Liverpool*	68
1	2007–08*b*	Manchester U	87	Chelsea	85	Arsenal	83
1	2008–09*b*	Manchester U	90	Liverpool	86	Chelsea	83
1	2009–10*b*	Chelsea	86	Manchester U	85	Arsenal	75
1	2010–11*b*	Manchester U	80	Chelsea*	71	Manchester C	71
1	2011–12*b*	Manchester C*	89	Manchester U	89	Arsenal	70
1	2012–13*b*	Manchester U	89	Manchester C	78	Chelsea	75
1	2013–14*b*	Manchester C	86	Liverpool	84	Chelsea	82
1	2014–15*b*	Chelsea	87	Manchester C	79	Arsenal	75
1	2015–16*b*	Leicester C	81	Arsenal	71	Tottenham H	70
1	2016–17*b*	Chelsea	93	Tottenham H	86	Manchester C	78
1	2017–18*b*	Manchester C	100	Manchester U	81	Tottenham H	77
1	2018–19*b*	Manchester C	98	Liverpool	97	Chelsea	72
1	2019–20*b*	Liverpool	99	Manchester C	81	Mancheser U*	66
1	2020–21*b*	Manchester C	86	Manchester U	74	Liverpool	69
1	2021–22*b*	Manchester C	93	Liverpool	92	Chelsea	74

DIVISION 2 (1892–93 to 1991–92) – TIER 2

MAXIMUM POINTS: *a* 44; *b* 56; *c* 60; *d* 68; *e* 76; *f* 84; *g* 126; *h* 132; *k* 138.

2	1892–93*a*	Small Heath	36	Sheffield U	35	Darwen	30
2	1893–94*b*	Liverpool	50	Small Heath	42	Notts Co	39
2	1894–95*c*	Bury	48	Notts Co	39	Newton Heath*	38
2	1895–96*c*	Liverpool*	46	Manchester C	46	Grimsby T*	42
2	1896–97*c*	Notts Co	42	Newton Heath	39	Grimsby T	38
2	1897–98*c*	Burnley	48	Newcastle U	45	Manchester C	39
2	1898–99*d*	Manchester C	52	Glossop NE	46	Leicester Fosse	45
2	1899–1900*d*	The Wednesday	54	Bolton W	52	Small Heath	46
2	1900–01*d*	Grimsby T	49	Small Heath	48	Burnley	44
2	1901–02*d*	WBA	55	Middlesbrough	51	Preston NE*	42
2	1902–03*d*	Manchester C	54	Small Heath	51	Woolwich Arsenal	48
2	1903–04*d*	Preston NE	50	Woolwich Arsenal	49	Manchester U	48
2	1904–05*d*	Liverpool	58	Bolton W	56	Manchester U	53
2	1905–06*e*	Bristol C	66	Manchester U	62	Chelsea	53
2	1906–07*e*	Nottingham F	60	Chelsea	57	Leicester Fosse	48
2	1907–08*e*	Bradford C	54	Leicester Fosse	52	Oldham Ath	50
2	1908–09*e*	Bolton W	52	Tottenham H*	51	WBA	51
2	1909–10*e*	Manchester C	54	Oldham Ath*	53	Hull C*	53
2	1910–11*e*	WBA	53	Bolton W	51	Chelsea	49

Div	Season	First	Pts	Second	Pts	Third	Pts
2	1911–12*e*	Derby Co*	54	Chelsea	54	Burnley	52
2	1912–13*e*	Preston NE	53	Burnley	50	Birmingham	46
2	1913–14*e*	Notts Co	53	Bradford PA*	49	Woolwich Arsenal	49
2	1914–15*e*	Derby Co	53	Preston NE	50	Barnsley	47
2	1919–20*f*	Tottenham H	70	Huddersfield T	64	Birmingham	56
2	1920–21*f*	Birmingham*	58	Cardiff C	58	Bristol C	51
2	1921–22*f*	Nottingham F	56	Stoke*	52	Barnsley	52
2	1922–23*f*	Notts Co	53	West Ham U*	51	Leicester C	51
2	1923–24*f*	Leeds U	54	Bury*	51	Derby Co	51
2	1924–25*f*	Leicester C	59	Manchester U	57	Derby Co	55
2	1925–26*f*	The Wednesday	60	Derby Co	57	Chelsea	52
2	1926–27*f*	Middlesbrough	62	Portsmouth*	54	Manchester C	54
2	1927–28*f*	Manchester C	59	Leeds U	57	Chelsea	54
2	1928–29*f*	Middlesbrough	55	Grimsby T	53	Bradford PA*	48
2	1929–30*f*	Blackpool	58	Chelsea	55	Oldham Ath	53
2	1930–31*f*	Everton	61	WBA	54	Tottenham H	51
2	1931–32*f*	Wolverhampton W	56	Leeds U	54	Stoke C	52
2	1932–33*f*	Stoke C	56	Tottenham H	55	Fulham	50
2	1933–34*f*	Grimsby T	59	Preston NE	52	Bolton W*	51
2	1934–35*f*	Brentford	61	Bolton W*	56	West Ham U	56
2	1935–36*f*	Manchester U	56	Charlton Ath	55	Sheffield U*	52
2	1936–37*f*	Leicester C	56	Blackpool	55	Bury	52
2	1937–38*f*	Aston Villa	57	Manchester U*	53	Sheffield U	53
2	1938–39*f*	Blackburn R	55	Sheffield U	54	Sheffield W	53
2	1946–47*f*	Manchester C	62	Burnley	58	Birmingham C	55
2	1947–48*f*	Birmingham C	59	Newcastle U	56	Southampton	52
2	1948–49*f*	Fulham	57	WBA	56	Southampton	55
2	1949–50*f*	Tottenham H	61	Sheffield W*	52	Sheffield U*	52
2	1950–51*f*	Preston NE	57	Manchester C	52	Cardiff C	50
2	1951–52*f*	Sheffield W	53	Cardiff C*	51	Birmingham C	51
2	1952–53*f*	Sheffield U	60	Huddersfield T	58	Luton T	52
2	1953–54*f*	Leicester C*	56	Everton	56	Blackburn R	55
2	1954–55*f*	Birmingham C*	54	Luton T*	54	Rotherham U	54
2	1955–56*f*	Sheffield W	55	Leeds U	52	Liverpool*	48
2	1956–57*f*	Leicester C	61	Nottingham F	54	Liverpool	53
2	1957–58*f*	West Ham U	57	Blackburn R	56	Charlton Ath	55
2	1958–59*f*	Sheffield W	62	Fulham	60	Sheffield U*	53
2	1959–60*f*	Aston Villa	59	Cardiff C	58	Liverpool*	50
2	1960–61*f*	Ipswich T	59	Sheffield U	58	Liverpool	52
2	1961–62*f*	Liverpool	62	Leyton Orient	54	Sunderland	53
2	1962–63*f*	Stoke C	53	Chelsea*	52	Sunderland	52
2	1963–64*f*	Leeds U	63	Sunderland	61	Preston NE	56
2	1964–65*f*	Newcastle U	57	Northampton T	56	Bolton W	50
2	1965–66*f*	Manchester C	59	Southampton	54	Coventry C	53
2	1966–67*f*	Coventry C	59	Wolverhampton W	58	Carlisle U	52
2	1967–68*f*	Ipswich T	59	QPR*	58	Blackpool	58
2	1968–69*f*	Derby Co	63	Crystal Palace	56	Charlton Ath	50
2	1969–70*f*	Huddersfield T	60	Blackpool	53	Leicester C	51
2	1970–71*f*	Leicester C	59	Sheffield U	56	Cardiff C*	53
2	1971–72*f*	Norwich C	57	Birmingham C	56	Millwall	55
2	1972–73*f*	Burnley	62	QPR	61	Aston Villa	50
2	1973–74*f*	Middlesbrough	65	Luton T	50	Carlisle U	49
2	1974–75*f*	Manchester U	61	Aston Villa	58	Norwich C	53
2	1975–76*f*	Sunderland	56	Bristol C*	53	WBA	53
2	1976–77*f*	Wolverhampton W	57	Chelsea	55	Nottingham F	52
2	1977–78*f*	Bolton W	58	Southampton	57	Tottenham H*	56
2	1978–79*f*	Crystal Palace	57	Brighton & HA*	56	Stoke C	56
2	1979–80*f*	Leicester C	55	Sunderland	54	Birmingham C*	53
2	1980–81*f*	West Ham U	66	Notts Co	53	Swansea C*	50
2	1981–82*g*	Luton T	88	Watford	80	Norwich C	71
2	1982–83*g*	QPR	85	Wolverhampton W	75	Leicester C	70
2	1983–84*g*	Chelsea*	88	Sheffield W	88	Newcastle U	80
2	1984–85*g*	Oxford U	84	Birmingham C	82	Manchester C*	74
2	1985–86*g*	Norwich C	84	Charlton Ath	77	Wimbledon	76
2	1986–87*g*	Derby Co	84	Portsmouth	78	Oldham Ath‡	75
2	1987–88*h*	Millwall	82	Aston Villa*	78	Middlesbrough	78
2	1988–89*k*	Chelsea	99	Manchester C	82	Crystal Palace	81
2	1989–90*k*	Leeds U*	85	Sheffield U	85	Newcastle U‡	80
2	1990–91*k*	Oldham Ath	88	West Ham U	87	Sheffield W	82
2	1991–92*k*	Ipswich T	84	Middlesbrough	80	Derby Co	78

FIRST DIVISION (1992–93 to 2003–04)

MAXIMUM POINTS: 138

Div	Season	First	Pts	Second	Pts	Third	Pts
2	1992–93	Newcastle U	96	West Ham U*	88	Portsmouth‡	88
2	1993–94	Crystal Palace	90	Nottingham F	83	Millwall‡	74
2	1994–95	Middlesbrough	82	Reading‡	79	Bolton W	77
2	1995–96	Sunderland	83	Derby Co	79	Crystal Palace‡	75
2	1996–97	Bolton W	98	Barnsley	80	Wolverhampton W‡	76
2	1997–98	Nottingham F	94	Middlesbrough	91	Sunderland‡	90
2	1998–99	Sunderland	105	Bradford C	87	Ipswich T‡	86
2	1999–2000	Charlton Ath	91	Manchester C	89	Ipswich T	87
2	2000–01	Fulham	101	Blackburn R	91	Bolton W	87

2	2001–02	Manchester C	99	WBA	89	Wolverhampton W‡	86
2	2002–03	Portsmouth	98	Leicester C	92	Sheffield U‡	80
2	2003–04	Norwich C	94	WBA	86	Sunderland‡	79

FOOTBALL LEAGUE CHAMPIONSHIP (2004–05 to 2021–22)

MAXIMUM POINTS: 138

2	2004–05	Sunderland	94	Wigan Ath	87	Ipswich T‡	85
2	2005–06	Reading	106	Sheffield U	90	Watford	81
2	2006–07	Sunderland	88	Birmingham C	86	Derby Co	84
2	2007–08	WBA	81	Stoke C	79	Hull C	75
2	2008–09	Wolverhampton W	90	Birmingham C	83	Sheffield U‡	80
2	2009–10	Newcastle U	102	WBA	91	Nottingham F‡	79
2	2010–11	QPR	88	Norwich C	84	Swansea C*	80
2	2011–12	Reading	89	Southampton	88	West Ham U	86
2	2012–13	Cardiff C	87	Hull C	79	Watford‡	77
2	2013–14	Leicester C	102	Burnley	93	Derby Co‡	85
2	2014–15	Bournemouth	90	Watford	89	Norwich C	86
2	2015–16	Burnley	93	Middlesbrough*	89	Brighton & HA‡	89
2	2016–17	Newcastle U	94	Brighton & HA	93	Reading‡	85
2	2017–18	Wolverhampton W	99	Cardiff C	90	Fulham	88
2	2018–19	Norwich C	94	Sheffield U	89	Leeds U‡	83
2	2019–20	Leeds U	93	WBA	83	Brentford*‡	81
2	2020–21	Norwich C	97	Watford	91	Brentford	87
2	2021–22	Fulham	90	Bournemouth	88	Huddersfield T‡	82

DIVISION 3 (1920–1921) – TIER 3

MAXIMUM POINTS: ***a*** **84.**

3	1920–21*a*	Crystal Palace	59	Southampton	54	QPR	53

DIVISION 3—SOUTH (1921–22 to 1957–58)

MAXIMUM POINTS: ***a*** **84;** ***b*** **92.**

3	1921–22*a*	Southampton*	61	Plymouth Arg	61	Portsmouth	53
3	1922–23*a*	Bristol C	59	Plymouth Arg*	53	Swansea T	53
3	1923–24*a*	Portsmouth	59	Plymouth Arg	55	Millwall	54
3	1924–25*a*	Swansea T	57	Plymouth Arg	56	Bristol C	53
3	1925–26*a*	Reading	57	Plymouth Arg	56	Millwall	53
3	1926–27*a*	Bristol C	62	Plymouth Arg	60	Millwall	56
3	1927–28*a*	Millwall	65	Northampton T	55	Plymouth Arg	53
3	1928–29*a*	Charlton Ath*	54	Crystal Palace	54	Northampton T*	52
3	1929–30*a*	Plymouth Arg	68	Brentford	61	QPR	51
3	1930–31*a*	Notts Co	59	Crystal Palace	51	Brentford	50
3	1931–32*a*	Fulham	57	Reading	55	Southend U	53
3	1932–33*a*	Brentford	62	Exeter C	58	Norwich C	57
3	1933–34*a*	Norwich C	61	Coventry C*	54	Reading*	54
3	1934–35*a*	Charlton Ath	61	Reading	53	Coventry C	51
3	1935–36*a*	Coventry C	57	Luton T	56	Reading	54
3	1936–37*a*	Luton T	58	Notts Co	56	Brighton & HA	53
3	1937–38*a*	Millwall	56	Bristol C	55	QPR*	53
3	1938–39*a*	Newport Co	55	Crystal Palace	52	Brighton & HA	49
3	1946–47*a*	Cardiff C	66	QPR	57	Bristol C	51
3	1947–48*a*	QPR	61	Bournemouth	57	Walsall	51
3	1948–49*a*	Swansea T	62	Reading	55	Bournemouth	52
3	1949–50*a*	Notts Co	58	Northampton T*	51	Southend U	51
3	1950–51*b*	Nottingham F	70	Norwich C	64	Reading*	57
3	1951–52*b*	Plymouth Arg	66	Reading*	61	Norwich C	61
3	1952–53*b*	Bristol R	64	Millwall*	62	Northampton T	62
3	1953–54*b*	Ipswich T	64	Brighton & HA	61	Bristol C	56
3	1954–55*b*	Bristol C	70	Leyton Orient	61	Southampton	59
3	1955–56*b*	Leyton Orient	66	Brighton & HA	65	Ipswich T	64
3	1956–57*b*	Ipswich T*	59	Torquay U	59	Colchester U	58
3	1957–58*b*	Brighton & HA	60	Brentford*	58	Plymouth Arg	58

DIVISION 3—NORTH (1921–22 to 1957–58)

MAXIMUM POINTS: ***a*** **76;** ***b*** **84;** ***c*** **80;** ***d*** **92.**

3	1921–22*a*	Stockport Co	56	Darlington*	50	Grimsby T	50
3	1922–23*a*	Nelson	51	Bradford PA	47	Walsall	46
3	1923–24*b*	Wolverhampton W	63	Rochdale	62	Chesterfield	54
3	1924–25*b*	Darlington	58	Nelson*	53	New Brighton	53
3	1925–26*b*	Grimsby T	61	Bradford PA	60	Rochdale	59
3	1926–27*b*	Stoke C	63	Rochdale	58	Bradford PA	55
3	1927–28*b*	Bradford PA	63	Lincoln C	55	Stockport Co	54
3	1928–29*b*	Bradford C	63	Stockport Co	62	Wrexham	52
3	1929–30*b*	Port Vale	67	Stockport Co	63	Darlington*	50
3	1930–31*b*	Chesterfield	58	Lincoln C	57	Wrexham*	54
3	1931–32*c*	Lincoln C*	57	Gateshead	57	Chester	50
3	1932–33*b*	Hull C	59	Wrexham	57	Stockport Co	54
3	1933–34*b*	Barnsley	62	Chesterfield	61	Stockport Co	59
3	1934–35*b*	Doncaster R	57	Halifax T	55	Chester	54
3	1935–36*b*	Chesterfield	60	Chester*	55	Tranmere R	55
3	1936–37*b*	Stockport Co	60	Lincoln C	57	Chester	53
3	1937–38*b*	Tranmere R	56	Doncaster R	54	Hull C	53

3	1938–39*b*	Barnsley	67	Doncaster R	56	Bradford C	52
3	1946–47*b*	Doncaster R	72	Rotherham U	64	Chester	56
3	1947–48*b*	Lincoln C	60	Rotherham U	59	Wrexham	50
3	1948–49*b*	Hull C	65	Rotherham U	62	Doncaster R	50
3	1949–50*b*	Doncaster R	55	Gateshead	53	Rochdale*	51
3	1950–51*d*	Rotherham U	71	Mansfield T	64	Carlisle U	62
3	1951–52*d*	Lincoln C	69	Grimsby T	66	Stockport Co	59
3	1952–53*d*	Oldham Ath	59	Port Vale	58	Wrexham	56
3	1953–54*d*	Port Vale	69	Barnsley	58	Scunthorpe U	57
3	1954–55*d*	Barnsley	65	Accrington S	61	Scunthorpe U*	58
3	1955–56*d*	Grimsby T	68	Derby Co	63	Accrington S	59
3	1956–57*d*	Derby Co	63	Hartlepools U	59	Accrington S*	58
3	1957–58*d*	Scunthorpe U	66	Accrington S	59	Bradford C	57

DIVISION 3 (1958–59 to 1991–92)

MAXIMUM POINTS: 92; 138 FROM 1981–82.

3	1958–59	Plymouth Arg	62	Hull C	61	Brentford*	57
3	1959–60	Southampton	61	Norwich C	59	Shrewsbury T*	52
3	1960–61	Bury	68	Walsall	62	QPR	60
3	1961–62	Portsmouth	65	Grimsby T	62	Bournemouth*	59
3	1962–63	Northampton T	62	Swindon T	58	Port Vale	54
3	1963–64	Coventry C*	60	Crystal Palace	60	Watford	58
3	1964–65	Carlisle U	60	Bristol C*	59	Mansfield T	59
3	1965–66	Hull C	69	Millwall	65	QPR	57
3	1966–67	QPR	67	Middlesbrough	55	Watford	54
3	1967–68	Oxford U	57	Bury	56	Shrewsbury T	55
3	1968–69	Watford*	64	Swindon T	64	Luton T	61
3	1969–70	Orient	62	Luton T	60	Bristol R	56
3	1970–71	Preston NE	61	Fulham	60	Halifax T	56
3	1971–72	Aston Villa	70	Brighton & HA	65	Bournemouth*	62
3	1972–73	Bolton W	61	Notts Co	57	Blackburn R	55
3	1973–74	Oldham Ath	62	Bristol R*	61	York C	61
3	1974–75	Blackburn R	60	Plymouth Arg	59	Charlton Ath	55
3	1975–76	Hereford U	63	Cardiff C	57	Millwall	56
3	1976–77	Mansfield T	64	Brighton & HA	61	Crystal Palace*	59
3	1977–78	Wrexham	61	Cambridge U	58	Preston NE*	56
3	1978–79	Shrewsbury T	61	Watford*	60	Swansea C	60
3	1979–80	Grimsby T	62	Blackburn R	59	Sheffield W	58
3	1980–81	Rotherham U	61	Barnsley*	59	Charlton Ath	59
3	1981–82	Burnley*	80	Carlisle U	80	Fulham	78
3	1982–83	Portsmouth	91	Cardiff C	86	Huddersfield T	82
3	1983–84	Oxford U	95	Wimbledon	87	Sheffield U*	83
3	1984–85	Bradford C	94	Millwall	90	Hull C	87
3	1985–86	Reading	94	Plymouth Arg	87	Derby Co	84
3	1986–87	Bournemouth	97	Middlesbrough	94	Swindon T	87
3	1987–88	Sunderland	93	Brighton & HA	84	Walsall	82
3	1988–89	Wolverhampton W	92	Sheffield U*	84	Port Vale	84
3	1989–90	Bristol R	93	Bristol C	91	Notts Co	87
3	1990–91	Cambridge U	86	Southend U	85	Grimsby T*	83
3	1991–92	Brentford	82	Birmingham C	81	Huddersfield T‡	78

SECOND DIVISION (1992–93 to 2003–04)

MAXIMUM POINTS: 138

3	1992–93	Stoke C	93	Bolton W	90	Port Vale‡	89
3	1993–94	Reading	89	Port Vale	88	Plymouth Arg*‡	85
3	1994–95	Birmingham C	89	Brentford‡	85	Crewe Alex‡	83
3	1995–96	Swindon T	92	Oxford U	83	Blackpool‡	82
3	1996–97	Bury	84	Stockport Co	82	Luton T‡	78
3	1997–98	Watford	88	Bristol C	85	Grimsby T	72
3	1998–99	Fulham	101	Walsall	87	Manchester C	82
3	1999–2000	Preston NE	95	Burnley	88	Gillingham	85
3	2000–01	Millwall	93	Rotherham U	91	Reading‡	86
3	2001–02	Brighton & HA	90	Reading	84	Brentford*‡	83
3	2002–03	Wigan Ath	100	Crewe Alex	86	Bristol C*‡	83
3	2003–04	Plymouth Arg	90	QPR	83	Bristol C‡	82

FOOTBALL LEAGUE ONE (2004–05 to 2021–22)

MAXIMUM POINTS: 138

3	2004–05	Luton T	98	Hull C	86	Tranmere R‡	79
3	2005–06	Southend U	82	Colchester U	79	Brentford‡	76
3	2006–07	Scunthorpe U	91	Bristol C	85	Blackpool	83
3	2007–08	Swansea C	92	Nottingham F	82	Doncaster R*	80
3	2008–09	Leicester C	96	Peterborough U	89	Milton Keynes D‡	87
3	2009–10	Norwich C	95	Leeds U	86	Millwall	85
3	2010–11	Brighton & HA	95	Southampton	92	Huddersfield T‡	87
3	2011–12	Charlton Ath	101	Sheffield W	93	Sheffield U‡	90
3	2012–13	Doncaster R	84	Bournemouth	83	Brentford‡	79
3	2013–14	Wolverhampton W	103	Brentford	94	Leyton Orient‡	86
3	2014–15	Bristol C	99	Milton Keynes D	91	Preston NE	89
3	2015–16	Wigan Ath	87	Burton Alb	85	Walsall‡	84
3	2016–17	Sheffield U	100	Bolton W	86	Scunthorpe U*‡	82
3	2017–18	Wigan Ath	98	Blackburn R	96	Shrewsbury T‡	87

3	2018–19	Luton T	94	Barnsley	91	Charlton Ath*	88		
3	2019–20[2]	Coventry C	67	Rotherham U	62	Wycombe W	59		

[2] *Season curtailed due to COVID-19 pandemic. League positions decided on points-per-game basis.*

3	2020–21	Hull C	89	Peterborough U	87	Blackpool	80
3	2021–22	Wigan Ath	92	Rotherham U	90	Milton Keynes D‡	89

DIVISION 4 (1958–59 to 1991–92) – TIER 4

MAXIMUM POINTS: 92; 138 FROM 1981–82.

4	1958–59	Port Vale	64	Coventry C*	60	York C	60	Shrewsbury T	58
4	1959–60	Walsall	65	Notts Co*	60	Torquay U	60	Watford	57
4	1960–61	Peterborough U	66	Crystal Palace	64	Northampton T*	60	Bradford PA	60
4	1961–62[3]	Millwall	56	Colchester U	55	Wrexham	53	Carlisle U	52
4	1962–63	Brentford	62	Oldham Ath*	59	Crewe Alex	59	Mansfield T*	57
4	1963–64	Gillingham*	60	Carlisle U	60	Workington	59	Exeter C	58
4	1964–65	Brighton & HA	63	Millwall*	62	York C	62	Oxford U	61
4	1965–66	Doncaster R*	59	Darlington	59	Torquay U	58	Colchester U*	56
4	1966–67	Stockport Co	64	Southport*	59	Barrow	59	Tranmere R	58
4	1967–68	Luton T	66	Barnsley	61	Hartlepools U	60	Crewe Alex	58
4	1968–69	Doncaster R	59	Halifax T	57	Rochdale*	56	Bradford C	56
4	1969–70	Chesterfield	64	Wrexham	61	Swansea C	60	Port Vale	59
4	1970–71	Notts Co	69	Bournemouth	60	Oldham Ath	59	York C	56
4	1971–72	Grimsby T	63	Southend U	60	Brentford	59	Scunthorpe U	57
4	1972–73	Southport	62	Hereford U	58	Cambridge U	57	Aldershot*	56
4	1973–74	Peterborough U	65	Gillingham	62	Colchester U	60	Bury	59
4	1974–75	Mansfield T	68	Shrewsbury T	62	Rotherham U	59	Chester*	57
4	1975–76	Lincoln C	74	Northampton T	68	Reading	60	Tranmere R	58
4	1976–77	Cambridge U	65	Exeter C	62	Colchester U*	59	Bradford C	59
4	1977–78	Watford	71	Southend U	60	Swansea C*	56	Brentford	56
4	1978–79	Reading	65	Grimsby T*	61	Wimbledon*	61	Barnsley	61
4	1979–80	Huddersfield T	66	Walsall	64	Newport Co	61	Portsmouth*	60
4	1980–81	Southend U	67	Lincoln C	65	Doncaster R	56	Wimbledon	55
4	1981–82	Sheffield U	96	Bradford C*	91	Wigan Ath	91	Bournemouth	88
4	1982–83	Wimbledon	98	Hull C	90	Port Vale	88	Scunthorpe U	83
4	1983–84	York C	101	Doncaster R	85	Reading*	82	Bristol C	82
4	1984–85	Chesterfield	91	Blackpool	86	Darlington	85	Bury	84
4	1985–86	Swindon T	102	Chester C	84	Mansfield T	81	Port Vale	79
4	1986–87	Northampton T	99	Preston NE	90	Southend U	80	Wolverhampton W‡	79
4	1987–88	Wolverhampton W	90	Cardiff C	85	Bolton W	78	Scunthorpe U*‡	77
4	1988–89	Rotherham U	82	Tranmere R	80	Crewe Alex	78	Scunthorpe U*‡	77
4	1989–90	Exeter C	89	Grimsby T	79	Southend U	75	Stockport Co‡	74
4	1990–91	Darlington	83	Stockport Co*	82	Hartlepool U	82	Peterborough U	80
4	1991–92[4]	Burnley	83	Rotherham U*	77	Mansfield T	77	Blackpool	76

[3] *Maximum points: 88 owing to Accrington Stanley's resignation.*
[4] *Maximum points: 126 owing to Aldershot being expelled (and only 23 teams started the competition).*

THIRD DIVISION (1992–93 to 2003–04)

MAXIMUM POINTS: *a* 126; *b* 138.

4	1992–93*a*	Cardiff C	83	Wrexham	80	Barnet	79	York C	75
4	1993–94*a*	Shrewsbury T	79	Chester C	74	Crewe Alex	73	Wycombe W	70
4	1994–95*a*	Carlisle U	91	Walsall	83	Chesterfield	81	Bury‡	80
4	1995–96*b*	Preston NE	86	Gillingham	83	Bury	79	Plymouth Arg*	78
4	1996–97*b*	Wigan Ath*	87	Fulham	87	Carlisle U	84	Northampton T	72
4	1997–98*b*	Notts Co	99	Macclesfield T	82	Lincoln C	75	Colchester U*	74
4	1998–99*b*	Brentford	85	Cambridge U	81	Cardiff C	80	Scunthorpe U	74
4	1999–2000*b*	Swansea C	85	Rotherham U	84	Northampton T	82	Darlington‡	79
4	2000–01*b*	Brighton & HA	92	Cardiff C	82	Chesterfield[5]	80	Hartlepool U‡	77
4	2001–02*b*	Plymouth Arg	102	Luton T	97	Mansfield T	79	Cheltenham T*	78
4	2002–03*b*	Rushden & D	87	Hartlepool U	85	Wrexham	84	Bournemouth	74
4	2003–04*b*	Doncaster R	92	Hull C	88	Torquay U*	81	Huddersfield T	81

[5] *Chesterfield deducted 9pts for irregularities.*

FOOTBALL LEAGUE TWO (2004–05 to 2021–22)

MAXIMUM POINTS: 138

4	2004–05	Yeovil T	83	Scunthorpe U*	80	Swansea C	80	Southend U	78
4	2005–06	Carlisle U	86	Northampton T	83	Leyton Orient	81	Grimsby T‡	78
4	2006–07	Walsall	89	Hartlepool U	88	Swindon T	85	Milton Keynes D‡	84
4	2007–08	Milton Keynes D	97	Peterborough U	92	Hereford U	88	Stockport Co	82
4	2008–09	Brentford	85	Exeter C	79	Wycombe W*	78	Bury‡	78
4	2009–10	Notts Co	93	Bournemouth	83	Rochdale	82	Morecambe*‡	73
4	2010–11	Chesterfield	86	Bury	81	Wycombe W	80	Shrewsbury T‡	79
4	2011–12	Swindon T	93	Shrewsbury T	88	Crawley T	84	Southend U‡	83
4	2012–13	Gillingham	83	Rotherham U	79	Port Vale	78	Burton Alb	76
4	2013–14	Chesterfield	84	Scunthorpe U*	81	Rochdale	81	Fleetwood T	76
4	2014–15	Burton Alb	94	Shrewsbury T	89	Bury	85	Wycombe W*‡	84
4	2015–16	Northampton T	99	Oxford U	86	Bristol R*	85	Accrington S‡	85
4	2016–17	Portsmouth*	87	Plymouth Arg	87	Doncaster R	85	Luton T‡	77
4	2017–18	Accrington S	93	Luton T	88	Wycombe W	84	Exeter C‡	80
4	2018–19	Lincoln C	85	Bury*	79	Milton Keynes D	79	Mansfield T‡	76
4	2019–20[6]	Swindon T*	69	Crewe Alex	69	Plymouth Arg	68	Cheltenham T‡	64

[6] *Season curtailed due to COVID-19 pandemic. League positions decided on points-per-game basis.*

4	2020–21	Cheltenham T	82	Cambridge U	80	Bolton W	79	Morecambe	78
4	2021–22	Forest Green R*	84	Exeter C	84	Bristol R*	80	Northampton T‡	80

LEAGUE TITLE WINS

DIVISION 1 (1888–89 to 1991–92) – TIER 1
Liverpool 18, Arsenal 10, Everton 9, Aston Villa 7, Manchester U 7, Sunderland 6, Newcastle U 4, Sheffield W 4 (3 as The Wednesday), Huddersfield T 3, Leeds U 3, Wolverhampton W 3, Blackburn R 2, Burnley 2, Derby Co 2, Manchester C 2, Portsmouth 2, Preston NE 2, Tottenham H 2, Chelsea 1, Ipswich T 1, Nottingham F 1, Sheffield U 1, WBA 1.

PREMIER LEAGUE (1992–93 to 2021–22) – TIER 1
Manchester U 13, Manchester C 6, Chelsea 5, Arsenal 3, Blackburn R 1, Leicester C 1, Liverpool 1.

DIVISION 2 (1892–93 TO 1991–92) – TIER 2
Leicester C 6, Manchester C 6, Sheffield W 5 (1 as The Wednesday), Birmingham C 4 (1 as Small Heath), Derby Co 4, Liverpool 4, Ipswich T 3, Leeds U 3, Middlesbrough 3, Notts Co 3, Preston NE 3, Aston Villa 2, Bolton W 2, Burnley 2, Chelsea 2, Grimsby T 2, Manchester U 2, Norwich C 2, Nottingham F 2, Stoke C 2, Tottenham H 2, WBA 2, West Ham U 2, Wolverhampton W 2, Blackburn R 1, Blackpool 1, Bradford C 1, Brentford 1, Bristol C 1, Bury 1, Coventry C 1, Crystal Palace 1, Everton 1, Fulham 1, Huddersfield T 1, Luton T 1, Millwall 1, Newcastle U 1, Oldham Ath 1, Oxford U 1, QPR 1, Sheffield U 1, Sunderland 1.

FIRST DIVISION (1992–93 to 2003–04) – TIER 2
Sunderland 1, Bolton W 1, Charlton Ath 1, Crystal Palace 1, Fulham 1, Manchester C 1, Middlesbrough 1, Newcastle U 1, Norwich C 1, Nottingham F 1, Portsmouth 1.

FOOTBALL LEAGUE CHAMPIONSHIP (2004–05 to 2021–22) – TIER 2
Newcastle U 2, Norwich C 2, Reading 2, Sunderland 2, Wolverhampton W 2, Bournemouth 1, Burnley 1, Cardiff C 1, Fulham 1, Leeds U 1, Leicester C 1, QPR 1, WBA 1.

DIVISION 3—SOUTH (1920–21 to 1957–58) – TIER 3
Bristol C 3, Charlton Ath 2, Ipswich T 2, Millwall 2, Notts Co 2, Plymouth Arg 2, Swansea T 2, Brentford 1, Brighton & HA 1, Bristol R 1, Cardiff C 1, Coventry C 1, Crystal Palace 1, Fulham 1, Leyton Orient 1, Luton T 1, Newport Co 1, Norwich C 1, Nottingham F 1, Portsmouth 1, QPR 1, Reading 1, Southampton 1.

DIVISION 3—NORTH (1921–22 to 1957–58) – TIER 3
Barnsley 3, Doncaster R 3, Lincoln C 3, Chesterfield 2, Grimsby T 2, Hull C 2, Port Vale 2, Stockport Co 2, Bradford C 1, Bradford PA 1, Darlington 1, Derby Co 1, Nelson 1, Oldham Ath 1, Rotherham U 1, Scunthorpe U 1, Stoke C 1, Tranmere R 1, Wolverhampton W 1.

DIVISION 3 (1958–59 to 1991–92) – TIER 3
Oxford U 2, Portsmouth 2, Aston Villa 1, Blackburn R 1, Bolton W 1, Bournemouth 1, Bradford C 1, Brentford 1, Bristol R 1, Burnley 1, Bury 1, Cambridge U 1, Carlisle U 1, Coventry C 1, Grimsby T 1, Hereford U 1, Hull C 1, Mansfield T 1, Northampton T 1, Oldham Ath 1, Orient 1, Plymouth Arg 1, Preston NE 1, QPR 1, Reading 1, Rotherham U 1, Shrewsbury T 1, Southampton 1, Sunderland 1, Watford 1, Wolverhampton W 1, Wrexham 1.

SECOND DIVISION (1992–93 to 2003–04) – TIER 3
Birmingham C 1, Brighton & HA 1, Bury 1, Fulham 1, Millwall 1, Plymouth Arg 1, Preston NE 1, Reading 1, Stoke C 1, Swindon T 1, Watford 1, Wigan Ath 1.

FOOTBALL LEAGUE ONE (2004–05 to 2021–22) – TIER 3
Luton T 2, Wigan Ath 2, Brighton & HA 1, Bristol C 1, Charlton Ath 1, Coventry C 1, Doncaster R 1, Hull C 1, Leicester C 1, Norwich C 1, Scunthorpe U 1, Sheffield U 1, Southend U 1, Swansea C 1, Wigan Ath 1, Wolverhampton W 1.

DIVISION 4 (1958–59 to 1991–92) – TIER 4
Chesterfield 2, Doncaster R 2, Peterborough U 2, Brentford 1, Brighton & HA 1, Burnley 1, Cambridge U 1, Darlington 1, Exeter C 1, Gillingham 1, Grimsby T 1, Huddersfield T 1, Lincoln C 1, Luton T 1, Mansfield T 1, Millwall 1, Northampton T 1, Notts Co 1, Port Vale 1, Reading 1, Rotherham U 1, Sheffield U 1, Southend U 1, Southport 1, Stockport Co 1, Swindon T 1, Walsall 1, Watford 1, Wimbledon 1, Wolverhampton W 1, York C 1.

THIRD DIVISION (1992–93 to 2003–04) – TIER 4
Brentford 1, Brighton & HA 1, Cardiff C 1, Carlisle U 1, Doncaster R 1, Notts Co 1, Plymouth Arg 1, Preston NE 1, Rushden & D 1, Shrewsbury T 1, Swansea C 1, Wigan Ath 1.

FOOTBALL LEAGUE TWO (2004–05 to 2021–22) – TIER 4
Chesterfield 2, Swindon T 2, Accrington S 1, Brentford 1, Burton Alb 1, Carlisle U 1, Cheltenham T 1, Forest Green R 1, Gillingham 1, Lincoln C 1, Milton Keynes D 1, Northampton T 1, Notts Co 1, Portsmouth 1, Walsall 1, Yeovil T 1.

PROMOTED AFTER PLAY-OFFS

1986–87	Charlton Ath to Division 1; Swindon T to Division 2; Aldershot to Division 3
1987–88	Middlesbrough to Division 1; Walsall to Division 2; Swansea C to Division 3
1988–89	Crystal Palace to Division 1; Port Vale to Division 2; Leyton Orient to Division 3
1989–90	Sunderland to Division 1; Notts Co to Division 2; Cambridge U to Division 3
1990–91	Notts Co to Division 1; Tranmere R to Division 2; Torquay U to Division 3
1991–92	Blackburn R to Premier League; Peterborough U to First Division; Blackpool to Second Division
1992–93	Swindon T to Premier League; WBA to First Division; York C to Second Division
1993–94	Leicester C to Premier League; Burnley to First Division; Wycombe W to Second Division
1994–95	Bolton W to Premier League; Huddersfield T to First Division; Wycombe W to Second Division
1995–96	Leicester C to Premier League; Bradford C to First Division; Plymouth Arg to Second Division
1996–97	Crystal Palace to Premier League; Crewe Alex to First Division; Northampton T to Second Division
1997–98	Charlton Ath to Premier League; Grimsby T to First Division; Colchester U to Second Division
1998–99	Watford to Premier League; Manchester C to First Division; Scunthorpe U to Second Division
1999–2000	Ipswich to Premier League; Gillingham to First Division; Peterborough U to Second Division
2000–01	Bolton W to Premier league; Walsall to First Division; Blackpool to Second Division
2001–02	Birmingham C to Premier League; Stoke C to First Division; Cheltenham T to Second Division
2002–03	Wolverhampton W to Premier League; Cardiff C to First Division; Bournemouth to Second Division
2003–04	Crystal Palace to Premier League; Brighton & HA to First Division; Huddersfield T to Second Division
2004–05	West Ham U to Premier League; Sheffield W to Championship; Southend U to Football League One
2005–06	Watford to Premier League; Barnsley to Championship; Cheltenham T to Football League One
2006–07	Derby Co to Premier League; Blackpool to Championship; Bristol R to Football League One
2007–08	Hull C to Premier League; Doncaster R to Championship; Stockport Co to Football League One
2008–09	Burnley to Premier League; Scunthorpe U to Championship; Gillingham to Football League One
2009–10	Blackpool to Premier League; Millwall to Championship; Dagenham & R to Football League One
2010–11	Swansea C to Premier League; Peterborough U to Championship; Stevenage to Football League One
2011–12	West Ham U to Premier League; Huddersfield T to Championship; Crewe Alex to Football League One
2012–13	Crystal Palace to Premier League; Yeovil T to Championship; Bradford C to Football League One
2013–14	QPR to Premier League; Rotherham U to Championship; Fleetwood T to Football League One
2014–15	Norwich C to Premier League; Preston NE to Championship; Southend U to Football League One
2015–16	Hull C to Premier League; Barnsley to Championship; AFC Wimbledon to Football League One
2016–17	Huddersfield T to Premier League; Millwall to Championship; Blackpool to Football League One
2017–18	Fulham to Premier League; Rotherham U to Championship; Coventry C to Football League One
2018–19	Aston Villa to Premier League; Charlton Ath to Championship; Tranmere R to Football League One
2019–20	Fulham to Premier League; Wycombe W to Championship; Northampton T to Football League One
2020–21	Brentford to Premier League; Blackpool to Championship; Morecambe to Football League One
2021–22	Nottingham F to Premier League; Sunderland to Championship; Port Vale to Football League One

RELEGATED CLUBS

1891–92 League extended. Newton Heath, Sheffield W and Nottingham F admitted. *Second Division formed* including Darwen.
1892–93 In Test matches, Sheffield U and Darwen won promotion in place of Notts Co and Accrington S.
1893–94 In Tests, Liverpool and Small Heath won promotion. Newton Heath and Darwen relegated.
1894–95 After Tests, Bury promoted, Liverpool relegated.
1895–96 After Tests, Liverpool promoted, Small Heath relegated.
1896–97 After Tests, Notts Co promoted, Burnley relegated.
1897–98 Test system abolished after success of Stoke C and Burnley. League extended. Blackburn R and Newcastle U elected to First Division. *Automatic promotion and relegation introduced.*

DIVISION 1 TO DIVISION 2 (1898–99 to 1991–92)

1898–99 Bolton W and Sheffield W
1899–1900 Burnley and Glossop NE
1900–01 Preston NE and WBA
1901–02 Small Heath and Manchester C
1902–03 Grimsby T and Bolton W
1903–04 Liverpool and WBA
1904–05 League extended. Bury and Notts Co, two bottom clubs in First Division, re-elected.
1905–06 Nottingham F and Wolverhampton W
1906–07 Derby Co and Stoke C
1907–08 Bolton W and Birmingham C
1908–09 Manchester C and Leicester Fosse
1909–10 Bolton W and Chelsea
1910–11 Bristol C and Nottingham F
1911–12 Preston NE and Bury
1912–13 Notts Co and Woolwich Arsenal
1913–14 Preston NE and Derby Co
1914–15 Tottenham H and Chelsea*
1919–20 Notts Co and Sheffield W
1920–21 Derby Co and Bradford PA
1921–22 Bradford C and Manchester U
1922–23 Stoke C and Oldham Ath
1923–24 Chelsea and Middlesbrough
1924–25 Preston NE and Nottingham F
1925–26 Manchester C and Notts Co
1926–27 Leeds U and WBA
1927–28 Tottenham H and Middlesbrough
1928–29 Bury and Cardiff C
1929–30 Burnley and Everton
1930–31 Leeds U and Manchester U
1931–32 Grimsby T and West Ham U
1932–33 Bolton W and Blackpool
1933–34 Newcastle U and Sheffield U
1934–35 Leicester C and Tottenham H
1935–36 Aston Villa and Blackburn R
1936–37 Manchester U and Sheffield W
1937–38 Manchester C and WBA
1938–39 Birmingham C and Leicester C
1946–47 Brentford and Leeds U
1947–48 Blackburn R and Grimsby T
1948–49 Preston NE and Sheffield U
1949–50 Manchester C and Birmingham C
1950–51 Sheffield W and Everton
1951–52 Huddersfield T and Fulham
1952–53 Stoke C and Derby Co
1953–54 Middlesbrough and Liverpool
1954–55 Leicester C and Sheffield W
1955–56 Huddersfield T and Sheffield U
1956–57 Charlton Ath and Cardiff C
1957–58 Sheffield W and Sunderland
1958–59 Portsmouth and Aston Villa
1959–60 Luton T and Leeds U
1960–61 Preston NE and Newcastle U
1961–62 Chelsea and Cardiff C
1962–63 Manchester C and Leyton Orient
1963–64 Bolton W and Ipswich T
1964–65 Wolverhampton W and Birmingham C
1965–66 Northampton T and Blackburn R
1966–67 Aston Villa and Blackpool
1967–68 Fulham and Sheffield U
1968–69 Leicester C and QPR
1969–70 Sunderland and Sheffield W
1970–71 Burnley and Blackpool
1971–72 Huddersfield T and Nottingham F
1972–73 Crystal Palace and WBA
1973–74 Southampton, Manchester U, Norwich C
1974–75 Luton T, Chelsea, Carlisle U
1975–76 Wolverhampton W, Burnley, Sheffield U
1976–77 Sunderland, Stoke C, Tottenham H
1977–78 West Ham U, Newcastle U, Leicester C
1978–79 QPR, Birmingham C, Chelsea
1979–80 Bristol C, Derby Co, Bolton W
1980–81 Norwich C, Leicester C, Crystal Palace
1981–82 Leeds U, Wolverhampton W, Middlesbrough
1982–83 Manchester C, Swansea C, Brighton & HA
1983–84 Birmingham C, Notts Co, Wolverhampton W
1984–85 Norwich C, Sunderland, Stoke C
1985–86 Ipswich T, Birmingham C, WBA
1986–87 Leicester C, Manchester C, Aston Villa
1987–88 Chelsea**, Portsmouth, Watford, Oxford U
1988–89 Middlesbrough, West Ham U, Newcastle U
1989–90 Sheffield W, Charlton Ath, Millwall
1990–91 Sunderland and Derby Co
1991–92 Luton T, Notts Co, West Ham U

***Relegated after play-offs.*

**Subsequently re-elected to Division 1 when League was extended after the War.*

PREMIER LEAGUE TO DIVISION 1 (1992–93 to 2003–04)

1992–93 Crystal Palace, Middlesbrough, Nottingham F
1993–94 Sheffield U, Oldham Ath, Swindon T
1994–95 Crystal Palace, Norwich C, Leicester C, Ipswich T
1995–96 Manchester C, QPR, Bolton W
1996–97 Sunderland, Middlesbrough, Nottingham F
1997–98 Bolton W, Barnsley, Crystal Palace
1998–99 Charlton Ath, Blackburn R, Nottingham F
1999–2000 Wimbledon, Sheffield W, Watford
2000–01 Manchester C, Coventry C, Bradford C
2001–02 Ipswich T, Derby Co, Leicester C
2002–03 West Ham U, WBA, Sunderland
2003–04 Leicester C, Leeds U, Wolverhampton W

PREMIER LEAGUE TO CHAMPIONSHIP (2004–05 to 2021–22)

2004–05 Crystal Palace, Norwich C, Southampton
2005–06 Birmingham C, WBA, Sunderland
2006–07 Sheffield U, Charlton Ath, Watford
2007–08 Reading, Birmingham C, Derby Co
2008–09 Newcastle U, Middlesbrough, WBA
2009–10 Burnley, Hull C, Portsmouth
2010–11 Birmingham C, Blackpool, West Ham U
2011–12 Bolton W, Blackburn R, Wolverhampton W
2012–13 Wigan Ath, Reading, QPR
2013–14 Norwich C, Fulham, Cardiff C
2014–15 Hull C, Burnley, QPR
2015–16 Newcastle U, Norwich C, Aston Villa
2016–17 Hull C, Middlesbrough, Sunderland
2017–18 Swansea C, Stoke C, WBA
2018–19 Cardiff C, Fulham, Huddersfield T
2019–20 Bournemouth, Watford, Norwich C
2020–21 Fulham, WBA, Sheffield U
2021–22 Burnley, Watford, Norwich C

DIVISION 2 TO DIVISION 3 (1920–21 to 1991–92)

1920–21 Stockport Co
1921–22 Bradford PA and Bristol C
1922–23 Rotherham Co and Wolverhampton W
1923–24 Nelson and Bristol C
1924–25 Crystal Palace and Coventry C
1925–26 Stoke C and Stockport Co
1926–27 Darlington and Bradford C
1927–28 Fulham and South Shields
1928–29 Port Vale and Clapton Orient
1929–30 Hull C and Notts Co
1930–31 Reading and Cardiff C
1931–32 Barnsley and Bristol C
1932–33 Chesterfield and Charlton Ath
1933–34 Millwall and Lincoln C
1934–35 Oldham Ath and Notts Co
1935–36 Port Vale and Hull C
1936–37 Doncaster R and Bradford C
1937–38 Barnsley and Stockport Co
1938–39 Norwich C and Tranmere R
1946–47 Swansea T and Newport Co
1947–48 Doncaster R and Millwall
1948–49 Nottingham F and Lincoln C
1949–50 Plymouth Arg and Bradford PA
1950–51 Grimsby T and Chesterfield
1951–52 Coventry C and QPR
1952–53 Southampton and Barnsley
1953–54 Brentford and Oldham Ath
1954–55 Ipswich T and Derby Co
1955–56 Plymouth Arg and Hull C
1956–57 Port Vale and Bury
1957–58 Doncaster R and Notts Co
1958–59 Barnsley and Grimsby T
1959–60 Bristol C and Hull C
1960–61 Lincoln C and Portsmouth
1961–62 Brighton & HA and Bristol R
1962–63 Walsall and Luton T
1963–64 Grimsby T and Scunthorpe U
1964–65 Swindon T and Swansea T
1965–66 Middlesbrough and Leyton Orient
1966–67 Northampton T and Bury
1967–68 Plymouth Arg and Rotherham U
1968–69 Fulham and Bury
1969–70 Preston NE and Aston Villa
1970–71 Blackburn R and Bolton W
1971–72 Charlton Ath and Watford
1972–73 Huddersfield T and Brighton & HA
1973–74 Crystal Palace, Preston NE, Swindon T
1974–75 Millwall, Cardiff C, Sheffield W
1975–76 Oxford U, York C, Portsmouth
1976–77 Carlisle U, Plymouth Arg, Hereford U
1977–78 Blackpool, Mansfield T, Hull C
1978–79 Sheffield U, Millwall, Blackburn R
1979–80 Fulham, Burnley, Charlton Ath
1980–81 Preston NE, Bristol C, Bristol R
1981–82 Cardiff C, Wrexham, Orient
1982–83 Rotherham U, Burnley, Bolton W
1983–84 Derby Co, Swansea C, Cambridge U
1984–85 Notts Co, Cardiff C, Wolverhampton W
1985–86 Carlisle U, Middlesbrough, Fulham
1986–87 Sunderland**, Grimsby T, Brighton & HA
1987–88 Huddersfield T, Reading, Sheffield U**
1988–89 Shrewsbury T, Birmingham C, Walsall
1989–90 Bournemouth, Bradford C, Stoke C
1990–91 WBA and Hull C
1991–92 Plymouth Arg, Brighton & HA, Port Vale

FIRST DIVISION TO SECOND DIVISION (1992–93 to 2003–04)

1992–93 Brentford, Cambridge U, Bristol R
1993–94 Birmingham C, Oxford U, Peterborough U
1994–95 Swindon T, Burnley, Bristol C, Notts Co
1995–96 Millwall, Watford, Luton T
1996–97 Grimsby T, Oldham Ath, Southend U
1997–98 Manchester C, Stoke C, Reading
1998–99 Bury, Oxford U, Bristol C
1999–2000 Walsall, Port Vale, Swindon T
2000–01 Huddersfield T, QPR, Tranmere R
2001–02 Crewe Alex, Barnsley, Stockport Co
2002–03 Sheffield W, Brighton & HA, Grimsby T
2003–04 Walsall, Bradford C, Wimbledon

FOOTBALL LEAGUE CHAMPIONSHIP TO FOOTBALL LEAGUE ONE (2004–05 to 2021–22)

2004–05 Gillingham, Nottingham F, Rotherham U
2005–06 Crewe Alex, Millwall, Brighton & HA
2006–07 Southend U, Luton T, Leeds U
2007–08 Leicester C, Scunthorpe U, Colchester U
2008–09 Norwich C, Southampton, Charlton Ath
2009–10 Sheffield W, Plymouth Arg, Peterborough U
2010–11 Preston NE, Sheffield U, Scunthorpe U
2011–12 Portsmouth, Coventry C, Doncaster R
2012–13 Peterborough U, Wolverhampton W, Bristol C
2013–14 Doncaster R, Barnsley, Yeovil T
2014–15 Millwall, Wigan Ath, Blackpool
2015–16 Charlton Ath, Milton Keynes D, Bolton W
2016–17 Blackburn R, Wigan Ath, Rotherham U
2017–18 Barnsley, Burton Alb, Sunderland
2018–19 Rotherham U, Bolton W, Ipswich T
2019–20 Charlton Ath, Wigan Ath, Hull C
2020–21 Wycombe W, Rotherham U, Sheffield W
2021–22 Peterborough U, Derby Co, Barnsley

DIVISION 3 TO DIVISION 4 (1958–59 to 1991–92)

1958–59 Stockport Co, Doncaster R, Notts Co, Rochdale
1959–60 York C, Mansfield T, Wrexham, Accrington S
1960–61 Tranmere R, Bradford C, Colchester U, Chesterfield
1961–62 Torquay U, Lincoln C, Brentford, Newport Co
1962–63 Bradford PA, Brighton & HA, Carlisle U, Halifax T
1963–64 Millwall, Crewe Alex, Wrexham, Notts Co
1964–65 Luton T, Port Vale, Colchester U, Barnsley
1965–66 Southend U, Exeter C, Brentford, York C
1966–67 Swansea T, Darlington, Doncaster R, Workington
1967–68 Grimsby T, Colchester U, Scunthorpe U, Peterborough U (demoted)
1968–69 Northampton T, Hartlepool, Crewe Alex, Oldham Ath
1969–70 Bournemouth, Southport, Barrow, Stockport Co
1970–71 Reading, Bury, Doncaster R, Gillingham
1971–72 Mansfield T, Barnsley, Torquay U, Bradford C
1972–73 Rotherham U, Brentford, Swansea C, Scunthorpe U
1973–74 Cambridge U, Shrewsbury T, Southport, Rochdale
1974–75 Bournemouth, Tranmere R, Watford, Huddersfield T
1975–76 Aldershot, Colchester U, Southend U, Halifax T
1976–77 Reading, Northampton T, Grimsby T, York C
1977–78 Port Vale, Bradford C, Hereford U, Portsmouth
1978–79 Peterborough U, Walsall, Tranmere R, Lincoln C
1979–80 Bury, Southend U, Mansfield T, Wimbledon
1980–81 Sheffield U, Colchester U, Blackpool, Hull C
1981–82 Wimbledon, Swindon T, Bristol C, Chester
1982–83 Reading, Wrexham, Doncaster R, Chesterfield
1983–84 Scunthorpe U, Southend U, Port Vale, Exeter C
1984–85 Burnley, Orient, Preston NE, Cambridge U
1985–86 Lincoln C, Cardiff C, Wolverhampton W, Swansea C
1986–87 Bolton W**, Carlisle U, Darlington, Newport Co
1987–88 Rotherham U**, Grimsby T, York C, Doncaster R
1988–89 Southend U, Chesterfield, Gillingham, Aldershot
1989–90 Cardiff C, Northampton T, Blackpool, Walsall
1990–91 Crewe Alex, Rotherham U, Mansfield T
1991–92 Bury, Shrewsbury T, Torquay U, Darlington

*** Relegated after play-offs.*

SECOND DIVISION TO THIRD DIVISION (1992–93 to 2003–04)

1992–93 Preston NE, Mansfield T, Wigan Ath, Chester C
1993–94 Fulham, Exeter C, Hartlepool U, Barnet
1994–95 Cambridge U, Plymouth Arg, Cardiff C, Chester C, Leyton Orient
1995–96 Carlisle U, Swansea C, Brighton & HA, Hull C
1996–97 Peterborough U, Shrewsbury T, Rotherham U, Notts Co
1997–98 Brentford, Plymouth Arg, Carlisle U, Southend U
1998–99 York C, Northampton T, Lincoln C, Macclesfield T
1999–2000 Cardiff C, Blackpool, Scunthorpe U, Chesterfield
2000–01 Bristol R, Luton T, Swansea C, Oxford U
2001–02 Bournemouth, Bury, Wrexham, Cambridge U
2002–03 Cheltenham T, Huddersfield T, Mansfield T Northampton T
2003–04 Grimsby T, Rushden & D, Notts Co, Wycombe W

FOOTBALL LEAGUE ONE TO FOOTBALL LEAGUE TWO (2004–05 to 2021–22)

2004–05 Torquay U, Wrexham, Peterborough U, Stockport Co
2005–06 Hartlepool U, Milton Keynes D, Swindon T, Walsall
2006–07 Chesterfield, Bradford C, Rotherham U, Brentford
2007–08 Bournemouth, Gillingham, Port Vale, Luton T
2008–09 Northampton T, Crewe Alex, Cheltenham T, Hereford U
2009–10 Gillingham, Wycombe W, Southend U, Stockport Co
2010–11 Dagenham & R, Bristol R, Plymouth Arg, Swindon T
2011–12 Wycombe W, Chesterfield, Exeter C, Rochdale
2012–13 Scunthorpe U, Bury, Hartlepool U, Portsmouth
2013–14 Tranmere R, Carlisle U, Shrewsbury T, Stevenage
2014–15 Notts Co, Crawley T, Leyton Orient, Yeovil T
2015–16 Doncaster R, Blackpool, Colchester U, Crewe Alex
2016–17 Port Vale, Swindon T, Coventry C, Chesterfield
2017–18 Oldham Ath, Northampton T, Milton Keynes D, Bury
2018–19 Plymouth Arg, Walsall, Scunthorpe U, Bradford C
2019–20 Tranmere R, Southend U, Bolton W
2020–21 Rochdale, Northampton T, Swindon T, Bristol R
2021–22 Gillingham, Doncaster R, AFC Wimbledon, Crewe Alex

LEAGUE STATUS FROM 1986–87

RELEGATED FROM LEAGUE

1986–87 Lincoln C
1987–88 Newport Co
1988–89 Darlington
1989–90 Colchester U
1990–91 —
1991–92 —
1992–93 Halifax T
1993–94 —
1994–95 —
1995–96 —
1996–97 Hereford U
1997–98 Doncaster R
1998–99 Scarborough
1999–2000 Chester C
2000–01 Barnet
2001–02 Halifax T
2002–03 Shrewsbury T, Exeter C
2003–04 Carlisle U, York C
2004–05 Kidderminster H, Cambridge U
2005–06 Oxford U, Rushden & D
2006–07 Boston U, Torquay U
2007–08 Mansfield T, Wrexham
2008–09 Chester C, Luton T
2009–10 Grimsby T, Darlington
2010–11 Lincoln C, Stockport Co
2011–12 Hereford U, Macclesfield T
2012–13 Barnet, Aldershot T
2013–14 Bristol R, Torquay U
2014–15 Cheltenham T, Tranmere R
2015–16 Dagenham & R, York C
2016–17 Hartlepool U, Leyton Orient
2017–18 Barnet, Chesterfield
2018–19 Notts Co, Yeovil T
2019–20 Macclesfield T
2020–21 Southend U, Grimsby T
2021–22 Oldham Ath, Scunthorpe U

PROMOTED TO LEAGUE

1986–87 Scarborough
1987–88 Lincoln C
1988–89 Maidstone U
1989–90 Darlington
1990–91 Barnet
1991–92 Colchester U
1992–93 Wycombe W
1993–94 —
1994–95 —
1995–96 —
1996–97 Macclesfield T
1997–98 Halifax T
1998–99 Cheltenham T
1999–2000 Kidderminster H
2000–01 Rushden & D
2001–02 Boston U
2002–03 Yeovil T, Doncaster R
2003–04 Chester C, Shrewsbury T
2004–05 Barnet, Carlisle U
2005–06 Accrington S, Hereford U
2006–07 Dagenham & R, Morecambe
2007–08 Aldershot T, Exeter C
2008–09 Burton Alb, Torquay U
2009–10 Stevenage B, Oxford U
2010–11 Crawley T, AFC Wimbledon
2011–12 Fleetwood T, York C
2012–13 Mansfield T, Newport Co
2013–14 Luton T, Cambridge U
2014–15 Barnet, Bristol R
2015–16 Cheltenham T, Grimsby T
2016–17 Lincoln C, Forest Green R
2017–18 Macclesfield T, Tranmere R
2018–19 Leyton Orient, Salford C
2019–20 Barrow, Harrogate T
2020–21 Sutton U, Hartlepool U
2021–22 Stockport Co, Grimsby T

APPLICATIONS FOR RE-ELECTION

FOURTH DIVISION

Eleven: Hartlepool U.
Seven: Crewe Alex.
Six: Barrow (lost League place to Hereford U 1972), Halifax T, Rochdale, Southport (lost League place to Wigan Ath 1978), York C.
Five: Chester C, Darlington, Lincoln C, Stockport Co, Workington (lost League place to Wimbledon 1977).
Four: Bradford PA (lost League place to Cambridge U 1970), Newport Co, Northampton T.
Three: Doncaster R, Hereford U.
Two: Bradford C, Exeter C, Oldham Ath, Scunthorpe U, Torquay U.
One: Aldershot, Colchester U, Gateshead (lost League place to Peterborough U 1960), Grimsby T, Swansea C, Tranmere R, Wrexham, Blackpool, Cambridge U, Preston NE.

Accrington S resigned and Oxford U were elected 1962.
Port Vale were forced to re-apply following expulsion in 1968.
Aldershot expelled March 1992. Maidstone U resigned August 1992.

THIRD DIVISIONS NORTH & SOUTH

Seven: Walsall.
Six: Exeter C, Halifax T, Newport Co.
Five: Accrington S, Barrow, Gillingham, New Brighton, Southport.
Four: Rochdale, Norwich C.
Three: Crystal Palace, Crewe Alex, Darlington, Hartlepool U, Merthyr T, Swindon T.
Two: Aberdare Ath, Aldershot, Ashington, Bournemouth, Brentford, Chester, Colchester U, Durham C, Millwall, Nelson, QPR, Rotherham U, Southend U, Tranmere R, Watford, Workington.
One: Bradford C, Bradford PA, Brighton & HA, Bristol R, Cardiff C, Carlisle U, Charlton Ath, Gateshead, Grimsby T, Mansfield T, Shrewsbury T, Torquay U, York C.

ENGLISH LEAGUE ATTENDANCES 2021–22

PREMIER LEAGUE ATTENDANCES

	Average Gate			*Season 2021–22*	
	2019–20	*2021–22*	*+/–%*	*Highest*	*Lowest*
Arsenal	60,279	59,776	–0.83	60,223	58,729
Aston Villa	41,661	41,681	+0.05	42,045	40,290
Brentford	11,699	16,912	+44.56	17,094	16,479
Brighton & HA	30,358	30,943	+1.93	31,637	29,485
Burnley	20,260	19,438	–4.06	22,000	16,910
Chelsea	40,563	37,812	–6.78	40,113	31,478
Crystal Palace	25,060	24,282	–3.11	25,434	22,445
Everton	39,150	38,968	–0.47	40,000	38,203
Leeds U	35,321	36,308	+2.79	36,715	35,558
Leicester C	32,061	31,941	–0.38	32,236	30,892
Liverpool	53,143	52,998	–0.27	53,213	52,550
Manchester C	54,361	52,774	–2.92	53,395	51,437
Manchester U	72,726	73,150	+0.58	73,564	72,732
Newcastle U	48,251	51,487	+6.71	52,281	44,017
Norwich C	27,025	26,810	–0.80	27,066	26,361
Southampton	29,675	29,939	+0.89	31,588	26,951
Tottenham H	59,384	56,523	–4.82	62,027	40,539
Watford	20,837	20,598	–1.14	21,142	20,012
West Ham U	59,896	58,367	–2.55	59,972	41,027
Wolverhampton W	31,360	30,765	–1.90	31,842	29,658

TOTAL ATTENDANCES:	15,037,940 (380 games) Average 39,574 (+0.65%)
HIGHEST:	73,564 Manchester U v Chelsea
LOWEST:	16,479 Brentford v Arsenal
HIGHEST AVERAGE:	73,150 Manchester U
LOWEST AVERAGE:	16,912 Brentford

SKY BET ENGLISH FOOTBALL LEAGUE CHAMPIONSHIP ATTENDANCES

	Average Gate			*Season 2021–22*	
	2019–20	*2021–22*	*+/–%*	*Highest*	*Lowest*
Barnsley	14,061	13,235	–5.87	16,961	11,322
Birmingham C	20,412	16,162	–20.82	18,659	9,922
Blackburn R	13,873	14,218	+2.48	30,428	9,038
Blackpool	8,770	12,104	+38.01	15,298	9,745
Bournemouth	10,510	9,594	–8.72	11,094	8,293
Bristol C	21,810	19,183	–12.05	21,942	16,878
Cardiff C	22,822	18,869	–17.32	27,280	16,882
Coventry C	6,677	19,541	+192.68	24,492	15,587
Derby Co	26,727	23,010	–13.91	32,211	16,123
Fulham	18,204	17,774	–2.36	19,538	15,789
Huddersfield T	21,748	17,325	–20.34	20,535	14,613
Hull C	11,553	12,888	+11.55	18,399	10,189
Luton T	10,048	9,857	–1.90	10,073	9,101
Middlesbrough	19,933	21,825	+9.49	29,832	17,931
Millwall	13,734	12,950	–5.70	16,734	10,183
Nottingham F	27,724	27,137	–2.11	29,293	23,830
Peterborough U	7,371	10,088	+36.87	12,870	6,832
Preston NE	13,579	12,608	–7.16	18,740	9,838
QPR	13,721	14,437	+5.21	17,648	11,591
Reading	14,407	13,193	–8.43	22,692	9,611
Sheffield U	30,869	27,611	–10.55	30,813	25,345
Stoke C	22,828	20,921	–8.35	26,384	17,720
Swansea C	16,151	17,389	+7.66	19,288	15,927
WBA	24,053	21,875	–9.06	24,870	19,659

TOTAL ATTENDANCES:	9,268,320 (552 games) Average 16,821 (–9.64%)
HIGHEST:	32,211 Derby Co v Birmingham C
LOWEST:	6,832 Peterborough U v Swansea C
HIGHEST AVERAGE:	27,611 Sheffield U
LOWEST AVERAGE:	9,594 Bournemouth

Due to the COVID-19 pandemic, the majority of matches in 2020–21 were played behind closed doors. The comparison here is from the 2019–20 season.

SKY BET ENGLISH FOOTBALL LEAGUE ONE ATTENDANCES

	Average Gate			Season 2021–22	
	2019–20	2021–22	+/–%	Highest	Lowest
Accrington S	2,862	2,915	+1.83	4,870	1,746
AFC Wimbledon	4,383	7,688	+75.39	8,502	6,138
Bolton W	11,511	15,439	+34.12	20,892	12,501
Burton Alb	2,986	3,229	+8.11	4,763	1,946
Cambridge U	4,178	5,668	+35.65	7,944	4,019
Charlton Ath	18,017	15,592	–13.46	26,376	8,807
Cheltenham T	3,203	4,239	+32.34	5,744	2,762
Crewe Alex	4,580	4,523	–1.25	6,325	3,285
Doncaster R	8,252	6,906	–16.31	11,217	5,396
Fleetwood T	3,130	3,228	+3.12	5,019	2,226
Gillingham	5,148	5,139	–0.18	8,542	3,115
Ipswich T	19,549	21,779	+11.41	29,005	18,111
Lincoln C	8,986	8,773	–2.37	10,346	7,571
Milton Keynes D	9,246	9,255	+0.10	15,311	6,564
Morecambe	2,264	4,310	+90.37	5,831	3,173
Oxford U	7,636	8,463	+10.82	11,690	5,654
Plymouth Arg	10,338	13,130	+27.01	16,087	10,453
Portsmouth	17,804	15,003	–15.73	17,418	11,470
Rotherham U	8,906	9,337	+4.84	11,522	8,004
Sheffield W	23,733	22,470	–5.32	33,394	18,581
Shrewsbury T	6,059	6,216	+2.59	8,369	4,510
Sunderland	30,118	30,847	+2.42	38,395	26,516
Wigan Ath	11,347	10,343	–8.85	20,136	8,098
Wycombe W	5,521	5,662	+2.54	9,005	3,391

TOTAL ATTENDANCES: 5,523,493 (552 games)
Average 10,006 (+14.32%)
HIGHEST: 38,395 Sunderland v Doncaster R
LOWEST: 1,746 Accrington S v AFC Wimbledon
HIGHEST AVERAGE: 30,847 Sunderland
LOWEST AVERAGE: 2,915 Accrington S

SKY BET ENGLISH FOOTBALL LEAGUE TWO ATTENDANCES

	Average Gate			Season 2021–22	
	2019–20	2021–22	+/–%	Highest	Lowest
Barrow	2,010	3,202	+59.32	4,658	2,116
Bradford C	14,309	15,450	+7.97	18,283	13,646
Bristol R	7,348	7,512	+2.23	9,790	6,005
Carlisle U	4,140	4,966	+19.95	8,514	3,172
Colchester U	3,634	2,813	–22.61	6,140	2,028
Crawley T	2,232	2,277	+2.03	3,572	1,483
Exeter C	4,847	5,312	+9.59	8,147	3,823
Forest Green R	2,542	2,678	+5.36	4,128	1,829
Harrogate T	1,301	2,312	+77.74	3,180	1,564
Hartlepool U	3,355	5,195	+54.85	6,112	4,214
Leyton Orient	5,504	5,116	–7.06	6,623	3,413
Mansfield T	4,419	5,107	+15.57	7,374	3,695
Newport Co	3,867	4,194	+8.46	6,237	1,687
Northampton T	5,101	5,366	+5.20	7,764	4,059
Oldham Ath	3,466	4,976	+43.56	8,199	3,492
Port Vale	4,862	6,104	+25.55	10,840	4,311
Rochdale	3,632	2,918	–19.66	5,234	2,041
Salford C	2,997	2,152	–28.19	3,765	1,290
Scunthorpe U	3,546	2,781	–21.58	5,014	2,009
Stevenage	2,906	2,893	–0.46	4,642	1,808
Sutton U	1,722	3,088	+79.35	4,010	2,427
Swindon T	7,788	9,603	+23.31	13,355	7,306
Tranmere R	6,777	6,427	–5.16	10,924	3,500
Walsall	4,664	5,067	+8.64	9,089	3,609

TOTAL ATTENDANCES: 2,698,518 (552 games)
Average 4,897 (+4.58%)
HIGHEST: 18,283 Bradford C v Carlisle U
LOWEST: 1,290 Salford C v Crawley T
HIGHEST AVERAGE: 15,450 Bradford C
LOWEST AVERAGE: 2,152 Salford C

LEAGUE ATTENDANCES SINCE 1946–47

Season	*Matches*	*Total*	*Div. 1*	*Div. 2*	*Div. 3 (S)*	*Div. 3 (N)*
1946–47	1848	35,604,606	15,005,316	11,071,572	5,664,004	3,863,714
1947–48	1848	40,259,130	16,732,341	12,286,350	6,653,610	4,586,829
1948–49	1848	41,271,414	17,914,667	11,353,237	6,998,429	5,005,081
1949–50	1848	40,517,865	17,278,625	11,694,158	7,104,155	4,440,927
1950–51	2028	39,584,967	16,679,454	10,780,580	7,367,884	4,757,109
1951–52	2028	39,015,866	16,110,322	11,066,189	6,958,927	4,880,428
1952–53	2028	37,149,966	16,050,278	9,686,654	6,704,299	4,708,735
1953–54	2028	36,174,590	16,154,915	9,510,053	6,311,508	4,198,114
1954–55	2028	34,133,103	15,087,221	8,988,794	5,996,017	4,051,071
1955–56	2028	33,150,809	14,108,961	9,080,002	5,692,479	4,269,367
1956–57	2028	32,744,405	13,803,037	8,718,162	5,622,189	4,601,017
1957–58	2028	33,562,208	14,468,652	8,663,712	6,097,183	4,332,661
		Total	*Div. 1*	*Div. 2*	*Div. 3*	*Div. 4*
1958–59	2028	33,610,985	14,727,691	8,641,997	5,946,600	4,276,697
1959–60	2028	32,538,611	14,391,227	8,399,627	5,739,707	4,008,050
1960–61	2028	28,619,754	12,926,948	7,033,936	4,784,256	3,874,614
1961–62	2015	27,979,902	12,061,194	7,453,089	5,199,106	3,266,513
1962–63	2028	28,885,852	12,490,239	7,792,770	5,341,362	3,261,481
1963–64	2028	28,535,022	12,486,626	7,594,158	5,419,157	3,035,081
1964–65	2028	27,641,168	12,708,752	6,984,104	4,436,245	3,512,067
1965–66	2028	27,206,980	12,480,644	6,914,757	4,779,150	3,032,429
1966–67	2028	28,902,596	14,242,957	7,253,819	4,421,172	2,984,648
1967–68	2028	30,107,298	15,289,410	7,450,410	4,013,087	3,354,391
1968–69	2028	29,382,172	14,584,851	7,382,390	4,339,656	3,075,275
1969–70	2028	29,600,972	14,868,754	7,581,728	4,223,761	2,926,729
1970–71	2028	28,194,146	13,954,337	7,098,265	4,377,213	2,764,331
1971–72	2028	28,700,729	14,484,603	6,769,308	4,697,392	2,749,426
1972–73	2028	25,448,642	13,998,154	5,631,730	3,737,252	2,081,506
1973–74	2027	24,982,203	13,070,991	6,326,108	3,421,624	2,163,480
1974–75	2028	25,577,977	12,613,178	6,955,970	4,086,145	1,992,684
1975–76	2028	24,896,053	13,089,861	5,798,405	3,948,449	2,059,338
1976–77	2028	26,182,800	13,647,585	6,250,597	4,152,218	2,132,400
1977–78	2028	25,392,872	13,255,677	6,474,763	3,332,042	2,330,390
1978–79	2028	24,540,627	12,704,549	6,153,223	3,374,558	2,308,297
1979–80	2028	24,623,975	12,163,002	6,112,025	3,999,328	2,349,620
1980–81	2028	21,907,569	11,392,894	5,175,442	3,637,854	1,701,379
1981–82	2028	20,006,961	10,420,793	4,750,463	2,836,915	1,998,790
1982–83	2028	18,766,158	9,295,613	4,974,937	2,943,568	1,552,040
1983–84	2028	18,358,631	8,711,448	5,359,757	2,729,942	1,557,484
1984–85	2028	17,849,835	9,761,404	4,030,823	2,667,008	1,390,600
1985–86	2028	16,488,577	9,037,854	3,551,968	2,490,481	1,408,274
1986–87	2028	17,379,218	9,144,676	4,168,131	2,350,970	1,715,441
1987–88	2030	17,959,732	8,094,571	5,341,599	2,751,275	1,772,287
1988–89	2036	18,464,192	7,809,993	5,887,805	3,035,327	1,791,067
1989–90	2036	19,445,442	7,883,039	6,867,674	2,803,551	1,891,178
1990–91	2036	19,508,202	8,618,709	6,285,068	2,835,759	1,768,666
1991–92	2064*	20,487,273	9,989,160	5,809,787	2,993,352	1,694,974
		Total	*Premier*	*Div. 1*	*Div. 2*	*Div. 3*
1992–93	2028	20,657,327	9,759,809	5,874,017	3,483,073	1,540,428
1993–94	2028	21,683,381	10,644,551	6,487,104	2,972,702	1,579,024
1994–95	2028	21,856,020	11,213,168	6,044,293	3,037,752	1,560,807
1995–96	2036	21,844,416	10,469,107	6,566,349	2,843,652	1,965,308
1996–97	2036	22,783,163	10,804,762	6,931,539	3,195,223	1,851,639
1997–98	2036	24,692,608	11,092,106	8,330,018	3,503,264	1,767,220
1998–99	2036	25,435,542	11,620,326	7,543,369	4,169,697	2,102,150
1999–2000	2036	25,341,090	11,668,497	7,810,208	3,700,433	2,161,952
2000–01	2036	26,030,167	12,472,094	7,909,512	3,488,166	2,160,395
2001–02	2036	27,756,977	13,043,118	8,352,128	3,963,153	2,398,578
2002–03	2036	28,343,386	13,468,965	8,521,017	3,892,469	2,460,935
2003–04	2036	29,197,510	13,303,136	8,772,780	4,146,495	2,975,099
		Total	*Premier*	*Championship*	*League One*	*League Two*
2004–05	2036	29,245,870	12,878,791	9,612,761	4,270,674	2,483,644
2005–06	2036	29,089,084	12,871,643	9,719,204	4,183,011	2,315,226
2006–07	2036	29,541,949	13,058,115	10,057,813	4,135,599	2,290,422
2007–08	2036	29,914,212	13,708,875	9,397,036	4,412,023	2,396,278
2008–09	2036	29,881,966	13,527,815	9,877,552	4,171,834	2,304,765
2009–10	2036	30,057,892	12,977,251	9,909,882	5,043,099	2,127,660
2010–11	2036	29,459,105	13,406,990	9,595,236	4,150,547	2,306,332
2011–12	2036	29,454,401	13,148,465	9,784,100	4,091,897	2,429,939
2012–13	2036	29,225,443	13,653,958	9,662,232	3,485,290	2,423,963
2013–14	2036	29,629,309	13,930,810	9,168,922	4,126,701	2,402,876
2014–15	2036	30,052,575	13,746,753	9,838,940	3,884,414	2,582,468
2015–16	2036	30,207,923	13,852,291	9,705,865	3,955,385	2,694,382
2016–17	2036	31,727,248	13,612,316	11,106,918	4,385,178	2,622,836
2017–18	2036	32,656,695	14,560,349	11,313,826	4,303,525	2,478,995
2018–19	2035†	32,911,714	14,515,181	11,119,775	4,811,797	2,464,961
2019–20	1572‡	25,151,300	11,323,981	8,265,475	3,501,237	2,060,607
2020–21	*Due to the COVID-19 pandemic, the majority of matches were played behind closed doors.*					
2021–22	2036	32,528,271	15,037,940	9,268,320	5,523,493	2,698,518

**Figures include matches played by Aldershot. †The Championship match between Bolton W v Brentford on 7 May 2019 was not played. ‡Premier League and Championship games behind closed doors from 17 June 2020. League 1 and 2 curtailed from 9 June 2020. Football League official total for their three divisions in 2001–02 was 14,716,162.*

LEAGUE CUP FINALS 1961–2022

*Played as a two-leg final until 1966. All subsequent finals played at Wembley except between 2001 and 2007 (inclusive) which were played at Millennium Stadium, Cardiff. *After extra time.*

FOOTBALL LEAGUE CUP

1961	Rotherham U v Aston Villa	2-0
	Aston Villa v Rotherham U	3-0*
	Aston Villa won 3-2 on aggregate.	
1962	Rochdale v Norwich C	0-3
	Norwich C v Rochdale	1-0
	Norwich C won 4-0 on aggregate.	
1963	Birmingham C v Aston Villa	3-1
	Aston Villa v Birmingham C	0-0
	Birmingham C won 3-1 on aggregate.	
1964	Stoke C v Leicester C	1-1
	Leicester C v Stoke C	3-2
	Leicester C won 4-3 on aggregate.	
1965	Chelsea v Leicester C	3-2
	Leicester C v Chelsea	0-0
	Chelsea won 3-2 on aggregate.	
1966	West Ham U v WBA	2-1
	WBA v West Ham U	4-1
	WBA won 5-3 on aggregate.	
1967	QPR v WBA	3-2
1968	Leeds U v Arsenal	1-0
1969	Swindon T v Arsenal	3-1*
1970	Manchester C v WBA	2-1*
1971	Tottenham H v Aston Villa	2-0
1972	Stoke C v Chelsea	2-1
1973	Tottenham H v Norwich C	1-0
1974	Wolverhampton W v Manchester C	2-1
1975	Aston Villa v Norwich C	1-0
1976	Manchester C v Newcastle U	2-1
1977	Aston Villa v Everton	0-0
Replay	Aston Villa v Everton *(at Hillsborough)*	1-1*
Replay	Aston Villa v Everton *(at Old Trafford)*	3-2*
1978	Nottingham F v Liverpool	0-0*
Replay	Nottingham F v Liverpool *(at Old Trafford)*	1-0
1979	Nottingham F v Southampton	3-2
1980	Wolverhampton W v Nottingham F	1-0
1981	Liverpool v West Ham U	1-1*
Replay	Liverpool v West Ham U *(at Villa Park)*	2-1

MILK CUP

1982	Liverpool v Tottenham H	3-1*
1983	Liverpool v Manchester U	2-1*
1984	Liverpool v Everton	0-0*
Replay	Liverpool v Everton *(at Maine Road)*	1-0
1985	Norwich C v Sunderland	1-0
1986	Oxford U v QPR	3-0

LITTLEWOODS CUP

1987	Arsenal v Liverpool	2-1
1988	Luton T v Arsenal	3-2
1989	Nottingham F v Luton T	3-1
1990	Nottingham F v Oldham Ath	1-0

RUMBELOWS LEAGUE CUP

1991	Sheffield W v Manchester U	1-0
1992	Manchester U v Nottingham F	1-0

COCA-COLA CUP

1993	Arsenal v Sheffield W	2-1
1994	Aston Villa v Manchester U	3-1
1995	Liverpool v Bolton W	2-1
1996	Aston Villa v Leeds U	3-0
1997	Leicester C v Middlesbrough	1-1*
Replay	Leicester C v Middlesbrough *(at Hillsborough)*	1-0*
1998	Chelsea v Middlesbrough	2-0*

WORTHINGTON CUP

1999	Tottenham H v Leicester C	1-0
2000	Leicester C v Tranmere R	2-1
2001	Liverpool v Birmingham C	1-1*
	Liverpool won 5-4 on penalties.	
2002	Blackburn R v Tottenham H	2-1
2003	Liverpool v Manchester U	2-0

CARLING CUP

2004	Middlesbrough v Bolton W	2-1
2005	Chelsea v Liverpool	3-2*
2006	Manchester U v Wigan Ath	4-0
2007	Chelsea v Arsenal	2-1
2008	Tottenham H v Chelsea	2-1*
2009	Manchester U v Tottenham H	0-0*
	Manchester U won 4-1 on penalties.	
2010	Manchester U v Aston Villa	2-1
2011	Birmingham C v Arsenal	2-1
2012	Liverpool v Cardiff C	2-2*
	Liverpool won 3-2 on penalties.	

CAPITAL ONE CUP

2013	Swansea C v Bradford C	5-0
2014	Manchester C v Sunderland	3-1
2015	Chelsea v Tottenham H	2-0
2016	Manchester C v Liverpool	1-1*
	Manchester C won 3-1 on penalties.	

EFL CUP

2017	Manchester U v Southampton	3-2

CARABAO CUP

2018	Manchester C v Arsenal	3-0
2019	Manchester C v Chelsea	0-0*
	Manchester C won 4-3 on penalties.	
2020	Manchester C v Aston Villa	2-1
2021	Manchester C v Tottenham H	1-0
2022	Liverpool v Chelsea	0-0*
	Liverpool won 11-10 on penalties.	

LEAGUE CUP WINS

Liverpool 9, Manchester C 8, Aston Villa 5, Chelsea 5, Manchester U 5, Nottingham F 4, Tottenham H 4, Leicester C 3, Arsenal 2, Birmingham C 2, Norwich C 2, Wolverhampton W 2, Blackburn R 1, Leeds U 1, Luton T 1, Middlesbrough 1, Oxford U 1, QPR 1, Sheffield W 1, Stoke C 1, Swansea C 1, Swindon T 1, WBA 1.

APPEARANCES IN FINALS

Liverpool 13, Aston Villa 9, Chelsea 9, Manchester C 9, Manchester U 9, Tottenham H 9, Arsenal 8, Nottingham F 6, Leicester C 5, Norwich C 4, Birmingham C 3, Middlesbrough 3, WBA 3, Bolton W 2, Everton 2, Leeds U 2, Luton T 2, QPR 2, Sheffield W 2, Southampton 2, Stoke C 2, Sunderland 2, West Ham U 2, Wolverhampton W 2, Blackburn R 1, Bradford C 1, Cardiff C 1, Newcastle U 1, Oldham Ath 1, Oxford U 1, Rochdale 1, Rotherham U 1, Swansea C 1, Swindon T 1, Tranmere R 1, Wigan Ath 1.

APPEARANCES IN SEMI-FINALS

Liverpool 18, Tottenham H 17, Manchester U 16, Arsenal 16, Aston Villa 15, Chelsea 15, Manchester C 13, West Ham U 9, Blackburn R 6, Leicester C 6, Nottingham F 6, Birmingham C 5, Everton 5, Leeds U 5, Middlesbrough 5, Norwich C 5, Bolton W 4, Burnley 4, Crystal Palace 4, Ipswich T 4, Sheffield W 4, Sunderland 4, WBA 4, Bristol C 3, QPR 3, Southampton 3, Stoke C 3, Swindon T 3, Wolverhampton W 3, Cardiff C 2, Coventry C 2, Derby Co 2, Luton T 2, Oxford U 2, Plymouth Arg 2, Sheffield U 2, Tranmere R 2, Watford 2, Wimbledon 2, Blackpool 1, Bradford C 1, Brentford 1, Burton Alb 1, Bury 1, Carlisle U 1, Chester C 1, Huddersfield T 1, Hull C 1, Newcastle U 1, Oldham Ath 1, Peterborough U 1, Rochdale 1, Rotherham U 1, Shrewsbury T 1, Stockport Co 1, Swansea C 1, Walsall 1, Wigan Ath 1, Wycombe W 1.

CARABAO CUP 2021–22

▪ *Denotes player sent off.*

FIRST ROUND NORTH

Sunday, 1 August 2021

Sheffield W (0) 0

Huddersfield T (0) 0 12,860

Sheffield W: (433) Peacock-Farrell; Hunt J, Iorfa, Hutchinson, Palmer; Adeniran, Wing, Bannan (Luongo 84); Green (Dele-Bashiru 75), Paterson, Shodipo (Brown 34).
Huddersfield T: (433) Nicholls; Turton, Pearson, Colwill, Toffolo; High (Sinani 90), Hogg, O'Brien; Koroma (Thomas 57), Ward (Rhodes 81), Holmes.
Huddersfield T won 4-2 on penalties.
Referee: Darren Bond.

Tuesday, 10 August 2021

Barrow (0) 1 *(Sea 50)*

Scunthorpe U (0) 0 1320

Barrow: (352) Farman; Arthur (Grayson 70), Ellis, Ntlhe (Brown 78); Hutton, White, Banks, Devitt, Brough; Gordon (Zanzala 68), Sea.
Scunthorpe U: (532) Watson; Pugh, Davis (Wilson 81), Onariase, Taft, O'Malley; Perry, Kenyon (Beestin 68), Hippolyte; Loft, Bunn (Green 68).
Referee: Oliver Langford.

Blackburn R (1) 1 *(Dolan 22)*

Morecambe (0) 2 *(Stockton 52, Phillips 84 (pen))* 5283

Blackburn R: (352) Kaminski; Magloire (Davenport 65), Lenihan, Carter; Nyambe, Travis, Buckley (Butterworth 46), Rothwell (Gallagher 66), Pickering; Brereton, Dolan.
Morecambe: (433) Andresson; Mellor (Diagouraga 46), Lavelle, O'Connor, Leigh; Phillips, McLoughlin, Jones; Ayunga, Stockton, McDonald (Gibson 46 (Mensah 78)).
Referee: Tom Nield.

Bolton W (0) 0

Barnsley (0) 0 7147

Bolton W: (4231) Dixon; Jones, Santos, Johnston, Gordon; Williams, Lee (Sheehan 79); Isgrove, Sarcevic, Delfouneso (Bakayoko 55); Doyle (Kachunga 65).
Barnsley: (343) Walton; Moon, Helik, Halme; Miller, Styles (Kane 60), Benson, Williams; Oduor, Woodrow (Cole 60), Adeboyejo (Thompson 56).
Bolton W won 5-4 on penalties. Referee: Ollie Yates.

Derby Co (1) 3 *(Hutchinson 43, Kazim-Richards 71 (pen), Morrison 82)*

Salford C (2) 3 *(Turnbull 8, Morris 14, 74 (pen))* 4747

Derby Co: (4231) Allsop; Ebosele, Brown, Forsyth, Williams; Watson, Hutchinson (Kazim-Richards 66); Sibley, Morrison (Shinnie 88), Jozwiak; Stretton.
Salford C: (442) King; Golden, Eastham, Turnbull, Touray I; Morris, Lowe, Willock, Hunter (Burgess 65); McAleny (Lund 81), Elliott (Henderson 64).
Derby Co won 5-3 on penalties. Referee: James Bell.

Harrogate T v Rochdale
Tie awarded to Rochdale due to positive Covid tests at Harrogate T.

Hartlepool U (0) 0

Crewe Alex (0) 1 *(Ainley 50)* 3149

Hartlepool U: (532) Mitchell; Sterry, Byrne, Liddle (Ferguson 70), Odusina, Francis-Angol; Daly, Featherstone, Smith (Cullen 60); Molyneux (Olomola 60), Burey.
Crewe Alex: (433) Jaaskelainen; Ramsay, Sass-Davies▪, Offord, McFadzean; Lundstram, MacDonald, Ainley (Murphy 78); Long (Daniels 15), Porter (Mandron 46), Dale.
Referee: Thomas Bramall.

Hull C (0) 1 *(Lewis-Potter 55)*

Wigan Ath (0) 1 *(Humphrys 50)* 4139

Hull C: (433) Baxter; Emmanuel, Bernard, Greaves (Smith A 61), Fleming; Cannon, Smith M, Moncur (Wood 74); Scott, Eaves, Lewis-Potter (Jarvis 61).
Wigan Ath: (4231) Jamie Jones; Power (Lloyd 68), Naylor, Watts (Carragher 74), Robinson; Smith, Cousins; Aasgaard, Keane, Jordan Jones; Humphrys (Massey 68).
Wigan Ath won 8-7 on penalties. Referee: Martin Coy.

Mansfield T (0) 0

Preston NE (1) 3 *(Sinclair 45, 81, Jakobsen 71)* 2526

Mansfield T: (41212) Bishop; Gordon, Rawson, McLaughlin, Burke; Maris (Law 74); Clarke O (Johnson 78), Stirk; Lapslie; Bowery, Oates (Sinclair 65).
Preston NE: (3412) Iversen; Storey, Bauer, Hughes; van den Berg, Whiteman, Johnson, Cunningham; Potts (Thomas 83); Sinclair (Rodwell-Grant 82), Maguire (Jakobsen 67).
Referee: Ross Joyce.

Oldham Ath (0) 2 *(Bahamboula 59, Davies 68 (og))*

Tranmere R (1) 2 *(Foley 40, Nevitt 51)* 2684

Oldham Ath: (3421) Rogers; Jameson, Piergianni, Hart; Fage (Adams 63), Bowden, Cisse, Stobbs; Bahamboula (Vaughan 70), Keillor-Dunn; Blyth (Luamba 66).
Tranmere R: (4231) Doohan; Dacres-Cogley, Davies, Clarke, Maguire; Watson (Spearing 65), Foley; Morris, McManaman (Feeney 79), Glatzel; Nevitt (Dieseruvwe 60).
Oldham Ath won 4-3 on penalties. Referee: Scott Oldham.

Port Vale (0) 1 *(Proctor 67)*

Sunderland (1) 2 *(Hawkes 40, O'Brien 50 (pen))* 3267

Port Vale: (532) Stone; Worrall, Smith, Legge, Jones D (Cass 65), Benning; Garrity, Walker (Amoo 65), Pett; Wilson (Bailey 75), Proctor.
Sunderland: (4231) Patterson; Younger, Flanagan, Wright, Taylor (Doyle 74); Neil, O'Nien; Diamond (McGeady 65), Pritchard (Grigg 65), Hawkes; O'Brien.
Referee: Sam Allison.

Rotherham U (0) 1 *(Sadlier 76)*

Accrington S (1) 2 *(Charles 38, Bishop 86)* 3131

Rotherham U: (352) Johansson; Edmonds-Green, Ihiekwe, Mattock; Sadlier, Barlaser (Ogbene 46), Odofin (Wiles 68), Rathbone, Ferguson; Kayode, Ladapo (Smith 60).
Accrington S: (532) Savin; Rodgers, Sykes, Nottingham, Burgess, Pritchard; Pell (McConville 78), Morgan, Butcher; Charles, Bishop.
Referee: Will Finnie.

Sheffield U (1) 1 *(Brewster 24)*

Carlisle U (0) 0 6778

Sheffield U: (343) Verrips; Basham, Lopata, Gordon (Norwood 65); Bogle, Freeman, Brunt, Norrington-Davies; Brewster, Sharp (McBurnie 46), Smith (Jebbison 65).
Carlisle U: (3421) Jensen; Tanner, Feeney, Armer; Riley, Guy, Dixon (Dickenson 63), Charters (Mellish 63); Bell (Abrahams 72), Toure; Mampala.
Referee: James Oldham.

Shrewsbury T (0) 2 *(Udoh 69, 79)*

Lincoln C (0) 2 *(Hopper 49, Bishop 52)* 2069

Shrewsbury T: (3412) Marosi; Pennington, Pierre, Nurse; Bennett, Davis, Ogbeta, Leahy (Daniels 64); Vela; Bowman (Udoh 65), Pyke (Bloxham 85).
Lincoln C: (433) Griffiths; Poole, Montsma (Sorensen 68), Melbourne, Bramall; McGrandles, Sanders, Bishop (Fiorini 72); Adelakun (Longdon 72), Hopper, Scully.
Shrewsbury T won 4-2 on penalties. Referee: Andy Haines.

Stoke C (1) 2 *(Surridge 45, Souttar 77)*

Fleetwood T (0) 1 *(Chester 90 (og))* 4694

Stoke C: (3142) Davies; Souttar, Chester, Ostigard; Thompson; Ince, Porter (Vrancic 70), Clucas, Doughty; Surridge (Fletcher 70), Brown (Norton 76).
Fleetwood T: (352) Cairns; Hill, Holgate, Andrew; Halliday, Batty (Biggins 77), Matete, Camps, Clark; Pilkington (Morris 65), Edmondson (Morton 70).
Referee: Anthony Backhouse.

Walsall (0) 0

Doncaster R (0) 0 2384

Walsall: (4231) Rushworth; Leak (Ward 79), Taylor, Menayese, Mills; Osadebe, Labadie (Kinsella 56); Shade (Earing 70), Phillips, Kiernan; Wilkinson.
Doncaster R: (4231) Dahlberg; Knoyle, Williams R, Anderson, John (Horton 61); Bostock (Greaves▪ 72), Close; Williams E, Barlow, Gardner; Bogle (Cukur 75).
Doncaster R won 4-3 on penalties. Referee: John Busby.

Wednesday, 11 August 2021

Blackpool (1) 3 *(Connolly 31, Lavery 76, Anderson 78)*

Middlesbrough (0) 0 5836

Blackpool: (442) Grimshaw; Connolly, Ekpiteta, Casey, Husband; Bowler, James, Dougall (Ward 46), Hamilton (Anderson 63); Carey, Lavery (Yates 81).
Middlesbrough: (433) Lumley; Peltier, Wood-Gordon, Bamba, Robinson; Malley, Morsy (Sivi 63), Jones; Spence, Coburn (Ikpeazu 63), Payero (Hackney 71).
Referee: Robert Madley.

Nottingham F (2) 2 *(Joao Carvalho 39, 41)*

Bradford C (0) 1 *(Cooke 54)* 9514

Nottingham F: (4231) Horvath; Back, Fernandes (Yates 69), Harbottle (Tobias Figueiredo 67), Richardson; Fornah, Cafu; Zinckernagel (Nuno Da Costa 51), Joao Carvalho, Konate; Mighten.
Bradford C: (4231) O'Donnell; Cousin-Dawson, O'Connor, Canavan, Ridehalgh; Cooke, Watt; Gilliead (Crankshaw 83), Sutton (Eisa 34), Angol; Cook (Vernam 84).
Referee: Peter Wright.

FIRST ROUND SOUTH

Saturday, 31 July 2021

Bournemouth (1) 5 *(Brooks 35, 83, Solanke 47, Billing 72, Saydee 80)*

Milton Keynes D (0) 0 5746

Bournemouth: (433) Travers; Stacey (Zemura 41), Rossi, Kelly, Smith; Marcondes (Stanislas 66), Kilkenny, Billing; Brooks, Solanke (Saydee 76), Anthony.
Milton Keynes D: (352) Ravizzoli; Darling, O'Hora, Baldwin; Watson (Martin 75), O'Riley, Twine, Kasumu, Harvie; Brown (Robson 54), Eisa.
Referee: Sam Purkiss.

Tuesday, 10 August 2021

Birmingham C (0) 1 *(Oakley 75)*

Colchester U (0) 0 6199

Birmingham C: (41212) Trueman; Oakley, Gordon (Campbell 73), Friend, Castillo; Sunjic; Ivan Sanchez, Lakin; Graham; Aneke (McGree 74), Leko.
Colchester U: (4231) George; Welch-Hayes, Eastman, Smith, Clampin; Sarpong-Wiredu, Skuse (Kennedy 66); Coxe, Chilvers, Jasper (Judge 82); Nouble (Sears 72).
Referee: Declan Bourne.

Bristol R (0) 0

Cheltenham T (0) 2 *(May 58, Vassell 71)* 2409

Bristol R: (433) Belshaw; Kilgour, Taylor, Baldwin, Anderton; Westbrooke (Spence 70), Grant, Liddle (Langlais 70); Thomas (Jones 78), Saunders, Anderson H.
Cheltenham T: (352) Flinders; Horton, Tozer, Boyle; Long, Perry (Sercombe 66), Wright, Chapman (Hussey 80), Freestone; May (Vassell 65), Lloyd.
Referee: Lee Swabey.

Cambridge U (0) 0

Swindon T (0) 0 1825

Cambridge U: (4231) Mitov; Williams, Jones (Digby 73), Okedina (Taylor 58), Iredale; Weir, May; Knibbs (Ironside 72), Worman, Dunk; Smith.
Swindon T: (4231) Ward; Odimayo (Grant 63), Baudry (Hunt 40), Crichlow-Noble, Iandolo; Reed, East; McKirdy, Parsons, Payne; Simpson (Aguiar 69).
Cambridge U won 3-1 on penalties. Referee: Trevor Kettle.

Cardiff C (1) 3 *(Watkins 44, 50, Murphy 84)*

Sutton U (1) 2 *(Wilson 4, Rowe 90)* 3500

Cardiff C: (343) Smithies; Morrison, Flint, Nelson; Sang, Wintle, Vaulks, Davies T; Watkins (Colwill 78), Moore (Collins 86), Harris (Murphy 78).
Sutton U: (442) Bouzanis; Barden, Goodliffe, Rowe, Milsom; Ajiboye, Eastmond, Davis (Smith 85), Beautyman; Bugiel (Bennett 80), Wilson (Boldewijn 77).
Referee: Antony Coggins.

Charlton Ath (0) 0

AFC Wimbledon (1) 1 *(Osew 26)* 3372

Charlton Ath: (433) MacGillivray; Gunter, Elerewe, Pearce, Roddy; Morgan, Watson (Dobson 68), Clare; Ghandour (Stockley 68), Davison, Clayden (Powell 82).
AFC Wimbledon: (3412) Tzanev; Kalambayi, Heneghan (Rudoni 78), Csoka; Lawrence, Marsh, Hartigan, Osew (Alexander 75); Chislett; Pressley (Palmer 82), Mebude (Assal 64).
Referee: Robert Lewis.

Crawley T (0) 2 *(Ashford 55, Davies 90)*

Gillingham (1) 2 *(Sithole 3, Phillips 90)* 1904

Crawley T: (442) Nna Noukeu; Francomb, Francillette, Craig, Dallison; Frost (Tilley 69), Hessenthaler, Payne (Powell 88), Ferry; Ashford (Davies 80), Nadesan.
Gillingham: (41212) Chapman; Lintott, Maghoma, Ehmer, Akehurst (Tutonda 80); Bennett (Lloyd 61); Phillips, O'Keefe; Lee; Sithole, Carayol (Oliver 69).
Gillingham won 10-9 on penalties. Referee: Paul Howard.

Exeter C (0) 0

Wycombe W (0) 0 2555

Exeter C: (3412) Dawson; Sweeney, Ray (Grounds 67), Dyer; Caprice, Kite, Atangana (Dieng 56), Sparkes; Jay (Dodd 63); Brown, Seymour.
Wycombe W: (3421) Stockdale; Grimmer, Burley, Jacobson (Vokes 62); Freeman, Thompson (Horgan 46), Bloomfield (Pendlebury 45), Obita (McCarthy 46); KaiKai, Mehmeti; Samuel.
Wycombe W won 4-3 on penalties. Referee: David Rock.

Forest Green R (1) 2 *(Matt 11, Hendry 90)*

Bristol C (1) 2 *(Janneh 40, 67)* 2554

Forest Green R: (3412) Thomas; Godwin-Malife (Stevenson 46), Moore-Taylor (Bernard 46), Sweeney; Wilson, Hendry, Diallo, Cadden; Adams; Aitchison (Young 70), Matt.
Bristol C: (4231) O'Leary; Simpson, Kalas, Moore, Pring; Williams (Bakinson 39), Nagy (Palmer 63); Janneh, Massengo, Bell (Conway 69); Wells.
Forest Green R won 6-5 on penalties.
Referee: Darren Drysdale.

Ipswich T (0) 0

Newport Co (1) 1 *(Abraham 4)* 6144

Ipswich T: (442) Holy; Donacien, Woolfenden, Ndaba, Clements; Aluko (Fraser 58), El Mizouni, Humphreys, Dobra; Barry (Norwood 64), Bonne (Jackson 64).
Newport Co: (4231) Townsend; Lewis A, Woodiwiss, Clarke, Hall; Missilou, Livermore (Upson 54); Abraham, Azaz (Collins 64), Ellison (Telford 73); Greenidge.
Referee: Neil Hair.

Millwall (2) 2 *(Malone 21, Saville 27)*

Portsmouth (1) 1 *(Hackett-Fairchild 4)* 4021

Millwall: (352) Long; Leonard, Hutchinson, Cooper; Romeo, Wallace J (Mahoney 67), Kieftenbeld, Saville, Malone (Thompson 79); Bradshaw (Smith 66), Afobe.
Portsmouth: (4231) Bass; Johnson■, Raggett, Robertson, Ogilvie; Tunnicliffe, Williams (Jacobs 61); Hackett-Fairchild, Ahadme (Freeman 52), Curtis; Marquis (Hirst 46).
Referee: Charles Breakspear.

Peterborough U (0) 0

Plymouth Arg (2) 4 *(Hardie 23, 33, Jephcott 66, Camara 84)* 4021

Peterborough U: (4411) Cornell; Knight, Edwards, Kent, Burrows; Tomlinson, Hamilton (Barker 59), Grant, Randall; Poku (Ward 58); Jade-Jones (Kanu 18).
Plymouth Arg: (352) Cooper M; Wilson, Scarr, Galloway; Edwards, Camara, Houghton (Randell 78), Mayor (Law 42), Grant; Jephcott (Shirley 85), Hardie.
Referee: Ben Toner.

Reading (0) 0

Swansea C (1) 3 *(Latibeaudiere 18, Cabango 60, Piroe 83)* 4989

Reading: (4231) Southwood; Sackey, Holmes, McIntyre (Stickland 46), Abbey; Tetek, Osorio; Leavy (Bristow 64), Camara, Ehibhationham (Clarke 55); Puscas.
Swansea C: (3421) Benda; Cabango, Naughton (Joseph 65), Cooper; Latibeaudiere, Williams D, Grimes (Manning 65), Bidwell (McFayden 65); Whittaker, Dhanda; Piroe.
Referee: Sam Barrott.

Stevenage (2) 2 *(List 2, Coker 26)*

Luton T (2) 2 *(Jerome 5, Muskwe 40)* 3052

Stevenage: (442) Anang; Wildin, Vancooten, Cuthbert, Coker; Osborne, Taylor, Reeves, Carter (Smith J 78); List (Lines 70), Reid (Norris 59).
Luton T: (4231) Shea; Kioso, Osho, Lockyer, Beckwith; Lansbury, Rea; Muskwe (Pereira 72), Lee (Campbell 79), Mendes Gomes; Jerome (Cornick 72).
Stevenage won 3-0 on penalties. Referee: Gavin Ward.

Wednesday, 11 August 2021

Burton Alb (0) 1 *(Mousinho 90 (og))*

Oxford U (0) 1 *(Holland 85)* 1868

Burton Alb: (4231) Garratt; Brayford, Shaughnessy, Leak, Hamer; Oshilaja (Taylor 51), O'Connor; Akins, Powell, Smith (Rowe 78); Patrick (Blake-Tracy 90).
Oxford U: (4231) Eastwood; Forde, McNally, Thorniley, Chambers (Mousinho 87); Sykes, Gorrin; Bodin, McGuane (Johnson 76), Agyei; Winnall (Holland 70).
Oxford U won 4-2 on penalties.
Referee: Sebastian Stockbridge.

Coventry C (1) 1 *(Walker 13)*

Northampton T (0) 2 *(Etete 52, 70)* 5284

Coventry C: (4231) Wilson; Da Costa, Drysdale, Rose (Pask 63), Reid; Howley (Maatsen 63), Allen; Enobakhare (Waghorn 63), Jones, Shipley; Walker.
Northampton T: (532) Maxted; Hoskins, Nelson (Connolly 72), Horsfall, Guthrie, Koiki; Lewis, McWilliams, Pollock (Pinnock 56); Etete, Rose (Kabamba 60).
Referee: Ben Speedie.

Leyton Orient (0) 1 *(Drinan 74)*

QPR (1) 1 *(Dickie 16)* 4071

Leyton Orient: (4231) Vigouroux; James, Beckles, Happe, Wood; Pratley, Kyprianou; Sotiriou, Kemp, Archibald; Drinan.
QPR: (541) Archer; Kakay, Dickie, Dunne, Barbet (Kelman 61), Wallace (Odubajo 46); Adomah, Dozzell, Bettache (Ball 83), Thomas; Dykes.
QPR won 5-3 on penalties. Referee: Craig Hicks.

SECOND ROUND NORTH

Tuesday, 24 August 2021

Barrow (0) 0

Aston Villa (3) 6 *(Archer 10, 62, 88, El Ghazi 24 (pen), 45, Guilbert 75)* 5349

Barrow: (352) Farman; Brown, Ellis (Arthur 70), Grayson; Hutton, White (Williams 65), Taylor, Banks, Brough; Gordon (Kay 60), Zanzala.
Aston Villa: (4231) Steer; Guilbert (Lindley 82), Tuanzebe, Hause, Targett; Hourihane, Nakamba; Philogene-Bidace, Carney Chukwuemeka (Caleb Chukwuemeka 73), El Ghazi (Ramsey A 63); Archer.
Referee: Ivan Stankovic.

Blackpool (1) 2 *(Lavery 9, Bowler 87)*

Sunderland (1) 3 *(O'Brien 12, 57, 90)* 5756

Blackpool: (4231) Grimshaw; Casey, Keogh, Gretarsson, Garbutt; James, Antwi (Bowler 69); Hamilton (Anderson 78), Carey, John-Jules; Lavery (Yates 78).
Sunderland: (4231) Patterson; Huggins, Alves (Doyle 77), Wright, Cirkin; Winchester, Neil; Diamond, Pritchard (Embleton 73), O'Brien; Broadhead (Stewart 74).
Referee: Peter Wright.

Huddersfield T (1) 1 *(Lees 45)*

Everton (1) 2 *(Iwobi 26, Townsend 79)* 10,459

Huddersfield T: (352) Nicholls; Pearson, Lees (Turton 69), Sarr; Thomas, High (Koroma 80), Vallejo, Holmes, Toffolo; Sinani (O'Brien 69), Campbell.
Everton: (343) Begovic; Holgate, Keane, Branthwaite (Andre Gomes 57); Kenny, Gbamin, Davies (Digne 64), Nkounkou (Gray 75); Townsend, Kean■, Iwobi.
Referee: Matthew Donohue.

Leeds U (0) 3 *(Phillips 79, Harrison 85, 90)*

Crewe Alex (0) 0 34,154

Leeds U: (4231) Meslier; Shackleton, Llorente (Ayling 46), Struijk, Firpo; Forshaw (Klich 61), Phillips; Helder Costa, Roberts, Harrison; Rodrigo (Bamford 69).
Crewe Alex: (433) Jaaskelainen; Adebisi, Ramsay, Sass-Davies, Thomas T; Lundstram, Murphy (Griffiths 89), McFadzean; Knight (Johnson 76), Mandron, Finney (Ainley 69).
Referee: Ben Speedie.

Millwall (2) 3 *(Wallace M 39, 42, Smith 54)*

Cambridge U (1) 1 *(Williams 33)* 4005

Millwall: (343) Long; Ballard (Mitchell A 80), Pearce, Cooper; Mitchell B, Thompson (Saville 72), Evans, Wallace M; Mahoney, Smith (Bodvarsson 72), Bradshaw.
Cambridge U: (41212) Mitov; Williams, Jones (Digby 75), Masterson, Iredale; Weir; Worman, May; Tracey (Lankester 70); Smith, Knibbs (Ironside 75).
Referee: Neil Hair.

Morecambe (1) 2 *(O'Connor 45, Stockton 61)*

Preston NE (2) 4 *(Jakobsen 7, 33, Ledson 64, van den Berg 79)* 4334

Morecambe: (442) Andresson; Cooney, Lavelle, O'Connor, Leigh; Duffus (Phillips 80), McLoughlin (McPake 80), Diagouraga, McCalmont; Stockton, Gnahoua (McDonald 76).
Preston NE: (352) Rudd; van den Berg, Storey, Hughes; Rafferty (Bauer 75), Potts, Ledson, Johnson (Bayliss 83), Cunningham; Sinclair (Maguire 59), Jakobsen.
Referee: James Oldham.

Nottingham F (0) 0

Wolverhampton W (0) 4 *(Saiss 58, Daniel Podence 60, Trincao 86, Gibbs-White 88)* 10,769

Nottingham F: (4231) Horvath; Back, Fernandes, Harbottle, Richardson; Fornah, Colback; Hammond (Mighten 73), Garner (Cafu 73), Konate; Grabban (Taylor L 61).
Wolverhampton W: (3412) Ruddy; Kilman, Coady, Saiss; Hoever, Dendoncker, Joao Moutinho, Ait Nouri (Traore 82); Gibbs-White; Silva (Cundle 89), Daniel Podence (Trincao 66).
Referee: Andy Davies.

Oldham Ath (0) 0

Accrington S (0) 0 2362

Oldham Ath: (352) Walker; Clarke, Piergianni, Hart; Fage, Vaughan (Keillor-Dunn 61), Whelan, Diarra (Adams 69), Bahamboula; Hope (Dearnley 61), Luamba.
Accrington S: (352) Savin; Sherring, Sykes, Rodgers (Procter 57); Perritt (Charles 54), Pritchard (Leigh 54), Morgan, Butcher, Nolan; Mumbongo, Bishop.
Oldham Ath won 5-4 on penalties.
Referee: Sebastian Stockbridge.

Sheffield U (0) 2 *(Freeman 53, Sharp 76)*

Derby Co (1) 1 *(Sibley 44)* 7973

Sheffield U: (352) Verrips; Gordon, Lopata, Robinson; Bogle, McGoldrick (Ndiaye 62), Brunt, Freeman, Osborn; Jebbison (Fleck 46), Burke (Sharp 69).
Derby Co: (4231) Allsop; McDonald, Stearman, Forsyth, Williams; Watson, Brown; Sibley, Hutchinson, Jozwiak (Buchanan 63); Stretton (Borkovic 67).
Referee: Anthony Backhouse.

Shrewsbury T (0) 0

Rochdale (0) 2 *(Beesley 68 (pen), Cashman 77)* 2229

Shrewsbury T: (442) Marosi; Bennett, Pennington■, Ebanks-Landell, Nurse; Whalley (Daniels 78), Vela, Leshabela, Leahy; Cosgrove (Bloxham 72), Pyke (Udoh 65).
Rochdale: (343) Coleman; Taylor, O'Connell, Dorsett; O'Keeffe, Morley, Dooley (Brierley 90), Keohane; Cashman (Andrews 81), Beesley, Odoh (Newby 75).
Referee: Scott Oldham.

Stoke C (1) 2 *(Ince 38, Surridge 48)*

Doncaster R (0) 0 6193

Stoke C: (352) Davies; Chester, Batth, Fox; Ince, Porter (Vrancic 73), Sawyers, Thompson, Doughty; Surridge (Fletcher 66), Norton (Brown 66).
Doncaster R: (433) Jones; Knoyle, Blythe, John (Seaman 13), Horton; Smith (Harrison 81), Close (Rowe 46), Greaves; Williams E, Gardner, Barlow.
Referee: Marc Edwards.

Wigan Ath (0) 0

Bolton W (0) 0 11,660

Wigan Ath: (4231) Jamie Jones; Darikwa (Aasgaard 70), Naylor, Watts, Pearce; Smith, Power; Massey, Edwards (Lang 66), McClean (Jordan Jones 86); Humphrys.
Bolton W: (4231) Gilks; Brockbank (Jones 72), Baptiste, Johnston, Gordon; Lee, Thomason (Sarcevic 68); Delfouneso, Sheehan, Afolayan; Kachunga (Doyle 65).
Wigan Ath won 5-4 on penalties. Referee: Thomas Bramall.

Wednesday, 25 August 2021

Newcastle U (0) 0

Burnley (0) 0 30,082

Newcastle U: (532) Woodman; Manquillo (Saint-Maximin 76), Krafth, Lascelles, Clark, Lewis; Hendrick, Longstaff S, Fraser (Almiron 83); Joelinton, Gayle (Willock 76).
Burnley: (442) Hennessey; Bardsley, Collins, Mee, Pieters; Lennon (Taylor 59), Brownhill, Cork, McNeil; Wood, Rodriguez (Barnes 68).
Burnley won 4-3 on penalties. Referee: Oliver Langford.

SECOND ROUND SOUTH

Tuesday, 24 August 2021

Birmingham C (0) 0

Fulham (1) 2 *(Stansfield 26, Robinson 90)* 4783

Birmingham C: (343) Etheridge; Sanderson (Chang 73), Friend, Mitchell Roberts; Oakley, Sunjic (Lakin 61), McGree, Castillo; Leko, Aneke (Simmonds 62), Graham.
Fulham: (3421) Rodak; Odoi, Hector, Mawson; Knockaert, Pajaziti, Francois, Bryan; Reid (Onomah 90), Kebano (Ivan Cavaleiro 73); Stansfield (Robinson 86).
Referee: Sam Barrott.

Brentford (0) 3 *(Wissa 60, Mbeumo 75, Forss 86)*

Forest Green R (1) 1 *(Aitchison 8)* 12,137

Brentford: (4231) Fernandez; Roerslev (Canos 46), Sorensen (Ajer 45), Pinnock, Thompson; Bidstrup (Onyeka 46), Janelt; Dervisoglu (Mbeumo 68), Ghoddos, Wissa; Forss.
Forest Green R: (352) Thomas; Bernard, Cargill, Moore-Taylor; Edwards (Matt 79), Hendry, Diallo (March 34), Adams■, Cadden (Allen 74); Young (Wilson 59), Aitchison.
Referee: Will Finnie.

Cardiff C (0) 0

Brighton & HA (1) 2 *(Moder 9, Zeqiri 55)* 6013

Cardiff C: (532) Smithies; d'Almeida, Morrison (Denham 34), Flint, Nelson, Ng; Wintle, Vaulks, Bowen; Collins (Moore 67), Murphy (Colwill 67).
Brighton & HA: (4231) Steele; Mwepu (Ferguson 81), Tsoungui, Roberts, Karbownik; Alzate, Caicedo; Leonard (Moran 68), Richards (Offiah 68), Moder; Zeqiri.
Referee: James Bell.

Gillingham (1) 1 *(Oliver 20)*

Cheltenham T (1) 1 *(May 24)* 2151

Gillingham: (41212) Chapman; McKenzie, Ehmer, Bennett, Tutonda (Akehurst 37); Adshead; O'Keefe, Reeves (Carayol 76); Lee; Lloyd, Oliver (Tucker 46).
Cheltenham T: (532) Evans; Blair, Horton, Tozer, Long (Boyle 46), Freestone; Sercombe (Wright 60), Chapman, Perry; May (Thomas 66), Lloyd.
Cheltenham T won 5-4 on penalties. Referee: David Rock.

Northampton T (0) 0

AFC Wimbledon (0) 1 *(Hartigan 90)* 3257

Northampton T: (442) Maxted; McGowan, Guthrie, Horsfall, Mills; Connolly (Hoskins 76), Flores (Pinnock 66), Lewis, Koiki; Rose (Ashley-Seal 82), Etete.
AFC Wimbledon: (3412) Tzanev; Kalambayi, Heneghan, Csoka; Osew, Marsh, Hartigan, Guinness-Walker (Lawrence 63); Rudoni; Pressley (Palmer 74), Mebude (McCormick 73).
Referee: Andy Davies.

Norwich C (3) 6 *(Tzolis 12, 66, McLean 26, Rupp 34, Sargent 49, 75)*

Bournemouth (0) 0 20,090

Norwich C: (433) Gunn; Mumba, Zimmermann, Omobamidele, Williams (Giannoulis 76); Rupp (Idah 77), Sorensen, McLean (Gilmour 71); Dowell, Sargent, Tzolis.
Bournemouth: (433) Nyland; Camp, Rossi, Cook S, Davis; Kilkenny, Pearson, Taylor; Brooks (Mepham 64), Marcondes (Glover 64), Rogers (Saydee 82).
Referee: Charles Breakspear.

QPR (2) 2 *(Dickie 26, Chambers 40 (og))*

Oxford U (0) 0 8154

QPR: (3421) Archer; Kakay, Dickie (Gubbins 88), Dunne; Odubajo, Thomas, Dozzell, McCallum (Duke-Mckenna 64); Willock, Chair (Alfa 75); Kelman.
Oxford U: (433) Eastwood; Chambers, McNally, Moore, Seddon; Sykes, Gorrin, McGuane (Brannagan 46); Agyei, Winnall (Johnson 69), Holland (Whyte 46).
Referee: Tom Nield.

Stevenage (0) 2 *(List 50, Reid 77)*

Wycombe W (1) 2 *(Akinfenwa 23, De Barr 90)* 1934

Stevenage: (442) Anang; Wildin, Marshall, Prosser, Coker; Smith J, Taylor, Reeves, Read (Norris 67); List (Daly 66), Reid (Vancooten 80).
Wycombe W: (3421) Przybek; Ram, Tafazolli (Stewart 46), Jacobson; KaiKai, Burley (Horgan 66), Pendlebury, Obita; Samuel, Mehmeti; Akinfenwa (De Barr 71).
Wycombe W won 5-3 on penalties.
Referee: Declan Bourne.

Swansea C (1) 4 *(Lowe 29, Whittaker 79, 86, 90)*

Plymouth Arg (0) 1 *(Shirley 63)* 7491

Swansea C: (3421) Hamer; Latibeaudiere, Bennett (Naughton 68), Manning (Cooper 46); Joseph (Laird 78), Williams D, Fulton, Bidwell; Whittaker, Dhanda; Lowe.
Plymouth Arg: (532) Burton; Edwards, Tomlinson, Scarr, Gillesphey, Law (Cooper G 70); Camara (Houghton 61), Randell, Broom; Jephcott, Hardie (Shirley 58).
Referee: Robert Madley.

Watford (0) 1 *(Fletcher 86)*

Crystal Palace (0) 0 9011

Watford: (433) Foster; Ngakia (Femenia 62), Troost-Ekong, Sierralta, Rose; Louza, Etebo, Sema (Cleverley 76); Fletcher, King (Dennis 46), Hernandez.
Crystal Palace: (433) Butland; Tomkins (Mitchell 81), Andersen, Guehi, Ward; Gallagher (McArthur 63), Kouyate, Schlupp; Ayew, Mateta (Benteke 63), Zaha.
Referee: Tim Robinson.

Wednesday, 25 August 2021

Newport Co (0) 0

Southampton (3) 8 *(Broja 9, 57, Tella 25, Walker-Peters 44, Elyounoussi 48, 55, 90, Redmond 69)* 7002

Newport Co: (4231) Townsend; Lewis A, Farquharson, Clarke, Hall; Bennett (Greenidge 65), Dolan (Upson 46); Willmott, Azaz (Ellison 46), Missilou; Abraham.
Southampton: (442) Forster; Valery, Stephens, Bednarek, Walker-Peters; Elyounoussi, Diallo, Ward-Prowse (Walcott 70), Tella (Obafemi 65); Redmond, Broja (Long 65).
Referee: Darren Drysdale.

WBA (0) 0

Arsenal (3) 6 *(Aubameyang 17, 45, 62, Pepe 45, Saka 50, Lacazette 69)* 17,016

WBA: (343) Palmer; Kipre, Taylor (Richards 82), Shotton; Ingram, Castro, Snodgrass (King 74), Reach; Fellows, Zohore (Faal 64), Gardner-Hickman.
Arsenal: (4231) Ramsdale; Chambers, Holding, Kolasinac, Tavares; Elneny, Xhaka (Lacazette 67); Pepe, Odegaard (Maitland-Niles 61), Saka; Aubameyang (Martinelli 76).
Referee: David Webb.

THIRD ROUND

Tuesday, 21 September 2021

Brentford (5) 7 *(Forss 3 (pen), 16, 44, 60, Wissa 38, 87, Diarra 43 (og))*

Oldham Ath (0) 0 12,819

Brentford: (3511) Fernandez; Jorgensen, Goode, Thompson; Roerslev (Bidstrup 71), Ghoddos, Jensen, Onyeka (Peart-Harris 72), Fosu (Stevens 71); Wissa; Forss.

Oldham Ath: (451) Leutwiler; Fage, Clarke, Piergianni (Da Silva 46), Jameson; Keillor-Dunn, Bowden, Whelan, Diarra, Bahamboula (Couto 46); Dearnley (Vaughan 46).
Referee: Simon Hooper.

Burnley (0) 4 *(Rodriguez 50, 60, 62, 77)*
Rochdale (0) 1 *(Beesley 47)* 9125
Burnley: (442) Pope; Bardsley, Collins, Tarkowski, Pieters; Lennon, Cork, Westwood (Lowton 78), Cornet; Rodriguez (Wood 77), Vydra.
Rochdale: (343) Lynch; Taylor, O'Connell, Dorsett; O'Keeffe, Dooley (Broadbent 75), Morley, Keohane; Beesley, Odoh (Andrews 74), Cashman (Kelly L 83).
Referee: Geoff Eltringham.

Fulham (0) 0
Leeds U (0) 0 11,299
Fulham: (4231) Rodak; Christie, Hector, Mawson, Bryan; Reed (Adarabioyo 83), Onomah; Knockaert (Ivan Cavaleiro 71), Quina (Reid 71), Kebano; Rodrigo Muniz.
Leeds U: (4231) Meslier; Dallas, Cresswell, Phillips, Firpo; Shackleton, Klich (Gelhardt 68); Summerville (McKinstry 75), Rodrigo, James; Roberts (Forshaw 55).
Leeds U won 6-5 on penalties. Referee: Tim Robinson.

Manchester C (3) 6 *(De Bruyne 29, Mahrez 43, 83, Foden 45, Torres 71, Palmer 88)*
Wycombe W (1) 1 *(Hanlan 22)* 30,959
Manchester C: (433) Steffen; Egan-Riley, Burns, Mbete-Tabu, Wilson-Esbrand (McAtee 72); De Bruyne, Lavia, Foden; Mahrez, Torres (Palmer 72), Sterling.
Wycombe W: (3142) Stockdale; Stewart, Tafazolli, Jacobson; Gape (Scowen 75); McCarthy, Wheeler, KaiKai (Horgan 68), Obita; Akinfenwa (Vokes 65), Hanlan.
Referee: Robert Jones.

Norwich C (0) 0
Liverpool (1) 3 *(Minamino 4, 80, Origi 50)* 26,353
Norwich C: (3142) Gunn; Omobamidele, Hanley, Gibson; Rupp; Mumba (Rashica 69), Gilmour, Lees-Melou (Dowell 77), Giannoulis; Tzolis (Pukki 69), Idah.
Liverpool: (433) Kelleher; Bradley, Konate, Gomez, Tsimikas (Robertson 66); Oxlade-Chamberlain, Jones (Henderson 87), Keita (Morton 46); Gordon, Origi, Minamino.
Referee: Darren England.

Preston NE (2) 4 *(Hughes 25, Rafferty 37, Maguire 82, Jakobsen 90)*
Cheltenham T (0) 1 *(Vassell 56)* 6561
Preston NE: (3412) Rudd; Storey, Lindsay (van den Berg 31), Hughes; Rafferty, McCann, Whiteman, Cunningham; Potts (Browne 80); Jakobsen, Wickham (Maguire 7).
Cheltenham T: (3412) Evans; Horton, Pollock, Freestone; Blair (Bonds 78), Thomas (Raglan 79), Barkers, Chapman; Perry; May, Williams A (Vassell 54).
Referee: Dean Whitestone.

QPR (2) 2 *(Austin 18, 34)*
Everton (1) 2 *(Digne 30, Townsend 47)* 12,888
QPR: (3412) Dieng; Dickie, Dunne, Barbet; Adomah, Dozzell (Amos 63), Ball, McCallum (Kakay 66); Chair (Duke-Mckenna 76); Austin, Willock.
Everton: (4231) Begovic; Kenny, Holgate, Godfrey, Digne (Keane 80); Davies, Andre Gomes (Doucoure 58); Townsend, Iwobi, Gordon; Rondon (Gray 73).
QPR won 8-7 on penalties. Referee: Kevin Friend.

Sheffield U (1) 2 *(Stevens 8, McBurnie 66)*
Southampton (1) 2 *(Diallo 23, Salisu 53)* 8934
Sheffield U: (4231) Foderingham; Bogle, Basham, Robinson, Stevens; Norwood, Guedioura; Freeman (Osborn 46), Ndiaye (Fleck 78), Burke (Brewster 46); McBurnie.
Southampton: (4231) Forster; Valery, Lyanco (Bednarek 74), Salisu, Perraud; Diallo, Romeu; Tella (Adams 81), Redmond (Ward-Prowse 46), Djenepo; Broja.
Southampton won 4-2 on penalties.
Referee: John Brooks.

Watford (0) 1 *(Fletcher 61)*
Stoke C (1) 3 *(Powell 24, Clucas 80, Tymon 85)* 8421
Watford: (433) Elliot; Ngakia, Kabasele, Sierralta, Masina; Tufan, Louza (Sissoko 74), Gosling (Dennis 80); Hernandez, Fletcher, Sema.
Stoke C: (343) Davies; Wilmot, Batth, Chester; Duhaney, Thompson, Tymon, Doughty (Clucas 68); Powell (Sawyers 74), Surridge (Sima 67), Brown.
Referee: Tony Harrington.

Wigan Ath (0) 0
Sunderland (1) 2 *(Broadhead 26, O'Nien 54)* 6511
Wigan Ath: (4231) Amos; Lloyd, Kerr, Tilt, Pearce; Cousins (Lang 67), Smith; Edwards (Sze 90), Massey (Adeeko 85), Jordan Jones; Humphrys.
Sunderland: (4231) Burge; Huggins (Neil 79), Alves, Wright, Cirkin; Evans, O'Nien; Dajaku (Stewart 71), Pritchard (Embleton 71), O'Brien; Broadhead.
Referee: Leigh Doughty.

Wednesday, 22 September 2021

Arsenal (1) 3 *(Lacazette 11 (pen), Smith Rowe 77, Nketiah 80)*
AFC Wimbledon (0) 0 56,276
Arsenal: (4321) Leno; Cedric, Holding, Pablo Mari, Tavares; Maitland-Niles, Partey (Smith Rowe 60), Sambi Lokonga; Martinelli (Saka 76), Nketiah (Balogun 83); Lacazette.
AFC Wimbledon: (4411) Tzanev; Lawrence, Heneghan, Nightingale, Guinness-Walker; McCormick (Mebude 60), Woodyard, Hartigan, Rudoni (Chislett 68); Palmer (Pressley 54); Assal.
Referee: Jarred Gillett.

Brighton & HA (2) 2 *(Connolly 33, 38)*
Swansea C (0) 0 8838
Brighton & HA: (442) Steele; Lamptey (Gross 46), Turns, Roberts, Burn; Richards, Alzate, Leonard, Connolly (Locadia 76); Mac Allister (Sarmiento 69), Moder.
Swansea C: (3421) Benda; Williams R, Cooper, Cabango (Manning 46); Latibeaudiere, Walsh (Downes 64), Fulton, Bidwell; Smith (Dhanda 64), Whittaker; Cullen.
Referee: Michael Salisbury.

Chelsea (0) 1 *(Werner 54)*
Aston Villa (0) 1 *(Archer 64)* 35,892
Chelsea: (433) Arrizabalaga; James, Chalobah, Sarr, Chilwell; Kante (Mount 46), Loftus-Cheek, Saul (Lukaku 76); Hudson-Odoi, Werner, Ziyech (Barkley 76).
Aston Villa: (4231) Steer; Cash (Konsa 77), Tuanzebe, Hause, Young; Sanson (Carney Chukwuemeka 42), Nakamba; Traore (Philogene-Bidace 64), Buendia, El Ghazi; Archer.
Chelsea won 4-3 on penalties.
Referee: Graham Scott.

Manchester U (0) 0
West Ham U (1) 1 *(Lanzini 9)* 72,568
Manchester U: (433) Henderson; Dalot, Bailly, Lindelof, Alex Telles (Elanga 73); van de Beek, Matic, Mata (Greenwood 62); Lingard (Bruno Fernandes 72), Martial, Sancho.
West Ham U: (4231) Areola; Fredericks (Coufal 17), Dawson, Diop, Johnson; Kral, Noble; Yarmolenko, Lanzini (Fornals 69), Masuaku (Vlasic 69); Bowen.
Referee: Jonathan Moss.

Millwall (0) 0
Leicester C (0) 2 *(Lookman 50, Iheanacho 88)* 9985
Millwall: (3421) Long; Hutchinson (Ballard 65), Pearce (Afobe 72), Cooper; Leonard, Mitchell B, Evans, Wallace M; Mahoney, Thompson (Smith 72); Bradshaw.
Leicester C: (352) Ward; Amartey, Soyuncu, Evans; Albrighton (Vestergaard 72), Tielemans, Ndidi, Dewsbury-Hall, Thomas; Iheanacho, Lookman (Daka 69).
Referee: Andrew Madley.

Wolverhampton W (1) 2 *(Dendoncker 38, Daniel Podence 58)*

Tottenham H (2) 2 *(Ndombele 14, Kane 23)* 28,798

Wolverhampton W: (343) Ruddy; Mosquera (Coady 9), Boly, Kilman; Hoever, Neves, Dendoncker, Ait Nouri (Nelson Semedo 75); Daniel Podence (Joao Moutinho 84), Silva (Traore 46), Hwang.
Tottenham H: (433) Gollini; Tanganga (Reguilon 90), Romero, Sanchez, Davies; Alli (Hojbjerg 82), Skipp, Ndombele; Lo Celso (Son 62), Kane, Gil Salvatierra.
Tottenham H won 3-2 on penalties. Referee: Peter Bankes.

FOURTH ROUND

Tuesday, 26 October 2021

Arsenal (0) 2 *(Chambers 55, Nketiah 69)*

Leeds U (0) 0 59,126

Arsenal: (4231) Leno; Cedric, White (Chambers 55), Holding (Tavares 76), Kolasinac; Elneny (Sambi Lokonga 72), Maitland-Niles; Pepe, Smith Rowe (Lacazette 72), Martinelli; Nketiah.
Leeds U: (4231) Meslier; Drameh, Llorente (Cooper 59), Struijk, Dallas; Phillips, Forshaw (Klich 46); Harrison, Roberts (Gelhardt 53), James (Summerville 70); Rodrigo (Greenwood 70).
Referee: Andre Marriner.

Chelsea (1) 1 *(Havertz 44)*

Southampton (0) 1 *(Adams 47)* 39,766

Chelsea: (3421) Arrizabalaga; James, Chalobah, Sarr; Hudson-Odoi, Kovacic, Saul, Alonso; Ziyech (Mount 67), Barkley (Chilwell 67); Havertz.
Southampton: (343) Forster; Valery, Lyanco, Salisu; Walker-Peters, Diallo (Romeu 77), Armstrong S (Smallbone 77), Djenepo (Livramento 83); Tella (Walcott 67), Adams (Long 66), Armstrong A.
Chelsea won 4-3 on penalties. Referee: Kevin Friend.

QPR (0) 0

Sunderland (0) 0 15,372

QPR: (3412) Dieng; Dickie, De Wijs, Barbet; Kakay (Adomah 72), Amos (Duke-Mckenna 84), Chair, Odubajo; Willock (Dozzell 73); Dykes, Gray (Austin 62).
Sunderland: (4231) Burge; Winchester, Alves (Doyle 69), Wright, Hume (Cirkin 24); Neil, Evans (O'Brien 65); Gooch (McGeady 65), O'Nien, Dajaku (Pritchard 69); Stewart.
Sunderland won 3-1 on penalties. Referee: Keith Stroud.

Wednesday, 27 October 2021

Burnley (0) 0

Tottenham H (0) 1 *(Lucas Moura 68)* 14,637

Burnley: (442) Pope; Roberts, Collins, Mee, Pieters; Gudmundsson (Lennon 75), Brownhill, Cork, McNeil (Cornet 75); Rodriguez (Barnes 60), Vydra (Wood 60).
Tottenham H: (4231) Gollini; Emerson, Romero, Sanchez, Davies; Hojbjerg, Skipp (Ndombele 66); Gil Salvatierra (Lucas Moura 25), Lo Celso (Rodon 89), Bergwijn (Son 66); Kane.
Referee: Peter Bankes.

Leicester C (2) 2 *(Barnes 6, Lookman 45)*

Brighton & HA (1) 2 *(Webster 45, Mwepu 71)* 21,163

Leicester C: (3421) Ward; Soyuncu, Vestergaard, Bertrand (Mendy 59); Daley-Campbell (Ricardo Pereira 73), Dewsbury-Hall (Maddison 59), Choudhury (Soumare 66), Thomas; Lookman (Iheanacho 73), Barnes; Daka.
Brighton & HA: (343) Steele; Webster (Bissouma 63), Duffy, Roberts (Cucurella 69); Veltman (Dunk 63), Gross, Mac Allister, Burn (Mwepu 46); Sarmiento (Maupay 69), Connolly, Locadia.
Leicester C won 4-2 on penalties. Referee: Jarred Gillett.

Preston NE (0) 0

Liverpool (0) 2 *(Minamino 62, Origi 84)* 22,131

Preston NE: (3412) Rudd; van den Berg, Lindsay, Hughes; Rafferty, McCann (Johnson 78), Ledson (Whiteman 79), Cunningham (Earl 69); Potts; Barkhuizen (Jakobsen 63), Maguire (Sinclair 79).
Liverpool: (433) Adrian; Williams N, Matip (Phillips 46), Gomez, Tsimikas; Oxlade-Chamberlain (Dixon-Bonner 90), Jones (Beck 90), Morton; Blair (Bradley 55), Origi, Minamino.
Referee: David Coote.

Stoke C (0) 1 *(Sawyers 57)*

Brentford (2) 2 *(Canos 22, Toney 40)* 9584

Stoke C: (343) Bursik; Ostigard (Brown 82), Souttar, Wilmot; Duhaney, Sawyers, Thompson (Ince 82), Tymon; Campbell (Sima 63), Fletcher (Surridge 63), Doughty (Vrancic 56).
Brentford: (3511) Fernandez; Ajer, Goode, Jorgensen; Roerslev, Ghoddos, Bidstrup (Norgaard 62), Jensen (Onyeka 72), Canos (Henry 72); Forss (Fosu 72); Toney.
Referee: Michael Salisbury.

West Ham U (0) 0

Manchester C (0) 0 60,000

West Ham U: (4231) Areola; Johnson, Dawson, Diop, Cresswell; Soucek, Noble; Vlasic (Benrahma 62), Lanzini (Coufal 82), Masuaku (Fornals 62); Yarmolenko (Bowen 62).
Manchester C: (433) Steffen; Walker (Joao Cancelo 46), Stones, Ake, Zinchenko; De Bruyne (Grealish 83), Fernandinho, Gundogan; Mahrez (Foden 71), Palmer (Gabriel Jesus 76), Sterling.
West Ham U won 5-3 on penalties.
Referee: Jonathan Moss.

QUARTER-FINALS

Tuesday, 21 December 2021

Arsenal (2) 5 *(Nketiah 17, 49, 58, Pepe 27, Patino 90)*

Sunderland (1) 1 *(Broadhead 31)* 59,027

Arsenal: (4141) Leno; Cedric, White (Gabriel 73), Holding, Tavares; Elneny; Pepe, Odegaard (Martinelli 73), Smith Rowe (Patino 80), Balogun (Xhaka 56); Nketiah.
Sunderland: (3412) Burge; Wright, Flanagan, Doyle; Winchester, Embleton (O'Brien 78), Neil, Gooch (Evans 78); Pritchard; Stewart (Mbunga-Kimpioka 90), Broadhead (Hume 45).
Referee: Simon Hooper.

Wednesday, 22 December 2021

Brentford (0) 0

Chelsea (0) 2 *(Jansson 80 (og), Jorginho 85 (pen))* 16,577

Brentford: (352) Fernandez; Pinnock, Jansson, Sorensen; Canos, Jensen (Forss 81), Janelt (Norgaard 66), Baptiste (Onyeka 74), Henry (Ghoddos 73); Mbeumo, Wissa (Toney 65).
Chelsea: (3412) Arrizabalaga; Azpilicueta, Chalobah, Sarr; Simons (James 65), Kovacic (Jorginho 46), Saul, Alonso; Barkley (Kante 76); Vale (Mount 65), Soonsup-Bell (Pulisic 46).
Referee: Peter Bankes.

Liverpool (1) 3 *(Oxlade-Chamberlain 19, Jota 68, Minamino 90)*

Leicester C (3) 3 *(Vardy 9, 13, Maddison 33)* 52,020

Liverpool: (433) Kelleher; Bradley (Jota 46), Gomez, Koumetio (Konate 46), Tsimikas (Beck 80); Henderson (Keita 59), Morton (Milner 46), Oxlade-Chamberlain; Williams N, Firmino, Minamino.
Leicester C: (4312) Schmeichel; Ricardo Pereira (Albrighton 42), Ndidi, Soyuncu (Vestergaard 60), Thomas; Tielemans, Soumare, Dewsbury-Hall (Bertrand 60); Maddison; Vardy, Daka (Iheanacho 56).
Liverpool won 5-4 on penalties. Referee: Andrew Madley.

Tottenham H (2) 2 *(Bergwijn 29, Lucas Moura 34)*

West Ham U (1) 1 *(Bowen 32)* 40,031

Tottenham H: (3421) Lloris; Sanchez, Dier, Davies; Doherty (Tanganga 83), Hojbjerg, Skipp (Alli 77), Reguilon (Emerson 83); Lucas Moura (Winks 61), Bergwijn (Son 61); Kane.
West Ham U: (3421) Areola; Johnson, Dawson, Diop; Ashby (Yarmolenko 80), Soucek, Rice, Masuaku; Vlasic (Benrahma 68), Lanzini (Fornals 68); Bowen.
Referee: Chris Kavanagh.

SEMI-FINALS FIRST LEG

Wednesday, 5 January 2022

Chelsea (2) 2 *(Havertz 5, Davies 34 (og))*

Tottenham H (0) 0 37,868

Chelsea: (4231) Arrizabalaga; Azpilicueta (Vale 90), Rudiger, Sarr, Alonso; Saul (Loftus-Cheek 73), Jorginho; Ziyech (Pulisic 79), Mount (Kovacic 73), Havertz (Werner 46); Lukaku.
Tottenham H: (343) Lloris; Tanganga, Sanchez, Davies; Emerson, Skipp (Winks 73), Hojbjerg, Doherty (Ndombele 46); Lucas Moura (Gil Salvatierra 79), Kane, Son (Lo Celso 79).
Referee: Craig Pawson.

Thursday, 13 January 2022

Liverpool (0) 0

Arsenal (0) 0 52,377

Liverpool: (433) Alisson; Alexander-Arnold (Williams N 75), Matip (Gomez 76), van Dijk, Robertson; Henderson, Fabinho (Oxlade-Chamberlain 75), Milner (Jones 61); Jota, Firmino, Minamino.
Arsenal: (4231) Ramsdale; Cedric (Chambers 11), White, Gabriel, Tierney; Sambi Lokonga, Xhaka■; Saka (Tavares 81), Lacazette, Martinelli; Nketiah (Holding 28).
Referee: Michael Oliver.

SEMI-FINALS SECOND LEG

Wednesday, 12 January 2022

Tottenham H (0) 0

Chelsea (1) 1 *(Rudiger 18)* 45,603

Tottenham H: (532) Gollini; Emerson, Tanganga, Sanchez, Davies, Doherty (Sessegnon 65); Lo Celso (Gil Salvatierra 71), Winks (Skipp 81), Hojbjerg; Kane, Lucas Moura.
Chelsea: (4222) Arrizabalaga; Azpilicueta, Christensen (Thiago Silva 66), Rudiger, Sarr; Jorginho (Loftus-Cheek 82), Kovacic (Kante 77); Mount (Ziyech 66), Hudson-Odoi; Lukaku, Werner (Alonso 66).
Chelsea won 3-0 on aggregate.
Referee: Andre Marriner.

Thursday, 20 January 2022

Arsenal (0) 0

Liverpool (1) 2 *(Jota 19, 77)* 59,360

Arsenal: (4141) Ramsdale; Tomiyasu, White, Gabriel, Tierney; Sambi Lokonga; Saka, Odegaard, Smith Rowe (Partey■ 74), Martinelli; Lacazette (Nketiah 74).
Liverpool: (433) Kelleher; Alexander-Arnold, Matip (Konate 46), van Dijk, Robertson; Henderson (Milner 75), Fabinho, Jones; Gordon (Minamino 63), Firmino (Williams N 84), Jota.
Liverpool won 2-0 on aggregate.
Referee: Martin Atkinson.

CARABAO CUP FINAL 2021–22

Sunday, 27 February 2022

(at Wembley Stadium, attendance 85,512)

Chelsea (0) 0 Liverpool (0) 0

Chelsea: (3421) Mendy (Arrizabalaga 120); Chalobah, Thiago Silva, Rudiger; Azpilicueta (James 57), Kante, Kovacic (Jorginho 106), Alonso; Mount (Lukaku 74), Pulisic (Werner 74); Havertz.

Liverpool: (433) Kelleher; Alexander-Arnold, Matip (Konate 91), van Dijk, Robertson; Henderson (Elliott 79), Fabinho, Keita (Milner 80); Salah, Mane (Jota 80), Diaz (Origi 97).

aet; Liverpool won 11-10 on penalties.

Referee: Stuart Attwell.

Chelsea's goalkeeper Kepa Arrizabalaga misses the crucial penalty in the shoot-out to hand Liverpool victory in the Carabao Cup Final in February. (Action Images via Reuters/John Sibley)

LEAGUE CUP ATTENDANCES 1960–2022

Season	*Attendances*	*Games*	*Average*
1960–61	1,204,580	112	10,755
1961–62	1,030,534	104	9,909
1962–63	1,029,893	102	10,097
1963–64	945,265	104	9,089
1964–65	962,802	98	9,825
1965–66	1,205,876	106	11,376
1966–67	1,394,553	118	11,818
1967–68	1,671,326	110	15,194
1968–69	2,064,647	118	17,497
1969–70	2,299,819	122	18,851
1970–71	2,035,315	116	17,546
1971–72	2,397,154	123	19,489
1972–73	1,935,474	120	16,129
1973–74	1,722,629	132	13,050
1974–75	1,901,094	127	14,969
1975–76	1,841,735	140	13,155
1976–77	2,236,636	147	15,215
1977–78	2,038,295	148	13,772
1978–79	1,825,643	139	13,134
1979–80	2,322,866	169	13,745
1980–81	2,051,576	161	12,743
1981–82	1,880,682	161	11,681
1982–83	1,679,756	160	10,498
1983–84	1,900,491	168	11,312
1984–85	1,876,429	167	11,236
1985–86	1,579,916	163	9,693
1986–87	1,531,498	157	9,755
1987–88	1,539,253	158	9,742
1988–89	1,552,780	162	9,585
1989–90	1,836,916	168	10,934
1990–91	1,675,496	159	10,538
1991–92	1,622,337	164	9,892
1992–93	1,558,031	161	9,677
1993–94	1,744,120	163	10,700
1994–95	1,530,478	157	9,748
1995–96	1,776,060	162	10,963
1996–97	1,529,321	163	9,382
1997–98	1,484,297	153	9,701
1998–99	1,555,856	153	10,169
1999–2000	1,354,233	153	8,851
2000–01	1,501,304	154	9,749
2001–02	1,076,390	93	11,574
2002–03	1,242,478	92	13,505
2003–04	1,267,729	93	13,631
2004–05	1,313,693	93	14,216
2005–06	1,072,362	93	11,531
2006–07	1,098,403	93	11,811
2007–08	1,332,841	94	14,179
2008–09	1,329,753	93	14,298
2009–10	1,376,405	93	14,800
2010–11	1,197,917	93	12,881
2011–12	1,209,684	93	13,007
2012–13	1,210,031	93	13,011
2013–14	1,362,360	93	14,649
2014–15	1,274,413	93	13,690
2015–16	1,430,554	93	15,382
2016–17	1,462,722	93	15,728
2017–18	1,454,912	93	15,644
2018–19	1,275,575	93	13,716
2019–20	1,337,845	92	14,542
2020–21	*Due to the COVID-19 pandemic all games played behind closed doors until the final.*		
2021–22	1,415,787	92	15,389

CARABAO CUP 2021–22

Round	*Aggregate*	*Games*	*Average*
One	145,042	34	4,266
Two	234,364	25	9,375
Three	346,227	16	21,639
Four	241,779	8	30,222
Quarter-finals	167,655	4	41,914
Semi-finals	195,208	4	48,802
Final	85,512	1	85,512
Total	1,415,787	92	15,389

FOOTBALL LEAGUE TROPHY FINALS 1984–2022

The 1984 final was played at Boothferry Park, Hull. All subsequent finals played at Wembley except between 2001 and 2007 (inclusive) which were played at Millennium Stadium, Cardiff.

ASSOCIATE MEMBERS' CUP

1984	Bournemouth v Hull C	2-1

FREIGHT ROVER TROPHY

1985	Wigan Ath v Brentford	3-1
1986	Bristol C v Bolton W	3-0
1987	Mansfield T v Bristol C	1-1*
	Mansfield T won 5-4 on penalties	

SHERPA VANS TROPHY

1988	Wolverhampton W v Burnley	2-0
1989	Bolton W v Torquay U	4-1

LEYLAND DAF CUP

1990	Tranmere R v Bristol R	2-1
1991	Birmingham C v Tranmere R	3-2

AUTOGLASS TROPHY

1992	Stoke C v Stockport Co	1-0
1993	Port Vale v Stockport Co	2-1
1994	Swansea C v Huddersfield T	1-1*
	Swansea C won 3-1 on penalties	

AUTO WINDSCREENS SHIELD

1995	Birmingham C v Carlisle U	1-0*
1996	Rotherham U v Shrewsbury T	2-1
1997	Carlisle U v Colchester U	0-0*
	Carlisle U won 4-3 on penalties	
1998	Grimsby T v Bournemouth	2-1
1999	Wigan Ath v Millwall	1-0
2000	Stoke C v Bristol C	2-1

LDV VANS TROPHY

2001	Port Vale v Brentford	2-1
2002	Blackpool v Cambridge U	4-1
2003	Bristol C v Carlisle U	2-0
2004	Blackpool v Southend U	2-0
2005	Wrexham v Southend U	2-0*

FOOTBALL LEAGUE TROPHY

2006	Swansea C v Carlisle U	2-1

JOHNSTONE'S PAINT TROPHY

2007	Doncaster R v Bristol R	3-2*
2008	Milton Keynes D v Grimsby T	2-0
2009	Luton T v Scunthorpe U	3-2*
2010	Southampton v Carlisle U	4-1
2011	Carlisle U v Brentford	1-0
2012	Chesterfield v Swindon T	2-0
2013	Crewe Alex v Southend U	2-0
2014	Peterborough U v Chesterfield	3-1
2015	Bristol C v Walsall	2-0
2016	Barnsley v Oxford U	3-2

EFL CHECKATRADE TROPHY

2017	Coventry C v Oxford U	2-1
2018	Lincoln C v Shrewsbury T	1-0
2019	Portsmouth v Sunderland	2-2*
	Portsmouth won 5-4 on penalties	

PAPA JOHN'S EFL TROPHY

2020†	Salford C v Portsmouth	0-0*
	Salford C won 4-2 on penalties	
2021	Sunderland v Tranmere R	1-0
2022	Rotherham U v Sutton U	4-2*

**After extra time. †Due to the COVID-19 pandemic, the final due to be played on Sunday 5 April 2020 was postponed and played on Saturday 13 March 2021.*

FOOTBALL LEAGUE TROPHY WINS

Bristol C 3, Birmingham C 2, Blackpool 2, Carlisle U 2, Port Vale 2, Rotherham U 2, Stoke C 2, Swansea C 2, Wigan Ath 2, Barnsley 1, Bolton W 1, Bournemouth 1, Chesterfield 1, Coventry C 1, Crewe Alex 1, Doncaster R 1, Grimsby T 1, Lincoln C 1, Luton T 1, Mansfield T 1, Milton Keynes D 1, Peterborough U 1, Portsmouth 1, Salford C 1, Southampton 1, Sunderland 1, Tranmere R 1, Wolverhampton W 1, Wrexham 1.

APPEARANCES IN FINALS

Carlisle U 6, Bristol C 5, Brentford 3, Southend U 3, Tranmere R 3, Birmingham C 2, Blackpool 2, Bolton W 2, Bournemouth 2, Bristol R 2, Chesterfield 2, Grimsby T 2, Oxford U 2, Port Vale 2, Portsmouth 2, Rotherham U 2, Shrewsbury T 2, Stockport Co 2, Stoke C 2, Sunderland 2, Swansea C 2, Wigan Ath 2, Barnsley 1, Burnley 1, Cambridge U 1, Colchester U 1, Coventry C 1, Crewe Alex 1, Doncaster R 1, Huddersfield T 1, Hull C 1, Lincoln C 1, Luton T 1, Mansfield T 1, Millwall 1, Milton Keynes D 1, Peterborough U 1, Salford C 1, Scunthorpe U 1, Southampton 1, Sutton U 1, Swindon T 1, Torquay U 1, Walsall 1, Wolverhampton W 1, Wrexham 1.

EFL TROPHY ATTENDANCES 2021–22

Round	*Aggregate*	*Games*	*Average*
One	159,106	96	1,657
Two	28,024	16	1,752
Three	11,607	8	1,451
Quarter-finals	11,000	4	2,750
Semi-finals	14,083	2	7,042
Final	30,688	1	30,688
Total	254,508	127	2,004

PAPA JOHN'S EFL TROPHY 2021–22

■ *Denotes player sent off.*
In the group stages drawn matches were decided on a penalty shoot-out. Two points were awarded to the team that won on penalties (DW). The team that lost on penalties were awarded one point (DL).

NORTHERN SECTION GROUP A

Tuesday, 31 August 2021

Carlisle U (1) 3 *(Charters 11, Mampala 59, Abrahams 78)*

Hartlepool U (1) 3 *(Daly 18, Molyneux 81, Olomola 89 (pen))* 1360

Carlisle U: (433) Jensen; Devine (Riley 71), Feeney, Mellish, Armer; Dixon, Alessandra (Abrahams 60), Charters; Mampala, Young, Dickenson (Clough 60).
Hartlepool U: (532) Mitchell; Ogle, Hendrie, Lawlor, Odusina, Ferguson (Crawford 79); Molyneux, Smith, Daly; Goodwin (Olomola 62), Cullen (Burey 62).
Carlisle U won 4-3 on penalties.

Tuesday, 14 September 2021

Morecambe (0) 0

Everton U21 (0) 1 *(McAllister 64)* 1004

Morecambe: (433) Letheren; McLaughlin (Cooney 60), Wootton, Mensah, Gibson; McCalmont, Wildig, Jones (McLoughlin 82); McDonald, Price (Gnahoua 72), McPake.
Everton U21: (3412) Leban; Welch, Astley, Anderson; Mills, Butterfield, Price, Campbell; Whitaker; Cannon (Warrington 82), Dobbin (McAllister 57).

Tuesday, 28 September 2021

Carlisle U (1) 2 *(Young 44, 67)*

Everton U21 (0) 0 875

Carlisle U: (442) Jensen; Riley, Feeney, Dinzeyi, Armer; Bell, Devine (Whelan 64), Charters, Toure; Clough (Fishburn 68), Young (Mampala 68).
Everton U21: (352) Barrett; Welch, Astley, Anderson; John, McAllister, Price (Warrington 46), Whitaker (Butterfield 46), Campbell; Dobbin, Garcia (Kouyate 66).

Tuesday, 5 October 2021

Hartlepool U (1) 2 *(Daly 8, 83)*

Morecambe (2) 2 *(McLoughlin 33, Jones 40 (pen))* 1572

Hartlepool U: (4312) Mitchell; Ogle, Byrne, Odusina, Ferguson; Crawford, Smith, Daly; Cook (Fondop-Talom 77); Goodwin, Cullen (Molyneux 72).
Morecambe: (451) Andresson; Cooney, Mensah, Wootton, Delaney; McLoughlin, Jones, Pye (McDonald 74), Wildig, Price (Gnahoua 74); Ayunga.
Hartlepool U won 4-2 on penalties.

Tuesday, 2 November 2021

Hartlepool U (0) 1 *(Daly 71)*

Everton U21 (0) 0 1990

Hartlepool U: (532) Mitchell; Ogle, Odusina, Byrne, Francis-Angol (Molyneux 60), Jones; Shelton, Smith, Crawford; Goodwin (Cullen 80), Grey (Daly 70).
Everton U21: (451) Tyrer; John, Astley, Welch, Campbell; Hughes, Price (Whitaker 73), Warrington (McAllister 83), Onyango, Dobbin; Cannon (Mills 46).

Tuesday, 9 November 2021

Morecambe (0) 0

Carlisle U (0) 2 *(Gibson 49, Mellor 54)* 945

Morecambe: (433) Andre Mendes; Cooney, O'Connor, Wootton, Gibson; Jones, Diagouraga (Phillips 78), Wildig (Harrison 78); Ayunga, Stockton, Gnahoua (McDonald 55).
Carlisle U: (433) Howard; Mellor, Feeney, Dinzeyi, Charters; Mampala (Riley 67), Whelan, Devine; Young (Fishburn 76), Abrahams, Clough (Gibson 46).

North Group A	P	W	PW	PL	L	F	A	GD	Pts
Carlisle U	3	2	1	0	0	7	3	4	8
Hartlepool U	3	1	1	1	0	6	5	1	6
Everton U21	3	1	0	0	2	1	3	–2	3
Morecambe	3	0	0	1	2	2	5	–3	1

NORTHERN SECTION GROUP B

Tuesday, 31 August 2021

Oldham Ath (1) 1 *(Piergianni 43)*

Salford C (0) 0 1915

Oldham Ath: (4411) Leutwiler; Fage, Piergianni, Jameson, Couto; Adams (Hope 69), Whelan, Bowden, Bettache (Luamba 76); Keillor-Dunn; Dearnley (Da Silva 46).
Salford C: (4231) Jeacock; Golden, Smith A, Turnbull, Touray I (Ndaba 63); Melhado, Denny (Campbell 62); N'Mai, Sargent, Hunter (Willock 46); Thomas-Asante.

Tuesday, 14 September 2021

Tranmere R (3) 4 *(Maynard 7, 41, Foley 34, 87)*

Leeds U U21 (0) 1 *(Miller 63)* 1209

Tranmere R: (451) Doohan; O'Connor, Clarke, Knight-Percival, MacDonald (Maguire 58); Glatzel, Duffy (Hawkes 75), Merrie, Foley, Walker; Maynard (Dieseruvwe 58).
Leeds U U21: (4411) van den Heuvel; Suttcliffe (Carole 46), Mullen, Moore, Snowdon; Miller, Kenneh, Allen, McGirk; Gray; Dean.

Tuesday, 28 September 2021

Oldham Ath (0) 2 *(Dearnley 78, Keillor-Dunn 90)*

Leeds U U21 (1) 3 *(Summerville 42 (pen), McGahey 58 (og), Jameson 80 (og))* 732

Oldham Ath: (352) Leutwiler; Fage, McGahey, Jameson; Stobbs (Keillor-Dunn 46), Vaughan, Bowden, Bettache (Whelan 65), Couto (Diarra 46); Da Silva, Dearnley.
Leeds U U21: (4231) Klaesson; Suttcliffe, Moore, Hjelde (Kenneh 46), McCarron (Drameh 46); Allen, Bate; Summerville (McKinstry 46), McGirk, Miller; Dean.

Tuesday, 5 October 2021

Salford C (0) 0

Tranmere R (1) 2 *(Watson 16, Walker 86)* 720

Salford C: (442) Jeacock; Rydel, Smith A, Turnbull (Ndaba 60), Golden; Loughlin, Love (Denny 61), Sargent, N'Mai; Thomas-Asante, Oteh.
Tranmere R: (451) Murphy; MacDonald, Davies, Knight-Percival, Maguire; Glatzel (Walker 66), Duffy (Nevitt 88), Merrie, Watson, Feeney; Maynard (Dieseruvwe 64).

Tuesday, 2 November 2021

Salford C (3) 5 *(Thomas-Asante 26, 59, Touray I 32, Oteh 39, Turnbull 69)*

Leeds U U21 (2) 3 *(Dean 9, Greenwood 35, Bate 68)* 427

Salford C: (4231) Ripley (Jeacock 67); Shephard, Smith A, Turnbull, Touray I; Love, Golden; Wright, Willock (Denny 52), Oteh; Thomas-Asante.
Leeds U U21: (4231) van den Heuvel; Moore, Cresswell (Kenneh 46), Mullen, McCarron; Jenkins (Bate 46), McKinstry; Miller, Greenwood, Dean; Gelhardt (McGirk 46).

Tuesday, 9 November 2021

Tranmere R (1) 3 *(Glatzel 45, 75, Maynard 55)*

Oldham Ath (2) 2 *(Dearnley 15, 43)* 1405

Tranmere R: (4231) Murphy; Stratulis, Davies, Knight-Percival, Maguire; Duffy, Foley; Glatzel, Morris (MacDonald 89), Walker (Watson 67); Maynard (Dieseruvwe 89).
Oldham Ath: (3421) Leutwiler; Clarke (Whelan 46), Piergianni, McGahey; Adams (Fage 63), Diarra, Bettache, Couto; Bahamboula, Keillor-Dunn (Hope 63); Dearnley.

North Group B	P	W	PW	PL	L	F	A	GD	Pts
Tranmere R	3	3	0	0	0	9	3	6	9
Oldham Ath	3	1	0	0	2	5	6	–1	3
Salford C	3	1	0	0	2	5	6	–1	3
Leeds U U21	3	1	0	0	2	7	11	–4	3

NORTHERN SECTION GROUP C

Tuesday, 31 August 2021

Shrewsbury T (0) 0

Crewe Alex (0) 1 *(Knight 90)* 1680

Shrewsbury T: (4231) Burgoyne; Daniels, Pennington, Ebanks-Landell, Ogbeta; Leshabela (Bennett 88), Davis; Pyke (Nurse 29), Caton (Leahy 84), Whalley; Bowman.
Crewe Alex: (3421) Richards; Ramsay, Daniels, Johnson; Ainley, Robertson, Lowery, McFadzean; Griffiths (Lundstram 82), Finney (Knight 61); Porter.

Wigan Ath (0) 0

Wolverhampton W U21 (0) 0 1240

Wigan Ath: (4231) Jamie Jones; Lloyd, Carragher, Long, Robinson; Bayliss, Smith; Massey, Aasgaard, Edwards; Humphrys.
Wolverhampton W U21: (352) Moulden; Mabete, Kandola, Richards; Birtwhistle, Bugarin (Griffiths 45 (Rees 88)), Cundle, Hasketh (Roberts 63), Keto-Diyawa; Carty, Campbell.
Wolverhampton W U21 won 4-2 on penalties.

Tuesday, 5 October 2021

Crewe Alex (1) 2 *(Finney 14, Smith 60 (og))*

Wigan Ath (0) 0 925

Crewe Alex: (442) Richards; Johnson, Offord, Thomas T, McFadzean; Griffiths, Gomes, Lundstram, Finney; Mandron, Porter.
Wigan Ath: (4231) Tickle; Lloyd, Kerr, Tilt, Pearce; Smith, Bayliss; Massey, Sze (Robinson 76), Edwards; Humphrys.

Shrewsbury T (0) 3 *(Bloxham 72, Lloyd 78, Pyke 90)*

Wolverhampton W U21 (1) 1 *(Hasketh 31)* 1334

Shrewsbury T: (433) Burgoyne; Wilson, Ebanks-Landell (Nurse 46), Pierre (Pennington 46), Ogbeta; Lloyd (Leahy 90), Leshabela, Caton; Bloxham, Cosgrove, Pyke.
Wolverhampton W U21: (343) Moulden; Agboola (Mabete 46), Estrada, Nya (Harkin 81); Birtwhistle, Cundle, Hasketh, Lembikisa; Hodnett, Campbell, Carty.

Tuesday, 9 November 2021

Crewe Alex (2) 3 *(Mandron 12, 36, Robbins 79)*

Wolverhampton W U21 (0) 0 598

Crewe Alex: (532) Jaaskelainen; Lundstram, Thomas T (Tabiner 68), Woodthorpe, Williams, McFadzean; Robbins, Finney, Griffiths; Bennett (Knight 68), Mandron (Long 68).
Wolverhampton W U21: (352) Ruddy; Rasmussen (Richards 64), Tipton, Nya; Birtwhistle, Hasketh, Cundle, Hodnett, Lembikisa (Bueno 64); Carty (Harkin 64), Campbell.

Wednesday, 10 November 2021

Wigan Ath (1) 2 *(Long 9, Sze 53)*

Shrewsbury T (0) 0 1121

Wigan Ath: (3412) Jamie Jones; Carragher (Baningime 22), Robinson, Long; Massey, Smith, Aasgaard, Pearce; Adeeko (Costello 77); Edwards, Sze (McHugh 77).
Shrewsbury T: (451) Burgoyne; Wilson, Ebanks-Landell, Pierre (Nurse 46), Ogbeta (Whalley 46); Bloxham, Vela, Davis, Leshabela, Leahy; Cosgrove (Caton 74).

North Group C	P	W	PW	PL	L	F	A	GD	Pts
Crewe Alex	3	3	0	0	0	6	0	6	9
Wigan Ath	3	1	0	1	1	2	2	0	4
Shrewsbury T	3	1	0	0	2	3	4	–1	3
Wolverhampton W U21	3	0	1	0	2	1	6	–5	2

NORTHERN SECTION GROUP D

Tuesday, 31 August 2021

Bolton W (1) 3 *(Doyle 28, Delfouneso 54, Afolayan 77)*

Port Vale (2) 2 *(Conlon 35, Amoo 43)* 2926

Bolton W: (4231) Gilks; Brockbank, Santos, Baptiste, Gordon; Thomason, Tutte; Isgrove (Afolayan 67), Delfouneso, Kachunga (Henry 90); Doyle (Sarcevic 67).
Port Vale: (352) Stone; Cass, Smith, Johnson; Gibbons (Taylor 55), Pett, Garrity, Conlon (Worrall 55), Benning; Amoo (Lloyd 68), Rodney.

Rochdale (1) 4 *(Kelly L 33, O'Keeffe 50 (pen), 72, Andrews 78)*

Liverpool U21 (0) 0 1107

Rochdale: (352) Coleman; Taylor, McNulty, Dunne; O'Keeffe (Keohane 75), Grant, Broadbent, Kelly L (Brierley 61), White (Dorsett 70); Andrews, Cashman.
Liverpool U21: (433) Davies; Wilson, Clayton, Koumetio, Chambers; Dixon-Bonner, Ritaccio (Stephenson 68), Morton; Bearne, O'Rourke (Musialowski 16), Woltman (McLaughlin-Miles 82).

Tuesday, 5 October 2021

Bolton W (1) 4 *(Delfouneso 27, Bakayoko 58, 81 (pen), Quansah 66 (og))*

Liverpool U21 (0) 1 *(Dixon-Bonner 72)* 2299

Bolton W: (4231) Gilks; Brockbank, Aimson, Baptiste, Gordon; Comley, Sheehan (Pettifer 72); Isgrove (Henry 67), Thomason, Delfouneso; Kachunga (Bakayoko 46).
Liverpool U21: (433) Marcelo; Wilson (Koumetio 67), Phillips, Quansah, Gallacher; Corness, Morton, Ritaccio (Mabaya 25); Bearne, Dixon-Bonner, Woltman (Cannonier 75).

Port Vale (0) 1 *(Taylor 90 (og))*

Rochdale (0) 0 1727

Port Vale: (3421) Stone; Gibbons (Cass 46), Johnson, Amos; Hurst, Walker (Jones E 46), Taylor, Benning; Amoo, Politic; Lloyd.
Rochdale: (343) Lynch; Taylor, McNulty, White; O'Keeffe (Dorsett 64), Kelly, Broadbent (Brierley 90), Keohane; Grant, Done (Cashman 80), Newby.

Tuesday, 2 November 2021

Rochdale (0) 0

Bolton W (3) 3 *(Afolayan 16, John 19, Doyle 45 (pen))* 1116

Rochdale: (343) Lynch; Taylor, Graham, Dorsett; O'Keeffe, Broadbent, Dooley, White; Cashman (Odoh 44), Done, Grant.
Bolton W: (4231) Dixon; Isgrove (Edwards 90), Santos, Baptiste, John; Williams, Sheehan; Kachunga, Thomason, Afolayan (Delfouneso 72); Doyle (Henry 90).

Tuesday, 9 November 2021

Port Vale (2) 5 *(Lloyd 15, Politic 26, Benning 51, Martin 63, Taylor 77)*

Liverpool U21 (0) 0 2349

Port Vale: (3412) Stone; Cass (Johnson 46), Martin, Amos; Worrall (Legge 62), Walker, Taylor, Benning; Garrity (Amoo 46); Lloyd, Politic.
Liverpool U21: (433) Marcelo; Norris, Quansah, Bajcetic, Gallacher; Corness, Musialowski, Clark (Pilling 80); Bearne, Gordon (Cannonier 76), Woltman.

North Group D	P	W	PW	PL	L	F	A	GD	Pts
Bolton W	3	3	0	0	0	10	3	7	9
Port Vale	3	2	0	0	1	8	3	5	6
Rochdale	3	1	0	0	2	4	4	0	3
Liverpool U21	3	0	0	0	3	1	13	–12	0

NORTHERN SECTION GROUP E

Tuesday, 24 August 2021

Scunthorpe U (0) 0

Manchester C U21 (2) 3 *(Palmer 6, Bolton 24, McAtee 84)* 860

Scunthorpe U: (541) Collins; Rowe, Davis, Onariase, Thompson, O'Malley; Wilson (Poulter 46), Gallimore, Shrimpton, Hippolyte (Lobley 80); Jessop (Moore-Billam 76).
Manchester C U21: (433) Slicker; Egan-Riley, Burns, Mbete-Tabu (Robinson 46), Wilson-Esbrand (Larios 60); Palmer, Lavia, McAtee; Bolton, Sodje (Oduroh 71), Hamilton.

Tuesday, 7 September 2021

Doncaster R (0) 0

Rotherham U (3) 6 *(Miller 13, Ladapo 15, Jones 16 (og), Grigg 49, Hull 67, Mattock 85)* 1765

Doncaster R: (433) Jones; Seaman, Williams R, Horton, Rowe; Smith, Bostock, Close; Vilca (Gardner 63), Dodoo (Greaves 63), Hiwula (Knoyle 63).
Rotherham U: (3412) Vickers; Edmonds-Green, Hull, Mattock; Miller, Barlaser, Odofin, Bola; Sadlier (Rathbone 46); Grigg (Gratton 65), Ladapo (Smith 65).

Tuesday, 21 September 2021

Doncaster R (1) 2 *(Dodoo 14, 58)*

Manchester C U21 (1) 1 *(Edozie 8)* 1802

Doncaster R: (433) Jones; Seaman, Olowu, Williams R, Horton; Barlow, Bostock (Rowe 82), Gardner; Hiwula (Galbraith 64), Cukur, Dodoo (Vilca 61).
Manchester C U21: (433) Slicker; Bolton (Mebude 81), Katongo, Smith, Larios; Hamilton, Charles, Gyabi (Sodje 18); Bobb, Delap (Oduroh 61), Edozie.

Tuesday, 5 October 2021

Rotherham U (2) 4 *(Grigg 8, Ladapo 20, Odofin 82, Smith 90)*

Scunthorpe U (0) 1 *(Loft 65)* 1439

Rotherham U: (3412) Vickers; Edmonds-Green, Hull (Rathbone 61), Ihiekwe; Harding, Barlaser (Wiles 61), Odofin, Bola; Sadlier; Grigg (Smith 61), Ladapo.
Scunthorpe U: (442) Watson; Millen, Onariase, Davis, Thompson; Green, Wood (Pugh 75), Beestin, Hippolyte; Hallam (Hackney 84), Loft (Jarvis 71).

Tuesday, 26 October 2021

Rotherham U (0) 5 *(Grigg 51, Sadlier 63 (pen), 81, 90, Hull 66)*

Manchester C U21 (0) 0 1908

Rotherham U: (3412) Johansson; Hull, Wood (McGuckin 66), Bola; Gratton, Durose (Warne 66), Odofin, Miller; Sadlier; Kayode, Ladapo (Grigg 46).
Manchester C U21: (433) Slicker; Lewis, Burns, Mbete-Tabu, Wilson-Esbrand (Tarensi 87); Charles, Lavia, McAtee; Bobb, Delap (O'Reilly 46), Hamilton (Kayky 46).

Tuesday, 9 November 2021

Scunthorpe U (0) 2 *(Loft 88, Scrimshaw 90)*

Doncaster R (2) 3 *(Vilca 5, Dodoo 16, 58)* 1011

Scunthorpe U: (433) Watson; Pugh, Rowe, Taft, Thompson; Wood, Perry, Hackney (Kenyon 66); Green (Loft 36), Jarvis (Scrimshaw 73), Hippolyte.
Doncaster R: (4231) Jones; Knoyle, Anderson, Blythe, Horton; Smith, Hasani; Kuleya (Hollings 82), Rowe, Vilca; Dodoo (Goodman 87).

North Group E	*P*	*W*	*PW*	*PL*	*L*	*F*	*A*	*GD*	*Pts*
Rotherham U	3	3	0	0	0	15	1	14	9
Doncaster R	3	2	0	0	1	5	9	−4	6
Manchester C U21	3	1	0	0	2	4	7	−3	3
Scunthorpe U	3	0	0	0	3	3	10	−7	0

NORTHERN SECTION GROUP F

Tuesday, 24 August 2021

Lincoln C (2) 3 *(Scully 23, 32, 57)*

Manchester U U21 (0) 2 *(McNeill 68, Hardley 89)* 3510

Lincoln C: (433) Long; Poole, Montsma, Eyoma, Bramall; Bishop (Sorensen 64), Fiorini, McGrandles; Longdon, N'Lundulu, Scully (Brooks 80).
Manchester U U21: (4231) Mee; Wellens, Svidersky, Hardley, Fernandez; Mejbri■, Savage; Bughail-Mellor (Iqbal 74), Shoretire, Hoogerwerf (Mather 74); McNeill.

Tuesday, 31 August 2021

Bradford C (0) 0

Lincoln C (2) 3 *(Hopper 14, Adelakun 36, Scully 49)* 1739

Bradford C: (4231) Hornby; Threlkeld (Foulds 73), Kelleher, O'Connor, Ridehalgh; Watt (Sutton 59), Cooke; Gilliead, Evans, Vernam; Cook (Lavery 59).
Lincoln C: (4231) Long; Poole, Eyoma, Montsma, Bramall; Fiorini, Bridcutt (McGrandles 72); Adelakun (Longdon 79), Bishop (Sorensen 62), Scully; Hopper.

Tuesday, 21 September 2021

Bradford C (0) 0

Manchester U U21 (0) 3 *(Songo'o 47 (og), Hugill 57, Hoogerwerf 82)* 2022

Bradford C: (4231) Hornby; Cousin-Dawson, Sikora (Cook 64), Staunton, Foulds; Songo'o, Sutton; Crankshaw, Evans (Threlkeld 46), Scales; Gilliead (Vernam 46).
Manchester U U21: (4231) Kovar; Fernandez, Mengi, McShane, Hardley (Hoogerwerf 46); Svidersky, Savage; Wellens, Shoretire, Iqbal (Garnacho 86); Hugill (Emeran 81).

Tuesday, 5 October 2021

Lincoln C (0) 1 *(Montsma 90)*

Sunderland (1) 2 *(Neil 2, Wearne 72)* 3060

Lincoln C: (433) Long; Poole, Montsma, Walsh (Eyoma 46), Robson; Longdon (N'Lundulu 69), Sorensen, Sanders; Maguire (Bramall 69), Adelakun, Scully.
Sunderland: (4231) Burge; Richardson, Alves, Younger, Hume; Neil, Sohna; Taylor (Wearne 62), Pritchard, O'Brien; Harris (O'Nien 75 (Embleton 81)).

Wednesday, 13 October 2021

Sunderland (0) 2 *(Dyce 50, Wearne 66)*

Manchester U U21 (0) 1 *(Iqbal 57)* 3960

Sunderland: (4231) Carney; Richardson, Almond, Younger, Hume (Kachosa 71); Scott, Sohna; Taylor (Kelly 90), Wearne (Johnson 90), Dyce; Harris.
Manchester U U21: (442) Mee; Wellens (Jurado 90), McShane, Hardley, Fernandez; Hoogerwerf (Forson 81), Iqbal, Savage, Mather; McNeill, Hugill (Norkett 80).

Tuesday, 9 November 2021

Sunderland (0) 1 *(Broadhead 52)*

Bradford C (1) 1 *(Robinson 36)* 1800

Sunderland: (4231) Hoffmann; Richardson, Alves, Younger, Gooch; O'Nien, Sohna (Winchester 73); Dajaku, Pritchard, Embleton (Taylor 73); Broadhead (Harris 57).
Bradford C: (433) Hornby; Threlkeld, Kelleher, Staunton, Foulds; Evans, Cooke, Scales; Vernam (Sutton 61), Robinson (Gilliead 61), Angol (Watt 46).
Bradford C won 4-2 on penalties.

North Group F	*P*	*W*	*PW*	*PL*	*L*	*F*	*A*	*GD*	*Pts*
Sunderland	3	2	0	1	0	5	3	2	7
Lincoln C	3	2	0	0	1	7	4	3	6
Manchester U U21	3	1	0	0	2	6	5	1	3
Bradford C	3	0	1	0	2	1	7	−6	2

NORTHERN SECTION GROUP G

Tuesday, 31 August 2021

Accrington S (1) 2 *(Bishop 32, 50)*

Barrow (0) 2 *(Arthur 48, Banks 72 (pen))* 930

Accrington S: (352) Savin; Sherring, Amankwah (Nottingham 46), Procter; Clark, Leigh, Morgan (Moonan 66), Scully, Nolan; Mumbongo, Bishop.
Barrow: (352) Maloney; Jones J (Banks 59), Ellis, Grayson (Zanzala 74); Hutton, Taylor, Arthur, White, Ntlhe (Brough 39); Gordon, Williams.
Accrington S won 5-4 on penalties.

Fleetwood T (2) 4 *(Morton 6, 42, 48, Edmondson 60)*

Leicester C U21 (0) 1 *(Wakeling 75)* 566

Fleetwood T: (3412) Crellin; Hill, Johnson D (Garner G 72), Holgate; Johnson C, Camps (Biggins 72), Matete, Clark; Pilkington (Morris 85); Edmondson, Morton (Hayes 59).
Leicester C U21: (4231) Young; Daley-Campbell, Brunt, Nelson R, Hughes; Hulme, McAteer (Pennant 71); Fitzhugh (Godsmark-Ford 46), Suengchitthawon (Alves 75), Maswanhise (Marcal-Madivadua 81); Wakeling.

Tuesday, 5 October 2021

Accrington S (2) 5 *(Leigh 24, Nottingham 31, Nolan 51, O'Sullivan 53, Malcolm 62)*

Leicester C U21 (0) 0 885

Accrington S: (352) Savin; Sykes, Nottingham, Procter; O'Sullivan (Clark 56), Leigh, Coyle, Scully, Nolan (Carson 65); Malcolm (Stowe 65), Bishop.
Leicester C U21: (352) Young; Nelson R, Nelson B (Russ 46), Brunt; Daley-Campbell, Marcal-Madivadua, McAteer, Suengchitthawon, Flynn; Fitzhugh (Alves 53), Maswanhise (Pennant 54).

Barrow (1) 1 *(Zanzala 28)*

Fleetwood T (0) 3 *(Matete 48, Edmondson 55, McMillan 67)* 1281

Barrow: (4312) Lillis; Arthur, Jones J, Grayson, Brough; Gotts (Stevens 46), Taylor, White; Williams (Gordon 76); Zanzala, Kay (Maloney 90).
Fleetwood T: (3412) Crellin; Johnson C, Teale, Andrew (Raffie 81); Thiam (Bird 90), Thompson (Hayes 81), Matete, Clark; Batty; McMillan, Edmondson.

Tuesday, 9 November 2021

Barrow (0) 1 *(Stevens 90)*

Leicester C U21 (0) 0 575

Barrow: (352) Lillis; Brown, Ellis, Arthur; Hutton, White, Taylor, Jones M (Stevens 81), Kay; James, Williams (Zanzala 30).
Leicester C U21: (3412) Odunze; Spencer-Adams, Brunt, Flynn; Hughes (Maswanhise 74), Ewing, Suengchitthawon, McAteer; Fitzhugh; Wakeling (Alves 81), Russ (Pennant 66).

Fleetwood T (1) 1 *(Garner G 37 (pen))*

Accrington S (2) 4 *(Pell 23, Hamilton 42, Leigh 50, Nottingham 86)* 633

Fleetwood T: (352) Crellin; Johnson C, McLaughlin, Andrew; Thiam (Morton 58), Biggins, Matete, Batty, Clark; Garner G, Edmondson (Morris 58).
Accrington S: (3421) Savin; Sherring, Nottingham, Procter; Rodgers, Coyle, Conneely (Scully 46), Hamilton; Pell (Malcolm 78), Leigh; Mansell (Mumbongo 46).

North Group G	P	W	PW	PL	L	F	A	GD	Pts
Accrington S	3	2	1	0	0	11	3	8	8
Fleetwood T	3	2	0	0	1	8	6	2	6
Barrow	3	1	0	1	1	4	5	–1	4
Leicester C U21	3	0	0	0	3	1	10	–9	0

NORTHERN SECTION GROUP H

Tuesday, 31 August 2021

Harrogate T (1) 3 *(Orsi-Dadomo 44, 53, 69)*

Mansfield T (0) 1 *(Lapslie 66)* 825

Harrogate T: (442) Cracknell; Fallowfield, Smith, Hall (Burrell 64), Sheron; Thomson (Muldoon 78), Pattison (Falkingham 77), Kerry, Power; Orsi-Dadomo, Martin.
Mansfield T: (41212) Shelvey; Clarke J, Rawson (Oates 54), Ward, Burke; Hill; Charsley, Law; Lapslie (Caine 68); Bowery, Sinclair (Cooper 77).

Sheffield W (1) 3 *(Sow 41, Johnson 52, Palmer 54)*

Newcastle U U21 (0) 0 6593

Sheffield W: (4231) Wildsmith; Palmer, Iorfa (Hunt J 68), Brennan, Johnson; Wing, Adeniran (Byers 60); Corbeanu, Dele-Bashiru, Sow (Adedoyin 74); Kamberi.
Newcastle U U21: (4231) Langley; Oliver, Wiggett, Savage, Bondswell; Turner-Cook (Miley 63), Cross; Allan (Longelo 80), Young, Scott (Wilson 56); Stephenson.

Tuesday, 5 October 2021

Harrogate T (2) 2 *(Kerry 6, Orsi-Dadomo 45)*

Newcastle U U21 (0) 0 920

Harrogate T: (442) Cracknell; Fallowfield, Smith, Burrell, Sheron; Thomson (Williams 88), Kerry, Falkingham (Tweed 88), Diamond; Muldoon (Ilesanmi 84), Orsi-Dadomo.
Newcastle U U21: (4231) Gillespie; Oliver, Wiggett, Savage, Cross; Young, Brookwell (De Bolle 79); White (Turner-Cook 46), Anderson, Scott; Stephenson (Wilson 78).

Mansfield T (0) 1 *(Quinn 68)*

Sheffield W (0) 2 *(Wing 63, Kamberi 90)* 2836

Mansfield T: (41212) Shelvey; Clarke J, Cooper (Hewitt 46), Rawson, Burke; Ward; Charsley (Lapslie 72), Quinn; Law (Oates 79); Johnson, Sinclair.
Sheffield W: (4231) Wildsmith; Hunt J (Brown 61), Dunkley, Gibson (Palmer 46), Johnson; Dele-Bashiru, Wing; Corbeanu, Kamberi, Sow; Berahino (Shodipo 46).

Tuesday, 9 November 2021

Mansfield T (2) 6 *(Johnson 16, 53, 70 (pen), O'Toole 45, Sinclair 78 (pen), Caine 90)*

Newcastle U U21 (2) 3 *(Stephenson 5, White 23, Ndiweni 90)* 805

Mansfield T: (433) Shelvey; Clarke J, Rawson (Cooper 80), Forrester, Law; Sinclair, Ward, O'Toole (Stirk 46); Gale, Bowery, Johnson (Caine 71).
Newcastle U U21: (4231) Langley; Barrett, Wiggett, Brookwell (Carlyon 65), Bondswell; De Bolle, Young; Stephenson, White, Scott (Crossley 61); Ferguson (Ndiweni 73).

Sheffield W (1) 4 *(Berahino 17, Byers 57, Sow 60, Adedoyin 68 (pen))*

Harrogate T (0) 0 5433

Sheffield W: (4231) Wildsmith; Hunt J, Brennan, Agbontohoma, Brown; Luongo (Dele-Bashiru 72), Byers (Adeniran 73); Waldock, Berahino (Adedoyin 61), Shodipo; Sow.
Harrogate T: (442) Oxley; Fallowfield, Burrell, Hall■, Page; Power, Pattison, Falkingham, Diamond (Thomson 73); Muldoon (Martin 8), Orsi-Dadomo (Smith 74).

North Group H	P	W	PW	PL	L	F	A	GD	Pts
Sheffield W	3	3	0	0	0	9	1	8	9
Harrogate T	3	2	0	0	1	5	5	0	6
Mansfield T	3	1	0	0	2	8	8	0	3
Newcastle U U21	3	0	0	0	3	3	11	–8	0

SOUTHERN SECTION GROUP A

Tuesday, 7 September 2021

Colchester U (0) 0

Gillingham (0) 1 *(McKenzie 90)* 731

Colchester U: (4231) Turner; Coxe, Beadle, Eastman, Tchamadeu; Sarpong-Wiredu (Judge 46), Kennedy; Jasper (Hannant 63), Chilvers, Dobra; Nouble (Sears 46).
Gillingham: (352) Chapman; McKenzie, Ehmer, Tucker; Lintott (Reeves 46), MacDonald (Carayol 82), O'Keefe, Phillips, Tutonda; Kelman, Lloyd (Sithole 85).

Tuesday, 14 September 2021

Ipswich T (1) 1 *(Norwood 2)*

West Ham U U21 (1) 2 *(Appiah-Forson 12, Okoflex 89 (pen))* 4231

Ipswich T: (4231) Holy; Vincent-Young, Woolfenden, Armin, Penney; Morsy, Carroll; Jackson (Chaplin 57), El Mizouni (Pigott 78), Barry (Siziba 66); Norwood.
West Ham U U21: (343) Hegyi; Baptiste, Laing, Alese; Ashby, Ekwah■, Appiah-Forson, Longelo; Chesters (Rosa 88), Swyer (Perkins 70), Okoflex.

Tuesday, 28 September 2021

Colchester U (1) 1 *(Dobra 7)*

West Ham U U21 (0) 0 962

Colchester U: (4231) Gerken; Tchamadeu, Chambers, Eastman, Clampin; Chilvers, Sarpong-Wiredu; Tovide (Sears 82), Cooper (Jasper 70), Dobra; Nouble (Hannant 55).
West Ham U U21: (433) Hegyi; Ashby, Baptiste, Alese, Greenidge (Dju 84); Chesters, Appiah-Forson, Swyer; Longelo, Perkins, Diallo (Ashley 46 (Rosa 55)).

Tuesday, 5 October 2021

Gillingham (0) 0

Ipswich T (1) 2 *(Pigott 43, Chaplin 72)* 1116

Gillingham: (4231) Chapman; Bennett, Ehmer (Lintott 60), Tucker, Akehurst; O'Keefe, McKenzie; Reeves (Lloyd 73), Lee, Kelman; Akinde (Sithole 72).
Ipswich T: (4231) Holy; Vincent-Young, Nsiala, Woolfenden, Kenlock; Harper, El Mizouni; Jackson, Chaplin (Siziba 85), Edwards (Barry 73); Pigott (Norwood 73).

Tuesday, 26 October 2021

Gillingham (0) 0

West Ham U U21 (2) 2 *(Ashby 22, Nevers 33)* 819

Gillingham: (4141) Chapman; Jackson (McKenzie 55), Tucker, Bennett, Akehurst; Adshead; Lloyd (Carayol 66), Lee, Reeves, Kelman (Sithole 46); Oliver.
West Ham U U21: (433) Hegyi; Ashby, Baptiste, Alese, Longelo; Appiah-Forson, Ekwah, Potts; Chesters, Nevers (Swyer 76), Okoflex.

Tuesday, 9 November 2021

Ipswich T (0) 0

Colchester U (0) 0 8100

Ipswich T: (4231) Hladky; Vincent-Young (Burns 46), Woolfenden, Burgess, Kenlock (Clements 46); Harper, Fraser; Aluko, Barry (Celina 71), Chaplin; Pigott.
Colchester U: (433) Turner; Tchamadeu (Welch-Hayes 67), Chambers, Eastman, Daniels (Coxe 84); Chilvers, Kennedy (Cooper 60), Sarpong-Wiredu; Hannant, Sears, Nouble.
Ipswich T won 4-3 on penalties.

South Group A	P	W	PW	PL	L	F	A	GD	Pts
Ipswich T	3	1	1	0	1	3	2	1	5
Colchester U	3	1	0	1	1	1	1	0	4
West Ham U U21*	3	2	0	0	1	4	2	2	3
Gillingham	3	1	0	0	2	1	4	–3	3

**Deducted 3 points for fielding an ineligible player.*

SOUTHERN SECTION GROUP B

Tuesday, 31 August 2021

Sutton U (1) 3 *(Sho-Silva 31, Smith 52, Korboa 81)*

Crystal Palace U21 (0) 0 1504

Sutton U: (4411) House; Kizzi, Goodliffe, Rowe, Wyatt; Boldewijn, Barden (Eastmond 18), Smith, Korboa; Bennett (Dundas 73); Sho-Silva (Wilson 59).
Crystal Palace U21: (4231) Matthews; Boateng D, Rich-Baghuelou, Jach, Hannam; Taylor, Boateng M; Rak-Sakyi (Roles 83), Banks, Omilabu (Robertson 64); Street (Gordon 70).

Tuesday, 7 September 2021

AFC Wimbledon (2) 5 *(Kalambayi 2, Pressley 43, 80 (pen), Nightingale 87, McCormick 90)*

Portsmouth (1) 3 *(Harrison 45, 52, 78)* 3560

AFC Wimbledon: (4231) Oualah; Alexander, Kalambayi, Nightingale, Guinness-Walker; Marsh, Hartigan; Assal (McCormick 70), Chislett (Rudoni 70), Mebude (Lawrence 57); Pressley.
Portsmouth: (442) Eastwood; Romeo, Mnoga, Downing, Ogilvie; Hackett-Fairchild, Thompson (Jewitt-White 71), Jacobs, Ahadme; Harrison, Hirst.

Tuesday, 12 October 2021

Portsmouth (0) 0

Sutton U (0) 2 *(Olaofe 55, John 71)* 2490

Portsmouth: (3412) Bass; Downing (Freeman 43), Raggett, Brown; Romeo, Thompson, Mnoga (Williams 46), Hackett-Fairchild; Jacobs; Ahadme (Harrison 56), Hirst.
Sutton U: (442) Bouzanis; Kizzi, Rowe, John, Wyatt; Korboa, Beautyman (Eastmond 74), Smith, Randall; Sho-Silva (Bennett 65), Olaofe (Boldewijn 61).

Tuesday, 26 October 2021

AFC Wimbledon (0) 0

Crystal Palace U21 (0) 2 *(Rak-Sakyi 57, Street 83)* 2397

AFC Wimbledon: (343) Oualah; Jenkins (Sutcliffe 53), Charles, Csoka; Osew, Lawrence, Olaniyan (Campbell 63), Hallard; Chislett, Bartley (Sasu 77), Mebude.
Crystal Palace U21: (433) Whitworth; Robertson, O'Brien, Rich-Baghuelou, Adaramola; Wells-Morrison (Boateng D 90), Boateng M, Kirby (Gordon 74); Rak-Sakyi, Street, Omilabu (Banks 66).

Tuesday, 9 November 2021

Portsmouth (1) 3 *(Azeez 32, Ahadme 54, Hirst 90)*

Crystal Palace U21 (0) 0 1660

Portsmouth: (442) Bass; Freeman, Raggett, Ogilvie, Hughes; Payce (Bridgman 88), Thompson (Jewitt-White 46), Azeez, Jacobs; Hirst, Ahadme (Kaba 90).
Crystal Palace U21: (4231) Goodman; Boateng D, Quick, Rich-Baghuelou, Watson (Imray 77); Boateng M, Roles (Taylor 57); Omilabu, Kirby (Mooney 76), Gordon; Street.

Sutton U (0) 1 *(Wilson 47)*

AFC Wimbledon (0) 0 2458

Sutton U: (442) House; Kizzi, Goodliffe, Rowe, Wyatt; Boldewijn, Smith, Davis (Milsom 64), Korboa (Ajiboye 74); Wilson, Bennett (Sho-Silva 57).
AFC Wimbledon: (3511) Tzanev; Alexander (Palmer 61), Charles (Jenkins 61), Guinness-Walker; Biler, McCormick, Hartigan, Chislett (Assal 72), Currie; Rudoni; Cosgrave.

South Group B	P	W	PW	PL	L	F	A	GD	Pts
Sutton U	3	3	0	0	0	6	0	6	9
Portsmouth	3	1	0	0	2	6	7	–1	3
AFC Wimbledon	3	1	0	0	2	5	6	–1	3
Crystal Palace U21	3	1	0	0	2	2	6	–4	3

SOUTHERN SECTION GROUP C

Tuesday, 31 August 2021

Burton Alb (0) 1 *(O'Riley 67 (og))*

Milton Keynes D (0) 2 *(Bird 58, Darling 63)* 690

Burton Alb: (4231) Balcombe; Hamer, Shaughnessy, Leak, Blake-Tracy; Morris (Powell 64), Borthwick-Jackson (Gilligan 74); Rowe, Williams (Taylor 63), Patrick; Holloway.
Milton Keynes D: (3412) Walker; Baldwin, Darling, Jules; Watson (O'Hora 89), Boateng, McEachran (O'Riley 57), Harvie (Ilunga 73); Bird; Martin, Brown.

Wycombe W (1) 1 *(Parsons 11)*

Aston Villa U21 (1) 3 *(Archer 42, Philogene-Bidace 68, 90)* 1409

Wycombe W: (3421) Przybek; Burley (Obita 81), Joseph, Ram; Wheeler (Clark 62), Thompson, Pendlebury, Parsons; McCleary, Linton; Hanlan (KaiKai 69).
Aston Villa U21: (433) Zych; Zito, Bogarde, Appiah, Swinkels; Iroegbunam, Sanson (Lindley 46), Thorndike (Abldeen-Goodridge 90); Archer, Caleb Chukwuemeka (Jay-Hart 85), Philogene-Bidace.

Tuesday, 5 October 2021

Burton Alb (2) 2 *(Jebbison 19, Hemmings 23)*

Aston Villa U21 (1) 4 *(Archer 35, 61, 71, Abldeen-Goodridge 51)* 1108

Burton Alb: (4231) Balcombe; Blake-Tracy, Shaughnessy, Leak, Borthwick-Jackson (Gilligan 67); Morris, Powell; Hemmings, Maddox, Patrick; Jebbison (Holloway 67).
Aston Villa U21: (433) Zych; Ealing, Bogarde, Feeney, Swinkels; Iroegbunam, Lindley, Jay-Hart (Thorndike 57); Archer (Reddi 83), Abldeen-Goodridge (Patterson 90), Caleb Chukwuemeka.

Milton Keynes D (1) 2 *(Boateng 4, Jules 64)*

Wycombe W (1) 1 *(Hanlan 8)* 1320

Milton Keynes D: (3412) Ravizzoli; Baldwin, O'Hora, Jules; Watson, Kasumu (Robson 86), McEachran, Ilunga (Kioso 67); Boateng; Martin, Eisa (Brown 63).
Wycombe W: (4132) Przybek; McCarthy, Grimmer, Jacobson, Obita; Gape (Thompson 83); Pendlebury, Mehmeti, Parsons; Hanlan (De Barr 67), Wheeler.

Tuesday, 26 October 2021

Milton Keynes D (2) 2 *(Parrott 16, Watters 25)*

Aston Villa U21 (2) 4 *(Davis 13, Archer 45, 90, Ramsey A 58)* 2683

Milton Keynes D: (3412) Ravizzoli; Watson, Baldwin, Jules; Martin, McEachran, Boateng (O'Riley 77), Ilunga (Johnson 86); Parrott (Eisa 66); Watters, Brown.

Aston Villa U21: (433) Sinisalo; Lindley, Bogarde, Swinkels, Ealing; Iroegbunam, Ramsey A, Carney Chukwuemeka; Archer, Davis (Abldeen-Goodridge 72), Thorndike.

Tuesday, 9 November 2021

Wycombe W (0) 0

Burton Alb (0) 5 *(Holloway 50, 71, 90, Lakin 75, Smith 76)* 593

Wycombe W: (3412) Przybek; Ram, Joseph, Burley; Parsons, Pendlebury, Leathers, Obita (Wakely 46); Mehmeti; Hanlan (Clark 46), Linton.
Burton Alb: (352) Balcombe; Hamer, Leak, Blake-Tracy; Maddox, Morris, Chapman (O'Connor 72), Lakin, Rowe (Smith 72); Holloway, Patrick (Borthwick-Jackson 62).

South Group C	P	W	PW	PL	L	F	A	GD	Pts
Aston Villa U21	3	3	0	0	0	11	5	6	9
Milton Keynes D	3	2	0	0	1	6	6	0	6
Burton Alb	3	1	0	0	2	8	6	2	3
Wycombe W	3	0	0	0	3	2	10	–8	0

SOUTHERN SECTION GROUP D

Tuesday, 31 August 2021

Forest Green R (1) 1 *(Harriman 14 (og))*

Northampton T (0) 1 *(Pollock 51)* 892

Forest Green R: (352) Thomas; Sweeney, Moore-Taylor, Bernard; Allen, Stevenson (Aitchison 67), Adams, Diallo, Evans; March (Stevens 78), Young (Matt 76).
Northampton T: (433) Maxted; Hoskins (Horsfall 69), Nelson, Harriman, Flores (Koiki 63); Sowerby (Rose 68), McWilliams, Pollock; Connolly, Ashley-Seal, Kabamba.
Northampton T won 4-2 on penalties.

Tuesday, 14 September 2021

Walsall (1) 1 *(Phillips 44)*

Brighton & HA U21 (0) 0 1229

Walsall: (4231) Rose; White, Taylor, Menayese, Mills; Labadie, Bates (Perry 61); Willis (Miller 61), Osadebe, Shade (Earing 82); Phillips.
Brighton & HA U21: (433) McGill; Packham (Offiah 84), Turns, Roberts, Furlong; Spong, Dicker■, Leonard; Peupion (Tolaj 80), Ferguson, Sarmiento (Moran 68).

Tuesday, 5 October 2021

Northampton T (0) 1 *(Connolly 72 (pen))*

Walsall (1) 1 *(Osadebe 4)* 1285

Northampton T: (442) Maxted; Harriman, Revan, Horsfall (Dyche 68), Koiki; Connolly, Flores, Pollock (McWilliams 68), Pinnock; Etete, Kabamba (Ashley-Seal 68).
Walsall: (4231) Rose; Leak, Menayese, Monthe, Mills; Bates (Earing 64), Perry (Labadie 76); Shade, Osadebe, Kiernan; Miller (Phillips 61).
Walsall won 4-2 on penalties.

Tuesday, 12 October 2021

Forest Green R (1) 2 *(Stevens 27 (pen), 56)*

Brighton & HA U21 (1) 2 *(Miller 34, Tolaj 63)* 604

Forest Green R: (3412) Thomas; McIntosh (Bennett 86), Bernard, Cargill; Edwards, Diallo, Evans (Bell 90), Allen; Young ; Stevens (Aitchison 58), March.
Brighton & HA U21: (343) McGill; Offiah, Tsoungui■, Turns; Packham, Leonard, Spong, Furlong; Peupion, Tolaj, Miller (Ifill 82).
Forest Green R won 5-3 on penalties.

Tuesday, 2 November 2021

Northampton T (1) 1 *(Kabamba 37)*

Brighton & HA U21 (0) 2 *(Ferguson 71, Tolaj 90)* 1014

Northampton T: (442) Woods; Hoskins, Tomlinson, Revan, Flanagan; Cross, Pollock, Abimbola, Ngwa (Curry 72); Kabamba, Ashley-Seal.
Brighton & HA U21: (4231) McGill; Packham, Offiah, Turns, Furlong; Spong, Leonard; Peupion (Ferguson 57), Moran, Miller (Ella 82); Tolaj.

Wednesday, 10 November 2021

Walsall (0) 0

Forest Green R (1) 2 *(Stevens 15, Young 88)* 1778

Walsall: (433) Rose; Leak, Taylor, Menayese, Ward (Miller 69); Labadie, Bates, Perry (Osadebe 55); Khan, Phillips, Kiernan (Shade 62).
Forest Green R: (352) McGee; Bernard, Bunker (Godwin-Malife 73), Cargill; Edwards, Diallo, Hendry, Evans, Allen; Aitchison (Cadden 80), Stevens (Young 58).

South Group D	P	W	PW	PL	L	F	A	GD	Pts
Forest Green R	3	1	1	1	0	5	3	2	6
Walsall	3	1	1	0	1	2	3	–1	5
Brighton & HA U21	3	1	0	1	1	4	4	0	4
Northampton T	3	0	1	1	1	3	4	–1	3

SOUTHERN SECTION GROUP E

Tuesday, 24 August 2021

Exeter C (0) 1 *(Jay 90 (pen))*

Chelsea U21 (1) 1 *(Fiabema 45)* 1669

Exeter C: (3412) Lee; Key, Pond (Jay 78), Grounds; Caprice (Lilley 62), Dodd, Dyer, Rowe; Edwards (Brown 74); Seymour, Nombe.
Chelsea U21: (343) Sharman-Lowe; Mbuyamba, McClelland, Humphreys; Rankine (Frith 88), Elliott, McEachran, Nunn; Soonsup-Bell (Hall 84), Fiabema, Vale.
Chelsea U21 won 4-3 on penalties.

Tuesday, 31 August 2021

Bristol R (0) 2 *(Nicholson 61, Saunders 70)*

Cheltenham T (0) 0 889

Bristol R: (3421) Ward; Taylor, Kilgour, Harries; Anderson H, Finley (Hargreaves 75), Grant, Saunders; Spence (Jones 75), Nicholson (Westbrooke 74); Collins.
Cheltenham T: (343) Evans; Horton, Pollock (Jakeways 75), Freestone; Hunt (Chapman 60), Thomas, Bonds, Taylor; Miles (Vassell 60), Williams A, Perry.

Tuesday, 5 October 2021

Cheltenham T (1) 2 *(Chapman 37, Miles 70)*

Exeter C (2) 2 *(Daniel 8, Collins 38)* 987

Cheltenham T: (41212) Evans; Horton, Armitage, Freestone, Hussey; Barkers; Bonds, Chapman (Miles 62); Crowley; Vassell, Norton.
Exeter C: (451) Lee; Caprice, Sweeney, Grounds, Daniel; Coley (Kite 62), Atangana, Rowe, Collins (Cox 49), Edwards (Pond 74); Amond.
Exeter C won 3-2 on penalties.

Wednesday, 13 October 2021

Bristol R (1) 1 *(Thomas 17)*

Chelsea U21 (1) 2 *(Lovelock 39 (og), Baker 48)* 1149

Bristol R: (4231) Ward; Martinez, Lovelock, Harries, Clarke T (Mbuenimo 62); Mehew, Hargreaves; Thomas (Langlais 74), Westbrooke, Nicholson (Phillips 62); Walker.
Chelsea U21: (343) Wady; Brooking, Mbuyamba, Gilchrist (Tobin 85); Rankine, Simons, Baker, Nunn; Haigh (Flower 70), Wareham, McEachran.

Tuesday, 26 October 2021

Cheltenham T (0) 0

Chelsea U21 (0) 0 2932

Cheltenham T: (4231) Evans; Hunt (Jakeways 90), Armitage, Horton, Freestone; Thomas (Chapman 61), Barkers; Miles, May, Norton; Williams A (Guinan 88).
Chelsea U21: (343) Wady; Brooking, Mbuyamba, Hughes; Andersson (Thomas 82), Baker, Simons, Nunn; McEachran, Soonsup-Bell (Wareham 67), Webster (Haigh 67).
Cheltenham T won 5-4 on penalties.

Wednesday, 10 November 2021

Exeter C (5) 5 *(Coley 1, 44, Dieng 4, Amond 12, 38)*

Bristol R (0) 3 *(Westbrooke 61, Jones 72, Anderton 88)* 1479

Exeter C: (451) Lee; Caprice, Stubbs (Sweeney 46), Grounds, Sparkes; Coley (Daniel 69), Dieng, Kite, Taylor K (Cox 52), Edwards; Amond.
Bristol R: (4231) Ward; Mbuenimo, Hoole, Martinez, Anderton; Westbrooke, Hargreaves; Walker, Spence, Jones; Collins.

South Group E	P	W	PW	PL	L	F	A	GD	Pts
Exeter C	3	1	1	1	0	8	6	2	6
Chelsea U21	3	1	1	1	0	3	2	1	6
Bristol R	3	1	0	0	2	6	7	–1	3
Cheltenham T	3	0	1	1	1	2	4	–2	3

SOUTHERN SECTION GROUP F

Tuesday, 31 August 2021

Newport Co (0) 2 *(Telford 58, Abraham 84)*

Plymouth Arg (0) 0 1032

Newport Co: (433) Townsend; Bright, Woodiwiss, Dolan (Evans 46), Lewis A; Cain (Hillier 61), Livermore, Cooper; Willmott (Maher 46), Abraham, Telford.
Plymouth Arg: (352) Burton; Tomlinson, Wilson, Pursall; Garrick, Craske (Garside 81), Randell, Wariuh (Davies 63), Law; Massey (Issaka 69), Shirley.

Tuesday, 7 September 2021

Swindon T (1) 2 *(Dabre 17, Taylor-Hart 69 (og))*

Arsenal U21 (1) 1 *(Ideho 34)* 2452

Swindon T: (442) Ward; Hunt, Odimayo, Crichlow-Noble (Conroy 63), Iandolo; Dabre, Aguiar, East, Parsons; Mitchell-Lawson (Simpson 63), Gilbert (Payne 64).
Arsenal U21: (3421) Ejeheri; Monlouis, Kirk, Ogungbo; Walters, Francis (Oulad M'hand 46), Patino, Lopez; Ideho (Butler-Oyedeji 71), Taylor-Hart (Cozier-Duberry 70); Biereth.

Tuesday, 12 October 2021

Newport Co (1) 3 *(Greenidge 19, Abraham 62, Fisher 68)*

Arsenal U21 (1) 4 *(Hutchinson 33, Oulad M'hand 53, Olayinka 86, Sagoe Junior 90)* 1426

Newport Co: (3412) Townsend; Missilou, Woodiwiss, Hall; Lewis A, Cain (Twamley 87), Livermore, Collins; Hylton (Abraham 46); Greenidge (Fisher 46), Ellison.
Arsenal U21: (343) Ejeheri; Monlouis (Foran 74), Swanson, Ogungbo; Alebiosu, Olayinka, Oulad M'hand, Lopez; Ideho (Sagoe Junior 87), Hutchinson, Taylor-Hart (Edwards 78).

Plymouth Arg (1) 1 *(Agard 24)*

Swindon T (1) 3 *(Gillesphey 20 (og), Mitchell-Lawson 74, McKirdy 84)* 1556

Plymouth Arg: (352) Burton; Tomlinson, Wilson, Gillesphey; Edwards, Camara, Randell, Mayor (Davies 46), Law; Agard (Garrick 66), Shirley (Hardie 79).
Swindon T: (532) Ward; Hunt (Cowmeadow 63), Odimayo (Iandolo 64), Baudry, Crichlow-Noble, Dabre; Lyden (McKirdy 64), East, Aguiar; Mitchell-Lawson, Parsons.

Tuesday, 2 November 2021

Plymouth Arg (1) 1 *(Agard 24)*

Arsenal U21 (0) 1 *(Balogun 56)* 1795

Plymouth Arg: (352) Burton; Tomlinson, Gillesphey, Pursall; Garrick (Craske 65), Davies, Houghton (Garside 46), Mayor (Roberts 56), Law; Shirley, Agard.
Arsenal U21: (343) Okonkwo; Norton-Cuffy, Swanson, Rekik (Walters 74); Alebiosu (Foran 51), Olayinka, Akinola, Lopez (Ideho 88); Balogun, Biereth, Taylor-Hart.
Plymouth Arg won 5-4 on penalties.

Tuesday, 9 November 2021

Swindon T (0) 1 *(Lyden 57)*

Newport Co (0) 0 2125

Swindon T: (3412) Ward; Hunt, Minturn, Winchcombe; Parsons, Lyden, East, Dabre; Gilbert; McKirdy, Mitchell-Lawson.
Newport Co: (3412) Townsend; Bright, Dolan (Woodiwiss 62), Haynes; Ellison, Upson, Missilou, Collins; Hylton (Hall 75); Fisher, Abraham (Greenidge 58).

South Group F	P	W	PW	PL	L	F	A	GD	Pts
Swindon T	3	3	0	0	0	6	2	4	9
Arsenal U21	3	1	0	1	1	6	6	0	4
Newport Co	3	1	0	0	2	5	5	0	3
Plymouth Arg	3	0	1	0	2	2	6	–4	2

SOUTHERN SECTION GROUP G

Tuesday, 31 August 2021

Charlton Ath (3) 6 *(Davison 6, 90, Blackett-Taylor 18, Lee 22, Francomb 54 (og), Burstow 82)*

Crawley T (0) 1 *(Appiah 75 (pen))* 1404

Charlton Ath: (442) Harness; Barker, Elerewe, Pearce, Roddy; Blackett-Taylor (Kirk 64), Dobson, Clare (Dempsey 64), Clayden; Davison, Lee (Burstow 81).
Crawley T: (442) Nna Noukeu; Francomb, Dallison (Frost 13), Craig, Gallacher (Hessenthaler 46); Tilley, Powell, Payne, Tsaroulla; Ashford, Nadesan (Appiah 56).

Tuesday, 14 September 2021

Leyton Orient (0) 1 *(Papadopoulos 82)*

Southampton U21 (0) 0 634

Leyton Orient: (343) Byrne; Mitchell, Beckles, Happe; Papadopoulos, Reilly (Tanga 72), Kyprianou, Sweeney; Sotiriou (Nkrumah 43), Omotoye, Kemp.
Southampton U21: (343) Bycroft; Otseh-Taiwo (Hewlett 84), Lancashire, Simeu; Payne, Doyle, Chauke, Lett; Watts, Mitchell (Smith 71), Olaigbe.

Tuesday, 5 October 2021

Charlton Ath (3) 4 *(Stockley 28, 34 (pen), Purrington 45, Pearce 90)*

Southampton U21 (0) 1 *(Lancashire 75)* 689

Charlton Ath: (433) Harness; Matthews, Elerewe, Pearce, Purrington; Morgan, Dobson, Clare (Dempsey 77); Jaiyesimi (Clayden 61), Stockley, Kirk (Blackett-Taylor 75).
Southampton U21: (343) Bycroft; Olufunwa, Lancashire, Simeu; Otseh-Taiwo (Davey 82), Smallbone (Hewlett 46), Chauke, Payne; Watts, Mitchell, Doyle.

Crawley T (0) 0

Leyton Orient (2) 4 *(Sotiriou 7, 59, Happe 30, Kemp 77)* 810

Crawley T: (4411) Henry; Davies, Dallison, Craig, Gallacher; Tilley (Frost 60), Bansal-McNulty (Kevser-Junior 85), Powell, Marshall; Khaleel (Appiah 60); Battle.
Leyton Orient: (343) Byrne; Ogie, Sweeney, Happe; James, Kyprianou, Clay, Papadopoulos; Sotiriou, Omotoye (Nkrumah 80), Kemp.

Tuesday, 9 November 2021

Crawley T (0) 0

Southampton U21 (2) 4 *(Olaigbe 28, 58, Mitchell 41, Small 89)* 385

Crawley T: (4141) Nna Noukeu; Davies, Francillette, Craig, Dallison; Payne (Marshall 46); Ashford, Powell, Bansal-McNulty, Frost (Matthews 81); Rodari (Grego-Cox 64).
Southampton U21: (442) Bycroft; Payne, Olufunwa, Lancashire, Small; Watts, Doyle (Finnigan 64), Chauke (Burnett 64), Olaigbe; Hewlett (Turner 70), Mitchell.

Leyton Orient (0) 1 *(Smyth 78)*

Charlton Ath (0) 0 2295

Leyton Orient: (3412) Byrne; Mitchell, Ogie (Thompson 71), Happe; Papadopoulos■, Kyprianou, Young, Wood; Smyth (Kemp 85); Sotiriou, Omotoye (Nkrumah 90).
Charlton Ath: (352) Harness; Elerewe, Bakrin, Souare; Chin (Viggars 76), Morgan, Dempsey, Henry, Clayden; Burstow (Powell 70), Davison (Aouachira 46).

South Group G	P	W	PW	PL	L	F	A	GD	Pts
Leyton Orient	3	3	0	0	0	6	0	6	9
Charlton Ath	3	2	0	0	1	10	3	7	6
Southampton U21	3	1	0	0	2	5	5	0	3
Crawley T	3	0	0	0	3	1	14	–13	0

SOUTHERN SECTION GROUP H

Tuesday, 31 August 2021

Cambridge U (2) 4 *(Smith 45, 45, Knibbs 80, Yearn 90)*
Oxford U (0) 1 *(Agyei 71)* 1390

Cambridge U: (442) McKenzie-Lyle; Bennett, Digby, Jobe, Dunk; Lankester (Yearn 69), May, Weir, Worman; Knibbs, Smith (Brophy 77).
Oxford U: (4231) Eastwood; Chambers (Nosakhare 46), McNally■, Mousinho, Elechi; Johnson, Kane (Anifowose 86); Cooper, Goodrham, Holland (O'Donkor 61); Agyei.

Stevenage (1) 3 *(Daly 42, Marshall 63, Omole 88 (og))*
Tottenham H U21 (2) 4 *(White 8, 50, Alonso 24, Lyons-Foster 73)* 1235

Stevenage: (442) Bastien; Barry (Wildin 51), Marshall, Cuthbert, Coker; Read, Smith J, Lines, Andrade (Taylor 52); Norris (Reid 74), Daly.
Tottenham H U21: (433) Oluwayemi; Walcott, Muir, Omole, Lavinier; Markanday (Pedder 89), Lyons-Foster, White; Cesay, Alonso, Clarke.

Tuesday, 21 September 2021

Cambridge U (0) 1 *(Smith 72)*
Tottenham H U21 (0) 0 2025

Cambridge U: (442) McKenzie-Lyle; Williams (Davies 63), Okedina, Jones (Iredale 77), Dunk; Worman, Weir, May (Yearn 63), Lankester; Knibbs, Smith.
Tottenham H U21: (442) Oluwayemi; Matthew Craig, Muir, Omole, Cesay (Michael Craig 87); Markanday, Lyons-Foster (Alonso 70), White, Clarke; John, Devine.

Tuesday, 5 October 2021

Oxford U (1) 1 *(Agyei 11)*
Stevenage (0) 2 *(Reid 75, Norris 90)* 1712

Oxford U: (433) Eastwood; Forde, Moore, Thorniley (Long 46), Seddon; Henry (Davis 73), Brannagan, Sykes; Williams, Agyei, Cooper (Holland 62).
Stevenage: (4222) Anang; Wildin, Vancooten, Prosser, Melbourne (Townsend-West 75); Reeves, Smith J (List 85); Osborne, Andrade (Taylor 74); Reid, Norris.

Tuesday, 26 October 2021

Oxford U (2) 3 *(Cooper 2, 28, Gorrin 65)*
Tottenham H U21 (1) 2 *(Scarlett 24 (pen), Clarke 90)* 1702

Oxford U: (433) Eastwood; Forde, McNally■, Mousinho, Hanson (Golding 78); Johnson, Gorrin, McGuane (O'Donkor 78); Bodin (Anifowose 87), Agyei, Cooper.
Tottenham H U21: (433) Lo-Tutala; Michael Craig (Lavinier 85), Paskotsi, Walcott, Cesay; John (Alonso 77), Lyons-Foster, White; Clarke, Scarlett, Markanday.

Tuesday, 9 November 2021

Stevenage (1) 1 *(List 40)*
Cambridge U (0) 0 967

Stevenage: (442) Smith A; Wildin, Vancooten, Prosser, Melbourne; Osborne, Taylor (Lines 80), Reeves, Barry (Read 65); List (Daly 65), Reid.
Cambridge U: (4231) McKenzie-Lyle; Davies, Okedina, Masterson, Dunk; Simper (Ironside 80), May; Bennett (Brophy 64), Yearn (Weir 64), Worman; Knibbs.

South Group H	P	W	PW	PL	L	F	A	GD	Pts
Cambridge U	3	2	0	0	1	5	2	3	6
Stevenage	3	2	0	0	1	6	5	1	6
Tottenham H U21	3	1	0	0	2	6	7	–1	3
Oxford U	3	1	0	0	2	5	8	–3	3

NORTHERN SECTION SECOND ROUND

Tuesday, 30 November 2021

Accrington S (1) 1 *(Pell 18)*
Wigan Ath (0) 1 *(Humphrys 53)* 1131

Accrington S: (4411) Savin; Sherring (Amankwah 88), Sykes, Nottingham, Rodgers; Hamilton, Scully (Mumbongo 57), Coyle, McConville (Nolan 61); Pell; Bishop.
Wigan Ath: (4231) Jamie Jones; Massey, Kerr, Watts, Bennett (Robinson 68); Smith (Adeeko 45), Bayliss; Edwards (Sze 81), Aasgaard (McHugh 81), Jordan Jones; Humphrys (Baningime 82).
Wigan Ath won 5-4 on penalties.

Bolton W (1) 1 *(Lee 34)*
Fleetwood T (0) 0 1773

Bolton W: (4231) Dixon; Gordon, Baptiste, Aimson, John (Delfouneso 70); Johnston, Lee (Pettifer 70); Amaechi (Henry 84), Thomason, Afolayan (Tweedley 84); Doyle (Kachunga 70).
Fleetwood T: (433) Crellin; Johnston, Bird, McLaughlin (Teale 46), Clark; Boyle, Baggley, Biggins (Raffie 75); Hayes, Edmondson, McMillan (Conn-Clarke 61).

Carlisle U (0) 1 *(Armer 69)*
Lincoln C (1) 1 *(Maguire 45)* 884

Carlisle U: (442) Howard; Mellor, Feeney, McDonald, Armer; Gibson (Charters 63), Guy, Mellish, Clough (Whelan 85); Abrahams (Young 46), Fishburn (Mampala 63).
Lincoln C: (433) Griffiths; Poole, Montsma, Eyoma, Bramall (Robson 69); McGrandles, N'Lundulu, Sanders (Bishop 78); Fiorini, Adelakun, Maguire.
Carlisle U won 4-3 on penalties.

Rotherham U (0) 1 *(Smith 56)*
Port Vale (0) 1 *(Amoo 87)* 1560

Rotherham U: (3142) Johansson; Harding, Ihiekwe (Edmonds-Green 64), Mattock; Rathbone (Miller 64); Sadlier, Odofin, Lindsay, Bola (Ferguson 46); Kayode (Ladapo 77), Grigg (Smith 46).
Port Vale: (352) Stone; Smith, Legge (Amos 74), Johnson (Martin 60); Cass, Garrity (Burgess 60), Conlon, Walker, Jones D (Benning 61); Politic (Amoo 60), Rodney.
Rotherham U won 5-3 on penalties.

Wednesday, 1 December 2021

Crewe Alex (1) 2 *(Knight 33, Finney 72)*
Doncaster R (0) 0 699

Crewe Alex: (532) Jaaskelainen; Ainley (Johnson 46), O'Riordan, Thomas T, Offord, Woodthorpe (Tabiner 77); Gomes (Lundstram 46), Murphy, Finney; Mandron, Knight.
Doncaster R: (4231) Jones; Knoyle, Anderson, Olowu, Horton (Rowe 46); Smith, Galbraith; Barlow (Hasani 57), Cukur (Kuleya 68), Hiwula; Dodoo.

Sheffield W (0) 0
Hartlepool U (2) 3 *(Shelton 11, Brown 14 (og), Goodwin 59)* 5109

Sheffield W: (352) Wildsmith; Paterson, Brennan (Adedoyin 85), Brown; Corbeanu, Byers (Hunt 46), Dele-Bashiru, Wing (Agbontohoma 70), Shodipo (Bannan 46); Berahino, Sow (Windass 46).
Hartlepool U: (532) Mitchell; Sterry, Odusina, Hendrie, Francis-Angol (Byrne 86), Jones; Shelton, Smith, Crawford; Goodwin (Fondop-Talom 86), Grey (Olomola 80).

Sunderland (0) 0
Oldham Ath (0) 1 *(Vaughan 53)* 3498

Sunderland: (343) Burge; Xhemajli, Alves, Younger; Dajaku (Kachosa 46), Embleton (Wearne 46), Wilding, Dunne (Dyce 73); O'Brien, Harris, Mbunga-Kimpioka.
Oldham Ath: (4231) Leutwiler; Adams, Clarke, Piergianni, Couto; Cisse (Hopcutt 80), Whelan (Bowden 81); Stobbs (Dearnley 59), Vaughan (Diarra 64), Keillor-Dunn; Hope (Bahamboula 80).

Tuesday, 21 December 2021

Tranmere R (1) 1 *(Maynard 11)*
Harrogate T (0) 2 *(Muldoon 53, Pattison 71)* 400

Tranmere R: (4141) Murphy; Hayde, Davies, Maguire (Clarke 90), MacDonald; Merrie (O'Connor 72); McManaman, Watson, Duffy (Foley 62), Feeney (Jolley 71); Maynard (Nevitt 72).
Harrogate T: (433) Oxley; Fallowfield, Sheron, Burrell, Page; Pattison, Falkingham, Kerry (Muldoon 46); Thomson, Armstrong, Diamond.

SOUTHERN SECTION SECOND ROUND

Tuesday, 30 November 2021

Cambridge U (1) 2 *(Smith 18 (pen), Tracey 80)*

Walsall (0) 0 718

Cambridge U: (442) McKenzie-Lyle; Bennett, Okedina, Masterson, Iredale (Dunk 62); Lankester (Brophy 74), Weir, Simper (Digby 73), Worman (Yearn 90); Smith (Tracey 62), Knibbs.
Walsall: (4231) Rose; Khan, Taylor, Monthe, White (Mills 60); Earing (Willock 73), Kinsella (Bates 83); Wilkinson (Miller 60), Osadebe (Perry 83), Shade; Phillips.

Charlton Ath (2) 2 *(Burstow 15, Stockley 43 (pen))*

Aston Villa U21 (1) 1 *(Thorndike 40)* 1283

Charlton Ath: (3142) Harness; Bakrin, Elerewe, Gunter; Watson; Clayden (Blackett-Taylor 38), Morgan, Arter (Henry 74), Kirk; Burstow (Davison 64), Stockley (Leko 65).
Aston Villa U21: (4231) Zych; Ealing, Feeney, Swinkels, Chrisene (Barber 61); Bogarde, Iroegbunam; Caleb Chukwuemeka (Ableen-Goodridge 77), Thorndike, Philogene-Bidace; Archer.

Forest Green R (0) 1 *(March 64)*

Chelsea U21 (0) 1 *(Uwakwe 65)* 1270

Forest Green R: (3412) Thomas; Godwin-Malife, Sweeney, Bunker; Edwards, Evans, Diallo (Aitchison 80), Allen; Hendry; March, Young (Stevens 86).
Chelsea U21: (343) Bergstrom; Hughes, Mbuyamba, Gilchrist; Haigh, Simons, Baker, Hall; McEachran, Fiabema (Mothersille 62), Uwakwe (Nunn 79).
Chelsea U21 won 4-1 on penalties.

Leyton Orient (0) 0

Milton Keynes D (0) 0 990

Leyton Orient: (3412) Byrne; Mitchell, Thompson, Happe; Archibald, Kyprianou, Young, Wood (James 77); Nkrumah (Smith 76); Sotiriou, Omotoye (Tanga 62).
Milton Keynes D: (343) Ravizzoli; Baldwin, Darling, Jules; Watson, McEachran (Martin 57), Robson, Ilunga; Boateng, Brown (Eisa 78), Parrott■.
Milton Keynes D won 5-4 on penalties.

Sutton U (0) 0

Stevenage (0) 0 770

Sutton U: (442) House (Bouzanis 69); Barden, Goodliffe, John (Boldewijn 73), Wyatt (Milsom 50); Korboa, Eastmond, Davis, Randall; Wilson (Olaofe 73), Bennett (Bugiel 69).
Stevenage: (352) Anang; Marshall, Vancooten, Melbourne; Barry (Wildin 75), Taylor, Lines (Reeves 75), Read (List 75), Smith J (Osborne 63); Daly (Reid 63), Norris.
Sutton U won 4-3 on penalties.

Swindon T (1) 1 *(Crichlow-Noble 45)*

Colchester U (2) 2 *(Chambers 6, 11)* 1728

Swindon T: (532) Ward; Francis (Gordon 57), Minturn (Dworzak 89), Grant, Crichlow-Noble, Dabre; Lyden, Gilbert, East; Mitchell-Lawson, McKirdy (Fox 63).
Colchester U: (4231) Turner; Welch-Hayes, Chambers, Smith, Coxe; Judge (Hannant 64), Skuse; Jasper (Tovide 64), Chilvers, Dobra (Tchamadeu 87); Sears (McCoulsky 65).

Wednesday, 1 December 2021

Ipswich T (2) 2 *(Jackson 31, 43)*

Arsenal U21 (0) 2 *(Vincent-Young 68 (og), Balogun 71)* 4065

Ipswich T: (4231) Hladky; Vincent-Young (Donacien 79), Woolfenden, Burgess, Penney; Carroll, El Mizouni (Chaplin 90); Jackson, Harper (Evans 78), Edwards (Celina 78); Pigott.
Arsenal U21: (532) Ejeheri; Swanson (Alebiosu 89), Norton-Cuffy, Rekik, Ogungbo, Lopez; Hutchinson, Akinola, Patino (Oulad M'hand 46); Biereth, Balogun.
Arsenal U21 won 4-3 on penalties.

Friday, 7 January 2022

Exeter C (1) 2 *(Jay 6, Collins 76)*

Portsmouth (1) 3 *(Hirst 5, Curtis 89, 90)* 2146

Exeter C: (3421) Dawson; Sweeney (Kite 46), Stubbs, Diabate; Key, Collins, Taylor K (Dieng 55), Caprice; Jay (Coley 79), Edwards (Amond 71); Seymour (Brown J 55).
Portsmouth: (3412) Bass; Freeman, Raggett, Ogilvie; Romeo, Azeez (Thompson 63), Morrell (Jewitt-White 88), Brown; Harness (Jacobs 63); Hirst (Hackett-Fairchild 63), Marquis (Curtis 63).

NORTHERN SECTION THIRD ROUND

Tuesday, 4 January 2022

Crewe Alex (1) 2 *(Mandron 11, Robertson 71)*

Rotherham U (1) 4 *(Sadlier 41, Smith 57, Kayode 82, Ladapo 90)* 771

Crewe Alex: (343) Jaaskelainen; O'Riordan, Daniels, Thomas T; Ramsay (Tabiner 69), Griffiths (Salisbury 85), Robertson, Johnson; Finney (Murphy 68), Mandron (Porter 85), Ainley.
Rotherham U: (3412) Vickers; Edmonds-Green, Ihiekwe, Mattock (Ogbene 78); Harding, Lindsay (Ferguson 71), Odofin, Bola (Rathbone 71); Sadlier; Smith (Kayode 62), Grigg (Ladapo 78).

Harrogate T (1) 1 *(Armstrong 7)*

Carlisle U (0) 0 928

Harrogate T: (433) Oxley; Sheron, McArdle, Hall, Page; Diarra (Beck 81), Falkingham, Austerfield (Kerry 73); Muldoon, Armstrong, Diamond.
Carlisle U: (442) Howard; Mellor (Mampala 80), Feeney, McDonald, Armer; Gibson, Whelan, Guy (Senior 80), Dickenson (Charters 86); Fishburn (Riley 46), Mellish (Abrahams 80).

Hartlepool U (0) 1 *(Daly 84)*

Bolton W (0) 0 2529

Hartlepool U: (433) Killip; Jones, Byrne, Odusina, Francis-Angol; Crawford, Smith (Featherstone 76), Daly; Olomola (Fondop-Talom 82), Molyneux, Grey (Ferguson 90).
Bolton W: (433) Dixon; Fossey, Santos, Johnston, John (Gordon 85); Thomason, Williams, Delfouneso; Kachunga (Bakayoko 55), Charles (Doyle 61), Afolayan.

Oldham Ath (0) 0

Wigan Ath (3) 6 *(Naylor 28, Keane 34, Power 36, Massey 47, Edwards 64, 67)* 1831

Oldham Ath: (4231) Rogers; Adams, McGahey, Hart, Couto; Turner, Cisse (Bowden 54); Bahamboula (Hope 81), Vaughan, Hopcutt (Fage 53); Luamba (Keillor-Dunn 54).
Wigan Ath: (4231) Amos; Darikwa, Whatmough (Kerr 78), Tilt, Pearce (Robinson 69); Power, Naylor; Massey (Aasgaard 68), Lang (Jordan Jones 61), Edwards; Keane (Humphrys 62).

SOUTHERN SECTION THIRD ROUND

Tuesday, 4 January 2022

Charlton Ath (0) 1 *(Leko 90)*

Milton Keynes D (0) 0 1653

Charlton Ath: (343) Harness; Matthews (Elerewe 66), Inniss (Ness 77), Gunter; Blackett-Taylor (Williams 67), Henry (Dempsey 87), Watson, Souare; Leko, Burstow, Kirk (Davison 87).
Milton Keynes D: (343) Ravizzoli; O'Hora, Darling, Jules; Watson, Kasumu, Robson (McEachran 88), Ilunga; Boateng, Eisa, Bird (Martin 60).

Sutton U (1) 2 *(Turner 7 (og), Wilson 52)*

Colchester U (1) 1 *(Sears 45)* 977

Sutton U: (442) Bouzanis; Kizzi, Goodliffe, John, Wyatt; Boldewijn, Smith, Barden, Olaofe; Wilson (Milsom 81), Bennett (Sho-Silva 77).
Colchester U: (541) Turner; Tchamadeu (Tovide 81), Eastman, Chambers, Smith, Coxe; Judge, Skuse, Sarpong-Wiredu, Dobra (Hannant 68); Sears.

Tuesday, 11 January 2022

Arsenal U21 (2) 4 *(Olayinka 10, Biereth 42, Hutchinson 61, Flores 67)*

Chelsea U21 (1) 1 *(Wareham 38)* 1610

Arsenal U21: (343) Hein; Norton-Cuffy, Awe, Ogungbo; Alebiosu (Ideho 82), Francis, Oulad M'hand (Walters 62), Lopez (Edwards 82); Hutchinson (Flores 62), Biereth, Olayinka (Akinola 23).
Chelsea U21: (343) Sharman-Lowe; Brooking, Mbuyamba■, Gilchrist (Hughes 75); Simons, Elliott (Rankine 46), Baker, Vale (Fiabema 75); Haigh, Wareham (Nunn 63), Soonsup-Bell (Webster 63).

Cambridge U (0) 2 *(Knibbs 50, 59)*

Portsmouth (0) 1 *(Jacobs 76)* 1308

Cambridge U: (4231) Mitov; Bennett, Okedina, Iredale, Dunk; O'Neil (Worman 46), May (Digby 71); Lankester (Dickens 90), Hoolahan (Brophy 71), Knibbs (Ironside 83); Smith.
Portsmouth: (3412) Bass; Freeman, Robertson (Raggett 46), Ogilvie; Romeo, Thompson (Tunnicliffe 60), Morrell, Hackett-Fairchild (Brown 61); Jacobs; Curtis (Marquis 61), Hirst (Harness 61).

QUARTER-FINALS

Tuesday, 25 January 2022

Hartlepool U (1) 2 *(Grey 7, Molyneux 73)*

Charlton Ath (2) 2 *(Burstow 17, Gilbey 32)* 3615

Hartlepool U: (4411) Killip; Sterry, Hendrie, Odusina, Francis-Angol; Olomola (Molyneux 70), Smith, Shelton, Grey (Ogle 85); Crawford; Cullen.
Charlton Ath: (352) MacGillivray; Matthews, Pearce, Famewo; Leko (Blackett-Taylor 71), Morgan (Lee 80), Watson (Clare 80), Gilbey, Purrington (Castillo 88); Burstow (Aneke 70), Washington.
Hartlepool U won 5-4 on penalties.

Rotherham U (1) 1 *(Harding 9)*

Cambridge U (1) 1 *(Digby 40)* 2239

Rotherham U: (3142) Johansson; Edmonds-Green, Ihiekwe, Mattock; Odofin; Harding (Ogbene 65), Lindsay, Sadlier (Wiles 65), Bola (Miller 66); Grigg (Ladapo 65), Kayode (Ferguson 86).
Cambridge U: (4231) Mitov; Bennett, Williams, Okedina, Dunk; Digby, Worman; Knibbs, May, Brophy; Smith.
Rotherham U won 7-6 on penalties.

Sutton U (0) 1 *(Eastmond 80)*

Harrogate T (0) 0 1499

Sutton U: (442) Bouzanis; Kizzi, Goodliffe, John, Wyatt; Boldewijn, Davis (Smith 59), Eastmond, Randall (Ajiboye 65); Wilson (Olaofe 60), Bennett (Bugiel 60).
Harrogate T: (3421) Oxley; Sheron, McArdle, Burrell; Thomson, Falkingham, Kerry (Beck 82), Page (Smith 53); Muldoon, Diarra (Pattison 66); Armstrong.

Wigan Ath (0) 1 *(Baningime 83)*

Arsenal U21 (0) 0 3647

Wigan Ath: (3421) Jamie Jones; Carragher, Long, Bennett (Baningime 73); Lloyd, Power (Robinson 15), Bayliss, Pearce (Hughes 33); McHugh, Aasgaard; Sze.
Arsenal U21: (3421) Ejeheri; Kirk (Edwards 89), Awe, Ogungbo; Swanson, Patino (Walters 46), Francis (Ideho 66), Lopez; Hutchinson, Oulad M'hand; Biereth.

SEMI-FINALS

Tuesday, 8 March 2022

Wigan Ath (1) 1 *(McClean 39)*

Sutton U (1) 1 *(Randall 29)* 6541

Wigan Ath: (4231) Jamie Jones; Darikwa, Kerr, Watts, Pearce (Keane 65); Bayliss (Power 66), Shinnie; Massey (Edwards 65), McGrath, McClean; Magennis.
Sutton U: (442) Bouzanis; Kizzi, Goodliffe, John, Milsom; Ajiboye, Eastmond, Beautyman, Randall (Korboa 83); Wilson (Boldewijn 75), Bugiel (Bennett 78).
Sutton U won 7-6 on penalties.

Wednesday, 9 March 2022

Hartlepool U (1) 2 *(Grey 29, Molyneux 55)*

Rotherham U (0) 2 *(Smith 50, 63)* 7542

Hartlepool U: (433) Killip; Sterry, Byrne, Odusina, Ferguson; Shelton, Featherstone, Crawford; Molyneux, Bogle, Grey (Carver 85).
Rotherham U: (3142) Johansson; Edmonds-Green, Wood (Ihiekwe 46), MacDonald; Barlaser; Osei-Tutu (Ferguson 90), Lindsay (Miller 34), Odofin (Rathbone 46), Bola (Ogbene 61); Wiles, Smith.
Rotherham U won 5-4 on penalties.

PAPA JOHN'S EFL TROPHY FINAL 2021–22

Sunday, 3 April 2022

(at Wembley Stadium, attendance 30,688)

Rotherham U (1) 4 **Sutton U (1) 2**

Rotherham U: (3142) Johansson; Ihiekwe, Wood, Mattock (Ferguson 80); Barlaser (Lindsay 90); Ogbene, Rathbone (Harding 61), Wiles, Miller (Osei-Tutu 80); Smith, Kayode (Ladapo 60).
Scorers: Wiles 42, Osei-Tutu 90, Ogbene 96, Ihiekwe 112.

Sutton U: (442) Bouzanis; Kizzi, Goodliffe (Rowe 73), John, Milsom (Wyatt 82); Ajiboye, Eastmond (Davis 82), Beautyman, Randall; Bugiel (Bennett 82), Wilson (Olaofe 67).
Scorers: Wilson 30, Eastmond 48.

aet.

Referee: Sebastian Stockbridge.

FA CUP FINALS 1872–2022

VENUES

1872 and 1874–92	Kennington Oval
1873	Lillie Bridge
1893	Fallowfield, Manchester
1894	Everton
1923–2000	Wembley Stadium (old)
1895–1914	Crystal Palace
1915	Old Trafford, Manchester
1920–22	Stamford Bridge
2001–06	Millennium Stadium, Cardiff
2007 to date	Wembley Stadium (new)

THE FA CUP

1872	Wanderers v Royal Engineers	1-0
1873	Wanderers v Oxford University	2-0
1874	Oxford University v Royal Engineers	2-0
1875	Royal Engineers v Old Etonians	1-1*
Replay	Royal Engineers v Old Etonians	2-0
1876	Wanderers v Old Etonians	1-1*
Replay	Wanderers v Old Etonians	3-0
1877	Wanderers v Oxford University	2-1*
1878	Wanderers v Royal Engineers	3-1

Wanderers won the cup outright, but it was restored to the Football Association.

1879	Old Etonians v Clapham R	1-0
1880	Clapham R v Oxford University	1-0
1881	Old Carthusians v Old Etonians	3-0
1882	Old Etonians v Blackburn R	1-0
1883	Blackburn Olympic v Old Etonians	2-1*
1884	Blackburn R v Queen's Park, Glasgow	2-1
1885	Blackburn R v Queen's Park, Glasgow	2-0
1886	Blackburn R v WBA	0-0
Replay	Blackburn R v WBA	2-0
	(at Racecourse Ground, Derby Co)	

A special trophy was awarded to Blackburn R for third consecutive win.

1887	Aston Villa v WBA	2-0
1888	WBA v Preston NE	2-1
1889	Preston NE v Wolverhampton W	3-0
1890	Blackburn R v The Wednesday	6-1
1891	Blackburn R v Notts Co	3-1
1892	WBA v Aston Villa	3-0
1893	Wolverhampton W v Everton	1-0
1894	Notts Co v Bolton W	4-1
1895	Aston Villa v WBA	1-0

FA Cup was stolen from a shop window in Birmingham and never found.

1896	The Wednesday v Wolverhampton W	2-1
1897	Aston Villa v Everton	3-2
1898	Nottingham F v Derby Co	3-1
1899	Sheffield U v Derby Co	4-1
1900	Bury v Southampton	4-0
1901	Tottenham H v Sheffield U	2-2
Replay	Tottenham H v Sheffield U	3-1
	(at Burnden Park, Bolton W)	
1902	Sheffield U v Southampton	1-1
Replay	Sheffield U v Southampton	2-1
1903	Bury v Derby Co	6-0
1904	Manchester C v Bolton W	1-0
1905	Aston Villa v Newcastle U	2-0
1906	Everton v Newcastle U	1-0
1907	The Wednesday v Everton	2-1
1908	Wolverhampton W v Newcastle U	3-1
1909	Manchester U v Bristol C	1-0
1910	Newcastle U v Barnsley	1-1
Replay	Newcastle U v Barnsley	2-0
	(at Goodison Park, Everton)	
1911	Bradford C v Newcastle U	0-0
Replay	Bradford C v Newcastle U	1-0
	(at Old Trafford, Manchester U)	

Trophy was given to Lord Kinnaird – he made nine FA Cup Final appearances – for services to football.

1912	Barnsley v WBA	0-0
Replay	Barnsley v WBA	1-0
	(at Bramall Lane, Sheffield U)	
1913	Aston Villa v Sunderland	1-0
1914	Burnley v Liverpool	1-0
1915	Sheffield U v Chelsea	3-0
1920	Aston Villa v Huddersfield T	1-0*
1921	Tottenham H v Wolverhampton W	1-0
1922	Huddersfield T v Preston NE	1-0
1923	Bolton W v West Ham U	2-0
1924	Newcastle U v Aston Villa	2-0
1925	Sheffield U v Cardiff C	1-0
1926	Bolton W v Manchester C	1-0
1927	Cardiff C v Arsenal	1-0
1928	Blackburn R v Huddersfield T	3-1
1929	Bolton W v Portsmouth	2-0
1930	Arsenal v Huddersfield T	2-0
1931	WBA v Birmingham	2-1
1932	Newcastle U v Arsenal	2-1
1933	Everton v Manchester C	3-0
1934	Manchester C v Portsmouth	2-1
1935	Sheffield W v WBA	4-2
1936	Arsenal v Sheffield U	1-0
1937	Sunderland v Preston NE	3-1
1938	Preston NE v Huddersfield T	1-0*
1939	Portsmouth v Wolverhampton W	4-1
1946	Derby Co v Charlton Ath	4-1*
1947	Charlton Ath v Burnley	1-0*
1948	Manchester U v Blackpool	4-2
1949	Wolverhampton W v Leicester C	3-1
1950	Arsenal v Liverpool	2-0
1951	Newcastle U v Blackpool	2-0
1952	Newcastle U v Arsenal	1-0
1953	Blackpool v Bolton W	4-3
1954	WBA v Preston NE	3-2
1955	Newcastle U v Manchester C	3-1
1956	Manchester C v Birmingham C	3-1
1957	Aston Villa v Manchester U	2-1
1958	Bolton W v Manchester U	2-0
1959	Nottingham F v Luton T	2-1
1960	Wolverhampton W v Blackburn R	3-0
1961	Tottenham H v Leicester C	2-0
1962	Tottenham H v Burnley	3-1
1963	Manchester U v Leicester C	3-1
1964	West Ham U v Preston NE	3-2
1965	Liverpool v Leeds U	2-1*
1966	Everton v Sheffield W	3-2
1967	Tottenham H v Chelsea	2-1
1968	WBA v Everton	1-0*
1969	Manchester C v Leicester C	1-0
1970	Chelsea v Leeds U	2-2*
Replay	Chelsea v Leeds U	2-1
	(at Old Trafford, Manchester U)	
1971	Arsenal v Liverpool	2-1*
1972	Leeds U v Arsenal	1-0
1973	Sunderland v Leeds U	1-0
1974	Liverpool v Newcastle U	3-0
1975	West Ham U v Fulham	2-0
1976	Southampton v Manchester U	1-0
1977	Manchester U v Liverpool	2-1
1978	Ipswich T v Arsenal	1-0
1979	Arsenal v Manchester U	3-2
1980	West Ham U v Arsenal	1-0
1981	Tottenham H v Manchester C	1-1*
Replay	Tottenham H v Manchester C	3-2

1982	Tottenham H v QPR	1-1*
Replay	Tottenham H v QPR	1-0
1983	Manchester U v Brighton & HA	2-2*
Replay	Manchester U v Brighton & HA	4-0
1984	Everton v Watford	2-0
1985	Manchester U v Everton	1-0*
1986	Liverpool v Everton	3-1
1987	Coventry C v Tottenham H	3-2*
1988	Wimbledon v Liverpool	1-0
1989	Liverpool v Everton	3-2*
1990	Manchester U v Crystal Palace	3-3*
Replay	Manchester U v Crystal Palace	1-0
1991	Tottenham H v Nottingham F	2-1*
1992	Liverpool v Sunderland	2-0
1993	Arsenal v Sheffield W	1-1*
Replay	Arsenal v Sheffield W	2-1*
1994	Manchester U v Chelsea	4-0

THE FA CUP SPONSORED BY LITTLEWOODS POOLS

1995	Everton v Manchester U	1-0
1996	Manchester U v Liverpool	1-0
1997	Chelsea v Middlesbrough	2-0
1998	Arsenal v Newcastle U	2-0

THE AXA-SPONSORED FA CUP

1999	Manchester U v Newcastle U	2-0
2000	Chelsea v Aston Villa	1-0
2001	Liverpool v Arsenal	2-1
2002	Arsenal v Chelsea	2-0

THE FA CUP

2003	Arsenal v Southampton	1-0
2004	Manchester U v Millwall	3-0
2005	Arsenal v Manchester U *Arsenal won 5-4 on penalties.*	0-0*
2006	Liverpool v West Ham U *Liverpool won 3-1 on penalties.*	3-3*

THE FA CUP SPONSORED BY E.ON

2007	Chelsea v Manchester U	1-0*
2008	Portsmouth v Cardiff C	1-0
2009	Chelsea v Everton	2-1
2010	Chelsea v Portsmouth	1-0
2011	Manchester C v Stoke C	1-0

THE FA CUP WITH BUDWEISER

2012	Chelsea v Liverpool	2-1
2013	Wigan Ath v Manchester C	1-0
2014	Arsenal v Hull C	3-2*

THE FA CUP

2015	Arsenal v Aston Villa	4-0

THE EMIRATES FA CUP

2016	Manchester U v Crystal Palace	2-1*
2017	Arsenal v Chelsea	2-1
2018	Chelsea v Manchester U	1-0
2019	Manchester C v Watford	6-0
2020	Arsenal v Chelsea	2-1
2021	Leicester C v Chelsea	1-0
2022	Liverpool v Chelsea *Liverpool won 6-5 on penalties.*	0-0*

**After extra time.*

FA CUP WINS

Arsenal 14, Manchester U 12, Chelsea 8, Liverpool 8, Tottenham H 8, Aston Villa 7, Blackburn R 6, Manchester C 6, Newcastle U 6, Everton 5, The Wanderers 5, WBA 5, Bolton W 4, Sheffield U 4, Wolverhampton W 4, Sheffield W 3 (2 as The Wednesday), West Ham U 3, Bury 2, Nottingham F 2, Old Etonians 2, Portsmouth 2, Preston NE 2, Sunderland 2, Barnsley 1, Blackburn Olympic 1, Blackpool 1, Bradford C 1, Burnley 1, Cardiff C 1, Charlton Ath 1, Clapham R 1, Coventry C 1, Derby Co 1, Huddersfield T 1, Ipswich T 1, Leeds U 1, Leicester C 1, Notts Co 1, Old Carthusians 1, Oxford University 1, Royal Engineers 1, Southampton 1, Wigan Ath 1, Wimbledon 1.

APPEARANCES IN FINALS

Arsenal 21, Manchester U 20, Chelsea 16, Liverpool 15, Everton 13, Newcastle U 13, Aston Villa 11, Manchester C 11, WBA 10, Tottenham H 9, Blackburn R 8, Wolverhampton W 8, Bolton W 7, Preston NE 7, Old Etonians 6, Sheffield U 6, Sheffield W 6, Huddersfield T 5, Leicester C 5, Portsmouth 5, *The Wanderers 5, West Ham U 5, Derby Co 4, Leeds U 4, Oxford University 4, Royal Engineers 4, Southampton 4, Sunderland 4, Blackpool 3, Burnley 3, Cardiff C 3, Nottingham F 3, Barnsley 2, Birmingham C 2, *Bury 2, Charlton Ath 2, Clapham R 2, Crystal Palace 2, Notts Co 2, Queen's Park (Glasgow) 2, Watford 2, *Blackburn Olympic 1, *Bradford C 1, Brighton & HA 1, Bristol C 1, *Coventry C 1, Fulham 1, Hull C 1, *Ipswich T 1, Luton T 1, Middlesbrough 1, Millwall 1, *Old Carthusians 1, QPR 1, Stoke C 1, *Wigan Ath 1, *Wimbledon 1.
** Denotes undefeated in final.*

APPEARANCES IN SEMI-FINALS

Arsenal 30, Manchester U 30, Chelsea 26, Everton 26, Liverpool 25, Aston Villa 21, Tottenham H 21, WBA 20, Blackburn R 18, Manchester C 17, Newcastle U 17, Sheffield W 16, Wolverhampton W 15, Bolton W 14, Sheffield U 14, Derby Co 13, Southampton 13, Nottingham F 12, Sunderland 12, Preston NE 10, Birmingham C 9, Burnley 8, Leeds U 8, Leicester C 8, Huddersfield T 7, Portsmouth 7, West Ham U 7, Watford 7, Fulham 6, Old Etonians 6, Oxford University 6, Crystal Palace (professional club) 5, Millwall 5, Notts Co 5, The Wanderers 5, Cardiff C 4, Luton T 4, Queen's Park (Glasgow) 4, Royal Engineers 4, Stoke C 4, Barnsley 3, Blackpool 3, Clapham R 3, Ipswich T 3, Middlesbrough 3, Norwich C 3, Old Carthusians 3, Oldham Ath 3, The Swifts 3, Blackburn Olympic 2, Brighton & HA 2, Bristol C 2, Bury 2, Charlton Ath 2, Grimsby T 2, Hull C 2, Reading 2, Swansea T 2, Swindon T 2, Wigan Ath 2, Wimbledon 2, Bradford C 1, Cambridge University 1, Chesterfield 1, Coventry C 1, Crewe Alex 1, Crystal Palace (amateur club) 1, Darwen 1, Derby Junction 1, Glasgow Rangers 1, Marlow 1, Old Harrovians 1, Orient 1, Plymouth Arg 1, Port Vale 1, QPR 1, Shropshire W 1, Wycombe W 1, York C 1.

THE EMIRATES FA CUP 2021–22

PRELIMINARY AND QUALIFYING ROUNDS

**After extra time.*

EXTRA PRELIMINARY ROUND

Ashington v Newcastle Benfield	3-4
Shildon v Garforth T	1-0
Redcar Ath v Hemsworth MW	4-1
Penrith v Guisborough T	1-2
Whitley Bay v North Ferriby	1-1
Replay: North Ferriby v Whitley Bay	2-5
Whickham v Consett	2-3
Billingham T v West Allotment Celtic	2-3
Seaham Red Star v Crook T	3-1
Newton Aycliffe v Thornaby	4-3
Sunderland RCA v Bishop Auckland	5-1
North Shields v West Auckland T	3-1
Goole v Sunderland Ryhope CW	1-1
Replay: Sunderland Ryhope CW v Goole *(1-1 at the end of normal time)*	2-3*
Knaresborough T v Northallerton T	2-1
Irlam v Albion Sports	3-0
Macclesfield v Burscough	4-0
Athersley Recreation v Campion	1-4
Glossop North End v Widnes	3-0
Lower Breck v Penistone Church	0-0
Replay: Penistone Church v Lower Breck	1-2
Longridge T v Northwich Vic	1-2
Barnoldswick T v Runcorn T	6-1
Padiham v AFC Liverpool	2-3
Ashton Ath v Squires Gate	0-2
West Didsbury & Chorlton v Avro	1-3
Prestwich Heys v Litherland Remyca	3-1
Vauxhall Motors v Skelmersdale U	0-0
Replay: Skelmersdale U v Vauxhall Motors	2-0
Thackley v Wythenshawe T	2-3
Silsden v Eccleshill U	0-4
Winsford U v Charnock Richard	0-2
Emley v Congleton T	3-2
Tividale v Shifnal T	2-0
Sporting Khalsa v Coventry Sphinx	4-3
Lye T v Hanley T	2-3
Rugby T v Boldmere St Michaels	1-0
Coventry U v Worcester C	4-1
Highgate U v Malvern T	3-1
Westfields v Heather St Johns	3-0
Hereford Lads Club v Haughmond	0-0
Replay: Haughmond v Hereford Lads Club	1-0
Walsall Wood v Hinckley LR	0-2
Whitchurch Alport v Wolverhampton Casuals	2-1
Racing Club Warwick v Stone Old Alleynians	0-4
Gresley R v Bewdley T	3-0
Romulus v Uttoxeter T	1-2
AFC Wulfrunians v Heanor T	2-1
Stourport Swifts v Lichfield C	0-4
Quorn v Selston	5-1
Barton T v Maltby Main	2-3
Pinchbeck U v Skegness T	0-1
GNG Oadby T v Stamford	0-2
Sherwood Colliery v Boston T	1-1
Replay: Boston T v Sherwood Colliery	0-1
Newark v Lutterworth T	0-0
Replay: Lutterworth T v Newark	1-3
Bottesford T v Eastwood Community (walkover)	
Anstey Nomads v Sleaford T	1-0
Long Eaton U v Holbeach U	4-1
Winterton Rangers v Grimsby Bor	6-2
Leicester Nirvana v Deeping Rangers	1-1
Replay: Deeping Rangers v Leicester Nirvana	3-1
Handsworth v AFC Mansfield	2-0
Staveley MW v Loughborough Students	1-2
Cleethorpes T v Melton T	4-0
Lakenheath v Mulbarton W	2-2
Replay: Mulbarton W v Lakenheath	3-1
Swaffham T v Walsham Le Willows	0-3
Mildenhall T v Wroxham	1-0
Fakenham T v Ely C	1-0
Cogenhoe U v Haverhill R	0-0
Replay: Haverhill R v Cogenhoe U	0-2
Harborough T v Rothwell Corinthians	2-0
Newport Pagnell T v Peterborough Northern Star	4-1
Corby T v Woodbridge T	3-1
Potton U v Eynesbury R	2-1
Norwich U v Long Buckby	2-1
Brantham Ath v Gorleston	4-3
Hadleigh U v Desborough T	2-0
Kirkley & Pakefield v Long Melford	1-1
Replay: Long Melford v Kirkley & Pakefield	0-4
Arlesey T v Thetford T	4-3
Bugbrooke St Michaels v March Town U (walkover)	
Kempston R v Whitton U	1-1
Replay: Whitton U v Kempston R	2-1
Godmanchester R v Northampton ON Chenecks	1-1
Replay: Northampton ON Chenecks v Godmanchester R	1-0
Wellingborough T v Newmarket T	1-3
Harpenden T v Romford	1-1
Replay: Romford v Harpenden T	3-1
Ware v Takeley	2-1
Sporting Bengal U v White Ensign	0-3
Redbridge v Ilford	1-2
Stanway R v Leverstock Green	1-0
Baldock T v Wembley	1-0
Biggleswade U v Saffron Walden T	0-7
Little Oakley v St Margaretsbury	2-0
Edgware T v Hadley	0-3
Walthamstow v Crawley Green	4-1
West Essex v St Panteleimon	4-2
Witham T v Woodford T	3-2
FC Clacton v Leighton T	0-1
Enfield v Milton Keynes Irish	2-1
Sawbridgeworth T v Cockfosters	0-3
Basildon U v Stansted	4-0
Dunstable T v North Greenford U	1-5
Southend Manor v London Colney	1-0
Hoddesdon T v Clapton	0-1
New Salamis v Kensington & Ealing Bor	1-3
Easington Sports v Wokingham & Emmbrook	1-1
Replay: Wokingham & Emmbrook v Easington Sports	0-0*
Easington Sports won 4-3 on penalties	
Bishop's Cleeve v Clevedon T	6-1
Brislington v Brimscombe & Thrupp	3-3
Replay: Brimscombe & Thrupp v Brislington	3-1
Shrivenham v Burnham	1-1
Replay: Burnham v Shrivenham	4-0
Chipping Sodbury T v Harefield U	1-2
Risborough Rangers v Lydney T	1-0
Aylesbury Vale Dynamos v Longlevens	0-1
Thornbury T v Royal Wootton Bassett T	0-4
Ascot U v Holyport	3-0
Aylesbury U v Fairford T	2-0
Tuffley R v Windsor	3-2
Broadfields U v Cribbs	4-1
Ardley U v Ashton & Backwell U	2-0
Oxhey Jets v Bitton	2-0
Cadbury Heath v Flackwell Heath	0-2
Tring Ath v Keynsham T	3-0
Reading C v Hallen	3-1
Roman Glass St George v Holmer Green	2-1
K Sports v Rushtall	3-1
Walton & Hersham v Tunbridge Wells	2-1
Beckenham T v Colliers Wood U	0-0
Replay: Colliers Wood U v Beckenham T	1-3
AFC Varndeanians v Farnham T	1-2
Steyning T Community v Pagham	2-2
Replay: Pagham v Steyning T Community	2-3

Badshot Lea v East Preston 3-3
Replay: East Preston v Badshot Lea 0-2
Jersey Bulls v Horsham YMCA 10-1
Chatham T v Eastbourne U 6-2
Hollands & Blair v Holmesdale 3-0
Staines T v Little Common 1-2
Cobham v Sevenoaks T 2-2
Replay: Sevenoaks T v Cobham 3-1
CB Hounslow U v Redhill 0-3
Kennington v Horley T 5-0
Broadbridge Heath v Littlehampton T 2-6
Glebe v Abbey Rangers 2-3
Deal T v Southall 1-0
Eastbourne T v Guildford C 2-4
Newhaven v Camberley T 6-1
Bexhill U v Peacehaven & Telscombe 0-1
Lingfield v Egham T 2-1
Hassocks v Spelthorne Sports 1-2
Ashford T (Middlesex) v AFC Uckfield T 2-1
Tower Hamlets v Sheppey U 1-4
Hanworth Villa v Loxwood 1-3
Virginia Water v Athletic Newham 1-1
Replay: Athletic Newham v Virginia Water 3-1
Lordswood v Knaphill 0-0
Replay: Knaphill v Lordswood 2-2*
Knaphill won 4-3 on penalties
East Grinstead T v Alfold 1-2
Sheerwater v Erith T 0-2
Crawley Down Gatwick v Welling T 3-2
Tooting & Mitcham U v Erith & Belvedere 1-1
Replay: Erith & Belvedere v Tooting & Mitcham U 3-1*
(1-1 at the end of normal time)
Fisher v Raynes Park Vale 0-1
Molesey v Phoenix Sports 0-1
Saltdean U v Frimley Green 4-0
Mile Oak v Punjab U 0-2
Balham v Canterbury C 3-0
Crowborough Ath v AFC Croydon Ath 1-3
Banstead Ath v Bearsted 2-2
Replay: Bearsted v Banstead Ath 2-1
AFC Portchester v Horndean 4-2
Amesbury T v Shaftesbury 1-4
Westbury U v Christchurch 4-2
Hythe & Dibden v Bradford T 1-7
Blackfield & Langley v Cowes Sports 5-1
Portland U v Bournemouth 2-2
Replay: Bournemouth v Portland U 3-1
Calne T v Bashley 1-1
Replay: Bashley v Calne T 2-1
Moneyfields v AFC Stoneham 1-3
Brockenhurst v Hamworthy U 1-2
United Services Portsmouth v Alton 0-3
Larkhall Ath v Lymington T 1-2
Bridport v Fleet T 1-2
Alresford T v Odd Down 3-0
Tadley Calleva v Baffins Milton R 0-2
Shepton Mallet v Andover New Street 0-0
Replay: Andover New Street v Shepton Mallet 0-4
Hamble Club v Corsham T 2-3
Fareham T v Street 8-0
Millbrook (Cornwall) v Saltash U 2-2
Replay: Saltash U v Millbrook (Cornwall) 4-6
Mousehole v Helston Ath 3-1
Bridgwater U v Brixham 2-1
Replay: Bridgwater U v Brixham 2-1
(Tie ordered to be replayed due to refereeing decision)
Buckland Ath v Exmouth T 1-2
AFC St Austell v Tavistock 2-3
Ilfracombe T v Wellington 4-3

PRELIMINARY ROUND
Marske U v Pickering T 7-0
Goole v Pontefract Collieries 0-1
Stockton T v Ossett U 1-0
Newcastle Benfield v Dunston UTS 1-2
Liversedge v Knaresborough T 5-0
North Shields v Guisborough T 2-0
Shildon v Brighouse T 2-1
West Allotment Celtic v Whitley Bay 4-2
Consett v Bridlington T 2-3
Seaham Red Star v Redcar Ath 2-2
Replay: Redcar Ath v Seaham Red Star 1-3
Frickley Ath v Sunderland RCA 0-3
Tadcaster Alb v Newton Aycliffe 1-2
Yorkshire Amateur v Hebburn T 0-7
Avro v Runcorn Linnets 1-1
Replay: Runcorn Linnets v Avro 4-1*
(1-1 at the end of normal time)
Prescot Cables v Campion 3-2
Northwich Vic v Clitheroe 1-2
Squires Gate v Macclesfield 6-4
Glossop North End v Kendal T 0-1
Lower Breck v Mossley 2-2
Replay: Mossley v Lower Breck 2-0
Eccleshill U v Charnock Richard 1-1
Replay: Charnock Richard v Eccleshill U 5-1
Wythenshawe T v 1874 Northwich 1-2
City of Liverpool v Emley 2-0
Workington v Marine 1-1
Replay: Marine v Workington 2-1*
(1-1 at the end of normal time)
Barnoldswick T v Ramsbottom U 5-4
Prestwich Heys v Warrington Rylands 0-3
AFC Liverpool v Bootle 2-3
Irlam v Skelmersdale U 1-5
Trafford v Colne 2-2
Replay: Colne v Trafford 2-1
Halesowen T v Sutton Coldfield T 3-0
Gresley R v Leek T 0-2
Bedworth U v Kidsgrove Ath 2-1
Tividale v AFC Wulfrunians 2-1
Chasetown v Uttoxeter T 7-0
Stone Old Alleynians v Rugby T 4-2
Sporting Khalsa v Market Drayton T 3-2
Westfields v Coventry U 0-1
Highgate U v Coleshill T 1-4
Haughmond v Hanley T 0-5
Belper T v Whitchurch Alport 3-1
Newcastle T v Hinckley LR 0-1
Evesham U v Lichfield C 2-4
Loughborough Students v Newark 3-2
Maltby Main v Carlton T 1-1
Replay: Carlton T v Maltby Main 1-0
Cleethorpes T v Loughborough Dynamo 3-1
Quorn v Ilkeston T 1-2
Handsworth v Stocksbridge Park Steels 5-2
Worksop T v Eastwood Community 4-4
Replay: Eastwood Community v Worksop T 2-5
Sheffield v Sherwood Colliery 1-2
Winterton Rangers v Deeping Rangers 4-1
Lincoln U v Stamford 0-3
Long Eaton U v Shepshed Dynamo 4-0
Anstey Nomads v Skegness T 2-1
Norwich U v Newmarket T 1-0
Yaxley v Mildenhall T 1-1
Replay: Mildenhall T v Yaxley 1-0*
(0-0 at the end of normal time)
Harborough T v Biggleswade 0-3
Potton U v Walsham Le Willows 5-1
Fakenham T v Bury T 0-1
Cogenhoe U v Dereham T 0-2
Arlesey T v March T U 3-2
Kirkley & Pakefield v Northampton ON Chenecks 1-0
Wisbech T v Whitton U 2-0
Bedford T v St Neots T 3-0
Newport Pagnell T v Histon 4-1
Brantham Ath v Spalding U 0-3
Corby T v Soham T Rangers 3-3
Replay: Soham T Rangers v Corby T 2-4*
(2-2 at the end of normal time)
Mulbarton W v Hadleigh U 1-0
Daventry T v Cambridge C 1-5
Brentwood T v Leighton T 1-0
FC Romania v Welwyn Garden C 1-1
Replay: Welwyn Garden C v FC Romania 3-2
Coggeshall T v Berkhamsted 0-1
Walthamstow v Hullbridge Sports 2-0
Canvey Island v Waltham Abbey 2-1

Great Wakering R v Heybridge Swifts 3-1
Felixstowe & Walton U v Southend Manor 5-3
Little Oakley v Hertford T 0-0
Replay: Hertford T v Little Oakley 1-2
Baldock T v Grays Ath 2-1
Saffron Walden T v Hadley 0-4
Maldon & Tiptree v Aveley 0-1
Barton R v West Essex 3-0
Kensington & Ealing Bor v Romford 0-1
Cockfosters v AFC Sudbury 1-2
Barking v Ilford 2-3
Replay: Barking v Ilford 3-2
(Tie ordered to be replayed after Ilford fielded an ineligible player)
Ware v Hashtag U 1-0
Stowmarket T v Witham T 4-0
Colney Heath v Harlow T 3-0
Stanway R v Enfield 1-1
Replay: Enfield v Stanway R 2-1
Clapton v AFC Dunstable 1-3
Basildon U v White Ensign 1-0
North Greenford U v Tilbury 0-7
Marlow v Slimbridge 3-0
Bishop's Cleeve v Tring Ath 2-0
Wantage T v Highworth T 1-2
Longlevens v Chalfont St Peter 3-2
Roman Glass St George v Cirencester T 0-2
Aylesbury U v Brimscombe & Thrupp 8-0
Northwood v Burnham 1-1
Replay: Burnham v Northwood 1-4
Tuffley R v Flackwell Heath 2-2
Replay: Flackwell Heath v Tuffley R 6-0
Royal Wootton Bassett T v Ardley U 2-2
Replay: Ardley U v Royal Wootton Bassett T 3-1
Oxhey Jets v Didcot T 1-0
Broadfields U v Reading C 0-0
Replay: Reading C v Broadfields U 1-3
Harefield U v Binfield 2-1
Thame U v Thatcham T 2-0
North Leigh v Kidlington 1-2
Risborough Rangers v Ascot U 1-1
Replay: Ascot U v Risborough Rangers 3-2
Cinderford T v Easington Sports 3-3
Replay: Easington Sports v Cinderford T 2-2*
Easington Sports won 4-2 on penalties
Lingfield v Chertsey T 1-4
Sheppey U (walkover) v Saltdean U
Hanwell T v Athletic Newham 5-0
Newhaven v Jersey Bulls 0-4
Farnham T v Spelthorne Sports 2-3
Ashford T (Middlesex) v Knaphill 1-1
Replay: Knaphill v Ashford T (Middlesex) 1-2*
(1-1 at the end of normal time)
Whyteleafe v Whitehawk (walkover)
South Park v Three Bridges 3-3
Replay: Three Bridges v South Park 2-4
Chipstead v Faversham T 3-0
Raynes Park Vale v VCD Ath 2-3
Erith & Belvedere v AFC Croydon Ath 0-0
Replay: AFC Croydon Ath v Erith & Belvedere 2-3
Steyning T Community v Sutton Common R 0-0
Replay: Sutton Common R v Steyning T Community 4-0
Walton & Hersham v Guildford C 2-0
Abbey Rangers v Loxwood 1-0
Beckenham T v Hastings U 0-3
Peacehaven & Telscombe v Crawley Down Gatwick 2-1
Hythe T v Westfield 3-3
Replay: Westfield v Hythe T 1-3
Redhill v Deal T 1-1
Replay: Deal T v Redhill 0-1
Chatham T v Ashford U 1-1
Replay: Ashford U v Chatham T 1-1*
Chatham T won 6-5 on penalties
Balham v K Sports 3-0
Hollands & Blair v Ramsgate 1-2
Bedfont Sports Club v Herne Bay 3-1
Sevenoaks T v Erith T 2-2
Replay: Erith T v Sevenoaks T 1-2
Bearsted v Burgess Hill T 0-3
Badshot Lea v Corinthian 2-4
Sittingbourne v Littlehampton T 2-2
Replay: Littlehampton T v Sittingbourne 4-0
Phoenix Sports v Punjab U 7-0
Kennington v Little Common 2-0
Lancing v Haywards Heath T 0-4
Whitstable T v Alfold 5-0
Uxbridge v Cray Valley (PM) 1-0
Bracknell T v Bashley 1-0
Shaftesbury v AFC Stoneham 6-1
Westbury U v Hamworthy U 0-2
Corsham T v Fleet T 1-5
Winchester C v Chichester C 1-3
Basingstoke T v AFC Totton 2-1
Bradford T v Alton 1-1
Replay: Alton v Bradford T 3-0
Blackfield & Langley v AFC Portchester 1-1
Replay: AFC Portchester v Blackfield & Langley 1-3
Alresford T v Fareham T 1-0
Lymington T v Bournemouth 2-1
Baffins Milton R v Sholing 2-4
Melksham T v Shepton Mallet 0-1
Mangotsfield U v Tavistock 3-0
Bridgwater U v Ilfracombe T 3-0
Willand R v Millbrook (Cornwall) 3-3
Replay: Millbrook (Cornwall) v Willand R 1-2
Exmouth T v Bristol Manor Farm 2-1
Frome T v Paulton R 3-1
Bideford v Barnstaple T 1-3
Mousehole v Plymouth Parkway 1-3

FIRST QUALIFYING ROUND

Squires Gate v North Shields 1-0
Ashton U v Hebburn T 0-1
West Allotment Celtic v Bamber Bridge 2-7
Bootle v FC United of Manchester 2-2
Replay: FC United of Manchester v Bootle 3-2
Radcliffe v Skelmersdale U 2-0
Runcorn Linnets v Liversedge 2-0
Barnoldswick T v Pontefract Collieries 0-3
Marske U v Seaham Red Star 6-0
Sunderland RCA v Stockton T 2-4
Atherton Collieries v Bridlington T 1-1
Replay: Bridlington T v Atherton Collieries 1-3
Warrington Rylands v Whitby T 0-4
Shildon v South Shields 1-3
Lancaster C v 1874 Northwich 1-0
Scarborough Ath v Witton Alb 0-2
Mossley v Newton Aycliffe 1-0
City of Liverpool v Clitheroe 1-0
Kendal T v Warrington T 0-1
Stalybridge Celtic v Colne 0-1
Charnock Richard v Prescot Cables 2-3
Dunston UTS v Marine 1-2
Morpeth T v Hyde U 6-1
Sherwood Colliery v Buxton 2-2
Replay: Buxton v Sherwood Colliery 5-1
Stamford v Redditch U 2-0
Worksop T v Newport Pagnell T 3-0
Basford U v Stourbridge 1-0
Rushall Olympic v Stafford Rangers 2-2
Replay: Stafford Rangers v Rushall Olympic 0-2
Leek T v Mickleover 0-2
Halesowen T v Ilkeston T 2-1
Anstey Nomads v Stone Old Alleynians 0-1
Nantwich T v Grantham T 2-0
Hinckley LR v Hanley T 1-1
Replay: Hanley T v Hinckley LR 2-1
Bromsgrove Sporting v Loughborough Students 2-0
Sporting Khalsa v Gainsborough Trinity 2-1
Carlton T v Stratford T 1-3
Matlock T v Belper T 0-3
Bedworth U v Winterton Rangers 4-1
Chasetown v Barwell 2-1
Hednesford T v Cleethorpes T 1-1
Replay: Cleethorpes T v Hednesford T 2-1
Tamworth v Alvechurch 3-1
Long Eaton U v Coleshill T 2-1
Coalville T v AFC Rushden & Diamonds 5-2

Handsworth v Coventry U 2-0
Lichfield C v Nuneaton Bor 1-3
Tividale v Spalding U 0-1
Hadley v Enfield 1-1
Replay: Enfield v Hadley 2-3*
(2-2 at the end of normal time)
Cambridge C v East Thurrock U 1-3
Enfield T v Dereham T 2-1
Bury T v Norwich U 1-4
Wingate & Finchley v Basildon U 1-1
Replay: Basildon U v Wingate & Finchley 1-6
Potton U v AFC Sudbury 0-1
Colney Heath v Ware 0-4
Corby T v Hendon 1-0
Felixstowe & Walton U v Great Wakering R 1-3
Biggleswade v AFC Dunstable 0-1
Leiston v Brightlingsea Regent 3-2
Barking v Aveley 1-1
Replay: Aveley v Barking 1-1*
Barking won 5-4 on penalties
Hornchurch v Barton R 1-1
Replay: Barton R v Hornchurch 1-4
Biggleswade T v Hitchin T 0-3
Kings Langley v Romford 3-2
Little Oakley v Kirkley & Pakefield 2-1
Stowmarket T v Potters Bar T 2-1
Mulbarton W v Welwyn Garden C 2-2
Replay: Welwyn Garden C v Mulbarton W 2-1
Arlesey T v Bowers & Pitsea 0-5
Walthamstow v Berkhamsted 1-0
Baldock T v Wisbech T 1-0
Peterborough Sports v Haringey Bor 2-1
Brentwood T v Cheshunt 0-2
Needham Market v St Ives T 1-0
Royston T v Mildenhall T 1-2
Bedford T v Canvey Island 0-0
Replay: Canvey Island v Bedford T 2-3
Bishop's Stortford v Lowestoft T 3-0
Walton Casuals v Hartley Wintney 2-1
Abbey Rangers v Chatham T 5-0
Phoenix Sports v Chipstead 2-1
Redhill v Sevenoaks T 1-1
Replay: Sevenoaks T v Redhill 3-4
Whitstable T v Leatherhead 2-2
Replay: Leatherhead v Whitstable T 1-0
Kennington v Carshalton Ath 0-3
Harefield U v Hastings U 0-4
Haywards Heath T v Horsham 1-1
Replay: Horsham v Haywards Heath T 2-0
Harrow Bor v Ramsgate 4-2
Balham v Merstham 0-2
Margate v Thame U 2-2
Replay: Thame U v Margate 2-4
Hythe T v Ascot U 1-0
Uxbridge v Chesham U 2-2
Replay: Chesham U v Uxbridge 2-1
Corinthian v Folkestone Invicta 2-3
Northwood v Chichester C 2-3
Littlehampton T v Whitehawk 4-5
Fleet T v Hanwell T 0-2
Farnborough v Peacehaven & Telscombe 4-0
Jersey Bulls v VCD Ath 5-1
Sheppey U v Marlow 0-1
Ashford T (Middlesex) v Tilbury 2-1
Cray W v Sutton Common R 1-3
Hayes & Yeading U v Bognor Regis T 4-3
Beaconsfield T v Walton & Hersham 2-2
Replay: Walton & Hersham v Beaconsfield T 2-5
Lewes v Metropolitan Police 1-2
Broadfields U v South Park 2-2
Replay: South Park v Broadfields U 1-2
Oxhey Jets v Kingstonian 2-2
Replay: Kingstonian v Oxhey Jets 8-1
Worthing v Corinthian Casuals 1-1
Replay: Corinthian Casuals v Worthing 3-1
Burgess Hill T v Bracknell T 2-0
Spelthorne Sports v Bedfont Sports Club 1-1
Replay: Bedfont Sports Club v Spelthorne Sports 2-0
Erith & Belvedere v Chertsey T 0-4
Merthyr T v Hamworthy U 0-0
Replay: Hamworthy U v Merthyr T 2-0
Frome T v Mangotsfield U 1-0
Aylesbury U v Willand R 4-1
Kidlington v Bishop's Cleeve 2-3
Basingstoke T v Bridgwater U 4-1
Highworth T v Shaftesbury 1-1
Replay: Shaftesbury v Highworth T 4-2
Weston-super-Mare v Flackwell Heath 2-2
Replay: Flackwell Heath v Weston-super-Mare 0-1
Banbury U v Ardley U 1-0
Gosport Bor v Plymouth Parkway 2-1
Shepton Mallet v Taunton T 1-8
Barnstaple T v Lymington T 0-1
Poole T v Swindon Supermarine 5-0
Dorchester T v Yate T 1-3
Longlevens v Alresford T 2-1
Cirencester T v Easington Sports 3-0
Blackfield & Langley v Wimborne T 0-3
Truro C v Exmouth T 3-1
Alton v Sholing 1-3
Salisbury v Tiverton T 0-2

SECOND QUALIFYING ROUND

Chorley v Southport 2-2
Replay: Southport v Chorley 1-0
York C v Hebburn T 3-0
Marine v Warrington T 3-0
Atherton Collieries v Witton Alb 3-1
Squires Gate v Pontefract Collieries 2-3
Gateshead v Bradford (Park Avenue) 6-2
Blyth Spartans v FC United of Manchester 1-1
Replay: FC United of Manchester v Blyth Spartans 0-2
Colne v Guiseley 0-1
Darlington v Chester 0-0
Replay: Chester v Darlington 1-0
Curzon Ashton v Stockton T 4-0
AFC Fylde v Spennymoor T 1-1
Replay: Spennymoor T v AFC Fylde 1-0
City of Liverpool v Farsley Celtic 3-0
Morpeth T v Lancaster C 4-1
Mossley v Radcliffe 1-2
Prescot Cables v Whitby T 0-3
Runcorn Linnets v Bamber Bridge 3-1
Marske U v South Shields 3-0
Leamington v Stone Old Alleynians 3-1
Belper T v Tamworth 0-5
Bromsgrove Sporting v Worksop T 6-0
Brackley T v Coalville T 4-2
Sporting Khalsa v Kidderminster H 1-3
Buxton v Rushall Olympic 4-0
Boston U v Corby T 6-0
Nantwich T v Banbury U 1-2
AFC Telford U v Stamford 1-2
Spalding U v Kettering T 1-1
Replay: Kettering T v Spalding U 2-0
Hanley T v Chasetown 2-1
Bedworth U v Long Eaton U 1-3
Halesowen T v Handsworth 1-3
Cleethorpes T v Alfreton T 1-0
Mickleover v Basford U 1-3
Stratford T v Nuneaton Bor 4-0
Braintree T v Billericay T 1-2
Hornchurch v Walthamstow 4-1
Bishop's Stortford v Bowers & Pitsea 0-2
Barking v AFC Dunstable 1-3
Norwich U v Mildenhall T 3-2
East Thurrock U v Needham Market 2-2
Replay: Needham Market v East Thurrock U 2-3
AFC Sudbury v Stowmarket T 0-0
Replay: Stowmarket T v AFC Sudbury 0-1
Wingate & Finchley v Baldock T 3-0
Concord Rangers v St Albans C 0-0
Replay: St Albans C v Concord Rangers 2-0
Chelmsford C v Little Oakley 2-1
Kings Langley v Leiston 1-1
Replay: Leiston v Kings Langley 3-1
Ware v Hemel Hempstead T 2-2
Replay: Hemel Hempstead T v Ware 0-1

Bedford T v Welwyn Garden C	1-3
Enfield T v Hadley	1-1
Replay: Hadley v Enfield T	1-2
Hitchin T v Cheshunt	0-3
Great Wakering R v Peterborough Sports	3-5
Ashford T (Middlesex) v Folkestone Invicta	2-7
Abbey Rangers v Marlow	0-2
Chertsey T v Chesham U	1-0
Carshalton Ath v Ebbsfleet U	1-2
Chichester C v Maidstone U	1-3
Phoenix Sports v Redhill	1-3
Broadfields U v Hastings U	2-3
Burgess Hill T v Dorking W	0-4
Kingstonian v Horsham	1-1
Replay: Horsham v Kingstonian	1-0
Merstham v Margate	4-1
Hanwell T v Eastbourne Bor	0-2
Sutton Common R v Jersey Bulls	2-2
Replay: Jersey Bulls v Sutton Common R	3-2
Beaconsfield T v Havant & Waterlooville	3-5
Slough T v Whitehawk	1-3
Dartford v Hythe T	5-1
Metropolitan Police v Farnborough	1-1
Replay: Farnborough v Metropolitan Police	0-1
Dulwich Hamlet v Bedfont Sports Club	0-1
Hayes & Yeading U v Tonbridge Angels	5-0
Walton Casuals v Hampton & Richmond Bor	0-3
Leatherhead v Corinthian Casuals	0-0
Replay: Corinthian Casuals v Leatherhead	3-0
Welling U v Harrow Bor	0-2
Aylesbury U v Bishop's Cleeve	5-1
Cirencester T v Hamworthy U	3-1
Longlevens v Gloucester C	1-3
Tiverton T v Sholing	1-3
Basingstoke T v Wimborne T	3-4
Frome T v Oxford C	2-1
Poole T v Chippenham T	1-1
Replay: Chippenham T v Poole T	1-0
Weston-super-Mare v Taunton T	5-1
Shaftesbury v Bath C	0-1
Hungerford T v Truro C	1-0
Yate T v Gosport Bor	2-0
Lymington T v Hereford	2-2
Replay: Hereford v Lymington T	4-0

THIRD QUALIFYING ROUND

Radcliffe v Morpeth T	1-3
Atherton Collieries v Marine	0-0
Replay: Marine v Atherton Collieries	3-2*
(2-2 at the end of normal time)	
Pontefract Collieries v Handsworth	6-0
Marske U v Chester	0-0
Replay: Chester v Marske U	0-4
City of Liverpool v Buxton	1-6
Curzon Ashton v Cleethorpes T	4-0
Runcorn Linnets v Gateshead	2-3
York C v Whitby T	2-0
Guiseley v Blyth Spartans	1-0
Spennymoor T v Southport	0-0
Replay: Southport v Spennymoor T	3-2
Ware v Kidderminster H	1-1
Replay: Kidderminster H v Ware	3-0
Stamford v Norwich U	2-1
Boston U v East Thurrock U	4-0
Leamington v Kettering T	3-3
Replay: Kettering T v Leamington	2-0
Leiston v Tamworth	1-3
Stratford T v Long Eaton U	3-2
AFC Sudbury v Cheshunt	1-0
Hanley T v Brackley T	1-1
Replay: Brackley T v Hanley T	1-0
AFC Dunstable v Peterborough Sports	2-3
Chelmsford C v Enfield T	1-0
Bromsgrove Sporting v Welwyn Garden C	1-0
Basford U v Banbury U	0-1
Merstham v Hereford	0-2
Metropolitan Police v St Albans C	0-0
Replay: St Albans C v Metropolitan Police	3-1
Hungerford T v Cirencester T	3-2
Maidstone U v Dartford	0-3
Folkestone Invicta v Gloucester C	1-0
Hayes & Yeading U v Whitehawk	3-2
Bedfont Sports Club v Sholing	3-3
Replay: Sholing v Bedfont Sports Club	1-2
Havant & Waterlooville v Billericay T	3-2
Chippenham T v Hastings U	0-1
Harrow Bor v Marlow	2-1
Jersey Bulls v Chertsey T	0-1
Horsham v Eastbourne Bor	2-2
Replay: Eastbourne Bor v Horsham	0-1
Hampton & Richmond Bor v Wimborne T	3-1
Bowers & Pitsea v Hornchurch	2-2
Replay: Hornchurch v Bowers & Pitsea	0-2
Corinthian Casuals v Wingate & Finchley	1-1
Replay: Wingate & Finchley v Corinthian Casuals	0-3
Yate T v Redhill	3-0
Aylesbury U v Ebbsfleet U	0-1
Dorking W v Weston-super-Mare	1-0
Bath C v Frome T	5-0

FOURTH QUALIFYING ROUND

Marine v Wrexham	1-1
Replay: Wrexham v Marine	2-0
Marske U v Gateshead	0-0
Replay: Gateshead v Marske U	3-2
Curzon Ashton v Chesterfield	0-4
Brackley T v Guiseley	1-1
Replay: Guiseley v Brackley T	2-1
Hereford v Solihull Moors	0-1
Pontefract Collieries v FC Halifax T	0-0
Replay: FC Halifax T v Pontefract Collieries	1-0
York C v Morpeth T	1-1
Replay: Morpeth T v York C	1-3
Kettering T v Buxton	2-2
Replay: Buxton v Kettering T	3-1*
(1-1 at the end of normal time)	
Boston U v Stratford T	1-1
Replay: Stratford T v Boston U	3-2
King's Lynn T v Peterborough Sports	2-1
Bromsgrove Sporting v Grimsby T	0-5
Stockport Co v Stamford	3-0
Southport v Altrincham	2-3
Tamworth v Notts Co	0-0
Replay: Notts Co v Tamworth	4-0
Ebbsfleet U v Hampton & Richmond Bor	2-0
Horsham v Woking	1-0
Dorking W v Hayes & Yeading U	2-2
Replay: Hayes & Yeading U v Dorking W	2-2*
Hayes & Yeading U won 4-3 on penalties	
Corinthian Casuals v St Albans C	1-1
Replay: St Albans C v Corinthian Casuals	1-1*
St Albans C won 4-2 on penalties	
Maidenhead U v Hastings U	3-1
Bedfont Sports Club v Kidderminster H	0-1
Hungerford T v Bromley	1-2
Harrow Bor v Chelmsford C	4-2
Wealdstone v Dagenham & R	1-2
AFC Sudbury v Dartford	3-1
Banbury U v Bath C	1-0
Barnet v Boreham Wood	0-1
Yeovil T v Weymouth	1-1
Replay: Weymouth v Yeovil T	1-1*
Yeovil T won 2-1 on penalties	
Eastleigh v Folkestone Invicta	3-3
Replay: Folkestone Invicta v Eastleigh	2-3
Bowers & Pitsea v Aldershot T	2-1
Dover Ath v Yate T	1-1
Replay: Yate T v Dover Ath	1-0
Torquay U v Havant & Waterlooville	2-2
Replay: Havant & Waterlooville v Torquay U	4-2
Southend U v Chertsey T	4-2

THE EMIRATES FA CUP 2021–22

COMPETITION PROPER

▪ *Denotes player sent off.*

FIRST ROUND

Friday, 5 November 2021

AFC Sudbury (0) 0

Colchester U (2) 4 *(Sarpong-Wiredu 35, Sears 39, Jasper 71, McCoulsky 90)* 2000

AFC Sudbury: (4231) Blunkell; Keys, Shaw (Gilchrist 78), Grimwood, Harris; Turner, Frimpong; Nyadzayo, O'Malley, Andrews (Hipkin 69); Temple (Clowsley 54).
Colchester U: (433) George; Tchamadeu, Chambers, Eastman, Clampin (Coxe 12); Chilvers, Skuse (Cooper 73), Sarpong-Wiredu; Jasper (Hannant 78), Sears (McCoulsky 73), Dobra (Nouble 73).
Referee: James Bell.

Saturday, 6 November 2021

AFC Wimbledon (1) 1 *(Palmer 44)*

Guiseley (0) 0 4973

AFC Wimbledon: (4231) Tzanev; Alexander (Lawrence 81), Heneghan, Csoka, Guinness-Walker; Woodyard, Hartigan; Rudoni (Mebude 86), McCormick (Chislett 81), Assal; Palmer (Pressley 65).
Guiseley: (343) Wade; Hull, Bencherif (Hollins 69), Cantrill; Hutchinson, Spencer, Ekpolo, Nicholson; Mbeka, Thewlis (Tuton 64), Hey (Gratton 53).
Referee: Martin Woods.

Banbury U (0) 0

Barrow (1) 4 *(Gordon 8, Zanzala 55, Banks 80 (pen), Stevens 83)* 2400

Banbury U: (442) Taylor; Roberts C, Sharpe (Johnston 78), Langmead, Brown; Roberts M (Reilly 90), Rasulo, Babos, Acquaye; Wreh, Stevens (Landers 56).
Barrow: (3421) Farman; Jones J, Platt, Grayson; Hutton (Brown 54), Banks, Gotts (White 88), Brough; Stevens (Taylor 87), Zanzala (James 83); Gordon (Kay 82).
Referee: Robert Madley.

Boreham Wood (1) 2 *(Boden 45, 61)*

Eastleigh (0) 0 931

Boreham Wood: (352) Ashby-Hammond; Evans, Fyfield, Ilesanmi; Smith K, Rees, Ricketts, Mafuta, Mendy; Boden, Marsh (Clifton 86).
Eastleigh: (4222) McDonnell; Harper, Maghoma, Boyce, Kelly (Hare 69); Miley (Hill 69), Pritchard (Whitehall 78); Whelan, Hesketh (Smart 85); Barnett, House.
Referee: Sunny Gill.

Bradford C (1) 1 *(Robinson 28)*

Exeter C (0) 1 *(Nombe 86)* 3236

Bradford C: (3412) O'Donnell; O'Connor, Songo'o, Canavan; Threlkeld, Sutton, Watt, Foulds; Gilliead; Robinson (Angol 77), Vernam (Cooke 68).
Exeter C: (3412) Dawson; Sweeney, Ray (Grounds 46), Hartridge (Sparkes 73); Caprice (Key 56), Collins, Atangana (Dieng 56), Daniel (Edwards 56); Jay; Nombe, Brown J.
Referee: Sebastian Stockbridge.

Carlisle U (0) 2 *(Young 69, Clough 90)*

Horsham (0) 0 2581

Carlisle U: (433) Howard; Riley, McDonald, Whelan, Armer; Mellish, Guy, Gibson (Charters 78); Alessandra (Fishburn 62), Abrahams (Young 61), Clough.
Horsham: (442) Howes; Metcalf (Richards 76), Miles (Dudley 75), Harris (Rodrigues 75), Sparks; Kavanagh, Brivio, Harding, Hester-Cook; O'Toole (Smith 78), Dsane (Fenelon 49).
Referee: Lewis Smith.

Charlton Ath (0) 4 *(Davison 72, Stockley 76 (pen), 85, Burstow 90)*

Havant & Waterlooville (0) 0 3865

Charlton Ath: (442) Henderson; Clare, Elerewe, Famewo, Souare (Clayden 87); Blackett-Taylor, Arter (Watson 71), Morgan (Lee 71), Kirk; Stockley (Burstow 86), Davison (Washington 90).
Havant & Waterlooville: (451) Mannion; Magri (Rooney 63), Collins (Bell-Baggie 77), Oastler, Green; Passley, Chambers (Searle 81), McCarthy, Gobern, Newton (Rendell 77); Roberts.
Referee: Carl Brook.

Chesterfield (2) 3 *(Khan 6, Croll 14, Tshimanga 79)*

Southend U (1) 1 *(Murphy 4)* 4713

Chesterfield: (3421) Minter; Kerr, Croll, Whittle; King, Oyeleke, McCourt (Weston 76), Miller▪; Mandeville (Tshimanga 76), Khan (Kellermann 64); Payne (Tyson 66).
Southend U: (3412) Arnold; White, Lopata, Hobson; Howard (Walsh 79), Dunne, Ferguson (Rush 73), Bridge; Brunt▪; Dalby, Murphy (Dennis 87).
Referee: Scott Simpson.

Crawley T (0) 0

Tranmere R (1) 1 *(McManaman 38)* 1765

Crawley T: (4312) Morris; Davies (Frost 71), Francillette, Craig, Dallison; Hessenthaler, Payne, Powell (Ferry 71); Nichols; Appiah, Nadesan (Bansal-McNulty 85).
Tranmere R: (4231) Doohan; Dacres-Cogley, Knight-Percival, Clarke, MacDonald; Spearing, O'Connor; McManaman, Watson (Davies 81), Feeney (Foley 73); Nevitt (Dieseruvwe 81).
Referee: Charles Breakspear.

Crewe Alex (0) 0

Swindon T (1) 3 *(Reed 25, 79, Simpson 52)* 2303

Crewe Alex: (352) Richards; Thomas T (Lundstram 64), Sass-Davies, Daniels (Bennett 46); Offord, Lowery, Murphy (Finney 75), Gomes (Robertson 75), Adebisi; Kashket, Porter (Mandron 63).
Swindon T: (532) Wollacott; Kesler, Baudry (Hunt 14), Conroy, Odimayo, Iandolo; Williams (Gladwin 71), Reed (East 85), Payne; Simpson (Gilbert 84), McKirdy (Mitchell-Lawson 84).
Referee: Trevor Kettle.

FC Halifax T (4) 7 *(Warren 10, Warburton 17, Spence 37, Waters 42, 59, Slew 56, Newby 73)*

Maidenhead U (3) 4 *(Kelly 13, 61, Acquah 20, 44)* 1514

FC Halifax T: (3412) Johnson; Bradbury, Spence, Maher; Senior, Warburton (Summerfield 67), Green, Warren (Swaby-Neavin 80); Waters; Vale (Newby 71), Slew.
Maidenhead U: (352) Holden; Beckwith, Parry, Massey; Barratt (Sparkes 63), Adams (Burley 46), Ferdinand, Upward (Asonganyi 74), Mingi; Acquah (Smith 74), Kelly (Blissett 67).
Referee: Jacob Miles.

Fleetwood T (1) 1 *(Garner J 12)*

Burton Alb (1) 2 *(Powell 14, Jebbison 77)* 1362

Fleetwood T: (352) Cairns; McLaughlin (Johnson C 76), Clarke, Andrew; Morris, Matete, Camps (Batty 66), Biggins, Lane; Morton (Garner G 76), Garner J (Edmondson 88).
Burton Alb: (3412) Garratt; Shaughnessy, Oshilaja, Leak; Hamer, Mancienne, Taylor, Borthwick-Jackson; Powell; Hemmings (Holloway 85), Jebbison (Patrick 85).
Referee: Tom Reeves.

Gateshead (0) 2 *(Campbell 47, Olley 79)*

Altrincham (0) 2 *(Dinanga 83, Moult 90)* 1066

Gateshead: (4231) Chapman; Bailey, Williamson, Storey, Nicholson; Ward, Jacob; Campbell (Hunter 85), Olley, Scott (Blackett 90); Langstaff.

Altrincham: (451) Gould; Senior, Mullarkey, Digie, Fitzpatrick; Whitehead (Porter 71), Hancock (Walker 77), Moult, Colclough, Peers (Dinanga 78); Baggley (Kosylo 46).
Referee: Thomas Parsons.

Gillingham (0) 1 *(Sithole 59)*
Cheltenham T (1) 1 *(Pollock 34)* 2555
Gillingham: (41212) Chapman; Jackson (Lintott 80), Bennett (Akinde 72), Ehmer, McKenzie (Akehurst 56); Tucker; Adshead (Sithole 46), Reeves; Dempsey; Lloyd, Oliver.
Cheltenham T: (343) Flinders; Long, Pollock, Freestone; Blair, Thomas, Chapman, Hussey; May (Sercombe 67), Vassell (Crowley 77), Norton (Joseph 76).
Referee: Ollie Yates.

Harrogate T (0) 2 *(Power 73, Orsi-Dadomo 78)*
Wrexham (1) 1 *(Ponticelli 38)* 2403
Harrogate T: (433) Oxley; Sheron, Burrell, Hall, Page (Fallowfield 46); Pattison, Falkingham, Kerry (Muldoon 62); Thomson (Power 57), Martin (Orsi-Dadomo 61), Diamond.
Wrexham: (352) Lainton; Hayden, Tozer, Brisley (Angus 82); French, Jones J (Hall-Johnson 83), Young, McAlinden (Hosannah 69), Green (Jarvis 83); Davies, Ponticelli.
Referee: Scott Oldham.

Hartlepool U (1) 2 *(Cullen 45, Molyneux 65)*
Wycombe W (0) 2 *(Joseph 63, Jacobson 74 (pen))* 4271
Hartlepool U: (532) Mitchell; Ogle (Odusina 90), Hendrie, Liddle, Byrne, Ferguson; Featherstone, Daly, Holohan (Shelton 76); Molyneux, Cullen (Grey 77).
Wycombe W: (343) Przybek; KaiKai (Mehmeti 70), Joseph, Jacobson; McCarthy, Thompson, Gape (Scowen 70), Obita; Wheeler, Vokes (Hanlan 84), Horgan (De Barr 90).
Referee: Darren Drysdale.

Hayes & Yeading U (0) 0
Sutton U (0) 1 *(Randall 71)* 1201
Hayes & Yeading U: (352) Dickinson; Frempah, McDevitt, Robinson; Nasha (Rowe 69), Goodrham, Odelusi, Jalloh (Hippolyte-Patrick 80), Connors (Norville-Williams 46); Emmanuel, Amartey.
Sutton U: (442) Bouzanis; Kizzi, Goodliffe, Rowe, Wyatt; Ajiboye, Smith, Milsom, Randall (Boldewijn 90); Olaofe (Wilson 68), Bugiel (Sho-Silva 81).
Referee: Sam Allison.

Ipswich T (1) 1 *(Burns 8)*
Oldham Ath (1) 1 *(Keillor-Dunn 41)* 8845
Ipswich T: (4231) Walton; Vincent-Young (Donacien 46), Nsiala, Edmundson, Burgess (Penney 46); Morsy, Evans (Harper 83); Burns (Aluko 83), Celina, Edwards (Chaplin 53); Bonne.
Oldham Ath: (3412) Leutwiler; Clarke, Piergianni, McGahey; Fage (Adams 87), Bowden, Whelan, Couto; Keillor-Dunn; Hope, Bahamboula (Vaughan 78).
Referee: Neil Hair.

Kidderminster H (0) 1 *(Hemmings 72 (pen))*
Grimsby T (0) 0 2791
Kidderminster H: (442) Simpson; Penny, Lowe, Cameron, Richards; Sterling-James, Carrington, Bonds, Hemmings (Martin 80); Austin, Morgan-Smith (Freemantle 65).
Grimsby T: (352) Crocombe; Waterfall (Grant 74), Longe-King, Towler; Efete, Clifton, Fox, Coke, Revan; Bapaga (John-Lewis 60), Taylor.
Referee: Garreth Rhodes.

King's Lynn T (0) 0
Walsall (1) 1 *(Kiernan 15)* 1934
King's Lynn T: (3412) Jones P; Bowry, Callan-McFadden, Fernandez (Bird 59); Jones A, Coleman, Clunan, Barrows (Omotayo 46); Davis (McGavin 79); Morias, Linton (Barrett 63).
Walsall: (433) Rushworth; White, Menayese, Monthe, Ward; Osadebe (Perry 83), Earing, Labadie; Shade, Miller, Kiernan (Phillips 65).
Referee: Robert Lewis.

Leyton Orient (1) 1 *(Drinan 24)*
Ebbsfleet U (0) 0 3451
Leyton Orient: (3412) Vigouroux; Clay, Beckles, Ogie; James, Pratley, Kyprianou, Archibald; Kemp; Drinan, Smith.
Ebbsfleet U: (3412) Gould; Chapman (Egan 72), Kahraman, Martin J; Paxman, Solly, Tanner (Krasniqi 85), Cundle; Martin L (West 88); Bingham (Monlouis 85), Poleon (Romain 72).
Referee: Will Finnie.

Lincoln C (0) 1 *(Sanders 66)*
Bowers & Pitsea (0) 0 5800
Lincoln C: (4231) Long; Eyoma, Montsma, Roughan (Draper 51), Bramall; Sanders, McGrandles; Adelakun, Maguire, Bishop; N'Lundulu.
Bowers & Pitsea: (541) Beeney; Bentley, Thomas (Trendall 58), Leahy, White, Stephen; Monville, Cornhill, Dicks (Ademiluyi 83), Norton (Albon 41); Manor (Sach 83).
Referee: Marc Edwards.

Milton Keynes D (1) 2 *(Darling 34, Watters 76)*
Stevenage (0) 2 *(Barry 70, List 73)* 2860
Milton Keynes D: (3412) Fisher; O'Hora, Darling, Lewington; Baldwin, McEachran, O'Riley, Ilunga; Twine (Brown 87); Watters, Parrott.
Stevenage: (442) Anang; Wildin, Cuthbert, Vancooten, Coker (Melbourne 67); Reeves, Taylor, Read (Lines 90), Barry; Osborne (Reid 66), List.
Referee: Simon Mather.

Morecambe (0) 1 *(Wildig 68)*
Newport Co (0) 0 1879
Morecambe: (433) Andresson; McLaughlin (Cooney 83), O'Connor, Wootton, Leigh; Jones, Phillips (Wildig 67), McCalmont; Ayunga, Stockton, Gnahoua (Diagouraga 79).
Newport Co: (41212) Day; Norman, Clarke, Demetriou, Lewis A (Collins 83); Willmott; Azaz, Cain (Ellison 77); Cooper (Fisher 90); Baker-Richardson, Telford.
Referee: Tom Nield.

Northampton T (2) 2 *(Etete 6, Lewis 35)*
Cambridge U (1) 2 *(Smith 14, Masterson 66)* 3792
Northampton T: (4411) Roberts; Revan, Guthrie, Horsfall, Koiki; Hoskins (Kabamba 88), Sowerby (Connolly 74), McWilliams, Pinnock (Rose 74); Lewis; Etete.
Cambridge U: (4231) Mitov; Williams, Okedina, Masterson, Iredale; May (Weir 63), Digby; Tracey (Brophy 46), Worman (Knibbs 63), Smith; Ironside.
Referee: Martin Coy.

Port Vale (1) 5 *(Wilson 30, 73, 79, Cass 85, Lloyd 90)*
Accrington S (0) 1 *(Hamilton 85)* 4605
Port Vale: (343) Lucas Covolan; Cass, Smith, Jones D; Worrall (Martin 76), Pett (Walker 84), Conlon (Taylor 81), Gibbons; Politic (Garrity 46), Wilson (Lloyd 81), Amoo.
Accrington S: (3511) Savin; Sykes, Nottingham, Amankwah (Malcolm 78); O'Sullivan, Conneely, Morgan (Mansell 54), Hamilton, Nolan; Pell (Mumbongo 78); Bishop■.
Referee: Ben Speedie.

Portsmouth (1) 1 *(Harness 28)*
Harrow Bor (0) 0 6869
Portsmouth: (4411) Bazunu; Romeo, Raggett, Ogilvie, Brown; Harness (Hackett-Fairchild 83), Morrell, Williams (Thompson 73), Curtis; Azeez (Ahadme 60); Marquis (Jacobs 83).
Harrow Bor: (4231) Strizovic; Adenola, Mansfield, Preddie (Cole 71), Taylor; Donnellan, Uche; Keita (Wynter 79), Moore, Bryan (Otudeko 74); Ewington.
Referee: Scott Tallis.

Rotherham U (2) 3 *(Wiles 43, Ladapo 45, Grigg 80)*
Bromley (0) 0 4064
Rotherham U: (3142) Johansson; Ihiekwe (Edmonds-Green 46), Wood, Harding; Barlaser; Ogbene (Sadlier 53), Rathbone, Odofin (Wiles 17), Ferguson (Bola 60); Grigg, Ladapo (Kayode 60).
Bromley: (3412) Charles-Cook (Cousins 46); Sowunmi, Webster, Bush; Coulson (Sablier 77), Bingham (Cawley 19), Trotter (Arthurs 46), Forster (Mnoga■ 46); Cheek (Lovatt 81); Alexander (Dennis 46), Alabi.
Referee: Declan Bourne.

Scunthorpe U (0) 0
Doncaster R (1) 1 *(Rowe 38)* 3301
Scunthorpe U: (433) Watson; Rowe, Taft, Onariase, O'Malley; Hackney, Pugh (Wood 76), Beestin (Perry 61); Scrimshaw (Green 61), Loft, Bunn (Hippolyte 22 (Jarvis 76)).
Doncaster R: (433) Dahlberg; Knoyle, Anderson, Olowu (Horton 13), Rowe; Bostock (Barlow 46 (Blythe 90)), Smith, Galbraith; Dodoo, Cukur (Hasani 85), Hiwula.
Referee: Carl Boyeson.

Sunderland (0) 0
Mansfield T (1) 1 *(Oates 5)* 8620
Sunderland: (4231) Burge; Alves (Winchester 46), Wright, Flanagan (Doyle 46), Cirkin (O'Nien 71); Evans, Neil; Dajaku (Pritchard 46), Embleton, O'Brien (Gooch 46); Broadhead.
Mansfield T: (4231) Bishop; Hewitt, O'Toole, Hawkins, McLaughlin; Charsley (Forrester 90), Clarke O; Maris, Quinn, Lapslie (Sinclair 84); Oates (Bowery 63).
Referee: James Oldham.

Wigan Ath (0) 0
Solihull Moors (0) 0 2843
Wigan Ath: (4231) Jamie Jones; Darikwa, Kerr, Watts (Tilt 20 (Robinson 46)), Pearce; Bayliss (Jordan Jones 69), Power; Lang, Keane (Aasgaard 69), Edwards (Humphrys 82); Wyke.
Solihull Moors: (4231) Boot; Williams, Gudger, Howe, Boyes; Maynard, Maycock; Donawa, Osborne, Sbarra; Dallas (Rooney 77).
Referee: Daniel Middleton.

Yate T (0) 0
Yeovil T (3) 5 *(Worthington 7, Wakefield 14, Gorman 29 (pen), Yussuf 48, Lo-Everton 62)* 1600
Yate T: (442) Hannah; Turl, Angel, Lewis (Bower 65), Tunnicliff (Thuo 73); Tumelty (Hall 65), Adams, Kamara (Mehew 54), Rees; Harding (Williams 72), Sims-Burgess.
Yeovil T: (4231) Smith G; Moss, Staunton, Williams (Wilkinson 53), Robinson (Lo-Everton 53); Gorman (Stephens 76), Barnett; Wakefield, Worthington (Bradley 66), Knowles; Yussuf (Quigley 67).
Referee: Matthew Russell.

York C (0) 0
Buxton (0) 1 *(De Girolamo 85)* 3791
York C: (442) Jameson; Fielding, Brown, Wright, Newton; Hopper, McLaughlin, Heaney, Dyson (Gilchrist 71); Donaldson, Willoughby (Beck 61).
Buxton: (4231) Richardson; Curley, Middleton, Granite, Fox; Meikle, Dawson; Clarke, Elliot (Hurst 89), Ward (Chambers 74); De Girolamo.
Referee: Aaron Jackson.

Sunday, 7 November 2021

Bolton W (2) 2 *(Doyle 33, Kachunga 36)*
Stockport Co (2) 2 *(Quigley 23, Whitfield 45)* 11,183
Bolton W: (433) Dixon; Isgrove, Santos, Baptiste, John (Gordon 46); Lee, Williams, Thomason (Delfouneso 69); Kachunga (Bakayoko 76), Doyle, Afolayan.
Stockport Co: (4231) Ross; Minihan (Collar 60), Hogan, Palmer, Kitching (Pye 70); Rooney, Croasdale (Keane 79); Crankshaw, Madden, Whitfield (Rydel 46); Quigley (Reid 79).
Referee: Christopher Sarginson.

Oxford U (1) 2 *(Taylor 11, McGuane 51)*
Bristol R (1) 2 *(Finley 45, Evans 87 (pen))* 5083
Oxford U: (433) Eastwood; Long, Moore, Thorniley, Seddon; Brannagan, Gorrin (Williams 22), McGuane (Hanson 79); Sykes (Bodin 71), Taylor (Agyei 71), Whyte (Forde 71).
Bristol R: (352) Belshaw; Kilgour, Taylor, Harries; Anderson H (Collins 82), Finley, Whelan, Coutts (Spence 82), Grant (Hoole 68); Nicholson, Evans.
Referee: Paul Howard.

Rochdale (1) 1 *(O'Keeffe 45)*
Notts Co (0) 1 *(Wootton 62)* 2587
Rochdale: (343) Lynch; Graham, O'Connell, Dorsett; O'Keeffe, Morley, Kelly L, Keohane; Dooley (Grant 64), Beesley, Odoh.
Notts Co: (352) Patterson; Brindley, Cameron, Chicksen; Kelly-Evans (Nemane 58), Roberts (Vincent 78), Palmer M, O'Brien, Taylor; Rodrigues, Wootton.
Referee: Ross Joyce.

Sheffield W (0) 0
Plymouth Arg (0) 0 7261
Sheffield W: (352) Peacock-Farrell; Palmer, Dunkley, Johnson; Paterson (Hunt J 60), Adeniran (Dele-Bashiru 60), Bannan, Wing, Corbeanu (Shodipo 76); Kamberi (Gregory 60), Berahino (Sow 85).
Plymouth Arg: (532) Cooper M; Edwards (Agard 85), Wilson, Scarr, Galloway, Grant; Camara, Houghton, Mayor (Broom 63); Jephcott (Shirley 90), Hardie (Garrick 46).
Referee: Anthony Backhouse.

St Albans C (2) 3 *(Weiss 25, Banton 29, Jeffers 78)*
Forest Green R (2) 2 *(Stevens 18, Aitchison 45)* 4100
St Albans C: (433) Johnson; Diedhiou, Mukena, Adebiyi, Lankshear; Noble (Dawson 79), Wiltshire, Weiss (Sole 90); Goddard (Brown 79), Jeffers, Banton.
Forest Green R: (4231) McGee; Wilson, Godwin-Malife, Moore-Taylor, Cadden; Adams, Stevenson; Aitchison, March, Young (Diallo 65); Stevens.
Referee: Rebecca Welch.

Stratford T (1) 1 *(Grocott 5)*
Shrewsbury T (1) 5 *(Bowman 25, 54, Leahy 57, Bennett 62, Bloxham 90)* 2800
Stratford T: (4231) O'Brien; Wilson, Vann, Williams, Isaac; Fry, Sammons; Obeng (James 45), Grocott, Dawes (Power 83); Gordon (Andoh 76).
Shrewsbury T: (352) Burgoyne; Ebanks-Landell, Pierre, Nurse; Bennett, Udoh (Bloxham 86), Davis, Leahy, Ogbeta (Caton 89); Pyke (Leshabela 89), Bowman (Cosgrove 86).
Referee: Ben Toner.

Monday, 8 November 2021

Dagenham & R (0) 0
Salford C (1) 1 *(Turnbull 3)* 2330
Dagenham & R: (352) Justham; Wright, Clark, Reynolds; Ling (Akanbi 71), Sagaf, Rance (Jones 67), Robinson, Weston; Vilhete (Saunders 80), Balanta.
Salford C: (3412) Ripley; Smith A, Eastham, Turnbull; Shephard, Lowe, Lund, Touray I; Morris (Love 79); Oteh (McAleny 62), Henderson (N'Mai 79).
Referee: David Rock.

FIRST ROUND REPLAYS

Tuesday, 16 November 2021

Altrincham (1) 2 *(Hancock 30, Mooney 79)*
Gateshead (1) 3 *(Langstaff 22, 90, Ward 57)* 1390
Altrincham: (4141) Thompson; Senior, Mullarkey, Hannigan, Fitzpatrick; Moult; Peers (Dinanga 64), Colclough, Porter (Whitehead 63), Kosylo (Pringle 78); Hancock (Mooney 54).

Gateshead: (4231) Chapman; Nicholson, Williamson, Storey, Jacob; Bailey, Ward (Hunter 85); Scott, Olley, Campbell (Williams 84); Langstaff (Tinkler 90).
Referee: Martin Woods.

Bristol R (0) 4 *(Finley 48, Spence 110, 118, Collins 115)*
Oxford U (0) 3 *(Taylor 57 (pen), Bodin 91, Seddon 93)* 4918

Bristol R: (4312) Belshaw; Anderson H, Taylor, Harries, Anderton; Coutts, Finley (Martinez 98), Westbrooke (Spence 97); Thomas (Grant 73); Nicholson (Collins 80), Evans (Jones 97).
Oxford U: (343) Eastwood; McNally, Mousinho (Moore 91), Thorniley (Long 55); Forde, Sykes (Seddon 71), McGuane, Williams; Bodin, Agyei (Taylor 55), Kane (Henry 54).
aet.
Referee: Neil Hair.

Cambridge U (2) 3 *(Knibbs 13, Smith 40, Worman 48)*
Northampton T (0) 1 *(Rose 75)* 3068

Cambridge U: (433) Mitov; Williams, Iredale, Okedina, Dunk; Digby, Worman (Weir 73), May; Knibbs (Lankester 88), Ironside, Smith (Brophy 73).
Northampton T: (4411) Roberts; Harriman (McGowan 42), Guthrie, Horsfall, Koiki; Hoskins (Kabamba 67), McWilliams, Connolly (Pinnock 67), Rose; Lewis; Etete.
Referee: Darren Drysdale.

Cheltenham T (1) 1 *(Pollock 11)*
Gillingham (0) 0 2651

Cheltenham T: (442) Flinders; Long, Blair, Hussey, Pollock; Thomas, Freestone, Sercombe (Barkers 90), Norton (Joseph 71); Vassell, Crowley (May 71).
Gillingham: (442) Chapman; Jackson, Akehurst, Phillips (Lintott 84), Ehmer; Adshead, Tucker, O'Keefe, Akinde; Reeves (Gbode 62), Lloyd (Sithole 34).
Referee: Lee Swabey.

Notts Co (0) 1 *(White 63 (og))*
Rochdale (1) 2 *(Andrews 15, Beesley 90)* 4416

Notts Co: (352) Patterson; Brindley, Rawlinson, Chicksen; Nemane (Kelly-Evans 76), Vincent (Francis 89), Palmer M, Rodrigues, Taylor; Mitchell (Roberts 57), Wootton.
Rochdale: (343) Lynch; Taylor, O'Connell, Dorsett; O'Keeffe, Kelly L, Morley (Broadbent 81), White (Done 67); Beesley, Andrews (Dooley 68), Newby (Odoh 81).
Referee: James Bell.

Oldham Ath (1) 1 *(McGahey 29)*
Ipswich T (1) 2 *(Chaplin 36, El Mizouni 81)* 2801

Oldham Ath: (3412) Leutwiler; Clarke (Dearnley 86), Piergianni, McGahey; Fage, Bowden, Whelan, Couto (Hart 69); Keillor-Dunn (Hopcutt 68); Bahamboula (Adams 86), Hope.
Ipswich T: (4231) Walton; Burns (Vincent-Young 76), Woolfenden (Burgess 46), Edmundson, Clements; Harper (Edwards 75), El Mizouni; Aluko, Chaplin, Fraser; Pigott (Jackson 84).
Referee: Carl Boyeson.

Plymouth Arg (2) 3 *(Garrick 20, 67, Hardie 36)*
Sheffield W (0) 0 11,094

Plymouth Arg: (352) Cooper M; Wilson, Scarr, Gillesphey; Edwards, Camara, Houghton (Randell 84), Broom (Mayor 76), Grant; Garrick (Agard 71), Hardie.
Sheffield W: (3412) Wildsmith; Paterson, Dunkley, Palmer; Adeniran (Sow 28), Dele-Bashiru, Wing, Brown; Bannan (Luongo 74); Kamberi (Shodipo 75), Berahino (Corbeanu 59).
Referee: Christopher Sarginson.

Solihull Moors (0) 1 *(Rooney 48 (pen))*
Wigan Ath (0) 2 *(Kerr 66, Lang 104)* 3703

Solihull Moors: (343) Boot; Maynard, Howe, Ball; Barnett (Hudlin 98), Maycock, Storer, Boyes; Rooney (Donawa 73), Newton (Dallas 72), Sbarra (Osborne 79).
Wigan Ath: (4231) Jamie Jones; Darikwa, Kerr, Watts, Pearce (Robinson 115); Bayliss (Smith 96), Power; Massey (Whatmough 110), Lang (Sze 110), Edwards; Wyke.
aet.
Referee: Charles Breakspear.

Stevenage (0) 2 *(Reid 61, Norris 120 (pen))*
Milton Keynes D (1) 1 *(Darling 37)* 1876

Stevenage: (41212) Smith A; Wildin, Cuthbert (Vancooten 106), Prosser, Coker; Lines (Melbourne 61); Reeves, Taylor (Osborne 114); Andrade (Norris 82); List, Reid.
Milton Keynes D: (343) Fisher; O'Hora, Darling■, Baldwin; Watson (Parrott 46), Robson (Kasumu 67), McEachran (Twine 79), Harvie; Boateng, Eisa (Watters 78), Martin■.
aet.
Referee: Alan Young.

Wycombe W (0) 0
Hartlepool U (1) 1 *(Cullen 20)* 1582

Wycombe W: (343) Stockdale; Grimmer (McCarthy 86), Stewart, Jacobson; Horgan, Scowen (Wheeler 72), Thompson, Obita; Akinfenwa (Mehmeti 78), Vokes, Hanlan.
Hartlepool U: (532) Killip; Sterry, Byrne, Liddle, Francis-Angol, Ferguson; Shelton (Smith 87), Featherstone, Daly (Crawford 87); Molyneux (Fondop-Talom 90), Cullen (Grey 73).
Referee: Chris Pollard.

Wednesday, 17 November 2021

Stockport Co (2) 5 *(Madden 24 (pen), Quigley 45, 95, Palmer 85, Crankshaw 119)*
Bolton W (3) 3 *(Kachunga 2, Palmer 6 (og), Bakayoko 28)* 10,084

Stockport Co: (352) Ross; Keane (Minihan 90), Palmer, Kitching; Southam-Hales (Barclay 103), Collar (Raikhy 68), Croasdale, Sarcevic (Crankshaw 75), Rydel; Madden, Quigley (Reid 106).
Bolton W: (433) Dixon; Isgrove, Santos, Johnston, John (Gordon 100); Sheehan (Aimson 45), Thomason, Lee; Kachunga, Bakayoko (Delfouneso 74), Afolayan (Amaechi 77).
aet.
Referee: Sam Barrott.

FIRST ROUND SECOND REPLAY

Tuesday, 30 November 2021

Exeter C (0) 2 *(Dieng 51, Canavan 80 (og))*
Bradford C (1) 1 *(Angol 11)* 3228

Exeter C: (451) Dawson; Key, Stubbs (Ray 69), Hartridge, Daniel; Coley (Nombe 69), Taylor K (Collins 56), Kite, Dieng, Edwards (Jay 68); Brown J (Grounds 90).
Bradford C: (4231) O'Donnell; Threlkeld (Cousin-Dawson 89), Canavan, O'Connor, Ridehalgh; Songo'o, Sutton (Robinson 84); Gilliead, Cooke (Foulds 89), Watt; Angol (Evans 89).
Referee: Charles Breakspear.
Reply original played on 16 November but was declared void after too many substitutes were played by Exeter C. The first replay finished 3-0 to Exeter C.

SECOND ROUND

Friday, 3 December 2021

Gateshead (0) 0
Charlton Ath (1) 2 *(Stockley 30, 54)* 3746

Gateshead: (433) Chapman; Tinkler, Williamson, Storey, Nicholson; Bailey (Hunter 86), Ward (Williams 68), Olley; Langstaff (Pani 82), Scott, Campbell (Blackett 68).
Charlton Ath: (3142) Henderson; Clare, Elerewe, Famewo; Dobson; Jaiyesimi (Leko 73), Gilbey, Lee (Morgan 66), Purrington (Souare 82); Washington (Davison 73), Stockley.
Referee: Tom Reeves.

Rotherham U (1) 1 *(Smith 43)*

Stockport Co (0) 0 6466

Rotherham U: (352) Vickers; Edmonds-Green, Wood (Harding 46), Ihiekwe; Ogbene, Wiles, Barlaser (Odofin 81), Miller (Mattock 81), Rathbone (Lindsay 65); Ladapo, Smith (Grigg 75).
Stockport Co: (3412) Hinchliffe; Barclay (Hogan 77), Palmer, Kitching (Raikhy 85); Southam-Hales, Collar (Madden 55), Croasdale (Rooney 85), Rydel; Sarcevic; Crankshaw (Jennings C 77), Quigley.
Referee: Ollie Yates.

Saturday, 4 December 2021

AFC Wimbledon (2) 4 *(Assal 36, 55, Palmer 41, 65)*

Cheltenham T (1) 3 *(May 2, Williams A 73, Heneghan 81 (og))* 4322

AFC Wimbledon: (4231) Tzanev; Osew (Lawrence 86), Heneghan, Csoka, Guinness-Walker; Woodyard, Hartigan (Marsh 68); Assal (Kaja 69), McCormick, Rudoni; Palmer (Pressley 68).
Cheltenham T: (4231) Flinders; Horton, Long (Raglan 62), Pollock, Hussey; Sercombe, Chapman; Joseph (Williams A 62), Crowley (Blair 46), May (Norton 61); Wright (Barkers 72).
Referee: Alan Young.

Bristol R (0) 2 *(Collins 57 (pen), Anderton 60)*

Sutton U (0) 1 *(Randall 52)* 4456

Bristol R: (3412) Belshaw; Taylor, Harries, Anderton; Anderson H, Whelan, Coutts, Finley; Collins; Nicholson (Pitman 76), Evans.
Sutton U: (442) Bouzanis; Barden, Goodliffe, John, Milsom; Randall (Korboa 70), Davis, Eastmond, Ajiboye (Boldewijn 83); Olaofe (Wilson 36), Bugiel (Bennett 83).
Referee: Darren Drysdale.

Burton Alb (1) 1 *(Leak 23)*

Port Vale (0) 2 *(Politic 79, 82)* 3539

Burton Alb: (343) Garratt; Shaughnessy, Leak, Oshilaja; Hamer, Taylor (Chapman 87), O'Connor (Mancienne 64), Borthwick-Jackson; Smith, Jebbison (Holloway 87), Hemmings.
Port Vale: (352) Stone; Smith, Martin (Worrall 62), Jones D; Gibbons, Garrity, Conlon, Pett, Benning (Cass 62); Amoo (Politic 74), Rodney (Walker 90).
Referee: Martin Coy.

Buxton (0) 0

Morecambe (1) 1 *(Stockton 29)* 3642

Buxton: (4141) Richardson; Curley, Hurst, Middleton, Fox; Meikle; Clarke, Dawson (Tear 81), Elliot, Ward; De Girolamo (Chambers 48).
Morecambe: (433) Letheren; McLaughlin, O'Connor, Delaney, Leigh; McLoughlin, Diagouraga, McCalmont (Jones 68); McDonald, Stockton, Gnahoua (Ayunga 67).
Referee: Lee Swabey.

Cambridge U (1) 2 *(May 23, Knibbs 88)*

Exeter C (1) 1 *(Nombe 10 (pen))* 2834

Cambridge U: (4231) Mitov; Williams, Okedina, Iredale, Dunk (Masterson 80); Digby, May (Weir 80); Tracey (Smith 62), Hoolahan, Brophy (Knibbs 80); Ironside.
Exeter C: (3412) Dawson; Sweeney (Coley 63), Ray (Amond 90), Grounds (Hartridge 62); Key, Collins, Kite (Edwards 90), Caprice; Jay; Nombe (Taylor K 55), Brown J.
Referee: David Rock.

Carlisle U (0) 1 *(Gibson 90)*

Shrewsbury T (1) 2 *(Bloxham 10, Bowman 78)* 2794

Carlisle U: (442) Howard; Mellor (Devine 27), McDonald, Feeney, Armer; Young (Charters 61), Guy, Whelan, Dickenson (Fishburn 62); Abrahams (Mampala 62), Clough (Gibson 35).
Shrewsbury T: (3412) Marosi; Pennington, Leahy, Ebanks-Landell (Daniels 21); Nurse, Bennett, Vela, Ogbeta (Caton 85); Udoh (Cosgrove 85); Bloxham (Leshabela 89), Bowman.
Referee: Sam Barrott.

Doncaster R (1) 2 *(Horton 7, Rowe 84)*

Mansfield T (0) 3 *(Forrester 48, Lapslie 60, 71)* 7040

Doncaster R: (433) Jones; Knoyle, Anderson, Horton, Rowe; Smith, Hasani, Ravenhill (Blythe 57); Hiwula, Dodoo, Barlow (Cukur 64).
Mansfield T: (442) Bishop; Hewitt, O'Toole, Forrester, McLaughlin (Bowery 46); Lapslie, Stirk, Clarke O (Charsley 90), Quinn; Oates (Sinclair 80), Maris.
Referee: Sebastian Stockbridge.

Ipswich T (0) 0

Barrow (0) 0 6425

Ipswich T: (4231) Walton; Donacien, Nsiala, Burgess, Clements; Morsy, El Mizouni (Pigott 46); Jackson (Aluko 74), Chaplin (Humphreys 85), Fraser; Bonne.
Barrow: (352) Farman; Jones J, Ellis, Grayson; Brown, Banks (Taylor 90), White (Zanzala 63), Gotts, Brough; Gordon, Kay (Stevens 86).
Referee: Sam Purkiss.

Leyton Orient (2) 4 *(Smith 22, 83, Beckles 36, Drinan 60 (pen))*

Tranmere R (0) 0 3248

Leyton Orient: (3412) Vigouroux; Thompson, Beckles, Ogie (Happe 85); James, Kyprianou, Clay (Pratley 56), Archibald; Kemp (Young 70); Smith, Drinan.
Tranmere R: (532) Doohan; Dacres-Cogley, O'Connor, Clarke, Knight-Percival, MacDonald (McManaman 56); Morris, Spearing (Foley 46), Hawkes (Watson 46); Glatzel (Nevitt 72), Maynard (Dieseruvwe 56).
Referee: James Oldham.

Lincoln C (0) 0

Hartlepool U (0) 1 *(Fiorini 52 (og))* 5506

Lincoln C: (433) Long; Poole (Sanders 63), Montsma, Jackson, Robson (Bramall 74); McGrandles, Fiorini, Maguire; Bishop, N'Lundulu, Adelakun.
Hartlepool U: (532) Killip; Ogle, Byrne, Liddle, Odusina, Ferguson; Shelton, Featherstone, Daly (Holohan 87); Molyneux, Cullen (Goodwin 76).
Referee: Robert Madley.

Portsmouth (1) 1 *(Harrison 45)*

Harrogate T (1) 2 *(Armstrong 44, Diamond 90)* 7857

Portsmouth: (343) Bazunu; Freeman (Brown 57), Raggett, Ogilvie; Romeo, Williams, Azeez, Hackett-Fairchild (Marquis 75); Harness, Jacobs, Harrison (Curtis 60).
Harrogate T: (433) Oxley; Sheron, Burrell, Hall, Page; Pattison, Falkingham, Kerry; Thomson, Armstrong, Diamond.
Referee: Simon Mather.

Walsall (1) 1 *(Osadebe 37)*

Swindon T (1) 2 *(Simpson 16, Kesler 67)* 4331

Walsall: (4231) Rushworth; White, Menayese, Monthe, Mills (Khan 73); Labadie, Earing; Wilkinson, Osadebe (Kinsella 66), Phillips; Miller (Shade 73).
Swindon T: (3511) Wollacott; Conroy, Odimayo, Hunt; Kesler, Payne, Reed, Williams (Gladwin 66), Iandolo (Crichlow-Noble 84); McKirdy (Mitchell-Lawson 75); Simpson.
Referee: Peter Wright.

Yeovil T (0) 1 *(Wakefield 51)*

Stevenage (0) 0 2754

Yeovil T: (433) Smith G; Moss, Wilkinson, Hunt, Williams; Gorman, Staunton, Worthington; Wakefield (Bradley 90), Yussuf (Knowles 66), Lo-Everton (Reid 81).
Stevenage: (442) Smith A; Wildin, Vancooten, Prosser (Norris 57), Melbourne; Osborne (Barry 73), Taylor, Reeves, Andrade; List, Reid (Read 73).
Referee: Craig Hicks.

Sunday, 5 December 2021

Colchester U (1) 1 *(Sears 45)*

Wigan Ath (1) 2 *(Lang 24, 75)* 2056

Colchester U: (4231) Turner; Tchamadeu, Chambers, Smith, Coxe; Skuse (Cooper 83), Chilvers; Jasper, Judge (Sarpong-Wiredu 72), Dobra (Tovide 83); Sears.

Wigan Ath: (3412) Jamie Jones; Kerr (Darikwa 65), Whatmough, Watts; Massey (Edwards 76), Cousins (Naylor 65), Power, Pearce (McClean 76); Lang; Keane, Humphrys (Jordan Jones 76).
Referee: Carl Brook.

Kidderminster H (2) 2 *(Morgan-Smith 3, Hemmings 17)*

FC Halifax T (0) 0 4290

Kidderminster H: (4231) Simpson; Penny, Cameron, Bajrami, Richards; Bonds, Carrington; Hemmings, Austin, Sterling-James; Morgan-Smith.
FC Halifax T: (442) Johnson; Warren, Debrah (Bradbury 46), Maher, Senior; Vale (Newby 59), Green, Spence (Woods 67), Slew (Gilmour 84); Warburton (Summerfield 59), Waters.
Referee: Brett Huxtable.

Rochdale (0) 1 *(Morley 55)*

Plymouth Arg (1) 2 *(Garrick 17, Jephcott 86)* 2687

Rochdale: (343) Lynch; Taylor, O'Connell, Dorsett; O'Keeffe (Cashman 89), Morley (Broadbent 90), Kelly L, Odoh; Beesley, Andrews (Dooley 73), Grant (White 46).
Plymouth Arg: (352) Cooper M; Wilson, Scarr, Gillesphey; Edwards, Broom (Camara 70), Houghton, Mayor, Cooper G (Law 55); Garrick (Ennis 84), Hardie (Jephcott 84).
Referee: Andrew Kitchen.

Salford C (0) 0

Chesterfield (1) 2 *(Mandeville 28, Kellermann 86)* 1997

Salford C: (442) King; Shephard (Wright 79), Eastham, Turnbull, Touray I; Love, Lowe, Lund, Morris; Thomas-Asante (Oteh 79), Elliott (Dackers 79).
Chesterfield: (3421) Loach; Kerr, Grimes, Croll (Khan 51); Miller, Oyeleke, Weston, Whittle; Kellermann, Mandeville (Clarke 90); Tshimanga (Payne 90).
Referee: Ross Joyce.

Monday, 6 December 2021

Boreham Wood (1) 4 *(Rees 25, 49, Mafuta 64, Clifton 81)*

St Albans C (0) 0 4101

Boreham Wood: (352) Ashby-Hammond; Evans, Stephens, Fyfield; Smith K (Clifton 79), Mafuta (Raymond 77), Ricketts, Rees, Mendy; Marsh (Comley 88), Boden (Ranger 87).
St Albans C: (433) Boyce-Clarke; Diedhiou (Bender 66), Mukena, Adebiyi, Lankshear (Sole 78); Weiss (Akinola 88), Wiltshire (Brown 77), Dawson (Noble 66); Goddard, Jeffers, Banton.
Referee: Ben Speedie.

SECOND ROUND REPLAY

Wednesday, 15 December 2021

Barrow (2) 2 *(Stevens 26, Gotts 35)*

Ipswich T (0) 0 2756

Barrow: (3421) Farman; Jones J, Platt, Grayson; Brown (Hutton 79), Banks, White, Brough; Stevens (Kay 79), Gotts (Ellis 90); Gordon (Zanzala 82).
Ipswich T: (442) Walton; Vincent-Young, Nsiala (Donacien 76), Burgess, Penney; Aluko (Chaplin 75), El Mizouni, Carroll (Woolfenden 46), Fraser (Morsy 46); Jackson, Norwood (Pigott 68).
Referee: James Bell.

THIRD ROUND

Friday, 7 January 2022

Swindon T (0) 1 *(McKirdy 78)*

Manchester C (2) 4 *(Bernardo Silva 14, Gabriel Jesus 28, Gundogan 59, Palmer 82)* 14,753

Swindon T: (3142) Ward; Hunt, Conroy, Odimayo (Crichlow-Noble 71); Reed (East 87); Kesler, Lyden, Gladwin (Williams 71), Iandolo; McKirdy (Dabre 87), Simpson (Parsons 83).
Manchester C: (433) Steffen; Walker, Dias, Ake (Mbete-Tabu 86), Joao Cancelo; De Bruyne (McAtee 66), Rodri, Gundogan (Lavia 83); Palmer (Kayky 86), Bernardo Silva, Gabriel Jesus.
Referee: Darren England.

Saturday, 8 January 2022

Barnsley (2) 5 *(Andersen 23, Williams 42, Cole 83, Morris 88, 102)*

Barrow (0) 4 *(Banks 61, Driscoll-Glennon 78, Jones J 86, Kay 90)* 4755

Barnsley: (442) Walton; Williams, Moon (Hondermarck 65), Andersen, Kitching; Brittain, Vita, Styles, Cole; Adeboyejo (Morris 65), Palmer (Ackroyd 106).
Barrow: (352) Farman; Jones J, Platt, Brough; Hutton, Banks (Arthur 87), Beadling■, White (Devitt 87), Driscoll-Glennon (Brown 106); Stevens (James 58), Sea (Kay 32).
aet.
Referee: Ross Joyce.

Birmingham C (0) 0

Plymouth Arg (0) 1 *(Law 104)* 9823

Birmingham C: (41212) Etheridge; Colin (Williams 106), Mengi, Friend■, Pedersen; Woods (Sunjic 90); James (Bellingham 70), Gardner (Chang 106); Campbell; Hogan (Aneke 88), Deeney.
Plymouth Arg: (532) Cooper M; Edwards, Bolton, Scarr, Gillesphey, Grant; Randell (Law 97), Houghton, Mayor; Garrick (Lewis 119), Hardie (Ennis 53).
aet.
Referee: Rebecca Welch.

Boreham Wood (1) 2 *(Marsh 10, Clifton 86)*

AFC Wimbledon (0) 0 3501

Boreham Wood: (352) Ashby-Hammond; Evans, Stephens, Fyfield; Smith K, Rees, Ricketts, Mafuta, Mendy (Raymond 90); Marsh (Clifton 85), Boden (Ranger 90).
AFC Wimbledon: (3412) Tzanev; Lawrence (Nightingale 57), Heneghan, Guinness-Walker; Osew, Woodyard, Hartigan, Rudoni (Kaja 65); McCormick (Chislett 80); Assal (Mebude 65), Palmer.
Referee: James Bell.

Bristol C (0) 0

Fulham (0) 1 *(Wilson 105)* 7304

Bristol C: (3412) O'Leary; Kalas, Atkinson, Pring; Scott (Weimann 106), Massengo, King (Dasilva 71), O'Dowda; Benarous (Palmer 78); Wells (Conway 91), Martin (Semenyo 89).
Fulham: (4231) Gazzaniga; Odoi, Adarabioyo, Hector, Bryan; Francois (Reed 71), Chalobah (Wilson 91); Reid, Carvalho (Cairney 86), Quina (Kebano 71); Rodrigo Muniz (Mitrovic 70).
aet.
Referee: Jonathan Moss.

Burnley (1) 1 *(Rodriguez 28)*

Huddersfield T (0) 2 *(Koroma 74, Pearson 86)* 7654

Burnley: (442) Pope; Bardsley, Tarkowski, Mee, Lowton; Brownhill, Stephens (Dodgson 82), Westwood, Lennon; Rodriguez, Wood (Cork 46).
Huddersfield T: (3421) Schofield (Bilokapic 40); Pearson, Lees, Sarr; Pipa (Thomas 69), Hogg (O'Brien 56), Russell, Ruffels; Sinani (Holmes 57), Koroma; Rhodes (Ward 70).
Referee: Andre Marriner.

Chelsea (4) 5 *(Werner 6, Hudson-Odoi 18, Lukaku 20, Christensen 39, Ziyech 55 (pen))*

Chesterfield (0) 1 *(Asante 80)* 39,795

Chelsea: (3421) Bettinelli; Sarr, Christensen (Baker 59), Hall; Ziyech, Saul, Kovacic (Loftus-Cheek 46), Hudson-Odoi (Barkley 66); Pulisic (Vale 59), Werner; Lukaku (Havertz 46).
Chesterfield: (343) Loach; Kerr, Gunning (Grimes 60), Croll; King (Miller 46), Weston, Oyeleke (Maguire 73), Whittle; Kellermann (Asante 66), Tshimanga, Khan (Mandeville 46).
Referee: Jarred Gillett.

Coventry C (1) 1 *(Hyam 42)*
Derby Co (0) 0 8896
Coventry C: (3421) Wilson; Clarke-Salter, Hyam, Rose; Kane, Sheaf, Allen (O'Hare 90), Dabo; Hamer (Eccles 66), Shipley (Jones 66); Godden (Gyokeres 90).
Derby Co: (4411) Allsop; Ebosele, Jagielka, Davies, Forsyth (Stretton 85); Morrison (Baldock 79), Bird, Thompson, Knight (Shinnie 80); Lawrence (Jozwiak 79); Kazim-Richards (Plange 79).
Referee: Kevin Friend.

Hartlepool U (0) 2 *(Ferguson 48, Grey 61)*
Blackpool (1) 1 *(Anderson 8)* 4932
Hartlepool U: (352) Killip; Byrne, Liddle, Odusina; Sterry, Crawford, Featherstone, Holohan, Ferguson; Cullen (Grey 59), Molyneux (Fondop-Talom 90).
Blackpool: (442) Grimshaw; Sterling, Ekpiteta (Yates 78), Keogh, Husband (Garbutt 41); Bowler (Mitchell 79), Connolly, Dougall, Anderson (Hamilton 34); Madine, Lavery.
Referee: Matthew Donohue.

Hull C (1) 2 *(Smith T 1, Longman 71)*
Everton (2) 3 *(Gray 21, Andre Gomes 31, Townsend 99)* 16,282
Hull C: (352) Baxter; Bernard, McLoughlin, Greaves; Williams (Longman 63), Honeyman, Smallwood (Huddlestone 63), Docherty (Moncur 63), Lewis-Potter; Smith T (Hinds 109), Eaves.
Everton: (343) Begovic; Coleman, Keane, Godfrey; Kenny (Doucoure 74), Allan, Andre Gomes (Gbamin 88), Mykolenko; Gordon (Townsend 66), Rondon (Tosun 117), Gray (Dobbin 106).
aet.
Referee: Andrew Madley.

Kidderminster H (0) 2 *(Austin 69, Morgan-Smith 82)*
Reading (1) 1 *(Puscas 45)* 5178
Kidderminster H: (4231) Simpson; Penny, Cameron, Bajrami, Richards; Martin (Montrose 90), Carrington; Hemmings, Austin, Sterling-James (White 90); Morgan-Smith (Freemantle 84).
Reading: (4231) Rafael Cabral; Tetek (Felipe Araruna 59 (Stickland 64)), Holmes (Laurent 46), Holzman, Bristow; Drinkwater (Rinomhota 58), Osorio; Camara, Dele-Bashiru, Halilovic (Azeez 40); Puscas.
Referee: Gavin Ward.

Leicester C (2) 4 *(Tielemans 7 (pen), Maddison 25, Barnes 54, Albrighton 85)*
Watford (1) 1 *(Joao Pedro 27)* 25,710
Leicester C: (4231) Ward; Albrighton, Choudhury, Vestergaard, Daley-Campbell (Marcal-Madivadua 46); Tielemans, Brunt; Perez (McAteer 74), Maddison, Barnes; Lookman (Alves 86).
Watford: (4231) Bachmann; Ngakia, Cathcart, Sierralta, Morris; Cleverley (Gosling 63), Sissoko (Conteh 74); Fletcher (Sema 58), Tufan (Kucka 64), Joao Pedro (Forde 74); Hernandez.
Referee: Mike Dean.

Mansfield T (0) 2 *(Hawkins 67, Oates 85)*
Middlesbrough (2) 3 *(Ikpeazu 4, Boyd-Munce 14, Hewitt 90 (og))* 7297
Mansfield T: (41212) Bishop; Hewitt, O'Toole, Hawkins, McLaughlin (Lapslie 61); Maris; Clarke O (Johnson 61), Stirk (Law 72); Quinn; Bowery, Oates.
Middlesbrough: (352) Lumley; Peltier, Wood-Gordon, Bamba; Gibson (Crooks 58), McNair, Howson, Boyd-Munce (Tavernier 58), Kokolo (Jones 77); Ikpeazu (Dijksteel 78), Coburn (Hernandez 62).
Referee: Keith Stroud.

Millwall (1) 1 *(Afobe 17)*
Crystal Palace (0) 2 *(Olise 46, Mateta 58)* 16,646
Millwall: (3421) Long; Hutchinson, Pearce (Bennett 62), Cooper; McNamara, Mitchell B, Saville (Kieftenbeld 50), Malone; Ojo (Boateng 81), Afobe (Burey 81); Bradshaw (Smith 81).
Crystal Palace: (433) Butland; Ward, Andersen, Guehi, Mitchell; Gallagher, Hughes (Milivojevic 81), Schlupp (Riedewald 88); Olise (Clyne 88), Mateta (Edouard 65), Eze (Benteke 64).
Referee: Anthony Taylor.

Newcastle U (0) 0
Cambridge U (0) 1 *(Ironside 56)* 51,395
Newcastle U: (433) Dubravka; Trippier, Krafth, Schar, Ritchie (Manquillo 79); Shelvey, Joelinton, Longstaff S (Almiron 60); Fraser, Saint-Maximin, Murphy (Willock 60).
Cambridge U: (4231) Mitov; Williams, Okedina, Iredale, Dunk; Digby, Worman (Hoolahan 62); Brophy, May (O'Neil 90), Knibbs (Lankester 76); Ironside.
Referee: Tony Harrington.

Peterborough U (1) 2 *(Szmodics 20, Mumba 63)*
Bristol R (1) 1 *(Coutts 30 (pen))* 4937
Peterborough U: (442) Cornell; Thompson, Knight, Edwards, Tomlinson (Mumba 46); Grant, Norburn, Jack Taylor, Burrows (Clarke-Harris 88); Szmodics, Dembele (Jade-Jones 90).
Bristol R: (4231) Belshaw; Hoole, Connolly, Anderton, Clarke T (Jones 63); Westbrooke, Coutts; Thomas (Edwards 90), Evans, Spence (Pitman 69); Nicholson.
Referee: Andy Davies.

Port Vale (0) 1 *(Harratt 69)*
Brentford (1) 4 *(Forss 26, Mbeumo 65, 76, 87 (pen))* 8069
Port Vale: (3412) Stone; Smith, Cass, Martin; Worrall, Pett (Walker 81), Garrity, Gibbons (Benning 59); Conlon; Amoo (Politic 59), Wilson (Harratt 54).
Brentford: (352) Lossl; Ajer (Roerslev 62), Sorensen, Pinnock; Stevens, Bidstrup, Janelt (Baptiste 71), Ghoddos (Peart-Harris 82), Thompson (Toney 82); Forss, Wissa (Mbeumo 62).
Referee: Thomas Bramall.

QPR (0) 1 *(Dykes 115)*
Rotherham U (0) 1 *(Ihiekwe 98)* 7157
QPR: (3412) Archer; Dickie, Dunne, Barbet; Adomah, Ball (Amos 70), Johansen, Wallace (Odubajo 59 (Drewe 91)); Thomas (Dozzell 71); Austin (Dykes 59), Gray.
Rotherham U: (3142) Vickers; Edmonds-Green (Ogbene 58), Wood, Ihiekwe; Barlaser (Odofin 79); Harding, Rathbone, Sadlier (Lindsay 58), Ferguson (Bola 79); Smith, Grigg (Kayode 65).
aet; QPR won 8-7 on penalties.
Referee: Michael Salisbury.

Swansea C (0) 2 *(Piroe 77, Bednarek 94 (og))*
Southampton (1) 3 *(Redmond 8, Elyounoussi 95, Long 102)*
Swansea C: (433) Hamer; Naughton, Bennett, Cooper (Ntcham 62), Manning; Smith (Williams 114), Downes, Walsh (Grimes 61); Obafemi (Fulton 91), Piroe, Cullen (Dhanda 85).
Southampton: (442) Forster; Valery■, Stephens, Bednarek, Perraud; Armstrong S (Diallo 65), Ward-Prowse, Romeu, Tella (Elyounoussi 77); Redmond (Armstrong A 65), Broja (Long 77).
aet. Played behind closed doors.
Referee: Graham Scott.

WBA (0) 1 *(Robinson 47)*
Brighton & HA (0) 2 *(Moder 81, Maupay 98)* 8208
WBA: (343) Button; Kipre■, Bartley, Townsend; Furlong, Livermore (Cleary 100), Gardner-Hickman (Ashworth 68), Reach; Robinson (Taylor 79), Phillips (Diangana 64), Ahearne-Grant (Fellows 79).
Brighton & HA: (352) Scherpen; Veltman (Ferguson 76), Duffy, Burn; Offiah (Cucurella 55), Gross, Mwepu (Mac Allister 28), Alzate (Moder 76), March; Welbeck (Trossard 56), Maupay.
aet.
Referee: Robert Jones.

Wigan Ath (0) 3 *(Power 61, Pears 75 (og), Aasgaard 90)*
Blackburn R (0) 2 *(Khadra 49, Ayala 89)* 9892
Wigan Ath: (343) Jamie Jones; Kerr, Whatmough, Watts; Darikwa (Massey 63), Naylor (Aasgaard 79), Power, Pearce (McClean 62); Lang (Jordan Jones 87), Keane (Humphrys 79), Edwards.
Blackburn R: (343) Pears; Lenihan (Johnson 46), Ayala, van Hecke; Dolan, Travis, Rothwell, Edun; Gallagher (Khadra 30), Buckley (Butterworth 70), Brereton.
Referee: Tim Robinson.

Yeovil T (0) 1 *(Quigley 48)*
Bournemouth (2) 3 *(Marcondes 19, 43, 70)* 7818
Yeovil T: (442) Barnes; Moss, Hunt, Wilkinson, Williams (Wakefield 69); Gorman (Reid 86), Worthington (Lo-Everton 80), Staunton, Barnett; Knowles, Quigley (Yussuf 80).
Bournemouth: (433) Nyland; Moriah-Welsh, Mepham, Rossi, Davis (Saydee 84); Marcondes, Pearson (Camp 90), Anthony (Brady 64); Kilkenny, Lowe, Rogers.
Referee: Jeremy Simpson.

Sunday, 9 January 2022

Cardiff C (1) 2 *(Davies I 42, Harris 116)*
Preston NE (0) 1 *(Johnson 54 (pen))* 30,720
Cardiff C: (3421) Phillips; Nelson, Morrison, Brown (Harris 68); Ng, Vaulks, Pack (Sang 100), Bagan; Colwill (Wintle 75), Davies I (Evans 91); Collins.
Preston NE: (3412) Iversen; van den Berg, Bauer, Cunningham; Potts, Ledson (Whiteman 80), McCann (Harrop 80), Earl; Johnson (Browne 104); Maguire (Evans 93), Jakobsen (Sinclair 58).
aet.
Referee: Simon Hooper.

Charlton Ath (0) 0
Norwich C (0) 1 *(Rashica 79)* 13,835
Charlton Ath: (3241) Henderson; Clare, Pearce, Inniss (Gunter 70); Leko, Jaiyesimi (Blackett-Taylor 71); Lee, Dobson, Gilbey (Kirk 87), Purrington; Burstow (Davison 70).
Norwich C: (451) Krul; Kabak, Hanley, Giannoulis (Williams 46), Byram (Aarons 71); Sorensen, Tzolis (Pukki 46), Sargent (Idah 85), McLean, Lees-Melou; Dowell (Rashica 46).
Referee: Josh Smith.

Liverpool (2) 4 *(Gordon 34, Fabinho 44 (pen), 90, Firmino 78)*
Shrewsbury T (1) 1 *(Udoh 27)* 52,226
Liverpool: (433) Kelleher; Bradley, Konate, van Dijk, Robertson (Tsimikas 90); Dixon-Bonner (Firmino 64), Fabinho, Morton (Norris 90); Gordon (Frauendorf 81), Woltman (Minamino 46), Jones.
Shrewsbury T: (352) Marosi; Pennington, Ebanks-Landell, Nurse; Bennett (Daniels 88), Vela, Davis, Leahy (Caton 90), Ogbeta (Pierre 83); Bowman (Bloxham 83), Udoh (Janneh 83).
Referee: David Coote.

Luton T (1) 4 *(Adebayo 18, Jerome 50, Naismith 82, Berry 88)*
Harrogate T (0) 0 4834
Luton T: (343) Shea; Burke, Naismith, Bradley; Bree, Lansbury (Berry 60), Mendes Gomes, Bell (Mpanzu 71); Clark (Onyedinma 71), Adebayo (Hylton 77), Jerome (Campbell 61).
Harrogate T: (433) Oxley; Fallowfield (Burrell 52), McArdle, Sheron, Page; Diarra, Falkingham, Thomson; Muldoon, Armstrong, Kerry (Austerfield 61).
Referee: James Linington.

Nottingham F (0) 1 *(Grabban 83)*
Arsenal (0) 0 24,938
Nottingham F: (343) Samba; Worrall, Cook, McKenna; Spence, Yates, Garner, Colback; Johnson, Davis (Grabban 67), Zinckernagel (Cafu 75).
Arsenal: (4231) Leno; Cedric (Kolasinac 90), White, Holding, Tavares (Tierney 35); Sambi Lokonga, Patino (Lacazette 69); Saka, Odegaard, Martinelli; Nketiah.
Referee: Craig Pawson.

Stoke C (1) 2 *(Ince 43, Campbell 89)*
Leyton Orient (0) 0 5269
Stoke C: (352) Bonham; Wilmot, Chester, Fox; Duhaney, Ince, Allen, Clucas (Vrancic 70), Doughty (Tymon 71); Wright-Phillips (Tezgel 84), Brown (Campbell 75).
Leyton Orient: (3412) Vigouroux; Mitchell, Beckles, Ogie; Clay (Young 65), Kyprianou, Pratley, Wood; Smyth; Smith, Drinan (Sotiriou 73).
Referee: Sam Barrott.

Tottenham H (0) 3 *(Winks 74, Lucas Moura 85, Kane 88)*
Morecambe (1) 1 *(O'Connor 33)* 40,310
Tottenham H: (532) Gollini; Doherty, Tanganga, Rodon, Davies, Sessegnon (Emerson 86); Lo Celso (Scarlett 88), Winks, Ndombele (Skipp 69); Gil Salvatierra (Lucas Moura 69), Alli (Kane 69).
Morecambe: (532) Carson; Cooney (Jones 77), McLaughlin, O'Connor, Bedeau (Gibson 65), Leigh; McLoughlin, Diagouraga (Wildig 77), McCalmont; Ayunga (Obika 58), Stockton.
Referee: John Brooks.

West Ham U (1) 2 *(Lanzini 34, Bowen 90)*
Leeds U (0) 0 54,303
West Ham U: (4231) Areola; Fredericks, Dawson, Diop, Johnson; Rice, Soucek; Bowen, Lanzini (Fornals 76), Vlasic (Masuaku 88); Antonio (Yarmolenko 90).
Leeds U: (4231) Meslier; Ayling (Forshaw 60), Llorente, Hjelde (Summerville 78), Firpo (Drameh 69); Koch, Bate (Dallas 46); Harrison, Klich, James; Greenwood (Raphinha 46).
Referee: Stuart Attwell.

Wolverhampton W (1) 3 *(Daniel Podence 14, 80, Nelson Semedo 72)*
Sheffield U (0) 0 27,004
Wolverhampton W: (343) Ruddy; Kilman, Coady, Marcal (Joao Moutinho 46); Nelson Semedo, Dendoncker, Neves (Bruno Jordao 86), Ait Nouri; Traore (Trincao 68), Silva (Jimenez 68), Daniel Podence (Cundle 86).
Sheffield U: (532) Foderingham; Bogle, Basham, Gordon, Robinson (Freeman 46), Norrington-Davies; Berge (Norwood 80), Hourihane, Osborn; McGoldrick (Burke 65), Sharp (Ndiaye 79).
Referee: Paul Tierney.

Monday, 10 January 2022

Manchester U (1) 1 *(McTominay 8)*
Aston Villa (0) 0 72,911
Manchester U: (442) de Gea; Lindelof, Varane, Dalot, Shaw; McTominay, Fred, Bruno Fernandes (Lingard 85), Rashford (Elanga 85); Greenwood, Cavani (van de Beek 72).
Aston Villa: (442) Martinez; Cash, Konsa, Mings, Targett; McGinn, Douglas Luiz, Ramsey A (Philogene-Bidace 86), Buendia (El Ghazi 79); Ings, Watkins.
Referee: Michael Oliver.

FOURTH ROUND

Friday, 4 February 2022

Manchester U (1) 1 *(Sancho 25)*
Middlesbrough (0) 1 *(Crooks 64)* 71,871
Manchester U: (4231) Henderson; Dalot, Varane (Jones 91), Maguire, Shaw; Pogba (Fred 82), McTominay; Rashford (Elanga 82), Bruno Fernandes, Sancho (Mata 100); Ronaldo.
Middlesbrough: (352) Lumley; Dijksteel, Fry, McNair; Jones (Bamba 118), Crooks (Payero 78), Howson, Tavernier, Taylor (Peltier 91); Sporar (Connolly 91), Balogun (Watmore 62).
aet; Middlesbrough won 8-7 on penalties.
Referee: Anthony Taylor.

Saturday, 5 February 2022

Cambridge U (0) 0

Luton T (2) 3 *(Burke 14, Mendes Gomes 23, Muskwe 88)* 7937

Cambridge U: (4231) Mitov; Williams, Okedina, Sherring, Dunk; Digby, May (Worman 75); Knibbs (Tolaj 75), Hoolahan, Brophy (Lankester 75); Smith.
Luton T: (352) Steer; Lockyer, Osho, Burke; Kioso, Mendes Gomes (Campbell 85), Thorpe (Hylton 69), Muskwe, Potts; Onyedinma (Bell 85), Jerome (Cornick 78).
Referee: Thomas Bramall.

Chelsea (1) 2 *(Azpilicueta 41, Alonso 105)*

Plymouth Arg (1) 1 *(Gillesphey 8)* 39,959

Chelsea: (433) Arrizabalaga; Azpilicueta (Chalobah 112), Christensen (Alonso 46), Rudiger, Sarr; Mount (Saul 97), Jorginho, Kovacic (Werner 82); Ziyech, Lukaku, Hudson-Odoi (Havertz 64).
Plymouth Arg: (532) Cooper M; Edwards, Wilson, Scarr, Gillesphey, Grant (Law 95); Camara (Broom 94), Houghton, Mayor (Randell 77); Garrick (Hardie 68), Jephcott (Ennis 58).
aet.
Referee: Simon Hooper.

Crystal Palace (2) 2 *(Guehi 4, Olise 22)*

Hartlepool U (0) 0 22,114

Crystal Palace: (433) Butland; Ward (Adaramola 86), Kelly, Guehi, Mitchell (Clyne 71); Gallagher, Milivojevic, Schlupp (Hughes 71); Olise, Mateta (Benteke 80), Eze (Edouard 71).
Hartlepool U: (541) Killip; Sterry, Byrne, Liddle (Grey 59), Odusina, Ferguson (Fletcher 90); Shelton (White 60), Morris, Crawford (Holohan 82), Molyneux; Bogle (Cullen 90).
Referee: Peter Bankes.

Everton (1) 4 *(Mina 31, Richarlison 48, Holgate 62, Townsend 90)*

Brentford (0) 1 *(Toney 54 (pen))* 37,310

Everton: (343) Pickford; Holgate, Keane, Godfrey (Mina 14); Coleman, Allan, Andre Gomes, Mykolenko (Kenny 73); Gordon (Townsend 73), Richarlison (Tosun 88), Gray (Iwobi 88).
Brentford: (352) Raya; Ajer, Jansson, Sorensen; Roerslev (Dasilva 72), Jensen, Norgaard, Janelt (Baptiste 62), Henry (Stevens 83); Toney, Canos (Ghoddos 72).
Referee: Michael Oliver.

Huddersfield T (1) 1 *(Holmes 19)*

Barnsley (0) 0 16,607

Huddersfield T: (433) Blackman; Pipa (Turton 30), Pearson, Sarr, Ruffels; Holmes (Lees 84), Eiting (O'Brien 60), Russell; Thomas, Rhodes (Ward 84), Koroma (Sinani 60).
Barnsley: (433) Walton; Williams, Andersen, Halme (Helik 46), Kitching; Palmer (Cole 78), Gomes, Bassi; Marsh (Benson 46), Iseka (Morris 46), Styles.
Referee: Jeremy Simpson.

Kidderminster H (1) 1 *(Penny 19)*

West Ham U (0) 2 *(Rice 90, Bowen 120)* 5327

Kidderminster H: (4231) Simpson; Penny, Preston, Cameron, Richards; Bajrami (Lowe 112), Carrington (Montrose 71); Hemmings (White 101), Austin (Redmond 78), Sterling-James; Morgan-Smith (Martin 106).
West Ham U: (4231) Areola; Fredericks, Diop (Dawson 46), Zouma, Johnson (Cresswell 63); Kral (Rice 46), Noble (Soucek 63); Yarmolenko, Benrahma, Vlasic (Fornals 77); Bowen.
aet.
Referee: Jonathan Moss.

Manchester C (2) 4 *(Gundogan 6, Stones 13, Mahrez 53 (pen), 57)*

Fulham (1) 1 *(Carvalho 4)* 53,400

Manchester C: (433) Steffen; Walker, Stones, Ake, Joao Cancelo (Zinchenko 67); De Bruyne (Sterling 68), Fernandinho, Gundogan; Mahrez (McAtee 78), Grealish (Delap 77), Foden (Bernardo Silva 78).
Fulham: (4231) Gazzaniga; Williams, Adarabioyo, Ream, Bryan; Chalobah, Reed (Seri 67); Wilson (Cairney 75), Carvalho (Ivan Cavaleiro 88), Kebano (Knockaert 67); Mitrovic (Rodrigo Muniz 75).
Referee: Jarred Gillett.

Peterborough U (1) 2 *(Ward 25, Jade-Jones 71)*

QPR (0) 0 10,119

Peterborough U: (3412) Benda; Kent, Edwards, Beevers; Ward (Coulson 65), Fuchs, Norburn, Mumba (Thompson 90); Poku (Brown 57); Clarke-Harris (Szmodics 46), Marriott (Jade-Jones 65).
QPR: (3412) Marshall; Sanderson, Dickie, Dunne; Odubajo, Amos (Hendrick 46), Johansen (Dozzell 62), Wallace (Adomah 46); Chair (Thomas 62); Austin, Dykes.
Referee: David Webb.

Southampton (0) 2 *(Armstrong S 63, Walker-Peters 112)*

Coventry C (1) 1 *(Gyokeres 22)* 30,512

Southampton: (343) Caballero; Valery, Lyanco (Redmond 34), Stephens; Livramento (Romeu 90), Diallo, Ward-Prowse, Small (Walker-Peters 46); Walcott (Broja 64), Long, Armstrong A (Armstrong S 46).
Coventry C: (343) Moore; Hyam, Rose, Clarke-Salter; Eccles (Kane 73), Hamer (Allen 73), Sheaf, Bidwell (Waghorn 73); O'Hare (Jones 89), Gyokeres, Maatsen (Shipley 64).
aet.
Referee: Tony Harrington.

Stoke C (1) 2 *(Maja 14, Brown 62)*

Wigan Ath (0) 0 12,641

Stoke C: (4231) Bursik; Wilmot, Harwood-Bellis, Moore, Tymon; Allen, Thompson (Clucas 61); Campbell (Tezgel 77), Powell (Fox 70), Wright-Phillips (Brown 61); Maja (Fletcher 78).
Wigan Ath: (4231) Jamie Jones; Power (Darikwa 46), Watts, Kerr, Bennett; Rea, Bayliss; Edwards■, McGrath, Massey; Magennis (Humphrys 63).
Referee: Geoff Eltringham.

Tottenham H (2) 3 *(Kane 13, 66, March 24 (og))*

Brighton & HA (0) 1 *(Bissouma 63)* 54,697

Tottenham H: (343) Lloris; Sanchez, Romero (Rodon 77), Davies; Emerson (Doherty 87), Winks (Bentancur 77), Hojbjerg, Reguilon; Lucas Moura (Kulusevski 68), Kane, Son (Bergwijn 69).
Brighton & HA: (3511) Sanchez; Webster, Dunk, Cucurella; Lamptey (Welbeck 70), Gross, Lallana (Veltman 46), Bissouma, March (Caicedo 61); Moder (Ferguson 79); Maupay.
Referee: Stuart Attwell.

Wolverhampton W (0) 0

Norwich C (1) 1 *(McLean 45)* 30,736

Wolverhampton W: (352) Ruddy; Kilman, Coady, Gomes (Jimenez 64); Nelson Semedo, Dendoncker (Chiquinho 74), Neves, Joao Moutinho, Ait Nouri; Silva, Daniel Podence.
Norwich C: (433) McGovern; Byram, Hanley, Gibson, Williams; Lees-Melou, Gilmour (Dowell 72), McLean (Normann 66); Placheta, Idah (Pukki 66), Rashica (Rowe 82).
Referee: David Coote.

Sunday, 6 February 2022

Bournemouth (0) 0

Boreham Wood (1) 1 *(Ricketts 38)* 9548

Bournemouth: (433) Woodman; Moriah-Welsh (Billing 66), Phillips, Hill (Solanke 76), Davis; Cook (Christie 46), Pearson (Cantwell 46), Kilkenny; Anthony, Lowe, Marcondes (Stacey 65).
Boreham Wood: (3412) Ashby-Hammond; Evans, Stephens, Stevens; Smith K, Ricketts (Comley 87), Raymond, Mendy; Rees; Marsh (Clifton 85), Boden (Ranger 90).
Referee: Graham Scott.

Liverpool (0) 3 *(Jota 53, Minamino 68, Elliott 76)*

Cardiff C (0) 1 *(Colwill 80)* 51,268

Liverpool: (433) Kelleher; Alexander-Arnold, Konate, van Dijk, Tsimikas (Robertson 70); Henderson (Thiago 78), Keita (Elliott 58), Jones (Diaz 58); Minamino (Milner 69), Firmino, Jota.
Cardiff C: (352) Phillips; Denham, Flint, McGuinness; Ng (Semenyo 90), King (Colwill 69), Pack, Vaulks (Doyle 69), Bagan; Harris (Davies 58), Collins (Hugill 58).
Referee: Andrew Madley.

Nottingham F (3) 4 *(Zinckernagel 23, Johnson 24, Worrall 32, Spence 61)*

Leicester C (1) 1 *(Iheanacho 40)* 28,762

Nottingham F: (3412) Samba; Worrall, Cook, McKenna; Spence, Yates, Garner (Cafu 88), Lowe; Zinckernagel (Colback 63); Johnson (Xande Silva 88), Davis (Surridge 71).
Leicester C: (4231) Ward; Justin, Amartey, Soyuncu, Thomas; Tielemans (Dewsbury-Hall 65), Ndidi; Lookman (Ricardo Pereira 65), Maddison, Barnes (Daka 46); Iheanacho.
Referee: Paul Tierney.

FIFTH ROUND

Tuesday, 1 March 2022

Crystal Palace (0) 2 *(Kouyate 53, Riedewald 82)*

Stoke C (0) 1 *(Tymon 58)* 22,100

Crystal Palace: (4231) Butland; Clyne, Andersen, Guehi, Adaramola (Schlupp 65); Kouyate (Riedewald 78), Hughes (Milivojevic 78); Olise, Ayew (Gallagher 64), Zaha; Mateta (Benteke 90).
Stoke C: (352) Bonham; Moore, Chester (Fletcher 86), Harwood-Bellis; Smith, Sawyers (Vrancic 79), Allen, Thompson, Tymon; Powell (Campbell 86), Maja (Brown 67).
Referee: Robert Jones.

Middlesbrough (0) 1 *(Coburn 107)*

Tottenham H (0) 0 31,135

Middlesbrough: (352) Lumley; Dijksteel, Fry, McNair (Peltier 106); Jones, Crooks, Howson (Bamba 118), Tavernier, Taylor (Bola 96); Sporar (Coburn 96), Watmore (Balogun 75).
Tottenham H: (3421) Lloris; Romero, Dier, Davies (Scarlett 115); Doherty (Emerson 81), Hojbjerg, Winks, Sessegnon (Bergwijn 81); Kulusevski (Reguilon 106), Son; Kane.
aet.
Referee: Darren England.

Peterborough U (0) 0

Manchester C (0) 2 *(Mahrez 60, Grealish 67)* 13,405

Peterborough U: (343) Benda; Knight, Edwards, Kent; Ward (Mumba 79), Fuchs, Grant, Coulson (Burrows 79); Poku (Marriott 71), Jade-Jones (Clarke-Harris 71), Szmodics (Brown 71).
Manchester C: (433) Ederson; Joao Cancelo, Dias (Stones 46), Ake (Laporte 46), Zinchenko; Foden, Fernandinho, Gundogan; Mahrez, Gabriel Jesus, Grealish.
Referee: Andrew Madley.

Wednesday, 2 March 2022

Liverpool (2) 2 *(Minamino 27, 39)*

Norwich C (0) 1 *(Rupp 76)* 52,231

Liverpool: (433) Alisson; Milner, Konate, Gomez, Tsimikas; Oxlade-Chamberlain, Henderson (Morton 61), Jones (Elliott 46); Minamino, Origi (Mane 84), Jota (Diaz 84).
Norwich C: (433) Krul; Byram, Zimmermann, Gibson, Giannoulis; Rupp (McLean 77), Normann (Gilmour 61), Lees-Melou; Placheta (Sargent 46), Pukki (Dowell 61), Rashica (Rowe 61).
Referee: Martin Atkinson.

Luton T (2) 2 *(Burke 2, Cornick 40)*

Chelsea (1) 3 *(Saul 27, Werner 68, Lukaku 78)* 10,140

Luton T: (352) Steer (Isted 14); Burke, Lockyer, Potts; Kioso, Mendes Gomes (Hylton 76), Osho, Berry (Campbell 63), Bell; Cornick (Jerome 62), Muskwe (Snodgrass 76).
Chelsea: (343) Arrizabalaga; Rudiger, Loftus-Cheek, Sarr; Hudson-Odoi (Vale 62), Jorginho (James 76), Saul, Kenedy (Pulisic 61); Mount, Lukaku, Werner.
Referee: Peter Bankes.

Southampton (1) 3 *(Perraud 31, Ward-Prowse 69 (pen), Broja 90)*

West Ham U (0) 1 *(Antonio 60)* 28,383

Southampton: (442) Caballero; Walker-Peters (Livramento 58), Valery, Stephens, Perraud; Smallbone (Redmond 81), Ward-Prowse, Diallo (Romeu 90), Djenepo (Armstrong S 46); Long (Broja 46), Armstrong A.
West Ham U: (3412) Areola; Dawson, Zouma, Diop; Johnson, Soucek (Benrahma 53), Rice, Fornals (Vlasic 76); Lanzini; Bowen, Antonio.
Referee: Andre Marriner.

Thursday, 3 March 2022

Everton (0) 2 *(Rondon 57, 84)*

Boreham Wood (0) 0 38,836

Everton: (343) Begovic; Kenny, Keane (Price 89), Branthwaite; Patterson (Richarlison 46), Allan (Welch 89), Doucoure, Mykolenko (Coleman 59); Townsend, Rondon, Gordon (Dobbin 86).
Boreham Wood: (3412) Ashby-Hammond; Evans, Stephens, Stevens; Smith K (Smith C 73), Ricketts (Comley 69), Raymond, Mendy; Rees; Boden (Ranger 89), Marsh (Clifton 90).
Referee: Tony Harrington.

Monday, 7 March 2022

Nottingham F (2) 2 *(Surridge 29, Yates 37)*

Huddersfield T (1) 1 *(Lees 13)* 27,417

Nottingham F: (3412) Horvath; Worrall, Cook, McKenna; Spence, Yates, Garner, Lowe; Zinckernagel (Colback 64); Johnson, Surridge (Davis 67).
Huddersfield T: (343) Blackman; Pearson, Lees, Sarr (Ward 55); Pipa, Eiting, Hogg, Ruffels (Toffolo 55); Holmes (Rhodes 67), Sinani (Anjorin 79), Thomas.
Referee: Graham Scott.

SIXTH ROUND

Saturday, 19 March 2022

Middlesbrough (0) 0

Chelsea (2) 2 *(Lukaku 15, Ziyech 31)* 31,422

Middlesbrough: (352) Lumley; Dijksteel, Fry (Bamba 46), McNair (Peltier 53); Jones, Crooks, Howson, Tavernier, Taylor (Bola 58); Balogun (Coburn 74), Connolly (Watmore 58).
Chelsea: (4231) Mendy; Azpilicueta, Thiago Silva, Rudiger, Sarr; Kovacic (Kante 69), Loftus-Cheek; Ziyech (Kenedy 81), Mount, Pulisic (Werner 68); Lukaku (Vale 84).
Referee: Paul Tierney.

Sunday, 20 March 2022

Crystal Palace (2) 4 *(Guehi 25, Mateta 41, Zaha 79, Hughes 87)*

Everton (0) 0 25,306

Crystal Palace: (433) Butland; Clyne, Andersen, Guehi, Mitchell; Gallagher, Kouyate (Hughes 83), Eze (Milivojevic 71); Olise (Benteke 83), Mateta (Edouard 71), Zaha.
Everton: (343) Pickford; Godfrey, Keane, Holgate; Coleman (Iwobi 73), Andre Gomes, Doucoure, Kenny (Calvert-Lewin 46); Townsend (Gray 17), Richarlison, Gordon.
Referee: Stuart Attwell.

Nottingham F (0) 0

Liverpool (0) 1 *(Jota 78)* 28,584

Nottingham F: (4231) Horvath; Spence, Worrall, Tobias Figueiredo, Colback (Xande Silva 90); Yates, Garner; Lolley (Cafu 65), Zinckernagel (Mighten 78), Johnson; Davis (Surridge 77).
Liverpool: (433) Alisson; Gomez, Konate, van Dijk, Tsimikas; Keita (Henderson 64), Fabinho (Thiago 64), Oxlade-Chamberlain (Diaz 64); Elliott (Minamino 64), Firmino, Jota.
Referee: Craig Pawson.

Southampton (1) 1 *(Laporte 45 (og))*

Manchester C (1) 4 *(Sterling 12, De Bruyne 62 (pen), Foden 75, Mahrez 78)* 29,702

Southampton: (442) Forster; Livramento, Stephens, Salisu, Walker-Peters; Armstrong S (Djenepo 83), Romeu (Smallbone 88), Ward-Prowse, Elyounoussi (Diallo 88); Armstrong A (Adams 63), Long (Broja 63).
Manchester C: (433) Steffen; Walker, Stones, Laporte (Ake 82), Joao Cancelo (Zinchenko 82); De Bruyne, Rodri (Fernandinho 82), Gundogan; Gabriel Jesus (Mahrez 64), Grealish (Foden 63), Sterling.
Referee: Mike Dean.

SEMI-FINALS

Wembley, Saturday, 16 April 2022

Manchester C (0) 2 *(Grealish 47, Bernardo Silva 90)*

Liverpool (3) 3 *(Konate 9, Mane 17, 45)* 73,793

Manchester C: (433) Steffen; Joao Cancelo, Stones, Ake, Zinchenko; Bernardo Silva, Fernandinho, Foden; Gabriel Jesus (Mahrez 83), Grealish, Sterling.
Liverpool: (433) Alisson; Alexander-Arnold, Konate, van Dijk, Robertson; Keita (Henderson 73), Fabinho, Thiago (Jones 87); Salah, Mane (Jota 85), Diaz (Firmino 85).
Referee: Michael Oliver.

Wembley, Sunday, 17 April 2022

Chelsea (0) 2 *(Loftus-Cheek 65, Mount 76)*

Crystal Palace (0) 0 76,238

Chelsea: (3412) Mendy; James, Christensen (Thiago Silva 82), Rudiger; Azpilicueta, Jorginho (Kante 77), Kovacic (Loftus-Cheek 26), Alonso; Mount (Ziyech 77); Havertz (Lukaku 76), Werner.
Crystal Palace: (352) Butland; Kouyate (Milivojevic 85), Andersen, Guehi; Ward, Eze, McArthur (Olise 72), Schlupp (Benteke 72), Mitchell; Mateta (Ayew 55), Zaha.

THE EMIRATES FA CUP FINAL 2021–22

Saturday, 14 May 2022

(at Wembley Stadium, attendance 84,897)

Chelsea (0) 0 **Liverpool (0) 0**

Chelsea: (3421) Mendy; Chalobah (Azpilicueta 106), Thiago Silva, Rudiger; James, Jorginho, Kovacic (Kante 66), Alonso; Mount, Pulisic (Loftus-Cheek 106 (Barkley 120)); Lukaku (Ziyech 85).

Liverpool: (433) Alisson; Alexander-Arnold, Konate, van Dijk (Matip 91), Robertson (Tsimikas 111); Keita (Milner 74), Henderson, Thiago; Salah (Jota 33), Mane, Diaz (Firmino 98).

aet; Liverpool won 6-5 on penalties.

Referee: Craig Pawson.

Konstantinos Tsimikas of Liverpool scores the winning penalty in the shoot-out that decided the FA Cup Final against Chelsea. (Action Images via Reuters/Peter Cziborra)

FA CUP ATTENDANCES 1969–2022

	1st Round	*2nd Round*	*3rd Round*	*4th Round*	*5th Round*	*6th Round*	*Semi-finals & Final*	*Total*	*No. of matches*	*Average per match*
1969–70	345,229	195,102	925,930	651,374	319,893	198,537	390,700	3,026,765	170	17,805
1970–71	329,687	230,942	956,683	757,852	360,687	304,937	279,644	3,220,432	162	19,879
1971–72	277,726	236,127	986,094	711,399	486,378	230,292	248,546	3,158,562	160	19,741
1972–73	259,432	169,114	938,741	735,825	357,386	241,934	226,543	2,928,975	160	18,306
1973–74	214,236	125,295	840,142	747,909	346,012	233,307	273,051	2,779,952	167	16,646
1974–75	283,956	170,466	914,994	646,434	393,323	268,361	291,369	2,968,903	172	17,261
1975–76	255,533	178,099	867,880	573,843	471,925	206,851	205,810	2,759,941	161	17,142
1976–77	379,230	192,159	942,523	631,265	373,330	205,379	258,216	2,982,102	174	17,139
1977–78	258,248	178,930	881,406	540,164	400,751	137,059	198,020	2,594,578	160	16,216
1978–79	243,773	185,343	880,345	537,748	243,683	263,213	249,897	2,604,002	166	15,687
1979–80	267,121	204,759	804,701	507,725	364,039	157,530	355,541	2,661,416	163	16,328
1980–81	246,824	194,502	832,578	534,402	320,530	288,714	339,250	2,756,800	169	16,312
1981–82	236,220	127,300	513,185	356,987	203,334	124,308	279,621	1,840,955	160	11,506
1982–83	191,312	150,046	670,503	452,688	260,069	193,845	291,162	2,209,625	154	14,348
1983–84	192,276	151,647	625,965	417,298	181,832	185,382	187,000	1,941,400	166	11,695
1984–85	174,604	137,078	616,229	320,772	269,232	148,690	242,754	1,909,359	157	12,162
1985–86	171,142	130,034	486,838	495,526	311,833	184,262	192,316	1,971,951	168	11,738
1986–87	209,290	146,761	593,520	349,342	263,550	119,396	195,533	1,877,400	165	11,378
1987–88	204,411	104,561	720,121	443,133	281,461	119,313	177,585	2,050,585	155	13,229
1988–89	212,775	121,326	690,199	421,255	206,781	176,629	167,353	1,966,318	164	12,173
1989–90	209,542	133,483	683,047	412,483	351,423	123,065	277,420	2,190,463	170	12,885
1990–91	194,195	121,450	594,592	530,279	276,112	124,826	196,434	2,038,518	162	12,583
1991–92	231,940	117,078	586,014	372,576	270,537	155,603	201,592	1,935,340	160	12,095
1992–93	241,968	174,702	612,494	377,211	198,379	149,675	293,241	2,047,670	161	12,718
1993–94	190,683	118,031	691,064	430,234	172,196	134,705	228,233	1,965,146	159	12,359
1994–95	219,511	125,629	640,017	438,596	257,650	159,787	174,059	2,015,249	161	12,517
1995–96	185,538	115,669	748,997	391,218	274,055	174,142	156,500	2,046,199	167	12,252
1996–97	209,521	122,324	651,139	402,293	199,873	67,035	191,813	1,843,998	151	12,211
1997–98	204,803	130,261	629,127	455,557	341,290	192,651	172,007	2,125,696	165	12,883
1998–99	191,954	132,341	609,486	431,613	359,398	181,005	202,150	2,107,947	155	13,599
1999–2000	181,485	127,728	514,030	374,795	182,511	105,443	214,921	1,700,913	158	10,765
2000–01	171,689	122,061	577,204	398,241	256,899	100,663	177,778	1,804,535	151	11,951
2001–02	198,369	119,781	566,284	330,434	249,190	173,757	171,278	1,809,093	148	12,224
2002–03	189,905	104,103	577,494	404,599	242,483	156,244	175,498	1,850,326	150	12,336
2003–04	162,738	117,967	624,732	347,964	292,521	156,780	167,401	1,870,103	149	12,551
2004–05	161,197	98,702	602,152	477,472	339,082	127,914	193,233	1,999,752	146	13,697
2005–06	188,876	107,456	654,570	388,339	286,225	163,449	177,723	1,966,638	160	12,291
2006–07	168,884	113,924	708,628	478,924	340,612	230,064	177,810	2,218,846	158	14,043
2007–08	175,195	99,528	704,300	356,404	276,903	142,780	256,210	2,011,320	152	13,232
2008–09	161,526	96,923	631,070	529,585	297,364	149,566	264,635	2,131,669	163	13,078
2009–10	147,078	100,476	613,113	335,426	288,604	144,918	254,806	1,884,421	151	12,480
2010–11	169,259	101,291	637,202	390,524	284,311	164,092	250,256	1,996,935	150	13,313
2011–12	155,858	92,267	640,700	391,214	250,666	194,971	262,064	1,987,740	151	13,164
2012–13	135,642	115,965	645,676	373,892	288,509	221,216	234,210	2,015,110	156	12,917
2013–14	144,709	75,903	668,242	346,706	254,084	156,630	243,350	1,889,624	149	12,682
2014–15	156,621	111,434	609,368	515,229	208,908	233,341	258,780	2,093,681	153	13,684
2015–16	134,914	94,855	755,187	397,217	235,433	227,262	253,793	2,098,661	149	14,085
2016–17	147,448	97,784	685,467	409,084	212,842	163,620	261,552	1,977,797	156	12,678
2017–18	125,978	87,075	712,036	371,650	210,328	140,641	245,730	1,893,438	149	12,708
2018–19	146,449	92,928	655,501	402,836	146,476	86,028	237,467	1,767,685	150	11,785
2019–20*	160,471	91,200	697,152	489,571	233,190			1,671,584	149	11,219
2020–21	*Due to the COVID-19 pandemic most games were played behind closed doors.*									
2021–22	199,848	86,847	596,352	482,808	223,647	115,014	234,928	1,939,444	137	14,157

**Due to the COVID-19 pandemic, the 6th Round, Semi-finals and Final were played behind closed doors.*

NATIONAL LEAGUE 2021–22

NATIONAL LEAGUE TABLE 2021–22

(R) Relegated into division at end of 2020–21 season. No teams promoted into division at end of 2020–21 season.

			Home					Away					Total						
		P	W	D	L	F	A	W	D	L	F	A	W	D	L	F	A	GD	Pts
1	Stockport Co	44	15	3	4	44	17	15	1	6	43	21	30	4	10	87	38	49	94
2	Wrexham	44	15	6	1	47	18	11	4	7	44	28	26	10	8	91	46	45	88
3	Solihull Moors	44	14	5	3	51	24	11	7	4	32	21	25	12	7	83	45	38	87
4	FC Halifax T	44	17	2	3	37	11	8	7	7	25	24	25	9	10	62	35	27	84
5	Notts Co	44	15	5	2	47	22	9	5	8	34	30	24	10	10	81	52	29	82
6	Grimsby T (R)¶	44	15	2	5	38	19	8	6	8	30	27	23	8	13	68	46	22	77
7	Chesterfield	44	11	7	4	36	26	9	7	6	33	25	20	14	10	69	51	18	74
8	Dagenham & R	44	10	6	6	46	29	12	1	9	34	24	22	7	15	80	53	27	73
9	Boreham Wood	44	11	8	3	28	14	7	5	10	21	26	18	13	13	49	40	9	67
10	Bromley	44	11	7	4	36	23	7	6	9	25	30	18	13	13	61	53	8	67
11	Torquay U	44	11	6	5	39	23	7	6	9	27	31	18	12	14	66	54	12	66
12	Yeovil T	44	7	7	8	20	25	8	7	7	23	21	15	14	15	43	46	–3	59
13	Southend U (R)	44	10	5	7	26	27	6	5	11	19	34	16	10	18	45	61	–16	58
14	Altrincham	44	10	4	8	39	27	5	6	11	23	42	15	10	19	62	69	–7	55
15	Woking	44	8	0	14	28	36	8	5	9	31	25	16	5	23	59	61	–2	53
16	Wealdstone	44	8	7	7	24	24	6	4	12	27	41	14	11	19	51	65	–14	53
17	Maidenhead U	44	9	5	8	32	35	4	7	11	16	32	13	12	19	48	67	–19	51
18	Barnet	44	6	6	10	28	42	7	5	10	31	47	13	11	20	59	89	–30	50
19	Eastleigh	44	8	6	8	33	33	4	4	14	19	41	12	10	22	52	74	–22	46
20	Aldershot T	44	4	5	13	19	40	7	5	10	27	33	11	10	23	46	73	–27	43
21	King's Lynn T	44	4	4	14	22	38	4	6	12	25	41	8	10	26	47	79	–32	34
22	Weymouth	44	3	7	12	21	38	3	3	16	19	50	6	10	28	40	88	–48	28
23	Dover Ath*	44	1	3	18	13	41	1	4	17	24	60	2	7	35	37	101	–64	1

**Dover Ath deducted 12 points for failing to fulfil fixtures in the 2020–21 season. ¶Grimsby T promoted via play-offs.*

NATIONAL LEAGUE PLAY-OFFS 2021–22

NATIONAL LEAGUE PLAY-OFF ELIMINATORS

Monday, 23 May 2022

Notts Co (0) 1 *(Rodrigues 73 (pen))*

Grimsby T (0) 2 *(Holohan 90, Dieseruvwe 119)* 12,023

Notts Co: (442) Slocombe; Cameron, Lacey, Brindley, Chicksen; Richardson J (Kelly-Evans 113), Palmer M, O'Brien (Francis 60), Roberts (Sam 22); Rodrigues (Brunt 82), Wootton.
Grimsby T: (442) Crocombe; Cropper (Dieseruvwe 87), Waterfall, Smith, Amos; Fox, Clifton, Sousa, Holohan (Coke 109); McAtee (Maguire-Drew 81), Taylor (Abrahams 81).
aet.
Referee: Sunny Gill.

Tuesday, 24 May 2022

FC Halifax T (0) 1 *(Stenson 68)*

Chesterfield (1) 2 *(Rowe 19, King 66)* 5661

FC Halifax T: (442) Johnson; Warren, Maher, Senior, Woods; Green (Stenson 56), Gilmour, Warburton, Waters; Slew (Dearnley 77), Debrah.
Chesterfield: (442) Loach; Miller (Whittle 77), Maguire, Grimes, Williams; King, Kellermann, Whelan, Khan (McCourt 89); Mandeville, Rowe (Tyson 72).
Referee: Scott Tallis.

NATIONAL LEAGUE PLAY-OFF SEMI-FINALS

Saturday, 28 May 2022

Wrexham (1) 4 *(Mullin 13 (pen), 65, Tozer 63, Davies 80)*

Grimsby T (1) 5 *(McAtee 15, Waterfall 47, 119, Taylor 72, Dieseruvwe 78)* 9734

Wrexham: (3412) Dibble; French (Jarvis 120), Tozer, Cleworth (O'Connor 91); Hosannah (McAlinden 73), Jones J, Young, McFadzean; Davies; Palmer (Hyde 106), Mullin.
Grimsby T: (442) Crocombe; Cropper, Waterfall, Smith, Amos (Pearson 91); Fox, Clifton, Sousa, Holohan (Raikhy 102); McAtee (Abrahams 87), Taylor (Dieseruvwe 75).
aet.
Referee: Adam Herczeg.

Sunday, 29 May 2022

Solihull Moors (2) 3 *(Dallas 15, Gudger 35, Howe 59)*

Chesterfield (1) 1 *(Quigley 7)* 4026

Solihull Moors: (442) McDonnell; Clarke, Storer, Howe, Gudger; Sbarra (Reilly 77), Maycock, Barnett, Boyes; Dallas, Hudlin (Newton 68).
Chesterfield: (442) Loach; Maguire (Rowley 59), Grimes, Williams, King; Kellermann (Whittle 59), Whelan, Khan, Miller; Mandeville (Denton 81), Quigley.
Referee: Thomas Kirk.

NATIONAL LEAGUE PLAY-OFF FINAL

Sunday, 5 June 2022

Grimsby T (0) 2 *(McAtee 69, Maguire-Drew 111)*

Solihull Moors (1) 1 *(Hudlin 45)* 22,897

Grimsby T: (442) Crocombe; Cropper, Waterfall, Smith, Amos; Fox, Clifton, Sousa (Maguire-Drew 66), Holohan (Abrahams 101); McAtee (Raikhy 90), Taylor (Dieseruvwe 81).
Solihull Moors: (442) McDonnell; Clarke, Howe, Gudger, Storer; Sbarra (Reilly 109), Maycock (Ellis 113), Barnett, Boyes; Dallas (McNally 116), Hudlin (Newton 58).
aet.
Referee: Martin Woods.

NATIONAL LEAGUE ATTENDANCES BY CLUB 2021–22

	Aggregate 2021–22	Average 2021–22	Highest Attendance 2021–22
Notts Co	149,602	6,800	12,843 v Solihull Moors
Chesterfield	140,859	6,403	9,198 v Stockport Co
Southend U	127,020	5,774	8,070 v Bromley
Grimsby T	125,485	5,704	7,818 v Stockport Co
Woking	59,445	2,702	5,171 v Aldershot T
Torquay U	56,680	2,576	3,830 v Yeovil T
Eastleigh	56,454	2,566	3,499 v Grimsby T
Yeovil T	52,322	2,378	3,936 v Weymouth
FC Halifax T	46,870	2,130	3,344 v Wrexham
Altrincham	46,621	2,119	3,900 v Stockport Co
Bromley	43,169	1,962	3,759 v Southend U
Aldershot T	40,123	1,824	3,699 v Woking
Solihull Moors	39,130	1,779	3,219 v Wealdstone
Dagenham & R	38,946	1,770	3,673 v Southend U
Barnet	34,441	1,566	2,438 v Grimsby T
Maidenhead U	31,004	1,409	2,324 v Boreham Wood
Wealdstone	29,449	1,339	2,662 v Barnet
Weymouth	25,870	1,176	2,609 v Yeovil T
King's Lynn T	25,477	1,158	3,111 v Grimsby T
Boreham Wood	23,275	1,058	2,053 v Wrexham
Dover Ath	18,267	830	2,657 v Southend U

NATIONAL LEAGUE LEADING GOALSCORERS 2021–22

Player	*League*	*FA Cup*	*FA Trophy*	*Play-offs*	*Total*
Paul Mullin (Wrexham)	26	2	2	2	32
Kabongo Tshimanga (Chesterfield)	24	1	0	0	25
Paddy Madden (Stockport Co)	23	2	0	0	25
Michael Cheek (Bromley)	17	1	5	0	23
Ruben Rodrigues (Notts Co)	19	0	2	1	22
Kyle Wootton (Notts Co)	19	2	1	0	22
Andrew Dallas (Solihull Moors)	18	0	3	1	22
Jordan Davies (Wrexham)	15	1	4	1	21
Paul McCallum (Dagenham & R)	18	0	2	0	20
Billy Waters (FC Halifax T)	17	2	1	0	20
Adam Marriott (Barnet)	19	0	0	0	19
Ollie Palmer (Wrexham)	15	3	1	0	19
Includes 3 goals in FA Cup for AFC Wimbledon.					
Joe Sbarra (Solihull Moors)	18	0	0	0	18
Josh Kelly (Maidenhead U)	15	2	0	0	17
Callum Roberts (Notts Co)	16	0	0	0	16
Josh Umerah (Wealdstone)	16	0	0	0	16
John McAtee (Grimsby T)	14	0	0	2	16
Armani Little (Torquay U)	15	0	0	0	15
Tahvon Campbell (Woking)	13	0	1	0	14
Matthew Warburton (FC Halifax T)	13	1	0	0	14
Junior Morias (Dagenham & R)	12	0	2	0	14
Includes 1 league goal for King's Lynn T.					
Inih Effiong (Woking)	13	0	0	0	13
Max Kretzschmar (Woking)	13	0	0	0	13
Dan Mooney (Altrincham)	12	1	0	0	13

NATIONAL LEAGUE NORTH LEADING GOALSCORERS 2021–22

League goals only

Macaulay Langstaff (Gateshead)	28
Nick Haughton (AFC Fylde)	26
Glen Taylor (Spennymoor T)	25
Cedwyn Scott (Gateshead)	24
Daniel Elliott (Boston U)	19
Jordan Archer (Southport)	16
Ashley Hemmings (Kidderminster H)	15
Lee Ndlovu (Brackley T)	14
JJ O'Donnell (Blyth Spartans)	14
Jason Oswell (AFC Telford U)	13
Tom Owen-Evans (Hereford)	13
Adam Campbell (Gateshead)	12
Marcus Carver (Southport)	12
Luke Charman (Darlington)	12
Matt Rhead (Alfreton T)	12

NATIONAL LEAGUE SOUTH LEADING GOALSCORERS 2021–22

League goals only

Alfie Rutherford (Dorking W)	30
Shaun Jeffers (St Albans C)	27
Ryan Seager (Hungerford T)	27
Charley Kendall (Eastbourne Bor)	24
Joe Iaciofano (Oxford C)	22
Joan Luque (Maidstone U)	20
Dipo Akinyemi (Welling U)	18
Jack Barham (Maidstone U)	18
Dominic Poleon (Ebbsfleet U)	17
Alex Fletcher (Bath C)	16
Cody Cooke (Bath C)	14
Marcus Dinanga (Dartford)	13
James McShane (Dorking W)	13
Danny Mills (Dulwich Hamlet)	13
Rakish Bingham (Ebbsfleet U)	12
Tommy Wood (Tonbridge Angels)	12
Adebayo Azeez (Dartford)	11
Simeon Jackson (Chelmsford C)	11
Jake Robinson (Dartford)	10

NATIONAL LEAGUE NORTH 2021–22

NATIONAL LEAGUE NORTH TABLE 2021–22

Due to COVID-19 pandemic, no teams were promoted or relegated into division at end of 2020–21 season.

			Home					*Away*					*Total*						
		P	*W*	*D*	*L*	*F*	*A*	*W*	*D*	*L*	*F*	*A*	*W*	*D*	*L*	*F*	*A*	*GD*	*Pts*
1	Gateshead	42	18	1	2	53	19	11	6	4	46	28	29	7	6	99	47	52	94
2	Brackley T	42	15	3	3	23	9	10	9	2	30	14	25	12	5	53	23	30	87
3	AFC Fylde	42	14	3	4	36	18	10	5	6	32	19	24	8	10	68	37	31	80
4	Kidderminster H	42	14	3	4	50	12	7	8	6	22	23	21	11	10	72	35	37	74
5	York C¶	42	11	4	6	32	20	8	5	8	26	30	19	9	14	58	50	8	66
6	Chorley	42	12	5	4	44	25	5	9	7	18	24	17	14	11	62	49	13	65
7	Boston U	42	10	5	6	39	28	8	4	9	24	29	18	9	15	63	57	6	63
8	Kettering T	42	9	7	5	30	21	7	6	8	24	27	16	13	13	54	48	6	61
9	Alfreton T	42	7	9	5	30	26	10	1	10	28	33	17	10	15	58	59	–1	61
10	Spennymoor T	42	10	6	5	32	21	7	3	11	23	30	17	9	16	55	51	4	60
11	Southport	42	8	11	2	35	20	6	4	11	25	35	14	15	13	60	55	5	57
12	Hereford	42	10	5	6	28	23	5	5	11	23	29	15	10	17	51	52	–1	55
13	Darlington	42	9	4	8	29	24	5	7	9	28	34	14	11	17	57	58	–1	53
14	Curzon Ashton	42	7	7	7	24	27	6	6	9	27	36	13	13	16	51	63	–12	52
15	Leamington	42	10	5	6	25	20	2	7	12	14	27	12	12	18	39	47	–8	48
16	Chester	42	9	6	6	43	27	3	5	13	27	44	12	11	19	70	71	–1	47
17	Gloucester C	42	6	9	6	28	24	4	7	10	19	36	10	16	16	47	60	–13	46
18	Bradford (Park Avenue)	42	7	6	8	26	32	4	5	12	20	38	11	11	20	46	70	–24	44
19	Blyth Spartans	42	8	3	10	23	30	4	4	13	18	46	12	7	23	41	76	–35	43
20	AFC Telford U	42	7	7	7	31	25	0	9	12	17	40	7	16	19	48	65	–17	37
21	Farsley Celtic	42	7	6	8	23	34	2	4	15	14	44	9	10	23	37	78	–41	37
22	Guiseley	42	6	6	9	18	33	3	2	16	13	36	9	8	25	31	69	–38	35

¶York C promoted via play-offs.

NATIONAL LEAGUE NORTH PLAY-OFFS 2021–22

NATIONAL LEAGUE NORTH PLAY-OFF ELIMINATORS

Wednesday 11 May 2022

York C (1) 2 *(John-Lewis 10, Hancox 49)*

Chorley (1) 1 *(Hall 25)* 6394

York C: Jameson; Dyson, Kougun, Sanders, Barrow, Wright, Hancox, McLaughlin, Kouhyar (Willoughby 83), John-Lewis (Brown 90), McKay (Donaldson 62).
Chorley: Urwin; Henley, Leather, Baines, Whitehouse (Holmes 76), Calveley, Sampson, Tomlinson, Blakeman (Halls 67), Alli (Ustabasi 76), Hall.
Referee: James Westgate.

Thursday 12 May 2022

Kidderminster H (0) 1 *(Hemmings 65)*

Boston U (1) 2 *(Elliott 45, Penny 76 (og))* 3921

Kidderminster H: Simpson, Penny, Richards, Cameron, Carrington (Freemantle 86), Morgan-Smith, Hemmings, Sterling, Foulkes, Martin, Bajrami.
Boston U: Dewhurst; Duxbury (Ferguson 22), Garner, Shiels, Green, Wright JD (Massanka 79), Elliott, Wright JM, Abbott, Byrne, Seriki.
Referee: Aaron Bannister.

NATIONAL LEAGUE NORTH PLAY-OFF SEMI-FINALS

Saturday 14 May 2022

Brackley T (0) 0

York C (1) 1 *(John-Lewis 44)* 1745

Brackley T: Lewis; Myles (York 74), Dean, Cullinane-Liburd, Franklin (Gordon 69), Walker, Murombedzi, Armson (Yusuf 87), Richards, Lowe, Ndlovu.
York C: Jameson; Dyson, Kouogun, Sanders, Barrow, Wright, Hancox (Brown 63), McLaughlin, Kouhyar, John-Lewis (Willoughby 46), Donaldson.
Referee: Richie Watkins.

Sunday 15 May 2022

AFC Fylde (0) 0

Boston U (0) 2 *(Elliott 80, 90 (pen))* 2050

AFC Fylde: Neal; Davis, Morrison, Whitmore, Philliskirk, Hatfield (Whitehead 40), Walker (Dobbie 80), Conlan (Burke 69), Haughton, Osborne, Taylor.
Boston U: Dewhurst; Garner, Shiels, Green, Ferguson, Elliott, Dimaio, Abbott, Byrne, Massanka (Wright JD 59), Seriki.
Referee: Ben Atkinson.

NATIONAL LEAGUE NORTH PLAY-OFF FINAL

Saturday 21 May 2022

York C (1) 2 *(John-Lewis 5, Kouhyar 86)*

Boston U (0) 0 7448

York C: Jameson; Dyson, Kouogun, Sanders, Barrow (Brown 71), Wright, Hancox, McLaughlin, Kouhyar, John-Lewis, Donaldson.
Boston U: Dewhurst; Seriki, Shiels, Garner, Ferguson, Byrne, Abbott (Massanka 60), Green, Dimaio (Preston 83), Wright JD (Hanson 75), Elliott.
Referee: Matt Corlett.

NATIONAL LEAGUE SOUTH 2021–22

NATIONAL LEAGUE SOUTH TABLE 2021–22

Due to COVID-19 pandemic, no teams were promoted or relegated into division at end of 2020–21 season.

			Home					*Away*					*Total*						
		P	*W*	*D*	*L*	*F*	*A*	*W*	*D*	*L*	*F*	*A*	*W*	*D*	*L*	*F*	*A*	*GD*	*Pts*
1	Maidstone U	40	16	1	3	44	18	11	5	4	36	20	27	6	7	80	38	42	87
2	Dorking W¶	40	17	1	2	61	23	8	5	7	40	30	25	6	9	101	53	48	81
3	Ebbsfleet U	40	13	3	4	45	18	11	1	8	33	35	24	4	12	78	53	25	76
4	Dartford	40	10	8	2	32	18	11	3	6	43	24	21	11	8	75	42	33	74
5	Oxford C	40	10	6	4	40	24	9	6	5	31	22	19	12	9	71	46	25	69
6	Eastbourne Bor	40	10	4	6	43	36	7	5	8	30	31	17	9	14	73	67	6	60
7	Chippenham T	40	10	3	7	39	30	6	8	6	22	20	16	11	13	61	50	11	59
8	Havant & Waterlooville	40	8	5	7	37	24	7	7	6	21	31	15	12	13	58	55	3	57
9	St Albans C	40	8	3	9	30	28	7	4	9	25	30	15	7	18	55	58	–3	52
10	Dulwich Hamlet	40	7	6	7	29	26	6	6	8	34	34	13	12	15	63	60	3	51
11	Hampton & Richmond Bor	40	9	4	7	30	22	5	5	10	26	34	14	9	17	56	56	0	51
12	Hungerford T	40	7	3	10	27	34	8	1	11	32	34	15	4	21	59	68	–9	49
13	Slough T	40	8	6	6	30	31	4	7	9	21	38	12	13	15	51	69	–18	49
14	Concord Rangers	40	9	5	6	28	31	4	5	11	25	41	13	10	17	53	72	–19	49
15	Hemel Hempstead T	40	6	6	8	26	42	7	3	10	23	30	13	9	18	49	72	–23	48
16	Tonbridge Angels	40	6	6	8	21	20	5	6	9	22	33	11	12	17	43	53	–10	45
17	Braintree T	40	6	6	8	20	24	5	6	9	18	30	11	12	17	38	54	–16	45
18	Bath C	40	7	5	8	21	26	6	1	13	24	42	13	6	21	45	68	–23	45
19	Chelmsford C	40	4	9	7	18	21	5	5	10	28	32	9	14	17	46	53	–7	41
20	Welling U	40	7	3	10	24	40	3	5	12	22	47	10	8	22	46	87	–41	38
21	Billericay T	40	4	5	11	23	38	5	4	11	18	30	9	9	22	41	68	–27	36

¶Dorking W promoted via play-offs.

NATIONAL LEAGUE SOUTH PLAY-OFFS 2021–22

NATIONAL LEAGUE SOUTH PLAY-OFF ELIMINATORS

Wednesday 11 May 2022

Oxford C (1) 2 *(Benyon 23, Harmon 76)*

Eastbourne Bor (0) 0 1349

Oxford C: Dudzinski; Harmon, Asare, Rowan, Fleet, Ashby, Carroll, Clark, Benyon (Owusu 90), McEachran (Coyle 89), Iaciofano (Bancroft 85).
Eastbourne Bor: Worgan; Dickinson, Mahorn (Elliott 80), Currie, Whelpdale (Hutchinson 61), Nippard, Vaughan, Hammond, Walker, Luer (Gravata 78), Kendall.
Referee: Dale Wooton.

Thursday 12 May 2022

Dartford (0) 0

Chippenham T (0) 0 1325

Dartford: Charles-Cook; Durojaiye, Meade, Campbell, Roberts (Leonard 85), Bonner, Kalala (Azeez 110), Carruthers (Allen 90), Dinanga (Greenidge 116), Jebb, Roberts.
Chippenham T: Henry; Hamilton, Greenslade, Richards, Parselle, Russe, Mehew, D'Abadia, Hanks (Bradbury 73), Dabre (Coppin 119), Young.
Referee: Callum Walchester.
aet; Chippenham T won 3-2 on penalties.

NATIONAL LEAGUE SOUTH PLAY-OFF SEMI-FINALS

Saturday 14 May 2022

Dorking W (2) 3 *(Prior 8, Fuller 19, Rutherford 48)*

Oxford C (0) 0 3000

Dorking W: Lincoln; Fuller, Harris (Gallagher 54), Cheadle, Wheeler, Moore, Prior, Rutherford (Ottaway 64), Taylor J, Muit, McShane (Fogden 54).
Oxford C: Dudzinski; Harmon, Asare, Rowan, Fleet, Ashby, Carroll, Clark (Coyle 67), Benyon (Bancroft 45), McEachran (Owusu 67), Iaciofano.
Referee: Dean Watson.

Sunday 15 May 2022

Ebbsfleet U (0) 1 *(Martin L 97)*

Chippenham T (0) 0 2166

Ebbsfleet U: Moulden; Jombati, N'Guessan, Bingham (Domi 112), Poleon (Mekki 100), Romain (Martin L 76), Solly, Paxman, Chapman, Finney, Coulthirst (Egan 63).
Chippenham T: Henry; Hamilton (Bradbury 113), Greenslade, Richards, Parselle, Russe, Mehew (King 89), Hanks, Dabre (Al-Hussein 104), D'Abadia, Young (Coppin 60).
Referee: Sam Mulhall.
aet.

NATIONAL LEAGUE SOUTH PLAY-OFF FINAL

Saturday 21 May 2022

Dorking W (1) 3 *(McShane 44, Moore 90, Rutherford 97)*

Ebbsfleet U (1) 2 *(Bingham 22, Tanner 90)* 3000

Dorking W: Lincoln; Fuller, Gallagher, Cheadle (Wills 90), Muitt (Taylor B 73), Wheeler (Harris 88), Moore, Taylor J, McShane, Rutherford, Prior (Oldaker 88).
Ebbsfleet U: Moulden; Martin J (Tanner 78), Solly, Finney, Jombati, Chapman, N'Guessan, Egan, Paxman, Romain (Martin L 60 (Coulthirst 98)), Bingham (Poleon 87).
Referee: Jason Richardson.
aet; 2-2 at the end of normal time.

ALDERSHOT TOWN

Ground: The EBB Stadium at the Recreation Ground, High Street, Aldershot, Hampshire GU11 1TW.
Tel: (01252) 320 211. *Website:* www.theshots.co.uk *Email:* admin@theshots.co.uk *Year Formed:* 1926.
Record Attendance: 19,138 v Carlisle U, FA Cup 4th rd (replay), 28 January 1970. *Nickname:* 'The Shots'.
Manager: Mark Molesley. *Colours:* Red shirts with blue trim, blue shorts with red trim, red socks with blue trim.

ALDERSHOT TOWN – NATIONAL LEAGUE 2021–22 LEAGUE RECORD

Match No.	Date	Venue	Opponents	Result		H/T Score	Lg Pos.	Goalscorers	Attendance
1	Aug 21	H	Chesterfield	L	0-2	0-0	16		2393
2	28	A	Boreham Wood	L	0-1	0-0	21		602
3	30	H	Yeovil T	L	1-2	0-1	21	Andrews 75	2073
4	Sept 4	A	Notts Co	L	2-3	1-1	22	Andrews 2 44, 50	5921
5	11	H	Solihull Moors	L	1-2	1-1	22	Phillips 26	1354
6	14	A	Southend U	W	3-2	1-1	21	Demetriou (og) 37, Bettamer 50, Berkeley-Agyepong 88	5004
7	18	A	Wealdstone	D	2-2	0-1	21	Andrews 2 48, 68	1106
8	25	H	FC Halifax T	L	0-1	0-1	22		1622
9	Oct 5	A	Dover Ath	W	2-1	1-0	21	Willard 23, Edser 74	648
10	9	A	Stockport Co	L	0-1	0-1	22		6132
11	23	H	Bromley	L	2-3	2-2	22	Ndjoli 4, Kinsella 25	1354
12	26	H	Weymouth	L	0-2	0-1	22		1510
13	30	A	Barnet	L	1-2	0-1	22	Sylla 56	1336
14	Nov 9	H	Wrexham	L	0-5	0-2	22		1639
15	13	H	Grimsby T	W	2-1	1-1	21	Willard 12, Whittingham 60	2343
16	23	H	Torquay U	W	1-0	0-0	20	Kinsella 85	1582
17	27	A	King's Lynn T	W	1-0	0-0	18	Whittingham 80	785
18	Dec 4	H	Altrincham	D	2-2	2-1	18	Whittingham 28, Sylla 40	1596
19	11	A	Eastleigh	W	3-0	0-0	18	Andrews 2 64, 85, Kinsella 77	2784
20	26	H	Woking	D	1-1	0-0	17	Andrews (pen) 86	3699
21	28	A	Dagenham & R	L	0-1	0-1	17		1879
22	Jan 2	A	Woking	W	3-2	0-1	17	Harris 46, Andrews (pen) 88, Ndjoli 90	5171
23	8	H	Maidenhead U	D	1-1	0-1	17	Edser 65	1714
24	22	A	Chesterfield	D	0-0	0-0	17		6422
25	25	H	Southend U	D	1-1	1-0	15	Glover 5	2141
26	29	A	Weymouth	W	1-0	0-0	15	Goodship (og) 90	1571
27	Feb 5	H	Barnet	L	1-3	0-2	16	Willard 90	1887
28	12	A	Grimsby T	L	1-3	0-2	18	Glover 90	5177
29	22	H	Dover Ath	D	0-0	0-0	17		1420
30	26	A	Wrexham	L	1-4	0-1	20	Phillips 90	8475
31	Mar 5	H	Stockport Co	L	0-2	0-2	20		1552
32	19	H	King's Lynn T	L	0-3	0-1	20		1660
33	22	A	Torquay U	L	0-4	0-3	20		1832
34	26	A	Altrincham	L	0-1	0-0	20		2341
35	Apr 2	H	Eastleigh	L	0-2	0-2	20		1590
36	9	H	Boreham Wood	W	2-1	1-0	20	Ndjoli 22, Berkeley-Agyepong 74	1092
37	15	A	Yeovil T	W	2-0	0-0	20	Phillips 65, Glover 69	2528
38	18	H	Dagenham & R	L	0-2	0-2	20		1528
39	23	A	Solihull Moors	L	1-2	0-1	20	Kinsella 90	1974
40	26	A	Bromley	D	1-1	0-0	20	Ndjoli 71	1151
41	30	H	Notts Co	W	3-1	2-1	20	Ndjoli 8, Willard 34, Armstrong 88	1969
42	May 2	A	Maidenhead U	D	2-2	1-2	20	Armstrong 27, Panayiotou 78	1676
43	7	A	FC Halifax T	D	1-1	0-0	20	Ndjoli 86	2662
44	15	H	Wealdstone	L	1-3	1-1	20	Harris 29	2405

Final League Position: 20

GOALSCORERS

League (46): Andrews 9 (2 pens), Ndjoli 6, Kinsella 4, Willard 4, Glover 3, Phillips 3, Whittingham 3, Armstrong 2, Berkeley-Agyepong 2, Edser 2, Harris 2, Sylla 2, Bettamer 1, Panayiotou 1, own goals 2.
FA Cup (1): Fowler 1.
FA Trophy (2): Berkeley-Agyepong 1, own goal 1.

Walker M 17+1	Fowler 3+2	Kinsella 32+1	Lokko 7	Lyons-Foster 35+2	Phillips 34	Edser 16+3	Berkeley-Agyepong 23+11	Harris 27+6	Willard 26+8	Andrews 19+1	Oxlade-Chamberlain 38+2	Akanbi 2+6	Watts 1+5	Whittingham 18+11	Aouachria 2+4	Bettamer 8+8	Vennings 9+4	Ndjoli 14+9	Wagstaff 5+3	Glover 21+6	Toure 1+2	Jordan 25+1	Walker L 10	Sylla 28+2	Saunders 16+1	Angell —+1 / Ngalo —+2	Gubbins 3	Webb 6	Shroll 2+1	Fawole 1+2 / Armstrong 2+1	Panayiotou 9+5	Wilson —+2	Barnes 4	Matthews 1+4	Daniel 6+4	Ross 9	Hall 4	Match No.
1	2^{1}	3	4	5	6	7^{2}	8	9	10	11^{3}	12	13	14																									1
1		2	3	4	5	6	7	9^{2}	10^{3}	11^{1}	8	12	13	14																								2
1		2	3	4	5	6	7	11^{1}		9	8	10		12																								3
1		2	3	4	10	6	7^{1}	11	13	8^{2}		9^{3}	14	5	12																							4
1		2		3	4	6	8^{2}	11		9^{3}	7	14	13	5	10^{1}	12																						5
1	2	3		4	5	7	12	9		11^{1}	8	13		6		10^{2}																						6
1	2	3		4	10	6	13	11		8	9			5^{1}	12	7^{2}																						7
1	13	2		3	4	6	7	9	12	11	8^{1}			5^{2}	14	10^{3}																						8
1	14	2		3	4	6			9^{2}	11^{1}	7			5	13	10^{3}	8	12																				9
1		2		3	9	5			11^{1}	6	7			4^{2}	8^{3}	13	10	12	14																			10
1		2		3	4	6					7	13				11^{3}	9	10^{1}	5^{2}	8	12	14																11
1		2		3		6				10	7^{3}	13		14			9	11^{1}	5	8^{2}	12	4																12
		2		4		5				12	7					6^{1}	10^{3}	9	3	14	11^{2}	8	1	13														13
		2		3			13		14	10	6^{3}			12			9	11^{1}	5	7		4	1	8^{2}														14
		2		3			13		10	11^{2}	7			6				12		8^{1}		4	1	9^{3}	5	14												15
		2		3^{1}			13		10	11	7			6^{2}			12			8		4	1	9	5													16
		2							10	4^{1}	5			3			13	12		6		7	1	8	9^{2}		11											17
								12	10	11	7			6				13		8^{1}		2	1	9	3		5	4^{2}										18
		5					13	12	10^{3}	11	7			6					14	8^{1}		4	1	9	3		2^{2}											19
		2			4		7^{1}	12	14	11^{3}	8			6						9^{2}		3	1	10	5■				13									20
		2					13	9	10		7		4^{1}					11^{3}	6	12		3	1	14				5^{2}	8									21
		2			10		4	11	13	5	6			3^{2}				12^{3}	14	7^{1}		8	1	9														22
1		2			4	12	6	11			7			5^{1}						8		3		9					10^{2}	13								23
1		2		3	6		7	11^{2}			8			13				14		9^{1}		5		10						4^{3}	12							24
1				2	4	12	6^{2}	10			7			13						8		3		9				5^{3}		14	11^{1}							25
1				2	4	5	12	9	10^{1}		6							13		7^{2}		3		8							11							26
1				2^{2}	4	5	6^{1}	9^{3}	10		7						13			12		3		8							11	14						27
				2^{2}	8	13	14	9	10		3						12	7^{3}		4		5		6^{1}				11					1					28
				14	3	5	12		9		6						8			7^{1}		2^{3}						4			11^{2}	13	1	10				29
				14	7			13	10		3						8			4		5^{3}		6	9^{1}						2^{2}		1	12	11			30
				2^{1}	8		3^{3}	9^{2}	13		4						10			5		6		7							14		1	12	11			31
			2	3^{2}			6	10^{1}	13		7			14						8^{3}		4		9							11			12	5	1		32
				2	4				10		8			7		14				12		3		9	5^{3}			6^{2}			11^{1}			13		1		33
		2^{2}	3	4	5			12	10		14			7		13				8^{1}				9	6						11^{3}					1		34
12^{3}		2	3^{2}	4	6		14	13	10					8		11				9		5			7											1^{1}		35
		2		3	4		6^{1}	9	10		7			12				11^{2}						8	5										13		1	36
		2^{2}		3	4		6	9	10^{1}		7			14				11^{3}		12■				8	5										13	1		37
		2^{1}		4	3		6	9	10		7					13		11						8	5^{2}	12										1		38
		2		3	8		4	9^{2}	11^{3}		5					14		7		12				6	10^{1}	13										1		39
		2		3	5		6	9	12^{3}		7							10^{1}				4		8						11^{2}	13				14	1		40
		2		3	9		4^{2}	10	11^{1}		5			13				8^{3}				6		7						12					14	1		41
				2	7		3	8^{2}	9		4^{1}					13		6						5	12					11^{3}	14				10		1	42
		5		6	3		7	9^{3}	10^{2}				12			14		11						8	2						13				4^{1}		1	43
		13		2	7		4	8	10					14		3^{1}		12						6	9^{2}						5				11^{3}		1	44

FA Cup

Fourth Qualifying	Bowers & Pitsea	(a)	1-2

FA Trophy

Third Round	Kingstonian	(h)	2-1
Fourth Round	Bromley	(h)	0-2

ALTRINCHAM

Ground: J. Davidson Stadium, Moss Lane, Altrincham WA15 8AP. *Tel:* (0161) 928 1045. *Website:* www.altrinchamfc.co.uk *Email:* see website. *Year Formed:* 1903. *Record Attendance:* 10,275 Altrincham Boys v Sunderland Boys, ESFA Shield, 28 February 1925 at Moss Lane; 35,175 v Everton, FA Cup 3rd rd replay, 7 January 1975 at Old Trafford. *Nickname:* 'The Robins'. *Manager:* Philip Parkinson. *Colours:* Red and white striped shirts with red sleeves and white trim, black shorts with white trim, white socks with black trim.

ALTRINCHAM – NATIONAL LEAGUE 2021–22 LEAGUE RECORD

Match No.	*Date*	*Venue*	*Opponents*	*Result*		*H/T Score*	*Lg Pos.*	*Goalscorers*	*Attendance*
1	Aug 21	A	Torquay U	W	3-1	2-0	2	Dinanga [14], Kirby [19], Mullarkey [84]	2599
2	30	A	FC Halifax T	L	0-2	0-0	12		1941
3	Sept 4	H	Dover Ath	W	3-2	1-1	8	Mooney [21], Leitch-Smith [71], Colclough (pen) [86]	1871
4	11	A	Wealdstone	L	0-1	0-0	12		1013
5	25	H	Notts Co	W	1-0	1-0	12	Dinanga [29]	2569
6	28	H	King's Lynn T	W	4-1	1-0	8	Colclough [12], Moult [52], Mooney [86], Hancock [89]	1009
7	Oct 2	A	Dagenham & R	W	3-2	1-2	6	Reynolds (og) [10], Hancock [87], Mooney [90]	1360
8	5	H	Grimsby T	L	2-3	0-1	9	Mooney [65], Moult [75]	2882
9	9	H	Maidenhead U	W	2-0	0-0	8	Kosylo [56], Peers [90]	2091
10	12	A	Yeovil T	D	1-1	0-0	7	Leitch-Smith [65]	1640
11	23	A	Eastleigh	L	1-2	1-0	9	Moult [5]	2046
12	26	H	Solihull Moors	L	1-2	1-0	9	Baggley [15]	3683
13	30	A	Woking	L	2-3	1-1	10	Peers [19], Hancock [66]	2985
14	Nov 13	H	Boreham Wood	D	1-1	0-0	12	Hancock [76]	2283
15	20	A	Weymouth	W	4-1	1-0	11	Colclough 2 [34, 60], Kosylo 2 [57, 89]	932
16	23	A	Chesterfield	D	2-2	0-2	11	Kosylo [84], Leitch-Smith [90]	5273
17	27	H	Southend U	L	1-2	0-2	12	Mooney [68]	1288
18	Dec 4	A	Aldershot T	D	2-2	1-2	12	Mullarkey [45], Colclough [90]	1596
19	11	H	Bromley	L	0-1	0-1	12		1405
20	26	A	Stockport Co	L	1-5	1-4	13	Croasdale (og) [31]	8896
21	28	H	Wrexham	L	0-2	0-2	15		3145
22	Jan 8	A	Barnet	D	1-1	0-0	16	Pringle [62]	1150
23	11	H	Stockport Co	L	1-4	0-2	16	Leitch-Smith [90]	3900
24	15	A	Grimsby T	L	0-2	0-0	16		4573
25	22	H	Torquay U	L	1-2	1-1	16	Mullarkey [30]	1744
26	29	A	Solihull Moors	L	0-5	0-4	18		2090
27	Feb 5	H	Woking	D	2-2	0-2	18	Colclough 2 [67, 84]	1334
28	12	A	King's Lynn T	W	1-0	1-0	17	Colclough [45]	905
29	15	A	Boreham Wood	L	0-2	0-1	18		1413
30	26	H	Dagenham & R	W	3-0	2-0	17	Mooney [19], Hulme [30], Hancock [53]	1642
31	Mar 5	A	Maidenhead U	D	0-0	0-0	17		1113
32	8	H	Weymouth	W	5-0	4-0	14	Kosylo 2 [10, 15], Cooper [27], Colclough [45], Mooney [87]	1613
33	12	H	Eastleigh	W	4-0	2-0	13	Colclough 2 (1 pen) [25 (p), 47], Hulme [29], Mooney [57]	1614
34	19	A	Southend U	L	0-2	0-2	15		5976
35	22	H	Chesterfield	W	1-0	0-0	15	Kosylo [48]	2042
36	26	H	Aldershot T	W	1-0	0-0	14	Mooney [87]	2341
37	Apr 15	H	FC Halifax T	D	1-1	0-1	13	Perritt [51]	2521
38	18	A	Wrexham	L	0-4	0-4	15		10,022
39	23	H	Wealdstone	W	4-2	1-0	15	Kosylo 2 [8, 46], Marriott [52], Mooney [56]	1657
40	30	A	Dover Ath	W	1-0	1-0	14	Hancock [38]	465
41	May 2	H	Barnet	D	1-1	1-0	14	Mooney [22]	1864
42	7	A	Notts Co	L	0-3	0-0	14		6581
43	10	A	Bromley	D	1-1	0-1	14	Mooney [87]	1098
44	15	H	Yeovil T	L	0-1	0-1	14		2123

Final League Position: 14

GOALSCORERS

League (62): Mooney 12, Colclough 11 (2 pens), Kosylo 9, Hancock 6, Leitch-Smith 4, Moult 3, Mullarkey 3, Dinanga 2, Hulme 2, Peers 2, Baggley 1, Cooper 1, Kirby 1, Marriott 1, Perritt 1, Pringle 1, own goals 2.
FA Cup (7): Hancock 2, Dinanga 1, Kosylo 1, Mooney 1, Moult 1, Peers 1.
FA Trophy (1): Hannigan 1.

Thompson 37	Hannigan 25	Moult 26 + 6	Mooney 33 + 3	Dinanga 14 + 1	Hancock 23 + 11	Colclough 36 + 2	Kirby 4	Fitzpatrick 8 + 1 / Drench 3	Senior 21	Mullarkey 39	Jackson 4 + 3	Peers 5 + 9 / Ferguson 8 + 1	Sutton 2 + 2	Bunney 3 + 1 / Hall K 3 + 3	Leitch-Smith 4 + 15	Pringle 12 + 23	Kosylo 28 + 4	Furman 3 + 6	Densmore 6 + 5	Hampson 4 + 3	Gould 4	Whitehead 4 + 2	Baggley 2	Walker 2 / Campbell — + 3	Porter 7 + 1	Digie 6 + 2 / Morton — + 1	Marriott 18 + 3	Morgan 6 + 1	White 11 + 5	Osborne 22 + 1	Hulme 12 + 1	Berkoe 2 + 1	Jones 12 + 1	Cooper 11 + 1	Conn-Clarke 2	Mudimu 1 + 1	Perritt 11 + 1	*Match No.*
1	2	3	4^{2}	5^{1}	6	7	8	9^{3}	10	11	12	13	14																									1
1	2	5	9^{1}	10	6^{2}	11	7		3	8	12			4^{3}	13	14																						2
1	2	4^{2}	8	9^{3}		10	5		3	7	6	14			12	13	11^{1}																					3
1	2^{2}	3	4	5^{3}		6	7^{1}		10	11	9■	14		12		13	8																					4
1	2	5	8^{2}	9	13	10^{1}			3	7		14		4		6^{3}	11	12																				5
1	2	5	8	9^{2}	14	10^{3}		12	3	7				4^{1}		6	11	13																				6
1	2	5	8	9^{1}	13	10		3^{3}	4	6					14		11^{2}	7	12																			7
1	2	3	4	5^{1}	6^{3}	7			9	10	8				13	12	14	11^{2}																				8
1	2	5	9	10^{1}	6				3	8	14	12				7^{2}	11^{3}	13	4																			9
1^{2}	2	3	4		5				9	10^{3}	7	14			11	8	6^{1}	13		12																		10
	3	4		5^{2}	6	13			10	11		9	12			8^{3}	7		2^{1}		1	14																11
	5	6			8			3	2			11	4			12		7^{1}			1		9	10														12
	3	4			5			7	9			8	2			6■			12		1		10^{1}	11														13
1	2^{2}	5		9^{3}	7	10		3	4	8		12					11					13			6^{1}	14												14
1	2		3^{2}	5		6^{3}		8^{1}	9	10		12				14	7			13		11			4													15
1	3			4^{3}		5			9	10		12			13	14	6			2		11			8^{2}	7^{1}												16
1	3	13	12		14	9			4	7		11				6^{2}	10^{1}			2		8			5^{3}													17
1	3	5	8^{1}		12	9			4	6					11	14	10^{2}			2		7^{3}			13													18
1	4	5		13	8	9			2	6					11^{1}	12	10^{2}			3					7													19
1	2	6^{2}			8	10		4^{3}	5	9					13		11	14							7^{1}	3	12											20
1		5	14		7	10		3	4	8					13		11^{2}	12							6^{1}	2	9^{3}											21
1	2	5	10^{2}		7	12				8						13	11^{3}									14		3^{1}	4	6	9							22
1	2	3	4^{3}		6	7^{1}				11					14	13			12							8		9	10^{2}	5								23
1	2	5	9^{3}		7	10				8					12	13												3	4^{1}	6	11^{2}	14						24
1		5	9^{3}		7^{1}	10				8					12	13										2	14	3		6	11^{2}	4						25
1					6^{1}	10				8		11				7^{2}	13■		12							2	9	3		5		4■						26
1		4	8^{3}			9				7					13	12	14											2		5	10^{1}		3	6	11^{2}			27
1		3	4^{3}			6^{1}				9							12		2								14		8	5	10			7	11^{2}	13		28
1			14		13	9				6					11^{1}	5^{2}	10^{3}		2								7		3	4	12					8		29
1			9		5	10^{2}				7					12												8		13	4	11^{1}		3	6			2	30
			2^{1}			4		1		8						13	6^{3}		14								11		12	3	10		9^{2}	5			7	31
			8			9		1		6					13	14	10^{2}										7		12	4	11^{1}		3	5			2^{3}	32
			8^{2}		12	9^{3}		1		6						14	10										7		13	4^{1}	11		3	5			2	33
1			8		13	9				6					12	14	10^{3}										7^{2}			4	11^{1}		3	5			2	34
1		13	9^{3}		6^{1}	11				7		4		12			10^{2}										8		2	5				14			3	35
1		14	10		6	9				7		4			13	12	11^{2}										8^{1}		2	5^{3}							3	36
1			8^{2}		12	10^{1}				6		4				13	11										7		2	5	9^{3}		14				3	37
1			9		12	10				5		4				14	11^{1}										7		13	6	8^{3}		3^{2}				2	38
1		12	9		6	10				7		3		13			11^{2}										8^{1}		2	5			4					39
1			2		4^{3}	5^{2}						9		12		14	7^{1}							13			11			3			10	6			8	40
1		14	9		6^{1}	10^{2}				7		3		11		13											8		2^{3}	5			4				12	41
1		14	11							8		2		10^{1}		7								13			9^{3}	12		5			4	6			3^{2}	42
	3^{1}	5	10									12		11^{2}		8			2		1			13		14	9^{3}			6			4	7				43
1	3	4	5	6^{1}	12	7^{3}										9			2	13							11		10^{2}	14				8				44

FA Cup

Fourth Qualifying	Southport	(a)	3-2
First Round	Gateshead	(a)	2-2
Replay	Gateshead	(h)	2-3

FA Trophy

Third Round	Notts Co	(a)	1-2

BARNET

Ground: The Hive Stadium, Camrose Avenue, Edgware, London HA8 6AG. *Tel:* (020) 8381 3800.
Website: www.barnetfc.com *Email:* tellus@barnetfc.com *Year Formed:* 1888.
Record Attendance: 11,026 v Wycombe Wanderers, FA Amateur Cup 4th rd, 2 February 1952 (at Underhill); 6,215 v Brentford, FA Cup 4th rd, 28 January 2019 (at The Hive Stadium). *Nickname:* 'The Bees'.
Manager: Dean Brennan. *Colours:* Amber shirts with black trim, black shorts with amber trim, black socks.

BARNET – NATIONAL LEAGUE 2021–22 LEAGUE RECORD

Match No.	*Date*	*Venue*	*Opponents*	*Result*		*H/T Score*	*Lg Pos.*	*Goalscorers*	*Attendance*
1	Aug 21	H	Notts Co	L	0-5	0-0	18		2067
2	28	A	Solihull Moors	D	1-1	0-1	16	Powell [80]	1271
3	30	H	Dagenham & R	L	0-2	0-2	20		1728
4	Sept 4	A	Grimsby T	L	3-4	2-1	21	Tasdemir [33], Bloomfield [43], Widdowson [62]	5030
5	11	H	Eastleigh	D	1-1	1-0	21	Bloomfield [24]	959
6	14	A	Chesterfield	L	2-4	2-2	22	Tasdemir [45], Marriott [45]	4538
7	18	A	Bromley	L	0-2	0-1	22		1451
8	25	H	Weymouth	W	3-1	1-0	20	Brundle [33], Marriott [79], Richards-Everton [85]	1269
9	Oct 2	H	FC Halifax T	D	0-0	0-0	20		1302
10	5	A	King's Lynn T	D	1-1	1-1	22	Widdowson [4]	1007
11	9	A	Dover Ath	W	2-1	1-0	17	Bloomfield [10], Powell [59]	885
12	23	H	Wrexham	L	0-3	0-2	18		2237
13	26	A	Stockport Co	W	2-1	1-1	18	Widdowson [21], Greenidge [51]	4363
14	30	H	Aldershot T	W	2-1	1-0	14	Flanagan [27], Hall [86]	1336
15	Nov 13	A	Wealdstone	L	0-1	0-0	17		2662
16	20	H	Torquay U	W	2-1	1-0	15	Marriott [42], Mason-Clarke (pen) [65]	1498
17	27	A	Woking	W	2-1	1-1	15	Marriott 2 [28, 90]	1779
18	Dec 4	H	Maidenhead U	W	3-0	1-0	13	Hall [31], Brundle [48], Mason-Clarke [55]	906
19	11	A	Yeovil T	L	0-1	0-1	13		2024
20	Jan 2	A	Boreham Wood	D	0-0	0-0	15		1283
21	8	H	Altrincham	D	1-1	0-0	15	Brundle [90]	1150
22	15	H	Chesterfield	L	1-4	0-0	15	Richards-Everton [90]	1777
23	29	H	Stockport Co	L	0-5	0-1	17		2183
24	Feb 1	A	Southend U	L	1-2	1-2	17	Marriott [36]	6036
25	5	A	Aldershot T	W	3-1	2-0	17	Marriott 2 [5, 53], Beard [16]	1887
26	8	A	Notts Co	L	1-6	0-3	17	Mason-Clarke [66]	5657
27	12	H	Wealdstone	L	1-3	0-2	19	Richards-Everton [48]	2248
28	19	A	Torquay U	D	2-2	1-2	17	Marriott [37], Mason-Clarke [60]	2221
29	22	H	King's Lynn T	D	0-0	0-0	16		1137
30	26	A	FC Halifax T	L	0-1	0-1	19		1799
31	Mar 5	H	Dover Ath	W	6-0	1-0	15	Grego-Cox 2 [5, 87], Marriott 2 [51, 55], Greenidge [67], Woods [90]	1168
32	15	H	Boreham Wood	W	1-0	1-0	16	Mason-Clarke [13]	1580
33	19	H	Woking	L	0-2	0-1	17		1501
34	26	A	Maidenhead U	W	2-1	0-0	16	Marriott [61], Grego-Cox [79]	1194
35	Apr 2	H	Yeovil T	D	2-2	1-1	16	Mason-Clarke [23], Marriott [70]	1393
36	5	A	Wrexham	L	0-6	0-3	16		8868
37	9	H	Solihull Moors	L	0-2	0-1	17		1016
38	15	A	Dagenham & R	L	3-7	0-5	18	Powell 2 [54, 55], Reynolds (og) [64]	2010
39	18	H	Southend U	L	1-3	0-2	18	Marriott [62]	2202
40	23	A	Eastleigh	W	3-2	0-1	18	Marriott 2 (1 pen) [48 (p), 50], De Havilland [90]	2514
41	30	H	Grimsby T	D	2-2	1-0	18	Marriott [37], Waterfall (og) [52]	2438
42	May 2	A	Altrincham	D	1-1	0-1	18	Marriott [53]	1864
43	7	A	Weymouth	W	2-1	1-0	18	Marriott (pen) [45], Powell [48]	1081
44	15	H	Bromley	L	2-4	1-1	18	Powell [10], Richards-Everton [72]	1346

Final League Position: 18

GOALSCORERS

League (59): Marriott 19 (2 pens), Mason-Clarke 6 (1 pen), Powell 6, Richards-Everton 4, Bloomfield 3, Brundle 3, Grego-Cox 3, Widdowson 3, Greenidge 2, Hall 2, Tasdemir 2, Beard 1, De Havilland 1, Flanagan 1, Woods 1, own goals 2.
FA Cup (0).
FA Trophy (2): Fonguck 1, Hall 1.

Sargeant 10	Thomas 21 + 6	Doherty 3	Payne 6 + 6	Turley 13	Richards-Everton 34 + 5	Brundle 22	Bloomfield 12 + 8	Mason-Clarke 34 + 5	Flanagan 17 + 5	Taylor H 37	Nugent — + 2	Tasdemir 8 + 11	Granville 4 + 7	Powell 18 + 7	Beard 22 + 2	Sesay 6	Widdowson 8 + 1	Marriott 28 + 8	Hall 27 + 7	Fonguck 24 + 8	Oxborough 22	Woods 19 + 1	Greenidge 22 + 2	Howe 12 + 6	De Havilland 14 + 4	Marshall 16	Grego-Cox 12 + 1	Walsh 1 + 8	Azaze 7	Askew 5	*Match No.*
1	2	3■	4^{1}	5	6	7	8^{2}	9	10	11^{3}	12	13	14																		1
1	12				2	3	4	13	6	8		9	7	5	10^{2}	11^{1}															2
1	2^{1}	3	6		4	7	11	12	9	5		10	13	8^{2}																	3
1	14	2■	12			3	4	5^{2}	6	8	13	9^{1}	7			11^{3}	10														4
1	2		13		3	6	10	12	7			9^{1}	8^{3}		14	5	4^{2}	11													5
1	13				2	6	10	12	7^{2}	3		9^{1}	8		14	5	4	11^{3}													6
1					2	3	4	12	6^{2}	7		8^{1}	14	13	10^{3}	11	9	5													7
1	2		6		3	7	11^{2}	8^{3}	9	4				12	10	5^{1}		14	13												8
1	2		5		3	6	14	8	9^{1}	4				7	10^{2}		12	11^{3}	13												9
1	2		12		3	6	11	7^{1}	8	4				13			5	14	10^{3}	9^{2}											10
	2		6		3	7	11^{2}	9	12	4				8			5		10^{1}	13	1										11
	2		7^{1}		3	8	11^{3}	9		4							5	12	10^{2}	14	1	6	13								12
	2■				13	3	12	4	7	9		14					10^{3}	5^{2}		8^{1}	1	11	6								13
					2^{2}	3		4	7	9		13			10			5	12	8^{1}	1	11	6								14
				7		3	13	5	2^{2}	8					11			6	4^{1}	12	1	9	10								15
	12			2		6	13	7	8^{1}	4					10			11	14	9^{2}	1	5^{3}	3								16
	2			3	14	6	13	7		5		12			9			11^{2}	10^{1}	8^{3}	1		4								17
	2			3		6	13	7^{1}		5		14		12	9			11^{2}	10^{3}	8	1		4								18
	2		13	3	12	5		6■		9		10^{1}			11				4	8^{2}	1		7								19
	2			3	4	7	10			5		12			8			11^{1}	9^{2}	13	1	6									20
	2^{3}			3	4	7	13			5		8^{2}			9			11	10	12	1	6^{1}	14								21
	13			2	12	6		8		4				7^{2}	10			14	11^{3}	9	1	5^{1}	3								22
				3	12			8	14	5				7	10			13	11	9^{3}	1	6^{2}	4^{1}	2							23
	2		14		4		12	8^{1}	13					7				11	10^{2}	9^{3}	1	5	6	3							24
	2				3				14	5		12		7	9^{3}			11^{1}	10	8^{2}	1	6	4	13							25
			13		3			7	8^{2}	4		12		6	10				11^{1}	9	1	5		2							26
	2				4				12	6		13		8				11	10^{1}	9	1	7^{2}	5	3^{3}	14						27
					3			5^{1}	7	8				12				6			1	9		2	10	4^{2}	11	13			28
					3			7	8^{3}	4				14				11	13	12	1	5		2	9^{2}	6	10^{1}				29
								7		4				6^{3}	9			12	10^{2}	8^{1}	1		3	2	13	5	11	14			30
					2			6		4					7			11	10^{2}	13	1	12	3		8	5^{1}	9				31
				2	3			7							8			11^{1}			1	5	4	12	9	6	10				32
				2	3			7							8			11	10^{2}			5	4	13	9	6^{1}		12	1		33
				2	3			5					14	13	9			6	4^{2}	8^{1}		10	7		12		11^{3}			1	34
					2			6							8			10	9^{2}	7		4^{3}	3	13	12	5^{1}	11	14		1	35
	12				3			7											10	8			4	2^{1}	9	5	11	6		1	36
	2				3			8		5^{2}								10	9^{1}	13			4		7	6	11	12		1	37
	2^{2}				3			8		5				7				14	12	9^{3}			4	13	10^{1}	6	11			1	38
	2				3			8		5				7^{2}				13	12	9			4^{1}		10	6	11		1		39
	2				3			7		10			14	6^{3}				8^{1}	4^{2}	9				13	11	5	12■		1		40
					3			7		10		13	12	6				8	4^{2}	9^{1}				2	11	5			1		41
					3			7		4				6				11	10^{1}	8				2	9	5		12	1		42
					4			7		2		13		6^{2}				10	11^{1}	8				3	9	5		12	1		43
					4					2			13	6				10	11^{1}	7^{2}				3	8	5	9	12	1		44

FA Cup
Fourth Qualifying Boreham Wood (h) 0-1

FA Trophy
Third Round Boreham Wood (h) 2-3

BOREHAM WOOD

Ground: LV Bet Stadium, Meadow Park, Broughinge Road, Borehamwood, Hertfordshire WD6 5AL.
Tel: (02089) 535 097. *Website:* borehamwoodfootballclub.co.uk *Email:* see website. *Year Formed:* 1948.
Record Attendance: 4,101 v St Albans C, FA Cup 2nd rd, 6 December 2021. *Nickname:* 'The Wood'.
Manager: Luke Garrard. *Colours:* White shirts, white shorts, white socks.

BOREHAM WOOD – NATIONAL LEAGUE 2021–22 LEAGUE RECORD

Match No.	Date	Venue	Opponents		Result	H/T Score	Lg Pos.	Goalscorers	Attendance
1	Aug 21	A	Weymouth	W	2-0	2-0	4	Smith, K 9, Marsh 40	1195
2	28	H	Aldershot T	W	1-0	0-0	4	Fyfield 65	602
3	30	A	Dover Ath	W	1-0	1-0	3	Goodman (og) 41	1517
4	Sept 4	H	Stockport Co	D	0-0	0-0	3		782
5	11	A	Bromley	W	3-2	1-0	2	Boden 16, Rees 55, Marsh 90	1311
6	14	H	FC Halifax T	D	2-2	2-1	3	Rees 27, Boden 38	503
7	18	A	Solihull Moors	L	1-3	1-2	5	Mendy 36	1021
8	25	H	Yeovil T	W	2-1	1-1	4	Staunton (og) 26, Rees 60	658
9	Oct 2	A	Eastleigh	D	1-1	1-1	4	Boden (pen) 33	1789
10	5	H	Torquay U	W	2-0	1-0	2	Smith, K 42, Boden (pen) 46	701
11	9	H	Dagenham & R	W	2-0	0-0	2	Fyfield 49, Rees 58	1111
12	23	A	Chesterfield	L	1-2	0-2	3	Evans 67	5477
13	26	A	King's Lynn T	W	1-0	1-0	3	Boden 7	1160
14	30	H	Southend U	W	1-0	0-0	1	Marsh 83	1501
15	Nov 13	A	Altrincham	D	1-1	0-0	2	Fyfield 57	2283
16	20	H	Maidenhead U	W	4-0	2-0	2	Boden 2 18, 46, Rees 24, Mendy 79	601
17	23	H	Notts Co	D	1-1	0-1	2	Marsh 64	821
18	Dec 11	A	Woking	W	2-0	2-0	2	Smith, K 1, Mafuta 13	1687
19	Jan 2	H	Barnet	D	0-0	0-0	4		1283
20	11	H	Wealdstone	W	1-0	0-0	3	Orsi-Dadomo 67	1298
21	22	H	Weymouth	D	1-1	1-1	5	Raymond 27	811
22	25	A	FC Halifax T	W	1-0	1-0	5	Rees 37	2256
23	29	H	King's Lynn T	W	3-1	1-1	5	Rees 2 41, 50, Marsh 61	907
24	Feb 15	H	Altrincham	W	2-0	1-0	3	Smith, K 19, Boden 57	1413
25	19	A	Maidenhead U	L	0-2	0-1	3		2324
26	22	A	Torquay U	D	0-0	0-0	3		2251
27	26	H	Eastleigh	W	1-0	1-0	3	Marsh 5	1236
28	Mar 8	A	Wrexham	L	2-4	1-1	5	Boden 38, Marsh 68	8705
29	12	H	Chesterfield	D	1-1	0-0	5	Clifton 88	1621
30	15	A	Barnet	L	0-1	0-1	5		1580
31	19	H	Grimsby T	D	0-0	0-0	6		1670
32	22	A	Notts Co	L	0-1	0-1	7		5010
33	Apr 2	H	Woking	L	0-1	0-0	8		901
34	5	A	Dagenham & R	D	0-0	0-0	8		1278
35	9	A	Aldershot T	L	1-2	0-1	9	Orsi-Dadomo 60	1092
36	15	H	Dover Ath	L	1-2	1-2	9	Boden 9	880
37	18	A	Wealdstone	L	0-2	0-1	10		1181
38	23	H	Bromley	W	2-0	1-0	9	Marsh 5, Boden 72	821
39	26	A	Southend U	L	0-1	0-0	9		4756
40	30	A	Stockport Co	W	2-1	1-0	9	Lewis 24, Fyfield 61	8778
41	May 2	H	Wrexham	D	1-1	0-0	9	Marsh (pen) 89	2053
42	7	A	Yeovil T	D	2-2	2-0	9	Marsh 11, Lewis 27	2599
43	10	A	Grimsby T	L	0-1	0-1	9		6010
44	15	H	Solihull Moors	L	0-3	0-2	9		1101

Final League Position: 9

GOALSCORERS

League (49): Boden 11 (2 pens), Marsh 10 (1 pen), Rees 8, Fyfield 4, Smith, K 4, Lewis 2, Mendy 2, Orsi-Dadomo 2, Clifton 1, Evans 1, Mafuta 1, Raymond 1, own goals 2.
FA Cup (10): Boden 2, Clifton 2, Rees 2, Evans 1, Mafuta 1, Marsh 1, Ricketts 1.
FA Trophy (4): Marsh 4 (2 pens).

Ashmore 19	Ilesanmi 14 + 1	Ricketts 24 + 2	Evans 41	Rees 33 + 1	Mafuta 26 + 2	Boden 39 + 5	Marsh 43 + 1	Fyfield 34	Mendy 44	Smith K 32	Smith C 3 + 11	Munns — + 1	Raymond 28 + 6	Stephens 27 + 7	Clifton 3 + 35	Oluwabori — + 3	Ashby-Hammond 25	Lewis 17 + 6	Comley 14 + 5	Orsi-Dadomo 7 + 17	Reckord 3 + 3	Stevens 8	Match No.
1	2	3	4	5^{1}	6	7	8^{2}	9	10	11	12	13											1
1	2	7	3	8		10	11	4	5	6	12		9^{1}										2
1	4	7	3	5^{1}		11	10^{2}	2	9	6	12		8	13									3
1	2	7	3	8^{1}		10^{2}	11	4	5	6	12		9		13								4
1	2	7	3	8^{3}		10^{1}	11	4	5	6	12		9^{2}	14	13								5
1	2	7	3	8^{3}		10^{1}	11	4	5	6	12		9^{2}	14	13								6
1	2	7	3	8^{2}		10	11	4	5	6	12		9^{1}		13								7
1	2	7	3	8^{3}		10	11^{2}	4	5	6	12		9^{1}	14	13								8
1	2	7	3	8^{3}	12	10	11^{2}	4	5	6	13		9^{1}		14								9
1	2	7	3	13	8^{2}	10^{1}	11^{3}	4	5	6	9			14	12								10
1	2		3	7	8^{1}	10	11^{2}	4	5	6			9	13	12								11
1	2	7	3■	8	9^{2}	10^{1}	11^{3}	4	5	6				14	13	12							12
	2	7		8^{1}	9	10^{3}	11^{2}	4	5	6			12	3	13	14	1						13
	2		3	7^{1}	8	10^{2}	11	4	5	6			9		13	12	1						14
		7	2	8^{2}	9	10^{1}	11^{3}	4	5	6			12	3	14		1	13					15
		7	2	8	9^{1}	10^{3}	11^{2}	4	5	6			13	3	12		1	14					16
		7	2		8^{1}	10^{2}	11	4	5	6			9	3	13		1	12					17
		7	2■	8	9	10^{1}	11^{2}	4	5	6			12	3	13		1						18
		4		5^{1}	6	9	10	2	3				7				1	11	8	12			19
		12	2	7^{1}	8^{2}	10^{3}	13	4	5	6			9	3	14		1			11			20
			3	7		10	11		5	6			9^{1}	4			1		8	12	2		21
			2	4		5^{1}	6^{3}	8^{2}	10	11			7	3	14		1		9	13	12		22
			3	7^{1}		12	10		5	6			8	4	13		1		9	11^{2}	2		23
		7	2^{2}	8		10^{3}	11^{1}		5	6				3	14		1		9	13	12	4	24
		7	2	8		10^{1}	11		5	6^{2}				3	14		1	12	9^{3}	13		4	25
		3^{2}	4	5		13	6^{3}		9				7		14		1	8	12	11^{1}	2	10	26
			2	7		10^{1}	11^{2}		5				8	3	13		1	6	9	12		4	27
			2	4		5^{3}	6		9		10^{1}		7	3	14		1	8	12	13		11^{2}	28
			2	6	12	10^{2}	11	4	5		8^{3}		7^{1}	3	14		1	9		13			29
		7^{1}	2	8^{2}	9	10^{3}	11	4	5				12	3	14		1	6		13			30
			2	6	7	13	9^{2}	4	5				8^{3}	3	14		1	11	12	10^{1}			31
			2	7	8	12	10	4	6				9^{1}	3	13		1	5		11^{2}			32
			2	7	8	12	10	4	5	6			9^{3}	3^{2}	13		1	14		11^{1}			33
			2	7	8	10^{1}	11	3	5	6							1		9	12		4	34
			2	7^{3}	8	10^{1}	11	3	5	6^{2}					14		1	13	9	12		4	35
		6^{3}	2		7	8^{2}	10	4	5				14	3	12		1	9		11^{1}	13		36
		12			6	10^{1}	11	3	5				7■	2	8^{3}		1	9	14	13		4^{2}	37
1		6	2		7^{2}	10	11	4	5					3	8^{1}			9	12	13			38
1		6	2		7	10	11	4	5					3	8^{1}			9		12			39
1			2		7	9^{1}	10	4	5	6				3	12			11	8				40
1			2			9^{1}	10	4■	5	6	12		7	3	13			11^{3}	8^{2}	14			41
1			2		7	9^{1}	10		5	6			8	3	12			11	4				42
1			2		7	9^{2}	10		5	6	13		8^{3}	3	12			11	4^{1}	14			43
1	14		2^{2}		6	9^{3}	10		4	5			8	3	13			11	7^{1}	12			44

FA Cup

Fourth Qualifying	Barnet	(a)	1-0
First Round	Eastleigh	(h)	2-0
Second Round	St Albans C	(h)	4-0
Third Round	AFC Wimbledon	(h)	2-0
Fourth Round	Bournemouth	(a)	1-0
Fifth Round	Everton	(a)	0-2

FA Trophy

Third Round	Barnet	(a)	3-2
Fourth Round	Maidstone U	(h)	1-1
(Boreham Wood won 5-4 on penalties)			
Fifth Round	Wrexham	(a)	0-3

BROMLEY

Ground: The Stadium, Hayes Lane, Bromley, Kent BR2 9EF. *Tel:* (02084) 605 291.
Website: bromleyfc.tv *Email:* info@bromleyfc.co.uk *Year Formed:* 1892.
Record Attendance: 10,798 v Nigeria, Friendly, 24 September 1949. *Nickname:* 'The Ravens', 'The Lillywhites'.
Manager: Andy Woodman. *Colours:* White shirts, white shorts, white socks.

BROMLEY – NATIONAL LEAGUE 2021–22 LEAGUE RECORD

Match No.	*Date*	*Venue*	*Opponents*	*Result*		*H/T Score*	*Lg Pos.*	*Goalscorers*	*Attendance*
1	Aug 28	A	Dagenham & R	L	2-4	1-1	18	Webster ^{7}, Cheek ^{90}	1423
2	30	H	Eastleigh	W	3-0	1-0	10	Alabi ^{25}, Whitely ^{49}, Cheek ^{87}	1521
3	Sept 4	A	Chesterfield	D	2-2	1-1	15	Cheek 2 (1 pen) $^{36 (p), 90}$	5229
4	11	H	Boreham Wood	L	2-3	0-1	17	Bingham ^{48}, Cheek ^{66}	1311
5	18	H	Barnet	W	2-0	1-0	12	Cheek (pen) ^{19}, Bush ^{62}	1451
6	25	A	Dover Ath	W	1-0	1-0	10	Whitely ^{7}	927
7	28	H	Grimsby T	W	3-1	0-1	7	Cheek ^{57}, Alabi ^{67}, Whitely ^{81}	1927
8	Oct 5	H	Weymouth	W	3-0	2-0	6	Cheek ^{10}, Bush ^{45}, Alabi ^{77}	1334
9	9	H	Torquay U	W	2-0	2-0	5	Sablier ^{17}, Sowunmi ^{36}	2523
10	23	A	Aldershot T	W	3-2	2-2	6	Alexander ^{9}, Walker, M (og) ^{33}, Cheek (pen) ^{65}	1354
11	26	A	Notts Co	D	1-1	0-0	6	Cheek ^{80}	5331
12	30	H	FC Halifax T	D	0-0	0-0	7		2005
13	Nov 2	A	Woking	W	2-0	0-0	4	Alexander ^{78}, Cawley ^{86}	1843
14	13	A	Stockport Co	D	1-1	0-0	4	Hogan (og) ^{89}	5515
15	20	H	King's Lynn T	W	3-2	1-1	4	Cheek 2 $^{43, 70}$, Alabi ^{62}	1910
16	23	H	Yeovil T	L	1-2	1-2	4	Cheek (pen) ^{44}	1910
17	27	A	Wrexham	L	0-2	0-1	6		8156
18	Dec 4	H	Wealdstone	W	3-2	2-1	3	Alexander ^{25}, Sablier ^{29}, Webster ^{90}	1747
19	11	A	Altrincham	W	1-0	1-0	3	Sowunmi ^{31}	1405
20	26	H	Southend U	D	1-1	0-0	4	Cheek ^{64}	3759
21	28	A	Maidenhead U	L	0-1	0-0	5		1303
22	Jan 8	H	Solihull Moors	W	2-1	2-0	3	Wagstaff ^{36}, Cheek ^{45}	1411
23	22	A	Grimsby T	W	2-1	1-1	4	Alexander ^{39}, Arthurs ^{83}	5854
24	25	H	Woking	W	1-0	1-0	4	Arthurs ^{23}	1663
25	29	H	Notts Co	W	1-0	1-0	4	Arthurs ^{45}	3606
26	Feb 8	A	Southend U	L	0-2	0-0	4		8070
27	15	H	Stockport Co	L	1-3	0-0	5	Webster ^{90}	2753
28	22	A	Weymouth	D	2-2	0-1	7	Parsons ^{55}, Cheek ^{75}	1003
29	Mar 5	A	Torquay U	D	0-0	0-0	9		2350
30	15	A	FC Halifax T	L	0-1	0-0	10		1693
31	19	H	Wrexham	D	0-0	0-0	9		3123
32	22	A	Yeovil T	L	1-2	1-1	10	Alexander ^{24}	1732
33	26	A	Wealdstone	D	1-1	0-0	10	Webster ^{74}	1161
34	Apr 5	A	King's Lynn T	L	0-1	0-0	10		857
35	9	H	Dagenham & R	L	0-2	0-0	11		1674
36	15	A	Eastleigh	W	2-0	1-0	11	Bingham ^{40}, Vennings ^{79}	2564
37	18	H	Maidenhead U	D	0-0	0-0	11		1549
38	23	A	Boreham Wood	L	0-2	0-1	11		821
39	26	H	Aldershot T	D	1-1	0-0	11	Webster ^{88}	1151
40	30	H	Chesterfield	W	4-2	3-2	10	Al-Hamadi 2 $^{12, 36}$, Coulson ^{29}, Whitely ^{50}	1827
41	May 2	A	Solihull Moors	L	0-3	0-1	11		2259
42	7	H	Dover Ath	D	2-2	1-0	11	Bush ^{26}, Whitely ^{90}	1916
43	10	H	Altrincham	D	1-1	1-0	11	Bloomfield ^{17}	1098
44	15	A	Barnet	W	4-2	1-1	10	Bloomfield ^{12}, Dennis ^{49}, Al-Hamadi ^{52}, Cheek ^{80}	1346

Final League Position: 10

GOALSCORERS

League (61): Cheek 17 (4 pens), Alexander 5, Webster 5, Whitely 5, Alabi 4, Al-Hamadi 3, Arthurs 3, Bush 3, Bingham 2, Bloomfield 2, Sablier 2, Sowunmi 2, Cawley 1, Coulson 1, Dennis 1, Parsons 1, Vennings 1, Wagstaff 1, own goals 2.
FA Cup (2): Alabi 1, Cheek 1.
FA Trophy (11): Cheek 5, Alabi 2, Alexander 1, Francis 1, Lovatt 1, Partingdon 1.

Cousins 28	Bush 38 + 3	Sowunmi 27 + 2	Webster 40	Partington 21 + 7	Bingham 38	Trotter 14 + 17	Arthurs 33 + 4	Whitely 35 + 3	Cheek 41 + 1	Dennis 10 + 11	Forster 16 + 7	Alabi 10 + 30	O'Brien — + 1	Coulson 32 + 4	Skeffington 2 + 1	Stevenson — + 1	Mnoga 1 + 5	Sablier 13 + 2	Alexander 25 + 3	Cawley 6 + 10	Tormey — + 1	Charles-Cook 1	Francis — + 2	Wagstaff 8 + 2	Parsons 6 + 5	Bloomfield 4 + 4	Balcombe 15	Vennings 11 + 1	Al-Hamadi 8 + 2	Margetson 1	*Match No.*
1	2	3	4	5	6	7	8^{1}	9^{3}	10	11^{2}	12	13	14																		1
1	13	4	10	2	3	12	6^{2}	11	7			8^{3}		5■	9^{1}	14															2
1		3	4	2	6	13	7^{2}	9	10	12	14	11			8^{1}		5^{3}														3
1	13	3^{3}	4	2	7	12	8^{2}	5	9	11	6^{1}	10					14														4
1	4		9	2	3	8	5^{1}	10	6	7^{2}	11^{3}	12					14	13													5
1	4		8	2	3	12	6^{3}	9^{2}	7	13				5			14	11^{1}	10												6
1	2	3	5		8	13	9	7	10	14		12		4^{2}				6^{3}	11^{1}												7
1	3	13	5	2^{2}	7	12	8^{1}	9	10			14		4				6	11^{3}												8
1	2	3	5		7	8^{2}		9	10	13		12		4	14			6^{1}	11^{3}												9
1	2	3	5		7	8	12	9	10^{2}	14		13		4				6^{3}	11^{1}												10
1	3	4	9		2	8^{3}	6	10^{1}	7	14	12	13		5					11^{2}												11
1	2	3	5		7	12	8^{2}		10		9^{1}	13		4			14	6^{3}	11												12
1	2	3	5		6^{3}	7	14		9		8	10		4^{2}			12		11^{1}	13											13
1	3	4	2			7	6		9	13	8^{2}	10		5				12^{3}	11^{1}	14											14
1	2	3	5^{1}	12		7	6		9	10^{3}	8	13		4					11^{2}	14											15
1	4	5		2	3	13	7^{2}		8	9^{3}	11	12		6					10^{1}	14											16
1	3	4	11		2	9■		8^{3}	6		10	7^{1}		5^{2}					14	12	13										17
1	2	3	5	14	8		7	13	11		9^{3}	12		4				6^{1}	10^{2}												18
	3	4	6		2		7	8^{3}	11		12	13		5				9^{1}	10^{2}	14		1									19
1	2	3	5			8	7	13	10	11^{2}	9^{1}	14		4				6^{3}	12												20
1	3	4	9	13	2		6^{1}	10^{3}	7		12	8		5					11^{2}				14								21
1	2	3	5	13	7		6	9	10^{1}			14		4					11^{3}				12	8^{2}							22
1	3	4	11	14	2		6^{2}	10	7		8^{1}	12		5					9^{3}	13											23
1	2	3	5	12	6		7^{3}	9	11		8^{2}	13		4					10^{1}	14											24
1	2	3	5		6		7	8	11^{3}		9^{2}	13		4					10^{1}	14				12							25
1	2	3	5		8	14	6^{1}	7	10			12		4					11^{2}						9^{3}	13					26
1	2	3	5		6	12	7^{1}	9	11			13		4					10^{2}	14				8^{3}							27
1	3	4	2	13		7		8	11	10^{1}				5					12^{3}					6	9^{2}	14					28
		3	7		2	13	4^{2}	8^{3}	5			12		14					9^{1}	10				6	11		1				29
	4		5	2	6		12	8	11			13		3^{3}										7	14		1	9^{2}	10^{1}		30
	4		9	2	3		6	10	7			13		5										8^{1}	12		1		11^{2}		31
			9	2		12	4^{3}	6	5			13		3					8^{2}	10					11^{1}	14	1	7			32
	3		4	2	5	13		7	10	14	8^{2}	11		12										6^{3}			1	9^{1}			33
	4		8	2	3		5	9	13	12		14												6^{2}	11	7^{3}	1		10^{1}		34
	3		4	2	5		6^{2}	7	9	10		13							11^{1}						12		1	8			35
	4			2	3	13	5	8	6^{3}	7^{1}		12							10^{2}	11							1	9	14		36
	3			2	5	14	6^{3}	7	9	10^{2}		13								4					12		1	8	11^{1}		37
	3			2	5	7^{2}	6^{1}	8	10			13		12						4				14			1	9	11^{3}		38
	3		5	2	7			8	10			11^{1}		4				6^{2}							12		1	9	13		39
	4		7	2	3	12	14	8	6^{1}			13		5				10^{3}									1	9^{2}	11		40
1	14		7	2		6	4^{3}				13			3^{2}				9	8	10					11^{1}	5		12			41
	3		6		8			7	11^{1}		12	13		4				2^{3}								14	1	9	10^{2}	5	42
	3	13	5	2^{1}	6	7	9^{3}	14		12	8^{2}	10		4												11	1				43
	2	3	4		5^{1}	12		7	11	13	8^{3}			14												10^{2}	1	6	9		44

FA Cup

Fourth Qualifying	Hungerford T	(a)	2-1
First Round	Rotherham U	(a)	0-3

FA Trophy

Third Round	Dover Ath	(a)	1-0
Fourth Round	Aldershot T	(a)	2-0
Fifth Round	Tonbridge Angels	(a)	1-1
(Bromley won 3-2 on penalties)			
Quarter-Final	Solihull Moors	(h)	3-1
Semi-Final	York C	(h)	3-1
Final	Wrexham	(Wembley)	1-0

CHESTERFIELD

Ground: Technique Stadium, 1866 Sheffield Road, Whittington Moor, Chesterfield, Derbyshire S41 8NZ.
Tel: (01246) 269 300. *Website:* www.chesterfield-fc.co.uk *Email:* reception@chesterfield-fc.co.uk *Year Formed:* 1866.
Record Attendance: 30,968 v Newcastle U, Division 2, 7 April 1939 (at Saltergate); 10,089 v Rotherham U, FL 2, 18 March 2011 (at b2net Stadium (now called the Technique Stadium)). *Nickname:* 'The Blues', 'The Spireites'.
Manager: Paul Cook. *Colours:* Blue shirts with white trim, white shorts with blue trim, blue socks.

CHESTERFIELD – NATIONAL LEAGUE 2021–22 LEAGUE RECORD

Match No.	Date	Venue	Opponents	Result		H/T Score	Lg Pos.	Goalscorers	Attendance
1	Aug 21	A	Aldershot T	W	2-0	0-0	4	Rowe (pen) ^{72}, Tshimanga ^{76}	2393
2	28	H	Wealdstone	W	2-0	1-0	2	Khan ^{5}, Carline ^{81}	5356
3	30	A	King's Lynn T	W	2-0	1-0	2	Tshimanga 2 (1 pen) $^{16 (p), 48}$	1806
4	Sept 4	H	Bromley	D	2-2	1-1	2	Carline ^{38}, Oyeleke ^{71}	5229
5	11	A	Dover Ath	D	0-0	0-0	3		1024
6	14	H	Barnet	W	4-2	2-2	2	Tshimanga 3 (2 pens) $^{6, 9 (p), 64 (p)}$, Gunning ^{77}	4538
7	18	A	Yeovil T	W	2-0	2-0	1	Oyeleke ^{19}, Tshimanga ^{36}	2356
8	25	H	Torquay U	D	2-2	0-0	2	Tshimanga 2 $^{58, 73}$	5127
9	28	A	Woking	L	1-3	1-0	2	Khan ^{12}	1855
10	Oct 5	A	Wrexham	D	1-1	1-0	5	Kerr ^{5}	9147
11	9	A	Southend U	W	4-0	2-0	4	Rowe 3 (1 pen) $^{19, 40, 73 (p)}$, Khan ^{49}	4625
12	23	H	Boreham Wood	W	2-1	2-0	2	Rowe (pen) ^{20}, Tshimanga ^{43}	5477
13	26	H	Eastleigh	W	1-0	1-0	2	Tshimanga ^{34}	5086
14	30	A	Dagenham & R	D	2-2	0-2	3	Grimes ^{50}, Tshimanga ^{52}	1711
15	Nov 13	H	Weymouth	W	4-0	2-0	1	Tshimanga 3 (1 pen) $^{23 (p), 45, 58}$, Khan ^{73}	5862
16	20	A	Solihull Moors	W	2-0	2-0	1	Whittle ^{36}, Tshimanga ^{45}	1950
17	23	H	Altrincham	D	2-2	2-0	1	Mandeville ^{11}, Tshimanga ^{44}	5273
18	Dec 11	A	Grimsby T	W	1-0	0-0	1	Tshimanga ^{84}	6504
19	28	H	FC Halifax T	D	1-1	0-1	1	Clarke ^{85}	8106
20	Jan 1	H	King's Lynn T	W	1-0	0-0	1	Mandeville ^{51}	6328
21	15	A	Barnet	W	4-1	0-0	2	Tshimanga 2 $^{48, 70}$, Asante ^{59}, King ^{90}	1777
22	18	A	Maidenhead U	L	2-3	1-2	2	King ^{45}, Tshimanga ^{55}	1232
23	22	H	Aldershot T	D	0-0	0-0	1		6422
24	29	A	Eastleigh	W	1-0	0-0	2	Weston ^{89}	3076
25	Feb 5	H	Dagenham & R	W	2-1	1-1	2	Tshimanga 2 (2 pens) $^{44, 62}$	6063
26	8	A	Stockport Co	D	2-2	2-0	2	Tshimanga ^{16}, Asante ^{21}	10,236
27	12	A	Weymouth	D	1-1	0-0	2	Whittle ^{70}	1299
28	19	H	Solihull Moors	L	2-3	2-1	2	Whittle ^{14}, Asante ^{21}	7391
29	22	H	Wrexham	L	0-2	0-0	2		7854
30	26	H	Yeovil T	W	1-0	1-0	2	Kellermann ^{45}	5371
31	Mar 1	H	Notts Co	W	3-1	0-1	2	Maguire 2 $^{60, 86}$, Asante (pen) ^{90}	7912
32	5	H	Southend U	D	2-2	1-0	2	King ^{9}, Miller ^{77}	6625
33	12	A	Boreham Wood	D	1-1	0-0	2	Asante (pen) ^{82}	1621
34	19	H	Maidenhead U	W	1-0	0-0	2	Asante ^{76}	5518
35	22	A	Altrincham	L	0-1	0-0	2		2042
36	26	A	Notts Co	D	1-1	1-1	3	Whittle ^{13}	10,334
37	Apr 2	H	Grimsby T	L	1-4	1-2	5	Maguire ^{6}	7819
38	9	A	Wealdstone	W	2-1	1-0	5	Grimes ^{35}, Quigley ^{68}	1337
39	18	A	FC Halifax T	L	0-2	0-0	5		3294
40	23	H	Dover Ath	W	3-2	1-1	5	Khan 2 $^{24, 82}$, King ^{85}	5291
41	30	A	Bromley	L	2-4	2-3	7	Maguire ^{39}, Denton ^{43}	1827
42	May 2	H	Stockport Co	L	0-1	0-1	7		9198
43	7	A	Torquay U	L	0-2	0-0	7		3075
44	15	H	Woking	D	0-0	0-0	7		9013

Final League Position: 7

GOALSCORERS

League (69): Tshimanga 24 (6 pens), Asante 6 (2 pens), Khan 6, Rowe 5 (3 pens), King 4, Maguire 4, Whittle 4, Carline 2, Grimes 2, Mandeville 2, Oyeleke 2, Clarke 1, Denton 1, Gunning 1, Kellermann 1, Kerr 1, Miller 1, Quigley 1, Weston 1.
FA Cup (10): Mandeville 2, Asante 1, Croll 1, Kellermann 1, Khan 1, King 1, Payne 1 (pen), Tshimanga 1, Tyson 1.
FA Trophy (0).
National League Play-offs (3): King 1, Quigley 1, Rowe 1.

Loach 44	Miller 27 + 7	Maguire 24	Gunning 19 + 1	Grimes 32 + 6	King 32 + 1	Oyeleke 20 + 4	Weston 31 + 4	Mandeville 34 + 9	Rowe 8 + 5	Tshimanga 27	Clarke 2 + 4	Carline 6 + 3	Khan 22 + 15	Kerr 19 + 1	McCourt 8 + 13	Payne 7 + 9	Whittle 28 + 7	Kellermann 25 + 5	Williams 19 + 1	Croll 9	Tyson — + 3	Asante 18 + 6	Quigley 9 + 7	Denton 5 + 4	Whelan 8 + 4	Rowley 1 + 5	*Match No.*
1	2	3	4	5	6^{2}	7^{3}	8	9^{1}	10	11	12	13	14														1
1	2	3	4		6^{3}		8		10^{2}	11	9	12	7^{1}	5	13	14											2
1	2	3	4	14			7	9^{3}	12	11	13	6		5^{2}	8	10^{1}											3
1	2	3	4	5		12	7	13	10^{2}	11	9^{1}	6	8^{3}			14											4
1	2	3^{3}	4	13		8	12	9^{1}	10	11		6	14	5	7^{2}												5
1	2^{2}		4	5	6	7	8^{3}	12		11			9^{1}	3	14	10	13										6
1	2^{2}		4^{3}	3	12	8^{1}	7	9		11		6		5	14	10	13										7
1	5^{3}	4	3				6	9^{2}	13	11		7	12	2	8	10^{1}	14										8
1	2		3	4	7^{3}		6	9^{2}	13	10		12	8	5	14	11^{1}											9
1		3	2		6		5	12	10^{3}	11		9^{2}	7^{1}	4		13	14	8									10
1	2	3	4	12	6	14	7^{2}	13	10	11			9^{3}	5^{1}				8									11
1	6^{2}	5	4		2	7		9	10^{1}	11				3	14	13	12	8^{3}									12
1	5	4	3^{3}	12	7	6		9		11			14	2	13	10^{1}		8^{2}									13
1	12	3^{1}		4■	6	8		13		11			9^{3}	5	14	10^{2}	2	7									14
1				4	6	8^{3}	7	14		11^{2}			10		12	13	2	9^{1}	3	5							15
1				4	6	8^{1}	7	13		11			10^{3}		12	14	2	9^{2}	5	3							16
1				9		2^{3}	3	4		7			10^{2}		12	13	11	6^{1}	5	8	14						17
1	2			5		8^{1}	7	9^{2}		11^{3}	12		13	4		14	6	10	3								18
1	2		4			8	7^{1}	12		10	14		13	5^{2}			6	9	3			11^{3}					19
1	2		4^{1}	12	6	7^{2}	8	9		11^{3}			10				3	13	5			14					20
1	2^{2}			4	6	8	7	9^{1}		10			14				12	13	5	3		11^{3}					21
1				4^{1}	6	8	7	10^{2}		11			13			14	2	9^{3}	3	5		12					22
1	2^{2}	4			6		7	13		10			8				12		3	5		11^{3}	9^{1}	14			23
1		5		13			7	9		11^{1}				3			6	8	2	4		12	10^{2}				24
1				4	6	12		9		10			8^{1}	5	7^{2}		2	13		3		11					25
1	14			4	6■	7^{1}		9		10				5	8		2	13	12	3^{3}		11^{2}					26
1	2^{3}			4		8^{2}	12	9		10^{1}			13	3	7		5	6				11	14				27
1	14			4			6■	9					13	3^{3}	7		8	5^{1}	2			11	10^{2}		12		28
1	2	3		4				9^{1}					14				6	7	5^{3}			11	10^{2}	12	8	13	29
1	2	4		5	6			9					13				3	7				11^{1}	10^{2}	12	8		30
1	5	3		4	6			10					8				2^{1}	7				11	12^{2}		9	13	31
1	5^{1}	4		3	6		7	10						14			2	8^{2}				11^{3}	13		9	12	32
1	5	4		3	6			10					8				2	7				12	11		9^{1}		33
1	10^{2}	4		3	2		14	8					9^{1}				5	6				13	11		7^{3}	12	34
1	12	4		3	5		14	9					7				2	6^{3}				11	10^{2}		13	8^{1}	35
1	10	4	12	3^{2}	2		6	8^{1}					9				5					11	13		7		36
1	5^{2}	3		4	6	12	7	10					8^{3}				2					11	13		9^{1}	14	37
1	14		4	3	6		7	9^{1}					13				2	8	5			11^{2}	12	10^{3}			38
1	12		4^{2}	3	6		7	9							14		2	8^{1}	5			11	13	10^{3}			39
1		3		4	6	8^{1}	7	10^{2}					9		13		2		5			11^{3}		12	14		40
1	14	5		4	6		8	10					9^{1}		7^{3}		2^{2}		3		12			11	13		41
1	2^{3}		4	5	6	7	9	10	14				12					8^{1}	3			13		11^{2}			42
1			4	5	6	7^{2}	8^{1}	9	13				14				2	12	3			11^{3}	10				43
1				4	5		6^{2}	9	10				8		12		2	7	3		13			11^{1}			44

FA Cup

Fourth Qualifying	Curzon Ashton	(a)	4-0
First Round	Southend U	(h)	3-1
Second Round	Salford C	(a)	2-0
Third Round	Chelsea	(a)	1-5

National League Play-offs

Quarter-Final	FC Halifax T	(a)	2-1
Semi-Final	Solihull Moors	(a)	1-3

FA Trophy

Third Round	Guiseley	(h)

(Chesterfield withdrew due to positive COVID-19 tests)

DAGENHAM & REDBRIDGE

Ground: Chigwell Construction Stadium, Victoria Road, Dagenham, Essex RM10 7XL.
Tel: (020) 8592 1549. *Website:* www.daggers.co.uk *Email:* info@daggers.co.uk *Year Formed:* 1992.
Record Attendance: 5,949 v Ipswich T, FA Cup 3rd rd, 5 January 2002. *Nickname:* 'The Daggers'.
Manager: Daryl McMahon. *Colours:* Red shirts with white trim, blue shorts with white trim, blue socks.

DAGENHAM & REDBRIDGE – NATIONAL LEAGUE 2021–22 LEAGUE RECORD

Match No.	*Date*	*Venue*	*Opponents*	*Result*		*H/T Score*	*Lg Pos.*	*Goalscorers*	*Attendance*
1	Aug 21	A	Stockport Co	W	3-1	1-1	2	Wright [40], Walker [56], Robinson [58]	5265
2	28	H	Bromley	W	4-2	1-1	1	Walker [36], McCallum [61], Robinson [72], Weston [86]	1423
3	30	A	Barnet	W	2-0	2-0	1	McCallum [21], Walker [38]	1728
4	Sept 4	H	Wealdstone	D	2-2	1-1	1	McCallum [35], Saunders [80]	1735
5	11	A	King's Lynn T	W	2-1	0-0	1	Walker [46], Weston [88]	859
6	14	H	Weymouth	W	4-2	1-2	1	Vilhete [21], Wright 2 [54, 78], McCallum [84]	1240
7	18	A	Wrexham	L	0-1	0-1	2		8033
8	25	H	Solihull Moors	W	5-1	2-1	1	McCallum 2 (1 pen) [36, 90 (p)], Walker (pen) [39], Wilson [76], Vilhete [80]	1175
9	Oct 2	H	Altrincham	L	2-3	2-1	2	Vilhete [34], Robinson [41]	1360
10	5	A	Woking	L	0-1	0-1	4		2226
11	9	A	Boreham Wood	L	0-2	0-0	6		1111
12	23	H	Southend U	W	3-0	0-0	5	Sagaf [52], Ling 2 [56, 58]	3673
13	26	A	FC Halifax T	L	0-1	0-1	7		1761
14	30	H	Chesterfield	D	2-2	2-0	8	Balanta [13], Saunders [23]	1711
15	Nov 13	A	Maidenhead U	W	4-1	2-0	7	Balanta 3 [28, 39, 66], Akanbi [72]	1331
16	20	H	Yeovil T	L	0-1	0-1	7		1642
17	23	H	Eastleigh	L	0-1	0-0	10		1306
18	27	A	Notts Co	L	1-2	1-1	10	Balanta [42]	4889
19	Dec 4	H	Grimsby T	W	3-2	1-1	10	Rance [20], Akanbi [51], Balanta [53]	1734
20	26	A	Dover Ath	W	2-0	2-0	9	Robinson 2 [10, 36]	697
21	28	H	Aldershot T	W	1-0	1-0	8	Balanta [39]	1879
22	Jan 2	H	Dover Ath	W	3-1	2-0	5	Morias [29], Walker [36], Weston [54]	1631
23	8	A	Torquay U	D	2-2	1-2	4	Walker [29], Balanta [71]	2339
24	22	H	Stockport Co	L	0-2	0-2	8		1749
25	25	A	Weymouth	W	2-1	0-1	7	Walker [71], McCallum [83]	901
26	29	H	FC Halifax T	L	1-3	0-2	9	Robinson [62]	2460
27	Feb 5	A	Chesterfield	L	1-2	1-1	9	Walker [35]	6063
28	22	H	Woking	D	1-1	1-0	10	McCallum [45]	1358
29	26	A	Altrincham	L	0-3	0-2	10		1642
30	Mar 1	H	Maidenhead U	W	3-0	3-0	10	Morias [11], McCallum 2 [44, 45]	1057
31	8	A	Yeovil T	W	3-0	2-0	10	McCallum 2 [5, 22], Morias [63]	1836
32	15	A	Southend U	W	3-0	2-0	9	Atkinson (og) [5], Arnold (og) [28], Robinson [67]	7542
33	19	H	Notts Co	L	1-2	1-1	10	Morias [5]	1846
34	22	A	Eastleigh	W	1-0	1-0	9	McCallum [33]	2250
35	26	A	Grimsby T	L	1-2	0-2	9	Reynolds [90]	4804
36	Apr 5	H	Boreham Wood	D	0-0	0-0	9		1278
37	9	A	Bromley	W	2-0	0-0	8	McCallum [47], Morias [76]	1674
38	15	H	Barnet	W	7-3	5-0	8	Morias 3 [14, 24, 26], McCallum 2 [44, 90], Weston [45], Robinson [84]	2010
39	18	A	Aldershot T	W	2-0	2-0	8	Morias [27], Vilhete [35]	1528
40	23	H	King's Lynn T	D	1-1	0-1	8	McCallum [90]	1457
41	30	A	Wealdstone	W	2-1	1-0	8	Morias [23], Onariase [47]	1321
42	May 2	H	Torquay U	D	0-0	0-0	8		1752
43	7	A	Solihull Moors	L	1-3	0-3	8	Walker [55]	2061
44	15	H	Wrexham	W	3-0	0-0	8	Morias [55], McCallum [80], Robinson [90]	3470

Final League Position: 8

GOALSCORERS

League (80): McCallum 18 (1 pen), Morias 11, Walker 10 (1 pen), Robinson 9, Balanta 8, Vilhete 4, Weston 4, Wright 3, Akanbi 2, Ling 2, Saunders 2, Onariase 1, Rance 1, Reynolds 1, Sagaf 1, Wilson 1, own goals 2.
FA Cup (2): Balanta 2.
FA Trophy (6): McCallum 2, Morias 2, Sagaf 1, Walker 1.

Justham 44	Wright 43	Reynolds 36	Johnson 27 + 1	Ling 25 + 7	Sagaf 30 + 7	Jones 14	Robinson 38 + 2	Vilhete 29 + 8	Balanta 16 + 6	McCallum 34 + 2	Walker 18 + 14	Weston 29 + 12	Saunders 5 + 10	Phipps 1 + 3	Scott 1 + 3	Rance 19 + 4	Wilson 3 + 4	Clark 8 + 2	Akanbi 3 + 6	Zouma 6	Morias 22 + 2	Comley 16 + 1	Hare 8 + 2	Onariase 9 + 1	Match No.
1	2	3	4	5	6	7	8	9^{2}	10^{1}	11	12	13													1
1	2	3	4	5^{1}	6^{2}	7	8	9		11	10^{3}	12	13	14											2
1	2	3	4	12	7	5^{1}	8	9		11^{2}	10^{3}	6	14	13											3
1	2	3	4	7			8	9		11	10	5	12		6^{1}										4
1	2	3	4	7			8	9		11	10^{2}	12	5	6^{1}		13									5
1	2	3	4	6	12		7	8		11	10^{1}	9	5^{2}				13								6
1	2	3	4	7^{2}	6		8	9		11^{1}	10	5	12				13								7
1	2	3	4	13	6	7^{1}	8	9		11	10^{2}	5					12								8
1	2	3	4	13	7	5^{2}	8	9	12	11	10^{1}	6													9
1	2	3	4	5	7^{1}	6	8	9^{2}	12	11	10	13													10
1	2		4	5	12	6^{2}	7		9	11^{1}	10	8					13	3							11
1	2	3	4	5	6^{1}	7	8^{2}	13	10^{3}			9			14	12	11								12
1	4	2	3	10^{1}	5	11	8^{3}	12	6			7	14			13	9^{2}								13
1	2	3	4^{2}		7			9	10			8	5^{1}		14	6	11^{3}	12	13						14
1	2	4		5	7		8	9	10			12				6		3	11^{1}						15
1		2	4■	5	7		8	9^{2}	10	11		12	13			6^{1}		3							16
1	2	3		4	6^{2}		8	13	10	11		5	9^{1}			7			12						17
1	2	3		4	6^{2}		8	9	10	11^{1}		5	13			7			12						18
1	2	3		4			7	9^{1}	10			5	8		12	6			11						19
1	2	4		5	7		6	13	9		11^{1}	8							12	3	10^{2}				20
1	2	4		5	7		6	8	9^{2}		12	13							11^{1}	3	10				21
1	2	3		12	7		6	8^{2}	9^{1}		11	5		13						4	10				22
1	2	3		5^{1}	7	6		13	9	12	11^{2}	8								4	10				23
1	2	3	4	5^{3}	7	6^{1}	14	13	9	12	11	8									10^{2}				24
1	2				14	9^{2}	7	8^{1}		10	13	5	12			6		3		4	11^{3}				25
1	2			5^{1}			7			10	11	8	12			6		3		4	9				26
1	2	4		5^{1}		6	8			10	11	9	13			7^{3}		3^{2}			14	12			27
1	2	4			12		8^{1}	9		10	11^{3}	13				6		3			14	7	5^{2}		28
1	2	4			13	8^{1}		9		10	11	12				6		3				7	5^{2}		29
1	2	3^{1}	4		8					10^{2}	12	9				6		13	14		11^{3}	7	5		30
1	2	3	4		8^{2}		13			10^{3}	12	9				6			14		11^{1}	7	5		31
1	2	3	4	12	5		8^{2}		13	10		9				6					11^{1}	7			32
1	2	3	4		5		8	14	13	10		9^{2}				6^{3}					11	7^{1}	12		33
1	2	3	4		12		7	8^{2}	9^{1}	10		13				6					11^{3}		5	14	34
1	2	3	4				8	13	12	10	14	9^{3}				6					11^{2}	7^{1}	5		35
1	2	4		5	6		8	9		10											11	7		3	36
1	2	4	13		6		8	9^{1}		10	12	5									11^{2}	7		3	37
1	2	4		12	6		8	9		10	13	5^{2}									11^{1}	7		3	38
1	2	4		14	6^{3}		8	9		10	12	5^{1}				13					11^{2}	7		3	39
1	2		4	5^{2}	6^{1}		8	9		10	12										11	7	13	3	40
1	2		4	9	13		8			10^{1}	12					6					11^{2}	7	5	3	41
1	2		4		6^{2}		8	9		10	13	12									11	7	5^{1}	3	42
1	2		4	5^{1}	6^{2}		8	9		10	12	13									11	7		3	43
1	2		4				8	9	13	10^{1}	12	5				7					11^{2}	6		3	44

FA Cup

Fourth Qualifying	Wealdstone	(a)	2-1
First Round	Salford C	(h)	0-1

FA Trophy

Third Round	Truro C	(a)	1-1
(Dagenham & R won 4-2 on penalties)			
Fourth Round	Southend U	(h)	2-0
Fifth Round	Spennymoor T	(h)	2-0
Quarter-Final	York C	(h)	1-1
(York C won 7-6 on penalties)			

DOVER ATHLETIC

Ground: Crabble Athletic Ground, Lewisham Road, Dover, Kent CT17 0JB. *Tel:* (01304) 822 373.
Website: doverathletic.com *Email:* enquiries@doverathletic.com *Year Formed:* 1894 as Dover FC, reformed as Dover Ath 1983. *Record Attendance:* 7,000 v Folkestone, 13 October 1951 (Dover FC); 5,645 v Crystal Palace, FA Cup 3rd rd, 4 January 2015 (Dover Ath). *Nickname:* 'The Whites'. *Manager:* Andy Hessenthaler.
Colours: White shirts with black trim, black shorts with white trim, black socks.

DOVER ATHLETIC – NATIONAL LEAGUE 2021–22 LEAGUE RECORD

Match No.	*Date*	*Venue*	*Opponents*	*Result*		*H/T Score*	*Lg Pos.*	*Goalscorers*	*Attendance*
1	Aug 28	A	Maidenhead U	L	0-2	0-2	23		1060
2	30	H	Boreham Wood	L	0-1	0-1	23		1517
3	Sept 4	A	Altrincham	L	2-3	1-1	23	Arthur [8], Cosgrave [57]	1871
4	11	H	Chesterfield	D	0-0	0-0	23		1024
5	14	A	Eastleigh	L	1-4	0-4	23	Cosgrave [64]	1745
6	18	A	Weymouth	D	1-1	1-1	23	Arthur [22]	1028
7	21	H	Solihull Moors	D	0-0	0-0	23		809
8	25	H	Bromley	L	0-1	0-1	23		927
9	Oct 2	A	Grimsby T	L	0-6	0-5	23		5913
10	5	H	Aldershot T	L	1-2	0-1	23	Cosgrave [50]	648
11	9	H	Barnet	L	1-2	0-1	23	Cosgrave [64]	885
12	30	H	Stockport Co	L	2-5	1-2	23	Williamson (pen) [32], Arthur [50]	635
13	Nov 2	A	Southend U	L	1-4	0-2	23	Hanson [69]	4996
14	13	A	Torquay U	L	1-2	1-1	23	Gregory [4]	2892
15	20	H	FC Halifax T	L	1-3	0-1	23	Williamson [77]	595
16	23	H	Wealdstone	L	2-3	1-2	23	Ransom [11], Woods [63]	399
17	27	A	Yeovil T	D	1-1	1-0	23	Bramble [2]	2062
18	Dec 4	H	Wrexham	L	0-1	0-0	23		838
19	11	A	King's Lynn T	L	1-2	1-1	23	Pavey [31]	591
20	26	H	Dagenham & R	L	0-2	0-2	23		697
21	28	A	Woking	L	2-3	1-2	23	Goodman [11], Hanson [87]	2248
22	Jan 2	A	Dagenham & R	L	1-3	0-2	23	Pavey [50]	1631
23	15	A	Wealdstone	L	1-2	1-0	23	Pavey [23]	940
24	22	A	Solihull Moors	L	0-5	0-4	23		1393
25	25	H	Eastleigh	W	1-0	0-0	23	Pavey [59]	486
26	29	H	Southend U	L	0-1	0-0	23		2657
27	Feb 5	A	Stockport Co	L	0-1	0-0	23		7263
28	12	H	Torquay U	L	1-3	1-1	23	Goodman [25]	783
29	22	A	Aldershot T	D	0-0	0-0	23		1420
30	26	H	Grimsby T	L	1-3	1-2	23	Goodman [40]	831
31	Mar 5	A	Barnet	L	0-6	0-1	23		1168
32	12	A	FC Halifax T	L	1-2	1-1	23	Pavey [10]	1828
33	19	H	Yeovil T	L	0-2	0-1	23		822
34	26	A	Wrexham	L	5-6	2-2	23	Wilkinson [22], Pavey [28], Gyasi 3 [51, 54, 63]	8572
35	Apr 2	H	King's Lynn T	D	1-1	1-0	23	Arthur [28]	511
36	9	H	Maidenhead U	L	0-1	0-0	23		475
37	15	A	Boreham Wood	W	2-1	2-1	23	Gyasi (pen) [7], Arthur [30]	880
38	18	H	Woking	L	1-4	0-2	23	Nikaj [78]	655
39	23	A	Chesterfield	L	2-3	1-1	23	Gyasi [14], Goodman [81]	5291
40	26	H	Notts Co	L	0-3	0-0	23		845
41	30	H	Altrincham	L	0-1	0-1	23		465
42	May 2	A	Notts Co	L	0-1	0-1	23		6523
43	7	A	Bromley	D	2-2	0-1	23	Collinge 2 [81, 90]	1916
44	15	H	Weymouth	L	1-2	0-1	23	Nelson [76]	763

Final League Position: 23 (Deducted 12pts for failing to fulfil fixtures in the 2021–22 season)

GOALSCORERS

League (37): Pavey 6, Arthur 5, Gyasi 5 (1 pen), Cosgrave 4, Goodman 4, Collinge 2, Hanson 2, Williamson 2 (1 pen), Bramble 1, Gregory 1, Nelson 1, Nikaj 1, Ransom 1, Wilkinson 1, Woods 1.
FA Cup (1): Miller 1.
FA Trophy (0).

Bexon 10	Johnson 4	Goodman 35 + 3	Collinge 38	Wood 16 + 2	Bramble 21 + 1	Woods 37 + 3	Hanson 24 + 2	Miller 7 + 3	Williamson 23	Cosgrave 18 + 1	Gregory 9 + 2	Arthur 23 + 9	Nana Ofori-Twumasi 16 + 1	Caton 1 + 11	Green — + 1	Da Costa 3 + 12	Ransom 35 + 2	Carney 1 + 6	Parkes 22	Tiensia 12 + 1	Bentley 2 + 7	Drais 2 + 2	Wratten 1 + 4	Pavey 18	Andre 12	Judd 15	Wilkinson 17 + 5	Gyasi 17 + 2	Moses 10 + 3	Krasniqi 17 + 1	Parfitt-Williams 2 + 7	Baptiste 10 + 2	Byford 4 + 2	Agbebi — + 4	Nelson 1 + 7	Nikaj 1 + 6	Match No.
1	2	3	4	5	6	7	8^1	9	10^2	11	12	13																									1
1		4^1	2	5^2	7	8		10^3	9	11	6	12	3	13	14																						2
1			3	4	5	6		8^2	9	10^1	11	7	2	12		13																					3
1		4	11	2	3^1	9	12	13	5	6	8	10^2	7																								4
1		4^3	11	2	3	9		5^1	6	7^2		10	8	13			12	14																			5
			11	13	2	8		12	3	4^1	7^2	10^3	5			14	6		1	9																	6
		2	5		7^1	6		8^2	9	10			3			13	11		1	4	12																7
		4^2	11	2	3	10		5^3	6	7^1		13	8			14	9		1		12																8
		14	10	2	3	8^1			5	13		9	6			4^3	7		1		11^2	12															9
		14	3	4	5	6^3		8^2	9	10		7	2				11^1		1		12	13															10
		4	5	2^1	8			13	7	11	3	9^3				12			1		10^2	6	14														11
	4^3		3				7		10	11	12	8^2	2			14	5		1	6	13	9^1															12
	2^3		4		5^2	12	7		8^1	9	11	6	13				10		1	3	14																13
	3^3	4	2		6^1	7	8		11	10	9^2	13					12		1	5	14																14
		4	2		7	8^2	6		11	10^1	9			12			3		1	5	13																15
1		3		4^2	6	7	5		11^1	10	8	12					9	13		2																	16
1		5	3	6	8	9	7			10^1				13			4	12		2				11^2													17
1		3		2^2	7	8	6		10^1	9		13	4	12						5				11													18
1		2	3		6^3	7	5		9^1	8		13		12		14	11^2			4				10													19
1		3	4			7	6		8			13	5^1			12	9	11^2		2				10													20
		4	5	2^3		8	6		10			7^2		14		9^1	3	13		12				11	1												21
		4^1	5			8	6		9			7	3	12^2		13	10			2				11	1												22
				4		5	7		8^1			6	2			12	9	13	1					10		3	11^2										23
		12		4		5	7		9			6^1	2^2			13	10	14	1					11		3	8^3										24
		2		13		6	8					7	3^2			5^1	10		1					9		4	11^3	12	14								25
		3		2^2		5	7					6				13	4		1					8		9	12	11^1		10							26
		2	3			5	7					6^1					10		1					11		4▮	12	9		8							27
		2	3		12	4	6					5					10		1					11			7^1	9		8							28
		3	2		7	6^3	5					8^2		12			11		1					10^1			14	9		4	13						29
		2	3		4	5^1	7					6^2		14			10		1					11			12	9		8^3	13						30
		2^2	3		5	6						8^1		9			10		1					11		4	7^3	13	14		12						31
		3	4			12											10		1					11		5^1	6^3	8	2	7^2	9	13	14				32
		2	3									12					4		1					10		5	7^2	9	6	8^3	11^1	14		13			33
		3	6			12						5					4		1					7		10	8	11^2	2^1	14	13	9^3					34
		2	6			4^3						5^1					3								1	9	7			10	13	8		14	11^2	12	35
		4	2			8^1											5								1		10	11	7	6	12	9▮	3				36
		2	4			7						9^1					11						13		1	3	6	10^3	5	8^2	14				12		37
		4	2			7											3^2						13		1	5	9^1	11	8^3	6		10			12	14	38
		3	2			7^1	12										11								1	4	8^2	10	5	6		9				13	39
		3	4			7^3	8																6^2		1	5▮	13	11^1	2	10		9			14	12	40
			4				6^2										3						14		1		7	10	2^1	9		8	5	13	12	11^3	41
		3	5			8	7										4								1		9^3	11^1		6		10^2	2	13	12	14	42
		2	3			5	6^1										11								1	4^3	7	10	14	9		8^2	12		13		43
		3	6			5											4								1		8▮	11	2	10		9^1	7^2		12	13	44

FA Cup

Fourth Qualifying	Yate T	(h)	1-1
Replay	Yate T	(a)	0-1

FA Trophy

Third Round	Bromley	(h)	0-1

EASTLEIGH

Ground: The Silverlake Stadium, Ten Acres, Stoneham Lane, Eastleigh, Hampshire SO50 9HT. *Tel:* (02380) 613 361.
Website: eastleighfc.com *Email:* admin@eastleighfc.com *Year Formed:* 1946.
Record Attendance: 5,025 v Bolton W, FA Cup 3rd rd, 9 January 2016. *Nickname:* 'Spitfires'.
Manager: Lee Bradbury. *Colours:* Blue shirts with white trim, blue shorts with white trim, blue socks.

EASTLEIGH – NATIONAL LEAGUE 2021–22 LEAGUE RECORD

Match No.	Date	Venue	Opponents	Result		H/T Score	Lg Pos.	Goalscorers	Attendance
1	Aug 28	H	Wrexham	L	0-2	0-2	19		2572
2	30	A	Bromley	L	0-3	0-1	22		1521
3	Sept 4	H	King's Lynn T	D	3-3	2-0	20	Bird (og) 1, Pritchard 9, House 79	1789
4	11	A	Barnet	D	1-1	0-1	20	House 71	959
5	14	H	Dover Ath	W	4-1	4-0	15	Hill 20, Pritchard 21, House 41, Hare 45	1745
6	18	A	Grimsby T	L	0-2	0-1	18		6051
7	25	H	Woking	W	3-2	1-2	14	Whitehall 30, Whelan 2 (2 pens) 63, 73	2521
8	Oct 2	H	Boreham Wood	D	1-1	1-1	15	Pritchard 31	1789
9	5	A	Southend U	L	0-1	0-0	16		3349
10	9	A	Wealdstone	W	2-1	1-0	13	Barnett 36, House 88	1267
11	23	H	Altrincham	W	2-1	0-1	13	Hollands 52, Whelan 61	2046
12	26	A	Chesterfield	L	0-1	0-1	13		5086
13	30	H	Maidenhead U	W	1-0	1-0	12	Barnett 38	2034
14	Nov 13	A	Yeovil T	L	1-2	0-1	15	Pritchard 68	2494
15	20	H	Notts Co	W	2-0	1-0	14	Barnett 40, Boyce 68	2817
16	23	A	Dagenham & R	W	1-0	0-0	14	Whitehall 66	1306
17	Dec 11	H	Aldershot T	L	0-3	0-0	15		2784
18	14	H	Solihull Moors	D	0-0	0-0	13		2085
19	28	H	Torquay U	W	2-1	0-1	13	Whelan (pen) 53, Barnett 67	2730
20	Jan 2	H	Weymouth	W	3-2	1-0	12	Barnett 40, Maghoma 64, Whitehall 90	2839
21	8	A	FC Halifax T	L	0-4	0-1	13		1822
22	18	A	Stockport Co	L	0-3	0-2	13		4634
23	25	A	Dover Ath	L	0-1	0-0	14		486
24	29	H	Chesterfield	L	0-1	0-0	14		3076
25	Feb 5	A	Maidenhead U	D	2-2	0-1	14	Whitehall 72, Hill 79	1159
26	12	H	Yeovil T	D	0-0	0-0	14		2760
27	15	A	Weymouth	L	0-1	0-0	14		1053
28	19	A	Notts Co	L	0-2	0-2	14		5692
29	22	H	Southend U	D	1-1	1-0	14	Pritchard 9	3062
30	26	A	Boreham Wood	L	0-1	0-1	15		1236
31	Mar 5	H	Wealdstone	W	4-1	1-0	14	Whitehall 10, Hill 52, Broadbent 63, Hollands 65	2615
32	12	A	Altrincham	L	0-4	0-2	17		1614
33	19	A	Solihull Moors	L	3-5	1-3	18	Pitman 44, Hesketh 49, Whitehall 81	1272
34	22	H	Dagenham & R	L	0-1	0-1	19		2250
35	26	H	Stockport Co	L	0-2	0-0	19		3295
36	Apr 2	A	Aldershot T	W	2-0	2-0	17	Camp 22, Barnett 45	1590
37	9	A	Wrexham	L	2-3	1-1	19	Whitehall 2 26, 65	9163
38	15	H	Bromley	L	0-2	0-1	19		2564
39	18	A	Torquay U	D	0-0	0-0	19		3646
40	23	H	Barnet	L	2-3	1-0	19	Smart 15, Whitehall 55	2514
41	30	A	King's Lynn T	D	3-3	0-1	19	Barnett 64, Harper 76, Kelly (pen) 90	968
42	May 2	H	FC Halifax T	L	1-2	0-2	19	Pritchard 49	3068
43	7	A	Woking	W	2-1	0-0	19	Whitehall 65, Smith 90	2492
44	15	H	Grimsby T	D	4-4	0-2	19	Whitehall 54, Smart 56, Hesketh 71, Barnett (pen) 90	3499

Final League Position: 19

GOALSCORERS

League (52): Whitehall 11, Barnett 8 (1 pen), Pritchard 6, House 4, Whelan 4 (3 pens), Hill 3, Hesketh 2, Hollands 2, Smart 2, Boyce 1, Broadbent 1, Camp 1, Hare 1, Harper 1, Kelly 1 (1 pen), Maghoma 1, Pitman 1, Smith 1, own goal 1.
FA Cup (6): Barnet 1, Hesketh 1, Hill 1 (pen), House 1, Maghoma 1, Whelan 1.
FA Trophy (6): Hesketh 3, Boyce 1, Hare 1, Pritchard 1.

McDonnell 42	Hare 24	Low 8	Boyce 42	Maghoma 15 + 2	Kelly 26 + 5	Miley 26 + 1	Whelan 26	Hesketh 24 + 7	House 17	Barnett 22 + 14	Hill 24 + 7	Whitehall 21 + 20	Pritchard 36 + 3	Smart 10 + 16	Harper 29 + 7	Hollands 16 + 6	Broadbent 29 + 1	Bradshaw — + 1	Bragg 3 + 1	Smith 4 + 7	Pitman 8 + 9	De Barr 3 + 1	Camp 15	Silva 7 + 3	Wilson 3 + 1	Simpson 1 + 3	Yang 1 + 1	Flitney 2	*Match No.*
1	2	3	4	5[3]	6	7	8	9[2]	10	11[1]	12	13	14																1
1	2	4[2]	3	5[3]	6	7	9	10[1]	11		8	12	14	13															2
1	2		3	4	5	6	7	8[2]	10		11[1]	12	9	13															3
1	2	4[3]	3		5	7	8[2]	9	11		10[1]	13	6	14	12														4
1	2	4	3		5	8	7	14	10[2]		11[3]	12	9	13	6[1]														5
1	2	4[1]	3		5	8	7	14	10		11[3]	12	9	13	6[2]														6
1	2	4	3	14	5	6	7[1]		11	13	9[2]	10[3]	8		12														7
1	2	4	3		5		7		11	12	9	10[1]	8			6													8
1	2	4	3		5		7	13	11[3]	12	9[1]	10[2]	8	14		6													9
1	2		4	10		12	9		7	6[1]	14	13	5[3]		11	8[2]	3												10
1			4	3	14	7	8	9[1]	11	10[3]		13	6		2	12	5[2]												11
1			4	3	5[1]	6	7	8[3]	11	12	13	10[2]	9	14	2														12
1			4	3	5	7	8	9[3]	11	10[2]	13	14	6[1]		2	12													13
1	2		3		5[3]	6	8	7[2]	11	10	13	14	9[1]		12		4												14
1	2		4	10	14		9		8[2]	6[3]	7[1]	13	5	12	11		3												15
1	2		4	3	12		7			10	9	11[2]	8	13	6[1]		5												16
1	2		4	3[1]			7		10	11	9[3]	14	8[2]	13	6	12	5												17
1	2		4	10			9		7		12	6[1]	5		11	8	3												18
1	2		3	13	5		7	9[2]		10[3]	11[1]	12	8	14		6	4												19
1	2		3	7	5			9■		10[3]	11[1]	12	8	6[2]			4	13	14										20
1	2		4	3	6		8			10[1]		11[3]	9[2]	12	13	7	5			14									21
1	2		4	3■	6		9			12	11		10	7[1]	5[2]	8	13												22
1	2[3]		3		5		7	13		10[2]	6	12	9		14	8[1]	4			11									23
1	2		4	3			7	13		11[2]	10		9		6	8[1]	5			12									24
1	2		3			8	7	12		13	6	10[1]	9		5		4				11[2]								25
1	2		3			8	7	13		14	6	10[3]	9[1]		5		4				11[2]	12							26
1	2		3			8[2]	7	9[1]		10[3]	6	12	14		5		4				13	11							27
1			3		2	6		7			9	12	8[1]		5	13	4				10[2]	11							28
1			3[2]		5	6		7		13	9	10[1]	8		12		4				14	11[3]	2						29
1					2	7				11[1]	6	12	9		5	8	4				10		3						30
1			4		5	7[2]		9		12	10[1]	11[3]	6			8	3				14		2	13					31
1			4		5			9[2]		12	10	11[3]	6[1]		14	8	3				13		2	7					32
1			3			8		9		11[2]		12		6[1]	5					13	10[3]		2	7	4	14			33
1			4			7		9[2]		13		10		12	6	14	5		3		11		2[3]	8[1]					34
1			2		6[3]	7		9		12		10[2]		5	4		3			11[1]	13			8	14				35
1			3			7		9		11[1]		10[3]	8[2]	6	5	13	4			14	12		2						36
1			5			3		9[1]		8		10[2]	7	6	11		4			13			2	12					37
1			3		13	6				11[1]		10	7[3]	5[2]	8		4			12	9		2				14		38
1			3		6					13		11	10[1]	8[2]	5	7	4			12			2	9					39
1			3		5	8		9[2]		13		11	10	7[1]	6		4				12		2						40
1					12					11			9[2]	6	5	7	4		3		10[1]		2	8		13			41
1			3		5	7		10				11	8	12[3]	9		4[2]			6[1]	13		2	14					42
			3					4[3]		10[1]		9[2]		12	7	5				11	13		2	6	8	14		1	43
			4					9[3]		10	14	12		13	6	7			3[1]				2		5	11[2]	8	1	44

FA Cup

Fourth Qualifying	Folkestone Invicta	(h)	3-3
Replay *(aet)*	Folkestone Invicta	(a)	3-2
First Round	Boreham Wood	(a)	0-2

FA Trophy

Third Round	Enfield T	(h)	5-0
Fourth Round	Notts Co	(a)	1-2

FC HALIFAX TOWN

Ground: The Shay Stadium, Halifax HX1 2YT. *Tel:* (01422) 341 222.
Website: fchalifaxtown.com *Email:* tonyallan@fchalifaxtown.com *Year Formed:* 1911 (Reformed 2008).
Record Attendance: 36,855 v Tottenham H, FA Cup 5th rd, 15 February 1953. *Nickname:* 'The Shaymen'.
Manager: Chris Millington. *Colours:* Blue shirts with white trim, blue shorts with white trim, blue socks with white trim.

FC HALIFAX TOWN – NATIONAL LEAGUE 2021–22 LEAGUE RECORD

Match No.	Date	Venue	Opponents	Result		H/T Score	Lg Pos.	Goalscorers	Attendance
1	Aug 21	H	Maidenhead U	L	1-2	1-0	11	Waters [26]	1547
2	28	A	Woking	W	3-2	2-1	9	Debrah [24], Woods [44], Waters [46]	3068
3	30	H	Altrincham	W	2-0	0-0	5	Slew [59], Waters [84]	1941
4	Sept 4	A	Yeovil T	L	0-1	0-1	8		1899
5	11	H	Southend U	W	3-1	1-0	7	Slew [39], Waters [48], Maher [73]	1959
6	14	A	Boreham Wood	D	2-2	1-2	6	Bradbury [22], Waters [79]	503
7	18	H	Stockport Co	W	3-0	1-0	6	Warburton [41], Bradbury [78], Waters [90]	2661
8	25	A	Aldershot T	W	1-0	1-0	5	Waters [27]	1622
9	Oct 2	A	Barnet	D	0-0	0-0	5		1302
10	5	H	Notts Co	W	3-2	0-1	3	Slew [79], Waters [86], Warburton [90]	2023
11	9	H	Weymouth	W	2-0	1-0	3	Slew [33], Spence [83]	2241
12	23	A	Solihull Moors	L	0-1	0-0	4		1594
13	26	H	Dagenham & R	W	1-0	1-0	4	Green [12]	1761
14	30	A	Bromley	D	0-0	0-0	4		2005
15	Nov 20	A	Dover Ath	W	3-1	1-0	5	Waters 2 [9, 88], Green [80]	595
16	23	H	Wrexham	L	1-2	0-0	5	Slew [67]	3344
17	27	A	Torquay U	W	3-2	1-0	3	Slew 2 [30, 46], Waters [50]	2269
18	Dec 11	A	Wealdstone	W	1-0	1-0	5	Warburton (pen) [34]	958
19	14	H	King's Lynn T	W	2-0	0-0	2	Warburton [63], Vale [90]	1604
20	28	A	Chesterfield	D	1-1	1-0	2	Warburton [18]	8106
21	Jan 3	A	Grimsby T	D	1-1	0-0	2	Spence [54]	5027
22	8	H	Eastleigh	W	4-0	1-0	1	Slew 2 [22, 65], Allen [73], Warburton [80]	1822
23	11	H	Grimsby T	W	1-0	0-0	1	Warburton (pen) [69]	2933
24	22	A	Maidenhead U	L	0-1	0-1	2		1221
25	25	H	Boreham Wood	L	0-1	0-1	3		2256
26	29	A	Dagenham & R	W	3-1	2-0	3	Warburton [19], Waters 2 [43, 90]	2460
27	Feb 22	A	Notts Co	D	1-1	1-1	6	Martin [18]	5603
28	26	H	Barnet	W	1-0	1-0	5	Maher [41]	1799
29	Mar 5	A	Weymouth	W	2-0	0-0	4	Bradbury [53], Dearnley [90]	1026
30	12	H	Dover Ath	W	2-1	1-1	4	Waters [40], Warburton [69]	1828
31	15	H	Bromley	W	1-0	0-0	3	Summerfield [64]	1693
32	19	H	Torquay U	W	2-0	0-0	3	Waters [60], McDonagh [71]	2192
33	22	A	Wrexham	L	1-3	0-2	3	Dearnley [88]	8711
34	26	A	King's Lynn T	L	0-2	0-0	4		921
35	Apr 2	H	Wealdstone	W	2-0	0-0	2	Waters 2 [60, 75]	1850
36	5	H	Solihull Moors	D	0-0	0-0	3		1750
37	9	H	Woking	W	2-1	1-0	3	Warburton 2 (1 pen) [10 (p), 62]	1763
38	15	A	Altrincham	D	1-1	1-0	3	Spence [14]	2521
39	18	H	Chesterfield	W	2-0	0-0	3	Slew [77], Warburton [80]	3294
40	23	A	Southend U	L	0-1	0-1	3		5620
41	30	H	Yeovil T	W	1-0	0-0	3	Dearnley [83]	1947
42	May 2	A	Eastleigh	W	2-1	2-0	3	Spence [39], Warburton [43]	3068
43	7	H	Aldershot T	D	1-1	0-0	4	Woods [59]	2662
44	15	A	Stockport Co	L	0-2	0-1	4		10,307

Final League Position: 4

GOALSCORERS

League (62): Waters 17, Warburton 13 (3 pens), Slew 10, Spence 4, Bradbury 3, Dearnley 3, Green 2, Maher 2, Woods 2, Allen 1, Debrah 1, Martin 1, McDonagh 1, Summerfield 1, Vale 1.
FA Cup (8): Waters 2, Newby 1, Slew 1, Spence 1, Vale 1, Warburton 1, Warren 1.
FA Trophy (5): Bradbury 1, Spence 1, Summerfield 1, Vale 1, Waters 1.
National League Play-offs (1): Stenson 1.

Johnson 43	Benn 10	Senior 29 + 4	Maher 40	Bradbury 33	Woods 18 + 15	Summerfield 13 + 11	Warburton 38 + 3	Waters 43 + 1	Slew 32 + 6	Gilmour 20 + 12	Allen 13 + 11	McDonagh 5 + 8	Green 29 + 5	Debrah 23 + 1	Warren 38 + 3	Spence 31 + 6	Vale 6 + 4	Swaby-Neavin 4	Tear — + 2	Newby 2 + 9	Stenson 2 + 5	Scott 1	Martin 4	Thomas 2 + 6	Dearnley 1 + 12	Bird 4 + 1	*Match No.*
1	2	3	4	5	6	7	8^{3}	9	10^{1}	11^{2}	12	13	14														1
1	6^{1}	5	4	3	7	8^{3}	10	9	11^{2}		13		12	2	14												2
1	2	3	4	5	6^{3}	7	8^{1}	9	10^{2}	11	12		13			14											3
1	5		4	3	7	8^{2}	9	10^{3}	11	13	14		12	2	6^{1}												4
1	2^{2}		5	3	6		8	9	10^{3}	11^{1}	13		7	4	12		14										5
1			5	4	6^{3}		9	10	11^{1}	8^{2}	13		7		3	14	12	2									6
1		3	5	4	13		8	10	9^{2}	11^{1}	12		7		2	6^{3}			14								7
1		3	5	4	12		9	10	11^{3}	8^{2}	13		7		2	6^{1}	14										8
1		3	5	4				10	11^{3}	8^{1}	9^{2}	14	7		2	6			13	12							9
1		3	5	4■			13	10	11^{3}	8^{1}	9^{2}	14	7		2	6				12							10
1		3	4		14		9^{3}	10^{1}	11	7^{2}	13		5	8	2	6				12							11
1		3	5	4	14		8^{1}	9	13		11^{3}		7		2	6	10^{2}			12							12
1		2	11	3			6^{1}	7	13	14	4^{3}		5		9	8	10^{2}			12							13
1		3	5	4			8^{3}	9	12	14	11^{2}		7		2	6	10^{1}			13							14
1		5	4			13	8^{2}	9	10	14			7	3	2	6^{3}	11^{1}			12							15
1		3	5				8	9	10^{1}	13			7	4	2	6	11^{2}			12							16
1		3	5		14	12	8^{2}	9	10				7	4	2	6^{3}	11^{1}			13							17
1		3	4	5	13	14	8^{3}	9	10^{1}	12			6		2	7^{2}				11							18
1		3	5	4	14	12	8	9^{1}	10				7		2	6^{3}	13			11^{2}							19
1		3	5	4	13	12	9^{2}	11	10	8			7		2	6^{1}											20
1	3		5	4	12		8^{1}	10	9^{2}	11			7		2	6					13						21
1	3^{1}	13	5	4			8	9	10		12		7		2	6					11^{2}						22
1	2^{2}	13	11	3		12	6	7	10		4^{1}		5		9	8											23
	2	3	11	4	10		7	8		13	5		6^{2}	12	9^{1}							1					24
1	2^{2}	3	11^{3}	5	10	13	7	8		9^{1}	14			4	12								6				25
1		3		4	6^{2}	7	8^{1}	9		13	11	12		5	2								10^{3}	14			26
1		5■	4^{1}	3	8	7		11^{2}		12	6	14		2		9							10^{3}	13			27
1			4	3	7	6		9^{3}	12		11^{1}	13		5	2	8							10^{2}	14			28
1			5	3	6^{3}	7	13	9	10^{1}		11^{2}			4	2	8								14	12		29
1		12	4	3	5^{2}	6	13	8	9^{3}		10			11^{1}	2	7									14		30
1		2	4	3	6^{3}	7	8	11	10^{2}		9^{1}				5	13								12	14		31
1		2	5	4	6	7^{2}	8	10	11^{1}			13			3	12								9^{3}	14		32
1		2	11	3	10		4	5^{1}	9			12			8	7								6^{2}	13		33
1		3^{1}	5	4	6		8	10^{3}	11^{2}	12		9	14		2	7									13		34
1			4	5	14	13	8	12		9		10	6^{1}	3	2	7^{2}									11^{3}		35
1			4	5	13	12	8^{2}	11	14	9		10	6^{1}	3	2	7^{3}											36
1			11		13■	12	4	5		9		6^{2}	3^{1}	2	10	7^{3}		8								14	37
1			4			12	9	10	13	7^{1}		11^{2}	5^{3}	8	2	6		3							14		38
1		13	4	3		6	9^{1}	10^{3}	11	7^{2}			5	8	2	12									14		39
1		3	4^{3}			7	8^{2}	9	10	11^{1}			6	5	2	13					12				14		40
1		2			13		8	9	10^{3}	11^{1}			6^{2}	4	3	7					12				14	5	41
1		2			13		8^{2}	9^{3}	10	12			6	4	3	7					11^{1}				14	5	42
1					12		11	10	8^{1}	7^{3}			5^{2}	9	2	6		3			14				13	4	43
1		3	5		6^{2}		9	11	10	12				8	2	7^{1}					13			14		4^{3}	44

FA Cup

Fourth Qualifying	Pontefract Collieries	(a)	0-0
Replay	Pontefract Collieries	(h)	1-0
First Round	Maidenhead U	(h)	7-4
Second Round	Kidderminster H	(a)	0-2

National League Play-offs

Quarter-Final	Chesterfield	(h)	1-2

FA Trophy

Third Round	Bradford (Park Avenue)	(a)	3-3
(FC Halifax T won 5-3 on penalties)			
Fourth Round	Alfreton T	(a)	1-1
(FC Halifax T won 3-2 on penalties)			
Fifth Round	Notts Co	(h)	1-2

GRIMSBY TOWN

Ground: Blundell Park, Cleethorpes, North East Lincolnshire DN35 7PY. *Tel:* (01472) 605 050.
Website: www.gtfc.co.uk *Email:* enquiries@gtfc.co.uk *Year Formed:* 1878.
Record Attendance: 31,651 v Wolverhampton W, FA Cup 5th rd, 20 February 1937. *Nickname:* 'The Mariners'.
Manager: Paul Hurst. *Colours:* Black and white striped shirts with white sleeves and red trim, black shorts with red and white trim, red socks with black and white trim.

GRIMSBY TOWN – NATIONAL LEAGUE 2021–22 LEAGUE RECORD

Match No.	Date	Venue	Opponents	Result		H/T Score	Lg Pos.	Goalscorers	Attendance
1	Aug 28	H	Weymouth	W	1-0	0-0	8	McAtee [74]	5034
2	31	A	Stockport Co	D	0-0	0-0	9		6452
3	Sept 4	H	Barnet	W	4-3	1-2	5	McAtee 2 (2 pens) [5, 65], Taylor [75], Hunt [90]	5030
4	11	A	Torquay U	W	3-1	2-1	4	Efete [24], Coke [33], Clifton [90]	2364
5	14	H	Wrexham	W	3-1	2-1	4	Taylor [27], Waterfall [34], Wright [90]	6663
6	18	H	Eastleigh	W	2-0	1-0	3	Efete [45], Fox [74]	6051
7	25	A	Maidenhead U	D	1-1	0-0	3	Sousa [73]	1976
8	28	A	Bromley	L	1-3	1-0	3	McAtee [43]	1927
9	Oct 2	H	Dover Ath	W	6-0	5-0	1	Waterfall 2 [26, 70], McAtee [31], Taylor 2 (1 pen) [33 (p), 45], Bapaga [45]	5913
10	5	A	Altrincham	W	3-2	1-0	1	Bapaga [27], Taylor [48], Clifton [55]	2882
11	9	A	Woking	W	1-0	0-0	1	Clifton [87]	4478
12	23	H	Yeovil T	W	2-0	1-0	1	John-Lewis (pen) [20], McAtee [90]	6470
13	26	A	Wealdstone	L	0-1	0-1	1		1892
14	30	H	Notts Co	L	0-1	0-0	2		7213
15	Nov 13	A	Aldershot T	L	1-2	1-1	3	Clifton [17]	2343
16	19	H	Southend U	W	1-0	1-0	2	Taylor [3]	5836
17	23	A	Solihull Moors	L	0-2	0-1	3		1772
18	Dec 4	A	Dagenham & R	L	2-3	1-1	6	McAtee [45], Bell [68]	1734
19	11	H	Chesterfield	L	0-1	0-0	8		6504
20	Jan 3	H	FC Halifax T	D	1-1	0-0	10	Maguire-Drew [90]	5027
21	11	A	FC Halifax T	L	0-1	0-0	10		2933
22	15	H	Altrincham	W	2-0	0-0	9	McAtee [47], Maguire-Drew [83]	4573
23	22	H	Bromley	L	1-2	1-1	10	Maguire-Drew [23]	5854
24	25	A	Wrexham	L	0-1	0-1	10		8434
25	29	H	Wealdstone	W	2-1	1-0	10	Pearson [34], Efete [51]	4747
26	Feb 5	A	Notts Co	W	2-1	0-1	10	Taylor [76], Waterfall [90]	9305
27	8	H	King's Lynn T	D	0-0	0-0	9		4631
28	12	H	Aldershot T	W	3-1	2-0	8	Sousa [10], McAtee 2 [39, 60]	5177
29	26	A	Dover Ath	W	3-1	2-1	9	Pearson [27], Abrahams [36], McAtee [72]	831
30	Mar 5	H	Woking	W	1-0	0-0	8	Dieseruvwe [90]	5423
31	8	A	Southend U	L	0-1	0-0	8		7205
32	12	A	Yeovil T	W	2-0	1-0	7	Scannell [9], Dieseruvwe [57]	2422
33	19	A	Boreham Wood	D	0-0	0-0	8		1670
34	22	H	Solihull Moors	L	1-2	1-0	8	Clifton [43]	4498
35	26	H	Dagenham & R	W	2-1	2-0	7	Maguire-Drew [30], Waterfall [45]	4804
36	Apr 2	A	Chesterfield	W	4-1	2-1	7	McAtee [27], Holohan [31], Clifton [50], Taylor [78]	7819
37	9	A	Weymouth	D	0-0	0-0	7		1228
38	15	H	Stockport Co	W	2-1	0-1	7	McAtee [64], Holohan [77]	7818
39	18	A	King's Lynn T	W	1-0	1-0	6	Abrahams [45]	3111
40	23	H	Torquay U	W	2-1	1-1	6	Clifton [39], Abrahams (pen) [90]	5826
41	30	A	Barnet	D	2-2	0-1	6	Waterfall [89], Smith [81]	2438
42	May 7	H	Maidenhead U	L	1-3	0-2	6	Abrahams (pen) [76]	6383
43	10	H	Boreham Wood	W	1-0	1-0	6	McAtee [19]	6010
44	15	A	Eastleigh	D	4-4	2-0	6	Maguire-Drew [31], Dieseruvwe 3 (1 pen) [44 (p), 60, 86]	3499

Final League Position: 6

GOALSCORERS

League (68): McAtee 14 (2 pens), Taylor 8 (1 pen), Clifton 7, Waterfall 6, Dieseruvwe 5 (1 pen), Maguire-Drew 5, Abrahams 4 (2 pens), Efete 3, Bapaga 2, Holohan 2, Pearson 2, Sousa 2, Bell 1, Coke 1, Fox 1, Hunt 1, John-Lewis 1 (1 pen), Scannell 1, Smith 1, Wright 1.
FA Cup (5): Revan 2, Bapaga 1, John-Lewis 1 (pen), Longe-King 1.
FA Trophy (0).
National League Play-offs (9): Dieseruvwe 2, McAtee 2, Waterfall 2, Maguire-Drew 1, Holohan 1, Taylor 1.

McKeown 17	Efete 28	Longe-King 4 + 1	Pearson 19 + 7	Crookes 24	Fox 22 + 10	Hunt 16 + 2	Clifton 38 + 2	Sousa 27 + 6	McAtee 33 + 3	Taylor 34 + 3	John-Lewis 3 + 12	Wright 2 + 11	Waterfall 41 + 1	Coke 20 + 3	Revan 2 + 4	Bapaga 7 + 3	Essel — + 2	Towler 13	Sears 6	Khouri 1 + 1 / Tomlinson — + 1	Bell 2 + 2	Crocombe 26	Maguire-Drew 12 + 4	Scannell 6 + 6	Grant — + 1	Smith 15 + 2	Amos 18	Burgess 7 + 7	Abrahams 6 + 12	Raikhy 5 + 2	Dieseruvwe 3 + 10	Jones C 3	Holohan 9	Cropper 7 + 1	Jones J 6	Battersby 1	Bramwell 1	*Match No.*
1	2	3	4	5	6	7^{2}	8	9^{3}	10	11^{1}	12	13	14																									1
1	2	3^{1}	12	5	14	8	7		10	11^{3}	13		4	6	9^{2}																							2
1	2		4	5	14	6^{3}	13	8	10	11			3	7^{2}		9^{1}	12																					3
1	2			5	12	8^{3}	7	9^{1}	10^{2}	11		13	3	6			14	4																				4
1	2		13	5	14	8^{1}	7	9^{3}	10^{2}	11		12	3	6				4																				5
1	2			5	6	8^{3}	7	9^{1}	12	11^{2}	13		3		14	10		4																				6
1	2		13	5	12	7^{1}	8	9^{3}	10	11	14		4	6^{2}				3																				7
1	2■			5	6		8	9^{1}	10	12	13		3	7		11^{2}		4																				8
1				5	6^{1}	7	8	13	10^{2}	11^{3}	12		3	14		9		4	2																			9
1				5	6	7	8	12	10^{2}	11^{1}	13		4			9■		3	2																			10
1			14	5	6	7^{3}	8	9	10^{2}	11^{1}	12	13	3					4	2																			11
1				5	6	8^{1}	7^{3}	13	10		11		3	12	14	9^{2}		4	2																			12
1				5	7	13		8	10^{1}		11	12	3	6^{2}		9		4	2																			13
1				5	6	9	8	10		13	11^{3}		3	7^{2}	12	14		4	2^{1}																			14
1	2				10^{1}	9	6	8		11	12		3		5	13		4		7^{2}																		15
1	2		3	5	9	7^{2}	8	10^{1}	12	11			4	6	13																							16
1	2		3	5	8	7	6	9^{2}	12	11			4			13					10^{1}																	17
	2	5			9	7	6		8■	11^{2}	13		4					3			12	1	10^{1}															18
	2	5^{2}	3	6	9		8			11^{1}	12		4	7							10^{3}	1	13	14														19
	2		3	5	8^{1}	12	9	10^{2}		11		13	4	7^{3}							14	1	6															20
	2^{3}	12	5	3	10		11	8^{1}	9	6		13	4									1	7^{2}		14													21
			4		6			8^{1}	10^{2}	11		12	2	7						14		1	9^{3}			3	5	13										22
			3		8^{1}		12	13	9	11		14	4	7								1	6^{2}			2	5		10^{3}									23
			3	5	6^{2}			8^{3}	9	11	14		4	7^{1}								1				2		13	10	12								24
	2		3		13		8	10	9	11^{2}			4	7								1					5		12	6^{1}								25
	2		3		12^{3}		8	10	9^{1}	11		13	4	7^{2}								1					5		14	6								26
	2		3				8	9	10	11^{2}			4	7^{3}								1		13			5	14	12	6^{1}								27
	2		3				8	10^{2}	9	11^{3}			4^{1}									1		12		14	5	7	13	6								28
	2		3				7	9	11				4	12								1				14	5^{2}	8	10^{1}	6^{3}	13							29
	2		3	5			7	9^{1}	11				4									1						8	10		12	6						30
	2		3	5			7	9^{2}	11				4	8^{1}								1						13	10		12	6						31
	2						8	12	11	13			4									1		9^{3}		3	5	7	14		10^{1}	6^{2}						32
	2						8	9^{1}	11	10^{2}			4	6								1	13			3	5	7			12							33
	2^{1}		12				9	13	11	10			4									1	6^{3}			3	5	7^{2}	14				8					34
							8		11^{1}	10^{2}			4									1	6^{3}	9		3	5	13	14		12		7	2				35
					13		9		11^{3}	10^{2}			4									1	7^{1}	12		3	5				14		8	2	6			36
							8		11	10^{1}			4									1	6^{2}	12		3	5		14		13		7	2^{3}	9			37
	2				13		8^{1}		11^{3}	10^{2}			4									1	12	6		3	5				14		7		9			38
					7		8		11^{1}			6^{3}	4									1	9^{2}	13		3	5	14	12		10			2				39
	2		14				8			11^{3}		12	4									1	10^{1}	7		3	5		13				9		6^{2}			40
	2^{1}			5	14		9	7		10			4									1		6		3			13				11^{2}	12	8^{3}			41
			13		6		8			11^{1}			4■									1	12	7^{3}		3	5		10		14		9	2^{2}				42
			4		6		8	7	10^{1}	11^{2}												1				3	5	13			12		9	2				43
			3	5								9^{1}		8^{2}						14			10^{3}					7	13	12	11			2	6	1	4	44

FA Cup

Fourth Qualifying	Bromsgrove Sporting	(a)	5-0
First Round	Kidderminster H	(a)	0-1

National League Play-offs

Quarter-Final	Notts Co	(a)	2-1
Semi-Final	Wrexham	(a)	5-4
Final	Solihull Moors (London Stadium)		2-1

FA Trophy

Third Round	Stockport Co	(a)	0-4

KING'S LYNN TOWN

Ground: The Walks Stadium, Tennyson Road, King's Lynn PE30 5PB. *Tel:* (01553) 760 060.
Website: www.kltown.co.uk *Email:* office@kltown.co.uk *Year Formed:* 1881 (reformed 2010).
Record Attendance: 12,937 v Exeter C, FA Cup First Round, 24 November 1951.
Nickname: 'The Linnets'. *Manager:* Tommy Widdrington.
Colours: Blue shirts with yellow trim, yellow shorts with blue trim, blue socks.

KING'S LYNN TOWN – NATIONAL LEAGUE 2021–22 LEAGUE RECORD

Match No.	Date	Venue	Opponents	Result		H/T Score	Lg Pos.	Goalscorers	Attendance
1	Aug 21	H	Southend U	L	0-1	0-1	13		2683
2	28	A	Yeovil T	W	2-1	0-1	11	Coleman [71], Sundire [85]	2024
3	30	H	Chesterfield	L	0-2	0-1	16		1806
4	Sept 4	A	Eastleigh	D	3-3	0-2	16	Clunan [49], Coleman [68], McGavin [85]	1789
5	11	H	Dagenham & R	L	1-2	0-0	18	Reynolds (og) [90]	859
6	25	H	Wealdstone	L	0-1	0-1	21		885
7	28	A	Altrincham	L	1-4	0-1	22	Morias [87]	1009
8	Oct 2	A	Maidenhead U	W	3-2	0-1	19	Linton [46], Barrows [50], McGavin [90]	1039
9	5	H	Barnet	D	1-1	1-1	19	Clunan [22]	1007
10	9	H	Solihull Moors	L	0-1	0-0	19		1009
11	23	A	Torquay U	L	0-2	0-1	20		2506
12	26	H	Boreham Wood	L	0-1	0-1	20		1160
13	30	A	Weymouth	L	0-1	0-0	20		1056
14	Nov 13	H	Wrexham	L	2-6	1-1	22	Clunan [12], Linton [86]	1070
15	20	A	Bromley	L	2-3	1-1	22	Davis [6], Barrows [51]	1910
16	23	A	Stockport Co	L	0-5	0-2	22		4568
17	27	H	Aldershot T	L	0-1	0-0	22		785
18	Dec 11	H	Dover Ath	W	2-1	1-1	22	Barrett 2 [20, 49]	591
19	14	A	FC Halifax T	L	0-2	0-0	22		1604
20	Jan 1	A	Chesterfield	L	0-1	0-0	22		6328
21	11	H	Notts Co	L	2-4	1-0	22	Omotayo [9], Clunan [82]	1505
22	21	A	Southend U	L	1-2	1-0	22	Phipps [27]	6122
23	29	A	Boreham Wood	L	1-3	1-1	22	Linton [12]	907
24	Feb 5	H	Weymouth	W	3-0	1-0	22	Linton (pen) [25], Clunan [70], Barrett [74]	847
25	8	A	Grimsby T	D	0-0	0-0	22		4631
26	12	H	Altrincham	L	0-1	0-1	22		905
27	22	A	Barnet	D	0-0	0-0	22		1137
28	26	H	Maidenhead U	L	1-4	1-1	22	Omotayo [15]	863
29	Mar 1	A	Wrexham	L	0-2	0-2	22		8178
30	5	A	Solihull Moors	D	2-2	1-0	22	Linton [10], Fernandez [52]	1533
31	8	H	Woking	D	0-0	0-0	22		713
32	12	H	Torquay U	L	2-3	1-2	22	Linton [45], McGavin [57]	870
33	19	A	Aldershot T	W	3-0	1-0	22	Linton 2 [20, 56], Omotayo [90]	1660
34	22	H	Stockport Co	L	0-3	0-2	22		914
35	26	H	FC Halifax T	W	2-0	0-0	21	Barrett [53], Omotayo [90]	921
36	Apr 2	A	Dover Ath	D	1-1	0-1	21	Barrett [66]	511
37	5	H	Bromley	W	1-0	0-0	21	Widdrington [59]	857
38	9	H	Yeovil T	D	2-2	2-1	21	Clunan [38], Omotayo [45]	1148
39	15	A	Notts Co	L	1-4	1-2	21	Omotayo [11]	6722
40	18	H	Grimsby T	L	0-1	0-1	21		3111
41	23	A	Dagenham & R	D	1-1	1-0	21	Coulson [12]	1457
42	30	H	Eastleigh	D	3-3	1-0	21	Omotayo 2 [40, 90], Barrows [89]	968
43	May 2	A	Woking	W	3-0	1-0	21	Omotayo [45], Denton [85], Charles [90]	2484
44	7	A	Wealdstone	L	1-2	1-0	21	Omotayo [36]	1324

Final League Position: 21

GOALSCORERS

League (47): Omotayo 10, Linton 8 (1 pen), Clunan 6, Barrett 5, Barrows 3, McGavin 3, Coleman 2, Charles 1, Coulson 1, Davis 1, Denton 1, Fernandez 1, Morias 1, Phipps 1, Sundire 1, Widdrington 1, own goal 1.
FA Cup (2): McGavin 1, Omotayo 1.
FA Trophy (3): Barrett 3 (1 pen).

Jones P 44	Fernandez 14 + 8	Denton 26 + 1	Callan-McFadden 14	Bird 12 + 1	Clunan 37 + 5	Coleman 20	Omotayo 36 + 2	Morias 6 + 1	Barrows 35 + 4	Rowley 9	Linton 20 + 8	Gyasi 3 + 9	Sundire 18 + 15	McGavin 25 + 11	Bowry 19 + 2	Gascoigne — + 1	Walker 3 + 8	Jones A 29 + 4	Taylor — + 1	Davis 3 + 1	Barrett 21 + 8	Ionton 2 + 1	Charles 1 + 13	Rasberry — + 1	Widdrington 15 + 2	Scott 18 + 2	Kurran-Browne — + 8	Phipps 8	Coulson 21	Hargreaves 17 + 2	Hickman 8 + 2	Match No.
1	2^3	3	4	5	6^1	7	8	9▪	10	11^2	12	13	14																			1
1	3^1	2	4	5	7^3	8^2	9		6	11	10	12	13	14																		2
1	12	2	3	4	6	7	8		11			9^1	10^3	13	5^2	14																3
1	14	2	3	4^1	12	6	7^3		10	11	8		9	13	5^2																	4
1	2	3		4	13	6		7	9	11	12		14	8^2	5^3		10^1															5
1		2	3		5	6^3		7	9^2	11	12		14	8	4		10^1	13														6
1		2	3		6			11	12	10	13	7	14	8^3	4		9^1	5^2														7
1	2		3		5^1	6	7	8^2	10	11	12			13	4			9														8
1	2		3		5^2	6	7		10	11^3	8^1	13		12	4		14	9														9
1	2		3		7	8	10		6^2	9^3	11^1	14		13	4			5	12													10
1	2	3	4		5	6	7		11		8^2	12	13	9				10^1														11
1	2	3	4		6	7	8	12	13		9^3			14	5^2			10^1		11												12
1	13	2^1	3		5	6	7	8^3	12			14▪	10^2		4			9		11												13
1			2^2	3^1	5	6	7		10		8		14	12	4			9		13	11^3											14
1	2			3	8^3	9	11		7^1		14		6		4			5		10^2	13	12										15
1	2			3	7	8^2	10				11^3	13	6	12	4			5			14	9^1										16
1			3	14	4		5				7^3	6	10^1	8	2			9			12	11^2	13									17
1				2	6	7	9		13		10^1	14	5^2	8	3			4			11^3		12									18
1				9	8	11	6				7^2	14	10^3	4	2			3			5^1		12	13								19
1	2^3					4	5		10				8^1	13	3			7			9		12		6^2	11	14					20
1				3	6	7	10		5		12				2^1			4			11^3		14		8^2	9	13					21
1		13^3			4	5	11		2				12	7^2			14	3			10				6	8^1		9				22
1	2			3	5						10		14	7^3			12	4			13		11^2		6^1	8		9				23
1					9^1				2		10^3		13	7			14	3			11				8^2	6		5	4	12		24
1		3^2			8				6		11^3			13				2			14				9^1	7		10	5	4	12	25
1					9		12		2		10^3			7^2				3			11		14		8^1	6		4	5	13		26
1					12		11		3					9^2				13			10				8	6		7	4	5	2^1	27
1					12		11		5				13	8^1							10^2		14		7^3	3		4	6	9	2	28
1	14	2^2					11		6		12		5					4			13					10		9^1	8	7	3^3	29
1	12	2			13		14		8^3		4		6		3			5			7^1					9^2			11	10		30
1	2	3			8		9				10^1		12	7^2							11		13						4	5	6	31
1					7		10		2		9^1		13	8^2				3			11		14				12		4	5	6^3	32
1		2			7		9		4		10		14	8^1				12			11^2					13			6	5	3^3	33
1	13	5			7		10^2		2		9^1		11					4▪			12					6^3	14		3	8		34
1		4			5		10		2				7	8							11^1					6	12		3	9		35
1		5			9		11		3				2	8^2							10				13	6^1	12		4	7		36
1	13	4			6		9		2				10	8							11^2				5^1	12			3	7		37
1		4			6		9		2				10▪	8				13			11^1				5^2		12		3	7		38
1		2			8		11		5					10	12		13	4^2							9^1		14		7	6	3^3	39
1	5^2	8			7		10		3				6^1	4			12				11		13		9				2			40
1	12	2			3		5		9				8					7					13		6^2	10^1			11		4	41
1		4			8		11		3				12	5			14	7^1			13				10^3	6			2	9^2		42
1		4			9		11		3					7^2	12			5			10^1		14			8^3			2	6	13	43
1		3			9^3		11		4					7			13	2			10^1		12		14	8^2			5	6		44

FA Cup

Fourth Qualifying	Peterborough Sports	(h)	2-1
First Round	Walsall	(h)	0-1

FA Trophy

Third Round	Nantwich T	(h)	2-1
Fourth Round	Tonbridge Angels	(a)	1-1

(Tonbridge Angels won 4-3 on penalties)

MAIDENHEAD UNITED

Ground: York Road, Maidenhead, Berkshire SL6 1SF. *Tel:* (01628) 636 314.
Website: pitchero.com/clubs/maidenheadunited *Email:* social@maidenheadunitedfc.org *Year Formed:* 1870.
Record Attendance: 7,920 v Southall, FA Amateur Cup quarter-final, 7 March 1936. *Nickname:* 'The Magpies'.
Manager: Alan Devonshire. *Colours:* Black and white striped shirts with white sleeves and red trim, black shorts with white trim, white socks.

MAIDENHEAD UNITED – NATIONAL LEAGUE 2021–22 LEAGUE RECORD

Match No.	Date	Venue	Opponents	Result		H/T Score	Lg Pos.	Goalscorers	Attendance
1	Aug 21	A	FC Halifax T	W	2-1	0-1	6	Barratt [61], Ferdinand [90]	1547
2	28	H	Dover Ath	W	2-0	2-0	3	Kelly [14], Barratt [19]	1060
3	30	A	Weymouth	L	1-3	0-2	6	Kelly [61]	849
4	Sept 4	H	Torquay U	L	3-4	0-4	11	Clerima [46], Massey [54], Acquah [66]	1495
5	14	H	Stockport Co	L	0-2	0-1	14		1082
6	18	A	Notts Co	L	0-1	0-0	17		5748
7	25	H	Grimsby T	D	1-1	0-0	17	Ferdinand [83]	1976
8	Oct 2	H	King's Lynn T	L	2-3	1-0	18	Ferdinand [4], Barratt (pen) [90]	1039
9	5	A	Yeovil T	D	0-0	0-0	17		2031
10	9	A	Altrincham	L	0-2	0-0	18		2091
11	23	H	Woking	W	3-2	1-1	16	Barratt 2 [38, 90], Kelly [76]	1165
12	26	H	Wrexham	W	3-2	2-1	16	Ferdinand [17], Mingi [23], Kelly [77]	1692
13	30	A	Eastleigh	L	0-1	0-1	18		2034
14	Nov 13	H	Dagenham & R	L	1-4	0-2	19	Kelly [58]	1331
15	20	A	Boreham Wood	L	0-4	0-2	19		601
16	Dec 4	A	Barnet	L	0-3	0-1	21		906
17	7	A	Southend U	D	1-1	0-1	20	Ferdinand [72]	4928
18	11	H	Solihull Moors	L	0-4	0-3	21		1006
19	28	H	Bromley	W	1-0	0-0	19	Blissett [68]	1303
20	Jan 8	A	Aldershot T	D	1-1	1-0	20	Kelly [45]	1714
21	18	H	Chesterfield	W	3-2	2-1	20	Kelly 2 [7, 80], Sparkes [20]	1232
22	22	H	FC Halifax T	W	1-0	1-0	19	Kelly [29]	1221
23	25	A	Stockport Co	L	0-3	0-0	20		5352
24	29	A	Wrexham	D	1-1	0-1	19	McCoulsky [90]	8759
25	Feb 5	H	Eastleigh	D	2-2	1-0	19	Adams [42], Smith [87]	1159
26	19	H	Boreham Wood	W	2-0	1-0	20	Kelly [32], Blissett [84]	2324
27	22	H	Yeovil T	D	1-1	1-1	19	Ferdinand [44]	1153
28	26	A	King's Lynn T	W	4-1	1-1	14	Sparkes [18], Kelly 2 [53, 56], Upward [75]	863
29	Mar 1	A	Dagenham & R	L	0-3	0-3	15		1057
30	5	H	Altrincham	D	0-0	0-0	16		1113
31	8	H	Wealdstone	L	0-2	0-0	18		1029
32	12	A	Woking	L	0-1	0-0	19		2188
33	19	A	Chesterfield	L	0-1	0-0	19		5518
34	22	H	Southend U	W	2-1	0-0	18	De Havilland [72], Upward [82]	1624
35	26	H	Barnet	L	1-2	0-0	18	McCoulsky [89]	1194
36	Apr 2	A	Solihull Moors	L	1-3	0-2	19	Kelly [52]	1458
37	5	A	Wealdstone	D	0-0	0-0	19		1222
38	9	A	Dover Ath	W	1-0	0-0	16	Kelly [90]	475
39	15	H	Weymouth	W	2-0	0-0	16	Donnellan [55], Kelly [90]	2056
40	18	A	Bromley	D	0-0	0-0	17		1549
41	30	A	Torquay U	D	1-1	0-0	16	Barratt [55]	2148
42	May 2	H	Aldershot T	D	2-2	2-1	16	Sparkes [26], Acquah [34]	1676
43	7	A	Grimsby T	W	3-1	2-0	16	Waterfall (og) [25], Barratt (pen) [27], Upward [68]	6383
44	15	H	Notts Co	L	0-1	0-0	17		2074

Final League Position: 17

GOALSCORERS

League (48): Kelly 15, Barratt 7 (2 pens), Ferdinand 6, Sparkes 3, Upward 3, Acquah 2, Blissett 2, McCoulsky 2, Adams 1, Clerima 1, De Havilland 1, Donnellan 1, Massey 1, Mingi 1, Smith 1, own goal 1.
FA Cup (7): Acquah 2, Kelly 2, Barratt 1, Blissett 1, Ferdinand 1.
FA Trophy (0).

Holden 8	Massey 41	Wells 17 + 5	Clerima 29 + 2	Senga-Ngoyi 2 + 2	Sheckelford 25 + 2	De Havilland 27	Adams 30 + 6	Barratt 17 + 4	Kelly 34 + 5	Blissett 23 + 8	Ferdinand 35 + 3	Acquah 21 + 10	Smith 10 + 21	Asonganyi 1 + 7	Parry 11 + 1	Upward 26 + 6	Beckwith 27 + 3	Lovett 10	Donnellan 23 + 5	Mingi Jay 7 + 1	Sparkes 14 + 8	Burley 2 + 1	Sendles-White 3	Gyollai 16	Smile 2 + 6	McCoulsky 6 + 13	Palmer 2	Ashmore 8	Wakely 6 + 1	Keetch 1 + 1	Match No.
1	2	3	4	5[1]	6	7	8	9	10[2]	11[3]	12	13	14																		1
1	2	3	4	8	5[1]	6	7	9[2]	10[3]	11	13		14	12																	2
1		2[1]	4		5	6	7[3]		10		9	11	14	8[2]	3	12	13														3
1	2	3	4		5	6	7[2]		9[1]	11	8	10	12	13																	4
1■	2		4■	14	5		6	13	10[2]	11[3]	7	9[1]			3	12	8														5
	2				3	4	5[3]	8	10[1]	11[2]	6	13	14	12		7	9	1													6
	2					3	4[1]	7	11[3]	13	5	10[2]	12	14		6	8	1	9												7
	2			13		3[1]	4	7	11[2]	14	5	10			12	6[3]	8	1	9												8
	2	3	5					9[1]	12	11[2]	7	13	10[3]		4	8	14	1		6■											9
	2	3	5				9[2]	8	13	11[3]	7	14	10[1]		4	6	12	1													10
	2		4					8	10	11[2]	6	14	12		3	7	9[3]	1		5[1]	13										11
	2				3[1]	4	13		10[2]		6	11	7			8	9	1	12	5[3]	14										12
	10					2	13	11	12	4	5		7[3]			8[2]	6	1	3	9[1]	14										13
	10	2	4					11	9		5	7		12	3			1		8[1]		6									14
1	4	5	3				14		11	10	7		9[2]						13	8[3]	12	6[1]	2								15
	3	5	2						11[1]	10	6	13	12			9		1		7[2]	8		4								16
1	3	5	2				6		11	13	7	10[2]	8[1]		4	9					12										17
1	3		2[2]				6		11		8	10[1]	9[3]	12		14	7		5			13	4								18
	4	14	12			3	5		11[1]	10	7[2]			13		9[3]	2		6		8			1							19
	4		2		14	3	7		11[1]	10[3]		12				9	6		5[2]	13	8			1							20
	4	12	2		5	3	8		11			10[3]	14			13	7		6[1]		9[2]			1							21
	5	7[1]	3		6	4	8		11[2]			10	12			9	2							1	13						22
	6	12	3		5	2	9[2]		11[3]			10	7[1]				4		8					1	14	13					23
	2		5		3[1]	4	8	13	10			11[2]				7	6		14					1	9[3]	12					24
	5				4	2	9	8[2]	11	10[3]		12	13			7[1]			3		6			1		14					25
	11		3		7	2	10[3]		9[2]	4	12					8[1]	6		14		5			1		13					26
	6		3		5	2			11	10[2]	7		12				9		4		8[1]			1		13					27
		14	3			2			11[3]		6	9			4	10	8		5[1]		7[2]			1	13	12					28
	5				4	2	9		11	10[1]	6		12			14	8		3[2]		7[3]			1		13					29
	10				7	2	11[3]		9	3[2]	4[1]		13			8	6		14		5			1		12					30
	5				4				11[1]	10[3]	6	13	12		2	9	8		3		7[2]					14	1				31
	11		3		7				10		5[2]	8[1]			2	9	6		4		12					13		1			32
	11	12	3		7		14				5	8	9[1]		2		6[2]		4[3]		13					10		1			33
	10	2			5	3	11		13	14	4	7[3]	6[2]			8									12	9[1]		1			34
		3	12		7	4	10[2]		13	5[3]	6		14			8									11[1]	9	1		2		35
	11		3		8	2	14	12	10[2]		5					9[1]	7		4		6[3]					13		1			36
	5		3			2	9	8[1]	11	10	6		12				7		4									1			37
	9		3[2]		12	2	11	10	8		5	7[3]					6		4[1]						14	13		1			38
	9				6	2	11	10[3]	8	13	4						5		3[2]						12	7[1]		1	14		39
	5				4		9		11[2]	10[3]	6	13	14			8	7		3[1]							12		1	2		40
	9	3			7[2]		11	10[1]		5	6		13			8			4		12			1					2		41
	11	3	4				13	12		14	5	8[1]				9					6			1		10[3]			2	7[2]	42
	2	4	5				10	9[3]		14	7	11[1]	13			12			6[2]		8			1					3		43
	9	3	4				11[3]	10[2]		13	6	7[1]	12						5					1		8			2	14	44

FA Cup

Fourth Qualifying	Hastings U	(h)	3-1
First Round	FC Halifax T	(a)	4-7

FA Trophy

Third Round	Maidstone U	(h)

(Maidenhead U withdrew due to positive COVID-19 tests)

NOTTS COUNTY

Ground: Meadow Lane Stadium, Meadow Lane, Nottingham NG2 3HJ. *Tel:* (0115) 952 9000.
Website: www.nottscountyfc.co.uk *Email:* office@nottscountyfc.co.uk *Year Formed:* 1862.
Record Attendance: 47,310 v York C, FA Cup 6th rd, 12 March 1955. *Nickname:* 'The Magpies'.
Manager: Ian Burchnall. *Colours:* Black and white striped shirts, black shorts with white trim, black socks with white trim.

NOTTS COUNTY – NATIONAL LEAGUE 2021–22 LEAGUE RECORD

Match No.	*Date*	*Venue*	*Opponents*	*Result*		*H/T Score*	*Lg Pos.*	*Goalscorers*	*Attendance*
1	Aug 21	A	Barnet	W	5-0	0-0	1	Rodrigues 2 [47, 54], Roberts (pen) [68], Wootton [79], O'Brien [90]	2067
2	28	H	Torquay U	D	1-1	0-1	5	Wootton [68]	6934
3	30	A	Wrexham	D	1-1	1-0	7	Wootton [44]	5454
4	Sept 4	H	Aldershot T	W	3-2	1-1	4	Wootton [38], Cameron [52], Roberts [64]	5921
5	11	A	Weymouth	D	1-1	0-0	5	Roberts [59]	1783
6	14	H	Wealdstone	W	3-2	2-1	5	Roberts [41], Wootton [45], Cameron [57]	5213
7	18	H	Maidenhead U	W	1-0	0-0	4	Lacey [48]	5748
8	25	A	Altrincham	L	0-1	0-1	6		2569
9	Oct 2	H	Woking	L	1-4	1-0	7	Rodrigues [29]	5807
10	5	A	FC Halifax T	L	2-3	1-0	10	Rodrigues [30], Lacey [57]	2023
11	9	A	Yeovil T	W	2-0	1-0	9	Rodrigues 2 [16, 81]	2438
12	23	H	Stockport Co	W	2-1	0-0	8	Wootton [54], Vincent [68]	7418
13	26	H	Bromley	D	1-1	0-0	8	Cameron [46]	5331
14	30	A	Grimsby T	W	1-0	0-0	6	Rodrigues [90]	7213
15	Nov 13	H	Solihull Moors	W	2-0	0-0	5	Wootton [55], Mitchell [83]	12,843
16	20	A	Eastleigh	L	0-2	0-1	6		2817
17	23	A	Boreham Wood	D	1-1	1-0	6	Rodrigues [31]	821
18	27	H	Dagenham & R	W	2-1	1-1	5	Vincent [35], Wootton [73]	4889
19	Dec 11	H	Southend U	W	4-1	1-1	6	Roberts [31], Wootton 2 [63, 71], Cameron [88]	6206
20	Jan 2	H	Wrexham	W	3-1	2-1	6	Wootton 2 (1 pen) [10 (p), 39], Richardson, J [67]	8890
21	11	A	King's Lynn T	W	4-2	0-1	4	Roberts 3 [52, 57, 67], Vincent [78]	1505
22	25	A	Wealdstone	D	0-0	0-0	8		1547
23	29	A	Bromley	L	0-1	0-1	8		3606
24	Feb 5	H	Grimsby T	L	1-2	1-0	8	Roberts [15]	9305
25	8	H	Barnet	W	6-1	3-0	8	Sam 2 [7, 29], Roberts [11], Rodrigues [48], Wootton [72], Palmer, M [90]	5657
26	19	H	Eastleigh	W	2-0	2-0	8	Roberts [35], Wootton [41]	5692
27	22	H	FC Halifax T	D	1-1	1-1	8	Sam [43]	5603
28	26	A	Woking	W	2-0	1-0	7	Rodrigues [44], Sam [76]	3141
29	Mar 1	A	Chesterfield	L	1-3	1-0	7	Sam [40]	7912
30	5	H	Yeovil T	D	1-1	0-0	7	Lacey [90]	6943
31	8	A	Solihull Moors	D	3-3	1-1	7	Rodrigues 2 [18, 73], Lacey [56]	2120
32	15	A	Stockport Co	L	0-3	0-1	8		7951
33	19	A	Dagenham & R	W	2-1	1-1	7	Lacey [29], Wright (og) [64]	1846
34	22	H	Boreham Wood	W	1-0	1-0	6	Palmer, M [13]	5010
35	26	H	Chesterfield	D	1-1	1-1	6	Wootton (pen) [45]	10,334
36	Apr 2	A	Southend U	W	3-0	1-0	6	Rodrigues 3 [19, 61, 80]	6338
37	9	A	Torquay U	L	1-5	0-2	6	Wootton [74]	3130
38	15	H	King's Lynn T	W	4-1	2-1	6	Wootton [24], Roberts [39], Nemane [60], Sam [81]	6722
39	23	H	Weymouth	W	3-1	2-0	7	Wootton [8], Nemane [13], Rodrigues [48]	6032
40	26	A	Dover Ath	W	3-0	0-0	5	Francis [60], Roberts [83], Rodrigues [90]	845
41	30	A	Aldershot T	L	1-3	1-2	5	Roberts (pen) [24]	1969
42	May 2	H	Dover Ath	W	1-0	1-0	5	Rodrigues [17]	6523
43	7	H	Altrincham	W	3-0	0-0	5	Roberts (pen) [46], Wootton [75], Rodrigues [83]	6581
44	15	A	Maidenhead U	W	1-0	0-0	5	Roberts (pen) [71]	2074

Final League Position: 5

GOALSCORERS

League (81): Rodrigues 19, Wootton 19 (2 pens), Roberts 16 (4 pens), Sam 6, Lacey 5, Cameron 4, Vincent 3, Nemane 2, Palmer, M 2, Francis 1, Mitchell 1, O'Brien 1, Richardson, J 1, own goal 1.
FA Cup (6): Mitchell 2, Wootton 2, Vincent 1, own goal 1.
FA Trophy (7): Rodriguez 2 (1 pen), Sam 2, Mitchell 1, Rawlinson 1, Wootton 1.
National League Play-offs (1): Rodriguez.

Slocombe 20	Cameron 25 + 2	Rawlinson 19 + 4	Brindley 32	Taylor 19 + 1	Kelly-Evans 20 + 8	Francis 17 + 15	Roberts 31 + 5	Rodrigues 41 + 1	Palmer M 43	Wootton 42 + 1	O'Brien 12 + 12	Chicksen 28 + 3	Nemane 8 + 12	Mitchell 6 + 20	Lacey 26 + 1	Sam 8 + 15	Patterson 9	Brennan 4	Knight — + 1	Vincent 18 + 5	Parsons 1 + 2	Richardson J 24	Brunt 4 + 9	Jaros 15	Arter 8 + 1	Graham 4	*Match No.*
1	2	3[3]	4	5	6[1]	7	8	9[2]	10	11	12	13	14														1
1	2	3	4		6[3]	7[2]	9	10[1]	8	11	13	5	12	14													2
1	2	3[3]	4	5	6	7[2]	13	12	9	11	8	14		10[1]													3
1	2	13	4[3]	5	6	14	9	10	7	11	8[1]			12	3[2]												4
1	2		4	5	6[1]	14	9[3]	10	7	11	8[2]		12	13	3												5
1	2		4	5	13	6	8[1]	9[3]	7	11	12			10[2]	3	14											6
1	2[3]		4	5	14	6	8[1]	9	7	11	13	12		10[2]	3												7
			4	5[2]	6[1]	7[3]	9	10	8	11	12	2	13	14			1	3									8
			5		14			8	7	10	6[2]	2	11[1]	9	3		1	4	12[3]	13							9
			5[3]		12		8	10[2]	7	11	6	2	9[1]	13	3	14	1	4									10
	3		5		12	14	8	9	7	11[1]	6	2[2]	10[3]	13			1	4									11
	2	3	4	5	6		12	10[1]	7	11	8[2]			13			1			9							12
	2	3	4	5	6		12	10[2]	7	11	8			13			1			9[1]							13
	2	3	4	5	6[1]	14	13	10	7	11	8[3]		12				1			9[2]							14
		12	4	5	6	14	9[3]	10	7	11		2		13	3[2]		1			8[1]							15
1	14	3[3]	4	5	6[1]	12	8	10	7	11		2	13							9[2]							16
1	2		4	5	6		8[1]	10	7	11				12	3					9							17
1	2		4	5		13	8	10[1]	7	11	12			14	3					9[2]	6[3]						18
1	2		4	5[2]		14	8[3]	10	7	11	13				3					9[1]	12	6					19
	2		4			8			7	11		5		10[1]	3	12	1			9		6					20
1			4			7[1]	6[2]	10[3]	8	11		2		13	3	14				9		5	12				21
1	2		4				9	10[1]	7	11		5[2]			3	14				8[3]	13	6	12				22
1	2		4[2]	5			9[3]	10	7	11				12	3	14				13		6	8[1]				23
	2		4	5			9	10[2]	7	11					3	13				12		6	8[1]	1			24
	3		4			6	7	9[2]	8	10[3]		2	13	14		11[1]						5	12	1			25
	3		4			6	10[2]	8	7	11		2	13	12		9[1]						5		1			26
	3		4			6[1]	10	8	7	11		2		13		9[2]				14		5	12[3]	1			27
	3		4			6[2]		8	7	11		2	9[1]	13		10				12		5		1			28
	3		4				9	8	6	10[2]		2	14	13		11[1]				7[3]		5	12	1			29
	3[2]	4			13	6[3]	10	8	7	11		2		14	12	9						5[1]		1			30
		2		13	4[1]	3	7	9		11		5	12		6					8[2]			10	1			31
		3		5[1]	14	7	9[3]	10	8	11		2	12	13	4							6[2]		1			32
		3	4[1]		12	14			8	11		5		10	2[3]	13				9		6		1	7[2]		33
1		4			5	12		10	7	11		2			3					9		6			8[1]		34
1		4			5	13		10	9	11	12	2			3					8[2]		6			7[1]		35
		4			5			10[1]	9	11	12	2			3	14				8[3]		6	13	1	7[2]		36
		4			5[2]			10	9	11	14	2	12		3	13				8[1]		6		1	7[3]		37
		4				14	10	8	7	11[2]		2	9[1]			12						5	13	1	6[3]	3	38
		4				12	10	8	7	11[2]	13	2	9[1]			14						5		1	6[3]	3	39
1		12				6	9	10	7		14	2	8[1]		3[3]	11[2]						5	13			4	40
		4[3]			5	6	10	11	7	12		2	9[2]			14							8[1]	1	13	3	41
1		4		2		13	12	9	7	11	8[1]				3	10						5			6[2]		42
1	12		4		5[2]	13	9[1]	10	7	11	8[3]	2			3	14						6					43
1	2[3]	13	4		5		9[1]	10	7	11[2]	8				3	12						6	14				44

FA Cup

Fourth Qualifying	Tamworth	(a)	0-0
Replay	Tamworth	(a)	4-0
First Round	Rochdale	(a)	1-1
Replay	Rochdale	(h)	1-2

FA Trophy

Third Round	Altrincham	(h)	2-1
Fourth Round	Eastleigh	(h)	2-1
Fifth Round	FC Halifax T	(a)	2-1
Quarter-Final	Wrexham	(h)	1-2

National League Play-offs

Quarter-Final	Grimsby T	(h)	1-2

SOLIHULL MOORS

Ground: The ARMCO Arena, Damson Parkway, Solihull, West Midlands B91 2PP (satnav B92 9EJ).
Tel: (0121) 705 6770. *Website:* www.solihullmoorsfc.co.uk *Email:* info@solihullmoorsfc.co.uk *Year Formed:* 2007.
Record Attendance: 3,703 v Wigan Ath, FA Cup 1st rd replay, 16 November 2021.
Nickname: 'Moors'. *Manager:* Neil Ardley.
Colours: Yellow shirts with thin blue stripes and blue trim, blue shorts with yellow trim, yellow socks with blue trim.

SOLIHULL MOORS – NATIONAL LEAGUE 2021–22 LEAGUE RECORD

Match No.	*Date*	*Venue*	*Opponents*	*Result*		*H/T Score*	*Lg Pos.*	*Goalscorers*	*Attendance*
1	Aug 21	H	Wrexham	D	2-2	1-2	9	Sbarra 2 [18, 90]	2196
2	28	H	Barnet	D	1-1	1-0	14	Dallas [42]	1271
3	Sept 4	H	Weymouth	L	3-4	1-3	18	Sbarra 2 [37, 70], Dallas [90]	1383
4	11	A	Aldershot T	W	2-1	1-1	13	Maynard [45], Sbarra [88]	1354
5	14	H	Torquay U	W	2-1	1-0	9	Dallas [32], Sbarra [48]	1232
6	18	H	Boreham Wood	W	3-1	2-1	8	Sbarra [8], Newton 2 [29, 48]	1021
7	21	A	Dover Ath	D	0-0	0-0	7		809
8	25	A	Dagenham & R	L	1-5	1-2	8	Ball [25]	1175
9	Oct 2	H	Southend U	W	2-0	1-0	8	Hobson (og) [29], Ball (pen) [54]	1527
10	5	A	Wealdstone	D	0-0	0-0	7		1501
11	9	A	King's Lynn T	W	1-0	0-0	7	Newton [86]	1009
12	23	H	FC Halifax T	W	1-0	0-0	7	Maycock [52]	1594
13	26	A	Altrincham	W	2-1	0-1	5	Donawa [46], Sbarra [72]	3683
14	30	H	Yeovil T	D	0-0	0-0	5		1607
15	Nov 13	A	Notts Co	L	0-2	0-0	8		12,843
16	20	H	Chesterfield	L	0-2	0-2	8		1950
17	23	H	Grimsby T	W	2-0	1-0	7	Rooney [7], Sbarra [68]	1772
18	Dec 4	H	Woking	W	2-0	1-0	8	Sbarra [28], Rooney (pen) [78]	1214
19	11	A	Maidenhead U	W	4-0	3-0	7	Sbarra [12], Boyes [40], Osborne [45], Donawa [58]	1006
20	14	A	Eastleigh	D	0-0	0-0	6		2085
21	28	H	Stockport Co	L	0-1	0-0	7		2984
22	Jan 8	A	Bromley	L	1-2	0-2	9	Ball [72]	1411
23	22	H	Dover Ath	W	5-0	4-0	9	Dallas 5 [8, 10, 35, 39, 54]	1393
24	25	A	Torquay U	W	2-0	0-0	9	Hudlin [84], Dallas [90]	2469
25	29	H	Altrincham	W	5-0	4-0	7	Dallas [18], Osborne [26], Densmore (og) [35], Maycock [42], Barnett [81]	2090
26	Feb 5	A	Yeovil T	D	0-0	0-0	6		1955
27	19	A	Chesterfield	W	3-2	1-2	6	Clarke [37], Maycock [51], Boyes [55]	7391
28	22	H	Wealdstone	W	2-1	1-1	4	Dallas [6], Maynard [81]	3219
29	26	A	Southend U	D	1-1	1-1	6	Maycock [44]	6607
30	Mar 5	H	King's Lynn T	D	2-2	0-1	6	Gudger [60], Howe [88]	1533
31	8	H	Notts Co	D	3-3	1-1	6	Dallas 2 (1 pen) [7 (p), 71], Barnett [86]	2120
32	19	H	Eastleigh	W	5-3	3-1	5	Sbarra 3 [9, 40, 79], Howe [15], Newton [90]	1272
33	22	A	Grimsby T	W	2-1	0-1	5	Hudlin 2 [78, 89]	4498
34	26	A	Woking	W	3-2	1-1	5	Boyes [40], Rooney [62], Barnett [72]	2198
35	Apr 2	H	Maidenhead U	W	3-1	2-0	4	Dallas 2 [12, 40], Boyes [90]	1458
36	5	A	FC Halifax T	D	0-0	0-0	4		1750
37	9	A	Barnet	W	2-0	1-0	4	Dallas [7], Richards-Everton (og) [85]	1016
38	15	A	Wrexham	D	1-1	0-0	4	Sbarra [56]	9949
39	18	A	Stockport Co	L	0-1	0-0	4		9211
40	23	H	Aldershot T	W	2-1	1-0	4	Sbarra [37], Newton [51]	1974
41	30	A	Weymouth	W	4-2	2-0	4	Boyes [7], Harfield (og) [41], Clarke [69], Dallas [90]	756
42	May 2	H	Bromley	W	3-0	1-0	4	Rooney [7], Sbarra [75], Dallas (pen) [84]	2259
43	7	H	Dagenham & R	W	3-1	3-0	3	Howe [13], Maycock [21], Gudger [42]	2061
44	15	A	Boreham Wood	W	3-0	2-0	3	Hudlin [14], Sbarra [42], Rooney (pen) [75]	1101

Final League Position: 3

GOALSCORERS

League (83): Dallas 18 (2 pens), Sbarra 18, Boyes 5, Maycock 5, Newton 5, Rooney 5 (2 pens), Hudlin 4, Ball 3 (1 pen), Barnett 3, Howe 3, Clarke 2, Donawa 2, Gudger 2, Maynard 2, Osborne 2, own goals 4.
FA Cup (2): Newton 1, Rooney 1 (pen).
FA Trophy (6): Dallas 3, Maycock 1, Newton 1, own goal 1.
National League Play-offs (4): Dallas 1, Gudger 1, Howe 1, Hudlin 1.

Dewhurst 3	Williams 8 + 3	Storer 21 + 8	Howe 32	Sbarra 41 + 3	Maycock 41 + 3	Barnett 34 + 6	Boyes 30 + 1	Dallas 35 + 8	Preston 6 + 1	Newton 22 + 13	Hudlin 5 + 18	Donawa 8 + 6	Maynard 26 + 4	Cranston 15 + 6	Boot 39	Gudger 28 + 2	Ball 12 + 4	Rooney 15 + 8	Osborne 21 + 10	Clarke 28	McNally 1 + 2	Lundstram 1	Ellis 7	Malcolm 1 + 1	Reilly 2 + 7	McDonnell 2	*Match No.*
1	2	3	4	5	6	7^{1}	8	9^{2}	10	11	12	13															1
1	2	3	4	5^{2}	6	7^{3}	8	9	10	11^{1}	12	13	14														2
1	2^{1}	3	4	5	6	7	8^{2}	9	10	12	11^{3}	13		14													3
	2^{1}	8	4	7	9	10^{3}		11	13	12		14	5^{2}	3	1	6											4
	13	6	3	7^{1}	8			10	5	11		9^{2}		2	1	4	12										5
	12	7	3	6^{3}	8			10^{1}	5	11		9^{2}		2	1	4	13	14									6
		7	3	8^{2}	14	9		12	5	11			6^{3}	2	1	4	13	10^{1}									7
	2^{1}	4	5	7	8	9		10		11^{2}				3	1	6	12	13									8
	14		3	5	6			9^{2}		10^{1}	12	7	11	2	1	4	8^{3}		13								9
			3	6^{1}	7	13		10^{2}		11^{3}	12	9	5	2	1	4	8		14								10
			3	5^{2}	7	8		11^{1}		13	14		6	2	1	4	9	10^{3}	12								11
	2	13	4	6^{3}	7	8		10^{2}		12		14	11	3	1	5	9^{1}										12
	2	6	4	12	7			13		11^{1}		10	5	3	1			9	8^{2}								13
	2	4	5	6^{2}	7	8		10					11	3■	1		9^{1}	13	12								14
		2	3	5	6	13	8	10^{3}			14	9	11		1	4^{1}		12	7^{2}								15
		3■	4	5^{2}	13	8	12	14		10			11	2	1		9	6^{3}	7^{1}								16
			4^{1}	13	5	7	8	10^{2}					11	3	1		9	6		2	12						17
			4^{3}	5	6	8^{2}	9					13	2	14	1	12	10	11	7^{1}	3							18
				5^{2}	6^{3}	8	9	13		14		10	4	12	1	3		11	7^{1}	2							19
				4	5	7^{1}	8	13		14		9^{2}	11	12	1	3	10	6^{3}		2							20
				4	5	8	9	13		12					1	3	10	6^{2}	7^{1}	2		11					21
				5	6	7	8	11		12			4		1	3^{1}	9	10^{2}	13	2							22
				5^{3}	6	12	8	11^{1}		13			4		1	3	9	10	7	2^{2}	14						23
				4	5	6^{1}	7	8		10^{2}	13		11		1	3			12	2			9				24
				6	7^{3}	12	9^{2}	10^{1}		11	14		5	13	1	3			8	2			4				25
		13		7	8^{2}	12		10		11			6	3■	1	4			9^{1}	2			5				26
		12		4	5	7	8	9^{1}		11^{2}					1	3		13	6^{3}	2			10	14			27
		3		5^{2}	6	13	7	9^{1}		11	14		12		1	4				2			10■	8^{3}			28
		5		6	7	8	9	10^{1}		11^{3}	12			14	1	3			13	2	4^{2}						29
		3^{2}	4	6	7	8	9	10		11^{1}					1	5		12	13	2							30
		5^{1}		6	7	9	10	11			12				1	3			8	2			4				31
		12	3	5^{1}	6^{3}	9	10	11^{2}		13			14		1	4		7	8	2							32
		5	3	6	7	9	10	12			13		4		1			11^{1}	8^{2}	2							33
			3	5^{1}	6	8	9	11			12		4		1			10^{2}	7	2					13		34
			3	4^{2}	5	7	8	9		12	11^{1}		10		1				6	2					13		35
		13	3	4	5	7	8	9^{2}		10^{1}	12		11		1				6	2							36
		6	4	14	7	8		10^{1}		11^{2}	13		5	3	1				12	2					9^{3}		37
		5	3	6^{3}	7	9	10	11^{1}		12	13		4		1				8^{2}	2					14		38
		14	3	5^{1}	6	8^{2}	9	10^{3}		11	13				1	4			7	2					12		39
			3	4^{2}	5	7	8	9		10^{1}	12		11		1				6	2					13		40
		5	3	6^{2}	7	8^{1}	9^{3}	10			11				1	14			13	2			4		12		41
		14	3	5	13	8	9	12		11^{1}					1	4		6	7^{2}	2					10^{3}		42
		12	3	5^{2}	6	8	9	10^{1}			11^{3}		13			4		14	7■	2						1	43
		6	3	5^{2}	7	8	9	10^{3}		12	11^{1}					4		13		2					14	1	44

FA Cup

Fourth Qualifying	Hereford	(a)	1-0
First Round	Wigan Ath	(a)	0-0
Replay	Wigan Ath	(h)	1-2
(aet)			

FA Trophy

Third Round	AFC Fylde	(a)	1-0
Fourth Round	Southport	(a)	3-0
Fifth Round	Stourbridge	(a)	1-0
Quarter-Final	Bromley	(a)	1-3

National League Play-offs

Semi-Final	Chesterfield	(h)	3-1
Final	Grimsby T (London Stadium)		1-2

SOUTHEND UNITED

Ground: Roots Hall Stadium, Victoria Avenue, Southend-on-Sea, Essex SS2 6NQ. *Tel:* (01702) 304 050.
Website: www.southendunited.co.uk *Email:* info@southend-united.co.uk *Year Formed:* 1906.
Record Attendance: 31,090 v Liverpool, FA Cup 3rd rd, 10 January 1979 (at Roots Hall). *Nickname:* 'The Shrimpers'.
Manager: Kevin Maher. *Colours:* Navy blue shirts with white trim, navy blue shorts, white socks.

SOUTHEND UNITED – NATIONAL LEAGUE 2021–22 LEAGUE RECORD

Match No.	*Date*	*Venue*	*Opponents*	*Result*		*H/T Score*	*Lg Pos.*	*Goalscorers*	*Attendance*
1	Aug 21	A	King's Lynn T	W	1-0	1-0	8	Dalby [9]	2683
2	28	H	Stockport Co	L	0-1	0-1	12		5678
3	30	A	Wealdstone	D	0-0	0-0	9		2151
4	Sept 4	H	Wrexham	D	2-2	1-0	13	Dalby [25], Murphy [52]	6036
5	11	A	FC Halifax T	L	1-3	0-1	14	Murphy [88]	1959
6	14	H	Aldershot T	L	2-3	1-1	16	Murphy [17], Demetriou [90]	5004
7	18	A	Torquay U	L	0-1	0-0	19		2301
8	Oct 2	A	Solihull Moors	L	0-2	0-1	21		1527
9	5	H	Eastleigh	W	1-0	0-0	18	Ferguson [69]	3349
10	9	H	Chesterfield	L	0-4	0-2	20		4625
11	23	A	Dagenham & R	L	0-3	0-0	21		3673
12	30	A	Boreham Wood	L	0-1	0-0	21		1501
13	Nov 2	H	Dover Ath	W	4-1	2-0	20	Murphy 2 (1 pen) [30, 35 (p)], Dalby [59], Bridge [73]	4996
14	13	H	Woking	L	0-2	0-1	20		5821
15	19	A	Grimsby T	L	0-1	0-1	20		5836
16	27	A	Altrincham	W	2-1	2-0	21	Murphy [1], Dalby [34]	1288
17	Dec 7	H	Maidenhead U	D	1-1	1-0	19	Murphy [44]	4928
18	11	A	Notts Co	L	1-4	1-1	19	Dalby [10]	6206
19	26	A	Bromley	D	1-1	0-0	19	Dennis [67]	3759
20	Jan 8	A	Weymouth	W	1-0	1-0	19	Dennis [5]	1335
21	11	H	Yeovil T	W	2-1	1-0	18	Demetriou [29], Clifford [60]	4845
22	21	H	King's Lynn T	W	2-1	0-1	18	Dennis [49], Dalby (pen) [90]	6122
23	25	A	Aldershot T	D	1-1	0-1	18	Cardwell [87]	2141
24	29	A	Dover Ath	W	1-0	0-0	16	Husin [72]	2657
25	Feb 1	H	Barnet	W	2-1	2-1	13	Dennis 2 [4, 27]	6036
26	8	H	Bromley	W	2-0	0-0	13	Dennis [47], Hobson [50]	8070
27	12	A	Woking	W	3-2	2-0	12	Demetriou [8], Powell [11], Cardwell [76]	3819
28	22	A	Eastleigh	D	1-1	0-1	12	Husin [60]	3062
29	26	H	Solihull Moors	D	1-1	1-1	12	Dalby [31]	6607
30	Mar 5	A	Chesterfield	D	2-2	0-1	12	Dalby (pen) [53], Kerr (og) [88]	6625
31	8	H	Grimsby T	W	1-0	0-0	12	Dalby (pen) [62]	7205
32	15	H	Dagenham & R	L	0-3	0-2	12		7542
33	19	H	Altrincham	W	2-0	2-0	12	Ralph [35], Dennis [41]	5976
34	22	A	Maidenhead U	L	1-2	0-0	12	Clifford [63]	1624
35	26	A	Yeovil T	L	0-2	0-2	13		2475
36	Apr 2	H	Notts Co	L	0-3	0-1	13		6338
37	9	A	Stockport Co	L	0-5	0-2	13		7738
38	15	H	Wealdstone	L	0-1	0-0	14		5849
39	18	A	Barnet	W	3-1	2-0	13	Cardwell (pen) [5], Demetriou [15], Dunne [90]	2202
40	23	H	FC Halifax T	W	1-0	1-0	13	Clark [12]	5620
41	26	H	Boreham Wood	W	1-0	0-0	12	Bridge [77]	4756
42	30	A	Wrexham	L	0-1	0-0	12		9269
43	May 2	H	Weymouth	D	1-1	0-1	12	Powell [49]	5323
44	15	H	Torquay U	D	1-1	0-1	13	Dunne [76]	6294

Final League Position: 13

GOALSCORERS

League (45): Dalby 9 (3 pens), Dennis 7, Murphy 7 (1 pen), Demetriou 4, Cardwell 3 (1 pen), Bridge 2, Clifford 2, Dunne 2, Husin 2, Powell 2, Clark 1, Ferguson 1, Hobson 1, Ralph 1, own goal 1.
FA Cup (5): Murphy 2, Ferguson 1, Ralph 1, Walsh 1.
FA Trophy (2): Dalby 1, Dennis 1.

Arnold 41	Ralph 27 + 1	Ogogo 6	Coulson 7 + 1	Bridge 22 + 5	Murphy 18 + 3	Dalby 38 + 5	Ferguson 11 + 9	Phillips 7 + 2	Demetriou 32 + 1	White 13 + 2	Hobson 38 + 3	Dennis 15 + 12	Egbri 4 + 6	Kargbo 2 + 3	Rush — + 9	Dunne 18 + 5	Seaden 2	Atkinson 27 + 6	Walsh 4 + 3	Benton Jon — + 1	Sayers 4 + 2	Mbunga-Kimpioka 2	Akinola 1	Howard 3	Lopata 17	Brunt 8	Gard 2 + 3	Clifford 18 + 1	Neal 19 + 3	Kensdale 11 + 4	Davies 13 + 3	Cardwell 13 + 1	Husin 16 + 1	Powell 9 + 8	Wood — + 5	Clark 6	Gubbins 9 + 1	Andeng-Ndi 1	Match No.
1	2	3	4	5^1	6^2	7	8	9	10	11	12	13																											1
1	5	6^1	2	7^2	10	11	8	9^3	3	4		13	12	14																									2
1	2			4^1	5^2	6	8	9		11	3	10	7	13	12																								3
1	2^1		3	4	6	7	8^3	9	10	11	12	13	14			5^2																							4
	2		3	4	6	7	8^3	9^2	10	11^1	13		12			5	1	14																					5
1	2		4^3	6	10	11^2			5	12	3		8^1		14	7		9	13																				6
1	2	3	4	5^2	7^1	8				11		12	9	13		6		10																					7
1		2	11	4	6^1	12	14		9		3	13				5			7^3		8	10^2																	8
1	2			6	13	12	8		4		5			11^1		7		9			3		10^2																9
1	2			4	13	14	6		10		3		12	9^3		5		7^2			8	11^1																	10
		3		5^2	7	8	10^1	12		11	4		9			6	1				13			2															11
1		7▮			10	11^2	12			6	3					8			13		4			2	5	9^1													12
1				6^2	10	11^3	12	8^1		5	3				13	7					14			2	4	9													13
1	12			3^3	5	6		7^2	9^1	11	2				14	4			13						8	10													14
1					11	14	7		5	4	2	13	12			6^1		9^3	8^2						3	10													15
1	2				10^2	11	6	12	5		3				13			8	7^1						4	9													16
1	2				4	5	6		10		3		12					8^2	7^1						9	11	13												17
1^1	2				10	11	12		5	6	3				13	7		14								9	8^3	4^2											18
1	2		13		14	10			4	5^3	3	11^1				7^2		8								9	12	6											19
1	2				9^2	10	13		6		3	11^1			12			7							5			4	8										20
1	2				9^2	10	12		6		3	11^3			13			7^1							5			4	8	14									21
1	5					11	13				6	9^2						7							3			4	8		2	10^1	12						22
1	2					11	14		13		3				12			7^2							5			4	8		6^3	10	9^1						23
1	2					4	13		8		3	9^1						6							7			5				11^2	10	12					24
1	2					9			6		3	11				12		7							5			4					8	10^1					25
1	2					9			6^1		3	10^2						7							5			4	12		13	11	8						26
1	3					9			2^1		4					14		6^2							7			5	12		13	10	8	11^3					27
1	2					4			9		3	13						7							8			6^2	14		12	11^1	10	5^3					28
1	2			12		10			4		3	11^1						7^2											8	6	5		9	13					29
1	2			13		10					3	11^2						7							4				8	6^1	5		9	12					30
1	2			12		10			5		3							7							4				8	6			9	11^1					31
1	2			12		4			8^2		3	14						6^1										13	7	10	9		11	5^3					32
1	2^3			7^1		10					3	11				13		12										4	8	6	5		9^2		14				33
1				3^1		5					2	10				4▮		7										6	8	11	9			12					34
1				3^3		4					2	10^1						6										5	7	11^2	9	13		14		8	12		35
1				12		3			9		2	10^1						6^2										4	7				11	13		8	5		36
						2			8			9^1						5^2										3	6	12		11^3	10	14	13	7	4	1	37
1				7^2		14			6		2	12																3	8			11	9	10^1	13	5	4^3		38
1						9			6		2	13				14		7										3^3		12		11^2	8	10^1		5	4		39
1				3^2		4			8		2					14		12											6	13	9	11	10^3			7^1	5		40
1				7^1		10			4		2					8											12		9	6	5	11					3		41
1				7		11			4		2	14				8^3		12											9	6	5^1	10^2		13			3		42
1				3							2	12						7		13							5^2		8	10	9	11^3		4^1	14		6		43
1				7^1		10			4▮	13	2					8		12											9	6	5^3			11^2	14		3		44

FA Cup

Fourth Qualifying	Chertsey T	(h)	4-1
First Round	Chesterfield	(a)	1-3

FA Trophy

Third Round	Dorking W	(h)	2-1
Fourth Round	Dagenham & R	(a)	0-2

STOCKPORT COUNTY

Ground: Edgeley Park, Hardcastle Road, Edgeley, Stockport, Cheshire SK3 9DD. *Tel:* (0161) 286 8888.
Website: www.stockportcounty.com *Email:* see website *Year Formed:* 1883.
Record Attendance: 27,833 v Liverpool, FA Cup 5th rd, 11 February 1950. *Nickname:* 'County' or 'The Hatters'.
Manager: Dave Challinor. *Colours:* Blue shirts, blue shorts, white socks.

STOCKPORT COUNTY – NATIONAL LEAGUE 2021–22 LEAGUE RECORD

Match No.	*Date*	*Venue*	*Opponents*	*Result*	*H/T Score*	*Lg Pos.*	*Goalscorers*	*Attendance*
1	Aug 21	H	Dagenham & R	L 1-3	1-1	14	Rooney[9]	5265
2	28	A	Southend U	W 1-0	1-0	13	Rooney[16]	5678
3	31	H	Grimsby T	D 0-0	0-0	11		6452
4	Sept 4	A	Boreham Wood	D 0-0	0-0	14		782
5	11	H	Yeovil T	L 0-3	0-1	16		5231
6	14	A	Maidenhead U	W 2-0	1-0	10	Rooney[17], Reid[59]	1082
7	18	A	FC Halifax T	L 0-3	0-1	11		2661
8	25	H	Wrexham	W 2-1	0-1	9	Madden[48], Rydel[80]	7771
9	Oct 2	A	Weymouth	W 2-1	0-1	9	Madden[72], Crankshaw[88]	872
10	9	H	Aldershot T	W 1-0	1-0	10	Madden[45]	6132
11	23	A	Notts Co	L 1-2	0-0	10	Whitfield (pen)[90]	7418
12	26	H	Barnet	L 1-2	1-1	10	Crankshaw[40]	4363
13	30	A	Dover Ath	W 5-2	2-1	9	Quigley[22], Madden[42], Crankshaw[66], Hogan[76], Whitfield[90]	635
14	Nov 13	H	Bromley	D 1-1	0-0	11	Quigley[49]	5515
15	20	A	Woking	W 2-1	2-0	10	Madden 2[5, 29]	2753
16	23	H	King's Lynn T	W 5-0	2-0	9	Keane[34], Rydel[45], Crankshaw[48], Barclay[77], Jennings, C[90]	4568
17	27	A	Wealdstone	W 4-1	1-0	8	Quigley[26], Crankshaw 3[62, 67, 81]	1382
18	Dec 11	A	Torquay U	L 1-2	1-2	10	Collar[21]	2156
19	26	H	Altrincham	W 5-1	4-1	8	Sarcevic[4], Madden[10], Quigley[13], Collar[37], Crankshaw[82]	8896
20	28	A	Solihull Moors	W 1-0	0-0	6	Madden[73]	2984
21	Jan 11	A	Altrincham	W 4-1	2-0	7	Sarcevic[6], Collar[44], Madden (pen)[50], Croasdale[67]	3900
22	18	H	Eastleigh	W 3-0	2-0	3	Boyce (og)[14], Madden[40], Jennings, C[74]	4634
23	22	A	Dagenham & R	W 2-0	2-0	3	Palmer[3], Collar[5]	1749
24	25	H	Maidenhead U	W 3-0	0-0	1	Sarcevic[53], Croasdale[62], Rooney[90]	5352
25	29	A	Barnet	W 5-0	1-0	1	Collar[45], Johnson, R 2[54, 90], Hogan[67], Jennings, C[90]	2183
26	Feb 5	H	Dover Ath	W 1-0	0-0	1	Madden[84]	7263
27	8	H	Chesterfield	D 2-2	0-2	1	Collar[56], Croasdale[65]	10,236
28	15	A	Bromley	W 3-1	0-0	1	Madden 2[64, 85], Quigley[71]	2753
29	19	H	Woking	W 1-0	0-0	1	Palmer[72]	6820
30	26	H	Weymouth	W 1-0	1-0	1	Murray (og)[23]	7418
31	Mar 5	A	Aldershot T	W 2-0	2-0	1	Crankshaw[14], Collar[26]	1552
32	15	H	Notts Co	W 3-0	1-0	1	Madden 2[28, 71], Crankshaw[48]	7951
33	19	H	Wealdstone	W 4-2	0-2	1	Madden (pen)[55], Johnson, R[57], Palmer[61], Sarcevic[90]	7453
34	22	A	King's Lynn T	W 3-0	2-0	1	Newby[17], Hogan[29], Madden[61]	914
35	26	A	Eastleigh	W 2-0	0-0	1	Hippolyte[50], Hogan[84]	3295
36	Apr 9	H	Southend U	W 5-0	2-0	1	Collar[21], Hippolyte[25], Madden 2[50, 63], Cannon[89]	7738
37	15	A	Grimsby T	L 1-2	1-0	1	Quigley[14]	7818
38	18	H	Solihull Moors	W 1-0	0-0	1	Madden[90]	9211
39	23	A	Yeovil T	L 1-2	0-1	1	Hippolyte[70]	2783
40	30	H	Boreham Wood	L 1-2	0-1	1	Newby[90]	8778
41	May 2	A	Chesterfield	W 1-0	1-0	1	Madden (pen)[35]	9198
42	8	A	Wrexham	L 0-3	0-2	2		10,118
43	11	H	Torquay U	W 1-0	0-0	1	Madden[64]	9407
44	15	H	FC Halifax T	W 2-0	1-0	1	Madden[10], Collar[54]	10,307

Final League Position: 1

GOALSCORERS

League (87): Madden 23 (3 pens), Crankshaw 10, Collar 9, Quigley 6, Hogan 4, Rooney 4, Sarcevic 4, Croasdale 3, Hippolyte 3, Jennings, C 3, Johnson, R 3, Palmer 3, Newby 2, Rydel 2, Whitfield 2 (1 pen), Barclay 1, Cannon 1, Keane 1, Reid 1, own goals 2.
FA Cup (10): Quigley 4, Madden 2 (2 pens), Crankshaw 1, Crossdale 1, Palmer 1, Whitfield 1.
FA Trophy (11): Collar 2, Jennings C 2, Reid 2, Crossdale 1, Hippolyte 1, Johnson R 1, Keane 1, Palmer 1.

Hinchliffe 37	Hogan 26 + 7	Barclay 8 + 3	Southam-Hales 30	Rooney 15 + 4	Madden 42 + 1	Whitfield 8 + 7	Collar 30 + 6	Croasdale 44	Walker 1 + 5	Fish 1 + 1	Reid 6 + 7	Rydel 24 + 8	Newby 6 + 10	Keane 17 + 2	Palmer 40	Raikhy 4 + 1	Quigley 24 + 7	Fryers 4 + 1	Dunnwald — + 1	Kitching 21 + 5	Ross 7	Pye 2	Crankshaw 14 + 18	Sarcevic 23 + 2	Minihan 7 + 5	Jennings C 4 + 13	Johnson R 17 + 4	Hippolyte 14 + 4	Cannon 5 + 4	Duffus 1	Francis-Angol 2	*Match No.*
1	2	3	4	5	6	7	8^{1}	9	10^{3}	11^{2}	12	13	14																			1
1		5	6	7^{3}	11	14	13	9			12	2		3	4	8^{2}	10^{1}															2
1		3		6	10	7^{2}	14	9	12		11^{1}	5	13	4	2	8^{3}																3
1		3	5	6	11	7^{3}	8^{1}	10	13		12	14		4	2	9^{2}																4
1	2	4^{1}	5	6	7	8		10	12		11^{2}				3■	9^{3}		13	14													5
1	3	4	5	6	7	14	8^{3}	9		13	10	12						11^{2}		2^{1}												6
1	3	4	5	6	7	13	8^{2}	9	12		10							11^{1}		2												7
	12	4^{1}	5	7	11	8	14	9			10^{3}	13			3			6		2^{2}	1											8
	3		5	6	7	8^{1}	14	9			10^{3}	13			4					2^{2}	1	11	12									9
	12		4	5	6	7^{3}		9				13		8^{2}	3		14	10		2^{1}	1		11									10
	3		5	6	7^{2}	13		9						8	4		10^{1}			2	1		11	12								11
	3		5■	6	7	8^{1}		9^{3}			14	13			4		12			2^{2}	1		11	10								12
	2			3	4	12	13	7^{2}			14	6		5			8				1	11	10^{1}	9^{3}								13
	14			7^{3}	10^{1}		13	6				5		4	3		11			2	1		9^{2}	8	12							14
1		14	4	5^{2}	6			9				8		7	3	13	10^{3}			2			12	11^{1}								15
1		13	6				7	8			12	5		4^{3}	3		11^{2}			2			10^{1}	9		14						16
1		13	6		12		7	8				5		4^{2}	3		11^{1}			2			10^{3}	9		14						17
1			10		11		7^{2}	6	14		13	5		4^{3}	3					2^{1}			9	8	12							18
1	12		6		9^{3}		7	8				5^{2}		4	3		11^{1}			2			13	10		14						19
1	3		5	13	6^{2}		7^{3}	9				8		14	4		10^{1}			2			11			12						20
1	3		5		6^{2}		7	9				8			4		10^{1}			2^{3}			13	11		14	12					21
1	3		7	13	10		8^{1}	6				5	14		4		11^{3}			2				9^{2}		12						22
1	3		5		6^{1}		8	10				9^{3}	14		4					2			12	11		7^{2}	13					23
1	3		5	14	6		8	10				9^{1}			4					2			12	11^{2}		7^{3}	13					24
1	2		6	13	10^{1}		7	8				5			3		11^{2}						12	9^{3}		14	4					25
1	2^{3}		6		10		7	8^{1}				5	12		3		11^{2}						9			13	4	14				26
1	2^{1}		6		10		7	8				5	13		3		11						12				4	9^{2}				27
1	2		6		11		7	8				5^{1}			3		10^{2}			12						13	4	9				28
1	2■		4		5		6	9				8^{3}	13		3		11^{1}			14			12				7	10^{2}				29
1			3		4		5	9				8^{1}	14	7	2		10^{2}			12■			11				6^{3}	13				30
1			3		4	14	6	8							2		13						11	10^{3}	12	5^{1}	7	9^{2}				31
1			4^{3}		5		6^{2}	8					13		3		12			2			11^{1}	10	14		7	9				32
1	13		5^{3}		11		6	7							3		12			2^{2}			10^{1}	9	14		4	8				33
1	4				6^{1}		7^{2}	9^{3}					10	12	5		11			3			14	13	2		8					34
1	3				10		6	7							4		11^{2}			13				9	2		5	8^{1}	12			35
1	3				5^{3}		6^{1}	8					14		4		10						13	11^{2}	2		7	9	12			36
1	3				5		6	8							4		10^{2}			12			13	11■	2		7^{3}	9^{1}	14			37
1	3^{3}				10		8	9				6			4		11^{2}						13		2	14	5	12	7^{1}			38
1	3^{2}				6		7■	10				9			4		11^{1}						12		2	14	8	13	5^{3}			39
1	3				10			7^{2}				6	8		4^{3}		14						13		2	11^{1}	5	9	12			40
1	14				11			6				12	7	4	2		13							9			3	8^{3}	5^{2}	10^{1}		41
1	2				10			6				5^{2}	7	4	3		11^{1}						13	9		12		8				42
1	14				11		6	7					8	3	2								12	10^{2}		13		9^{1}	5^{3}		4	43
1					11	14	6	7					8	3^{3}	2								13	10			12	9	5^{2}		4^{1}	44

FA Cup

Fourth Qualifying	Stamford	(h)	3-0
First Round	Bolton W	(a)	2-2
Replay	Bolton W	(h)	5-3
(aet)			
Second Round	Rotherham U	(a)	0-1

FA Trophy

Third Round	Grimsby T	(h)	4-0
Fourth Round	Larkhall Ath	(h)	3-0
Fifth Round	Cheshunt	(h)	1-0
Quarter-Final	Needham Market	(a)	3-0
Semi-Final	Wrexham	(a)	0-2

TORQUAY UNITED

Ground: Plainmoor, Marnham Road, Torquay, Devon TQ1 3PS. *Tel:* (01803) 328 666.
Website: www.torquayunited.com *Email:* reception@torquayunited.com *Year Formed:* 1899.
Record Attendance: 21,908 v Huddersfield T, FA Cup 4th rd, 29 January 1955. *Nickname:* 'The Gulls'.
Manager: Gary Johnson. *Colours:* Yellow shirts with blue trim, blue shorts, blue socks.

TORQUAY UNITED – NATIONAL LEAGUE 2021–22 LEAGUE RECORD

Match No.	Date	Venue	Opponents	Result		H/T Score	Lg Pos.	Goalscorers	Attendance
1	Aug 21	H	Altrincham	L	1-3	0-2	14	Moult (og) [74]	2599
2	28	A	Notts Co	D	1-1	1-0	15	Wright [36]	6934
3	30	H	Woking	L	0-4	0-2	19		2486
4	Sept 4	A	Maidenhead U	W	4-3	4-0	17	Little 2 [14, 20], Hall [44], Lemonheigh-Evans [45]	1495
5	11	H	Grimsby T	L	1-3	1-2	19	Little [11]	2364
6	14	A	Solihull Moors	L	1-2	0-1	20	Lolos [80]	1232
7	18	H	Southend U	W	1-0	0-0	13	Lemonheigh-Evans [90]	2301
8	25	A	Chesterfield	D	2-2	0-0	16	Little [88], Lapslie [90]	5127
9	Oct 2	H	Wealdstone	W	5-0	4-0	13	Lapslie [11], Holman 2 [17, 68], Little [30], Lewis [45]	2097
10	5	A	Boreham Wood	L	0-2	0-1	13		701
11	9	A	Bromley	L	0-2	0-2	14		2523
12	23	H	King's Lynn T	W	2-0	1-0	14	Armstrong [41], Lewis [77]	2506
13	30	A	Wrexham	D	1-1	0-1	16	Lemonheigh-Evans [84]	9813
14	Nov 13	H	Dover Ath	W	2-1	1-1	14	Little 2 [34, 90]	2892
15	20	A	Barnet	L	1-2	0-1	16	Little [59]	1498
16	23	A	Aldershot T	L	0-1	0-0	17		1582
17	27	H	FC Halifax T	L	2-3	0-1	17	Lolos [88], Little [90]	2269
18	Dec 4	A	Weymouth	W	2-1	0-0	16	Lewis [65], Armstrong [70]	1559
19	11	H	Stockport Co	W	2-1	2-1	16	Collar (og) [19], Hall (pen) [45]	2156
20	26	H	Yeovil T	W	3-0	0-0	12	Wynter [66], Sparkes [70], Lewis [86]	3830
21	28	A	Eastleigh	L	1-2	1-0	14	Little [32]	2730
22	Jan 2	A	Yeovil T	W	2-1	0-0	13	Lemonheigh-Evans [75], Holman [89]	3866
23	8	H	Dagenham & R	D	2-2	2-1	12	Hall [1], Wright [12]	2339
24	22	A	Altrincham	W	2-1	1-1	11	Lemonheigh-Evans [6], Wearne [49]	1744
25	25	H	Solihull Moors	L	0-2	0-0	11		2469
26	Feb 5	H	Wrexham	W	1-0	1-0	11	Hall [8]	3181
27	12	A	Dover Ath	W	3-1	1-1	11	Hall [2], Lewis [78], Duke-McKenna [90]	783
28	19	H	Barnet	D	2-2	2-1	11	Lemonheigh-Evans 2 [8, 27]	2221
29	22	H	Boreham Wood	D	0-0	0-0	11		2251
30	26	A	Wealdstone	D	1-1	0-0	11	Wynter [81]	0
31	Mar 5	H	Bromley	D	0-0	0-0	11		2350
32	12	A	King's Lynn T	W	3-2	2-1	11	Wright 2 [29, 34], Duke-McKenna [52]	870
33	19	A	FC Halifax T	L	0-2	0-0	11		2192
34	22	H	Aldershot T	W	4-0	3-0	11	Moxey [13], Wearne [16], Webb (og) [24], Lemonheigh-Evans [47]	1832
35	26	H	Weymouth	W	3-0	2-0	11	Wearne [12], Little (pen) [19], Wright [46]	2538
36	Apr 9	H	Notts Co	W	5-1	2-0	10	Little 2 [11, 90], Lemonheigh-Evans 3 [14, 77, 85]	3130
37	15	A	Woking	W	1-0	1-0	10	Little [19]	3344
38	18	H	Eastleigh	D	0-0	0-0	9		3646
39	23	A	Grimsby T	L	1-2	1-1	10	Hall [28]	5826
40	30	H	Maidenhead U	D	1-1	0-0	11	Lewis [90]	2148
41	May 2	A	Dagenham & R	D	0-0	0-0	10		1752
42	7	H	Chesterfield	W	2-0	0-0	10	Duke-McKenna [70], Little (pen) [81]	3075
43	11	A	Stockport Co	L	0-1	0-0	10		9407
44	15	A	Southend U	D	1-1	1-0	11	Johnson [45]	6294

Final League Position: 11

GOALSCORERS

League (66): Little 15 (2 pens), Lemonheigh-Evans 11, Hall 6 (1 pen), Lewis 6, Wright 5, Duke-McKenna 3, Holman 3, Wearne 3, Armstrong 2, Lapslie 2, Lolos 2, Wynter 2, Johnson 1, Moxey 1, Sparkes 1, own goals 3.
FA Cup (4): Andrews 1, Johnson 1, Lolos 1, Wynter 1.
FA Trophy (1): Wright 1.

Halstead 7 + 1	Wynter 44	Lapslie 29 + 2	Omar 13 + 12	Wright 30 + 3	Little 38	O'Connell 11 + 17	Rogers 4 + 3	Moxey 37	Holman 14 + 15	Lewis 41	Hall 26 + 4	Johnson 20 + 9	Lolos 11 + 17	Martin 25 + 6	Lemonheigh-Evans 37 + 2	Brzozowski — + 1	Addai — + 4	MacDonald 37	Perritt 7 + 1	Armstrong 6 + 2	Moore 3 + 2	Andrews 1 + 2	Sparkes 3	Felix 3 + 6	Wearne 14	Duke-McKenna 20 + 1	Edwards 3 + 3	Koszela — + 3	Moyse — + 1	Match No.
1	2	3^2	4	5	6	7^3	8^1	9	10	11	12	13	14																	1
1	2	7	3■	10	8	9^1		5	11^3	6	14	4^2		12	13															2
1	2			6	7	12	14	9	10^3	11	5	8■	13	3^2	4^1															3
1	2	3	4	7	8	12		9	10	11	6^1				5															4
1	2		3	6	7^2	13		9^3	10^1	11	5	8	14	12	4															5
1^3	2		3	10			8	6	11^2	5	7	4^1	13		9	12	14													6
	2		14	5		7^1	8^3	10	13	11	4	6	9^2		3		12	1												7
	2	13		11	7	8	9^2	4	12	5	6	3^3	10^1				14	1												8
	2	4	14		7	8	13	9^1	10	11	6^2		12	3	5^3			1												9
	2	4	14		7	8^2		9	10	11	6^3	12	13	3^1	5			1												10
	2	7	14		9	13		4	11^3	6	8	5^1	12	3^2	10			1												11
	2				4	12		8	10^1	11		5	7		3			1	6	9										12
	2	12			7			6	11^1	3		4	10^3		9		14	1	5^2	8	13									13
	2	3			4	6	14	8	10^1	11		12^3	7					1	5		9^2	13								14
	2	6	12		7	8^2		4	13	5			10					1	3^1	11	9^3	14								15
	2	7^3	14		8			5	13	6				3	9			1	4^1	11	12	10^2								16
	2	4			7	13		9^3	12	11	6^2		14	3	5			1	8^1	10										17
	4	6			8	12		3	10^1	2	7		11	5				1		13	9^2									18
	2	6		13	8			4		5	7		11^3	3	14			1	12	9^2			10^1							19
	2	6	14	10	7	13		4^2		5		12	11^1	3	9			1					8^3							20
	2	4^1		6	7			9	14	11	12	13	8^2	3	5			1					10^3							21
	2			6		13		9^2	14	11	5	7	8^1	3	4			1		12				10^3						22
	2			11		9		5	12	6	7^1		13	3	10			1	4						8^2					23
	2		4	11^2	7	14			12		6	5		3	10			1						13	8^1	9^3				24
	2		4	7^1	8	14			12		6	10	13	3	5			1							9^3	11^2				25
	2	4	13		7^2			10	12	11	6			3	5			1							8	9^1				26
	2	6		13	8			4	11^1	5	7			3	10			1							9^2	12				27
	2	4^2		12	7			10		11	6		13	3^3	5			1						14	8^1	9				28
	2	4		7^2				10		11	6	12	13	3^1	5			1							8	9				29
	3	7		11^2	9	13		5		2		4^1	12^3		10			1						14	8	6				30
	2	3	12	5^2	6^1			10		11■		8			4			1						13	7	9				31
	2	6	5	11	7			4	12			3			10			1							8^1	9				32
	2	3		5^1	6			9	13	11		14		12	4			1							7^3	8	10^2			33
	2	5^2	14	11^3	6			3^1	13	4				12	10			1							7	8	9			34
	2	5		11^3	6	13		3	14	4				12	10			1							7	8^2	9^1			35
	2	3		5	6	14		10		11	13	8^3		12	4			1							7^2	9^1				36
	2			11	8	13		5		6	7	4^2		3	10			1								9^1	12			37
	2		12	11	7	9^2		4^1		5	6		13	3	10			1								8				38
	2	4^1	13	7	8			10^2		11	6		12	3	5			1								9				39
	2	4	5^3	8	9	13				11	7	12	14	3^1	6			1								10^2				40
	2	3^2	4	7^3	8					11	6^1	9	13		5			1						12		10	14			41
	2	6^3	4	11^2	8					5	7^1	12		3	10			1						13		9		14		42
12	2		4	11^2	8	13				7		5		3	10			1^3						6^1		9		14		43
1	2		4	11		9^2				7		5		3^3	10									6^1		8	12	13	14	44

FA Cup

Fourth Qualifying	Havant & Waterlooville	(h)	2-2
Replay	Havant & Waterlooville	(a)	2-4

FA Trophy

Third Round	Tonbridge Angels	(a)	1-2

WEALDSTONE

Ground: Grosvenor Vale, Ruislip, Middlesex HA4 6JQ. *Tel:* (07790) 038 095. *Website:* www.wealdstone-fc.com
Email: see website. *Year Formed:* 1899. *Record Attendance:* 13,504 v Leytonstone, FA Amateur Cup, 4th rd replay, 5 March 1949 at Lower Mead; 2,662 v Barnet, National League, 13 November 2021 at Grosvenor Vale.
Nicknames: 'The Stones', 'The Royals'. *Manager:* Stuart Maynard.
Colours: Royal blue shirts with white trim, white shorts with royal blue trim, white socks with royal blue trim.

WEALDSTONE – NATIONAL LEAGUE 2021–22 LEAGUE RECORD

Match No.	Date	Venue	Opponents	Result		H/T Score	Lg Pos.	Goalscorers	Attendance
1	Aug 21	H	Woking	L	1-2	0-2	11	Umerah 69	1405
2	28	A	Chesterfield	L	0-2	0-1	20		5356
3	30	H	Southend U	D	0-0	0-0	18		2151
4	Sept 4	A	Dagenham & R	D	2-2	1-1	19	Umerah 8, Lewis 75	1735
5	11	H	Altrincham	W	1-0	0-0	14	Elito (pen) 90	1013
6	14	A	Notts Co	L	2-3	1-2	16	Umerah 2 31, 64	5213
7	18	H	Aldershot T	D	2-2	1-0	16	Jackson 26, Umerah 62	1106
8	25	A	King's Lynn T	W	1-0	1-0	13	Cooper 32	885
9	Oct 2	A	Torquay U	L	0-5	0-4	16		2097
10	5	H	Solihull Moors	D	0-0	0-0	15		1501
11	9	H	Eastleigh	L	1-2	0-1	16	Umerah 84	1267
12	23	A	Weymouth	D	1-1	0-1	17	McAvoy 62	1024
13	26	H	Grimsby T	W	1-0	1-0	17	Buse 29	1892
14	Nov 13	H	Barnet	W	1-0	0-0	16	Browne 77	2662
15	20	A	Wrexham	D	0-0	0-0	17		8592
16	23	A	Dover Ath	W	3-2	2-1	15	Sweeney 2 4, 72, Umerah 24	399
17	27	H	Stockport Co	L	1-4	0-1	16	Jackson 87	1382
18	Dec 4	A	Bromley	L	2-3	1-2	17	Umerah 8, Cook 72	1747
19	11	H	FC Halifax T	L	0-1	0-1	17		958
20	Jan 11	A	Boreham Wood	L	0-1	0-0	19		1298
21	15	H	Dover Ath	W	2-1	0-1	18	Stevens 63, Charles 70	940
22	22	A	Woking	L	0-2	0-1	20		2667
23	25	H	Notts Co	D	0-0	0-0	19		1547
24	29	A	Grimsby T	L	1-2	0-1	20	Mascoll 55	4747
25	Feb 8	H	Yeovil T	W	2-1	2-0	18	Umerah 38, Tavares 43	1175
26	12	A	Barnet	W	3-1	2-0	16	Ferguson 12, Umerah 30, Mundle-Smith 51	2248
27	19	H	Wrexham	L	1-2	0-0	16	Browne (pen) 71	1901
28	22	A	Solihull Moors	L	1-2	1-1	18	Okimo 22	3219
29	26	H	Torquay U	D	1-1	0-0	18	Mundle-Smith 72	0
30	Mar 5	A	Eastleigh	L	1-4	0-1	19	Clayden 56	2615
31	8	A	Maidenhead U	W	2-0	0-0	16	Cook 65, Browne 75	1029
32	12	H	Weymouth	W	3-2	0-1	15	Browne 2 50, 74, Cook 53	1003
33	19	A	Stockport Co	L	2-4	2-0	16	Cook 13, Henry 33	7453
34	26	H	Bromley	D	1-1	0-0	17	Umerah 89	1161
35	Apr 2	A	FC Halifax T	L	0-2	0-0	18		1850
36	5	H	Maidenhead U	D	0-0	0-0	17		1222
37	9	H	Chesterfield	L	1-2	0-1	18	Umerah 52	1337
38	15	A	Southend U	W	1-0	0-0	17	Browne 68	5849
39	18	H	Boreham Wood	W	2-0	1-0	16	Henry 35, Umerah 51	1181
40	23	A	Altrincham	L	2-4	0-1	16	Cooper 71, Mullarkey (og) 77	1657
41	30	H	Dagenham & R	L	1-2	0-1	17	Umerah 90	1321
42	May 2	A	Yeovil T	D	0-0	0-0	17		2210
43	7	H	King's Lynn T	W	2-1	0-1	17	Umerah 59, Jackson 87	1324
44	15	A	Aldershot T	W	3-1	1-1	16	McAvoy 14, Umerah 69, Jackson 90	2405

Final League Position: 16

GOALSCORERS

League (51): Umerah 16, Browne 6 (1 pen), Cook 4, Jackson 4, Cooper 2, Henry 2, McAvoy 2, Mundle-Smith 2, Sweeney 2, Buse 1, Charles 1, Clayden 1, Elito 1 (1 pen), Ferguson 1, Lewis 1, Mascoll 1, Okimo 1, Stevens 1, Tavares 1, own goal 1.
FA Cup (1): Bird 1.
FA Trophy (1): Buse 1.

Wickens 40	Cook 40	Okimo 33 + 3	Fasanmade 7 + 6	Buse 8 + 6	Umerah 38 + 5	Browne 20 + 9	Lewis 10 + 3	Eleftheriou 11	Tavares 23 + 3	Cooper 31 + 5	Dyer 18 + 10	Elito 13 + 12	Charles 28 + 4	Cawley 5	Wishart 3 + 2	Jackson 9 + 14	Barker 3	Bird 4 + 4	Stevens 6 + 2	Mundle-Smith 24 + 7	McAvoy 28	Dronfield 1 + 2	Mascoll 8 + 9	Sweeney 5	Marigliani — + 1	Dennis 1	Sargeant 1	James-Taylor 2 + 2	Sesay 10 + 3	Ferguson 17	Henry 20	Clayden 15 + 3	Howes 2	*Match No.*
1	2	3	4[1]	5[2]	6	7	8	9	10	11	12	13																						1
1	2	3	4[2]	14	11	7	8	5	6	10[3]	9[1]	12	13																					2
1	2	4	12		5	6[1]	7[2]	8		10	9		3	11	13																			3
1	2	5	6[2]		7	12	13	8	14	10	9		4	11[1]	3[3]																			4
1	2	4	12		5[2]	6[1]	7	8		10	9[3]	14	3	11		13																		5
1	2	4	14		5[3]	12	6[1]	7		10	8[2]	9	3	11		13																		6
1	2	4	13	12	5[1]		6	7		10		9[2]	3	11		8																		7
1	2			14	5[3]	12	13	6	8	11		9[2]	4		3	7■	10[1]																	8
1	2			13	5		6	7	8[3]	11		9[1]	4		3[2]		10	12	14															9
1	2			12	10		7	3	4	9	8[1]	13	6[2]				5	11																10
1	2				12		5	6[1]	7	11	8[2]	9	3		13			10	4[3]	14														11
1	4	5	14	13	11[3]		7		3	9	8[2]		6			12		10[1]			2													12
1	2	3	14	8	10[3]		13		6				7			11[2]		12		5	4	9[1]												13
1	2	14		4[3]	5	13			8	10	12		3			7[1]				9	6		11[2]											14
1	2	12			4	5[1]			7[2]	10	8		3					13		9	6			11										15
1	2	3		7[1]	11	8[2]				10	9							12		5	4	13		6										16
1	2	3		7[1]	10					9	8					12		11[2]		5[3]	4	14	13	6										17
1■	2	3			10					9	8		7			11[1]					4		5	6	12									18
	4	6	7[1]		11					10	9		5			12			13		8		2[2]	3		1								19
		4	5[2]	6[3]	7				8		9	13	2			14			3	10			11[1]				1	12						20
1	2	4	5						6	10	8	13	9			12			3	7[1]								11[2]						21
1	3	7[2]	6[1]		11				5	10[3]	9	12	8						4	13			2					14■						22
1	2[2]	12		5	6					10		8[1]	3						4	9	7		11						13					23
1		4		5	13					10[1]	14	7	2						3	9[3]	6		11					8[2]	12					24
1	2	3			10	14			5	12		8[2]				11[3]				13	4		6[1]							7	9			25
1	2	3			11	12			5[1]	10	14	8[3]								6[2]	4								13	7	9			26
1	2■	3			5	12[3]				11		8[1]								10	7		14						6[2]	4	9	13		27
1		3			5[1]	6						14	2[2]			12				11	8		13						7[3]	4	10	9		28
1	2				10	8			5	13	14		6							12	4								3[2]	7[1]	9[3]	11		29
1	2				10	8[1]			5[3]	13			6[2]			14				12	4								3	7	9	11		30
1	2	3			14	7[3]				9[1]		12				10[2]				5	4		13							6	8	11		31
1	2	3			5[1]	6				11[2]	13	12								10	7									4	9	8		32
1	2	3			10	7				9[3]		13	14							5			12						4[1]	6	8[2]	11		33
1	2	3			13	7			14	9[3]	12					10[1]				5	4[2]									6	8	11		34
1	2	3			5	6[1]			8		9[2]		13			14				12	7[3]									4	11	10		35
1	2	3			12	8							6[1]			10				5	4									7	9	11		36
1		3			5	6[2]						12	2[1]			13				11	8		14						7[3]	4	10	9		37
1	2	3			10	13						8[3]	6							12	5		14						4[1]	7	9[2]	11		38
1	2	3			11	8			5[2]		12	9[1]				14				6	4									7[3]	10	13		39
1	4	5			11	10			2[1]	12	14	9[2]								3	6									8[3]	7	13		40
	2	3			5	6			12	11[2]	13									10	7[1]									4	9	8	1	41
	2	3			10[1]	13			5	9	7■		12							6									4		8	11[2]	1	42
1	2				10				5	9			7			12				6	4		13						3[2]		8	11[1]		43
1	2				4	5[1]			8	12			3[2]			13				11[3]	7		14						6		10	9		44

FA Cup
Fourth Qualifying Dagenham & R (h) 1-2

FA Trophy
Third Round Needham Market (a) 1-2

WEYMOUTH

Ground: Bob Lucas Stadium, Radipole Lane, Weymouth, Dorset DT4 9XJ. *Tel:* (01305) 785 558.
Year formed: 1890. *Website:* www.uptheterrars.co.uk *Email:* info@theterrars.co.uk
Record Attendance: 6,680 v Nottingham F, FA Cup 1st rd replay, 14 November 2005.
Nickname: The Terras. *Manager:* David Oldfield.
Colours: Claret shirts with sky blue sleeves, sky blue shorts with white trim, sky blue socks with white trim.

WEYMOUTH – NATIONAL LEAGUE 2021–22 LEAGUE RECORD

Match No.	*Date*	*Venue*	*Opponents*	*Result*		*H/T Score*	*Lg Pos.*	*Goalscorers*	*Attendance*
1	Aug 21	H	Boreham Wood	L	0-2	0-2	16		1195
2	28	A	Grimsby T	L	0-1	0-0	21		5034
3	30	H	Maidenhead U	W	3-1	2-0	14	Murray [28], Cordner [41], McQuoid [64]	849
4	Sept 4	A	Solihull Moors	W	4-3	3-1	12	Leslie-Smith [8], Ash 2 [21, 45], McQuoid [48]	1383
5	11	H	Notts Co	D	1-1	0-0	9	Robinson [69]	1783
6	14	A	Dagenham & R	L	2-4	2-1	11	Leslie-Smith [6], Ash (pen) [40]	1240
7	18	H	Dover Ath	D	1-1	1-1	10	McQuoid [42]	1028
8	25	A	Barnet	L	1-3	0-1	15	Goodship [70]	1269
9	Oct 2	H	Stockport Co	L	1-2	1-0	17	Shields [39]	872
10	5	A	Bromley	L	0-3	0-2	20		1334
11	9	A	FC Halifax T	L	0-2	0-1	21		2241
12	23	H	Wealdstone	D	1-1	1-0	19	Thomson [40]	1024
13	26	A	Aldershot T	W	2-0	1-0	19	Thomson [9], Leslie-Smith [62]	1510
14	30	H	King's Lynn T	W	1-0	0-0	17	Mussa [50]	1056
15	Nov 13	A	Chesterfield	L	0-4	0-2	18		5862
16	20	H	Altrincham	L	1-4	0-1	18	Olomowewe [62]	932
17	23	H	Woking	L	2-3	0-1	18	Cordner [66], Robinson [90]	789
18	Dec 4	H	Torquay U	L	1-2	0-0	19	Goodship [68]	1559
19	11	A	Wrexham	L	0-1	0-1	20		7530
20	Jan 2	A	Eastleigh	L	2-3	0-1	21	McQuoid [79], Goodship [88]	2839
21	8	H	Southend U	L	0-1	0-1	21		1335
22	22	A	Boreham Wood	D	1-1	1-1	21	Reckord (og) [42]	811
23	25	H	Dagenham & R	L	1-2	1-0	21	McQuoid [38]	901
24	29	H	Aldershot T	L	0-1	0-0	21		1571
25	Feb 1	A	Yeovil T	D	1-1	1-0	21	Shields [4]	3936
26	5	A	King's Lynn T	L	0-3	0-1	21		847
27	12	H	Chesterfield	D	1-1	0-0	21	Rose, A [90]	1299
28	15	H	Eastleigh	W	1-0	0-0	21	Goodship [71]	1053
29	22	H	Bromley	D	2-2	1-0	21	Bearwish [34], Murray [73]	1003
30	26	A	Stockport Co	L	0-1	0-1	21		7418
31	Mar 5	H	FC Halifax T	L	0-2	0-0	21		1026
32	8	A	Altrincham	L	0-5	0-4	21		1613
33	12	A	Wealdstone	L	2-3	1-0	21	Ash [45], McQuoid [85]	1003
34	22	A	Woking	L	0-2	0-1	21		1826
35	26	A	Torquay U	L	0-3	0-2	22		2538
36	Apr 9	H	Grimsby T	D	0-0	0-0	22		1228
37	15	A	Maidenhead U	L	0-2	0-0	22		2056
38	18	H	Yeovil T	D	0-0	0-0	22		2609
39	23	A	Notts Co	L	1-3	0-2	22	Bearwish [54]	6032
40	26	H	Wrexham	L	1-6	1-0	22	Bearwish [20]	921
41	30	H	Solihull Moors	L	2-4	0-2	22	Cordner [79], Blair [90]	756
42	May 2	A	Southend U	D	1-1	1-0	22	McQuoid [40]	5323
43	7	H	Barnet	L	1-2	0-1	22	Carlyle [72]	1081
44	15	A	Dover Ath	W	2-1	1-0	22	Goodship (pen) [9], Blair [90]	763

Final League Position: 22

GOALSCORERS

League (40): McQuoid 7, Goodship 5 (1 pen), Ash 4 (1 pen), Bearwish 3, Cordner 3, Leslie-Smith 3, Blair 2, Murray 2, Robinson 2, Shields 2, Thomson 2, Carlyle 1, Mussa 1, Olomowewe 1, Rose, A 1, own goal 1.
FA Cup (2): Bearwish 1, McQuoid 1.
FA Trophy (1): McQuoid 1.

Fitzsimons 43	Cordner 41	Goodship 21 + 15	Mussa 28 + 6	McQuoid 33 + 5	Ash 18 + 8	Robinson 20 + 6	Brooks 5 + 2	Harfield 35 + 2	Olomowewe 18 + 1	Shields 28 + 5	Rose A 4 + 13	Bearwish 23 + 14	Morgan 15 + 2	Leslie-Smith 14 + 3	Murray 31 + 4	Thomson 7 + 5	McBurnie 3 + 2	Yarney 1	Taylor-Crossdale 2 + 6	Blair 9 + 14	Davies 2	Solance 2	Solanke 3	Mnoga 19	Greenidge 3 + 2	Drewe 19	Mampala 5 + 6	Bunker 6	Smith 4 + 1	Greenwood 8	Carlyle 6 + 1	Buse 7 + 1	Scott 1	*Match No.*
1	2	3	4^{1}	5^{2}	6	7	8	9	10	11	12	13																						1
1	3	7	13	8^{3}	12	6	4^{1}	5		11	10^{2}	9	2	14																				2
1	3	13	4^{3}	5^{1}	6	12		9	10	11		14	2^{2}	7	8																			3
1	3		4^{3}	5^{1}	6	14		9	10	11	13	12	2	7^{2}	8																			4
1	3	12	4^{1}		5	8	13	10		11		6^{2}	2	7	9																			5
1	3	13	4^{2}	14	5	12		9	10	11		6	2^{3}	7	8^{1}																			6
1	2	3	4	5^{1}	6	7	8^{2}	10	11			12	13		9																			7
1	2	12	8	9	10^{2}	6		4	5	11		13		3	7^{1}																			8
1	2	3	4^{2}	5^{1}	12	7		9	10	11		13		6	8^{3}	14																		9
1	2	7	8	9^{2}	10^{1}	6	3	4	5^{3}	11	14			12		13																		10
1	2	8	9	13	14	6^{1}	4	5		11^{3}		10		3	7^{2}		12																	11
1	4	11^{3}	13	10	14	6	12	2		8				5	7	9^{1}		3^{2}																12
1	2	12	8^{3}	10^{2}		6		4	5		14	11		3	7	9^{1}			13															13
1		2^{2}	3^{1}	5	14	8		10	11	12		6		7	9	4^{3}			13															14
1	3		8^{3}	10		7		5■	6	12		11	2^{2}	4	13	9^{1}			14															15
1	2	3	14	4^{3}	12				10	11^{2}	13	5■		6	9				7^{1}	8														16
1	3	14	8	9	10^{2}	7		5	6	11^{3}			2	4^{1}					13	12														17
1	4	5	6^{1}	7				10	11	12			3^{2}	14	9				8^{3}	13	2													18
1	4	5^{3}	12	6^{1}		7		10	11	14			3						13	8^{2}	2	9												19
1	2	12	3^{3}	4		6		10	11			13		5^{2}	8				14	7			9^{1}											20
1	3	9^{2}	10	11^{1}	13	6		5				12	2		8					7				4										21
1	2	12	8^{3}	9^{2}				4	5	11^{1}		13			6					14			7	3	10									22
1	2	12		3^{2}				8	10^{1}	11	14				6					13			7	4	9^{3}	5								23
1	2	12	7	8^{2}				5		11	13	9			6									3	10^{1}	4								24
1	2		7■	8^{2}				5		11^{3}	12	9			6					13				3	14	4	10^{1}							25
1	2	14		8				5		11	12	9			6^{2}					13		7^{3}		3		4	10^{1}							26
1	2	14	3					9		11	12	5^{2}			8					13				4		6		7^{3}	10^{1}					27
1	2	3	4^{3}	13				9		11	10^{2}				8					12				5		6^{1}	14	7						28
1	5	10^{1}		13				3		9		11^{2}			7					12				4		2		6	8					29
1	2	3	4	5^{2}				11				7			10					12				6		8^{1}	14	9^{3}	13					30
1	2		3	4	5			10				14								12				6	13	7^{1}	8^{2}	9^{3}	11					31
1	4	10	12	14				5			13	9			7					8^{1}				3		2		6^{3}	11^{2}					32
1	2	14	3	4	5^{1}			9^{2}		11	10^{3}	12			8					13				6		7								33
1	3	13	7^{1}	8	9				14	11		10^{3}	2		6^{2}	12				5■						4								34
1	4	7		9	10					11^{1}		14	3^{2}		6	8^{3}										5				2	12	13		35
1	4	5^{1}			6					11		8^{2}			12	13	3^{3}							7		9	14			2		10		36
1	4	5			6	13				11		8^{2}	14		3^{3}	12								7		9				2^{1}		10		37
1	4			9^{1}	10	14				12		11	3^{2}			8										5	13			2	6	7^{3}		38
1	4			6^{3}	7			14				8	3^{2}			5				12						9	13			2	11^{1}	10		39
1				9	10	6^{3}		14				11	3		12					7^{2}				4		5	13			2^{1}		8		40
1	2	8^{2}	12	9^{1}		13		4		11	14	10^{3}			7					6				3							5			41
1	3		4^{1}	5^{2}		7					12	13					14							6		8	9^{3}			2	11	10		42
1	2	13	6^{1}		12	7		3		11	10^{2}	9			14		5			8^{3}											4			43
		4^{2}				6		10				13			8		3			12				5			7^{1}			2	11	9	1	44

FA Cup

Fourth Qualifying	Yeovil T	(a)	1-1
Replay	Yeovil T	(h)	1-1

(aet; Yeovil T won 2-1 on penalties)

FA Trophy

Third Round	Hungerford T	(a)	1-0
Fourth Round	Dartford	(a)	0-1

WOKING

Ground: The Laithwaite Community Stadium, Kingfield, Woking, Surrey GU22 9AA. *Tel:* (01483) 722 470.
Website: wokingfc.co.uk *Email:* see website *Year Formed:* 1889.
Record Attendance: 7,020 v Finchley, FA Amateur Cup 4th rd, 1957–58. *Nickname:* 'The Cardinals'.
Manager: Darren Sarll. *Colours:* Red and white halved shirts with black trim, black shorts with white trim, black socks with white trim.

WOKING – NATIONAL LEAGUE 2021–22 LEAGUE RECORD

Match No.	*Date*	*Venue*	*Opponents*	*Result*		*H/T Score*	*Lg Pos.*	*Goalscorers*	*Attendance*
1	Aug 21	A	Wealdstone	W	2-1	2-0	6	Kretzschmar 2 [20, 24]	1405
2	28	H	FC Halifax T	L	2-3	1-2	9	Maguire-Drew (pen) [39], Oakley [68]	3068
3	30	A	Torquay U	W	4-0	2-0	4	Campbell 2 [2, 55], Ince [4], Thompson-Sommers [90]	2486
4	Sept 11	A	Wrexham	L	0-1	0-1	10		8242
5	25	A	Eastleigh	L	2-3	2-1	18	Campbell 2 [3, 16]	2521
6	28	H	Chesterfield	W	3-1	0-1	12	Campbell 2 [64, 87], Effiong [89]	1855
7	Oct 2	A	Notts Co	W	4-1	0-1	11	Effiong [70], Diarra [75], Campbell 2 [78, 90]	5807
8	5	H	Dagenham & R	W	1-0	1-0	8	Kretzschmar (pen) [30]	2226
9	9	H	Grimsby T	L	0-1	0-0	11		4478
10	23	A	Maidenhead U	L	2-3	1-1	12	Effiong [25], McNerney [50]	1165
11	26	A	Yeovil T	L	0-2	0-1	12		2024
12	30	H	Altrincham	W	3-2	1-1	11	Kretzschmar [39], Effiong [63], Campbell [78]	2985
13	Nov 2	H	Bromley	L	0-2	0-0	11		1843
14	13	A	Southend U	W	2-0	1-0	10	Campbell [22], Kretzschmar (pen) [88]	5821
15	20	H	Stockport Co	L	1-2	0-2	12	Campbell [66]	2753
16	23	A	Weymouth	W	3-2	1-0	12	Campbell 2 [34, 81], Ince [61]	789
17	27	H	Barnet	L	1-2	1-1	13	McNerney [2]	1779
18	Dec 4	A	Solihull Moors	L	0-2	0-1	14		1214
19	11	H	Boreham Wood	L	0-2	0-2	14		1687
20	26	A	Aldershot T	D	1-1	0-0	14	Kretzschmar (pen) [90]	3699
21	28	H	Dover Ath	W	3-2	2-1	12	Kretzschmar (pen) [6], Effiong 2 [34, 60]	2248
22	Jan 2	H	Aldershot T	L	2-3	1-0	14	Kretzschmar 2 (1 pen) [7, 71 (p)]	5171
23	22	H	Wealdstone	W	2-0	1-0	12	Effiong [20], Loza [76]	2667
24	25	A	Bromley	L	0-1	0-1	12		1663
25	29	H	Yeovil T	L	0-1	0-1	13		2496
26	Feb 5	A	Altrincham	D	2-2	2-0	13	Effiong [1], Lofthouse [33]	1334
27	12	H	Southend U	L	2-3	0-2	15	Effiong 2 (1 pen) [47, 58 (p)]	3819
28	19	A	Stockport Co	L	0-1	0-0	15		6820
29	22	A	Dagenham & R	D	1-1	0-1	15	Effiong [82]	1358
30	26	H	Notts Co	L	0-2	0-1	16		3141
31	Mar 5	A	Grimsby T	L	0-1	0-0	18		5423
32	8	A	King's Lynn T	D	0-0	0-0	19		713
33	12	H	Maidenhead U	W	1-0	0-0	16	Kabamba [90]	2188
34	19	A	Barnet	W	2-0	1-0	14	Diarra [15], Loza [86]	1501
35	22	H	Weymouth	W	2-0	1-0	14	Johnson [17], Kretzschmar (pen) [90]	1826
36	26	H	Solihull Moors	L	2-3	1-1	15	Effiong 2 [16, 49]	2198
37	Apr 2	A	Boreham Wood	W	1-0	0-0	14	Kretzschmar (pen) [75]	901
38	9	A	FC Halifax T	L	1-2	0-1	14	Kretzschmar (pen) [75]	1763
39	15	H	Torquay U	L	0-1	0-1	15		3344
40	18	A	Dover Ath	W	4-1	2-0	14	Woods (og) [6], Kabamba 2 [26, 48], Longe-King [55]	655
41	23	H	Wrexham	W	2-1	0-1	14	Kretzschmar (pen) [65], Loza [86]	2697
42	May 2	H	King's Lynn T	L	0-3	0-1	15		2484
43	7	H	Eastleigh	L	1-2	0-0	15	Roles [68]	2492
44	15	A	Chesterfield	D	0-0	0-0	15		9013

Final League Position: 15

GOALSCORERS

League (59): Campbell 13, Effiong 13 (1 pen), Kretzschmar 13 (9 pens), Kabamba 3, Loza 3, Diarra 2, Ince 2, McNerney 2, Johnson 1, Lofthouse 1, Longe-King 1, Maguire-Drew 1 (1 pen), Oakley 1, Roles 1, Thompson-Sommers 1, own goal 1.
FA Cup (0).
FA Trophy (1): Campbell 1.

Ross 33	Lofthouse 26 + 3	Casey 38 + 2	McNerney 21 + 3	Diarra 39	Nwabuokei 33 + 8	Effiong 32 + 8	Kretzschmar 29 + 5	Maguire-Drew 5 + 2	Campbell 21	Ince 34 + 1	Allarakhia 10 + 10	Champion 34 + 2	Oakley 10 + 7	Thompson-Sommers — + 11	Johnson 29 + 7	Loza 11 + 19	Block 4	Annesley 14 + 4	Smith M 11	Anderson 13 + 3	Britton 3 + 1	Longe-King 15	Kabamba 12 + 9	Roles 4 + 6	Pendlebury 3 + 1	*Match No.*
1	2	3	4	5	6	7	8^{2}	9^{1}	10^{3}	11	12	13	14													1
1	2	3	4	5	6			9	10^{1}	11		7^{2}	8	12	13											2
1	2	3	5	6	7			9^{1}	10^{2}	11^{3}	13	4	8	12	14											3
1	2	3	4	5	7^{3}	13		8	11	9^{1}	12	6	10^{2}	14												4
1	2	3	5		6^{3}	7	12	9^{2}	10	11		4	13	14	8^{1}											5
1	5	2	3	4	7	12	8		11	9		6	10^{1}													6
1	2	3	5	6	7^{2}	8	9^{3}		10	11	14	4^{1}		13	12											7
1	5	2	3	4	7	10	8^{1}		11	9		6		12												8
1	5	2	3	4	7	11			10	9^{1}	8^{2}	6		12		13										9
1	2	3	5■	6	7^{3}	8	9^{2}		10^{1}	11		4		13	12	14										10
1	12	2		3	5^{1}	9	6^{3}		11	8	13	4		14	10		7^{2}									11
1	2	3		5	6	7	8		10	11^{1}		4		12				9								12
1	6	3^{2}		2	7	10^{1}	8^{3}	14	11	9		5			13	12		4								13
1	2	3		5	7	12	8		10	11		4		13	9^{1}	6^{2}										14
1	2	3		5	7^{2}	13	8	14	10	11		4			9^{3}	6^{1}		12								15
	2	3	4	5	6^{1}	10	7^{2}		11	8	13	12				9^{3}		14	1							16
	5	2	3	4	12	11	7^{3}			9^{2}	8	6			14	10^{1}		13	1							17
	6	4^{2}	3	2	8				11		9^{1}	5			12	13■			1	7	10					18
				3		12	4		8	11		2			5		9	6	1	10	7^{1}					19
1	13	2^{2}	3^{1}		12	9	6		11			5			10		7^{3}	4		8	14					20
1	2	13		4	5	6	7^{2}					3			8	12		9		11	10^{1}					21
1	12	2		4	5	6	7		9			3			8^{1}	13	10^{2}			11						22
	5			3		9^{1}	6		10^{2}	8	7				11	13		2	1			4	12			23
	5			2	12	9	6^{2}			8	7^{1}				10	13		3■	1			4	11			24
	5	12	2^{3}	3	6^{2}	10				8	13				11^{1}	9			1	7		4	14			25
	5	2		3	13	10				8	6^{2}				11	9^{3}		4	1	7^{1}			12	14		26
	2	4		5	6^{2}	9				8	12				10	14		3	1	13			11^{1}	7^{3}		27
1	11	2		4		5^{2}				10	7	3	14			13		6		9^{3}			8^{1}	12		28
1	2			4	5	6	13			11■	9	3^{2}			7	12		8					10^{1}			29
1	2^{3}	3	12	5	6^{1}	7	13				10	4			8	14		9					11^{2}			30
1		2	14	4	5	6^{3}	12				9^{2}	3	13		7			8^{1}					10		11	31
1		2		3	6	9	7^{1}				13	5			10^{2}	12						4	11		8	32
1		2		4	6	7^{1}	8			11		3	12		9^{2}	5						10	13			33
1		2		3	6	13	7^{1}			8		5	10^{2}		9^{3}	12						4	11		14	34
1		2	13	3	6	14	12			7		5	11^{3}		10^{1}	9						4■			8^{2}	35
1		2	3	4^{2}	6	9	7			8^{3}		5	13		10	12							11^{1}	14		36
1		4	3		6	9	7			8■		5	10^{2}		11^{1}	13						2	12			37
1		2	4		5	6	7					3	9^{3}		8^{1}	13				11^{2}		10	12	14		38
1		2	3		6^{3}	9	7					5	11^{2}		10	12				8^{1}		4	13	14		39
		2	3	4	13		6^{1}			8^{2}					10	9		14	1	12		5^{3}	11	7		40
1		2	3	4	13	10^{1}	6^{3}			8					11^{2}	9				14		5	12	7		41
		2		3	5	13				12		6	10^{1}		9^{3}	8			1	7^{2}		4	11	14		42
1		4		2	12	10	6			9^{1}		5			11^{3}	13■				8^{2}		3	14	7		43
1		2		3	14	9^{1}	6^{3}			8	13		12		10^{2}			4		7		5	11			44

FA Cup
Fourth Qualifying Horsham (a) 0-1

FA Trophy
Third Round Yeovil T (a) 1-3

WREXHAM

Ground: Racecourse Ground, Mold Road, Wrexham, Wales LL11 2AH. *Tel:* (01978) 891 864.
Website: wrexhamafc.co.uk *Email:* info@wrexhamfc.tv *Year Formed:* 1872.
Record Attendance: 34,445 v Manchester U, FA Cup 4th rd, 26 January 1957. *Nickname:* 'Red Dragons'.
Manager: Phil J. Parkinson. *Colours:* Red shirts with white sleeves, white shorts with red trim, white socks with red trim.

WREXHAM – NATIONAL LEAGUE 2021–22 LEAGUE RECORD

Match No.	*Date*	*Venue*	*Opponents*	*Result*		*H/T Score*	*Lg Pos.*	*Goalscorers*	*Attendance*
1	Aug 21	A	Solihull Moors	D	2-2	2-1	9	Mullin (pen) [26], David Jones [30]	2196
2	28	A	Eastleigh	W	2-0	2-0	6	Hyde 2 [12, 42]	2572
3	30	H	Notts Co	D	1-1	0-1	8	Mullin [53]	5454
4	Sept 4	A	Southend U	D	2-2	0-1	7	Reckord [54], Angus [66]	6036
5	11	H	Woking	W	1-0	1-0	8	Davies [40]	8242
6	14	A	Grimsby T	L	1-3	1-2	8	Hyde [22]	6663
7	18	H	Dagenham & R	W	1-0	1-0	7	Mullin [8]	8033
8	25	A	Stockport Co	L	1-2	1-0	7	Mullin [2]	7771
9	Oct 5	H	Chesterfield	D	1-1	0-1	12	Mullin [84]	9147
10	23	A	Barnet	W	3-0	2-0	11	Mullin [24], Hayden [28], Brisley [55]	2237
11	26	A	Maidenhead U	L	2-3	1-2	11	Mullin [45], Davies [57]	1692
12	30	H	Torquay U	D	1-1	1-0	13	Lennon [4]	9813
13	Nov 9	A	Aldershot T	W	5-0	2-0	9	Hayden [40], Lennon [43], Hall-Johnson [58], Ponticelli [61], Davies [68]	1639
14	13	A	King's Lynn T	W	6-2	1-1	9	Hayden [22], Davies [52], Mullin [63], Ponticelli [76], Green [90], Jarvis [90]	1070
15	20	H	Wealdstone	D	0-0	0-0	9		8592
16	23	A	FC Halifax T	W	2-1	0-0	8	Jones, J [83], Mullin [90]	3344
17	27	H	Bromley	W	2-0	1-0	7	Hall-Johnson [33], Mullin [60]	8156
18	30	H	Yeovil T	L	0-2	0-0	7		8057
19	Dec 4	A	Dover Ath	W	1-0	0-0	4	Davies [84]	838
20	11	H	Weymouth	W	1-0	1-0	4	Davies [29]	7530
21	28	A	Altrincham	W	2-0	2-0	3	Hayden [24], Hosannah [38]	3145
22	Jan 2	A	Notts Co	L	1-3	1-2	3	Hall-Johnson [4]	8890
23	22	A	Yeovil T	W	2-1	0-1	6	Mullin [59], Williams (og) [79]	2988
24	25	H	Grimsby T	W	1-0	1-0	6	Palmer [35]	8434
25	29	H	Maidenhead U	D	1-1	1-0	6	Hayden [17]	8759
26	Feb 5	A	Torquay U	L	0-1	0-1	7		3181
27	19	A	Wealdstone	W	2-1	0-0	7	Davies [88], Hall-Johnson [90]	1901
28	22	A	Chesterfield	W	2-0	0-0	5	Palmer 2 [58, 68]	7854
29	26	H	Aldershot T	W	4-1	1-0	4	Mullin 2 [35, 68], Davies [49], Palmer [57]	8475
30	Mar 1	H	King's Lynn T	W	2-0	2-0	3	Davies [11], Mullin [31]	8178
31	8	H	Boreham Wood	W	4-2	1-1	3	Palmer [15], Hayden [61], Jones, J [66], Mullin [70]	8705
32	19	A	Bromley	D	0-0	0-0	4		3123
33	22	H	FC Halifax T	W	3-1	2-0	4	Mullin (pen) [6], Palmer [28], Jones, J [86]	8711
34	26	H	Dover Ath	W	6-5	2-2	2	Mullin [6], Jones, J [20], Palmer 2 [65, 69], Davies 2 [90, 90]	8572
35	Apr 5	H	Barnet	W	6-0	3-0	2	Palmer [14], Mullin [27], Davies [44], Tozer [50], Hall-Johnson [73], McAlinden [85]	8868
36	9	H	Eastleigh	W	3-2	1-1	2	Hayden [27], Mullin 2 (1 pen) [77, 90 (p)]	9163
37	15	H	Solihull Moors	D	1-1	0-0	2	Palmer [58]	9949
38	18	H	Altrincham	W	4-0	4-0	2	Davies [2], Mullin 2 [28, 33], Palmer [35]	10,022
39	23	A	Woking	L	1-2	1-0	2	Johnson (og) [44]	2697
40	26	A	Weymouth	W	6-1	0-1	2	Davies 2 [47, 64], Mullin 2 [49, 83], Jones, J [54], Palmer [84]	921
41	30	H	Southend U	W	1-0	0-0	2	Palmer [47]	9269
42	May 2	A	Boreham Wood	D	1-1	0-0	2	Mullin [54]	2053
43	8	H	Stockport Co	W	3-0	2-0	1	Palmer 2 [34, 46], Mullin [45]	10,118
44	15	A	Dagenham & R	L	0-3	0-0	2		3470

Final League Position: 2

GOALSCORERS

League (91): Mullin 26 (3 pens), Davies 15, Palmer 15, Hayden 7, Hall-Johnson 5, Jones, J 5, Hyde 3, Lennon 2, Ponticelli 2, Angus 1, Brisley 1, Green 1, Hosannah 1, Jarvis 1, David Jones 1, McAlinden 1, Reckord 1, Tozer 1, own goals 2.
FA Cup (4): Mullin 2, Davies 1, Ponticelli 1.
FA Trophy (17): Davies 4, Jones J 2, Mullin 2, Ponticelli 2, Thomas 2, Cleworth 1, Hayden 1, Hosannah 1, Jarvis 1, Palmer 1.
National League Play-offs (4): Mullin 2 (1 pen), Davies 1, Tozer 1.

Dibble 16 + 2	Hall-Johnson 30 + 2	Reckord 12	Hayden 39	Davies 38 + 1	Young 40 + 1	Hyde 10 + 4	Mullin 38	French 17 + 4	Jones David 1 + 3	Cleworth 25 + 3	McAlinden 12 + 20	Lennon 16 + 1	Lainton 28	Tozer 43	Jones J 37 + 3	Angus 3 + 13	Ponticelli 10 + 17	Redmond 2 + 1	Green — + 7	Hosannah 19 + 4	Brisley 3	Jarvis 5 + 12	Thomas 1 + 5	Palmer 21	O'Connor 3 + 3	McFadzean 15	*Match No.*
1	2^{1}	3	4	5	6	7^{2}	8	9	10	11	12	13															1
		6	3	9	7	10	11^{1}	2				5	1	4	8	12											2
		6	3	9	7	10^{1}	11	2		5	13		1	4	8^{2}	12											3
		6	3	9	7	10^{3}		2		13	14	5^{1}	1	4	8	11^{2}	12										4
		6	3	9^{1}	7	10	11^{2}	2	12■		13	5	1	4	8												5
		6	3		8	10^{3}	11	2		5^{2}	12		1	4	7	13		9^{1}	14								6
		2	3		5		6	8	14	13	7^{2}	10^{3}	1	4	11	12	9^{1}										7
		6	3		7		11	2			9^{2}	5	1	4	8	12	10^{1}	13									8
		6^{2}	3	7		10	11	12			13	5^{3}	1	4	9	14		8^{1}		2							9
1		5	3	7^{2}			10^{3}	2			9			6	13	11^{1}	12			8	4	14					10
1		5	3	7			10	2			8^{2}			6	14	11^{3}	12			9■	4^{1}	13					11
		6	3	8	14			2			10	4	1	5	7^{3}	12	11^{1}			9^{2}		13					12
12	7^{2}		2	6	8							4	1^{1}	3	9	14	11^{3}		13	5		10					13
1	2^{2}		3	9	8		10^{1}					5		4	7		11		12	6		13					14
	2		3	5	6	13	7					10	1	4	11^{1}		9^{3}		12	8^{2}		14					15
	2		3	9	8	12	11						1	5	7		13		14	6^{1}	4^{3}	10^{2}					16
	2			8	7	10	11	5				3	1	4			12			6		9^{1}					17
	2		3	8	7	14	11				9■	5^{2}	1	4	12		10^{1}		13	6^{3}							18
	2		3	8	7	10	11		13			5^{2}	1	4	9^{1}		12			6							19
	2		3	8	7	10^{1}	11			5			1	4	9		12			6							20
	8		2	6^{2}	7		11			12		4	1	3	9		10^{1}			5			13				21
	2		3	9^{3}	8		10					5■	1	4	7	13	11^{2}		12	6^{1}			14				22
	2		3	9	8		10				13	5	1	4	7		12			6^{2}			11^{1}				23
	2		3	9	8		10^{2}	12		5	6		1	4	7^{3}		14						13	11^{1}			24
	7		3	5	8		9■			2	10		1	4	6								12	11^{1}			25
	2		3		8					5^{1}	12		1	4	9^{2}	13	10^{3}			6			14	11	7		26
	2		4	6	7					10^{3}	13		1	5			12			14		8		11	9^{2}	3^{1}	27
	8		2	6	9					4	12		1	3						5		10^{1}		11	7		28
	2^{2}		3	9	8		10			5	13		1	4	7		14			12				11^{1}		6^{3}	29
	7		2	6^{1}	9		10			4	12		1	3	8					13				11		5^{2}	30
	2		3		9		10^{1}			5	8		1	4	7		12							11		6	31
14	2		3^{1}	13	8		10	12		5	9^{3}		1^{2}	4	7									11		6	32
1	2		3	9^{1}	7		10			5	12			4	8									11		6	33
1	2^{1}		4	6	7		8			10^{2}	13			5	9^{3}	14						12		11		3	34
1	7		2	6^{2}	8		10^{3}			4	12			3	9	13						14		11^{1}		5	35
1	2		4	6	7		8			10^{2}	13			5	9^{3}	14						12		11		3^{1}	36
1	7^{1}		2	6	8		10			4	12			3	9									11		5	37
1	2		3^{3}	9^{2}	7		10^{1}	12		5	13			4	8							14		11		6	38
1	8		2	6	7		11			4^{2}	12			3	9^{3}		14					13		10		5^{1}	39
1	12		5^{3}	6^{2}	8		10^{1}	2		3	9			4	7		14							11	13		40
1	7^{1}			5^{2}	6		9^{3}	2		4	11			3	8		14			12				10	13		41
1	12			7	8	14	10^{1}	3^{2}		5				4	9					2^{3}		13		11		6	42
1				7^{1}	8		10	3		5				4	9		13			2				11^{2}	12	6	43
1	7			6	9		10	2^{3}		4	13			3	8^{2}		14					12		11		5^{1}	44

FA Cup

Fourth Qualifying	Marine	(a)	1-1
Replay	Marine	(h)	2-0
First Round	Harrogate T	(a)	1-2

National League Play-offs

Semi-Final	Grimsby T	(h)	4-5

FA Trophy

Third Round	Gloucester C	(h)	5-0
Fourth Round	Folkestone Invicta	(h)	5-1
Fifth Round	Boreham Wood	(h)	3-0
Quarter-Final	Notts Co	(a)	2-1
Semi-Final	Stockport Co	(h)	2-0
Final	Bromley	(Wembley)	0-1

YEOVIL TOWN

Ground: Huish Park, Lufton Way, Yeovil, Somerset BA22 8YF. *Tel:* (01935) 423 662. *Website:* www.ytfc.net
Email: info@ytfc.net *Year Formed:* 1895. *Record Attendance:* 16,318 v Sunderland, FA Cup 4th rd, 29 January 1949 (at Huish); 9,527 v Leeds U, FL 1, 25 April 2008 (at Huish Park). *Nickname:* 'The Glovers'.
Manager: Chris Hargreaves. *Colours:* Green shirts with white trim, white shorts with green trim, white socks with green trim.

YEOVIL TOWN – NATIONAL LEAGUE 2021–22 LEAGUE RECORD

Match No.	*Date*	*Venue*	*Opponents*	*Result*		*H/T Score*	*Lg Pos.*	*Goalscorers*	*Attendance*
1	Aug 28	H	King's Lynn T	L	1-2	1-0	17	Quigley [15]	2024
2	30	A	Aldershot T	W	2-1	1-0	12	Quigley 2 (1 pen) [14, 83 (p)]	2073
3	Sept 4	H	FC Halifax T	W	1-0	1-0	10	Quigley (pen) [14]	1899
4	11	A	Stockport Co	W	3-0	1-0	6	Wakefield [26], Quigley (pen) [53], Yussuf [86]	5231
5	18	H	Chesterfield	L	0-2	0-2	9		2356
6	25	A	Boreham Wood	L	1-2	1-1	11	Gorman [15]	658
7	Oct 5	H	Maidenhead U	D	0-0	0-0	14		2031
8	9	H	Notts Co	L	0-2	0-1	15		2438
9	12	H	Altrincham	D	1-1	0-0	14	Quigley [57]	1640
10	23	A	Grimsby T	L	0-2	0-1	15		6470
11	26	H	Woking	W	2-0	1-0	14	Wakefield [4], Knowles [47]	2024
12	30	A	Solihull Moors	D	0-0	0-0	15		1607
13	Nov 13	H	Eastleigh	W	2-1	1-0	13	Knowles [42], Yussuf [76]	2494
14	20	A	Dagenham & R	W	1-0	1-0	13	McCallum (og) [45]	1642
15	23	A	Bromley	W	2-1	2-1	13	Knowles [18], Wakefield [45]	1910
16	27	H	Dover Ath	D	1-1	0-1	11	Yussuf [77]	2062
17	30	A	Wrexham	W	2-0	0-0	10	Staunton [64], Lo-Everton [83]	8057
18	Dec 11	H	Barnet	W	1-0	1-0	9	Yussuf [9]	2024
19	26	A	Torquay U	L	0-3	0-0	11		3830
20	Jan 2	H	Torquay U	L	1-2	0-0	11	Barnett [66]	3866
21	11	A	Southend U	L	1-2	0-1	11	Reid [90]	4845
22	22	H	Wrexham	L	1-2	1-0	13	Knowles [14]	2988
23	29	A	Woking	W	1-0	1-0	11	Wakefield [15]	2496
24	Feb 1	H	Weymouth	D	1-1	0-1	11	Yussuf [52]	3936
25	5	H	Solihull Moors	D	0-0	0-0	12		1955
26	8	A	Wealdstone	L	1-2	0-2	12	Gorman (pen) [62]	1175
27	12	A	Eastleigh	D	0-0	0-0	13		2760
28	22	A	Maidenhead U	D	1-1	1-1	13	Olomola [18]	1153
29	26	A	Chesterfield	L	0-1	0-1	13		5371
30	Mar 5	A	Notts Co	D	1-1	0-0	13	Bradley [47]	6943
31	8	H	Dagenham & R	L	0-3	0-2	13		1836
32	12	H	Grimsby T	L	0-2	0-1	14		2422
33	19	A	Dover Ath	W	2-0	1-0	13	Barclay [19], Gorman [56]	822
34	22	H	Bromley	W	2-1	1-1	13	D'Ath [10], Knowles [71]	1732
35	26	H	Southend U	W	2-0	2-0	12	Reid [4], Knowles [8]	2475
36	Apr 2	A	Barnet	D	2-2	1-1	12	Knowles [8], Reid [82]	1393
37	9	A	King's Lynn T	D	2-2	1-2	12	Gorman (pen) [6], Wakefield [90]	1148
38	15	H	Aldershot T	L	0-2	0-0	12		2528
39	18	A	Weymouth	D	0-0	0-0	12		2609
40	23	H	Stockport Co	W	2-1	1-0	12	Knowles [39], Neufville [55]	2783
41	30	A	FC Halifax T	L	0-1	0-0	13		1947
42	May 2	H	Wealdstone	D	0-0	0-0	13		2210
43	7	H	Boreham Wood	D	2-2	0-2	13	Williams [58], Wilkinson [65]	2599
44	15	A	Altrincham	W	1-0	1-0	12	Knowles [16]	2123

Final League Position: 12

GOALSCORERS

League (43): Knowles 9, Quigley 6 (3 pens), Wakefield 5, Yussuf 5, Gorman 4 (2 pens), Reid 3, Barclay 1, Barnett 1, Bradley 1, D'Ath 1, Lo-Everton 1, Neufville 1, Olomola 1, Staunton 1, Wilkinson 1, Williams 1, own goal 1.
FA Cup (9): Wakefield 3, Worthington 2, Gorman 1 (pen), Lo-Everton 1, Quigley 1, Yussuf 1,
FA Trophy (4): Yussuf 2, Knowles 1, Williams 1.

Smith G 37	Wilkinson 31 + 2	Williams 27 + 6	Hunt 24	Barnett 31 + 6	Worthington 29 + 2	Staunton 32 + 1	Gorman 39 + 1	Wakefield 36 + 4	Knowles 38 + 4	Quigley 10 + 6	Moss 19 + 1	Yussuf 17 + 18	Lo-Everton 18 + 15	Bradley 5 + 17	Stephens — + 1	Robinson 12 + 5	Rose 1 + 2	Seymour 2 + 2	Pereira 1	Simper — + 1	Dyer — + 1	Reid 10 + 13	Barnes 1	Little 19	Barclay 18 + 2	D'Ath 11 + 6	Olomola 4 + 4	Cann 5	Neufville 6 + 5	Evans 1	Haste — + 1	Match No.
1	2	3	4	5^{3}	6■	7	8^{1}	9	10^{2}	11	12	13	14																			1
1	3	13	4	5		6	7	8^{2}	9	11	2	12	10^{1}																			2
1	3		4	5		6	7	9	10^{2}	11	2	12	8^{1}	13																		3
1	3		4	5		6	7	10^{3}	8^{2}	11	2	13	9^{1}	12	14																	4
1	3^{2}	12	4	5		6	7	9	10	11	2	13	8^{1}																			5
1			4	5^{1}	6^{3}	3	7	8^{2}	9	11	2	10■	13			12	14															6
1			3	13		4	7	9	8^{3}	10	2^{2}		12	14		5	6	11^{1}														7
1			4		6	3	7^{1}	12	9^{2}	11	2		10^{3}			5	14	13	8													8
1			4	5	6^{1}	3	7	12	8^{3}	9	2^{2}	11		13		14		10														9
1			4	6^{1}	8	3	7	11	13	10^{3}	2	12	9^{2}			5				14												10
1			4	6	8^{3}	3	7	10	9^{1}	12	2	11^{2}				5		13			14											11
1			4■	8	6	3	7	10^{3}	9^{2}	12	2	11^{1}	13	14		5																12
1	3	14	4	5	8^{3}	6	7	11^{2}	9^{1}	13	2	10	12																			13
1	3	14	4	5	8^{2}	6	7	10	9^{3}	12	2	11^{1}	13																			14
1	3	12	4	5	7	6		11	9^{1}		2	10	8^{2}	13																		15
1	3	12	4^{2}	5	8^{3}	6	7	11	9		2^{1}	10	13	14																		16
1	13	5	4	6	8	3	7	9			2	11^{1}	10^{2}	12																		17
1	3	5	4		8	6	7^{3}	11^{1}	12		2	10^{2}	9	14								13										18
1■	3	5^{3}	4	13	8	6	7^{1}	9	12		2	11^{2}	10■									14										19
		2^{3}	4	5	8^{2}	6	7	11	9	12		10^{1}	13			3						14	1									20
1	3		4	5^{1}		6	7	9	8	13	2	11^{3}	10^{2}			14						12										21
1		3		6^{1}	8^{3}	4^{2}	7	11	9			13	10	12		5						14		2								22
1	3	5		6^{1}	8		7	10	9^{3}			13	11^{2}	14		12								2■	4							23
1	3	5		6^{3}	8^{1}		7	9				11	10^{2}	14		2						12			4	13						24
1	3	5		6^{2}	9^{1}	7	8	11	10							14						13		2^{3}	4	12						25
1	3	2^{1}			8^{3}	6	7	10	9			12	13	14		5						11^{2}			4							26
1	3	5		7^{3}		6	8	10	9^{1}			13	12	14										2	4		11^{2}					27
1	3	5		13		6		11	9			14		8^{3}								12		2	4	7^{2}	10^{1}					28
1	3	5		7^{1}	8^{2}	6		10	9			11^{3}	13									14		2	4	12						29
1	3	5		10^{2}	13	6	7	11	9^{1}					8^{3}								14		2	4	12						30
1	3	5		2	14	6^{3}	7	11	9			13		8^{2}											4	12	10^{1}					31
1	3^{2}	5		14	9	6	7^{3}	11	12				13											2	4	8^{1}	10					32
		5		6	8	3	7	11^{2}	9^{3}			10^{1}										14		2	4		13	1	12			33
	13	5			8	3^{2}	7	11^{1}	9													10		2	4	6^{3}	14	1	12			34
	3	5			8		7	11^{2}	9					14								10^{3}		2	4	6^{1}	13	1	12			35
	3	5			7		6	10^{2}	9				12									11^{1}		2	4	8^{3}	14	1	13			36
	3	5		12	6■		8	13	9			14	7^{3}									11		2^{2}	4			1	10^{1}			37
1	3			5			7	12	8			14	9	6^{1}								10		2^{3}	4	13			11^{2}			38
1	3	5		6			7	10^{1}	9			14	13									11^{2}		2	4	8^{3}			12			39
1	3	5	4	6			7		9			12		13								10^{1}		2		8^{2}			11			40
1	3	5	4	7			6		9^{3}			12	14									10^{1}		2^{2}	13	8			11			41
1	3	2			6^{2}		13		8			10^{3}	9^{1}	14		5						12			4	7			11			42
1	3	5	4^{3}	14	8^{2}		7		11							6						12		2^{1}	13	9			10			43
		2		7		13		10^{2}	6			12	8^{3}	5^{1}		4						11		3		9				1	14	44

FA Cup

Fourth Qualifying	Weymouth	(h)	1-1
Replay	Weymouth	(a)	1-1
(aet; Yeovil T won 2-1 on penalties)			
First Round	Yate T	(a)	5-0
Second Round	Stevenage	(h)	1-0
Third Round	Bournemouth	(h)	1-3

FA Trophy

Third Round	Woking	(h)	3-1
Fourth Round	Needham Market	(h)	1-1
(Needham Market won 8-7 on penalties)			

SCOTTISH LEAGUE TABLES 2021–22

(P) Promoted into division at end of 2020–21 season. (R) Relegated into division at end of 2020–21 season.

CINCH PREMIERSHIP 2021–22

		Home						Away					Total						
		P	W	D	L	F	A	W	D	L	F	A	W	D	L	F	A	GD	Pts
1	Celtic[1]	38	16	3	0	55	6	13	3	3	37	16	29	6	3	92	22	70	93
2	Rangers[2]	38	14	4	1	40	12	13	4	2	40	19	27	8	3	80	31	49	89
3	Hearts (P)[3]	38	11	4	4	32	16	6	6	7	22	28	17	10	11	54	44	10	61
4	Dundee U[4]	38	8	4	7	21	23	4	8	7	16	21	12	12	14	37	44	–7	48
5	Motherwell[5]	38	9	4	6	26	28	3	6	10	16	33	12	10	16	42	61	–19	46
6	Ross Co	38	5	7	7	28	30	5	4	10	19	31	10	11	17	47	61	–14	41
7	Livingston	38	7	5	7	22	23	6	5	8	19	23	13	10	15	41	46	–5	49
8	Hibernian	38	7	7	5	22	16	4	5	10	16	26	11	12	15	38	42	–4	45
9	St Mirren	38	4	8	7	14	20	6	6	7	19	31	10	14	14	33	51	–18	44
10	Aberdeen	38	8	5	6	25	19	2	6	11	16	27	10	11	17	41	46	–5	41
11	St Johnstone	38	5	5	9	15	21	3	6	10	9	30	8	11	19	24	51	–27	35
12	Dundee (P)	38	4	7	8	20	29	2	4	13	14	35	6	11	21	34	64	–30	29

Top 6 teams split after 33 games, teams in the bottom six cannot pass teams in the top six after the split. St Johnstone not relegated after play-offs. [1]Celtic qualify for Champions League Group Stage. [2]Rangers qualify for Champions League third qualifying round. [3]Hearts qualify for Europa League play-off round. [4]Dundee U qualify for Europa Conference League third qualifying round. [5]Motherwell qualify for Europa Conference League second qualifying round.

CINCH PREMIERSHIP TOP GOALSCORERS 2021–22 (LEAGUE ONLY)

Regan Charles-Cook (Ross Co)	13
Giorgos Giakoumakis (Celtic)	13
Kyogo Furuhashi (Celtic)	12
Bruce Anderson (Livingston)	11
Lewis Ferguson (Aberdeen)	11
Alfredo Morelos (Rangers)	11
Liel Abada (Celtic)	10
Liam Boyce (Hearts)	10
Jota (Celtic)	10
Christian Ramirez (Aberdeen)	10
Kemar Roofe (Rangers)	10
Tony Watt (Dundee U)	10
Includes 9 League goals for Motherwell.	
Fashion Sakala (Rangers)	9
James Tavernier (Rangers)	9
Kevin van Veen (Motherwell)	9
Joe Aribo (Rangers)	8
Nicky Clark (Dundee U)	8
Callum Hendry (St Johnstone)	8
Martin Boyle (Hibernian)	7
Eamonn Brophy (St Mirren)	7
Joseph Hungbo (Ross Co)	7
Daniel Mullen (Dundee)	7
Connor Ronan (St Mirren)	7
Alan Forrest (Livingston)	6
Stephen Kingsley (Hearts)	6
Daizen Maeda (Celtic)	6
Tomas Rogic (Celtic)	6
David Turnbull (Celtic)	6
Josh Ginnelly (Hearts)	5
Dylan Levitt (Dundee U)	5
Kevin Nisbet (Hibernian)	5
Ellis Simms (Hearts)	5
Blair Spittal (Ross Co)	5
Jordan White (Ross Co)	5

CINCH CHAMPIONSHIP 2021–22

		Home						Away					Total						
		P	W	D	L	F	A	W	D	L	F	A	W	D	L	F	A	GD	Pts
1	Kilmarnock (R)	36	12	1	5	28	14	8	6	4	22	13	20	7	9	50	27	23	67
2	Arbroath	36	9	8	1	32	14	8	6	4	22	14	17	14	5	54	28	26	65
3	Inverness CT	36	10	3	5	30	17	6	8	4	23	17	16	11	9	53	34	19	59
4	Partick Thistle (P)	36	9	4	5	17	13	5	6	7	29	27	14	10	12	46	40	6	52
5	Raith R	36	5	8	5	23	26	7	6	5	21	18	12	14	10	44	44	0	50
6	Hamilton A (R)	36	5	5	8	16	28	5	7	6	22	25	10	12	14	38	53	–15	42
7	Greenock Morton	36	3	9	6	23	27	6	4	8	13	20	9	13	14	36	47	–11	40
8	Ayr U	36	5	7	6	21	25	4	5	9	18	27	9	12	15	39	52	–13	39
9	Dunfermline Ath®	36	5	8	5	22	24	2	6	10	14	29	7	14	15	36	53	–17	35
10	Queen of the South	36	4	5	9	13	19	4	4	10	23	35	8	9	19	36	54	–18	33

®Dunfermline relegated after play-offs.

CINCH CHAMPIONSHIP TOP GOALSCORERS 2021–22 (LEAGUE ONLY)

Michael McKenna (Arbroath)	15
Oli Shaw (Kilmarnock)	14
Brian Graham (Partick Thistle)	13
Tomi Adeloye (Ayr U)	11
Shane Sutherland (Inverness CT)	10
Billy Mckay (Inverness CT)	9
Andrew Ryan (Hamilton A)	9
Aidan Connolly (Raith R)	8
Kyle Lafferty (Kilmarnock)	8
David Moyo (Hamilton A)	8
Dario Zanatta (Raith R)	8
Lee Connelly (Queen of the South)	7
Jack Hamilton (Arbroath)	7
Matej Poplatnik (Raith R)	7
Zak Rudden (Partick Thistle)	7
Chigozie Ugwu (Greenock Morton)	7
Ross Docherty (Partick Thistle)	6
Kevin O'Hara (Dunfermline Ath)	6
Gary Oliver (Greenock Morton)	6
Logan Chalmers (Inverness CT)	5
Anton Dowds (Arbroath)	5
Michael Gardyne (Inverness CT)	5
James Maxwell (Ayr U)	5
Gavin Reilly (Greenock Morton)	5
Ethan Ross (Raith R)	5
Scott Tiffoney (Partick Thistle)	5

CINCH LEAGUE ONE 2021–22

		Home						Away					Total						
		P	*W*	*D*	*L*	*F*	*A*	*W*	*D*	*L*	*F*	*A*	*W*	*D*	*L*	*F*	*A*	*GD*	*Pts*
1	Cove Rangers	36	13	5	0	43	13	10	5	3	30	19	23	10	3	73	32	41	79
2	Airdrieonians	36	12	3	3	36	21	9	6	3	32	16	21	9	6	68	37	31	72
3	Montrose	36	6	9	3	25	20	9	5	4	28	16	15	14	7	53	36	17	59
4	Queen's Park (P)¶	36	8	8	2	29	15	3	10	5	22	21	11	18	7	51	36	15	51
5	Alloa Ath (R)	36	6	4	8	26	30	6	5	7	23	27	12	9	15	49	57	–8	45
6	Falkirk	36	5	3	10	23	31	7	5	6	26	24	12	8	16	49	55	–6	44
7	Peterhead	36	8	4	6	24	17	3	5	10	22	34	11	9	16	46	51	–5	42
8	Clyde	36	6	5	7	23	36	3	7	8	16	26	9	12	15	39	62	–23	39
9	Dumbarton®	36	3	6	9	21	31	6	1	11	27	40	9	7	20	48	71	–23	34
10	East Fife	36	4	5	9	17	26	1	3	14	14	44	5	8	23	31	70	–39	23

¶Queen's Park promoted after play-offs. ®Dumbarton relegated after play-offs.

CINCH LEAGUE ONE TOP GOALSCORERS 2021–22 (LEAGUE ONLY)

Mitch Megginson (Cove Rangers)	18	Craig Johnston (Montrose)	7
Rory McAllister (Cove Rangers)	16	Scott Brown (Peterhead)	6
Calum Gallagher (Airdrieonians)	15	Conner Duthie (Dumbarton)	6
David Goodwillie (Clyde)	15	Louis Longridge (Queen's Park)	6
Graham Webster (Montrose)	15	Blair Lyons (Montrose)	6
Euan Henderson (Alloa Ath)	13	Harry Milne (Cove Rangers)	6
Russell McLean (Peterhead)	12	Hamish Ritchie (Peterhead)	6
Callum Smith (Airdrieonians)	12	Grant Savoury (Peterhead)	6
Steven Boyd (Alloa Ath)	8	Lewis Jamieson (Clyde)	5
Kyle Connell (East Fife)	8	Aidan Keena (Falkirk)	5
Dylan Easton (Airdrieonians)	8	Robbie Leitch (Cove Rangers)	5
Fraser Fyvie (Cove Rangers)	8	Alistair Love (Clyde)	5
Bob McHugh (Queen's Park)	8	Rhys McCabe (Airdrieonians)	5
Callumn Morrison (Falkirk)	8	Gabriel McGill (Airdrieoians)	5
Stuart Carswell (Dumbarton)	7	Simon Murray (Queen's Park)	5
Luca Connell (Queen's Park)	7	Conor Sammon (Alloa Ath)	5
Anton Dowds (Falkirk)	7	Charles Telfer (Falkirk)	5

CINCH LEAGUE TWO 2021–22

		Home						Away					Total						
		P	*W*	*D*	*L*	*F*	*A*	*W*	*D*	*L*	*F*	*A*	*W*	*D*	*L*	*F*	*A*	*GD*	*Pts*
1	Kelty Hearts (P)	36	13	5	0	36	12	11	4	3	32	16	24	9	3	68	28	40	81
2	Forfar Ath (R)	36	10	5	3	34	17	6	7	5	23	19	16	12	8	57	36	21	60
3	Annan Ath	36	7	4	7	33	29	11	1	6	31	22	18	5	13	64	51	13	59
4	Edinburgh C¶	36	7	5	6	23	25	7	5	6	20	24	14	10	12	43	49	–6	52
5	Stenhousemuir	36	5	4	9	22	27	8	6	4	25	19	13	10	13	47	46	1	49
6	Stranraer	36	6	4	8	18	26	7	4	7	32	28	13	8	15	50	54	–4	47
7	Stirling Alb	36	6	2	10	22	26	5	7	6	19	20	11	9	16	41	46	–5	42
8	Albion R	36	5	5	8	17	26	5	4	9	20	32	10	9	17	37	58	–21	39
9	Elgin C	36	6	6	6	20	21	3	4	11	13	30	9	10	17	33	51	–18	37
10	Cowdenbeath®	36	3	5	10	13	21	4	3	11	15	28	7	8	21	28	49	–21	29

¶Edinburgh C promoted after play-offs. ®Cowdenbeath relegated after play-offs.

CINCH LEAGUE TWO TOP GOALSCORERS 2021–22 (LEAGUE ONLY)

Nathan Austin (Kelty Hearts)	17	Ryan Shanley (Edinburgh C)	7
Kane Hester (Elgin C)	13	Alfredo Agyeman (Kelty Hearts)	6
Thomas Orr (Stenhousemuir)	13	Adam Brown (Stenhousemuir)	6
Tony Wallace (Annan Ath)	13	Liam Buchanan (Cowdenbeath)	6
Joe Cardle (Kelty Hearts)	12	Dominic Docherty (Annan Ath)	6
Tommy Goss (Annan Ath)	12	James Hilton (Stranraer)	6
Dale Carrick (Stirling Alb)	11	*Includes 3 League goals for Edinburgh C.*	
Stefan McCluskey (Forfar Ath)	11	Owen Moxon (Annan Ath)	6
Matthew Aitken (Forfar Ath)	10	Charlie Reilly (Albion R)	6
Jamie Barjonas (Kelty Hearts)	9	Scott Shephard (Forfar Ath)	6
Andy Munro (Forfar Ath)	9	Craig Slater (Forfar Ath)	6
Matt Yates (Stranraer)	9	Adam Corbett (Stenhousemuir)	5
Tommy Muir (Stranraer)	8	Fraser Mullen (Cowdenbeath)	5
Aidan Smith (Annan Ath)	8	Innes Murray (Edinburgh C)	5
Daniel Handling (Edinburgh C)	7	Craig Ross (Stranraer)	5
Kallum Higginbotham (Kelty Hearts)	7	Ousman See (Edinburgh C)	5
Darryl McHardy (Elgin C)	7	Paul Woods (Stranraer)	5
John Robertson (Edinburgh C)	7		

ABERDEEN

Year Formed: 1903. *Ground & Address:* Pittodrie Stadium, Pittodrie St, Aberdeen AB24 5QH. *Telephone:* 01224 650400. *Fax:* 01224 644173. *E-mail:* feedback@afc.co.uk *Website:* afc.co.uk
Ground Capacity: 20,866 (all seated). *Size of Pitch:* 105m × 66m.
Chairman: Dave Cormack.
Manager: Jim Goodwin. *Assistant Manager:* Lee Sharp.
Club Nicknames: 'The Dons'; 'The Reds'; 'The Dandies'.
Record Attendance: 45,061 v Hearts, Scottish Cup 4th rd, 13 March 1954.
Record Transfer Fee received: £4,200,000 from Liverpool for Calvin Ramsay (June 2022).
Record Transfer Fee paid: £1,000,000 to Oldham Ath for Paul Bernard (September 1995).
Record Victory: 13-0 v Peterhead, Scottish Cup 3rd rd, 10 February 1923.
Record Defeat: 0-9 v Celtic, Premier League, 6 November 2010.
Most Capped Player: Alex McLeish, 77 (Scotland).
Most League Appearances: 556: Willie Miller, 1973-90.
Most League Goals in Season (Individual): 38: Benny Yorston, Division I, 1929-30.
Most Goals Overall (Individual): 199: Joe Harper, 1969-72; 1976-81.

ABERDEEN – CINCH PREMIERSHIP 2021–22 LEAGUE RECORD

Match No.	*Date*	*Venue*	*Opponents*	*Result*		*H/T Score*	*Lg Pos.*	*Goalscorers*	*Attendance*
1	Aug 1	H	Dundee U	W	2-0	1-0	2	Hayes 27, Ramirez 51	6305
2	8	A	Livingston	W	2-1	0-1	2	Jenks 47, MacKenzie 90	1710
3	22	A	Hearts	D	1-1	0-0	2	Ojo 71	17,449
4	29	H	Ross Co	D	1-1	0-1	4	Ramirez 88	14,434
5	Sept 11	A	Motherwell	L	0-2	0-1	6		5623
6	18	H	St Johnstone	L	0-1	0-0	6		13,007
7	26	A	St Mirren	L	2-3	2-1	7	Brown 18, Ramirez 34	4513
8	Oct 3	H	Celtic	L	1-2	0-1	9	Ferguson 56	14,522
9	16	A	Dundee	L	1-2	0-0	9	Ramirez 67	6876
10	23	H	Hibernian	W	1-0	1-0	8	Ramirez 27	9431
11	27	A	Rangers	D	2-2	2-1	8	Ramirez 8, Brown 16	49,760
12	30	H	Hearts	W	2-1	0-1	6	Watkins 49, Ferguson 69	9736
13	Nov 6	H	Motherwell	L	0-2	0-0	7		9666
14	20	A	Dundee U	L	0-1	0-0	8		10,500
15	28	A	Celtic	L	1-2	1-1	8	Ferguson (pen) 33	58,469
16	Dec 1	H	Livingston	W	2-0	1-0	7	Hedges 23, Bates 75	6295
17	4	H	St Mirren	W	4-1	3-1	6	Watkins 2 6, 43, Ramirez 2 9, 71	8002
18	11	A	St Johnstone	W	1-0	0-0	6	Jenks 83	3791
19	22	A	Hibernian	L	0-1	0-0	7		14,314
20	26	H	Dundee	W	2-1	1-1	6	Hedges 12, Ferguson 70	500
21	Jan 18	H	Rangers	D	1-1	0-1	6	Ferguson (pen) 73	16,731
22	25	A	St Mirren	L	0-1	0-0	6		4829
23	Feb 1	A	Ross Co	D	1-1	0-0	6	Hayes 48	3343
24	5	A	Livingston	L	1-2	0-1	7	Ramirez 66	4276
25	9	H	Celtic	L	2-3	0-2	9	Ramirez 56, Ferguson 61	15,291
26	15	H	St Johnstone	D	1-1	0-1	8	Ferguson (pen) 71	12,973
27	19	A	Motherwell	D	1-1	1-0	8	Besuijen 34	5171
28	26	H	Dundee U	D	1-1	1-1	9	Edwards (og) 16	18,719
29	Mar 2	A	Hearts	L	0-2	0-1	10		16,703
30	5	A	Rangers	L	0-1	0-0	10		50,010
31	19	H	Hibernian	W	3-1	1-1	10	Ferguson 2 (2 pens) 37, 64, Besuijen 80	15,321
32	Apr 2	A	Dundee	D	2-2	1-0	9	Ramsay 41, McCrorie 81	7815
33	9	H	Ross Co	L	0-1	0-0	9		15,162
34	23	H	Livingston	L	1-2	0-1	9	Ferguson (pen) 90	12,338
35	30	H	Dundee	W	1-0	0-0	9	Ferguson (pen) 73	13,747
36	May 7	A	Hibernian	D	1-1	0-0	10	Bates 55	14,509
37	11	A	St Johnstone	L	0-1	0-1	10		3421
38	15	H	St Mirren	D	0-0	0-0	10		14,906

Final League Position: 10

Honours
League Champions: Division I 1954-55; Premier Division 1979-80, 1983-84, 1984-85.
Runners-up: Premiership 2014-15, 2015-16, 2016-17, 2017-18; Division I 1910-11, 1936-37, 1955-56, 1970-71, 1971-72; Premier Division 1977-78, 1980-81, 1981-82, 1988-89, 1989-90, 1990-91, 1992-93, 1993-94.
Scottish Cup Winners: 1947, 1970, 1982, 1983, 1984, 1986, 1990; *Runners-up:* 1937, 1953, 1954, 1959, 1967, 1978, 1993, 2000, 2017.
League Cup Winners: 1955-56, 1976-77, 1985-86, 1989-90, 1995-96, 2013-14; *Runners-up:* 1946-47, 1978-79, 1979-80, 1987-88, 1988-89, 1992-93, 1999-2000, 2016-17, 2018-19.
Drybrough Cup Winners: 1971, 1980.

European: *European Cup:* 12 matches (1980-81, 1984-85, 1985-86); *Cup Winners' Cup:* 39 matches (1967-68, 1970-71, 1978-79, 1982-83 winners, 1983-84 semi-finals, 1986-87, 1990-91, 1993-94); *UEFA Cup:* 56 matches (*Fairs Cup:* 1968-69. *UEFA Cup:* 1971-72, 1972-73, 1973-74, 1977-78, 1979-80, 1981-82, 1987-88, 1988-89, 1989-90, 1991-92, 1994-95, 1996-97, 2000-01, 2002-03, 2007-08). *Europa League:* 35 matches (2009-10, 2014-15, 2015-16, 2016-17, 2017-18, 2018-19, 2019-20, 2020-21). *Europa Conference League*: 6 matches (2021-22).

Club colours: All: Red with blue and white trim.

Goalscorers: *League (41):* Ferguson 11 (7 pens), Ramirez 10, Watkins 3, Bates 2, Besuijen 2, Brown 2, Hayes 2, Hedges 2, Jenks 2, MacKenzie 1, McCrorie 1, Ojo 1, Ramsay 1, own goal 1.
Scottish FA Cup (4): Ramirez 2, Ferguson 1, Hedges 1.
Premier Sports Scottish League Cup (1): Emmanuel-Thomas 1. *SPFL Trust Trophy (2):* Ruth 2.
UEFA Europa Conference League (11): Ferguson 4 (2 pens), Ramirez 3, Hedges 2, Considine 1, McLennan 1.

Lewis J 34	Ramsay C 20 + 4	McCrorie R 30	Considine A 3 + 1	MacKenzie J 14 + 6	Ojo F 26 + 4	Ferguson L 36	Brown S 23 + 1	Hayes J 28 + 7	Emmanuel-Thomas J 7 + 8	Ramirez C 33 + 3	McLennan C 5 + 14	McGeouch D 8 + 6	Gurr J 3 + 1	Gallagher D 20 + 2	Hedges R 16	McGinn N 1 + 8	Jenks T 7 + 11	Campbell D 7 + 5	Longstaff M 3 + 2	Samuels A 3 + 4	Watkins M 16 + 5	Bates D 32 + 1	Woods G 4	Kennedy M 3 + 5	Besuijen V 15 + 1	Montgomery A 4 + 3	Barron C 13	Ruth M 1 + 2	Polvara D 3 + 2	Harvey L — + 2	*Match No.*
1	2	3	4	5	6^{1}	7	8	9^{2}	10	11^{3}	12	13	14																		1
1	14		4	5			12	10^{2}	11	13		6	2^{1}	3	7	8^{3}	9														2
1	2	4			8	7	6	5^{2}	12	11	10^{1}			3			9	13													3
1	2	4			9	6^{3}	7	14	13	10				3				5	8^{1}	11^{2}	12										4
1	2^{3}	4		5	9^{1}	6	7		14	10	13			3					8^{2}		11	12									5
1	2	4		5	6	8	7	12	11^{1}	10				14		13				9^{2}		3^{3}									6
1	2	4		5		7	6	10	13	11^{2}					8^{1}		9▮			12		3									7
	2	4		5		10	8^{2}	6		11	13	12						14	7^{3}	9^{1}		3	1								8
	2			5	6^{1}	8^{2}	7	11^{3}	14	10				3	9	13					12	4	1								9
1	2^{3}	5			7	8	6	12		10				4^{2}	9	14			13		11^{1}	3									10
1		5			2	8	4	7^{1}		11^{2}		9			10			6		13	12	3									11
1		4			5	7	3	12		11		6^{1}			9	13		8			10^{2}	2									12
1		4			5	7	3	13		11		6^{1}			9	12		8^{2}			10	2									13
1		2		4^{2}	7▮		3	12		11		6^{3}	5^{1}		9		13	8	14		10										14
1		3				6	7^{3}	5		10		8^{2}	2		9		13	12		14	11^{1}	4									15
1		3			2	6	7	5	8	10^{2}	13				9^{1}	12				14	11^{3}	4									16
1		3			2	6	7	5	8^{2}	11	13				9^{1}	14	12				10^{3}	4									17
1		3			2	6	7	5	8^{2}	11	13				9		12				10^{1}	4									18
1	12				2	6		5	9^{3}	11	14			3	8		13	7^{2}			10^{1}	4									19
1	2^{3}	3			6	7		5		10	12				9	13	8^{1}	14			11^{2}	4									20
1	2^{2}	3			9^{1}	7	8	5		11	12				6		10	13				4									21
1	2^{1}	3			10	7	6		12	11	13				8^{3}		9^{2}	5				4		14							22
1	2	3		13	10^{1}	9	6	5		11		7^{2}					12					4			8						23
	2^{1}	3		12	7	6		10	14	11							9^{2}					4	1	13	8	5^{3}					24
	5^{2}	2			13	8	7	9		11		6^{1}		3								4	1	12	10						25
1	2			5^{1}	14	9	7^{2}	10	15	11				3^{3}								4		8^{4}	12	13	6				26
1	2	7				9		5		11	12			3								4			8	10^{1}	6				27
1					7	9				11	2^{1}	12		3			13					4		10^{2}	8	5^{3}	6	14			28
1				15	2	9	7^{2}	5^{3}		11	12	14		3			13					4		10^{4}	8		6^{1}				29
1	13	7^{2}		12	2	9		5^{3}		10	11^{1}			3								4			6		8		14		30
1	2^{2}	8				9		5		11^{5}	10^{3}	12		3			15				13	4			7^{1}		6^{4}	14	16		31
1	2^{2}	8		13		9		5		11	10^{1}			3							12	4			7		6				32
1		7^{1}		13	2	6		5		11	12			3							8^{2}	4			10		9				33
1	14	9▮		5^{3}	2	6		10		12				3^{2}			13				11^{1}	4			8		7				34
1	2			5		7		10^{2}		9^{1}				3			12				11	4			8	13	6				35
1		2^{4}	16	5^{2}	13	7		10		12		14		3							11^{5}	4			8	15	6^{3}		9^{1}		36
1				5	2	7		12^{4}			14			3								4		13	8	10^{3}	6	11^{1}	9^{2}	15	37
1		2	4^{2}	5	14	7		10^{3}						12							11^{1}	3		15	8		9		6^{4}	13	38

AIRDRIEONIANS

Year Formed: 2002. *Ground & Address:* The Penny Cars Stadium, New Broomfield, Craigneuk Avenue, Airdrie ML6 8QZ. *Telephone:* (Stadium) 01236 622000. *Fax:* 01236 622001.
E-mail: enquiries@airdriefc.com *Website:* airdriefc.com
Ground Capacity: 10,101 (all seated). *Size of Pitch:* 105m × 67m.
Chairman: Martin Ferguson.
Player/Manager: Rhys McCabe. *Assistant Manager:* Scott Agnew. *Player/Assistant Manager:* Callum Fordyce.
Club Nickname: 'The Diamonds'.
Record Attendance: 9,044 v Rangers, League 1, 23 August 2013.
Record Victory: 11-0 v Gala Fairydean, Scottish Cup 3rd rd, 19 November 2011.
Record Defeat: 0-7 v Partick Thistle, First Division, 20 October 2012.
Most Capped Player: Simon Vella, 3 (Malta).
Most League Appearances: 222: Paul Lovering, 2004-12.
Most League Goals in Season (Individual): 23: Andy Ryan, 2016-17.
Most Goals Overall (Individual): 43: Bryan Prunty, 2005-08, 2015-16.

AIRDRIEONIANS – CINCH LEAGUE ONE 2021–22 LEAGUE RECORD

Match No.	Date	Venue	Opponents	Result		H/T Score	Lg Pos.	Goalscorers	Attendance
1	July 31	H	Montrose	L	0-3	0-1	9		529
2	Aug 7	A	Dumbarton	D	2-2	1-0	9	McGill, G [17], McCabe (pen) [49]	532
3	14	H	Falkirk	L	1-2	0-2	9	McGill, G [50]	1314
4	21	A	Peterhead	W	3-2	1-0	7	McCabe 2 (1 pen) [24, 70 (p)], McGill, G [75]	536
5	Sept 11	A	Queen's Park	D	0-0	0-0	9		446
6	14	H	Alloa Ath	W	2-1	1-0	6	Gallagher [12], Frizzell [51]	529
7	18	H	East Fife	W	3-0	1-0	5	Gallagher 2 [4, 80], McGill, S [59]	546
8	25	A	Cove R	L	0-1	0-0	7		652
9	Oct 2	H	Clyde	W	2-1	1-1	4	Smith [10], Gallagher [57]	736
10	16	A	Falkirk	W	3-0	1-0	3	Easton [35], Smith [67], Kerr [81]	3525
11	23	H	Dumbarton	W	3-2	1-1	3	McCabe (pen) [8], Easton [90], Kouider-Aisser [90]	653
12	30	A	Alloa Ath	L	1-2	0-1	4	Fordyce [85]	858
13	Nov 6	H	Peterhead	W	3-1	1-0	1	Easton [44], McInroy [57], Smith [64]	547
14	13	A	East Fife	W	1-0	1-0	1	Gallagher [35]	651
15	20	H	Cove R	L	0-2	0-0	2		819
16	Dec 7	A	Montrose	L	1-2	1-1	4	McInroy [36]	193
17	26	H	Alloa Ath	W	3-1	2-0	3	Smith [2], Gallagher [7], McInroy [61]	438
18	29	H	Queen's Park	W	1-0	0-0	3	McInroy [71]	500
19	Jan 2	A	Dumbarton	W	1-0	0-0	3	Easton [69]	312
20	8	H	East Fife	W	3-0	3-0	3	Allan [3], Frizzell [17], Easton [43]	500
21	15	H	Falkirk	W	3-2	2-0	2	Fordyce [35], McGill, S [43], Gallagher [86]	500
22	25	A	Clyde	D	2-2	0-0	2	Easton [72], Allan [84]	743
23	29	A	Queen's Park	D	1-1	1-1	2	McGill, S [28]	832
24	Feb 5	A	Cove R	D	1-1	0-1	2	Smith [73]	835
25	12	H	Montrose	W	4-1	2-1	2	Gallagher 2 [34, 36], Watson [63], Frizzell [69]	649
26	19	A	Peterhead	W	1-0	1-0	2	Afolabi [28]	553
27	26	H	Clyde	D	1-1	0-1	2	McGill, G [74]	824
28	Mar 5	A	Alloa Ath	W	2-0	1-0	2	Smith 2 [21, 84]	807
29	12	A	Falkirk	W	4-1	1-0	2	Smith 2 [6, 62], Gallagher [74], McGill, S [83]	3646
30	19	H	Queen's Park	W	2-0	2-0	2	Smith [38], Easton [45]	883
31	26	H	Cove R	D	1-1	1-0	2	McGill, G [2]	1650
32	Apr 2	A	East Fife	W	2-0	1-0	2	Gallagher 2 [41, 72]	644
33	9	A	Montrose	D	2-2	1-1	2	Smith [26], Gallagher [73]	784
34	16	H	Dumbarton	W	3-2	2-1	2	Easton [24], Gallagher [27], Allan [88]	902
35	23	A	Clyde	W	5-0	1-0	2	McCabe (pen) [36], Smith [55], Gallagher [63], MacDonald [71], Afolabi [86]	1378
36	30	H	Peterhead	D	1-1	0-1	2	Ferry (og) [60]	1116

Final League Position: 2

Honours
League Champions: Second Division 2003-04.
Runners-up: Second Division 2007-08; League One 2020-21.
League Challenge Cup Winners: 2008-09; *Runners-up:* 2003-04.

Club colours: Shirt: White with red diamond and black piping. Shorts: Black. Socks: Red with white trim.

Goalscorers: *League (68):* Gallagher 15, Smith 12, Easton 8, McCabe 5 (4 pens), McGill G 5, McGill S 4, McInroy 4, Allan 3, Frizzell 3, Afolabi 2, Fordyce 2, Kerr 1, Kouider-Aisser 1, MacDonald 1, Watson 1, own goal 1.
Scottish FA Cup (2): Frizzell 1, Smith 1.
Premier Sports Scottish League Cup (4): McCabe 1, McDonald 1, McGill G 1, McGill S 1.
SPFL Trust Trophy (1): Smith 1.
Scottish League Play-offs (8): Smith 3, McCabe 2 (1 pen), Afolabi 1, Gallagher 1, McGill G 1.

Currie M 35	Watson C 26 + 1	Kerr J 15 + 6	Fordyce C 32	McCabe R 32	McGill S 22 + 12	Agnew S 25 + 5	McDonald M 5 + 4	Quitongo R 10	Gallagher C 31 + 3	Kouider-Aisser S 3 + 5	McGill G 14 + 5	Allan J 5 + 21	Easton D 34 + 1	Wardrop S 1 + 1	Frizzell A 31	Smith C 29 + 2	Walker S 8 + 5	Caves R — + 2	Ritchie D 1 + 5	McInroy K 12	Lyons L 1 + 1	MacDonald K 6	Paterson B 12 + 2	Afolabi J 3 + 9	Devenny J 2 + 7	Cantley J 1 + 1	Match No.
1	2	3	4	5	6^{1}	7	8^{3}	9	10	11^{2}	12	13	14														1
1	3		4	7	13		12	5	10^{2}		9^{1}	14	8^{3}	2■	6	11											2
1	3		4	7	14	12		5	10^{2}		9^{1}	13	8		6	11	2^{3}										3
1			2	6	7	3	4		11^{1}	12	5		10		8	9											4
1	2		4	3	9	6		5	11^{2}		7^{1}	12	10	13	8												5
1	2		4	3	10	6		5	11^{2}	13	7^{1}		9		8			12									6
1	5	4^{1}	3		2	8	12		11	10^{2}		13	7		6	9^{3}			14								7
1	4	3			2	8		5^{1}	11	10		12	7		9	6											8
1	2	4		3	6^{1}	12		5	11^{2}	13			7		9	10				8							9
1		4	5	3	6	12			11		13		8^{1}		9	10^{2}	2^{3}	14		7							10
1	2	4^{1}	5	3	6^{3}				11	13	12	14	8		9	10				7^{2}							11
1	2^{1}		3	4	5^{3}	12			11	13	10^{2}	14	8		6	9				7							12
1	2		3	4	12	8			11^{1}				10		6	9	5^{2}			7	13						13
1	2		4	3	12	8		5	11				10		6	9				7^{1}							14
1	2^{3}		4	3	13	8		5^{2}	11		12	14	10		6^{1}	9				7							15
1	2		4	6	10^{2}			5	14		11		9		8^{3}	12	13			7	3^{1}						16
1	2		4	3	5	6	13		11^{1}			12	8		7	10^{2}				9							17
1	2		4	3	9^{3}	7	6^{1}		11^{2}			14	8			10	12		13	5							18
1	2	13	4	3		6	7^{2}		10^{1}			12	8			11	5			9							19
1	2	13	3	4	7^{1}	6						10	8		9^{2}	11^{3}	12		14	5							20
1	2	13	4	3	9^{1}	6			12			10^{2}	8		7	11	5										21
1	2	3	4^{2}	6	8^{1}				10			12	9		7	11						5	13				22
1	2	4		3	9^{2}	6			10^{1}			13	8		7	11						5	12				23
1		3	4	7	13	6			12			10^{2}	8		9	11^{1}						2	5				24
1	12	3	4	7	14	6			10^{3}			16	8^{2}		9^{5}	11^{1}						2^{4}	5	13	15		25
1	2	3	4	8	12	6			10^{3}			13	9^{2}		7								5	11^{1}	14		26
1	2		4	3	9^{3}	6^{2}			10		13	14	8		7	12							5^{1}	11			27
1	2		3	7	12	8			10^{3}		9^{2}		6		5	11^{1}							4	13	14		28
1	2	15	4	3	12	7^{3}			11^{4}		6^{2}	13	8		9^{5}	10^{1}	16						5	14			29
1		15	4	3	12	7			11^{2}		6^{3}		8^{1}		9	10	2^{4}						5	14	13		30
1	2	14	4	3	12	7			10^{3}		9^{1}		8^{2}		6	11							5	13			31
1		3	4		2	7^{2}			10^{1}		9^{3}	12	8		6	11^{4}			15				5	13	14		32
1			4	2	3^{3}	6^{2}			10		9^{1}	13	8		7	11							5	12	14		33
1		4	3	6	9^{3}				10^{2}			14	8		7■	11	2^{1}						5	12	13		34
1^{3}		3	4^{4}	6^{5}			16		10^{2}			7	9^{1}			11	12		15			2	5	13	8	14	35
		3			6	12	8				10	7					4		5^{1}			2		11	9	1	36

ALBION ROVERS

Year Formed: 1882. *Ground & Address:* Reigart Stadium, Main St, Coatbridge ML5 3RB. *Telephone/Fax:* 01236 606334.
E-mail: secretary@albionroversfc.com *Website:* albionroversfc.com
Ground capacity: 1,572 (seated: 489). *Size of Pitch:* 101m × 66m.
Chairman (Interim): Ian Benton.
Manager: Brian Reid. *Assistant Manager:* Scott MacKenzie.
Club Nickname: 'The Wee Rovers'.
Previous Grounds: Cowheath Park, Meadow Park, Whifflet.
Record Attendance: 27,381 v Rangers, Scottish Cup 2nd rd, 8 February 1936.
Record Transfer Fee received: £40,000 from Motherwell for Bruce Cleland (1979).
Record Transfer Fee paid: £7,000 to Stirling Alb for Gerry McTeague (September 1989).
Record Victory: 12-0 v Airdriehill, Scottish Cup 1st rd, 3 September 1887.
Record Defeat: 1-11 v Partick Thistle, League Cup 2nd rd, 11 August 1993.
Most Capped Player: Jock White, 1 (2), Scotland.
Most League Appearances: 399: Murdy Walls, 1921-36.
Most League Goals in Season (Individual): 41: Jim Renwick, Division II, 1932-33.
Most Goals Overall (Individual): 105: Bunty Weir, 1928-31.

ALBION ROVERS – CINCH LEAGUE TWO 2021–22 LEAGUE RECORD

Match No.	*Date*	*Venue*	*Opponents*	*Result*		*H/T Score*	*Lg Pos.*	*Goalscorers*	*Atten-dance*
1	July 31	H	Edinburgh C	W	2-0	2-0	1	Byrne (pen) 4, Doherty 39	275
2	Aug 7	H	Stenhousemuir	D	2-2	0-0	3	Roberts 49, Wilson, D 90	317
3	14	A	Elgin C	L	0-3	0-2	5		488
4	21	H	Annan Ath	L	0-1	0-1	7		303
5	28	A	Stirling Alb	L	1-2	0-0	8	Reilly 75	527
6	Sept 11	H	Cowdenbeath	W	2-1	1-1	6	Wright 21, Doherty 82	230
7	18	H	Kelty Hearts	L	0-3	0-2	7		427
8	25	A	Forfar Ath	L	1-3	0-1	8	Melingui 82	425
9	Oct 2	A	Stranraer	L	0-1	0-1	8		275
10	16	H	Elgin C	W	2-0	0-0	7	Wilson, C 75, Morton 80	267
11	Nov 5	A	Edinburgh C	W	4-0	3-0	6	Wright 22, McGowan 29, Wilson, C 44, O'Donnell 62	263
12	9	A	Stenhousemuir	L	1-3	1-1	7	Reilly 19	431
13	13	H	Stirling Alb	W	1-0	1-0	7	Doherty 26	417
14	20	A	Annan Ath	D	1-1	1-1	7	Wilson, C 42	284
15	Dec 4	H	Forfar Ath	L	2-3	0-1	8	Dolan 64, Reilly 74	213
16	11	A	Kelty Hearts	L	1-6	1-2	8	O'Donnell 27	554
17	18	A	Cowdenbeath	D	0-0	0-0	8		266
18	26	H	Stranraer	W	3-2	1-2	8	Reilly 8, Dolan 51, Wilson, L 90	251
19	Jan 8	H	Stenhousemuir	L	1-2	1-1	9	Wright 13	349
20	15	A	Elgin C	D	1-1	1-1	9	Fagan 45	500
21	29	H	Cowdenbeath	L	0-1	0-1	9		292
22	Feb 5	A	Forfar Ath	L	0-2	0-1	9		423
23	15	A	Edinburgh C	W	2-1	0-0	8	Travis (og) 72, Doherty 84	321
24	26	A	Stranraer	D	0-0	0-0	9		303
25	Mar 2	H	Annan Ath	L	1-4	0-1	9	Wilson, D (pen) 77	151
26	5	H	Edinburgh C	L	0-1	0-0	9		262
27	12	A	Kelty Hearts	L	1-3	0-2	9	Wilson, C 59	635
28	16	H	Kelty Hearts	D	0-0	0-0	9		277
29	19	H	Forfar Ath	D	0-0	0-0	9		220
30	22	A	Stirling Alb	W	1-0	0-0	8	Fagan 89	368
31	26	A	Annan Ath	W	4-2	2-1	8	Malcolm 23, Roberts 31, Fagan 85, Dolan 90	388
32	Apr 2	H	Elgin C	D	0-0	0-0	8		289
33	9	H	Stranraer	L	0-5	0-1	8		223
34	16	A	Stenhousemuir	L	1-4	1-4	9	Reilly (pen) 40	446
35	23	H	Stirling Alb	D	1-1	0-1	9	Wilson, D 60	307
36	30	A	Cowdenbeath	W	1-0	0-0	8	Reilly 46	411

Final League Position: 8

Honours
League Champions: Division II 1933-34; Second Division 1988-89; League Two 2014-15.
Runners-up: Division II 1913-14, 1937-38, 1947-48; Third Division 2010-11.
Promoted via play-offs: 2010-11 (to Second Division).
Scottish Cup Runners-up: 1920.

Club colours: Shirt: Red with vertical yellow stripes. Shorts: Red. Socks: Red.

Goalscorers: *League (37):* Reilly 6 (1 pen), Doherty 4, Wilson C 4, Dolan 3, Fagan 3, Wilson D 3 (1 pen), Wright 3, O'Donnell 2, Roberts 2, Byrne 1 (1 pen), Malcolm 1, McGowan 1, Melingui 1, Morton 1, Wilson L 1, own goal 1.
Scottish FA Cup (2): Wilson D 1 (1 pen), Wright 1.
Premier Sports Scottish League Cup (4): Byrne 1, Reilly 1, Wilson D 1, Wright 1.
SPFL Trust Trophy (7): Doherty 4 (1 pen), Dolan 1, Wright 1, own goal 1.

Binnie C 26	Lynas A 32 + 2	El-Zubaidi A 9	Robinson A 6 + 7	Leslie J 33	Wilson C 29	Wilson D 31 + 2	McKernon J 6	Reilly C 26 + 2	Doherty K 23 + 5	Byrne D 8 + 5	Roberts S 14 + 14	McGowan J 27	Wilson L 16 + 7	Stevenson R 1 + 3	Dolan K 5 + 9	Fagan S 31 + 1	Wright M 13 + 6	Morton J — + 6	Sweeney P — + 1	Melingui B 1 + 1	Mullen M 1 + 6	O'Donnell C 7 + 3	Fernie A 18 + 3	McVey J — + 2	Malcolm B 11 + 3	Jack J 8 + 8	Watson P 1	Stone H 10	Leighton T 3 + 3	*Match No.*
1	2	3	4	5	6	7	8	9^{1}	10	11	12																			1
1	2	4		5	7	8		9^{1}	10^{2}	11	6	3	12	13																2
1	2	4^{1}	15	5	8	7			10^{2}	11	6	3^{4}	9^{3}	12	13	14														3
1	2	3	12	7	6^{3}	8		9	10^{1}	11^{4}	15	4^{2}		13		5	14													4
1	2	3	4	5	6	7	8	9	12	10^{2}	13			11^{1}																5
1	2	5		7	6	13	8	14	10	12	9^{3}		3^{1}			4	11^{2}													6
1	2	7^{1}	14	5^{3}	6^{2}	8	4		11		9		12			3	10^{4}	13	15											7
1	2	5	4	6		8	7		10^{1}		9^{2}		12		14	3	11^{3}			13										8
1	2	5^{3}		9^{4}	6	7	8		10^{2}		14	3	12			4				11^{1}	13	15								9
1	2			7	6	8			10			3				4		12			11^{1}	9	5							10
1	2			8	6^{4}	7		9^{3}				3			14	4	10^{2}	12			13	11^{1}	5	15						11
1	2			8	6^{4}	7		9^{1}	12			3			14	4	10^{3}	15			13	11^{2}	5							12
1	2■		12	8	6	7		9	10^{1}			3				4	11^{2}					13	5							13
1			2	8	6	7		9	10^{1}			3			13	4	11^{2}					12	5							14
1	2			8		7		9	11			3			12	4	10^{1}					6	5							15
1	8		2^{4}			7		9^{2}			12	4	6		10^{1}	3		15			14	11^{3}	5	13						16
1	2			8^{2}		7		9			13	3	6		11	4					12	10^{1}	5							17
1	2		12		7	8		9			6^{1}	3^{4}	14		10^{2}	4		15			13	11^{3}	5							18
1	2				6	7		9^{2}				5	12		10	4	11^{1}						3		8	13				19
1	2			8	6			9		14	12		5			3	10^{2}						13		7^{3}	11^{1}	4■			20
1	2			7^{4}	6	8		9^{3}	12	13	14	3	5			4	10^{2}								15	11^{1}				21
1	2			8	6	7		9^{2}	11^{3}	13	12	3				4	14								5	10^{1}				22
	2			8	6^{2}	7		9	12	10^{1}	14	3				4	11^{3}								5	13		1		23
	2			8	9^{3}	7		6^{2}	11	10^{1}	14					4	12								5	13		1	3	24
	2			7	6^{3}	8		9	11^{1}	10^{4}	14		12			4	15						16		5^{5}	13		1	3^{2}	25
1	2			7				6	12	13	9	3	5			4	11^{2}								8	10^{1}				26
1	2^{3}			8	11	13		6	10		9^{2}	3	5			4							12		7^{1}	14				27
				7	6^{2}	8		9	10		12	3	5			4							2		13	11^{1}		1		28
	13			6	7	9		10^{3}	11		12	4	5			3	14						2^{2}			8^{1}		1		29
	13			6^{2}	7	9			11■		10	4	5			3							2		12	8^{1}		1		30
	7		13	6^{2}	11^{1}	8					10	3^{4}	5^{3}		14	4							2		9	15		1	12	31
	6			7		8					9	3	5		11^{1}	4							2		10			1	12	32
	6		14	7^{3}	9^{4}	8		12	11		10	3^{2}	5		16	4^{5}							2^{1}			15		1	13	33
1	8		2	9				6	11						12	4■							5		7	10			3^{1}	34
1	2			8	9	7		6	11		10	3	5										4							35
	2			8	10	7		6	11^{2}		9^{1}	3	5			4	12									13		1		36

ALLOA ATHLETIC

Year Formed: 1878. *Ground & Address:* Indodrill Stadium, Recreation Park, Clackmannan Rd, Alloa FK10 1RY.
Telephone: 01259 722695. *Fax:* 01259 210886. *E-mail:* fcadmin@alloaathletic.co.uk *Website:* alloaathletic.co.uk
Ground Capacity: 3,100 (seated: 905). *Size of Pitch:* 102m × 69m.
Chairman: Mike Mulraney. *Vice-Chairman:* Martin Ross.
Manager: Brian Rice. *Assistant Manager:* Paddy Connolly.
Club Nicknames: 'The Wasps'; 'The Hornets'.
Previous Grounds: West End Public Park: Gabberston Park; Bellevue Park.
Record Attendance: 15,467 v Celtic, Scottish Cup 5th rd, 5 February 1955.
Record Transfer Fee received: £100,000 from Bristol R for Martin Cameron (July 2000); £100,000 from Celtic for Greig Spence (August 2009).
Record Transfer Fee paid: £26,000 to Stenhousemuir for Ross Hamilton (July 2000).
Record Victory: 9-0 v Selkirk, Scottish Cup 1st rd, 28 November 2005.
Record Defeat: 0-10 v Dundee, Division II, 8 March 1947; v Third Lanark, League Cup, 8 August 1953.
Most Capped Player: Jock Hepburn, 1, Scotland.
Most League Appearances: 324: Kevin Cawley 2011-15; 2016-.
Most League Goals in Season (Individual): 49: 'Wee' Willie Crilley, Division II, 1921-22.

ALLOA ATHLETIC – CINCH LEAGUE ONE 2021–22 LEAGUE RECORD

Match No.	*Date*	*Venue*	*Opponents*	*Result*		*H/T Score*	*Lg Pos.*	*Goalscorers*	*Attendance*
1	July 31	A	Peterhead	L	0-2	0-1	8		242
2	Aug 7	H	East Fife	W	3-1	1-0	6	Boyd 2 29, 66, Sammon 65	516
3	14	A	Clyde	L	1-2	0-0	8	Scougall 72	512
4	21	H	Queen's Park	D	1-1	0-0	5	Boyd 78	610
5	Sept 11	H	Falkirk	W	2-0	1-0	6	Henderson 30, Sammon 64	1385
6	14	A	Airdrieonians	L	1-2	0-1	7	Sammon 62	529
7	18	A	Montrose	W	2-0	2-0	6	Niang 26, King 45	532
8	25	A	Dumbarton	D	1-1	1-0	5	Boyd 45	573
9	Oct 2	H	Cove R	L	1-3	0-0	7	Yule (og) 76	554
10	16	H	Peterhead	L	2-4	2-2	8	Boyd 10, Gilmour 39	414
11	24	A	Queen's Park	W	4-3	1-1	6	Cawley 1, Howie 54, Henderson 2 90, 90	681
12	30	H	Airdrieonians	W	2-1	1-0	6	Henderson 2 33, 50	858
13	Nov 6	A	Falkirk	D	1-1	0-0	6	Henderson 90	3514
14	13	H	Montrose	D	2-2	0-0	6	Durnan 2 53, 64	742
15	20	H	Dumbarton	L	1-2	0-0	6	Sammon 72	609
16	Dec 4	A	East Fife	D	1-1	0-0	6	Henderson 51	427
17	11	H	Clyde	L	0-1	0-0	6		667
18	18	A	Cove R	L	0-3	0-1	7		585
19	26	A	Airdrieonians	L	1-3	0-2	8	Henderson 64	438
20	Jan 8	A	Montrose	D	1-1	1-0	8	Boyd 44	463
21	15	H	Queen's Park	D	1-1	0-1	8	Cawley 58	484
22	29	A	Clyde	L	1-2	0-1	8	Scougall 90	648
23	Feb 5	A	Peterhead	W	1-0	1-0	7	Henderson 14	538
24	8	H	Falkirk	L	0-3	0-0	7		1504
25	12	H	East Fife	L	1-3	1-2	8	Durnan 3	638
26	19	A	Dumbarton	W	2-1	1-1	7	Cawley 22, King 82	678
27	26	H	Cove R	D	2-2	2-0	7	Graham 6, Boyd 19	612
28	Mar 5	H	Airdrieonians	L	0-2	0-1	7		807
29	12	A	Queen's Park	D	1-1	0-0	7	Durnan 49	750
30	19	H	Peterhead	W	1-0	0-0	7	Cawley 69	651
31	26	A	East Fife	W	3-0	0-0	6	Cawley 62, Scougall (pen) 66, Boyd 76	517
32	Apr 2	H	Dumbarton	L	2-3	0-0	6	Riley-Snow 82, Scougall (pen) 90	676
33	9	H	Clyde	W	1-0	0-0	6	MacIver 57	677
34	16	A	Cove R	L	0-3	0-0	6		1281
35	23	A	Falkirk	W	2-1	1-0	6	Cawley 8, Sammon 56	3366
36	30	H	Montrose	W	4-1	1-1	5	Henderson 4 26, 47, 49, 66	668

Final League Position: 5

Most Goals Overall (Individual): 91: Willie Irvine, 1996-2001.

Honours
League Champions: Division II 1921-22; Third Division 1997-98, 2011-12.
Runners-up: Division II 1938-39; Second Division 1976-77, 1981-82, 1984-85, 1988-89, 1999-2000, 2001-02, 2009-10, 2012-13; League One 2016-17.
Promoted via play-offs: 2012-13 (to First Division); 2017-18 (to Championship).
League Challenge Cup Winners: 1999-2000; *Runners-up:* 2001-02, 2014-15.

Club colours: Shirt: Gold and black hoops. Shorts: Black. Socks: Gold and black hoops.

Goalscorers: *League (49):* Henderson 13, Boyd 8, Cawley 6, Sammon 5, Durnan 4, Scougall 4 (2 pens), King 2, Gilmour 1, Graham 1, Howie 1, MacIver 1, Niang 1, Riley-Snow 1, own goal 1.
Scottish FA Cup (6): Henderson 3, Niang 2, Sammon 1.
Premier Sports Scottish League Cup (2): Taggart 1, Trouten 1 (1 pen).
SPFL Trust Trophy (4): Boyd 1, Niang 1, Scougall 1, Trouten 1.

Hutton D 26	Howie C 17 + 3	Mendy F 16 + 2	Graham A 24 + 1	Armstrong J 1 + 1	King A 19 + 10	Trouten A 2 + 3	Scougall S 27 + 5	Boyd S 29 + 5	Sammon C 20 + 15	Church D 20 + 4	O'Donnel C 2 + 16	Webster R — + 1	Lamont M — + 1	Durnan M 33	Taggart S 30	Niang M 26 + 4	Robertson J 22 + 5	Armour B — + 3	Cawley K 25 + 6	Henderson E 27 + 1	Gilmour C 11	Burt L — + 1	Wright K 1	Riley-Snow B 5 + 3	Morrison Peter 9	MacIver R 4 + 5	*Match No.*
1	2	3	4	5^1	6	7^3	8	9	10	11^2	12	13	14														1
1	10	4	3		9		6	7	11	8				2	5												2
1	6	4^1	3		10^2		9	8^3	11		14			2	5	7	12	13									3
1	6■	14	4		12		8	10	11^2		13			3	5^3	7	2		9^1								4
1		3			6	9^2		10^1	13	14	12			4	2	7	5		8	11^3							5
1		3	14		6		9^2	11	12	13				4	2	7^3	5		8^1	10							6
1		3			8			9^1	10	5	13			4	2	7	6		12	11^2							7
1		3			6		9^3	11^2	13	5	12			4	2	7	8		14	10^1							8
1	14	3			9^3		6	10	11^1	5^2				4	2	7■	13		12		8						9
1■		3			9		6	10	13	5				4	2^1		14		7^2	11^3	8	12					10
	6	3				13	8^1	10	11^2					4	2		5		9	12	7		1				11
1	6	3				12	8	10^2	13					4	2	5			9	11^1	7						12
1	6^2	3					8^1	10	13					4	2	9	5		12	11	7						13
1	12	3					9	11^1	13					4	2	6	5		8	10^2	7						14
1	14	3■				12	9^1	10	13					4	2	7^2	5		8	11^3	6						15
1	3■		4		7		9^1	13	12						2	6	5		8	11^2	10						16
1			3				8	10^1	12					4	2	7	5		9	11	6						17
1			3		13		8^1	10	12					4	2	6	5		9^2	11	7						18
1		13	3^1		14				12	5	10^2			4	2	9	7^3		8	11	6						19
1			3		6			8	11^1	5	12			4		7	2		10	9							20
1	9		3		7		12	10^2	13	5				4	2	6^1			8	11							21
1			4		9		12	10	11	5	13			3	2		8^2		6^1					7			22
1		3	4		12		8^2	13	11	5					2	9			7^1	10				6			23
1		3			9^1		12	10^3	11	5	13			4	2	8			14	7				6^2			24
1			3		7^3		10^2	12		5	14			4	2	9^1	13	15	8	11■				6^4			25
1			3		7		12	11^2	10	5	13			4	2	6	8		9^1								26
1			3		7^2		9^3	10	11^1	5				4	2	6	12■	14	8					13			27
			3		8		7^1	10^3	12	5^2	13			4	2	6			9	11					1	14	28
	2		3		6^1		16	13	10^5	12	9^2			4	5	8			14	11^4				7^3	1	15	29
	4		3		13		7^2	9^3	11^1					2	8	14	6		5	10					1	12	30
	4		2		13		6^2	7^4	10^1		14			3	5	15	8		9^3	11					1	12	31
	2		3		15		8	9^1	10	5^4	13			4			7^2		6^3	11				14	1	12	32
	5		3		13		7^4	8^2	11^1	12	15			4	2^3	14	6			10					1	9	33
	3		4				7	12	11	9				2		5	6			10					1	8^1	34
	2		3		14		7^3	8^2	12	9				4		13	6		5	11					1	10^1	35
	2		3■	15	13		9^3		11^1	5	12			4		7^4			8	10^2				14	1	6	36

ANNAN ATHLETIC

Year Formed: 1942. *Ground & Address:* Galabank, North Street, Annan DG12 5DQ. *Telephone:* 01461 204108.
E-mail: annanathletic.enquiries@btconnect.com *Website:* annanathleticfc.com
Ground capacity: 2,517 (seated: 500). *Size of Pitch:* 100m × 62m.
Chairman: Philip Jones. *Vice-Chairman:* Russell Brown.
Secretary: Alan Irving.
Manager: Peter Murphy.
Assistant Manager: Colin McMenamin.
Club Nicknames: 'Galabankies'; 'Black and Golds'.
Previous Ground: Mafeking Park.
Record attendance: 2,517, v Rangers, Third Division, 15 September 2012.
Record Victory: 6-0 v Elgin C, Third Division, 7 March 2009; 6-0 v Berwick Rangers, League Two, 6 April 2019.
Record Defeat: 1-8 v Inverness CT, Scottish Cup 3rd rd, 24 January 1998.
Most League Appearances: 209: Steven Swinglehurst, 2012-.
Most League Goals in Season (Individual): 22: Peter Weatherson, 2014-15.
Most Goals Overall (Individual): 56: Peter Weatherson, 2013-17.

ANNAN ATHLETIC – CINCH LEAGUE TWO 2021–22 LEAGUE RECORD

Match No.	Date	Venue	Opponents	Result		H/T Score	Lg Pos.	Goalscorers	Attendance
1	July 31	H	Forfar Ath	L	0-2	0-2	8		300
2	Aug 7	A	Stranraer	W	3-0	1-0	4	Johnston [14], Smith [51], Moxon [72]	255
3	14	H	Stirling Alb	W	3-1	2-0	3	Johnston [22], Anderson [23], Goss [85]	295
4	21	A	Albion R	W	1-0	1-0	2	Anderson [45]	303
5	28	A	Cowdenbeath	W	3-1	0-1	2	Wallace 2 (1 pen) [49 (p), 81], Anderson [53]	282
6	Sept 11	H	Stenhousemuir	L	1-2	0-0	2	Robert McCartney [86]	435
7	18	A	Elgin C	W	2-0	1-0	2	Moxon [3], Douglas [85]	467
8	25	H	Edinburgh C	L	1-3	0-2	3	Robert McCartney [79]	324
9	Oct 2	A	Kelty Hearts	L	1-2	1-1	3	Wallace [43]	674
10	16	A	Forfar Ath	L	0-2	0-1	4		351
11	30	H	Cowdenbeath	W	1-0	0-0	4	Hunter [57]	187
12	Nov 6	H	Stranraer	D	2-2	1-1	4	Smith [38], Moxon [87]	305
13	13	A	Stenhousemuir	L	0-2	0-1	4		502
14	20	H	Albion R	D	1-1	1-1	4	Docherty [24]	284
15	Dec 3	A	Edinburgh C	W	1-0	1-0	3	Goss [11]	219
16	11	H	Elgin C	W	4-1	1-1	3	Docherty 3 [29, 64, 68], Smith [75]	221
17	18	A	Stirling Alb	W	3-2	2-1	3	Johnston [30], Goss [33], Robert McCartney [76]	464
18	26	H	Kelty Hearts	W	5-1	1-1	3	Moxon [44], Garrity [46], Wallace 3 (1 pen) [76, 87 (p), 90]	372
19	Jan 2	A	Stranraer	D	1-1	0-1	3	Goss [88]	337
20	8	A	Cowdenbeath	W	3-1	2-1	3	Wallace (pen) [7], Goss [45], Smith (pen) [85]	243
21	15	H	Forfar Ath	D	2-2	1-2	3	Goss [4], Smith [57]	341
22	29	H	Stirling Alb	D	0-0	0-0	3		395
23	Feb 5	H	Stenhousemuir	L	0-2	0-1	3		295
24	15	A	Elgin C	W	2-0	2-0	3	Hunter [8], Smith [41]	347
25	19	H	Edinburgh C	W	2-1	0-0	3	Docherty [52], Moxon [76]	305
26	26	A	Kelty Hearts	L	1-3	0-2	3	Robert McCartney [78]	617
27	Mar 2	A	Albion R	W	4-1	1-0	2	Wallace [14], Smith (pen) [58], Moxon [70], Anderson [82]	151
28	5	H	Stranraer	W	4-1	3-1	2	Wallace [22], Barnes [44], Garrity [45], Clark [89]	323
29	12	H	Elgin C	W	2-1	0-0	2	Goss 2 [46, 80]	271
30	19	A	Stirling Alb	W	3-0	1-0	2	Smith [44], Goss 2 [72, 76]	411
31	26	H	Albion R	L	2-4	1-2	2	Goss [45], Wallace [68]	388
32	Apr 2	A	Stenhousemuir	W	1-0	1-0	2	Goss [26]	384
33	9	H	Cowdenbeath	L	2-3	1-2	2	Wallace 2 (1 pen) [32, 83 (p)]	263
34	16	A	Forfar Ath	L	1-5	0-5	2	Wallace [79]	472
35	22	A	Edinburgh C	L	1-2	1-2	2	Docherty [42]	264
36	30	H	Kelty Hearts	L	1-2	1-2	3	Reilly (og) [22]	441

Final League Position: 3

Honours
League Two Runners-up: 2013-14.
League Challenge Cup: Semi-finals: 2009-10, 2011-12.

Club colours: Shirt: Gold with black trim. Shorts: Black with gold trim. Socks: Gold with black tops.

Goalscorers: *League (64):* Wallace 13 (4 pens), Goss 12, Smith 8 (2 pens), Docherty 6, Moxon 6, Anderson 4, Robert McCartney 4, Johnston 3, Garrity 2, Hunter 2, Barnes 1, Clark 1, Douglas 1, own goal 1.
Scottish FA Cup (8): Moxon 2, Wallace 2 (1 pen), Anderson 1, Douglas 1, Robert McCartney 1, Smith 1.
Premier Sports Scottish League Cup (3): Fleming K 1, Wallace 1 (1 pen), own goal 1.
SPFL Trust Trophy (0).
Scottish League Play-offs (4): Wallace 2 (2 pens), Garrity 1, Goss 1.

Fleming G 35	Steele R 15 + 5	Douglas M 31	Swinglehurst S 27 + 1	Lowdon J 22 + 3	Johnston C 30 + 4	Docherty D 24 + 10	Hunter L 19 + 8	Goss T 19 + 10	Smith A 29 + 6	Wallace T 28 + 6	Anderson I 11 + 15	McCartney Robert 3 + 22	Birch C 3 + 4	Barnes C 22 + 4	Moxon O 33 + 1	Fleming K 5 + 18	Purdue J — + 7	Garrity M 15 + 11	Adamson R 1	Clark C 16 + 1	Hooper S 8	Match No.
1	2	3	4	5	6^{3}	7^{1}	8	9^{2}	10	11	12	13	14									1
1		3	4	5	6^{3}	7^{2}	12	13	10	11^{1}	9^{4}	16	14	2	8^{5}	15						2
1		3	4	5	6^{2}	8^{1}	13	12	10	9	11			2	7							3
1		3	4	5	6	8^{1}	12		10	9	11^{2}	13		2	7							4
1	12	4	3	5	6	8^{3}		13	11^{5}	9^{4}	10^{2}	16	15	2^{1}	7	14						5
1	2^{2}	3	4	5	6^{3}	8		13	10	9^{1}	11	12		14	7							6
1	2	3	4	5	6^{3}	8^{4}	15		10	9^{1}	11^{2}	12			7	14	13					7
1	2	3■	4^{2}	5	6^{3}	7		12	10	9^{1}	11^{4}	13	14		8		15					8
1	3		4	5	6^{4}	8^{3}		12	10^{1}	9	11^{2}	15	2		7	13		14				9
	2	3	4^{1}	5	6^{3}	7			15	9^{4}	11^{2}	10		12	8		14	13	1			10
1	2	3	4	5	13	12	7^{2}		11	9^{3}		10			8	14		6^{1}				11
1	4	3		5^{1}	6	13	7		11	9^{2}	12		2		8			10				12
1	2^{2}	3	4	5	6	14	7^{1}	13		9	11^{4}			12	8		15	10^{3}				13
1		3	4		6^{3}	7^{2}	8	11^{1}	10	9^{4}	13		5	2	14	15		12				14
1		3	4		6^{1}	7^{2}	9	11^{4}	10^{3}	12	14			2	8	15		13		5		15
1		3	4		6^{2}	7^{1}	9^{3}	11^{5}	10^{4}	12	14			2	8	15	16	13		5		16
1		3	4		9^{2}	8	6^{1}	11^{3}	10			12		2	7	13		14		5		17
1		3	4^{2}	15	6^{5}	7^{4}	9	13	10^{1}	12				2	8^{3}	16	14	11		5		18
1	12	3	4^{1}		6		7	13	10^{2}	9^{3}		14		2■	8			11		5		19
1	2	3	4		6	15	7^{5}	11^{1}	10^{3}	9^{2}	16	13			8^{4}	14	12			5		20
1	2	3		5	6	12	7^{1}	10^{2}	11	9	13				8					4		21
1	2^{2}	3		5	6	9^{4}	8^{3}	11^{5}	14		13	15		12	7	16		10^{1}		4		22
1		3	4^{1}		6^{4}	14	7^{2}	11^{3}	13	9	10	12		2	8			15		5		23
1		3	4	5		12	9	11^{2}	8	13		14		2	6	7^{1}		10^{3}				24
1		3	4	5	6	7^{2}	13	11	10^{3}	9^{1}				2	8	14		12				25
1		3	4	5	9^{4}	8	6^{3}	12	10^{2}	13	15	14		2	7			11^{1}				26
1	2	3			15	13	9		11	8^{1}	12	7^{3}			6^{2}	14		10^{4}		5	4	27
1		3			6	7^{2}	13		10^{4}	9^{3}	14	12		2	8	15		11^{1}		5	4	28
1		3			12	7^{3}	14	11	13	6^{1}				2	8	9		10^{2}		5	4	29
1		3		12	9^{5}	14	7^{2}	11^{1}	10	6^{4}		16		2	8	15		13		5^{3}	4	30
1	14	3		16		7^{5}	13	11^{2}	10^{3}	6	12	15		2^{4}	8			9^{1}		5	4	31
1		4^{2}	13	5	9		8^{1}	10	11^{3}	6				2	7	14		12			3	32
1	2^{1}		4		12	8^{2}		10	9^{3}	6		14			7	13		11		5	3	33
1	3^{3}		4	5	6^{5}	13		11^{1}	10^{2}	8	16	15		2	9^{4}	7		14		12		34
1	13		4	5	6^{2}	7		11^{1}	14	8	12	15		2		9		10^{4}		3^{3}		35
1	12		4^{1}	5	6^{5}	7		10^{3}	15	13	14	16		2	8^{2}	9		11^{4}			3	36

ARBROATH

Year Formed: 1878. *Ground & Address:* Gayfield Park, Arbroath DD11 1QB. *Telephone:* 01241 872157. *Fax:* 01241 431125. *E-mail:* office@arbroathfc.co.uk *Website:* arbroathfc.co.uk
Ground Capacity: 6,600 (seated: 861). *Size of Pitch:* 105m × 65m.
Chairman: Mike Caird. *Secretary:* Dr Gary Callon.
Manager: Dick Campbell. *Assistant Manager:* Ian Campbell.
Club Nickname: 'The Red Lichties'.
Previous Ground: Lesser Gayfield.
Record Attendance: 13,510 v Rangers, Scottish Cup 3rd rd, 23 February 1952.
Record Transfer Fee received: £120,000 from Dundee for Paul Tosh (August 1993).
Record Transfer Fee paid: £20,000 to Montrose for Douglas Robb (1981).
Record Victory: 36-0 v Bon Accord, Scottish Cup 1st rd, 12 September 1885.
Record Defeat: 0-8 v Kilmarnock, Division II, 3 January 1949; 1-9 v Celtic, League Cup 3rd rd, 25 August 1993.
Most Capped Player: Ned Doig, 2 (5), Scotland.
Most League Appearances: 445: Tom Cargill, 1966-81.
Most League Goals in Season (Individual): 45: Dave Easson, Division II, 1958-59.
Most Goals Overall (Individual): 120: Jimmy Jack, 1966-71.

ARBROATH – CINCH CHAMPIONSHIP 2021–22 LEAGUE RECORD

Match No.	*Date*	*Venue*	*Opponents*	*Result*		*H/T Score*	*Lg Pos.*	*Goalscorers*	*Attendance*
1	July 31	H	Inverness CT	L	0-1	0-0	8		1008
2	Aug 7	A	Ayr U	D	2-2	2-0	7	Nouble 10, McKenna 28	1244
3	21	H	Partick Thistle	W	3-1	1-1	4	McKenna 2 45, 54, Low 58	1585
4	28	A	Dunfermline Ath	W	3-0	2-0	4	McKenna 2 12, 67, Gold 44	2928
5	Sept 11	H	Hamilton A	W	4-0	1-0	3	Stewart 45, McKenna 57, Nouble 80, Low 85	1234
6	18	A	Queen of the South	W	2-0	1-0	3	O'Brien 16, Nouble 79	1174
7	24	H	Kilmarnock	D	0-0	0-0	3		2410
8	Oct 2	A	Greenock Morton	D	2-2	1-0	3	Colin Hamilton 43, McKenna (pen) 87	1126
9	16	A	Raith R	L	1-2	0-2	5	Dowds 90	1748
10	23	H	Ayr U	D	1-1	0-0	5	McKenna 56	1415
11	26	A	Inverness CT	W	1-0	0-0	3	McKenna 54	1909
12	30	H	Dunfermline Ath	W	4-2	2-2	3	O'Brien 15, Nouble 37, Linn 77, McKenna (pen) 85	1359
13	Nov 6	A	Hamilton A	D	1-1	0-1	3	O'Brien 90	1107
14	13	H	Queen of the South	D	1-1	0-0	5	McKenna 67	1408
15	20	A	Kilmarnock	W	1-0	0-0	5	Dowds 85	4242
16	Dec 4	H	Raith R	D	0-0	0-0	5		1539
17	11	A	Partick Thistle	W	2-0	1-0	3	Dowds 45, Henderson 78	2285
18	18	H	Greenock Morton	W	2-1	0-0	1	Colin Hamilton 48, Dowds 80	1220
19	26	A	Dunfermline Ath	W	3-0	2-0	1	Breen (og) 6, McKenna 45, Dowds 81	3405
20	Jan 2	H	Inverness CT	D	0-0	0-0	1		494
21	8	A	Ayr U	L	0-1	0-1	1		500
22	15	A	Raith R	W	2-1	0-1	1	Hamilton, J 47, Low (pen) 82	500
23	Feb 4	H	Kilmarnock	W	1-0	0-0	1	Hamilton, J 56	2803
24	9	H	Hamilton A	D	2-2	1-2	1	Low (pen) 38, McKenna (pen) 90	1213
25	19	A	Queen of the South	D	0-0	0-0	1		1067
26	26	A	Greenock Morton	D	0-0	0-0	1		1696
27	Mar 1	H	Partick Thistle	D	1-1	1-0	1	Colin Hamilton 6	1648
28	5	H	Dunfermline Ath	W	1-0	1-0	1	Gold 9	2141
29	12	A	Inverness CT	L	0-3	0-2	2		2149
30	19	H	Ayr U	W	1-0	0-0	2	Hamilton, J 50	1727
31	26	H	Raith R	D	3-3	1-1	2	Hamilton, J 1, Hilson 67, McKenna 70	2118
32	Apr 2	A	Partick Thistle	D	0-0	0-0	2		2810
33	9	A	Hamilton A	W	1-0	0-0	2	Hamilton, J 59	911
34	16	H	Queen of the South	W	5-1	2-1	2	Colin Hamilton 25, Hamilton, J 2 37, 59, Cameron (og) 54, Craigen 90	2413
35	22	A	Kilmarnock	L	1-2	1-0	2	Craigen 9	11,500
36	29	H	Greenock Morton	W	3-0	1-0	2	Thomson 16, Craigen 78, McKenna 85	3121

Final League Position: 2

Honours
League Champions: League One 2018-19. Third Division 2010-11; League Two 2016-17.
Runners-up: Championship 1921-22; Division II 1934-35, 1958-59, 1967-68, 1971-72; Second Division 2000-01; Third Division 1997-98, 2006-07.
Promoted via play-offs: 2007-08 (to Second Division).
Scottish Cup: Semi-finals 1947, Quarter-finals 1993.

Club colours: Shirt: Maroon. Shorts: White. Socks: Maroon.

Goalscorers: *League (54):* McKenna 15 (3 pens), Hamilton J 7, Dowds 5, Colin Hamilton 4, Low 4 (2 pens), Nouble 4, Craigen 3, O'Brien 3, Gold 2, Henderson 1, Hilson 1, Linn 1, Stewart 1, Thomson 1, own goals 2.
Scottish FA Cup (7): Hamilton J 3, Donnelly 1, Little 1, Thomson 1, Wighton 1.
Premier Sports Scottish League Cup (8): Donnelly 3, Colin Hamilton 1, Hilson 1, Low 1 (1 pen), Nouble 1, O'Brien 1.
SPFL Trust Trophy (1): Henderson 1.
Scottish League Play-offs (0).

Gaston D 33	Stewart S 33 + 2	Little R 34	O'Brien T 35	Hamilton Colin 35	McKenna M 33 + 1	Low N 16 + 3	Clark H 7 + 1	Linn B 5 + 18	Donnelly L 12 + 12	Nouble J 20	Hilson D 5 + 18	Craigen J 16 + 17	Swankie G 1 + 5	Hamilton Chris 27 + 1	Henderson L 20 + 5	Gold D 10 + 15	Dowds A 9 + 8	Paterson D — + 2	Thomson J 17 + 4	Hamilton J 14 + 2	Wighton C 9 + 4	Ford S 1 + 4	Bakare M 1 + 1	Antell C 3	*Match No.*
1	2^{3}	3	4	5	6	7	8^{2}	9^{1}	10	11	12	13	14												1
1	6	3	4^{1}	5	9^{3}	7	8^{2}			11	13	12	14	2	10										2
1	2	3	4	5	7^{2}	8		12		11		10			9^{1}	6^{3}	13	14							3
1	2^{3}	3	4	5	7	8		14	13	11^{1}	12	10			9^{2}	6									4
1	2	3	4	5	7	8				11^{3}	13	10			9^{2}	6^{1}	14	12							5
1	2	3	4	5^{1}	7	8	12			11^{3}	13	10^{2}			9	6■	14								6
1	6^{2}	3	4	5	7	8^{3}		13		11	12	10		2	9^{1}		14								7
1	6	3	4	5	7			14	11^{3}		10^{1}	9		2^{2}	8		12		13						8
1	6	3	4	5	7			12		10	11^{2}	9^{3}	14		8^{1}		13		2						9
1	7	3	4	5	8		6^{3}		9^{1}	10				14	13	12	11^{2}		2						10
1	7^{1}	3	4	5	8		6		9^{3}	10	12	13		2		14	11^{2}								11
1	7	3	4	5	8		6^{3}	13	9^{2}	11	12	14		2			10^{1}								12
1	7^{1}	3	4	5	8		6^{3}	12	9^{2}	11	13	14		2			10								13
1	7^{1}	3	4	5	8		6^{3}	13	9	11		12		2		14	10^{2}								14
1	7^{3}	3	4	5	8				10^{1}	11		12		6	9^{2}	14	13		2						15
1	7^{1}	3^{2}	4	5	11			14	9^{3}	10		8^{4}		6	15	12	13		2						16
1	7^{2}		4	5	11					10	12	8		6	3	13	9^{1}		2						17
1	7	3		5				9^{1}		10		8	12	6	4		11		2						18
1	7	3	4	5^{1}	8					11				6	9	12	10		2						19
1		3	4	5	7			13		11	14	8^{3}		6		9^{1}	10^{2}		2	12					20
1	6^{1}	3	4	5	7	12		13		11	14	9^{3}		8		2^{2}				10					21
1	6	3	4	5		8^{1}			10^{2}			13	14	7	9^{3}				2	11	12				22
1	7^{1}	3	4	5	8^{4}	9^{3}		16	14		15	13■		6	12				2	11^{5}	10^{2}				23
1	6^{4}	3	4^{3}	5	7	9^{1}		14	15		13			8^{2}	12	16			2	11	10^{5}				24
1	6	3	4	5	8			12	10^{2}		13	9^{1}				7			2		11^{3}	14			25
1	7^{5}	3	4	5	8			13	14			15		6	9^{3}	12			2^{1}	11^{4}	10^{2}	16			26
1	2	3	4	5	8^{3}			7^{4}	13		12	14		6	9					11^{2}	10^{1}	15			27
1	2	3	4	5	9			7^{1}	15		14	13		6	10^{2}	8^{3}			12	11^{4}					28
1	2^{1}	3	4	5	9^{5}	12		13				14		6^{3}		8^{2}			7	11	10^{4}	15	16		29
	14	3	4	5	8	9^{1}			12			6^{2}		7		13			2	11	10^{3}			1	30
	14	3	4	5	7^{2}	8		15	13		12	9^{3}		6^{5}		16			2^{1}	11	10^{4}			1	31
1	2	3	4	5	6	8^{4}			14		11^{3}	13		7^{1}	9^{2}	12				10	15				32
1	2	3	4	5	6	8^{1}			12		11^{2}	15		7^{4}	9^{3}	13				10	14				33
1	2	3^{3}	4	5	7	8^{5}		16	12		11^{4}	14		6^{1}	9^{2}	13			15	10					34
1	2	3	4	5	7^{1}	8^{2}			11^{3}			9^{4}		6	14	12			15	10	13				35
	2^{4}		4		16	13		9	14			15	6^{3}		5	7			3	12	10^{5}	11^{1}	8^{2}	1	36

AYR UNITED

Year Formed: 1910. *Ground & Address:* Somerset Park, Tryfield Place, Ayr KA8 9NB. *Telephone:* 01292 263435. *Fax:* 01292 281314. *E-mail:* info@ayrunitedfc.co.uk *Website:* ayrunitedfc.co.uk
Ground Capacity: 10,185 (seated: 1,597). *Size of Pitch:* 101m × 66m.
Chairman: David Smith.
Head Coach: Lee Bullen. *Assistant Head Coach:* David Timmins.
Club Nickname: 'The Honest Men'.
Record Attendance: 25,225 v Rangers, Division I, 13 September 1969.
Record Transfer Fee received: £300,000 from Liverpool for Steve Nicol (October 1981).
Record Transfer Fee paid: £90,000 to Stranraer for Mark Campbell (March 1999).
Record Victory: 11-1 v Dumbarton, League Cup, 13 August 1952.
Record Defeat: 0-9 in Division I v Rangers (1929); v Hearts (1931); B Division v Third Lanark (1954).
Most Capped Player: Jim Nisbet, 3, Scotland.
Most League Appearances: 459: John Murphy, 1963-78.
Most League League and Cup Goals in Season (Individual): 66: Jimmy Smith, 1927-28.
Most League and Cup Goals Overall (Individual): 213: Peter Price, 1955-61.

AYR UNITED – CINCH CHAMPIONSHIP 2021–22 LEAGUE RECORD

Match No.	Date	Venue	Opponents	Result		H/T Score	Lg Pos.	Goalscorers	Attendance
1	Aug 2	A	Kilmarnock	L	0-2	0-0	10		3692
2	7	H	Arbroath	D	2-2	0-2	8	Adeloye 70, McKenzie 87	1244
3	21	A	Inverness CT	L	0-1	0-0	9		2032
4	Sept 7	H	Raith R	L	0-2	0-2	9		1204
5	11	H	Dunfermline Ath	W	3-1	2-1	7	Adeloye 2 3, 63, Salkeld 25	1553
6	18	A	Hamilton A	W	2-0	0-0	6	Bradley 64, Adeloye 78	1365
7	25	H	Greenock Morton	D	0-0	0-0	5		1638
8	Oct 2	A	Partick Thistle	L	0-4	0-2	7		2667
9	16	H	Queen of the South	W	2-1	0-0	6	Muirhead (pen) 73, Maxwell 79	1663
10	23	A	Arbroath	D	1-1	0-0	6	Afolabi 80	1415
11	26	H	Kilmarnock	L	0-1	0-0	6		6052
12	30	A	Raith R	L	1-2	0-2	6	Baird, J 71	1602
13	Nov 6	H	Inverness CT	D	2-2	1-2	6	Chalmers 15, Reading 53	1289
14	13	H	Partick Thistle	L	0-4	0-2	6		2037
15	20	A	Dunfermline Ath	L	0-3	0-2	7		3503
16	Dec 4	A	Greenock Morton	D	2-2	0-1	7	Bradley 73, Adeloye 77	1335
17	10	H	Hamilton A	D	1-1	0-1	7	Adeloye 48	951
18	18	A	Queen of the South	L	0-3	0-2	8		997
19	26	H	Raith R	W	2-0	1-0	7	Adeloye 22, McKenzie 76	472
20	Jan 8	H	Arbroath	W	1-0	1-0	7	Maxwell 18	500
21	15	H	Greenock Morton	L	0-2	0-1	7		500
22	29	A	Hamilton A	D	1-1	0-1	8	Ashford 66	1230
23	Feb 1	A	Partick Thistle	L	0-1	0-0	8		2207
24	5	H	Dunfermline Ath	D	1-1	1-1	9	Martin (og) 17	1611
25	9	A	Kilmarnock	W	2-1	1-1	7	Maxwell 14, Reading 80	7560
26	19	A	Inverness CT	W	2-1	1-0	7	McGinty 35, Adeloye 64	1850
27	26	H	Queen of the South	L	0-1	0-1	8		1875
28	Mar 5	A	Raith R	W	4-0	3-0	6	Adeloye 3, Maxwell 2 32, 38, Ashford 65	1513
29	11	H	Kilmarnock	L	1-3	1-3	6	McInroy 38	6136
30	19	A	Arbroath	L	0-1	0-0	8		1727
31	26	A	Greenock Morton	D	1-1	0-1	8	Adeloye 79	1815
32	Apr 1	H	Hamilton A	D	1-1	0-1	8	McInroy 90	1618
33	9	H	Inverness CT	D	2-2	0-2	8	Bryden 54, Fjortoft 76	1756
34	16	A	Dunfermline Ath	L	1-2	1-0	8	Muirhead (pen) 35	4855
35	23	A	Queen of the South	D	1-1	0-0	8	East (og) 87	2271
36	29	H	Partick Thistle	W	3-1	2-0	8	Muirhead 2 (2 pens) 5, 61, Adeloye 30	3426

Final League Position: 8

Honours
League Champions: Division II 1911-12, 1912-13, 1927-28, 1936-37, 1958-59, 1965-66; Second Division 1987-88, 1996-97; League One 2017-18.
Runners-up: Division II 1910-11, 1955-56, 1968-69; Second Division 2008-09; League One 2015-16.
Promoted via play-offs: 2008-09 (to First Division); 2010-11 (to First Division); 2015-16 (to Championship).
Scottish Cup: Semi-finals 2002.
League Cup: Runners-up: 2001-02.
League Challenge Cup Runners-up: 1990-91, 1991-92.

Club colours: Shirt: White with black trim. Shorts: Black. Socks: White.

Goalscorers: *League (39):* Adeloye 11, Maxwell 5, Muirhead 4 (4 pens), Ashford 2, Bradley 2, McInroy 2, McKenzie 2, Reading 2, Afolabi 1, Baird J 1, Bryden 1, Chalmers 1, Fjortoft 1, McGinty 1, Salkeld 1, own goals 2.
Scottish FA Cup (2): Maxwell 1, Moffat 1.
Premier Sports Scottish League Cup (5): Adeloye 3, Murdoch 1, Salkeld 1.
SPFL Trust Trophy (0).

Albinson C 9	Houston J 26	Baird J 24 + 3	McGinty S 28	Reading P 35	Hewitt M 2 + 1	Muirhead A 27 + 1	Murdoch A 32	McKenzie M 20 + 8	Salkeld C 8 + 7	Adeloye T 24 + 8	O'Connor D 13 + 11	Afolabi J 5 + 9	Maxwell J 29 + 5	Fjortoft M 14 + 6	Chalmers J 13 + 3	McAdams A 27	McAllister Nicholas 11 + 1	Bradley S 6 + 7	Moffat M 4 + 14	Ecrepont F — + 1	Bryden F 3 + 8	Gondoh R 1 + 5	Dempsey B 6 + 1	Ashford S 12 + 1	Rowe B — + 3	McInroy K 13 + 1	Smith P 1 + 4	Kenyon A 3	*Match No.*
1	2	3	4	5	6^3	7^1	8	9^2	10	11	12	13	14																1
1	5	3	4	9		12	7	14	6^2	11	10^3	13	8	2^1															2
1	5	4	2		7^3	6	9^1	11	14	10	13	12		3	8^2														3
	2	3		5		7■		10^2	14	11		13■	9	4	8^1	1	6^3	12											4
1		3	4	9			7	14	6^3	11	8		5	12			2^1	10^2	13										5
1	2^3	3	4	5		7	6		14	10^1	11			12	8			9^2	13										6
1		4	3	5		8	7	14	6^3	11	9^1		12	2				10^2	13										7
1		3	4	5		8	7		13	11		14	12	2^3	9^2		6		10^1										8
		4		5		7	8		6^2	10^1		11^3	9	3	13	1	2	12	14										9
		3		5		2	7		6^2	10^1		13	9	4	8	1		11	12										10
		3		5		2	7		13	10		14	9^2	4	8	1	6^1	11^3	12										11
	2^3	3		5			7	12	11^2	10^1		13	9	4	8	1	6		14										12
		4		5			7	9		10^1	12	11	6	3	8	1	2												13
		4		5			7	6^3		10^2	12	11	9^1	3	8	1	2	13	14										14
	2	3		5		6	8	7^2	12		10^1	11	13	4	9^3	1		14											15
1	2^2	3	4	5			7			13	9	11^1	6				8	12	10										16
1	2		4	5			7		13	11	9^3		6	3	14		8^1	12	10^2										17
	2		4	5			7		10	11^2	9^1		6	3	12	1	8^3	13	14										18
	2	3	4	5			7	6^2		11^1		13	9		8	1		10^3	12	14									19
	2	3	4	5		6	9	7^1			13		10^2		8	1	14		11^3		12								20
	2	3	4	5		6	8	7		11^3	13		10^1		9^2	1					14	12							21
	2	3	4	5		6	8	13		11^2	10^3		14			1					15	7^4	9^1	12					22
	2^4	3	4	5		6^3	8	7		15			10			1					12		9^1	11^2	13	14			23
	2		3	5		4	7	6			12		9^1			1							8	11		10			24
	2		4	5		3	7	6		12			9^2			1							10	11^1	13	8			25
	2^2		4	5		3	7	6^4		13	14		9^3			1						16	10^1	11^5	12	8	15		26
	2	4^2	3	5		7		6^3		13	12		9^1			1						14	10	11		8			27
	2		5^2	3		4	7^1	6^4		10^3	15		9^5	12		1			13			16		11		8	14		28
	2^1	14	4	5		3	7	6^2		11^4			9^3	13■		1					15		12	10		8			29
	2	13	4	5		3	7	6					9^1			1					12			11■		8		10^2	30
	2		4	5		3	8	7^1		12			10			1			13		11					9		6^2	31
	2		4	5		3	7	6^1		12	9^2		10			1			13		11					8			32
	2^2	16	3^3	5		4		6^4		13	12		9^1	15		1					10			11		8	14	7^5	33
	2^1		3	5		8	4	13		10	6^2		9	12		1								11		7			34
		3	2	5		4	7^3	13		10	6^1		9^2			1					12	15		11^4		8	14		35
		3	4	5	14	2		15		10^4	6^2		9^3			1			12		13			11^1		8	7		36

CELTIC

Year Formed: 1888. *Ground & Address:* Celtic Park, Glasgow G40 3RE. *Telephone:* 0871 226 1888. *Fax:* 0141 551 8106.
E-mail: customerservices@celticfc.co.uk *Website:* celticfc.com
Ground Capacity: 60,832 (all seated). *Size of Pitch:* 105m × 68m.
Chairman: Ian Bankier. *Chief Executive:* Michael Nicholson.
Manager: Ange Postecoglou. *Assistant Manager:* John Kennedy.
Club Nicknames: 'The Bhoys'; 'The Hoops'; 'The Celts'.
Record Attendance: 92,000 v Rangers, Division I, 1 January 1938.
Record Transfer Fee received: £25,000,000 from Arsenal for Kieran Tierney (August 2019).
Record Transfer Fee paid: £9,000,000 to Paris Saint-Germain for Odsonne Édouard (June 2018).
Record Victory: 11-0 Dundee, Division I, 26 October 1895. *Record Defeat:* 0-8 v Motherwell, Division I, 30 April 1937.
Most Capped Player: Pat Bonner, 80, Republic of Ireland. *Most League Appearances:* 486: Billy McNeill, 1957-75.
Most League Goals in Season (Individual): 50: James McGrory, Division I, 1935-36.
Most League Goals Overall (Individual): 397: James McGrory, 1922-39.

Honours
League Champions: (52 times) Division I 1892-93, 1893-94, 1895-96, 1897-98, 1904-05, 1905-06, 1906-07, 1907-08, 1908-09, 1909-10, 1913-14, 1914-15, 1915-16, 1916-17, 1918-19, 1921-22, 1925-26, 1935-36, 1937-38, 1953-54, 1965-66, 1966-67, 1967-68, 1968-69, 1969-70, 1970-71, 1971-72, 1972-73, 1973-74; Premier Division 1976-77, 1978-79, 1980-81, 1981-82, 1985-86, 1987-88, 1997-98, 2000-01, 2001-02, 2003-04, 2005-06, 2006-07, 2007-08, 2011-12, 2012-13; Premiership 2013-14, 2014-15, 2015-16, 2016-17, 2017-18, 2018-19, 2019-20, 2021-22. *Runners-up:* 32 times.
Scottish Cup Winners: (40 times) 1892, 1899, 1900, 1904, 1907, 1908, 1911, 1912, 1914, 1923, 1925, 1927, 1931, 1933, 1937, 1951, 1954, 1965, 1967, 1969, 1971, 1972, 1974, 1975, 1977, 1980, 1985, 1988, 1989, 1995, 2001, 2004, 2005, 2007, 2011, 2013, 2017, 2018, 2019, 2020. *Runners-up:* 18 times.
League Cup Winners: (20 times) 1956-57, 1957-58, 1965-66, 1966-67, 1967-68, 1968-69, 1969-70, 1974-75, 1982-83, 1997-98, 1999-2000, 2000-01, 2005-06, 2008-09, 2014-15, 2016-17, 2017-18, 2018-19, 2019-20, 2021-22. *Runners-up:* 15 times.

CELTIC – CINCH PREMIERSHIP 2021–22 LEAGUE RECORD

Match No.	*Date*	*Venue*	*Opponents*	*Result*		*H/T Score*	*Lg Pos.*	*Goalscorers*	*Attendance*
1	July 31	A	Hearts	L	1-2	0-1	7	Ralston [54]	5272
2	Aug 8	H	Dundee	W	6-0	2-0	4	Furuhashi 3 [20, 25, 67], Rogic [49], Ralston [84], Edouard (pen) [90]	24,500
3	21	H	St Mirren	W	6-0	4-0	1	Abada 2 [17, 22], Turnbull 3 [28, 44, 84], Edouard [62]	56,052
4	29	A	Rangers	L	0-1	0-0	6		49,402
5	Sept 11	H	Ross Co	W	3-0	0-0	5	Carter-Vickers [64], Ajeti 2 [70, 85]	56,511
6	19	A	Livingston	L	0-1	0-1	6		8573
7	26	H	Dundee U	D	1-1	1-1	6	Abada [16]	56,403
8	Oct 3	A	Aberdeen	W	2-1	1-0	6	Furuhashi [11], Jota [84]	14,522
9	16	A	Motherwell	W	2-0	1-0	4	Jota [17], Turnbull [52]	8446
10	23	H	St Johnstone	W	2-0	1-0	4	Giakoumakis [34], Juranovic (pen) [80]	57,434
11	27	A	Hibernian	W	3-1	3-1	2	Ralston [10], Carter-Vickers [14], Furuhashi [30]	17,580
12	30	H	Livingston	D	0-0	0-0	2		57,388
13	Nov 7	A	Dundee	W	4-2	2-1	2	Jota 2 [8, 47], Furuhashi 2 [19, 50]	8604
14	28	H	Aberdeen	W	2-1	1-1	2	Jota [20], McGregor [60]	58,469
15	Dec 2	H	Hearts	W	1-0	1-0	2	Furuhashi [33]	57,578
16	5	A	Dundee U	W	3-0	2-0	2	Rogic [19], Turnbull [40], Scales [81]	8311
17	12	H	Motherwell	W	1-0	1-0	2	Rogic [45]	57,705
18	15	A	Ross Co	W	2-1	1-0	2	Abada [21], Ralston [90]	5592
19	22	A	St Mirren	D	0-0	0-0	2		6596
20	26	A	St Johnstone	W	3-1	2-0	2	Abada 2 [9, 22], Bitton [82]	500
21	Jan 17	H	Hibernian	W	2-0	2-0	2	Maeda [4], Juranovic (pen) [25]	58,296
22	26	A	Hearts	W	2-1	2-0	2	Hatate [27], Giakoumakis [35]	17,967
23	29	H	Dundee U	W	1-0	0-0	2	Abada [90]	58,188
24	Feb 2	H	Rangers	W	3-0	3-0	1	Hatate 2 [5, 42], Abada [44]	59,077
25	6	A	Motherwell	W	4-0	3-0	1	Abada [28], Rogic 2 [31, 45], Maeda [71]	7421
26	9	A	Aberdeen	W	3-2	2-0	1	Jota 2 [16, 62], O'Riley [20]	15,291
27	20	H	Dundee	W	3-2	2-1	1	Giakoumakis 3 [34, 38, 86]	58,030
28	27	A	Hibernian	D	0-0	0-0	1		17,374
29	Mar 2	H	St Mirren	W	2-0	0-0	1	Carter-Vickers [55], McGregor [81]	57,360
30	6	A	Livingston	W	3-1	1-0	1	Maeda [17], Devlin (og) [46], Forrest [55]	8922
31	19	H	Ross Co	W	4-0	3-0	1	Giakoumakis 3 (1 pen) [11, 18, 61 (p)], Maeda [26]	58,432
32	Apr 3	A	Rangers	W	2-1	2-1	1	Rogic [7], Carter-Vickers [42]	50,023
33	9	H	St Johnstone	W	7-0	3-0	1	Hatate [8], Giakoumakis [22], Maeda [36], Juranovic (pen) [52], O'Riley 2 [70, 73], Abada [78]	58,321
34	24	A	Ross Co	W	2-0	1-0	1	Furuhashi [12], Jota [87]	6698
35	May 1	H	Rangers	D	1-1	1-0	1	Jota [21]	58,247
36	7	H	Hearts	W	4-1	2-1	1	Maeda [30], Furuhashi [37], O'Riley [69], Giakoumakis [90]	58,554
37	11	A	Dundee U	D	1-1	0-0	1	Giakoumakis [53]	9401
38	14	H	Motherwell	W	6-0	3-0	1	Furuhashi 2 [21, 43], Turnbull [40], Jota [59], Giakoumakis 2 [68, 90]	58,953

Final League Position: 1

European: *European Cup/Champions League:* 216 matches (1966-67 winners, 1967-68, 1968-69, 1969-70 runners-up, 1970-71, 1971-72, 1972-73, 1973-74 semi-finals, 1974-75, 1977-78, 1979-80, 1981-82, 1982-83, 1986-87, 1988-89, 1998-99, 2001-02, 2002-03, 2003-04, 2004-05, 2005-06, 2006-07, 2007-08, 2008-09, 2009-10, 2010-11, 2012-13, 2013-14, 2014-15, 2015-16, 2016-17, 2017-18, 2018-19, 2019-20, 2020-21, 2021-22). *Cup Winners' Cup:* 38 matches (1963-64 semi-finals, 1965-66 semi-finals, 1975-76, 1980-81, 1984-85, 1985-86, 1989-90, 1995-96). *UEFA Cup:* 75 matches (*Fairs Cup:* 1962-63, 1964-65. *UEFA Cup:* 1976-77, 1983-84, 1987-88, 1991-92, 1992-93, 1993-94, 1996-97, 1997-98, 1998-99, 1999-2000, 2000-01, 2001-02, 2002-03 runners-up, 2003-04 quarter-finals). *Europa League:* 70 matches (2009-10, 2010-11, 2011-12, 2014-15, 2015-16, 2017-18, 2018-19, 2019-20, 2020-21, 2021-22). *Europa Conference League:* 2 matches (2021-22).

Club colours: Shirt: Green and white hoops. Shorts: White. Socks: White with green hoops.

Goalscorers: *League (92):* Giakoumakis 13 (1 pen), Furuhashi 12, Abada 10, Jota 10, Maeda 6, Rogic 6, Turnbull 6, Carter-Vickers 4, Hatate 4, O'Riley 4, Ralston 4, Juranovic 3 (3 pens), Ajeti 2, Edouard 2 (1 pen), McGregor 2, Bitton 1, Forrest 1, Scales 1, own goal 1.
Scottish FA Cup (10): Giakoumakis 4, Abada 1, Bitton 1, Maeda 1, McGregor 1, Scales 1, Taylor 1.
Premier Sports Scottish League Cup (9): Furuhashi 3, Abada 1, Edouard 1, Forrest 1, Jota 1, Turnbull 1, Welsh 1.
SPFL Trust Trophy (3): Dickson 1, O'Connor 1, Robertson 1.
UEFA Champions League (2): Abada 1, McGregor 1.
UEFA Europa League (23): Furuhashi 5, Turnbull 3 (1 pen), Abada 2, Forrest 2, Jota 2, Juranovic 2 (2 pens), Ajeti 1, Christie 1, Henderson 1, Ralston 1, Welsh 1, own goals 2.
UEFA Europa Conference League (1): Maeda 1.

Bain S 2	Ralston A 25 + 3	Bitton N 11 + 13	Starfelt C 34	Taylor G 22 + 2	Soro I 1 + 7	McGregor C 33	Abada L 24 + 12	Turnbull D 20 + 5	Forrest J 9 + 10	Edouard O 3 + 1	Christie R 3 + 1	Furuhashi K 16 + 4	Rogic T 20 + 12	Hart J 35	Welsh S 9 + 1	Montgomery A 2 + 6	Ajeti A 3 + 4	Juranovic J 23 + 3	Carter-Vickers C 33	Jota J 25 + 4	McCarthy J 4 + 6	Bolingoli Mbombo B 2	Johnston M 3 + 9	Giakoumakis G 11 + 10	Scales L 4 + 1	Moffat O 1 + 1	Shaw L — + 1	Barkas V 1	Dawson J — + 1	Hatate R 15 + 2	Maeda D 14 + 2	Ideguchi Y — + 3	O'Riley M 10 + 6	Doak B — + 2	Dembele K — + 1	Match No.
1	2	3	4	5	6^{3}	7	8^{2}	9^{1}	10	11	12	13	14																							1
	2		4	5^{1}		7	9	6	12	13	11	10^{3}	8^{2}	1	3	14																				2
	2		3	5	12	7^{3}	9	8		10^{1}	6	11^{2}	13	1	4		14																			3
	2		4		12	7	9^{2}	8^{1}		10^{3}	6	11	13	1	3	14		5																		4
			4	5^{3}	13	7^{2}	9	8					6^{1}	1		12	10	2	3	11	14															5
		14			12		9	8					6^{1}	1	4^{3}		10	2	3	11	7^{2}	5	13													6
	2		4		13		9	8					6	1		12	10	5^{1}	3	11	7^{2}															7
	2	7^{1}	4			8	9^{2}	6				10	13	1		5	12		3	11																8
	2	13	4			6	9^{3}	8				10^{1}	7^{2}	1					3	11		5	14	12												9
	2		4			7	13	8				9^{3}	6	1			14	5	3	11^{2}			12	10^{1}												10
	2	12	4			7	14	8				10^{3}	6^{1}	1				5	3	9			11^{2}	13												11
	2	7	4^{1}			6	9^{3}	8	14			13		1				5	3	11^{2}			12	10												12
	2	6				9	7^{3}	8	12			11^{2}		1	4			5	3	10^{1}			14	13												13
	2					8	9^{2}	6	12			10^{3}		1	4		14	5	3	11^{1}	7		13													14
	2^{1}	14	4			7		8	9			10	6	1	3^{3}	12		5		11^{2}			13													15
		13	4	5^{1}		7	12	11	6^{2}			10	9^{3}	1				2	3				8		14											16
	13	7	4	5		8	9	10	11^{1}				6	1				2	3				12^{2}													17
	2	7^{2}	4■			8	10	6					13	1		11^{1}		9	3						5	12										18
1	2	6^{2}		14		8	11						9		4			12	3				10		5^{1}	7^{3}	13									19
		7	4				10					11^{1}	9		2	13		6	3		8				5^{2}			1	12							20
			4	5		7	9^{3}		11^{1}				6	1				2	3	15			14	12						8^{2}	10^{4}	13				21
		7	4	5	14		12		9					1				2	3	11^{3}	13			10						8^{1}			6^{2}			22
	2^{1}	7■	4	14			9		11^{2}					1				13	3	12	16			10^{5}	5^{3}					8^{4}			6	15		23
			4	5	15	7	9^{2}		12					1				2	3	11^{4}	14			10^{5}						8^{3}	13		6^{1}	16		24
	2	13	4	5^{4}		7^{1}	9^{3}		12				6	1				16	3	14				10^{2}						8^{5}	11		15			25
	2	13	4	5		7	9^{3}		14				15	1					3	11				12						8^{1}	10^{4}		6^{2}			26
	2	14	4			7	12						13	1				5	3	9				10						8^{2}	11^{3}		6^{1}			27
			4	5		7	9						6^{1}	1				2	3	11										8	10		12			28
		14	4	5		7^{2}	9^{1}		13				12	1				2	3	11^{3}										8^{4}	10	16	6^{5}		15	29
	2	7	4	5		8^{2}	12		9^{1}				6^{4}	1					3	11				13						15	10^{3}		14			30
	14	16	4	5		7^{2}	13	15					8^{4}	1				2^{3}	3	9^{1}				10						6^{5}	11		12			31
	14	13	4	5^{1}		7	16	15					6^{3}	1				2	3	9^{4}				10						8^{2}	11		12^{5}			32
			4	5		7^{1}	12	14				16	6^{3}	1				2	3	9^{2}	15			10^{4}						8^{5}	11		13			33
	2		4	5		7	12	15	16			10^{3}	14	1					3	9^{2}				13						8^{5}	11^{1}		6^{4}			34
	2	13	4	5		7	15					10^{3}	14	1					3	9				12						8^{2}	11^{4}		6^{1}			35
	2		4	5		7	12	8^{5}	16			10^{2}	15	1					3	9^{3}				13						14	11^{4}		6^{1}			36
	2		4	5		7	9^{4}	13	11^{3}			16	14	1					3	12				10^{1}						8^{2}	15		6^{5}			37
	2	16	4	5^{1}		7^{3}		8^{2}				10^{5}	6^{4}	1	15				3	9	14			12							11	13				38

CLYDE

Year Formed: 1877. *Ground & Address:* New Douglas Park, Cadzow Avenue, Hamilton ML3 0FT (groundshare with Hamilton A for 2022-23). *Telephone:* 01236 341711. *Fax:* 01236 733490. *E-mail:* info@clydefc.co.uk *Website:* clydefc.co.uk
Ground Capacity: 6,078 (all seated). *Size of Pitch:* 105m × 68m.
Chairman: Gordon Thomson. *Vice-Chairman:* David MacPherson.
Manager: Danny Lennon. *Assistant Manager:* Allan Moore.
Club Nickname: 'The Bully Wee'.
Previous Grounds: Barrowfield Park 1877-98; Shawfield Stadium 1898-1986; Firhill Stadium 1986-91; Douglas Park 1991-94.
Record Attendance: 52,000 v Rangers, Division I, 21 November 1908.
Record Transfer Fee received: £200,000 from Blackburn R for Gordon Greer (May 2001).
Record Transfer Fee paid: £14,000 to Sunderland for Harry Hood (1966).
Record Victory: 11-1 v Cowdenbeath, Division II, 6 October 1951.
Record Defeat: 0-11 v Dumbarton, Scottish Cup 4th rd, 22 November, 1879; v Rangers, Scottish Cup 4th rd, 13 November 1880.
Most Capped Player: Tommy Ring, 12, Scotland.
Most League Appearances: 420: Brian Ahern, 1971-81; 1983-87.
Most League Goals in Season (Individual): 32: Bill Boyd, 1932-33.
Most League Goals Overall (Individual): 124: Tommy Ring, 1950-60.

CLYDE – CINCH LEAGUE ONE 2021–22 LEAGUE RECORD

Match No.	Date	Venue	Opponents	Result		H/T Score	Lg Pos.	Goalscorers	Attendance
1	July 31	H	Dumbarton	L	0-3	0-2	9		746
2	Aug 7	A	Montrose	D	2-2	0-0	9	Jones 88, Love 90	613
3	14	H	Alloa Ath	W	2-1	0-0	6	Goodwillie 2 59, 89	512
4	21	A	Falkirk	L	0-3	0-0	8		3545
5	28	H	Cove R	W	2-1	2-0	6	Goodwillie 2 8, 43	550
6	Sept 11	A	Peterhead	L	2-3	2-3	7	Goodwillie 2 (1 pen) 9 (p), 41	488
7	18	H	Queen's Park	D	2-2	1-0	8	Goodwillie 2 36, 90	651
8	25	A	East Fife	W	2-0	0-0	8	Cunningham 2 73, 77	481
9	Oct 2	A	Airdrieonians	L	1-2	1-1	8	Goodwillie (pen) 34	736
10	16	H	Montrose	L	0-5	0-3	9		640
11	23	A	Cove R	L	0-3	0-1	9		505
12	30	H	Falkirk	L	1-3	0-1	9	Goodwillie (pen) 74	1163
13	Nov 6	A	Dumbarton	D	1-1	0-0	9	Goodwillie 90	562
14	13	A	Queen's Park	D	0-0	0-0	9		839
15	20	H	East Fife	W	3-1	0-0	9	Goodwillie 67, Cunningham 2 69, 88	604
16	Dec 4	H	Peterhead	D	2-2	1-2	9	Goodwillie 2 (1 pen) 45 (p), 52	483
17	11	A	Alloa Ath	W	1-0	0-0	7	Love 57	667
18	26	A	Falkirk	W	2-1	0-0	5	Love (pen) 61, Splaine 75	400
19	Jan 8	H	Cove R	L	0-1	0-0	6		500
20	15	A	Peterhead	D	1-1	1-0	6	Elsdon 32	497
21	22	H	Queen's Park	D	1-1	0-0	6	Goodwillie (pen) 70	811
22	25	H	Airdrieonians	D	2-2	0-0	6	Jones 80, Mortimer 88	743
23	29	H	Alloa Ath	W	2-1	1-0	5	Splaine 17, Tade 88	648
24	Feb 5	A	East Fife	D	0-0	0-0	5		443
25	12	H	Dumbarton	L	1-3	1-3	6	Jones 34	612
26	19	A	Montrose	D	1-1	1-1	6	McAllister 28	722
27	26	A	Airdrieonians	D	1-1	1-0	6	Jamieson 42	824
28	Mar 5	H	Falkirk	D	1-1	0-1	6	Jamieson 90	1331
29	12	A	Cove R	L	1-4	1-2	6	Love (pen) 35	766
30	19	H	East Fife	W	2-0	1-0	6	Love 19, Jamieson 59	633
31	26	A	Queen's Park	L	0-1	0-0	7		896
32	Apr 2	H	Peterhead	L	0-3	0-1	7		597
33	9	A	Alloa Ath	L	0-1	0-0	7		677
34	16	H	Montrose	W	2-1	2-1	7	Jamieson 15, McAllister 41	502
35	23	H	Airdrieonians	L	0-5	0-1	8		1378
36	30	A	Dumbarton	L	1-2	1-1	8	Jamieson 45	655

Final League Position: 8

Honours
League Champions: Division II 1904-05, 1951-52, 1956-57, 1961-62, 1972-73; Second Division 1977-78, 1981-82, 1992-93, 1999-2000.
Runners-up: Division II 1903-04, 1905-06, 1925-26, 1963-64; First Division 2002-03, 2003-04; League Two 2018-19.
Promoted via play-offs: 2018-19 (to League Two).
Scottish Cup Winners: 1939, 1955, 1958; *Runners-up:* 1910, 1912, 1949.
League Cup: Semi-finals 1956, 1957, 1968.
League Challenge Cup Runners-up: 2006-07.

Club colours: Shirt: White with red trim. Shorts: White. Socks: White with red trim.

Goalscorers: *League (39):* Goodwillie 15 (5 pens), Jamieson 5, Love 5 (2 pens), Cunningham 4, Jones 3, McAllister 2, Splaine 2, Elsdon 1, Mortimer 1, Tade 1.
Scottish FA Cup (0).
Premier Sports Scottish League Cup (5): Goodwillie 2 (1 pen), Love 2 (1 pen), Jones 1.
SPFL Trust Trophy (0).

Mitchell D 4	Cuddihy B 18 + 3	Balatoni C 9 + 1	Rumsby S 30 + 1	Docherty M 20 + 7	Love A 25 + 4	Gomis M 30 + 3	Splaine A 28 + 2	Cunningham R 17 + 3	Goodwillie D 18 + 3	Jones R 18 + 13	Mortimer W 4 + 16	Livingstone A 29 + 5	Kennedy P 12 + 3	Munro M 7	Nicoll K 13 + 9	Elsdon M 27 + 2	Andrew O 2 + 8	Bradley-Hurst J 5	Blair R — + 1	Parry N 25	Deveney E 3 + 5	Tade G 3 + 21	Page J 19	Brunton M — + 1	Osei-Bonsu A — + 2	Jamieson L 13	McAllister N 13	Maley G 2	Samuel M 2 + 4	Cassidy A — + 1	*Match No.*
1	2	3	4	5^{2}	6	7^{1}	8	9	10	11^{3}	12	13	14																		1
1	6■	3	4		13	9^{2}	7	14	11	12		5	10^{3}	2	8^{1}																2
1			4	12		8	9	11	10	14	13	5^{3}	6^{1}	2	7^{2}	3															3
1	6^{2}		4	14		8		11	10	12	5		9^{1}	2	7^{3}	3	13														4
		3	2^{2}	15		7	14	10	11		12	9	8^{4}	6^{1}	5^{3}	4■		1	13												5
	4	2	3			6	12	11	10	13	14	9	8^{3}	5^{1}	7^{2}					1											6
	8	2	4^{2}				7^{1}	9	11	10		13	6^{3}			3	14			1	5	12									7
	6	2	4^{3}			13	7	9	11	10^{1}		12	8			3				1	5^{2}	14									8
	7	4	2		14	12	8^{2}	6	10	11^{1}		5^{3}	9			3				1		13									9
	6	4	2^{2}		13	7	8	10^{3}	11	14		5^{1}				3				1	9	12									10
			3		10^{2}	7	9^{1}	8	11	13		5	12	2	6^{3}	4				1	14										11
				5		7	9	12	11	10	14		8^{2}	2^{1}	6^{3}	4				1		13	3								12
	5			4	13	7	6	8	11	10^{1}		9^{2}				2				1		12	3								13
			2	5	9^{3}	8^{1}	7	6	10	11^{2}		13	12			3				1	14		4								14
	2		3	5	11^{1}	7^{3}	8	6	10			14	9^{2}		13	4				1		12									15
				5	8^{2}	7	6	9^{1}	11	10^{3}		2				3				1	12	13	4	14							16
			13	2	9^{1}	7	6		10	11^{2}	12	5	8^{3}			3				1	14		4								17
			3	5	11	6	9^{2}	8^{1}		10		7			12	4				1	13		2								18
	12		2	4	9^{1}	6				10		8			7^{3}	3	11^{2}			1		13	5		14						19
	12		2	4	9^{3}	6	7		13	10^{2}		8			14	3	11^{1}			1			5								20
			4	2	11^{1}	7^{3}	6		12	9		8			13	3				1		10^{2}	5		14						21
			3	5	6		8		10^{1}	12	14	9			7^{3}	4				1		13	2			11^{2}					22
		16	3	2	9^{4}		8^{5}		13	10^{1}	14	6			12	4^{2}				1		15	5			11^{3}	7				23
			3	5	6^{2}	12	8			11^{4}	14	9				4	15			1		13	2			10^{3}	7^{1}				24
	15	3^{1}		5^{4}	6^{3}	7^{2}				11	13	9				4	14			1		12	2			10■	8				25
	2		3	5	10^{1}	7	8^{3}	12		13	14	9								1		11^{2}	4				6				26
	2^{3}		3		9^{1}	7	8	11^{2}			14	5				13		1				12	4			10	6				27
	2		3	15	9^{4}	7^{2}	8	11^{1}		13	14	5										12	4			10	6^{3}	1			28
	8		3	12	10	7^{4}	9			13	2^{2}	5			15	4^{3}	14					11^{1}					6	1			29
	9^{2}		3	4	10	8^{3}	7			12		5			13		14	1					2			11^{1}	6				30
			3		10	6	7			13	2	5^{3}			9^{1}	4		1				12				11	8^{2}		14		31
			3	5^{3}	8	7	9			13		2			6^{1}	4	14	1				12				11			10^{2}		32
	7^{1}		3	15	11^{3}	6^{4}				10^{5}	13	5			16	4				1		12	2^{2}			9	8		14		33
	2			5^{1}	9	7	8^{3}				14	11			6	4				1		12				10^{2}	3		13		34
	2^{4}		4^{3}	5	9^{1}	7					12	11			6^{2}	13	15			1		14				10	3		8		35
			3	14	9^{2}	8				11^{3}	2^{4}	5	7^{1}		13■					1		12	4			10	6^{5}		16	15	36

COVE RANGERS

Year Formed: 1922. *Ground & Address:* Balmoral Stadium, Wellington Circle, Altens, Aberdeen AB12 3JG.
Telephone: 01224 392 111. *Fax:* 01224 392 858. *E-mail:* info@coverangersfc.com *Website:* coverangersfc.com
Ground Capacity: 2322 (356 seated). *Size of Pitch:* 105yd × 68yd.
Chairman: Keith Moorhouse. *Vice-Chairman:* Graeme Reid. *Secretary:* Duncan Little.
Manager: Jim McIntyre. *Assistant Manager:* Jimmy Boyle.
Club Nickname: 'Wee Rangers', 'Toonsers'.
Previous Grounds: Allan Park.
Record Attendance: 2,100 v Deveronvale, 2009, Highland League.
Record Transfer Fee received: £25,000 from Liverpool for Scott Paterson (March 1992).
Record Victory: 7-1 v Stirling Albion, League Two, 10 March 2020.
Record Defeat: 0-7 v Ross County, League Cup Group rd, 30 July 2016.
Most League Appearances: 91: Connor Scully 2019-22.
Most League Goals in Season (Individual): 24: Mitch Megginson, 2019-20.
Most Goals Overall (Individual): 80: Mitch Megginson, 2016-22.

COVE RANGERS – CINCH LEAGUE ONE 2021–22 LEAGUE RECORD

Match No.	*Date*	*Venue*	*Opponents*	*Result*		*H/T Score*	*Lg Pos.*	*Goalscorers*	*Attendance*
1	July 31	H	Falkirk	D	1-1	0-0	4	McAllister [78]	672
2	Aug 7	A	Queen's Park	L	0-2	0-0	8		401
3	14	H	East Fife	W	5-2	2-0	4	Leitch [19], Megginson 3 [42, 77, 82], McAllister (pen) [47]	541
4	21	A	Dumbarton	W	3-1	2-0	4	Megginson [23], Leitch [24], McAllister (pen) [84]	456
5	28	A	Clyde	L	1-2	0-2	4	McAllister (pen) [84]	550
6	Sept 11	H	Montrose	D	1-1	-	5	McAllister [49]	679
7	18	A	Peterhead	W	1-0	0-0	3	McAllister (pen) [79]	625
8	25	H	Airdrieonians	W	1-0	0-0	3	Neill [89]	652
9	Oct 2	A	Alloa Ath	W	3-1	0-0	1	McAllister 3 (1 pen) [52, 83, 89 (p)]	554
10	16	A	East Fife	L	2-4	0-3	2	Leitch [46], Neill [72]	409
11	23	H	Clyde	W	3-0	1-0	2	Scully [45], Masson [51], Leitch [90]	505
12	30	H	Queen's Park	D	3-3	1-2	2	McAllister [5], Megginson [69], Morrison (og) [77]	531
13	Nov 6	A	Montrose	D	0-0	0-0	3		711
14	13	H	Peterhead	W	3-0	0-0	2	Strachan [49], Megginson 2 (1 pen) [79, 90 (p)]	925
15	20	A	Airdrieonians	W	2-0	0-0	1	Megginson [79], Fyvie [82]	819
16	Dec 4	H	Dumbarton	W	2-0	0-0	1	Fyvie [69], Vigurs [85]	371
17	11	A	Falkirk	W	3-0	2-0	1	Neill [20], McAllister [39], McIntosh [90]	3258
18	18	H	Alloa Ath	W	3-0	1-0	1	Masson [41], McAllister (pen) [60], Megginson [85]	585
19	26	H	East Fife	W	4-2	0-0	1	McIntosh [54], Megginson [59], Yule [65], Leitch [83]	499
20	Jan 2	A	Peterhead	W	1-0	0-0	1	McKenzie [87]	494
21	8	A	Clyde	W	1-0	0-0	1	Vigurs [71]	500
22	15	H	Montrose	W	1-0	1-0	1	McAllister [10]	499
23	29	A	Dumbarton	D	2-2	0-1	1	McAllister (pen) [52], Scully [54]	447
24	Feb 5	H	Airdrieonians	D	1-1	1-0	1	Milne [7]	835
25	12	H	Queen's Park	D	0-0	0-0	1		544
26	19	H	Falkirk	W	2-0	1-0	1	Megginson [25], Fyvie [64]	1101
27	26	A	Alloa Ath	D	2-2	0-2	1	Adeyemo [82], McAllister [87]	612
28	Mar 5	H	Peterhead	W	5-2	3-1	1	McAllister (pen) [8], Megginson 2 [10, 21], Milne 2 [47, 76]	819
29	12	H	Clyde	W	4-1	2-1	1	Megginson [30], Fyvie [44], Reynolds [51], McIntosh [70]	766
30	19	A	Montrose	W	2-1	2-1	1	Megginson [6], Fyvie [32]	848
31	26	A	Airdrieonians	D	1-1	0-1	1	Fyvie [90]	1650
32	Apr 3	A	Queen's Park	D	1-1	0-0	1	McIntosh [90]	723
33	9	A	Falkirk	W	2-0	0-0	1	Milne 2 [54, 60]	3113
34	16	H	Alloa Ath	W	3-0	0-0	1	Fyvie 2 [57, 83], Milne [89]	1281
35	23	H	Dumbarton	W	1-0	0-0	1	Megginson [75]	1645
36	30	A	East Fife	W	3-2	1-2	1	Megginson 2 (1 pen) [38 (p), 55], Reynolds [62]	449

Final League Position: 1

Honours
League Champions: League One: 2021-22; League Two 2019-20.
Scottish Highland League Champions: 2000-01, 2007-08, 2008-09, 2012-13, 2015-16, 2017-18, 2018-19.
Promoted via play-offs: 2018-19.

Club colours: All: Royal blue with gold trim.

Goalscorers: *League (73):* Megginson 18 (2 pens), McAllister 16 (8 pens), Fyvie 8, Milne 6, Leitch 5, McIntosh 4, Neill 3, Masson 2, Reynolds 2, Scully 2, Vigurs 2, Adeyemo 1, McKenzie 1, Strachan 1, Yule 1, own goal 1.
Scottish FA Cup (5): Megginson 2, Fyvie 1, McAllister 1, Vigurs 1.
Premier Sports Scottish League Cup (6): Fyvie 2, Megginson 2, McIntosh 1, Yule 1.
SPFL Trust Trophy (9): Fyvie 2, Masson 2, McAllister 2, Megginson 2 (1 pen), McIntosh 1.

Gourlay K 5	Logan S 24	Ross Scott 30	Neill M 35	Milne H 27 + 2	Yule B 30 + 3	Draper R 1	Vigurs I 32	Leitch R 11 + 12	Fyvie F 27 + 2	Megginson M 33	Scully C 29 + 4	McAllister R 27 + 5	Strachan R 14 + 1	McIntosh L 6 + 21	Anderson J 3 + 4	Masson J 12 + 16	Watson B — + 1	McKenzie S 31	Robertson F 4 + 6	Adeyemo O 1 + 10	Reynolds M 14	Fotheringham K — + 5	*Match No.*
1	2	3	4	5	6	7	8	9[1]	10[2]	11	12	13											1
1	2		4[2]	5	6		8	9[1]	7■	10	13	12	3	11[3]	14								2
1	2	3		5	6		8	9[2]		10[1]	7	11[3]	4	13		12	14						3
1		3	2[3]	5	6		8	9[1]		10	7[2]	11	4	12	13	14							4
1		2	4		7		6	8[1]		11	9	10	3	13	5[2]	12							5
	2	3	4	13	6■		8	9[2]	7	10	5[1]	11[3]		14		12		1					6
	2	3	4	5			7	12	6[2]	10	8	11		13		9[1]		1					7
	2	3	4	5			8	13	7[3]	11	6[1]	10		14		9[2]		1	12				8
	2	3	4	5	6[3]		8	9[1]	12	11		10		14		13		1	7[2]				9
	2	3[2]	4				8	9[1]	6	10	7	11	12			5[3]		1	14	13			10
	2		4		13		8	12	6	10	5	11	3			9[2]		1	7[1]				11
	2[2]		4	12	13		6		8	10	5[1]	11	3	14		9[3]		1	7				12
		3	2	5	12		6	13	8[3]	10		11[1]	4			9		1	7[2]	14			13
	5[1]	2	4	8	6		7	14		10	13	11[3]	3	12		9[2]		1					14
			2	8	5		7		12	9[2]	6	10[1]	3	13	4	11[3]		1	14				15
	5	2[3]	4		6		7		9	10[1]	8	11[2]	3	13		12		1	14				16
	2■	3	4	5	6		7		9	10	8	11[1]		12				1					17
		2	3	4	5		7[2]	14	6	10	8	11[1]		12		9[3]		1	13				18
	2	4	3	5	8			12		11	7	10[2]		6		9[1]		1		13			19
	5	2	4		6			9[2]	7		8	11[1]	3	10	13			1		12			20
	5		3	4	6		7	11[2]				10	2	9[1]	8	12		1	13				21
	6[3]	2	4	9	7		8[2]		5	10[1]	14	11	3	12	13			1					22
		2	4	5	6		8		7	11	9	10						1			3		23
		2	3	8	5		6		9[1]	10	7	11[2]				13		1			4	12	24
		2	3	8	5[3]		6		9	10	7[1]	12		11[2]		13		1			4	14	25
		5	2	9	6		7		10	11	8		4					1			3		26
		2[1]	3	5	6		8	15	11[4]	10[3]	7[5]	12		14		9[2]		1		16	4	13	27
		2	3	8	5		6	13	9[1]	10[3]	7	11[2]						1		14	4	12	28
	2[4]		3	8■	5[2]		6	13	9	10[3]	7	11[1]		12		15		1		14	4		29
	5	2	3		6		7		9	10[2]	8	11[1]		13		12		1			4		30
	5	2	3	8[4]	6[2]		7		10	11[3]	9[1]	12		14		13		1		15	4		31
	5	2	3		6			12	7	9[2]	8[1]	10		13		14		1		11[3]	4		32
	5	2	3	8[3]	6		7	15	10		9[2]	11[1]		12[4]		13		1		14	4		33
	5	2[1]	3	9	6		7		11	10	8					12		1			4		34
	5	2	3	9	6		7		11	10[2]	8[1]			12		13		1			4		35
		2	3	5	6			9[2]		11	7			8[1]		10		1		13	4	12	36

COWDENBEATH

Year Formed: 1882. *Ground & Address:* Central Park, Cowdenbeath KY4 9QQ. *Telephone:* 01383 610166. *Fax:* 01383 512132.
E-mail: office@cowdenbeathfc.com *Website:* cowdenbeathfc.com
Ground Capacity: 4,370 (seated: 1,431). *Size of Pitch:* 95m × 60m.
Chairman: Donald Findlay QC. *Finance Director and Secretary:* David Allan.
Club Nicknames: 'The Blue Brazil'; 'Cowden'; 'The Miners'.
Manager: Maurice Ross. *Assistant Manager:* Colin Jack.
Previous Ground: North End Park.
Record Attendance: 25,586 v Rangers, League Cup quarter-final, 21 September 1949.
Record Transfer Fee received: £30,000 from Falkirk for Nicky Henderson (March 1994).
Record Victory: 12-0 v Johnstone, Scottish Cup 1st rd, 21 January 1928.
Record Defeat: 1-11 v Clyde, Division II, 6 October 1951; 0-10 v Hearts, Championship, 28 February 2015.
Most Capped Player: Jim Paterson, 3, Scotland.
Most League and Cup Appearances: 491, Ray Allan 1972-75, 1979-89.
Most League Goals in Season (Individual): 54, Rab Walls, Division II, 1938-39.
Most Goals Overall (Individual): 127, Willie Devlin, 1922-26, 1929-30.

COWDENBEATH – CINCH LEAGUE TWO 2021–22 LEAGUE RECORD

Match No.	Date	Venue	Opponents	Result		H/T Score	Lg Pos.	Goalscorers	Attendance
1	July 31	A	Kelty Hearts	L	0-2	0-1	8		1202
2	Aug 7	H	Elgin C	W	3-1	2-1	5	Buchanan, L 2 (2 pens) 13, 25, Mahady 82	307
3	21	A	Stenhousemuir	D	1-1	0-0	6	Renton 76	324
4	28	H	Annan Ath	L	1-3	1-0	7	Buchanan, R 4	282
5	31	H	Stranraer	L	1-2	0-0	8	Buchanan, L 50	282
6	Sept 11	A	Albion R	L	1-2	1-1	10	Clarke 45	230
7	18	H	Forfar Ath	D	1-1	0-1	9	Thomson 82	323
8	25	A	Stirling Alb	L	0-4	0-2	10		586
9	Oct 1	A	Edinburgh C	D	1-1	0-1	9	Renton 83	314
10	16	H	Stenhousemuir	L	0-2	0-2	10		293
11	30	A	Annan Ath	L	0-1	0-0	10		187
12	Nov 6	H	Kelty Hearts	L	0-1	0-0	10		727
13	13	A	Elgin C	L	0-1	0-0	10		650
14	20	A	Forfar Ath	L	0-3	0-0	10		474
15	Dec 4	H	Stirling Alb	W	1-0	0-0	10	Mullen 48	313
16	11	A	Stranraer	L	0-2	0-2	10		258
17	18	H	Albion R	D	0-0	0-0	10		266
18	22	H	Edinburgh C	L	1-2	0-0	10	Buchanan, L 75	221
19	Jan 8	H	Annan Ath	L	1-3	1-2	10	Buchanan, L 32	243
20	15	A	Stenhousemuir	W	2-0	0-0	10	Buchanan, R 48, Barr, B 58	344
21	22	H	Stranraer	L	0-1	0-0	10		331
22	29	A	Albion R	W	1-0	1-0	10	Mullen (pen) 9	292
23	Feb 19	H	Elgin C	W	2-0	1-0	10	Mullen (pen) 2, Barrowman 90	441
24	22	A	Kelty Hearts	L	0-1	0-0	10		1092
25	25	A	Edinburgh C	L	0-1	0-1	10		424
26	Mar 5	H	Kelty Hearts	L	0-1	0-1	10		475
27	8	A	Stirling Alb	L	1-2	0-1	10	Buchanan, L 90	378
28	12	A	Stranraer	L	0-3	0-2	10		283
29	15	H	Forfar Ath	L	1-2	1-1	10	Mullen 36	246
30	19	H	Stenhousemuir	D	1-1	0-0	10	Mullen (pen) 79	455
31	26	A	Forfar Ath	D	1-1	1-0	10	Ompreon 45	434
32	Apr 2	H	Stirling Alb	D	0-0	0-0	10		416
33	9	A	Annan Ath	W	3-2	2-1	10	Barrowman 12, Barr, C 38, Ompreon 59	263
34	16	H	Edinburgh C	D	0-0	0-0	10		328
35	23	A	Elgin C	W	4-1	0-0	10	Ompreon 56, Dunn 64, Barrowman 81, Cooper (og) 84	665
36	30	H	Albion R	L	0-1	0-0	10		411

Final League Position: 10

Honours
League Champions: Division II 1913-14, 1914-15, 1938-39; Second Division 2011-12; Third Division 2005-06.
Runners-up: Division II 1921-22, 1923-24, 1969-70; Second Division 1991-92; Third Division 2000-01, 2008-09.
Promoted via play-offs: 2009-10 (to First Division).
Scottish Cup: Quarter-finals 1931.
League Cup: Semi-finals 1959, 1970.

Club colours: Shirt: Royal blue with white sleeves. Shorts: White. Socks: Red.

Goalscorers: *League (28):* Buchanan L 6 (2 pens), Mullen 5 (3 pens), Barrowman 3, Ompreon 3, Buchanan R 2, Renton 2, Barr C 1, Barr B 1, Clarke 1, Dunn 1, Mahady 1, Thomson 1, own goal 1.
Scottish FA Cup (2): Buchanan L 1, Renton 1.
Premier Sports Scottish League Cup (5): Buchanan L 3 (1 pen), Renton 2.
SPFL Trust Trophy (1): Buchanan L 1.
Scottish League Play-offs (0).

Gill C 32 + 1	Mullen F 30 + 1	Barr C 35	Todd J 30 + 1	Thomson C 25 + 2	Buchanan R 30 + 2	Hutton K 16 + 2	Miller K 24 + 3	Barr B 13 + 14	Renton K 10 + 1	Buchanan L 23 + 11	Coulson Q 13 + 14	Mahady L 1 + 6	Pollock R 1	Clarke R 4 + 1	Watson L — + 1	Swan H 15 + 13	O'Conner K 10	Morrison G 19 + 3	McGurn D 1	Glass J 3	Barrowman A 12 + 1	Denham S 15	Carty D 5 + 5	Moore J — + 7	Dunn S 8 + 2	Ferguson A 10 + 2	Ompreon S 8 + 2	Aikamhenze C — + 3	McDowall C 3	*Match No.*
1	2	3	4	5	6	7	8^{1}	9	10	11	12																			1
1	2	3	4	5	6	8	7	9	10^{2}	11^{1}	13	12																		2
1		4		3	7	8		9	11	10^{1}	6		2	5■	12															3
1	2	4	3	5	9	8	7^{2}		11	10	6^{1}	13				12														4
1	2	3	4	5	6	8	7		10	11						9														5
1	5	3	4^{1}	2	8	7^{2}	6	12	10	11		13		9																6
1	2^{2}	3	4	5	7	8		14	11^{3}	10	6^{1}	13		9		12														7
1	9	4	3	2	6^{2}	7	13	11	12	10	14			5^{3}		8^{1}														8
1	2	3		5	6	7	8		11	10	12					9^{1}	4													9
1	2^{2}	3		5	6^{1}	7^{3}	8	13	11	10	14					9	4	12												10
1	5	3		2	6	12		8^{3}	10	11^{1}	13	14				9	4	7^{2}												11
1		4	7	2	6	9		13		11	12	10^{1}				5	3	8^{2}												12
1	12	3^{1}	4	5^{2}	10^{4}	7	15	14		9	11	13				8	2	6^{3}												13
1	5	3	2	14	10	6	7^{3}	13		9^{1}	11^{2}					8	4	12												14
1	5	3	2	8	13	7	6	9^{3}		10^{1}	14					11^{2}	4	12												15
1	5	3	2	8	12	7^{2}	6	9^{1}		10^{3}	13					14	4	11												16
1	8	3	4	5	11		6	13		10^{2}	9^{1}					12	2	7												17
1	8	3	4	5	9	12	6^{2}	11		14	10^{1}					13	2^{3}	7												18
	9	3■	4	5	8	7		11		12	14			13				6^{3}	1	2^{1}	10^{2}									19
1	8		2	5	9		6	10^{2}		12	11^{1}					13		7		4		3								20
1	8	3		5	9^{3}		6	10^{1}		13	11^{2}					12		7		2		4	14							21
1	8	3	4	5	10		6■	11^{1}			9^{2}					14		7				2	13	12^{3}						22
1	5	3	12		9											8		7			11	4	10		2^{1}	6				23
1	5	3	4	7	9^{1}			12		14						8					11^{2}	2	10^{3}	13		6				24
1	8^{4}	3	4	5	9^{1}		7			13	12					14					11^{3}	2	10^{2}	15		6				25
1	8	3	4		9^{4}		6	12		14						15		7				2	10^{2}	13	5^{3}		11^{1}			26
1	8^{2}	3	2	5	9^{4}			11^{3}		13	12					15		7				4	14			6	10^{1}			27
1	9	3	4	5^{2}	11^{4}			14		10						13		7			8^{3}	2^{1}		15	12	6				28
1	8	3	2		9		6			11	5^{1}							7			10^{2}				4		13	12		29
	8	3	4		5		6^{1}			10^{2}	11^{4}							7			9^{3}		15		2	14	12	13	1	30
		3	4		8		6	13		10^{1}								7			11^{2}	2			5	12	9		1	31
12	8	3	4		10^{2}		6^{1}			13						14		7			15	2			5^{4}	9	11		1^{3}	32
1	5	3	4				12	13		14	10^{1}					8		7			11^{3}	2				9^{2}	6			33
1		3	4				7			10^{1}						8					11	2	13		5^{2}	9	6	12		34
1		2	3				7^{2}	13		12	15					4					11	9	6^{3}	14	5^{4}	8	10^{1}			35
1	5^{2}	3	4^{1}	15			7	13		10^{4}	12					8					9^{3}	2		16	14	6	11^{5}			36

DUMBARTON

Year Formed: 1872. *Ground:* C&G Systems Stadium, Castle Road, Dumbarton G82 1JJ. *Telephone/Fax:* 01389 762569.
E-mail: office@dumbartonfc.com *Website:* dumbartonfootballclub.com
Ground Capacity: total: 2,025 (all seated). *Size of Pitch:* 98m × 67m.
Chairman: Dr Neil MacKay. *Vice-Chairman:* Colin Hosie.
Manager: Stevie Farrell. *Assistant Manager:* Frank McKeown.
Club Nicknames: 'The Sons'; 'Sons of the Rock'.
Previous Grounds: Broadmeadow; Ropework Lane; Townend Ground; Boghead Park; Cliftonhill Stadium.
Record Attendance: 18,000 v Raith R, Scottish Cup, 2 March 1957.
Record Transfer Fee received: £300,000 from Sunderland for Neill Collins (July 2004).
Record Transfer Fee paid: £50,000 to Stirling Alb for Charlie Gibson (1989).
Record Victory: 13-1 v Kirkintilloch Central, Scottish Cup 1st rd, 1 September 1888.
Record Defeat: 1-11 v Albion R, Division II, 30 January 1926: v Ayr U, League Cup, 13 August 1952.
Most Capped Player: James McAulay, 9, Scotland.
Most League Appearances: 298: Andy Jardine, 1957-67.
Most Goals in Season (Individual): 38: Kenny Wilson, Division II, 1971-72. *(League and Cup):* 46 Hughie Gallacher, 1955-56.
Most Goals Overall (Individual): 202: Hughie Gallacher, 1954-62

DUMBARTON – CINCH LEAGUE ONE 2021–22 LEAGUE RECORD

Match No.	*Date*	*Venue*	*Opponents*	*Result*		*H/T Score*	*Lg Pos.*	*Goalscorers*	*Atten-dance*
1	July 31	A	Clyde	W	3-0	2-0	1	Balatoni (og) [11], MacLean [34], Duthie [80]	746
2	Aug 7	H	Airdrieonians	D	2-2	0-1	1	McGeever [80], Geggan [87]	532
3	14	A	Queen's Park	L	0-3	0-1	5		613
4	21	H	Cove R	L	1-3	0-2	6	Carswell [47]	456
5	28	A	Montrose	W	2-1	2-0	5	Buchanan [20], Orsi [30]	599
6	Sept 11	H	East Fife	W	5-0	2-0	3	MacLean [12], Buchanan 2 [41, 66], McGeever [73], Stokes [87]	469
7	18	A	Falkirk	W	2-1	0-0	2	Orsi [60], Wilson [68]	3518
8	25	H	Alloa Ath	D	1-1	0-1	2	Boyle [80]	573
9	Oct 2	A	Peterhead	L	0-5	0-1	5		545
10	16	H	Queen's Park	L	0-3	0-0	6		652
11	23	A	Airdrieonians	L	2-3	1-1	6	MacLean [25], Paton [90]	653
12	30	A	East Fife	L	1-2	0-1	8	Duthie [90]	442
13	Nov 6	H	Clyde	D	1-1	0-0	7	Stokes [89]	562
14	13	H	Falkirk	L	0-3	0-1	7		886
15	20	A	Alloa Ath	W	2-1	0-0	7	Carswell (pen) [63], Stokes [82]	609
16	Dec 4	A	Cove R	L	0-2	0-0	8		371
17	11	H	Montrose	L	1-3	1-2	9	Duthie [15]	386
18	18	H	Peterhead	L	2-3	2-2	9	Geggan [17], Duthie [28]	336
19	Jan 2	H	Airdrieonians	L	0-1	0-0	9		312
20	8	A	Falkirk	L	2-6	0-3	9	Paton [56], Carswell (pen) [66]	500
21	15	H	East Fife	W	2-0	0-0	9	Oyinsan [55], Wylde [65]	481
22	29	H	Cove R	D	2-2	1-0	9	Carswell 2 (2 pens) [40, 85]	447
23	Feb 5	A	Montrose	D	1-1	1-1	9	Oyinsan [44]	531
24	8	A	Queen's Park	L	1-2	1-2	9	Carswell (pen) [27]	428
25	12	A	Clyde	W	3-1	3-1	7	MacLean 2 [8, 21], Carswell [19]	612
26	19	H	Alloa Ath	L	1-2	1-1	8	Paton [45]	678
27	26	A	Peterhead	L	3-4	0-3	9	MacLean [64], Lyle (og) [78], Pignatiello [90]	534
28	Mar 5	H	Queen's Park	L	0-3	0-2	9		584
29	12	A	East Fife	L	0-2	0-0	9		858
30	19	H	Falkirk	L	0-2	0-2	9		685
31	26	H	Montrose	D	0-0	0-0	9		492
32	Apr 2	A	Alloa Ath	W	3-2	0-0	9	Duthie 2 (1 pen) [86 (p), 88], Syvertsen [90]	676
33	9	H	Peterhead	D	1-1	1-1	9	Oyinsan [5]	527
34	16	A	Airdrieonians	L	2-3	1-2	9	Stanger [39], McCabe (og) [70]	902
35	23	A	Cove R	L	0-1	0-0	9		1645
36	30	H	Clyde	W	2-1	1-1	9	Syvertsen [11], Wylde [82]	655

Final League Position: 9

Honours
League Champions: Division I 1890-91 (shared with Rangers), 1891-92; Division II 1910-11, 1971-72; Second Division 1991-92; Third Division 2008-09.
Runners-up: First Division 1983-84; Division II 1907-08; Second Division 1994-95; Third Division 2001-02.
Promoted via play-offs: 2011-12 (Second Division).
Scottish Cup Winners: 1883; *Runners-up:* 1881, 1882, 1887, 1891, 1897.
League Challenge Cup: Runners-up: 2017-18.

Club colours: Shirt: Yellow with black trim. Shorts: Black. Socks: Yellow.

Goalscorers: *League (48):* Carswell 7 (5 pens), Duthie 6 (1 pen), MacLean 6, Buchanan 3, Oyinsan 3, Paton 3, Stokes 3, Geggan 2, McGeever 2, Orsi 2, Syvertsen 2, Wylde 2, Boyle 1, Pignatiello 1, Stanger 1, Wilson 1, own goals 3.
Scottish FA Cup (3): McKee 1, Pignatiello 1, Schiavone 1.
Premier Sports Scottish League Cup (2): MacLean 2.
SPFL Trust Trophy (2): Buchanan 1, Stokes 1.
Scottish League Play-offs (2): MacLean 1, Syvertsen 1.

Ramsbottom S 22	Lynch E 18	McGeever R 11	Buchanan G 32	Muir S 6	Carswell S 29 + 2	Pignatiello C 34 + 1	Hopkirk D 4 + 3	McKee J 13 + 8	MacLean R 26 + 2	Orsi K 26 + 10	Duthie C 25 + 10	Syvertsen K 1 + 7	Erskine C 1	Geggan A 11 + 3	Wilson C 14 + 21	Boyle P 29	Schiavone R 5 + 11	Paton P 22	Stokes E 6 + 18	Maley E — + 1	Wylde G 12 + 2	Bronsky S 11 + 1	Oyinsan J 9 + 1	Wright K 13	Hutchinson A 6 + 1	Stanger G 10	0	Match No.
1	2	3	4	5	6	7^{3}	8^{2}	9^{1}	10	11	12	14			13													1
	2^{2}	3	4	5^{3}	6	7	8		10	11	9^{1}	13	1	12	14													2
1		3	4		6	7	8	9	10	11^{3}	14			2^{2}	13	5^{1}	12											3
1	2	3	4		6^{3}		10^{2}		8^{1}	11	12				9	5	14	7	13									4
1	2	3	4		7	6			10^{1}	11	13				9^{2}	5	12	8										5
1	2	3	4		6	7		13	10^{1}	11	8^{3}				9^{2}	5	12		14									6
1	2	3	4		6	7		10^{2}		11^{1}	8			13	9^{3}	5	12		14									7
1	2	4	3		6	7	14	9^{3}	12	11^{1}	8^{2}				10	5	13											8
1	5	4	3		8	7	12		10	11^{2}	9^{3}			13	6^{1}	2	14											9
1	2	3	4		7	8	13	9^{1}	10	11^{3}	14			6^{2}	12	5												10
1		3^{3}	4■		12	7		8	11■	14	13			2■	9^{2}	5	10^{1}	6										11
1	2			9^{2}	3	5		6		13	10				8^{1}	4	11	7	12									12
1			4		3	2		9^{2}	8	10^{3}	13			6	14	5	11^{1}	7	12									13
1			4		3	2		9	10^{3}	8	14			7	13	5	11^{2}	6^{1}	12									14
1	2		4		3	6		13		10	7			8^{2}	9	5	11^{1}		12									15
1	2		4		8	7		13		6^{1}	11			3	9^{2}	5	12		10									16
1	3		4			8		14	12	9	10			5^{3}	6^{1}	2	13	7	11^{2}									17
1	3		4	5		7^{3}		9	10	11^{1}	8^{2}			2	14		12	6	13									18
1	3			5		7			11	10^{1}				2	6	4	12	8	9^{2}	13								19
1	3		4		6	8			10	11	9			2^{1}	12			7			5							20
1			4		7	2			10^{3}	12	6				13	5		8	14		9^{2}	3	11^{1}					21
1			3		7	2			11	12	6				13	5		8			9^{1}	4	10^{2}					22
			4		7	2		15		11^{2}	6				12	5		8^{3}	13		9^{4}	3	10^{1}	1	14			23
			4		7	2				12	6				13	5			9^{1}		10^{2}	3	11	1	8			24
			4		7	9^{1}			11^{2}	12	6^{3}				13	5		8	14		10	3		1	2			25
			3			6^{3}		13	10	14	11				12	5		7			9^{2}	4		1	8	2^{1}		26
			3^{4}		8	6		13	10■	15	11^{2}				14	5^{3}		7■	12		9^{1}	4		1		2		27
			4		7	6		8		11^{2}	10				12				13		9	3		1	5^{1}	2		28
					7■	6		8		13	11				12	5		3	10^{2}		9^{1}	4		1		2		29
	2^{2}		4			7		13	11	6	10				12				14		9^{1}	3		1	8^{3}	5		30
			3		4	7			11^{1}	6	9	12				5		8	13				10^{2}	1		2		31
			3		4^{1}	8			11	6^{2}	9	12			13	5		7	14				10^{3}	1		2		32
			4		7	2			10	6^{1}	9^{2}	12			13	5		8	14				11^{3}	1		3		33
			4		8	2			10	6^{1}	9	14			12	5^{4}		7^{3}	13		15		11^{2}	1		3		34
			4^{1}		8^{2}	2			10^{5}	16	12	13			6	5		7	9^{4}		15	14	11^{3}	1		3		35
1	2			5	12	15		8	11^{1}	6^{4}	13	10			7^{2}						9	3	14		4^{3}			36

DUNDEE

Year Formed: 1893. *Ground & Address:* Kilmac Stadium at Dens Park, Sandeman St, Dundee DD3 7JY. *Telephone:* 01382 889966. *Fax:* 01382 832284. *E-mail:* reception@dundeefc.co.uk *Website:* dundeefc.co.uk
Ground Capacity: 11,850 (all seated). *Size of Pitch:* 101m × 66m.
Chairmain: Tim Keyes. *Managing Director:* John Nelms. *Technical Director:* Gordon Strachan.
Manager: Gary Bowyer. *Assistant Manager:* Billy Barr.
Club Nicknames: 'The Dark Blues'; 'The Dee'.
Previous Ground: Carolina Port 1893-98.
Record Attendance: 43,024 v Rangers, Scottish Cup 2nd rd, 7 February 1953.
Record Transfer Fee received: £1,500,000 from Celtic for Jack Hendry (January 2018); £1,500,000 from Celtic for Robert Douglas (October 2000).
Record Transfer Fee paid: £600,000 to Sol de América (Paraguay) for Fabian Caballero (July 2000).
Record Victory: 10-0 Division II v Alloa Ath, 9 March 1947 and v Dunfermline Ath, 22 March 1947.
Record Defeat: 0-11 v Celtic, Division I, 26 October 1895.
Most Capped Player: Alex Hamilton, 24, Scotland.
Most League Appearances: 400: Barry Smith, 1995-2006.
Most League Goals in Season (Individual): 32: Alan Gilzean, 1963-64.
Most Goals Overall (Individual): 169: Alan Gilzean 1960-64.

DUNDEE – CINCH PREMIERSHIP 2021–22 LEAGUE RECORD

Match No.	*Date*	*Venue*	*Opponents*	*Result*		*H/T Score*	*Lg Pos.*	*Goalscorers*	*Attendance*
1	July 31	H	St Mirren	D	2-2	1-1	3	Shaughnessy (og) 44, Cummings 60	2300
2	Aug 8	A	Celtic	L	0-6	0-2	11		24,500
3	22	H	Hibernian	D	2-2	1-1	9	Cummings 11, McGowan 83	5295
4	28	A	Motherwell	L	0-1	0-1	9		4998
5	Sept 11	H	Livingston	D	0-0	0-0	9		5015
6	19	A	Dundee U	L	0-1	0-0	12		12,806
7	25	H	Rangers	L	0-1	0-1	12		8574
8	Oct 2	A	St Johnstone	L	1-3	0-2	12	Sweeney 74	5097
9	16	H	Aberdeen	W	2-1	0-0	11	Griffiths 49, McCowan 62	6876
10	23	A	Hearts	D	1-1	0-1	11	Cummings 83	17,557
11	27	H	Ross Co	L	0-5	0-4	11		4883
12	30	A	St Mirren	W	1-0	1-0	11	Anderson 11	3582
13	Nov 7	H	Celtic	L	2-4	1-2	11	Mullen 23, Ashcroft 67	8604
14	27	H	Motherwell	W	3-0	2-0	11	McCowan 19, Mullen 26, Sweeney 49	4747
15	Dec 1	H	St Johnstone	W	1-0	1-0	9	Mullen 39	5196
16	4	A	Rangers	L	0-3	0-1	9		49,628
17	11	A	Ross Co	L	2-3	2-1	10	McCowan 2 15, 38	3122
18	14	A	Hibernian	L	0-1	0-1	10		13,516
19	18	H	Hearts	L	0-1	0-0	10		5874
20	26	A	Aberdeen	L	1-2	1-1	11	Griffiths 7	500
21	Jan 18	A	Livingston	L	0-2	0-0	11		1612
22	26	A	St Johnstone	D	0-0	0-0	11		4135
23	Feb 1	H	Dundee U	D	0-0	0-0	12		11,273
24	5	H	Ross Co	L	1-2	1-1	12	Rudden 24	4621
25	9	A	Hearts	W	2-1	0-1	11	Sibbick (og) 51, Mullen 78	15,527
26	20	A	Celtic	L	2-3	1-2	12	Mullen 26, Sweeney 60	58,030
27	26	H	Livingston	L	0-4	0-3	12		4679
28	Mar 2	H	Hibernian	D	0-0	0-0	12		5237
29	5	A	Motherwell	D	1-1	1-1	12	McMullan 6	4435
30	9	H	St Mirren	L	0-1	0-0	12		5069
31	20	H	Rangers	L	1-2	1-0	12	Elliot 6	7669
32	Apr 2	H	Aberdeen	D	2-2	0-1	12	McGhee 62, Mullen 86	7815
33	9	A	Dundee U	D	2-2	0-1	12	Mullen 59, Adam 61	10,307
34	23	H	St Johnstone	D	1-1	1-0	12	Marshall 10	7937
35	30	A	Aberdeen	L	0-1	0-0	12		13,747
36	May 7	A	St Mirren	L	0-2	0-1	12		5564
37	10	H	Hibernian	W	3-1	1-1	12	McGinn 3, Mulligan 67, Adam 86	5452
38	15	A	Livingston	L	1-2	0-0	12	Mulligan 59	1629

Final League Position: 12

Honours

League Champions: Division I 1961-62; First Division 1978-79, 1991-92, 1997-98; Championship 2013-14; Division II 1946-47, 1947-48.
Runners-up: Division I 1902-03, 1906-07, 1908-09, 1948-49; First Division 1980-81, 2007-08, 2009-10, 2011-12; Championship: 2020-21.
Promoted via play-offs: 2020-21 (to Premiership).
Scottish Cup Winners: 1910; *Runners-up:* 1925, 1952, 1964, 2003.
League Cup Winners: 1951-52, 1952-53, 1973-74; *Runners-up:* 1967-68, 1980-81, 1995-96.
League Challenge Cup Winners: 1990-91, 2009-10; *Runners-up:* 1994-95.

European: *European Cup:* 8 matches (1962-63 semi-finals). *Cup Winners' Cup:* 2 matches: (1964-65).
UEFA Cup: 22 matches: (*Fairs Cup:* 1967-68 semi-finals. *UEFA Cup:* 1971-72, 1973-74, 1974-75, 2003-04).

Club colours: Shirt: Navy blue with blue and white trim. Shorts: White. Socks: Navy blue.

Goalscorers: *League (34):* Mullen 7, McCowan 4, Cummings 3, Sweeney 3, Adam 2, Griffiths 2, Mulligan 2, Anderson 1, Ashcroft 1, Elliot 1, Marshall 1, McGhee 1, McGinn 1, McGowan 1, McMullan 1, Rudden 1, own goals 2.
Scottish FA Cup (4): Adam 1 (1 pen), Griffiths 1 (1 pen), McGinn 1, Mulligan 1.
Premier Sports Scottish League Cup (12): Cummings 3 (2 pens), McMullan 2, Adam 1, Ashcroft 1, Elliot 1, Jakubiak 1, McCowan 1, McGowan 1, Panter 1.
SPFL Trust Trophy (1): Panter 1.

Legzdins A 24	Elliot C 9 + 4	Ashcroft L 15 + 1	McGhee J 30 + 4	Marshall J 29 + 1	Anderson M 28 + 5	Robertson F 1 + 1	Adam C 21 + 6	McMullan P 34 + 2	Mullen D 19 + 6	McGowan P 23 + 5	Cummings J 4 + 10	Sweeney R 33 + 2	Sheridan C 2 + 7	Byrne S 21 + 3	McCowan L 17 + 12	Fontaine L 15 + 4	McDaid D 3 + 4	Kerr C 35	Griffiths L 9 + 6	Jakubiak A 2 + 5	Panter C 1	Mulligan J 5 + 6	McGinn N 8 + 7	Daley-Campbell V 5 + 4	Rudden Z 8 + 5	Chapman J — + 2	Lawlor I 8	Rossi Z 3	Sharp H 6	*Match No.*
1	2^{3}	3	4	5	6■	7^{1}	8	9	10^{2}	11	12	13	14																	1
1	2^{2}	3	7	5■		12	9^{1}	6		10	14	4	11^{3}	8	13															2
1	2	3	5		7^{1}		8^{3}	9		12	10	14		6	11	4^{2}	13													3
1		3	5		7		9^{1}	6		12	11		13	8^{2}	10^{3}	4	14	2												4
1		3	6	5	8^{2}					14	13	4		7	9^{3}		12	2	10	11^{1}										5
1		3	6	5	8^{1}			9		11^{2}	14	4^{4}	15	7		12		2^{3}	10	13										6
1		2	8	9	6^{3}			10		13	12	4		7^{1}		3		5	11^{2}	14										7
1		2	8^{2}	9	14			10		6	11	4	12	7^{1}	13	3^{3}		5												8
1		3	6	5	14		7	11	13			4	12	8^{2}	9^{1}			2	10^{3}											9
1		3	6	5	8		7	9^{2}	12		13	4	14		11^{1}			2	10^{3}											10
1		3	6	5			7	11^{1}	12	8^{3}	9^{2}	4	13		14			2	10											11
1	14	3	13	5	8^{3}		9	6	12	7^{1}		4	11^{2}		10			2												12
1	2^{3}	4	13	6	10		9^{2}	7	11^{1}	8	14	5			12			3												13
1	14	3^{2}		5	7^{1}		8	6	11	10^{3}		4			9	12		2	13											14
1				5	7		8	6	11	10^{1}		4			9	3		2	12											15
1	6			5			7^{1}	10	11^{2}	9	13	4			8	3		2	12											16
1			12	5	7		8^{3}	9	11	10^{2}	14	4			6	3^{1}		2	13											17
1			7	5	6^{1}			8^{2}	11	9	12	4■			10	3		2	13											18
1	2		4		8			6	11	7					9^{1}	3		5	10	12										19
1			7	9						8		4			6	3		5	11	10	2									20
1	12		3	5^{2}	8		7^{4}	9^{3}	10	6^{1}					11	4		2	15	14		13								21
1	2				6		12	8		9^{2}		4		7	10^{1}	3		5	11^{3}	14			13							22
1			12		6		9^{1}	8	11^{3}			4		7	14	3		5					10^{4}	2^{2}	13	15				23
1			8		7^{1}		14	9	13			4		6	12	3		5					11^{3}	2■	10^{2}					24
			2		12		6	5	11			4		7		3		9				8^{1}	13		10^{2}		1			25
			4		7^{2}			11^{3}	10			5		8	12	14		6				9^{4}	13	2	15		1	3^{1}		26
			4	15	9^{1}		13	12	10	16		5		7^{5}				6				8^{3}	14	2	11^{4}		1	3^{2}		27
		13	3	5^{1}	7		8^{2}	6	10	11		4		12				2					9^{3}	14			1			28
		3	7	5	9			10				4		8			11^{1}	2				13		6^{2}		12			1	29
			8	5	7^{3}			6				4		13	10^{2}		11^{1}	2					9	14	12			3	1	30
	2		4	6	12			7		9^{2}		5		8	14		10^{3}	3					13		11^{1}		1			31
	2^{1}		4	6			12	7	10	9		5		8			13	3							11^{2}		1			32
	14		3	5^{1}	6		8^{3}	9	10	11^{2}		4		7				2				13	12				1			33
			3	5	7^{2}		9	6^{3}	11	10^{1}		4		8^{4}	12			2				15	14		13		1			34
			3	5	6^{1}		7^{4}	9	10	8		4			14			2^{2}				12	11^{3}	15	13				1	35
			3	5	15		7^{3}	12	11	6^{1}		4		14	8^{4}			2				13	9		10^{2}				1	36
			3	5	9		12	7^{2}				4		6^{3}	13	14		2				8	10		11^{1}				1	37
			3	5^{1}	9^{2}		14	7^{3}	13			4		6	12			2				8	10	15	11^{4}				1	38

DUNDEE UNITED

Year Formed: 1909 (1923). *Ground & Address:* Tannadice Park, Tannadice St, Dundee DD3 7JW. *Telephone:* 01382 833166. *Fax:* 01382 889398. *E-mail:* admin@dundeeunited.co.uk *Website:* dundeeunitedfc.co.uk
Ground Capacity: 14,223 (all seated). *Size of Pitch:* 100m × 66m.
Chairman: Mark Ogren. *Sporting Director:* Tony Asghar.
Head Coach: Jack Ross. *Assistant Head Coach:* Liam Fox.
Club Nicknames: 'The Terrors'; 'The Arabs'.
Previous Name: Dundee Hibernian (up to 1923).
Record Attendance: 28,000 v Barcelona, Fairs Cup, 16 November 1966.
Record Transfer Fee received: £4,000,000 from Rangers for Duncan Ferguson (July 1993).
Record Transfer Fee paid: £750,000 to Coventry C for Steven Pressley (July 1995).
Record Victory: 14-0 v Nithsdale Wanderers, Scottish Cup 1st rd, 17 January 1931.
Record Defeat: 1-12 v Motherwell, Division II, 23 January 1954.
Most Capped Player: Maurice Malpas, 55, Scotland.
Most League Appearances: 618: Maurice Malpas, 1980-2000.
Most Appearances in European Matches: 76: Dave Narey (record for Scottish player at the time).
Most League Goals in Season (Individual): 40: John Coyle, Division II, 1955-56.
Most Goals Overall (Individual): 199: Peter McKay, 1947-54.

DUNDEE UNITED – CINCH PREMIERSHIP 2021–22 LEAGUE RECORD

Match No.	Date		Venue	Opponents	Result		H/T Score	Lg Pos.	Goalscorers	Attendance
1	Aug	1	A	Aberdeen	L	0-2	0-1	11		6305
2		7	H	Rangers	W	1-0	0-0	5	Robson, J 64	4600
3		22	A	St Johnstone	W	1-0	0-0	6	Pawlett 60	5716
4		28	H	Hearts	L	0-2	0-1	7		9234
5	Sept	11	A	St Mirren	D	0-0	0-0	7		4894
6		19	H	Dundee	W	1-0	0-0	5	Harkes 81	12,806
7		26	A	Celtic	D	1-1	1-1	5	Harkes 18	56,403
8	Oct	2	H	Ross Co	W	1-0	1-0	5	Niskanen 31	6548
9		16	A	Hibernian	W	3-0	1-0	3	Clark 44, Edwards 52, Freeman 74	15,114
10		23	H	Motherwell	W	2-1	1-0	3	Edwards 35, Mulgrew 77	6854
11		27	A	Livingston	D	1-1	1-1	4	Pawlett 43	2586
12		30	H	St Johnstone	L	0-1	0-1	4		7580
13	Nov	6	A	Hearts	L	2-5	1-2	4	Edwards 34, Clark 62	18,129
14		20	H	Aberdeen	W	1-0	0-0	4	Harkes 80	10,500
15		27	A	Ross Co	D	1-1	0-0	4	Appere 49	3214
16		30	A	Motherwell	L	0-1	0-1	4		4287
17	Dec	5	H	Celtic	L	0-3	0-2	4		8311
18		11	H	Livingston	L	0-1	0-0	5		4552
19		18	A	Rangers	L	0-1	0-0	5		49,252
20		26	H	Hibernian	L	1-3	0-1	7	Glass 90	500
21	Jan	18	H	St Mirren	L	1-2	0-1	7	Power (og) 73	4978
22		26	H	Ross Co	W	2-1	0-0	7	Clark 2 (1 pen) 74 (p), 90	4519
23		29	A	Celtic	L	0-1	0-0	7		58,188
24	Feb	1	A	Dundee	D	0-0	0-0	7		11,273
25		5	A	St Johnstone	D	0-0	0-0	6		5005
26		9	H	Motherwell	W	2-0	1-0	4	Levitt 29, Watt 59	4591
27		20	H	Rangers	D	1-1	1-0	5	Graham 29	9993
28		26	A	Aberdeen	D	1-1	1-1	4	McNulty (pen) 4	18,719
29	Mar	2	A	Livingston	L	1-2	1-1	6	Smith, L 2	1864
30		5	H	Hearts	D	2-2	0-1	7	Smith, L 46, Clark (pen) 57	7172
31		19	A	St Mirren	W	2-1	0-1	4	Levitt 57, McNulty 90	5710
32	Apr	2	A	Hibernian	D	1-1	1-1	4	Graham 10	16,707
33		9	H	Dundee	D	2-2	1-0	4	Clark 12, Mulgrew 55	10,307
34		24	H	Hearts	L	2-3	1-1	4	Levitt 4, Edwards 65	6421
35		30	H	Motherwell	W	1-0	1-0	4	Levitt 37	6250
36	May	8	A	Rangers	L	0-2	0-0	4		49,340
37		11	H	Celtic	D	1-1	0-0	5	Levitt 72	9401
38		14	A	Ross Co	W	2-1	0-0	4	Clark 2 (1 pen) 70 (p), 89	5165

Final League Position: 4

Honours: *League Champions:* Premier Division 1982-83; Championship 2019-20; Division II 1924-25, 1928-29.
Runners-up: Division II 1930-31, 1959-60; First Division 1995-96; Championship 2018-19.
Scottish Cup Winners: 1994, 2010; *Runners-up:* 1974, 1981, 1985, 1987, 1988, 1991, 2005, 2014.
League Cup Winners: 1979-80, 1980-81; *Runners-up:* 1981-82, 1984-85, 1997-98, 2007-08, 2014-15.
League Challenge Cup Winners, 2016-17; *Runners-up:* 1995-96.

European: *European Cup:* 8 matches (1983-84, semi-finals). *Cup Winners' Cup:* 10 matches (1974-75, 1988-89, 1994-95). *UEFA Cup:* 86 matches (*Fairs Cup:* 1966-67, 1969-70, 1970-71. *UEFA Cup:* 1975-76, 1977-78, 1978-79, 1979-80, 1980-81, 1981-82, 1982-83, 1984-85, 1985-86, 1986-87 runners-up, 1987-88, 1989-90, 1990-91, 1993-94, 1997-98, 2005-06). *Europa League:* 6 matches (2010-2011, 2011-12, 2012-13).

Club colours: Shirt: Tangerine with black trim. Shorts: Black. Socks: Tangerine and black hoops.

Goalscorers: *League (37):* Clark 8 (3 pens), Levitt 5, Edwards 4, Harkes 3, Graham 2, McNulty 2 (1 pen), Mulgrew 2, Pawlett 2, Smith L 2, Appere 1, Freeman 1, Glass 1, Niskanen 1, Robson J 1, Watt 1, own goal 1.
Scottish FA Cup (3): Harkes 1, Levitt 1, McNulty 1.
Premier Sports Scottish League Cup (11): Pawlett 3, Shankland 3, Clark 2 (1 pen), Freeman 1, Mochrie 1, Mulgrew 1.
SPFL Trust Trophy (0).

Siegrist B 34	Edwards R 36	Mulgrew C 30 + 1	Reynolds M 1	Smith L 19 + 1	Harkes I 27 + 1	Butcher C 14 + 3	Clark N 26 + 11	Robson J 4	Pawlett P 19 + 3	Shankland L 1	Fuchs J 16 + 2	Chalmers L 2 + 3	Mochrie C 4 + 5	Sporle A 7 + 9	Watson D 2 + 4	Carson T 4	Levitt D 23 + 2	McNulty M 16 + 3	McMann S 25 + 4	Niskanen I 25 + 8	Appere L 4 + 9	Connolly M — + 1	Smith K 3 + 2	Freeman K 17 + 6	Glass D 6 + 4	Hoti F 2 + 3	Biamou M — + 3	Meekison A 7 + 2	Moore C 1	Neilson L 5 + 1	Watt T 15 + 2	Graham R 13 + 2	Akinola T 1	McDonald K 6 + 3	Macleod R 1 + 2	Thomson M 1	Cudjoe M 1 + 1	*Match No.*
1	2	3	4^{3}	5	6	7	8^{2}	9	10	11^{1}	12	13	14																									1
1	3	4		2	8	6	10	5	11^{2}		7	9^{1}		12	13																							2
	3	4		2			11	5	6■		8			9		1	7	10																				3
	3	4		2	12	13	11^{2}	5			8		6	9^{1}	14	1	7^{3}	10																				4
	3^{1}	4		2^{2}	8	7			10^{3}		6					1	12	11	5	9	13	14																5
1	3	4			7	8^{4}	15		10		9						12	11^{1}	5	6^{2}	13		2^{3}	14														6
1	4				6		10		7^{2}		8			12			9		5	11^{1}	13		3	2														7
1	3	4			9		11		6		7						8		5	10^{1}	12			2														8
1	3	4			8		11^{2}		6		7								5	9				2	10^{1}	12	13											9
1	3	4			9		11^{1}		6		7						8		5	10	12			2														10
1	3	4			9		11^{1}		6		12	13					7		5	10^{3}				2	8^{2}		14											11
1	3	4			6		10		13		8	9^{2}					7		5	12	11^{1}		2^{3}	14														12
1	3	4^{2}			7		11		6		9								5	10			12	2	8^{1}		13											13
1	3	4			9	8■	11		6^{3}		7^{1}								5	10^{2}	12			2	14	13												14
1	3	4			7		10		6					12					5	9^{1}	11			2		8												15
1	3	4			8		12		7					14	13				5^{3}	10^{2}	11			2	6^{1}	9												16
1	3	4			8	12	11^{1}		7		9			5	13					6	10^{2}			2														17
1	3	4			6		11^{1}		10		8			12					5	9	13			2^{3}	7^{2}			14										18
	2	3					11						6^{3}	9	5	1			4		12		14		10^{2}	13		8	7^{1}									19
1		4			7		11					14	9^{1}	6	10^{3}				5	12				2^{2}	13			8		3								20
1	3	4			10		14		6^{1}		8^{3}						7	11	5	9^{4}				13	15					2^{2}	12							21
1	3				8	4	12		9^{1}		6^{2}						7	10^{3}	5	13	14			2							11							22
1					8	3	10^{4}		15					9			7	13	4^{2}	5					14			6^{3}		2	11^{1}	12						23
1	3			12	7	2	9		14								6	11^{1}	8^{3}	13				5^{2}							10	4						24
1	3			2	9	4	10^{4}		6^{3}				15				8^{2}	14	13	12											11	5	7^{1}					25
1	3			5	6	2	12										8	11	13	9^{1}											10^{2}	4		7^{3}	14			26
1	2	3		5	6	7^{1}	13										8	11		9				12							10^{2}	4						27
1	2	3		5	6	12	13										8^{3}	10		9				14							11^{2}	4		7^{1}				28
1	2	3		6	9	7^{4}	12						14					11	13	8				5^{2}							10^{3}	4^{1}		15				29
1	2^{1}			6	7	4	11							13				10	9^{2}	5										12		3		8				30
1	3	4		2		8	13										7	11	5^{1}	9											10	12				6^{2}		31
1	2	3		5			9^{3}							12			6	11^{1}		8											10^{2}	4		7	14		13	32
1	2	3		5			9										7	11		8											10	4		6				33
1	2	3		6			11^{3}						7^{1}	15			8	14	9^{2}	5^{4}				12				13			10	4						34
1	3	7		5			13							14			8	10^{3}	9^{2}	12								6		2	11^{1}	4						35
1	3	7		5			13						16	9			6		15	14								8^{2}		2^{4}	11^{1}	4^{3}		12			10^{5}	36
1	3	12		2			10						14				8		4	9				5				6^{2}			13			7^{1}	11^{3}			37
1	3	7		2			10										8		9^{1}	12				5				6^{2}			11	4		13				38

DUNFERMLINE ATHLETIC

Year Formed: 1885. *Ground & Address:* East End Park, Halbeath Road, Dunfermline KY12 7RB.
Telephone: 01383 724295. *Fax:* 01383 745 959. *E-mail:* enquiries@dafc.co.uk
Website: dafc.co.uk
Ground Capacity: 11,380 (all seated). *Size of Pitch:* 105m × 65m.
Chairman and CEO: David Cook. *Vice-Chairman:* Billy Braisby.
Manager: James McPake. *First Team Coach:* Greg Shields.
Club Nickname: 'The Pars'.
Record Attendance: 27,816 v Celtic, Division I, 30 April 1968.
Record Transfer Fee received: £650,000 from Celtic for Jackie McNamara (October 1995).
Record Transfer Fee paid: £540,000 to Bordeaux for Istvan Kozma (September 1989).
Record Victory: 11-2 v Stenhousemuir, Division II, 27 September 1930.
Record Defeat: 1-13 v St. Bernard's, Scottish Cup 1st rd, 15 September 1883.
Most Capped Player: Colin Miller 16 (61), Canada.
Most League Appearances: 497: Norrie McCathie, 1981-96.
Most League Goals in Season (Individual): 53: Bobby Skinner, Division II, 1925-26.
Most Goals Overall (Individual): 212: Charles Dickson, 1954-64.

DUNFERMLINE ATHLETIC – CINCH CHAMPIONSHIP 2021–22 LEAGUE RECORD

Match No.	Date	Venue	Opponents	Result	H/T Score	Lg Pos.	Goalscorers	Attendance
1	July 31	A	Greenock Morton	D 2-2	0-1	5	Todorov [50], O'Hara [74]	821
2	Aug 7	H	Partick Thistle	L 0-3	0-2	9		2000
3	28	H	Arbroath	L 0-3	0-2	10		2928
4	Sept 11	A	Ayr U	L 1-3	1-2	10	Todorov [28]	1553
5	18	H	Inverness CT	D 0-0	0-0	10		3158
6	25	H	Hamilton A	D 0-0	0-0	10		3150
7	29	A	Raith R	D 1-1	0-1	10	O'Hara [79]	2876
8	Oct 2	A	Queen of the South	L 0-1	0-0	10		1071
9	16	H	Kilmarnock	D 2-2	0-0	10	Thomas [74], Comrie [90]	4095
10	23	A	Partick Thistle	D 0-0	0-0	10		3333
11	26	H	Raith R	D 1-1	0-0	10	Thomas [50]	4450
12	30	A	Arbroath	L 2-4	2-2	10	O'Hara 2 [8, 12]	1359
13	Nov 6	H	Greenock Morton	L 1-3	1-1	10	Todd [35]	3531
14	13	A	Inverness CT	W 2-1	0-1	10	Devine (og) [51], Thomas [64]	2111
15	20	H	Ayr U	W 3-0	2-0	6	McCann 2 [14, 52], Dow [40]	3503
16	Dec 4	A	Hamilton A	L 0-1	0-0	9		1175
17	11	H	Queen of the South	D 3-3	1-1	8	Kennedy [21], Connolly [54], McCann [88]	3425
18	26	H	Arbroath	L 0-3	0-2	9		3405
19	Jan 2	A	Raith R	D 0-0	0-0	9		500
20	8	A	Greenock Morton	L 0-5	0-3	10		429
21	15	H	Hamilton A	W 1-0	1-0	10	Dow [32]	556
22	22	H	Inverness CT	D 1-1	0-1	9	Lawless (pen) [80]	3138
23	29	A	Queen of the South	W 2-0	2-0	7	Dorrans [22], Pybus [29]	947
24	Feb 5	A	Ayr U	D 1-1	1-1	8	Donaldson [10]	1611
25	12	A	Kilmarnock	L 1-2	0-0	9	Lawless [59]	3698
26	26	H	Kilmarnock	D 0-0	0-0	9		4083
27	Mar 5	A	Arbroath	L 0-1	0-1	10		2141
28	12	A	Hamilton A	D 2-2	1-1	10	Donaldson [6], Lawless (pen) [52]	1369
29	18	H	Greenock Morton	D 1-1	0-1	10	McCann [88]	4593
30	22	H	Partick Thistle	W 4-1	3-1	9	Mayo (og) [10], Todd [22], Edwards [27], Thomas [82]	3380
31	26	A	Inverness CT	L 0-2	0-0	9		2171
32	Apr 6	H	Raith R	W 2-0	1-0	9	O'Hara 2 [33, 79]	5199
33	9	A	Kilmarnock	L 0-2	0-1	9		5013
34	16	H	Ayr U	W 2-1	0-1	8	Cole [79], Todorov [86]	4855
35	23	A	Partick Thistle	L 0-1	0-1	9		3428
36	29	H	Queen of the South	L 1-2	1-0	9	Edwards [6]	5406

Final League Position: 9

Honours
League Champions: First Division 1988-89, 1995-96, 2010-11; Division II 1925-26; Second Division 1985-86; League One 2015-16.
Runners-up: First Division 1986-87, 1993-94, 1994-95, 1999-2000; Division II 1912-13, 1933-34, 1954-55, 1957-58, 1972-73; Second Division 1978-79; League One 2013-14.
Scottish Cup Winners: 1961, 1968; *Runners-up:* 1965, 2004, 2007.
League Cup Runners-up: 1949-50, 1991-92, 2005-06.
League Challenge Cup Runners-up: 2007-08.

European: *Cup Winners' Cup:* 14 matches (1961-62, 1968-69 semi-finals). *UEFA Cup:* 32 matches (*Fairs Cup:* 1962-63, 1964-65, 1965-66, 1966-67, 1969-70. *UEFA Cup:* 2004-05, 2007-08).

Club colours: Shirt: Black and white stripes. Shorts: Black. Socks: Black with white tops.

Goalscorers: *League (36):* O'Hara 6, McCann 4, Thomas 4, Lawless 3 (2 pens), Todorov 3, Donaldson 2, Dow 2, Edwards 2, Todd 2, Cole 1, Comrie 1, Connolly 1, Dorrans 1, Kennedy 1, Pybus 1, own goals 2.
Scottish FA Cup (0).
Premier Sports Scottish League Cup (13): O'Hara 3, Todorov 3, Wighton 3, Comrie 1, MacDonald 1, Thomas 1, own goal 1.
Scottish League Play-offs (0).

Mehmet D 5	Comrie A 27 + 3	Watson P 6	Graham R 3 + 1	MacDonald K 7 + 2	Thomas D 16 + 9	Dorrans G 17 + 2	Edwards J 36	Wighton C 7 + 7	Todorov N 9 + 12	O'Hara K 21 + 11	Cole R 3 + 7	Kennedy K 8 + 6	Pybus D 27 + 5	Dow R 26 + 4	Gaspuitis V 11	Fon Williams O 20	Jones L 2	Connolly M 13	Allan P 11 + 2	McCann L 14 + 8	Breen R 7 + 4	Wilson I — + 3	Todd M 18 + 2	Lawless S 18	Donaldson C 16	Martin L 4 + 2	Chalmers J 14	Kamwa B — + 7	Stolarczyk J 11	Ambrose E 12	Polworth L 7 + 2	*Match No.*
1	2	3	4	5	6^2	7	8	9^1	10^3	11	12	13	14																			1
1	2^2	3	4	5	7^3	6	8	12	11	10	9^1		13	14																		2
1		3		2	12	8	5	13	10^1	11	14	9	7^3	6^2	4																	3
	2	4	5			7	8	13	11	10		12	9	6^1		1	3^2															4
	2	3			13	8	5	12	10^1	11^2	14	9	7^3	6	4	1																5
	2	3			14	8	5	11^1	10^3	12	13	9^2	7	6	4	1																6
	2				14	8	5	12	11^1	13	10^3	9	7^2	6	4	1		3														7
	2				13		5	11^1	12	10		9	7	6^2	4	1		3	8^3	14												8
	2				6		5	11	14	10		12	7^3	9^1	4^2	1		3	8		13											9
	2				6		5	11^2	14	10^3		13	7	9^1	4	1		3	8			12										10
	2				6		5	11^1	13	10^3		14	8^2	9	4	1		3	7			12										11
	2				6		5		11	10			8^1	9	3	1			7^2	13	4	12										12
	2			13	10^1		5	12	14	11^2		9		6		1		3	7		4		8^3									13
	2		13	6	9	7	5			10			12	14		1		3		11^2	4^3		8^1									14
	2			6^2	9	8	5	13		14				10	4	1		3	12	11^3			7^1									15
	2			7^1		6■	5		14	12		10^3	13	8	4	1		3		11			9^2									16
	2			7^2		6	5		14	13		10	12	8^1		1		3		11	4		9^3									17
	2					6	5	11^2		12		13		7		1		3	8	10	4		9^1									18
	2						5			12			9	8		1		3	6	11	4		7^1	10								19
	2						5		12				6	9		1			7	11			10^1	8	3	4						20
	2			13			5						6	11^1		1		3	7^2	10			8	9	4	12						21
	2					13	5			12	14		6	11^3		1			7^1	10			8^2	9	3	4						22
	2					8^1	3						6	4		1				9				10	5	7	11	12				23
	2					7	5						6^1	9						11				10	3	4	8	12	1			24
	2■					9	5			13	7^1			10						11^2			12	8	3		6		1	4		25
					13	9^1	5			12			6	10						11^2			2	8	3		7		1	4		26
	2^2				12	9^4	5			11			6^5	10^3						16	15			8	3	13	7		1	4^1	14	27
	2				13		5			11			7^2	9^1						12				10	3		8		1	4	6	28
					10		5			11			6							12			2^1	8	4		7		1	3	9	29
1	16				10^3		5		13	11^5			6	12					14		15		2^2	8	4^4		7			3	9^1	30
1	15				10^2		5		14	11	16		6	13									2^1	8^4	4		7	12		3^3	9^5	31
					10		5			11^1			6										2	8	4		7	12	1	3	9	32
	13				10^5		5		14	11^2			6^3	9						12	15		2	8^1	4		7^4	16	1	3		33
					10^3		5		15	11^4	13		6							12			2	8	3^1		7^2	14	1	4	9	34
	5^4				15		9		11	14			6^3				2^1			10^2	4		12	7			8		1	3	13	35
					10^2	12	5			11			6^1							13			2	8	4^3		7	14	1	3	9	36

EAST FIFE

Year Formed: 1903. *Ground & Address:* Locality Hub Bayview Stadium, Harbour View, Methil, Fife KY8 3RW. *Telephone:* 01333 426323. *Fax:* 01333 426376. *E-mail:* office@eastfifefc.info. *Website:* eastfifefc.info
Ground Capacity: 1,992. *Size of Pitch:* 105m × 65m.
Chairman: Jim Stevenson. *Vice-Chairman:* John Barclay.
Manager: Stevie Crawford. *Assistant Manager:* Greig McDonald.
Club Nickname: 'The Fifers'.
Previous Ground: Bayview Park.
Record Attendance: 22,515 v Raith Rovers, Division I, 2 January 1950 (Bayview Park); 4,700 v Rangers, League One, 26 October 2013 (Bayview Stadium).
Record Transfer Fee received: £150,000 from Hull C for Paul Hunter (March 1990).
Record Transfer Fee paid: £70,000 to Kilmarnock for John Sludden (July 1991).
Record Victory: 13-2 v Edinburgh C, Division II, 11 December 1937.
Record Defeat: 0-9 v Hearts, Division I, 5 October 1957.
Most Capped Player: George Aitken, 5 (8), Scotland.
Most League Appearances: 517: David Clarke, 1968-86.
Most League Goals in Season (Individual): 41: Jock Wood, Division II; 1926-27 and Henry Morris, Division II, 1947-48.
Most Goals Overall (Individual): 225: Phil Weir, 1922-35.

EAST FIFE – CINCH LEAGUE ONE 2021–22 LEAGUE RECORD

Match No.	Date	Venue	Opponents	Result		H/T Score	Lg Pos.	Goalscorers	Attendance
1	July 31	H	Queen's Park	D	1-1	1-0	4	Watt 8	320
2	Aug 7	A	Alloa Ath	L	1-3	0-1	7	Semple 48	516
3	14	A	Cove R	L	2-5	0-2	10	McManus (pen) 58, Smith, K 80	541
4	21	H	Montrose	L	0-2	0-1	10		488
5	28	H	Peterhead	W	3-0	0-0	9	Smith, K 48, McManus (pen) 69, Denholm 87	373
6	Sept 11	A	Dumbarton	L	0-5	0-2	10		469
7	18	A	Airdrieonians	L	0-3	0-1	10		546
8	25	H	Clyde	L	0-2	0-0	10		481
9	Oct 2	A	Falkirk	L	1-2	1-0	10	Millar 21	3250
10	16	H	Cove R	W	4-2	3-0	10	Steele 12, Connell 2 17, 49, Mercer 45	409
11	23	A	Montrose	L	1-4	0-0	10	Mercer 88	606
12	30	H	Dumbarton	W	2-1	1-0	10	Newton 36, Connell 71	442
13	Nov 6	A	Queen's Park	D	1-1	0-0	10	Millar 90	597
14	13	H	Airdrieonians	L	0-1	0-1	10		651
15	20	A	Clyde	L	1-3	0-0	10	Connell 57	604
16	Dec 4	H	Alloa Ath	D	1-1	0-0	10	Semple 79	427
17	11	A	Peterhead	D	1-1	0-0	10	Connell 48	470
18	26	A	Cove R	L	2-4	0-0	10	Milne (og) 72, Millar 90	499
19	Jan 2	H	Montrose	L	0-2	0-0	10		497
20	8	A	Airdrieonians	L	0-3	0-3	10		500
21	15	A	Dumbarton	L	0-2	0-0	10		481
22	22	H	Falkirk	L	0-2	0-0	10		1020
23	29	H	Peterhead	D	0-0	0-0	10		568
24	Feb 5	H	Clyde	D	0-0	0-0	10		443
25	12	A	Alloa Ath	W	3-1	2-1	10	Wallace (pen) 36, Connell 41, Denholm 81	638
26	19	H	Queen's Park	D	1-1	1-1	10	Ferrie (og) 6	481
27	26	A	Falkirk	L	1-3	1-1	10	Wallace 25	4104
28	Mar 5	A	Montrose	D	0-0	0-0	10		705
29	12	H	Dumbarton	W	2-0	0-0	10	Connell 3, Denholm 61	858
30	19	A	Clyde	L	0-2	0-1	10		633
31	26	H	Alloa Ath	L	0-3	0-0	10		517
32	Apr 2	H	Airdrieonians	L	0-2	0-1	10		644
33	9	A	Queen's Park	L	0-1	0-0	10		580
34	16	H	Falkirk	L	1-3	0-1	10	Semple (pen) 84	562
35	23	A	Peterhead	L	0-1	0-1	10		676
36	30	H	Cove R	L	2-3	2-1	10	Denholm 14, Connell 19	449

Final League Position: 10

Honours
League Champions: Division II 1947-48; Third Division 2007-08; League Two 2015-16.
Runners-up: Division II 1929-30, 1970-71; Second Division 1983-84, 1995-96; Third Division 2002-03.
Scottish Cup Winners: 1938; *Runners-up:* 1927, 1950.
League Cup Winners: 1947-48, 1949-50, 1953-54.

Club colours: Shirt: Gold with black checks. Shorts: Black. Socks: Black.

Goalscorers: *League (31):* Connell 8, Denholm 4, Millar 3, Semple 3 (1 pen), McManus 2 (2 pens), Mercer 2, Smith K 2, Wallace 2 (1 pen), Newton 1, Steele 1, Watt 1, own goals 2.
Scottish FA Cup (1): Semple 1.
Premier Sports Scottish League Cup (2): McManus 1 (1 pen), Smith K 1.
SPFL Trust Trophy (3): Mercer 2, Denholm 1.

Gallacher S 10 + 1	Mercer S 35	Dunlop R 13 + 2	Higgins C 31	Slattery P 17 + 5	Denholm D 23 + 7	Newton L 19 + 4	McManus C 16 + 3	Watt L 13 + 4	Brown S 1 + 7	Smith K 12 + 8	Cunningham M — + 7	Steele A 24 + 4	Dow C — + 2	Semple J 10 + 18	Connell K 27 + 1	Smith J 24 + 1	Dunsmore A 11 + 3	Higgins D 11 + 7	Osei-Bonsu A 3 + 6	Murdoch S 12 + 2	Millar K 23 + 3	Wallace R 15 + 1	Davidson R 4	Campbell L 2	Mansouri A — + 1	Anderson L — + 1	Blair R 16 + 1	Watson L 7	Healy J 4 + 10	Watson D 4 + 1	Swanson D 4 + 6	Pollock F 5 + 2	Walls B — + 4	*Match No.*
1	2^1	3	4	5	6	7	8	9	10^2	11^3	12	13	14																					1
1	2	3	4	5	8^3	6	7	10	12		13		14	9^1	11^2																			2
1^1	2	3	4	5	8	6	7	10^2		13				9^3	11	12	14																	3
1	2	3	4	5			6	10^1	14	9^3				12	11^2		8	7	13															4
1	5	3	4^1	10	13		7			11^2				9			8	12	14	2^3	6													5
1	5	3		9^2	12		7	13	14	10^1				11^3			2	4	6		8													6
1	2	4			9^3	7			14	11^1		13		12			5	10■	6	3^2	8													7
	5	14	4		9^3	6	7		13	11^2		3		12		1	2		10^1		8													8
	5		4		10^3	6	7	13	14	9^1		3		11^2		1	2		12		8													9
	5	4^2	3	9		8	7	6	14			2		13	11^3	1		12				10^1												10
	5		3	9		8^2	7	6				2			11	1		4^1	12		13	10												11
	5		3	12	9^2	6	7	8				2		14	11^1	1		4^3			13	10												12
	5		3^1	4	9^2	6	7	8		14		2		13	11	1					12	10^3												13
	5			9		6	3	8^1				2		13	10^2	1			12	4	7■	11												14
	9			14	13	6	3	8^1				2		7^3	11	1	5^2		12	4		10												15
	2		4		10	7^1	14	6^3		11^2				12	13	1		3		5	9		8											16
	8^3		3		14		12	9^2		11^1		2		13	10	1	5	4			6		7											17
	2		4	5	11^1	10^3		8^2				3					7	13			6		9	1	12	14								18
1	2^2		4	5^3	9		8^1	14				3			11■		6	13			7	12					10							19
1	2		4	5	9^1		8	14		11^3		3		13			6^2	12				10					7							20
1			4		9^3	6^1	12			14		3		13	10			2				11	8^2				7	5						21
12	2		4	7	8					9^1		3		13	11^2	1■		5				10					6^3		14					22
	5	14	4	7		16				9^1		3		13	11^3		15	2^2				10		1			6^4	8^5		12				23
	5	4	3	12						16		2		9^1	11^3	1	13				6^4	10^5					7		15	8^2	14			24
	5^4	3	4		12							2		9^2	10^3	1				13	8	11^1					7		14	6	15			25
	8	3	4		10^4					15		2		9^1	11^3	1				12	7						6		13	5^2	14			26
	2^3	3	4		9^5	16				14		12			10^1	1				5	7	11^2					8		13	6^4	15			27
	2	3^1	4	15	9^4							12		14	10	1				5	7	11					8^3		6^2		13			28
	2			4	10					15					11^2	1		12		3^3	7	9^4					6	5	8^1		13	14		29
	2		4		10					15	13	3		14	11^2	1					7						6^3	5	8^1		9^4	12		30
	2		4		10^1	15					14			12	11^2	1				3	7						6	5^3	13		9	8^4		31
	6^1		4	14	13	12						2			11	1				3	7						9^3	5	15		8^4	10^2		32
	6		4		12	9^1						2		13	11^3	1				3	7						8	5^4	14			10^2	15	33
	2^4		4		7	9					15	3		12	11^3	1		14		5^2	8								6			10^1	13	34
	5		4		7^3	9					14	2		6^2	11	1		3^1			8						13		12^4		10		15	35
	2		4	5^3	10	9					13	3			11^2	1					8						7		12			6^1	14	36

ELGIN CITY

Year Formed: 1893. *Ground and Address:* Borough Briggs, Borough Briggs Road, Elgin IV30 1AP.
Telephone: 01343 551114. *Fax:* 01343 547921. *E-mail:* elgincityfc@btconnect.com *Website:* elgincity.net
Ground Capacity: 3,927 (seated: 478). *Size of pitch:* 102m × 68m.
Chairman: Graham Tatters.
Manager: Gavin Price. *Assistant Manager:* Steven McKay.
Previous name: Elgin City United 1900-03.
Club Nicknames: 'City'; 'The Black & Whites'.
Previous Grounds: Association Park 1893-95; Milnfield Park 1895-1909; Station Park 1909-19; Cooper Park 1919-21.
Record Attendance: 12,608 v Arbroath, Scottish Cup, 17 February 1968.
Record Transfer Fee received: £32,000 from Dundee for Michael Teasdale (January 1994).
Record Transfer Fee paid: £10,000 to Fraserburgh for Russell McBride (July 2001).
Record Victory: 18-1 v Brora Rangers, North of Scotland Cup, 6 February 1960.
Record Defeat: 1-14 v Hearts, Scottish Cup, 4 February 1939.
Most League Appearances: 306: Mark Nicholson, 2007-17.
Most League Goals in Season (Individual): 21: Craig Gunn, 2015-16.
Most Goals Overall (Individual): 128: Craig Gunn, 2009-17.

ELGIN CITY – CINCH LEAGUE TWO 2021–22 LEAGUE RECORD

Match No.	Date	Venue	Opponents	Result		H/T Score	Lg Pos.	Goalscorers	Attendance
1	July 31	H	Stranraer	D	1-1	1-0	5	McHardy 23	405
2	Aug 7	A	Cowdenbeath	L	1-3	1-2	8	McHardy 37	307
3	14	H	Albion R	W	3-0	2-0	4	Hester 3 17, 22, 46	488
4	21	H	Forfar Ath	D	1-1	0-0	5	O'Keefe 47	688
5	27	A	Edinburgh C	L	0-2	0-2	6		338
6	Sept 11	A	Kelty Hearts	D	1-1	1-0	7	MacPhee (pen) 30	608
7	18	H	Annan Ath	L	0-2	0-1	8		467
8	25	A	Stenhousemuir	W	2-1	1-0	6	McHardy 4, Dingwall, R 76	391
9	Oct 2	H	Stirling Alb	L	0-2	0-1	7		652
10	16	A	Albion R	L	0-2	0-0	9		267
11	Nov 6	A	Forfar Ath	L	1-2	1-1	9	MacEwan 32	469
12	13	H	Cowdenbeath	W	1-0	0-0	9	MacPhee 53	650
13	20	A	Stranraer	L	0-1	0-0	9		235
14	23	H	Edinburgh C	D	1-1	0-0	9	Wilson, J 66	378
15	Dec 11	A	Annan Ath	L	1-4	1-1	9	Cooper 4	221
16	18	H	Stenhousemuir	D	2-2	1-2	9	Hester (pen) 37, McHardy 90	518
17	21	A	Stirling Alb	W	1-0	0-0	9	Mailer 68	383
18	Jan 2	H	Forfar Ath	W	1-0	0-0	9	McHardy 90	499
19	7	A	Edinburgh C	D	2-2	1-1	9	Cooper 14, Hester 59	258
20	15	H	Albion R	D	1-1	1-1	8	Hester (pen) 25	500
21	25	H	Kelty Hearts	W	2-0	1-0	8	Hester 2 36, 75	531
22	29	A	Stenhousemuir	L	1-2	1-2	8	Hester 38	348
23	Feb 5	A	Kelty Hearts	L	0-4	0-2	8		433
24	12	H	Stranraer	L	1-2	0-1	8	McHardy 89	539
25	15	H	Annan Ath	L	0-2	0-2	9		347
26	19	A	Cowdenbeath	L	0-2	0-1	9		441
27	26	H	Stirling Alb	W	3-1	2-0	7	McHardy 10, Omar 26, Hester 82	561
28	Mar 5	A	Forfar Ath	D	0-0	0-0	7		482
29	12	A	Annan Ath	L	1-2	0-0	8	Hester 55	271
30	19	H	Kelty Hearts	D	0-0	0-0	8		733
31	26	H	Edinburgh C	W	2-0	2-0	9	Peters 9, Hester 17	667
32	Apr 2	A	Albion R	D	0-0	0-0	9		289
33	9	H	Stenhousemuir	L	0-2	0-1	9		585
34	16	A	Stirling Alb	W	2-0	0-0	8	MacEwan 52, Cooper 78	443
35	23	H	Cowdenbeath	L	1-4	0-0	8	Hester 75	665
36	30	A	Stranraer	L	0-2	0-0	9		235

Final League Position: 9

Honours
League Runners-up: League Two 2015-16.
Scottish Cup: Quarter-finals 1968.
Highland League Champions: winners 15 times.

Club colours: Shirt: Black and white stripes. Shorts: Black. Socks: White with black tops.

Goalscorers: *League (33):* Hester 13 (2 pens), McHardy 7, Cooper 3, MacEwan 2, MacPhee 2 (1 pen), Dingwall R 1, Mailer 1, O'Keefe 1, Omar 1, Peters 1, Wilson J 1.
Scottish FA Cup (2): Cameron 1, MacEwan 1.
Premier Sports Scottish League Cup (5): Hester 2, Dingwall T 1, Little 1, Mailer 1.
SPFL Trust Trophy (4): Hester 2, Cameron 1, Grivosti 1.

Hoban D 17	Cooper M 20	Little C 6 + 1	McHardy D 27 + 1	Spark E 20 + 1	Mailer A 29 + 5	MacPhee A 11 + 4	Dingwall R 35 + 1	Dingwall T 15 + 10	Sopel A 17 + 11	Hester K 26 + 4	MacEwan R 22 + 9	O'Keefe C 8 + 13	Peters J 8 + 20	Cameron B 23 + 2	Lawrence D — + 1	MacBeath J — + 2	McHale T 19	Cooney N 6 + 2	Allen F 3 + 9	Nicolson H — + 2	Machado M 4 + 13	Grivosti T 12	Hamilton O — + 1	Wilson J 5 + 3	Draper R 18 + 2	Towler E 16 + 1	Omar R 16 + 1	Hanratty K — + 3	El-Zubaidi A 2	O'Connor K 8 + 3	Anderson J 3	Mykyta T — + 3	Hamilton J — + 1	*Match No.*
1	2^{3}	3	4	5	6	7	8	9^{1}	10^{2}	11	12	13	14																					1
1		3	4	5	2^{3}	6^{4}	8	9^{2}	10^{1}	11^{5}	14	12	13	7	15	16																		2
		3	4	5	14	12	8	6^{3}	15	11^{5}	7^{1}	9^{4}	13	10^{2}			1	2	16															3
		3^{3}	4	5	13		7	6^{4}	14	11	8^{2}	9^{1}		10		15	1	2		12														4
		3^{4}	4	5	8^{3}	13	7	6	12	11		9^{1}	10^{2}				1	2		14	15													5
		4	5	6	2	9	7	10^{2}	13		8^{3}		14	11			1	12				3^{1}												6
1■		14	6	5		11	7		9^{3}	12^{5}	4^{1}	10	15	8				2^{4}	16			3^{2}	13											7
			4	5	2	9	8	12	13		7	10^{2}		11			1	3^{1}				6												8
			4	2	7^{1}	5	8	10^{4}	14		6^{2}	11^{3}		9			1		15		13	3		12										9
			3	5	2^{4}	9^{3}	7	12			14	10^{1}	13	8			1		15		16	4		11^{5}	6^{2}									10
	5^{1}			2		6	7	12	10^{3}		8		14	9			1				13	3		11^{2}	4									11
	3		4	5	13	8^{3}	9^{4}	14	11^{2}	12	6	15		7			1					2		10^{1}										12
	4		3	5	13	9^{3}	6	7^{2}	11^{1}	10■		14		8			1					2		12										13
	3		4	5	6^{1}	8	9	14	11^{3}			12		7^{2}			1		13			2		10										14
	8		4		5		6	14	12	10	7^{2}	11^{1}	13				1	2^{4}			15	3		9^{3}										15
	2		4	5	14		8	9^{1}	10^{2}	11	7	13					1					3■		12	6^{3}									16
	2		3	5^{1}	9		7	14	10^{2}	11^{4}	8	12	15				1	13	6^{3}						4									17
	6		4	5^{1}	8		14	13		11	7^{2}		10^{3}				1				9	2			3	12								18
1	3^{3}		4		7	15	6	13		10	8	14	11^{1}								9^{2}				12	5	2^{4}							19
1			4	2^{2}	7	15	6	10^{4}		11	8^{1}	13	14								12				3	5	9^{3}							20
			5	3	2		7	9^{1}		11^{3}	8		12				1		14						4	6	10^{2}	13						21
			14	2^{2}	8		6	9		11	7		12				1								3	5	10^{3}	13	4^{1}					22
					5		6	7^{2}	12	11^{1}	8		15				1		13		14				3^{3}	9	10^{4}		4	2				23
			4		2^{4}		6	9^{2}	15	10	8		14	12			1		11^{3}		13				3	5	7^{1}							24
1			4		2		6	8^{1}	12	10^{3}	7^{4}		15	13					11^{2}						3	9	5	14						25
1	3		4		2		8	12		13	9^{1}		11	6							10^{2}					5	7							26
1	2		3^{4}		7		8		12	11^{3}	13			6							10^{1}					5	9^{2}			14	4	15		27
1	2		3	12^{4}	6		10		8^{2}	11^{1}	15		13	7												5^{3}	9			14	4			28
1	2		3		7		8^{2}		10^{3}	11	13		14	6											12	5	9^{4}			15	4^{1}			29
1	9		4^{2}		5		6		8^{3}	11^{1}	12^{4}	13	14	7											3		10■			2		15		30
1	2				8		6^{3}		9^{2}	10	14	12	11^{1}	7											4	5				3		13		31
1	2				8		6		9^{1}	10			11^{2}	7							13				4	5	12			3				32
1	2				7		6^{2}			11		13	10^{3}	8					14		12				3	5	9^{1}			4				33
1	2				7^{3}		6		11^{2}	10^{1}	12		13	8							14				3	5	9			4				34
1	2				6^{3}		7		10^{2}	11^{1}	3		12	8							13				4		9			5			14	35
1					7		6		10^{4}	14	2	13	11^{1}	8^{3}					15		12				4	5	9^{2}			3				36

FALKIRK

Year Formed: 1876. *Ground & Address:* The Falkirk Stadium, 4 Stadium Way, Falkirk FK2 9EE. *Telephone:* 01324 624121. *Fax:* 01324 612418. *Email:* post@falkirkfc.co.uk *Website:* falkirkfc.co.uk
Ground Capacity: 8,750 (all seated). *Size of Pitch:* 105m × 68m.
Directors: Kenny Jamieson, Keith Gourlay.
Manager: John McGlynn. *Assistant Manager:* Paul Smith.
Club Nickname: 'The Bairns'.
Previous Grounds: Randyford 1876-81; Blinkbonny Grounds 1881-83; Brockville Park 1883-2003.
Record Attendance: 23,100 v Celtic, Scottish Cup 3rd rd, 21 February 1953.
Record Transfer Fee received: £945,000 from Norwich C for Conor McGrandles (August 2014).
Record Transfer Fee paid: £225,000 to Chelsea for Kevin McAllister (August 1991).
Record Victory: 11-1 v Tillicoultry, Scottish Cup 1st rd, 7 Sep 1889.
Record Defeat: 1-11 v Airdrieonians, Division I, 28 April 1951.
Most Capped Player: Alex Parker, 14 (15), Scotland.
Most League Appearances: 451: Tom Ferguson, 1919-32.
Most League Goals in Season (Individual): 43: Evelyn Morrison, Division I, 1928-29.
Most Goals Overall (Individual): 154: Kenneth Dawson, 1934-51.

FALKIRK – CINCH LEAGUE ONE 2021–22 LEAGUE RECORD

Match No.	*Date*	*Venue*	*Opponents*	*Result*	*H/T Score*	*Lg Pos.*	*Goalscorers*	*Attendance*
1	July 31	A	Cove R	D 1-1	0-0	4	Nesbitt [65]	672
2	Aug 7	H	Peterhead	W 2-1	1-0	4	McGuffie [14], Dixon [54]	2806
3	14	A	Airdrieonians	W 2-1	2-0	3	Morrison [28], Keena [30]	1314
4	21	H	Clyde	W 3-0	0-0	2	Dixon [57], Morrison 2 (1 pen) [67 (p), 90]	3545
5	28	H	Queen's Park	L 0-1	0-1	3		4043
6	Sept 11	A	Alloa Ath	L 0-2	0-1	4		1385
7	18	H	Dumbarton	L 1-2	0-0	7	Telfer [90]	3518
8	25	A	Montrose	D 2-2	0-0	6	Keena [79], Ruth [90]	918
9	Oct 2	H	East Fife	W 2-1	0-1	3	Ruth [60], Keena [74]	3250
10	16	H	Airdrieonians	L 0-3	0-1	5		3525
11	23	A	Peterhead	D 0-0	0-0	5		743
12	30	A	Clyde	W 3-1	1-0	5	Ruth [45], McGuffie [67], Telfer [90]	1163
13	Nov 6	H	Alloa Ath	D 1-1	0-0	5	Morrison (pen) [88]	3514
14	13	A	Dumbarton	W 3-0	1-0	5	Ruth [11], Nesbitt [54], Telfer [71]	886
15	20	H	Montrose	L 0-1	0-1	5		3365
16	Dec 4	A	Queen's Park	L 0-6	0-2	5		1119
17	11	H	Cove R	L 0-3	0-2	5		3258
18	26	H	Clyde	L 1-2	0-0	7	Keena (pen) [50]	400
19	Jan 8	H	Dumbarton	W 6-2	3-0	5	Dowds 3 [8, 45, 88], Morrison [13], Taylor-Sinclair [54], Keena [72]	500
20	15	A	Airdrieonians	L 2-3	0-2	5	McKay [47], Dowds [89]	500
21	22	A	East Fife	W 2-0	0-0	5	Kabia 2 [52, 90]	1020
22	29	A	Montrose	L 1-2	1-2	6	Fleming (og) [34]	1036
23	Feb 5	H	Queen's Park	D 1-1	0-1	6	Dowds [49]	3427
24	8	A	Alloa Ath	W 3-0	0-0	5	Kabia [50], McGuffie [58], Watson [78]	1504
25	19	A	Cove R	L 0-2	0-1	5		1101
26	22	H	Peterhead	D 1-1	1-1	5	Dowds [41]	3187
27	26	H	East Fife	W 3-1	1-1	5	McGuffie [16], Watson [89], Griffiths (pen) [90]	4104
28	Mar 5	A	Clyde	D 1-1	1-0	5	Watson [27]	1331
29	12	H	Airdrieonians	L 1-4	0-1	5	Griffiths [76]	3646
30	19	A	Dumbarton	W 2-0	2-0	5	Kabia [4], Telfer [27]	685
31	26	A	Peterhead	L 0-1	0-1	5		705
32	Apr 2	H	Montrose	L 0-3	0-1	5		3158
33	9	H	Cove R	L 0-2	0-0	5		3113
34	16	A	East Fife	W 3-1	1-0	5	Morrison 2 [34, 90], Telfer [56]	562
35	23	H	Alloa Ath	L 1-2	0-1	5	Dowds [77]	3366
36	30	A	Queen's Park	D 1-1	0-1	6	Morrison [84]	922

Final League Position: 6

Honours

League Champions: Division II 1935-36, 1969-70, 1974-75; First Division 1990-91, 1993-94, 2002-03, 2004-05; Second Division 1979-80;
Runners-up: Division I 1907-08, 1909-10; First Division 1985-86, 1988-89, 1997-98, 1998-99; Division II 1904-05, 1951-52, 1960-61; Championship: 2015-16, 2016-17; League One 2019-20.
Scottish Cup Winners: 1913, 1957; *Runners-up:* 1997, 2009, 2015.
League Cup Runners-up: 1947-48.
League Challenge Cup Winners: 1993-94, 1997-98, 2004-05, 2011-12.

European: *Europa League:* 2 matches (2009-10).

Club colours: Shirts: Navy blue with white pinstripes. Shorts: White. Socks: Red.

Goalscorers: *League (49):* Morrison 8 (2 pens), Dowds 7, Keena 5 (1 pen), Telfer 5, Kabia 4, McGuffie 4, Ruth 4, Watson 3, Dixon 2, Griffiths 2 (1 pen), Nesbitt 2, McKay 1, Taylor-Sinclair 1, own goal 1.
Scottish FA Cup (1): Morrison 1.
Premier Sports Scottish League Cup (6): Morrison 2, Dixon 1, Nesbitt 1, Telfer 1, Weekes 1.
SPFL Trust Trophy (4): Keena 1, Nesbitt 1, Ross 1, own goal 1.

Mutch R 23	Miller G 30 + 4	Hall B 17 + 1	Dixon P 20 + 1	Williamson C 2 + 1	Nesbitt A 23 + 11	Telfer C 36	Ross S 6 + 14	Morrison C 15 + 5	Wilson J 2 + 6	McGuffie C 29 + 5	Keena A 8 + 13	McCann L 21 + 6	Hetherington S 22 + 5	Ompreon S 1 + 10	Weekes B — + 2	Lemon M 5 + 2	Krasniqi E — + 5	Ruth M 11 + 1	McKay B 15	McDaid D 8 + 1	Williamson R 19 + 3	Martin P 13	Taylor-Sinclair A 15 + 1	Dowds A 11 + 2	Kabia J 8 + 4	Mills J 6	Watson P 10	Jacobs K 9 + 3	Griffiths L 11 + 2	Malcolm F — + 1	*Match No.*
1	2	3	4	5^{3}	6	7	8^{2}	9	10^{1}	11	12	13	14																		1
1	2	3	4		8^{3}	6	13	9		11^{1}	10^{2}	5	7	12	14																2
1	2	3			9	6		8^{2}	14	10^{1}	11^{3}	5	7■	13		4	12														3
1	2	3	4		8	7	6^{1}	9	13	11^{3}	10^{2}	5			14		12														4
1	2	3	4		8	7	11	9^{1}	14	13	10^{3}	5	6^{2}	12																	5
1	4	3	2		7	11	9			8^{1}	13	5	6	12				10^{2}													6
1	2^{1}		4		9	6				10^{2}	14	5	7	8^{3}				11	3	12	13										7
1	12		4	5^{3}	9^{1}	7	14			10	13		6					11	3	8	2^{2}										8
	2	13	5^{3}		9^{1}	7				10^{2}	12		6			4	14	11	3	8		1									9
	5				6	8^{2}	14			13	11^{1}	2	7	12		3		10	4	9^{3}		1									10
	2	3	4		7	8^{1}				11^{3}	12	5^{2}	6	14		13		10		9		1									11
	2	3	4		7	8				11^{1}	12	5	6■	14			13	10^{2}		9^{3}		1									12
	2^{3}	3	4		7	8		13		11^{2}	12	5	6					10^{1}		9	14	1									13
	2	3	4		8	6		12		9^{3}	13	5	7				14	10^{2}		11^{1}		1									14
	2^{2}	3	4		8	6^{1}	14	9		11^{3}	12	5	7					10			13	1									15
	14	3			8	6	13	9			12	5	7^{3}			4		10^{2}		11^{1}	2	1									16
	7	3			6	8	11^{1}	9		14	10	5^{2}		12				13	4		2^{3}	1									17
	7	2			6	8	11^{1}	5		9	10			12		4			3			1									18
	6	3			13	11	14	9^{1}		7^{3}	12	8							5		2	1	4	10^{2}							19
	7	3			12	8^{2}		10^{1}		6	13	9							2		5	1	4	11							20
	8	3^{1}		14	7	5				9	11^{3}	13							2		6^{2}	1	4	10	12						21
1	7				8^{2}	6^{1}	14	13		9^{3}		15									5		4^{4}	10	11	2	3	12			22
1	15		9^{4}		12■	6^{3}				8^{2}		13	14	16					2		5		4	10^{1}	11		3	7^{5}			23
1	14					8^{2}	15		16	6^{1}		9	12						2		5^{3}		4	10	11^{4}		3	7^{5}	13		24
1					14	6				12		9	8^{3}						4■		5		2	11	13		3	7^{1}	10^{2}		25
1	7		4^{1}		8^{3}	6				9						15					5		13	11	10^{2}	2	3^{4}	14	12		26
1	7		13		12	6	14			11^{3}											2		5^{1}	9		3	4	8^{2}	10		27
1	7				12	6				11^{3}		5	14								2			9^{1}	13	3	4	8^{2}	10		28
1					9^{2}	6	13	12		8^{3}		5	14						4		2				11	7	3		10^{1}		29
1	7				13	9^{4}	14		12	10			8^{1}								2		5		6^{2}	4	3	15	11^{3}		30
1	6				13	9	14		12■	8^{3}			7^{2}						3		2		5		10^{1}		4		11		31
1	7^{1}		4		11^{2}	6	13	12		14			8						3		2		5		9^{3}				10		32
1	2		3		13	6^{1}		10^{2}		9			7								5		4		12^{3}			8	11	14	33
1	2		3			6^{1}	14	10		9^{2}		13	7								5		4	12				8	11^{3}		34
1	2		3		12	6^{1}		11	5	9^{2}		14	7										4	13				8	10^{3}		35
1	2		3		12	7		5				9	6										4	11				8	10^{1}		36

FC EDINBURGH

Year formed: 1928 (disbanded 1955, reformed from Postal United in 1986; name changed from Edinburgh City in June 2022).
Ground & Address: Meadowbank Stadium, Edinburgh EH7 6AE. *Telephone:* 0845 463 1932.
E-mail: admin@edinburghcityfc.com *Website:* edinburghcityfc.com
Ground Capacity: 500 (seated 500). *Size of Pitch:* 96m × 66m
Chairman: Jim Brown.
Manager: Alan Maybury. *Assistant Manager:* Mark Kerr.
Previous name: Postal United, Edinburgh City.
Club Nickname: 'The Citizens'.
Previous Grounds: City Park 1928-55; Fernieside 1986-95; Meadowbank Stadium 1996-2017; Ainslie Park 2018-2020.
Record victory: 5-0 v King's Park, Division II (1935-36); 6-1 and 7-2 v Brechin City, Division II (1937-38).
Record defeat: 1-11 v Rangers, Scottish Cup, 19 January 1929.
Most League Appearances: 129: Marc Laird, 2016-21.
Most League Goals in Season (Individual): 30: Blair Henderson, League Two, 2018-19.
Most Goals Overall (Individual): 56: Blair Henderson, 2018-21.

EDINBURGH CITY – CINCH LEAGUE TWO 2021–22 LEAGUE RECORD

Match No.	Date	Venue	Opponents	Result		H/T Score	Lg Pos.	Goalscorers	Attendance
1	July 31	A	Albion R	L	0-2	0-2	8		275
2	Aug 7	A	Forfar Ath	L	0-2	0-1	10		465
3	13	H	Stenhousemuir	W	1-0	1-0	7	Shanley 31	313
4	21	A	Kelty Hearts	L	0-1	0-0	8		677
5	27	H	Elgin C	W	2-0	2-0	5	Handling 2 1, 7	338
6	Sept 11	A	Stranraer	W	1-0	0-0	5	See 80	299
7	17	H	Stirling Alb	D	2-2	1-1	4	Murray 40, Hilton 60	479
8	25	A	Annan Ath	W	3-1	2-0	5	See 10, Hilton 32, Robertson 68	324
9	Oct 1	H	Cowdenbeath	D	1-1	1-0	4	Handling 8	314
10	15	H	Kelty Hearts	L	2-3	1-2	5	See 16, Murray 88	726
11	Nov 5	H	Albion R	L	0-4	0-3	5		263
12	12	H	Stranraer	W	3-1	2-0	5	Robertson 2 22, 40, Hilton 90	218
13	20	A	Stirling Alb	W	2-1	1-1	5	Robertson (pen) 38, Murray 79	528
14	23	A	Elgin C	D	1-1	0-0	4	Murray 62	378
15	Dec 3	H	Annan Ath	L	0-1	0-1	5		219
16	11	A	Stenhousemuir	D	2-2	1-0	5	Bronsky 44, Robertson 86	321
17	17	H	Forfar Ath	L	0-4	0-3	5		273
18	22	A	Cowdenbeath	W	2-1	0-0	4	Robertson 51, Reekie 83	221
19	Jan 7	H	Elgin C	D	2-2	1-1	4	Tapping, C 37, Travis 71	258
20	15	A	Kelty Hearts	D	2-2	0-1	4	Handling 75, Brydon 90	500
21	31	A	Forfar Ath	W	3-2	2-0	4	McDonald 22, Handling 28, Murray 55	441
22	Feb 5	A	Stranraer	W	2-0	1-0	4	See 2, Handling 74	302
23	11	H	Stirling Alb	W	1-0	0-0	4	Hamilton 59	498
24	15	H	Albion R	L	1-2	0-0	4	Robertson 75	321
25	19	A	Annan Ath	L	1-2	0-0	4	Shanley 90	305
26	25	H	Cowdenbeath	W	1-0	1-0	4	Shanley 42	424
27	Mar 2	H	Stenhousemuir	D	1-1	1-1	4	Brydon 38	182
28	5	A	Albion R	W	1-0	0-0	4	Shanley (pen) 90	262
29	12	A	Stenhousemuir	D	0-0	0-0	4		476
30	18	H	Stranraer	L	1-2	0-2	4	McDonald 66	525
31	26	A	Elgin C	L	0-2	0-2	4		667
32	Apr 1	H	Kelty Hearts	D	1-1	0-0	4	Shanley (pen) 66	487
33	9	H	Forfar Ath	W	2-0	1-0	4	Handling 28, Shanley (pen) 69	197
34	16	A	Cowdenbeath	D	0-0	0-0	4		328
35	22	H	Annan Ath	W	2-1	2-1	4	Shanley 13, See 20	264
36	30	A	Stirling Alb	L	0-5	0-4	4		508

Final League Position: 4

Honours
League Champions: Scottish Lowland League Champions: 2014-15, 2015-16. *Runners-up:* League Two 2019-20, 2020-21.
Promoted via play-offs: 2021-22 (to League One); 2015-16 (to League Two).
League Challenge Cup: Semi-finals 2018-19.

Club colours: Shirt: White with black trim. Shorts: White. Socks: White.

Goalscorers: *League (43):* Handling 7, Robertson 7 (1 pen), Shanley 7 (3 pens), Murray 5, See 5, Hilton 3, Brydon 2, McDonald 2, Bronsky 1, Hamilton 1, Reekie 1, Tapping C 1, Travis 1.
Scottish FA Cup (4): Handling 1, Murray 1, Robertson 1, Shanley 1.
Premier Sports Scottish League Cup (1): Hilton 1.
SPFL Trust Trophy (0).
Scottish League Play-offs (8): Murray 2, See 2, Shanley 2, Robertson 1, own goal 1.

Goodfellow R 2	Reekie S 10 + 5	Toshney L 5 + 1	McIntyre R 9	Crane C 17	Jardine D 8 + 4	Hilton J 11 + 6	Tapping C 22 + 1	Handling D 27 + 3	Kidd L 7	See O 27 + 7	Robertson J 20 + 7	Bronsky S 12 + 5	Shanley R 16 + 12	McFarlane M — + 5	Brian C 18 + 11	Schwake B 33 + 1	Kane C 7 + 6	Hamilton L 11 + 3	Murray I 30 + 1	Berry L 8 + 13	Ferguson A 5 + 4	McKay D 9	Jarron J 3 + 2	Farrell J 6 + 7	Smith A — + 3	Fraser C 1 + 1	Boyle L — + 2	Logan C 18	Brydon J 10	Travis M 15 + 1	McDonald A 12	Stirling B 16 + 1	Leighfield J 1	Mitchell Q — + 1	*Match No.*
1	2	3^{4}	4	5	6^{1}	7^{2}	8	9	10	11^{3}	12	13	14	15																					1
1^{2}	5	4	6	2	9^{3}	13	8	7			10^{1}		11	14	3	12																			2
		4	9	5	7	6^{2}	8	13		12	10^{1}	3	11^{3}		2	1	14																		3
	16	4	9^{3}	5	7^{1}	12	8	13		6	10	15	11^{4}		2^{2}	1	14	3^{5}																	4
	12	4^{2}		5	6^{3}	8	7	10		11		3			2	1	13		9^{1}	14															5
	5			9		6	8			11^{2}	10^{1}	3	13	12	2	1		4	7																6
	5	12^{3}		9	13^{4}	6	8			11	10^{1}	3	15		2	1	14	4^{2}	7																7
	5					6^{2}	7	8		10^{1}	9^{3}	3	12	14	2	1	4		11		13														8
	5					9^{2}	7	8		10	11^{1}	3	13			1	4		6		12	2													9
	5^{3}					14	8^{4}	6	2	10	11^{1}		13			1	4		9	15	7^{2}	3	12												10
	5^{2}					6^{1}	8	9	2	12	11	13	10^{4}	14		1	4^{3}			7		3		15											11
						14	8	9	2	10^{2}	11	4	13		12	1			6^{1}	7		3	5^{3}												12
						13	8	9^{1}	2	10	11	4			12	1	14		6	7^{2}		3	5^{3}												13
						12	8	9	2	10^{3}	11^{4}	4	14		5^{2}	1	15		6	7^{1}	13	3													14
	15					9^{3}			6	11	7	3			5	1	4^{1}		10	8^{4}	12	2^{2}		14	13										15
	2					7				10^{3}	11^{2}	3			5^{1}	1	8		9	13	6	4		14	12										16
	5					7^{4}				10^{2}	11	4			9^{1}	1	2		6^{3}	12	8		15	3	13	14									17
	12									10^{1}	11	14			5	1			9	7	6	4	2^{2}	3		8^{3}	13								18
							8	9		11		15			5	1			6	13	7^{1}			12			14	2^{3}	3	4^{4}	10^{2}				19
	13						8	9		11	12				5	1			10									2	3	4	6^{1}	7^{2}			20
				8^{2}			7	9		10^{1}	12		16		13	1		14	11	15								2^{5}	3	4	6^{4}	5^{3}			21
				8			7	9^{2}		11^{1}	6^{5}		14		13	1		12	10	16				15				2	3	4^{4}		5^{3}			22
				5	13			10^{3}		11^{2}	7^{1}		12			1		4	8	14								2	6	3		9			23
					12			9		13	10		11^{1}		5	1			8									2	3	4	6^{2}	7			24
					7^{2}			9		14	12		11		13	1			10					3^{1}				5	2	4	6^{3}	8			25
				5^{2}	7^{1}			9		12			11^{3}		15	1			10	14				13				2	3	4	6^{4}	8			26
					7^{2}			9		13			11^{1}		14	1			10	12				3^{3}				2	5	4	6	8			27
								8		11			10		12	1			9	13				6				2	3^{1}	4	5^{2}	7			28
				5				7^{3}		8^{2}			11		14	1		12	9	13				3■				2		4	10^{1}	6			29
								9					11		5	1		3	10	7								2		4	6	8			30
				5■			7^{3}	9^{1}		11			10^{2}		14	1		3	8					12				2		4■	6	13			31
			4				7	6^{2}		12			10		5	1		3	11	13								2			9^{1}	8			32
			4	5			7^{2}	9		11	14		10^{3}		13	1		3	6^{1}									2		12		8			33
			4	5				9		11	12		10			1		3	6									2^{1}		7		8			34
			4	8			12	9		10^{2}	13		11^{1}			1		2	6									5		3		7			35
			4	9^{1}	15		7^{5}	14		10^{4}	11		13		8			2^{2}	16	6								5				3^{3}	1	12	36

FORFAR ATHLETIC

Year Formed: 1885. *Ground & Address:* Station Park, Carseview Road, Forfar DD8 3BT. *Telephone:* 01307 463576. *Fax:* 01307 466956. *E-mail:* alan.shepherd@forfarathletic.co.uk *Website:* forfarathletic.co.uk
Ground Capacity: 6,777 (seated: 739). *Size of Pitch:* 103m × 64m.
Chairman: Scott Murdie. *Secretary:* Alan Shepherd.
Player/Manager: Gary Irvine. *Assistant Manager:* Scott Robinson.
Club Nicknames: 'The Loons'; 'The Sky Blues'.
Record Attendance: 10,780 v Rangers, Scottish Cup 2nd rd, 2 February 1970.
Record Transfer Fee received: £65,000 from Dunfermline Ath for David Bingham (September 1995).
Record Transfer Fee paid: £50,000 to Airdrieonians for Ian McPhee (1991).
Record Victory: 14-1 v Lindertis, Scottish Cup 1st rd, 1 September 1888.
Record Defeat: 2-12 v King's Park, Division II, 2 January 1930.
Most League Appearances: 463: Ian McPhee, 1978-88 and 1991-98.
Most League Goals in Season (Individual): 46: Dave Kilgour, Division II, 1929-30.
Most Goals Overall: 125: John Clark, 1978-91.

FORFAR ATHLETIC – CINCH LEAGUE TWO 2021–22 LEAGUE RECORD

Match No.	Date	Venue	Opponents	Result		H/T Score	Lg Pos.	Goalscorers	Attendance
1	July 31	A	Annan Ath	W	2-0	2-0	1	McCluskey [26], Shepherd [43]	300
2	Aug 7	H	Edinburgh C	W	2-0	1-0	2	Aitken [3], Gallagher [90]	465
3	14	H	Kelty Hearts	D	2-2	2-1	2	Aitken (pen) [17], Thomson, C [45]	623
4	21	A	Elgin C	D	1-1	0-0	3	McCluskey [20]	688
5	28	H	Stranraer	D	1-1	0-0	3	Slater [54]	445
6	Sept 11	A	Stirling Alb	L	0-1	0-0	4		508
7	18	A	Cowdenbeath	D	1-1	1-0	4	Aitken [24]	323
8	25	H	Albion R	W	3-1	1-0	4	McCluskey [11], Shepherd [64], Aitken [68]	425
9	Oct 2	A	Stenhousemuir	D	1-1	1-0	4	Thomson, C [5]	371
10	16	H	Annan Ath	W	2-0	1-0	3	Munro [42], McCluskey [60]	351
11	30	A	Stranraer	W	3-2	1-1	3	Aitken (pen) [44], Thomson, C [56], Ness [88]	312
12	Nov 6	H	Elgin C	W	2-1	1-1	2	Munro [26], Anderson, G [58]	469
13	13	A	Kelty Hearts	L	0-1	0-0	2		856
14	20	H	Cowdenbeath	W	3-0	0-0	2	Munro [77], Anderson, G [85], Aitken [90]	474
15	Dec 4	A	Albion R	W	3-2	1-0	2	McCluskey [26], Crossan [62], Anderson, S [82]	213
16	11	H	Stirling Alb	W	2-0	0-0	2	Slater [48], McCluskey [90]	473
17	17	A	Edinburgh C	W	4-0	3-0	2	Munro [29], McCluskey [36], Anderson, S [40], Aitken [48]	273
18	26	H	Stenhousemuir	L	3-4	1-4	2	Fisher [11], Shepherd [54], Munro [57]	411
19	Jan 2	A	Elgin C	L	0-1	0-0	2		499
20	8	H	Stranraer	W	3-2	1-1	2	Shepherd 2 (2 pens) [42, 64], Anderson, G [60]	436
21	15	A	Annan Ath	D	2-2	2-1	2	Munro [29], Slater [44]	341
22	31	H	Edinburgh C	L	2-3	0-2	2	Slater [53], Aitken [60]	441
23	Feb 5	H	Albion R	W	2-0	1-0	2	Munro 2 [7, 73]	423
24	15	A	Stirling Alb	D	1-1	1-0	2	Slater [13]	449
25	19	H	Kelty Hearts	W	1-0	0-0	2	Aitken [73]	670
26	26	A	Stenhousemuir	L	0-2	0-1	2		348
27	Mar 5	H	Elgin C	D	0-0	0-0	3		482
28	12	H	Stirling Alb	L	0-1	0-1	3		496
29	15	A	Cowdenbeath	W	2-1	1-1	3	Thomson, C [13], Munro [84]	246
30	19	A	Albion R	D	0-0	0-0	3		220
31	26	H	Cowdenbeath	D	1-1	0-1	3	Shepherd [77]	434
32	Apr 2	A	Stranraer	W	2-0	0-0	3	Slater [83], McCluskey [86]	257
33	9	A	Edinburgh C	L	0-2	0-1	3		197
34	16	H	Annan Ath	W	5-1	5-0	3	Aitken [12], Warnock [23], McCluskey 3 (1 pen) [26, 34, 37 (p)]	472
35	23	A	Kelty Hearts	D	1-1	0-1	2	Warnock [47]	903
36	30	H	Stenhousemuir	D	0-0	0-0	2		490

Final League Position: 2

Honours
League Champions: Second Division 1983-84; Third Division 1994-95; C Division 1948-49.
Runners-up: League One 2018-19; Third Division 1996-97, 2009-10; League Two 2016-17, 2021-22.
Promoted via play-offs: 2009-10 (to Second Division); 2016-17 (to League One).
Scottish Cup: Semi-finals 1982.
League Cup: Semi-finals 1977-78.
League Challenge Cup: Semi-finals 2004-05.

Club colours: Shirt: Sky blue. Shorts: Navy blue. Socks: Sky blue and navy blue hoops.

Goalscorers: *League (57):* McCluskey 11 (1 pen), Aitken 10 (2 pens), Munro 9, Shepherd 6 (2 pens), Slater 6, Thomson C 4, Anderson G 3, Anderson S 2, Warnock 2, Crossan 1, Fisher 1, Gallagher 1, Ness 1.
Scottish FA Cup (2): Anderson G 1, Shepherd 1 (1 pen).
Premier Sports Scottish League Cup (3): Anderson G 1, Gallagher 1, McCluskey 1.
SPFL Trust Trophy (1): Aitken 1.
Scottish League Play-offs (1): McCluskey 1.

McCallum M 35	Meechan R 34	Fisher S 7 + 3	Munro A 32	Strachan L 24 + 3	Crossan P 18 + 11	Gallagher M 6 + 6	Slater C 36	Thomson C 21 + 5	Aitken M 33 + 1	McCluskey S 28 + 2	Shepherd S 18 + 18	Doris S — + 12	Anderson G 8 + 21	Thomas A 7 + 9	Irvine G 2	Anderson S 18 + 1	Travis M 1 + 2	Ness J 6	Harkins G 9 + 8	Hussain Y 2 + 4	Moore C 11 + 7	Whyte D 13 + 3	Hutton K 10 + 3	Brindley T 11 + 1	Warnock S 5 + 2	Sanderson L 1	Match No.
1	2	3	4	5	6	7^{1}	8	9^{3}	10^{4}	11^{2}	12	13	14	15													1
1	5		4	2	9^{1}	7	8	6	11		10^{2}	12	13		3												2
1	2		4	5^{2}	9		8	6	10^{1}	12	11^{3}	14		7	3	13											3
1	2		4	5	9^{1}		7	6	10^{2}	11^{3}	12	14	13	8		3											4
1	2		3	5	6^{1}		7	9	11^{2}	10	13		12	8		4											5
1	2			5	12	14	7	6^{1}	10^{2}	11	13	15	9^{3}			4	3	8^{4}									6
1	2		4	5		12	7	6	10		11^{1}		9			3		8^{2}	13								7
1	2		4	5	14	8^{1}	7	6^{2}	11	9^{3}	10		13			3			12								8
1	2		3^{1}	5^{3}	12	8	7	6	11^{4}	9	10^{2}		13			4	15			14							9
1	2		3	5	13	8^{4}	7	6	10^{1}	9^{3}	11			12		4^{2}	15		14								10
1	2		3	5	12		7	6^{1}	11	9^{2}	10^{3}	13	14			4		8									11
1	2		4	5	9^{2}	12	8		10^{1}	6	11		13	14		3		7^{3}									12
1	2		4	5	12		6	7	10^{1}	9	11^{2}	13		8		3											13
1	2		4	5	9	8^{2}	6		11		10^{1}	13	12	7		3											14
1	2		3	5	9^{3}	14	7		11^{2}	10	12		6^{1}	13		4		8									15
1	2	5^{1}	4		9		8		11^{3}	10	14		6	12		3		7^{2}		13							16
1	2		3	5^{1}	9^{4}	13	6		11^{2}	10^{3}	12	14		8		4				15	7						17
1		2	3	5	9^{1}		8		10		11	13	6^{2}	7		4			12								18
1	2		3	5	10^{4}	14	6			8	11^{2}	13	15			4^{1}			7		9^{3}	12					19
1	2	14	3	5	10		6				11^{2}	15	8^{4}	12		4			7^{1}		9^{3}	13					20
1	2		3	5	9^{3}		7		10^{2}	6	11		14	13		4^{4}			8^{1}		15	12					21
1	2		3	5^{1}	7^{3}		8		10	11	14		15						6^{2}		9^{4}	4	12	13			22
1	2		3		12		7	13	10^{4}	6^{2}	11		9^{1}								14	4	8^{3}	5	15		23
1		2	3				7	6^{2}	10^{1}	9	13		12						14		11	4	8^{3}	5			24
1	2	13	3^{2}	12	9		7	6^{1}	10^{3}	11	15		14									4	8	5^{4}			25
	2		3		9		7^{1}	6	10^{2}	11	13										12	4	8	5		1	26
1	2		3		9^{2}		8	6	11^{1}	10	13		12								14	4	7^{3}	5			27
1	2		3		13		7	6^{2}	14	10	11^{3}		9^{4}						15	4	12		8^{1}	5			28
1	3		2				8	6^{2}	10	11^{3}	12		13						14	4	7		9^{1}	5			29
1	2		3		12		7	6	11^{1}	14	10^{2}								13		9^{3}	4	8	5			30
1	2		3	5			10	6^{4}	11	9^{1}	15		12						7^{2}		14	4	8^{3}		13		31
1	2		3	5			10	13	11	9^{3}	6^{1}		12	14					7^{2}		15	4			8^{4}		32
1	2	14	3^{2}	5			10	12	11	9^{4}	13		15						7		8^{3}	4			6^{1}		33
1	2	3			13		8^{4}	12	11^{5}	9^{2}	14		16						6^{1}		10	4	15	5	7^{3}		34
1	2	4		14	12		8	16	11^{3}	9■	13								7^{4}		10^{1}	3	15	5^{2}	6^{5}		35
1	2	4		15			6^{1}	11	10^{3}		12		14	13						16	8^{5}	3	7	5^{2}	9^{4}		36

GREENOCK MORTON

Year Formed: 1874. *Ground & Address:* Cappielow Park, Sinclair St, Greenock PA15 2TU. *Telephone:* 01475 723571. *Fax:* 01475 781084. *E-mail:* admin@gmfc.net *Website:* gmfc.net
Ground Capacity: 11,612 (seated: 6,062). *Size of Pitch:* 100m × 65m.
Chairman: Crawford Rae.
Manager: Dougie Imrie. *Assistant Manager:* Andy Millen.
Club Nickname: 'The Ton'.
Previous Grounds: Grant Street 1874; Garvel Park 1875; Cappielow Park 1879; Ladyburn Park 1882; Cappielow Park 1883.
Record Attendance: 23,500 v Celtic, 29 April 1922.
Record Transfer Fee received: £500,000 from Leeds U for Derek Lilley (March 1997).
Record Transfer Fee paid: £250,000 to MyPa (Finland) for Janne Lindberg and Marko Rajamäki (November 1994).
Record Victory: 11-0 v Carfin Shamrock, Scottish Cup 4th rd, 13 November 1886.
Record Defeat: 1-10 v Port Glasgow Ath, Division II, 5 May, 1894 and v St Bernards, Division II, 14 October 1933.
Most Capped Player: Jimmy Cowan, 25, Scotland.
Most League Appearances: 534: Derek Collins, 1987-98, 2001-05.
Most League Goals in Season (Individual): 58: Allan McGraw, Division II, 1963-64.
Most Goals Overall (Individual): 136: Andy Ritchie, 1976-83.

GREENOCK MORTON – CINCH CHAMPIONSHIP 2021–22 LEAGUE RECORD

Match No.	*Date*	*Venue*	*Opponents*	*Result*		*H/T Score*	*Lg Pos.*	*Goalscorers*	*Attendance*
1	July 31	H	Dunfermline Ath	D	2-2	1-0	5	Oliver (pen) [23], McGrattan [81]	821
2	Aug 7	A	Hamilton A	W	1-0	1-0	4	Ugwu [40]	935
3	21	H	Queen of the South	L	2-3	1-1	5	Jacobs [31], Brynn (og) [83]	1429
4	28	A	Partick Thistle	L	0-3	0-1	6		3034
5	Sept 11	A	Kilmarnock	L	0-1	0-0	8		4189
6	18	H	Raith R	L	0-1	0-1	8		1420
7	25	A	Ayr U	D	0-0	0-0	8		1638
8	Oct 2	H	Arbroath	D	2-2	0-1	9	Oliver [47], Blues [55]	1126
9	16	A	Inverness CT	L	0-2	0-1	9		1900
10	23	A	Queen of the South	D	0-0	0-0	9		1093
11	26	H	Partick Thistle	D	0-0	0-0	9		1867
12	30	H	Hamilton A	D	1-1	0-1	9	Mimnaugh (og) [90]	1529
13	Nov 6	A	Dunfermline Ath	W	3-1	1-1	8	Oliver 2 (1 pen) [13, 87 (p)], Ugwu [60]	3531
14	13	H	Kilmarnock	L	0-2	0-2	8		2878
15	20	A	Raith R	L	1-2	1-1	9	Ledger [5]	1640
16	Dec 4	H	Ayr U	D	2-2	1-0	8	Ugwu 2 [26, 84]	1335
17	11	H	Inverness CT	L	1-6	1-3	10	Ugwu (pen) [45]	1192
18	18	A	Arbroath	L	1-2	0-0	10	Oliver [74]	1220
19	29	A	Kilmarnock	D	1-1	0-1	10	Lithgow [68]	500
20	Jan 8	H	Dunfermline Ath	W	5-0	3-0	8	Oliver [35], Blues [40], Reilly [45], Donaldson (og) [72], Muirhead [79]	429
21	15	A	Ayr U	W	2-0	1-0	8	Reilly 2 [27, 61]	500
22	28	H	Raith R	D	2-2	1-2	7	Ugwu [25], Muirhead [75]	1404
23	Feb 5	A	Inverness CT	W	1-0	1-0	7	Strapp [24]	1808
24	12	H	Queen of the South	W	2-1	0-0	6	Reilly [80], Blues [81]	1445
25	19	A	Hamilton A	L	0-1	0-0	8		1360
26	22	A	Partick Thistle	W	1-0	0-0	6	McEntee [80]	2345
27	26	H	Arbroath	D	0-0	0-0	6		1696
28	Mar 5	A	Queen of the South	L	0-3	0-2	7		1217
29	12	H	Partick Thistle	W	2-1	0-1	6	Reilly [76], Muirhead [86]	2294
30	18	A	Dunfermline Ath	D	1-1	1-0	6	Wilson [42]	4593
31	26	H	Ayr U	D	1-1	1-0	7	Blues [38]	1815
32	Apr 1	H	Kilmarnock	D	1-1	0-0	7	Ugwu [59]	2650
33	9	A	Raith R	W	1-0	0-0	6	Muirhead [65]	1660
34	16	H	Hamilton A	L	0-1	0-1	7		1808
35	23	H	Inverness CT	L	0-1	0-1	7		1717
36	29	A	Arbroath	L	0-3	0-1	7		3121

Final League Position: 7

Honours
League Champions: First Division 1977-78, 1983-84, 1986-87; Division II 1949-50, 1963-64, 1966-67; Second Division 1994-95, 2006-07; League One 2014–15; Third Division 2002-03.
Runners-up: Division 1 1916-17; First Division 2012-13; Second Division 2005-06;. Division II 1899-1900, 1928-29, 1936-37.
Scottish Cup Winners: 1922; *Runners-up:* 1948.
League Cup Runners-up: 1963-64.
League Challenge Cup Runners-up: 1992-93.

European: *UEFA Cup:* 2 matches (*Fairs Cup:* 1968-69).

Club colours: Shirt: Blue and white hoops. Shorts: White. Socks: Blue.

Goalscorers: *League (36):* Ugwu 7 (1 pen), Oliver 6 (2 pens), Reilly 5, Blues 4, Muirhead 4, Jacobs 1, Ledger 1, Lithgow 1, McEntee 1, McGrattan 1, Strapp 1, Wilson 1, own goals 3.
Scottish FA Cup (3): Muirhead 2, Reilly 1.
Premier Sports Scottish League Cup (3): Muirhead 2, McGregor 1.
SPFL Trust Trophy (4): Blues 1, Garrity 1, Lithgow 1, Muirhead 1.

Hamilton J 36	Hynes D 11 + 3	Ledger M 21 + 4	Lithgow A 32	Strapp L 27 + 2	Blues C 26 + 3	Jacobs K 14 + 4	McGregor L 6 + 1	Oliver G 24 + 11	Ugwu G 29 + 2	Muirhead R 16 + 15	Russell Mark 14 + 12	McGrattan L 2 + 13	Lyon R 18 + 12	Knowles J 3 + 7	King A 1 + 8	McLean B 20	Oksanen J 12 + 1	Allan T 7 + 1	Reilly G 27 + 2	McEntee O 24 + 1	Garrity M — + 2	Easdale A 1 + 4	Brandon J 14	Wilson I 11 + 2	*Match No.*
1	2^{3}	3	4	5	6	7	8^{1}	9	10	11^{2}	12	13	14												1
1	2	3	4	5	8■	7	9^{1}	6	10	11^{2}	12		13												2
1	2^{2}	3	4	5		6		9	10	11^{1}	8	13	7^{3}	12	14										3
1		2	3	5	7^{1}	6^{3}	8^{2}	9	11	13	10		12		14	4									4
1		2	3	5	7			6^{1}	12	11				13		4	8	9^{2}	10						5
1	5		3	9				13		10^{2}			6	14		4	7	8^{3}	11^{1}	2	12				6
1			4	14	13	6^{1}	9^{2}	12	11				7			2	8	5	10^{3}	3					7
1			3	4	8	6	9^{1}	5	7^{2}		13			12			10		11	2					8
1			3	4	5	6		9		13	12		14	10^{2}			7	8^{1}	11^{3}	2					9
1			3		7			13		10^{2}	4	14	9	12		8	6	5^{3}	11^{1}	2					10
1		12	3		5^{2}	6		11			8	14	9	13		4	7		10^{1}	2^{3}					11
1			3		6^{3}			11	12	14	5		7	13		4	8	9^{1}	10^{2}	2					12
1		12	4					9	10	8^{2}	5	13	6	11^{3}		3^{1}	7		14	2					13
1		2	3	4	7	8		9^{3}	10	6^{2}	5	14		11^{1}	13				12						14
1		2	3■	5		7^{3}		14	11			9^{1}	13		12		8	6^{2}	10	4					15
1	2^{2}	3		5	7			14	10	6^{1}	9^{3}				13		8	12	11	4					16
1	2		3	4	12		13	9	10	6^{2}	5		7^{1}				8		11^{3}			14			17
1	2^{2}	3	4			8		9	10	13	6		7^{1}				12		11	5					18
1	2	3	4	12	13	8^{1}		7	10	14	6^{2}		9			5^{3}			11						19
1	5	2	3	9	7^{1}	13		8^{3}	10	12			6			4			11^{2}		14				20
1	12	2	3	9	7			8	11	13			6			4			10^{1}				5^{2}		21
1		2^{2}	3	9	7			8^{4}	11	13	14	15	6^{1}			4^{3}			10	12			5		22
1			4	6	9	14		7^{1}	10	13			8^{2}			5			11^{3}	3			2	12	23
1		12	3	9	6			8^{1}	10	14	15	16	7^{5}			4^{4}			11^{2}	2			5^{3}	13	24
1		14	3	9^{5}	6^{4}			12	10	13	15		8^{2}			4^{1}			11^{3}	2		16	5	7	25
1			3	9^{1}	6^{2}			8^{3}	10	11	12	14	13			4				2			5	7	26
1		4	3	9^{2}	6			8^{1}	10	15	14		12						11^{4}	2		13	5^{3}	7	27
1		4^{1}	3	9^{3}	6	16		8^{5}	10	14	12		13		15				11^{2}	2			5	7^{4}	28
1		4^{2}	3	9		6^{1}			10	12	13	14	8^{3}						11	2			5	7	29
1		2	3	9	6^{2}	12		8^{3}	11^{1}	13			14						10	4			5	7	30
1	5	2	3	4	6			13	10	9^{2}	8		12						11^{1}					7	31
1			3	8	6			12	10	9^{1}					13	4			11^{2}	2			5	7	32
1	14		3	8^{2}	6			11^{1}	10	9^{4}	13	12	15			4				2			5^{3}	7	33
1		2^{2}			6			12	10	9	8^{1}	14			13	4			11^{3}	3			5	7	34
1	12	2^{3}		8	6			16	10	9^{2}		15	13			3			11^{5}	4		14	5^{4}	7^{1}	35
1	2	3				7	6^{1}	12			5	10	8		9					4		11			36

HAMILTON ACADEMICAL

Year Formed: 1874. *Ground:* Hope Stadium, New Douglas Park, Cadzow Avenue, Hamilton ML3 0FT. *Telephone:* 01698 368652. *Fax:* 01698 285422. *E-mail:* office@acciesfc.co.uk *Website:* hamiltonacciesfc.co.uk
Ground Capacity: 6,078 (all seated). *Size of Pitch:* 105m × 68m.
Chairman: Allan Maitland. *Vice-Chairman:* Les Gray.
Head Coach: John Rankin.
Club Nickname: 'The Accies'.
Previous Grounds: Bent Farm; South Avenue; South Haugh; Douglas Park; Cliftonhill Stadium; Firhill Stadium.
Record Attendance: 28,690 v Hearts, Scottish Cup 3rd rd, 3 March 1937 (at Douglas Park); 5,895 v Rangers, 28 February 2009 (at New Douglas Park).
Record Transfer Fee received: £1,200,000 (rising to £3,200,000) from Wigan Ath for James McCarthy (July 2009).
Record Transfer Fee paid: £180,000 to Sigma Olomouc for Tomas Cerny (July 2009).
Record Victory: 10-2 v Greenock Morton, Scottish Championship, 3 May 2014.
Record Defeat: 1-11 v Hibernian, Division I, 6 November 1965.
Most Capped Player: Colin Miller, 29 (61), Canada, 1988-94.
Most League Appearances: 452: Rikki Ferguson, 1974-88.
Most League Goals in Season (Individual): 35: David Wilson, Division I; 1936-37.
Most Goals Overall (Individual): 246: David Wilson, 1928-39.

HAMILTON ACADEMICAL – CINCH CHAMPIONSHIP 2021–22 LEAGUE RECORD

Match No.	Date	Venue	Opponents	Result		H/T Score	Lg Pos.	Goalscorers	Attendance
1	July 31	A	Raith R	D	4-4	0-2	3	MacDonald 2 68, 83, Ryan 78, Want 90	1569
2	Aug 7	H	Greenock Morton	L	0-1	0-1	5		935
3	21	H	Kilmarnock	L	0-2	0-0	8		2595
4	28	A	Queen of the South	W	2-1	0-0	5	Ryan 46, Smith, L 74	1232
5	Sept 11	A	Arbroath	L	0-4	0-1	9		1234
6	18	H	Ayr U	L	0-2	0-0	9		1365
7	25	A	Dunfermline Ath	D	0-0	0-0	9		3150
8	Oct 2	H	Inverness CT	W	2-1	2-0	8	Smith, L 5, Ryan 26	1088
9	15	H	Partick Thistle	L	1-6	0-1	8	Moyo 89	1775
10	23	A	Kilmarnock	L	1-2	1-1	8	Hamilton 8	3969
11	26	H	Queen of the South	W	1-0	0-0	7	Ryan 76	942
12	30	A	Greenock Morton	D	1-1	1-0	7	Smith, L 39	1529
13	Nov 6	H	Arbroath	D	1-1	1-0	7	Ryan (pen) 16	1107
14	13	H	Raith R	L	0-3	0-3	7		1303
15	20	A	Partick Thistle	L	0-1	0-0	8		2886
16	Dec 4	H	Dunfermline Ath	W	1-0	0-0	6	Moyo (pen) 61	1175
17	10	A	Ayr U	D	1-1	1-0	6	Smith, L 40	951
18	18	A	Inverness CT	W	2-1	0-0	6	Moyo 79, Winter 82	1862
19	26	H	Kilmarnock	L	2-3	1-2	6	Hughes 3, Mullin 84	420
20	Jan 2	A	Queen of the South	W	3-0	1-0	6	Moyo 20, Hamilton 70, Mullin 77	437
21	8	H	Partick Thistle	D	2-2	0-1	6	Ryan (pen) 55, Popescu 67	532
22	15	A	Dunfermline Ath	L	0-1	0-1	6		556
23	29	H	Ayr U	D	1-1	1-0	6	Kennedy 7	1230
24	Feb 5	A	Raith R	D	0-0	0-0	6		1196
25	9	A	Arbroath	D	2-2	2-1	6	O'Reilly 25, Ryan 45	1213
26	19	H	Greenock Morton	W	1-0	0-0	6	Spence 47	1360
27	25	H	Inverness CT	D	1-1	1-1	6	Mullin 13	1187
28	Mar 5	A	Kilmarnock	L	0-2	0-1	8		4083
29	12	H	Dunfermline Ath	D	2-2	1-1	8	Moyo 2 25, 77	1369
30	19	A	Partick Thistle	W	4-0	2-0	7	Ryan 2 19, 50, Moyo 45, Winter 63	2567
31	26	H	Queen of the South	W	1-0	0-0	6	Winter 65	1214
32	Apr 1	A	Ayr U	D	1-1	1-0	6	Winter 6	1618
33	9	H	Arbroath	L	0-1	0-0	7		911
34	16	A	Greenock Morton	W	1-0	1-0	6	Moyo 6	1808
35	23	H	Raith R	L	0-2	0-1	6		1478
36	29	A	Inverness CT	L	0-4	0-4	6		2131

Final League Position: 6

Honours
League Champions: Division II 1903-04; First Division 1985-86, 1987-88, 2007-08; Third Division 2000-01.
Runners-up: Division II 1952-53, 1964-65; Second Division 1996-97, 2003-04; Championship 2013-14.
Promoted via play-offs: 2013-14 (to Premiership).
Scottish Cup Runners-up: 1911, 1935. *League Cup:* Semi-finalists three times.
League Challenge Cup Winners: 1991-92, 1992-93; *Runners-up:* 2005-06, 2011-12.

Club colours: Shirt: Red and white hoops. Shorts: White. Socks: White.

Goalscorers: *League (38):* Ryan 9 (2 pens), Moyo 8 (1 pen), Smith L 4, Winter 4, Mullin 3, Hamilton 2, MacDonald 2, Hughes 1, Kennedy 1, O'Reilly 1, Popescu 1, Spence 1, Want 1.
Scottish FA Cup (0).
Premier Sports Scottish League Cup (5): Hughes 2 (2 pens), Smith C 2, Hamilton 1.
SPFL Trust Trophy (7): Ryan 2 (1 pen), McGowan 1, Moyo 1, Munro 1, Spence 1, Virtanen 1.

Fulton R 20	Stirling B 1 + 3	Hamilton J 26 + 1	Want S 6	MacDonald K 31 + 1	Mimnaugh R 24 + 3	Spence L 18 + 2	Redfern M 16 + 6	Smith L 22 + 6	Smith C 1	Moyo D 26 + 3	Ryan A 24 + 8	McMann S 3 + 1	Templeton D 1 + 2	Virtanen M 8 + 7	Stanger G 2	Mullin J 28 + 4	Easton B 19 + 3	Matheson L 8 + 1	Munro K 3 + 3	McGowan A — + 5	Popescu M 30 + 1	Hughes R 10 + 4	Hilton J 16	Martin S 5 + 8	Winter A 7 + 8	Shiels M 5 + 3	O'Reilly D 17	Brown E 3 + 7	Kennedy K 6 + 1	Lawson S 10 + 1	Nicolson S — + 1	*Match No.*
1	2	3	4	5	6	7	8^{1}	9	10^{3}	11^{2}	12	13	14																			1
1		8	4	9		7	13	6^{2}			10	5	11	2	3^{1}	12																2
1		3		5	13	7		10^{2}		14	11^{1}	9	12	8^{3}	2	6	4															3
1		4			10	7	8^{1}	12		9	11	5				6	3	2														4
1		3■		5	10^{2}	7	8^{3}	13			11					6	4	2	9^{1}	12	14											5
1				5	8^{1}	7	10^{2}	12			11			13		9	4	2	6		3											6
1			4^{2}	5	8	7^{1}	10	6^{3}			11			12		9	14	2		13	3											7
1			3^{2}	5	8■		10^{1}	7		13	11^{3}			6		9	14	2			4	12										8
1		13	3	5			10^{1}	7		12	11			8		9		2^{2}			4	6										9
1		2		5	6		12	10^{2}		11	7					9	4			13	3	8^{1}										10
		2		5	6		10	7		11^{1}	12					9	4				3	8	1									11
		2		5	6		10	7^{2}		11	13					9	4	12			3^{1}	8	1									12
	14	3^{3}		5^{2}	6		12	10^{1}		11	7					8	4	2	13			9	1									13
	14			5	6		7^{3}	10			11			13		9	4	2^{2}			3	8^{1}	1	12								14
	13		2^{2}	5	6		14	10^{1}		11	7			12		9	4				3		1	8^{3}								15
		2^{1}		5	6		10^{2}	7		11				12		9	4		13		3		1	8								16
		2^{3}		5	6		10^{1}	7		11	13			12		9	4				3	14	1	8^{2}								17
		2		5	7			6		10	11^{1}			13		8	4		9^{2}		3		1		12							18
		3		2			13	10^{2}		11	7			6		9					4	8	1		12	5^{1}						19
		2					10^{1}	7^{3}		11	12			6		9					3	8^{2}	1		13	5	4	14				20
		6			12		5^{1}	9			10			7			3				2		1		11	8	4					21
		2		12	7			9^{1}			10			8					14		3	6	1		11^{2}	5^{3}	4		13			22
		2		5	8^{2}			6^{3}		11	12					9					3	7^{1}	1	13			4	14	10			23
		2		5	7	12	13			10	11					6					3		1	9^{1}			4		8^{2}			24
		2		9	6	12				10	11^{2}					7	4				3		1	8^{1}	13		5					25
		2^{2}		5	6	8^{3}	9^{1}	13		11						7					3		1	14			4		10	12		26
1				5	7^{2}	8^{3}	9^{1}			11	14					6					3			12	15		4	13	10^{4}	2		27
1				5	7^{3}	8^{2}		14		11	9^{1}					6^{5}					3	16		12	15		4	13	10^{4}	2		28
1		2		8		7		13		11	14					5^{2}					3				12		4	10^{1}	9^{3}	6		29
1		2		8		6^{1}				11	9					13	4				3				10^{2}		5	12		7		30
1		2		8^{2}		6				11	9					13	4^{3}				3				10^{1}	12	5	14		7		31
1		2		8^{1}		6				11	10						4				3			12	9^{2}	13	5			7		32
1		2		5		7^{2}				11	10					8^{1}					3			12	9		4	13		6		33
1		2^{2}		8^{1}	14	6				11	9^{3}					13	4				3			12^{4}	10	15	5			7		34
1				5	6	8		7		11^{2}						2				12	3						4	10^{1}		9	13	35
1					6^{4}	8^{3}		7		11^{1}						2	12			15	3	13			14	5	4	10^{2}		9		36

HEART OF MIDLOTHIAN

Year Formed: 1874. *Ground & Address:* Tynecastle Stadium, McLeod Street, Edinburgh EH11 2NL. *Telephone:* 0333 043 1874. *Fax:* 0131 200 7222. *E-mail:* supporterservices@homplc.co.uk *Website:* heartsfc.co.uk
Ground Capacity: 20,099. *Size of Pitch:* 100m × 64m.
Chairwoman: Ann Budge. *Chief Executive:* Andrew McKinlay
Manager: Robbie Neilson. *Assistant Managers:* Gordon Forrest, Lee McCulloch.
Club Nicknames: 'Hearts'; 'Jam Tarts'; 'Jambos'.
Previous Grounds: The Meadows 1874; Powderhall 1878; Old Tynecastle 1881; Tynecastle Park 1886.
Record Attendance: 53,396 v Rangers, Scottish Cup 3rd rd, 13 February 1932 (57,857 v Barcelona, 28 July 2007 at Murrayfield).
Record Transfer Fee received: £9,000,000 from Sunderland for Craig Gordon (August 2008).
Record Transfer Fee paid: £850,000 to Genk for Mirsad Beslija (January 2006).
Record Victory: 15-0 v King's Park, Scottish Cup 2nd rd, 13 February 1937 (21-0 v Anchor, EFA Cup, 30 October 1880).
Record Defeat: 1-8 v Vale of Leven, Scottish Cup 3rd rd, 1883; 0-7 v Celtic, Scottish Cup 4th rd, 1 December 2013.
Most Capped Player: Steven Pressley, 32, Scotland.
Most League Appearances: 515: Gary Mackay, 1980-97.
Most League Goals in Season (Individual): 44: Barney Battles, 1930-31.
Most Goals Overall (Individual): 214: John Robertson, 1983-98.

HEART OF MIDLOTHIAN – CINCH PREMIERSHIP 2021–22 LEAGUE RECORD

Match No.	Date	Venue	Opponents	Result		H/T Score	Lg Pos.	Goalscorers	Attendance
1	July 31	H	Celtic	W	2-1	1-0	2	Mackay-Steven [8], Souttar [89]	5272
2	Aug 7	A	St Mirren	W	2-1	1-0	1	Halliday [16], Boyce [73]	1039
3	22	H	Aberdeen	D	1-1	0-0	3	Boyce (pen) [56]	17,449
4	28	A	Dundee U	W	2-0	1-0	2	Boyce [45], Gnanduillet [90]	9234
5	Sept 12	H	Hibernian	D	0-0	0-0	3		18,177
6	18	A	Ross Co	D	2-2	1-2	3	Boyce [9], Kingsley [66]	3802
7	25	H	Livingston	W	3-0	2-0	2	Smith, M [25], Boyce (pen) [33], Cochrane [64]	16,175
8	Oct 2	H	Motherwell	W	2-0	2-0	1	Boyce (pen) [5], Kingsley [22]	17,028
9	16	A	Rangers	D	1-1	0-1	2	Halkett [90]	49,650
10	23	H	Dundee	D	1-1	1-0	1	Souttar [37]	17,557
11	27	A	St Johnstone	D	1-1	1-1	3	Ginnelly [40]	6083
12	30	A	Aberdeen	L	1-2	1-0	3	Souttar (pen) [45]	9736
13	Nov 6	H	Dundee U	W	5-2	2-1	2	Woodburn 2 [22, 50], Cochrane [25], Kingsley [76], McEneff [86]	18,129
14	20	A	Motherwell	L	0-2	0-1	3		7908
15	27	H	St Mirren	W	2-0	0-0	2	Mackay-Steven [61], Kingsley [75]	17,311
16	Dec 2	A	Celtic	L	0-1	0-1	3		57,578
17	5	A	Livingston	W	1-0	0-0	3	Boyce [49]	5597
18	12	H	Rangers	L	0-2	0-2	3		18,593
19	18	A	Dundee	W	1-0	0-0	3	Walker [75]	5874
20	26	H	Ross Co	W	2-1	2-0	3	Smith, M [4], Woodburn [42]	0
21	Jan 18	H	St Johnstone	W	2-0	0-0	3	Ginnelly 2 [46, 75]	16,589
22	26	H	Celtic	L	1-2	0-2	3	Boyce [62]	17,967
23	29	H	Motherwell	W	2-0	1-0	3	Halliday [37], Simms [58]	17,699
24	Feb 1	A	Hibernian	D	0-0	0-0	3		20,419
25	6	A	Rangers	L	0-5	0-1	3		49,708
26	9	H	Dundee	L	1-2	1-0	3	Simms [21]	15,527
27	19	A	St Johnstone	L	1-2	1-1	3	Atkinson [6]	4409
28	26	A	St Mirren	W	2-0	0-0	3	Simms [64], Devlin [67]	5767
29	Mar 2	H	Aberdeen	W	2-0	1-0	3	Souttar [38], Kingsley [60]	16,703
30	5	A	Dundee U	D	2-2	1-0	3	Boyce [1], Halkett [81]	7172
31	19	H	Livingston	W	2-0	1-0	3	Baningime [3], McKay [58]	17,957
32	Apr 2	A	Ross Co	D	1-1	1-1	3	McKay [39]	5210
33	9	H	Hibernian	W	3-1	1-1	3	Halliday 2 [45, 58], Kingsley [47]	19,041
34	24	A	Dundee U	W	3-2	1-1	3	Boyce [44], Ginnelly [59], Simms [83]	6421
35	30	H	Ross Co	D	0-0	0-0	3		16,699
36	May 7	A	Celtic	L	1-4	1-2	3	Simms [3]	58,554
37	11	A	Motherwell	L	1-2	1-1	3	Ginnelly [9]	5769
38	14	H	Rangers	L	1-3	1-2	3	Haring [24]	16,969

Final League Position: 3

Honours
League Champions: Division I 1894-95, 1896-97, 1957-58, 1959-60; First Division 1979-80; Championship 2014-15, 2020-21
Runners-up: Division I 1893-94, 1898-99, 1903-04, 1905-06, 1914-15, 1937-38, 1953-54, 1956-57, 1958-59, 1964-65; Premier Division 1985-86, 1987-88, 1991-92, 2005-06; First Division 1977-78, 1982-83.
Scottish Cup Winners: 1891, 1896, 1901, 1906, 1956, 1998, 2006, 2012; *Runners-up:* 1903, 1907, 1968, 1976, 1986, 1996, 2019, 2020, 2022.
League Cup Winners: 1954-55, 1958-59, 1959-60, 1962-63; *Runners-up:* 1961-62, 1996-97, 2012-13.

European: *European Cup:* 8 matches (1958-59, 1960-61, 2006-07). *Cup Winners' Cup:* 10 matches (1976-77, 1996-97, 1998-99). *UEFA Cup:* 46 matches (*Fairs Cup:* 1961-62, 1963-64, 1965-66. *UEFA Cup:* 1984-85, 1986-87, 1988-89, 1990-91, 1992-93, 1993-94, 2000-01, 2003-04, 2004-05, 2006-07). *Europa League:* 12 matches (2010-11, 2011-12, 2012-13, 2016-17).

Club colours: Shirt: Maroon with white trim. Shorts: Maroon. Socks: Maroon.

Goalscorers: *League (54):* Boyce 10 (3 pens), Kingsley 6, Ginnelly 5, Simms 5, Halliday 4, Souttar 4 (1 pen), Woodburn 3, Cochrane 2, Halkett 2, Mackay-Steven 2, McKay 2, Smith M 2, Atkinson 1, Baningime 1, Devlin 1, Gnanduillet 1, Haring 1, McEneff 1, Walker 1.
Scottish FA Cup (11): Boyce 2 (1 pen), Haring 2, Simms 2, Baningime 1, Cochrane 1, Halliday 1, Kingsley 1, McEneff 1.
Premier Sports Scottish League Cup (10): Boyce 4 (1 pen), Mackay-Steven 2, Halliday 1, McEneff 1, Pollock 1, Walker 1.
SPFL Trust Trophy (3): Denholm 1, Henderson 1 (1 pen), Kirk 1.

Gordon C 36	Souttar J 26 + 1	Halkett C 27 + 1	Kingsley S 31 + 2	Smith M 19 + 1	Baningime B 23 + 1	Halliday A 15 + 12	Cochrane A 25 + 6	Ginnelly J 16 + 15	Boyce L 29 + 2	Mackay-Steven G 19 + 13	Haring P 20 + 11	Gnanduillet A 3 + 11	McEneff A 7 + 7	Henderson E — + 2	Walker J — + 4	Woodburn B 16 + 12	Moore T 16 + 6	McKay B 30 + 3	Devlin C 23 + 2	Atkinson N 13 + 2	Simms E 11 + 6	Sibbick T 11 + 3	Stewart R 2	Kirk M — + 1	Thomas M — + 2	*Match No.*
1	2	3	4	5	6	7	8	9^{1}	10	11^{2}	12	13														1
1	2	3		5	7	8	4	9^{2}	11^{1}	10^{3}	6	12	13	14												2
1	2	3		5	6	8^{2}	4	9^{1}	10	11^{3}	7		13	14	12											3
1	2	3		5	6	8^{3}	4	12	11	10^{2}	7	13				9^{1}	14									4
1	2	3	4	5^{2}	6		8	12	10	11^{3}	7					9^{1}	13	14								5
1	4	3	8		7				10	9^{2}		11			13	6^{1}	2	5	12							6
1		3^{2}	4^{1}	5	6	13	8		10^{3}	14	15	12				11	2	9^{4}	7							7
1		3^{1}	4	5	6	12	8		10	13	14					11^{3}	2	9^{2}	7							8
1	2	3	4	5	6		8^{2}	12	11	14		13				10^{3}		9^{1}	7							9
1	2	3	4	5	7		8	14	10^{1}	12		13				11^{2}		9^{3}	6							10
1	2	3	4	5	7	8		9^{2}		13		10				12		11^{1}	6							11
1	2	3	4	5	7	14■	8^{3}	9^{1}		11^{2}		10				13		12	6							12
1	2	3	4		7		8	10^{2}		12		13	14			11^{1}	5	9^{3}	6							13
1	3		4	5	6^{1}		8	11^{3}	12			13	14			10^{2}	2■	9	7							14
1	2	3	4	5	6^{3}	8		12	10^{2}	11^{1}	14	13						9	7							15
1	3	4	5	2				11	12	13	7		9^{1}			8^{2}		10	6							16
1	2	3	4	5^{3}			8		10^{2}		13	14	6			11^{1}	12	9	7							17
1	3	4	5					8■	11	10^{1}	6	13				12	2	9	7^{2}							18
1	2	3	4^{1}			8	12			9^{2}	6		14		13	10^{3}	5	11	7							19
1	2	3^{3}	12	6		8	4			14	7		9^{2}		13	10^{1}	5	11								20
1	2	3^{2}	4	5		14	8	10		11^{1}	7		12				13	9^{3}	6							21
1	2	3^{2}	4	5^{4}	15	16	8^{1}	9^{5}	10	14	7							11	6^{3}	12	13					22
1	3^{5}		4		7	8^{4}	16		9^{3}	11^{1}	14					13	2	15	6^{2}	5	10	12				23
1			4		7	8^{2}	13	14	11^{1}		15					12	2	9^{3}	6^{4}	5	10	3				24
1			4		6^{4}	16	8	13	11^{3}		14		9^{1}			15	2	10	7^{5}	5^{2}	12	3				25
1	2		4		7^{3}	8^{1}		12	10	14	6					13	5	9^{2}			11	3				26
	3		4			12	8^{1}	9^{3}		13	7					14		11	6^{2}	5	10	2	1			27
1	2	3	4^{1}		6	16	14	13	10	8^{2}	15					9^{5}		11	7^{4}	5^{3}	12					28
1	3	4	5		7	14		12	9^{1}	10^{2}	13							8	6^{3}	2	11					29
1	3^{4}	4	5		7	14	12^{5}	15	9	10^{3}	13							8	6^{2}	2^{1}	11	16				30
1		3	4		7^{3}	5^{2}	12	13	9		6		8^{5}			16	15	10^{1}		2^{4}	11	14				31
1		3	4			7	8	12	9^{2}		6		5^{1}			13		11			10^{3}	2		14		32
1		3	4			7^{4}	8	14	9	15	6		12				13	10^{3}		5^{1}	11^{2}	2				33
1							4	9^{2}	10	8	7		6^{1}			12	2	11		5	13	3				34
1						13	4	9	10	8^{2}	6					7^{1}	2	11		5	12	3				35
1			4				5	8^{3}	9	12	6					13	3	10^{1}		2	11^{2}	7			14	36
			13	15		7^{3}	4	10	11^{2}	9	6					8^{4}	2		14	5^{5}	12	3^{1}	1		16	37
1	14	16	3	5^{1}		15	4	12	11^{4}	9	6^{5}							8	7^{3}	13	10^{2}	2				38

HIBERNIAN

Year Formed: 1875. *Ground & Address:* Easter Road Stadium, 12 Albion Place, Edinburgh EH7 5QG. *Telephone:* 0131 661 2159. *Fax:* 0131 659 6488. *E-mail:* club@hibernianfc.co.uk *Website:* hibernianfc.co.uk
Ground Capacity: 20,421 (all seated). *Size of Pitch:* 105m × 68m.
Chairman: Ronald Gordon. *CEO:* Ben Kensell.
Manager: Lee Johnson. *Assistant Managers:* Jamie McAllister and Adam Owen.
Club Nickname: 'Hibs'; 'Hibees'.
Previous Grounds: Meadows 1875-78; Powderhall 1878-79; Mayfield 1879-80; First Easter Road 1880-92; Second Easter Road 1892.
Record Attendance: 65,860 v Hearts, Division I, 2 January 1950.
Record Transfer Fee received: £4,400,000 from Celtic for Scott Brown (July 2007).
Record Transfer Fee paid: £700,000 to LDU Quito for Ulises de la Cruz (2001).
Record Victory: 15-1 v Pebbles Rovers, Scottish Cup 2nd rd, 11 February 1961.
Record Defeat: 0-10 v Rangers, Division I, 24 December 1898.
Most Capped Player: Lawrie Reilly, 38, Scotland.
Most League Appearances: 446: Arthur Duncan, 1969-84.
Most League Goals in Season (Individual): 42: Joe Baker, 1959-60.
Most Goals Overall (Individual): 233: Lawrie Reilly, 1945-58.

HIBERNIAN – CINCH PREMIERSHIP 2021–22 LEAGUE RECORD

Match No.	Date	Venue	Opponents	Result	H/T Score	Lg Pos.	Goalscorers	Attendance
1	Aug 1	A	Motherwell	W 3-2	1-2	3	Magennis [17], Doidge [56], Boyle (pen) [70]	5230
2	8	H	Ross Co	W 3-0	3-0	1	Boyle [22], Magennis [26], Doidge [33]	5600
3	22	A	Dundee	D 2-2	1-1	1	Boyle (pen) [39], Porteous [59]	5295
4	28	H	Livingston	W 2-0	0-0	1	Nisbet [51], Boyle [89]	13,431
5	Sept 12	A	Hearts	D 0-0	0-0	2		18,177
6	18	H	St Mirren	D 2-2	0-1	1	McGinn [56], Boyle (pen) [61]	13,501
7	26	H	St Johnstone	W 1-0	0-0	2	Boyle (pen) [61]	13,263
8	Oct 3	A	Rangers	L 1-2	1-0	3	Nisbet [8]	49,125
9	16	H	Dundee U	L 0-3	0-1	5		15,114
10	23	A	Aberdeen	L 0-1	0-1	5		9431
11	27	H	Celtic	L 1-3	1-3	5	Boyle [37]	17,580
12	Nov 24	A	Ross Co	L 0-1	0-0	7		3316
13	27	A	St Johnstone	W 2-1	0-1	6	Nisbet [83], Murphy [86]	3362
14	Dec 1	H	Rangers	L 0-1	0-0	6		17,209
15	4	H	Motherwell	D 1-1	1-0	7	Nisbet [33]	15,266
16	8	A	Livingston	L 0-1	0-1	7		2363
17	11	A	St Mirren	D 1-1	0-0	7	Campbell [52]	4698
18	14	H	Dundee	W 1-0	1-0	7	McMullan (og) [34]	13,516
19	22	H	Aberdeen	W 1-0	0-0	5	Porteous [64]	14,314
20	26	A	Dundee U	W 3-1	1-0	5	Nisbet [38], Cadden [78], Murphy [90]	500
21	Jan 17	A	Celtic	L 0-2	0-2	5		58,296
22	26	A	Motherwell	D 0-0	0-0	5		5202
23	29	H	Livingston	L 2-3	2-1	5	Mitchell [6], Cadden [32]	15,480
24	Feb 1	H	Hearts	D 0-0	0-0	5		20,419
25	5	H	St Mirren	L 0-1	0-0	5		13,227
26	9	A	Rangers	L 0-2	0-1	7		49,700
27	19	H	Ross Co	W 2-0	0-0	4	Doyle-Hayes 2 [50, 78]	14,149
28	27	H	Celtic	D 0-0	0-0	4		17,374
29	Mar 2	A	Dundee	D 0-0	0-0	5		5237
30	5	H	St Johnstone	D 0-0	0-0	4		19,585
31	19	A	Aberdeen	L 1-3	1-1	5	Ramsay (og) [20]	15,321
32	Apr 2	H	Dundee U	D 1-1	1-1	6	Clarke [45]	16,707
33	9	A	Hearts	L 1-3	1-1	7	Wright [5]	19,041
34	23	A	St Mirren	W 1-0	0-0	7	Henderson [74]	4992
35	30	A	Livingston	L 0-1	0-0	8		2840
36	May 7	H	Aberdeen	D 1-1	0-0	8	McGinn [83]	14,509
37	10	A	Dundee	L 1-3	1-1	9	Scott [29]	5452
38	15	H	St Johnstone	W 4-0	1-0	8	McGinn [44], Scott 3 [48, 61, 88]	14,233

Final League Position: 8

Honours

League Champions: Division I 1902-03, 1947-48, 1950-51, 1951-52; First Division 1980-81, 1998-99; Championship 2016-17; Division II 1893-94, 1894-95, 1932-33.
Runners-up: Division I 1896-97, 1946-47, 1949-50, 1952-53, 1973-74, 1974-75; Championship 2014-15.
Scottish Cup Winners: 1887, 1902, 2016; *Runners-up:* 1896, 1914, 1923, 1924, 1947, 1958, 1972, 1979, 2001, 2012, 2013, 2021.
League Cup Winners: 1972-73, 1991-92, 2006-07; *Runners-up:* 1950-51, 1968-69, 1974-75, 1985-86, 1993-94, 2003-04, 2015-16, 2021-22. *Drybrough Cup Winners:* 1972-73, 1973-74.

European: *European Cup:* 6 matches (1955-56 semi-finals). *Cup Winners' Cup:* 6 matches (1972-73). *UEFA Cup:* 64 matches (*Fairs Cup:* 1960-61 semi-finals, 1961-62, 1962-63, 1965-66, 1967-68, 1968-69, 1970-71. *UEFA Cup:* 1973-74, 1974-75, 1975-76, 1976-77, 1978-79, 1989-90, 1992-93, 2001-02, 2005-06). *Europa League:* 10 matches (2010-11, 2013-14, 2018-19). *Europa Conference League:* 4 matches (2021-22).

Club colours: Shirt: Green with white sleeves. Shorts: White. Socks: Green.

Goalscorers: *League (38):* Boyle 7 (4 pens), Nisbet 5, Scott 4, McGinn 3, Cadden 2, Doidge 2, Doyle-Hayes 2, Magennis 2, Murphy 2, Porteous 2, Campbell 1, Clarke 1, Henderson 1, Mitchell 1, Wright 1, own goals 2.
Scottish FA Cup (7): Melkersen 2, Nisbet 2, Cadden 1, Mitchell 1, Mueller 1.
Premier Sports Scottish League Cup (9): Boyle 4 (2 pens), Allan 1, Hanlon 1, Magennis 1, Newell 1, Nisbet 1.
SPFL Trust Trophy (1): Aiken 1.
UEFA Europa Conference League (7): Boyle 3 (1 pen), Mackay 1, Magennis 1, Murphy 1, Nisbet 1.

Macey M 32	McGinn P 25	Porteous R 29	Hanlon P 23+1	Stevenson L 19+4	Newell J 27	Gogic A 4+5	Boyle M 20	Magennis K 7	Murphy J 8+10	Nisbet K 26 / Blaney J —+1	Doidge C 6+11	Doyle-Hayes J 31+3	Campbell J 20+6	Doig J 31+3	McGregor D 6+5	Mackay D —+2	Allan S 4+13	Scott J 7+9	Wright D 7+10	Gullan J 2+4	Cadden C 28	Wood-Gordon N 1	Bushiri R 12+2	Bradley S —+1	Mueller C 5+6	Mitchell D 3+3	Henderson E 10+6	Dabrowski M 6	Jasper S 5+8	Melkersen E 7+3	Hauge R —+2	O'Connor J —+1	Clarke H 7	Aiken M —+1	Hamilton R —+1	Macintyre O —+1	Delferriere A —+1	*Match No.*
1	2	3	4	5	6	7^1	8	9^2	10^3	11	12	13	14																									1
1	2	3	4^3		7		8^1	9	10^2		11	6		5	12	13	14																					2
1	2^1	3		12		7	8	9	10^3			6		5	4			11^2	13	14																		3
1	2	3					8	7	10^3	11^1		6		5	4	14	12	9^2	13																			4
1	2	3	4		7	12	10	6		11				8				9^1	13		5^2																	5
1	2	3	4		9	13	10	6		11		7^2		8			12				5^1																	6
1	2	3	4	13	6		10	7^1		11		12		5^3			9^2			14	8																	7
1	2	3■	4		8	13	10		14	11		6^2		9	12		7^1				5^3																	8
1			4		7		8		10	11		6		5			9^1	12			2	3																9
1	2		4	8	6		10		12	9		7^2			3■		13		14	11^1	5^3																	10
1	2	3	4		9	8^1	6		10^2	11^3		7	12	5					13	14																		11
1	2		4		8		11■			10^3	12■	6	7^1	9^2	3		13			14	5																	12
1	2^2	3	4		7				12	10		6^3	9	8			13	14		11^1	5																	13
1	2	3	4		7		10		12	11		6	9^1	8			13				5^2																	14
1	2	3	4		8^3		10		12	11	13	7^1	9	5			14				6^2																	15
1	2■	3^2	4■		8		6		9^1	11	13	7	10^3	5	14		12																					16
1		3		5	7	6	8		10^2	11^1	13		9		4				12		2																	17
1	2	3	4	8	7	14	10		13	11^3	12	6^2	9								5^1																	18
1	2	3	4			12	10		13	11^3	14	6^2	7	8			9^1				5																	19
1		2	3	4			10		12	11^3	14	6	7	8^2	13				9^1		5																	20
1			3	14	6^2		10		12	11^5		7	8^3	4^1			16	13	9^4		5		2	15														21
1	2			4^2	7^4					10	15	6	9^3	8					12		5		3		11^1	13	14											22
1	2^4	3		4^5					13	10	11^3	7	6^1	16				15			5		12		14	8^2	9											23
		3		4	7^2					10	11^1	6	14	8^3					13		5		2		9^4	12	15	1										24
		3		4^1						10	11^2	6^4	7^5	15			16	14			5		2		9	8^3	12	1	13									25
1	2^3	3		7^2						11	15	8	14	5							6		4		13	9^4	10^1		12									26
1		3		4						11^1		6	7^3	8	15			13	14		5		2		12		9^4		10^2									27
1		3		8^1						11^3	12	6	7	4			14		9^2		5		2		13				10									28
		3		4							11^2	6	7	8					10^3		5		2■				9^1	1	12	13	14							29
		3		8							11^3	6	7	4			13		5^2		2						9^1	1	10	12	14							30
		4■	14	8^3	7^4								6	5					9^2		2		3		12		15	1	11	10^1		13						31
			3		7^3							6		4				14	13		5		2^1		10		12	1	9^2	11			8					32
1			3		7							6^4	12	4^2				13	9^1		5		2		10		15		14	11^3			8					33
1	2		3	4	7							6	15	12				11^3			5^1				13		9^2		14	10^4			8					34
1	2		3	4^1	7							6		8				11^2								13	9		12	10			5					35
1	2	3	4^4	15	7							6	10^1	8				13					14				9^3		12	11^2			5					36
1	2	4^3		6	7							14	10^2	5				11					3				9^1		12	13			8					37
1	2^5	4^3		7	6					16				8	3			11									9^1			10^4			5^2	12	13	14	15	38

INVERNESS CALEDONIAN THISTLE

Year Formed: 1994. *Ground & Address:* Caledonian Stadium, Stadium Road, Inverness IV1 1FF. *Telephone:* 01463 222880. *Fax:* 01463 227479. *E-mail:* info@ictfc.co.uk *Website:* ictfc.com
Ground Capacity: 7,780 (all seated). *Size of Pitch:* 105m × 68m.
Chairman: Ross Morrison. *Chief Executive:* Scot Gardiner.
Manager: Billy Dodds. *Assistant Manager:* Scott Kellacher.
Club Nicknames: 'Caley Thistle'; 'Caley Jags'; 'ICT'.
Record Attendance: 7,753 v Rangers, SPL, 20 January 2008.
Record Transfer Fee received: £400,000 from Dinamo Bucharest for Marius Niculae (July 2008).
Record Transfer Fee paid: £65,000 to Ross Co for John Rankin (July 2006).
Record Victory: 8-1 v Annan Ath, Scottish Cup 3rd rd, 24 January 1998; 7-0 v Ayr U, First Division, 24 April 2010; 7-0 v Arbroath, League Cup Northern Section Group C, 30 July 2016.
Record Defeats: 0-6 v Airdrieonians, First Division, 21 Sep 2000; 0-6 v Celtic, League Cup 3rd rd, 22 Sep 2010; 0-6 v Celtic, Scottish Premiership, 27 April 2014; 0-6 v Celtic, Scottish Cup 5th rd, 11 February 2017.
Most Capped Player: Richard Hastings, 38 (59), Canada.
Most League Appearances: 490: Ross Tokely, 1995-2012.
Most League Goals in Season: 27: Iain Stewart, 1996-97; Denis Wyness, 2002-03.
Most Goals Overall (Individual): 118: Denis Wyness, 2000-03, 2005-08.

INVERNESS CALEDONIAN TH – CINCH CHAMPIONSHIP 2021–22 LEAGUE RECORD

Match No.	Date	Venue	Opponents	Result		H/T Score	Lg Pos.	Goalscorers	Attendance
1	July 31	A	Arbroath	W	1-0	0-0	2	Sutherland [66]	1008
2	Aug 7	H	Raith R	W	1-0	0-0	3	MacGregor [80]	1675
3	21	H	Ayr U	W	1-0	0-0	2	Walsh [54]	2032
4	28	A	Kilmarnock	W	1-0	1-0	1	Gardyne [5]	5004
5	Sept 11	H	Partick Thistle	W	3-1	0-1	1	Broadfoot [51], Sutherland [68], Doran [71]	2148
6	18	A	Dunfermline Ath	D	0-0	0-0	1		3158
7	25	H	Queen of the South	W	2-1	1-0	1	Welsh [12], Gardyne [81]	1884
8	Oct 2	A	Hamilton A	L	1-2	0-2	1	Gardyne [90]	1088
9	16	H	Greenock Morton	W	2-0	1-0	1	McKay [20], Gardyne [49]	1900
10	23	A	Raith R	D	1-1	0-0	1	Welsh [79]	1900
11	26	H	Arbroath	L	0-1	0-0	2		1909
12	30	A	Partick Thistle	D	0-0	0-0	2		2527
13	Nov 6	A	Ayr U	D	2-2	2-1	2	Welsh [13], Gardyne [26]	1289
14	13	H	Dunfermline Ath	L	1-2	1-0	3	McKay [22]	2111
15	19	A	Queen of the South	W	2-1	1-0	2	McKay 2 (1 pen) [19 (p), 50]	942
16	Dec 3	H	Kilmarnock	W	1-0	0-0	1	Welsh [69]	2296
17	11	A	Greenock Morton	W	6-1	3-1	1	Hamilton (og) [15], Sutherland 2 [33, 60], McKay [43], McAlear [51], Jamieson [78]	1192
18	18	H	Hamilton A	L	1-2	0-0	2	Harper [65]	1862
19	Jan 2	A	Arbroath	D	0-0	0-0	2		494
20	8	H	Raith R	D	1-1	0-1	2	McAlear [86]	478
21	15	H	Queen of the South	D	2-2	0-1	2	McKay [62], Walsh [73]	479
22	22	A	Dunfermline Ath	D	1-1	1-0	2	Sutherland [39]	3138
23	29	A	Kilmarnock	L	0-1	0-1	3		4790
24	Feb 5	H	Greenock Morton	L	0-1	0-1	3		1808
25	9	H	Partick Thistle	D	3-3	2-2	3	McKay [21], Sutherland [45], Broadfoot [90]	1781
26	19	H	Ayr U	L	1-2	0-1	3	Nicolson, L [86]	1850
27	25	A	Hamilton A	D	1-1	1-1	3	Pearson [30]	1187
28	Mar 4	A	Partick Thistle	L	0-1	0-0	4		2099
29	12	H	Arbroath	W	3-0	2-0	4	Sutherland [5], McAlear [11], McKay [68]	2149
30	19	A	Raith R	W	3-2	1-2	3	Sutherland [27], Chalmers 2 [89, 90]	1591
31	26	H	Dunfermline Ath	W	2-0	0-0	3	McAlear [58], Samuels [77]	2171
32	Apr 9	A	Ayr U	D	2-2	2-0	3	Sutherland [6], Chalmers [13]	1756
33	15	H	Kilmarnock	W	2-1	0-0	3	McKay [76], Chalmers [82]	3829
34	19	A	Queen of the South	L	1-2	1-2	3	Chalmers [17]	631
35	23	A	Greenock Morton	W	1-0	1-0	3	MacGregor [29]	1717
36	29	H	Hamilton A	W	4-0	4-0	3	Walsh 2 [4, 22], Sutherland [15], Hardy [28]	2131

Final League Position: 3

Honours
League Champions: First Division 2003-04, 2009-10; Third Division 1996-97.
Runners-up: Championship 2019-20; Second Division 1998-99.
Scottish Cup Winners: 2015; Semi-finals 2003, 2004, 2019.
League Cup Runners-up: 2013-14.
League Challenge Cup Winners: 2003-04, 2017-18; *Runners-up:* 1999-2000, 2009-10.

European: *Europa League:* 4 matches (2015-16).

Club colours: Shirt: Blue and red vertical panels. Shorts: Blue. Socks: Blue.

Goalscorers: *League (53):* Sutherland 10, McKay, Billy 9 (1 pen), Chalmers 5, Gardyne 5, McAlear 4, Walsh 4, Welsh 4, Broadfoot 2, MacGregor 2, Doran 1, Hardy 1, Harper 1, Jamieson 1, Nicolson L 1, Pearson 1, Samuels 1, own goal 1.
Scottish FA Cup (2): Devine 1, McKay 1.
Premier Sports Scottish League Cup (5): Duku 2 (1 pen), Doran 1, MacGregor 1, Sutherland 1.
SPFL Trust Trophy (8): McKay 5, Jamieson 2, Harper 1.
Scottish League Play-offs (5): McAlear 2, Samuels 2, Sutherland 1.

Ridgers M 29	Carson D 26 + 3	Broadfoot K 34	Devine D 27 + 1	Deas R 36	MacGregor R 15 + 6	McAlear R 22 + 6	Allardice S 20	Walsh T 20 + 6	Sutherland S 27 + 3	Duku I 10 + 10	Harper C 6 + 18	McKay B 25 + 7	Hyde L 2 + 4	Gardyne M 10 + 1	Doran A 19 + 7	Welsh S 22 + 6	Jamieson L — + 8	Duffy W 16 + 2	McDonald A — + 2	Chalmers L 7 + 5	Pearson S 6 + 2	Hardy J 4 + 8	Samuels A 6 + 7	Nicolson L — + 3	Mackay C 7 + 1	*Match No.*
1	2	3	4	5	6^{1}	7	8	9^{2}	10	11^{3}	12	13	14													1
1	2	7	5	3	12	6^{3}	4	8^{1}	10	9^{2}			14	11	13											2
1	2	3	4	5	7		8	6^{2}	10^{1}	11^{3}		12		9	14	13										3
1	2	3	4	5	8		7	6^{2}	10^{1}	11^{3}		14		9	13	12										4
1	2	3	4	5	8^{2}	14	7	6^{3}	10	11^{1}	12				9	13										5
1	2	3	4	5	7		8	6	10^{3}	11^{2}	13	12			9^{1}	14										6
1	2	3	4	5	10^{3}	12	8^{2}	6		11^{1}		13		9		7	14									7
1		3		4	10		8	6^{3}	12	11^{1}	5	13		9		7		2^{2}	14							8
1		3	4	5	8	6^{1}	2		10^{3}	12		11^{2}		9	13	7	14									9
1		3	4	5	6		8^{1}		10^{2}	13		11^{3}		9	12	7	14	2								10
1		3	4	5	7^{1}	14	2	6		10^{3}		11		12	9^{2}	8	13									11
1		3	4	5	13		7	6^{1}				11		9	10^{2}	8	12	2								12
1		3	4	5	13		8	6^{2}		12		11		9	10	7^{1}		2								13
1	2^{1}	3	4	5	13	7^{2}	8	6^{3}				11		9	10		12		14							14
1	2	3	4	5	8	6	7		9	13	12	11^{1}			10^{2}											15
1	2	3	4	5	6^{2}	14	7	12	10		13	11^{1}			9^{3}	8										16
1	2	3	4	5		8	7	6	10^{2}	13	12	11^{1}			9^{3}		14									17
1	2	3	4	5^{2}		8	7^{1}	6	10	14	12	11			9^{3}		13									18
1	8	3	4	5			7	6^{1}	11	13	12	10^{3}	14		9^{2}			2								19
1	8^{3}	3	4	5		13	7^{2}	6	10	12	9	11				14		2^{1}								20
1	2	3	4	5	9^{1}	8		6	10	12		11				7										21
1	2	3	4^{3}	5		8		6	10	11^{1}	9^{2}					7		12		13	14					22
1	15	3		4		8		9^{1}	11^{5}	16	5^{2}					7		2^{4}		10	6^{3}	12	13	14		23
1	12	3		4^{2}		7			9^{3}		14	10				6		2		5^{1}	8^{4}	13	11	15		24
1	2	4		3^{2}		8			6		13	11				7		5		12	9^{3}	14	10^{1}			25
	7■	4		3		8			10^{4}		5^{1}	11	15		16			2^{3}		9^{5}	6^{2}	13	12	14	1	26
		3	4^{1}	5		9			13		12	10	2		8^{2}	7					6^{3}	14	11		1	27
	2	3	4	5		7			13			11			9^{2}	6				14	8^{1}	12	10^{3}		1	28
	2	3^{2}	4	5		7		14	6		13	11^{4}			10^{1}	8		12			15	9^{3}			1	29
	2	3	4^{4}	5		7		15	9^{2}		13	10			6^{1}	8				14		11^{3}	12		1	30
	2	3		4		7		14	8		12	11^{3}			9^{2}	6		5		10^{1}			13		1	31
	2^{3}	3	16	5	13	7^{4}			8		12	11^{2}			9^{5}	6		4		10^{1}		15	14		1	32
1	13	3	4	5		7^{2}			6		14	10^{1}			12	8		2		9^{3}		15	11^{4}			33
1	2		4	5^{1}	16	7		15	8^{5}		13	12			9^{2}	6^{3}		3		10		11^{4}	14			34
1	2	4		5	9	7		12			13	11			8^{1}	6		3					10^{2}			35
1^{5}	2			4^{2}	7	15		9	6^{4}		5	10^{1}	8			12		3^{3}		16		11	14		13	36

KELTY HEARTS

Year Formed: 1975. *Ground & Address:* New Central Park, Bath Street, Kelty KY4 0LZ.
Email: enquiries@keltyhearts.co.uk *Website:* keltyhearts.co.uk
Ground Capacity: 2,181 (353 seated). *Size of Pitch:* 100m × 60m.
Chairman: Derek Hodgson.
Managing Director: Dean McKenzie.
Manager: John Potter.
Club Nicknames: 'Maroon Machine', 'Hearts'.
Record Attendance: 2,300 v Rangers, Friendly, 7 October 2012.
Record Victory: 6-1 v Albion R, League Two, 11 December 2021.
Record Defeat: 5-1 v Annan Ath, League Two, 26 December 2021.
Most Capped Player: Kieran Mgwenya, 1, Malawi.
Most League Appearances: 36: Joe Cardle, 2021-22.
Most League Goals in Season (Individual): 17: Nathan Austin, 2021-22.
Most Goals Overall (Individual): 21: Nathan Austin, 2021-22.

KELTY HEARTS – CINCH LEAGUE TWO 2021–22 LEAGUE RECORD

Match No.	Date	Venue	Opponents	Result		H/T Score	Lg Pos.	Goalscorers	Attendance
1	July 31	H	Cowdenbeath	W	2-0	1-0	1	Cardle [38], Philp [69]	1202
2	Aug 7	A	Stirling Alb	W	3-1	2-0	1	Forster [39], Cardle [40], Higginbotham [56]	601
3	14	A	Forfar Ath	D	2-2	1-2	1	Austin 2 [22, 64]	623
4	21	H	Edinburgh C	W	1-0	0-0	1	Barjonas [54]	677
5	28	A	Stenhousemuir	W	4-1	2-1	1	Agyeman 2 [13, 71], Cardle [33], Barjonas [66]	436
6	Sept 11	H	Elgin C	D	1-1	0-1	1	Higginbotham [90]	608
7	18	A	Albion R	W	3-0	2-0	1	Austin 3 [11, 20, 63]	427
8	25	H	Stranraer	W	1-0	1-0	1	Austin [8]	528
9	Oct 2	H	Annan Ath	W	2-1	1-1	1	Barjonas [37], Higginbotham [74]	674
10	15	A	Edinburgh C	W	3-2	2-1	1	Austin 2 [22, 48], Tidser [37]	726
11	30	H	Stirling Alb	D	1-1	0-0	1	Cardle [62]	937
12	Nov 6	A	Cowdenbeath	W	1-0	0-0	1	Cardle [76]	727
13	13	H	Forfar Ath	W	1-0	0-0	1	Agyeman [47]	856
14	20	H	Stenhousemuir	W	2-0	1-0	1	Barron [7], Cardle [50]	571
15	Dec 11	H	Albion R	W	6-1	2-1	1	Austin 2 [5, 48], Finlayson [37], Biabi 2 [52, 75], Barjonas [79]	554
16	18	A	Stranraer	W	4-0	3-0	1	Burns (og) [10], Forster [42], Austin 2 [45, 54]	272
17	26	A	Annan Ath	L	1-5	1-1	1	Austin [36]	372
18	Jan 8	A	Stirling Alb	W	3-0	1-0	1	Austin [4], Cardle 2 [58, 78]	483
19	15	H	Edinburgh C	D	2-2	1-0	1	Cardle 2 [27, 55]	500
20	25	A	Elgin C	L	0-2	0-1	1		531
21	29	H	Stranraer	W	3-2	2-0	1	O'Ware [21], Barjonas [22], Austin [89]	559
22	Feb 5	H	Elgin C	W	4-0	2-0	1	Higginbotham (pen) [8], Agyeman 2 [29, 56], Tidser [52]	433
23	19	A	Forfar Ath	L	0-1	0-0	1		670
24	22	H	Cowdenbeath	W	1-0	0-0	1	Higginbotham (pen) [82]	1092
25	26	H	Annan Ath	W	3-1	2-0	1	Moxon (og) [5], Barjonas [16], Cardle [72]	617
26	Mar 5	A	Cowdenbeath	W	1-0	1-0	1	Cardle [37]	475
27	8	A	Stenhousemuir	W	1-0	0-0	1	Austin [90]	458
28	12	H	Albion R	W	3-1	2-0	1	Austin [1], Barjonas 2 [36, 84]	635
29	16	A	Albion R	D	0-0	0-0	1		277
30	19	A	Elgin C	D	0-0	0-0	1		733
31	26	H	Stenhousemuir	W	1-0	0-0	1	Kucheriavyi [84]	812
32	Apr 1	A	Edinburgh C	D	1-1	0-0	1	Barjonas [48]	487
33	9	H	Stirling Alb	D	1-1	1-1	1	Biabi [8]	519
34	16	A	Stranraer	W	3-0	0-0	1	McNab [62], Reilly [64], Higginbotham [81]	301
35	23	H	Forfar Ath	D	1-1	1-0	1	Hill [31]	903
36	30	A	Annan Ath	W	2-1	2-1	1	Higginbotham [30], Agyeman [45]	441

Final League Position: 1

Honours
League Champions: League Two 2021-22. Promoted to League Two via play-offs: 2020-21.

Club colours: Shirts: Maroon with white trim. Shorts: White. Socks: Maroon.

Goalscorers: *League (68):* Austin 17, Cardle 12, Barjonas 9, Higginbotham 7 (2 pens), Agyeman 6, Biabi 3, Forster 2, Tidser 2, Barron 1, Finlayson 1, Hill 1, Kucheriavyi 1, McNab 1, O'Ware 1, Philp 1, Reilly 1, own goals 2.
Scottish FA Cup (6): Cardle 3, Higginbotham 1, O'Ware 1, Philp 1.
Premier Sports Scottish League Cup (8): Austin 4, Agyeman 1, Cardle 1, Higginbotham 1, Russell 1.
SPFL Trust Trophy (1): Tidser 1.

Jamieson D 35	Philp R 18 + 14	Forster J 22 + 1	O'Ware T 27 + 1	Peggie R 1 + 2	Tidser M 32 + 1	Reilly T 8 + 5	Higginbotham K 35	Barjonas J 30	Cardle J 29 + 7	Agyeman A 15 + 19	Hooper S 11 + 2	Biabi B 8 + 18	McNab R 12 + 10	Russell C — + 3	Hill D 16 + 2	Barron C 12 + 1	Austin N 19 + 7	Black A 14 + 8	Finnan B — + 1	Finlayson D 19 + 4	Ngwenya K 22 + 3	Donaldson J 1	Clark H 1 + 2	Kucheriavyi M 9 + 4	Cameron S — + 2	*Match No.*
1	2	3	4	5^{1}	6	7^{4}	8	9	10^{2}	11^{3}	12	13	14	15												1
1	14	3	4		6		10	7^{3}	9	12	2	11^{2}	13		5^{1}	8										2
1		3	4		6		11	7	9^{1}	13	2	10^{2}	5			8	12									3
1	2		4		6		8	9	10^{2}	12	3		5	14		7^{1}	11^{3}	13								4
1	2		4	12	7		9	8	11^{2}	10	3		5					6^{1}	13							5
1	6	3	15	14			9	8	11	10^{4}	2^{2}		5^{1}	13	4		12	7^{3}								6
1	6	3	4				9	8	11		2	12	5				10^{1}	7								7
1	2	3	4		7		9	8^{4}	11^{3}	15		14	12		5^{1}	13	10^{2}	6								8
1		3	4		7		9	8	12	11^{1}		14	5			6^{2}	10^{3}	13		2						9
1	14		4		7		9	8	11^{1}		3	12				6^{3}	10^{2}	13		2	5					10
1	14	3	4		7		9		11	13					5^{2}	8	10^{1}	6^{3}		2	12					11
1	13	3	4		7		9		11	14					5^{2}	8	10^{3}	6		2^{1}	12					12
1	12	3	5		7		9		11^{4}	13		15			4^{2}	8	10^{3}	6		2^{1}	14					13
1	2	3			7		9		11^{2}	10^{1}		13	14		4	8^{3}	12	6			5					14
1	16	3			7^{3}	14	9^{2}	6^{1}	12	13		11			4	8^{4}	10^{5}	15		2	5					15
1	12	3			7^{1}	16	9	6^{5}	11^{2}	13		14	15		4	8^{4}	10^{3}			2	5					16
	2^{3}	3■			7	14	9	8	11^{2}	12		13				6	10			4^{1}	5	1				17
1	13		4		7	8^{1}	11	6^{2}	9	15			2		3^{3}		10^{4}	12			5		14			18
1	14	3	4		6		9		8	13		10^{2}	12				11^{3}			2	5		7^{1}			19
1	12	3	4^{2}		7		11	8	9^{3}	13		14	2^{1}				10	6^{4}		15	5					20
1	6^{2}	3^{1}	4		8		9	7	11^{3}	10	15				12^{4}		14	13		2	5					21
1	14		4		7^{2}	12	9^{3}	8^{1}	11	10	3	13						6		2	5					22
1	6^{1}		4		7	12	9^{3}	8	13	11^{2}	3	14					10			2	5					23
1	2		3		7		9	8^{1}	11^{2}	13	4						10	6			5			12		24
1	2		3		7		9^{2}	8^{3}	12	10^{1}	4						13	6		14	5			11		25
1	2		4		7			8^{2}	9^{3}	12		6^{1}	13		14		10			3	5			11		26
1	2		4		7		9	8	11	10^{1}							12			3	5			6		27
1	2		4		12	7^{1}	9^{5}	8	11^{4}	15		14	16		3^{3}		10			13	5			6^{2}		28
1	2		4		7		9	8	11^{2}	10^{3}		14	12				13			3	5■			6^{1}		29
1	2		4		7	6^{1}	9	8	12	14		11^{2}	5				10^{3}			3				13		30
1		14	3		7	6^{5}	9	8^{1}	11^{4}	10^{3}		16	15		4^{2}			13		2	5			12		31
1	2	3	4^{2}		7		11	8	13	10^{1}		9	5							12				6		32
1	12	4			7		9	6	11^{2}	14		10			3			8^{3}		2^{1}	5			13		33
1		4			7	8^{3}	9		11	10^{2}		12	2		3^{1}			13			5			6	14	34
1	13	4			7^{3}	6	9	8	10^{1}	12		14	2^{2}		3						5			11		35
1	12	3				6^{3}	11	7	13	10^{2}		14			4^{4}			8^{5}		2^{1}	5		15	9	16	36

KILMARNOCK

Year Formed: 1869. *Ground & Address:* The BBSP Stadium, Rugby Park, Kilmarnock KA1 2DP. *Telephone:* 01563 545300. *Fax:* 01563 522181. *E-mail:* info@kilmarnockfc.co.uk *Website:* kilmarnockfc.co.uk
Ground Capacity: 18,128 (all seated). *Size of Pitch:* 102m × 67m.
Director: Billy Bowie.
Manager: Derek McInnes. *Assistant Managers:* Tony Docherty and Paul Sheerin.
Club Nickname: 'Killie'.
Previous Grounds: Rugby Park (Dundonald Road); The Grange; Holm Quarry; Rugby Park 1899.
Record Attendance: 35,995 v Rangers, Scottish Cup Quarter-final, 10 March 1962.
Record Transfer Fee received: £2,200,000 from Celtic for Greg Taylor (August 2019).
Record Transfer Fee paid: £340,000 to St Johnstone for Paul Wright (1995).
Record Victory: 11-1 v Paisley Academical, Scottish Cup 1st rd, 18 January 1930.
Record Defeat: 1-9 v Celtic, Division I, 13 August 1938.
Most Capped Player: Joe Nibloe, 11, Scotland.
Most League Appearances: 481: Alan Robertson, 1972-88.
Most League Goals in Season (Individual): 34: Harry 'Peerie' Cunningham 1927-28; Andy Kerr 1960-61.
Most Goals Overall (Individual): 148: Willy Culley, 1912-23.

KILMARNOCK – CINCH CHAMPIONSHIP 2021–22 LEAGUE RECORD

Match No.	*Date*	*Venue*	*Opponents*	*Result*	*H/T Score*	*Lg Pos.*	*Goalscorers*	*Attendance*
1	Aug 2	H	Ayr U	W 2-0	0-0	1	Polworth [56], Cameron (pen) [86]	3692
2	7	A	Queen of the South	W 1-0	0-0	2	Naismith [90]	1195
3	21	A	Hamilton A	W 2-0	0-0	1	Robinson 2 [60, 70]	2595
4	28	H	Inverness CT	L 0-1	0-1	3		5004
5	Sept 11	H	Greenock Morton	W 1-0	0-0	2	McKenzie [75]	4189
6	18	A	Partick Thistle	W 2-0	0-0	2	Holt (og) [52], Shaw [65]	4315
7	24	A	Arbroath	D 0-0	0-0	1		2410
8	Oct 2	H	Raith R	L 1-3	0-1	2	Hendry [76]	4008
9	16	A	Dunfermline Ath	D 2-2	0-0	3	Hendry [68], Shaw [75]	4095
10	23	H	Hamilton A	W 2-1	1-1	2	Shaw [5], Armstrong [74]	3969
11	26	A	Ayr U	W 1-0	0-0	1	Shaw (pen) [89]	6052
12	30	H	Queen of the South	W 4-0	1-0	1	Shaw 2 [17, 59], Hendry [90], Burke [90]	3992
13	Nov 6	H	Partick Thistle	L 0-1	0-1	1		4560
14	13	A	Greenock Morton	W 2-0	2-0	1	Alston [34], Shaw [43]	2878
15	20	H	Arbroath	L 0-1	0-0	1		4242
16	Dec 3	A	Inverness CT	L 0-1	0-0	3		2296
17	11	A	Raith R	L 0-1	0-0	4		2426
18	26	A	Hamilton A	W 3-2	2-1	4	Hendry (pen) [8], Stokes [35], Murray, F [54]	420
19	29	H	Greenock Morton	D 1-1	1-0	3	McKenzie [27]	500
20	Jan 8	A	Queen of the South	W 2-0	1-0	2	Stokes [43], Shaw (pen) [71]	492
21	14	A	Partick Thistle	D 1-1	0-0	2	Shaw (pen) [59]	500
22	29	H	Inverness CT	W 1-0	1-0	2	Lafferty [9]	4790
23	Feb 4	A	Arbroath	L 0-1	0-0	2		2803
24	9	H	Ayr U	L 1-2	1-1	2	Murray, F [7]	7560
25	12	H	Dunfermline Ath	W 2-1	0-0	2	Lafferty 2 [67, 83]	3698
26	19	H	Raith R	W 3-0	2-0	2	McGinn [5], Lafferty 2 [12, 63]	4080
27	26	A	Dunfermline Ath	D 0-0	0-0	2		4083
28	Mar 5	H	Hamilton A	W 2-0	1-0	2	Murray, F [44], Alston [55]	4083
29	11	A	Ayr U	W 3-1	3-1	1	McKenzie [3], Shaw [12], Sanders [16]	6136
30	19	H	Queen of the South	W 2-1	1-0	1	Taylor [42], Shaw [81]	4074
31	26	H	Partick Thistle	W 2-1	1-0	1	Lafferty 2 [22, 46]	5003
32	Apr 1	A	Greenock Morton	D 1-1	0-0	1	Shaw (pen) [64]	2650
33	9	H	Dunfermline Ath	W 2-0	1-0	1	Lafferty [26], Shaw [76]	5013
34	15	A	Inverness CT	L 1-2	0-0	1	Taylor [60]	3829
35	22	H	Arbroath	W 2-1	0-1	1	Taylor [78], Alston [90]	11,500
36	29	A	Raith R	D 1-1	0-1	1	Shaw [50]	3417

Final League Position: 1

Honours
League Champions: Division I 1964-65; Championship 2021-22; Division II 1897-98, 1898-99.
Runners-up: Division I 1959-60, 1960-61, 1962-63, 1963-64; First Division 1975-76, 1978-79, 1981-82, 1992-93; Division II 1953-54, 1973-74; Second Division 1989-90.
Scottish Cup Winners: 1920, 1929, 1997; *Runners-up:* 1898, 1932, 1938, 1957, 1960.
League Cup Winners: 2011-12; *Runners-up:* 1952-53, 1960-61, 1962-63, 2000-01, 2006-07.

European: *European Cup:* 4 matches (1965-66). *Cup Winners' Cup:* 4 matches (1997-98). *UEFA Cup:* 32 matches (*Fairs Cup:* 1964-65, 1966-67 semi-finals, 1969-70, 1970-71. *UEFA Cup:* 1998-99, 1999-2000, 2001-02).

Club colours: Shirt: Blue with white stripes. Shorts: White. Socks: White with blue tops.

Goalscorers: *League (50):* Shaw 14 (4 pens), Lafferty 8, Hendry 4 (1 pen), Alston 3, McKenzie 3, Murray F 3, Taylor 3, Robinson 2, Stokes 2, Armstrong 1, Burke 1, Cameron 1 (1 pen), McGinn 1, Naismith 1, Polworth 1, Sanders 1, own goal 1.
Scottish FA Cup (2): McKenzie 1, Murray E 1.
Premier Sports Scottish League Cup (7): Murray F 2, Alston 1, Burke 1, Cameron 1 (1 pen), Connell 1, Naismith 1.
SPFL Trust Trophy (10): Murray F 2, Sanders 2, Shaw 2 (1 pen), Armstrong 1, Hendry 1, Murray E 1, Naismith 1.

Hemming Z 36	Naismith J 14 + 2	Murray E 23 + 5	Stokes C 18 + 1	Haunstrup B 17	Burke C 15 + 14	McGinn S 29 + 3	Alston B 27 + 4	Murray F 24 + 10	Polworth L 13 + 1	Cameron I 2 + 4	Lyons B 8 + 11	McGowan D 17 + 3	Armstrong D 3 + 12	Robinson S 11 + 5	Burrell R — + 6	McKenzie R 26 + 2	Sanders J 10 + 4	Shaw O 26 + 3	Waters C 15 + 1	Hendry C 9 + 4	Hodson L 18	Walker S — + 1	Warnock S — + 1	Taylor A 10 + 1	Mackay D 3 + 7	Tait D 2 + 5	Lafferty K 13 + 1	Campbell D 6 + 2	Glass D — + 6	McArthur C 1	Match No.
1	2	3	4	5	6^{1}	7^{3}	8	9	10^{2}	11	12	13	14																		1
1	2	3	4	5	6^{3}	7	8	9^{1}	10	11^{2}			13	12	14																2
1	2	4		5	8^{3}	7	6	13	9^{1}	14	12	3		11^{2}		10															3
1	2	4		5	8	6	7	13	9^{1}	12		3	14	11^{3}		10^{2}															4
1	2	4		5		7^{3}	6	10	9^{1}		13	14		12		8^{2}	3	11													5
1	2	4		5		7	6	10^{3}		14	12	3		9^{1}		8		11^{2}	13												6
1	2	4		5		13	6	10		12	7	3		9^{1}		8^{2}		11													7
1	2	4		5^{1}	13	6	7		10			3	14	9^{3}		8^{2}		11		12											8
1	2	4		5	12	7	8	9^{3}			14	3		13		6^{2}		10		11^{1}											9
1	2	4			6^{2}	7	8	9^{1}	12		14	3	13					10	5	11^{3}											10
1	2	4				12	7^{3}	13	8		14	3	9^{1}			6^{2}		10	5	11											11
1	2	4			13	7			8		14	3	6^{2}	11^{3}		9		10^{1}	5	12											12
1	2	4			12	7		14	8^{1}			3	6^{2}	13		9		10	5	11^{3}											13
1		4			6^{2}	7	9	12	8^{1}			3	14			13		10	5	11^{3}	2										14
1		4			6^{1}	7^{2}	9	12	8			3	14	13				10	5	11^{3}	2										15
1		4			6		13	12	8^{3}		7	3		10^{2}	14	9^{1}		11	5		2										16
1		4		9	13		6^{3}	8			7^{1}	3		10^{2}		12	2	11		14	5										17
1■			4	9		7	12	8^{2}				3		10^{1}	14	6	2			11^{3}	5	13									18
1			4	9		7		8				3		10^{3}	13	6	2■	12		11^{2}	5^{1}		14								19
1		3	4	9	5^{2}	7	13	14	8^{3}					11^{1}		6		10		12	2										20
1		13	4	5	6^{3}	8^{1}	7	14								9		10		11^{2}	2			3	12						21
1		12		5	13	15	14	6								7	3^{3}	10			2			4	9^{1}	8^{2}	11^{4}				22
1	2^{5}	15	4	5^{2}	12			6					16			9		14						3^{4}	10^{1}	8^{3}	11	7	13		23
1	13		4	5^{3}	6			9				3				7		11^{1}			2^{2}				14	12	10	8			24
1		3^{4}	4		12	7	6^{3}	9^{2}								11	14		5		2				13	15	10	8^{1}			25
1		3	4		7^{5}	6^{4}	8	10^{2}					13			9^{1}			5^{3}		2				16	12	11	15	14		26
1	12	3	4		10^{3}	7^{1}	8^{4}	6								9	2^{5}	16	5						14	13	11^{2}		15		27
1		4			7^{3}	6^{4}	8^{2}	10					12		14	9	3	11^{1}	5		2					13		15			28
1			4		12	6^{2}	7	5			14					9	3^{1}	10	8		2			13			11^{3}				29
1		15	4		13	8^{1}	7	6^{4}			14					9	12	10	5		2^{2}			3^{3}			11				30
1			4		13	8^{4}	7	9^{3}			12					6^{2}		11	5		2			3	15		10^{1}		14		31
1			4		12	7^{2}	6	5^{1}			8						2	10	9					3			11		13		32
1			4		13	5^{1}	8	6^{3}			7	14	15		16		12	11			2^{2}			3			10^{5}	9^{4}			33
1			4			5^{1}	8	6^{2}			7							11			2			3	13		10	9	12		34
1		2^{1}	4		12	7	8	9			5^{2}					6	13	11						3			10				35
1		16	12		5^{1}	7	6	15			10^{3}		14				2	11						3^{2}	8^{5}		13	9		4^{4}	36

LIVINGSTON

Year Formed: 1974. *Ground:* Tony Macaroni Arena, Almondvale Stadium, Alderstone Road, Livingston EH54 7DN.
Telephone: 01506 417000. *Fax:* 01506 429948.
E-mail: lfcreception@livingstonfc.co.uk *Website:* livingstonfc.co.uk
Ground Capacity: 9,865 (all seated). *Size of Pitch:* 98m × 69m.
Chairman: Robert Wilson. *Chief Executive:* John Ward.
Manager: David Martindale. *Assistant Manager:* Marvin Bartley.
Club Nickname: 'Livi Lions'.
Previous Ground: Meadowbank Stadium (as Meadowbank Thistle).
Record Attendance: 10,024 v Celtic, Premier League, 18 August 2001.
Record Transfer Fee received: £2,000,000 from QPR for Lyndon Dykes (August 2020).
Record Transfer Fee paid: £225,000 to Queen of the South for Lyndon Dykes (January 2019).
Record Victory: 8-0 v Stranraer, League Cup, 1st rd, 31 July 2012.
Record Defeat: 0-8 v Hamilton A. Division II, 14 December 1974.
Most League Appearances: 446: Walter Boyd, 1979-89.
Most League Goals in Season (Individual): 22: Leigh Griffiths, 2008-09; Iain Russell, 2010-11; Liam Buchanan, 2016-17.
Most Goals Overall (Individual): 64: David Roseburgh, 1986-93.

LIVINGSTON – CINCH PREMIERSHIP 2021–22 LEAGUE RECORD

Match No.	*Date*	*Venue*	*Opponents*	*Result*		*H/T Score*	*Lg Pos.*	*Goalscorers*	*Attendance*
1	July 31	A	Rangers	L	0-3	0-1	8		23,000
2	Aug 8	H	Aberdeen	L	1-2	1-0	12	Anderson 35	1710
3	21	H	Motherwell	L	1-2	1-0	12	Forrest 38	1718
4	28	A	Hibernian	L	0-2	0-0	12		13,431
5	Sept 11	A	Dundee	D	0-0	0-0	12		5015
6	19	H	Celtic	W	1-0	1-0	9	Shinnie 25	8573
7	25	A	Hearts	L	0-3	0-2	10		16,175
8	Oct 2	H	St Mirren	L	0-1	0-1	10		1627
9	16	A	St Johnstone	W	3-0	2-0	10	Bailey 3, Anderson 29, Pitman 66	4274
10	23	A	Ross Co	W	3-2	2-1	9	Anderson 31, Bailey 43, Parkes 90	2566
11	27	H	Dundee U	D	1-1	1-1	9	Clark (og) 36	2586
12	30	A	Celtic	D	0-0	0-0	10		57,388
13	Nov 20	A	St Mirren	D	1-1	0-0	10	Devlin 88	3016
14	28	H	Rangers	L	1-3	1-2	10	Anderson 30	8825
15	Dec 1	A	Aberdeen	L	0-2	0-1	11		6295
16	5	H	Hearts	L	0-1	0-0	11		5597
17	8	H	Hibernian	W	1-0	1-0	9	McMillan 16	2363
18	11	A	Dundee U	W	1-0	0-0	8	Obileye (pen) 66	4552
19	18	H	Ross Co	D	1-1	0-1	8	Obileye 89	2554
20	26	A	Motherwell	L	1-2	0-1	8	Anderson 87	500
21	Jan 18	H	Dundee	W	2-0	0-0	8	Anderson 2 46, 56	1612
22	26	A	Rangers	L	0-1	0-0	9		48,343
23	29	A	Hibernian	W	3-2	1-2	8	Obileye 18, Fitzwater 53, Forrest 59	15,480
24	Feb 1	H	St Johnstone	L	1-2	1-1	8	Anderson 34	1319
25	5	H	Aberdeen	W	2-1	1-0	8	Obileye 8, Forrest 49	4276
26	9	A	Ross Co	D	1-1	0-0	8	Forrest 50	2224
27	19	H	St Mirren	D	1-1	0-0	9	Anderson 55	4228
28	26	A	Dundee	W	4-0	3-0	6	Anderson 2 6, 21, Pitman 18, Fitzwater 65	4679
29	Mar 2	H	Dundee U	W	2-1	1-1	4	Pitman 23, Edwards (og) 83	1864
30	6	H	Celtic	L	1-3	0-1	5	Shinnie 56	8922
31	19	A	Hearts	L	0-2	0-1	6		17,957
32	Apr 2	A	St Johnstone	L	0-1	0-1	8		3321
33	9	H	Motherwell	D	2-2	1-0	8	Bailey 26, Forrest 58	3848
34	23	A	Aberdeen	W	2-1	1-0	8	Devlin 41, Holt (pen) 70	12,338
35	30	H	Hibernian	W	1-0	0-0	7	Pitman 57	2840
36	May 7	H	St Johnstone	D	1-1	0-0	7	Fitzwater 90	1499
37	11	A	St Mirren	D	0-0	0-0	7		4554
38	15	H	Dundee	W	2-1	0-0	7	Shinnie 78, Forrest 84	1629

Final League Position: 7

Honours

League Champions: First Division 2000-01; Second Division 1986-87, 1998-99, 2010-11; League One 2016-17; Third Division 1995-96, 2009-10.
Runners-up: Second Division 1982-83; First Division 1987-88; Championship 2017-18.
Promoted via play-offs: 2017-18 (to Premiership).
Scottish Cup: Semi-finals 2001, 2004.
League Cup Winners: 2003-04. *Runners-up:* 2020-21. *Semi-finals:* 1984-85.
League Challenge Cup Winners: 2014-15; *Runners-up:* 2000-01.

European: *UEFA Cup:* 4 matches (2002-03).

Club colours: All: Black with amber trim.

Goalscorers: *League (41):* Anderson 11, Forrest 6, Obileye 4 (1 pen), Pitman 4, Bailey 3, Fitzwater 3, Shinnie 3, Devlin 2, Holt 1 (1 pen), McMillan 1, Parkes 1, own goals 2.
Scottish FA Cup (1): Obileye 1 (1 pen).
Premier Sports Scottish League Cup (8): Anderson 2, Forrest 1, Longridge 1, Obileye 1, Parkes 1, Sibbald 1, own goal 1.

Stryjek M 35	McMillan J 11 + 5	Obileye A 32 + 2	Fitzwater J 38	Lewis A 6 + 3	Pitman S 22 + 6	Holt J 37	Sibbald C 10 + 4	Forrest A 26 + 10	Anderson B 20 + 8	Penrice J 24 + 2	Kabia J — + 2	Devlin N 34 + 3	Hamilton J — + 8	Longridge J 9 + 7	Kelly S 9 + 6	Reilly G — + 1	Bailey O 22 + 9	Shinnie A 18 + 12	Jacobs K — + 2	Williamson B 4 + 1	Omeonga S 25 + 2	Montano C 7 + 7	Parkes T 6 + 2	Panayiotou H — + 4	Chukwuemeka C 1 + 7	Nouble J 13 + 3	Boyes M 4 + 5	Soto S 2 + 10	Konovalov I 3	Maley G — + 1	*Match No.*
1	2	3	4	5^{2}	6	7	8^{1}	9	10^{3}	11	12	13	14																		1
1		3	4		6	7	9^{1}	11^{2}	10^{3}	8		2	12	5	13	14															2
1		4^{1}	3		7	6	8^{3}	11	10			2	14	5	13		9^{2}	12													3
1		3	4^{1}			6	8^{2}	10	11^{3}	5		2	12		13		7	9	14												4
1		3	4			6	8^{2}	10	11^{3}	5		2	13				12	9	14	7^{1}											5
1	8^{1}	3	4	7	12	9		14		10		2		5^{2}			13	11		6^{3}											6
1	6	3	4	9^{2}		7			14	5		2		12			11^{1}	10		8^{3}	13										7
1	2^{3}	4	3			7		9	12	8		13	14	5			11^{1}	10^{2}			6										8
1	13	4	3		9	6	15	14	11^{3}	5^{2}		2		12			8^{4}				7^{1}	10									9
1	14	4	3^{1}		9	6		12	11			2			5		8^{4}			15	7^{2}	10^{3}	13								10
1		4	3		9	6		10^{2}	11^{3}			2	14		5		8^{1}			7■		12	13								11
1		4■	3			8		12	11^{3}			2		14	6^{1}		7	10^{2}			9		5	13							12
1	5		3			6		12	11^{2}			2		14			10	9^{3}			7	8^{1}	4	13							13
1	5^{1}		3			6		8	11^{3}	13	14	2					9^{2}	12			7	10	4								14
1		3^{2}	2			6		10^{3}	11^{1}	14		5	13	8■			9	12			7		4								15
1	8^{3}		3			6	9^{2}	10	12	5		2						11			7^{1}	13	4	14							16
1	6^{3}	12	3		14	7	9^{2}	11		5		2						10			8	13	4^{1}								17
1	6	4	3		13	7		9	10^{2}	5		2					12	14			8^{3}	11^{1}									18
1	6^{2}	4	3		13	7	9^{1}	11	14	5		2					12	10^{3}			8										19
1	14	3	2			7	6^{3}	10^{1}	12	9				4	5			11			8^{2}			13							20
1		4	3		7	6		13	10^{1}	5^{4}		2		15			9^{2}	11^{3}			8	14			12						21
1	14	4	3		6	7		13	10^{4}			2		5^{3}			9^{2}	11^{1}			8				15	12					22
1		4	3		6^{4}	7		11^{1}	14			2		5^{3}			9	13			8	12				10^{2}	15				23
1		4	3		6^{3}	7		11	10^{1}	5		2					9^{2}	13			8				12	14■					24
1		4	3	8^{3}	12	7		11^{2}	10^{1}	5		2					15				6	9■			13^{4}		14				25
1		4	3		6	7		11^{2}	12	5		2					9^{3}	13			8					10^{1}	14				26
1		4^{1}	3		6	7		9	10^{3}	5		2						12			8					11^{2}	14	13			27
1		4	3		6^{4}	7		11^{2}	10^{1}	5^{5}		2		15			12	16			8				14	9^{3}		13			28
1		4	3		6	7		11^{1}	10^{2}	5		2					13				8	14				9^{3}		12			29
1		4	3		8^{3}	7	15	10	12	5		2			14			9^{4}			6^{2}					11^{1}		13			30
1		4	3	15	7^{5}	6		8^{1}		5^{3}		2			14		10^{4}	16			9^{2}				12	11		13			31
1		4	3	14	7^{2}	6		11		5^{1}		2			12		13	15			8^{3}					9		10^{4}			32
1		4	3	12	7^{4}	6		11^{2}		5^{3}		2			8		9^{1}	13								10	14	15			33
1	13	4	3	5^{2}	7	6						2		12	8^{4}		9^{3}	11^{1}				14				10		15			34
		4	3		7	6	13	12				2			8		9^{2}	11^{1}								10^{3}	5	14	1		35
		4	3		7	6		12				2			8^{2}		9^{1}	11^{3}							13	10	5	14	1		36
		16	3		9^{4}	6^{2}	15	10^{3}				2		5^{1}	7		12				14				8^{5}	11	4	13	1		37
1^{4}	2^{5}		3	5	15		9^{1}	14				13					8	7			6	10^{2}				12	4	11^{3}		16	38

MONTROSE

Year Formed: 1879. *Ground & Address:* Links Park, Wellington St, Montrose DD10 8QD. *Telephone:* 01674 673200. *Fax:* 01674 677311. *E-mail:* office@montrosefc.co.uk *Website:* montrosefc.co.uk
Ground Capacity: total: 4,936, (seated: 1,338). *Size of Pitch:* 100m × 64m.
Chairman: John Crawford. *Secretary:* Brian Petrie.
Manager: Stewart Petrie. *Assistant Manager:* Ross Campbell.
Club Nickname: 'The Gable Endies'.
Record Attendance: 8,983 v Dundee, Scottish Cup 3rd rd, 17 March 1973.
Record Transfer Fee received: £50,000 from Hibernian for Gary Murray (December 1980).
Record Transfer Fee paid: £17,500 to Airdrieonians for Jim Smith (February 1992).
Record Victory: 12-0 v Vale of Leithen, Scottish Cup 2nd rd, 4 January 1975.
Record Defeat: 0-13 v Aberdeen, 17 March 1951.
Most Capped Player: Alexander Keillor, 2 (6), Scotland.
Most League Appearances: 432: David Larter, 1987-98.
Most League Goals in Season (Individual): 28: Brian Third, Division II, 1972-73.
Most Goals Overall (Individual): 126: Bobby Livingstone, 1967-79.

MONTROSE – CINCH LEAGUE ONE 2021–22 LEAGUE RECORD

Match No.	*Date*	*Venue*	*Opponents*	*Result*		*H/T Score*	*Lg Pos.*	*Goalscorers*	*Attendance*
1	July 31	A	Airdrieonians	W	3-0	1-0	1	Masson [10], Milne [50], Webster (pen) [74]	529
2	Aug 7	H	Clyde	D	2-2	0-0	1	Webster (pen) [50], Steeves [57]	613
3	14	H	Peterhead	W	1-0	0-0	2	Webster (pen) [55]	552
4	21	A	East Fife	W	2-0	1-0	1	Webster [29], Cammy Ballantyne [77]	488
5	28	H	Dumbarton	L	1-2	0-2	2	Webster (pen) [84]	599
6	Sept 11	A	Cove R	D	1-1	-	2	Webster (pen) [61]	679
7	18	H	Alloa Ath	L	0-2	0-2	4		532
8	25	H	Falkirk	D	2-2	0-0	4	Webster 2 [60, 76]	918
9	Oct 3	A	Queen's Park	D	1-1	0-0	6	Milne [68]	596
10	16	A	Clyde	W	5-0	3-0	4	Milne 2 [2, 66], Balatoni (og) [5], Cameron Ballantyne [26], Johnston [81]	640
11	23	H	East Fife	W	4-1	0-0	4	Keatings [52], Webster [55], Johnston 2 [76, 79]	606
12	30	A	Peterhead	D	0-0	0-0	3		560
13	Nov 6	H	Cove R	D	0-0	0-0	4		711
14	13	A	Alloa Ath	D	2-2	0-0	4	Allan 2 [77, 90]	742
15	20	A	Falkirk	W	1-0	1-0	3	Cammy Ballantyne [37]	3365
16	Dec 7	H	Airdrieonians	W	2-1	1-1	2	Johnston [20], Webster [66]	193
17	11	A	Dumbarton	W	3-1	2-1	2	Webster 2 (1 pen) [32 (p), 35], Callaghan [60]	386
18	18	H	Queen's Park	D	1-1	0-1	2	Webster (pen) [49]	594
19	22	H	Peterhead	W	2-0	1-0	2	Steeves [6], Lyons [75]	498
20	Jan 2	A	East Fife	W	2-0	0-0	2	Mercer (og) [60], Lyons [63]	497
21	8	H	Alloa Ath	D	1-1	0-1	2	Callaghan [51]	463
22	15	A	Cove R	L	0-1	0-1	3		499
23	29	H	Falkirk	W	2-1	2-1	3	Lyons [40], Johnston [45]	1036
24	Feb 5	H	Dumbarton	D	1-1	1-1	3	Johnston [24]	531
25	12	A	Airdrieonians	L	1-4	1-2	3	Webster (pen) [45]	649
26	19	H	Clyde	D	1-1	1-1	3	Lyons [32]	722
27	26	A	Queen's Park	W	1-0	1-0	3	Quinn [45]	680
28	Mar 5	H	East Fife	D	0-0	0-0	3		705
29	12	A	Peterhead	W	1-0	0-0	3	Gardyne [68]	573
30	19	H	Cove R	L	1-2	1-2	3	Johnston [38]	848
31	26	A	Dumbarton	D	0-0	0-0	3		492
32	Apr 2	A	Falkirk	W	3-0	1-0	3	Cameron [13], Gardyne (pen) [71], Campbell, R [89]	3158
33	9	H	Airdrieonians	D	2-2	1-1	3	Lyons 2 [2, 69]	784
34	16	A	Clyde	L	1-2	1-2	3	Gardyne [3]	502
35	23	H	Queen's Park	W	2-1	0-1	3	Doyle (og) [78], Dillon [81]	720
36	30	A	Alloa Ath	L	1-4	1-1	3	Webster (pen) [22]	668

Final League Position: 3

Honours
League Champions: Second Division 1984-85; League Two 2017-18.
Runners-up: Second Division 1990-91; Third Division 1994-95.
Scottish Cup: Quarter-finals 1973, 1976.
League Cup: Semi-finals 1975-76.
League Challenge Cup: Semi-finals 1992-93, 1996-97.

Club colours: Shirt: Blue with white sleeves. Shorts: Blue. Socks: White.

Goalscorers: *League (53):* Webster 15 (9 pens), Johnston 7, Lyons 6, Milne 4, Gardyne 3 (1 pen), Allan 2, Cammy Ballantyne 2, Callaghan 2, Steeves 2, Cameron Ballantyne 1, Cameron 1, Campbell R 1, Dillon 1, Keatings 1, Masson 1, Quinn 1, own goals 3.
Scottish FA Cup (1): Johnston 1.
Premier Sports Scottish League Cup (4): Johnston 1, Lyons 1, Milne 1 (1 pen), Rennie 1.
SPFL Trust Trophy (1): Webster 1 (1 pen).
Scottish League Play-offs (5): Cameron Ballantyne 2, Johnston 1, Milne 1, Rennie 1.

Fleming A 17 + 1	Waddell K 9 + 3	Dillon S 30 + 2	Allan M 20 + 2	Webster G 28 + 1	Masson T 26 + 5	Whatley M 23 + 9	Callaghan L 9 + 7	Steeves A 35	Rennie M 1 + 1	Milne L 20 + 6	Lyons B 26 + 5	Quinn A 12 + 4	Watson P 9 + 17	Ballantyne Cammy 28 + 1	Johnston C 17 + 12	Brown C 2 + 10	Antoniazzi C 4 + 6	Keatings J 7 + 3	Lennox A 19	Ballantyne Cameron 26 + 2	Campbell R 1 + 8	Simpson E 6 + 7	Gardyne M 14	Baxter T 1 + 1	Cameron L 6 + 3	Giacomini L — + 1	Grant C — + 1	Middleton C — + 1	Match No.
1	2^{3}	3	4	5	6	7	8	9^{1}	10^{2}	11	12	13	14																1
1	4	3	2^{1}	9	6	7	8^{3}	5		11	10^{2}			12	13	14													2
1		4	3	9	6^{1}	7^{3}	12	5		8	11^{2}		14	2	10		13												3
1	12	4	3	9	6^{3}	7	13	5		11^{1}	10		14	2			8^{2}												4
1	12	4	3	9	6^{2}	7		5		8	11^{1}		14	2	13		10^{3}												5
1	3	4	2^{3}	9	14	7^{1}	12	8		11	13		6^{2}	5	10														6
1	3	4^{3}			6	7^{2}	13	5		8	11		12	2	10	9^{1}	14												7
1	4^{1}	13	3	6	7	12		5		8	9^{3}	14		2	11			10^{2}											8
	12	4	3	6^{2}	7	8^{1}		5		10				2	13	14		11^{3}	1	9									9
	3	4		6	7^{2}	12		5		9	10^{1}			2	14		13	11^{3}	1	8									10
	3^{1}	4		9	7^{3}	13		5		8	11^{2}	12		2	14			10	1	6									11
		4■	14	6	8	12		5		7^{1}		3		2	11^{3}	13	9^{2}		1	10									12
	3			11	6	7		5		9	13	4		2	12			10^{1}	1	8^{2}									13
			3	11	6	7^{2}		5			13	4	14	2	12	10^{1}	9^{3}		1	8									14
	3			9^{1}	6	13		5		7	11^{3}	4	12	2	10^{2}		14		1	8									15
		13	4	9^{3}		7	8^{1}	5			11	3	12	2	10^{2}				1	6	14								16
		3	4	8^{3}		5	6	2			10^{2}		9		11^{1}	12	14	13	1	7									17
		4	3	9		2	8	5			11		7^{2}			12	13	10^{1}	1	6									18
		4	3	9	13	7^{3}	8^{1}	5			11	12	14	2■				10^{2}	1	6									19
		3	4	9	2		6	5			11^{2}		7^{3}			12		13	1	8	14	10^{1}							20
1		4	3		8		12	5			11		7^{3}	2	13			14		9		10^{1}	6^{2}						21
12		3	2^{2}	9^{4}	13		7^{3}	8			11	4	15	5					1^{1}	6		14	10						22
1		4		9	7	12		5			11^{1}	3	14	2	10^{3}	15				8^{2}		13	6^{4}						23
1		4		9	7^{3}			5		12	11^{4}	3	14■	2	10^{2}	15				8^{1}		13	6						24
1		4	3	9^{2}	7^{1}	14		5		6^{3}	11			2	10^{4}	13				8^{5}	16	12		15					25
		4		12	7^{4}	14		5		8^{3}	11■	3		2	9^{5}	15			1	13	16	10^{1}	6^{2}						26
		4	14	9	7^{2}	8		5		13		3		2	12				1	11		10^{1}	6^{3}						27
		4		9^{3}	6^{4}	7		5^{1}		15		3■	14	2	13				1	11		10^{2}	8		12				28
		4	3		14	8		5			9^{3}		13	2■	10^{2}				1	7^{4}	15	12	11■		6^{1}				29
1		4	3		6^{3}	8		5		12	11^{2}		7^{1}		10					2	14	13			9				30
1		3	4^{1}		7	2		5		11	13		8^{2}		12					9^{3}		14■	10		6				31
1		3			7	8		5		13	9	4^{1}	14	2	10^{4}					12	15		11^{2}		6^{3}				32
1		3				4	13	5		8	10^{2}		12	2	11					7^{1}			6		9				33
1		4		6^{3}	13	3^{1}		5		8	10		9^{2}	2	12					7			11		14				34
		3		2	7^{4}	14	15	4		13	11^{2}		12	5	10^{5}				1	8^{3}	16		6		9^{1}				35
				2		7	5		15	6^{5}			4						1^{1}	8^{4}	3	10^{2}	11^{3}	9	12	13	14	16	36

MOTHERWELL

Year Formed: 1886. *Ground & Address:* Fir Park Stadium, Motherwell ML1 2QN. *Telephone:* 01698 333333. *Fax:* 01698 338001.
E-mail: mfcenquiries@motherwellfc.co.uk *Website:* motherwellfc.co.uk
Ground Capacity: 13,742 (all seated). *Size of Pitch:* 105m × 65m.
Chairman: James McMahon. *Chief Executive:* Alan Burrows.
Manager: Graham Alexander. *Assistant Manager:* Keith Lasley.
Club Nicknames: 'The Well'; 'The Steelmen'.
Previous Grounds: The Meadows; Dalziel Park.
Record Attendance: 35,632 v Rangers, Scottish Cup 4th rd replay, 12 March 1952.
Record Transfer Fee received: £3,000,000 (rising to £3,250,000) from Celtic for David Turnbull (August 2020).
Record Transfer Fee paid: £500,000 to Everton for John Spencer (January 1999).
Record Victory: 12-1 v Dundee U, Division II, 23 January 1954.
Record Defeat: 0-8 v Aberdeen, Premier Division, 26 March 1979.
Most Capped Player: Stephen Craigan, 54, Northern Ireland.
Most League Appearances: 626: Bobby Ferrier, 1918-37.
Most League Goals in Season (Individual): 52: Willie McFadyen, Division I, 1931-32.
Most Goals Overall (Individual): 283: Hugh Ferguson, 1916-25.

MOTHERWELL – CINCH PREMIERSHIP 2021–22 LEAGUE RECORD

Match No.	Date	Venue	Opponents	Result		H/T Score	Lg Pos.	Goalscorers	Attendance
1	Aug 1	H	Hibernian	L	2-3	2-1	9	van Veen [12], Mugabi [29]	5230
2	8	A	St Johnstone	D	1-1	0-1	9	Watt [80]	2169
3	21	A	Livingston	W	2-1	0-1	5	Watt [48], Grimshaw [79]	1718
4	28	H	Dundee	W	1-0	1-0	4	Watt [34]	4998
5	Sept 11	H	Aberdeen	W	2-0	1-0	4	van Veen [26], Ojala [59]	5623
6	19	A	Rangers	D	1-1	0-1	4	Woolery [66]	48,961
7	25	H	Ross Co	W	2-1	1-1	3	Slattery [2], Watt [80]	4477
8	Oct 2	A	Hearts	L	0-2	0-2	4		17,028
9	16	H	Celtic	L	0-2	0-1	6		8446
10	23	A	Dundee U	L	1-2	0-1	6	Watt (pen) [70]	6854
11	27	H	St Mirren	D	2-2	0-0	6	Watt 2 (1 pen) [48, 52 (p)]	4576
12	31	H	Rangers	L	1-6	1-2	7	Mugabi [13]	7740
13	Nov 6	A	Aberdeen	W	2-0	0-0	5	van Veen 2 [50, 57]	9666
14	20	H	Hearts	W	2-0	1-0	5	Shields [23], Lamie [66]	7908
15	27	A	Dundee	L	0-3	0-2	5		4747
16	30	H	Dundee U	W	1-0	1-0	5	Watt [12]	4287
17	Dec 4	A	Hibernian	D	1-1	0-1	5	Watt [60]	15,266
18	12	A	Celtic	L	0-1	0-1	5		57,705
19	18	H	St Johnstone	W	2-0	1-0	4	Cornelius [17], van Veen [55]	3920
20	26	H	Livingston	W	2-1	1-0	4	van Veen 2 [13, 69]	500
21	Jan 18	A	Ross Co	L	1-3	0-1	4	Roberts [55]	2523
22	26	H	Hibernian	D	0-0	0-0	4		5202
23	29	A	Hearts	L	0-2	0-1	4		17,699
24	Feb 1	A	St Mirren	D	1-1	0-0	4	Tierney [90]	4987
25	6	H	Celtic	L	0-4	0-3	4		7421
26	9	A	Dundee U	L	0-2	0-1	5		4591
27	19	H	Aberdeen	D	1-1	0-1	5	O'Hara [68]	5171
28	27	A	Rangers	D	2-2	0-2	6	Roberts [52], Woolery [76]	49,318
29	Mar 2	H	Ross Co	L	0-1	0-1	7		3587
30	5	H	Dundee	D	1-1	1-1	8	Efford [18]	4435
31	19	A	St Johnstone	L	1-2	1-1	8	van Veen [12]	3772
32	Apr 2	H	St Mirren	W	4-2	3-2	5	Goss [20], Shields [21], Cornelius [45], Tait (og) [78]	4441
33	9	A	Livingston	D	2-2	0-1	6	Slattery [72], Lamie [90]	3848
34	23	H	Rangers	L	1-3	1-1	6	Tierney [35]	8036
35	30	A	Dundee U	L	0-1	0-1	6		6250
36	May 7	A	Ross Co	W	1-0	0-0	5	van Veen (pen) [68]	3067
37	11	H	Hearts	W	2-1	1-1	4	Efford [3], Lamie [56]	5769
38	14	A	Celtic	L	0-6	0-3	5		58,953

Final League Position: 5

Honours
League Champions: Division I 1931-32;. First Division 1981-82, 1984-85; Division II 1953-54, 1968-69.
Runners-up: Premier Division 1994-95, 2012-13; Premiership 2013-14; Division I 1926-27, 1929-30, 1932-33, 1933-34; Division II 1894-95, 1902-03.
Scottish Cup: 1952, 1991; *Runners-up:* 1931, 1933, 1939, 1951, 2011, 2018.
League Cup Winners: 1950-51; *Runners-up:* 1954-55, 2004-05, 2017-18.

European: *Champions League:* 2 matches (2012-13). *Cup Winners' Cup:* 2 matches (1991-92). *UEFA Cup:* 8 matches (1994-95, 1995-96, 2008-09). *Europa League:* 21 matches (2009-10, 2010-11, 2012-13, 2013-14, 2014-15, 2020-21).

Club colours: Shirt: Amber with maroon band. Shorts: Maroon with amber trim. Socks: Amber with maroon tops.

Goalscorers: *League (42):* van Veen 9 (1 pen), Watt 9 (2 pens), Lamie 3, Cornelius 2, Efford 2, Mugabi 2, Roberts 2, Shields 2, Slattery 2, Tierney 2, Woolery 2, Goss 1, Grimshaw 1, O'Hara 1, Ojala 1, own goal 1.
Scottish FA Cup (5): van Veen 2 (1 pen), Donnelly 1, Efford 1, Shields 1.
Premier Sports Scottish League Cup (6): Amaluzor 1, Lamie 1, Lawless 1, Maguire 1, Watt 1, Woolery 1.

Kelly L 38	O'Donnell S 26 + 2	Mugabi B 29 + 2	Lamie R 20 + 5	Carroll J 19 + 6	Slattery C 27 + 4	Donnelly L 16 + 7	Maguire B 11 + 2	Woolery K 24 + 7	van Veen K 24 + 8	Watt T 18 + 1	Amaluzor J 2 + 8	Lawless S — + 2	Shields C 17 + 8	Ojala J 18 + 3	Grimshaw L 10 + 4	O'Hara M 14 + 5	McGinley N 22 + 2	O'Connor D — + 1	Goss S 26 + 3	Johansen S 21 + 1	Roberts J 7 + 11	Cornelius D 10 + 2	Tierney R 5 + 9	Shaw L 2 + 5	Efford J 11 + 3	Nirennold V 1 + 2	Match No.
1	2	3	4	5	6^1	7	8	9^2	10	11	12	13															1
1	2	3	4	5	6	7^1	8	9	10	12		13	11^2														2
1		2	4	5	7			11^2		10	9^1			3	6	8	12	13									3
1		2	4	5■	7			11^1	12	10^2	9^3			3	6	8	14		13								4
1		2	12		7		14	9^1	11^3	10^2				4	6	8	5		13	3							5
1	2	3	12		7	14		9	11^1	10^3				4^2	6	8	5				13						6
1	2		4	14	7	12		9^1	11^2	10				3	6^3	8	5				13						7
1	2	3			7			9	11^2	10	12		13	4	6^1	8	5										8
1	2	3			7			11	12	10	13			4	6^1		5		8		9^2						9
1	2	3			8^3			9^1	11^2	10			13	4	7	12	5		6		14						10
1	2	12		14	8^3			9^2		11			10	4^1	7	13	5		6	3							11
1	2■	3	13		6^3		14		12	11			10^1			7	5		8	4	9^2						12
1		2	12	13			8	14	10^3	11^1				4^2		6	5		7	3	9						13
1	12	2	4		8		6	9^2		11	13		10^3		14		5		7^1	3							14
1		2	4		6		7	9	13	11			10^1		8^2		5			3	12						15
1	12	2	4	13	6		7■	9^2	10^3	11					14		5		8	3^1							16
1	2	3	4^2	13	6			9^1	10^3	11			14				5		8		12	7					17
1	2	3		4	6^2	12	7	9^1	10^3	11			13				5		8		14						18
1	2	3		13		7		9^1	10^2	11^3			12				5		8	4	14	6					19
1	2	3				6	7	9^3	10				11^1	12	13		5		8	4^2	14						20
1	2	3				6	7^1	9^2	10		13		12				5		8	4	11						21
1	2			4	14	6■	7		10				11^1				5		8	3	9^2		12^3	13			22
1	2			4	6		7^1		10		14		13				5		12^3	3	11^2		9	8			23
1	5	2		4	9^3	6		13	11								8^1		10	3	14		12	7^2			24
1	5	2		8^2	9^1	6		13	10^4						16		4		11^5	3^3		7	14		12	15	25
1		2			6^3	7^4		11^1	13				15	4			5		8	3	10^2	14	12		9		26
1		2	13	5		7		12	10				11	4		6			8	3^1					9^2		27
1	2	3	4	5		8		9^4			13^5			16		7^1				15	14	6	11^3	12	10^2		28
1	2		4	5	14	7		9	10				11^2			6			8^3	3^1	13				12		29
1	2		5		13	7		9	10					4		6^1			8^2	3			12		11		30
1	5		3	8^1		7		12	10				11	2						4		6			9		31
1	5	2	4		7	13			10^1				9						8^3	3		6	12	14	11^2		32
1		2	4	5^3	7^4	15		13	10^1				9	16		12			8	3		6^5	14		11^2		33
1		2^2	4	5	7			13			14		10	3		12			8^1			6	9		11^3		34
1		2	4	8	6	13		9^1					11	3^2		5			7				10		12		35
1	5		4	8	12	2			13				9^4	3^1		6			7			15	10^2	14	11^3		36
1	5	15	4	8	9^1	2			12				11^3	3^4					7^5			6	14	13	10^2	16	37
1	8	2^3	3	4	9	13			12				10^4			15			7^1			6	14		11	5^2	38

PARTICK THISTLE

Year Formed: 1876. *Ground & Address:* Energy Check Stadium at Firhill, 80 Firhill Rd, Glasgow G20 7AL. *Telephone:* 0141 579 1971. *Fax:* 0141 945 1525. *E-mail:* mail@ptfc.co.uk *Website:* ptfc.co.uk
Ground Capacity: 10,102 (all seated). *Size of Pitch:* 105m × 68m.
Chairman: Jacqui Low. *Chief Executive:* Gerry Britton.
Manager: Ian McCall. *Assistant Managers:* Alan Archibald and Neil Scally.
Club Nickname: 'The Jags'.
Previous Grounds: Overnewton Park; Jordanvale Park; Muirpark; Inchview; Meadowside Park.
Record Attendance: 49,838 v Rangers, Division I, 18 February 1922. *Ground Record:* 54,728, Scotland v Ireland, 25 February 1928.
Record Transfer Fee received: £350,000 from Barnsley for Liam Lindsay (June 2017); £350,000 from Norwich C for Aidan Fitzpatrick (July 2019).
Record Transfer Fee paid: £85,000 to Celtic for Andy Murdoch (February 1991).
Record Victory: 16-0 v Royal Albert, Scottish Cup 1st rd, 17 January 1931.
Record Defeat: 0-10 v Queen's Park, Scottish Cup 5th rd, 3 December 1881.
Most Capped Player: Alan Rough, 51 (53), Scotland.
Most League Appearances: 410: Alan Rough, 1969-82.
Most League Goals in Season (Individual): 41: Alex Hair, Division I, 1926-27.
Most Goals Overall (Individual): 229: Willie Sharp, 1939-57.

PARTICK THISTLE – CINCH CHAMPIONSHIP 2021–22 LEAGUE RECORD

Match No.	*Date*	*Venue*	*Opponents*	*Result*	*H/T Score*	*Lg Pos.*	*Goalscorers*	*Attendance*
1	July 31	H	Queen of the South	W 3-2	2-1	1	Graham 2 [16, 30], Tiffoney [85]	1534
2	Aug 7	A	Dunfermline Ath	W 3-0	2-0	1	Docherty [7], Holt [22], Graham (og) [78]	2000
3	21	A	Arbroath	L 1-3	1-1	3	Colin Hamilton (og) [33]	1585
4	28	H	Greenock Morton	W 3-0	1-0	2	Holt [9], Rudden [47], Graham [55]	3034
5	Sept 11	A	Inverness CT	L 1-3	1-0	4	Tiffoney [17]	2148
6	18	H	Kilmarnock	L 0-2	0-0	4		4315
7	26	A	Raith R	L 2-3	0-1	5	Graham [86], Rudden [90]	1781
8	Oct 2	H	Ayr U	W 4-0	2-0	5	Rudden [34], Smith [45], McGinty (og) [72], Graham [85]	2667
9	15	A	Hamilton A	W 6-1	1-0	4	Rudden 2 [7, 58], Graham 2 [53, 74], Tiffoney [61], Murray [72]	1775
10	23	H	Dunfermline Ath	D 0-0	0-0	4		3333
11	26	A	Greenock Morton	D 0-0	0-0	5		1867
12	30	H	Inverness CT	D 0-0	0-0	5		2527
13	Nov 6	A	Kilmarnock	W 1-0	1-0	5	Rudden [3]	4560
14	13	A	Ayr U	W 4-0	2-0	4	Docherty [30], Graham 2 [33, 81], Gordon [90]	2037
15	20	H	Hamilton A	W 1-0	0-0	4	Mayo [57]	2886
16	Dec 4	A	Queen of the South	D 0-0	0-0	4		1308
17	11	H	Arbroath	L 0-2	0-1	5		2285
18	18	H	Raith R	W 1-0	0-0	4	Turner [90]	2229
19	Jan 8	A	Hamilton A	D 2-2	1-0	5	Tiffoney [45], Rudden [64]	532
20	14	H	Kilmarnock	D 1-1	0-0	5	Docherty [87]	500
21	Feb 1	H	Ayr U	W 1-0	0-0	5	Graham [51]	2207
22	9	A	Inverness CT	D 3-3	2-2	5	Graham 3 (1 pen) [8, 27, 72 (p)]	1781
23	22	H	Greenock Morton	L 0-1	0-0	5		2345
24	26	A	Raith R	D 0-0	0-0	5		1759
25	Mar 1	A	Arbroath	D 1-1	0-1	4	McKenna [60]	1648
26	4	H	Inverness CT	W 1-0	0-0	3	Holt [85]	2099
27	8	H	Queen of the South	W 1-0	0-0	3	Holt (pen) [82]	2044
28	12	A	Greenock Morton	L 1-2	1-0	3	Turner [5]	2294
29	19	H	Hamilton A	L 0-4	0-2	4		2567
30	22	A	Dunfermline Ath	L 1-4	1-3	4	Docherty [5]	3380
31	26	A	Kilmarnock	L 1-2	0-1	4	Docherty [87]	5003
32	Apr 2	H	Arbroath	D 0-0	0-0	4		2810
33	8	A	Queen of the South	W 1-0	0-0	4	Tiffoney [62]	1099
34	16	H	Raith R	L 0-1	0-0	4		2644
35	23	H	Dunfermline Ath	W 1-0	1-0	4	Docherty [15]	3428
36	29	A	Ayr U	L 1-3	0-2	4	Jakubiak [81]	3426

Final League Position: 4

Honours
League Champions: First Division 1975-76, 2001-02, 2012-13; League One: 2020-21; Division II 1896-97, 1899-1900, 1970-71; Second Division 2000-01.
Runners-up: First Division 1991-92, 2008-09; Division II 1901-02.
Promoted via play-offs: 2005-06 (to First Division).
Scottish Cup Winners: 1921; *Runners-up:* 1930.
League Cup Winners: 1971-72; *Runners-up:* 1953-54, 1956-57, 1958-59.
League Challenge Cup Runners-up: 2012-13.

European: *Fairs Cup:* 4 matches (1963-64). *UEFA Cup:* 2 matches (1972-73). *Intertoto Cup:* 4 matches (1995-96).

Club colours: Shirt: Yellow with red stripes. Shorts: Black with red and yellow trim. Socks: Red with yellow hoop.

Goalscorers: *League (46):* Graham 13 (1 pen), Rudden 7, Docherty 6, Tiffoney 5, Holt 4 (1 pen), Turner 2, Gordon 1, Jakubiak 1, Mayo 1, McKenna 1, Murray 1, Smith 1, own goals 3.
Scottish FA Cup (2): Docherty 1, Graham 1.
Premier Sports Scottish League Cup (6): Graham 4, Rudden 2.
SPFL Trust Trophy (2): Akinola 1, Holt 1.
Scottish League Play-offs (1): Crawford 1.

Sneddon J 34	Mayo L 33	Bell S 1 + 6	Holt K 33 + 1	McKenna C 22 + 1	Turner K 22 + 9	Docherty R 34	Bannigan S 34 + 1	Foster R 26 + 1	Graham B 27 + 5	Rudden Z 17 + 2	Smith C 20 + 15	Tiffoney S 28 + 1	Stone H 2	Murray C 5 + 13	MacIver R 1 + 16	Akinola T 25 + 3	Gordon S 1 + 7	Hastie J — + 6	Hendrie S 6 + 7	Crawford Robert 11 + 5	Jakubiak A 7 + 4	McAllister K 2 + 1	Alegria J 5 + 5	Stanway B — + 1	Match No.
1	2	3	4	5	6[2]	7	8	9	10	11[1]	12	13													1
	3		4	2	6	7	8	5	10[3]	11[1]	12	9[2]	1	13	14										2
	3		4	2[2]	7		8	5	10	11[1]	14	9	1		6[3]	12	13								3
1			4		6	7[3]	8	5	10	11[2]	12	9[1]		13		3	2	14							4
1	2		4		6[1]	7	8	5	10[3]	12	11[2]	9			14	3		13							5
1	2		4	3	6[3]	7	8	5	10[2]	11[1]	13	9			14		12								6
1	5		4	3[2]	7	6	9[3]	2	11	13	8[1]	10				12	14								7
1	3		4		14	7[3]	8	5	10	11[2]	6[1]	9		13		2		12							8
1	4		5[2]	12		7	8	2	10[1]	11	6[3]	9		13		3		14							9
1	4		5			7	8	2	11[2]	10[1]	6[3]	9		12	14	3		13							10
1	4		5		6	7[1]	8	2	10[2]	11[3]	12	9			14	3	13								11
1	4		5			7	8	2	10[1]	11	9[2]	6[3]		14		3	13	12							12
1	4		5		6	7	8	2	13	11[3]	12	9[2]		10[1]	14	3									13
1			4	2	6[3]	8	7	5	11	10[1]	12	9[2]		13		3	14								14
1	4		5	2	6	7	8		10[1]	11[2]	12	9			13	3									15
1	4		5		6[3]	7	8	2	12	11[1]	13	9		10[2]	14	3									16
1	4		5		6	7	8[2]	2	11		10[1]	9[3]			12	3	14		13						17
1	4		5		12	7	8	2	10	11[1]	6[2]	9			13	3									18
1	4		5		6	8		2	11[2]	10[3]	12	9		13	14	3				7[1]					19
1	4		5		13	10	8	2	12	11[1]	6[2]	9			14	3				7[3]					20
1	4			2	15	7	8	5[4]	11[1]		10[2]	9			14	3			12	6[3]	13				21
1	4		5	2		7	8		11[3]		10[1]	9[2]			14	3			13	6	12				22
1	4		5	2	15	7	8		10[3]		6[2]			13	14	3				9[1]	11[4]	12			23
1	3				13	7	8	2	12		10[4]			14	15	4			5	9[2]	11[1]	6[3]			24
1	4		5	2	9[1]	6	8	14	11		7[2]	10[4]		15		3[3]				12			13		25
1	3	15	4	2	12	7	8[4]	5	10		13			9[1]						6[3]	14		11[2]		26
1	3		4	2	14	7	8	5	12		13			9[2]						6[1]	10		11[3]		27
1	3		4	2	6	7	8	5	10		9[2]								13		11[1]		12		28
1	4	12	5	2	6	7	8				10[2]					3			13	9[1]			11[3]	14	29
1	3	16	4	2[1]	14	7	8	5[4]			10[3]	9[2]		12		15			13	6			11[5]		30
1			4	2	6	7	8				12	9		10		3			5				11[1]		31
1	7		4	2	6		8[3]		10[2]		9[1]	11		13		3			5	12			14		32
1	3	14	4	2	6[2]	7	8		10		9[1]	11[3]							5	13	12				33
1	7		4	2		6	8		10			11				3[1]			5	12	9[2]		13		34
1	3	14	4	2	6[2]	7	8		10		13	11[3]							5	12	9[1]				35
1	3[2]	16	13	2	8[5]	7	12	5[1]			11[3]					4			14	6	10	9[4]	15		36

PETERHEAD

Year Formed: 1891. *Ground and Address:* Balmoor Stadium, Balmoor Terrace, Peterhead AB42 1EQ.
Telephone: 01779 478256. *Fax:* 01779 490682. *E-mail:* office@peterheadfc.co.uk *Website:* peterheadfc.org
Ground Capacity: 3,150 (seated: 1,000). *Size of Pitch:* 101m × 64m.
Chairman: Rodger Morrison.
Manager: Jim McInally. *Assistant Manager:* David Nicholls.
Club Nickname: 'Blue Toon'.
Previous Ground: Recreation Park.
Record Attendance: 8,643 v Raith R, Scottish Cup 4th rd replay, 25 February 1987 (Recreation Park); 4,855 v Rangers, Third Division, 19 January 2013 (at Balmoor).
Record Victory: 9-0 v Colville Park, Scottish Cup 2nd rd, 14 October 2017.
Record Defeat: 0-13 v Aberdeen, Scottish Cup 3rd rd, 10 February 1923.
Most League Appearances: 275: Martin Bavidge, 2003-13.
Most League Goals in Season (Individual): 32: Rory McAllister, 2013-14.
Most Goals Overall (Individual): 194: Rory McAllister, 2008, 2011-19.

PETERHEAD – CINCH LEAGUE ONE 2021–22 LEAGUE RECORD

Match No.	*Date*	*Venue*	*Opponents*	*Result*		*H/T Score*	*Lg Pos.*	*Goalscorers*	*Attendance*
1	July 31	H	Alloa Ath	W	2-0	1-0	3	McLean [8], Payne [63]	242
2	Aug 7	A	Falkirk	L	1-2	0-1	5	Jordon Brown [90]	2806
3	14	A	Montrose	L	0-1	0-0	7		552
4	21	H	Airdrieonians	L	2-3	0-1	9	Brown, S [81], McLean [90]	536
5	28	A	East Fife	L	0-3	0-0	10		373
6	Sept 11	H	Clyde	W	3-2	3-2	8	McCarthy [5], Brown, S [18], McLean [19]	488
7	18	H	Cove R	L	0-1	0-0	9		625
8	25	A	Queen's Park	L	2-3	0-1	9	Ritchie [51], Lyle [54]	546
9	Oct 2	H	Dumbarton	W	5-0	1-0	9	Conroy [4], Ritchie [48], Jason Brown [53], Mulligan [80], Brown, S (pen) [82]	545
10	16	A	Alloa Ath	W	4-2	2-2	7	Payne [29], Brown, S (pen) [37], McLean [58], Mulligan [84]	414
11	23	H	Falkirk	D	0-0	0-0	7		743
12	30	H	Montrose	D	0-0	0-0	7		560
13	Nov 6	A	Airdrieonians	L	1-3	0-1	8	Currie (og) [90]	547
14	13	A	Cove R	L	0-3	0-0	8		925
15	20	H	Queen's Park	W	2-1	0-1	8	Brown, S (pen) [55], McLean [76]	527
16	Dec 4	A	Clyde	D	2-2	2-1	7	McLean [20], Savoury [26]	483
17	11	H	East Fife	D	1-1	0-0	8	Duncan [74]	470
18	18	A	Dumbarton	W	3-2	2-2	5	Mulligan [25], McLean 2 [37, 66]	336
19	22	A	Montrose	L	0-2	0-1	5		498
20	Jan 2	H	Cove R	L	0-1	0-0	6		494
21	15	H	Clyde	D	1-1	0-1	7	Brown, S [90]	497
22	29	A	East Fife	D	0-0	0-0	7		568
23	Feb 5	H	Alloa Ath	L	0-1	0-1	8		538
24	19	H	Airdrieonians	L	0-1	0-1	9		553
25	22	A	Falkirk	D	1-1	1-1	9	Duncan [9]	3187
26	26	H	Dumbarton	W	4-3	3-0	8	Ritchie 2 [3, 42], McLean [8], Savoury [87]	534
27	Mar 1	A	Queen's Park	L	1-2	0-1	8	McLean [90]	350
28	5	A	Cove R	L	2-5	1-3	8	Ritchie [15], McLean [83]	819
29	12	H	Montrose	L	0-1	0-0	8		573
30	19	A	Alloa Ath	L	0-1	0-0	8		651
31	26	H	Falkirk	W	1-0	1-0	8	Jack Brown [36]	705
32	Apr 2	A	Clyde	W	3-0	1-0	8	Savoury 2 [15, 62], Ritchie [54]	597
33	9	A	Dumbarton	D	1-1	1-1	8	McLean [44]	527
34	16	H	Queen's Park	W	2-1	1-0	8	Duncan [4], Savoury [49]	615
35	23	H	East Fife	W	1-0	1-0	7	Jack Brown [11]	676
36	30	A	Airdrieonians	D	1-1	1-0	7	Savoury [45]	1116

Final League Position: 7

Honours
League Champions: League Two 2013-14, 2018-19.
Runners up: Third Division 2004-05, 2012-13; League Two 2017-18.
Scottish Cup: Quarter-finals 2001.
League Challenge Cup: Runners up: 2015-16.

Club colours: All: Royal blue with white trim.

Goalscorers: *League (46):* McLean 12, Brown S 6 (3 pens), Ritchie 6, Savoury 6, Duncan 3, Mulligan 3, Jack Brown 2, Payne 2, Jason Brown 1, Jordon Brown, Conroy 1, Lyle 1, McCarthy 1, own goal 1.
Scottish FA Cup (5): McLean 2 (1 pen), Brown S 1, Cameron 1, McCarthy 1.
Premier Sports Scottish League Cup (4): Brown S 2 (1 pen), Cameron 1, McLean 1.
SPFL Trust Trophy (2): Payne 2.

Long B 36	McCarthy A 29	Mulligan J 19	McDonald A 31 + 2	Conroy R 9 + 6	Ritchie H 28 + 2	Ferry S 19	Brown S 33 + 1	Cameron L 6 + 7	McLean R 25 + 5	Payne N 29 + 4	Brown Jordon — + 19	Strachan D 5 + 5	Lyle D 3 + 21	Brown Jason 25 + 1	Kesson D — + 1	Cook A — + 7	Duffy F 23 + 3	Wilson D 12 + 1	Savoury G 20 + 5	Duncan R 9 + 6	Cusick S 1	Quitongo R 14 + 1	Cairns O 3 + 6	Brown Jack 6 + 7	Want S 10	Fraser G 1 + 7	*Match No.*
1	2^{1}	3	4	5	6	7	8	9^{2}	10	11^{3}	12	13	14														1
1	2	6^{2}	4	5	11	7^{1}	8	12	10	9^{3}	14	13		3													2
1	7^{3}	9	4	5	6^{1}		8		10	11	13	2	12	3^{2}	14												3
1		8	4	5	9^{3}	7^{2}	6	12	13	10	14	2	11^{1}	3													4
1	5	2	4		9^{3}	6^{1}	7	8^{2}	11	10	13	14	12	3													5
1	4^{3}	2	3	9	6	8^{2}	7	12	11	13		5	10^{1}			14											6
1	2	3	4	5	7	6^{1}	9		10	11^{2}			12	13		14	8^{3}										7
1	2^{2}	3		5	7^{1}	6	9	14	10^{3}	11			13	4			8	12									8
1	9^{3}	5	14	8	10	7^{2}	6	12		11^{1}			13	3			2	4									9
1	9	2	10^{3}	5^{2}	8	7	6		13	11^{1}				4			12	3	14								10
1	7^{1}	2	14		8	6^{2}	9	13	11	10^{3}				4			5	3	12								11
1	8	5	4	13	6		7		10				11^{1}	3			9^{2}	2	12								12
1	8	5	4		6^{1}		7	13	10				12	3			9	2	11^{2}								13
1	6	5	4	12		7^{2}	8		10^{1}	11			13	3^{3}			9	2	14								14
1		6	4				7	9^{1}	13	11^{2}	14	5	12	3			8	2	10^{3}								15
1	6	5	4		8^{1}		7		10	12				3			9	2	11								16
1	7^{1}	6	4		12	5^{2}	8		10	13				3			9	2^{3}	11	14							17
1		2	4		9^{3}		8	7	10	11^{1}	13	12	14	3			5^{2}		6								18
1		8	4		7			6	10	11^{2}	14	2^{1}	13	3			5		9^{3}	12							19
1	7		4		8		2	6^{1}	10	9^{2}	14	12	13	3■						11	5^{3}						20
1	6		4		8	2^{3}	7		10^{1}	11^{2}	14		13				5	3	12	9							21
1	6		2			7^{2}			10	8^{3}			14	3			5^{1}	4	11	9		12	13				22
1	6		4	14			13		10^{1}	11^{4}	15		16	3			8^{3}	2^{5}		9		5	12	7^{2}			23
1	7		4		10^{1}		6		12	11	14			3			2^{3}		9	8^{2}		5		13			24
1	6		4		10		7		12	11							2		9	8		5		3^{1}			25
1	6		4		10^{1}		7		11^{2}	8^{4}	15		14			16	2^{5}		9^{3}			5	13	12	3		26
1	6		4		10		7		11	8^{3}			13				2^{2}		9^{1}			5	12	14	3		27
1	6^{5}		4	14	9		7^{4}		11		12					16	15		10^{2}			5^{1}	2	8^{3}	3	13	28
1	6		3		9		7		10	11^{1}							5^{2}		8	12		2			4	13	29
1			4■		7^{1}		8		10^{4}	12	15		16	2^{2}					9^{3}	11^{5}		5	6	13	3	14	30
1			5		8^{4}	6^{1}	7			11^{3}	13		15	4		14			9			2		10^{2}	3	12	31
1	10				8^{4}	6^{5}	7			11^{3}	16			4		14	5		9^{2}	15		2^{1}	12	13	3		32
1	6^{2}						8		11	10	15			4			5		9^{1}	7^{3}		2^{4}	14	12	3	13	33
1	8		5			6	7			11^{3}				4■			12		9^{1}	10^{2}		2		13	3	14	34
1	8^{1}		5	15	13	6^{4}	7			11^{3}			16						9	12		2^{5}	4	10^{2}	3	14	35
1			3	16	7^{5}	4	8			11^{2}	15		14			13	5^{3}		9	12		2		10^{4}		6^{1}	36

QUEEN OF THE SOUTH

Year Formed: 1919. *Ground & Address:* Palmerston Park, Dumfries DG2 9BA. *Telephone:* 01387 254853.
Fax: 01387 240470. *E-mail:* admin@qosfc.com *Website:* qosfc.com
Ground Capacity: 8,690 (seated: 3,377) *Size of Pitch:* 102m × 66m.
Chairman: Billy Hewitson. *Vice-Chairman:* Craig Paterson.
Player/Manager: Wullie Gibson. *Assistant Manager:* Grant Murray.
Club Nickname: 'The Doonhamers'.
Record Attendance: 26,552 v Hearts, Scottish Cup 3rd rd, 23 February 1952.
Record Transfer Fee received: £250,000 from Southend U for Andy Thomson (July 1994).
Record Transfer Fee paid: £30,000 to Alloa Ath for Jim Butter (1995).
Record Victory: 11-1 v Stranraer, Scottish Cup 1st rd, 16 January 1932.
Record Defeat: 2-10 v Dundee, Division I, 1 December 1962.
Most Capped Player: Billy Houliston, 3, Scotland.
Most League Appearances: 731: Allan Ball, 1963-82.
Most League Goals in Season (Individual): 37: Jimmy Gray, Division II, 1927-28.
Most Goals in Season: 43: Stephen Dobbie, 2018-19.
Most Goals Overall (Individual): 251: Jim Patterson, 1949-63.

QUEEN OF THE SOUTH – CINCH CHAMPIONSHIP 2021–22 LEAGUE RECORD

Match No.	*Date*	*Venue*	*Opponents*	*Result*		*H/T Score*	*Lg Pos.*	*Goalscorers*	*Attendance*
1	July 31	A	Partick Thistle	L	2-3	1-2	7	Gibson [10], Paton [74]	1534
2	Aug 7	H	Kilmarnock	L	0-1	0-0	10		1195
3	21	A	Greenock Morton	W	3-2	1-1	6	Roy [24], Jacobs (og) [55], Soares-Junior [72]	1429
4	28	H	Hamilton A	L	1-2	0-0	7	Paton [54]	1232
5	Sept 11	A	Raith R	W	1-0	1-0	5	Connelly [12]	1640
6	18	H	Arbroath	L	0-2	0-1	7		1174
7	25	A	Inverness CT	L	1-2	0-1	7	Connelly [74]	1884
8	Oct 2	H	Dunfermline Ath	W	1-0	0-0	6	Connelly [85]	1071
9	16	A	Ayr U	L	1-2	0-0	7	Connelly [68]	1663
10	23	H	Greenock Morton	D	0-0	0-0	7		1093
11	26	A	Hamilton A	L	0-1	0-0	8		942
12	30	A	Kilmarnock	L	0-4	0-1	8		3992
13	Nov 6	H	Raith R	D	1-1	0-0	9	Johnston [49]	964
14	13	A	Arbroath	D	1-1	0-0	9	Cameron [55]	1408
15	19	H	Inverness CT	L	1-2	0-1	9	Connelly [75]	942
16	Dec 4	H	Partick Thistle	D	0-0	0-0	10		1308
17	11	A	Dunfermline Ath	D	3-3	1-1	9	Cooper [3], Connelly [48], Cameron [65]	3425
18	18	H	Ayr U	W	3-0	2-0	7	East [9], Cameron [29], Todd [48]	997
19	Jan 2	H	Hamilton A	L	0-3	0-1	8		437
20	8	H	Kilmarnock	L	0-2	0-1	9		492
21	15	A	Inverness CT	D	2-2	1-0	9	Connelly [39], Roy [77]	479
22	29	H	Dunfermline Ath	L	0-2	0-2	10		947
23	Feb 1	A	Raith R	D	3-3	1-2	10	Liddle [17], Cooper [48], Gordon [85]	1005
24	12	A	Greenock Morton	L	1-2	0-0	10	East [59]	1445
25	19	H	Arbroath	D	0-0	0-0	10		1067
26	26	A	Ayr U	W	1-0	1-0	10	Fitzpatrick [32]	1875
27	Mar 5	H	Greenock Morton	W	3-0	2-0	9	Johnston [19], Fitzpatrick [31], Paton (pen) [52]	1217
28	8	A	Partick Thistle	L	0-1	0-0	9		2044
29	12	H	Raith R	L	0-1	0-1	9		1091
30	19	A	Kilmarnock	L	1-2	0-1	9	Roy [66]	4074
31	26	A	Hamilton A	L	0-1	0-0	10		1214
32	Apr 8	H	Partick Thistle	L	0-1	0-0	10		1099
33	16	A	Arbroath	L	1-5	1-2	10	Roy [12]	2413
34	19	H	Inverness CT	W	2-1	2-1	10	Todd [6], East [40]	631
35	23	H	Ayr U	D	1-1	0-0	10	East [80]	2271
36	29	A	Dunfermline Ath	W	2-1	0-1	10	Chalmers (og) [51], O'Connor [71]	5406

Final League Position: 10

Honours
League Champions: Division II 1950-51; Second Division 2001-02, 2012-13.
Runners-up: Division II 1932-33, 1961-62, 1974-75; Second Division 1980-81, 1985-86; Division Three 1924-25.
Scottish Cup Runners-up: 2007-08.
League Cup: semi-finals 1950-51, 1960-61.
League Challenge Cup Winners: 2002-03, 2012-13; *Runners-up:* 1997-98, 2010-11, 2021-22.

European: *UEFA Cup:* 2 matches (2008-09).

Club colours: Shirt: Royal blue with white trim. Shorts: White. Socks: Royal blue.

Goalscorers: *League (36):* Connelly 7, East 4, Roy 4, Cameron 3, Paton 3 (1 pen), Cooper 2, Fitzpatrick 2, Johnston 2, Todd 2, Gibson 1, Gordon 1, Liddle 1, O'Connor 1, Soares-Junior 1, own goals 2.
Scottish FA Cup (2): Paton 1, Soares-Junior 1.
Premier Sports Scottish League Cup (9): Roy 6, Paton 2, Soares-Junior 1.
SPFL Trust Trophy (9): Connelly 2, Paton 2 (1 pen), Roy 2, Fitzpatrick 1, Gibson 1 (1 pen), own goal 1.

Rae J 20	Nditi R 23 + 4	McKay P 16	East E 24 + 2	Paton R 23 + 11	McGrory C 23 + 1	Todd J 21 + 4	Gibson W 35	Connelly L 28 + 2	Soares-Junior R 15 + 7	Roy A 12 + 14	Cochrane H 14 + 7	Debayo J 21 + 2	Chima U — + 1	Cowie C — + 1	Joseph N 2 + 8	Brynn S 16	Johnston M 24 + 1	Liddle B 9 + 8	Fitzpatrick A 3 + 9	Cooper A 18 + 2	Cameron I 23	Gordon S 9 + 3	O'Connor D 15	Folarin S 1 + 6	McKechnie K 1 + 5	Match No.
1	2	3^{1}	4	5	6	7^{2}	8	9	10^{3}	11	12	13	14													1
1^{2}	3	2	4	8	7^{1}	6	5		11	10^{3}	13	9		12	14											2
	4	2		9	7^{1}	8	5	12	11	10	6^{2}	3			13	1										3
	4	2	13	9	6^{2}	12	5	8	11^{1}	10^{3}	7	3			14	1										4
	5	3	14	9	8		6	10^{3}	11		7^{1}	4			13	1	2^{2}	12								5
	2^{1}	3	8	9	7^{2}		5	10	11^{3}		6	4				1	14	13	12							6
	7	3	5	14	9^{1}		6	10	12			4			11	1	2^{2}	8^{3}	13							7
	7	3		14			6	9^{1}	10^{3}		8	4				1	2	13	12	5^{2}	11					8
	4	2					6	9^{2}	10^{1}	13	7	3				1	5		12	8	11					9
	3	2		14			6	9	11^{2}	13	7	4				1	5	12		8^{3}	10^{1}					10
	3	2		14		13	8	9^{2}	12	10^{1}	7	4				1	5	6			11^{3}					11
	4	3		11	12	8^{1}	9	10			7	5				1	2			6						12
	3	2		9	6^{2}		7	10^{3}		13	12	4				1	5^{1}	8		14	11					13
	3	2		9	6	13	7	11^{2}		12		4				1	5	8^{1}			10					14
	5	3		7	6^{3}		2	10		14	13	4^{1}				1	8	9^{2}		12	11					15
	4	3		6		9^{1}	2	10	12	13	8					1	7			5	11^{2}					16
	4		3	6	7	9	2	10		12						1	8			5^{1}	11					17
	6		4	7	8	10	3	9^{2}	12	14		5^{3}			13	1	2				11^{1}					18
1	6		4		8	7	3■	10^{3}	9^{2}	11^{1}		5			13			12	14	2						19
1	7		4	6^{2}	8^{1}	9		10	11^{3}	14		3					2	12	13	5						20
1	3		5	11^{2}	7		4^{1}	10		14		12					2	8	13	9		6^{3}				21
1	7^{1}		4	14		12	3	6		11^{2}							8	13		5		10	2	9^{3}		22
1	13		4	12		9^{1}	2	10^{3}									6	7^{2}	14	5	11	8	3			23
1			4	13	8	7^{2}	6										2^{1}	10^{3}	12	5	11	9	3	14		24
1			4	6^{2}	7	8	5	10^{1}		14							2		9^{3}		11	13	3		12	25
1	13		3	6^{2}	7	10	5			12							2		9^{1}		11	8	4			26
1			4	12		9	7^{1}		11^{2}	13		5					2		6^{3}		10	8	3		14	27
1			3	6		7	8		11^{2}	12		4					5			9^{1}	10		2	13		28
1			4	9^{2}		6	3		12	11^{3}							5			8	10	7^{1}	2	13	14	29
1	4		3	9^{2}		6	7	14		10	12				11^{3}		5	13				8^{1}	2			30
1	13		3	15		8	7	9^{3}		10^{4}	12							6■		4^{1}	11		2	14	5^{2}	31
1			4	6	7^{2}		2	9^{1}	13	10	8^{3}	5			14						11		3		12	32
1			4	6^{1}	7		2	9		10^{2}	13	5									11	8^{3}	3	12	14	33
1			4	13	7^{1}	6	2	9	11		8									5	10^{2}	12	3			34
1			4	12	8^{1}	9	2	6	11^{2}		7^{3}									5	10	13	3	14		35
1	12		4^{3}	6	8	9	2	10	14		7^{2}				13					5	11^{1}		3			36

QUEEN'S PARK

Year Formed: 1867. *Ground & Address:* Lesser Hampden, Mount Florida, Glasgow G42 9BA (2022-23 groundshare at Ochilview Park, Stenhousemuir). *Telephone:* 0141 632 1275. *Fax:* 0141 636 1612. *E-mail:* secretary@queensparkfc.co.uk
Website: queensparkfc.co.uk
Ground Capacity: 3,746 (seated: 626) (Ochilview Park). *Size of Pitch:* 101m × 66m.
President: David Hunter. *Chief Executive:* Leeann Dempster.
Head Coach: Owen Coyle. *Assistant Head Coach:* Sandy Stewart.
Club Nickname: 'The Spiders'.
Previous Grounds: 1st Hampden (Recreation Ground); (Titwood Park was used as an interim measure between 1st & 2nd Hampdens); 2nd Hampden (Cathkin); 3rd Hampden, Hampden Park; Falkirk Stadium (2020-21); Firhill (2021-22).
Record Attendance: 95,772 v Rangers, Scottish Cup 1st rd, 18 January 1930.
Record for Ground: 149,547 Scotland v England, 1937.
Record Transfer Fees: Not applicable due to amateur status from 1867-2019. No transfer fees paid or received since 2019.
Record Victory: 16-0 v St. Peter's, Scottish Cup 1st rd, 12 Sep 1885.
Record Defeat: 0-9 v Motherwell, Division I, 26 April 1930.
Most Capped Player: Walter Arnott, 14, Scotland.
Most League Appearances: 532: Ross Caven, 1982-2002.
Most League Goals in Season (Individual): 30: William Martin, Division I, 1937-38.
Most Goals Overall (Individual): 163: James B. McAlpine, 1919-33.

QUEEN'S PARK – CINCH LEAGUE ONE 2021–22 LEAGUE RECORD

Match No.	Date	Venue	Opponents	Result		H/T Score	Lg Pos.	Goalscorers	Attendance
1	July 31	A	East Fife	D	1-1	0-1	4	Fox [47]	320
2	Aug 7	H	Cove R	W	2-0	0-0	3	Murray [53], McHugh [54]	401
3	14	H	Dumbarton	W	3-0	1-0	1	Murray [24], Longridge [49], Brown [88]	613
4	21	A	Alloa Ath	D	1-1	0-0	3	Murray [56]	610
5	28	A	Falkirk	W	1-0	1-0	1	Murray [36]	4043
6	Sept 11	H	Airdrieonians	D	0-0	0-0	1		446
7	18	A	Clyde	D	2-2	0-1	1	Longridge [55], Gillespie (pen) [58]	651
8	25	H	Peterhead	W	3-2	1-0	1	Robson [5], Connell [76], Thomson [80]	546
9	Oct 3	H	Montrose	D	1-1	0-0	1	Smith [54]	596
10	16	A	Dumbarton	W	3-0	0-0	1	Gillespie [49], McHugh [74], Longstaff [79]	652
11	24	H	Alloa Ath	L	3-4	1-1	1	McHugh 2 [34, 49], Connell [88]	681
12	30	A	Cove R	D	3-3	2-1	1	McHugh [40], Longridge [45], Doyle [83]	531
13	Nov 6	H	East Fife	D	1-1	0-0	2	Kilday [86]	597
14	13	H	Clyde	D	0-0	0-0	3		839
15	20	A	Peterhead	L	1-2	1-0	4	Connell [10]	527
16	Dec 4	H	Falkirk	W	6-0	2-0	2	Longridge [4], Brown 2 [35, 65], Connell [68], Fox [77], Longstaff [84]	1119
17	18	A	Montrose	D	1-1	1-0	3	Longridge [26]	594
18	29	A	Airdrieonians	L	0-1	0-0	4		500
19	Jan 15	A	Alloa Ath	D	1-1	1-0	4	Smith [38]	484
20	22	A	Clyde	D	1-1	0-0	4	Doyle [65]	811
21	29	H	Airdrieonians	D	1-1	1-1	4	Fox [27]	832
22	Feb 5	A	Falkirk	D	1-1	1-0	4	Smith [15]	3427
23	8	H	Dumbarton	W	2-1	2-1	4	Longstaff 2 [7, 45]	428
24	12	A	Cove R	D	0-0	0-0	4		544
25	19	A	East Fife	D	1-1	1-1	4	Brown [20]	481
26	26	H	Montrose	L	0-1	0-1	4		680
27	Mar 1	H	Peterhead	W	2-1	1-0	4	McHugh [1], Thomson [46]	350
28	5	A	Dumbarton	W	3-0	2-0	4	Connell 2 [5, 36], Longridge [75]	584
29	12	H	Alloa Ath	D	1-1	0-0	4	Darcy [84]	750
30	19	A	Airdrieonians	L	0-2	0-2	4		883
31	26	H	Clyde	W	1-0	0-0	4	McHugh [59]	896
32	Apr 3	H	Cove R	D	1-1	0-0	4	McHugh [54]	723
33	9	H	East Fife	W	1-0	0-0	4	Connell (pen) [90]	580
34	16	A	Peterhead	L	1-2	0-1	4	Murray [64]	615
35	23	A	Montrose	L	1-2	1-0	4	Smith [1]	720
36	30	H	Falkirk	D	1-1	1-0	4	Quitongo [30]	922

Final League Position: 4

Honours
League Champions: Division II 1922-23; B Division 1955-56; Second Division 1980-81; Third Division 1999-2000; League Two: 2020-21.
Runners-up: Third Division 2011-12; League Two 2014-15.
Promoted via play-offs: 2021-22 (to Championship); 2015-16 (to League One); 2006-07 (to Second Division).
Scottish Cup Winners: 1874, 1875, 1876, 1880, 1881, 1882, 1884, 1886, 1890, 1893; *Runners-up:* 1892, 1900.
FA Cup Runners-up: 1884, 1885.
FA Charity Shield: 1899 (shared with Aston Villa).

Club colours: Shirt: Black and white thin hoops. Shorts: White. Socks: Black with white tops.

Goalscorers: *League (51):* McHugh 8, Connell 7 (1 pen), Longridge 6, Murray 5, Brown 4, Longstaff 4, Smith 4, Fox 3, Doyle 2, Gillespie 2 (1 pen), Thomson 2, Darcy 1, Kilday 1, Quitongo 1, Robson 1.
Scottish FA Cup (0).
Premier Sports Scottish League Cup (3): Biggar 1, Murray 1, own goal 1.
SPFL Trust Trophy (3): Gillespie 3 (3 pens).
Scottish League Play-offs (4): Murray 3 (1 pen), Smith 1.

Muir W 12	Doyle M 32 + 2	Morrison S 11 + 1	Fox C 29 + 2	Robson T 35	Gillespie G 19 + 2	Davidson J 9 + 9	Moore L 6 + 6	Brown L 29	Biggar C 2 + 2	Murray S 14 + 4	Longridge L 29 + 3	Thomson J 21 + 5	McHugh B 24 + 6	Lyon D 6 + 4	Nicol G — + 1	Kilday L 21 + 1	Smith C 21 + 8	Gillies M 2 + 4	Longstaff L 9 + 19	Connell L 22 + 5	Ferrie C 23	Herraghty J 1	Quitongo J 1 + 14	McBride C 5 + 9	Darcy R 4 + 6	Reid D — + 2	Grant P 8 + 2	Bruce C 1 + 1	Match No.
1	2	3	4	5	6	7^{2}	8	9	10^{1}	11	12	13																	1
1	2	3	4	5	6	7^{3}		9	10^{1}	11^{2}	8	12	13	14															2
1	2	3	4	5	7		8^{2}	9^{3}		11^{1}	10	6	12	13	14														3
1	2	3	4	5	7		8^{1}	9		11	10	6	12																4
1	2	3^{2}	12	5	7		8^{3}	9		11	10^{1}	6	14			4	13												5
1	3		12	5	6		8^{1}	9^{2}		11	10	7				4^{3}	14	2	13										6
1	3		4	5	7			9^{1}		11^{2}	10	6	8^{3}				13	2	14	12									7
1	2		4	5	8^{1}		14	9		11^{3}		7	10			3	6^{2}		13	12									8
1	2		4	5	12			7^{1}		11	14	6	10			3	9^{3}		13	8^{2}									9
1	2		4	5	6	14	12	8			10	7^{1}	11^{2}			3	9^{3}		13										10
1	2		4	5	8^{1}		12	7^{3}		13	9	6	11			3	10^{2}			14									11
1	2	4		5	13	14		6^{2}		11■	8	7	10^{1}			3			12	9^{3}									12
	2	4		5	7^{1}		10^{3}	8^{2}			9	6	11			3	12		14	13	1								13
	2	3		5	6			9			10		11			4	12		8^{1}	7	1								14
	2	3		5	7		14	6		10	11^{3}		12			4	13		9^{2}	8^{1}	1								15
		3^{1}	4	5		2^{3}		6			11	7	10			12	9	14	13	8^{2}	1								16
	2		4	5	6	3				10^{1}	11	7					9		12	8	1								17
		4^{1}	3	9	7	2						6■	10			5		12^{2}	11	8		1	13						18
	2		4	5	8			7^{1}	13				10			3	11		9^{2}	6	1		12						19
	2		4	5	8			7	12			14	10^{3}			3^{1}	11		9^{2}	6	1		13						20
	2^{2}		4	5	7	15	13	6^{1}			9^{3}	14	10			3	11		12	8^{4}	1								21
	2		4	5	6						10^{1}	12	14			3	9		8^{3}	7^{4}	1		15	11^{2}	13				22
	2		4	5				7			9^{2}	6	11			3	10^{1}		8^{3}		1		14	12	13				23
	2		4	5		12		7^{1}			9^{3}	6^{5}	11^{4}			3	10^{2}		8■		1		14	13	16	15			24
	2^{2}		4	5		15	14^{4}	7			9	6^{1}				3	10			12	1			11	8^{3}	13			25
	2		4	5				8			9^{3}	6^{4}				3^{2}	10		14	7	1		15	13	11^{1}		12		26
	2		4^{4}	5		13		9			8^{1}	6	11^{3}				10^{2}		15	7	1		12	14			3		27
	2^{3}			5		4		9^{2}			8	7	11^{1}	15			10^{4}	16	12	6^{5}	1		14		13		3		28
	2^{4}		4	5^{3}				6^{2}			8^{1}	7	11				10^{5}	12	13	9	1			15	14		3	16	29
	2		4			14		6			8^{5}		11^{3}	13			9		12	7	1		16	15	10^{2}		3^{1}	5^{4}	30
	2		4	5		14		6^{2}			8^{3}		11	7					12	9	1		13	10^{1}			3■		31
	2		4	5		13				14	8		10	6^{1}		3	9^{2}		12	7	1			11^{3}					32
	2		4	5						12	8^{4}		11	6		3^{1}	9^{3}		13	7	1		14	10^{2}			15		33
	2		4	5		6^{1}				11^{3}	8^{4}			7			13		12	9	1		14	15	10^{2}		3		34
	13		4	5		2				10^{1}	12		11	8^{4}			6^{3}		9^{5}	7^{2}	1		14	15	16		3		35
	16	14	4	5^{1}		2		9		15	10		11^{5}	6^{4}			12			7	1		8^{2}	13			3^{3}		36

RAITH ROVERS

Year Formed: 1883. *Ground & Address:* Stark's Park, Pratt St, Kirkcaldy KY1 1SA. *Telephone:* 01592 263514. *Fax:* 01592 642833. *E-mail:* info@raithrovers.net *Website:* raithrovers.net
Ground Capacity: 8,473 (all seated). *Size of Pitch:* 103m × 64m.
Chairman: Steven MacDonald. *Chief Executive:* Karen Macartney.
Manager: Ian Murray. *Assistant Manager:* Scott Agnew.
Club Nickname: 'Rovers'.
Previous Grounds: Robbie's Park.
Record Attendance: 31,306 v Hearts, Scottish Cup 2nd rd, 7 February 1953.
Record Transfer Fee received: £900,000 from Bolton W for Steve McAnespie (September 1995).
Record Transfer Fee paid: £225,000 to Airdrieonians for Paul Harvey (July 1996).
Record Victory: 10-1 v Coldstream, Scottish Cup 2nd rd, 13 February 1954.
Record Defeat: 2-11 v Morton, Division II, 18 March 1936.
Most Capped Player: David Morris, 6, Scotland.
Most League Appearances: 430: Willie McNaught, 1946-51.
Most League Goals in Season (Individual): 38: Norman Haywood, Division II, 1937-38.
Most Goals Overall (Individual): 154: Gordon Dalziel (League), 1987-94.

RAITH ROVERS – CINCH CHAMPIONSHIP 2021–22 LEAGUE RECORD

Match No.	Date	Venue	Opponents	Result		H/T Score	Lg Pos.	Goalscorers	Attendance
1	July 31	H	Hamilton A	D	4-4	2-0	3	Vaughan 2 (1 pen) [13 (p), 65], Zanatta [25], Connolly [52]	1569
2	Aug 7	A	Inverness CT	L	0-1	0-0	5		1675
3	Sept 7	A	Ayr U	W	2-0	2-0	5	Varian [14], Zanatta [25]	1204
4	11	H	Queen of the South	L	0-1	0-1	6		1640
5	18	A	Greenock Morton	W	1-0	1-0	5	Zanatta [33]	1420
6	26	H	Partick Thistle	W	3-2	1-0	4	Zanatta [22], Benedictus 2 (1 pen) [64 (p), 78]	1781
7	29	H	Dunfermline Ath	D	1-1	1-0	4	Zanatta [11]	2876
8	Oct 2	A	Kilmarnock	W	3-1	1-0	4	Dick [20], Poplatnik 2 [82, 90]	4008
9	16	H	Arbroath	W	2-1	2-0	2	Tait [3], Matthews [45]	1748
10	23	H	Inverness CT	D	1-1	0-0	3	Connolly [62]	1900
11	26	A	Dunfermline Ath	D	1-1	0-0	4	Spencer [88]	4450
12	30	H	Ayr U	W	2-1	2-0	4	Ross [12], Zanatta [27]	1602
13	Nov 6	A	Queen of the South	D	1-1	0-0	4	Connolly [72]	964
14	13	A	Hamilton A	W	3-0	3-0	2	MacDonald (og) [6], Ross 2 [34, 45]	1303
15	20	H	Greenock Morton	W	2-1	1-1	2	Connolly [31], Ross [67]	1640
16	Dec 4	A	Arbroath	D	0-0	0-0	2		1539
17	11	H	Kilmarnock	W	1-0	0-0	2	Zanatta (pen) [58]	2426
18	18	A	Partick Thistle	L	0-1	0-0	3		2229
19	26	A	Ayr U	L	0-2	0-1	3		472
20	Jan 2	H	Dunfermline Ath	D	0-0	0-0	3		500
21	8	A	Inverness CT	D	1-1	1-0	4	Ross [24]	478
22	15	H	Arbroath	L	1-2	1-0	4	Tumilty [42]	500
23	28	A	Greenock Morton	D	2-2	2-1	4	Gullan (pen) [42], Tumilty [45]	1404
24	Feb 1	H	Queen of the South	D	3-3	2-1	4	Zanatta [9], Connolly [13], Poplatnik [83]	1005
25	5	H	Hamilton A	D	0-0	0-0	4		1196
26	19	A	Kilmarnock	L	0-3	0-2	4		4080
27	26	H	Partick Thistle	D	0-0	0-0	4		1759
28	Mar 5	H	Ayr U	L	0-4	0-3	5		1513
29	12	A	Queen of the South	W	1-0	1-0	5	Poplatnik [21]	1091
30	19	H	Inverness CT	L	2-3	2-1	5	Connolly [13], Poplatnik [30]	1591
31	26	A	Arbroath	D	3-3	1-1	5	Poplatnik [31], Connolly [48], Varian [65]	2118
32	Apr 6	A	Dunfermline Ath	L	0-2	0-1	5		5199
33	9	H	Greenock Morton	L	0-1	0-0	5		1660
34	16	A	Partick Thistle	W	1-0	0-0	5	Poplatnik [90]	2644
35	23	A	Hamilton A	W	2-0	1-0	5	Williamson 2 [11, 58]	1478
36	29	H	Kilmarnock	D	1-1	1-0	5	Connolly [30]	3417

Final League Position: 5

Honours
League Champions: First Division 1992-93, 1994-95; League One 2019-20; Second Division 2002-03, 2008-09; Division II 1907-08, 1909-10 (shared with Leith Ath), 1937-38, 1948-49.
Runners-up: Division II 1908-09, 1926-27, 1966-67;. Second Division 1975-76, 1977-78, 1986-87; League One 2017-18.
Scottish Cup Runners-up: 1913.
League Cup Winners: 1994-95; *Runners-up:* 1948-49.
League Challenge Cup Winners: 2013-14, 2021-22.

European: *UEFA Cup:* 6 matches (1995-96).

Club colours: Shirt: Navy and white halves. Shorts: Navy. Socks: Navy with red tops.

Goalscorers: *League (44):* Connolly 8, Zanatta 8 (1 pen), Poplatnik 7, Ross 5, Benedictus 2 (1 pen), Tumilty 2, Varian 2, Vaughan 2 (1 pen), Williamson 2, Dick 1, Gullan 1 (1 pen), Matthews 1, Spencer 1, Tait 1, own goal 1.
Scottish FA Cup (5): Connolly 1, Matthews 1, Poplatnik 1, Ross 1, Stanton 1.
Premier Sports Scottish League Cup (7): Spencer 2, Vaughan 2, Zanatta 2, Varian 1.
SPFL Trust Trophy (9): Poplatnik 3, Connolly 1, Matthews 1, Riley-Snow 1, Ross 1, Tait 1, own goal 1.

MacDonald J 35	Tumilty R 33 + 2	Benedictus K 28 + 1	Berra C 26	Dick L 26 + 1	Connolly A 26 + 6	Spencer B 17 + 2	Tait D 19 + 1	Zanatta D 23 + 8	Vaughan L 1	Poplatnik M 14 + 17	Fotheringham K 1 + 4	Varian E 21 + 11	Riley-Snow B 2 + 7	Lang T 12 + 4	Matthews R 27 + 4	Keatings J — + 3	Arnott A 1 + 10	McKay D 5 + 3	Mitchell K — + 3	Ross E 19 + 6	Musonda F 16 + 2	Young G 1 + 3	Williamson B 13 + 1	Stanton S 17	Gullan J 7 + 2	Mackie S 5 + 2	Thomson R 1 + 1	*Match No.*
1	2	3	4	5	6	7	8	9^3	10^1	11^2	12	13	14															1
1	5	2	3	9	6		8^2	10^1		11^3		12	13	4	7	14												2
1	2	3	4	5	7^2		8^3	10^1			12	11	6■		9	13	14											3
1	2	3	4	5		7^2	8	11		12	9^3	10^1			6	14		13										4
1	2	3	4	5	12	7^1	8^3	10			13	11^2	6	14	9													5
1	2	3	4	5	8	6^1	9	10^2		13		11^3	12		7				14									6
1	2	3	4	5	9	8	7^1	11		12	13	10^2			6													7
1	8	3	4	5	12	6	9^1	10^2		13		11^3	14	2	7													8
1	2	4	3	5	9^2	8	7	11^1		13		10^3		14	6					12								9
1	2	4^1	3	5	9^2	8	7	11		12		10^3		13	6■					14								10
1	2		4	5	8^1	6	7	10		11			13	3					12	9^2								11
1	2		4	5	6	7^1	8	9		11^2		13	12	3			14			10^3								12
1	2		4		6	7	8^2	9		13		11		3	12					10^1	5							13
1	2	14	4		6	7^3	8	9		13		11^2		3	12					10^1	5							14
1	2		3		6	8	7	9^1		13		11		4	12					10^2	5							15
1	14	2	4	9		7^1	6	11^3				10		3	8		13			12	5^2							16
1	2		4	5	8		7^2	10^3		13		11	14	3	6		12			9^1								17
1	2	3	4■	5	9^3		7	11^1							6		8		13	10^2	12	14						18
1	2	4		5	6		7	9^1		12		11		3	8					10								19
1	2	4		5	14		13	12		11^1		10		3	6					9^3			7^2	8				20
1	2	3	4	5						13		9^1			6		14			10^2	7		8^3	11	12			21
1	2	4	3^3	5	13			12		14					6^1					9^2	7		8	11	10			22
1	5	4	3^3	8						13				12	6		14			11^2	2		7^1	9	10			23
1	2	4		5	6^1			9^2		14		13			7^3					10	3		12	8	11			24
1	2	4		5	6^4			15		13		14		3^3	7					10	12		9^2	8	11^1			25
1	5		3	4	13			14				12			8					10	2		6^1	7	11^2	9^3		26
1	2	4	3	5	8			10		12		11^2			9		13						6^1	7				27
1	2	3	4	5^2	9^1					10^4		15			7		14			11			6^3	8	13	12		28
1		4	3		6					10^3		9					12	14			2	13	7^2	8	11^1	5		29
1^4	13	4■	3^2	14	6					10^3		11			15					9^1	2		8■	7		5	12	30
	2			5	6			13		10^1		9			8			3		12				7	11^2	4	1	31
1	2	4			6	7^1		10^2		11		13			8			3		12	5			9				32
1	2	4			14	7^3		13		10		11^2			8			3		12	6	5^1		9				33
1	2	4			8	14		13		11		12			6			3		10^2	5		9^3	7^1				34
1	2	4			8	12		13		11^4		14			6			3		10^3	5^1		9^2	7		15		35
1	2	4			8	6		10^1		11^4		12					14	13			3^2	15	9^3	7		5		36

RANGERS

Year Formed: 1873. *Ground & Address:* Ibrox Stadium, 150 Edmiston Drive, Glasgow G51 2XD.
Telephone: 0871 702 1972. *Fax:* 0870 600 1978. *Website:* rangers.co.uk
Ground Capacity: 51,082 (all seated). *Size of Pitch:* 105m × 68m.
Chairman: Douglas Park. *Deputy Chairman:* John Bennett.
Manager: Giovanni van Bronckhorst. *Assistant Manager:* Dave Vos.
Club Nickname: 'The Gers'; 'The Teddy Bears'.
Previous Grounds: Flesher's Haugh, Burnbank, Kinning Park, Old Ibrox.
Record Attendance: 118,567 v Celtic, Division I, 2 January 1939.
Record Transfer Fee received: £12,000,000 from Everton for Nathan Patterson (January 2022).
Record Transfer Fee paid: £12,000,000 to Chelsea for Tore Andre Flo (November 2000).
Record Victory: 13-0 v Possilpark, Scottish Cup 1st rd, 6 October 1877; v Uddingston, Scottish Cup 3rd rd, 10 November 1877; v Kelvinside Athletic, Scottish Cup 2nd rd, 28 September 1889.
Record Defeat: 1-7 v Celtic, League Cup Final, 19 October 1957.
Most Capped Player: Ally McCoist, 61, Scotland. *Most League Appearances:* 496: John Greig, 1962-78.
Most League Goals in Season (Individual): 44: Sam English, Division I, 1931-32.
Most Goals Overall (Individual): 355: Ally McCoist; 1985-98.

Honours
League Champions: (55 times) Division I 1890-91 (shared with Dumbarton), 1898-99, 1899-1900, 1900-01, 1901-02, 1910-11, 1911-12, 1912-13, 1917-18, 1919-20, 1920-21, 1922-23, 1923-24, 1924-25, 1926-27, 1927-28, 1928-29, 1929-30, 1930-31, 1932-33, 1933-34, 1934-35, 1936-37, 1938-39, 1946-47, 1948-49, 1949-50, 1952-53, 1955-56, 1956-57, 1958-59, 1960-61, 1962-63, 1963-64, 1974-75. Premier Division: 1975-76, 1977-78, 1986-87, 1988-89, 1989-90, 1990-91, 1991-92, 1992-93, 1993-94, 1994-95, 1995-96, 1996-97, 1998-99, 1999-2000, 2002-03, 2004-05, 2008-09, 2009-10, 2010-11; Premiership: 2020-21. *Runners-up, tier 1:* 33 times. Championship 2015-16. League One 2013-14. Third Division 2012-13.
Scottish Cup Winners: (34 times) 1894, 1897, 1898, 1903, 1928, 1930, 1932, 1934, 1935, 1936, 1948, 1949, 1950, 1953, 1960, 1962, 1963, 1964, 1966, 1973, 1976, 1978, 1979, 1981, 1992, 1993, 1996, 1999, 2000, 2002, 2003, 2008, 2009, 2022; *Runners-up:* 18 times.

RANGERS – CINCH PREMIERSHIP 2021–22 LEAGUE RECORD

Match No.	Date	Venue	Opponents	Result		H/T Score	Lg Pos.	Goalscorers	Attendance
1	July 31	H	Livingston	W	3-0	1-0	1	Hagi 8, Wright, S 78, Roofe 90	23,000
2	Aug 7	A	Dundee U	L	0-1	0-0	2		4600
3	22	A	Ross Co	W	4-2	2-1	5	Aribo 15, Goldson 19, Morelos 56, Arfield 84	6450
4	29	H	Celtic	W	1-0	0-0	3	Helander 66	49,402
5	Sept 11	A	St Johnstone	W	2-1	0-0	1	Roofe (pen) 58, Tavernier 79	7319
6	19	H	Motherwell	D	1-1	1-0	1	Sakala 12	48,961
7	25	A	Dundee	W	1-0	1-0	1	Aribo 16	8574
8	Oct 3	H	Hibernian	W	2-1	0-1	1	Roofe 60, Morelos 78	49,125
9	16	H	Hearts	D	1-1	1-0	1	Lundstram 40	49,650
10	24	A	St Mirren	W	2-1	2-1	1	Roofe (pen) 42, Morelos 43	6100
11	27	H	Aberdeen	D	2-2	1-2	1	Morelos 20, Tavernier (pen) 81	49,760
12	31	A	Motherwell	W	6-1	2-1	1	Tavernier 43, Sakala 3 45, 63, 85, Kamara 75, Roofe 90	7740
13	Nov 7	H	Ross Co	W	4-2	2-1	1	Aribo 19, Kent 30, Bacuna 49, Iacovitti (og) 60	49,222
14	28	A	Livingston	W	3-1	2-1	1	Arfield 8, Aribo 16, Sakala 78	8825
15	Dec 1	A	Hibernian	W	1-0	0-0	1	Roofe (pen) 85	17,209
16	4	H	Dundee	W	3-0	1-0	1	Aribo 36, Sweeney (og) 55, Morelos 70	49,628
17	12	A	Hearts	W	2-0	2-0	1	Morelos 9, Aribo 13	18,593
18	15	H	St Johnstone	W	2-0	1-0	1	Morelos 43, Kent 49	47,561
19	18	H	Dundee U	W	1-0	0-0	1	Tavernier (pen) 71	49,252
20	26	H	St Mirren	W	2-0	2-0	1	Wright, S 14, Morelos 26	500
21	Jan 18	A	Aberdeen	D	1-1	1-0	1	Hagi 20	16,731
22	26	H	Livingston	W	1-0	0-0	1	Arfield 75	48,343
23	29	A	Ross Co	D	3-3	1-2	1	Diallo 5, Tavernier 49, Goldson 72	6401
24	Feb 2	A	Celtic	L	0-3	0-3	2		59,077
25	6	H	Hearts	W	5-0	1-0	2	Morelos 2 11, 64, Kamara 72, Arfield 75, Sakala 84	49,708
26	9	H	Hibernian	W	2-0	1-0	2	Tavernier (pen) 5, Morelos 57	49,700
27	20	A	Dundee U	D	1-1	0-1	2	Aribo 76	9993
28	27	H	Motherwell	D	2-2	2-0	2	Mugabi (og) 22, Sakala 24	49,318
29	Mar 2	A	St Johnstone	W	1-0	1-0	2	Kamara 3	6869
30	5	H	Aberdeen	W	1-0	0-0	2	Roofe 81	50,010
31	20	A	Dundee	W	2-1	0-1	2	Ramsey 64, Goldson 86	7669
32	Apr 3	H	Celtic	L	1-2	1-2	2	Ramsey 3	50,023
33	10	A	St Mirren	W	4-0	2-0	2	Roofe 3 2, 45, 50, Aribo 76	6583
34	23	A	Motherwell	W	3-1	1-1	2	Kelly (og) 14, Wright, S 47, Tavernier (pen) 62	8036
35	May 1	A	Celtic	D	1-1	0-1	2	Sakala 67	58,247
36	8	H	Dundee U	W	2-0	0-0	2	Tavernier (pen) 55, Diallo 78	49,340
37	11	H	Ross Co	W	4-1	2-0	2	Wright, S 13, Tavernier (pen) 29, Sakala 82, Diallo 90	48,474
38	14	A	Hearts	W	3-1	2-1	2	Itten 32, Lowry 45, McKinnon 81	16,969

Final League Position: 2

League Cup Winners: (27 times) 1946-47, 1948-49, 1960-61, 1961-62, 1963-64, 1964-65, 1970-71, 1975-76, 1977-78, 1978-79, 1981-82, 1983-84, 1984-85, 1986-87, 1987-88, 1988-89, 1990-91, 1992-93, 1993-94, 1996-97, 1998-99, 2001-02, 2002-03, 2004-05, 2007-08, 2009-10, 2010-11; *Runners-up:* 8 times.
League Challenge Cup Winners: 2015-16; *Runners-up:* 2013-14.

European: *European Cup:* 163 matches (1956-57, 1957-58, 1959-60 semi-finals, 1961-62, 1963-64, 1964-65, 1975-76, 1976-77, 1978-79, 1987-88, 1989-90, 1990-91, 1991-92, 1992-93 final pool, 1993-94, 1994-95, 1995-96; 1996-97, 1997-98, 1999-2000, 2000-01, 2001-02, 2003-04, 2004-05, 2005-06, 2007-08, 2008-09, 2009-10, 2010-11, 2011-12, 2021-22).
Cup Winners' Cup: 54 matches (1960-61 runners-up, 1962-63, 1966-67 runners-up, 1969-70, 1971-72 winners, 1973-74, 1977-78, 1979-80, 1981-82, 1983-84).
UEFA Cup: 88 matches (*Fairs Cup:* 1967-68, 1968-69 semi-finals, 1970-71. *UEFA Cup:* 1982-83, 1984-85, 1985-86, 1986-87, 1988-89, 1997-98, 1998-99, 1999-2000, 2000-01, 2001-02, 2002-03, 2004-05, 2006-07, 2007-08 runners-up). *Europa League:* 48 matches (2010-11, 2011-12, 2017-18, 2019-20, 2020-21, 2021-22 runners-up).

Club colours: Shirt: Royal blue with red and white trim. Shorts: White. Socks: Black with red tops.

Goalscorers: *League (80):* Morelos 11, Roofe 10 (3 pens), Sakala 9, Tavernier 9 (6 pens), Aribo 8, Arfield 4, Wright S 4, Diallo 3, Goldson 3, Kamara 3, Hagi 2, Kent 2, Ramsey 2, Bacuna 1, Helander 1, Itten 1, Lowry 1, Lundstram 1, McKinnon 1, own goals 4. *Scottish FA Cup (14):* Sakala 3, Tavernier 2 (2 pens), Arfield 1, Goldson 1, Helander 1, Itten 1, Jack 1, Lowry 1, Roofe 1, Wright S 1, own goal 1. *Premier Sports Scottish League Cup (8):* Roofe 3 (1 pen), Arfield 1, Hagi 1, Lundstram 1, Morelos 1, Wright S 1. *SPFL Trust Trophy (7):* Alegria 3, Fraser 1, Hastie 1, Lowry 1, Weston 1. *UEFA Champions League (2):* Davis 1, Morelos 1. *UEFA Europa League (24):* Tavernier 7 (4 pens), Morelos 5, Balogun 2, Lundstram 2, Roofe 2, Aribo 1, Hagi 1, Kamara 1, Kent 1, Wright S 1, own goal 1.

McLaughlin J 8	Tavernier J 35	Goldson C 36	Balogun L 17 + 4	Bassey C 28 + 1	Kamara G 28 + 3	Davis S 13 + 5	Aribo J 31 + 3	Hagi I 15	Sakala F 13 + 17	Kent R 26	Wright S 9 + 10	Lundstram J 18 + 9	Roofe K 9 + 12	Helander F 6	Barisic B 22 + 1	Morelos A 25 + 1	Itten C 3 + 3	Defoe J — + 2	McGregor A 29	Arfield S 18 + 11	McCrorie R 1	Simpson J 1 + 3	Bacuna J 1 + 5	Patterson N 2 + 4	Jack R 4 + 5	Sands J 5 + 2	Lowry A 3 + 1	Diallo A 4 + 6	Ramsey A 5 + 2	King L 2 + 2	Devine A 1 + 1	McCann C — + 2	McKinnon C — + 1	McCausland R — + 1	Weston T — + 1	*Match No.*
1	2	3	4	5	6	7	8^{2}	9^{3}	10^{1}	11	12	13	14																							1
1	2	3			8	7	9			11^{3}	12	6^{2}		4	5	10^{1}	13	14																		2
	2	3	4	5	8^{2}	7	6^{3}	9^{1}		11		12	14			10			1	13																3
		3	2		8	7	6		13	11^{3}		12	9^{2}	4	5	10^{1}				14	1															4
1	2		3	5	8	7	6		13	11^{2}		14	9	4^{1}		10^{3}						12														5
	2	3			8	7^{1}	6		10^{2}		11^{3}		9		5	12			1	14		4	13													6
1	2	3	4	5	6		8	9^{1}	12		13	7	11^{2}			10^{3}							14													7
		3	4		7^{1}	14	9^{3}	8			10^{2}	6	12		5	11			1				13	2												8
	2	3	4		7	14	9^{2}	8^{3}			10^{1}	6	13		5	11			1				12													9
1	2	3	4			7	6	9^{3}	12			8	11^{1}		5	10^{2}				13				14												10
1	2	3	4	5	8		6^{2}	11	13		14	7^{3}	9^{1}			10				12																11
	2	3	4^{1}	5	8	7	9^{2}		11		14		12			10^{3}			1	6		13														12
	2	3	4^{2}	5			6	11	10	9^{3}		7^{1}	12						1				8	14	13											13
	2	3		4	6		7	8^{1}	12	10^{2}					5	11^{3}		14	1	9				13												14
	2	3		4	7	6^{2}	8	9		10^{1}		14	12		5	11^{3}			1	13																15
	2	3		4	8^{2}		6^{3}	9^{1}	11		12				5	10			1	7			14		13											16
	2	3		4	6		7		10^{1}	8	12	13			5	11^{2}			1	9																17
	2	3		4	7		6	9	12	11^{1}					5^{2}	10			1	8				13												18
	2	3		4	8		13	9		11	12	7^{1}				10			1	6^{2}				5												19
	2	3		4	7		8	6^{2}	12	11^{1}	9				5	10			1	13																20
	2	3		4	7			6^{1}	13	11▮	9^{3}	12			5	10^{2}	14		1							8										21
	2	3		4	7				10		8^{2}		12		5		11^{3}		1	13					14	6^{1}	9									22
	2	3		4	7		8		13	11		14	12		5		10^{3}		1	6^{1}								9^{2}								23
	2	3	14	4	7^{3}		8		13	11			10		5^{2}				1	6					12			9^{1}								24
	2	3	4	5	12	15	10^{2}		14	9^{3}		7^{1}				11			1	8^{4}					6^{5}			16	13							25
	2	3	4^{1}	5	6		10^{3}		14	9		7			12	11			1	8^{2}									13							26
	2	3		5			9		12	10		7		4^{2}		11			1	8^{1}					6			13								27
	2	3		5	7		8		9^{1}	11		4	12			10			1	6																28
	2	3	4	5	7		9			10		6				11			1	8																29
	2	3	12	4	7		9		8^{3}	10		15	14		5^{1}	11^{2}			1	13					6^{4}											30
	2	3	16	5	15		13		12	10		7	14	4^{4}		11^{1}			1	9^{2}						6^{3}			8^{5}							31
	2	3	4	5			8		12	10		6	11						1	13					7^{2}				9^{1}							32
	2	3				12	8		9	11^{3}	15	7^{1}	10^{5}	4^{2}	5				1							14		16	6^{4}	13						33
	2	3	4▮	12	7^{3}	6^{4}	14		11		8^{2}				5		15		1	9^{1}						13		10^{5}		16						34
	2	3		4		7^{3}	11^{1}		8	10	13	6			5				1	9^{2}					12			14								35
1	2^{2}	3			16	7			10		8^{5}				5^{1}					11^{3}						6	13	12	9^{4}	4	14	15				36
	2	3	13	4	8	14	10^{2}		15	11^{5}	9^{3}	6^{4}			5^{1}				1	16							7	12								37
1			4^{5}			6^{4}											10			8^{2}		15				3	11	9^{1}	7^{3}	5	2	12	13	14	16	38

ROSS COUNTY

Year Formed: 1929. *Ground & Address:* The Global Energy Stadium, Victoria Park, Dingwall IV15 9QZ. *Telephone:* 01349 860860. *Fax:* 01349 866277. *E-mail:* info@rosscountyfootballclub.co.uk
Website: rosscountyfootballclub.co.uk
Ground Capacity: 6,700 (all seated). *Size of Ground:* 105 × 68m.
Chairman: Roy MacGregor. *Chief Executive:* Steven Ferguson.
Manager: Malky Mackay. *Assistant Manager:* Don Cowie.
Club Nickname: 'The Staggies'.
Record Attendance: 6,110 v Celtic, Premier League, 18 August 2012.
Record Transfer Fee received: £500,000 from Burton Albion for Liam Boyce (June 2017).
Record Transfer Fee paid: £100,000 to Inverness CT for Ross Draper (August 2017).
Record Victory: 11-0 v St Cuthbert Wanderers, Scottish Cup 1st rd, 11 December 1993.
Record Defeat: 0-7 v Kilmarnock, Scottish Cup 3rd rd, 17 February 1962.
Most League Appearances: 353: Michael Gardyne, 2006-07, 2008-12, 2014-21.
Most League Goals in Season: 24: Andrew Barrowman, 2007-08.
Most League Goals (Overall): 48: Liam Boyce, 2014-17; Micheal Gardyne, 2006-07, 2008-12, 2014-21.

ROSS COUNTY – CINCH PREMIERSHIP 2021–22 LEAGUE RECORD

Match No.	*Date*	*Venue*	*Opponents*	*Result*		*H/T Score*	*Lg Pos.*	*Goalscorers*	*Attendance*
1	July 31	H	St Johnstone	D	0-0	0-0	5		1990
2	Aug 8	A	Hibernian	L	0-3	0-3	10		5600
3	22	H	Rangers	L	2-4	1-2	10	Clarke 40, White (pen) 77	6450
4	29	A	Aberdeen	D	1-1	1-0	9	Charles-Cook 33	14,434
5	Sept 11	A	Celtic	L	0-3	0-0	11		56,511
6	18	H	Hearts	D	2-2	2-1	11	Spittal 2 11, 45	3802
7	25	A	Motherwell	L	1-2	1-1	11	Charles-Cook 39	4477
8	Oct 2	A	Dundee U	L	0-1	0-1	11		6548
9	16	H	St Mirren	L	2-3	1-3	12	Spittal 37, Iacovitti 66	3882
10	23	H	Livingston	L	2-3	1-2	12	Clarke 7, Callachan (pen) 67	2566
11	27	A	Dundee	W	5-0	4-0	12	Clarke 18, Callachan 27, Hungbo 34, Charles-Cook 2 40, 71	4883
12	Nov 7	A	Rangers	L	2-4	1-2	12	Hungbo 5, White 87	49,222
13	24	H	Hibernian	W	1-0	0-0	12	Spittal 72	3316
14	27	H	Dundee U	D	1-1	0-0	12	Baldwin 90	3214
15	Dec 1	A	St Mirren	D	0-0	0-0	12		3806
16	11	H	Dundee	W	3-2	1-2	11	Samuel, D 23, Mullen (og) 64, Charles-Cook 78	3122
17	15	H	Celtic	L	1-2	0-1	11	Baldwin 57	5592
18	18	A	Livingston	D	1-1	1-0	11	Cancola 45	2554
19	22	A	St Johnstone	W	2-1	1-1	10	Charles-Cook 16, Callachan 69	2249
20	26	A	Hearts	L	1-2	0-2	10	White 72	0
21	Jan 18	H	Motherwell	W	3-1	1-0	10	Johansen (og) 45, Charles-Cook 2 (1 pen) 72, 79 (p)	2523
22	26	A	Dundee U	L	1-2	0-0	10	Charles-Cook 53	4519
23	29	H	Rangers	D	3-3	2-1	10	White 25, Charles-Cook 29, Wright 90	6401
24	Feb 1	H	Aberdeen	D	1-1	0-0	10	Callachan 53	3343
25	5	A	Dundee	W	2-1	1-1	10	Hungbo 45, Charles-Cook 80	4621
26	9	H	Livingston	D	1-1	0-0	10	Ramsay 90	2224
27	19	A	Hibernian	L	0-2	0-0	10		14,149
28	26	H	St Johnstone	W	3-1	1-1	10	Charles-Cook 2 35, 53, Hungbo 66	3161
29	Mar 2	A	Motherwell	W	1-0	1-0	8	Hungbo (pen) 15	3587
30	5	H	St Mirren	W	1-0	0-0	6	Hungbo (pen) 49	3229
31	19	A	Celtic	L	0-4	0-3	7		58,432
32	Apr 2	H	Hearts	D	1-1	1-1	7	Iacovitti 31	5210
33	9	A	Aberdeen	W	1-0	0-0	5	Hungbo (pen) 86	15,162
34	24	H	Celtic	L	0-2	0-1	5		6698
35	30	A	Hearts	D	0-0	0-0	5		16,699
36	May 7	H	Motherwell	L	0-1	0-0	6		3067
37	11	A	Rangers	L	1-4	0-2	6	White 72	48,474
38	14	H	Dundee U	L	1-2	0-0	6	Spittal 65	5165

Final League Position: 6

Honours
League Champions: First Division 2011-12; Championship 2018-19; Second Division 2007-08; Third Division 1998-99.
Scottish Cup Runners-up: 2010.
League Cup Winners: 2015-16.
League Challenge Cup Winners: 2006-07, 2010-11, 2018-19; *Runners-up:* 2004-05, 2008-09.

Club colours: Shirt: Navy blue with red and white pinstripes. Shorts: Navy blue. Socks: Navy blue.

Goalscorers: *League (47):* Charles-Cook 13 (1 pen), Hungbo 7 (3 pens), Spittal 5, White 5 (1 pen), Callachan 4 (1 pen), Clarke 3, Baldwin 2, Iacovitti 2, Cancola 1, Ramsay 1, Samuel D 1, Wright 1, own goals 2.
Scottish FA Cup (0).
Premier Sports Scottish League Cup (5): Iacovitti 2, Spittal 2, White 1.

Laidlaw R 20	Donaldson C 2	Watson K 13 + 11	Iacovitti A 31	Randall C 27 + 2	Callachan R 33 + 2	Tillson J 29 + 3	Spittal B 27 + 7	Charles-Cook R 36 + 1	White J 31 + 7	Samuel D 9 + 19	Shaw O — + 1	Paton H 23 + 8	Burroughs J 7 + 10	Clarke H 15 + 2	Cancola D 12 + 6	Paton B 6 + 4	Hungbo J 21 + 12	Baldwin J 27 + 3	Samuel A 3 + 2	Maynard-Brewer A 17	Robertson A — + 3	Vokins J 19 + 1	Drysdale D 3 + 2	Ramsay K 5 + 3	Wright M — + 4	Mackinnon A 1 + 2	Munro R 1	Sims J — + 1	Match No.
1	2	3	4	5	6	7	8[1]	9	10	11[2]	12	13																	1
1	3[1]	4	5	2	10[3]	8	9	6	11			7[2]	12	13	14														2
1			4	2	8	7	10	9[1]	11	13				3	6[2]	5	12												3
1		14	4	2[1]	9	6	10	8[3]	11			12		3	7[2]	5		13											4
1		14			9	7	6	10	11[1]	13		12	2[3]	3		5		4	8[2]										5
		13	3		9[3]	7	6[1]	11[2]	10			4	5			8	14	2		1	12								6
		5[3]	3		9	7	11	8[2]	10			6[1]	4	13			12	2		1	14								7
			4		13	6[3]	8	9[2]	12	14		7	5	2			11	3	10[1]	1									8
			4		8		9	11	13			7	5[2]	2	6[3]	12	14	3	10[1]	1									9
			4		6		9[1]	10	11[2]	13		7		2		5	8	3		1	12								10
			4	5[3]	9	6	12	10[2]	11			7	14	2		13	8[1]	3		1									11
			4	5	7[1]	8	12	10	13	14		9	11[2]	2			6[3]	3		1									12
		14	4	5	10	7[3]	13	9[2]	11[1]			8		2	12		6	3		1									13
		12	4[2]	5		6[3]	8	10[1]	11	14		9		2■	7		13	3		1									14
		12	4[2]	2	9[1]	14	10		13	11[3]		6			7		8	3		1		5							15
		3		5[1]	9		14	10	13	11		6[3]		2	7[2]		8	4		1		12							16
		3			9[2]	7	11	10	13	12		6[1]	14	2			8[3]	4		1		5							17
		14		2	12	7	9[2]	6[3]	11	10[1]			13	3	8			4		1		5							18
		3[2]		12	9	14	6	10[1]	11	13				2	7[3]		8	4		1		5							19
1				2			6	10	11	9[1]			12	3	7[2]		8	4	13			5							20
			4	2	9	13■	7	10[1]	11[2]	12			15		6[3]		8[4]			1		5	3	14					21
			4	2	8		6[2]	10	11	7[3]		9[1]					13	12		1		5	3	14					22
		13	4		9[3]	6		8	11[1]	12		7[2]	15				10	3		1		5[4]		2	14				23
1		3	4	12	8	7		6	11	10		13					9[2]					5		2[1]					24
1		3	4	2	9	8	6[2]	10[1]	11	12		13					7[3]					5	14						25
1		3	4[2]	2[1]	9	7[3]	6	8	11			12					10[4]	13				5		14	15				26
1			4	2	10	7[2]		8	11	9[1]		6					12	3	13			5							27
1		2	4	5	6	7		10[1]	11	13		9[2]	12				8[3]	3								14			28
1			4	5	6	7	12	10[1]	11	14		9[3]	13				8[2]	3						2					29
1			4	5	6	7	12	10[2]	11	14		9[1]					8[3]	3					13	2					30
1		12	4	5	7	6[4]	13	10[3]	11[2]			9[5]	14		16	15	8[1]	3						2■					31
1			4	2	6	7	8	10[1]	11	12		9[2]					13	3				5							32
1		15	4	2	6	7	8[4]	10[3]	11[2]	12		9[1]			13		14	3				5							33
1		3	4	2	7	6[2]	8	10[3]	11	14		9[1]			13		12					5							34
1		3	4	2	9[2]	7	8	10[3]	11[1]	13		14			6		12					5							35
1		13	4	2[1]	9	7[2]	8	10	11	14					6[3]		12	3				5[4]			15				36
1		2	4		10[2]	8	7[4]	15	13	11			9[1]		12[5]	14	6[3]	3				5				16			37
				2[1]			9	10[3]	11			13				6	8	4				5	3		14	7[2]	1	12	38

ST JOHNSTONE

Year Formed: 1884. *Ground & Address:* McDiarmid Park, Crieff Road, Perth PH1 2SJ. *Telephone:* 01738 459090. *Fax:* 01738 625 771. *E-mail:* enquiries@perthsaints.co.uk *Website:* perthstjohnstonefc.co.uk
Ground Capacity: 10,673 (all seated). *Size of Pitch:* 105m × 68m.
Chairman: Steve Brown. *Vice-Chairman:* Charlie Fraser.
Manager: Callum Davidson. *Assistant Manager:* Alec Cleland.
Club Nickname: 'Saints'.
Previous Grounds: Recreation Grounds; Muirton Park.
Record Attendance: 29,972 v Dundee, Scottish Cup 2nd rd, 10 February 1951 (Muirton Park): 10,545 v Dundee, Premier Division, 23 May 1999 (McDiarmid Park).
Record Transfer Fee received: £1,750,000 from Blackburn R for Callum Davidson (March 1998).
Record Transfer Fee paid: £400,000 to Dundee for Billy Dodds (January 1994).
Record Victory: 9-0 v Albion R, League Cup, 9 March 1946.
Record Defeat: 1-10 v Third Lanark, Scottish Cup 1st rd, 24 January 1903.
Most Capped Player: Nick Dasovic, 26, Canada.
Most League Appearances: 362: Steven Anderson, 2004-19.
Most League Goals in Season (Individual): 36: Jimmy Benson, Division II, 1931-32.
Most Goals Overall (Individual): 140: John Brogan, 1977-83.

ST JOHNSTONE – CINCH PREMIERSHIP 2021–22 LEAGUE RECORD

Match No.	*Date*	*Venue*	*Opponents*	*Result*		*H/T Score*	*Lg Pos.*	*Goalscorers*	*Attendance*
1	July 31	A	Ross Co	D	0-0	0-0	5		1990
2	Aug 8	H	Motherwell	D	1-1	1-0	7	O'Donnell, S (og) 34	2169
3	22	H	Dundee U	L	0-1	0-0	8		5716
4	29	A	St Mirren	D	0-0	0-0	8		4326
5	Sept 11	H	Rangers	L	1-2	0-0	8	O'Halloran 51	7319
6	18	A	Aberdeen	W	1-0	0-0	8	May 84	13,007
7	26	A	Hibernian	L	0-1	0-0	9		13,263
8	Oct 2	H	Dundee	W	3-1	2-0	8	Kane 2 31, 39, May 46	5097
9	16	H	Livingston	L	0-3	0-2	8		4274
10	23	A	Celtic	L	0-2	0-1	10		57,434
11	27	H	Hearts	D	1-1	1-1	10	Gordon 11	6083
12	30	A	Dundee U	W	1-0	1-0	9	Crawford 17	7580
13	Nov 6	H	St Mirren	D	0-0	0-0	9		3482
14	27	H	Hibernian	L	1-2	1-0	9	Porteous (og) 40	3362
15	Dec 1	A	Dundee	L	0-1	0-1	10		5196
16	11	H	Aberdeen	L	0-1	0-0	12		3791
17	15	A	Rangers	L	0-2	0-1	12		47,561
18	18	A	Motherwell	L	0-2	0-1	12		3920
19	22	H	Ross Co	L	1-2	1-1	12	Butterfield 19	2249
20	26	H	Celtic	L	1-3	0-2	12	Kane 69	500
21	Jan 18	A	Hearts	L	0-2	0-0	12		16,589
22	26	H	Dundee	D	0-0	0-0	12		4135
23	Feb 1	A	Livingston	W	2-1	1-1	11	Hendry 11, Crawford 90	1319
24	5	H	Dundee U	D	0-0	0-0	11		5005
25	9	A	St Mirren	L	1-2	1-1	12	Hendry (pen) 28	4286
26	15	A	Aberdeen	D	1-1	1-0	12	Hendry 6	12,973
27	19	H	Hearts	W	2-1	1-1	11	Crawford 1, McCart 56	4409
28	26	A	Ross Co	L	1-3	1-1	11	Hendry 24	3161
29	Mar 2	H	Rangers	L	0-1	0-1	11		6869
30	5	A	Hibernian	D	0-0	0-0	11		19,585
31	19	H	Motherwell	W	2-1	1-1	11	Hendry 2 21, 90	3772
32	Apr 2	H	Livingston	W	1-0	1-0	11	Hendry (pen) 3	3321
33	9	A	Celtic	L	0-7	0-3	11		58,321
34	23	A	Dundee	D	1-1	0-1	11	Rooney 68	7937
35	30	H	St Mirren	L	0-1	0-0	11		4253
36	May 7	A	Livingston	D	1-1	0-0	11	Middleton 76	1499
37	11	H	Aberdeen	W	1-0	1-0	11	Hendry 17	3421
38	15	A	Hibernian	L	0-4	0-1	11		14,233

Final League Position: 11

Honours
League Champions: First Division 1982-83, 1989-90, 1996-97, 2008-09; Division II 1923-24, 1959-60, 1962-63.
Runners-up: Division II 1931-32; First Division 2005-06, 2006-07; Second Division 1987-88.
Scottish Cup Winners: 2014, 2021.
League Cup Winners: 2020-21; *Runners-up:* 1969-70, 1998-99.
League Challenge Cup Winners: 2007-08; *Runners-up:* 1996-97.

European: *UEFA Cup:* 10 matches (1971-72, 1999-2000). *Europa League:* 16 matches (2012-13, 2013-14, 2014-15, 2015-16, 2017-18, 2021-22). *Europa Conference League:* 2 matches (2021-22).

Club colours: Shirt: Blue with white trim. Shorts: White with blue trim. Socks: Blue with white tops.

Goalscorers: *League (24):* Hendry 8 (2 pens), Crawford 3, Kane 3, May 2, Butterfield 1, Gordon 1, McCart 1, Middleton 1, O'Halloran 1, Rooney 1, own goals 2.
Scottish FA Cup (0).
Premier Sports Scottish League Cup (4): Crawford 1, McCart 1, Middleton 1, Rooney 1.
SPFL Trust Trophy (0).
Scottish League Play-offs (6): Rooney 2, Hallberg 1, Hendry 1, MacPherson 1, May 1.
UEFA Europa League (3): Kerr 2 (1 pen), O'Halloran 1.
UEFA Europa Conference League (1): Kane 1.

Clark Z 32	Kerr J 3	Gordon L 30 + 1	McCart J 37	Rooney S 22 + 1	McCann A 4	Davidson M 19 + 4	Wotherspoon D 9 + 1	Devine R 4 + 2	O'Halloran M 13 + 8	Hendry C 18 + 1	Kane C 12 + 6	May S 13 + 17	Craig L 9 + 7	Muller H 7 + 1	Booth C 25 + 2	Middleton G 16 + 12	Brown J 16 + 6	Crawford A 24 + 4	Vertainen E 3 + 4	Ambrose E 4 + 2	Northcott J 1	Gilmour C 1 + 5	Dendoncker L 5 + 1	MacPherson C 11 + 9	Bryson C 8 + 1	Solomon-Otabor V 2 + 5	Butterfield J 12 + 6	Parish E 6 + 1	Cleary D 15	Ciftci N 8 + 3	Hallberg M 14	McGinty E 1 + 2	Gallacher T 7 + 2	Sang T 7 + 2	Bair T — + 7	*Match No.*
1	2	3	4	5	6	7	8^{3}	9	10^{1}	11^{2}	12	13	14																							1
1		3	4	5	6	14	10		13		12	11^{2}	7^{3}	2	8	9^{1}																				2
1	3		4	5	6	7			12	13	11	10^{1}	14	2^{2}	9^{3}	8																				3
1	3		4	5	6		10	8^{2}		9^{1}	13	11^{3}	7	2	14	12																				4
1			5	2			7	6	10		11	13	8	4^{1}			3	9^{2}	12																	5
1			4	5		7	6		9^{1}		10^{3}	13			8	11^{2}	2	12	14	3																6
1			4▮	5			6		9		11^{3}	14	7^{2}	2^{1}	8	12		10			3	13														7
1				3			9		2^{1}		10	11^{3}	8	14	6	13		7^{2}		4			5	12												8
1			4	2^{3}		15	9^{4}		5^{2}		10	11	7		8	13	14			3^{1}			12	6												9
1		3	4				11^{2}				10^{3}	13			8	9^{1}	5	12	14	2				6	7											10
1		3	4			7		12			11	10^{2}			9	14	5^{1}	8		13			2^{3}	6												11
1		3	4					12	5^{1}		11	13		2^{3}	8	10^{2}		9		14				6	7											12
1		3	4	13		6	14		5^{1}		11▮	12		2	8	9^{2}		10^{3}							7											13
1		3	4	5^{1}		6^{2}			9						8		13	10	11^{3}				2	12	7▮	14										14
1		3	4	2		7^{1}			9		11		12		8			5	10^{2}					6		13										15
1		3	4	5^{1}					13		11		7		8	10^{3}	2	9^{2}	12						6	14										16
1		3	4	5				8	10^{1}			12	7				2	9	11^{2}						14	13	6^{3}									17
1		3	4	5					13			11	7^{2}		8	9	2^{1}								6	10	12									18
		3	4			6			9^{3}			11			8^{1}	13	5	14					2		10^{2}	12	7	1								19
		3	4								12	11^{2}	13		8	14	5	9^{3}					2		6^{1}	10	7	1								20
1		3	4			6^{2}			5		12	11^{4}			9	14		15				13		8			7^{3}		2	10^{1}						21
1		3	4			6				11^{1}	12	13			9		5							8			7		2	10^{2}						22
1		3^{2}	4			13				11		10^{3}			9	14	5	8									7		2		6^{1}	12				23
1		3	4			12				11^{1}		10^{4}			9^{3}	15	5	8^{2}						13			7		2		6▮		14			24
1		3	4^{2}			7^{5}				11		16				10	14	9				15		6^{1}			12		2				8^{3}	5^{4}	13	25
1^{2}		3	4							11^{4}		13	15		8^{1}	9	5	10									7	12	2		6^{3}		14			26
		3	4			7				11^{1}						10^{3}		9^{4}				12					13	1	2	14	6^{2}		8	5	15	27
		3	4^{4}						15	11						10		9^{1}				13					7^{3}	1	2	12	6		8^{2}	5	14	28
		3	4						14	11^{2}		12					2	9^{4}						13			7	1		10^{3}	6^{1}		8	5	15	29
1		3	4^{3}						13	11						10^{2}	12^{4}	9						7					2	14	6	15	8	5^{1}		30
1		2	3	6^{1}		5^{3}				11		12					14	8									13		4	10^{2}	7		9			31
1		3	4	5		7				10		13			12			9^{4}						14			15		2	11^{3}	6^{2}		8^{1}			32
1		4	5	2^{5}		7^{3}				11^{1}		14			6	9^{2}	3	10						13			16				8^{4}			12	15	33
1		3	4	5		7				10		14			8			9^{2}						13					2^{1}	11^{3}	6			12		34
1		3	4	2		7^{4}				10		14			8	13		9^{3}						12						11^{2}	6			5^{1}	15	35
1		3	4	5		6				11		10^{1}			8^{2}	13	12							9					2		7					36
1		3	4	6		7				10^{1}			14			11	9							13			5^{2}		2		8^{3}				12	37
		14	4	5^{1}					12				13			10						6		9			7^{3}	1	2	11		3^{2}		8		38

ST MIRREN

Year Formed: 1877. *Ground & Address:* The Simple Digital Arena, St Mirren Park, Greenhill Road, Paisley PA3 1RU. *Telephone:* 0141 889 2558. *Fax:* 0141 848 6444. *E-mail:* info@stmirren.com *Website:* stmirren.com
Ground Capacity: 7,937 (all seated). *Size of Pitch:* 105m × 68m.
Chairman: John Needham. *Chief Operating Officer:* Keith Lasley.
Manager: Stephen Robinson. *Assistant Manager:* Diarmuid O'Carroll.
Club Nickname: 'The Buddies'.
Previous Grounds: Shortroods 1877-79, Thistle Park Greenhill 1879-83, Westmarch 1883-94, Love Street 1894-2009.
Record Attendance: 47,438 v Celtic, League Cup, 20 August 1949.
Record Transfer Fee received: £850,000 from Rangers for Ian Ferguson (February 1988).
Record Transfer Fee paid: £400,000 to Bayer Uerdingen for Thomas Stickroth (March 1990).
Record Victory: 15-0 v Glasgow University, Scottish Cup 1st rd, 30 January 1960.
Record Defeat: 0-9 v Rangers, Division I, 4 December 1897.
Most Capped Player: Godmundur Torfason, 29, Iceland.
Most League Appearances: 403: Hugh Murray, 1997-2012.
Most League Goals in Season (Individual): 45: Dunky Walker, Division I, 1921-22.
Most League Goals Overall (Individual): 222: David McCrae, 1923-34.

ST MIRREN – CINCH PREMIERSHIP 2021–22 LEAGUE RECORD

Match No.	Date	Venue	Opponents	Result		H/T Score	Lg Pos.	Goalscorers	Attendance
1	July 31	A	Dundee	D	2-2	1-1	3	Brophy [4], McGrath (pen) [54]	2300
2	Aug 7	H	Hearts	L	1-2	0-1	9	Shaughnessy [85]	1039
3	21	A	Celtic	L	0-6	0-4	11		56,052
4	29	H	St Johnstone	D	0-0	0-0	11		4326
5	Sept 11	H	Dundee U	D	0-0	0-0	10		4894
6	18	A	Hibernian	D	2-2	1-0	9	Brophy [42], Shaughnessy [88]	13,501
7	26	H	Aberdeen	W	3-2	1-2	8	Ronan 2 [14, 58], Main [61]	4513
8	Oct 2	A	Livingston	W	1-0	1-0	7	Erhahon [29]	1627
9	16	A	Ross Co	W	3-2	3-1	7	Brophy [15], Fraser [34], Tanser [38]	3882
10	24	H	Rangers	L	1-2	1-2	7	Ronan [4]	6100
11	27	A	Motherwell	D	2-2	0-0	7	Brophy 2 (1 pen) [74, 78 (p)]	4576
12	30	H	Dundee	L	0-1	0-1	8		3582
13	Nov 6	A	St Johnstone	D	0-0	0-0	8		3482
14	20	H	Livingston	D	1-1	0-0	6	McGrath [68]	3016
15	27	A	Hearts	L	0-2	0-0	7		17,311
16	Dec 1	H	Ross Co	D	0-0	0-0	8		3806
17	4	A	Aberdeen	L	1-4	1-3	8	Tanser [42]	8002
18	11	H	Hibernian	D	1-1	0-0	9	Shaughnessy [87]	4698
19	22	H	Celtic	D	0-0	0-0	9		6596
20	26	A	Rangers	L	0-2	0-2	9		500
21	Jan 18	A	Dundee U	W	2-1	1-0	9	Henderson [15], Brophy [60]	4978
22	25	H	Aberdeen	W	1-0	0-0	8	Ronan [61]	4829
23	Feb 1	H	Motherwell	D	1-1	0-0	9	Gogic [80]	4987
24	5	A	Hibernian	W	1-0	0-0	9	Ronan [62]	13,227
25	9	H	St Johnstone	W	2-1	1-1	6	Ronan (pen) [42], Greive [49]	4286
26	19	A	Livingston	D	1-1	0-0	7	Kiltie [78]	4228
27	26	H	Hearts	L	0-2	0-0	8		5767
28	Mar 2	A	Celtic	L	0-2	0-0	9		57,360
29	5	A	Ross Co	L	0-1	0-0	9		3229
30	9	A	Dundee	W	1-0	0-0	9	Ronan [90]	5069
31	19	H	Dundee U	L	1-2	1-0	9	Henderson [3]	5710
32	Apr 2	A	Motherwell	L	2-4	2-3	10	Brophy [14], McCarthy [38]	4441
33	10	H	Rangers	L	0-4	0-2	10		6583
34	23	H	Hibernian	L	0-1	0-0	10		4992
35	30	A	St Johnstone	W	1-0	0-0	10	Kiltie [53]	4253
36	May 7	H	Dundee	W	2-0	1-0	9	Greive [4], Main [55]	5564
37	11	H	Livingston	D	0-0	0-0	8		4554
38	15	A	Aberdeen	D	0-0	0-0	9		14,906

Final League Position: 9

Honours
League Champions: First Division 1976-77, 1999-2000, 2005-06; Division II 1967-68; Championship 2017-18.
Runners-up: First Division 2004-05; Division II 1935-36.
Scottish Cup Winners: 1926, 1959, 1987; *Runners-up:* 1908, 1934, 1962.
League Cup Winners: 2012-13; *Runners-up:* 1955-56, 2009-10.
League Challenge Cup Winners: 2005-06; *Runners-up:* 2016-17.
B&Q Cup Runners-up: 1993-94. *Anglo-Scottish Cup:* 1979-80.

European: *Cup Winners' Cup:* 4 matches (1987-88). *UEFA Cup:* 10 matches (1980-81, 1983-84, 1985-86).

Club colours: Shirt: Black and white stripes. Shorts: Black. Socks: Black with white tops.

Goalscorers: *League (33):* Brophy 7 (1 pen), Ronan 7 (1 pen), Shaughnessy 3, Greive 2, Henderson 2, Kiltie 2, Main 2, McGrath 2 (1 pen), Tanser 2, Erhahon 1, Fraser 1, Gogic 1, McCarthy 1.
Scottish FA Cup (8): Kiltie 3, Brophy 1, Greive 1, Jones 1, McAllister 1, Ronan 1.
Premier Sports Scottish League Cup (7): Main 2, Dennis 1, Erwin 1, McCarthy 1, McGrath 1 (1 pen), Shaughnessy 1.
SPFL Trust Trophy (1): Jack 1.

Alnwick J 33	Fraser M 35 + 1	Shaughnessy J 36	Dunne C 21 + 1	Henderson J 11 + 8	McGrath J 18	Power A 32 + 2	Tanser S 30 + 1	Erhahon E 14 + 9	Main C 16 + 15	Brophy E 23 + 8	Kiltie G 19 + 6	Tait R 21 + 6	Dennis K 1 + 12	MacPherson C — + 2	McCarthy C 20 + 2	Flynn R 10 + 13	McAllister K 3 + 8	Erwin L — + 3	Reid D 3	Millar M 9 + 3	Ronan C 26 + 1	Lyness D 5 + 1	Offord K 1 + 1	McManus D — + 1	Greive A 9 + 8	Jones J 10 + 1	Gogic A 12 + 1	Gilmartin A — + 1	Match No.
1	2	3	4	5^2	6	7	8	9^3	10	11^1	12	13	14																1
1	2	3	4	12	6	7	8		10	11^1	9^3	5^2	14■	13															2
1	2	4			7	6■	9	8	11^1	13	10^3			12	3	5^2	14												3
1	2	3	4		7		9	8■	10^2	11^1		6	12		5			13											4
1	2	3			8		9		10	11		13			4	14	12		5^2	6^1	7^3								5
1	2	4			10	8	9	13	12	11					3		14		5^2	6^3	7^1								6
1	2^4	4			10	8	9	5^2	12	11^1			15		3	14	13			6^3	7								7
1	4	2			9	6	8	7	12	11^2					3		13	14		5^1	10^3								8
1	2	4			9^1	6	8^3	7^2	14	11		13			3	12				5	10								9
1	2	4			9	6	8^2	7^1	14	11		13			3	12				5^3	10								10
1	4	2				6	8		10^1	11	12	14	13		3	7^2	5^3				9								11
1	4	2				6	8		10^2	11	12	14	13		3	7^3	5^1				9								12
1	4	2			11	6	8		10^2	12		5	13		3	7^1					9								13
1	4	2	12		11	6	8		14	10^2		5	13		3^3	7					9^1								14
1	4	2■	3		9	7	8^1			11	14	5	13			6^3	12				10^2								15
1	4		3		9	7	8^1		12	11^3	13	2	10				5			14	6^2								16
1	4	2	3		10	6	8	14	12	11^2			13			7				5^3	9^1								17
1	4	2	3		9	7	8		11		10^2		12			6^3	14			5^1	13								18
	5	3	4	10			6		11		8								9	2		1	7^1	12					19
1	3	4	5	7	10^2	8	6	9	11^1		13		12			2^3							14						20
1	2	3	4	5^1		6	9	7		11^2	10^3					12	14				8				13				21
1	2	3	4	8	10	6	5	13		11^1	9										7^2				12				22
1	2	3	4	8^2		6		15		11^3	9	5				14		13			7^4					10^1	12		23
1	2	3	4	8^4		6^1		14	13		9	5				12				15	7				11^2	10^3			24
1	2	3	4			6					8	5^1				12					9				11	10	7		25
1	2	3	4■	12		6	14		13		8	5									9				11^2	10^3	7^1		26
1	2	3	4			6^1			12	14	8^2	5				13					9■				11^3	10	7		27
1	15	4	5	14		8^4	6^1	16	11^3	13	7^5	2			3										12	10^2	9		28
		4	5	15		8^3	6	13	12	14	7^1	2			3^2							1			11^4	10	9		29
		3	4	12		8	5			11^1	6^2	2									7	1			13	10	9		30
1■	2	3	4	9^1		7^3		15	14	10^4	11^2	5			13						6	16			12^5		8		31
	2	4		9		7		8^2	13	10		5^1			3						6	1			12	11			32
	2	3	4^1	9^3		7		15	14	10^2		5			12						8	1			13	11^4	6		33
1	2	3		12		6^1	9	8^2	10	11^3		4^4			5	14					7				13	15			34
1	2	3					8		10	13	9^2	5			4	12					7				11^1		6		35
1	2	3		14		12	8	7^4	10^1	15	9^3	5			4	13									11^2		6		36
1	2	3		12		13	8	7^1	10		9				4	5^2									11		6		37
1	2			6^1		7	9	8^2		13	10	5^3			4	14				12					11^4		3	15	38

STENHOUSEMUIR

Year Formed: 1884. *Ground & Address:* Ochilview Park, Gladstone Rd, Stenhousemuir FK5 4QL. *Telephone:* 01324 562992. *Fax:* 01324 562980. *E-mail:* info@stenhousemuirfc.com *Website:* stenhousemuirfc.com
Ground Capacity: 3,746 (seated: 626). *Size of Pitch:* 101m × 66m.
Chairman: Iain McMenemy. *Vice-Chairman:* David Reid.
Manager: Stephen Swift. *Assistant Manager:* Frazer Wright.
Club Nickname: 'The Warriors'.
Previous Grounds: Tryst Ground 1884-86; Goschen Park 1886-90.
Record Attendance: 12,500 v East Fife, Scottish Cup quarter-final, 11 March 1950.
Record Transfer Fee received: £70,000 from St Johnstone for Euan Donaldson (May 1995).
Record Transfer Fee paid: £20,000 to Livingston for Ian Little (June 1995); £20,000 to East Fife for Paul Hunter (September 1995).
Record Victory: 9-2 v Dundee U, Division II, 16 April 1937.
Record Defeat: 2-11 v Dunfermline Ath, Division II, 27 September 1930.
Most League Appearances: 434: Jimmy Richardson, 1957-73.
Most League Goals in Season (Individual): 32: Robert Taylor, Division II, 1925-26.

STENHOUSEMUIR – CINCH LEAGUE TWO 2021–22 LEAGUE RECORD

Match No.	Date	Venue	Opponents	Result		H/T Score	Lg Pos.	Goalscorers	Attendance
1	July 31	H	Stirling Alb	L	0-1	0-0	7		440
2	Aug 7	A	Albion R	D	2-2	0-0	7	Orr [63], Thomson [69]	317
3	13	A	Edinburgh C	L	0-1	0-1	8		313
4	21	H	Cowdenbeath	D	1-1	0-0	9	Christie [67]	324
5	28	H	Kelty Hearts	L	1-4	1-2	9	Brown, A [23]	436
6	Sept 11	A	Annan Ath	W	2-1	0-0	8	Orr [55], Brown, A [81]	435
7	18	A	Stranraer	L	0-2	0-1	10		280
8	25	H	Elgin C	L	1-2	0-1	9	Jamieson [69]	391
9	Oct 2	H	Forfar Ath	D	1-1	0-1	9	Crighton [90]	371
10	16	A	Cowdenbeath	W	2-0	2-0	8	Thomson (og) [6], Thomson [28]	293
11	Nov 6	A	Stirling Alb	W	3-1	3-0	8	Cummins (og) [10], Orr [21], Christie [35]	734
12	9	H	Albion R	W	3-1	1-1	5	O'Reilly [4], Graham [64], Crighton [82]	431
13	13	H	Annan Ath	W	2-0	1-0	5	Brown, A (pen) [32], O'Reilly [80]	502
14	20	A	Kelty Hearts	L	0-2	0-1	6		571
15	Dec 4	H	Stranraer	L	1-4	1-3	7	Orr [5]	364
16	11	H	Edinburgh C	D	2-2	0-1	7	Bronsky (og) [74], Crighton [50]	321
17	18	A	Elgin C	D	2-2	2-1	7	Miller [17], Orr [21]	518
18	26	A	Forfar Ath	W	4-3	4-1	5	Corbett 2 [5, 32], Forbes 2 (1 pen) [24, 43 (p)]	411
19	Jan 2	H	Stirling Alb	L	1-2	1-0	6	Orr [25]	500
20	8	A	Albion R	W	2-1	1-1	4	Orr 2 [18, 56]	349
21	15	H	Cowdenbeath	L	0-2	0-0	5		344
22	29	H	Elgin C	W	2-1	2-1	4	Orr 2 [4, 13]	348
23	Feb 5	A	Annan Ath	W	2-0	1-0	5	Orr [31], Jamieson [56]	295
24	19	A	Stranraer	D	1-1	0-1	5	Orr [68]	326
25	26	H	Forfar Ath	W	2-0	1-0	5	Thomson [26], Corbett [50]	348
26	Mar 2	A	Edinburgh C	D	1-1	1-1	5	Orr [45]	182
27	5	A	Stirling Alb	W	1-0	0-0	5	Brown, A [67]	571
28	8	H	Kelty Hearts	L	0-1	0-0	5		458
29	12	H	Edinburgh C	D	0-0	0-0	5		476
30	19	A	Cowdenbeath	D	1-1	0-0	5	Christie [90]	455
31	26	A	Kelty Hearts	L	0-1	0-0	5		812
32	Apr 2	H	Annan Ath	L	0-1	0-1	5		384
33	9	A	Elgin C	W	2-0	1-0	5	Corbett [15], Miller [84]	585
34	16	H	Albion R	W	4-1	4-1	5	Corbett [1], O'Reilly [8], Thomson [20], Brown, A [24]	446
35	23	H	Stranraer	L	1-3	0-2	5	Brown, A [72]	557
36	30	A	Forfar Ath	D	0-0	0-0	5		490

Final League Position: 5

Honours
League Runners-up: Third Division 1998-99.
Promoted via play-offs: 2008-09 (to Second Division); 2017-18 (to League One).
Scottish Cup: Semi-finals 1902-03. Quarter-finals 1948-49, 1949-50, 1994-95.
League Cup: Quarter-finals 1947-48, 1960-61, 1975-76.
League Challenge Cup Winners: 1995-96.

Club colours: Shirt: Maroon with white trim. Shorts: White. Socks: Maroon.

Goalscorers: *League (47):* Orr 13, Brown A 6 (1 pen), Corbett 5, Thomson 4, Christie 3, Crighton 3, O'Reilly 3, Forbes 2 (1 pen), Jamieson 2, Miller 2, Graham 1, own goals 3.
Scottish FA Cup (4): Brown A 2, Lyon R 1, Orr 1.
Premier Sports Scottish League Cup (5): Orr 2 (1 pen), Thomson 2, Lyon J 1.
SPFL Trust Trophy (3): Graham 1, Jamieson 1, Tierney 1.

Marshall R 7	Lyon R 20 + 7	Crighton S 32 + 1	Jamieson N 32	Mills J 1	Forbes R 23 + 9	Christie D 21 + 10	Wedderburn N 33 + 1	Lyon J 7 + 10	Orr T 28 + 4	Thomson R 21 + 4	O'Reilly E 23 + 7	Brown A 18 + 13	Tierney R — + 11	Coll B 7 + 7	Andersen M 14 + 8	Reid C 1	Graham C 1 + 13	Corbett A 23 + 1	Hughes D 6 + 1	Wilson David 19	Miller M 28	Tapping J 7 + 1	Moreland J — + 2	Urminsky P 10	Yeats C 14	Match No.
1	2	3	4	5	6	7	8^{1}	9^{3}	10^{2}	11	12	13	14													1
1	2	4	3		6^{3}	13	7	8^{2}	10^{1}	11	12	9		5	14											2
1		3	4		15	7^{2}	8	12	10^{4}	11	6^{1}	9^{3}	14	5		2	13									3
1	2		4		9^{1}	6^{3}	8		14	11^{2}	13	10		5			12	3	7							4
1	2		3		7	6^{1}	8^{3}		12	11	9^{2}	10		5	14		13	4								5
	2^{2}	13	3		7		15		10^{4}	11^{1}		12	14	5	8		9^{3}	4		1	6					6
	13	4	3		6			12	10^{4}	11	15	9^{3}	14	5	8^{1}			2^{2}		1	7					7
	5		3		6^{3}		7	10^{2}	11	13	9	12	14						8^{1}	1	2	4				8
	5	4	3		6^{4}	15	7	10^{3}	11^{1}	13	9	12	14						8^{2}	1	2					9
	5	4	3		6^{1}	13	7			11^{2}	9	10	12						8	1	2					10
	5	3	4		6	8^{1}	7		11		10^{2}	9		13	12					1	2					11
	5^{5}	4	3		6^{4}	8^{2}	7	12	11^{1}		10	9^{3}	15	14			13		16	1	2					12
	5	4	3			8^{1}	6		11^{2}		10	9	13	12			14		7^{3}	1	2					13
	5	4	3		9^{2}	8		13			10	11		14	6		12		7^{1}	1	2^{3}					14
	2^{4}	4	3		6^{2}	7	9	15	11		10	8^{1}		5^{3}	14		12	13		1						15
	5	3	4^{2}		14	8^{3}	7	9^{1}	11		10	13			6			2		1		12				16
	5	3			9	8^{2}	7	12	11^{3}		10		15	13	14			2		1	6^{1}	4^{4}				17
	5	4			9	8^{2}	6		11		10	13		12				2		1	7	3^{1}				18
	5	4			9	8^{2}	6		11		10■	12					13	2		1	7^{1}	3				19
1	5	4	7		9	8^{2}	6		11			12			13			2^{1}			10	3				20
1	5	2	4^{2}		9^{3}	10	6^{1}	13	11^{4}			8^{5}	15	12			16				7	3	14			21
		4			13	12	8		10^{2}	11^{1}	9				7			2			6	3■		1	5	22
		3	4		13	12	8		10^{2}	11^{1}	9				7			2			6			1	5	23
		3	4			12	8	13	11^{2}	10	9				7^{1}			2			6			1	5	24
	12	4	3		6		8^{1}		10	11					7			2			9			1	5	25
		4	3		6^{2}	14	8		10	11^{3}	13	12			7^{1}			2			9			1	5	26
		3	4		14	6^{3}	8		10	11^{1}	9^{2}	13			12			2		1	7				5	27
		3	4		6^{2}	13	8		10	11^{1}		12			9			2		1	7				5	28
	12	3	4		14	13	8^{1}		10	11		9			7^{2}			2^{3}			6			1	5	29
	13	3	4		6^{2}	12	8	14	10^{4}	11	15	9^{1}						2			7			1	5^{3}	30
	13	3	4		15	7^{2}	6	10^{3}	11^{1}	12		8^{4}	14		9			2						1	5	31
		4	3		14	7^{4}	6	10^{3}		11	12	13			8^{1}		15	2		1	9^{2}				5	32
	13	3	4			11^{1}	8	12		10	6	9^{2}						2		1	7				5	33
		3	4			11^{2}	8		12	10^{1}	6	9					13	2			7			1	5	34
	13	3	4		14	8^{2}	7^{3}		12	11	10^{5}	9			16		15	2^{4}			6			1■	5^{1}	35
	5	3	4		8^{2}		7^{3}		11^{1}	14	10	9			6		13			1	2		12			36

STIRLING ALBION

Year Formed: 1945. *Ground & Address:* Forthbank Stadium, Springkerse, Stirling FK7 7UJ. *Telephone:* 01786 450399. *Fax:* 01786 448592. *E-mail:* office@stirlingalbionfc.co.uk *Website:* stirlingalbionfc.co.uk
Ground Capacity: 3,808 (seated: 2,508). *Size of Pitch:* 101m × 68m.
Chairman and Operations Director: Stuart Brown.
Manager: Darren Young. *Assistant Manager:* James Creaney.
Club Nickname: 'The Binos'.
Previous Ground: Annfield 1945-92.
Record Attendance: 26,400 v Celtic, Scottish Cup 4th rd, 14 March 1959 (Annfield); 3,808 v Aberdeen, Scottish Cup 4th rd, 15 February 1996 (Forthbank).
Record Transfer Fee received: £90,000 from Motherwell for Stephen Nicholas (March 1999).
Record Transfer Fee paid: £25,000 to Falkirk for Craig Taggart (August 1994).
Record Victory: 20-0 v Selkirk, Scottish Cup 1st rd, 8 December 1984.
Record Defeat: 0-9 v Dundee U, Division I, 30 December 1967; 0-9 v Ross Co, Scottish Cup 5th rd, 6 February 2010.
Most League Appearances: 504: Matt McPhee, 1967-81.
Most League Goals in Season (Individual): 27: Joe Hughes, Division II, 1969-70.
Most Goals Overall (Individual): 129: Billy Steele, 1971-83.

STIRLING ALBION – CINCH LEAGUE TWO 2021–22 LEAGUE RECORD

Match No.	Date	Venue	Opponents	Result		H/T Score	Lg Pos.	Goalscorers	Attendance
1	July 31	A	Stenhousemuir	W	1-0	0-0	4	McNiff [72]	440
2	Aug 7	H	Kelty Hearts	L	1-3	0-2	6	Forster (og) [67]	601
3	14	A	Annan Ath	L	1-3	0-2	7	Roberts, K [73]	295
4	21	A	Stranraer	W	3-0	2-0	4	Mackin [39], Grant, R [41], McGeachie [67]	275
5	28	H	Albion R	W	2-1	0-0	4	Roberts, K [62], Carrick (pen) [79]	527
6	Sept 11	H	Forfar Ath	W	1-0	0-0	3	Bikey [81]	508
7	17	A	Edinburgh C	D	2-2	1-1	2	Leitch [13], Mackin [69]	479
8	25	H	Cowdenbeath	W	4-0	2-0	2	Leitch [7], Mackin [34], Carrick [83], Heaver [89]	586
9	Oct 2	A	Elgin C	W	2-0	1-0	2	McNiff [45], Carrick [86]	652
10	16	H	Stranraer	D	1-1	0-0	2	Cummins [71]	625
11	30	A	Kelty Hearts	D	1-1	0-0	2	Scally [65]	937
12	Nov 6	H	Stenhousemuir	L	1-3	0-3	3	Bikey [59]	734
13	13	A	Albion R	L	0-1	0-1	3		417
14	20	H	Edinburgh C	L	1-2	1-1	3	Carrick [22]	528
15	Dec 4	A	Cowdenbeath	L	0-1	0-0	4		313
16	11	A	Forfar Ath	L	0-2	0-0	6		473
17	18	H	Annan Ath	L	2-3	1-2	6	Scally 2 [7, 90]	464
18	21	H	Elgin C	L	0-1	0-0	6		383
19	Jan 2	A	Stenhousemuir	W	2-1	0-1	5	Tapping (og) [76], Flanagan [80]	500
20	8	H	Kelty Hearts	L	0-3	0-1	6		483
21	15	A	Stranraer	D	3-3	1-1	6	Leitch [23], Moore [74], Cummins [79]	337
22	29	A	Annan Ath	D	0-0	0-0	7		395
23	Feb 11	A	Edinburgh C	L	0-1	0-0	7		498
24	15	H	Forfar Ath	D	1-1	0-1	7	Carrick [65]	449
25	26	A	Elgin C	L	1-3	0-2	8	Mackin [54]	561
26	Mar 5	H	Stenhousemuir	L	0-1	0-0	8		571
27	8	H	Cowdenbeath	W	2-1	1-0	7	Carrick 2 [11, 84]	378
28	12	A	Forfar Ath	W	1-0	1-0	7	Francis [32]	496
29	19	H	Annan Ath	L	0-3	0-1	7		411
30	22	H	Albion R	L	0-1	0-0	7		368
31	26	H	Stranraer	W	1-0	0-0	7	Dunsmore [65]	501
32	Apr 2	A	Cowdenbeath	D	0-0	0-0	7		416
33	9	A	Kelty Hearts	D	1-1	1-1	7	Moore [2]	519
34	16	H	Elgin C	L	0-2	0-0	7		443
35	23	A	Albion R	D	1-1	1-0	7	Carrick [33]	307
36	30	H	Edinburgh C	W	5-0	4-0	7	Banner [14], Carrick 3 (1 pen) [17 (p), 19, 28], Leitch [67]	508

Final League Position: 7

Honours
League Champions: Division II 1952-53, 1957-58, 1960-61, 1964-65; Second Division 1976-77, 1990-91, 1995-96, 2009-10; Division C 1946-47.
Runners-up: Division II 1948-49, 1950-51; Second Division 2006-07; Third Division 2003-04.
Promoted via play-offs: 2006-07 (to First Division); 2013-14 (to League One).
League Cup: Semi-finals 1961-62.
League Challenge Cup: Semi-finals 1995-96, 1999-2000.

Club colours: All: Red.

Goalscorers: *League (41):* Carrick 11 (2 pens), Leitch 4, Mackin 4, Scally 3, Bikey 2, Cummins 2, McNiff 2, Moore 2, Roberts K 2, Banner 1, Dunsmore 1, Flanagan 1, Francis 1, Grant R 1, Heaver 1, McGeachie 1, own goals 2.
Scottish FA Cup (6): Mackin 3 (1 pen), McGregor 2, Leitch 1.
Premier Sports Scottish League Cup (8): Flanagan 2, Leitch 1, Mackin 1, McGregor 1, McNiff 1, Moore 1, Omar 1.
SPFL Trust Trophy (0).

Currie B 35	McGeachie R 29 + 1	McGregor J 25 + 1	Banner K 25 + 4	McNiff M 20 + 4	Laird M 15 + 5	Roberts K 28 + 7	Leitch J 28 + 1	Flanagan N 22 + 9	Mackin D 22 + 9	Carrick D 24 + 8	Grant R 20 + 3	Cummins A 20 + 4	Moore K 15 + 17	Bikey D 9 + 8	Omar R 3 + 4	Heaver S 2 + 13	Summers C 1 + 1	Scally D 7 + 5	Watson L 5 + 3	Creaney J 3 + 1	Hancock M 12 + 1	Francis A 8 + 4	Paterson D 4 + 8	Dunsmore A 11	Grant J — + 3	McLean P 2	Law C 1	Match No.
1	2	3	4	5	6^{2}	7^{4}	8^{1}	9^{3}	10■	11	12	13	14	15														1
1	2	3	4	5	6^{1}	12		7		11^{3}	8		13	10	9^{2}	14												2
1	2	3		5		12		9^{1}	11	10^{2}	8	4	7	13	6^{3}	14												3
1	2	3	14	5^{2}		6	10^{1}	8^{5}	11^{3}	9	7^{4}	4		16		15	12	13										4
1			5	2		8	9^{3}	6^{4}	10^{1}	11^{2}	7	3	15		14	13	4	12										5
1	2	3		5	14	7	9		11^{1}	10^{4}	8^{3}	4	12	13		15		6^{2}										6
1	2	3		5		7	11	12	10	9^{1}	8	4		6														7
1	2	3		5^{1}	6	9	8^{4}	7^{2}	11^{5}	14		4	13	10^{3}	12	16			15									8
1	2	3^{4}	12	5	6	7	9^{2}	8	11^{1}	14		4	15	10^{3}	13													9
1		3	2	5	6	8	9^{2}	7	11^{3}	13		4		12	10^{1}	14												10
1	2	3		5	8	6	9^{1}	7^{2}	10^{4}	12		4	14	11^{3}	15			13										11
1	2	3		5^{5}	7^{1}	6^{3}	8	13	10^{2}		16	4	15	11		14		9^{4}	12									12
1	2		3			6^{4}	8	9^{3}	15	10^{2}	7	4■	12	11		13		14		5^{1}								13
1	4	3	2		5	14	7	15	12	11^{2}	8■		6^{4}	9^{1}		10^{3}			13									14
1	2	3	5^{3}		6	7^{4}	8	12	10	9^{1}		4	15			11^{2}		14		13								15
1		3	2		7^{2}	12	10^{1}	13	11	9	8	4		14				6^{3}	5									16
1	2^{2}	4	3			8^{1}	6■	9^{4}	10^{3}	13	7		15	12		14		11	5									17
1			3			9		8	12	10^{2}	7	4	2	11^{1}		13		6	5									18
1	2	3	4			6		9^{1}		10^{2}	7		14	13		12		11^{3}	8	5								19
1	5	3	2	4		7	12	11^{5}	13	10^{2}	6^{1}		16			15		9^{4}	8^{3}		14							20
1	2	3	15	4^{4}		7	9^{1}	6^{3}	13	11	8	12	14								5	10^{2}						21
1	2		3			8	9^{1}	6^{2}	10	12	7	4	14								5	11^{3}	13					22
1		4	3			8	9	6^{2}	10	12	7		2								5	11^{1}	13					23
1		3	4		13	8	9	12	10	11	7^{2}		2								5		6^{1}					24
1	12	4■	3		13	8	9	14	11^{2}	10^{4}	7^{3}		2								5	15	6^{1}					25
1	2		3	14	6■	7	8	10^{1}	13	11^{4}			12							4^{3}		15	9^{2}	5				26
1	2		5^{1}	3		8	7	12	13	11^{3}			6								4^{2}	10	14	9				27
1	3			4	12	6	7^{2}	8	10^{1}	9			5									11	13	2				28
1	4	12	14	3^{1}	6^{2}	7		8^{5}	10	11^{4}		16	5									9^{3}	13	2	15			29
1	5	3	7		13	8		10^{2}	11■			4	9									12	6^{1}	2				30
1	2	3^{1}	8	12		7	9					4	10								5	11		6				31
1	2		7	3	8	9^{1}	10			12		4	11^{2}								5		13	6				32
1	2		7	3	8^{3}	12	9	13		11^{4}		4	10^{1}								5	14	15	6^{2}				33
1	2		6	4	7^{1}	13		8^{2}	12		14	3	11								9	10^{3}		5				34
1	2	4	8	12		13	7^{1}		11^{3}	10	6^{4}		14								9		16	5^{5}	15	3^{2}		35
	2	3^{4}	8	13			10		14	11^{3}	7	12	9								5			6^{2}	15	4^{1}	1	36

STRANRAER

Year Formed: 1870. *Ground & Address:* Stair Park, London Rd, Stranraer DG9 8BS. *Telephone and Fax:* 01776 703271.
E-mail: secretary@stranraerfc.org *Website:* stranraerfc.org
Ground Capacity: 4,178 (seated: 1,830). *Size of Pitch:* 103m × 64m.
Chairman: Iain Dougan.
Manager: Jamie Hamill. *Assistant Manager:* Daryl Duffy.
Club Nicknames: 'The Blues'; 'The Clayholers'.
Record Attendance: 6,500 v Rangers, Scottish Cup 1st rd, 24 January 1948.
Record Transfer Fee received: £90,000 from Ayr U for Mark Campbell (1999).
Record Transfer Fee paid: £35,000 to St Johnstone for Michael Moore (March 2005).
Record Victory: 9-0 v St Cuthbert Wanderers, Scottish Cup 2nd rd, 23 October 2010; 9-0 v Wigtown & Bladnoch, Scottish Cup 2nd rd, 22 October 2011.
Record Defeat: 1-11 v Queen of the South, Scottish Cup 1st rd, 16 January 1932.
Most League Appearances: 301: Keith Knox, 1986-90; 1999-2001.
Most League Goals in Season (Individual): 27: Derek Frye, 1977-78.
Most Goals Overall (Individual): 136: Jim Campbell, 1965-75.

STRANRAER – CINCH LEAGUE TWO 2021–22 LEAGUE RECORD

Match No.	Date	Venue	Opponents	Result		H/T Score	Lg Pos.	Goalscorers	Attendance
1	July 31	A	Elgin C	D	1-1	0-1	5	Gallagher [55]	405
2	Aug 7	H	Annan Ath	L	0-3	0-1	9		255
3	21	H	Stirling Alb	L	0-3	0-2	10		275
4	28	A	Forfar Ath	D	1-1	0-0	10	Duffy [69]	445
5	31	A	Cowdenbeath	W	2-1	0-0	7	Rennie [83], Gallagher [90]	282
6	Sept 11	H	Edinburgh C	L	0-1	0-0	9		299
7	18	H	Stenhousemuir	W	2-0	1-0	6	Yates [6], Watson [49]	280
8	25	A	Kelty Hearts	L	0-1	0-1	7		528
9	Oct 2	H	Albion R	W	1-0	1-0	6	Woods [35]	275
10	16	A	Stirling Alb	D	1-1	0-0	6	Yates [67]	625
11	30	H	Forfar Ath	L	2-3	1-1	6	Muir [40], Josh Walker [64]	312
12	Nov 6	A	Annan Ath	D	2-2	1-1	7	Smith, R [24], Woods [86]	305
13	12	A	Edinburgh C	L	1-3	0-2	8	Yates [53]	218
14	20	H	Elgin C	W	1-0	0-0	8	Ross, C [47]	235
15	Dec 4	A	Stenhousemuir	W	4-1	3-1	6	Robertson [22], Brady [31], Sonkur [33], Muir (pen) [47]	364
16	11	H	Cowdenbeath	W	2-0	2-0	4	Yates [19], Muir [39]	258
17	18	H	Kelty Hearts	L	0-4	0-3	4		272
18	26	A	Albion R	L	2-3	2-1	6	Woods [15], Muir [28]	251
19	Jan 2	H	Annan Ath	D	1-1	1-0	7	Watson [17]	337
20	8	A	Forfar Ath	L	2-3	1-1	7	Josh Walker [34], Muir [70]	436
21	15	H	Stirling Alb	D	3-3	1-1	7	Muir [34], Duffy [59], Yates (pen) [90]	337
22	22	A	Cowdenbeath	W	1-0	0-0	5	Yates (pen) [85]	331
23	29	A	Kelty Hearts	L	2-3	0-2	6	Muir [53], Hilton [56]	559
24	Feb 5	H	Edinburgh C	L	0-2	0-1	6		302
25	12	A	Elgin C	W	2-1	1-0	6	Yates (pen) [11], Mullen [75]	539
26	19	H	Stenhousemuir	D	1-1	1-0	6	Duffy [11]	326
27	26	H	Albion R	D	0-0	0-0	6		303
28	Mar 5	A	Annan Ath	L	1-4	1-3	6	Hawkshaw [1]	323
29	12	H	Cowdenbeath	W	3-0	2-0	6	Burns [13], Ross, C [17], Woods [68]	283
30	18	A	Edinburgh C	W	2-1	2-0	6	Ross, C [12], Burns [28]	525
31	26	A	Stirling Alb	L	0-1	0-0	6		501
32	Apr 2	H	Forfar Ath	L	0-2	0-0	6		257
33	9	A	Albion R	W	5-0	1-0	6	Yates [3], Muir [52], Sonkur [84], Ross, C [88], Woods [90]	223
34	16	H	Kelty Hearts	L	0-3	0-0	6		301
35	23	A	Stenhousemuir	W	3-1	2-0	6	Ross, C [24], Hilton 2 [27, 67]	557
36	30	H	Elgin C	W	2-0	0-0	6	Yates (pen) [64], Ellis [86]	235

Final League Position: 6

Honours
League Champions: Second Division 1993-94, 1997-98; Third Division 2003-04.
Runners-up: Second Division 2004-05; Third Division 2007-08; League One 2014-15.
Promoted via play-offs: 2011-12 (to Second Division).
Scottish Cup: Quarter-finals 2003.
League Cup: Quarter-finals 1968-69.
League Challenge Cup Winners: 1996-97. Semi-finals: 2000-01, 2014-15.

Club colours: Shirt: Blue with white trim. Shorts: White with blue trim. Socks: Blue with red tops.

Goalscorers: *League (50):* Yates 9 (4 pens), Muir 8 (1 pen), Ross C 5, Woods 5, Duffy 3, Hilton 3, Burns 2, Gallagher 2, Sonkur 2, Josh Walker 2, Watson 2, Brady 1, Ellis 1, Hawkshaw 1, Mullen 1, Rennie 1, Robertson 1, Smith R 1.
Scottish FA Cup (0).
Premier Sports Scottish League Cup (2): Walker 1, Yates 1.
SPFL Trust Trophy (0).

Lyle C 3	McIntosh S 24 + 1	Ross C 34	Robertson S 32	Burns S 29 + 1	Gallagher G 29	Millar K 2	Woods P 21 + 14	Walker Josh 13 + 16	Hawkshaw D 14 + 7	Yates M 28 + 6	Rennie J — + 11	Moore J — + 10	Langan R 2 + 9	Irving R 2 + 7	Ngoy E 2 + 4	Duffy D 6 + 3	Baker J 10	Sonkur A 27 + 1	Smith R 11 + 10	Watson B 19 + 10	Scullion L 23	Brady A 23 + 5	Ellis S 14 + 5	Muir T 19 + 7	Hamill J 1	Hilton J 8 + 4	Mullen M — + 10	Match No.
1	2	3	4	5	6	7	8^{3}	9^{2}	10	11^{1}	12	13	14															1
1	2	3	4	5	7	6^{1}	8^{4}	10^{2}	9^{3}	11	15	14	12	13														2
1	2	3	4	5	7		10^{1}	8		9^{2}	14	13	6		11^{3}	12												3
	2		4	5	8		9				12	13		10		11^{1}	1	3	6^{2}	7								4
	2		4	5	8		9^{1}	13		15	12	14		10^{2}	11^{3}		1	3	7^{4}	6								5
		2	4	5^{3}	6		10^{1}	13		11			12	14				3	9^{2}	8	1	7^{4}	15					6
		2	4	5	7		10^{4}	14		11^{1}		13	12	15	16			3	9^{3}	8^{2}	1	6^{5}						7
		2	4	5	7		10^{4}	12		11^{3}				15	13			3	9	8^{2}	1	6^{1}		14				8
		2	3	5	7		10^{5}	15		11^{4}		14	12	13				4	9^{2}	8^{1}	1	6^{3}		16				9
		2	3	5	7^{1}		10^{2}	13		11^{4}			14		15			4	9	8^{3}	1	6		12				10
		2	3	5	7		12	9^{3}		11^{2}			15		14			4	13	6^{4}	1	8^{1}		10				11
		2	4	5■	8^{4}		13	6^{2}		10			15					3	7^{3}	14	1	9	12	11^{1}				12
	14	2	4				12	6^{3}	15	10			8^{4}					3^{1}	9^{2}	13	1	7	5	11				13
	2	3	7				12		8^{2}	11	14			15			1	4	13	6^{1}		9^{4}	5	10^{3}				14
	2	3	8	12				16	7^{5}	10^{2}	14	15		17			1	4^{5}	13	6^{3}		9^{1}	5	11^{4}				15
	2	3	7	4			12	14	9^{3}	6^{2}	15								13	10^{1}	1	8^{4}	5	11				16
		2	6^{2}	4			14	16	9^{1}	7	15	12					1	3	13	10^{4}		8^{3}	5	11^{5}				17
	2	3	7	4			9^{2}	15		6	14	12					1	13		11^{1}		8^{4}	5■	10^{3}				18
		2	7		6^{3}		8	9^{2}	13	10	14		12				1	4	5	11					3^{1}			19
	2	3	7		6		8	9^{2}	15	10						12	1	4^{1}	5^{3}	11^{4}		14		13				20
	2	3	8		7		6^{4}	9^{1}	13	12						10^{3}	1	4		14		15	5	11^{2}				21
	2	3	8		7		9^{3}			6						10^{1}	1	4				14	5	11^{2}		12	13	22
		3	8^{2}	2	7		9^{1}	13	12	6								4		14	1		5^{4}	11		10^{3}	15	23
		3	8	2	7		9^{3}		15	6^{1}						14		4		13	1		5^{2}	11■		10^{4}	12	24
	4	3	8^{2}	2	7		14	15	10^{4}	6^{3}						11^{1}				12	1	9	5				13	25
	2	3	8	4	7		12		9^{1}	10						11^{2}				13	1	6^{3}	5				14	26
	2	3	7	4	8		14		9^{1}	11^{4}						10^{3}				15	1	6^{2}	5	12		13		27
	2	3	7^{5}	4	8		14	12	9^{4}	13									16		1	6^{1}	5	11^{2}		10^{3}	15	28
	2	3^{1}		5	8		6		9^{2}									4		10	1	7	13	11		12		29
	2	3		5	8		9^{1}	12	6^{4}	13								4		10^{2}	1	7		11^{3}		14	15	30
	2	3		5			9^{2}	12	6^{3}	13								4	14	10	1	7		11^{1}		8^{4}	15	31
	2	3		5	7		9^{2}	13	6	12								4		10^{3}	1	8^{1}		11			14	32
	5	2	3^{1}	9	7		13	10^{3}		8								4	14		1	12		11		6^{2}		33
	2	3	8^{2}	5	7^{1}		12	10^{3}		6								4	15	13	1	14		11^{5}		9^{4}	16	34
	2^{2}	3	6^{3}	5	7		12	11^{1}		10^{4}								4		15	1	8	14	13		9		35
	2	3^{1}	6^{4}	5	7		12	11^{3}	15	10								4	16		1	8^{2}	14	13		9^{5}		36

SCOTTISH LEAGUE ATTENDANCES 2021–22

CINCH PREMIERSHIP ATTENDANCES

	Average Gate			*Season 2021–22*	
	2019–20	*2021–22*	*+/–%*	*Highest*	*Lowest*
Aberdeen	13,836	11,952	–13.62	18,719	500
Celtic	57,944	56,079	–3.22	59,077	24,500
Dundee	5,277	6,164	+16.81	11,273	2,300
Dundee U	8,496	7,111	–16.30	12,806	500
Hearts	16,751	16,713	–0.22	19,041	5,272
Hibernian	16,729	14,972	–10.50	20,419	5,600
Livingston	3,542	3,557	+0.43	8,922	1,319
Motherwell	5,575	5,356	–3.92	8,446	500
Rangers	49,238	45,315	–7.97	50,023	500
Ross Co	4,664	3,945	–15.42	6,698	1,990
St Johnstone	4,091	4,170	+1.92	7,319	500
St Mirren	5,376	4,729	–12.05	6,596	1,039

CINCH CHAMPIONSHIP ATTENDANCES

	Average Gate			*Season 2021–22*	
	2019–20	*2021–22*	*+/–%*	*Highest*	*Lowest*
Arbroath	1,462	1,714	+17.25	3,121	494
Ayr U	1,778	1,974	+11.01	6,136	472
Dunfermline Ath	4,152	3,603	–13.21	5,406	556
Greenock Morton	1,607	1,603	–0.25	2,878	429
Hamilton A	2,565	1,221	–52.38	2,595	420
Inverness CT	2,117	1,916	–9.47	3,829	478
Kilmarnock	5,856	4,664	–20.35	11,500	500
Partick Thistle	2,699	2,525	–6.43	4,315	500
Queen of the South	1,396	1,068	–23.50	2,271	437
Raith R	1,839	1,685	–8.40	3,417	500

CINCH LEAGUE ONE ATTENDANCES

	Average Gate			*Season 2021–22*	
	2019–20	*2021–22*	*+/–%*	*Highest*	*Lowest*
Airdrieonians	1,038	758	–27.01	1,650	438
Alloa Ath	1,125	726	–35.47	1,504	414
Clyde	947	728	–23.14	1,378	483
Cove R	765	747	–2.31	1,645	371
Dumbarton	663	540	–18.58	886	312
East Fife	824	535	–35.06	1,020	320
Falkirk	3,713	3,096	–16.63	4,104	400
Montrose	664	646	–2.70	1,036	193
Peterhead	687	551	–19.71	743	242
Queen's Park	583	667	+14.38	1,119	350

CINCH LEAGUE TWO ATTENDANCES

	Average Gate			*Season 2021–22*	
	2019–20	*2021–22*	*+/–%*	*Highest*	*Lowest*
Albion R	301	282	–6.35	427	151
Annan Ath	347	319	–8.02	441	187
Cowdenbeath	350	353	+0.87	727	221
Edinburgh C	324	350	+7.89	726	182
Elgin C	636	549	–13.74	733	347
Forfar Ath	645	471	–26.95	670	351
Kelty Hearts	N/A	704	N/A	1,202	433
Stenhousemuir	554	413	–25.42	557	321
Stirling Alb	563	504	–10.58	734	368
Stranraer	350	286	–18.46	337	235

SCOTTISH LEAGUE HONOURS 1890–2022

*=Until 1921–22 season teams were equal if level on points, unless a play-off took place. §Not promoted after play-offs. *Won or placed on goal average (ratio), goal difference or most goals scored (goal average from 1921–22 until 1971–72 when it was replaced by goal difference). No official competition during 1939–46; regional leagues operated.*

DIVISION 1 (1890–91 to 1974–75) – TIER 1

Tier	Season	Max Pts	First	Pts	Second	Pts	Third	Pts
1	1890–91	36	Dumbarton=	29	Rangers=	29	Celtic	21
	Dumbarton and Rangers held title jointly after indecisive play-off ended 2-2. Celtic deducted 4 points for fielding an ineligible player.							
1	1891–92	44	Dumbarton	37	Celtic	35	Hearts	34
1	1892–93	36	Celtic	29	Rangers	28	St Mirren	20
1	1893–94	36	Celtic	29	Hearts	26	St Bernard's	23
1	1894–95	36	Hearts	31	Celtic	26	Rangers	22
1	1895–96	36	Celtic	30	Rangers	26	Hibernian	24
1	1896–97	36	Hearts	28	Hibernian	26	Rangers	25
1	1897–98	36	Celtic	33	Rangers	29	Hibernian	22
1	1898–99	36	Rangers	36	Hearts	26	Celtic	24
1	1899–1900	36	Rangers	32	Celtic	25	Hibernian	24
1	1900–01	40	Rangers	35	Celtic	29	Hibernian	25
1	1901–02	36	Rangers	28	Celtic	26	Hearts	22
1	1902–03	44	Hibernian	37	Dundee	31	Rangers	29
1	1903–04	52	Third Lanark	43	Hearts	39	Celtic / Rangers=	38
1	1904–05	52	Celtic=	41	Rangers=	41	Third Lanark	35
	Celtic won title after beating Rangers 2-1 in play-off.							
1	1905–06	60	Celtic	49	Hearts	43	Airdrieonians	38
1	1906–07	68	Celtic	55	Dundee	48	Rangers	45
1	1907–08	68	Celtic	55	Falkirk	51	Rangers	50
1	1908–09	68	Celtic	51	Dundee	50	Clyde	48
1	1909–10	68	Celtic	54	Falkirk	52	Rangers	46
1	1910–11	68	Rangers	52	Aberdeen	48	Falkirk	44
1	1911–12	68	Rangers	51	Celtic	45	Clyde	42
1	1912–13	68	Rangers	53	Celtic	49	Hearts / Airdrieonians=	41
1	1913–14	76	Celtic	65	Rangers	59	Hearts / Morton=	54
1	1914–15	76	Celtic	65	Hearts	61	Rangers	50
1	1915–16	76	Celtic	67	Rangers	56	Morton	51
1	1916–17	76	Celtic	64	Morton	54	Rangers	53
1	1917–18	68	Rangers	56	Celtic	55	Kilmarnock / Morton=	43
1	1918–19	68	Celtic	58	Rangers	57	Morton	47
1	1919–20	84	Rangers	71	Celtic	68	Motherwell	57
1	1920–21	84	Rangers	76	Celtic	66	Hearts	50
1	1921–22	84	Celtic	67	Rangers	66	Raith R	51
1	1922–23	76	Rangers	55	Airdrieonians	50	Celtic	46
1	1923–24	76	Rangers	59	Airdrieonians	50	Celtic	46
1	1924–25	76	Rangers	60	Airdrieonians	57	Hibernian	52
1	1925–26	76	Celtic	58	Airdrieonians*	50	Hearts	50
1	1926–27	76	Rangers	56	Motherwell	51	Celtic	49
1	1927–28	76	Rangers	60	Celtic*	55	Motherwell	55
1	1928–29	76	Rangers	67	Celtic	51	Motherwell	50
1	1929–30	76	Rangers	60	Motherwell	55	Aberdeen	53
1	1930–31	76	Rangers	60	Celtic	58	Motherwell	56
1	1931–32	76	Motherwell	66	Rangers	61	Celtic	48
1	1932–33	76	Rangers	62	Motherwell	59	Hearts	50
1	1933–34	76	Rangers	66	Motherwell	62	Celtic	47
1	1934–35	76	Rangers	55	Celtic	52	Hearts	50
1	1935–36	76	Celtic	66	Rangers*	61	Aberdeen	61
1	1936–37	76	Rangers	61	Aberdeen	54	Celtic	52
1	1937–38	76	Celtic	61	Hearts	58	Rangers	49
1	1938–39	76	Rangers	59	Celtic	48	Aberdeen	46
1	1946–47	60	Rangers	46	Hibernian	44	Aberdeen	39
1	1947–48	60	Hibernian	48	Rangers	46	Partick Thistle	36
1	1948–49	60	Rangers	46	Dundee	45	Hibernian	39
1	1949–50	60	Rangers	50	Hibernian	49	Hearts	43
1	1950–51	60	Hibernian	48	Rangers*	38	Dundee	38
1	1951–52	60	Hibernian	45	Rangers	41	East Fife	37
1	1952–53	60	Rangers*	43	Hibernian	43	East Fife	39
1	1953–54	60	Celtic	43	Hearts	38	Partick Thistle	35
1	1954–55	60	Aberdeen	49	Celtic	46	Rangers	41
1	1955–56	68	Rangers	52	Aberdeen	46	Hearts*	45
1	1956–57	68	Rangers	55	Hearts	53	Kilmarnock	42
1	1957–58	68	Hearts	62	Rangers	49	Celtic	46

1	1958–59	68	Rangers	50	Hearts	48	Motherwell	44
1	1959–60	68	Hearts	54	Kilmarnock	50	Rangers*	42
1	1960–61	68	Rangers	51	Kilmarnock	50	Third Lanark	42
1	1961–62	68	Dundee	54	Rangers	51	Celtic	46
1	1962–63	68	Rangers	57	Kilmarnock	48	Partick Thistle	46
1	1963–64	68	Rangers	55	Kilmarnock	49	Celtic*	47
1	1964–65	68	Kilmarnock*	50	Hearts	50	Dunfermline Ath	49
1	1965–66	68	Celtic	57	Rangers	55	Kilmarnock	45
1	1966–67	68	Celtic	58	Rangers	55	Clyde	46
1	1967–68	68	Celtic	63	Rangers	61	Hibernian	45
1	1968–69	68	Celtic	54	Rangers	49	Dunfermline Ath	45
1	1969–70	68	Celtic	57	Rangers	45	Hibernian	44
1	1970–71	68	Celtic	56	Aberdeen	54	St Johnstone	44
1	1971–72	68	Celtic	60	Aberdeen	50	Rangers	44
1	1972–73	68	Celtic	57	Rangers	56	Hibernian	45
1	1973–74	68	Celtic	53	Hibernian	49	Rangers	48
1	1974–75	68	Rangers	56	Hibernian	49	Celtic*	45

PREMIER DIVISION (1975–76 to 1997–98)

1	1975–76	72	Rangers	54	Celtic	48	Hibernian	43
1	1976–77	72	Celtic	55	Rangers	46	Aberdeen	43
1	1977–78	72	Rangers	55	Aberdeen	53	Dundee U	40
1	1978–79	72	Celtic	48	Rangers	45	Dundee U	44
1	1979–80	72	Aberdeen	48	Celtic	47	St Mirren	42
1	1980–81	72	Celtic	56	Aberdeen	49	Rangers*	44
1	1981–82	72	Celtic	55	Aberdeen	53	Rangers	43
1	1982–83	72	Dundee U	56	Celtic*	55	Aberdeen	55
1	1983–84	72	Aberdeen	57	Celtic	50	Dundee U	47
1	1984–85	72	Aberdeen	59	Celtic	52	Dundee U	47
1	1985–86	72	Celtic*	50	Hearts	50	Dundee U	47
1	1986–87	88	Rangers	69	Celtic	63	Dundee U	60
1	1987–88	88	Celtic	72	Hearts	62	Rangers	60
1	1988–89	72	Rangers	56	Aberdeen	50	Celtic	46
1	1989–90	72	Rangers	51	Aberdeen*	44	Hearts	44
1	1990–91	72	Rangers	55	Aberdeen	53	Celtic*	41
1	1991–92	88	Rangers	72	Hearts	63	Celtic	62
1	1992–93	88	Rangers	73	Aberdeen	64	Celtic	60
1	1993–94	88	Rangers	58	Aberdeen	55	Motherwell	54
1	1994–95	108	Rangers	69	Motherwell	54	Hibernian	53
1	1995–96	108	Rangers	87	Celtic	83	Aberdeen*	55
1	1996–97	108	Rangers	80	Celtic	75	Dundee U	60
1	1997–98	108	Celtic	74	Rangers	72	Hearts	67

PREMIER LEAGUE (1998–99 to 2012–13)

1	1998–99	108	Rangers	77	Celtic	71	St Johnstone	57
1	1999–2000	108	Rangers	90	Celtic	69	Hearts	54
1	2000–01	114	Celtic	97	Rangers	82	Hibernian	66
1	2001–02	114	Celtic	103	Rangers	85	Livingston	58
1	2002–03	114	Rangers*	97	Celtic	97	Hearts	63
1	2003–04	114	Celtic	98	Rangers	81	Hearts	68
1	2004–05	114	Rangers	93	Celtic	92	Hibernian*	61
1	2005–06	114	Celtic	91	Hearts	74	Rangers	73
1	2006–07	114	Celtic	84	Rangers	72	Aberdeen	65
1	2007–08	114	Celtic	89	Rangers	86	Motherwell	60
1	2008–09	114	Rangers	86	Celtic	82	Hearts	59
1	2009–10	114	Rangers	87	Celtic	81	Dundee U	63
1	2010–11	114	Rangers	93	Celtic	92	Hearts	63
1	2011–12	114	Celtic	93	Rangers	73	Motherwell	62
	Rangers deducted 10 points for entering administration.							
1	2012–13	114	Celtic	79	Motherwell	63	St Johnstone	56

SPFL SCOTTISH PREMIERSHIP (2013–14 to 2021–22)

1	2013–14	114	Celtic	99	Motherwell	70	Aberdeen	68
1	2014–15	114	Celtic	92	Aberdeen	75	Inverness CT	65
1	2015–16	114	Celtic	86	Aberdeen	71	Hearts	65
1	2016–17	114	Celtic	106	Aberdeen	76	Rangers	67
1	2017–18	114	Celtic	82	Aberdeen	73	Rangers	70
1	2018–19	114	Celtic	87	Rangers	78	Kilmarnock*	67
1	2019–20	114	Celtic	80	Rangers	67	Motherwell	46
	The 2019–20 season was curtailed due to the COVID-19 pandemic and positions awarded on a points-per-game basis.							
1	2020–21	114	Rangers	102	Celtic	77	Hibernian	63
1	2021–22	114	Celtic	93	Rangers	89	Hearts	61

DIVISION 2 (1893–93 to 1974–75) – TIER 2

Tier	Season	Max Pts	First	Pts	Second	Pts	Third	Pts
2	1893–94	36	Hibernian	29	Cowlairs	27	Clyde	24
2	1894–95	36	Hibernian	30	Motherwell	22	Port Glasgow Ath	20
2	1895–96	36	Abercorn	27	Leith Ath	23	Renton / Kilmarnock=	21
2	1896–97	36	Partick Thistle	31	Leith Ath	27	Airdrieonians / Kilmarnock=	21
2	1897–98	36	Kilmarnock	29	Port Glasgow Ath	25	Morton	22
2	1898–99	36	Kilmarnock	32	Leith Ath	27	Port Glasgow Ath	25
2	1899–1900	36	Partick Thistle	29	Morton	28	Port Glasgow Ath	20
2	1900–01	36	St Bernard's	26	Airdrieonians	23	Abercorn	21
2	1901–02	44	Port Glasgow Ath	32	Partick Thistle	30	Motherwell	26
2	1902–03	44	Airdrieonians	35	Motherwell	28	Ayr U / Leith Ath=	27
2	1903–04	44	Hamilton A	37	Clyde	29	Ayr U	28
2	1904–05	44	Clyde	32	Falkirk	28	Hamilton A	27
2	1905–06	44	Leith Ath	34	Clyde	31	Albion R	27
2	1906–07	44	St Bernard's	32	Vale of Leven=	27	Arthurlie=	27
2	1907–08	44	Raith R	30	Dumbarton=	27	Ayr U=	27

Dumbarton deducted 2 points for registration irregularities.

Tier	Season	Max Pts	First	Pts	Second	Pts	Third	Pts
2	1908–09	44	Abercorn	31	Raith R=	28	Vale of Leven=	28
2	1909–10	44	Leith Ath=	33	Raith R=	33	St Bernard's	27

Leith Ath and Raith R held title jointly, no play-off game played.

Tier	Season	Max Pts	First	Pts	Second	Pts	Third	Pts
2	1910–11	44	Dumbarton	31	Ayr U	27	Albion R	25
2	1911–12	44	Ayr U	35	Abercorn	30	Dumbarton	27
2	1912–13	52	Ayr U	34	Dunfermline Ath	33	East Stirlingshire	32
2	1913–14	44	Cowdenbeath	31	Albion R	27	Dunfermline Ath / Dundee Hibernian=	26
2	1914–15	52	Cowdenbeath=	37	St Bernard's=	37	Leith Ath=	37

Cowdenbeath won title after a round robin tournament between the three tied clubs.

Tier	Season	Max Pts	First	Pts	Second	Pts	Third	Pts
2	1921–22	76	Alloa Ath	60	Cowdenbeath	47	Armadale	45
2	1922–23	76	Queen's Park	57	Clydebank	50	St Johnstone	48

Clydebank and St Johnstone both deducted 2 points for fielding an ineligible player.

Tier	Season	Max Pts	First	Pts	Second	Pts	Third	Pts
2	1923–24	76	St Johnstone	56	Cowdenbeath	55	Bathgate	44
2	1924–25	76	Dundee U	50	Clydebank	48	Clyde	47
2	1925–26	76	Dunfermline Ath	59	Clyde	53	Ayr U	52
2	1926–27	76	Bo'ness	56	Raith R	49	Clydebank	45
2	1927–28	76	Ayr U	54	Third Lanark	45	King's Park	44
2	1928–29	72	Dundee U	51	Morton	50	Arbroath	47
2	1929–30	76	Leith Ath*	57	East Fife	57	Albion R	54
2	1930–31	76	Third Lanark	61	Dundee U	50	Dunfermline Ath	47
2	1931–32	76	East Stirlingshire*	55	St Johnstone	55	Raith R*	46
2	1932–33	68	Hibernian	54	Queen of the South	49	Dunfermline Ath	47

Armadale and Bo'ness were expelled for failing to meet match guarantees. Their records were expunged.

Tier	Season	Max Pts	First	Pts	Second	Pts	Third	Pts
2	1933–34	68	Albion R	45	Dunfermline Ath*	44	Arbroath	44
2	1934–35	68	Third Lanark	52	Arbroath	50	St Bernard's	47
2	1935–36	68	Falkirk	59	St Mirren	52	Morton	48
2	1936–37	68	Ayr U	54	Morton	51	St Bernard's	48
2	1937–38	68	Raith R	59	Albion R	48	Airdrieonians	47
2	1938–39	68	Cowdenbeath	60	Alloa Ath*	48	East Fife	48
2	1946–47	52	Dundee	45	Airdrieonians	42	East Fife	31
2	1947–48	60	East Fife	53	Albion R	42	Hamilton A	40
2	1948–49	60	Raith R*	42	Stirling Alb	42	Airdrieonians*	41
2	1949–50	60	Morton	47	Airdrieonians	44	Dunfermline Ath*	36
2	1950–51	60	Queen of the South*	45	Stirling Alb	45	Ayr U*	36
2	1951–52	60	Clyde	44	Falkirk	43	Ayr U	39
2	1952–53	60	Stirling Alb	44	Hamilton A	43	Queen's Park	37
2	1953–54	60	Motherwell	45	Kilmarnock	42	Third Lanark*	36
2	1954–55	60	Airdrieonians	46	Dunfermline Ath	42	Hamilton A	39
2	1955–56	72	Queen's Park	54	Ayr U	51	St Johnstone	49
2	1956–57	72	Clyde	64	Third Lanark	51	Cowdenbeath	45
2	1957–58	72	Stirling Alb	55	Dunfermline Ath	53	Arbroath	47
2	1958–59	72	Ayr U	60	Arbroath	51	Stenhousemuir	46
2	1959–60	72	St Johnstone	53	Dundee U	50	Queen of the South	49
2	1960–61	72	Stirling Alb	55	Falkirk	54	Stenhousemuir	50
2	1961–62	72	Clyde	54	Queen of the South	53	Morton	44
2	1962–63	72	St Johnstone	55	East Stirlingshire	49	Morton	48
2	1963–64	72	Morton	67	Clyde	53	Arbroath	46
2	1964–65	72	Stirling Alb	59	Hamilton A	50	Queen of the South	45
2	1965–66	72	Ayr U	53	Airdrieonians	50	Queen of the South	47
2	1966–67	76	Morton	69	Raith R	58	Arbroath	57
2	1967–68	72	St Mirren	62	Arbroath	53	East Fife	49
2	1968–69	72	Motherwell	64	Ayr U	53	East Fife*	48
2	1969–70	72	Falkirk	56	Cowdenbeath	55	Queen of the South	50

2	1970–71	72	Partick Thistle	56	East Fife	51	Arbroath	46
2	1971–72	72	Dumbarton*	52	Arbroath	52	Stirling Alb*	50
2	1972–73	72	Clyde	56	Dumfermline Ath	52	Raith R*	47
2	1973–74	72	Airdrieonians	60	Kilmarnock	58	Hamilton A	55
2	1974–75	76	Falkirk	54	Queen of the South*	53	Montrose	53

Elected to First Division: 1894 Clyde; 1895 Hibernian; 1896 Abercorn; 1897 Partick Thistle; 1899 Kilmarnock; 1900 Morton and Partick Thistle; 1902 Port Glasgow and Partick Thistle; 1903 Airdrieonians and Motherwell; 1905 Falkirk and Aberdeen; 1906 Clyde and Hamilton A; 1910 Raith R; 1913 Ayr U and Dumbarton.

FIRST DIVISION (1975–76 to 2012–13)

2	1975–76	52	Partick Thistle	41	Kilmarnock	35	Montrose	30
2	1976–77	78	St Mirren	62	Clydebank	58	Dundee	51
2	1977–78	78	Morton*	58	Hearts	58	Dundee	57
2	1978–79	78	Dundee	55	Kilmarnock*	54	Clydebank	54
2	1979–80	78	Hearts	53	Airdrieonians	51	Ayr U*	44
2	1980–81	78	Hibernian	57	Dundee	52	St Johnstone	51
2	1981–82	78	Motherwell	61	Kilmarnock	51	Hearts	50
2	1982–83	78	St Johnstone	55	Hearts	54	Clydebank	50
2	1983–84	78	Morton	54	Dumbarton	51	Partick Thistle	46
2	1984–85	78	Motherwell	50	Clydebank	48	Falkirk	45
2	1985–86	78	Hamilton A	56	Falkirk	45	Kilmarnock*	44
2	1986–87	88	Morton	57	Dunfermline Ath	56	Dumbarton	53
2	1987–88	88	Hamilton A	56	Meadowbank Thistle	52	Clydebank	49
2	1988–89	78	Dunfermline Ath	54	Falkirk	52	Clydebank	48
2	1989–90	78	St Johnstone	58	Airdrieonians	54	Clydebank	44
2	1990–91	78	Falkirk	54	Airdrieonians	53	Dundee	52
2	1991–92	88	Dundee	58	Partick Thistle*	57	Hamilton A	57
2	1992–93	88	Raith R	65	Kilmarnock	54	Dunfermline Ath	52
2	1993–94	88	Falkirk	66	Dunfermline Ath	65	Airdrieonians	54
2	1994–95	108	Raith R	69	Dunfermline Ath*	68	Dundee	68
2	1995–96	108	Dunfermline Ath	71	Dundee U*	67	Greenock Morton	67
2	1996–97	108	St Johnstone	80	Airdrieonians	60	Dundee*	58
2	1997–98	108	Dundee	70	Falkirk	65	Raith R*	60
2	1998–99	108	Hibernian	89	Falkirk	66	Ayr U	62
2	1999–2000	108	St Mirren	76	Dunfermline Ath	71	Falkirk	68
2	2000–01	108	Livingston	76	Ayr U	69	Falkirk	56
2	2001–02	108	Partick Thistle	66	Airdrieonians	56	Ayr U*	52
2	2002–03	108	Falkirk	81	Clyde	72	St Johnstone	67
2	2003–04	108	Inverness CT	70	Clyde	69	St Johnstone	57
2	2004–05	108	Falkirk	75	St Mirren*	60	Clyde	60
2	2005–06	108	St Mirren	76	St Johnstone	66	Hamilton A	59
2	2006–07	108	Gretna	66	St Johnstone	65	Dundee*	53
2	2007–08	108	Hamilton A	76	Dundee	69	St Johnstone	58
2	2008–09	108	St Johnstone	65	Partick Thistle	55	Dunfermline Ath	51
2	2009–10	108	Inverness CT	73	Dundee	61	Dunfermline Ath	58
2	2010–11	108	Dunfermline Ath	70	Raith R	60	Falkirk	58
2	2011–12	108	Ross Co	79	Dundee	55	Falkirk	52
2	2012–13	108	Partick Thistle	78	Greenock Morton	67	Falkirk	53

SPFL SCOTTISH CHAMPIONSHIP (2013–14 to 2021–22)

2	2013–14	108	Dundee	69	Hamilton A	67	Falkirk§	66
2	2014–15	108	Hearts	91	Hibernian§	70	Rangers§	67
2	2015–16	108	Rangers	81	Falkirk*§	70	Hibernian§	70
2	2016–17	108	Hibernian	71	Falkirk§	60	Dundee U§	57
2	2017–18	108	St Mirren	74	Livingston	62	Dundee U§	61
2	2018–19	108	Ross Co	71	Dundee U§	65	Inverness CT§	56
2	2019–20	108	Dundee U	59	Inverness CT	45	Dundee	41
	The 2019–20 season was curtailed due to the COVID-19 pandemic and positions awarded on a points-per-game basis.							
2	2020–21	81	Hearts	57	Dundee	45	Raith R§	43
2	2021–22	108	Kilmarnock	67	Arbroath§	65	Inverness CT§	59

SECOND DIVISION (1975–76 to 2012–13) – TIER 3

Tier	*Season*	*Max Pts*	*First*	*Pts*	*Second*	*Pts*	*Third*	*Pts*
3	1975–76	52	Clydebank*	40	Raith R	40	Alloa Ath	35
3	1976–77	78	Stirling Alb	55	Alloa Ath	51	Dunfermline Ath	50
3	1977–78	78	Clyde*	53	Raith R	53	Dunfermline Ath*	48
3	1978–79	78	Berwick Rangers	54	Dunfermline Ath	52	Falkirk	50
3	1979–80	78	Falkirk	50	East Stirlingshire	49	Forfar Ath	46
3	1980–81	78	Queen's Park	50	Queen of the South	46	Cowdenbeath	45
3	1981–82	78	Clyde	59	Alloa Ath*	50	Arbroath	50
3	1982–83	78	Brechin C	55	Meadowbank Thistle	54	Arbroath	49
3	1983–84	78	Forfar Ath	63	East Fife	47	Berwick Rangers	43
3	1984–85	78	Montrose	53	Alloa Ath	50	Dunfermline Ath	49
3	1985–86	78	Dunfermline Ath	57	Queen of the South	55	Meadowbank Thistle	49

3	1986–87	78	Meadowbank Thistle	55	Raith R*	52	Stirling Alb*	52
3	1987–88	78	Ayr U	61	St Johnstone	59	Queen's Park	51
3	1988–89	78	Albion R	50	Alloa Ath	45	Brechin C	43
3	1989–90	78	Brechin C	49	Kilmarnock	48	Stirling Alb	47
3	1990–91	78	Stirling Alb	54	Montrose	46	Cowdenbeath	45
3	1991–92	78	Dumbarton	52	Cowdenbeath	51	Alloa Ath	50
3	1992–93	78	Clyde	54	Brechin C*	53	Stranraer	53
3	1993–94	78	Stranraer	56	Berwick Rangers	48	Stenhousemuir*	47
3	1994–95	108	Greenock Morton	64	Dumbarton	60	Stirling Alb	58
3	1995–96	108	Stirling Alb	81	East Fife	67	Berwick Rangers	60
3	1996–97	108	Ayr U	77	Hamilton A	74	Livingston	64
3	1997–98	108	Stranraer	61	Clydebank	60	Livingston	59
3	1998–99	108	Livingston	77	Inverness CT	72	Clyde	53
3	1999–2000	108	Clyde	65	Alloa Ath	64	Ross Co	62
3	2000–01	108	Partick Thistle	75	Arbroath	58	Berwick Rangers*	54
3	2001–02	108	Queen of the South	67	Alloa Ath	59	Forfar Ath	53
3	2002–03	108	Raith R	59	Brechin C	55	Airdrie U	54
3	2003–04	108	Airdrie U	70	Hamilton A	62	Dumbarton	60
3	2004–05	108	Brechin C	72	Stranraer	63	Greenock Morton	62
3	2005–06	108	Gretna	88	Greenock Morton§	70	Peterhead*§	57
3	2006–07	108	Greenock Morton	77	Stirling Alb	69	Raith R§	62
3	2007–08	108	Ross Co	73	Airdrie U	66	Raith R§	60
3	2008–09	108	Raith R	76	Ayr U	74	Brechin C§	62
3	2009–10	108	Stirling Alb*	65	Alloa Ath§	65	Cowdenbeath	59
3	2010–11	108	Livingston	82	Ayr U*	59	Forfar Ath§	59
3	2011–12	108	Cowdenbeath	71	Arbroath§	63	Dumbarton	58
3	2012–13	108	Queen of the South	92	Alloa Ath	67	Brechin C§	61

SPFL SCOTTISH LEAGUE ONE (2013–14 to 2021–22)

3	2013–14	108	Rangers	102	Dunfermline Ath§	63	Stranraer§	51
3	2014–15	108	Greenock Morton	69	Stranraer§	67	Forfar Ath	66
3	2015–16	108	Dunfermline Ath	79	Ayr U	61	Peterhead§	59
3	2016–17	108	Livingston	81	Alloa Ath§	62	Airdrieonians§	52
3	2017–18	108	Ayr U	76	Raith R§	75	Alloa Ath	60
3	2018–19	108	Arbroath	70	Forfar Ath§	63	Raith R§	60
3	2019–20	108	Raith R	53	Falkirk	52	Airdrieonians	48
	The 2019–20 season was curtailed due to the COVID-19 pandemic and positions awarded on a points-per-game basis.							
3	2020–21	66	Partick Thistle	40	Airdrieonians§	38	Cove Rangers§	36
3	2021–22	108	Cove Rangers	79	Airdrieonians§	72	Montrose§	59

THIRD DIVISION (1994–95 to 2012–13) – TIER 4

Tier	*Season*	*Max Pts*	*First*	*Pts*	*Second*	*Pts*	*Third*	*Pts*
4	1994–95	108	Forfar Ath	80	Montrose	67	Ross Co	60
4	1995–96	108	Livingston	72	Brechin C	63	Inverness CT	57
4	1996–97	108	Inverness CT	76	Forfar Ath*	67	Ross Co	67
4	1997–98	108	Alloa Ath	76	Arbroath	68	Ross Co	67
4	1998–99	108	Ross Co	77	Stenhousemuir	64	Brechin C	59
4	1999–2000	108	Queen's Park	69	Berwick Rangers	66	Forfar Ath	61
4	2000–01	108	Hamilton A*	76	Cowdenbeath	76	Brechin C	72
4	2001–02	108	Brechin C	73	Dumbarton	61	Albion R	59
4	2002–03	108	Greenock Morton	72	East Fife	71	Albion R	70
4	2003–04	108	Stranraer	79	Stirling Alb	77	Gretna	68
4	2004–05	108	Gretna	98	Peterhead	78	Cowdenbeath	51
4	2005–06	108	Cowdenbeath*	76	Berwick Rangers§	76	Stenhousemuir§	73
4	2006–07	108	Berwick Rangers	75	Arbroath§	70	Queen's Park	68
4	2007–08	108	East Fife	88	Stranraer	65	Montrose§	59
4	2008–09	108	Dumbarton	67	Cowdenbeath	63	East Stirlingshire§	61
4	2009–10	108	Livingston	78	Forfar Ath	63	East Stirlingshire§	61
4	2010–11	108	Arbroath	66	Albion R	61	Queen's Park*§	59
4	2011–12	108	Alloa Ath	77	Queen's Park§	63	Stranraer	58
4	2012–13	108	Rangers	83	Peterhead§	59	Queen's Park§	56

SPFL SCOTTISH LEAGUE TWO (2013–14 to 2021–22)

4	2013–14	108	Peterhead	76	Annan Ath§	63	Stirling Alb	57
4	2014–15	108	Albion R	71	Queen's Park§	61	Arbroath§	56
4	2015–16	108	East Fife	62	Elgin C§	59	Clyde§	57
4	2016–17	108	Abroath	66	Forfar Ath	64	Annan Ath§	58
4	2017–18	108	Montrose	77	Peterhead§	76	Stirling Alb§	55
4	2018–19	108	Peterhead	79	Clyde	74	Edinburgh C§	67
4	2019–20	108	Cove Rangers	68	Edinburgh C	55	Elgin C	43
	The 2019–20 season was curtailed due to the COVID-19 pandemic and positions awarded on a points-per-game basis.							
4	2020–21	66	Queen's Park	54	Edinburgh C*§	38	Elgin C*§	38
4	2021–22	108	Kelty Hearts	81	Forfar Ath	60	Annan Ath§	59

RELEGATED CLUBS

RELEGATED FROM DIVISION I (1921–22 to 1973–74)

1921–22 *Dumbarton, Queen's Park, Clydebank
1922–23 Albion R, Alloa Ath
1923–24 Clyde, Clydebank
1924–25 Ayr U, Third Lanark
1925–26 Raith R, Clydebank
1926–27 Morton, Dundee U
1927–28 Bo'ness, Dunfermline Ath
1928–29 Third Lanark, Raith R
1929–30 Dundee U, St Johnstone
1930–31 Hibernian, East Fife
1931–32 Dundee U, Leith Ath
1932–33 Morton, East Stirlingshire
1933–34 Third Lanark, Cowdenbeath
1934–35 St Mirren, Falkirk
1935–36 Airdrieonians, Ayr U
1936–37 Dunfermline Ath, Albion R
1937–38 Dundee, Morton
1938–39 Queen's Park, Raith R
1946–47 Kilmarnock, Hamilton A
1947–48 Airdrieonians, Queen's Park
1948–49 Morton, Albion R
1949–50 Queen of the South, Stirling Alb
1950–51 Clyde, Falkirk
1951–52 Morton, Stirling Alb
1952–53 Motherwell, Third Lanark
1953–54 Airdrieonians, Hamilton A
1954–55 *No clubs relegated as league extended to 18 teams*
1955–56 Clyde, Stirling Alb
1956–57 Dunfermline Ath, Ayr U
1957–58 East Fife, Queen's Park
1958–59 Falkirk, Queen of the South
1959–60 Stirling Alb, Arbroath
1960–61 Clyde, Ayr U
1961–62 St Johnstone, Stirling Alb
1962–63 Clyde, Raith R
1963–64 Queen of the South, East Stirlingshire
1964–65 Airdrieonians, Third Lanark
1965–66 Morton, Hamilton A
1966–67 St Mirren, Ayr U
1967–68 Motherwell, Stirling Alb
1968–69 Falkirk, Arbroath
1969–70 Raith R, Partick Thistle
1970–71 St Mirren, Cowdenbeath
1971–72 Clyde, Dunfermline Ath
1972–73 Kilmarnock, Airdrieonians
1973–74 East Fife, Falkirk

**Season 1921–22 – only 1 club promoted, 3 clubs relegated.*

RELEGATED FROM PREMIER DIVISION (1974–75 to 1997–98)

1974–75 *No relegation due to League reorganisation*
1975–76 Dundee, St Johnstone
1976–77 Hearts, Kilmarnock
1977–78 Ayr U, Clydebank
1978–79 Hearts, Motherwell
1979–80 Dundee, Hibernian
1980–81 Kilmarnock, Hearts
1981–82 Partick Thistle, Airdrieonians
1982–83 Morton, Kilmarnock
1983–84 St Johnstone, Motherwell
1984–85 Dumbarton, Morton
1985–86 *No relegation due to League reorganisation*
1986–87 Clydebank, Hamilton A
1987–88 Falkirk, Dunfermline Ath, Morton
1988–89 Hamilton A
1989–90 Dundee
1990–91 *No clubs relegated*
1991–92 St Mirren, Dunfermline Ath
1992–93 Falkirk, Airdrieonians
1993–94 St Johnstone, Raith R, Dundee
1994–95 Dundee U
1995–96 Partick Thistle, Falkirk
1996–97 Raith R
1997–98 Hibernian

RELEGATED FROM PREMIER LEAGUE (1998–99 to 2012–13)

1998–99 Dunfermline Ath
1999–2000 *No relegation due to League reorganisation*
2000–01 St Mirren
2001–02 St Johnstone
2002–03 *No clubs relegated*
2003–04 Partick Thistle
2004–05 Dundee
2005–06 Livingston
2006–07 Dunfermline Ath
2007–08 Gretna
2008–09 Inverness CT
2009–10 Falkirk
2010–11 Hamilton A
2011–12 Dunfermline Ath, Rangers (demoted to Third Division)
2012–13 Dundee

RELEGATED FROM SPFL SCOTTISH PREMIERSHIP (2013–14 to 2021–22)

2013–14 Hibernian, Hearts
2014–15 St Mirren
2015–16 Dundee U
2016–17 Inverness CT
2017–18 Ross Co, Partick Thistle
2018–19 Dundee
2019–20 Hearts
2020–21 Hamilton A, Kilmarnock
2021–22 Dundee

RELEGATED FROM FIRST DIVISION (1975–76 to 2012–13)

1975–76 Dunfermline Ath, Clyde
1976–77 Raith R, Falkirk
1977–78 Alloa Ath, East Fife
1978–79 Montrose, Queen of the South
1979–80 Arbroath, Clyde
1980–81 Stirling Alb, Berwick Rangers
1981–82 East Stirlingshire, Queen of the South
1982–83 Dunfermline Ath, Queen's Park
1983–84 Raith R, Alloa Ath
1984–85 Meadowbank Thistle, St Johnstone
1985–86 Ayr U, Alloa Ath
1986–87 Brechin C, Montrose
1987–88 East Fife, Dumbarton
1988–89 Kilmarnock, Queen of the South
1989–90 Albion R, Alloa Ath
1990–91 Clyde, Brechin C
1991–92 Montrose, Forfar Ath
1992–93 Meadowbank Thistle, Cowdenbeath
1993–94 Dumbarton, Stirling Alb, Clyde, Morton, Brechin C
1994–95 Ayr U, Stranraer
1995–96 Hamilton A, Dumbarton
1996–97 Clydebank, East Fife
1997–98 Partick Thistle, Stirling Alb
1998–99 Hamilton A, Stranraer
1999–2000 Clydebank

2000–01 Greenock Morton, Alloa Ath
2001–02 Raith R
2002–03 Alloa Ath, Arbroath
2003–04 Ayr U, Brechin C
2004–05 Partick Thistle, Raith R
2005–06 Stranraer, Brechin C
2006–07 Airdrie U, Ross Co
2007–08 Stirling Alb
2008–09 Livingstone *(for breaching rules)*, Clyde
2009–10 Airdrie U, Ayr U
2010–11 Cowdenbeath, Stirling Alb
2011–12 Ayr U, Queen of the South
2012–13 Dunfermline Ath, Airdrie U

RELEGATED FROM SPFL SCOTTISH CHAMPIONSHIP (2013–14 to 2021–22)

2013–14 Greenock Morton
2014–15 Cowdenbeath
2015–16 Livingston, Alloa Ath
2016–17 Raith R, Ayr U
2017–18 Brechin C, Dumbarton
2018–19 Falkirk
2019–20 Partick Thistle
2020–21 Alloa Ath
2021–22 Dunfermline Ath, Queen of the South

RELEGATED FROM SECOND DIVISION (1993–94 to 2012–13)

1993–94 Alloa Ath, Forfar Ath, East Stirlingshire, Montrose, Queen's Park, Arbroath, Albion R, Cowdenbeath *(all relegated to new third division for 1994–95 season)*
1994–95 Meadowbank Thistle, Brechin C
1995–96 Forfar Ath, Montrose
1996–97 Dumbarton, Berwick Rangers
1997–98 Stenhousemuir, Brechin C
1998–99 East Fife, Forfar Ath
1999–2000 Hamilton A *(after being deducted 15 points)*
2000–01 Queen's Park, Stirling Alb
2001–02 Greenock Morton
2002–03 Stranraer, Cowdenbeath
2003–04 East Fife, Stenhousemuir
2004–05 Arbroath, Berwick Rangers
2005–06 Dumbarton
2006–07 Stranraer, Forfar Ath
2007–08 Cowdenbeath, Berwick Rangers
2008–09 Queen's Park, Stranraer
2009–10 Arbroath, Clyde
2010–11 Alloa Ath, Peterhead
2011–12 Stirling Alb
2012–13 Albion R

RELEGATED FROM SPFL SCOTTISH LEAGUE ONE (2013–14 to 2021–22)

2013–14 East Fife, Arbroath
2014–15 Stirling Alb
2015–16 Cowdenbeath, Forfar Ath
2016–17 Peterhead, Stenhousmuir
2017–18 Albion R, Queen's Park
2018–19 Stenhousemuir, Brechin C
2019–20 Stranraer
2020–21 Forfar Ath
2021–22 Dumbarton, East Fife

RELEGATED FROM SPFL SCOTTISH LEAGUE TWO (2015–16 to 2021–22)

2015–16 East Stirlingshire (replaced by Edinburgh C)
2016–17 None
2017–18 None
2018–19 Berwick Rangers (replaced by Cove Rangers)
2019–20 None
2020–21 Brechin C (replaced by Kelty Hearts)
2021–22 Cowdenbeath (replaced by Bonnyrigg Rose Ath)

SCOTTISH LEAGUE CHAMPIONSHIP WINS

Rangers 55, Celtic 52, Aberdeen 4, Hearts 4, Hibernian 4, Dumbarton 2, Dundee 1, Dundee U 1, Kilmarnock 1, Motherwell 1, Third Lanark 1.

The totals for Rangers and Dumbarton each include the shared championship of 1890–91.

Since the formation of the Scottish Football League in 1890, there have been periodic reorganisations of the leagues to allow for expansion, improve competition and commercial aspects of the game. The table below lists the league names by tier and chronology. This table can be used to assist when studying the records.

Tier	Division	
1	Scottish League Division I	1890–1939
	Scottish League Division A	1946–1956
	Scottish League Division I	1956–1975
	Premier Division	1975–1998
	Scottish Premier League	1998–2013
	SPFL Premiership	2013–
2	Scottish League Division II	1893–1939
	Scottish League Division B	1946–1956
	Scottish League Division II	1956–1975
	First Division	1975–2013
	SPFL Championship	2013–
3	Scottish League Division III	1923–1926
	Scottish League Division C	1946–1949
	Second Division	1975–2013
	SPFL League One	2013–
4	Third Division	1994–2013
	SPFL League Two	2013–

In 2013–14 the SPFL introduced play-offs to determine a second promotion/relegation place for the Premiership, Championship and League One.

The team finishing second bottom of the Premiership plays two legs against the team from the Championship that won the eliminator games played between the teams finishing second, third and fourth.

For both the Championship and League One, the team finishing second bottom joins the teams from second, third and fourth places of the lower league in a play-off series of two-legged semi-finals and finals.

In 2014–15 a play-off was introduced for promotion/relegation from League Two. The team finishing bottom of League Two plays two legs against the victors of the eliminator games between the winners of the Highland and Lowland leagues.

SCOTTISH LEAGUE PLAY-OFFS 2021–22

▪ *Denotes player sent off.*

PREMIERSHIP QUARTER-FINAL FIRST LEG

Tuesday, 3 May 2022

Partick Thistle (0) 1 *(Crawford 54)*

Inverness CT (0) 2 *(Sutherland 71, Samuels 82)* 2919

Partick Thistle: (433) Sneddon; McKenna, Akinola, Holt, Hendrie; Crawford, Docherty, Bannigan; Jakubiak (Alegria 74), Graham (Smith 86), Tiffoney.
Inverness CT: (4231) Ridgers; Carson, Broadfoot, Devine, Deas; Welsh, McAlear; Sutherland, Walsh (Hyde 19 (Samuels 60)), Chalmers (Harper 75); McKay (Hardy 75).
Referee: Steven McLean.

PREMIERSHIP QUARTER-FINAL SECOND LEG

Friday, 6 May 2022

Inverness CT (1) 1 *(Samuels 29)*

Partick Thistle (0) 0 2470

Inverness CT: (4231) Ridgers; Carson, Broadfoot, Devine, Deas; Welsh, McAlear (Hyde 90); Sutherland (Allardice 90), Samuels (Doran 66), Chalmers (Harper 66); McKay (Hardy 79).
Partick Thistle: (433) Sneddon; Foster, Akinola, Holt (Bell 66), Hendrie; Crawford (Murray 82), Docherty, Bannigan (Turner 46); Smith (Jakubiak 46), Graham (Alegria 66), Tiffoney.
Inverness CT won 3-1 on aggregate.
Referee: Kevin Clancy.

PREMIERSHIP SEMI-FINAL FIRST LEG

Tuesday, 10 May 2022

Inverness CT (0) 0

Arbroath (0) 0 2201

Inverness CT: (4231) Ridgers; Carson, Devine, Broadfoot, Deas; Welsh, McAlear; Sutherland (Harper 71), McKay (Doran 63), Chalmers (Hardy 79); Samuels.
Arbroath: (4141) Gaston; Thomson, Little, O'Brien, Colin Hamilton; Chris Hamilton; Stewart, Low (Henderson 84), McKenna, Craigen; Hamilton J (Donnelly 84).
Referee: Euan Anderson.

PREMIERSHIP SEMI-FINAL SECOND LEG

Friday, 13 May 2022

Arbroath (0) 0

Inverness CT (0) 0 5154

Arbroath: (4141) Gaston; Thomson (Donnelly 90), Little, O'Brien (Henderson 106), Colin Hamilton; Chris Hamilton (Gold 106); Stewart, McKenna, Low, Craigen (Linn 76); Hamilton J (Wighton 111).
Inverness CT: (4231) Ridgers; Carson, Broadfoot, Devine▪, Deas; McAlear (Duffy▪ 74), Welsh; Sutherland (Hyde 91), Doran (Hardy 60), Chalmers (Harper 68); Samuels (McKay 46).
Aggregate 0-0 aet; Inverness CT won 5-3 on penalties.
Referee: Alan Muir.

PREMIERSHIP FINAL FIRST LEG

Friday, 20 May 2022

Inverness CT (0) 2 *(McAlear 73, 80)*

St Johnstone (2) 2 *(Rooney 18, Hallberg 24)* 4811

Inverness CT: (352) Ridgers; Broadfoot, Welsh, Deas; Carson, Hyde (Allardice 56), Doran (Chalmers 46), McAlear, Harper; Hardy (Samuels 46), McKay.
St Johnstone: (352) Clark; Cleary, Gordon, McCart; Rooney, Hallberg (Butterfield 69), Davidson, MacPherson, Brown; Middleton (May 69), Hendry.
Referee: Steven McLean.

PREMIERSHIP FINAL SECOND LEG

Monday, 23 May 2022

St Johnstone (0) 4 *(May 46, MacPherson 53, Hendry 87, Rooney 90)*

Inverness CT (0) 0 7355

St Johnstone: (3412) Clark; Cleary, Gordon, Mahon; Rooney, MacPherson, Davidson, Brown; Hallberg; Middleton (May 46), Hendry.
Inverness CT: (433) Ridgers; Duffy, Broadfoot, Devine (Hardy 82), Deas; Carson (Harper 74), Welsh (Allardice 81), McAlear; Samuels, McKay, Chalmers (Doran 65).
St Johnstone won 6-2 on aggregate.
Referee: Nick Walsh.

CHAMPIONSHIP SEMI-FINALS FIRST LEG

Tuesday, 3 May 2022

Montrose (1) 1 *(Johnston 8)*

Airdrieonians (0) 0 1362

Montrose: (433) Fleming; Cammy Ballantyne, Steeves, Dillon, Webster; Cameron (Cameron Ballantyne 73), Whatley (Watson 84), Masson; Lyons (Milne 55), Johnston, Gardyne.
Airdrieonians: (4141) Currie; MacDonald, McCabe, Fordyce, Paterson; Agnew; McGill G (Allan 75), Frizzell, Easton, Smith; Gallagher.
Referee: Graham Grainger.

Wednesday, 4 May 2022

Queen's Park (0) 0

Dunfermline Ath (0) 0 1403

Queen's Park: (4231) Ferrie; Doyle, Grant, Fox, Robson; Brown (Thomson 70), Davidson; Longridge (Quitongo 70), Lyon, Smith; McHugh (Murray 80).
Dunfermline Ath: (4411) Stolarczyk; Todd, Ambrose, Donaldson, Edwards; Lawless, Polworth, Chalmers, Dow; Dorrans (Comrie 90); O'Hara (McCann 75).
Referee: David Munro.

CHAMPIONSHIP SEMI-FINALS SECOND LEG

Saturday, 7 May 2022

Airdrieonians (0) 6 *(Smith 53, 70, 75, Gallagher 86, Afolabi 105, McGill G 119)*

Montrose (2) 4 *(Cameron Ballantyne 12, 26, Milne 69, Rennie 120)* 2080

Airdrieonians: (4141) Currie; MacDonald (Watson 31), McCabe (Devenny 118), Fordyce, Paterson (Allan 46); Agnew (Afolabi 70); McGill S (McGill G 31), Frizzell, Easton, Smith; Gallagher (Kerr 116).
Montrose: (4141) Fleming; Webster, Dillon, Steeves, Cammy Ballantyne; Masson (Callaghan 91); Gardyne (Lyons 59), Milne, Cameron Ballantyne (Whatley 59), Cameron (Quinn 46 (Rennie 106)); Johnston (Watson 72).
aet; Airdrieonians won 6-5 on aggregate.
Referee: Alan Newlands.

Dunfermline Ath (0) 0

Queen's Park (0) 1 *(Murray 89)* 3179

Dunfermline Ath: (4411) Stolarczyk; Todd, Ambrose▪, Donaldson, Martin; Lawless (Kamwa 90), Polworth, Chalmers (Comrie 62), Dow (Pybus 63); Dorrans (McCann 90); O'Hara.
Queen's Park: (4231) Ferrie; Doyle, Grant, Fox, Robson; Davidson (Longridge 67), Connell; Quitongo (Murray 55), Brown (Thomson 67), Smith (McBride 81); McHugh.
Queen's Park won 1-0 on aggregate.
Referee: Craig Napier.

CHAMPIONSHIP FINAL FIRST LEG

Thursday, 12 May 2022

Queen's Park (0) 1 *(Murray 64)*

Airdrieonians (0) 1 *(McCabe 87 (pen))* 1899

Queen's Park: (4231) Ferrie; Doyle, Grant, Fox, Robson; Davidson (Thomson 72), Lyon (Brown 78); Quitongo (Longridge 59), Connell, Smith; Murray (McHugh 79).
Airdrieonians: (4141) Currie; Watson, McCabe, Fordyce, Paterson; Agnew; McGill G (McGill S 59), Frizzell, Easton, Smith; Gallagher (Afolabi 67).
Referee: Gavin Duncan.

CHAMPIONSHIP FINAL SECOND LEG

Sunday, 15 May 2022

Airdrieonians (1) 1 *(McCabe 13)*

Queen's Park (1) 2 *(Smith 17, Murray 112 (pen))* 3770

Airdrieonians: (4141) Currie; Watson, McCabe, Fordyce, Paterson; Agnew (Kerr 113); Afolabi (McGill G 77), Frizzell, Easton, Smith (McGill S 99); Gallagher (Allan 90).
Queen's Park: (4231) Ferrie; Doyle, Grant (Kilday 98), Fox, Robson; Brown, Lyon (Thomson 78); Longridge (McHugh 68), Connell (Quitongo 90), Smith; Murray.
aet; Queen's Park won 3-2 on aggregate.
Referee: Andrew Dallas.

LEAGUE ONE SEMI-FINALS FIRST LEG

Tuesday, 3 May 2022

Annan Ath (1) 1 *(Garrity 31)*

Forfar Ath (0) 0 608

Annan Ath: (442) Fleming G; Barnes, Hooper, Swinglehurst (Steele 79), Lowdon; Johnston, Docherty (Fleming K 89), Moxon, Wallace; Garrity, Goss (Smith 79).
Forfar Ath: (442) McCallum; Meechan, Fisher, Whyte, Brindley; Thomson C (Crossan 60), Slater, Harkins (Hutton 70), Warnock (Anderson G 71); McCluskey, Aitken (Shepherd 75).
Referee: Lloyd Wilson.

Edinburgh C (2) 4 *(See 11, 71, Buchanan 27 (og), Robertson 90)*

Dumbarton (0) 1 *(MacLean 61)* 630

Edinburgh C: (3412) Schwake; Hamilton (Brian 34), Travis, McIntyre; Logan (Jardine 72), Murray, Tapping C, Crane; Handling; See, Shanley (Robertson 78).
Dumbarton: (4411) Wright; Pignatiello, Stanger, Buchanan, Boyle (Wylde 82); Duthie, Paton, Carswell, Syvertsen (Wilson 46); MacLean; Oyinsan (Orsi 46).
Referee: Chris Graham.

LEAGUE ONE SEMI-FINALS SECOND LEG

Saturday, 7 May 2022

Dumbarton (0) 1 *(Syvertsen 59)*

Edinburgh C (0) 1 *(Shanley 64)* 637

Dumbarton: (433) Wright; Bronsky, Stanger, Buchanan, Muir; Pignatiello, Paton (Carswell 57), Wilson (Syvertsen 55); Duthie (McKee 57), Oyinsan (Orsi 55), MacLean.
Edinburgh C: (3412) Schwake; Hamilton, Travis, Jardine (Berry 78); Logan, Murray, Tapping C, Crane (Robertson 85); Handling (Brian 61); Shanley, See.
Edinburgh C won 5-2 on aggregate.
Referee: Gavin Duncan.

Forfar Ath (1) 1 *(McCluskey 32)*

Annan Ath (0) 1 *(Wallace 88 (pen))* 886

Forfar Ath: (451) McCallum; Meechan, Fisher, Whyte, Brindley; Moore, McCluskey, Harkins (Crossan 90), Slater, Warnock; Aitken (Shepherd 90).
Annan Ath: (451) Fleming G; Barnes, Hooper, Swinglehurst (Clark 29), Lowdon; Johnston (Smith 46), Wallace, Docherty, Moxon, Garrity (Fleming K 90); Goss.
Annan Ath won 2-1 on aggregate.
Referee: Steven Kirkland.

LEAGUE ONE FINAL FIRST LEG

Tuesday, 10 May 2022

Edinburgh C (0) 2 *(Murray 50, Shanley 62)*

Annan Ath (0) 0 1008

Edinburgh C: (3412) Schwake; Hamilton, Travis, McIntyre; Logan, Murray, Tapping C, Crane; Handling (Jardine 64); See, Shanley (Robertson 75).
Annan Ath: (433) Fleming G; Barnes, Hooper, Clark, Lowdon; Smith, Docherty, Moxon; Goss, Wallace, Garrity (Johnston 64).
Referee: Colin Steven.

LEAGUE ONE FINAL SECOND LEG

Friday, 13 May 2022

Annan Ath (2) 2 *(Wallace 6 (pen), Goss 20)*

Edinburgh C (0) 1 *(Murray 53)* 1152

Annan Ath: (442) Fleming G; Barnes, Hooper, Clark, Lowdon (Steele 73); Johnston (Robert McCartney 83), Docherty, Moxon, Wallace (Garrity 67); Smith, Goss.
Edinburgh C: (3412) Schwake; Hamilton, Travis, McIntyre; Logan (Brian 71), Murray, Tapping C, Crane; Handling (Jardine 83); See, Shanley (Robertson 83).
Edinburgh C won 3-2 on aggregate.
Referee: Euan Anderson.

LEAGUE TWO FINAL FIRST LEG

Saturday, 7 May 2022

Bonnyrigg Rose Ath (2) 3 *(Brown 40, Martyniuk 44 (pen), Brett 74)*

Cowdenbeath (0) 0 2202

Bonnyrigg Rose Ath: (442) Weir; Brett, Young, Horne, Martyniuk; Connelly, Stewart, Currie, Gray R (Hall 72); Barrett, Brown.
Cowdenbeath: (442) Gill; Dunn (Thomson 68), Barr C, Todd, Swan■; Morrison, Miller, Denham, Barrowman; Buchanan (Ferguson 37), Ompreon.
Referee: Grant Irvine.

LEAGUE TWO FINAL SECOND LEG

Saturday, 14 May 2022

Cowdenbeath (0) 0

Bonnyrigg Rose Ath (0) 1 *(Martyniuk 62 (pen))* 2117

Cowdenbeath: (442) Gill; Thomson, Denham, Barr C, Mullen; Ferguson, Morrison, Todd, Barrowman (Buchanan 53); Ompreon, Barr B (Coulson 60).
Bonnyrigg Rose Ath: (442) Weir; Brett (Turner 75), Young, Horne, Martyniuk; Connelly, Stewart (Gray S 75), Currie, Barrett; Brown (Hall 68), Gray R (Hunter 68).
Bonnyrigg Rose Ath won 4-0 on aggregate.
Referee: David Munro.

SCOTTISH LEAGUE CUP FINALS 1946–2022

SCOTTISH LEAGUE CUP

1946–47	Rangers v Aberdeen	4-0
1947–48	East Fife v Falkirk	0-0*
Replay	East Fife v Falkirk	4-1
1948–49	Rangers v Raith R	2-0
1949–50	East Fife v Dunfermline Ath	3-0
1950–51	Motherwell v Hibernian	3-0
1951–52	Dundee v Rangers	3-2
1952–53	Dundee v Kilmarnock	2-0
1953–54	East Fife v Partick Thistle	3-2
1954–55	Hearts v Motherwell	4-2
1955–56	Aberdeen v St Mirren	2-1
1956–57	Celtic v Partick Thistle	0-0*
Replay	Celtic v Partick Thistle	3-0
1957–58	Celtic v Rangers	7-1
1958–59	Hearts v Partick Thistle	5-1
1959–60	Hearts v Third Lanark	2-1
1960–61	Rangers v Kilmarnock	2-0
1961–62	Rangers v Hearts	1-1*
Replay	Rangers v Hearts	3-1
1962–63	Hearts v Kilmarnock	1-0
1963–64	Rangers v Morton	5-0
1964–65	Rangers v Celtic	2-1
1965–66	Celtic v Rangers	2-1
1966–67	Celtic v Rangers	1-0
1967–68	Celtic v Dundee	5-3
1968–69	Celtic v Hibernian	6-2
1969–70	Celtic v St Johnstone	1-0
1970–71	Rangers v Celtic	1-0
1971–72	Partick Thistle v Celtic	4-1
1972–73	Hibernian v Celtic	2-1
1973–74	Dundee v Celtic	1-0
1974–75	Celtic v Hibernian	6-3
1975–76	Rangers v Celtic	1-0
1976–77	Aberdeen v Celtic	2-1*
1977–78	Rangers v Celtic	2-1*
1978–79	Rangers v Aberdeen	2-1

BELL'S LEAGUE CUP

1979–80	Dundee U v Aberdeen	0-0*
Replay	Dundee U v Aberdeen	3-0
1980–81	Dundee U v Dundee	3-0

SCOTTISH LEAGUE CUP

1981–82	Rangers v Dundee U	2-1
1982–83	Celtic v Rangers	2-1
1983–84	Rangers v Celtic	3-2*

SKOL CUP

1984–85	Rangers v Dundee U	1-0
1985–86	Aberdeen v Hibernian	3-0
1986–87	Rangers v Celtic	2-1
1987–88	Rangers v Aberdeen *Rangers won 5-3 on penalties.*	3-3*
1988–89	Rangers v Aberdeen	3-2
1989–90	Aberdeen v Rangers	2-1*
1990–91	Rangers v Celtic	2-1*
1991–92	Hibernian v Dunfermline Ath	2-0
1992–93	Rangers v Aberdeen	2-1*

SCOTTISH LEAGUE CUP

1993–94	Rangers v Hibernian	2-1

COCA-COLA CUP

1994–95	Raith R v Celtic *Raith R won 6-5 on penalties.*	2-2*
1995–96	Aberdeen v Dundee	2-0
1996–97	Rangers v Hearts	4-3
1997–98	Celtic v Dundee U	3-0

SCOTTISH LEAGUE CUP

1998–99	Rangers v St Johnstone	2-1

CIS INSURANCE CUP

1999–2000	Celtic v Aberdeen	2-0
2000–01	Celtic v Kilmarnock	3-0
2001–02	Rangers v Ayr U	4-0
2002–03	Rangers v Celtic	2-1
2003–04	Livingston v Hibernian	2-0
2004–05	Rangers v Motherwell	5-1
2005–06	Celtic v Dunfermline Ath	3-0
2006–07	Hibernian v Kilmarnock	5-1
2007–08	Rangers v Dundee U *Rangers won 3-2 on penalties.*	2-2*

CO-OPERATIVE INSURANCE CUP

2008–09	Celtic v Rangers	2-0*
2009–10	Rangers v St Mirren	1-0
2010–11	Rangers v Celtic	2-1*

SCOTTISH COMMUNITIES LEAGUE CUP

2011–12	Kilmarnock v Celtic	1-0
2012–13	St Mirren v Hearts	3-2
2013–14	Aberdeen v Inverness CT *Aberdeen won 4-2 on penalties.*	0-0*

SCOTTISH LEAGUE CUP PRESENTED BY QTS

2014–15	Celtic v Dundee U	2-0
2015–16	Ross Co v Hibernian	2-1

BETFRED SCOTTISH LEAGUE CUP

2016–17	Celtic v Aberdeen	3-0
2017–18	Celtic v Motherwell	2-0
2018–19	Celtic v Aberdeen	1-0
2019–20	Celtic v Rangers	1-0
2020–21	St Johnstone v Livingston	1-0

PREMIER SPORTS SCOTTISH LEAGUE CUP

2021–22	Celtic v Hibernian	2-1

**After extra time.*

SCOTTISH LEAGUE CUP WINS

Rangers 27, Celtic 20, Aberdeen 6, Hearts 4, Dundee 3, East Fife 3, Hibernian 3, Dundee U 2, Kilmarnock 1, Livingston 1, Motherwell 1, Partick Thistle 1, Raith R 1, Ross Co 1, St Johnstone 1, St Mirren 1.

APPEARANCES IN FINALS

Celtic 35, Rangers 35, Aberdeen 15, Hibernian 11, Dundee U 7, Hearts 7, Dundee 6, Kilmarnock 6, Motherwell 4, Partick Thistle 4, Dunfermline Ath 3, East Fife 3, St Johnstone 3, St Mirren 3, Livingston 2, Raith R 2, Ayr U 1, Falkirk 1, Inverness CT 1, Morton 1, Ross Co 1, Third Lanark 1.

PREMIER SPORTS SCOTTISH LEAGUE CUP 2021–22

■ *Denotes player sent off.*
PW = Drawn match won on penalties (2 pts).
PL = Drawn match lost on penalties (1 pt).
* *Qualified for Second Round as best runners-up.*

NORTHERN SECTION

FIRST ROUND – GROUP A

Saturday, 10 July 2021

Cove R (0) 2 *(Fyvie 69, 82)*

Stirling Alb (1) 3 *(Omar 28, Flanagan 55, 90)* 298

Cove R: (4411) McKenzie; Ross, Neill, Strachan (Scully 20), Milne (Thomas 67); Yule, Vigurs, Draper, Watson; Fyvie; McAllister (Megginson 63).
Stirling Alb: (4141) Currie; Cummins (Banner 55), McLean, McGregor, McNiff; Laird; Moore (Heaver 90), Omar, Leitch, Flanagan; Mackin (Bikey 75).

Peterhead (0) 0

Hearts (1) 2 *(Mackay-Steven 31, Boyce 58)* 246

Peterhead: (442) Wilson; Strachan (Jordon Brown 63), Mulligan (Cook 60), McDonald, Conroy; Ritchie, Ferry, McCarthy, Cameron; McLean, Payne (Lyle 72).
Hearts: (343) Gordon; Souttar, Halkett, Kingsley; Smith M, McEneff (Pollock 60), Haring, Cochrane (Halliday 83); Ginnelly (Walker 59), Boyce (Henderson 83), Mackay-Steven (Roberts 70).

Tuesday, 13 July 2021

Hearts (2) 3 *(Halliday 12, Boyce 45, Mackay-Steven 55)*

Cove R (0) 0 1873

Hearts: (343) Gordon; Souttar, Halkett, Kingsley (Haring 59); Smith M, Pollock (McEneff 58), Halliday (Smith C 77), Cochrane; Ginnelly (Henderson 71), Boyce, Mackay-Steven (Denholm 77).
Cove R: (4411) Gourlay; Ross (Watson 60), Draper, Neill, Milne (Thomas 78); Yule, Scully (McAllister 63), Vigurs, McIntosh; Fyvie; Megginson.

Inverness CT (0) 2 *(Duku 50, Doran 54)*

Peterhead (0) 0 679

Inverness CT: (4411) Ridgers; Carson, Broadfoot (Devine 65), Fyffe, Harper; Walsh (Hyde 78), McAlear (MacGregor 57), Welsh, Doran (Gardyne 57); Sutherland; Duku (Allardice 66).
Peterhead: (4141) Long; Mulligan, McDonald, Jason Brown, Conroy; Brown S; Kesson (Cameron 46), Jordon Brown (Payne 55), Ritchie (Strachan 86), Cook (Ferry 55); Lyle (McLean 55).

Saturday, 17 July 2021

Inverness CT (1) 2 *(MacGregor 27, Sutherland 49)*

Stirling Alb (2) 2 *(Mackin 4, Moore 20)* 650

Inverness CT: (4411) Mackay; Carson, Broadfoot (Devine 63), Fyffe (Deas 46), Harper; Walsh, Welsh (Allardice 38), MacGregor, Gardyne (Doran 63); Sutherland; Duku (McAlear 83).
Stirling Alb: (4141) Currie; Cummins (McGeachie 74), McLean, McGregor, McNiff; Laird (Banner 83); Moore (Heaver 90), Omar, Leitch, Flanagan; Mackin (Carrick 74).
Stirling Alb won 3-2 on penalties.

Peterhead (2) 3 *(Brown S 3, Cameron 44, McLean 54)*

Cove R (1) 1 *(Megginson 12)* 236

Peterhead: (433) Long; Mulligan (Strachan 63), Jason Brown, McDonald, Conroy; Ritchie, Ferry (Lyle 74), Brown S; Cameron (Mushanu 83), McLean (Kesson 74), Payne (Jordon Brown 63).
Cove R: (343) McKenzie; Ross, Neill, Higgins (Milne 46); Yule, Vigurs, Draper, Scully; Megginson (McIntosh 68), McAllister (Watson 73), Leitch (Fyvie 46).

Tuesday, 20 July 2021

Cove R (2) 3 *(McIntosh 35, Megginson 38, Yule 85)*

Inverness CT (0) 1 *(Duku 90 (pen))* 491

Cove R: (4411) Gourlay; Yule, Draper, Neill, Milne; McIntosh (McAllister 72), Vigurs, Scully, Leitch (Watson 46); Fyvie; Megginson.
Inverness CT: (4411) Ridgers; Duffy, Broadfoot, Deas, Harper; Gardyne (Walsh 60), McAlear, Allardice (MacGregor 60), Doran; Sutherland; Duku.

Stirling Alb (0) 0

Hearts (1) 2 *(Boyce 31, Pollock 74)* 211

Stirling Alb: (4132) Currie; McGeachie, McGregor (Cummins 75), Banner, McNiff (Creaney 82); Laird (McLean 65); Bikey, Roberts K (Johnston 82), Leitch (Flanagan 75); Carrick, Heaver.
Hearts: (3421) Gordon; Souttar, Halkett, Kingsley; Smith M, Haring (Gnanduillet 68), Halliday, Cochrane (Smith C 85); Ginnelly (Pollock 68), Mackay-Steven (Walker 80); Boyce (McEneff 80).

Saturday, 24 July 2021

Stirling Alb (2) 3 *(McGregor 6, McNiff 12, Leitch 47)*

Peterhead (1) 1 *(Brown S 7 (pen))* 273

Stirling Alb: (442) Currie; McGeachie (Grant R 82), McGregor, Cummins, McNiff; Omar (Banner 65), Laird (Roberts K 65), Leitch, Flanagan; Carrick (Moore 54), Mackin (Bikey 83).
Peterhead: (433) Wilson; Strachan, Jason Brown (Mushanu 77), McDonald, Conroy; Ritchie, Kesson (Lyle 59), Brown S; Mulligan, Jordon Brown (Cameron 60), Payne.

Sunday, 25 July 2021

Hearts (0) 1 *(Walker 75)*

Inverness CT (0) 0 2989

Hearts: (433) Gordon; Smith M, Halkett, Kingsley, Cochrane; Pollock (Walker 66), Halliday (Haring 66), Boyce; Ginnelly, Gnanduillet (Henderson 84), Mackay-Steven.
Inverness CT: (4411) Ridgers; Duffy, Broadfoot, Devine (Fyffe 76), Deas (Harper 76); Walsh (McDonald 81), McAlear, MacGregor, Gardyne■; Sutherland (Jamieson 81); Duku (Allardice 70).

Group A Table	P	W	PW	PL	L	F	A	GD	Pts
Hearts	4	4	0	0	0	8	0	8	12
Stirling Alb	4	2	1	0	1	8	7	1	8
Inverness CT	4	1	0	1	2	5	6	–1	4
Cove Rangers	4	1	0	0	3	6	10	–4	3
Peterhead	4	1	0	0	3	4	8	–4	3

FIRST ROUND – GROUP B

Friday, 9 July 2021

Kelty Hearts (0) 0

Dundee U (0) 1 *(Shankland 77)* 500

Kelty Hearts: (4231) Jamieson; Philp, Hill, McNab, Peggie; Tidser, Reilly (Biabi 56); Higginbotham, Barjonas, Cardle; Austin (Agyeman 72).
Dundee U: (352) Siegrist; Reynolds, Mulgrew, Butcher; Freeman, Pawlett (Chalmers 59), Fuchs, Harkes, Duffy (Neilson 68); Shankland, Clark (Mochrie 78).

Saturday, 10 July 2021

Elgin C (0) 0

Arbroath (0) 1 *(Donnelly 80)* 220

Elgin C: (4231) Hoban; Mailer, Little, McHardy, MacPhee; Dingwall R, MacEwan; Dingwall T (O'Keefe 63), Cameron (Allen 70), Sopel (Peters 65); Hester.
Arbroath: (442) Antell; Stewart (Paterson 64), Little, Colin Hamilton, Gold; McKenna (Swankie 64), Craigen, Low (Clark 70), Linn; Hilson, Donnelly.

Wednesday, 14 July 2021

Arbroath (0) 2 *(Hilson 71, Donnelly 89)*

East Fife (0) 0 460

Arbroath: (442) Antell■; Gold, Little, O'Brien (Linn 25), Colin Hamilton; Stewart (Hilson 59), Henderson, Clark (Donnelly 58), Low; Swankie (Craigen 58), Nouble (McKenna 58).
East Fife: (442) Gallacher; Murdoch, Dunlop, Higgins C, Mercer; Dunsmore (Brown 64), Davidson, McManus, Watt (Slattery 83); Wallace, Smith K (Cunningham 77).

Dundee U (4) 6 *(Shankland 19, 32, Clark 24, Pawlett 40, Freeman 54, Mochrie 64)*

Elgin C (1) 1 *(Hester 4)* 268

Dundee U: (352) Siegrist; Smith K (Neilson 59), Edwards (Butcher 46), Reynolds; Freeman, Pawlett, Fuchs (Robson F 68), Hoti (Harkes 68), Duffy; Shankland (Mochrie 58), Clark.
Elgin C: (4231) McHale; Mailer, Little, McHardy, MacPhee (Peters 69); Dingwall R, MacEwan (Allen 82); Dingwall T (Sopel 63), Cameron, O'Keefe (Cooper 46); Hester (Lawrence 82).

Saturday, 17 July 2021

Dundee U (1) 1 *(Mulgrew 21)*

Arbroath (0) 0 286

Dundee U: (343) Siegrist; Mulgrew, Edwards, Neilson (Freeman 70); Smith L, Harkes (Meekison 66), Butcher, Robson J; Chalmers (Clark 65), Shankland (Watson 59), Mochrie.
Arbroath: (442) Gaston; Stewart, Henderson, Little, Colin Hamilton; Hilson, Clark (Gold 75), Low, Linn (McKenna 60); Craigen (Swankie 75), Donnelly (Paterson 87).

Kelty Hearts (2) 3 *(Austin 13, 25, Agyeman 87)*

East Fife (0) 0 392

Kelty Hearts: (451) Jamieson; Philp, Hill (Forster 46), McNab, Peggie; Higginbotham, Tidser, Barjonas, Reilly (Black 67), Cardle (Biabi 57); Austin (Agyeman 67).
East Fife: (442) Gallacher; Murdoch (Dunsmore 37), Dunlop, Higgins C, Mercer; Denholm (Watt 76), Davidson, McManus (Smith K 79), Wallace; Brown (Cunningham 76), Newton (Slattery 76).

Tuesday, 20 July 2021

East Fife (0) 0

Dundee U (1) 1 *(Pawlett 40)* 362

East Fife: (442) Gallacher; Mercer, Dunlop, Higgins C, Slattery; Dunsmore (Watt 68), Davidson (Newton 72), McManus, Denholm (Dow 79); Brown, Smith K (Cunningham 79).
Dundee U: (352) Siegrist; Smith L, Edwards (Smith K 61), Mulgrew (Reynolds 46); Freeman, Harkes (Chalmers 61), Butcher, Fuchs (Hoti 73), Duffy; Pawlett, Clark (Shankland 61).

Elgin C (1) 1 *(Little 5)*

Kelty Hearts (0) 3 *(Russell 52, Austin 76, 87)* 220

Elgin C: (442) McHale; Mailer (Lawrence 82), Cooper, Little, McHardy; Dingwall T (Allen 82), Dingwall R, MacPhee (MacEwan 62), Sopel (O'Keefe 62); Peters (MacBeath 70), Hester.
Kelty Hearts: (4141) Jamieson; Black (Cardle 72), Forster, McNab, Peggie; Tidser; Russell (Higginbotham 62), Philp, Barjonas, Biabi (Austin 62); Agyeman (Reilly 78).

Saturday, 24 July 2021

Arbroath (1) 3 *(Donnelly 31, Colin Hamilton 52, Low 58 (pen))*

Kelty Hearts (2) 2 *(Higginbotham 20, Cardle 27)* 626

Arbroath: (442) Gaston; Stewart (Chris Hamilton 80), Little, Henderson, Colin Hamilton; McKenna, Clark, Low, Linn (Swankie 75); Hilson (Gold 46), Donnelly (Nouble 68).
Kelty Hearts: (4321) Jamieson; Black, Forster, McNab, Peggie; Philp, Tidser, Reilly (Barjonas 55); Higginbotham (Agyeman 59), Cardle (Biabi 59); Austin.

East Fife (2) 2 *(Smith K 2, McManus 34 (pen))*

Elgin C (2) 3 *(Mailer 15, Hester 42, Dingwall T 48)* 199

East Fife: (442) Gallacher; Mercer (Denholm 18), Higgins, Steele, Slattery; Dunsmore (Dunlop 46), Watt (Brown 73), McManus, Newton (Anderson 84); Smith K (Dow 73), Cunningham.
Elgin C: (4411) Hoban; Nicolson (Sopel 59), Little, McHardy, Spark; Dingwall R, Mailer, MacEwan, O'Keefe (Peters 66); Dingwall T; Hester (Allen 84).

Group B Table	P	W	PW	PL	L	F	A	GD	Pts
Dundee U	4	4	0	0	0	9	1	8	12
Arbroath*	4	3	0	0	1	6	3	3	9
Kelty Hearts	4	2	0	0	2	8	5	3	6
Elgin C	4	1	0	0	3	5	12	–7	3
East Fife	4	0	0	0	4	2	9	–7	0

FIRST ROUND – GROUP C

Saturday, 10 July 2021

Forfar Ath v Ross Co

Due to positive COVID-19 results in the Ross Co squad the game was unable to be played. Forfar Ath were awarded a 3-0 win.

Montrose (2) 3 *(Rennie 20, Lyons 22, Milne 88 (pen))*

Brora R (0) 0 231

Montrose: (433) Fleming; Ballantyne, Waddell (Allan 46), Dillon, Steeves; Masson (Brown 61), Whatley (Watson 73), Callaghan (Milne 73); Webster (Antoniazzi 49), Rennie, Lyons.
Brora R: (442) Malin; Pickles, Nicolson, Gamble, Williamson; Kelly (MacRae J 65), Gillespie, MacDonald G, Macdonald A; MacRae A (Sutherland 64), Wallace.

Tuesday, 13 July 2021

Dundee (2) 4 *(McGowan 24, McMullan 34, 49, Jakubiak 51)*

Brora R (0) 0 327

Dundee: (343) Legzdins; Fontaine, Ashcroft, McGhee (Anderson 69); Kerr, Byrne (Robertson 69), Adam (McCowan 54), Marshall; McGowan, Jakubiak (Cummings 59), McMullan (McDaid 69).
Brora R: (442) Beattie (Stephen 85); Pickles, Nicolson, Gamble, Williamson; Kelly, Gillespie, MacDonald G, Macdonald A; MacRae A (Sutherland 50), Wallace (MacRae J 59).

Forfar Ath (0) 0

Montrose (0) 0 142

Forfar Ath: (433) McCallum; Meechan, Travis, Munro, Strachan; Thomas (Irvine 89), Slater, Thomson C; Crossan (Harkins 77), Shepherd, Gallagher.
Montrose: (433) Lennox; Ballantyne, Waddell, Dillon, Steeves; Masson, Whatley, Callaghan (Brown 73); Antoniazzi (Milne 59), Rennie (Johnston 59), Lyons (Watson 78).
Forfar Ath won 5-4 on penalties.

Saturday, 17 July 2021

Brora R (0) 0

Forfar Ath (0) 1 *(Gallagher 80)* 150

Brora R: (3412) Malin; Gamble, Nicolson, Williamson; Pickles (Kelly 49), Gillespie (Maclean 51), MacDonald G, Macdonald A; Wallace; MacRae J (MacRae A 67), Sutherland.
Forfar Ath: (433) McCallum; Meechan, Fisher (Hussain 90), Munro, Strachan; Thomson C, McCluskey (Harkins 90), Thomas (Gallagher 62); Crossan (Anderson G 77), Shepherd (Aitken 63), Slater.

Sunday, 18 July 2021

Ross Co v Dundee

Due to positive COVID-19 results in the Ross Co squad the game was unable to be played. Dundee were awarded a 3-0 win.

Wednesday, 21 July 2021

Brora R (0) 0

Ross Co (0) 1 *(Iacovitti 53)* 135

Brora R: (4411) Malin; Kelly, Nicolson, Gamble, Macdonald A; Sutherland, Maclean (Gillespie 72), MacDonald G, MacRae A; Wallace; MacRae J.
Ross Co: (352) Laidlaw; Donaldson, Watson, Iacovitti; Randall, Spittal, Callachan, Tillson, Vokins (Robertson 66); Shaw, Samuel D (White 70).

Montrose (0) 0

Dundee (0) 2 *(Cummings 70 (pen), McCowan 73)* 1090

Montrose: (433) Fleming; Allan, Waddell, Dillon, Steeves; Masson (Rennie 80), Whatley (Antoniazzi 73), Callaghan (Johnston 64); Webster (Watson 73), Milne, Brown (Lyons 64).

Dundee: (433) Legzdins; Kerr (Elliot 46), Fontaine, Ashcroft, Marshall; McGhee (Robertson 82), Byrne, Adam (Anderson 63); McMullan, Jakubiak (Cummings 46), McGowan (McCowan 63).

Saturday, 24 July 2021

Dundee (3) 5 *(Adam 12, Panter 31, Elliot 42, Cummings 75 (pen), 88)*

Forfar Ath (0) 2 *(McCluskey 62, Anderson G 81)* 771

Dundee: (433) Legzdins; Elliot, Fontaine (McDaid 17), Ashcroft, Panter; Anderson, Robertson, Adam (McGowan 36); McMullan, Cummings, Mullen (Sheridan 63).
Forfar Ath: (433) McCallum; Meechan, Munro, Travis (Irvine 39), Hussain (Gallagher 63); Thomson C, McCluskey, Thomas (Anderson G 77); Crossan (Aitken 63), Shepherd (Doris 76), Slater.

Ross Co (2) 4 *(Spittal 6, 56, Iacovitti 35, White 53)*

Montrose (0) 1 *(Johnston 61)* 620

Ross Co: (352) Laidlaw; Donaldson, Iacovitti, Watson; Spittal, Robertson (Randall 46), Tillson, Callachan (Shaw 54), Vokins (Williamson 84); White (Wright 62), Samuel D (MacLeman 84).
Montrose: (442) Lennox; Webster, Waddell, Allan, Steeves; Brown (Rennie 57), Watson (Antoniazzi 62), Callaghan (Masson 62), Lyons (Dillon 57); Johnston, Milne (Whatley 80).

Group C Table	P	W	PW	PL	L	F	A	GD	Pts
Dundee	4	4	0	0	0	14	2	12	12
Forfar Ath	4	2	1	0	1	6	5	1	8
Ross Co	4	2	0	0	2	5	7	−2	6
Montrose	4	1	0	1	2	4	6	−2	4
Brora Rangers	4	0	0	0	4	0	9	−9	0

FIRST ROUND – GROUP D

Saturday, 10 July 2021

Brechin C (0) 0

Livingston (1) 3 *(Parkes 1, Obileye 61, Longridge 90)* 250

Brechin C: (541) Wills; Docherty, Jordan, Wood, Bollan, Bain; MacKintosh, Inglis (Scott 77), Paton, Currie (Golasso 64); Cox.
Livingston: (4231) Stryjek; McMillan, Fitzwater, Parkes, Longridge; Obileye (Reilly 69), Pitman; Lewis, Kabia (Mullin 35), Penrice (Forrest 77); Anderson (Hamilton 69).

Cowdenbeath (0) 0

Raith R (1) 1 *(Vaughan 21)* 778

Cowdenbeath: (442) Gill; Pollock (Clarke 62), Todd, Barr C, Thomson; Buchanan R (Collins 80), Hutton, Miller, Barr B (Swan 68); Renton, Buchanan L.
Raith R: (4411) MacDonald; Tumilty, Benedictus, Berra, Dick; Connolly (McKay 86), Spencer, Tait, Zanatta (Mitchell 85); Vaughan; Poplatnik (Keatings 71).

Tuesday, 13 July 2021

Alloa Ath (0) 0

Cowdenbeath (0) 1 *(Buchanan L 54)* 224

Alloa Ath: (4231) Parry; Taggart, Graham, Howie, Church (Armstrong 65); King, Robertson; Cawley (Armour 74), Scougall, Boyd; Sammon.
Cowdenbeath: (4132) Gill; Mullen, Thomson, Todd, Clarke (Pollock 76); Hutton; Barr B, Miller, Swan (Buchanan R 70); Renton (Mahady 63), Buchanan L.

Raith R (1) 4 *(Vaughan 43, Spencer 62, 83, Zanatta 66)*

Brechin C (0) 0 594

Raith R: (4411) MacDonald; Tumilty, Berra, Benedictus, Dick; Connolly (Mitchell 79), Spencer, Tait, Zanatta; Vaughan (Arnott 73); Poplatnik (Keatings 67).
Brechin C: (541) Wills; Docherty, Jordan (Scott 46), Wood, Bollan, Bain; MacKintosh, Milne (Currie 63), Paton, Inglis; Cox (Golasso 78).

Saturday, 17 July 2021

Alloa Ath (0) 2 *(Taggart 82, Trouten 86 (pen))*

Livingston (0) 1 *(Anderson 63)* 294

Alloa Ath: (4231) McDowall; Taggart, Graham, Howie, Church; King (Trouten 62), Robertson; Boyd, Scougall, O'Donnel (Armstrong 90); Sammon (Armour 70).
Livingston: (433) Stryjek; McMillan (Reilly 84), Fitzwater, Parkes, Longridge; Pitman, Williamson (Obileye 65), Lewis; Sibbald (Montano 55), Anderson, Penrice.

Cowdenbeath (2) 3 *(Renton 26, 89, Buchanan L 28 (pen))*

Brechin C (0) 2 *(Wood 67, Inglis 77 (pen))* 245

Cowdenbeath: (442) Gill; Mullen, Barr C, Todd, Thomson; Buchanan R, Miller, Hutton, Barr B (Swan 84); Renton (Mahady 90), Buchanan L.
Brechin C: (4132) Wills; Jordan, Davidson■, Bollan (Inglis 46), Bain; Paton; Scott (Golasso 69), Milne, Kucheriavyi; Cox (Currie 81), Wood.

Tuesday, 20 July 2021

Brechin C (0) 1 *(Scott 55)*

Alloa Ath (0) 0 245

Brechin C: (541) Wills; Inglis, Jordan, Wood, Bollan, Bain; Kucheriavyi, Milne, Paton, Currie (Golasso 68); Cox (Scott 51).
Alloa Ath: (4231) McDowall; Taggart, Howie, Graham, Armstrong; Robertson, Scougall; Boyd, O'Donnel (McCall 84), Church (King 61); Armour (Sammon 53).

Wednesday, 21 July 2021

Livingston (0) 0

Raith R (0) 0 853

Livingston: (433) Stryjek; McMillan (Obileye 57), Fitzwater, Parkes, Longridge; Holt (Williamson 67), Pitman, Penrice (Montano 59); Shinnie, Anderson, Lewis (Sibbald 57).
Raith R: (433) MacDonald; Tumilty, Benedictus, Berra, Dick; Spencer, Riley-Snow (McKay 71), Tait; Connolly (Arnott 85), Vaughan, Zanatta (Varian 71).
Livingston won 6-5 on penalties.

Saturday, 24 July 2021

Livingston (2) 3 *(Todd 21 (og), Anderson 38, Sibbald 53)*

Cowdenbeath (1) 1 *(Buchanan L 9)* 545

Livingston: (433) Barden; Fitzwater (McMillan 65), Obileye, Kelly, Longridge (Penrice 5); Holt (Lewis 65), Pitman, Sibbald; Shinnie (Kabia 32), Anderson (Reilly 65), Montano.
Cowdenbeath: (442) Gill; Mullen, Barr C, Todd, Clarke (Pollock 85); Buchanan R, Miller (Swan 75), Hutton, Barr B (Coulson 62); Renton (Mahady 75), Buchanan L.

Raith R (0) 0

Alloa Ath (0) 0 958

Raith R: (4411) MacDonald; Tumilty, Berra, Benedictus, Dick; Connolly, Spencer, Tait (Riley-Snow 81), Zanatta (Varian 71); Vaughan; Poplatnik (Keatings 71).
Alloa Ath: (4231) Hutton; Taggart, Graham, Howie, Church; King, Robertson; Boyd, Scougall, O'Donnel (Armour 56); Sammon.
Raith R won 5-4 on penalties.

Group D Table	P	W	PW	PL	L	F	A	GD	Pts
Raith R	4	2	1	1	0	5	0	5	9
Livingston*	4	2	1	0	1	7	3	4	8
Cowdenbeath	4	2	0	0	2	5	6	−1	6
Alloa Ath	4	1	0	1	2	2	3	−1	4
Brechin C	4	1	0	0	3	3	10	−7	3

SOUTHERN SECTION

FIRST ROUND – GROUP E

Friday, 9 July 2021

Edinburgh C (0) 0

Hamilton A (1) 1 *(Smith C 25)* 300

Edinburgh C: (442) Goodfellow; Reekie, Bronsky (McFarlane 26), McIntyre, Crane; Hilton, Jardine, Tapping C, Handling; See (Fraser 87), Ferguson (Shanley 76).
Hamilton A: (4231) Hilton; Stirling, Want (Hamilton 62), Easton, MacDonald; Odofin, Mimnaugh; Smith L (Munro 58), Hughes, Smith C; Moyo (Redfern 80).

Saturday, 10 July 2021

Albion R (0) 0

Ayr U (0) 0 150

Albion R: (451) Binnie; Robinson, McGowan, Fagan, Fernie (Leslie 30); Wilson C (Roberts 74), Wilson D, Byrne (Stevenson 73), McKernon, Reilly; Doherty (Wright 73).
Ayr U: (352) McAdams; Baird J, Muirhead, McGinty; Houston, Salkeld, Michael Miller, Murdoch, Reading; McKenzie (Ecrepont 81), Adeloye.
Albion R won 4-2 on penalties.

Tuesday, 13 July 2021

Ayr U (1) 3 *(Adeloye 37, 49, Murdoch 84)*

Edinburgh C (0) 0 439

Ayr U: (4312) Albinson; Houston, McGinty, Baird J (Ecrepont 85), Reading; McKenzie, Muirhead, Murdoch; Hewitt; Salkeld (Smith 86), Adeloye (Michael Miller 74).
Edinburgh C: (4411) Goodfellow; Reekie, Hamilton (Kane 65), McIntyre, Crane; Jardine, Ferguson (Kidd 46), Tapping C, Handling (McFarlane 46); Hilton (Toshney 70); See (Fraser 89).

Falkirk (3) 5 *(Morrison 23, 29, Dixon 36, Telfer 85, Weekes 87)*

Albion R (1) 1 *(Wright 11)* 686

Falkirk: (433) Mutch; Williamson R, McKay, Dixon, McCann (Williamson C 87); Miller, Ross (Nesbitt 61), Telfer; Morrison, Wilson (Dowds 62), McGuffie (Weekes 79).
Albion R: (442) Binnie; Lynas, Fagan, McGowan (Leslie 46), Robinson; Roberts (Dolan 52), Wilson C, McKernon (Fee 78), Reilly; Byrne (Doherty 61), Wright (Stevenson 61).

Saturday, 17 July 2021

Albion R (1) 1 *(Byrne 4)*

Edinburgh C (0) 1 *(Hilton 70)* 120

Albion R: (442) Binnie; Lynas, Fagan, Robinson, Leslie (Fernie 72); Wilson C (Roberts 80), Wilson D, McKernon, Reilly; Doherty, Byrne.
Edinburgh C: (4411) Goodfellow; Kidd, Hamilton, Reekie, Crane; McFarlane (Hilton 58), Jardine, Tapping C, McIntyre; Handling (Ferguson 76); See.
Albion R won 5-4 on penalties.

Falkirk (0) 1 *(Nesbitt 46)*

Hamilton A (0) 2 *(Hughes 79 (pen), Hamilton 87)* 723

Falkirk: (451) Mutch; Williamson R, Miller■, Dixon, McCann; Morrison (Keena 90), Hetherington, Nesbitt (Hall 80), Telfer, McGuffie (Wilson 61); Dowds (Ross 61).
Hamilton A: (4321) Hilton; Stirling, Want, Hamilton, MacDonald; Mimnaugh (Redfern 76), Spence, Hughes; Smith L, Smith C (Munro 58); Moyo (Ryan 76).

Tuesday, 20 July 2021

Hamilton A (0) 0

Ayr U (1) 1 *(Salkeld 27)* 801

Hamilton A: (433) Hilton; Stirling, Hamilton, Easton (McGowan 88), MacDonald; Mimnaugh (Redfern 75), Spence, Hughes; Smith L, Smith C (Moyo 74), Munro.
Ayr U: (451) Albinson; Houston, Baird J, McGinty, Reading; Salkeld, Murdoch, Muirhead, Hewitt (Chalmers 71), McKenzie (Michael Miller 88); Adeloye (Fjortoft 68).

Wednesday, 21 July 2021

Edinburgh C v Falkirk

Due to positive COVID-19 results in the Falkirk squad the game was unable to be played. Edinburgh C were awarded a 3-0 win.

Saturday, 24 July 2021

Hamilton A (0) 2 *(Hughes 55 (pen), Smith C 79)*

Albion R (2) 2 *(Wilson D 37, Reilly 39)* 488

Hamilton A: (433) Hilton; Stirling, Hamilton, Easton, McGinn (Moyo 86); Mimnaugh, Meikle (Smith C 46), Hughes; Smith L (McGowan 83), Munro, Redfern.
Albion R: (442) Binnie; Lynas (Fernie 82), McGowan, Fagan (Robinson 62), Leslie; Wilson C, Wilson D, McKernon (Roberts 73), Reilly; Byrne, Doherty (Wright 73).
Hamilton A won 6-5 on penalties.

Ayr U v Falkirk

Due to positive COVID-19 results in the Falkirk squad the game was unable to be played. Ayr U were awarded a 3-0 win.

Group E Table	P	W	PW	PL	L	F	A	GD	Pts
Ayr U	4	3	0	1	0	7	0	7	10
Hamilton A	4	2	1	0	1	5	4	1	8
Albion R	4	0	2	1	1	4	8	–4	5
Edinburgh C	4	1	0	1	2	4	5	–1	4
Falkirk	4	1	0	0	3	6	9	–3	3

FIRST ROUND – GROUP F

Saturday, 10 July 2021

Airdrieonians (0) 1 *(McDonald 90)*

Annan Ath (0) 1 *(Wallace 67 (pen))* 233

Airdrieonians: (3412) Currie; Watson, Fordyce, Lyons; Wardrop, Quitongo, Agnew, McCabe; Easton (McDonald 45); Allan (Kouider-Aisser 60), Gallagher.
Annan Ath: (433) Adamson; Barnes, Moxon, Douglas, Birch; Docherty (Hunter 82), Swinglehurst, Fleming K; Johnston (Anderson 64), Smith, Wallace.
Annan Ath won 5-4 on penalties.

Queen of the South (0) 0

Queen's Park (0) 1 *(Biggar 54)* 336

Queen of the South: (3421) Rae; Gibson, Nditi, Cooper (Roy 68); East, Todd, McGrory, Joseph (McMahon 78); Paton, Connelly; Soares-Junior.
Queen's Park: (4231) Muir; Doyle, Morrison, Davidson, Robson; Lyon (Gillies 84), Gillespie; Moore, Brown, Biggar (Murray 64); Baynham.

Tuesday, 13 July 2021

Annan Ath (0) 1 *(Fleming K 74)*

Queen of the South (1) 3 *(Paton 29, Roy 49, 84)* 239

Annan Ath: (433) Fleming G; Barnes (Steele 65), Douglas, Swinglehurst, Birch (Lowdon 65); Docherty (Anderson 37), Moxon, Hunter (Fleming K 65); Johnston (Goss 52), Smith, Wallace.
Queen of the South: (352) Rae; Nditi, Dunn (McMahon 71), East; Paton, Joseph, Connelly, McGrory, Gibson; Soares-Junior, Roy.

Wednesday, 14 July 2021

Queen's Park (0) 0

Motherwell (1) 1 *(Lawless 15)* 117

Queen's Park: (4231) Muir; Doyle, Morrison, Davidson, Robson; Gillespie, Lyon; Moore, Brown, Biggar; Murray (Nicol 72).
Motherwell: (433) Kelly; O'Donnell S, O'Connor, Lamie, Carroll; Cornelius (Donnelly 79), Crawford, Maguire; Lawless, Woolery, Watt (van Veen 86).

Saturday, 17 July 2021

Motherwell (0) 3 *(Watt 49, Lamie 72, Woolery 75)*

Queen of the South (2) 2 *(Paton 40, Roy 45)* 1539

Motherwell: (433) Kelly; O'Donnell S, O'Connor, Lamie, Carroll; Cornelius, Donnelly (Woolery 66), Maguire; Watt, van Veen (McGinley 83), Lawless (Crawford 89).
Queen of the South: (532) Rae; Paton, Nditi, Dunn, East, Gibson; Joseph (McMahon 89), Connelly, Todd; Soares-Junior, Roy.

Queen's Park (0) 0

Airdrieonians (0) 0 224

Queen's Park: (4231) Muir; Doyle, Morrison, Fox, Robson; Gillespie, Davidson; Moore (McHugh 79), Brown, Biggar; Murray.
Airdrieonians: (343) Currie; Watson, Lyons (Ritchie 74), Fordyce; Wardrop, McDonald, Agnew, Quitongo; Gallagher, Allan (Kerr 64), Kouider-Aisser.
Airdrieonians won 4-3 on penalties.

Tuesday, 20 July 2021

Annan Ath (1) 1 *(Davidson 22 (og))*

Queen's Park (1) 2 *(Swinglehurst 13 (og), Murray 81)* 134

Annan Ath: (442) Fleming G; Steele, Douglas, Swinglehurst, Lowdon; Johnston (Birch 72), Hunter, Fleming K, Wallace; Goss (Robert McCartney 85), Anderson.
Queen's Park: (4231) Ferrie; Doyle, Morrison, Davidson, Robson; Gillespie, Brown; Moore (Nicol 84), McHugh (Yeats 77), Biggar; Murray (Gillies 90).

Wednesday, 21 July 2021

Airdrieonians (0) 2 *(McCabe 66, McGill S 79)*

Motherwell (0) 0 1377

Airdrieonians: (352) Currie; Watson, Kerr, Fordyce; Wardrop (McGill S 65), McCabe, McDonald, Agnew (Ritchie 89), Quitongo; Gallagher (McGill G 74), Kouider-Aisser (Allan 89).
Motherwell: (433) Kelly; O'Donnell S, O'Connor, Lamie, McGinley; Cornelius, Maguire, Crawford (van Veen 66); Woolery, Watt, Lawless.

Saturday, 24 July 2021

Motherwell (1) 2 *(Amaluzor 39, Maguire 56)*

Annan Ath (0) 0 1624

Motherwell: (343) Kelly; O'Connor, Lamie, McGinley; O'Donnell S, Donnelly, Maguire (Slattery 77), Carroll; Woolery, van Veen (Watt 65), Amaluzor.
Annan Ath: (442) Fleming G; Steele, Douglas (Hunter 86), Swinglehurst (Barnes 86), Lowdon; Fleming K (Goss 59), Docherty, Moxon, Johnston (Birch 76); Smith, Anderson (Robert McCartney 76).

Queen of the South (2) 4 *(Roy 23, 35, 58, Soares-Junior 55)*

Airdrieonians (0) 1 *(McGill G 90)* 362

Queen of the South: (352) Rae; Nditi (McKay 61), Dunn, East; Paton, McGrory, Todd (McMahon 77), Connelly (Potts 77), Gibson; Soares-Junior (Muir 77), Roy (Joseph 64).
Airdrieonians: (352) Currie; Watson, Kerr, Fordyce; Wardrop (McGill G 46), McGill S (Ritchie 60), Agnew, McDonald, Quitongo; Gallagher (Allan 60), Kouider-Aisser.

Group F Table	P	W	PW	PL	L	F	A	GD	Pts
Motherwell	4	3	0	0	1	6	4	2	9
Queen's Park	4	2	0	1	1	3	2	1	7
Queen of the South	4	2	0	0	2	9	6	3	6
Airdrieonians	4	1	1	1	1	4	5	–1	6
Annan Ath	4	0	1	0	3	3	8	–5	2

FIRST ROUND – GROUP G

Saturday, 10 July 2021

East Kilbride (0) 0

Kilmarnock (0) 2 *(Murray F 49, Naismith 62)* 270

East Kilbride: (433) Brennan; Stevenson, Saunders, Old, Wylde; Malcolm B (Stewart 84), Millar, McLaughlin (Brady 74); Elliott, Malcolm C (Rodgers 82), Vitoria.
Kilmarnock: (4231) Hemming; Naismith, Sanders (Stokes 82), Murray E, Haunstrup; McGinn, Alston (McKenzie 72); Burke (Armstrong 72), Lyons (Smith 82), Murray F; Cameron (Connell 82).
Kilmarnock fielded ineligible player – East Kilbride awarded 3-0 win.

Stranraer v Greenock Morton

Due to positive COVID-19 results in the Greenock Morton squad the game was unable to be played. Stranraer were awarded a 3-0 win.

Tuesday, 13 July 2021

Clyde (1) 1 *(Goodwillie 24 (pen))*

Stranraer (0) 0 419

Clyde: (433) Mitchell; Mortimer, Balatoni, Rumsby, Docherty; Cuddihy (Jones 57), Gomis (Kennedy 57), Splaine; Love (Andrew 71), Goodwillie (McGrath 78), Cunningham (Livingstone 78).
Stranraer: (4231) Lyle; McIntosh, Robertson, Ross C, Burns; Millar, Gallagher; Moore (Irving 85), Josh Walker (Hawkshaw 71), Yates (Woods 71); Muir (Rennie 60).

Greenock Morton (0) 0

East Kilbride (0) 0 334

Greenock Morton: (352) Hamilton; Ledger, Lithgow, Stafford; McGregor (Aitken 90), Oliver, Jacobs, King (Cooper 68), Muirhead; Ugwu, Garrity.
East Kilbride: (433) Brennan; Stevenson, Saunders, Old, Wylde; Brady (Erskine 75), Millar (Rodgers 79), Malcolm B; Vitoria (Stewart 75), McLaughlin (Malcolm C 68), Elliott.
Greenock Morton won 5-4 on penalties.

Saturday, 17 July 2021

Clyde (0) 1 *(Love 57 (pen))*

Kilmarnock (2) 2 *(Alston 1, Cameron 19 (pen))* 467

Clyde: (433) Mitchell; Cuddihy, Balatoni, Rumsby, Docherty (Livingstone 46); Kennedy (Mortimer 46), Gomis, Splaine (Andrew 60); Love, Jones (McGrath 60), Cunningham.
Kilmarnock: (4231) Walker; Naismith, Stokes (Sanders 65), Murray E, Haunstrup; McGinn, Alston; Burke (Lyons 65), McKenzie, Murray F; Cameron.

Stranraer (1) 1 *(Yates 26)*

East Kilbride (0) 0 179

Stranraer: (4231) Lyle; McIntosh, Ross C, Robertson, Burns; Millar (Langan 71), Gallagher; Moore (Woods 71), Yates, Josh Walker (Rennie 56); Muir (Hawkshaw 57).
East Kilbride: (433) Brennan; Stevenson, Kenny, Old, Brady; Rodgers (Erskine 63), Stewart, McLaughlin; Elliott, Malcolm C, Vitoria (McAninch 80).

Tuesday, 20 July 2021

East Kilbride (2) 2 *(Erskine 4, Vitoria 30)*

Clyde (2) 2 *(Jones 11, Goodwillie 26)* 270

East Kilbride: (433) Brennan; Stevenson (Connor 79), Kenny, Old, Brady; Stewart, Erskine (McAninch 46), McLaughlin; Malcolm C (Richardson 81), Elliott (Rodgers 75), Vitoria.
Clyde: (442) Mitchell; Cuddihy, Balatoni, Rumsby, Livingstone (McGrath 85); Cunningham, Gomis (Andrew 85), Splaine (Kennedy 77), Love (Docherty 68); Goodwillie, Jones (Mortimer 77).
Clyde won 4-3 on penalties.

Kilmarnock (0) 1 *(Connell 90)*

Greenock Morton (1) 1 *(McGregor 16)* 2000

Kilmarnock: (4231) Hemming; Naismith, Murray E, Stokes, Haunstrup; Lyons (Polworth 64), McGinn (Connell 79); Burke, McKenzie (Alston 24), Murray F; Cameron (Armstrong 64).
Greenock Morton: (4141) Hamilton; Ledger, Lithgow, McLean, Strapp; Blues; Muirhead (Lyon 79), Jacobs, Oliver, McGregor (Garrity 60); Ugwu.
Kilmarnock won 4-3 on penalties.

Saturday, 24 July 2021

Greenock Morton (0) 2 *(Muirhead 63, 68)*

Clyde (0) 1 *(Love 56)* 339

Greenock Morton: (41212) Hamilton; Hynes, Lithgow, McLean (Ledger 46), Strapp; Blues; Jacobs, McGrattan (Garrity 63); Lyon (Oliver 76); Ugwu, Muirhead (McGregor 85).
Clyde: (442) Mitchell; Mortimer (Docherty 69), Balatoni, Page, Livingstone (McGrath 80); Cuddihy, Kennedy (Love 49), Gomis, Splaine; Goodwillie, Andrew (Jones 49).

Kilmarnock (1) 2 *(Murray F 38, Burke 66)*

Stranraer (0) 1 *(Josh Walker 53)* 2000

Kilmarnock: (4141) Walker; Naismith, McGowan, Stokes, Haunstrup; McGinn (Murray E 63); Armstrong (Burke 64), Alston, Polworth (Lyons 78), Murray F; Cameron (Connell 64).
Stranraer: (4231) Scullion; McIntosh, Ross C, Robertson, Burns; Millar, Gallagher; Moore (Hawkshaw 48), Josh Walker (Irving 90), Yates; Rennie (Woods 46).

Group G Table	P	W	PW	PL	L	F	A	GD	Pts
Kilmarnock	4	2	1	0	1	5	6	–1	8
Stranraer	4	2	0	0	2	5	3	2	6
Greenock Morton	4	1	1	1	1	3	5	–2	6
East Kilbride	4	1	0	2	1	5	3	2	5
Clyde	4	1	1	0	2	5	6	–1	5

FIRST ROUND – GROUP H

Saturday, 10 July 2021

Partick Thistle (1) 2 *(Graham 16, Rudden 64)*

Dunfermline Ath (3) 4 *(Todorov 30, 53, Comrie 35, MacDonald 43)* 665

Partick Thistle: (433) Sneddon; Foster (McKenna 83), O'Ware, Bell, Holt; Turner, Docherty, Bannigan (MacIver 74); Murray, Graham, Tiffoney (Rudden 57).
Dunfermline Ath: (352) Mehmet; Comrie, Watson (Gaspuitis 84), Graham; MacDonald, O'Hara, Allan, Thomas, Edwards; Todorov (Pybus 71), Wighton (Todd 89).

Dumbarton v St Mirren

Due to positive COVID-19 results in the Dumbarton squad the game was unable to be played. St Mirren were awarded a 3-0 win.

Tuesday, 13 July 2021

Dumbarton (1) 1 *(MacLean 40)*

Stenhousemuir (0) 2 *(Lyon J 63, Thomson 79)* 200

Dumbarton: (4231) Ramsbottom; Geggan, McGeever, Buchanan, Muir; Carswell, Wilson (McKnight 84); Duthie, Stokes (Syvertsen 68), MacLean; Hopkirk.
Stenhousemuir: (433) Marshall; Andersen (Lyon R 46), Crighton, Reid (Mills 64), Coll; Forbes, Wedderburn, Brown A; Orr (Christie 76), Lyon J, Thomson.

St Mirren (1) 1 *(Main 30)*

Dunfermline Ath (0) 0 500

St Mirren: (352) Alnwick; Fraser, Shaughnessy, Dunne; Henderson, McGrath (MacPherson 67), Power, Kiltie (Erhahon 67), Tanser (McAllister 73); Brophy (Dennis 67), Main (Erwin 67).
Dunfermline Ath: (3142) Fon Williams; Comrie, Watson, Graham; Allan; MacDonald, Pybus, Thomas (Wighton 63), Edwards; O'Hara, Todorov.

Saturday, 17 July 2021

Dunfermline Ath (3) 5 *(Todorov 2, Thomas 4, Wighton 29, Buchanan 51 (og), O'Hara 71)*

Dumbarton (0) 1 *(MacLean 56)* 953

Dunfermline Ath: (343) Mehmet; Comrie, Watson (Gaspuitis 46), Graham; MacDonald, Allan (Pybus 46), Thomas, Edwards (Fenton 82); Wighton, Todorov (Todd 77), O'Hara.
Dumbarton: (4231) Ramsbottom; McKnight, McGeever, Buchanan, Muir; Carswell, Stokes (Wilson 67); Hopkirk, Duthie, MacLean; Syvertsen.

Stenhousemuir (1) 1 *(Orr 32 (pen))*

Partick Thistle (0) 2 *(Rudden 52, Graham 73)* 290

Stenhousemuir: (451) Marshall; Lyon R, Crighton, Jamieson, Mills; Christie (Andersen 72), Hughes (Brown A 58), Forbes, Wedderburn, Graham (Thomson 59); Orr.
Partick Thistle: (442) Stone; McKenna, Bell, Holt, Foster; Murray (Tiffoney 46), Turner, Docherty, Bannigan; Rudden (MacIver 70), Graham.

Tuesday, 20 July 2021

Partick Thistle (1) 2 *(Graham 45, 52)*

Dumbarton (0) 0 755

Partick Thistle: (442) Sneddon; McKenna, Niang (Bell 46), Holt, Foster; MacIver, Turner (Owens 69), Bannigan (Docherty 46), Tiffoney (Murray 46); Graham (Ocholi 79), Rudden.
Dumbarton: (4321) Ramsbottom; Lynch, Buchanan, McGeever, Muir; McKee (Wilson 74), Carswell (Duthie 46), Pignatiello; Hopkirk (Stokes 81), MacLean (Lamont 74); Orsi (Syvertsen 69).

Stenhousemuir (0) 1 *(Orr 76)*

St Mirren (0) 3 *(Main 50, Dennis 66, Erwin 90)* 412

Stenhousemuir: (451) Marshall; Lyon R, Crighton, Jamieson, Coll; Forbes, Lyon J (O'Reilly 57), Wedderburn, Mills (Brown A 83), Thomson (Christie 74); Orr.
St Mirren: (352) Lyness; Fraser, McCarthy, Finlayson; Flynn, MacPherson (Erwin 67), Erhahon, Kiltie (McGrath 67), Tanser (Henderson 76); Dennis (Brophy 67), Main (Power 68).

Saturday, 24 July 2021

Dunfermline Ath (3) 4 *(Wighton 15, 44, O'Hara 36, 49)*

Stenhousemuir (0) 1 *(Thomson 67)* 1570

Dunfermline Ath: (343) Fon Williams; Comrie, Gaspuitis, Graham; MacDonald, Thomas (Allan 76), Cole (Pybus 64), Edwards; Wighton (Kennedy 46), Todorov, O'Hara (Todd 86).
Stenhousemuir: (352) David Wilson; Jamieson, Crighton, Coll (Reid 46); Christie, Forbes (Andersen 63), Wedderburn, Brown A, Graham (Mills 46); Orr (Thomson 63), O'Reilly (Lyon J 46).

Sunday, 25 July 2021

St Mirren (1) 2 *(McGrath 25 (pen), Shaughnessy 90)*

Partick Thistle (0) 0 1023

St Mirren: (3412) Alnwick; Dunne, Fraser, Shaughnessy; Henderson, McGrath, Power (MacPherson 81), Tanser; Kiltie (Erhahon 69); Main, Brophy (Erwin 66).
Partick Thistle: (442) Stone; McKenna, Bell, Holt (Niang 60), Foster; Turner (Owens 79), Docherty, Bannigan (Murray 73), MacIver; Graham, Rudden (Gordon 74).

Group H Table	*P*	*W*	*PW*	*PL*	*L*	*F*	*A*	*GD*	*Pts*
St Mirren	4	4	0	0	0	9	1	8	12
Dunfermline Ath*	4	3	0	0	1	13	5	8	9
Partick Thistle	4	2	0	0	2	6	7	–1	6
Stenhousemuir	4	1	0	0	3	5	10	–5	3
Dumbarton	4	0	0	0	4	2	12	–10	0

SECOND ROUND

Friday, 13 August 2021

Rangers (4) 5 *(Lundstram 3, Wright S 17, Hagi 19, Roofe 33, 58 (pen))*

Dunfermline Ath (0) 0 41,467

Rangers: (433) McLaughlin; Patterson, Goldson, Simpson, Bassey; Kamara (Kelly 78), Lundstram, Aribo; Hagi (Arfield 70), Roofe, Wright S (Morelos 64).
Dunfermline Ath: (352) Mehmet; Comrie, Watson, Graham; MacDonald (Dow 46), Pybus, O'Hara (Thomas 46), Dorrans, Edwards; Todorov, Wighton (Cole 56).

Saturday, 14 August 2021

Ayr U (0) 1 *(Adeloye 56)*

Dundee U (0) 1 *(Clark 80 (pen))* 2196

Ayr U: (442) McAdams; Houston (Michael Miller 110), Baird J■, Fjortoft, Reading; Hewitt (Chalmers 111), Murdoch (Nicholas McAllister 103), Muirhead, Maxwell (Salkeld 91); McKenzie (Afolabi 103), Adeloye (McGinty 81).
Dundee U: (433) Siegrist; Smith L, Edwards, Mulgrew, Robson J; Harkes (Mochrie 77), Fuchs, Pawlett; Watson (Hoti 88), Clark, Sporle (McNulty 64).
aet; Dundee U won 4-3 on penalties.

Dundee (0) 1 *(Ashcroft 78)*

Motherwell (0) 0 3603

Dundee: (433) Legzdins; Elliot, Fontaine, Ashcroft, Marshall; McGhee, Byrne (McGowan 82), Adam; McMullan, Cummings (McDaid 89), McCowan (Jakubiak 76).
Motherwell: (442) Kelly; Grimshaw, Ojala, Lamie, Carroll; Slattery, Maguire (Amaluzor 74), Donnelly (O'Hara 65), Lawless; Woolery, Shields (Watt 66).

Livingston (1) 1 *(Forrest 41)*

St Mirren (0) 1 *(McCarthy 82)* 1855

Livingston: (433) Stryjek; Devlin, Fitzwater, Obileye, Longridge (Jacobs 103); Holt, Pitman, Sibbald; Bailey (Kelly 62), Anderson (Panayiotou 67), Forrest (Hamilton 66).
St Mirren: (352) Alnwick; Fraser (McAllister 73), Shaughnessy, Dunne (McCarthy 27); Tait (Henderson 59), Kiltie (MacPherson 59), McGrath, Erhahon, Tanser; Main, Brophy (Erwin 91).
aet; Livingston won 4-3 on penalties.

Sunday, 15 August 2021

Arbroath (1) 2 *(Nouble 31, O'Brien 93)*

St Johnstone (0) 2 *(Middleton 59, McCart 105)* 1842

Arbroath: (451) Gaston; Chris Hamilton, Little, O'Brien, Colin Hamilton; Stewart (Paterson 72), Clark (Gold 46), McKenna (Hilson 86), Low, Craigen (Linn 71); Nouble (Donnelly 86).
St Johnstone: (343) Parish (Clark 120); Rooney, Kerr, McCart; Brown (Davidson 106), McCann, Craig, Devine (Booth 79); Middleton (O'Halloran 84), May (Ballantyne 71), Hendry.
aet; St Johnstone won 3-2 on penalties.

Celtic (2) 3 *(Edouard 29, Welsh 34, Furuhashi 63)*

Hearts (0) 2 *(Boyce 57 (pen), McEneff 90)* 42,361

Celtic: (433) Hart; Ralston, Welsh, Starfelt, Taylor; Rogic (McCarthy 75), McGregor, Turnbull (Soro 88); Forrest, Edouard (Ajeti 88), Furuhashi (Montgomery 75).
Hearts: (532) Gordon; Smith M, Souttar, Halkett, Kingsley, Cochrane (Walker 75); Baningime, Haring (McEneff 68), Halliday (Ginnelly 46); Boyce, Mackay-Steven.

Hibernian (0) 2 *(Magennis 51, Nisbet 73)*

Kilmarnock (0) 0 5990

Hibernian: (4231) Macey; McGinn, McGregor, Porteous, Doig (Stevenson 56); Newell, Doyle-Hayes; Boyle (Wright 85), Magennis, Murphy (Allan 67); Nisbet (Mackay 85).
Kilmarnock: (4231) Walker; Naismith, Murray E, Stokes (McGinn 56), Haunstrup; Alston (Lyons 79), McGowan; Burke, Polworth, McKenzie (Armstrong 74); Robinson (Cameron 74).

Raith R (0) 2 *(Varian 48, Zanatta 71)*

Aberdeen (1) 1 *(Emmanuel-Thomas 13)* 3297

Raith R: (451) MacDonald; Tumilty, Benedictus, Berra, Dick; Connolly, Matthews, Riley-Snow (Arnott 83), Tait, Zanatta (Fotheringham 89); Varian (Poplatnik 80).
Aberdeen: (4141) Lewis; Gurr, McCrorie, Gallagher, Hayes; McGeouch (Brown 70); McLennan (Ramsay 75), Jenks (Ferguson 70), Ojo, McGinn (Ramirez 60); Emmanuel-Thomas (Hedges 70).

QUARTER-FINALS

Wednesday, 22 September 2021

Dundee (0) 0

St Johnstone (0) 2 *(Rooney 70, Crawford 84)* 4707

Dundee: (433) Legzdins; Kerr, Fontaine, Ashcroft, Marshall; Anderson (McCowan 81), Byrne, McGhee (Sheridan 75); McMullan, Griffiths, McGowan.
St Johnstone: (343) Clark; Brown (O'Halloran 45), Ambrose, McCart; Rooney, Wotherspoon, Craig, Booth; Crawford (Gilmour 90), Kane (Hendry 90), Middleton (May 65).

Rangers (0) 2 *(Roofe 48, Morelos 63)*

Livingston (0) 0 35,779

Rangers: (433) McLaughlin; Patterson (Tavernier 62), Goldson, Balogun, Bassey; Kamara, Lundstram, Aribo (Arfield 77); Wright S (Hagi 46), Morelos (Bacuna 70), Roofe (Sakala 77).
Livingston: (451) Stryjek; Devlin, Obileye, Fitzwater, Penrice; Bailey, Omeonga, Holt, Lewis (McMillan 45), Montano (Forrest 59); Shinnie (Anderson 70).

Thursday, 23 September 2021

Celtic (2) 3 *(Jota 26, Abada 40, Turnbull 47)*

Raith R (0) 0 42,367

Celtic: (4231) Hart; Ralston, Carter-Vickers, Starfelt, Montgomery; McCarthy (Bitton 69), Turnbull; Abada (Juranovic 61), Rogic (Soro 69), Jota; Ajeti (Scales 61).
Raith R: (451) MacDonald; Tumilty, Benedictus, Berra, Dick; Connolly (Fotheringham 71), Tait (McKay 71), Riley-Snow (Arnott 80), Matthews (Spencer 63), Zanatta■; Varian (Poplatnik 63).

Dundee U (0) 1 *(Pawlett 58)*

Hibernian (3) 3 *(Newell 3, Allan 37, Boyle 45 (pen))* 5395

Dundee U: (433) Carson; Freeman, Edwards, Mulgrew (Reynolds 17), McMann; Harkes, Levitt, Fuchs (Hoti 83); Pawlett (Appere 83), Clark, McNulty (Mochrie 70).
Hibernian: (4231) Macey; McGinn, Porteous, Hanlon, Stevenson; Doyle-Hayes (Gogic 77), Newell; Boyle, Magennis (Scott 85), Allan (Cadden 65); Nisbet (Gullan 85).

SEMI-FINALS

Saturday, 20 November 2021

Celtic (0) 1 *(Forrest 73)*

St Johnstone (0) 0 42,298

Celtic: (433) Hart; Ralston, Carter-Vickers, Welsh (McCarthy 78), Juranovic; Turnbull (Soro 90), Bitton, McGregor; Abada (Forrest 69), Furuhashi (Ajeti 90), Jota (Johnston 90).
St Johnstone: (352) Clark; Brown (Vertainen 80), Gordon, McCart; Rooney (Dendoncker 90), Wotherspoon (Crawford 52), Davidson, Bryson (Craig 80), Booth; O'Halloran, Kane.

Sunday, 21 November 2021

Rangers (1) 1 *(Arfield 40)*

Hibernian (3) 3 *(Boyle 9, 21, 38 (pen))* 45,014

Rangers: (433) McGregor; Tavernier, Goldson, Balogun (Bassey 80), Barisic; Arfield (Hagi 69), Davis, Kamara (Wright S 80); Aribo (Jack 69), Morelos, Kent (Sakala 61).
Hibernian: (352) Macey; McGinn, Porteous (McGregor 80), Hanlon; Cadden, Doyle-Hayes, Campbell, Newell, Doig (Stevenson 59); Nisbet (Doidge 81), Boyle.

PREMIER SPORTS SCOTTISH LEAGUE CUP FINAL 2021–22

Sunday, 19 December 2021

(at Hampden Park, attendance 48,540)

Hibernian (0) 1 Celtic (0) 2

Hibernian: (4231) Macey; McGinn, Porteous, Hanlon, Stevenson (Doig 81); Newell, Doyle-Hayes; Boyle, Campbell (Allan 73), Murphy (Doidge 81); Nisbet.
Scorer: Hanlon 51.

Celtic: (4141) Hart; Juranovic, Carter-Vickers, Starfelt, Taylor (Ralston 75); McGregor; Abada, Rogic, Turnbull (Bitton 27), Johnston (Scales 83); Furuhashi (Moffat 83).
Scorer: Furuhashi 52, 72.

Referee: John Beaton.

SPFL TRUST TROPHY 2021–22

■ *Denotes player sent off.*

FIRST ROUND – NORTH

Tuesday, 10 August 2021

Brora R (0) 0

Aberdeen U21 (0) 1 *(Ruth 70)* 86

Brora R: (433) Malin; Gamble, Nicolson, Williamson, Macdonald A; MacDonald G (Riddle 65), Gillespie, Maclean; Sutherland, MacRae J, MacRae A.
Aberdeen U21: (4231) Ritchie; Yeats■, Hancock (Fatona 76), Turner, Ngwenya; Milne, MacIver; Hanratty, Mykyta, Duncan; Ruth.
Referee: Dan McFarlane.

East Fife (1) 1 *(Mercer 33)*

St Johnstone U21 (0) 0 190

East Fife: (4231) Gallacher; Mercer, Steele, Slattery, Dow; Newton, McManus (Anderson 85); Watt, Semple (Dair 76), Smith K (Cunningham 70); Connell.
St Johnstone U21: (541) Sinclair; Innes (Pert 46), Denham, Parker, Falconer, Lowndes (Regan 87); Northcott, Ballantyne, Moreland, Kucheriavyi; Steven.
Referee: Mike Roncone.

Forfar Ath (1) 1 *(Aitken 12)*

Formartine U (0) 0 255

Forfar Ath: (352) McCallum; Meechan, Anderson S (Munro 64), Irvine; Shepherd, Gallagher (Crossan 4), Harkins, Thomas, Anderson G; Aitken (Thomson C 64), Doris.
Formartine U: (4411) Demus; Crawford (Lawson 79), Paterson, Lynch, Smith S; Rodger, Anderson, Strachan, Lisle; Greig (McGinlay 56); Smith J.
Referee: Alan Newlands.

Fraserburgh (0) 0

Cowdenbeath (0) 1 *(Buchanan L 90)* 250

Fraserburgh: (433) Flinn; Cowie, Beagrie, Campbell G, Davidson; Sargent (Hay 74), West, Watt (Young 52); Duncan, Harris (Barbour 67), Campbell P.
Cowdenbeath: (442) Gill; Mullen, Barr C, Todd, Clarke; Coulson (Miller 46), Buchanan R, Hutton, Barr B (Collins 83); Buchanan L, Mahady (Swan 46).
Referee: Chris Fordyce.

Hibernian U21 (0) 1 *(Aiken 89)*

Elgin C (1) 2 *(Hester 30, 51)* 100

Hibernian U21: (4141) Johnson; McCullock, Blaney, Fairley, Macintyre; Murray; Aiken, Fordyce (Laidlaw 65), Hamilton, Young; O'Connor.
Elgin C: (4411) McHale; Spark, Nicolson, McHardy, Little (Sopel 73); MacBeath (Dingwall T 65), Dingwall R, MacEwan, O'Keefe (Allen 84); Peters (Mailer 74); Hester (Lawrence 84).
Referee: Calum Scott.

Stenhousemuir (2) 3 *(Jamieson 31, Tierney 37, Graham 77)*

Dundee U U21 (0) 0 164

Stenhousemuir: (442) David Wilson; Lyon R (Lyon J 46), Reid, Jamieson, Craig; Christie (Graham 54), Hughes (Thomson 68), Andersen, O'Reilly (Brown A 60); Orr (Wedderburn 68), Tierney.
Dundee U U21: (442) Newman; Freeman, Hutchinson■, Cooney, Duffy; Caves, Mochrie, Neilson, Walker (Brown 75); Watson, Fotheringham (Heenan 75).
Referee: Barry Cook.

Wednesday, 11 August 2021

Brechin C (0) 1 *(Bollan 51)*

Buckie Thistle (1) 3 *(Morrison 34, Urquhart 75, Murray C 90)* 285

Brechin C: (343) Wills; Bollan, Davidson, Jordan; Bain, MacKintosh, Paton, Currie (Wade 46); Scott, Wood, Golasso (Inglis 76).
Buckie Thistle: (4321) Main; Munro, Morrison■, Murray J, McLauchlan; Pugh, Fraser, Barry (Cowie 88); MacAskill (Wood 85), Urquhart; MacLeod (Murray C 68).
Referee: Graham Grainger.

Dundee U21 (1) 1 *(Panter 35)*

Peterhead (1) 2 *(Payne 37, 70)* 258

Dundee U21: (442) Lawlor; Strachan, Wilkie, Panter, Murray; Robertson, Lamb (Richardson 90), Anderson, Mulligan; Cameron, Blacklock (White 63).
Peterhead: (3412) Wilson; Mushanu, Jason Brown, McDonald; Kesson (Long 87), Ritchie, Brown S, Conroy; Jordon Brown; Payne (McCarthy 72), Lyle (McLean 64).
Referee: Scott Lambie.

Ross Co U21

Stirling Alb (walkover)

Ross Co U21 were unable to field a team and withdrew from the competition. Walkover to Stirling Alb.

FIRST ROUND – SOUTH

Tuesday, 10 August 2021

Queen's Park (0) 1 *(Gillespie 75 (pen))*

Bonnyrigg Rose Ath (0) 1 *(Hoskins 61)* 318

Queen's Park: (4231) Muir; Doyle, Morrison, Fox, Yeats (Robson 71); Thomson (Murray 71), Gillespie; Lyon (Moore 83), Brown, Longridge; McHugh.
Bonnyrigg Rose Ath: (352) Andrews; Young, Horne, Martyniuk (Wilson 51); Gray S, Connelly (Turner 82), Stewart, Currie, Hoskins (Barrett 64); Gray R (Evans 83), Hunter.
Queen's Park won 5-4 on penalties.
Referee: Lloyd Wilson.

St Mirren U21 (0) 1 *(Jack 89)*

Kelty Hearts (0) 1 *(Tidser 69)* 372

St Mirren U21: (4231) Urminsky; McDonald, Kenny, Finlayson, Ellis (Thomson 81); Reid (Gallagher 46), McMaster; Struthers, Jack, Taylor (Donaldson 75); Offord.
Kelty Hearts: (433) Donaldson; McNab, Hooper, Hill (Philp 46), Peggie; Black, Tidser (Finnan 78), Barron (Barjonas 51); Russell (Higginbotham 51), Agyeman (Biabi 51), Cardle.
St Mirren U21 won 3-0 on penalties.
Referee: Chris Graham.

Wednesday, 11 August 2021

Broomhill (1) 1 *(Alexander 21)*

Clyde (0) 0 144

Broomhill: (4411) Barr; Duncan (Chaudry 84), MacCalman, O'Sullivan, Crawford; Gray (MacNair 72), Sinnamon, Alexander, Cusick; Monk (Slaven 60); McNab (Lavelle 60).
Clyde: (4231) Bradley-Hurst; Mortimer (Kennedy 75), Balatoni, Elsdon, Docherty (Livingstone 75); Nicoll (Cuddihy 46), Love; Cunningham, Andrew (Gomis 46), McGrath (Splaine 46); Jones.
Referee: Duncan Williams.

Celtic U21 (1) 2 *(O'Connor 3, Robertson 75)*

Annan Ath (0) 0 285

Celtic U21: (4141) Mullen; O'Connor, Lawal, Murray, Paterson; Connell; McInroy, Robertson, Shaw, Moffat (Wylie 84); Brooks (Dawson 54).
Annan Ath: (4141) Fleming G; Fleming K, Douglas, Barnes, Lowdon (Birch 68); Moxon; Robert McCartney (Anderson 61), Wallace, Docherty, Smith; Goss.
Referee: Matthew MacDermid.

Dumbarton (0) 2 *(Buchanan 88, Stokes 89)*

Rangers U21 (2) 3 *(Hastie 20, Lowry 25, Weston 76)* 259

Dumbarton: (4231) Erskine; Lynch (Schiavone 61), McGeever, Buchanan, Boyle; Carswell (Paton 60), Geggan; Hopkirk (Wilson 72), Pignatiello, MacLean (Stokes 80); Orsi (Syvertsen 72).
Rangers U21: (433) Budinauckas; Devine, McClelland, Katic (King 72), Fraser; McKinnon (Miller 79), McCann, Lindsay (Ritchie-Hosler 87); Hastie (Lyall 79), Weston, Lowry (McKee 71).
Referee: Steven Reid.

Falkirk (1) 3 *(Old 31 (og), Ross 57, Keena 72)*

East Kilbride (0) 0 1120

Falkirk: (433) Martin; Williamson C, Hall (Telfer 61), Lemon, McCann (Miller 61); Ross, Krasniqi, Nesbitt (Hetherington 61); Ompreon (Morrison 74), Weekes, Wilson (Keena 68).
East Kilbride: (4411) Kean; Stevenson, Saunders (Mcluckie 66), Old, Wylde (Peacock 46); McAninch, Millar, Stewart (Rodgers 12), Brady; Erskine (Fellowes 72); Malcolm (Vezza 72).
Referee: Lorraine Watson.

Tuesday, 17 August 2021

Edinburgh C (0) 0

Hearts U21 (1) 1 *(Henderson 44 (pen))* 272

Edinburgh C: (433) Schwake; Reekie, Bronsky, Hamilton, McIntyre (Fraser 73); McFarlane (Brian 62), See, Jardine; Hilton, Handling, Crane (Tapping C 25).
Hearts U21: (433) MacFarlane; Docherty (Thomas 65), Watson, Darge, Popescu; Rathie, Smith C, Denholm; McGill, Henderson, Kirk (Hambrook 85).
Referee: Lloyd Wilson.

Stranraer 3

Motherwell U21 0

Motherwell U21 were unable to field a team due to positive COVID-19 tests in the camp. Stranraer awarded 3-0 win.

Livingston U21

Albion R (walkover)

Livingston U21 were unable to field a team and withdrew from the competition. Walkover to Albion R.

SECOND ROUND – NORTH

Saturday, 4 September 2021

Aberdeen U21 (0) 1 *(Ruth 74)*

Arbroath (0) 1 *(Henderson 90)* 650

Aberdeen U21: (4231) Ritchie; Gurr, Towler, Hancock, Ngwenya; Milne, MacIver; Hanratty, Mykyta, Duncan; Harvey (Ruth 66).
Arbroath: (442) Antell; Chris Hamilton (O'Brien 72), Thomson, Henderson, Gold (Colin Hamilton 63); Paterson, Clark (Stewart 72), Low (Craigen 71), Hilson; Donnelly (McKenna 64), Dowds.
Aberdeen U21 won 4-1 on penalties.
Referee: Chris Graham.

Cove R (0) 0

Stenhousemuir (0) 0 324

Cove R: (433) McKenzie; Logan, Neill, Ross, Scully; Fyvie, Yule, Masson; McAllister, Megginson, McIntosh (Leitch 68).
Stenhousemuir: (433) David Wilson; Lyon R, Jamieson, Corbett, Coll; Forbes, Miller (Wedderburn 68), Andersen (Brown A 90); Thomson (Tierney 62), Orr, Graham (O'Reilly 62).
Cove R won 4-2 on penalties.
Referee: Barry Cook.

Cowdenbeath (0) 0

Alloa Ath (1) 2 *(Boyd 45, Scougall 79)* 292

Cowdenbeath: (442) Gill; Mullen, Barr C, Todd, Thomson; Buchanan R, Miller (Barr B 73), Hutton, Clarke; Renton (Mahady 55), Buchanan L.
Alloa Ath: (433) Hutton; Robertson, Mendy, Durnan, Church; King, Niang (Howie 80), Scougall; Cawley (Lamont 90), Trouten, Boyd.
Referee: Dan McFarlane.

Inverness CT (1) 4 *(Jamieson 24, Harper 67, McKay 81, 90)*

Buckie Thistle (0) 0 902

Inverness CT: (4411) Mackay; Hyde (Allardice 86), Duffy, Deas, Harper; McDonald (Walsh 65), Welsh, McAlear, Doran; Jamieson; McKay.
Buckie Thistle: (532) Main; Wood (Goodall 80), Pugh, MacKinnon (Cowie 60), Murray J, McLauchlan; Fraser, Barry, Urquhart; MacAskill, MacLeod (Murray C 68).
Referee: Calum Scott.

Montrose (1) 1 *(Webster 4 (pen))*

Stirling Alb (0) 0 491

Montrose: (433) Lennox; Webster, Quinn, Steeves, Callaghan; Masson, Watson, Brown; Antoniazzi (Whatley 61), Johnston, Lyons.
Stirling Alb: (442) Law; Greenhorn (Drydon 80), Banner, Cummins, Creaney; Moore, Laird, Roberts K (Grant R 81), Scally; Bikey, Heaver (Carey 86).
Referee: Chris Fordyce.

Peterhead (0) 0

East Fife (1) 1 *(Denholm 10)* 358

Peterhead: (442) Wilson; Jason Brown, Mushanu, McDonald, Conroy (Ritchie 60); Kesson, Brown S, McCarthy (Payne 60), Jordon Brown (Cook 78); McLean, Lyle.
East Fife: (4231) Smith J; Dunsmore, Steele, Higgins D, Mercer; Newton (McManus 82), Millar; Denholm (Anderson 88), Osei-Bonsu (Brown 69), Watt (Slattery 68); Semple.
Referee: Stewart Luke.

Raith R (1) 1 *(Riley-Snow 25)*

Forfar Ath (0) 0 842

Raith R: (433) MacDonald; Tumilty, Benedictus, Berra (Lang 87), Dick; Tait, Riley-Snow, Matthews; Varian (Mitchell 71), Poplatnik (Keatings 71), Zanatta (Connolly 78).
Forfar Ath: (4411) McCallum; Meechan, Travis (Irvine 66), Anderson S, Strachan; Thomson C, Slater, Ness (Gallagher 72), Anderson G (Crossan 72); Harkins (McCluskey 55); Doris (Aitken 55).
Referee: Matthew MacDermid.

Elgin C 3

Dunfermline Ath 0

Dunfermline Ath were unable to field a team due to positive COVID-19 tests in the camp. Elgin C awarded 3-0 win.

SECOND ROUND – SOUTH

Tuesday, 31 August 2021

Hamilton A (1) 3 *(Virtanen 5, Spence 71, Ryan 78)*

Hearts U21 (0) 2 *(Kirk 61, Denholm 63)* 409

Hamilton A: (433) Fulton; Stirling, Want (Matheson 45), Stanger, MacDonald; Mullin, Virtanen (Spence 52), Mimnaugh; Smith L (Redfern 69), Moyo (Ryan 62), Munro.
Hearts U21: (343) Stewart; Rathie, Flatman, Docherty; Smith C, McGill, Denholm, Watson; Pollock, Kirk (Tait 86), Henderson.
Referee: Chris Graham.

Friday, 3 September 2021

Airdrieonians (0) 1 *(Smith 49)*

Queen's Park (0) 1 *(Gillespie 86 (pen))* 460

Airdrieonians: (4132) Cantley; Wardrop (Walker 82), Watson, Fordyce, Quitongo; McCabe; Smith, Easton, Frizzell; Allan (Agnew 74), McGill G.
Queen's Park: (4231) Ferrie; Gillies, Doyle, Kilday, Yeats (Robson 79); Brown, Lyon (Gillespie 84); Moore (Longridge 68), Longstaff (Thomson 79), Biggar (Murray 68); McHugh.
Queen's Park won 5-4 on penalties.
Referee: Grant Irvine.

Saturday, 4 September 2021

Albion R (3) 6 *(Clocherty 3 (og), Doherty 23, 44 (pen), 59, 64, Dolan 90)*

St Mirren U21 (0) 0 317

Albion R: (442) Binnie; Lynas, Fagan, El-Zubaidi (Fernie 80), Wilson L; Wilson C (Reilly 67), Roberts, McKernon, Leslie; Doherty (McVey 80), Wright (Dolan 67).
St Mirren U21: (3412) Thackery; McDonald, Clocherty, Ellis; Taylor (Gilmartin 57), McMaster, McManus, Thomson (Donaldson 46); Jack; Offord, Struthers (Czapla 73).
Referee: Lloyd Wilson.

Celtic U21 (1) 1 *(Dickson 29)*

Greenock Morton (2) 3 *(Garrity 16, Muirhead 26, Blues 66)* 482

Celtic U21: (433) Mullen; Murphy, Urhoghide, Corr, Anderson (Letsosa 61); McInroy, Dickson, Shaw; Davidson, Brooks, Carse.
Greenock Morton: (442) Wylie; Hynes, Ledger, Lithgow, Russell (Strapp 71); Blues, McGrattan (Allan 71), Garrity, Lyon; Muirhead (Knowles 68), Reilly (Oliver 88).
Referee: Mike Roncone.

Kilmarnock (1) 3 *(Murray F 4, 78, Naismith 55)*

Falkirk (1) 1 *(Nesbitt 8)* 2457

Kilmarnock: (4231) Walker; Naismith, Sanders, Murray E, Waters; Lyons, Alston; Armstrong (McKenzie 77), Polworth (Watson 84), Murray F (Warnock 83); Shaw (Cameron 81).
Falkirk: (433) Martin; Williamson C, McKay (Hall 46), Lemon (Dixon 77), McCann; Ross (Telfer 64), Krasniqi (Hetherington 64), Nesbitt; Wilson (Weekes 69), Ompreon, McGuffie.
Referee: Alan Newlands.

Stranraer (0) 0

Partick Thistle (1) 2 *(Akinola 12, Holt 90)* 598

Stranraer: (4231) Scullion; Ross C, Sonkur, Robertson, Burns; Watson (Moore 84), Gallagher; Smith R, Rennie (Josh Walker 84), Woods; Irving (Yates 57).
Partick Thistle: (442) Sneddon; Gordon, Akinola, Holt, Foster; MacIver (Graham 65), Docherty, Bannigan (Stanway 90), Tiffoney (Stevenson 90); Smith, Murray (Turner 65).
Referee: Craig Napier.

Sunday, 5 September 2021

Queen of the South (1) 3 *(Paton 7 (pen), Connelly 62, Gibson 78 (pen))*

Broomhill (0) 0 717

Queen of the South: (3421) Brynn; Nditi, McKay, Debayo; Johnston, Cochrane (McGrory 80), Todd (Joseph 69), Gibson; Paton (Liddle 69), Connelly (McMahon 87); Soares-Junior (East 80).
Broomhill: (4411) Smith; Crawford, Cassidy (O'Connor 79), O'Sullivan, Moss (Dunlop 65); Gray, Sinnamon, Devenny, Cusick (Chiedu 79); Kavanagh (Slaven 59); Frizzell (McNab 65).
Referee: Peter Stuart.

Tuesday, 14 September 2021

Rangers U21 3

Ayr U 0

Rangers: (433) Wright; Devine, King (Ewen 77), Mackinnon, Fraser; McKinnon, Miller (Ritchie-Hosler 51), Lindsay; McCausland (Ure 83), Weston McCann.
Ayr U: (442) McAdams; Houston (Jeanes 82), Fjortoft, McGinty, Ecrepont; Chalmers, Muirhead (Salkeld 58), Murdoch (Bradley 69), O'Connor (Adeloy 69); McKenzie (Bilham 82), Moffat.
Rangers U21 awarded 3-0 won after Ayr U had fielded two ineligible players. The original match ended in a 3-0 win to Ayr U.

THIRD ROUND

Wednesday, 6 October 2021

Hamilton A (1) 2 *(McGowan 37, Munro 67)*

Aberdeen U21 (0) 0 363

Hamilton A: (4141) Hilton; Stirling, Hamilton, Easton, McGinn; Mimnaugh; Munro, Hughes (Smith L 46), Virtanen, McGowan; Moyo (Ryan 46).
Aberdeen U21: (4231) Ritchie; Gurr (Fatona 74), Milne, Hancock, Towler; Yeats, Campbell■; Mykyta, MacIver (Lobban 77), Hanratty; Ruth.
Referee: Steven Kirkland.

Friday, 8 October 2021

Kilmarnock (1) 3 *(Shaw 14, Murray E 53, Hendry 61)*

Queen's Park (0) 1 *(Gillespie 50 (pen))* 2149

Kilmarnock: (442) Walker; Hodson, Murray E, McArthur, Waters; Burke (Armstrong 64), Lyons (Brindley 80), McGinn, McKenzie (Warnock 86); Shaw (Burrell 85), Hendry (Robinson 64).
Queen's Park: (4231) Ferrie; Doyle, Kilday, Fox (Gillies 89), Robson (Yeats 89); Gillespie, Thomson (Brown 74); Moore (Biggar 74), Longstaff, Longridge; McHugh.
Referee: Alan Muir.

Queen of the South (0) 2 *(Connelly 69, Roy 90)*

Partick Thistle (0) 0 1043

Queen of the South: (3421) Brynn; Nditi, McKay, Debayo; Johnston, Gibson, Liddle (Cochrane 87), Cooper; Fitzpatrick (Roy 76), Connelly (East 81); Paton (Soares-Junior 81).
Partick Thistle: (4231) Sneddon; Akinola, McKenna, Holt, Hendrie; Docherty, Turner (Gordon 72); Smith (Murray 67), Rudden (Bannigan 66), Tiffoney; Graham (MacIver 82).
Referee: Alan Newlands.

Saturday, 9 October 2021

Cove R (0) 4 *(Megginson 79, McAllister 82, 89, Masson 86)*

Albion R (0) 1 *(Wright 90)* 327

Cove R: (442) Gourlay; Yule, Ross, Neill, Milne; McIntosh (Masson 56), Fyvie, Scully, Leitch (Adeyemo 56); Megginson, McAllister.
Albion R: (442) Binnie; Lynas, McGowan, Fagan, Wilson L (El-Zubaidi 58); Wilson C, Leslie, Wilson D, O'Donnell (Sweeney 80); Doherty, Mullen (Wright 65).
Referee: Graham Grainger.

Elgin C (2) 2 *(Grivosti 9, Cameron 22)*

Inverness CT (2) 4 *(McKay 38, 40, 68, Jamieson 72)* 1348

Elgin C: (4231) McHale; Spark, Grivosti, McHardy, MacPhee (Peters 85); MacEwan (Allen 76), Mailer; Dingwall R, Cameron, Dingwall T (Lawrence 76); O'Keefe (Machado 58).
Inverness CT: (4312) Mackay; Duffy, Devine (Doran 76), Deas, Harper (Allardice 50); McAlear, Welsh, MacGregor; Sutherland (Duku 76); McKay, Jamieson.
Referee: Barry Cook.

Montrose (0) 0

Greenock Morton (0) 0 476

Montrose: (4411) Lennox; Allan (Webster 46), Quinn (Masson 76), Waddell, Steeves; Brown (Milne 69), Watson, Whatley, Lyons; Antoniazzi (Dillon 69); Johnston.
Greenock Morton: (352) Hamilton; Ledger, Lithgow, Strapp; Russell (Blues 68), Jacobs (King 68), Lyon, McGrattan, Allan (Reilly 81); Knowles, Oliver.
Greenock Morton won 4-2 on penalties.
Referee: Lloyd Wilson.

Raith R (2) 3 *(Tait 35, Connolly 39, Poplatnik 62)*

East Fife (1) 1 *(Mercer 37)* 1177

Raith R: (433) MacDonald; Tumilty, Benedictus, Berra, Dick (Young 88); Tait (Riley-Snow 88), Matthews, Spencer; Connolly (Arnott 82), Varian (Poplatnik 58), Zanatta (Mitchell 82).
East Fife: (352) Smith J; Dunlop, Higgins C, Steele; Mercer, Millar, McManus (Newton 71), Watt, Slattery (Denholm 58); Brown (Connell 58), Osei-Bonsu (Smith K 77).
Referee: Mike Roncone.

Wednesday, 27 October 2021

Alloa Ath (2) 2 *(Niang 8, Trouten 40)*

Rangers U21 (2) 3 *(Alegria 30, 34, 62)* 234

Alloa Ath: (4231) Hutton; Leighton, Graham, Armstrong, Church (Williamson 52); King, Niang (Howie 60); Lamont (Scougall 60), Trouten (Taggart 79), O'Donnel; Sammon (Armour 46).
Rangers U21: (433) Budinauckas; Devine, Mackinnon, McKinnon, Fraser; Kelly, McCann, Lindsay (Weston 90); McCausland (Miller 90), Alegria (Ure 74), Lowry (Ritchie-Hosler 82).
Referee: Calum Scott.

QUARTER-FINALS

Tuesday, 30 November 2021

Cove R (4) 5 *(Fyvie 3, 35, Megginson 5 (pen), Masson 14, McIntosh 67)*

Rangers U21 (1) 1 *(Fraser 10)* 562

Cove R: (4231) Gourlay; Logan, Ross (Strachan 69), Neill, Milne■; Vigurs, Scully; Yule, Fyvie, Masson (McIntosh 65); Megginson (Adeyemo 72).
Rangers U21: (433) Budinauckas; Devine, Mackinnon (McClelland 25), King (Ritchie-Hosler 46), Fraser; McCann, Kelly, McKinnon; Lowry, Weston (McKee 87), McCausland (Alegria 48).
Referee: Mike Roncone.

Hamilton A (0) 2 *(Moyo 68, Ryan 86 (pen))*

Kilmarnock (0) 3 *(Armstrong 53, Sanders 89, 90)* 829

Hamilton A: (4141) Hilton; Want (Stirling 22 (Matheson 46)), Hamilton (Shiels 73), Easton, MacDonald; Mimnaugh; Ryan, Mullin, Virtanen (Martin 54), Smith L; Moyo.
Kilmarnock: (3412) Walker; Sanders, Stokes, McArthur; Murray F (Lyons 69), McGinn, Alston, Haunstrup; Hendry (Shaw 77); Burrell (Robinson 77), Armstrong (Warnock 63).
Referee: Steven Kirkland.

Inverness CT (0) 0

Raith R (0) 0 670

Inverness CT: (442) Mackay; Carson (Carnihan 77), Welsh (Allardice 61), Deas, Harper; Walsh, McAlear (Doran 77), MacGregor (MacInnes 61), McDonald; McKay (Sutherland 46), Jamieson.
Raith R: (4411) Thomson; Tumilty, Benedictus (Lang 79), Berra, Dick; Connolly, Matthews, Tait, Zanatta (Mitchell 57); Ross (Riley-Snow 35 (Arnott 79)); Poplatnik (Varian 56).
Raith R won 5-4 on penalties.
Referee: Barry Cook.

Wednesday, 1 December 2021

Queen of the South (1) 2 *(Hamilton 27 (og), Paton 88)*

Greenock Morton (0) 1 *(Lithgow 86)* 525

Queen of the South: (4141) Brynn; Johnston, McKay, Gibson, Cooper; McGrory; Paton, Cochrane, Todd (Joseph 80), Connelly; Soares-Junior (Roy 80).
Greenock Morton: (442) Hamilton; Ledger, Lithgow, McEntee, Strapp; Oliver (Muirhead 56), Jacobs (Reilly 56), Oksanen (Allan 73), McGrattan (King 46); Lyon, Ugwu (Easdale 73).
Referee: Alan Newlands.

SEMI-FINALS

Tuesday, 1 March 2022

Cove R (0) 0

Queen of the South (1) 1 *(Fitzpatrick 2)* 728

Cove R: (3412) Gourlay; Ross, Neill, Reynolds; Yule, Fyvie (Adeyemo 78), Vigurs, Scully (McIntosh 78); Leitch (Masson 69); Megginson, McAllister.
Queen of the South: (352) Rae; O'Connor, East, Debayo (Cooper 85); Johnston, Fitzpatrick (Joseph 86), McGrory, Todd, Gibson; Soares-Junior, Roy (Paton 90).
Referee: David Dickinson.

Wednesday, 2 March 2022

Kilmarnock (1) 1 *(Shaw 43 (pen))*

Raith R (0) 2 *(Matthews 66, Waters 87 (og))* 2118

Kilmarnock: (433) Walker; Naismith (Hodson 76), Murray E, Stokes (McArthur 46), Waters; Murray F, Alston, Glass (McGinn 76); Armstrong (McKenzie 63), Shaw, Mackay (Burke 85).
Raith R: (4231) MacDonald; Tumilty, Benedictus, Berra, Dick; Matthews, Stanton; Connolly (Ross 71), Williamson, Zanatta (Arnott 80); Varian (Poplatnik 46).
Referee: Grant Irvine.

SPFL TRUST TROPHY FINAL 2021–22

Sunday, 3 April 2022

(at Airdrieonians, attendance 4452)

Raith R (1) 3 Queen of the South (1) 1

Raith R: (442) MacDonald; Tumilty, Musonda, Dick (McKay 83), Mackie; Connolly, Stanton, Matthews, Ross (Arnott 87); Poplatnik, Varian (Zanatta 56).
Scorers: Poplatnik 16, 70, Ross 78.

Queen of the South: (442) Rae; Cooper, East, O'Connor, Gibson; Todd, Cochrane, McGrory, Connelly (McKechnie 81); Roy, Paton (Soares-Junior 81).
Scorer: Roy 45.

Referee: Grant Irvine.

SCOTTISH FA CUP FINALS 1874–2022

SCOTTISH FA CUP

1874	Queen's Park v Clydesdale	2-0
1875	Queen's Park v Renton	3-0
1876	Queen's Park v Third Lanark	1-1
Replay	Queen's Park v Third Lanark	2-0
1877	Vale of Leven v Rangers	1-1
Replay	Vale of Leven v Rangers	1-1
2nd Replay	Vale of Leven v Rangers	3-2
1878	Vale of Leven v Third Lanark	1-0
1879	Vale of Leven v Rangers	1-1
	Vale of Leven awarded cup, Rangers failing to appear for replay.	
1880	Queen's Park v Thornliebank	3-0
1881	Queen's Park v Dumbarton	2-1
Replay	Queen's Park v Dumbarton	3-1
	After Dumbarton protested the first game.	
1882	Queen's Park v Dumbarton	2-2
Replay	Queen's Park v Dumbarton	4-1
1883	Dumbarton v Vale of Leven	2-2
Replay	Dumbarton v Vale of Leven	2-1
1884	Queen's Park v Vale of Leven	
	Queen's Park awarded cup, Vale of Leven failing to appear.	
1885	Renton v Vale of Leven	0-0
Replay	Renton v Vale of Leven	3-1
1886	Queen's Park v Renton	3-1
1887	Hibernian v Dumbarton	2-1
1888	Renton v Cambuslang	6-1
1889	Third Lanark v Celtic	3-0
Replay	Third Lanark v Celtic	2-1
	Replay by order of Scottish FA because of playing conditions in first match.	
1890	Queen's Park v Vale of Leven	1-1
Replay	Queen's Park v Vale of Leven	2-1
1891	Hearts v Dumbarton	1-0
1892	Celtic v Queen's Park	1-0
Replay	Celtic v Queen's Park	5-1
	After mutually protested first match.	
1893	Queen's Park v Celtic	0-1
Replay	Queen's Park v Celtic	2-1
	Replay by order of Scottish FA because of playing conditions in first match.	
1894	Rangers v Celtic	3-1
1895	St Bernard's v Renton	2-1
1896	Hearts v Hibernian	3-1
1897	Rangers v Dumbarton	5-1
1898	Rangers v Kilmarnock	2-0
1899	Celtic v Rangers	2-0
1900	Celtic v Queen's Park	4-3
1901	Hearts v Celtic	4-3
1902	Hibernian v Celtic	1-0
1903	Rangers v Hearts	1-1
Replay	Rangers v Hearts	0-0
2nd Replay	Rangers v Hearts	2-0
1904	Celtic v Rangers	3-2
1905	Third Lanark v Rangers	0-0
Replay	Third Lanark v Rangers	3-1
1906	Hearts v Third Lanark	1-0
1907	Celtic v Hearts	3-0
1908	Celtic v St Mirren	5-1
1909	Celtic v Rangers	2-2
Replay	Celtic v Rangers	1-1
	Owing to riot, the cup was withheld.	
1910	Dundee v Clyde	2-2
Replay	Dundee v Clyde	0-0*
2nd Replay	Dundee v Clyde	2-1
1911	Celtic v Hamilton A	0-0
Replay	Celtic v Hamilton A	2-0
1912	Celtic v Clyde	2-0
1913	Falkirk v Raith R	2-0
1914	Celtic v Hibernian	0-0
Replay	Celtic v Hibernian	4-1
1920	Kilmarnock v Albion R	3-2
1921	Partick Thistle v Rangers	1-0
1922	Morton v Rangers	1-0
1923	Celtic v Hibernian	1-0
1924	Airdrieonians v Hibernian	2-0
1925	Celtic v Dundee	2-1
1926	St Mirren v Celtic	2-0
1927	Celtic v East Fife	3-1
1928	Rangers v Celtic	4-0
1929	Kilmarnock v Rangers	2-0
1930	Rangers v Partick Thistle	0-0
Replay	Rangers v Partick Thistle	2-1
1931	Celtic v Motherwell	2-2
Replay	Celtic v Motherwell	4-2
1932	Rangers v Kilmarnock	1-1
Replay	Rangers v Kilmarnock	3-0
1933	Celtic v Motherwell	1-0
1934	Rangers v St Mirren	5-0
1935	Rangers v Hamilton A	2-1
1936	Rangers v Third Lanark	1-0
1937	Celtic v Aberdeen	2-1
1938	East Fife v Kilmarnock	1-1
Replay	East Fife v Kilmarnock	4-2*
1939	Clyde v Motherwell	4-0
1947	Aberdeen v Hibernian	2-1
1948	Rangers v Morton	1-1*
Replay	Rangers v Morton	1-0*
1949	Rangers v Clyde	4-1
1950	Rangers v East Fife	3-0
1951	Celtic v Motherwell	1-0
1952	Motherwell v Dundee	4-0
1953	Rangers v Aberdeen	1-1
Replay	Rangers v Aberdeen	1-0
1954	Celtic v Aberdeen	2-1
1955	Clyde v Celtic	1-1
Replay	Clyde v Celtic	1-0
1956	Hearts v Celtic	3-1
1957	Falkirk v Kilmarnock	1-1
Replay	Falkirk v Kilmarnock	2-1*
1958	Clyde v Hibernian	1-0
1959	St Mirren v Aberdeen	3-1
1960	Rangers v Kilmarnock	2-0
1961	Dunfermline Ath v Celtic	0-0
Replay	Dunfermline Ath v Celtic	2-0
1962	Rangers v St Mirren	2-0
1963	Rangers v Celtic	1-1
Replay	Rangers v Celtic	3-0
1964	Rangers v Dundee	3-1
1965	Celtic v Dunfermline Ath	3-2
1966	Rangers v Celtic	0-0
Replay	Rangers v Celtic	1-0
1967	Celtic v Aberdeen	2-0
1968	Dunfermline Ath v Hearts	3-1
1969	Celtic v Rangers	4-0
1970	Aberdeen v Celtic	3-1
1971	Celtic v Rangers	1-1
Replay	Celtic v Rangers	2-1
1972	Celtic v Hibernian	6-1
1973	Rangers v Celtic	3-2
1974	Celtic v Dundee U	3-0
1975	Celtic v Airdrieonians	3-1
1976	Rangers v Hearts	3-1
1977	Celtic v Rangers	1-0
1978	Rangers v Aberdeen	2-1
1979	Rangers v Hibernian	0-0
Replay	Rangers v Hibernian	0-0*
2nd Replay	Rangers v Hibernian	3-2*
1980	Celtic v Rangers	1-0*
1981	Rangers v Dundee U	0-0*
Replay	Rangers v Dundee U	4-1
1982	Aberdeen v Rangers	4-1*
1983	Aberdeen v Rangers	1-0*
1984	Aberdeen v Celtic	2-1*
1985	Celtic v Dundee U	2-1
1986	Aberdeen v Hearts	3-0
1987	St Mirren v Dundee U	1-0*
1988	Celtic v Dundee U	2-1
1989	Celtic v Rangers	1-0

TENNENTS SCOTTISH CUP

1990	Aberdeen v Celtic	0-0*
	Aberdeen won 9-8 on penalties.	
1991	Motherwell v Dundee U	4-3*
1992	Rangers v Airdrieonians	2-1
1993	Rangers v Aberdeen	2-1
1994	Dundee U v Rangers	1-0
1995	Celtic v Airdrieonians	1-0
1996	Rangers v Hearts	5-1
1997	Kilmarnock v Falkirk	1-0
1998	Hearts v Rangers	2-1
1999	Rangers v Celtic	1-0
2000	Rangers v Aberdeen	4-0
2001	Celtic v Hibernian	3-0
2002	Rangers v Celtic	3-2
2003	Rangers v Dundee	1-0
2004	Celtic v Dunfermline Ath	3-1
2005	Celtic v Dundee U	1-0
2006	Hearts v Gretna	1-1*
	Hearts won 4-2 on penalties.	
2007	Celtic v Dunfermline Ath	1-0

SCOTTISH FA CUP

2008	Rangers v Queen of the South	3-2

HOMECOMING SCOTTISH CUP

2009	Rangers v Falkirk	1-0

ACTIVE NATION SCOTTISH CUP

2010	Dundee U v Ross Co	3-0

SCOTTISH FA CUP

2011	Celtic v Motherwell	3-0

WILLIAM HILL SCOTTISH CUP

2012	Hearts v Hibernian	5-1
2013	Celtic v Hibernian	3-0
2014	St Johnstone v Dundee U	2-0
2015	Inverness CT v Falkirk	2-1
2016	Hibernian v Rangers	3-2
2017	Celtic v Aberdeen	2-1
2018	Celtic v Motherwell	2-0
2019	Celtic v Hearts	2-1
2020	Celtic v Hearts	3-3*
	Celtic won 4-3 on penalties	

SCOTTISH FA CUP

2021	St Johnstone v Hibernian	1-0
2022	Rangers v Hearts	2-0*

**After extra time.*

SCOTTISH CUP WINS

Celtic 40†, Rangers 34†, Queen's Park 10, Hearts 8, Aberdeen 7, Clyde 3, Hibernian 3, Kilmarnock 3, St Mirren 3, Vale of Leven 3, Dundee U 2, Dunfermline Ath 2, Falkirk 2, Motherwell 2, Renton 2, St Johnstone 2, Third Lanark 2, Airdrieonians 1, Dumbarton 1, Dundee 1, East Fife 1, Inverness CT 1, Morton 1, Partick Thistle 1, St Bernard's 1.
†*The 1909 final between Celtic and Rangers is not included. Owing to a riot the cup was withheld.*

APPEARANCES IN FINAL

Celtic 59, Rangers 53, Hearts 17, Aberdeen 16, Hibernian 15, Queen's Park 12, Dundee U 10, Kilmarnock 8, Motherwell 8, Vale of Leven 7, Clyde 6, Dumbarton 6, St Mirren 6, Third Lanark 6, Dundee 5, Dunfermline Ath 5, Falkirk 5, Renton 5, Airdrieonians 4, East Fife 3, Hamilton A 2, Morton 2, Partick Thistle 2, St Johnstone 2, Albion R 1, Cambuslang 1, Clydesdale 1, Gretna 1, Inverness CT 1, Queen of the South 1, Raith R 1, Ross Co 1, St Bernard's 1, Thornliebank 1.

LEAGUE CHALLENGE FINALS 1990–2022

B&Q CENTENARY CUP

1990–91	Dundee v Ayr U	3-2*

B&Q CUP

1991–92	Hamilton A v Ayr U	1-0
1992–93	Hamilton A v Morton	3-2
1993–94	Falkirk v St Mirren	3-0
1994–95	Airdrieonians v Dundee	3-2*

SCOTTISH LEAGUE CHALLENGE CUP

1995–96	Stenhousemuir v Dundee U	0-0*
	Stenhousemuir won 5-4 on penalties.	
1996–97	Stranraer v St Johnstone	1-0
1997–98	Falkirk v Queen of the South	1-0
1998–99	*No competition.*	
	Suspended due to lack of sponsorship.	

BELL'S CHALLENGE CUP

1999–2000	Alloa Ath v Inverness CT	4-4*
	Alloa Ath won 5-4 on penalties.	
2000–01	Airdrieonians v Livingston	2-2*
	Airdrieonians won 3-2 on penalties.	
2001–02	Airdrieonians v Alloa Ath	2-1

BELL'S CUP

2002–03	Queen of the South v Brechin C	2-0
2003–04	Inverness CT v Airdrie U	2-0
2004–05	Falkirk v Ross Co	2-1
2005–06	St Mirren v Hamilton A	2-1

SCOTTISH LEAGUE CHALLENGE CUP

2006–07	Ross Co v Clyde	1-1*
	Ross Co won 5-4 on penalties.	
2007–08	St Johnstone v Dunfermline Ath	3-2

ALBA CHALLENGE CUP

2008–09	Airdrie U v Ross Co	2-2*
	Airdrie U won 3-2 on penalties.	
2009–10	Dundee v Inverness CT	3-2
2010–11	Ross Co v Queen of the South	2-0

RAMSDENS CUP

2011–12	Falkirk v Hamilton A	1-0
2012–13	Queen of the South v Partick Thistle	1-1*
	Queen of the South won 6-5 on penalties.	
2013–14	Raith R v Rangers	1-0*

PETROFAC TRAINING SCOTTISH LEAGUE CHALLENGE CUP

2014–15	Livingston v Alloa Athletic	4-0
2015–16	Rangers v Peterhead	4-0

IRN-BRU SCOTTISH LEAGUE CHALLENGE CUP

2016–17	Dundee U v St Mirren	2-1
2017–18	Inverness CT v Dumbarton	1-0
2018–19	Ross Co v Connah's Quay Nomads	3-1

TUNNOCK'S CARAMEL WAFER SCOTTISH LEAGUE CHALLENGE CUP

2019–20†	Raith R v Inverness CT	Joint winners
2020–21	*No competition due to COVID-19 pandemic*	

SPFL TRUST TROPHY

2021–22	Raith R v Queen of the South	3-1

**After extra time.* †*Due to the COVID-19 pandemic, the final due to be played on Sunday 8 March 2020 was postponed.*

SCOTTISH FA CUP 2021–22

■ *Denotes player sent off.*

PRELIMINARY ROUND

Blackburn U v Easthouses Lily Miners Welfare	2-1
Burntisland Shipyard v Dalkeith Thistle	1-1
Dunbar U v Broxburn Ath	3-1
Dundonald Bluebell v Penicuik Ath	1-3
Hawick Royal Albert U v Golspie Sutherland	0-2
Irvine Meadow v Musselburgh Ath	2-1
Jeanfield Swifts v Whitehill Welfare	4-1
Linlithgow Rose v Banks O' Dee	1-2
Newton Stewart v Coldstream	1-3
Preston Ath v Threave R	2-0
Tynecastle v Girvan	4-2

PRELIMINARY ROUND REPLAY

Dalkeith Thistle v Burntisland Shipyard	3-3
(Dalkeith Thistle won 6-5 on penalties)	

FIRST ROUND

Banks O' Dee v Turriff U	1-0
Berwick Rangers v Gretna 2008	2-1
Blackburn U v Rothes	1-2
Brechin C v Vale Of Leithen	5-0
Broomhill v Glasgow University	6-0
Caledonian Braves v Stirling University	0-1
Clachnacuddin v Dunipace	1-2
Clydebank v Dalkeith Thistle	7-0
Coldstream v East Kilbride	1-10
Cumbernauld Colts v Buckie Thistle	1-1
Deveronvale v Haddington Ath	2-2
Dunbar U v Camelon Juniors	2-0
East Stirlingshire v Fort William	3-0
Formartine U v Cumnock Juniors	2-2
Forres Mechanics v Bonnyrigg Rose Ath	0-2
Fraserburgh v Sauchie Juniors	1-2
Golspie Sutherland v Civil Service Strollers	0-3
Huntly v Hill Of Beath Hawthorn	3-0
Inverurie Loco Works v Jeanfield Swifts	0-3
Irvine Meadow v Auchinleck Talbot	1-3
Keith v Darvel	1-2
Lossiemouth v Preston Ath	0-3
Lothian Thistle v Edinburgh University	2-2
Nairn Co v Strathspey Thistle	4-0
Newtongrange Star v Dalbeattie Star	1-1
Penicuik Ath v Tranent Juniors	1-3
Spartans v Gala Fairydean R	0-1
Tynecastle v Brora Rangers	0-6
Wick Academy v Bo'ness U	2-2
Wigtown & Bladnoch v St Cuthbert W	0-8

FIRST ROUND REPLAYS

Bo'ness U v Wick Academy	4-1
Buckie Thistle v Cumbernauld Colts	4-1
Cumnock Juniors v Formartine U	1-5
Dalbeattie Star v Newtongrange Star	3-2
Edinburgh University v Lothian Thistle	0-3
Haddington Ath v Deveronvale	1-1
(Haddington Ath won 5-3 on penalties)	

SECOND ROUND

Saturday, 23 October 2021

Annan Ath (0) 3 *(Wallace 50 (pen), 60, Moxon 85)*
Jeanfield Swifts (0) 1 *(McLeish 89)* 395

Annan Ath: (442) Adamson; Birch, Barnes, Douglas, Lowdon; Purdue (Robert McCartney 72), Moxon (Docherty 87), Hunter, Wallace; Fleming K, Smith.
Jeanfield Swifts: (442) Mitchell; Reid (Smith F 75), Whitehead, Dolzanski, Smith S; McLaren, Stewart, Fergus (Simpson 63), Dodd (Struthers 63); McLeish, Scott.
Referee: Steven Reid.

Banks O' Dee (3) 5 *(Buglass 15, Winton 23, Philipson 29, MacLeod 56, 59)*
Nairn Co (0) 0 196

Banks O' Dee: (442) Hobday; Young, Allan, Lewecki, Lawrie; Buglass, Gilmour, Winton (Alexander 71), Armstrong; MacLeod (Henderson 64), Philipson (Watson 80).
Nairn Co: (433) Maclean; Gordon (Mitchell 73), Fyffe, Treasurer, Williamson B; Williamson R (Gethins 46), Maclennan, Porritt; Young (McConaghy 59), Main, MacKenzie.
Referee: Daniel Graves.

Berwick R (1) 1 *(Denholm 33)*
Stirling Alb (1) 2 *(Mackin 25, McGregor 90)* 519

Berwick R: (442) McNeil; Nelson, Pyper, Cook, Ferguson; Taylor, Denholm, Sinclair, Stewart; Smith, McGrath.
Stirling Alb: (442) Currie; Banner, McGregor, Cummins (Watson 45), McNiff; Moore (Flanagan 82), Roberts K, Leitch, Omar (Scally 67); Mackin, Bikey.
Referee: Mike Roncone.

Brechin C (0) 2 *(Denham 55, Robertson 90 (og))*
Haddington Ath (1) 1 *(McGarry 22)* 401

Brechin C: (442) Ross; Denham, Davidson, Cruickshank (Booth 68), Thomson; Paton, Inglis, Cox, MacKintosh; Wade, Currie (Wood 79).
Haddington Ath: (352) Cornet; Aitchison, Watson C, Simpson (Eddington 70); Robertson, McGarry, Hill, King, Russell; Watson E, Auriemma (Jones 86).
Referee: Alastair Grieve.

Broomhill (0) 0
Tranent Juniors (1) 2 *(Rutherford 15, Miller 83)* 202

Broomhill: (352) Smith; Sinnamon, O'Sullivan, Dunlop; Gray, Devenny, Dunn, Alexander (Chaudry 46), Moss (Cusick 27); Kavanagh, Scally (Monk 72).
Tranent Juniors: (352) Swain; Stevenson, Donaldson, Rutherford; Mitchell, Greig, Murphy, Anderson, Knox; Wringe (Somerville 85), Docherty (Watson 44 (Miller 64)).
Referee: David Milton.

Brora Rangers (0) 0
Albion R (0) 0 287

Brora Rangers: (442) Malin; Kelly, Williamson, Nicolson, Macdonald A; MacDonald G, Gillespie, Mackinnon, Sutherland; MacRae A (MacRae J 57), Wright (Ewan 76).
Albion R: (442) Binnie; Lynas, McGowan, Fagan, Fernie; Wilson C, Leslie, Wilson D, O'Donnell (Reilly 76); Doherty, Mullen (Morton 46).
Referee: Iain Snedden.

Cowdenbeath (2) 2 *(Renton 13, Buchanan L 35)*
Civil Service Strollers (2) 4 *(Valentine 17, Faye 38, 65, Irving 76)* 282

Cowdenbeath: (442) Gill; Mullen (Hutton 66), Barr C, O'Conner, Thomson; Buchanan R■, Morrison, Barr B, Swan; Buchanan L■, Renton.
Civil Service Strollers: (541) Whyte; Shaw, Brydon, McConnell, Duffy, Valentine; Joao Balde, Fairley (Irving 52), Young (Dukuray 76), Cole (Makovora 88); Faye.
Referee: Jordan Curran.

Dalbeattie Star (0) 0
Rothes (0) 0 210

Dalbeattie Star: (451) Holt; Brotherston, McChesney, Dickinson, Muir; Orsi, McMahon, Todd, Cairnie, Sloan (Cowie 68); Currie (Park 80).
Rothes: (352) McCarthy; McRitchie, Milne, Johnstone; Stark, Mackintosh, Pollock, Brown, Finnis; Kerr (Wilson 66), Hyde (Gunn 76).
Referee: Colin Whyte.

Dunbar U (0) 1 *(Devlin 72 (pen))*
Lothian Thistle (0) 1 *(Douglas 90)* 858

Dunbar U: (433) Laing; Fleming, Weir, McFarlane, Berry; Handling, Ingram, Smith; Jones (Bathgate 61), McLaren (Devlin 61), Edmond (Neave 88).
Lothian Thistle: (433) Adams; Moore, Lally, Deland, Penker (Signorini 27); Cunningham, Doherty, Daniel; O'Brien (Cummings 74), Douglas, Viola.
Referee: Paul Timmons.

East Kilbride (1) 4 *(McManus 23, Malcolm B 60, Stainrod 83, 87)*

Stirling University (0) 0 170

East Kilbride: (4132) Brennan; Elliott, Stevenson, Old, Wylde; McLaughlin N; Owens (Malcolm C 54), Malcolm B (Stainrod 81), McManus (Finlay 74); Vitoria, Erskine.
Stirling University: (532) Fry; Burrows, Taylor (McArthur 75), Hutchinson, Lavery, Downie (Kennedy 64); Davidson (McGill 64), Berry, Doan; Penker, Stokes.
Referee: Ryan Kennedy.

East Stirlingshire (0) 0

Bonnyrigg Rose Ath (2) 3 *(Young 8, Barrett 23, Hunter 77)* 421

East Stirlingshire: (3511) Connelly; Fulton, Greene, Kay (Hodge 70); Crooks (Barr 46), Gibbons, Churchill, Hamilton (Young 70), Rodden; Healy; Watson.
Bonnyrigg Rose Ath: (352) Andrews; Young, Horne, Martyniuk; Brett (Gray S 89), Stewart, Connelly, Currie, Barrett; Hall (McGachie 71), Hunter (Evans 81).
Referee: Greg Soutar.

Edinburgh C (1) 2 *(Shanley 45, Robertson 76)*

Bo'ness U (1) 1 *(Anderson 10)* 352

Edinburgh C: (442) Schwake; Kidd, McKay, Kane, Jarron; Hilton, Ferguson (Handling 46), Tapping C, Murray (Berry 54); Shanley (Robertson 66), See.
Bo'ness U: (4231) Murphy; Stevenson, Skinner, Hunter (Hawkins 46), Jacobs; Peggie, Gemmell (Flynn 80); Nicol, Galbraith, Locke; Anderson.
Referee: Lloyd Wilson.

Formartine U (0) 0

Forfar Ath (1) 2 *(Shepherd 33 (pen), Anderson G 61)* 382

Formartine United: (442) MacDonald; Crawford, Spink, Norris (Greig 85), Smith S; Rodger, Lawrence, Anderson (Park 82), Hanratty; Lisle, Mykyta.
Forfar Ath: (4411) McCallum; Meechan, Travis, Munro■, Hussain; Anderson G (Thomson C 77), Thomas, Ness (Slater 68), McCluskey; Crossan; Shepherd (Anderson S 71).
Referee: Calum Scott.

Kelty Hearts (2) 4 *(O'Ware 34, Cardle 36, 77, Philp 86)*

Buckie Thistle (0) 1 *(Urquhart 79)* 608

Kelty Hearts: (433) Jamieson; Finlayson (Cameron 89), Hill, O'Ware, Philp; Higginbotham, Tidser, Barjonas (McNab 83); Cardle, Austin, Biabi (Black 61).
Buckie Thistle: (433) Main; Wood (MacKinnon 71), Murray J, Morrison, McLauchlan; Pugh, Fraser, Barry (MacLeod 71); MacAskill, Goodall (Adams 79), Urquhart.
Referee: Steven Kirkland.

Preston Ath (0) 0

Auchinleck Talbot (0) 2 *(Glasgow 77, Samson 82)* 316

Preston Ath: (442) Newman; Austin, Prior, Currie■, Innes; Jack (Young 52), O'Connor, Archibald, Somers; Malloy (Stokes 83), Grotlin (Hamilton 72).
Auchinleck Talbot: (442) Leishman; Stafford, McCracken C, Armstrong (Glasgow 46), Wilson A; Healy, McPherson, Hyslop (Shankland 68), Samson; Boylan (Boyd 68), Wilson G.
Referee: Chris Gentles.

Sauchie Juniors (1) 2 *(Smith 31 (pen), 65 (pen))*

Dunipace (0) 1 *(Grant D 60)* 678

Sauchie Juniors: (433) Clarke; Greenhorn, Tully, Carroll, Cross; Docherty, Dickie (Kelly K 87), Morgan; Sam Davidson (Collumbine 83), Kelly C (Craunall 87), Smith.
Dunipace: (442) Kane; McCroary, Ashe■, Grant A, Galloway; Langton (Colley■ 72), Herron, Morrison, France (Denham 72); Wright (Stevenson 85), Grant D.
Referee: Stephen Gill.

St Cuthbert W (1) 1 *(Kelly 25)*

Gala Fairydean R (2) 3 *(Berry 36, Murray 44 (pen), Healy 71)* 250

St Cuthbert W: (433) Gemmell; Black (Harris 82), McMurtrie, Taylor, Renwick (Currie 89); Meechan (O'Rourke 75), Williamson, Kelly; Milligan, Hunter, Ballantyne.
Gala Fairydean R: (442) Spratt; Docherty, Grant, Jordan, Hall C; Healy, Darge, Chalmers (Gray 90), Berry (Hall L 86); Murray■, Aitchison (Touray 89).
Referee: Alex Shepherd.

Stenhousemuir (1) 4 *(Brown A 30, 71, Orr 48, Lyon R 68)*

Huntly (1) 1 *(MacIver 45)* 324

Stenhousemuir: (451) Marshall; Jamieson, Miller, Crighton, Lyon R; Forbes, Andersen (Christie 72), Wedderburn, Brown A (Tierney 86), O'Reilly; Orr (Graham 85).
Huntly: (4411) Storrier; Thoirs, Johnstone, Clark, Jack; Buchan, MacIver, Murison, Elphinstone (Heslop 74); Dangana (Imbert-Thomas 39); MacBeath (McKeown 87).
Referee: Connor Ashwood.

Stranraer (0) 0

Darvel (1) 1 *(Allan 38)* 357

Stranraer: (4231) Scullion; Ross C, Sonkur, Ellis, Burns; Brady, Gallagher; Watson (Muir 46), Smith R (Josh Walker 46), Woods (Rennie 77); Yates.
Darvel: (352) Truesdale; Reid, Little, Meggatt; Miller, McShane, Stirling (Thomson 89), Monaghan, Allan; Ferguson (Mackenzie 62), Kirkpatrick (Caldwell 79).
Referee: Greg Soutar.

Monday, 25 October 2021

Clydebank (0) 1 *(Little 69 (pen))*

Elgin C (1) 1 *(MacEwan 14)* 1040

Clydebank: (532) Donnelly; Hodge, Darroch, Niven, McLean, Byrne (McGonigle 59); Black, Slattery, Gallacher; Little (Mulcahy 79), McKinlay (Lynass 83).
Elgin C: (4141) McHale; Spark, Cooper, McHardy, MacPhee; MacEwan (Peters 87); Dingwall R, Cameron, Dingwall T, Lawrence (Machado 56); O'Keefe (Mailer 67).
Referee: Matthew MacDermid.

SECOND ROUND REPLAYS

Saturday, 30 October 2021

Albion R (0) 1 *(Wilson D 83 (pen))*

Brora Rangers (0) 0 276

Albion R: (442) Binnie; Lynas, McGowan, Fagan, Fernie; Wilson C, Wilson D, Leslie, Morton (Reilly 63); Wright (O'Donnell 63), Doherty■.
Brora Rangers: (451) Malin; Pickles (Hennem 81), Williamson, Nicolson, Macdonald A; Kelly, Gillespie, Mackinnon, Meekings (Wright 46), MacDonald G; MacRae J (MacRae A 72).
Referee: Iain Snedden.

Elgin C (0) 1 *(Cameron 79)*

Clydebank (1) 2 *(McGonigle 14, Little 67)* 1118

Elgin C: (4231) McHale; Spark, Cooper, Cooney (Peters 55), MacPhee; Dingwall R, MacEwan (Mailer 70); Dingwall T, Cameron, O'Keefe (Sopel 70); Wilson J.
Clydebank: (4231) Donnelly; Hodge, Niven, Darroch, McLean; Black (Holmes 52), Slattery; Gallacher, Little, McGonigle (Byrne 72); McPherson (McKinlay 63).
Referee: Matthew MacDermid.

Lothian Thistle (1) 2 *(Cunningham 16 (pen), 49)*

Dunbar U (1) 1 *(Devlin 3)* 282

Lothian Thistle: (433) Adams; Moore, Deland, Crawford, Daniel; Signorini, Doherty, Cunningham; O'Brien (Murray 85), Douglas, Viola (Cumming 68).
Dunbar U: (433) Laing; Berry, McFarlane, Weir, Fleming; Smith, Ingram (Hay 46), Handling; Edmond (McLaren 65), Devlin■, Jones (Thomson 46).
Referee: Chris Gentles.

Rothes (0) 0

Dalbeattie Star (0) 1 *(Orsi 81)* 194

Rothes: (442) McCarthy; Stark (Harkness 82), Milne, Finnis, McRitchie; Mackintosh (Cormack 59), Robertson, Pollock, Brown; Kerr (Gunn 69), Wilson.
Dalbeattie Star: (451) Holt; Brotherston, McChesney, Dickinson, Muir; Orsi, McMahon, Todd (Graham 70), Cairnie (Degnan 79), Sloan (Park 79); Currie.
Referee: Colin Whyte.

THIRD ROUND

Friday, 26 November 2021

Partick Thistle (0) 1 *(Docherty 82)*

Dunfermline Ath (0) 0 3198

Partick Thistle: (442) Sneddon; McKenna, Akinola, Holt, Hendrie; Turner (Gordon 73), Docherty, Bannigan, Tiffoney; Smith (Murray 80), Rudden (MacIver 68).

Dunfermline Ath: (4141) Fon Williams; Comrie, Connolly, Gaspuitis, Edwards; Dorrans; MacDonald, Dow, Todd (Todorov 69), Thomas (O'Hara 84); McCann.
Referee: John Beaton.

Saturday, 27 November 2021

Alloa Ath (2) 5 *(Niang 13, 90, Henderson 20, 70, 83)*
Bonnyrigg Rose Ath (0) 0 513

Alloa Ath: (4231) Hutton; Taggart, Mendy, Graham, Robertson; King, Niang; Scougall, Cawley, Boyd; Henderson (Sammon 85).
Bonnyrigg Rose Ath: (352) Andrews; Horne, Young, Martyniuk; Brett, Currie, Stewart (Connelly 75), Gray R, Barrett; Hunter (Evans 83), McGachie (Hall 75).
Referee: Mike Roncone.

Arbroath (2) 3 *(Thomson 12, Little 20, Donnelly 53)*
Forfar Ath (0) 0 1280

Arbroath: (451) Gaston; Thomson, Little, O'Brien, Colin Hamilton (Clark 74); Stewart, Chris Hamilton, McKenna, Craigen, Linn (Hilson 74); Donnelly (Swankie 74).
Forfar Ath: (442) McCallum; Meechan, Fisher, Anderson S, Hussain (Strachan 74); Thomson C (Anderson G 51), Slater, Thomas, Crossan; Aitken, Shepherd (McCluskey 61).
Referee: Calum Scott.

Auchinleck Talbot (0) 1 *(Wilson G 60)*
Hamilton A (0) 0 1778

Auchinleck Talbot: (4411) Leishman; McCracken R, McPherson, McCracken C, Wilson A; Glasgow (Samson 57), Armstrong, Healy, Shankland (Boyd 70); Wilson G; Boylan (McDowall 88).
Hamilton A: (451) Hilton; Stirling, Want, Popescu, Shiels; Munro, Martin (Virtanen 73), Mimnaugh, Hughes (Smith L 77), Redfern (Moyo 63); Ryan.
Referee: Matthew MacDermid.

Ayr U (0) 2 *(Maxwell 54, Moffat 65)*
Albion R (0) 1 *(Wright 46)* 986

Ayr U: (442) McAdams; Houston, McGinty, Baird J, Reading; Maxwell (Bradley 77), Murdoch, Muirhead, O'Connor; Moffat, Afolabi (Salkeld 85).
Albion R: (442) Binnie; Robinson (Dolan 68), McGowan, Fagan, Fernie; Wilson C (Wilson L 61), Wilson D, Leslie, Reilly; O'Donnell, Wright.
Referee: William Collum.

Banks O' Dee (1) 2 *(Higgins C 28 (og), Gilmour 81)*
East Fife (1) 1 *(Semple 13)* 328

Banks O' Dee: (4231) Hobday; Beattie, Kelly, Lewecki, Lawrie; Winton, Young (Crosbie 72); Gilmour, Philipson, Armstrong (Alexander 82); MacLeod (Henderson 71).
East Fife: (442) Smith J; Dunsmore■, Higgins C, Murdoch, Mercer■; Semple, McManus, Newton (Davidson 67), Watt (Slattery 75); Denholm, Connell (Smith K 61).
Referee: Chris Fordyce.

Civil Service Strollers (0) 0
Peterhead (0) 3 *(McLean 55 (pen), Brown S 59, Cameron 90)* 180

Civil Service Strollers: (343) Whyte; McConnell, Brydon, Duffy; Irving (Makovora 78), Clapperton (Fairley 69), Young, Valentine; Faye (Johnstone 69), Jaciz Balde■, Cole.
Peterhead: (343) Long; Wilson, Jason Brown, McDonald; Ritchie (Lyle 63), McCarthy, Brown S, Duffy; McLean, Savoury (Jordon Brown 88), Payne (Cameron 75).
Referee: Chris Graham.

Clydebank (1) 2 *(Darroch 44, Little 64)*
Clyde (0) 0 1040

Clydebank: (4231) Donnelly; Hodge, Niven, Darroch, Byrne; Black, Slattery; Gallacher (Holmes 86), Little, McGonigle (Lynass 80); McPherson (McKinlay 69).
Clyde: (433) Parry; Cuddihy (Mortimer 39), Page, Elsdon, Docherty; Splaine, Nicoll (Tade 50), Gomis (Kennedy 63); Cunningham, Goodwillie, Love.
Referee: Alan Newlands.

Cove Rangers (1) 2 *(Vigurs 33, McAllister 90)*
Queen of the South (1) 2 *(Soares-Junior 32, Paton 72)* 468

Cove Rangers: (3412) McKenzie; Neill, Ross, Anderson (Logan 68); Yule, Scully, Vigurs, Milne (Masson 76); Fyvie; Megginson, McIntosh (McAllister 68).
Queen of the South: (4141) Brynn; Gibson, McKay, Nditi■, Cooper; McGrory; Connelly (Todd 81), Johnston, Cochrane, Soares-Junior; Roy (Paton 71).
Referee: Scott Lambie.

Dalbeattie Star (0) 1 *(Degnan 69)*
East Kilbride (1) 2 *(McLaughlin N 42 (pen), Saunders 64)* 196

Dalbeattie Star: (352) Holt; Brotherston, McChesney, Dickinson; Muir, Todd (Cowie 88), McMahon, Sloan, Cairnie (Currie 64); Orsi (Park 81), Degnan.
East Kilbride: (442) Brennan; Stevenson, Saunders, Old, Wylde; McLaughlin N, Blair, Owens, Erskine (McManus 75); Stainrod (Vitoria 73), Elliott (Malcolm B 90).
Referee: Iain Snedden.

Dumbarton (1) 3 *(Pignatiello 24, Schiavone 90, McKee 90)*
Sauchie Juniors (0) 1 *(Smith 58 (pen))* 571

Dumbarton: (442) Ramsbottom; Lynch, Geggan (Carswell 62), Buchanan, Boyle; Orsi (Schiavone 77), Pignatiello, McKee, Wilson; Stokes, Duthie.
Sauchie Juniors: (4231) Clarke; Greenhorn (Finlayson 80), Scott Davidson, Carroll, Cross; Dickie, Collumbine (Kelly K 83); Smith, Morgan, Docherty; Crawford (Kelly C 87).
Referee: Peter Stuart.

Falkirk (0) 1 *(Morrison 50)*
Raith R (1) 2 *(Matthews 27, Ross 84)* 2512

Falkirk: (433) Martin; Williamson R (Miller 68), Hall, Dixon, McCann (Keena 80); Telfer, Hetherington (Krasniqi 54), Nesbitt; Morrison, Ruth, McGuffie.
Raith R: (4411) MacDonald; Tumilty■, Lang, Berra, Dick; Connolly (Musonda 23), Matthews, Spencer, Zanatta (Poplatnik 73); Ross (Benedictus 90); Varian.
Referee: Nick Walsh.

Gala Fairydean R (0) 0
Annan Ath (0) 1 *(Smith 51)* 300

Gala Fairydean R: (4231) Spratt; Docherty, Jordan, Rodger, Hall C; Hall L, Chalmers (Grant 79); Healy, Darge, Berry (Campbell 85); Murray (Scott 56).
Annan Ath: (442) Fleming G; Barnes, Douglas, Clark, Birch (Swinglehurst 46); Johnston, Docherty, Moxon, Fleming K (Anderson 85); Smith, Goss (Wallace 71).
Referee: George Calder.

Inverness CT (1) 1 *(McKay 12)*
Greenock Morton (0) 1 *(Reilly 81)* 790

Inverness CT: (4231) Ridgers; Carson, Broadfoot, Devine, Deas; McAlear (Welsh 71), Allardice; MacGregor (Walsh 70), Sutherland, Doran; McKay.
Greenock Morton: (442) Hamilton; Ledger, Lithgow, McEntee, Strapp; Blues (Reilly 75), Oliver, Oksanen, McGrattan (King 68); Lyon, Ugwu.
Referee: Colin Steven.

Kelty Hearts (0) 0
Montrose (0) 0 805

Kelty Hearts: (433) Jamieson; Philp, Forster, Hill (Hooper 73), Finlayson; Black, Tidser, Higginbotham (McNab 38); Agyeman, Austin, Cardle (Barjonas 86).
Montrose: (433) Lennox; Ballantyne, Quinn, Waddell, Steeves; Masson (Callaghan 76), Whatley, Watson; Milne (Brown 45), Johnston (Antoniazzi 79), Lyons.
Referee: Barry Cook.

Lothian Thistle (0) 1 *(Douglas 82)*
Edinburgh C (2) 2 *(Handling 35, Murray 42)* 216

Lothian Thistle: (433) Adams; Moore, Lally, Douglas, Deland; Doherty (Viola 61), Renton (Murray 69), Cunningham; Findlay, O'Brien, Kemp (Cumming 79).
Edinburgh C: (4231) Schwake; Brian, McKay, Bronsky, Jarron (Kane 62); Tapping C (Berry 56), Ferguson; Robertson, Murray, Handling (Smith 78); See.
Referee: Dan McFarlane.

Queen's Park (0) 0

Kilmarnock (1) 1 *(Murray E 45)* 1153

Queen's Park: (433) Ferrie; Doyle■, Morrison, Davidson, Robson; Brown (Moore 66), Gillespie (Biggar 89), Connell; Smith (Longstaff 65), McHugh, Longridge.
Kilmarnock: (4411) Walker; Hodson, McGowan, Murray E (Sanders 46), Waters; Burke (Armstrong 84), Lyons, Polworth, McKenzie; Robinson (Burrell 75); Shaw.
Referee: Grant Irvine.

Stenhousemuir (0) 0

Airdrieonians (1) 2 *(Frizzell 37, Smith 55)* 597

Stenhousemuir: (4141) David Wilson; Lyon R, Jamieson, Crighton, Coll; Corbett (Tapping 85); Christie (Lyon J 60), Forbes, Brown A (Graham 60), O'Reilly; Tierney.
Airdrieonians: (442) Currie; Watson, Lyons, Fordyce, Quitongo (Walker 90); McGill S (McInroy 73), Easton, McCabe, Frizzell; McGill G (Agnew 88), Smith.
Referee: Steven Kirkland.

Stirling Alb (2) 4 *(Mackin 20, 63 (pen), Leitch 30, McGregor 81)*

Tranent Juniors (0) 0 701

Stirling Alb: (352) Currie; McGregor, Banner, McGeachie; Moore (Cummins 58), Grant R, Laird (Roberts K 77), Leitch (Scally 68), Flanagan; Heaver, Mackin.
Tranent Juniors: (433) Swain; Stevenson, Donaldson, Mitchell, Rutherford; Murphy, Miller, Anderson (Greig 69); Thomson (Knox 46), Wringe, Docherty (Somerville 80).
Referee: Lloyd Wilson.

Monday, 29 November 2021

Brechin C (0) 1 *(Cox 56)*

Darvel (1) 1 *(Kirkpatrick 32)* 577

Brechin C: (442) Ross; Bain, Davidson, Thomson, McHattie; Scott (Booth 90), Kucheriavyi, MacKintosh, Inglis; Cox, Wood (Wade 71).
Darvel: (352) Truesdale; Reid, Little, Meggatt; Miller (Thomson 90), McShane, Stirling, Monaghan, Allan; Ferguson (Mackenzie 67), Kirkpatrick (Galt 82).
Referee: Graham Grainger.

THIRD ROUND REPLAYS

Saturday, 4 December 2021

Montrose (1) 1 *(Johnston 42)*

Kelty Hearts (1) 1 *(Cardle 6)* 690

Montrose: (433) Lennox; Ballantyne, Quinn, Waddell (Allan 67), Steeves; Whatley, Watson (Callaghan 71), Masson; Lyons, Antoniazzi (Brown 77), Johnston.
Kelty Hearts: (433) Jamieson; McNab, Hooper, Hill, Finlayson; Philp (Barjonas 56), Tidser (Reilly 87), Black (Agyeman 78); Higginbotham, Austin, Cardle.
Kelty Hearts won 3-1 on penalties.
Referee: Barry Cook.

Tuesday, 7 December 2021

Greenock Morton (1) 1 *(Muirhead 42)*

Inverness CT (0) 1 *(Devine 47)* 700

Greenock Morton: (442) Hamilton; Hynes, Lithgow, Strapp, Russell; Muirhead, Lyon, Oksanen, Oliver; Ugwu, Reilly.
Inverness CT: (4411) Ridgers; Carson, Broadfoot, Devine, Deas; MacGregor (McAlear 61), Welsh (Walsh 30), Allardice, Doran; Sutherland; McKay (Jamieson 72).
Greenock Morton won 5-4 on penalties.
Referee: David Dickinson.

Queen of the South (0) 0

Cove Rangers (1) 3 *(Fyvie 38, Megginson 80, 83)* 527

Queen of the South: (4141) Brynn; Johnston, McKay, Gibson, Cooper; McGrory; Paton, Joseph (East 70), Connelly, Todd (Roy 63); Soares-Junior.
Cove Rangers: (3412) Gourlay; Ross, Strachan, Neill; Yule, Scully, Masson (Adeyemo 90), Milne; Fyvie; Megginson (Anderson 85), McIntosh.
Referee: Scott Lambie.

Tuesday, 14 December 2021

Darvel (1) 2 *(Meggatt 45, Thomson 80)*

Brechin C (1) 2 *(Inglis 38, MacKintosh 88)* 781

Darvel: (343) Truesdale; Meggatt, Little, Monaghan; Miller, McShane, Kirkpatrick (Ferguson 12), Allan; Stirling (Thomson 20), Mackenzie (Caldwell 68), Galt.
Brechin C: (3142) Ross; Bain, Davidson, Thomson; Paton (Milne 83); Inglis, Kucheriavyi, MacKintosh, Scott (Wood 76); Wade (Cox 83), Booth.
Darvel won 5-4 on penalties.
Referee: Graham Grainger.

FOURTH ROUND

Thursday, 20 January 2022

Hibernian (0) 1 *(Nisbet 112)*

Cove Rangers (0) 0 5849

Hibernian: (3412) Macey; Hallberg (Doyle-Hayes 82), Hanlon, Stevenson; Cadden, Campbell, Newell, Doig; Henderson (Murphy 59); Mueller (Scott 91), Doidge (Nisbet 59).
Cove Rangers: (343) Gourlay; Neill, Strachan (Anderson 91), Milne; Ross, Yule, Fyvie (Leitch 82), Scully; McIntosh (Reynolds 68), Megginson, Masson (McAllister 68).
aet. Referee: Euan Anderson.

Friday, 21 January 2022

Rangers (2) 4 *(Lowry 31, Tavernier 37 (pen), Itten 59, Sakala 86)*

Stirling Alb (0) 0 37,916

Rangers: (433) McLaughlin; Tavernier, Goldson, Balogun (King 60), Simpson; Hagi (Lowry 15), Lundstram, Bacuna; Barker (Roofe 67), Itten, Sakala.
Stirling Alb: (451) Currie; McGeachie, McGregor, Cummins, Hancock (Creaney 86); Moore (Banner 71), Roberts K, Grant R, Leitch, Flanagan; Francis (Mackin 75).
Referee: John Beaton.

Saturday, 22 January 2022

Aberdeen (2) 3 *(Hedges 23, Ramirez 44, Ferguson 90)*

Edinburgh C (0) 0 9019

Aberdeen: (4411) Lewis; Ramsay, McCrorie (Barron 46), Bates, Hayes; Hedges (Gallagher 59), Jenks, Brown, Ojo; Ferguson; Ramirez (Emmanuel-Thomas 73).
Edinburgh C: (442) Schwake; Logan, Hamilton (Reekie 63), Robertson (Crane 46), Brian; Murray, Farrell, Tapping C, Handling (Berry 79); McDonald, See.
Referee: Alan Muir.

Alloa Ath (0) 1 *(Sammon 78)*

Celtic (2) 2 *(Giakoumakis 14, Abada 45)* 3022

Alloa Ath: (4231) Hutton; Taggart, Graham, Durnan, Church; King (Trouten 77), Howie (Robertson 46); Cawley (Scougall 77), Niang, Boyd; Sammon.
Celtic: (4141) Hart; Ralston, Welsh, Starfelt, Scales; Ideguchi (Bitton 63); Abada (Jota 52), Rogic, McGregor (McCarthy 45), Maeda; Giakoumakis.
Referee: Don Robertson.

Arbroath (1) 3 *(Hamilton J 28, 68, 90)*

Darvel (0) 0 1106

Arbroath: (442) Gaston; Thomson, Little, O'Brien, Colin Hamilton; Stewart (Linn 67), McKenna, Chris Hamilton, Henderson (Craigen 71); Hamilton J, Wighton (Donnelly 71).
Darvel: (343) Truesdale; Meggatt, Thomson, Little; Miller, McShane, Monaghan (Kirkpatrick 67), Allan; Galt (Mackenzie 55), Ferguson (Caldwell 68), Stirling.
Referee: David Dickinson.

Auchinleck Talbot (0) 0

Hearts (2) 5 *(Halliday 14, Boyce 39 (pen), 51, Haring 80, Cochrane 83)* 3500

Auchinleck Talbot: (451) Leishman; Stafford, McPherson, McCracken C, Wilson A; Samson, Armstrong, Healy (Boyd 81), Wilson G (Mason 68), Glasgow; Boylan (McDowall 69).
Hearts: (4411) Gordon; Smith M, Halkett, Kingsley, Cochrane; Atkinson, Haring, Devlin, Halliday (McEneff 69); McKay (Mackay-Steven 78); Boyce (Ginnelly 82).
Referee: Greg Aitken.

Ayr U (0) 0

St Mirren (2) 2 *(McAllister 7, Kiltie 24)* 3423

Ayr U: (352) McAdams; Muirhead, Baird J, McGinty; Houston, Gondoh (Bryden 73), Murdoch, Maxwell (O'Connor 46), Reading; McKenzie, Moffat (Adeloye 72).
St Mirren: (4231) Alnwick; Fraser, Shaughnessy, Dunne, Tanser; Ronan, Erhahon (Flynn 54); Henderson, Kiltie (Power 68), McAllister; Dennis (Greive 63).
Referee: Gavin Duncan.

Banks O' Dee (0) 0

Raith R (0) 3 *(Stanton 67, Poplatnik 90, Connolly 90)* 870

Banks O' Dee: (4231) Hobday; Young, Kelly, Lewecki, Lawrie; Duff (Allan 52), Gilmour; Henderson (Crosbie 59), Philipson, Alexander (Armstrong 73); MacLeod.
Raith R: (433) MacDonald; Musonda, Lang, Berra, Dick; Matthews, Stanton, Williamson; Ross, Gullan (Poplatnik 89), Zanatta (Connolly 63).
Referee: Craig Napier.

Clydebank (1) 3 *(McKinlay 45, Black 68, Mulcahy 94)*

Annan Ath (1) 4 *(Moxon 9, Douglas 54, Robert McCartney 119, Anderson 120)* 1200

Clydebank: (451) Donnelly; Hodge, Niven (McLean 78), Darroch, Byrne; Gallacher, Little, Slattery (Johnstone 67), Black, McKinlay (McGonigle 81); Mulcahy (McPherson 108).
Annan Ath: (4141) Fleming G; Steele, Douglas, Swinglehurst, Clark (Docherty 107); Moxon; Johnston, Wallace (Anderson 101), Hunter, Smith; Goss (Robert McCartney 88).
aet. Referee: Grant Irvine.

Dumbarton (0) 0

Dundee (0) 1 *(Griffiths 63 (pen))* 1198

Dumbarton: (4231) Ramsbottom; Pignatiello, Buchanan, Boyle, Muir; Carswell, Paton; Duthie, McKee (Wilson 69), MacLean■; Oyinsan.
Dundee: (4231) Lawlor; Elliot, Sweeney, McGhee (Griffiths 46), Kerr; Byrne, Anderson; Mulligan (Adam 60), McGowan (McMullan 46), McCowan; Mullen.
Referee: Colin Steven.

Kelty Hearts (0) 1 *(Higginbotham 103)*

St Johnstone (0) 0 2183

Kelty Hearts: (4231) Jamieson; Finlayson, Forster, O'Ware, Ngwenya; Philp, Tidser (Black 97); Barjonas (McNab 105), Higginbotham, Cardle (Agyeman 78); Austin (Biabi 90).
St Johnstone: (3142) Clark; Gordon, Cleary, McCart; Butterfield; Brown (O'Halloran 92 (Craig 105)), Gilmour, Crawford, Gallacher; Ciftci (May 79), Kane (Middleton 73).
aet. Referee: Kevin Clancy.

Kilmarnock (1) 1 *(McKenzie 20)*

Dundee U (1) 2 *(McNulty 4, Levitt 111)* 5380

Kilmarnock: (3511) Hemming; Sanders, Taylor, Stokes (Murray E 39); Murray F, McKenzie, Tait, Alston (Polworth 96), Haunstrup (Burke 84); Mackay (Lafferty 53); Shaw.
Dundee U: (3412) Siegrist; Edwards, Mulgrew (Harkes 91), McMann; Freeman, Butcher, Levitt, Sporle (Niskanen 66); Clark (Pawlett 72); McNulty (Appere 79), Watt.
aet. Referee: William Collum.

Livingston (1) 1 *(Obileye 16 (pen))*

Ross Co (0) 0 1227

Livingston: (433) Stryjek; Devlin, Fitzwater, Obileye, Longridge; Pitman, Holt, Omeonga (McMillan 52); Bailey, Anderson (Nouble 60), Chukwuemeka (Forrest 46).
Ross Co: (442) Laidlaw; Randall, Drysdale, Ramsay, Vokins; Burroughs (Paton H 86), Callachan, Paton B, Spittal; Samuel A (White 60), Samuel D.
Referee: Bobby Madden.

Motherwell (0) 2 *(van Veen 111 (pen), Donnelly 120)*

Greenock Morton (0) 1 *(Muirhead 105)* 4735

Motherwell: (433) Kelly; O'Donnell S, Johansen, McGinley, Carroll; Maguire (Slattery 106), Donnelly, Goss; Woolery (van Veen 61), Shields (Tierney 76), Roberts (Amaluzor 107).
Greenock Morton: (352) Hamilton; Ledger, Lithgow, McLean; Brandon (McEntee 76), Lyon (Jacobs 96), Blues, Oliver (Muirhead 95), Strapp; Reilly, Ugwu (King 106).
aet. Referee: Nick Walsh.

Partick Thistle (1) 1 *(Graham 25)*

Airdrieonians (0) 0 2895

Partick Thistle: (442) Sneddon; McKenna, Mayo, Akinola■, Holt; Smith (Crawford 60), Bannigan, Docherty, Tiffoney (MacIver 90); Graham, Rudden (Hendrie 53).
Airdrieonians: (4132) Currie; Watson, McCabe, Fordyce, Walker (Gallagher 73); Agnew; Frizzell, Easton, McGill S (Kerr 79); Smith, Allan.
Referee: David Munro.

Peterhead (2) 2 *(McLean 43, McCarthy 45)*

East Kilbride (1) 2 *(Vitoria 11, 65)* 629

Peterhead: (343) Long; Jason Brown, Ferry, McDonald; Wilson (Payne 71), Ritchie (Jordon Brown 97), McCarthy, Duffy; Duncan, McLean, Savoury (Lyle 71).
East Kilbride: (343) Brennan; Kenny, Old, McManus; Stevenson, Owens (Stainrod 59), Millar (Mclaughlin R 76), Smith (McAninch 91); Vitoria (Finlay 81), Elliott, McLaughlin N.
aet; Peterhead won 5-3 on penalties. Referee: Chris Graham.

FIFTH ROUND

Saturday, 12 February 2022

Annan Ath (0) 0

Rangers (3) 3 *(Helander 7, Roofe 22, Sakala 32)* 2500

Annan Ath: (442) Fleming G; Barnes, Douglas, Clark, Lowdon (Swinglehurst 74); Johnston (Goss 82), Docherty (Hunter 75), Moxon, Wallace (Fleming K 74); Anderson (Garrity 64), Smith.
Rangers: (4231) McLaughlin; Zukowski, Sands, Helander (Lowry 61), Barisic; Diallo (McCann 70), Davis (King 61); Wright S, Ramsey (Simpson 61), Sakala (Itten 70); Roofe.
Referee: Alan Muir.

Hearts (0) 0

Livingston (0) 0 12,232

Hearts: (343) Gordon; Sibbick, Souttar, Kingsley; Smith M (Atkinson 71), Devlin, Baningime (Haring 71), Cochrane (Mackay-Steven 59); McKay (Woodburn 106), Simms, Halliday (Boyce 59).
Livingston: (352) Stryjek; Devlin, Obileye, Fitzwater; Forrest (Bailey 100), Pitman (McMillan 119), Omeonga (Kelly 119), Holt, Penrice; Anderson (Montano 64), Nouble (Shinnie 95).
aet; Hearts won 4-3 on penalties. Referee: Nick Walsh.

Motherwell (2) 2 *(van Veen 34, Shields 45)*

Aberdeen (1) 1 *(Ramirez 3)* 5892

Motherwell: (433) Kelly; Ojala, Johansen, Mugabi, Carroll; Donnelly, O'Hara, Goss (Shaw 78); Efford (Cornelius 84), Shields (Lamie 79), van Veen.
Aberdeen: (4231) Woods; McCrorie (Ramsay 38), Gallagher, Bates, Montgomery (Kennedy 52); Brown, Ojo (Barron 79); Besuijen (Emmanuel-Thomas 79), Ferguson, Hayes (MacKenzie 46); Ramirez.
Referee: Greg Aitken.

Partick Thistle (0) 0

Dundee U (1) 1 *(Harkes 34)* 4632

Partick Thistle: (442) Sneddon; McKenna, Mayo, Holt, Hendrie; Crawford (Murray 88), Docherty, Bannigan (Turner 79), Tiffoney; Graham (MacIver 68), Jakubiak (Smith 79).
Dundee U: (352) Siegrist; Butcher (Meekison 83), Edwards, Graham; Smith, Harkes, McDonald (McMann 53), Levitt (Clark 74), Niskanen; McNulty, Watt.
Referee: John Beaton.

St Mirren (1) 4 *(Greive 15, Jones 50, Kiltie 58, 85)*

Kelty Hearts (0) 0 3398

St Mirren: (4231) Alnwick; Fraser (Flynn 46), Shaughnessy (McCarthy 68), Dunne, Tait (Tanser 46); Gogic, Power (Erhahon 68); Kiltie, Ronan, Jones (Henderson 72); Greive.
Kelty Hearts: (433) Jamieson; Philp, Forster (McNab 69), O'Ware, Ngwenya; Barjonas, Tidser, Black (Agyeman 51); Higginbotham, Austin (Biabi 64), Cardle (Reilly 51).
Referee: Andrew Dallas.

Sunday, 13 February 2022

Arbroath (1) 1 *(Wighton 6)*

Hibernian (1) 3 *(Mitchell 20, Nisbet 71, Mueller 87)* 4049

Arbroath: (4312) Gaston; Thomson, Little, O'Brien, Colin Hamilton; Stewart, Chris Hamilton (Ford 89), Henderson (Low 70); McKenna; Hamilton J (Bakare 89), Wighton (Donnelly 89).
Hibernian: (3421) Macey; Bushiri, Porteous, Doig; Cadden, Stevenson, Doyle-Hayes, Mitchell (Campbell 78); Henderson (Wright 83), Jasper (Mueller 65); Nisbet (Doidge 83).
Referee: William Collum.

Celtic (1) 4 *(Scales 22, Giakoumakis 68, Maeda 71, Bitton 88)*

Raith R (0) 0 14,737

Celtic: (433) Hart; Ralston, Carter-Vickers (Jullien 74), Welsh, Scales; Rogic (Ideguchi 69), Bitton, Hatate; Forrest (Abada 69), Giakoumakis (Maeda 69), Johnston (Jota 55).
Raith R: (4231) MacDonald; Tumilty, Musonda, Benedictus (Mackie 80), Dick; Williamson (Zanatta 46), Stanton; Connolly (Varian 64), Matthews, Ross (Arnott 85); Gullan (Poplatnik 64).
Referee: Steven McLean.

Monday, 14 February 2022

Peterhead (0) 0

Dundee (1) 3 *(Adam 33 (pen), McGinn 53, Mulligan 88)* 1598

Peterhead: (433) Long; Conroy (McLean 67), Jason Brown, McDonald, Duffy; McCarthy, Brown S, Ritchie (Jordon Brown 82); Duncan (Cook 82), Savoury, Payne (Lyle 76).
Dundee: (433) Lawlor; McGhee, Sweeney, Rossi, Kerr; Byrne (Mulligan 57), Adam (McGowan 75), Anderson; McMullan (McCowan 57), Mullen (Elliot 85), McGinn.
Referee: David Munro.

QUARTER-FINALS

Saturday, 12 March 2022

Hearts (2) 4 *(Baningime 16, Haring 29, McEneff 67, Simms 85)*

St Mirren (1) 2 *(Brophy 36, Ronan 62)* 13,899

Hearts: (4231) Gordon; Atkinson, Halkett, Kingsley, Halliday; Haring, Baningime; Woodburn (McEneff 67), Boyce, McKay (Sibbick 90); Simms.
St Mirren: (451) Alnwick; Tait, Shaughnessy, Dunne, Tanser (Fraser 53); Kiltie (Henderson 75), Ronan, Power, Gogic (Greive 75), Jones; Brophy.
Referee: Bobby Madden.

Sunday, 13 March 2022

Dundee (0) 0

Rangers (2) 3 *(Goldson 9, Tavernier 25 (pen), Sakala 87)* 5536

Dundee: (4411) Sharp; Kerr, Ashcroft (Daley-Campbell 44), Sweeney, Marshall (McDaid 77); McMullan (Byrne 61), Anderson, McGhee, McGinn (McCowan 60); McGowan; Mullen.
Rangers: (4231) McLaughlin; Tavernier, Goldson, Helander, Bassey; Sands, Jack (Lowry 86); Ramsey (McCann 79), Kamara (Sakala 46), Kent (Diallo 67); Morelos (Roofe 46).
Referee: Steven McLean.

Motherwell (1) 1 *(Efford 43)*

Hibernian (2) 2 *(Melkersen 15, 37)* 8126

Motherwell: (343) Kelly; Ojala (O'Donnell S 46), Lamie, Johansen; Mugabi■, Cornelius (Shields 90), Donnelly, McGinley; Efford, van Veen, Roberts (Woolery 81).
Hibernian: (3421) Macey; Cadden, Porteous, Doig (Mueller 9 (McGregor 76)); Wright, Campbell, Newell, Stevenson; Henderson (Allan 53), Jasper; Melkersen (Doidge 75).
Referee: William Collum.

Monday, 14 March 2022

Dundee U (0) 0

Celtic (1) 3 *(McGregor 12, Giakoumakis 58, 88)* 8553

Dundee U: (352) Siegrist; Butcher, Edwards, Graham; Freeman (Sporle 66), Smith, Levitt (Meekison 72), Harkes (McDonald 28), Niskanen; Clark, McNulty (Thomson 71).
Celtic: (433) Hart; Juranovic, Carter-Vickers, Starfelt, Taylor; O'Riley (McCarthy 76), McGregor (Ideguchi 87), Hatate (Rogic 46); Forrest (Johnston 76), Giakoumakis, Maeda (Dembele 76).
Referee: John Beaton.

SEMI-FINALS

Saturday, 16 April 2022

Hearts (2) 2 *(Simms 16, Kingsley 21)*

Hibernian (1) 1 *(Cadden 22)* 37,783

Hearts: (3421) Gordon; Sibbick, Halkett (Moore 50), Kingsley (Devlin 87); Atkinson, Haring, Halliday (McEneff 39), Cochrane; Boyce, McKay; Simms.
Hibernian: (3142) Macey; McGinn (Campbell 74), Porteous, Hanlon; Stevenson (Melkersen 74); Cadden, Doyle-Hayes, Newell■, Clarke; Henderson (Mueller 90), Scott (Jasper 90).
Referee: John Beaton.

Sunday, 17 April 2022

Celtic (0) 1 *(Taylor 64)*

Rangers (0) 2 *(Arfield 78, Starfelt 114 (og))* 50,072

Celtic: (433) Hart; Juranovic (Ralston 67), Carter-Vickers, Starfelt, Taylor (Welsh 91); Rogic (Furuhashi 58), McGregor, Hatate (Turnbull 109); Abada (O'Riley 58), Maeda (Forrest 91), Jota.
Rangers: (4231) McLaughlin; Tavernier, Goldson, Bassey, Barisic (Balogun 109); Jack (Davis 75), Lundstram (Kamara 102); Ramsey (Wright S 43), Aribo (Arfield 75), Kent; Roofe (Sakala 109).
aet.
Referee: Bobby Madden.

SCOTTISH FA CUP FINAL 2021–22

Saturday, 21 May 2022

(at Hampden Park, attendance 50,319)

Rangers (0) 2 Hearts (0) 0

Rangers: (433) McLaughlin (McGregor 119); Tavernier, Goldson, Balogun, Bassey; Davis (Jack 81), Lundstram, Arfield (Kamara 81); Diallo (Wright S 63), Aribo (Sakala 106), Kent.
Scorers: Jack 94, Wright S 97.

Hearts: (3412) Gordon; Souttar, Halkett, Kingsley; Atkinson, Haring, Devlin (McEneff 106), Cochrane (Mackay-Steven 100); Boyce (Halliday 76); Simms, McKay (Ginnelly 82).

aet.

Referee: William Collum.

BARCLAYS FA WOMEN'S SUPER LEAGUE 2021–22

			Home					*Away*					*Total*						
		P	*W*	*D*	*L*	*F*	*A*	*W*	*D*	*L*	*F*	*A*	*W*	*D*	*L*	*F*	*A*	*GD*	*Pts*
1	Chelsea*	22	10	1	0	29	4	8	1	2	33	7	18	2	2	62	11	51	56
2	Arsenal†	22	10	1	0	40	6	7	3	1	25	4	17	4	1	65	10	55	55
3	Manchester C§	22	7	1	3	31	11	8	1	2	29	11	15	2	5	60	22	38	47
4	Manchester U	22	8	1	2	29	11	4	5	2	16	11	12	6	4	45	22	23	42
5	Tottenham H	22	5	3	3	12	8	4	2	5	12	15	9	5	8	24	23	1	32
6	West Ham U	22	3	4	4	14	15	4	2	5	9	18	7	6	9	23	33	–10	27
7	Brighton & HA	22	4	2	5	11	18	4	0	7	13	20	8	2	12	24	38	–14	26
8	Reading	22	5	1	5	12	18	2	3	6	9	22	7	4	11	21	40	–19	25
9	Aston Villa	22	1	2	8	5	17	5	1	5	8	23	6	3	13	13	40	–27	21
10	Everton	22	2	3	6	11	22	3	2	6	7	19	5	5	12	18	41	–23	20
11	Leicester C	22	3	1	7	9	26	1	0	10	5	27	4	1	17	14	53	–39	13
12	Birmingham C	22	1	1	9	5	20	2	1	8	10	31	3	2	17	15	51	–36	11

**Chelsea qualify for Women's Champions League Group Stage, †Arsenal qualify for Women's Champions League Round 2, §Manchester C qualifying for Women's Champions League Round 1.*

BARCLAYS FA WOMEN'S SUPER LEAGUE LEADING GOALSCORERS 2021–22

Player (Team)	*Goals*
Sam Kerr (Chelsea)	20
Vivianne Miedema (Arsenal)	14
Beth Mead (Arsenal)	11
Lauren Hemp (Manchester C)	10
Alessia Russo (Manchester U)	9
Khadija Shaw (Manchester C)	9
Bethany England (Chelsea)	8
Leah Galton (Manchester U)	8
Georgia Stanway (Manchester C)	8
Guro Reiten (Chelsea)	7
Ella Toone (Manchester U)	7
Stina Blackstenius (Arsenal)	6
Natasha Dowie (Reading)	6
Jessie Fleming (Chelsea)	6
Pernille Harder (Chelsea)	6
Fran Kirby (Chelsea)	6
Kim Little (Arsenal)	6
Caroline Weir (Manchester C)	6

FA WOMEN'S CHAMPIONSHIP 2021–22

			Home					*Away*					*Total*						
		P	*W*	*D*	*L*	*F*	*A*	*W*	*D*	*L*	*F*	*A*	*W*	*D*	*L*	*F*	*A*	*GD*	*Pts*
1	Liverpool	22	7	3	1	20	3	9	1	1	29	8	16	4	2	49	11	38	52
2	London City Lionesses	22	7	2	2	20	12	6	0	5	15	10	13	2	7	35	22	13	41
3	Bristol C	22	6	1	4	23	16	5	3	3	20	12	11	4	7	43	28	15	37
4	Crystal Palace	22	6	2	3	19	20	5	2	4	16	19	11	4	7	35	39	–4	37
5	Charlton Ath	22	7	1	3	15	6	3	3	5	12	12	10	4	8	27	18	9	34
6	Durham	22	6	2	3	16	11	4	2	5	14	17	10	4	8	30	28	2	34
7	Sheffield U	22	6	2	3	20	14	3	4	4	14	17	9	6	7	34	31	3	33
8	Lewes	22	7	1	3	15	9	2	1	8	8	15	9	2	11	23	24	–1	29
9	Sunderland	22	3	4	4	12	14	3	2	6	11	18	6	6	10	23	32	–9	24
10	Blackburn R	22	5	0	6	14	20	0	2	9	3	21	5	2	15	17	41	–24	17
11	Coventry U*	22	3	3	5	8	13	2	4	5	10	19	5	7	10	18	32	–14	12
12	Watford	22	1	4	6	9	23	1	1	9	9	23	2	5	15	18	46	–28	11

**Coventry U deducted 10 points for entering voluntary liquidation.*

FA WOMEN'S CHAMPIONSHIP LEADING GOALSCORERS 2021–22

Player (Team)	*Goals*
Abi Harrison (Bristol C)	17
Leanne Kiernan (Liverpool)	13
Courtney Sweetman-Kirk (Sheffield U)	11
Beth Hepple (Durham)	10
Katie Stengel (Liverpool)	8
Lucy Watson (Sheffield U)	8
Katie Wilkinson (Coventry U)	7
Chloe Bull (Bristol C)	6
Rio Hardy (Durham)	6
Amy Rodgers (London C)	6
Agnes Beever-Jones (Bristol C)	5
Millie Farrow (Crystal Palace)	5
Emma Follis (Charlton Ath)	5
Rachel Furness (Liverpool)	5
Coral-Jade Haines (Crystal Palace)	5
Elise Hughes (Charlton Ath)	5
Aimee Palmer (Bristol C)	5
Mollie Sharpe (Crystal Palace)	5
Siobhan Wilson (Crystal Palace)	5

FA WOMEN'S CONTINENTAL TYRES LEAGUE CUP 2021–22

GROUP STAGE

Drawn games were decided by a penalty shoot-out.
WP = match won on penalties (2 pts);
LP = match lost on penalties (1 pt).

GROUP A

Liverpool v Aston Villa 1-1
Liverpool won 5-4 on penalties
Sheffield U v Sunderland 1-1
Sunderland won 4-2 on penalties
Sheffield U v Liverpool 0-0
Liverpool won 5-3 on penalties
Blackburn R v Sunderland 1-2
Liverpool v Blackburn R 2-1
Aston Villa v Sheffield U 1-2
Blackburn R v Sheffield U 1-0
Sunderland v Aston Villa 0-7
Sunderland v Liverpool 0-0
Sunderland won 4-2 on penalties
Aston Villa v Blackburn R 0-1

Group A Table	P	W	WP	LP	L	F	A	GD	Pts
Liverpool	4	1	2	1	0	3	2	1	8
Sunderland	4	1	2	0	1	3	9	−6	7
Blackburn R	4	2	0	0	2	4	4	0	6
Sheffield U	4	1	0	2	1	3	3	0	5
Aston Villa	4	1	0	1	2	9	4	5	4

GROUP B

Manchester C v Everton 5-1
Durham v Manchester U 2-2
Manchester U won 5-3 on penalties
Leicester C v Everton 1-3
Manchester C v Durham 3-0
Durham v Leicester C 1-2
Manchester U v Manchester C 2-1
Manchester U v Leicester C 2-2
Leicester C won 4-3 on penalties
Everton v Durham 1-0
Everton v Manchester U 0-2
Leicester C v Manchester C 0-5

Group B Table	P	W	WP	LP	L	F	A	GD	Pts
Manchester C	4	3	0	0	1	14	3	11	9
Manchester U	4	2	1	1	0	8	5	3	9
Everton	4	2	0	0	2	5	8	−3	6
Leicester C	4	1	1	0	2	5	11	−6	5
Durham	4	0	0	1	3	3	8	−5	1

GROUP C

Tottenham H v Charlton Ath 1-0
Coventry U v Watford 3-0
Charlton Ath v Coventry U 3-1
Watford v Tottenham H 0-11
Watford v Charlton Ath 0-5
Coventry U v Tottenham H 2-3

Group C Table	P	W	WP	LP	L	F	A	GD	Pts
Tottenham H	3	3	0	0	0	15	2	13	9
Charlton Ath	3	2	0	0	1	8	2	6	6
Coventry U	3	1	0	0	2	6	6	0	3
Watford	3	0	0	0	3	0	19	−19	0

GROUP D

Reading v Bristol C 0-1
Lewes v Crystal Palace 1-1
Crystal Palace won 4-3 on penalties
Bristol C v Lewes 3-1
Crystal Palace v Reading 1-3
Lewes v Reading 1-1
Lewes won 6-5 on penalties
Crystal Palace v Bristol C 0-0
Bristol C won 5-4 on penalties

Group D Table	P	W	WP	LP	L	F	A	GD	Pts
Bristol C	3	2	1	0	0	4	1	3	8
Reading	3	1	0	1	1	4	3	1	4
Crystal Palace	3	0	1	1	1	2	4	−2	3
Lewes	3	0	1	1	1	3	5	−2	3

GROUP E

London C Lionesses v West Ham U 0-1
Birmingham C v Brighton & HA 0-1
Brighton & HA v London C Lionesses 0-1
Birmingham C v West Ham U 0-4
London C Lionesses v Birmingham C 2-2
London C Lionesses won 5-4 on penalties
West Ham U v Brighton & HA 3-0

Group E Table	P	W	WP	LP	L	F	A	GD	Pts
West Ham U	3	3	0	0	0	8	0	8	9
London C Lionesses	3	1	1	0	1	3	3	0	5
Brighton & HA	3	1	0	0	2	1	4	−3	3
Birmingham C	3	0	0	1	2	2	7	−5	1

KNOCK-OUT ROUNDS

QUARTER-FINALS

West Ham U v Chelsea 2-4
Tottenham H v Liverpool 1-0
Manchester C v Bristol C 3-1
Arsenal v Manchester U 0-1

SEMI-FINALS

Chelsea v Manchester U 3-1
Manchester C v Tottenham H 3-0

WOMEN'S CONTINENTAL TYRES CUP FINAL 2021–22

Saturday, 5 March 2022

(at AFC Wimbledon, attendance 8004)

Chelsea (1) 1 Manchester C (0) 3

Chelsea: Berger; Nouwen, Bright, Ingle, Carter, Ji So-yun (Spence 79), Reiten (James 68), Kerr, Charles (England 79), Harder, Andersson (Abdullina 90).

Manchester C: Roebuck, Stokes, Greenwood, Stanway, Raso (Blakstad 81), Hemp, White (Shaw 89), Weir, Bronze, Walsh, Kennedy.

Referee: Lisa Benn.

FA WOMEN'S NATIONAL LEAGUE 2021–22

FA WOMEN'S NATIONAL LEAGUE NORTHERN PREMIER DIVISION 2021–22

			Home					Away					Total						
		P	W	D	L	F	A	W	D	L	F	A	W	D	L	F	A	GD	Pts
1	Wolverhampton W	24	9	3	0	28	9	9	2	1	33	7	18	5	1	61	16	45	59
2	Derby Co	24	7	3	2	24	7	9	0	3	24	12	16	3	5	48	19	29	51
3	AFC Fylde	24	9	1	2	32	14	5	4	3	15	14	14	5	5	47	28	19	47
4	Burnley	24	8	1	3	39	14	6	3	3	31	13	14	4	6	70	27	43	46
5	Nottingham F	24	7	3	2	16	9	6	2	4	24	8	13	5	6	40	17	23	44
6	Huddersfield T	24	6	3	3	24	13	7	1	4	30	15	13	4	7	54	28	26	43
7	Brighouse T	24	6	2	4	22	13	5	5	2	29	18	11	7	6	51	31	20	40
8	WBA	24	5	4	3	20	22	2	3	7	9	22	7	7	10	29	44	–15	28
9	Stoke C	24	4	1	7	19	25	4	0	8	17	29	8	1	15	36	54	–18	25
10	Loughborough Lightning	24	4	2	6	22	33	2	3	7	13	30	6	5	13	35	63	–28	23
11	Middlesbrough	24	3	0	9	12	35	2	3	7	15	32	5	3	16	27	67	–40	18
12	Hull C	24	1	2	9	8	34	1	1	10	10	38	2	3	19	18	72	–54	9
13	Sheffield	24	2	2	8	7	28	0	0	12	6	35	2	2	20	13	63	–50	8

FA WOMEN'S NATIONAL LEAGUE SOUTHERN PREMIER DIVISION 2021–22

		P	W	D	L	F	A	W	D	L	F	A	W	D	L	F	A	GD	Pts
1	Southampton FC Women	26	10	2	1	58	9	12	1	0	41	4	22	3	1	99	13	86	69
2	Oxford U	26	12	1	0	49	6	7	2	4	22	9	19	3	4	71	15	56	60
3	Ipswich T	26	8	3	2	34	7	10	1	2	35	7	18	4	4	69	14	55	58
4	Bridgwater U	26	9	1	3	32	7	6	4	3	16	9	15	5	6	48	16	32	50
5	Crawley Wasps	26	9	0	4	29	16	6	0	7	28	24	15	0	11	57	40	17	45
6	Gillingham	26	8	2	3	17	11	5	4	4	20	22	13	6	7	37	33	4	45
7	Portsmouth	26	6	3	4	23	13	7	1	5	28	16	13	4	9	51	29	22	43
8	London Bees	26	4	3	6	27	25	5	0	8	19	26	9	3	14	46	51	–5	30
9	Milton Keynes D	26	5	3	5	20	16	3	2	8	14	26	8	5	13	34	42	–8	29
10	Plymouth Arg	26	6	1	6	26	28	3	1	9	20	33	9	2	15	46	61	–15	29
11	Cardiff C*	26	5	0	8	18	27	3	2	8	15	25	8	2	16	33	52	–19	24
12	Chichester & Selsey	26	6	1	6	15	21	1	2	10	16	39	7	3	16	31	60	–29	24
13	Keynsham T	26	5	0	8	21	42	1	0	12	10	68	6	0	20	31	110	–79	18
14	Hounslow	26	0	0	13	2	59	0	0	13	3	63	0	0	26	5	122	–117	0

**Cardiff C deducted 2 points for failing to fulfil fixtures.*

CHAMPIONSHIP PLAY-OFF

Southampton FC Women v Wolverhampton W 1-0

FA WOMEN'S NATIONAL LEAGUE DIVISION ONE NORTH 2021–22

		P	W	D	L	F	A	W	D	L	F	A	W	D	L	F	A	GD	Pts
1	Liverpool Feds	22	10	1	0	37	4	9	1	1	23	7	19	2	1	60	11	49	59
2	Newcastle U	22	9	2	0	50	8	9	0	2	35	8	18	2	2	85	16	69	56
3	Durham Cestria	22	5	1	4	29	16	8	1	3	36	19	13	2	7	65	35	30	41
4	Leeds U	22	6	3	2	30	14	6	1	4	21	20	12	4	6	51	34	17	40
5	Chorley	22	4	5	2	22	17	4	5	2	17	17	8	10	4	39	34	5	34
6	Stockport Co	22	5	0	6	24	23	2	6	3	20	19	7	6	9	44	42	2	27
7	Bradford C	22	5	2	4	21	19	2	3	6	18	29	7	5	10	39	48	–9	26
8	Norton & Stockton Ancients	22	2	3	6	16	19	5	2	4	19	26	7	5	10	35	45	–10	26
9	Barnsley*	22	2	2	7	16	23	6	0	5	25	28	8	2	12	41	51	–10	23
10	FC United of Manchester	22	3	2	6	20	30	3	1	7	14	42	6	3	13	34	72	–38	21
11	Chester-le-Street T	22	2	2	8	17	38	1	3	6	11	24	3	5	14	28	62	–34	14
12	Alnwick T	22	0	1	10	13	39	0	1	10	11	56	0	2	20	24	95	–71	2

**Barnsley deducted 3 points.*

FA WOMEN'S NATIONAL LEAGUE DIVISION ONE MIDLANDS 2021–22

		P	W	D	L	F	A	W	D	L	F	A	W	D	L	F	A	GD	Pts
1	Boldmere St Michaels	22	8	2	1	30	9	8	1	2	29	11	16	3	3	59	20	39	51
2	Doncaster R Belles	22	8	2	1	29	12	7	2	2	26	9	15	4	3	55	21	34	49
3	Lincoln C	22	8	1	2	30	11	7	2	2	38	19	15	3	4	68	30	38	48
4	Long Eaton U	22	7	2	2	22	11	4	3	4	22	16	11	5	6	44	27	17	38
5	Leek T	22	5	2	4	27	23	5	1	5	24	29	10	3	9	51	52	–1	33
6	Sporting Khalsa	22	2	1	7	12	21	7	4	1	25	16	9	5	8	37	37	0	32
7	Solihull Moors	22	5	1	5	34	32	4	2	5	21	15	9	3	10	55	47	8	30
8	Peterborough U	22	2	4	5	17	32	6	1	4	28	18	8	5	9	45	50	–5	29
9	Leafield Ath	22	4	3	4	15	16	3	2	6	20	29	7	5	10	35	45	–10	26
10	Wem T	22	2	3	6	14	28	1	3	7	10	19	3	6	13	24	47	–23	15
11	Burton Alb	22	2	1	9	10	38	2	2	6	16	25	4	3	15	26	63	–37	15
12	Bedworth U	22	1	1	9	9	40	1	0	10	14	43	2	1	19	23	83	–60	7
13	Holwell Sports*	0	0	0	0	0	0	0	0	0	0	0	0	0	0	0	0	0	0

**Holwell Sports withdrew from the league.*

FA WOMEN'S NATIONAL LEAGUE DIVISION ONE SOUTH EAST 2021–22

		P	W	D	L	F	A	W	D	L	F	A	W	D	L	F	A	GD	Pts
1	Billericay T	24	11	1	0	39	9	9	2	1	38	6	20	3	1	77	15	62	63
2	Hashtag U	24	11	0	1	44	9	9	2	1	39	5	20	2	2	83	14	69	62
3	AFC Wimbledon	24	8	3	1	31	6	8	2	2	31	9	16	5	3	62	15	47	53
4	QPR	24	7	2	3	28	21	5	3	4	18	19	12	5	7	46	40	6	41
5	Actonians	24	8	4	0	34	7	3	3	6	18	19	11	7	6	52	26	26	40
6	London Seaward	24	3	4	5	14	21	4	4	4	17	22	7	8	9	31	43	–12	29
7	Cambridge C	24	3	4	5	15	22	4	1	7	21	26	7	5	12	36	48	–12	26
8	Norwich C	24	4	1	7	17	31	4	1	7	16	25	8	2	14	33	56	–23	26
9	Cambridge U	24	3	1	8	9	33	5	1	6	20	27	8	2	14	29	60	–31	26
10	Enfield T	24	3	4	5	19	20	3	2	7	17	17	6	6	12	36	37	–1	24
11	Stevenage	24	2	2	8	11	32	4	2	6	8	29	6	4	14	19	61	–42	22
12	Harlow T	24	1	1	10	9	35	4	1	7	18	38	5	2	17	27	73	–46	17
13	Kent	24	2	0	10	7	27	1	3	8	12	35	3	3	18	19	62	–43	12

FA WOMEN'S NATIONAL LEAGUE DIVISION ONE SOUTH WEST 2021–22

			Home					Away					Total						
		P	W	D	L	F	A	W	D	L	F	A	W	D	L	F	A	GD	Pts
1	Cheltenham T	18	7	1	1	25	9	7	2	0	19	3	14	3	1	44	12	32	45
2	Bournemouth	18	7	2	0	32	6	5	2	2	20	8	12	4	2	52	14	38	40
3	Exeter C	18	7	0	2	29	7	5	2	2	23	12	12	2	4	52	19	33	38
4	Southampton Women's FC	18	4	4	1	25	6	7	0	2	22	8	11	4	3	47	14	33	37
5	Chesham U	18	5	0	4	12	11	3	2	4	19	21	8	2	8	31	32	−1	26
6	Maidenhead U	18	2	2	5	11	17	4	2	3	15	15	6	4	8	26	32	−6	22
7	Swindon T	18	3	1	5	18	16	2	3	4	12	15	5	4	9	30	31	−1	19
8	Portishead*	18	1	3	5	11	19	3	1	5	12	25	4	4	10	23	44	−21	15
9	Larkhall Ath	18	2	2	5	14	24	0	2	7	6	28	2	4	12	20	52	−32	10
10	Poole T	18	0	1	8	1	35	0	0	9	2	43	0	1	17	3	78	−75	1
11	Buckland Ath†	0	0	0	0	0	0	0	0	0	0	0	0	0	0	0	0	0	0

**Portishead deducted 1 point. †Buckland Ath withdrew from the league.*

FA WOMEN'S NATIONAL LEAGUE CUP 2021–22

**After extra time.*

DETERMINING ROUND

AFC Wimbledon v Oxford U 1-2
Alnwick T v Chorley 2-6
Barnsley v Sporting Khalsa 2-0
Bedworth U v Burton Alb 2-5
Bridgwater U v Maidenhead U 2-1
Brighouse T v Holwell Sports 4-1
Cambridge C v Buckland Ath 17-0
Cambridge U v Portishead 4-0
Cardiff C v Actonians 2-0
Cheltenham T v Southampton FC Women 2-3
Chesham U v Kent 1-2
Chester-le-Street T v Leafield Ath 3-0
Crawley Wasps v London Seaward 11-0
Derby Co v Lincoln C 7-0
Durham Cestria v Stockport Co 3-1*
Enfield T v QPR 4-1
Exeter C v Plymouth Arg 0-2
Gillingham v Norwich C 6-0
Harlow T v Billericay T 0-5
Hashtag U v Stevenage 7-0
Hounslow v Bournemouth 0-1
Huddersfield T v Boldmere St Michaels 7-2
Hull C (walkover) v Burnley
Ipswich T v London Bees 1-0
Liverpool Feds v Nottingham F 1-0
Long Eaton U v Peterborough U 4-1
Loughborough Lightning v Doncaster Belles 2-1
Milton Keynes D v Keynsham T 7-1
Newcastle U v Leek T Ladies 6-0
Norton & Stockton v Wem T 10-2
Poole T v Swindon T 0-1
Portsmouth v Chichester & Selsey 0-2
Sheffield v Bradford C 1-0
Southampton Women's FC v Larkhall Ath 3-1
Stoke C v Solihull Moors 7-0
United of Manchester v Fylde 0-9
WBA v Middlesbrough 2-3*
Wolverhampton W v Leeds U 3-1

PRELIMINARY ROUND

Bournemouth v Kent 5-0
Brighouse T v Stoke C 5-2
Derby Co v Barnsley 5-0
Long Eaton U v Norton & Stockton 3-4
Sheffield v Fylde 2-5
Oxford U v Swindon T 5-0
Byes: Milton Keynes D, Cambridge C, Ipswich T, Southampton FC Women, Chichester & Selsey, Plymouth Arg, Hashtag U, Southampton Women's FC, Cardiff C, Gillingham, Crawley Wasps, Bridgwater U, Billericay T, Enfield T, Chester-le-Street T, Durham Cestria, Liverpool Feds, Chorley, Wolverhampton W, Hull C, Burton Alb, Newcastle U, Cambridge U, Loughborough Lightning, Huddersfield T, Middlesbrough.

FIRST ROUND

Huddersfield T v Middlesbrough 3-2
Wolverhampton W v Hull C 7-0
Southampton Women's FC v Cardiff C 5-1
Oxford U v Bridgwater U 2-0
Norton & Stockton v Chester-le-Street T 5-0
Newcastle U v Brighouse T 1-3*
Milton Keynes D v Cambridge C 2-1
Liverpool Feds v Chorley 3-0
Ipswich T v Southampton FC Women 0-1
Hashtag U v Bournemouth 0-0*
Hashtag U won 3-0 on penalties
Gillingham v Crawley Wasps 0-1
Durham Cestria v Fylde 1-2
Derby Co v Burton Alb 7-0
Chichester & Selsey v Plymouth Arg 3-1
Cambridge U v Loughborough Lightning 1-2
Billericay T v Enfield T 2-2*
Billericay T won 3-1 on penalties

SECOND ROUND

Chichester & Selsey v Hashtag U 2-2*
Hashtag U won 5-4 on penalties
Oxford U v Billericay T 2-0
Southampton FC Women v Milton Keynes D 2-1
Norton & Stockton v Fylde 2-3*
Loughborough Lightning v Huddersfield T 1-3
Derby Co v Brighouse T 1-4*
Liverpool Feds v Wolverhampton W 3-3*
Liverpool Feds won 3-2 on penalties
Southampton Women's FC v Crawley Wasps 0-4

QUARTER-FINALS

Crawley Wasps v Oxford U 1-0
Fylde v Liverpool Feds 0-2
Southampton FC Women v Hashtag U 1-0
Brighouse T v Huddersfield T 1-4

SEMI-FINALS

Southampton FC Women v Crawley Wasps 2-0
Liverpool Feds v Huddersfield T 0-1

FA WOMEN'S NATIONAL LEAGUE CUP FINAL 2021–22

Sunday, 24 April 2022

(at Armco Arena, Solihull)

Southampton FC Women (1) 3 Huddersfield T (0) 0

Southampton FC Women: Rendell; Morris, Parnell, Rafferty, Freeland (Williams 75), Pusey (Watling 75), Ware, Pharoah, Kendall, Mott, Rutherford.
Scorers: Ware 45, Kendall 71, 83.

Huddersfield T: Davies; Ibbotson (Fletcher 38), Mallin, Griffiths, Stanley, Montgomery (Laughton 87), Elford, Sanderson, Housely (Abbott 87), Marshall, Parry.

THE VITALITY WOMEN'S FA CUP 2020–21

QUARTER-FINALS

Manchester C v Leicester C	6-0
Birmingham C v Chelsea	0-4
Arsenal v Tottenham H	5-1
Brighton & HA v Charlton Ath	1-0

SEMI-FINALS

Manchester C v Chelsea	0-3
Arsenal v Brighton & HA	3-0

THE VITALITY WOMEN'S FA CUP FINAL 2020–21

Sunday, 5 December 2021

(at Wembley Stadium, attendance 40,942)

Chelsea (1) 3 Arsenal (0)

Chelsea: Berger; Bright, Carter, Eriksson, Cuthbert, Leupolz (Ji 86), Ingle (Nouwen 90), Reiten (Spence 87), Fleming, Kerr (England 86), Kirby (Harder 74).
Scorers: Kirby 3, Kerr 56, 78.

Arsenal: Zinsberger; Maritz, Wubben-Moy (Boye Sorensen 87), Beattie (Foord 70), Catley, Little, Walti (Iwabuchi 61), Maanum (Parris 80), Mead, Miedema, McCabe.

Referee: Helen Conley (Durham).

THE VITALITY WOMEN'S FA CUP 2021–22

* *After extra time.*

FIRST ROUND QUALIFYING

Birtley T v Hartlepool Pools Youth	2-5
Darlington v CLS Amazons	4-2
Penrith v Leam Rangers	7-2
Stanwix v Bishop Auckland	2-2
Bishop Auckland won 5-4 on penalties	
West Allotment Celtic v Carlisle U	9-0
Guisborough T v Gateshead	0-12
Durham U v Workington Reds	1-4
Thornaby v Boro Rangers	3-8
Epworth T Colts Belles v St Joseph's Rockware of Worksop (walkover)	
Dronfield T v Barnsley	2-1
South Cave Sporting Club v Altofts	0-10
Appleby Frodingham v Grimsby Bor	0-7
Yorkshire Amateur v Hull U	1-4
Ripon C v Hepworth U	3-2
Harworth Colliery v Cleethorpes T	3-0
Silsden v Farsley Celtic Juniors	1-4
Ashton U v Hindley Juniors	2-3
Didsbury v Nantwich T	2-1
Macclesfield T v Pilkington	6-4
Penwortham T v Northwich Vixens	1-2
Warrington Wolves Foundation v Blackburn Community Sports Club	2-4
Ashton T Lionesses v West Kirby	3-1
Sandbach U v BRNESC	2-3
Alder v Haslingden	3-4
Runcorn Linnets v Preston North End	4-1
Salford C Lionesses v Curzon Ashton	5-4
Wythenshawe Amateurs v Egerton	4-0
Hinckley v Nottingham Trent University	0-10
Bugbrooke St Michaels v Rugby T	4-4
Bugbrooke St Michaels won 5-4 on penalties	
Sherwood v Kettering T	0-3
Coalville T v Leicester Road	1-3
Anstey Nomads v Ketton	6-0
Thrapston T v Rugby Bor & Girls	2-0
Arnold Eagles v Nuneaton Bor	6-1
Westfields (walkover) v Staffordshire Vic	
Solihull Sporting (walkover) v Balls To Cancer	
Walsall v Shrewsbury T	1-4
Tie ordered to be replayed due to error by officials in first match by playing extra-time. The first match score was 7-3 to Shrewsbury T after extra time (3-3 at end of normal time).	
Droitwich Spa v AFC Telford U	1-3
Kingfisher v Port Vale	3-1
Walsall Wood v Sedgley & Gornal U	6-1
Sandwell v Redditch Bor	2-1
Shifnal T v Wyrley	10-1
Doveridge v Cookley Sports	3-1
Knowle v Darlaston T	1-1
Knowle won 7-6 on penalties	
March T U v Haverhill R	0-6
Newmarket T v AFC Sudbury	3-1
Wootton Blue Cross v Garston	0-2
Rayleigh T v Southend U Community SC	1-5
Chelmsford C v Houghton Ath	10-0
Herts Vipers v Hemel Hempstead T	9-0
Sutton U v Meridian	1-0
Cray Valley (PM) v Tunbridge Wells Foresters	1-3
Bexhill U v Glebe	0-0
Glebe won 4-3 on penalties	
Hastings U v Regents Park Rangers	9-0
Phoenix Sports v Bromley	1-9
Borough Green (walkover) v Ramsgate	
Eversley & California (walkover) v Wokingham & Emmbrook	
Caversham U v Warminster T	3-1
AFC Acorns v Leatherhead	2-2
AFC Acorns won 4-3 on penalties	
Badshot Lea v Burgess Hill T	4-0
Woking v Abbey Rangers	2-1
Steyning T Community v Eastbourne T	9-0
Woodingdean v Seaford T	1-8
Chichester C v Montpelier Villa	2-2
Chichester C won 3-1 on penalties	
Hassocks v Eastbourne U	0-4
QK Southampton v Shanklin	1-1
Shanklin won 5-4 on penalties	
Fleet T (walkover) v Shaftesbury	
Bursledon v AFC Stoneham	0-6
Gloucester C v Weston Super Mare	3-2
Almondsbury (walkover) v Olveston U	
Downend Flyers v Paulton R	3-3
Paulton R won 5-3 on penalties	
Chipping Sodbury T v AEK Boco	2-4
Pucklechurch Sports v Bristol R	1-1
Pucklechurch Sports won 3-1 on penalties	
Ottery St Mary (walkover) v RNAS Culdrose	
Feniton v Signal Box Oak Villa	12-0
Liskeard Ath v Callington T	28-0

SECOND ROUND QUALIFYING

Gateshead Rutherford v Penrith	0-2
Wallsend Boys Club v Sunderland West End	2-2
Sunderland West End won 5-4 on penalties	
Washington v West Allotment Celtic	3-1
Hartlepool Pools Youth v Darlington	1-3
Bishop Auckland v Blyth T	2-1
Hartlepool U v Workington Reds	7-2
Gateshead v Spennymoor T	2-1
South Shields v Chester-le-Street U	3-2

Boro Rangers v Redcar T (walkover)	
St Joseph's Rockware of Worksop v Thackley	1-2
Harworth Colliery v Wakefield Trinity	1-6
Oughtibridge War Memorial v Hull U	1-2
Ossett U v Farsley Celtic Juniors	5-2
York C v Brighouse Sports	9-2
Grimsby Bor v Chesterfield	1-3
Harrogate T v Ripon C	4-1
Rotherham U v Sheffield Wednesday	4-2
Bradford Park Avenue v Millmoor Juniors	1-2
Dronfield T v Grimsby T	3-2
Altofts v Farsley Celtic	1-2
Altrincham v Ashton T Lionesses	4-2
Sir Tom Finney v Marine	6-1
Merseyrail v Wythenshawe Amateurs	10-0
West Didsbury & Chorlton v Tranmere R	0-1
Morecambe v Macclesfield T	7-1
Chester v Salford C Lionesses	4-5
Blackburn Community Sports Club v Sale U	5-0
Fleetwood T Wrens v Accrington	1-0
Northwich Vixens v Cheadle T Stingers	1-2
AFC Darwen v Didsbury	11-0
Hindley Juniors v Mossley Hill	1-3
BRNESC v Runcorn Linnets	4-2
Haslingden v Crewe Alex	3-5
Notts Co v Kettering T	2-0
Rise Park v Northampton T	0-7
Woodlands v Anstey Nomads	0-5
Nottingham Trent University v Bugbrooke St Michaels	10-1
Leicester Road v Leicester C	4-0
Loughborough Students v Arnold Eagles	4-2
Thrapston T (walkover) v Stewarts & Lloyds Corby	
Lincoln U v Oadby & Wigston	5-0
Allexton & New Parks v Mansfield T	0-10
Kingfisher v Lichfield C	0-1
Sutton Coldfield T v Redditch U	2-0
Stourbridge v Kidderminster H	6-1
Tamworth Academy v Lye T	1-3
Leamington Lions v Coventry Sphinx	3-2
Westfields v Shrewsbury T	1-6
Coundon Court v Knowle	0-2
Worcester C v Shifnal T	1-2
Walsall Wood v AFC Telford U	0-3
Crusaders v Hereford Pegasus	8-0
Tamworth v Doveridge	7-0
Sandwell v Solihull Sporting	3-10
Peterborough Northern Star v East Bergholt U (walkover)	
Needham Market v Sprowston	5-1
St Ives T v Newmarket T	3-2
Histon v Whittlesey Ath (walkover)	
Wroxham (walkover) v Bury T	
Netherton U v Bungay T	5-2
Haverhill R v Wymondham T	0-10
Brett Vale v King's Lynn T	1-5
Watford Development v Chelmsford C	2-5
Royston T v Bowers & Pitsea	1-2
Headstone Manor v Biggleswade U	2-3
Garston v Southend U Community SC	2-3
Herts Vipers v AFC Dunstable	7-1
Bedford v Hutton	2-0
Frontiers v Wodson Park	1-1
Frontiers won 3-0 on penalties	
Luton T v Oaklands Wolves	12-1
Leigh Ramblers v Colney Heath	3-0
Margate v Sutton U	1-10
Dulwich Hamlet v Herne Bay	1-1
Herne Bay won 3-2 on penalties	
Haringey Bor v Clapton Community	3-6
Glebe v Millwall Lionesses	0-4
Maidstone U v Bromley	0-7
Ashford v Hackney	1-1
Hackney won 4-1 on penalties	
Islington Bor v Hastings U	1-2
Welling U v Borough Green	5-0
New London Lionesses v Aylesford	4-0
Dartford v Tunbridge Wells Foresters	11-1
Abingdon T v Long Crendon	6-0
Royal Wootton Bassett T v Denham U	4-5
Ascot U v Tilehurst Panthers	3-0
Eversley & California v Caversham U	2-4
Milton U v Woodley U	7-2
Wycombe W v Sport London e Benfica	6-0
Brentford v Abingdon U	2-5
Ashford T (Middlesex) v Highworth T	25-0
FC Chippenham v Oxford C	1-2
Walton Casuals v Woking	1-1
Walton Casuals won 5-4 on penalties	
Worthing v Newhaven	6-0
Lancing v Seaford T	0-0
Seaford T won 5-3 on penalties	
AFC Acorns v Badshot Lea	1-0
Steyning T Community v Roffey	7-1
Fulham v Eastbourne U	3-1
Chichester C v AFC Littlehampton	2-3
Whyteleafe v Dorking W	0-4
Ashmount Leigh v Saltdean U	2-2
Saltdean U won 10-9 on penalties	
Fleet T (walkover) v Holt U	
Shanklin v Bournemouth Sports	0-2
Winchester C Flyers v New Milton T	2-6
Weymouth v Alton	5-1
Merley Cobham Sports v AFC Stoneham (walkover)	
Moneyfields (walkover) v Redlands	
United Services Portsmouth v Eastleigh In The Community	0-7
Middlezoy R v Oldland Abbotonians	5-4
Sherborne T v Pucklechurch Sports	4-1
Forest Green R v Almondsbury	5-1
Paulton R v AEK Boco	1-2
Brislington v Longwell Green (walkover)	
Bristol Union v Longlevens	3-0
Gloucester C v Ilminster T	0-11
Frampton Rangers v Bishops Lydeard	0-2
Ottery St Mary v Liskeard Ath	0-11
Torquay U v Helston Ath	3-0
Axminster T v Budleigh Salterton	3-2
Saltash U (walkover) v Halwill	
Bideford v Feniton	2-5
AFC St Austell v Marine Academy Plymouth	7-0

THIRD ROUND QUALIFYING

Morecambe v South Shields	0-5
Durham Cestria v Merseyrail	3-0
Sir Tom Finney (walkover) v Bolton	
Alnwick T v Penrith	6-0
Bradford C v Ossett U	2-0
Tranmere R v Cheadle T Stingers	2-2
Cheadle T Stingers won 4-2 on penalties	
Farsley Celtic v Darlington	8-2
Crewe Alex v Sunderland West End	1-0
Mossley Hill v Bishop Auckland	4-0
Redcar T v Leeds U	0-4
Wakefield Trinity v Hull U	2-2
Wakefield Trinity won 4-3 on penalties	
Washington v Fleetwood T Wrens	0-4
Chester-le-Street T v Chorley	0-2
FC United of Manchester v BRNESC	12-1
York C v Newcastle U	0-3
Barnsley v Salford C Lionesses	3-0
Tie awarded to Salford C Lionesses due to player registration issue – Barnsley removed	
Stockport Co v Liverpool Feds	1-2
Gateshead v Harrogate T	0-2
Altrincham v Norton & Stockton Ancients	0-7
Hartlepool U v AFC Darwen	3-3
Hartlepool U won 6-5 on penalties	
Blackburn Community Sports Club v Thackley	6-0
Lye T v Whittlesey Ath	9-0
Knowle v Loughborough Students	3-3
Knowle won 5-4 on penalties	
Leicester Road v Leafield Ath	1-12
Holwell Sports v Lincoln C	2-3
Netherton U v Anstey Nomads	3-2
AFC Telford U v Rotherham U	3-0
Crusaders v Solihull Moors	0-5
Thrapston T v Sporting Khalsa	1-5
Shifnal T v Notts Co	2-1
Leek T v Sutton Coldfield T	3-3
Sutton Coldfield T won 5-4 on penalties	
Doncaster R Belles v Nottingham Trent University	3-0
Lincoln U v Millmoor Juniors	6-1
Chesterfield v Bedworth U	1-2
Shrewsbury T v Wem T	3-2
Dronfield T v Peterborough U	2-10
Lichfield C v Boldmere St Michaels	2-1
Tamworth v Northampton T	0-1
Burton Alb v Mansfield T	2-1
Solihull Sporting v Stourbridge	1-9
Leamington Lions v Long Eaton U	0-4
Biggleswade U v Clapton Community	0-2

Southend U Community SC v Frontiers 3-0
Luton T v Wroxham 3-2
Harlow T v Norwich C 0-2
Hashtag U v Enfield T 2-1
Leigh Ramblers v Wymondham T 1-5
St Ives T v Cambridge C 0-5
King's Lynn T v Cambridge U 0-3
Needham Market v Billericay T 3-6
London Seaward v Chelmsford C 8-0
Bedford v Bowers & Pitsea 2-2
Bedford won 4-3 on penalties
Hackney v Stevenage 2-5
East Bergholt U v Herts Vipers 3-4
Queens Park Rangers v Caversham U 4-0
Herne Bay v Wycombe W 2-1
Steyning T Community v Milton U 3-1
Dorking W v Seaford T 5-0
AFC Acorns v Southampton Women FC 1-5
Abingdon U v Moneyfields 2-1
Bromley v Hastings U 2-0
New London Lionesses v Ashford T (Middlesex) 1-2
Kent Football U v Denham U 0-0
Kent Football U won 5-4 on penalties
Chesham U v Maidenhead U 3-0
AFC Wimbledon v Walton Casuals 7-1
Saltdean U v Actonians 1-3
Fulham v Dartford 1-1
Fulham won 6-5 on penalties
Millwall Lionesses v Fleet T 5-1
Ascot U v Oxford C 4-0
Welling U v Sutton U 1-2
Worthing v AFC Littlehampton 5-0
AFC Stoneham v Feniton 4-0
AFC Bournemouth (walkover) v Saltash U
Abingdon T v Portishead T 2-2
Abingdon T won 8-7 on penalties
Swindon T v Longwell Green 8-0
Weymouth v Sherborne T 0-13
Poole T v Torquay U 0-6
Cheltenham T v Larkhall Ath 3-1
Liskeard Ath v Axminster T 4-0
Bristol Union v Ilminster T 0-8
Exeter C (walkover) v Buckland Ath
AEK Boco v AFC St Austell 3-4
Middlezoy R v New Milton T 0-3
Eastleigh In The Community v Forest Green R 2-0
Bournemouth Sports v Bishops Lydeard 3-3
Bournemouth Sports won 5-4 on penalties

FIRST ROUND

Farsley Celtic v Mossley Hill 2-0
Huddersfield T v Sir Tom Finney 20-0
Hartlepool U v Leeds U 0-4
Cheadle T Stingers v Bradford C 1-2
Salford C Lionesses v Alnwick T 4-0
Blackburn Community Sports Club v Hull C 0-1
Wakefield Trinity v AFC Fylde 1-4
Chorley v Middlesbrough 4-4*
Chorley won 4-1 on penalties
Liverpool Feds v Fleetwood T Wrens 2-0
FC United of Manchester v Brighouse T 0-1
South Shields v Norton & Stockton Ancients 1-4
Burnley v Durham Cestria 2-0
Newcastle U v Harrogate T 5-1
Northampton T v Bedworth U 2-2*
Northampton T won 4-2 on penalties
Long Eaton U v Peterborough U 4-0
Crewe Alex v WBA 0-5
Shifnal T v Lincoln U 0-4
Sporting Khalsa v Wolverhampton W 1-7
AFC Telford U v Leafield Ath 0-4
Solihull Moors v Loughborough Lightning 0-3
Shrewsbury T v Lye T 1-2
Stoke C v Doncaster R Belles 5-3
Nottingham Forest v Lichfield C 4-0
Netherton U v Knowle 3-2*
(2-2 at the end of normal time)
Sheffield v Sutton Coldfield T 1-1*
Sheffield won 4-2 on penalties
Burton Alb v Lincoln C 0-4
Derby Co v Stourbridge 2-3
MK Dons v Ipswich T 0-2
Chesham U v Cambridge U 3-2
Billericay T v Luton T 5-1
Herts Vipers v Stevenage 3-6*
(3-3 at the end of normal time)
Wymondham T v Norwich C 0-2
Hashtag U v Southend U Community SC 17-0
London Seaward v Cambridge C 0-2
Clapton Community v Bedford 1-1*
Clapton Community won 4-3 on penalties
Herne Bay v Actonians 1-8
Fulham v Oxford U 0-3
Queens Park Rangers v Bromley 11-0
Worthing v Hounslow 1-1*
Hounslow won 4-3 on penalties
Portsmouth v Dorking W 13-0
Crawley Wasps v London Bees 3-2
Millwall Lionesses v AFC Wimbledon 0-2
Ascot U v Chichester & Selsey 0-4
Steyning T Community v Kent Football U 0-3
Abingdon U v Southampton Women FC 0-3
Abingdon T v Gillingham 1-4
Sutton U v Ashford T (Middlesex) 0-6
Cheltenham T v Liskeard Ath 4-0
New Milton T v Bridgwater U 0-4
AFC St Austell v Torquay U 2-0
Ilminster T v Sherborne T 3-0
Bournemouth Sports v AFC Bournemouth 1-2
Southampton FC Women v Swindon T 1-0
AFC Stoneham v Eastleigh In The Community 0-6
Keynsham T v Plymouth Arg 3-5
Exeter C v Cardiff C 3-1

SECOND ROUND

Norton & Stockton Ancients v Leeds U 1-2
Salford C Lionesses v Newcastle U 0-4
Chorley v Bradford C 5-0
Hull C v Liverpool Feds 1-2
Brighouse T v Farsley Celtic 8-0
AFC Fylde v Burnley 2-3
Sheffield v Huddersfield T 0-3
Long Eaton U v Netherton U A-A
Match abandoned after 80 minutes due to bad weather. Tie awarded to Long Eaton U who were winning 6-0 when the match was abandoned.
Stoke C v Norwich C 5-1
Stevenage v Loughborough Lightning 0-2
Cambridge C v Stourbridge 1-2
WBA v Lincoln U 4-1
Lye T v Northampton T 1-2
Wolverhampton W v Nottingham F 0-4
Leafield Ath v Lincoln C 2-3
Queens Park Rangers v Billericay T 0-3
Ipswich T v Crawley Wasps 4-0
Gillingham v Actonians A-A
Match abandoned after 88 minutes due to a series injury. Tie awarded to Gillingham who were winning 2-0 when the match was abandoned.
Ashford T (Middlesex) v Oxford U 3-0
Hashtag U v AFC Wimbledon 0-1
Hounslow v Clapton Community 0-0*
Clapton Community won 3-1 on penalties
Kent Football U v Chesham U 1-6
Portsmouth v AFC Bournemouth 2-1
Eastleigh In The Community v Exeter C 0-5
Ilminster T v Southampton FC Women 0-7
Plymouth Arg v AFC St Austell 4-2
Cheltenham T v Southampton Women FC 3-3*
Southampton Women FC won 6-5 on penalties
Chichester & Selsey v Bridgwater U 0-3

THIRD ROUND

Chorley v Newcastle U 0-3
Leeds U v Durham 0-6
Brighouse T v Sunderland 0-1
Burnley v Liverpool 0-4
Liverpool Feds v Blackburn R 0-1
Huddersfield T v Loughborough Lightning 3-1
Lincoln C v Northampton T 4-2*
(2-2 at the end of normal time)
Stoke C v Nottingham F 1-2
WBA v Long Eaton U 5-1
Stourbridge v Sheffield U 0-3
Watford v Coventry U 0-4
Gillingham v Charlton Ath 0-1
Ashford T (Middlesex) v London C Lionesses 1-6
Bristol C v Lewes 5-0
Bridgwater U v Crystal Palace 1-0
Plymouth Arg v Clapton Community 5-0

Chesham U v Billericay T 0-10
Portsmouth v Southampton FC Women 1-2*
(1-1 at the end of normal time)
Southampton Women FC v Exeter C 0-3
AFC Wimbledon v Ipswich T 0-2

FOURTH ROUND
Southampton FC Women v Bristol C 1-0*
(0-0 at the end of normal time)
Newcastle U v Ipswich T 0-1
Plymouth Arg v Charlton Ath 0-6
Liverpool v Lincoln C 6-0
Brighton & HA v Reading 2-3
Nottingham F v Manchester C 0-8
Aston Villa v Chelsea 1-3
Billericay T v Coventry U 1-1*
Coventry U won 4-2 on penalties
Durham v Blackburn R 3-1
WBA v Exeter C 0-0*
WBA won 4-2 on penalties
Sheffield U v West Ham U 1-4
Birmingham C v Sunderland 2-1*
(1-1 at the end of normal time)
Bridgwater U v Manchester U 0-2
Huddersfield T v Everton 0-4
Tottenham H v Leicester C 1-3*
(1-1 at the end of normal time)
Arsenal v London C Lionesses 1-0

FIFTH ROUND
Charlton Ath v Everton 0-2
Durham v Birmingham C 0-1
WBA v Coventry U 2-4
Reading v West Ham U 0-1*
(0-0 at the end of normal time)
Chelsea v Leicester C 7-0
Manchester U v Manchester C 1-4
Ipswich T v Southampton FC Women 1-1*
Ipswich T won 4-2 on penalties
Liverpool v Arsenal 0-4

QUARTER-FINALS
Chelsea v Birmingham C 5-0
Arsenal v Coventry U 4-0
Manchester C v Everton 4-0
Ipswich T v West Ham U 0-1

SEMI-FINALS
West Ham U v Manchester C 1-4
Arsenal v Chelsea 0-2

THE VITALITY WOMEN'S FA CUP FINAL 2021–22

Sunday, 15 May 2022

(at Wembley Stadium, attendance 49,094)

Chelsea (1) 3 Manchester C (1) 2

Chelsea: Berger; Bright, Nouwen (Charles 70), Eriksson; Carter, Ingle, Cuthbert, Reiten (Andersson 90); England (Ji So-Yun 70 (Mjelde 119)), Kerr, Harder (Fleming 80).
Scorers: Kerr 33, 99, Cuthbert 63.

Manchester C: Roebuck; Bronze, Kennedy, Greenwood, Stokes (Blakstad 83); Stanway (Coombs 80), Walsh (Losada 119), Weir; Kelly (Raso 70), Shaw (White 80), Hemp.
Scorers: Hemp 42, Raso 89.

Referee: Kirsty Dowle (Kent).

aet.

Chelsea's Sam Kerr scores her side's third goal against Manchester City in the Women's FA Cup Final at Wembley in May. Chelsea won 3-2 in front of very nearly 50,000 spectators. (John Walton/PA Images/Alamy)

UEFA WOMEN'S CHAMPIONS LEAGUE 2021–22

**After extra time.*

QUALIFYING STAGE

CHAMPIONS PATH

GROUP 1 SEMI-FINALS
Breidablik v KI 7-0
Gintra Universitetas v Flora 2-0

THIRD-PLACE PLAY-OFF
KI v Flora 0-1

FINAL
Gintra Universitetas v Breidablik 1-8

GROUP 2 SEMI-FINALS
Glasgow C v Birkirkara 3-0
BIIK Kazygurt v Slovan Bratislava 4-0

THIRD-PLACE PLAY-OFF
Slovan Bratislava v Birkirkara 1-0*

FINAL
BIIK Kazygurt v Glasgow C 0-1

GROUP 3 SEMI-FINALS
Anderlecht v Hayasa 3-0
Osijek v Breznica Pljevlja 5-0

THIRD-PLACE PLAY-OFF
Breznica Pljevlja v Hayasa 3-2

FINAL
Anderlecht v Osijek 0-1

GROUP 4 SEMI-FINALS
SFK 2000 v Racing FC 0-1
Benfica v Kiryat Gat 4-0

THIRD-PLACE PLAY-OFF
SFK 2000 v Kiryat Gat 1-1*
SFK 2000 won 4-2 on penalties.

FINAL
Benfica v Racing FC 7-0

GROUP 5 SEMI-FINALS
Servette Chenois v Glentoran 1-0
Olimpia Cluj v Aland U 0-4

THIRD-PLACE PLAY-OFF
Olimpia Cluj v Glentoran 0-2

FINAL
Servette Chenois v Aland U 1-0

GROUP 6 SEMI-FINALS
Apollon v Dinamo-BGU Minsk 2-0*
CSKA Moscow v Swansea C 4-1*

THIRD-PLACE PLAY-OFF
Dinamo-BGU Minsk v Swansea C 2-0

FINAL
Apollon v CSKA Moscow 2-1

GROUP 7 SEMI-FINALS
PAOK v Agarista Anenii Noi 6-0
Valerenga v Mitrovica 5-0

THIRD-PLACE PLAY-OFF
Mitrovica v Agarista Anenii Noi 3-0

FINAL
Valerenga v PAOK 2-0

GROUP 8 SEMI-FINALS
Juventus v Kamenica Sasa 12-0
St Polten v Besiktas 7-0

THIRD-PLACE PLAY-OFF
Besiktas v Kamenica Sasa 4-0

FINAL
St Polten v Juventus 1-4

GROUP 9 SEMI-FINALS
Spartak Subotica v Peamount U 5-2
Twente v Tbilisi Nike 9-0

THIRD-PLACE PLAY-OFF
Peamount U v Tbilisi Nike 3-0
Match awarded due to a positive COVID-19 test in the Tbilisi Nike squad.

FINAL
Twente v Spartak Subotica 5-3*

GROUP 10 SEMI-FINALS
Zhytlobud-1 Kharkiv v NSA Sofia 5-1
Pomurje v Rigas FS 6-1

THIRD-PLACE PLAY-OFF
NSA Sofia v Rigas FS 2-1

FINAL
Zhytlobud-1 Kharkiv v Pomurje 4-1

GROUP 11 SEMI-FINALS
Ferencvaros v Czarni Sosnowiec 2-1

FINAL
Vllaznia v Ferencvaros 0-0*
Vllaznia won 3-1 on penalties.

LEAGUE PATH

GROUP 1 SEMI-FINALS
TSG 1899 Hoffenheim v Valur 1-0
Zurich v AC Milan 1-2

THIRD-PLACE PLAY-OFF
Zurich v Valur 1-3

FINAL
TSG 1899 Hoffenheim v AC Milan 2-0

GROUP 2 SEMI-FINALS
Brondby v Kristianstad 0-1
Bordeaux v Slovacko 2-1

THIRD-PLACE PLAY-OFF
Brondby v Slovacko 2-1

FINAL
Bordeaux v Kristianstad 3-1

GROUP 3 SEMI-FINALS
FC Minsk v Rosenborg 1-2
Levante v Celtic 2-1

THIRD-PLACE PLAY-OFF
FC Minsk v Celtic 3-2*

FINAL
Levante v Rosenborg 4-3*

GROUP 4 SEMI-FINALS
Arsenal v Okzhetpes 4-0
PSV Eindhoven v Lokomotiv Moscow 3-1

THIRD-PLACE PLAY-OFF
Okzhetpes v Lokomotiv Moscow 0-4

FINAL
Arsenal v PSV Eindhoven 3-1

ROUND 2 FIRST LEG

CHAMPIONS PATH
Sparta Prague v Koge 0-1
Osijek v Breidablik 1-1
Vllaznia v Juventus 0-2
FC Twente v Benfica 1-1
Apollon v Zhytlobud-1 Kharkiv 1-2
Servette Chenois v Glasgow C 1-1
Valerenga v Hacken 1-3

LEAGUE PATH

Levante v Lyon	1-2
Arsenal v Slavia Prague	3-0
Real Madrid v Manchester C	1-1
VfL Wolfsburg v Bordeaux	3-2
Rosengard v TSG 1899 Hoffenheim	0-3

ROUND 2 SECOND LEG

CHAMPIONS PATH

		(agg)
Koge v Sparta Prague	2-0	3-0
Breidablik v Osijek	3-0	4-1
Juventus v Vllaznia	1-0	3-0
Benfica v FC Twente	4-0	5-1
Zhytlobud-1 Kharkiv v Apollon	3-1	5-2
Glasgow C v Servette Chenois	1-2	2-3
Hacken v Valerenga	3-2	6-3

LEAGUE PATH

		(agg)
Lyon v Levante	2-1	4-2
Slavia Prague v Arsenal	0-4	0-7
Manchester C v Real Madrid	0-1	1-2
Bordeaux v VfL Wolfsburg	3-2*	5-5
VfL Wolfsburg won 3-0 on penalties		
TSG 1899 Hoffenheim v Rosengard	3-3	6-3

GROUP STAGE

GROUP A

Servette Chenois v Juventus	0–3
Chelsea v VfL Wolfsburg	3–3
VfL Wolfsburg v Servette Chenois	5–0
Juventus v Chelsea	1–2
Servette Chenois v Chelsea	0–7
Juventus v VfL Wolfsburg	2–2
VfL Wolfsburg v Juventus	0–2
Chelsea v Servette Chenois	1–0
Servette Chenois v VfL Wolfsburg	0–3
Chelsea v Juventus	0–0
VfL Wolfsburg v Chelsea	4–0
Juventus v Servette Chenois	4–0

Group A Table	P	W	D	L	F	A	GD	Pts
VfL Wolfsburg	6	3	2	1	17	7	10	11
Juventus	6	3	2	1	12	4	8	11
Chelsea	6	3	2	1	13	8	5	11
Servette Chenois	6	0	0	6	0	23	–23	0

GROUP B

Zhytlobud-1 Kharkiv v Real Madrid	0–1
Breidablik v Paris Saint-Germain	0–2
Paris Saint-Germain v Zhytlobud-1 Kharkiv	5–0
Real Madrid v Breidablik	5–0
Zhytlobud-1 Kharkiv v Breidablik	0–0
Paris Saint-Germain v Real Madrid	4–0
Breidablik v Zhytlobud-1 Kharkiv	0–2
Real Madrid v Paris Saint-Germain	0–2
Zhytlobud-1 Kharkiv v Paris Saint-Germain	0–6
Breidablik v Real Madrid	0–3
Paris Saint-Germain v Breidablik	6–0
Real Madrid v Zhytlobud-1 Kharkiv	3–0

Group B Table	P	W	D	L	F	A	GD	Pts
Paris Saint-Germain	6	6	0	0	25	0	25	18
Real Madrid	6	4	0	2	12	6	6	12
Zhytlobud-1 Kharkiv	6	1	1	4	2	15	–13	4
Breidablik	6	0	1	5	0	18	–18	1

GROUP C

TSG 1899 Hoffenheim v Koge	5–0
Barcelona v Arsenal	4–1
Koge v Barcelona	0–2
Arsenal v TSG 1899 Hoffenheim	4–0
Koge v Arsenal	1–5
Barcelona v TSG 1899 Hoffenheim	4–0
TSG 1899 Hoffenheim v Barcelona	0–5
Arsenal v Koge	3–0
Koge v TSG 1899 Hoffenheim	1–2
Arsenal v Barcelona	0–4
TSG 1899 Hoffenheim v Arsenal	4–1
Barcelona v Koge	5–0

Group C Table	P	W	D	L	F	A	GD	Pts
Barcelona	6	6	0	0	24	1	23	18
Arsenal	6	3	0	3	14	13	1	9
TSG 1899 Hoffenheim	6	3	0	3	11	15	–4	9
Koge	6	0	0	6	2	22	–20	0

GROUP D

Hacken v Lyon	0–3
Benfica v Bayern Munich	0–0
Bayern Munich v Hacken	4–0
Lyon v Benfica	5–0
Lyon v Bayern Munich	2–1
Benfica v Hacken	0–1
Hacken v Benfica	1–2
Bayern Munich v Lyon	1–0
Hacken v Bayern Munich	1–5
Benfica v Lyon	0–5
Lyon v Hacken	4–0
Bayern Munich v Benfica	4–0

Group D Table	P	W	D	L	F	A	GD	Pts
Lyon	6	5	0	1	19	2	17	15
Bayern Munich	6	4	1	1	15	3	12	13
Benfica	6	1	1	4	2	16	–14	4
Hacken	6	1	0	5	3	18	–15	3

KNOCKOUT STAGE

QUARTER-FINALS FIRST LEG

Bayern Munich v Paris Saint-Germain	1-2
Juventus v Lyon	2-1
Arsenal v VfL Wolfsburg	1-1
Real Madrid v Barcelona	1-3

QUARTER-FINALS SECOND LEG

		(agg)
Paris Saint-Germain v Bayern Munich	2-2*	4-3
Lyon v Juventus	3-1	4-3
VfL Wolfsburg v Arsenal	2-0	3-1
Barcelona v Real Madrid	5-2	8-3

SEMI-FINALS FIRST LEG

Barcelona v VfL Wolfsburg	5-1
Lyon v Paris Saint-Germain	3-2

SEMI-FINALS SECOND LEG

		(agg)
VfL Wolfsburg v Barcelona	2-0	3-5
Paris Saint-Germain v Lyon	1-2	3-5

UEFA WOMEN'S CHAMPIONS LEAGUE FINAL 2021–22

Saturday 21 May 2022

(at Juventus Stadium, Turin, attendance 32,257)

Barcelona (1) 1 Lyon (3) 3

Barcelona: Panos; Torrejon (Crnogorcevic 59), Paredes, Leon, Rolfo (Pina 75), Bonmati, Guijarro, Putellas, Hansen, Hermoso (Oshoala 46), Caldentey (Martens 59).
Scorer: Putellas 41.

Lyon: Endler; Carpenter (Buchanan 14), Renard, Mbock Bathy (Cayman 81), Bacha, Horan, Henry, Macario, Cascarino (Morroni 81), Hegerberg, Malard (Le Sommer 72).
Scorers: Henry 6, Hegerberg 23, Macario 33.

Referee: Lina Lehtovaara (Finland).

UEFA WOMEN'S CHAMPIONS LEAGUE FINALS

**After extra time.*

EUROPEAN CUP FINALS

Year (leg)	Winners v Runners-up	Score (agg)	Venue	Attendance	Referee
2001–02	Frankfurt v Umea	2-0	Frankfurt	12,106	Katrina Elovirta (Finland)
2002–03 (1)	Umea v Fortuna Hjorring	4-1	Umea	7,648	Elke Gunthner (Germany)
2002–03 (2)	Fortuna Hjorring v Umea	0-3 (1-7)	Hjorring	2,119	Wendy Toms (England)
2003–04 (1)	Umea v Frankfurt	3-0	Stockholm	5,409	Floarea Ionescu (Romania)
2003–04 (2)	Frankfurt v Umea	0-5 (0-8)	Frankfurt	9,500	Claudine Brohet (Belgium)
2004–05 (1)	Djurgarden v Turbine Potsdam	0-2	Stockholm	1,382	Anna De Toni (Italy)
2004–05 (2)	Turbine Potsdam v Djurgarden	3-1 (5-1)	Potsdam	8,677	Lale Orta (Turkey)
2005–06 (1)	Turbine Potsdam v Frankfurt	0-4	Potsdam	4,431	Eva Oediun (Sweden)
2005–06 (2)	Frankfurt v Turbine Potsdam	3-2 (7-2)	Frankfurt	13,200	Dagmar Damkova (Czech Republic)
2006–07 (1)	Umea v Arsenal	0-1	Umea	6,265	Christine Beck (Germany)
2006–07 (2)	Arsenal v Umea	0-0 (1-0)	Borehamwood	3,467	Nicole Petignat (Switzerland)
2007–08 (1)	Umea v Frankfurt	1-1	Umea	4,128	Gyongyi Gaal (Hungary)
2007–08 (2)	Frankfurt v Umea	3-2 (4-3)	Frankfurt	27,640	Alexandra Ihringova (Slovakia)
2008–09 (1)	Zvezda Perm v Duisburg	0-6	Kazan	700	Claudine Brohet (Belgium)
2008–09 (2)	Duisburg v Zvezda Perm	1-1 (7-1)	Duisburg	28,112	Jenny Palmqvist (Sweden)

EUROPEAN CHAMPIONS LEAGUE FINALS

Year	Winners v Runners-up	Score	Venue	Attendance	Referee
2009–10	Turbine Potsdam v Lyon	0-0*	Getafe	10,372	Kirsi Heikkinen (Finland)
	Turbine Potsdam won 7-6 on penalties				
2010–11	Lyon v Turbine Potsdam	2-0	London	14,303	Dagmar Damkova (Czech Republic)
2011–12	Lyon v Frankfurt	2-0	Munich	50,212	Jenny Palmqvist (Sweden)
2012–13	Wolfsburg v Lyon	1-0	London	19,278	Teodora Albon (Romania)
2013–14	Wolfsburg v Tyreso	4-3	Lisbon	11,217	Kateryna Monzul (Ukraine)
2014–15	Frankfurt v Paris Saint-Germain	2-1	Berlin	17,147	Esther Staubli (Switzerland)
2015–16	Lyon v Wolfsburg	1-1*	Reggio Emilia	15,117	Katalin Kulcsar (Hungary)
	Lyon won 4-3 on penalties				
2016–17	Lyon v Paris Saint-Germain	0-0*	Cardiff	22,433	Bibiana Steinhaus (Germany)
	Lyon won 7-6 on penalties				
2017–18	Lyon v Wolfsburg	4-1*	Kiev	14,237	Jane Adamkova (Czech Republic)
2018–19	Lyon v Barcelona	4-1	Budapest	19,487	Anastasia Pustovoitova (Russia)
2019–20	Lyon v Wolfsburg	3-1	San Sebastian	0	Esther Staubli (Switzerland)
2020–21	Barcelona v Chelsea	4-0	Gothenburg	0	Riem Hussein (Germany)
2021–22	Lyon v Barcelona	3-1	Turin	32,257	Lina Lehtovaara (Finland)

WOMEN'S EUROPEAN CHAMPIONSHIP FINALS

UNOFFICIAL FINALS

Year (leg)	Winners v Runners-up	Score	Venue	Attendance	Referee
1969	Italy v Denmark	3-1	Turin	10,000	Nino Cosentino (Italy)
1979	Denmark v Italy	2-0	Naples	15,000	Anna Pancani (Italy)

OFFICIAL FINALS

Year (leg)	Winners v Runners-up	Score	Venue	Attendance	Referee
1984 (1)	Sweden v England	1-0	Gothenburg	5,662	Cees Bakker (Netherlands)
1984 (2)	Engand v Sweden	1-0	Luton	2,567	Ignace Gorice (Belgium)
	1-1 on aggregate; Sweden won 4-3 on penalties				
1987	Norway v Sweden	2-1	Oslo	8,408	Eero Aho (Finland)
1989	West Germany v Norway	4-1	Osnabruck	22,000	Carlos Valente (Portugal)
1991	Germany v Norway	3-1*	Aalborg	6,000	James McCluskey (Scotland)
1993	Norway v Italy	1-0	Cesena	7,000	Alfred Woeser (Austria)
1995	Germany v Sweden	3-2	Kaiserslautern	8,500	Ilkka Koho (Finland)
1997	Germany v Italy	2-0	Oslo	2,221	Gitte Lyngo-Nielsen (Denmark)
2001	Germany v Sweden	1-0*	Ulm	18,000	Nicole Petignat (Switzerland)
	Golden goal				
2005	Germany v Norway	3-1	Blackburn	21,105	Alexandra Ihringova (Slovakia)
2009	Germany v England	6-2	Helsinki	15,877	Dagmar Damkova (Czech Republic)
2013	Germany v Norway	1-0	Solna	41,301	Cristina Dorcioman (Romania)
2017	Netherlands v Denmark	4-2	Enschede	28,182	Esther Staubli (Switzerland)

FIFA WOMEN'S WORLD CUP FINALS

Year	Winners v Runners-up	Score	Venue	Attendance	Referee
1991	USA v Norway	2-1	Guangzhou	63,000	Vadim Zhuk (Soviet Union)
1995	Norway v Germany	2-0	Stockholm	17,158	Ingrid Jonsson (Sweden)
1999	USA v China PR	0-0*	Pasadena	90,185	Nicole Petignat (Switzerland)
	USA won 5-4 on penalties				
2003	Germany v Sweden	2-1*	Los Angeles	26,137	Cristina Ionescu (Romania)
2007	Germany v Brazil	2-0	Shanghai	31,000	Tammy Ogston (Australia)
2011	Japan v USA	2-2	Frankfurt	48,817	Bibiana Steinhaus (Germany)
	Japan won 3-1 on penalties				
2015	USA v Japan	5-2	Vancouver	53,341	Kateryna Monzul (Ukraine)
2019	USA v Netherlands	2-0	Lyon	57,900	Stephanie Frappart (France)

FIFA WOMEN'S WORLD CUP 2021–23

QUALIFYING EUROPE

GROUP A

Slovakia v Sweden 0-1
Finland v Slovakia 2-1
Sweden v Georgia 4-0
Georgia v Finland 0-3
Republic of Ireland v Sweden 0-1
Slovakia v Georgia 2-0
Finland v Republic of Ireland 1-2
Sweden v Finland 2-1
Republic of Ireland v Slovakia 1-1
Sweden v Slovakia 3-0
Republic of Ireland v Georgia 11-0
Georgia v Sweden 0-15
Slovakia v Finland 1-1
Finland v Georgia 6-0
Sweden v Republic of Ireland 1-1
Georgia v Republic of Ireland 0-9

Group A Table	*P*	*W*	*D*	*L*	*F*	*A*	*GD*	*Pts*
Sweden	7	6	1	0	27	2	25	19
Republic of Ireland	6	3	2	1	24	4	20	11
Finland	6	3	1	2	14	6	8	10
Slovakia	6	1	2	3	5	8	–3	5
Georgia	7	0	0	7	0	50	–50	0

GROUP B

Faroe Islands v Spain 0-10
Hungary v Scotland 0-2
Hungary v Spain 0-7
Scotland v Faroe Islands 7-1
Ukraine v Faroe Islands 4-0
Scotland v Hungary 2-1
Ukraine v Spain 0-6
Faroe Islands v Hungary 1-7
Spain v Faroe Islands 12-0
Scotland v Ukraine 1-1
Hungary v Ukraine 4-2
Spain v Scotland 8-0
Hungary v Faroe Islands 7-0
Scotland v Spain 0-2
Ukraine v Scotland 0-4
Ukraine v Hungary 2-0

Group B Table	*P*	*W*	*D*	*L*	*F*	*A*	*GD*	*Pts*
Spain	6	6	0	0	45	0	45	18
Scotland	7	4	1	2	16	13	3	13
Hungary	7	3	0	4	19	16	3	9
Ukraine	6	2	1	3	9	15	–6	7
Faroe Islands	6	0	0	6	2	47	–45	0

GROUP C

Belarus v Cyprus 4-1
Netherlands v Czech Republic 1-1
Czech Republic v Cyprus 8-0
Iceland v Netherlands 0-2
Cyprus v Netherlands 0-8
Iceland v Czech Republic 4-0
Belarus v Netherlands 0-2
Iceland v Cyprus 5-0
Cyprus v Belarus 1-1
Czech Republic v Netherlands 2-2
Cyprus v Iceland 0-4
Belarus v Iceland 0-5
Netherlands v Cyprus 12-0
Czech Republic v Iceland 0-1
Belarus v Czech Republic 2-1
Netherlands v Belarus 3-0

Group C Table	*P*	*W*	*D*	*L*	*F*	*A*	*GD*	*Pts*
Netherlands	7	5	2	0	30	3	27	17
Iceland	6	5	0	1	19	2	17	15
Belarus	6	2	1	3	7	13	–6	7
Czech Republic	6	1	2	3	12	10	2	5
Cyprus	7	0	1	6	2	42	–40	1

GROUP D

Latvia v Austria 1-8
England v North Macedonia 8-0
Northern Ireland v Luxembourg 4-0
North Macedonia v Austria 0-6
Northern Ireland v Latvia 4-0
Luxembourg v England 0-10
Latvia v North Macedonia 1-4
Austria v Luxembourg 5-0
England v Northern Ireland 4-0
North Macedonia v Luxembourg 2-3
Latvia v England 0-10
Northern Ireland v Austria 2-2
North Macedonia v Northern Ireland 0-11
England v Austria 1-0
Northern Ireland v North Macedonia 9-0
England v Latvia 20-0
Luxembourg v Austria 0-8
North Macedonia v England 0-10
Austria v Northern Ireland 3-1
Luxembourg v Latvia 3-2
Luxembourg v North Macedonia 2-1
Austria v Latvia 8-0
Northern Ireland v England 0-5
Latvia v Luxembourg 1-0

Group D Table	*P*	*W*	*D*	*L*	*F*	*A*	*GD*	*Pts*
England	8	8	0	0	68	0	68	24
Austria	8	6	1	1	40	5	35	19
Northern Ireland	8	4	1	3	31	14	17	13
Luxembourg	8	3	0	5	8	33	–25	9
North Macedonia	8	1	0	7	7	50	–43	3
Latvia	8	1	0	7	5	57	–52	3

GROUP E

Denmark v Malta 7-0
Bosnia-Herzegovina v Montenegro 2-3
Russia v Azerbaijan *2-0*
Russia v Montenegro *5-0*
Azerbaijan v Denmark 0-8
Malta v Bosnia-Herzegovina 2-2
Montenegro v Azerbaijan 2-0
Russia v Malta *3-0*
Denmark v Bosnia-Herzegovina 8-0
Bosnia-Herzegovina v Russia 0-4
Azerbaijan v Malta 1-2
Montenegro v Denmark 1-5
Bosnia-Herzegovina v Denmark 0-3
Azerbaijan v Russia *0-4*
Malta v Montenegro 0-2
Bosnia-Herzegovina v Malta 1-0
Azerbaijan v Montenegro 1-0
Denmark v Russia *3-1*
Montenegro v Russia Cancelled
Bosnia-Herzegovina v Azerbaijan 1-0
Malta v Denmark 0-2
Montenegro v Bosnia-Herzegovina 0-2
Denmark v Azerbaijan 2-0
Malta v Russia Cancelled

Group E Table	*P*	*W*	*D*	*L*	*F*	*A*	*GD*	*Pts*
Denmark	7	7	0	0	35	1	34	21
Bosnia-Herzegovina	7	3	1	3	8	16	–8	10
Montenegro	6	3	0	3	8	10	–2	9
Malta	6	1	1	4	4	15	–11	4
Azerbaijan	6	1	0	5	2	15	–13	3
Russia*	0	0	0	0	0	0	0	0

**Due to the Russian invasion of Ukraine, FIFA and UEFA suspended Russian national teams from all competitions. All fixtures were voided (italics) or cancelled.*

GROUP F

Norway v Armenia 10-0
Albania v Kosovo 1-1
Poland v Belgium 1-1
Armenia v Poland 0-1
Kosovo v Norway 0-3
Belgium v Albania 7-0
Albania v Armenia 5-0
Belgium v Kosovo 7-0
Poland v Norway 0-0
Armenia v Kosovo 0-1
Norway v Belgium 4-0
Poland v Albania 2-0
Kosovo v Poland 1-2
Belgium v Armenia 19-0
Albania v Norway 0-7

Armenia v Norway 0-10
Kosovo v Albania 1-3
Belgium v Poland 4-0
Norway v Kosovo 5-1
Albania v Belgium 0-5
Poland v Armenia 12-0
Armenia v Albania 0-4
Norway v Poland 2-1
Kosovo v Belgium 1-6

Group F Table	P	W	D	L	F	A	GD	Pts
Norway	8	7	1	0	41	2	39	22
Belgium	8	6	1	1	49	6	43	19
Poland	8	4	2	2	19	8	11	14
Albania	8	3	1	4	13	23	–10	10
Kosovo	8	1	1	6	6	27	–21	4
Armenia	8	0	0	8	0	62	–62	0

GROUP G

Italy v Moldova 3-0
Switzerland v Lithuania 4-1
Romania v Croatia 2-0
Croatia v Italy 0-5
Moldova v Switzerland 0-6
Romania v Lithuania 3-0
Italy v Croatia 3-0
Switzerland v Romania 2-0
Lithuania v Italy 0-5
Switzerland v Croatia 5-0
Croatia v Lithuania 0-0
Italy v Switzerland 1-2
Romania v Moldova 3-0
Croatia v Moldova 4-0
Lithuania v Switzerland 0-7
Romania v Italy 0-5
Moldova v Croatia 0-1
Romania v Switzerland 1-1
Italy v Lithuania 7-0
Croatia v Romania 0-1
Lithuania v Moldova 4-0
Switzerland v Italy 0-1
Moldova v Romania 0-4
Moldova v Lithuania 1-1

Group G Table	P	W	D	L	F	A	GD	Pts
Italy	8	7	0	1	30	2	28	21
Switzerland	8	6	1	1	27	4	23	19
Romania	8	5	1	2	14	8	6	16
Croatia	8	2	1	5	5	16	–11	7
Lithuania	8	1	2	5	6	27	–21	5
Moldova	8	0	1	7	1	26	–25	1

GROUP H

Turkey v Portugal 1-1
Germany v Bulgaria 7-0
Israel v Portugal 0-4
Germany v Serbia 5-1
Turkey v Bulgaria 1-0
Israel v Germany 0-1
Portugal v Serbia 2-1
Germany v Israel 7-0
Bulgaria v Portugal 0-5
Serbia v Turkey 2-0
Serbia v Bulgaria 3-0
Portugal v Israel 4-0
Germany v Turkey 8-0
Bulgaria v Serbia 1-4
Turkey v Israel 3-2
Portugal v Germany 1-3
Turkey v Serbia 2-5
Bulgaria v Turkey 0-2
Serbia v Israel 4-0
Germany v Portugal 3-0
Serbia v Germany 3-2
Israel v Turkey 1-0
Portugal v Bulgaria 3-0
Bulgaria v Israel 0-2

Group H Table	P	W	D	L	F	A	GD	Pts
Germany	8	7	0	1	36	5	31	21
Serbia	8	6	0	2	23	12	11	18
Portugal	8	5	1	2	20	8	12	16
Turkey	8	3	1	4	9	19	–10	10
Israel	8	2	0	6	5	23	–18	6
Bulgaria	8	0	0	8	1	27	–26	0

GROUP I

Greece v France 0-10
Estonia v Slovenia 0-4
Wales v Kazakhstan 6-0
Estonia v Wales 0-1
Greece v Kazakhstan 3-2
Slovenia v France 2-3
Kazakhstan v Greece 0-1
Slovenia v Wales 1-1
France v Estonia 11-0
Kazakhstan v France 0-5
Greece v Slovenia 1-4
Wales v Estonia 4-0
Slovenia v Estonia 6-0
Wales v Greece 5-0
France v Kazakhstan 6-0
Slovenia v Greece 0-0
France v Wales 2-0
Kazakhstan v Slovenia 0-2
Estonia v Greece 1-3
Wales v France 1-2
Kazakhstan v Wales 0-3
Greece v Estonia 3-0
France v Slovenia 1-0
Estonia v Kazakhstan 4-2

Group I Table	P	W	D	L	F	A	GD	Pts
France	8	8	0	0	40	3	37	24
Wales	8	5	1	2	21	5	16	16
Slovenia	8	4	2	2	19	6	13	14
Greece	8	4	1	3	11	22	–11	13
Estonia	8	1	0	7	5	34	–29	3
Kazakhstan	8	0	0	8	4	30	–26	0

ENGLAND WOMEN'S INTERNATIONALS 2021–22

FIFA WORLD CUP 2023 QUALIFYING – GROUP D

Southampton, Friday 17 September 2021

England (3) 8 *(Toone 12, White 42, 67 (pen), Zivikj 45 (og), England 77, 90, Kolarovska 79 (og), Mead 90)*

North Macedonia (0) 0 8214

England: Earps; Daly (Charles 82), Bright (Wubben-Moy 63), Greenwood, Stokes, Stanway (England 71), Williamson, Toone, Mead, Hemp (Parris 63), White (Scott 72).

Luxembourg, Tuesday 21 September 2021

Luxembourg (0) 0

England (4) 10 *(White 12, 17, Parris 27, Greenwood 37, 47, Berscheid 61 (og), Bright 78, 90, Daly, 90, England 90)*

England: Earps; Daly, Bright, Greenwood (Wubben-Moy 59), Stokes, Kirby (Stanway 71), Williamson, Toone (Scott 81), Parris, Hemp (Mead 59), White (England 59).

Wembley, Saturday 23 October 2021

England (0) 4 *(Mead 64, 74, 78, England 72)*

Northern Ireland (0) 0 23,225

England: Earps; Daly (Mead 64), Stokes (Walsh 46), Williamson, Bright, Greenwood (Staniforth 80), Parris (England 63), Kirby (Wubben-Moy 80), White, Toone, Hemp.

Northern Ireland: Burns; McKenna, Nelson, McFadden, Burrows (Watling 73), Vance, Hamilton (McGuinness 64), McCarron, Furness (McDaniel 74), Wade (Beattie 81), Callaghan (Wilson 81).

Liepaja, Tuesday 26 October 2021

Latvia (0) 0

England (4) 10 *(Toone 8, 12, 68, White 25, Bright 32, Mead 55, Daly 70, 82, Williamson 79, Stanway 81)*

England: Earps; Bright, Williamson, Walsh, Greenwood (Stokes 46), Toone (Wubben-Moy 69), Mead, Kirby (Stanway 46), White (Daly 46), England, Hemp (Paris 46).

Sunderland, Saturday 27 November 2021

England (1) 1 *(White 39)*

Austria (0) 0 9159

England: Earps; Daly, Bright, Greenwood, Stokes (Carter 90), Kirby, Walsh, Toone (Stanway 63), Mead (Parris 70), White, Hemp.

Doncaster, Tuesday 30 November 2021

England (8) 20 *(Mead 3, 12, 23, White 6, 9, 49, Hemp 18, 44, 76, 88, Toone 42, Stanway 52 (pen), Carter 56, England 61, 84, Scott 67, Russo 71, 81, 82, Nobbs 80)*

Latvia (0) 0 10,402

England: Earps; Bright (Carter 46), Wubben-Moy, Greenwood, Mead, Stanway (Scott 59), Walsh (Zelem 71), Toone (Nobbs 46), Hemp, White (Russo 59), England.

Skopje, Friday 8 April 2022

North Macedonia (0) 0

England (5) 10 *(Mead 5, 12, 47, 53, Toone 24, 74, 78, White 41, Stanway 45, 56)*

England: Hampton; Bronze (Daly 71), Bright, Carter, Stokes, Stanway (Scott 61), Walsh (Zelem 71), Toone, Mead, White (Russo 71), Hemp (Parris 60).

Belfast, Tuesday 12 April 2022

Northern Ireland (0) 0

England (1) 5 *(Hemp 26, 60, Toone 52, Stanway 70, 79)* 15,348

England: Earps; Bronze, Carter (Daly 66), Walsh, Williamson, Bright, Mead (Parris 71), Stanway (Nobbs 87), White (England 65), Toone, Hemp.

Northern Ireland: Burns; Magee (Hamilton 82), Nelson, McFadden, Vance, Burrows (McKenna 75), Callaghan, Furness (McCarron 61), Andrews (Caldwell 75), Magill, Wade (McGuinness 61).

ARNOLD CLARK CUP

Middlesbrough, Thursday 17 February 2022

England (1) 1 *(Bright 22)*

Canada (0) 1 *(Beckie 55)* 8769

England: Earps; Daly (Bronze 65), Bright, Greenwood (Carter 65), Stokes, Williamson (Parris 65), Toone (Stanway 46), Walsh; Kirby, Russo (White 75), Hemp (Mead 65).

Norwich, Sunday 20 February 2022

England (0) 0

Spain (0) 0 14,284

England: Hampton; Bronze; Carter; Greenwood, Daly, Nobbs (Walsh 62), Scott (Williamson 62), Stanway (Toone 80), Parris (Hemp 46), White, Mead (Kirby 72).

Wolverhampton, Wednesday 23 February 2022

England (1) 3 *(White 15, Bright 84, Kirby 90)*

Germany (1) 1 *(Magull 41)* 14,463

England: Roebuck; Bronze (Bronze 82), Bright, Greenwood, Carter (Daly 34), Williamson, Walsh (Parris 61), Stanway, Kirby, White (Russo 82), Hemp.

FRIENDLIES

Wolverhampton, Thursday 16 June 2022

England (0) 3 *(Kelly 62, Daly 66, Evrard 83 (og))*

Belgium (0) 0 9598

England: Earps; Bronze, Bright, Wubben-Moy (Greenwood 46), Stokes (Daly 46), Williamson, Walsh, Mead (Kelly 46), Stanway (Kirby 61), Hemp (Parris 81), White (England 61).

Leeds, Friday 24 June 2022

England (1) 5 *(Bronze 32, Mead 53, 90, Toone 72, Hemp 74)*

Netherlands (1) 1 *(Martens 22)* 19,365

England: Earps; Bronze, Bright, Greenwood (Stanway 64), Daly (Carter 82), Walsh, Williamson, Kelly (Mead 46), Kirby (Toone 64), Hemp (Parris 82), England (Russo 64).

Zurich, Thursday 30 June 2022

Switzerland (0) 0

England (0) 4 *(Russo 56, Stanway 74 (pen), England 76, Scott 90)* 10,022

England: Earps; Daly, Bright, Williamson, Greenwood (Carter 62), Stanway (Scott 79), Walsh, Mead (Kelly 62), Kirby (Toone 61), Hemp (Parris 75), Russo (England 61).

ENGLAND WOMEN'S INTERNATIONAL MATCHES 1972–2022

Note: In the results that follow, WC = World Cup; EC = European (UEFA) Championships; M = Mundialito; CC = Cyprus Cup; AC = Algarve Cup. * = After extra time. Games were organised by the Women's Football Association from 1971 to 1992 and the Football Association from 1993 to date. **Bold type** indicates matches played in season 2021–22.

v ARGENTINA

WC2007	17 Sept	Chengdu	6-1
WC2019	14 June	Le Havre	1-0

v AUSTRALIA

2003	3 Sept	Burnley	1-0
CC2015	6 Mar	Nicosia	3-0
2015	27 Oct	Yongchuan	1-0
2018	9 Oct	Fulham	1-1

v AUSTRIA

WC2005	1 Sept	Amstetten	4-1
WC2006	20 Apr	Gillingham	4-0
WC2010	25 Mar	Shepherd's Bush	3-0
WC2010	21 Aug	Krems	4-0
2017	10 Apr	Milton Keynes	3-0
2018	8 Nov	Vienna	3-0
WC2021	**27 Nov**	**Sunderland**	**1-0**
EC2022	**6 July**	**Old Trafford**	**1-0**

v BELARUS

EC2007	27 Oct	Walsall	4-0
EC2008	8 May	Minsk	6-1
WC2013	21 Sept	Bournemouth	6-0
WC2014	14 June	Minsk	3-0

v BELGIUM

1978	31 Oct	Southampton	3-0
1980	1 May	Ostende	1-2
M1984	20 Aug	Jesolo	1-1
M1984	25 Aug	Caorle	2-1
1989	14 May	Epinal	2-0
EC1990	17 Mar	Ypres	3-0
EC1990	7 Apr	Sheffield	1-0
EC1993	6 Nov	Koksijde	3-0
EC1994	13 Mar	Nottingham	6-0
EC2016	8 Apr	Rotherham	1-1
EC2016	20 Sept	Leuven	2-0
2019	29 Aug	Leuven	3-3
2022	**16 June**	**Wolverhampton**	**3-0**

v BOSNIA-HERZEGOVINA

EC2015	29 Nov	Bristol	1-0
EC2016	12 Apr	Zenica	1-0
WC2017	24 Nov	Walsall	4-0
WC2018	10 Apr	Zenica	2-0

v BRAZIL

2018	6 Oct	Nottingham	1-0
2019	27 Feb	Philadelphia	2-1
2019	5 Oct	Middlesbrough	1-2

v CAMEROON

WC2019	23 June	Valenciennes	3-0

v CANADA

WC1995	6 June	Helsingborg	3-2
2003	19 May	Montreal	0-4
2003	22 May	Ottawa	0-4
CC2009	12 Mar	Nicosia	3-1
CC2010	27 Feb	Nicosia	0-1
CC2011	7 Mar	Nicosia	0-2
CC2013	13 Mar	Nicosia	1-0
2013	7 Apr	Rotherham	1-0
CC2014	10 Mar	Nicosia	2-0
CC2015	11 Mar	Larnaca	1-0
2015	29 May	Hamilton	0-1
WC2015	27 June	Vancouver	2-1
2019	5 Apr	Manchester	0-1
2021	13 Apr	Stoke	0-2
2022	**17 Feb**	**Middlesbrough**	**1-1**

v CHINA PR

AC2005	15 Mar	Guia	0-0*
2007	26 Jan	Guangzhou	0-2
2015	9 Apr	Manchester	2-1
2015	23 Oct	Yongchuan	1-2

v COLOMBIA

WC2015	17 June	Montreal	2-1

v CROATIA

EC1995	19 Nov	Charlton	5-0
EC1996	18 Apr	Osijek	2-0
EC2012	31 Mar	Vrbovec	6-0
EC2012	19 Sept	Walsall	3-0

v CZECH REPUBLIC

2005	26 May	Walsall	4-1
EC2008	20 Mar	Doncaster	0-0
EC2008	28 Sept	Prague	5-1
2019	12 Nov	Ceske Budejovice	3-2

v DENMARK

1979	19 May	Hvidovre	1-3
1979	13 Sept	Hull	2-2
1981	9 Sept	Tokyo	0-1
EC1984	8 Apr	Crewe	2-1
EC1984	28 Apr	Hjorring	1-0
M1985	19 Aug	Caorle	0-1
EC1987	8 Nov	Blackburn	2-1
EC1988	8 May	Herning	0-2
1991	28 June	Nordby	0-0
1991	30 June	Nordby	3-3
1999	22 Aug	Odense	1-0
2001	23 Aug	Northampton	0-3
2004	19 Feb	Portsmouth	2-0
EC2005	8 June	Blackburn	1-2
2009	22 July	Swindon	1-0
2017	1 July	Copenhagen	2-1
2019	25 May	Walsall	2-0

v ESTONIA

2015	21 Sept	Tallinn	8-0
EC2016	15 Sept	Nottingham	5-0

v FINLAND

1979	19 July	Sorrento	3-1
EC1987	25 Oct	Kirkkonummi	2-1
EC1988	4 Sept	Millwall	1-1
EC1989	1 Oct	Brentford	0-0
EC1990	29 Sept	Tampere	0-0
2000	28 Sept	Leyton	2-1
EC2005	5 June	Manchester	3-2
2009	9 Feb	Larnaca	2-2
2009	11 Feb	Larnaca	4-1
EC2009	3 Sept	Turku	3-2
CC2012	28 Feb	Nicosia	3-1
CC2014	7 Mar	Larnaca	3-0
CC2015	4 Mar	Larnaca	3-1

v FRANCE

1973	22 Apr	Brion	3-0
1974	7 Nov	Wimbledon	2-0
1977	26 Feb	Longjumeau	0-0
M1988	22 July	Riva del Garda	1-1
1998	15 Feb	Alencon	2-3
1999	15 Sept	Yeovil	0-1
2000	16 Aug	Marseilles	0-1
WC2002	17 Oct	Crystal Palace	0-1
WC2002	16 Nov	St Etienne	0-1
WC2006	26 Mar	Blackburn	0-0
WC2006	30 Sept	Rennes	1-1
CC2009	7 Mar	Paralimni	2-2
WC2011	9 July	Leverkusen	1-1*
CC2012	4 Mar	Paralimni	0-3
2012	20 Oct	Paris	2-2
EC2013	18 July	Linkoping	0-3
CC2014	12 Mar	Nicosia	0-2
WC2015	9 June	Moncton	0-1
2016	9 Mar	Boca Raton	0-0
2016	21 Oct	Doncaster	0-0
2017	1 Mar	Pennsylvania	1-2
2017	30 July	Deventer	1-0
2017	20 Oct	Valenciennes	0-1
2018	1 Mar	Columbus	4-1
2021	9 Apr	Caen	1-3

v GERMANY

EC1990	25 Nov	High Wycombe	1-4
EC1990	16 Dec	Bochum	0-2
EC1994	11 Dec	Watford	1-4
EC1995	23 Feb	Bochum	1-2
WC1995	13 June	Vasteras	0-3
1997	27 Feb	Preston	4-6
WC1997	25 Sept	Dessau	0-3
WC1998	8 Mar	Millwall	0-1
EC2001	30 June	Jena	0-3
WC2001	27 Sept	Kassel	1-3
WC2002	19 May	Crystal Palace	0-1
2003	11 Sept	Darmstadt	0-4
2006	25 Oct	Aalen	1-5
2007	30 Jan	Guangzhou	0-0
WC2007	14 Sept	Shanghai	0-0
2008	17 July	Unterhaching	0-3
EC2009	10 Sept	Helsinki	2-6
2014	23 Nov	Wembley	0-3
WC2015	4 July	Vancouver	1-0*
2015	26 Nov	Duisburg	0-0
2016	6 Mar	Nashville	1-2
2017	7 Mar	Washington	0-1
2018	4 Mar	New Jersey	2-2
2019	9 Nov	Wembley	1-2
2022	**23 Feb**	**Wolverhampton**	**3-1**

v HUNGARY

WC2005	27 Oct	Tapolca	13-0
WC2006	11 May	Southampton	2-0

v ICELAND

EC1992	17 May	Yeovil	4-0
EC1992	19 July	Kopavogur	2-1
EC1994	8 Oct	Reykjavik	2-1
EC1994	30 Oct	Brighton	2-1
WC2002	16 Sept	Reykjavik	2-2
WC2002	22 Sept	Birmingham	1-0
2004	14 May	Peterborough	1-0
2006	9 Mar	Norwich	1-0
2007	17 May	Southend	4-0
2009	16 July	Colchester	0-2

v ITALY

1976	2 June	Rome	0-2
1976	4 June	Cesena	1-2
1977	15 Nov	Wimbledon	1-0
1979	25 July	Naples	1-3
1982	11 June	Pescara	0-2
M1984	24 Aug	Jesolo	1-1
M1985	20 Aug	Caorle	1-1
M1985	25 Aug	Caorle	3-2
EC1987	13 June	Drammen	1-2
M1988	30 July	Arco di Trento	2-1
1989	1 Nov	High Wycombe	1-1
1990	18 Aug	Wembley	1-4
EC1992	17 Oct	Solofra	2-3
EC1992	7 Nov	Rotherham	0-3
1995	25 Jan	Florence	1-1
EC1995	1 Nov	Sunderland	1-1
EC1996	16 Mar	Cosenza	1-2
1997	23 Apr	Turin	0-2
1998	21 Apr	West Bromwich	1-2
1999	26 May	Bologna	1-4
2003	25 Feb	Viareggio	0-1
2005	17 Feb	Milton Keynes	4-1
EC2009	25 Aug	Lahti	1-2
CC2010	3 Mar	Nicosia	3-2
CC2011	2 Mar	Larnaca	2-0
CC2012	6 Mar	Paralimni	1-3
CC2013	6 Mar	Nicosia	4-2
EC2014	5 Mar	Larnaca	2-0
2017	7 Apr	Port Vale	1-1

v JAPAN

1981	6 Sept	Kobe	4-0
WC2007	11 Sept	Shanghai	2-2
WC2011	5 July	Augsburg	2-0
2013	26 June	Burton	1-1
WC2015	1 July	Edmonton	1-2
2019	5 Mar	Tampa	3-0
WC2019	19 June	Nice	2-0
2020	8 Mar	New Jersey	1-0

v KAZAKHSTAN

WC2017	28 Nov	Colchester	5-0
WC2018	4 Sept	Pavlodar	6-0

v KOREA REPUBLIC

2010	19 Oct	Suwon	0-0
CC2011	9 Mar	Larnaca	2-0

v LATVIA

WC**2021**	**26 Oct**	**Liepaja**	**10-0**
WC**2021**	**30 Nov**	**Doncaster**	**20-0**

v LUXEMBOURG

WC**2021**	**21 Sept**	**Luxembourg**	**10-0**

v MALTA

WC2009	25 Oct	Blackpool	8-0
WC2010	20 May	Ta'Qali	6-0

v MEXICO

AC2005	13 Mar	Lagos	5-0
WC2011	27 June	Wolfsburg	1-1
WC2015	13 June	Moncton	2-1

v MONTENEGRO

WC2014	5 Apr	Brighton	9-0
WC2014	17 Sept	Petrovac	10-0

v NETHERLANDS

1973	9 Nov	Reading	1-0
1974	31 May	Groningen	0-3
1976	2 May	Blackpool	2-0
1978	30 Sept	Vlissingen	1-3
1989	13 May	Epinal	0-0
wc1997	30 Oct	West Ham	1-0
wc1998	23 May	Waalwijk	1-2
wc2001	4 Nov	Grimsby	0-0
wc2002	23 Mar	Den Haag	4-1
2004	18 Sept	Heerhugowaard	2-1
2004	22 Sept	Tuitjenhoorn	1-0
wc2005	17 Nov	Zwolle	1-0
wc2006	31 Aug	Charlton	4-0
2007	14 Mar	Swindon	0-1
EC2009	6 Sept	Tampere	2-1*
EC2011	27 Oct	Zwolle	0-0
EC2012	17 June	Salford	1-0
cc2015	9 Mar	Nicosia	1-1
2016	29 Nov	Tilburg	1-0
2017	3 Aug	Enschede	0-3
2022	**24 June**	**Leeds**	**5-1**

v NEW ZEALAND

2010	21 Oct	Suwon	0-0
wc2011	1 July	Dresden	2-1
cc2013	11 Mar	Larnaca	3-1
2019	1 June	Brighton	0-1

v NIGERIA

wc1995	10 June	Karlstad	3-2
2002	23 July	Norwich	0-1
2004	22 Apr	Reading	0-3

v NORTHERN IRELAND

1973	7 Sept	Bath	5-1
EC1982	19 Sept	Crewe	7-1
EC1983	14 May	Belfast	4-0
EC1985	25 May	Antrim	8-1
EC1986	16 Mar	Blackburn	10-0
1987	11 Apr	Leeds	6-0
AC2005	9 Mar	Paderne	4-0
EC2007	13 May	Gillingham	4-0
EC2008	6 Mar	Lurgan	2-0
2021	23 Feb	Burton	6-0
wc2021	**23 Oct**	**Wembley**	**4-0**
wc2022	**12 Apr**	**Belfast**	**5-0**
EC2022	**15 July**	**Southampton**	**5-0**

v NORTH MACEDONIA

wc2021	**17 Sept**	**Southampton**	**8-0**
wc2022	**8 Apr**	**Skopje**	**10-0**

v NORWAY

1981	25 Oct	Cambridge	0-3
EC1988	21 Aug	Klep-pe	0-2
EC1988	18 Sept	Blackburn	1-3
EC1990	27 May	Klep-pe	0-2
EC1990	2 Sept	Old Trafford	0-0
wc1995	8 June	Karlstad	3-2
1997	8 June	Lillestrom	0-4
wc1998	14 May	Oldham	1-2
wc1998	15 Aug	Lillestrom	0-2
EC2000	7 Mar	Norwich	0-3
EC2000	4 June	Moss	0-8
AC2002	1 Mar	Albufeira	1-3
2005	6 May	Barnsley	1-0
2008	14 Feb	Larnaca	2-1
2009	23 Apr	Shrewsbury	3-0
2014	17 Jan	La Manga	1-1
wc2015	22 June	Ottawa	2-1
2017	22 Jan	La Manga	0-1
wc2019	27 June	Le Havre	3-0
2019	3 Sept	Bergen	1-2
EC2022	**11 July**	**Brighton**	**8-0**

v PORTUGAL

EC1996	11 Feb	Benavente	5-0
EC1996	19 May	Brentford	3-0
EC2000	20 Feb	Barnsley	2-0
EC2000	22 Apr	Sacavem	2-2
wc2001	24 Nov	Gafanha da Nazare	1-1
wc2002	24 Feb	Portsmouth	3-0
AC2005	11 Mar	Faro	4-0
2017	27 July	Tilburg	2-1
2019	8 Oct	Setubal	1-0

v REPUBLIC OF IRELAND

1978	2 May	Exeter	6-1
1981	2 May	Dublin	5-0
EC1982	7 Nov	Dublin	1-0
EC1983	11 Sept	Reading	6-0
EC1985	22 Sept	Cork	6-0
EC1986	27 Apr	Reading	4-0
1987	29 Mar	Dublin	1-0

v ROMANIA

EC1998	12 Sept	Campina	4-1
EC1998	11 Oct	High Wycombe	2-1

v RUSSIA

EC2001	24 June	Jena	1-1
2003	21 Oct	Moscow	2-2
2004	19 Aug	Bristol	1-2
2007	8 Mar	Milton Keynes	6-0
EC2009	28 Aug	Helsinki	3-2
EC2013	15 July	Linkoping	1-1
wc2017	19 Sept	Tranmere	6-0
wc2018	8 June	Moscow	3-1

v SCOTLAND

1972	18 Nov	Greenock	3-2
1973	23 June	Nuneaton	8-0
1976	23 May	Enfield	5-1
1977	29 May	Dundee	1-2
EC1982	3 Oct	Dumbarton	4-0
EC1983	22 May	Leeds	2-0
EC1985	17 Mar	Preston	4-0
EC1986	12 Oct	Kirkcaldy	3-1
1989	30 Apr	Kirkcaldy	3-0
1990	6 May	Paisley	4-0
1990	12 May	Wembley	4-0
1991	20 Apr	High Wycombe	5-0
EC1992	17 Apr	Walsall	1-0
EC1992	23 Aug	Perth	2-0
1997	9 Mar	Sheffield	6-0
1997	23 Aug	Livingston	4-0
2001	27 May	Bolton	1-0
AC2002	7 Mar	Quarteira	4-1
2003	13 Nov	Preston	5-0
2005	21 Apr	Tranmere	2-1
2007	11 Mar	High Wycombe	1-0
cc2009	10 Mar	Larnaca	3-0
cc2011	4 Mar	Nicosia	0-2
cc2013	8 Mar	Larnaca	4-4
EC2017	19 July	Utrecht	6-0
wc2019	9 June	Nice	2-1

v SERBIA

EC2011	17 Sept	Belgrade	2-2
EC2011	23 Nov	Doncaster	2-0
EC2016	4 June	Wycombe	7-0
EC2016	7 June	Stara Pazova	7-0

v SLOVENIA

EC1993	25 Sept	Ljubljana	10-0
EC1994	17 Apr	Brentford	10-0
EC2011	22 Sept	Swindon	4-0
EC2012	21 June	Velenje	4-0

v SOUTH AFRICA

cc2009	5 Mar	Larnaca	6-0
cc2010	24 Feb	Larnaca	1-0

v SPAIN

EC1993	19 Dec	Osuna	0-0
EC1994	20 Feb	Bradford	0-0
EC1996	8 Sept	Montilla	1-2
EC1996	29 Sept	Tranmere	1-1
2001	22 Mar	Luton	4-2
EC2007	25 Nov	Shrewsbury	1-0
EC2008	2 Oct	Zamora	2-2
wc2010	1 Apr	Millwall	1-0
wc2010	19 June	Aranda de Duero	2-2
EC2013	12 July	Linkoping	2-3
2016	25 Oct	Guadalajara	2-1
EC2017	23 July	Breda	2-0
2019	9 Apr	Swindon	2-1
2020	11 Mar	Frisco (Texas)	0-1
2022	**20 Feb**	**Norwich**	**0-0**

v SWEDEN

1975	15 June	Gothenburg	0-2
1975	7 Sept	Wimbledon	1-3
1979	27 July	Scafati	0-0*
1980	17 Sept	Leicester	1-1
1982	26 May	Kinna	1-1
1983	30 Oct	Charlton	2-2
EC1984	12 May	Gothenburg	0-1
EC1984	27 May	Luton	1-0
EC1987	11 June	Moss	2-3*
1989	23 May	Wembley	0-2
1995	13 May	Halmstad	0-4
1998	26 July	Dagenham	0-1
EC2001	27 June	Jena	0-4
2002	25 Jan	La Manga	0-5
AC2002	5 Mar	Lagos	3-6
EC2005	11 June	Blackburn	0-1
2006	7 Feb	Larnaca	0-0
2006	9 Feb	Achna	1-1
2008	12 Feb	Larnaca	0-2
EC2009	31 Aug	Turku	1-1
2011	17 May	Oxford	2-0
2013	4 July	Ljungskile	1-4
2014	3 Aug	Hartlepool	4-0
2017	24 Jan	La Manga	0-0
2018	11 Nov	Rotherham	0-2
wc2019	6 July	Nice	1-2

v SWITZERLAND

1975	19 Apr	Basel	3-1
1977	28 Apr	Hull	9-1
1979	23 July	Sorrento	2-0
EC1999	16 Oct	Zofingen	3-0
EC2000	13 May	Bristol	1-0
cc2010	1 Mar	Nicosia	2-2
wc2010	12 Sept	Shrewsbury	2-0
wc2010	16 Sept	Wohlen	3-2
cc2012	1 Mar	Larnaca	1-0
2017	10 June	Biel	4-0
2022	**30 June**	**Zurich**	**4-0**

v TURKEY

wc2009	26 Nov	Izmir	3-0
wc2010	29 July	Walsall	3-0
wc2013	26 Sept	Portsmouth	8-0
wc2013	31 Oct	Adana	4-0

v UKRAINE

EC2000	30 Oct	Kiev	2-1
EC2000	28 Nov	Leyton	2-0
wc2014	8 May	Shrewsbury	4-0
wc2014	19 June	Lviv	2-1

v USA

M1985	23 Aug	Caorle	3-1
M1988	27 July	Riva del Garda	2-0
1990	9 Aug	Blaine	0-3
1991	25 May	Hirson	1-3
1997	9 May	San Jose	0-5
1997	11 May	Portland	0-6
AC2002	3 Mar	Ferreiras	0-2
2003	17 May	Birmingham (Alabama)	0-6
2007	28 Jan	Guangzhou	1-1
wc2007	22 Sept	Tianjin	0-3
2011	2 Apr	Leyton	2-1
2015	13 Feb	Milton Keynes	0-1
2016	4 Mar	Tampa	0-1
2017	4 Mar	New Jersey	1-0
2018	8 Mar	Orlando	0-1
2019	2 Mar	Nashville	2-2
wc2019	2 July	Lyon	1-2
2020	5 Mar	Orlando	0-2

v USSR

1990	11 Aug	Blaine	1-1
1991	20 July	Dmitrov	2-1
1991	21 July	Kashira	2-0
1991	7 Sept	Southampton	2-0
1991	8 Sept	Brighton	1-3

v WALES

1974	17 Mar	Slough	5-0
1976	22 May	Bedford	4-0
1976	17 Oct	Ebbw Vale	2-1
1977	18 Sept	Warminster	5-0
1980	1 June	Warminster	6-1
1985	17 Aug	Ramsey (Isle of Man)	6-0
wc2013	26 Oct	Millwall	2-0
wc2014	21 Aug	Cardiff	4-0
wc2018	6 Apr	Southampton	0-0
wc2018	31 Aug	Newport	3-0

v WEST GERMANY

M1984	22 Aug	Jesolo	0-2
1990	5 Aug	Blaine	1-3

OTHER MATCHES

v ITALY B

1984	27 Aug	Monfalcone	3-1
M1988	20 July	Riva del Garda	3-0

v USA B

1990	7 Aug	Blaine	1-0

WELSH FOOTBALL 2021–22

JD CYMRU PREMIER LEAGUE 2021–22

			Home					Away					Total						
		P	*W*	*D*	*L*	*F*	*A*	*W*	*D*	*L*	*F*	*A*	*W*	*D*	*L*	*F*	*A*	*GD*	*Pts*
1	The New Saints[1]	32	14	1	1	53	15	11	4	1	33	11	25	5	2	86	26	60	80
2	Bala T[2]	32	8	6	2	40	22	8	5	3	27	15	16	11	5	67	37	30	59
3	Newtown[2]	32	7	3	6	23	21	8	3	5	27	14	15	6	11	50	35	15	51
4	Caernarfon T[3]	32	5	2	9	20	30	8	2	6	26	23	13	4	15	46	53	–7	43
5	Flint Town U	32	7	4	5	30	23	5	2	9	21	30	12	6	14	51	53	–2	42
6	Penybont	32	6	5	5	26	23	4	5	7	23	34	10	10	12	49	57	–8	40
7	Cardiff Met University	32	5	7	4	23	20	5	5	6	12	18	10	12	10	35	38	–3	42
8	Aberystwyth T	32	6	1	9	22	24	5	6	5	16	21	11	7	14	38	45	–7	40
9	Connah's Quay Nomads*	32	9	3	4	24	8	6	8	2	20	10	15	11	6	44	18	26	38
10	Haverfordwest Co	32	5	7	4	19	12	5	1	10	26	34	10	8	14	45	46	–1	38
11	Barry Town U	32	5	4	7	11	15	3	3	10	20	32	8	7	17	31	47	–16	31
12	Cefn Druids	32	2	2	12	15	45	0	1	15	7	64	2	3	27	22	109	–87	9

*Top 6 teams split after 22 games. [1]The New Saints qualify for the UEFA Champions League first qualifying round. [2]Bala T and Newtown qualify for the Europa Conference League first qualifying round. [2]Caernarfon T qualify for the Scottish Challenge Cup after play-offs. *Connah's Quay Nomads deducted 18 points for fielding an ineligible player in 6 matches.*

PREVIOUS WELSH LEAGUE WINNERS

1993 Cwmbran Town
1994 Bangor City
1995 Bangor City
1996 Barry Town
1997 Barry Town
1998 Barry Town
1999 Barry Town
2000 TNS
2001 Barry Town
2002 Barry Town
2003 Barry Town
2004 Rhyl
2005 TNS
2006 TNS
2007 TNS
2008 Llanelli
2009 Rhyl
2010 The New Saints
2011 Bangor C
2012 The New Saints
2013 The New Saints
2014 The New Saints
2015 The New Saints
2016 The New Saints
2017 The New Saints
2018 The New Saints
2019 The New Saints
2020 Connah's Quay Nomads
2021 Connah's Quay Nomads
2022 The New Saints

JD CYMRU NORTH LEAGUE 2021–22

			Home					Away					Total						
		P	*W*	*D*	*L*	*F*	*A*	*W*	*D*	*L*	*F*	*A*	*W*	*D*	*L*	*F*	*A*	*GD*	*Pts*
1	Airbus UK Broughton	28	13	1	0	51	11	10	2	2	34	12	23	3	2	85	23	62	72
2	Llandudno	28	11	1	2	29	5	9	2	3	26	16	20	3	5	55	21	34	63
3	Guilsfield	28	7	6	1	28	9	7	4	3	23	15	14	10	4	51	24	27	52
4	Holywell T	28	7	2	5	38	18	8	3	3	30	18	15	5	8	68	36	32	50
5	Ruthin T	28	10	0	4	36	17	5	4	5	15	17	15	4	9	51	34	17	49
6	Colwyn Bay	28	8	1	5	30	22	7	2	5	30	18	15	3	10	60	40	20	48
7	Holyhead Hotspur	28	7	4	3	23	10	4	4	6	18	24	11	8	9	41	34	7	41
8	Buckley T	28	5	5	4	27	24	6	2	6	21	24	11	7	10	48	48	0	40
9	Penrhyncoch	28	5	4	5	16	18	4	4	6	23	39	9	8	11	39	57	–18	35
10	Conwy Bor	28	3	5	6	17	30	5	3	6	25	29	8	8	12	42	59	–17	32
11	Gresford Ath	28	7	4	3	27	12	1	3	10	12	30	8	7	13	39	42	–3	31
12	Llanidloes T	28	5	4	5	26	30	2	3	9	18	29	7	7	14	44	59	–15	28
13	Prestatyn T	28	3	4	7	14	21	2	1	11	20	47	5	5	18	34	68	–34	20
14	Llangefni T	28	2	1	11	11	41	1	5	8	8	29	3	6	19	19	70	–51	15
15	Llanrhaeadr Ym Mochnant	28	1	2	11	14	44	1	2	11	9	40	2	4	22	23	84	–61	10
16	Bangor C*	0	0	0	0	0	0	0	0	0	0	0	0	0	0	0	0	0	0

**Bangor C withdrew from the league.*

JD CYMRU SOUTH LEAGUE 2021–22

			Home					Away					Total						
		P	*W*	*D*	*L*	*F*	*A*	*W*	*D*	*L*	*F*	*A*	*W*	*D*	*L*	*F*	*A*	*GD*	*Pts*
1	Llantwit Major*	30	12	1	2	33	10	12	1	2	40	21	24	2	4	73	31	42	74
2	Pontypridd T	30	11	3	1	49	14	10	3	2	30	16	21	6	3	79	30	49	69
3	Briton Ferry	30	10	2	3	37	14	7	3	5	39	22	17	5	8	76	36	40	56
4	Cambrian & Clydach	30	10	4	1	45	12	5	2	8	28	30	15	6	9	73	42	31	51
5	Carmarthen T†	30	9	3	3	30	11	6	6	3	22	14	15	9	6	52	25	27	51
6	Goytre U	30	8	3	4	33	17	7	3	5	22	19	15	6	9	55	36	19	51
7	Taffs Well	30	7	3	5	30	23	7	4	4	27	24	14	7	9	57	47	10	49
8	Swansea University	30	6	3	6	28	23	5	4	6	16	20	11	7	12	44	43	1	40
9	Llanelli	30	5	5	5	21	26	6	2	7	22	28	11	7	12	43	54	–11	40
10	Afan Lido	30	5	1	9	22	35	7	2	6	23	32	12	3	15	45	67	–22	39
11	Trefelin BGC	30	4	5	6	28	24	5	5	5	30	27	9	10	11	58	51	7	37
12	Ammanford	30	5	2	8	34	32	5	2	8	24	24	10	4	16	58	56	2	34
13	Cwmbran Celtic	30	6	2	7	20	30	4	2	9	23	44	10	4	16	43	74	–31	34
14	Risca U	30	4	5	6	25	21	3	5	7	18	30	7	10	13	43	51	–8	31
15	Undy Ath	30	2	2	11	23	40	3	0	12	18	44	5	2	23	41	84	–43	17
16	Port Talbot T	30	0	0	15	2	56	0	0	15	6	65	0	0	30	8	121	–113	0

**Llantwit Major refused a Tier 1 licence, Pontypridd T promoted to JD Welsh Premier League.*
†Carmarthen T deducted 3 points for failing to fulfil a fixture.

JD WELSH FA CUP 2021–22

**After extra time.*

QUALIFYING ROUND 2 – NORTH

Chirk AAA v Rhos Aelwyd	2-2
Rhos Aelwyd won 4-3 on penalties	
Llandudno Alb v Glantraeth	4-1
Llysfaen v Llanelwy Ath	0-4
Amlwch T v Llanrwst U	1-2
Brickfield Rangers v Saltney T	0-3
Bro Cernyw v Llanfairfechan T	1-5
Caergybi v Llangoed	5-0
Llanberis v Nantlle Vale	2-2
Llanberis won 4-2 on penalties	
Llanerch Y Medd (walkover) v Bangor 1876	
Bangor 1876 forfeited the match due to positive COVID-19 test	
Y Fali v Bodedern Ath	1-6
Y Rhyl 1879 v Prestatyn Sports	2-0
Denbigh T v Rhudddlan T	12-2
FC Queens Park v Cefn Alb	1-4
Hawarden Rangers v Llay Welfare	0-4
Llandyrnog U v Llansannan	4-1
Llanuwchllyn v Pwllheli	1-0
Meliden v Rhydymwyn	2-3
Mold Alex v Connahs Quay T	3-0
Penrhyndeudraeth v Dolgellau	3-0
Penycae v Brymbo	1-1
Brymbo won 4-2 on penalties	
Porthmadog v Mountain Rangers	9-0
Rhostyllen v Corwen	5-0
Y Felinheli v Waunfawr	2-0

QUALIFYING ROUND 2 – CENTRAL

Aberaeron v Builth Wells	3-1
Berriew (walkover) v Knighton T	
Brecon Corries v Llandrindod Wells	3-0
Four Crosses v Llanfair U	0-3
Llanymynech v Caersws	0-6
Llansantffraid Village v Welshpool T	2-2
Llansantffraid Village won 4-2 on penalties	
Presteigne St Andrews v Bow Street	1-4
Tywyn Bryncrug v Penparcau	0-4

QUALIFYING ROUND 2 – SOUTH

Canton Liberal v Dinas Powys	1-1
Dinas Powys won 3-0 on penalties	
Merthyr Saints v Penydarren BGC	0-3
Ynyshir Albions v Cwmbach Royal Stars	2-0
Aberbargoed Buds v AC Pontymister	1-4
Aberfan v Penrhiwceiber Rangers	0-6
Abertillery Bluebirds v Caldicot T	2-2
Caldicot T won 7-6 on penalties	
Abertillery Excelsiors v Monmouth T	1-3
Bryn R v Pencoed Ath	2-7
Caerau Ely v Canton Rangers	3-1
Cardiff Airport v Ynysddu Welfare	4-0
Chepstow T v Rogerstone	1-0
Clwb Cymric v Fairwater	3-4
Cwmamman U v South Gower	2-1
FC Tredegar v Trethomas Bluebirds	0-5
Garden Village v Newcastle Emlyn	6-2
Garw SBGC v Ynysygerwn	2-8
Goytre v Newport C	1-1
Goytre won 5-3 on penalties	
Morriston T v Pontardawe T	0-6
Newport Corinthians v Abergavenny T	0-1
Pontyclun v AFC Whitchurch	4-0
Porthcawl Town Ath v Maesteg Park	3-1
Treharris Ath v Baglan Dragons	3-2
Treowen Stars v Aber Valley	1-2
Trostre v Penlan Club	1-4
West End v Seven Sisters Onllwyn	4-2

ROUND 1 – NORTH

Llandudno Alb v Llanerch-Y-Medd	5-1
Bodedern Ath v Llandyrnog U	5-1
Bow Street v Llanidloes T	2-3
Brymbo v Llansantffraid Village	3-1
Buckley T v Mold Alex	2-1
Y Rhyl 1879 v Rhydymwyn	1-0
Caergybi v Cefn Alb	1-4
Caersws v Rhostyllen	2-2
Rhostyllen won 5-4 on penalties	
Holyhead Hotspur v Rhos Aelwyd	1-0
Holywell T v Gresford Ath	2-3
Llanelwy Ath v Berriew	2-7
Llanfair U v Penrhyndeudraeth	2-3
Llanfairfechan T v Llanrwst U	1-2
Llangefni T v Ruthin T	0-1
Llanuwchllyn v Denbigh T	2-4
Llay Welfare v Llandudno	2-4
Porthmadog v Llanberis	3-0
Saltney T v Y Felinheli	3-1

ROUND 1 – SOUTH

Caldicot T v Penparcau	6-3
Penydarren BGC v Cwmbran Celtic	1-0
Undy Ath v Chepstow T	3-0
AC Pontymister v Dinas Powys	1-2
Aberaeron v Ynyshir Albions	1-3
Abergavenny T v Taff's Well	1-3
Caerau Ely v Brecon Corries	3-8
Cardiff Airport v Trethomas Bluebirds	2-2
Trethomas Bluebirds won 3-1 on penalties	
Cwmamman U v Monmouth T	1-3
Garden Village v Goytre	2-2
Goytre won 3-0 on penalties	
Llantwit Major v Risca U	4-0
Pencoed Ath v Treharris Ath	5-0
Penlan Club v Ynysygerwn	0-2
Pontyclun v Pontardawe T	0-3
Port Talbot T v Afan Lido	0-6
Porthcawl Town Ath v Aber Valley	0-2
Trefelin BGC v Fairwater	8-1
West End v Penrhiwceiber Rangers	2-12

ROUND 2 – NORTH

Llandudno v Airbus UK Broughton	1-2
Connah's Quay Nomads v Y Rhyl 1879	5-0
Denbigh T v Caernarfon T	0-4
Gresford Ath v Colwyn Bay	1-2
Bala T v Brymbo	17-1
Bodedern Ath v Ruthin T	4-5
Buckley T v Porthmadog	3-1
Cefn Druids v Holyhead Hotspur	0-0
Cefn Druids won 4-2 on penalties	
Conwy Borough v Cefn Alb	3-2
Flint Town U v Penrhyndeudraeth	5-0
Llandudno Alb v Guilsfield	3-5
Llanidloes T v Bangor C	1-4
Llanrhaeadr v Saltney T	3-5
Newtown v Berriew	6-1
Prestatyn T v Rhostyllen	6-0
The New Saints v Llanrwst U	6-0

ROUND 2 – SOUTH

Ammanford v Penrhiwceiber Rangers	1-2
Briton Ferry Llansawel v Trefelin BGC	5-0
Aberystwyth T v Aber Valley	0-4
Barry Town U v Goytre	1-2
Carmarthen T v Trethomas Bluebirds	17-1
Dinas Powys v Afan Lido	4-5
Goytre U v Taff's Well	3-1
Haverfordwest Co v Brecon Corries	0-0
Monmouth T v Llanelli T	3-2
Llantwit Major v Pencoed Ath	5-0
Penrhyncoch v Ynyshir Albions	3-5
Penybont v Undy Ath	1-4

Pontardawe T v Cardiff Metropolitan University 3-5
Pontypridd T v Penydarren BGC 6-1
Swansea University v Caldicot T 6-0
Ynysygerwn v Cambrian & Clydach Vale BGC 6-0

ROUND 3
Caernarfon T v Prestatyn T 3-0
Cambrian & Clydach Vale BGC v Penybont 1-3
Colwyn Bay v Ruthin T 5-1
Conwy Borough v The New Saints 0-1
Taff's Well v Llantwit Major 2-1
Aberystwyth T v Cefn Druids 4-1
Airbus UK Broughton v Haverfordwest Co 1-2
Bala T v Pontypridd T 5-0
Buckley T v Monmouth T 2-0
Cardiff Met University v Barry Town U 3-0
Dinas Powys v Guilsfield 2-4
Newtown v Carmarthen T 0-0
Carmarthen T won 5-4 on penalties
Penrhiwceiber Rangers v Flint Town U 1-3
Saltney T v Penrhyncoch 0-0
Saltney T won 4-2 on penalties
Swansea University v Bangor C 1-0
Trefelin BGC v Connah's Quay Nomads 0-4

ROUND 4
Flint Town U v Connah's Quay Nomads 0-2
Buckley T v Taff's Well 0-2
Carmarthen T v The New Saints 0-0
The New Saints won 5-4 on penalties
Colwyn Bay v Cardiff Met University 1-0
Haverfordwest Co v Bala T 1-3
Penybont v Caernarfon T 0-0
Penybont won 3-1 on penalties
Saltney T v Aberystwyth T 0-0
Aberystwyth T won 5-4 on penalties
Swansea University v Guilsfield 1-2

QUARTER-FINALS
Bala T v Aberystwyth T 2-1
Connah's Quay Nomads v Colwyn Bay 0-2
Penybont v Taff's Well 3-2
The New Saints v Guilsfield 2-0

SEMI-FINALS
Penybont v Bala T 0-0
Penybont won 5-3 on penalties
The New Saints v Colwyn Bay 1-0

JD WELSH FA CUP FINAL 2021–22

Cardiff, Sunday 1 May 2022, attendance 2417

The New Saints (2) 3 Penybont (0) 2

The New Saints: Roberts; Marriott, Davies K, Astles, Routledge, Brobbel, McManus (Robles 81), Redmond (Cieslewicz 79), Williams, Smith (Clark 67), Davies D.
Scorers: Williams 31, 32, McManus 59 (pen).

Penybont: Morris; Owen, Evans, Jefferies, Georgievsky (Walsh 67), Ahmun (Watts 56), Wood, Whitmore, Snaith, Borge (Reynolds, 46), MacDonald.
Scorers: MacDonald 84, Jefferies 89.*Referee:* Rob Jenkins.

PREVIOUS WELSH CUP WINNERS

1878 Wrexham
1879 Newtown White Stars
1880 Druids
1881 Druids
1882 Druids
1883 Wrexham
1884 Oswestry White Stars
1885 Druids
1886 Druids
1887 Chirk
1888 Chirk
1889 Bangor
1890 Chirk
1891 Shrewsbury T
1892 Chirk
1893 Wrexham
1894 Chirk
1895 Newtown
1896 Bangor
1897 Wrexham
1898 Druids
1899 Druids
1900 Aberystwyth T
1901 Oswestry U
1902 Wellington T
1903 Wrexham
1904 Druids
1905 Wrexham
1906 Wellington T
1907 Oswestry U
1908 Chester
1909 Wrexham
1910 Wrexham
1911 Wrexham
1912 Cardiff C
1913 Swansea T
1914 Wrexham
1915 Wrexham
1920 Cardiff C
1921 Wrexham
1922 Cardiff C
1923 Cardiff C
1924 Wrexham
1925 Wrexham
1926 Ebbw Vale
1927 Cardiff C
1928 Cardiff C
1929 Connah's Quay
1930 Cardiff C
1931 Wrexham
1932 Swansea T
1933 Chester
1934 Bristol C
1935 Tranmere R
1936 Crewe Alex
1937 Crewe Alex
1938 Shrewsbury T
1939 South Liverpool
1940 Wellington T
1947 Chester
1948 Lovell's Ath
1949 Merthyr Tydfil
1950 Swansea T
1951 Merthyr Tydfil
1952 Rhyl
1953 Rhyl
1954 Flint Town U
1955 Barry T
1956 Cardiff C
1957 Wrexham
1958 Wrexham
1959 Cardiff C
1960 Wrexham
1961 Swansea T
1962 Bangor C
1963 Borough U
1964 Cardiff C
1965 Cardiff C
1966 Swansea T
1967 Cardiff C
1968 Cardiff C
1969 Cardiff C
1970 Cardiff C
1971 Cardiff C
1972 Wrexham
1973 Cardiff C
1974 Cardiff C
1975 Wrexham
1976 Cardiff C
1977 Shrewsbury T
1978 Wrexham
1979 Shrewsbury T
1980 Newport Co
1981 Swansea C
1982 Swansea C
1983 Swansea C
1984 Shrewsbury T
1985 Shrewsbury T
1986 Wrexham
1987 Merthyr Tydfil
1988 Cardiff C
1989 Swansea C
1990 Hereford U
1991 Swansea C
1992 Cardiff C
1993 Cardiff C
1994 Barry T
1995 Wrexham
1996 TNS
1997 Barry T
1998 Bangor C
1999 Inter Cable-Tel
2000 Bangor C
2001 Barry T
2002 Barry T
2003 Barry T
2004 Rhyl
2005 TNS
2006 Rhyl
2007 Carmarthen T
2008 Bangor C
2009 Bangor C
2010 Bangor C
2011 Llanelli
2012 The New Saints
2013 Prestatyn T
2014 The New Saints
2015 The New Saints
2016 The New Saints
2017 Bala T
2018 Connah's Quay Nomads
2019 The New Saints
2020 Not completed
2021 Not completed
2022 The New Saints

NATHANIEL MG WELSH LEAGUE CUP 2021–22

FIRST ROUND – NORTH

Airbus UK Broughton v Guilsfield	1-1
Airbus UK Broughton won 6-5 on penalties	
Bangor C v Holyhead Hotspur	5-0
Holywell T v Colwyn Bay	2-1
Llandudno v Denbigh T	3-3
Llandudno won 3-0 on penalties	
Llangefni T v Prestatyn T	1-2
Llanidloes T v Gresford Ath	2-3
Llanrhaeadr Ym Mochnant v Penrhyncoch	1-4

FIRST ROUND – SOUTH

Briton Ferry Llansawel v Pontypridd T	2-2
Pontypridd T won 4-3 on penalties	
Cambrian and Clydach Vale v Carmarthen T	4-1
Cwmbran Celtic v Afan Lido	3-0
Llanelli T v Newport Co	5-0
Llantwit Major v Risca U	3-3
Risca U won 4-2 on penalties	
Port Talbot T v Swansea University (walkover)	
Trefelin BGC v Taff's Well	2-0

SECOND ROUND – NORTH

Airbus UK Broughton v Buckley T	3-2
Connah's Quay Nomads v Llandudno	2-0
Conwy Bor v Holywell T	1-3
Flint Town U v Bala T	1-1
Bala T won 3-1 on penalties	
Gresford Ath v Bangor C	0-1
Penrhyncoch v The New Saints	2-1
Prestatyn T v Cefn Druids	3-0
Ruthin T v Caernarfon T	0-3

SECOND ROUND – SOUTH

Aberystwyth T v Penybont	1-1
Aberystwyth T won 5-4 on penalties	
Ammanford v Cardiff Met University	0-4
Barry Town U v Llanelli T	5-0
Cambrian and Clydach Vale v Newtown	2-4
Cwmbran Celtic v Pontypridd T	1-2
Haverfordwest Co v Goytre U	3-0
Trefelin BGC v Risca U	2-0
Undy Ath v Swansea University	1-1
Undy Ath won 5-3 on penalties	

THIRD ROUND – NORTH

Bangor C v Bala T	0-0
Bala T won 8-7 on penalties	
Connah's Quay Nomads v Airbus UK Broughton	6-3
Newtown v Caernarfon T	5-0
Prestatyn T v Holywell T	3-4

THIRD ROUND – SOUTH

Aberystwyth T v Cardiff Met University	2-5
Barry Town U v Trefelin BGC	3-0
Haverfordwest Co v Undy Ath	5-0
Penrhyncoch v Pontypridd T	1-3

QUARTER-FINALS – NORTH

Bala T v Newtown	3-1
Connah's Quay Nomads v Holywell T	4-0

QUARTER-FINALS – SOUTH

Barry Town U v Pontypridd T	7-1
Haverfordwest Co v Cardiff Met University	0-2

SEMI-FINALS

Bala T v Connah's Quay Nomads	1-4
Cardiff Met University v Barry Town U	3-2

NATHANIEL MG WELSH LEAGUE CUP FINAL 2021–22

Bridgend, Sunday 6 February 2022, attendance 822

Cardiff Met University (0) 0 Connah's Quay Nomads (0) 0

Cardiff Met University: Lang; Chubb, McCarthy, Lewis, Price, Evans E, Baker, Roscrow (Craven 82), Owen (Warman 87), Rees (Jones 59), Evans J.

Connah's Quay Nomads: Byrne; Horan, Fernandes Mendes, Mullan (Insall 69), Morris, Poole, Holmes, Owens, Eardley, Edwards, Simpson (Curran 62).

Connah's Quay Nomads won 10-9 on penalties.

NATHANIEL MG LEAGUE CUP FINALS 1992–93 to 2021–22

**After extra time.*

1992–93	Afan Lido v Caersws	1-1
	Afan Lido won 4-3 on penalties	
1993–94	Afan Lido v Bangor C	1-0
1994–95	Llansantffraid v Ton Pentre	2-1
1995–96	Connah's Quay Nomads v Ebbw Vale	1-0
1996–97	Barry T v Bangor C	2-2
	Barry T won 4-2 on penalties	
1997–98	Barry T v Bangor C	1-1
	Barry T won 5-4 on penalties	
1998–99	Barry T v Caernarfon T	3-0
1999–2000	Barry T v Bangor C	6-0
2000–01	Caersws v Barry T	2-0
2001–02	Caersws v Cwmbran T	2-1
2002–03	Rhyl v Bangor C	2-2
	Rhyl won 4-3 on penalties	
2003–04	Rhyl v Carmarthen T	4-0
2004–05	Carmarthen T v Rhyl	2-0*
2005–06	Total Network Solutions v Port Talbot T	4-0
2006–07	Caersws v Rhyl	1-1
	Caersws won 3-1 on penalties	
2007–08	Llanelli v Rhyl	2-0
2008–09	The New Saints v Bangor C	2-0
2009–10	The New Saints v Rhyl	3-1
2010–11	The New Saints v Llanelli	4-3*
2011–12	Afan Lido v Newtown	1-1
	Afan Lido won 3–2 on penalties	
2012–13	Carmarthen T v The New Saints	3-3
	Carmarthen T won 3-1 on penalties	
2013–14	Carmarthen T v Bala T	0-0
	Carmarthen T won 3-1 on penalties	
2014–15	The New Saints v Bala T	3-0
2015–16	The New Saints v Denbigh T	2-0
2016–17	The New Saints v Barry Town U	4-0
2017–18	The New Saints v Cardiff Met University	1-0
2018–19	Cardiff Met University v Cambrian & Clydach Vale	2-0
2019–20	Connah's Quay Nomads v STM Sports	3-0
2020–21	*Cancelled due to COVID-19 pandemic.*	
2021–22	Cardiff Met University v Connah's Quay Nomads	0-0
	Connah's Quay Nomads won 10-9 on penalties	

THE FAW TROPHY 2021–22

ROUND 3 – NORTH

Aberffraw v Berriew	1-4
Bangor 1876 v Halkyn & Flint Mountain	5-2
Caersws v Rhostyllen	2-0
Cefn Alb v Chirk AAA	2-1
Gwalchmai v Llanrwst U	3-4
Llangollen T v Welshpool T	2-0
Machynlleth v Menai Bridge Tigers	1-3
Meliden v Llandudno Alb	1-5
Mold Alex v Queens Park	4-0
Mynydd Llandegai v Bontnewydd	2-1
New Brighton Villa v Bodedern Ath	0-7
Penrhyndeudraeth v Denbigh T	5-3
Radnor Valley v Llay Welfare	2-1
Rhayader T v Llannefydd	1-3
Porthmadog v Tywyn Bryncrug	4-1

ROUND 3 – SOUTH

Rockspur v Seven Sisters Onllwyn	2-0
AFC Llwydcoed v Caerau Ely	2-4
AFC Porth v Tredegar T	3-2
Cardiff Draconians v Ynyshir Albions	0-3
Cefn Cribwr v Porthcawl Town Ath	3-1
Fairwater v Cefn Fforest	4-3
FC Cwmaman v Croesyceiliog	5-1
Garden Village v Hakin U	1-2
Goytre v Newport Corinthians	2-0
Grange Alb v Monmouth T	0-5
Lliswerry v Treowen Stars	3-0
Mumbles Rangers v Pontardawe T	2-5
Penlan AFC v Baglan Dragons	1-4
Pontyclun v C K Swiss Valley	7-1
Ynysygerwn v Clase Social	4-2
Canton Liberal v Cardiff Corinthians	0-1
Penydarren BGC v Abertillery Bluebirds	1-2

ROUND 4 – NORTH

Berriew v Mynydd Llandegai	2-2
Berriew won 4-3 on penalties	
Bodedern Ath v Penrhyndeudraeth	7-0
Cefn Alb v Porthmadog	2-0
Llandudno Alb v Llanrwst U	1-0
Llangollen T v Mold Alex	1-2
Llannefydd v Bangor 1876	3-1
Menai Bridge Tigers v Caersws	0-3

ROUND 4 – SOUTH

Baglan Dragons v Ynysygerwn	3-2
Fairwater v Cardiff Corinthians	0-8
Lliswerry v Cefn Cribwr	3-3
Lliswerry won 6-5 on penalties	
Monmouth T v Hakin U	1-0
Pontardawe T v Radnor Valley	2-0
Pontyclun v Caerau Ely	2-1
Rockspur v AFC Porth	3-1
Ynyshir Albions v FC Cwmaman	2-0
Goytre v Abertillery Bluebirds	2-0

ROUND 5 – NORTH

Bodedern Ath v Berriew	5-3
Cefn Albion v Llannefydd	3-0
Mold Alex v Llandudno Alb	2-2
Mold Alex won 3-1 on penalties	

ROUND 5 – SOUTH

Baglan Dragons v Cardiff Corinthians	2-0
Caersws v Ynyshir Albions	1-2
Goytre v Rockspur	2-3
Monmouth T v Pontardawe T	4-0
Pontyclun v Lliswerry	2-2
Pontyclun won 4-3 on penalties	

QUARTER-FINALS

Baglan Dragons v Bodedern Ath	2-0
Pontyclun v Mold Alex	0-1
Rockspur v Cefn Alb	3-0
Ynyshir Albions v Monmouth T	2-0

SEMI-FINALS

Baglan Dragons v Ynyshir Albions	3-0
Rockspur v Mold Alex	0-3

FAW TROPHY FINAL 2021–22

Caersws, Saturday 23 April 2022

Mold Alex (0) 1 *(Warren 48)*

Baglan Dragons (0) 0

THE FAW TROPHY FINALS 1993–94 to 2021–22

1993–94	Barry T v Aberaman	2-1
1994–95	Rhydymwyn v Taffs Well	1-0
1995–96	Rhydymwyn v Penrhyncoch	2-1
1996–97	Cambrian U Sky Blues v Rhyl Delta	2-1
1997–98	Dinas Powys v Llanrwst	2-0
1998–99	Ragged School v Barry Ath	3-1
1999-00	Trefelin BGC v Bryntirion Ath	6-2
2000–01	Ragged School v Gresford Ath	1-0
2001–02	Cefn U v Llangeinor	2-0
2002–03	Rhydyfelin Zenith v Tillery	4-1
2003–04	Penycae v Llanrhaeadr	3-2
2004–05	West End v Rhydymwyn	3-1
2005–06	West End v Cefn U	4-2
2006–07	Brymbo v Glan Conwy	6-2
2007–08	Rhos Aelwyd v Corwen	4-2
2008–09	Ragged School v Penycae	1-0
2009–10	Glan Conwy v Clydach Wasps	5-1
2010–11	Holywell T v Conwy U	3-2
2011–12	Sully Sports v Holyhead Hotspur	2-1
2012–13	Caernarfon T v Kilvey Fords	6-0
2013–14	Llanrug U v Chirk AAA	3-2
2014–15	Holywell T v Penrhyndeudraeth	4-2
2015-16	Abergavenny T v Sully Sports	1-0
2016-17	Chirk AAA v Penlan Club	2-1
2017-18	Conwy Borough v Rhos Aelwyd	4-1
2018-19	Cefn Albion v Pontardawe T	4-0
2019–20	*Cancelled due to COVID-19 pandemic.*	
2020–21	*Cancelled due to COVID-19 pandemic.*	
2021–22	Mold Alex v Baglan Dragons	1-0

NORTHERN IRISH FOOTBALL 2021–22

NIFL DANSKE BANK PREMIERSHIP 2021–22

			Home					Away					Total						
		P	*W*	*D*	*L*	*F*	*A*	*W*	*D*	*L*	*F*	*A*	*W*	*D*	*L*	*F*	*A*	*GD*	*Pts*
1	Linfield[1]	38	1	2	0	3	1	1	1	0	2	1	24	11	3	67	24	43	83
2	Cliftonville[2]	38	0	2	0	0	0	2	1	0	7	5	24	10	4	61	29	32	82
3	Glentoran	38	0	1	2	1	6	0	1	1	3	4	21	8	9	68	44	24	71
4	Crusaders	38	0	1	2	5	7	2	0	0	8	1	21	5	12	60	36	24	68
5	Larne¶	38	1	0	0	3	0	1	3	0	2	1	17	11	10	61	39	22	62
6	Coleraine	38	1	0	2	5	8	0	0	2	0	5	14	9	15	55	45	10	51
7	Glenavon	38	2	0	1	5	3	1	0	1	3	3	15	9	14	54	50	4	54
8	Ballymena U	38	2	0	1	5	2	1	0	1	3	4	16	5	17	46	52	–6	53
9	Dungannon Swifts	38	2	0	1	6	4	0	1	1	0	1	11	2	25	46	86	–40	35
10	Carrick Rangers	38	1	0	1	1	1	2	0	1	7	4	9	7	22	41	67	–26	34
11	Portadown*	38	0	1	2	0	6	0	0	2	1	3	5	10	23	29	72	–43	25
12	Warrenpoint T	38	0	0	1	1	2	3	0	1	4	3	6	3	29	35	79	–44	21

Top 6 teams split after 33 games. [1]*Linfield qualify for Champions League first qualifying round.*
[2]*Cliftonville qualify for Europa Conference League first qualifying round.*
¶Larne qualify for Europa Conference League first qualifying round after play-offs.
**Portadown not relegated after play-offs.*

UEFA CONFERENCE LEAGUE PLAY-OFF SEMI-FINALS

Glentoran v Glenavon 2-0
Larne v Coleraine 2-0

UEFA CONFERENCE LEAGUE PLAY-OFF FINAL

Glentoran v Larne 2-4
aet; Larne qualify for UEFA Europa Conference League First Qualifying Round.

PREMIERSHIP PROMOTION/RELEGATION PLAY-OFF FIRST LEG

Annagh U v Portadown 2-3

PREMIERSHIP PROMOTION/RELEGATION PLAY-OFF SECOND LEG

Portadown v Annagh U 1-0
Portadown won 4-2 on aggregate.

LEADING GOALSCORERS (League goals only)

Player (Club)	*Goals*
Jay Donnelly (Glentoran)	25
Conor McMenamin (Glentoran)	20
Ryan Curran (Cliftonville)	19
Christy Manzinga (Linfield)	17
Matthew Fitzpatrick (Glenavon)	13
Joe Gormley (Cliftonville)	13
Matthew Shevlin (Coleraine)	13
Peter Campbell (Glenavon)	12
Ben Kennedy (Crusaders)	12
David McDaid (Larne)	12
Paul Heatley (Crusaders)	10
Paul McElroy (Ballymena United)	10
Lee Bonis (Portadown, Larne)	9
Rhyss Campbell (Dungannon Swifts)	9
Jordan Gibson (Carrick Rangers)	8
Adam Lecky (Crusaders)	8
Lee Lynch (Larne)	8
Darragh McBrien (Dungannon Swifts)	8
David Cushley (Carrick Rangers)	7
Ryan Mayse (Dungannon Swifts)	7
Jamie McDonagh (Cliftonville)	6
David Parkhouse (Ballymena United)	6
Alan O'Sullivan (Warrenpoint Town)	6
Adam Salley (Portadown)	6

IRISH LEAGUE CHAMPIONSHIP WINNERS

1891	Linfield	1915	Belfast Celtic	1951	Glentoran	1976	Crusaders	2001	Linfield
1892	Linfield	1920	Belfast Celtic	1952	Glenavon	1977	Glentoran	2002	Portadown
1893	Linfield	1921	Glentoran	1953	Glentoran	1978	Linfield	2003	Glentoran
1894	Glentoran	1922	Linfield	1954	Linfield	1979	Linfield	2004	Linfield
1895	Linfield	1923	Linfield	1955	Linfield	1980	Linfield	2005	Glentoran
1896	Distillery	1924	Queen's Island	1956	Linfield	1981	Glentoran	2006	Linfield
1897	Glentoran	1925	Glentoran	1957	Glentoran	1982	Linfield	2007	Linfield
1898	Linfield	1926	Belfast Celtic	1958	Ards	1983	Linfield	2008	Linfield
1899	Distillery	1927	Belfast Celtic	1959	Linfield	1984	Linfield	2009	Glentoran
1900	Belfast Celtic	1928	Belfast Celtic	1960	Glenavon	1985	Linfield	2010	Linfield
1901	Distillery	1929	Belfast Celtic	1961	Linfield	1986	Linfield	2011	Linfield
1902	Linfield	1930	Linfield	1962	Linfield	1987	Linfield	2012	Linfield
1903	Distillery	1931	Glentoran	1963	Distillery	1988	Glentoran	2013	Cliftonville
1904	Linfield	1932	Linfield	1964	Glentoran	1989	Linfield	2014	Cliftonville
1905	Glentoran	1933	Belfast Celtic	1965	Derry City	1990	Portadown	2015	Crusaders
1906	Cliftonville/	1934	Linfield	1966	Linfield	1991	Portadown	2016	Crusaders
	Distillery (shared)	1935	Linfield	1967	Glentoran	1992	Glentoran	2017	Linfield
1907	Linfield	1936	Belfast Celtic	1968	Glentoran	1993	Linfield	2018	Crusaders
1908	Linfield	1937	Belfast Celtic	1969	Linfield	1994	Linfield	2019	Linfield
1909	Linfield	1938	Belfast Celtic	1970	Glentoran	1995	Crusaders	2020	Linfield
1910	Cliftonville	1939	Belfast Celtic	1971	Linfield	1996	Portadown	2021	Linfield
1911	Linfield	1940	Belfast Celtic	1972	Glentoran	1997	Crusaders	2022	Linfield
1912	Glentoran	1948	Belfast Celtic	1973	Crusaders	1998	Cliftonville		
1913	Glentoran	1949	Linfield	1974	Coleraine	1999	Glentoran		
1914	Linfield	1950	Linfield	1975	Linfield	2000	Linfield		

NIFL LOUGH 41 CHAMPIONSHIP 2021–22

			Home					Away					Total						
		P	W	D	L	F	A	W	D	L	F	A	W	D	L	F	A	GD	Pts
1	Newry C	38	1	0	1	6	3	1	1	1	4	2	22	7	9	70	32	38	73
2	Annagh U	38	0	1	0	1	1	1	1	2	5	18	20	7	11	73	64	9	67
3	Loughgall	38	1	0	1	12	2	2	0	1	4	2	19	6	13	68	41	27	63
4	Ballinamallard U	38	2	0	1	7	4	0	2	0	3	3	17	9	12	69	56	13	60
5	H&W Welders	38	1	1	2	4	7	0	1	0	2	2	18	5	15	62	57	5	59
6	Dergview	38	0	3	0	3	3	1	0	1	2	6	14	13	11	57	53	4	55
7	Ards	38	0	0	1	0	1	2	1	1	7	6	16	7	15	64	55	9	55
8	Dundela	38	2	1	0	7	3	1	0	1	3	3	15	8	15	65	56	9	53
9	Institute	38	3	0	0	7	4	1	0	1	2	4	13	6	19	44	71	–27	45
10	Ballyclare Comrades	38	1	1	1	5	5	0	1	1	3	4	11	9	18	51	72	–21	42
11	Knockbreda*	38	1	0	1	2	3	0	1	2	4	6	8	10	20	61	94	–33	34
12	Queen's University	38	0	1	2	5	7	1	0	1	4	3	8	7	23	37	70	–33	31

**Championship Play-offs: Bangor 2, 0 v Knockbreda 2, 2. Knockbreda not relegated.*

NIFL CHAMPIONSHIP WINNERS

1996 Coleraine
1997 Ballymena United
1998 Newry Town
1999 Distillery
2000 Omagh Town
2001 Ards
2002 Lisburn Distillery
2003 Dungannon Swifts
2004 Loughgall
2005 Armagh City
2006 Crusaders
2007 Institute
2008 Loughgall
2009 Portadown
2010 Loughgall
2011 Carrick Rangers
2012 Ballinamallard U
2013 Ards
2014 Institute
2015 Carrick Rangers
2016 Ards
2017 Warrenpoint T
2018 Institute
2019 Larne
2020 Portadown
2021 No competition
2022 Newry C

NIFL LOUGH 41 PREMIER INTERMEDIATE LEAGUE 2021–22

			Home					Away					Total						
		P	W	D	L	F	A	W	D	L	F	A	W	D	L	F	A	GD	Pts
1	Newington	25	3	0	0	13	2	2	0	0	8	2	18	3	4	67	28	39	57
2	Bangor	25	1	0	1	3	6	1	1	1	6	6	16	2	7	48	27	21	50
3	Armagh C	25	1	0	1	2	3	0	1	2	2	9	14	4	7	48	34	14	46
4	Limavady U	25	1	1	1	7	6	0	0	2	2	4	13	4	8	47	27	20	43
5	Banbridge T	25	1	1	1	3	2	1	0	1	2	6	12	5	8	28	25	3	41
6	Dollingstown	25	0	1	1	4	5	1	1	1	4	5	12	4	9	46	34	12	40
7	Portstewart	24	2	0	0	10	0	0	1	1	3	4	10	2	12	42	28	14	32
8	Lisburn Distillery	24	2	0	0	8	2	1	0	1	6	5	10	2	12	38	39	–1	32
9	Moyola Park	24	1	1	0	5	4	0	1	1	2	3	4	8	12	31	54	–23	20
10	PSNI	24	0	1	1	3	7	1	0	1	5	8	5	1	18	27	72	–45	16
11	Tobermore U	24	0	1	1	2	6	0	1	1	3	8	0	7	17	16	70	–54	7

IFA DEVELOPMENT LEAGUES 2021–22

PREMIERSHIP DEVELOPMENT LEAGUE (U20)

	P	W	D	L	F	A	GD	Pts
Crusaders	33	20	9	4	68	33	35	69
Cliftonville Olympic	33	16	6	11	80	68	12	54
Ballymena U	33	16	5	12	66	59	7	53
Dungannon Swifts	33	15	6	12	74	59	15	51
Linfield Swifts	33	16	3	14	68	70	–2	51
Carrick Rangers	33	13	6	14	56	64	–8	45
Portadown	33	12	8	13	58	67	–9	44
Glenavon	33	12	6	15	80	72	8	42
Glentoran	33	12	4	17	70	76	–6	40
Coleraine	33	12	4	17	61	67	–6	40
Larne Olympic	33	10	8	15	46	59	–13	38
Warrenpoint T	33	8	7	18	46	79	–33	31

CHAMPIONSHIP DEVELOPMENT LEAGUE (U20)

	P	W	D	L	F	A	GD	Pts
Queen's University	30	26	2	2	104	24	80	80
Dundela	30	21	3	6	75	34	41	66
Loughgall	30	18	7	5	80	39	41	61
H&W Welders	30	20	1	9	85	53	32	61
Newry C	30	18	2	10	71	48	23	56
Ballinamallard U	30	17	4	9	83	43	40	55
Bangor	30	13	5	12	59	43	16	44
Limavady U	30	13	3	14	62	54	8	42
Ards	30	12	5	13	70	76	–6	41
Institute	30	13	1	16	59	54	5	40
Knockbreda	30	12	1	17	56	70	–14	37
Ballyclare Comrades	30	10	6	14	54	56	–2	36
Newington	30	6	3	21	43	74	–31	21
Lisburn Distillery	30	5	6	19	41	86	–45	21
Moyola Park Olympic	30	4	4	22	22	119	–97	16
PSNI Olympic	30	4	3	23	28	119	–91	15

ACADEMY LEAGUE (U18)

Section A	P	W	D	L	F	A	GD	Pts
Coleraine	28	21	4	3	89	31	58	67
Cliftonville Strollers	28	18	4	6	85	48	37	58
Crusaders	27	15	5	7	61	25	36	50
Ballinamallard U	28	13	5	10	60	51	9	44
Portadown	28	14	1	13	58	60	–2	43
Larne Youth	28	13	0	15	47	48	–1	39
Ballymena U	28	12	1	15	56	68	–12	37
Warrenpoint T	27	9	3	15	55	57	–2	30
Section B	P	W	D	L	F	A	GD	Pts
Dungannon Swifts	28	15	7	6	69	35	34	52
Linfield Rangers	28	16	3	9	60	42	18	51
Glentoran Colts	28	13	5	10	68	39	29	44
Carrick Rangers	28	12	5	11	54	57	–3	41
Ards	28	10	0	18	42	69	–27	30
Glenavon	28	7	8	13	55	58	–3	29
Institute	28	7	2	19	32	82	–50	23
Newry C	28	1	1	26	5	126	–121	4

ACADEMY LEAGUE (U16)

Section A	P	W	D	L	F	A	GD	Pts
Dungannon Swifts	28	21	4	3	87	32	55	67
Linfield	28	19	2	7	68	28	40	59
Cliftonville	28	16	4	8	60	39	21	52
Ballymena U	28	15	4	9	57	32	25	49
Coleraine	28	15	3	10	50	46	4	48
Glenavon	28	13	5	10	66	48	18	44
Glentoran	28	11	5	12	56	48	8	38
Warrenpoint T	28	10	1	17	40	62	–22	31
Section B	P	W	D	L	F	A	GD	Pts
Crusaders	26	13	3	10	53	38	15	42
Ballinamallard U	26	13	1	12	45	49	–4	40
Larne	26	10	6	10	31	39	–8	36
Portadown	26	11	2	13	49	52	–3	35
Institute	26	8	6	12	39	47	–8	30
Carrick Rangers	26	6	3	17	27	63	–36	21
Newry C	26	3	3	20	22	85	–63	12

Ards withdrew, record expunged.

IRISH CUP FINALS 1880–81 to 2021–22

**After extra time.*

1880–81	Moyola Park v Cliftonville	1-0
1881–82	Queen's Island (1881) v Cliftonville	1-0
1882–83	Cliftonville v Ulster	5-0
1883–84	Distillery v Wellington Park	5-0
1884–85	Distillery v Limavady	3-0
1885–86	Distillery v Limavady	1-0
1886–87	Ulster v Cliftonville	3-0
1887–88	Cliftonville v Distillery	2-1
1888–89	Distillery v YMCA	5-4
1889–90	Gordon Highlanders v Cliftonville	2-2
Replay	Gordon Highlanders v Cliftonville	3-1
1890–91	Linfield v Ulster	4-2
1891–92	Linfield v The Black Watch	7-0
1892–93	Linfield v Cliftonville	5-1
1893–94	Distillery v Linfield	2-2
Replay	Distillery v Linfield	3-2
1894–95	Linfield v Bohemians	10-1
1895–96	Distillery v Glentoran	3-1
1896–97	Cliftonville v Sherwood Foresters	3-1
1897–98	Linfield v St Columb's Hall Celtic	2-0
1898–99	Linfield v Glentoran	2-1
1899–00	Cliftonville v Bohemians	2-1
1900–01	Cliftonville v Freebooters	1-0
1901–02	Linfield v Distillery	5-1
1902–03	Distillery v Bohemians	3-1
1903–04	Linfield v Derry Celtic	5-1
1904–05	Distillery v Shelbourne	3-0
1905–06	Shelbourne v Belfast Celtic	2-0
1906–07	Cliftonville v Shelbourne	0-0
Replay	Cliftonville v Shelbourne	1-0
1907–08	Bohemians v Shelbourne	1-1
Replay	Bohemians v Shelbourne	3-1
1908–09	Cliftonville v Bohemians	0-0
Replay	Cliftonville v Bohemians	2-1
1909–10	Distillery v Cliftonville	1-0
1910–11	Shelbourne v Bohemians	0-0
Replay	Shelbourne v Bohemians	2-1
1911–12	*Linfield were awarded the trophy after Cliftonville, Glentoran and Shelbourne resigned from the IFA at the semi-final stage.*	
1912–13	Linfield v Glentoran	2-0
1913–14	Glentoran v Linfield	3-1
1914–15	Linfield v Belfast Celtic	1-0
1915–16	Linfield v Glentoran	1-1
Replay	Linfield v Glentoran	1-0
1916–17	Glentoran v Belfast Celtic	2-0
1917–18	Belfast Celtic v Linfield	0-0
Replay	Belfast Celtic v Linfield	0-0
2nd replay	Belfast Celtic v Linfield	2-0
1918–19	Linfield v Glentoran	1-1
Replay	Linfield v Glentoran	0-0
2nd replay	Linfield v Glentoran	2-1
1919–20	*Shelbourne were awarded the trophy after Belfast Celtic and Glentoran were removed from the competition at the semi-final stage.*	
1920–21	Glentoran v Glenavon	2-0
1921–22	Linfield v Glenavon	2-0
1922–23	Linfield v Glentoran	2-0
1923–24	Queen's Island (1920) v Willowfield	1-0
1924–25	Distillery v Glentoran	2-1
1925–26	Belfast Celtic v Linfield	3-2
1926–27	Ards v Cliftonville	3-2
1927–28	Willowfield v Larne	1-0
1928–29	Ballymena v Belfast Celtic	2-1
1929–30	Linfield v Ballymena	4-3
1930–31	Linfield v Ballymena	3-0
1931–32	Glentoran v Linfield	2-1
1932–33	Glentoran v Distillery	1-1
Replay	Glentoran v Distillery	1-1
2nd replay	Glentoran v Distillery	3-1
1933–34	Linfield v Cliftonville	5-0
1934–35	Glentoran v Larne	0-0
Replay	Glentoran v Larne	0-0
2nd replay	Glentoran v Larne	1-0
1935–36	Linfield v Derry C	0-0
Replay	Linfield v Derry C	2-0
1936–37	Belfast Celtic v Linfield	3-0
1937–38	Belfast Celtic v Bangor	0-0
Replay	Belfast Celtic v Bangor	2-0
1938–39	Linfield v Ballymena U	2-0
1939–40	Ballymena U v Glenavon	2-0
1940–41	Belfast Celtic v Linfield	1-0
1941–42	Linfield v Glentoran	3-1
1942–43	Belfast Celtic v Glentoran	1-0
1943–44	Belfast Celtic v Linfield	3-1
1944–45	Linfield v Glentoran	4-2
1945–46	Linfield v Distillery	3-0
1946–47	Belfast Celtic v Glentoran	1-0
1947–48	Linfield v Coleraine	3-0
1948–49	Derry C v Glentoran	3-1
1949–50	Linfield v Distillery	2-1
1950–51	Glentoran v Ballymena U	3-1
1951–52	Ards v Glentoran	1-0
1952–53	Linfield v Coleraine	5-0
1953–54	Derry C v Glentoran	2-2
Replay	Derry C v Glentoran	0-0
2nd replay	Derry C v Glentoran	1-0
1954–55	Dundela v Glenavon	3-0
1955–56	Distillery v Glentoran	2-2
Replay	Distillery v Glentoran	0-0
2nd replay	Distillery v Glentoran	1-0
1956–57	Glenavon v Derry C	2-0
1957–58	Ballymena U v Linfield	2-0
1958–59	Glenavon v Ballymena U	1-1
Replay	Glenavon v Ballymena U	2-0
1959–60	Linfield v Ards	5-1
1960–61	Glenavon v Linfield	5-1
1961–62	Linfield v Portadown	4-0
1962–63	Linfield v Distillery	2-1
1963–64	Derry C v Glentoran	2-0
1964–65	Coleraine v Glenavon	2-1
1965–66	Glentoran v Linfield	2-0
1966–67	Crusaders v Glentoran	3-1
1967–68	Crusaders v Linfield	2-0
1968–69	Ards v Distillery	0-0
Replay	Ards v Distillery	4-2
1969–70	Linfield v Ballymena U	2-1
1970–71	Distillery v Derry C	3-0
1971–72	Coleraine v Portadown	2-1
1972–73	Glentoran v Linfield	3-2
1973–74	Ards v Ballymena U	2-1
1974–75	Coleraine v Linfield	1-1
Replay	Coleraine v Linfield	0-0
2nd replay	Coleraine v Linfield	1-0
1975–76	Carrick Rangers v Linfield	2-1
1976–77	Coleraine v Linfield	4-1
1977–78	Linfield v Ballymena U	3-1
1978–79	Cliftonville v Portadown	3-2
1979–80	Linfield v Crusaders	2-0
1980–81	Ballymena U v Glenavon	1-0
1981–82	Linfield v Coleraine	2-1
1982–83	Glentoran v Linfield	1-1
Replay	Glentoran v Linfield	2-1
1983–84	Ballymena U v Carrick Rangers	4-1
1984–85	Glentoran v Linfield	1-1
Replay	Glentoran v Linfield	1-0
1985–86	Glentoran v Coleraine	2-1
1986–87	Glentoran v Larne	1-0
1987–88	Glentoran v Glenavon	1-0
1988–89	Ballymena U v Larne	1-0
1989–90	Glentoran v Portadown	3-0
1990–91	Portadown v Glenavon	2-1
1991–92	Glenavon v Linfield	2-1
1992–93	Bangor v Ards	1-1*
Replay	Bangor v Ards	1-1*
2nd replay	Bangor v Ards	1-0
1993–94	Linfield v Bangor	2-0
1994–95	Linfield v Carrick Rangers	3-1
1995–96	Glentoran v Glenavon	1-0
1996–97	Glenavon v Cliftonville	1-0
1997–98	Glentoran v Glenavon	1-0*
1998–99	*Portadown awarded the trophy after Cliftonville were removed from the competition for fielding an ineligible player in the semi-final.*	
1999–2000	Glentoran v Portadown	1-0
2000–01	Glentoran v Linfield	1-0*
2001–02	Linfield v Portadown	2-1
2002–03	Coleraine v Glentoran	1-0
2003–04	Glentoran v Coleraine	1-0
2004–05	Portadown v Larne	5-1
2005–06	Linfield v Glentoran	2-1
2006–07	Linfield v Dungannon Swifts	2-2*
Linfield won 3-2 on penalties		
2007–08	Linfield v Coleraine	2-1
2008–09	Crusaders v Cliftonville	1-0
2009–10	Linfield v Portadown	2-1
2010–11	Linfield v Crusaders	2-1
2011–12	Linfield v Crusaders	4-1
2012–13	Glentoran v Cliftonville	3-1*
2013–14	Glenavon v Ballymena U	2-1
2014–15	Glentoran v Portadown	1-0
2015–16	Glenavon v Linfield	2-0
2016–17	Linfield v Coleraine	3-0
2017–18	Coleraine v Cliftonville	3-1
2018–19	Crusaders v Ballinamallard U	3-0
2019–20	Glentoran v Ballymena U	2-1*
2020–21	Linfield v Larne	2-1
2021–22	Crusaders v Ballymena U	2-1*

SAMUEL GELSTON'S WHISKEY IRISH FA CUP 2021–22

**After extra time.*

SECOND QUALIFYING ROUND

Glebe Rangers v Colin Valley 0-3
18th Newtownabbey Old Boys v Shankill U 3-4
Aquinas v Crewe U 1-5
Match abandoned after 74 minutes due to serious injury.
Ards Rangers v Crumlin U 3-1
Armagh C v Dollingstown 3-0
Ballynahinch Olympic v Immaculata 1-1*
Ballynahinch Olympic won 5-3 on penalties
Banbridge Rangers v Desertmartin 5-0
Banbridge T v Tobermore U 2-3*
Bangor v Killyleagh Youth 2-1
Bangor Amateurs v Windmill Stars 2-4
Coagh U v Ballymacash Rangers 1-8
Comber Recreation v Kilmore Recreation 1-2
Craigavon C v Dromara Village 3-4
Derriaghy Cricket Club v Bloomfield 2-0
Match abandoned after 50 minutes due to serious injury.
Downshire Young Men v Newington 0-3
Drumaness Mills v Fivemiletown U 2-2*
Drumaness Mills won 4-2 on penalties
Dunloy v Markethill Swifts 2-1
Dunmurry Young Men v St Mary's 1-3
Greenisland v Ardstraw 1-0
Hanover v Tandragee Rovers 0-1
Islandmagee v Ballynure Old Boys 5-3
Limavady U v PSNI 3-0*
Lisburn Distillery v Ballymoney U 2-1
Lower Maze v Laurelvale 6-2
Maiden C v Portstewart 0-3
Oxford Sunnyside v Chimney Corner 3-3*
Oxford Sunnyside won 8-7 on penalties
Rathfriland Rangers v Abbey Villa 3-0
Rosario Youth v Lisburn Rangers 3-2
Sirocco Works (walkover) v Newtowne
St Oliver Plunkett v St James' Swifts 1-1*
St James' Swifts won 4-3 on penalties
Strabane Athletic v Holywood 3-3*
Holywood won 3-0 on penalties
Mossley received a bye.

THIRD QUALIFYING ROUND

Ards Rangers v Banbridge Rangers 3-2*
Armagh C v Windmill Stars 0-1
Ballymacash Rangers v Portstewart 0-3
Ballynahinch Olympic v Newington 0-2
Bangor v St James' Swifts 2-0
Colin Valley v Crewe U 4-1
Dromara Village v Rathfriland Rangers 2-3
Dunloy v Derriaghy Cricket Club 2-2*
Derriaghy Cricket Club won 4-3 on penalties
Greenisland v Lisburn Distillery 2-1
Holywood v Limavady U 3-5
Islandmagee v Drumaness Mills 1-1*
Islandmagee won 3-0 on penalties
Kilmore Recreation v Lower Maze 3-2
Mossley v Shankill U 4-4*
Mossley won 3-0 on penalties
Oxford Sunnyside v Rosario Youth 3-0
Sirocco Works v Tobermore U 2-4
Tandragee Rovers v St Mary's 2-1

FOURTH QUALIFYING ROUND

Ards Rangers v Greenisland 2-2*
Ards Rangers won 6-5 on penalties
Colin Valley v Bangor 0-2
Kilmore Recreation v Islandmagee 1-1*
Islandmagee won 5-4 on penalties
Limavady U v Rathfriland Rangers 4-1
Mossley v Portstewart 1-3
Newington v Derriaghy Cricket Club 3-1
Oxford Sunnyside v Tandragee Rovers 2-1
Windmill Stars v Tobermore U 2-1

FIRST ROUND

Glenavon v Crusaders 0-4
Ballinamallard U v Ards Rangers 2-0*
Ballyclare Comrades v Carrick Rangers 0-2
Ballymena U v Loughgall 2-0
Bangor v Larne 0-5
Cliftonville v Islandmagee 5-0
Coleraine v Windmill Stars 6-0
Dergview v Glentoran 2-3
Dundela v Ards 3-2
Dundella expelled from the competition for fielding an uneligible player. Ards reinstated for the second round.
Harland & Wolff Welders v Annagh U 1-2
Institute v Portstewart 0-1
Knockbreda v Dungannon Swifts 0-2
Linfield v Oxford Sunnyside 4-0
Portadown v Limavady U 2-0
Queen's University v Newington 2-0
Warrenpoint T v Newry C 1-2

SECOND ROUND

Larne v Linfield 2-0
Newry C v Ards 1-0
Ballinamallard U v Crusaders 0-1
Carrick Rangers v Cliftonville 0-1
Coleraine v Portadown 2-0
Dungannon Swifts v Annagh U 4-1
Queen's University v Glentoran 0-4
Ballymena U v Portstewart 3-0

QUARTER-FINALS

Cliftonville v Coleraine 2-1
Ballymena U v Larne 3-3*
Ballymena U won 4-3 on penalties
Crusaders v Dungannon Swifts 4-2
Glentoran v Newry C 1-0
Glentoran expelled from the competition for fielding an ineligible player. Newry C reinstated for the semi-finals.

SEMI-FINALS

Cliftonville v Crusaders 1-2
Newry C v Ballymena U 0-1

SAMUEL GELSTON'S WHISKEY IRISH FA CUP FINAL 2021–22

Windsor Park Belfast, Saturday 7 May 2022

Crusaders (0) 2 Ballymena U (1) 1

Crusaders: Tuffey; Burns (Doyle 88), Weir (Robinson 46), Lowry (Owens 81), Forsythe, Heatley, Clarke (McMurray 67), O'Rourke, Lecky (Caddell 67), Kennedy, Larmour (Wilson 109).
Scorers: Robinson 90, McMurray 120.

Ballymena U: Williamson; Redman, McCullough, Keeley (Loughran 78), Graham, McGrory, Millar, Kelly (Henderson 82), Barr (McElroy 71), Parkhouse (Kane 78), Waide (Place 91).
Scorer: Weir 9 (og).

Referee: Tony Clarke.

aet.

BETMcLEAN NORTHERN IRISH LEAGUE CUP 2021–22

**After extra time.*

FIRST ROUND

Ballyclare Comrades v Queen's University	2-1
Newry C v Tobermore U	2-1
Annagh U v Knockbreda	4-1

SECOND ROUND

Annagh U v Ballymena U	2-4
Ballyclare Comrades v Linfield	0-4
Bangor v Coleraine	0-5
Carrick Rangers v Dergview	2-1*
Cliftonville v H&W Welders	2-0
Crusaders v Moyola Park	5-0
Dundela v Ballinamallard U	0-4*
Dungannon Swifts v Armagh C	3-0
Glenavon v Portstewart	5-1
Glentoran v Banbridge T	5-0
Institute v PSNI	4-3
Institute expelled for fielding an ineligible player. PSNI advance to the third round.	
Larne v Limavady U	4-0
Larne expelled for fielding an ineligible player. Limavady U advance to the third round.	
Loughgall v Lisburn Distillery	6-2
Newry C v Warrenpoint T	1-2*
Portadown v Newington	2-0
Ards v Dollingstown	4-0

THIRD ROUND

Carrick Rangers v Coleraine	0-2
Crusaders v Ballymena U	2-3*
Glenavon v Glentoran	2-2*
Glentoran won 5-4 on penalties	
Warrenpoint T v Loughgall	1-0
Ards v Cliftonville	1-4
Portadown v Ballinamallard U	1-0
Limavady U v Dungannon Swifts	3-2
Linfield v PSNI	11-0

QUARTER-FINALS

Ballymena U v Linfield	3-1
Coleraine v Glentoran	2-0
Portadown v Cliftonville	1-2
Warrenpoint T v Limavady U	6-1

SEMI-FINALS

Coleraine v Warrenpoint T	6-1
Cliftonville v Ballymena U	3-0

BETMcLEAN NORTHERN IRISH LEAGUE CUP FINAL 2021–22

Windsor Park, Belfast, Sunday 13 March 2022, attendance 11,103

Cliftonville (0) 4 Coleraine (0) 3

Cliftonville: McNicholas; Ives, Hale (Curran C 53), Curran R, McDonagh (Coates 118), Lowe, Addis, Doherty (O'Neill 70), Turner, Gallagher, Kearns (Gormley 61).
Scorers: Gormley 74, 107, O'Neill 90, 104.

Coleraine: Deane; Kane, Brown, McKendry (Wilson 73), Lowry, Carson, O'Donnell, Glackin (McLaughlin 78), Traynor (Allen 106), Kelly, Shevlin (Bradley 88).
Scorers: Shelvin 58, Lowry 63, Allen 119.

aet; 2-2 after normal time. Referee: Andrew Davy.

NIFWA AWARDS 2021–22

NIFWA PREMIERSHIP PLAYER OF THE MONTH 2021–22

Month	*Player*	*Team*
September	Chris Shields	Linfield
October	Jay Donnelly	Glentoran
November	Gareth Dean	Coleraine
December	Chris Shields	Linfield
January	Jamie McDonagh	Cliftonville
February	Colin McMenamin	Glentoran
March	Joe Gormley	Cliftonville
April	Ryan Curran	Cliftonville

NIFWA MANAGER OF THE MONTH 2021–22

Month	*Player*	*Team*
September	Paddy McLaughlin	Cliftonville
October	David Healy	Linfield
November	Mick McDermott	Glentoran
December	Mick McDermott	Glentoran
January	Dean Shiels	Dungannon Swifts
February	Paddy McLaughlin	Cliftonville
March	Paddy McLaughlin	Cliftonville
April	David Healy	Linfield

NIFWA CHAMPIONSHIP PLAYER OF THE MONTH 2021–22

Month	*Player*	*Team*
August	Thomas Lockhart	Newry C
September	Brendan McLauglin	Institute
October	Richard Purcell	Ballyclare
November	Craig Taylor	Annagh U
December	Nedas Maciulaitis	Loughall
January	Noel Healy	Newry C
February	Adam Carroll	Annagh U
March	Philip Donnelly	Newry C
April	Jamie Dunne	Institute

AKTIVORA MANAGER OF THE YEAR
David Healy (Linfield)

DANSKE BANK PLAYER OF THE YEAR
Chris Shields (Linfield)

DANSKE BANK WOMEN'S PLAYER OF THE YEAR
Kerry Beattie (Glentoran)

CHAMPIONSHIP PLAYER OF THE YEAR
Noel Healy (Newry C)

PREMIER INTERMEDIATE PLAYER OF THE YEAR
Richard Gowdy (Newington)

YOUNG PLAYER OF THE YEAR
Luke Turner (Cliftonville on loan from Aberdeen)

NORTHERN IRELAND ROLL OF HONOUR SEASON 2021–22

NIFL Danske Bank Premiership: Linfield
Samuel Gelston's Whiskey Irish FA Cup: Crusaders
NIFL Lough 41 Championship: Newry C
NIFL Lough 41 Premier Intermediate: Newington
BetMcLean Northern Ireland League Cup: Cliftonville
McComb's Coach Travel Intermediate Cup: Rathfriland Rangers
NIFL Danske Bank Women's Premiership 2021: Glentoran
Steel & Sons Cup: Linfield Swifts
Co Antrim Senior Shield: Larne
Co Antrim Junior Shield: Harryville Homers
fonaCAB Irish Junior Cup: Coalisland Ath
Mid Ulster Cup (Senior): Warrenpoint T
Harry Cavan Youth Cup: Dungannon Swifts
North West Senior Cup: Dergview

EUROPEAN CUP FINALS

EUROPEAN CUP FINALS 1956–1992

Year	Winners v Runners-up		Venue	Attendance	Referee
1956	Real Madrid v Reims	4-3	Paris	38,239	A. Ellis (England)
1957	Real Madrid v Fiorentina	2-0	Madrid	124,000	L. Horn (Netherlands)
1958	Real Madrid v AC Milan	3-2*	Brussels	67,000	A. Alsteen (Belgium)
1959	Real Madrid v Reims	2-0	Stuttgart	72,000	A. Dutsch (West Germany)
1960	Real Madrid v Eintracht Frankfurt	7-3	Glasgow	127,621	J. Mowat (Scotland)
1961	Benfica v Barcelona	3-2	Berne	26,732	G. Dienst (Switzerland)
1962	Benfica v Real Madrid	5-3	Amsterdam	61,257	L. Horn (Netherlands)
1963	AC Milan v Benfica	2-1	Wembley	45,715	A. Holland (England)
1964	Internazionale v Real Madrid	3-1	Vienna	71,333	J. Stoll (Austria)
1965	Internazionale v Benfica	1-0	Milan	89,000	G. Dienst (Switzerland)
1966	Real Madrid v Partizan Belgrade	2-1	Brussels	46,745	R. Kreitlein (West Germany)
1967	Celtic v Internazionale	2-1	Lisbon	45,000	K. Tschenscher (West Germany)
1968	Manchester U v Benfica	4-1*	Wembley	92,225	C. Lo Bello (Italy)
1969	AC Milan v Ajax	4-1	Madrid	31,782	J. Ortiz de Mendibil (Spain)
1970	Feyenoord v Celtic	2-1*	Milan	53,187	C. Lo Bello (Italy)
1971	Ajax v Panathinaikos	2-0	Wembley	90,000	J. Taylor (England)
1972	Ajax v Internazionale	2-0	Rotterdam	61,354	R. Helies (France)
1973	Ajax v Juventus	1-0	Belgrade	89,484	M. Guglovic (Yugoslavia)
1974	Bayern Munich v Atletico Madrid	1-1	Brussels	48,722	V. Loraux (Belgium)
Replay	Bayern Munich v Atletico Madrid	4-0	Brussels	23,325	A. Delcourt (Belgium)
1975	Bayern Munich v Leeds U	2-0	Paris	48,374	M. Kitabdjian (France)
1976	Bayern Munich v Saint-Etienne	1-0	Glasgow	54,864	K. Palotai (Hungary)
1977	Liverpool v Borussia Moenchengladbach	3-1	Rome	52,078	R. Wurtz (France)
1978	Liverpool v Club Brugge	1-0	Wembley	92,500	C. Corver (Netherlands)
1979	Nottingham F v Malmo	1-0	Munich	57,500	E. Linemayr (Austria)
1980	Nottingham F v Hamburg	1-0	Madrid	51,000	A. Garrido (Portugal)
1981	Liverpool v Real Madrid	1-0	Paris	48,360	K. Palotai (Hungary)
1982	Aston Villa v Bayern Munich	1-0	Rotterdam	46,000	G. Konrath (France)
1983	Hamburg v Juventus	1-0	Athens	73,500	N. Rainea (Romania)
1984	Liverpool v Roma	1-1*	Rome	69,693	E. Fredriksson (Sweden)
	(Liverpool won 4-2 on penalties)				
1985	Juventus v Liverpool	1-0	Brussels	58,000	A. Daina (Switzerland)
1986	Steaua Bucharest v Barcelona	0-0*	Seville	70,000	M. Vautrot (France)
	(Steaua won 2-0 on penalties)				
1987	FC Porto v Bayern Munich	2-1	Vienna	57,500	A. Ponnet (Belgium)
1988	PSV Eindhoven v Benfica	0-0*	Stuttgart	68,000	L. Agnolin (Italy)
	(PSV Eindhoven won 6-5 on penalties)				
1989	AC Milan v Steaua Bucharest	4-0	Barcelona	97,000	K.-H. Tritschler (West Germany)
1990	AC Milan v Benfica	1-0	Vienna	57,500	H. Kohl (Austria)
1991	Red Star Belgrade v Marseille	0-0*	Bari	56,000	T. Lanese (Italy)
	(Red Star Belgrade won 5-3 on penalties)				
1992	Barcelona v Sampdoria	1-0*	Wembley	70,827	A. Schmidhuber (Germany)

UEFA CHAMPIONS LEAGUE FINALS 1993–2022

Year	Winners v Runners-up		Venue	Attendance	Referee
1993	Marseille† v AC Milan	1-0	Munich	64,400	K. Rothlisberger (Switzerland)
1994	AC Milan v Barcelona	4-0	Athens	70,000	P. Don (England)
1995	Ajax v AC Milan	1-0	Vienna	49,730	I. Craciunescu (Romania)
1996	Juventus v Ajax	1-1*	Rome	70,000	M. D. Vega (Spain)
	(Juventus won 4-2 on penalties)				
1997	Borussia Dortmund v Juventus	3-1	Munich	59,000	S. Puhl (Hungary)
1998	Real Madrid v Juventus	1-0	Amsterdam	48,500	H. Krug (Germany)
1999	Manchester U v Bayern Munich	2-1	Barcelona	90,245	P. Collina (Italy)
2000	Real Madrid v Valencia	3-0	Paris	80,000	S. Braschi (Italy)
2001	Bayern Munich v Valencia	1-1*	Milan	79,000	D. Jol (Netherlands)
	(Bayern Munich won 5-4 on penalties)				
2002	Real Madrid v Bayer Leverkusen	2-1	Glasgow	50,499	U. Meier (Switzerland)
2003	AC Milan v Juventus	0-0*	Manchester	62,315	M. Merk (Germany)
	(AC Milan won 3-2 on penalties)				
2004	FC Porto v Monaco	3-0	Gelsenkirchen	53,053	K. M. Nielsen (Denmark)
2005	Liverpool v AC Milan	3-3*	Istanbul	65,000	M. M. González (Spain)
	(Liverpool won 3-2 on penalties)				
2006	Barcelona v Arsenal	2-1	Paris	79,610	T. Hauge (Norway)
2007	AC Milan v Liverpool	2-1	Athens	74,000	H. Fandel (Germany)
2008	Manchester U v Chelsea	1-1*	Moscow	67,310	L. Michel (Slovakia)
	(Manchester U won 6-5 on penalties)				
2009	Barcelona v Manchester U	2-0	Rome	62,467	M. Busacca (Switzerland)
2010	Internazionale v Bayern Munich	2-0	Madrid	73,490	H. Webb (England)
2011	Barcelona v Manchester U	3-1	Wembley	87,695	V. Kassai (Hungary)
2012	Chelsea v Bayern Munich	1-1*	Munich	62,500	P. Proença (Portugal)
	(Chelsea won 4-3 on penalties)				
2013	Bayern Munich v Borussia Dortmund	2-1	Wembley	86,298	N. Rizzoli (Italy)
2014	Real Madrid v Atletico Madrid	4-1*	Lisbon	60,000	B. Kuipers (Netherlands)
2015	Barcelona v Juventus	3-1	Berlin	70,442	C. Cakir (Turkey)
2016	Real Madrid v Atletico Madrid	1-1*	Milan	71,942	M. Clattenburg (England)
	(Real Madrid won 5-3 on penalties)				
2017	Real Madrid v Juventus	4-1	Cardiff	65,842	F. Brych (Germany)
2018	Real Madrid v Liverpool	3-1	Kiev	61,561	M. Mazic (Serbia)
2019	Liverpool v Tottenham H	2-0	Madrid	63,272	D. Skomina (Slovenia)
2020	Bayern Munich v Paris Saint-Germain	1-0	Lisbon	0	D. Orsato (Italy)
2021	Chelsea v Manchester C	1-0	Porto	14,110	A. Lahoz (Spain)
2022	Real Madrid v Liverpool	1-0	Paris	73,000	C. Turpin (France)

*†Subsequently stripped of title. *After extra time.*

UEFA CHAMPIONS LEAGUE 2021–22

**After extra time. ■ Denotes player sent off.*

QUALIFYING STAGE

PRELIMINARY ROUND – SEMI-FINALS

Tuesday, 22 June 2021

Folgore Falciano v Prishtina	0-2
HB Torshavn v Inter Club d'Escaldes	0-1

PRELIMINARY ROUND – FINAL

Friday, 25 June 2021

Prishtina v Inter Club d'Escaldes	2-0

FIRST QUALIFYING ROUND FIRST LEG

Tuesday, 6 July 2021

CFR Cluj v Borac Banja Luka	3-1
Ferencvaros v Prishtina	3-0
Flora v Hibernians	2-0
Fola Esch v Lincoln Red Imps	2-2
HJK v Buducnost Podgorica	3-1
Shkendija v Mura	0-1
Zalgiris Vilnius v Linfield	3-1

Wednesday, 7 July 2021

Bodo/Glimt v Legia Warsaw	2-3
Connah's Quay Nomads v Alashkert	2-2
Dinamo Tbilisi v Neftchi	1-2
Dinamo Zagreb v Valur	3-2
Ludogorets Razgrad v Shakhtyor Soligorsk	1-0
Maccabi Haifa v Kairat	1-1
Malmo v Riga FC	1-0
Slovan Bratislava v Shamrock R	2-0
Teuta v Sheriff Tiraspol	0-4

Tuesday, 6 July 2021

Zalgiris Vilnius (2) 3 *(Videmont 38, Kis 45 (pen), Johns 66 (og))*

Linfield (0) 1 *(Manzinga 54)* 1500

Zalgiris Vilnius: (433) Gertmonas; Mikoliunas, Diaw, Ljubisavljevic, Bopesu; Verbickas (Onazi 59), Kis, Gamakov (Uzela 83); Kyeremeh (Karamarko 84), Sylvestr (Tadic 83), Videmont.
Linfield: (433) Johns; Clarke M, Newbury, Callacher, Pepper; Fallon, Mulgrew, Shields; Palmer, Manzinga (Nasseri 78), Quinn (Stewart 77).

Wednesday, 7 July 2021

Connah's Quay Nomads (1) 2 *(Curran 19, Horan 79)*

Alashkert (2) 2 *(Khurtsidze 21, 44)* 145

Connah's Quay Nomads: Byrne, Disney, Horan, Holmes (Moore 58), Morris, Owen J (Edwards 46), Harrison (Owens 46), Poole, Mullan, Wilde, Curran.
Alashkert: Cancarevic, Tiago Cameta, Voskanyan, Kadio, Boljevic, James, Khurtsidze, Hovsepyan (Yedigaryan 67), Grigoryan, Davidyan (Mihajlovic 90), Jose Embalo (Glisic 68).

Slovan Bratislava (1) 2 *(Rafael Ratao 28, 47)*

Shamrock R (0) 0 500

Slovan Bratislava: Chovan, Medvedev, Kashia, Bozhikov, De Marco, de Kamps, Cavric (Hrncar 74), Kankava (Zmrhal 74), Ibrahim (Lichy 90), Rafael Ratao (Strelec 90), Henty (Weiss 63).
Shamrock R: Mannus, Hoare, Lopes, Grace, Gannon (Mandroiu 68), Towell (Burke 68), Finn, O'Neill, Scales, Gaffney, Greene (Watts 68).

FIRST QUALIFYING ROUND SECOND LEG

Tuesday, 13 July 2021

		(agg)
Borac Banja Luka v CFR Cluj	2-1*	3-4
Buducnost Podgorica v HJK	0-4	1-7
Hibernians v Flora	0-3	0-5
Lincoln Red Imps v Fola Esch	5-0	7-2
Linfield v Zalgiris Vilnius	1-2	2-5
Mura v Shkendija	5-0	6-0
Prishtina v Ferencvaros	1-3	1-6
Riga FC v Malmo	1-1	1-2
Shakhtyor Soligorsk v Ludogorets Razgrad	0-1	0-2
Shamrock R v Slovan Bratislava	2-1	2-3
Sheriff Tiraspol v Teuta	1-0	5-0
Valur v Dinamo Zagreb	0-2	2-5

Wednesday, 14 July 2021

Alashkert v Connah's Quay Nomads	1-0*	3-2
Kairat v Maccabi Haifa	2-0	3-1
Legia Warsaw v Bodo/Glimt	2-0	5-2
Neftchi v Dinamo Tbilisi	2-1	4-2

Tuesday, 13 July 2021

Linfield (0) 1 *(Shields 66 (pen))*

Zalgiris Vilnius (2) 2 *(Mikoliunas 17, Onazi 44)* 888

Linfield: Johns, Hume, Newbury, Callacher, Clarke M (Stewart 46), Shields, Mulgrew (Palmer 72), Millar, Fallon, Quinn (Nasseri 72), Manzinga (Clarke A 86).
Zalgiris Vilnius: Gertmonas, Mikoliunas, Ljubisavljevic, Diaw■, Bopesu, Onazi (Verbickas 78), Gamakov (Uzela■ 86), Tatomirovic, Kyeremeh (Karamarko 86), Sylvestr (Tadic 70), Videmont.
Zalgiris Vilnius won 5-2 on aggregate.

Shamrock R (1) 2 *(Burke 16 (pen), Towell 64)*

Slovan Bratislava (0) 1 *(Weiss 72)* 1500

Shamrock R: Mannus, O'Brien (Hoare 81), Lopes, Grace, Finn, Towell (Greene 84), O'Neill (Watts 71), Mandroiu, Scales, Burke, Gaffney.
Slovan Bratislava: Chovan, Medvedev, Kashia, Bozhikov, De Marco, Hrncar (Cavric 59), Kankava, de Kamps (Abena 90), Rafael Ratao (Zmrhal 82), Weiss (Mustafic 90), Henty (Ibrahim 59).
Slovan Bratislava won 3-2 on aggregate.

Wednesday, 14 July 2021

Alashkert (0) 1 *(Bezecourt 112)*

Connah's Quay Nomads (0) 0 4000

Alashkert: (442) Yurchenko; James (Mihajlovic 62), Kadio, Tiago Cameta, Voskanyan; Davidyan (Tankov 90), Khurtsidze (Bezecourt 111), Yedigaryan, Grigoryan (Gome 120); Jose Embalo (Aghekyan 62), Glisic (Hovsepyan 46).
Connah's Quay Nomads: (352) Byrne; Disney, Owens, Edwards; Curran, Morris, Poole, Davies, Moore; Mullan (Owen H 120), Insall (Williams 106).
aet; Alashkert won 3-2 on aggregate.

SECOND QUALIFYING ROUND FIRST LEG

Tuesday, 20 July 2021

Alashkert v Sheriff Tiraspol	0-1
Celtic v FC Midtjylland	1-1
Dinamo Zagreb v Omonia Nicosia	2-0
Ferencvaros v Zalgiris Vilnius	2-0
Lincoln Red Imps v CFR Cluj	1-2
Rapid Vienna v Sparta Prague	2-1

Wednesday, 21 July 2021

Kairat v Red Star Belgrade	2-1
Legia Warsaw v Flora	2-1
Malmo v HJK	2-1
Mura v Ludogorets Razgrad	0-0
Olympiacos v Neftchi	1-0
PSV Eindhoven v Galatasaray	5-1
Slovan Bratislava v Young Boys	0-0

Tuesday, 20 July 2021

Celtic (1) 1 *(Abada 39)*

FC Midtjylland (0) 1 *(Evander 66)* 9000

Celtic: (433) Barkas; Ralston, Welsh, Bitton■, Taylor; Turnbull (Rogic 78), Soro, McGregor; Abada (Murray 45), Edouard (Ajeti 77), Christie.
FC Midtjylland: (433) Lossl; Dalsgaard, Sviatchenko, Hoegh, Paulinho (Andersson 88); Anderson (Mabil 72), Evander, Nwadike (Madsen 82); Dreyer■, Junior Brumado (Hansen 87), Sisto.

SECOND QUALIFYING ROUND SECOND LEG

Tuesday, 27 July 2021		*(agg)*
Flora v Legia Warsaw	0-1	1-3
HJK v Malmo	2-2	3-4
Omonia Nicosia v Dinamo Zagreb	0-1	0-3
Zalgiris Vilnius v Ferencvaros	1-3	1-5
Wednesday, 28 July 2021		
CFR Cluj v Lincoln Red Imps	2-0	4-1
FC Midtjylland v Celtic	2-1*	3-2
Galatasaray v PSV Eindhoven	1-2	2-7
Ludogorets Razgrad v Mura	3-1	3-1
Neftchi v Olympiacos	0-1	0-2
Red Star Belgrade v Kairat	5-0	6-2
Sheriff Tiraspol v Alashkert	3-1	4-1
Sparta Prague v Rapid Vienna	2-0	3-2
Young Boys v Slovan Bratislava	3-2	3-2

Wednesday, 28 July 2021

FC Midtjylland (0) 2 *(Mabil 61, Nwadike 94)*

Celtic (0) 1 *(McGregor 48)* 4890

FC Midtjylland: (343) Lossl; Dalsgaard, Sviatchenko, Juninho (Nicolaisen 112); Andersson (Cools 106), Charles (Nwadike 59), Evander, Paulinho (Dyhr 89); Mabil (Lind 89), Junior Brumado (Hansen 77), Sisto.
Celtic: (433) Bain; Ralston, Welsh, Murray, Taylor (Montgomery 106); Turnbull (Ajeti 106), Soro (Rogic 98), McGregor; Abada (Forrest 59), Edouard, Christie.
aet; Celtic won 3-2 on aggregate.

THIRD QUALIFYING ROUND FIRST LEG

Tuesday, 3 August 2021	
CFR Cluj v Young Boys	1-1
Genk v Shakhtar Donetsk	1-2
Malmo v Rangers	2-1
Olympiacos v Ludogorets Razgrad	1-1
PSV Eindhoven v FC Midtjylland	3-0
Red Star Belgrade v Sheriff Tiraspol	1-1
Sparta Prague v Monaco	0-2
Wednesday, 4 August 2021	
Dinamo Zagreb v Legia Warsaw	1-1
Ferencvaros v Slavia Prague	2-0
Spartak Moscow v Benfica	0-2

Tuesday, 3 August 2021

Malmo (0) 2 *(Rieks 47, Birmancevic 49)*

Rangers (0) 1 *(Davis 90)* 5820

Malmo: (532) Dahlin; Berget, Ahmedhodzic, Nielsen, Moisander, Rieks (Beijmo 88); Lewicki, Innocent, Christiansen (Rakip 89); Colak (Malik 88), Birmancevic (Nalic 74).
Rangers: (433) McGregor; Tavernier, Helander, Goldson, Barisic; Arfield, Davis, Lundstram; Wright S, Itten (Sakala 63), Kent.

THIRD QUALIFYING ROUND SECOND LEG

Tuesday, 10 August 2021		*(agg)*
Benfica v Spartak Moscow	2-0	4-0
FC Midtjylland v PSV Eindhoven	0-1	0-4
Legia Warsaw v Dinamo Zagreb	0-1	1-2
Ludogorets Razgrad v Olympiacos	2-2*	3-3
(Ludogorets Razgrad won 4-1 on penalties.)		
Monaco v Sparta Prague	3-1	5-1
Rangers v Malmo	1-2	2-4
Shakhtar Donetsk v Genk	2-1	4-2
Sheriff Tiraspol v Red Star Belgrade	1-0	2-1
Slavia Prague v Ferencvaros	1-0	1-2
Young Boys v CFR Cluj	3-1	4-2

Tuesday, 10 August 2021

Rangers (1) 1 *(Morelos 18)*

Malmo (0) 2 *(Colak 53, 57)* 47,021

Rangers: (433) McGregor; Tavernier, Goldson, Balogun, Barisic; Davis, Aribo, Arfield (Hagi 70); Wright S (Sakala 62), Morelos, Kent.
Malmo: (442) Dahlin; Lewicki, Ahmedhodzic, Nielsen, Moisander; Birmancevic (Rakip 74), Innocent■, Christiansen, Rieks; Berget (Beijmo 83), Colak (Malik 90).
Malmo won 4-2 on aggregate.

PLAY-OFF ROUND FIRST LEG

Tuesday, 17 August 2021	
Monaco v Shakhtar Donetsk	0-1
Red Bull Salzburg v Brondby	2-1
Sheriff Tiraspol v Dinamo Zagreb	3-0
Wednesday, 18 August 2021	
Benfica v PSV Eindhoven	2-1
Malmo v Ludogorets Razgrad	2-0
Young Boys v Ferencvaros	3-2

PLAY-OFF ROUND SECOND LEG

Tuesday, 24 August 2021		*(agg)*
Ferencvaros v Young Boys	2-3	4-6
Ludogorets Razgrad v Malmo	2-1	2-3
PSV Eindhoven v Benfica	0-0	1-2
Wednesday, 25 August 2021		
Brondby v Red Bull Salzburg	1-2	2-4
Dinamo Zagreb v Sheriff Tiraspol	0-0	0-3
Shakhtar Donetsk v Monaco	2-2*	3-2

GROUP STAGE

GROUP A

Wednesday, 15 September 2021

Club Brugge (1) 1 *(Vanaken 27)*

Paris Saint-Germain (1) 1 *(Ander Herrera 15)* 27,546

Club Brugge: (4411) Mignolet; Mata, Hendry, N'Soki, Sobol; Sowah (Maouassa 90), Rits, Balanta, Lang; Vanaken; De Ketelaere.
Paris Saint-Germain: (433) Navas; Hakimi, Marquinhos, Kimpembe, Diallo (Nuno Mendes 75); Ander Herrera, Paredes (Danilo Pereira 46), Wijnaldum (Draxler 46); Messi, Mbappe-Lottin (Icardi 51), Neymar.

Manchester C (3) 6 *(Ake 16, Mukiele 28 (og), Mahrez 45 (pen), Grealish 56, Joao Cancelo 75, Gabriel Jesus 85)*

RB Leipzig (1) 3 *(Nkunku 42, 51, 73)* 38,062

Manchester C: (433) Ederson; Joao Cancelo, Dias, Ake, Zinchenko; De Bruyne (Foden 71), Rodri (Fernandinho 59), Bernardo Silva (Gundogan 59); Mahrez, Torres (Sterling 72), Grealish (Gabriel Jesus 81).
RB Leipzig: (4231) Gulacsi; Mukiele, Klostermann, Orban, Angelino■; Adams, Laimer (Haidara 60); Nkunku (Gvardiol 81), Olmo (Brobbey 72), Forsberg (Szoboszlai 61); Andre Silva (Poulsen 60).

Tuesday, 28 September 2021

Paris Saint-Germain (1) 2 *(Gueye 8, Messi 74)*

Manchester C (0) 0 37,350

Paris Saint-Germain: (433) Donnarumma; Hakimi, Marquinhos, Kimpembe, Nuno Mendes; Ander Herrera, Verratti (Wijnaldum 78), Gueye (Danilo Pereira 90); Messi, Mbappe-Lottin, Neymar.
Manchester C: (433) Ederson; Walker, Dias, Laporte, Joao Cancelo; Bernardo Silva, Rodri, De Bruyne; Mahrez, Sterling (Gabriel Jesus 78), Grealish (Foden 68).

RB Leipzig (1) 1 *(Nkunku 5)*

Club Brugge (2) 2 *(Vanaken 22, Rits 41)* 23,500

RB Leipzig: (343) Gulacsi; Simakan (Adams 78), Orban, Klostermann; Mukiele (Gvardiol 46), Laimer (Haidara 46), Kampl, Szoboszlai (Andre Silva 58); Nkunku, Poulsen (Brobbey 78), Forsberg.
Club Brugge: (4411) Mignolet; Mata, Hendry, N'Soki, Sobol (Ricca 79); Sowah (van der Brempt 68), Rits (Vormer 79), Balanta, Lang; Vanaken; De Ketelaere (Wesley 72).

Tuesday, 19 October 2021

Club Brugge (0) 1 *(Vanaken 81)*

Manchester C (2) 5 *(Joao Cancelo 30, Mahrez 43 (pen), 84, Walker 53, Palmer 67)* 24,915

Club Brugge: (4411) Mignolet; Mata, Hendry, N'Soki (Mechele 79), Sobol; Sowah (van der Brempt 56), Rits (Vormer 56), Balanta (Mbamba 68), Lang; Vanaken; De Ketelaere (Dost 79).
Manchester C: (433) Ederson; Walker, Dias, Laporte (Ake 57), Joao Cancelo; De Bruyne (Palmer 64), Rodri (Fernandinho 71), Bernardo Silva (Gundogan 57); Mahrez, Foden (Sterling 64), Grealish.

Paris Saint-Germain (1) 3 *(Mbappe-Lottin 9, Messi 67, 74 (pen))*

RB Leipzig (1) 2 *(Andre Silva 28, Mukiele 57)* 47,359

Paris Saint-Germain: (433) Navas; Hakimi, Marquinhos, Kimpembe, Nuno Mendes; Ander Herrera (Wijnaldum 61), Gueye (Danilo Pereira 61), Verratti; Messi, Mbappe-Lottin, Draxler (Kehrer 90).
RB Leipzig: (352) Gulacsi; Simakan (Poulsen 83), Orban, Klostermann (Gvardiol 70); Mukiele, Laimer, Adams, Haidara (Moriba 62), Angelino (Henrichs 83); Nkunku, Andre Silva (Forsberg 83).

Wednesday, 3 November 2021

Manchester C (1) 4 *(Foden 15, Mahrez 54, Sterling 72, Gabriel Jesus 90)*

Club Brugge (1) 1 *(Stones 17 (og))* 50,228

Manchester C: (433) Ederson; Walker (Zinchenko 80), Stones, Laporte, Joao Cancelo; Gundogan, Rodri, Bernardo Silva (De Bruyne 75); Mahrez (Sterling 69), Foden (Palmer 80), Grealish (Gabriel Jesus 68).
Club Brugge: (532) Mignolet; Mata (van der Brempt 78), Hendry, Mechele, N'Soki, Sobol (Ricca 73); Vormer, Rits (Mbamba 78), Vanaken; Lang (Dost 78), De Ketelaere (Sowah 87).

RB Leipzig (1) 2 *(Nkunku 8, Szoboszlai 90 (pen))*

Paris Saint-Germain (2) 2 *(Wijnaldum 21, 39)* 39,794

RB Leipzig: (3421) Gulacsi; Orban (Haidara 46), Simakan, Gvardiol; Mukiele, Laimer (Henrichs 85), Adams (Olmo 74), Angelino; Nkunku, Forsberg (Szoboszlai 59); Andre Silva (Poulsen 59).
Paris Saint-Germain: (433) Donnarumma; Hakimi, Marquinhos, Kimpembe, Nuno Mendes; Wijnaldum (Ander Herrera 85), Danilo Pereira, Gueye; Di Maria (Draxler 85), Mbappe-Lottin (Icardi 90), Neymar.

Wednesday, 24 November 2021

Club Brugge (0) 0

RB Leipzig (4) 5 *(Nkunku 12, 90, Forsberg 17 (pen), 45, Andre Silva 26)* 24,072

Club Brugge: (343) Mignolet; Mata, Hendry, N'Soki (Ricca 46); van der Brempt (Mechele 60), Balanta, Vanaken, Sowah (Izquierdo 82); De Ketelaere (Wesley 82), Dost (Rits 46), Lang.
RB Leipzig: (41212) Martinez; Mukiele, Klostermann (Henrichs 62), Gvardiol (Bonnah 80), Angelino; Kampl; Laimer (Moriba 62), Forsberg; Nkunku; Brobbey (Novoa 66), Andre Silva.

Manchester C (0) 2 *(Sterling 63, Gabriel Jesus 76)*

Paris Saint-Germain (0) 1 *(Mbappe-Lottin 50)* 52,030

Manchester C: (433) Ederson; Walker, Stones, Dias, Joao Cancelo; Gundogan, Rodri, Zinchenko (Gabriel Jesus 54); Mahrez, Bernardo Silva, Sterling.
Paris Saint-Germain: (433) Navas; Hakimi, Marquinhos, Kimpembe, Nuno Mendes (Kehrer 67); Ander Herrera (Danilo Pereira 61), Paredes, Gueye (Di Maria 67); Messi, Mbappe-Lottin, Neymar.

Tuesday, 7 December 2021

Paris Saint-Germain (3) 4 *(Mbappe-Lottin 2, 7, Messi 38, 76 (pen))*

Club Brugge (0) 1 *(Rits 68)* 47,492

Paris Saint-Germain: (433) Donnarumma; Hakimi, Marquinhos, Diallo, Nuno Mendes (Kehrer 50); Wijnaldum, Verratti (Ebimbe 83), Gueye (Paredes 71); Di Maria (Ander Herrera 71), Messi, Mbappe-Lottin (Icardi 83).
Club Brugge: (4231) Mignolet; Mata, Hendry, N'Soki, Ricca; Rits (Vormer 69), Balanta (Mbamba 69); Sandra (van der Brempt 57), Vanaken, Lang; De Ketelaere.

RB Leipzig (1) 2 *(Szoboszlai 24, Andre Silva 71)*

Manchester C (0) 1 *(Mahrez 76)* 0

RB Leipzig: (4231) Gulacsi; Mukiele (Henrichs 79), Klostermann (Simakan 46), Gvardiol, Angelino; Laimer (Adams 63), Kampl; Nkunku, Forsberg (Brobbey 80), Szoboszlai; Andre Silva (Moriba 86).
Manchester C: (433) Steffen; Walker■, Stones, Ake (Dias 87), Zinchenko; Gundogan, Fernandinho, De Bruyne (Palmer 87); Mahrez, Grealish, Foden (Sterling 46).
Behind closed doors due to COVID-19 pandemic.

Group A Table	P	W	D	L	F	A	GD	Pts
Manchester C	6	4	0	2	18	10	8	12
Paris Saint-Germain	6	3	2	1	13	8	5	11
RB Leipzig	6	2	1	3	15	14	1	7
Club Brugge	6	1	1	4	6	20	−14	4

GROUP B

Wednesday, 15 September 2021

Atletico Madrid (0) 0

Porto (0) 0 40,098

Atletico Madrid: (3142) Oblak; Gimenez, Felipe (Herrera 75), Hermoso (Renan Lodi 56); Kondogbia; Llorente, Koke (Correa 56), Lemar (De Paul 36), Carrasco; Suarez, Joao Felix (Griezmann 56).
Porto: (442) Costa D; Corona, Mbemba■, Pepe K (Marcano 53), Sanusi (Wendell 46); Otavio, Grujic, Uribe (Vitinha 66), Diaz (Pepe E 84); Martinez (Sergio Oliveira 66), Taremi.

Liverpool (1) 3 *(Tomori 9 (og), Salah 48, Henderson 69)*

AC Milan (2) 2 *(Rebic 42, Diaz 44)* 51,445

Liverpool: (433) Alisson; Alexander-Arnold, Matip, Gomez, Robertson; Henderson (Milner 84), Fabinho, Keita (Thiago 71); Salah (Oxlade-Chamberlain 84), Origi (Mane 63), Jota (Jones 71).
AC Milan: (4231) Maignan; Calabria, Kjaer, Tomori, Hernandez; Bennacer (Tonali 71), Kessie; Saelemaekers (Florenzi 62), Diaz, Leao (Giroud 62); Rebic (Maldini 83).

Tuesday, 28 September 2021

AC Milan (1) 1 *(Leao 20)*

Atletico Madrid (0) 2 *(Griezmann 84, Suarez 90 (pen))* 35,374

AC Milan: (4231) Maignan; Calabria, Tomori, Romagnoli, Hernandez; Bennacer (Florenzi 81), Kessie■; Saelemaekers (Kalulu Kyatengwa 82), Diaz (Toure 57), Leao (Giroud 57); Rebic (Tonali 34).
Atletico Madrid: (442) Oblak; Trippier (Joao Felix 40), Felipe, Gimenez, Hermoso (Renan Lodi 46); Llorente, Kondogbia (Lemar 64), Koke (Griezmann 61), Carrasco (De Paul 46); Correa, Suarez.

Porto (0) 1 *(Taremi 74)*

Liverpool (2) 5 *(Salah 18, 60, Mane 45, Firmino 77, 81)* 23,520

Porto: (442) Costa D; Corona, Fabio Cardoso, Marcano, Sanusi (Wendell 56); Otavio (Vieira 14), Sergio Oliveira (Pepe E 67), Uribe (Vitinha 56), Diaz; Taremi, Martinez (Grujic 46).
Liverpool: (433) Alisson; Milner (Gomez 66), Matip, van Dijk, Robertson; Henderson (Oxlade-Chamberlain 73), Fabinho, Jones; Salah (Firmino 67), Jota (Origi 88), Mane (Minamino 67).

Tuesday, 19 October 2021

Atletico Madrid (2) 2 *(Griezmann 20, 34)*

Liverpool (2) 3 *(Salah 8, 78 (pen), Keita 13)* 60,725

Atletico Madrid: (3142) Oblak; Felipe, Kondogbia (Gimenez 46), Hermoso (Llorente 80); Koke; Trippier, De Paul (Renan Lodi 80), Lemar (Suarez 80), Carrasco; Joao Felix (Correa 80), Griezmann■.
Liverpool: (433) Alisson; Alexander-Arnold (Gomez 85), Matip, van Dijk, Robertson; Keita (Fabinho 46), Henderson, Milner (Oxlade-Chamberlain 63); Salah (Williams 90), Firmino, Mane (Jota 62).

Porto (0) 1 *(Diaz 65)*

AC Milan (0) 0 32,130

Porto: (442) Costa D; Joao Mario, Mbemba, Pepe K, Wendell (Sanusi 46); Otavio (Grujic 90), Uribe, Sergio Oliveira (Vitinha 67), Diaz; Taremi (Martinez 84), Evanilson (Corona 67).
AC Milan: (4231) Tatarusanu; Calabria, Kjaer, Tomori (Romagnoli 58), Toure (Kalulu Kyatengwa 58); Tonali (Bakayoko 66), Bennacer; Saelemaekers, Krunic (Maldini 82), Leao; Giroud (Ibrahimovic 58).

Wednesday, 3 November 2021

AC Milan (0) 1 *(Mbemba 61 (og))*

Porto (1) 1 *(Diaz 6)* 39,675

AC Milan: (4231) Tatarusanu; Calabria (Kalulu Kyatengwa 46), Tomori, Romagnoli, Hernandez; Tonali (Kessie 68), Bennacer; Saelemaekers, Diaz (Krunic 68), Leao (Maldini 85); Giroud (Ibrahimovic 76).
Porto: (442) Costa D; Joao Mario, Pepe K, Mbemba, Sanusi; Otavio (Martinez 85), Grujic, Sergio Oliveira (Vitinha 70), Diaz (Costa B 79); Taremi (Pepe E 86), Evanilson (Francisco Conceicao 79).

Liverpool (2) 2 *(Jota 13, Mane 21)*

Atletico Madrid (0) 0 51,347

Liverpool: (433) Alisson; Alexander-Arnold (Phillips 90), Matip, van Dijk, Tsimikas; Henderson, Fabinho (Thiago 59), Oxlade-Chamberlain (Minamino 78); Salah, Jota, Mane (Firmino 46 (Origi 78)).
Atletico Madrid: (3421) Oblak; Felipe■, Gimenez, Hermoso; Trippier, Koke (Matheus Cunha 69), De Paul, Carrasco (Vrsaljko 69); Correa (Serrano 75), Joao Felix (Renan Lodi 59); Suarez (Herrera 59).

Wednesday, 24 November 2021

Atletico Madrid (0) 0

AC Milan (0) 1 *(Messias 87)* 61,019

Atletico Madrid: (3142) Oblak; Savic, Gimenez, Hermoso (Renan Lodi 64); Koke; Llorente, De Paul (Vrsaljko 77), Lemar (Correa 64), Carrasco; Griezmann (Kondogbia 81), Suarez (Matheus Cunha 77).
AC Milan: (4231) Tatarusanu; Kalulu Kyatengwa (Florenzi 65), Kjaer, Romagnoli, Hernandez; Tonali (Bakayoko 65), Kessie; Saelemaekers, Diaz (Bennacer 78), Krunic (Messias 65); Giroud (Ibrahimovic 66).

Liverpool (0) 2 *(Thiago 52, Salah 70)*

Porto (0) 0 52,209

Liverpool: (433) Alisson; Williams, Matip, Konate, Tsimikas (Robertson 63); Oxlade-Chamberlain (Milner 82), Morton, Thiago (Henderson 63); Salah (Fabinho 71), Minamino, Mane (Origi 72).
Porto: (442) Costa D; Joao Mario, Mbemba, Pepe K (Fabio Cardoso 25), Sanusi; Otavio, Sergio Oliveira (Vitinha 64), Uribe (Grujic 77), Diaz; Evanilson (Martinez 77), Taremi (Francisco Conceicao 64).

Tuesday, 7 December 2021

AC Milan (1) 1 *(Tomori 28)*

Liverpool (1) 2 *(Salah 36, Origi 55)* 56,237

AC Milan: (4231) Maignan; Kalulu Kyatengwa (Florenzi 64), Tomori, Romagnoli, Hernandez; Tonali (Saelemaekers 59), Kessie; Messias, Diaz (Bennacer 59), Krunic (Bakayoko 83); Ibrahimovic.
Liverpool: (433) Alisson; Williams (Bradley 90), Phillips, Konate, Tsimikas; Oxlade-Chamberlain, Morton, Minamino (Woltman 90); Salah (Keita 64), Origi (Fabinho 80), Mane (Gomez 64).

Porto (0) 1 *(Sergio Oliveira 90 (pen))*

Atletico Madrid (0) 3 *(Griezmann 56, Correa 90, De Paul 90)* 38,830

Porto: (442) Costa D; Joao Mario (Sergio Oliveira 81), Mbemba, Pepe K, Sanusi (Wendell■ 63); Otavio (Vieira 82), Vitinha, Grujic (Corona 81), Diaz; Taremi (Martinez 82), Evanilson.
Atletico Madrid: (3421) Oblak; Vrsaljko, Kondogbia, Hermoso; Llorente, Koke, De Paul, Carrasco■; Lemar (Correa 66), Griezmann; Suarez (Matheus Cunha 13 (Renan Lodi 83)).

Group B Table	P	W	D	L	F	A	GD	Pts
Liverpool	6	6	0	0	17	6	11	18
Atletico Madrid	6	2	1	3	7	8	−1	7
Porto	6	1	2	3	4	11	−7	5
AC Milan	6	1	1	4	6	9	−3	4

GROUP C

Wednesday, 15 September 2021

Besiktas (0) 1 *(Montero 90)*

Borussia Dortmund (2) 2 *(Bellingham 20, Haaland 45)* 22,445

Besiktas: (4141) Destanoglu; Rosier, Welinton, Montero, N'Sakala; Josef; Ghezzal (Tore 89), Pjanic, Hutchinson (Ucan 78), Larin (Karaman 61); Batshuayi.
Borussia Dortmund: (4231) Kobel; Meunier, Akanji, Hummels (Pongracic 70), Guerreiro; Dahoud, Brandt (Witsel 46); Bellingham (Wolf 69), Reus, Malen (Moukoko 70); Haaland (Knauff 86).

Sporting Lisbon (1) 1 *(Paulinho 33)*

Ajax (3) 5 *(Haller 2, 9, 51, 63, Berghuis 39)* 20,382

Sporting Lisbon: (343) Adan; Neto, Inacio (Ricardo Esgaio 21), Feddal; Porro, Joao Palhinha, Matheus Luiz, Ruben Vinagre (Matheus Reis 46); Cabral (Sarabia 46), Paulinho (Braganca 78), Nuno Santos (Tomas 60).
Ajax: (4231) Pasveer; Mazraoui (Rensch 70), Timber, Martinez, Blind (Schuurs 80); Alvarez, Gravenberch; Antony (Neres 70), Berghuis (Taylor 77), Tadic; Haller.

Tuesday, 28 September 2021

Ajax (2) 2 *(Berghuis 17, Haller 43)*

Besiktas (0) 0 52,628

Ajax: (4231) Pasveer; Mazraoui, Timber, Martinez, Blind; Alvarez, Gravenberch; Antony (Neres 71), Berghuis (Klaassen 72), Tadic; Haller.
Besiktas: (4141) Destanoglu; Rosier, Saatci, N'Sakala, Meras (Vardar 73); Josef; Karaman, Bozdogan, Ucan (Ozyakup 46), Yilmaz (Tore 46); Batshuayi.

Borussia Dortmund (1) 1 *(Malen 37)*

Sporting Lisbon (0) 0 25,000

Borussia Dortmund: (4231) Kobel; Meunier, Akanji, Hummels, Guerreiro (Schulz 75); Dahoud (Brandt 8), Witsel; Bellingham, Reus, Hazard (Wolf 71); Malen (Reinier 75).
Sporting Lisbon: (3421) Adan; Neto, Coates, Feddal; Porro (Tabata 84), Matheus Luiz, Joao Palhinha (Braganca 84), Matheus Reis (Ricardo Esgaio 84); Sarabia (Cabral 74), Tomas (Nuno Santos 58); Paulinho.

Tuesday, 19 October 2021

Ajax (2) 4 *(Reus 11 (og), Blind 25, Antony 57, Haller 72)*

Borussia Dortmund (0) 0 54,029

Ajax: (4231) Pasveer; Mazraoui (Rensch 83), Timber, Martinez, Blind; Alvarez, Gravenberch; Antony (Neres 76), Berghuis (Klaassen 69), Tadic; Haller (Daramy 83).
Borussia Dortmund: (433) Kobel; Meunier (Wolf 79), Akanji, Hummels (Pongracic 79), Schulz (Can 46); Bellingham, Witsel, Brandt (Knauff 88); Reus, Haaland, Malen (Hazard 53).

Besiktas (1) 1 *(Larin 24)*

Sporting Lisbon (3) 4 *(Coates 15, 27, Sarabia 44 (pen), Paulinho 89)* 22,936

Besiktas: (4231) Destanoglu; Rosier, Welinton, Vida, N'Sakala; Pjanic, Josef; Ghezzal, Alex Teixeira (Karaman 80), Larin (Tore 73); Batshuayi.
Sporting Lisbon: (3421) Adan; Inacio, Coates, Feddal (Neto 90); Porro, Joao Palhinha, Matheus Luiz (Braganca 90), Matheus Reis (Ricardo Esgaio 73); Goncalves (Nuno Santos 90), Sarabia (Tomas 84); Paulinho.

Wednesday, 3 November 2021

Borussia Dortmund (1) 1 *(Reus 37 (pen))*

Ajax (0) 3 *(Tadic 72, Haller 83, Klaassen 90)* 54,820

Borussia Dortmund: (433) Kobel; Meunier, Akanji, Hummels■, Wolf (Passlack 58); Brandt, Witsel, Bellingham; Hazard (Pongracic 34), Tigges (Malen 76), Reus (Knauff 76).
Ajax: (4231) Pasveer; Mazraoui, Timber, Martinez, Blind; Alvarez (Klaassen 46), Gravenberch; Antony, Berghuis (Kudus 67), Tadic; Haller.

Sporting Lisbon (3) 4 *(Goncalves 31 (pen), 38, Paulinho 41, Sarabia 56)*

Besiktas (0) 0 40,836

Sporting Lisbon: (3421) Adan; Inacio, Coates, Feddal; Porro (Ricardo Esgaio 17), Joao Palhinha, Matheus Luiz (Braganca 60), Matheus Reis (Ruben Vinagre 72); Sarabia, Goncalves (Cabral 72); Paulinho (Nuno Santos 60).
Besiktas: (433) Destanoglu; Uysal, Welinton, Montero (Alex Teixeira 46), Yilmaz; Josef■, Topal, Hutchinson (Ucan 61); Ghezzal (Tore 78), Karaman, Larin (Bozdogan 61 (Ozyakup 83)).

Wednesday, 24 November 2021

Besiktas (1) 1 *(Ghezzal 22 (pen))*

Ajax (0) 2 *(Haller 54, 69)* 11,712

Besiktas: (4231) Gunok; Rosier, Vida, Montero (Uysal 81), Meras; Pjanic (Ucan 81), Topal (Hutchinson 81); Ghezzal (Batshuayi 67), Alex Teixeira (Bozdogan 59), Nkoudou; Larin.
Ajax: (4231) Onana; Mazraoui (Timber 72), Schuurs (Rensch 77), Martinez, Tagliafico (Blind 77); Klaassen, Gravenberch; Neres, Berghuis (Taylor 83), Daramy (Haller 46); Tadic.

Sporting Lisbon (2) 3 *(Goncalves 30, 39, Porro 81)*

Borussia Dortmund (0) 1 *(Malen 90)* 41,341

Sporting Lisbon: (3421) Adan; Inacio, Coates, Feddal; Porro (Ugarte 88), Joao Palhinha, Matheus Luiz, Matheus Reis (Ricardo Esgaio 67); Goncalves (Nazinho 88), Sarabia (Nuno Santos 67); Paulinho (Tomas 82).
Borussia Dortmund: (4231) Kobel; Meunier, Akanji, Pongracic (Tigges 67), Schulz (Can■ 46); Bellingham, Witsel (Dahoud 66); Reus, Reinier (Zagadou 66), Brandt; Malen.

Tuesday, 7 December 2021

Ajax (2) 4 *(Haller 8 (pen), Antony 42, Neres 58, Berghuis 62)*

Sporting Lisbon (1) 2 *(Nuno Santos 22, Tabata 78)* 0

Ajax: (4231) Pasveer; Mazraoui (Timber 77), Schuurs (Rensch 59), Martinez, Blind (Tagliafico 46); Alvarez (Taylor 72), Gravenberch; Antony, Berghuis, Neres (Klaassen 60); Haller.
Sporting Lisbon: (3421) Virginia; Neto, Inacio, Matheus Reis; Esteves (Nazinho 73), Braganca (Essugo 81), Ugarte (Sarabia 73), Ricardo Esgaio; Tomas (Goncalves 60), Nuno Santos (Paulinho 60); Tabata.
Behind closed doors due to COVID-19 pandemic.

Borussia Dortmund (2) 5 *(Malen 29, Reus 45 (pen), 53, Haaland 68, 81)*

Besiktas (0) 0 15,000

Borussia Dortmund: (433) Kobel; Meunier (Reinier 46), Hummels, Zagadou (Pongracic 73), Schulz; Bellingham (Guerreiro 73), Witsel, Dahoud; Wolf (Passlack 62), Malen, Reus (Haaland 63).
Besiktas: (4231) Destanoglu; Uysal, Welinton■, Montero, Meras; Topal, Josef (Hutchinson 82); Karaman (Rosier 46), Bozdogan (Ucan 76), Larin (Ghezzal 69); Batshuayi.

Group C Table	*P*	*W*	*D*	*L*	*F*	*A*	*GD*	*Pts*
Ajax	6	6	0	0	20	5	15	18
Sporting Lisbon	6	3	0	3	14	12	2	9
Borussia Dortmund	6	3	0	3	10	11	−1	9
Besiktas	6	0	0	6	3	19	−16	0

GROUP D

Wednesday, 15 September 2021

Internazionale (0) 0

Real Madrid (0) 1 *(Rodrygo 89)* 37,082

Internazionale: (352) Handanovic; Skriniar, de Vrij, Bastoni; Darmian (Dumfries 55), Barella (Vecino 84), Brozovic, Calhanoglu (Vidal 65), Perisic (Dimarco 55); Dzeko, Martinez (Correa 65).
Real Madrid: (433) Courtois; Carvajal, Eder Militao, Alaba, Nacho; Valverde, Casemiro, Modric (Camavinga 80); Lucas (Rodrygo 66), Benzema, Vinicius Junior (Asensio 90).

Sheriff Tiraspol (1) 2 *(Traore 16, Yansane 62)*

Shakhtar Donetsk (0) 0 5205

Sheriff Tiraspol: (433) Athanasiadis; Fernando, Arboleda, Dulanto, Cristiano; Kolovos (Yansane 55), Addo (Radeljic 85), Thill; Traore, Yakhshiboev (Bruno 67), Castaneda (Nikolov 85).
Shakhtar Donetsk: (4231) Pyatov; Dodo, Marlon, Matviyenko, Ismaily; Maycon, Marcos Antonio (Alan Patrick 64); Tete (Marlos 46), Pedrinho, Fernando (Mudryk 65); Traore.

Tuesday, 28 September 2021

Real Madrid (0) 1 *(Benzema 65 (pen))*

Sheriff Tiraspol (1) 2 *(Yakhshiboev 25, Thill 89)* 24,522

Real Madrid: (433) Courtois; Nacho (Rodrygo 66), Eder Militao, Alaba, Gutierrez (Kroos 66); Valverde, Casemiro (Modric 66), Camavinga; Hazard (Jovic 66), Benzema, Vinicius Junior.
Sheriff Tiraspol: (4231) Athanasiadis; Fernando, Arboleda, Dulanto, Cristiano; Addo, Thill; Traore, Kolovos (Nikolov 90), Castaneda (Julien 78); Yakhshiboev (Bruno 57).

Shakhtar Donetsk (0) 0

Internazionale (0) 0 26,170

Shakhtar Donetsk: (4141) Pyatov; Dodo, Marlon, Matviyenko, Ismaily (Kryvtsov 78); Stepanenko; Pedrinho, Maycon, Alan Patrick (Marlos 85), Solomon (Mudryk 78); Traore (Tete 11).
Internazionale: (352) Handanovic; Skriniar, de Vrij, Bastoni; Dumfries, Vecino (Gagliardini 81), Brozovic (Calhanoglu 55), Barella, Dimarco (Perisic 81); Martinez (Sanchez 72), Dzeko (Correa 55).

Tuesday, 19 October 2021

Internazionale (1) 3 *(Dzeko 34, Vidal 58, de Vrij 67)*

Sheriff Tiraspol (0) 1 *(Thill 52)* 43,305

Internazionale: (352) Handanovic; Skriniar, de Vrij, Dimarco (Bastoni 53); Dumfries, Barella, Brozovic (Sensi 85), Vidal (Gagliardini 75), Perisic (Kolarov 85); Dzeko (Sanchez 75), Martinez.
Sheriff Tiraspol: (4231) Celeadnic; Fernando, Arboleda, Dulanto, Cristiano; Addo (Nikolov 75), Thill; Kolovos (Cojocaru M 84), Castaneda (Radeljic 46), Bruno; Traore (Cojocaru S 90).

Shakhtar Donetsk (0) 0

Real Madrid (1) 5 *(Kryvtsov 37 (og), Vinicius Junior 51, 56, Rodrygo 65, Benzema 90)* 34,037

Shakhtar Donetsk: (4231) Trubin; Dodo, Kryvtsov, Marlon, Ismaily (Korniyenko 75); Maycon, Alan Patrick (Stepanenko 79); Tete (Marlos 46), Pedrinho, Solomon (Marcos Antonio 46); Fernando (Mudryk 74).
Real Madrid: (433) Courtois; Lucas, Eder Militao (Vallejo 87), Alaba, Mendy (Marcelo 69); Modric (Camavinga 78), Casemiro, Kroos (Valverde 78); Rodrygo (Asensio 78), Benzema, Vinicius Junior.

Wednesday, 3 November 2021

Real Madrid (1) 2 *(Benzema 14, 61)*

Shakhtar Donetsk (1) 1 *(Fernando 39)* 38,105

Real Madrid: (433) Courtois; Carvajal (Nacho 66), Eder Militao, Alaba, Mendy; Kroos, Casemiro, Modric; Lucas, Benzema (Jovic 79), Vinicius Junior.
Shakhtar Donetsk: (4231) Trubin; Dodo, Marlon, Matviyenko, Ismaily; Maycon, Stepanenko (Sudakov 80); Tete (Marlos 80), Alan Patrick (Marcos Antonio 79), Mudryk (Solomon 71); Fernando (Dentinho 86).

Sheriff Tiraspol (0) 1 *(Traore 90)*

Internazionale (0) 3 *(Brozovic 54, Skriniar 65, Sanchez 82)* 5930

Sheriff Tiraspol: (4231) Athanasiadis; Fernando, Arboleda, Dulanto, Cristiano; Addo (Radeljic 62), Thill; Traore, Kolovos (Bruno 73), Castaneda; Yakhshiboev (Julien 82).
Internazionale: (352) Handanovic; Skriniar, de Vrij (Ranocchia 85), Bastoni; Darmian (Dumfries 46), Barella, Brozovic, Vidal, Dimarco (Perisic 64); Dzeko (Correa 81), Martinez (Sanchez 81).

Wednesday, 24 November 2021

Internazionale (0) 2 *(Dzeko 61, 67)*

Shakhtar Donetsk (0) 0 46,225

Internazionale: (352) Handanovic; Skriniar, Ranocchia, Bastoni; Darmian (D'Ambrosio 79), Barella (Vidal 78), Brozovic, Calhanoglu (Sensi 86), Perisic (Dimarco 86); Martinez (Correa 68), Dzeko.
Shakhtar Donetsk: (4231) Trubin; Dodo, Vitao, Marlon, Matviyenko; Maycon, Stepanenko (Marcos Antonio 46); Tete (Marlos 80), Pedrinho (Bondarenko 73), Solomon; Fernando (Mudryk 80).

Sheriff Tiraspol (0) 0

Real Madrid (2) 3 *(Alaba 30, Kroos 45, Benzema 55)* 5932

Sheriff Tiraspol: (4231) Athanasiadis; Fernando, Arboleda, Dulanto, Cristiano; Addo, Thill; Bruno (Julien 59), Kolovos (Nikolov 60), Castaneda (Yansane 60); Traore (Cojocaru M 81).
Real Madrid: (433) Courtois; Carvajal (Lucas 65), Eder Militao, Alaba (Nacho 65), Mendy (Marcelo 60); Modric, Casemiro (Blanco 84), Kroos; Rodrygo (Asensio 84), Benzema, Vinicius Junior.

Tuesday, 7 December 2021

Real Madrid (1) 2 *(Kroos 17, Asensio 79)*

Internazionale (0) 0 46,887

Real Madrid: (433) Courtois; Carvajal, Eder Militao, Alaba, Mendy; Modric, Casemiro (Camavinga 71), Kroos (Valverde 78); Rodrygo (Asensio 78), Jovic (Mariano 78), Vinicius Junior (Hazard 81).
Internazionale: (352) Handanovic; D'Ambrosio, Skriniar, Bastoni; Dumfries (Dimarco 46), Barella■, Brozovic (Vidal 60), Calhanoglu (Vecino 60), Perisic; Martinez (Gagliardini 66), Dzeko (Sanchez 60).

Shakhtar Donetsk (1) 1 *(Fernando 42)*

Sheriff Tiraspol (0) 1 *(Nikolov 90)* 6841

Shakhtar Donetsk: (4141) Pyatov (Shevchenko 86); Dodo, Bondar, Kryvtsov, Korniyenko (Ismaily 67); Marcos Antonio; Marlos, Bondarenko (Maycon 67), Sudakov (Tete 46), Solomon; Fernando (Mudryk 46).
Sheriff Tiraspol: (4321) Athanasiadis; Fernando, Arboleda, Dulanto, Cristiano; Traore, Addo, Bruno; Kolovos (Nikolov 46), Thill; Yansane.

Group D Table	P	W	D	L	F	A	GD	Pts
Real Madrid	6	5	0	1	14	3	11	15
Internazionale	6	3	1	2	8	5	3	10
Sheriff Tiraspol	6	2	1	3	7	11	–4	7
Shakhtar Donetsk	6	0	2	4	2	12	–10	2

GROUP E

Tuesday, 14 September 2021

Barcelona (0) 0

Bayern Munich (1) 3 *(Muller 34, Lewandowski 56, 85)* 39,737

Barcelona: (3142) ter Stegen; Araujo, Pique, Garcia (Mingueza 66); Busquets (Gavi 59); Sergi Roberto (Demir 59), de Jong F, Gonzalez P, Jordi Alba (Balde 74); de Jong L (Coutinho 66), Depay.
Bayern Munich: (4231) Neuer; Pavard (Lucas 66), Upamecano, Sule (Stanisic 82), Davies; Kimmich, Goretzka; Musiala (Gnabry 69), Muller (Sabitzer 82), Sane (Coman 82); Lewandowski.

Dynamo Kyiv (0) 0

Benfica (0) 0 21,657

Dynamo Kyiv: (4411) Boyko; Kedziora, Zabarnyi, Syrota, Mykolenko; Tsygankov (Karavayev 76), Sydorchuk, Shaparenko, De Pena (Verbic 76); Buyalsky; Shkurin (Harmash 60).
Benfica: (3421) Vlachodimos; Otamendi, Vertonghen, Morato; Gilberto (Lazaro 59), Joao Mario (Taarabt 85), Weigl, Grimaldo; Rafa Silva (Pizzi 90), Everton (Radonjic 59); Yaremchuk (Nunez 59).

Wednesday, 29 September 2021

Bayern Munich (2) 5 *(Lewandowski 12 (pen), 27, Gnabry 68, Sane 74, Choupo-Moting 87)*

Dynamo Kyiv (0) 0 25,000

Bayern Munich: (4231) Neuer; Sule, Upamecano, Lucas, Davies (Pavard 69); Kimmich, Goretzka (Sabitzer 79); Gnabry (Musiala 69), Muller, Sane (Sarr 79); Lewandowski (Choupo-Moting 79).
Dynamo Kyiv: (4231) Bushchan; Tymchyk (Kedziora 46), Zabarnyi, Shabanov, Mykolenko; Sydorchuk, Andrievsky; Tsygankov (Karavayev 70), Shaparenko (Shepelev 46), De Pena; Harmash (Supriaga 70).

Benfica (1) 3 *(Nunez 3, 79 (pen), Rafa Silva 69)*

Barcelona (0) 0 29,454

Benfica: (343) Vlachodimos; Lucas Verissimo, Otamendi, Vertonghen; Lazaro (Gilberto 45), Weigl, Joao Mario, Grimaldo (Andre Almeida 75); Rafa Silva (Pizzi 86), Yaremchuk (Taarabt 76), Nunez (Goncalo Ramos 86).
Barcelona: (3412) ter Stegen; Araujo, Pique (Gavi 33), Garcia■; Sergi Roberto (Mingueza 89), de Jong F, Busquets (Gonzalez N 68), Dest; Gonzalez P (Coutinho 68); de Jong L (Fati 68), Depay.

Wednesday, 20 October 2021

Barcelona (1) 1 *(Pique 36)*

Dynamo Kyiv (0) 0 45,968

Barcelona: (433) ter Stegen; Mingueza (Coutinho 46), Pique, Lenglet, Jordi Alba; de Jong F, Busquets, Gavi (Sergi Roberto 69); Dest, de Jong L (Fati 46), Depay (Aguero 75).
Dynamo Kyiv: (4411) Bushchan; Kedziora (Tymchyk 78), Zabarnyi, Syrota, Mykolenko; Tsygankov (Karavayev 85), Sydorchuk, Shaparenko, De Pena (Vitinho 61); Buyalsky (Ramirez 85); Supriaga (Harmash 61).

Benfica (0) 0

Bayern Munich (0) 4 *(Sane 70, 84, Everton 80 (og), Lewandowski 82)* 55,201

Benfica: (343) Vlachodimos; Lucas Verissimo, Otamendi, Vertonghen; Andre Almeida (Goncalves 40), Joao Mario (Taarabt 81), Weigl, Grimaldo; Rafa Silva (Pizzi 80), Yaremchuk (Everton 76), Nunez (Goncalo Ramos 81).
Bayern Munich: (4231) Neuer; Pavard (Gnabry 66), Sule, Upamecano, Lucas (Richards 85); Kimmich, Sabitzer (Tolisso 86); Muller (Stanisic 77), Sane, Coman (Musiala 86); Lewandowski.

Tuesday, 2 November 2021

Bayern Munich (2) 5 *(Lewandowski 26, 61, 84, Gnabry 32, Sane 49)*

Benfica (1) 2 *(Morato 38, Nunez 74)* 50,000

Bayern Munich: (4231) Neuer; Pavard, Upamecano, Kouassi, Davies (Richards 65); Goretzka, Kimmich (Sabitzer 72); Coman (Musiala 64), Gnabry (Sarr 85), Sane (Muller 72); Lewandowski.
Benfica: (3421) Vlachodimos; Lucas Verissimo, Vertonghen, Morato; Gilberto, Meite, Joao Mario (Bernardo 77), Grimaldo (Goncalo Ramos 77); Pizzi (Rafa Silva 64), Everton (Goncalves 64); Yaremchuk (Nunez 64).

Dynamo Kyiv (0) 0

Barcelona (0) 1 *(Fati 70)* 31,378

Dynamo Kyiv: (4231) Bushchan; Kedziora (Tymchyk 77), Zabarnyi, Syrota, Karavayev; Sydorchuk, Shaparenko (Shepelev 81); Tsygankov, Buyalsky (Lednev 81), De Pena (Verbic 77); Harmash (Vitinho 71).
Barcelona: (433) ter Stegen; Mingueza, Garcia, Lenglet (Araujo 79), Jordi Alba; Gonzalez N, Busquets, de Jong F; Gavi (Dembele 65), Depay, Fati (Balde 87).

Tuesday, 23 November 2021

Barcelona (0) 0

Benfica (0) 0 49,572

Barcelona: (3421) ter Stegen; Araujo (Garcia 86), Pique, Lenglet (Dest 86); Demir (Dembele 66), Busquets, de Jong F, Jordi Alba; Gonzalez N, Gavi; Depay.
Benfica: (3421) Vlachodimos; Andre Almeida, Otamendi, Vertonghen; Gilberto, Weigl, Joao Mario (Taarabt 59), Grimaldo (Seferovic 81); Rafa Silva (Lazaro 70), Everton (Pizzi 70); Yaremchuk (Nunez 59).

Dynamo Kyiv (0) 1 *(Harmash 70)*

Bayern Munich (2) 2 *(Lewandowski 14, Coman 42)* 28,732

Dynamo Kyiv: (4231) Bushchan; Kedziora (Karavayev 76), Zabarnyi, Syrota, Mykolenko; Sydorchuk, Shaparenko; Tsygankov, Buyalsky, De Pena (Harmash 46); Shkurin (Vitinho 46).
Bayern Munich: (4231) Neuer; Pavard, Kouassi (Tillman 85), Lucas (Sarr 46), Davies; Tolisso, Goretzka; Coman (Roca 67), Muller, Sane (Richards 87); Lewandowski.

Wednesday, 8 December 2021

Bayern Munich (2) 3 *(Muller 34, Sane 43, Musiala 62)*

Barcelona (0) 0 0

Bayern Munich: (4231) Neuer; Pavard, Upamecano, Sule (Kouassi 78), Davies (Richards 71); Tolisso (Roca 60), Musiala; Coman (Sarr 71), Muller, Sane; Lewandowski (Tillman 77).
Barcelona: (433) ter Stegen; Araujo, Pique, Lenglet, Jordi Alba (Mingueza 31); de Jong F (Puig 73), Busquets, Gavi (Demir 86); Dest (Gonzalez N 46), Depay, Dembele (Coutinho 73).
Behind closed doors due to COVID-19 pandemic.

Benfica (2) 2 *(Yaremchuk 16, Gilberto 22)*

Dynamo Kyiv (0) 0 36,591

Benfica: (343) Vlachodimos; Andre Almeida, Otamendi, Vertonghen; Gilberto (Lazaro 73), Weigl, Joao Mario (Taarabt 73), Grimaldo; Pizzi (Everton 59), Yaremchuk (Nunez 82), Rafa Silva (Bernardo 82).
Dynamo Kyiv: (442) Bushchan; Tymchyk, Zabarnyi, Syrota, Mykolenko; Tsygankov (Karavayev 79), Sydorchuk (Andrievsky 86), Shaparenko, Verbic (De Pena 64); Harmash (Ramirez 79), Buyalsky.

Group E Table	*P*	*W*	*D*	*L*	*F*	*A*	*GD*	*Pts*
Bayern Munich	6	6	0	0	22	3	19	18
Benfica	6	2	2	2	7	9	−2	8
Barcelona	6	2	1	3	2	9	−7	7
Dynamo Kyiv	6	0	1	5	1	11	−10	1

GROUP F

Tuesday, 14 September 2021

Villarreal (1) 2 *(Trigueros 39, Danjuma 73)*

Atalanta (1) 2 *(Freuler 6, Gosens 83)* 12,918

Villarreal: (442) Rulli; Foyth, Albiol, Torres, Pedraza (Mario 88); Pino (Moreno 72), Capoue (Coquelin■ 60), Parejo, Trigueros (Moi Gomez 60); Gerard, Dia (Danjuma 61).
Atalanta: (3421) Musso; Toloi, Palomino, Djimsiti (Demiral 61); Zappacosta, de Roon (Koopmeiners 70), Freuler, Gosens; Malinovsky (Pasalic 71), Pessina (Miranchuk 79); Zapata (Ilicic 70).

Young Boys (0) 2 *(Ngamaleu 66, Siebatcheu 90)*

Manchester U (1) 1 *(Ronaldo 13)* 31,120

Young Boys: (4231) von Ballmoos; Hefti (Sulejmani 83), Camara, Lauper (Zesiger 90), Garcia; Martins Pereira (Rieder 82), Sierro (Siebatcheu 46); Fassnacht, Aebischer, Ngamaleu; Elia (Kanga 90).
Manchester U: (4231) de Gea; Wan-Bissaka■, Lindelof, Maguire, Shaw; van de Beek (Varane 46), Fred (Martial 89); Sancho (Dalot 37), Bruno Fernandes (Matic 72), Pogba; Ronaldo (Lingard 72).

Wednesday, 29 September 2021

Atalanta (0) 1 *(Pessina 68)*

Young Boys (0) 0 8536

Atalanta: (3421) Musso; Toloi, Demiral, Djimsiti; Zappacosta (Pezzella 90), de Roon, Freuler (Koopmeiners 90), Gosens (Maehle 11); Malinovsky (Muriel 75), Pessina (Pasalic 75); Zapata.
Young Boys: (433) von Ballmoos; Hefti (Maceiras 83), Camara, Lauper, Garcia; Aebischer (Spielmann 83), Martins Pereira, Sierro (Mambimbi 69); Elia (Rieder 66), Siebatcheu (Kanga 66), Ngamaleu.

Manchester U (0) 2 *(Alex Telles 60, Ronaldo 90)*

Villarreal (0) 1 *(Alcacer 53)* 73,130

Manchester U: (4231) de Gea; Dalot, Lindelof, Varane, Alex Telles (Fred 89); Pogba (Cavani 75), McTominay; Greenwood (Lingard 89), Bruno Fernandes, Sancho (Matic 75); Ronaldo.
Villarreal: (433) Rulli; Foyth, Albiol (Mandi 73), Torres, Moreno (Pena 73); Parejo, Capoue, Trigueros (Estupinan 61); Pino (Moi Gomez 73), Alcacer (Dia 58), Danjuma.

Wednesday, 20 October 2021

Manchester U (0) 3 *(Rashford 53, Maguire 75, Ronaldo 81)*

Atalanta (2) 2 *(Pasalic 15, Demiral 28)* 72,279

Manchester U: (4231) de Gea; Wan-Bissaka, Lindelof, Maguire, Shaw; McTominay (Pogba 66), Fred (Matic 88); Greenwood (Sancho 73), Bruno Fernandes, Rashford (Cavani 67); Ronaldo.
Atalanta: (3412) Musso; de Roon, Demiral (Lovato 46), Palomino; Zappacosta, Koopmeiners (Pezzella 80), Freuler, Maehle; Pasalic (Malinovsky 68); Ilicic (Miranchuk 68), Muriel (Zapata 56).

Young Boys (0) 1 *(Elia 77)*

Villarreal (2) 4 *(Pino 6, Gerard 16, Moreno 88, Chukwueze 90)* 27,398

Young Boys: (532) von Ballmoos; Ngamaleu, Camara, Lauper, Lefort (Hefti 62), Garcia; Aebischer, Martins Pereira (Rieder 70), Fassnacht (Mambimbi 90); Siebatcheu (Kanga 70), Elia.
Villarreal: (352) Rulli; Foyth, Albiol (Mandi 83), Torres; Pino (Moi Gomez 89), Parejo, Capoue, Coquelin (Moreno 69), Pedraza; Gerard, Danjuma (Chukwueze 90).

Tuesday, 2 November 2021

Atalanta (1) 2 *(Ilicic 12, Zapata 56)*

Manchester U (1) 2 *(Ronaldo 45, 90)* 14,443

Atalanta: (3412) Musso; de Roon, Demiral, Palomino; Zappacosta, Koopmeiners, Freuler, Maehle; Pasalic (Djimsiti 46); Ilicic (Muriel 71), Zapata.
Manchester U: (3421) de Gea; Bailly, Varane (Greenwood 38), Maguire; Wan-Bissaka, Pogba (Matic 69), McTominay (Sancho 87), Shaw; Bruno Fernandes (van de Beek 87), Rashford (Cavani 69); Ronaldo.

Villarreal (1) 2 *(Capoue 36, Danjuma 89)*

Young Boys (0) 0 14,890

Villarreal: (442) Rulli; Mario, Albiol, Torres, Pedraza (Estupinan 75); Pino (Chukwueze 59), Parejo (Moi Gomez 90), Capoue, Coquelin (Moreno 75); Dia (Trigueros 59), Danjuma.
Young Boys: (442) Faivre; Hefti (Maceiras 75), Burgy, Lauper, Garcia (Lefort 75); Fassnacht, Aebischer, Sierro (Mambimbi 75), Ngamaleu (Siebatcheu 82); Elia, Rieder.

Tuesday, 23 November 2021

Villarreal (0) 0

Manchester U (0) 2 *(Ronaldo 78, Sancho 90)* 20,875

Villarreal: (442) Rulli; Foyth, Albiol, Torres, Estupinan (Raba 79); Pino (Chukwueze 73), Capoue, Parejo, Moi Gomez (Dia 84); Trigueros (Moreno 73), Danjuma.
Manchester U: (4231) de Gea; Wan-Bissaka, Lindelof, Maguire, Alex Telles; Fred, McTominay; Sancho (Mata 90), van de Beek (Bruno Fernandes 66), Martial (Rashford 66); Ronaldo (Matic 90).

Young Boys (1) 3 *(Siebatcheu 39, Sierro 80, Hefti 84)*

Atalanta (1) 3 *(Zapata 10, Palomino 51, Muriel 88)* 31,120

Young Boys: (433) Faivre; Hefti, Burgy, Lauper, Garcia; Aebischer, Martins Pereira (Kanga 88), Rieder (Sierro 67); Elia (Mambimbi 67), Siebatcheu, Ngamaleu.
Atalanta: (3412) Musso; Toloi, Demiral (Djimsiti 71), Palomino; Zappacosta (Pezzella 46), de Roon, Freuler (Pessina 78), Maehle (Muriel 87); Pasalic (Koopmeiners 71); Malinovsky, Zapata.

Wednesday, 8 December 2021

Manchester U (1) 1 *(Greenwood 9)*

Young Boys (1) 1 *(Rieder 42)* 73,156

Manchester U: (4141) Henderson (Heaton 68); Wan-Bissaka, Bailly, Matic, Shaw (Mengi 61); van de Beek; Diallo (Shoretire 68), Mata (Savage 89), Lingard (Iqbal 89), Elanga; Greenwood.
Young Boys: (442) Faivre; Maceiras, Camara (Lauper 77), Lustenberger, Lefort; Ngamaleu, Aebischer (Sierro 62), Martins Pereira, Rieder (Hefti 62); Elia (Maier 87), Siebatcheu (Kanga 62).

Thursday, 9 December 2021

Atalanta (0) 2 *(Malinovsky 71, Zapata 80)*

Villarreal (2) 3 *(Danjuma 3, 51, Capoue 42)* 11,690

Atalanta: (3412) Musso; Toloi, Demiral (Djimsiti 46), Palomino; Hateboer, de Roon (Muriel 54), Freuler, Maehle (Zappacosta 90); Pessina (Malinovsky 46); Ilicic, Zapata.
Villarreal: (442) Rulli; Foyth, Albiol, Torres, Estupinan; Moi Gomez (Pena 90), Capoue, Parejo (Trigueros 90), Moreno (Pedraza 87); Gerard (Iborra 80), Danjuma (Dia 88).

Group F Table	P	W	D	L	F	A	GD	Pts
Manchester U	6	3	2	1	11	8	3	11
Villarreal	6	3	1	2	12	9	3	10
Atalanta	6	1	3	2	12	13	–1	6
Young Boys	6	1	2	3	7	12	–5	5

GROUP G

Tuesday, 14 September 2021

Lille (0) 0

VfL Wolfsburg (0) 0 34,314

Lille: (442) Grbic; Celik, Fonte, Botman, Mandava; Ikone (Lihadji 74), Andre, Xeka (Onana 83), Gomes (Yazici 74); David, Yilmaz.
VfL Wolfsburg: (4231) Casteels; Mbabu, Lacroix, Brooks■, Roussillon (Gerhardt 84); Guilavogui, Arnold; Baku (Lukebakio 61), Philipp (Bornauw 66), Steffen (Waldschmidt 61); Weghorst (Nmecha L 66).

Sevilla (1) 1 *(Rakitic 42 (pen))*

Red Bull Salzburg (1) 1 *(Sucic 21 (pen))* 18,373

Sevilla: (433) Bounou; Jesus Navas (Montiel 87), Kounde, Diego Carlos, Acuna; Jordan (Delaney 46), Fernando, Rakitic (Mir 65); Suso (Ocampos 46), En-Nesyri■, Gomez (Lamela 58).
Red Bull Salzburg: (41212) Kohn; Kristensen, Solet, Wober (Piatkowski 51), Ulmer; Camara; Sucic, Seiwald (Capaldo 80); Aaronson; Sesko (Adamu 67), Adeyemi (Okafor 80).

Wednesday, 29 September 2021

Red Bull Salzburg (1) 2 *(Adeyemi 35 (pen), 53 (pen))*

Lille (0) 1 *(Yilmaz 62)* 24,207

Red Bull Salzburg: (4312) Kohn; Kristensen, Onguene, Wober, Ulmer; Seiwald, Camara, Sucic (Capaldo 71); Aaronson; Okafor (Sesko 62), Adeyemi (Adamu 75).
Lille: (442) Grbic; Djalo, Fonte, Botman, Gudmundsson (Mandava 84); Weah (Bamba 59), Andre, Xeka (Onana 60), Gomes (Ikone 59); David (Lihadji 84), Yilmaz.

VfL Wolfsburg (0) 1 *(Steffen 48)*

Sevilla (0) 1 *(Rakitic 87 (pen))* 11,733

VfL Wolfsburg: (4231) Casteels; Mbabu (Nmecha L 62), Lacroix, Bornauw, Roussillon; Guilavogui■, Arnold; Baku, Lukebakio, Steffen (Waldschmidt 74); Weghorst (Gerhardt 90).
Sevilla: (4231) Bounou; Jesus Navas, Kounde, Diego Carlos, Acuna (Rekik 46); Fernando, Jordan (Romero 70); Suso (Lamela 52), Gomez, Ocampos (Munir 74); Mir (Rakitic 53).

Wednesday, 20 October 2021

Lille (0) 0

Sevilla (0) 0 34,362

Lille: (442) Grbic; Celik, Fonte, Djalo, Mandava; Sanches (Ikone 71), Andre, Onana (Xeka 71), Bamba; David (Weah 82), Yilmaz.
Sevilla: (4231) Bounou; Jesus Navas, Diego Carlos, Rekik (Jordan 57), Acuna (Augustinsson 65); Fernando, Delaney; Suso (Rakitic 74), Torres (Gomez 64), Ocampos (Lamela 74); Mir.

Red Bull Salzburg (1) 3 *(Adeyemi 3, Okafor 65, 77)*

VfL Wolfsburg (1) 1 *(Nmecha L 15)* 29,520

Red Bull Salzburg: (41212) Kohn; Kristensen, Onguene, Wober (Bernardo 72), Ulmer (Guindo 86); Camara (Capaldo 66); Sucic, Seiwald; Aaronson; Okafor (Simic 87), Adeyemi (Adamu 87).
VfL Wolfsburg: (4231) Casteels; Mbabu, Lacroix, Brooks, Roussillon (Paulo Otavio 70); Vranckx, Arnold; Baku (Nmecha F 70), Lukebakio, Steffen; Nmecha L.

Tuesday, 2 November 2021

Sevilla (1) 1 *(Ocampos 15)*

Lille (1) 2 *(David 43 (pen), Ikone 51)* 29,369

Sevilla: (4231) Bounou; Jesus Navas (Montiel 65), Kounde, Diego Carlos, Acuna; Fernando, Delaney (Lamela 57); Suso (Jordan 57), Torres (Munir 72), Ocampos; Mir (En-Nesyri 57).
Lille: (442) Grbic; Celik, Fonte, Djalo, Mandava; Ikone, Andre, Sanches (Onana 75), Bamba; David (Xeka 86), Weah (Yazici 72).

VfL Wolfsburg (1) 2 *(Baku 3, Nmecha L 60)*

Red Bull Salzburg (1) 1 *(Wober 30)* 16,112

VfL Wolfsburg: (343) Casteels; Lacroix, Guilavogui, Brooks; Baku, Vranckx (Mbabu 82), Arnold, Paulo Otavio (Steffen 73); Nmecha L, Weghorst (Lukebakio 63), Gerhardt (Roussillon 73).
Red Bull Salzburg: (41212) Kohn; Kristensen, Onguene (Solet 77), Wober, Ulmer; Camara (Kjaergaard 89); Seiwald, Sucic (Adamu 77); Aaronson; Okafor, Adeyemi (Sesko 63).

Tuesday, 23 November 2021

Lille (1) 1 *(David 31)*

Red Bull Salzburg (0) 0 33,573

Lille: (442) Grbic; Celik, Fonte, Djalo, Mandava; Weah (Yazici 84), Sanches, Xeka, Bamba; Yilmaz (Onana 70), David (Lihadji 90).
Red Bull Salzburg: (41212) Kohn; Kristensen, Onguene, Wober, Ulmer; Camara; Sucic (Capaldo 59), Seiwald (Bernardo 85); Aaronson (Kjaergaard 85); Sesko (Adamu 59), Adeyemi.

Sevilla (1) 2 *(Jordan 12, Mir 90)*

VfL Wolfsburg (0) 0 28,663

Sevilla: (433) Bounou; Montiel, Kounde, Diego Carlos (Augustinsson 90), Acuna; Jordan (Delaney 82), Fernando, Rakitic (Rekik 90); Ocampos, Munir (Mir 80), Gomez (Torres 80).
VfL Wolfsburg: (433) Pervan; Baku (Mbabu 75), Lacroix, Brooks (Ginczek 88), Roussillon (Paulo Otavio 75); Vranckx (Lukebakio 75), Guilavogui, Arnold; Gerhardt (Philipp 66), Weghorst, Nmecha L.

Wednesday, 8 December 2021

Red Bull Salzburg (0) 1 *(Okafor 50)*

Sevilla (0) 0 0

Red Bull Salzburg: (41212) Kohn; Kristensen, Onguene, Solet, Ulmer; Camara; Sucic (Capaldo 75), Seiwald; Aaronson; Okafor (Adamu 84), Adeyemi (Sesko 66).
Sevilla: (433) Bounou; Montiel (Rekik 68), Kounde, Diego Carlos, Augustinsson (Mir 53); Jordan■, Fernando, Rakitic (Torres 68); Ocampos, Munir, Gomez (Rodriguez 68).
Behind closed doors due to COVID-19 pandemic.

VfL Wolfsburg (0) 1 *(Steffen 89)*

Lille (1) 3 *(Yilmaz 11, David 72, Gomes 78)* 6544

VfL Wolfsburg: (4231) Casteels; Mbabu (Baku 63), Lacroix, Bornauw, Paulo Otavio (Roussillon 63); Arnold, Guilavogui (Nmecha F 75); Vranckx, Waldschmidt (Steffen 74), Gerhardt (Lukebakio 46); Weghorst.

Lille: (442) Grbic; Celik (Djalo 83), Fonte, Botman, Mandava; Ikone (Yazici 84), Andre, Sanches, Gudmundsson (Gomes 68); David, Yilmaz (Onana 75).

Group G Table	P	W	D	L	F	A	GD	Pts
Lille	6	3	2	1	7	4	3	11
Red Bull Salzburg	6	3	1	2	8	6	2	10
Sevilla	6	1	3	2	5	5	0	6
VfL Wolfsburg	6	1	2	3	5	10	–5	5

GROUP H

Tuesday, 14 September 2021

Chelsea (0) 1 *(Lukaku 69)*

Zenit St Petersburg (0) 0 39,252

Chelsea: (3421) Mendy; Azpilicueta (Thiago Silva 83), Christensen, Rudiger; James, Kovacic, Jorginho, Alonso (Chilwell 83); Mount (Loftus-Cheek 90), Ziyech (Havertz 63); Lukaku.
Zenit St Petersburg: (541) Kritsyuk; Sutormin, Barrios, Chistyakov, Rakitskiy (Krugovoy 88), Douglas Santos; Malcom (Dzyuba 75), Wendel (Erokhin 76), Kuzyaev (Kravtsov 82), Claudinho (Mostovoy 88); Azmoun.

Malmo (0) 0

Juventus (3) 3 *(Alex Sandro 23, Dybala 45 (pen), Morata 45)* 5832

Malmo: (532) Diawara; Berget, Ahmedhodzic, Nielsen, Brorsson, Rieks (Olsson 75); Innocent (Nanasi 75), Christiansen, Rakip (Nalic 59); Birmancevic (Malik 59), Colak.
Juventus: (442) Szczesny; Danilo, Bonucci, de Ligt (Rugani 87), Alex Sandro; Cuadrado (Kulusevski 82), Bentancur (McKennie 68), Locatelli, Rabiot; Dybala (Ramsey 82), Morata (Kean 67).

Wednesday, 29 September 2021

Juventus (0) 1 *(Chiesa 46)*

Chelsea (0) 0 19,934

Juventus: (433) Szczesny; Danilo, Bonucci, de Ligt, Alex Sandro; Bentancur (Chiellini 83), Locatelli, Rabiot (McKennie 76); Cuadrado, Bernardeschi (Kulusevski 65), Chiesa (Kean 77).
Chelsea: (3421) Mendy; Christensen (Barkley 75), Thiago Silva, Rudiger; Azpilicueta (Loftus-Cheek 62), Jorginho (Chalobah 62), Kovacic, Alonso (Chilwell 46); Havertz, Ziyech (Hudson-Odoi 62); Lukaku.

Zenit St Petersburg (1) 4 *(Claudinho 9, Kuzyaev 49, Sutormin 80, Wendel 90)*

Malmo (0) 0 15,339

Zenit St Petersburg: (343) Kritsyuk; Barrios, Chistyakov, Rakitskiy; Sutormin (Kravtsov 83), Kuzyaev (Azmoun 75), Wendel, Douglas Santos (Krugovoy 84); Malcom, Dzyuba (Mostovoy 84), Claudinho (Erokhin 75).
Malmo: (532) Dahlin; Larsson, Ahmedhodzic■, Nielsen, Brorsson (Eile 87), Berget; Innocent (Pena 62), Rakip (Olsson 55), Christiansen; Colak (Malik 63), Birmancevic (Nalic 88).

Wednesday, 20 October 2021

Chelsea (2) 4 *(Christensen 9, Jorginho 21 (pen), 57 (pen), Havertz 48)*

Malmo (0) 0 39,095

Chelsea: (3421) Mendy; Christensen, Thiago Silva, Rudiger; Azpilicueta (James 66), Kante (Saul 65), Jorginho, Chilwell (Alonso 66); Mount, Werner (Hudson-Odoi 44); Lukaku (Havertz 23).
Malmo: (352) Dahlin (Diawara 46); Larsson, Nielsen, Brorsson; Berget (Moisander 84), Pena (Rakip 59), Innocent, Christiansen (Nalic 58), Olsson; Colak, Birmancevic (Malik 46).

Zenit St Petersburg (0) 0

Juventus (0) 1 *(Kulusevski 86)* 18,717

Zenit St Petersburg: (3421) Kritsyuk; Lovren, Chistyakov (Krugovoy 88), Rakitskiy; Karavaev (Sutormin 61), Wendel, Barrios, Douglas Santos; Malcom (Kuzyaev 69), Claudinho (Erokhin 88); Dzyuba (Azmoun 60).

Juventus: (433) Szczesny; De Sciglio, Bonucci, de Ligt, Alex Sandro (Cuadrado 58); McKennie, Locatelli (Arthur 58), Bentancur (Ramsey 84); Bernardeschi (Kulusevski 58), Morata (Kean 76), Chiesa.

Tuesday, 2 November 2021

Juventus (1) 4 *(Dybala 11, 58 (pen), Chiesa 73, Morata 82)*

Zenit St Petersburg (1) 2 *(Bonucci 26 (og), Azmoun 90)* 20,053

Juventus: (442) Szczesny; Danilo, Bonucci (Rugani 85), de Ligt, Alex Sandro; Chiesa, McKennie, Locatelli (Arthur 80), Bernardeschi (Rabiot 80); Dybala (Kulusevski 85), Morata.
Zenit St Petersburg: (3421) Kritsyuk; Lovren, Chistyakov, Rakitskiy (Dzyuba 74); Sutormin, Barrios, Wendel (Kuznetsov 88), Karavaev (Malcom 59); Mostovoy (Krugovoy 58), Claudinho (Erokhin 74); Azmoun.

Malmo (0) 0

Chelsea (0) 1 *(Ziyech 56)* 19,551

Malmo: (352) Dahlin; Ahmedhodzic, Nielsen, Brorsson; Berget (Larsson 86), Rakip (Birmancevic 86), Innocent, Pena (Lewicki 58), Rieks (Olsson 57); Colak, Nanasi (Nalic 74).
Chelsea: (3421) Mendy; Christensen, Thiago Silva, Rudiger; Azpilicueta, Loftus-Cheek, Jorginho, Alonso; Ziyech (Barkley 74), Hudson-Odoi (Pulisic 74); Havertz.

Tuesday, 23 November 2021

Chelsea (1) 4 *(Chalobah 25, James 55, Hudson-Odoi 58, Werner 90)*

Juventus (0) 0 39,513

Chelsea: (3421) Mendy; Chalobah, Thiago Silva, Rudiger; James, Kante (Loftus-Cheek 37), Jorginho (Saul 76), Chilwell (Azpilicueta 71); Ziyech, Hudson-Odoi (Mount 76); Pulisic (Werner 72).
Juventus: (442) Szczesny; Cuadrado (De Winter 80), Bonucci, de Ligt, Alex Sandro; McKennie, Bentancur (Dybala 59), Locatelli (Arthur 67), Rabiot; Chiesa (Kulusevski 80), Morata (Kean 67).

Malmo (1) 1 *(Rieks 28)*

Zenit St Petersburg (0) 1 *(Rakitskiy 90 (pen))* 15,520

Malmo: (541) Dahlin; Larsson, Ahmedhodzic, Brorsson, Moisander, Rieks; Pena (Rakip 78), Lewicki, Innocent, Birmancevic (Olsson 69); Colak.
Zenit St Petersburg: (3421) Kerzhakov; Lovren (Erokhin 46), Chistyakov■, Rakitskiy; Karavaev, Barrios, Wendel, Douglas Santos; Malcom (Krugovoy 90), Claudinho (Mostovoy 46); Dzyuba.

Wednesday, 8 December 2021

Juventus (1) 1 *(Kean 18)*

Malmo (0) 0 17,501

Juventus: (4231) Perin; De Winter (De Sciglio 71), Bonucci, Rugani, Alex Sandro; Rabiot, Arthur; Bernardeschi (Cuadrado 82), Dybala (Morata 46), Bentancur (Miretti 90); Kean (Marco Da Graca 90).
Malmo: (541) Diawara; Berget, Ahmedhodzic, Nielsen, Moisander, Olsson; Rakip (Pena 30), Innocent (Nalic 89), Christiansen, Birmancevic; Colak (Malik 78).

Zenit St Petersburg (2) 3 *(Claudinho 38, Azmoun 41, Ozdoev 90)*

Chelsea (1) 3 *(Werner 2, 85, Lukaku 62)* 29,349

Zenit St Petersburg: (4141) Kerzhakov; Karavaev, Lovren, Rakitskiy (Krugovoy 65), Douglas Santos; Barrios; Malcom (Erokhin 80), Kuzyaev (Ozdoev 80), Wendel (Mostovoy 51), Claudinho; Azmoun (Dzyuba 79).
Chelsea: (3412) Arrizabalaga; Azpilicueta, Christensen, Sarr; Hudson-Odoi (Pulisic 65), James, Barkley (Ziyech 65), Saul (Alonso 76); Mount; Lukaku (Havertz 75), Werner.

Group H Table	P	W	D	L	F	A	GD	Pts
Juventus	6	5	0	1	10	6	4	15
Chelsea	6	4	1	1	13	4	9	13
Zenit St Petersburg	6	1	2	3	10	10	0	5
Malmo	6	0	1	5	1	14	–13	1

KNOCK-OUT STAGE

ROUND OF 16 FIRST LEG

Tuesday, 15 February 2022

Paris Saint-Germain (0) 1 *(Mbappe 90)*

Real Madrid (0) 0 47,443

Paris Saint-Germain: (433) Donnarumma; Hakimi, Marquinhos, Kimpembe, Nuno Mendes; Danilo Pereira (Gueye 87), Paredes, Verratti; Di Maria (Neymar 73), Messi, Mbappe.
Real Madrid: (433) Courtois; Carvajal (Lucas 72), Eder Militao, Alaba, Mendy; Modric (Valverde 82), Casemiro, Kroos; Asensio (Rodrygo 72), Benzema (Bale 87), Vinicius Junior (Hazard 82).
Referee: Daniele Orsato.

Sporting Lisbon (0) 0

Manchester C (4) 5 *(Mahrez 7, Bernardo Silva 17, 44, Foden 32, Sterling 58)* 48,129

Sporting Lisbon: (3421) Adan; Inacio, Coates, Matheus Reis; Porro (Neto 82), Joao Palhinha, Matheus Luiz, Ricardo Esgaio; Sarabia (Tabata 75), Goncalves (Ugarte 51); Paulinho (Slimani 75).
Manchester C: (433) Ederson; Stones (Zinchenko 61), Dias, Laporte (Ake 85), Joao Cancelo; De Bruyne, Rodri (Fernandinho 73), Bernardo Silva (Delap 85); Mahrez, Foden (Gundogan 61), Sterling.
Referee: Srdjan Jovanovic.

Wednesday, 16 February 2022

Internazionale (0) 0

Liverpool (0) 2 *(Firmino 75, Salah 83)* 37,918

Internazionale: (352) Handanovic; Skriniar, de Vrij (Ranocchia 87), Bastoni (Dimarco 90); Dumfries (Darmian 87), Vidal (Gagliardini 87), Brozovic, Calhanoglu, Perisic; Martinez (Sanchez 70), Dzeko.
Liverpool: (433) Alisson; Alexander-Arnold, Konate, van Dijk, Robertson; Elliott (Keita 59), Fabinho (Henderson 60), Thiago (Milner 86); Salah, Jota (Firmino 46), Mane (Diaz 59).
Referee: Szymon Marciniak.

Red Bull Salzburg (1) 1 *(Adamu 21)*

Bayern Munich (0) 1 *(Coman 90)* 29,520

Red Bull Salzburg: (4312) Kohn; Kristensen, Solet, Wober, Ulmer; Capaldo, Camara, Seiwald (Sucic 80); Aaronson; Okafor (Adamu 12), Adeyemi (Kjaergaard 87).
Bayern Munich: (3241) Ulreich; Pavard, Sule, Hernandez; Kimmich, Tolisso (Sabitzer 80); Gnabry (Choupo-Moting 77), Muller, Sane, Coman; Lewandowski.
Referee: Michael Oliver.

Tuesday, 22 February 2022

Chelsea (1) 2 *(Havertz 8, Pulisic 63)*

Lille (0) 0 38,832

Chelsea: (343) Mendy; Christensen, Thiago Silva, Rudiger; Azpilicueta, Kante, Kovacic (Loftus-Cheek 51), Alonso (Sarr 80); Ziyech (Saul 60), Havertz, Pulisic (Werner 80).
Lille: (4231) Leo Jardim; Celik, Fonte, Botman, Djalo (Gudmundsson 76); Xeka, Andre; Sanches (Ben Arfa 81), Onana (Yilmaz 65), Bamba; David (Zhegrova 81).
Referee: Jesus Gil Manzano.

Villarreal (0) 1 *(Parejo 66)*

Juventus (1) 1 *(Vlahovic 1)* 17,686

Villarreal: (442) Rulli; Foyth, Albiol, Torres, Pedraza (Estupinan 79); Chukwueze (Pino 90), Capoue, Parejo, Moreno (Trigueros 79); Lo Celso, Danjuma (Dia 90).
Juventus: (352) Szczesny; Danilo, de Ligt, Alex Sandro (Bonucci 46); Cuadrado, McKennie (Zakaria 81), Locatelli (Arthur 71), Rabiot, De Sciglio (Pellegrini 87); Vlahovic, Morata.
Referee: Daniel Siebert.

Wednesday, 23 February 2022

Atletico Madrid (1) 1 *(Joao Felix 7)*

Manchester U (0) 1 *(Elanga 80)* 63,273

Atletico Madrid: (352) Oblak; Savic, Gimenez, Mandava; Vrsaljko, Llorente, Kondogbia, Herrera, Renan Lodi (Lemar 76); Correa, Joao Felix (Griezmann 76).
Manchester U: (4231) de Gea; Lindelof (Wan-Bissaka 66), Varane, Maguire, Shaw (Alex Telles 67); Fred, Pogba (Matic 66); Rashford (Elanga 75), Bruno Fernandes, Sancho (Lingard 82); Ronaldo.
Referee: Ovidiu Alin Hategan.

Benfica (1) 2 *(Haller 26 (og), Yaremchuk 72)*

Ajax (2) 2 *(Tadic 18, Haller 29)* 54,760

Benfica: (4411) Vlachodimos; Gilberto (Goncalves 90), Otamendi, Vertonghen, Grimaldo; Rafa Silva, Taarabt (Bernardo 85), Weigl, Everton (Yaremchuk 62); Goncalo Ramos; Nunez (Lazaro 90).
Ajax: (4231) Pasveer; Mazraoui (Rensch 90), Timber, Martinez, Blind (Tagliafico 73); Alvarez, Gravenberch (Klaassen 73); Antony, Berghuis, Tadic; Haller.
Referee: Slavko Vincic.

ROUND OF 16 SECOND LEG

Tuesday, 8 March 2022

Bayern Munich (4) 7 *(Lewandowski 12 (pen), 21 (pen), 23, Gnabry 31, Muller 54, 83, Sane 85)*

Red Bull Salzburg (0) 1 *(Kjaergaard 70)* 25,000

Bayern Munich: (3241) Neuer; Pavard, Sule (Kouassi 66), Hernandez (Upamecano 60); Kimmich, Musiala (Roca 66); Gnabry (Sarr 46), Muller, Sane, Coman (Choupo-Moting 66); Lewandowski.
Red Bull Salzburg: (4312) Kohn; Kristensen, Solet (Piatkowski 46), Wober, Ulmer; Capaldo, Camara (Tijani 67), Seiwald (Sucic 46); Aaronson; Adamu (Kjaergaard 61), Adeyemi (Sesko 62).
Bayern Munich won 8-2 on aggregate.
Referee: Clement Turpin.

Liverpool (0) 0

Internazionale (0) 1 *(Martinez 61)* 51,747

Liverpool: (433) Alisson; Alexander-Arnold, Matip, van Dijk, Robertson; Jones (Keita 65), Fabinho, Thiago (Henderson 65); Salah, Jota (Diaz 83), Mane.
Internazionale: (352) Handanovic; Skriniar, de Vrij (D'Ambrosio 46), Bastoni; Dumfries (Darmian 75), Vidal, Brozovic (Gagliardini 75), Calhanoglu (Vecino 83), Perisic; Martinez (Correa 75), Sanchez■.
Liverpool won 2-1 on aggregate.
Referee: Antonio Miguel Mateu Lahoz.

Wednesday, 9 March 2022

Manchester C (0) 0

Sporting Lisbon (0) 0 51,213

Manchester C: (433) Ederson (Carson 73); Egan-Riley, Stones, Laporte (Mbete-Tabu 84), Zinchenko; Bernardo Silva (Mahrez 46), Fernandinho, Gundogan; Gabriel Jesus, Foden (McAtee 46), Sterling.
Sporting Lisbon: (3421) Adan; Neto (Feddal 89), Coates, Inacio; Porro (Ricardo Esgaio 78), Tabata, Ugarte, Matheus Reis; Sarabia (Edwards 58), Paulinho (Nuno Santos 78); Slimani (Duarte Ribeiro 89).
Manchester C won 5-0 on aggregate.
Referee: Halil Meler.

Real Madrid (0) 3 *(Benzema 61, 76, 78)*

Paris Saint-Germain (1) 1 *(Mbappe 39)* 59,895

Real Madrid: (433) Courtois; Carvajal (Lucas 66), Eder Militao, Alaba, Nacho; Valverde, Kroos (Camavinga 57), Modric; Asensio (Rodrygo 57), Benzema, Vinicius Junior.
Paris Saint-Germain: (433) Donnarumma; Hakimi (Draxler 88), Marquinhos, Kimpembe, Nuno Mendes; Danilo Pereira (Di Maria 80), Paredes (Gueye 71), Verratti; Messi, Neymar, Mbappe.
Real Madrid won 3-2 on aggregate.
Referee: Danny Makkelie.

Tuesday, 15 March 2022

Ajax (0) 0

Benfica (0) 1 *(Nunez 77)* 54,066

Ajax: (4231) Onana; Mazraoui, Timber (Kudus 90), Martinez, Blind; Gravenberch, Alvarez (Brobbey 81); Antony, Berghuis (Klaassen 81), Tadic; Haller.
Benfica: (4231) Vlachodimos; Gilberto (Lazaro 90), Otamendi, Vertonghen, Grimaldo; Taarabt (Meite 46), Weigl; Rafa Silva, Goncalo Ramos (Bernardo 90), Everton (Yaremchuk 72); Nunez (Goncalves 81).
Benfica won 3-2 on aggregate.
Referee: Carlos del Cerro Grande.

Manchester U (0) 0

Atletico Madrid (1) 1 *(Renan Lodi 41)* 73,008

Manchester U: (4231) de Gea; Dalot, Varane, Maguire (Mata 84), Alex Telles; Fred (Cavani 75), McTominay (Matic 67); Elanga (Rashford 67), Bruno Fernandes (Pogba 67), Sancho; Ronaldo.
Atletico Madrid: (3142) Oblak; Savic, Gimenez, Mandava; Herrera; Llorente, De Paul, Koke (Kondogbia 80), Renan Lodi; Griezmann (Correa 90), Joao Felix (Felipe 90).
Atletico Madrid won 2-1 on aggregate.
Referee: Slavko Vincic.

Wednesday, 16 March 2022

Juventus (0) 0

Villarreal (0) 3 *(Gerard 78 (pen), Torres 85, Danjuma 90 (pen))* 30,385

Juventus: (352) Szczesny; Danilo, de Ligt, Rugani (Dybala 79); Cuadrado, Locatelli (Bernardeschi 83), Arthur, Rabiot, De Sciglio; Vlahovic, Morata (Kean 86).
Villarreal: (4411) Rulli; Aurier, Albiol, Torres, Estupinan; Pino (Chukwueze 65), Capoue, Parejo (Pedraza 86), Trigueros (Coquelin 64); Lo Celso (Gerard 74); Danjuma.
Villarreal won 4-1 on aggregate.
Referee: Szymon Marciniak.

Lille (1) 1 *(Yilmaz 38 (pen))*

Chelsea (1) 2 *(Pulisic 45, Azpilicueta 71)* 49,048

Lille: (442) Leo Jardim; Celik (Weah 58), Fonte, Botman (Onana 58), Djalo; Bamba (Gomes 78), Andre, Xeka, Gudmundsson (Bradaric 77); Yilmaz, David (Ben Arfa 77).
Chelsea: (352) Mendy; Christensen (Chalobah 33), Thiago Silva, Rudiger; Azpilicueta, Kante, Jorginho (Loftus-Cheek 74), Kovacic (Mount 46), Alonso; Havertz (Ziyech 83), Pulisic (Lukaku 74).
Chelsea won 4-1 on aggregate.
Referee: Davide Massa.

QUARTER-FINALS FIRST LEG

Tuesday, 5 April 2022

Benfica (0) 1 *(Nunez 49)*

Liverpool (2) 3 *(Konate 17, Mane 34, Diaz 87)* 59,633

Benfica: (4231) Vlachodimos; Gilberto, Otamendi, Vertonghen, Grimaldo; Weigl, Taarabt (Meite 70); Rafa Silva, Goncalo Ramos (Joao Mario 87), Everton (Yaremchuk 82); Nunez.
Liverpool: (433) Alisson; Alexander-Arnold (Gomez 89), Konate, van Dijk, Robertson; Keita (Milner 89), Fabinho, Thiago (Henderson 61); Salah (Jota 61), Mane (Firmino 61), Diaz.
Referee: Jesus Gil Manzano.

Manchester C (0) 1 *(De Bruyne 70)*

Atletico Madrid (0) 0 52,018

Manchester C: (433) Ederson; Joao Cancelo, Stones, Laporte, Ake; De Bruyne, Rodri, Gundogan (Grealish 68); Mahrez (Foden 68), Bernardo Silva, Sterling (Gabriel Jesus 68).
Atletico Madrid: (532) Oblak; Vrsaljko, Savic, Felipe, Mandava, Renan Lodi; Llorente (Matheus Cunha 60), Koke (De Paul 60), Kondogbia; Griezmann (Correa 60), Joao Felix (Lemar 81).
Referee: Istvan Kovacs.

Wednesday, 6 April 2022

Chelsea (1) 1 *(Havertz 40)*

Real Madrid (2) 3 *(Benzema 21, 24, 46)* 38,689

Chelsea: (3421) Mendy; Christensen (Kovacic 46), Thiago Silva, Rudiger; James, Kante (Ziyech 46), Jorginho (Loftus-Cheek 64), Azpilicueta; Mount, Pulisic (Lukaku 64); Havertz.
Real Madrid: (433) Courtois; Carvajal, Eder Militao (Nacho 64), Alaba, Mendy; Modric, Casemiro, Kroos (Camavinga 74); Valverde (Ceballos 86), Benzema (Bale 86), Vinicius Junior.
Referee: Clement Turpin.

Villarreal (1) 1 *(Danjuma 8)*

Bayern Munich (0) 0 21,626

Villarreal: (442) Rulli; Foyth (Aurier 81), Albiol, Torres, Estupinan; Lo Celso, Capoue, Parejo, Coquelin (Pedraza 59); Gerard, Danjuma (Chukwueze 81).
Bayern Munich: (4231) Neuer; Pavard (Sule 71), Upamecano, Hernandez, Davies; Kimmich, Musiala; Coman, Muller (Goretzka 62 (Roca 90)), Gnabry (Sane 62); Lewandowski.
Referee: Anthony Taylor.

QUARTER-FINALS SECOND LEG

Tuesday, 12 April 2022

Bayern Munich (0) 1 *(Lewandowski 52)*

Villarreal (0) 1 *(Chukwueze 88)* 70,000

Bayern Munich: (3241) Neuer; Pavard, Upamecano, Hernandez (Davies 87); Kimmich, Goretzka; Sane, Muller (Choupo-Moting 90), Musiala (Gnabry 82), Coman; Lewandowski.
Villarreal: (442) Rulli; Foyth, Albiol, Torres, Estupinan; Lo Celso, Capoue, Parejo (Aurier 90), Coquelin (Chukwueze 84); Gerard, Danjuma (Pedraza 84).
Villarreal won 2-1 on aggregate.
Referee: Slavko Vincic.

Real Madrid (0) 2 *(Rodrygo 80, Benzema 96)*

Chelsea (1) 3 *(Mount 15, Rudiger 51, Werner 75)* 59,839

Real Madrid: (433) Courtois; Carvajal, Nacho (Lucas 88), Alaba, Mendy (Marcelo 78); Modric, Casemiro (Rodrygo 78), Kroos (Camavinga 73); Valverde, Benzema, Vinicius Junior (Ceballos 115).
Chelsea: (3412) Mendy; James, Thiago Silva, Rudiger; Loftus-Cheek (Saul 106), Kante (Ziyech 99), Kovacic (Jorginho 106), Alonso; Mount; Havertz, Werner (Pulisic 83).
aet; Real Madrid won 5-4 on aggregate.
Referee: Szymon Marciniak.

Wednesday, 13 April 2022

Atletico Madrid (0) 0

Manchester C (0) 0 65,675

Atletico Madrid: (541) Oblak; Llorente, Savic, Felipe■, Mandava, Renan Lodi (Correa 70); Griezmann (Carrasco 69), Koke (De Paul 69), Kondogbia, Lemar (Suarez 82); Joao Felix (Matheus Cunha 82).
Manchester C: (433) Ederson; Walker (Ake 73), Stones, Laporte, Joao Cancelo; De Bruyne (Sterling 65), Rodri, Gundogan; Mahrez, Foden, Bernardo Silva (Fernandinho 79).
Manchester C won 1-0 on aggregate.
Referee: Daniel Siebert.

Liverpool (1) 3 *(Konate 21, Firmino 55, 65)*

Benfica (1) 3 *(Goncalo Ramos 32, Yaremchuk 73, Nunez 82)* 51,373

Liverpool: (433) Alisson; Gomez, Matip, Konate, Tsimikas; Keita, Henderson (Fabinho 58), Milner (Thiago 58); Diaz (Mane 66), Firmino (Origi 90), Jota (Salah 57).
Benfica: (4231) Vlachodimos; Gilberto (Gil Dias 90), Otamendi, Vertonghen, Grimaldo; Taarabt (Joao Mario 66), Weigl; Everton (Andre Almeida 90), Goncalo Ramos (Bernardo 78), Goncalves (Yaremchuk 46); Nunez.
Liverpool won 6-4 on aggregate.
Referee: Serdar Gozubuyuk.

SEMI-FINALS FIRST LEG

Tuesday, 26 April 2022

Manchester C (2) 4 *(De Bruyne 2, Gabriel Jesus 11, Foden 53, Bernardo Silva 74)*

Real Madrid (1) 3 *(Benzema 33, 82 (pen), Vinicius Junior 55)* 52,217

Manchester C: (433) Ederson; Stones (Fernandinho 36), Dias, Laporte, Zinchenko; Bernardo Silva, Rodri, De Bruyne; Mahrez, Gabriel Jesus (Sterling 83), Foden.
Real Madrid: (433) Courtois; Carvajal, Eder Militao, Alaba (Nacho 46), Mendy; Valverde, Kroos, Modric (Ceballos 79); Rodrygo (Camavinga 70), Benzema, Vinicius Junior (Asensio 88).
Referee: Istvan Kovacs.

Wednesday, 27 April 2022

Liverpool (0) 2 *(Estupinan 53 (og), Mane 55)*

Villarreal (0) 0 51,586

Liverpool: (433) Alisson; Alexander-Arnold (Gomez 81), Konate, van Dijk, Robertson; Henderson (Keita 72), Fabinho, Thiago; Salah, Mane (Jota 73), Diaz (Origi 81).
Villarreal: (442) Rulli; Foyth, Albiol, Torres, Estupinan (Trigueros 72); Lo Celso, Capoue, Parejo (Aurier 71), Coquelin (Pedraza 57); Chukwueze (Dia 72), Danjuma (Alcacer 86).
Referee: Szymon Marciniak.

SEMI-FINALS SECOND LEG

Tuesday, 3 May 2022

Villarreal (2) 2 *(Dia 3, Coquelin 41)*

Liverpool (0) 3 *(Fabinho 62, Diaz 67, Mane 74)* 21,872

Villarreal: (442) Rulli; Foyth, Albiol (Aurier 79), Torres, Estupinan (Trigueros 79); Lo Celso, Parejo, Capoue■, Coquelin (Pedraza 68); Gerard (Chukwueze 68), Dia (Alcacer 79).
Liverpool: (433) Alisson; Alexander-Arnold, Konate, van Dijk, Robertson (Tsimikas 79); Keita (Henderson 79), Fabinho (Milner 84), Thiago (Jones 80); Salah, Jota (Diaz 46), Mane.
Liverpool won 5-2 on aggregate.
Referee: Danny Makkelie.

Wednesday, 4 May 2022

Real Madrid (0) 3 *(Rodrygo 90, 90, Benzema 95 (pen))*

Manchester C (0) 1 *(Mahrez 73)* 61,416

Real Madrid: (4231) Courtois; Carvajal, Eder Militao (Vallejo 115), Nacho, Mendy; Casemiro (Asensio 75), Kroos (Rodrygo 68); Valverde, Modric (Camavinga 75), Vinicius Junior (Lucas 115); Benzema (Ceballos 104).
Manchester C: (433) Ederson; Walker (Zinchenko 72), Dias, Laporte, Joao Cancelo; Bernardo Silva, Rodri (Sterling 99), De Bruyne (Gundogan 72); Mahrez (Fernandinho 85), Gabriel Jesus (Grealish 78), Foden.
aet; Real Madrid won 6-5 on aggregate.
Referee: Daniele Orsato.

UEFA CHAMPIONS LEAGUE FINAL 2021–22

Saturday, 28 May 2022

(at Stade de France, St Denis, Paris, attendance 80,698)

Liverpool (0) 0 Real Madrid (0) 1

Liverpool: (433) Alisson; Alexander-Arnold, Konate, van Dijk, Robertson; Henderson (Keita 77), Fabinho, Thiago (Firmino 77); Salah, Mane, Diaz (Jota 65).

Real Madrid: (433) Courtois; Carvajal, Eder Militao, Alaba, Mendy; Modric (Ceballos 90), Casemiro, Kroos; Valverde (Camavinga 85), Benzema, Vinicius Junior (Rodrygo 90).
Scorer: Vinicius Junior 59.

Referee: Clement Turpin.

Real Madrid's Vinicius Junior scores the only goal of the game against Liverpool in the Champions League Final in Paris. (Gonzalo Fuentes/REUTERS/Alamy)

EUROPEAN CUP-WINNERS' CUP FINALS 1961–99

Year	Winners v Runners-up		Venue	Attendance	Referee
1961	1st Leg Rangers v Fiorentina	0-2	Glasgow	80,000	C. E. Steiner (Austria)
	2nd Leg Fiorentina v Rangers	2-1	Florence	50,000	V. Hernadi (Hungary)
1962	Atletico Madrid v Fiorentina	1-1	Glasgow	27,389	T. Wharton (Scotland)
Replay	Atletico Madrid v Fiorentina	3-0	Stuttgart	38,000	K. Tschenscher (West Germany)
1963	Tottenham Hotspur v Atletico Madrid	5-1	Rotterdam	49,000	A. van Leuwen (Netherlands)
1964	Sporting Lisbon v MTK Budapest	3-3*	Brussels	3,208	L. van Nuffel (Belgium)
Replay	Sporting Lisbon v MTK Budapest	1-0	Antwerp	13,924	G. Versyp (Belgium)
1965	West Ham U v Munich 1860	2-0	Wembley	7,974	I. Zsolt (Hungary)
1966	Borussia Dortmund v Liverpool	2-1*	Glasgow	41,657	P. Schwinte (France)
1967	Bayern Munich v Rangers	1-0*	Nuremberg	69,480	C. Lo Bello (Italy)
1968	AC Milan v Hamburg	2-0	Rotterdam	53,000	J. Ortiz de Mendibil (Spain)
1969	Slovan Bratislava v Barcelona	3-2	Basel	19,000	L. van Ravens (Netherlands)
1970	Manchester C v Gornik Zabrze	2-1	Vienna	7,968	P. Schiller (Austria)
1971	Chelsea v Real Madrid	1-1*	Athens	45,000	R. Scheurer (Switzerland)
Replay	Chelsea v Real Madrid	2-1	Athens	19,917	R. Scheurer (Switzerland)
1972	Rangers v Dynamo Moscow	3-2	Barcelona	24,701	J. Ortiz de Mendibil (Spain)
1973	AC Milan v Leeds U	1-0	Salonika	40,154	C. Mihas (Greece)
1974	Magdeburg v AC Milan	2-0	Rotterdam	4,641	A. van Gemert (Netherlands)
1975	Dynamo Kyiv v Ferencvaros	3-0	Basel	13,000	R. Davidson (Scotland)
1976	Anderlecht v West Ham U	4-2	Brussels	51,296	R. Wurtz (France)
1977	Hamburg v Anderlecht	2-0	Amsterdam	66,000	P. Partridge (England)
1978	Anderlecht v Austria/WAC	4-0	Paris	48,679	H. Adlinger (West Germany)
1979	Barcelona v Fortuna Dusseldorf	4-3*	Basel	58,000	K. Palotai (Hungary)
1980	Valencia v Arsenal *(Valencia won 5-4 on penalties)*	0-0*	Brussels	40,000	V. Christov (Czechoslovakia)
1981	Dinamo Tbilisi v Carl Zeiss Jena	2-1	Dusseldorf	4,750	R. Lattanzi (Italy)
1982	Barcelona v Standard Liege	2-1	Barcelona	80,000	W. Eschweiler (West Germany)
1983	Aberdeen v Real Madrid	2-1*	Gothenburg	17,804	G. Menegali (Italy)
1984	Juventus v Porto	2-1	Basel	55,000	A. Prokop (Egypt)
1985	Everton v Rapid Vienna	3-1	Rotterdam	38,500	P. Casarin (Italy)
1986	Dynamo Kyiv v Atletico Madrid	3-0	Lyon	50,000	F. Wohrer (Austria)
1987	Ajax v Lokomotiv Leipzig	1-0	Athens	35,107	L. Agnolin (Italy)
1988	Mechelen v Ajax	1-0	Strasbourg	39,446	D. Pauly (West Germany)
1989	Barcelona v Sampdoria	2-0	Berne	42,707	G. Courtney (England)
1990	Sampdoria v Anderlecht	2-0*	Gothenburg	20,103	B. Galler (Switzerland)
1991	Manchester U v Barcelona	2-1	Rotterdam	43,500	B. Karlsson (Sweden)
1992	Werder Bremen v Monaco	2-0	Lisbon	16,000	P. D'Elia (Italy)
1993	Parma v Antwerp	3-1	Wembley	37,393	K.-J. Assenmacher (Germany)
1994	Arsenal v Parma	1-0	Copenhagen	33,765	V. Krondl (Czech Republic)
1995	Real Zaragoza v Arsenal	2-1	Paris	42,424	P. Ceccarini (Italy)
1996	Paris Saint-Germain v Rapid Vienna	1-0	Brussels	37,000	P. Pairetto (Italy)
1997	Barcelona v Paris Saint-Germain	1-0	Rotterdam	52,000	M. Merk (Germany)
1998	Chelsea v VfB Stuttgart	1-0	Stockholm	30,216	S. Braschi (Italy)
1999	Lazio v Mallorca	2-1	Villa Park	33,021	G. Benko (Austria)

INTER-CITIES FAIRS CUP FINALS 1958–71

Year	1st Leg		Attendance	2nd Leg	Attendance	Agg	Winner
1958	London XI v Barcelona	2-2	45,466	0-6	70,000	2-8	Barcelona
1960	Birmingham C v Barcelona	0-0	40,524	1-4	70,000	1-4	Barcelona
1961	Birmingham C v Roma	2-2	21,005	0-2	60,000	2-4	Roma
1962	Valencia v Barcelona	6-2	65,000	1-1	60,000	7-3	Valencia
1963	Dinamo Zagreb v Valencia	1-2	40,000	0-2	55,000	1-4	Valencia
1964	Real Zaragoza v Valencia	2-1	50,000	(in Barcelona, one match only)			Real Zaragoza
1965	Ferencvaros v Juventus	1-0	25,000	(in Turin, one match only)			Ferencvaros
1966	Barcelona v Real Zaragoza	0-1	70,000	4-2*	70,000	4-3	Barcelona
1967	Dinamo Zagreb v Leeds U	2-0	40,000	0-0	35,604	2-0	Dynamo Zagreb
1968	Leeds U v Ferencvaros	1-0	25,368	0-0	70,000	1-0	Leeds U
1969	Newcastle U v Ujpest Dozsa	3-0	60,000	3-2	37,000	6-2	Newcastle U
1970	Anderlecht v Arsenal	3-1	37,000	0-3	51,612	3-4	Arsenal
1971	Juventus v Leeds U	0-0	*(abandoned 51 minutes)*		42,000		
	Juventus v Leeds U	2-2	42,000	1-1	42,483	3-3	Leeds U
	Leeds U won on away goals rule.						

Trophy Play-Off – *between first and last winners to decide who would have possession of the original trophy*

1971	Barcelona v Leeds U	2-1	50,000	(in Barcelona, one match only)

**After extra time.*

UEFA CUP FINALS 1972–97

Year	1st Leg		Attendance	2nd Leg	Attendance	Agg	Winner
1972	Wolverhampton W v Tottenham H	1-2	38,562	1-1	54,303	2-3	Tottenham H
1973	Liverpool v Moenchengladbach	0-0	*(abandoned after 27 minutes)*		44,967		
	Liverpool v Moenchengladbach	3-0	41,169	0-2	35,000	3-2	Liverpool
1974	Tottenham H v Feyenoord	2-2	46,281	0-2	59,317	2-4	Feyenoord
1975	Moenchengladbach v FC Twente	0-0	42,368	5-1	21,767	5-1	Moenchengladbach
1976	Liverpool v Club Brugge	3-2	49,981	1-1	29,423	4-3	Liverpool
1977	Juventus v Athletic Bilbao	1-0	66,000	1-2	39,700	2-2	Juventus
	Juventus won on away goals rule.						
1978	Bastia v PSV Eindhoven	0-0	8,006	0-3	28,000	0-3	PSV Eindhoven
1979	RS Belgrade v Moenchengladbach	1-1	65,000	0-1	45,000	1-2	Moenchengladbach
1980	Moenchengladbach v E. Frankfurt	3-2	25,000	0-1	59,000	3-3	E. Frankfurt
	Eintracht Frankfurt won on away goals rule.						
1981	Ipswich T v AZ 67 Alkmaar	3-0	27,532	2-4	22,291	5-4	Ipswich T
1982	IFK Gothenburg v Hamburg	1-0	42,548	3-0	57,312	4-0	IFK Gothenburg
1983	Anderlecht v Benfica	1-0	55,000	1-1	70,000	2-1	Anderlecht
1984	Anderlecht v Tottenham H	1-1	33,000	1-1*	46,258	2-2	Tottenham H
	Tottenham H won 4-3 on penalties.						
1985	Videoton v Real Madrid	0-3	30,000	1-0	80,000	1-3	Real Madrid
1986	Real Madrid v Cologne	5-1	60,000	0-2	22,000	5-3	Real Madrid
1987	IFK Gothenburg v Dundee U	1-0	48,614	1-1	20,900	2-1	IFK Gothenburg
1988	Espanol v Bayer Leverkusen	3-0	31,180	0-3*	21,600	3-3	Bayer Leverkusen
	Bayer Leverkusen won 3-2 on penalties.						
1989	Napoli v VfB Stuttgart	2-1	81,093	3-3	64,000	5-4	Napoli
1990	Juventus v Fiorentina	3-1	47,519	0-0	30,999	3-1	Juventus
1991	Internazionale v Roma	2-0	68,887	0-1	70,901	2-1	Internazionale
1992	Torino v Ajax	2-2	65,377	0-0	40,000	2-2	Ajax
	Ajax won on away goals rule.						
1993	Borussia Dortmund v Juventus	1-3	37,000	0-3	62,781	1-6	Juventus
1994	Salzburg v Internazionale	0-1	43,000	0-1	80,345	0-2	Internazionale
1995	Parma v Juventus	1-0	22,057	1-1	80,000	2-1	Parma
1996	Bayern Munich v Bordeaux	2-0	63,000	3-1	30,000	5-1	Bayern Munich
1997	Schalke 04 v Internazionale	1-0	57,000	0-1*	81,675	1-1	Schalke 04
	Schalke 04 won 4-1 on penalties.						

UEFA CUP FINALS 1998–2009

Year	Winners v Runners-up		Venue	Attendance	Referee
1998	Internazionale v Lazio	3-0	Paris	44,412	A. L. Nieto (Spain)
1999	Parma v Marseille	3-0	Moscow	61,000	H. Dallas (Scotland)
2000	Galatasaray v Arsenal	0-0*	Copenhagen	38,919	A. L. Nieto (Spain)
	Galatasaray won 4-1 on penalties.				
2001	Liverpool v Alaves	5-4*	Dortmund	48,050	G. Veissiere (France)
	Liverpool won on sudden death 'golden goal'.				
2002	Feyenoord v Borussia Dortmund	3-2	Rotterdam	45,611	V. M. M. Pereira (Portugal)
2003	FC Porto v Celtic	3-2*	Seville	52,140	L. Michel (Slovakia)
2004	Valencia v Marseille	2-0	Gothenburg	39,000	P. Collina (Italy)
2005	CSKA Moscow v Sporting Lisbon	3-1	Lisbon	47,085	G. Poll (England)
2006	Sevilla v Middlesbrough	4-0	Eindhoven	32,100	H. Fandel (Germany)
2007	Sevilla v Espanyol	2-2*	Glasgow	47,602	M. Busacca (Switzerland)
	Sevilla won 3-1 on penalties.				
2008	Zenit St Petersburg v Rangers	2-0	Manchester	43,878	P. Fröjdfeldt (Sweden)
2009	Shakhtar Donetsk v Werder Bremen	2-1*	Istanbul	37,357	L. M. Chantalejo (Spain)

UEFA EUROPA LEAGUE FINALS 2010–22

Year	Winners v Runners-up		Venue	Attendance	Referee
2010	Atletico Madrid v Fulham	2-1*	Hamburg	49,000	N. Rizzoli (Italy)
2011	FC Porto v Braga	1-0	Dublin	45,391	V. Carballo (Spain)
2012	Atletico Madrid v Athletic Bilbao	3-0	Bucharest	52,347	W. Stark (Germany)
2013	Chelsea v Benfica	2-1	Amsterdam	46,163	B. Kuipers (Netherlands)
2014	Sevilla v Benfica	0-0*	Turin	33,120	F. Brych (Germany)
	Sevilla won 4-2 on penalties.				
2015	Sevilla v Dnipro Dnipropetrovsk	3-2	Warsaw	45,000	M. Atkinson (England)
2016	Sevilla v Liverpool	3-1	Basel	34,429	J. Eriksson (Sweden)
2017	Manchester U v Ajax	2-0	Stockholm	46,961	D. Skomina (Slovenia)
2018	Atletico Madrid v Marseille	3-0	Lyon	55,768	B. Kuipers (Netherlands)
2019	Chelsea v Arsenal	4-1	Baku	51,370	G. Rocchi (Italy)
2020	Sevilla v Internazionale	3-2	Cologne	0	D. Makkelie (Netherlands)
2021	Villareal v Manchester U	1-1*	Gdansk	9,412	C. Turpin (France)
	Villareal won 11-10 on penalties.				
2022	Eintracht Frankfurt v Rangers	1-1*	Seville	38,842	S. Vincic (Slovenia)
	Eintracht Frankfurt won 5-4 on penalties.				

**After extra time.*

UEFA EUROPA LEAGUE 2021–22

**After extra time. ■ Denotes player sent off.*

QUALIFYING STAGE

THIRD QUALIFYING ROUND FIRST LEG

Tuesday, 3 August 2021

Neftchi v HJK	2-2

Thursday, 5 August 2021

Galatasaray v St Johnstone	1-1
Jablonec v Celtic	2-4
Kairat v Alashkert	0-0
Lincoln Red Imps v Slovan Bratislava	1-3
Mura v Zalgiris Vilnius	0-0
Omonia Nicosia v Flora	1-0
Rapid Vienna v Anorthosis Famagusta	3-0

Thursday, 5 August 2021

Galatasaray (0) 1 *(Boey 60)*

St Johnstone (0) 1 *(Kerr 58 (pen))* 6216

Galatasaray: (451) Muslera■; van Aanholt (Bayram 46), Luyindama, Marcao, Boey; Babel (Turan 46), Kara (Balaban 57), Antalyali, Kutlu (Sekidika 86), Akturkoglu; Mohamed (Diagne 46).
St Johnstone: (352) Clark; Gordon, Kerr, McCart; Wotherspoon, Davidson, Rooney (Brown 88), McCann, Devine (Booth 88); O'Halloran (Hendry 76), Kane (May 62).

Jablonec (1) 2 *(Pilar 17, Bitton 85 (og))*

Celtic (2) 4 *(Abada 12, Furuhashi 16, Forrest 64, Christie 90)* 4805

Jablonec: (451) Hanus; Surzyn, Martinec, Zeleny, Krob; Plestil (Malinsky 73), Kubista (Cvancara 86), Povazanec (Hubschman 86), Kratochvil (Houska 73), Pilar (Holik 78); Dolezal.
Celtic: (433) Hart; Ralston, Bitton, Starfelt, Taylor; Soro, Turnbull (Christie 65), McGregor; Abada (Rogic 65), Furuhashi (Edouard 65), Forrest.

THIRD QUALIFYING ROUND SECOND LEG

Tuesday, 10 August 2021

		(agg)
Flora v Omonia Nicosia	2-1*	2-2
(Omonia Nicosia won 5-4 on penalties.)		
Slovan Bratislava v Lincoln Red Imps	1-1	4-2

Thursday, 12 August 2021

Alashkert v Kairat	3-2*	3-2
Anorthosis Famagusta v Rapid Vienna	2-1	2-4
Celtic v Jablonec	3-0	7-2
HJK v Neftchi	3-0	5-2
St Johnstone v Galatasaray	2-4	3-5
Zalgiris Vilnius v Mura	0-1	0-1

Thursday, 12 August 2021

Celtic (1) 3 *(Turnbull 25, 55, Forrest 72)*

Jablonec (0) 0 50,076

Celtic: (433) Hart; Starfelt, Ralston, Taylor, Welsh; McGregor (Bitton 84), Rogic (Soro 73), Turnbull (Ajeti 74); Forrest, Christie (Montgomery 74), Furuhashi (Edouard 66).
Jablonec: (451) Hanus; Krob, Zeleny, Kubista, Holik; Pilar (Smejkal 87), Povazanec (Martinec 87), Houska, Plestil (Malinsky 70), Kratochvil; Dolezal (Cvancara 70).
Celtic won 7-2 on aggregate.

St Johnstone (1) 2 *(Kerr 36, O'Halloran 90)*

Galatasaray (1) 4 *(Diagne 29, Akturkoglu 64, Feghouli 70, Kilinc 90)* 9106

St Johnstone: (352) Clark; Gordon, Kerr, McCart; Craig (Hendry 71), Davidson, Booth (Devine 82), McCann, Brown (Rooney 67); O'Halloran, Kane (May 66).
Galatasaray: (433) Cipe; van Aanholt, Luyindama, Marcao, Boey; Turan (Babel 73), Antalyali (Ozturk 89), Kutlu; Feghouli (Kilinc 88), Diagne (Kara 83), Akturkoglu (Mohamed 82).
Galatasaray won 5-3 on aggregate.

PLAY-OFF ROUND FIRST LEG

Tuesday, 17 August 2021

Red Star Belgrade v CFR Cluj	4-0

Wednesday, 18 August 2021

Celtic v AZ Alkmaar	2-0

Thursday, 19 August 2021

Fenerbahce v HJK	1-0
Mura v Sturm Graz	1-3
Olympiacos v Slovan Bratislava	3-0
Omonia Nicosia v Antwerp	4-2
Randers v Galatasaray	1-1
Rangers v Alashkert	1-0
Rapid Vienna v Zorya Luhansk	3-0
Slavia Prague v Legia Warsaw	2-2

Wednesday, 18 August 2021

Celtic (1) 2 *(Furuhashi 11, Letschert 61 (og))*

AZ Alkmaar (0) 0 52,000

Celtic: (433) Hart; Starfelt, Ralston, Taylor, Welsh; McGregor, Rogic (McCarthy 75), Turnbull (Soro 88); Forrest, Furuhashi (Montgomery 75), Abada (Edouard 58).
AZ Alkmaar: (451) Verhulst; Martins Indi, Letschert, Oosting, Sugawara; Midtsjoe (Clasie 72), Gudmundsson (Evjen 72), de Wit, Koopmeiners, Aboukhlal; Pavlidis (Poku 80).

Thursday, 19 August 2021

Rangers (0) 1 *(Morelos 67)*

Alashkert (0) 0 42,649

Rangers: (433) McGregor; Tavernier, Goldson, Helander, Bassey; Davis, Lundstram■, Aribo (Arfield 81); Morelos (Itten 83), Hagi (Kelly 90), Kent (Wright S 46).
Alashkert: (451) Cancarevic; Voskanyan, Kadio, Tiago Cameta, Boljevic; Grigoryan, Hovsepyan, Papikyan (Gome 8 (Bezecourt 75)), Khurtsidze (Glisic 80), James (Yedigaryan 75); Jose Embalo.

PLAY-OFF ROUND SECOND LEG

Thursday, 26 August 2021

		(agg)
Alashkert v Rangers	0-0	0-1
Antwerp v Omonia Nicosia	2-0*	4-4
(Antwerp won 3-2 on penalties.)		
AZ Alkmaar v Celtic	2-1	2-3
CFR Cluj v Red Star Belgrade	1-2	1-6
Galatasaray v Randers	2-1	3-2
HJK v Fenerbahce	2-5	2-6
Legia Warsaw v Slavia Prague	2-1	4-3
Slovan Bratislava v Olympiacos	2-2	2-5
Sturm Graz v Mura	2-0	5-1
Zorya Luhansk v Rapid Vienna	2-3	2-6

Thursday, 26 August 2021

Alashkert (0) 0

Rangers (0) 0 6800

Alashkert: (433) Cancarevic; Kryuchkov, Voskanyan, Tiago Cameta, Boljevic; Grigoryan (Gome 75), Hovsepyan (Bezecourt 46), Khurtsidze (Fofana 88); Jose Embalo (Aghekyan 88), Glisic (Tankov 61), James■.
Rangers: (451) McCrorie; Goldson, Helander, Barisic, Patterson; Davis, Arfield, Kamara, Aribo, Hagi (Itten 64); Morelos.
Rangers won 1-0 on aggregate.

AZ Alkmaar (2) 2 *(Aboukhlal 6, Starfelt 26 (og))*

Celtic (1) 1 *(Furuhashi 3)* 10,041

AZ Alkmaar: (433) Verhulst; Martins Indi, Letschert, Witry, Sugawara; Midtsjoe (Beukema 75), de Wit, Koopmeiners; Karlsson, Pavlidis (Gudmundsson 71), Aboukhlal (Poku 71).
Celtic: (451) Hart; Starfelt, Ralston, Taylor (Montgomery 24), Welsh; McGregor, Christie, Rogic (Edouard 60), Turnbull, Abada; Furuhashi (Soro 86).
Celtic won 3-2 on aggregate.

GROUP STAGE

GROUP A

Thursday, 16 September 2021

Brondby (0) 0

Sparta Prague (0) 0 18,867

Brondby: (352) Hermansen; Rosted (Borkeeiet 75), Maxso, Tshiembe; Bruus, Frendrup, Radosevic, Ben Slimane (Cappis 69), Mensah (Gammelby 85); Uhre (Divkovic 69), Hedlund (Pavlovic 75).
Sparta Prague: (433) Nita; Wiesner, Celustka, Hancko, Polidar (Vindheim 38); Soucek, Pavelka, Sacek (Drchal 90); Pesek, Hlozek, Haraslin (Moberg Karlsson 64).

Rangers (0) 0

Lyon (1) 2 *(Toko Ekambi 23, Tavernier 55 (og))* 44,906

Rangers: (433) McGregor; Tavernier, Goldson, Balogun, Barisic; Lundstram, Davis (Wright S 60), Kamara; Aribo (Sakala 76), Morelos, Kent (Roofe 70).
Lyon: (433) Lopes; Gusto, Boateng (Diomande 65), Denayer, Emerson Palmieri; Caqueret, Bruno Guimaraes, Aouar; Lucas Paqueta, Slimani, Toko Ekambi (Shaqiri 71).

Thursday, 30 September 2021

Lyon (0) 3 *(Toko Ekambi 64, 71, Aouar 86)*

Brondby (0) 0 25,466

Lyon: (4231) Lopes; Dubois (Gusto 83), Da Silva, Diomande, Emerson Palmieri; Caqueret (Kadewere 83), Thiago Mendes; Shaqiri (Cherki 65), Aouar, Toko Ekambi; Lucas Paqueta (Keita 83).
Brondby: (541) Hermansen; Bruus, Heggheim (Tshiembe 62), Maxso, Rosted, Gammelby (Mensah 62); Greve (Ben Slimane 63), Frendrup, Radosevic (Borkeeiet 84), Hedlund (Cappis 73); Pavlovic.

Sparta Prague (1) 1 *(Hancko 29)*

Rangers (0) 0 10,879

Sparta Prague: (4231) Nita; Wiesner, Panak, Celustka, Hancko; Sacek, Pavelka; Pesek, Hlozek (Dockal 90), Haraslin (Moberg Karlsson 75); Minchev (Drchal 69).
Rangers: (433) McGregor; Tavernier, Balogun, Bassey, Barisic; Davis, Bacuna (Hagi 38), Kamara■; Aribo (Lundstram 77), Sakala, Roofe (Morelos 66).

Thursday, 21 October 2021

Rangers (2) 2 *(Balogun 18, Roofe 30)*

Brondby (0) 0 46,842

Rangers: (433) McGregor; Tavernier, Goldson, Balogun (Bassey 64), Barisic; Aribo, Lundstram (Arfield 78), Davis; Hagi (Wright S 78), Morelos (Sakala 71), Roofe (Bacuna 78).
Brondby: (352) Mikkelsen; Heggheim, Maxso, Rosted; Gammelby, Cappis (Greve 81), Frendrup (Borkeeiet 73), Ben Slimane (Radosevic 46), Mensah (Riveros 62); Uhre (Hedlund 63), Pavlovic.

Sparta Prague (2) 3 *(Haraslin 4, 19, Krejci II 90)*

Lyon (1) 4 *(Toko Ekambi 42, 88, Aouar 53, Lucas Paqueta 67)* 12,427

Sparta Prague: (4411) Nita; Wiesner, Panak, Celustka, Hancko; Pesek (Polidar 84), Sacek (Krejci II 73), Pavelka (Karabec 84), Haraslin; Hlozek; Minchev (Dockal 63).
Lyon: (4231) Lopes; Gusto■, Boateng (Diomande 69), Denayer, Henrique (Emerson Palmieri 46); Thiago Mendes, Bruno Guimaraes; Shaqiri (Dubois 75), Aouar (Caqueret 90), Toko Ekambi; Kadewere (Lucas Paqueta 46).

Thursday, 4 November 2021

Brondby (1) 1 *(Balogun 45 (og))*

Rangers (0) 1 *(Hagi 77)* 20,462

Brondby: (3142) Hermansen; Rosted, Maxso, Tshiembe; Radosevic; Bruus (Riveros 64), Frendrup, Cappis (Ben Slimane 63), Mensah; Uhre (Greve 75), Hedlund (Pavlovic 86).
Rangers: (433) McGregor; Tavernier, Goldson, Balogun, Barisic (Bassey 81); Arfield (Hagi 56), Davis (Bacuna 72), Kamara; Aribo, Morelos (Roofe 56), Sakala (Kent 56).

Lyon (0) 3 *(Slimani 61, 63, Toko Ekambi 90)*

Sparta Prague (0) 0 33,934

Lyon: (4231) Lopes; Diomande, Da Silva, Denayer, Henrique; Caqueret (Bruno Guimaraes 68), Thiago Mendes; Cherki (Barcola 82), Shaqiri, Aouar (Toko Ekambi 69); Slimani (Lucas Paqueta 69).
Sparta Prague: (433) Nita; Wiesner, Panak, Celustka (Vindheim 7), Hancko; Sacek (Dockal 68), Pavelka, Krejci II; Pesek (Pulkrab 68), Minchev, Haraslin (Karabec 82).

Thursday, 25 November 2021

Brondby (0) 1 *(Uhre 50)*

Lyon (0) 3 *(Cherki 57, 66, Slimani 76)* 16,645

Brondby: (352) Hermansen; Heggheim (Rosted 81), Maxso, Tshiembe; Bruus, Greve (Ben Slimane 63), Radosevic (Cappis 75), Frendrup, Riveros (Mensah 63); Uhre (Divkovic 75), Hedlund.
Lyon: (442) Lopes; Gusto (Vogel 87), Da Silva, Lukeba, Henrique; Cherki, Keita (Caqueret 75), Thiago Mendes (Bruno Guimaraes 75), Kadewere (Toko Ekambi 75); Dembele (Lucas Paqueta 75), Slimani.

Rangers (1) 2 *(Morelos 15, 49)*

Sparta Prague (0) 0 48,370

Rangers: (4231) McGregor; Tavernier, Goldson, Bassey, Barisic; Davis (Lundstram 89), Kamara; Hagi (Patterson 66), Aribo (Arfield 81), Kent (Sakala 81); Morelos.
Sparta Prague: (4231) Holec; Wiesner, Panak, Krejci II, Hancko; Pavelka, Sacek; Haraslin (Moberg Karlsson 59), Hlozek (Pulkrab 85), Krejci (Karabec 59); Minchev (Dockal 58).

Thursday, 9 December 2021

Lyon (0) 1 *(Bassey 48 (og))*

Rangers (1) 1 *(Wright S 41)* 26,842

Lyon: (4231) Pollersbeck; Vogel (Dubois 62), Da Silva, Lukeba, Henrique; Keita, Caqueret (Bruno Guimaraes 76); Cherki, Shaqiri (Aouar 62), Toko Ekambi (Kadewere 44); Dembele (Slimani 76).
Rangers: (4231) McLaughlin; Patterson, Goldson, Bassey, Barisic; Lundstram, Kamara (Davis 46); Wright S (Arfield 61), Hagi (Bacuna 61), Kent; Roofe (Aribo 73).

Sparta Prague (1) 2 *(Hancko 43, Hlozek 49)*

Brondby (0) 0 976

Sparta Prague: (4231) Holec; Wiesner■, Panak, Krejci II, Hancko; Pavelka, Soucek; Pesek (Krejci 69), Hlozek, Haraslin (Minchev 86); Pulkrab (Vindheim 60).
Brondby: (352) Hermansen; Heggheim (Greve 46), Maxso, Rosted; Mensah, Frendrup, Radosevic (Cappis 61), Ben Slimane■, Riveros (Bruus 61); Hedlund (Sidhu 72), Uhre (Kvistgaarden 80).

Group A Table	*P*	*W*	*D*	*L*	*F*	*A*	*GD*	*Pts*
Lyon	6	5	1	0	16	5	11	16
Rangers	6	2	2	2	6	5	1	8
Sparta Prague	6	2	1	3	6	9	–3	7
Brondby	6	0	2	4	2	11	–9	2

GROUP B

Thursday, 16 September 2021

Monaco (0) 1 *(Diatta 66)*

Sturm Graz (0) 0 2500

Monaco: (4222) Nubel; Aguilar, Maripan, Pavlovic, Jakobs (Henrique 46); Matazo (Fofana 73), Tchouameni; Diatta, Gelson Martins (Golovin 46); Volland (Ben Yedder 60), Isidor (Fabregas 46).
Sturm Graz: (41212) Siebenhandl; Gazibegovic (Jager 71), Affengruber, Wuthrich (Geyrhofer 78), Dante; Stankovic; Hierlander, Kiteishvili (Prass 71); Ljubic; Yeboah (Niangbo 71), Jantscher (Sarkaria 61).

PSV Eindhoven (1) 2 *(Gotze 31, Gakpo 54)*

Real Sociedad (2) 2 *(Januzaj 34, Isak 39)* 23,135

PSV Eindhoven: (4231) Drommel; Mwene (Teze 68), Ramalho, Obispo, Max; Boscagli, van Ginkel (Thomas 63); Madueke (Vertessen 63), Gotze, Gakpo (Bruma 89); Zahavi (Vinicius 63).

Real Sociedad: (433) Remiro; Zaldua (Romero 79), Elustondo, Le Normand (Zubeldia 61), Munoz (Pacheco 61); Guevara, Zubimendi, Merino; Januzaj (Gorosabel 79), Isak (Sorloth 83), Oyarzabal.

Thursday, 30 September 2021

Real Sociedad (0) 1 *(Merino 53)*

Monaco (1) 1 *(Disasi 16)* 23,765

Real Sociedad: (433) Remiro; Zaldua (Gorosabel 71), Elustondo, Zubeldia, Munoz; Merino, Zubimendi, Guevara (Turrientes 61); Januzaj, Portu (Barrenetxea 71), Oyarzabal (Karrikaburu 90).
Monaco: (451) Nubel; Sidibe (Aguilar 46), Disasi, Badiashile, Henrique (Pavlovic 90); Diatta, Fofana (Golovin 65), Tchouameni, Jean Lucas, Diop (Maripan 74); Boadu (Volland 65).

Sturm Graz (0) 1 *(Stankovic 55)*

PSV Eindhoven (1) 4 *(Sangare 32, Zahavi 51, Max 74, Vertessen 78)* 15,026

Sturm Graz: (41212) Siebenhandl; Gazibegovic, Affengruber, Wuthrich, Dante; Stankovic; Hierlander (Lang 82), Kiteishvili (Prass 82); Ljubic (Kuen 46); Yeboah (Niangbo 78), Jantscher (Sarkaria 68).
PSV Eindhoven: (433) Drommel; Mwene, Ramalho, Boscagli, Max; van Ginkel (Obispo 81), Sangare■, Gotze (Gutierrez 81); Doan (Vertessen 65), Zahavi (Vinicius 65), Gakpo (Junior 90).

Thursday, 21 October 2021

PSV Eindhoven (0) 1 *(Gakpo 59)*

Monaco (1) 2 *(Boadu 19, Diop 89)* 33,000

PSV Eindhoven: (433) Drommel; Mwene, Ramalho, Obispo, Max; van Ginkel, Gotze, Boscagli; Madueke (Vertessen 56), Vinicius (Zahavi 87), Gakpo (Bruma 64).
Monaco: (352) Nubel; Disasi (Gelson Martins 74), Maripan, Badiashile; Aguilar, Fofana (Matazo 70), Tchouameni, Jean Lucas (Diop 75), Henrique; Volland, Boadu (Ben Yedder 70).

Sturm Graz (0) 0

Real Sociedad (0) 1 *(Isak 68)* 14,809

Sturm Graz: (4312) Siebenhandl; Gazibegovic (Jager 73), Affengruber, Wuthrich, Dante; Kuen (Geyrhofer 66), Stankovic■, Prass (Hierlander 38); Niangbo (Ljubic 66); Yeboah (Sarkaria 73), Jantscher.
Real Sociedad: (4231) Remiro; Gorosabel (Zaldua 62), Zubeldia, Le Normand, Munoz; Zubimendi (Guevara 19), Merino; Portu, Silva (Sorloth 62), Januzaj (Turrientes 77); Isak (Lobete 77).

Thursday, 4 November 2021

Monaco (0) 0

PSV Eindhoven (0) 0 5840

Monaco: (352) Nubel; Disasi (Sidibe 46), Maripan, Badiashile; Aguilar (Golovin 46), Fofana, Tchouameni, Jean Lucas (Diop 46), Henrique; Volland (Diatta 75), Boadu (Ben Yedder 66).
PSV Eindhoven: (442) Drommel; Teze, Ramalho, Boscagli, Max; Mwene, Gutierrez, Sangare, Vertessen (Bruma 45); Zahavi (Romero 89), Vinicius (Doan 58).

Real Sociedad (0) 1 *(Sorloth 53)*

Sturm Graz (1) 1 *(Jantscher 38)* 25,010

Real Sociedad: (4231) Remiro; Gorosabel, Zubeldia, Le Normand, Munoz (Rico 83); Zubimendi, Merino; Portu (Barrenetxea 65), Silva, Januzaj; Sorloth (Isak 83).
Sturm Graz: (3412) Siebenhandl; Geyrhofer, Affengruber, Wuthrich; Jager, Ljubic, Prass, Dante; Niangbo (Wels 83); Sarkaria, Jantscher (Kuen 72).

Thursday, 25 November 2021

Monaco (2) 2 *(Volland 28, Fofana 37)*

Real Sociedad (1) 1 *(Isak 35)* 3834

Monaco: (4231) Nubel; Sidibe, Maripan, Badiashile (Disasi 68), Henrique; Fofana■, Jean Lucas; Golovin (Matazo 90), Volland (Matsima 90), Diop (Gelson Martins 76); Ben Yedder (Boadu 76).
Real Sociedad: (433) Ryan; Zaldua (Gorosabel 46), Elustondo, Le Normand, Munoz; Silva (Barrenetxea 46), Zubimendi, Merino (Turrientes 66); Januzaj (Portu 75), Isak (Sorloth 73), Oyarzabal.

PSV Eindhoven (1) 2 *(Vinicius 45 (pen), Bruma 55)*

Sturm Graz (0) 0 0

PSV Eindhoven: (4231) Drommel; Mwene, Ramalho, Boscagli (Obispo 58), Junior; Gutierrez (Propper 70), Sangare; Doan (Antonisse 87), Gotze (van Ginkel 70), Bruma; Vinicius (Vertessen 58).
Sturm Graz: (4321) Siebenhandl; Jager, Affengruber, Wuthrich (Geyrhofer 75), Dante (Gazibegovic 46); Ljubic, Stankovic (Borkovic 62), Kuen (Prass 62); Sarkaria, Jantscher; Yeboah (Niangbo 62).
Behind closed doors due to COVID-19 pandemic.

Thursday, 9 December 2021

Real Sociedad (1) 3 *(Oyarzabal 43 (pen), 62, Sorloth 90)*

PSV Eindhoven (0) 0 24,950

Real Sociedad: (442) Remiro; Zaldua, Elustondo, Le Normand, Munoz; Portu (Barrenetxea 70), Zubeldia, Zubimendi (Gorosabel 86), Januzaj (Turrientes 70); Oyarzabal (Pacheco 85), Isak (Sorloth 81).
PSV Eindhoven: (4231) Drommel; Mwene (Teze 68), Ramalho, Boscagli, Junior (Max 85); Gutierrez, Sangare■; Doan (Madueke 62 (Vertessen 68)), Gakpo (Vinicius 62), Bruma; Gotze.

Sturm Graz (1) 1 *(Jantscher 6 (pen))*

Monaco (1) 1 *(Volland 30)* 0

Sturm Graz: (4321) Siebenhandl; Gazibegovic (Jager 81), Affengruber, Wuthrich, Dante; Ljubic (Stuckler 87), Stankovic, Prass; Sarkaria (Wels 82), Niangbo (Huspek 73); Jantscher (Yeboah 46).
Monaco: (4231) Majecki; Aguilar, Matsima, Pavlovic, Henrique (Jakobs 46); Matazo, Tchouameni (Jean Lucas 46); Golovin (Diop 57), Volland, Isidor (Gelson Martins 80); Ben Yedder (Boadu 46).
Behind closed doors due to COVID-19 pandemic.

Group B Table	P	W	D	L	F	A	GD	Pts
Monaco	6	3	3	0	7	4	3	12
Real Sociedad	6	2	3	1	9	6	3	9
PSV Eindhoven	6	2	2	2	9	8	1	8
Sturm Graz	6	0	2	4	3	10	–7	2

GROUP C

Wednesday, 15 September 2021

Spartak Moscow (0) 0

Legia Warsaw (0) 1 *(Kastrati 90)* 6832

Spartak Moscow: (343) Maksimenko; Rasskazov, Gigot, Dzhikija; Moses (Bakaev 82), Umiarov, Zobnin (Hendrix 23), Ayrton (Lomovitskiy 69); Larsson (Sobolev 82), Ponce, Promes.
Legia Warsaw: (3511) Boruc; Jedrzejczyk, Wieteska, Nawrocki; Johansson, Slisz, Kharatin (Kastrati 59), Luquinhas (Muci 83), Mladenovic; Josue (Rafael Lopes 90); Emreli (Pekhart 83).

Thursday, 16 September 2021

Leicester C (1) 2 *(Perez 9, Barnes 64)*

Napoli (0) 2 *(Osimhen 69, 87)* 29,579

Leicester C: (433) Schmeichel; Castagne, Evans (Soyuncu 46), Vestergaard, Bertrand; Perez (Tielemans 46), Ndidi■, Soumare (Maddison 78); Daka (Lookman 71), Iheanacho (Vardy 88), Barnes.
Napoli: (433) Ospina; Malcuit (Juan Jesus 84), Rrahmani, Koulibaly, Di Lorenzo; Zambo (Petagna 84), Fabian, Zielinski (Elmas 64); Lozano (Politano 63), Osimhen, Insigne (Ounas 74).

Thursday, 30 September 2021

Legia Warsaw (1) 1 *(Emreli 31)*

Leicester C (0) 0 27,087

Legia Warsaw: (3511) Miszta; Jedrzejczyk, Wieteska, Nawrocki; Johansson (Abu Hanna 78), Slisz, Kharatin, Andre Martins (Kastrati 70), Mladenovic; Josue (Rafael Lopes 82); Emreli (Pekhart 84).
Leicester C: (3142) Schmeichel; Amartey (Lookman 78), Vestergaard, Soyuncu; Tielemans; Castagne, Soumare, Dewsbury-Hall (Maddison 67), Thomas; Perez (Barnes 67), Daka (Vardy 82).

Napoli (1) 2 *(Elmas 1, Osimhen 90)*

Spartak Moscow (0) 3 *(Promes 55, 90, Ignatov 80)* 13,373

Napoli: (433) Meret; Di Lorenzo, Manolas, Koulibaly, Mario Rui■; Elmas (Ounas 82), Fabian, Zielinski (Zambo 46); Politano (Lozano 73), Petagna (Osimhen 46), Insigne (Malcuit 41).
Spartak Moscow: (352) Maksimenko; Caufriez■, Gigot, Dzhikija; Moses, Litvinov (Ignatov 73), Bakaev (Lomovitskiy 89), Umiarov, Ayrton; Ponce (Sobolev 45), Promes.

Wednesday, 20 October 2021

Spartak Moscow (2) 3 *(Sobolev 11, 86, Larsson 44)*

Leicester C (1) 4 *(Daka 45, 48, 54, 78)* 11,366

Spartak Moscow: (3421) Maksimenko; Rasskazov, Gigot, Dzhikija; Moses, Litvinov, Zobnin (Ignatov 68), Ayrton; Larsson (Lomovitskiy 90), Bakaev (Promes 68); Sobolev.
Leicester C: (3412) Schmeichel; Amartey, Evans (Vestergaard 82), Soyuncu; Ricardo Pereira (Albrighton 59), Tielemans (Choudhury 65), Soumare, Thomas (Bertrand 82); Maddison; Iheanacho, Daka.

Thursday, 21 October 2021

Napoli (0) 3 *(Insigne 76, Osimhen 80, Politano 90)*

Legia Warsaw (0) 0 10,346

Napoli: (433) Meret; Di Lorenzo, Manolas (Politano 72), Koulibaly, Juan Jesus; Zambo (Fabian 57), Demme, Elmas; Lozano (Osimhen 57), Mertens (Petagna 72), Insigne (Rrahmani 81).
Legia Warsaw: (3511) Miszta; Jedrzejczyk, Wieteska, Nawrocki; Johansson, Josue, Andre Martins (Kharatin 77), Luquinhas (Kastrati 71), Mladenovic; Rafael Lopes (Slisz 59); Muci (Emreli 71).

Thursday, 4 November 2021

Legia Warsaw (1) 1 *(Emreli 10)*

Napoli (0) 4 *(Zielinski 51 (pen), Mertens 75 (pen), Lozano 78, Ounas 90)* 25,706

Legia Warsaw: (343) Miszta; Johansson, Wieteska, Jedrzejczyk; Yuri Ribeiro, Josue, Slisz (Andre Martins 70), Mladenovic; Kastrati (Muci 67), Emreli (Rafael Lopes 80), Luquinhas.
Napoli: (4231) Meret; Di Lorenzo, Rrahmani, Koulibaly, Juan Jesus; Zambo, Demme (Lobotka 65); Lozano (Ounas 83), Zielinski (Mertens 73), Elmas (Politano 65); Petagna (Zanoli 83).

Leicester C (0) 1 *(Amartey 58)*

Spartak Moscow (0) 1 *(Moses 51)* 30,222

Leicester C: (352) Schmeichel; Amartey, Evans, Soyuncu; Castagne, Soumare (Dewsbury-Hall 83), Perez (Ndidi 58), Tielemans, Bertrand (Lookman 58); Daka (Vardy 71), Iheanacho.
Spartak Moscow: (3412) Selikhov; Caufriez, Gigot, Dzhikija; Moses, Litvinov (Kutepov 90), Zobnin, Ayrton; Ignatov (Lomovitskiy 87); Sobolev (Bakaev 77), Promes (Umiarov 77).

Wednesday, 24 November 2021

Spartak Moscow (2) 2 *(Sobolev 3 (pen), 28)*

Napoli (0) 1 *(Elmas 64)* 10,852

Spartak Moscow: (352) Selikhov; Caufriez, Gigot, Dzhikija; Moses (Rasskazov 83), Umiarov, Ignatov (Lomovitskiy 72), Litvinov, Ayrton; Sobolev, Promes (Larsson 90).
Napoli: (4231) Meret; Di Lorenzo, Koulibaly, Juan Jesus, Mario Rui; Zielinski, Lobotka (Rrahmani 79); Lozano, Mertens, Elmas; Petagna.

Thursday, 25 November 2021

Leicester C (3) 3 *(Daka 11, Maddison 21, Ndidi 33)*

Legia Warsaw (1) 1 *(Mladenovic 26)* 30,658

Leicester C: (433) Schmeichel; Castagne, Amartey, Soyuncu, Thomas; Soumare (Dewsbury-Hall 62), Ndidi, Maddison (Perez 63); Lookman (Albrighton 84), Daka (Iheanacho 85), Barnes.
Legia Warsaw: (343) Miszta; Johansson (Holownia 46), Wieteska, Jedrzejczyk; Yuri Ribeiro, Andre Martins (Celhaka 71), Slisz, Mladenovic (Skibicki 71); Muci, Emreli (Wlodarczyk 78), Luquinhas (Pekhart 78).

Thursday, 9 December 2021

Legia Warsaw (0) 0

Spartak Moscow (1) 1 *(Bakaev 17)* 21,629

Legia Warsaw: (4231) Boruc; Johansson, Wieteska, Nawrocki, Yuri Ribeiro; Andre Martins (Wlodarczyk 72), Slisz (Kharatin 65); Kastrati (Skwierczynski 90), Josue (Rafael Lopes 65), Luquinhas; Emreli (Pekhart 72).
Spartak Moscow: (3421) Selikhov; Caufriez, Gigot, Dzhikija; Moses, Umiarov, Zobnin (Hendrix 77), Ayrton; Ignatov (Melkadze 77), Promes; Bakaev (Lomovitskiy 88).

Napoli (2) 3 *(Ounas 4, Elmas 24, 53)*

Leicester C (2) 2 *(Evans 27, Dewsbury-Hall 33)* 14,646

Napoli: (4231) Meret; Di Lorenzo, Rrahmani, Juan Jesus, Mario Rui; Demme (Manolas 78), Zielinski; Lozano (Malcuit 45), Ounas (Mertens 63), Elmas; Petagna.
Leicester C: (4231) Schmeichel; Castagne, Evans, Soyuncu, Bertrand; Tielemans (Soumare 77), Ndidi; Maddison, Dewsbury-Hall (Albrighton 89), Barnes (Daka 72); Vardy.

Group C Table	*P*	*W*	*D*	*L*	*F*	*A*	*GD*	*Pts*
Spartak Moscow	6	3	1	2	10	9	1	10
Napoli	6	3	1	2	15	10	5	10
Leicester C	6	2	2	2	12	11	1	8
Legia Warsaw	6	2	0	4	4	11	–7	6

GROUP D

Thursday, 16 September 2021

Eintracht Frankfurt (1) 1 *(Lammers 41)*

Fenerbahce (1) 1 *(Ozil 10)* 25,000

Eintracht Frankfurt: (442) Trapp; Da Costa, N'Dicka, Hinteregger, Durm; Kamada, Sow, Jakic, Kostic; Borre (Hauge 72), Lammers.
Fenerbahce: (343) Bayindir; Aziz, Kim, Szalai; Samuel, Yandas (Meyer 77), Gustavo, Kadioglu (Gumuskaya 77); Ozil (Pelkas 77), Rossi, Valencia (Berisha 76).

Olympiacos (0) 2 *(El Arabi 52, Reabciuk 87)*

Antwerp (0) 1 *(Samatta 74)* 15,615

Olympiacos: (442) Vaclik; Karbownik, Papastathopoulos, Cisse, Reabciuk; Camara A (Vrousai 81), M'Vila (Valbuena 76), Bouchalakis, Onyekuru (Tiquinho Soares 81); Camara M (Kunde 81), El Arabi (Ba 88).
Antwerp: (442) Butez; Buta, Dinis Almeida, De Laet, Bataille■; Miyoshi (Benson 67), Verstraete, Nainggolan (Gerkens 67), Fischer; Samatta, Frey (Eggestein 80).

Thursday, 30 September 2021

Antwerp (0) 0

Eintracht Frankfurt (0) 1 *(Paciencia 90 (pen))* 13,000

Antwerp: (442) Butez; Buta, Dinis Almeida, Dessoleil, De Laet; Benson (Miyoshi 77), Verstraete, Nainggolan, Fischer; Eggestein (Frey 46), Samatta (Gerkens 67).
Eintracht Frankfurt: (3412) Trapp; Toure, Hasebe (Ilsanker 72), Hinteregger; Chandler, Sow (Tuta 90), Jakic, Kostic; Hrustic (Kamada 46); Borre (Paciencia 86), Lammers (Lindstrom 72).

Fenerbahce (0) 0

Olympiacos (1) 3 *(Tiquinho Soares 6, Masouras 62, 68)* 22,160

Fenerbahce: (3421) Bayindir; Novak, Kim, Szalai; Samuel, Yandas (Meyer 75), Gustavo (Zajc 70), Kadioglu (Sanliturk 84); Pelkas, Rossi (Berisha 70); Valencia (Gumuskaya 75).
Olympiacos: (4141) Vaclik; Ba (Lala 46), Papastathopoulos, Cisse, Reabciuk; Bouchalakis; Masouras (Valbuena 89), Camara M (Vrousai 89), Camara A, Onyekuru (Kunde 64); Tiquinho Soares (El Arabi 86).

Thursday, 21 October 2021

Eintracht Frankfurt (2) 3 *(Borre 26 (pen), Toure 45, Kamada 59)*

Olympiacos (1) 1 *(El Arabi 30 (pen))* 35,000

Eintracht Frankfurt: (3412) Trapp; Tuta (N'Dicka 60), Hasebe, Hinteregger; Toure (Durm 82), Jakic, Sow (Hauge 88), Kostic; Kamada; Borre, Paciencia (Rode 82).

Olympiacos: (433) Vaclik; Lala (Androutsos 77), Papastathopoulos, Cisse, Reabciuk; Camara M (Kunde 65), M'Vila (Onyekuru 61), Bouchalakis; Masouras (Lopes 77), El Arabi (Tiquinho Soares 65), Camara A.

Fenerbahce (2) 2 *(Valencia 20, 45 (pen))*
Antwerp (1) 2 *(Samatta 2, Gerkens 62)* 16,629
Fenerbahce: (3412) Bayindir; Tisserand, Kim, Szalai (Novak 87); Samuel, Sosa (Zajc 67), Gustavo, Kadioglu (Sangare 67); Ozil (Pelkas 66); Berisha (Rossi 66), Valencia.
Antwerp: (433) Butez; Bataille, Dinis Almeida, De Laet, Vines; Gerkens, Verstraete, Yusuf (Dwomoh 63); Samatta, Frey (Benson 70), Fischer (Balikwisha 46).

Thursday, 4 November 2021

Antwerp (0) 0
Fenerbahce (3) 3 *(Yandas 9, Meyer 16, Berisha 29)* 0
Antwerp: (433) Butez; Bataille (Balikwisha 77), Dinis Almeida, De Laet, Vines; Gerkens (Dwomoh 68), Verstraete, Yusuf (Dessoleil 46); Benson (Miyoshi 62), Frey, Fischer (Samatta 61).
Fenerbahce: (352) Ozer; Tisserand (Szalai 73), Kim, Novak; Kadioglu (Sangare 73), Yandas (Zajc 65), Sosa (Pelkas 80), Meyer, Samuel; Kahveci (Rossi 64), Berisha.
Played behind closed doors due to crowd trouble at the match against Eintracht Frankfurt on 30 September 2021.

Olympiacos (1) 1 *(El Arabi 12)*
Eintracht Frankfurt (1) 2 *(Kamada 17, Hauge 90)* 23,050
Olympiacos: (4231) Vaclik; Lala, Papastathopoulos, Ba, Reabciuk; Camara M (Kunde 89), M'Vila; Masouras (Lopes 83), Camara A, Onyekuru (Valbuena 71); El Arabi (Tiquinho Soares 83).
Eintracht Frankfurt: (3412) Trapp; Tuta, Hasebe, N'Dicka; Barkok (Toure 58), Sow (Ilsanker 82), Jakic (Rode 78), Chandler; Kamada; Borre (Hauge 78), Lammers (Lindstrom 58).

Thursday, 25 November 2021

Eintracht Frankfurt (1) 2 *(Kamada 13, Paciencia 90)*
Antwerp (1) 2 *(Nainggolan 33, Samatta 88)* 30,000
Eintracht Frankfurt: (3421) Trapp; Tuta, Hasebe, N'Dicka; Chandler, Jakic (Rode 90), Sow, Kostic; Lindstrom (Hauge 78), Kamada (Paciencia 90); Borre (Lammers 69).
Antwerp: (4312) Butez; De Laet, Dinis Almeida, Dessoleil, Vines; Dwomoh (Yusuf 66), Verstraete, Nainggolan; Fischer (Eggestein 76); Frey, Samatta.

Olympiacos (0) 1 *(Tiquinho Soares 89)*
Fenerbahce (0) 0 22,405
Olympiacos: (4231) Vaclik; Lala, Papastathopoulos (Ba 25), Cisse, Reabciuk; Camara M (Bouchalakis 46), M'Vila; Masouras (Valbuena 68), Camara A, Onyekuru (Lopes 46); El Arabi (Tiquinho Soares 81).
Fenerbahce: (433) Ozer; Samuel, Tisserand, Kim, Novak (Szalai 78); Yandas (Gumuskaya 90), Sosa, Zajc (Meyer 65); Kahveci (Pelkas 65), Berisha, Rossi (Kadioglu 78).

Thursday, 9 December 2021

Antwerp (1) 1 *(Balikwisha 6)*
Olympiacos (0) 0 7992
Antwerp: (41212) Butez; De Laet (Quirynen 57), Dinis Almeida, Dessoleil (Engels 57), Bataille; Verstraete; Dwomoh, Gerkens; Eggestein (Frey 73); Benson (Samatta 73), Balikwisha (Yusuf 87).
Olympiacos: (4231) Vaclik; Lala (Androutsos 66), Papastathopoulos, Cisse, Reabciuk; M'Vila, Bouchalakis (Camara A 46); Lopes (Masouras 46), Camara M, Onyekuru (Vrousai 60); Tiquinho Soares (El Arabi 46).

Fenerbahce (1) 1 *(Berisha 42)*
Eintracht Frankfurt (1) 1 *(Sow 29)* 8932
Fenerbahce: (343) Ozer; Aziz, Kim, Szalai; Sangare, Sosa (Gustavo 72), Zajc (Meyer 76), Novak (Samuel 72); Kahveci (Rossi 76), Berisha, Pelkas (Gumuskaya 81).
Eintracht Frankfurt: (3421) Trapp; Tuta, Hasebe, N'Dicka; Chandler (Da Costa 69), Jakic (Rode 69), Sow (Hrustic 78), Kostic; Hauge (Lammers 69), Kamada; Borre (Paciencia 60).

Group D Table	P	W	D	L	F	A	GD	Pts
Eintracht Frankfurt	6	3	3	0	10	6	4	12
Olympiacos	6	3	0	3	8	7	1	9
Fenerbahce	6	1	3	2	7	8	−1	6
Antwerp	6	1	2	3	6	10	−4	5

GROUP E

Thursday, 16 September 2021

Galatasaray (0) 1 *(Strakosha 66 (og))*
Lazio (0) 0 15,353
Galatasaray: (4231) Muslera; Yedlin, Nelsson, Marcao, van Aanholt; Kutlu, Antalyali (Kilinc 78); Morutan (Feghouli 85), Cicaldau (Luyindama 90), Akturkoglu (Babel 79); Dervisoglu (Mohamed 90).
Lazio: (433) Strakosha; Lazzari, Felipe, Acerbi, Hysaj; Akpa Akpro (Milinkovic-Savic 56), Lucas (Cataldi 83), Luis Alberto (Basic 65); Felipe Anderson (Pedro 66), Immobile (Muriqi 56), Zaccagni.

Lokomotiv Moscow (0) 1 *(Anjorin 89)*
Marseille (0) 1 *(Under 59 (pen))* 8100
Lokomotiv Moscow: (433) Guilherme; Jedvaj, Magkeev, Murilo, Tiknizyan■; Kulikov (Maradishvili 56), Barinov, Beka Beka (Silyanov 64); Zhemaletdinov (Anjorin 63), Smolov (Lisakovich 75), Kamano (Kerk 75).
Marseille: (3331) Pau Lopez; Saliba, Alvaro, Luan Peres; Rongier, Kamara, Gerson (Gueye 83); Under, Guendouzi (Lirola 83), Dieng (Luis Henrique 82); Harit (de la Fuente 56).

Thursday, 30 September 2021

Lazio (2) 2 *(Basic 13, Patric Gil 38)*
Lokomotiv Moscow (0) 0 6767
Lazio: (433) Strakosha; Lazzari (Marusic 74), Patric Gil, Acerbi, Hysaj; Luis Alberto (Milinkovic-Savic 60), Cataldi (Lucas 60), Basic; Felipe Anderson, Immobile (Muriqi 41), Pedro (Moro 74).
Lokomotiv Moscow: (433) Guilherme; Zhivoglyadov, Barinov, Pablo Castro, Rybchinsky; Maradishvili (Kerk 72), Kulikov, Beka Beka; Smolov, Zhemaletdinov (Lisakovich 82), Anjorin (Petrov 82).

Marseille (0) 0
Galatasaray (0) 0 49,870
Marseille: (3331) Pau Lopez; Saliba, Alvaro, Luan Peres; Lirola, Gueye, Guendouzi; Under, Harit (de la Fuente 79), Dieng (Milik 61); Payet.
Galatasaray: (4231) Muslera; Boey (Yedlin 65), Nelsson, Marcao, van Aanholt; Kutlu (Luyindama 87), Antalyali; Morutan (Kilinc 72), Cicaldau, Akturkoglu (Babel 87); Dervisoglu (Diagne 72).

Thursday, 21 October 2021

Lazio (0) 0
Marseille (0) 0 8329
Lazio: (433) Strakosha; Lazzari, Felipe, Acerbi, Marusic; Milinkovic-Savic (Akpa Akpro 56), Cataldi (Lucas 77), Basic (Luis Alberto 57); Felipe Anderson (Pedro 56), Immobile, Zaccagni (Moro 77).
Marseille: (4231) Pau Lopez; Rongier (Balerdi 85), Saliba, Caleta-Car, Luan Peres; Guendouzi (Gueye 73), Kamara; Under, Payet, Lirola (Dieng 61); Milik (Gerson 73).

Lokomotiv Moscow (0) 0
Galatasaray (0) 1 *(Akturkoglu 82)* 8100
Lokomotiv Moscow: (442) Guilherme; Rybus (Zhivoglyadov 89), Jedvaj, Pablo Castro, Tiknizyan; Kerk, Barinov, Beka Beka, Maradishvili; Zhemaletdinov, Smolov.
Galatasaray: (4231) Muslera; Yedlin, Nelsson, Marcao, van Aanholt (Bayram 90); Antalyali, Kutlu; Yilmaz (Akturkoglu 67), Cicaldau (Luyindama 90), Babel (Morutan 76); Mohamed (Diagne 76).

Thursday, 4 November 2021

Galatasaray (1) 1 *(Feghouli 43)*

Lokomotiv Moscow (0) 1 *(Kamano 72)* 27,776

Galatasaray: (4141) Muslera; Yedlin, Nelsson, Marcao, van Aanholt (Bayram 76); Kutlu; Feghouli (Yilmaz 71), Morutan (Mohamed 76), Cicaldau, Akturkoglu; Dervisoglu (Diagne 89).
Lokomotiv Moscow: (442) Guilherme; Nenakhov (Zhivoglyadov 46), Barinov, Jedvaj, Rybus; Kerk, Maradishvili, Beka Beka (Murilo 85), Rybchinsky (Kamano 65); Zhemaletdinov, Lisakovich (Smolov 46).

Marseille (1) 2 *(Milik 33 (pen), Payet 82)*

Lazio (1) 2 *(Felipe Anderson 45, Immobile 49)* 59,163

Marseille: (4411) Pau Lopez; Rongier, Saliba, Caleta-Car, Luan Peres; Under, Guendouzi, Kamara (Harit 55), Lirola (Gueye 85); Payet; Milik.
Lazio: (433) Strakosha; Lazzari (Marusic 26), Felipe, Acerbi, Hysaj; Luis Alberto (Akpa Akpro 75), Lucas (Cataldi 52), Basic (Milinkovic-Savic 52); Felipe Anderson (Moro 75), Immobile, Pedro.

Thursday, 25 November 2021

Galatasaray (2) 4 *(Cicaldau 12, Caleta-Car 30 (og), Feghouli 64, Babel 83)*

Marseille (0) 2 *(Milik 68, 85)* 39,758

Galatasaray: (4141) Muslera; Yedlin, Nelsson, Marcao, van Aanholt; Antalyali; Feghouli (Luyindama 82), Cicaldau (Morutan 51), Kutlu (Elmaz 90), Akturkoglu (Babel 82); Diagne (Mohamed 90).
Marseille: (4132) Pau Lopez; Lirola, Saliba, Caleta-Car, Luan Peres; Kamara; Guendouzi, Gerson, Gueye (de la Fuente 63); Dieng, Milik.

Lokomotiv Moscow (0) 0

Lazio (0) 3 *(Immobile 56 (pen), 63 (pen), Pedro 87)* 8100

Lokomotiv Moscow: (442) Khudiakov; Nenakhov (Silyanov 28), Jedvaj, Murilo, Rybus; Maradishvili (Zinovich 77), Barinov, Beka Beka, Rybchinsky (Smolov 59); Lisakovich, Kamano (Borisenko 77).
Lazio: (433) Strakosha; Patric Gil, Felipe, Acerbi, Hysaj; Luis Alberto (Milinkovic-Savic 59), Lucas (Cataldi 59), Basic; Felipe Anderson (Pedro 46), Immobile (Muriqi 66), Zaccagni (Lazzari 82).

Thursday, 9 December 2021

Lazio (0) 0

Galatasaray (0) 0 13,178

Lazio: (433) Strakosha; Hysaj (Lazzari 63), Felipe, Acerbi, Marusic; Milinkovic-Savic, Lucas (Cataldi 73), Basic (Luis Alberto 73); Pedro (Felipe Anderson 63), Immobile, Zaccagni.
Galatasaray: (433) Muslera; Yedlin, Nelsson, Marcao, van Aanholt; Feghouli (Morutan 63), Antalyali, Kutlu (Luyindama 88); Akturkoglu (Mohamed 88), Diagne (Bayram 69), Babel (Kilinc 63).

Marseille (1) 1 *(Milik 35)*

Lokomotiv Moscow (0) 0 42,614

Marseille: (433) Mandanda; Rongier■, Balerdi, Saliba, Luan Peres; Guendouzi (Lirola 69), Gueye (Kamara 68), Gerson; Under (Luis Henrique 86), Milik (Payet 68), de la Fuente (Dieng 82).
Lokomotiv Moscow: (442) Khudiakov; Nenakhov, Jedvaj, Pablo Castro (Lisakovich 84), Rybus; Babkin, Maradishvili (Tiknizyan 56), Beka Beka, Petrov; Smolov, Kamano (Rybchinsky 32).

Group E Table	P	W	D	L	F	A	GD	Pts
Galatasaray	6	3	3	0	7	3	4	12
Lazio	6	2	3	1	7	3	4	9
Marseille	6	1	4	1	6	7	–1	7
Lokomotiv Moscow	6	0	2	4	2	9	–7	2

GROUP F

Thursday, 16 September 2021

FC Midtjylland (1) 1 *(Isaksen 3)*

Ludogorets Razgrad (1) 1 *(Despodov 32)* 6568

FC Midtjylland: (343) Olafsson; Dalsgaard, Sviatchenko, Juninho; Andersson, Nwadike, Evander, Paulinho (Cools 85); Isaksen (Lind 75), Sisto (Charles 86), Junior Brumado (Mabil 75).
Ludogorets Razgrad: (433) Kahlina; Cicinho, Plastun, Josue Sa, Nedyalkov (Pinas 54); Alex Santana (Yankov 74), Goncalves, Badji; Tekpetey (Verdon 74), Manu (Sotiriou 54), Despodov (Tchibota 60).

Red Star Belgrade (0) 2 *(Rodic 74, Katai 85 (pen))*

Braga (0) 1 *(Galeno 76)* 24,671

Red Star Belgrade: (4231) Borjan; Gobeljic, Degenek, Dragovic, Rodic; Sanogo (Pankov 87), Ivanic; Ben (Diony 39), Kanga, Katai (Srnic 87); Zivkovic (Krsticic 65).
Braga: (352) Matheus Magalhaes; Vitor Tormena, Paulo Oliveira (Nuno Sequeira 87), Diogo Leite; Fabiano (Yan Couto 86), Piazon (Fabio Martins 78), Lucas Mineiro (Andre Horta 78), Al Musrati, Galeno; Ruiz (Gonzalez 70), Ricardo Horta.

Thursday, 30 September 2021

Braga (0) 3 *(Galeno 55 (pen), 90, Ricardo Horta 62)*

FC Midtjylland (1) 1 *(Evander 19 (pen))* 5449

Braga: (343) Matheus Magalhaes; Paulo Oliveira, Diogo Leite, Nuno Sequeira (Moura 46); Yan Couto, Castro (Gonzalez 46), Al Musrati (Lucas Mineiro 72), Galeno; Piazon (Iuri Medeiros 61), Chiquinho, Ricardo Horta (Andre Horta 82).
FC Midtjylland: (343) Olafsson; Dalsgaard, Sviatchenko, Juninho■; Andersson, Nwadike (Cajuste 70), Evander, Paulinho; Isaksen (Marrony 71), Sisto (Lind 79), Junior Brumado.

Ludogorets Razgrad (0) 0

Red Star Belgrade (0) 1 *(Kanga 64)* 3078

Ludogorets Razgrad: (3412) Kahlina; Josue Sa (Despodov 71), Plastun, Verdon; Cicinho■, Badji (Show 88), Alex Santana (Tchibota 78), Pinas (Ikoko 71); Goncalves; Tekpetey, Sotiriou.
Red Star Belgrade: (3412) Popovic; Erakovic, Sanogo, Pankov; Gobeljic, Kanga (Stanic 71 (Krsticic 86)), Srnic, Rodic; Ivanic; Ben (Zivkovic 86), Diony (Pavkov 57).

Thursday, 21 October 2021

FC Midtjylland (0) 1 *(Dyhr 78)*

Red Star Belgrade (0) 1 *(Ivanic 58)* 8438

FC Midtjylland: (3412) Olafsson; Dalsgaard, Sviatchenko, Paulinho; Andersson, Cajuste (Lind 62), Nwadike, Dyhr (Mabil 90); Evander; Isaksen (Marrony 73), Sisto.
Red Star Belgrade: (4231) Borjan; Gobeljic, Dragovic, Degenek, Rodic; Srnic (Krsticic 46), Sanogo; Falco (Diony 56), Kanga (Pankov 81), Ivanic; Ben (Gajic 90).

Ludogorets Razgrad (0) 0

Braga (1) 1 *(Ricardo Horta 7)* 2280

Ludogorets Razgrad: (4231) Kahlina; Ikoko, Josue Sa, Verdon (Plastun 46), Pinas; Badji (Mitkov 87), Goncalves (Alex Santana 70); Tekpetey (Tchibota 59), Yankov (Manu 59), Despodov; Sotiriou.
Braga: (433) Matheus Magalhaes; Fabiano, Paulo Oliveira, Diogo Leite, Nuno Sequeira; Castro (Chiquinho 77), Al Musrati, Ricardo Horta (Lucas Mineiro 77); Iuri Medeiros (Piazon 60), Ruiz (Gonzalez 60), Galeno (Moura 90).

Thursday, 4 November 2021

Braga (3) 4 *(Al Musrati 25, Iuri Medeiros 37, Galeno 40, Gonzalez 73)*

Ludogorets Razgrad (1) 2 *(Sotiriou 33, Plastun 79)* 6221

Braga: (442) Matheus Magalhaes; Yan Couto, Paulo Oliveira, Diogo Leite, Nuno Sequeira (Bruno Rodrigues 74); Iuri Medeiros, Castro (Andre Horta 70), Al Musrati (Lucas Mineiro 62), Galeno (Moura 70); Vitor Oliveira (Gonzalez 61), Ricardo Horta.

Ludogorets Razgrad: (4231) Kahlina; Ikoko, Plastun, Verdon, Cicinho; Goncalves, Show (Badji 65); Despodov, Yankov, Tchibota (Tekpetey 65); Sotiriou (Manu 75).

Red Star Belgrade (0) 0

FC Midtjylland (0) 1 *(Kanga 56 (og))* 23,070

Red Star Belgrade: (4231) Borjan; Gobeljic■, Dragovic, Degenek■, Rodic (Erakovic 83); Kanga (Zivkovic 74), Sanogo; Ben (Diony 83), Katai (Pankov 63), Ivanic; Pavkov.
FC Midtjylland: (3412) Lossl; Dalsgaard, Sviatchenko, Paulinho; Andersson (Cools 75), Charles (Cajuste 66), Nwadike, Dyhr (Juninho 84); Evander; Isaksen (Hansen 85), Sisto (Lind 75).

Thursday, 25 November 2021

FC Midtjylland (1) 3 *(Sviatchenko 2, Isaksen 48, Evander 90 (pen))*

Braga (1) 2 *(Ricardo Horta 43, Galeno 85)* 7189

FC Midtjylland: (343) Lossl; Dalsgaard, Sviatchenko, Juninho; Andersson, Nwadike (Cajuste 88), Evander, Paulinho (Dyhr 72); Isaksen, Sisto (Lind 88), Junior Brumado (Charles 72).
Braga: (433) Tiago Sa; Yan Couto, Paulo Oliveira, Bruno Rodrigues (Moura 72), Diogo Leite; Castro (Chiquinho 58), Lucas Mineiro, Galeno; Iuri Medeiros (Ruiz 71), Vitor Oliveira (Gonzalez 72), Ricardo Horta.

Red Star Belgrade (0) 1 *(Ivanic 57)*

Ludogorets Razgrad (0) 0 11,252

Red Star Belgrade: (532) Borjan; Gajic, Pankov, Dragovic, Erakovic, Srnic; Kanga (Sanogo 82), Petrovic (Krsticic 67), Ivanic; Katai (Ben 46), Pavkov (Lazetic 81).
Ludogorets Razgrad: (4231) Padt; Ikoko, Terziev, Plastun, Pinas; Goncalves (Show 65), Badji (Mitkov 88); Despodov (Manu 65), Yankov, Tchibota (Rotariu 77); Sotiriou.

Thursday, 9 December 2021

Braga (0) 1 *(Galeno 52 (pen))*

Red Star Belgrade (0) 1 *(Katai 70 (pen))* 5344

Braga: (3421) Matheus Magalhaes; Paulo Oliveira, Raul Silva, Diogo Leite (Piazon 83); Yan Couto, Al Musrati, Andre Horta (Ruiz 71), Galeno (Moura 65); Iuri Medeiros (Lucas Mineiro 71), Ricardo Horta; Vitor Oliveira (Gonzalez 83).
Red Star Belgrade: (3421) Borjan; Erakovic, Dragovic, Pankov (Degenek 77); Gobeljic (Gajic 62), Kanga, Srnic (Ben 62), Rodic; Ivanic, Katai (Krsticic 77); Zivkovic (Pavkov 62).

Ludogorets Razgrad (0) 0

FC Midtjylland (0) 0 556

Ludogorets Razgrad: (4231) Padt; Ikoko, Plastun, Verdon, Cicinho; Goncalves, Badji; Yankov (Rotariu 76), Show (Pinas 90), Despodov; Sotiriou (Manu 63).
FC Midtjylland: (3421) Lossl; Dalsgaard, Juninho, Paulinho (Sviatchenko 88); Andersson, Charles, Evander, Dyhr (Cools 78); Isaksen, Junior Brumado (Sorensen 68); Sisto (Lind 78).

Group F Table	P	W	D	L	F	A	GD	Pts
Red Star Belgrade	6	3	2	1	6	4	2	11
Braga	6	3	1	2	12	9	3	10
FC Midtjylland	6	2	3	1	7	7	0	9
Ludogorets Razgrad	6	0	2	4	3	8	–5	2

GROUP G

Thursday, 16 September 2021

Bayer Leverkusen (1) 2 *(Palacios 37, Wirtz 69)*

Ferencvaros (1) 1 *(Mmaee R 8)* 11,013

Bayer Leverkusen: (4231) Hradecky; Frimpong, Kossounou, Tah, Sinkgraven (Hincapie 67); Palacios (Aranguiz 50), Demirbay; Diaby, Wirtz (Amiri 81), Adli (Bellarabi 67); Alario (Schick 66).
Ferencvaros: (532) Dibusz; Wingo, Blazic, Mmaee S, Civic, Zubkov (Cabraja 86); Zachariassen, Vecsei (Uzuni 66), Loncar (Gavric 76); Mmaee R, Nguen.

Real Betis (2) 4 *(Miranda 32, Juanmi 34, 53, Iglesias 50)*

Celtic (2) 3 *(Ajeti 13, Juranovic 27 (pen), Ralston 87)* 30,893

Real Betis: (4231) Bravo; Montoya, Gonzalez E, Victor Ruiz, Miranda (Alex Moreno 69); Canales (Gonzalez R 82), Guardado (William Carvalho 69); Joaquin (Ruibal 54), Fekir (Rodriguez 68), Juanmi; Iglesias.
Celtic: (433) Hart; Ralston, Carter-Vickers, Starfelt, Juranovic; Rogic, Soro (McCarthy 56), Turnbull; Jota, Ajeti, Montgomery.

Thursday, 30 September 2021

Celtic (0) 0

Bayer Leverkusen (2) 4 *(Hincapie 25, Wirtz 35, Alario 58 (pen), Adli 90)* 55,436

Celtic: (4231) Hart; Ralston, Carter-Vickers, Starfelt, Montgomery; McGregor (McCarthy 66), Turnbull (Giakoumakis 74); Abada, Rogic (Bitton 66), Jota; Furuhashi (Ajeti 74).
Bayer Leverkusen: (4231) Hradecky; Frimpong, Tah, Hincapie, Bakker; Aranguiz (Amiri 65), Demirbay; Diaby (Bellarabi 65), Wirtz (Adli 74), Paulinho (Retsos 79); Alario (Schick 74).

Ferencvaros (1) 1 *(Uzuni 44)*

Real Betis (1) 3 *(Fekir 17, Wingo 75 (og), Tello 90)* 16,759

Ferencvaros: (3421) Dibusz; Blazic, Mmaee S, Botka (Zubkov 81); Wingo, Laidouni (Loncar 89), Vecsei, Civic; Zachariassen (Nguen 61), Uzuni; Mmaee R.
Real Betis: (4231) Rui Silva; Montoya, Pezzella, Bartra, Alex Moreno; Akouokou (Rodriguez 57), Guardado; Sanchez (Gonzalez R 81), Fekir, Joaquin (Tello 57); Iglesias (Willian Jose 57).

Tuesday, 19 October 2021

Celtic (0) 2 *(Furuhashi 57, Vecsei 81 (og))*

Ferencvaros (0) 0 50,427

Celtic: (433) Hart; Ralston, Carter-Vickers, Starfelt, Montgomery (Scales 75); Rogic (Bitton 71), McGregor, Turnbull; Abada (Giakoumakis 71), Furuhashi (Johnston 86), Jota.
Ferencvaros: (433) Dibusz; Wingo, Blazic, Mmaee S, Civic; Zachariassen (Loncar 66), Vecsei, Laidouni (Somalia 67); Uzuni, Mmaee R, Nguen (Mak 83).

Thursday, 21 October 2021

Real Betis (0) 1 *(Iglesias 75 (pen))*

Bayer Leverkusen (0) 1 *(Andrich 82)* 39,230

Real Betis: (4231) Bravo; Montoya, Pezzella, Gonzalez E, Miranda (Alex Moreno 46); Rodriguez, William Carvalho; Joaquin (Lainez 46), Fekir (Canales 64), Ruibal (Juanmi 71); Iglesias (Willian Jose 85).
Bayer Leverkusen: (4231) Hradecky; Frimpong, Tah, Tapsoba, Hincapie (Bakker 76); Demirbay, Andrich; Bellarabi (Paulinho 76), Adli (Wirtz 69), Diaby (Palacios 90); Alario (Schick 69).

Thursday, 4 November 2021

Bayer Leverkusen (1) 4 *(Diaby 42, 52, Wirtz 86, Amiri 90)*

Real Betis (0) 0 15,208

Bayer Leverkusen: (442) Hradecky; Frimpong (Retsos 88), Tah, Tapsoba, Hincapie (Sinkgraven 77); Paulinho (Palacios 69), Andrich, Demirbay■, Diaby; Adli (Amiri 77), Wirtz (Kossounou 88).
Real Betis: (4231) Rui Silva; Bellerin, Bartra, Victor Ruiz, Miranda (Alex Moreno 46); Rodriguez, William Carvalho (Canales 46); Joaquin (Juanmi 79), Fekir■, Ruibal (Sanchez 59); Iglesias (Willian Jose 72).

Ferencvaros (1) 2 *(Juranovic 11 (og), Uzuni 86)*

Celtic (2) 3 *(Furuhashi 3, Jota 23, Abada 60)* 16,501

Ferencvaros: (4231) Bogdan; Somalia, Blazic, Mmaee S, Civic (Cabraja 73); Vecsei (Loncar 73), Laidouni; Zubkov (Szantho 81), Zachariassen (Mak 67), Nguen (Mmaee R 67); Uzuni.
Celtic: (4141) Hart; Ralston, Carter-Vickers, Welsh (Scales 89), Juranovic; Bitton (McCarthy 78); Abada (Forrest 70), Turnbull, McGregor, Jota (Johnston 70); Furuhashi (Giakoumakis 70).

Thursday, 25 November 2021

Bayer Leverkusen (1) 3 *(Andrich 16, 82, Diaby 87)*

Celtic (1) 2 *(Juranovic 40 (pen), Jota 56)* 19,830

Bayer Leverkusen: (442) Hradecky; Frimpong, Kossounou, Tah, Hincapie (Sinkgraven 75); Diaby, Andrich, Palacios, Paulinho (Amiri 75); Adli, Wirtz (Tapsoba 89).
Celtic: (4141) Hart; Ralston, Carter-Vickers, Welsh, Juranovic; Bitton (McCarthy 76); Forrest (Abada 72), Turnbull, McGregor, Jota (Johnston 72); Furuhashi (Ajeti 76).

Real Betis (1) 2 *(Tello 5, Canales 52)*

Ferencvaros (0) 0 30,137

Real Betis: (4231) Bravo (Rui Silva 71); Bellerin, Bartra, Gonzalez E, Miranda; Rodriguez, Canales; Joaquin (Lainez 72), Gonzalez R (Guardado 67), Tello; Iglesias.
Ferencvaros: (532) Dibusz; Botka (Wingo 79), Blazic, Kovacevic, Mmaee S, Cabraja; Zachariassen (Gavric 88), Vecsei (Laidouni 71), Loncar; Nguen (Szantho 88), Mmaee R (Mak 71).

Thursday, 9 December 2021

Celtic (1) 3 *(Welsh 3, Henderson 72, Turnbull 78 (pen))*

Real Betis (0) 2 *(Bain 69 (og), Iglesias 74)* 54,548

Celtic: (4231) Bain; Urhoghide, Bitton, Welsh, Scales; Soro (Turnbull 65), McCarthy; Abada, Shaw (McGregor 65), Montgomery (Johnston 65); Ajeti (Furuhashi 28 (Henderson 71)).
Real Betis: (4231) Rui Silva; Ruibal (Montoya 75), Pezzella, Gonzalez E, Miranda (Alex Moreno 75); Akouokou, William Carvalho (Willian Jose 79); Lainez (Canales 63), Joaquin, Tello (Juanmi 79); Iglesias.

Ferencvaros (0) 1 *(Laidouni 82)*

Bayer Leverkusen (0) 0 12,127

Ferencvaros: (3142) Dibusz; Blazic, Mmaee S, Kovacevic; Laidouni; Botka, Zachariassen (Somalia 71), Loncar (Vecsei 81), Zubkov (Cabraja 88); Uzuni, Nguen (Mmaee R 46).
Bayer Leverkusen: (4231) Lunev; Retsos, Kossounou, Tapsoba (Tah 46), Sinkgraven; Aranguiz (Frimpong 71), Palacios (Andrich 64); Bellarabi (Diaby 71), Amiri, Paulinho; Alario (Adli 81).

Group G Table	P	W	D	L	F	A	GD	Pts
Bayer Leverkusen	6	4	1	1	14	5	9	13
Real Betis	6	3	1	2	12	12	0	10
Celtic	6	3	0	3	13	15	–2	9
Ferencvaros	6	1	0	5	5	12	–7	3

GROUP H

Thursday, 16 September 2021

Dinamo Zagreb (0) 0

West Ham U (1) 2 *(Antonio 21, Rice 50)* 12,344

Dinamo Zagreb: (3421) Livakovic; Theophile-Catherine (Juric 46), Lauritsen, Sutalo; Ristovski (Moharrami 63), Misic (Tolic 75), Franjic, Orsic (Menalo 83); Ademi, Ivanusec (Gojak 84); Petkovic.
West Ham U: (4231) Fabianski; Fredericks, Diop, Zouma, Cresswell; Rice (Noble 82), Soucek; Vlasic (Bowen 69), Lanzini (Benrahma 52), Fornals (Masuaku 83); Antonio (Yarmolenko 83).

Rapid Vienna (0) 0

Genk (0) 1 *(Onuachu 90)* 18,400

Rapid Vienna: (442) Gartler; Stojkovic, Greiml (Wimmer 83), Hofmann, Ullmann (Auer 74); Arase (Schick 58), Aiwu, Grahovac (Petrovic 58), Grull; Fountas (Knasmullner 74), Kara.
Genk: (433) Vandevoordt; Munoz, Cuesta, Lucumi, Arteaga; Thorstvedt, Eiting (McKenzie 90), Heynen; Ito, Onuachu, Bongonda (Ndayishimiye 46).

Thursday, 30 September 2021

Genk (0) 0

Dinamo Zagreb (2) 3 *(Ivanusec 10, Petkovic 45 (pen), 67 (pen))* 11,262

Genk: (433) Vandevoordt; Munoz■, Cuesta, Lucumi, Arteaga; Toma (Preciado 70), Heynen, Thorstvedt (Bongonda 64); Ito (Eiting 70), Onuachu (Ugbo 76), Paintsil (Ndayishimiye 64).
Dinamo Zagreb: (4411) Livakovic; Ristovski, Lauritsen, Theophile-Catherine, Franjic (Leovac 70); Ivanusec (Baturina 83), Misic, Ademi (Gojak 64), Orsic; Petkovic (Andric 83); Cop (Menalo 70).

West Ham U (1) 2 *(Rice 29, Benrahma 90)*

Rapid Vienna (0) 0 58,000

West Ham U: (4231) Areola; Johnson, Dawson, Diop, Cresswell; Noble (Soucek 62), Rice; Yarmolenko (Fornals 76), Vlasic (Lanzini 62), Benrahma; Antonio (Bowen 62).
Rapid Vienna: (4231) Gartler; Aiwu, Greiml (Stojkovic 62), Wimmer, Ullmann (Auer 74); Petrovic (Ljubicic 81), Grahovac; Arase, Knasmullner, Fountas (Kitagawa 62); Kara (Grull 62).

Thursday, 21 October 2021

Rapid Vienna (2) 2 *(Grull 9, Hofmann 34)*

Dinamo Zagreb (1) 1 *(Orsic 24)* 22,300

Rapid Vienna: (3421) Gartler; Stojkovic, Greiml, Hofmann (Wimmer 90); Arase (Schick 89), Aiwu, Ljubicic, Ullmann; Fountas (Ballo 70), Grull; Kara (Kitagawa 89).
Dinamo Zagreb: (4411) Livakovic; Ristovski (Moharrami 78), Lauritsen (Sutalo 46), Theophile-Catherine, Franjic; Menalo, Misic, Gojak (Baturina 46), Orsic; Ivanusec (Tolic 78); Petkovic (Andric 39).

West Ham U (1) 3 *(Dawson 45, Diop 57, Bowen 58)*

Genk (0) 0 45,980

West Ham U: (4231) Areola; Johnson, Dawson, Diop, Cresswell (Fredericks 67); Soucek, Rice (Noble 67); Yarmolenko, Lanzini (Chesters 89), Vlasic (Fornals 83); Bowen (Benrahma 83).
Genk: (433) Vandevoordt; Preciado, Cuesta (Sadick 46), Lucumi, Arteaga; Hrosovsky, Heynen, Thorstvedt (Toma 83); Ito (Oyen 83), Onuachu (Ugbo 73), Bongonda (Ndayishimiye 73).

Thursday, 4 November 2021

Dinamo Zagreb (2) 3 *(Petkovic 12, Andric 34, Sutalo 83)*

Rapid Vienna (1) 1 *(Knasmullner 8)* 7835

Dinamo Zagreb: (4231) Livakovic; Moharrami (Ristovski 89), Sutalo, Theophile-Catherine, Franjic; Gojak, Misic; Ivanusec (Menalo 73), Petkovic, Orsic (Spikic 89); Andric (Bulat 79).
Rapid Vienna: (4231) Gartler; Aiwu, Hofmann, Moormann (Querfeld 21), Ullmann; Grahovac (Bosnjak 81), Ljubicic; Arase (Schick 46), Knasmullner, Grull (Ballo 69); Kara (Kitagawa 69).

Genk (1) 2 *(Paintsil 4, Soucek 87 (og))*

West Ham U (0) 2 *(Benrahma 59, 82)* 12,239

Genk: (4231) Vandevoordt; Munoz (Preciado 87), Sadick, Lucumi, Arteaga; Thorstvedt (Ugbo 87), Hrosovsky; Ito, Heynen, Paintsil (Oyen 90); Onuachu.
West Ham U: (4231) Areola; Coufal, Dawson, Diop, Cresswell; Noble (Soucek 58), Rice; Benrahma, Lanzini (Kral 85), Masuaku (Fornals 58); Antonio (Bowen 58).

Thursday, 25 November 2021

Dinamo Zagreb (1) 1 *(Menalo 35)*

Genk (1) 1 *(Ugbo 45)* 6892

Dinamo Zagreb: (4411) Livakovic; Moharrami (Bulat 86), Sutalo, Theophile-Catherine, Franjic; Menalo (Spikic 69), Misic, Ademi (Gojak 76), Orsic (Andric 76); Ivanusec; Petkovic (Cop 86).
Genk: (433) Vandevoordt; Preciado, Sadick, McKenzie, Arteaga; Heynen, Hrosovsky, Eiting (Thorstvedt 66); Ito (Paintsil 67), Ugbo, Bongonda.

Rapid Vienna (0) 0

West Ham U (2) 2 *(Yarmolenko 39, Noble 45 (pen))* 0

Rapid Vienna: (4231) Gartler; Stojkovic, Aiwu, Hofmann, Moormann; Petrovic, Ljubicic (Grahovac 90); Arase (Ballo 75), Knasmullner (Grull 59), Kitagawa (Kara 59); Fountas (Strunz 90).
West Ham U: (4231) Areola; Coufal, Dawson, Diop, Masuaku (Fredericks 77); Noble, Soucek (Kral 65); Yarmolenko, Lanzini (Fornals 65), Vlasic (Perkins 78); Bowen (Benrahma 65).
Behind closed doors due to COVID-19 pandemic.

Thursday, 9 December 2021

Genk (0) 0

Rapid Vienna (1) 1 *(Ljubicic 29)* 10,018

Genk: (433) Vandevoordt; Preciado (Oyen 78), Sadick (Lucumi 46), McKenzie, Arteaga (Juklerod 69); Thorstvedt, Hrosovsky, Paintsil; Bongonda, Ugbo (Onuachu 46), Ito (Cuesta 46).
Rapid Vienna: (4231) Gartler; Stojkovic, Aiwu, Moormann, Ullmann (Dijakovic 89); Petrovic, Ljubicic (Grahovac 75); Schick, Knasmullner (Kitagawa 46), Grull (Auer 75); Kara (Strunz 40).

West Ham U (0) 0

Dinamo Zagreb (1) 1 *(Orsic 3)* 49,401

West Ham U: (4231) Areola; Ashby, Baptiste, Alese, Longelo; Kral, Noble; Yarmolenko (Potts 87), Fornals (Benrahma 46), Vlasic; Perkins (Appiah-Forson 87).
Dinamo Zagreb: (352) Livakovic; Theophile-Catherine, Sutalo, Peric; Ristovski, Gojak, Ademi (Bulat 71), Ivanusec, Stefulj (Dilaver 80); Andric (Juric 64), Orsic (Misic 64).

Group H Table	P	W	D	L	F	A	GD	Pts
West Ham U	6	4	1	1	11	3	8	13
Dinamo Zagreb	6	3	1	2	9	6	3	10
Rapid Vienna	6	2	0	4	4	9	–5	6
Genk	6	1	2	3	4	10	–6	5

KNOCK-OUT STAGE

PLAY-OFFS FIRST LEG

Thursday, 17 February 2022

Atalanta (0) 2 *(Djimsiti 61, 63)*

Olympiacos (1) 1 *(Tiquinho Soares 16)* 9448

Atalanta: (3421) Musso; Toloi, Demiral, Djimsiti; Maehle (Hateboer 87), de Roon (Freuler 72), Pessina (Koopmeiners 46), Pezzella; Malinovsky (Mihaila 66), Pasalic; Muriel (Boga 46).
Olympiacos: (343) Vaclik; Papastathopoulos, Manolas, Cisse; Lala, M'Vila (Bouchalakis 85), Camara A, Reabciuk; Masouras (Camara M 64), Tiquinho Soares (El Arabi 72), Onyekuru (Lopes 85).

Barcelona (0) 1 *(Torres 59 (pen))*

Napoli (1) 1 *(Zielinski 29)* 73,525

Barcelona: (433) ter Stegen; Mingueza (Dest 81), Pique, Garcia, Jordi Alba; Gonzalez N (Gavi 65), de Jong F (Busquets 65), Gonzalez P; Traore (Dembele 65), Aubameyang (de Jong L 85), Torres.
Napoli: (4231) Meret; Di Lorenzo, Rrahmani, Koulibaly, Juan Jesus; Fabian, Zambo (Malcuit 84); Elmas (Mario Rui 84), Zielinski (Demme 80), Insigne (Ounas 72); Osimhen (Mertens 80).

Borussia Dortmund (0) 2 *(Bellingham 51, Guerreiro 82)*

Rangers (2) 4 *(Tavernier 38 (pen), Morelos 41, Lundstram 49, Zagadou 54 (og))* 10,000

Borussia Dortmund: (4231) Kobel; Akanji (Schulz 55), Hummels, Zagadou, Guerreiro; Dahoud, Witsel (Reyna 46); Brandt (Moukoko 46), Reus (Reinier 82), Bellingham; Malen (Tigges 68).
Rangers: (4231) McGregor; Tavernier, Goldson, Bassey, Barisic; Jack (Kamara 86), Lundstram; Arfield (Sands 66), Aribo (Ramsey 86), Kent; Morelos (Wright S 90).

Porto (1) 2 *(Martinez 37, 49)*

Lazio (1) 1 *(Zaccagni 23)* 32,929

Porto: (442) Costa D; Joao Mario (Costa B 88), Mbemba, Pepe K, Sanusi; Otavio, Uribe, Grujic (Galeno 46), Pepe E (Stephen Eustaquio 88); Vieira (Vitinha 46), Martinez (Evanilson 69).
Lazio: (433) Strakosha; Marusic, Felipe, Patric Gil, Radu (Hysaj 72); Milinkovic-Savic, Lucas (Cataldi 68), Luis Alberto (Basic 84); Felipe Anderson, Pedro (Cabral 84), Zaccagni (Moro 84).

RB Leipzig (1) 2 *(Nkunku 30, Forsberg 82 (pen))*

Real Sociedad (1) 2 *(Le Normand 8, Oyarzabal 64 (pen))* 21,113

RB Leipzig: (3412) Gulacsi; Simakan, Adams (Henrichs 46), Gvardiol; Klostermann, Laimer (Forsberg 63), Kampl (Haidara 86), Angelino; Olmo (Poulsen 79); Nkunku (Szoboszlai 80), Andre Silva.
Real Sociedad: (541) Ryan; Zaldua, Elustondo, Le Normand, Zubeldia, Rico (Munoz 61); Portu, Merino (Illarramendi 90), Rafinha (Pacheco 78), Oyarzabal (Martin 90); Sorloth.

Sevilla (3) 3 *(Rakitic 13 (pen), Ocampos 44, Martial 45)*

Dinamo Zagreb (1) 1 *(Orsic 41)* 28,372

Sevilla: (4231) Bounou; Kounde, Diego Carlos, Rekik (Gudelj 50), Acuna; Rakitic, Fernando (Torres 61); Ocampos (Jesus Navas 84), Gomez, Munir (Delaney 61); Martial (En-Nesyri 61).
Dinamo Zagreb: (343) Livakovic; Theophile-Catherine (Lauritsen 46), Sutalo, Franjic; Ristovski (Moharrami 77), Gojak, Ademi, Bockaj (Stefulj 70); Juric (Emreli 58), Petkovic (Spikic 76), Orsic.

Sheriff Tiraspol (1) 2 *(Thill 43 (pen), Traore 82)*

Braga (0) 0 3062

Sheriff Tiraspol: (343) Athanasiadis; Evangelou, Radeljic, Petro; Bruno, Nikolov (Kyabou 89), Thill (Cojocaru 90), Julien; Traore, Yakhshiboev (Belousov 89), Yansane (Basit 78).
Braga: (3421) Matheus Magalhaes; Bruno Rodrigues, Paulo Oliveira, Vitor Tormena; Yan Couto, Al Musrati, Castro (Andre Horta 64), Rodrigo Gomes (Moura 64); Iuri Medeiros (Fernandes 79 (Fale 86)), Ricardo Horta; Vitor Oliveira (Ruiz 64).

Zenit St Petersburg (2) 2 *(Dzyuba 25, Malcom 28)*

Real Betis (3) 3 *(Rodriguez 8, Willian Jose 18, Guardado 41)* 28,936

Zenit St Petersburg: (4411) Kerzhakov; Karavaev (Mostovoy 46), Chistyakov (Erokhin 88), Rakitskiy (Krugovoy 46), Douglas Santos; Malcom, Barrios, Wendel, Claudinho (Yuri Alberto 65); Kuzyaev; Dzyuba (Sergeev 73).
Real Betis: (4231) Rui Silva; Sabaly, Pezzella, Gonzalez, Alex Moreno; Rodriguez, Guardado; Ruibal (Bellerin 86), Joaquin (William Carvalho 58), Juanmi (Tello 58); Willian Jose (Iglesias 78).

PLAY-OFFS SECOND LEG

Thursday, 24 February 2022

Braga (2) 2 *(Iuri Medeiros 17, Ricardo Horta 43)*

Sheriff Tiraspol (0) 0 9423

Braga: (3421) Matheus Magalhaes; Fabiano, Carmo, Vitor Tormena; Yan Couto (Bruno Rodrigues 89), Al Musrati, Andre Horta (Castro 90), Rodrigo Gomes (Moura 64); Iuri Medeiros (Ruiz 74), Ricardo Horta; Vitor Oliveira (Fale 109).
Sheriff Tiraspol: (352) Athanasiadis; Petro, Radeljic, Dulanto; Bruno, Traore, Addo, Thill, Julien; Yansane (Nikolov 46), Yakhshiboev (Basit 111).
aet; Braga won 3-2 on penalties.

Dinamo Zagreb (0) 1 *(Orsic 65 (pen))*

Sevilla (0) 0 9788

Dinamo Zagreb: (3412) Livakovic; Theophile-Catherine, Sutalo, Franjic; Ristovski (Spikic 62), Tolic (Bulat 53), Misic, Stefulj (Bockaj 62); Gojak (Menalo 75); Petkovic (Emreli 62), Orsic.
Sevilla: (433) Bounou; Montiel (Jesus Navas 46), Kounde, Diego Carlos (Delaney■ 46), Acuna; Rakitic (Jordan 71), Fernando, Gomez; Ocampos, Mir (En-Nesyri 81), Corona (Torres 71).
Sevilla won 3-2 on aggregate.

Lazio (1) 2 *(Immobile 19, Cataldi 90)*

Porto (1) 2 *(Taremi 31 (pen), Uribe 68)* 24,948

Lazio: (433) Strakosha; Marusic, Felipe, Patric Gil, Radu (Hysaj 54); Milinkovic-Savic, Lucas (Cataldi 54), Luis Alberto; Felipe Anderson, Immobile, Pedro (Moro 71).
Porto: (442) Costa D; Costa B, Mbemba, Pepe K, Sanusi; Otavio, Uribe, Vitinha (Grujic 78), Pepe E (Joao Mario 69); Taremi (Evanilson 79), Martinez (Galeno 56).
Porto won 4-3 on aggregate.

Napoli (1) 2 *(Insigne 23 (pen), Politano 87)*

Barcelona (3) 4 *(Jordi Alba 8, de Jong F 13, Pique 45, Aubameyang 59)* 37,858

Napoli: (4231) Meret; Di Lorenzo, Rrahmani, Koulibaly, Mario Rui; Fabian (Ounas 74), Demme (Politano 46); Elmas, Zielinski (Mertens 73), Insigne (Petagna 82); Osimhen (Ghoulam 74).
Barcelona: (433) ter Stegen; Dest, Araujo, Pique, Jordi Alba; Gonzalez P (Gonzalez N 75), Busquets (Gavi 62), de Jong F; Traore (Dembele 74), Aubameyang (de Jong L 75), Torres (Puig 82).
Barcelona won 5-3 on aggregate.

Olympiacos (0) 0

Atalanta (1) 3 *(Maehle 40, Malinovsky 66, 69)* 15,835

Olympiacos: (3421) Vaclik; Manolas, Papastathopoulos, Cisse (Masouras 46); Lala (El Arabi 67), Camara M, M'Vila (Vrousai 67), Reabciuk; Camara A, Onyekuru (Valbuena 60); Tiquinho Soares (Fadiga 74).
Atalanta: (3421) Musso; Toloi, Demiral (Cittadini 90), Djimsiti; Hateboer, de Roon, Freuler, Maehle (Pezzella 83); Pessina (Koopmeiners 57), Pasalic (Boga 56); Malinovsky (Mihaila 84).
Atalanta won 5-1 on aggregate.

Rangers (1) 2 *(Tavernier 22 (pen), 57)*

Borussia Dortmund (2) 2 *(Bellingham 31, Malen 42)* 47,709

Rangers: (4231) McGregor; Tavernier, Goldson, Bassey, Barisic (Balogun 46); Jack, Lundstram; Arfield (Kamara 69), Aribo, Kent; Morelos.
Borussia Dortmund: (4231) Kobel; Meunier (Wolf 46), Can, Hummels, Schulz; Dahoud, Bellingham; Brandt (Moukoko 69), Reus (Witsel 86), Hazard (Reinier 69); Malen (Tigges 77).
Rangers won 6-4 on aggregate.

Real Betis (0) 0

Zenit St Petersburg (0) 0 44,236

Real Betis: (4231) Rui Silva; Bellerin, Pezzella, Gonzalez, Alex Moreno; Rodriguez, Guardado (Tello 90); Canales (William Carvalho 70), Fekir (Joaquin 83), Ruibal; Willian Jose (Iglesias 83).
Zenit St Petersburg: (343) Odoevskiy; Barrios, Chistyakov, Douglas Santos; Sutormin (Mostovoy 86), Claudinho, Wendel, Krugovoy; Malcom, Dzyuba (Sergeev 64), Yuri Alberto (Erokhin 84).
Real Betis won 3-2 on aggregate.

Real Sociedad (0) 1 *(Zubimendi 65)*

RB Leipzig (1) 3 *(Orban 39, Andre Silva 59, Forsberg 89 (pen))* 30,113

Real Sociedad: (541) Ryan; Zaldua, Elustondo, Le Normand (Silva 62), Zubeldia, Munoz; Portu (Januzaj 62), Rafinha (Sorloth 84), Zubimendi, Oyarzabal; Isak (Djouahra 90).
RB Leipzig: (3412) Gulacsi; Simakan, Orban, Gvardiol; Klostermann, Laimer (Haidara 64), Kampl (Adams 90), Henrichs (Angelino 64); Olmo (Poulsen 79); Andre Silva (Forsberg 64), Nkunku.
RB Leipzig won 5-3 on aggregate.

ROUND OF 16 FIRST LEG

Wednesday, 9 March 2022

Porto (0) 0

Lyon (0) 1 *(Lucas Paqueta 59)* 26,309

Porto: (442) Costa D; Joao Mario (Galeno 80), Mbemba, Pepe K (Semedo 46), Sanusi; Otavio (Francisco Conceicao 88), Vitinha, Uribe, Pepe E; Evanilson (Martinez 72), Taremi (Vieira 80).
Lyon: (4231) Lopes; Dubois (Gusto 83), Thiago Mendes, Lukeba, Emerson Palmieri; Caqueret, Ndombele; Faivre (Aouar 80), Lucas Paqueta, Toko Ekambi; Dembele.

Real Betis (1) 1 *(Fekir 30)*

Eintracht Frankfurt (2) 2 *(Kostic 14, Kamada 32)* 36,574

Real Betis: (4231) Bravo; Sabaly, Pezzella, Gonzalez, Ruibal (Tello 77); Rodriguez, William Carvalho (Miranda 61); Canales, Fekir, Juanmi (Joaquin 61); Willian Jose (Iglesias 77).
Eintracht Frankfurt: (343) Trapp; Tuta, Hinteregger, N'Dicka; Knauff, Jakic, Sow, Kostic; Lindstrom (Hauge 73), Borre (Lammers 86), Kamada (Lenz 78).

Thursday, 10 March 2022

Atalanta (2) 3 *(Malinovsky 23, Muriel 25, 49)*

Bayer Leverkusen (1) 2 *(Aranguiz 11, Diaby 63)* 13,134

Atalanta: (3412) Musso; Toloi, Demiral, Djimsiti (Palomino 69); Hateboer, de Roon, Freuler, Zappacosta (Maehle 77); Koopmeiners; Malinovsky (Boga 69), Muriel (Miranchuk 77).
Bayer Leverkusen: (4231) Hradecky; Frimpong (Fosu-Mensah 80), Tah, Tapsoba, Bakker; Aranguiz, Palacios; Diaby, Wirtz (Azmoun 85), Adli (Paulinho 80); Alario (Kossounou 61).

Barcelona (0) 0

Galatasaray (0) 0 61,740

Barcelona: (433) ter Stegen; Dest, Araujo (Pique 46), Garcia, Jordi Alba; Gonzalez N (Busquets 46), de Jong F, Gonzalez P; Traore (de Jong L 80), Torres (Dembele 46), Depay (Aubameyang 61).
Galatasaray: (4231) Pena; Boey, Nelsson, Marcao, van Aanholt; Antalyali, Kulu; Babel (Kilinc 68), Feghouli (Cicaldau 79), Akturkoglu (Yilmaz 90); Mohamed (Gomis 68).

Braga (1) 2 *(Ruiz 3, Vitor Oliveira 89)*

Monaco (0) 0 10,228

Braga: (3421) Matheus Magalhaes; Fabiano, Carmo, Vitor Tormena; Yan Couto (Paulo Oliveira 65), Al Musrati, Andre Horta (Castro 74), Rodrigo Gomes (Fale 80); Iuri Medeiros (Moura 65), Ricardo Horta; Ruiz (Vitor Oliveira 65).
Monaco: (4231) Nubel; Vanderson, Disasi, Matsima (Badiashile 46), Henrique; Matazo (Golovin 58), Tchouameni; Jean Lucas, Volland (Diop 83), Gelson Martins; Ben Yedder (Boadu 77).

Rangers (2) 3 *(Tavernier 11 (pen), Morelos 15, Balogun 51)*

Red Star Belgrade (0) 0 48,589

Rangers: (4231) McGregor; Tavernier, Goldson, Balogun, Bassey; Lundstram, Jack (Sands 75); Aribo (Sakala 75), Kamara, Kent; Morelos.
Red Star Belgrade: (4231) Borjan; Piccini (Gajic 72), Erakovic, Dragovic, Rodic; Srnic (Ben 61), Sanogo; Katai (Motika 84), Kanga, Ivanic; Omoijuanfo (Pavkov 61).

Sevilla (0) 1 *(Munir 60)*

West Ham U (0) 0 34,728

Sevilla: (4231) Bounou; Jesus Navas, Kounde, Gudelj, Acuna; Torres, Jordan; Corona (Augustinsson 87), Munir (Martial 75), Ocampos; En-Nesyri (Mir 90).
West Ham U: (433) Areola; Johnson, Dawson, Zouma, Cresswell; Soucek, Rice, Lanzini (Noble 83); Vlasic (Benrahma 67), Antonio, Fornals (Masuaku 90).

ROUND OF 16 SECOND LEG

Thursday, 17 March 2022

Bayer Leverkusen (0) 0

Atalanta (0) 1 *(Boga 90)* 19,871

Bayer Leverkusen: (3412) Hradecky; Tah, Tapsoba, Hincapie; Fosu-Mensah (Bellarabi 61), Palacios (Azmoun 61), Aranguiz (Alario 82), Bakker; Demirbay (Andrich 61); Diaby, Adli.
Atalanta: (3421) Musso; Toloi (Djimsiti 10), Demiral, Palomino; Hateboer, de Roon, Freuler, Zappacosta (Pezzella 78); Malinovsky (Boga 65), Koopmeiners; Muriel (Pessina 79).
Atalanta won 4-2 on aggregate.

Eintracht Frankfurt (0) 1 *(Rodriguez 120 (og))*
Real Betis (0) 1 *(Iglesias 90)* 25,000

Eintracht Frankfurt: (343) Trapp; Tuta, Hinteregger, N'Dicka; Knauff, Jakic, Sow (Rode 104), Kostic; Lindstrom (Lammers 104), Borre (Paciencia 83), Kamada (Hauge 66).
Real Betis: (4231) Rui Silva; Sabaly, Pezzella, Bartra, Miranda (Juanmi 46); Rodriguez, Canales (William Carvalho 67); Joaquin (Lainez 67), Fekir (Sanchez 111), Ruibal; Willian Jose (Iglesias 79).
aet; Eintracht Frankfurt won 3-2 on aggregate.

Galatasaray (1) 1 *(Marcao 28)*
Barcelona (1) 2 *(Gonzalez P 37, Aubameyang 49)* 50,110

Galatasaray: (4231) Pena; Boey, Nelsson, Marcao, van Aanholt (Bayram 85); Antalyali, Kulu; Babel (Dervisoglu 74), Cicaldau (Morutan 74), Akturkoglu; Gomis (Mohamed 63).
Barcelona: (433) ter Stegen; Dest (Araujo 56), Garcia, Pique (Lenglet 81), Jordi Alba; de Jong F (Gavi 68), Busquets, Gonzalez P; Traore (Dembele 46), Aubameyang (Depay 82), Torres.
Barcelona won 2-1 on aggregate.

Lyon (1) 1 *(Dembele 13)*
Porto (1) 1 *(Pepe E 27)* 54,551

Lyon: (4231) Lopes; Dubois, Thiago Mendes, Lukeba, Emerson Palmieri; Caqueret, Ndombele; Faivre (Aouar 65), Lucas Paqueta, Toko Ekambi; Dembele (Kadewere 65).
Porto: (433) Costa D; Costa B (Joao Mario 56), Mbemba, Pepe K, Sanusi; Vieira, Grujic (Vitinha 79), Stephen Eustaquio (Uribe 57); Pepe E, Martinez (Taremi 74), Galeno (Evanilson 74).
Lyon won 2-1 on aggregate.

Monaco (0) 1 *(Disasi 90)*
Braga (1) 1 *(Ruiz 19)* 3892

Monaco: (442) Nubel; Vanderson (Aguilar 84), Disasi, Badiashile, Henrique (Jakobs 62); Diop (Golovin 52), Tchouameni, Jean Lucas (Maripan 52), Gelson Martins (Boadu 52); Ben Yedder, Volland.
Braga: (352) Matheus Magalhaes; Paulo Oliveira, Carmo, Vitor Tormena; Fabiano, Castro (Iuri Medeiros 76), Al Musrati, Andre Horta (Lucas Mineiro 69), Rodrigo Gomes (Moura 62); Ruiz (Vitor Oliveira 76), Ricardo Horta.
Braga won 3-1 on aggregate.

Red Star Belgrade (1) 2 *(Ivanic 10, Ben 90 (pen))*
Rangers (0) 1 *(Kent 56)* 47,024

Red Star Belgrade: (41212) Borjan; Piccini (Gajic 57), Erakovic, Dragovic, Rodic (Falco 72); Sanogo; Kanga, Ivanic (Motika 72); Katai; Omoijuanfo (Ben 63), Pavkov.
Rangers: (4231) McGregor; Tavernier, Goldson, Balogun, Bassey; Lundstram (Barisic 81), Jack (Sands 69); Aribo (Arfield 68), Kamara, Kent (Wright S 90); Morelos (Roofe 80).
Rangers won 4-2 on aggregate.

West Ham U (1) 2 *(Soucek 39, Yarmolenko 112)*
Sevilla (0) 0 59,981

West Ham U: (433) Areola; Johnson, Dawson, Zouma, Cresswell; Soucek, Rice, Lanzini (Noble 115); Fornals (Diop 119), Antonio (Fredericks 120), Benrahma (Yarmolenko 87).
Sevilla: (433) Bounou; Jesus Navas (Montiel 106), Kounde, Gudelj (Carmona 111), Augustinsson; Jordan, Delaney, Rakitic (Torres 56); Corona (Munir 96), En-Nesyri (Mir 91), Martial (Cruz 102).
aet; West Ham U won 2-1 on aggregate.

QUARTER-FINALS FIRST LEG

Thursday, 7 April 2022

Braga (1) 1 *(Ruiz 40)*
Rangers (0) 0 20,331

Braga: (343) Matheus Magalhaes; Fabiano, Carmo, Vitor Tormena; Yan Couto (Paulo Oliveira 89), Al Musrati (Castro 83), Andre Horta (Lucas Mineiro 82), Rodrigo Gomes; Iuri Medeiros (Fale 75), Ruiz (Vitor Oliveira 75), Ricardo Horta.
Rangers: (433) McGregor; Tavernier, Goldson, Balogun (Barisic 62), Bassey; Kamara, Lundstram, Jack (Aribo 63); Arfield, Sakala (Roofe 62), Kent.

Eintracht Frankfurt (0) 1 *(Knauff 48)*
Barcelona (0) 1 *(Torres 66)* 48,000

Eintracht Frankfurt: (3421) Trapp; Tuta■, Hinteregger, N'Dicka; Knauff, Jakic (Rode 89), Sow, Kostic; Lindstrom (Hauge 73), Kamada (Toure 81); Borre (Ache 89).
Barcelona: (433) ter Stegen; Araujo, Pique (Lenglet 23), Garcia, Jordi Alba; Gonzalez P, Busquets, Gavi (de Jong F 61); Traore (Dembele 62), Aubameyang, Torres.

RB Leipzig (0) 1 *(Zappacosta 58 (og))*
Atalanta (1) 1 *(Muriel 17)* 36,029

RB Leipzig: (3412) Gulacsi; Klostermann, Orban, Gvardiol (Halstenberg 73); Henrichs (Mukiele 87), Laimer, Kampl, Angelino; Olmo (Szoboszlai 73); Nkunku (Novoa 87), Andre Silva (Forsberg 62).
Atalanta: (4231) Musso; Hateboer, Demiral, Palomino, Zappacosta (Pezzella 89); de Roon, Freuler (Miranchuk 67); Pessina (Scalvini 61), Koopmeiners, Pasalic (Boga 61); Muriel (Zapata 61).

West Ham U (0) 1 *(Bowen 52)*
Lyon (0) 1 *(Ndombele 66)* 59,978

West Ham U: (4231) Areola; Fredericks, Dawson, Zouma, Cresswell■; Soucek, Rice; Bowen, Fornals, Benrahma (Johnson 46); Antonio.
Lyon: (4411) Lopes; Gusto, Boateng (Toko Ekambi 64), Lukeba, Emerson Palmieri; Faivre (Tete 63), Thiago Mendes (Denayer 90), Ndombele, Aouar; Lucas Paqueta; Dembele.

QUARTER-FINALS SECOND LEG

Thursday, 14 April 2022

Atalanta (0) 0
RB Leipzig (1) 2 *(Nkunku 18, 87 (pen))* 25,000

Atalanta: (3421) Musso; de Roon, Demiral (Scalvini 70), Palomino; Hateboer, Koopmeiners, Freuler (Pasalic 88), Zappacosta; Malinovsky (Muriel 58), Boga (Miranchuk 70); Zapata.
RB Leipzig: (3421) Gulacsi; Simakan, Orban, Gvardiol (Poulsen 79); Henrichs (Klostermann 73), Laimer (Adams 73), Kampl (Halstenberg 79), Angelino; Olmo, Nkunku; Andre Silva (Szoboszlai 63).
RB Leipzig won 3-1 on aggregate.

Barcelona (0) 2 *(Depay 90 (pen), Busquets 90)*
Eintracht Frankfurt (2) 3 *(Kostic 4 (pen), 67, Borre 36)* 79,468

Barcelona: (433) ter Stegen; Mingueza (Dest 62), Araujo, Garcia (de Jong L 70), Jordi Alba; Gonzalez P (de Jong F 46), Busquets, Gavi; Dembele, Aubameyang (Traore 61), Torres (Depay 80).
Eintracht Frankfurt: (3421) Trapp; Toure (Hasebe 90), Hinteregger, N'Dicka■; Knauff (Chandler 90), Jakic, Rode (Hrustic 80), Kostic; Lindstrom (Hauge 80), Kamada; Borre (Ache 90).
Eintracht Frankfurt won 4-3 on aggregate.

Lyon (0) 0
West Ham U (2) 3 *(Dawson 38, Rice 44, Bowen 48)* 50,065

Lyon: (4231) Pollersbeck; Gusto, Denayer (Reine-Adelaide 89), Lukeba, Emerson Palmieri; Thiago Mendes, Ndombele (Lucas Paqueta 46); Faivre (Tete 46), Aouar (Barcola 71), Toko Ekambi; Dembele.
West Ham U: (4231) Areola; Coufal, Dawson, Diop, Johnson; Soucek, Rice (Benrahma 90); Bowen, Lanzini (Noble 77), Fornals; Antonio (Yarmolenko 84).
West Ham U won 4-1 on aggregate.

Rangers (2) 3 *(Tavernier 2, 44 (pen), Roofe 101)*
Braga (0) 1 *(Carmo 83)* 48,894

Rangers: (4231) McGregor; Tavernier, Goldson, Bassey, Barisic (Balogun 90); Jack (Kamara 80), Lundstram; Ramsey (Wright S 80), Aribo (Sakala 106), Kent; Roofe (Arfield 106).
Braga: (352) Matheus Magalhaes; Paulo Oliveira, Carmo (Fale 118), Vitor Tormena■; Fabiano, Castro (Gorby 106), Al Musrati (Lucas Mineiro 100), Andre Horta (Moura 46), Rodrigo Gomes (Iuri Medeiros■ 61); Ruiz (Vitor Oliveira 61), Ricardo Horta.
aet; Rangers won 3-2 on aggregate.

SEMI-FINALS FIRST LEG
Thursday, 28 April 2022

RB Leipzig (0) 1 *(Angelino 85)*
Rangers (0) 0 40,303

RB Leipzig: (3412) Gulacsi; Klostermann, Gvardiol, Halstenberg; Henrichs (Mukiele 90), Laimer, Adams, Angelino; Olmo (Forsberg 71); Szoboszlai (Andre Silva 71), Nkunku (Poulsen 89).
Rangers: (532) McGregor; Tavernier, Goldson, Lundstram, Bassey, Barisic; Jack (Sands 83), Aribo (Arfield 83), Kamara; Wright S (Sakala 69), Kent.

West Ham U (1) 1 *(Antonio 21)*
Eintracht Frankfurt (1) 2 *(Knauff 1, Kamada 54)* 60,000

West Ham U: (4231) Areola; Johnson, Dawson, Zouma, Cresswell; Soucek, Rice; Bowen, Lanzini (Benrahma 66), Fornals; Antonio.
Eintracht Frankfurt: (3421) Trapp; Tuta, Hinteregger, Toure; Knauff, Sow, Rode, Kostic; Lindstrom (Hauge 62), Kamada; Borre (Ache 90).

SEMI-FINALS SECOND LEG
Thursday, 5 May 2022

Eintracht Frankfurt (1) 1 *(Borre 26)*
West Ham U (0) 0 48,000

Eintracht Frankfurt: (343) Trapp; Tuta, Hinteregger (Toure 8), N'Dicka; Knauff, Sow, Rode (Jakic 76), Kostic; Hauge (Hrustic 82), Borre (Paciencia 83), Kamada.
West Ham U: (4231) Areola; Coufal (Yarmolenko 87), Dawson, Zouma, Cresswell■; Soucek, Rice; Bowen, Lanzini (Johnson 22), Fornals (Benrahma 74); Antonio.
Eintracht Frankfurt won 3-1 on aggregate

Rangers (2) 3 *(Tavernier 18, Kamara 24, Lundstram 80)*
RB Leipzig (0) 1 *(Nkunku 70)* 49,397

Rangers: (541) McGregor; Tavernier, Lundstram, Goldson, Bassey, Barisic; Wright S (Arfield 59), Jack (Balogun 59), Kamara, Kent; Aribo (Sakala 45).
RB Leipzig: (3421) Gulacsi; Klostermann, Orban, Gvardiol; Henrichs, Kampl, Laimer, Angelino (Halstenberg 81); Olmo (Szoboszlai 62), Nkunku; Poulsen (Andre Silva 82).
Rangers won 3-2 on aggregate.

UEFA EUROPA LEAGUE FINAL 2021–22

Wednesday, 18 May 2022

(in Seville, attendance 38,842)

Eintracht Frankfurt (0) 1 Rangers (0) 1

Eintracht Frankfurt: (3421) Trapp; Toure, Tuta (Hasebe 58), N'Dicka (Lenz 100); Knauff, Rode (Jakic 90), Sow (Hrustic 106), Kostic; Lindstrom (Hauge 71), Kamada; Borre.
Scorer: Borre 69.

Rangers: (433) McGregor; Tavernier, Goldson, Bassey, Barisic (Roofe 117); Jack (Davis 74), Lundstram, Kamara (Arfield 91); Wright S (Sakala 74 (Ramsey 118)), Aribo (Sands 101), Kent.
Scorer: Vinicius Junior 59.

aet; Eintracht Frankfurt won 5-4 on penalties.

Referee: Slavko Vincic.

Glen Kamara of Rangers finds the net against RB Leipzig in their Europa League semi-final second leg at Ibrox. (Andrew Milligan/PA Images/Alamy)

UEFA EUROPA CONFERENCE LEAGUE 2021–22

**After extra time. ▪ Denotes player sent off.*

QUALIFYING STAGE

FIRST QUALIFYING ROUND FIRST LEG

Tuesday, 6 July 2021

FK Podgorica v Laci	1-0
Mons Calpe v FC Santa Coloma	1-1
Mosta v Spartak Trnava	3-2

Thursday, 8 July 2021

Bala T v Larne	0-1
Birkirkara v La Fiorita	1-0
Domzale v Swift Hesperange	1-0
Drita v Decic	2-1
Dundalk v Newtown	4-0
Europa v Kauno Zalgiris	0-0
FC Honka v NSI Runavik	0-0
FCI Levadia v St Joseph's	3-1
Fehervar v Ararat Yerevan	1-1
FH Hafnarfjordur v Sligo R	1-0
FK Liepaja v Struga	1-1
FK RFS v KI Klaksvik	2-3
Glentoran v The New Saints	1-1
Inter Turku v Puskas Akademia	1-1
Maribor v Urartu	1-0
Milsami Orhei v Sarajevo	0-0
Noah v KuPS Kuopio	1-0
Paide Linnameeskond v Slask Wroclaw	1-2
Partizani Tirana v Sfintul Gheorghe	5-2
Racing-Union v Breidablik	2-3
Sant Julia v Gzira United	0-0
Shkupi v Llapi	2-0
Sileks v Petrocub-Hincesti	1-1
Siroki Brijeg v Vllaznia	3-1
Stjarnan v Bohemians	1-1
Suduva v Valmiera	2-1
Sutjeska v Gagra	1-0
Tre Penne v Dinamo Batumi	0-4
Velez Mostar v Coleraine	2-1
Zilina v Dila Gori	5-1

Thursday, 8 July 2021

Bala T (0) 0

Larne (1) 1 *(McDaid 2)* 197

Bala T: (442) Ramsay; Woods (Smith S 73), Stephens, Spittle, Smith K (Peate 90); Edwards, Mendes (Leslie 77), Evans (Bauress 77), Shannon; Rutherford, Venables.
Larne: (433) Ferguson; Cosgrove, Bolger, Balmer (Watson 74), Hughes; Sule, Mitchell, Jarvis; Randall (McKendry 61), Lynch, McDaid (Hale 74).

Dundalk (2) 4 *(Duffy 34, McMillan 39, Patching 62, Han 90)*

Newtown (0) 0 120

Dundalk: (442) Abibi; Jurkovskis, Boyle, Nattestad, Leahy; Patching (Zahibo 81), McEleney, Stanton, Duffy; McMillan (Midtskogen 81), Kelly (Han 75).
Newtown: (433) Jones D; Williams T, Mills-Evans, Roberts, Evans; Davies (Jones A 89), Rowland (McAllister 68), Fletcher; Rushton (Downs 89), Williams A, Breese (Hesden 89).

FH Hafnarfjordur (0) 1 *(Lennon 85)*

Sligo R (0) 0 412

FH Hafnarfjordur: (4132) Nielsen; Kristjansson, Vidarsson, Thorisson, Gunnarsson; Sverrisson; Jonsson E, Jonsson J (Gudlaugsson 90), Helgason (Dimitrijevic 82); Lennon (Heidarsson 90), Vilhjalmsson.
Sligo R: (433) McNicholas; Buckley, Banks, Blaney, Horgan; Parkes, Morahan, Bolger▪; Gibson, de Vries (Figueira 64), Byrne (Cawley 64).

Glentoran (0) 1 *(McDonagh 82)*

The New Saints (1) 1 *(Smith 13)* 1021

Glentoran: (352) Coleing; Marron, McCullough, McClean; Marshall, Smith (McDonagh 73), Bigirimana, McMenamin, Kane; McDaid, Donnelly (Mitchell 73).
The New Saints: (433) Harrison; Ebbe, Routledge, Astles, Davies K; Clarke (Williams 71), Cieslewicz (Cornish 90), McManus (Robles 80); Daykin, Davies D, Smith.

Stjarnan (1) 1 *(Atlason 25)*

Bohemians (0) 1 *(Wilson 63)* 720

Stjarnan: (433) Haraldur Bjornsson; Aegisson, Gudjonsson, Hedinsson, Bjornsson E; Ingvarsson (Halldor Bjornsson 66), Anbo, Gudmundsson (Sloth 66); Ragnarsson (Oli 86) Atlason (Haurits 66), Halldorsson.
Bohemians: (442) Talbot; Lyons, Feely, Kelly C, Wilson; Coote, Devoy, Buckley, Burt; Tierney, Kelly G.

Velez Mostar (1) 2 *(De Souza 37 (pen), 66 (pen))*

Coleraine (1) 1 *(Doherty 9)* 5000

Velez Mostar: (442) Bogdanovic; Cosic, Zvonic (Isic 46), Zeljkovic, Radovic (Zubanovic 82); Hasanovic (Prses 46), Radovac, Ovcina, Andjusic (Vehabovic 58); De Souza (Georgijevic 67), Zaimovic.
Coleraine: (433) Deane; Kane▪, Brown, Canning, Traynor (McLaughlin 83); Carson, Lowry, Wilson; Doherty, Shevlin (Jarvis 69), Glackin.

FIRST QUALIFYING ROUND SECOND LEG

Tuesday, 13 July 2021		*(agg)*
Newtown v Dundalk	0-1	0-5
Thursday, 15 July 2021		
Ararat Yerevan v Fehervar	2-0	3-1
Bohemians v Stjarnan	3-0	4-1
Breidablik v Racing-Union	2-0	5-2
Coleraine v Velez Mostar	1-2	2-4
Decic v Drita	0-1	1-3
Dila Gori v Zilina	2-1	3-6
Dinamo Batumi v Tre Penne	3-0	7-0
FC Santa Coloma v Mons Calpe	4-0	5-1
Gagra v Sutjeska	1-1	1-2
Gzira United v Sant Julia	1-1*	1-1
(Gzira United won 5-3 on penalties.)		
Kauno Zalgiris v Europa	2-0	2-0
KI Klaksvik v FK RFS	2-4*	5-6
KuPS Kuopio v Noah	5-0	5-1
La Fiorita v Birkirkara	1-1	1-2
Laci v FK Podgorica	3-0*	3-1
Larne v Bala T	1-0	2-0
Llapi v Shkupi	1-1	1-3
NSI Runavik v FC Honka	1-3	1-3
Petrocub-Hincesti v Sileks	1-0	2-1
Puskas Akademia v Inter Turku	2-0	3-1
Sarajevo v Milsami Orhei	0-1	0-1
Sfintul Gheorghe v Partizani Tirana	2-3	4-8
Slask Wroclaw v Paide Linnameeskond	2-0	4-1
Sligo R v FH Hafnarfjordur	1-2	1-3
Spartak Trnava v Mosta	2-0	4-3
St Joseph's v FCI Levadia	1-1	2-4
Struga v FK Liepaja	1-4	2-5
Swift Hesperange v Domzale	1-1	1-2
The New Saints v Glentoran	2-0	3-1
Urartu v Maribor	0-1	0-2
Valmiera v Suduva	0-0	1-2
Vllaznia v Siroki Brijeg	3-0	4-3

Tuesday, 13 July 2021

Newtown (0) 0

Dundalk (0) 1 *(Duffy 52)* 174

Newtown: (4312) Jones D; Williams T, Mills-Evans, Roberts, Arsan; Fletcher, Rowland (Rushton 61), Hughes (McAllister 86); Davies (Evans 73); Williams A, Mwandwe (Breese 73).
Dundalk: (442) Abibi; Jurkovskis, Boyle, Nattestad, Leahy (Adedokun 57); McEleney (Han 77), Patching, Stanton, Duffy (Zahibo 57); McMillan (Midtskogen 69), Kelly (O'Kane 69).

Thursday, 15 July 2021

Bohemians (1) 3 *(Kelly G 34, 54, Burt 75)*

Stjarnan (0) 0 6000

Bohemians: (442) Talbot; Lyons, Feely (Cornwall 46), Kelly C, Wilson (Breslin 71); Coote, Devoy (Mullins 88), Buckley, Burt (Ward 79); Tierney (Levingston 71), Kelly G.

Stjarnan: (433) Haraldur Bjornsson; Aegisson, Laxdal, Gudjonsson, Bjornsson E; Anbo (Ingvarsson 69), Hedinsson (Gudmundsson 80), Sloth (Ingolfsson 88); Atlason (Haurits 69), Ragnarsson (Halldor Bjornsson 69), Halldorsson.

Coleraine (1) 1 *(Shevlin 33)*

Velez Mostar (0) 2 *(Brandao 54, Andjusic 71)* 500

Coleraine: (442) Deane; Wilson, Brown, O'Donnell, Traynor; Glackin, Lowry, Carson, McLaughlin (Bradley 69); Shevlin, Allen.
Velez Mostar: (433) Bogdanovic; Cosic, Isic, Zeljkovic, Ferreyra; Hasanovic (Zvonic 46), Radovac, Ovcina (Andjusic 46); Brandao (Radovic 79), Zaimovic (Georgijevic 73), Vehabovic (Prses 73).

Larne (0) 1 *(Hale 84)*

Bala T (0) 0 850

Larne: (442) Ferguson; Cosgrove, Balmer (Watson 78), Bolger, Hughes; Jarvis, Randall (Donnelly 66), Herron, Sule; Lynch (McKendry 55), McDaid (Hale 78).
Bala T: (433) Ramsay; Rutherford (Bauress 67), Shannon, Spittle, Woods (Smith S 83); Edwards, Kay, Mendes (Leslie 73); Venables, Evans, Smith K (Walker-Rice 83).

Sligo R (0) 1 *(Kenny 84 (pen))*

FH Hafnarfjordur (1) 2 *(Lennon 44, 49 (pen))* 400

Sligo R: (433) McNicholas; Donelon (Kane 71), Buckley, Blaney, Banks; Cawley (Horgan 71), Morahan (McDonnell 80), Gibson (Keogh 79); de Vries (Kenny 59), Parkes, Figueira.
FH Hafnarfjordur: (433) Nielsen; Vidarsson, Thorisson, Kristjansson, Gunnarsson; Dimitrijevic (Gudlaugsson 73), Sverrisson (Robertsson 82), Jonsson E; Lennon (Heidarsson 90), Vilhjalmsson, Jonsson J (Arnarsson 90).

The New Saints (2) 2 *(McManus 26 (pen), Smith 27)*

Glentoran (0) 0 198

The New Saints: (532) Harrison; McManus (Rees 87), Routledge, Astles, Davies K (Ebbe 75), Marriott; Smith, Clarke, Williams (Robles 67); Cieslewicz, Davies D.
Glentoran: (442) Coleing; Marron (Smith 67), McCullough, McClean, Kane; Bigirimana (Cushnie 81), Marshall, Clucas (Mitchell 57), McDaid; McMenamin, Donnelly (McDonagh 67).

SECOND QUALIFYING ROUND FIRST LEG

Shamrock R received a bye.

Tuesday, 20 July 2021

Domzale v FC Honka	1-1
Folgore Falciano v Hibernians	1-3
Kauno Zalgiris v The New Saints	0-5
Prishtina v Connah's Quay Nomads	4-1

Wednesday, 21 July 2021

Cukaricki v Sumqayit	0-0

Thursday, 22 July 2021

Aberdeen v Hacken	5-1
AEL Limassol v Vllaznia	1-0
Apollon Limassol v Zilina	1-3
Ararat Yerevan v Slask Wroclaw	2-4
Arda v Hapoel Be'er Sheva	0-2
Astana v Aris	2-0
Austria Vienna v Breidablik	1-1
CSKA Sofia v FK Liepaja	0-0
Dinamo Batumi v BATE Borisov	0-1
Dinamo Tbilisi v Maccabi Haifa	1-2
Drita v Feyenoord	0-0
Dundalk v FCI Levadia	2-2
Elfsborg v Milsami Orhei	4-0
F91 Dudelange v Bohemians	0-1
FC Basel v Partizani Tirana	3-0
FC Copenhagen v Torpedo-BelAZ Zhodino	4-1
FCSB v Shakhter Karagandy	1-0
FH Hafnarfjordur v Rosenborg	0-2
FK RFS v Puskas Akademia	3-0
Gent v Valerenga	4-0
Gzira United v Rijeka	0-2
Hajduk Split v Tobol	2-0
Hammarby v Maribor	3-1
HB Torshavn v Buducnost Podgorica	4-0
Hibernian v FC Santa Coloma	3-0
KuPS Kuopio v Vorskla Poltava	2-2
Laci v Universitatea Craiova	1-0
Larne v AGF Aarhus	2-1
Linfield v Borac Banja Luca	4-0
Lokomotiv Plovdiv v Slovacko	1-0
Molde v Servette	3-0
Olimpija Ljubljana v Birkirkara	1-0
Panevezys v Vojvodina	0-1
Partizan Belgrade v DAC Dunajska Streda	1-0
Petrocub-Hincesti v Sivasspor	0-1
Pogon Szczecin v Osijek	0-0
Qarabag v Ashdod	0-0
Riga FC v Shkendija	2-0
Shakhtyor Soligorsk v Fola Esch	1-2
Shkupi v Santa Clara	0-3
Sochi v Keshla	3-0
Spartak Trnava v Sepsi Sfantu Gheorghe	0-0
Suduva v Rakow Czestochowa	0-0
Sutjeska v Maccabi Tel Aviv	0-0
Teuta v Inter Club d'Escaldes	0-2
Ujpest v Vaduz	2-1
Valur v Bodo/Glimt	0-3
Velez Mostar v AEK Athens	2-1
Viktoria Plzen v Dinamo Brest	2-1

Tuesday, 20 July 2021

Kauno Zalgiris (0) 0

The New Saints (4) 5 *(Smith 8, Davies D 35, 38, McManus 40, Williams 87)* 550

Kauno Zalgiris: (433) Mikelionis; Choco, Dapkus (Sadauskas 71), Thicot, Vaitkunas; Naah, Kloniunas (David 46), Silkaitis; Sesplaukis, Pilibaitis (Thuique 63), Otele (Opeyemi 84).
The New Saints: (442) Harrison; Routledge, Astles, Davies K, Marriott; Clarke (Cornish 84), Robles (Williams 71), Cieslewicz (Rees 71), McManus (Ebbe 78); Davies D, Smith.

Prishtina (1) 4 *(Bekteshi 41, John 53, Krasniqi E 79, John 90)*

Connah's Quay Nomads (0) 1 *(Moore 75)* 1268

Prishtina: (343) Nika; Krasniqi B, Bekteshi, Mici; Mankenda, Boshnjaku, Bardhoku (Vangjeli 90), Hoti (Tolaj 74); Shabani, Kryeziu (John 28), Krasniqi E.
Connah's Quay Nomads: (433) Calderbank-Park; Disney, Owens, Curran (Williams 74), Morris; Edwards, Moore, Horan; Davies, Insall (Bibby 90), Mullan.

Thursday, 22 July 2021

Aberdeen (2) 5 *(Considine 28, Ferguson 45 (pen), 53, Ramirez 84, McLennan 90)*

Hacken (0) 1 *(Jeremejeff 59)* 5665

Aberdeen: (433) Lewis; Ramsay (Gurr 77), McCrorie, Considine, Hayes (McLennan 76); Ferguson, Brown, Ojo (MacKenzie 66); Emmanuel-Thomas, Ramirez (Jenks 90), Hedges.
Hacken: (433) Abrahamsson; Ekpolo, Toivio, Hammar, Sverrisson; Berggren, Friberg (Faltsetas 55), Bengtsson (Heintz 46); Walemark (Milovanovic 82), Jeremejeff, Youssef (Maarouf 54).

Dundalk (2) 2 *(Patching 3, McMillan 27)*

FCI Levadia (2) 2 *(Vastuk 2, 19)* 880

Dundalk: (433) Abibi; Jurkovskis, Boyle, Nattestad, Leahy; Patching, Zahibo (Sloggett 58), Stanton (Murray 75); Kelly, McMillan (Midtskogen 86), McEleney.
FCI Levadia: (4141) Vallner; Antonov (Elhi 56), Ugge, Podholjuzin, Ilic (Peetson 46); Lepistu; Liivak (Oigus 79), Putincanin, Vastuk, Agyiri (Roosnupp 66); Beglarishvili (Kirss 67).

F91 Dudelange (0) 0

Bohemians (1) 1 *(Tierney 11)* 625

F91 Dudelange: (4312) Joubert; Van Den Kerkhof, Delgado (Bojic 73), Cools, Diouf; Da Cruz, Morren, Kirch; Sinani (Gashi 73); Hadji (Hassan 61), Bettaieb (Muratovic 66).
Bohemians: (442) Talbot; Lyons, Cornwall, Kelly C (Feely 79), Breslin; Coote, Devoy, Buckley, Burt (Finnerty 83); Tierney (Levingston 68), Kelly G.

Hibernian (1) 3 *(Boyle 14 (pen), 47, Nisbet 81)*

FC Santa Coloma (0) 0 4697

Hibernian: (4231) Macey; McGinn, Porteous, Hanlon, Stevenson; Newell■, Gogic; Boyle (Campbell 88), Allan (Magennis 31), Mackay (Wright 46); Nisbet (Doidge 85).
FC Santa Coloma: (442) Ramos M; Torres, Miranda, Ramos R■, Cistero; Puerto Bellart (Pi 78), Blanco (Rodriguez 78), Santos, Bouharma■; Fernandez (Ramos A 74), Lopez (Tizon 90).

Larne (2) 2 *(McDaid 3, Jarvis 30)*

AGF Aarhus (0) 1 *(Ammitzboll 85)* 850

Larne: (433) Ferguson; Cosgrove, Watson, Bolger, Jarvis; Hughes, Sule, Herron (Mitchell 75); Lynch, McDaid (Hale 69), Randall (McKendry 63).
AGF Aarhus: (433) Hansen; Munksgaard (Juelsgaard 46), Hausner, Tingager (Bisseck 46), Lund (Ammitzboll 74); Gronbaek, Poulsen, Olsen; Jevtovic (Tengstedt 38), Kurminowski, Thorsteinsson (Gersbach 49).

Linfield (2) 4 *(Newberry 2, Manzinga 25, Mulgrew 75, Callacher 90)*

Borac Banja Luca (0) 0 995

Linfield: (4231) Johns; Hume, Newberry, Callacher (Roscoe 90), Clarke M; Mulgrew, Shields; Millar, Palmer, Fallon (Quinn 82); Manzinga (Clarke A 82).
Borac Banja Luca: (4231) Pavlovic; Coric, Milojevic (Subic 46), Jovanovic, Cosic; Vojnovic (Kulasin 67), Begic (Molls 46); Zakaric, Vranjes, Meleg (Vusurovic 79); Moraitis (Zivkovic 78).

SECOND QUALIFYING ROUND SECOND LEG

Tuesday, 27 July 2021		*(agg)*
Buducnost Podgorica v HB Torshavn	0-2	0-6
Hibernians v Folgore Falciano	4-2	7-3
Inter Club d'Escaldes v Teuta	0-3*	2-3
Thursday, 29 July 2021		
AEK Athens v Velez Mostar	1-0*	2-2
(Velez Mostar won 3-2 on penalties.)		
AGF Aarhus v Larne	1-1	3-2
Aris v Astana	2-1	2-3
Ashdod v Qarabag	0-1	0-1
BATE Borisov v Dinamo Batumi	1-4	2-4
Birkirkara v Olimpija Ljubljana	1-0*	1-1
(Olimpija Ljubljana won 5-4 on penalties.)		
Bodo/Glimt v Valur	3-0	6-0
Bohemians v F91 Dudelange	3-0	4-0
Borac Banja Luca v Linfield	0-0	0-4
Breidablik v Austria Vienna	2-1	3-2
Connah's Quay Nomads v Prishtina	4-2	5-6
DAC Dunajska Streda v Partizan Belgrade	0-2	0-3
Dinamo Brest v Viktoria Plzen	1-2	2-4
FC Honka v Domzale	0-1	1-2
FC Santa Coloma v Hibernian	1-2	1-5
FCI Levadia v Dundalk	1-2	3-4
Feyenoord v Drita	3-2	3-2
FK Liepaja v CSKA Sofia	0-0*	0-0
(CSKA Sofia won 3-1 on penalties.)		
Fola Esch v Shakhtyor Soligorsk	1-0	3-1
Hacken v Aberdeen	2-0	3-5
Hapoel Be'er Sheva v Arda	4-0	6-0
Keshla v Sochi	2-4	2-7
Maccabi Haifa v Dinamo Tbilisi	5-1	7-2
Maccabi Tel Aviv v Sutjeska	3-1	3-1
Maribor v Hammarby	0-1	1-4
Milsami Orhei v Elfsborg	0-5	0-9
Osijek v Pogon Szczecin	1-0	1-0
Partizani Tirana v FC Basel	0-2	0-5
Puskas Akademia v FK RSF	0-2	0-5
Rakow Czestochowa v Suduva	0-0*	0-0
(Rakow Czestochowa won 4-3 on penalties.)		
Rijeka v Gzira United	1-0	3-0
Rosenborg v FH Hafnarfjordur	4-1	6-1
Santa Clara v Shkupi	2-0	5-0
Sepsi Sfantu Gheorghe v Spartak Trnava	1-1*	1-1
(Spartak Trnava won 4-3 on penalties.)		
Servette v Molde	2-0	2-3
Shakhter Karagandy v FCSB	2-1*	2-2
(Shakhter Karagandy won 5-3 on penalties.)		
Shkendija v Riga FC	0-1	0-3
Sivasspor v Petrocub-Hincesti	1-0	2-0
Slask Wroclaw v Ararat Yerevan	3-3	7-5
Slovacko v Lokomotiv Plovdiv	1-0*	1-1
(Lokomotiv Plovdiv won 3-2 on penalties.)		
Sumqayit v Cukaricki	0-2	0-2
The New Saints v Kauno Zalgiris	5-1	10-1
Tobol v Hajduk Split	4-1*	4-3
Torpedo-BelAZ Zhodino v FC Copenhagen	0-5	1-9
Universitatea Craiova v Laci	0-0	0-1
Vaduz v Ujpest	1-3	2-5
Valerenga v Gent	2-0	2-4
Vllaznia v AEL Limassol	0-1	0-2
Vojvodina v Panevezys	1-0	2-0
Vorskla Poltava v KuPS Kuopio	2-3	4-5
Zilina v Apollon Limassol	2-2	5-3

Thursday, 29 July 2021

AGF Aarhus (0) 1 *(Olsen 72 (pen))*

Larne (1) 1 *(Hale 45)* 5170

AGF Aarhus: (433) Hansen; Munksgaard (D'Alberto 61), Tingager (Kristensen 87), Bisseck, Lund (Gersbach 69); Gronbaek, Poulsen, Olsen; Links, Kurminowski (Ammitzboll 69), Thorsteinsson■.
Larne: (433) Ferguson; Cosgrove (Robinson 71), Watson, Bolger, Jarvis; Sule (Mitchell 87), Herron, Hughes; Randall (Kelly 87), McDaid, Lynch (Hale 42).

Bohemians (1) 3 *(Cornwall 35, Kelly G 69, 73)*

F91 Dudelange (0) 0 6500

Bohemians: (442) Talbot; Lyons, Cornwall, Kelly C, Breslin; Coote, Buckley (Levingston 74), Devoy, Burt (Ward 83); Tierney, Kelly G (Finnerty 87).
F91 Dudelange: (343) Joubert; Delgado (Bojic 38), Cools, Diouf; Van Den Kerkhof, Morren (Kabore 80), Da Cruz, Kirch; Bettaieb (Ninte 79), Sinani (Muratovic 64), Hadji (Hassan 64).

Borac Banja Luca (0) 0

Linfield (0) 0 5208

Borac Banja Luca: (4231) Pavlovic; Coric (Vusurovic 76), Jovanovic, Cosic, Subic; Vojnovic (Kulasin 67), Begic; Zakaric (Cavic 75), Vranjes (Zivkovic 75), Meleg; Moraitis (Lukic 55).
Linfield: (433) Johns; Hume, Newberry, Callacher, Clarke M; Fallon (Pepper 79), Mulgrew, Palmer; Millar, Manzinga (Chadwick 49), Quinn (Nasseri 84).

Connah's Quay Nomads (1) 4 *(Insall 3, 57, Horan 47, Morris 82 (pen))*

Prishtina (2) 2 *(Krasniqi E 29, 36)* 108

Connah's Quay Nomads: (442) Byrne; Morris, Horan, Disney (Williams 46), Wilde; Poole, Edwards, Moore, Mullan (Davies 74); Owens, Insall.
Prishtina: (433) Nika; Mankenda, Krasniqi B, Bekteshi, Mici; Bardhoku, Boshnjaku, Krasniqi E (Tolaj 45); Shabani (Muca 72), John, Hoti (Vangjeli 90).

FC Santa Coloma (0) 1 *(Lopez 70)*

Hibernian (0) 2 *(Murphy 73, Mackay 76)* 80

FC Santa Coloma: (433) Ramos M; Torres (Pi 79), Miranda, Santos, Cistero (Tizon 80); Blanco, Rebes, Puerto Bellart; Fernandez (Cervos 80), Lopez, Rodriguez.
Hibernian: (442) Macey; McGinn, Porteous, Hanlon (McGregor 72), Doig; Magennis (Wright 81), Gogic, Doyle-Hayes (Mackay 72), Campbell; Boyle (Doidge 60), Nisbet (Murphy 60).

FCI Levadia (1) 1 *(Agyiri 17)*

Dundalk (1) 2 *(McMillan 44, Patching 90)* 1875

FCI Levadia: (4141) Vallner; Podholjuzin, Ugge, Mitrovic, Ilic (Elhi 71); Lepistu; Liivak, Putincanin, Vastuk (Roosnupp 34), Agyiri (Oigus 71); Beglarishvili (Kirss 65).
Dundalk: (433) Abibi; Jurkovskis, Boyle, Nattestad, Leahy; Patching, Stanton (Zahibo 90), Sloggett; Kelly (Murray 70), McMillan (Hoban 63), McEleney.

Hacken (0) 2 *(Olsson 51, Bengtsson 68 (pen))*

Aberdeen (0) 0 823

Hacken: (433) Abrahamsson; Ekpolo, Carlsson, Hammar, Olsson (Sverrisson 76); Berggren (Milovanovic 80), Faltsetas, Heintz (Maarouf 80); Traore (Walemark■ 46), Jeremejeff (Mohammed 40), Bengtsson.
Aberdeen: (433) Lewis; Ramsay (Gurr 82), McCrorie, Considine, Hayes (MacKenzie 65); Ferguson, Brown, Ojo (McLennan 65); Hedges (Gallagher 82), Ramirez, Emmanuel-Thomas (Jenks 50).

The New Saints (3) 5 *(Redmond 13, Robles 20, McManus 25, Smith 69, Davies D 74)*

Kauno Zalgiris (0) 1 *(Thuique 85)* 362

The New Saints: (4231) Harrison; Routledge (Rees 75), Astles, Davies K, Marriott (Clarke 77); Redmond (Cornish 67), McManus (Ebbe 67); Smith, Robles, Williams; Davies D (Cieslewicz 75).
Kauno Zalgiris: Mikelionis, Choco, Sadauskas, Thicot, Vaitkunas (Suwa 46), Dapkus (Putrius 46), Pilibaitis, Sesplaukis, David (Opeyemi 70), Thuique, Otele.

THIRD QUALIFYING ROUND FIRST LEG

Tuesday, 3 August 2021

Bohemians v PAOK	2-1
Linfield v Fola Esch	1-2

Thursday, 5 August 2021

AEL Limassol v Qarabag	1-1
Breidablik v Aberdeen	2-3
CSKA Sofia v Osijek	4-2
Cukaricki v Hammarby	3-1
Dinamo Batumi v Sivasspor	1-2
Elfsborg v Velez Mostar	1-1
Gent v FK RFS	2-2
Hibernian v Rijeka	1-1
Kolos Kovalivka v Shakhter Karagandy	0-0
KuPS Kuopio v Astana	1-1
Laci v Anderlecht	0-3
Lokomotiv Plovdiv v FC Copenhagen	1-1
Luzern v Feyenoord	0-3
Maccabi Haifa v HB Torshavn	7-2
Pacos de Ferreira v Larne	4-0
Prishtina v Bodo/Glimt	2-1
Rakow Czestochowa v Rubin Kazan	0-0
Riga FC v Hibernians	0-1
Rosenborg v Domzale	6-1
Santa Clara v Olimpija Ljubljana	2-0
Shamrock R v Teuta	1-0
Slask Wroclaw v Hapoel Be'er Sheva	2-1
Sochi v Partizan Belgrade	1-1
Spartak Trnava v Maccabi Tel Aviv	0-0
The New Saints v Viktoria Plzen	4-2
Tobol v Zilina	0-1
Trabzonspor v Molde	3-3
Ujpest v FC Basel	1-2
Vitesse v Dundalk	2-2
Vojvodina v LASK	0-1

Tuesday, 3 August 2021

Bohemians (1) 2 *(Coote 23, 52)*

PAOK (0) 1 *(Oliveira 77)* 6500

Bohemians: (442) Talbot; Lyons, Cornwall (Finnerty 82), Kelly C, Breslin; Coote (Ward 87), Buckley, Devoy (Levingston 76), Burt (Wilson 89); Tierney, Kelly G.
PAOK: (4231) Paschalakis; Rodrigo, Varela, Michailidis, Vieirinha; Esiti (Kurtic 63), Schwab; Zivkovic (Murg 69), Kagawa (Biseswar 64), El Kaddouri (Tzolis 64); Oliveira (Swiderski 82).

Linfield (1) 1 *(Chadwick 9)*

Fola Esch (0) 2 *(Bensi 69, Caron 88)* 2227

Linfield: (4231) Johns; Hume, Newberry (Salam 90), Callacher, Clarke M; Mulgrew, Shields; Millar, Fallon (Nasseri 90), Palmer (Quinn 65); Chadwick (Manzinga 64).
Fola Esch: (433) Cabral; Ouassiero, Klein, Delgardo, Grisez; Pimentel, Mustafic (Dragovic 90), Freire; Diallo (Boutrif 62), Omosanya (Caron 63), Bensi (Correia 90).

Thursday, 5 August 2021

Breidablik (2) 2 *(Eyjolfsson 16, Vilhjalmsson 43 (pen))*

Aberdeen (2) 3 *(Ramirez 3, 49, Ferguson 11)* 1197

Breidablik: (442) Einarsson A; Gunnlaugsson, Muminovic, Margeirsson V, Ingvarsson; Einarsson V, Sigurdarson (Atlason 88), Sigurjonsson (Yeoman 82), Eyjolfsson (Mikkelsen 82); Steindorsson (Svanthorsson 64), Vilhjalmsson.
Aberdeen: (433) Lewis; Ramsay (Gurr 65), McCrorie, Considine, MacKenzie; Ferguson (McGeouch 46), Brown, Ojo; Emmanuel-Thomas (Gallagher 46), Ramirez (Hedges 83), Hayes (McLennan 46).

Hibernian (0) 1 *(Boyle 67)*

Rijeka (0) 1 *(Ampem 61)* 5600

Hibernian: (442) Macey; McGinn, Porteous, Hanlon, Stevenson; Magennis (Allan 81), Newell (Gogic 81), Doyle-Hayes, Murphy (Doidge 63); Nisbet (Mackay 81), Boyle.
Rijeka: (523) Labrovic; Tomecak, Escoval, Galovic, Smolcic, Vukcevic (Kresic 80); Pavicic (Obregon 90), Liber (Selahi 63); Ampem (Muric 62), Drmic (Lepinjica 90), Abass.

Pacos de Ferreira (1) 4 *(Denilson 44, 70, Stephen Eustaquio 73, Uilton 90)*

Larne (0) 0 1577

Pacos de Ferreira: (4231) Ferreira A; Jorge Silva, Marco Baixinho, Maracas, Joao Vigario (Antunes 45); Luiz Carlos, Stephen Eustaquio; Delgado (Uilton 67), Nuno Santos (Djalo 74), Lucas Silva (Ferreira H 67); Denilson (Douglas Tanque 74).
Larne: (442) Ferguson; Hughes, Bolger, Watson, Balmer; Cosgrove, Sule (Mitchell 67), Herron, Jarvis; McDaid (Hale 76), Randall (Kelly 76).

Shamrock R (0) 1 *(Emakhu 90)*

Teuta (0) 0 1500

Shamrock R: (352) Mannus; O'Brien (Kavanagh 70), Lopes, Grace; Finn (Gannon 83), Watts, Towell (Greene 77), O'Neill (Burke 71), Scales; Mandroiu, Gaffney (Emakhu 83).
Teuta: (4231) Frasheri; Todorovski, Dragarski, Arapi, Kotobelli; Daja (Plaku 88), Karabeci; Vila, Kallaku (Gruda 69), Jackson; Seferi (Gorgiev 69).

The New Saints (2) 4 *(Hudson 19, McManus 30 (pen), 54 (pen), 76)*

Viktoria Plzen (0) 2 *(Beauguel 89, Ba Loua 90)* 345

The New Saints: (433) Harrison; Davies D (Baker 79), Davies K, Hudson, Marriott; Smith, Routledge, Redmond (Clarke 83); Robles, McManus, Cieslewicz (Williams 72).
Viktoria Plzen: (4141) Hruska; Reznik, Hejda, Brabec, Hybs (Chory 80); N'Diaye; Kayamba (Ba Loua 66), Kacer (Mosquera 46), Bucha (Janosek 74), Sulc; Beauguel.

Vitesse (1) 2 *(Bero 20, Openda 89)*

Dundalk (0) 2 *(McEleney 65, 76)* 8756

Vitesse: (433) Schubert; Doekhi, Bazoer (Von Moos 77), Hajek, Wittek; Gboho (Tannane 68), Tronstad, Bero; Frederiksen (Darfalou 68), Openda■, Manhoef (Oroz 83).
Dundalk: (442) Abibi; Jurkovskis (Murray 84), Boyle, Nattestad, Leahy; McEleney (Zahibo 84), Stanton, Sloggett, Duffy; McMillan (Hoban 59), Kelly (Dummigan 48).

THIRD QUALIFYING ROUND SECOND LEG

Tuesday, 10 August 2021		*(agg)*
Domzale v Rosenborg	1-2	2-8
Shakhter Karagandy v Kolos Kovalivka	0-0*	0-0
(Shakhter Karagandy won 3-1 on penalties.)		

Thursday, 12 August 2021		
Aberdeen v Breidablik	2-1	5-3
Anderlecht v Laci	2-1	5-1
Astana v KuPS Kuopio	3-4	4-5
Bodo/Glimt v Prishtina	2-0	3-2
Dundalk v Vitesse	1-2	3-4
FC Basel v Ujpest	4-0	6-1
FC Copenhagen v Lokomotiv Plovdiv	4-2	5-3
Feyenoord v Luzern	3-0	6-0
FK RFS v Gent	0-1	2-3
Fola Esch v Linfield	2-1	4-2
Hammarby v Cukaricki	5-1	6-4
Hapoel Be'er Sheva v Slask Wroclaw	4-0	5-2
HB Torshavn v Maccabi Haifa	1-0	3-7
Hibernians v Riga FC	1-4	2-4
Larne v Pacos de Ferreira	1-0	1-4
LASK v Vojvodina	6-1	7-1
Maccabi Tel Aviv v Spartak Trnava	1-0	1-0
Molde v Trabzonspor	1-1*	4-4
(Trabzonspor won 4-3 on penalties.)		
Olimpija Ljubljana v Santa Clara	0-1	0-3
Osijek v CSKA Sofia	1-1	3-5
PAOK v Bohemians	2-0	3-2
Partizan Belgrade v Sochi	2-2*	3-3
(Partizan Belgrade won on 4-2 penalties.)		
Qarabag v AEL Limassol	1-0	2-1
Rijeka v Hibernian	4-1	5-2

Rubin Kazan v Rakow Czestochowa	0-1	0-1
Sivasspor v Dinamo Batumi	1-1	3-2
Teuta v Shamrock R	0-2	0-3
Velez Mostar v Elfsborg	1-4	2-5
Viktoria Plzen v The New Saints	3-1*	5-5
(Viktoria Plzen won 4-1 on penalties.)		
Zilina v Tobol	5-0	6-0

Thursday, 12 August 2021

Aberdeen (0) 2 *(Hedges 47, 71)*

Breidablik (0) 1 *(Eyjolfsson 59)* 15,107

Aberdeen: (352) Lewis; McCrorie, Gallagher (McLennan 46), Considine; Ramsay, McGeouch (Ojo 46), Brown, Ferguson, MacKenzie (Hayes 79); Ramirez (Emmanuel-Thomas 78), Hedges (Jenks 88).
Breidablik: (343) Einarsson A; Atlason (Steindorsson 55), Muminovic, Margeirsson V; Svanthorsson (Gudbjargarson 87), Einarsson V (Margeirsson F 87), Sigurjonsson (Sigurdarson 55), Ingvarsson; Gunnlaugsson, Vilhjalmsson, Eyjolfsson.

Dundalk (0) 1 *(Hoban 70 (pen))*

Vitesse (2) 2 *(Bero 28, Gboho 38)* 1475

Dundalk: (442) Abibi; Dummigan, Boyle, Nattestad (Jurkovskis 73), Leahy; McEleney, Stanton (Kelly 58), Sloggett, Duffy; Hoban, Patching (McMillan 72).
Vitesse: (343) Schubert; Bazoer, Doekhi (Domgjoni 83), Oroz; Wittek, Gboho (Hajek 63), Tronstad, Manhoef (Vroegh 78); Bero, Darfalou, Frederiksen (Von Moos 63).

Fola Esch (0) 2 *(Correia Mendes 69, Rodrigo Parreira 90 (pen))*

Linfield (0) 1 *(Roscoe 90)* 730

Fola Esch: (4411) Cabral; Ouassiero, Klein, Delgardo, Grisez; Boutrif (Correia Mendes 62), Pimentel, Freire, Bensi (Caron 40); Mustafic (Rodrigo Parreira 79); Omosanya (Dragovic 62).
Linfield: (433) Johns; Hume, Newberry, Roscoe, Clarke M; Fallon, Mulgrew (Clarke A 73), Shields; Millar, Chadwick (Manzinga 61), Quinn (Salam 73).

Larne (0) 1 *(Randall 83)*

Pacos de Ferreira (0) 0 1150

Larne: (442) Ferguson; Balmer, Watson, Bolger, Hughes; Cosgrove, Mitchell (Scott 63), Herron (Lynch 85), Jarvis; Randall, Hale (Lusty 79).
Pacos de Ferreira: (4231) Ferreira A; Jorge Silva, Flavio Ramos, Marco Baixinho, Bastos; Stephen Eustaquio, Ibrahim (Pires 60); Ferreira H (Lucas Silva 70), Djalo (Nuno Santos 60), Uilton (Delgado 69); Joao Pedro (Douglas Tanque 70).

PAOK (2) 2 *(Schwab 4, Biseswar 28)*

Bohemians (0) 0 0

PAOK: (4231) Paschalakis; Rodrigo (Taylor 85), Varela, Michailidis, Vieirinha; Kurtic (Esiti 73), Schwab; Zivkovic, Biseswar (Murg 85), El Kaddouri; Oliveira (Swiderski 74).
Bohemians: (4141) Talbot; Lyons (Feely 86), Cornwall, Finnerty, Breslin; Buckley; Coote (Ward 62), Devoy (Mallon 85), Tierney (Levingston 78), Burt; Kelly G.
Behind closed doors due to COVID-19 pandemic.

Rijeka (1) 4 *(Pavicic 37, Abass 68, McGinn 73 (og), Busnja 90)*

Hibernian (0) 1 *(Magennis 56)* 4077

Rijeka: (4231) Prskalo; Tomecak, Galovic, Kresic, Smolcic; Pavicic, Cerin (Liber 66); Muric, Abass, Ampem (Vukcevic 90); Obregon (Busnja 77).
Hibernian: (442) Macey; McGinn, Porteous, McGregor■, Doig; Magennis, Doyle-Hayes, Newell (Campbell 86), Murphy (Gogic 71); Boyle, Nisbet.

Teuta (0) 0

Shamrock R (1) 2 *(Gaffney 20, 62)* 300

Teuta: (4231) Neziri; Todorovski (Beqja 82), Aleksi, Arapi, Jackson (Kotobelli 69); Daja, Karabeci (Gruda 69); Vila, Kallaku, Plaku (Zogaj 74); Seferi (Gorgiev 69).
Shamrock R: (352) Mannus; O'Brien (Hoare 77), Lopes, Grace; Finn (Gannon 70), Watts (McCann 78), Towell (Burke 58), O'Neill, Scales; Mandroiu, Gaffney (Greene 69).

Viktoria Plzen (0) 3 *(Bucha 56, Chory 85, Beauguel 90)*

The New Saints (1) 1 *(Robles 4)* 6079

Viktoria Plzen: (4141) Hruska; Havel (Falta 68), Pernica, Brabec, Hybs (Kayamba 68); N'Diaye (Janosek 30); Ba Loua (Kacer 113), Bucha, Sulc (Cermak 77), Mosquera (Chory 30); Beauguel.
The New Saints: (433) Harrison; Davies D, Davies K, Hudson, Marriott; Smith, Routledge (Clarke 108), Redmond; Robles (Baker 89), McManus (Ebbe 80), Cieslewicz (Williams 65).
aet; Viktoria Plzen won 4-1 on penalties.

PLAY-OFF ROUND FIRST LEG

Thursday, 19 August 2021

Anderlecht v Vitesse	3-3
FC Basel v Hammarby	3-1
Feyenoord v Elfsborg	5-0
Flora v Shamrock R	4-2
Fola Esch v Kairat	1-4
Hapoel Be'er Sheva v Anorthosis Famagusta	0-0
Jablonec v Zilina	5-1
KuPS Kuopio v Union Berlin	0-4
LASK v St Johnstone	1-1
Neftchi v Maccabi Haifa	3-3
Pacos de Ferreira v Tottenham H	1-0
PAOK v Rijeka	1-1
Qarabag v Aberdeen	1-0
Rakow Czestochowa v Gent	1-0
Rennes v Rosenborg	2-0
Riga FC v Lincoln Red Imps	1-1
Santa Clara v Partizan Belgrade	2-1
Shakhter Karagandy v Maccabi Tel Aviv	1-2
Sivasspor v FC Copenhagen	1-2
Trabzonspor v Roma	1-2
Viktoria Plzen v CSKA Sofia	2-0
Zalgiris Vilnius v Bodo/Glimt	2-2

Thursday, 19 August 2021

Flora (2) 4 *(Zenjov 13, Miller 27, 87, Sappinen 76)*

Shamrock R (1) 2 *(Burke 44, Scales 86)* 1129

Flora: (4141) Igonen; Lilander, Purg (Tougjas 90), Seppik, Kallaste; Soomets; Zenjov, Vassiljev, Miller, Ojamaa; Sappinen (Alliku 89).
Shamrock R: (352) Mannus; O'Brien, Lopes, Hoare; Finn, Watts, Towell (Mandroiu 68), O'Neill, Scales; Burke, Gaffney (Greene 54).

LASK (0) 1 *(Karamoko 60 (pen))*

St Johnstone (1) 1 *(Kane 17)* 550

LASK: (343) Schlager; Boller, Andrade, Filipovic; Flecker (Potzmann 69), Grgic (Nakamura 84), Michorl (Hyun-seok 69), Renner; Balic (Schmidt 46), Karamoko (Raguz 69), Goiginger.
St Johnstone: (352) Clark; Kerr, Gordon, McCart; Rooney, McCann, Davidson, Middleton, Booth; O'Halloran (Hendry 90), Kane (May 87).

Pacos de Ferreira (1) 1 *(Lucas Silva 45)*

Tottenham H (0) 0 2284

Pacos de Ferreira: (4231) Ferreira A; Fonseca, Flavio Ramos, Marco Baixinho, Antunes; Stephen Eustaquio, Luiz Carlos; Ferreira H (Uilton 71), Nuno Santos (Djalo 62), Lucas Silva (Delgado 71); Denilson (Joao Pedro 88).
Tottenham H: (541) Gollini; Doherty, Carter-Vickers (Paskotsi 87), Romero, John (Clarke 46), Davies; Sessegnon (Bennett 81), Lo Celso, Winks, Gil Salvatierra; Scarlett.

Qarabag (1) 1 *(Romero 30)*

Aberdeen (0) 0 9756

Qarabag: (4231) Mahammadaliyev; Huseynov, Medvedev, Medina, Bayramov; Qarayev (Ibrahhimli 87), Andrade P; Romero (Vesovic 87), Kady (Ozobic 78), Zoubir; Sheydayev.
Aberdeen: (343) Lewis; McCrorie, Gallagher, Considine (Hayes 14); Ramsay, Brown, Ferguson, MacKenzie; Emmanuel-Thomas (McLennan 46), Ramirez, Ojo.

PLAY-OFF ROUND SECOND LEG

Thursday, 26 August 2021		*(agg)*
Aberdeen v Qarabag	1-3	1-4
Anorthosis Famagusta v Hapoel Be'er Sheva	3-1	3-1

Bodo/Glimt v Zalgiris Vilnius	1-0	3-2
CSKA Sofia v Viktoria Plzen	3-0*	3-2
Elfsborg v Feyenoord	3-1	3-6
FC Copenhagen v Sivasspor	5-0	7-1
Gent v Rakow Czestochowa	3-0	3-1
Hammarby v FC Basel	3-1*	4-4
(FC Basel won 4-3 on penalties.)		
Kairat v Fola Esch	3-1	7-2
Lincoln Red Imps v Riga FC	3-1*	4-2
Maccabi Haifa v Neftchi	4-0	7-3
Maccabi Tel Aviv v Shakhter Karagandy	2-0	4-1
Partizan Belgrade v Santa Clara	2-0	3-2
Rijeka v PAOK	0-2	1-3
Roma v Trabzonspor	3-0	5-1
Rosenborg v Rennes	1-3	1-5
Shamrock R v Flora	0-1	2-5
St Johnstone v LASK	0-2	1-2
Tottenham H v Pacos de Ferreira	3-0	3-1
Union Berlin v KuPS Kuopio	0-0	4-0
Vitesse v Anderlecht	2-1	5-4
Zilina v Jablonec	0-3	1-8

Thursday, 26 August 2021

Aberdeen (0) 1 *(Ferguson 90 (pen))*

Qarabag (2) 3 *(Bayramov 8, Kady 18, Zoubir 72)* 15,533

Aberdeen: (433) Lewis; Ramsay, Gallagher, McCrorie, MacKenzie; Jenks (Emmanuel-Thomas 46), Brown, Ferguson; Ojo, Ramirez (Campbell 82), Hayes (McGinn 75).
Qarabag: (4231) Mahammadaliyev; Bayramov, Medvedev, Medina (Mustafazada 87), Huseynov; Qarayev (Almeida 86), Ibrahhimli; Romero (Vesovic 82), Kady (Ozobic 74), Zoubir; Sheydayev (Qurbanly 81).

Shamrock R (0) 0

Flora (0) 1 *(Sappinen 57)* 3500

Shamrock R: (352) Mannus; O'Brien, Lopes, Hoare (Gannon 33); Finn, Watts (Gaffney 62), Mandroiu (Towell 59), O'Neill, Scales; Burke, Greene.
Flora: (433) Igonen; Lilander, Seppik, Kuusk, Kallaste (Lukka 82); Soomets, Vassiljev, Miller; Zenjov, Sappinen (Reinkort 87), Ojamaa (Alliku 74).

St Johnstone (0) 0

LASK (0) 2 *(Balic 72, Raguz 85 (pen))* 8845

St Johnstone: (352) Clark; Rooney■, Kerr, McCart; Brown (Wotherspoon■ 75), McCann (Gilmour 90), Davidson, Middleton (Craig 88), Booth (Devine 88); O'Halloran, Kane (May 88).
LASK: (343) Schlager; Wiesinger (Balic 60), Andrade, Filipovic (Maresic 86); Flecker, Hyun-seok, Michorl, Renner (Potzmann 87); Nakamura (Boller 60), Goiginger, Karamoko (Raguz 74).

Tottenham H (2) 3 *(Kane 9, 35, Lo Celso 70)*

Pacos de Ferreira (0) 0 30,215

Tottenham H: (433) Gollini; Doherty, Romero, Dier, Davies; Lo Celso, Winks, Sessegnon (Hojbjerg 63); Lucas Moura (Alli 84), Kane (Son 72), Gil Salvatierra (Bergwijn 72).
Pacos de Ferreira: (433) Ferreira A; Jorge Silva, Marco Baixinho, Flavio Ramos, Antunes (Fonseca 76); Stephen Eustaquio (Nuno Santos 76), Maracas, Pires; Lucas Silva (Uilton 76), Denilson (Douglas Tanque 69), Delgado (Ferreira H 69).

GROUP STAGE

GROUP A

Tuesday, 14 September 2021

Maccabi Tel Aviv (3) 4 *(Perica 13, Kanichowsky 32, Bitton 45 (pen), Hozez 72)*

Alashkert (1) 1 *(Jose Embalo 17)* 16,364

Maccabi Tel Aviv: (433) Peretz; Andre Geraldes, Hernandez, Nacmias, Davidadze; Glazer, Kanichowsky (Kuwas 68), Yeini (Piven 68); Biton (Rikan 46), Perica (Khalaila 80), Guerrero (Hozez 46).
Alashkert: (4312) Cancarevic; Kadio Didier, Voskanyan, Tiago Cameta, Boljevic; Bezecourt (Yedigaryan 60), Grigoryan (Alessandro 76), Gome (Khurtsidze 40); Mihajlovic (Milinkovic 46); Glisic (Nixon 77), Jose Embalo.

Thursday, 16 September 2021

HJK (0) 0

LASK (1) 2 *(Maresic 17, Monschein 89)* 5000

HJK: (433) Keto; Moren, Tenho, O'Shaughnessy, Murillo (Olusanya 86); Lingman, Vaananen (Riku Riski 46), Jair; Roope Riski, Valencic, Hostikka (Browne 70).
LASK: (343) Schlager; Boller, Maresic (Renner 79), Luckeneder; Flecker, Holland (Grgic 64), Michorl, Potzmann; Hyun-seok (Horvath 55), Karamoko (Monschein 64), Goiginger (Balic 79).

Thursday, 30 September 2021

Alashkert (1) 2 *(Jose Embalo 23, Glisic 90)*

HJK (1) 4 *(Riku Riski 8, Valencic 57, Roope Riski 63, Olusanya 90)* 2000

Alashkert: (4411) Yurchenko; Kadio, Voskanyan, Tiago Cameta (Kryuchkov 65), Boljevic; Gome, Grigoryan■, Khurtsidze (Bezecourt 72), James (Papikyan 59); Mihajlovic (Milinkovic 59); Jose Embalo (Glisic 72).
HJK: (442) Keto; Peltola, Moren, Tenho, Murillo (Saksela 66); Vaananen, Sparv (Hostikka 66), Jair (Djalo 76), Riku Riski (Terho 66); Roope Riski (Olusanya 84), Valencic.

LASK (1) 1 *(Horvath 11)*

Maccabi Tel Aviv (0) 1 *(Shamir 87)* 700

LASK: (343) Schlager; Letard (Boller 30), Maresic, Filipovic (Hyun-seok 71); Potzmann, Holland, Michorl, Renner; Horvath (Balic 71), Schmidt (Raguz 56), Goiginger (Monschein 71).
Maccabi Tel Aviv: (433) Peretz; Andre Geraldes, Hernandez, Piven, Davidadze; Glazer, Biton (Guerrero 63), Yeini (Shamir 73); Kuwas (Hozez 63), Perica (Khalaila 73), Kanichowsky (Shahar 90).

Thursday, 21 October 2021

Alashkert (0) 0

LASK (1) 3 *(Hyun-seok 35, Goiginger 68, Michorl 90)* 1500

Alashkert: (4231) Cancarevic; Tiago Cameta (Nixon 78), Boljevic, Kadio, Kryuchkov; Hovsepyan, James (Yedigaryan 66); Khurtsidze, Bezecourt (Gome 58), Papikyan (Matheus Alessandro 78); Jose Embalo.
LASK: (343) Schlager; Luckeneder, Maresic, Boller (Holland 57); Potzmann, Renner, Hyun-seok (Grgic 57), Michorl; Monschein (Schmidt 57), Karamoko (Balic 70), Goiginger (Gruber 79).

HJK (0) 0

Maccabi Tel Aviv (1) 5 *(Kanichowsky 28, 59, Perica 49 (pen), Saborit 87 (pen), Shamir 90)* 4883

HJK: (4141) Keto; Moren, Tenho, O'Shaughnessy, Murillo; Djalo (Kouassivi-Benissan 67); Valencic (Terho 60), Lingman, Jair (Peltola 82), Hostikka (Riku Riski 46); Roope Riski (Olusanya 82).
Maccabi Tel Aviv: (4141) Peretz; Andre Geraldes, Hernandez, Piven, Saborit; Glazer; Kuwas (Guerrero 77), Golasa (Shamir 64), Yeini (Shahar 88), Kanichowsky (Hozez 88); Perica (Khalaila 77).

Thursday, 4 November 2021

LASK (1) 2 *(Nakamura 12, 87)*

Alashkert (0) 0 400

LASK: (442) Schlager; Potzmann, Luckeneder, Renner, Hyun-seok; Goiginger, Michorl, Horvath (Flecker 60), Nakamura; Schmidt (Gruber 61), Monschein (Letard 86).
Alashkert: (4312) Yurchenko; Tiago Cameta, Kryuchkov, Voskanyan, Boljevic; Bezecourt (Milinkovic 60), Grigoryan, Papikyan (Glisic 51); Hovsepyan (Yedigaryan 83); Jose Embalo, Mihajlovic (James 60).

Maccabi Tel Aviv (1) 3 *(Kuwas 22, Lingman 65 (og), Hozez 90)*

HJK (0) 0 8029

Maccabi Tel Aviv: (433) Peretz; Andre Geraldes, Hernandez, Piven, Saborit; Yeini, Glazer (Shahar 78), Kanichowsky (Golasa 66); Kuwas (Hozez 78), Perica (Khalaila 66), Ben Haim II (Almog 58).
HJK: (3412) Keto; Moren, Tenho, O'Shaughnessy; Peltola (Murillo 46), Vaananen (Hostikka 72), Jair, Browne; Lingman; Tanaka (Valencic 58), Roope Riski (Riku Riski 72).

Thursday, 25 November 2021

HJK (0) 1 *(Tanaka 48)*

Alashkert (0) 0 4424

HJK: (433) Keto; Moren, Tenho, O'Shaughnessy, Murillo; Tanaka, Jair, Lingman; Valencic (Vaananen 83), Roope Riski, Browne (Riku Riski 73).
Alashkert: (4141) Cancarevic; Tiago Cameta, Kadio, Voskanyan, Kryuchkov (Nixon 83); Grigoryan; Papikyan (Glisic 64), Milinkovic (Bezecourt 80), Gome (Hovsepyan 83), Yedigaryan (James 64); Jose Embalo.

Maccabi Tel Aviv (0) 0

LASK (0) 1 *(Horvath 89)* 12,203

Maccabi Tel Aviv: (3421) Peretz; Piven, Hernandez, Saborit; Andre Geraldes, Golasa (Shamir 84), Yeini, Hozez (Davidadze 69); Kuwas (Guerrero 81), Kanichowsky; Perica (Khalaila 69).
LASK: (4231) Schlager; Flecker (Potzmann 61), Boller, Luckeneder (Wiesinger 46), Renner; Hyun-seok (Holland 60), Grgic; Goiginger (Gruber 77), Horvath, Nakamura; Karamoko (Schmidt 77).

Thursday, 9 December 2021

Alashkert (0) 1 *(Boljevic 78)*

Maccabi Tel Aviv (0) 1 *(Almog 89)* 700

Alashkert: (451) Cancarevic; Tiago Cameta, Kadio, Kryuchkov, Boljevic; Bezecourt (Jose Embalo 58), Gome, Grigoryan (Hovsepyan 72), Khurtsidze, James (Yedigaryan 72); Milinkovic (Nixon 83).
Maccabi Tel Aviv: (433) Daniel; Kandil (Andre Geraldes 71), Nachmias, Baltaxa, Saborit (Davidadze 46); Shahar (Kanichowsky 64), Shamir, Rikan (Biton 64); Hozez (Kuwas 64), Khalaila, Almog.

LASK (1) 3 *(Balic 41, Nakamura 63, Gruber 81)*

HJK (0) 0 0

LASK: (343) Gebauer; Letard (Wiesinger 60), Maresic, Luckeneder; Flecker (Horvath 77), Holland (Grgic 46), Michorl, Renner; Gruber, Balic (Goiginger 60), Hyun-seok (Nakamura 46).
HJK: (433) Keto; Kouassivi-Benissan (Peltola 88), Moren, Halsti, Tenho; Lingman, Tanaka (Vaananen 63), Browne (Murillo 87); Olusanya, Roope Riski (Valencic 77), Hostikka (Riku Riski 88).
Behind closed doors due to COVID-19 pandemic.

Group A Table	*P*	*W*	*D*	*L*	*F*	*A*	*GD*	*Pts*
LASK	6	5	1	0	12	1	11	16
Maccabi Tel Aviv	6	3	2	1	14	4	10	11
HJK	6	2	0	4	5	15	−10	6
Alashkert	6	0	1	5	4	15	−11	1

GROUP B

Thursday, 16 September 2021

Anorthosis Famagusta (0) 0

Partizan Belgrade (1) 2 *(Menig 42, Gomes 68)* 5000

Anorthosis Famagusta: (343) Loria; Korrea (Kaltsas 72), Arajuuri, Risvanis; Warda (Kacharava 65), Artymatas, Husbauer (Busuladzic 46), Anderson Correia (Avraam 50); Roushias (Deletic 46), Popovic, Christodoulopoulos.
Partizan Belgrade: (4231) Popovic; Miljkovic, Vujacic, Sanicanin, Obradovic; Scekic, Zdjelar; Markovic (Holender 72), Natcho (Jojic 64), Menig (Jovic 64); Gomes (Terzic 83).

Flora (0) 0

Gent (0) 1 *(Lemajic 54)* 2666

Flora: (451) Igonen; Lilander, Seppik (Kallaste 18), Kuusk, Lukka; Zenjov, Vassiljev, Poom, Miller, Alliku (Ojamaa 68); Sappinen.
Gent: (3412) Bolat; Hanche-Olsen, Ngadeu Ngadjui, Godeau; Castro-Montes, Kums (de Sart 63), Owusu, Operi (Nurio Fortuna 83); Bezus (Tissoudali 63); Lemajic (Oladoye 90), Depoitre (M'Boyo 64).

Thursday, 30 September 2021

Gent (1) 2 *(Korrea 28 (og), Kums 81)*

Anorthosis Famagusta (0) 0 10,209

Gent: (3421) Bolat; Hanche-Olsen, Ngadeu Ngadjui, Okumu; Nurio Fortuna, Owusu (Oladoye 84), Kums (de Sart 84), Castro-Montes (Samoise 84); Bezus (Odjidja-Ofoe 70), Tissoudali; Lemajic (Depoitre 70).
Anorthosis Famagusta: (4231) Tzur; Korrea, Risvanis, Arajuuri, Antoniades (Anderson Correia 70); Artymatas, Husbauer; Kaltsas (Deletic 46), Popovic (Christodoulopoulos 59), Warda (Kacharava 78); Lafferty (Christofi 69).

Partizan Belgrade (2) 2 *(Markovic 19, 42)*

Flora (0) 0 4845

Partizan Belgrade: (4231) Popovic; Zivkovic, Vujacic, Miletic, Obradovic; Zdjelar, Jojic (Scekic 82); Natcho (Pantic 62), Markovic (Holender 82), Gomes (Terzic 89); Menig (Jovic 62).
Flora: (4231) Igonen; Lilander (Kallaste 46), Seppik (Purg 74), Kuusk, Lukka; Vassiljev, Soomets; Poom (Shein 90), Zenjov, Alliku (Miller 69); Ojamaa (Kuraksin 69).

Thursday, 21 October 2021

Anorthosis Famagusta (2) 2 *(Deletic 25, Popovic 28)*

Flora (1) 2 *(Sappinen 38, 80)* 4322

Anorthosis Famagusta: (4231) Tzur; Hambardzumyan (Korrea 46), Antoniades (Avraam 75), Risvanis, Arajuuri; Husbauer, Deletic (Kaltsas 60); Artymatas, Popovic (Ioannou 69), Warda; Kacharava (Christodoulopoulos 60).
Flora: (4411) Igonen; Lilander, Kallaste, Purg, Kuusk; Soomets, Zenjov, Poom (Miller 70), Ojamaa (Alliku 66); Sappinen (Kuraksin 84); Vassiljev.

Partizan Belgrade (0) 0

Gent (0) 1 *(Kums 59)* 8943

Partizan Belgrade: (4231) Popovic; Zivkovic, Vujacic, Sanicanin, Obradovic (Urosevic 64); Scekic (Lutovac 76), Zdjelar; Markovic (Holender 58), Natcho (Jojic 64), Menig (Pantic 64); Gomes.
Gent: (3421) Bolat; Hanche-Olsen, Ngadeu Ngadjui, Okumu; Samoise, Owusu (Oladoye 90), Kums (de Sart 77), Nurio Fortuna (Godeau 90); Odjidja-Ofoe (Bezus 77), Chakvetadze (M'Boyo 80); Depoitre.

Thursday, 4 November 2021

Flora (0) 2 *(Sappinen 55, Zenjov 58)*

Anorthosis Famagusta (2) 2 *(Christofi 28, Popovic 33)* 2023

Flora: (433) Igonen; Lilander (Hussar 56), Purg, Kuusk, Kallaste (Lukka 46); Poom, Vassiljev, Soomets; Zenjov (Alliku 81), Sappinen, Ojamaa (Miller 90).
Anorthosis Famagusta: (4231) Tzur; Hambardzumyan, Risvanis (Arajuuri 46), Antoniades, Avraam (Anderson Correia 62); Artymatas, Husbauer; Christofi (Deletic 63), Popovic (Christodoulopoulos 81), Warda; Kacharava.

Gent (0) 1 *(Tissoudali 80)*

Partizan Belgrade (0) 1 *(Urosevic 66)* 10,595

Gent: (352) Bolat; Hanche-Olsen, Ngadeu Ngadjui, Okumu; Castro-Montes (Samoise 90), Owusu (de Sart 71), Odjidja-Ofoe (Chakvetadze 71), Kums, Nurio Fortuna; Bezus (Tissoudali 71), Depoitre.
Partizan Belgrade: (3142) Popovic; Miletic, Vujacic, Sanicanin; Natcho (Smiljanic 77); Miljkovic, Jojic, Pantic (Jovic 90), Urosevic (Obradovic 87); Menig (Lutovac 87), Gomes.

Thursday, 25 November 2021

Anorthosis Famagusta (1) 1 *(Christodoulopoulos 27)*

Gent (0) 0 2573

Anorthosis Famagusta: (4231) Tzur; Hambardzumyan, Risvanis, Arajuuri, Anderson Correia; Ioannou, Husbauer; Deletic (Christofi 71), Popovic (Chrysostomou 57), Warda (Korrea 81); Christodoulopoulos (Roushias 81).
Gent: (3421) Bolat; Hanche-Olsen, Ngadeu Ngadjui, Godeau; Castro-Montes (Samoise 63), de Sart, Owusu (M'Boyo 81), Operi; Bezus (Tissoudali 63), Bruno (Odjidja-Ofoe 62); Lemajic (Depoitre 62).

Flora (1) 1 *(Miller 44)*

Partizan Belgrade (0) 0 1503

Flora: (4411) Igonen; Lilander, Purg, Kuusk, Lukka (Kallaste 79); Zenjov, Poom, Soomets (Shein 79), Kuraksin (Ojamaa 58); Miller (Vassiljev 72); Alliku (Sappinen 59).
Partizan Belgrade: (4231) Popovic; Miljkovic, Miletic, Sanicanin, Urosevic; Scekic (Jojic 57), Zdjelar; Menig (Markovic 57), Pantic (Pavlovic 56), Jovic (Lutovac 58); Gomes (Milovanovic 74).

Thursday, 9 December 2021

Gent (0) 1 *(Bruno 51)*

Flora (0) 0 7421

Gent: (3421) Roef; Hanche-Olsen, Ngadeu Ngadjui (Cisse 61), Godeau; Castro-Montes, de Sart (Odjidja-Ofoe 61), Owusu, Operi; Bruno (Tissoudali 70), Chakvetadze (Bezus 71); M'Boyo (Depoitre 70).
Flora: (433) Igonen; Lukka (Lilander 77), Purg, Kuusk, Kallaste (Hussar 46); Vassiljev, Soomets (Shein 77), Poom (Miller 56); Zenjov, Alliku (Kuraksin 65), Ojamaa.

Partizan Belgrade (1) 1 *(Milovanovic 20)*

Anorthosis Famagusta (1) 1 *(Christodoulopoulos 33 (pen))* 4493

Partizan Belgrade: (4231) Popovic; Miljkovic, Vujacic, Sanicanin, Urosevic (Zivkovic 88); Jojic (Miletic 89), Zdjelar; Menig (Holender 62), Pavlovic (Scekic 46), Jovic (Lutovac 62); Milovanovic.
Anorthosis Famagusta: (433) Tzur; Hambardzumyan, Arajuuri, Antoniades (Korrea 78), Anderson Correia; Husbauer, Artymatas, Ioannou (Popovic 46); Deletic (Christofi 71), Christodoulopoulos (Kacharava 69), Warda.

Group B Table	P	W	D	L	F	A	GD	Pts
Gent	6	4	1	1	6	2	4	13
Partizan Belgrade	6	2	2	2	6	4	2	8
Anorthosis Famagusta	6	1	3	2	6	9	–3	6
Flora	6	1	2	3	5	8	–3	5

GROUP C

Thursday, 16 September 2021

Bodo/Glimt (0) 3 *(Saltnes 48, Solbakken 49, Pellegrino 60)*

Zorya Luhansk (0) 1 *(Gromov 90)* 2703

Bodo/Glimt: (433) Haikin; Sampsted, Moe, Lode (Hoibraten 89), Bjorkan (Konradsen 79); Fet (Vetlesen 67), Berg, Saltnes; Solbakken (Mugisha 88), Botheim, Pellegrino (Koomson 79).
Zorya Luhansk: (442) Matsapura; Khomchenovskiy (Alefirenko 90), Vernydub, Cvek (Imerekov 90), Snurnitsyn; Gromov, Buletsa (Lunov 70), Nazaryna, Kochergin; Sayyadmanesh (Cristian 70), Kabayev (Owusu 90).

Roma (2) 5 *(Pellegrini 25, 62, El Shaarawy 38, Mancini 82, Abraham 84)*

CSKA Sofia (1) 1 *(Carey 10)* 29,876

Roma: (4231) Rui Patricio; Karsdorp (Ibanez 46), Mancini, Smalling, Calafiori (Kumbulla 77); Diawara (Cristante 58), Villar (Veretout 58); Perez, Pellegrini (Abraham 75), El Shaarawy; Shomurodov.
CSKA Sofia: (442) Busatto; Turitsov (Donchev 74), Galabov, Mattheij, Mazikou; Yomov (Bai 67), Muhar, Lam, Wildschut■; Carey, Krastev (Ahmedov 87).

Thursday, 30 September 2021

CSKA Sofia (0) 0

Bodo/Glimt (0) 0 7291

CSKA Sofia: (4231) Busatto; Turitsov, Lam, Mattheij, Mazikou; Yomov (Youga 82), Muhar; Geferson, Bai (Varela 68), Carey; Caicedo.
Bodo/Glimt: (433) Haikin; Sampsted, Lode, Hoibraten, Bjorkan; Fet, Berg, Saltnes (Konradsen 90); Pellegrino, Botheim, Solbakken.

Zorya Luhansk (0) 0

Roma (1) 3 *(El Shaarawy 6, Smalling 66, Abraham 68)* 7622

Zorya Luhansk: (433) Matsapura; Favorov (Snurnitsyn 90), Imerekov, Cvek, Khomchenovskiy; Buletsa (Cristian 69), Nazaryna, Kochergin; Kabayev (Lunov 83), Gromov (Owusu 90), Sayyadmanesh (Zahedi 69).
Roma: (4231) Rui Patricio; Ibanez, Kumbulla, Smalling, Calafiori; Darboe (Diawara 70), Cristante; Perez (Zaniolo 62), Pellegrini (Villar 77), El Shaarawy (Borja Mayoral 78); Shomurodov (Abraham 62).

Thursday, 21 October 2021

Bodo/Glimt (2) 6 *(Botheim 8, 52, Berg 20, Solbakken 71, 80, Pellegrino 78)*

Roma (1) 1 *(Perez 28)* 5652

Bodo/Glimt: (433) Haikin; Sampsted, Bjorkan, Moe, Lode (Hoibraten 82); Berg, Fet (Vetlesen 81), Konradsen (Hagen 90); Botheim, Solbakken (Koomson 87), Pellegrino (Mugisha 87).
Roma: (4231) Rui Patricio; Reynolds, Calafiori, Ibanez, Kumbulla; Diawara (Pellegrini 60), Perez; Darboe (Cristante 46), Villar (Mkhitaryan 46), El Shaarawy (Abraham 60); Borja Mayoral (Shomurodov 46).

CSKA Sofia (0) 0

Zorya Luhansk (0) 1 *(Sayyadmanesh 64)* 3158

CSKA Sofia: (4411) Busatto; Turitsov, Mattheij, Lam, Mazikou; Yomov (Krastev 83), Muhar, Geferson (Vion■ 73), Wildschut (Bai 73); Carey (Varela 57); Caicedo.
Zorya Luhansk: (442) Matsapura; Favorov, Cvek, Imerekov, Snurnitsyn; Sayyadmanesh, Gromov, Khomchenovskiy, Zahedi; Buletsa (Cristian 87), Gladky.

Thursday, 4 November 2021

Roma (0) 2 *(El Shaarawy 54, Ibanez 84)*

Bodo/Glimt (1) 2 *(Solbakken 45, Botheim 65)* 41,031

Roma: (4231) Rui Patricio; Karsdorp, Mancini, Cristante, Ibanez; Darboe (Villar 46), Veretout; Zaniolo (Shomurodov 66), Mkhitaryan (Perez 46), El Shaarawy (Zalewski 88); Abraham (Borja Mayoral 81).
Bodo/Glimt: (433) Haikin; Sampsted, Moe, Lode, Bjorkan; Fet, Hagen, Konradsen (Vetlesen 88); Solbakken, Botheim, Pellegrino (Mugisha 88).

Zorya Luhansk (0) 2 *(Zahedi 87, Sayyadmanesh 90)*

CSKA Sofia (0) 0 1122

Zorya Luhansk: (442) Matsapura; Favorov, Vernydub, Imerekov, Snurnitsyn (Juninho 71); Lunov (Cristian 79), Cvek, Khomchenovskiy, Buletsa (Alefirenko 90); Zahedi, Sayyadmanesh.
CSKA Sofia: (4411) Busatto; Turitsov, Mattheij, Lam, Mazikou; Yomov, Youga (Krastev 89), Geferson, Wildschut (Bai 72); Carey; Caicedo (Ahmedov 83).

Thursday, 25 November 2021

Bodo/Glimt (1) 2 *(Fet 25, Botheim 85)*

CSKA Sofia (0) 0 5339

Bodo/Glimt: (433) Haikin; Sampsted, Moe, Lode, Hoibraten; Fet (Hagen 83), Berg (Moberg 90), Vetlesen (Konradsen 46); Solbakken, Botheim (Nordas 90), Pellegrino (Mugisha 90).
CSKA Sofia: (4312) Busatto; Turitsov (Galabov 88), Mattheij, Lam, Mazikou; Vion, Geferson (Varela 62), Youga (Muhar 62); Yomov (Wildschut 62); Caicedo (Krastev 82), Carey.

Roma (2) 4 *(Perez 15, Zaniolo 33, Abraham 46, 75)*

Zorya Luhansk (0) 0 24,000

Roma: (343) Rui Patricio; Mancini, Smalling (Ibanez 70), Kumbulla; Karsdorp, Veretout, Mkhitaryan (Missori 79), El Shaarawy (Zalewski 70); Perez, Abraham (Borja Mayoral 76), Zaniolo (Shomurodov 70).
Zorya Luhansk: (442) Matsapura; Favorov, Vernydub, Imerekov, Juninho (Snurnitsyn 70); Sayyadmanesh (Owusu 83), Kabayev, Cvek, Buletsa (Cristian 83); Gromov (Nazaryna 46), Zahedi (Gladky 46).

Thursday, 9 December 2021

CSKA Sofia (0) 2 *(Catakovic 75, Wildschut 90)*

Roma (2) 3 *(Abraham 15, 53, Borja Mayoral 34)* 4640

CSKA Sofia: (433) Busatto; Galabov, Mattheij, Lam, Mazikou; Geferson, Vion (Catakovic 64), Muhar; Yomov (Wildschut 46), Caicedo (Krastev 63), Bai (Charles 90).
Roma: (3412) Fuzato; Ibanez, Kumbulla, Mancini; Karsdorp, Veretout, Cristante, Vina; Bove (Villar 57); Borja Mayoral (Shomurodov 68), Abraham (Zaniolo 67 (Darboe 85)).

Zorya Luhansk (1) 1 *(Nazaryna 18)*

Bodo/Glimt (0) 1 *(Vernydub 68 (og))* 1134

Zorya Luhansk: (433) Matsapura; Favorov, Vernydub, Imerekov, Juninho; Cvek, Khomchenovskiy, Nazaryna; Sayyadmanesh, Gladky (Owusu 72), Gromov (Zahedi 82).
Bodo/Glimt: (433) Haikin; Sampsted, Moe, Lode, Konradsen (Hoibraten 88); Fet (Vetlesen 46), Berg, Saltnes; Solbakken, Botheim, Pellegrino (Pernambuco 65 (Mugisha 89)).

Group C Table	P	W	D	L	F	A	GD	Pts
Roma	6	4	1	1	18	11	7	13
Bodo/Glimt	6	3	3	0	14	5	9	12
Zorya Luhansk	6	2	1	3	5	11	–6	7
CSKA Sofia	6	0	1	5	3	13	–10	1

GROUP D

Thursday, 16 September 2021

Jablonec (0) 1 *(Pilar 52 (pen))*

CFR Cluj (0) 0 2470

Jablonec: (451) Hanus; Holik, Kubista, Zeleny, Krob; Plestil (Malinsky 77), Kratochvil (Hubschman 90), Houska (Vanicek 88), Povazanec, Pilar (Martinec 77); Dolezal (Nespor 77).
CFR Cluj: (433) Balgradean; Manea, Burca, Cestor, Camora■; Deac (Adjei-Boateng 61), Bordeianu, Culio (Bouhenna 55); Omrani, Debeljuh (Paun 80), Petrila (Costache 62).

Randers (1) 2 *(Piesinger 27, Graves Jensen 68)*

AZ Alkmaar (2) 2 *(Clasie 24, Pavlidis 34)* 3365

Randers: (442) Carlgren; Kallesoe (Kristensen 75), Piesinger, Marxen, Kopplin; Kehinde (Klysner 78), Johnsen, Lauenborg (Graves Jensen 62), Ankersen (Tibbling 62); Hammershoj-Mistrati, Kamara (Odey 62).
AZ Alkmaar: (4231) Vindahl-Jensen; Witry (Sugawara 63), Chatzidiakos, Martins Indi, Wijndal; Clasie (Evjen 85), Midtsjoe; Gudmundsson (Reijnders 76), de Wit, Karlsson; Pavlidis (Aboukhlal 76).

Thursday, 30 September 2021

AZ Alkmaar (0) 1 *(Gudmundsson 53)*

Jablonec (0) 0 9071

AZ Alkmaar: (433) Vindahl-Jensen; Sugawara, Chatzidiakos, Martins Indi, Wijndal (Witry 78); Midtsjoe, de Wit, Clasie; Gudmundsson (Beukema 90), Pavlidis (Aboukhlal 66), Karlsson.
Jablonec: (451) Hanus; Holik, Kubista, Zeleny, Krob; Plestil (Malinsky 69), Houska, Povazanec (Vanicek 85), Kratochvil, Pilar; Cvancara (Nespor 46).

CFR Cluj (0) 1 *(Petrila 68)*

Randers (1) 1 *(Kamara 40)* 3825

CFR Cluj: (433) Figueiredo; Stefan, Cestor, Burca, Manea; Deac, Rodriguez (Bordeianu 46), Adjei-Boateng (Culio 82); Costache (Petrila 63), Debeljuh (Alibec 63), Paun (Gidea 90).
Randers: (442) Carlgren; Kopplin, Piesinger, Graves Jensen, Bundgaard O; Ankersen (Tibbling 69), Johnsen, Hammershoj-Mistrati (Klysner 86), Kehinde; Odey (Brock-Madsen 69), Kamara (Lauenborg 63).

Thursday, 21 October 2021

CFR Cluj (0) 0

AZ Alkmaar (1) 1 *(Karlsson 18)* 3628

CFR Cluj: (433) Balgradean; Manea, Burca, Cestor, Camora; Deac, Bordeianu (Sigurjonsson 82), Culio (Adjei-Boateng 46); Paun (Alibec 73), Debeljuh (Petrila 61), Omrani (Costache 82).
AZ Alkmaar: (433) Vindahl-Jensen; Sugawara, Chatzidiakos, Martins Indi, Wijndal (Witry 69); Midtsjoe, de Wit (Evjen 63), Clasie; Gudmundsson (Reijnders 82), Pavlidis (Duin 64), Karlsson.

Jablonec (1) 2 *(Cvancara 35, 53)*

Randers (1) 2 *(Odey 36, 90 (pen))* 3678

Jablonec: (4411) Hanus; Holik, Kubista, Zeleny, Krob; Plestil (Malinsky 74), Kratochvil, Povazanec, Pilar (Vanicek 77); Cvancara (Nespor 59); Dolezal (Hubschman 78).
Randers: (442) Carlgren; Kopplin, Piesinger, Marxen (Graves Jensen 77), Kristensen (Kallesoe 46); Kehinde, Hammershoj-Mistrati, Johnsen (Egho 83), Tibbling (Ankersen 61); Odey, Brock-Madsen (Onovo 61).

Thursday, 4 November 2021

AZ Alkmaar (1) 2 *(Gudmundsson 5, Pavlidis 86)*

CFR Cluj (0) 0 10,554

AZ Alkmaar: (433) Vindahl-Jensen; Sugawara, Chatzidiakos (Beukema 89), Martins Indi, Wijndal; Midtsjoe (Reijnders 46), de Wit (Evjen 77), Clasie; Gudmundsson, Pavlidis (Duin 89), Karlsson.
CFR Cluj: (541) Balgradean; Susic (Manea 83), Graovac, Bouhenna, Burca, Camora; Deac, Bordeianu (Adjei-Boateng 65), Culio (Costache 78), Paun (Petrila 65); Alibec (Debeljuh 46).

Randers (0) 2 *(Hammershoj-Mistrati 46, Kubista 53 (og))*

Jablonec (0) 2 *(Cvancara 73, Kratochvil 83)* 4071

Randers: (442) Carlgren; Kallesoe, Piesinger, Marxen, Kopplin; Tibbling (Lauenborg 72), Hammershoj-Mistrati (Egho 78), Johnsen, Kehinde; Kamara (Ankersen 73), Odey■.
Jablonec: (451) Hanus; Holik, Kubista■, Zeleny, Krob; Plestil (Vanicek 88), Povazanec (Surzyn 90), Hubschman, Kratochvil, Malinsky (Smejkal 90); Dolezal (Cvancara 63).

Thursday, 25 November 2021

Jablonec (1) 1 *(Kratochvil 7)*

AZ Alkmaar (1) 1 *(Evjen 44)* 2650

Jablonec: (451) Hanus; Holik, Surzyn, Zeleny, Krob; Plestil (Malinsky 18), Kratochvil (Hubschman 82), Houska (Dolezal 74), Povazanec, Pilar; Cvancara.
AZ Alkmaar: (433) Vindahl-Jensen; Witry (Sugawara 78), Chatzidiakos, Martins Indi, Wijndal; Midtsjoe (Aboukhlal 90), de Wit, Clasie; Evjen (Reijnders 63), Pavlidis (Gudmundsson 79), Karlsson.

Randers (0) 2 *(Kamara 68, Piesinger 75)*

CFR Cluj (0) 1 *(Deac 72)* 4309

Randers: (442) Carlgren; Kallesoe, Piesinger, Marxen, Kopplin (Kristensen 53); Tibbling, Lauenborg (Hammershoj-Mistrati 66), Johnsen, Ankersen (Onovo 84); Egho (Kamara 66), Bundgaard F (Kehinde 46).
CFR Cluj: (433) Balgradean; Manea (Susic 71), Graovac, Burca, Camora; Bordeianu (Sigurjonsson 46), Adjei-Boateng (Rodriguez 84), Deac; Omrani, Debeljuh (Alibec 71), Paun (Costache 84).

Thursday, 9 December 2021

AZ Alkmaar (0) 1 *(Oosting 87)*

Randers (0) 0 0

AZ Alkmaar: (433) Vindahl-Jensen; Witry (Sugawara 46), Beukema, Martins Indi, Wijndal; Midtsjoe (Aboukhlal 60), Reijnders, Clasie (Oosting 78); Gudmundsson, de Wit (Pavlidis 46), Karlsson (Taabouni 78).
Randers: (442) Carlgren; Kallesoe, Piesinger, Marxen, Kopplin; Kehinde (Kristensen 80), Johnsen, Lauenborg (Onovo 80), Tibbling (Klysner 88); Hammershoj-Mistrati (Ankersen 67), Kamara (Brock-Madsen 88).
Behind closed doors due to COVID-19 pandemic.

CFR Cluj (1) 2 *(Debeljuh 45, 82)*

Jablonec (0) 0 2400

CFR Cluj: (433) Balgradean; Manea, Graovac, Burca, Camora; Paun (Alibec 73), Adjei-Boateng, Bordeianu (Rodriguez 73); Deac (Stefan 87), Debeljuh (Bouhenna 87), Omrani (Costache 57).
Jablonec: (451) Hanus; Holik, Martinec, Zeleny, Surzyn; Malinsky (Kubista 67), Kratochvil, Hubschman (Povazanec 79), Houska (Smejkal 88), Pilar (Vanicek 88); Cvancara (Dolezal 68).

Group D Table	*P*	*W*	*D*	*L*	*F*	*A*	*GD*	*Pts*
AZ Alkmaar	6	4	2	0	8	3	5	14
Randers	6	1	4	1	9	9	0	7
Jablonec	6	1	3	2	6	8	−2	6
CFR Cluj	6	1	1	4	4	7	−3	4

GROUP E

Tuesday, 14 September 2021

Maccabi Haifa (0) 0

Feyenoord (0) 0 6934

Maccabi Haifa: (4321) Cohen; Meir, Planic, Arad (Dahan 64), Menachem; Mohamed, Jose Rodriguez, Jaber (Lavi 82); Chery, Abu Fani (Haziza 60); David (Donyoh 59).
Feyenoord: (433) Bijlow; Pedersen, Trauner, Senesi, Malacia; Auranes, Orkun Kokcu, Til; Toornstra (Geertruida 82), Linssen (Dessers 76), Sinisterra.

Thursday, 16 September 2021

Slavia Prague (1) 3 *(Bah 18, Kuchta 84, Schranz 88)*

Union Berlin (0) 1 *(Behrens 70)* 15,286

Slavia Prague: (4231) Mandous; Bah, Ousou, Kacharaba (Takacs 53), Dorley; Sevcik, Traore (Krmencik 82); Ekpai, Lingr (Stanciu 69), Masopust (Schranz 69); Tecl (Kuchta 53).

Union Berlin: (352) Luthe; Friedrich, Knoche, Jackel■; Trimmel, Oztunali (Becker 59), Khedira (Promel 59), Haraguchi, Puchacz (Ryerson 76); Kruse (Voglsammer 59), Awoniyi (Behrens 59).

Thursday, 30 September 2021

Feyenoord (2) 2 *(Kokcu 13, Linssen 24)*
Slavia Prague (0) 1 *(Holes 63)* 38,505
Feyenoord: (433) Bijlow; Pedersen, Trauner, Senesi, Malacia; Toornstra, Kokcu (Aursnes 64), Til; Jahanbakhsh (Geertruida 78), Linssen, Sinisterra (Dessers 64).
Slavia Prague: (4231) Mandous; Bah, Ousou, Holes, Masopust (Schranz 69); Sevcik (Krmencik 76), Traore; Ekpai (Plavsic 46), Stanciu (Lingr 46), Dorley; Tecl (Kuchta 46).

Union Berlin (1) 3 *(Voglsammer 33, Behrens 48, Awoniyi 76)*
Maccabi Haifa (0) 0 23,342
Union Berlin: (4141) Ronnow; Trimmel, Friedrich, Knoche, Giesselmann; Khedira (Ryerson 82); Becker (Oztunali 78), Mohwald (Promel 72), Haraguchi, Voglsammer (Puchacz 78); Behrens (Awoniyi 72).
Maccabi Haifa: (541) Cohen; Meir, Planic (Arad 80), Gershon, Menachem, Dahan (David 46); Rodriguez, Mohamed (Jaber 72), Chery, Donyoh (Sahar 62); Atzili (Haziza 62).

Thursday, 21 October 2021

Feyenoord (2) 3 *(Jahanbakhsh 11, Linssen 29, Sinisterra 76)*
Union Berlin (1) 1 *(Awoniyi 35)* 36,100
Feyenoord: (433) Bijlow; Pedersen, Trauner, Geertruida, Malacia; Toornstra, Kokcu (Aursnes 83), Til; Jahanbakhsh (Nelson 83), Linssen (Dessers 83), Sinisterra.
Union Berlin: (352) Luthe; Jackel, Knoche, Baumgartl (Voglsammer 77); Trimmel, Mohwald (Teuchert 77), Khedira, Promel, Puchacz (Giesselmann 77); Awoniyi (Behrens 66), Kruse (Becker 67).

Maccabi Haifa (1) 1 *(Donyoh 24)*
Slavia Prague (0) 0 10,000
Maccabi Haifa: (433) Cohen; Meir, Planic, Goldberg, Tawatha (Menachem 62); Mohamed, Rodriguez, Jaber (Gershon 84); Atzili (Sahar 69), Donyoh (Chery 70), David (Haziza 62).
Slavia Prague: (4231) Kolar; Bah, Ousou, Kacharaba, Dorley; Traore, Stanciu (Lingr 67); Olayinka, Schranz (Ekpai 76), Plavsic (Samek 46); Kuchta (Krmencik 67).

Thursday, 4 November 2021

Slavia Prague (0) 1 *(Kuchta 49)*
Maccabi Haifa (0) 0 13,646
Slavia Prague: (4141) Mandous; Bah, Ousou, Kacharaba, Dorley (Ekpai 82); Sevcik; Masopust (Plavsic 72), Samek (Traore 57), Lingr (Krmencik 57), Olayinka; Kuchta (Holes 72).
Maccabi Haifa: (343) Cohen; Rodriguez (Arad 46), Gershon, Goldberg; Meir, Mohamed (Levi 83), Chery, Menachem (Abu Fani 69); David (Donyoh 61), Sahar (Atzili 62), Haziza.

Union Berlin (1) 1 *(Trimmel 41)*
Feyenoord (1) 2 *(Sinisterra 15, Dessers 72)* 30,000
Union Berlin: (532) Luthe; Trimmel■, Jackel (Voglsammer 77), Knoche, Friedrich, Puchacz (Giesselmann 83); Oztunali (Teuchert■ 83), Khedira (Promel 77), Haraguchi; Becker (Awoniyi 59), Behrens.
Feyenoord: (433) Bijlow; Geertruida, Trauner, Senesi (Hendriks 83), Malacia; Aursnes, Kokcu, Til; Toornstra (Pedersen 74), Linssen (Dessers 64), Sinisterra.

Thursday, 25 November 2021

Maccabi Haifa (0) 0
Union Berlin (0) 1 *(Ryerson 66)* 22,150
Maccabi Haifa: (532) Cohen; Meir, Planic, Gershon, Goldberg (Levi 85), Haziza (Tawatha 70); Abu Fani (Mohamed 61), Rodriguez, Chery; Donyoh (Atzili 61), David (Sahar 70).
Union Berlin: (532) Ronnow; Ryerson (Jackel 86), Friedrich, Knoche, Baumgartl, Puchacz (Giesselmann 63); Haraguchi (Promel 64), Khedira, Mohwald (Becker 64); Kruse, Awoniyi (Voglsammer 74).

Slavia Prague (1) 2 *(Olayinka 12, Kuchta 66)*
Feyenoord (1) 2 *(Dessers 31, 90)* 14,562
Slavia Prague: (4231) Mandous; Bah (Traore 90), Ousou, Kacharaba, Dorley; Holes, Lingr (Ekpai 78); Masopust (Kuchta 46), Stanciu, Olayinka; Schranz (Sevcik 62).
Feyenoord: (4231) Marciano; Pedersen, Trauner, Senesi (Geertruida 85), Malacia; Aursnes, Kokcu; Toornstra (Jahanbakhsh 78), Til■, Sinisterra (Nelson 85); Linssen (Dessers 19).

Thursday, 9 December 2021

Feyenoord (1) 2 *(Dessers 38, Nelson 65)*
Maccabi Haifa (0) 1 *(David 90)* 0
Feyenoord: (4231) Bijlow; Pedersen (Benita 46), Geertruida, Senesi (Valk 56), Hendriks; Aursnes (Hartjes 56), Diemers; Teixeira (Milambo 71), Bannis, Nelson (Balde 79); Dessers.
Maccabi Haifa: (532) Mishpati; Meir (Azruel 59), Rodriguez (David 59), Arad, Gershon, Tawatha (Goldberg 46); Ashkenazi, Abu Fani (Mohamed 46), Levi; Haziza, Sahar (Donyoh 71).
Behind closed doors due to COVID-19 pandemic.

Union Berlin (0) 1 *(Kruse 64)*
Slavia Prague (0) 1 *(Schranz 50)* 4380
Union Berlin: (352) Ronnow; Friedrich, Knoche, Baumgartl (Oztunali 84); Trimmel (Ryerson 69), Becker (Voglsammer 74), Khedira (Haraguchi 69), Promel, Giesselmann; Awoniyi (Behrens 69), Kruse.
Slavia Prague: (532) Mandous; Bah (Ekpai 74), Masopust, Ousou, Kacharaba, Dorley; Samek (Traore 79), Holes, Lingr (Stanciu 74); Schranz, Olayinka (Plavsic 88).

Group E Table	*P*	*W*	*D*	*L*	*F*	*A*	*GD*	*Pts*
Feyenoord	6	4	2	0	11	6	5	14
Slavia Prague	6	2	2	2	8	7	1	8
Union Berlin	6	2	1	3	8	9	–1	7
Maccabi Haifa	6	1	1	4	2	7	–5	4

GROUP F

Thursday, 16 September 2021

Lincoln Red Imps (0) 0
PAOK (1) 2 *(Akpom 45, Mitrita 56)* 668
Lincoln Red Imps: (433) Soler; Wiseman, Chipolina R, Lopes, Toscano; Torrilla (Chipolina J 67), Rosa, Araiza (Peacock 81); Carralero (Sergeant 81), Gomez (Ocran 62), Anon (Ronan 62).
PAOK: (4231) Paschalakis; Taylor, Mihaj, Crespo (Michailidis 44), Sidcley; Esiti, Kurtic; Murg (Vieirinha 83), Biseswar (Swiderski 73), Mitrita (Konstantelias 73); Akpom (Koutsias 82).

Slovan Bratislava (1) 1 *(Henty 21)*
FC Copenhagen (2) 3 *(Wind 18, 68 (pen), Stage 41)* 9833
Slovan Bratislava: (4411) Chovan; Pauschek (Da Silva 78), Kashia, Bozhikov, Zmrhal; Cavric (Drazic 69), Agbo, Kankava, Green; Mraz; Henty (Lichy 83).
FC Copenhagen: (433) Grabara; Diks, Khocholava, Boilesen, Kristiansen; Stage (Baldursson 86), Zeca, Lerager (Johannesson 79); Biel (Wilczek 86), Wind (Hojlund 79), Boving Vick (Ankersen 70).

Thursday, 30 September 2021

FC Copenhagen (2) 3 *(Chipolina R 4 (og), Wind 45 (pen), Stage 52)*
Lincoln Red Imps (1) 1 *(Rosa 33)* 13,418
FC Copenhagen: (433) Grabara; Diks (Ankersen 67), Kristiansen, Khocholava (Gabrielsen 80), Boilesen; Zeca, Biel (Arnar Haraldsson 80), Lerager (Johannesson 60); Wind, Stage, Boving Vick (Singh 68).
Lincoln Red Imps: (4411) Soler; Wiseman, Toscano, Chipolina R, Lopes; Yahaya, Araiza (Ronan 78), Rosa (Anon 73), Britto (Torrilla 62); Gomez (Casciaro 73); Walker (Carralero 62).

PAOK (1) 1 *(Akpom 9)*
Slovan Bratislava (1) 1 *(Green 14)* 7537
PAOK: (4231) Paschalakis; Taylor, Mihaj, Michailidis, Sidcley (Vieirinha 68); Esiti, Schwab (Kurtic 68); Zivkovic, Douglas (Biseswar 59), Mitrita (Konstantelias 74); Akpom (Swiderski 74).

Slovan Bratislava: (442) Chovan; Medvedev (Abena 83), Kashia, Bozhikov, Pauschek; Drazic (Zmrhal 70), de Kamps (Agbo 33), Kankava, Green (Cavric 82); Da Silva (Mraz 70), Henty.

Thursday, 21 October 2021

FC Copenhagen (0) 1 *(Biel 80)*

PAOK (2) 2 *(Sidcley 19, Zivkovic 38)* 19,552

FC Copenhagen: (433) Grabara■; Ankersen, Khocholava, Boilesen, Diks; Lerager, Baldursson (Singh 46 (Hojlund 83)), Johannesson (Jelert 74); Biel, Wind, Boving Vick (Johnsson 12).
PAOK: (4231) Paschalakis; Taylor, Mihaj, Michailidis (Varela 74), Sidcley; Esiti, Schwab (El Kaddouri 65); Zivkovic, Biseswar (Douglas 74), Mitrita (Murg 83); Swiderski (Akpom 83).

Slovan Bratislava (0) 2 *(Green 46, Henty 84)*

Lincoln Red Imps (0) 0 6108

Slovan Bratislava: (442) Chovan; Medvedev (Hrncar 90), Kashia, Bozhikov, Zmrhal; Cavric (Ibrahim 74), Agbo, Kankava, Green (Drazic 67); Mraz (Da Silva 67), Henty (Lichy 90).
Lincoln Red Imps: (433) Coleing; Wiseman (Sergeant 51), Chipolina R, Lopes, Toscano; Yahaya, Rosa, Torrilla (Anon 71); Carralero (Ronan 82), Gomez (Casciaro 82), Britto (Chipolina J 71).

Thursday, 4 November 2021

Lincoln Red Imps (1) 1 *(Chipolina R 45)*

Slovan Bratislava (2) 4 *(Green 17, 25, Cavric 67, Mraz 71)* 553

Lincoln Red Imps: (433) Soler; Wiseman, Chipolina R (Sergeant 86), Chipolina J (Yahaya 75), Toscano; Torrilla, Rosa, Walker; Carralero (Araiza 74), Gomez (Ocran 86), Britto (Anon 54).
Slovan Bratislava: (541) Chovan; Medvedev, Kashia, Abena, Bozhikov (Hrncar 84), Zmrhal; Cavric (Da Silva 84), Ibrahim (Agbo 76), Kankava, Green (Weiss 76); Henty (Mraz 59).

PAOK (1) 1 *(Zivkovic 7)*

FC Copenhagen (1) 2 *(Ankersen 34, Biel 50)* 11,166

PAOK: (4231) Paschalakis; Crespo (Taylor 62), Mihaj, Michailidis■, Vieirinha; Schwab (Koutsias 86), Kurtic; Zivkovic, Biseswar (Murg 86), El Kaddouri; Swiderski (Akpom 71).
FC Copenhagen: (433) Johnsson; Ankersen (Gabrielsen 75), Khocholava, Boilesen, Kristiansen; Diks, Lerager, Stage; Biel (Baldursson 86), Wind (Hojlund 86), Boving Vick (Johannesson 62).

Thursday, 25 November 2021

Lincoln Red Imps (0) 0

FC Copenhagen (2) 4 *(Johannesson 5, Lerager 7, Boving Vick 63, Hojlund 73)* 1008

Lincoln Red Imps: (433) Coleing; Wiseman, Lopes, Chipolina R, Toscano; Torrilla (Peacock 79), Rosa, Walker (Anon 78); Carralero (Ronan 42), Gomez (Ocran 61), Britto (Yahaya 62).
FC Copenhagen: (433) Grabara; Ankersen (Jelert 64), Khocholava, Boilesen (Oikonomou 76), Kristiansen (Bengtsson 72); Johannesson, Lerager (Hojlund 64), Stage; Biel, Arnar Haraldsson, Boving Vick (Bisgard Haarbo 72).

Slovan Bratislava (0) 0

PAOK (0) 0 200

Slovan Bratislava: (4132) Chovan; Medvedev, Kashia, Bozhikov, De Marco (Da Silva 90); Agbo; Zmrhal (Drazic 70), Ibrahim (Mraz 90), Green (Cavric 71); Weiss, Henty.
PAOK: (4231) Paschalakis; Taylor, Varela, Crespo (Mihaj 46), Sidcley; Esiti (Schwab 64), Kurtic; Zivkovic, El Kaddouri (Murg 72), Biseswar (Mitrita 86); Akpom (Swiderski 71).

Thursday, 9 December 2021

FC Copenhagen (1) 2 *(Wind 30, Hojlund 53)*

Slovan Bratislava (0) 0 13,021

FC Copenhagen: (442) Grabara; Jelert, Oikonomou (Jakobsen 72), Khocholava, Kristiansen (Oviedo 54); Arnar Haraldsson (Bisgard Haarbo 72), Biel, Johannesson, Boving Vick; Hojlund (Wilczek 77), Wind.
Slovan Bratislava: (4231) Chovan; Medvedev, Abena, Bozhikov, De Marco (Da Silva 78); Agbo, Kankava; Drazic (Green 62), Weiss (Ibrahim 72), Zmrhal (Cavric 62); Henty (Mraz 72).

PAOK (1) 2 *(Zivkovic 17, Schwab 55)*

Lincoln Red Imps (0) 0 4684

PAOK: (4231) Paschalakis; Taylor (Lyratzis 61), Mihaj, Crespo, Sidcley; Kurtic, Schwab (Tsingaras 74); Murg, Douglas (Biseswar 68), Zivkovic; Swiderski (Akpom 68).
Lincoln Red Imps: (442) Coleing; Sergeant, Chipolina R, Lopes, Toscano; Walker (Ocran 65), Yahaya, Ronan (Carralero 72), Britto (Araiza 78); Gomez, Anon.

Group F Table	P	W	D	L	F	A	GD	Pts
FC Copenhagen	6	5	0	1	15	5	10	15
PAOK	6	3	2	1	8	4	4	11
Slovan Bratislava	6	2	2	2	8	7	1	8
Lincoln Red Imps	6	0	0	6	2	17	–15	0

GROUP G

Thursday, 16 September 2021

Mura (0) 0

Vitesse (1) 2 *(Tronstad 30, Doekhi 69)* 3300

Mura: (4231) Obradovic; Kous, Karnicnik, Gorenc, Sturm; Kozar (Lorbek 79), Horvat; Mandic (Cipot K 70), Lotric (Cipot T 46), Skoflek (Marosa 79); Klepac (Pucko 46).
Vitesse: (343) Schubert; Doekhi, Bazoer (Rasmussen 84), Hajek; Yapi, Tronstad, Bero (Vroegh 90), Wittek; Tannane (Openda 66), Gboho (Huisman 66), Frederiksen (Darfalou 65).

Rennes (1) 2 *(Tait 23, Laborde 71)*

Tottenham H (1) 2 *(Bade 11 (og), Hojbjerg 76)* 22,000

Rennes: (4141) Salin; Traore, Bade, Aguerd, Truffert (Meling 79); Santamaria (Martin 86); Laborde, Bourigeaud, Tait, Sulemana (Ugochukwu 79); Guirassy (Tel 90).
Tottenham H: (4231) Gollini; Doherty, Tanganga, Rodon, Davies; Ndombele (Alli 79), Skipp; Lucas Moura (Scarlett 54), Gil Salvatierra, Bergwijn (Hojbjerg 30); Kane (Emerson 54).

Thursday, 30 September 2021

Tottenham H (2) 5 *(Alli 4 (pen), Lo Celso 8, Kane 68, 76, 87)*

Mura (0) 1 *(Kous 52)* 25,121

Tottenham H: (433) Gollini; Doherty, Rodon, Romero, Reguilon (Emerson 80); Alli (Son 59), Skipp (Hojbjerg 68), Winks; Lo Celso, Scarlett (Kane 59), Gil Salvatierra (Lucas Moura 60).
Mura: (3412) Obradovic; Karnicnik, Marusko, Gorenc; Kous (Mandic 75), Lorbek (Ouro 75), Horvat (Lotric 74), Kozar; Sturm; Mulahusejnovic (Skoflek 62), Marosa (Cipot K 84).

Vitesse (1) 1 *(Wittek 30)*

Rennes (0) 2 *(Guirassy 54 (pen), Sulemana 70)* 14,571

Vitesse: (343) Schubert; Dasa, Doekhi, Rasmussen; Wittek, Bero, Bazoer (Hajek 58), Tronstad; Openda, Frederiksen (Darfalou 71), Gboho (Manhoef 71).
Rennes: (442) Gomis; Traore (Assignon 73), Bade■, Aguerd, Truffert; Tait (Martin 73), Santamaria, Bourigeaud (Sulemana 46), Laborde (Terrier 46); Guirassy (Omari 77), Tchaouna.

Thursday, 21 October 2021

Mura (1) 1 *(Lotric 20)*

Rennes (2) 2 *(Guirassy 17 (pen), Laborde 41)* 3500

Mura: (352) Obradovic; Gorenc, Marusko, Karnicnik; Kous, Sturm, Pucko (Mandic 71), Lorbek (Ouro 72), Horvat (Klepac 87); Lotric (Marosa 80), Mulahusejnovic (Cipot K 87).

Rennes: (442) Gomis; Traore, Truffert, Omari, Aguerd; Santamaria, Bourigeaud (Tchaouna 63), Tait (Majer 63), Sulemana (Terrier 46); Guirassy (Ugochukwu 87), Laborde (Assignon 77).

Vitesse (0) 1 *(Wittek 78)*

Tottenham H (0) 0 23,931

Vitesse: (343) Schubert; Doekhi, Bazoer, Rasmussen; Dasa, Bero, Tronstad, Wittek (Hajek 87); Frederiksen (Buitink 85), Darfalou, Openda (Oroz 90).
Tottenham H: (4231) Gollini; Tanganga, Sanchez, Rodon, Davies; Lo Celso, Winks; Gil Salvatierra, Alli, Bergwijn; Scarlett (Markanday 75).

Thursday, 4 November 2021

Rennes (0) 1 *(Bade 76)*

Mura (0) 0 23,115

Rennes: (442) Salin; Assignon, Bade, Aguerd, Truffert; Bourigeaud (Tel 75), Santamaria (Tait 66), Majer, Sulemana (Tchaouna 88); Terrier (Laborde 67), Guirassy (Abline 75).
Mura: (541) Obradovic; Kous, Karnicnik, Marusko, Karamarko, Sturm (Bucek 88); Pucko, Lorbek (Kozar 88), Horvat (Cipot T 88), Lotric (Ouro 68); Mulahusejnovic (Marosa 82).

Tottenham H (3) 3 *(Son 14, Lucas Moura 22, Rasmussen 28 (og))*

Vitesse (2) 2 *(Rasmussen 32, Bero 39)* 36,132

Tottenham H: (343) Lloris; Romero■, Dier, Davies; Emerson, Skipp (Winks 73), Hojbjerg (Lo Celso 87), Reguilon; Lucas Moura (Sanchez 73), Kane, Son (Ndombele 72).
Vitesse: (343) Schubert■; Doekhi■, Bazoer, Rasmussen; Dasa, Bero, Tronstad (Oroz 90), Wittek; Frederiksen (Darfalou 74), Buitink (Houwen 86), Gboho (Openda 46).

Thursday, 25 November 2021

Mura (1) 2 *(Horvat 11, Marosa 90)*

Tottenham H (0) 1 *(Kane 72)* 6100

Mura: (3421) Obradovic; Karnicnik, Gorenc, Karamarko; Kous, Lorbek, Kozar (Ouro 62), Sturm (Lotric 78); Horvat (Cipot K 87), Pucko; Mulahusejnovic (Marosa 62).
Tottenham H: (3421) Gollini; Tanganga, Rodon (Dier 54), Sanchez; Doherty (Davies 53), Ndombele (Hojbjerg 76), Skipp, Sessegnon■; Gil Salvatierra (Lucas Moura 54), Alli (Son 54); Kane.

Rennes (2) 3 *(Laborde 9, 39, 69)*

Vitesse (1) 3 *(Huisman 43, Buitink 75, Openda 90)* 23,081

Rennes: (433) Gomis; Traore, Omari, Aguerd, Meling; Majer (Doku 73), Santamaria, Tait (Ugochukwu 62); Bourigeaud (Sulemana 63), Laborde (Guirassy 73), Terrier (Truffert 82).
Vitesse: (532) Houwen; Yapi (Dasa 53), Oroz, Bazoer (Frederiksen 83), Rasmussen, Wittek; Bero, Tronstad, Gboho (Buitink 46); Openda, Huisman (Manhoef 79).

Thursday, 9 December 2021

Vitesse (3) 3 *(Buitink 3, Openda 35, Huisman 40)*

Mura (0) 1 *(Marosa 81)* 0

Vitesse: (352) Houwen; Doekhi, Bazoer (Oroz 65), Rasmussen; Dasa, Bero, Tronstad, Huisman (Gboho 60), Wittek; Openda, Buitink (Frederiksen 59).
Mura: (3421) Zalokar; Karnicnik, Marusko, Karamarko; Kous, Kozar (Ouro 63), Lorbek, Sturm (Marosa 46); Horvat (Bobicanec 73), Pucko (Scernjavic 83); Mulahusejnovic (Cipot K 46).
Behind closed doors due to COVID-19 pandemic.

Group G Table	*P*	*W*	*D*	*L*	*F*	*A*	*GD*	*Pts*
Rennes	6	4	2	0	13	7	6	14
Vitesse	6	3	1	2	12	9	3	10
Tottenham H	6	2	1	3	11	11	0	7
Mura	6	1	0	5	5	14	–9	3

Due to a number of positive COVID-19 tests in the Tottenham H squad, the match v Rennes was awarded as a 0-3 win to Rennes.

GROUP H

Thursday, 16 September 2021

Kairat (0) 0

Omonia Nicosia (0) 0 7038

Kairat: (532) Pokatilov; Mikanovic, Bagnack, Dugalic, Alip, Hovhannisyan; Kosovic, Polyakov, Alves; Kante (Shushenachev 63), Vagner Love (Alykulov 80).
Omonia Nicosia: (532) Fabiano; Psaltis (Abdullahi 90), Lang, Yuste, Panagiotou, Lecjaks; Atiemwen (Loizou 46), Bachirou, Gomez; Kakoullis, Papoulis (Zachariou 45).

Qarabag (0) 0

FC Basel (0) 0 17,586

Qarabag: (4231) Mahammadaliyev; Huseynov, Medvedev, Medina, Bayramov; Garayev, Andrade P; Romero (Vesovic 46), Borges Malinowski, Zoubir; Wadji (Sheydayev 73).
FC Basel: (442) Lindner; Lopez (Lang 70), Comert (Durrer 81), Pelmard, Petretta (Tavares 82); Ndoye (Millar 58), Burger (Xhaka 69), Kasami, Stocker; Males, Arthur Cabral.

Thursday, 30 September 2021

FC Basel (3) 4 *(Arthur Cabral 15, Lang 21, 39, Ndoye 49)*

Kairat (0) 2 *(Kante 65, Alves 69 (pen))* 8712

FC Basel: (433) Lindner; Lang, Comert (Djiga 46), Pelmard, Tavares; Kasami, Frei (Burger 60), Ndoye (Quintilla 86); Palacios, Millar (Zhegrova 60), Arthur Cabral (Esposito 60).
Kairat: (532) Pokatilov; Mikanovic (Vorogovskiy 66), Bagnack, Dugalic, Alip, Hovhannisyan; Kosovic (Shushenachev 86), Polyakov, Alves; Kante, Vagner Love (Alykulov 66).

Omonia Nicosia (1) 1 *(Lecjaks 40)*

Qarabag (0) 4 *(Kady 52, 90, Sheydayev 73, Medvedev 79 (pen))* 8345

Omonia Nicosia: (442) Fabiano; Psaltis, Hubocan, Lang, Lecjaks (Kiko 81); Zachariou (Scepovic 64), Bachirou (Abdullahi 31), Gomez, Tzionis; Papoulis (Loizou 46), Kakoullis (Bautheac 64).
Qarabag: (4231) Mahammadaliyev; Huseynov, Medvedev, Medina, Bayramov; Garayev, Andrade P (Almeida 85); Ozobic (Vesovic 74), Kady, Wadji (Sheydayev 66); Zoubir.

Thursday, 21 October 2021

FC Basel (2) 3 *(Millar 19, Arthur Cabral 41 (pen), Zhegrova 88)*

Omonia Nicosia (1) 1 *(Gomez 26 (pen))* 10,056

FC Basel: (4231) Lindner; Lang, Comert, Pelmard, Tavares; Kasami, Frei (Quintilla 64); Zhegrova (Stocker 89), Males (Esposito 89), Millar (Ndoye 72); Arthur Cabral (Palacios 72).
Omonia Nicosia: (433) Uzoho; Psaltis, Lang, Panagiotou, Lecjaks (Kiko 46); Loizou (Papoulis 66), Gomez (Bachirou 46), Diskerud (Abdullahi 46); Duris, Scepovic (Kakoullis 46), Tzionis.

Qarabag (0) 2 *(Sheydayev 79, Huseynov 90)*

Kairat (1) 1 *(Kante 19 (pen))* 17,252

Qarabag: (4231) Mahammadaliyev; Huseynov, Medvedev, Medina, Bayramov; Garayev (Richard 86), Andrade P; Borges Malinowski, Ozobic (Vesovic 87), Zoubir (Mustafazade 90); Wadji (Sheydayev 70).
Kairat: (532) Pokatilov; Mikanovic, Bagnack, Dugalic, Alip, Vorogovskiy; Kosovic (Goralski 72), Polyakov, Alves (Abiken 84); Kante (Shushenachev 84), Joao Paulo (Alykulov 75).

Thursday, 4 November 2021

Kairat (0) 1 *(Kante 68)*

Qarabag (0) 2 *(Wadji 57, Zoubir 72)* 2638

Kairat: (532) Pokatilov; Hovhannisyan, Bagnack, Dugalic, Alip (Polyakov 78), Vorogovskiy (Mikanovic 73); Kosovic (Shushenachev 81), Goralski, Alves; Kante, Vagner Love.
Qarabag: (4231) Mahammadaliyev; Huseynov (Vesovic 61), Medvedev, Medina, Bayramov; Garayev, Andrade P; Borges Malinowski (Sheydayev 61), Ozobic (Richard 85), Zoubir (Qurbanly 90); Wadji (Mustafazade 90).

Omonia Nicosia (1) 1 *(Kakoullis 16)*

FC Basel (0) 1 *(Millar 57)* 4597

Omonia Nicosia: (442) Fabiano (Uzoho 46); Psaltis, Hubocan, Panagiotou (Lang 15), Kiko; Zachariou, Charalambous (Diskerud 67), Gomez, Atiemwen (Tzionis 46); Duris, Kakoullis (Loizou 81).
FC Basel: (4141) Lindner; Lang, Comert, Pelmard, Tavares (Petretta 61); Burger (Males 46); Ndoye (Fernandes 55), Kasami (Palacios 46), Frei, Millar (Stocker 85); Arthur Cabral.

Thursday, 25 November 2021

Kairat (1) 2 *(Vagner Love 23, Hovhannisyan 56)*

FC Basel (1) 3 *(Arthur Cabral 45 (pen), Zhegrova 69, Kasami 72)* 4159

Kairat: (3421) Pokatilov; Polyakov, Bagnack, Alip; Mikanovic (Hovhannisyan 55), Goralski, Alves (Abiken 55), Vorogovskiy■; Kante (Shushenachev 55), Joao Paulo (Alykulov 70); Vagner Love (Seidakhmet 80).
FC Basel: (4231) Lindner; Lang (Lopez 64), Frei, Pelmard, Tavares; Kasami, Burger (Xhaka 88); Ndoye (Males 88), Stocker (Palacios 64), Millar (Zhegrova 64); Arthur Cabral.

Qarabag (0) 2 *(Psaltis 49 (og), Andrade P 88)*

Omonia Nicosia (1) 2 *(Duris 43 (pen), Gomez 90)* 17,231

Qarabag: (4231) Mahammadaliyev; Huseynov, Medvedev, Medina, Bayramov; Garayev, Andrade P; Borges Malinowski, Ozobic, Zoubir; Wadji (Sheydayev 69).
Omonia Nicosia: (343) Uzoho; Psaltis, Panagiotou, Lang; Zachariou (Hubocan 80), Asimenos (Gomez 63), Charalambous (Diskerud 63), Kiko■; Bautheac (Loizou 46), Kakoullis, Duris (Lecjaks 69).

Thursday, 9 December 2021

FC Basel (1) 3 *(Arthur Cabral 33, 74, Kasami 62)*

Qarabag (0) 0 10,059

FC Basel: (4231) Lindner; Lopez (Tavares 46), Frei, Djiga, Petretta; Kasami, Burger; Zhegrova (Ndoye 46), Palacios (Males 84), Stocker (Millar 62); Arthur Cabral (Quintilla 90).
Qarabag: (4231) Mahammadaliyev; Huseynov, Medvedev, Medina, Bayramov (Dzhafarquliyev 84); Garayev (Ibrahhimli 78), Andrade P (Richard 84); Borges Malinowski, Ozobic (Vesovic 65), Zoubir; Wadji (Sheydayev 65).

Omonia Nicosia (0) 0

Kairat (0) 0 3239

Omonia Nicosia: (442) Uzoho; Psaltis, Lang, Panagiotou, Lecjaks (Hubocan 57); Bautheac (Atiemwen 58), Bachirou (Gomez 58), Charalambous (Diskerud 76), Zachariou (Loizou 65); Kakoullis, Duris.
Kairat: (541) Pokatilov; Mikanovic (Buranchiev 86), Bagnack, Dugalic, Alip, Keiler; Kosovic, Goralski, Abiken (Kante 73), Joao Paulo (Seidakhmet 86); Shushenachev.

Group H Table	*P*	*W*	*D*	*L*	*F*	*A*	*GD*	*Pts*
FC Basel	6	4	2	0	14	6	8	14
Qarabag	6	3	2	1	10	8	2	11
Omonia	6	0	4	2	5	10	–5	4
Kairat	6	0	2	4	6	11	–5	2

KNOCK-OUT STAGE

KNOCK-OUT PLAY-OFFS FIRST LEG

Thursday, 17 February 2022

Celtic (0) 1 *(Maeda 79)*

Bodo/Glimt (1) 3 *(Espejord 6, Pellegrino 55, Vetlesen 81)* 54,926

Celtic: (4231) Hart; Juranovic, Carter-Vickers, Starfelt, Taylor; McGregor, O'Riley (Forrest 74); Abada (Giakoumakis 59), Rogic (Hatate 59), Jota; Maeda.
Bodo/Glimt: (433) Haikin; Sampsted, Moe, Hoibraten, Wembangomo (Sery Larsen 90); Vetlesen, Hagen, Saltnes (Konradsen 77); Solbakken (Mugisha 90), Espejord (Boniface 69), Pellegrino (Koomson 69).

FC Midtjylland (1) 1 *(Andersson 20)*

PAOK (0) 0 7088

FC Midtjylland: (3421) Olafsson; Dalsgaard, Sviatchenko, Juninho; Andersson, Nwadike, Evander (Meyer 60), Dyhr (Paulinho 60); Isaksen (Charles 69), Junior Brumado (Lind 70); Sisto (Marrony 82).
PAOK: (4231) Paschalakis; Lyratzis, Ingason, Crespo, Sidcley (El Kaddouri 79); Tsingaras, Schwab (Vieirinha 69); Zivkovic, Douglas (Filipe Soares 79), Mitrita (Biseswar 46); Akpom (Colak 84).

Fenerbahce (0) 2 *(Pelkas 58, Kadioglu 83)*

Slavia Prague (1) 3 *(Traore 45, Dorley 62, Lingr 63)* 30,094

Fenerbahce: (4231) Bayindir; Sangare, Kim (Tisserand 46), Szalai, Kadioglu; Yandas (Tufan 59), Sosa; Samuel, Zajc (Guler 75), Pelkas (Berisha 88); Valencia (Dursun 74).
Slavia Prague: (352) Mandous; Ousou, Holes, Kacharaba; Schranz, Sevcik, Plavsic (Lingr 46), Traore (Samek 75), Dorley (Tecl 80); Sor (Horsky 85), Olayinka.

Leicester C (1) 4 *(Ndidi 23, Barnes 49, Daka 54, Dewsbury-Hall 74)*

Randers (1) 1 *(Hammershoj-Mistrati 45)* 25,242

Leicester C: (433) Schmeichel; Amartey, Soyuncu, Vestergaard, Albrighton; Tielemans, Ndidi (Maddison 64 (Choudhury 83)), Dewsbury-Hall (Soumare 83); Lookman, Daka (Iheanacho 64), Barnes (Perez 83).
Randers: (442) Carlgren; Kallesoe, Piesinger, Graves Jensen, Kopplin; Kehinde (Klysner 76), Johnsen, Lauenborg (Tibbling 65), Ankersen (Bundgaard O 46); Kamara (Brock-Madsen 65), Hammershoj-Mistrati (Enggard 87).

Marseille (2) 3 *(Milik 41, 44, Payet 90)*

Qarabag (0) 1 *(Borges Malinowski 85)* 25,713

Marseille: (433) Mandanda; Lirola, Balerdi, Alvaro, Luan Peres; Kamara, Gueye, Gerson (Guendouzi 69); Under (Dieng 69), Milik (Payet 68), de la Fuente (Bakambu 69).
Qarabag: (4231) Gugeshashvili; Vesovic, Medvedev, Medina, Bayramov; Garayev (Ibrahhimli 90), Andrade P; Borges Malinowski, Ozobic (Sheydayev 74), Zoubir (Andrade L 90); Wadji (Qurbanly 88).

PSV Eindhoven (1) 1 *(Gakpo 11)*

Maccabi Tel Aviv (0) 0 14,280

PSV Eindhoven: (4231) Drommel; Mwene (Doan 46), Teze, Max, Junior; Gutierrez, Veerman; Madueke (Vertessen 61), Gotze, Gakpo; Zahavi (Bruma 87).
Maccabi Tel Aviv: (442) Peretz; Andre Geraldes, Nachmias, Saborit, Baltaxa (Davidadza 88); Biton (Ben Haim II 74), Shamir (Yeini 63), Glazer (Golasa 74), Kanichowsky; Jovanovic (Kuwas 63), Perica.

Rapid Vienna (2) 2 *(Druijf 1, Grull 15)*

Vitesse (0) 1 *(Openda 74)* 10,700

Rapid Vienna: (433) Gartler; Stojkovic■, Aiwu, Moormann (Wimmer 61), Auer; Grahovac (Querfeld 84), Demir (Fountas 62), Ljubicic; Kitagawa (Arase 69), Druijf (Petrovic 69), Grull.
Vitesse: (3142) Houwen; Doekhi, Oroz, Rasmussen; Tronstad; Dasa, Gboho (Frederiksen 55), Domgjoni, Wittek; Openda, Grbic (Buitink 86).

Sparta Prague (0) 0

Partizan Belgrade (0) 1 *(Menig 78)* 1000

Sparta Prague: (433) Holec; Suchomel, Vitik, Celustka (Panak 79), Hancko; Sacek, Pavelka, Karabec (Haraslin 56); Pesek (Krejci 66), Cvancara (Dockal 66), Hlozek.
Partizan Belgrade: (4231) Popovic; Miljkovic (Zivkovic 58), Miletic, Vujacic, Urosevic; Jojic, Zdjelar; Markovic (Jovic 63), Natkho (Jevtovic 46), Menig (Terzic 83); Gomes (Milovanovic 63).

KNOCK-OUT PLAY-OFFS SECOND LEG

Thursday, 24 February 2022

Bodo/Glimt (1) 2 *(Solbakken 9, Vetlesen 69)*

Celtic (0) 0 5801

Bodo/Glimt: (433) Smits; Sampsted, Moe, Hoibraten, Wembangomo (Sery Larsen 77); Vetlesen (Mugisha 77), Hagen, Saltnes (Konradsen 64); Solbakken, Espejord (Boniface 64), Pellegrino (Koomson 90).
Celtic: (433) Hart; Ralston, Welsh, Starfelt, Scales; Rogic (McGregor 46), Bitton, O'Riley (Abada 46); Forrest, Giakoumakis (McCarthy 76), Maeda.
Bodo/Glimt won 5-1 on aggregate.

Maccabi Tel Aviv (0) 1 *(Saborit 90)*

PSV Eindhoven (0) 1 *(Vertessen 84)* 28,058

Maccabi Tel Aviv: (4141) Peretz; Yeini, Nachmias (Kandil 81), Saborit, Baltaxa (Davidadza 88); Glazer; Kuwas (Golasa 85), Biton (Ben Haim II 86), Kanichowsky, Jovanovic; Perica.
PSV Eindhoven: (4312) Drommel; Junior, Teze, Boscagli, Max; Doan (Bruma 65), Gutierrez, Sangare; Gotze; Madueke (Vertessen 75), Zahavi (Vinicius 66).
PSV Eindhoven won 2-1 on aggregate.

PAOK (2) 2 *(Zivkovic 20, Vieirinha 26)*

FC Midtjylland (0) 1 *(Hoegh 80)* 7468

PAOK: (4231) Paschalakis; Lyratzis, Ingason, Crespo, Vieirinha (Sidcley 71); Tsingaras (Filipe Soares 90), Kurtic; Zivkovic (Schwab 104), Douglas (El Kaddouri 74), Biseswar (Mitrita 71); Colak.
FC Midtjylland: (352) Olafsson; Thychosen, Sviatchenko, Juninho (Hoegh 46); Andersson, Nwadike, Sisto (Meyer 46), Evander, Paulinho (Dyhr 46); Isaksen (Charles 99), Junior Brumado (Lind 73).
aet; PAOK won 5-3 on penalties.

Partizan Belgrade (2) 2 *(Gomes 7, 24)*

Sparta Prague (0) 1 *(Hlozek 85)* 10,120

Partizan Belgrade: (4231) Popovic; Miletic, Vujacic, Sanicanin, Urosevic; Jojic (Terzic 78), Zdjelar; Markovic (Jovic 61), Natkho (Jevtovic 61), Menig (Holender 78); Gomes▪.
Sparta Prague: (4231) Holec; Wiesner, Panak, Vitik, Hancko; Sacek (Dockal 62), Krejci II; Pesek (Minchev 46), Hlozek, Haraslin (Karabec 70); Cvancara (Krejci 62).
Partizan Belgrade won 3-1 on aggregate.

Qarabag (0) 0

Marseille (1) 3 *(Gueye 12, Guendouzi 77, de la Fuente 90)* 27,783

Qarabag: (4231) Gugeshashvili; Vesovic, Medvedev, Medina, Bayramov; Garayev (Ibrahhimli 81), Andrade P; Borges Malinowski, Ozobic (Sheydayev 54), Zoubir (Qurbanly 81); Wadji (Akhmedzade 68).
Marseille: (541) Mandanda; Rongier, Saliba, Kamara, Caleta-Car, Luan Peres; Dieng (de la Fuente 83), Gueye (Lirola 83), Guendouzi, Bakambu (Under 59); Payet (Harit 82).
Marseille won 6-1 on aggregate.

Randers (0) 1 *(Odey 84)*

Leicester C (1) 3 *(Barnes 2, Maddison 70, 74)* 8948

Randers: (442) Carlgren; Kallesoe (Bundgaard O 61), Piesinger, Graves Jensen (Andersson 61), Kopplin; Ankersen (Tibbling 76), Johnsen, Lauenborg (Bundgaard F 67), Kehinde; Odey, Hammershoj-Mistrati (Klysner 77).
Leicester C: (433) Schmeichel; Albrighton (Choudhury 60), Amartey, Vestergaard, Thomas; Tielemans (Soumare 60), Ndidi, Maddison; Lookman, Iheanacho, Barnes (Perez 60).
Leicester C won 7-2 on aggregate.

Slavia Prague (2) 3 *(Schranz 19, Sor 27, 63)*

Fenerbahce (1) 2 *(Yandas 39, Berisha 90)* 10,120

Slavia Prague: (4231) Mandous; Bah (Lingr 46), Ousou, Kacharaba (Kudela 90), Dorley; Traore (Taloverov 78), Holes; Schranz, Plavsic (Pudil M 90), Olayinka; Sor (Tecl 83).
Fenerbahce: (3421) Bayindir; Tisserand (Kim 81), Aziz, Szalai; Samuel, Yandas, Sosa (Tufan 57), Kadioglu (Sangare 28); Valencia, Pelkas (Guler 57); Dursun (Berisha 81).
Slavia Prague won 6-4 on aggregate.

Vitesse (2) 2 *(Grbic 3, Bero 19)*

Rapid Vienna (0) 0 13,517

Vitesse: (3142) Houwen; Oroz, Doekhi, Rasmussen; Tronstad; Dasa, Bero, Domgjoni (Vroegh 80), Wittek; Frederiksen (Huisman 69), Grbic (Yapi 90).
Rapid Vienna: (343) Hedl; Aiwu, Wimmer, Moormann; Schick (Kitagawa 57), Grahovac (Petrovic 81), Ljubicic, Auer (Schobesberger 81); Demir (Knasmullner 57), Druijf, Grull.
Vitesse won 3-2 on aggregate.

ROUND OF 16 FIRST LEG

Thursday, 10 March 2022

Bodo/Glimt (1) 2 *(Pellegrino 39, Solbakken 90 (pen))*

AZ Alkmaar (0) 1 *(Aboukhlal 73)* 5724

Bodo/Glimt: (433) Haikin; Sampsted, Moe, Hoibraten, Wembangomo; Vetlesen, Hagen, Saltnes; Solbakken, Espejord (Boniface 84), Pellegrino (Koomson 88).
AZ Alkmaar: (433) Vindahl-Jensen; Witry (Sowah 60), Chatzidiakos, Martins Indi, Wijndal; Reijnders, de Wit, Sugawara; Evjen, Pavlidis (Aboukhlal 60), Karlsson.

Leicester C (1) 2 *(Albrighton 30, Iheanacho 90)*

Rennes (0) 0 25,848

Leicester C: (433) Schmeichel; Justin (Choudhury 62), Amartey, Soyuncu, Thomas; Tielemans, Ndidi, Dewsbury-Hall (Maddison 80); Albrighton, Daka (Iheanacho 62), Barnes (Lookman 80).
Rennes: (442) Gomis; Traore, Omari, Aguerd, Truffert (Meling 77); Bourigeaud, Martin (Majer 64), Santamaria, Doku (Tait 64); Laborde (Guirassy 77), Terrier.

Marseille (1) 2 *(Milik 19 (pen), 68)*

FC Basel (0) 1 *(Esposito 79)* 22,992

Marseille: (433) Mandanda; Rongier, Saliba, Caleta-Car, Kolasinac (Luan Peres 78); Guendouzi, Kamara, Gerson; Under, Milik, Payet (Harit 78).
FC Basel: (4231) Lindner; Tavares, Frei, Pelmard, Katterbach; Xhaka (Burger 70), Kasami; Ndoye, Esposito, Millar (Fernandes 70); Chalov (Males 70).

PAOK (0) 1 *(Kurtic 58)*

Gent (0) 0 9098

PAOK: (4231) Paschalakis; Lyratzis, Ingason, Crespo, Vieirinha (Sidcley 80); Tsingaras, Kurtic (Schwab 80); Zivkovic (Murg 86), Douglas, Biseswar (El Kaddouri 71); Akpom (Colak 86).
Gent: (3421) Roef; Hanche-Olsen, Ngadeu Ngadjui, Okumu (Torunarigha 46); Samoise, de Sart, Kums, Castro-Montes; Odjidja-Ofoe, Hjulsager (Tissoudali 82); Depoitre.

Partizan Belgrade (1) 2 *(Natkho 13, Jovic 46)*

Feyenoord (1) 5 *(Toornstra 20, 77, Dessers 51, Geertruida 64, Sinisterra 71)* 13,564

Partizan Belgrade: (4231) Popovic; Zivkovic (Lutovac 75), Vujacic, Sanicanin, Urosevic; Zdjelar, Jojic (Holender 75); Markovic (Bazdar 75), Natkho (Jovic 17), Menig (Jevtovic 57); Milovanovic.
Feyenoord: (433) Bijlow; Geertruida, Trauner, Senesi, Malacia; Toornstra, Aursnes, Kokcu; Nelson (Jahanbakhsh 81), Dessers (Linssen 87), Sinisterra.

PSV Eindhoven (1) 4 *(Gakpo 21, 70, Doan 50, Zahavi 85)*

FC Copenhagen (3) 4 *(Johannesson 6, Biel 22, 78, Lerager 43)* 26,000

PSV Eindhoven: (433) Drommel; Junior, Teze, Obispo, Max; Gutierrez, Sangare (Vinicius 83), Veerman (Doan 46); Madueke (Zahavi 46), Gotze, Gakpo.
FC Copenhagen: (433) Grabara; Ankersen, Vavro, Boilesen, Kristiansen; Stage, Jensen, Lerager (Hojlund 86); Johannesson (Diks 64), Biel, Boving Vick (Bardagji 75).

Slavia Prague (2) 4 *(Sor 3, 29, Olayinka 82, Traore 85)*
LASK (0) 1 *(Balic 67)* 16,754
Slavia Prague: (4231) Mandous; Bah, Ousou, Holes, Plavsic; Traore, Taloverov; Pudil A (Pudil M 46 (Masopust 82)), Madsen (Samek 57), Olayinka; Sor (Tecl 70).
LASK: (541) Schlager; Potzmann, Boller, Holland, Wiesinger (Twardzik 81), Renner; Flecker (Schmidt 61), Hyun-seok, Michorl, Goiginger; Balic (Nakamura 81).

Vitesse (0) 0
Roma (1) 1 *(Sergio Oliveira 45)* 24,022
Vitesse: (3142) Houwen; Oroz (Buitink 83), Doekhi, Rasmussen; Tronstad; Dasa, Bero, Domgjoni (Bazoer 82), Wittek; Grbic, Openda (Frederiksen 82).
Roma: (3412) Rui Patricio; Mancini, Ibanez, Kumbulla; Maitland-Niles (Karsdorp 46), Sergio Oliveira■, Veretout (El Shaarawy 46), Vina (Cristante 46); Mkhitaryan (Smalling 88); Zaniolo (Pellegrini 66), Abraham.

ROUND OF 16 SECOND LEG

Thursday, 17 March 2022

AZ Alkmaar (2) 2 *(Pavlidis 18, 30)*
Bodo/Glimt (1) 2 *(Pellegrino 25, Sampsted 105)* 15,024
AZ Alkmaar: (4231) Vindahl-Jensen; Witry, Beukema, Martins Indi, Wijndal; Reijnders, Clasie (Evjen 81); Sugawara (Chatzidiakos 120), de Wit (Sowah 81), Karlsson; Pavlidis (Aboukhlal 76).
Bodo/Glimt: (433) Haikin; Sampsted, Moe, Hoibraten (Kvile 106), Wembangomo (Kongsro 116); Vetlesen, Hagen, Saltnes; Solbakken, Espejord (Boniface 91), Pellegrino (Koomson 91).
aet; Bodo/Glimt won 4-3 on aggregate.

FC Basel (0) 1 *(Ndoye 62)*
Marseille (0) 2 *(Under 74, Rongier 90)* 22,081
FC Basel: (4231) Lindner; Lang (Katterbach 68), Frei, Pelmard, Tavares; Xhaka (Palacios 81), Burger (Kasami 68); Ndoye (Males 87), Esposito, Millar; Chalov (Chipperfield 81).
Marseille: (4231) Mandanda; Lirola (Kamara 73), Saliba, Caleta-Car, Luan Peres; Rongier, Gueye; Under (Balerdi 90), Guendouzi, Harit (Gerson 63); Bakambu (Milik 64).
Marseille won 4-2 on aggregate.

FC Copenhagen (0) 0
PSV Eindhoven (2) 4 *(Zahavi 10, 79, Gotze 38, Madueke 90)* 30,337
FC Copenhagen: (433) Johnsson; Ankersen (Jelert 46), Vavro, Boilesen, Diks; Stage (Hojlund 83), Lerager, Johannesson; Bardagji (Sahsah 75), Biel (Baldursson 82), Boving Vick (Khocholava 46).
PSV Eindhoven: (4231) Drommel; Junior, Teze, Boscagli, Max; Sangare, Gutierrez (Bruma 90); Doan (Madueke 84), Gotze (Vertessen 90), Gakpo (Veerman 53); Zahavi (Vinicius 83).
PSV Eindhoven won 8-4 on aggregate,

Feyenoord (1) 3 *(Dessers 45, Nelson 59, Linssen 90)*
Partizan Belgrade (0) 1 *(Gomes 61)* 44,298
Feyenoord: (3421) Marciano; Aursnes (Benita 80), Senesi, Hendriks; Geertruida, Toornstra, Kokcu, Sinisterra (Jahanbakhsh 80); Nelson (Walemark 62), Til (Hendrix 72); Dessers (Linssen 62).
Partizan Belgrade: (4231) Stevanovic; Lutovac, Miletic, Sanicanin, Urosevic; Jevtovic (Smiljanic 84), Zdjelar; Markovic (Bazdar 84), Jojic (Terzic 72), Menig (Jovic 78); Gomes (Holender 78).
Feyenoord won 8-3 on aggregate.

Gent (1) 1 *(Depoitre 40)*
PAOK (1) 2 *(Crespo 20, Douglas 77)* 12,388
Gent: (3412) Roef; Okumu, Ngadeu Ngadjui, Torunarigha; Samoise (Nurio Fortuna 85), Owusu, Kums, Castro-Montes (Hanche-Olsen 85); Odjidja-Ofoe (Hjulsager 82); Depoitre, Tissoudali (Bezus 82).
PAOK: (4231) Paschalakis; Lyratzis, Ingason, Crespo (Mihaj 46), Vieirinha; Tsingaras, Schwab (Mitrita 85); Murg (Taylor 70), Douglas, Biseswar (Sidcley 57); Akpom (Colak 85).
PAOK won 3-1 on aggregate.

LASK (1) 4 *(Wiesinger 36, 76, Gruber 88, Schmidt 89)*
Slavia Prague (2) 3 *(Olayinka 24, Bah 37, Sor 62)* 8000
LASK: (4231) Schlager; Potzmann, Letard (Sako 57), Wiesinger, Renner; Michorl (Hyun-seok 80), Holland; Flecker (Schmidt 46), Horvath, Goiginger (Nakamura 46); Balic (Gruber 72).
Slavia Prague: (4231) Mandous; Bah, Ousou■, Holes, Plavsic■; Traore, Taloverov; Schranz (Tecl 80), Lingr (Masopust 77), Olayinka (Kudela 84); Sor.
Slavia Prague won 7-5 on aggregate.

Rennes (1) 2 *(Bourigeaud 8, Tait 75)*
Leicester C (0) 1 *(Fofana 51)* 27,000
Rennes: (433) Alemdar; Traore, Omari, Aguerd, Truffert (Meling 76); Majer, Martin (Tait 58), Santamaria; Bourigeaud, Laborde (Tchaouna 76), Terrier (Guirassy 68).
Leicester C: (433) Schmeichel; Justin, Amartey, Fofana (Vestergaard 78), Thomas; Tielemans, Ndidi (Maddison 60), Dewsbury-Hall; Albrighton (Lookman 12 (Ricardo Pereira 79)), Iheanacho, Barnes.
Leicester C won 3-2 on aggregate.

Roma (0) 1 *(Abraham 90)*
Vitesse (0) 1 *(Wittek 62)* 40,435
Roma: (343) Rui Patricio; Ibanez, Smalling, Kumbulla; Maitland-Niles (El Shaarawy 66), Mkhitaryan, Veretout (Cristante 66), Vina (Karsdorp 66); Zaniolo (Afena-Gyan 79), Abraham, Pellegrini (Bove 90).
Vitesse: (532) Houwen; Dasa, Doekhi, Bazoer (Buitink 90), Rasmussen, Wittek; Tronstad, Huisman (Gboho 60), Domgjoni (Frederiksen 90); Grbic, Openda.
Roma won 2-1 on aggregate,

QUARTER-FINALS FIRST LEG

Thursday, 7 April 2022

Bodo/Glimt (0) 2 *(Saltnes 56, Vetlesen 89)*
Roma (1) 1 *(Pellegrini 43)* 7739
Bodo/Glimt: (433) Haikin; Sampsted, Moe (Kvile 90), Hoibraten, Wembangomo; Vetlesen, Hagen, Saltnes; Koomson (Mugisha 82), Espejord (Boniface 76), Pellegrino.
Roma: (3421) Rui Patricio; Mancini (Smalling 69), Kumbulla, Ibanez; Karsdorp, Cristante, Sergio Oliveira, Zalewski (Vina 65); Mkhitaryan (Shomurodov 65), Pellegrini; Abraham.

Feyenoord (1) 3 *(Sinisterra 10, Senesi 74, Kokcu 86)*
Slavia Prague (1) 3 *(Olayinka 41, Sor 67, Traore 90)* 45,000
Feyenoord: (433) Marciano; Pedersen, Trauner, Senesi, Malacia; Nelson (Jahanbakhsh 77), Aursnes, Kokcu (Hendrix 89); Til (Toornstra 64), Linssen (Dessers 64), Sinisterra.
Slavia Prague: (4231) Kolar; Bah, Kudela, Kacharaba, Dorley; Taloverov (Lingr 67), Holes (Madsen 90); Schranz, Traore, Olayinka (Tecl 83); Sor.

Leicester C (0) 0
PSV Eindhoven (0) 0 31,327
Leicester C: (433) Schmeichel; Ricardo Pereira (Justin 67), Fofana, Evans, Castagne; Maddison, Tielemans, Dewsbury-Hall; Albrighton (Daka 81), Iheanacho (Lookman 67), Barnes.
PSV Eindhoven: (433) Mvogo; Junior (Teze 90), Ramalho, Boscagli, Max; Sangare, Gotze, Veerman; Madueke (Bruma 82), Zahavi (Doan 69), Gakpo (van Ginkel 90).

Marseille (2) 2 *(Gerson 13, Payet 45)*
PAOK (0) 1 *(El Kaddouri 48)* 45,182
Marseille: (433) Mandanda; Lirola (Rongier 63), Saliba, Caleta-Car, Kolasinac (Kamara 63); Guendouzi, Gueye, Gerson■; Under, Bakambu (Dieng 46), Payet.
PAOK: (4231) Paschalakis; Lyratzis, Ingason, Crespo, Vieirinha; Tsingaras (El Kaddouri 46), Kurtic; Zivkovic, Douglas, Biseswar (Mitrita 75); Akpom (Colak 75).

QUARTER-FINALS SECOND LEG

Thursday, 14 April 2022

PAOK (0) 0

Marseille (1) 1 *(Payet 34)* 27,648

PAOK: (4231) Paschalakis; Lyratzis, Ingason, Crespo, Vieirinha (Sidcley 68); Tsingaras (Mitrita 57), Kurtic; Zivkovic (Murg 77), Douglas, Biseswar (Schwab 77); Akpom (Colak 68).
Marseille: (433) Mandanda; Lirola, Saliba, Caleta-Car, Luan Peres; Guendouzi, Rongier, Gueye; Harit, Bakambu (Under 72), Payet (Kolasinac 88).
Marseille won 3-1 on aggregate.

PSV Eindhoven (1) 1 *(Zahavi 27)*

Leicester C (0) 2 *(Maddison 77, Ricardo Pereira 88)* 35,000

PSV Eindhoven: (433) Mvogo; Junior, Teze, Ramalho, Max (Oppegard 74); Gutierrez (Bruma 90), Gotze, Sangare; Veerman (Doan 82), Zahavi (Vinicius 82), Gakpo.
Leicester C: (433) Schmeichel; Ricardo Pereira, Fofana, Evans, Castagne; Maddison, Tielemans, Dewsbury-Hall; Albrighton (Daka 46), Iheanacho (Perez 65), Barnes (Lookman 46).
Leicester C won 2-1 on aggregate.

Roma (3) 4 *(Abraham 5, Zaniolo 23, 29, 49)*

Bodo/Glimt (0) 0 61,942

Roma: (3412) Rui Patricio; Mancini, Smalling, Ibanez; Karsdorp, Cristante, Mkhitaryan (Veretout 85), Zalewski (Maitland-Niles 86); Pellegrini (Sergio Oliveira 76); Zaniolo (Afena-Gyan 60), Abraham (Perez 85).
Bodo/Glimt: (433) Haikin; Sampsted, Moe (Sery Larsen 61), Hoibraten, Wembangomo (Kvile 89); Vetlesen, Hagen, Saltnes; Koomson (Mugisha 73), Espejord (Boniface 61), Solbakken (Nordas 89).
Roma won 5-2 on aggregate.

Slavia Prague (1) 1 *(Traore 14)*

Feyenoord (1) 3 *(Dessers 2, 59, Sinisterra 78)* 19,370

Slavia Prague: (4231) Mandous; Bah, Ousou (Sevcik 77), Kacharaba■, Dorley; Traore (Tecl 89), Taloverov; Lingr (Samek 82), Schranz (Plavsic 77), Olayinka; Sor.
Feyenoord: (433) Marciano; Geertruida (Pedersen 83), Trauner, Senesi, Malacia; Toornstra (Walemark 55), Aursnes, Kokcu; Nelson (Hendrix 67), Dessers, Sinisterra (Linssen 83).
Feyenoord won 6-4 on aggregate.

SEMI-FINALS FIRST LEG

Thursday, 28 April 2022

Feyenoord (2) 3 *(Dessers 18, 46, Sinisterra 20)*

Marseille (2) 2 *(Dieng 28, Gerson 40)* 24,500

Feyenoord: (4231) Marciano; Geertruida, Trauner, Senesi, Malacia; Aursnes, Kokcu (Hendrix 82); Nelson (Linssen 65), Til (Pedersen 89), Sinisterra; Dessers (Jahanbakhsh 82).
Marseille: (433) Mandanda; Rongier (Lirola 85), Saliba, Caleta-Car (Harit 69), Luan Peres; Guendouzi, Kamara, Gerson; Bakambu (Gueye 46), Payet, Dieng (Milik 85).

Leicester C (0) 1 *(Mancini 67 (og))*

Roma (1) 1 *(Pellegrini 15)* 31,659

Leicester C: (433) Schmeichel; Ricardo Pereira, Fofana, Evans, Castagne (Justin 21); Maddison, Tielemans, Dewsbury-Hall; Albrighton (Barnes 63), Vardy (Iheanacho 62), Lookman (Perez 84).
Roma: (352) Rui Patricio; Mancini, Smalling, Ibanez; Karsdorp, Mkhitaryan (Veretout 57), Cristante, Pellegrini (Afena-Gyan 85), Zalewski (Vina 85); Zaniolo (Sergio Oliveira 69), Abraham.

SEMI-FINALS SECOND LEG

Thursday, 5 May 2022

Marseille (0) 0

Feyenoord (0) 0 49,315

Marseille: (3241) Mandanda; Saliba, Kamara, Luan Peres; Rongier, Gueye (Lirola 46); Dieng (Bakambu 62), Guendouzi, Harit (Under 80), Gerson; Payet (Milik 33).
Feyenoord: (4231) Marciano; Geertruida, Trauner, Senesi, Malacia; Aursnes, Kokcu; Nelson (Jahanbakhsh 88), Til (Hendrix 81), Sinisterra (Linssen 74); Dessers.
Feyenoord won 3-2 on aggregate.

Roma (1) 1 *(Abraham 11)*

Leicester C (0) 0 63,940

Roma: (3421) Rui Patricio; Mancini, Smalling, Ibanez; Karsdorp, Cristante, Sergio Oliveira, Zalewski (Vina 84); Zaniolo (Veretout 78), Pellegrini; Abraham (Shomurodov 88).
Leicester C: (433) Schmeichel; Ricardo Pereira (Castagne 69), Fofana, Evans, Justin; Maddison, Tielemans, Dewsbury-Hall (Perez 77); Lookman (Amartey 46), Vardy, Barnes (Iheanacho 46).
Roma won 2-1 on aggregate.

UEFA EUROPA CONFERENCE LEAGUE FINAL 2021–22

Wednesday, 25 May 2022

(in Tirana, attendance 19,597)

Roma (1) 1 Feyenoord (0) 0

Roma: (3412) Rui Patricio; Mancini, Smalling, Ibanez; Karsdorp (Vina 89), Mkhitaryan (Sergio Oliveira 17), Cristante, Zalewski (Spinazzola 67); Pellegrini; Zaniolo (Veretout 66), Abraham (Shomurodov 89).
Scorer: Zaniolo 32.

Feyenoord: (4231) Bijlow; Geertruida, Trauner (Pedersen 74), Senesi, Malacia (Jahanbakhsh 88); Aursnes, Kokcu (Walemark 88); Nelson (Linssen 74), Til (Toornstra 59), Sinisterra; Dessers.

Referee: Istvan Kovacs.

BRITISH AND IRISH CLUBS IN EUROPE

SUMMARY OF APPEARANCES

EUROPEAN CUP AND CHAMPIONS LEAGUE 1955–2022

(Winners in brackets) (SE = seasons entered).

ENGLAND	SE	P	W	D	L	F	A
Manchester U (3)	30	293	160	69	64	533	284
Liverpool (6)	26	240	147	51	54	483	229
Arsenal	21	201	101	43	57	332	218
Chelsea (2)	18	191	99	52	40	330	172
Manchester C	12	106	58	19	29	213	126
Tottenham H	6	55	25	10	20	108	83
Leeds U	4	40	22	6	12	76	41
Newcastle U	3	24	11	3	10	33	33
Nottingham F (2)	3	20	12	4	4	32	14
Everton	3	10	2	5	3	14	10
Aston Villa (1)	2	15	9	3	3	24	10
Derby Co	2	12	6	2	4	18	12
Wolverhampton W	2	8	2	2	4	12	16
Leicester C	1	10	5	2	3	11	10
Blackburn R	1	6	1	1	4	5	8
Ipswich T	1	4	3	0	1	16	5
Burnley	1	4	2	0	2	8	8
SCOTLAND							
Celtic (1)	36	216	101	37	78	333	255
Rangers	31	163	62	40	61	234	222
Aberdeen	3	12	5	4	3	14	12
Hearts	3	8	2	1	5	8	16
Dundee U	1	8	5	1	2	14	5
Dundee	1	8	5	0	3	20	14
Hibernian	1	6	3	1	2	9	5
Kilmarnock	1	4	1	2	1	4	7
Motherwell	1	2	0	0	2	0	5
WALES							
The New Saints	13	36	9	5	22	36	63
Barry Town U	6	14	4	1	9	11	38
Rhyl	2	4	0	0	4	1	19
Cwmbran T	1	2	1	0	1	4	4
Llanelli	1	2	1	0	1	1	4
Bangor C	1	2	0	0	2	0	13
Connah's Quay Nomads	2	3	0	1	2	2	5
NORTHERN IRELAND							
Linfield	31	73	8	23	42	60	130
Glentoran	12	28	3	7	18	20	59
Crusaders	6	14	1	2	11	7	52
Cliftonville	3	6	0	1	5	1	20
Portadown	3	6	0	1	5	3	24
Glenavon	1	2	0	1	1	0	3
Lisburn Distillery	1	2	0	1	1	3	8
Ards	1	2	0	0	2	3	10
Coleraine	1	2	0	0	2	1	11
REPUBLIC OF IRELAND							
Dundalk	12	33	4	12	17	24	60
Shamrock R	10	22	2	6	14	11	36
Shelbourne	6	20	4	8	8	21	31
Bohemians	6	18	4	4	10	13	29
Waterford U	6	14	3	0	11	15	47
Derry C	4	9	1	1	7	9	26
St Patrick's Ath	4	8	0	3	5	2	23
Cork C	3	10	2	1	7	7	16
Dublin C	3	6	1	0	5	3	25
Athlone T	2	4	0	2	2	7	14
Sligo R	2	4	0	0	4	0	9
Limerick	2	4	0	0	4	4	16
Drogheda U	1	4	2	1	1	6	5
Cork Hibernians	1	2	0	0	2	1	7
Cork Celtic	1	2	0	0	2	1	7

UEFA CUP AND EUROPA LEAGUE 1971–2022

ENGLAND	SE	P	W	D	L	F	A
Tottenham H (2)	16	153	88	37	28	315	134
Liverpool (3)	14	124	66	34	24	186	94
Aston Villa	13	56	24	14	18	77	60
Manchester U (1)	11	64	31	19	14	101	50
Arsenal	10	76	44	13	19	154	79
Ipswich T (1)	10	52	30	10	12	98	53
Everton	9	52	27	8	17	87	64
Newcastle U	8	72	42	17	13	123	60
Manchester C	8	52	28	13	11	84	51
Leeds U	8	46	20	10	16	66	48
Southampton	7	22	6	9	7	23	20
Blackburn R	6	22	7	8	7	27	26
Wolverhampton W	5	37	25	5	7	79	37
Chelsea (2)	5	32	22	5	5	64	30
West Ham U	5	28	12	5	11	37	24
Fulham	3	39	21	10	8	64	31
Nottingham F	3	20	10	5	5	18	16
Stoke C	3	16	8	4	4	21	16
WBA	3	12	5	2	5	15	13
Leicester C	4	18	6	5	7	29	26
Middlesbrough	2	25	13	4	8	36	24
Bolton W	2	18	6	10	2	18	14
QPR	2	12	8	1	3	39	18
Derby Co	2	10	5	2	3	32	17
Birmingham C	1	8	4	2	2	11	8
Burnley	1	6	2	3	1	7	6
Norwich C	1	6	2	2	2	6	4
Portsmouth	1	6	2	2	2	11	10
Watford	1	6	2	1	3	10	12
Wigan Ath	1	6	1	2	3	6	7
Sheffield W	1	4	2	1	1	13	7
Hull C	1	4	2	1	1	4	3
Millwall	1	2	0	1	1	2	4
SCOTLAND							
Celtic	24	139	60	29	50	219	176
Aberdeen	23	87	29	27	31	116	109
Rangers	21	140	63	43	34	208	169
Dundee U	19	82	33	25	24	134	89
Hearts	14	50	21	10	19	61	62
Hibernian	13	40	15	11	14	57	63
Motherwell	9	29	9	3	17	40	40
St Johnstone	8	26	7	8	11	28	35
Dundee	4	14	6	0	8	24	24
Kilmarnock	4	14	5	2	7	9	17
St Mirren	3	10	2	3	5	9	12
Dunfermline Ath	2	4	0	2	2	4	6
Raith R	1	6	2	1	3	10	8
Livingston	1	4	1	2	1	7	9
Falkirk	1	2	1	0	1	1	2
Inverness CT	1	2	0	1	1	0	1
Gretna	1	2	0	1	1	3	7
Queen of the South	1	2	0	0	2	2	4
Partick Thistle	1	2	0	0	2	0	4
WALES							
The New Saints	11	26	3	4	19	21	68
Bangor C	10	22	2	2	18	10	61
Bala T	6	12	4	0	8	8	21
Connah's Quay Nomads	5	13	3	1	9	7	18
Llanelli	5	12	3	3	6	12	24
Barry Town U	4	11	2	3	6	11	25
Cardiff Met Univ	4	8	2	0	6	3	20
Rhyl	3	8	2	1	5	9	12
Newtown	3	8	2	1	5	6	21
Air UK Broughton	3	6	0	4	2	6	9
Cwmbran T	3	6	0	0	6	0	21
Carmarthen T	2	6	1	0	5	8	21
Cefn Druids	2	4	0	2	2	1	7
Swansea C	1	12	4	4	4	17	10
Prestatyn T	1	4	1	0	3	3	11
Afan Lido	1	2	0	1	1	1	2
Haverfordwest Co	1	2	0	0	2	1	4
Neath	1	2	0	0	2	1	6
Port Talbot T	1	2	0	0	2	1	7
Llandudno T	1	2	0	0	2	1	7
Aberystwith T	1	2	0	0	2	0	9
NORTHERN IRELAND							
Glentoran	19	42	4	8	30	24	102
Linfield	14	41	13	9	19	49	73
Portadown	11	28	3	7	18	16	62
Crusaders	11	26	6	4	16	27	62
Coleraine	10	21	2	7	12	13	49
Glenavon	9	20	2	2	16	10	49
Cliftonville	7	20	4	4	12	15	37
Ballymena U	3	8	2	1	5	4	20
Dungannon Swifts	1	2	1	0	1	1	4
Ards	1	2	1	0	1	4	8
Bangor	1	2	0	0	2	0	6
Lisburn Distillery	1	2	0	0	2	1	11

REPUBLIC OF IRELAND							
Bohemians	15	31	3	10	18	17	57
St Patrick's Ath	11	40	10	7	23	35	61
Shamrock R	11	38	9	7	22	36	68
Cork C	11	32	7	7	18	23	46
Dundalk	10	37	9	5	23	34	73
Derry C	10	27	7	5	15	32	48
Shelbourne	6	12	0	2	10	8	28
Drogheda U	4	12	3	4	5	10	24
Sligo R	4	10	2	4	4	11	13
Longford T	3	6	1	1	4	6	12
Finn Harps	3	6	0	0	6	3	33
Athlone T	1	4	1	2	1	4	5
University College Dublin	1	4	1	0	3	3	8
Limerick	1	2	0	1	1	1	4
Sporting Fingal	1	2	0	0	2	4	6
Galway U	1	2	0	0	2	2	8
Bray W	1	2	0	0	2	0	8

UEFA CONFERENCE LEAGUE 2021–22

ENGLAND	*SE*	*P*	*W*	*D*	*L*	*F*	*A*
Tottenham H	1	7	3	1	3	14	9
Leicester C	1	8	4	2	2	13	7
SCOTLAND							
Hibernian	1	4	2	1	1	7	6
Abderdeen	1	6	3	0	3	11	10
St Johnstone	1	2	0	1	1	1	3
Celtic	1	2	0	0	1	1	5
WALES							
The New Saints	1	6	4	1	1	18	7
Bala T	1	2	0	0	2	0	2
Newtown	1	2	0	0	2	0	5
Connah's Quay Nomads	1	2	1	0	1	5	6
NORTHERN IRELAND							
Coleraine	1	2	0	0	2	2	4
Glentoran	1	2	0	1	1	1	3
Larne	1	6	4	1	1	6	6
Linfield	1	4	1	1	2	6	4
REPUBLIC OF IRELAND							
Dundalk	1	6	3	2	1	12	7
Bohemians	1	6	4	1	1	10	4
Sligo R	1	2	0	0	2	1	3
Shamrock R	1	4	2	0	2	5	5

EUROPEAN CUP WINNERS' CUP 1960–1999

ENGLAND	*SE*	*P*	*W*	*D*	*L*	*F*	*A*
Tottenham H (1)	6	33	20	5	8	65	34
Chelsea (2)	5	39	23	10	6	81	28
Liverpool	5	29	16	5	8	57	29
Manchester U (1)	5	31	16	9	6	55	35
West Ham U (1)	4	30	15	6	9	58	42
Arsenal (1)	3	27	15	10	2	48	20
Everton (1)	3	17	11	4	2	25	9
Manchester C (1)	2	18	11	2	5	32	13
Ipswich T	1	6	3	2	1	6	3
Leeds U	1	9	5	3	1	13	3
Leicester C	1	4	2	1	1	8	5
Newcastle U	1	2	1	0	1	2	2
Southampton	1	6	4	0	2	16	8
Sunderland	1	4	3	0	1	5	3
WBA	1	6	2	2	2	8	5
Wolverhampton W	1	4	1	1	2	6	5
SCOTLAND							
Rangers (1)	10	54	27	11	16	100	62
Aberdeen (1)	8	39	22	5	12	79	37
Celtic	8	38	21	4	13	75	37
Dundee U	3	10	3	3	4	9	10
Hearts	3	10	3	3	4	16	14
Dunfermline Ath	2	14	7	2	5	34	14
Airdrieonians	1	2	0	0	2	1	3
Dundee	1	2	0	1	1	3	4
Hibernian	1	6	3	1	2	19	10
Kilmarnock	1	4	1	2	1	5	6
Motherwell	1	2	1	0	1	3	3
St Mirren	1	4	1	2	1	1	2
WALES							
Cardiff C	14	49	16	14	19	67	61
Wrexham	8	28	10	8	10	34	35
Swansea C	7	18	3	4	11	32	37
Bangor C	3	9	1	2	6	5	12
Barry T	1	2	0	0	2	0	7
Borough U	1	4	1	1	2	2	4
Cwmbran T	1	2	0	0	2	2	12
Merthyr Tydfil	1	2	1	0	1	2	3
Newport Co	1	6	2	3	1	12	3
The New Saints (Llansantfraid)	1	2	0	1	1	1	6
NORTHERN IRELAND							
Glentoran	9	22	3	7	12	18	46
Glenavon	5	10	1	3	6	11	25
Ballymena U	4	8	0	0	8	1	25
Coleraine	4	8	0	1	7	7	34
Crusaders	3	6	0	2	4	5	18
Derry C	3	6	1	1	4	1	11
Linfield	3	6	2	0	4	6	11
Ards	2	4	0	1	3	2	17
Bangor	2	4	0	1	3	2	8
Carrick Rangers	1	4	1	0	3	7	12
Cliftonville	1	2	0	0	2	0	8
Distillery	1	2	0	0	2	1	7
Portadown	1	2	1	0	1	4	7
REPUBLIC OF IRELAND							
Shamrock R	6	16	5	2	9	19	27
Shelbourne	4	10	1	1	8	9	20
Bohemians	3	8	2	2	4	6	13
Dundalk	3	8	2	1	5	7	14
Limerick U	3	6	0	1	5	2	11
Waterford U	3	8	1	1	6	6	14
Cork C	2	4	1	0	3	2	9
Cork Hibernians	2	6	2	1	3	7	8
Galway U	2	4	0	0	4	2	11
Sligo R	2	6	1	1	4	5	11
Bray W	1	2	0	1	1	1	3
Cork Celtic	1	2	0	1	1	1	3
Finn Harps	1	2	0	1	1	2	4
Home Farm	1	2	0	1	1	1	7
St Patrick's Ath	1	2	0	0	2	1	8
University College Dublin	1	2	0	1	1	0	1

INTER-CITIES FAIRS CUP 1955–1970

ENGLAND	*SE*	*P*	*W*	*D*	*L*	*F*	*A*
Leeds U (2)	5	53	28	17	8	92	40
Birmingham C	4	25	14	6	5	51	38
Liverpool	4	22	12	4	6	46	15
Arsenal (1)	3	24	12	5	7	46	19
Chelsea	3	20	10	5	5	33	24
Everton	3	12	7	2	3	22	15
Newcastle U (1)	3	24	13	6	5	37	21
Nottingham F	2	6	3	0	3	8	9
Sheffield W	2	10	5	0	5	25	18
Burnley	1	8	4	3	1	16	5
Coventry C	1	4	3	0	1	9	8
London XI	1	8	4	1	3	14	13
Manchester U	1	11	6	3	2	29	10
Southampton	1	6	2	3	1	11	6
WBA	1	4	1	1	2	7	9
SCOTLAND							
Hibernian	7	36	18	5	13	66	60
Dunfermline Ath	5	28	16	3	9	49	31
Kilmarnock	4	20	8	3	9	34	32
Dundee U	3	10	5	1	4	11	12
Hearts	3	12	4	4	4	20	20
Rangers	3	18	8	4	6	27	17
Celtic	2	6	1	3	2	9	10
Aberdeen	1	4	2	1	1	4	4
Dundee	1	8	5	1	2	14	6
Morton	1	2	0	0	2	3	9
Partick Thistle	1	4	3	0	1	10	7
NORTHERN IRELAND							
Glentoran	4	8	1	1	6	7	22
Coleraine	2	8	2	1	5	15	23
Linfield	2	4	1	0	3	3	11
REPUBLIC OF IRELAND							
Drumcondra	2	6	2	0	4	8	19
Dundalk	2	6	1	1	4	4	25
Shamrock R	2	4	0	2	2	4	6
Cork Hibernians	1	2	0	0	2	1	6
Shelbourne	1	5	1	2	2	3	4
St Patrick's Ath	1	2	0	0	2	4	9

FIFA CLUB WORLD CUP 2021

Formerly known as the FIFA Club World Championship, this tournament is played annually between the champion clubs from all 6 continental confederations, although since 2007 the champions of Oceania must play a qualifying play-off against the champion club of the host country.

(Finals in United Arab Emirates)

FIRST ROUND

Al Jazira v AS Pirae	4-1

SECOND ROUND

Al Ahly v Monterrey	1-0
Al Hilal v Al Jazira	6-1

SEMI-FINALS

Palmeiras v Al Ahly	2-0
Al Hilal v Chelsea	0-1

MATCH FOR FIFTH PLACE

Monterrey v Al Jazira	3-1

MATCH FOR THIRD PLACE

Al Hilal v Al Ahly	0-4

FIFA CLUB WORLD CUP FINAL 2021

Abu Dhabi, Saturday 12 February 2022

Chelsea (0) 2 *(Lukaku 54, Havertz 117 (pen))*

Palmeiras (0) 1 *(Veiga 64 (pen))* 32,871

Chelsea: Mendy; Christensen (Sarr 91), Thiago Silva, Rudiger, Azpilicueta, Kante, Kovacic (Ziyech 91), Hudson-Odoi (Saul 76), Mount (Pulisic 31), Havertz, Lukaku (Werner 76).

Palmerias: Weverton; Rocha (Deyverson 118), Gomez, Luan■, Piquerez, Gustavo Scarpa, Rony (Wesley 77), Danilo, Ze Rafael (Jailson 60), Dudu (Navarro 103), Veiga (Atiesta 78).

aet. Referee: Chris Beath (Australia).

PREVIOUS FINALS

2000 Corinthians beat Vasco da Gama 4-3 on penalties after 0-0 draw
2001–04 Not contested
2005 Sao Paulo beat Liverpool 1-0
2006 Internacional beat Barcelona 1-0
2007 AC Milan beat Boca Juniors 4-2
2008 Manchester U beat Liga De Quito 1-0
2009 Barcelona beat Estudiantes 2-1
2010 Internazionale beat TP Mazembe Englebert 3-0
2011 Barcelona beat Santos 4-0
2012 Corinthians beat Chelsea 1-0
2013 Bayern Munich beat Raja Casablanca 2-0
2014 Real Madrid beat San Lorenzo 2-0
2015 Barcelona beat River Plate 3-0
2016 Real Madrid beat Kashima Antlers 4-2 (*aet.*)
2017 Real Madrid beat Gremio 1-0
2018 Real Madrid beat Al-Ain 4-1
2019 Liverpool beat Flamengo 1-0 (*aet.*)
2020 Bayern Munich beat Tigres UANL 1-0
2021 Chelsea beat Palmeiras 2-1

EUROPEAN SUPER CUP 2021

Played annually between the winners of the European Champions' Cup and the European Cup-Winners' Cup (UEFA Cup from 2000; UEFA Europa League from 2010). AC Milan replaced Marseille in 1993–94. Match played in Monaco 1998–2012; various venues from 2013.

Belfast, Wednesday 11 August 2021, attendance 10,435

Chelsea (1) 1 *(Ziyech 27)* **Villareal (0) 1** *(Gerard Moreno 73)*

Chelsea: Mendy (Arrizabalaga 119); Zouma (Christensen 66), Chalobah, Rudiger, Kante (Jorginho 65), Kovacic, Hudson-Odoi (Azpilicueta 82), Alonso, Ziyech (Pulisic 43), Havertz, Werner (Mount 65).

Villarreal: Asenjo; Foyth, Albiol, Pau Torres, Pedraza (Estupinan 58), Trigueros (Gomez 70), Capoue (Gaspar 70), Alberto Moreno (Morlanes 85), Pino (Mandi 91), Gerard Moreno, Dia (Raba 85).

Referee: Sergei Karasev (Russia).

aet; Chelsea won 6-5 on penalties.

PREVIOUS MATCHES

1972 Ajax beat Rangers 3-1, 3-2
1973 Ajax beat AC Milan 0-1, 6-0
1974 Not contested
1975 Dynamo Kyiv beat Bayern Munich 1-0, 2-0
1976 Anderlecht beat Bayern Munich 4-1, 1-2
1977 Liverpool beat Hamburg 1-1, 6-0
1978 Anderlecht beat Liverpool 3-1, 1-2
1979 Nottingham F beat Barcelona 1-0, 1-1
1980 Valencia beat Nottingham F 1-0, 1-2
1981 Not contested
1982 Aston Villa beat Barcelona 0-1, 3-0
1983 Aberdeen beat Hamburg 0-0, 2-0
1984 Juventus beat Liverpool 2-0
1985 Juventus v Everton not contested due to UEFA ban on English clubs
1986 Steaua Bucharest beat Dynamo Kyiv 1-0
1987 FC Porto beat Ajax 1-0, 1-0
1988 KV Mechelen beat PSV Eindhoven 3-0, 0-1
1989 AC Milan beat Barcelona 1-1, 1-0
1990 AC Milan beat Sampdoria 1-1, 2-0
1991 Manchester U beat Crvena Zvezda 1-0
1992 Barcelona beat Werder Bremen 1-1, 2-1
1993 Parma beat AC Milan 0-1, 2-0
1994 AC Milan beat Arsenal 0-0, 2-0
1995 Ajax beat Zaragoza 1-1, 4-0
1996 Juventus beat Paris Saint-Germain 6-1, 3-1
1997 Barcelona beat Borussia Dortmund 2-0, 1-1
1998 Chelsea beat Real Madrid 1-0
1999 Lazio beat Manchester U 1-0
2000 Galatasaray beat Real Madrid 2-1
2001 Liverpool beat Bayern Munich 3-2
2002 Real Madrid beat Feyenoord 3-1
2003 AC Milan beat Porto 1-0
2004 Valencia beat Porto 2-1
2005 Liverpool beat CSKA Moscow 3-1
2006 Sevilla beat Barcelona 3-0
2007 AC Milan beat Sevilla 3-1
2008 Zenit beat Manchester U 2-1
2009 Barcelona beat Shakhtar Donetsk 1-0
2010 Atletico Madrid beat Internazionale 2-0
2011 Barcelona beat Porto 2-0
2012 Atletico Madrid beat Chelsea 4-1
2013 Bayern Munch beat Chelsea 5-4 on penalties after 2-2 draw
2014 Real Madrid beat Sevilla 2-0
2015 Barcelona beat Sevilla 5-4
2016 Real Madrid beat Sevilla 3-2
2017 Real Madrid beat Manchester U 2-1
2018 Atletico Madrid beat Real Madrid 4-2 after extra time
2019 Liverpool beat Chelsea 5-4 on penalties after 2-2 draw
2020 Bayern Munich beat Sevilla 2-1
2021 Chelsea beat Villarreal 6-5 on penalties after 1-1 draw

INTERNATIONAL DIRECTORY

The directory provides the latest available information on international and club football in the 211 national associations in the six Confederations of FIFA, the world governing body. This includes addresses, foundation dates and team colours. FIFA-recognised internationals played in season 2021–22 (i.e., *12 July 2021 to 11 July 2022*) are listed as well as league and cup champions at club level. In Europe, the latest league tables, cup winners and top scorers for the 55 UEFA nations are given, together with all-time league and cup honours. (Key to table symbols used: (C) league champions; [1] Champions League qualifier; [2] Europa League qualifier; [3] Europa Conference League qualifier; * team relegated; +* team relegated after play-offs; + team not relegated after play-offs.)

The four home nations, England, Scotland, Northern Ireland and Wales, are dealt with elsewhere in the Yearbook, but basic details appear in this directory. Gozo is included here for its close links with Maltese football, the Channel Islands for their proximity to England. Northern Cyprus is not a member of UEFA or FIFA and is the subject of an international territorial dispute. Gibraltar became the 54th member of UEFA in 2013 and joined FIFA in 2016. Kosovo was granted full membership of both UEFA (its 55th member) and FIFA in May 2016. FYR Macedonia's historic results are now credited to North Macedonia, its new name from February 2019. Swaziland was renamed Eswatini in April 2018. Due to the invasion of Ukraine, from 28 February 2022 all Russian representative and club teams were suspended from FIFA and UEFA competitions until further notice. Ukrainian league and cup competitions were abandoned.
International match venues are indicated as follows: home (h), away (a), neutral (n); in multi-nation tournaments the host nation is deemed to be playing at home and all others are on neutral territory; where a nation is unable to play a qualifier at home the neutral venue is stated in a note.

FIFA currently has 11 associate members who have affiliation to their Confederations: AFC: Northern Mariana Islands; CAF: Reunion, Zanzibar; CONCACAF: Bonaire, French Guiana, Guadeloupe, Martinique, Saint-Martin, Sint Maarten; OFC: Kiribati, Tuvalu. Matches between full members and associate members are indicated with †.

N.B. Final league rankings for clubs tied on points are decided on goal difference unless otherwise stated.

EUROPE (UEFA)

ALBANIA

Football Association of Albania, Rruga e Elbasanit, 1000 Tirana.
Founded: 1930. *FIFA:* 1932; *UEFA:* 1954. *National Colours:* Red shirts, black shorts, red socks.

International matches 2021–22

Poland (a) 1-4, Hungary (h) 1-0, San Marino (h) 5-0, Hungary (a) 1-0, Poland (h) 0-1, England (a) 0-5, Andorra (h) 1-0, Spain (a) 1-2, Georgia (h) 0-0, Iceland (a) 1-1, Israel (h) 1-2, Estonia (h) 0-0.

League Championship wins (1930–37; 1945–2022)

KF Tirana 26 (formerly SK Tirana; includes 17 Nentori 8); Dinamo Tirana 18; Partizani Tirana 16; Vllaznia Shkoder 9; Skenderbeu Korce 8; Elbasani 2 (incl. Labinoti 1); Teuta 2; Flamurtari Vlore 1; Kukesi 1.

Cup wins (1948–2022)

KF Tirana 16 (formerly SK Tirana; includes 17 Nentori 8); Partizani Tirana 15; Dinamo Tirana 13; Vllaznia 8; Flamurtari Vlore 4; Teuta 4; Elbasani 2 (incl. Labinoti 1); Besa 2; Laci 2; Kukesi 2; Apolonia Fier 1; Skenderbeu Korce 1.

Albanian Kategoria Superiore 2021–22

	P	*W*	*D*	*L*	*F*	*A*	*GD*	*Pts*
KF Tirana (C)[1]	36	22	7	7	64	27	37	73
Laci[3]	36	18	9	9	52	33	19	63
Partizani Tirana[3]	36	15	13	8	52	30	22	58
Kukesi	36	15	10	11	50	44	6	55
Vllaznia[3]	36	13	16	7	47	38	9	55
Teuta	36	13	11	12	39	44	–5	50
Kastrioti	36	13	4	19	30	54	–24	43
Egnatia+	36	8	11	17	30	49	–19	35
Dinamo Tirana*	36	6	11	19	21	46	–25	29
Skenderbeu Korce*	36	4	14	18	23	43	–20	26

Top scorers (joint): Guindo (Laci), Seferi (KF Tirana) 19.
Cup Final: Vllaznia 2, Kukesi 1 *(aet)*.

ANDORRA

Federacio Andorrana de Futbol, Avda Carlemany 67, 3er Pis, Apartado postal 65, Escaldes-Engordany.
Founded: 1994. *FIFA:* 1996; *UEFA:* 1996. *National Colours:* Red shirts with blue and yellow trim, red shorts with blue trim, red socks with blue and yellow trim.

International matches 2021–22

San Marino (h) 2-0, England (a) 0-4, Hungary (a) 1-2, England (h) 0-5, San Marino (a) 3-0, Poland (h) 1-4, Albania (a) 0-1, St Kitts & Nevis (h) 1-0, Grenada (h) 1-0, Latvia (a) 0-3, Moldova (h) 0-0, Liechtenstein (h) 2-1, Moldova (a) 0-0.

League Championship wins (1996–2022)

FC Santa Coloma 13; Principat 3; Inter Club d'Escaldes 3; Encamp 2; Sant Julia 2; Ranger's 2; Lusitanos 2; Constel-lacio Esportiva 1.

Cup wins (1991, 1994–2022)

FC Santa Coloma 10*; Principat 6*; Sant Julia 6; UE Santa Coloma 3; Constel-lacio Esportiva 1; Lusitanos 1; UE Engordany 1; Inter Club d'Escaldes 1; Atletic Club d'Escaldes 1.
* *Includes one unofficial title.*

Andorran Primera Divisio Qualifying Table 2021–22

	P	*W*	*D*	*L*	*F*	*A*	*GD*	*Pts*
Inter Club d'Escaldes	21	12	6	3	42	15	27	42
UE Santa Coloma	21	11	6	4	29	19	10	39
Sant Julia	21	10	7	4	33	21	12	37
Atletic Club d'Escaldes	21	10	7	4	36	19	17	37
FC Santa Coloma	21	10	7	4	41	26	15	37
Ordino	21	5	4	12	19	39	–20	19
Engordany	21	4	5	12	23	37	–14	17
CE Carroi	21	1	0	20	15	62	–47	3

Championship Round 2021–22

	P	*W*	*D*	*L*	*F*	*A*	*GD*	*Pts*
Inter Club d'Escaldes (C)[1]	27	14	8	5	54	24	30	50
UE Santa Coloma[3]	27	13	8	6	37	26	11	47
Sant Julia	27	12	10	5	41	30	11	46
Atletic Club d'Escaldes[3]	27	11	10	6	44	30	14	43

Relegation Round 2021–22

	P	*W*	*D*	*L*	*F*	*A*	*GD*	*Pts*
FC Santa Coloma	27	15	7	5	64	34	30	52
Ordino	27	7	6	14	30	49	–19	27
Engordany+	27	5	5	17	29	55	–26	20
CE Carroi*	27	3	2	22	22	73	–51	11

Top scorer: G. Lopez (FC Santa Coloma) 21.
Cup Final: Atletic Club d'Escaldes 4, Extremenya 1.

ARMENIA

Football Federation of Armenia, Khanjyan Street 27, 0010 Yerevan.
Founded: 1992. *FIFA:* 1992; *UEFA:* 1993. *National Colours:* Red shirts with white trim, red shorts, red socks with grey tops.

International matches 2021–22

North Macedonia (a) 1-0, Germany (a) 0-6, Liechtenstein (h) 1-1, Iceland (a) 1-1, Romania (a) 0-1, North Macedonia (h) 0-5, Germany (h) 1-4, Montenegro (h) 1-0, Norway (h) 0-9, Republic of Ireland (h) 1-0, Scotland (a) 0-2, Ukraine (a) 0-3, Scotland (h) 1-4.

League Championship wins (1992–2022)

Pyunik 15 (incl. Homenetmen 1*); Shirak 4*; Alashkert 4; Araks 2 (incl. Tsement 1); Ararat-Armenia 2; Ararat Yerevan 1; FK Yerevan 1; Ulisses 1; Banants (now Urartu) 1.
* *Includes one unofficial shared title.*

Cup wins (1992–2022)

Pyunik (incl. Homenetmen 1) 8; Ararat Yerevan 6; Mika 6; Banants (now Urartu) 3; Tsement 2; Shirak 2; Gandzasar Kapan 1; Alashkert 1; Noah 1; Noravank 1.
See also Russia section for Armenian club honours in Soviet era 1936–91.

Armenian Premier League 2021–22

	P	*W*	*D*	*L*	*F*	*A*	*GD*	*Pts*
Pyunik (C)[1]	32	23	6	3	52	25	27	75
Ararat-Armenia[3]	32	23	5	4	56	20	36	74
Alashkert[3]	32	14	9	9	38	30	8	51
Ararat Yerevan[3]	32	13	7	12	47	36	11	46
Urartu	32	9	13	10	37	32	5	40
Noah	32	9	12	11	38	43	–5	39
Noravank	32	7	7	18	36	55	–19	28
Van	32	6	7	19	19	47	–28	25

BKMA+	32	4	6	22	25	60	–35	18
Sevan*	0	0	0	0	0	0	0	0

** Sevan expelled for failing to fulfil fixtures, record expunged. Cup winners Noravank did not meet the requirements to hold an UEFA licence and were replaced in the Europa Conference League by Ararat Yerevan.*
Top scorer: Deble (Pyunik, incl. 14 for Ararat Yerevan) 22.
Cup Final: Noravank 2, Urartu 0.

AUSTRIA

Oesterreichischer Fussball-Bund, Ernst-Happel Stadion, Sektor A/F, Meiereistrasse 7, Wien 1021.
Founded: 1904. *FIFA:* 1905; *UEFA:* 1954. *National Colours:* Red shirts with white sleeves, white shorts, red socks.

International matches 2021–22

Moldova (a) 2-0, Israel (a) 2-5, Scotland (h) 0-1, Faroe Islands (a) 2-0, Denmark (a) 0-1, Israel (h) 4-2, Moldova (h) 4-1, Wales (a) 1-2, Scotland (h) 2-2, Croatia (a) 3-0, Denmark (h) 1-2, France (h) 1-1, Denmark (a) 0-2.

League Championship wins (1912–2022)

Rapid Vienna 32; Austria Vienna (formerly Amateure) 24; Red Bull Salzburg 16 (incl. Austria Salzburg 3); Wacker Innsbruck 10 (incl. Swarovski Tirol 2 [now WSG Tirol], Tirol Innsbruck 3); Admira Vienna (now Admira Wacker Modling) 9 (incl. Wacker Vienna 1); First Vienna 6; Wiener Sportklub 3; Sturm Graz 3; WAF 1; WAC 1; Floridsdorfer 1; Hakoah 1; LASK (Linz) 1; Voest Linz 1; GAK (Graz) 1.

Cup wins (1919–2022)

Austria Vienna (formerly Amateure) 27; Rapid Vienna 14; Red Bull Salzburg 9; Wacker Innsbruck 7 (incl. Swarovski Tirol 1); Admira Vienna (now Admira Wacker Modling) 6 (incl. Wacker Vienna 1); Sturm Graz 5; GAK Graz 4; First Vienna 3; WAC 3 (incl. Schwarz-Rot Wien 1); Ried 2; WAF 1; Wiener Sportklub 1; LASK (Linz) 1; Kremser 1; Stockerau 1; Karnten 1; Horn 1; Pasching 1.

Austrian Bundesliga Qualifying Table 2021–22

	P	*W*	*D*	*L*	*F*	*A*	*GD*	*Pts*
Red Bull Salzburg	22	17	4	1	50	13	37	55
Sturm Graz	22	10	7	5	46	32	14	37
Wolfsberg	22	11	4	7	34	32	2	37
Austria Vienna	22	8	9	5	31	23	8	33
Rapid Vienna	22	8	7	7	35	31	4	31
Austria Klagenfurt	22	7	9	6	31	33	–2	30
Ried	22	7	8	7	31	41	–10	29
LASK	22	6	7	9	28	29	–1	25
WSG Tirol	22	5	8	9	30	42	–12	23
Hartberg	22	5	7	10	29	35	–6	22
Admira Wacker Modling	22	4	8	10	25	31	–6	20
Rheindorf Altach	22	3	4	15	10	38	–28	13

NB: Points earned in Qualifying phase are halved and rounded down at start of Championship and Relegation Play-off phase.

Championship Round 2021–22

	P	*W*	*D*	*L*	*F*	*A*	*GD*	*Pts*
Red Bull Salzburg (C)[1]	32	25	5	2	77	19	58	52
Sturm Graz[1]	32	16	8	8	62	46	16	37
Austria Vienna[2]	32	11	13	8	44	39	5	29
Wolfsberg[3]	32	14	5	13	48	53	–5	28
Rapid Vienna†[3]	32	10	11	11	48	45	3	25
Austria Klagenfurt	32	8	12	12	43	57	–14	21

† Qualified for Europa Conference League Play-offs final.

Relegation Round 2021–22

	P	*W*	*D*	*L*	*F*	*A*	*GD*	*Pts*
WSG Swarovski Tirol†	32	10	10	12	46	58	–12	28
LASK†	32	9	12	11	44	42	2	26
Rheindorf Altach	32	7	8	17	24	49	–25	22
Ried	32	8	13	11	40	54	–14	22
Hartberg	32	7	12	13	43	47	–4	22
Admira Wacker Modling*	32	6	13	13	36	46	–10	21

† Qualified for Europa Conference League Play-offs semi-final.

Europa Conference League Play-offs

Semi-final
WSG Swarovski Tirol 2, LASK 1.
Final
WSG Swarovski Tirol 1, 0, Rapid Vienna 2, 2 (agg. 1-4)
Top scorer: Adeyemi (Red Bull Salzburg) 19.
Cup Final: Red Bull Salzburg 3, Ried 0.

AZERBAIJAN

Association of Football Federations of Azerbaijan, 2208 Nobel prospekti, 1025 Baku.
Founded: 1992. *FIFA:* 1994; *UEFA:* 1994. *National Colours:* All blue.

International matches 2021–22

Luxembourg (a) 1-2, Republic of Ireland (a) 1-1, Portugal (h) 0-3, Republic of Ireland (h) 0-3, Serbia (a) 1-3, Luxembourg (h) 1-3, Qatar (h) 2-2, Malta (a) 0-1, Latvia (h) 1-0, Kazakhstan (a) 0-2, Belarus (a) 0-0, Slovakia (h) 0-1, Belarus (h) 2-0.

League Championship wins (1992–2022)

Neftchi 9; Qarabag 9; Kapaz 3; Shamkir 3*; FK Baku 2; Inter Baku (now Keshla) 2; Turan 1; Khazar Lankaran 1.
** Includes one unofficial title.*

Cup wins (1992–2022)

Qarabag 7; Neftchi 7*; Kapaz 4; FK Baku 3; Khazar Lankaran 3; Keshla (formerly Inter Baku) 2; Inshatchi 1; Shafa 1; Gabala 1.
*No winner in 2019–20. * Includes one unofficial title.*

Azerbaijani Premyer Liqası 2021–22

	P	*W*	*D*	*L*	*F*	*A*	*GD*	*Pts*
Qarabag (C)[1]	28	21	6	1	72	13	59	69
Neftchi[3]	28	15	5	8	42	31	11	50
Zira[3]	28	13	8	7	33	27	6	47
Gabala[3]	28	12	9	7	38	34	4	45
Sabah	28	12	5	11	42	34	8	41
Sumqayit†	28	5	7	16	22	46	–24	22
Shamakhi†	28	5	7	16	25	49	–24	22
Sabail	28	4	3	21	17	57	–40	15

† Ranking decided on head-to-head points.
Top scorer: Kadi (Qarabag) 12.
Cup Final: Qarabag 1, Zira 1 (aet; Qarabag won 4-3 on penalties).

BELARUS

Belarus Football Federation, Prospekt Pobeditelei 20/3, 220020 Minsk.
Founded: 1989. *FIFA:* 1992; *UEFA:* 1993. *National Colours:* All maroon with white trim.

International matches 2021–22

Czech Republic (a) 0-1, Wales (h) 2-3, Belgium (h) 0-1, Estonia (a) 0-2, Czech Republic (h) 0-2, Wales (a) 1-5, Jordan (h) 1-0, India (n) 3-0, Bahrain (a) 1-0, Slovakia (h) 0-1, Azerbaijan (h) 0-0, Kazakhstan (h) 1-1, Azerbaijan (a) 0-2.

League Championship wins (1992–2021)

BATE Borisov 15; Dinamo Minsk 7; Shakhtyor Soligorsk 3; Slavia Mozyr (incl. MPKC 1) 2; Dnepr Mogilev 1; Belshina Bobruisk 1; Gomel 1; Dinamo Brest 1.

Cup wins (1992–2022)

BATE Borisov 5; Dinamo Minsk 3; Belshina Bobruisk 3; Shakhtyor Soligorsk 3; Gomel 3; Dinamo Brest 3; Slavia Mozyr (incl. MPKC 1) 2; MTZ-RIPA 2; Naftan Novopolotsk 2; Neman Grodno 1; Dinamo 93 Minsk 1; Lokomotiv 96 1; FC Minsk 1; Torpedo-BelAZ Zhodino 1.
See also Russia section for Belarusian club honours in Soviet era 1936–91.

Belarusian Vysheyshaya Liga 2021

	P	*W*	*D*	*L*	*F*	*A*	*GD*	*Pts*
Shakhtyor Soligorsk (C)[1]	30	24	3	3	62	18	44	75
BATE Borisov[3]	30	19	8	3	61	27	34	65
Dinamo Minsk[3]	30	19	5	6	55	20	35	62
Gomel[3]	30	17	8	5	57	23	34	59
Ruh Brest	30	16	10	4	52	28	24	58
Dinamo Brest	30	8	14	8	32	32	0	38
Vitebsk	30	9	10	11	37	41	–4	37
Torpedo BelAZ Zhodino	30	10	6	14	38	43	–5	36
Slutsk	30	9	8	13	36	44	–8	35
Isloch	30	9	7	14	38	47	–9	34
Neman Grodno	30	9	7	14	36	36	0	34
FC Minsk	30	8	9	13	32	52	–20	33
Energetyk-BGU Minsk	30	8	9	13	35	42	–7	33
Slavia Mozyr+	30	8	8	14	42	50	–8	32
Smorgon*	30	4	9	17	26	66	–40	21
Sputnik Rechitsa†*	30	2	1	27	12	82	–70	7

† Sputnik Rechitsa withdrew from the league due to financial difficulties. All subsequent games were awarded a 3-0 win to their opponents.
Top scorer: Darboe (Shakhtyor Soligorsk) 19.
Cup Final: Gomel 2, BATE Borisov 1.

BELGIUM

Union Royale Belge des Societes de Football-Association, 145 Avenue Houba de Strooper, B-1020 Bruxelles.
Founded: 1895. *FIFA:* 1904; *UEFA:* 1954. *National Colours:* All red with black trim.

International matches 2021–22

Estonia (a) 5-2, Czech Republic (h) 3-0, Belarus (a) 1-0, France (n) 2-3, Italy (a) 1-2, Estonia (h) 3-1, Wales (a) 1-1, Republic of Ireland (a) 2-2, Burkina Faso (h) 3-0, Netherlands (h) 1-4, Poland (h) 6-1, Wales (a) 1-1, Poland (a) 1-0.

League Championship wins (1896–2022)

Anderlecht 34; Club Brugge 18; Union St Gilloise 11; Standard Liege 10; Beerschot VAC (became Germinal) 7; RC Brussels 6; RFC Liege 5; Daring Brussels 5; Antwerp 4;

Lierse 4; Mechelen 4; Genk 4; Cercle Brugge 3; Beveren 2; RWD Molenbeek 1; Gent 1.

Cup wins (1912–14; 1927; 1935; 1954–2022)
Club Brugge 11; Anderlecht 9; Standard Liege 8; Genk 5; Gent 4; Antwerp 3; Union Saint-Gilloise 2; Cercle Brugge 2; Lierse 2; Beerschot VAC (became Germinal) 2; Beveren 2; Waterschei (became Racing Genk) 2; Mechelen 2; Beerschot Antwerpen Club (incl. Germinal Ekeren) 2; Zulte Waregem 2; Lokeren 2; Racing 1; Daring 1; Tournai 1; KFC Waregem 1; RFC Liege 1; Westerlo 1; La Louviere 1.

Belgian First Division A Final Table 2021–22

	P	*W*	*D*	*L*	*F*	*A*	*GD*	*Pts*
Union Saint-Gilloise†	34	24	5	5	78	27	51	77
Club Brugge	34	21	9	4	72	37	35	72
Anderlecht	34	18	10	6	72	36	36	64
Antwerp	34	19	6	9	55	38	17	63
Gent	34	18	8	8	56	30	26	62
Sporting Charleroi‡	34	15	9	10	55	46	9	54
Mechelen§	34	15	7	12	57	61	–4	52
Genk	34	15	6	13	66	47	19	51
Sint-Truiden	34	15	6	13	42	40	2	51
Cercle Brugge	34	12	9	13	49	46	3	45
Leuven§	34	10	11	13	47	58	–11	41
Oostende	34	10	7	17	34	61	–27	37
Kortrijk	34	9	10	15	43	48	–5	37
Standard Liege‡	34	9	9	16	32	51	–19	36
Eupen	34	8	8	18	37	61	–24	32
Zulte-Waregem	34	8	8	18	42	69	–27	32
RFC Seraing+	34	8	4	22	30	68	–38	28
Beerschot†*	34	4	4	26	33	76	–43	16

†Union Saint-Gilloise v Beerschot was abandoned due to disruption by away supporters with the score at 0-0. The match was awarded a 5-0 win to Union Saint-Gilloise.
‡Standard Liege v Sporting Charleroi was abandoned due to disruption by home supporters with the score at 0-3. The result stood.
**Leuven v Mechelen awarded a 5-0 win to Leuven; Mechelen failed to fulfil fixture.*
NB: Points earned in Qualifying phase are halved and rounded up at start of Champions League Play-off phase.

Champions League Play-off I 2021–22

	P	*W*	*D*	*L*	*F*	*A*	*GD*	*Pts*
Club Brugge (C)[1]	6	4	2	0	8	2	6	50
Union Saint-Gilloise[1]	6	2	1	3	5	5	0	46
Anderlecht[3]	6	2	2	2	8	7	1	40
Antwerp[3]	6	1	1	4	3	10	–7	36

Europa Conference League Play-off II 2021–22

	P	*W*	*D*	*L*	*F*	*A*	*GD*	*Pts*
Gent[2]	6	4	0	2	9	5	4	43
Genk	6	3	2	1	10	8	2	37
Sporting Charleroi	6	2	1	3	10	12	–2	34
Mechelen	6	1	1	4	6	10	–4	30

Top scorer: Undav (Union Saint-Gilloise) 26.
Cup Final: Gent 0, Anderlecht 0 *(aet; Gent won 4-3 on penalties).*

BOSNIA-HERZEGOVINA

Football Federation of Bosnia & Herzegovina, Ferhadija 30, 71000 Sarajevo.
Founded: 1992. *FIFA:* 1996; *UEFA:* 1998. *National Colours:* All blue with white trim.

International matches 2021–22
France (a) 1-1, Kuwait (h) 1-0, Kazakhstan (h) 2-2, Kazakhstan (a) 2-0, Ukraine (a) 1-1, Finland (h) 1-3, Ukraine (h) 0-2, USA (a) 0-1, Georgia (h) 0-1, Luxembourg (h) 1-0, Finland (a) 1-1, Romania (h) 1-0, Montenegro (a) 1-1, Finland (h) 3-2.

League Championship wins (1998–2022)
Zrinjski Mostar 7; Zeljeznicar 6; Sarajevo 5; Siroki Brijeg 2; Borac Banja Luka 2; Brotnjo 1; Leotar 1; Modrica 1.

Cup wins (1998–2022)
Sarajevo 7; Zeljeznicar 6; Siroki Brijeg 3; Bosna Visoko 1; Modrica 1; Orasje 1; Zrinjski Mostar 1; Slavija 1; Borac Banja Luka 1; Olimpik Sarajevo 1; Radnik Bijeljina 1; Velez Mostar 1.
No winner in 2019–20.
See also Serbia section for Bosnian-Herzogovinian club honours in Yugoslav Republic era 1947–91.

Premijer Liga Bosne i Hercegovine 2021–22

	P	*W*	*D*	*L*	*F*	*A*	*GD*	*Pts*
Zrinjski Mostar (C)[1]	33	26	6	1	74	14	60	84
Tuzla City[3]	33	15	12	6	49	36	13	57
Borac Banja Luka[3]	33	13	15	5	44	34	10	54
Sarajevo	33	13	7	13	37	33	4	46
Velez Mostar[3] (–3)	33	13	8	12	42	37	5	44
Zeljeznicar	33	9	16	8	28	29	–1	43
Siroki Brijeg	33	8	15	10	31	35	–4	39
Posusje	33	8	13	12	33	51	–18	37
Leotar	33	9	7	17	25	46	–21	34
Sloboda Tuzla	33	7	12	14	26	35	–9	33
Radnik Bijeljina*	33	5	12	16	34	53	–19	27
Rudar Prijedor*	33	5	11	17	28	48	–20	26

Velez Mostar deducted 3pts due to crowd disturbance in the match against Borac Banja Luka. Borac, who were leading 0-2 at the time of the disturbance, were later awarded the match 0-3.
Top scorer: Bilbija (Zrinjski Mostar) 33.
Cup Final: Sarajevo 0, Velez Mostar 0 *(Velez Mostar won 4-3 on penalties).*

BULGARIA

Bulgarian Football Union, 26 Tzar Ivan Assen II Str., 1124 Sofia.
Founded: 1923. *FIFA:* 1992; *UEFA:* 1954. *National Colours:* White shirts with green and red trim, green shorts with red and white trim, white socks with green and red trim.

International matches 2021–22
Italy (a) 1-1, Lithuania (h) 1-0, Georgia (h) 4-1, Lithuania (a) 1-3, Northern Ireland (h) 2-1, Ukraine (a) 1-1, Switzerland (a) 0-4, Qatar (a) 1-2, Croatia (n) 1-2, North Macedonia (h) 1-1, Georgia (h) 2-5, Gibraltar (a) 1-1, Georgia (a) 0-0.

League Championship wins (1925–2022)
CSKA Sofia 31; Levski Sofia 26; Ludogorets Razgrad 11; Slavia Sofia 7; Lokomotiv Sofia 4; Litex Lovech 4; Vladislav Varna (now Cherno More Varna) 3; Botev Plovdiv (includes Trakija) 2; Athletic Slava 1923 1; Sokol Varna (now Spartak Varna) 1; Sportklub Sofia (now Septemvri Sofia) 1; Ticha Varna (now Cherno More Varna) 1; Spartak Plovdiv 1; Beroe Stara Zagora 1; Etar 1; Lokomotiv Plovdiv 1.

Cup wins (1938–42; 1946–2021)
Levski Sofia (incl. Vitosha 1) 26; CSKA Sofia (incl. Sredets 3) 21; Slavia Sofia 8; Lokomotiv Sofia 4; Litex Lovech 4; Botev Plovdiv (includes Trakija) 3; FK 13 Sofia 2; Beroe Stara Zagora 2; Ludogorets Razgrad 2; Lokomotiv Plovdiv 2; Shipka Sofia 1; AS 23 Sofia 1; Spartak Plovdiv 1; Septemvri Sofia 1; Spartak Sofia 1; Marek Dupnitsa 1; Sliven 1; Cherno More Varna 1.

Bulgarian First League Qualifying Table 2021–22

	P	*W*	*D*	*L*	*F*	*A*	*GD*	*Pts*
Ludogorets Razgrad	26	21	1	4	64	23	41	64
CSKA Sofia	26	15	7	4	39	25	14	52
Botev Plovdiv	26	13	7	6	34	28	6	46
Cherno More	26	12	9	5	35	18	17	45
Levski Sofia	26	12	6	8	33	25	8	42
Slavia Sofia	26	9	9	8	30	26	4	36
Lokomotiv Plovdiv	26	9	7	10	30	35	–5	34
Beroe	26	9	5	12	23	27	–4	32
CSKA 1948 Sofia	26	8	6	12	36	37	–1	30
Arda	26	7	8	11	27	34	–7	29
Pirin Blagoevgrad	26	7	6	13	34	41	–7	27
Lokomotiv Sofia	26	6	7	13	22	42	–20	25
Botev Vratsa	26	5	7	14	23	48	–25	22
Tsarsko Selo	26	3	7	16	15	36	–21	16

Championship Round 2021–22

	P	*W*	*D*	*L*	*F*	*A*	*GD*	*Pts*
Ludogorets Razgrad (C)[1]	31	26	1	4	77	25	52	79
CSKA Sofia[3]	31	16	10	5	42	31	11	58
Botev Plovdiv‡[3]	31	15	8	8	38	33	5	53
Levski Sofia[3]	31	15	7	9	38	27	11	52
Cherno More	31	12	11	8	36	22	14	47
Slavia Sofia	31	9	10	12	35	38	–3	37

‡ Qualified for Europa Conference League Play-off.

Europa Conference League Round 2021–22

	P	*W*	*D*	*L*	*F*	*A*	*GD*	*Pts*
Beroe†‡[3]	32	11	8	13	30	33	–3	41
CSKA 1948 Sofia†	32	11	8	13	51	45	6	41
Lokomotiv Plovdiv	32	9	11	12	36	43	–7	38
Arda	32	8	11	13	38	51	–13	35

† Ranking decided on head-to-head points. ‡ Qualified for Europa Conference League Play-off.

Relegation Round 2021–22

	P	*W*	*D*	*L*	*F*	*A*	*GD*	*Pts*
Lokomotiv Sofia	32	8	10	14	27	46	–19	34
Pirin Blagoevgrad	32	9	6	17	40	53	–13	33
Botev Vratsa+	32	6	10	16	30	55	–25	28
Tsarsko Selo*	32	5	11	16	22	38	–16	26

Europa Conference League Play-off
Botev Plovdiv 2, Beroe 1
Top scorer: Sotiriou (Ludogorets Razgrad) 17.
Cup Final: Levski Sofia 1, CSKA Sofia 0.

CHANNEL ISLANDS

Guernsey

League Championship wins (1894–2022)
Northerners 32; Guernsey Rangers 17; St Martin's 16; Vale Recreation 15; Sylvans 10; Belgrave Wanderers 8; 2nd Bn Manchesters 3; 2nd Bn Wiltshires 2; 2nd Bn Royal Irish Regt 2; Guernsey Rovers 2; Band Comp 2nd Bn Royal Fusiliers 1; G&H Comp Royal Fusiliers 1; 10th Comp W Div Royal Artillery 1; 2nd Bn PA Somerset Light Infantry 1; Grange 1; 2nd Bn Leicesters 1; 2nd Middlesex Regt 1; Yorkshire Regt (Green Howards); Athletics 1.
No winner in 2019–20.

Guernsey Priaulx League 2021–22

	P	W	D	L	F	A	GD	Pts
St Martin's (C)	24	22	2	0	91	20	71	68
Northerners	24	17	2	5	88	33	55	53
Guernsey Rovers	24	14	3	7	53	41	12	45
Sylvans	24	13	4	7	66	44	22	43
Belgrave Wanderers	24	11	1	12	47	50	0	34
Alderney	24	9	2	13	48	49	–1	29
Vale Recreation	24	5	7	12	38	63	–25	22
Manzur	24	2	3	19	33	105	–72	9
Guernsey Rangers	24	2	2	20	25	84	–59	8

Top scorer: Murray (Northerners) 30.

Jersey

League Championship wins (1904–2022)
Jersey Wanderers 21; St Paul's 21; First Tower United 19; Jersey Scottish 11; Beeches Old Boys 5; Magpies 4; 2nd Bn King's Own Regt 3; Oaklands 3; St Peter 3; 1st Batt Devon Regt 2; 1st Bn East Surrey Regt 2; Georgetown 2; Mechanics 2; YMCA 2; 2nd Bn East Surrey Regt 1; 20th Comp Royal Garrison Artillery 1; National Rovers 1; Sporting Academics 1; Trinity 1; St Clement 1.

Jersey Football Combination 2021–22

	P	W	D	L	F	A	GD	Pts
St Clement (C)	16	11	2	3	50	20	30	35
St Peter	16	10	4	2	31	13	18	34
Grouville	16	10	2	4	39	22	17	32
St Brelade	16	8	2	6	36	26	10	26
St Pauls	16	6	1	9	32	35	–3	19
JTC Jersey Wanderers	16	5	4	7	35	40	–5	19
St Ouen	16	4	4	8	26	39	–13	16
Sporting Academics	16	4	1	11	26	52	–26	13
Rozel Rovers	16	3	2	11	19	47	–28	11
St Clement (C)	16	11	2	3	50	20	30	35

Top scorer: Moon (Grouville) 18.

Upton Park Trophy 2022 (For Guernsey & Jersey League Champions)
St Martin's 2, St Clement 0.

Upton Park Trophy wins (1907–2022)
Northerners 17 (incl. 1 shared); First Tower United 12; St Martin's 12; St Paul's 12; Jersey Wanderers 11 (incl. 1 shared); Jersey Scottish 6; Guernsey Rangers 5; Belgrave Wanderers 4; Vale Recreation 4; Old St Paul's 3; Beeches Old Boys 3; Magpies 3; Sylvans 3; St Peter 2; National Rovers 1; Jersey Mechanics 1; Jersey YMCA 1; Sporting Academics 1; Trinity 1.
No winner in 2019–20 and 2020–21.

CROATIA

Croatian Football Federation, Vukovarska 269A, 10000 Zagreb.
Founded: 1912. *FIFA:* 1992; *UEFA:* 1993. *National Colours:* Red and white check shirts with blue trim, white shorts with blue trim, red socks.

International matches 2021–22
Russia (a) 0-0, Slovakia (a) 1-0, Slovenia (h) 3-0, Cyprus (a) 3-0, Slovakia (h) 2-2, Malta (a) 7-1, Russia (h) 1-0, Slovenia (n) 1-1, Bulgaria (n) 2-1, Austria (h) 0-3, France (h) 1-1, Denmark (a) 1-0, France (a) 1-0.

League Championship wins (1992–2022)
Dinamo Zagreb (incl. Croatia Zagreb 3) 23; Hajduk Split 6; NK Zagreb 1; Rijeka 1.

Cup wins (1992–2021)
Dinamo Zagreb (incl. Croatia Zagreb 4) 16; Hajduk Split 7; Rijeka 6; Inter Zapresic 1; Osijek 1.
See also Serbia section for Croatian club honours in Yugoslav Republic era 1947–92.

Croatian Prva HNL 2021–22

	P	W	D	L	F	A	GD	Pts
Dinamo Zagreb (C)[1]	36	24	7	5	68	22	46	79
Hajduk Split[3]	36	21	9	6	64	31	33	72
Osijek[3]	36	19	12	5	49	29	20	69
Rijeka[3]	36	20	5	11	71	51	20	65
Lokomotiva Zagreb	36	12	13	11	55	50	5	49
Gorica	36	12	9	15	43	50	–7	45
Slaven Koprivnica	36	9	9	18	35	54	–19	36
Sibenik	36	9	5	22	46	75	–29	32
Istra 1961	36	7	10	19	42	67	–25	31
Hrvatski Dragovoljiac*	36	4	7	25	31	75	–44	19

Top scorer: Livaja (Hajduk Split) 28.
Cup Final: Hajduk Split 3, Rijeka 1.

CYPRUS

Cyprus Football Association, 10 Achaion Street, 2413 Engomi, PO Box 25071, 1306 Nicosia.
Founded: 1934. *FIFA:* 1948; *UEFA:* 1962. *National Colours:* All blue with white trim.

International matches 2021–22
Malta (a) 0-3, Russia (h) 0-2, Slovakia (a) 0-2, Croatia (h) 0-3, Malta (h) 2-2, Russia (a) 0-6, Slovenia (a) 1-2, Estonia (a) 0-0, Estonia (h) 2-0, Kosovo (h) 0-2, Northern Ireland (h) 0-0, Greece (a) 0-3, Northern Ireland (a) 2-2.

League Championship wins (1935–2022)
APOEL (Nicosia) 28; Omonia Nicosia 21; Anorthosis Famagusta 13; AEL Limassol 6; Apollon Limassol 4; EPA Larnaca 3; Olympiakos Nicosia 3; Pezoporikos Larnaca 2; Trust 1; Cetinkaya 1.
No winner in 2019–20.

Cup wins (1935–2022)
APOEL (Nicosia) 21; Omonia Nicosia 15; Anorthosis Famagusta 11; Apollon Limassol 9; AEL Limassol 7; EPA Larnaca 5; Trust 3; Cetinkaya 2; AEK Larnaca 2; Pezoporikos Larnaca 1; Olympiakos Nicosia 1; Nea Salamis Famagusta 1; APOP Kinyras 1.
No winner in 2019–20.

Cypriot First Division Qualifying Table 2021–22

	P	W	D	L	F	A	GD	Pts
Apollon Limassol	22	14	4	4	37	21	16	46
APOEL	22	11	6	5	35	25	10	39
AEK Larnaca	22	10	9	3	31	17	14	39
Anorthosis Famagusta	22	11	5	6	36	26	10	38
Aris Limassol	22	10	6	6	23	20	3	36
Paphos	22	8	10	4	27	19	8	34
Omonia Nicosia	22	9	4	9	25	25	0	31
AEL Limassol	22	7	4	11	26	28	–2	25
Olympiakos Nicosia	22	5	7	10	14	23	–9	22
Doxa Katokopia	22	5	7	10	18	30	–12	22
PAEEK	22	3	6	13	17	35	–18	15
Ethnikos Achna	22	3	4	15	13	33	–20	13

Championship Round 2021–22

	P	W	D	L	F	A	GD	Pts
Apollon (C)[1]	32	16	10	6	50	33	17	58
AEK Larnaca[1]	32	14	12	6	44	29	15	54
APOEL (Nicosia)[3]	32	14	10	8	48	41	7	52
Aris Limassol[3]	32	13	11	8	37	32	5	50
Anorthosis Famagusta	32	13	10	9	48	40	8	49
Paphos	32	11	13	8	39	30	9	46

Relegation Round 2021–22

	P	W	D	L	F	A	GD	Pts
Omonia Nicosia	32	14	8	10	44	38	6	50
AEL Limassol	32	14	5	13	43	39	4	47
Olympiakos Nicosia	32	10	10	12	30	31	–1	40
Doxa Katokopia	32	7	11	14	27	41	–14	32
Ethnikos Achna*	32	5	8	19	21	41	–20	23
PAEEK*	32	3	8	21	25	61	–36	17

Top scorer: Trichkovski (AEK Larnaca) 15.
Cup Final: Omonia Nicosia 0, Ethnikos Achna 0 *(aet; Omonia Nicosia won 5-4 on penalties).*

CZECH REPUBLIC

Fotbalova Asociace Ceske Republiky, Diskarska 2431/4, PO Box 11, Praha 6 16017.
Founded: 1901. *FIFA:* 1907; *UEFA:* 1954. *National Colours:* Red shirts, dark blue shorts, red socks.

International matches 2021–22
Belarus (h) 2-0, Belgium (a) 0-3, Ukraine (h) 1-1, Wales (h) 2-2, Belarus (a) 2-0*, Kuwait (h) 7-0, Estonia (h) 2-0, Sweden (a) 0-1, Wales (a) 1-1, Switzerland (h) 2-1, Spain (h) 2-2, Portugal (a) 0-2, Spain (a) 0-2.
* *Match played in Russia.*

League Championship wins – Czechoslovakia (1925–93)
Sparta Prague 21; Slavia Prague 13; Dukla Prague (prev. UDA, now Marila Pribram) 11; Slovan Bratislava (formerly NV Bratislava) 8; Spartak Trnava 5; Banik Ostrava 3; Viktoria Zizkov 1; Inter Bratislava 1; Spartak Hradec Kralove 1; Zbrojovka Brno 1; Bohemians 1; Vitkovice 1.

Cup wins – Czechoslovakia (1961–93)
Dukla Prague 8; Sparta Prague 8; Slovan Bratislava 5; Spartak Trnava 4; Banik Ostrava 3; Lokomotiva Kosice 2; TJ Gottwaldov 1; DAC 1904 Dunajska Streda 1; 1.FC Kosice 1.

League Championship wins – Czech Republic (1994–2022)
Sparta Prague 12; Slavia Prague 7; Viktoria Plzen 6; Slovan Liberec 3; Banik Ostrava 1.

Cup wins – Czech Republic (1994–2022)
Sparta Prague 7; Slavia Prague 6; Viktoria Zizkov 2; Jablonec 2; Slovan Liberec 2; Teplice 2; Mlada Boleslav 2; Hradec Kralove (formerly Spartak) 1; Banik Ostrava 1; Viktoria Plzen 1; Sigma Olomouc 1; FC Fastav Zlin 1; Slovacko 1.

Czech First League Qualifying Table 2021–22

	P	*W*	*D*	*L*	*F*	*A*	*GD*	*Pts*
Slavia Prague	30	23	4	3	71	19	52	73
Viktoria Plzen	30	22	6	2	53	19	34	72
Sparta Prague	30	20	6	4	65	32	33	66
Slovacko	30	18	5	7	50	30	20	59
Banik Ostrava	30	14	9	7	54	39	15	51
Hradec Kralove	30	9	13	8	38	40	–2	40
Mlada Boleslav	30	11	5	14	45	48	–3	38
Slovan Liberec	30	10	7	13	29	38	–9	37
Sigma Olomouc	30	9	10	11	39	37	2	37
Ceske Budejovice	30	9	9	12	40	46	–6	36
FC Fastav Zlin	30	8	6	16	36	53	–17	30
Teplice	30	8	3	19	29	49	–20	27
Jablonec	30	4	14	12	22	45	–23	26
Bohemians 1905	30	6	8	16	34	56	–22	26
Pardubice	30	5	9	16	35	67	–32	24
Karvina	30	3	8	19	30	52	–22	17
Slavia Prague	30	23	4	3	71	19	52	73
Viktoria Plzen	30	22	6	2	53	19	34	72

Championship Round 2021–22

	P	*W*	*D*	*L*	*F*	*A*	*GD*	*Pts*
Viktoria Plzen (C)[1]	35	26	7	2	61	21	+40	85
Slavia Prague[3]	35	24	6	5	79	26	+53	78
Sparta Prague[3]	35	22	7	6	71	38	+33	73
Slovacko[2]	35	21	5	9	57	37	+20	68
Banik Ostrava	35	15	10	10	59	47	+12	55
Hradec Kralove	35	10	14	11	44	50	–6	44

Relegation Round 2021–22

	P	*W*	*D*	*L*	*F*	*A*	*GD*	*Pts*
Pardubice	35	9	10	16	42	68	–26	37
Zlin	35	9	9	17	43	60	–17	36
Jablonec	35	6	16	13	27	48	–21	34
Bohemians 1905+	35	8	10	17	45	61	–16	34
Teplice+	35	8	5	22	33	59	–26	29
Karvina*	35	3	10	22	33	63	–30	19

Top scorer: Beauguel (Viktoria Plzen) 19.
Cup Final: Slovacko 3, Sparta Prague 1.

DENMARK

Dansk Boldspil-Union, Idraettens Hus, DBU Alle 1, DK-2605, Brondby.
Founded: 1889. *FIFA:* 1904; *UEFA:* 1954. *National Colours:* Red shirts with white sleeves, white shorts with red trim, red socks.

International matches 2021–22
Russia (a) 4-1*, Scotland (h) 2-0, Faroe Islands (a) 1-0, Israel (h) 5-0, Moldova (a) 4-0, Austria (h) 1-0, Faroe Islands (h) 3-1, Scotland (a) 0-2, Netherlands (a) 2-4, Serbia (h) 3-0, France (a) 2-1, Austria (a) 2-1, Croatia (h) 0-1, Austria (h) 2-0.
**Match played 21.06.21; result incorrect in last edition.*

League Championship wins (1913–2022)
KB (Copenhagen) 15; FC Copenhagen 14; Brondby 11; B 93 (Copenhagen) 9; AB (Akademisk) 9; B 1903 (Copenhagen) 7; Frem 6; AGF (Aarhus) 5; Vejle 5; Esbjerg 5; AaB (Aalborg) 4; Hvidovre 3; OB (Odense) 3; FC Midtjylland 3; Koge 2; B 1909 (Odense) 2; Lyngby 2; Silkeborg 1; Herfolge 1; FC Nordsjaelland 1.

Cup wins (1955–2022)
AGF (Aarhus) 9; FC Copenhagen 8; Brondby 7; Vejle 6; OB (Odense) 5; Esbjerg 3; AaB (Aalborg) 3; Randers Freja 3; Lyngby 3; Frem 2; B 1909 (Odense) 2; B 1903 (Copenhagen) 2; Randers 2; Nordsjaelland 2; FC Midtjylland 2; B 1913 (Odense) 1; KB (Copenhagen) 1; Vanlose 1; Hvidovre 1; B 93 (Copenhagen) 1; AB (Akademisk) 1; Viborg 1; Silkeborg 1; SonderjyskE 1.

Danish Superliga Qualifying Table 2021–22

	P	*W*	*D*	*L*	*F*	*A*	*GD*	*Pts*
FC Copenhagen	22	14	6	2	43	13	30	48
FC Midtjylland	22	13	3	6	37	22	15	42
Brondby	22	11	7	4	30	24	6	40
AaB	22	11	5	6	36	26	10	38
Randers	22	9	6	7	26	25	1	33
Silkeborg	22	7	10	5	34	21	13	31
Viborg	22	6	9	7	31	33	–2	27
AGF	22	6	8	8	24	29	–5	26
OB	22	4	9	9	31	35	–4	21
Nordsjaelland	22	5	6	11	24	37	–13	21
Vejle	22	4	4	14	21	48	–27	16
SonderjyskE	22	2	7	13	17	41	–24	13

Championship Round 2021–22

	P	*W*	*D*	*L*	*F*	*A*	*GD*	*Pts*
FC Copenhagen (C)[1]	32	20	8	4	56	19	37	68
FC Midtjylland[1]	32	20	5	7	59	33	26	65
Silkeborg[2]	32	13	10	9	54	37	17	49
Brondby[3]	32	13	9	10	40	41	–1	48
AaB†	32	13	6	13	47	45	2	45
Randers	32	12	7	13	36	42	–6	43

† Qualified for Europa Conference League Play-off.

Relegation Round 2021–22

	P	*W*	*D*	*L*	*F*	*A*	*GD*	*Pts*
Viborg†[3]	32	10	14	8	45	43	2	44
OB	32	8	14	10	45	46	–1	38
Nordsjaelland	32	8	12	12	38	47	–9	36
AGF	32	6	12	14	31	43	–12	30
Vejle*	32	7	8	17	31	60	–29	29
SonderjyskE*	32	4	11	17	28	54	–26	23

† Qualified for Europa Conference League Play-off.

Europa Conference League Play-off
AaB 1, Viborg 1 *(aet; Viborg won 3-1 on penalties).*
Top scorer: Helenius (Silkeborg) 17.
Cup Final: OB 0, FC Midtjylland 0 *(aet; FC Midtjylland won 4-3 on penalties).*

ENGLAND

The Football Association, Wembley Stadium, PO Box 1966, London SW1P 9EQ.
Founded: 1863. *FIFA:* 1905; *UEFA:* 1954. *National Colours:* White shirts with blue trim, blue shorts, white socks.

ESTONIA

Eesti Jalgpalli Liit, A. Le Coq Arena, Asula 4c, 11312 Tallinn.
Founded: 1921. *FIFA:* 1923; *UEFA:* 1992. *National Colours:* Blue shirts, black shorts, white socks.

International matches 2021–22
Belgium (h) 2-5, Northern Ireland (h) 0-1, Wales (a) 0-0, Belarus (h) 2-0, Wales (h) 0-1, Belgium (a) 1-3, Czech Republic (a) 0-2, Cyprus (h) 0-0, Cyprus (a) 0-2, San Marino (h) 2-0, Argentina (n) 0-5, Malta (h) 2-1, Albania (a) 0-0.

League Championship wins (1921–40; 1992–2021)
Flora 13; FCI Levadia (formerly Levadia Maardu) 10; Sport 9; Estonia 5; Sillamae Kalev 2; Tallinna JK 2; Norma 2; Lantana (formerly Nikol) 2; Nomme Kalju 2; Olimpia Tartu 1; TVMK Tallinn 1; FCI Tallinn 1.

Cup wins (1993–2022)
FCI Levadia (incl. Levadia Maardu 2) 10; Flora 8; Tallinna Sadam 2; Narva Trans 2; TVMK Tallinn 2; Lantana (formerly Nikol) 1; Norma 1; Levadia Tallinn (pre-2004) 1; Nomme Kalju 1; FCI Tallinn 1; Paide Linnameeskond 1.

Estonian Meistriliiga 2021

	P	*W*	*D*	*L*	*F*	*A*	*GD*	*Pts*
FCI Levadia	27	22	1	4	75	33	42	67
Flora	27	19	7	1	80	21	59	64
Paide Linnameeskond	27	15	8	4	52	27	25	53
Nomme Kalju	27	13	4	10	51	34	17	43
Legion	27	11	5	11	45	36	9	38
Nava Trans	27	8	5	14	33	52	–19	29
Kuressaare	27	8	4	15	33	46	–13	28
Viljandi Tulevik*	27	8	3	16	37	57	–20	27
Tammeka	27	5	4	18	29	69	–40	19
Vaprus*	27	4	3	20	20	80	–60	15

**Vaprus v Viljandi Tulevik, 1-0. Match awarded to Vaprus as Viljandi Tulevik fielded an ineligible player.*

Championship Round 2021

	P	*W*	*D*	*L*	*F*	*A*	*GD*	*Pts*
FCI Levadia (C)[1]	32	25	3	4	84	38	46	78
Flora[3]	32	23	8	1	90	23	67	77
Paide Linnameeskond[3]	32	18	8	6	66	35	31	62
Nomme Kalju	32	13	6	13	57	44	13	45
Legion	32	11	7	14	49	48	1	40
Nava Trans	32	9	6	17	36	61	–25	33

Relegation Round 2021

	P	*W*	*D*	*L*	*F*	*A*	*GD*	*Pts*
Kuressaare	30	10	4	16	39	47	–8	34
Viljandi Tulevik†*	30	9	3	18	39	62	–23	30
Tammeka+	30	7	4	19	34	72	–38	25
Vaprus*	30	5	3	22	24	88	–64	18

†Viljandi Tulevik announced voluntary relegation due to financial difficulties.
Top scorer: Anier (Paide Linnameeskond) 26.
Cup Final: Paide Linnameeskond 1, Nomme Kalju 0 *(aet).*

FAROE ISLANDS

Fotboltssamband Foroya, Gundadalur, PO Box 3028, 110 Torshavn.
Founded: 1979. *FIFA:* 1988; *UEFA:* 1990. *National Colours:* White shirts with blue trim, blue shorts with white trim, white socks with blue and red trim.

International matches 2021–22
Israel (h) 0-4, Denmark (h) 0-1, Moldova (h) 2-1, Austria (h) 0-2, Scotland (h) 0-1, Denmark (a) 1-3, Israel (a) 2-3, Gibraltar (a) 0-0, Liechtenstein (n) 1-0, Turkey (a) 0-4, Luxembourg (h) 0-1, Lithuania (h) 2-1, Luxembourg (a) 2-2.

League Championship wins (1942–2021)
HB (Torshavn) 24; KI (Klaksvik) 19; B36 Torshavn 11; TB (Tvoroyri) (includes FC Suduroy and Royn) 7; GI (Gota) 6; B68 Toftir 3; EB/Streymur 2; Vikingur 2; SI (Sorvagur) 1; IF (Fuglafjordur) 1; B71 (Sandur) 1; VB Vagur 1; NSI Runavik 1.

Cup wins (1955–2021)
HB (Torshavn) 28; B36 Torshavn 7; KI (Klaksvik) 6; GI (Gota) 6; TB (Tvoroyri) (includes FC Suduroy and Royn) 5; Vikingur 5; EB/Streymur 4; NSI Runavik 3; VB Vagur (now FC Suduroy) 1; B71 (Sandur) 1.

Faroese Premier League 2021

	P	W	D	L	F	A	GD	Pts
KI (C)[1]	27	23	3	1	99	12	87	72
HB[3]	27	19	4	4	87	22	65	61
Vikingur[3]	27	18	6	3	59	27	32	60
NSI Runavik	27	14	5	8	54	38	16	47
B36 Torshavn[3]	27	12	9	6	51	33	18	45
07 Vestur	27	8	4	15	36	74	–38	28
EB/Streymur	27	7	4	16	28	53	–25	25
B68 Toftir	27	7	4	16	33	66	–33	25
IF	27	4	4	19	26	70	–44	16
TB*	27	0	3	24	17	95	–78	3

Top scorer: Dahl (HB) 27.
Cup Final: NSI Runavik 1, B36 Torshavn 1 *(aet; B36 Torshavn won 4-3 on penalties).*

FINLAND

Suomen Palloliitto Finlands Bollfoerbund, Urheilukatu 5, PO Box 191, 00251 Helsinki.
Founded: 1907. *FIFA:* 1908; *UEFA:* 1954. *National Colours:* White shirts with blue trim, white shorts, white socks.

International matches 2021–22
Wales (h) 0-0, Kazakhstan (h) 1-0, France (a) 0-2, Ukraine (h) 1-2, Kazakhstan (a) 2-0, Bosnia-Herzegovina (a) 3-1, France (a) 0-2, Iceland (n) 1-1, Slovakia (n) 0-2, Bosnia-Herzegovina (h) 1-1, Montenegro (h) 2-0, Romania (a) 0-1, Bosnia-Herzegovina (a) 2-3.

League Championship wins (1908–2021)
HJK (Helsinki) 31; HPS (Helsinki) 9; FC Haka (Valkeakoski) 9; TPS (Turku) 8; HIFK (Helsinki) 7; KuPS (Kuopio) 6; Kuusysi Lahti 5; KIF Helsinki 4; AIFK Turku 3; VIFK Vaasa 3; Reipas Lahti 3; Tampere United 3; VPS (Vaasa) 2; KTP (Kotka) 2; OPS Oulu 2; Jazz Pori 2; Unitas Helsinki 1; PUS Helsinki 1; Sudet Viipuri 1; HT (Helsinki) 1; Ilves-Kissat 1; Pyrkiva Turku 1; KPV (Kokkola) 1; Ilves (Tampere) 1; TPV Tampere 1; MyPa Anjalankoski (renamed MYPA-47) 1; Inter Turku 1; SJK (Seinajoki) 1; IFK Mariehamn 1.

Cup wins (1955–2021)
HJK (Helsinki) 14; FC Haka (Valkeakoski) 12; Reipas Lahti 7; KTP (Kotka) 4; KuPS (Kuopio) 3; Ilves (Tampere) 3; TPS (Turku) 3; MyPa Anjalankoski (renamed MYPA-47) 3; Mikkeli 2; Kuusysi Lahti 2; RoPS (Rovaniemi) 2; Inter Turku 2; Pallo-Pojat 1; Drott (renamed Jaro) 1; HPS (Helsinki) 1; AIFK Turku 1; Jokerit (formerly PK-35) 1; Atlantis 1; Tampere United 1; FC Honka 1; IFK Mariehamn 1; SJK (Seinajoki) 1.

Finnish Veikkausliiga 2021

	P	W	D	L	F	A	GD	Pts
KuPS	22	15	4	3	38	14	24	49
HJK	22	15	4	3	32	12	20	49
Inter Turku	22	12	3	7	36	22	14	39
SJK	22	11	4	7	29	24	5	37
HIFK	22	9	6	7	23	23	0	33
Ilves Tampere	22	10	3	9	21	23	–2	33
FC Lahti	22	8	8	6	27	25	2	32
FC Honka	22	7	5	10	28	29	–1	26
FC Haka	22	7	3	12	21	26	–5	24
IFK Mariehamn	22	7	2	13	20	32	–12	23
Oulu	22	5	3	14	17	35	–18	18
KTP	22	1	5	16	18	45	–27	8

Championship Round 2021

	P	W	D	L	F	A	GD	Pts
HJK (C)[1]	27	18	5	4	41	19	22	59
KuPS[3]	27	17	7	3	46	20	26	58
SJK[3]	27	14	6	7	45	34	11	48
Inter Turku[3]	27	14	3	10	45	32	13	45
Ilves Tampere	27	11	3	13	29	34	–5	36
HIFK	27	9	8	10	25	31	–6	35

Relegation Round 2021

	P	W	D	L	F	A	GD	Pts
FC Lahti	27	10	10	7	35	30	5	40
FC Haka	27	10	5	12	30	29	1	35
FC Honka	27	9	6	12	38	37	1	33
IFK Mariehamn	27	9	3	15	28	40	–12	30
Oulu+	27	6	5	16	21	44	–23	23
KTP*	27	2	5	20	25	58	–33	11

Top scorers (joint): Kallman (Inter Turku), Ngueukam (SJK) 14.
Cup Final: Competition still being played.

FRANCE

Federation Francaise de Football, 87 Boulevard de Grenelle, 75738 Paris Cedex 15.
Founded: 1919. *FIFA:* 1904; *UEFA:* 1954. *National Colours:* Blue shirts with red trim, blue shorts, red socks.

International matches 2021–22
Bosnia-Herzegovina (h) 1-1, Ukraine (a) 1-1, Finland (h) 2-0, Belgium (n) 3-2, Spain (n) 2-1, Kazakhstan (h) 8-0, Finland (a) 2-0, Ivory Coast (h) 2-1, South Africa (h) 5-0, Denmark (h) 1-2, Croatia (a) 1-1, Austria (a) 1-1, Croatia (h) 0-1.

League Championship wins (1933–2022)
Saint-Etienne 10; Paris Saint-Germain 10; Olympique Marseille 9; AS Monaco 8; Nantes 8; Olympique Lyonnais (Lyon) 7; Stade de Reims 6; Bordeaux 6; Lille OSC 4; OGC Nice 4; FC Sete 2; Sochaux 2; Olympique Lillois 1; Racing Club Paris 1; Roubaix-Tourcoing 1; Strasbourg 1; Auxerre 1; Lens 1; Montpellier 1.

Cup wins (1918–2022)
Paris Saint-Germain 14; Olympique Marseille 10; Lille OSC 6; Saint-Etienne 6; Red Star 5; Racing Club Paris 5; AS Monaco 5; Olympique Lyonnais (Lyon) 5; Bordeaux 4; Nantes 4; Auxerre 4; Strasbourg 3; OGC Nice 3; Stade Rennais (Rennes) 3; CAS Genereaux 2; Montpellier 2; FC Sete 2; Sochaux 2; Stade de Reims 2; Sedan 2; Metz 2; Guingamp 2; Olympique de Pantin 1; CA Paris 1; Club Français 1; AS Cannes 1; Excelsior Roubaix 1; EF Nancy-Lorraine 1; Toulouse 1; Le Havre 1; AS Nancy 1; Bastia 1; Lorient 1.

French Ligue 1 2021–22

	P	W	D	L	F	A	GD	Pts
Paris Saint-Germain (C)[1]	38	26	8	4	90	36	54	86
Marseille[1]	38	21	8	9	63	38	25	71
Monaco[1]	38	20	9	9	65	40	25	69
Rennes[2]	38	20	6	12	82	40	42	66
Nice[3] (–1)	38	20	7	11	52	36	16	66
Strasbourg	38	17	12	9	60	43	17	63
Lens	38	17	11	10	62	48	14	62
Lyon (–1)	38	17	11	10	66	51	15	61
Nantes[3]	38	15	10	13	55	48	7	55
Lille	38	14	13	11	48	48	0	55
Brest	38	13	9	16	49	57	–8	48
Reims	38	11	13	14	43	44	–1	46
Montpellier	38	12	7	19	49	61	–12	43
Angers	38	10	11	17	44	55	–11	41
Troyes	38	9	11	18	37	53	–16	38
Lorient	38	8	12	18	35	63	–28	36
Clermont	38	9	9	20	38	69	–31	36
Saint-Etienne+*	38	7	11	20	42	77	–35	32
Metz*	38	6	13	19	35	69	–34	31
Bordeaux*	38	6	13	19	52	91	–39	31

Both Nice v Marseille and Lyon v Marseille matches were abandoned due to crowd disturbances. Nice and Lyon were each deducted 1pt with a further 1pt suspended and the matches were ordered to be replayed at a later date.
Bordeaux relegated to the third tier for financial issues.
Top scorer: Mbappe (Paris Saint-Germain) 28.
Cup Final: Nantes 1, Nice 0.

GEORGIA

Georgian Football Federation, 76A Chavchavadze Avenue, 0179 Tbilisi.
Founded: 1990. *FIFA:* 1992; *UEFA:* 1992. *National Colours:* All red with white trim.

International matches 2021–22
Kosovo (h) 0-1, Spain (a) 0-4, Bulgaria (a) 1-4, Greece (h) 0-2, Kosovo (a) 2-1, Sweden (h) 2-0, Uzbekistan (h) 1-0, Bosnia-Herzegovina (a) 1-0, Albania (a) 0-0, Gibraltar (h) 4-0, Bulgaria (a) 5-2, North Macedonia (a) 3-0, Bulgaria (h) 0-0.

League Championship wins (1990–2021)
Dinamo Tbilisi 18; Torpedo Kutaisi 4; WIT Georgia 2; Olimpi Rustavi (now FC Rustavi) 2; Zestafoni 2; Sioni Bolnisi 1; Dila Gori 1; Samtredia 1; Saburtalo 1; Dinamo Batumi 1.

Cup wins (1990–2021)
Dinamo Tbilisi 13; Torpedo Kutaisi 4; Locomotive Tbilisi 3; Ameri Tbilisi 2; Gagra 2; Saburtalo 2; Guria Lanchkhuti 1; Dinamo Batumi 1; Zestafoni 1; WIT Georgia 1; Dila Gori 1; Chikhura Sachkhere 1.
See also Russia section for Georgian club honours in Soviet era 1936–91.

Georgian Erovnuli Liga 2021

	P	*W*	*D*	*L*	*F*	*A*	*GD*	*Pts*
Dinamo Batumi (C)[1]	36	21	12	3	73	27	46	75
Dinamo Tbilisi[3]	36	21	7	8	59	28	31	70
Dila Gori[3]	36	17	10	9	48	35	13	61
Saburtalo[3]	36	15	12	9	52	40	12	57
Locomotive Tbilisi	36	15	8	13	57	59	–2	53
Telavi	36	12	8	16	35	53	–18	44
Samgurali Tsqaltubo	36	9	14	13	34	46	–12	41
Torpedo Kutaisi+	36	9	13	14	38	44	–6	40
Shukura Kobuleti+*	36	5	12	19	28	49	–21	27
Samtredia*	36	5	6	25	33	76	–43	21

Top scorer: Marusic (Dinamo Tbilisi) 16.
Cup Final: Saburtalo 1, Samgurali Tsqaltubo 0.

GERMANY

Deutscher Fussball-Bund, Hermann-Neuberger-Haus, Otto-Fleck-Schneise 6, 60528 Frankfurt Am Main.
Founded: 1900. *FIFA:* 1904; *UEFA:* 1954. *National Colours:* White shirts with red and black trim, black shorts, white socks with black trim.

International matches 2021–22
Liechtenstein (a) 2-0*, Armenia (h) 6-0, Iceland (a) 4-0, Romania (h) 2-1, North Macedonia (a) 4-0, Liechtenstein (h) 9-0, Armenia (a) 4-1, Israel (h) 2-0, Netherlands (a) 1-1, Italy (a) 1-1, England (h) 1-1, Hungary (a) 1-1, Italy (h) 5-2.
** Match played in Switzerland.*

League Championship wins (1903–2022)
Bayern Munich 32; 1.FC Nuremberg 9; Borussia Dortmund 8; Schalke 04 7; Hamburger SV 6; VfB Stuttgart 5; Borussia Moenchengladbach 5; 1.FC Kaiserslautern 4; Werder Bremen 4; 1.FC Lokomotive Leipzig 3; SpVgg Greuther Furth 3; 1.FC Cologne 3; Viktoria Berlin 2; Hertha Berlin 2; Hannover 96 2; Dresden SC 2; Union Berlin 1; Freiburger FC 1; Phoenix Karlsruhe 1; Karlsruher FV 1; Holstein Kiel 1; Fortuna Dusseldorf 1; Rapid Vienna 1; VfR Mannheim 1; Rot-Weiss Essen 1; Eintracht Frankfurt 1; Munich 1860 1; Eintracht Braunschweig 1; VfL Wolfsburg 1.

Cup wins (1935–2022)
Bayern Munich 20; Werder Bremen 6; Schalke 04 5; Borussia Dortmund 5; Eintracht Frankfurt 5; 1.FC Nuremberg 4; 1.FC Cologne 4; VfB Stuttgart 3; Borussia Moenchengladbach 3; Hamburger SV 3; Dresden SC 2; Munich 1860 2; Karlsruhe SC 2; Fortuna Dusseldorf 2; 1.FC Kaiserslautern 2; 1.FC Lokomotive Leipzig 1; Rapid Vienna 1; First Vienna 1; Rot-Weiss Essen 1; SW Essen 1; Kickers Offenbach 1; Bayer Uerdingen 1; Hannover 96 1; Bayer Leverkusen 1; VfLWolfsburg 1; RB Leipzig 1.

German Bundesliga 2021–22

	P	*W*	*D*	*L*	*F*	*A*	*GD*	*Pts*
Bayern Munich (C)[1]	34	24	5	5	97	37	60	77
Borussia Dortmund[1]	34	22	3	9	85	52	33	69
Bayer Leverkusen[1]	34	19	7	8	80	47	33	64
RB Leipzig[1]	34	17	7	10	72	37	35	58
Union Berlin[2]	34	16	9	9	50	44	6	57
Freiburg[2]	34	15	10	9	58	46	12	55
Cologne[3]	34	14	10	10	52	49	3	52
Mainz	34	13	7	14	50	45	5	46
TSG 1899 Hoffenheim	34	13	7	14	58	60	–2	46
Borussia M'gladbach	34	12	9	13	54	61	–7	45
Eintracht Frankfurt†[1]	34	10	12	12	45	49	–4	42
VfL Wolfsburg	34	12	6	16	43	54	–11	42
Bochum	34	12	6	16	38	52	–14	42
Augsburg	34	10	8	16	39	56	–17	38
Stuttgart	34	7	12	15	41	59	–18	33
Hertha Berlin+	34	9	6	19	37	71	–34	33
Arminia Bielefeld*	34	5	13	16	27	53	–26	28
Greuther Furth*	34	3	9	22	28	82	–54	18

†Eintracht Frankfurt qualified for the Champions League by winning the 2021–22 Europa League.
Top scorer: Lewandowski (Bayern Munich) 35.
Cup Final: Freiburg 1, RB Leipzig 1 *(aet; RB Leipzig won 4-2 on penalties).*

GIBRALTAR

Gibraltar Football Association, Bayside Sports Complex, PO Box 513, Gibraltar GX11 1AA.
Founded: 1895. *FIFA:* 2016; *UEFA:* 2013. *National Colours:* All red.

International matches 2021–22
Latvia (a) 1-3, Turkey (h) 0-3, Norway (a) 1-5, Montenegro (h) 0-3, Netherlands (a) 0-6, Turkey (a) 0-6, Latvia (h) 1-3, Grenada (h) 0-0, Faroe Islands (h) 0-0, Georgia (a) 0-4, North Macedonia (h) 0-2, Bulgaria (h) 1-1, North Macedonia (a) 0-4.

League Championship wins (1896–2022)
Lincoln Red Imps (incl. Newcastle United 5; 1 title shared) 26; Prince of Wales 19; Glacis United 17 (incl. 1 shared); Britannia (now Britannia XI) 14; Gibraltar United 11; Europa 7; Manchester United (now Manchester 62) 7; St Theresa's 3; Chief Construction 2; Jubilee 2; Exiles 2; South United 2; Gibraltar FC 2; Albion 1; Athletic 1; Royal Sovereign 1; Commander of the Yard 1; St Joseph's 1.
No winner in 2019–20.

Cup wins (1895–2022)
Lincoln Red Imps (incl. Newcastle United 4) 19; St Joseph's 10; Europa 8; Glacis United 5; Britannia (now Britannia XI) 3; Gibraltar United 4; Manchester United (now Manchester 62) 3; Gibraltar FC 1; HMS Hood 1; 2nd Bn The King's Regt 1; AARA 1; RAF New Camp 1; 4th Bn Royal Scots 1; Prince of Wales 1; Manchester United Reserves 1; 2nd Bn Royal Green Jackets 1; RAF Gibraltar 1; St Theresa's 1.
No winner in 2019–20.

Gibraltarian Premier Division Qualifying Table 2021–22

	P	*W*	*D*	*L*	*F*	*A*	*GD*	*Pts*
Lincoln Red Imps	10	10	0	0	40	5	35	30
Europa	10	9	0	1	36	7	29	27
St Joseph's	10	7	1	2	25	9	16	22
Glacis United	10	6	1	3	26	14	12	19
Mons Calpe	10	5	1	4	25	13	12	16
Bruno's Magpies	10	4	2	4	18	15	3	14
Manchester 62	10	4	1	5	11	21	–10	13
Lynx	10	3	1	6	15	25	–10	10
College 1975	10	2	0	8	5	21	–16	6
Europa Point	10	1	0	9	8	49	–41	3
Lions Gibraltar	10	0	1	9	6	36	–30	1

Championship Group 2021–22

	P	*W*	*D*	*L*	*F*	*A*	*GD*	*Pts*
Lincoln Red Imps (C)[1]	20	19	1	0	65	17	48	58
Europa[3]	20	15	2	3	57	21	36	47
St Joseph's[3]	20	11	2	7	45	27	18	35
Bruno's Magpies[3]	20	10	3	7	36	25	11	33
Glacis United	20	7	1	12	32	36	–4	22
Mons Calpe*	20	6	2	12	34	36	–2	20

**Mons Calpe banned from all UEFA club competitions for the 2022–23 season for breach of financial rules.*

Challenge Group 2021–22

	P	*W*	*D*	*L*	*F*	*A*	*GD*	*Pts*
Manchester 62	18	7	5	6	25	28	–3	26
College 1975	18	6	2	10	17	28	–11	20
Lynx	18	6	1	11	25	38	–13	19
Europa Point	18	4	2	12	17	65	–48	14
Lions Gibraltar	18	1	5	12	13	45	–32	8

Top scorer: Juanfri (St Joseph's) 14.
Cup Final: Lincoln Red Imps 2, Bruno's Magpies 1.

GOZO

Gozo Football Association, GFA Headquarters, Mgarr Road, Xewkija, XWK 9014, Malta. (Not a member of FIFA or UEFA.)
Founded: 1936.

League Championship wins (1938–2022)
Victoria Hotspurs 13; Nadur Youngsters 13; Sannat Lions 10; Xewkija Tigers 8; Ghajnsielem 7; Xaghra United 6 (incl. Xaghra Blue Stars 1, Xaghra Young Stars 1); Salesian Youths (renamed Oratory Youths) 6; Victoria Athletics 4; Victoria Stars 1; Victoria City 1; Calypcians 1; Victoria United (renamed Victoria Wanderers) 1; Kercem Ajax 1; Zebbug Rovers 1.

Cup wins (1972–2022)
Xewkija Tigers 11; Sannat Lions 9; Nadur Youngsters 9; Ghajnsielem 6; Xaghra United 4; Victoria Hotspurs 2; Kercem Ajax 2; Calypsians 1; Calypsians Bosco Youths 1; Qala St Joseph 1; Victoria Wanderers 1.

Gozitan L-Ewwel Divizjoni 2021–22

	P	*W*	*D*	*L*	*F*	*A*	*GD*	*Pts*
Nadur Youngsters (C)	21	18	2	1	70	14	56	56
Ghajnsielem	21	11	5	5	45	27	18	38
Kercem Ajax	21	10	4	7	47	48	–1	34
Victoria Hotspurs	21	8	6	7	36	33	3	30
Xewkija Tigers	21	6	5	10	35	50	–15	23
Oratory Youths	21	5	6	10	25	32	–7	21
Sannat Lions+	21	4	5	12	21	56	–35	17

Top scorer: Barbosa (Nadur Youngsters) 24.
Cup Final: Nadur Youngsters 3, Ghajnsielem 2.

GREECE

Hellenic Football Federation, Parko Goudi, PO Box 14161, 11510 Athens.
Founded: 1926. *FIFA:* 1927; *UEFA:* 1954. *National Colours:* White shirts with blue sash, white shorts, white socks with blue trim.

International matches 2021–22
Switzerland (a) 1-2, Kosovo (a) 1-1, Sweden (h) 2-1, Georgia (a) 2-0, Sweden (a) 0-2, Spain (h) 0-1, Kosovo (h) 1-1, Romania (a) 1-0, Montenegro (a) 0-1, Northern Ireland (a) 1-0, Kosovo (a) 1-0, Cyprus (h) 3-0, Kosovo (h) 2-0.

League Championship wins (1927–2022)
Olympiacos 47; Panathinaikos 20; AEK Athens 12; Aris 3; PAOK (Thessaloniki) 3; AEL (Larissa) 1.

Cup wins (1932–2022)
Olympiacos 28; Panathinaikos 19; AEK Athens 15; PAOK (Thessaloniki) 8; Panionios 2; AEL (Larissa) 2; Ethnikos 1; Aris 1; Iraklis 1; Kastoria 1; OFI Crete 1.

Greek Super League Qualifying Table 2021–22

	P	W	D	L	F	A	GD	Pts
Olympiacos	26	20	5	1	47	14	33	65
PAOK	26	16	5	5	50	24	26	53
AEK Athens	26	14	4	8	42	28	14	46
Aris	26	13	6	7	28	21	7	45
Panathinaikos	26	13	3	10	41	21	20	42
PAS Giannina	26	11	7	8	28	24	4	40
OFI Crete	26	9	10	7	33	32	1	37
Asteras Tripolis	26	10	5	11	27	29	–2	35
Panaitolikos	26	9	5	12	27	39	–12	32
Volos	26	8	6	12	35	42	–7	30
Ionikos	26	6	8	12	26	34	–8	26
Atromitos	26	6	5	15	27	47	–20	23
Lamia	26	4	6	16	19	37	–18	18
Apollon Smirnis	26	2	7	17	9	47	–38	13

Championship Round 2021–22

	P	W	D	L	F	A	GD	Pts
Olympiacos (C)[1]	36	25	8	3	62	26	36	83
PAOK[3]	36	19	7	10	58	33	25	64
Aris[3]	36	18	8	10	39	28	11	62
Panathinaikos[3]	36	18	7	11	52	26	26	61
AEK Athens	36	16	8	12	56	42	14	56
PAS Giannina	36	12	10	14	34	42	–8	46

Relegation Round 2021–22

	P	W	D	L	F	A	GD	Pts
Ionikos	33	12	9	12	44	42	2	45
OFI Crete	33	11	11	11	40	45	–5	44
Asteras Tripolis	33	11	8	14	33	37	–4	41
Volos	33	10	10	13	47	48	–1	40
Panaitolikos	33	10	7	16	32	48	–16	37
Atromitos	33	8	9	16	33	52	–19	33
Lamia+	33	6	8	19	24	44	–20	26
Apollon Smirnis*	33	4	10	19	16	57	–41	22

Top scorer: VanWeert (Volos) 17.
Cup Final: Panathinaikos 1, PAOK 0.

HUNGARY

Magyar Labdarugo Szovetseg, Kanai ut 2. D, 1112 Budapest.
Founded: 1901. *FIFA:* 1907; *UEFA:* 1954. *National Colours:* Red shirts with white trim, white shorts with red trim, green socks with white trim.

International matches 2021–22
England (h) 0-4, Albania (a) 0-1, Andorra (h) 2-1, Albania (h) 0-1, England (a) 1-1, San Marino (h) 4-0, Poland (a) 2-1, Serbia (h) 0-1, Northern Ireland (a) 1-0, England (h) 1-0, Italy (a) 1-2, Germany (h) 1-1, England (a) 4-0.

League Championship wins (1901–2022)
Ferencvaros 33; MTK Budapest 23; Ujpest 20; Budapest Honved 14 (incl. Kispest Honved); Debrecen 7; Vasas 6; Csepel 4; Gyor 4; Videoton (renamed Fehervar) 3; Budapesti TC 2; Nagyvarad 1; Vac 1; Dunaferr (renamed Dunaujvaros) 1; Zalaegerszeg 1.

Cup wins (1910–2022)
Ferencvaros 24; MTK Budapest 12; Ujpest 11; Budapest Honved 8 (inc. Kispest Honved); Debrecen 6; Vasas 4; Gyor 4; Diosgyor 2; Fehervar (incl. Videoton 1, Vidi 1) 2; Bocskai 1; III Keruleti TUE 1; Soroksar 1; Szolnoki MAV 1; Siofoki Banyasz 1; Bekescsaba 1; Pecsi 1; Sopron 1; Kecskemet 1.
Cup not regularly held until 1964.

Hungarian Nemzeti Bajnoksag I 2021–22

	P	W	D	L	F	A	GD	Pts
Ferencvaros (C)[1]	33	22	5	6	60	31	29	71
Kisvarda[3]	33	16	11	6	50	34	16	59
Puskas Akademia[3]	33	14	12	7	43	34	9	54
Fehervar[3]	33	13	9	11	48	43	5	48
Ujpest	33	12	8	13	50	48	2	44
Paks	33	12	7	14	75	63	12	43
Debrecen	33	10	9	14	45	52	–7	39
Zalaegerszegi	33	10	9	14	44	58	–14	39
Budapest Honved	33	10	8	15	48	51	–3	38
Mezokovesd	33	10	8	15	37	49	–12	38
MTK Budapest*	33	9	9	15	28	50	–22	36
Gyirmot*	33	7	11	15	34	49	–15	32

Top scorer: Adam (Paks) 31.
Cup Final: Ferencvaros 3, Paks 0.

ICELAND

Knattspyrnusamband Islands, Laugardal, 104 Reykjavik.
Founded: 1947. *FIFA:* 1947; *UEFA:* 1954. *National Colours:* All blue.

International matches 2021–22
Romania (h) 0-2, North Macedonia (h) 2-2, Germany (h) 0-4, Armenia (h) 1-1, Liechtenstein (h) 4-0, Romania (a) 0-0, North Macedonia (a) 1-3, Uganda (n) 1-1, Korea Republic (n) 1-5, Finland (a) 1-1, Spain (a) 0-5, Israel (a) 2-2, Albania (h) 1-1, San Marino (a) 1-0, Israel (h) 2-2.

League Championship wins (1912–2021)
KR (Reykjavik) 27; Valur 23; Fram 18; IA (Akranes) 18; FH (Hafnarfjordur) 8; Vikingur 6; Keflavik 4; IBV (Vestmannaeyjar) 3; KA (Akureyri) 1; Breidablik 1; Stjarnan 1.

Cup wins (1960–2021)
KR (Reykjavik) 14; Valur 11; IA (Akranes) 9; Fram 8; IBV (Vestmannaeyjar) 5; Keflavik 4; Vikingur 3; Fylkir 2; FH (Hafnarfjordur) 2; IBA Akureyri 1; Breidablik 1; Stjarnan 1.

Icelandic Besta-deild karla 2021

	P	W	D	L	F	A	GD	Pts
Vikingur (C)[1]	22	14	6	2	38	21	17	48
Breidablik[3]	22	15	2	5	55	21	34	47
KR[3]	22	12	5	5	35	19	16	41
KA	22	12	4	6	36	20	16	40
Valur	22	12	3	7	37	26	11	39
FH	22	9	6	7	39	26	13	33
Stjarnan	22	6	4	12	24	36	–12	22
Leiknir	22	6	4	12	18	32	–14	22
IA	22	6	3	13	29	44	–15	21
Keflavik	22	6	3	13	23	38	–15	21
HK*	22	5	5	12	21	39	–18	20
Fylkir*	22	3	7	12	18	51	–33	16

Top scorer: Hansen (Vikingur) 16.
Cup Final: Vikingur 3, IA 0.

ISRAEL

Israel Football Association, Ramat Gan Stadium, 299 Aba Hilell Street, PO Box 3591, Ramat Gan 52134.
Founded: 1928. *FIFA:* 1929; *UEFA:* 1994. *National Colours:* Grey and white patterned shirts, white shorts, white socks.

International matches 2021–22
Faroe Islands (a) 4-0, Austria (h) 5-2, Denmark (a) 0-5, Scotland (a) 2-3, Moldova (h) 2-1, Austria (a) 2-4, Faroe Islands (h) 3-2, Germany (a) 0-2, Romania (h) 2-2, Iceland (h) 2-2, Albania (a) 2-1, Iceland (a) 2-2.

League Championship wins (1932–2022)
Maccabi Tel Aviv 23; Hapoel Tel Aviv 14 (incl. 1 shared); Maccabi Haifa 14; Hapoel Petah Tikva 6; Beitar Jerusalem 6; Maccabi Netanya 5; Hapoel Be'er Sheva 5; Hakoah Amidar Ramat Gan 2; British Police 1; Beitar Tel Aviv 1 (shared); Hapoel Ramat Gan 1; Hapoel Kfar Saba 1; Bnei Yehuda 1; Hapoel Haifa 1; Ironi Kiryat Shmona 1.

Cup wins (1928–2022)
Maccabi Tel Aviv 24; Hapoel Tel Aviv 15; Beitar Jerusalem 7; Maccabi Haifa 6; Hapoel Haifa 4; Bnei Yehuda 4; Hapoel Kfar Saba 3; Hapoel Be'er Sheva 3; Maccabi Petah Tikva 2; Beitar Tel Aviv 2; Hapoel Petah Tikva 2; Hakoah Amidar Ramat Gan 2; Hapoel Ramat Gan 2; Maccabi Hashmonai Jerusalem 1; British Police 1; Hapoel Jerusalem 1; Maccabi Netanya 1; Hapoel Yehud 1; Hapoel Lod 1; Bnei Sakhnin 1; Ironi Kiryat Shmona 1.

Israeli Premier League Qualifying Table 2021–22

	P	W	D	L	F	A	GD	Pts
Maccabi Haifa	26	18	5	3	62	19	43	59
Hapoel Be'er Sheva	26	16	7	3	39	17	22	55
Maccabi Tel Aviv	26	16	5	5	48	31	17	53
Bnei Sakhnin	26	12	6	8	28	29	–1	42
Maccabi Netanya	26	10	10	6	34	27	7	40
Hapoel Tel Aviv	26	10	8	8	36	31	5	38
Hapoel Hadera	26	9	9	8	22	28	–6	36
Ironi Kiryat Shmona	26	9	6	11	29	32	–3	33
Hapoel Haifa	26	8	6	12	33	37	–4	30
Ashdod	26	8	3	15	28	44	–16	27
Hapoel Jerusalem	26	5	8	13	19	35	–16	23
Beitar Jerusalem	26	5	7	14	23	36	–13	22
Maccabi Petah Tikva	26	5	6	15	27	37	–10	21
Hapoel Nof HaGalil	26	4	8	14	20	45	–25	20

Championship Round 2021–22

	P	W	D	L	F	A	GD	Pts
Maccabi Haifa (C)[1]	36	24	6	6	79	27	52	78
Hapoel Be'er Sheva[3]	36	20	10	6	53	30	23	70
Maccabi Tel Aviv[3]	36	20	9	7	63	38	25	69
Maccabi Netanya[3]	36	13	13	10	47	41	6	52
Hapoel Tel Aviv	36	13	11	12	44	47	–3	50
Bnei Sakhnin	36	13	10	13	33	43	–10	49

Relegation Round 2021–22

	P	W	D	L	F	A	GD	Pts
Ironi Kiryat Shmona	33	14	8	11	48	39	9	50
Hapoel Hadera	33	11	9	13	34	43	–9	42
Ashdod	33	12	3	18	37	52	–15	39
Beitar Jerusalem	33	9	10	14	35	43	–8	37
Hapoel Haifa	33	9	8	16	36	47	–11	35
Hapoel Jerusalem	33	8	9	16	25	41	–16	33
Maccabi Petah Tikva*	33	6	9	18	34	49	–15	27
Hapoel Nof HaGalil*	33	6	9	18	25	53	–28	27

Top scorer: Atzili (Maccabi Haifa) 20.
Cup Final: Hapoel Be'er Sheva 2, Maccabi Haifa 2 *(aet; Hapoel Be'er Sheva won 3-1 on penalties).*

ITALY

Federazione Italiana Giuoco Calcio, Via Gregorio Allegri 14, 00198 Roma.
Founded: 1898. *FIFA:* 1905; *UEFA:* 1954. *National Colours:* Blue shirts, white shorts, blue socks.

International matches 2021–22

Bulgaria (h) 1-1, Switzerland (a) 0-0, Lithuania (h) 5-0, Spain (h) 1-2, Belgium (h) 2-1, Switzerland (h) 1-1, Northern Ireland (a) 0-0, North Macedonia (h) 0-1, Turkey (a) 3-2, Argentina (n) 1-1, Germany (h) 1-1, Hungary (h) 2-1, England (a) 0-0, Germany (a) 2-5.

League Championship wins (1898–2022)

Juventus 36 (excludes two titles revoked); AC Milan 19; Internazionale 19 (includes one title awarded); Genoa 9; Pro Vercelli 7; Bologna 7; Torino 7 (excludes one title revoked); Roma 3; Fiorentina 2; Lazio 2; Napoli 2; Casale 1; Novese 1; Cagliari 1; Hellas Verona 1; Sampdoria 1.

Cup wins (1928–2022)

Juventus 14; Roma 9; Internazionale 8; Lazio 7; Fiorentina 6; Napoli 6; Torino 5; AC Milan 5; Sampdoria 4; Parma 3; Bologna 2; Vado 1; Genoa 1; Venezia 1; Atalanta 1; Vicenza 1.

Italian Serie A 2021–22

	P	W	D	L	F	A	GD	Pts
AC Milan (C)[1]	38	26	8	4	69	31	38	86
Internazionale[1]	38	25	9	4	84	32	52	84
Napoli[1]	38	24	7	7	74	31	43	79
Juventus[1]	38	20	10	8	57	37	20	70
Lazio[2]	38	18	10	10	77	58	19	64
Roma[2]	38	18	9	11	59	43	16	63
Fiorentina[3]	38	19	5	14	59	51	8	62
Atalanta	38	16	11	11	65	48	17	59
Hellas Verona	38	14	11	13	65	59	6	53
Torino	38	13	11	14	46	41	5	50
Sassuolo	38	13	11	14	64	66	–2	50
Udinese	38	11	14	13	61	58	3	47
Bologna	38	12	10	16	44	55	–11	46
Empoli	38	10	11	17	50	70	–20	41
Sampdoria	38	10	6	22	46	63	–17	36
Spezia	38	10	6	22	41	71	–30	36
Salernitana	38	7	10	21	33	78	–45	31
Cagliari*	38	6	12	20	34	68	–34	30
Genoa*	38	4	16	18	27	60	–33	28
Venezia*	38	6	9	23	34	69	–35	27

Top scorer: Immobile (Lazio) 27.
Cup Final: Internazionale 4, Juventus 2 *(aet).*

KAZAKHSTAN

Football Federation of Kazakhstan, 29 Syganak Street, 9th floor, 010000 Astana.
Founded: 1914. *FIFA:* 1994; *UEFA:* 2002. *National Colours:* All yellow with light blue trim.

International matches 2021–22

Ukraine (h) 2-2, Finland (a) 0-1, Bosnia-Herzegovina (a) 2-2, Bosnia-Herzegovina (h) 0-2, Finland (h) 0-2, France (a) 0-8, Tajikistan (h) 1-0, Moldova (a) 2-1, Moldova (h) 0-1 (5-4p), Azerbaijan (h) 2-0, Slovakia (a) 1-0, Belarus (a) 1-1, Slovakia (h) 2-1.

League Championship wins (1992–2021)

Astana 6; Irtysh Pavlodar (includes Ansat) 5; Aktobe 5; Kairat 3; Yelimay (renamed Spartak Semey) 3; FC Astana-64 (includes Zhenis) 3; Tobol 2; Shakhter Karagandy 2; Taraz 1.

Cup wins (1992–2021)

Kairat 10; FC Astana-64 (incl. Zhenis) 3; Astana (incl. Lokomotiv) 3; Kaisar 2; Dostyk 1; Vostok 1; Yelimay (renamed Spartak Semey) 1; Irtysh Pavlodar 1; Taraz 1; Almaty 1; Tobol 1; Aktobe 1; Atyrau 1; Ordabasy 1; Shakhter Karagandy 1.
No winner in 2020.

Kazakh Premer Ligasy 2021

	P	W	D	L	F	A	GD	Pts
Tobol (C)[1]	26	18	7	1	54	18	36	61
Astana[3]	26	17	6	3	53	25	28	57
Kairat[3]	26	14	9	3	52	21	31	51
Kyzyl-Zhar[3]	26	11	6	9	32	24	8	39
Ordabasy	26	10	8	8	36	35	1	38
Aktobe	26	9	6	11	35	40	–5	33
Shakhter Karagandy	26	9	6	11	25	34	–9	33
Kaspiy	26	8	8	10	35	35	0	32
Akzhayik	26	9	5	12	25	31	–6	32
Taraz	26	7	8	11	27	34	–7	29
Atyrau	26	7	7	12	25	40	–15	28
Turan Turkistan	26	5	11	10	22	40	–18	26
Kaisar*	26	4	7	15	24	44	–20	19
Zhetysu* (–3)	26	5	4	17	23	47	–24	16

Zhetysu deducted 3pts for failing a stadium inspection.
Top scorer: Tomasov (Astana) 17.
Cup Final: Kairat 3, Shakhter Karagandy 3 *(aet; Kairat won 9-8 on penalties).*

KOSOVO

Football Federation of Kosovo, Rruga Agim Ramadani 45, Prishtina, Kosovo 10000. *Founded:* 1946. *FIFA:* 2016; *UEFA:* 2016. *National Colours:* All blue.

International matches 2019–20

Georgia (a) 1-0, Greece (h) 1-1, Spain (h) 0-2, Sweden (a) 0-3, Georgia (h) 1-2, Jordan (h) 0-2, Greece (a) 1-1, Burkina Faso (h) 5-0, Switzerland (a) 1-1, Cyprus (a) 2-0, Greece (h) 0-1, Northern Ireland (h) 3-2, Greece (a) 0-2.

League Championship wins (1945–97; 1999–2022)

Prishtina 15; Vellaznimi 9; KF Trepca 7; Liria 5; Buduqnosti 4; Rudari 3; Red Star 3; Drita 3; Besa Peje 3; Feronikeli 3; Jedinstvo 2; Kosova Prishtina 2; Slloga 2; Obiliqi 2; Fushe-Kosova 2; Proletari 1; KXEK Kosova 1; Rudniku 1; KNI Ramiz Sadiku 1; Dukagjini 1; Besiana 1; Hysi 1; Vushtrria 1; Trepca'89 1; Ballkani 1.

Cup wins (1992–97; 1999–2022)

Prishtina 7; Liria 3; Besa Peje 3; Feronikeli 3; Flamurtari 2; Llapi 2; KF Trepca 1; KF 2 Korriku 1; Gjilani 1; Drita 1; Besiana 1; KEK-u 1; Kosova Prishtina 1; Vellaznimi 1; Hysi 1; Trepca'89 1.

Kosovar Superliga 2021–22

	P	W	D	L	F	A	GD	Pts
Ballkani (C)[1]	36	23	7	6	61	26	35	76
Drita[3]	36	18	10	8	56	25	31	64
Gjilani[3]	36	16	14	6	57	36	21	62
Llapi[3]	36	15	9	12	57	44	13	54
Prishtina	36	14	9	13	49	37	12	51
Drenica Skenderaj†	36	14	8	14	51	48	3	50
Dukagjini†	36	12	14	10	37	34	3	50
Malisheva+	36	13	9	14	45	43	2	48
Ulpiana*	36	6	9	21	34	72	–38	27
Feronikeli*	36	3	3	30	16	98	–82	12

†Ranking decided on head-to-head points.
Top scorer: Progni (Gjilani) 21.
Cup Final: Llapi 2, Drita 1.

LATVIA

Latvijas Futbola Federacija, Olympic Sports Centre, Grostonas Street 6B, 1013 Riga.
Founded: 1921. *FIFA:* 1922; *UEFA:* 1992. *National Colours:* All carmine red with white trim.

International matches 2021–22

Gibraltar (h) 3-1, Norway (h) 0-2, Montenegro (a) 0-0, Netherlands (h) 0-1, Turkey (h) 1-2, Norway (a) 0-0, Gibraltar (a) 3-1, Kuwait (n) 1-1, Azerbaijan (n) 1-0, Andorra (h) 3-0, Liechtenstein (h) 1-0, Moldova (a) 4-2, Liechtenstein (a) 2-0.

League Championship wins (1922–2021)

Skonto Riga 15; ASK Riga (incl. AVN 2) 11; Sarkanais Metalurgs Liepaja 9; RFK Riga 8; Olympija Liepaya 7; VEF Riga 6; Ventspils 6; Energija Riga (incl. ESR Riga 2) 4; Elektrons Riga (incl. Alfa 1) 4; Riga FC 3; Torpedo Riga 3; Keisermezhs (Kaiserwald) Riga 2; Khimikis Daugavpils 2; RAF Yelgava 2; Daugava Liepaja 2; Liepajas Metalurgs 2; JPFS/Spartaks Jurmala 2; Dinamo Riga 1; Zhmilyeva Team 1; Darba Rezervi 1; RER Riga 1; Starts Brotseni 1; Venta Ventspils 1; Jumieks Riga 1; Gauja Valmiera 1; Daugava Daugavpils 1; FK Liepaja 1; FK RFS 1.

Cup wins (1937–2021)

Skonto Riga 8; ASK Riga 7 (includes AVN 3); Elektrons Riga 7; Ventspils 7; Sarkanais Metalurgs Liepaja 4; Jelgava 4; VEF Riga 3; Tseltnieks Riga 3; RAF Yelgava 3; RFK Riga 2; Daugava Liepaja 2; Starts Brotseni 2; Selmash Liepaya 2;

Yurnieks Riga 2; Khimikis Daugavpils 2; FK Liepaja 2; FK RFS 2; Rigas Vilki 1; Dinamo Liepaya 1; Dinamo Riga 1; RER Riga 1; Voulkan Kouldiga 1; Baltika Liepaja 1; Venta Ventspils 1; Pilots Riga 1; Lielupe Yurmala 1; Energija Riga (formerly ESR Riga) 1; Torpedo Riga 1; Daugava SKIF Riga 1; Tseltnieks Daugavpils 1; Olympija Riga 1; FK Riga 1; Liepajas Metalurgs 1; Daugava Daugavpils 1; Riga FC 1.

Latvian Virsliga 2021

	P	W	D	L	F	A	GD	Pts
FK RFS (C)[1]	28	20	6	2	65	22	43	66
Valmiera[3]	28	19	5	4	54	19	35	62
FK Liepaja[3]	28	16	3	9	47	26	21	51
Riga FC[3]	28	14	8	6	54	26	28	50
Spartaks Jurmala	28	11	2	15	40	41	–1	35
BFC Daugavpils	28	9	5	14	37	53	–16	32
Metta/LU	28	5	5	18	33	55	–22	20
Noah Jurmala†	28	1	0	27	8	96	–88	3
Ventspils†	0	0	0	0	0	0	0	0

†Withdrew from the league following bans for match fixing; no further relegations.
Top scorer: Wamba (Spartaks Jurmala) 14.
Cup Final: FK RFS 1, FK Liepaja 0.

LIECHTENSTEIN

Liechtensteiner Fussballverband, Landstrasse 149, 9494 Schaan.
Founded: 1934. *FIFA:* 1974; *UEFA:* 1974. *National Colours:* All blue with white trim.

International matches 2021–22
Germany (h) 2-0*, Romania (a) 0-2, Armenia (a) 1-1, North Macedonia (h) 0-4, Iceland (a) 0-4, Germany (a) 0-9, Romania (h) 0-2, Cape Verde (n) 0-6, Faroe Islands (n) 0-1, Moldova (h) 0-2, Latvia (a) 0-1, Andorra (a) 1-2, Latvia (h) 0-2.
* *Match played in Switzerland.*
Liechtenstein has no national league. Teams compete in Swiss regional leagues.

Cup wins (1937–2022)
Vaduz 48; FC Balzers 11; FC Triesen 8; USV Eschen/Mauren 5; FC Schaan 3.
No winner in 2019–20, 2020–21.
Cup Final: Vaduz 3, USV Eschen/Mauren 1.

LITHUANIA

Lietuvos Futbolo Federacija, Stadiono g. 2, 02106 Vilnius.
Founded: 1922. *FIFA:* 1923; *UEFA:* 1992. *National Colours:* All yellow with green trim.

International matches 2021–22
Northern Ireland (h) 1-4, Bulgaria (a) 0-1, Italy (a) 0-5, Bulgaria (h) 3-1, Switzerland (h) 0-4, Northern Ireland (a) 0-1, Kuwait (h) 1-1, San Marino (a) 2-1, Republic of Ireland (a) 0-1, Luxembourg (h) 0-2, Turkey (h) 0-6, Faroe Islands (a) 1-2, Turkey (a) 0-2.

League Championship wins (1990–2021)
Zalgiris Vilnius 9; FBK Kaunas 8 (incl. Zalgiris Kaunas 1); Ekranas 7; Suduva 3; Inkaras Kaunas 2; Kareda 2; Sirijus Klaipeda 1; ROMAR Mazeikiai 1.

Cup wins (1990–2021)
Zalgiris Vilnius 13; Ekranas 4; FBK Kaunas 4; Suduva 3; Kareda 2; Atlantas 2; Sirijus Klaipeda 1; Lietuvos Makabi Vilnius (renamed Neris Vilnius) 1; Inkaras Kaunas 1; Stumbras 1; Panevezys 1.

Lithuanian A Lyga Qualifying Table 2020

	P	W	D	L	F	A	GD	Pts
Zalgiris Vilnius (C)[1]	36	23	10	3	76	28	48	79
Suduva[3]	36	21	7	8	64	33	31	70
Kauno Zalgiris[3]	36	18	9	9	55	39	16	63
Panevezys[3]	36	16	12	8	55	40	15	60
Hegelmann Litauen	36	14	11	11	53	38	15	53
Riteriai	36	10	16	10	49	37	12	46
Banga	36	10	6	20	40	71	–31	36
Dziugas Telsiai	36	8	12	16	47	60	–13	36
Dainava* (–3)	36	9	11	16	39	56	–17	35
Nevezis*	36	2	4	30	15	91	–76	10

Dainava deducted 3pts at the start of the season for failing to meet licensing criteria.
Top scorer: Videmont (Zalgiris Vilnius) 17.
Cup Final: Zalgiris Vilnius 5, Panevezys 1.

LUXEMBOURG

Federation Luxembourgeoise de Football, BP 5 Rue de Limpach, 3932 Mondercange.
Founded: 1908. *FIFA:* 1910; *UEFA:* 1954. *National Colours:* Red shirts with blue and white trim, red shorts, red socks.

International matches 2021–22
Azerbaijan (h) 2-1, Serbia (a) 1-4, Qatar (h) 1-1, Serbia (h) 0-1, Portugal (a) 0-5, Azerbaijan (a) 3-1, Republic of Ireland (a) 0-3, Northern Ireland (h) 1-3, Bosnia-Herzegovina (a) 0-1, Lithuania (a) 2-0, Faroe Islands (a) 1-0, Turkey (h) 0-2, Faroe Islands (h) 2-2.

League Championship wins (1910–2022)
Jeunesse Esch 28; F91 Dudelange 16; Spora Luxembourg 11; Stade Dudelange 10; Fola Esch 8; Red Boys Differdange 6; Union Luxembourg 6; Avenir Beggen 6; US Hollerich-Bonnevoie 5; Progres NiederKorn 3; Aris Bonnevoie 3; Sporting Club 2; Racing Club 1; National Schifflange 1; Grevenmacher 1.
No winner in 2019–20.

Cup wins (1922–2022)
Red Boys Differdange 15; Jeunesse Esch 13; Union Luxembourg 10; Spora Luxembourg 8; F91 Dudelange 8; Avenir Beggen 7; Progres Niederkorn 4; Stade Dudelange 4; Grevenmacher 4; Differdange 03 4; Fola Esch 3; Alliance Dudelange 2; US Rumelange 2; Racing-Union 2; Racing Club 1; US Dudelange 1; SC Tetange 1; National Schifflange 1; Aris Bonnevoie 1; Jeunesse Hautcharage 1; Swift Hesperange 1; Etzella Ettelbruck 1; CS Petange (renamed Union Titus Petange) 1.
No winner in 2019–20, 2020–21.

Luxembourg Nationaldivisioun 2021–22

	P	W	D	L	F	A	GD	Pts
F91 Dudelange (C)[1]	30	21	4	5	78	27	51	67
Differdange 03[3]	30	19	5	6	58	28	30	62
Fola Esch[3]	30	18	8	4	64	37	27	62
Swift Hesperange	30	18	6	6	61	26	35	60
Progres Niederkorn	30	16	7	7	68	37	31	55
UNA Strassen	30	14	9	7	53	36	17	51
Racing-Union[3]	30	15	4	11	56	48	8	49
Jeunesse Esch	30	14	5	11	44	30	14	47
Mondorf-les-Bains	30	10	7	13	38	44	–6	37
Etzella Ettelbruck	30	12	1	17	45	66	–21	37
Union Titus Petange	30	10	5	15	40	41	–1	35
Victoria Rosport	30	8	9	13	45	59	–14	33
Wiltz+	30	9	4	17	42	53	–11	31
Hostert+	30	8	6	16	42	63	–21	30
Rodange 91*	30	6	1	23	23	70	–47	19
RM Hamm Benfica*	30	1	1	28	13	105	–92	4

Top scorer: Stolz (Swift Hesperange) 23.
Cup Final: Racing-Union 3, F91 Dudelange 2.

MALTA

Malta Football Association, Millennium Stand, Floor 2, National Stadium, Ta'Qali ATD4000.
Founded: 1900. *FIFA:* 1959; *UEFA:* 1960. *National Colours:* All red with white trim.

International matches 2021–22
Cyprus (h) 3-0, Slovenia (a) 0-1, Russia (a) 0-2, Slovenia (h) 0-4, Cyprus (a) 2-2, Croatia (h) 1-7, Slovakia (h) 0-6, Azerbaijan (h) 1-0, Kuwait (h) 2-0, Venezuela (h) 0-1, San Marino (a) 2-0, Estonia (h) 1-2, San Marino (h) 1-0.

League Championship wins (1910–2022)
Floriana 26; Sliema Wanderers 26; Valletta 25; Hibernians 13; Hamrun Spartans 8; Birkirkara 4; Rabat Ajax 2; St George's 1; KOMR 1; Marsaxlokk 1.

Cup wins (1935–2022)
Sliema Wanderers 21; Floriana 21; Valletta 14; Hibernians 10; Hamrun Spartans 6; Birkirkara 5; Melita 1; Gzira United 1; Zurrieq 1; Rabat Ajax 1; Balzan 1.
No winner in 2019–20, 2020–21.

Maltese Premier League 2021–22

	P	W	D	L	F	A	GD	Pts
Hibernians	22	13	8	1	39	18	21	47
Floriana	22	13	6	3	36	19	17	45
Birkirkara	22	9	9	4	30	22	8	36
Hamrun Spartans	22	10	5	7	28	22	6	35
Gzira United	22	9	6	7	39	33	6	33
Gudja United	22	9	2	11	26	25	1	29
Sirens	22	7	6	9	28	38	–10	27
Valletta	22	7	5	10	28	34	–6	26
Mosta	22	6	7	9	32	41	–9	25
Balzan	22	7	2	13	30	33	–3	23
St Lucia	22	4	10	8	28	38	–10	22
Sliema Wanderers	22	2	6	14	12	33	–21	12

Championship Round 2021–22

	P	W	D	L	F	A	GD	Pts
Hibernians (C)[1]	27	15	9	3	46	23	23	54
Floriana[3]	27	14	9	4	38	21	17	51
Hamrun Spartans[3]	27	13	6	8	33	24	9	45
Gzira United[3]	27	12	7	8	46	38	8	43
Birkirkara	27	10	11	6	35	27	8	41
Gudja United	27	10	2	15	29	35	–6	32

Relegation Round 2021–22

	P	W	D	L	F	A	GD	Pts
Valletta	27	10	6	11	39	40	–1	36
Sirens	27	9	7	11	40	48	–8	34

	P	W	D	L	F	A	GD	Pts
Mosta	27	8	8	11	41	50	−9	32
Balzan	27	9	3	15	37	42	−5	30
St Lucia*†	27	5	12	10	36	45	−9	27
Sliema Wanderers*	27	4	6	17	16	43	−27	18

†*St Lucia reprieved from relegation due to financial problems of Tier 2 champions.*
Top scorer: Maxuell (Gzira United) 17.
Cup Final: Floriana 2, Valletta 1 *(aet).*

MOLDOVA

Federatia Moldoveneasca de Fotbal, Str. Tricolorului 39, 2012 Chisinau.
Founded: 1990. *FIFA:* 1994; *UEFA:* 1993. *National Colours:* All blue with white trim.

International matches 2021–22

Austria (h) 0-2, Scotland (a) 0-1, Faroe Islands (a) 1-2, Denmark (h) 0-4, Israel (a) 1-2, Scotland (h) 0-2, Austria (a) 1-4, Uganda (n) 2-3, Korea Republic (n) 0-4, Kazakhstan (h) 1-2, Kazakhstan (a) 1-0 (4-5p), Liechtenstein (a) 2-0, Andorra (a) 0-0, Latvia (h) 2-4, Andorra (h) 2-1.

League Championship wins (1992–2022)

Sheriff (Tiraspol) 20; Zimbru Chisinau 8; Constructorul (renamed FC Tiraspol) 1; Dacia Chisinau 1; Milsami Orhei 1.

Cup wins (1992–2022)

Sheriff (Tiraspol) 11; Zimbru Chisinau 6; Tiligul-Tiras 3; FC Tiraspol 3 (incl. Constructorul 2); Milsami Orhei 2; Comrat 1; Nistru Otaci 1; Iskra-Stal 1; Zaria Balti (now Balti) 1; Petrocub-Hincesti 1; Sfîntul Gheorghe 1.

Moldovan Super Liga 2021–22

	P	W	D	L	F	A	GD	Pts
Sheriff (C)[1]	28	22	4	2	75	8	67	70
Petrocub-Hincesti[3]	28	20	4	4	62	20	42	64
Milsami Orhei[3]	28	15	6	7	50	31	19	51
Sfintul Gheorghe[3]	28	10	8	10	38	39	−1	38
Balti	28	11	3	14	39	39	0	36
Dinamo-Auto	28	9	5	14	35	72	−37	32
Zimbru Chisinau+	28	7	6	15	32	46	−14	27
Floresti* (−6)	28	0	0	28	12	88	−76	−6

* *Floresti were excluded from the league on 17 January 2022 and relegated after being found guilty of match fixing. Their remaining 9 matches were awarded a 3-0 victory to their opponents.*
Top scorer: Ambros (Petrocub) 17.
Cup Final: Sheriff 1, Sfîntul Gheorghe 0.

MONTENEGRO

Fudbalski Savez Crne Gore, Ulica 19. Decembar 13, PO Box 275, 81000 Podgorica.
Founded: 1931 *FIFA:* 2007; *UEFA:* 2007. *National Colours:* All red with gold trim.

International matches 2021–22

Turkey (a) 2-2, Netherlands (a) 0-4, Latvia (h) 0-0, Gibraltar (a) 3-0, Norway (a) 0-2, Netherlands (h) 2-2, Turkey (h) 1-2, Armenia (a) 0-1, Greece (h) 1-0, Romania (h) 2-0, Finland (a) 0-2, Bosnia-Herzegovina (h) 1-1, Romania (a) 3-0.

League Championship wins (2006–22)

Buducnost Podgorica 5; Sutjeska 5; Mogren 2; Rudar (Pljevlja) 2; Zeta 1; Mladost Podgorica (renamed OFK Titograd) 1.

Cup wins (2006–22)

Rudar (Pljevlja) 4; Buducnost Podgorica 4; Mladost Podgorica (renamed OFK Titograd) 2; Mogren 1; Petrovac 1; Celik 1; Lovcen 1: Sutjeska 1.
No winner in 2019–20.

Montenegrin Prva CFL 2021–22

	P	W	D	L	F	A	GD	Pts
Sutjeska (C)[1]	36	22	9	5	64	29	35	75
Buducnost Podgorica[3]	36	20	7	9	78	45	33	67
Decic[3]	36	15	11	10	54	44	10	56
Iskra[3]	36	15	6	15	48	45	3	51
Mornar	36	13	11	12	35	39	−4	50
Jezero	36	14	6	16	42	46	−4	48
Petrovac	36	10	13	13	47	60	−13	43
Rudar+	36	9	9	18	35	56	−21	36
FK Podgorica†+*	36	8	10	18	38	61	−23	34
Zeta†*	36	8	10	18	36	52	−16	34

† *Ranking decided on head-to-head points.*
Top scorer: Basic (Perovac) 14.
Cup Final: Buducnost Podgorica 3, Decic 1.

NETHERLANDS

Koninklijke Nederlandse Voetbalbond, Woudenbergseweg 56–58, Postbus 515, 3700 AM Zeist.
Founded: 1889. *FIFA:* 1904; *UEFA:* 1954. *National Colours:* All orange with black trim.

International matches 2021–22

Norway (a) 1-1, Montenegro (h) 4-0, Turkey (h) 6-1, Latvia (a) 0-1, Gibraltar (h) 6-0, Montenegro (a) 2-2, Norway (h) 2-0, Denmark (h) 4-2, Germany (h) 1-1, Belgium (a) 4-1, Wales (a) 2-1, Poland (h) 2-2, Wales (h) 3-2.

League Championship wins (1889–2022)

Ajax 36; PSV Eindhoven 24; Feyenoord 15; HVV The Hague 10; Sparta Rotterdam 6; RAP Amsterdam 5; Go Ahead Eagles Deventer 4; HFC Haarlem 3; HBS Craeyenhout 3; Willem II 3; RCH Heemstede 2; Heracles 2; ADO Den Haag 2; AZ 67 Alkmaar 2; VV Concordia 1; Quick Den Haag 1; Be Quick Groningen 1; NAC Breda 1; SC Enschede 1; Volewijckers Amsterdam 1; HFC Haarlem 1; BVV Den Bosch 1; Schiedam 1; Limburgia 1; EVV Eindhoven 1; SVV Rapid JC Den Heerlen (renamed Roda JC Kerkrade) 1; VV DOS (renamed FC Utrecht) 1; DWS Amsterdam 1; FC Twente 1.
No winner in 2019–20.

Cup wins (1899–2022)

Ajax 20; Feyenoord 13; PSV Eindhoven 10; Quick The Hague 4; AZ 67 Alkmaar 4; HFC Haarlem 3; Sparta Rotterdam 3; FC Twente 3; FC Utrecht 3; Haarlem 2; VOC 2; HBS Craeyenhout 2; DFC 2; RCH Haarlem 2; Wageningen 2; Willem II 2; Fortuna 54 2; FC Den Haag (includes ADO) 2; Roda JC 2; RAP Amsterdam 1; Velocitas Breda 1; HVV Den Haag 1; Concordia Delft 1; CVV 1; Schoten 1; ZFC Zaandam 1; Longa 1; VUC 1; Velocitas Groningen 1; Roermond 1; FC Eindhoven 1; VSV 1; Quick 1888 Nijmegen 1; VVV Groningen 1; NAC Breda 1; Heerenveen 1; PEC Zwolle 1; FC Groningen 1; Vitesse 1.
No winner in 2019–20.

Dutch Eredivisie 2021–22

	P	W	D	L	F	A	GD	Pts
Ajax (C)[1]	34	26	5	3	98	19	79	83
PSV Eindhoven[1]	34	26	3	5	86	42	44	81
Feyenoord[2]	34	22	5	7	76	34	42	71
FC Twente[3]	34	20	8	6	55	37	18	68
AZ Alkmaar[3]†	34	18	7	9	64	44	20	61
Vitesse†	34	15	6	13	42	51	−9	51
Utrecht†	34	12	11	11	51	46	5	47
Heerenveen†	34	11	8	15	37	50	−13	41
Cambuur	34	11	6	17	53	70	−17	39
RKC Waalwijk	34	9	11	14	40	51	−11	38
NEC	34	10	8	16	38	52	−14	38
FC Groningen	34	9	9	16	41	55	−14	36
Go Ahead Eagles	34	10	6	18	37	51	−14	36
Sparta Rotterdam	34	8	11	15	30	48	−18	35
Fortuna Sittard	34	10	5	19	36	67	−31	35
Heracles Almelo+*	34	9	7	18	33	49	−16	34
Willem II Tilberg*	34	9	6	19	32	57	−25	33
PEC Zwolle*	34	7	6	21	26	52	−26	27

† *Qualified for Europa Conference League Play-offs.*

Europa Conference League Play-offs

Semi-finals First Leg
Heerenveen 3, AZ Alkmaar 2
Utrecht 3, Vitesse 1
Semi-finals Second Leg
AZ Alkmaar 2, Heerenveen 0 *(AZ Alkmaar won 4-3 on aggregate)*
Vitesse 3, Utrecht 0 *(Vitesse won 4-3 on aggregate)*
Final First Leg
Vitesse 2, AZ Alkmaar 1
Final Second Leg
AZ Alkmaar 6, Vitesse 1 *(AZ Alkmaar won 7-3 on aggregate)*
Top scorer: Haller (Ajax) 21.
Cup Final: PSV Eindhoven 2, Ajax 1.

NORTH MACEDONIA

Football Federation of North Macedonia, 8-ma Udarna Brigada 31-A, PO Box 84, 1000 Skopje.
Founded: 1948. *FIFA:* 1994; *UEFA:* 1994. *National Colours:* All red with yellow trim.

International matches 2021–22

Armenia (h) 0-0, Iceland (a) 2-2, Romania (h) 0-0, Liechtenstein (a) 4-0, Germany (h) 0-4, Armenia (a) 5-0, Iceland (h) 3-1, Italy (a) 1-0, Portugal (a) 0-2, Bulgaria (a) 1-1, Gibraltar (a) 2-0, Georgia (h) 0-3, Gibraltar (h) 4-0.

League Championship wins (1992–2022)

Vardar 11*; Rabotnicki 4; Shkendija 4; Sileks 3; Sloga Jugomagnat 3; Pobeda 2; Makedonija GjP 1; Renova 1; Shkupi 1.

Cup wins (1992–2022)

Vardar 5; Rabotnicki 4; Sileks 3; Sloga Jugomagnat 3; Pelister 2; Makedonija GjP 2; Teteks 2; Shkendija 2; Pobeda 1; Cementarnica 55 1; Bashkimi 1; Metalurg 1; Renova 1; Akademija Pandev 1.
No winner in 2019–20.

North Macedonian Prva Liga Table 2021–22

	P	W	D	L	F	A	GD	Pts
Shkupi (C)[1]	33	23	7	3	66	21	45	76
Akademija Pandev[3]	33	19	7	7	55	32	23	64
Shkendija[3]	33	16	13	4	49	25	24	61
Makedonija GjP[3]	33	17	6	10	46	44	2	57
Renova	33	12	12	9	42	29	13	48
Struga	33	12	11	10	33	33	0	47
Bregalnica Stip	33	12	9	12	45	47	–2	45
Rabotnicki	33	13	4	16	29	35	–6	43
Skopje+	33	9	8	16	27	45	–18	35
Tikves+	33	9	7	17	36	38	–2	34
Borec*	33	5	6	22	25	66	–41	21
Pelister*	33	2	8	23	16	54	–38	14

Top scorer: Adetunji (Shkupi) 20.
Cup Final: Makedonija GjP 0, Sileks 0 *(aet; Makedonija GjP won 4-3 on penalties).*

NORTHERN CYPRUS

Cyprus Turkish Football Federation, 7 Memduh Asaf Street, 107 Koskluciftlik, Lefkosa. (Not a member of FIFA or UEFA.)
Founded: 1955; *National Colours:* Red shirts with white trim, red shorts, red socks.

League Championship wins (1956–63; 1969–74; 1976–2022)
Cetinkaya 14; Magusa Turk Gucu 11; Yenicami Agdelen 9; Gonyeli 9; Dogan Turk Birligi 7; Baf Ulku Yurdu 4; Kucuk Kaymakli 4; Akincilar 1; Binatli 1.
No winner in 2020–21.

Cup wins (1956–2022)
Cetinkaya 17; Yenicami Agdelen 8; Gonyeli 8; Magusa Turk Gucu 7; Kucuk Kaymakli 7; Turk Ocagi Limasol 5; Lefke 2; Dogan Turk Birligi 2; Genclik Gucu 1; Yalova 1; Binatli 1; Cihangir 1.
No winner in 2020–21.

Northern Cyprus Super Lig Table 2021–22

	P	W	D	L	F	A	GD	Pts
Magusa Turk Gucu (C)	30	22	3	5	80	32	48	69
Merit Alsancak Yesilov	30	14	9	7	58	43	15	51
Dogan Turk Birligi	30	14	9	7	50	38	12	51
Yenicami Agdelen	30	14	8	8	72	40	32	50
Lefke	30	13	11	6	41	31	10	50
Gonyeli	30	14	8	8	45	35	10	50
Mesarya	30	15	4	11	43	25	18	49
Cihangir	30	13	9	8	55	46	9	48
Yonpas Dumlupinar	30	14	6	10	53	33	20	48
Kucuk Kaymakli	30	10	12	8	41	34	7	42
Gocmenkoy+	30	11	6	13	36	44	–8	39
Turk Ocagi Limasol+	30	11	6	13	36	46	–10	39
Hamitkoy+	30	10	5	15	44	51	–7	35
Baf Ulku Yurdu+*	30	5	7	18	19	58	–39	22
Binatli*	30	4	4	22	28	75	–47	16
Girne Halk Evi*	30	1	3	26	25	95	–70	6

Top scorer: Betmezoglu (Mesarya) 25.
Cup Final: Magusa Turk Gucu 2, Dogan Turk Birligi 0.

NORTHERN IRELAND

Irish Football Association, Donegall Avenue, Belfast BT12 6LU.
Founded: 1880. *FIFA:* 1911; *UEFA:* 1954. *National Colours:* Green shirts with white trim, white shorts with green trim, green socks with white and blue trim.

NORWAY

Norges Fotballforbund, Ullevaal Stadion, Serviceboks 1, 0840 Oslo.
Founded: 1902. *FIFA:* 1908; *UEFA:* 1954. *National Colours:* Red shirts, white shorts, dark blue socks.

International matches 2021–22
Netherlands (h) 1-1, Latvia (a) 2-0, Gibraltar (h) 5-1, Turkey (a) 1-1, Montenegro (h) 2-0, Latvia (h) 0-0, Netherlands (a) 0-2, Slovakia (h) 2-0, Armenia (h) 9-0, Serbia (a) 1-0, Sweden (a) 2-1, Slovenia (h) 0-0, Sweden (h) 3-2.

League Championship wins (1938–2021)
Rosenborg 26; Fredrikstad 9; Viking Stavanger 8; Lillestrom 5; Valerenga 5; Molde 4; Larvik Turn 3; Brann 3; Lyn Oslo 2; Stromsgodset 2; IK Start 2; Bodo/Glimt 2; Freidig 1; Fram 1; Skeid 1; Moss 1; Stabaek 1.

Cup wins (1902–2022)
Odd Grenland 12; Rosenborg 12; Fredrikstad 11; Lyn Oslo 8; Skeid 8; Sarpsborg 6; Brann 6; Viking Stavanger 6; Lillestrom 6; Stromsgodset 5; Molde 5; Orn-Horten 4; Valerenga 4; Frigg 3; Mjondalen 3; Mercantile 2; Bodo/Glimt 2; Tromso 2; Aalesund 2; Grane Nordstrand 1; Kvik Halden 1; Sparta 1; Gjovik/Lyn 1; Moss 1; Bryne 1; Stabaek 1; Hodd 1.
(Known as the Norwegian Championship for HM The King's Trophy.)
No winner in 2020.

Norwegian Eliteserien 2021

	P	W	D	L	F	A	GD	Pts
Bodo/Glimt (C)[1]	30	18	9	3	59	25	34	63
Molde[3]	30	18	6	6	70	40	30	60
Viking[3]	30	17	6	7	60	47	13	57
Lillestrom[3]	30	14	7	9	49	40	9	49
Rosenborg	30	13	9	8	58	42	16	48
Kristiansund	30	14	4	12	41	46	–5	46
Valerenga	30	11	12	7	46	37	9	45
Sarpsborg 08	30	11	6	13	39	44	–5	39
Stromsgodset	30	9	9	12	43	43	0	36
Sandefjord	30	10	6	14	38	52	–14	36
Haugesund	30	9	8	13	46	45	1	35
Tromso	30	8	11	11	33	44	–11	35
Odd	30	8	9	13	44	58	–14	33
Brann+*	30	5	11	14	38	55	–17	26
Stabaek*	30	6	7	17	35	62	–27	25
Mjondale*	30	4	10	16	33	52	–19	22

Top scorer: Omoijuanfo (Molde) 27.
Cup Final: Molde 1, Bodo/Glimt 0.

POLAND

Polski Zwiazek Pilki Noznej, ul. Bitwy Warszawskiej 1920r. 7, 02-366 Warszawa.
Founded: 1919. *FIFA:* 1923; *UEFA:* 1954. *National Colours:* White shirts with red trim, red shorts with white trim, white socks with red trim.

International matches 2021–22
Albania (h) 4-1, San Marino (a) 7-1, England (h) 1-1, San Marino (h) 5-0, Albania (a) 1-0, Andorra (a) 4-1, Hungary (h) 1-2, Russia (a) w-o*, Scotland (a) 1-1, Sweden (h) 2-0, Wales (h) 2-1, Belgium (a) 1-6, Netherlands (a) 2-2, Poland (a) 0-1.
* *Russia suspended by UEFA following invasion of Ukraine; Poland walkover.*

League Championship wins (1921–23; 1925–38; 1946–2022)
Legia Warsaw 15; Ruch Chorzow 14; Gornik Zabrze 14; Wisla Krakow 13; Lech Poznan 8; Cracovia 5; Pogon Lwow 4; Widzew Lodz 4; Warta Poznan 2; Polonia Warsaw 2; Polonia Bytom 2; LKS Lodz 2; Stal Mielec 2; Slask Wroclaw 2; Zaglebie Lubin 2; Garbarnia Krakow 1; Szombierki Bytom 1; Piast Gliwice 1.

Cup wins (1926; 1951–2022)
Legia Warsaw 19; Gornik Zabrze 6; Lech Poznan 5; Wisla Krakow 4; Zaglebie Sosnowiec 4; Ruch Chorzow 3; GKS Katowice 3; Amica Wronki 3; Polonia Warsaw 2; Slask Wroclaw 2; Arka Gdynia 2; Lechia Gdansk 2; Dyskobolia Grodzisk 2; Rakow Czestochowa 2; Gwardia Warsaw 1; LKS Lodz 1; Stal Rzeszow 1; Widzew Lodz 1; Miedz Legnica 1; Wisla Plock 1; Jagiellonia Bialystok 1; Zawisza Bydgoszcz 1; Cracovia 1.

Polish Ekstraklasa Table 2021–22

	P	W	D	L	F	A	GD	Pts
Lech Poznan (C)[1]	34	22	8	4	67	24	43	74
Rakow Czestochowa[3]	34	20	9	5	60	30	30	69
Pogon Szczecin[3]	34	18	11	5	63	31	32	65
Lechia Gdansk[3]	34	16	9	9	52	39	13	57
Piast Gliwice	34	15	9	10	45	37	8	54
Wisla Plock†	34	15	3	16	48	51	–3	48
Radomiak Radom†	34	11	15	8	42	40	2	48
Gornik Zabrze	34	13	8	13	55	55	0	47
Cracovia	34	12	10	12	40	42	–2	46
Legia Warsaw	34	13	4	17	46	48	–2	43
Warta Poznan	34	11	9	14	35	38	–3	42
Jagiellonia Bialystok	34	9	13	12	39	50	–11	40
Zaglebie Lubin	34	11	5	18	43	59	–16	38
Stal Mielec	34	9	10	15	39	52	–13	37
Slask Wroclaw	34	7	14	13	42	52	–10	35
Niecieza*	34	7	11	16	36	56	–20	32
Wisla Krakow*	34	7	10	17	37	54	–17	31
Gornik Leczna*	34	6	10	18	29	60	–31	28

† *Ranking decided on head-to-head points.*
Top scorer: Ivi Lopez (Rakow Czestochowa) 20.
Cup Final: Rakow Czestochowa 3, Lech Poznan 1.

PORTUGAL

Federacao Portuguesa de Futebol, Rua Alexandre Herculano No. 58, Apartado postal 24013, Lisboa 1250-012.
Founded: 1914. *FIFA:* 1923; *UEFA:* 1954. *National Colours:* Carmine shirts with green and black trim, green shorts with carmine trim, carmine socks with green and black trim.

International matches 2021–22
Republic of Ireland (h) 2-1, Qatar (n) 3-1, Azerbaijan (a) 3-0, Qatar (h) 3-0, Luxembourg (h) 5-0, Republic of Ireland (a) 0-0, Serbia (h) 1-2, Turkey (h) 3-1, North Macedonia (h) 2-0, Spain (a) 1-1, Switzerland (h) 4-0, Czech Republic (h) 2-0, Switzerland (a) 0-1.

League Championship wins (1935–2022)
Benfica 37; Porto 30; Sporting Lisbon 19; Belenenses 1; Boavista 1.

Cup wins (1939–2022)
Benfica 26; Porto 18; Sporting Lisbon 17; Boavista 5; Belenenses 3; Vitoria de Setubal 3; Braga 3; Academica de Coimbra 2; Leixoes 1; Estrela da Amadora 1; Beira-Mar 1; Vitoria de Guimaraes 1; Desportivo das Aves 1.

Portuguese Primeira Liga 2021–22

	P	*W*	*D*	*L*	*F*	*A*	*GD*	*Pts*
Porto (C)[1]	34	29	4	1	86	22	64	91
Sporting Lisbon[1]	34	27	4	3	73	23	50	85
Benfica[1]	34	23	5	6	78	30	48	74
Sporting Braga[2]	34	19	8	7	52	31	21	65
Gil Vicente[3]	34	13	12	9	47	42	5	51
Vitoria de Guimaraes[3]	34	13	9	12	50	41	9	48
Santa Clara	34	9	13	12	38	54	–16	40
Famalicao†	34	9	12	13	45	51	–6	39
Estoril†	34	9	12	13	36	43	–7	39
Maritimo†	34	9	11	14	39	44	–5	38
Pacos de Ferreira†	34	9	11	14	29	44	–15	38
Boavista†	34	7	17	10	39	52	–13	38
Portimonense†	34	10	8	16	31	45	–14	38
Vizela	34	7	12	15	37	58	–21	33
Arouca	34	7	10	17	30	54	–24	31
Moreirense+*	34	7	8	19	33	51	–18	29
Tondela*	34	7	7	20	41	67	–26	28
Belenenses*	34	5	11	18	23	55	–32	26

† Ranking decided on head-to-head points.
Top scorer: Nunez (Benfica) 26.
Cup Final: Porto 3, Tondela 1.

REPUBLIC OF IRELAND

Football Association of Ireland (Cumann Peile na hEireann), National Sports Campus, Abbotstown, Dublin 15.
Founded: 1921. *FIFA:* 1923; *UEFA:* 1954. *National Colours:* Green shirts with white trim, white shorts, green socks with white trim.

League Championship wins (1922–2021)
Shamrock R 18; Dundalk 14; Shelbourne 13; Bohemians 11; St Patrick's Ath 8; Waterford U 6; Cork U 5; Drumcondra 5; Sligo R 3; Cork C 3; St James's Gate 2; Cork Ath 2; Limerick 2; Athlone T 2; Derry C 2; Dolphin 1; Cork Hibernians 1; Cork Celtic 1; Drogheda U 1.

Cup wins (1922–2021)
Shamrock R 25; Dundalk 12; Bohemians 7; Shelbourne 7; Drumcondra 5; Sligo R 5; Derry C 5; St Patrick's Ath 4; Cork C 4; St James's Gate 2; Cork (incl. Fordsons 1) 2; Waterford U 2; Cork U 2; Cork Ath 2; Limerick 2; Cork Hibernians 2; Bray W 2; Longford T 2; Alton U 1; Athlone T 1; Transport 1; Finn Harps 1; Home Farm 1; UC Dublin 1; Galway U 1; Drogheda U 1; Sporting Fingal 1.

League of Ireland Premier Division 2020

	P	*W*	*D*	*L*	*F*	*A*	*GD*	*Pts*
Shamrock R (C)[1]	36	24	6	6	59	28	31	78
St Patrick's Ath[3]	36	18	8	10	56	42	14	62
Sligo Rovers[3]	36	16	9	11	43	32	11	57
Derry C[3]	36	14	12	10	49	42	7	54
Bohemians	36	14	10	12	60	46	14	52
Dundalk	36	13	9	14	44	46	–2	48
Drogheda U	36	12	8	16	45	43	2	44
Finn Harps	36	11	11	14	44	52	–8	44
Waterford+*	36	12	6	18	36	56	–20	42
Longford T*	36	2	9	25	22	71	–49	15

Top scorer: G. Kelly (Bohemians) 21.
Cup Final: St Patrick's Ath 1, Bohemians 1 *(St Patrick's Ath won 4-3 on penalties).*

ROMANIA

Federatia Romana de Fotbal, House of Football, Str. Sergent Serbanica Vasile 12, 22186 Bucuresti.
Founded: 1909. *FIFA:* 1923; *UEFA:* 1954. *National Colours:* Yellow shirts, white shorts with red and blue trim, yellow socks with white tops.

International matches 2021–22
Iceland (a) 2-0, Liechtenstein (h) 2-0, North Macedonia (a) 0-0, Germany (a) 1-2, Armenia (h) 1-0, Iceland (h) 0-0, Liechtenstein (a) 2-0, Greece (h) 0-1, Israel (a) 2-2, Montenegro (a) 0-2, Bosnia-Herzegovina (a) 0-1, Finland (h) 1-0, Montenegro (h) 0-3.

League Championship wins (1910–2022)
Steaua Bucharest (renamed FCSB)* 26; Dinamo Bucharest 18; CFR Cluj 8; Venus Bucharest 7†; Chinezul Timisoara 6; UTA Arad 6; Petrolul Ploiesti 4; Ripensia Timisoara 4; Universitatea Craiova 4; Rapid Bucharest 3; Olimpia Bucharest 2; United Ploiesti 2 (incl. Prahova Ploiesti 1); Colentina Bucharest 2; Arges Pitesti 2; Romano-Americana Bucharest 1; Coltea Brasov 1; Metalul Resita (renamed CSM Resita) 1; Unirea Tricolor 1; CA Oradea 1; Unirea Urziceni 1; Otelul Galati 1; Astra Giurgiu 1; Viitorul Constanta 1.
† The validity of Venus Bucharest's first two titles is disputed.

Cup wins (1934–43; 1947–2022)
Steaua Bucharest (renamed FCSB)* 24; Rapid Bucharest 13; Dinamo Bucharest 13; Universitatea Craiova (incl. FC U Craiova 1948 1) 8; CFR Cluj 4; Petrolul Ploiesti 3; Ripensia Timisoara 2; UTA Arad 2; Politehnica Timisoara 2; CFR Turnu Severin 1; Metalul Resita (renamed CSM Resita) 1; Universitatea Cluj (includes Stiinta) 1; Progresul Oradea (formerly ICO) 1; Progresul Bucharest 1; Ariesul Turda 1; Chimia Ramnicu Vilcea 1; Jiul Petrosani 1; Gloria Bistrita 1; Astra Giurgiu 1; Voluntari 1; Viitorul Constanta 1; Sepsi Sfantu Gheorghe 1.
** Club involved in protracted legal dispute about right to name, brand and historical honours; UEFA currently recognises FCSB as essentially the same entity as Steaua Bucharest.*

Romanian Liga 1 Qualifying Table 2021–22

	P	*W*	*D*	*L*	*F*	*A*	*GD*	*Pts*
CFR Cluj	30	24	4	2	48	16	32	76
FCSB	30	18	8	4	54	28	26	62
Universitatea Craiova	30	16	6	8	55	29	26	54
Arges Pitesti†	30	14	6	10	28	22	6	48
Farul Constanta†	30	14	6	10	42	21	21	48
Voluntari	30	13	8	9	31	27	4	47
Botosani	30	11	13	6	33	28	5	46
Rapid Bucharest†	30	9	13	8	34	31	3	40
UTA Arad†	30	9	13	8	24	20	4	40
Sepsi Sfantu Gheorghe	30	9	12	9	33	29	4	39
Chindia Targoviste	30	8	11	11	23	23	0	35
FC U Craiova 1948	30	8	9	13	31	35	–4	33
Mioveni	30	6	11	13	19	36	–17	29
Dinamo Bucurest	30	4	5	21	24	66	–42	17
Academica Clinceni	30	3	5	22	21	64	–43	14
Gaz Metan Medias (–22)	30	6	6	*18*	*21*	*46*	–25	*2*

Gaz Metan Medias deducted 22pts for financial reasons.
† Ranking decided on head-to-head points.
NB: Points earned in Qualifying phase are halved and rounded up at start of Championship and Relegation Play-off phase.

Championship Round 2021–22

	P	*W*	*D*	*L*	*F*	*A*	*GD*	*Pts*
CFR Cluj (C)[1]	10	6	1	3	18	9	9	57
FCSB[3]	10	8	1	1	24	7	17	56
Universitatea Craiova†[3]	10	7	0	3	22	9	13	48
Voluntari	10	3	2	5	9	14	–5	35
Farul Constanta	10	2	2	6	5	16	–11	32
Arges Pitesti	10	1	0	9	3	26	–23	27

† Qualified for Europa Conference League Play-offs.

Relegation Round 2021–22

	P	*W*	*D*	*L*	*F*	*A*	*GD*	*Pts*
Sepsi Sfantu Gheorghe[3]	9	7	1	1	21	4	17	42
Botosani†	9	6	0	3	18	9	9	41
Rapid Bucharest	9	6	1	2	22	7	15	39
U Craiova 1948	9	5	2	2	14	11	3	34
UTA Arad	9	4	1	4	10	6	4	33
Mioveni	9	5	1	3	12	10	2	31
Chindia Targoviste+	9	2	2	5	8	8	0	26
Dinamo Bucurest+*	9	4	2	3	14	11	3	23
Academica Clinceni* (–26)	9	0	0	9	4	32	–28	–23
Gaz Metan Medias* (–42)	9	1	0	8	6	31	–25	–42

Points deductions for financial reasons: Academica Clinceni 26 pts, Gaz Metan Medias 42pts. † Qualified for Europa Conference League Play-offs.

Europa Conference League Play-off
Universitatea Craiova 2, Botosani 0
Top scorer: Tanase (FCSB) 20.
Cup Final: Sepsi Sfantu Gheorghe 2, Voluntari 1.

RUSSIA

Russian Football Union, Ulitsa Narodnaya 7, 115 172 Moscow.
Founded: 1912. *FIFA:* 1912; *UEFA:* 1954. *National Colours:* All brick red with white trim.

International matches 2021–22
Croatia (h) 0-0, Cyprus (a) 2-0, Malta (h) 2-0, Slovakia (h) 1-0, Slovenia (a) 2-1, Cyprus (h) 6-0, Croatia (a) 0-1, Poland (h) w-o*.
** Russia suspended by UEFA following invasion of Ukraine; Poland walkover.*

USSR League Championship wins (1936–91)
Dynamo Kyiv 13; Spartak Moscow 12; Dynamo Moscow 11; CSKA Moscow 7; Torpedo Moscow 3; Dinamo Tbilisi 2; Dnepr Dnepropetrovsk 2; Zorya Voroshilovgrad 1; Ararat Yerevan 1; Dinamo Minsk 1; Zenit Leningrad 1.

Russian League Championship wins (1992–2022)
Spartak Moscow 10; Zenit St Petersburg 8; CSKA Moscow 6;

Lokomotiv Moscow 3; Rubin Kazan 2; Spartak Vladikavkaz (formerly Alania) 1.

USSR Cup wins (1936–91)
Spartak Moscow 10; Dynamo Kyiv 9; Dynamo Moscow 6; Torpedo Moscow 6; CSKA Moscow 5; Shakhtar Donetsk 4; Lokomotiv Moscow 2; Ararat Yerevan 2; Dinamo Tbilisi 2; Zenit Leningrad 1; Karpaty Lvov 1; SKA Rostov-on-Don 1; Metalist Kharkov 1; Dnepr Dnepropetrovsk 1.

Russian Cup wins (1992–2022)
Lokomotiv Moscow 9; CSKA Moscow 7; Spartak Moscow 4; Zenit St Petersburg 4; Torpedo Moscow 1; Dynamo Moscow 1; Terek Grozny (renamed Akhmat Grozny) 1; Rubin Kazan 1; Rostov 1; Tosno 1.

Russian Premier Liga 2021–22

	P	*W*	*D*	*L*	*F*	*A*	*GD*	*Pts*
Zenit St Petersburg (C)	30	19	8	3	66	28	38	65
Sochi	30	17	5	8	54	30	24	56
Dinamo Moscow	30	16	5	9	53	41	12	53
Krasnodar†	30	14	8	8	42	30	12	50
CSKA Moscow†	30	15	5	10	42	29	13	50
Lokomotiv Moscow	30	13	9	8	43	39	4	48
Akhmat Grozny	30	13	3	14	36	38	–2	42
Krylya Sovetov	30	12	5	13	39	36	3	41
Rostov†	30	10	8	12	47	51	–4	38
Spartak Moscow†	30	10	8	12	37	41	–4	38
Nizhny Novgorod†	30	8	9	13	26	39	–13	33
Ural Yekaterinburg†	30	8	9	13	27	35	–8	33
Khimki+	30	7	11	12	34	47	–13	32
Ufa+*	30	6	12	12	29	40	–11	30
Rubin Kazan*	30	8	5	17	34	56	–22	29
Arsenal Tula*	30	5	8	17	30	59	–29	23

Russian clubs excluded from international competitions until further notice.
† Ranking decided on head-to-head points.
Top scorer: Agalarov (Ufa) 19.
Cup Final: Spartak Moscow 2, Dynamo Moscow 1.

SAN MARINO

Federazione Sammarinese Giuoco Calcio, Strada di Montecchio 17, 47890 San Marino.
Founded: 1931. *FIFA:* 1988; *UEFA:* 1988. *National Colours:* All cobalt blue.

International matches 2021–22
Andorra (a) 0-2, Poland (h) 1-7, Albania (a) 0-5, Poland (a) 0-5, Andorra (h) 0-3, Hungary (a) 0-4, England (h) 0-10, Lithuania (h) 1-2, Cape Verde (n) 0-2, Estonia (a) 0-2, Malta (h) 0-2, Iceland (h) 0-1, Malta (a) 0-1.

League Championship wins (1986–2022)
Tre Fiori 8; La Fiorita 6; Folgore Falciano 5; Domagnano 4; Tre Penne 4; Faetano 3; Murata 3; Montevito 1; Libertas 1; Cosmos 1; Pennarossa 1.

Cup wins (1937–2022)
Libertas 11; Tre Fiori 8; Domagnano 8; Tre Penne 6; La Fiorita 6; Juvenes 5; Cosmos 4; Faetano 3; Murata 3; Dogana 2; Pennarossa 2; Juvenes/Dogana 2; Folgore Falciano 1.
No winner in 2019–20.

Campionato Sammarinese 2021–22

First Phase

	P	*W*	*D*	*L*	*F*	*A*	*GD*	*Pts*
La Fiorita (C)[1]	28	17	9	2	43	16	27	60
Tre Penne	28	17	8	3	65	29	36	59
Tre Fiori[3]	28	14	10	4	46	28	18	52
Virtus	28	15	7	6	32	18	14	52
Pennarossa	28	12	11	5	30	22	8	47
Faetano	28	13	7	8	39	26	13	46
Libertas	28	13	5	10	48	40	8	44
Folgore Falciano	28	10	10	8	36	23	13	40
Fiorentino	28	9	9	10	43	37	6	36
Domagnano	28	8	6	14	28	40	–12	30
San Giovanni	28	6	11	11	29	34	–5	29
Murata	28	5	10	13	20	32	–12	25
Cailungo	28	4	10	14	26	46	–20	22
Juvenes/Dogana	28	5	6	17	24	63	–39	21
Cosmos	28	0	5	23	9	64	–55	5

Top four qualify for Second Phase quarter-finals; clubs placed fifth to twelfth play off for remaining quarter-final spots. Winners of drawn matches decided by record in regular season.

Second Phase

Play-offs
Pennarossa 1, Murata 1
Murata 1, Pennarossa 2
Pennarossa won 3-2 on aggregate
Faetano 1, San Giovanni 1
San Giovanni 1, Faetano 2
Faetano won 3-2 on aggregate
Libertas 5, Domagnano 0
Domagnano 0, Libertas 3
Libertas won 8-0 on aggregate
Folgore Falciano 0, Fiorentino 2
Fiorentino 1, Folgore Falciano 2
Fiorentino won 3-2 on aggregate

Quarter-finals
La Fiorita 0, Fiorentino 1
Fiorentino 0, La Fiorita 2
La Fiorita won 2-1 on aggregate
Tre Penne 2, Libertas 0
Libertas 1, Tre Penne 0
Tre Penne won 2-1 on aggregate
Tre Fiori 1, Faetano 1
Faetano 1, Tre Fiori 1
aggregate 2-2; Tre Fiori won on regular season record
Virtus 0, Pennarossa 1
Pennarossa 1, Virtus 1
Pennarossa won 2-1 on aggregate

Semi-finals
La Fiorita 2, Pennarossa 1
Pennarossa 1, La Fiorita 0
aggregate 2-2; La Fiorita won on regular season record
Tre Fiori 0, Tre Penne 1
Tre Penne 2, Tre Fiori 1
Tre Penne won 3-1 on aggregate

Third Place Final
Pennarossa 1, Tre Fiori 2

Final
La Fiorita 2, Tre Penne 0
Top scorer: Baldassi (Folgore Falciano) 13.
Cup Final: Tre Fiori 0, La Fiorita 0.
aet; La Fiorita won 10-9 on penalties.
Top scorer: Badalassi (Tre Penne) 24.
Cup Final: Tre Fiori 3, Folgore Falciano 1.

SCOTLAND

Scottish Football Association, Hampden Park, Glasgow G42 9AY.
Founded: 1873. *FIFA:* 1910; *UEFA:* 1954. *National Colours:* Dark blue shirts with red and white trim, dark blue shorts with white trim, dark blue socks with white trim.

SERBIA

Football Association of Serbia, Terazije 35, PO Box 263, 11000 Beograd.
Founded: 1919. *FIFA:* 1921; *UEFA:* 1954. *National Colours:* Red shirts with yellow trim, red shorts, red socks with yellow trim.

International matches 2021–22
Qatar (n) 4-0, Luxembourg (h) 4-1, Republic of Ireland (a) 1-1, Luxembourg (a) 1-0, Azerbaijan (h) 3-1, Qatar (h) 4-0, Portugal (a) 2-1, Hungary (a) 1-0, Denmark (a) 0-3, Norway (h) 0-1, Slovenia (h) 4-1, Sweden (a) 1-0, Slovenia (a) 2-2.

Yugoslav League Championship wins (1923–40; 1946–91)
Red Star Belgrade (Crvena Zvezda) 19; Partizan Belgrade 11*; Hajduk Split 9; Gradjanski Zagreb 5; BSK Belgrade (renamed OFK) 5; Dinamo Zagreb 4; Jugoslavija Belgrade 2; Concordia Zagreb 2; Vojvodina Novi Sad 2; FC Sarajevo 2; HASK Zagreb 1; Zeljeznicar 1.
** Total includes 1 League Championship (1986–87) originally awarded to Macedonian club Vardar.*

Serbian League Championship wins (1992–2022)
Partizan Belgrade 16; Red Star Belgrade (Crvena zvezda) 14; Obilic 1.

Yugoslav Cup wins (1923–41; 1947–91)
Red Star Belgrade (Crvena zvezda) 12; Hajduk Split 9; Dinamo Zagreb 7; Partizan Belgrade 6; OFK Belgrade (incl. BSK 3) 5; Rijeka 2; Velez Mostar 2; HASK Zagreb 1; Jugoslavija Belgrade 1; Vardar Skopje 1; Borac Banjaluka 1.

Serbian and Serbia-Montenegro Cup wins (1991–2022)
Red Star Belgrade (Crvena zvezda) 14; Partizan Belgrade 11; Vojvodina 2; Sartid 1; Zeleznik 1; Jagodina 1; Cukaricki 1.

Serbian SuperLiga Qualifying Table 2021–22

	P	*W*	*D*	*L*	*F*	*A*	*GD*	*Pts*
Red Star Belgrade	30	26	3	1	79	17	62	81
Partizan Belgrade	30	25	4	1	68	10	58	79
Cukaricki	30	14	12	4	48	27	21	54
TSC Backa Topola	30	11	8	11	44	41	3	41
Vozdovac	30	11	7	12	41	37	4	40
Radnicki Nis	30	9	13	8	32	33	–1	40
Vojvodina	30	11	6	13	38	40	–2	39
Napredak	30	10	7	13	31	36	–5	37
Mladost Lucani	30	10	6	14	38	44	–6	36
Radnik Surdulica	30	8	12	10	24	31	–7	36
Spartak Subotica	30	9	7	14	35	49	–14	34
Kolubara	30	10	4	16	32	56	–24	34
Radnicki Kragujevac	30	8	6	16	27	50	–23	30
Proleter Novi Sad	30	8	5	17	23	49	–26	29

Metalac GM	30	7	6	17	36	52	–16	27
Novi Pazar	30	5	10	15	25	49	–24	25

Championship Round 2021–22

	P	*W*	*D*	*L*	*F*	*A*	*GD*	*Pts*
Red Star Belgrade (C)[1]	37	32	4	1	95	19	76	100
Partizan Belgrade[2]	37	31	5	1	85	13	72	98
Cukaricki[3]	37	15	15	7	54	34	20	60
Radnicki Nis[3]	37	12	15	10	40	39	1	51
Vozdovac	37	13	10	14	48	45	3	49
TSC Backa Topola	37	13	9	15	51	56	–5	48
Vojvodina	37	13	6	18	44	51	–7	45
Napredak	37	10	8	19	31	51	–20	38

Relegation Round 2021–22

	P	*W*	*D*	*L*	*F*	*A*	*GD*	*Pts*
Radnik Surdulica	37	12	15	10	37	37	0	51
Kolubara	37	14	4	19	42	65	–23	46
Mladost Lucani	37	12	9	16	46	52	–6	45
Spartak Subotica	37	12	8	17	45	60	–15	44
Novi Pazar+	37	10	11	16	39	54	–15	41
Radnicki Kragujevac+	37	9	8	20	34	60	–26	35
Metalac GM*	37	8	9	20	42	65	–23	33
Proleter Novi Sad*	37	8	8	21	25	57	–32	32

Top scorer: Gomes (Partizan Belgrade) 29.
Cup Final: Red Star Belgrade 2, Partizan Belgrade 1.

SLOVAKIA

Slovensky Futbalovy Zvaz, Trnavska cesta 100, 821 01 Bratislava.
Founded: 1938. *FIFA:* 1994; *UEFA:* 1993. *National Colours:* Blue patterned shirts with dark blue trim, dark blue shorts with blue trim, dark blue socks.

International matches 2021–22

Slovenia (a) 1-1, Croatia (h) 0-1, Cyprus (h) 2-0, Russia (a) 0-1, Croatia (a) 2-2, Slovenia (h) 2-2, Malta (a) 6-0, Norway (a) 0-2, Finland (n) 2-0, Belarus (a) 1-0, Kazakhstan (h) 0-1, Azerbaijan (a) 1-0, Kazakhstan (a) 1-2.

League Championship wins (1938–44; 1993–2022)

Slovan Bratislava (incl. 4 as SK Bratislava) 16; Zilina 7; Kosice 2; Inter Bratislava 2; Artmedia Petrzalka 2; Trencin 2; Sparta Povazska Bystrica 1; OAP Bratislava 1; Ruzomberok 1; Spartak Trnava 1.

Cup wins (1961; 1969–93; 1993–2022)

Slovan Bratislava 17; Spartak Trnava 7; Inter Bratislava 6; VSS Kosice 5; Lokomotiva Kosice 3; Trencin 3; Zilina 2; Dukla Banska Bystrica 2; Artmedia Petrzalka 2; DAC 1904 Dunajska Streda 1; Tatran Presov 1; Chemlon Humenne 1; Koba Senec 1; Matador Puchov 1; Ruzomberok 1; ViOn Zlate Moravce 1.
See also Czech Republic section for Slovak club honours in Czechoslovak era 1925–93.

Slovak Super Liga Qualifying Table 2021–22

	P	*W*	*D*	*L*	*F*	*A*	*GD*	*Pts*
Slovan Bratislava	22	16	5	1	52	16	36	53
Spartak Trnava	22	13	6	3	29	12	17	45
Ruzomberok	22	11	8	3	39	17	22	41
DAC Dunajska Streda	22	10	6	6	28	23	5	36
Sered'	22	9	5	8	28	28	0	32
Zilina	22	8	6	8	34	33	1	30
Senica	22	7	6	9	21	32	–11	27
Trencin	22	6	7	9	32	33	–1	25
Zemplin Michalovce	22	7	2	13	20	31	–11	23
Tatran Liptovsky Mikulas	22	5	6	11	27	43	–16	21
Zlate Moravce	22	4	7	11	22	36	–14	19
Pohronie	22	2	4	16	19	47	–28	10

Championship Round 2021–22

	P	*W*	*D*	*L*	*F*	*A*	*GD*	*Pts*
Slovan Bratislava (C)[1]	32	22	8	2	71	25	46	74
Ruzomberok[3]	32	17	12	3	58	23	35	63
Spartak Trnava[3]	32	17	9	6	36	17	19	60
DAC Dunajska Streda†[3]	32	12	10	10	39	37	2	46
Sered'*	32	10	9	13	34	46	–12	39
Zilina†[3]	32	8	10	14	43	52	–9	34

** Sered' failed in their licence application for 2022–23 and were relegated. † Qualified for Europa Conference League play-offs.*

Relegation Round 2021–22

	P	*W*	*D*	*L*	*F*	*A*	*GD*	*Pts*
Trencin†	32	13	9	10	58	43	15	48
Tatran Liptovsky Mikulas§†	32	11	7	14	42	57	–15	40
Zemplin Michalovce§	32	12	4	16	32	42	–10	40
Senica*	32	9	7	16	29	51	–22	34
Zlate Moravce	32	7	9	16	33	50	–17	30
Pohronie*	32	4	6	22	27	59	–32	18

** Senica failed in their licence application for 2022–23 and were relegated. † Qualified for Europa Conference League play-offs. § Ranking decided on head-to-head points.*

Europa Conference League Play-offs

Semi-finals

Zilina 0, Trencin 2
DAC 1904 4, Tatran Liptovsky Mikulas 2

Final

DAC 1904 2, Trencin 1
Top scorer: Kadak (Trencin) 13.
Cup Final: Spartak Trnava 2, Slovan Bratislava 1 *(aet)*.

SLOVENIA

Nogometna Zveza Slovenije, Brnciceva 41g, PP 3986, 1001 Ljubljana.
Founded: 1920. *FIFA:* 1992; *UEFA:* 1992. *National Colours:* White shirts with blue trim, white shorts, white socks.

International matches 2021–22

Slovakia (h) 1-1, Malta (h) 1-0, Croatia (a) 0-3, Malta (a) 4-0, Russia (h) 1-2, Slovakia (a) 2-2, Cyprus (h) 2-1, Croatia (a) 1-1, Qatar (a) 0-0, Sweden (h) 0-2, Serbia (a) 1-4, Norway (a) 0-0, Serbia (h) 2-2.

League Championship wins (1991–2022)

Maribor 16; Olimpija (pre-2005) 4; Gorica 4; Domzale 2; Olimpija Ljubljana (post-2005) 2; Koper 1; Celje 1; Mura (post-2012) 1.

Cup wins (1991–2022)

Maribor 9; Olimpija (pre-2005) 4; Koper 4; Gorica 3; Olimpija Ljubljana (post-2005) 3; Interblock 2; Domzale 2; NK Mura (pre-2005) 1; Rudar Velenje 1; Celje 1; Mura (post-2012) 1.

Slovenian PrvaLiga 2021–22

	P	*W*	*D*	*L*	*F*	*A*	*GD*	*Pts*
Maribor (C)[1]	36	21	7	8	57	37	20	70
Koper[3]	36	19	10	7	54	38	16	67
Olimpija Ljubljana[3]	36	18	8	10	53	38	15	62
Mura[3]	36	15	12	9	57	50	7	57
Bravo	36	13	10	13	33	33	0	49
Radomlje	36	12	10	14	47	52	–5	46
Domzale	36	11	12	13	47	46	1	45
Celje	36	12	6	18	46	50	–4	42
Tabor Sezana+	36	7	9	20	30	41	–11	30
Aluminij*	36	4	12	20	33	72	–39	24

Top scorer: Mudrinski (Maribor) 17.
Cup Final: Koper 3, Bravo 1.

SPAIN

Real Federacion Espanola de Futbol, Calle Ramon y Cajal s/n, Apartado postale 385, 28230 Las Rozas, Madrid.
Founded: 1913. *FIFA:* 1913; *UEFA:* 1954. *National Colours:* Red shirts with yellow trim, blue shorts with yellow trim, red socks with yellow trim.

International matches 2021–22

Sweden (a) 1-2, Georgia (h) 4-0, Kosovo (a) 2-0, Italy (a) 2-1, France (n) 1-2, Greece (a) 1-0, Sweden (h) 1-0, Albania (h) 2-1, Iceland (h) 5-0, Portugal (h) 1-1, Czech Republic (a) 2-2, Switzerland (a) 1-0, Czech Republic (h) 2-0.

League Championship wins (1929–36; 1940–2022)

Real Madrid 35; Barcelona 26; Atletico Madrid 11; Athletic Bilbao 8; Valencia 6; Real Sociedad 2; Real Betis 1; Sevilla 1; Deportivo La Coruna 1.

Cup wins (1903–2022)

Barcelona 31; Athletic Bilbao (includes Vizcaya Bilbao 1) 23; Real Madrid 19; Atletico Madrid 10; Valencia 8; Real Zaragoza 6; Sevilla 5; Espanyol 4; Real Union de Irun 3; Real Sociedad (includes Ciclista) 3; Real Betis 3; Deportivo La Coruna 2; Racing de Irun 1; Arenas 1; Mallorca 1.
No winner in 2019–20.

Spanish La Liga 2021–22

	P	*W*	*D*	*L*	*F*	*A*	*GD*	*Pts*
Real Madrid (C)[1]	38	26	8	4	80	31	49	86
Barcelona[1]	38	21	10	7	68	38	30	73
Atletico Madrid[1]	38	21	8	9	65	43	22	71
Sevilla[1]	38	18	16	4	53	30	23	70
Real Betis[2]	38	19	8	11	62	40	22	65
Real Sociedad[2]	38	17	11	10	40	37	3	62
Villarreal[3]	38	16	11	11	63	37	26	59
Athletic Bilbao	38	14	13	11	43	36	7	55
Valencia	38	11	15	12	48	53	–5	48
Osasuna	38	12	11	15	37	51	–14	47
Celta Vigo	38	12	10	16	43	43	0	46
Rayo Vallecano	38	11	9	18	39	50	–11	42
Elche	38	11	9	18	40	52	–12	42
Espanyol	38	10	12	16	40	53	–13	42
Getafe	38	8	15	15	33	41	–8	39
Mallorca	38	10	9	19	36	63	–27	39
Cadiz	38	8	15	15	35	51	–16	39
Granada*	38	8	14	16	44	61	–17	38
Levante*	38	8	11	19	51	76	–25	35
Alaves*	38	8	7	23	31	65	–34	31

Top scorer: Benzema (Real Madrid) 27.

Cup Final: Real Betis 1, Valencia 1 *(aet; Real Betis won 5-4 on penalties).*

SWEDEN

Svenska Fotbollfoerbundet, Evenemangsgatan 31, PO Box 1216, SE-171 23 Solna.
Founded: 1904. *FIFA:* 1904; *UEFA:* 1954. *National Colours:* Yellow shirts with blue trim, blue shorts with yellow trim, yellow socks with blue trim.

International matches 2021–22

Spain (h) 2-1, Uzbekistan (h) 2-1, Greece (a) 1-2, Kosovo (h) 3-0, Greece (h) 2-0, Georgia (a) 0-2, Spain (a) 0-1, Czech Republic (h) 1-0, Poland (a) 0-2, Slovenia (a) 2-0, Norway (h) 1-2, Serbia (h) 0-1, Norway (a) 2-3.

League Championship wins (1896–2021)

Malmo 22; IFK Goteborg 18; IFK Norrkoping 13; Orgryte 12; AIK (Solna) 12; Djurgaarden 12; Elfsborg 6; Helsingborg 5; GAIS (Gothenburg) 4; Oster Vaxjo 4; Halmstad 4; Atvidaberg 2; Goteborgs IF 1; IFK Eskilstuna 1; Fassbergs 1; Brynas IF 1; IK Sleipner 1; Hammarby 1; Kalmar 1.
(Played in cup format from 1896–1925.)

Cup wins (1941–2022)

Malmo 15; AIK (Solna) 8; IFK Goteborg 8; IFK Norrkoping 6; Helsingborg 5; Djurgaarden 5; Kalmar 3; Elfsborg 3; Atvidaberg 2; Hacken 2; GAIS (Gothenburg) 1; Raa IF 1; Landskrona 1; Oster Vaxjo 1; Degerfors 1; Halmstad 1; Orgryte 1; Ostersund 1; Hammarby 1.

Allsvenskan 2021

	P	*W*	*D*	*L*	*F*	*A*	*GD*	*Pts*
Malmo (C)[1]	30	17	8	5	58	30	28	59
AIK[3]	30	18	5	7	45	25	20	59
Djurgarden[3]	30	17	6	7	46	30	16	57
Elfsborg[3]	30	17	4	9	51	35	16	55
Hammarby	30	15	8	7	54	41	13	53
Kalmar	30	13	8	9	41	39	2	47
IFK Norrkoping	30	13	5	12	45	41	4	44
IFK Goteborg	30	11	8	11	42	39	3	41
Mjallby	30	9	11	10	34	27	7	38
Varberg	30	9	10	11	35	38	–3	37
Sirius	30	10	7	13	39	53	–14	37
Hacken	30	9	9	12	46	46	0	36
Degerfors	30	10	4	16	34	51	–17	34
Halmstad+*	30	6	14	10	21	26	–5	32
Orebro*	30	4	6	20	23	58	–35	18
Ostersund*	30	3	5	22	24	59	–35	14

Top scorer: Adegbenro (IFK Norrkoping) 17.
Cup Final: Hammarby 0, Malmo 0 *(aet; Malmo won 4-3 on penalties).*

SWITZERLAND

Schweizerisher Fussballverband, Worbstrasse 48, Postfach 3000, Bern 15.
Founded: 1895. *FIFA:* 1904; *UEFA:* 1954. *National Colours:* All red with white trim.

International matches 2021–22

Greece (h) 2-1, Italy (h) 0-0, Northern Ireland (a) 0-0, Northern Ireland (h) 2-0, Lithuania (a) 4-0, Italy (a) 1-1, Bulgaria (h) 4-0, England (a) 1-2, Kosovo (h) 1-1, Czech Republic (a) 1-2, Portugal (a) 0-4, Spain (h) 0-1, Portugal (h) 1-0.

League Championship wins (1897–2022)

Grasshoppers 27; FC Basel 20; Servette 17; Young Boys 15; FC Zurich 13; Lausanne-Sport 7; Winterthur 3; Aarau 3; Lugano 3; La Chaux-de-Fonds 3; St Gallen 2; Neuchatel Xamax 2; Sion 2; Anglo-American Club 1; Brühl 1; Cantonal-Neuchatel 1; Etoile La Chaux-de-Fonds 1; Biel-Bienne 1; Bellinzona 1; Luzern 1.

Cup wins (1926–2022)

Grasshoppers 19; FC Basel 13; Sion 13; FC Zurich 10; Lausanne-Sport 9; Servette 7; Young Boys 7; La Chaux-de-Fonds 6; Lugano 4; Luzern 3; Urania Geneva Sport 1; Young Fellows Zurich (renamed Young Fellows Juventus) 1; FC Grenchen 1; St Gallen 1; Aarau 1; Wil 1.

Swiss Super League 2021–22

	P	*W*	*D*	*L*	*F*	*A*	*GD*	*Pts*
FC Zurich (C)[1]	36	23	7	6	78	46	32	76
FC Basel[3]	36	15	17	4	70	41	29	62
Young Boys[3]	36	16	12	8	80	50	30	60
Lugano[3]	36	16	6	14	50	54	–4	54
St Gallen	36	14	8	14	68	63	5	50
Servette	36	12	8	16	50	66	–16	44
Sion	36	11	8	17	46	67	–21	41
Grasshopper	36	9	13	14	54	58	–4	40
Luzern+	36	9	13	14	52	64	–12	40
Lausanne Sport*	36	4	10	22	37	76	–39	22

Top scorer: Pefok (Young Boys) 22.
Cup Final: Lugano 4, St Gallen 1.

TURKEY

Turkiye Futbol Federasyonu, Hasan Dogan Milli Takimlar, Kamp ve Egitim Tesisleri, Riva, Beykoz, Istanbul.
Founded: 1923. *FIFA:* 1923; *UEFA:* 1962. *National Colours:* All white with red trim.

International matches 2021–22

Montenegro (h) 2-2, Gibraltar (a) 3-0, Netherlands (a) 1-6, Norway (h) 1-1, Latvia (a) 2-1, Gibraltar (h) 6-0, Montenegro (a) 2-1, Portugal (a) 1-3, Italy (h) 2-3, Faroe Islands (h) 4-0, Lithuania (a) 6-0, Luxembourg (a) 2-0, Lithuania (h) 2-0.

League Championship wins (1959–2022)

Galatasaray 22; Fenerbahce 19; Besiktas 14; Trabzonspor 7; Bursaspor 1; Istanbul Basaksehir 1.

Cup wins (1963–2022)

Galatasaray 18; Besiktas 10; Trabzonspor 9; Fenerbahce 6; Altay Izmir 2; Goztepe Izmir 2; Ankaragucu 2; Genclerbirligi 2; Kocaelispor 2; Eskisehirspor 1; Bursaspor 1; Sakaryaspor 1; Kayseri 1; Konyaspor 1; Akhisar Belediyespor 1; Sivasspor 1.

Turkish Super Lig 2021–22

	P	*W*	*D*	*L*	*F*	*A*	*GD*	*Pts*
Trabzonspor (C)[1]	38	23	12	3	69	36	33	81
Fenerbahce[1]	38	21	10	7	73	38	35	73
Konyaspor[3]	38	20	8	10	66	45	21	68
Istanbul Basaksehir[3]	38	19	8	11	56	36	20	65
Alanyaspor	38	19	7	12	67	58	9	64
Besiktas	38	15	14	9	56	48	8	59
Antalyaspor	38	16	11	11	54	47	7	59
Fatih Karagumruk	38	16	9	13	47	52	–5	57
Adana Demirspor	38	15	10	13	60	47	13	55
Sivasspor[2]	38	14	12	12	52	50	2	54
Kasimpasa	38	15	8	15	67	57	10	53
Hatayspor	38	15	8	15	56	60	–4	53
Galatasaray	38	14	10	14	51	53	–2	52
Kayserispor	38	12	11	15	54	61	–7	47
Gaziantep	38	12	10	16	48	56	–8	46
Giresunspor	38	12	9	17	41	47	–6	45
Rizespor*	38	10	6	22	44	71	–27	36
Altay*	38	9	7	22	39	57	–18	34
Goztepe*	38	7	7	24	40	77	–37	28
Yeni Malatyaspor*	38	5	5	28	27	71	–44	20

Top scorer: Bozok (Kasimpasa) 20.
Cup Final: Sivasspor 3, Kayserispor 2 *(aet).*

UKRAINE

Football Federation of Ukraine, Provulok Laboratornyi 7-A, PO Box 55, 01133 Kyiv.
Founded: 1991. *FIFA:* 1992; *UEFA:* 1992. *National Colours:* All yellow with blue trim.

International matches 2021–22

Kazakhstan (a) 2-2, France (h) 1-1, Czech Republic (a) 1-1, Finland (a) 2-1, Bosnia-Herzegovina (h) 1-1, Bulgaria (h) 1-1, Bosnia-Herzegovina (a) 2-0, Scotland (a) 3-1, Wales (a) 0-1, Republic of Ireland (a) 1-0, Armenia (h) 3-0, Republic of Ireland (a) 1-1*.
* *Match played in Poland.*

League Championship wins (1992–2022)*

Dynamo Kyiv 16; Shakhtar Donetsk 13; Tavriya Simferopol 1.
* *No winner in 2021–22.*

Cup wins (1992–2022)

Dynamo Kyiv 13; Shakhtar Donetsk 13; Chornomorets Odesa 2; Vorskla Poltava 1; Tavriya Simferopol 1.
* *No winner in 2021–22. See also Russia section for Ukrainian club honours in Soviet era 1936–91.*

Ukrainian Premier League Qualifying Table 2021–22*

	P	*W*	*D*	*L*	*F*	*A*	*GD*	*Pts*
Shakhtar Donetsk (C)[1]	18	15	2	1	49	10	39	47
Dinamo Kiev[1]	18	14	3	1	47	9	38	45
SC Dnipro-1[2]	18	13	1	4	35	17	18	40
Zorya Luhansk[3]	18	11	3	4	37	19	18	36
Vorskla Poltava[3]	18	9	6	3	30	18	12	33
Oleksandria	18	7	5	6	19	16	3	26
Desna Chernihiv†	18	7	4	7	22	27	–5	25
Kolos Kovalivka	18	7	3	8	14	23	–9	24
Veres Rivne	18	6	5	7	15	20	–5	23
Metalist 1925 Kharkiv	18	6	1	11	17	29	–12	19
Rukh Lviv	17	4	6	7	16	21	–5	18
FC Lviv	18	4	5	9	14	30	–16	17
Chornomorets Odesa	18	3	5	10	20	40	–20	14
Inhulets	17	3	4	10	13	28	–15	13

**Due to the military invasion by Russia and the subsequent war, the season was suspended at week 18 then abandoned on 26 April 2022. No champion declared; league standings at suspension used to determine qualification for UEFA competitions in 2022–23.*

†*Due to the destruction of the infrastructure of their cities, Desna Chernihiv and Mariupol had their league membership suspended for 2022–23.*
Top scorer: Dovbyk (SC Dnipro-1) 14.
Cup Final: Competition abandoned.

WALES

Football Association of Wales, 11/12 Neptune Court, Vanguard Way, Cardiff CF24 5PJ.
Founded: 1876. *FIFA:* 1910; *UEFA:* 1954. *National Colours:* All red with yellow and green trim.

SOUTH AMERICA (CONMEBOL)

ARGENTINA

Asociacion del Futbol Argentina, Viamonte 1366/76, Buenos Aires 1053.
Founded: 1893. FIFA: 1912; CONMEBOL: 1916. National Colours: Light blue and white striped shirts, white shorts, white socks with blue trim.
International matches 2021–22
Venezuela (a) 3-1, Bolivia (h) 3-0, Paraguay (a) 0-0, Uruguay (h) 3-0, Peru (h) 1-0, Uruguay (a) 1-0, Brazil (h) 0-0, Chile (a) 2-1, Colombia (h) 1-0, Venezuela (h) 3-0, Ecuador (a) 1-1, Italy (n) 3-0, Estonia (n) 5-0.
League champions 2021: River Plate; *2022:* Competition still being played. *Cup winners 2019–20:* Boca Juniors; *2020–21:* Not contested; 2021–22: Competition still being played.

BOLIVIA

Federacion Boliviana de Futbol, Avenida Libertador Bolivar 1168, Casilla 484, Cochabamba.
Founded: 1925. *FIFA:* 1926; *CONMEBOL:* 1926. *National Colours:* Green shirts, white shorts, white socks with green tops.
International matches 2021–22
Colombia (h) 1-1, Uruguay (a) 2-4, Argentina (a) 0-3, Ecuador (a) 0-3, Peru (h) 1-0, Paraguay (h) 4-0, El Salvador (n) 1-0, Peru (a) 0-3, Uruguay (h) 3-0, Trinidad & Tobago (h) 5-0, Venezuela (a) 1-4, Chile (h) 2-3, Colombia (a) 0-3, Brazil (h) 0-4.
League champions 2021: Independiente Petrolero; *2022:* Bolivar (Apertura). *Cup winners: 2016:* Club Destroyers; *2017–21:* Not contested; competition resumes in 2022.

BRAZIL

Confederacao Brasileira de Futebol, Avenida Luis Carlos Prestes 130, Barra da Tijuca, Rio de Janeiro 22775-055.
Founded: 1914. *FIFA:* 1923; *CONMEBOL:* 1916. *National Colours:* Yellow shirts with green trim, blue shorts, white socks.
International matches 2021–22
Chile (a) 1-0, Peru (h) 2-0, Venezuela (a) 3-1, Colombia (a) 0-0, Uruguay (h) 4-1, Colombia (h) 1-0, Argentina (a) 0-0, Ecuador (a) 1-1, Paraguay (h) 4-0, Chile (h) 4-0, Bolivia (a) 4-0, Korea Republic (a) 5-1, Japan (a) 1-0.
League champions 2021: Atletico Mineiro; *2022:* Competition still being played. *Cup winners 2021:* Atletico Mineiro; *2022:* Competition still being played.

CHILE

Federacion de Futbol de Chile, Avenida Quilin 5635, Comuna Penalolen, Santiago de Chile.
Founded: 1895. *FIFA:* 1913; *CONMEBOL:* 1916. *National Colours:* Red shirts with blue trim, blue shorts, blue socks.
International matches 2021–22
Brazil (h) 0-1, Ecuador (a) 0-0, Colombia (a) 1-3, Peru (a) 0-2, Paraguay (h) 2-2, Venezuela (h) 3-0, Paraguay (a) 1-0, Ecuador (h) 0-2, Mexico (n) 2-2, El Salvador (n) 1-0, Argentina (h) 1-2, Bolivia (h) 3-2, Brazil (a) 0-4, Uruguay (h) 0-2, Korea Republic (a) 0-2, Tunisia (n) 0-2, Ghana (n) 0-0 (1-3p).
League champions 2021: Universidad Catolica; *2022:* Competition still being played. *Cup winners 2021:* Colo-Colo; *2022:* Competition still being played.

COLOMBIA

Federacion Colombiana de Futbol, Carrera 45A No. 94–06, Bogota.
Founded: 1924. *FIFA:* 1936; *CONMEBOL:* 1936. *National Colours:* Yellow shirts with red trim, blue shorts with yellow trim, red socks with yellow trim.
International matches 2021–22
Bolivia (a) 1-1, Paraguay (a) 1-1, Chile (h) 3-1, Uruguay (a) 0-0, Brazil (h) 0-0, Ecuador (h) 0-0, Brazil (a) 0-1, Paraguay (h) 0-0, Honduras (a) 2-1, Peru (h) 0-1, Argentina (a) 0-1, Bolivia (h) 3-0, Venezuela (a) 1-0, Saudi Arabia (a) 1-0.
League champions 2021: Deportes Tolima (Apertura), Deportes Cali (Finalizacion); *2022:* Atletico Nacional (Apertura). *Cup winners 2021:* Atletico Nacional; *2022:* Competition still being played.

ECUADOR

Federacion Ecuatoriana del Futbol, Avenida Las Aguas y Calle Alianza, PO Box 09-01-7447, Guayaquil 593.
Founded: 1925. *FIFA:* 1926; *CONMEBOL:* 1927. *National Colours:* Yellow shirts with dark blue sleeves, dark blue shorts, dark blue socks.
International matches 2021–22
Paraguay (h) 2-0, Chile (h) 0-0, Uruguay (a) 0-1, Bolivia (h) 3-0, Venezuela (a) 1-2, Colombia (a) 0-0, Mexico (a) 3-2, Venezuela (h) 1-0, Chile (a) 2-0, El Salvador (n) 1-1, Brazil (h) 1-1, Peru (a) 1-1, Paraguay (h) 1-3, Argentina (a) 1-1, Nigeria (n) 1-0, Mexico (n) 0-0, Cape Verde (n) 1-0.
League champions 2021: Independiente del Valle; *2022:* Competition still being played. *Cup winners 2019:* LDU Quito; *2020–21:* No competition; *2022:* Competition still being played.

PARAGUAY

Asociacion Paraguaya de Futbol, Avenida Medallistas Olimpicos No.1, Parque Olimpico, Nu Guasu, Ciudad de Luque.
Founded: 1906. *FIFA:* 1925; *CONMEBOL:* 1921. *National Colours:* Red and white striped shirts, blue shorts, blue socks.
International matches 2021–22
Ecuador (a) 0-2, Colombia (h) 1-1, Venezuela (h) 2-1, Argentina (h) 0-0, Chile (a) 0-2, Bolivia (a) 0-4, Chile (h) 0-1, Colombia (a) 0-0, Uruguay (h) 0-1, Brazil (a) 0-4, Ecuador (h) 3-1, Peru (a) 0-2, Japan (a) 1-4, Korea Republic (a) 2-2.
League champions 2021: Libertad (Apertura), Cerro Porteno (Clausura); *2022:* Libertad (Apertura). *Cup winners 2021:* Olimpia; *2022:* Competition still being played.

PERU

Federacion Peruana de Futbol, Avenida Aviacion 2085, San Luis, Lima 30.
Founded: 1922. *FIFA:* 1924; *CONMEBOL:* 1925. *National Colours:* White shirts with red sash, white shorts, white socks.
International matches 2021–22
Uruguay (h) 1-1, Venezuela (h) 1-0, Brazil (a) 0-2, Chile (h) 2-0, Bolivia (a) 0-1, Argentina (a) 0-1, Bolivia (h) 3-0, Venezuela (a) 2-1, Panama (h) 1-1, Jamaica (h) 3-0, Colombia (a) 1-0, Ecuador (h) 1-1, Uruguay (a) 0-1, Paraguay (h) 2-0, New Zealand (n) 1-0, Australia (n) 0-0 (4-5p).
League champions 2021: Alianza Lima; *2022:* Competition still being played. *Cup winners 2021:* Sporting Cristal.

URUGUAY

Asociacion Uruguaya de Futbol, Guayabo 1531, Montevideo 11200.
Founded: 1900. *FIFA:* 1923; *CONMEBOL:* 1916. *National Colours:* Sky blue shirts, black shorts, black socks with sky blue tops.
International matches 2021–22
Peru (a) 1-1, Bolivia (h) 4-2, Ecuador (h) 1-0, Colombia (h) 0-0, Argentina (a) 0-3, Brazil (a) 1-4, Argentina (h) 0-1, Bolivia (a) 0-3, Paraguay (a) 1-0, Venezuela (h) 4-1, Peru (h) 1-0, Chile (a) 2-0, Mexico (n) 3-0, USA (a) 0-0, Panama (h) 5-0.
League champions 2021: Penarol; *2022:* Competition still being played (Apertura). *Cup winners:* No competition.

VENEZUELA

Federacion Venezolana de Futbol, Avenida Santos Erminy, 1a Calle las Delicias Torre Mega II, Sabana Grande, 1050 Caracas.
Founded: 1926. *FIFA:* 1952; *CONMEBOL:* 1953. *National Colours:* All burgundy.
International matches 2021–22
Argentina (h) 1-3, Peru (a) 0-1, Paraguay (a) 1-2, Brazil (h) 1-3, Ecuador (h) 2-1, Chile (a) 0-3, Ecuador (a) 0-1, Peru (h) 1-2, Bolivia (h) 4-1, Uruguay (a) 1-4, Argentina (a) 0-3, Colombia (h) 0-1, Malta (a) 1-0, Saudi Arabia (n) 1-0.
League champions 2021: Deportivo Tachira; *2022:* Competition still being played. *Cup winners 2019:* Zamora; *2020–:* Not contested.

ASIA (AFC)

AFGHANISTAN

Afghanistan Football Federation, PO Box 128, Kabul.
Founded: 1933. *FIFA:* 1948; *AFC:* 1954. *National Colours:* All red.
International matches 2021–22
Indonesia (n) 1-0, Vietnam (a) 0-2, Hong Kong (n) 1-2, India (a) 1-2, Cambodia (n) 2-2.
**Match played in India.*
League champions 2020: Shaheen Asmayee; *2021–:* Not contested. *Cup winners:* No competition.

AUSTRALIA

Football Federation Australia Ltd, Locked Bag A4071, Sydney South, NSW 1235.

Founded: 1961. *FIFA:* 1963; *AFC:* 2006. *National Colours:* Gold shirts with green trim, green shorts, gold socks with green tops.
International matches 2021–22
China PR (h) 3-0*, Vietnam (a) 1-0, Oman (h) 3-1*, Japan (a) 1-2, Saudi Arabia (h) 0-0, China PR (a) 1-1‡, Vietnam (a) 4-0, Oman (a) 2-2, Japan (h) 0-2, Saudi Arabia (a) 0-1, Jordan (n) 2-1, UAE (n) 2-1, Peru (n) 0-0 (5-4p).
* *Match played in Qatar.* ‡ *Match played in UAE.*
League champions 2021–22: Western United. *Cup winners 2021–22:* Melbourne Victory.

BAHRAIN

Bahrain Football Association, Building 317, Road 3407, Block 934, North Riffa.
Founded: 1957. *FIFA:* 1968; *AFC:* 1969. *National Colours:* All red with gold trim.
International matches 2021–22
Haiti (h) 6-1, Jordan (h) 1-2, Curacao (h) 4-0, New Zealand (h) 0-1, Kyrgyz Republic (h) 4-2, Qatar (a) 0-1, Iraq (n) 0-0, Oman (n) 0-3, Uganda (h) 3-1, DR Congo (h) 1-0, India (h) 2-1, Burundi (h) 1-0, Belarus (h) 0-1, Myanmar (n) 2-0, Thailand (a) 2-1, Bangladesh (n) 2-0, Malaysia (a) 2-1, Turkmenistan (n) 1-0.
League champions 2021–22: Al-Riffa. *Cup winners 2021–22:* Al-Khaldiya.

BANGLADESH

Bangladesh Football Federation, BFF House, Motijheel Commercial Area, Dhaka 1000.
Founded: 1972. *FIFA:* 1976; *AFC:* 1974. *National Colours:* Green shirts with red trim, white shorts, green socks.
International matches 2021–22
Palestine (n) 0-2, Kyrgyz Republic (a) 1-4, Sri Lanka (n) 1-0, India (n) 1-1, Maldives (a) 0-2, Nepal (n) 1-1, Maldives (a) 0-2, Mongolia (h) 0-0, Indonesia (a) 0-0, Bahrain (n) 0-2, Turkmenistan (n) 1-2, Malaysia (a) 1-4.
League champions 2020–21: Bashundhara Kings; *2022:* Competition still being played. *Cup winners 2021–22:* Abahani Dhaka.

BHUTAN

Bhutan Football Federation, PO Box 365, Changlimthang, Thimphu 11001.
Founded: 1983. *FIFA:* 2000; *AFC:* 1993. *National Colours:* Orange shirts with yellow trim, orange shorts, orange socks.
International matches 2021–22
None played.
League champions 2021: Paro; *2022:* Competition still being played. *Cup winners:* No competition.

BRUNEI

Football Association of Brunei Darussalam, FABD House, Jalan Pusat Persidangan, Bandar Seri Begawan BB4313. (Succeeded BAFA which was banned by FIFA and AFC in 2009.)
Founded: 2011 (BAFA 1953). *FIFA:* 2011 (BAFA 1972); *AFC:* 2011 (BAFA 1969). *National Colours:* Yellow shirts with black trim, yellow shorts with black trim, black socks with yellow trim.
International matches 2021–22
Laos (a) 2-3, Malaysia (a) 0-4.
League champions 2018–19: MS ABDB; *2020:* Competition abandoned; *2021:* Competition suspended. *Cup winners 2019:* Kota Rangers; *2020–:* Not contested.

CAMBODIA

Football Federation of Cambodia, National Football Centre, Road Kabsrov Sangkat Samrongkrom, Khan Dangkor, Phnom Penh 2327 PPT3.
Founded: 1933. *FIFA:* 1954; *AFC:* 1954. *National Colours:* Blue and black broad stripes with blue sleeves, black shorts, black socks.
International matches 2021–22
Guam (n) 1-0, Guam (n) 2-1, Malaysia (n) 1-3, Indonesia (n) 2-4, Laos (n) 3-0, Vietnam (n) 0-4, Timor-Leste (h) 2-1, India (a) 0-2, Hong Kong (n) 0-3, Afghanistan (n) 2-2.
League champions 2021: Phnom Penh Crown; *2022:* Competition still being played. *Cup winners 2020:* Visakha; *2021:* Visakha.

CHINA PR

Chinese Football Association, Easton Centre Tower A, 18 Guangqu Road, Chaoyang District, Beijing 100022.
Founded: 1924. *FIFA:* 1931, rejoined 1980; *AFC:* 1974. *National Colours:* Red shirts with yellow trim, red shorts, red socks with yellow trim.
International matches 2021–22
Australia (a) 0-3*, Japan (h) 0-1*, Vietnam (h) 3-2‡, Saudi Arabia (a) 2-3, Oman (h) 1-1‡, Australia (h) 1-1‡, Japan (a) 0-2, Vietnam (a) 1-3, Saudi Arabia (h) 1-1‡, Oman (a) 0-2.
* *Match played in Qatar.* ‡ *Match played in UAE.*
League champions 2021–22: Shandong Taishan. *Cup winners 2021:* Shandong Taishan.

CHINESE TAIPEI

Chinese Taipei Football Association, 2nd Floor, No. 730 Zhongyang Road, Xinzhuang District, New Taipei City 242030.
Founded: 1924. *FIFA:* 1954; *AFC:* 1954. *National Colours:* All blue with red and white trim.
International matches 2021–22
Indonesia (n) 1-2, Indonesia (n) 0-3.
League champions 2021: Taiwan Steel (Tainan City); *2022:* Competition still being played. *Cup winners:* No competition.

GUAM

Guam Football Association, PO Box 20008, Barrigada, Guam 96921.
Founded: 1975. *FIFA:* 1996; *AFC:* 1996. *National Colours:* All dark blue with white trim.
International matches 2021–22
Cambodia (n) 0-1, Cambodia (n) 1-2, Northern Mariana Islands† (h) 2-0, Northern Mariana Islands† (h) 3-2.
League champions 2018–19: Rovers; *2019–20:* Competition abandoned; *2020–:* Not contested. *Cup winners 2019:* Bank of Guam Strykers; *2020–:* Not contested.

HONG KONG

Hong Kong Football Association Ltd, 55 Fat Kwong Street, Ho Man Tin, Kowloon, Hong Kong.
Founded: 1914. *FIFA:* 1954; *AFC:* 1954. *National Colours:* All red.
International matches 2021–22
Malaysia (a) 0-2, Afghanistan (n) 2-1, Cambodia (n) 3-0, India (a) 0-4.
League champions 2020–21: Kitchee, *2021–22:* Competition abandoned. *Cup winners 2019–20:* Eastern; *2020–:* Not contested.

INDIA

All India Football Federation, Football House, Sector 19, Phase 1 Dwarka, New Delhi 110075.
Founded: 1937. *FIFA:* 1948; *AFC:* 1954. *National Colours:* Blue shirts with orange trim, blue shorts, blue socks with orange tops.
International matches 2021–22
Nepal (a) 1-1, Nepal (a) 2-1, Bangladesh (n) 1-1, Sri Lanka (n) 0-0, Nepal (n) 1-0, Maldives (a) 3-1, Nepal (n) 3-0, Bahrain (n) 1-2, Belarus (n) 0-3, Jordan (n) 0-2, Cambodia (h) 2-0, Afghanistan (h) 2-1, Hong Kong (h) 4-0.
League champions 2021–22: I-League: Gokulam Kerala; Super League: Hyderabad. *Cup winners 2019:* FC Goa; *2020–:* Not contested.

INDONESIA

Football Association of Indonesia, Menara Olahraga Senayan (MOS) Building, FX Sudirman Office Tower 14th Floor, Jl. General Sudirman, Gelora Senayan, Jakarta 10270.
Founded: 1930. *FIFA:* 1952; *AFC:* 1954. *National Colours:* Red shirts, white shorts with red trim, red socks with white tops.
International matches 2021–22
Chinese Taipei (n) 2-1, Chinese Taipei (n) 3-0, Afghanistan (n) 0-1, Myanmar (n) 4-1, Cambodia (n) 4-2, Laos (n) 5-1, Vietnam (n) 0-0, Malaysia (n) 4-1, Singapore (a) 1-1, Singapore (a) 4-2, Thailand (n) 0-4, Thailand (n) 2-2, Timor-Leste (h) 4-1, Timor-Leste (h) 3-0, Bangladesh (h) 0-0, Kuwait (a) 2-1, Jordan (n) 0-1, Nepal (n) 7-0.
League champions 2021–22: Bali United. *Cup winners 2018–19:* PSM Makassar; *2020–:* Not contested.

IRAN

Football Federation Islamic Republic of Iran, No. 4 Third 12-meter St., Seoul Avenue, Tehran 19958-73591.
Founded: 1920. *FIFA:* 1948; *AFC:* 1954. *National Colours:* All white with red and green trim.
International matches 2021–22
Syria (h) 1-0, Iraq (a) 3-0*, UAE (a) 1-0, Korea Republic (h) 1-1, Lebanon (a) 2-1, Syria (a) 3-0‡, Iraq (h) 1-0, UAE (h) 1-0, Korea Republic (a) 0-2, Lebanon (h) 2-0, Algeria (n) 1-2.
* *Match played in Qatar.* ‡ *Match played in Lebanon.*
League champions 2021–22: Esteghlal. *Cup winners 2021:* Foolad; *2021–22:* Nassaji Massandaran.

IRAQ

Iraq Football Association, Al-Shaab Stadium, PO Box 484, Baghdad.
Founded: 1948. *FIFA:* 1950; *AFC:* 1970. *National Colours:* Green shirts, white shorts, green socks.
International matches 2021–22
Korea Republic (a) 0-0, IR Iran (h) 0-3*, Lebanon (h) 0-0*, UAE (a) 2-2, Syria (h) 1-1*, Korea Republic (h) 0-3*, Oman (n) 1-1*, Bahrain (n) 0-0, Qatar (a) 0-3, Uganda (n) 1-0*, IR Iran (a) 0-1, Lebanon (a) 1-1, Zambia (h) 3-1, UAE (a) 1-0‡, Syria (h) 1-1**.
* *Match played in Qatar.* ‡ *Match played in Saudi Arabia.* ** *Match played in UAE.*

League champions 2021–22: Al-Shorta. *Cup winners 2021–22:* Al-Karkh.

JAPAN

Japan Football Association, JFA House, Football Avenue, Bunkyo-ku, Tokyo 113-8311.
Founded: 1921. *FIFA:* 1929, rejoined 1950; *AFC:* 1954. *National Colours:* Blue patterned shirts with red trim, dark blue shorts with red trim, blue socks with red and white trim.
International matches 2021–22
Oman (h) 0-1, China PR (a) 1-0*, Saudi Arabia (a) 0-1, Australia (h) 2-1, Vietnam (a) 1-0, Oman (a) 1-0, China PR (h) 2-0, Saudi Arabia (h) 2-0, Australia (a) 2-0, Vietnam (h) 1-1, Paraguay (h) 4-1, Brazil (h) 0-1, Ghana (h) 4-1, Tunisia (h) 0-3.
* *Match played in Qatar.*
League champions 2021: Kawasaki Frontale; *2022:* Competition still being played. *Cup winners 2021:* Urawa Red Diamonds; *2022:* Competition still being played.

JORDAN

Jordan Football Association, PO Box 962024, Al-Hussein Youth City, Amman 11196.
Founded: 1949. *FIFA:* 1958; *AFC:* 1975. *National Colours:* White shirts with red trim, white shorts, white socks with black tops.
International matches 2021–22
Haiti (n) 0-2, Bahrain (a) 2-1, Malaysia (h) 4-0, Uzbekistan (h) 3-0, Kosovo (a) 2-0, Belarus (a) 0-1, Saudi Arabia (n) 1-0, Morocco (n) 0-4, Palestine (n) 5-1, Egypt (a) 1-3, New Zealand (n) 3-1, India (n) 2-0, Australia (n) 1-2, Nepal (n) 2-0, Indonesia (n) 1-0, Kuwait (a) 3-0.
League champions 2021: Al-Ramtha; *2022:* Competition still being played. *Cup winners 2021:* Al-Faisaly.

KOREA DPR

DPR Korea Football Association, Kumsongdong, Kwangbok Street, Mangyongdae, PO Box 818, Pyongyang.
Founded: 1945. *FIFA:* 1958; *AFC:* 1974. *National Colours:* All white with red trim.
International matches 2021–22
None played. Korea DPR withdrew from World Cup 2022 Qualifying; earlier results in AFC Group H were annulled.
League champions 2018–19: April 25; *2019–20:* Competition apparently abandoned; *2020–:* Not contested. *Cup winners 2019:* Ryomyong; *2020–:* Not contested.

KOREA REPUBLIC

Korea Football Association, KFA House 21, Gyeonghuigung-gil 46, Jongno-Gu, Seoul 110-062.
Founded: 1933, 1948. *FIFA:* 1948; *AFC:* 1954. *National Colours:* All red with black trim.
International matches 2021–22
Iraq (h) 0-0, Lebanon (h) 1-0, Syria (h) 2-1, IR Iran (a) 1-1, UAE (h) 1-0, Iraq (a) 3-0*, Iceland (n) 5-1, Moldova (n) 4-0, Lebanon (a) 1-0, Syria (a) 2-0‡, IR Iran (h) 2-0, UAE (a) 0-1, Brazil (h) 1-5, Chile (h) 2-0, Paraguay (h) 2-2, Egypt (h) 4-1.
* *Match played in Qatar.* ‡ *Match played in UAE.*
League champions 2021: Jeonbuk Hyundai Motors; *2022:* Competition still being played. *Cup winners 2021:* Jeonnam Dragons; *2022:* Competition still being played.

KUWAIT

Kuwait Football Association, Udailiya, Block 4, Sami Ahmad Al Manayes Street, PO Box 2029, Kuwait City 13021.
Founded: 1952. *FIFA:* 1964; *AFC:* 1964. *National Colours:* All blue with white trim.
International matches 2021–22
Bosnia-Herzegovina (a) 0-1, Czech Republic (a) 0-7, Lithuania (a) 1-1, Libya (h) 2-0, Libya (h) 0-2, Latvia (n) 1-1, Malta (a) 0-2, Singapore (n) 2-0, Indonesia (h) 1-2, Nepal (h) 4-1, Jordan (h) 0-3.
League champions 2021–22: Al-Kuwait. *Cup winners 2021:* Al-Kuwait; *2022:* Kazma.

KYRGYZ REPUBLIC

Football Federation of Kyrgyz Republic, Mederova Street 1 'B', PO Box 1484, Bishkek 720082.
Founded: 1992. *FIFA:* 1994; *AFC:* 1994. *National Colours:* All red.
International matches 2021–22
Palestine (h) 1-0, Bangladesh (h) 4-1, Singapore (n) 2-1, Bahrain (a) 2-4, Uzbekistan (a) 1-3, Tajikistan (a) 0-1, Singapore (h) 2-1, Myanmar (h) 2-0, Tajikistan (h) 0-0.
League champions 2021: Dordoi Bishkek; *2022:* Competition still being played. *Cup winners 2021:* Neftchi Kochkor-Ata.

LAOS

Lao Football Federation, Ban Houay Hong, Chanthabouly District, PO Box 1800, Vientiane.
Founded: 1951. *FIFA:* 1952; *AFC:* 1968. *National Colours:* All red shirts with blue trim.
International matches 2021–22
Vietnam (n) 0-2, Malaysia (n) 0-4, Indonesia (n) 1-5, Cambodia (n) 0-3, Mongolia (h) 1-0, Brunei (h) 3-2.
League champions 2020: FC Chanthabouly (formerly Lao Toyota); *2021:* Competition abandoned; *2022:* Competition still being played. *Cup winners 2020:* Young Elephant; *2021:* Competition abandoned.

LEBANON

Lebanese Football Association, Verdun Street, Bristol Radwan Centre, PO Box 4732, Beirut.
Founded: 1933. *FIFA:* 1936; *AFC:* 1964. *National Colours:* All red with white trim.
International matches 2021–22
UAE (a) 0-0, Korea Republic (a) 0-1, Iraq (a) 0-0*, Syria (a) 3-2‡, IR Iran (h) 1-2, UAE (h) 0-1, Egypt (n) 0-1, Algeria (n) 0-2, Sudan (n) 1-0, Korea Republic (h) 0-1, Iraq (h) 1-1, Syria (h) 0-3, IR Iran (a) 0-2.
* *Match played in Qatar.* ‡ *Match played in Jordan.*
League champions 2021–22: Al-Ahed. *Cup winners 2021–22:* Al-Nijmeh.

MACAU

Associacao de Futebol de Macau, Avenida Olimpica, Taipa Olympic Sports Centre – Stadium (Room GS 10–11), Taipa.
Founded: 1939. *FIFA:* 1978; *AFC:* 1978. *National Colours:* All green with white trim.
International matches 2021–22
None played.
League champions 2021: Chao Pak Kei; *2022:* Competition still being played. *Cup winners 2021:* Chao Pak Kei.

MALAYSIA

Football Association of Malaysia, 3rd Floor, Wisma FAM, Jalan SS5A/9, Kelana Jaya, Petaling Jaya 47301, Selangor Darul Ehsan.
Founded: 1933. *FIFA:* 1954; *AFC:* 1954. *National Colours:* All yellow with black trim.
International matches 2021–22
Jordan (a) 0-4, Uzbekistan (n) 1-5, Cambodia (n) 3-1, Laos (n) 4-0, Vietnam (n) 0-3, Indonesia (n) 1-4, Philippines (n) 2-0, Singapore (a) 1-2, Brunei (h) 4-0, Hong Kong (h) 2-0, Turkmenistan (h) 3-1, Bahrain (h) 1-2, Bangladesh (h) 4-1.
League champions 2021: Johor Darul Ta'zim; *2022:* Competition still being played. *Cup winners 2019:* Johor Darul Ta'zim; *2020:* Competition abandoned; *2021:* Kuala Lumpur City.

MALDIVES

Football Association of Maldives, Ma. Oliveena, Ground Floor, Chaandhanee Magu, Male 20195.
Founded: 1982. *FIFA:* 1986; *AFC:* 1986. *National Colours:* Red patterned shirts, red shorts with grey trim, grey socks.
International matches 2021–22
Nepal (h) 0-1, Bangladesh (h) 2-0, Sri Lanka (h) 1-0, India (h) 1-3, Sri Lanka (a) 4-4, Bangladesh (n) 1-2, Seychelles (n) 0-0, Bangladesh (h) 2-0, Thailand (n) 0-3, Uzbekistan (a) 04, Sri Lanka (n) 1-0.
League champions 2020–21: Maziya; *2022:* Competition still being played. *Cup winners 2017:* New Radiant; *2018–:* Not contested.

MONGOLIA

Mongolian Football Federation, PO Box 259, 15th Khoroo, Khan-Uul, Ulaanbaatar 210646.
Founded: 1959. *FIFA:* 1998; *AFC:* 1998. *National Colours:* White shirts with red trim, white shorts, white socks.
International matches 2021–22
Laos (a) 0-1, Bangladesh (a) 0-0, Palestine (h) 0-1, Philippines (h) 0-1, Yemen (h) 2-0.
League champions 2021: Athletic 220; *2021–22:* Khaan Khuns-Erchim. *Cup winners 2019:* Erchim; *2020–:* Not contested.

MYANMAR

Myanmar Football Federation, National Football Training Centre, Waizayanta Road, Thuwunna, Thingankyun Township, Yangon 11070.
Founded: 1947. *FIFA:* 1952; *AFC:* 1954. *National Colours:* All red.
International matches 2021–22
Burundi (n) 1-2, Indonesia (n) 1-4, Singapore (a) 0-3, Timor-Leste (n) 2-0, Thailand (n) 0-4, Philippines (n) 2-3, Bahrain (n) 0-2, Tajikistan (n) 0-4, Kyrgyz Republic (a) 0-2, Singapore (n) 2-6.
League champions 2020: Shan United; *2021–:* Not contested. *Cup winners 2019:* Yangon United; *2020–:* Not contested.

NEPAL

All Nepal Football Association, ANFA House, Satdobato, Lalitpur-17, PO Box 12582, Kathmandu.
Founded: 1951. *FIFA:* 1972; *AFC:* 1954. *National Colours:* All dark blue with white trim.

International matches 2021–22
India (h) 1-1, India (h) 1-2, Oman (n) 2-7, Maldives (a) 1-0, Sri Lanka (n) 3-2, India (n) 0-1, Bangladesh (n) 1-1, India (n) 0-3, Mauritius (h) 1-0, Mauritius (h) 1-0, Thailand (n) 0-2, Timor-Leste (n) 2-2, Oman (n) 0-2, Jordan (n) 0-2, Kuwait (a) 1-4, Indonesia (n) 0-7.
League champions 2021: Kathmandu RayZRs. *Cup winners 2021:* Sankata Club; *2022:* Nepal APF Club.

NORTHERN MARIANA ISLANDS

Northern Mariana Islands Football Association, PMB 338 Box 10001, Saipan, MP 96950.
Founded: 2005. *AFC:* 2020. *National Colours:* Dark blue shirts with sky blue trim, dark blue shiorts, dark blue socks.
International matches 2021–22
Guam (a) 0-2, Guam (a) 2-3.
League champions 2021: Tan Holdings (Spring), All Blue (Fall). *Cup winners:* No competition.

OMAN

Oman Football Association, Seeb Sports Stadium, PO Box 1188, 132 Al Khoudh.
Founded: 1978. *FIFA:* 1980; *AFC:* 1980. *National Colours:* All red with green and white trim.
International matches 2021–22
Japan (a) 1-0, Saudi Arabia (h) 0-1, Nepal (n) 7-2, Australia (a) 1-3*, Vietnam (h) 3-1, China PR (a) 1-1‡, Japan (h) 0-1, Iraq (n) 1-1, Qatar (a) 1-2*, Bahrain (n) 3-0*, Tunisia (n) 1-2, Saudi Arabia (a) 0-1, Australia (h) 2-2, Vietnam (a) 1-0, China PR (h) 2-0, Nepal (h) 2-0, New Zealand (n) 0-0.
** Match played in UAE. ‡ Match played in Qatar.*
League champions 2021–22: Al-Seeb. *Cup winners 2021–22:* Al-Seeb.

PAKISTAN

Pakistan Football Federation, Football House, Ferozepur Road, Lahore 54600, Punjab.
Founded: 1947. *FIFA:* 1948; *AFC:* 1954. *National Colours:* White shirts with green sleeves and side panel, white shorts, white socks.
International matches 2021–22
None played.
League champions 2019–21: Not contested; *2021–22* WAPDA. *Cup winners 2020:* WAPDA; *2021–:* Not contested.

PALESTINE

Palestinian Football Association, Nr. Faisal Al-Husseini Stadium, PO Box 4373, Jerusalem-al-Ram.
Founded: 1928. *FIFA:* 1998; *AFC:* 1998. *National Colours:* All red.
International matches 2021–22
Kyrgyz Republic (a) 0-1, Bangladesh (n) 2-0, Morocco (n) 0-4, Saudi Arabia (n) 1-1, Jordan (n) 1-5, Mongolia (a) 1-0, Yemen (n) 5-0, Philippines (n) 4-0
League champions 2021–22: West Bank: Shabab Al-Khalil, Gaza Strip: Shabab Rafah; *2021–22:* West Bank: Shabab Al-Khalil, Gaza Strip: Shabab Rafah. *Cup winners 2018–19:* West Bank: Markez Balata; *2019–:* Not contested; Gaza Strip: *2019–20:* Shabab Rafah; *2020–:* Not contested.

PHILIPPINES

Philippine Football Federation, 27 Danny Floro–corner Capt. Henry Javier Streets, Oranbo, Pasig City 1600.
Founded: 1907. *FIFA:* 1930; *AFC:* 1954. *National Colours:* All white with grey and blue trim.
International matches 2021–22
Singapore (a) 1-2, Timor-Leste (n) 7-0, Thailand (n) 1-2, Myanmar (n) 3-2, Malaysia (n) 0-2, Singapore (a) 0-2, Yemen (n) 0-0, Mongolia (a) 1-0, Palestine (n) 0-4.
League champions 2020: United City (formerly Ceres-Negros); *2021–:* Not contested. *Cup winners 2021:* Kaya-Iloilo; *2022:* United City.

QATAR

Qatar Football Association, 28th Floor, Al Bidda Tower, Corniche Street, West Bay, PO Box 5333, Doha.
Founded: 1960. *FIFA:* 1972; *AFC:* 1974. *National Colours:* All maroon.
International matches 2021–22
Panama (n) 3-3, Grenada (n) 4-0, Honduras (n) 2-0, El Salvador (n) 3-2, USA (a) 0-1, Serbia (n) 0-4, Portugal (n) 1-3, Luxembourg (a) 1-1, Portugal (a) 0-3, Republic of Ireland (a) 0-4, Serbia (a) 0-4, Azerbaijan (a) 2-2, Bahrain (h) 1-0, Oman (h) 2-1, Iraq (h) 3-0, UAE (h) 5-0, Algeria (n) 1-2, Egypt (a) 0-0 (5-4p), Bulgaria (h) 2-1, Slovenia (h) 0-0.
League champions 2021–22: Al-Sadd. *Cup winners 2021:* Al-Sadd; *2022:* Al-Duhail.

SAUDI ARABIA

Saudi Arabian Football Federation, Al Mather Quarter, Prince Faisal Bin Fahad Street, PO Box 5844, Riyadh 11432.
Founded: 1956. *FIFA:* 1956; *AFC:* 1972. *National Colours:* White shirts with green trim, green shorts, white socks.
International matches 2021–22
Vietnam (h) 3-1, Oman (a) 2-1, Japan (h) 1-0, China PR (h) 3-2, Australia (a) 0-0, Vietnam (a) 1-0, Jordan (n) 0-1, Palestine (n) 1-1, Morocco (n) 0-1, Oman (h) 1-0, Japan (a) 0-2, China PR (a) 1-1*, Australia (h) 1-0, Colombia (n) 0-1, Venezuela (n) 0-1.
**Match played in UAE.*
League champions 2021–22: Al-Ittihad. *Cup winners 2021–22: Al-Feiha.*

SINGAPORE

Football Association of Singapore, Jalan Besar Stadium 01-02, 100 Tyrwhitt Road, Singapore 207542.
Founded: 1892. *FIFA:* 1956; *AFC:* 1954. *National Colours:* All red.
International matches 2021–22
Kyrgyz Republic (n) 1-2, Myanmar (h) 3-0, Philippines (h) 2--1, Timor-Leste (h) 2-0, Thailand (h) 0-2, Indonesia (h) 1-1, Indonesia (h) 2-4, Malaysia (h) 2-1, Philippines (h) 2-0, Kuwait (n) 0-2, Kyrgyz Republic (a) 1-2, Tajikistan (n) 0-1, Myanmar (n) 6-2.
League champions 2021: Lion City Sailors; *2022:* Competition still being played. *Cup winners 2019:* Tampines Rovers; 2020–: Not contested.

SRI LANKA

Football Federation of Sri Lanka, 100/9 Independence Avenue, Colombo 07.
Founded: 1939. *FIFA:* 1952; *AFC:* 1954. *National Colours:* Yellow shirts, black shorts with yellow trim, yellow socks.
International matches 2021–22
Bangladesh (n) 0-1, Nepal (n) 2-3, India (n) 0-0, Maldives (a) 0-1, Maldives (h) 4-4, Seychelles (h) 0-1, Bangladesh (h) 2-1, Seychelles (h) 3-3 (1-3p), Uzbekistan (a) 0-3, Thailand (n) 0-2, Maldives (n) 0-1.
League champions 2019–21: Not contested. *2021–22:* Blue Star. *Cup winners 2019–20:* Police; *2020–:* Not contested.

SYRIA

Syrian Arab Federation for Football, Al Faihaa Sports Complex, PO Box 421, Damascus.
Founded: 1936. *FIFA:* 1937; *AFC:* 1970. *National Colours:* All red with gold trim.
International matches 2021–22
IR Iran (a) 0-1, UAE (h) 1-1*, Korea Republic (a) 1-2, Lebanon (h) 2-3*, Iraq (a) 1-1‡, IR Iran (h) 0-3*, UAE (n) 1-2, Tunisia (n) 2-0, Mauritania (n) 1-2, UAE (a) 0-2, Korea Republic (h) 0-2**, Lebanon (a) 3-0, Iraq (h) 1-1**, Tajikistan (n) 1-0.
**Match played in Jordan. ‡Match played in Qatar. **Match played in UAE.*
League champions 2021–22: Tishreen. *Cup winners 2020–21:* Jabala.

TAJIKISTAN

Tajikistan Football Federation, 14/3 Ayni Street, Dushanbe 734 025.
Founded: 1936. *FIFA:* 1994; *AFC:* 1994. *National Colours:* Red shirts with white trim, white shorts with red trim, green socks.
International matches 2021–22
Kazakhstan (a) 0-1, Uganda (n) 1-1 (4-5p), Kyrgyz Republic (n) 1-0, Syria (n) 0-1, Myanmar (n) 4-0, Singapore (n) 1-0, Kyrgyz Republic (a) 0-0.
League champions 2021: Istiklol; *2022:* Competition still being played. *Cup winners 2021:* Khujand.

THAILAND

Football Association of Thailand, 40th Anniversary Building (Building 2), 286, Ramkhamhaeng Road, Huamark, Bangkapi, Bangkok 10240.
Founded: 1916. *FIFA:* 1925; *AFC:* 1954. *National Colours:* All blue.
International matches 2021–22
Oman (n) 0-1*, Tajikistan (n) 2-2*, Indonesia (h) 2-2*‡, UAE (a) 1-3*‡, Malaysia (h) 0-1*‡, Timor-Leste (n) 2-0, Myanmar (n) 4-0, Philippines (n) 2-1, Singapore (a) 2-0, Vietnam (n) 2-0, Vietnam (n) 0-0, Indonesia (n) 4-0, Indonesia (n) 2-2, Nepal (h) 2-0, Suriname (h) 1-0, Turkmenistan (h) 1-0, Bahrain (h) 1-2, Maldives (n) 3-0, Sri Lanka (n) 2-0, Uzbekistan (a) 0-2.
** Results from 25.05.21 to 15.06.21 omitted from last edition. ‡ Match played in UAE.*
League champions 2020–21: BG Pathum United; *2021–22:* Buriram United. *Cup winners 2020:* Chiangrai United; *2021–22:* Buriram United.

TIMOR-LESTE

Federacao Futebol de Timor-Leste, Campo Democracia, Avenida Bairo Formosa, Dili.
Founded: 2002. *FIFA:* 2005; *AFC:* 2005. *National Colours:* Red shirts with black and yellow trim, black shorts with red and yellow trim, black socks.
International matches 2021–22
Thailand (n) 0-2, Myanmar (n) 0-2, Philippines (n) 0-7, Singapore (a) 0-2, Indonesia (a) 1-4, Indonesia (a) 0-3, Nepal (n) 2-2, Cambodia (a) 1-2.
League champions 2021: Karketu Dili. *Cup winners 2019:* Lalenok United; *2020–:* Not contested.

TURKMENISTAN

Football Federation of Turkmenistan, G. Kuliyev Street 68, Ashgabat 744 001.
Founded: 1992. *FIFA:* 1994; *AFC:* 1994. *National Colours:* All green.
International matches 2021–22
Thailand (a) 0-1, Malaysia (a) 1-3, Bangladesh (n) 2-1, Bahrain (n) 0-1.
League champions 2021: Altyn Asyr. *Cup winners 2021:* Sagadam.

UNITED ARAB EMIRATES (UAE)

United Arab Emirates Football Association, Al Khaleej Al Arabi Street, Zayed Sports City, PO Box 916, Abu Dhabi.
Founded: 1971. *FIFA:* 1974; *AFC:* 1974. *National Colours:* All white with red trim.
International matches 2021–22
Lebanon (h) 0-0, Syria (a) 1-1*, IR Iran (h) 0-1, Iraq (h) 2-2, Korea Republic (a) 0-1, Lebanon (a) 1-0, Syria (n) 2-1, Mauritania (n) 1-0, Tunisia (n) 0-1, Qatar (h) 0-5, Syria (h) 2-0, IR Iran (a) 0-1, Iraq (a) 0-1‡, Korea Republic (h) 1-0, Gambia (h) 1-1, Australia (n) 1-2.
** Match played in Jordan. ‡ Match played in Jordan.*
League champions 2021–22: Al-Ain. *Cup winners 2020–21:* Al-Shabab Al-Ahli; *2021–22:* Competition still being played.

UZBEKISTAN

Uzbekistan Football Federation, Islam Karimov Street 98A, Tashkent 100011.
Founded: 1946. *FIFA:* 1994; *AFC:* 1994. *National Colours:* White shirts with blue trim, white shorts, white and blue socks.
International matches 2021–22
Sweden (a) 1-2, Malaysia (n) 5-1, Jordan (a) 0-3, Georgia (a) 0-1, South Sudan (n) 3-0, Kyrgyz Republic (h) 3-1, Uganda (h) 4-2, Sri Lanka (h) 3-0, Maldives (h) 4-0, Thailand (h) 2-0. [14/6]
League champions 2021: Pakhtakor; *2022:* Competition still being played. *Cup winners 2021:* Nasaf; *2022:* Competition still being played.

VIETNAM

Vietnam Football Federation, Le Quang Dao Street, Phu Do Ward, Nam Tu Liem District, Hanoi 844.
Founded: 1960 (NV). *FIFA:* 1952 (SV), 1964 (NV); *AFC:* 1954 (SV), 1978 (SRV). *National Colours:* All red with yellow trim.
International matches 2021–22
Saudi Arabia (a) 1-3, Australia (h) 0-1, China PR (a) 2-3*, Oman (a) 1-3, Japan (h) 0-1, Saudi Arabia (h) 0-1, Morocco (n) 0-1, Laos (n) 2-0, Malaysia (n) 3-0, Indonesia (n) 0-0, Cambodia (n) 4-0, Thailand (n) 0-2, Thailand (n) 0-0, Australia (a) 0-4, China PR (h) 3-1, Oman (h) 0-1, Japan (a) 0-1, Afghanistan (h) 2-0.
** Match played in UAE.*
League champions 2020: Viettel; *2021:* Competition abandoned; *2022:* Competition still being played. *Cup winners 2020:* Ha Noi; *2021–:* Not contested.

YEMEN

Yemen Football Association, Quarter of Sport Al Jeraf (Ali Mohsen Al-Muraisi Stadium), PO Box 908, Al-Thawra City, Sana'a.
Founded: 1940 (SY), 1962 (NY). *FIFA:* 1967 (SY), 1980 (NY); *AFC:* 1972 (SY), 1980 (NY). *National Colours:* Red shirts, red shorts, black socks.
International matches 2021–22
Philippines (n) 0-0, Palestine (n) 0-5, Mongolia (a) 0-2.
League champions 2019–20: Al-Sha'ab Hadramaut; *2020:* Not contested. *2021:* Fahman. *Cup winners 2017:* Al-Wahda. *2018–:* Not contested.

NORTH AND CENTRAL AMERICA AND CARIBBEAN (CONCACAF)

ANGUILLA

Anguilla Football Association, 2 Queen Elizabeth Avenue, PO Box 1318, The Valley, AI-2640.
Founded: 1990. *FIFA:* 1996; *CONCACAF:* 1996. *National Colours:* Orange shirts with dark blue trim, orange shorts with dark blue trim, dark blue socks.
International matches 2021–22
US Virgin Islands* (a) 0-0, British Virgin Islands (n) 2-1, Saint-Martin† (a) 2-1, Dominica (h) 0-0, Dominica (a) 1-1, St Lucia (a) 0-2.
** Match played 21.03.21; result omitted from last edition.*
League champions 2021: Roaring Lions; *2022:* Competition still being played. *Cup winners:* No competition.

ANTIGUA & BARBUDA

Antigua & Barbuda Football Association, Vendors Mall Heritage Quay, Suite No. 19, PO Box 773, St John's.
Founded: 1928. *FIFA:* 1970; *CONCACAF:* 1972. *National Colours:* Black shirts with yellow trim, yellow shorts, yellow socks.
International matches 2021–22
Barbados (n) 1-0, Guadeloupe† (n) 1-0, Cuba (n) 0-2, Cuba (a) 1-3.
League champions 2018–19: Liberta Black Hawks; *2019–:* Not contested. *Cup winners:* No competition.

ARUBA

Arubaanse Voetbal Bond, Technical Centre Angel Botta, Shaba 24, PO Box 376, Noord.
Founded: 1932. *FIFA:* 1988; *CONCACAF:* 1986. *National Colours:* Yellow shirts with sky blue sleeves, yellow shorts, yellow socks.
International matches 2021–22
Sint Maarten† (h) 5-0, Saint-Martin† (a) 0-0, Saint-Martin† (h) 3-0, St Kitts & Nevis (h) 2-3.
League champions 2021: Racing Club Aruba; *2021–22:* Dakota. *Cup winners 2022:* Racing Club Aruba.

BAHAMAS

Bahamas Football Association, Rosetta Street, PO Box N-8434, Nassau, NP.
Founded: 1967. *FIFA:* 1968; *CONCACAF:* 1981. *National Colours:* Yellow shirts with blue sash, black shorts, black socks.
International matches 2021–22
Saint-Martin† (a) 0-2, Turks & Caicos Islands (h) 4-2, Turks & Caicos Islands (h) 1-2, St Vincent/Grenadines (h) 1-0, Trinidad & Tobago (a) 0-1, Nicaragua (h) 0-2, Nicaragua (a) 0-4.
League champions 2018–19: Dynamos; *2020–:* Not contested. *Cup winners 2017–18:* Western Warriors; *2019–:* Not contested.

BARBADOS

Barbados Football Association, PO Box 1362, BB11000, Bridgetown.
Founded: 1910. *FIFA:* 1968; *CONCACAF:* 1967. *National Colours:* All gold with royal blue trim.
International matches 2021–22
Bermuda (n) 1-8*, Suriname (a) 0-1, Martinique† (a) 1-3, Trinidad & Tobago (a) 0-9, Guyana (n) 0-5, Antigua & Barbuda (h) 0-1, Cuba (a) 0-3, Guadeloupe† (h) 0-1, Guadeloupe† (a) 1-2.
**Match played 2.07.2021; result omitted from last edition*
League champions 2018–19: Barbados Defence Force; *2020–:* Competition suspended. *Cup winners 2019:* Weymouth Wales; *2020–:* Not contested.

BELIZE

Football Federation of Belize, 26 Hummingbird Highway, Belmopan, PO Box 1742, Belize City.
Founded: 1980. *FIFA:* 1986; *CONCACAF:* 1986. *National Colours:* Blue shirts with red trim, blue shorts, blue socks.
International matches 2021–22
Nicaragua (a) 0-4, Nicaragua (a) 1-1, Cuba (h) 0-3, Dominican Republic (h) 0-2, Guatemala (a) 0-2, French Guiana† (h) 1-1, French Guiana† (a) 0-1.
League champions 2020–21: Competition suspended; *2021–22:* Verdes (Opening). *Cup winners:* No competition.

BERMUDA

Bermuda Football Association, 1 BFA Way, Devonshire DV 01, PO Box HM 745, Hamilton HM CX.
Founded: 1928. *FIFA:* 1962; *CONCACAF:* 1967. *National Colours:* Royal blue shirts, white shorts, royal blue socks.
International matches 2021–22
Guyana (n) 0-1*, Barbados (n) 8-1*, Haiti (h) 1-4, Haiti (h) 0-0, Guyana (a) 1-2, Montserrat (a) 2-3‡, Montserrat (a) 3-0**.
**Match played in 2021; result omitted from last edition. ‡ Match played in Dominican Republic. ** Match awarded to Bermuda; Montserrat failed to fulfil fixture.*
League champions 2021–22: Dandy Town Hornets. *Cup winners 2021–22:* Dandy Town Hornets.

BONAIRE

Federashon de Futbol Boneriano, Kaya Grandi 32B, Bonaire.
Founded: 1960. *CONCACAF:* 2014. *National Colours:* Blue and yellow shirts with white sash, white shorts, white socks with yellow tops.
International matches 2021–22
Curacao (a) 0-1, Turks & Caicos Islands (a) 4-1, Sint Maarten† (h) 2-2*, US Virgin Islands (a) 2-0, US Virgin Islands (h) 2-0*.
**Match played in Curacao.*
League champions 2021: Real Rincon; *2022:* Competition still being played. *Cup winners:* No competition.

BRITISH VIRGIN ISLANDS

British Virgin Islands Football Association, Botanic Station, PO Box 4269, Road Town, Tortola VG 1110.
Founded: 1974. *FIFA:* 1996; *CONCACAF:* 1996. *National Colours:* All green with white trim.
International matches 2021–22
Anguilla (n) 1-2, Cayman Islands (h) 1-1, Cayman Islands (a) 1-1, Puerto Rico (a) 0-6.
League champions 2021: Sugar Boys; *2021–22:* Sugar Boys. *Cup winners:* No competition.

CANADA

Canadian Soccer Association, Place Soccer Canada, 237 Metcalfe Street, Ottawa, Ontario K2P 1R2.
Founded: 1912. *FIFA:* 1912; *CONCACAF:* 1961. *National Colours:* All red.
International matches 2021–22
Haiti (n) 4-1, Haiti (n) 4-1, USA (a) 0-1, Costa Rica (n) 2-0, Mexico (n) 1-2, Honduras (h) 1-1, USA (a) 1-1, El Salvador (h) 3-0, Mexico (a) 1-1, Jamaica (a) 0-0, Panama (h) 4-1, Costa Rica (h) 1-0, Mexico (h) 2-1, Honduras (a) 2-0, USA (h) 2-0, El Salvador (a) 2-0, Costa Rica (a) 0-1, Jamaica (h) 4-0, Panama (a) 0-1, Curacao (h) 4-0, Honduras (a) 1-2.
League champions 2021: Pacific. *Cup winners 2020 (delayed final):* Toronto; *2021:* CF Montreal. *2022:* Competition still being played. (N.B. Canadian teams also compete in MLS and USL.)

CAYMAN ISLANDS

Cayman Islands Football Association, PO Box 178, Poindexter Road, Prospect, George Town, Grand Cayman KY1-1104.
Founded: 1966. *FIFA:* 1992; *CONCACAF:* 1990. *National Colours:* All red with white trim.
International matches 2021–22
British Virgin Islands (a) 1-1, British Virgin Islands (h) 1-1, Puerto Rico (h) 0-3.
League champions 2020–21: Scholar's International; *2021–22* Competition still being played. *Cup winners 2020–21:* Bodden Town; *2021–22* Competition still being played.

COSTA RICA

Federacion Costarricense de Futbol, 600 mts sur del Cruce de la Panasonic, San Rafael de Alajuela, Radial a Santa Ana, San Jose 670-1000.
Founded: 1921. *FIFA:* 1927; *CONCACAF:* 1961. *National Colours:* Red shirts, blue shorts, white socks.
International matches 2021–22
Guadeloupe† (n) 3-1, Suriname (n) 2-1, Jamaica (n) 1-0, Canada (n) 0-2, El Salvador (n) 0-0, Panama (a) 0-0, Mexico (h) 0-1, Jamaica (h) 1-1, Honduras (a) 0-0, El Salvador (h) 2-1, USA (a) 1-2, Canada (a) 0-1, Honduras (h) 2-1, Panama (h) 1-0, Mexico (a) 0-1, Jamaica (a) 1-0, Canada (h) 1-0, El Salvador (a) 2-1, USA (h) 2-0, Panama (a) 0-2, Martinique† (h) 2-0, New Zealand (n) 1-0.
League champions 2021–22: Herediano (Apertura), Cartagines (Clausura). *Cup winners:* No competition.

CUBA

Asociacion de Futbol de Cuba, Estadio Pedro Marrero, Escuela Nacional de Futbol – Mario Lopez, Avenida 41, 44 y 46 Municipio Playa, Havana.
Founded: 1924. *FIFA:* 1932; *CONCACAF:* 1961. *National Colours:* All red with black and white trim.
International matches 2021–22
Nicaragua (h) 3-0, Nicaragua (h) 0-2, Guatemala (a) 0-1, Belize (a) 3-0, Guadeloupe† (a) 1-2, Barbados (h) 3-0, Antigua & Barbuda (a) 2-0, Antigua & Barbuda (h) 3-1.
League champions 2019: Santiago de Cuba; *2020–:* Not contested. *Cup winners:* No competition.

CURACAO

Federashon Futbol Korsou, Bonamweg 49, PO Box 341, Willemstad.
Founded: 1921 (Netherlands Antilles), 2010. *FIFA:* 1932, 2010; *CONCACAF:* 1961, 2010. *National Colours:* All white with blue trim.
International matches 2021–22
Bonaire† (h) 1-0, Bahrain (a) 0-4, New Zealand (n) 1-2, Honduras (h) 0-1, Honduras (a) 2-1, Canada (a) 0-4.
League champions 2021: Jong Holland; *2022:* Competition still being played. *Cup winners:* No competition.

DOMINICA

Dominica Football Association, Patrick John Football House, Bath Estate, PO Box 1080, Roseau.
Founded: 1970. *FIFA:* 1994; *CONCACAF:* 1994. *National Colours:* Emerald shirts with yellow sleeves, black shorts, emerald socks.
International matches 2021–22
St Vincent/Grenadines (h) 2-1, St Vincent/Grenadines (h) 3-1, Anguilla (a) 0-0, Anguilla (h) 1-1, St Lucia (h) 0-1.
League champions 2020: Sagicor South East United; *2021:* Competition abandoned. *Cup winners 2021:* Sagicor South East United.

DOMINICAN REPUBLIC

Federacion Dominicana de Futbol, Centro Olimpico Juan Pablo Duarte, Apartado Postal 1953, Santo Domingo.
Founded: 1953. *FIFA:* 1958; *CONCACAF:* 1964. *National Colours:* All white with blue trim.
International matches 2021–22
Belize (a) 2-0, French Guiana† (h) 2-3, Guatemala (h) 1-1, Guatemala (a) 0-2.
League champions 2021: Cibao; *2022:* Competition still being played. *Cup winners:* No competition.

EL SALVADOR

Federacion Salvadorena de Futbol, Avenida Jose Matias Delgado, Frente al Centro Espanol Colonia Escalon, Zona 10, San Salvador 1029.
Founded: 1935. *FIFA:* 1938; *CONCACAF:* 1961. *National Colours:* Blue shirts, black shorts, blue socks.
International matches 2021–22
Trinidad & Tobago (n) 2-0, Mexico (n) 0-1, Qatar (n) 2-3, Costa Rica (n) 0-0, USA (h) 0-0, Honduras (h) 0-0, Canada (a) 0-3, Guatemala (n) 0-2, Panama (h) 1-0, Costa Rica (a) 1-2, Mexico (h) 0-2, Bolivia (n) 0-1, Jamaica (h) 1-1, Panama (a) 1-2, Ecuador (n) 1-1, Chile (n) 0-1, USA (a) 0-1, Honduras (a) 2-0, Canada (h) 0-2, Jamaica (a) 1-1, Costa Rica (h) 1-2, Mexico (a) 0-2, Guatemala (n) 0-4, Panama (n) 3-2, Grenada (h) 3-1, Grenada (a) 2-2, USA (h) 1-1.
League champions 2021–22: Alianza (Apertura), Alianza (Clausura). *Cup winners: 2018–19:* Santa Tecla; *2019–:* Not contested.

FRENCH GUIANA

Ligue de Football de la Guyane, BP 765, Stade de Baduel, Cayenne 97322 CEDEX.
Founded: 1962. *CONCACAF:* 2013. *National Colours:* Yellow shirts with black trim, blue shorts, green socks.
International matches 2021–22
Guyana (h) 2-1, Guyana (h) 1-2, Suriname (n) 3-1, Guatemala (h) 2-0, Dominican Republic (a) 3-2, Belize (a) 1-1, Belize (h) 1-1.
League champions 2019–20: Olympique de Cayenne; *2020–21:* Competition abandoned; *2021–22:* Competition still being played. *Cup winners 2018–19:* AS Etoile Matoury; *2019–21:* Not contested; *2021–22:* Competition still being played.

GRENADA

Grenada Football Association, National Stadium, Queens Park, PO Box 326, St George's.
Founded: 1924. *FIFA:* 1978; *CONCACAF:* 1969. *National Colours:* Red and yellow hooped shirts with red sleeves, red shorts, red and yellow hooped socks.
International matches 2021–22
Honduras (n) 0-4, Qatar (n) 0-4, Panama (n) 1-3, Gibraltar (a) 0-0, Andorra (a) 0-1, El Salvador (n) 1-3, El Salvador (n) 2-2, USA (n) 0-5.
League champions 2020–21: Competition abandoned; *2021–22:* Competition still being played. *Cup winners 2020:* Camerhogne; *2021–:* Not contested.

GUADELOUPE

Ligue Guadelopeenne de Football, Rue de la Ville d'Orly, Bergevin 97110, Pointe-a-Pitre.
Founded: 1958. *CONCACAF:* 2013. *National Colours:* Red shirts with maroon sleeves, red shorts, red socks.
International matches 2021–22
Bahamas (n) 2-0, Guatemala (n) 1-1 (10-9p), Costa Rica (n) 1-3, Jamaica (n) 1-2, Suriname (n) 1-2, Cape Verde (n) 0-2, Martinique† (n) 3-4, Cuba (h) 2-1, Antigua & Barbuda (a) 0-1, Barbados (a) 1-0, Barbados (h) 2-1.
League champions 2020–21: AS Gosier; *2021–22:* Solidarite-Scolaire. *Cup winners 2020:* Phare du Canal; 2021: Solidarite-Scolaire.

GUATEMALA

Federacion Nacional de Futbol de Guatemala, 2a Calle 15-57, Zona 15, Boulevard Vista Hermosa, Guatemala City 01015.
Founded: 1919. *FIFA:* 1946; *CONCACAF:* 1961. *National Colours:* White shirts with blue sash, white shorts with blue trim, white socks.
International matches 2021-22
Mexico (n) 0-3, Trinidad & Tobago (n) 1-1, Nicaragua (h) 2-2, El Salvador (n) 2-0, Cuba (h) 1-0, Haiti (n) 2-1, El Salvador (n) 4-0, Mexico (n) 0-0, French Guiana† (a) 0-2, Belize (h) 2-0, Dominican Republic (a) 1-1, Dominican Republic (h) 2-0.
League champions 2021–22 Malacateco (Apertura); Comunicaciones (Clausura). *Cup winners 2018–19:* Coban Imperial; *2019–:* Not contested.

GUYANA

Guyana Football Federation, Lot 17, Dadanawa Street Section 'K', Campbellville, PO Box 10727, Georgetown.
Founded: 1902. *FIFA:* 1970; *CONCACAF:* 1961. *National Colours:* All yellow.
International matches 2021–22
Bermuda (a) 1-0*, Suriname (a) 1-2, Barbados (n) 5-0, Trinidad & Tobago (a) 1-1, French Guiana† (a) 1-2, French Guiana† (a) 2-1, Montserrat (a) 2-1‡, Bermuda (h) 2-1, Haiti (h) 2-6, Haiti (a) 0-6‡.
** Match played in USA 28.06.21; result omitted from last edition. ‡ Match played in Dominican Republic.*
League champions 2019: Fruta Conquerors; *2020–:* Not contested. *Cup winners 2015:* Slingerz. *2016–:* Not contested.

HAITI

Federation Haitienne de Football, Stade Sylvio Cator, Rue Oswald Durand, Port-au-Prince.
Founded: 1904. *FIFA:* 1933; *CONCACAF:* 1961. *National Colours:* Blue shirts with white sleeves, blue shorts, blue socks.
International matches 2021–22
Canada (n) 1-4, Martinique† (n) 2-1, Bahrain (a) 1-6, Jordan (n) 2-0, Guatemala (n) 1-2, Bermuda (a) 0-0, Montserrat (h) 3-2, Guyana (a) 6-2, Guyana (h) 6-0.
League champions 2020–21: Violette (Ouverture), Competition abandoned (Cloture). *Cup winners:* No competition.

HONDURAS

Federacion Nacional Autonoma de Futbol de Honduras, Colonia Florencia Norte, Edificio Plaza America, Ave. Roble, 1 y 2 Nivle, PO Box 827, Tegucigalpa 504.
Founded: 1935. *FIFA:* 1946; *CONCACAF:* 1961. *National Colours:* All white with blue trim.
International matches 2021-22
Grenada (n) 4-0, Panama (n) 3-2, Qatar (n) 0-2, Mexico (n) 0-3, Canada (a) 1-1, El Salvador (a) 0-0, USA (h) 1-4, Costa Rica (h) 0-0, Mexico (a) 0-3, Jamaica (h) 0-2, Panama (h) 2-3, Costa Rica (a) 1-2, Colombia (n) 1-2, Canada (h) 0-2, El Salvador (h) 0-2, USA (a) 0-3, Panama (a) 1-1, Mexico (h) 0-1, Jamaica (a) 1-2, Curacao (a) 1-0, Curacao (h) 1-2, Canada (h) 2-1.
League champions 2021–22: Olimpia (Apertura), Motagua (Clausura). *Cup winners 2018:* Platense; *2019–:* Not contested.

JAMAICA

Jamaica Football Federation Ltd, 20 St Lucia Crescent, Kingston 5.
Founded: 1910. *FIFA:* 1962; *CONCACAF:* 1963. *National Colours:* Gold shirts with black trim, black shorts, gold socks.
International matches 2021–22
Suriname (n) 2-0, Guadeloupe† (n) 2-1, Costa Rica (n) 0-1, USA (a) 0-1, Mexico (a) 1-2, Panama (h) 0-3, Costa Rica (a) 1-1, USA (a) 0-2, Canada (h) 0-0, Honduras (a) 2-0, El Salvador (a) 1-1, USA (h) 1-1, Peru (a) 0-3, Mexico (h) 1-2, Panama (a) 2-3, Costa Rica (h) 0-1, El Salvador (h) 1-1, Canada (a) 0-4, Honduras (h) 2-1, Suriname (a) 1-1, Suriname (h) 3-1, Mexico (h) 1-1.
League champions 2021: Cavalier; *2022:* Harbour View. *Cup winners 2014:* Reno; *2015–:* Not contested.

MARTINIQUE

Ligue de Football de la Martinique, 2 rue Saint-John Perse, Boite Postale 307, Morne Tartenson 97203, Fort-de-France.
Founded: 1953. *CONCACAF:* 2013. *National Colours:* White shirts with blue trim shirts, white shorts, white socks.
International matches 2021–22
Canada (n) 1-4, USA (a) 1-6, Haiti (n) 1-2, Barbados (h) 3-1, Guadeloupe† (n) 4-3, Costa Rica (a) 0-2, Panama (h) 0-5, Panama (a) 0-0.
League champions 2020–21: Golden Lion; *2021–22:* Golden Lion. *Cup winners 2020:* Club Franciscain; *2021–22:* CO Trenelle.

MEXICO

Federacion Mexicana de Futbol Asociacion, Avenida Arboleda 101, Ex Hacienda Santin, San Mateo Otzacatipan, C.P. 50210 Toluca, Estado de Mexico.
Founded: 1927. *FIFA:* 1929; *CONCACAF:* 1961. *National Colours:* Green shirts with red trim white shorts with red trim, red socks with white trim.
International matches 2021-22
Guatemala (n) 3-0, El Salvador (n) 1-0, Honduras (n) 3-0, Canada (n) 2-1, USA (a) 0-1, Jamaica (h) 2-1, Costa Rica (a) 1-0, Panama (a) 1-1, Canada (h) 1-1, Honduras (h) 3-0, El Salvador (a) 2-0, Ecuador (n) 2-3, USA (a) 0-2, Canada (a) 1-2, Chile (n) 2-2, Jamaica (a) 2-1, Costa Rica (h) 0-0, Panama (h) 1-0, USA (h) 0-0, Honduras (a) 1-0, El Salvador (h) 2-0, Guatemala (n) 0-0, Nigeria (n) 2-1, Uruguay (n) 0-3, Ecuador (n) 0-0, Suriname (h) 3-0, Jamaica (a) 1-0.
League champions 2021–22: Atlas (Apertura), Atlas (Clausura). *Cup winners 2019–20:* Monterrey; *2020–:* Not contested.

MONTSERRAT

Montserrat Football Association Inc., PO Box 505, 1250 Blakes, Plymouth.
Founded: 1994. *FIFA:* 1996; *CONCACAF:* 1996. *National Colours:* Green shirts with white trim, green shorts, green socks.
International matches 2021–22
US Virgin Islands (h) 4-0*, Guyana (h) 1-2, Haiti (a) 2-3, Bermuda (h) 3-2, Bermuda (a) 0-3‡.
** Match played in Dominican Republic; result incorrect in last edition. ‡ Match awarded to Bermuda; Montserrat failed to fulfil fixture.*
League champions: 2016: Royal Montserrat Police Force; 2017–: Not contested. *Cup winners:* No competition.

NICARAGUA

Federacion Nicaraguense de Futbol, Porton Principal del Hospital Bautista 1 Cuadra Abajo, 1 Cuadra al Sur y 1/2 Cuadra Abajo, Apartado Postal 976, Managua.
Founded: 1931. *FIFA:* 1950; *CONCACAF:* 1961. *National Colours:* All blue with white trim.
International matches 2021–22
Guatemala (a) 2-2, Cuba (h) 0-3, Cuba (h) 2-0, Belize (h) 4-0, Belize (h) 1-1, Trinidad & Tobago (h) 2-1, St Vincent/Grenadines (a) 2-2, Bahamas (a) 2-0, Bahamas (h) 4-0.
League champions 2021–22: Diriangen (Apertura), Diriangen (Clausura). *Cup winners 2020:* Diriangen; *2021:* Walter Ferreti; *2022:* Competition still being played.

PANAMA

Federacion Panamena de Futbol, Ciudad Deportiva Irving Saladino, Corregimiento de Juan Diaz, Apartado Postal 0835-394, Zona 10, Ciudad de Panama.
Founded: 1937. *FIFA:* 1938; *CONCACAF:* 1961. *National Colours:* All red.
International matches 2021–22
Curacao (a) 0-0*, Qatar (n) 3-3, Honduras (n) 2-3, Grenada (n) 3-1, Costa Rica (h) 0-0, Jamaica (a) 3-0, Mexico (h) 1-1, El Salvador (a) 0-1, USA (h) 1-0, Canada (a) 1-4, Honduras (a) 3-2, El Salvador (h) 2-1, Peru (a) 1-1, Costa Rica (a) 0-1, Jamaica (h) 3-2, Mexico (a) 0-1, Honduras (h) 1-1, USA (a) 1-5, Canada (h) 1-0, El Salvador (n) 2-3, Costa Rica (h) 2-0, Martinique† (h) 5-0, Uruguay (h)0-5, Martinique† (h) 0-0.
** Match played 15.06.21; result omitted from last edition.*
League champions 2021: Plaza Amador (Apertura), Tauro (Clausura); *2022:* Alianza (Apertura). *Cup winners:* No competition.

PUERTO RICO

Federacion Puertorriquena de Futbol, Calle Los Angeles Final, Plaza de Santurce, Apartado Postal 367567, San Juan 00936.
Founded: 1940. *FIFA:* 1960; *CONCACAF:* 1961. *National Colours:* Red and white striped shirts, blue shorts with white trim, white socks.
International matches 2021–22
Cayman Islands (a) 3-0, British Virgin Islands (h) 6-0.
League champions 2021: Bayamon; *2022:* Metropolitan FA. *Cup winners 2019:* Bayamon; *2020–:* Not contested.

SAINT-MARTIN

Saint-Martin Football Association, PO Box 811-97059, Sandy Ground, Saint-Martin CEDEX.
Founded: 1986. *CONCACAF:* 2013. *National Colours:* Blue shirts with red and white trim, blue shorts, blue socks.
International matches 2021–22
Anguilla (h) 1-2, Bahamas (h) 2-0, Aruba (h) 0-0, Aruba (a) 0-3, St Kitts & Nevis (a) 1-1.
League champions 2021: Concordia. *Cup winners 2021:* Junior.

SINT MAARTEN

Sint Maarten Soccer Association, Airport Road 69, Philipsburg.
Founded: 1986. *CONCACAF:* 2013. *National Colours:* Red shirts, blue shorts, white socks.
International matches 2021–22
Aruba (a) 0-5, US Virgin Islands (h) 1-1, Bonaire† (a) 2-2, Turks & Caicos Islands (h) 8-2*, Turks & Caicos Islands (a) 0-2.
* *Match played in Curacao.*
League champions 2020–21: Flames United; *2021–22:* SCSA Eagles. *Cup winners 2021:* SCSA Eagles; *2022:* SCSA Eagles.

ST KITTS & NEVIS

St Kitts & Nevis Football Association, PO Box 465, Lozack Road, Basseterre.
Founded: 1932. *FIFA:* 1992; *CONCACAF:* 1992. *National Colours:* Red shirts with white trim, green shorts, red socks.
International matches 2021–22
Andorra (a) 0-1, Aruba (a) 3-2, Saint-Martin† (h) 1-1.
League champions 2019–20: St Paul's United Strikers; *2021:* Competition still being played. *Cup winners 2020:* St Paul's United Strikers; *2021–:* Not contested.

ST LUCIA

St Lucia National Football Association, Barnard Hill, PO Box 255, Castries.
Founded: 1979. *FIFA:* 1988; *CONCACAF:* 1986. *National Colours:* Blue shirts with yellow sleeves, blue shorts, blue socks.
International matches 2021–22
Dominica (a) 1-0, Anguilla (h) 2-0.
League champions 2021: Platinum; *2022:* Competition still being played. *Cup winners 2019:* Gros Islet; *2020–:* Not contested.

ST VINCENT & THE GRENADINES

St Vincent & the Grenadines Football Federation, Corner of Grenville and Higginson Street, PO Box 1278, Kingstown.
Founded: 1979. *FIFA:* 1988; *CONCACAF:* 1986. *National Colours:* Yellow shirts, blue shorts with yellow trim, blue socks with yellow trim.
International matches 2021–22
Dominica (a) 1-2, Dominica (a) 1-3, Bahamas (a) 0-1, Nicaragua (h) 2-2, Trinidad & Tobago (h) 0-2, Trinidad & Tobago (a) 1-4.
League champions 2019–20: Hope International; *2020–21:* Competition abandoned. *Cup winners:* No competition.

SURINAME

Surinaamse Voetbal Bond, Letitia Vriesdelaan 7, PO Box 1223, Paramaribo.
Founded: 1920. *FIFA:* 1929; *CONCACAF:* 1961. *National Colours:* White shirts with red and green trim, white shorts, white socks with green tops.
International matches 2021–22
Jamaica (n) 0-2, Costa Rica (n) 1-2, Guadeloupe (n) 2-1, Barbados (h) 1-0, Guyana (h) 2-1, Thailand (a) 0-1, French Guiana† (a) 1-1, Jamaica (h) 1-1, Jamaica (a) 1-3, Mexico (a) 0-3.
League champions 2018–19: Inter Moengotapoe; *2019–21:* Not contested; *2022:* Competition still being played. *Cup winners 2019:* Inter Moengotapoe; *2020–:* Not contested.

TRINIDAD & TOBAGO

Trinidad & Tobago Football Association, 24–26 Dundonald Street, PO Box 400, Port of Spain.
Founded: 1908. *FIFA:* 1964; *CONCACAF:* 1962. *National Colours:* Red shirts with black trim, black shorts, red socks with white tops.
International matches 2021–22
El Salvador (n) 0-2, Guatemala (n) 1-1, Bolivia (a) 0-5, Barbados (h) 9-0, Guyana (h) 1-1, Nicaragua (a) 1-2, Bahamas (h) 1-0, St Vincent/Grenadines (a) 2-0, St Vincent/Grenadines (h) 4-1.
League champions 2019–20: Defence Force; *2021–:* Not contested. *Cup winners 2017:* Williams Connection; *2018–:* Not contested.

TURKS & CAICOS ISLANDS

Turks & Caicos Islands Football Association, TCIFA National Academy, Venetian Road, PO Box 626, Providenciales.
Founded: 1996. *FIFA:* 1998; *CONCACAF:* 1996. *National Colours:* All dark blue with white trim.
International matches 2021–22
Bahamas (a) 2-4, Bahamas (a) 2-1, Bonaire† (h) 1-4, US Virgin Islands (a) 2-3, Sint Maarten† (a) 2-8*, Sint Maarten† (h) 2-0.
* *Match played in Curacao.*
League champions 2021–22: Blue Hills (Apertura); SWA Sharks (Clausura). *Cup winners: 2020:* No competition; *2021:* SWA Sharks.

UNITED STATES OF AMERICA (USA)

US Soccer Federation, US Soccer House, 1801 South Prairie Avenue, Chicago, IL 60616.
Founded: 1913. *FIFA:* 1914; *CONCACAF:* 1961. *National Colours:* White shirts with red and blue trim, blue shorts, white socks with red and blue trim.
International matches 2021–22
Martinique† (n) 1-6, Canada (h) 1-0, Jamaica (h) 1-0, Qatar (h) 1-0, Mexico (h) 1-1, El Salvador (a) 0-0, Canada (h) 1-1, Honduras (a) 4-1, Jamaica (h) 2-0, Panama (a) 0-1, Costa Rica (h) 2-1, Mexico (h) 2-0, Jamaica (a) 1-1, Bosnia-Herzegovina (h) 1-0, El Salvador (h) 1-0, Canada (a) 0-2, Honduras (h) 3-0, Mexico (a) 0-0, Panama (h) 5-1, Costa Rica (a) 0-2, Morocco (h) 3-0, Uruguay (h) 0-0, Grenada (h) 5-0, El Salvador (a) 1-1.
MSL champions 2021: New York City; *2022:* Competition still being played. *Cup winners 2019:* Atlanta United; *2020–:* Not contested. (N.B. Teams from USA and Canada compete in MLS and USL.)

US VIRGIN ISLANDS

USVI Soccer Federation Inc., 23-1 Bethlehem, PO Box 2346, 00851 Christiansted, St Croix.
Founded: 1987. *FIFA:* 1998; *CONCACAF:* 1987. *National Colours:* All royal blue with gold trim.
International matches 2021–22
Anguilla (h) 0-0*, Sint Maarten† (a) 1-1, Turks & Caicos Islands (h) 3-2, Bonaire† (h) 0-2, Bonaire† (a) 0-2.
* *Match played 21.03.21; result omitted from last edition.*
League champions 2018–19: Helenites; *2019–:* Not contested. *Cup winners:* No competition.

OCEANIA (OFC)

AMERICAN SAMOA

Football Federation American Samoa, Pago Park, PO Box 982 413, Pago Pago AS 96799.
Founded: 1984. *FIFA:* 1998; *OFC:* 1998. *National Colours:* All blue with white trim.
International matches 2021–22
None played.
League champions 2020: Not contested; *2021:* Vaiala Tongan. *Cup winners 2014:* Utelai Youth; *2015–:* Not contested.

COOK ISLANDS

Cook Islands Football Association, Matavera Main Road, PO Box 29, Avarua, Rarotonga.
Founded: 1971. *FIFA:* 1994; *OFC:* 1994. *National Colours:* Green shirts with white trim, green shorts, white socks.
International matches 2021–22
Solomon Islands (h) 0-2*.
* *Match played in Qatar.*
League champions 2021: Nikao Sokattack; *2022:* Competition still being played. *Cup winners 2021:* Nikao Sokattack.

FIJI

Fiji Football Association, Taramati Street, Vatuwaqa, PO Box 2514, Suva.
Founded: 1938. *FIFA:* 1964; *OFC:* 1966. *National Colours:* White shirts, black shorts, white socks.
International matches 2021–22
Vanuatu (n) 3-0, New Caledonia (a) 2-1*, New Zealand (a) 0-4*, Papua New Guinea (h) 1-2*, Vanuatu (n) 2-1.
* *Match played in Qatar.*
League champions 2021: Lautoka; *2022:* Competition still being played. *Cup winners 2020:* Suva; *2021–:* Not contested.

KIRIBATI

Kiribati Islands Football Federation, PO Box 416, Betio, Tarawa.
Founded: 1980. *OFC:* 2007. *National Colours:* All red with yellow trim.
International matches 2021–22
None played.
League champions 2019: Betio Town Council; *2020–:* Not contested. *Cup winners:* No competition.

NEW CALEDONIA

Federation Caledonienne de Football, 7 bis, Rue Suffrien, Quartien latin, BP 560, Noumea 99845.
Founded: 1928. *FIFA:* 2004; *OFC:* 2004. *National Colours:* All red with white trim.
International matches 2021–22
Fiji (h) 1-2*, Papua New Guinea (a) 0-1*, New Zealand (a) 1-7*.
* *Match played in Qatar.*
League champions 2021: Hienghene Sport; *2022:* Competition still being played. *Cup winners 2020:* Hienghene Sport; *2021:* Competition abandoned.

NEW ZEALAND

New Zealand Football, Football House, North Harbour Stadium, Stadium Drive, PO Box 301-043, Albany, Auckland.
Founded: 1891. *FIFA:* 1948; *OFC:* 1966. *National Colours:* All white.
International matches 2021–22
Curacao (n) 2-1, Bahrain (a) 1-0, Gambia (n) 2-0, Jordan (n) 1-3, Papua New Guinea (a) 1-0*, Fiji (h) 4-0*, New Caledonia (h) 7-1*, Tahiti (h) 1-0*, Solomon Islands (a) 5-0*, Peru (n) 0-1, Oman (n) 0-0, Costa Rica (n) 0-1.
* *Match played in Qatar.*
League champions 2021: Miramar Rangers. *Cup winners 2021:* Cashmere Technical.

PAPUA NEW GUINEA

Papua New Guinea Football Association, PO Box 371, Port Moresby, National Capital District.
Founded: 1962. *FIFA:* 1966; *OFC:* 1966. *National Colours:* Grey shirts with red with white trim, white shorts with black trim, black socks.
International matches 2021–22
New Zealand (h) 0-1*, New Caledonia (h) 1-0*, Fiji (a) 2-1*, Solomon Islands (a) 2-3*.
* *Match played in Qatar.*
League champions 2019–20: Lae City (formerly Toti City); *2021:* Competition abandoned. *Cup winners:* Not contested since 2006.

SAMOA

Football Federation Samoa, PO Box 1682, Tuana'imato, Apia.
Founded: 1968. *FIFA:* 1986; *OFC:* 1986. *National Colours:* Blue shirts with white trim, white shorts with blue trim, blue socks with white trim.
International matches 2021–22
None played.
League champions 2021: Lupe ole Soaga; *2022:* Competition still being played. *Cup winners: 2018:* Manu-fili; *2019–:* Not contested.

SOLOMON ISLANDS

Solomon Islands Football Federation, Allan Boso Complex, Ranadi Highway, PO Box 584, Honiara.
Founded: 1978. *FIFA:* 1988; *OFC:* 1988. *National Colours:* Yellow shirt, blue shorts, green socks.
International matches 2021–22
Cook Islands (a) 2-0*, Tahiti (h) 3-1*, Papua New Guinea (h) 3-2*, New Zealand (h) 0-5*.
* *Match played in Qatar.*
League champions 2021: Central Coast. *Cup winners:* No competition.

TAHITI

Federation Tahitienne de Football, 751 rue Paul Berniere a Pirae, PO Box 50358, Pirae 98716.
Founded: 1989. *FIFA:* 1990; *OFC:* 1990. *National Colours:* White shirts with red sleeves, white shorts, white socks.
International matches 2021–22
Solomon Islands (a) 1-3*, New Zealand (a) 0-1*.
* *Match played in Qatar.*
League champions 2020–21: AS Pirae; *2021–22:* Competition still being played. *Cup winners 2021:* AS Venus.

TONGA

Tonga Football Association, Loto-Tonga Soko Centre, Valungafulu Road, Atele, PO Box 852, Nuku'alofa.
Founded: 1965. *FIFA:* 1994; *OFC:* 1994. *National Colours:* All red with white trim.
International matches 2021–22
None played.
League champions 2019: Veitongo; *2020–:* Not contested. *Cup winners 2020:* Veitongo; *2021–:* Not contested.

TUVALU

Tuvalu Island Football Association, Tuvalu Sports Ground, Funafuti, tnfatu8@gmail.com.
Founded: 1979. *OFC:* 2006. *National Colours:* Blue shirts with thin white stripes, black shorts, black socks.
International matches 2021–22
None played.
League champions 2021: FC Tofaga; *2022:* Nauti. *Cup winners 2021:* Nanumea; *2022:* Competition still being played.

VANUATU

Vanuatu Football Federation, VFF House, Anabrou, PO Box 266, Port Vila.
Founded: 1934. *FIFA:* 1988; *OFC:* 1988. *National Colours:* Gold shirts with black trim, black shorts with gold trim, gold socks.
International matches 2021–22
Fiji (n) 0-3, Fiji (n) 1-2.
League champions 2020–21: Galaxy; *2021–22:* Competition still being played. *Cup winners: 2019:* Tafea; *2020–:* Not contested.

AFRICA (CAF)

ALGERIA

Federation Algerienne De Football, Chemin Ahmed Ouaked, BP 39, Dely-Ibrahim, Algiers 16000.
Founded: 1962. *FIFA:* 1963; *CAF:* 1964. *National Colours:* All white with green trim.
International matches 2021–22
Djibouti (h) 8-0, Burkina Faso (a) 1-1, Niger (h) 6-1, Niger (a) 0-4, Djibouti (a) 4-0‡, Burkina Faso (h) 2-2, Sudan (n) 4-0, Lebanon (n) 2-0, Egypt (n) 1-1, Morocco (n) 2-2 (5-3p), Qatar (a) 2-1, Tunisia (n) 2-0, Ghana (n) 3-0, Sierra Leone (n) 0-0, Equatorial Guinea (n) 0-1, Ivory Coast (a) 1-3, Cameroon (a) 1-0, Cameroon (h) 1-2, Uganda (h) 2-0, Tanzania (a) 2-0, IR Iran (n) 2-1.
* *Match played in Morocco.* ‡ *Match played in Egypt.*
League champions 2020–21: CR Belouizdad; *2021–22:* CR Belouizdad. *Cup winners 2018–19:* CR Belouizdad; *2019–:* No competition.

ANGOLA

Federacao Angolana de Futetbol, Senado de Compl. da Cidadela Desportiva, BP 3449, Luanda.
Founded: 1979. *FIFA:* 1980; *CAF:* 1980. *National Colours:* Red shirts with yellow trim, black shorts, red socks.
International matches 2021–22
Egypt (a) 0-1, Libya (h) 0-1, Gabon (h) 3-1, Gabon (a) 0-2, Egypt (h) 2-2, Libya (a) 1-1, Guinea-Bissau (n) 3-2, Equatorial Guinea (n) 0-0, Central African Republic (h) 2-1, Madagascar (a) 1-1, Comoros (n) 3-1, Seychelles (n) 3-0, Botswana (n) 0-1.
League champions 2020–21: Sagrada Esperanca. *2021–22:* Petro de Luanda. *Cup winners 2021:* Petro de Luanda; *2021:* Petro de Luanda.

BENIN

Federation Beninoise de Football, Rue du boulevard Djassain, BP 112, 3-eme Arrondissement de Porto-Novo 01.
Founded: 1962. *FIFA:* 1962; *CAF:* 1962. *National Colours:* All yellow with red and green trim.
International matches 2021–22
Madagascar (a) 1-0, DR Congo (h) 1-1, Tanzania (a) 1-0, Tanzania (h) 0-1, Madagascar (h) 2-0, DR Congo (a) 0-2, Liberia (n) 4-0, Zambia (n) 2-1, Togo (n) 1-1, Senegal (a) 1-3, Mozambique (h) 0-1.
League champions 2021–22: Coton Sport. *Cup winners 2019:* ESAE; *2020–:* No competition.

BOTSWANA

Botswana Football Association, PO Box 1396, Gaborone.
Founded: 1970. *FIFA:* 1978; *CAF:* 1976. *National Colours:* Blue shirts with thin black stripes and white sleeves, blue shorts, blue socks.
International matches 2021–22
Zambia (n) 1-2, Eswatini (n) 1-1, Libya (a) 0-1, Tunisia (h) 0-0, Seychelles (n) 1-0, Comoros (n) 1-0, Angola (n) 1-0.
League champions 2021–22: Gaborone United. *Cup winners 2020:* Gaborone United; *2021:* No competition; *2022:* Gaborone United.

BURKINA FASO

Federation Burkinabe de Foot-Ball, Centre Technique National Ouaga 2000, BP 57, Ouagadougou 01.
Founded: 1960. *FIFA:* 1964; *CAF:* 1964. *National Colours:* Green shirts with white trim, green shorts, green socks.
International matches 2021–22
Niger (a) 2-0*, Algeria (h) 1-1*, Djibouti (a) 4-0*, Djibouti (h) 2-0*, Niger (h) 1-1*, Algeria (a) 2-2, Mauritania (n) 0-0, Gabon (n) 3-0, Cameroon (a) 1-2, Cape Verde (n) 1-0, Ethiopia (n) 1-1, Gabon (n) 1-1 (7-6p), Tunisia (n) 1-0, Senegal (n) 1-3, Cameroon (a) 3-3 (3-5p), Kosovo (a) 0-5, Belgium (a) 0-3, Cape Verde (h) 2-0*, Eswatini (a) 3-1‡.
* *Match played in Morocco.* ‡ *Match played in South Africa.*
League champions 2021–22: Rail Club de Kadiogo. *Cup winners 2022:* AS Douanes.

BURUNDI

Federation de Football du Burundi, Avenue Muyinga, BP 3426, Bujumbura.
Founded: 1948. *FIFA:* 1972; *CAF:* 1972. *National Colours:* Red shirts with white trim, white shorts, green socks.
International matches 2021–22
Seychelles (n) 8-1, Comoros (a) 0-1, Myanmar (n) 2-1, Bahrain (a) 0-1, Liberia (n) 2-1, Namibia (a) 1-1*, Cameroon (a) 0-1‡.
* *Match played in South Africa.* ‡ *Match played in Tanzania.*
League champions 2021–22: Flambeau du Centre. *Cup winners 2022:* Bumamuru.

CAMEROON

Federation Camerounaise de Football, Avenue du 27 aout 1940, Tsinga-Yaounde, BP 1116, Yaounde.

Founded: 1959. *FIFA:* 1962; *CAF:* 1963. *National Colours:* Green shirts, red shorts, yellow socks.
International matches 2021–22
Malawi (h) 2-0, Ivory Coast (a) 1-2, Mozambique (h) 3-1, Mozambique (a) 1-0*, Malawi (a) 4-0‡, Ivory Coast (h) 1-0, Burkina Faso (h) 2-1, Ethiopia (h) 4-1, Cape Verde (h) 1-1, Comoros (h) 2-1, Gambia (h) 2-0, Egypt (h) 0-0 (1-3p), Burkina Faso (h) 3-3 (3-5p), Algeria (h) 0-1, Algeria (a) 2-1, Burundi (a) 1-0**.
* *Match played in Morocco.* ‡ *Match played in South Africa.* ***Match played in Tanzania.*
League champions 2021: Coton Sport; *2022:* Coton Sport. *Cup winners 2021–22:* PWD Bamenda.

CAPE VERDE

Federacao Caboverdiana de Futebol, Praia Cabo Verde, FCF CX, PO Box 234, Praia.
Founded: 1982. *FIFA:* 1986; *CAF:* 2000. *National Colours:* All blue with yellow trim.
International matches 2021–22
Central African Republic (a) 1-1*, Nigeria (h) 1-2, Liberia (a) 2-1‡, Liberia (h) 1-0, Central African Republic (h) 2-1, Nigeria (a) 1-1, Ethiopia (n) 1-0, Burkina Faso (n) 0-1, Cameroon (a) 1-1, Senegal (n) 0-2, Guadeloupe† (n) 2-0, Liechtenstein (n) 6-0, San Marino (n) 2-0, Burkina Faso (n) 0-2**, Togo (h) 2-0**, Ecuador (n) 0-1.
* *Match played in Cameroon.* ‡ *Match played in Ghana.* ** *Match played in Morocco.*
League champions 2020, 2021: Competition cancelled; *2022:* Academica de Mindelo. *Cup winners 2020, 2021:* Competition cancelled; *2022:* Competition still being played.

CENTRAL AFRICAN REPUBLIC

Federation Centrafricaine de Football, Avenue des Martyrs, BP 344, Bangui.
Founded: 1961. *FIFA:* 1964; *CAF:* 1965. *National Colours:* All white with blue trim.
International matches 2021–22
Cape Verde (h) 1-1*, Liberia (h) 0-1*, Nigeria (a) 1-0, Nigeria (h) 0-2*, Cape Verde (a) 1-2*, Liberia (a) 1-3‡, Tanzania (a) 1-3, Sudan (n) 0-0, Angola (a) 1-2, Ghana (h) 1-1**.
* *Match played in Cameroon.* ‡ *Match played in Morocco.* ** *Match played in Angola.*
League champions 2021–22: Olympique Real. *Cup winners 2021*: Castel Foot.

CHAD

Federation Tchadienne de Football, BP 886, N'Djamena.
Founded: 1962. *FIFA:* 1964; *CAF:* 1964. *National Colours:* Blue shirts with red and yellow trim, yellow shorts with red and blue trim, red socks.
International matches 2021–22
Gambia (a) 0-1*, Gambia (h) 2-2‡.
* *Match played in Cameroon.* ‡ *Match played in Morocco.*
League champions 2020: Gazelle; *2021–:* Not contested. *Cup winners 2015:* Renaissance; *2016–:* Not contested.

COMOROS

Federation Comorienne de Football, Route d'Itsandra, BP 798, Moroni.
Founded: 1979. *FIFA:* 2005; *CAF:* 2003. *National Colours:* Emerald shirts with dark green sleeves, emerald shorts, emerald socks.
International matches 2021–22
Seychelles (h) 7-1, Burundi (h) 1-0, Sierra Leone (n) 2-0, Malawi (n) 1-2, Gabon (n) 0-1, Morocco (n) 0-2, Ghana (n) 3-2, Cameroon (a) 1-2, Ethiopia (h) 2-1, Lesotho (h) 2-0, Zambia (a) 1-2, Angola (n) 1-1, Botswana (n) 4-1, Seychelles (n) 2-1.
League champions 2020–21: US Zilimadjou; *2021–22:* Volcan Club. *Cup winners 2022:* Gombessa Sport.

CONGO

Federation Congolaise de Football, 80 Rue Eugene Etienne, Centre Ville, BP Box 11, Brazzaville 00 242.
Founded: 1962. *FIFA:* 1964; *CAF:* 1965. *National Colours:* All red with yellow trim.
International matches 2021–22
Namibia (a) 1-1*, Senegal (h) 1-3, Togo (a) 1-1, Togo (h) 1-2, Namibia (h) 1-1, Senegal (a) 0-2, Zambia (n) 1-3, Sierra Leone (n) 1-2, Mali (a) 0-4, Gambia (h) 1-0.
**Match played in South Africa.*
League champions 2021–22: AS Otoho. *Cup winners 2019:* Etoile du Congo; *2020, 2021*: Not contested; *2022:* Competition still being played.

DR CONGO

Federation Congolaise de Football-Association, 31 Avenue de la Justice Kinshasa-Gombe, BP 1284, Kinshasa 1.
Founded: 1919. *FIFA:* 1964; *CAF:* 1964. *National Colours:* Blue shirts with red trim, blue shorts with red trim, red socks.
International matches 2021–22
Tanzania (h) 1-1, Benin (a) 1-1, Madagascar (h) 2-0, Madagascar (a) 0-1, Tanzania (a) 3-0, Benin (h) 2-0, Bahrain (a) 0-1, Morocco (h) 1-1, Morocco (a) 1-4, Gabon (h) 0-1, Sudan (a) 1-2.
League champions 2020–21: AS Vita Club; *2021–22:* TP Mazembe. *Cup winners 2022:* DC Motema Pembe.

DJIBOUTI

Federation Djiboutienne de Football, Centre Technique National, BP 2694, Ville de Djibouti.
Founded: 1979. *FIFA:* 1994; *CAF:* 1994. *National Colours:* Sky blue shirts with green trim, white shorts with sky blue trim, white socks.
International matches 2021–22
Algeria (a) 0-8, Niger (h) 2-4*, Burkina Faso (h) 0-4*, Burkina Faso (a) 0-2*, Algeria (h) 0-4‡, Niger (a) 2-7, South Sudan (h) 2-4‡, South Sudan (a) 0-1**.
* *Match played in Morocco.* ‡ *Match played in Egypt.* ** *Match played in Uganda.*
League champions 2021–22: AS Arta/Solar7. *Cup winners 2022:* AS Arta/Solar7.

EGYPT

Egyptian Football Association, 5 Gabalaya Street, Gezira El Borg Post Office, Cairo.
Founded: 1921. *FIFA:* 1923; *CAF:* 1957. *National Colours:* Red shirts with black and white trim, white shorts, black socks.
International matches 2021–22
Angola (h) 1-0, Gabon (a) 1-1, Liberia (h) 2-0, Libya (h) 1-0, Libya (a) 3-0, Angola (a) 2-2, Gabon (h) 2-1, Lebanon (n) 1-0, Sudan (n) 5-0, Algeria (n) 1-1, Jordan (n) 3-1, Tunisia (n) 0-1, Qatar (a) 0-0 (4-5p), Nigeria (n) 0-1, Guinea-Bissau (n) 1-0, Sudan (n) 1-0, Ivory Coast (a) 0-0 (4-5p), Morocco (n) 2-1, Cameroon (a) 0-0 (1-3p), Senegal (h) 0-0 (2-4p), Senegal (h) 1-0, Senegal (a) 0-1 (1-3p), Guinea (h) 1-0, Ethiopia (a) 0-2*, Korea Republic (a) 1-4.
* *Match played in Malawi.*
League champions 2020–21: Zemalek; *2021–22:* Competition still being played. *Cup winners 2019–20:* Al-Ahly; *2020–21:* Delayed competition still being played.

EQUATORIAL GUINEA

Federacion Ecuatoguineana de Futbol, Avenida de Hassan II, Apartado de correo 1017, Malabo.
Founded: 1957. *FIFA:* 1986; *CAF:* 1986. *National Colours:* Red shirts with white trim, red shorts with white trim, blue socks.
International matches 2021–22
Tunisia (a) 0-3, Mauritania (h) 1-0, Zambia (h) 2-0, Zambia (a) 1-1, Tunisia (h) 1-0, Mauritania (a) 1-1, Ivory Coast (n) 0-1, Algeria (n) 1-0, Sierra Leone (n) 1-0, Mali (n) 0-0 (6-5p), Senegal (n) 1-3, Guinea-Bissau (n) 0-3, Angola (n) 0-0, Tunisia (a) 0-4, Libya (h) 2-0.
League champions 2020, 2021: Not contested; *2021–22:* Deportivo Mongomo. *Cup winners 2019:* Akonangui; *2020, 2021:* Not contested; *2022:* Competition still being played.

ERITREA

Eritrean National Football Federation, Sematat Avenue 29–31, PO Box 3665, Asmara.
Founded: 1996. *FIFA:* 1998; *CAF:* 1998. *National Colours:* All blue with red trim.
International matches 2021–22
None played.
League champions 2019: Red Sea; *2020–:* Not contested. *Cup winners 2013*: Maitemanai; *2013–:* Not contested.

ESWATINI (SWAZILAND)

Eswatini Football Association, Sigwaca House, Plot 582, Sheffield Road, PO Box 641, Mbabane H100.
Founded: 1968. *FIFA:* 1978; *CAF:* 1976. *National Colours:* All blue.
International matches 2021–22
Botswana (n) 1-1, Senegal (n) 2-2 (0-3p), Mozambique (n) 1-1 (4-2p), Somalia (a) 3-0*, Somalia (a) 2-1‡, Mozambique (a) 1-0, Togo (a) 2-2, Burkina Faso (n) 1-3‡, Mauritius (n) 3-0, Malawi (n) 1-1, Lesotho (n) 2-0.
* *Match played in Tanzania.* ‡ *Match played in South Africa.*
League champions 2020–21: Royal Leopards; *2021–22:* Royal Leopards. *Cup winners 2019:* Young Buffaloes; *2020–:* Not contested.

ETHIOPIA

Ethiopia Football Federation, Addis Ababa Stadium, PO Box 1080, Addis Ababa.
Founded: 1943. *FIFA:* 1952; *CAF:* 1957. *National Colours:* Green shirts with yellow and red trim, yellow shorts with green trim, red socks.
International matches 2021–22
Sierra Leone (h) 0-0, Uganda (h) 2-1, Ghana (a) 0-1, Zimbabwe (h) 1-0, South Africa (h) 1-3, South Africa (a) 0-1,

Ghana (h) 1-1*, Zimbabwe (a) 1-1, Sudan (n) 3-2, Cape Verde (n) 0-1, Cameroon (a) 1-4, Burkina Faso (n) 1-1, Comoros (a) 1-2, Lesotho (h) 1-1, Lesotho (h) 1-1, Malawi (a) 1-2, Egypt (h) 2-0‡.
* *Match played in South Africa.* ‡ *Match played in Malawi.*
League champions 2021–22: St George. *Cup winners 2019:* Fasil Kenema; *2020–:* Not contested.

GABON

Federation Gabonaise de Football, BP 181, Libreville.
Founded: 1962. *FIFA:* 1966; *CAF:* 1967. *National Colours:* Yellow shirts with green trim, blue shorts with yellow trim, blue socks.
International matches 2021–22
Libya (a) 1-2, Egypt (h) 1-1, Angola (a) 1-3, Angola (h) 2-0, Libya (h) 1-0, Egypt (a) 1-2, Burkina Faso (n) 0-3, Mauritania (n) 1-1, Comoros (n) 1-0, Ghana (n) 1-1, Morocco (n) 2-2, Burkina Faso (n) 1-1 (6-7p), DR Congo (a) 1-0, Mauritania (h) 0-0.
League champions 2019: Cercle Mberie Sportif; *2020, 2021:* Not contested; *2022:* Competition still being played. *Cup winners: 2019 (League Cup):* Mangasport; *2020–:* Not contested.

GAMBIA

Gambia Football Association, Kafining Layout, Bakau, PO Box 523, Banjul.
Founded: 1952. *FIFA:* 1968; *CAF:* 1966. *National Colours:* Red shirts, blue shorts, green socks.
International matches 2021–22
Sierra Leone (n) 1-2, South Sudan (a) 2-1, New Zealand (n) 0-2, Mauritania (n) 1-0, Mali (n) 1-1, Tunisia (n) 1-0, Guinea (n) 1-0, Cameroon (h) 0-2, Chad (a) 1-0*, Chad (h) 2-2†, UAE (a) 1-1, South Sudan (h) 1-0**, Congo (a) 0-1.
* *Match played in Cameroon.* † *Match played in Morocco.* ** *Match played in Senegal.*
League champions 2021: Fortune; *2021–22:* Competition still being played. *Cup winners 2019:* Real Banjul; *2020, 2021:* Not contested. *2021–22:* Competition still being played.

GHANA

Ghana Football Association, General Secretariat, South East Ridge, PO Box AN 19338, Accra.
Founded: 1957 (dissolved 2018, reconvened 2019). *FIFA:* 1958; *CAF:* 1958. *National Colours:* White shirts with red, yellow and green trim, white shorts, white socks.
International matches 2021–22
Ethiopia (h) 1-0, South Africa (a) 0-1, Zimbabwe (h) 3-1, Zimbabwe (a) 1-0, Ethiopia (a) 1-1*, South Africa (h) 1-0, Algeria (n) 0-3, Morocco (n) 0-1, Gabon (n) 1-1, Comoros (n) 2-3, Nigeria (h) 0-0, Nigeria (a) 1-1, Madagascar (h) 3-0, Central African Republic (h) 1-1‡, Japan (a) 1-4, Chile (n) 0-0 (3-1p).
* *Match played in South Africa.* ‡ *Match played in Angola.*
League champions 2021–22: Asante Kotoko. *Cup winners: 2017–20:* Not contested; *2021:* Hearts of Oak; *2021–22:* Hearts of Oak.

GUINEA

Federation Guinéenne de Football, Annexe 1 du Palais du Peuple, PO Box 3645, Conakry.
Founded: 1960. *FIFA:* 1962; *CAF:* 1963. *National Colours:* Red shirts with yellow trim, yellow shorts with red trim, green socks.
International matches 2021–22
Guinea-Bissau (a) 1-1*, Sudan (a) 1-1‡, Sudan (h) 2-2‡, Morocco (h) 1-4‡, Guinea-Bissau (h) 0-0, Morocco (a) 0-3, Rwanda (a) 0-3, Rwanda (a) 2-0, Malawi (n) 1-0, Senegal (n) 0-0, Zimbabwe (n) 1-2, Gambia (n) 0-1, South Africa (n) 0-0, Egypt (a) 0-1, Malawi (h) 1-0.
* *Match played in Mauritania.* ‡ *Match played in Morocco.*
League champions 2021–22: Horoya. *Cup winners 2019:* Horoya; *2020–:* Not contested.

GUINEA-BISSAU

Federacao de Futebol da Guiné-Bissau, Alto Bandim (Nova Sede), BP 375, Bissau 1035.
Founded: 1974. *FIFA:* 1986; *CAF:* 1986. *National Colours:* All red with green and yellow trim.
International matches 2021–22
Guinea (h) 1-1*, Sudan (a) 4-2, Morocco (a) 0-5, Morocco (h) 0-3‡, Guinea (a) 0-0, Sudan (h) 0-0‡, Sudan (n) 0-0, Egypt (n) 0-1, Nigeria (n) 0-2, Equatorial Guinea (n) 3-0, Angola (n) 2-3, Sao Tome & Principe (h) 5-1‡, Sierra Leone (a) 0-2**.
* *Match played in Mauritania.* ‡ *Match played in Morocco.* ** *Match played in Guinea.*
League champions 2020–21: Sporting de Guiné-Bissau; *2021–22:* Competition still being played. *Cup winners 2021:* Benfica de Bissau; *2022:* Competition still being played.

IVORY COAST

Federation Ivoirienne de Football, Treichville Avenue 1, 01, BP 1202, Abidjan 01.
Founded: 1960. *FIFA:* 1964; *CAF:* 1960. *National Colours:* Orange shirts with white trim, orange shorts, orange socks.
International matches 2021–22
Mozambique (a) 0-0, Cameroon (h) 2-1, Malawi (n) 3-0*, Malawi (n) 2-1‡, Mozambique (h) 3-0‡, Cameroon (a) 0-1, Equatorial Guinea (n) 1-0, Sierra Leone (n) 2-2, Algeria (n) 3-1, Egypt (n) 0-0 (4-5p), France (a) 1-2, England (a) 0-3, Zambia (h) 3-1, Lesotho (a) 0-0*.
* *Match played in South Africa.* ‡ *Match played in Benin.*
League champions 2021–22: ASEC Mimosas. *Cup winners 2019:* FC San Pedro; *2020–:* Not contested.

KENYA

Football Kenya Federation, Nyayo Sports Complex, Kasarani, PO Box 12705, 00400 Nairobi. (FKF suspended by FIFA from February 2022 for political interference.)
Founded: 1960 (KFF); 2011 (FKF). *FIFA:* 1960 (2012); *CAF:* 1968 (2012). *National Colours:* All red with black and white trim.
International matches 2021–22
Uganda (h) 0-0, Rwanda (a) 1-1, Mali (h) 0-5*, Mali (h) 0-1, Uganda (a) 1-1, Rwanda (h) 2-1.
* *Match played in Morocco.*
League champion 2020–21: Tusker; *2021–22:* Tusker. *Cup winners 2021:* Gor Mahia. *2022:* Competition still being played.

LESOTHO

Lesotho Football Association, Bambatha Tsita Sports Arena, Old Polo Ground, PO Box 1879, Maseru 100.
Founded: 1932. *FIFA:* 1964; *CAF:* 1964. *National Colours:* White shirts with blue and green trim, white shorts with green trim, white socks.
International matches 2021–22
South Africa (a) 0-4, Seychelles (h) 0-0*, Seychelles (h) 3-1‡, Ethiopia (a) 1-1, Ethiopia (a) 1-1, Comoros (a) 0-2, Ivory Coast (h) 0-0‡, Malawi (n) 2-1, Mauritius (n) 2-1, Eswatini (n) 0-2.
* *Match played in Mauritius.* ‡ *Match played in South Africa.*
League champion 2021–22: Matlama. *Cup winners 2019:* Matlama; *2020–:* Not contested.

LIBERIA

Liberia Football Association, Professional Building, Benson Street, PO Box 10-1066, Monrovia 1000.
Founded: 1936. *FIFA:* 1964; *CAF:* 1960. *National Colours:* Red and white striped shirts with red sleeves, red shorts, red socks.
International matches 2021–22
Nigeria (a) 0-2, Central African Republic (a) 1-0*, Egypt (a) 0-2, Cape Verde (h) 1-2‡, Cape Verde (a) 0-1, Nigeria (h) 0-2**, Central African Republic (h) 3-1**, Benin (n) 0-4, Sierra Leone (n) 0-1, Burundi (n) 1-2, Morocco (h) 0-2**.
* *Match played in Cameroon.* ‡ *Match played in Ghana.* ** *Match played in Morocco.*
League champions 2021–22: Watanga. *Cup winners 2021–22:* LISCR.

LIBYA

Libyan Football Federation, General Sports Federation Building, Sports City, Goriji, PO Box 5137, Tripoli.
Founded: 1962. *FIFA:* 1964; *CAF:* 1965. *National Colours:* Red shirts, black shorts, green socks.
International matches 2021–22
Gabon (h) 2-1, Angola (a) 1-0, Egypt (a) 0-1, Egypt (h) 0-3, Gabon (a) 0-1, Angola (h) 1-1, Kuwait (a) 0-2, Kuwait (a) 2-0, Niger (n) 2-1, Mauritania (a) 0-2, Botswana (h) 1-0, Equatorial Guinea (a) 0-2.
League champions 2021: Al-Ittihad; *2021–22:* Competition still being played. *Cup winners: 2018:* Al-Ittihad; *2019–21:* Not contested; *2022:* Competition still being played.

MADAGASCAR

Federation Malagasy de Football, 29 Rue de Russie Isoraka, PO Box 4409, Antananarivo 101.
Founded: 1961. *FIFA:* 1964; *CAF:* 1963. *National Colours:* Green shirts with red trim, white shorts with red trim, green socks.
International matches 2021–22
Benin (h) 0-1, Tanzania (a) 2-3, DR Congo (a) 0-2, DR Congo (h) 1-0, Benin (a) 0-2, Tanzania (a) 1-1, Ghana (a) 0-3, Angola (h) 1-1.
League champions 2021–22: CFFA. *Cup winners 2021:* CFFA; *2022:* AS St Michel.

MALAWI

Football Association of Malawi, Chiwembe Technical Centre, Off Chiwembe Road, PO Box 51657, Limbe.
Founded: 1966. *FIFA:* 1968; *CAF:* 1968. *National Colours:* All red with green trim.

International matches 2021–22
Namibia (n) 1-1, Senegal (n) 1-2, Cameroon (a) 0-2, Mozambique (h) 1-0*, Ivory Coast (h) 0-3*, Ivory Coast (a) 1-2‡, Cameroon (h) 0-4*, Mozambique (a) 0-1‡, Comoros (n) 2-1, Guinea (n) 0-1, Zimbabwe (n) 2-1, Senegal (n) 0-0, Morocco (n) 1-2, Ethiopia (h) 2-1, Guinea (a) 0-1, Lesotho (n) 1-2, Malawi (n) 1-1*, Mauritius (n) 2-0.
* *Match played in South Africa.* ‡ *Match played in Benin.*
League champions 2020–21: Nyasa Big Bullets; *2021–22:* Competition still being played. *Cup winners 2015:* CIVO United; *2016–20:* Not contested; *2021:* Silver Strikers.

MALI

Federation Malienne de Football, Avenue du Mali, Hamdallaye ACI 2000, BP 1020, Bamako 0000.
Founded: 1960. *FIFA:* 1964; *CAF:* 1963. *National Colours:* Green shirts with red and yellow trim, yellow shorts, yellow socks.
International matches 2021–22
Rwanda (h) 1-0*, Uganda (a) 0-0, Kenya (h) 5-0*, Kenya (a) 1-0, Rwanda (a) 3-0, Uganda (h) 1-0*, Tunisia (n) 1-0, Gambia (n) 1-1, Mauritania (n) 2-0, Equatorial Guinea (n) 0-0 (5-6p), Tunisia (h) 0-1, Tunisia (a) 0-0, Congo (h) 4-0, South Sudan (a) 3-1‡.
* *Match played in Morocco.* ‡ *Match played in Uganda.*
League champions 2021–22: Djoliba AC. *Cup winners 2022:* Djoliba AC.

MAURITANIA

Federation de Foot-Ball de la Rep. Islamique de Mauritanie, Route de l'Espoire, BP 566, Nouakchott.
Founded: 1961. *FIFA:* 1970; *CAF:* 1968. *National Colours:* Green shirts with yellow and red trim, green shorts, green socks with yellow trim.
International matches 2021–22
Zambia (h) 1-2, Equatorial Guinea (a) 0-1, Tunisia (a) 0-3, Tunisia (h) 0-0, Zambia (a) 0-4, Equatorial Guinea (h) 1-1, Tunisia (n) 1-5, UAE (n) 0-1, Syria (n) 2-1, Burkina Faso (h) 0-0, Gabon (n) 1-1, Gambia (n) 0-1, Tunisia (n) 0-4, Mali (n) 0-2, Mozambique (h) 2-1, Libya (h) 2-0, Sudan (h) 3-0, Gabon (a) 0-0.
League champions 2021–22: FC Nouadhibou. *Cup winners 2021:* ASAC Concorde; *2022:* Competition still being played.

MAURITIUS

Mauritius Football Association, Sepp Blatter House, Trianon.
Founded: 1952. *FIFA:* 1964; *CAF:* 1963. *National Colours:* All red with white trim.
International matches 2021–22
Nepal (a) 0-1, Nepal (a) 0-1, Seychelles (h) 0-0, Sao Tome & Principe (a) 0-1*, Sao Tome & Principe (h) 3-3*, Eswatini (n) 0-3, Lesotho (n) 1-2, Malawi (n) 0-2.
* *Match played in Mauritius.*
League champions 2018–19: Pamplemousses; *2019–:* Not contested. *Cup winners 2019:* Roche-Bois Bolton City; *2020–:* Not contested.

MOROCCO

Federation Royale Marocaine de Football, 51 bis, Avenue Ibn Sina, Agdal BP 51, Rabat 10 000.
Founded: 1955. *FIFA:* 1960; *CAF:* 1959. *National Colours:* Red shirts with green trim, green shorts, red socks.
International matches 2021–22
Sudan (h) 2-0, Guinea-Bissau (h) 5-0, Guinea-Bissau (a) 3-0*, Guinea (a) 4-1*, Sudan (a) 3-0*, Guinea (h) 3-0, Palestine (n) 4-0, Jordan (n) 4-0, Saudi Arabia (n) 1-0, Algeria (n) 2-2 (3-5p), Ghana (n) 1-0, Comoros (n) 2-0, Gabon (n) 2-2, Malawi (n) 2-1, Egypt (h) 1-2, DR Congo (a) 1-1, DR Congo (h) 4-1, USA (a) 0-3, South Africa (h) 2-1, Liberia (a) 2-0*.
* *Match played in Morocco.*
League champions 2021–22: Wydad AC. *Cup winners 2020:* AS FAR; *2021–:* Not contested.

MOZAMBIQUE

Federacao Mocambicana de Futebol, Avenida Samora Machel 11, Caixa Postal 1467, Maputo.
Founded: 1976. *FIFA:* 1980; *CAF:* 1980. *National Colours:* Red shirts with black trim, black shorts, red socks.
International matches 2021–22
Namibia (n) 1-0, South Africa (a) 0-3, Eswatini (n) 1-1 (2-4p), Ivory Coast (h) 0-0, Malawi (a) 0-1*, Cameroon (a) 1-3, Cameroon (a) 0-1‡, Ivory Coast (h) 0-3**, Malawi (n) 1-0**, Niger (n) 1-1, Mauritania (a) 1-2, Eswatini (h) 0-1, Rwanda (h) 1-1*, Benin (a) 1-0.
* *Match played in South Africa.* ‡ *Match played in Morocco.*
** *Match played in Benin.*
League champions 2021: Associacao Black Bulls; *2022:* Competition still being played. *Cup winners 2019:* Uniao Desportiva do Songo; *2020, 2021:* Not contested; *2022:* Competition still being played.

NAMIBIA

Namibia Football Association, Richard Kamuhuka Str., Soccer House, Katutura, PO Box 1345, Windhoek 9000.
Founded: 1990. *FIFA:* 1992; *CAF:* 1992. *National Colours:* Red shirts with white trim, red shorts, red socks with white tops.
International matches 2021–22
Malawi (n) 1-1, Mozambique (n) 0-1, Congo (h) 1-1*, Togo (a) 1-0, Senegal (a) 1-4, Senegal (h) 1-3*, Congo (a) 1-1, Togo (h) 0-1*, Lesotho (n) 1-2, Burundi (h) 1-1*.
* *Match played in South Africa.*
League champions 2018–19: Black Africa; *2019–20:* Not contested; *2021:* Transitional competition abandoned. *Cup winners 2021:* Civics.

NIGER

Federation Nigerienne de Football, Avenue Francois Mitterand, BP 10299, Niamey.
Founded: 1961. *FIFA:* 1964; *CAF:* 1964. *National Colours:* All orange.
International matches 2021–22
Sudan (n) 2-1, Sudan (n) 0-3, Burkina Faso (h) 0-2*, Djibouti (a) 4-2*, Algeria (a) 1-6, Algeria (h) 0-4, Burkina Faso (a) 1-1*, Djibouti (h) 7-2, Mozambique (n) 1-1, Libya (n) 1-2, Tanzania (h) 1-1‡, Uganda (a) 1-1.
* *Match played in Morocco.* ‡ *Match played in Benin.*
League champions 2021–22: ASN Nigelec. *Cup winners 2021:* US Gendarmerie Nationale; *2022:* Competition still being played.

NIGERIA

Nigeria Football Federation, Plot 2033, Olusegun Obasanjo Way, Zone 7, Wuse Abuja, PO Box 5101 Garki, Abuja.
Founded: 1945. *FIFA:* 1960; *CAF:* 1960. *National Colours:* Green shirts with white trim, green shorts, green socks with white trim.
International matches 2021–22
Liberia (h) 2-0, Cape Verde (a) 2-1, Central African Republic (h) 0-1, Central African Republic (a) 2-0*, Liberia (h) 2-0‡, Cape Verde (h) 1-1, Egypt (n) 1-0, Sudan (n) 3-1, Guinea-Bissau (n) 2-0, Tunisia (n) 0-1, Ghana (n) 0-0, Ghana (h) 1-1, Mexico (n) 1-2, Ecuador (n) 0-1, Sierra Leone (h) 2-1, Sao Tome & Principe (a) 10-0‡.
* *Match played in Cameroon.* ‡ *Match played in Morocco.*
League champions 2020–21: Akwa United; *2021–22:* Rivers United. *Cup winners 2021:* Bayelsa United; *2022:* Competition still being played.

RWANDA

Federation Rwandaise de Football Association, BP 2000, Kigali.
Founded: 1972. *FIFA:* 1978; *CAF:* 1976. *National Colours:* Yellow shirts with green trim, green shorts with yellow trim, green socks.
International matches 2021–22
Mali (a) 0-1, Kenya (h) 1-1, Uganda (h) 0-1, Uganda (a) 0-1, Mali (h) 0-3, Kenya (a) 1-2, Guinea (h) 3-0, Guinea (h) 0-2, Mozambique (h) 1-1*, Senegal (h) 0-1‡.
* *Match played in South Africa.* ‡ *Match played in Senegal.*
League champions 2021–22: APR. *Cup winners 2022:* AS Kigali.

SAO TOME & PRINCIPE

Federacao Santomense de Futebol, Rua Ex-Joao de Deus No. QXXIII-426/26, BP 440, Sao Tome.
Founded: 1975. *FIFA:* 1986; *CAF:* 1986. *National Colours:* Yellow shirts with green trim, yellow shorts, yellow socks.
International matches 2021–22
Mauritius (h) 1-0, Mauritius (a) 3-3, Guinea-Bissau (h) 1-5*, Nigeria (h) 0-10*.
* *Match played in Morocco.*
League champions 2019: Agrosport; *2020:* Not contested; *2021–22:* Competition still being played. *Cup winners 2019:* FC Porto Real; *2020:* Not contested; *2021–22:* Competition still being played.

SENEGAL

Federation Senegalaise de Football, VDN Ouest-Foire en face du Cicesi, BP 13021, Dakar.
Founded: 1960. *FIFA:* 1964; *CAF:* 1964. *National Colours:* All white with green, yellow and red trim.
International matches 2021–22
Zimbabwe (n) 2-1, Malawi (n) 2-1, Eswatini (n) 2-2 (3-0p), South Africa (a) 0-0 (4-5p), Togo (h) 2-0, Congo (a) 3-1, Namibia (h) 4-1, Namibia (a) 3-1*, Togo (a) 1-1, Congo (h) 2-0, Zimbabwe (n) 1-0, Guinea (n) 0-0, Malawi (n) 0-0, Cape Verde (n) 2-0, Equatorial Guinea (n) 3-1, Burkina Faso (n) 3-1, Egypt (h) 0-0 (4-2p), Egypt (a) 0-1, Egypt (h) 1-0 (3-1p), Benin (h) 3-1, Rwanda (h) 1-0.
* *Match played in South Africa.*
League champions 2022: Casa Sports. *Cup winners 2021:* Casa Sports; *2022:* Casa Sports.

SEYCHELLES

Seychelles Football Federation, Maison Football, Roche Caiman, PO Box 843, Mahé.
Founded: 1979. *FIFA:* 1986; *CAF:* 1986. *National Colours:* Red shirts with brown sleeves, brown shorts, red socks.
International matches 2021–22
Comoros (n) 1-7, Burundi (n) 1-8, Bangladesh (n) 1-1, Sri Lanka (a) 1-0, Maldives (n) 0-0, Sri Lanka (a) 3-3 (3-1p), Mauritius (a) 0-0, Lesotho (h) 0-0*, Lesotho (h) 1-3‡, Botswana (n) 0-1, Angola (n) 0-3, Comoros (n) 1-2.
* *Match played in Mauritius.* ‡ *Match played in South Africa.*
League champion 2021–22: La Passe. *Cup winners 2020:* Foresters; *2021–:* Not contested.

SIERRA LEONE

Sierra Leone Football Association, 21 Battery Street, Kingtom, PO Box 672, Freetown.
Founded: 1960. *FIFA:* 1960; *CAF:* 1960. *National Colours:* All blue.
International matches
Ethiopia (a) 0-0, South Sudan (n) 1-1, Gambia (n) 2-1, Comoros (n) 0-2, Algeria (n) 0-0, Ivory Coast (n) 2-2, Equatorial Guinea (n) 0-1, Togo (n) 0-3, Liberia (n) 1-0, Congo (n) 2-1, Nigeria (a) 1-2, Guinea-Bissau (h) 2-2*.
* *Match played in Guinea.*
League champions 2021–22: Bo Rangers. *Cup winners: 2016:* FC Johansen; *2017–:* Not contested.

SOMALIA

Somali Football Federation, Mogadishu BN 03040 (DHL only).
Founded: 1951. *FIFA:* 1962; *CAF:* 1968. *National Colours:* Sky blue and white striped shirts, sky blue shorts, royal blue socks.
International matches 2021–22
Eswatini (h) 0-3*, Eswatini (a) 1-2‡.
* *Match played in Tanzania.* ‡ *Match played in South Africa.*
League champions 2021: Horseed; *2022:* Competition still being played. *Cup winners 2020:* Horseed; *2021–:* Not contested.

SOUTH AFRICA

South African Football Association, 76 Nasrec Road, Nasrec, Johannesburg 2000.
Founded: 1991. *FIFA:* 1992; *CAF:* 1992. *National Colours:* Yellow shirts with green trim, green shorts, yellow socks.
International matches 2021–22
Lesotho (h) 4-0, Zambia (h) 0-0, Mozambique (h) 3-0, Senegal (h) 0-0 (5-4p), Zimbabwe (a) 0-0, Ghana (h) 1-0, Ethiopia (a) 3-1, Ethiopia (h) 1-0, Zimbabwe (h) 1-0, Ghana (a) 0-1, Guinea (n) 0-0, France (n) 0-5, Morocco (a) 1-2.
League champions 2021–22: Mamelodi Sundowns. *Cup winners 2021–22:* Mamelodi Sundowns.

SOUTH SUDAN

South Sudan Football Association, Juba National Stadium, Hai Himra, Talata, Juba.
Founded: 2011. *FIFA:* 2012; *CAF:* 2012. *National Colours:* White shirts with red trim, white shorts, white socks.
International matches 2021–22
Sierra Leone (n) 1-1, Gambia (n) 1-2, Uzbekistan (n) 0-3, Djibouti (n) 4-2*, Djibouti (n) 1-0‡, Gambia (n) 0-1**, Mali (n) 1-3‡.
* *Match played in Egypt.* ‡ *Match played in Uganda.* ** *Match played in Senegal.*
League champions 2019: Atlabara; *2020–:* Not contested. *Cup winners 2022:* Al-Hilal (Wau).

SUDAN

Sudan Football Association, Baladia Street, PO Box 437, 11111 Khartoum.
Founded: 1936. *FIFA:* 1948; *CAF:* 1957. *National Colours:* All red with white trim.
International matches 2021–22
Niger (n) 1-2, Niger (h) 3-0, Morocco (a) 0-2, Guinea-Bissau (h) 2-4, Guinea (h) 1-1*, Guinea (a) 2-2*, Morocco (h) 0-3*, Guinea-Bissau (a) 0-0*, Algeria (n) 0-4, Egypt (n) 0-5, Lebanon (n) 0-1, Ethiopia (n) 2-3, Zimbabwe (n) 0-0, Guinea-Bissau (n) 0-0, Nigeria (n) 1-3, Egypt (n) 0-1, Central African Republic (n) 0-0, Tanzania (a) 1-1, Mauritania (a) 0-3, DR Congo (a) 2-1.
**Match played in Morocco.*
League champions 2020–21: Al-Hilal (Omdurman); *2021–22:* Competition still being played. *Cup winners 2018:* Al-Merrikh; *2019–:* Not contested.

TANZANIA

Tanzania Football Federation, Karume Memorial Stadium, Uhuru/Shauri Moyo Road, PO Box 1574, Ilala/Dar Es Salaam.
Founded: 1930. *FIFA:* 1964; *CAF:* 1964. *National Colours:* Blue shirts, black shorts, black socks.
International matches 2021–22
DR Congo (a) 1-1, Madagascar (h) 3-2, Benin (h) 0-1, Benin (a) 1-0, DR Congo (h) 0-3, Madagascar (a) 1-1, Uganda (h) 0-2, Central African Republic (h) 3-1, Sudan (h) 1-1, Niger (n) 1-1*, Algeria (h) 0-2.
* *Match played in Benin.*
League champions 2021–22: Young Africans. *Cup winners 2020–21:* Simba; *2021–22:* Young Africans.

TOGO

Federation Togolaise de Football, Route de Kegoue, BP 05, Lome.
Founded: 1960. *FIFA:* 1964; *CAF:* 1964. *National Colours:* Yellow shirts with green trim, yellow shorts, yellow socks.
International matches 2021–22
Senegal (a) 0-2, Namibia (h) 0-1, Congo (h) 1-1, Congo (a) 2-1, Senegal (h) 0-2, Namibia (a) 0-1*, Sierra Leone (n) 3-0, Benin (n) 1-1, Eswatini (h) 2-2, Cape Verde (h) 0-2‡.
* *Match played in South Africa.*
League champions 2021–22: ASKO de Kara. *Cup winners 2018:* Gomido; *2019–:* Not contested.

TUNISIA

Federation Tunisienne de Football, Stade Annexe d'El Menzah, Cite Olympique, El Menzah 1003.
Founded: 1957. *FIFA:* 1960; *CAF:* 1960. *National Colours:* All white with red trim.
International matches 2021–22
Equatorial Guinea (h) 3-0, Zambia (a) 2-0, Mauritania (h) 3-0, Mauritania (a) 0-0, Equatorial Guinea (a) 0-1, Zambia (h) 3-1, Mauritania (n) 5-1, Syria (n) 0-2, UAE (n) 1-0, Oman (n) 2-1, Egypt (n) 1-0, Algeria (n) 0-2, Mali (n) 0-1, Mauritania (n) 4-0, Gambia (n) 0-1, Nigeria (n) 1-0, Burkina Faso (n) 0-1, Mali (a) 1-0, Mali (n) 0-0, Equatorial Guinea (h) 4-0, Botswana (a) 0-0, Chile (n) 2-0, Japan (a) 3-0.
League champions 2021–22: Esperance de Tunis. *Cup winners 2020–21:* CS Sfaxien; *2021–22:* Competition still being played.

UGANDA

Federation of Uganda Football Associations, FUFA House, Plot No. 879, Wakaliga Road, Mengo, PO Box 22518, Kampala.
Founded: 1924. *FIFA:* 1960; *CAF:* 1960. *National Colours:* Red shirts with yellow and black trim, black shorts, red socks.
International matches 2021–22
Ethiopia (a) 1-2, Kenya (a) 0-0, Mali (h) 0-0, Rwanda (a) 1-0, Rwanda (h) 1-0, Kenya (h) 1-1, Mali (a) 0-1*, Tanzania (a) 2-0, Iceland (n) 1-1, Moldova (n) 3-2, Iraq (a) 0-1, Bahrain (h) 1-3, Tajikistan (n) 1-1 (5-4p), Uzbekistan (a) 2-4, Algeria (a) 0-2, Niger (a) 1-1.
* *Match played in Morocco.*
League champions 2021–22: Vipers. *Cup winners 2021:* Vipers; *2022:* BUL Jinja.

ZAMBIA

Football Association of Zambia, Football House, Alick Nkhata Road, Long Acres, PO Box 34751, Lusaka.
Founded: 1929. *FIFA:* 1964; *CAF:* 1964. *National Colours:* All green.
International matches 2021–22
Botswana (n) 2-1, South Africa (a) 0-0, Mauritania (a) 2-1, Tunisia (h) 0-2, Equatorial Guinea (a) 0-2, Equatorial Guinea (h) 1-1, Mauritania (h) 4-0, Tunisia (a) 1-3, Iraq (a) 1-3, Congo (n) 3-1, Benin (n) 1-2, Ivory Coast (a) 1-3, Comoros (h) 2-1.
League champions 2021–22: Red Arrows. *Cup winners 2007:* Red Arrows; *2008–:* Not contested.

ZIMBABWE

Zimbabwe Football Association, ZIFA House, 53 Livingston Avenue, PO Box CY 114, Causeway, Harare. (ZIFA suspended by FIFA from February 2022 for political interference.)
Founded: 1965. *FIFA:* 1965; *CAF:* 1980. *National Colours:* All gold.
International matches 2021–22
Senegal (n) 1-2, South Africa (h) 0-0, Ethiopia (a) 0-1, Ghana (a) 1-3, Ghana (h) 0-1, South Africa (a) 0-1, Ethiopia (h) 1-1, Sudan (n) 0-0, Senegal (n) 0-1, Malawi (n) 1-2, Guinea (n) 2-1.
League champions 2019: FC Platinum; *2020, 2021:* Not contested; *2021–22:* Competition still being played. *Cup winners 2021:* FC Platinum.

OLYMPIC FOOTBALL 2021 – TOKYO

MEN'S COMPETITION

**After extra time.*

GROUP A
Mexico v France 4-1
Japan v South Africa 1-0
France v South Africa 4-3
Japan v Mexico 2-1
France v Japan 0-4
South Africa v Mexico 0-3

Group A Table	P	W	D	L	F	A	GD	Pts
Japan	3	3	0	0	7	1	6	9
Mexico	3	2	0	1	8	3	5	6
France	3	1	0	2	5	11	–6	3
South Africa	3	0	0	3	3	8	–5	0

GROUP B
New Zealand v Korea Republic 1-0
Honduras v Romania 0-1
New Zealand v Honduras 2-3
Romania v Korea Republic 0-4
Romania v New Zealand 0-0
Korea Republic v Honduras 6-0

Group B Table	P	W	D	L	F	A	GD	Pts
Korea Republic	3	2	0	1	10	1	9	6
New Zealand	3	1	1	1	3	3	0	4
Romania	3	1	1	1	1	4	–3	4
Honduras	3	1	0	2	3	9	–6	3

GROUP C
Egypt v Spain 0-0
Argentina v Australia 0-2
Egypt v Argentina 0-1
Australia v Spain 0-1
Australia v Egypt 0-2
Spain v Argentina 1-1

Group C Table	P	W	D	L	F	A	GD	Pts
Spain	3	1	2	0	2	1	1	5
Egypt	3	1	1	1	2	1	1	4
Argentina	3	1	1	1	2	3	–1	4
Australia	3	1	0	2	2	3	–1	3

GROUP D
Ivory Coast v Saudi Arabia 2-1
Brazil v Germany 4-2
Brazil v Ivory Coast 0-0
Saudi Arabia v Germany 2-3
Saudi Arabia v Brazil 1-3
Germany v Ivory Coast 1-1

Group D Table	P	W	D	L	F	A	GD	Pts
Brazil	3	2	1	0	7	3	4	7
Ivory Coast	3	1	2	0	3	2	1	5
Germany	3	1	1	1	6	7	–1	4
Saudi Arabia	3	0	0	3	4	8	–4	0

QUARTER-FINALS
Spain v Ivory Coast 5-2*
Japan v New Zealand 0-0*
Japan won 4-2 on penalties
Brazil v Egypt 1-0
Korea Republic v Mexico 3-6

SEMI-FINALS
Mexico v Brazil 0-0*
Brazil won 4-1 on penalties
Japan v Spain 0-1*

BRONZE MEDAL MATCH
Mexico v Japan 3-1

GOLD MEDAL MATCH
Yokohama, Saturday 7 August 2021

Brazil (1) 2 *(Cunha 45, Malcom 108)*

Spain (0) 1 *(Oyarzabal 61)*

Brazil: Santos; Carlos, Arana, Alves, Nino, Douglas Luiz, Guimaraes, Cunha (Malcom 91), Antony (Menino 112), Claudinho (Reinier 106), Richarlison (Paulinho 114).
Spain: Simon; Cucurella (Miranda 91), Torres, Garcia, Gil O (Vallejo 91), Zubimendi (Moncayola 112), Merino (Soler 46), Gonzalez, Asensio (Gil B 46), Oyarzabal (Mir 104), Olmo.
aet. Referee: Chris Beath (Australia).

WOMEN'S COMPETITION

GROUP E
Great Britain v Chile 2-0
Japan v Canada 1-1
Chile v Canada 1-2
Japan v Great Britain 0-1
Chile v Japan 0-1
Canada v Great Britain 1-1

Group E Table	P	W	D	L	F	A	GD	Pts
Great Britain	3	2	1	0	4	1	3	7
Canada	3	1	2	0	4	3	1	5
Japan	3	1	1	1	2	2	0	4
Chile	3	0	0	3	1	5	–4	0

GROUP F
China PR v Brazil 0-5
Zambia v Netherlands 3-10
China PR v Zambia 4-4
Netherlands v Brazil 3-3
Netherlands v China PR 8-2
Brazil v Zambia 1-0

Group F Table	P	W	D	L	F	A	GD	Pts
Netherlands	3	2	1	0	21	8	13	7
Brazil	3	2	1	0	9	3	6	7
Zambia	3	0	1	2	7	15	–8	1
China PR	3	0	1	2	6	17	–11	1

GROUP G
Sweden v United States 3-0
Australia v New Zealand 2-1
Sweden v Australia 4-2
New Zealand v United States 1-6
New Zealand v Sweden 0-2
United States v Australia 0-0

Group G Table	P	W	D	L	F	A	GD	Pts
Sweden	3	3	0	0	9	2	7	9
United States	3	1	1	1	6	4	2	4
Australia	3	1	1	1	4	5	–1	4
New Zealand	3	0	0	3	2	10	–8	0

QUARTER-FINALS
Canada v Brazil 0-0*
Canada won 4-3 on penalties
Great Britain v Australia 3-4*
Sweden v Japan 3-1
Netherlands v United States 2-2*
USA won 4-2 on penalties

SEMI-FINALS
United States v Canada 0-1
Australia v Sweden 0-1

BRONZE MEDAL MATCH
Australia v United States 3-4

GOLD MEDAL MATCH
Yokohama, Friday 6 August 2021

Sweden (1) 1 *(Blackstenius 34)*

Canada (0) 1 *(Fleming 68 pen)*

Sweden: Lindahl; Glas, Eriksson (Andersson 75), Ilestedt (Kullberg 120), Bjorn, Asllani, Jakobsson (Hurtig 75), Angeldal (Bennison 75), Seger, Rolfo (Schough 106), Blackstenius (Anvegard 106).
Canada: Labbe; Chapman (Riviere 93), Buchanan, Lawrence, Gilles, Quinn (Grosso 46), Scott (Zadorsky 120), Sinclair (Huitema 86), Fleming, Prince (Rose 63), Beckie (Leon 46).
aet; Canada won 3-2 on penalties
Referee: Anastasia Pustovoitova (Russia).

EUROPEAN FOOTBALL CHAMPIONSHIP 1960–2020

Year	Winners v Runners-up		Venue	Attendance	Referee
1960	USSR v Yugoslavia	2-1*	Paris	17,966	A. E. Ellis (England)
	Winning Coach: Gavriil Kachalin				
1964	Spain v USSR	2-1	Madrid	79,115	A. E. Ellis (England)
	Winning Coach: Jose Villalonga				
1968	Italy v Yugoslavia	1-1	Rome	68,817	G. Dienst (Switzerland)
Replay	Italy v Yugoslavia	2-0	Rome	32,866	J. M. O. de Mendibil (Spain)
	Winning Coach: Ferruccio Valcareggi				
1972	West Germany v USSR	3-0	Brussels	43,066	F. Marschall (Austria)
	Winning Coach: Helmut Schon				
1976	Czechoslovakia v West Germany	2-2	Belgrade	30,790	S. Gonella (Italy)
	Czechoslovakia won 5-3 on penalties.				
	Winning Coach: Vaclav Jezek				
1980	West Germany v Belgium	2-1	Rome	47,860	N. Rainea (Romania)
	Winning Coach: Jupp Derwall				
1984	France v Spain	2-0	Paris	47,368	V. Christov (Slovakia)
	Winning Coach: Michel Hidalgo				
1988	Netherlands v USSR	2-0	Munich	62,770	M. Vautrot (France)
	Winning Coach: Rinus Michels				
1992	Denmark v Germany	2-0	Gothenburg	37,800	B. Galler (Switzerland)
	Winning Coach: Richard Moller Nielsen				
1996	Germany v Czech Republic	2-1*	Wembley	73,611	P. Pairetto (Italy)
	Germany won on sudden death 'golden goal'.				
	Winning Coach: Berti Vogts				
2000	France v Italy	2-1*	Rotterdam	48,200	A. Frisk (Sweden)
	France won on sudden death 'golden goal'.				
	Winning Coach: Roger Lemerre				
2004	Greece v Portugal	1-0	Lisbon	62,865	M. Merk (Germany)
	Winning Coach: Otto Rehhagel				
2008	Spain v Germany	1-0	Vienna	51,428	R. Rosetti (Italy)
	Winning Coach: Luis Aragones				
2012	Spain v Italy	4-0	Kyiv	63,170	P. Proenca (Portugal)
	Winning Coach: Vicente del Bosque				
2016	Portugal v France	1-0*	Paris	75,868	M. Clattenburg (England)
	Winning Coach: Fernando Santos				
2020†	Italy v England	1-1*	Wembley	67,173	B. Kuipers (Netherlands)
	Italy won 3-2 on penalties.				
	Winning Coach: Roberto Mancini				

**After extra time. †Postponed until 2021 due to COVID-19 pandemic.*

UEFA NATIONS LEAGUE 2020–21

■ *Denotes player sent off.*

SEMI-FINALS LEAGUE A

Wednesday, 6 October 2021

Italy (0) 1 *(Pellegrini 83)*

Spain (2) 2 *(Torres F 17, 45)* 33,524

Italy: (433) Donnarumma; Di Lorenzo, Bonucci■, Bastoni, Emerson Palmieri; Barella (Calabria 72), Jorginho (Pellegrini 64), Verratti (Locatelli 58); Chiesa, Bernardeschi (Chiellini 46), Insigne (Kean 58).
Spain: (433) Simon; Azpilicueta, Laporte, Torres P, Alonso; Gavi (Sergi Roberto 83), Busquets, Koke (Merino 75); Torres F (Pino 49), Sarabia (Gil B 75), Oyarzabal.
Referee: Sergei Karasev.

Thursday, 7 October 2021

Belgium (2) 2 *(Carrasco 37, Lukaku 40)*

France (0) 3 *(Benzema 62, Mbappe-Lottin 69 (pen), Hernandez T 90)* 12,409

Belgium: (343) Courtois; Alderweireld, Denayer, Vertonghen; Castagne (Batshuayi 90), Witsel, Tielemans (Vanaken 70), Carrasco; De Bruyne, Lukaku, Hazard E (Trossard 74).
France: (3412) Lloris; Kounde, Varane, Hernandez L; Pavard (Dubois 90), Pogba, Rabiot (Tchouameni 75), Hernandez T; Griezmann; Benzema (Veretout 90), Mbappe-Lottin.
Referee: Daniel Siebert.

THIRD PLACE PLAY-OFF

Sunday, 10 October 2021

Italy (0) 2 *(Barella 46, Berardi 65 (pen))*

Belgium (0) 1 *(De Ketelaere 86)* 16,724

Italy: (433) Donnarumma; Di Lorenzo, Acerbi, Bastoni, Emerson Palmieri; Barella (Cristante 70), Locatelli, Pellegrini (Jorginho 70); Berardi (Insigne 90), Raspadori (Kean 65), Chiesa (Bernardeschi 90).
Belgium: (343) Courtois; Alderweireld, Denayer, Vertonghen; Castagne, Witsel, Tielemans (De Bruyne 59), Carrasco (Trossard 87); Saelemaekers (De Ketelaere 59), Batshuayi, Vanaken.
Referee: Srdjan Jovanovic.

FINAL

Sunday, 10 October 2021

Spain (0) 1 *(Oyarzabal 64)*

France (0) 2 *(Benzema 66, Mbappe-Lottin 80)* 31,511

Spain: (433) Simon; Azpilicueta, Garcia, Laporte, Alonso; Gavi (Koke 75), Busquets, Rodri (Fornals 84); Torres F (Merino 84), Oyarzabal, Sarabia (Pino 61).
France: (3412) Lloris; Kounde, Varane (Upamecano 43), Kimpembe; Pavard (Dubois 80), Tchouameni, Pogba, Hernandez T; Griezmann (Veretout 90); Mbappe-Lottin, Benzema.
Referee: Anthony Taylor.

FIFA WORLD CUP 2022 QUALIFYING – EUROPE

▪ *Denotes player sent off.*

GROUP A

Wednesday, 1 September 2021

Luxembourg (2) 2 *(Mica Pinto 8, Rodrigues 28 (pen))*
Azerbaijan (0) 1 *(Mahmudov 67)* 2000

Luxembourg: (4132) Moris; Jans, Mahmutovic, Carlson, Mica Pinto (Veiga 76); Martins Pereira; Barreiro, Thill S (Deville 90), Thill O (Bohnert 74); Sinani (Skenderovic 90), Rodrigues.
Azerbaijan: (532) Mahammadaliyev; Huseynov A (Krivotsyuk 46), Haghverdi, Medvedev, Salahli (Sadikhov 68), Bayramov; Ibrahhimli (Alasgarov 46), Garayev (Nuriyev 74), Mahmudov; Ozobic, Ghorbani (Emreli 46).

Portugal (0) 2 *(Ronaldo 89, 90)*
Republic of Ireland (1) 1 *(Egan 45)* 7831

Portugal: (433) Rui Patricio; Joao Cancelo (Goncalo Guedes 82), Pepe, Dias, Guerreiro (Nuno Mendes 62); Bernardo Silva, Joao Palhinha (Joao Moutinho 73), Bruno Fernandes (Joao Mario 62); Rafa Silva (Andre Silva 46), Ronaldo, Jota.
Republic of Ireland: (3421) Bazunu; O'Shea (Omobamidele 35), Duffy, Egan; Coleman, Hendrick, Cullen, Doherty; McGrath (Molumby 90), Connolly (McClean 72); Idah (Collins 90).

Saturday, 4 September 2021

Republic of Ireland (0) 1 *(Duffy 87)*
Azerbaijan (1) 1 *(Mahmudov 45)* 21,287

Republic of Ireland: (3421) Bazunu; Coleman, Duffy, Egan; Doherty (Collins 80), Molumby (Hourihane 63), Cullen (Browne 88), McClean; Parrott (Robinson 63), Connolly (Horgan 46); Idah.
Azerbaijan: (433) Mahammadaliyev; Medvedev (Huseynov A 70), Badalov, Haghverdi, Krivotsyuk; Mahmudov, Garayev, Bayramov (Salahli 70); Alasgarov (Akhmedzade 71), Emreli (Sheydayev 79), Ozobic (Nuriyev 80).

Serbia (2) 4 *(Mitrovic A 22, 35, Chanot 81 (og), Milenkovic 90)*
Luxembourg (0) 1 *(Thill O 77)* 10,078

Serbia: (343) Rajkovic; Milenkovic, Nastasic (Veljkovic 84), Pavlovic; Lazovic (Vlahovic 70), Lukic (Radonjic 70), Gudelj, Kostic; Tadic (Nemanja Maksimovic 90), Mitrovic A (Jovic 84), Milinkovic-Savic S.
Luxembourg: (532) Moris; Jans, Mahmutovic (Thill O 46), Chanot (Skenderovic 89), Carlson, Mica Pinto; Barreiro, Martins Pereira, Thill S (Borges Sanches 90); Sinani (Deville 89), Rodrigues▪.

Tuesday, 7 September 2021

Azerbaijan (0) 0
Portugal (2) 3 *(Bernardo Silva 26, Andre Silva 31, Jota 75)* 20,574

Azerbaijan: (541) Mahammadaliyev; Huseynov A, Badalov, Haghverdi, Salahli (Sadikhov 76), Khalilzade (Ghorbani 46); Mahmudov, Emreli (Bayramov 63), Garayev (Nuriyev 46), Ozobic (Mustafayev 62); Alasgarov.
Portugal: (4231) Rui Patricio; Joao Cancelo, Pepe, Dias, Guerreiro (Nuno Mendes 71); Joao Palhinha (Neves 46), Joao Moutinho (Joao Mario 78); Bernardo Silva (Otavio 78), Bruno Fernandes, Jota (Goncalo Guedes 78); Andre Silva.

Republic of Ireland (0) 1 *(Milenkovic 86 (og))*
Serbia (1) 1 *(Milinkovic-Savic S 20)* 25,415

Republic of Ireland: (3511) Bazunu; Omobamidele, Duffy, Egan; Doherty, McGrath (Horgan 66), Cullen (Molumby 66), Hendrick (Hourihane 78), McClean; Browne (Robinson 58); Idah (Collins 78).
Serbia: (3412) Rajkovic; Milenkovic, Veljkovic, Pavlovic; Djuricic (Radonjic 71), Milinkovic-Savic S, Gudelj, Kostic (Lazovic 87); Tadic (Nemanja Maksimovic 83); Vlahovic (Jovic 70), Mitrovic A.

Saturday, 9 October 2021

Azerbaijan (0) 0
Republic of Ireland (2) 3 *(Robinson 7, 39, Ogbene 90)* 6852

Azerbaijan: (541) Mahammadaliyev; Huseynov A, Haghverdi, Medvedev, Krivotsyuk (Dadashov 79), Bayramov (Abdullayev 63); Alasgarov (Sheydayev 63), Mahmudov (Sadikhov 86), Garayev, Ozobic; Emreli.
Republic of Ireland: (3421) Bazunu; Omobamidele, Duffy, Egan; Doherty, Cullen (Hourihane 90), Hendrick, McClean; Robinson (Parrott 90), Horgan (McGrath 46); Idah (Ogbene 59).

Luxembourg (0) 0
Serbia (0) 1 *(Vlahovic 68)* 2000

Luxembourg: (4141) Moris; Jans, Chanot, Carlson, Mica Pinto; Thill O (Muratovic 90); Deville (Omosanya 74), Barreiro, Thill S, Borges Sanches; Sinani.
Serbia: (3412) Rajkovic; Veljkovic, Nastasic, Pavlovic (Spajic 46); Djuricic (Radonjic 46), Milinkovic-Savic S, Gudelj (Lukic 70), Kostic (Lazovic 70); Tadic; Vlahovic, Mitrovic A (Nemanja Maksimovic 87).

Tuesday, 12 October 2021

Portugal (3) 5 *(Ronaldo 8 (pen), 13 (pen), 87, Bruno Fernandes 17, Joao Palhinha 69)*
Luxembourg (0) 0 18,553

Portugal: (433) Rui Patricio; Joao Cancelo, Pepe, Dias, Nuno Mendes; Bruno Fernandes (Goncalo Guedes 80), Joao Palhinha (Neves 73), Joao Moutinho (Joao Mario 65); Bernardo Silva (Matheus Luiz 80), Ronaldo, Andre Silva (Leao 73).
Luxembourg: (451) Moris; Jans, Chanot, Carlson, Mica Pinto (Muratovic 87); Thill O (Borges Sanches 46), Barreiro, Martins Pereira, Thill S (Deville 46), Rodrigues; Sinani (Veiga 88).

Serbia (1) 3 *(Vlahovic 30 (pen), 52, Tadic 83 (pen))*
Azerbaijan (1) 1 *(Mahmudov 45)* 5890

Serbia: (3412) Rajkovic; Veljkovic, Mitrovic S, Nastasic; Lazovic (Mladenovic 88), Grujic (Tadic 66), Lukic, Kostic (Radonjic 75); Milinkovic-Savic S; Jovic (Mitrovic A 65), Vlahovic (Nemanja Maksimovic 88).
Azerbaijan: (3412) Mahammadaliyev; Medvedev, Haghverdi, Krivotsyuk; Huseynov A (Mutallimov 63), Mahmudov (Mustafayev 84), Garayev, Salahli; Ozobic (Alasgarov 73); Dadashov (Sheydayev 73), Abdullayev (Nuriyev 73).

Thursday, 11 November 2021

Azerbaijan (0) 1 *(Salahli 82)*
Luxembourg (0) 3 *(Rodrigues 67, 90, Thill S 78)* 2986

Azerbaijan: (3412) Mahammadaliyev; Medvedev, Mustafazade, Krivotsyuk; Mutallimov▪, Mahmudov, Garayev, Salahli (Abdullayev 83); Ozobic (Akhmedzade 68); Emreli (Alasgarov 83), Sheydayev (Dadashov 68).
Luxembourg: (451) Schon; Jans (Bohnert 72), Chanot, Carlson, Mica Pinto; Sinani (Thill S 72), Barreiro, Martins Pereira, Thill O (Olesen 88), Borges Sanches (Deville 57); Rodrigues.

Republic of Ireland (0) 0
Portugal (0) 0 50,737

Republic of Ireland: (343) Bazunu; Coleman, Duffy, Egan; Doherty, Hendrick (Hourihane 78), Cullen, Stevens (McClean 78); Ogbene (Keane 90), Robinson, McGrath (Idah 61).
Portugal: (433) Rui Patricio; Nelson Semedo, Pepe▪, Danilo Pereira, Dalot; Joao Palhinha, Matheus Luiz (Joao Moutinho 57), Bruno Fernandes (Sanches 75); Goncalo Guedes (Leao 56 (Fonte 83)), Andre Silva (Joao Felix 75), Ronaldo.

Sunday, 14 November 2021

Luxembourg (0) 0

Republic of Ireland (0) 3 *(Duffy 67, Ogbene 75, Robinson 88)* 9268

Luxembourg: (4141) Schon; Jans, Chanot, Selimovic, Mica Pinto; Martins Pereira (Thill S 86); Sinani, Barreiro, Thill O, Borges Sanches (Deville 52); Rodrigues.
Republic of Ireland: (3421) Bazunu; Coleman, Duffy, Egan; Doherty (Parrott 90), Hendrick, Cullen (Hourihane 90), McClean; Ogbene (Browne 82), Robinson (Omobamidele 90); Idah (Knight 62).

Portugal (1) 1 *(Sanches 2)*

Serbia (1) 2 *(Tadic 33, Mitrovic A 90)* 58,873

Portugal: (433) Rui Patricio; Joao Cancelo, Fonte, Dias, Nuno Mendes; Sanches (Neves 84), Danilo Pereira (Andre Silva 90), Joao Moutinho (Joao Palhinha 64); Bernardo Silva (Bruno Fernandes 64), Ronaldo, Jota (Joao Felix 83).
Serbia: (3511) Rajkovic; Milenkovic, Veljkovic (Spajic 65), Pavlovic; Zivkovic (Radonjic 69), Lukic, Gudelj (Mitrovic A 46), Milinkovic-Savic S, Kostic (Jovic 89); Tadic; Vlahovic.

Group A Table	P	W	D	L	F	A	GD	Pts
Serbia	8	6	2	0	18	9	9	20
Portugal	8	5	2	1	17	6	11	17
Republic of Ireland	8	2	3	3	11	8	3	9
Luxembourg	8	3	0	5	8	18	−10	9
Azerbaijan	8	0	1	7	5	18	−13	1

GROUP B

Thursday, 2 September 2021

Georgia (0) 0

Kosovo (1) 1 *(Muriqi 18)* 122

Georgia: (4231) Loria; Chabradze, Kashia, Khocholava, Azarovi; Kankava, Aburjania (Davitashvili 77); Tsitaishvili, Qazaishvili (Mikautadze 60), Kiteishvili L (Azouz 12); Kvilitaia (Chakvetadze 77).
Kosovo: (433) Muric; Vojvoda, Rrahmani, Aliti, Hadergjonaj; Halimi (Loshaj 68), Dresevic, Berisha V (Kryeziu 90); Kastrati (Bytyqi 68), Muriqi, Rashani (Shala 90).

Sweden (1) 2 *(Isak 5, Claesson 57)*

Spain (1) 1 *(Carlos Soler 4)* 16,901

Sweden: (442) Olsen; Krafth, Lindelof, Helander, Augustinsson; Claesson, Olsson K, Ekdal (Cajuste 69), Forsberg (Svanberg 90); Kulusevski (Quaison 85), Isak (Thelin 85).
Spain: (433) Simon; Azpilicueta, Garcia, Laporte, Jordi Alba; Carlos Soler (Mendez 85), Busquets (Rodri 85), Koke (Llorente M 75); Torres F, Morata (Sarabia 75), Gerard (Traore 64).

Sunday, 5 September 2021

Kosovo (0) 1 *(Muriqi 90)*

Greece (1) 1 *(Douvikas 45)* 1200

Kosovo: (433) Muric; Vojvoda, Rrahmani, Aliti (Fazliji 78), Hadergjonaj; Halimi (Muslija 84), Dresevic, Berisha V (Loshaj 78); Kastrati (Bytyqi 46), Muriqi, Rashica.
Greece: (532) Vlachodimos; Androutsos, Mavropanos, Tzavelas, Giannoulis, Tsimikas (Papadopoulos 89); Bakasetas, Bouchalakis, Siopis; Douvikas (Mandalos 63), Pavlidis (Fountas 80).

Spain (3) 4 *(Gaya 14, Carlos Soler 25, Torres F 41, Sarabia 63)*

Georgia (0) 0 8444

Spain: (433) Simon (Sanchez 74); Azpilicueta, Garcia (Merino 61), Laporte (Albiol 46), Gaya (Mendez 73); Llorente M, Rodri, Carlos Soler; Torres F (Fornals 60), Ruiz, Sarabia.
Georgia: (451) Loria; Chabradze, Kashia, Lochoshvili, Giorbelidze (Kakabadze 76); Davitashvili (Chakvetadze 69), Mamuchashvili, Kankava, Aburjania (Altunashvili 69), Azarovi (Qazaishvili 57); Zaria (Mikautadze 57).

Wednesday, 8 September 2021

Greece (0) 2 *(Bakasetas 62, Pavlidis 74)*

Sweden (0) 1 *(Quaison 80)* 3475

Greece: (343) Vlachodimos; Chatzidiakos, Mavropanos, Tzavelas; Androutsos, Zeca, Bouchalakis, Tsimikas; Bakasetas, Pavlidis (Vrousai 90), Douvikas (Tzolis 71).
Sweden: (442) Olsen; Johansson (Krafth 76), Lindelof, Helander (Danielson 88), Augustinsson; Claesson (Karlsson 77), Olsson K, Svanberg (Quaison 66), Forsberg; Kulusevski (Thelin 88), Isak.

Kosovo (0) 0

Spain (1) 2 *(Fornals 32, Torres F 88)* 1200

Kosovo: (442) Muric; Hadergjonaj, Rrahmani, Fazliji, Vojvoda; Rashani, Loshaj, Dresevic, Bytyqi; Muriqi, Rashica.
Spain: (433) Simon; Llorente M (Merino 86), Laporte, Martinez, Reguilon (Albiol 86); Koke, Busquets, Carlos Soler (Azpilicueta 58); Torres F, Morata (Sarabia 72), Fornals (Traore 59).

Saturday, 9 October 2021

Georgia (0) 0

Greece (0) 2 *(Bakasetas 90 (pen), Pelkas 90)*

Georgia: (4231) Loria; Kakabadze, Khocholava, Dvali, Giorbelidze; Aburjania (Davitashvili 90), Kankava; Lobzhanidze (Kvilitaia 90), Chakvetadze (Gvilia 60), Kvaratskhelia; Mikautadze (Okriashvili 60).
Greece: (352) Vlachodimos; Chatzidiakos, Mavropanos, Tzavelas; Androutsos, Bakasetas, Siopis (Mandalos 85), Bouchalakis, Tsimikas; Masouras (Tzolis 78), Pavlidis (Pelkas 46).

Sweden (1) 3 *(Forsberg 29 (pen), Isak 62, Quaison 79)*

Kosovo (0) 0 44,213

Sweden: (442) Olsen; Krafth, Danielson, Nilsson, Augustinsson; Claesson, Olsson K (Eriksson 90), Ekdal (Cajuste 85), Forsberg (Svanberg 85); Kulusevski (Gyokeres 90), Isak (Quaison 75).
Kosovo: (442) Muric; Hadergjonaj, Rrahmani, Aliti, Vojvoda (Domgjoni 73); Rashani (Muslija 87), Loshaj (Fazliji 87), Dresevic, Bytyqi (Selmani 70); Muriqi, Rashica.

Tuesday, 12 October 2021

Kosovo (1) 1 *(Muriqi 45 (pen))*

Georgia (1) 2 *(Okriashvili 11, Davitashvili 82)* 3550

Kosovo: (433) Muric; Vojvoda, Rrahmani, Fazliji, Aliti (Selmani 86); Halimi (Loshaj 74), Dresevic, Celina (Muslija 86); Rashani (Kastrati 59), Muriqi, Rashica (Bytyqi 73).
Georgia: (343) Loria; Kakabadze, Kashia, Dvali; Lobzhanidze (Mamuchashvili 90), Gvilia, Kvekveskiri, Giorbelidze (Azarovi 80); Tsitaishvili (Chabradze 72), Okriashvili (Kvilitaia 72), Kvaratskhelia (Davitashvili 72).

Sweden (0) 2 *(Forsberg 59 (pen), Isak 69)*

Greece (0) 0 47,314

Sweden: (442) Olsen; Krafth, Lindelof, Danielson, Augustinsson; Claesson (Svanberg 82), Olsson K, Ekdal (Cajuste 82), Forsberg (Olsson M 87); Quaison (Gyokeres 87), Isak.
Greece: (352) Vlachodimos; Chatzidiakos■, Mavropanos, Tsimikas; Androutsos, Bakasetas, Siopis (Pelkas 71), Bouchalakis, Giannoulis (Limnios 84); Masouras (Tzolis 71), Pavlidis (Douvikas 75).

Thursday, 11 November 2021

Georgia (0) 2 *(Kvaratskhelia 61, 77)*

Sweden (0) 0 6800

Georgia: (3421) Loria; Kakabadze, Kashia, Khocholava; Lobzhanidze (Chabradze 81), Gvilia, Kvekveskiri (Aburjania 90), Azarovi; Tsitaishvili (Davitashvili 70), Kvaratskhelia (Qazaishvili 80); Okriashvili (Volkovi 70).
Sweden: (442) Olsen; Krafth, Lindelof, Nilsson, Augustinsson; Claesson (Kulusevski 74), Svanberg (Quaison 78), Olsson K, Forsberg; Isak (Karlsson 87), Ibrahimovic.

Greece (0) 0

Spain (1) 1 *(Sarabia 26 (pen))* 7825

Greece: (541) Vlachodimos; Androutsos, Goutas, Tzavelas, Tsimikas, Giannoulis (Limnios 67); Masouras (Tzolis 46), Siopis, Bouchalakis (Pelkas 78), Mandalos; Pavlidis (Douvikas 46).
Spain: (433) Simon; Carvajal, Laporte, Martinez (Azpilicueta 89), Gaya; Koke, Rodri, Gavi (Busquets 65); Sarabia (Olmo 57), Morata (Fornals 65), De Tomas (Rodrigo 57).

Sunday, 14 November 2021

Greece (1) 1 *(Masouras 44)*

Kosovo (0) 1 *(Rrahmani 76)* 7825

Greece: (352) Vlachodimos; Chatzidiakos, Goutas, Tzavelas (Pavlidis 80); Androutsos, Pelkas (Vrousai 80), Bouchalakis, Mandalos, Tsimikas; Masouras (Limnios 86), Douvikas (Tzolis 66).
Kosovo: (442) Muric; Vojvoda, Rrahmani, Fazliji, Aliti; Idrizi (Kastrati 86), Shala (Halimi 70), Loshaj (Zhegrova 46), Berisha V; Muriqi, Rashica (Selmani 80).

Spain (0) 1 *(Morata 86)*

Sweden (0) 0 51,844

Spain: (433) Simon; Azpilicueta, Laporte, Torres P, Jordi Alba; Gavi (Rodri 89), Busquets, Carlos Soler (Merino 73); Sarabia (Morata 59), De Tomas (Rodrigo 60), Olmo (Mendez 89).
Sweden: (442) Olsen; Krafth (Olsson M 85), Lindelof, Nilsson, Augustinsson; Claesson, Olsson K, Ekdal, Forsberg (Svanberg 63); Kulusevski (Quaison 64), Isak (Ibrahimovic 73).

Group B Table	P	W	D	L	F	A	GD	Pts
Spain	8	6	1	1	15	5	10	19
Sweden	8	5	0	3	12	6	6	15
Greece	8	2	4	2	8	8	0	10
Georgia	8	2	1	5	6	12	–6	7
Kosovo	8	1	2	5	5	15	–10	5

GROUP C

Thursday, 2 September 2021

Italy (1) 1 *(Chiesa 16)*

Bulgaria (1) 1 *(Iliev A 39)* 14,366

Italy: (433) Donnarumma; Florenzi (Toloi 64), Bonucci, Acerbi, Emerson Palmieri (Pellegrini 90); Barella (Cristante 63), Jorginho, Verratti; Chiesa, Immobile (Raspadori 75), Insigne (Berardi 74).
Bulgaria: (433) Georgiev; Hristov A, Hristov P, Antov, Nedyalkov; Kostadinov, Vitanov (Malinov 75), Yankov (Chochev 57); Yomov (Delev 46), Iliev A (Krastev 70), Despodov (Kirilov 75).

Lithuania (0) 1 *(Baravykas 54)*

Northern Ireland (1) 4 *(Ballard 20, Washington 52 (pen), Lavery 67, McNair 82 (pen))* 1612

Lithuania: (4231) Setkus; Baravykas, Satkus, Utkus, Slavickas (Barauskas 74); Megelaitis, Verbickas (Uzela 80); Novikovas, Cernych (Jankauskas 80), Lasickas; Dubickas (Kazlauskas 74).
Northern Ireland: (352) Peacock-Farrell; McNair, Catheart, Ballard; Smith (Flanagan 89), McCann, Davis, Thompson (McCalmont 83), Lewis; Washington (Jones 83), Lavery (Lafferty 83).

Sunday, 5 September 2021

Bulgaria (0) 1 *(Chochev 82)*

Lithuania (0) 0 2503

Bulgaria: (4231) Georgiev; Turitsov, Hristov P, Antov, Nedyalkov; Kostadinov (Chochev 58), Malinov (Hristov A 90); Yomov (Delev 75), Nedelev (Iliev D 58), Despodov; Iliev A (Krastev 90).
Lithuania: (4231) Setkus; Lasickas, Satkus, Utkus, Baravykas; Slivka (Simkus 81), Megelaitis (Klimavicius L 87); Novikovas, Cernych, Kazlauskas (Verbickas 72); Dubickas (Jankauskas 46).

Switzerland (0) 0

Italy (0) 0 31,500

Switzerland: (4321) Sommer; Widmer, Akanji, Elvedi, Rodriguez (Garcia 63); Aebischer, Frei, Sow (Zakaria 63); Steffen (Fassnacht 71), Zuber (Vargas 63); Seferovic (Zeqiri 86).
Italy: (433) Donnarumma; Di Lorenzo, Bonucci, Chiellini, Emerson Palmieri; Barella (Pessina 90), Jorginho, Locatelli (Verratti 77); Berardi (Chiesa 59), Immobile (Zaniolo 59), Insigne (Raspadori 90).

Wednesday, 8 September 2021

Italy (4) 5 *(Kean 11, 29, Utkus 14 (og), Raspadori 24, Di Lorenzo 54)*

Lithuania (0) 0 10,578

Italy: (433) Donnarumma (Sirigu 46); Di Lorenzo, Acerbi, Bastoni, Biraghi (Calabria 46); Pessina, Jorginho (Castrovilli 61), Cristante; Bernardeschi (Scamacca 62), Raspadori, Kean (Berardi 73).
Lithuania: (4231) Setkus; Lasickas, Utkus (Satkus 46), Klimavicius L (Tutyskinas 83), Slavickas (Barauskas 46); Dapkus (Megelaitis 46), Slivka; Novikovas, Verbickas, Kazlauskas; Dubickas (Uzela 73).

Northern Ireland (0) 0

Switzerland (0) 0 15,660

Northern Ireland: (532) Peacock-Farrell; Smith (Bradley 67), Ballard, Cathcart, Brown, Lewis; McCann, Davis, Thompson (Saville 74); Lavery (Jones 86), Washington (Charles 68).
Switzerland: (4321) Sommer; Widmer (Lotomba 86), Akanji, Elvedi, Rodriguez; Freuler, Frei (Steffen 59), Zakaria (Aebischer 86); Fassnacht (Zuber 59), Vargas; Seferovic (Zeqiri 77).

Saturday, 9 October 2021

Lithuania (1) 3 *(Lasickas 18, Cernych 82, 84)*

Bulgaria (0) 1 *(Despodov 64)* 2526

Lithuania: (4231) Setkus; Vaitkunas, Satkus, Klimavicius L, Baravykas; Megelaitis (Verbickas 67), Slivka; Lasickas, Cernych (Dapkus 90), Novikovas; Laukzemis (Kazlauskas 74).
Bulgaria: (4231) Lukov; Hristov A, Hristov P, Antov, Bozhikov; Vitanov (Chochev 60), Malinov (Iliev I 60); Despodov, Nedelev (Yankov 87), Yomov (Delev 72); Iliev D (Krastev 72).

Switzerland (1) 2 *(Zuber 45, Fassnacht 90)*

Northern Ireland (0) 0 19,129

Switzerland: (4231) Sommer; Mbabu (Widmer 80), Akanji (Schar 53), Elvedi, Rodriguez; Zakaria, Freuler; Steffen, Shaqiri (Sow 90), Zuber (Fassnacht 81); Embolo (Itten 90).
Northern Ireland: (541) Peacock-Farrell; McNair, Ballard, Cathcart, Brown (Ferguson 80), Lewis■; Dallas (Bradley 86), Davis, Thompson (Jones 80), Saville; Washington (Magennis 62).

Tuesday, 12 October 2021

Bulgaria (0) 2 *(Nedelev 53, 63)*

Northern Ireland (1) 1 *(Washington 35)* 822

Bulgaria: (4312) Karadzhov; Turitsov, Hristov P, Hristov A, Velkovski; Tsonev R (Iliev I 46), Chochev, Tsonev B (Malinov 73); Nedelev (Yankov 73); Iliev A (Krastev 80), Despodov (Bozhikov 90).
Northern Ireland: (532) Peacock-Farrell; Bradley (Jones 67), Ballard (McGinn 82), Cathcart, Flanagan, Ferguson; McNair, Davis, Thompson; Washington (Charles 82), Magennis (Dallas 67).

Lithuania (0) 0

Switzerland (3) 4 *(Embolo 31, 45, Steffen 42, Gavranovic 90)* 1806

Lithuania: (4231) Setkus; Baravykas, Satkus, Girdvainis (Gaspuitis 89), Barauskas; Slivka (Verbickas 46), Megelaitis (Armanavicius 89); Lasickas, Cernych (Veliulis 83), Novikovas; Laukzemis (Kazlauskas 46).
Switzerland: (4231) Sommer; Widmer, Schar, Elvedi, Rodriguez (Garcia 46); Sow, Freuler; Steffen (Fassnacht 68), Shaqiri (Gavranovic 76), Zuber (Vargas 68); Embolo (Itten 89).

Friday, 12 November 2021

Italy (1) 1 *(Di Lorenzo 36)*

Switzerland (1) 1 *(Widmer 11)* 45,699

Italy: (433) Donnarumma; Di Lorenzo, Bonucci, Acerbi, Emerson Palmieri (Calabria 80); Barella (Cristante 69), Jorginho, Locatelli (Tonali 58); Chiesa, Belotti (Berardi 58), Insigne (Raspadori 79).
Switzerland: (4231) Sommer; Widmer, Schar, Akanji, Rodriguez (Garcia 68); Zakaria, Freuler; Steffen (Imeri 69), Shaqiri (Sow 80), Vargas (Zeqiri 87); Okafor (Frei 79).

Northern Ireland (1) 1 *(Satkus 17 (og))*

Lithuania (0) 0 14,336

Northern Ireland: (352) Peacock-Farrell; McNair, Evans J, Cathcart; Dallas, McCann, Davis, Saville (Evans C 70), Ferguson (Lewis 70); Magennis (Taylor 78), Washington (Jones 88).
Lithuania: (4231) Setkus; Vaitkunas, Satkus, Dapkus (Gaspuitis 75), Barauskas; Megelaitis (Armanavicius 86), Cernych; Lasickas, Verbickas (Simkus 86), Novikovas; Laukzemis (Kazlauskas 80).

Monday, 15 November 2021

Northern Ireland (0) 0

Italy (0) 0 15,969

Northern Ireland: (532) Peacock-Farrell; Dallas, Flanagan, Evans J, Cathcart, Lewis; McCann, Davis, Saville (Evans C 72); Whyte (Washington 72), Magennis.
Italy: (433) Donnarumma; Di Lorenzo, Bonucci, Acerbi, Emerson Palmieri (Scamacca 80); Tonali (Cristante 46), Jorginho (Locatelli 68), Barella (Belotti 64); Berardi, Insigne (Bernardeschi 68), Chiesa.

Switzerland (0) 4 *(Okafor 48, Vargas 57, Itten 72, Freuler 90)*

Bulgaria (0) 0 14,300

Switzerland: (4231) Sommer; Mbabu, Schar (Sow 90), Frei, Widmer; Freuler, Zakaria; Okafor (Steffen 68), Shaqiri (Aebischer 90), Vargas (Zeqiri 79); Gavranovic (Itten 68).
Bulgaria: (442) Karadzhov; Turitsov (Velkovski 46), Dimitrov, Hristov A, Tsvetanov; Nedelev, Kostadinov, Chochev (Iliev I 65), Kirilov (Tsonev R 70); Iliev A (Minchev G 46), Despodov (Yankov 80).

Group C Table	P	W	D	L	F	A	GD	Pts
Switzerland	8	5	3	0	15	2	13	18
Italy	8	4	4	0	13	2	11	16
Northern Ireland	8	2	3	3	6	7	–1	9
Bulgaria	8	2	2	4	6	14	–8	8
Lithuania	8	1	0	7	4	19	–15	3

GROUP D

Wednesday, 1 September 2021

France (1) 1 *(Griezmann 39)*

Bosnia-Herzegovina (1) 1 *(Dzeko 36)* 21,754

France: (433) Lloris; Kounde■, Varane, Kimpembe, Digne; Pogba, Veretout (Dubois 54), Lemar (Tchouameni 46); Griezmann (Coman 76), Benzema (Martial 76), Mbappe-Lottin (Diaby 90).
Bosnia-Herzegovina: (352) Sehic; Ahmedhodzic, Hadzikadunic, Sanicanin; Susic (Cipetic 64), Pjanic, Hadziahmetovic, Cimirot (Loncar 72), Kolasinac (Civic 54); Demirovic (Prevljak 72), Dzeko.

Kazakhstan (0) 2 *(Valiullin 74, 90)*

Ukraine (1) 2 *(Yaremchuk 2, Sikan 90)* 6274

Kazakhstan: (532) Pokatilov; Bystrov, Maliy, Marochkin, Logvinenko, Valiullin; Vasiljev (Zhukov 90), Tagybergen (Orazov 90), Kuat (Vorogovskiy 84); Nurgaliev (Zaynutdinov 61), Shushenachev (Aimbetov 60).
Ukraine: (3421) Pyatov; Zabarnyi, Matviyenko, Mykolenko; Karavayev, Sydorchuk (Shaparenko 75), Zinchenko, Sobol (Sikan 82); Yarmolenko, Buyalsky (Malinovsky 59); Yaremchuk (Tsygankov 59).

Saturday, 4 September 2021

Finland (0) 1 *(Pohjanpalo 60)*

Kazakhstan (0) 0 10,167

Finland: (352) Hradecky; Vaisanen L, Arajuuri, O'Shaughnessy; Alho, Valakari (Nissila 78), Schuller (Sparv 90), Taylor (Kairinen 78), Uronen; Pohjanpalo (Jensen 80), Pukki (Forss 90).
Kazakhstan: (532) Shatski; Tapalov, Yerlanov, Marochkin, Alip, Taikenov (Kuat 72); Zhukov (Zharinbetov 81), Orazov (Tagybergen 63), Vorogovskiy; Tattybayev (Vasiljev 63), Aimbetov (Shushenachev 72).

Ukraine (1) 1 *(Shaparenko 44)*

France (0) 1 *(Martial 50)* 48,000

Ukraine: (3421) Pyatov; Zabarnyi, Kryvtsov, Matviyenko; Tymchyk, Stepanenko, Shaparenko (Sydorchuk 90), Mykolenko; Yarmolenko (Zubkov 90), Tsygankov (Malinovsky 82); Yaremchuk (Sikan 82).
France: (433) Lloris; Dubois, Zouma, Kimpembe, Digne; Pogba, Tchouameni (Veretout 83), Rabiot; Griezmann, Martial (Benzema 64), Coman (Diaby 64).

Tuesday, 7 September 2021

Bosnia-Herzegovina (0) 2 *(Pjanic 74 (pen), Menalo 85)*

Kazakhstan (0) 2 *(Kuat 51, Zaynutdinov 90)* 3980

Bosnia-Herzegovina: (352) Sehic; Ahmedhodzic, Hadzikadunic (Menalo 68), Sanicanin; Stevanovic, Pjanic, Cimirot, Nalic (Gojak 54), Kolasinac (Civic 46); Demirovic (Prevljak 79), Dzeko.
Kazakhstan: (532) Shatski; Bystrov, Maliy, Marochkin, Logvinenko (Yerlanov 88), Vorogovskiy (Taikenov 83); Vasiljev (Orazov 83), Tagybergen, Kuat (Zharinbetov 88); Zhukov, Shushenachev (Zaynutdinov 57).

France (1) 2 *(Griezmann 25, 53)*

Finland (0) 0 57,057

France: (3412) Lloris; Zouma, Varane, Kimpembe (Lenglet 90); Dubois (Mukiele 67), Pogba, Rabiot, Hernandez T; Griezmann (Tchouameni 90); Martial (Ben Yedder 80), Benzema.
Finland: (532) Hradecky; Alho (Raitala 80), Vaisanen L, Arajuuri, O'Shaughnessy, Uronen (Soiri 62); Nissila (Kairinen 73), Schuller (Valakari 62), Kamara; Pohjanpalo (Jensen 73), Pukki.

Saturday, 9 October 2021

Finland (1) 1 *(Pukki 29)*

Ukraine (2) 2 *(Yarmolenko 4, Yaremchuk 34)* 29,485

Finland: (532) Hradecky; Alho (Hamalainen 62), Toivio, Arajuuri, Vaisanen L, Raitala (Niskanen 78); Lod, Lam (Nissila 61), Kamara; Pukki, Pohjanpalo (Riski 77).
Ukraine: (3421) Pyatov; Zabarnyi, Kryvtsov, Matviyenko; Tymchyk, Stepanenko (Sydorchuk 77), Shaparenko, Sobol (Korniyenko 46); Yarmolenko (Buletsa 86), Tsygankov (Zubkov 77); Yaremchuk (Dovbyk 86).

Kazakhstan (0) 0

Bosnia-Herzegovina (1) 2 *(Prevljak 25, 66)* 12,897

Kazakhstan: (532) Pokatilov; Bystrov (Murtazaev 84), Logvinenko, Maliy, Alip, Shomko (Beysebekov 78); Zhukov (Zhaksylykov 61), Kuat, Vorogovskiy (Orazov 78); Zaynutdinov, Shchetkin (Omirtayev 61).
Bosnia-Herzegovina: (352) Sehic; Ahmedhodzic, Kovacevic, Civic; Stevanovic, Cimirot (Nalic 63), Hadziahmetovic, Gojak, Kolasinac; Dzeko, Prevljak (Demirovic 81).

Tuesday, 12 October 2021

Kazakhstan (0) 0

Finland (1) 2 *(Pukki 45, 47)* 8365

Kazakhstan: (532) Shatski; Bystrov (Tapalov 76), Beysebekov, Maliy, Alip, Vorogovskiy (Taikenov 73); Zhukov (Zhaksylykov 58), Kuat, Vasiljev (Tagybergen 58); Omirtayev (Shchetkin 58), Zaynutdinov.
Finland: (4132) Hradecky; Granlund (Raitala 79), Vaisanen L, Ivanov, Hamalainen; Schuller; Kamara, Lod (Taylor 90), Nissila (Riski 90); Pohjanpalo (Jensen 33), Pukki (Valakari 79).

Ukraine (1) 1 *(Yarmolenko 15)*

Bosnia-Herzegovina (0) 1 *(Ahmedhodzic 77)* 23,810

Ukraine: (3421) Pyatov; Zabarnyi, Kryvtsov, Matviyenko; Tymchyk, Stepanenko, Shaparenko (Sydorchuk 72), Sobol; Yarmolenko (Zubkov 82), Tsygankov (Buletsa 82); Yaremchuk (Sikan 72).
Bosnia-Herzegovina: (433) Sehic; Stevanovic, Hadzikadunic, Ahmedhodzic, Civic; Hadziahmetovic, Nalic (Saric 58), Kolasinac (Kovacevic 90); Gojak (Prcic 58), Dzeko, Prevljak (Demirovic 83).

Saturday, 13 November 2021

Bosnia-Herzegovina (0) 1 *(Menalo 69)*

Finland (1) 3 *(Forss 29, Lod 50, O'Shaughnessy 73)* 10,000

Bosnia-Herzegovina: (433) Sehic; Ahmedhodzic, Sanicanin, Civic, Kolasinac (Demirovic 39); Hadziahmetovic (Prcic 56), Pjanic (Susic 66), Cimirot (Gojak 56); Stevanovic, Prevljak, Krunic (Menalo 67).
Finland: (532) Hradecky; Raitala■, Vaisanen L, Ivanov (Arajuuri 80), O'Shaughnessy, Hamalainen; Lod (Uronen 76), Schuller, Kamara; Forss (Nissila 46), Pukki (Jensen 80).

France (3) 8 *(Mbappe-Lottin 6, 12, 32, 87, Benzema 55, 59, Rabiot 75, Griezmann 84 (pen))*

Kazakhstan (0) 0 45,551

France: (3412) Lloris; Kounde, Upamecano, Hernandez L (Lenglet 80); Coman (Pavard 79), Kante (Tchouameni 72), Rabiot, Hernandez T; Griezmann; Benzema (Diaby 71), Mbappe-Lottin (Ben Yedder 88).
Kazakhstan: (532) Pokatilov; Bystrov (Kairov 84), Yerlanov, Marochkin, Alip, Taikenov; Tapalov (Baytana 68), Kuat, Zharinbetov; Omirtayev (Vasiljev 60), Aimbetov (Zhaksylykov 59).

Tuesday, 16 November 2021

Bosnia-Herzegovina (0) 0

Ukraine (0) 2 *(Zinchenko 58, Dovbyk 79)* 3370

Bosnia-Herzegovina: (442) Vasilj; Ahmedhodzic, Kovacevic, Hadzikadunic, Susic; Stevanovic, Gojak (Cimirot 64), Prcic (Krunic 64), Hadziahmetovic (Nalic 71); Demirovic (Kodro 80), Menalo (Prevljak 71).
Ukraine: (433) Bushchan; Tymchyk, Zabarnyi, Matviyenko, Sobol (Shaparenko 64); Malinovsky (Sydorchuk 81), Stepanenko, Zinchenko; Yarmolenko (Karavayev 82), Yaremchuk (Dovbyk 74), Tsygankov (Zubkov 75).

Finland (0) 0

France (0) 2 *(Benzema 66, Mbappe-Lottin 76)* 31,890

Finland: (532) Hradecky; Uronen (Taylor 73), Vaisanen L, Ivanov, O'Shaughnessy (Pohjanpalo 82), Hamalainen; Kamara, Schuller (Forss 64), Nissila (Valakari 82); Pukki, Lod.
France: (3412) Lloris; Kounde (Coman 57), Zouma, Upamecano; Dubois (Pavard 46), Rabiot (Veretout 86), Tchouameni, Digne; Griezmann (Guendouzi 67); Diaby (Benzema 56), Mbappe-Lottin.

Group D Table	P	W	D	L	F	A	GD	Pts
France	8	5	3	0	18	3	15	18
Ukraine	8	2	6	0	11	8	3	12
Finland	8	3	2	3	10	10	0	11
Bosnia-Herzegovina	8	1	4	3	9	12	–3	7
Kazakhstan	8	0	3	5	5	20	–15	3

GROUP E

Thursday, 2 September 2021

Czech Republic (1) 1 *(Barak 34)*

Belarus (0) 0 7218

Czech Republic: (4231) Vaclik; Coufal, Kalas, Holes, Mateju; Soucek, Kral (Sadilek 63); Jankto (Zmrhal 78), Barak (Tecl 90), Hlozek (Pesek 78); Dolezal (Vydra 63).
Belarus: (541) Chernik; Begunov, Rakhmanov, Shvyatsow (Skavysh 89), Sachivko, Zolotov (Shevchenko 85); Antilevski (Yuzepchuk 64), Klimovich (Bykov 64), Korzun, Ebong (Kontsevoj 89); Lisakovich V.

Estonia (1) 2 *(Kait 2, Sorga 83)*

Belgium (2) 5 *(Vanaken 22, Lukaku 29, 52, Witsel 64, Foket 76)* 6685

Estonia: (532) Hein; Puri (Lilander 80), Tamm, Kuusk, Mets, Pikk (Kallaste 69); Vassiljev (Zenjov 86), Kreida, Kait; Anier (Sinyavskiy 80), Sappinen (Sorga 69).
Belgium: (343) Courtois; Alderweireld (Dendoncker 83), Boyata, Denayer; Saelemaekers (Foket 66), Vanaken, Witsel, Carrasco (Lukebakio 83); Trossard, Lukaku (Benteke 74), Hazard E (Sambi Lokonga 74).

Sunday, 5 September 2021

Belarus (2) 2 *(Lisakovich V 29 (pen), Sedko 30)*

Wales (1) 3 *(Bale 5 (pen), 69 (pen), 90)*

Belarus: (541) Chernik; Begunov (Shevchenko 78), Khadarkevich, Shvyatsow, Sachivko, Zolotov; Ebong (Podstrelov 73), Klimovich, Bykov, Sedko (Yuzepchuk 73); Lisakovich V (Skavysh 90).
Wales: (4231) Ward; Gunter, Mepham, Lawrence J, Davies B; Allen, Morrell; Bale, Johnson (Williams J 63), James; Colwill (Harris 57).

Belgium (2) 3 *(Lukaku 8, Hazard E 41, Saelemaekers 65)*

Czech Republic (0) 0 21,416

Belgium: (343) Courtois; Alderweireld, Denayer, Vertonghen; Castagne, Witsel, Tielemans (Dendoncker 81), Carrasco (Saelemaekers 57); Vanaken (Lukebakio 81), Lukaku (Batshuayi 81), Hazard E (Trossard 73).
Czech Republic: (4231) Vaclik (Stanek 14); Coufal, Kasa, Kalas, Mateju; Soucek, Holes; Pesek (Zmrhal 66), Barak (Kral 76), Hlozek (Wiesner 77); Vydra (Tecl 65).

Wednesday, 8 September 2021

Belarus (0) 0

Belgium (1) 1 *(Praet 33)*

Belarus: (532) Chernik; Shevchenko (Begunov 81), Shvyatsow, Rakhmanov, Sachivko, Zolotov (Podstrelov 81); Bykov, Lisakovich R (Ebong 70), Klimovich; Lisakovich V, Skavysh (Sedko 70).
Belgium: (343) Casteels; Alderweireld, Boyata, Denayer; Saelemaekers (Foket 84), Praet, Tielemans, Castagne; Trossard (Hazard E 60), Batshuayi (Dendoncker 84), Lukebakio (Benteke 76).

Wales (0) 0

Estonia (0) 0 21,624

Wales: (433) Ward; Gunter, Mepham, Ampadu, Davies B; Allen, Morrell, Wilson (Williams J 36); Bale, Roberts T (Harris 63), James.
Estonia: (532) Hein; Puri (Lilander 30), Paskotsi (Lukka 86), Kuusk, Mets, Pikk; Vassiljev, Kreida (Poom 86), Kait; Anier (Sinyavskiy 71), Sappinen (Sorga 71).

Friday, 8 October 2021

Czech Republic (1) 2 *(Pesek 38, Ward 49 (og))*

Wales (1) 2 *(Ramsey 36, James 69)* 16,856

Czech Republic: (4231) Vaclik; Mateju, Celustka, Kalas, Novak (Wiesner 84); Kral (Kuchta 83), Soucek; Pesek (Vydra 76), Barak (Sadilek 77), Hlozek (Zmrhal 90); Schick.
Wales: (532) Ward; Gunter (Roberts C 60), Mepham (Roberts T 86), Rodon, Ampadu, Williams N (Thomas 76); Allen, Morrell (Wilson 60), Ramsey; Moore, James.

Estonia (0) 2 *(Sorga 57, Zenjov 90)*

Belarus (0) 0 3597

Estonia: (532) Hein; Paskotsi (Kallaste 87), Kuusk, Tamm, Mets, Sinyavskiy (Teniste 80); Vassiljev, Kreida, Kait; Anier (Ojamaa 81), Sorga (Zenjov 69).
Belarus: (352) Pavlyuchenko; Selyava, Yudenkov, Bordachev (Pobudey 66); Begunov (Antilevski 81), Klimovich, Yablonskiy (Lisakovich R 81), Bykov, Shevchenko (Pechenin 66); Solovey (Sedko 46), Lisakovich V.

Monday, 11 October 2021

Belarus (0) 0

Czech Republic (1) 2 *(Schick 22, Hlozek 65)*

Belarus: (433) Pavlyuchenko; Begunov, Selyava (Sadovnichiy 46), Yudenkov, Pechenin; Bykov, Klimovich (Solovey 78), Antilevski (Lisakovich R 68); Sedko, Lisakovich V, Ebong.
Czech Republic: (4231) Vaclik; Wiesner, Celustka, Zima, Mateju; Sadilek (Zmrhal 88), Soucek; Pesek (Kopic 81), Hlozek (Kuchta 88), Vydra (Pavelka 46); Schick (Kral 90).

Estonia (0) 0

Wales (1) 1 *(Moore 12)* 5118

Estonia: (532) Hein; Teniste (Ojamaa 75), Paskotsi, Tamm, Kuusk, Pikk (Sinyavskiy 57); Poom, Mets, Kait (Kallaste 82); Zenjov (Vastsuk 82), Sorga (Kirss 81).
Wales: (352) Ward; Mepham, Rodon, Ampadu; Roberts C (Gunter 83), Ramsey (Morrell 80), Allen, Wilson (Johnson 83), Thomas; James, Moore (Harris 71).

Saturday, 13 November 2021

Belgium (1) 3 *(Benteke 11, Carrasco 53, Hazard T 74)*

Estonia (0) 1 *(Sorga 70)* 29,895

Belgium: (3421) Courtois; Castagne, Denayer, Vertonghen; Meunier (Saelemaekers 63), De Bruyne (De Ketelaere 83), Witsel, Carrasco (Mertens 71); Vanaken, Hazard E (Hazard T 62); Benteke (Origi 84).
Estonia: (352) Igonen; Paskotsi, Tamm, Mets; Teniste (Puri 79), Poom, Kreida, Vassiljev (Soomets 80), Ojamaa (Sinyavskiy 60); Zenjov (Sorga 67), Anier (Sappinen 59).

Wales (2) 5 *(Ramsey 2, 50 (pen), Williams N 20, Davies B 77, Roberts C 89)*

Belarus (0) 1 *(Kontsevoj 87)* 27,152

Wales: (442) Ward (Hennessey 90); Ampadu, Rodon, Davies B, Williams N; Roberts C, Ramsey (Morrell 71), Allen, Wilson; Bale (Johnson 46), James (Roberts T 76).
Belarus: (352) Chernik; Shvyatsow, Naumov, Yudenkov (Kontsevoj 82); Zolotov (Yuzepchuk 71), Klimovich (Ebong 70), Yablonskiy, Selyava, Pechenin; Sedko (Antilevski 60), Lisakovich V (Bakhar 81).

Tuesday, 16 November 2021

Czech Republic (0) 2 *(Brabec 59, Sykora 85)*

Estonia (0) 0 10,076

Czech Republic: (4231) Vaclik; Coufal, Zima, Brabec, Novak; Kral (Kuchta 60), Sadilek (Pavelka 69); Masopust (Krmencik 60), Barak, Pesek (Sykora 28); Vydra (Kopic 69).
Estonia: (532) Igonen; Paskotsi (Kirss 87), Kuusk, Tamm, Mets, Sinyavskiy (Ojamaa 61); Poom, Kreida, Vassiljev; Sappinen (Zenjov 76), Sorga (Anier 61).

Wales (1) 1 *(Moore 32)*

Belgium (1) 1 *(De Bruyne 12)* 32,343

Wales: (541) Ward; Roberts C, Mepham, Rodon, Davies B, Williams N; Morrell, Ramsey (Johnson 90), Allen, James; Moore.
Belgium: (3412) Casteels; Castagne (Dendoncker 58), Boyata, Theate (Vertonghen 85); Meunier (Trossard 85), Witsel, Vanaken, Hazard T; De Bruyne; De Ketelaere (Saelemaekers 58), Origi (Vanzeir 59).

Group E Table	*P*	*W*	*D*	*L*	*F*	*A*	*GD*	*Pts*
Belgium	8	6	2	0	25	6	19	20
Wales	8	4	3	1	14	9	5	15
Czech Republic	8	4	2	2	14	9	5	14
Estonia	8	1	1	6	9	21	–12	4
Belarus	8	1	0	7	7	24	–17	3

GROUP F

Wednesday, 1 September 2021

Denmark (2) 2 *(Wass 14, Maehle 15)*

Scotland (0) 0 34,562

Denmark: (541) Schmeichel; Wass (Stryger Larsen 85), Andersen, Kjaer, Christensen A, Maehle; Skov Olsen (Daramy 85), Hojbjerg, Delaney (Norgaard 85), Damsgaard (Lindstrom 90); Poulsen (Wind 68).
Scotland: (352) Gordon; Hanley, Cooper, McKenna (Dykes 46); Robertson, Gilmour (Ferguson 90), McLean (Turnbull 85), McGregor C, Tierney; Fraser, Adams (Christie 71).

Faroe Islands (0) 0

Israel (2) 4 *(Zahavi 11, 44, 90, Dabbur 52)* 2666

Faroe Islands: (451) Nielsen G; Sorensen, Faero, Nattestad, Joensen R; Vatnhamar S (Edmundsson 63), Vatnhamar G (Mohr 76), Andreasen (Hansson 64), Olsen B (Jensen 76), Olsen M; Olsen K (Johansen 76).
Israel: (3412) Marciano; Dgani (Arad 71), Tibi, Bitton (Abu Abaid 84); Dasa, Natcho (Abu Fani 62), Peretz, Menachem; Solomon (Abada 84); Zahavi, Dabbur (Weissman 71).

Moldova (0) 0

Austria (1) 2 *(Baumgartner 45, Arnautovic 90)* 3945

Moldova: (4231) Avram; Jardan, Posmac, Potirniche (Bolohan 84), Reabciuk; Dros, Ionita; Platica S (Antoniuc 84), Ginsari (Bogaciuc 59), Belousov (Marandici 73); Ghecev (Spataru 59).
Austria: (442) Bachmann; Trimmel, Lienhart, Hinteregger, Ulmer; Schaub (Kainz 77), Laimer (Schopf 62), Grillitsch (Ilsanker 82), Baumgartner (Alaba 83); Arnautovic, Gregoritsch (Kara 62).

Saturday, 4 September 2021

Faroe Islands (0) 0

Denmark (0) 1 *(Wind 85)* 4620

Faroe Islands: (4141) Gestsson; Sorensen, Faero, Nattestad (Vatnsdal 73), Joensen R■; Vatnhamar G (Olsen A 90); Vatnhamar S, Hansson, Olsen B, Olsen M (Knudsen 89); Edmundsson (Frederiksen 90).
Denmark: (4141) Schmeichel; Kristensen (Maehle 46), Nelsson, Christensen A, Stryger Larsen; Norgaard; Bruun Larsen (Damsgaard 53), Christiansen (Poulsen 76), Jensen (Hojbjerg 89), Daramy (Skov Olsen 46); Wind.

Israel (3) 5 *(Solomon 5, Dabbur 20, Zahavi 33, 90, Weissman 58)*

Austria (1) 2 *(Baumgartner 42, Arnautovic 55)* 13,500

Israel: (352) Marciano; Dgani, Tibi (Glazer 46), Bitton; Dasa, Elhamed, Natcho (Abu Fani 57), Solomon (Haziza 86), Menachem (Davidadze 74); Zahavi, Dabbur (Weissman 57).
Austria: (343) Bachmann; Posch, Dragovic (Schaub 46), Hinteregger; Mwene, Laimer (Kainz 79), Grillitsch (Ilsanker 79), Alaba; Schopf (Demir 67), Arnautovic, Baumgartner (Kara 79).

Scotland (1) 1 *(Dykes 14)*

Moldova (0) 0 40,869

Scotland: (3412) Gordon; Hendry, Hanley, Tierney; Patterson, Gilmour (McLean 73), McGinn J (McGregor C 65), Robertson (Cooper 74); Christie; Dykes (Turnbull 85), Nisbet (Adams 65).
Moldova: (352) Avram; Potirniche, Bolohan, Armas; Jardan, Platica S, Rata, Ionita (Clescenco 90), Reabciuk; Ghecev (Dros 46), Ginsari (Spataru 88).

Tuesday, 7 September 2021

Austria (0) 0

Scotland (1) 1 *(Dykes 30 (pen))* 18,800

Austria: (4231) Bachmann; Trimmel, Dragovic, Hinteregger, Alaba; Ilsanker (Gregoritsch 56), Grillitsch (Ulmer 76); Laimer (Kara 88), Schaub (Demir 76), Baumgartner; Arnautovic.
Scotland: (3412) Gordon; Hendry, Hanley, Tierney; O'Donnell (McGinn P 77), Gilmour (Ferguson 88), McGregor C, Robertson; McGinn J; Adams (Nisbet 88), Dykes (Christie 71).

Denmark (3) 5 *(Poulsen 28, Kjaer 31, Skov Olsen 41, Delaney 58, Cornelius 90)*

Israel (0) 0 35,158

Denmark: (343) Schmeichel; Andersen, Kjaer, Christensen A; Wass (Cornelius 86), Hojbjerg (Norgaard 83), Delaney, Maehle; Skov Olsen (Stryger Larsen 77), Poulsen (Daramy 77), Damsgaard (Wind 83).
Israel: (532) Marciano; Dasa (Kinda 80), Dgani (Davidadze 61), Tibi, Elhamed, Menachem; Glazer, Natcho (Abu Fani 46), Solomon (Atzili 70); Weissman (Haziza 46), Zahavi.

Faroe Islands (0) 2 *(Olsen K 68, Vatnsdal 71)*

Moldova (0) 1 *(Milinceanu 84)* 2714

Faroe Islands: (4141) Gestsson; Sorensen, Faero (Andreasen 65), Vatnsdal, Johansen; Vatnhamar G; Vatnhamar S, Hansson, Olsen B (Askham 87), Olsen M (Edmundsson 65); Olsen K (Olsen A 87).
Moldova: (343) Avram; Posmac, Bolohan (Clescenco 80), Armas; Jardan, Rata, Dros (Milinceanu 60), Reabciuk; Platica S (Spataru 74), Nicolaescu, Ginsari (Cotogoi 74).

Saturday, 9 October 2021

Faroe Islands (0) 0

Austria (1) 2 *(Laimer 26, Sabitzer 48)* 3021

Faroe Islands: (451) Gestsson; Sorensen, Faero (Olsen K 68), Nattestad, Davidsen V (Agnarsson 68); Joensen R (Bjartalid 68), Hansson, Vatnhamar G, Olsen B, Jonsson; Edmundsson (Frederiksen 86).
Austria: (4321) Bachmann; Trimmel, Ilsanker, Hinteregger (Posch 65), Alaba; Laimer (Ljubicic 77), Grillitsch, Sabitzer; Onisiwo (Schaub 77), Kainz (Demir 88); Kara (Gregoritsch 88).

Moldova (0) 0

Denmark (4) 4 *(Skov Olsen 23, Kjaer 34 (pen), Norgaard 39, Maehle 44)* 2642

Moldova: (451) Avram; Jardan, Posmac, Armas, Marandici; Ghecev (Potirniche 46), Ginsari (Dros 62), Rata, Ionita (Cotogoi 78), Iosipoi (Spataru 62); Nicolaescu (Puntus 79).
Denmark: (433) Schmeichel; Wass, Kjaer (Vestergaard 46), Christensen A, Maehle; Hojbjerg (Andersen 65), Norgaard, Delaney (Jensen 57); Skov Olsen (Dolberg 46), Poulsen (Cornelius 77), Damsgaard.

Scotland (1) 3 *(McGinn J 29, Dykes 55, McTominay 90)*

Israel (2) 2 *(Zahavi 5, Dabbur 31)* 50,585

Scotland: (352) Gordon; McTominay, Hendry, Tierney; Patterson, McGinn J, Gilmour (Cooper 90), McGregor C, Robertson; Adams (Christie 68), Dykes.
Israel: (3421) Marciano; Abu Abaid, Bitton, Arad (Kinda 74); Dasa, Peretz, Natcho (Glazer 66), Menachem (Davidadze 87); Dabbur (Weissman 66), Solomon; Zahavi.

Tuesday, 12 October 2021

Denmark (0) 1 *(Maehle 53)*

Austria (0) 0 35,843

Denmark: (343) Schmeichel; Christensen A, Kjaer, Vestergaard; Wass (Norgaard 90), Hojbjerg, Delaney (Jensen 90), Maehle; Skov Olsen (Stryger Larsen 77), Poulsen, Damsgaard (Dolberg 44).
Austria: (4231) Bachmann; Trimmel, Posch, Hinteregger, Alaba; Ilsanker (Onisiwo 72), Grillitsch; Laimer (Kainz 83), Sabitzer, Grull (Gregoritsch 83); Kara (Schaub 72).

Faroe Islands (0) 0

Scotland (0) 1 *(Dykes 86)* 4233

Faroe Islands: (343) Gestsson; Faero, Vatnsdal (Askham 59), Nattestad; Sorensen, Vatnhamar G, Olsen B, Davidsen V (Knudsen 59); Hansson (Frederiksen 90), Edmundsson (Olsen K 90), Jonsson.
Scotland: (3412) Gordon; Hendry (McGregor C 68), Hanley, Tierney; Fraser (Patterson 83), McTominay, Gilmour (Cooper 89), Robertson; McGinn J; Christie (Nisbet 83), Dykes.

Israel (1) 2 *(Zahavi 28, Dabbur 49)*

Moldova (0) 1 *(Nicolaescu 90)* 9000

Israel: (3421) Marciano; Abu Abaid, Bitton, Abu Hanna (Arad 46); Dasa (Podgoreanu 87), Peretz, Natcho (Kinda 64), Menachem; Dabbur (Abada 74), Solomon; Zahavi.
Moldova: (352) Avram; Potirniche (Bolohan 11), Posmac, Armas; Jardan, Dros (Spataru 64), Rata, Ionita, Reabciuk■; Puntus (Nicolaescu 46), Cociuc (Ginsari 46).

Friday, 12 November 2021

Austria (0) 4 *(Arnautovic 51 (pen), Schaub 62, 72, Sabitzer 84)*

Israel (1) 2 *(Bitton 32, Peretz 58)* 4300

Austria: (4231) Bachmann; Trimmel, Lienhart, Hinteregger (Dragovic 90), Alaba; Seiwald, Grillitsch; Schopf (Schaub 58), Sabitzer, Grull (Ulmer 90); Arnautovic (Adamu 89).
Israel: (3421) Marciano; Abu Abaid (Abu Fani 82), Bitton, Elhamed; Dasa, Peretz, Natcho (Gandelman 23), Menachem; Dabbur (Abada 82), Solomon; Zahavi (Weissman 65).

Denmark (1) 3 *(Skov Olsen 18, Bruun Larsen 63, Maehle 90)*

Faroe Islands (0) 1 *(Olsen K 89)* 35,531

Denmark: (3421) Schmeichel; Stryger Larsen, Kjaer, Christensen A; Wass, Norgaard (Jonsson 80), Lindstrom (Delaney 57), Maehle; Skov Olsen (Cornelius 67), Daramy (Bruun Larsen 57); Poulsen (Dreyer 68).
Faroe Islands: (541) Gestsson; Joensen R (Mohr 81), Faero, Askham, Nattestad, Davidsen V; Hansson, Vatnhamar G (Jensen 67), Andreasen, Vatnhamar S (Knudsen 80); Edmundsson (Olsen K 55).

Moldova (0) 0

Scotland (1) 2 *(Patterson 38, Adams 65)* 3642

Moldova: (352) Namasco; Jardan, Posmac, Bolohan (Razgoniuc 62); Revenco, Rata, Dros (Bogaciuc 61), Ionita, Marandici (Iosipoi 71); Nicolaescu (Puntus 71), Ginsari (Cojocaru 61).
Scotland: (343) Gordon; Hendry, Cooper, Tierney; Patterson, Gilmour (McLean 85), McGregor C, Robertson; McGinn J (Turnbull 90), Adams (Brown 85), Armstrong (Nisbet 76).

Monday, 15 November 2021

Austria (2) 4 *(Arnautovic 4, 55 (pen), Trimmel 21, Ljubicic 83)*

Moldova (0) 1 *(Nicolaescu 60)* 1800

Austria: (4231) Lindner; Trimmel, Lienhart, Dragovic (Posch 82), Ulmer; Seiwald (Ilsanker 72), Grillitsch (Ljubicic 58); Schaub (Onisiwo 58), Sabitzer, Grull (Kara 81); Arnautovic.
Moldova: (532) Namasco; Jardan, Razgoniuc (Iosipoi 46), Posmac, Bolohan (Iovu 88), Revenco; Ionita, Dros, Cociuc (Ginsari 59); Puntus (Nicolaescu 58), Spataru (Cojocaru 84).

Israel (1) 3 *(Dabbur 30 (pen), Weissman 58, Peretz 74)*

Faroe Islands (0) 2 *(Vatnhamar S 62, Olsen K 72)* 6800

Israel: (3412) Marciano; Dgani (Tibi 76), Bitton, Elhamed; Dasa, Avraham (Haziza 75), Peretz, Podgoreanu; Solomon; Weissman, Dabbur (Abada 81).
Faroe Islands: (541) Nielsen; Joensen R, Faero, Askham, Nattestad (Mohr 71), Davidsen V; Hansson (Olsen K 52), Andreasen (Jensen 70), Olsen B, Vatnhamar S (Knudsen 80); Edmundsson (Bjartalid 80).

Scotland (1) 2 *(Souttar 35, Adams 86)*

Denmark (0) 0 49,527

Scotland: (3421) Gordon; Souttar, Cooper, Tierney (Ralston 88); O'Donnell, Gilmour (McLean 74), McGregor C, Robertson (McKenna 79); McGinn J, Christie (Armstrong 80); Adams.
Denmark: (343) Schmeichel; Christensen A, Kjaer, Vestergaard; Kristensen (Bah 81), Wass (Dreyer 81), Jonsson (Stage 56), Maehle; Skov Olsen, Cornelius (Uhre 72), Bruun Larsen (Sisto 56).

Group F Table	P	W	D	L	F	A	GD	Pts
Denmark	10	9	0	1	30	3	27	27
Scotland	10	7	2	1	17	7	10	23
Israel	10	5	1	4	23	21	2	16
Austria	10	5	1	4	19	17	2	16
Faroe Islands	10	1	1	8	7	23	–16	4
Moldova	10	0	1	9	5	30	–25	1

GROUP G

Wednesday, 1 September 2021

Latvia (0) 3 *(Gutkowski 50 (pen), 85, Ciganiks 89)*

Gibraltar (0) 1 *(De Barr 71 (pen))* 1466

Latvia: (4231) Steinbors; Savavnieks, Cernomordijs, Dubra, Jurkovskis; Zjuzins (Karklins 90), Emsis; Ikaunieks J (Jaunzems 90), Uldrikis (Krollis 78), Ciganiks; Gutkowski.
Gibraltar: (541) Coleing; Sergeant, Chipolina R, Wiseman, Bosio (Mouelhi 64), Britto; Ronan (Chipolina J 89), Torrilla (Styche 89), Annesley (Anthony Hernandez 63), Valarino (Pons 64); De Barr.

Norway (1) 1 *(Haaland 20)*

Netherlands (1) 1 *(Klaassen 36)* 6711

Norway: (4222) Hansen; Pedersen (Ryerson 59), Strandberg, Hanche-Olsen, Meling; Thorsby, Normann (Berg 68); Odegaard, Hauge (Daehli 59); Elyounoussi M, Haaland.
Netherlands: (433) Bijlow; Timber (Dumfries 90), de Vrij, van Dijk, Blind; Wijnaldum, de Jong F, Klaassen; Berghuis (Malen 46), Depay, Gakpo.

Turkey (2) 2 *(Under 9, Yazici 30)*

Montenegro (1) 2 *(Marusic 40, Radunovic 90)* 12,472

Turkey: (4141) Bayindir; Celik, Ayhan, Demiral, Muldur; Yokuslu (Ozturk 82); Under (Unal 82), Yazici (Kokcu 66), Calhanoglu, Karaman (Akturkoglu 75); Burak Yilmaz.
Montenegro: (442) Mijatovic; Vesovic, Savic, Vujacic, Tomasevic (Radunovic 65); Marusic, Scekic, Kosovic (Raickovic 57), Haksabanovic (Osmajic 78); Bozovic (Ivanovic 66), Djurdjevic.

Saturday, 4 September 2021

Gibraltar (0) 0

Turkey (0) 3 *(Dervisoglu 54, Calhanoglu 65, Karaman 83)* 702

Gibraltar: (442) Coleing; Sergeant, Wiseman, Chipolina R, Britto (Pons 34); Ronan, Mouelhi, Torrilla, Valarino; De Barr (Styche 73), Anthony Hernandez (Coombes 69).
Turkey: (442) Cakir; Celik (Calhanoglu 46), Ayhan, Soyuncu (Yilmaz R 81), Muldur; Karaca, Antalyali (Karaman 46), Kokcu, Akturkoglu (Demiral 66); Yazici, Unal (Dervisoglu 46).

Netherlands (1) 4 *(Depay 38 (pen), 62, Wijnaldum 70, Gakpo 76)*

Montenegro (0) 0 20,458

Netherlands: (433) Bijlow; Dumfries, de Vrij, de Ligt, Malacia; Wijnaldum (de Roon 73), de Jong F (Til 84), Klaassen; Berghuis, Depay, Gakpo (Bergwijn 77).
Montenegro: (442) Sarkic; Vesovic (Vukcevic M 52), Savic (Simic 46), Tomasevic, Radunovic; Marusic (Haksabanovic 63), Scekic (Vujnovic 77), Lagator, Osmajic; Bozovic (Raickovic 63), Mugosa.

Latvia (0) 0

Norway (1) 2 *(Haaland 20 (pen), Elyounoussi M 66)* 2520

Latvia: (442) Steinbors (Ozols 43); Savavnieks, Tarasovs, Dubra, Jurkovskis; Kamess (Fyodorov 75), Emsis, Karklins (Zjuzins 70), Ciganiks (Krollis 75); Gutkowski (Uldrikis 70), Ikaunieks J.
Norway: (4231) Hansen; Pedersen, Strandberg, Ajer, Meling; Thorsby, Normann (Berg 60); Odegaard (Hauge 88), Thorstvedt (Sorloth 60), Elyounoussi M (Daehli 78); Haaland (King 88).

Tuesday, 7 September 2021

Netherlands (3) 6 *(Klaassen 1, Depay 16, 38 (pen), 54, Til 80, Malen 90)*

Turkey (0) 1 *(Under 90)* 31,389

Netherlands: (433) Bijlow; Dumfries (Rensch 71), de Vrij, van Dijk, Blind; Wijnaldum (Til 61), de Jong F (Koopmeiners 46), Klaassen (Gravenberch 71); Berghuis, Depay, Bergwijn (Malen 61).
Turkey: (4411) Cakir; Ayhan, Demiral, Soyuncu■, Muldur; Under, Yokuslu (Yazici 90), Kokcu (Tufan 46), Karaman (Kabak 46); Calhanoglu (Dervisoglu 86); Burak Yilmaz (Akturkoglu 65).

Montenegro (0) 0

Latvia (0) 0 2134

Montenegro: (442) Mijatovic; Vesovic, Vujacic, Tomasevic, Radunovic; Marusic, Scekic (Vukcevic N 72), Kosovic (Bozovic 79), Haksabanovic (Osmajic 79); Beciraj (Mugosa 60), Djurdjevic (Ivanovic 79).
Latvia: (4231) Ozols; Savavnieks, Cernomordijs, Dubra, Jurkovskis; Emsis, Zjuzins (Tarasovs 81); Kamess (Ciganiks 63), Uldrikis, Ikaunieks J; Gutkowski (Krollis 72).

Norway (3) 5 *(Thorstvedt 22, Haaland 27, 39, 90, Sorloth 59)*

Gibraltar (1) 1 *(Styche 43)* 9442

Norway: (433) Nyland; Pedersen, Hanche-Olsen, Ajer, Meling (Bjorkan 46); Odegaard, Berg (Donnum 63), Thorstvedt (Aursnes 80); Sorloth (King 63), Haaland, Elyounoussi M (Daehli 80).
Gibraltar: (541) Goldwin; Jolley (Chipolina J 83), Annesley (Chipolina R 80), Wiseman, Mouelhi, Sergeant; Anthony Hernandez (Pons 65), Torrilla, Ronan, Valarino (Bosio 65); Styche (Coombes 80).

Friday, 8 October 2021

Gibraltar (0) 0

Montenegro (2) 3 *(Marusic 7, Beciraj 44 (pen), 68)* 1351

Gibraltar: (541) Goldwin; Wiseman (Bosio 73), Annesley, Chipolina R, Olivero, Chipolina J (Britto 74); Walker (Badr 82), Ronan, Torrilla (Coombes 83), Valarino; Styche (Casciaro L 62).
Montenegro: (442) Mijatovic; Vesovic, Vujacic, Tomasevic, Radunovic; Marusic (Jankovic M 73), Scekic (Bozovic 51), Kosovic (Vukcevic N 73), Haksabanovic (Jovovic 73); Beciraj, Mugosa (Osmajic 45).

Latvia (0) 0

Netherlands (1) 1 *(Klaassen 19)* 4711

Latvia: (4231) Ozols; Savavnieks, Cernomordijs, Dubra, Jurkovskis; Zjuzins (Karklins 84), Emsis (Stuglis 89); Jaunzems (Ontuzans 81), Kigurs (Krollis 84), Ciganiks; Uldrikis (Tarasovs 89).
Netherlands: (433) Bijlow; Dumfries, de Vrij, van Dijk, Blind; Klaassen, de Jong F, Til (Gravenberch 62); Berghuis (Lang 62), Depay, Gakpo (Weghorst 76).

Turkey (1) 1 *(Akturkoglu 6)*

Norway (1) 1 *(Thorstvedt 41)* 21,408

Turkey: (4231) Cakir; Celik, Aziz (Ayhan 70), Demiral, Erkin; Tufan (Kutlu 58), Ozdemir (Antalyali 70); Under (Yazici 70), Calhanoglu, Akturkoglu (Karaman 84); Burak Yilmaz.
Norway: (433) Nyland; Pedersen (Ryerson 84), Strandberg, Hanche-Olsen, Meling; Odegaard, Berg (Aursnes 75), Thorsby; Hauge (Daehli 75), Thorstvedt (Berisha 75), Elyounoussi M.

Monday, 11 October 2021

Netherlands (3) 6 *(van Dijk 9, Depay 21, 45 (pen), Dumfries 48, Danjuma 75, Malen 86)*

Gibraltar (0) 0 31,583

Netherlands: (433) Bijlow; Dumfries, de Vrij, van Dijk, Blind; Wijnaldum, de Jong F (Weghorst 60), Klaassen; Berghuis (Danjuma 60), Depay, Lang (Malen 78).
Gibraltar: (541) Banda; Bosio (Ronan 46), Wiseman, Chipolina R, Olivero, Chipolina J (Britto 46); Walker (Badr 80), Annesley, Torrilla (Mouelhi 88), Valarino; Styche (Casciaro L 62).

Latvia (0) 1 *(Demiral 70 (og))*

Turkey (0) 2 *(Dursun 75, Burak Yilmaz 90 (pen))* 2453

Latvia: (4231) Ozols; Savavnieks, Cernomordijs, Dubra, Jurkovskis; Zjuzins (Tarasovs 60), Emsis; Jaunzems (Ontuzans 73), Uldrikis (Kigurs 60), Ciganiks; Gutkowski (Krollis 81).
Turkey: (4141) Cakir; Celik, Demiral, Soyuncu, Erkin (Yilmaz R 65); Ozdemir; Under, Kokcu (Dursun 65), Calhanoglu, Akturkoglu (Dervisoglu 74); Burak Yilmaz.

Norway (1) 2 *(Elyounoussi M 29, 90)*

Montenegro (0) 0 23,748

Norway: (4141) Nyland; Pedersen, Strandberg, Hanche-Olsen (Gabrielsen 88), Meling; Berg; Daehli (Johnsen 64), Odegaard (Gregersen 81), Elyounoussi M, Hauge (Aursnes 46); Thorstvedt (Berisha 64).
Montenegro: (4141) Sarkic; Vesovic■, Vujacic, Tomasevic, Radunovic (Beciraj 82); Scekic (Jovovic 76); Marusic, Kosovic (Osmajic 46), Jankovic M, Haksabanovic (Djurdjevic 67); Jovetic.

Saturday, 13 November 2021

Montenegro (0) 2 *(Vukotic 82, Vujnovic 86)*

Netherlands (1) 2 *(Depay 25 (pen), 54)* 1844

Montenegro: (541) Sarkic; Vukcevic M, Vujacic, Savic, Tomasevic (Raickovic 80), Radunovic; Jovovic (Vujnovic 62), Jankovic M (Bozovic 69), Haksabanovic (Vukotic 69), Osmajic; Djurdjevic (Beciraj 62).
Netherlands: (433) Bijlow; Dumfries, de Vrij (de Ligt 90), van Dijk, Blind; Wijnaldum (Koopmeiners 66), de Jong F (Gravenberch 78), Klaassen; Malen (Bergwijn 46), Depay, Danjuma (Lang 78).

Norway (0) 0

Latvia (0) 0 24,376

Norway: (4231) Nyland; Pedersen, Strandberg, Lode, Meling; Thorsby (King 46), Normann; Odegaard, Thorstvedt (Solbakken 82), Elyounoussi M; Sorloth.
Latvia: (4231) Ozols; Savavnieks, Cernomordijs, Dubra, Jurkovskis; Emsis, Kigurs (Karklins 89); Jaunzems (Kamess 59), Uldrikis (Tarasovs 75), Ciganiks; Gutkowski (Krollis 89).

Turkey (3) 6 *(Akturkoglu 11, Dervisoglu 38, 41, Demiral 65, Dursun 81, Muldur 84)*

Gibraltar (0) 0 8895

Turkey: (442) Cakir; Celik (Muldur 46), Demiral, Soyuncu, Erkin (Yilmaz R 46); Baris Yilmaz, Kokcu, Calhanoglu (Kutlu 82), Akturkoglu; Burak Yilmaz (Dursun 69), Dervisoglu (Karaman 69).
Gibraltar: (541) Coleing; Sergeant (Barnett 82), Chipolina R, Wiseman, Mouelhi, Olivero■; Walker (Badr 59), Jolley (Chipolina J 46), Annesley, Valarino (Casciaro L 46); De Barr (Styche 59).

Tuesday, 16 November 2021

Gibraltar (1) 1 *(Walker 7)*

Latvia (1) 3 *(Gutkowski 25, Uldrikis 55, Krollis 75)* 1130

Gibraltar: (532) Coleing; Sergeant, Wiseman, Chipolina R, Mouelhi, Britto; Torrilla, Annesley (Ronan 67), Valarino (Styche 76); De Barr (Casciaro L 45), Walker.
Latvia: (442) Ozols; Savavnieks, Cernomordijs, Dubra, Jurkovskis; Jaunzems (Kamess 46), Tarasovs, Kigurs (Krollis 69), Ciganiks (Varslavans 90); Gutkowski, Uldrikis (Karklins 69).

Netherlands (0) 2 *(Bergwijn 84, Depay 90)*

Norway (0) 0

Netherlands: (433) Cillessen; Dumfries, de Ligt, van Dijk, Blind; Wijnaldum, de Jong F, Klaassen (de Roon 74); Bergwijn, Depay, Danjuma (Ake 89).
Norway: (433) Nyland; Pedersen (Olsen 87), Strandberg, Hanche-Olsen, Meling; Odegaard, Normann (Gregersen 74), Thorsby (Thorstvedt 46); Solbakken (Hauge 46 (King 74)), Sorloth, Elyounoussi M.

Montenegro (1) 1 *(Beciraj 3)*

Turkey (1) 2 *(Akturkoglu 22, Kokcu 60)* 2885

Montenegro: (541) Sarkic; Vesovic, Vujacic, Savic (Simic 57), Tomasevic, Radunovic; Jovovic (Bozovic 67), Haksabanovic (Vukotic 57), Jankovic M (Raickovic 74), Osmajic; Beciraj (Vujnovic 66).
Turkey: (442) Cakir; Celik (Ayhan 90), Demiral, Soyuncu, Erkin; Omur (Kutlu 79), Ozdemir (Kokcu 46), Calhanoglu, Akturkoglu (Baris Yilmaz 79); Burak Yilmaz, Dervisoglu (Karaman 69).

Group G Table	P	W	D	L	F	A	GD	Pts
Netherlands	10	7	2	1	33	8	25	23
Turkey	10	6	3	1	27	16	11	21
Norway	10	5	3	2	15	8	7	18
Montenegro	10	3	3	4	14	15	–1	12
Latvia	10	2	3	5	11	14	–3	9
Gibraltar	10	0	0	10	4	43	–39	0

GROUP H

Wednesday, 1 September 2021

Malta (1) 3 *(Attard 43, 54, Mbong J 46)*

Cyprus (0) 0 2686

Malta: (3421) Bonello; Shaw (Muscat Z 59), Pepe, Borg S; Attard, Pisani, Teuma (Caruana 85), Camenzuli; Mbong J (Dimech 59), Mbong P (Grech 70); Montebello (Satariano 70).
Cyprus: (343) Michael; Karo, Soteriou■, Antoniades (Katelaris 64); Psaltis, Charis Kyriakou (Loizou 71), Artymatas, Ioannou N; Papoulis (Panagiotou 58), Christofi (Elia 59), Pittas (Kastanos 58).

Russia (0) 0

Croatia (0) 0 18,708

Russia: (433) Guilherme; Fernandes (Samoshnikov 78), Diveev, Dzhikija, Karavaev; Kuzyaev (Erokhin 84), Barinov, Golovin; Ionov (Bakaev 70), Aleksey Miranchuk (Zabolotny 46), Zakharyan (Cheryshev 70).
Croatia: (4312) Livakovic; Juranovic, Lovren, Caleta-Car (Skoric 84), Sosa; Pasalic (Ivanusec 70), Brozovic, Kovacic; Vlasic; Kramaric (Orsic 74), Perisic (Livaja 74).

Slovenia (1) 1 *(Stojanovic 42)*

Slovakia (1) 1 *(Bozenik 32)* 4034

Slovenia: (4231) Oblak; Stojanovic, Blazic, Mevlja, Balkovec; Lovric (Bijol 83), Stulac (Stankovic 70); Ilicic, Zajc (Cerin 70), Mlakar (Crnigoj 57); Sesko (Sporar 83).
Slovakia: (433) Rodak; Pekarik, Satka, Skriniar, Holubek; Hamsik, Lobotka, Kucka (Duda 90); Schranz (Strelec 76), Bozenik (Koscelnik 76), Weiss (Mak 64).

Saturday, 4 September 2021

Cyprus (0) 0

Russia (1) 2 *(Erokhin 6, Zhemaletdinov 55)* 1645

Cyprus: (541) Michael; Psaltis (Zachariou 77), Katelaris, Karo, Panagiotou (Avraam 61), Ioannou N; Loizou, Artymatas (Charis Kyriakou 73), Kastanos, Papoulis (Elia 72); Pittas (Tzionis 61).
Russia: (433) Guilherme; Karavaev, Diveev, Dzhikija, Samoshnikov; Erokhin, Barinov, Golovin (Kuzyaev 67); Aleksey Miranchuk (Bakaev 64), Smolov (Tyukavin 75), Cheryshev (Zhemaletdinov 46).

Slovakia (0) 0

Croatia (0) 1 *(Brozovic 86)* 9047

Slovakia: (433) Rodak; Pekarik (Strelec 89), Satka, Skriniar, Hancko; Kucka, Lobotka, Hamsik (Duda 63); Mak (Jirka 79), Schranz (Bozenik 62), Weiss (Koscelnik 80).
Croatia: (4231) Ivusic; Juranovic, Lovren, Vida, Sosa; Brozovic, Kovacic (Majer 84); Ivanusec (Perisic 55), Vlasic (Pasalic 55), Orsic (Kramaric 62); Colak (Livaja 55).

Slovenia (1) 1 *(Lovric 44 (pen))*

Malta (0) 0 4571

Slovenia: (4231) Oblak; Stojanovic, Bijol, Mevlja, Balkovec; Cerin, Kurtic; Mlakar (Zajc 61), Lovric (Stankovic 70), Bohar (Crnigoj 60); Sesko (Sporar 70).
Malta: (343) Bonello; Shaw, Pepe, Muscat Z; Attard, Caruana (Pisani 79), Teuma, Corbalan (Camenzuli 46); Mbong J (Gambin 73), Satariano (Montebello 58), Dimech (Mbong P 58).

Tuesday, 7 September 2021

Croatia (1) 3 *(Livaja 33, Pasalic 66, Vlasic 90)*

Slovenia (0) 0 16,237

Croatia: (4231) Ivusic; Juranovic, Lovren (Caleta-Car 77), Vida, Barisic; Brozovic, Kovacic (Ivanusec 76); Kramaric (Orsic 76), Pasalic, Perisic (Colak 86); Livaja (Vlasic 58).

Slovenia: (433) Oblak; Stojanovic (Zahovic 88), Bijol, Mevlja, Balkovec (Jurcevic 65); Cerin, Stankovic (Skubic 65), Kurtic; Ilicic (Mlakar 54), Sesko (Sporar 65), Lovric.

Russia (1) 2 *(Smolov 10, Bakaev 84 (pen))*
Malta (0) 0 10,508
Russia: (433) Guilherme; Kuzyaev, Diveev, Osipenko, Karavaev; Erokhin (Zobnin 46), Barinov, Aleksey Miranchuk (Samoshnikov 58); Ionov (Zhemaletdinov 79), Smolov (Zabolotny 71), Zakharyan (Bakaev 46).
Malta: (3421) Bonello; Muscat Z, Agius (Shaw 86), Borg S; Attard (Dimech 75), Pisani (Caruana 66), Teuma (Muscat N 86), Camenzuli; Mbong J, Mbong P; Montebello (Satariano 66).

Slovakia (0) 2 *(Schranz 55, Koscelnik 77)*
Cyprus (0) 0 6762
Slovakia: (4231) Rodak; Koscelnik, Satka, Skriniar, Hancko; Lobotka (Hrosovsky 53), Hamsik; Schranz (Suslov 79), Duda, Weiss (Jirka 59); Bozenik (Strelec 79).
Cyprus: (343) Michael; Katelaris, Soteriou, Ioannou N; Psaltis (Zachariou 75), Artymatas, Kastanos (Charis Kyriakou 75), Avraam (Roushias 88); Loizou (Pittas 75), Elia (Papoulis 60), Tzionis.

Friday, 8 October 2021

Cyprus (0) 0
Croatia (1) 3 *(Perisic 45, Gvardiol 80, Livaja 90)* 2333
Cyprus: (541) Michael; Psaltis, Andreou, Soteriou, Ioannou N, Avraam (Antoniades 60); Pittas (Tzionis 46), Artymatas (Charalambos Kyriakou 69), Kastanos, Papoulis (Loizou 69); Sotiriou (Kakoullis 86).
Croatia: (433) Livakovic; Stanisic, Caleta-Car, Gvardiol, Sosa; Modric (Ivanusec 84), Brozovic (Jakic 84), Kovacic (Pasalic 63); Vlasic (Brekalo 68), Kramaric (Livaja 68), Perisic.

Malta (0) 0
Slovenia (1) 4 *(Ilicic 27, 60, Sporar 49, Sesko 67)* 3967
Malta: (343) Bonello; Shaw, Pepe, Muscat Z; Mbong J (Overend 68), Pisani (Caruana 68), Teuma, Attard; Dimech (Gambin 57), Montebello (Degabriele 80), Mbong P (Satariano 57).
Slovenia: (4231) Oblak; Karnicnik, Bijol, Mevlja, Balkovec; Cerin, Kurtic (Elsnik 82); Ilicic (Zahovic 72), Lovric (Stankovic 71), Verbic (Crnigoj 61); Sporar (Sesko 61).

Russia (1) 1 *(Skriniar 24 (og))*
Slovakia (0) 0 9588
Russia: (433) Safonov; Sutormin, Diveev, Dzhikija, Terekhov (Kudryashov 80); Kuzyaev, Barinov, Erokhin (Chistyakov 63); Bakaev (Zhemaletdinov 73), Smolov (Fomin 46), Zakharyan (Zabolotny 46).
Slovakia: (4231) Rodak; Pekarik (Suslov 80), Satka, Skriniar, Hancko; Kucka (Hrosovsky 64), Hamsik; Schranz, Duda (Rusnak 64), Haraslin (Almasi 80); Bozenik (Strelec 64).

Monday, 11 October 2021

Croatia (1) 2 *(Kramaric 25, Modric 71)*
Slovakia (2) 2 *(Schranz 20, Haraslin 45)* 9926
Croatia: (4141) Livakovic; Stanisic (Livaja 67), Vida, Gvardiol, Barisic; Brozovic; Ivanusec (Vlasic 46), Modric, Pasalic (Brekalo 60), Perisic; Kramaric (Sucic 85).
Slovakia: (4141) Rodak; Pekarik, Satka, Skriniar, Hancko; Hrosovsky; Schranz, Kucka (Jirka 85), Hamsik (Bero 41), Haraslin (Koscelnik 72); Almasi.

Cyprus (1) 2 *(Papoulis 6, Sotiriou 80)*
Malta (0) 2 *(Muscat Z 53, Degabriele 90)* 1405
Cyprus: (343) Michael; Andreou (Pittas 79), Soteriou, Antoniades; Demetriou M (Psaltis 86), Charalambos Kyriakou (Gogic 79), Kastanos, Ioannou N; Loizou (Kakoullis 61), Sotiriou, Papoulis (Panagiotou 86).
Malta: (3421) Bonello (Galea 82); Borg S (Shaw 57), Pepe, Muscat Z; Attard, Caruana (Pisani 46), Teuma, Camenzuli; Grech (Degabriele 71), Mbong P (Dimech 71); Montebello.

Slovenia (1) 1 *(Ilicic 40)*
Russia (2) 2 *(Diveev 28, Dzhikija 32)* 6524
Slovenia: (4231) Oblak; Karnicnik (Rogelj 86), Bijol, Mevlja, Balkovec; Cerin (Zahovic 86), Kurtic; Ilicic, Lovric, Verbic (Sesko 53); Sporar (Crnigoj 72).
Russia: (433) Safonov; Sutormin, Diveev (Osipenko 36), Dzhikija, Kudryashov; Fomin (Erokhin 86), Barinov, Kuzyaev; Aleksey Miranchuk (Zabolotny 78), Smolov (Zakharyan 78), Bakaev (Chistyakov 86).

Thursday, 11 November 2021

Malta (1) 1 *(Brozovic 31 (og))*
Croatia (4) 7 *(Perisic 6, Caleta-Car 22, Pasalic 39, Modric 45, Majer 47, 64, Kramaric 53)* 4581
Malta: (343) Bonello; Shaw (Micallef 83), Agius, Pepe; Attard, Kristensen (Pisani 46), Teuma (Guillaumier 63), Camenzuli; Mbong J (Dimech 69), Montebello (Satariano 62), Degabriele.
Croatia: (433) Grbic; Juranovic, Caleta-Car, Gvardiol, Sosa; Modric (Vlasic 54), Brozovic (Jakic 46), Pasalic (Livaja 62); Majer, Kramaric (Petkovic 54), Perisic (Orsic 54).

Russia (1) 6 *(Erokhin 4, 87, Smolov 55, Mostovoy 56, Sutormin 62, Zabolotny 81)*
Cyprus (0) 0 10,108
Russia: (433) Safonov; Sutormin, Diveev (Chistyakov 67), Osipenko, Terekhov; Erokhin, Fomin (Glebov 67), Golovin (Zobnin 57); Aleksey Miranchuk, Smolov (Zabolotny 57), Mostovoy (Ionov 72).
Cyprus: (343) Dimitriou D; Karo, Soteriou, Laifis; Psaltis (Demetriou M 46), Artymatas, Kastanos (Antoniades 83), Ioannou N; Tzionis (Mamas 68), Sotiriou (Kakoullis 74), Papoulis (Spoljaric 83).

Slovakia (0) 2 *(Duda 58 (pen), Strelec 74)*
Slovenia (1) 2 *(Zajc 18, Mevlja 62)* 2726
Slovakia: (4141) Rodak; Pekarik (Bozenik 88), Satka, Skriniar, Holubek; Lobotka; Mak (Suslov 71), Bero (Strelec 71), Hamsik (Duda 46), Haraslin (Jirka 65); Almasi.
Slovenia: (4231) Oblak; Stojanovic, Blazic■, Mevlja, Balkovec; Lovric, Stulac; Ilicic (Rogelj 85), Zajc (Vrhovec 71), Verbic (Karnicnik 59); Sporar.

Sunday, 14 November 2021

Croatia (0) 1 *(Kudryashov 81 (og))*
Russia (0) 0 30,257
Croatia: (433) Grbic; Juranovic (Brekalo 75), Lovren, Gvardiol, Sosa; Modric, Brozovic, Pasalic (Livaja 75); Vlasic (Petkovic 58), Kramaric (Stanisic 86), Perisic.
Russia: (433) Safonov; Karavaev, Diveev, Dzhikija, Kudryashov; Fomin (Glebov 80), Barinov, Golovin (Chistyakov 57); Ionov (Zobnin 57), Smolov (Zabolotny 57), Bakaev (Mostovoy 78).

Malta (0) 0
Slovakia (3) 6 *(Rusnak 6, 16, Duda 7, 69, 80, De Marco 71)* 4581
Malta: (343) Bonello; Muscat Z, Shaw, Borg J (Micallef 78); Attard, Guillaumier (Dimech 85), Teuma■, Camenzuli■; Mbong J (Caruana 85), Satariano (Montebello 55), Mbong P (Kristensen 55).
Slovakia: (4141) Dubravka; Koscelnik (Bozenik 77), Satka, Skriniar, Hancko (De Marco 70); Lobotka (Hromada 71); Suslov, Rusnak, Duda, Haraslin (Mak 61); Strelec (Almasi 62).

Slovenia (0) 2 *(Zajc 48, Cerin 84)*
Cyprus (0) 1 *(Kakoullis 89)* 5117
Slovenia: (4231) Oblak; Stojanovic, Karnicnik, Bijol, Balkovec; Cerin, Kurtic; Ilicic, Zajc (Stulac 84), Verbic (Lovric 31); Celar (Vrhovec 90).
Cyprus: (343) Michael; Andreou, Laifis, Antoniades; Demetriou M, Artymatas, Kastanos, Avraam (Spoljaric 90); Papoulis (Kakoullis 81), Sotiriou, Tzionis (Efrem 74).

Group H Table	*P*	*W*	*D*	*L*	*F*	*A*	*GD*	*Pts*
Croatia	10	7	2	1	21	4	17	23
Russia	10	7	1	2	19	6	13	22
Slovakia	10	3	5	2	17	10	7	14
Slovenia	10	4	2	4	13	12	1	14
Cyprus	10	1	2	7	4	21	–17	5
Malta	10	1	2	7	9	30	–21	5

GROUP I

Thursday, 2 September 2021

Andorra (2) 2 *(Vales 18, 24)*

San Marino (0) 0 1400

Andorra: (442) Gomes; San Nicolas M, Llovera, Alavedra, Cervos; Alaez, Vales (Vieira X 73), Moreno (Vieira M 65), Martinez A (Jordi Rubio 86); Fernandez (Bernat 86), Pujol (Martinez C 73).
San Marino: (4231) Benedettini E; Manuel Battistini, Fabbri, Rossi (Cevoli 46), Palazzi; Lunadei (Mularoni 75), Golinucci E; Tomassini F (Vitaioli M 75), Tomassini D (Zafferani 46), Hirsch (Ceccaroli 75); Nanni N.

Hungary (0) 0

England (0) 4 *(Sterling 55, Kane 63, Maguire 69, Rice 87)* 58,260

Hungary: (3421) Gulacsi; Kecskes, Orban, Attila Szalai; Bolla (Varga K 70), Kleinheisler (Gazdag 82), Schafer, Fiola; Sallai (Salloi 66), Szoboszlai; Adam Szalai.
England: (4231) Pickford; Walker, Stones, Maguire, Shaw; Phillips, Rice (Henderson 87); Sterling, Mount (Lingard 84), Grealish (Saka 88); Kane.

Poland (2) 4 *(Lewandowski 12, Buksa 44, Krychowiak 54, Linetty 89)*

Albania (1) 1 *(Cikalleshi 25)* 38,254

Poland: (442) Szczesny; Bereszynski (Dawidowicz 33), Glik, Bednarek, Rybus (Puchacz 81); Jozwiak, Moder, Krychowiak, Frankowski (Linetty 62); Buksa (Swiderski 81), Lewandowski.
Albania: (352) Berisha; Ismajli, Kumbulla, Djimsiti; Hysaj, Bare, Gjasula, Abrashi (Cekici 74), Trashi (Roshi 67); Cikalleshi (Uzuni 83), Manaj (Balaj 68).

Sunday, 5 September 2021

Albania (0) 1 *(Broja 87)*

Hungary (0) 0 4135

Albania: (3412) Berisha; Ismajli, Kumbulla, Djimsiti; Doka (Hoxhallari 78), Gjasula, Abrashi (Cekici 69), Trashi (Roshi 46); Bajrami (Laci 63); Balaj (Broja 78), Uzuni.
Hungary: (3142) Gulacsi (Dibusz 46); Orban, Lang, Attila Szalai; Nagy A; Botka (Varga R 88), Kleinheisler (Nikolic 90), Gazdag (Salloi 67), Fiola; Sallai (Szabo 88), Szoboszlai.

England (1) 4 *(Lingard 18, 78, Kane 72 (pen), Saka 85)*

Andorra (0) 0 67,171

England: (433) Johnstone; James (Grealish 62), Coady, Mings, Trippier; Alexander-Arnold, Henderson, Bellingham (Mount 62); Lingard, Bamford (Kane 62), Saka.
Andorra: (541) Gomes; Jesus Rubio, Garcia C, Vales, Llovera, San Nicolas M (Cervos 86); Clemente (Martinez A 74), Rebes, Vieira M (Lima 86), Jordi Rubio (Garcia M 74); Sanchez A (Fernandez 66).

San Marino (0) 1 *(Nanni N 48)*

Poland (4) 7 *(Lewandowski 4, 21, Swiderski 16, Linetty 44, Buksa 67, 90, 90)* 500

San Marino: (532) Benedettini E; D'Addario, Fabbri (Conti 66), Brolli (Cevoli 46), Rossi (Tomassini F 39), Grandoni; Lunadei, Golinucci E, Mularoni; Nanni N (Palazzi 73), Vitaioli M (Hirsch 46).
Poland: (352) Szczesny (Skorupski 46); Piatkowski, Helik, Kedziora; Kaminski, Szymanski D, Linetty (Frankowski 79), Moder (Slisz 46), Puchacz (Zalewski 66); Swiderski, Lewandowski (Buksa 46).

Wednesday, 8 September 2021

Albania (1) 5 *(Manaj 32, Laci 58, Broja 61, Hysaj 68, Uzuni 80)*

San Marino (0) 0 3850

Albania: (3421) Strakosha; Mihaj, Kumbulla, Djimsiti; Hysaj (Doka 81), Bare, Laci (Ramadani 71), Trashi (Roshi 46); Uzuni (Cokaj 81), Bajrami (Broja 46); Manaj.
San Marino: (541) Benedettini E; Manuel Battistini, Fabbri (Conti 57), Brolli, Palazzi, Grandoni (Zafferani 69); Hirsch (Vitaioli 69), Golinucci E (Michael Battistini 75), Golinucci A, Tomassini D (Tomassini F 46); Nanni N.

Hungary (2) 2 *(Adam Szalai 9 (pen), Botka 18)*

Andorra (0) 1 *(Llovera 82)* 46,240

Hungary: (3142) Dibusz; Fiola, Lang, Attila Szalai; Nagy A (Gazdag 65); Botka (Tamas 90), Kleinheisler (Szoboszlai 46), Schafer, Schon (Nikolic 74); Adam Szalai, Sallai (Salloi 46).
Andorra: (541) Iker; San Nicolas M, Llovera, Garcia E, Alavedra, Garcia M; Alaez, Pujol (Lima 80), Vieira M (Martinez C 76), Cervos (Martinez A 75); Fernandez (Bernat 80).

Poland (0) 1 *(Szymanski D 90)*

England (0) 1 *(Kane 72)* 56,212

Poland: (3142) Szczesny; Dawidowicz, Glik (Helik 80), Bednarek; Krychowiak (Szymanski D 68); Jozwiak (Frankowski 80), Linetty, Moder, Puchacz (Rybus 80); Buksa (Swiderski 63), Lewandowski.
England: (4231) Pickford; Walker, Stones, Maguire, Shaw; Phillips, Rice; Sterling, Mount, Grealish; Kane.

Saturday, 9 October 2021

Andorra (0) 0

England (2) 5 *(Chilwell 17, Saka 40, Abraham 59, Ward-Prowse 79, Grealish 86)* 2285

Andorra: (541) Gomes; Jesus Rubio, Garcia C (Lima 31 (Garcia E 63)), Vales, Llovera, Garcia M; Martinez C (Alaez 64), Rebes, Vieira X, Jordi Rubio (Cervos 82); Sanchez A (Fernandez 64).
England: (433) Johnstone; Trippier, Stones (Tomori 60), Coady, Chilwell; Lingard (Mount 73), Ward-Prowse, Foden; Saka, Abraham (Watkins 80), Sancho (Grealish 72).

Hungary (0) 0

Albania (0) 1 *(Broja 79)* 273

Hungary: (3421) Gulacsi; Botka (Lang 83), Orban, Attila Szalai; Nego (Szabo 83), Nagy A (Kleinheisler 71), Schafer, Nagy Z; Sallai (Vecsei 71), Szoboszlai; Salloi (Schon 58).
Albania: (3412) Berisha; Ismajli, Kumbulla, Djimsiti (Veseli 29); Hysaj, Bare, Gjasula, Trashi (Balliu 86); Cekici (Bajrami 46); Uzuni (Broja 66), Cikalleshi (Manaj 66).

Poland (2) 5 *(Swiderski 10, Brolli 20 (og), Kedziora 50, Buksa 84, Piatek 90)*

San Marino (0) 0 56,128

Poland: (3412) Fabianski (Majecki 58); Gumny, Helik, Kedziora; Frankowski (Bereszynski 66), Klich (Piatek 46), Linetty, Placheta; Kozlowski; Lewandowski (Moder 66), Swiderski (Buksa 72).
San Marino: (433) Benedettini E; Manuel Battistini, Simoncini D, Brolli (Rossi 74), Palazzi (Fabbri 52); Golinucci A, Censoni (Grandoni 46), Golinucci E; Mularoni, Vitaioli M (Bernardi 75), Hirsch (Tomassini D 46).

Tuesday, 12 October 2021

Albania (0) 0

Poland (0) 1 *(Swiderski 77)* 21,000

Albania: (433) Berisha; Hysaj, Ismajli, Kumbulla, Veseli; Ramadani, Bare (Cokaj 77), Trashi (Lenjani 65); Roshi (Bajrami 77), Manaj, Uzuni (Broja 58).
Poland: (3142) Szczesny; Dawidowicz, Glik, Bednarek (Helik 90); Krychowiak; Jozwiak (Frankowski 71), Zielinski, Moder (Klich 46), Puchacz (Bereszynski 90); Buksa (Swiderski 71), Lewandowski.

England (1) 1 *(Stones 37)*

Hungary (1) 1 *(Sallai 24 (pen))* 69,380

England: (433) Pickford; Walker, Stones, Mings, Shaw; Foden, Rice, Mount; Sterling (Henderson 76), Kane (Abraham 76 (Watkins 90)), Grealish (Saka 62).
Hungary: (3421) Gulacsi; Kecskes, Lang, Attila Szalai; Nego (Bolla 90), Nagy A, Schafer (Vecsei 79), Nagy Z; Szoboszlai (Nikolic 90), Schon (Holender 68); Sallai (Szabo 79).

San Marino (0) 0

Andorra (1) 3 *(Pujol 10, Moreno 53, Fernandez 89)* 243

San Marino: (4141) Benedettini E; Manuel Battistini, Fabbri, Simoncini D, Grandoni; Censoni (Ceccaroli 68); Mularoni (Vitaioli M 60), Golinucci E, Golinucci A, Tomassini D (Hirsch 68); Nanni N.
Andorra: (442) Iker; San Nicolas M (De Pablos 90), Llovera, Alavedra, Cervos; Martinez C (Jordi Rubio 84), Vales, Moreno (Vieira M 77), Alaez; Fernandez (Rebes 90), Pujol (Vieira X 90).

Friday, 12 November 2021

Andorra (1) 1 *(Vales 45)*

Poland (3) 4 *(Lewandowski 5, 73, Jozwiak 11, Milik 45)* 1049

Andorra: (442) Iker; San Nicolas M (De Pablos 84), Llovera, Alavedra, Cervos; Vieira M, Vales (Garcia C 66), Clemente (Martinez A 66), Alaez (Garcia M 84); Fernandez■, Pujol (Rosas 62).
Poland: (3142) Szczesny; Bereszynski, Glik, Rybus; Krychowiak (Linetty 64); Jozwiak, Zielinski (Szymanski D 86), Klich (Piatek 64), Frankowski (Cash 64); Lewandowski, Milik (Swiderski 77).

England (5) 5 *(Maguire 9, Kane 18, 33, 45, Henderson 28)*

Albania (0) 0 80,366

England: (343) Pickford; Walker, Stones, Maguire; James (Alexander-Arnold 77), Henderson, Phillips (Bellingham 64), Chilwell; Foden (Grealish 63), Kane (Abraham 63), Sterling (Smith Rowe 77).
Albania: (343) Strakosha; Ismajli, Kumbulla (Dermaku 17), Veseli; Hysaj, Gjasula, Bare (Laci 12), Trashi (Mihaj 46); Uzuni (Roshi 86), Cikalleshi, Bajrami (Ramadani 46).

Hungary (2) 4 *(Szoboszlai 6, 83, Gazdag 22, Vecsei 88)*

San Marino (0) 0 12,800

Hungary: (3421) Dibusz; Botka (Balogh 85), Lang, Attila Szalai; Nego, Nagy A (Schàfer 57), Vecsei, Schon (Varga K 57); Gazdag (Kiss 73), Szoboszlai (Szabo 85); Adam Szalai.
San Marino: (442) Benedettini E; Manuel Battistini, Fabbri, Rossi (Zonzini 71), Grandoni (Golinucci A 60); Mularoni, Lunadei, Golinucci E, Tomassini D (Hirsch 36); Tomassini F (D'Addario 60), Nanni N (Vitaioli N 60).

Monday, 15 November 2021

Albania (0) 1 *(Cekici 73 (pen))*

Andorra (0) 0 75

Albania: (352) Strakosha; Mihaj, Dermaku, Hoxhallari (Lenjani 90); Roshi, Cekici, Ramadani (Bajrami 56), Laci, Hysaj; Uzuni, Sulejmanov (Muci 56).
Andorra: (541) Gomes; San Nicolas M, Llovera, Garcia C, Alavedra (Rodrigues 85), Cervos; Alaez, Pujol (Vieira X 85), Vieira M (Moreno 85), Martinez C (Garcia M 63); Rosas (Martinez A 74).

Poland (0) 1 *(Swiderski 61)*

Hungary (1) 2 *(Schafer 37, Gazdag 80)* 56,197

Poland: (3142) Szczesny; Dawidowicz, Bednarek, Kedziora; Linetty (Frankowski 65); Cash (Jozwiak 46), Klich, Moder (Zielinski 46), Puchacz (Placheta 83); Swiderski, Piatek (Milik 65).
Hungary: (3421) Dibusz; Fiola, Lang, Attila Szalai; Nego, Nagy A (Vecsei 90), Schafer, Nagy Z; Varga K (Gazdag 58), Schon (Kiss 72); Adam Szalai (Szabo 89).

San Marino (0) 0

England (6) 10 *(Maguire 6, Fabbri 15 (og), Kane 27 (pen), 31, 39 (pen), 42, Smith Rowe 58, Mings 69, Abraham 78, Saka 79)* 2775

San Marino: (352) Benedettini E; Manuel Battistini, Fabbri (Conti 81), Rossi■; Tomassini F (Vitaioli M 46), Lunadei (Grandoni 74), Golinucci E, Mularoni, D'Addario (Censoni 46); Nanni N, Hirsch (Golinucci A 46).
England: (343) Ramsdale; Maguire (Chilwell 46), Coady, Mings; Alexander-Arnold, Bellingham, Phillips (Gallagher 46), Saka; Foden (Abraham 46), Kane (James 63), Smith Rowe (Stones 73).

Group I Table	P	W	D	L	F	A	GD	Pts
England	10	8	2	0	39	3	36	26
Poland	10	6	2	2	30	11	19	20
Albania	10	6	0	4	12	12	0	18
Hungary	10	5	2	3	19	13	6	17
Andorra	10	2	0	8	8	24	–16	6
San Marino	10	0	0	10	1	46	–45	0

Harry Kane spectacularly scores the final goal as England thrash Albania 5-0 in a World Cup qualifier at Wembley in November. (Action Images via Reuters/Carl Recine)

GROUP J

Thursday, 2 September 2021

Iceland (0) 0

Romania (0) 2 *(Man 47, Stanciu 83)* 1961

Iceland: (433) Runarsson; Saevarsson, Hermannsson, Brynjar Ingi Bjarnason, Thorarinsson; Birkir Bjarnason, Palsson, Baldursson (Johannesson 67); Gudmundsson J, Kjartansson (Thorsteinsson 67), Gudmundsson A (Gudjohnsen A 79).
Romania: (4231) Nita; Ratiu (Manea 69), Chiriches, Nedelcearu, Camora; Cicaldau (Rus 88), Nedelcu; Man (Marin R 76), Stanciu, Sorescu (Hagi 68); Alibec (Markovic 76).

Liechtenstein (0) 0

Germany (1) 2 *(Werner 41, Sane 77)* 7958

Liechtenstein: (532) Buchel B; Wolfinger S (Yildiz 83), Malin (Kollmann 83), Kaufmann, Hofer, Goppel; Frick N (Kardesoglu 71), Frommelt, Hasler; Sele A (Wolfinger F 61), Frick Y (Grunenfelder 71).
Germany: (4231) Leno; Baku (Hofmann 60), Kehrer, Sule, Gosens; Gundogan (Goretzka 73), Kimmich (Wirtz 82); Musiala (Reus 60), Havertz (Gnabry 60), Sane; Werner.

North Macedonia (0) 0

Armenia (0) 0 3147

North Macedonia: (4141) Dimitrievski; Ristovski S, Velkovski, Musliu, Alioski; Bardhi; Churlinov, Kostadinov (Askovski 83), Elmas, Trajkovski (Spirovski 60); Jahovic (Ristovski M 81).
Armenia: (433) Yurchenko; Hambardzumyan, Voskanyan, Calisir, Hovhannisyan K; Bichakhchyan (Koryan 46 (Terteryan 90)), Grigoryan A, Udo; Vardanyan (Spertsyan 67), Adamyan (Shagoyan 72), Mkhitaryan.

Sunday, 5 September 2021

Germany (4) 6 *(Gnabry 6, 15, Reus 35, Werner 44, Hofmann 52, Adeyemi 90)*

Armenia (0) 0 18,086

Germany: (4231) Neuer; Hofmann, Sule, Rudiger, Kehrer (Raum 83); Kimmich (Gundogan 61), Goretzka; Gnabry (Adeyemi 71), Reus (Wirtz 61), Sane (Musiala 60); Werner.
Armenia: (442) Yurchenko; Hambardzumyan (Terteryan 57), Haroyan, Voskanyan, Hovhannisyan K; Adamyan (Geloyan 46), Grigoryan A, Wbeymar (Udo 46), Bayramyan (Avanesyan 82); Barseghyan (Bichakhchyan 70), Mkhitaryan.

Iceland (0) 2 *(Brynjar Ingi Bjarnason 78, Gudjohnsen A 84)*

North Macedonia (1) 2 *(Velkovski 11, Alioski 54)* 1862

Iceland: (451) Runarsson; Saevarsson, Arnason, Brynjar Ingi Bjarnason, Thorarinsson (Skulason A 66); Anderson (Thorsteinsson 60), Birkir Bjarnason, Baldursson (Helgason 60), Johannesson (Gudjohnsen A 82), Gudmundsson A; Kjartansson (Sigurdsson A 60).
North Macedonia: (442) Dimitrievski; Ristovski S, Velkovski (Ristevski 90), Musliu, Alioski; Churlinov, Spirovski, Kostadinov (Jahovic 80), Elmas; Bardhi (Trajkovski 72), Ristovski M (Avramovski 80).

Romania (2) 2 *(Tosca 11, Manea 18)*

Liechtenstein (0) 0 9404

Romania: (433) Nita; Manea, Rus, Nedelcearu (Ghita 79), Tosca; Stanciu (Cicaldau 64), Marin R, Olaru (Marin M 63); Cordea, Markovic (Man 64), Hagi (Sorescu 80).
Liechtenstein: (532) Buchel B; Wolfinger F (Kollmann 82), Grunenfelder, Malin, Hofer, Goppel; Frick N (Sele A 46), Frommelt, Hasler (Spirig 83); Kardesoglu (Ospelt P 64), Frick Y (Yildiz 71).

Wednesday, 8 September 2021

Armenia (1) 1 *(Mkhitaryan 45 (pen))*

Liechtenstein (0) 1 *(Frick N 80)* 14,400

Armenia: (41212) Yurchenko; Terteryan, Haroyan, Calisir (Geloyan 87), Hovhannisyan K; Udo; Barseghyan, Bayramyan (Shagoyan 46); Mkhitaryan; Adamyan, Karapetyan (Vardanyan 78).
Liechtenstein: (532) Buchel B; Wolfinger S (Spirig 75), Malin, Kaufmann, Hofer, Goppel; Sele A (Yildiz 61), Frommelt, Hasler; Kardesoglu (Wolfinger F 46), Frick Y (Frick N 42).

Iceland (0) 0

Germany (2) 4 *(Gnabry 4, Rudiger 24, Sane 56, Werner 88)* 3505

Iceland: (433) Halldorsson; Saevarsson, Brynjar Ingi Bjarnason, Fjoluson, Skulason A; Birkir Bjarnason, Palsson (Baldursson 90), Johannesson (Sigurdsson A 71); Gudmundsson J (Thorsteinsson 71), Gudmundsson A (Gudjohnsen A 80), Helgason.
Germany: (4231) Neuer; Hofmann (Klostermann 46), Sule (Gosens 60), Rudiger, Kehrer; Kimmich, Goretzka (Wirtz 80); Gnabry (Havertz 46), Gundogan, Sane (Musiala 59); Werner.

North Macedonia (0) 0

Romania (0) 0 5260

North Macedonia: (4231) Dimitrievski; Ristovski S, Velkovski (Ristevski 64), Musliu, Alioski; Kostadinov, Spirovski (Trajkovski 78); Elmas, Bardhi (Askovski 90), Churlinov (Nikolov 78); Ristovski M (Jahovic 64).
Romania: (433) Nita; Ratiu, Chiriches, Nedelcearu, Camora; Stanciu, Nedelcu (Marin R 63), Cicaldau; Man, Markovic (Cordea 63), Sorescu (Marin M 74).

Friday, 8 October 2021

Germany (0) 2 *(Gnabry 52, Muller 81)*

Romania (1) 1 *(Hagi 9)* 25,000

Germany: (4231) ter Stegen; Hofmann (Klostermann 85), Sule, Rudiger, Kehrer; Goretzka, Kimmich; Gnabry, Reus (Havertz 67), Sane (Adeyemi 89); Werner (Muller 67).
Romania: (541) Nita; Ratiu, Rus, Chiriches, Burca (Manea 50), Tosca; Hagi (Maxim 60), Marin R, Stanciu (Albu 82), Mihaila (Ivan 60); Puscas (Mitrita 82).

Iceland (0) 1 *(Johannesson 77)*

Armenia (1) 1 *(Hovhannisyan K 35)* 1697

Iceland: (433) Olafsson; Saevarsson, Hermannsson (Gudjohnsen S 68), Brynjar Ingi Bjarnason (Gretarsson 46), Skulason A; Birkir Bjarnason, Palsson, Helgason (Ellertsson 90); Gudmundsson A, Kjartansson (Johannesson 46), Thorsteinsson (Anderson 81).
Armenia: (442) Yurchenko; Terteryan, Haroyan, Voskanyan, Hovhannisyan K; Barseghyan (Geloyan 87), Udo, Spertsyan (Grigoryan A 78), Mkhitaryan; Adamyan (Karapetyan 78), Zelarrayan (Bayramyan 64).

Liechtenstein (0) 0

North Macedonia (1) 4 *(Velkovski 39, Alioski 66 (pen), Nikolov 74, Churlinov 83)* 1628

Liechtenstein: (532) Buchel B; Wolfinger S (Grunenfelder 79), Malin, Kaufmann, Hofer, Goppel; Sele A (Martin Buchel 75), Wolfinger F (Yildiz 61), Hasler; Frick N (Meier 46), Frick Y.
North Macedonia: (4141) Dimitrievski; Ristovski S (Rakip 76), Velkovski (Zajkov 76), Ristevski, Alioski (Nikolov 70); Spirovski; Churlinov, Ademi (Askovski 70), Elmas, Trajkovski; Ristovski M (Miovski 61).

Monday, 11 October 2021

Iceland (2) 4 *(Thordarson 19, Gudmundsson A 35 (pen), 79 (pen), Gudjohnsen A 89)*

Liechtenstein (0) 0 4461

Iceland: (433) Olafsson; Sampsted, Brynjar Ingi Bjarnason, Gretarsson (Hermannsson 32), Thorarinsson; Thordarson (Gudjohnsen A 80), Birkir Bjarnason, Helgason (Baldursson 65); Gudmundsson A, Kjartansson (Gudjohnsen S 65), Thorsteinsson (Ellertsson 65).
Liechtenstein: (532) Buchel B; Wolfinger S (Kardesoglu 84), Grunenfelder, (Marxer M■ 8), Hofer, Goppel; Sele (Yildiz 67), Frommelt, Hasler; Meier (Frick N 46), Frick Y (Brandle 84).

North Macedonia (0) 0

Germany (0) 4 *(Havertz 50, Werner 70, 73, Musiala 83)* 16,182

North Macedonia: (4231) Dimitrievski; Ristovski S (Askovski 77), Velkovski, Musliu, Alioski; Kostadinov (Ristevski 77), Ademi (Spirovski 29); Nikolov (Rakip 58), Elmas, Churlinov; Jahovic (Miovski 58).
Germany: (4231) Neuer; Klostermann, Sule, Kehrer, Raum; Goretzka (Wirtz 61), Kimmich; Gnabry (Hofmann 74), Muller (Neuhaus 80), Havertz (Adeyemi 61); Werner (Musiala 74).

Romania (1) 1 *(Mitrita 26)*

Armenia (0) 0 13,576

Romania: (433) Nita; Ratiu (Manea 66), Chiriches, Nedelcearu, Bancu; Cicaldau, Marin R, Stanciu (Nedelcu 81); Hagi (Mihaila 81), Keseru (Ivan 62), Mitrita (Morutan 62).
Armenia: (442) Yurchenko; Terteryan, Haroyan, Voskanyan, Hovhannisyan K; Bayramyan (Adamyan 46), Grigoryan A (Geloyan 46), Udo (Karapetyan 82), Mkhitaryan; Barseghyan (Zelarrayan 46), Spertsyan (Vardanyan 77).

Thursday, 11 November 2021

Armenia (0) 0

North Macedonia (2) 5 *(Trajkovski 22, Bardhi 36, 66 (pen), 90 (pen), Ristovski M 79)* 7200

Armenia: (4231) Yurchenko; Terteryan, Hambardzumyan, Calisir, Hovhannisyan K (Margaryan 46); Udo, Vardanyan (Grigoryan A 46); Barseghyan (Grigoryan N 73), Zelarrayan (Bichakhchyan 77), Mkhitaryan; Briasco (Geloyan 73).
North Macedonia: (4141) Dimitrievski; Askovski (Todoroski 83), Velkovski, Musliu, Alioski; Kostadinov (Atanasov 83); Churlinov (Ristevski 77), Elmas (Miovski 83), Bardhi, Trajkovski (Spirovski 64); Ristovski M.

Germany (4) 9 *(Gundogan 11 (pen), Kaufmann 20 (og), Sane 22, 49, Reus 23, Muller 76, 86, Baku 80, Goppel 89 (og))*

Liechtenstein (0) 0 25,984

Germany: (4231) Neuer; Hofmann (Nmecha 46), Kehrer (Ginter 72), Rudiger, Gunter; Goretzka (Neuhaus 46), Gundogan (Arnold 64); Baku, Reus, Sane (Volland 64); Muller.
Liechtenstein: (532) Buchel B; Wolfinger S (Brandle 83), Malin, Kaufmann, Hofer■, Goppel; Sele A (Martin Buchel 84), Frommelt, Hasler; Salanovic (Grunenfelder 69), Frick Y (Wolfinger F 29 (Meier 69)).

Romania (0) 0

Iceland (0) 0

Romania: (433) Nita; Ratiu, Chiriches, Nedelcearu, Tosca (Bancu 68); Cicaldau (Puscas 86), Marin R, Stanciu (Morutan 68); Hagi, Alibec (Ivan 68), Tanase (Maxim 77).
Iceland: (433) Olafsson; Sampsted, Brynjar Ingi Bjarnason, Gretarsson, Skulason A (Thorarinsson 15); Thordarson (Helgason 74), Birkir Bjarnason, Johannesson (Thrandarson 90); Gudmundsson A (Ellertsson 90), Gudjohnsen S (Gudjohnsen A 74), Thorsteinsson.

Sunday, 14 November 2021

Armenia (0) 1 *(Mkhitaryan 59 (pen))*

Germany (2) 4 *(Havertz 15, Gundogan 45 (pen), 50, Hofmann 64)* 7200

Armenia: (532) Buchnev; Terteryan, Haroyan, Voskanyan, Calisir, Margaryan; Udo (Grigoryan A 84), Spertsyan, Bayramyan (Zelarrayan 69); Mkhitaryan (Grigoryan N 76), Adamyan (Briasco 69).
Germany: (3421) ter Stegen; Kehrer, Ginter, Tah; Hofmann (Baku 84), Neuhaus (Volland 73), Gundogan (Arnold 60), Raum; Muller (Nmecha 60), Sane (Brandt 60); Havertz.

Liechtenstein (0) 0

Romania (1) 2 *(Man 7, Bancu 87)* 2237

Liechtenstein: (532) Buchel B; Wolfinger S (Yildiz 82), Grunenfelder, Frommelt, Goppel, Spirig; Meier (Kaufmann 71), Sele A (Martin Buchel 82), Hasler; Frick N (Kardesoglu 63), Frick Y (Wolfinger F 71).
Romania: (433) Nita; Manea, Rus, Burca, Bancu; Morutan (Cicaldau 73), Nedelcu, Stanciu (Maxim 63); Man (Hagi 74), Puscas (Alibec 63), Ivan (Sali 82).

North Macedonia (1) 3 *(Alioski 7, Elmas 65, 86)*

Iceland (0) 1 *(Thorsteinsson 54)* 15,986

North Macedonia: (433) Dimitrievski; Ristovski S (Zajkov 89), Velkovski, Musliu, Alioski; Bardhi, Kostadinov, Elmas; Churlinov (Askovski 63), Ristovski M (Miovski 78), Trajkovski (Spirovski 78).
Iceland: (433) Olafsson; Saevarsson, Brynjar Ingi Bjarnason, Gretarsson, Thorarinsson (Thrandarson 86); Thordarson (Helgason 72), Birkir Bjarnason, Johannesson■; Gudmundsson A (Ellertsson 86), Gudjohnsen S (Gudjohnsen A 72), Thorsteinsson (Traustason 78).

Group J Table	*P*	*W*	*D*	*L*	*F*	*A*	*GD*	*Pts*
Germany	10	9	0	1	36	4	32	27
North Macedonia	10	5	3	2	23	11	12	18
Romania	10	5	2	3	13	8	5	17
Armenia	10	3	3	4	9	20	–11	12
Iceland	10	2	3	5	12	18	–6	9
Liechtenstein	10	0	1	9	2	34	–32	1

FIFA WORLD CUP 2022 QUALIFYING – EUROPEAN PLAY-OFFS

PLAY-OFFS SEMI-FINALS

Thursday, 24 March 2022

Italy (0) 0

North Macedonia (0) 1 *(Trajkovski 90)*

Italy: (433) Donnarumma; Florenzi, Mancini (Chiellini 90), Bastoni, Emerson Palmieri; Barella (Tonali 77), Jorginho, Verratti; Berardi (Joao Pedro 89), Immobile (Pellegrini 77), Insigne (Raspadori 64).
North Macedonia: (4141) Dimitrievski; Ristovski S, Velkovski (Ristevski 86), Musliu, Alioski; Ademi (Askovski 59); Churlinov, Nikolov (Spirovski 59), Bardhi, Trajkovski; Ristovski M (Miovski 72).

Portugal (2) 3 *(Otavio 15, Jota 42, Matheus Luiz 90)*

Turkey (0) 1 *(Burak Yilmaz 65)*

Portugal: (4132) Costa; Dalot, Fonte, Danilo Pereira, Guerreiro (Nuno Mendes 88); Joao Moutinho (Matheus Luiz 88); Otavio (Leao 89), Bruno Fernandes (William Carvalho 80), Bernardo Silva; Ronaldo, Jota (Joao Felix 71).
Turkey: (3421) Cakir; Kabak, Demiral, Soyuncu; Celik (Yazici 80), Kokcu (Tokoz 80), Calhanoglu, Kutlu (Dursun 90); Under, Akturkoglu (Unal 66); Burak Yilmaz.

Sweden (0) 1 *(Quaison 110)*

Czech Republic (0) 0

Sweden: (442) Olsen; Danielson, Lindelof, Nilsson, Olsson M (Bengtsson 61); Claesson (Quaison 62), Olsson K (Karlstrom 107), Ekdal (Svanberg 72), Forsberg (Elanga 115); Kulusevski, Isak (Helander 115).
Czech Republic: (3241) Vaclik; Zima, Brabec, Holes; Soucek, Sadilek (Sykora 90); Masopust (Havel 76), Barak (Krejci II 90), Hlozek (Lingr 111), Jankto (Mateju 76); Kuchta (Pekhart 83).
aet.

Wednesday, 1 June 2022

Scotland (0) 1 *(McGregor C 79)*

Ukraine (1) 3 *(Yarmolenko 33, Yaremchuk 49, Dovbyk 90)*

Scotland: (3412) Gordon; McTominay, Hanley, Cooper (Hendry 68); Hickey, Gilmour (Armstrong 68), McGregor C, Robertson; McGinn J; Adams, Dykes (Christie 46).
Ukraine: (4141) Bushchan; Karavayev, Zabarnyi, Matviyenko, Mykolenko; Stepanenko (Sydorchuk 90); Yarmolenko (Zubkov 78), Malinovsky (Shaparenko 72), Zinchenko, Tsygankov (Mudryk 72); Yaremchuk (Dovbyk 78).

Wales (1) 2 *(Bale 25, 51)*

Austria (0) 1 *(Sabitzer 64)*

Wales: (352) Hennessey; Ampadu, Rodon, Davies B; Roberts C, Ramsey, Allen, Wilson, Williams N; Bale (Mepham 90), James (Johnson 88).
Austria: (4411) Lindner; Lainer (Gregoritsch 88), Dragovic, Hinteregger, Alaba; Laimer (Kalajdzic 55), Schlager X (Lazaro 77), Seiwald, Baumgartner (Weimann 77); Sabitzer; Arnautovic.

PLAY-OFFS FINALS

Tuesday, 29 March 2022

Poland (0) 2 *(Lewandowski 49 (pen), Zielinski 72)*

Sweden (0) 0

Poland: (4141) Szczesny; Cash, Glik, Bednarek, Bereszynski; Bielik; Zielinski (Buksa 89), Goralski (Krychowiak 46), Moder, Szymanski S; Lewandowski.
Sweden: (442) Olsen; Krafth, Lindelof, Danielson (Ibrahimovic 79), Augustinsson; Kulusevski, Olsson K (Karlsson 80), Karlstrom (Svanberg 67), Forsberg; Quaison (Elanga 66), Isak.

Portugal (1) 2 *(Bruno Fernandes 32, 65)*

North Macedonia (0) 0

Portugal: (433) Costa; Joao Cancelo, Pepe, Danilo Pereira, Nuno Mendes; Bruno Fernandes (Matheus Luiz 88), Joao Moutinho (Vitinha 90), Bernardo Silva (Joao Felix 87); Otavio (William Carvalho 77), Jota (Leao 77), Ronaldo.
North Macedonia: (4231) Dimitrievski; Ristovski S, Velkovski, Musliu, Alioski; Ademi, Bardhi; Kostadinov (Askovski 75), Elmas (Nikolov 87), Trajkovski (Churlinov 59); Ristovski M (Miovski 46).

Sunday, 5 June 2022

Wales (1) 1 *(Yarmolenko 34 (og))*

Ukraine (0) 0

Wales: (343) Hennessey; Ampadu, Rodon, Davies B; Roberts C, Allen, Ramsey, Williams N (Norrington-Davies 90); Bale (Wilson 83), Moore, James (Johnson 71).
Ukraine: (4141) Bushchan; Karavayev, Zabarnyi, Matviyenko, Mykolenko; Stepanenko (Sydorchuk 70); Yarmolenko, Malinovsky (Shaparenko 70), Zinchenko, Tsygankov (Mudryk 77); Yaremchuk (Dovbyk 77).

FIFA WORLD CUP 2022

QUALIFIED TEAMS

HOSTS
Qatar

ASIAN FOOTBALL CONFEDERATION (AFC)
Iran
Japan
Saudi Arabia
Korea Republic
Australia

CONFEDERATION OF AFRICAN FOOTBALL (CAF)
Cameroon
Ghana
Morocco
Senegal
Tunisia

CONFEDERATION OF NORTH, CENTRAL AMERICA AND CARIBBEAN (CONCACAF)
Canada
Mexico
USA
Peru

SOUTH AMERICAN FOOTBALL CONFEDERATION (CONMEBOL)
Argentina
Brazil
Ecuador
Uruguay

UNION OF EUROPEAN FOOTBALL ASSOCIATIONS (UEFA)
Belgium
Croatia
Denmark
England
France
Germany
Netherlands
Poland
Portugal
Serbia
Spain
Switzerland
Wales

FIFA WORLD CUP 2022

GROUP STAGE DRAW

GROUP A
Qatar
Ecuador
Senegal
Netherlands

GROUP B
England
Iran
USA
Wales

GROUP C
Argentina
Saudi Arabia
Mexico
Poland

GROUP D
France
Australia
Denmark
Tunisia

GROUP E
Spain
Costa Rica
Germany
Japan

GROUP F
Belgium
Canada
Morocco
Croatia

GROUP G
Brazil
Serbia
Switzerland
Cameroon

GROUP H
Portugal
Ghana
Uruguay
Korea Republic

THE WORLD CUP 1930–2018

Year	Winners v Runners-up		Venue	Attendance	Referee
1930	Uruguay v Argentina *Winning Coach:* Alberto Suppici	4-2	Montevideo	68,346	J. Langenus (Belgium)
1934	Italy v Czechoslovakia *Winning Coach:* Vittorio Pozzo	2-1*	Rome	55,000	I. Eklind (Sweden)
1938	Italy v Hungary *Winning Coach:* Vittorio Pozzo	4-2	Paris	45,000	G. Capdeville (France)
1950	Uruguay v Brazil *Winning Coach:* Juan Lopez	2-1	Rio de Janeiro	173,850	G. Reader (England)
1954	West Germany v Hungary *Winning Coach:* Sepp Herberger	3-2	Berne	62,500	W. Ling (England)
1958	Brazil v Sweden *Winning Coach:* Vicente Feola	5-2	Stockholm	49,737	M. Guigue (France)
1962	Brazil v Czechoslovakia *Winning Coach:* Aymore Moreira	3-1	Santiago	68,679	N. Latychev (USSR)
1966	England v West Germany *Winning Coach:* Alf Ramsey	4-2*	Wembley	96,924	G. Dienst (Sweden)
1970	Brazil v Italy *Winning Coach:* Mario Zagallo	4-1	Mexico City	107,412	R. Glockner (East Germany)
1974	West Germany v Netherlands *Winning Coach:* Helmut Schon	2-1	Munich	78,200	J. Taylor (England)
1978	Argentina v Netherlands *Winning Coach:* Cesar Luis Menotti	3-1*	Buenos Aires	71,483	S. Gonella (Italy)
1982	Italy v West Germany *Winning Coach:* Enzo Bearzot	3-1	Madrid	90,000	A. C. Coelho (Brazil)
1986	Argentina v West Germany *Winning Coach:* Carlos Bilardo	3-2	Mexico City	114,600	R. A. Filho (Brazil)
1990	West Germany v Argentina *Winning Coach:* Franz Beckenbauer	1-0	Rome	73,603	E. C. Mendez (Mexico)
1994	Brazil v Italy *Brazil won 3-2 on penalties.* *Winning Coach:* Carlos Alberto Parreira	0-0*	Los Angeles	94,194	S. Puhl (Hungary)
1998	France v Brazil *Winning Coach:* Aime Jacquet	3-0	Paris	80,000	S. Belqola (Morocco)
2002	Brazil v Germany *Winning Coach:* Luiz Felipe Scolari	2-0	Yokohama	69,029	P. Collina (Italy)
2006	Italy v France *Italy won 5-3 on penalties.* *Winning Coach:* Marcello Lippi	1-1*	Berlin	69,000	H. Elizondo (Argentina)
2010	Spain v Netherlands *Winning Coach:* Vicente del Bosque	1-0	Johannesburg	84,490	H. Webb (England)
2014	Germany v Argentina *Winning Coach:* Joachim Low	1-0*	Rio de Janeiro	74,738	N. Rizzoli (Italy)
2018	France v Croatia *Winning Coach:* Didier Deschamps	4-2	Moscow	78,011	N. Pitana (Argentina)

*(*After extra time)*

GOALSCORING AND ATTENDANCES IN WORLD CUP FINAL ROUNDS

Year	*Venue*	*Games*	*Goals (av)*	*Attendance (av)*
1930	Uruguay	18	70 (3.9)	590,549 (32,808)
1934	Italy	17	70 (4.1)	363,000 (21,352)
1938	France	18	84 (4.7)	375,700 (20,872)
1950	Brazil	22	88 (4.0)	1,045,246 (47,511)
1954	Switzerland	26	140 (5.4)	768,607 (29,562)
1958	Sweden	35	126 (3.6)	819,810 (23,423)
1962	Chile	32	89 (2.8)	893,172 (27,912)
1966	England	32	89 (2.8)	1,563,135 (48,848)
1970	Mexico	32	95 (3.0)	1,603,975 (50,124)
1974	West Germany	38	97 (2.6)	1,865,753 (49,098)
1978	Argentina	38	102 (2.7)	1,545,791 (40,678)
1982	Spain	52	146 (2.8)	2,109,723 (40,571)
1986	Mexico	52	132 (2.5)	2,394,031 (46,039)
1990	Italy	52	115 (2.2)	2,516,215 (48,388)
1994	USA	52	141 (2.7)	3,587,538 (68,991)
1998	France	64	171 (2.7)	2,785,100 (43,517)
2002	Japan/S. Korea	64	161 (2.5)	2,705,197 (42,268)
2006	Germany	64	147 (2.3)	3,359,439 (52,491)
2010	South Africa	64	145 (2.3)	3,178,856 (49,669)
2014	Brazil	64	171 (2.7)	3,367,727 (52,621)
2018	Russia	64	169 (2.6)	3,031,768 (47,371)
Total		900	2548 (2.8)	40,470,332 (44,967)

LEADING GOALSCORERS

Year	*Player*	*Goals*
1930	Guillermo Stabile (Argentina)	8
1934	Oldrich Nejedly (Czechoslovakia)	5
1938	Leonidas da Silva (Brazil)	7
1950	Ademir (Brazil)	8
1954	Sandor Kocsis (Hungary)	11
1958	Just Fontaine (France)	13
1962	Valentin Ivanov (USSR), Leonel Sanchez (Chile), Garrincha (Brazil), Vava (Brazil), Florian Albert (Hungary), Drazen Jerkovic (Yugoslavia)	4
1966	Eusebio (Portugal)	9
1970	Gerd Muller (West Germany)	10
1974	Grzegorz Lato (Poland)	7
1978	Mario Kempes (Argentina)	6
1982	Paolo Rossi (Italy)	6
1986	Gary Lineker (England)	6
1990	Salvatore Schillaci (Italy)	6
1994	Oleg Salenko (Russia) Hristo Stoichkov (Bulgaria)	6
1998	Davor Suker (Croatia)	6
2002	Ronaldo (Brazil)	8
2006	Miroslav Klose (Germany)	5
2010	Thomas Muller (Germany), David Villa (Spain), Wesley Sneijder (Netherlands), Diego Forlan (Uruguay)	5
2014	James Rodriguez (Colombia)	6
2018	Harry Kane (England)	6

UEFA NATIONS LEAGUE 2022–23

▪ *Denotes player sent off.*

GROUP A1

Friday, 3 June 2022

Croatia (0) 0

Austria (1) 3 *(Arnautovic 41, Gregoritsch 54, Sabitzer 57)*

Croatia: (4231) Ivusic; Juranovic, Caleta-Car, Pongracic, Sosa (Barisic 46); Brozovic, Kovacic (Orsic 71); Majer (Modric 58), Pasalic (Vlasic 58), Brekalo; Kramaric (Budimir 58).
Austria: (3142) Lindner; Danso, Trauner, Wober (Friedl 77); Sabitzer; Lainer (Trimmel 46), Laimer, Schlager X, Weimann (Baumgartner 72); Arnautovic (Seiwald 46), Onisiwo (Gregoritsch 46).

France (0) 1 *(Benzema 51)*

Denmark (0) 2 *(Cornelius 68, 88)*

France: (3412) Lloris; Kounde (Diaby 90), Varane (Saliba 61), Hernandez L; Coman (Clauss 90), Kante, Tchouameni, Hernandez T; Griezmann (Rabiot 78); Benzema, Mbappe (Nkunku 46).
Denmark: (3421) Schmeichel; Andersen, Vestergaard (Kristensen 60), Nelsson; Wass (Damsgaard 60), Delaney (Jensen M 85), Hojbjerg, Maehle; Skov Olsen (Braithwaite 84), Eriksen; Dolberg (Cornelius 60).

Monday, 6 June 2022

Austria (0) 1 *(Schlager X 67)*

Denmark (1) 2 *(Hojbjerg 28, Stryger Larsen 84)*

Austria: (4231) Pentz; Trimmel, Posch (Danso 63), Alaba, Friedl (Wober 78); Seiwald, Schlager X; Laimer, Baumgartner (Sabitzer 46), Ljubicic (Arnautovic 46); Kalajdzic (Gregoritsch 46).
Denmark: (3412) Schmeichel; Andersen, Vestergaard (Cornelius 52), Nelsson; Kristensen, Hojbjerg, Jensen M (Delaney 80), Maehle (Stryger Larsen 66); Eriksen; Poulsen (Damsgaard 52), Braithwaite (Skov Olsen 52).

Croatia (0) 1 *(Kramaric 83 (pen))*

France (0) 1 *(Rabiot 52)*

Croatia: (433) Livakovic; Juranovic, Erlic, Vida, Barisic; Modric (Sucic 79), Brozovic, Kovacic (Vlasic 79); Majer (Pasalic 63), Budimir (Kramaric 69), Brekalo (Orsic 63).
France: (4231) Maignan; Pavard, Saliba, Kimpembe, Digne; Tchouameni (Kamara 62), Guendouzi; Diaby (Clauss 79), Nkunku, Rabiot; Ben Yedder (Griezmann 62).

Friday, 10 June 2022

Austria (1) 1 *(Weimann 37)*

France (0) 1 *(Mbappe 83)*

Austria: (442) Pentz; Lainer (Lazaro 54), Trauner, Alaba (Danso 69), Wober; Laimer, Schlager X, Seiwald, Sabitzer; Weimann (Gregoritsch 64), Arnautovic (Onisiwo 64).
France: (4231) Lloris; Pavard, Saliba, Konate, Hernandez T; Tchouameni (Guendouzi 63), Kamara; Diaby, Griezmann (Mbappe 63), Coman (Nkunku 79); Benzema.

Denmark (0) 0

Croatia (0) 1 *(Pasalic 69)*

Denmark: (4231) Schmeichel; Wass (Kristensen 61), Andersen, Christensen, Maehle; Hojbjerg, Delaney; Skov Olsen (Poulsen 83 (Skov 90)), Eriksen, Damsgaard (Braithwaite 62); Cornelius (Wind 62).
Croatia: (4231) Livakovic; Vrsaljko (Stanisic 46), Erlic, Sutalo, Juranovic; Jakic (Kovacic 46), Brozovic; Ivanusec (Modric 46), Pasalic, Orsic (Vlasic 58); Kramaric (Budimir 77).

Monday, 13 June 2022

Denmark (2) 2 *(Wind 21, Skov Olsen 37)*

Austria (0) 0

Denmark: (3421) Schmeichel; Andersen (Nelsson 63), Christensen, Boilesen; Kristensen, Hojbjerg, Jensen M (Eriksen 76), Maehle (Stryger Larsen 49); Skov Olsen (Billing 46), Wind; Cornelius (Braithwaite 46).
Austria: (442) Lindner; Trimmel, Danso, Trauner, Lazaro (Lainer 46); Wimmer (Onisiwo 46), Schlager X (Laimer 46), Seiwald, Sabitzer; Kalajdzic (Arnautovic 65), Weimann (Gregoritsch 65).

France (0) 0

Croatia (1) 1 *(Modric 5 (pen))*

France: (433) Maignan; Kounde (Pavard 46), Konate, Kimpembe, Digne; Guendouzi (Griezmann 80), Kamara (Tchouameni 46), Rabiot; Nkunku (Coman 73), Benzema, Mbappe.
Croatia: (433) Ivusic; Stanisic, Erlic, Sutalo, Juranovic; Modric, Brozovic, Kovacic (Sucic 90); Pasalic (Majer 65), Budimir (Kramaric 73), Brekalo (Vlasic 73).

Group A1 Table	P	W	D	L	F	A	GD	Pts
Denmark	4	3	0	1	6	3	3	9
Croatia	4	2	1	1	3	4	−1	7
Austria	4	1	1	2	5	5	0	4
France	4	0	2	2	3	5	−2	2

GROUP A2

Thursday, 2 June 2022

Czech Republic (1) 2 *(Kuchta 11, Sow 58 (og))*

Switzerland (1) 1 *(Okafor 44)*

Czech Republic: (343) Vaclik; Zima, Brabec, Krejci II; Coufal, Soucek, Sadilek (Kalvach 84), Zeleny (Mateju 87); Jankto (Lingr 67), Kuchta (Pesek 68), Hlozek (Jurecka 87).
Switzerland: (442) Sommer; Widmer, Schar, Elvedi, Rodriguez (Lotomba 87); Sow (Zuber 68), Freuler, Xhaka, Vargas (Seferovic 87); Okafor (Shaqiri 68), Embolo (Gavranovic 90).

Spain (1) 1 *(Morata 25)*

Portugal (0) 1 *(Ricardo Horta 82)*

Spain: (433) Simon; Azpilicueta, Llorente D, Torres P, Jordi Alba; Carlos Soler (Koke 63), Busquets, Gavi (Llorente M 81); Torres F (Olmo 63), Morata (De Tomas 70), Sarabia.
Portugal: (433) Costa; Joao Cancelo, Pepe, Danilo Pereira, Guerreiro; Bruno Fernandes (Matheus Luiz 81), Joao Moutinho (Neves 46), Bernardo Silva; Otavio (Ronaldo 62), Andre Silva (Goncalo Guedes 62), Leao (Ricardo Horta 72).

Sunday, 5 June 2022

Czech Republic (1) 2 *(Pesek 4, Kuchta 66)*

Spain (1) 2 *(Gavi 45, Martinez 90)*

Czech Republic: (343) Vaclik; Zima, Brabec, Mateju; Coufal, Soucek, Sadilek, Zeleny (Jankto 24 (Havel 46)); Lingr (Cerny 59), Kuchta (Jurecka 78), Pesek (Hlozek 59).
Spain: (433) Simon; Carvajal, Garcia, Martinez, Alonso; Gavi, Rodri (Busquets 61), Koke (Llorente M 72); Sarabia (Torres F 46), De Tomas (Morata 61), Olmo (Asensio 61).

Portugal (3) 4 *(William Carvalho 15, Ronaldo 35, 39, Joao Cancelo 68)*

Switzerland (0) 0

Portugal: (433) Rui Patricio; Joao Cancelo, Pepe, Danilo Pereira, Nuno Mendes; Bruno Fernandes (Bernardo Silva 67), Neves (Joao Palhinha 77), William Carvalho (Matheus Luiz 84); Otavio (Leao 77), Ronaldo, Jota (Ricardo Horta 67).
Switzerland: (4231) Kobel; Mbabu, Schar, Frei, Rodriguez (Okafor 62); Sow (Gavranovic 81), Xhaka; Steffen (Bottani 70), Shaqiri (Freuler 69), Lotomba; Seferovic (Embolo 62).

Thursday, 9 June 2022

Portugal (2) 2 *(Joao Cancelo 33, Goncalo Guedes 38)*

Czech Republic (0) 0

Portugal: (4141) Costa; Joao Cancelo, Pepe, Danilo Pereira, Guerreiro; Neves (Joao Moutinho 88); Goncalo Guedes (Joao Palhinha 88), Bernardo Silva (Vitinha 68), William Carvalho (Bruno Fernandes 68), Jota (Leao 80); Ronaldo.
Czech Republic: (343) Stanek; Zima, Brabec, Mateju (Kral 80); Coufal, Soucek, Sadilek, Havel (Jemelka 46); Lingr (Pesek 46), Kuchta (Jurecka 46), Hlozek (Vlkanova 73).

Switzerland (0) 0

Spain (1) 1 *(Sarabia 13)*

Switzerland: (433) Sommer; Widmer, Akanji (Frei 79), Comert, Rodriguez (Sow 89); Freuler, Xhaka, Aebischer (Okafor 63); Shaqiri (Seferovic 80), Embolo, Zuber (Steffen 63).
Spain: (433) Simon; Azpilicueta, Llorente D, Torres P, Jordi Alba; Llorente M (Carlos Soler 80), Busquets, Gavi (Koke 73); Torres F, Morata (Asensio 73), Sarabia (Olmo 63).

Sunday, 12 June 2022

Spain (1) 2 *(Carlos Soler 24, Sarabia 75)*

Czech Republic (0) 0

Spain: (433) Simon; Carvajal, Garcia, Martinez, Alonso (Jordi Alba 78); Carlos Soler (Gavi 59), Rodri, Koke (Busquets 79); Asensio (Sarabia 72), Morata (Torres F 59), Olmo.
Czech Republic: (343) Mandous; Zima, Brabec, Jemelka; Coufal, Soucek, Sadilek (Kral 30), Zeleny (Kalvach 79); Cerny (Hlozek 59), Kuchta (Jurecka 59), Pesek (Tecl 79).

Switzerland (1) 1 *(Seferovic 1)*

Portugal (0) 0

Switzerland: (433) Omlin; Widmer (Steffen 46), Akanji, Elvedi, Rodriguez (Stergiou 79); Freuler, Xhaka, Sow (Aebischer 79); Shaqiri (Okafor 22), Seferovic, Embolo (Zuber 65).
Portugal: (433) Rui Patricio; Joao Cancelo, Pepe, Danilo Pereira, Nuno Mendes; Vitinha (Bernardo Silva 62), Neves (Ricardo Horta 82), Bruno Fernandes (Matheus Luiz 74); Otavio (Goncalo Guedes 46), Andre Silva, Leao (Jota 62).

Group A2 Table	P	W	D	L	F	A	GD	Pts
Spain	4	2	2	0	6	3	3	8
Portugal	4	2	1	1	7	2	5	7
Czech Republic	4	1	1	2	4	7	–3	4
Switzerland	4	1	0	3	2	7	–5	3

GROUP A3

Saturday, 4 June 2022

Hungary (0) 1 *(Szoboszlai 66 (pen))*

England (0) 0

Hungary: (3421) Gulacsi; Lang, Orban, Attila Szalai; Nego, Nagy A (Styles 82), Schafer, Nagy Z (Vecsei 88); Sallai (Kleinheisler 71), Szoboszlai (Fiola 82); Adam Szalai (Adam 88).
England: (343) Pickford; Walker (Stones 62), Coady (Phillips 79), Maguire; Alexander-Arnold (James 62), Bellingham, Rice, Justin (Saka 46); Bowen, Kane, Mount (Grealish 62).

Italy (0) 1 *(Pellegrini 70)*

Germany (0) 1 *(Kimmich 73)*

Italy: (433) Donnarumma; Florenzi, Acerbi, Bastoni, Biraghi (Dimarco 80); Frattesi (Ricci 86), Cristante, Tonali (Pobega 80); Politano (Gnonto 65), Scamacca (Cancellieri 85), Pellegrini.
Germany: (4231) Neuer; Henrichs (Hofmann 59), Sule, Rudiger, Kehrer; Kimmich, Goretzka (Gundogan 69); Gnabry (Raum 80), Muller (Havertz 70), Sane (Musiala 59); Werner.

Tuesday, 7 June 2022

Germany (0) 1 *(Hofmann 50)*

England (0) 1 *(Kane 88 (pen))*

Germany: (3421) Neuer; Klostermann, Rudiger, Schlotterbeck; Hofmann (Gnabry 65), Kimmich, Gundogan (Sane 83), Raum; Muller (Goretzka 76), Musiala (Werner 65); Havertz.
England: (4231) Pickford; Walker, Stones, Maguire, Trippier; Rice, Phillips (Bellingham 14); Saka (Bowen 80), Mount (Grealish 72), Sterling; Kane.

Italy (2) 2 *(Barella 30, Pellegrini 45)*

Hungary (0) 1 *(Mancini 61 (og))*

Italy: (433) Donnarumma; Calabria, Mancini, Bastoni, Spinazzola (Dimarco 75); Barella (Tonali 84), Cristante, Pellegrini (Locatelli 66); Politano (Belotti 75), Raspadori (Zerbin 84), Gnonto.
Hungary: (3421) Dibusz; Lang, Orban, Attila Szalai; Nego (Fiola 58), Nagy A (Styles 58), Schafer (Vancsa 87), Nagy Z (Bolla 81); Sallai, Szoboszlai; Adam Szalai (Adam 87).

Saturday, 11 June 2022

England (0) 0

Italy (0) 0

England: (4231) Ramsdale; James, Maguire, Tomori (Guehi 88), Trippier; Ward-Prowse, Rice (Phillips 65); Sterling (Saka 79), Mount (Bowen 65), Grealish; Abraham (Kane 65).
Italy: (433) Donnarumma; Di Lorenzo, Gatti, Acerbi, Dimarco (Florenzi 87); Frattesi, Locatelli (Gnonto 64), Tonali; Pessina (Cristante 88), Scamacca (Raspadori 77), Pellegrini (Esposito 64).

Hungary (1) 1 *(Nagy Z 6)*

Germany (1) 1 *(Hofmann 9)*

Hungary: (3421) Gulacsi; Lang, Orban, Attila Szalai; Fiola, Nagy A, Styles (Vecsei 87), Nagy Z (Nego 70); Sallai (Gazdag 76), Szoboszlai; Adam Szalai (Adam 69).
Germany: (3421) Neuer; Kehrer, Sule, Schlotterbeck; Hofmann (Nmecha 85), Kimmich, Goretzka (Gundogan 69), Raum; Havertz (Adeyemi 85), Musiala (Brandt 78); Werner (Muller 78).

Tuesday, 14 June 2022

England (0) 0

Hungary (1) 4 *(Sallai 16, 70, Nagy Z 80, Gazdag 89)*

England: (433) Ramsdale; Walker, Stones■, Guehi, James; Gallagher (Mount 56), Phillips, Bellingham (Foden 68); Bowen (Sterling 46), Kane, Saka (Maguire 85).
Hungary: (3421) Dibusz; Lang, Orban, Attila Szalai; Fiola, Schafer, Styles (Nagy A 56), Nagy Z; Sallai (Nego 78), Szoboszlai (Gazdag 56); Adam Szalai (Adam 68).

Germany (2) 5 *(Kimmich 10, Gundogan 45 (pen), Muller 51, Werner 68, 69)*

Italy (0) 2 *(Gnonto 78, Bastoni 90)*

Germany: (4231) Neuer; Klostermann, Sule (Tah 87), Rudiger, Raum; Gundogan (Stach 88), Kimmich; Hofmann (Gnabry 64), Muller (Musiala 75), Sane; Werner (Nmecha 75).
Italy: (433) Donnarumma; Calabria, Mancini (Scamacca 78), Bastoni, Spinazzola (Dimarco 65); Frattesi (Caprari 46), Cristante, Barella; Politano (Felipe 44), Raspadori (Scalvini 46), Gnonto.

Group A3 Table	P	W	D	L	F	A	GD	Pts
Hungary	4	2	1	1	7	3	4	7
Germany	4	1	3	0	8	5	3	6
Italy	4	1	2	1	5	7	–2	5
England	4	0	2	2	1	6	–5	2

GROUP A4

Wednesday, 1 June 2022

Poland (0) 2 *(Kaminski 72, Swiderski 85)*

Wales (0) 1 *(Williams J 52)*

Poland: (4312) Grabara; Bereszynski, Glik, Bednarek, Puchacz (Zalewski 74); Klich (Zurkowski 60), Krychowiak (Grosicki 81), Goralski (Kaminski 60); Zielinski; Lewandowski, Buksa (Swiderski 74).
Wales: (352) Ward (Hennessey 46); Gunter, Mepham, Norrington-Davies; Smith, Levitt, Morrell, Williams J (Thomas 77), Burns (Williams N 61); Moore (Harris 46), James (Matondo 46).

Friday, 3 June 2022

Belgium (0) 1 *(Batshuayi 90)*

Netherlands (1) 4 *(Bergwijn 40, Depay 51, 65, Dumfries 61)*

Belgium: (343) Mignolet; Alderweireld, Boyata, Vertonghen; Meunier (Carrasco 67), Vanaken (Onana 46), Witsel (Batshuayi 67), Castagne; Lukaku (Trossard 27), De Bruyne, Hazard E (Mertens 46).
Netherlands: (352) Cillessen; Timber, van Dijk, Ake (de Ligt 74); Dumfries, Berghuis (Koopmeiners 83), de Jong F, Klaassen, Blind; Bergwijn, Depay.

Wednesday, 8 June 2022

Belgium (1) 6 *(Witsel 42, De Bruyne 59, Trossard 73, 80, Dendoncker 83, Openda 90)*

Poland (1) 1 *(Lewandowski 28)*

Belgium: (343) Mignolet; Dendoncker, Alderweireld, Vertonghen; Castagne (Hazard T 84), Witsel (Faes 85), Tielemans, Carrasco; De Bruyne (De Ketelaere 75), Batshuayi (Openda 84), Hazard E (Trossard 66).
Poland: (451) Dragowski; Gumny, Glik, Bednarek, Puchacz (Bereszynski 46); Kaminski (Zalewski 81), Zurkowski, Krychowiak (Szymanski D 46), Zielinski, Szymanski S (Cash 66); Lewandowski (Buksa 69).

Wales (0) 1 *(Norrington-Davies 90)*

Netherlands (0) 2 *(Koopmeiners 50, Weghorst 90)*

Wales: (532) Ward (Davies A 46); Roberts C, Mepham, Rodon, Davies B, Norrington-Davies; Levitt (Smith 67), Morrell (Colwill 59), Wilson; Johnson (Bale 77), James (Matondo 77).
Netherlands: (3421) Flekken; Teze, de Vrij, de Ligt (Martins Indi 84); Hateboer, Koopmeiners, Schouten (de Jong F 67), Malacia; Lang (Til 90), Gakpo (Bergwijn 67); Weghorst.

Saturday, 11 June 2022

Netherlands (0) 2 *(Klaassen 51, Dumfries 54)*

Poland (1) 2 *(Cash 18, Zielinski 49)*

Netherlands: (352) Flekken; Timber (Teze 64), de Vrij, Ake; Dumfries, Berghuis (Koopmeiners 65), Klaassen (Gakpo 65), de Jong F, Blind; Bergwijn (Weghorst 77), Depay.
Poland: (4231) Skorupski; Cash, Bednarek, Kiwior, Bereszynski; Krychowiak, Goralski (Zurkowski 58); Frankowski (Glik 84), Zielinski, Zalewski; Piatek.

Wales (0) 1 *(Johnson 86)*

Belgium (0) 1 *(Tielemans 51)*

Wales: (3142) Hennessey; Mepham, Rodon, Davies B (Colwill 73); Ampadu; Roberts C (Norrington-Davies 61), Allen (Ramsey 38), Wilson (Burns 73), Williams N; Bale (Johnson 73), James.
Belgium: (3421) Casteels; Dendoncker, Boyata, Theate; Meunier, Witsel (Openda 90), Tielemans, Carrasco (Hazard T 61); De Bruyne (Hazard E 72), Trossard (Praet 72); Batshuayi.

Tuesday, 14 June 2022

Netherlands (2) 3 *(Lang 17, Gakpo 23, Depay 90)*

Wales (1) 2 *(Johnson 26, Bale 90 (pen))*

Netherlands: (343) Cillessen; Teze (de Vrij 46), de Ligt, Martins Indi; Hateboer (Dumfries 46), Koopmeiners, de Jong F, Malacia; Janssen (Depay 73), Gakpo, Lang (Bergwijn 73).
Wales: (532) Hennessey; Thomas, Mepham, Rodon (Gunter 67), Davies B, Burns (Roberts C 46); Smith (Ramsey 63), Ampadu, Wilson; Johnson, James (Bale 70).

Poland (0) 0

Belgium (1) 1 *(Batshuayi 16)*

Poland: (532) Szczesny; Cash, Wieteska (Grosicki 84), Glik, Kiwior, Zalewski (Frankowski 57); Zurkowski, Linetty (Goralski 84), Szymanski S (Klich 70); Zielinski (Swiderski 57), Lewandowski.
Belgium: (343) Mignolet; Dendoncker, Alderweireld, Vertonghen; Castagne, Tielemans, Witsel (Vanaken 46), Hazard T (Foket 62); Mertens (De Ketelaere 80), Batshuayi (Openda 67), Hazard E (Trossard 67).

Group A4 Table	P	W	D	L	F	A	GD	Pts
Netherlands	4	3	1	0	11	6	5	10
Belgium	4	2	1	1	9	6	3	7
Poland	4	1	1	2	5	10	–5	4
Wales	4	0	1	3	5	8	–3	1

GROUP B1

Saturday, 4 June 2022

Armenia (0) 1 *(Spertsyan 74)*

Republic of Ireland (0) 0

Armenia: (532) Yurchenko; Hambardzumyan, Mkoyan, Haroyan, Hovhannisyan A (Mkrtchyan R 61), Hovhannisyan K; Bayramyan, Grigoryan A, Spertsyan; Barseghyan (Dashyan 89), Bichakhchyan (Adamyan 56).
Republic of Ireland: (343) Kelleher; Collins N, Duffy, Egan; Coleman (Keane 81), Hendrick, Cullen (Browne 81), Stevens (McClean 73); Ogbene, Robinson (Knight 73), Parrott (Obafemi 65).

Wednesday, 8 June 2022

Republic of Ireland (0) 0

Ukraine (0) 1 *(Tsygankov 47)*

Republic of Ireland: (343) Kelleher; Collins N, Duffy, Egan (O'Shea 62); Christie (Browne 69), Hendrick, Cullen, Stevens (McClean 69); Robinson (Obafemi 69), Ogbene (Hamilton 78), Knight.
Ukraine: (3421) Lunin; Popov, Bondar, Syrota; Kacharaba (Karavayev 72), Sydorchuk (Ignatenko 88), Shaparenko, Mykolenko; Zubkov (Tsygankov 46), Mudryk (Pikhalyonok 72); Dovbyk (Sikan 80).

Scotland (2) 2 *(Ralston 28, McKenna 40)*

Armenia (0) 0

Scotland: (343) Gordon; Souttar, Hendry, McKenna; Ralston (Patterson 76), McGinn J, McGregor C, Robertson (Hickey 76); Armstrong (McTominay 75), Adams (Brown 87), Christie (Stewart 87).
Armenia: (4321) Yurchenko; Hambardzumyan, Mkoyan, Haroyan, Hovhannisyan A; Bayramyan (Dashyan 89), Grigoryan A (Wbeymar 46), Spertsyan (Udo 71); Barseghyan, Hovhannisyan K (Voskanyan 46); Adamyan (Bichakhchyan 46).

Saturday, 11 June 2022

Republic of Ireland (2) 3 *(Browne 20, Parrott 28, Obafemi 51)*

Scotland (0) 0

Republic of Ireland: (3142) Kelleher; Collins N, Duffy, Egan; Cullen; Browne, Molumby (Hendrick 84), Knight (Hourihane 72), McClean; Obafemi (Hogan 56), Parrott (Robinson 85).
Scotland: (3421) Gordon; Hendry (Gilmour 46), Hanley, McKenna (Souttar 74); Ralston, McTominay, McGregor C, Robertson; McGinn J (Armstrong 59), Christie (Brown 59); Adams (Stewart 59).

Ukraine (0) 3 *(Malinovsky 61, Karavayev 77, Mykolenko 84)*

Armenia (0) 0

Ukraine: (4141) Pyatov; Karavayev, Zabarnyi, Matviyenko, Zinchenko (Mykolenko 78); Sydorchuk (Ignatenko 85); Tsygankov, Malinovsky, Shaparenko (Pikhalyonok 70), Mudryk (Zubkov 78); Yaremchuk (Dovbyk 70).
Armenia: (541) Yurchenko; Monroy, Voskanyan, Mkoyan, Mkrtchyan S, Hovhannisyan K; Barseghyan (Harutyunyan 66), Dashyan (Malakyan 81), Udo, Bayramyan (Bichakhchyan 55); Babayan (Adamyan 55).

Tuesday, 14 June 2022

Armenia (1) 1 *(Bichakhchyan 6)*

Scotland (2) 4 *(Armstrong 14, 45, McGinn J 50, Adams 53)*

Armenia: (532) Yurchenko; Dashyan, Hambardzumyan, Haroyan, Mkoyan, Hovhannisyan A■; Grigoryan A (Mkrtchyan S 46), Spertsyan (Wbeymar 59), Bayramyan (Hovhannisyan K■ 59); Barseghyan (Serobyan 84), Bichakhchyan (Udo 59).
Scotland: (3421) Gordon; McTominay, Hanley (Campbell 86), Hendry; Patterson (Ralston 64), Gilmour (Ferguson 63), McGregor C, Taylor; McGinn J (Turnbull 64), Armstrong; Adams (Brown 74).

Ukraine (0) 1 *(Dovbyk 47)*

Republic of Ireland (1) 1 *(Collins N 31)*

Ukraine: (433) Riznyk; Karavayev, Zabarnyi, Matviyenko (Popov 72), Mykolenko; Malinovsky (Mudryk 28), Sydorchuk, Zinchenko; Yarmolenko, Dovbyk (Sikan 73), Shaparenko.
Republic of Ireland: (532) Kelleher; Browne, Lenihan, Collins N, O'Shea, McClean; Molumby (Hendrick 67), Cullen, Knight (Hourihane 67); Parrott (Ogbene 80), Hogan (Robinson 56).

Group B1 Table	P	W	D	L	F	A	GD	Pts
Ukraine	3	2	1	0	5	1	4	7
Scotland	3	2	0	1	6	4	2	6
Republic of Ireland	4	1	1	2	4	3	1	4
Armenia	4	1	0	3	2	9	–7	3

GROUP B2

Thursday, 2 June 2022

Israel (1) 2 *(Abada 25, Weissman 84)*

Iceland (1) 2 *(Helgason 42, Sigurdsson A 53)*

Israel: (433) Marciano; Dasa, Miguel Vitor, Goldberg, Leidner; Peretz (Glazer 74), Abu Fani (Jaber 61), Karzev (Baribo 73); Abada (Atzili 80), Dabbur (Weissman 61), Solomon.
Iceland: (433) Runarsson; Sampsted, Brynjar Ingi Bjarnason (Olafsson 46), Gretarsson, Magnusson; Helgason, Birkir Bjarnason (Thrandarson 89), Arnar Haraldsson (Thordarson 78); Sigurdsson A, Gudjohnsen S (Gudmundsson A 60), Thorsteinsson (Anderson 78).

Monday, 6 June 2022

Iceland (0) 1 *(Thorsteinsson 49)*

Albania (1) 1 *(Sulejmanov 30)*

Iceland: (433) Runarsson; Sampsted, Gretarsson, Magnusson, Olafsson; Helgason (Arnar Haraldsson 62), Bjarkason (Thrandarson 74), Johannesson; Sigurdsson A (Ellertsson 74), Gudjohnsen A (Gudjohnsen S 90), Thorsteinsson (Anderson 62).
Albania: (352) Berisha; Ismajli, Kumbulla, Djimsiti; Balliu (Veseli 82), Cekici (Asllani 73), Gjasula, Abrashi (Ramadani 79), Hysaj; Cikalleshi (Balaj 73), Sulejmanov (Vrioni 73).

Friday, 10 June 2022

Albania (1) 1 *(Broja 45 (pen))*

Israel (0) 2 *(Solomon 57, 73)*

Albania: (352) Berisha; Ismajli, Djimsiti, Veseli (Cekici 84); Balliu, Abrashi (Vrioni 84), Bajrami (Gjasula 67), Asllani (Ramadani 59), Hysaj; Uzuni (Balaj 84), Broja.
Israel: (433) Marciano; Dasa, Miguel Vitor, Goldberg, Leidner (Menachem 64); Peretz, Jaber, Karzev (Safouri 46); Abada, Weissman (Glazer 90), Solomon (Dabbur 81).

Monday, 13 June 2022

Iceland (1) 2 *(Thorsteinsson 9, Helgason 60)*

Israel (1) 2 *(Gretarsson 35 (og), Peretz 65)*

Iceland: (4141) Runarsson; Sampsted, Gretarsson, Magnusson, Olafsson; Birkir Bjarnason (Thrandarson 79); Sigurdsson A (Johannesson 61), Helgason (Gudmundsson A 90), Arnar Haraldsson, Thorsteinsson (Thordarson 79); Gudjohnsen A (Gudjohnsen S 62).
Israel: (433) Marciano; Dasa, Miguel Vitor (Abu Abaid 78 (Glazer 90)), Goldberg, Leidner (Menachem 46); Safouri, Peretz, Jaber; Abada (Atzili 78), Dabbur (Weissman 73), Solomon.

Group B2 Table	P	W	D	L	F	A	GD	Pts
Israel	3	1	2	0	6	5	1	5
Iceland	3	0	3	0	5	5	0	3
Albania	2	0	1	1	2	3	–1	1
Russia*	0	0	0	0	0	0	0	0

**Russia suspended.*

GROUP B3

Saturday, 4 June 2022

Finland (1) 1 *(Pukki 45 (pen))*

Bosnia-Herzegovina (0) 1 *(Prevljak 90)*

Finland: (532) Hradecky; Alho, Vaisanen L, Ivanov, O'Shaughnessy, Uronen; Nissila (Taylor 61), Schuller (Lam 61), Kamara; Lod (Forss 78), Pukki (Kallman 78).
Bosnia-Herzegovina: (433) Sehic; Gazibegovic (Hotic 67), Ahmedhodzic, Hadzikadunic, Kolasinac; Hadziahmetovic (Prevljak 82), Pjanic (Gojak 56), Prcic; Stevanovic, Dzeko, Krunic (Menalo 57).

Montenegro (0) 2 *(Mugosa 66, Vukcevic M 87)*

Romania (0) 0

Montenegro: (4411) Mijatovic; Vesovic, Vujacic, Tomasevic, Vukcevic A; Marusic (Vukcevic M 80), Jankovic M (Savicevic 84), Raickovic (Scekic 79), Jovovic (Bozovic 56); Haksabanovic (Radunovic 84); Mugosa.
Romania: (433) Nita; Ratiu, Chiriches, Rus, Bancu; Marin R (Cicaldau 78), Cristea (Cretu 13), Olaru (Maxim 46); Ivan, Tanase (Alibec 65), Mihaila (Mitrita 65).

Tuesday, 7 June 2022

Bosnia-Herzegovina (0) 1 *(Prevljak 68)*

Romania (0) 0

Bosnia-Herzegovina: (433) Sehic; Susic, Ahmedhodzic, Sanicanin, Civic (Kolasinac 67); Cimirot (Pjanic 46), Prcic (Hadziahmetovic 46), Gojak; Stevanovic (Besic 81), Dzeko (Prevljak 46), Duljevic.
Romania: (3421) Nita; Rus (Tanase 74), Chiriches, Burca; Manea (Hanca 81), Marin R (Popescu 74), Marin M, Camora; Maxim (Ivan 74), Cicaldau; Puscas (Alibec 74).

Finland (2) 2 *(Pohjanpalo 31, 37)*

Montenegro (0) 0

Finland: (352) Hradecky; Vaisanen L, Ivanov, Jensen (Vaisanen S 86); Granlund (Alho 79), Lod (Valakari 67), Kamara (Schuller 67), Lingman, Niskanen; Pohjanpalo, Pukki (Forss 67).
Montenegro: (352) Petkovic; Vujacic (Haksabanovic 67), Sipcic, Tomasevic; Vukcevic M, Savicevic (Marusic 78), Vukotic (Bozovic 46), Scekic, Radunovic; Beciraj (Camaj 46), Duranovic (Sekulic 46).

Saturday, 11 June 2022

Montenegro (0) 1 *(Marusic 77)*

Bosnia-Herzegovina (0) 1 *(Menalo 62)*

Montenegro: (442) Mijatovic; Vesovic (Vukcevic M 90), Vujacic, Tomasevic, Vukcevic A; Marusic, Raickovic (Bozovic 67), Jankovic M (Scekic 79), Jovovic (Krstovic 67); Mugosa, Haksabanovic (Radunovic 90).
Bosnia-Herzegovina: (442) Sehic; Susic, Ahmedhodzic, Hadzikadunic, Kolasinac (Civic 68); Hotic (Menalo 46), Pjanic (Prevljak 61), Hadziahmetovic, Gojak; Dzeko (Demirovic 79), Krunic.

Romania (1) 1 *(Bancu 30)*

Finland (0) 0

Romania: (4231) Nita; Ratiu, Chiriches, Burca, Bancu; Olaru (Cretu 69), Marin M; Sorescu (Mihaila 80), Cicaldau (Marin R 69), Popescu (Hanca 54); Puscas.
Finland: (532) Joronen; Alho (Soisalo 68), Vaisanen L (Kallman 80), Ivanov, O'Shaughnessy (Jensen 17), Uronen; Lod, Schuller, Kamara; Pohjanpalo, Pukki (Nissila 68).

Tuesday, 14 June 2022

Bosnia-Herzegovina (2) 3 *(Pjanic 5 (pen), Dzeko 29, 58)*

Finland (2) 2 *(Pukki 10, Kallman 18)*

Bosnia-Herzegovina: (433) Sehic; Stevanovic, Ahmedhodzic (Kovacevic 73), Hadzikadunic, Kolasinac (Civic 68); Krunic, Prcic (Hadziahmetovic 46), Pjanic (Gojak 77); Menalo, Dzeko, Duljevic (Milicevic 46).
Finland: (532) Hradecky; Soisalo, Vaisanen S (Ivanov 46), Tenho, Jensen, Niskanen (Taylor 81); Lingman, Schuller (Lod 59), Nissila (Kamara 46); Kallman (Pohjanpalo 73), Pukki.

Romania (0) 0

Montenegro (1) 3 *(Mugosa 42, 56, 63)*

Romania: (433) Nita; Manea, Chiriches, Burca, Bancu; Marin R (Olaru 57), Marin M (Paun 76), Maxim (Tanase 46); Stefanescu (Popescu 58), Puscas, Mihaila (Sorescu 58).
Montenegro: (4231) Mijatovic; Vesovic, Vujacic, Tomasevic (Sipcic 88), Radunovic; Jankovic M (Bozovic 63), Scekic (Raickovic 75); Jovovic (Vukcevic M 46), Krstovic (Djukanovic 88), Savicevic; Mugosa.

Group B3 Table	P	W	D	L	F	A	GD	Pts
Bosnia-Herzegovina	4	2	2	0	6	4	2	8
Montenegro	4	2	1	1	6	3	3	7
Finland	4	1	1	2	5	5	0	4
Romania	4	1	0	3	1	6	–5	3

GROUP B4

Thursday, 2 June 2022

Serbia (0) 0

Norway (1) 1 *(Haaland 26)*

Serbia: (3421) Milinkovic-Savic V; Milenkovic, Veljkovic (Erakovic 75), Pavlovic, Lazovic (Zivkovic 69), Lukic (Grujic 69), Gudelj (Jovic 46), Kostic (Radonjic 69); Tadic, Milinkovic-Savic S; Mitrovic A.
Norway: (4141) Nyland; Pedersen, Strandberg, Ostigard, Meling; Aursnes (Thorstvedt 76); Elyounoussi M (Ryerson 88), Odegaard, Berge (Daehli 75), King (Sorloth 46); Haaland (Thorsby 67).

Slovenia (0) 0

Sweden (1) 2 *(Forsberg 39 (pen), Kulusevski 88)*

Slovenia: (3412) Oblak; Blazic, Bijol, Mevlja (Verbic 76); Stojanovic, Cerin, Kurtic, Sikosek (Karnicnik 65); Zajc (Lovric 65); Celar (Zahovic 82), Sporar (Sesko 46).
Sweden: (433) Olsen; Andersson (Krafth 66), Starfelt (Milosevic 45), Nilsson, Augustinsson; Olsson K (Svanberg 65), Karlstrom (Cajuste 79), Forsberg; Kulusevski, Isak (Quaison 80), Claesson.

Sunday, 5 June 2022

Serbia (1) 4 *(Mitrovic A 24, Milinkovic-Savic S 56, Jovic 85, Radonjic 90)*

Slovenia (1) 1 *(Stojanovic 30)*

Serbia: (3412) Rajkovic; Milenkovic, Masovic, Mitrovic S; Zivkovic, Maksimovic, Ilic (Tadic 46), Ristic (Radonjic 46); Milinkovic-Savic S (Lukic 72); Jovanovic (Jovic 46), Mitrovic A (Racic 81).
Slovenia: (532) Oblak; Stojanovic, Blazic, Bijol, Mevlja (Sikosek 79), Karnicnik; Lovric (Celar 79), Stankovic (Cerin 63), Kurtic; Zajc (Zahovic 84), Sesko (Sporar 63).

Sweden (0) 1 *(Elanga 90)*

Norway (1) 2 *(Haaland 20 (pen), 69)*

Sweden: (433) Olsen; Krafth, Milosevic, Nilsson, Augustinsson; Svanberg, Cajuste (Karlstrom 78), Forsberg (Elanga 66); Kulusevski, Isak (Gyokeres 66), Claesson (Olsson K 78).
Norway: (433) Nyland; Pedersen (Hanche-Olsen 89), Strandberg, Ostigard, Meling; Odegaard, Berge (Hauge 89), Thorsby (Berg 61); Sorloth, Haaland (King 75), Elyounoussi M (Thorstvedt 75).

Thursday, 9 June 2022

Norway (0) 0

Slovenia (0) 0

Norway: (433) Nyland; Pedersen, Hanche-Olsen, Ostigard, Meling (Bjorkan 73); Odegaard, Aursnes (Thorstvedt 46), Berge; Elyounoussi M (Hauge 81), Haaland, King (Sorloth 46).
Slovenia: (442) Oblak; Karnicnik (Milec 81), Blazic■, Brekalo (Mevlja 80), Sikosek; Stojanovic, Cerin, Kurtic, Verbic (Bijol 66); Sesko (Sporar 66), Celar (Crnigoj 66).

Sweden (0) 0

Serbia (1) 1 *(Jovic 45)*

Sweden: (4141) Olsen; Andersson, Ekdal, Nilsson (Kurtulus 41), Augustinsson; Cajuste; Elanga (Gyokeres 86), Svanberg, Olsson K (Forsberg 77), Claesson (Gudmundsson 77); Quaison.
Serbia: (3421) Dmitrovic; Milenkovic, Veljkovic, Pavlovic (Mitrovic S 79); Lazovic (Radonjic 63), Milinkovic-Savic S, Gudelj, Terzic (Kostic 64); Tadic, Djuricic (Racic 70); Jovic (Lukic 77).

Sunday, 12 June 2022

Norway (1) 3 *(Haaland 10, 54 (pen), Sorloth 77)*

Sweden (0) 2 *(Forsberg 62, Gyokeres 90)*

Norway: (433) Nyland; Ryerson (Pedersen 66), Strandberg, Ostigard, Bjorkan; Odegaard (Thorstvedt 66), Berge, Thorsby (Berg 66); Sorloth, Haaland (Berisha 89), Daehli (Elyounoussi M 57).
Sweden: (433) Olsen; Krafth, Kurtulus (Papagiannopoulos 85), Ekdal, Gudmundsson; Karlstrom (Claesson 59), Cajuste (Eriksson 83), Forsberg; Kulusevski, Isak (Gyokeres 58), Quaison (Elanga 58).

Slovenia (0) 2 *(Cerin 48, Sesko 53)*

Serbia (2) 2 *(Zivkovic 8, Mitrovic A 35)*

Slovenia: (532) Oblak; Karnicnik, Bijol, Mevlja (Stankovic 84), Brekalo (Balkovec 46), Sikosek (Verbic 78); Zajc (Crnigoj 46), Cerin, Kurtic; Sesko, Celar (Sporar 46).
Serbia: (3421) Milinkovic-Savic V; Milenkovic, Veljkovic, Pavlovic; Zivkovic (Radonjic 46), Maksimovic (Racic 85), Grujic (Milinkovic-Savic S 65), Mladenovic (Jovic 56); Tadic, Lukic (Kostic 57); Mitrovic A.

Group B4 Table	*P*	*W*	*D*	*L*	*F*	*A*	*GD*	*Pts*
Norway	4	3	1	0	6	3	3	10
Serbia	4	2	1	1	7	4	3	7
Sweden	4	1	0	3	5	6	–1	3
Slovenia	4	0	2	2	3	8	–5	2

GROUP C1

Saturday, 4 June 2022

Lithuania (0) 0

Luxembourg (1) 2 *(Sinani 44, 78)*

Lithuania: (4231) Setkus; Baravykas, Satkus, Utkus, Barauskas; Megelaitis, Slivka (Dolznikov 84); Novikovas, Golubickas (Petkevicius 63), Lasickas; Klimavicius A (Kruzikas 63).
Luxembourg: (442) Moris; Da Graca, Chanot, Carlson, Mica Pinto; Thill V (Rodrigues 46), Barreiro, Martins Pereira, Borges Sanches (Olesen 60); Sinani (Thill S 89), Muratovic (Bohnert 69).

Turkey (1) 4 *(Under 37, Dervisoglu 47, Dursun 82, Demiral 85)*

Faroe Islands (0) 0

Turkey: (442) Cakir; Muldur, Demiral, Soyuncu (Sinik 46), Kadioglu; Under (Akgun 80), Tokoz (Ozcan 66), Calhanoglu, Akturkoglu (Ayhan 46); Unal, Dervisoglu (Dursun 65).
Faroe Islands: (451) Nielsen; Joensen R, Faero, Askham, Davidsen V; Sorensen (Agnarsson 53), Vatnhamar S, Vatnhamar G (Edmundsson 86), Hansson (Mikkelsen 86), Jonsson (Andreasen 53); Johannesen (Olsen K 53).

Tuesday, 7 June 2022

Faroe Islands (0) 0

Luxembourg (0) 1 *(Rodrigues 74 (pen))*

Faroe Islands: (442) Nielsen; Joensen R■, Faero, Askham (Nattestad 60), Davidsen V; Sorensen, Vatnhamar S■, Vatnhamar G (Andreasen 85), Olsen M (Jonsson 86); Hansson (Mikkelsen 78), Olsen K (Agnarsson 78).
Luxembourg: (433) Moris; Da Graca, Chanot, Carlson, Mica Pinto; Barreiro, Martins Pereira, Olesen (Gerson 90); Sinani, Rodrigues (Bohnert 90), Borges Sanches (Thill S 86).

Lithuania (0) 0

Turkey (2) 6 *(Sinik 2, 14, Dursun 56 (pen), 81, Akgun 89, Dervisoglu 90)*

Lithuania: (4231) Setkus; Mikoliunas, Satkus, Klimavicius L, Sirvys; Armanavicius, Megelaitis (Utkus 46); Novikovas (Petkevicius 64), Golubickas (Barauskas 76), Dolznikov (Cernych 46); Laukzemis (Klimavicius A 65).
Turkey: (4411) Alemdar; Muldur, Kabak (Ozkacar 76), Ayhan, Kadioglu (Elmali 58); Under (Akgun 46), Ozcan, Calhanoglu (Kokcu 46), Sinik (Akturkoglu 66); Dervisoglu; Dursun.

Saturday, 11 June 2022

Faroe Islands (2) 2 *(Davidsen V 20 (pen), Andreasen 45)*

Lithuania (1) 1 *(Cernych 6)*

Faroe Islands: (442) Nielsen; Sorensen, Faero (Nattestad 67), Askham (Vatnsdal 25), Davidsen V; Bjartalid, Vatnhamar G, Andreasen (Hansson 66), Olsen M (Jonsson 67); Olsen K, Johannesen (Edmundsson 83).
Lithuania: (4231) Bartkus; Baravykas (Kruzikas 82), Utkus, Klimavicius L, Barauskas (Sirvys 46); Slivka, Megelaitis (Armanavicius 82); Lasickas (Milasius 71), Cernych, Novikovas; Klimavicius A (Laukzemis 64).

Luxembourg (0) 0

Turkey (1) 2 *(Calhanoglu 37 (pen), Dursun 76)*

Luxembourg: (4141) Moris; Da Graca (Bohnert 81), Chanot, Carlson, Mica Pinto; Martins Pereira (Omosanya 63); Rodrigues, Olesen (Thill S 46), Barreiro, Borges Sanches (Thill V 54); Sinani (Gerson 81).
Turkey: (433) Cakir; Celik, Demiral, Soyuncu, Kadioglu (Elmali 68); Kokcu (Dursun 46), Tokoz (Kulu 81), Calhanoglu (Ozcan 68); Under, Dervisoglu (Akturkoglu 68), Sinik.

Tuesday, 14 June 2022

Luxembourg (1) 2 *(Rodrigues 12 (pen), Barreiro 49)*

Faroe Islands (0) 2 *(Bjartalid 56, 59)*

Luxembourg: (4141) Moris; Da Graca, Chanot (Ikene 75), Carlson, Mica Pinto; Gerson (Martins Pereira 46); Bohnert (Deville 67), Barreiro, Thill S (Borges Sanches 68), Rodrigues; Sinani.

Faroe Islands: (451) Nielsen; Sorensen (Hansen 89), Vatnsdal (Baldvinsson 60), Nattestad, Davidsen V; Bjartalid (Mikkelsen 89), Joensen R, Vatnhamar G, Hansson, Olsen M (Jonsson 73); Olsen K (Edmundsson 46).

Turkey (1) 2 *(Ayhan 37, Calhanoglu 54 (pen))*

Lithuania (0) 0

Turkey: (4411) Bayindir; Celik, Ayhan, Soyuncu, Kadioglu (Muldur 84); Under (Cukur 84), Ozcan, Calhanoglu (Kabak 84), Akturkoglu (Sinik 62); Dervisoglu (Akgun 62); Dursun.
Lithuania: (541) Bartkus; Baravykas (Sirvys 46), Girdvainis, Klimavicius L (Satkus 78), Barauskas, Milasius (Tutyskinas 85); Golubickas (Klimavicius A 71), Megelaitis, Uzela, Lasickas (Armanavicius 46); Cernych.

Group C1 Table	P	W	D	L	F	A	GD	Pts
Turkey	4	4	0	0	14	0	14	12
Luxembourg	4	2	1	1	5	4	1	7
Faroe Islands	4	1	1	2	4	8	–4	4
Lithuania	4	0	0	4	1	12	–11	0

GROUP C2

Thursday, 2 June 2022

Cyprus (0) 0

Kosovo (0) 2 *(Berisha V 65, Zhegrova 78)*

Cyprus: (352) Michael; Kyriakou (Katelaris 66), Gogic, Panagiotou; Antoniou (Panayiotou 67), Artymatas, Kastanos, Papoulis (Pittas 67), Ioannou N (Kakoullis 76); Tzionis (Loizou 71), Sotiriou.
Kosovo: (433) Muric; Kastrati L, Rrahmani, Kryeziu, Aliti; Idrizi (Loshaj 71), Fazliji, Berisha V (Dresevic 76); Zhegrova, Muriqi, Rashica (Bytyqi 87).

Northern Ireland (0) 0

Greece (1) 1 *(Bakasetas 39)*

Northern Ireland: (532) Peacock-Farrell; Bradley (McGinn 62), McNair, Evans J, Ballard, Lane (Hume 78); McCann, Davis, Saville (Charles S 79); Lavery (Lafferty 62), Whyte (Charles D 71).
Greece: (4231) Vlachodimos; Rota (Baldock 90), Mavropanos, Chatzidiakos, Tsimikas; Siopis (Tzavelas 82), Bouchalakis; Limnios (Pavlidis 69), Bakasetas (Kourbelis 69), Mandalos; Giakoumakis (Chatzigiovanis 69).

Sunday, 5 June 2022

Cyprus (0) 0

Northern Ireland (0) 0

Cyprus: (352) Michael; Katelaris (Panagiotou 46), Gogic, Korrea; Pittas, Loizou (Tzionis 56), Artymatas, Kastanos (Papoulis 66), Ioannou N; Christofi (Kyriakou 65), Sotiriou (Kakoullis 77).
Northern Ireland: (4141) Peacock-Farrell; McNair, Evans J, Brown, Lane (Spencer 64); Charles S (Donnelly 64); Whyte (McMenamin 64), Davis (Lavery 77), Saville (McCann 70), McGinn; Lafferty.

Kosovo (0) 0

Greece (1) 1 *(Bakasetas 36)*

Kosovo: (4231) Muric■; Kastrati L, Rrahmani, Kryeziu, Aliti■; Loshaj (Berisha V 75), Fazliji (Dresevic 75); Zhegrova (Ujkani 90), Zeneli (Kololli 57), Rashica (Bytyqi 57); Muriqi.
Greece: (433) Vlachodimos; Baldock, Mavropanos, Chatzidiakos, Tsimikas; Bakasetas, Kourbelis (Siopis 56), Mandalos (Bouchalakis 86); Limnios, Giakoumakis (Pavlidis 57), Masouras (Douvikas 78).

Thursday, 9 June 2022

Greece (2) 3 *(Bakasetas 8, Pavlidis 20, Limnios 48)*

Cyprus (0) 0

Greece: (433) Vlachodimos; Baldock, Mavropanos, Chatzidiakos (Tzavelas 24), Tsimikas; Bakasetas (Papanikolaou 81), Siopis (Alexandropoulos 52), Mandalos (Kourbelis 52); Limnios, Pavlidis, Douvikas (Masouras 46).
Cyprus: (343) Michael; Katelaris (Laifis 46), Gogic, Korrea; Pittas, Charalambos Kyriakou, Artymatas, Ioannou N (Panagiotou 64); Loizou (Tzionis 64), Sotiriou (Christofi 46), Papoulis (Spoljaric 74).

Kosovo (2) 3 *(Muriqi 9 (pen), 52, Bytyqi 19)*

Northern Ireland (1) 2 *(Lavery 44, Ballard 83)*

Kosovo: (433) Ujkani; Kastrati L, Rrahmani, Kryeziu, Rrudhani (Fazliji 75); Berisha V (Domgjoni 79), Dresevic, Muslija; Rashica (Sahiti 89), Muriqi, Bytyqi.
Northern Ireland: (4411) Peacock-Farrell; Spencer (Bradley 86), Ballard, Evans J, Brown; Lavery (Whyte 68), Davis, Saville (Thompson 73), McMenamin; McCann (Charles S 68); Lafferty (Charles D 68).

Sunday, 12 June 2022

Greece (0) 2 *(Giakoumakis 71, Mandalos 90)*

Kosovo (0) 0

Greece: (433) Vlachodimos; Baldock, Mavropanos, Chatzidiakos, Tsimikas; Bakasetas (Giannoulis 85), Siopis, Bouchalakis (Kourbelis 77); Chatzigiovanis (Mandalos 46), Pavlidis (Giakoumakis 58), Masouras (Alexandropoulos 85).
Kosovo: (442) Muric; Domgjoni, Rrahmani, Kryeziu, Aliti; Bytyqi (Zeneli 76), Berisha V, Muslija (Idrizi 58), Rrudhani (Loshaj 46); Muriqi, Rashica (Sahiti 90).

Northern Ireland (0) 2 *(McNair 71, Evans J 90)*

Cyprus (1) 2 *(Kakoullis 32, 51)*

Northern Ireland: (4141) Carson; Spencer (Bradley 69), Ballard, Evans J, Brown; Davis; Lavery (Whyte 59), McNair, Charles S (Thompson 59), McMenamin (McGinn 69); Lafferty (Charles D 69).
Cyprus: (3421) Christodoulou; Artymatas, Gogic, Laifis (Ioannou N 69); Pittas (Panayiotou 46), Charalambos Kyriakou, Kastanos, Panagiotou; Christofi, Tzionis (Papoulis 58); Kakoullis (Katelaris 78).

Group C2 Table	P	W	D	L	F	A	GD	Pts
Greece	4	4	0	0	7	0	7	12
Kosovo	4	2	0	2	5	5	0	6
Northern Ireland	4	0	2	2	4	6	–2	2
Cyprus	4	0	2	2	2	7	–5	2

GROUP C3

Friday, 3 June 2022

Belarus (0) 0

Slovakia (0) 1 *(Suslov 61)*

Belarus: (541) Pavlyuchenko; Begunov, Khadarkevich, Politevich, Yudenkov, Shevchenko; Klimovich (Bessmertny 71), Bocherov (Grechikho 82), Yablonskiy (Bykov 62), Ebong (Malkevich 72); Bakhar (Solovey 71).
Slovakia: (4141) Rodak; Pekarik, Satka, Skriniar, De Marco; Lobotka (Herc 89); Schranz (Suslov 59), Kucka (Hrosovsky 75), Duda (Rusnak 60), Weiss; Almasi (Bozenik 75).

Kazakhstan (0) 2 *(Aymbetov 50, 57)*

Azerbaijan (0) 0

Kazakhstan: (541) Shatski; Kairov, Akhnetov (Maliy 80), Marochkin, Alip, Vorogovskiy; Baytana (Orazov 46), Tagybergen (Zharinbetov 86), Darabayev, Astanov (Kuat 73); Aymbetov (Shushenachev 79).
Azerbaijan: (3142) Mahammadaliyev; Huseynov B (Bayramov 79), Mustafazade, Haghverdi; Eddy; Medvedev, Mahmudov (Nazarov 79), Isaev (Nuriyev 68), Salahli; Emreli (Sheydayev 79), Dadashov (Alasgarov 68).

Monday, 6 June 2022

Belarus (0) 0

Azerbaijan (0) 0

Belarus: (343) Pavlyuchenko; Khadarkevich, Politevich, Volkov (Ebong 33); Nechaev, Yablonskiy (Bessmertny 82), Bocherov (Klimovich 61), Shevchenko; Bykov, Solovey (Gromyko 61), Malkevich (Pechenin 82).
Azerbaijan: (352) Mahammadaliyev; Huseynov C, Mustafazade, Haghverdi; Medvedev (Aliyev■ 65), Mahmudov, Eddy, Richard (Garayev 75), Salahli; Dadashov (Alasgarov 59), Sheydayev (Emreli 59).

Slovakia (0) 0

Kazakhstan (1) 1 *(Darabayev 26)*

Slovakia: (4141) Rodak; Koscelnik (Strelec 83), Gyomber, Skriniar (Valjent 43), Chvatal; Lobotka; Schranz (Haraslin 46), Rusnak (Bozenik 71), Kucka, Weiss (Suslov 46); Almasi.

Kazakhstan: (3421) Shatski; Maliy, Marochkin, Alip; Gabyshev (Kairov 66), Darabayev (Zharinbetov 73), Kuat, Dosmagambetov; Astanov (Vasiljev 73), Orazov (Vorogovskiy 59); Aymbetov (Shushenachev 65).

Friday, 10 June 2022

Azerbaijan (0) 0

Slovakia (0) 1 *(Weiss 81)*

Azerbaijan: (352) Mahammadaliyev; Huseynov C, Mustafazade, Haghverdi; Medvedev (Huseynov B 65), Mahmudov (Huseynov A 79), Eddy, Richard (Garayev 55), Salahli; Dadashov (Emreli 46), Sheydayev (Nuriyev 65).
Slovakia: (442) Rodak; Pekarik, Satka, Valjent, De Marco; Suslov (Weiss 65), Lobotka (Bero 75), Hrosovsky, Haraslin; Rusnak (Schranz 90), Strelec (Duda 65).

Belarus (0) 1 *(Malkevich 84)*

Kazakhstan (1) 1 *(Aymbetov 13)*

Belarus: (352) Pavlyuchenko; Khadarkevich, Volkov, Yudenkov (Gromyko 46); Begunov (Shevchenko 76), Bykov, Yablonskiy (Klimovich 81), Ebong, Pechenin; Bakhar (Malkevich 65), Sedko (Bogomolskiy 46).
Kazakhstan: (3421) Shatski; Maliy, Marochkin, Alip; Kairov, Darabayev (Dosmagambetov 77), Kuat, Vorogovskiy (Suyumbayev 59); Orazov (Zharinbetov 67), Astanov (Vasiljev 77); Aymbetov (Shushenachev 68).

Monday, 13 June 2022

Azerbaijan (0) 2 *(Emreli 76, Sheydayev 90)*

Belarus (0) 0

Azerbaijan: (352) Mahammadaliyev; Huseynov C, Mustafazade, Huseynov B; Huseynov A (Alasgarov 73), Mahmudov, Eddy (Diniyev 59), Richard (Isaev 73), Salahli (Krivotsyuk 59); Dadashov (Emreli 59), Sheydayev.
Belarus: (4411) Pavlyuchenko; Shevchenko (Bessmertny 86), Politevich, Khadarkevich, Pechenin; Malkevich (Podstrelov 71), Yablonskiy, Bocherov (Gromyko 57), Ebong; Klimovich (Bykov 57); Bakhar (Bogomolskiy 70).

Kazakhstan (2) 2 *(Vorogovskiy 18, Astanov 39)*

Slovakia (0) 1 *(Bero 51)*

Kazakhstan: (541) Shatski; Gabyshev (Kairov 73), Maliy, Marochkin, Alip, Dosmagambetov; Astanov (Logvinenko 84), Darabayev (Yerlanov 88), Tagybergen, Vorogovskiy (Orazov 74); Aymbetov (Samorodov 88).
Slovakia: (442) Rodak; Pekarik, Gyomber, Valjent, Chvatal (De Marco 46); Kucka, Hrosovsky, Bero (Almasi 82), Haraslin (Suslov 88); Rusnak (Strelec 72), Duda■.

Group C3 Table	P	W	D	L	F	A	GD	Pts
Kazakhstan	4	3	1	0	6	2	4	10
Slovakia	4	2	0	2	3	3	0	6
Azerbaijan	4	1	1	2	2	3	–1	4
Belarus	4	0	2	2	1	4	–3	2

GROUP C4

Thursday, 2 June 2022

Bulgaria (1) 1 *(Despodov 13)*

North Macedonia (0) 1 *(Ristovski M 50)*

Bulgaria: (4231) Mihailov; Turitsov, Hristov P, Hristov A, Nedyalkov; Krastev (Kostadinov 59), Chochev; Milanov (Minchev M 87), Nedelev (Stefanov 71), Despodov; Iliev (Minchev G 46).
North Macedonia: (4231) Dimitrievski; Askovski, Velkovski (Ristevski 88), Musliu, Alioski; Spirovski (Nikolov 72), Bardhi; Churlinov (David Babunski 46), Elmas, Trajkovski (Miovski 46); Ristovski M (Dorian Babunski 73).

Georgia (2) 4 *(Kvaratskhelia 12, Kashia 33, Mikautadze 87, Qazaishvili 88)*

Gibraltar (0) 0

Georgia: (3421) Loria; Kakabadze, Kashia (Kobakhidze 63), Khocholava; Lobzhanidze, Mekvabishvili, Aburjania (Kiteishvili 63), Tsitaishvili (Giorbelidze 40); Chakvetadze (Kvekveskiri 78), Kvaratskhelia (Qazaishvili 63); Mikautadze.

Gibraltar: (541) Coleing; Jolley (Valarino 66), Chipolina R, Lopes, Wiseman, Britto; Walker (Anthony Hernandez 73), Ronan (Torrilla 46), Annesley (Mouelhi 66), Casciaro L; Styche (Coombes 46).

Sunday, 5 June 2022

Bulgaria (0) 2 *(Iliev 50, Stefanov 83)*

Georgia (2) 5 *(Davitashvili 4, Hristov A 31 (og), Zivzivadze 52, Kvaratskhelia 58 (pen), Qazaishvili 69)*

Bulgaria: (4231) Mihailov; Turitsov (Popov 64), Hristov A, Nedyalkov, Jordanov (Hristov P 46); Chochev, Milanov (Stefanov 46); Minchev M (Yankov 64), Nedelev (Krastev 64), Despodov; Iliev.
Georgia: (3421) Loria; Kvirkvelia, Kashia, Khocholava; Kakabadze (Kiteishvili 84), Kvekveskiri, Aburjania (Gvilia 75), Azarovi; Davitashvili (Mamuchashvili 74), Kvaratskhelia (Qazaishvili 67); Zivzivadze (Mikautadze 67).

Gibraltar (0) 0

North Macedonia (1) 2 *(Bardhi 21, Nikolov 84)*

Gibraltar: (352) Coleing; Jolley, Wiseman, Lopes; Valarino (Casciaro L 78), Torrilla, Annesley, Britto, Olivero; Walker (Pozo 87), Styche (Coombes 65).
North Macedonia: (4141) Iliev; Todoroski, Serafimov, Musliu, Alioski (Askovski 66); Spirovski (Ristevski 46); Elmas (David Babunski 65), Nikolov, Bardhi, Trajkovski (Miovski 57); Ristovski M (Dorian Babunski 57).

Thursday, 9 June 2022

Gibraltar (0) 1 *(Walker 61 (pen))*

Bulgaria (1) 1 *(Minchev G 45)*

Gibraltar: (442) Coleing; Wiseman, Chipolina R, Lopes, Olivero; Valarino (Ronan 85), Torrilla (Mouelhi 80), Annesley, Britto (Styche 75); Walker, Casciaro L.
Bulgaria: (442) Vutsov; Popov, Chorbadzhiyski, Hristov P, Jordanov; Milanov, Kraev, Krastev (Iliev 83), Minchev M (Despodov 71); Minchev G, Stefanov (Nedelev 72).

North Macedonia (0) 0

Georgia (0) 3 *(Zivzivadze 52, Kvaratskhelia 62, Kiteishvili 84)*

North Macedonia: (352) Dimitrievski; Velkovski, Musliu, Alioski; Askovski, Churlinov, Bardhi, Spirovski (Miovski 71), Trajkovski (Nikolov 60); Ristovski M (David Babunski 71), Elmas (Todoroski 79).
Georgia: (532) Mamardashvili; Kakabadze (Lobzhanidze 83), Kvirkvelia, Kashia, Khocholava, Tsitaishvili; Davitashvili (Mamuchashvili 71), Kvekveskiri, Aburjania (Kiteishvili 61); Zivzivadze (Mikautadze 71), Kvaratskhelia (Qazaishvili 83).

Sunday, 12 June 2022

Georgia (0) 0

Bulgaria (0) 0

Georgia: (532) Loria; Lobzhanidze, Khocholava, Kashia, Dvali, Azarovi (Kiteishvili 63); Mekvabishvili (Davitashvili 63), Kvekveskiri, Kvaratskhelia; Qazaishvili (Tsitaishvili 52), Mikautadze (Zivzivadze 80).
Bulgaria: (442) Mihailov; Turitsov, Galabov, Chorbadzhiyski, Nedyalkov; Minchev M (Chochev 85), Kraev, Kostadinov, Milanov; Stefanov (Malinov 65), Iliev (Minchev G 51).

North Macedonia (4) 4 *(Bardhi 4, Torrilla 14 (og), Miovski 16, Churlinov 31)*

Gibraltar (0) 0

North Macedonia: (3412) Siskovski; Serafimov, Zajkov, Ristevski; Todoroski, Nikolov, Elmas (Grozdanovski 80), Alioski (Ethemi 46); Bardhi (Fazlagic 46); Churlinov (Dimoski 46), Miovski (Dorian Babunski 62).
Gibraltar: (442) Banda; Wiseman, Chipolina R (Sergeant 60), Lopes, Olivero; Valarino (Jolley 74), Torrilla (Ronan 46), Annesley, Britto (Chipolina J 60); Casciaro L (Styche 59), Walker.

Group C4 Table	P	W	D	L	F	A	GD	Pts
Georgia	4	3	1	0	12	2	10	10
North Macedonia	4	2	1	1	7	4	3	7
Bulgaria	4	0	3	1	4	7	–3	3
Gibraltar	4	0	1	3	1	11	–10	1

GROUP D1

Friday, 3 June 2022

Latvia (1) 3 *(Uldrikis 9, 77, Ikaunieks J 85 (pen))*

Andorra (0) 0

Latvia: (4411) Steinbors; Savavnieks, Cernomordijs, Dubra, Jurkovskis; Ikaunieks J (Ikaunieks D 86), Tobers, Zjuzins (Emsis 86), Ciganiks (Jaunzems 67); Uldrikis; Gutkowski (Krollis 75).
Andorra: (532) Gomes; Jesus Rubio, Llovera, Garcia C, Alavedra (Vieira X 86), Garcia M; Rebes (Vieira M 78), Vales, Cervos (Bernat 78); Alaez (Jordi Rubio 90), Rosas (Sanchez A 86).

Liechtenstein (0) 0

Moldova (1) 2 *(Nicolaescu 5 (pen), Bolohan 90)*

Liechtenstein: (3421) Buchel B; Grunenfelder, Malin, Wolfinger S; Graber (Brandle 83), Sele A, Luchinger (Beck 72), Meier (Netzer 72); Yildiz (Frick N 62), Hasler; Frick Y (Wolfinger F 62).
Moldova: (343) Railean; Posmac (Craciun 57), Bolohan, Armas; Revenco, Rata, Platica M (Dros 57), Reabciuk; Caimacov (Stina 85), Nicolaescu (Platica S 83), Iosipoi (Mandricenco 46).

Monday, 6 June 2022

Andorra (0) 0

Moldova (0) 0

Andorra: (532) Gomes; De Pablos, Llovera, Garcia C, Vales (Alavedra 12), Cervos; Vieira X, Vieira M (Rebes 46), Jordi Rubio (Rosas 58); Alaez (Bernat 86), Fernandez (Martinez 58).
Moldova: (3421) Railean; Posmac, Bolohan (Dros 46), Armas; Revenco, Rata, Platica M (Cojocaru 61), Reabciuk; Mandricenco (Platica S 46), Stina■; Nicolaescu.

Latvia (0) 1 *(Zjuzins 73)*

Liechtenstein (0) 0

Latvia: (4411) Steinbors; Savavnieks, Cernomordijs, Dubra, Jurkovskis; Jaunzems (Ciganiks 57), Emsis (Zjuzins 57), Tobers, Ikaunieks J (Ikaunieks D 85); Uldrikis; Gutkowski (Krollis 62).
Liechtenstein: (343) Buchel B; Grunenfelder, Malin, Wolfinger S; Graber (Brandle 64), Sele A, Beck (Yildiz 77), Netzer (Wolfinger M 54); Meier (Frick N 78), Frick Y (Wolfinger F 54), Hasler.

Friday, 10 June 2022

Andorra (0) 2 *(Alaez 78 (pen), Jesus Rubio 82)*

Liechtenstein (0) 1 *(Meier 90)*

Andorra: (442) Gomes; Jesus Rubio, Llovera, Alavedra, Cervos; Alaez (Clemente 86), Rebes, Vieira X (Vieira M 79), Bernat (Garcia M 79); Pujol (Fernandez 58), Rosas (Lima 86).
Liechtenstein: (3421) Buchel B; Grunenfelder, Malin, Wolfinger S (Meier 40); Graber (Yildiz 89), Sele A (Frick N 46), Luchinger, Netzer (Marxer M 77); Beck, Hasler; Frick Y (Kollmann 77).

Moldova (1) 2 *(Nicolaescu 5 (pen), Motpan 64)*

Latvia (2) 4 *(Gutkowski 19, 60, Ikaunieks J 26, 75)*

Moldova: (541) Railean; Revenco, Posmac (Craciun 65), Bolohan, Armas, Reabciuk; Rata, Caimacov, Platica M (Motpan 53), Platica S (Cojocaru 80); Nicolaescu (Cobet 80).
Latvia: (4411) Steinbors; Savavnieks, Cernomordijs, Dubra, Jurkovskis; Ikaunieks J, Zjuzins (Emsis 80), Tobers (Tarasovs 90), Ciganiks (Jaunzems 61); Uldrikis (Krollis 61); Gutkowski (Ikaunieks D 79).

Tuesday, 14 June 2022

Liechtenstein (0) 0

Latvia (2) 2 *(Gutkowski 20, 28)*

Liechtenstein: (343) Buchel B; Grunenfelder, Malin, Beck; Meier, Sele A (Gassner 78), Luchinger (Marxer M 65), Netzer (Wolfinger F 65); Frick N (Brandle 77), Frick Y (Yildiz 46), Hasler.
Latvia: (442) Steinbors; Savavnieks, Cernomordijs, Dubra, Jurkovskis; Ikaunieks J (Jaunzems 67), Zjuzins (Emsis 71), Tobers, Ciganiks (Kamess 87); Gutkowski (Ikaunieks D 87), Uldrikis (Krollis 67).

Moldova (1) 2 *(Caimacov 26 (pen), Nicolaescu 50 (pen))*

Andorra (1) 1 *(Vieira M 45)*

Moldova: (343) Railean; Craciun, Bolohan (Posmac 61), Armas; Jardan (Revenco 53), Rata, Caimacov, Reabciuk; Motpan, Nicolaescu (Cobet 78), Cojocaru (Platica S 61).
Andorra: (532) Iker; Jesus Rubio, Llovera, Garcia C, Alavedra, Garcia M (Pujol 80); Vieira M (Bernat 87), Rebes, Jordi Rubio (Cervos 55); Fernandez (Rosas 54), Clemente (Alaez 54).

Group D1 Table	P	W	D	L	F	A	GD	Pts
Latvia	4	4	0	0	10	2	8	12
Moldova	4	2	1	1	6	5	1	7
Andorra	4	1	1	2	3	6	–3	4
Liechtenstein	4	0	0	4	1	7	–6	0

GROUP D2

Thursday, 2 June 2022

Estonia (2) 2 *(Kirss 24, Tamm 32)*

San Marino (0) 0

Estonia: (352) Hein; Kuusk (Paskotsi 69), Tamm, Mets; Zenjov (Teniste 85), Vassiljev (Puri 85), Kreida (Miller 46), Kait, Sinyavskiy; Kirss, Sorga (Anier 69).
San Marino: (3511) Benedettini E; Manuel Battistini (D'Addario 21), Palazzi, Fabbri; Zafferani (Hirsch 57), Golinucci A (Tomassini D 89), Michael Battistini, Mularoni, Grandoni (Rinaldi 57); Vitaioli M (Cevoli 57); Nanni N.

Sunday, 5 June 2022

San Marino (0) 0

Malta (0) 2 *(Busuttil 59, Guillaumier 75)*

San Marino: (3511) Benedettini E; Cevoli, Rossi, Palazzi; D'Addario (Zafferani 68), Lunadei, Michael Battistini (Censoni 85), Golinucci A, Ceccaroli (Tomassini F 68); Rinaldi (Hirsch 80); Nanni N (Bernardi 85).
Malta: (3412) Bonello; Borg S, Pepe (Apap 90), Borg J (Muscat Z 69); Mbong (Corbalan 46), Guillaumier (Muscat N 88), Vella (Busuttil 46), Overend; Paiber; Satariano, Degabriele.

Thursday, 9 June 2022

Malta (0) 1 *(Hein 56 (og))*

Estonia (1) 2 *(Vassiljev 21, Anier 90)*

Malta: (3412) Bonello; Borg S, Pepe, Borg J (Muscat Z 85); Mbong, Guillaumier (Vella 80), Paiber, Camenzuli; Teuma; Satariano (Montebello 69), Degabriele (Gambin 80).
Estonia: (352) Hein; Paskotsi, Tamm, Mets; Teniste, Vassiljev (Miller 90), Soomets, Kait, Kallaste; Kirss (Zenjov 60), Sorga (Anier 60).

Sunday, 12 June 2022

Malta (0) 1 *(Muscat Z 50)*

San Marino (0) 0

Malta: (3412) Bonello; Apap (Borg J 79), Pepe, Muscat Z; Mbong, Guillaumier, Paiber (Vella 78), Camenzuli; Teuma; Gambin (Degabriele 71), Montebello (Satariano 87).
San Marino: (532) Benedettini E; D'Addario (Zafferani 79), Palazzi, Rossi, Fabbri, Grandoni (Rinaldi 61); Lunadei (Vitaioli M 85), Michael Battistini, Tomassini D (Mularoni 61); Nanni N, Ceccaroli (Hirsch 79).

Group D2 Table	P	W	D	L	F	A	GD	Pts
Estonia	2	2	0	0	4	1	3	6
Malta	3	2	0	1	4	2	2	6
San Marino	3	0	0	3	0	5	–5	0

BRITISH AND IRISH INTERNATIONAL RESULTS 1872–2022

Note: In the results that follow, WC = World Cup, EC = European Championship, NL = Nations League UI = Umbro International Trophy. TF = Tournoi de France. NC = Nations Cup. Northern Ireland played as Ireland before 1921. *After extra time.

Bold type indicates matches played in season 2021–22.

ENGLAND v SCOTLAND

Played: 114; England won 48, Scotland won 41, Drawn 26. Goals: England 203, Scotland 174.

Year	Date	Venue	*E*	*S*
1872	30 Nov	Glasgow	0	0
1873	8 Mar	Kennington Oval	4	2
1874	7 Mar	Glasgow	1	2
1875	6 Mar	Kennington Oval	2	2
1876	4 Mar	Glasgow	0	3
1877	3 Mar	Kennington Oval	1	3
1878	2 Mar	Glasgow	2	7
1879	5 Apr	Kennington Oval	5	4
1880	13 Mar	Glasgow	4	5
1881	12 Mar	Kennington Oval	1	6
1882	11 Mar	Glasgow	1	5
1883	10 Mar	Sheffield U	2	3
1884	15 Mar	Glasgow	0	1
1885	21 Mar	Kennington Oval	1	1
1886	31 Mar	Glasgow	1	1
1887	19 Mar	Blackburn	2	3
1888	17 Mar	Glasgow	5	0
1889	13 Apr	Kennington Oval	2	3
1890	5 Apr	Glasgow	1	1
1891	6 Apr	Blackburn	2	1
1892	2 Apr	Glasgow	4	1
1893	1 Apr	Richmond	5	2
1894	7 Apr	Glasgow	2	2
1895	6 Apr	Everton	3	0
1896	4 Apr	Glasgow	1	2
1897	3 Apr	Crystal Palace	1	2
1898	2 Apr	Glasgow	3	1
1899	8 Apr	Aston Villa	2	1
1900	7 Apr	Glasgow	1	4
1901	30 Mar	Crystal Palace	2	2
1902	3 Mar	Aston Villa	2	2
1903	4 Apr	Sheffield U	1	2
1904	9 Apr	Glasgow	1	0
1905	1 Apr	Crystal Palace	1	0
1906	7 Apr	Glasgow	1	2
1907	6 Apr	Newcastle	1	1
1908	4 Apr	Glasgow	1	1
1909	3 Apr	Crystal Palace	2	0
1910	2 Apr	Glasgow	0	2
1911	1 Apr	Everton	1	1
1912	23 Mar	Glasgow	1	1
1913	5 Apr	Chelsea	1	0
1914	14 Apr	Glasgow	1	3
1920	10 Apr	Sheffield W	5	4
1921	9 Apr	Glasgow	0	3
1922	8 Apr	Aston Villa	0	1
1923	14 Apr	Glasgow	2	2
1924	12 Apr	Wembley	1	1
1925	4 Apr	Glasgow	0	2
1926	17 Apr	Manchester	0	1
1927	2 Apr	Glasgow	2	1
1928	31 Mar	Wembley	1	5
1929	13 Apr	Glasgow	0	1
1930	5 Apr	Wembley	5	2
1931	28 Mar	Glasgow	0	2
1932	9 Apr	Wembley	3	0
1933	1 Apr	Glasgow	1	2
1934	14 Apr	Wembley	3	0
1935	6 Apr	Glasgow	0	2
1936	4 Apr	Wembley	1	1
1937	17 Apr	Glasgow	1	3
1938	9 Apr	Wembley	0	1
1939	15 Apr	Glasgow	2	1
1947	12 Apr	Wembley	1	1
1948	10 Apr	Glasgow	2	0
1949	9 Apr	Wembley	1	3
WC1950	15 Apr	Glasgow	1	0
1951	14 Apr	Wembley	2	3
1952	5 Apr	Glasgow	2	1
1953	18 Apr	Wembley	2	2
WC1954	3 Apr	Glasgow	4	2
1955	2 Apr	Wembley	7	2
1956	14 Apr	Glasgow	1	1
1957	6 Apr	Wembley	2	1
1958	19 Apr	Glasgow	4	0
1959	11 Apr	Wembley	1	0
1960	9 Apr	Glasgow	1	1
1961	15 Apr	Wembley	9	3
1962	14 Apr	Glasgow	0	2
1963	6 Apr	Wembley	1	2
1964	11 Apr	Glasgow	0	1
1965	10 Apr	Wembley	2	2
1966	2 Apr	Glasgow	4	3
EC1967	15 Apr	Wembley	2	3
EC1968	24 Jan	Glasgow	1	1
1969	10 May	Wembley	4	1
1970	25 Apr	Glasgow	0	0
1971	22 May	Wembley	3	1
1972	27 May	Glasgow	1	0
1973	14 Feb	Glasgow	5	0
1973	19 May	Wembley	1	0
1974	18 May	Glasgow	0	2
1975	24 May	Wembley	5	1
1976	15 May	Glasgow	1	2
1977	4 June	Wembley	1	2
1978	20 May	Glasgow	1	0
1979	26 May	Wembley	3	1
1980	24 May	Glasgow	2	0
1981	23 May	Wembley	0	1
1982	29 May	Glasgow	1	0
1983	1 June	Wembley	2	0
1984	26 May	Glasgow	1	1
1985	25 May	Glasgow	0	1
1986	23 Apr	Wembley	2	1
1987	23 May	Glasgow	0	0
1988	21 May	Wembley	1	0
1989	27 May	Glasgow	2	0
EC1996	15 June	Wembley	2	0
EC1999	13 Nov	Glasgow	2	0
EC1999	17 Nov	Wembley	0	1
2013	14 Aug	Wembley	3	2
2014	18 Nov	Glasgow	3	1
WC2016	11 Nov	Wembley	3	0
WC2017	10 June	Glasgow	2	2
EC2021	18 June	Wembley	0	0

ENGLAND v WALES

Played: 102; England won 68, Wales won 14, Drawn 21. Goals: England 250, Wales 91.

Year	Date	Venue	*E*	*W*
1879	18 Jan	Kennington Oval	2	1
1880	15 Mar	Wrexham	3	2
1881	26 Feb	Blackburn	0	1
1882	13 Mar	Wrexham	3	5
1883	3 Feb	Kennington Oval	5	0
1884	17 Mar	Wrexham	4	0
1885	14 Mar	Blackburn	1	1
1886	29 Mar	Wrexham	3	1
1887	26 Feb	Kennington Oval	4	0
1888	4 Feb	Crewe	5	1
1889	23 Feb	Stoke	4	1
1890	15 Mar	Wrexham	3	1

			E	*W*
1891	7 May	Sunderland	4	1
1892	5 Mar	Wrexham	2	0
1893	13 Mar	Stoke	6	0
1894	12 Mar	Wrexham	5	1
1895	18 Mar	Queen's Club, Kensington	1	1
1896	16 Mar	Cardiff	9	1
1897	29 Mar	Sheffield	4	0
1898	28 Mar	Wrexham	3	0
1899	20 Mar	Bristol	4	0
1900	26 Mar	Cardiff	1	1
1901	18 Mar	Newcastle	6	0
1902	3 Mar	Wrexham	0	0
1903	2 Mar	Portsmouth	2	1
1904	29 Feb	Wrexham	2	2
1905	27 Mar	Liverpool	3	1
1906	19 Mar	Cardiff	1	0
1907	18 Mar	Fulham	1	1
1908	16 Mar	Wrexham	7	1
1909	15 Mar	Nottingham	2	0
1910	14 Mar	Cardiff	1	0
1911	13 Mar	Millwall	3	0
1912	11 Mar	Wrexham	2	0
1913	17 Mar	Bristol	4	3
1914	16 Mar	Cardiff	2	0
1920	15 Mar	Highbury	1	2
1921	14 Mar	Cardiff	0	0
1922	13 Mar	Liverpool	1	0
1923	5 Mar	Cardiff	2	2
1924	3 Mar	Blackburn	1	2
1925	28 Feb	Swansea	2	1
1926	1 Mar	Crystal Palace	1	3
1927	12 Feb	Wrexham	3	3
1927	28 Nov	Burnley	1	2
1928	17 Nov	Swansea	3	2
1929	20 Nov	Chelsea	6	0
1930	22 Nov	Wrexham	4	0
1931	18 Nov	Liverpool	3	1
1932	16 Nov	Wrexham	0	0
1933	15 Nov	Newcastle	1	2
1934	29 Sept	Cardiff	4	0
1936	5 Feb	Wolverhampton	1	2
1936	17 Oct	Cardiff	1	2
1937	17 Nov	Middlesbrough	2	1
1938	22 Oct	Cardiff	2	4
1946	13 Nov	Manchester	3	0

			E	*W*
1947	18 Oct	Cardiff	3	0
1948	10 Nov	Aston Villa	1	0
WC1949	15 Oct	Cardiff	4	1
1950	15 Nov	Sunderland	4	2
1951	20 Oct	Cardiff	1	1
1952	12 Nov	Wembley	5	2
WC1953	10 Oct	Cardiff	4	1
1954	10 Nov	Wembley	3	2
1955	27 Oct	Cardiff	1	2
1956	14 Nov	Wembley	3	1
1957	19 Oct	Cardiff	4	0
1958	26 Nov	Aston Villa	2	2
1959	17 Oct	Cardiff	1	1
1960	23 Nov	Wembley	5	1
1961	14 Oct	Cardiff	1	1
1962	21 Oct	Wembley	4	0
1963	12 Oct	Cardiff	4	0
1964	18 Nov	Wembley	2	1
1965	2 Oct	Cardiff	0	0
EC1966	16 Nov	Wembley	5	1
EC1967	21 Oct	Cardiff	3	0
1969	7 May	Wembley	2	1
1970	18 Apr	Cardiff	1	1
1971	19 May	Wembley	0	0
1972	20 May	Cardiff	3	0
WC1972	15 Nov	Cardiff	1	0
WC1973	24 Jan	Wembley	1	1
1973	15 May	Wembley	3	0
1974	11 May	Cardiff	2	0
1975	21 May	Wembley	2	2
1976	24 Mar	Wrexham	2	1
1976	8 May	Cardiff	1	0
1977	31 May	Wembley	0	1
1978	3 May	Cardiff	3	1
1979	23 May	Wembley	0	0
1980	17 May	Wrexham	1	4
1981	20 May	Wembley	0	0
1982	27 Apr	Cardiff	1	0
1983	23 Feb	Wembley	2	1
1984	2 May	Wrexham	0	1
WC2004	9 Oct	Old Trafford	2	0
WC2005	3 Sept	Cardiff	1	0
EC2011	26 Mar	Cardiff	2	0
EC2011	6 Sept	Wembley	1	0
EC2016	16 June	Lens	2	1
2020	8 Oct	Wembley	3	0

ENGLAND v NORTHERN IRELAND

Played: 98; England won 75, Northern Ireland won 7, Drawn 16. Goals: England 323, Northern Ireland 81.

			E	*NI*
1882	18 Feb	Belfast	13	0
1883	24 Feb	Liverpool	7	0
1884	23 Feb	Belfast	8	1
1885	28 Feb	Manchester	4	0
1886	13 Mar	Belfast	6	1
1887	5 Feb	Sheffield	7	0
1888	31 Mar	Belfast	5	1
1889	2 Mar	Everton	6	1
1890	15 Mar	Belfast	9	1
1891	7 Mar	Wolverhampton	6	1
1892	5 Mar	Belfast	2	0
1893	25 Feb	Birmingham	6	1
1894	3 Mar	Belfast	2	2
1895	9 Mar	Derby	9	0
1896	7 Mar	Belfast	2	0
1897	20 Feb	Nottingham	6	0
1898	5 Mar	Belfast	3	2
1899	18 Feb	Sunderland	13	2
1900	17 Mar	Dublin	2	0
1901	9 Mar	Southampton	3	0
1902	22 Mar	Belfast	1	0
1903	14 Feb	Wolverhampton	4	0
1904	12 Mar	Belfast	3	1
1905	25 Feb	Middlesbrough	1	1
1906	17 Feb	Belfast	5	0
1907	16 Feb	Everton	1	0
1908	15 Feb	Belfast	3	1
1909	13 Feb	Bradford	4	0
1910	12 Feb	Belfast	1	1
1911	11 Feb	Derby	2	1
1912	10 Feb	Dublin	6	1
1913	15 Feb	Belfast	1	2
1914	14 Feb	Middlesbrough	0	3

			E	*NI*
1919	25 Oct	Belfast	1	1
1920	23 Oct	Sunderland	2	0
1921	22 Oct	Belfast	1	1
1922	21 Oct	West Bromwich	2	0
1923	20 Oct	Belfast	1	2
1924	22 Oct	Everton	3	1
1925	24 Oct	Belfast	0	0
1926	20 Oct	Liverpool	3	3
1927	22 Oct	Belfast	0	2
1928	22 Oct	Everton	2	1
1929	19 Oct	Belfast	3	0
1930	20 Oct	Sheffield	5	1
1931	17 Oct	Belfast	6	2
1932	17 Oct	Blackpool	1	0
1933	14 Oct	Belfast	3	0
1935	6 Feb	Everton	2	1
1935	19 Oct	Belfast	3	1
1936	18 Nov	Stoke	3	1
1937	23 Oct	Belfast	5	1
1938	16 Nov	Manchester	7	0
1946	28 Sept	Belfast	7	2
1947	5 Nov	Everton	2	2
1948	9 Oct	Belfast	6	2
WC1949	16 Nov	Manchester	9	2
1950	7 Oct	Belfast	4	1
1951	14 Nov	Aston Villa	2	0
1952	4 Oct	Belfast	2	2
WC1953	11 Nov	Everton	3	1
1954	2 Oct	Belfast	2	0
1955	2 Nov	Wembley	3	0
1956	10 Oct	Belfast	1	1
1957	6 Nov	Wembley	2	3
1958	4 Oct	Belfast	3	3

			E	*NI*
1959	18 Nov	Wembley	2	1
1960	8 Oct	Belfast	5	2
1961	22 Nov	Wembley	1	1
1962	20 Oct	Belfast	3	1
1963	20 Nov	Wembley	8	3
1964	3 Oct	Belfast	4	3
1965	10 Nov	Wembley	2	1
EC1966	20 Oct	Belfast	2	0
EC1967	22 Nov	Wembley	2	0
1969	3 May	Belfast	3	1
1970	21 Apr	Wembley	3	1
1971	15 May	Belfast	1	0
1972	23 May	Wembley	0	1
1973	12 May	Everton	2	1
1974	15 May	Wembley	1	0
1975	17 May	Belfast	0	0
1976	11 May	Wembley	4	0
1977	28 May	Belfast	2	1
1978	16 May	Wembley	1	0
EC1979	7 Feb	Wembley	4	0
1979	19 May	Belfast	2	0
EC1979	17 Oct	Belfast	5	1
1980	20 May	Wembley	1	1
1982	23 Feb	Wembley	4	0
1983	28 May	Belfast	0	0
1984	24 Apr	Wembley	1	0
WC1985	27 Feb	Belfast	1	0
WC1985	13 Nov	Wembley	0	0
EC1986	15 Oct	Wembley	3	0
EC1987	1 Apr	Belfast	2	0
WC2005	26 Mar	Old Trafford	4	0
WC2005	7 Sept	Belfast	0	1

SCOTLAND v WALES

Played: 107; Scotland won 61, Wales won 23, Drawn 23. Goals: Scotland 243, Wales 124.

			S	*W*
1876	25 Mar	Glasgow	4	0
1877	5 Mar	Wrexham	2	0
1878	23 Mar	Glasgow	9	0
1879	7 Apr	Wrexham	3	0
1880	3 Apr	Glasgow	5	1
1881	14 Mar	Wrexham	5	1
1882	25 Mar	Glasgow	5	0
1883	12 Mar	Wrexham	3	0
1884	29 Mar	Glasgow	4	1
1885	23 Mar	Wrexham	8	1
1886	10 Apr	Glasgow	4	1
1887	21 Mar	Wrexham	2	0
1888	10 Mar	Easter Road	5	1
1889	15 Apr	Wrexham	0	0
1890	22 Mar	Paisley	5	0
1891	21 Mar	Wrexham	4	3
1892	26 Mar	Tynecastle	6	1
1893	18 Mar	Wrexham	8	0
1894	24 Mar	Kilmarnock	5	2
1895	23 Mar	Wrexham	2	2
1896	21 Mar	Dundee	4	0
1897	20 Mar	Wrexham	2	2
1898	19 Mar	Motherwell	5	2
1899	18 Mar	Wrexham	6	0
1900	3 Feb	Aberdeen	5	2
1901	2 Mar	Wrexham	1	1
1902	15 Mar	Greenock	5	1
1903	9 Mar	Cardiff	1	0
1904	12 Mar	Dundee	1	1
1905	6 Mar	Wrexham	1	3
1906	3 Mar	Tynecastle	0	2
1907	4 Mar	Wrexham	0	1
1908	7 Mar	Dundee	2	1
1909	1 Mar	Wrexham	2	3
1910	5 Mar	Kilmarnock	1	0
1911	6 Mar	Cardiff	2	2
1912	2 Mar	Tynecastle	1	0
1913	3 Mar	Wrexham	0	0
1914	28 Feb	Glasgow	0	0
1920	26 Feb	Cardiff	1	1
1921	12 Feb	Aberdeen	2	1
1922	4 Feb	Wrexham	1	2
1923	17 Mar	Paisley	2	0
1924	16 Feb	Cardiff	0	2
1925	14 Feb	Tynecastle	3	1
1925	31 Oct	Cardiff	3	0
1926	30 Oct	Glasgow	3	0
1927	29 Oct	Wrexham	2	2
1928	27 Oct	Glasgow	4	2
1929	26 Oct	Cardiff	4	2
1930	25 Oct	Glasgow	1	1
1931	31 Oct	Wrexham	3	2
1932	26 Oct	Tynecastle	2	5
1933	4 Oct	Cardiff	2	3
1934	21 Nov	Aberdeen	3	2
1935	5 Oct	Cardiff	1	1
1936	2 Dec	Dundee	1	2
1937	30 Oct	Cardiff	1	2
1938	9 Nov	Tynecastle	3	2
1946	19 Oct	Wrexham	1	3
1947	12 Nov	Glasgow	1	2
1948	23 Oct	Cardiff	3	1
WC1949	9 Nov	Glasgow	2	0
1950	21 Oct	Cardiff	3	1
1951	14 Nov	Glasgow	0	1
1952	18 Oct	Cardiff	2	1
WC1953	4 Nov	Glasgow	3	3
1954	16 Oct	Cardiff	1	0
1955	9 Nov	Glasgow	2	0
1956	20 Oct	Cardiff	2	2
1957	13 Nov	Glasgow	1	1
1958	18 Oct	Cardiff	3	0
1959	4 Nov	Glasgow	1	1
1960	20 Oct	Cardiff	0	2
1961	8 Nov	Glasgow	2	0
1962	20 Oct	Cardiff	3	2
1963	20 Nov	Glasgow	2	1
1964	3 Oct	Cardiff	2	3
EC1965	24 Nov	Glasgow	4	1
EC1966	22 Oct	Cardiff	1	1
1967	22 Nov	Glasgow	3	2
1969	3 May	Wrexham	5	3
1970	22 Apr	Glasgow	0	0
1971	15 May	Cardiff	0	0
1972	24 May	Glasgow	1	0
1973	12 May	Wrexham	2	0
1974	14 May	Glasgow	2	0
1975	17 May	Cardiff	2	2
1976	6 May	Glasgow	3	1
WC1976	17 Nov	Glasgow	1	0
1977	28 May	Wrexham	0	0
WC1977	12 Oct	Liverpool	2	0
1978	17 May	Glasgow	1	1
1979	19 May	Cardiff	0	3
1980	21 May	Glasgow	1	0
1981	16 May	Swansea	0	2
1982	24 May	Glasgow	1	0
1983	28 May	Cardiff	2	0
1984	28 Feb	Glasgow	2	1
WC1985	27 Mar	Glasgow	0	1
WC1985	10 Sept	Cardiff	1	1
1997	27 May	Kilmarnock	0	1
2004	18 Feb	Cardiff	0	4
2009	14 Nov	Cardiff	0	3
NC2011	25 May	Dublin	3	1
WC2012	12 Oct	Cardiff	1	2
WC2013	22 Mar	Glasgow	1	2

SCOTLAND v NORTHERN IRELAND

Played: 96; Scotland won 64, Northern Ireland won 15, Drawn 17. Goals: Scotland 261, Northern Ireland 81.

			S	*NI*
1884	26 Jan	Belfast	5	0
1885	14 Mar	Glasgow	8	2
1886	20 Mar	Belfast	7	2
1887	19 Feb	Glasgow	4	1
1888	24 Mar	Belfast	10	2
1889	9 Mar	Glasgow	7	0
1890	29 Mar	Belfast	4	1
1891	28 Mar	Glasgow	2	1

Year	Date	Venue	*S*	*NI*
1892	19 Mar	Belfast	3	2
1893	25 Mar	Glasgow	6	1
1894	31 Mar	Belfast	2	1
1895	30 Mar	Glasgow	3	1
1896	28 Mar	Belfast	3	3
1897	27 Mar	Glasgow	5	1
1898	26 Mar	Belfast	3	0
1899	25 Mar	Glasgow	9	1
1900	3 Mar	Belfast	3	0
1901	23 Feb	Glasgow	11	0
1902	1 Mar	Belfast	5	1
1902	9 Aug	Belfast	3	0
1903	21 Mar	Glasgow	0	2
1904	26 Mar	Dublin	1	1
1905	18 Mar	Glasgow	4	0
1906	17 Mar	Dublin	1	0
1907	16 Mar	Glasgow	3	0
1908	14 Mar	Dublin	5	0
1909	15 Mar	Glasgow	5	0
1910	19 Mar	Belfast	0	1
1911	18 Mar	Glasgow	2	0
1912	16 Mar	Belfast	4	1
1913	15 Mar	Dublin	2	1
1914	14 Mar	Belfast	1	1
1920	13 Mar	Glasgow	3	0
1921	26 Feb	Belfast	2	0
1922	4 Mar	Glasgow	2	1
1923	3 Mar	Belfast	1	0
1924	1 Mar	Glasgow	2	0
1925	28 Feb	Belfast	3	0
1926	27 Feb	Glasgow	4	0
1927	26 Feb	Belfast	2	0
1928	25 Feb	Glasgow	0	1
1929	23 Feb	Belfast	7	3
1930	22 Feb	Glasgow	3	1
1931	21 Feb	Belfast	0	0
1931	19 Sept	Glasgow	3	1
1932	12 Sept	Belfast	4	0
1933	16 Sept	Glasgow	1	2
1934	20 Oct	Belfast	1	2
1935	13 Nov	Tynecastle	2	1
1936	31 Oct	Belfast	3	1
1937	10 Nov	Aberdeen	1	1
1938	8 Oct	Belfast	2	0

Year	Date	Venue	*S*	*NI*
1946	27 Nov	Glasgow	0	0
1947	4 Oct	Belfast	0	2
1948	17 Nov	Glasgow	3	2
wc1949	1 Oct	Belfast	8	2
1950	1 Nov	Glasgow	6	1
1951	6 Oct	Belfast	3	0
1952	5 Nov	Glasgow	1	1
wc1953	3 Oct	Belfast	3	1
1954	3 Nov	Glasgow	2	2
1955	8 Oct	Belfast	1	2
1956	7 Nov	Glasgow	1	0
1957	5 Oct	Belfast	1	1
1958	5 Nov	Glasgow	2	2
1959	3 Oct	Belfast	4	0
1960	9 Nov	Glasgow	5	2
1961	7 Oct	Belfast	6	1
1962	7 Nov	Glasgow	5	1
1963	12 Oct	Belfast	1	2
1964	25 Nov	Glasgow	3	2
1965	2 Oct	Belfast	2	3
1966	16 Nov	Glasgow	2	1
1967	21 Oct	Belfast	0	1
1969	6 May	Glasgow	1	1
1970	18 Apr	Belfast	1	0
1971	18 May	Glasgow	0	1
1972	20 May	Glasgow	2	0
1973	16 May	Glasgow	1	2
1974	11 May	Glasgow	0	1
1975	20 May	Glasgow	3	0
1976	8 May	Glasgow	3	0
1977	1 June	Glasgow	3	0
1978	13 May	Glasgow	1	1
1979	22 May	Glasgow	1	0
1980	17 May	Belfast	0	1
wc1981	25 Mar	Glasgow	1	1
1981	19 May	Glasgow	2	0
wc1981	14 Oct	Belfast	0	0
1982	28 Apr	Belfast	1	1
1983	24 May	Glasgow	0	0
1983	13 Dec	Belfast	0	2
1992	19 Feb	Glasgow	1	0
2008	20 Aug	Glasgow	0	0
NC2011	9 Feb	Dublin	3	0
2015	25 Mar	Glasgow	1	0

WALES v NORTHERN IRELAND

Played: 96; Wales won 45, Northern Ireland won 27, Drawn 24. Goals: Wales 191, Northern Ireland 132.

Year	Date	Venue	*W*	*NI*
1882	25 Feb	Wrexham	7	1
1883	17 Mar	Belfast	1	1
1884	9 Feb	Wrexham	6	0
1885	11 Apr	Belfast	8	2
1886	27 Feb	Wrexham	5	0
1887	12 Mar	Belfast	1	4
1888	3 Mar	Wrexham	11	0
1889	27 Apr	Belfast	3	1
1890	8 Feb	Shrewsbury	5	2
1891	7 Feb	Belfast	2	7
1892	27 Feb	Bangor	1	1
1893	8 Apr	Belfast	3	4
1894	24 Feb	Swansea	4	1
1895	16 Mar	Belfast	2	2
1896	29 Feb	Wrexham	6	1
1897	6 Mar	Belfast	3	4
1898	19 Feb	Llandudno	0	1
1899	4 Mar	Belfast	0	1
1900	24 Feb	Llandudno	2	0
1901	23 Mar	Belfast	1	0
1902	22 Mar	Cardiff	0	3
1903	28 Mar	Belfast	0	2
1904	21 Mar	Bangor	0	1
1905	18 Apr	Belfast	2	2
1906	2 Apr	Wrexham	4	4
1907	23 Feb	Belfast	3	2
1908	11 Apr	Aberdare	0	1
1909	20 Mar	Belfast	3	2
1910	11 Apr	Wrexham	4	1
1911	28 Jan	Belfast	2	1
1912	13 Apr	Cardiff	2	3
1913	18 Jan	Belfast	1	0
1914	19 Jan	Wrexham	1	2
1920	14 Feb	Belfast	2	2
1921	9 Apr	Swansea	2	1

Year	Date	Venue	*W*	*NI*
1922	4 Apr	Belfast	1	1
1923	14 Apr	Wrexham	0	3
1924	15 Mar	Belfast	1	0
1925	18 Apr	Wrexham	0	0
1926	13 Feb	Belfast	0	3
1927	9 Apr	Cardiff	2	2
1928	4 Feb	Belfast	2	1
1929	2 Feb	Wrexham	2	2
1930	1 Feb	Belfast	0	7
1931	22 Apr	Wrexham	3	2
1931	5 Dec	Belfast	0	4
1932	7 Dec	Wrexham	4	1
1933	4 Nov	Belfast	1	1
1935	27 Mar	Wrexham	3	1
1936	11 Mar	Belfast	2	3
1937	17 Mar	Wrexham	4	1
1938	16 Mar	Belfast	0	1
1939	15 Mar	Wrexham	3	1
1947	16 Apr	Belfast	1	2
1948	10 Mar	Wrexham	2	0
1949	9 Mar	Belfast	2	0
wc1950	8 Mar	Wrexham	0	0
1951	7 Mar	Belfast	2	1
1952	19 Mar	Swansea	3	0
1953	15 Apr	Belfast	3	2
wc1954	31 Mar	Wrexham	1	2
1955	20 Apr	Belfast	3	2
1956	11 Apr	Cardiff	1	1
1957	10 Apr	Belfast	0	0
1958	16 Apr	Cardiff	1	1
1959	22 Apr	Belfast	1	4
1960	6 Apr	Wrexham	3	2
1961	12 Apr	Belfast	5	1
1962	11 Apr	Cardiff	4	0
1963	3 Apr	Belfast	4	1

			W	NI
1964	15 Apr	Swansea	2	3
1965	31 Mar	Belfast	5	0
1966	30 Mar	Cardiff	1	4
EC1967	12 Apr	Belfast	0	0
EC1968	28 Feb	Wrexham	2	0
1969	10 May	Belfast	0	0
1970	25 Apr	Swansea	1	0
1971	22 May	Belfast	0	1
1972	27 May	Wrexham	0	0
1973	19 May	Everton	0	1
1974	18 May	Wrexham	1	0
1975	23 May	Belfast	0	1
1976	14 May	Swansea	1	0
1977	3 June	Belfast	1	1
1978	19 May	Wrexham	1	0
1979	25 May	Belfast	1	1
1980	23 May	Cardiff	0	1
1982	27 May	Wrexham	3	0
1983	31 May	Belfast	1	0
1984	22 May	Swansea	1	1
WC2004	8 Sept	Cardiff	2	2
WC2005	8 Oct	Belfast	3	2
2007	6 Feb	Belfast	0	0
NC2011	27 May	Dublin	2	0
2016	24 Mar	Cardiff	1	1
EC2016	25 June	Paris	1	0

OTHER BRITISH INTERNATIONAL RESULTS 1908–2022

ENGLAND

v ALBANIA			E	A
WC1989	8 Mar	Tirana	2	0
WC1989	26 Apr	Wembley	5	0
WC2001	28 Mar	Tirana	3	1
WC2001	5 Sept	Newcastle	2	0
WC2021	28 Mar	Tirana	2	0
WC2021	**12 Nov**	**Wembley**	**5**	**0**

v ALGERIA			E	A
WC2010	18 June	Cape Town	0	0

v ANDORRA			E	A
EC2006	2 Sept	Old Trafford	5	0
EC2007	28 Mar	Barcelona	3	0
WC2008	6 Sept	Barcelona	2	0
WC2009	10 June	Wembley	6	0
WC2021	**5 Sept**	**Wembley**	**4**	**0**
WC2021	**9 Oct**	**Andorra La Vella**	**5**	**0**

v ARGENTINA			E	A
1951	9 May	Wembley	2	1
1953	17 May	Buenos Aires	0	0
(*abandoned after 21 mins*)				
WC1962	2 June	Rancagua	3	1
1964	6 June	Rio de Janeiro	0	1
WC1966	23 July	Wembley	1	0
1974	22 May	Wembley	2	2
1977	12 June	Buenos Aires	1	1
1980	13 May	Wembley	3	1
WC1986	22 June	Mexico City	1	2
1991	25 May	Wembley	2	2
WC1998	30 June	St Etienne	2	2
2000	23 Feb	Wembley	0	0
WC2002	7 June	Sapporo	1	0
2005	12 Nov	Geneva	3	2

v AUSTRALIA			E	A
1980	31 May	Sydney	2	1
1983	11 June	Sydney	0	0
1983	15 June	Brisbane	1	0
1983	18 June	Melbourne	1	1
1991	1 June	Sydney	1	0
2003	12 Feb	West Ham	1	3
2016	27 May	Sunderland	2	1

v AUSTRIA			E	A
1908	6 June	Vienna	6	1
1908	8 June	Vienna	11	1
1909	1 June	Vienna	8	1
1930	14 May	Vienna	0	0
1932	7 Dec	Chelsea	4	3
1936	6 May	Vienna	1	2
1951	28 Nov	Wembley	2	2
1952	25 May	Vienna	3	2
WC1958	15 June	Boras	2	2
1961	27 May	Vienna	1	3
1962	4 Apr	Wembley	3	1
1965	20 Oct	Wembley	2	3
1967	27 May	Vienna	1	0
1973	26 Sept	Wembley	7	0
1979	13 June	Vienna	3	4
WC2004	4 Sept	Vienna	2	2
WC2005	8 Oct	Old Trafford	1	0
2007	16 Nov	Vienna	1	0
2021	2 June	Middlesbrough	1	0

v AZERBAIJAN			E	A
WC2004	13 Oct	Baku	1	0
WC2005	30 Mar	Newcastle	2	0

v BELARUS			E	B
WC2008	15 Oct	Minsk	3	1
WC2009	14 Oct	Wembley	3	0

v BELGIUM			E	B
1921	21 May	Brussels	2	0
1923	19 Mar	Highbury	6	1
1923	1 Nov	Antwerp	2	2
1924	8 Dec	West Bromwich	4	0
1926	24 May	Antwerp	5	3
1927	11 May	Brussels	9	1
1928	19 May	Antwerp	3	1
1929	11 May	Brussels	5	1
1931	16 May	Brussels	4	1
1936	9 May	Brussels	2	3
1947	21 Sept	Brussels	5	2
1950	18 May	Brussels	4	1
1952	26 Nov	Wembley	5	0
WC1954	17 June	Basel	4	4*
1964	21 Oct	Wembley	2	2
1970	25 Feb	Brussels	3	1
EC1980	12 June	Turin	1	1
WC1990	27 June	Bologna	1	0*
1998	29 May	Casablanca	0	0
1999	10 Oct	Sunderland	2	1
2012	2 June	Wembley	1	0
WC2018	28 June	Kaliningrad	0	1
WC2018	14 July	St Petersburg	0	2
NL2020	11 Oct	Wembley	2	1
NL2020	15 Nov	Leuven	0	2

v BOHEMIA			E	B
1908	13 June	Prague	4	0

v BRAZIL			E	B
1956	9 May	Wembley	4	2
WC1958	11 June	Gothenburg	0	0
1959	13 May	Rio de Janeiro	0	2
WC1962	10 June	Vina del Mar	1	3
1963	8 May	Wembley	1	1
1964	30 May	Rio de Janeiro	1	5
1969	12 June	Rio de Janeiro	1	2
WC1970	7 June	Guadalajara	0	1
1976	23 May	Los Angeles	0	1
1977	8 June	Rio de Janeiro	0	0
1978	19 Apr	Wembley	1	1
1981	12 May	Wembley	0	1
1984	10 June	Rio de Janeiro	2	0
1987	19 May	Wembley	1	1
1990	28 Mar	Wembley	1	0
1992	17 May	Wembley	1	1
1993	13 June	Washington	1	1
UI1995	11 June	Wembley	1	3
TF1997	10 June	Paris	0	1
2000	27 May	Wembley	1	1
WC2002	21 June	Shizuoka	1	2
2007	1 June	Wembley	1	1
2009	14 Nov	Doha	0	1
2013	6 Feb	Wembley	2	1
2013	2 June	Rio de Janeiro	2	2
2017	14 Nov	Wembley	0	0

v BULGARIA			E	B
WC1962	7 June	Rancagua	0	0
1968	11 Dec	Wembley	1	1
1974	1 June	Sofia	1	0
EC1979	6 June	Sofia	3	0
EC1979	22 Nov	Wembley	2	0

			E	*B*
1996	27 Mar	Wembley	1	0
EC1998	10 Oct	Wembley	0	0
EC1999	9 June	Sofia	1	1
EC2010	3 Sept	Wembley	4	0
EC2011	2 Sept	Sofia	3	0
EC2019	7 Sept	Wembley	4	0
EC2019	14 Oct	Sofia	6	0

v CAMEROON

			E	*C*
WC1990	1 July	Naples	3	2*
1991	6 Feb	Wembley	2	0
1997	15 Nov	Wembley	2	0
2002	26 May	Kobe	2	2

v CANADA

			E	*C*
1986	24 May	Burnaby	1	0

v CHILE

			E	*C*
WC1950	25 June	Rio de Janeiro	2	0
1953	24 May	Santiago	2	1
1984	17 June	Santiago	0	0
1989	23 May	Wembley	0	0
1998	11 Feb	Wembley	0	2
2013	15 Nov	Wembley	0	2

v CHINA PR

			E	*CPR*
1996	23 May	Beijing	3	0

v CIS

			E	*C*
1992	29 Apr	Moscow	2	2

v COLOMBIA

			E	*C*
1970	20 May	Bogota	4	0
1988	24 May	Wembley	1	1
1995	6 Sept	Wembley	0	0
WC1998	26 June	Lens	2	0
2005	31 May	New Jersey	3	2
WC2018	3 July	Moscow	1	1

v COSTA RICA

			E	*C*
WC2014	26 June	Belo Horizonte	0	0
2018	7 June	Leeds	2	0

v CROATIA

			E	*C*
1996	24 Apr	Wembley	0	0
2003	20 Aug	Ipswich	3	1
EC2004	21 June	Lisbon	4	2
EC2006	11 Oct	Zagreb	0	2
EC2007	21 Nov	Wembley	2	3
WC2008	10 Sept	Zagreb	4	1
WC2009	9 Sept	Wembley	5	1
WC2018	11 July	Moscow	1	2*
NL2018	12 Oct	Rijeka	0	0
NL2018	18 Nov	Wembley	2	1
EC2021	13 June	Wembley	1	0

v CYPRUS

			E	*C*
EC1975	16 Apr	Wembley	5	0
EC1975	11 May	Limassol	1	0

v CZECHOSLOVAKIA

			E	*C*
1934	16 May	Prague	1	2
1937	1 Dec	Tottenham	5	4
1963	29 May	Bratislava	4	2
1966	2 Nov	Wembley	0	0
WC1970	11 June	Guadalajara	1	0
1973	27 May	Prague	1	1
EC1974	30 Oct	Wembley	3	0
EC1975	30 Oct	Bratislava	1	2
1978	29 Nov	Wembley	1	0
WC1982	20 June	Bilbao	2	0
1990	25 Apr	Wembley	4	2
1992	25 Mar	Prague	2	2

v CZECH REPUBLIC

			E	*C*
1998	18 Nov	Wembley	2	0
2008	20 Aug	Wembley	2	2
EC2019	22 Mar	Wembley	5	0
EC2019	11 Oct	Prague	1	2
EC2021	22 June	Wembley	1	0

v DENMARK

			E	*D*
1948	26 Sept	Copenhagen	0	0
1955	2 Oct	Copenhagen	5	1
WC1956	5 Dec	Wolverhampton	5	2
WC1957	15 May	Copenhagen	4	1
1966	3 July	Copenhagen	2	0
EC1978	20 Sept	Copenhagen	4	3
EC1979	12 Sept	Wembley	1	0
EC1982	22 Sept	Copenhagen	2	2
EC1983	21 Sept	Wembley	0	1
1988	14 Sept	Wembley	1	0
1989	7 June	Copenhagen	1	1
1990	15 May	Wembley	1	0
EC1992	11 June	Malmo	0	0
1994	9 Mar	Wembley	1	0
WC2002	15 June	Niigata	3	0
2003	16 Nov	Old Trafford	2	3
2005	17 Aug	Copenhagen	1	4
2011	9 Feb	Copenhagen	2	1
2014	5 Mar	Wembley	1	0
NL2020	8 Sept	Copenhagen	0	0
NL2020	14 Oct	Wembley	0	1
EC2021	7 July	Wembley	2	1

v ECUADOR

			E	*Ec*
1970	24 May	Quito	2	0
WC2006	25 June	Stuttgart	1	0
2014	4 June	Miami	2	2

v EGYPT

			E	*Eg*
1986	29 Jan	Cairo	4	0
WC1990	21 June	Cagliari	1	0
2010	3 Mar	Wembley	3	1

v ESTONIA

			E	*Es*
EC2007	6 June	Tallinn	3	0
EC2007	13 Oct	Wembley	3	0
EC2014	12 Oct	Tallinn	1	0
EC2015	9 Oct	Wembley	2	0

v FIFA

			E	*FIFA*
1938	26 Oct	Highbury	3	0
1953	21 Oct	Wembley	4	4
1963	23 Oct	Wembley	2	1

v FINLAND

			E	*F*
1937	20 May	Helsinki	8	0
1956	20 May	Helsinki	5	1
1966	26 June	Helsinki	3	0
WC1976	13 June	Helsinki	4	1
WC1976	13 Oct	Wembley	2	1
1982	3 June	Helsinki	4	1
WC1984	17 Oct	Wembley	5	0
WC1985	22 May	Helsinki	1	1
1992	3 June	Helsinki	2	1
WC2000	11 Oct	Helsinki	0	0
WC2001	24 Mar	Liverpool	2	1

v FRANCE

			E	*F*
1923	10 May	Paris	4	1
1924	17 May	Paris	3	1
1925	21 May	Paris	3	2
1927	26 May	Paris	6	0
1928	17 May	Paris	5	1
1929	9 May	Paris	4	1
1931	14 May	Paris	2	5
1933	6 Dec	Tottenham	4	1
1938	26 May	Paris	4	2
1947	3 May	Highbury	3	0
1949	22 May	Paris	3	1
1951	3 Oct	Highbury	2	2
1955	15 May	Paris	0	1
1957	27 Nov	Wembley	4	0
EC1962	3 Oct	Sheffield	1	1
EC1963	27 Feb	Paris	2	5
WC1966	20 July	Wembley	2	0
1969	12 Mar	Wembley	5	0
WC1982	16 June	Bilbao	3	1
1984	29 Feb	Paris	0	2
1992	19 Feb	Wembley	2	0
EC1992	14 June	Malmo	0	0
TF1997	7 June	Montpellier	1	0
1999	10 Feb	Wembley	0	2
2000	2 Sept	Paris	1	1
EC2004	13 June	Lisbon	1	2
2008	26 Mar	Paris	0	1
2010	17 Nov	Wembley	1	2
EC2012	11 June	Donetsk	1	1
2015	17 Nov	Wembley	2	0
2017	13 June	Paris	2	3

v GEORGIA

			E	*G*
WC1996	9 Nov	Tbilisi	2	0
WC1997	30 Apr	Wembley	2	0

v GERMANY

			E	*G*
1930	10 May	Berlin	3	3
1935	4 Dec	Tottenham	3	0
1938	14 May	Berlin	6	3

			E	*G*
1991	11 Sept	Wembley	0	1
1993	19 June	Detroit	1	2
EC1996	26 June	Wembley	1	1*
EC2000	17 June	Charleroi	1	0
WC2000	7 Oct	Wembley	0	1
WC2001	1 Sept	Munich	5	1
2007	22 Aug	Wembley	1	2
2008	19 Nov	Berlin	2	1
WC2010	27 June	Bloemfontein	1	4
2013	19 Nov	Wembley	0	1
2016	26 Mar	Berlin	3	2
2017	22 Mar	Dortmund	0	1
2017	10 Nov	Wembley	0	0
EC2021	29 June	Wembley	2	0
NL2022	**7 June**	**Munich**	**1**	**1**

v EAST GERMANY			*E*	*EG*
1963	2 June	Leipzig	2	1
1970	25 Nov	Wembley	3	1
1974	29 May	Leipzig	1	1
1984	12 Sept	Wembley	1	0

v WEST GERMANY			*E*	*WG*
1954	1 Dec	Wembley	3	1
1956	26 May	Berlin	3	1
1965	12 May	Nuremberg	1	0
1966	23 Feb	Wembley	1	0
WC1966	30 July	Wembley	4	2*
1968	1 June	Hanover	0	1
WC1970	14 June	Leon	2	3*
EC1972	29 Apr	Wembley	1	3
EC1972	13 May	Berlin	0	0
1975	12 Mar	Wembley	2	0
1978	22 Feb	Munich	1	2
WC1982	29 June	Madrid	0	0
1982	13 Oct	Wembley	1	2
1985	12 June	Mexico City	3	0
1987	9 Sept	Dusseldorf	1	3
WC1990	4 July	Turin	1	1*

v GHANA			*E*	*G*
2011	29 Mar	Wembley	1	1

v GREECE			*E*	*G*
EC1971	21 Apr	Wembley	3	0
EC1971	1 Dec	Piraeus	2	0
EC1982	17 Nov	Salonika	3	0
EC1983	30 Mar	Wembley	0	0
1989	8 Feb	Athens	2	1
1994	17 May	Wembley	5	0
WC2001	6 June	Athens	2	0
WC2001	6 Oct	Old Trafford	2	2
2006	16 Aug	Old Trafford	4	0

v HONDURAS			*E*	*H*
2014	7 June	Miami	0	0

v HUNGARY			*E*	*H*
1908	10 June	Budapest	7	0
1909	29 May	Budapest	4	2
1909	31 May	Budapest	8	2
1934	10 May	Budapest	1	2
1936	2 Dec	Highbury	6	2
1953	25 Nov	Wembley	3	6
1954	23 May	Budapest	1	7
1960	22 May	Budapest	0	2
WC1962	31 May	Rancagua	1	2
1965	5 May	Wembley	1	0
1978	24 May	Wembley	4	1
WC1981	6 June	Budapest	3	1
WC1982	18 Nov	Wembley	1	0
EC1983	27 Apr	Wembley	2	0
EC1983	12 Oct	Budapest	3	0
1988	27 Apr	Budapest	0	0
1990	12 Sept	Wembley	1	0
1992	12 May	Budapest	1	0
1996	18 May	Wembley	3	0
1999	28 Apr	Budapest	1	1
2006	30 May	Old Trafford	3	1
2010	11 Aug	Wembley	2	1
WC2021	**2 Sept**	**Budapest**	**4**	**0**
WC2021	**12 Oct**	**Wembley**	**1**	**1**
NL2022	**4 June**	**Budapest**	**0**	**1**
NL2022	**14 June**	**Wolverhampton**	**0**	**4**

v ICELAND			*E*	*I*
1982	2 June	Reykjavik	1	1
2004	5 June	City of Manchester	6	1
EC2016	27 June	Nice	1	2
NL2020	5 Sept	Reykjavik	1	0
NL2020	18 Nov	Wembley	4	0

v ISRAEL			*E*	*I*
1986	26 Feb	Ramat Gan	2	1
1988	17 Feb	Tel Aviv	0	0
EC2007	24 Mar	Tel Aviv	0	0
EC2007	8 Sept	Wembley	3	0

v ITALY			*E*	*I*
1933	13 May	Rome	1	1
1934	14 Nov	Highbury	3	2
1939	13 May	Milan	2	2
1948	16 May	Turin	4	0
1949	30 Nov	Tottenham	2	0
1952	18 May	Florence	1	1
1959	6 May	Wembley	2	2
1961	24 May	Rome	3	2
1973	14 June	Turin	0	2
1973	14 Nov	Wembley	0	1
1976	28 May	New York	3	2
WC1976	17 Nov	Rome	0	2
WC1977	16 Nov	Wembley	2	0
EC1980	15 June	Turin	0	1
1985	6 June	Mexico City	1	2
1989	15 Nov	Wembley	0	0
WC1990	7 July	Bari	1	2
WC1997	12 Feb	Wembley	0	1
TF1997	4 June	Nantes	2	0
WC1997	11 Oct	Rome	0	0
2000	15 Nov	Turin	0	1
2002	27 Mar	Leeds	1	2
EC2012	24 June	Kyiv	0	0
2012	15 Aug	Berne	2	1
WC2014	14 June	Manaus	1	2
2015	31 Mar	Turin	1	1
2018	27 Mar	Wembley	1	1
EC2021	11 July	Wembley	1	1*
NL2022	**11 June**	**Wolverhampton**	**0**	**0**

v IVORY COAST			*E*	*IC*
2022	**29 Mar**	**Wembley**	**3**	**0**

v JAMAICA			*E*	*J*
2006	3 June	Old Trafford	6	0

v JAPAN			*E*	*J*
UI1995	3 June	Wembley	2	1
2004	1 June	City of Manchester	1	1
2010	30 May	Graz	2	1

v KAZAKHSTAN			*E*	*K*
WC2008	11 Oct	Wembley	5	1
WC2009	6 June	Almaty	4	0

v KOREA REPUBLIC			*E*	*KR*
2002	21 May	Seoguipo	1	1

v KOSOVO			*E*	*K*
EC2019	10 Sept	Southampton	5	3
EC2019	17 Nov	Pristina	4	0

v KUWAIT			*E*	*K*
WC1982	25 June	Bilbao	1	0

v LIECHTENSTEIN			*E*	*L*
EC2003	29 Mar	Vaduz	2	0
EC2003	10 Sept	Old Trafford	2	0

v LITHUANIA			*E*	*L*
EC2015	27 Mar	Wembley	4	0
EC2015	12 Oct	Vilnius	3	0
WC2017	26 Mar	Wembley	2	0
WC2017	8 Oct	Vilnius	1	0

v LUXEMBOURG			*E*	*L*
1927	21 May	Esch-sur-Alzette	5	2
WC1960	19 Oct	Luxembourg	9	0
WC1961	28 Sept	Highbury	4	1
WC1977	30 Mar	Wembley	5	0
WC1977	12 Oct	Luxembourg	2	0
EC1982	15 Dec	Wembley	9	0
EC1983	16 Nov	Luxembourg	4	0
EC1998	14 Oct	Luxembourg	3	0
EC1999	4 Sept	Wembley	6	0
EC2006	7 Oct	Old Trafford	0	0

v MALAYSIA			*E*	*M*
1991	12 June	Kuala Lumpur	4	2

		v MALTA	E	M
EC1971	3 Feb	Valletta	1	0
EC1971	12 May	Wembley	5	0
2000	3 June	Valletta	2	1
WC2016	8 Oct	Wembley	2	0
WC2017	1 Sept	Ta'Qali	4	0

		v MEXICO	E	M
1959	24 May	Mexico City	1	2
1961	10 May	Wembley	8	0
WC1966	16 July	Wembley	2	0
1969	1 June	Mexico City	0	0
1985	9 June	Mexico City	0	1
1986	17 May	Los Angeles	3	0
1997	29 Mar	Wembley	2	0
2001	25 May	Derby	4	0
2010	24 May	Wembley	3	1

		v MOLDOVA	E	M
WC1996	1 Sept	Chisinau	3	0
WC1997	10 Sept	Wembley	4	0
WC2012	7 Sept	Chisinau	5	0
WC2013	6 Sept	Wembley	4	0

		v MONTENEGRO	E	M
EC1989	8 Mar	Tirana	2	0
2010	12 Oct	Wembley	0	0
EC2011	7 Oct	Podgorica	2	2
WC2013	26 Mar	Podgorica	1	1
WC2013	11 Oct	Wembley	4	1
EC2019	25 Mar	Podgorica	5	1
EC2019	14 Nov	Wembley	7	0

		v MOROCCO	E	M
WC1986	6 June	Monterrey	0	0
1998	27 May	Casablanca	1	0

		v NETHERLANDS	E	N
1935	18 May	Amsterdam	1	0
1946	27 Nov	Huddersfield	8	2
1964	9 Dec	Amsterdam	1	1
1969	5 Nov	Amsterdam	1	0
1970	14 June	Wembley	0	0
1977	9 Feb	Wembley	0	2
1982	25 May	Wembley	2	0
1988	23 Mar	Wembley	2	2
EC1988	15 June	Dusseldorf	1	3
WC1990	16 June	Cagliari	0	0
2005	9 Feb	Villa Park	0	0
WC1993	28 Apr	Wembley	2	2
WC1993	13 Oct	Rotterdam	0	2
EC1996	18 June	Wembley	4	1
2001	15 Aug	Tottenham	0	2
2002	13 Feb	Amsterdam	1	1
2006	15 Nov	Amsterdam	1	1
2009	12 Aug	Amsterdam	2	2
2012	29 Feb	Wembley	2	3
2016	29 Mar	Wembley	1	2
2018	23 Mar	Amsterdam	1	0
NL2019	6 June	Guimaraes	1	3

		v NEW ZEALAND	E	NZ
1991	3 June	Auckland	1	0
1991	8 June	Wellington	2	0

		v NIGERIA	E	N
1994	16 Nov	Wembley	1	0
WC2002	12 June	Osaka	0	0
2018	2 June	Wembley	2	1

		v NORTH MACEDONIA	E	M
EC2002	16 Oct	Southampton	2	2
EC2003	6 Sept	Skopje	2	1
EC2006	6 Sept	Skopje	1	0

		v NORWAY	E	N
1937	14 May	Oslo	6	0
1938	9 Nov	Newcastle	4	0
1949	18 May	Oslo	4	1
1966	29 June	Oslo	6	1
WC1980	10 Sept	Wembley	4	0
WC1981	9 Sept	Oslo	1	2
WC1992	14 Oct	Wembley	1	1
WC1993	2 June	Oslo	0	2
1994	22 May	Wembley	0	0
1995	11 Oct	Oslo	0	0
2012	26 May	Oslo	1	0
2014	3 Sept	Wembley	1	0

		v PANAMA	E	P
WC2018	24 June	Nizhny Novgorod	6	1

		v PARAGUAY	E	P
WC1986	18 June	Mexico City	3	0
2002	17 Apr	Liverpool	4	0
WC2006	10 June	Frankfurt	1	0

		v PERU	E	P
1959	17 May	Lima	1	4
1962	20 May	Lima	4	0
2014	30 May	Wembley	3	0

		v POLAND	E	P
1966	5 Jan	Everton	1	1
1966	5 July	Chorzow	1	0
WC1973	6 June	Chorzow	0	2
WC1973	17 Oct	Wembley	1	1
WC1986	11 June	Monterrey	3	0
WC1989	3 June	Wembley	3	0
WC1989	11 Oct	Katowice	0	0
EC1990	17 Oct	Wembley	2	0
EC1991	13 Nov	Poznan	1	1
WC1993	29 May	Katowice	1	1
WC1993	8 Sept	Wembley	3	0
WC1996	9 Oct	Wembley	2	1
WC1997	31 May	Katowice	2	0
EC1999	27 Mar	Wembley	3	1
EC1999	8 Sept	Warsaw	0	0
WC2004	8 Sept	Katowice	2	1
WC2005	12 Oct	Old Trafford	2	1
WC2012	17 Oct	Warsaw	1	1
WC2013	15 Oct	Wembley	2	0
WC2021	31 Mar	Wembley	2	1
WC2021	**8 Sept**	**Warsaw**	**1**	**1**

		v PORTUGAL	E	P
1947	25 May	Lisbon	10	0
1950	14 May	Lisbon	5	3
1951	19 May	Everton	5	2
1955	22 May	Oporto	1	3
1958	7 May	Wembley	2	1
WC1961	21 May	Lisbon	1	1
WC1961	25 Oct	Wembley	2	0
1964	17 May	Lisbon	4	3
1964	4 June	São Paulo	1	1
WC1966	26 July	Wembley	2	1
1969	10 Dec	Wembley	1	0
1974	3 Apr	Lisbon	0	0
EC1974	20 Nov	Wembley	0	0
EC1975	19 Nov	Lisbon	1	1
WC1986	3 June	Monterrey	0	1
1995	12 Dec	Wembley	1	1
1998	22 Apr	Wembley	3	0
EC2000	12 June	Eindhoven	2	3
2002	7 Sept	Villa Park	1	1
2004	18 Feb	Faro	1	1
EC2004	24 June	Lisbon	2	2*
WC2006	1 July	Gelsenkirchen	0	0
2016	2 June	Wembley	1	0

		v REPUBLIC OF IRELAND	E	RI
1946	30 Sept	Dublin	1	0
1949	21 Sept	Everton	0	2
WC1957	8 May	Wembley	5	1
WC1957	19 May	Dublin	1	1
1964	24 May	Dublin	3	1
1976	8 Sept	Wembley	1	1
EC1978	25 Oct	Dublin	1	1
EC1980	6 Feb	Wembley	2	0
1985	26 Mar	Wembley	2	1
EC1988	12 June	Stuttgart	0	1
WC1990	11 June	Cagliari	1	1
EC1990	14 Nov	Dublin	1	1
EC1991	27 Mar	Wembley	1	1
1995	15 Feb	Dublin	0	1
(abandoned after 27 mins)				
2013	29 May	Wembley	1	1
2015	7 June	Dublin	0	0
2020	12 Nov	Wembley	3	0

		v ROMANIA	E	R
1939	24 May	Bucharest	2	0
1968	6 Nov	Bucharest	0	0
1969	15 Jan	Wembley	1	1
WC1970	2 June	Guadalajara	1	0
WC1980	15 Oct	Bucharest	1	2
WC1981	29 April	Wembley	0	0
WC1985	1 May	Bucharest	0	0
WC1985	11 Sept	Wembley	1	1
1994	12 Oct	Wembley	1	1

			E	R
WC1998	22 June	Toulouse	1	2
EC2000	20 June	Charleroi	2	3
2021	6 June	Middlesbrough	1	0

v RUSSIA

			E	R
EC2007	12 Sept	Wembley	3	0
EC2007	17 Oct	Moscow	1	2
EC2016	11 June	Marseille	1	1

v SAN MARINO

			E	SM
WC1992	17 Feb	Wembley	6	0
WC1993	17 Nov	Bologna	7	1
WC2012	12 Oct	Wembley	5	0
WC2013	22 Mar	Serravalle	8	0
EC2014	9 Oct	Wembley	5	0
EC2015	5 Sept	Serravalle	6	0
WC2021	25 Mar	Wembley	5	0
WC2021	**15 Nov**	**Serravalle**	**10**	**0**

v SAUDI ARABIA

			E	SA
1988	16 Nov	Riyadh	1	1
1998	23 May	Wembley	0	0

v SERBIA-MONTENEGRO

			E	SM
2003	3 June	Leicester	2	1

v SLOVAKIA

			E	S
EC2002	12 Oct	Bratislava	2	1
EC2003	11 June	Middlesbrough	2	1
2009	28 Mar	Wembley	4	0
EC2016	20 June	Lille	0	0
WC2016	4 Sept	Trnava	1	0
WC2017	4 Sept	Wembley	2	1

v SLOVENIA

			E	S
2009	5 Sept	Wembley	2	1
WC2010	23 June	Port Elizabeth	1	0
EC2014	15 Nov	Wembley	3	1
EC2015	14 June	Ljubljana	3	2
WC2016	11 Oct	Ljubljana	0	0
WC2017	5 Oct	Wembley	1	0

v SOUTH AFRICA

			E	SA
1997	24 May	Old Trafford	2	1
2003	22 May	Durban	2	1

v SPAIN

			E	S
1929	15 May	Madrid	3	4
1931	9 Dec	Highbury	7	1
WC1950	2 July	Rio de Janeiro	0	1
1955	18 May	Madrid	1	1
1955	30 Nov	Wembley	4	1
1960	15 May	Madrid	0	3
1960	26 Oct	Wembley	4	2
1965	8 Dec	Madrid	2	0
1967	24 May	Wembley	2	0
EC1968	3 Apr	Wembley	1	0
EC1968	8 May	Madrid	2	1
1980	26 Mar	Barcelona	2	0
EC1980	18 June	Naples	2	1
1981	25 Mar	Wembley	1	2
WC1982	5 July	Madrid	0	0
1987	18 Feb	Madrid	4	2
1992	9 Sept	Santander	0	1
EC 1996	22 June	Wembley	0	0*
2001	28 Feb	Villa Park	3	0
2004	17 Nov	Madrid	0	1
2007	7 Feb	Old Trafford	0	1
2009	11 Feb	Seville	0	2
2011	12 Nov	Wembley	1	0
2015	13 Nov	Alicante	0	2
2016	15 Nov	Wembley	2	2
NL2018	8 Sept	Wembley	1	2
NL2018	15 Oct	Seville	3	2

v SWEDEN

			E	S
1923	21 May	Stockholm	4	2
1923	24 May	Stockholm	3	1
1937	17 May	Stockholm	4	0
1947	19 Nov	Highbury	4	2
1949	13 May	Stockholm	1	3
1956	16 May	Stockholm	0	0
1959	28 Oct	Wembley	2	3
1965	16 May	Gothenburg	2	1
1968	22 May	Wembley	3	1
1979	10 June	Stockholm	0	0
1986	10 Sept	Stockholm	0	1
WC1988	19 Oct	Wembley	0	0
WC1989	6 Sept	Stockholm	0	0
EC1992	17 June	Stockholm	1	2
UI1995	8 June	Leeds	3	3
EC1998	5 Sept	Stockholm	1	2
EC1999	5 June	Wembley	0	0
2001	10 Nov	Old Trafford	1	1
WC2002	2 June	Saitama	1	1
2004	31 Mar	Gothenburg	0	1
WC2006	20 June	Cologne	2	2
2011	15 Nov	Wembley	1	0
EC2012	15 June	Kyiv	3	2
2012	14 Nov	Stockholm	2	4
WC2018	7 July	Samara	2	0

v SWITZERLAND

			E	S
1933	20 May	Berne	4	0
1938	21 May	Zurich	1	2
1947	18 May	Zurich	0	1
1948	2 Dec	Highbury	6	0
1952	28 May	Zurich	3	0
WC1954	20 June	Berne	2	0
1962	9 May	Wembley	3	1
1963	5 June	Basel	8	1
EC1971	13 Oct	Basel	3	2
EC1971	10 Nov	Wembley	1	1
1975	3 Sept	Basel	2	1
1977	7 Sept	Wembley	0	0
WC1980	19 Nov	Wembley	2	1
WC1981	30 May	Basel	1	2
1988	28 May	Lausanne	1	0
1995	15 Nov	Wembley	3	1
EC1996	8 June	Wembley	1	1
1998	25 Mar	Berne	1	1
EC2004	17 June	Coimbra	3	0
2008	6 Feb	Wembley	2	1
EC1989	8 Mar	Tirana	2	0
EC2010	7 Sept	Basel	3	1
EC2011	4 June	Wembley	2	2
EC2014	8 Sept	Basel	2	0
EC2015	8 Sept	Wembley	2	0
2018	11 Sept	Leicester	1	0
NL2019	9 June	Guimaraes	0	0
2022	**26 Mar**	**Wembley**	**2**	**1**

v TRINIDAD & TOBAGO

			E	TT
WC2006	15 June	Nuremberg	2	0
2008	2 June	Port of Spain	3	0

v TUNISIA

			E	T
1990	2 June	Tunis	1	1
WC1998	15 June	Marseilles	2	0
WC2018	18 June	Volgograd	2	1

v TURKEY

			E	T
WC1984	14 Nov	Istanbul	8	0
WC1985	16 Oct	Wembley	5	0
EC1987	29 Apr	Izmir	0	0
EC1987	14 Oct	Wembley	8	0
EC1991	1 May	Izmir	1	0
EC1991	16 Oct	Wembley	1	0
WC1992	18 Nov	Wembley	4	0
WC1993	31 Mar	Izmir	2	0
EC2003	2 Apr	Sunderland	2	0
EC2003	11 Oct	Istanbul	0	0
2016	22 May	Etihad Stadium	2	1

v UKRAINE

			E	U
2000	31 May	Wembley	2	0
2004	18 Aug	Newcastle	3	0
WC2009	1 Apr	Wembley	2	1
WC2009	10 Oct	Dnepr	0	1
EC2012	19 June	Donetsk	1	0
WC2012	11 Sept	Wembley	1	1
WC2013	10 Sept	Kyiv	0	0
EC2021	3 July	Rome	4	0

v URUGUAY

			E	U
1953	31 May	Montevideo	1	2
WC1954	26 June	Basel	2	4
1964	6 May	Wembley	2	1
WC1966	11 July	Wembley	0	0
1969	8 June	Montevideo	2	1
1977	15 June	Montevideo	0	0
1984	13 June	Montevideo	0	2
1990	22 May	Wembley	1	2
1995	29 Mar	Wembley	0	0
2006	1 Mar	Liverpool	2	1
WC2014	19 June	Sao Paulo	1	2

v USA			*E*	*USA*
wc1950	29 June	Belo Horizonte	0	1
1953	8 June	New York	6	3

v USA			*E*	*USA*
1959	28 May	Los Angeles	8	1
1964	27 May	New York	10	0
1985	16 June	Los Angeles	5	0
1993	9 June	Foxboro	0	2
1994	7 Sept	Wembley	2	0
2005	28 May	Chicago	2	1
2008	28 May	Wembley	2	0
wc2010	12 June	Rustenburg	1	1
2018	15 Nov	Wembley	3	0

v USSR			*E*	*USSR*
1958	18 May	Moscow	1	1
wc1958	8 June	Gothenburg	2	2
wc1958	17 June	Gothenburg	0	1
1958	22 Oct	Wembley	5	0
1967	6 Dec	Wembley	2	2
EC1968	8 June	Rome	2	0
1973	10 June	Moscow	2	1
1984	2 June	Wembley	0	2
1986	26 Mar	Tbilisi	1	0
EC1988	18 June	Frankfurt	1	3
1991	21 May	Wembley	3	1

v YUGOSLAVIA			*E*	*Y*
1939	18 May	Belgrade	1	2
1950	22 Nov	Highbury	2	2
1954	16 May	Belgrade	0	1
1956	28 Nov	Wembley	3	0
1958	11 May	Belgrade	0	5
1960	11 May	Wembley	3	3
1965	9 May	Belgrade	1	1
1966	4 May	Wembley	2	0
EC1968	5 June	Florence	0	1
1972	11 Oct	Wembley	1	1
1974	5 June	Belgrade	2	2
EC1986	12 Nov	Wembley	2	0
EC1987	11 Nov	Belgrade	4	1
1989	13 Dec	Wembley	2	1

SCOTLAND

v ALBANIA			*S*	*A*
NL2018	10 Sept	Glasgow	2	0
NL2018	17 Nov	Shkoder	4	0

v ARGENTINA			*S*	*A*
1977	18 June	Buenos Aires	1	1
1979	2 June	Glasgow	1	3
1990	28 Mar	Glasgow	1	0
2008	19 Nov	Glasgow	0	1

v ARMENIA			*S*	*A*
NL2022	**8 June**	**Glasgow**	**2**	**0**
NL2022	**14 June**	**Yerevan**	**4**	**1**

v AUSTRALIA			*S*	*A*
*1967	28 May	Sydney	1	0
*1967	31 May	Adelaide	2	1
*1967	3 June	Melbourne	2	0
wc1985	20 Nov	Glasgow	2	0
wc1985	4 Dec	Melbourne	0	0
1996	27 Mar	Glasgow	1	0
2000	15 Nov	Glasgow	0	2
2012	15 Aug	Easter Road	3	1

**1967 tour upgraded to full internationals in October 2021.*

v AUSTRIA			*S*	*A*
1931	16 May	Vienna	0	5
1933	29 Nov	Glasgow	2	2
1937	9 May	Vienna	1	1
1950	13 Dec	Glasgow	0	1
1951	27 May	Vienna	0	4
wc1954	16 June	Zurich	0	1
1955	19 May	Vienna	4	1
1956	2 May	Glasgow	1	1
1960	29 May	Vienna	1	4
1963	8 May	Glasgow	4	1
(*abandoned after 79 mins*)				
wc1968	6 Nov	Glasgow	2	1
wc1969	5 Nov	Vienna	0	2
EC1978	20 Sept	Vienna	2	3
EC1979	17 Oct	Glasgow	1	1
1994	20 Apr	Vienna	2	1
wc1996	31 Aug	Vienna	0	0
wc1997	2 Apr	Celtic Park	2	0
2003	30 Apr	Glasgow	0	2
2005	17 Aug	Graz	2	2
2007	30 May	Vienna	1	0
wc2021	25 Mar	Glasgow	2	2
wc2021	**7 Sept**	**Vienna**	**1**	**0**
2022	**29 Mar**	**Vienna**	**2**	**2**

v BELARUS			*S*	*B*
wc1997	8 June	Minsk	1	0
wc1997	7 Sept	Aberdeen	4	1
wc2005	8 June	Minsk	0	0
wc2005	8 Oct	Glasgow	0	1

v BELGIUM			*S*	*B*
1946	23 Jan	Glasgow	2	2
1947	18 May	Brussels	1	2
1948	28 Apr	Glasgow	2	0
1951	20 May	Brussels	5	0
EC1971	3 Feb	Liege	0	3
EC1971	10 Nov	Aberdeen	1	0
1974	1 June	Brussels	1	2
EC1979	21 Nov	Brussels	0	2
EC1979	19 Dec	Glasgow	1	3
EC1982	15 Dec	Brussels	2	3
EC1983	12 Oct	Glasgow	1	1
EC1987	1 Apr	Brussels	1	4
EC1987	14 Oct	Glasgow	2	0
wc2001	24 Mar	Glasgow	2	2
wc2001	5 Sept	Brussels	0	2
wc2012	16 Oct	Brussels	0	2
wc2013	6 Sept	Glasgow	0	2
2018	7 Sept	Glasgow	0	4
EC2019	11 June	Brussels	0	3
EC2019	9 Sept	Glasgow	0	4

v BOSNIA-HERZEGOVINA			*S*	*BH*
EC1999	4 Sept	Sarajevo	2	1
EC1999	5 Oct	Ibrox	1	0

v BRAZIL			*S*	*B*
1966	25 June	Glasgow	1	1
1972	5 July	Rio de Janeiro	0	1
1973	30 June	Glasgow	0	1
wc1974	18 June	Frankfurt	0	0
1977	23 June	Rio de Janeiro	0	2
wc1982	18 June	Seville	1	4
1987	26 May	Glasgow	0	2
wc1990	20 June	Turin	0	1
wc1998	10 June	St Denis	1	2
2011	27 Mar	Emirates	0	2

v BULGARIA			*S*	*B*
1978	22 Feb	Glasgow	2	1
EC1986	10 Sept	Glasgow	0	0
EC1987	11 Nov	Sofia	1	0
EC1990	14 Nov	Sofia	1	1
EC1991	27 Mar	Glasgow	1	1
2006	11 May	Kobe	5	1

v CANADA			*S*	*C*
*1967	13 June	Winnipeg	7	2
1983	12 June	Vancouver	2	0
1983	16 June	Edmonton	3	0
1983	20 June	Toronto	2	0
1992	21 May	Toronto	3	1
2002	15 Oct	Easter Road	3	1
2017	22 Mar	Easter Road	1	1

**1967 tour upgraded to full internationals in October 2021.*

v CHILE			*S*	*C*
1977	15 June	Santiago	4	2
1989	30 May	Glasgow	2	0

v CIS			*S*	*C*
EC1992	18 June	Norrkoping	3	0

v COLOMBIA			*S*	*C*
1988	17 May	Glasgow	0	0
1996	29 May	Miami	0	1
1998	23 May	New York	2	2

v COSTA RICA

			S	*CR*
wc1990	11 June	Genoa	0	1
2018	23 Mar	Glasgow	0	1

v CROATIA

			S	*C*
wc2000	11 Oct	Zagreb	1	1
wc2001	1 Sept	Glasgow	0	0
2008	26 Mar	Glasgow	1	1
wc2013	7 June	Zagreb	1	0
wc2013	15 Oct	Glasgow	2	0
EC2021	22 June	Glasgow	1	3

v CYPRUS

			S	*C*
wc1968	11 Dec	Nicosia	5	0
wc1969	17 May	Glasgow	8	0
wc1989	8 Feb	Limassol	3	2
wc1989	26 Apr	Glasgow	2	1
2011	11 Nov	Larnaca	2	1
EC2019	8 June	Glasgow	2	1
EC2019	16 Nov	Nicosia	2	1

v CZECHOSLOVAKIA

			S	*C*
1937	15 May	Prague	3	1
1937	8 Dec	Glasgow	5	0
wc1961	14 May	Bratislava	0	4
wc1961	26 Sept	Glasgow	3	2
wc1961	29 Nov	Brussels	2	4*
1972	2 July	Porto Alegre	0	0
wc1973	26 Sept	Glasgow	2	1
wc1973	17 Oct	Bratislava	0	1
wc1976	13 Oct	Prague	0	2
wc1977	21 Sept	Glasgow	3	1

v CZECH REPUBLIC

			S	*C*
EC1999	31 Mar	Glasgow	1	2
EC1999	9 June	Prague	2	3
2008	30 May	Prague	1	3
2010	3 Mar	Glasgow	1	0
EC2010	8 Oct	Prague	0	1
EC2011	3 Sept	Glasgow	2	2
2016	24 Mar	Prague	1	0
NL2020	7 Sept	Olomouc	2	1
NL2020	14 Oct	Glasgow	1	0
EC2021	14 June	Glasgow	0	2

v DENMARK

			S	*D*
1951	12 May	Glasgow	3	1
1952	25 May	Copenhagen	2	1
1968	16 Oct	Copenhagen	1	0
EC1970	11 Nov	Glasgow	1	0
EC1971	9 June	Copenhagen	0	1
wc1972	18 Oct	Copenhagen	4	1
wc1972	15 Nov	Glasgow	2	0
EC1975	3 Sept	Copenhagen	1	0
EC1975	29 Oct	Glasgow	3	1
wc1986	4 June	Nezahualcoyotl	0	1
1996	24 Apr	Copenhagen	0	2
1998	25 Mar	Ibrox	0	1
2002	21 Aug	Glasgow	0	1
2004	28 Apr	Copenhagen	0	1
2011	10 Aug	Glasgow	2	1
2016	29 Mar	Glasgow	1	0
wc2021	**1 Sept**	**Copenhagen**	**0**	**2**
wc2021	**15 Nov**	**Glasgow**	**2**	**0**

v ECUADOR

			S	*E*
1995	24 May	Toyama	2	1

v EGYPT

			S	*E*
1990	16 May	Aberdeen	1	3

v ESTONIA

			S	*E*
wc1993	19 May	Tallinn	3	0
wc1993	2 June	Aberdeen	3	1
wc1997	11 Feb	Monaco	0	0
wc1997	29 Mar	Kilmarnock	2	0
EC1998	10 Oct	Tynecastle	3	2
EC1999	8 Sept	Tallinn	0	0
2004	27 May	Tallinn	1	0
2013	6 Feb	Aberdeen	1	0

v FAROE ISLANDS

			S	*F*
EC1994	12 Oct	Glasgow	5	1
EC1995	7 June	Toftir	2	0
EC1998	14 Oct	Aberdeen	2	1
EC1999	5 June	Toftir	1	1
EC2002	7 Sept	Toftir	2	2
EC2003	6 Sept	Glasgow	3	1
EC2006	2 Sept	Celtic Park	6	0
EC2007	6 June	Toftir	2	0
2010	16 Nov	Aberdeen	3	0
wc2021	31 Mar	Glasgow	4	0
wc2021	**12 Oct**	**Torshavn**	**1**	**0**

v FINLAND

			S	*F*
1954	25 May	Helsinki	2	1
wc1964	21 Oct	Glasgow	3	1
wc1965	27 May	Helsinki	2	1
1976	8 Sept	Glasgow	6	0
1992	25 Mar	Glasgow	1	1
EC1994	7 Sept	Helsinki	2	0
EC1995	6 Sept	Glasgow	1	0
1998	22 Apr	Easter Road	1	1

v FRANCE

			S	*F*
1930	18 May	Paris	2	0
1932	8 May	Paris	3	1
1948	23 May	Paris	0	3
1949	27 Apr	Glasgow	2	0
1950	27 May	Paris	1	0
1951	16 May	Glasgow	1	0
wc1958	15 June	Orebro	1	2
1984	1 June	Marseilles	0	2
wc1989	8 Mar	Glasgow	2	0
wc1989	11 Oct	Paris	0	3
1997	12 Nov	St Etienne	1	2
2000	29 Mar	Glasgow	0	2
2002	27 Mar	Paris	0	5
EC2006	7 Oct	Glasgow	1	0
EC2007	12 Sept	Paris	1	0
2016	4 June	Metz	0	3

v GEORGIA

			S	*G*
EC2007	24 Mar	Glasgow	2	1
EC2007	17 Oct	Tbilisi	0	2
EC2014	11 Oct	Ibrox	1	0
EC2015	4 Sept	Tblisi	0	1

v GERMANY

			S	*G*
1929	1 June	Berlin	1	1
1936	14 Oct	Glasgow	2	0
EC1992	15 June	Norrkoping	0	2
1993	24 Mar	Glasgow	0	1
1999	28 Apr	Bremen	1	0
EC2003	7 June	Glasgow	1	1
EC2003	10 Sept	Dortmund	1	2
EC2014	7 Sept	Dortmund	1	2
EC2015	7 Sept	Glasgow	2	3

v EAST GERMANY

			S	*EG*
1974	30 Oct	Glasgow	3	0
1977	7 Sept	East Berlin	0	1
EC1982	13 Oct	Glasgow	2	0
EC1983	16 Nov	Halle	1	2
1985	16 Oct	Glasgow	0	0
1990	25 Apr	Glasgow	0	1

v WEST GERMANY

			S	*WG*
1957	22 May	Stuttgart	3	1
1959	6 May	Glasgow	3	2
1964	12 May	Hanover	2	2
wc1969	16 Apr	Glasgow	1	1
wc1969	22 Oct	Hamburg	2	3
1973	14 Nov	Glasgow	1	1
1974	27 Mar	Frankfurt	1	2
wc1986	8 June	Queretaro	1	2

v GIBRALTAR

			S	*G*
EC2015	29 Mar	Glasgow	6	1
EC2015	11 Oct	Faro	6	0

v GREECE

			S	*G*
EC1994	18 Dec	Athens	0	1
EC1995	16 Aug	Glasgow	1	0

v HONG KONG XI

			S	*HK*
†2002	23 May	Hong Kong	4	0

†*match not recognised by FIFA*

v HUNGARY

			S	*H*
1938	7 Dec	Ibrox	3	1
1954	8 Dec	Glasgow	2	4
1955	29 May	Budapest	1	3
1958	7 May	Glasgow	1	1
1960	5 June	Budapest	3	3
1980	31 May	Budapest	1	3
1987	9 Sept	Glasgow	2	0
2004	18 Aug	Glasgow	0	3
2018	27 Mar	Budapest	1	0

		v ICELAND	S	I
wc1984	17 Oct	Glasgow	3	0
wc1985	28 May	Reykjavik	1	0
EC2002	12 Oct	Reykjavik	2	0
EC2003	29 Mar	Glasgow	2	1
wc2008	10 Sept	Reykjavik	2	1
wc2009	1 Apr	Glasgow	2	1

		v IRAN	S	I
wc1978	7 June	Cordoba	1	1

		v ISRAEL	S	I
*1967	16 May	Tel Aviv	2	1
wc1981	25 Feb	Tel Aviv	1	0
wc1981	28 Apr	Glasgow	3	1
1986	28 Jan	Tel Aviv	1	0
NL2018	11 Oct	Haifa	1	2
NL2018	20 Nov	Glasgow	3	2
NL2020	4 Sept	Glasgow	1	1
EC2020	8 Oct	Glasgow	0	0
NL2020	18 Nov	Netanya	0	1
wc2021	28 Mar	Tel Aviv	1	1
wc2021	**9 Oct**	**Glasgow**	**3**	**2**

**1967 tour upgraded to full internationals in October 2021.*

		v ITALY	S	I
1931	20 May	Rome	0	3
wc1965	9 Nov	Glasgow	1	0
wc1965	7 Dec	Naples	0	3
1988	22 Dec	Perugia	0	2
wc1992	18 Nov	Ibrox	0	0
wc1993	13 Oct	Rome	1	3
wc2005	26 Mar	Milan	0	2
wc2005	3 Sept	Glasgow	1	1
EC2007	28 Mar	Bari	0	2
EC2007	17 Nov	Glasgow	1	2
2016	29 May	Ta'Qali	0	1

		v JAPAN	S	J
1995	21 May	Hiroshima	0	0
2006	13 May	Saitama	0	0
2009	10 Oct	Yokohama	0	2

		v KAZAKHSTAN	S	K
EC2019	21 Mar	Astana	0	3
EC2019	19 Nov	Glasgow	3	1

		v KOREA REPUBLIC	S	KR
2002	16 May	Busan	1	4

		v LATVIA	S	L
wc1996	5 Oct	Riga	2	0
wc1997	11 Oct	Celtic Park	2	0
wc2000	2 Sept	Riga	1	0
wc2001	6 Oct	Glasgow	2	1

		v LIECHTENSTEIN	S	L
EC2010	7 Sept	Glasgow	2	1
EC2011	8 Oct	Vaduz	1	0

		v LITHUANIA	S	L
EC1998	5 Sept	Vilnius	0	0
EC1999	9 Oct	Glasgow	3	0
EC2003	2 Apr	Kaunas	0	1
EC2003	11 Oct	Glasgow	1	0
EC2006	6 Sept	Kaunas	2	1
EC2007	8 Sept	Glasgow	3	1
EC2010	3 Sept	Kaunas	0	0
EC2011	6 Sept	Glasgow	1	0
wc2016	8 Oct	Glasgow	1	1
wc2017	1 Sept	Vilnius	3	0

		v LUXEMBOURG	S	L
1947	24 May	Luxembourg	6	0
EC1986	12 Nov	Glasgow	3	0
EC1987	2 Dec	Esch	0	0
2012	14 Nov	Luxembourg	2	1
2021	6 June	Luxembourg	1	0

		v MALTA	S	M
1988	22 Mar	Valletta	1	1
1990	28 May	Valletta	2	1
wc1993	17 Feb	Ibrox	3	0
wc1993	17 Nov	Valletta	2	0
1997	1 June	Valletta	3	2
wc2016	4 Sept	Ta'Qali	5	1
wc2017	4 Sept	Glasgow	2	0

		v MEXICO	S	M
2018	3 June	Mexico City	0	1

		v MOLDOVA	S	M
wc2004	13 Oct	Chisinau	1	1
wc2005	4 June	Glasgow	2	0
wc2021	**4 Sept**	**Glasgow**	**1**	**0**
wc2021	**12 Nov**	**Chisinau**	**2**	**0**

		v MOROCCO	S	M
wc1998	23 June	St Etienne	0	3

		v NETHERLANDS	S	N
1929	4 June	Amsterdam	2	0
1938	21 May	Amsterdam	3	1
1959	27 May	Amsterdam	2	1
1966	11 May	Glasgow	0	3
1968	30 May	Amsterdam	0	0
1971	1 Dec	Amsterdam	1	2
wc1978	11 June	Mendoza	3	2
1982	23 Mar	Glasgow	2	1
1986	29 Apr	Eindhoven	0	0
EC1992	12 June	Gothenburg	0	1
1994	23 Mar	Glasgow	0	1
1994	27 May	Utrecht	1	3
EC1996	10 June	Villa Park	0	0
2000	26 Apr	Arnhem	0	0
EC2003	15 Nov	Glasgow	1	0
EC2003	19 Nov	Amsterdam	0	6
wc2009	28 Mar	Amsterdam	0	3
wc2009	9 Sept	Glasgow	0	1
2017	9 Nov	Aberdeen	0	1
2021	2 June	Faro	2	2

		v NEW ZEALAND	S	NZ
wc1982	15 June	Malaga	5	2
2003	27 May	Tynecastle	1	1

		v NIGERIA	S	N
2002	17 Apr	Aberdeen	1	2
2014	28 May	Craven Cottage	2	2

		v NORTH MACEDONIA	S	M
wc2008	6 Sept	Skopje	0	1
wc2009	5 Sept	Glasgow	2	0
wc2012	11 Sept	Glasgow	1	1
wc2013	10 Sept	Skopje	2	1

		v NORWAY	S	N
1929	26 May	Oslo	7	3
1954	5 May	Glasgow	1	0
1954	19 May	Oslo	1	1
1963	4 June	Bergen	3	4
1963	7 Nov	Glasgow	6	1
1974	6 June	Oslo	2	1
EC1978	25 Oct	Glasgow	3	2
EC1979	7 June	Oslo	4	0
wc1988	14 Sept	Oslo	2	1
wc1989	15 Nov	Glasgow	1	1
1992	3 June	Oslo	0	0
wc1998	16 June	Bordeaux	1	1
2003	20 Aug	Oslo	0	0
wc2004	9 Oct	Glasgow	0	1
wc2005	7 Sept	Oslo	2	1
wc2008	11 Oct	Glasgow	0	0
wc2009	12 Aug	Oslo	0	4
2013	19 Nov	Molde	1	0

		v PARAGUAY	S	P
wc1958	11 June	Norrkoping	2	3

		v PERU	S	P
1972	26 Apr	Glasgow	2	0
wc1978	3 June	Cordoba	1	3
1979	12 Sept	Glasgow	1	1
2018	30 May	Lima	0	2

		v POLAND	S	P
1958	1 June	Warsaw	2	1
1960	4 May	Glasgow	2	3
wc1965	23 May	Chorzow	1	1
wc1965	13 Oct	Glasgow	1	2
1980	28 May	Poznan	0	1
1990	19 May	Glasgow	1	1
2001	25 Apr	Bydgoszcz	1	1
2014	5 Mar	Warsaw	1	0
EC2014	14 Oct	Warsaw	2	2
EC2015	8 Oct	Glasgow	2	2
2022	**24 Mar**	**Glasgow**	**1**	**1**

		v PORTUGAL	S	P
1950	21 May	Lisbon	2	2
1955	4 May	Glasgow	3	0

			S	*P*
1959	3 June	Lisbon	0	1
1966	18 June	Glasgow	0	1
EC1971	21 Apr	Lisbon	0	2
EC1971	13 Oct	Glasgow	2	1
1975	13 May	Glasgow	1	0
EC1978	29 Nov	Lisbon	0	1
EC1980	26 Mar	Glasgow	4	1
WC1980	15 Oct	Glasgow	0	0
WC1981	18 Nov	Lisbon	1	2
WC1992	14 Oct	Ibrox	0	0
WC1993	28 Apr	Lisbon	0	5
2002	20 Nov	Braga	0	2
2018	14 Oct	Glasgow	1	3

v QATAR			*S*	*Q*
2015	5 June	Easter Road	1	0

v REPUBLIC OF IRELAND			*S*	*RI*
WC1961	3 May	Glasgow	4	1
WC1961	7 May	Dublin	3	0
1963	9 June	Dublin	0	1
1969	21 Sept	Dublin	1	1
EC1986	15 Oct	Dublin	0	0
EC1987	18 Feb	Glasgow	0	1
2000	30 May	Dublin	2	1
2003	12 Feb	Glasgow	0	2
NC2011	29 May	Dublin	0	1
EC2014	14 Nov	Glasgow	1	0
EC2015	13 June	Dublin	1	1
NL2022	**11 June**	**Dublin**	**0**	**3**

v ROMANIA			*S*	*R*
EC1975	1 June	Bucharest	1	1
EC1975	17 Dec	Glasgow	1	1
1986	26 Mar	Glasgow	3	0
EC1990	12 Sept	Glasgow	2	1
EC1991	16 Oct	Bucharest	0	1
2004	31 Mar	Glasgow	1	2

v RUSSIA			*S*	*R*
EC1994	16 Nov	Glasgow	1	1
EC1995	29 Mar	Moscow	0	0
EC2019	6 Sept	Glasgow	1	2
EC2019	10 Oct	Moscow	0	4

v SAN MARINO			*S*	*SM*
EC1991	1 May	Serravalle	2	0
EC1991	13 Nov	Glasgow	4	0
EC1995	26 Apr	Serravalle	2	0
EC1995	15 Nov	Glasgow	5	0
WC2000	7 Oct	Serravalle	2	0
WC2001	28 Mar	Glasgow	4	0
EC2019	24 Mar	Serravalle	2	0
EC2019	13 Oct	Glasgow	6	0

v SAUDI ARABIA			*S*	*SA*
1988	17 Feb	Riyadh	2	2

v SERBIA			*S*	*Se*
WC2012	8 Sept	Glasgow	0	0
WC2013	26 Mar	Novi Sad	0	2
EC2020	12 Nov	Belgrade	1	1

v SLOVAKIA			*S*	*Sl*
WC2016	11 Oct	Trnava	0	3
WC2017	5 Oct	Glasgow	1	0
NL2020	11 Oct	Glasgow	1	0
NL2020	15 Nov	Trnava	0	1

v SLOVENIA			*S*	*Sl*
WC2004	8 Sept	Glasgow	0	0
WC2005	12 Oct	Celje	3	0
2012	29 Feb	Koper	1	1
WC2017	26 Mar	Glasgow	1	0
WC2017	8 Oct	Ljubljana	2	2

v SOUTH AFRICA			*S*	*SA*
2002	20 May	Hong Kong	0	2
2007	22 Aug	Aberdeen	1	0

v SPAIN			*S*	*S*
WC1957	8 May	Glasgow	4	2
WC1957	26 May	Madrid	1	4
1963	13 June	Madrid	6	2
1965	8 May	Glasgow	0	0
EC1974	20 Nov	Glasgow	1	2
EC1975	5 Feb	Valencia	1	1
1982	24 Feb	Valencia	0	3
WC1984	14 Nov	Glasgow	3	1
WC1985	27 Feb	Seville	0	1
1988	27 Apr	Madrid	0	0
2004	3 Sept	Valencia	1	1
Match abandoned after 60 minutes; floodlight failure.				
EC2010	12 Oct	Glasgow	2	3
EC2011	11 Oct	Alicante	1	3

v SWEDEN			*S*	*Sw*
1952	30 May	Stockholm	1	3
1953	6 May	Glasgow	1	2
1975	16 Apr	Gothenburg	1	1
1977	27 Apr	Glasgow	3	1
WC1980	10 Sept	Stockholm	1	0
WC1981	9 Sept	Glasgow	2	0
WC1990	16 June	Genoa	2	1
1995	11 Oct	Stockholm	0	2
WC1996	10 Nov	Ibrox	1	0
WC1997	30 Apr	Gothenburg	1	2
2004	17 Nov	Easter Road	1	4
2010	11 Aug	Stockholm	0	3

v SWITZERLAND			*S*	*Sw*
1931	24 May	Geneva	3	2
1946	15 May	Glasgow	3	1
1948	17 May	Berne	1	2
1950	26 Apr	Glasgow	3	1
WC1957	19 May	Basel	2	1
WC1957	6 Nov	Glasgow	3	2
1973	22 June	Berne	0	1
1976	7 Apr	Glasgow	1	0
EC1982	17 Nov	Berne	0	2
EC1983	30 May	Glasgow	2	2
EC1990	17 Oct	Glasgow	2	1
EC1991	11 Sept	Berne	2	2
WC1992	9 Sept	Berne	1	3
WC1993	8 Sept	Aberdeen	1	1
WC1996	18 June	Villa Park	1	0
2006	1 Mar	Glasgow	1	3

v TRINIDAD & TOBAGO			*S*	*TT*
2004	30 May	Easter Road	4	1

v TURKEY			*S*	*T*
1960	8 June	Ankara	2	4

v UKRAINE			*S*	*U*
EC2006	11 Oct	Kyiv	0	2
EC2007	13 Oct	Glasgow	3	1
WC2022	**1 June**	**Glasgow**	**1**	**3**

v URUGUAY			*S*	*U*
WC1954	19 June	Basel	0	7
1962	2 May	Glasgow	2	3
1983	21 Sept	Glasgow	2	0
WC1986	13 June	Nezahualcoyotl	0	0

v USA			*S*	*USA*
1952	30 Apr	Glasgow	6	0
1992	17 May	Denver	1	0
1996	26 May	New Britain	1	2
1998	30 May	Washington	0	0
2005	12 Nov	Glasgow	1	1
2012	26 May	Jacksonville	1	5
2013	15 Nov	Glasgow	0	0

v USSR			*S*	*USSR*
1967	10 May	Glasgow	0	2
1971	14 June	Moscow	0	1
WC1982	22 June	Malaga	2	2
1991	6 Feb	Ibrox	0	1

v YUGOSLAVIA			*S*	*Y*
1955	15 May	Belgrade	2	2
1956	21 Nov	Glasgow	2	0
WC1958	8 June	Vasteras	1	1
1972	29 June	Belo Horizonte	2	2
WC1974	22 June	Frankfurt	1	1
1984	12 Sept	Glasgow	6	1
WC1988	19 Oct	Glasgow	1	1
WC1989	6 Sept	Zagreb	1	3

v ZAIRE			*S*	*Z*
WC1974	14 June	Dortmund	2	0

WALES

		v ALBANIA	*W*	*A*
EC1994	7 Sept	Cardiff	2	0
EC1995	15 Nov	Tirana	1	1
2018	20 Nov	Elbasan	0	1
2021	5 June	Cardiff	0	0

		v ANDORRA	*W*	*A*
EC2014	9 Sept	La Vella	2	1
EC2015	13 Oct	Cardiff	2	0

		v ARGENTINA	*W*	*A*
1992	3 June	Tokyo	0	1
2002	13 Feb	Cardiff	1	1

		v ARMENIA	*W*	*A*
WC2001	24 Mar	Erevan	2	2
WC2001	1 Sept	Cardiff	0	0

		v AUSTRALIA	*W*	*A*
2011	10 Aug	Cardiff	1	2

		v AUSTRIA	*W*	*A*
1954	9 May	Vienna	0	2
1955	23 Nov	Wrexham	1	2
EC1974	4 Sept	Vienna	1	2
1975	19 Nov	Wrexham	1	0
1992	29 Apr	Vienna	1	1
EC2005	26 Mar	Cardiff	0	2
EC2005	30 Mar	Vienna	0	1
2013	6 Feb	Swansea	2	1
WC2016	6 Oct	Vienna	2	2
WC2017	2 Sept	Cardiff	1	0
WC2022	**24 Mar**	**Cardiff**	**2**	**1**

		v AZERBAIJAN	*W*	*A*
EC2002	20 Nov	Baku	2	0
EC2003	29 Mar	Cardiff	4	0
WC2004	4 Sept	Baku	1	1
WC2005	12 Oct	Cardiff	2	0
WC2008	6 Sept	Cardiff	1	0
WC2009	6 June	Baku	1	0
EC2019	6 Sept	Cardiff	2	1
EC2019	16 Nov	Baku	2	0

		v BELARUS	*W*	*B*
EC1998	14 Oct	Cardiff	3	2
EC1999	4 Sept	Minsk	2	1
WC2000	2 Sept	Minsk	1	2
WC2001	6 Oct	Cardiff	1	0
2019	9 Sept	Cardiff	1	0
WC2021	**5 Sept**	**Kazan**	**3**	**2**
WC2021	**13 Nov**	**Cardiff**	**5**	**1**

		v BELGIUM	*W*	*B*
1949	22 May	Liege	1	3
1949	23 Nov	Cardiff	5	1
EC1990	17 Oct	Cardiff	3	1
EC1991	27 Mar	Brussels	1	1
WC1992	18 Nov	Brussels	0	2
WC1993	31 Mar	Cardiff	2	0
WC1997	29 Mar	Cardiff	1	2
WC1997	11 Oct	Brussels	2	3
WC2012	7 Sept	Cardiff	0	2
WC2013	15 Oct	Brussels	1	1
EC2014	16 Nov	Brussels	0	0
EC2015	12 June	Cardiff	1	0
EC2016	1 July	Lille	3	1
WC2021	24 Mar	Leuven	1	3
WC2021	**16 Nov**	**Cardiff**	**1**	**1**
NL2022	**11 June**	**Cardiff**	**1**	**1**

		v BOSNIA-HERZEGOVINA	*W*	*BH*
2003	12 Feb	Cardiff	2	2
2012	15 Aug	Llanelli	0	2
EC2014	10 Oct	Cardiff	0	0
EC2015	10 Oct	Zenica	0	2

		v BRAZIL	*W*	*B*
WC1958	19 June	Gothenburg	0	1
1962	12 May	Rio de Janeiro	1	3
1962	16 May	São Paulo	1	3
1966	14 May	Rio de Janeiro	1	3
1966	18 May	Belo Horizonte	0	1
1983	12 June	Cardiff	1	1
1991	11 Sept	Cardiff	1	0
1997	12 Nov	Brasilia	0	3
2000	23 May	Cardiff	0	3
2006	5 Sept	Cardiff	0	2

		v BULGARIA	*W*	*B*
EC1983	27 Apr	Wrexham	1	0
EC1983	16 Nov	Sofia	0	1
EC1994	14 Dec	Cardiff	0	3
EC1995	29 Mar	Sofia	1	3
2006	15 Aug	Swansea	0	0
2007	22 Aug	Burgas	1	0
EC2010	8 Oct	Cardiff	0	1
EC2011	12 Oct	Sofia	1	0
NL2020	6 Sept	Cardiff	1	0
NL2020	14 Oct	Sofia	1	0

		v CANADA	*W*	*C*
1986	10 May	Toronto	0	2
1986	20 May	Vancouver	3	0
2004	30 May	Wrexham	1	0

		v CHILE	*W*	*C*
1966	22 May	Santiago	0	2
2014	4 June	Valparaiso	0	2

		v CHINA	*W*	*C*
2018	22 Mar	Nanning	6	0

		v COSTA RICA	*W*	*CR*
1990	20 May	Cardiff	1	0
2012	29 Feb	Cardiff	0	1

		v CROATIA	*W*	*C*
2002	21 Aug	Varazdin	1	1
2010	23 May	Osijek	0	2
WC2012	16 Oct	Osijek	0	2
WC2013	26 Mar	Swansea	1	2
EC2019	8 June	Osijek	1	2
EC2019	13 Oct	Cardiff	1	1

		v CYPRUS	*W*	*C*
WC1992	14 Oct	Limassol	1	0
WC1993	13 Oct	Cardiff	2	0
2005	16 Nov	Limassol	0	1
EC2006	11 Oct	Cardiff	3	1
EC2007	13 Oct	Nicosia	1	3
EC2014	13 Oct	Cardiff	2	1
EC2015	3 Sept	Nicosia	1	0

		v CZECHOSLOVAKIA	*W*	*C*
WC1957	1 May	Cardiff	1	0
WC1957	26 May	Prague	0	2
EC1971	21 Apr	Swansea	1	3
EC1971	27 Oct	Prague	0	1
WC1977	30 Mar	Wrexham	3	0
WC1977	16 Nov	Prague	0	1
WC1980	19 Nov	Cardiff	1	0
WC1981	9 Sept	Prague	0	2
EC1987	29 Apr	Wrexham	1	1
EC1987	11 Nov	Prague	0	2
WC1993	28 Apr	Ostrava†	1	1
WC1993	8 Sept	Cardiff†	2	2

†*Czechoslovakia played as RCS (Republic of Czechs and Slovaks).*

		v CZECH REPUBLIC	*W*	*C*
WC2021	30 Mar	Cardiff	1	0
WC2021	**8 Oct**	**Prague**	**2**	**2**
2022	**29 Mar**	**Cardiff**	**1**	**1**

		v DENMARK		
WC1964	21 Oct	Copenhagen	0	1
WC1965	1 Dec	Wrexham	4	2
EC1987	9 Sept	Cardiff	1	0
EC1987	14 Oct	Copenhagen	0	1
1990	11 Sept	Copenhagen	0	1
EC1998	10 Oct	Copenhagen	2	1
EC1999	9 June	Liverpool	0	2
2008	19 Nov	Brondby	1	0
2018	9 Sept	Aarhus	0	2
NL2018	16 Nov	Cardiff	1	2
EC2021	26 June	Amsterdam	0	4

		v ESTONIA	*W*	*E*
1994	23 May	Tallinn	2	1
2009	29 May	Llanelli	1	0
WC2021	**8 Sept**	**Cardiff**	**0**	**0**
WC2021	**11 Oct**	**Tallinn**	**1**	**0**

		v FAROE ISLANDS	*W*	*F*
WC1992	9 Sept	Cardiff	6	0
WC1993	6 June	Toftir	3	0

v FINLAND			W	F
EC1971	26 May	Helsinki	1	0
EC1971	13 Oct	Swansea	3	0
EC1987	10 Sept	Helsinki	1	1
NL2020	3 Sept	Helsinki	1	0
NL2020	18 Nov	Cardiff	3	1
EC1987	1 Apr	Wrexham	4	0
WC1988	19 Oct	Swansea	2	2
WC1989	6 Sept	Helsinki	0	1
2000	29 Mar	Cardiff	1	2
EC2002	7 Sept	Helsinki	2	0
EC2003	10 Sept	Cardiff	1	1
WC2009	28 Mar	Cardiff	0	2
WC2009	10 Oct	Helsinki	1	2
2013	16 Nov	Cardiff	1	1
2021	**1 Sept**	**Helsinki**	**0**	**0**

v FRANCE			W	F
1933	25 May	Paris	1	1
1939	20 May	Paris	1	2
1953	14 May	Paris	1	6
1982	2 June	Toulouse	1	0
2017	10 Nov	Paris	0	2
2021	2 June	Nice	0	3

v GEORGIA			W	G
EC1994	16 Nov	Tbilisi	0	5
EC1995	7 June	Cardiff	0	1
2008	20 Aug	Swansea	1	2
WC2016	9 Oct	Cardiff	1	1
WC2017	6 Oct	Tbilisi	1	0

v GERMANY			W	G
EC1995	26 Apr	Dusseldorf	1	1
EC1995	11 Oct	Cardiff	1	2
2002	14 May	Cardiff	1	0
EC2007	8 Sept	Cardiff	0	2
EC2007	21 Nov	Frankfurt	0	0
WC2008	15 Oct	Moenchengladbach	0	1
WC2009	1 Apr	Cardiff	0	2

v EAST GERMANY			W	EG
WC1957	19 May	Leipzig	1	2
WC1957	25 Sept	Cardiff	4	1
WC1969	16 Apr	Dresden	1	2
WC1969	22 Oct	Cardiff	1	3

v WEST GERMANY			W	WG
1968	8 May	Cardiff	1	1
1969	26 Mar	Frankfurt	1	1
1976	6 Oct	Cardiff	0	2
1977	14 Dec	Dortmund	1	1
EC1979	2 May	Wrexham	0	2
EC1979	17 Oct	Cologne	1	5
WC1989	31 May	Cardiff	0	0
WC1989	15 Nov	Cologne	1	2
EC1991	5 June	Cardiff	1	0
EC1991	16 Oct	Nuremberg	1	4

v GREECE			W	G
WC1964	9 Dec	Athens	0	2
WC1965	17 Mar	Cardiff	4	1

v HUNGARY			W	H
WC1958	8 June	Sanviken	1	1
WC1958	17 June	Stockholm	2	1
1961	28 May	Budapest	2	3
EC1962	7 Nov	Budapest	1	3
EC1963	20 Mar	Cardiff	1	1
EC1974	30 Oct	Cardiff	2	0
EC1975	16 Apr	Budapest	2	1
1985	16 Oct	Cardiff	0	3
2004	31 Mar	Budapest	2	1
2005	9 Feb	Cardiff	2	0
EC2019	11 June	Budapest	0	1
EC2019	19 Nov	Cardiff	2	0

v ICELAND			W	I
WC1980	2 June	Reykjavik	4	0
WC1981	14 Oct	Swansea	2	2
WC1984	12 Sept	Reykjavik	0	1
WC1984	14 Nov	Cardiff	2	1
1991	1 May	Cardiff	1	0
2008	28 May	Reykjavik	1	0
2014	5 Mar	Cardiff	3	1

v IRAN			W	I
1978	18 Apr	Tehran	1	0

v ISRAEL			W	I
WC1958	15 Jan	Tel Aviv	2	0
WC1958	5 Feb	Cardiff	2	0
1984	10 June	Tel Aviv	0	0
1989	8 Feb	Tel Aviv	3	3
EC2015	28 Mar	Haifa	3	0
EC2015	6 Sept	Cardiff	0	0

v ITALY			W	I
1965	1 May	Florence	1	4
WC1968	23 Oct	Cardiff	0	1
WC1969	4 Nov	Rome	1	4
1988	4 June	Brescia	1	0
1996	24 Jan	Terni	0	3
EC1998	5 Sept	Liverpool	0	2
EC1999	5 June	Bologna	0	4
EC2002	16 Oct	Cardiff	2	1
EC2003	6 Sept	Milan	0	4
EC2021	20 June	Rome	0	1

v JAMAICA			W	J
1998	25 Mar	Cardiff	0	0

v JAPAN			W	J
1992	7 June	Matsuyama	1	0

v KUWAIT			W	K
1977	6 Sept	Wrexham	0	0
1977	20 Sept	Kuwait	0	0

v LATVIA			W	L
2004	18 Aug	Riga	2	0

v LIECHTENSTEIN			W	L
2006	14 Nov	Swansea	4	0
WC2008	11 Oct	Cardiff	2	0
WC2009	14 Oct	Vaduz	2	0

v LUXEMBOURG			W	L
EC1974	20 Nov	Swansea	5	0
EC1975	1 May	Luxembourg	3	1
EC1990	14 Nov	Luxembourg	1	0
EC1991	13 Nov	Cardiff	1	0
2008	26 Mar	Luxembourg	2	0
2010	11 Aug	Llanelli	5	1

v MALTA			W	M
EC1978	25 Oct	Wrexham	7	0
EC1979	2 June	Valletta	2	0
1988	1 June	Valletta	3	2
1998	3 June	Valletta	3	0

v MEXICO			W	M
WC1958	11 June	Stockholm	1	1
1962	22 May	Mexico City	1	2
2012	27 May	New Jersey	0	2
2018	29 May	Pasadena	0	0
2021	27 Mar	Cardiff	1	0

v MOLDOVA			W	M
EC1994	12 Oct	Kishinev	2	3
EC1995	6 Sept	Cardiff	1	0
WC2016	5 Sept	Cardiff	4	0
WC2017	5 Sept	Chisinau	2	0

v MONTENEGRO			W	M
2009	12 Aug	Podgorica	1	2
EC2010	3 Sept	Podgorica	0	1
EC2011	2 Sept	Cardiff	2	1

v NETHERLANDS			W	N
WC1988	14 Sept	Amsterdam	0	1
WC1989	11 Oct	Wrexham	1	2
1992	30 May	Utrecht	0	4
WC1996	5 Oct	Cardiff	1	3
WC1996	9 Nov	Eindhoven	1	7
2008	1 June	Rotterdam	0	2
2014	4 June	Amsterdam	0	2
2015	13 Nov	Cardiff	2	3
NL2022	**8 June**	**Cardiff**	**1**	**2**
NL2022	**14 June**	**Feyenoord**	**2**	**3**

v NEW ZEALAND			W	NZ
2007	26 May	Wrexham	2	2

v NORTH MACEDONIA			W	M
WC2013	6 Sept	Skopje	1	2
WC2013	11 Oct	Cardiff	1	0

v NORWAY			W	N
EC1982	22 Sept	Swansea	1	0
EC1983	21 Sept	Oslo	0	0
1984	6 June	Trondheim	0	1

			W	N
1985	26 Feb	Wrexham	1	1
1985	5 June	Bergen	2	4
1994	9 Mar	Cardiff	1	3
WC2000	7 Oct	Cardiff	1	1
WC2001	5 Sept	Oslo	2	3
2004	27 May	Oslo	0	0
2008	6 Feb	Wrexham	3	0
2011	12 Nov	Cardiff	4	1

v PANAMA			W	P
2017	14 Nov	Cardiff	1	1

v PARAGUAY			W	P
2006	1 Mar	Cardiff	0	0

v POLAND			W	P
WC1973	28 Mar	Cardiff	2	0
WC1973	26 Sept	Katowice	0	3
1991	29 May	Radom	0	0
WC2000	11 Oct	Warsaw	0	0
WC2001	2 June	Cardiff	1	2
WC2004	13 Oct	Cardiff	2	3
WC2005	7 Sept	Warsaw	0	1
2009	11 Feb	Vila Real	0	1
NL2022	**1 June**	**Wroclaw**	**1**	**2**

v PORTUGAL			W	P
1949	15 May	Lisbon	2	3
1951	12 May	Cardiff	2	1
2000	2 June	Chaves	0	3
EC2016	6 July	Lille	0	2

v QATAR			W	Q
2000	23 Feb	Doha	1	0

v REPUBLIC OF IRELAND			W	RI
1960	28 Sept	Dublin	3	2
1979	11 Sept	Swansea	2	1
1981	24 Feb	Dublin	3	1
1986	26 Mar	Dublin	1	0
1990	28 Mar	Dublin	0	1
1991	6 Feb	Wrexham	0	3
1992	19 Feb	Dublin	1	0
1993	17 Feb	Dublin	1	2
1997	11 Feb	Cardiff	0	0
EC2007	24 Mar	Dublin	0	1
EC2007	17 Nov	Cardiff	2	2
NC2011	8 Feb	Dublin	0	3
2013	14 Aug	Cardiff	0	0
WC2017	24 Mar	Dublin	0	0
WC2017	9 Oct	Cardiff	0	1
NL2018	6 Sept	Cardiff	4	1
NL2018	16 Oct	Dublin	1	0
NL2020	11 Oct	Dublin	0	0
NL2020	15 Nov	Cardiff	1	0

v ROMANIA			W	R
EC1970	11 Nov	Cardiff	0	0
EC1971	24 Nov	Bucharest	0	2
1983	12 Oct	Wrexham	5	0
WC1992	20 May	Bucharest	1	5
WC1993	17 Nov	Cardiff	1	2

v RUSSIA			W	R
EC2003	15 Nov	Moscow	0	0
EC2003	19 Nov	Cardiff	0	1
WC2008	10 Sept	Moscow	1	2
WC2009	9 Sept	Cardiff	1	3
EC2016	20 June	Toulouse	3	0

v SAN MARINO			W	SM
WC1996	2 June	Serravalle	5	0
WC1996	31 Aug	Cardiff	6	0
EC2007	28 Mar	Cardiff	3	0
EC2007	17 Oct	Serravalle	2	1

v SAUDI ARABIA			W	SA
1986	25 Feb	Dahran	2	1

v SERBIA			W	S
WC2012	11 Sept	Novi Sad	1	6
WC2013	10 Sept	Cardiff	0	3
WC2016	12 Nov	Cardiff	1	1
WC2017	11 June	Belgrade	1	1

v SERBIA-MONTENEGRO			W	SM
EC2003	20 Aug	Belgrade	0	1
EC2003	11 Oct	Cardiff	2	3

v SLOVAKIA			W	S
EC2006	7 Oct	Cardiff	1	5
EC2007	12 Sept	Trnava	5	2
EC2016	11 June	Bordeaux	2	1
EC2019	24 Mar	Cardiff	1	0
EC2019	10 Oct	Trnava	1	1

v SLOVENIA			W	Sl
2005	17 Aug	Swansea	0	0

v SPAIN			W	S
WC1961	19 Apr	Cardiff	1	2
WC1961	18 May	Madrid	1	1
1982	24 Mar	Valencia	1	1
WC1984	17 Oct	Seville	0	3
WC1985	30 Apr	Wrexham	3	0
2018	11 Oct	Cardiff	1	4

v SWEDEN			W	S
WC1958	15 June	Stockholm	0	0
1988	27 Apr	Stockholm	1	4
1989	26 Apr	Wrexham	0	2
1990	25 Apr	Stockholm	2	4
1994	20 Apr	Wrexham	0	2
2010	3 Mar	Swansea	0	1
2016	5 June	Stockholm	0	3

v SWITZERLAND			W	S
1949	26 May	Berne	0	4
1951	16 May	Wrexham	3	2
1996	24 Apr	Lugano	0	2
EC1999	31 Mar	Zurich	0	2
EC1999	9 Oct	Wrexham	0	2
EC2010	12 Oct	Basel	1	4
EC2011	8 Oct	Swansea	2	0
EC2021	12 June	Baku	1	1

v TRINIDAD & TOBAGO			W	TT
2006	27 May	Graz	2	1
2019	20 Mar	Wrexham	1	0

v TUNISIA			W	T
1998	6 June	Tunis	0	4

v TURKEY			W	T
EC1978	29 Nov	Wrexham	1	0
EC1979	21 Nov	Izmir	0	1
WC1980	15 Oct	Cardiff	4	0
WC1981	25 Mar	Ankara	1	0
WC1996	14 Dec	Cardiff	0	0
WC1997	20 Aug	Istanbul	4	6
EC2021	16 June	Baku	2	0

v UKRAINE			W	U
WC2001	28 Mar	Cardiff	1	1
WC2001	6 June	Kyiv	1	1
2016	28 Mar	Kyiv	0	1
WC2022	**5 June**	**Cardiff**	**1**	**0**

v REST OF UNITED KINGDOM			W	RUK
1951	5 Dec	Cardiff	3	2
1969	28 July	Cardiff	0	1

v URUGUAY			W	U
1986	21 Apr	Wrexham	0	0
2018	26 Mar	Nanning	0	1

v USA			W	USA
2003	27 May	San Jose	0	2
2020	12 Nov	Swansea	0	0

v USSR			W	USSR
WC1965	30 May	Moscow	1	2
WC1965	27 Oct	Cardiff	2	1
WC1981	30 May	Wrexham	0	0
WC1981	18 Nov	Tbilisi	0	3
1987	18 Feb	Swansea	0	0

v YUGOSLAVIA			W	Y
1953	21 May	Belgrade	2	5
1954	22 Nov	Cardiff	1	3
EC1976	24 Apr	Zagreb	0	2
EC1976	22 May	Cardiff	1	1
EC1982	15 Dec	Titograd	4	4
EC1983	14 Dec	Cardiff	1	1
1988	23 Mar	Swansea	1	2

NORTHERN IRELAND

v ALBANIA			*NI*	*A*
wc1965	7 May	Belfast	4	1
wc1965	24 Nov	Tirana	1	1
EC1982	15 Dec	Tirana	0	0
EC1983	27 Apr	Belfast	1	0
wc1992	9 Sept	Belfast	3	0
wc1993	17 Feb	Tirana	2	1
wc1996	14 Dec	Belfast	2	0
wc1997	10 Sept	Zurich	0	1
2010	3 Mar	Tirana	0	1

v ALGERIA			*NI*	*A*
wc1986	3 June	Guadalajara	1	1

v ARGENTINA			*NI*	*A*
wc1958	11 June	Halmstad	1	3

v ARMENIA			*NI*	*A*
wc1996	5 Oct	Belfast	1	1
wc1997	30 Apr	Erevan	0	0
EC2003	29 Mar	Erevan	0	1
EC2003	10 Sept	Belfast	0	1

v AUSTRALIA			*NI*	*A*
1980	11 June	Sydney	2	1
1980	15 June	Melbourne	1	1
1980	18 June	Adelaide	2	1

v AUSTRIA			*NI*	*A*
wc1982	1 July	Madrid	2	2
EC1982	13 Oct	Vienna	0	2
EC1983	21 Sept	Belfast	3	1
EC1990	14 Nov	Vienna	0	0
EC1991	16 Oct	Belfast	2	1
EC1994	12 Oct	Vienna	2	1
EC1995	15 Nov	Belfast	5	3
wc2004	13 Oct	Belfast	3	3
wc2005	12 Oct	Vienna	0	2
NL2018	12 Oct	Vienna	0	1
NL2018	18 Nov	Belfast	1	2
NL2020	11 Oct	Belfast	0	1
NL2020	15 Nov	Vienna	1	2

v AZERBAIJAN			*NI*	*A*
wc2004	9 Oct	Baku	0	0
wc2005	3 Sept	Belfast	2	0
wc2012	14 Nov	Belfast	1	1
wc2013	11 Oct	Baku	0	2
wc2016	11 Nov	Belfast	4	0
wc2017	10 June	Baku	1	0

v BARBADOS			*NI*	*B*
2004	30 May	Waterford	1	1

v BELARUS			*NI*	*B*
2016	27 May	Belfast	3	0
EC2019	24 Mar	Belfast	2	1
EC2019	11 June	Barysaw	1	0

v BELGIUM			*NI*	*B*
wc1976	10 Nov	Liege	0	2
wc1977	16 Nov	Belfast	3	0
1997	11 Feb	Belfast	3	0

v BOSNIA-HERZEGOVINA			*NI*	*B*
NL2018	8 Sept	Belfast	1	2
NL2018	15 Oct	Sarajevo	0	2
EC2020	8 Oct	Sarajevo	1	1

v BRAZIL			*NI*	*B*
wc1986	12 June	Guadalajara	0	3

v BULGARIA			*NI*	*B*
wc1972	18 Oct	Sofia	0	3
wc1973	26 Sept	Sheffield	0	0
EC1978	29 Nov	Sofia	2	0
EC1979	2 May	Belfast	2	0
wc2001	28 Mar	Sofia	3	4
wc2001	2 June	Belfast	0	1
2008	6 Feb	Belfast	0	1
wc2021	31 Mar	Belfast	0	0
wc2021	**12 Oct**	**Sofia**	**1**	**2**

v CANADA			*NI*	*C*
1995	22 May	Edmonton	0	2
1999	27 Apr	Belfast	1	1
2005	9 Feb	Belfast	0	1

v CHILE			*NI*	*C*
1989	26 May	Belfast	0	1
1995	25 May	Edmonton	1	2
2010	30 May	Chillan	0	1
2014	4 June	Valparaiso	0	2

v COLOMBIA			*NI*	*C*
1994	4 June	Boston	0	2

v COSTA RICA			*NI*	*CR*
2018	3 June	San Jose	0	3

v CROATIA			*NI*	*C*
2016	15 Nov	Belfast	0	3

v CYPRUS			*NI*	*C*
EC1971	3 Feb	Nicosia	3	0
EC1971	21 Apr	Belfast	5	0
wc1973	14 Feb	Nicosia	0	1
wc1973	8 May	London	3	0
2002	21 Aug	Belfast	0	0
2014	5 Mar	Nicosia	0	0
NL2022	**5 June**	**Larnaca**	**0**	**0**
NL2022	**12 June**	**Belfast**	**2**	**2**

v CZECHOSLOVAKIA			*NI*	*C*
wc1958	8 June	Halmstad	1	0
wc1958	17 June	Malmo	2	1*

**After extra time*

v CZECH REPUBLIC			*NI*	*C*
wc2001	24 Mar	Belfast	0	1
wc2001	6 June	Teplice	1	3
wc2008	10 Sept	Belfast	0	0
wc2009	14 Oct	Prague	0	0
wc2016	4 Sept	Prague	0	0
wc2017	4 Sept	Belfast	2	0
2019	14 Oct	Prague	3	2

v DENMARK			*NI*	*D*
EC1978	25 Oct	Belfast	2	1
EC1979	6 June	Copenhagen	0	4
1986	26 Mar	Belfast	1	1
EC1990	17 Oct	Belfast	1	1
EC1991	13 Nov	Odense	1	2
wc1992	18 Nov	Belfast	0	1
wc1993	13 Oct	Copenhagen	0	1
wc2000	7 Oct	Belfast	1	1
wc2001	1 Sept	Copenhagen	1	1
EC2006	7 Oct	Copenhagen	0	0
EC2007	17 Nov	Belfast	2	1

v ESTONIA			*NI*	*E*
2004	31 Mar	Tallinn	1	0
2006	1 Mar	Belfast	1	0
EC2011	6 Sept	Tallinn	1	4
EC2011	7 Oct	Belfast	1	2
EC2019	21 Mar	Belfast	2	0
EC2019	8 June	Tallinn	2	1
2021	**5 Sept**	**Tallin**	**1**	**0**

v FAROE ISLANDS			*NI*	*F*
EC1991	1 May	Belfast	1	1
EC1991	11 Sept	Landskrona	5	0
EC2010	12 Oct	Toftir	1	1
EC2011	10 Aug	Belfast	4	0
EC2014	11 Oct	Belfast	2	0
EC2015	4 Sept	Torshavn	3	1

v FINLAND			*NI*	*F*
wc1984	27 May	Pori	0	1
wc1984	14 Nov	Belfast	2	1
EC1998	10 Oct	Belfast	1	0
EC1998	9 Oct	Helsinki	1	4
2003	12 Feb	Belfast	0	1
2006	16 Aug	Helsinki	2	1
2012	15 Aug	Belfast	3	3
EC2015	29 Mar	Belfast	2	1
EC2015	11 Oct	Helsinki	1	1

v FRANCE			*NI*	*F*
1928	21 Feb	Paris	0	4
1951	12 May	Belfast	2	2
1952	11 Nov	Paris	1	3
wc1958	19 June	Norrkoping	0	4
1982	24 Mar	Paris	0	4
wc1982	4 July	Madrid	1	4
1986	26 Feb	Paris	0	0
1988	27 Apr	Belfast	0	0
1999	18 Aug	Belfast	0	1

v GEORGIA			*NI*	*G*
2008	26 Mar	Belfast	4	1

v GERMANY			*NI*	*G*
1992	2 June	Bremen	1	1
1996	29 May	Belfast	1	1
wc1996	9 Nov	Nuremberg	1	1
wc1997	20 Aug	Belfast	1	3
EC1999	27 Mar	Belfast	0	3
EC1999	8 Sept	Dortmund	0	4
2005	4 June	Belfast	1	4
EC2016	21 June	Paris	0	1
wc2016	11 Oct	Hanover	0	2
wc2017	5 Oct	Belfast	1	3
EC2019	9 Sept	Belfast	0	2
EC2019	19 Nov	Frankfurt	1	6

v WEST GERMANY			*NI*	*WG*
wc1958	15 June	Malmo	2	2
wc1960	26 Oct	Belfast	3	4
wc1961	10 May	Hamburg	1	2
1966	7 May	Belfast	0	2
1977	27 Apr	Cologne	0	5
EC1982	17 Nov	Belfast	1	0
EC1983	16 Nov	Hamburg	1	0

v GREECE			*NI*	*G*
wc1961	3 May	Athens	1	2
wc1961	17 Oct	Belfast	2	0
1988	17 Feb	Athens	2	3
EC2003	2 Apr	Belfast	0	2
EC2003	11 Oct	Athens	0	1
EC2014	14 Oct	Piraeus	2	0
EC2015	8 Oct	Belfast	3	1
NL2022	**2 June**	**Belfast**	**0**	**1**

v HONDURAS			*NI*	*H*
wc1982	21 June	Zaragoza	1	1

v HUNGARY			*NI*	*H*
wc1988	19 Oct	Budapest	0	1
wc1989	6 Sept	Belfast	1	2
2000	26 Apr	Belfast	0	1
2008	19 Nov	Belfast	0	2
EC2014	7 Sept	Budapest	2	1
EC2015	7 Sept	Belfast	1	1
2022	**29 Mar**	**Belfast**	**0**	**1**

v ICELAND			*NI*	*I*
wc1977	11 June	Reykjavik	0	1
wc1977	21 Sept	Belfast	2	0
wc2000	11 Oct	Reykjavik	0	1
wc2001	5 Sept	Belfast	3	0
EC2006	2 Sept	Belfast	0	3
EC2007	12 Sept	Reykjavik	1	2

v ISRAEL			*NI*	*I*
1968	10 Sept	Jaffa	3	2
1976	3 Mar	Tel Aviv	1	1
wc1980	26 Mar	Tel Aviv	0	0
wc1981	18 Nov	Belfast	1	0
1984	16 Oct	Belfast	3	0
1987	18 Feb	Tel Aviv	1	1
2009	12 Aug	Belfast	1	1
wc2013	26 Mar	Belfast	0	2
wc2013	15 Oct	Tel Aviv	1	1
2018	11 Sept	Belfast	3	0

v ITALY			*NI*	*I*
wc1957	25 Apr	Rome	0	1
1957	4 Dec	Belfast	2	2
wc1958	15 Jan	Belfast	2	1
1961	25 Apr	Bologna	2	3
1997	22 Jan	Palermo	0	2
2003	3 June	Campobasso	0	2
2009	6 June	Pisa	0	3
EC2010	8 Oct	Belfast	0	0
EC2011	11 Oct	Pescara	0	3
wc2021	25 Mar	Parma	0	2
wc2021	**15 Nov**	**Belfast**	**0**	**0**

v KOREA REPUBLIC			*NI*	*KR*
2018	24 Mar	Belfast	2	1

v KOSOVO			*NI*	*K*
NL2022	**9 June**	**Pristina**	**2**	**3**

v LATVIA			*NI*	*L*
wc1993	2 June	Riga	2	1
wc1993	8 Sept	Belfast	2	0
EC1995	26 Apr	Riga	1	0
EC1995	7 June	Belfast	1	2
EC2006	11 Oct	Belfast	1	0
EC2007	8 Sept	Riga	0	1
2015	13 Nov	Belfast	1	0

v LIECHTENSTEIN			*NI*	*L*
EC1994	20 Apr	Belfast	4	1
EC1995	11 Oct	Eschen	4	0
2002	27 Mar	Vaduz	0	0
EC2007	24 Mar	Vaduz	4	1
EC2007	22 Aug	Belfast	3	1

v LITHUANIA			*NI*	*L*
wc1992	28 Apr	Belfast	2	2
wc1993	25 May	Vilnius	1	0
wc2021	**2 Sept**	**Vilnius**	**4**	**1**
wc2021	**12 Nov**	**Belfast**	**1**	**0**

v LUXEMBOURG			*NI*	*L*
2000	23 Feb	Luxembourg	3	1
wc2012	11 Sept	Belfast	1	1
wc2013	10 Sept	Luxembourg	2	3
2019	5 Sept	Belfast	1	0
2022	**25 Mar**	**Luxembourg**	**3**	**1**

v MALTA			*NI*	*M*
wc1988	21 May	Belfast	3	0
wc1989	26 Apr	Valletta	2	0
2000	28 Mar	Valletta	3	0
wc2000	2 Sept	Belfast	1	0
wc2001	6 Oct	Valletta	1	0
2005	17 Aug	Ta'Qali	1	1
2013	6 Feb	Ta'Qali	0	0
2021	30 May	Klagenfurt	3	0

v MEXICO			*NI*	*M*
1966	22 June	Belfast	4	1
1994	11 June	Miami	0	3

v MOLDOVA			*NI*	*M*
EC1998	18 Nov	Belfast	2	2
EC1999	31 Mar	Chisinau	0	0

v MONTENEGRO			*NI*	*M*
2010	11 Aug	Podgorica	0	2

v MOROCCO			*NI*	*M*
1986	23 Apr	Belfast	2	1
2010	17 Nov	Belfast	1	1

v NETHERLANDS			*NI*	*N*
1962	9 May	Rotterdam	0	4
wc1965	17 Mar	Belfast	2	1
wc1965	7 Apr	Rotterdam	0	0
wc1976	13 Oct	Rotterdam	2	2
wc1977	12 Oct	Belfast	0	1
2012	2 June	Amsterdam	0	6
EC2019	10 Oct	Rotterdam	1	3
EC2019	16 Nov	Belfast	0	0

v NEW ZEALAND			*NI*	*N*
2017	2 June	Belfast	1	0

v NORWAY			*NI*	*N*
1922	25 May	Bergen	1	2
EC1974	4 Sept	Oslo	1	2
EC1975	29 Oct	Belfast	3	0
1990	27 Mar	Belfast	2	3
1996	27 Mar	Belfast	0	2
2001	28 Feb	Belfast	0	4
2004	18 Feb	Belfast	1	4
2012	29 Feb	Belfast	0	3
wc2017	26 Mar	Belfast	2	0
wc2017	8 Oct	Oslo	0	1
NL2020	7 Sept	Belfast	1	5
NL2020	14 Oct	Oslo	0	1

v PANAMA			*NI*	*P*
2018	30 May	Panama City	0	0

v POLAND			*NI*	*P*
EC1962	10 Oct	Katowice	2	0
EC1962	28 Nov	Belfast	2	0
1988	23 Mar	Belfast	1	1
1991	5 Feb	Belfast	3	1
2002	13 Feb	Limassol	1	4
EC2004	4 Sept	Belfast	0	3
EC2005	30 Mar	Warsaw	0	1
wc2009	28 Mar	Belfast	3	2
wc2009	5 Sept	Chorzow	1	1
EC2016	12 June	Nice	0	1

v PORTUGAL			NI	P
wc1957	16 Jan	Lisbon	1	1
wc1957	1 May	Belfast	3	0
wc1973	28 Mar	Coventry	1	1
wc1973	14 Nov	Lisbon	1	1
wc1980	19 Nov	Lisbon	0	1
wc1981	29 Apr	Belfast	1	0
EC1994	7 Sept	Belfast	1	2
EC1995	3 Sept	Lisbon	1	1
wc1997	29 Mar	Belfast	0	0
wc1997	11 Oct	Lisbon	0	1
2005	15 Nov	Belfast	1	1
wc2012	16 Oct	Porto	1	1
wc2013	6 Sept	Belfast	2	4

v QATAR			NI	Q
2015	31 May	Crewe	1	1

v REPUBLIC OF IRELAND			NI	RI
EC1978	20 Sept	Dublin	0	0
EC1979	21 Nov	Belfast	1	0
wc1988	14 Sept	Belfast	0	0
wc1989	11 Oct	Dublin	0	3
wc1993	31 Mar	Dublin	0	3
wc1993	17 Nov	Belfast	1	1
EC1994	16 Nov	Belfast	0	4
EC1995	29 Mar	Dublin	1	1
1999	29 May	Dublin	1	0
NC2011	24 May	Dublin	0	5
2018	15 Nov	Dublin	0	0

v ROMANIA			NI	R
wc1984	12 Sept	Belfast	3	2
wc1985	16 Oct	Bucharest	1	0
1994	23 Mar	Belfast	2	0
2006	27 May	Chicago	0	2
EC2014	14 Nov	Bucharest	0	2
EC2015	13 June	Belfast	0	0
NL2020	4 Sept	Bucharest	1	1
NL2020	18 Nov	Belfast	1	1

v RUSSIA			NI	R
wc2012	7 Sept	Moscow	0	2
wc2013	14 Aug	Belfast	1	0

v ST KITTS & NEVIS			NI	SK
2004	2 June	Basseterre	2	0

v SAN MARINO			NI	SM
wc2008	15 Oct	Belfast	4	0
wc2009	11 Feb	Serravalle	3	0
wc2016	8 Oct	Belfast	4	0
wc2017	1 Sept	Serravalle	3	0

v SERBIA			NI	S
2009	14 Nov	Belfast	0	1
EC2011	25 Mar	Belgrade	1	2
EC2011	2 Sept	Belfast	0	1

v SERBIA-MONTENEGRO			NI	SM
2004	28 Apr	Belfast	1	1

v SLOVAKIA			NI	S
1998	25 Mar	Belfast	1	0
wc2008	6 Sept	Bratislava	1	2
wc2009	9 Sept	Belfast	0	2
2016	4 June	Trnava	0	0
EC2020	12 Nov	Belfast	1	2

v SLOVENIA			NI	S
wc2008	11 Oct	Maribor	0	2
wc2009	1 Apr	Belfast	1	0
EC2010	3 Sept	Maribor	1	0
EC2011	29 Mar	Belfast	0	0
2016	28 Mar	Belfast	1	0

v SOUTH AFRICA			NI	SA
1924	24 Sept	Belfast	1	2

v SPAIN			NI	S
1958	15 Oct	Madrid	2	6
1963	30 May	Bilbao	1	1
1963	30 Oct	Belfast	0	1
EC1970	11 Nov	Seville	0	3
EC1972	16 Feb	Hull	1	1
wc1982	25 June	Valencia	1	0
1985	27 Mar	Palma	0	0
wc1986	7 June	Guadalajara	1	2
wc1988	21 Dec	Seville	0	4
wc1989	8 Feb	Belfast	0	2
wc1992	14 Oct	Belfast	0	0
wc1993	28 Apr	Seville	1	3
1998	2 June	Santander	1	4
2002	17 Apr	Belfast	0	5
EC2002	12 Oct	Albacete	0	3
EC2003	11 June	Belfast	0	0
EC2006	6 Sept	Belfast	3	2
EC2007	21 Nov	Las Palmas	0	1

v SWEDEN			NI	S
EC1974	30 Oct	Solna	2	0
EC1975	3 Sept	Belfast	1	2
wc1980	15 Oct	Belfast	3	0
wc1981	3 June	Solna	0	1
1996	24 Apr	Belfast	1	2
EC2007	28 Mar	Belfast	2	1
EC2007	17 Oct	Stockholm	1	1

v SWITZERLAND			NI	S
wc1964	14 Oct	Belfast	1	0
wc1964	14 Nov	Lausanne	1	2
1998	22 Apr	Belfast	1	0
2004	18 Aug	Zurich	0	0
wc2017	9 Nov	Belfast	0	1
wc2017	12 Nov	Basel	0	0
wc2021	**8 Sept**	**Belfast**	**0**	**0**
wc2021	**9 Oct**	**Geneva**	**0**	**2**

v THAILAND			NI	T
1997	21 May	Bangkok	0	0

v TRINIDAD & TOBAGO			NI	TT
2004	6 June	Bacolet	3	0

v TURKEY			NI	T
wc1968	23 Oct	Belfast	4	1
wc1968	11 Dec	Istanbul	3	0
2013	15 Nov	Adana	0	1
EC1983	30 Mar	Belfast	2	1
EC1983	12 Oct	Ankara	0	1
wc1985	1 May	Belfast	2	0
wc1985	11 Sept	Izmir	0	0
EC1986	12 Nov	Izmir	0	0
EC1987	11 Nov	Belfast	1	0
EC1998	5 Sept	Istanbul	0	3
EC1999	4 Sept	Belfast	0	3
2010	26 May	New Britain	0	2
2013	15 Nov	Adana	0	1

v UKRAINE			NI	U
wc1996	31 Aug	Belfast	0	1
wc1997	2 Apr	Kyiv	1	2
EC2002	16 Oct	Belfast	0	0
EC2003	6 Sept	Donetsk	0	0
EC2016	16 June	Lyon	2	0
2021	3 June	Dnipro	0	1

v URUGUAY			NI	U
1964	29 Apr	Belfast	3	0
1990	18 May	Belfast	1	0
2006	21 May	New Jersey	0	1
2014	30 May	Montevideo	0	1

v USA			NI	USA
2021	28 Mar	Belfast	1	2

v USSR			NI	USSR
wc1969	19 Sept	Belfast	0	0
wc1969	22 Oct	Moscow	0	2
EC1971	22 Sept	Moscow	0	1
EC1971	13 Oct	Belfast	1	1

v YUGOSLAVIA			NI	Y
EC1975	16 Mar	Belfast	1	0
EC1975	19 Nov	Belgrade	0	1
wc1982	17 June	Zaragoza	0	0
EC1987	29 Apr	Belfast	1	2
EC1987	14 Oct	Sarajevo	0	3
EC1990	12 Sept	Belfast	0	2
EC1991	27 Mar	Belgrade	1	4
2000	16 Aug	Belfast	1	2

REPUBLIC OF IRELAND

		v ALBANIA	*RI*	*A*
WC1992	26 May	Dublin	2	0
WC1993	26 May	Tirana	2	1
EC2003	2 Apr	Tirana	0	0
EC2003	7 June	Dublin	2	1

		v ALGERIA	*RI*	*A*
1982	28 Apr	Algiers	0	2
2010	28 May	Dublin	3	0

		v ANDORRA	*RI*	*A*
WC2001	28 Mar	Barcelona	3	0
WC2001	25 Apr	Dublin	3	1
EC2010	7 Sept	Dublin	3	1
EC2011	7 Oct	Andorra La Vella	2	0
2021	3 June	Andorra La Vella	4	1

		v ARGENTINA	*RI*	*A*
1951	13 May	Dublin	0	1
†1979	29 May	Dublin	0	0
1980	16 May	Dublin	0	1
1998	22 Apr	Dublin	0	2
2010	11 Aug	Dublin	0	1

†*Not considered a full international.*

		v ARMENIA	*RI*	*A*
EC2010	3 Sept	Erevan	1	0
EC2011	11 Oct	Dublin	2	1
NL2022	**4 June**	**Yerevan**	**0**	**1**

		v AUSTRALIA	*RI*	*A*
2003	19 Aug	Dublin	2	1
2009	12 Aug	Limerick	0	3

		v AUSTRIA	*RI*	*A*
1952	7 May	Vienna	0	6
1953	25 Mar	Dublin	4	0
1958	14 Mar	Vienna	1	3
WC2013	10 Sept	Vienna	0	1
1962	8 Apr	Dublin	2	3
EC1963	25 Sept	Vienna	0	0
EC1963	13 Oct	Dublin	3	2
1966	22 May	Vienna	0	1
1968	10 Nov	Dublin	2	2
EC1971	30 May	Dublin	1	4
EC1971	10 Oct	Linz	0	6
EC1995	11 June	Dublin	1	3
EC1995	6 Sept	Vienna	1	3
WC2013	26 Mar	Dublin	2	2
WC2013	10 Sept	Vienna	0	1
WC2016	12 Nov	Vienna	1	0
WC2017	11 June	Dublin	1	1

		v AZERBAIJAN	*RI*	*A*
WC2021	**4 Sept**	**Dublin**	**1**	**1**
WC2021	**9 Oct**	**Baku**	**3**	**0**

		v BELARUS	*RI*	*B*
2016	31 May	Cork	1	2

		v BELGIUM	*RI*	*B*
1928	12 Feb	Liege	4	2
1929	30 Apr	Dublin	4	0
1930	11 May	Brussels	3	1
WC1934	25 Feb	Dublin	4	4
1949	24 Apr	Dublin	0	2
1950	10 May	Brussels	1	5
1965	24 Mar	Dublin	0	2
1966	25 May	Liege	3	2
WC1980	15 Oct	Dublin	1	1
WC1981	25 Mar	Brussels	0	1
EC1986	10 Sept	Brussels	2	2
EC1987	29 Apr	Dublin	0	0
WC1997	29 Oct	Dublin	1	1
WC1997	16 Nov	Brussels	1	2
EC2016	18 June	Bordeaux	0	3
2022	**26 Mar**	**Dublin**	**2**	**2**

		v BOLIVIA	*RI*	*B*
1994	24 May	Dublin	1	0
1996	15 June	New Jersey	3	0
2007	26 May	Boston	1	1

		v BOSNIA-HERZEGOVINA	*RI*	*BH*
2012	26 May	Dublin	1	0
EC2015	13 Nov	Zenica	1	1
EC2015	16 Nov	Dublin	2	0

		v BRAZIL	*RI*	*B*
1974	5 May	Rio de Janeiro	1	2
1982	27 May	Uberlandia	0	7
1987	23 May	Dublin	1	0
2004	18 Feb	Dublin	0	0
2008	6 Feb	Dublin	0	1
2010	2 Mar	Emirates	0	2

		v BULGARIA	*RI*	*B*
WC1977	1 June	Sofia	1	2
WC1977	12 Oct	Dublin	0	0
EC1979	19 May	Sofia	0	1
EC1979	17 Oct	Dublin	3	0
WC1987	1 Apr	Sofia	1	2
WC1987	14 Oct	Dublin	2	0
2004	18 Aug	Dublin	1	1
WC2009	28 Mar	Dublin	1	1
WC2009	6 June	Sofia	1	1
2019	10 Sept	Dublin	3	1
NL2020	3 Sept	Sofia	1	1
NL2020	18 Nov	Dublin	0	0

		v CAMEROON	*RI*	*C*
WC2002	1 June	Niigata	1	1

		v CANADA	*RI*	*C*
2003	18 Nov	Dublin	3	0

		v CHILE	*RI*	*C*
1960	30 Mar	Dublin	2	0
1972	21 June	Recife	1	2
1974	12 May	Santiago	2	1
1982	22 May	Santiago	0	1
1991	22 May	Dublin	1	1
2006	24 May	Dublin	0	1

		v CHINA PR	*RI*	*CPR*
1984	3 June	Sapporo	1	0
2005	29 Mar	Dublin	1	0

		v COLOMBIA	*RI*	*C*
2008	29 May	Fulham	1	0

		v COSTA RICA	*RI*	*C*
2014	6 June	Philadelphia	1	1

		v CROATIA	*RI*	*C*
1996	2 June	Dublin	2	2
EC1998	5 Sept	Dublin	2	0
EC1999	4 Sept	Zagreb	0	1
2001	15 Aug	Dublin	2	2
2004	16 Nov	Dublin	1	0
2011	10 Aug	Dublin	0	0
EC2012	10 June	Poznan	1	3

		v CYPRUS	*RI*	*C*
WC1980	26 Mar	Nicosia	3	2
WC1980	19 Nov	Dublin	6	0
WC2001	24 Mar	Nicosia	4	0
WC2001	6 Oct	Dublin	4	0
WC2004	4 Sept	Dublin	3	0
WC2005	8 Oct	Nicosia	1	0
EC2006	7 Oct	Nicosia	2	5
EC2007	17 Oct	Dublin	1	1
2008	15 Oct	Dublin	1	0
WC2009	5 Sept	Nicosia	2	1

		v CZECHOSLOVAKIA	*RI*	*C*
1938	18 May	Prague	2	2
EC1959	5 Apr	Dublin	2	0
EC1959	10 May	Bratislava	0	4
WC1961	8 Oct	Dublin	1	3
WC1961	29 Oct	Prague	1	7
EC1967	21 May	Dublin	0	2
EC1967	22 Nov	Prague	2	1
WC1969	4 May	Dublin	1	2
WC1969	7 Oct	Prague	0	3
1979	26 Sept	Prague	1	4
1981	29 Apr	Dublin	3	1
1986	27 May	Reykjavik	1	0

		v CZECH REPUBLIC	*RI*	*C*
1994	5 June	Dublin	1	3
1996	24 Apr	Prague	0	2
1998	25 Mar	Olomouc	1	2
2000	23 Feb	Dublin	3	2
2004	31 Mar	Dublin	2	1
EC2006	11 Oct	Dublin	1	1
EC2007	12 Sept	Prague	0	1
2012	29 Feb	Dublin	1	1

v DENMARK			*RI*	*D*
WC1956	3 Oct	Dublin	2	1
WC1957	2 Oct	Copenhagen	2	0
WC1968	4 Dec	Dublin	1	1
(*abandoned after 51 mins*)				
WC1969	27 May	Copenhagen	0	2
WC1969	15 Oct	Dublin	1	1
EC1978	24 May	Copenhagen	3	3
EC1979	2 May	Dublin	2	0
WC1984	14 Nov	Copenhagen	0	3
WC1985	13 Nov	Dublin	1	4
WC1992	14 Oct	Copenhagen	0	0
WC1993	28 Apr	Dublin	1	1
2002	27 Mar	Dublin	3	0
2007	22 Aug	Copenhagen	4	0
WC2017	11 Nov	Copenhagen	0	0
WC2017	14 Nov	Dublin	1	5
NL2018	13 Oct	Dublin	0	0
NL2018	19 Nov	Aarhus	0	0
EC2019	7 June	Copenhagen	1	1
EC2019	18 Nov	Dublin	1	1

v ECUADOR			*RI*	*E*
1972	19 June	Natal	3	2
2007	23 May	New Jersey	1	1

v EGYPT			*RI*	*E*
WC1990	17 June	Palermo	0	0

v ENGLAND			*RI*	*E*
1946	30 Sept	Dublin	0	1
1949	21 Sept	Everton	2	0
WC1957	8 May	Wembley	1	5
WC1957	19 May	Dublin	1	1
1964	24 May	Dublin	1	3
1976	8 Sept	Wembley	1	1
EC1978	25 Oct	Dublin	1	1
EC1980	6 Feb	Wembley	0	2
1985	26 Mar	Wembley	1	2
EC1988	12 June	Stuttgart	1	0
WC1990	11 June	Cagliari	1	1
EC1990	14 Nov	Dublin	1	1
EC1991	27 Mar	Wembley	1	1
1995	15 Feb	Dublin	1	0
(*abandoned after 27 mins*)				
2013	29 May	Wembley	1	1
2015	7 June	Dublin	0	0
2020	12 Nov	Wembley	0	3

v ESTONIA			*RI*	*E*
WC2000	11 Oct	Dublin	2	0
WC2001	6 June	Tallinn	2	0
EC2011	11 Nov	Tallinn	4	0
EC2011	15 Nov	Dublin	1	1

v FAROE ISLANDS			*RI*	*F*
EC2004	13 Oct	Dublin	2	0
EC2005	8 June	Toftir	2	0
WC2012	16 Oct	Torshavn	4	1
WC2013	7 June	Dublin	3	0

v FINLAND			*RI*	*F*
WC1949	8 Sept	Dublin	3	0
WC1949	9 Oct	Helsinki	1	1
1990	16 May	Dublin	1	1
2000	15 Nov	Dublin	3	0
2002	21 Aug	Helsinki	3	0
NL2020	6 Sept	Dublin	0	1
NL2020	14 Oct	Helsinki	0	1

v FRANCE			*RI*	*F*
1937	23 May	Paris	2	0
1952	16 Nov	Dublin	1	1
WC1953	4 Oct	Dublin	3	5
WC1953	25 Nov	Paris	0	1
WC1972	15 Nov	Dublin	2	1
WC1973	19 May	Paris	1	1
WC1976	17 Nov	Paris	0	2
WC1977	30 Mar	Dublin	1	0
WC1980	28 Oct	Paris	0	2
WC1981	14 Oct	Dublin	3	2
1989	7 Feb	Dublin	0	0
WC2004	9 Oct	Paris	0	0
WC2005	7 Sept	Dublin	0	1
WC2009	14 Nov	Dublin	0	1
WC2009	18 Nov	Paris	1	1
EC2016	26 June	Lyon	1	2
2018	28 May	Paris	0	2

v GEORGIA			*RI*	*G*
EC2003	29 Mar	Tbilisi	2	1
EC2003	11 June	Dublin	2	0
WC2008	6 Sept	Mainz	2	1
WC2009	11 Feb	Dublin	2	1
2013	2 June	Dublin	3	0
EC2014	7 Sept	Tbilisi	2	1
EC2015	7 Sept	Dublin	1	0
WC2016	6 Oct	Dublin	1	0
WC2017	2 Sept	Tbilisi	1	1
EC2019	26 Mar	Dublin	1	0
EC2019	12 Oct	Tbilisi	0	0

v GERMANY			*RI*	*G*
1935	8 May	Dortmund	1	3
1936	17 Oct	Dublin	5	2
1939	23 May	Bremen	1	1
1994	29 May	Hanover	2	0
WC2002	5 June	Ibaraki	1	1
EC2006	2 Sept	Stuttgart	0	1
EC2007	13 Oct	Dublin	0	0
WC2012	12 Oct	Dublin	1	6
WC2013	11 Oct	Cologne	0	3
EC2014	14 Oct	Gelsenkirchen	1	1
EC2015	8 Oct	Dublin	1	0

v WEST GERMANY			*RI*	*WG*
1951	17 Oct	Dublin	3	2
1952	4 May	Cologne	0	3
1955	28 May	Hamburg	1	2
1956	25 Nov	Dublin	3	0
1960	11 May	Dusseldorf	1	0
1966	4 May	Dublin	0	4
1970	9 May	Berlin	1	2
1975	1 Mar	Dublin	1	0†
1979	22 May	Dublin	1	3
1981	21 May	Bremen	0	3†
1989	6 Sept	Dublin	1	1

†*v West Germany 'B'*

v GIBRALTAR			*RI*	*G*
EC2014	11 Oct	Dublin	7	0
EC2015	4 Sept	Faro	4	0
EC2019	23 Mar	Gibraltar	1	0
EC2019	10 June	Dublin	2	0

v GREECE			*RI*	*G*
2000	26 Apr	Dublin	0	1
2002	20 Nov	Athens	0	0
2012	14 Nov	Dublin	0	1

v HUNGARY			*RI*	*H*
1934	15 Dec	Dublin	2	4
1936	3 May	Budapest	3	3
1936	6 Dec	Dublin	2	3
1939	19 Mar	Cork	2	2
1939	18 May	Budapest	2	2
WC1969	8 June	Dublin	1	2
WC1969	5 Nov	Budapest	0	4
WC1989	8 Mar	Budapest	0	0
WC1989	4 June	Dublin	2	0
1991	11 Sept	Gyor	2	1
2012	4 June	Budapest	0	0
2021	8 June	Budapest	0	0

v ICELAND			*RI*	*I*
EC1962	12 Aug	Dublin	4	2
EC1962	2 Sept	Reykjavik	1	1
EC1982	13 Oct	Dublin	2	0
EC1983	21 Sept	Reykjavik	3	0
1986	25 May	Reykjavik	2	1
WC1996	10 Nov	Dublin	0	0
WC1997	6 Sept	Reykjavik	4	2
2017	28 Mar	Dublin	0	1

v IRAN			*RI*	*I*
1972	18 June	Recife	2	1
WC2001	10 Nov	Dublin	2	0
WC2001	15 Nov	Tehran	0	1

v ISRAEL			*RI*	*I*
1984	4 Apr	Tel Aviv	0	3
1985	27 May	Tel Aviv	0	0
1987	10 Nov	Dublin	5	0
EC2005	26 Mar	Tel Aviv	1	1
EC2005	4 June	Dublin	2	2

v ITALY			*RI*	*I*
1926	21 Mar	Turin	0	3
1927	23 Apr	Dublin	1	2

			RI	*I*
EC1970	8 Dec	Rome	0	3
EC1971	10 May	Dublin	1	2
1985	5 Feb	Dublin	1	2
WC1990	30 June	Rome	0	1
1992	4 June	Foxboro	0	2
WC1994	18 June	New York	1	0
2005	17 Aug	Dublin	1	2
WC2009	1 Apr	Bari	1	1
WC2009	10 Oct	Dublin	2	2
2011	7 June	Liege	2	0
EC2012	18 June	Poznan	0	2
2014	31 May	Craven Cottage	0	0
EC2016	22 June	Lille	1	0

v JAMAICA

			RI	*J*
2004	2 June	Charlton	1	0

v KAZAKHSTAN

			RI	*K*
WC2012	7 Sept	Astana	2	1
WC2013	15 Oct	Dublin	3	1

v LATVIA

			RI	*L*
WC1992	9 Sept	Dublin	4	0
WC1993	2 June	Riga	2	1
EC1994	7 Sept	Riga	3	0
EC1995	11 Oct	Dublin	2	1
2013	15 Nov	Dublin	3	0

v LIECHTENSTEIN

			RI	*L*
EC1994	12 Oct	Dublin	4	0
EC1995	3 June	Eschen	0	0
WC1996	31 Aug	Eschen	5	0
WC1997	21 May	Dublin	5	0

v LITHUANIA

			RI	*L*
WC1993	16 June	Vilnius	1	0
WC1993	8 Sept	Dublin	2	0
WC1997	20 Aug	Dublin	0	0
WC1997	10 Sept	Vilnius	2	1
2022	**29 Mar**	**Dublin**	**1**	**0**

v LUXEMBOURG

			RI	*L*
1936	9 May	Luxembourg	5	1
WC1953	28 Oct	Dublin	4	0
WC1954	7 Mar	Luxembourg	1	0
EC1987	28 May	Luxembourg	2	0
EC1987	9 Sept	Dublin	2	1
WC2021	27 Mar	Dublin	0	1
WC2021	**14 Nov**	**Luxembourg**	**3**	**0**

v MALTA

			RI	*M*
EC1983	30 Mar	Valletta	1	0
EC1983	16 Nov	Dublin	8	0
WC1989	28 May	Dublin	2	0
WC1989	15 Nov	Valletta	2	0
1990	2 June	Valletta	3	0
EC1998	14 Oct	Dublin	5	0
EC1999	8 Sept	Valletta	3	2

v MEXICO

			RI	*M*
1984	8 Aug	Dublin	0	0
WC1994	24 June	Orlando	1	2
1996	13 June	New Jersey	2	2
1998	23 May	Dublin	0	0
2000	4 June	Chicago	2	2
2017	2 June	New Jersey	1	3

v MOLDOVA

			RI	*M*
WC2016	9 Oct	Chisinau	3	1
WC2017	6 Oct	Dublin	2	0

v MONTENEGRO

			RI	*M*
WC2008	10 Sept	Podgorica	0	0
WC2009	14 Oct	Dublin	0	0

v MOROCCO

			RI	*M*
1990	12 Sept	Dublin	1	0

v NETHERLANDS

			RI	*N*
1932	8 May	Amsterdam	2	0
1934	8 Apr	Amsterdam	2	5
1935	8 Dec	Dublin	3	5
1955	1 May	Dublin	1	0
1956	10 May	Rotterdam	4	1
WC1980	10 Sept	Dublin	2	1
WC1981	9 Sept	Rotterdam	2	2
EC1982	22 Sept	Rotterdam	1	2
EC1983	12 Oct	Dublin	2	3
EC1988	18 June	Gelsenkirchen	0	1
WC1990	21 June	Palermo	1	1
1994	20 Apr	Tilburg	1	0
WC1994	4 July	Orlando	0	2
EC1995	13 Dec	Liverpool	0	2
1996	4 June	Rotterdam	1	3
WC2000	2 Sept	Amsterdam	2	2
WC2001	1 Sept	Dublin	1	0
2004	5 June	Amsterdam	1	0
2006	16 Aug	Dublin	0	4
2016	27 May	Dublin	1	1

v NEW ZEALAND

			RI	*N*
2019	14 Nov	Dublin	3	1

v NIGERIA

			RI	*N*
2002	16 May	Dublin	1	2
2004	29 May	Charlton	0	3
2009	29 May	Fulham	1	1

v NORTHERN IRELAND

			RI	*NI*
EC1978	20 Sept	Dublin	0	0
EC1979	21 Nov	Belfast	0	1
WC1988	14 Sept	Belfast	0	0
WC1989	11 Oct	Dublin	3	0
WC1993	31 Mar	Dublin	3	0
WC1993	17 Nov	Belfast	1	1
EC1994	16 Nov	Belfast	4	0
EC1995	29 Mar	Dublin	1	1
1999	29 May	Dublin	0	1
NC2011	24 May	Dublin	5	0
2018	15 Nov	Dublin	0	0

v NORTH MACEDONIA

			RI	*M*
WC1996	9 Oct	Dublin	3	0
WC1997	2 Apr	Skopje	2	3
EC1999	9 June	Dublin	1	0
EC1999	9 Oct	Skopje	1	1
EC2011	26 Mar	Dublin	2	1
EC2011	4 June	Podgorica	2	0

v NORWAY

			RI	*N*
WC1937	10 Oct	Oslo	2	3
WC1937	7 Nov	Dublin	3	3
1950	26 Nov	Dublin	2	2
1951	30 May	Oslo	3	2
1954	8 Nov	Dublin	2	1
1955	25 May	Oslo	3	1
1960	6 Nov	Dublin	3	1
1964	13 May	Oslo	4	1
1973	6 June	Oslo	1	1
1976	24 Mar	Dublin	3	0
1978	21 May	Oslo	0	0
WC1984	17 Oct	Oslo	0	1
WC1985	1 May	Dublin	0	0
1988	1 June	Oslo	0	0
WC1994	28 June	New York	0	0
2003	30 Apr	Dublin	1	0
2008	20 Aug	Oslo	1	1
2010	17 Nov	Dublin	1	2

v OMAN

			RI	*O*
2012	11 Sept	London	4	1
2014	3 Sept	Dublin	2	0
2016	31 Aug	Dublin	4	0

v PARAGUAY

			RI	*P*
1999	10 Feb	Dublin	2	0
2010	25 May	Dublin	2	1

v POLAND

			RI	*P*
1938	22 May	Warsaw	0	6
1938	13 Nov	Dublin	3	2
1958	11 May	Katowice	2	2
1958	5 Oct	Dublin	2	2
1964	10 May	Kracow	1	3
1964	25 Oct	Dublin	3	2
1968	15 May	Dublin	2	2
1968	30 Oct	Katowice	0	1
1970	6 May	Dublin	1	2
1970	23 Sept	Dublin	0	2
1973	16 May	Wroclaw	0	2
1973	21 Oct	Dublin	1	0
1976	26 May	Poznan	2	0
1977	24 Apr	Dublin	0	0
1978	12 Apr	Lodz	0	3
1981	23 May	Bydgoszcz	0	3
1984	23 May	Dublin	0	0
1986	12 Nov	Warsaw	0	1
1988	22 May	Dublin	3	1
EC1991	1 May	Dublin	0	0
EC1991	16 Oct	Poznan	3	3

			RI	*P*
2004	28 Apr	Bydgoszcz	0	0
2013	19 Nov	Poznan	0	0
2008	19 Nov	Dublin	2	3
2013	6 Feb	Dublin	2	0
2013	19 Nov	Poznan	0	0
EC2015	29 Mar	Dublin	1	1
EC2015	11 Oct	Warsaw	1	2
2018	11 Sept	Wroclaw	1	1

v PORTUGAL			*RI*	*P*
1946	16 June	Lisbon	1	3
1947	4 May	Dublin	0	2
1948	23 May	Lisbon	0	2
1949	22 May	Dublin	1	0
1972	25 June	Recife	1	2
1992	7 June	Boston	2	0
EC1995	26 Apr	Dublin	1	0
EC1995	15 Nov	Lisbon	0	3
1996	29 May	Dublin	0	1
WC2000	7 Oct	Lisbon	1	1
WC2001	2 June	Dublin	1	1
2005	9 Feb	Dublin	1	0
2014	10 June	New Jersey	1	5
WC2021	**1 Sept**	**Algarve**	**1**	**2**
WC2021	**11 Nov**	**Dublin**	**0**	**0**

v QATAR			*RI*	*Q*
2021	30 Mar	Dublin	1	1
2021	**12 Oct**	**Dublin**	**4**	**0**

v ROMANIA			*RI*	*R*
1988	23 Mar	Dublin	2	0
WC1990	25 June	Genoa	0	0*
WC1997	30 Apr	Bucharest	0	1
WC1997	11 Oct	Dublin	1	1
2004	27 May	Dublin	1	0

v RUSSIA			*RI*	*R*
1994	23 Mar	Dublin	0	0
1996	27 Mar	Dublin	0	2
2002	13 Feb	Dublin	2	0
EC2002	7 Sept	Moscow	2	4
EC2003	6 Sept	Dublin	1	1
EC2010	8 Oct	Dublin	2	3
EC2011	6 Sept	Moscow	0	0

v SAN MARINO			*RI*	*SM*
EC2006	15 Nov	Dublin	5	0
EC2007	7 Feb	Serravalle	2	1

v SAUDI ARABIA			*RI*	*SA*
WC2002	11 June	Yokohama	3	0

v SCOTLAND			*RI*	*S*
WC1961	3 May	Glasgow	1	4
WC1961	7 May	Dublin	0	3
1963	9 June	Dublin	1	0
1969	21 Sept	Dublin	1	1
EC1986	15 Oct	Dublin	0	0
EC1987	18 Feb	Glasgow	1	0
2000	30 May	Dublin	1	2
2003	12 Feb	Glasgow	2	0
NC2011	29 May	Dublin	1	0
EC2014	14 Nov	Glasgow	0	1
EC2015	13 June	Dublin	1	1
NL2022	**11 June**	**Dublin**	**3**	**0**

v SERBIA			*RI*	*S*
2008	24 May	Dublin	1	1
2012	15 Aug	Belgrade	0	0
2014	5 Mar	Dublin	1	2
WC2016	5 Sept	Belgrade	2	2
WC2017	5 Sept	Dublin	0	1
WC2021	24 Mar	Belgrade	2	3
WC2021	**7 Sept**	**Dublin**	**1**	**1**

v SLOVAKIA			*RI*	*S*
EC2007	28 Mar	Dublin	1	0
EC2007	8 Sept	Bratislava	2	2
EC2010	12 Oct	Zilina	1	1
EC2011	2 Sept	Dublin	0	0
2016	29 Mar	Dublin	2	2
EC2020	8 Oct	Bratislava	0	0

v SOUTH AFRICA			*RI*	*SA*
2000	11 June	New Jersey	2	1
2009	8 Sept	Limerick	1	0

v SPAIN			*RI*	*S*
1931	26 Apr	Barcelona	1	1
1931	13 Dec	Dublin	0	5
1946	23 June	Madrid	1	0
1947	2 Mar	Dublin	3	2
1948	30 May	Barcelona	1	2
1949	12 June	Dublin	1	4
1952	1 June	Madrid	0	6
1955	27 Nov	Dublin	2	2
EC1964	11 Mar	Seville	1	5
EC1964	8 Apr	Dublin	0	2
WC1965	5 May	Dublin	1	0
WC1965	27 Oct	Seville	1	4
WC1965	10 Nov	Paris	0	1
EC1966	23 Oct	Dublin	0	0
EC1966	7 Dec	Valencia	0	2
1977	9 Feb	Dublin	0	1
EC1982	17 Nov	Dublin	3	3
EC1983	27 Apr	Zaragoza	0	2
1985	26 May	Cork	0	0
WC1988	16 Nov	Seville	0	2
WC1989	26 Apr	Dublin	1	0
WC1992	18 Nov	Seville	0	0
WC1993	13 Oct	Dublin	1	3
WC2002	16 June	Suwon	1	1
EC2012	14 June	Gdansk	0	4
2013	11 June	New York	0	2

v SWEDEN			*RI*	*S*
WC1949	2 June	Stockholm	1	3
WC1949	13 Nov	Dublin	1	3
1959	1 Nov	Dublin	3	2
1960	18 May	Malmo	1	4
EC1970	14 Oct	Dublin	1	1
EC1970	28 Oct	Malmo	0	1
1999	28 Apr	Dublin	2	0
2006	1 Mar	Dublin	3	0
WC2013	22 Mar	Stockholm	0	0
WC2013	6 Sept	Dublin	1	2
EC2016	13 June	Paris	1	1

v SWITZERLAND			*RI*	*S*
1935	5 May	Basel	0	1
1936	17 Mar	Dublin	1	0
1937	17 May	Berne	1	0
1938	18 Sept	Dublin	4	0
1948	5 Dec	Dublin	0	1
EC1975	11 May	Dublin	2	1
EC1975	21 May	Berne	0	1
1980	30 Apr	Dublin	2	0
WC1985	2 June	Dublin	3	0
WC1985	11 Sept	Berne	0	0
1992	25 Mar	Dublin	2	1
EC2002	16 Oct	Dublin	1	2
EC2003	11 Oct	Basel	0	2
WC2004	8 Sept	Basel	1	1
WC2005	12 Oct	Dublin	0	0
2016	25 Mar	Dublin	1	0
EC2019	5 Sept	Dublin	1	1
EC2019	15 Oct	Geneva	0	2

v TRINIDAD & TOBAGO			*RI*	*TT*
1982	30 May	Port of Spain	1	2

v TUNISIA			*RI*	*T*
1988	19 Oct	Dublin	4	0

v TURKEY			*RI*	*T*
EC1966	16 Nov	Dublin	2	1
EC1967	22 Feb	Ankara	1	2
EC1974	20 Nov	Izmir	1	1
EC1975	29 Oct	Dublin	4	0
2014	25 May	Dublin	1	2
1976	13 Oct	Ankara	3	3
1978	5 Apr	Dublin	4	2
1990	26 May	Izmir	0	0
EC1990	17 Oct	Dublin	5	0
EC1991	13 Nov	Istanbul	3	1
EC1999	13 Nov	Dublin	1	1
EC1999	17 Nov	Bursa	0	0
2003	9 Sept	Dublin	2	2
2014	25 May	Dublin	1	2
2018	23 Mar	Antalya	0	1

v UKRAINE			*RI*	*U*
NL2022	**8 June**	**Dublin**	**0**	**1**
NL2022	**14 June**	**Lodz (Poland)**	**1**	**1**

		v URUGUAY	RI	U
1974	8 May	Montevideo	0	2
1986	23 Apr	Dublin	1	1
2011	29 Mar	Dublin	2	3
2017	4 June	Dublin	3	1

		v USA	RI	USA
1979	29 Oct	Dublin	3	2
1991	1 June	Boston	1	1
1992	29 Apr	Dublin	4	1
1992	30 May	Washington	1	3
1996	9 June	Boston	1	2
2000	6 June	Boston	1	1
2002	17 Apr	Dublin	2	1
2014	18 Nov	Dublin	4	1
2018	2 June	Dublin	2	1

		v USSR	RI	USSR
WC1972	18 Oct	Dublin	1	2
WC1973	13 May	Moscow	0	1
EC1974	30 Oct	Dublin	3	0
EC1975	18 May	Kyiv	1	2
WC1984	12 Sept	Dublin	1	0
WC1985	16 Oct	Moscow	0	2
EC1988	15 June	Hanover	1	1
1990	25 Apr	Dublin	1	0

		v WALES	RI	W
1960	28 Sept	Dublin	2	3
1979	11 Sept	Swansea	1	2
1981	24 Feb	Dublin	1	3
1986	26 Mar	Dublin	0	1
1990	28 Mar	Dublin	1	0
1991	6 Feb	Wrexham	3	0
1992	19 Feb	Dublin	0	1
1993	17 Feb	Dublin	2	1
1997	11 Feb	Cardiff	0	0
EC2007	24 Mar	Dublin	1	0
EC2007	17 Nov	Cardiff	2	2
NC2011	8 Feb	Dublin	3	0
2013	14 Aug	Cardiff	0	0
WC2017	24 Mar	Dublin	0	0
WC2017	9 Oct	Cardiff	1	0
NL2018	6 Sept	Cardiff	1	4
NL2018	16 Oct	Dublin	0	1
NL2020	11 Oct	Dublin	0	0
NL2020	15 Nov	Cardiff	0	1

		v YUGOSLAVIA	RI	Y
1955	19 Sept	Dublin	1	4
1988	27 Apr	Dublin	2	0
EC1998	18 Nov	Belgrade	0	1
EC1999	1 Sept	Dublin	2	1

OTHER BRITISH AND IRISH INTERNATIONAL MATCHES 2021–22

FRIENDLIES

■ *Denotes player sent off.*

ENGLAND

Saturday, 26 March 2022

England (1) 2 *(Shaw 45, Kane 78 (pen))*

Switzerland (1) 1 *(Embolo 22)*

England: (343) Pickford; Coady, White, Guehi; Walker-Peters (Sterling 61), Gallagher (Rice 61), Henderson, Shaw (Mitchell 61); Foden (Bellingham 80), Kane (Watkins 88), Mount (Grealish 62).
Switzerland: (4231) Omlin; Rodriguez, Akanji, Frei, Widmer (Mbabu 36); Freuler (Zuber 62), Xhaka; Steffen (Zeqiri 62), Shaqiri (Aebischer 80), Vargas (Sow 62); Embolo (Gavranovic 80).
Referee: Andreas Ekberg.

Tuesday, 29 March 2022

England (2) 3 *(Watkins 30, Sterling 45, Mings 90)*

Ivory Coast (0) 0

England: (433) Pope; White (Walker-Peters 46), Mings, Maguire, Mitchell (Shaw 61); Bellingham, Rice, Ward-Prowse (Gallagher 79); Sterling (Foden 62), Watkins (Kane 62), Grealish (Smith Rowe 62).
Ivory Coast: (4231) Sangare; Aurier■, Bailly (Agbadou 46), Deli, Kamara; Seri (Akouokou 90), Kessie; Gradel (Coulibaly 46), Cornet (Konan 63), Pepe (Boly 46); Haller (Boli 86).
Referee: Erik Lambrechts.

SCOTLAND

Thursday, 24 March 2022

Scotland (0) 1 *(Tierney 68)*

Poland (0) 1 *(Piatek 90 (pen))* 39,090

Scotland: (3421) Gordon; McTominay, Hanley, Tierney; Patterson (O'Donnell 66), Gilmour (McLean 77), McGregor C (Jack 77), Taylor (Hickey 66); McGinn J, Christie (Armstrong 76); Adams (Brown 90).
Poland: (343) Skorupski; Salamon (Bielik 44), Glik, Bednarek (Buksa 83); Cash, Zurkowski, Krychowiak (Szymanski S 61), Reca; Moder, Milik (Piatek 26), Zielinski (Grosicki 71).
Referee: Robert Hennessy.

Tuesday, 29 March 2022

Austria (0) 2 *(Gregoritsch 75, Schopf 82)*

Scotland (1) 2 *(Hendry 28, McGinn 56)*

Austria: (3412) Bachmann (Pentz 87); Ilsanker (Weimann 74), Hinteregger, Dragovic; Lazaro, Laimer (Grull 59), Baumgartner (Schopf 59), Ulmer (Ullmann 87); Sabitzer; Kalajdzic (Gregoritsch 74), Arnautovic.
Scotland: (3421) Gordon; Hendry, Hanley, Tierney; Patterson (O'Donnell 58), Ferguson (Gilmour 77), Jack (McTominay 57), Robertson (Hickey 58); McGinn J, Armstrong (Christie 77); Adams (Dykes 66).
Referee: Tamas Bognar.

WALES

Wednesday, 1 September 2021

Finland (0) 0

Wales (0) 0

Finland: (442) Eriksson; Raitala (Alho 73), Ivanov, Toivio, Hamalainen; Assehnoun (Nissila 46), Kairinen, Kamara, Hostikka (Soiri 63); Forss (Pohjanpalo 74), Jensen (Taylor 64).
Wales: (3412) Ward (Hennessey 46); Ampadu (Woodburn 73), Lockyer, Lawrence J (Davies B 46); Levitt, Smith, Williams J (Sheehan 64), Wilson; Norrington-Davies; Roberts T (Bale 82), Johnson (Colwill 64).
Referee: Kristo Tohver.

Tuesday, 29 March 2022

Wales (1) 1 *(Colwill 34)*

Czech Republic (1) 1 *(Soucek 32)*

Wales: (442) Hennessey (Davies A 60); Thomas, Cabango, Mepham, Gunter (Rodon 61); Norrington-Davies, Morrell, Colwill (Bale 81), Vaulks (Ampadu 61); Johnson (Harris 81), Matondo (Williams J 71).
Czech Republic: (3511) Stanek (Vaclik 46); Zima, Petrasek, Brabec; Masopust (Jankto 63), Lingr (Hlozek 81), Soucek, Sadilek (Barak 63), Zeleny; Pesek (Sykora 46); Kuchta (Jurecka 46).
Referee: Paul Tierney.

NORTHERN IRELAND

Sunday, 5 September 2021

Estonia (0) 0

Northern Ireland (0) 1 *(Ferguson 75)*

Estonia: (442) Igonen; Lilander (Puri 46), Lukka, Kuusk, Paskotsi; Vassiljev (Kait 46), Kreida (Mets 46), Poom, Sinyavskiy (Kirss 80); Sappinen (Anier 46), Sorga (Zenjov 76).
Northern Ireland: (442) Carson (Hazard 63); Flanagan, Brown, McNair, Lewis (Ferguson 55); McGinn, McCalmont, Donnelly (Bradley 63), Whyte; Jones, Lafferty (Charles D 55).
Referee: Mads-Kristoffer Kristoffersen.

Friday, 25 March 2022

Luxembourg (0) 1 *(Martins 58)*

Northern Ireland (1) 3 *(Magennis 16, Davis 83, Whyte 85)*

Luxembourg: (4141) Moris; Martins, Chanot, Carlson (Mahmutovic 46), Mica Pinto (Olesen 74); Martins Pereira; Thill O (Thill V 69), Sinani (Deville 87), Barreiro (Thill S 84), Jans; Rodrigues (Borges Sanches 84).
Northern Ireland: (352) Hazard (Southwood 46); Flanagan, Evans J (Brown 62), Cathcart; Dallas (McGinn 80), Evans C, Thompson (Davis 62), Saville, Ferguson; Lavery (Whyte 62), Magennis (Charles D 62).
Referee: Daniel Schlager.

Tuesday, 29 March 2022

Northern Ireland (0) 0

Hungary (0) 1 *(Sallai 55)*

Northern Ireland: (433) Peacock-Farrell; McNair, Cathcart, Ballard (Hume 82), Brown; McCann, Davis (Saville 61), Lane (Dallas 61); McGinn (Lavery 68), Magennis (Charles D 46), Whyte (Thompson 68).
Hungary: (3421) Dibusz; Orban, Lang (Kecskes 81), Fiola; Nego (Bolla 81), Styles (Vecsei 81), Schafer, Nagy Z; Szoboszlai (Nagy A 65), Sallai (Gazdag 72); Adam Szalai (Adam 72).
Referee: Rob Harvey.

REPUBLIC OF IRELAND

Tuesday, 12 October 2021

Republic of Ireland (2) 4 *(Robinson 4, 13 (pen), 53, Duffy 59)*

Qatar (0) 0

Republic of Ireland: (523) Kelleher; Doherty (Christie 46), Omobamidele, Duffy (Collins N 77), Egan, Stevens; Hendrick, Hourihane (Arter 87); Ogbene (Knight 69), Robinson (Parrott 77), McGrath (Collins J 88).
Qatar: (352) Barsham; Al-Rawi, Salman, Hassan; Deus Correia, Al-Haydos, Boudiaf, Hatem (Madibo 72), Mohammed; Ali (Alaaeldin 72), Afif.
Referee: Keith Kennedy.

Saturday, 26 March 2022

Republic of Ireland (1) 2 *(Ogbene 35, Browne 86)*

Belgium (1) 2 *(Batshuayi 12, Vanaken 58)*

Republic of Ireland: (343) Kelleher; Coleman, Duffy, Egan; Doherty, Cullen, Hendrick (Browne 76), McClean (Manning 80); Ogbene, Robinson (Parrott 90), Knight (Keane 76).
Belgium: (343) Mignolet; Denayer, Boyata, Theate (Mangala 75); Saelemaekers (Foket 46), Dendoncker, Tielemans, Hazard T; De Ketelaere (Januzaj 75), Batshuayi (Benteke 83), Vanaken.
Referee: Nick Walsh.

Tuesday, 29 March 2022

Republic of Ireland (0) 1 *(Parrott 90)*

Lithuania (0) 0

Republic of Ireland: (343) Kelleher; Collins N, Egan, O'Shea (McClean 63); Doherty, Browne (Hendrick 82), Hourihane, Manning; Ogbene (Knight 82), Keane (Parrott 62), Robinson (Hogan 77).
Lithuania: (4231) Bartkus; Baravykas, Klimavicius L, Satkus, Vaitkunas; Utkus, Slivka; Lasickas (Sirvys 82), Cernych (Sirgedas 87), Milasius (Kazlauskas 45); Klimavicius A (Kruzikas 61).
Referee: Bram van Driessche.

BRITISH AND IRISH INTERNATIONAL MANAGERS

England
Walter Winterbottom 1946–1962 (after period as coach); Alf Ramsey 1963–1974; Joe Mercer (caretaker) 1974; Don Revie 1974–1977; Ron Greenwood 1977–1982; Bobby Robson 1982–1990; Graham Taylor 1990–1993; Terry Venables (coach) 1994–1996; Glenn Hoddle 1996–1999; Kevin Keegan 1999–2000; Sven-Goran Eriksson 2001–2006; Steve McClaren 2006–2007; Fabio Capello 2008–2012; Roy Hodgson 2012–2016; Sam Allardyce 2016 for one match; Gareth Southgate from November 2016.

Northern Ireland
Peter Doherty 1951–1952; Bertie Peacock 1962–1967; Billy Bingham 1967–1971; Terry Neill 1971–1975; Dave Clements (player-manager) 1975–1976; Danny Blanchflower 1976–1979; Billy Bingham 1980–1994; Bryan Hamilton 1994–1998; Lawrie McMenemy 1998–1999; Sammy McIlroy 2000–2003; Lawrie Sanchez 2004–2007; Nigel Worthington 2007–2011; Michael O'Neill 2011–2020; Ian Baraclough from June 2020.

Scotland (since 1967)
Bobby Brown 1967–1971; Tommy Docherty 1971–1972; Willie Ormond 1973–1977; Ally MacLeod 1977–1978; Jock Stein 1978–1985; Alex Ferguson (caretaker) 1985–1986 Andy Roxburgh (coach) 1986–1993; Craig Brown 1993–2001; Berti Vogts 2002–2004; Walter Smith 2004–2007; Alex McLeish 2007; George Burley 2008–2009; Craig Levein 2009–2012; Gordon Strachan 2013–2017; Alex McLeish 2018–19; Steve Clarke from May 2019.

Wales (since 1974)
Mike Smith 1974–1979; Mike England 1980–1988; David Williams (caretaker) 1988; Terry Yorath 1988–1993; John Toshack 1994 for one match; Mike Smith 1994–1995; Bobby Gould 1995–1999; Mark Hughes 1999–2004; John Toshack 2004–2010; Gary Speed 2010–2011; Chris Coleman 2012–2017; Ryan Giggs from January 2018; Robert Page from November 2020 (caretaker).

Republic of Ireland
Liam Tuohy 1971–1972; Johnny Giles 1973–1980 (after period as player-manager); Eoin Hand 1980–1985; Jack Charlton 1986–1996; Mick McCarthy 1996–2002; Brian Kerr 2003–2006; Steve Staunton 2006–2007; Giovanni Trapattoni 2008–2013; Martin O'Neill 2013–2018; Mick McCarthy 2018–2020; Stephen Kenny from April 2020.

BRITISH AND IRISH INTERNATIONAL APPEARANCES 1872–2022

This is a list of full international appearances by Englishmen, Irishmen, Scotsmen and Welshmen in matches against the Home Countries and against foreign nations. It does not include unofficial matches against Commonwealth and Empire countries. The year indicated refers to the player's international debut season; i.e. 2022 is the 2021–22 season. **Bold** type indicates players who have made an international appearance in season 2021–22.

As at July 2022.

ENGLAND

Abbott, W. 1902 (Everton) 1
Abraham, K. O. T. (Tammy) 2018 (Chelsea, Roma) 11
A'Court, A. 1958 (Liverpool) 5
Adams, T. A. 1987 (Arsenal) 66
Adcock, H. 1929 (Leicester C) 5
Agbonlahor, G. 2009 (Aston Villa) 3
Alcock, C. W. 1875 (Wanderers) 1
Alderson, J. T. 1923 (Crystal Palace) 1
Aldridge, A. 1888 (WBA, Walsall Town Swifts) 2
Alexander-Arnold, T. J. 2018 (Liverpool) 17
Allen, A. 1888 (Aston Villa) 1
Allen, A. 1960 (Stoke C) 3
Allen, C. 1984 (QPR, Tottenham H) 5
Allen, H. 1888 (Wolverhampton W) 5
Allen, J. P. 1934 (Portsmouth) 2
Allen, R. 1952 (WBA) 5
Alli, B. J. (Dele) 2016 (Tottenham H) 37
Alsford, W. J. 1935 (Tottenham H) 1
Amos, A. 1885 (Old Carthusians) 2
Anderson, R. D. 1879 (Old Etonians) 1
Anderson, S. 1962 (Sunderland) 2
Anderson, V. A. 1979 (Nottingham F, Arsenal, Manchester U) 30
Anderton, D. R. 1994 (Tottenham H) 30
Angus, J. 1961 (Burnley) 1
Armfield, J. C. 1959 (Blackpool) 43
Armitage, G. H. 1926 (Charlton Ath) 1
Armstrong, D. 1980 (Middlesbrough, Southampton) 3
Armstrong, K. 1955 (Chelsea) 1
Arnold, J. 1933 (Fulham) 1
Arthur, J. W. H. 1885 (Blackburn R) 7
Ashcroft, J. 1906 (Woolwich Arsenal) 3
Ashmore, G. S. 1926 (WBA) 1
Ashton, C. T. 1926 (Corinthians) 1
Ashton, D. 2008 (West Ham U) 1
Ashurst, W. 1923 (Notts Co) 5
Astall, G. 1956 (Birmingham C) 2
Astle, J. 1969 (WBA) 5
Aston, J. 1949 (Manchester U) 17
Athersmith, W. C. 1892 (Aston Villa) 12
Atyeo, P. J. W. 1956 (Bristol C) 6
Austin, S. W. 1926 (Manchester C) 1

Bach, P. 1899 (Sunderland) 1
Bache, J. W. 1903 (Aston Villa) 7
Baddeley, T. 1903 (Wolverhampton W) 5
Bagshaw, J. J. 1920 (Derby Co) 1
Bailey, G. R. 1985 (Manchester U) 2
Bailey, H. P. 1908 (Leicester Fosse) 5
Bailey, M. A. 1964 (Charlton Ath) 2
Bailey, N. C. 1878 (Clapham R) 19
Baily, E. F. 1950 (Tottenham H) 9
Bain, J. 1877 (Oxford University) 1
Baines, L. J. 2010 (Everton) 30
Baker, A. 1928 (Arsenal) 1
Baker, B. H. 1921 (Everton, Chelsea) 2
Baker, J. H. 1960 (Hibernian, Arsenal) 8
Ball, A. J. 1965 (Blackpool, Everton, Arsenal) 72
Ball, J. 1928 (Bury) 1
Ball, M. J. 2001 (Everton) 1
Balmer, W. 1905 (Everton) 1
Bamber, J. 1921 (Liverpool) 1
Bambridge, A. L. 1881 (Swifts) 3
Bambridge, E. C. 1879 (Swifts) 18
Bambridge, E. H. 1876 (Swifts) 1
Bamford, P. J. 2022 (Leeds U) 1
Banks, G. 1963 (Leicester C, Stoke C) 73
Banks, H. E. 1901 (Millwall) 1
Banks, T. 1958 (Bolton W) 6
Bannister, W. 1901 (Burnley, Bolton W) 2
Barclay, R. 1932 (Sheffield U) 3
Bardsley, D. J. 1993 (QPR) 2
Barham, M. 1983 (Norwich C) 2
Barkas, S. 1936 (Manchester C) 5
Barker, J. 1935 (Derby Co) 11
Barker, R. 1872 (Hertfordshire Rangers) 1
Barker, R. R. 1895 (Casuals) 1
Barkley, R. 2013 (Everton, Chelsea) 33
Barlow, R. J. 1955 (WBA) 1
Barmby, N. J. 1995 (Tottenham H, Middlesbrough, Everton, Liverpool) 23
Barnes, H. L. 2021 (Leicester C) 1
Barnes, J. 1983 (Watford, Liverpool) 79
Barnes, P. S. 1978 (Manchester C, WBA, Leeds U) 22
Barnet, H. H. 1882 (Royal Engineers) 1
Barrass, M. W. 1952 (Bolton W) 3
Barrett, A. F. 1930 (Fulham) 1
Barrett, E. D. 1991 (Oldham Ath, Aston Villa) 3
Barrett, J. W. 1929 (West Ham U) 1
Barry, G. 2000 (Aston Villa, Manchester C) 53
Barry, L. 1928 (Leicester C) 5
Barson, F. 1920 (Aston Villa) 1
Barton, J. 1890 (Blackburn R) 1
Barton, J. 2007 (Manchester C) 1
Barton, P. H. 1921 (Birmingham) 7
Barton, W. D. 1995 (Wimbledon, Newcastle U) 3
Bassett, W. I. 1888 (WBA) 16
Bastard, S. R. 1880 (Upton Park) 1
Bastin, C. S. 1932 (Arsenal) 21
Batty, D. 1991 (Leeds U, Blackburn R, Newcastle U, Leeds U) 42
Baugh, R. 1886 (Stafford Road, Wolverhampton W) 2
Bayliss, A. E. J. M. 1891 (WBA) 1
Baynham, R. L. 1956 (Luton T) 3
Beardsley, P. A. 1986 (Newcastle U, Liverpool, Newcastle U) 59
Beasant, D. J. 1990 (Chelsea) 2
Beasley, A. 1939 (Huddersfield T) 1
Beats, W. E. 1901 (Wolverhampton W) 2
Beattie, J. S. 2003 (Southampton) 5
Beattie, T. K. 1975 (Ipswich T) 9
Beckham, D. R. J. 1997 (Manchester U, Real Madrid, LA Galaxy) 115
Becton, F. 1895 (Preston NE, Liverpool) 2
Bedford, H. 1923 (Blackpool) 2
Bell, C. 1968 (Manchester C) 48
Bellingham, J. V. W. 2021 (Borussia Dortmund) 15
Bennett, W. 1901 (Sheffield U) 2
Benson, R. W. 1913 (Sheffield U) 1
Bent, D. A. 2006 (Charlton Ath, Tottenham H, Sunderland, Aston Villa) 13
Bentley, D. M. 2008 (Blackburn R, Tottenham H) 7
Bentley, R. T. F. 1949 (Chelsea) 12
Beresford, J. 1934 (Aston Villa) 1
Berry, A. 1909 (Oxford University) 1
Berry, J. J. 1953 (Manchester U) 4
Bertrand, R. 2013 (Chelsea, Southampton) 19
Bestall, J. G. 1935 (Grimsby T) 1
Betmead, H. A. 1937 (Grimsby T) 1
Betts, M. P. 1877 (Old Harrovians) 1
Betts, W. 1889 (Sheffield W) 1
Beverley, J. 1884 (Blackburn R) 3
Birkett, R. H. 1879 (Clapham R) 1
Birkett, R. J. E. 1936 (Middlesbrough) 1
Birley, F. H. 1874 (Oxford University, Wanderers) 2
Birtles, G. 1980 (Nottingham F) 3
Bishop, S. M. 1927 (Leicester C) 4
Blackburn, F. 1901 (Blackburn R) 3
Blackburn, G. F. 1924 (Aston Villa) 1
Blenkinsop, E. 1928 (Sheffield W) 26
Bliss, H. 1921 (Tottenham H) 1

Blissett, L. L. 1983 (Watford, AC Milan)	14
Blockley, J. P. 1973 (Arsenal)	1
Bloomer, S. 1895 (Derby Co, Middlesbrough)	23
Blunstone, F. 1955 (Chelsea)	5
Bond, R. 1905 (Preston NE, Bradford C)	8
Bonetti, P. P. 1966 (Chelsea)	7
Bonsor, A. G. 1873 (Wanderers)	2
Booth, F. 1905 (Manchester C)	1
Booth, T. 1898 (Blackburn R, Everton)	2
Bothroyd, J. 2011 (Cardiff C)	1
Bould, S. A. 1994 (Arsenal)	2
Bowden, E. R. 1935 (Arsenal)	6
Bowen, J. 2022 (West Ham U)	**4**
Bower, A. G. 1924 (Corinthians)	5
Bowers, J. W. 1934 (Derby Co)	3
Bowles, S. 1974 (QPR)	5
Bowser, S. 1920 (WBA)	1
Bowyer, L. D. 2003 (Leeds U)	1
Boyer, P. J. 1976 (Norwich C)	1
Boyes, W. 1935 (WBA, Everton)	3
Boyle, T. W. 1913 (Burnley)	1
Brabrook, P. 1958 (Chelsea)	3
Bracewell, P. W. 1985 (Everton)	3
Bradford, G. R. W. 1956 (Bristol R)	1
Bradford, J. 1924 (Birmingham)	12
Bradley, W. 1959 (Manchester U)	3
Bradshaw, F. 1908 (Sheffield W)	1
Bradshaw, T. H. 1897 (Liverpool)	1
Bradshaw, W. 1910 (Blackburn R)	4
Brann, G. 1886 (Swifts)	3
Brawn, W. F. 1904 (Aston Villa)	2
Bray, J. 1935 (Manchester C)	6
Brayshaw, E. 1887 (Sheffield W)	1
Bridge W. M. 2002 (Southampton, Chelsea, Manchester C)	36
Bridges, B. J. 1965 (Chelsea)	4
Bridgett, A. 1905 (Sunderland)	11
Brindle, T. 1880 (Darwen)	2
Brittleton, J. T. 1912 (Sheffield W)	5
Britton, C. S. 1935 (Everton)	9
Broadbent, P. F. 1958 (Wolverhampton W)	7
Broadis, I. A. 1952 (Manchester C, Newcastle U)	14
Brockbank, J. 1872 (Cambridge University)	1
Brodie, J. B. 1889 (Wolverhampton W)	3
Bromilow, T. G. 1921 (Liverpool)	5
Bromley-Davenport, W. E. 1884 (Oxford University)	2
Brook, E. F. 1930 (Manchester C)	18
Brooking, T. D. 1974 (West Ham U)	47
Brooks, J. 1957 (Tottenham H)	3
Broome, F. H. 1938 (Aston Villa)	7
Brown, A. 1882 (Aston Villa)	3
Brown, A. 1971 (WBA)	1
Brown, A. S. 1904 (Sheffield U)	2
Brown, G. 1927 (Huddersfield T, Aston Villa)	9
Brown, J. 1881 (Blackburn R)	5
Brown, J. H. 1927 (Sheffield W)	6
Brown, K. 1960 (West Ham U)	1
Brown, W. 1924 (West Ham U)	1
Brown, W. M. 1999 (Manchester U)	23
Bruton, J. 1928 (Burnley)	3
Bryant, W. I. 1925 (Clapton)	1
Buchan, C. M. 1913 (Sunderland)	6
Buchanan, W. S. 1876 (Clapham R)	1
Buckley, F. C. 1914 (Derby Co)	1
Bull, S. G. 1989 (Wolverhampton W)	13
Bullock, F. E. 1921 (Huddersfield T)	1
Bullock, N. 1923 (Bury)	3
Burgess, H. 1904 (Manchester C)	4
Burgess, H. 1931 (Sheffield W)	4
Burnup, C. J. 1896 (Cambridge University)	1
Burrows, H. 1934 (Sheffield W)	3
Burton, F. E. 1889 (Nottingham F)	1
Bury, L. 1877 (Cambridge University, Old Etonians)	2
Butcher, T. 1980 (Ipswich T, Rangers)	77
Butland, J. 2013 (Birmingham C, Stoke C)	9
Butler, J. D. 1925 (Arsenal)	1
Butler, W. 1924 (Bolton W)	1
Butt, N. 1997 (Manchester U, Newcastle U)	39
Byrne, G. 1963 (Liverpool)	2
Byrne, J. J. 1962 (Crystal Palace, West Ham U)	11
Byrne, R. W. 1954 (Manchester U)	33
Cahill, G. J. 2011 (Bolton W, Chelsea)	61
Callaghan, I. R. 1966 (Liverpool)	4
Calvert-Lewin, D. N. 2021 (Everton)	11
Calvey, J. 1902 (Nottingham F)	1
Campbell, A. F. 1929 (Blackburn R, Huddersfield T)	8
Campbell, F. L. 2012 (Sunderland)	1
Campbell, S. 1996 (Tottenham H, Arsenal, Portsmouth)	73
Camsell, G. H. 1929 (Middlesbrough)	9
Capes, A. J. 1903 (Stoke)	1
Carr, J. 1905 (Newcastle U)	2
Carr, J. 1920 (Middlesbrough)	2
Carr, W. H. 1875 (Owlerton, Sheffield)	1
Carragher, J. L. 1999 (Liverpool)	38
Carrick, M. 2001 (West Ham U, Tottenham H, Manchester U)	34
Carroll, A. T. 2011 (Newcastle U, Liverpool)	9
Carson, S. P. 2008 (Liverpool, WBA)	4
Carter, H. S. 1934 (Sunderland, Derby Co)	13
Carter, J. H. 1926 (WBA)	3
Catlin, A. E. 1937 (Sheffield W)	5
Caulker, S. A. 2013 (Tottenham H)	1
Chadwick, A. 1900 (Southampton)	2
Chadwick, E. 1891 (Everton)	7
Chalobah, N. N. 2019 (Watford)	1
Chamberlain, M. 1983 (Stoke C)	8
Chambers, H. 1921 (Liverpool)	8
Chambers, C. 2015 (Arsenal)	3
Channon, M. R. 1973 (Southampton, Manchester C)	46
Chappell, F. 1872 (Oxford University)	1
Charles, G. A. 1991 (Nottingham F)	2
Charlton, J. 1965 (Leeds U)	35
Charlton, R. 1958 (Manchester U)	106
Charnley, R. O. 1963 (Blackpool)	1
Charsley, C. C. 1893 (Small Heath)	1
Chedgzoy, S. 1920 (Everton)	8
Chenery, C. J. 1872 (Crystal Palace)	3
Cherry, T. J. 1976 (Leeds U)	27
Chilton, A. 1951 (Manchester U)	2
Chilwell, B. J. 2019 (Leicester C, Chelsea)	**17**
Chippendale, H. 1894 (Blackburn R)	1
Chivers, M. 1971 (Tottenham H)	24
Christian, E. 1879 (Old Etonians)	1
Clamp, E. 1958 (Wolverhampton W)	4
Clapton, D. R. 1959 (Arsenal)	1
Clare, T. 1889 (Stoke)	4
Clarke, A. J. 1970 (Leeds U)	19
Clarke, H. A. 1954 (Tottenham H)	1
Clay, T. 1920 (Tottenham H)	4
Clayton, R. 1956 (Blackburn R)	35
Clegg, J. C. 1872 (Sheffield W)	1
Clegg, W. E. 1873 (Sheffield W, Sheffield Alb)	2
Clemence, R. N. 1973 (Liverpool, Tottenham H)	61
Clement, D. T. 1976 (QPR)	5
Cleverley, T. W. 2013 (Manchester U)	13
Clough, B. H. 1960 (Middlesbrough)	2
Clough, N. H. 1989 (Nottingham F)	14
Clyne, N. E. 2015 (Southampton, Liverpool)	14
Coady, C. D. 2021 (Wolverhampton W)	**10**
Coates, R. 1970 (Burnley, Tottenham H)	4
Cobbold, W. N. 1883 (Cambridge University, Old Carthusians)	9
Cock, J. G. 1920 (Huddersfield T, Chelsea)	2
Cockburn, H. 1947 (Manchester U)	13
Cohen, G. R. 1964 (Fulham)	37
Colclough, H. 1914 (Crystal Palace)	1
Cole, A. 2001 (Arsenal, Chelsea)	107
Cole, A. A. 1995 (Manchester U)	15
Cole, C. 2009 (West Ham U)	7
Cole, J. J. 2001 (West Ham U, Chelsea)	56
Coleman, E. H. 1921 (Dulwich Hamlet)	1
Coleman, J. 1907 (Woolwich Arsenal)	1
Collymore, S. V. 1995 (Nottingham F, Aston Villa)	3
Common, A. 1904 (Sheffield U, Middlesbrough)	3
Compton, L. H. 1951 (Arsenal)	2
Conlin, J. 1906 (Bradford C)	1
Connelly, J. M. 1960 (Burnley, Manchester U)	20
Cook, L. J. 2018 (Bournemouth)	1
Cook, T. E. R. 1925 (Brighton)	1
Cooper, C. T. 1995 (Nottingham F)	2
Cooper, N. C. 1893 (Cambridge University)	1
Cooper, T. 1928 (Derby Co)	15
Cooper, T. 1969 (Leeds U)	20
Coppell, S. J. 1978 (Manchester U)	42
Copping, W. 1933 (Leeds U, Arsenal, Leeds U)	20
Corbett, B. O. 1901 (Corinthians)	1
Corbett, R. 1903 (Old Malvernians)	1
Corbett, W. S. 1908 (Birmingham)	3
Cork, J. F. P. 2018 (Burnley)	1

Corrigan, J. T. 1976 (Manchester C) 9
Cottee, A. R. 1987 (West Ham U, Everton) 7
Cotterill, G. H. 1891 (Cambridge University, Old Brightonians) 4
Cottle, J. R. 1909 (Bristol C) 1
Cowan, S. 1926 (Manchester C) 3
Cowans, G. S. 1983 (Aston Villa, Bari, Aston Villa) 10
Cowell, A. 1910 (Blackburn R) 1
Cox, J. 1901 (Liverpool) 3
Cox, J. D. 1892 (Derby Co) 1
Crabtree, J. W. 1894 (Burnley, Aston Villa) 14
Crawford, J. F. 1931 (Chelsea) 1
Crawford, R. 1962 (Ipswich T) 2
Crawshaw, T. H. 1895 (Sheffield W) 10
Crayston, W. J. 1936 (Arsenal) 8
Creek, F. N. S. 1923 (Corinthians) 1
Cresswell, A. W. 2017 (West Ham U) 3
Cresswell, W. 1921 (South Shields, Sunderland, Everton) 7
Crompton, R. 1902 (Blackburn R) 41
Crooks, S. D. 1930 (Derby Co) 26
Crouch, P. J. 2005 (Southampton, Liverpool, Portsmouth, Tottenham H) 42
Crowe, C. 1963 (Wolverhampton W) 1
Cuggy, F. 1913 (Sunderland) 2
Cullis, S. 1938 (Wolverhampton W) 12
Cunliffe, A. 1933 (Blackburn R) 2
Cunliffe, D. 1900 (Portsmouth) 1
Cunliffe, J. N. 1936 (Everton) 1
Cunningham, L. 1979 (WBA, Real Madrid) 6
Curle, K. 1992 (Manchester C) 3
Currey, E. S. 1890 (Oxford University) 2
Currie, A. W. 1972 (Sheffield U, Leeds U) 17
Cursham, A. W. 1876 (Notts Co) 6
Cursham, H. A. 1880 (Notts Co) 8

Daft, H. B. 1889 (Notts Co) 5
Daley, A. M. 1992 (Aston Villa) 7
Danks, T. 1885 (Nottingham F) 1
Davenport, P. 1985 (Nottingham F) 1
Davenport, J. K. 1885 (Bolton W) 2
Davies, K. C. 2011 (Bolton W) 1
Davis, G. 1904 (Derby Co) 2
Davis, H. 1903 (Sheffield W) 3
Davison, J. E. 1922 (Sheffield W) 1
Dawson, J. 1922 (Burnley) 2
Dawson, M. R. 2011 (Tottenham H) 4
Day, S. H. 1906 (Old Malvernians) 3
Dean, W. R. 1927 (Everton) 16
Deane, B. C. 1991 (Sheffield U) 3
Deeley, N. V. 1959 (Wolverhampton W) 2
Defoe, J. C. 2004 (Tottenham H, Portsmouth, Tottenham H, Sunderland) 57
Delph, F. 2015 (Aston Villa, Manchester C) 20
Devey, J. H. G. 1892 (Aston Villa) 2
Devonshire, A. 1980 (West Ham U) 8
Dewhurst, F. 1886 (Preston NE) 9
Dewhurst, G. P. 1895 (Liverpool Ramblers) 1
Dickinson, J. W. 1949 (Portsmouth) 48
Dier, E. J. E. 2016 (Tottenham H) 45
Dimmock, J. H. 1921 (Tottenham H) 3
Ditchburn, E. G. 1949 (Tottenham H) 6
Dix, R. W. 1939 (Derby Co) 1
Dixon, J. A. 1885 (Notts Co) 1
Dixon, K. M. 1985 (Chelsea) 8
Dixon, L. M. 1990 (Arsenal) 22
Dobson, A. T. C. 1882 (Notts Co) 4
Dobson, C. F. 1886 (Notts Co) 1
Dobson, J. M. 1974 (Burnley, Everton) 5
Doggart, A. G. 1924 (Corinthians) 1
Dorigo, A. R. 1990 (Chelsea, Leeds U) 15
Dorrell, A. R. 1925 (Aston Villa) 4
Douglas, B. 1958 (Blackburn R) 36
Downing, S. 2005 (Middlesbrough, Aston Villa, Liverpool, West Ham U) 35
Downs, R. W. 1921 (Everton) 1
Doyle, M. 1976 (Manchester C) 5
Drake, E. J. 1935 (Arsenal) 5
Drinkwater, D. N. 2016 (Leicester C) 3
Dublin, D. 1998 (Coventry C, Aston Villa) 4
Ducat, A. 1910 (Woolwich Arsenal, Aston Villa) 6
Dunk, L. C. 2019 (Brighton & HA) 1
Dunn, A. T. B. 1883 (Cambridge University, Old Etonians) 4
Dunn, D. J. I. 2003 (Blackburn R) 1
Duxbury, M. 1984 (Manchester U) 10
Dyer, K. C. 2000 (Newcastle U, West Ham U) 33

Earle, S. G. J. 1924 (Clapton, West Ham U) 2
Eastham, G. 1963 (Arsenal) 19
Eastham, G. R. 1935 (Bolton W) 1
Eckersley, W. 1950 (Blackburn R) 17
Edwards, D. 1955 (Manchester U) 18
Edwards, J. H. 1874 (Shropshire Wanderers) 1
Edwards, W. 1926 (Leeds U) 16
Ehiogu, U. 1996 (Aston Villa, Middlesbrough) 4
Ellerington, W. 1949 (Southampton) 2
Elliott, G. W. 1913 (Middlesbrough) 3
Elliott, W. H. 1952 (Burnley) 5
Evans, R. E. 1911 (Sheffield U) 4
Ewer, F. H. 1924 (Casuals) 2

Fairclough, P. 1878 (Old Foresters) 1
Fairhurst, D. 1934 (Newcastle U) 1
Fantham, J. 1962 (Sheffield W) 1
Fashanu, J. 1989 (Wimbledon) 2
Felton, W. 1925 (Sheffield W) 1
Fenton, M. 1938 (Middlesbrough) 1
Fenwick, T. W. 1984 (QPR, Tottenham H) 20
Ferdinand, L. 1993 (QPR, Newcastle U, Tottenham H) 17
Ferdinand, R. G. 1998 (West Ham U, Leeds U, Manchester U) 81
Field, E. 1876 (Clapham R) 2
Finney, T. 1947 (Preston NE) 76
Flanagan, J. P. 2014 (Liverpool) 1
Fleming, H. J. 1909 (Swindon T) 11
Fletcher, A. 1889 (Wolverhampton W) 2
Flowers, R. 1955 (Wolverhampton W) 49
Flowers, T. D. 1993 (Southampton, Blackburn R) 11
Foden, P. W. 2021 (Manchester C) 16
Forman, Frank 1898 (Nottingham F 9
Forman, F. R. 1899 (Nottingham F) 3
Forrest, J. H. 1884 (Blackburn R) 11
Forster, F. G. 2013 (Celtic, Southampton) 6
Fort, J. 1921 (Millwall) 1
Foster, B. 2007 (Manchester U, Birmingham C, WBA) 8
Foster, R. E. 1900 (Oxford University, Corinthians) 5
Foster, S. 1982 (Brighton & HA) 3
Foulke, W. J. 1897 (Sheffield U) 1
Foulkes, W. A. 1955 (Manchester U) 1
Fowler, R. B. 1996 (Liverpool, Leeds U) 26
Fox, F. S. 1925 (Millwall) 1
Francis, G. C. J. 1975 (QPR) 12
Francis, T. 1977 (Birmingham C, Nottingham F, Manchester C, Sampdoria) 52
Franklin, C. F. 1947 (Stoke C) 27
Freeman, B. C. 1909 (Everton, Burnley) 5
Froggatt, J. 1950 (Portsmouth) 13
Froggatt, R. 1953 (Sheffield W) 4
Fry, C. B. 1901 (Corinthians) 1
Furness, W. I. 1933 (Leeds U) 1

Gallagher, C. J. 2022 (Chelsea) 4
Galley, T. 1937 (Wolverhampton W) 2
Gardner, A. 2004 (Tottenham H) 1
Gardner, T. 1934 (Aston Villa) 2
Garfield, B. 1898 (WBA) 1
Garraty, W. 1903 (Aston Villa) 1
Garrett, T. 1952 (Blackpool) 3
Gascoigne, P. J. 1989 (Tottenham H, Lazio, Rangers, Middlesbrough) 57
Gates, E. 1981 (Ipswich T) 2
Gay, L. H. 1893 (Cambridge University, Old Brightonians) 3
Geary, F. 1890 (Everton) 2
Geaves, R. L. 1875 (Clapham R) 1
Gee, C. W. 1932 (Everton) 3
Geldard, A. 1933 (Everton) 4
George, C. 1977 (Derby Co) 1
George, W. 1902 (Aston Villa) 3
Gerrard, S. G. 2000 (Liverpool) 114
Gibbins, W. V. T. 1924 (Clapton) 2
Gibbs, K. J. R. 2011 (Arsenal) 10
Gidman, J. 1977 (Aston Villa) 1
Gillard, I. T. 1975 (QPR) 3
Gilliat, W. E. 1893 (Old Carthusians) 1
Godfrey, B. M. 2021 (Everton) 2
Goddard, P. 1982 (West Ham U) 1
Gomez, J. D. 2018 (Liverpool) 11
Goodall, F. R. 1926 (Huddersfield T) 25

Goodall, J. 1888 (Preston NE, Derby Co) 14
Goodhart, H. C. 1883 (Old Etonians) 3
Goodwyn, A. G. 1873 (Royal Engineers) 1
Goodyer, A. C. 1879 (Nottingham F) 1
Gosling, R. C. 1892 (Old Etonians) 5
Gosnell, A. A. 1906 (Newcastle U) 1
Gough, H. C. 1921 (Sheffield U) 1
Goulden, L. A. 1937 (West Ham U) 14
Graham, L. 1925 (Millwall) 2
Graham, T. 1931 (Nottingham F) 2
Grainger, C. 1956 (Sheffield U, Sunderland) 7
Gray, A. A. 1992 (Crystal Palace) 1
Gray, M. 1999 (Sunderland) 3
Grealish, J. P. 2021 (Aston Villa, Manchester C) 23
Greaves, J. 1959 (Chelsea, Tottenham H) 57
Green, F. T. 1876 (Wanderers) 1
Green, G. H. 1925 (Sheffield U) 8
Green, R. P. 2005 (Norwich C, West Ham U) 12
Greenhalgh, E. H. 1872 (Notts Co) 2
Greenhoff, B. 1976 (Manchester U, Leeds U) 18
Greenwood, D. H. 1882 (Blackburn R) 2
Greenwood, M. W. J. 2021 (Manchester U) 1
Gregory, J. 1983 (QPR) 6
Grimsdell, A. 1920 (Tottenham H) 6
Grosvenor, A. T. 1934 (Birmingham) 3
Guehi, A, K. M-I. 2022 (Crystal Palace) 3
Gunn, W. 1884 (Notts Co) 2
Guppy, S. 2000 (Leicester C) 1
Gurney, R. 1935 (Sunderland) 1

Hacking, J. 1929 (Oldham Ath) 3
Hadley, H. 1903 (WBA) 1
Hagan, J. 1949 (Sheffield U) 1
Haines, J. T. W. 1949 (WBA) 1
Hall, A. E. 1910 (Aston Villa) 1
Hall, G. W. 1934 (Tottenham H) 10
Hall, J. 1956 (Birmingham C) 17
Halse, H. J. 1909 (Manchester U) 1
Hammond, H. E. D. 1889 (Oxford University) 1
Hampson, J. 1931 (Blackpool) 3
Hampton, H. 1913 (Aston Villa) 4
Hancocks, J. 1949 (Wolverhampton W) 3
Hapgood, E. 1933 (Arsenal) 30
Hardinge, H. T. W. 1910 (Sheffield U) 1
Hardman, H. P. 1905 (Everton) 4
Hardwick, G. F. M. 1947 (Middlesbrough) 13
Hardy, H. 1925 (Stockport Co) 1
Hardy, S. 1907 (Liverpool, Aston Villa) 21
Harford, M. G. 1988 (Luton T) 2
Hargreaves, F. W. 1880 (Blackburn R) 3
Hargreaves, J. 1881 (Blackburn R) 2
Hargreaves, O. 2002 (Bayern Munich, Manchester U) 42
Harper, E. C. 1926 (Blackburn R) 1
Harris, G. 1966 (Burnley) 1
Harris, P. P. 1950 (Portsmouth) 2
Harris, S. S. 1904 (Cambridge University, Old Westminsters) 6
Harrison, A. H. 1893 (Old Westminsters) 2
Harrison, G. 1921 (Everton) 2
Harrow, J. H. 1923 (Chelsea) 2
Hart, C. J. J. 2008 (Manchester C) 75
Hart, E. 1929 (Leeds U) 8
Hartley, F. 1923 (Oxford C) 1
Harvey, A. 1881 (Wednesbury Strollers) 1
Harvey, J. C. 1971 (Everton) 1
Hassall, H. W. 1951 (Huddersfield T, Bolton W) 5
Hateley, M. 1984 (Portsmouth, AC Milan, Monaco, Rangers) 32
Hawkes, R. M. 1907 (Luton T) 5
Haworth, G. 1887 (Accrington) 5
Hawtrey, J. P. 1881 (Old Etonians) 2
Haygarth, E. B. 1875 (Swifts) 1
Haynes, J. N. 1955 (Fulham) 56
Healless, H. 1925 (Blackburn R) 2
Heaton, T. 2016 (Burnley) 3
Hector, K. J. 1974 (Derby Co) 2
Hedley, G. A. 1901 (Sheffield U) 1
Hegan, K. E. 1923 (Corinthians) 4
Hellawell, M. S. 1963 (Birmingham C) 2
Henderson D. B. 2021 (Manchester U) 1
Henderson, J. B. 2011 (Sunderland, Liverpool) 69
Hendrie, L. A. 1999 (Aston Villa) 1
Henfrey, A. G. 1891 (Cambridge University, Corinthians) 5
Henry, R. P. 1963 (Tottenham H) 1
Heron, F. 1876 (Wanderers) 1
Heron, G. H. H. 1873 (Uxbridge, Wanderers) 5
Heskey, E. W. I. 1999 (Leicester C, Liverpool, Birmingham C, Wigan Ath, Aston Villa) 62
Hibbert, W. 1910 (Bury) 1
Hibbs, H. E. 1930 (Birmingham) 25
Hill, F. 1963 (Bolton W) 2
Hill, G. A. 1976 (Manchester U) 6
Hill, J. H. 1925 (Burnley, Newcastle U) 11
Hill, R. 1983 (Luton T) 3
Hill, R. H. 1926 (Millwall) 1
Hillman, J. 1899 (Burnley) 1
Hills, A. F. 1879 (Old Harrovians) 1
Hilsdon, G. R. 1907 (Chelsea) 8
Hinchcliffe, A. G. 1997 (Everton, Sheffield W) 7
Hine, E. W. 1929 (Leicester C) 6
Hinton, A. T. 1963 (Wolverhampton W, Nottingham F) 3
Hirst, D. E. 1991 (Sheffield W) 3
Hitchens, G. A. 1961 (Aston Villa, Internazionale) 7
Hobbis, H. H. F. 1936 (Charlton Ath) 2
Hoddle, G. 1980 (Tottenham H, Monaco) 53
Hodge, S. B. 1986 (Aston Villa, Tottenham H, Nottingham F) 24
Hodgetts, D. 1888 (Aston Villa) 6
Hodgkinson, A. 1957 (Sheffield U) 5
Hodgson, G. 1931 (Liverpool) 3
Hodkinson, J. 1913 (Blackburn R) 3
Hogg, W. 1902 (Sunderland) 3
Holdcroft, G. H. 1937 (Preston NE) 2
Holden, A. D. 1959 (Bolton W) 5
Holden, G. H. 1881 (Wednesbury OA) 4
Holden-White, C. 1888 (Corinthians) 2
Holford, T. 1903 (Stoke) 1
Holley, G. H. 1909 (Sunderland) 10
Holliday, E. 1960 (Middlesbrough) 3
Hollins, J. W. 1967 (Chelsea) 1
Holmes, R. 1888 (Preston NE) 7
Holt, J. 1890 (Everton, Reading) 10
Hopkinson, E. 1958 (Bolton W) 14
Hossack, A. H. 1892 (Corinthians) 2
Houghton, W. E. 1931 (Aston Villa) 7
Houlker, A. E. 1902 (Blackburn R, Portsmouth, Southampton) 5
Howarth, R. H. 1887 (Preston NE, Everton) 5
Howe, D. 1958 (WBA) 23
Howe, J. R. 1948 (Derby Co) 3
Howell, L. S. 1873 (Wanderers) 1
Howell, R. 1895 (Sheffield U, Liverpool) 2
Howey, S. N. 1995 (Newcastle U) 4
Huddlestone, T. A. 2010 (Tottenham H) 4
Hudson, A. A. 1975 (Stoke C) 2
Hudson, J. 1883 (Sheffield) 1
Hudson-Odoi C. J. 2019 (Chelsea) 3
Hudspeth, F. C. 1926 (Newcastle U) 1
Hufton, A. E. 1924 (West Ham U) 6
Hughes, E. W. 1970 (Liverpool, Wolverhampton W) 62
Hughes, L. 1950 (Liverpool) 3
Hulme, J. H. A. 1927 (Arsenal) 9
Humphreys, P. 1903 (Notts Co) 1
Hunt, G. S. 1933 (Tottenham H) 3
Hunt, Rev. K. R. G. 1911 (Leyton) 2
Hunt, R. 1962 (Liverpool) 34
Hunt, S. 1984 (WBA) 2
Hunter, J. 1878 (Sheffield Heeley) 7
Hunter, N. 1966 (Leeds U) 28
Hurst, G. C. 1966 (West Ham U) 49

Ince, P. E. C. 1993 (Manchester U, Internazionale, Liverpool, Middlesbrough) 53
Ings, D. 2016 (Liverpool, Southampton) 3
Iremonger, J. 1901 (Nottingham F) 2

Jack, D. N. B. 1924 (Bolton W, Arsenal) 9
Jackson, E. 1891 (Oxford University) 1
Jagielka, P. N. 2008 (Everton) 40
James. D. B. 1997 (Liverpool, Aston Villa, West Ham U, Manchester C, Portsmouth) 53
James, R. 2021 (Chelsea) 13
Jarrett, B. G. 1876 (Cambridge University) 3
Jarvis, M. T. 2011 (Wolverhampton W) 1
Jefferis, F. 1912 (Everton) 2
Jeffers, F. 2003 (Arsenal) 1
Jenas, J. A. 2003 (Newcastle U, Tottenham H) 21
Jenkinson, C. D. 2013 (Arsenal) 1
Jezzard, B. A. G. 1954 (Fulham) 2

Johnson, A. 2005 (Crystal Palace, Everton) 8
Johnson, A. 2010 (Manchester C) 12
Johnson, D. E. 1975 (Ipswich T, Liverpool) 8
Johnson, E. 1880 (Saltley College, Stoke) 2
Johnson, G. M. C. 2004 (Chelsea, Portsmouth, Liverpool) 54
Johnson, J. A. 1937 (Stoke C) 5
Johnson, S. A. M. 2001 (Derby Co) 1
Johnson, T. C. F. 1926 (Manchester C, Everton) 5
Johnson, W. H. 1900 (Sheffield U) 6
Johnston, H. 1947 (Blackpool) 10
Johnstone, S. L. 2021 (WBA) 3
Jones, A. 1882 (Walsall Swifts, Great Lever) 3
Jones, H. 1923 (Nottingham F) 1
Jones, H. 1927 (Blackburn R) 6
Jones, M. D. 1965 (Sheffield U, Leeds U) 3
Jones, P. A. 2012 (Manchester U) 27
Jones, R. 1992 (Liverpool) 8
Jones, W. 1901 (Bristol C) 1
Jones, W. H. 1950 (Liverpool) 2
Joy, B. 1936 (Casuals) 1
Justin, J. M. 2022 (Leicester C) 1

Kail, E. I. L. 1929 (Dulwich Hamlet) 3
Kane, H. E. 2015 (Tottenham H) 73
Kay, A. H. 1963 (Everton) 1
Kean, F. W. 1923 (Sheffield W, Bolton W) 9
Keane, M. V. 2017 (Burnley, Everton) 12
Keegan, J. K. 1973 (Liverpool, Hamburg, Southampton) 63
Keen, E. R. L. 1933 (Derby Co) 4
Kelly, M. R. 2012 (Liverpool) 1
Kelly, R. 1920 (Burnley, Sunderland, Huddersfield T) 14
Kennedy, A. 1984 (Liverpool) 2
Kennedy, R. 1976 (Liverpool) 17
Kenyon-Slaney, W. S. 1873 (Wanderers) 1
Keown, M. R. 1992 (Everton, Arsenal) 43
Kevan, D. T. 1957 (WBA) 14
Kidd, B. 1970 (Manchester U) 2
King, L. B. 2002 (Tottenham H) 21
King, R. S. 1882 (Oxford University) 1
Kingsford, R. K. 1874 (Wanderers) 1
Kingsley, M. 1901 (Newcastle U) 1
Kinsey, G. 1892 (Wolverhampton W, Derby Co) 4
Kirchen, A. J. 1937 (Arsenal) 3
Kirkland, C. E. 2007 (Liverpool) 1
Kirton, W. J. 1922 (Aston Villa) 1
Knight, A. E. 1920 (Portsmouth) 1
Knight, Z. 2005 (Fulham) 2
Knowles, C. 1968 (Tottenham H) 4
Konchesky, P. M. 2003 (Charlton Ath, West Ham U) 2

Labone, B. L. 1963 (Everton) 26
Lallana, A. D. 2013 (Southampton, Liverpool) 34
Lambert, R. L. 2013 (Southampton, Liverpool) 11
Lampard, F. J. 2000 (West Ham U, Chelsea) 106
Lampard, F. R. G. 1973 (West Ham U) 2
Langley, E. J. 1958 (Fulham) 3
Langton, R. 1947 (Blackburn R, Preston NE, Bolton W) 11
Latchford, R. D. 1978 (Everton) 12
Latheron, E. G. 1913 (Blackburn R) 2
Lawler, C. 1971 (Liverpool) 4
Lawton, T. 1939 (Everton, Chelsea, Notts Co) 23
Leach, T. 1931 (Sheffield W) 2
Leake, A. 1904 (Aston Villa) 5
Lee, E. A. 1904 (Southampton) 1
Lee, F. H. 1969 (Manchester C) 27
Lee, J. 1951 (Derby Co) 1
Lee, R. M. 1995 (Newcastle U) 21
Lee, S. 1983 (Liverpool) 14
Leighton, J. E. 1886 (Nottingham F) 1
Lennon, A. J. 2006 (Tottenham H) 21
Lescott, J. P. 2008 (Everton, Manchester C) 26
Le Saux, G. P. 1994 (Blackburn R, Chelsea) 36
Le Tissier, M. P. 1994 (Southampton) 8
Lilley, H. E. 1892 (Sheffield U) 1
Linacre, H. J. 1905 (Nottingham F) 2
Lindley, T. 1886 (Cambridge University, Nottingham F) 13
Lindsay, A. 1974 (Liverpool) 4
Lindsay, W. 1877 (Wanderers) 1
Lineker, G. 1984 (Leicester C, Everton, Barcelona, Tottenham H) 80
Lingard, J. E. 2017 (Manchester U) 32
Lintott, E. H. 1908 (QPR, Bradford C) 7
Lipsham, H. B. 1902 (Sheffield U) 1
Little, B. 1975 (Aston Villa) 1
Livermore, J. C. 2013 (Tottenham H, WBA) 7
Lloyd, L. V. 1971 (Liverpool, Nottingham F) 4
Lockett, A. 1903 (Stoke) 1
Lodge, L. V. 1894 (Cambridge University, Corinthians) 5
Lofthouse, J. M. 1885 (Blackburn R, Accrington, Blackburn R) 7
Lofthouse, N. 1951 (Bolton W) 33
Loftus-Cheek, R. I. 2018 (Chelsea) 10
Longworth, E. 1920 (Liverpool) 5
Lowder, A. 1889 (Wolverhampton W) 1
Lowe, E. 1947 (Aston Villa) 3
Lucas, T. 1922 (Liverpool) 3
Luntley, E. 1880 (Nottingham F) 2
Lyttelton, Hon. A. 1877 (Cambridge University) 1
Lyttelton, Hon. E. 1878 (Cambridge University) 1

Mabbutt, G. 1983 (Tottenham H) 16
Macaulay, R. H. 1881 (Cambridge University) 1
Macrae, S. 1883 (Notts Co) 5
Maddison, F. B. 1872 (Oxford University) 1
Maddison, J. D. 2020 (Leicester C) 1
Madeley, P. E. 1971 (Leeds U) 24
Magee, T. P. 1923 (WBA) 5
Maguire, J. H. 2018 (Leicester C, Manchester U) 46
Maitland Niles, A. C. 2021 (Arsenal) 5
Makepeace, H. 1906 (Everton) 4
Male, C. G. 1935 (Arsenal) 19
Mannion, W. J. 1947 (Middlesbrough) 26
Mariner, P. 1977 (Ipswich T, Arsenal) 35
Marsden, J. T. 1891 (Darwen) 1
Marsden, W. 1930 (Sheffield W) 3
Marsh, R. W. 1972 (QPR, Manchester C) 9
Marshall, T. 1880 (Darwen) 2
Martin, A. 1981 (West Ham U) 17
Martin, H. 1914 (Sunderland) 1
Martyn, A. N. 1992 (Crystal Palace, Leeds U) 23
Marwood, B. 1989 (Arsenal) 1
Maskrey, H. M. 1908 (Derby Co) 1
Mason, C. 1887 (Wolverhampton W) 3
Mason, R. G. 2015 (Tottenham H) 1
Matthews, R. D. 1956 (Coventry C) 5
Matthews, S. 1935 (Stoke C, Blackpool) 54
Matthews, V. 1928 (Sheffield U) 2
Maynard, W. J. 1872 (1st Surrey Rifles) 2
McCall, J. 1913 (Preston NE) 5
McCann, G. P. 2001 (Sunderland) 1
McCarthy, A. S. 2019 (Southampton) 1
McDermott, T. 1978 (Liverpool) 25
McDonald, C. A. 1958 (Burnley) 8
Macdonald, M. 1972 (Newcastle U) 14
McFarland, R. L. 1971 (Derby Co) 28
McGarry, W. H. 1954 (Huddersfield T) 4
McGuinness, W. 1959 (Manchester U) 2
McInroy, A. 1927 (Sunderland) 1
McMahon, S. 1988 (Liverpool) 17
McManaman, S. 1995 (Liverpool, Real Madrid) 37
McNab, R. 1969 (Arsenal) 4
McNeal, R. 1914 (WBA) 2
McNeil, M. 1961 (Middlesbrough) 9
Meadows, J. 1955 (Manchester C) 1
Medley, L. D. 1951 (Tottenham H) 6
Meehan, T. 1924 (Chelsea) 1
Melia, J. 1963 (Liverpool) 2
Mercer, D. W. 1923 (Sheffield U) 2
Mercer, J. 1939 (Everton) 5
Merrick, G. H. 1952 (Birmingham C) 23
Merson, P. C. 1992 (Arsenal, Middlesbrough, Aston Villa) 21
Metcalfe, V. 1951 (Huddersfield T) 2
Mew, J. W. 1921 (Manchester U) 1
Middleditch, B. 1897 (Corinthians) 1
Milburn, J. E. T. 1949 (Newcastle U) 13
Miller, B. G. 1961 (Burnley) 1
Miller, H. S. 1923 (Charlton Ath) 1
Mills, D. J. 2001 (Leeds U) 19
Mills, G. R. 1938 (Chelsea) 3
Mills, M. D. 1973 (Ipswich T) 42
Milne, G. 1963 (Liverpool) 14
Milner, J. P. 2010 (Aston Villa, Manchester C, Liverpool) 61
Milton, C. A. 1952 (Arsenal) 1
Milward, A. 1891 (Everton) 4

Mings, T. D. 2020 (Aston Villa) 17
Mitchell, C. 1880 (Upton Park) 5
Mitchell, J. F. 1925 (Manchester C) 1
Mitchell, T. K. 2022 (Crystal Palace) 2
Moffat, H. 1913 (Oldham Ath) 1
Molyneux, G. 1902 (Southampton) 4
Moon, W. R. 1888 (Old Westminsters) 7
Moore, H. T. 1883 (Notts Co) 2
Moore, J. 1923 (Derby Co) 1
Moore, R. F. 1962 (West Ham U) 108
Moore, W. G. B. 1923 (West Ham U) 1
Mordue, J. 1912 (Sunderland) 2
Morice, C. J. 1872 (Barnes) 1
Morley, A. 1982 (Aston Villa) 6
Morley, H. 1910 (Notts Co) 1
Morren, T. 1898 (Sheffield U) 1
Morris, F. 1920 (WBA) 2
Morris, J. 1949 (Derby Co) 3
Morris, W. W. 1939 (Wolverhampton W) 3
Morse, H. 1879 (Notts Co) 1
Mort, T. 1924 (Aston Villa) 3
Morten, A. 1873 (Crystal Palace) 1
Mortensen, S. H. 1947 (Blackpool) 25
Morton, J. R. 1938 (West Ham U) 1
Mosforth, W. 1877 (Sheffield W, Sheffield Alb, Sheffield W) 9
Moss, F. 1922 (Aston Villa) 5
Moss, F. 1934 (Arsenal) 4
Mosscrop, E. 1914 (Burnley) 2
Mount, M. T. 2020 (Chelsea) 31
Mozley, B. 1950 (Derby Co) 3
Mullen, J. 1947 (Wolverhampton W) 12
Mullery, A. P. 1965 (Tottenham H) 35
Murphy, D. B. 2002 (Liverpool) 9

Neal, P. G. 1976 (Liverpool) 50
Needham, E. 1894 (Sheffield U) 16
Neville, G. A. 1995 (Manchester U) 85
Neville, P. J. 1996 (Manchester U, Everton) 59
Newton, K. R. 1966 (Blackburn R, Everton) 27
Nicholls, J. 1954 (WBA) 2
Nicholson, W. E. 1951 (Tottenham H) 1
Nish, D. J. 1973 (Derby Co) 5
Norman, M. 1962 (Tottenham H) 23
Nugent, D. J. 2007 (Preston NE) 1
Nuttall, H. 1928 (Bolton W) 3

Oakley, W. J. 1895 (Oxford University, Corinthians) 16
O'Dowd, J. P. 1932 (Chelsea) 3
O'Grady, M. 1963 (Huddersfield T, Leeds U) 2
Ogilvie, R. A. M. M. 1874 (Clapham R) 1
Oliver, L. F. 1929 (Fulham) 1
Olney, B. A. 1928 (Aston Villa) 2
Osborne, F. R. 1923 (Fulham, Tottenham H) 4
Osborne, R. 1928 (Leicester C) 1
Osgood, P. L. 1970 (Chelsea) 4
Osman, L. 2013 (Everton) 2
Osman, R. 1980 (Ipswich T) 11
Ottaway, C. J. 1872 (Oxford University) 2
Owen, J. R. B. 1874 (Sheffield) 1
Owen, M. J. 1998 (Liverpool, Real Madrid, Newcastle U) 89
Owen, S. W. 1954 (Luton T) 3
Oxlade-Chamberlain, A. M. D. 2012 (Arsenal, Liverpool) 35

Page, L. A. 1927 (Burnley) 7
Paine, T. L. 1963 (Southampton) 19
Pallister, G. A. 1988 (Middlesbrough, Manchester U) 22
Palmer, C. L. 1992 (Sheffield W) 18
Pantling, H. H. 1924 (Sheffield U) 1
Paravicini, P. J. de 1883 (Cambridge University) 3
Parker, P. A. 1989 (QPR, Manchester U) 19
Parker, S. M. 2004 (Charlton Ath, Chelsea, Newcastle U, West Ham U, Tottenham H) 18
Parker, T. R. 1925 (Southampton) 1
Parkes, P. B. 1974 (QPR) 1
Parkinson, J. 1910 (Liverpool) 2
Parlour, R. 1999 (Arsenal) 10
Parr, P. C. 1882 (Oxford University) 1
Parry, E. H. 1879 (Old Carthusians) 3
Parry, R. A. 1960 (Bolton W) 2
Patchitt, B. C. A. 1923 (Corinthians) 2
Pawson, F. W. 1883 (Cambridge University, Swifts) 2
Payne, J. 1937 (Luton T) 1
Peacock, A. 1962 (Middlesbrough, Leeds U) 6
Peacock, J. 1929 (Middlesbrough) 3
Pearce, S. 1987 (Nottingham F, West Ham U) 78
Pearson, H. F. 1932 (WBA) 1
Pearson, J. H. 1892 (Crewe Alex) 1
Pearson, J. S. 1976 (Manchester U) 15
Pearson, S. C. 1948 (Manchester U) 8
Pease, W. H. 1927 (Middlesbrough) 1
Pegg, D. 1957 (Manchester U) 1
Pejic, M. 1974 (Stoke C) 4
Pelly, F. R. 1893 (Old Foresters) 3
Pennington, J. 1907 (WBA) 25
Pentland, F. B. 1909 (Middlesbrough) 5
Perry, C. 1890 (WBA) 3
Perry, T. 1898 (WBA) 1
Perry, W. 1956 (Blackpool) 3
Perryman, S. 1982 (Tottenham H) 1
Peters, M. 1966 (West Ham U, Tottenham H) 67
Phelan, M. C. 1990 (Manchester U) 1
Phillips, K. 1999 (Sunderland) 8
Phillips, K. M. 2021 (Leeds U) 23
Phillips, L. H. 1952 (Portsmouth) 3
Pickering, F. 1964 (Everton) 3
Pickering, J. 1933 (Sheffield U) 1
Pickering, N. 1983 (Sunderland) 1
Pickford, J. L. 2018 (Everton) 45
Pike, T. M. 1886 (Cambridge University) 1
Pilkington, B. 1955 (Burnley) 1
Plant, J. 1900 (Bury) 1
Platt, D. 1990 (Aston Villa, Bari, Juventus, Sampdoria, Arsenal) 62
Plum, S. L. 1923 (Charlton Ath) 1
Pointer, R. 1962 (Burnley) 3
Pope, N. D. 2018 (Burnley) 8
Porteous, T. S. 1891 (Sunderland) 1
Powell, C. G. 2001 (Charlton Ath) 5
Priest, A. E. 1900 (Sheffield U) 1
Prinsep, J. F. M. 1879 (Clapham R) 1
Puddefoot, S. C. 1926 (Blackburn R) 2
Pye, J. 1950 (Wolverhampton W) 1
Pym, R. H. 1925 (Bolton W) 3

Quantrill, A. 1920 (Derby Co) 4
Quixall, A. 1954 (Sheffield W) 5

Radford, J. 1969 (Arsenal) 2
Raikes, G. B. 1895 (Oxford University) 4
Ramsdale, A. C. 2022 (Arsenal) 3
Ramsey, A. E. 1949 (Southampton, Tottenham H) 32
Rashford, M. 2016 (Manchester U) 46
Rawlings, A. 1921 (Preston NE) 1
Rawlings, W. E. 1922 (Southampton) 2
Rawlinson, J. F. P. 1882 (Cambridge University) 1
Rawson, H. E. 1875 (Royal Engineers) 1
Rawson, W. S. 1875 (Oxford University) 2
Read, A. 1921 (Tufnell Park) 1
Reader, J. 1894 (WBA) 1
Reaney, P. 1969 (Leeds U) 3
Redknapp, J. F. 1996 (Liverpool) 17
Redmond, N. D. J. 2017 (Southampton) 1
Reeves, K. P. 1980 (Norwich C, Manchester C) 2
Regis, C. 1982 (WBA, Coventry C) 5
Reid, P. 1985 (Everton) 13
Revie, D. G. 1955 (Manchester C) 6
Reynolds, J. 1892 (WBA, Aston Villa) 8
Rice, D. 2019 (West Ham U) 32
Richards, C. H. 1898 (Nottingham F) 1
Richards, G. H. 1909 (Derby Co) 1
Richards, J. P. 1973 (Wolverhampton W) 1
Richards, M. 2007 (Manchester C) 13
Richardson, J. R. 1933 (Newcastle U) 2
Richardson, K. 1994 (Aston Villa) 1
Richardson, K. E. 2005 (Manchester U) 8
Richardson, W. G. 1935 (WBA) 1
Rickaby, S. 1954 (WBA) 1
Ricketts, M. B. 2002 (Bolton W) 1
Rigby, A. 1927 (Blackburn R) 5
Rimmer, E. J. 1930 (Sheffield W) 4
Rimmer, J. J. 1976 (Arsenal) 1
Ripley, S. E. 1994 (Blackburn R) 2
Rix, G. 1981 (Arsenal) 17
Robb, G. 1954 (Tottenham H) 1
Roberts, C. 1905 (Manchester U) 3
Roberts, F. 1925 (Manchester C) 4
Roberts, G. 1983 (Tottenham H) 6

Roberts, H. 1931 (Arsenal) 1
Roberts, H. 1931 (Millwall) 1
Roberts, R. 1887 (WBA) 3
Roberts, W. T. 1924 (Preston NE) 2
Robinson, J. 1937 (Sheffield W) 4
Robinson, J. W. 1897 (Derby Co, New Brighton Tower, Southampton) 11
Robinson, P. W. 2003 (Leeds U, Tottenham H, Blackburn R) 41
Robson, B. 1980 (WBA, Manchester U) 90
Robson, R. 1958 (WBA) 20
Rocastle, D. 1989 (Arsenal) 14
Rodriguez, J. E. 2013 (Southampton) 1
Rodwell, J. 2012 (Everton) 3
Rooney, W. M. 2003 (Everton, Manchester U, D.C. United) 120
Rose, D. L. 2016 (Tottenham H) 29
Rose, W. C. 1884 (Swifts, Preston NE, Wolverhampton W) 5
Rostron, T. 1881 (Darwen) 2
Rowe, A. 1934 (Tottenham H) 1
Rowley, J. F. 1949 (Manchester U) 6
Rowley, W. 1889 (Stoke) 2
Royle, J. 1971 (Everton, Manchester C) 6
Ruddlesdin, H. 1904 (Sheffield W) 3
Ruddock, N. 1995 (Liverpool) 1
Ruddy, J. T. G. 2013 (Norwich C) 1
Ruffell, J. W. 1926 (West Ham U) 6
Russell, B. B. 1883 (Royal Engineers) 1
Rutherford, J. 1904 (Newcastle U) 11

Sadler, D. 1968 (Manchester U) 4
Sagar, C. 1900 (Bury) 2
Sagar, E. 1936 (Everton) 4
Saka, B. A. T. M. 2021 (Arsenal) 18
Salako, J. A. 1991 (Crystal Palace) 5
Sancho, J. M. 2019 (Borussia Dortmund, Manchester U) 23
Sandford, E. A. 1933 (WBA) 1
Sandilands, R. R. 1892 (Old Westminsters) 5
Sands, J. 1880 (Nottingham F) 1
Sansom, K. G. 1979 (Crystal Palace, Arsenal) 86
Saunders, F. E. 1888 (Swifts) 1
Savage, A. H. 1876 (Crystal Palace) 1
Sayer, J. 1887 (Stoke) 1
Scales, J. R. 1995 (Liverpool) 3
Scattergood, E. 1913 (Derby Co) 1
Schofield, J. 1892 (Stoke) 3
Scholes, P. 1997 (Manchester U) 66
Scott, L. 1947 (Arsenal) 17
Scott, W. R. 1937 (Brentford) 1
Seaman, D. A. 1989 (QPR, Arsenal) 75
Seddon, J. 1923 (Bolton W) 6
Seed, J. M. 1921 (Tottenham H) 5
Settle, J. 1899 (Bury, Everton) 6
Sewell, J. 1952 (Sheffield W) 6
Sewell, W. R. 1924 (Blackburn R) 1
Shackleton, L. F. 1949 (Sunderland) 5
Sharp, J. 1903 (Everton) 2
Sharpe, L. S. 1991 (Manchester U) 8
Shaw, G. E. 1932 (WBA) 1
Shaw, G. L. 1959 (Sheffield U) 5
Shaw, L. P. H. 2014 (Southampton, Manchester U) 21
Shawcross, R. J. 2013 (Stoke C) 1
Shea, D. 1914 (Blackburn R) 2
Shearer, A. 1992 (Southampton, Blackburn R, Newcastle U) 63
Shellito, K. J. 1963 (Chelsea) 1
Shelton A. 1889 (Notts Co) 6
Shelton, C. 1888 (Notts Rangers) 1
Shelvey, J. 2013 (Liverpool, Swansea C) 6
Shepherd, A. 1906 (Bolton W, Newcastle U) 2
Sheringham, E. P. 1993 (Tottenham H, Manchester U, Tottenham H) 51
Sherwood, T. A. 1999 (Tottenham H) 3
Shilton, P. L. 1971 (Leicester C, Stoke C, Nottingham F, Southampton, Derby Co) 125
Shimwell, E. 1949 (Blackpool) 1
Shorey, N. 2007 (Reading) 2
Shutt, G. 1886 (Stoke) 1
Silcock, J. 1921 (Manchester U) 3
Sillett, R. P. 1955 (Chelsea) 3
Simms, E. 1922 (Luton T) 1
Simpson, J. 1911 (Blackburn R) 8
Sinclair, T. 2002 (West Ham U, Manchester C) 12
Sinton, A. 1992 (QPR, Sheffield W) 12
Slater, W. J. 1955 (Wolverhampton W) 12
Smalley, T. 1937 (Wolverhampton W) 1
Smalling, C. L. 2012 (Manchester U) 31
Smart, T. 1921 (Aston Villa) 5
Smith, A. 1891 (Nottingham F) 3
Smith, A. 2001 (Leeds U, Manchester U, Newcastle U) 19
Smith, A. K. 1872 (Oxford University) 1
Smith, A. M. 1989 (Arsenal) 13
Smith, B. 1921 (Tottenham H) 2
Smith, C. E. 1876 (Crystal Palace) 1
Smith, G. O. 1893 (Oxford University, Old Carthusians, Corinthians) 20
Smith, H. 1905 (Reading) 4
Smith, J. 1920 (WBA) 2
Smith, Joe 1913 (Bolton W) 5
Smith, J. C. R. 1939 (Millwall) 2
Smith, J. W. 1932 (Portsmouth) 3
Smith, Leslie 1939 (Brentford) 1
Smith, Lionel 1951 (Arsenal) 6
Smith, R. A. 1961 (Tottenham H) 15
Smith, S. 1895 (Aston Villa) 1
Smith, S. C. 1936 (Leicester C) 1
Smith, T. 1960 (Birmingham C) 2
Smith, T. 1971 (Liverpool) 1
Smith, W. H. 1922 (Huddersfield T) 3
Smith Rowe, E. 2022 (Arsenal) 3
Solanke, D. A. 2018 (Liverpool) 1
Sorby, T. H. 1879 (Thursday Wanderers, Sheffield) 1
Southgate, G. 1996 (Aston Villa, Middlesbrough) 57
Southworth, J. 1889 (Blackburn R) 3
Sparks, F. J. 1879 (Hertfordshire Rangers, Clapham R) 3
Spence, J. W. 1926 (Manchester U) 2
Spence, R. 1936 (Chelsea) 2
Spencer, C. W. 1924 (Newcastle U) 2
Spencer, H. 1897 (Aston Villa) 6
Spiksley, F. 1893 (Sheffield W) 7
Spilsbury, B. W. 1885 (Cambridge University) 3
Spink, N. 1983 (Aston Villa) 1
Spouncer, W. A. 1900 (Nottingham F) 1
Springett, R. D. G. 1960 (Sheffield W) 33
Sproston, B. 1937 (Leeds U, Tottenham H, Manchester C) 11
Squire, R. T. 1886 (Cambridge University) 3
Stanbrough, M. H. 1895 (Old Carthusians) 1
Staniforth, R. 1954 (Huddersfield T) 8
Starling, R. W. 1933 (Sheffield W, Aston Villa) 2
Statham, D. J. 1983 (WBA) 3
Steele, F. C. 1937 (Stoke C) 6
Stein, B. 1984 (Luton T) 1
Stephenson, C. 1924 (Huddersfield T) 1
Stephenson, G. T. 1928 (Derby Co, Sheffield W) 3
Stephenson, J. E. 1938 (Leeds U) 2
Stepney, A. C. 1968 (Manchester U) 1
Sterland, M. 1989 (Sheffield W) 1
Sterling, R. S. 2013 (Liverpool, Manchester C) 77
Steven, T. M. 1985 (Everton, Rangers, Marseille) 36
Stevens, G. A. 1985 (Tottenham H) 7
Stevens, M. G. 1985 (Everton, Rangers) 46
Stewart, J. 1907 (Sheffield W, Newcastle U) 3
Stewart, P. A. 1992 (Tottenham H) 3
Stiles, N. P. 1965 (Manchester U) 28
Stoker, J. 1933 (Birmingham) 3
Stone, S. B. 1996 (Nottingham F) 9
Stones, J. 2014 (Everton, Manchester C) 58
Storer, H. 1924 (Derby Co) 2
Storey, P. E. 1971 (Arsenal) 19
Storey-Moore, I. 1970 (Nottingham F) 1
Strange, A. H. 1930 (Sheffield W) 20
Stratford, A. H. 1874 (Wanderers) 1
Streten, B. 1950 (Luton T) 1
Sturgess, A. 1911 (Sheffield U) 2
Sturridge, D. A. 2012 (Chelsea, Liverpool) 26
Summerbee, M. G. 1968 (Manchester C) 8
Sunderland, A. 1980 (Arsenal) 1
Sutcliffe, J. W. 1893 (Bolton W, Millwall) 5
Sutton, C. R. 1998 (Blackburn R) 1
Swan, P. 1960 (Sheffield W) 19
Swepstone, H. A. 1880 (Pilgrims) 6
Swift, F. V. 1947 (Manchester C) 19

Tait, G. 1881 (Birmingham Excelsior) 1
Talbot, B. 1977 (Ipswich T, Arsenal) 6
Tambling, R. V. 1963 (Chelsea) 3
Tarkowski, J. A. 2018 (Burnley) 2

Tate, J. T. 1931 (Aston Villa) 3
Taylor, E. 1954 (Blackpool) 1
Taylor, E. H. 1923 (Huddersfield T) 8
Taylor, J. G. 1951 (Fulham) 2
Taylor, P. H. 1948 (Liverpool) 3
Taylor, P. J. 1976 (Crystal Palace) 4
Taylor, T. 1953 (Manchester U) 19
Temple, D. W. 1965 (Everton) 1
Terry, J. G. 2003 (Chelsea) 78
Thickett, H. 1899 (Sheffield U) 2
Thomas, D. 1975 (QPR) 8
Thomas, D. 1983 (Coventry C) 2
Thomas, G. R. 1991 (Crystal Palace) 9
Thomas, M. L. 1989 (Arsenal) 2
Thompson, A. 2004 (Celtic) 1
Thompson, P. 1964 (Liverpool) 16
Thompson, P. B. 1976 (Liverpool) 42
Thompson T. 1952 (Aston Villa, Preston NE) 2
Thomson, R. A. 1964 (Wolverhampton W) 8
Thornewell, G. 1923 (Derby Co) 4
Thornley, I. 1907 (Manchester C) 1
Tilson, S. F. 1934 (Manchester C) 4
Titmuss, F. 1922 (Southampton) 2
Todd, C. 1972 (Derby Co) 27
Tomori, O. O. (Fikayo) 2020 (Chelsea, AC Milan) 3
Toone, G. 1892 (Notts Co) 2
Topham, A. G. 1894 (Casuals) 1
Topham, R. 1893 (Wolverhampton W, Casuals) 2
Towers, M. A. 1976 (Sunderland) 3
Townley, W. J. 1889 (Blackburn R) 2
Townrow, J. E. 1925 (Clapton Orient) 2
Townsend, A. D. 2013 (Tottenham H, Newcastle U, Crystal Palace) 13
Tremelling, D. R. 1928 (Birmingham) 1
Tresadern, J. 1923 (West Ham U) 2
Trippier, K. J. 2017 (Tottenham H, Atletico Madrid, Newcastle U) 37
Tueart, D. 1975 (Manchester C) 6
Tunstall, F. E. 1923 (Sheffield U) 7
Turnbull, R. J. 1920 (Bradford) 1
Turner, A. 1900 (Southampton) 2
Turner, H. 1931 (Huddersfield T) 2
Turner, J. A. 1893 (Bolton W, Stoke, Derby Co) 3
Tweedy, G. J. 1937 (Grimsby T) 1

Ufton, D. G. 1954 (Charlton Ath) 1
Underwood, A. 1891 (Stoke C) 2
Unsworth, D. G. 1995 (Everton) 1
Upson, M. J. 2003 (Birmingham C, West Ham U) 21
Urwin, T. 1923 (Middlesbrough, Newcastle U) 4
Utley, G. 1913 (Barnsley) 1

Vardy, J. R. 2015 (Leicester C) 26
Vassell, D. 2002 (Aston Villa) 22
Vaughton, O. H. 1882 (Aston Villa) 5
Veitch, C. C. M. 1906 (Newcastle U) 6
Veitch, J. G. 1894 (Old Westminsters) 1
Venables, T. F. 1965 (Chelsea) 2
Venison, B. 1995 (Newcastle U) 2
Vidal, R. W. S. 1873 (Oxford University) 1
Viljoen, C. 1975 (Ipswich T) 2
Viollet, D. S. 1960 (Manchester U) 2
Von Donop 1873 (Royal Engineers) 2

Wace, H. 1878 (Wanderers) 3
Waddle, C. R. 1985 (Newcastle U, Tottenham H, Marseille) 62
Wadsworth, S. J. 1922 (Huddersfield T) 9
Wainscoat, W. R. 1929 (Leeds U) 1
Waiters, A. K. 1964 (Blackpool) 5
Walcott, T. J. 2006 (Arsenal) 47
Walden, F. I. 1914 (Tottenham H) 2
Walker, D. S. 1989 (Nottingham F, Sampdoria, Sheffield W) 59
Walker, I. M. 1996 (Tottenham H, Leicester C) 4
Walker, K. A. 2012 (Tottenham H, Manchester C) 68
Walker, W. H. 1921 (Aston Villa) 18
Walker-Peters, K. L. 2022 (Southampton) 2
Wall, G. 1907 (Manchester U) 7
Wallace, C. W. 1913 (Aston Villa) 3
Wallace, D. L. 1986 (Southampton) 1
Walsh, P. A. 1983 (Luton T) 5
Walters, A. M. 1885 (Cambridge University, Old Carthusians) 9
Walters, K. M. 1991 (Rangers) 1
Walters, P. M. 1885 (Oxford University, Old Carthusians) 13
Walton, N. 1890 (Blackburn R) 1
Ward, J. T. 1885 (Blackburn Olympic) 1
Ward, P. 1980 (Brighton & HA) 1
Ward, T. V. 1948 (Derby Co) 2
Ward-Prowse, J. M. E. 2017 (Southampton) 11
Waring, T. 1931 (Aston Villa) 5
Warner, C. 1878 (Upton Park) 1
Warnock, S. 2008 (Blackburn R, Aston Villa) 2
Warren, B. 1906 (Derby Co, Chelsea) 22
Waterfield, G. S. 1927 (Burnley) 1
Watkins, O. G. A. 2021 (Aston Villa) 7
Watson, D. 1984 (Norwich C, Everton) 12
Watson, D. V. 1974 (Sunderland, Manchester C, Werder Bremen, Southampton, Stoke C) 65
Watson, V. M. 1923 (West Ham U) 5
Watson, W. 1913 (Burnley) 3
Watson, W. 1950 (Sunderland) 4
Weaver, S. 1932 (Newcastle U) 3
Webb, G. W. 1911 (West Ham U) 2
Webb, N. J. 1988 (Nottingham F, Manchester U) 26
Webster, M. 1930 (Middlesbrough) 3
Wedlock, W. J. 1907 (Bristol C) 26
Weir, D. 1889 (Bolton W) 2
Welbeck, D. N. T. M. 2011 (Manchester U, Arsenal) 42
Welch, R. de C. 1872 (Wanderers, Harrow Chequers) 2
Weller, K. 1974 (Leicester C) 4
Welsh, D. 1938 (Charlton Ath) 3
West, G. 1969 (Everton) 3
Westwood, R. W. 1935 (Bolton W) 6
Whateley, O. 1883 (Aston Villa) 2
Wheeler, J. E. 1955 (Bolton W) 1
Wheldon, G. F. 1897 (Aston Villa) 4
White, B. W. 2021 (Brighton & HA, Arsenal) 4
White, D. 1993 (Manchester C) 1
White, T. A. 1933 (Everton) 1
Whitehead, J. 1893 (Accrington, Blackburn R) 2
Whitfeld, H. 1879 (Old Etonians) 1
Whitham, M. 1892 (Sheffield U) 1
Whitworth, S. 1975 (Leicester C) 7
Whymark, T. J. 1978 (Ipswich T) 1
Widdowson, S. W. 1880 (Nottingham F) 1
Wignall, F. 1965 (Nottingham F) 2
Wilcox, J. M. 1996 (Blackburn R, Leeds U) 3
Wilkes, A. 1901 (Aston Villa) 5
Wilkins, R. C. 1976 (Chelsea, Manchester U, AC Milan) 84
Wilkinson, B. 1904 (Sheffield U) 1
Wilkinson, L. R. 1891 (Oxford University) 1
Williams, B. F. 1949 (Wolverhampton W) 24
Williams, O. 1923 (Clapton Orient) 2
Williams, S. 1983 (Southampton) 6
Williams, W. 1897 (WBA) 6
Williamson, E. C. 1923 (Arsenal) 2
Williamson, R. G. 1905 (Middlesbrough) 7
Willingham, C. K. 1937 (Huddersfield T) 12
Willis, A. 1952 (Tottenham H) 1
Wilshaw, D. J. 1954 (Wolverhampton W) 12
Wilshere, J. A. 2011 (Arsenal) 34
Wilson, C. 2019 (Bournemouth) 4
Wilson, C. P. 1884 (Hendon) 2
Wilson, C. W. 1879 (Oxford University) 2
Wilson, G. 1921 (Sheffield W) 12
Wilson, G. P. 1900 (Corinthians) 2
Wilson, R. 1960 (Huddersfield T, Everton) 63
Wilson, T. 1928 (Huddersfield T) 1
Winckworth, W. N. 1892 (Old Westminsters) 2
Windridge, J. E. 1908 (Chelsea) 8
Wingfield-Stratford, C. V. 1877 (Royal Engineers) 1
Winks, H. B. 2018 (Tottenham H) 10
Winterburn, N. 1990 (Arsenal) 2
Wise, D. F. 1991 (Chelsea) 21
Withe, P. 1981 (Aston Villa) 11
Wollaston, C. H. R. 1874 (Wanderers) 4
Wolstenholme, S. 1904 (Everton, Blackburn R) 3
Wood, H. 1890 (Wolverhampton W) 3
Wood, R. E. 1955 (Manchester U) 3
Woodcock, A. S. 1978 (Nottingham F, Cologne, Arsenal) 42
Woodgate, J. S. 1999 (Leeds U, Newcastle U, Real Madrid, Tottenham H) 8
Woodger, G. 1911 (Oldham Ath) 1
Woodhall, G. 1888 (WBA) 2
Woodley, V. R. 1937 (Chelsea) 19

Woods, C. C. E. 1985 (Norwich C, Rangers, Sheffield W) 43
Woodward, V. J. 1903 (Tottenham H, Chelsea) 23
Woosnam, M. 1922 (Manchester C) 1
Worrall, F. 1935 (Portsmouth) 2
Worthington, F. S. 1974 (Leicester C) 8
Wreford-Brown, C. 1889 (Oxford University, Old Carthusians) 4
Wright, E. G. D. 1906 (Cambridge University) 1
Wright, I. E. 1991 (Crystal Palace, Arsenal, West Ham U) 33
Wright, J. D. 1939 (Newcastle U) 1
Wright, M. 1984 (Southampton, Derby Co, Liverpool) 45
Wright, R. I. 2000 (Ipswich T, Arsenal) 2
Wright, T. J. 1968 (Everton) 11
Wright, W. A. 1947 (Wolverhampton W) 105
Wright-Phillips, S. C. 2005 (Manchester C, Chelsea, Manchester C) 36
Wylie, J. G. 1878 (Wanderers) 1

Yates, J. 1889 (Burnley) 1
York, R. E. 1922 (Aston Villa) 2
Young, A. 1933 (Huddersfield T) 9
Young, A. S. 2008 (Aston Villa, Manchester U) 39
Young, G. M. 1965 (Sheffield W) 1
Young, L. P. 2005 (Charlton Ath) 7

Zaha, D. W. A. 2013 (Manchester U) 2
Zamora, R. L. 2011 (Fulham) 2

NORTHERN IRELAND

Addis, D. J. 1922 (Cliftonville) 1
Aherne, T. 1947 (Belfast Celtic, Luton T) 4
Alexander, T. E. 1895 (Cliftonville) 1
Allan, C. 1936 (Cliftonville) 1
Allen, J. 1887 (Limavady) 1
Anderson, J. 1925 (Distillery) 1
Anderson, T. 1973 (Manchester U, Swindon T, Peterborough U) 22
Anderson, W. 1898 (Linfield, Cliftonville) 4
Andrews, W. 1908 (Glentoran, Grimsby T) 3
Armstrong, G. J. 1977 (Tottenham H, Watford, Real Mallorca, WBA, Chesterfield) 63

Baird, C. P. 2003 (Southampton, Fulham, Reading, Burnley, WBA, Derby Co) 79
Baird, G. 1896 (Distillery) 3
Baird, H. C. 1939 (Huddersfield T) 1
Balfe, J. 1909 (Shelbourne) 2
Ballard, D. G. 2021 (Arsenal) 16
Bambrick, J. 1929 (Linfield, Chelsea) 11
Banks, S. J. 1937 (Cliftonville) 1
Barr, H. H. 1962 (Linfield, Coventry C) 3
Barron, J. H. 1894 (Cliftonville) 7
Barry, J. 1888 (Cliftonville) 3
Barry, J. 1900 (Bohemians) 1
Barton, A. J. 2011 (Preston NE) 1
Baxter, R. A. 1887 (Distillery) 1
Baxter, S. N. 1887 (Cliftonville) 1
Bennett, L. V. 1889 (Dublin University) 1
Best, G. 1964 (Manchester U, Fulham) 37
Bingham, W. L. 1951 (Sunderland, Luton T, Everton, Port Vale) 56
Black, K. T. 1988 (Luton T, Nottingham F) 30
Black, T. 1901 (Glentoran) 1
Blair, H. 1928 (Portadown, Swansea T) 4
Blair, J. 1907 (Cliftonville) 5
Blair, R. V. 1975 (Oldham Ath) 5
Blanchflower, J. 1954 (Manchester U) 12
Blanchflower, R. D. 1950 (Barnsley, Aston Villa, Tottenham H) 56
Blayney, A. 2006 (Doncaster R, Linfield) 5
Bookman, L. J. O. 1914 (Bradford C, Luton T) 4
Bothwell, A. W. 1926 (Ards) 5
Bowler, G. C. 1950 (Hull C) 3
Boyce, L. 2011 (Werder Bremen, Ross Co, Burton Alb, Hearts) 28
Boyle, P. 1901 (Sheffield U) 5
Bradley, C. 2021 (Liverpool) 8
Braithwaite, R. M. 1962 (Linfield, Middlesbrough) 10
Braniff, K. R. 2010 (Portadown) 2
Breen, T. 1935 (Belfast Celtic, Manchester U) 9
Brennan, B. 1912 (Bohemians) 1
Brennan, R. A. 1949 (Luton T, Birmingham C, Fulham) 5
Briggs, W. R. 1962 (Manchester U, Swansea T) 2
Brisby, D. 1891 (Distillery) 1
Brolly, T. H. 1937 (Millwall) 4
Brookes, E. A. 1920 (Shelbourne) 1
Brotherston, N. 1980 (Blackburn R) 27
Brown, C. M. 2020 (Cardiff C) 12
Brown, J. 1921 (Glenavon, Tranmere R) 3
Brown, J. 1935 (Wolverhampton W, Coventry C, Birmingham C) 10
Brown, N. M. 1887 (Limavady) 1
Brown, W. G. 1926 (Glenavon) 1
Browne, F. 1887 (Cliftonville) 5
Browne, R. J. 1936 (Leeds U) 6
Bruce, A. 1925 (Belfast Celtic) 1
Bruce, A. S. 2013 (Hull C) 2
Bruce, W. 1961 (Glentoran) 2
Brunt, C. 2005 (Sheffield W, WBA) 65
Bryan, M. A. 2010 (Watford) 2
Buckle, H. R. 1903 (Cliftonville, Sunderland, Bristol R) 3
Buckle, J. 1882 (Cliftonville) 1
Burnett, J. 1894 (Distillery, Glentoran) 5
Burnison, J. 1901 (Distillery) 2
Burnison, S. 1908 (Distillery, Bradford, Distillery) 8
Burns, J. 1923 (Glenavon) 1
Burns, W. 1925 (Glentoran) 1
Butler, M. P. 1939 (Blackpool) 1

Camp, L. M. J. 2011 (Nottingham F) 9
Campbell, A. C. 1963 (Crusaders) 2
Campbell, D. A. 1986 (Nottingham F, Charlton Ath) 10
Campbell, James 1897 (Cliftonville) 14
Campbell, John 1896 (Cliftonville) 1
Campbell, J. P. 1951 (Fulham) 2
Campbell, R. M. 1982 (Bradford C) 2
Campbell, W. G. 1968 (Dundee) 6
Capaldi, A. C. 2004 (Plymouth Arg, Cardiff C) 22
Carey, J. J. 1947 (Manchester U) 7
Carroll, E. 1925 (Glenavon) 1
Carroll, R. E. 1997 (Wigan Ath, Manchester U, West Ham U, Olympiacos, Notts Co, Linfield) 45
Carson, J. G. 2011 (Ipswich T) 4
Carson, S. 2009 (Coleraine) 1
Carson, T. 2018 (Motherwell, Dundee U) 8
Casement, C. 2009 (Ipswich T) 1
Casey, T. 1955 (Newcastle U, Portsmouth) 12
Caskey, W. 1979 (Derby Co, Tulsa Roughnecks) 7
Cassidy, T. 1971 (Newcastle U, Burnley) 24
Cathcart, C. G. 2011 (Blackpool, Watford) 69
Caughey, M. 1986 (Linfield) 2
Chambers, R. J. 1921 (Distillery, Bury, Nottingham F) 12
Charles, D. E. 2021 (Accrington S, Bolton W) 11
Charles, S. E. 2022 (Manchester C) 4
Chatton, H. A. 1925 (Partick Thistle) 3
Christian, J. 1889 (Linfield) 1
Clarke, C. J. 1986 (Bournemouth, Southampton, QPR, Portsmouth) 38
Clarke, R. 1901 (Belfast Celtic) 2
Cleary, J. 1982 (Glentoran) 5
Clements, D. 1965 (Coventry C, Sheffield W, Everton, New York Cosmos) 48
Clingan, S. G. 2006 (Nottingham F, Norwich C, Coventry C, Kilmarnock) 39
Clugston, J. 1888 (Cliftonville) 14
Clyde, M. G. 2005 (Wolverhampton W) 3
Coates, C. 2009 (Crusaders) 6
Cochrane, D. 1939 (Leeds U) 12
Cochrane, G. 1903 (Cliftonville) 1
Cochrane, G. T. 1976 (Coleraine, Burnley, Middlesbrough, Gillingham) 26
Cochrane, M. 1898 (Distillery, Leicester Fosse) 8
Collins, F. 1922 (Celtic) 1
Collins, R. 1922 (Cliftonville) 1
Condy, J. 1882 (Distillery) 3
Connell, T. E. 1978 (Coleraine) 1
Connor, J. 1901 (Glentoran, Belfast Celtic) 13
Connor, M. J. 1903 (Brentford, Fulham) 3
Cook, W. 1933 (Celtic, Everton) 15
Cooke, S. 1889 (Belfast YMCA, Cliftonville) 3
Coote, A. 1999 (Norwich C) 6
Coulter, J. 1934 (Belfast Celtic, Everton, Grimsby T, Chelmsford C) 11

Cowan, J. 1970 (Newcastle U) 1
Cowan, T. S. 1925 (Queen's Island) 1
Coyle, F. 1956 (Coleraine, Nottingham F) 4
Coyle, L. 1989 (Derry C) 1
Coyle, R. I. 1973 (Sheffield W) 5
Craig, A. B. 1908 (Rangers, Morton) 9
Craig, D. J. 1967 (Newcastle U) 25
Craigan, S. J. 2003 (Partick Thistle, Motherwell) 54
Crawford, A. 1889 (Distillery, Cliftonville) 7
Croft, T. 1922 (Queen's Island) 3
Crone, R. 1889 (Distillery) 4
Crone, W. 1882 (Distillery) 12
Crooks, W. J. 1922 (Manchester U) 1
Crossan, E. 1950 (Blackburn R) 3
Crossan, J. A. 1960 (Sparta-Rotterdam, Sunderland, Manchester C, Middlesbrough) 24
Crothers, C. 1907 (Distillery) 1
Cumming, L. 1929 (Huddersfield T, Oldham Ath) 3
Cunningham, W. 1892 (Ulster) 4
Cunningham, W. E. 1951 (St Mirren, Leicester C, Dunfermline Ath) 30
Curran, S. 1926 (Belfast Celtic) 4
Curran, J. J. 1922 (Glenavon, Pontypridd, Glenavon) 5
Cush, W. W. 1951 (Glenavon, Leeds U, Portadown) 26

Dallas, S. A. 2011 (Crusaders, Brentford, Leeds U) 62
Dalrymple, J. 1922 (Distillery) 1
Dalton, W. 1888 (YMCA, Linfield) 11
D'Arcy, S. D. 1952 (Chelsea, Brentford) 5
Darling, J. 1897 (Linfield) 22
Davey, H. H. 1926 (Reading, Portsmouth) 5
Davis, S. 2005 (Aston Villa, Fulham, Rangers, Southampton, Rangers) 138
Davis, T. L. 1937 (Oldham Ath) 1
Davison, A. J. 1996 (Bolton W, Bradford C, Grimsby T) 3
Davison, J. R. 1882 (Cliftonville) 8
Dennison, R. 1988 (Wolverhampton W) 18
Devine, A. O. 1886 (Limavady) 4
Devine, J. 1990 (Glentoran) 1
Dickson, D. 1970 (Coleraine) 4
Dickson, T. A. 1957 (Linfield) 1
Dickson, W. 1951 (Chelsea, Arsenal) 12
Diffin, W. J. 1931 (Belfast Celtic) 1
Dill, A. H. 1882 (Knock, Down Ath, Cliftonville) 9
Doherty, I. 1901 (Belfast Celtic) 1
Doherty, J. 1928 (Portadown) 1
Doherty, J. 1933 (Cliftonville) 2
Doherty, L. 1985 (Linfield) 2
Doherty, M. 1938 (Derry C) 1
Doherty, P. D. 1935 (Blackpool, Manchester C, Derby Co, Huddersfield T, Doncaster R) 16
Doherty, T. E. 2003 (Bristol C) 9
Donaghy, B. 1903 (Belfast Celtic) 1
Donaghy, M. M. 1980 (Luton T, Manchester U, Chelsea) 91
Donnelly, L. 1913 (Distillery) 1
Donnelly, L. F. P. D. 2014 (Fulham, Motherwell) 4
Donnelly, M. 2009 (Crusaders) 1
Doran, J. F. 1921 (Brighton) 3
Dougan, A. D. 1958 (Portsmouth, Blackburn R, Aston Villa, Leicester C, Wolverhampton W) 43
Douglas, J. P. 1947 (Belfast Celtic) 1
Dowd, H. O. 1974 (Glenavon, Sheffield W) 3
Dowie, I. 1990 (Luton T, West Ham U, Southampton, C Palace, West Ham U, QPR) 59
Duff, M. J. 2002 (Cheltenham T, Burnley) 24
Duggan, H. A. 1930 (Leeds U) 8
Dunlop, G. 1985 (Linfield) 4
Dunne, J. 1928 (Sheffield U) 7

Eames, W. L. E. 1885 (Dublin University) 3
Eglington, T. J. 1947 (Everton) 6
Elder, A. R. 1960 (Burnley, Stoke C) 40
Elleman, A. R. 1889 (Cliftonville) 2
Elliott, S. 2001 (Motherwell, Hull C) 39
Elwood, J. H. 1929 (Bradford) 2
Emerson, W. 1920 (Glentoran, Burnley) 11
English, S. 1933 (Rangers) 2
Enright, J. 1912 (Leeds C) 1
Evans, C. J. 2009 (Manchester U, Hull C, Blackburn R, Sunderland) 69
Evans, J. G. 2007 (Manchester U, WBA, Leicester C) 98

Falloon, E. 1931 (Aberdeen) 2
Farquharson, T. G. 1923 (Cardiff C) 7
Farrell, P. 1901 (Distillery) 2
Farrell, P. 1938 (Hibernian) 1
Farrell, P. D. 1947 (Everton) 7
Feeney, J. M. 1947 (Linfield, Swansea T) 2
Feeney, W. 1976 (Glentoran) 1
Feeney, W. J. 2002 (Bournemouth, Luton T, Cardiff C, Oldham Ath, Plymouth Arg) 46
Ferguson, G. 1999 (Linfield) 5
Ferguson, S. K. 2009 (Newcastle U, Millwall, Rotherham U) 54
Ferguson, W. 1966 (Linfield) 2
Ferris, J. 1920 (Belfast Celtic, Chelsea, Belfast Celtic) 6
Ferris, R. O. 1950 (Birmingham C) 3
Fettis, A. W. 1992 (Hull C, Nottingham F, Blackburn R) 25
Finney, T. 1975 (Sunderland, Cambridge U) 14
Fitzpatrick, J. C. 1896 (Bohemians) 2
Flack, H. 1929 (Burnley) 1
Flanagan, T. M. 2017 (Burton Alb, Sunderland, Shrewsbury T) 13
Fleming, J. G. 1987 (Nottingham F, Manchester C, Barnsley) 31
Forbes, G. 1888 (Limavady, Distillery) 3
Forde, J. T. 1959 (Ards) 4
Foreman, T. A. 1899 (Cliftonville) 1
Forsythe, J. 1888 (YMCA) 2
Fox, W. T. 1887 (Ulster) 2
Frame, T. 1925 (Linfield) 1
Fulton, R. P. 1928 (Larne, Belfast Celtic) 21

Gaffikin, G. 1890 (Linfield Ath) 15
Galbraith, E. S. W. (Manchester U) 2
Galbraith, W. 1890 (Distillery) 1
Gallagher, P. 1920 (Celtic, Falkirk) 11
Gallogly, C. 1951 (Huddersfield T) 2
Gara, A. 1902 (Preston NE) 3
Gardiner, A. 1930 (Cliftonville) 5
Garrett, J. 1925 (Distillery) 1
Garrett, R. 2009 (Linfield) 5
Gaston, R. 1969 (Oxford U) 1
Gaukrodger, G. 1895 (Linfield) 1
Gault, M. 2008 (Linfield) 1
Gaussen, A. D. 1884 (Moyola Park, Magherafelt) 6
Geary, J. 1931 (Glentoran) 2
Gibb, J. T. 1884 (Wellington Park, Cliftonville) 10
Gibb, T. J. 1936 (Cliftonville) 1
Gibson W. K. 1894 (Cliftonville) 14
Gillespie, K. R. 1995 (Manchester U, Newcastle U, Blackburn R, Leicester C, Sheffield U) 86
Gillespie, S. 1886 (Hertford) 6
Gillespie, W. 1889 (West Down) 1
Gillespie, W. 1913 (Sheffield U) 25
Goodall, A. L. 1899 (Derby Co, Glossop) 10
Goodbody, M. F. 1889 (Dublin University) 2
Gordon, H. 1895 (Linfield) 3
Gordon R. W. 1891 (Linfield) 7
Gordon, T. 1894 (Linfield) 2
Gorman, R. J. 2010 (Wolverhampton W) 9
Gorman, W. C. 1947 (Brentford) 4
Gough, J. 1925 (Queen's Island) 1
Gowdy, J. 1920 (Glentoran, Queen's Island, Falkirk) 6
Gowdy, W. A. 1932 (Hull C, Sheffield W, Linfield, Hibernian) 6
Graham, W. G. L. 1951 (Doncaster R) 14
Gray, P. 1993 (Luton T, Sunderland, Nancy, Luton T, Burnley, Oxford U) 26
Greer, W. 1909 (QPR) 3
Gregg, H. 1954 (Doncaster R, Manchester U) 25
Griffin, D. J. 1996 (St Johnstone, Dundee U, Stockport Co) 29
Grigg, W. D. 2012 (Walsall, Brentford, Milton Keynes D, Wigan Ath) 13

Hall, G. 1897 (Distillery) 1
Halligan, W. 1911 (Derby Co, Wolverhampton W) 2
Hamill, M. 1912 (Manchester U, Belfast Celtic, Manchester C) 7
Hamill, R. 1999 (Glentoran) 1
Hamilton, B. 1969 (Linfield, Ipswich T, Everton, Millwall, Swindon T) 50
Hamilton, G. 2003 (Portadown) 5
Hamilton, J. 1882 (Knock) 2
Hamilton, R. 1928 (Rangers) 5
Hamilton, W. D. 1885 (Dublin Association) 1
Hamilton, W. J. 1885 (Dublin Association) 1

Hamilton, W. J. 1908 (Distillery) 1
Hamilton, W. R. 1978 (QPR, Burnley, Oxford U) 41
Hampton, H. 1911 (Bradford C) 9
Hanna, J. 1912 (Nottingham F) 2
Hanna, J. D. 1899 (Royal Artillery, Portsmouth) 1
Hannon, D. J. 1908 (Bohemians) 6
Harkin, J. T. 1968 (Southport, Shrewsbury T) 5
Harland, A. I. 1922 (Linfield) 2
Harris, J. 1921 (Cliftonville, Glenavon) 2
Harris, V. 1906 (Shelbourne, Everton) 20
Harvey, M. 1961 (Sunderland) 34
Hastings, J. 1882 (Knock, Ulster) 7
Hatton, S. 1963 (Linfield) 2
Hayes, W. E. 1938 (Huddersfield T) 4
Hazard, C. 2018 (Celtic) 4
Healy, D. J. 2000 (Manchester U, Preston NE, Leeds U, Fulham, Sunderland, Rangers, Bury) 95
Healy, P. J. 1982 (Coleraine, Glentoran) 4
Hegan, D. 1970 (WBA, Wolverhampton W) 7
Hehir, J. C. 1910 (Bohemians) 1
Henderson, J. 1885 (Ulster) 3
Hewison, G. 1885 (Moyola Park) 2
Hill, C. F. 1990 (Sheffield U, Leicester C, Trelleborg, Northampton T) 27
Hill, M. J. 1959 (Norwich C, Everton) 7
Hinton, E. 1947 (Fulham, Millwall) 7
Hodson, L. J. S. 2011 (Watford, Milton Keynes D, Rangers) 24
Holmes, S. P. 2002 (Wrexham) 1
Hopkins, J. 1926 (Brighton) 1
Horlock, K. 1995 (Swindon T, Manchester C) 32
Houston, J. 1912 (Linfield, Everton) 6
Houston, W. 1933 (Linfield) 1
Houston, W. J. 1885 (Moyola Park) 2
Hughes, A. W. 1998 (Newcastle U, Aston Villa, Fulham, QPR, Brighton & HA, Melbourne C, Kerala Blasters, Hearts) 112
Hughes, J. 2006 (Lincoln C) 2
Hughes, M. A. 2006 (Oldham Ath) 2
Hughes, M. E. 1992 (Manchester C, Strasbourg, West Ham U, Wimbledon, Crystal Palace) 71
Hughes, P. A. 1987 (Bury) 3
Hughes, W. 1951 (Bolton W) 1
Hume, T. 2021 (Sunderland) 2
Humphries, W. M. 1962 (Ards, Coventry C, Swansea T) 14
Hunter, A. 1905 (Distillery, Belfast Celtic) 8
Hunter, A. 1970 (Blackburn R, Ipswich T) 53
Hunter, B. V. 1995 (Wrexham, Reading) 15
Hunter, R. J. 1884 (Cliftonville) 3
Hunter, V. 1962 (Coleraine) 2

Ingham, M. G. 2005 (Sunderland, Wrexham) 3
Irvine, R. J. 1962 (Linfield, Stoke C) 8
Irvine, R. W. 1922 (Everton, Portsmouth, Connah's Quay, Derry C) 15
Irvine, W. J. 1963 (Burnley, Preston NE, Brighton & HA) 23
Irving, S. J. 1923 (Dundee, Cardiff C, Chelsea) 18

Jackson, T. A. 1969 (Everton, Nottingham F, Manchester U) 35
Jamison, J. 1976 (Glentoran) 1
Jenkins, I. 1997 (Chester C, Dundee U) 6
Jennings, P. A. 1964 (Watford, Tottenham H, Arsenal, Tottenham H) 119
Johnson, D. M. 1999 (Blackburn R, Birmingham C) 56
Johnston, H. 1927 (Portadown) 1
Johnston, R. S. 1882 (Distillery) 5
Johnston, R. S. 1905 (Distillery) 1
Johnston, S. 1890 (Linfield) 4
Johnston, W. 1885 (Oldpark) 2
Johnston, W. C. 1962 (Glenavon, Oldham Ath) 2
Jones, J. 1930 (Linfield, Hibernian, Glenavon) 23
Jones, J. 1956 (Glenavon) 3
Jones, J. L. 2018 (Kilmarnock, Rangers, Sunderland, Wigan Ath) 18
Jones, S. 1934 (Distillery, Blackpool) 2
Jones, S. G. 2003 (Crewe Alex, Burnley) 29
Jordan, T. 1895 (Linfield) 2

Kavanagh, P. J. 1930 (Celtic) 1
Keane, T. R. 1949 (Swansea T) 1
Kearns, A. 1900 (Distillery) 6
Kee, P. V. 1990 (Oxford U, Ards) 9
Keith, R. M. 1958 (Newcastle U) 23
Kelly, H. R. 1950 (Fulham, Southampton) 4
Kelly, J. 1896 (Glentoran) 1
Kelly, J. 1932 (Derry C) 11
Kelly, P. J. 1921 (Manchester C) 1
Kelly, P. M. 1950 (Barnsley) 1
Kennedy, A. L. 1923 (Arsenal) 2
Kennedy, M. 2021 (Aberdeen) 3
Kennedy, P. H. 1999 (Watford, Wigan Ath) 20
Kernaghan, N. 1936 (Belfast Celtic) 3
Kirk, A. R. 2000 (Hearts, Boston U, Northampton T, Dunfermline Ath) 11
Kirkwood, H. 1904 (Cliftonville) 1
Kirwan, J. 1900 (Tottenham H, Chelsea, Clyde) 17

Lacey, W. 1909 (Everton, Liverpool, New Brighton) 23
Lafferty, D. P. 2012 (Burnley) 13
Lafferty, K. 2006 (Burnley, Rangers, Sion, Palermo, Norwich C, Hearts, Rangers, Kilmarnock) 89
Lane, P. J. 2022 (Fleetwood T) 3
Lavery, S. F. 2018 (Everton, Linfield, Blackpool) 15
Lawrie, J. 2009 (Port Vale) 3
Lawther, R. 1888 (Glentoran) 2
Lawther, W. I. 1960 (Sunderland, Blackburn R) 4
Leatham, J. 1939 (Belfast Celtic) 1
Ledwidge, J. J. 1906 (Shelbourne) 2
Lemon, J. 1886 (Glentoran, Belfast YMCA) 3
Lennon, N. F. 1994 (Crewe Alex, Leicester C, Celtic) 40
Leslie, W. 1887 (YMCA) 1
Lewis, J. 1899 (Glentoran, Distillery) 4
Lewis, J. P. 2018 (Norwich C, Newcastle U) 26
Little, A. 2009 (Rangers) 9
Lockhart, H. 1884 (Rossall School) 1
Lockhart, N. H. 1947 (Linfield, Coventry C, Aston Villa) 8
Lomas, S. M. 1994 (Manchester C, West Ham U) 45
Loyal, J. 1891 (Clarence) 1
Lund, M. C. 2017 (Rochdale) 3
Lutton, R. J. 1970 (Wolverhampton W, West Ham U) 6
Lynas, R. 1925 (Cliftonville) 1
Lyner, D. R. 1920 (Glentoran, Manchester U, Kilmarnock) 6
Lytle, J. 1898 (Glentoran) 1

Madden, O. 1938 (Norwich C) 1
Magee, G. 1885 (Wellington Park) 3
Magennis, J. B. D. 2010 (Cardiff C, Aberdeen, St Mirren, Kilmarnock, Charlton Ath, Bolton W, Hull C, Wigan Ath) 67
Magill, E. J. 1962 (Arsenal, Brighton & HA) 26
Magilton, J. 1991 (Oxford U, Southampton, Sheffield W, Ipswich T) 52
Maginnis, H. 1900 (Linfield) 8
Maguire, E. 1907 (Distillery) 1
Mahood, J. 1926 (Belfast Celtic, Ballymena) 9
Manderson, R. 1920 (Rangers) 5
Mannus, A. 2004 (Linfield, St Johnstone) 9
Mansfield, J. 1901 (Dublin Freebooters) 1
Martin, C. 1925 (Bo'ness) 1
Martin, C. J. 1947 (Glentoran, Leeds U, Aston Villa) 6
Martin, D. C. 1882 (Cliftonville) 3
Martin, D. K. 1934 (Belfast Celtic, Wolverhampton W, Nottingham F) 10
Mathieson, A. 1921 (Luton T) 2
Maxwell, J. 1902 (Linfield, Glentoran, Belfast Celtic) 7
McAdams, W. J. 1954 (Manchester C, Bolton W, Leeds U) 15
McAlery, J. M. 1882 (Cliftonville) 2
McAlinden, J. 1938 (Belfast Celtic, Portsmouth, Southend U) 4
McAllen, J. 1898 (Linfield) 9
McAlpine, S. 1901 (Cliftonville) 1
McArdle, R. A. 2010 (Rochdale, Aberdeen, Bradford C) 7
McArthur, A. 1886 (Distillery) 1
McAuley, G. 2005 (Lincoln C, Leicester C, Ipswich T, WBA, Rangers) 80
McAuley, J. L. 1911 (Huddersfield T) 6
McAuley, P. 1900 (Belfast Celtic) 1
McBride, S. D. 1991 (Glenavon) 4
McCabe, J. J. 1949 (Leeds U) 6
McCabe, W. 1891 (Ulster) 1
McCalmont, A. J. 2020 (Leeds U) 4
McCambridge, J. 1930 (Ballymena, Cardiff C) 4
McCandless, J. 1912 (Bradford) 5
McCandless, W. 1920 (Linfield, Rangers) 9
McCann, A. 2021 (St Johnstone, Preston NE) 14

McCann, G. S. 2002 (West Ham U, Cheltenham T, Barnsley, Scunthorpe U, Peterborough U) 39
McCann, P. 1910 (Belfast Celtic, Glentoran) 7
McCartan, S. V. 2017 (Accrington S, Bradford C) 2
McCarthy, J. D. 1996 (Port Vale, Birmingham C) 18
McCartney, A. 1903 (Ulster, Linfield, Everton, Belfast Celtic, Glentoran) 15
McCartney, G. 2002 (Sunderland, West Ham U, Sunderland) 34
McCashin, J. W. 1896 (Cliftonville) 5
McCavana, W. T. 1955 (Coleraine) 3
McCaw, J. H. 1927 (Linfield) 6
McClatchey, J. 1886 (Distillery) 3
McClatchey, T. 1895 (Distillery) 1
McCleary, J. W. 1955 (Cliftonville) 1
McCleery, W. 1922 (Cliftonville, Linfield) 10
McClelland, J. 1980 (Mansfield T, Rangers, Watford, Leeds U) 53
McClelland, J. T. 1961 (Arsenal, Fulham) 6
McClelland, S. 2021 (Chelsea) 1
McCluggage, A. 1922 (Cliftonville, Bradford, Burnley) 13
McClure, G. 1907 (Cliftonville, Distillery) 4
McConnell, E. 1904 (Cliftonville, Glentoran, Sunderland, Sheffield W) 12
McConnell, P. 1928 (Doncaster R, Southport) 2
McConnell, W. G. 1912 (Bohemians) 6
McConnell, W. H. 1925 (Reading) 8
McCourt, F. J. 1952 (Manchester C) 6
McCourt, P. J. 2002 (Rochdale, Celtic, Barnsley, Brighton & HA, Luton T) 18
McCoy, R. K. 1987 (Coleraine) 1
McCoy, S. 1896 (Distillery) 1
McCracken, E. 1928 (Barking) 1
McCracken, R. 1921 (Crystal Palace) 4
McCracken, R. 1922 (Linfield) 1
McCracken, W. R. 1902 (Distillery, Newcastle U, Hull C) 16
McCreery, D. 1976 (Manchester U, QPR, Tulsa Roughnecks, Newcastle U, Hearts) 67
McCrory, S. 1958 (Southend U) 1
McCullough, K. 1935 (Belfast Celtic, Manchester C) 5
McCullough, L. 2014 (Doncaster R) 6
McCullough, W. J. 1961 (Arsenal, Millwall) 10
McCurdy, C. 1980 (Linfield) 1
McDonald, A. 1986 (QPR) 52
McDonald, R. 1930 (Rangers) 2
McDonnell, J. 1911 (Bohemians) 4
McElhinney, G. M. A. 1984 (Bolton W) 6
McEvilly, L. R. 2002 (Rochdale) 1
McFaul, W. S. 1967 (Linfield, Newcastle U) 6
McGarry, J. K. 1951 (Cliftonville) 3
McGaughey, M. 1985 (Linfield) 1
McGibbon, P. C. G. 1995 (Manchester U, Wigan Ath) 7
McGinn, N. 2009 (Derry C, Celtic, Brentford, Aberdeen, Gwangju, Aberdeen, Dundee) 73
McGivern, R. 2009 (Manchester C, Hibernian, Port Vale, Shrewsbury) 24
McGovern, M. 2010 (Ross Co, Hamilton A, Norwich C) 33
McGrath, R. C. 1974 (Tottenham H, Manchester U) 21
McGregor, S. 1921 (Glentoran) 1
McGrillen, J. 1924 (Clyde, Belfast Celtic) 2
McGuire, J. 1928 (Linfield) 1
McIlroy, H. 1906 (Cliftonville) 1
McIlroy, J. 1952 (Burnley, Stoke C) 55
McIlroy, S. B. 1972 (Manchester U, Stoke C, Manchester C) 88
McIlvenny, P. 1924 (Distillery) 1
McIlvenny, R. 1890 (Distillery, Ulster) 2
McKay, W. R. 2013 (Inverness CT, Wigan Ath) 11
McKeag, W. 1968 (Glentoran) 2
McKeague, T. 1925 (Glentoran) 1
McKee, F. W. 1906 (Cliftonville, Belfast Celtic) 5
McKee, H. 1895 (Cliftonville) 3
McKelvey, H. 1901 (Glentoran) 2
McKenna, J. 1950 (Huddersfield T) 7
McKenzie, H. 1922 (Distillery) 2
McKenzie, R. 1967 (Airdrieonians) 1
McKeown, N. 1892 (Linfield) 7
Mackie, J. A. 1923 (Arsenal, Portsmouth) 3
McKinney, D. 1921 (Hull C, Bradford C) 2
McKinney, V. J. 1966 (Falkirk) 1
McKnight, A. D. 1988 (Celtic, West Ham U) 10
McKnight, J. 1912 (Preston NE, Glentoran) 2
McLaughlin, C. G. 2012 (Preston NE, Fleetwood T, Millwall, Sunderland) 43
McLaughlin, J. C. 1962 (Shrewsbury T, Swansea T) 12
McLaughlin, R. 2014 (Liverpool, Oldham Ath) 5
McLean, B. S. 2006 (Rangers) 1
McLean, T. 1885 (Limavady) 1
McMahon, G. J. 1995 (Tottenham H, Stoke C) 17
McMahon, J. 1934 (Bohemians) 1
McMaster, G. 1897 (Glentoran) 3
McMenamin, C. 2022 (Glentoran) 3
McMichael, A. 1950 (Newcastle U) 40
McMillan, G. 1903 (Distillery) 2
McMillan, S. T. 1963 (Manchester U) 2
McMillen, W. S. 1934 (Manchester U, Chesterfield) 7
McMordie, A. S. 1969 (Middlesbrough) 21
McMorran, E. J. 1947 (Belfast Celtic, Barnsley, Doncaster R) 15
McMullan, D. 1926 (Liverpool) 3
McNair, P. J. C. 2015 (Manchester U, Sunderland, Middlesbrough) 56
McNally, B. A. 1986 (Shrewsbury T) 5
McNinch, J. 1931 (Ballymena) 3
McPake, J. 2012 (Coventry C) 1
McParland, P. J. 1954 (Aston Villa, Wolverhampton W) 34
McQuoid, J. J. B. 2011 (Millwall) 5
McShane, J. 1899 (Cliftonville) 4
McVeigh, P. M. 1999 (Tottenham H, Norwich C) 20
McVicker, J. 1888 (Linfield, Glentoran) 2
McWha, W. B. R. 1882 (Knock, Cliftonville) 7
Meek, H. L. 1925 (Glentoran) 1
Mehaffy, J. A. C. 1922 (Queen's Island) 1
Meldon, P. A. 1899 (Dublin Freebooters) 2
Mercer, H. V. A. 1908 (Linfield) 1
Mercer, J. T. 1898 (Distillery, Linfield, Distillery, Derby Co) 12
Millar, W. 1932 (Barrow) 2
Miller, J. 1929 (Middlesbrough) 3
Milligan, D. 1939 (Chesterfield) 1
Milne, R. G. 1894 (Linfield) 28
Mitchell, E. J. 1933 (Cliftonville, Glentoran) 2
Mitchell, W. 1932 (Distillery, Chelsea) 15
Molyneux, T. B. 1883 (Ligoniel, Cliftonville) 11
Montgomery, F. J. 1955 (Coleraine) 1
Moore, C. 1949 (Glentoran) 1
Moore, P. 1933 (Aberdeen) 1
Moore, R. 1891 (Linfield Ath) 3
Moore, R. L. 1887 (Ulster) 2
Moore, W. 1923 (Falkirk) 1
Moorhead, F. W. 1885 (Dublin University) 1
Moorhead, G. 1923 (Linfield) 4
Moran, J. 1912 (Leeds C) 1
Moreland, V. 1979 (Derby Co) 6
Morgan, G. F. 1922 (Linfield, Nottingham F) 8
Morgan, S. 1972 (Port Vale, Aston Villa, Brighton & HA, Sparta Rotterdam) 18
Morrison, R. 1891 (Linfield Ath) 2
Morrison, T. 1895 (Glentoran, Burnley) 7
Morrogh, D. 1896 (Bohemians) 1
Morrow, S. J. 1990 (Arsenal, QPR) 39
Morrow, W. J. 1883 (Moyola Park) 3
Muir, R. 1885 (Oldpark) 2
Mulgrew, J. 2010 (Linfield) 2
Mulholland, T. S. 1906 (Belfast Celtic) 2
Mullan, G. 1983 (Glentoran) 4
Mulligan, J. 1921 (Manchester C) 1
Mulryne, P. P. 1997 (Manchester U, Norwich C, Cardiff C) 27
Murdock, C. J. 2000 (Preston NE, Hibernian, Crewe Alex, Rotherham U) 34
Murphy, J. 1910 (Bradford C) 3
Murphy, N. 1905 (QPR) 3
Murray, J. M. 1910 (Motherwell, Sheffield W) 3

Napier, R. J. 1966 (Bolton W) 1
Neill, W. J. T. 1961 (Arsenal, Hull C) 59
Nelis, P. 1923 (Nottingham F) 1
Nelson, S. 1970 (Arsenal, Brighton & HA) 51
Nicholl, C. J. 1975 (Aston Villa, Southampton, Grimsby T) 51
Nicholl, H. 1902 (Belfast Celtic) 3
Nicholl, J. M. 1976 (Manchester U, Toronto Blizzard, Sunderland, Toronto Blizzard, Rangers, Toronto Blizzard, WBA) 73
Nicholson, J. J. 1961 (Manchester U, Huddersfield T) 41
Nixon, R. 1914 (Linfield) 1
Nolan, I. R. 1997 (Sheffield W, Bradford C, Wigan Ath) 18

Nolan-Whelan, J. V. 1901 (Dublin Freebooters) 5
Norwood, O. J. 2011 (Manchester U, Huddersfield T, Reading, Brighton & HA) 57

O'Boyle, G. 1994 (Dunfermline Ath, St Johnstone) 13
O'Brien, M. T. 1921 (QPR, Leicester C, Hull C, Derby Co) 10
O'Connell, P. 1912 (Sheffield W, Hull C) 5
O'Connor, M. J. 2008 (Crewe Alex, Scunthorpe U, Rotherham U) 11
O'Doherty, A. 1970 (Coleraine) 2
O'Driscoll, J. F. 1949 (Swansea T) 3
O'Hagan, C. 1905 (Tottenham H, Aberdeen) 11
O'Hagan, W. 1920 (St Mirren) 2
O'Kane, W. J. 1970 (Nottingham F) 20
O'Mahoney, M. T. 1939 (Bristol R) 1
O'Neill, C. 1989 (Motherwell) 3
O'Neill, J. 1962 (Sunderland) 1
O'Neill, J. P. 1980 (Leicester C) 39
O'Neill, M. A. M. 1988 (Newcastle U, Dundee U, Hibernian, Coventry C) 31
O'Neill, M. H. M. 1972 (Distillery, Nottingham F, Norwich C, Manchester C, Norwich C, Notts Co) 64
O'Reilly, H. 1901 (Dublin Freebooters) 3
Owens, J. 2011 (Crusaders) 1

Parke, J. 1964 (Linfield, Hibernian, Sunderland) 14
Paterson, M. A. 2008 (Scunthorpe U, Burnley, Huddersfield T) 22
Paton, P. R. 2014 (Dundee U) 4
Patterson, D. J. 1994 (Crystal Palace, Luton T, Dundee U) 17
Patterson, R. 2010 (Coleraine, Plymouth Arg) 5
Peacock, R. 1952 (Celtic, Coleraine) 31
Peacock-Farrell, B. 2018 (Leeds U, Burnley) 33
Peden, J. 1887 (Linfield, Distillery) 24
Penney, S. 1985 (Brighton & HA) 17
Percy, J. C. 1889 (Belfast YMCA) 1
Platt, J. A. 1976 (Middlesbrough, Ballymena U, Coleraine) 23
Pollock, W. 1928 (Belfast Celtic) 1
Ponsonby, J. 1895 (Distillery) 9
Potts, R. M. C. 1883 (Cliftonville) 2
Priestley, T. J. M. 1933 (Coleraine, Chelsea) 2
Pyper, Jas. 1897 (Cliftonville) 7
Pyper, John 1897 (Cliftonville) 9
Pyper, M. 1932 (Linfield) 1

Quinn, J. M. 1985 (Blackburn R, Swindon T, Leicester C, Bradford C, West Ham U, Bournemouth, Reading) 46
Quinn, S. J. 1996 (Blackpool, WBA, Willem II, Sheffield W, Peterborough U, Northampton T) 50

Rafferty, P. 1980 (Linfield) 1
Ramsey, P. C. 1984 (Leicester C) 14
Rankin, J. 1883 (Alexander) 2
Rattray, D. 1882 (Avoniel) 3
Rea, R. 1901 (Glentoran) 1
Redmond, R. 1884 (Cliftonville) 1
Reeves, B. N. 2015 (Milton Keynes D) 2
Reid, G. H. 1923 (Cardiff C) 1
Reid, J. 1883 (Ulster) 6
Reid, S. E. 1934 (Derby Co) 3
Reid, W. 1931 (Hearts) 1
Reilly, M. M. 1900 (Portsmouth) 2
Renneville, W. T. J. 1910 (Leyton, Aston Villa) 4
Reynolds, J. 1890 (Distillery, Ulster) 5
Reynolds, R. 1905 (Bohemians) 1
Rice, P. J. 1969 (Arsenal) 49
Roberts, F. C. 1931 (Glentoran) 1
Robinson, P. 1920 (Distillery, Blackburn R) 2
Robinson, S. 1997 (Bournemouth, Luton T) 7
Rogan, A. 1988 (Celtic, Sunderland, Millwall) 18
Rollo, D. 1912 (Linfield, Blackburn R) 16
Roper, E. O. 1886 (Dublin University) 1
Rosbotham, A. 1887 (Cliftonville) 7
Ross, W. E. 1969 (Newcastle U) 1
Rowland, K. 1994 (West Ham U, QPR) 19
Rowley, R. W. M. 1929 (Southampton, Tottenham H) 6
Rushe, F. 1925 (Distillery) 1
Russell, A. 1947 (Linfield) 1
Russell, S. R. 1930 (Bradford C, Derry C) 3
Ryan, R. A. 1950 (WBA) 1

Sanchez, L. P. 1987 (Wimbledon) 3
Saville, G. A. 2018 (Millwall, Middlesbrough, Millwall) 40
Scott, E. 1920 (Liverpool, Belfast Celtic) 31
Scott, J. 1958 (Grimsby) 2
Scott, J. E. 1901 (Cliftonville) 1
Scott, L. J. 1895 (Dublin University) 2
Scott, P. W. 1975 (Everton, York C, Aldershot) 10
Scott, T. 1894 (Cliftonville) 13
Scott, W. 1903 (Linfield, Everton, Leeds C) 25
Scraggs, M. J. 1921 (Glentoran) 2
Seymour, H. C. 1914 (Bohemians) 1
Seymour, J. 1907 (Cliftonville) 2
Shanks, T. 1903 (Woolwich Arsenal, Brentford) 3
Sharkey, P. G. 1976 (Ipswich T) 1
Sheehan, Dr G. 1899 (Bohemians) 3
Sheridan, J. 1903 (Everton, Stoke C) 6
Sherrard, J. 1885 (Limavady) 3
Sherrard, W. C. 1895 (Cliftonville) 3
Sherry, J. J. 1906 (Bohemians) 2
Shields, R. J. 1957 (Southampton) 1
Shiels, D. 2006 (Hibernian, Doncaster R, Kilmarnock) 14
Silo, M. 1888 (Belfast YMCA) 1
Simpson, W. J. 1951 (Rangers) 12
Sinclair, J. 1882 (Knock) 2
Slemin, J. C. 1909 (Bohemians) 1
Sloan, A. S. 1925 (London Caledonians) 1
Sloan, D. 1969 (Oxford U) 2
Sloan, H. A. de B. 1903 (Bohemians) 8
Sloan, J. W. 1947 (Arsenal) 1
Sloan, T. 1926 (Cardiff C, Linfield) 11
Sloan, T. 1979 (Manchester U) 3
Small, J. M. 1887 (Clarence, Cliftonville) 4
Smith, A. W. 2003 (Glentoran, Preston NE) 18
Smith, E. E. 1921 (Cardiff C) 4
Smith, J. E. 1901 (Distillery) 2
Smith, M. 2016 (Peterborough U, Hearts) 19
Smyth, P. P. 2018 (QPR) 3
Smyth, R. H. 1886 (Dublin University) 1
Smyth, S. 1948 (Wolverhampton W, Stoke C) 9
Smyth, W. 1949 (Distillery) 4
Snape, A. 1920 (Airdrieonians) 1
Sonner, D. J. 1998 (Ipswich T, Sheffield W, Birmingham C, Nottingham F, Peterborough U) 13
Southwood, L. K. 2022 (Reading) 1
Spence, D. W. 1975 (Bury, Blackpool, Southend U) 29
Spencer, B. G. 2022 (Huddersfield T) 3
Spencer, S. 1890 (Distillery) 6
Spiller, E. A. 1883 (Cliftonville) 5
Sproule, I. 2006 (Hibernian, Bristol C) 11
Stanfield, O. M. 1887 (Distillery) 30
Steele, A. 1926 (Charlton Ath, Fulham) 4
Steele, J. 2013 (New York Red Bulls) 3
Stevenson, A. E. 1934 (Rangers, Everton) 17
Stewart, A. 1967 (Glentoran, Derby Co) 7
Stewart, D. C. 1978 (Hull C) 1
Stewart, I. 1982 (QPR, Newcastle U) 31
Stewart, R. K. 1890 (St Columb's Court, Cliftonville) 11
Stewart, T. C. 1961 (Linfield) 1
Swan, S. 1899 (Linfield) 1

Taggart, G. P. 1990 (Barnsley, Bolton W, Leicester C) 51
Taggart, J. 1899 (Walsall) 1
Taylor, D. 2022 (Nottingham F) 1
Taylor, M. S. 1999 (Fulham, Birmingham C, unattached) 88
Thompson, A. L. 2011 (Watford) 2
Thompson, F. W. 1910 (Cliftonville, Linfield, Bradford C, Clyde) 12
Thompson, J. 1897 (Distillery) 1
Thompson, J. A. 2018 (Rangers, Blackpool, Stoke C) 24
Thompson, P. 2006 (Linfield, Stockport Co) 8
Thompson, R. 1928 (Queen's Island) 1
Thompson, W. 1889 (Belfast Ath) 1
Thunder, P. J. 1911 (Bohemians) 1
Todd, S. J. 1966 (Burnley, Sheffield W) 11
Toner, C. 2003 (Leyton Orient) 2
Toner, J. 1922 (Arsenal, St Johnstone) 8
Torrans, R. 1893 (Linfield) 1
Torrans, S. 1889 (Linfield) 26
Trainor, D. 1967 (Crusaders) 1
Tuffey, J. 2009 (Partick Thistle, Inverness CT) 8
Tully, C. P. 1949 (Celtic) 10
Turner, A. 1896 (Cliftonville) 1
Turner, E. 1896 (Cliftonville) 1
Turner, W. 1886 (Cliftonville) 3
Twomey, J. F. 1938 (Leeds U) 2

Uprichard, W. N. M. C. 1952 (Swindon T, Portsmouth) 18

Vassell, K. T. 2019 (Rotherham U) 2
Vernon, J. 1947 (Belfast Celtic, WBA) 17

Waddell, T. M. R. 1906 (Cliftonville) 1
Walker, J. 1955 (Doncaster R) 1
Walker, T. 1911 (Bury) 1
Walsh, D. J. 1947 (WBA) 9
Walsh, W. 1948 (Manchester C) 5
Ward, J. J. 2012 (Derby Co, Nottingham F) 35
Waring, J. 1899 (Cliftonville) 1
Warren, P. 1913 (Shelbourne) 2
Washington, C. J. 2016 (QPR, Sheffield U, Hearts, Charlton Ath) 35
Watson, J. 1883 (Ulster) 9
Watson, P. 1971 (Distillery) 1
Watson, T. 1926 (Cardiff C) 1
Wattie, J. 1899 (Distillery) 1
Webb, C. G. 1909 (Brighton & HA) 3
Webb, S. M. 2006 (Ross Co) 4
Weir, E. 1939 (Clyde) 1
Welsh, E. 1966 (Carlisle U) 4
Whiteside, N. 1982 (Manchester U, Everton) 38
Whiteside, T. 1891 (Distillery) 1
Whitfield, E. R. 1886 (Dublin University) 1
Whitley, Jeff 1997 (Manchester C, Sunderland, Cardiff C) 20
Whitley, Jim 1998 (Manchester C) 3
Whyte, G. 2019 (Oxford U, Cardiff C) 27
Williams, J. R. 1886 (Ulster) 2
Williams, M. S. 1999 (Chesterfield, Watford, Wimbledon, Stoke C, Wimbledon, Milton Keynes D) 36
Williams, P. A. 1991 (WBA) 1
Williamson, J. 1890 (Cliftonville) 3
Willighan, T. 1933 (Burnley) 2
Willis, G. 1906 (Linfield) 4
Wilson, D. J. 1987 (Brighton & HA, Luton T, Sheffield W) 24
Wilson, H. 1925 (Linfield) 2
Wilson, K. J. 1987 (Ipswich T, Chelsea, Notts Co, Walsall) 42
Wilson, M. 1884 (Distillery) 3
Wilson, R. 1888 (Cliftonville) 1
Wilson, S. J. 1962 (Glenavon, Falkirk, Dundee) 12
Wilton, J. M. 1888 (St Columb's Court, Cliftonville, St Columb's Court) 7
Winchester, C. 2011 (Oldham Ath) 1
Wood, T. J. 1996 (Walsall) 1
Worthington, N. 1984 (Sheffield W, Leeds U, Stoke C) 66
Wright, J. 1906 (Cliftonville) 6
Wright, T. J. 1989 (Newcastle U, Nottingham F, Manchester C) 31

Young, S. 1907 (Linfield, Airdrieonians, Linfield) 9

SCOTLAND

Scottish appearances and goals include those made on the Scottish tour of 1967. In October 2021, the following matches were upgraded to full internationals: v Israel (Tel Aviv, 16 May 1967); v Australia (Sydney, 28 May 1967); v Australia (Adelaide, 31 May 1967); v Australia (Melbourne, 3 June 1967); v Canada (Winnipeg, 13 June 1967).

Adam, C. G. 2007 (Rangers, Blackpool, Liverpool, Stoke C) 26
Adams, C. Z. E. F. 2021 (Southampton) 19
Adams, J. 1889 (Hearts) 3
Agnew, W. B. 1907 (Kilmarnock) 3
Aird, J. 1954 (Burnley) 4
Aitken, A. 1901 (Newcastle U, Middlesbrough, Leicester Fosse) 14
Aitken, G. G. 1949 (East Fife, Sunderland) 8
Aitken, R. 1886 (Dumbarton) 2
Aitken, R. 1980 (Celtic, Newcastle U, St Mirren) 57
Aitkenhead, W. A. C. 1912 (Blackburn R) 1
Albiston, A. 1982 (Manchester U) 14
Alexander, D. 1894 (East Stirlingshire) 2
Alexander, G. 2002 (Preston NE, Burnley) 40
Alexander, N. 2006 (Cardiff C) 3
Allan, D. S. 1885 (Queen's Park) 3
Allan, G. 1897 (Liverpool) 1
Allan, H. 1902 (Hearts) 1
Allan, J. 1887 (Queen's Park) 2
Allan, T. 1974 (Dundee) 2
Ancell, R. F. D. 1937 (Newcastle U) 2
Anderson, A. 1933 (Hearts) 28
Anderson, F. 1874 (Clydesdale) 1
Anderson, G. 1901 (Kilmarnock) 1
Anderson, H. A. 1914 (Raith R) 1
Anderson, J. 1954 (Leicester C) 1
Anderson, K. 1896 (Queen's Park) 3
Anderson, R. 2003 (Aberdeen, Sunderland) 11
Anderson, W. 1882 (Queen's Park) 6
Andrews, P. 1875 (Eastern) 1
Anya, I. 2013 (Watford, Derby Co) 29
Archer, J. G. 2018 (Millwall) 1
Archibald, A. 1921 (Rangers) 8
Archibald, S. 1980 (Aberdeen, Tottenham H, Barcelona) 27
Armstrong, M. W. 1936 (Aberdeen) 3
Armstrong, S. 2017 (Celtic, Southampton) 36
Arnott, W. 1883 (Queen's Park) 14
Auld, J. R. 1887 (Third Lanark) 3
Auld, R. 1959 (Celtic) 3

Bain, S. 2018 (Celtic) 3
Baird, A. 1892 (Queen's Park) 2
Baird, D. 1890 (Hearts) 3
Baird, H. 1956 (Airdrieonians) 1
Baird, J. C. 1876 (Vale of Leven) 3
Baird, S. 1957 (Rangers) 7
Baird, W. U. 1897 (St Bernard) 1
Bannan, B. 2011 (Aston Villa, Crystal Palace, Sheffield W) 27
Bannon, E. J. 1980 (Dundee U) 11
Barbour, A. 1885 (Renton) 1
Bardsley, P. A. 2011 (Sunderland) 13
Barker, J. B. 1893 (Rangers) 2
Barr, D. 2009 (Falkirk) 1
Barrett, F. 1894 (Dundee) 2
Bates, D. 2019 (Hamburg) 4
Battles, B. 1901 (Celtic) 3
Battles, B. jun. 1931 (Hearts) 1
Bauld, W. 1950 (Hearts) 3
Baxter, J. C. 1961 (Rangers, Sunderland) 34
Baxter, R. D. 1939 (Middlesbrough) 3
Beattie, A. 1937 (Preston NE) 7
Beattie, C. 2006 (Celtic, WBA) 7
Beattie, R. 1939 (Preston NE) 1
Begbie, I. 1890 (Hearts) 4
Bell, A. 1912 (Manchester U) 1
Bell, C. 2011 (Kilmarnock) 1
Bell, J. 1890 (Dumbarton, Everton, Celtic) 10
Bell, M. 1901 (Hearts) 1
Bell, W. J. 1966 (Leeds U) 2
Bennett, A. 1904 (Celtic, Rangers) 11
Bennie, R. 1925 (Airdrieonians) 3
Bernard, P. R. J. 1995 (Oldham Ath) 2
Berra, C. D. 2008 (Hearts, Wolverhampton W, Ipswich T) 41
Berry, D. 1894 (Queen's Park) 3
Berry, W. H. 1888 (Queen's Park) 4
Bett, J. 1982 (Rangers, Lokeren, Aberdeen) 25
Beveridge, W. W. 1879 (Glasgow University) 3
Black, A. 1938 (Hearts) 3
Black, D. 1889 (Hurlford) 1
Black, E. 1988 (Metz) 2
Black, I. 2013 (Rangers) 1
Black, I. H. 1948 (Southampton) 1
Blackburn, J. E. 1873 (Royal Engineers) 1
Blacklaw, A. S. 1963 (Burnley) 3
Blackley, J. 1974 (Hibernian) 7
Blair, D. 1929 (Clyde, Aston Villa) 8
Blair, J. 1920 (Sheffield W, Cardiff C) 8
Blair, J. 1934 (Motherwell) 1
Blair, J. A. 1947 (Blackpool) 1
Blair, W. 1896 (Third Lanark) 1
Blessington, J. 1894 (Celtic) 4
Blyth, J. A. 1978 (Coventry C) 2
Bone, J. 1972 (Norwich C) 2
Booth, S. 1993 (Aberdeen, Borussia Dortmund, Twente) 21
Bowie, J. 1920 (Rangers) 2

Bowie, W. 1891 (Linthouse) 1
Bowman, D. 1992 (Dundee U) 6
Bowman, G. A. 1892 (Montrose) 1
Boyd, G. I. 2013 (Peterborough U, Hull C) 2
Boyd, J. M. 1934 (Newcastle U) 1
Boyd, K. 2006 (Rangers, Middlesbrough) 18
Boyd, R. 1889 (Mossend Swifts) 2
Boyd, T. 1991 (Motherwell, Chelsea, Celtic) 72
Boyd, W. G. 1931 (Clyde) 2
Bradshaw, T. 1928 (Bury) 1
Brand, R. 1961 (Rangers) 8
Brandon, T. 1896 (Blackburn R) 1
Brazil, A. 1980 (Ipswich T, Tottenham H) 13
Breckenridge, T. 1888 (Hearts) 1
Bremner, D. 1976 (Hibernian) 1
Bremner, W. J. 1965 (Leeds U) 54
Brennan, F. 1947 (Newcastle U) 7
Breslin, B. 1897 (Hibernian) 1
Brewster, G. 1921 (Everton) 1
Bridcutt, L. 2013 (Brighton & HA, Sunderland) 2
Broadfoot, K. 2009 (Rangers) 4
Brogan, J. 1971 (Celtic) 4
Brophy, E. 2019 (Kilmarnock) 1
Brown, A. 1890 (St Mirren) 2
Brown, A. 1904 (Middlesbrough) 1
Brown, A. D. 1950 (East Fife, Blackpool) 14
Brown, G. C. P. 1931 (Rangers) 19
Brown, H. 1947 (Partick Thistle) 3
Brown, J. B. 1939 (Clyde) 1
Brown, J. G. 1975 (Sheffield U) 1
Brown, J. S. 2022 (Stoke C) 5
Brown, R. 1884 (Dumbarton) 2
Brown, R. 1890 (Cambuslang) 1
Brown, R. 1947 (Rangers) 3
Brown, R. jun. 1885 (Dumbarton) 1
Brown, S. 2006 (Hibernian, Celtic) 55
Brown, W. D. F. 1958 (Dundee, Tottenham H) 28
Browning, J. 1914 (Celtic) 1
Brownlie, J. 1909 (Third Lanark) 16
Brownlie, J. 1971 (Hibernian) 7
Bruce, D. 1890 (Vale of Leven) 1
Bruce, R. F. 1934 (Middlesbrough) 1
Bryson, C. 2011 (Kilmarnock, Derby Co) 3
Buchan, M. M. 1972 (Aberdeen, Manchester U) 34
Buchanan, J. 1889 (Cambuslang) 1
Buchanan, J. 1929 (Rangers) 2
Buchanan, P. S. 1938 (Chelsea) 1
Buchanan, R. 1891 (Abercorn) 1
Buckley, P. 1954 (Aberdeen) 3
Buick, A. 1902 (Hearts) 2
Burchill, M. J. 2000 (Celtic) 6
Burke, C. 2006 (Rangers, Birmingham C) 7
Burke, O. J. 2016 (Nottingham F, RB Leipzig, WBA, Sheffield U) 13
Burley, C. W. 1995 (Chelsea, Celtic, Derby Co) 46
Burley, G. E. 1979 (Ipswich T) 11
Burns, F. 1970 (Manchester U) 1
Burns, K. 1974 (Birmingham C, Nottingham F) 20
Burns, T. 1981 (Celtic) 8
Busby, M. W. 1934 (Manchester C) 1

Cadden, C. 2018 (Motherwell) 2
Caddis, P. M. 2016 (Birmingham C) 1
Cairney, T. 2017 (Fulham) 2
Cairns, T. 1920 (Rangers) 8
Calderhead, D. 1889 (Q of S Wanderers) 1
Calderwood, C. 1995 (Tottenham H) 36
Calderwood, R. 1885 (Cartvale) 3
Caldow, E. 1957 (Rangers) 40
Caldwell, G. 2002 (Newcastle U, Hibernian, Celtic, Wigan Ath) 55
Caldwell, S. 2001 (Newcastle U, Sunderland, Burnley,Wigan Ath) 12
Callaghan, P. 1900 (Hibernian) 1
Callaghan, W. 1967 (Dunfermline Ath) 6
Cameron, C. 1999 (Hearts, Wolverhampton W) 28
Cameron, J. 1886 (Rangers) 1
Cameron, J. 1896 (Queen's Park) 1
Cameron, J. 1904 (St Mirren, Chelsea) 2
Campbell, A. 2022 (Luton T) 1
Campbell, C. 1874 (Queen's Park) 13
Campbell, H. 1889 (Renton) 1
Campbell, Jas 1913 (Sheffield W) 1
Campbell, J. 1880 (South Western) 1
Campbell, J. 1891 (Kilmarnock) 2
Campbell, John 1893 (Celtic) 12
Campbell, John 1899 (Rangers) 4
Campbell, K. 1920 (Liverpool, Partick Thistle) 8
Campbell, P. 1878 (Rangers) 2
Campbell, P. 1898 (Morton) 1
Campbell, R. 1947 (Falkirk, Chelsea) 5
Campbell, W. 1947 (Morton) 5
Canero, P. 2004 (Leicester C) 1
Carabine, J. 1938 (Third Lanark) 3
Carr, W. M. 1970 (Coventry C) 6
Cassidy, J. 1921 (Celtic) 4
Chalmers, S. 1965 (Celtic) 5
Chalmers, W. 1885 (Rangers) 1
Chalmers, W. S. 1929 (Queen's Park) 1
Chambers, T. 1894 (Hearts) 1
Chaplin, G. D. 1908 (Dundee) 1
Cheyne, A. G. 1929 (Aberdeen) 5
Christie, A. J. 1898 (Queen's Park) 3
Christie, R. 2018 (Celtic, Bournemouth) 31
Christie, R. M. 1884 (Queen's Park) 1
Clark, J. 1966 (Celtic) 4
Clark, R. B. 1968 (Aberdeen) 17
Clarke, S. 1988 (Chelsea) 6
Clarkson, D. 2008 (Motherwell) 2
Cleland, J. 1891 (Royal Albert) 1
Clements, R. 1891 (Leith Ath) 1
Clunas, W. L. 1924 (Sunderland) 2
Collier, W. 1922 (Raith R) 1
Collins, J. 1988 (Hibernian, Celtic, Monaco, Everton) 58
Collins, R. Y. 1951 (Celtic, Everton, Leeds U) 31
Collins, T. 1909 (Hearts) 1
Colman, D. 1911 (Aberdeen) 4
Colquhoun, E. P. 1967 (WBA, Sheffield U) 11
Colquhoun, J. 1988 (Hearts) 2
Combe, J. R. 1948 (Hibernian) 3
Commons, K. 2009 (Derby Co, Celtic) 12
Conn, A. 1956 (Hearts) 1
Conn, A. 1975 (Tottenham H) 2
Connachan, E. D. 1962 (Dunfermline Ath) 2
Connelly, G. 1974 (Celtic) 2
Connolly, J. 1973 (Everton) 1
Connor, J. 1886 (Airdrieonians) 1
Connor, J. 1930 (Sunderland) 4
Connor, R. 1986 (Dundee, Aberdeen) 4
Considine, A. 2021 (Aberdeen) 3
Conway, C. 2010 (Dundee U, Cardiff C) 7
Cook, W. L. 1934 (Bolton W) 3
Cooke, C. 1966 (Dundee, Chelsea) 16
Cooper, D. 1980 (Rangers, Motherwell) 22
Cooper, L. D. I. 2020 (Leeds U) 14
Cormack, P. B. 1966 (Hibernian, Nottingham F) 9
Cowan, J. 1896 (Aston Villa) 3
Cowan, J. 1948 (Morton) 25
Cowan, W, D. 1924 (Newcastle U) 1
Cowie, D. 1953 (Dundee) 20
Cowie, D. M. 2010 (Watford, Cardiff C) 10
Cox, C. J. 1948 (Hearts) 1
Cox, S. 1949 (Rangers) 24
Craig, A. 1929 (Motherwell) 3
Craig, J. 1977 (Celtic) 1
Craig, J. P. 1968 (Celtic) 1
Craig, T. 1927 (Rangers) 8
Craig, T. B. 1976 (Newcastle U) 1
Crainey, S. D. 2002 (Celtic, Southampton, Blackpool) 12
Crapnell, J. 1929 (Airdrieonians) 9
Crawford, D. 1894 (St Mirren, Rangers) 3
Crawford, J. 1932 (Queen's Park) 5
Crawford, S. 1995 (Raith R, Dunfermline Ath, Plymouth Arg) 25
Crerand, P. T. 1961 (Celtic, Manchester U) 16
Cringan, W. 1920 (Celtic) 5
Crosbie, J. A. 1920 (Ayr U, Birmingham) 2
Croal, J. A. 1913 (Falkirk) 3
Cropley, A. J. 1972 (Hibernian) 2
Cross, J. H. 1903 (Third Lanark) 1
Cruickshank, J. 1964 (Hearts) 9
Crum, J. 1936 (Celtic) 2
Cullen, M. J. 1956 (Luton T) 1
Cumming, D. S. 1938 (Middlesbrough) 1
Cumming, J. 1955 (Hearts) 9
Cummings, G. 1935 (Partick Thistle, Aston Villa) 9
Cummings, J. 2018 (Nottingham F) 2
Cummings, W. 2002 (Chelsea) 1
Cunningham, A. N. 1920 (Rangers) 12
Cunningham, W. C. 1954 (Preston NE) 8
Curran, H. P. 1970 (Wolverhampton W) 5

Dailly, C. 1997 (Derby Co, Blackburn R, West Ham U, Rangers) 67
Dalglish, K. 1972 (Celtic, Liverpool) 102
Davidson, C. I. 1999 (Blackburn R, Leicester C, Preston NE) 19
Davidson, D. 1878 (Queen's Park) 5
Davidson, J. A. 1954 (Partick Thistle) 8
Davidson, M. 2013 (St Johnstone) 1
Davidson, S. 1921 (Middlesbrough) 1
Dawson, A. 1980 (Rangers) 5
Dawson, J. 1935 (Rangers) 14
Deans, J. 1975 (Celtic) 2
Delaney, J. 1936 (Celtic, Manchester U) 13
Devine, A. 1910 (Falkirk) 1
Devlin, M. J. 2020 (Aberdeen) 3
Devlin, P. J. 2003 (Birmingham C) 10
Dewar, G. 1888 (Dumbarton) 2
Dewar, N. 1932 (Third Lanark) 3
Dick, J. 1959 (West Ham U) 1
Dickie, M. 1897 (Rangers) 3
Dickov, P. 2001 (Manchester C, Leicester C, Blackburn R) 10
Dickson, W. 1888 (Dundee Strathmore) 1
Dickson, W. 1970 (Kilmarnock) 5
Divers, J. 1895 (Celtic) 1
Divers, J. 1939 (Celtic) 1
Dixon, P. A. 2013 (Hudderfield T) 3
Dobie, R. S. 2002 (WBA) 6
Docherty, T. H. 1952 (Preston NE, Arsenal) 25
Dodds, D. 1984 (Dundee U) 2
Dodds, J. 1914 (Celtic) 3
Dodds, W. 1997 (Aberdeen, Dundee U, Rangers) 26
Doig, J. E. 1887 (Arbroath, Sunderland) 5
Donachie, W. 1972 (Manchester C) 35
Donaldson, A. 1914 (Bolton W) 6
Donnachie, J. 1913 (Oldham Ath) 3
Donnelly, S. 1997 (Celtic) 10
Dorrans, G. 2010 (WBA, Norwich C) 12
Dougal, J. 1939 (Preston NE) 1
Dougall, C. 1947 (Birmingham C) 1
Dougan, R. 1950 (Hearts) 1
Douglas, A. 1911 (Chelsea) 1
Douglas, B. 2018 (Wolverhampton W) 1
Douglas, J. 1880 (Renfrew) 1
Douglas, R. 2002 (Celtic, Leicester C) 19
Dowds, P. 1892 (Celtic) 1
Downie, R. 1892 (Third Lanark) 1
Doyle, D. 1892 (Celtic) 8
Doyle, J. 1976 (Ayr U) 1
Drummond, J. 1892 (Falkirk, Rangers) 14
Dunbar, M. 1886 (Cartvale) 1
Duncan, A. 1975 (Hibernian) 6
Duncan, D. 1933 (Derby Co) 14
Duncan, D. M. 1948 (East Fife) 3
Duncan, J. 1878 (Alexandra Ath) 2
Duncan, J. 1926 (Leicester C) 1
Duncanson, J. 1947 (Rangers) 1
Dunlop, J. 1890 (St Mirren) 1
Dunlop, W. 1906 (Liverpool) 1
Dunn, J. 1925 (Hibernian, Everton) 6
Durie, G. S. 1988 (Chelsea, Tottenham H, Rangers) 43
Durrant, I. 1988 (Rangers, Kilmarnock) 20
Dykes, J. 1938 (Hearts) 2
Dykes, L. J. 2021 (QPR) 22

Easson, J. F. 1931 (Portsmouth) 3
Elliott, M. S. 1998 (Leicester C) 18
Ellis, J. 1892 (Mossend Swifts) 1
Evans, A. 1982 (Aston Villa) 4
Evans, R. 1949 (Celtic, Chelsea) 48
Ewart, J. 1921 (Bradford C) 1
Ewing, T. 1958 (Partick Thistle) 2

Farm, G. N. 1953 (Blackpool) 10
Ferguson, A. 1967 (Dunfermline Ath) 4
Ferguson, B. 1999 (Rangers, Blackburn R, Rangers) 45
Ferguson, D. 1988 (Rangers) 2
Ferguson, D. 1992 (Dundee U, Everton) 7
Ferguson, I. 1989 (Rangers) 9
Ferguson, J. 1874 (Vale of Leven) 6
Ferguson, L. 2022 (Aberdeen) 4
Ferguson, R. 1966 (Kilmarnock) 7
Fernie, W. 1954 (Celtic) 12
Findlay, R. 1898 (Kilmarnock) 1
Findlay, S. J. 2020 (Kilmarnock) 1
Fitchie, T. T. 1905 (Woolwich Arsenal, Queen's Park) 4
Flavell, R. 1947 (Airdrieonians) 2
Fleck, J. A. 2020 (Sheffield U) 5
Fleck, R. 1990 (Norwich C) 4
Fleming, C. 1954 (East Fife) 1
Fleming, J. W. 1929 (Rangers) 3
Fleming, R. 1886 (Morton) 1
Fletcher, D. B. 2004 (Manchester U, WBA, Stoke C) 80
Fletcher, S. K. 2008 (Hibernian, Burnley, Wolverhampton W, Sunderland, Sheffield W) 33
Forbes, A. R. 1947 (Sheffield U, Arsenal) 14
Forbes, J. 1884 (Vale of Leven) 5
Ford, D. 1974 (Hearts) 3
Forrest, J. 1958 (Motherwell) 1
Forrest, J. 1966 (Rangers, Aberdeen) 5
Forrest, J. 2011 (Celtic) 38
Forsyth, A. 1972 (Partick Thistle, Manchester U) 10
Forsyth, C. 2014 (Derby Co) 4
Forsyth, R. C. 1964 (Kilmarnock) 4
Forsyth, T. 1971 (Motherwell, Rangers) 22
Fox, D. J. 2010 (Burnley, Southampton) 4
Foyers, R. 1893 (St Bernards) 2
Fraser, D. M. 1967 (WBA) 7
Fraser, J. 1891 (Moffat) 1
Fraser, J. 1907 (Dundee) 1
Fraser, M. J. E. 1880 (Queen's Park) 5
Fraser, R. 2017 (Bournemouth, Newcastle U) 22
Fraser, W. 1955 (Sunderland) 2
Freedman, D. A. 2002 (Crystal Palace) 2
Fulton, W. 1884 (Abercorn) 1
Fyfe, J. H. 1895 (Third Lanark) 1

Gabriel, J. 1961 (Everton) 2
Gallacher, H. K. 1924 (Airdrieonians, Newcastle U, Chelsea, Derby Co) 20
Gallacher, K. W. 1988 (Dundee U, Coventry C, Blackburn R, Newcastle U) 53
Gallacher, P. 1935 (Sunderland) 1
Gallacher, P. 2002 (Dundee U) 8
Gallagher, D. P. 2020 (Motherwell) 9
Gallagher, P. 2004 (Blackburn R) 1
Galloway, M. 1992 (Celtic) 1
Galt, J. H. 1908 (Rangers) 2
Gardiner, I. 1958 (Motherwell) 1
Gardner, D. R. 1897 (Third Lanark) 1
Gardner, R. 1872 (Queen's Park, Clydesdale) 5
Gemmell, T. 1955 (St Mirren) 2
Gemmell, T. 1966 (Celtic) 18
Gemmill, A. 1971 (Derby Co, Nottingham F, Birmingham C) 43
Gemmill, S. 1995 (Nottingham F, Everton) 26
Gibb, W. 1873 (Clydesdale) 1
Gibson, D. W. 1963 (Leicester C) 7
Gibson, J. D. 1926 (Partick Thistle, Aston Villa) 8
Gibson, N. 1895 (Rangers, Partick Thistle) 14
Gilchrist, J. E. 1922 (Celtic) 1
Gilhooley, M. 1922 (Hull C) 1
Gilks, M. 2013 (Blackpool) 3
Gillespie, G. 1880 (Rangers, Queen's Park) 7
Gillespie, G. T. 1988 (Liverpool) 13
Gillespie, Jas 1898 (Third Lanark) 1
Gillespie, John 1896 (Queen's Park) 1
Gillespie, R. 1927 (Queen's Park) 4
Gillick, T. 1937 (Everton) 5
Gilmour, B. C. 2021 (Chelsea) 15
Gilmour, J. 1931 (Dundee) 1
Gilzean, A. J. 1964 (Dundee, Tottenham H) 22
Glass, S. 1999 (Newcastle U) 1
Glavin, R. 1977 (Celtic) 1
Glen, A. 1956 (Aberdeen) 2
Glen, R. 1895 (Renton, Hibernian) 3
Goodwillie, D. 2011 (Dundee U, Blackburn R) 3
Goram, A. L. 1986 (Oldham Ath, Hibernian, Rangers) 43
Gordon, C. A. 2004 (Hearts, Sunderland, Celtic, Hearts) 70
Gordon, J. E. 1912 (Rangers) 10
Gossland, J. 1884 (Rangers) 1
Goudle, J. 1884 (Abercorn) 1
Gough, C. R. 1983 (Dundee U, Tottenham H, Rangers) 61
Gould, J. 2000 (Celtic) 2
Gourlay, J. 1886 (Cambuslang) 2
Govan, J. 1948 (Hibernian) 6
Gow, D. R. 1888 (Rangers) 1
Gow, J. J. 1885 (Queen's Park) 1
Gow, J. R. 1888 (Rangers) 1

Graham, A. 1978 (Leeds U) 11
Graham, G. 1972 (Arsenal, Manchester U) 12
Graham, J. 1884 (Annbank) 1
Graham, J. A. 1921 (Arsenal) 1
Grant, J. 1959 (Hibernian) 2
Grant, P. 1989 (Celtic) 2
Gray, A. 1903 (Hibernian) 1
Gray, A. D. 2003 (Bradford C) 2
Gray, A. M. 1976 (Aston Villa, Wolverhampton W, Everton) 20
Gray, D. 1929 (Rangers) 10
Gray, E. 1969 (Leeds U) 12
Gray, F. T. 1976 (Leeds U, Nottingham F, Leeds U) 32
Gray, W. 1886 (Pollokshields Ath) 1
Green, A. 1971 (Blackpool, Newcastle U) 6
Greer, G. 2013 (Brighton & HA) 11
Greig, J. 1964 (Rangers) 44
Griffiths, L. 2013 (Hibernian, Celtic) 22
Groves, W. 1888 (Hibernian, Celtic) 3
Gulliland, W. 1891 (Queen's Park) 4
Gunn, B. 1990 (Norwich C) 6

Haddock, H. 1955 (Clyde) 6
Haddow, D. 1894 (Rangers) 1
Haffey, F. 1960 (Celtic) 2
Hamilton, A. 1885 (Queen's Park) 4
Hamilton, A. W. 1962 (Dundee) 24
Hamilton, G. 1906 (Port Glasgow Ath) 1
Hamilton, G. 1947 (Aberdeen) 5
Hamilton, J. 1892 (Queen's Park) 3
Hamilton, J. 1924 (St Mirren) 1
Hamilton, R. C. 1899 (Rangers, Dundee) 11
Hamilton, T. 1891 (Hurlford) 1
Hamilton, T. 1932 (Rangers) 1
Hamilton, W. M. 1965 (Hibernian) 1
Hammell, S. 2005 (Motherwell) 1
Hanley, G. C. 2011 (Blackburn R, Newcastle U, Norwich C) 45
Hanlon, P. T. 2021 (Hibernian) 1
Hannah, A. B. 1888 (Renton) 1
Hannah, J. 1889 (Third Lanark) 1
Hansen, A. D. 1979 (Liverpool) 26
Hansen, J. 1972 (Partick Thistle) 2
Harkness, J. D. 1927 (Queen's Park, Hearts) 12
Harper, J. M. 1967 (Huddersfield T, Aberdeen, Hibernian, Aberdeen) 5
Harper, W. 1923 (Hibernian, Arsenal) 11
Harris, J. 1921 (Partick Thistle) 2
Harris, N. 1924 (Newcastle U) 1
Harrower, W. 1882 (Queen's Park) 3
Hartford, R. A. 1972 (WBA, Manchester C, Everton, Manchester C) 50
Hartley, P. J. 2005 (Hearts, Celtic, Bristol C) 25
Harvey, D. 1973 (Leeds U) 16
Hastings, A. C. 1936 (Sunderland) 2
Haughney, M. 1954 (Celtic) 1
Hay, D. 1970 (Celtic) 27
Hay, J. 1905 (Celtic, Newcastle U) 11
Hegarty, P. 1979 (Dundee U) 8
Heggie, C. 1886 (Rangers) 1
Henderson, G. H. 1904 (Rangers) 1
Henderson, J. G. 1953 (Portsmouth, Arsenal) 7
Henderson, W. 1963 (Rangers) 29
Hendry, E. C. J. 1993 (Blackburn R, Rangers, Coventry C, Bolton W) 51
Hendry, J. W. 2018 (Celtic, Oostende, Club Brugge) 17
Hepburn, J. 1891 (Alloa Ath) 1
Hepburn, R. 1932 (Ayr U) 1
Herd, A. C. 1935 (Hearts) 1
Herd, D. G. 1959 (Arsenal) 5
Herd, G. 1958 (Clyde) 5
Herriot, J. 1969 (Birmingham C) 8
Hewie, J. D. 1956 (Charlton Ath) 19
Hickey, A. B. 2022 (Bologna) 4
Higgins, A. 1885 (Kilmarnock) 1
Higgins, A. 1910 (Newcastle U) 4
Highet, T. C. 1875 (Queen's Park) 4
Hill, D. 1881 (Rangers) 3
Hill, D. A. 1906 (Third Lanark) 1
Hill, F. R. 1930 (Aberdeen) 3
Hill, J. 1891 (Hearts) 2
Hogg, G. 1896 (Hearts) 2
Hogg, J. 1922 (Ayr U) 1
Hogg, R. M. 1937 (Celtic) 1
Holm, A. H. 1882 (Queen's Park) 3
Holt, D. D. 1963 (Hearts) 5
Holt, G. J. 2001 (Kilmarnock, Norwich C) 10
Holton, J. A. 1973 (Manchester U) 15
Hood, H. 1967 (Clyde) 3
Hope, R. 1967 (WBA) 7
Hopkin, D. 1997 (Crystal Palace, Leeds U) 7
Houliston, W. 1949 (Queen of the South) 3
Houston, S. M. 1976 (Manchester U) 1
Howden, W. 1905 (Partick Thistle) 1
Howe, R. 1929 (Hamilton A) 2
Howie, H. 1949 (Hibernian) 1
Howie, J. 1905 (Newcastle U) 3
Howieson, J. 1927 (St Mirren) 1
Hughes, J. 1965 (Celtic) 8
Hughes, R. D. 2004 (Portsmouth) 5
Hughes, S. R. 2010 (Norwich C) 1
Hughes, W. 1975 (Sunderland) 1
Humphries, W. 1952 (Motherwell) 1
Hunter, A. 1972 (Kilmarnock, Celtic) 4
Hunter, J. 1909 (Dundee) 1
Hunter, J. 1874 (Third Lanark, Eastern, Third Lanark) 4
Hunter, W. 1960 (Motherwell) 3
Hunter, R. 1890 (St Mirren) 1
Husband, J. 1947 (Partick Thistle) 1
Hutchison, D. 1999 (Everton, Sunderland, West Ham U) 26
Hutchison, T. 1974 (Coventry C) 17
Hutton, A. 2007 (Rangers, Tottenham H, Aston Villa) 50
Hutton, J. 1887 (St Bernards) 1
Hutton, J. 1923 (Aberdeen, Blackburn R) 10
Hyslop, T. 1896 (Stoke, Rangers) 2

Imlach, J. J. S. 1958 (Nottingham F) 4
Imrie, W. N. 1929 (St Johnstone) 2
Inglis, J. 1883 (Rangers) 2
Inglis, J. 1884 (Kilmarnock Ath) 1
Irons, J. H. 1900 (Queen's Park) 1
Irvine, B. 1991 (Aberdeen) 9
Iwelumo, C. R. 2009 (Wolverhampton W, Burnley) 4

Jack, R. 2018 (Rangers) 12
Jackson, A. 1886 (Cambuslang) 2
Jackson, A. 1925 (Aberdeen, Huddersfield T) 17
Jackson, C. 1975 (Rangers) 8
Jackson, D. 1995 (Hibernian, Celtic) 28
Jackson, J. 1931 (Partick Thistle, Chelsea) 8
Jackson, T. A. 1904 (St Mirren) 6
James, A. W. 1926 (Preston NE, Arsenal) 8
Jardine, A. 1971 (Rangers) 38
Jarvie, A. 1971 (Airdrieonians) 3
Jenkinson, T. 1887 (Hearts) 1
Jess, E. 1993 (Aberdeen, Coventry C, Aberdeen) 18
Johnston, A. 1999 (Sunderland, Rangers, Middlesbrough) 18
Johnston, L. H. 1948 (Clyde) 2
Johnston, M. 1984 (Watford, Celtic, Nantes, Rangers) 38
Johnston, R. 1938 (Sunderland) 1
Johnston, W. 1966 (Rangers, WBA) 22
Johnstone, D. 1973 (Rangers) 14
Johnstone, J. 1888 (Abercorn) 1
Johnstone, J. 1965 (Celtic) 23
Johnstone, Jas 1894 (Kilmarnock) 1
Johnstone, J. A. 1930 (Hearts) 3
Johnstone, R. 1951 (Hibernian, Manchester C) 17
Johnstone, W. 1887 (Third Lanark) 3
Jordan, J. 1973 (Leeds U, Manchester U, AC Milan) 52

Kay, J. L. 1880 (Queen's Park) 6
Keillor, A. 1891 (Montrose, Dundee) 6
Keir, L. 1885 (Dumbarton) 5
Kelly, H. T. 1952 (Blackpool) 1
Kelly, J. 1888 (Renton, Celtic) 8
Kelly, J. C. 1949 (Barnsley) 2
Kelly, L. M. 2013 (Kilmarnock) 1
Kelso, R. 1885 (Renton, Dundee) 7
Kelso, T. 1914 (Dundee) 1
Kennaway, J. 1934 (Celtic) 1
Kennedy, A. 1875 (Eastern, Third Lanark) 6
Kennedy, J. 1897 (Hibernian) 1
Kennedy, J. 1964 (Celtic) 6
Kennedy, J. 2004 (Celtic) 1
Kennedy, S. 1905 (Partick Thistle) 1
Kennedy, S. 1975 (Rangers) 5
Kennedy, S. 1978 (Aberdeen) 8
Kenneth, G. 2011 (Dundee U) 2
Ker, G. 1880 (Queen's Park) 5

Ker, W. 1872 (Queen's Park) 2
Kerr, A. 1955 (Partick Thistle) 2
Kerr, B. 2003 (Newcastle U) 3
Kerr, P. 1924 (Hibernian) 1
Key, G. 1902 (Hearts) 1
Key, W. 1907 (Queen's Park) 1
King, A. 1896 (Hearts, Celtic) 6
King, J. 1933 (Hamilton A) 2
King, W. S. 1929 (Queen's Park) 1
Kingsley, S. 2016 (Swansea C) 1
Kinloch, J. D. 1922 (Partick Thistle) 1
Kinnaird, A. F. 1873 (Wanderers) 1
Kinnear, D. 1938 (Rangers) 1
Kyle, K. 2002 (Sunderland, Kilmarnock) 10

Lambert, P. 1995 (Motherwell, Borussia Dortmund, Celtic) 40
Lambie, J. A. 1886 (Queen's Park) 3
Lambie, W. A. 1892 (Queen's Park) 9
Lamont, W. 1885 (Pilgrims) 1
Lang, A. 1880 (Dumbarton) 1
Lang, J. J. 1876 (Clydesdale, Third Lanark) 2
Latta, A. 1888 (Dumbarton) 2
Law, D. 1959 (Huddersfield T, Manchester C, Torino, Manchester U, Manchester C) 55
Law, G. 1910 (Rangers) 3
Law, T. 1928 (Chelsea) 2
Lawrence, J. 1911 (Newcastle U) 1
Lawrence, T. 1963 (Liverpool) 3
Lawson, D. 1923 (St Mirren) 1
Leckie, R. 1872 (Queen's Park) 1
Leggat, G. 1956 (Aberdeen, Fulham) 18
Leighton, J. 1983 (Aberdeen, Manchester U, Hibernian, Aberdeen) 91
Lennie, W. 1908 (Aberdeen) 2
Lennox, R. 1967 (Celtic) 10
Leslie, L. G. 1961 (Airdrieonians) 5
Levein, C. 1990 (Hearts) 16
Liddell, W. 1947 (Liverpool) 28
Liddle, D. 1931 (East Fife) 3
Lindsay, D. 1903 (St Mirren) 1
Lindsay, J. 1880 (Dumbarton) 8
Lindsay, J. 1888 (Renton) 3
Linwood, A. B. 1950 (Clyde) 1
Little, R. J. 1953 (Rangers) 1
Livingstone, G. T. 1906 (Manchester C, Rangers) 2
Lochhead, A. 1889 (Third Lanark) 1
Logan, J. 1891 (Ayr) 1
Logan, T. 1913 (Falkirk) 1
Logie, J. T. 1953 (Arsenal) 1
Loney, W. 1910 (Celtic) 2
Long, H. 1947 (Clyde) 1
Longair, W. 1894 (Dundee) 1
Lorimer, P. 1970 (Leeds U) 21
Love, A. 1931 (Aberdeen) 3
Low, A. 1934 (Falkirk) 1
Low, J. 1891 (Cambuslang) 1
Low, T. P. 1897 (Rangers) 1
Low, W. L. 1911 (Newcastle U) 5
Lowe, J. 1887 (St Bernards) 1
Lundie, J. 1886 (Hibernian) 1
Lyall, J. 1905 (Sheffield W) 1

Macari, L. 1972 (Celtic, Manchester U) 24
Mackail-Smith, C. 2011 (Peterborough U, Brighton & HA) 7
Mackay-Steven, G. 2013 (Dundee U, Aberdeen) 2
Mackie, J. C. 2011 (QPR) 9
Madden, J. 1893 (Celtic) 2
Maguire, C. 2011 (Aberdeen) 2
Main, F. R. 1938 (Rangers) 1
Main, J. 1909 (Hibernian) 1
Maley, W. 1893 (Celtic) 2
Maloney, S. R. 2006 (Celtic, Aston Villa, Celtic, Wigan Ath, Chicago Fire, Hull C) 47
Malpas, M. 1984 (Dundee U) 55
Marshall, D. J. 2005 (Celtic, Cardiff C, Hull C, Wigan Ath. Derby Co) 47
Marshall, G. 1992 (Celtic) 1
Marshall, H. 1899 (Celtic) 2
Marshall, J. 1885 (Third Lanark) 4
Marshall, J. 1921 (Middlesbrough, Llanelly) 7
Marshall, J. 1932 (Rangers) 3
Marshall, R. W. 1892 (Rangers) 2
Martin, B. 1995 (Motherwell) 2
Martin, C. H. 2014 (Derby Co) 17
Martin, F. 1954 (Aberdeen) 6
Martin, N. 1965 (Hibernian, Sunderland) 3
Martin, R. K. A. 2011 (Norwich C) 29
Martis, J. 1961 (Motherwell) 1
Mason, J. 1949 (Third Lanark) 7
Massie, A. 1932 (Hearts, Aston Villa) 18
Masson, D. S. 1976 (QPR, Derby Co) 17
Mathers, D. 1954 (Partick Thistle) 1
Matteo, D. 2001 (Leeds U) 6
Maxwell, W. S. 1898 (Stoke C) 1
May, J. 1906 (Rangers) 5
May, S. 2015 (Sheffield W) 1
McAllister, J. R. 2004 (Livingston) 1
McAdam, J. 1880 (Third Lanark) 1
McAllister, B. 1997 (Wimbledon) 3
McAllister, G. 1990 (Leicester C, Leeds U, Coventry C) 57
McArthur, D. 1895 (Celtic) 3
McArthur, J. 2011 (Wigan Ath, Crystal Palace) 32
McAtee, A. 1913 (Celtic) 1
McAulay, J. 1884 (Arthurlie) 1
McAulay, J. D. 1882 (Dumbarton) 9
McAulay, R. 1932 (Rangers) 2
Macauley, A. R. 1947 (Brentford, Arsenal) 7
McAvennie, F. 1986 (West Ham U, Celtic) 5
McBain, E. 1894 (St Mirren) 1
McBain, N. 1922 (Manchester U, Everton) 3
McBride, J. 1967 (Celtic) 2
McBride, P. 1904 (Preston NE) 6
McBurnie, O. R. 2018 (Swansea C, Sheffield U) 16
McCall, A. 1888 (Renton) 1
McCall, A. S. M. 1990 (Everton, Rangers) 40
McCall, J. 1886 (Renton) 5
McCalliog, J. 1967 (Sheffield W, Wolverhampton W) 10
McCallum, N. 1888 (Renton) 1
McCann, N. 1999 (Hearts, Rangers, Southampton) 26
McCann, R. J. 1959 (Motherwell) 5
McCartney, W. 1902 (Hibernian) 1
McClair, B. 1987 (Celtic, Manchester U) 30
McClory, A. 1927 (Motherwell) 3
McCloy, P. 1924 (Ayr U) 2
McCloy, P. 1973 (Rangers) 4
McCoist, A. 1986 (Rangers, Kilmarnock) 61
McColl, I. M. 1950 (Rangers) 14
McColl, R. S. 1896 (Queen's Park, Newcastle U, Queen's Park) 13
McColl, W. 1895 (Renton) 1
McCombie, A. 1903 (Sunderland, Newcastle U) 4
McCorkindale, J. 1891 (Partick Thistle) 1
McCormack, R. 2008 (Motherwell, Cardiff C, Leeds U, Fulham) 13
McCormick, R. 1886 (Abercorn) 1
McCrae, D. 1929 (St Mirren) 2
McCreadie, A. 1893 (Rangers) 2
McCreadie, E. G. 1965 (Chelsea) 23
McCulloch, D. 1935 (Hearts, Brentford, Derby Co) 7
McCulloch, L. 2005 (Wigan Ath, Rangers) 18
MacDonald, A. 1976 (Rangers) 1
McDonald, J. 1886 (Edinburgh University) 1
McDonald, J. 1956 (Sunderland) 2
McDonald, K. D. 2018 (Fulham) 5
MacDougall, E. J. 1975 (Norwich C) 7
McDougall, J. 1877 (Vale of Leven) 5
McDougall, J. 1926 (Airdrieonians) 1
McDougall, J. 1931 (Liverpool) 2
McEveley, J. 2008 (Derby Co) 3
McFadden, J. 2002 (Motherwell, Everton, Birmingham C) 48
McFadyen, W. 1934 (Motherwell) 2
Macfarlane, A. 1904 (Dundee) 5
Macfarlane, W. 1947 (Hearts) 1
McFarlane, R. 1896 (Greenock Morton) 1
McGarr, E. 1970 (Aberdeen) 2
McGarvey, F. P. 1979 (Liverpool, Celtic) 7
McGeoch, A. 1876 (Dumbreck) 4
McGeouch, D. 2018 (Hibernian) 2
McGhee, J. 1886 (Hibernian) 1
McGhee, M. 1983 (Aberdeen) 4
McGinlay, J. 1994 (Bolton W) 13
McGinn, J. 2016 (Hibernian, Aston Villa) 48
McGinn, P. 2022 (Hibernian) 1
McGonagle, W. 1933 (Celtic) 6
McGrain, D. 1973 (Celtic) 62
McGregor, A. J. 2007 (Rangers, Besiktas, Hull C, Rangers) 42

McGregor, C. W. 2018 (Celtic) 46
McGregor, J. C. 1877 (Vale of Leven) 4
McGrory, J. 1928 (Celtic) 7
McGrory, J. E. 1965 (Kilmarnock) 6
McGuire, W. 1881 (Beith) 2
McGurk, F. 1934 (Birmingham) 1
McHardy, H. 1885 (Rangers) 1
McInally, A. 1989 (Aston Villa, Bayern Munich) 8
McInally, J. 1987 (Dundee U) 10
McInally, T. B. 1926 (Celtic) 2
McInnes, D. 2003 (WBA) 2
McInnes, T. 1889 (Cowlairs) 1
McIntosh, W. 1905 (Third Lanark) 1
McIntyre, A. 1878 (Vale of Leven) 2
McIntyre, H. 1880 (Rangers) 1
McIntyre, J. 1884 (Rangers) 1
MacKay, D. 1959 (Celtic) 14
Mackay, D. C. 1957 (Hearts, Tottenham H) 22
Mackay, G. 1988 (Hearts) 4
Mackay, M. 2004 (Norwich C) 5
McKay, B. 2016 (Rangers) 1
McKay, J. 1924 (Blackburn R) 1
McKay, R. 1928 (Newcastle U) 1
McKean, R. 1976 (Rangers) 1
McKenna, S. F. 2018 (Aberdeen, Nottingham F) 26
McKenzie, D. 1938 (Brentford) 1
Mackenzie, J. A. 1954 (Partick Thistle) 9
McKeown, M. 1889 (Celtic) 2
McKie, J. 1898 (East Stirling) 1
McKillop, T. R. 1938 (Rangers) 1
McKimmie, S. 1989 (Aberdeen) 40
McKinlay, D. 1922 (Liverpool) 2
McKinlay, T. 1996 (Celtic) 22
McKinlay, W. 1994 (Dundee U, Blackburn R) 29
McKinnon, A. 1874 (Queen's Park) 1
McKinnon, R. 1966 (Rangers) 28
McKinnon, R. 1994 (Motherwell) 3
MacKinnon, W. 1883 (Dumbarton) 4
MacKinnon, W. W. 1872 (Queen's Park) 9
McLaren, A. 1929 (St Johnstone) 5
McLaren, A. 1947 (Preston NE) 4
McLaren, A. 1992 (Hearts, Rangers) 24
McLaren, A. 2001 (Kilmarnock) 1
McLaren, J. 1888 (Hibernian, Celtic) 3
McLaughlin, J. P. 2018 (Hearts, Sunderland) 2
McLean, A. 1926 (Celtic) 4
McLean, D. 1896 (St Bernards) 2
McLean, D. 1912 (Sheffield W) 1
McLean, G. 1968 (Dundee) 1
McLean, K. 2016 (Aberdeen, Norwich C) 25
McLean, T. 1967 (Kilmarnock) 9
McLeish, A. 1980 (Aberdeen) 77
McLeod, D. 1905 (Celtic) 4
McLeod, J. 1888 (Dumbarton) 5
MacLeod, J. M. 1961 (Hibernian) 4
MacLeod, M. 1985 (Celtic, Borussia Dortmund, Hibernian) 20
McLeod, W. 1886 (Cowlairs) 1
McLintock, A. 1875 (Vale of Leven) 3
McLintock, F. 1963 (Leicester C, Arsenal) 9
McLuckie, J. S. 1934 (Manchester C) 1
McMahon, A. 1892 (Celtic) 6
McManus, S. 2007 (Celtic, Middlesbrough) 26
McMenemy, J. 1905 (Celtic) 12
McMenemy, J. 1934 (Motherwell) 1
McMillan, I. L. 1952 (Airdrieonians, Rangers) 6
McMillan, J. 1897 (St Bernards) 1
McMillan, T. 1887 (Dumbarton) 1
McMullan, J. 1920 (Partick Thistle, Manchester C) 16
McNab, A. 1921 (Morton) 2
McNab, A. 1937 (Sunderland, WBA) 2
McNab, C. D. 1931 (Dundee) 6
McNab, J. S. 1923 (Liverpool) 1
McNair, A. 1906 (Celtic) 15
McNamara, J. 1997 (Celtic, Wolverhampton W) 33
McNamee, D. 2004 (Livingston) 4
McNaught, W. 1951 (Raith R) 5
McNaughton, K. 2002 (Aberdeen, Cardiff C) 4
McNeill, W. 1961 (Celtic) 29
McNiel, H. 1874 (Queen's Park) 10
McNiel, M. 1876 (Rangers) 2
McNulty, M. 2019 (Reading) 2
McPhail, J. 1950 (Celtic) 5
McPhail, R. 1927 (Airdrieonians, Rangers) 17
McPherson, D. 1892 (Kilmarnock) 1
McPherson, D. 1989 (Hearts, Rangers) 27
McPherson, J. 1875 (Clydesdale) 1
McPherson, J. 1879 (Vale of Leven) 8
McPherson, J. 1888 (Kilmarnock, Cowlairs, Rangers) 9
McPherson, J. 1891 (Hearts) 1
McPherson, R. 1882 (Arthurlie) 1
McQueen, G. 1974 (Leeds U, Manchester U) 30
McQueen, M. 1890 (Leith Ath) 2
McRorie, D. M. 1931 (Morton) 1
McSpadyen, A. 1939 (Partick Thistle) 2
McStay, P. 1984 (Celtic) 76
McStay, W. 1921 (Celtic) 13
McSwegan, G. 2000 (Hearts) 2
McTavish, J. 1910 (Falkirk) 1
McTominay, S. F. 2018 (Manchester U) 34
McWattie, G. C. 1901 (Queen's Park) 2
McWilliam, P. 1905 (Newcastle U) 8
Meechan, P. 1896 (Celtic) 1
Meiklejohn, D. D. 1922 (Rangers) 15
Menzies, A. 1906 (Hearts) 1
Mercer, R. 1912 (Hearts) 2
Middleton, R. 1930 (Cowdenbeath) 1
Millar, J. 1897 (Rangers) 3
Millar, J. 1963 (Rangers) 2
Miller, A. 1939 (Hearts) 1
Miller, C. 2001 (Dundee U) 1
Miller, J. 1931 (St Mirren) 5
Miller, K. 2001 (Rangers, Wolverhampton W, Celtic, Derby Co, Rangers, Bursaspor, Cardiff C, Vancouver Whitecaps) 69
Miller, L. 2006 (Dundee U, Aberdeen) 3
Miller, P. 1882 (Dumbarton) 3
Miller, T. 1920 (Liverpool, Manchester U) 3
Miller, W. 1876 (Third Lanark) 1
Miller, W. 1947 (Celtic) 6
Miller, W. 1975 (Aberdeen) 65
Mills, W. 1936 (Aberdeen) 3
Milne, J. V. 1938 (Middlesbrough) 2
Mitchell, D. 1890 (Rangers) 5
Mitchell, J. 1908 (Kilmarnock) 3
Mitchell, R. C. 1951 (Newcastle U) 2
Mochan, N. 1954 (Celtic) 3
Moir, W. 1950 (Bolton W) 1
Moncur, R. 1968 (Newcastle U) 16
Morgan, H. 1898 (St Mirren, Liverpool) 2
Morgan, L. 2018 (St Mirren) 2
Morgan, W. 1967 (Burnley, Manchester U) 26
Morris, D. 1923 (Raith R) 6
Morris, H. 1950 (East Fife) 1
Morrison, J. C. 2008 (WBA) 46
Morrison, T. 1927 (St Mirren) 1
Morton, A. L. 1920 (Queen's Park, Rangers) 31
Morton, H. A. 1929 (Kilmarnock) 2
Mudie, J. K. 1957 (Blackpool) 17
Muir, W. 1907 (Dundee) 1
Muirhead, T. A. 1922 (Rangers) 8
Mulgrew, C. P. 2012 (Celtic, Blackburn R) 44
Mulhall, G. 1960 (Aberdeen, Sunderland) 3
Munro, A. D. 1937 (Hearts, Blackpool) 3
Munro, F. M. 1971 (Wolverhampton W) 9
Munro, I. 1979 (St Mirren) 7
Munro, N. 1888 (Abercorn) 2
Murdoch, J. 1931 (Motherwell) 1
Murdoch, R. 1966 (Celtic) 12
Murphy, F. 1938 (Celtic) 1
Murphy, J. 2018 (Rangers) 2
Murray, I. 2003 (Hibernian, Rangers) 6
Murray, J. 1895 (Renton) 1
Murray, J. 1958 (Hearts) 5
Murray, J. W. 1890 (Vale of Leven) 1
Murray, P. 1896 (Hibernian) 2
Murray, S. 1972 (Aberdeen) 1
Murty, G. S. 2004 (Reading) 4
Mutch, G. 1938 (Preston NE) 1

Naismith, S. J. 2007 (Kilmarnock, Rangers, Everton, Norwich C, Hearts) 51
Napier, C. E. 1932 (Celtic, Derby Co) 5
Narey, D. 1977 (Dundee U) 35
Naysmith, G. A. 2000 (Hearts, Everton, Sheffield U) 46
Neil, R. G. 1896 (Hibernian, Rangers) 2
Neill, R. W. 1876 (Queen's Park) 5
Neilson, R. 2007 (Hearts) 1
Nellies, P. 1913 (Hearts) 2
Nelson, J. 1925 (Cardiff C) 4
Nevin, P. K. F. 1986 (Chelsea, Everton, Tranmere R) 28

Niblo, T. D. 1904 (Aston Villa) 1
Nibloe, J. 1929 (Kilmarnock) 11
Nicholas, C. 1983 (Celtic, Arsenal, Aberdeen) 20
Nicholson, B. 2001 (Dunfermline Ath) 3
Nicol, S. 1985 (Liverpool) 27
Nisbet, J. 1929 (Ayr U) 3
Nisbet, K. 2021 (Hibernian) 10
Niven, J. B. 1885 (Moffat) 1

O'Connor, G. 2002 (Hibernian, Lokomotiv Moscow, Birmingham C) 16
O'Donnell, F. 1937 (Preston NE, Blackpool) 6
O'Donnell, P. 1994 (Motherwell) 1
O'Donnell, S. G. 2018 (Kilmarnock, Motherwell) 26
Ogilvie, D. H. 1934 (Motherwell) 1
O'Hare, J. 1970 (Derby Co) 13
O'Neil, B. 1996 (Celtic, Wolfsburg, Derby Co, Preston NE) 7
O'Neil, J. 2001 (Hibernian) 1
Ormond, W. E. 1954 (Hibernian) 6
O'Rourke, F. 1907 (Airdrieonians) 1
Orr, J. 1892 (Kilmarnock) 1
Orr, R. 1902 (Newcastle U) 2
Orr, T. 1952 (Morton) 2
Orr, W. 1900 (Celtic) 3
Orrock, R. 1913 (Falkirk) 1
Oswald, J. 1889 (Third Lanark, St Bernards, Rangers) 3

Palmer, L. J. 2019 (Sheffield W) 8
Parker, A. H. 1955 (Falkirk, Everton) 15
Parlane, D. 1973 (Rangers) 12
Parlane, R. 1878 (Vale of Leven) 3
Paterson, C. T. O. 2016 (Hearts, Cardiff C, Sheffield W) 17
Paterson, G. D. 1939 (Celtic) 1
Paterson, J. 1920 (Leicester C) 1
Paterson, J. 1931 (Cowdenbeath) 3
Paton, A. 1952 (Motherwell) 2
Paton, D. 1896 (St Bernards) 1
Paton, M. 1883 (Dumbarton) 5
Paton, R. 1879 (Vale of Leven) 2
Patrick, J. 1897 (St Mirren) 2
Patterson, N. K. 2021 (Rangers, Everton) 10
Paul, H. McD. 1909 (Queen's Park) 3
Paul, W. 1888 (Partick Thistle) 3
Paul, W. 1891 (Dykebar) 1
Pearson, S. P. 2004 (Motherwell, Celtic, Derby Co) 10
Pearson, T. 1947 (Newcastle U) 2
Penman, A. 1966 (Dundee, Rangers) 4
Pettigrew, W. 1976 (Motherwell) 5
Phillips, J. 1877 (Queen's Park) 3
Phillips, M. 2012 (Blackpool, QPR, WBA) 16
Plenderleith, J. B. 1961 (Manchester C) 1
Porteous, W. 1903 (Hearts) 1
Pressley, S. J. 2000 (Hearts) 32
Pringle, C. 1921 (St Mirren) 1
Provan, D. 1964 (Rangers) 5
Provan, D. 1980 (Celtic) 10
Pursell, P. 1914 (Queen's Park) 1

Quashie, N. F. 2004 (Portsmouth, Southampton, WBA) 14
Quinn, J. 1905 (Celtic) 11
Quinn, P. 1961 (Motherwell) 4

Rae, G. 2001 (Dundee, Rangers, Cardiff C) 14
Rae, J. 1889 (Third Lanark) 2
Raeside, J. S. 1906 (Third Lanark) 1
Raisbeck, A. G. 1900 (Liverpool) 8
Ralston, A. 2022 (Celtic) 4
Rankin, G. 1890 (Vale of Leven) 2
Rankin, R. 1929 (St Mirren) 3
Redpath, W. 1949 (Motherwell) 9
Reid, J. G. 1914 (Airdrieonians) 3
Reid, R. 1938 (Brentford) 2
Reid, W. 1911 (Rangers) 9
Reilly, L. 1949 (Hibernian) 38
Rennie, H. G. 1900 (Hearts, Hibernian) 13
Renny-Tailyour, H. W. 1873 (Royal Engineers) 1
Rhind, A. 1872 (Queen's Park) 1
Rhodes, J. L. 2012 (Huddersfield T, Blackburn R, Sheffield W) 14
Richmond, A. 1906 (Queen's Park) 1
Richmond, J. T. 1877 (Clydesdale, Queen's Park) 3
Ring, T. 1953 (Clyde) 12
Rioch, B. D. 1975 (Derby Co, Everton, Derby Co) 24
Riordan, D. G. 2006 (Hibernian) 3
Ritchie, A. 1891 (East Stirlingshire) 1
Ritchie, H. 1923 (Hibernian) 2
Ritchie, J. 1897 (Queen's Park) 1
Ritchie, M. T. 2015 (Bournemouth, Newcastle U) 16
Ritchie, P. S. 1999 (Hearts, Bolton W, Walsall) 7
Ritchie, W. 1962 (Rangers) 1
Robb, D. T. 1971 (Aberdeen) 5
Robb, W. 1926 (Rangers, Hibernian) 2
Robertson, A. 1955 (Clyde) 5
Robertson, A. 2014 (Dundee U, Hull C, Liverpool) 59
Robertson, D. 1992 (Rangers) 3
Robertson, G. 1910 (Motherwell, Sheffield W) 4
Robertson, G. 1938 (Kilmarnock) 1
Robertson, H. 1962 (Dundee) 1
Robertson, J. 1931 (Dundee) 2
Robertson, J. 1991 (Hearts) 16
Robertson, J. N. 1978 (Nottingham F, Derby Co) 28
Robertson, J. G. 1965 (Tottenham H) 1
Robertson, J. T. 1898 (Everton, Southampton, Rangers) 16
Robertson, P. 1903 (Dundee) 1
Robertson, S. 2009 (Dundee U) 2
Robertson, T. 1889 (Queen's Park) 4
Robertson, T. 1898 (Hearts) 1
Robertson, W. 1887 (Dumbarton) 2
Robinson, R. 1974 (Dundee) 4
Robson, B. G. G. 2008 (Dundee U, Celtic, Middlesbrough) 17
Ross, M. 2002 (Rangers) 13
Rough, A. 1976 (Partick Thistle, Hibernian) 53
Rougvie, D. 1984 (Aberdeen) 1
Rowan, A. 1880 (Caledonian, Queen's Park) 2
Russell, D. 1895 (Hearts, Celtic) 6
Russell, J. 1890 (Cambuslang) 1
Russell, J. S. S. 2015 (Derby Co, Kansas City) 14
Russell, W. F. 1924 (Airdrieonians) 2
Rutherford, E. 1948 (Rangers) 1

St John, I. 1959 (Motherwell, Liverpool) 21
Saunders, S. 2011 (Motherwell) 1
Sawers, W. 1895 (Dundee) 1
Scarff, P. 1931 (Celtic) 1
Schaedler, E. 1974 (Hibernian) 1
Scott, A. S. 1957 (Rangers, Everton) 16
Scott, J. 1966 (Hibernian) 1
Scott, J. 1971 (Dundee) 2
Scott, M. 1898 (Airdrieonians) 1
Scott, R. 1894 (Airdrieonians) 1
Scoular, J. 1951 (Portsmouth) 9
Sellar, W. 1885 (Battlefield, Queen's Park) 9
Semple, W. 1886 (Cambuslang) 1
Severin, S. D. 2002 (Hearts, Aberdeen) 15
Shankland, L. 2020 (Dundee U) 4
Shankly, W. 1938 (Preston NE) 5
Sharp, G. M. 1985 (Everton) 12
Sharp, J. 1904 (Dundee, Woolwich Arsenal, Fulham) 5
Shaw, D. 1947 (Hibernian) 8
Shaw, F. W. 1884 (Pollokshields Ath) 2
Shaw, J. 1947 (Rangers) 4
Shearer, D. 1994 (Aberdeen) 7
Shearer, R. 1961 (Rangers) 4
Shinnie, A. M. 2013 (Inverness CT) 1
Shinnie, G. 2018 (Aberdeen) 6
Sillars, D. C. 1891 (Queen's Park) 5
Simpson, J. 1895 (Third Lanark) 3
Simpson, J. 1935 (Rangers) 14
Simpson, N. 1983 (Aberdeen) 5
Simpson, R. C. 1967 (Celtic) 5
Sinclair, G. L. 1910 (Hearts) 3
Sinclair, J. W. E. 1966 (Leicester C) 1
Skene, L. H. 1904 (Queen's Park) 1
Sloan, T. 1904 (Third Lanark) 1
Smellie, R. 1887 (Queen's Park) 6
Smith, A. 1898 (Rangers) 20
Smith, D. 1966 (Aberdeen, Rangers) 2
Smith, G. 1947 (Hibernian) 18
Smith, H. G. 1988 (Hearts) 3
Smith, J. 1924 (Ayr U) 1
Smith, J. 1935 (Rangers) 2
Smith, J. 1968 (Aberdeen, Newcastle U) 4
Smith, J. 2003 (Celtic) 2
Smith, J. E. 1959 (Celtic) 2
Smith, Jas 1872 (Queen's Park) 1
Smith, John 1877 (Mauchline, Edinburgh University, Queen's Park) 10

Smith, N. 1897 (Rangers) 12
Smith, R. 1872 (Queen's Park) 2
Smith, T. M. 1934 (Kilmarnock, Preston NE) 2
Snodgrass, R. 2011 (Leeds U, Norwich C, Hull C, West Ham U) 28
Somers, P. 1905 (Celtic) 4
Somers, W. S. 1879 (Third Lanark, Queen's Park) 3
Somerville, G. 1886 (Queen's Park) 1
Souness, G. J. 1975 (Middlesbrough, Liverpool, Sampdoria) 54
Souttar, J. 2019 (Hearts) 6
Speedie, D. R. 1985 (Chelsea, Coventry C) 10
Speedie, F. 1903 (Rangers) 3
Speirs, J. H. 1908 (Rangers) 1
Spencer, J. 1995 (Chelsea, QPR) 14
Stanton, P. 1966 (Hibernian) 16
Stark, J. 1909 (Rangers) 2
Steel, W. 1947 (Morton, Derby Co, Dundee) 30
Steele, D. M. 1923 (Huddersfield) 3
Stein, C. 1969 (Rangers, Coventry C) 21
Stephen, J. F. 1947 (Bradford) 2
Stevenson, G. 1928 (Motherwell) 12
Stevenson, L. 2018 (Hibernian) 1
Stewart, A. 1888 (Queen's Park) 2
Stewart, A. 1894 (Third Lanark) 1
Stewart, D. 1888 (Dumbarton) 1
Stewart, D. 1893 (Queen's Park) 3
Stewart, D. S. 1978 (Leeds U) 1
Stewart, G. 1906 (Hibernian, Manchester C) 4
Stewart, J. 1977 (Kilmarnock, Middlesbrough) 2
Stewart, M. J. 2002 (Manchester U, Hearts) 4
Stewart, R. 1981 (West Ham U) 10
Stewart, R. C. 2022 (Sunderland) 2
Stewart, W. G. 1898 (Queen's Park) 2
Stockdale, R. K. 2002 (Middlesbrough) 5
Storrier, D. 1899 (Celtic) 3
Strachan, G. D. 1980 (Aberdeen, Manchester U, Leeds U) 50
Sturrock, P. 1981 (Dundee U) 20
Sullivan, N. 1997 (Wimbledon, Tottenham H) 28
Summers, W. 1926 (St Mirren) 1
Symon, J. S. 1939 (Rangers) 1

Tait, T. S. 1911 (Sunderland) 1
Taylor, G. J. 2019 (Kilmarnock, Celtic) 7
Taylor, J. 1872 (Queen's Park) 6
Taylor, J. D. 1892 (Dumbarton, St Mirren) 4
Taylor, W. 1892 (Hearts) 1
Teale, G. 2006 (Wigan Ath, Derby Co) 13
Telfer, P. N. 2000 (Coventry C) 1
Telfer, W. 1933 (Motherwell) 2
Telfer, W. D. 1954 (St Mirren) 1
Templeton, R. 1902 (Aston Villa, Newcastle U, Woolwich Arsenal, Kilmarnock) 11
Thompson, S. 2002 (Dundee U, Rangers) 16
Thomson, A. 1886 (Arthurlie) 1
Thomson, A. 1889 (Third Lanark) 1
Thomson, A. 1909 (Airdrieonians) 1
Thomson, A. 1926 (Celtic) 3
Thomson, C. 1904 (Hearts, Sunderland) 21
Thomson, C. 1937 (Sunderland) 1
Thomson, D. 1920 (Dundee) 1
Thomson, H. 1967 (Burnley) 2
Thomson, J. 1930 (Celtic) 4
Thomson, J. J. 1872 (Queen's Park) 3
Thomson, J. R. 1933 (Everton) 1
Thomson, K. 2009 (Rangers, Middlesbrough) 3
Thomson, R. 1932 (Celtic) 1
Thomson, R. W. 1927 (Falkirk) 1
Thomson, S. 1884 (Rangers) 2
Thomson, W. 1892 (Dumbarton) 4
Thomson, W. 1896 (Dundee) 1
Thomson, W. 1980 (St Mirren) 7
Thornton, W. 1947 (Rangers) 7
Tierney, K. 2016 (Celtic, Arsenal) 32
Tinney, H. 1967 (Bury) 1
Toner, W. 1959 (Kilmarnock) 2
Townsend, J. 1967 (Hearts) 4
Townsley, T. 1926 (Falkirk) 1
Troup, A. 1920 (Dundee, Everton) 5
Turnbull, D. 2021 (Celtic) 5
Turnbull, E. 1948 (Hibernian) 8
Turner, T. 1884 (Arthurlie) 1
Turner, W. 1885 (Pollokshields Ath) 2

Ure, J. F. 1962 (Dundee, Arsenal) 12
Urquhart, D. 1934 (Hibernian) 1

Vallance, T. 1877 (Rangers) 7
Venters, A. 1934 (Cowdenbeath, Rangers) 3

Waddell, T. S. 1891 (Queen's Park) 6
Waddell, W. 1947 (Rangers) 17
Wales, H. M. 1933 (Motherwell) 1
Walker, A. 1988 (Celtic) 3
Walker, F. 1922 (Third Lanark) 1
Walker, G. 1930 (St Mirren) 4
Walker, J. 1895 (Hearts, Rangers) 5
Walker, J. 1911 (Swindon T) 9
Walker, J. N. 1993 (Hearts, Partick Thistle) 2
Walker, R. 1900 (Hearts) 29
Walker, T. 1935 (Hearts) 20
Walker, W. 1909 (Clyde) 2
Wallace, I. A. 1978 (Coventry C) 3
Wallace, L. 2010 (Hearts, Rangers) 10
Wallace, R. 2010 (Preston NE) 1
Wallace, W. S. B. 1965 (Hearts, Celtic) 7
Wardhaugh, J. 1955 (Hearts) 2
Wark, J. 1979 (Ipswich T, Liverpool) 28
Watson, A. 1881 (Queen's Park) 3
Watson, J. 1903 (Sunderland, Middlesbrough) 6
Watson, J. 1948 (Motherwell, Huddersfield T) 2
Watson, J. A. K. 1878 (Rangers) 1
Watson, P. R. 1934 (Blackpool) 1
Watson, R. 1971 (Motherwell) 1
Watson, W. 1898 (Falkirk) 1
Watt, A. P. 2016 (Charlton Ath) 1
Watt, F. 1889 (Kilbirnie) 4
Watt, W. W. 1887 (Queen's Park) 1
Waugh, W. 1938 (Hearts) 1
Webster, A. 2003 (Hearts, Dundee U, Hearts) 28
Weir, A. 1959 (Motherwell) 6
Weir, D. G. 1997 (Hearts, Everton, Rangers) 69
Weir, J. 1887 (Third Lanark) 1
Weir, J. B. 1872 (Queen's Park) 4
Weir, P. 1980 (St Mirren, Aberdeen) 6
White, John 1922 (Albion R, Hearts) 2
White, J. A. 1959 (Falkirk, Tottenham H) 22
White, W. 1907 (Bolton W) 2
Whitelaw, A. 1887 (Vale of Leven) 2
Whittaker, S. G. 2010 (Rangers, Norwich C) 31
Whyte, D. 1988 (Celtic, Middlesbrough, Aberdeen) 12
Wilkie, L. 2002 (Dundee) 11
Williams, G. 2002 (Nottingham F) 5
Wilson, A. 1907 (Sheffield W) 6
Wilson, A. 1954 (Portsmouth) 1
Wilson, A. N. 1920 (Dunfermline, Middlesbrough) 12
Wilson, D. 1900 (Queen's Park) 1
Wilson, D. 1913 (Oldham Ath) 1
Wilson, D. 1961 (Rangers) 22
Wilson, D. 2011 (Liverpool) 5
Wilson, G. W. 1904 (Hearts, Everton, Newcastle U) 6
Wilson, Hugh 1890 (Newmilns, Sunderland, Third Lanark) 4
Wilson, I. A. 1987 (Leicester C, Everton) 5
Wilson, J. 1888 (Vale of Leven) 4
Wilson, M. 2011 (Celtic) 1
Wilson, P. 1926 (Celtic) 4
Wilson, P. 1975 (Celtic) 1
Wilson, R. P. 1972 (Arsenal) 2
Winters, R. 1999 (Aberdeen) 1
Wiseman, W. 1927 (Queen's Park) 2
Wood, G. 1979 (Everton, Arsenal) 4
Woodburn, W. A. 1947 (Rangers) 24
Wotherspoon, D. N. 1872 (Queen's Park) 2
Wright, K. 1992 (Hibernian) 1
Wright, S. 1993 (Aberdeen) 2
Wright, T. 1953 (Sunderland) 3
Wylie, T. G. 1890 (Rangers) 1

Yeats, R. 1965 (Liverpool) 2
Yorston, B. C. 1931 (Aberdeen) 1
Yorston, H. 1955 (Aberdeen) 1
Young, A. 1905 (Everton) 2
Young, A. 1960 (Hearts, Everton) 8
Young, G. L. 1947 (Rangers) 53
Young, J. 1906 (Celtic) 1
Younger, T. 1955 (Hibernian, Liverpool) 24

WALES

Adams, H. 1882 (Berwyn R, Druids) 4
Aizlewood, M. 1986 (Charlton Ath, Leeds U, Bradford C, Bristol C, Cardiff C) 39
Allchurch, I. J. 1951 (Swansea T, Newcastle U, Cardiff C, Swansea T) 68
Allchurch, L. 1955 (Swansea T, Sheffield U) 11
Allen, B. W. 1951 (Coventry C) 2
Allen, J. M. 2009 (Swansea C, Liverpool, Stoke C) 72
Allen, M. 1986 (Watford, Norwich C, Millwall, Newcastle U) 14
Ampadu, E. K. C. R. 2018 (Chelsea) 36
Arridge, S. 1892 (Bootle, Everton, New Brighton Tower) 8
Astley, D. J. 1931 (Charlton Ath, Aston Villa, Derby Co, Blackpool) 13
Atherton, R. W. 1899 (Hibernian, Middlesbrough) 9

Bailiff, W. E. 1913 (Llanelly) 4
Baker, C. W. 1958 (Cardiff C) 7
Baker, W. G. 1948 (Cardiff C) 1
Bale, G. F. 2006 (Southampton, Tottenham H, Real Madrid) 106
Bamford, T. 1931 (Wrexham) 5
Barnard, D. S. 1998 (Barnsley, Grimsby T) 22
Barnes, W. 1948 (Arsenal) 22
Bartley, T. 1898 (Glossop NE) 1
Bastock, A. M. 1892 (Shrewsbury T) 1
Beadles, G. H. 1925 (Cardiff C) 2
Bell, W. S. 1881 (Shrewsbury Engineers, Crewe Alex) 5
Bellamy, C. D. 1998 (Norwich C, Coventry C, Newcastle U, Blackburn R, Liverpool, West Ham U, Manchester C, Liverpool, Cardiff C) 78
Bennion, S. R. 1926 (Manchester U) 10
Berry, G. F. 1979 (Wolverhampton W, Stoke C) 5
Blackmore, C. G. 1985 (Manchester U, Middlesbrough) 39
Blake, D. J. 2011 (Cardiff C, Crystal Palace) 14
Blake, N. A. 1994 (Sheffield U, Bolton W, Blackburn R, Wolverhampton W) 29
Blew, H. 1899 (Wrexham) 22
Boden, T. 1880 (Wrexham) 1
Bodin, B. P. 2018 (Preston NE) 1
Bodin, P. J. 1990 (Swindon T, Crystal Palace, Swindon T) 23
Boulter, L. M. 1939 (Brentford) 1
Bowdler, H. E. 1893 (Shrewsbury T) 1
Bowdler, J. C. H. 1890 (Shrewsbury T, Wolverhampton W, Shrewsbury T) 4
Bowen, D. L. 1955 (Arsenal) 19
Bowen, E. 1880 (Druids) 2
Bowen, J. P. 1994 (Swansea C, Birmingham C) 2
Bowen, M. R. 1986 (Tottenham H, Norwich C, West Ham U) 41
Bowsher, S. J. 1929 (Burnley) 1
Boyle, T. 1981 (Crystal Palace) 2
Bradley, M. S. 2010 (Walsall) 1
Bradshaw, T. W. C. 2016 (Walsall, Barnsley) 3
Britten, T. J. 1878 (Parkgrove, Presteigne) 2
Brooks, D. R. 2018 (Sheffield U, Bournemouth) 21
Brookes, S. J. 1900 (Llandudno) 2
Brown, A. I. 1926 (Aberdare Ath) 1
Brown, J. R. 2006 (Gillingham, Blackburn R, Aberdeen) 3
Browning, M. T. 1996 (Bristol R, Huddersfield T) 5
Bryan, T. 1886 (Oswestry) 2
Buckland, T. 1899 (Bangor) 1
Burgess, W. A. R. 1947 (Tottenham H) 32
Burke, T. 1883 (Wrexham, Newton Heath) 8
Burnett, T. B. 1877 (Ruabon) 1
Burns, W. J. 2022 (Ipswich T) 3
Burton, A. D. 1963 (Norwich C, Newcastle U) 9
Butler, J. 1893 (Chirk) 3
Butler, W. T. 1900 (Druids) 2

Cabango, B. 2021 (Swansea C) 4
Cartwright, L. 1974 (Coventry C, Wrexham) 7
Carty, T. See McCarthy (Wrexham).
Challen, J. B. 1887 (Corinthians, Wellingborough GS) 4
Chapman, T. 1894 (Newtown, Manchester C, Grimsby T) 7
Charles, J. M. 1981 (Swansea C, QPR, Oxford U) 19
Charles, M. 1955 (Swansea T, Arsenal, Cardiff C) 31
Charles, W. J. 1950 (Leeds U, Juventus, Leeds U, Cardiff C) 38
Chester, J. G. 2014 (Hull C, WBA, Aston Villa) 35
Church, S. R. 2009 (Reading, Charlton Ath) 38
Clarke, R. J. 1949 (Manchester C) 22
Coleman, C. 1992 (Crystal Palace, Blackburn R, Fulham) 32
Collier, D. J. 1921 (Grimsby T) 1
Collins, D. L. 2005 (Sunderland, Stoke C) 12
Collins, J. M. 2004 (Cardiff C, West Ham U, Aston Villa, West Ham U) 51
Collins, W. S. 1931 (Llanelly) 1
Collison, J. D. 2008 (West Ham U) 16
Colwill, R. 2021 (Cardiff C) 6
Conde, C. 1884 (Chirk) 3
Cook, F. C. 1925 (Newport Co, Portsmouth) 8
Cornforth, J. M. 1995 (Swansea C) 2
Cotterill, D. R. G. B. 2006 (Bristol C, Wigan Ath, Sheffield U, Swansea C, Doncaster R, Birmingham C) 24
Coyne, D. 1996 (Tranmere R, Grimsby T, Leicester C, Burnley, Tranmere R) 16
Crofts, A. L. 2016 ((Gillingham, Brighton & HA, Norwich C, Scunthorpe U) 29
Crompton, W. 1931 (Wrexham) 3
Cross, E. A. 1876 (Wrexham) 2
Crosse, K. 1879 (Druids) 3
Crossley, M. G. 1997 (Nottingham F, Middlesbrough, Fulham) 8
Crowe, V. H. 1959 (Aston Villa) 16
Cumner, R. H. 1939 (Arsenal) 3
Curtis, A. T. 1976 (Swansea C, Leeds U, Swansea C, Southampton, Cardiff C) 35
Curtis, E. R. 1928 (Cardiff C, Birmingham) 3

Daniel, R. W. 1951 (Arsenal, Sunderland) 21
Darvell, S. 1897 (Oxford University) 2
Davies, A. 1876 (Wrexham) 2
Davies, A. 1904 (Druids, Middlesbrough) 2
Davies, A. 1983 (Manchester U, Newcastle U, Swansea C, Bradford C) 13
Davies, A. 2019 (Barnsley, Stoke C, Sheffield U) 4
Davies, A. O. 1885 (Barmouth, Swifts, Wrexham, Crewe Alex) 9
Davies, A. R. 2006 (Yeovil T) 1
Davies, A. T. 1891 (Shrewsbury T) 1
Davies, B. T. 2013 (Swansea C, Tottenham H) 74
Davies, C. 1972 (Charlton Ath) 1
Davies, C. M. 2006 (Oxford U, Verona, Oldham Ath, Barnsley) 7
Davies, D. 1904 (Bolton W) 3
Davies, D. C. 1899 (Brecon, Hereford) 2
Davies, D. W. 1912 (Treharris, Oldham Ath) 2
Davies, E. Lloyd 1904 (Stoke, Northampton T) 16
Davies, E. R. 1953 (Newcastle U) 6
Davies, G. 1980 (Fulham, Manchester C) 16
Davies, Rev. H. 1928 (Wrexham) 1
Davies, Idwal 1923 (Liverpool Marine) 1
Davies, J. E. 1885 (Oswestry) 1
Davies, Jas 1878 (Wrexham) 1
Davies, John 1879 (Wrexham) 1
Davies, Jos 1888 (Newton Heath, Wolverhampton W) 7
Davies, Jos 1889 (Everton, Chirk, Ardwick, Sheffield U, Manchester C, Millwall, Reading) 11
Davies, J. P. 1883 (Druids) 2
Davies, Ll. 1907 (Wrexham, Everton, Wrexham) 13
Davies, L. S. 1922 (Cardiff C) 23
Davies, O. 1890 (Wrexham) 1
Davies, R. 1883 (Wrexham) 3
Davies, R. 1885 (Druids) 1
Davies, R. O. 1892 (Wrexham) 2
Davies, R. T. 1964 (Norwich C, Southampton, Portsmouth) 29
Davies, R. W. 1964 (Bolton W, Newcastle U, Manchester C, Manchester U, Blackpool) 34
Davies, S. 2001 (Tottenham H, Everton, Fulham) 58
Davies, S. I. 1996 (Manchester U) 1
Davies, Stanley 1920 (Preston NE, Everton, WBA, Rotherham U) 18
Davies, T. 1886 (Oswestry) 1
Davies, T. 1903 (Druids) 4
Davies, W. 1884 (Wrexham) 1
Davies, W. 1924 (Swansea T, Cardiff C, Notts Co) 17
Davies, William 1903 (Wrexham, Blackburn R) 11
Davies, W. C. 1908 (Crystal Palace, WBA, Crystal Palace) 4
Davies, W. D. 1975 (Everton, Wrexham, Swansea C) 52
Davies, W. H. 1876 (Oswestry) 4

Davis, G. 1978 (Wrexham) 3
Davis, W. O. 1913 (Millwall Ath) 5
Day, A. 1934 (Tottenham H) 1
Deacy, N. 1977 (PSV Eindhoven, Beringen) 12
Dearson, D. J. 1939 (Birmingham) 3
Delaney, M. A. 2000 (Aston Villa) 36
Derrett, S. C. 1969 (Cardiff C) 4
Dewey, F. T. 1931 (Cardiff Corinthians) 2
Dibble, A. 1986 (Luton T, Manchester C) 3
Dorman, A. 2010 (St Mirren, Crystal Palace) 3
Doughty, J. 1886 (Druids, Newton Heath) 8
Doughty, R. 1888 (Newton Heath) 2
Duffy, R. M. 2006 (Portsmouth) 13
Dummett, P. 2014 (Newcastle U) 5
Durban, A. 1966 (Derby Co) 27
Dwyer, P. J. 1978 (Cardiff C) 10

Eardley, N. 2008 (Oldham Ath, Blackpool) 16
Earnshaw, R. 2002 (Cardiff C, WBA, Norwich C, Derby Co, Nottingham F, Cardiff C) 59
Easter, J. M. 2007 (Wycombe W, Plymouth Arg, Milton Keynes D, Crystal Palace, Millwall) 12
Eastwood, F. 2008 (Wolverhampton W, Coventry C) 11
Edwards, C. 1878 (Wrexham) 1
Edwards, C. N. H. 1996 (Swansea C) 1
Edwards, D. A. 2008 (Luton T, Wolverhampton W, Reading) 43
Edwards, G. 1947 (Birmingham C, Cardiff C) 12
Edwards, H. 1878 (Wrexham Civil Service, Wrexham) 8
Edwards, J. H. 1876 (Wanderers) 1
Edwards, J. H. 1895 (Oswestry) 3
Edwards, J. H. 1898 (Aberystwyth) 1
Edwards, L. T. 1957 (Charlton Ath) 2
Edwards, R. I. 1978 (Chester, Wrexham) 4
Edwards, R. O. 2003 (Aston Villa, Wolverhampton W) 15
Edwards, R. W. 1998 (Bristol C) 4
Edwards, T. 1932 (Linfield) 1
Egan, W. 1892 (Chirk) 1
Ellis, B. 1932 (Motherwell) 6
Ellis, E. 1931 (Nunhead, Oswestry) 3
Emanuel, W. J. 1973 (Bristol C) 2
England, H. M. 1962 (Blackburn R, Tottenham H) 44
Evans, B. C. 1972 (Swansea C, Hereford U) 7
Evans, C. M. 2008 (Manchester C, Sheffield U) 13
Evans, D. G. 1926 (Reading, Huddersfield T) 4
Evans, H. P. 1922 (Cardiff C) 6
Evans, I. 1976 (Crystal Palace) 13
Evans, J. 1893 (Oswestry) 3
Evans, J. 1912 (Cardiff C) 8
Evans, J. H. 1922 (Southend U) 4
Evans, L. 2018 (Wolverhampton W, Sheffield U, Wigan Ath) 4
Evans, Len 1927 (Aberdare Ath, Cardiff C, Birmingham) 4
Evans, M. 1884 (Oswestry) 1
Evans, P. S. 2002 (Brentford, Bradford C) 2
Evans, R. 1902 (Clapton) 1
Evans, R. E. 1906 (Wrexham, Aston Villa, Sheffield U) 10
Evans, R. O. 1902 (Wrexham, Blackburn R, Coventry C) 10
Evans, R. S. 1964 (Swansea T) 1
Evans, S. J. 2007 (Wrexham) 7
Evans, T. J. 1927 (Clapton Orient, Newcastle U) 4
Evans, W. 1933 (Tottenham H) 6
Evans, W. A. W. 1876 (Oxford University) 2
Evans, W. G. 1890 (Bootle, Aston Villa) 3
Evelyn, E. C. 1887 (Crusaders) 1
Eyton-Jones, J. A. 1883 (Wrexham) 4

Farmer, G. 1885 (Oswestry) 2
Felgate, D. 1984 (Lincoln C) 1
Finnigan, R. J. 1930 (Wrexham) 1
Fletcher, C. N. 2004 (Bournemouth, West Ham U, Crystal Palace) 36
Flynn, B. 1975 (Burnley, Leeds U, Burnley) 66
Fon Williams, O. 2016 (Inverness CT) 1
Ford, T. 1947 (Swansea T, Aston Villa, Sunderland, Cardiff C) 38
Foulkes, H. E. 1932 (WBA) 1
Foulkes, W. I. 1952 (Newcastle U) 11
Foulkes, W. T. 1884 (Oswestry) 2
Fowler, J. 1925 (Swansea T) 6
Freeman, K. S. 2019 (Sheffield U) 1
Freestone, R. 2000 (Swansea C) 1

Gabbidon, D. L. 2002 (Cardiff C, West Ham U, QPR, Crystal Palace) 49
Garner, G. 2006 (Leyton Orient) 1
Garner, J. 1896 (Aberystwyth) 1
Giggs, R. J. 1992 (Manchester U) 64
Giles, D. C. 1980 (Swansea C, Crystal Palace) 12
Gillam, S. G. 1889 (Wrexham, Shrewsbury, Clapton) 5
Glascodine, G. 1879 (Wrexham) 1
Glover, E. M. 1932 (Grimsby T) 7
Godding, G. 1923 (Wrexham) 2
Godfrey, B. C. 1964 (Preston NE) 3
Goodwin, U. 1881 (Ruthin) 1
Goss, J. 1991 (Norwich C) 9
Gough, R. T. 1883 (Oswestry White Star) 1
Gray, A. 1924 (Oldham Ath, Manchester C, Manchester Central, Tranmere R, Chester) 24
Green, A. W. 1901 (Aston Villa, Notts Co, Nottingham F) 8
Green, C. R. 1965 (Birmingham C) 15
Green, G. H. 1938 (Charlton Ath) 4
Green, R. M. 1998 (Wolverhampton W) 2
Grey, Dr D. 1876 (Druids) 2
Griffiths, A. T. 1971 (Wrexham) 17
Griffiths, F. J. 1900 (Blackpool) 2
Griffiths, G. 1887 (Chirk) 1
Griffiths, J. H. 1953 (Swansea T) 1
Griffiths, L. 1902 (Wrexham) 1
Griffiths, M. W. 1947 (Leicester C) 11
Griffiths, P. 1884 (Chirk) 6
Griffiths, P. H. 1932 (Everton) 1
Griffiths, T. P. 1927 (Everton, Bolton W, Middlesbrough, Aston Villa) 21
Gunter, C. R. 2007 (Cardiff C, Tottenham H, Nottingham F, Reading, Charlton Ath) 109

Hall, G. D. 1988 (Chelsea) 9
Hallam, J. 1889 (Oswestry) 1
Hanford, H. 1934 (Swansea T, Sheffield W) 7
Harrington, A. C. 1956 (Cardiff C) 11
Harris, C. S. 1976 (Leeds U) 24
Harris, M. T. 2022 (Cardiff C) 5
Harris, W. C. 1954 (Middlesbrough) 6
Harrison, W. C. 1899 (Wrexham) 5
Hartson, J. 1995 (Arsenal, West Ham U, Wimbledon, Coventry C, Celtic) 51
Haworth, S. O. 1997 (Cardiff C, Coventry C) 5
Hayes, A. 1890 (Wrexham) 2
Hedges, R. P. 2018 (Barnsley, Aberdeen) 3
Henley, A. D. 2016 (Blackburn R) 2
Hennessey, W. R. 2007 (Wolverhampton W, Crystal Palace, Burnley) 104
Hennessey, W. T. 1962 (Birmingham C, Nottingham F, Derby Co) 39
Hersee, A. M. 1886 (Bangor) 2
Hersee, R. 1886 (Llandudno) 1
Hewitt, R. 1958 (Cardiff C) 5
Hewitt, T. J. 1911 (Wrexham, Chelsea, South Liverpool) 8
Heywood, D. 1879 (Druids) 1
Hibbott, H. 1880 (Newtown Excelsior, Newtown) 3
Higham, G. G. 1878 (Oswestry) 2
Hill, M. R. 1972 (Ipswich T) 2
Hockey, T. 1972 (Sheffield U, Norwich C, Aston Villa) 9
Hoddinott, T. F. 1921 (Watford) 2
Hodges, G. 1984 (Wimbledon, Newcastle U, Watford, Sheffield U) 18
Hodgkinson, A. V. 1908 (Southampton) 1
Holden, A. 1984 (Chester C) 1
Hole, B. G. 1963 (Cardiff C, Blackburn R, Aston Villa, Swansea C) 30
Hole, W. J. 1921 (Swansea T) 9
Hollins, D. M. 1962 (Newcastle U) 11
Hopkins, I. J. 1935 (Brentford) 12
Hopkins, J. 1983 (Fulham, Crystal Palace) 16
Hopkins, M. 1956 (Tottenham H) 34
Horne, B. 1988 (Portsmouth, Southampton, Everton, Birmingham C) 59
Howell, E. G. 1888 (Builth) 3
Howells, R. G. 1954 (Cardiff C) 2
Hugh, A. R. 1930 (Newport Co) 1
Hughes, A. 1894 (Rhos) 2
Hughes, A. 1907 (Chirk) 1
Hughes, C. M. 1992 (Luton T, Wimbledon) 8
Hughes, E. 1899 (Everton, Tottenham H) 14
Hughes, E. 1906 (Wrexham, Nottingham F, Wrexham, Manchester C) 16

Hughes, F. W. 1882 (Northwich Victoria) 6
Hughes, I. 1951 (Luton T) 4
Hughes, J. 1877 (Cambridge University, Aberystwyth) 2
Hughes, J. 1905 (Liverpool) 3
Hughes, J. I. 1935 (Blackburn R) 1
Hughes, L. M. 1984 (Manchester U, Barcelona, Manchester U, Chelsea, Southampton) 72
Hughes, P. W. 1887 (Bangor) 3
Hughes, W. 1891 (Bootle) 3
Hughes, W. A. 1949 (Blackburn R) 5
Hughes, W. M. 1938 (Birmingham) 10
Humphreys, J. V. 1947 (Everton) 1
Humphreys, R. 1888 (Druids) 1
Hunter, A. H. 1887 (FA of Wales Secretary) 1
Huws, E. W. 2014 (Manchester C, Wigan Ath, Cardiff C) 11

Isgrove, L. J. 2016 (Southampton) 1

Jackett, K. 1983 (Watford) 31
Jackson, W. 1899 (St Helens Rec) 1
James, D. O. 2019 (Swansea C, Manchester U, Leeds U) 36
James, E. 1893 (Chirk) 8
James, E. G. 1966 (Blackpool) 9
James, L. 1972 (Burnley, Derby Co, QPR, Burnley, Swansea C, Sunderland) 54
James, R. M. 1979 (Swansea C, Stoke C, QPR, Leicester C, Swansea C) 47
James, W. 1931 (West Ham U) 2
Jarrett, R. H. 1889 (Ruthin) 2
Jarvis, A. L. 1967 (Hull C) 3
Jenkins, E. 1925 (Lovell's Ath) 1
Jenkins, J. 1924 (Brighton & HA) 8
Jenkins, R. W. 1902 (Rhyl) 1
Jenkins, S. R. 1996 (Swansea C, Huddersfield T) 16
Jenkyns, C. A. L. 1892 (Small Heath, Woolwich Arsenal, Newton Heath, Walsall) 8
Jennings, W. 1914 (Bolton W) 11
John, D. C. 2013 (Cardiff C, Rangers, Swansea C) 7
John, R. F. 1923 (Arsenal) 15
John, W. R. 1931 (Walsall, Stoke C, Preston NE, Sheffield U, Swansea T) 14
Johnson, A. J. 1999 (Nottingham F, WBA) 15
Johnson, B. P. 2021 (Nottingham F) 13
Johnson, M. G. 1964 (Swansea T) 1
Jones, A. 1987 (Port Vale, Charlton Ath) 6
Jones, A. F. 1877 (Oxford University) 1
Jones, A. T. 1905 (Nottingham F, Notts Co) 2
Jones, Bryn 1935 (Wolverhampton W, Arsenal) 17
Jones, B. S. 1963 (Swansea T, Plymouth Arg, Cardiff C) 15
Jones, Charlie 1926 (Nottingham F, Arsenal) 8
Jones, Cliff 1954 (Swansea T, Tottenham H, Fulham) 59
Jones, C. W. 1935 (Birmingham) 2
Jones, D. 1888 (Chirk, Bolton W, Manchester C) 14
Jones, D. E. 1976 (Norwich C) 8
Jones, D. O. 1934 (Leicester C) 7
Jones, Evan 1910 (Chelsea, Oldham Ath, Bolton W) 7
Jones, F. R. 1885 (Bangor) 3
Jones, F. W. 1893 (Small Heath) 1
Jones, G. P. 1907 (Wrexham) 2
Jones, H. 1902 (Aberaman) 1
Jones, Humphrey 1885 (Bangor, Queen's Park, East Stirlingshire, Queen's Park) 14
Jones, Ivor 1920 (Swansea T, WBA) 10
Jones, Jeffrey 1908 (Llandrindod Wells) 3
Jones, J. 1876 (Druids) 1
Jones, J. 1883 (Berwyn Rangers) 3
Jones, J. 1925 (Wrexham) 1
Jones, J. L. 1895 (Sheffield U, Tottenham H) 21
Jones, J. Love 1906 (Stoke, Middlesbrough) 2
Jones, J. O. 1901 (Bangor) 2
Jones, J. P. 1976 (Liverpool, Wrexham, Chelsea, Huddersfield T) 72
Jones, J. T. 1912 (Stoke, Crystal Palace) 15
Jones, K. 1950 (Aston Villa) 1
Jones, Leslie J. 1933 (Cardiff C, Coventry C, Arsenal 11
Jones, M. A. 2007 (Wrexham) 2
Jones, M. G. 2000 (Leeds U, Leicester C) 13
Jones, P. L. 1997 (Liverpool, Tranmere R) 2
Jones, P. S. 1997 (Stockport Co, Southampton, Wolverhampton W, QPR) 50
Jones, P. W. 1971 (Bristol R) 1
Jones, R. 1887 (Bangor, Crewe Alex) 3
Jones, R. 1898 (Leicester Fosse) 1
Jones, R. 1899 (Druids) 1
Jones, R. 1900 (Bangor) 2
Jones, R. 1906 (Millwall) 2
Jones, R. A. 1884 (Druids) 4
Jones, R. A. 1994 (Sheffield W) 1
Jones, R. S. 1894 (Everton) 1
Jones, S. 1887 (Wrexham, Chester) 2
Jones, S. 1893 (Wrexham, Burton Swifts, Druids) 6
Jones, T. 1926 (Manchester U) 4
Jones, T. D. 1908 (Aberdare) 1
Jones, T. G. 1938 (Everton) 17
Jones, T. J. 1932 (Sheffield W) 2
Jones, V. P. 1995 (Wimbledon) 9
Jones, W. E. A. 1947 (Swansea T, Tottenham H) 4
Jones, W. J. 1901 (Aberdare, West Ham U) 4
Jones, W. Lot 1905 (Manchester C, Southend U) 20
Jones, W. P. 1889 (Druids, Wynnstay) 4
Jones, W. R. 1897 (Aberystwyth) 1

Keenor, F. C. 1920 (Cardiff C, Crewe Alex) 32
Kelly, F. C. 1899 (Wrexham, Druids) 3
Kelsey, A. J. 1954 (Arsenal) 41
Kenrick, S. L. 1876 (Druids, Oswestry, Shropshire Wanderers) 5
Ketley, C. F. 1882 (Druids) 1
King, A. P. 2009 (Leicester C) 50
King, J. 1955 (Swansea T) 1
Kinsey, N. 1951 (Norwich C, Birmingham C) 7
Knill, A. R. 1989 (Swansea C) 1
Koumas, J. 2001 (Tranmere R, WBA, Wigan Ath) 34
Krzywicki, R. L. 1970 (WBA, Huddersfield T) 8

Lambert, R. 1947 (Liverpool) 5
Latham, G. 1905 (Liverpool, Southport Central, Cardiff C) 10
Law, B. J. 1990 (QPR) 1
Lawrence, E. 1930 (Clapton Orient, Notts Co) 2
Lawrence, J. A. 2019 (Anderlecht, St Pauli) 11
Lawrence, S. 1932 (Swansea T) 8
Lawrence, T. M. 2016 (Leicester C, Derby Co) 23
Lea, A. 1889 (Wrexham) 4
Lea, C. 1965 (Ipswich T) 2
Leary, P. 1889 (Bangor) 1
Ledley, J. C. 2006 (Cardiff C, Celtic, Crystal Palace, Derby Co) 77
Leek, K. 1961 (Leicester C, Newcastle U, Birmingham C, Northampton T) 13
Legg, A. 1996 (Birmingham C, Cardiff C) 6
Lever, A. R. 1953 (Leicester C) 1
Levitt, D. J. C. 2021 (Manchester U) 12
Lewis, B. 1891 (Chester, Wrexham, Middlesbrough, Wrexham) 10
Lewis, D. 1927 (Arsenal) 3
Lewis, D. 1983 (Swansea C) 1
Lewis, D. J. 1933 (Swansea T) 2
Lewis, D. M. 1890 (Bangor) 2
Lewis, J. 1906 (Bristol R) 1
Lewis, J. 1926 (Cardiff C) 1
Lewis, T. 1881 (Wrexham) 2
Lewis, W. 1885 (Bangor, Crewe Alex, Chester, Manchester C, Chester) 27
Lewis, W. L. 1927 (Swansea T, Huddersfield T) 6
Llewellyn, C. M. 1998 (Norwich C, Wrexham) 6
Lloyd, B. W. 1976 (Wrexham) 3
Lloyd, J. W. 1879 (Wrexham, Newtown) 2
Lloyd, R. A. 1891 (Ruthin) 2
Lockley, A. 1898 (Chirk) 1
Lockyer, T. A. 2018 (Bristol R, Charlton Ath, Luton T) 14
Lovell, S. 1982 (Crystal Palace, Millwall) 6
Lowndes, S. R. 1983 (Newport Co, Millwall, Barnsley) 10
Lowrie, G. 1948 (Coventry C, Newcastle U) 4
Lucas, P. M. 1962 (Leyton Orient) 4
Lucas, W. H. 1949 (Swansea T) 7
Lumberg, A. 1929 (Wrexham, Wolverhampton W) 4
Lynch, J. J. 2013 (Hudderfield T) 1

MacDonald, S. B. 2011 (Swansea C, Bournemouth) 4
Maguire, G. T. 1990 (Portsmouth) 7
Mahoney, J. F. 1968 (Stoke C, Middlesbrough, Swansea C) 51
Mardon, P. J. 1996 (WBA) 1
Margetson, M. W. 2004 (Cardiff C) 1
Marriott, A. 1996 (Wrexham) 5
Martin, T. J. 1930 (Newport Co) 1
Marustik, C. 1982 (Swansea C) 6

Mates, J. 1891 (Chirk) 3
Matondo, R. 2019 (Manchester C, Schalke 04) 11
Matthews, A. J. 2011 (Cardiff C, Celtic, Sunderland) 14
Matthews, R. W. 1921 (Liverpool, Bristol C, Bradford) 3
Matthews, W. 1905 (Chester) 2
Matthias, J. S. 1896 (Brymbo, Shrewsbury T, Wolverhampton W) 5
Matthias, T. J. 1914 (Wrexham) 12
Mays, A. W. 1929 (Wrexham) 1
McCarthy, T. P. 1889 (Wrexham) 1
McMillan, R. 1881 (Shrewsbury Engineers) 2
Medwin, T. C. 1953 (Swansea T, Tottenham H) 30
Melville, A. K. 1990 (Swansea C, Oxford U, Sunderland, Fulham, West Ham U) 65
Mepham, C. J. 2018 (Brentford, Bournemouth) 32
Meredith, S. 1900 (Chirk, Stoke, Leyton) 8
Meredith, W. H. 1895 (Manchester C, Manchester U) 48
Mielczarek, R. 1971 (Rotherham U) 1
Millership, H. 1920 (Rotherham Co) 6
Millington, A. H. 1963 (WBA, Crystal Palace, Peterborough U, Swansea C) 21
Mills, T. J. 1934 (Clapton Orient, Leicester C) 4
Mills-Roberts, R. H. 1885 (St Thomas' Hospital, Preston NE, Llanberis) 8
Moore, G. 1960 (Cardiff C, Chelsea, Manchester U, Northampton T, Charlton Ath) 21
Moore, K. R. F. 2020 (Wigan Ath, Cardiff C, Bournemouth) 26
Morgan, C. 2007 (Milton Keynes D, Peterborough U, Preston NE) 23
Morgan, J. R. 1877 (Cambridge University, Derby School Staff) 10
Morgan, J. T. 1905 (Wrexham) 1
Morgan-Owen, H. 1902 (Oxford University, Corinthians) 5
Morgan-Owen, M. M. 1897 (Oxford University, Corinthians) 12
Morison, S. W. 2011 (Millwall, Norwich C) 20
Morley, E. J. 1925 (Swansea T, Clapton Orient) 4
Morrell, J. J. 2020 (Bristol C, Luton T, Portsmouth) 28
Morris, A. G. 1896 (Aberystwyth, Swindon T, Nottingham F) 21
Morris, C. 1900 (Chirk, Derby Co, Huddersfield T) 27
Morris, E. 1893 (Chirk) 3
Morris, H. 1894 (Sheffield U, Manchester C, Grimsby T) 3
Morris, J. 1887 (Oswestry) 1
Morris, J. 1898 (Chirk) 1
Morris, R. 1900 (Chirk, Shrewsbury T) 6
Morris, R. 1902 (Newtown, Druids, Liverpool, Leeds C, Grimsby T, Plymouth Arg) 11
Morris, S. 1937 (Birmingham) 5
Morris, W. 1947 (Burnley) 5
Moulsdale, J. R. B. 1925 (Corinthians) 1
Murphy, J. P. 1933 (WBA) 15
Myhill, G. O. 2008 (Hull C, WBA) 19
Nardiello, D. 1978 (Coventry C) 2
Nardiello, D. A. 2007 (Barnsley, QPR) 3
Neal, J. E. 1931 (Colwyn Bay) 2
Neilson, A. B. 1992 (Newcastle U, Southampton) 5
Newnes, J. 1926 (Nelson) 1
Newton, L. F. 1912 (Cardiff Corinthians) 1
Nicholas, D. S. 1923 (Stoke, Swansea T) 3
Nicholas, P. 1979 (Crystal Palace, Arsenal, Crystal Palace, Luton T, Aberdeen, Chelsea, Watford) 73
Nicholls, J. 1924 (Newport Co, Cardiff C) 4
Niedzwiecki, E. A. 1985 (Chelsea) 2
Nock, W. 1897 (Newtown) 1
Nogan, L. M. 1992 (Watford, Reading) 2
Norman, A. J. 1986 (Hull C) 5
Norrington-Davies, R. L. 2021 (Sheffield U) 11
Nurse, M. T. G. 1960 (Swansea T, Middlesbrough) 12
Nyatanga, L. J. 2006 (Derby Co, Bristol C) 34
O'Callaghan, E. 1929 (Tottenham H) 11
Oliver, A. 1905 (Bangor, Blackburn R) 2
Oster, J. M. 1998 (Everton, Sunderland) 13
O'Sullivan, P. A. 1973 (Brighton & HA) 3
Owen, D. 1879 (Oswestry) 1
Owen, E. 1884 (Ruthin Grammar School) 3
Owen, G. 1888 (Chirk, Newton Heath, Chirk) 4
Owen, J. 1892 (Newton Heath) 1
Owen, T. 1879 (Oswestry) 1
Owen, Trevor 1899 (Crewe Alex) 2
Owen, W. 1884 (Chirk) 16
Owen, W. P. 1880 (Ruthin) 12
Owens, J. 1902 (Wrexham) 1
Page, M. E. 1971 (Birmingham C) 28
Page, R. J. 1997 (Watford, Sheffield U, Cardiff C, Coventry C) 41
Palmer, D. 1957 (Swansea T) 3
Parris, J. E. 1932 (Bradford) 1
Parry, B. J. 1951 (Swansea T) 1
Parry, C. 1891 (Everton, Newtown) 13
Parry, E. 1922 (Liverpool) 5
Parry, M. 1901 (Liverpool) 16
Parry, P. I. 2004 (Cardiff C) 12
Parry, T. D. 1900 (Oswestry) 7
Parry, W. 1895 (Newtown) 1
Partridge, D. W. 2005 (Motherwell, Bristol C) 7
Pascoe, C. 1984 (Swansea C, Sunderland) 10
Paul, R. 1949 (Swansea T, Manchester C) 33
Peake, E. 1908 (Aberystwyth, Liverpool) 11
Peers, E. J. 1914 (Wolverhampton W, Port Vale) 12
Pembridge, M. A. 1992 (Luton T, Derby Co, Sheffield W, Benfica, Everton, Fulham) 54
Perry, E. 1938 (Doncaster R) 3
Perry, J. 1994 (Cardiff C) 1
Phennah, E. 1878 (Civil Service) 1
Phillips, C. 1931 (Wolverhampton W, Aston Villa) 13
Phillips, D. 1984 (Plymouth Arg, Manchester C, Coventry C, Norwich C, Nottingham F) 62
Phillips, L. 1971 (Cardiff C, Aston Villa, Swansea C, Charlton Ath) 58
Phillips, T. J. S. 1973 (Chelsea) 4
Phoenix, H. 1882 (Wrexham) 1
Pipe, D. R. 2003 (Coventry C) 1
Poland, G. 1939 (Wrexham) 2
Pontin, K. 1980 (Cardiff C) 2
Powell, A. 1947 (Leeds U, Everton, Birmingham C) 8
Powell, D. 1968 (Wrexham, Sheffield U) 11
Powell, I. V. 1947 (QPR, Aston Villa) 8
Powell, J. 1878 (Druids, Bolton W, Newton Heath) 15
Powell, Seth 1885 (Oswestry, WBA) 7
Price, H. 1907 (Aston Villa, Burton U, Wrexham) 5
Price, J. 1877 (Wrexham) 12
Price, L. P. 2006 (Ipswich T, Derby Co, Crystal Palace) 11
Price, P. 1980 (Luton T, Tottenham H) 25
Pring, K. D. 1966 (Rotherham U) 3
Pritchard, H. K. 1985 (Bristol C) 1
Pryce-Jones, A. W. 1895 (Newtown) 1
Pryce-Jones, W. E. 1887 (Cambridge University) 5
Pugh, A. 1889 (Rhostyllen) 1
Pugh, D. H. 1896 (Wrexham, Lincoln C) 7
Pugsley, J. 1930 (Charlton Ath) 1
Pullen, W. J. 1926 (Plymouth Arg) 1

Ramsey, A. J. 2009 (Arsenal, Juventus, Rangers) 75
Rankmore, F. E. J. 1966 (Peterborough U) 1
Ratcliffe, K. 1981 (Everton, Cardiff C) 59
Rea, J. C. 1894 (Aberystwyth) 9
Ready, K. 1997 (QPR) 5
Reece, G. I. 1966 (Sheffield U, Cardiff C) 29
Reed, W. G. 1955 (Ipswich T) 2
Rees, A. 1984 (Birmingham C) 1
Rees, J. M. 1992 (Luton T) 1
Rees, R. R. 1965 (Coventry C, WBA, Nottingham F) 39
Rees, W. 1949 (Cardiff C, Tottenham H) 4
Ribeiro, C. M. 2010 (Bristol C) 2
Richards, A. 1932 (Barnsley) 1
Richards, A. D. J. (Jazz) 2012 (Swansea C, Cardiff C) 14
Richards, D. 1931 (Wolverhampton W, Brentford, Birmingham) 21
Richards, G. 1899 (Druids, Oswestry, Shrewsbury T) 6
Richards, R. W. 1920 (Wolverhampton W, West Ham U, Mold) 9
Richards, S. V. 1947 (Cardiff C) 1
Richards, W. E. 1933 (Fulham) 1
Ricketts, S. D. 2005 (Swansea C, Hull C, Bolton W, Wolverhampton W) 52
Roach, J. 1885 (Oswestry) 1
Robbins, W. W. 1931 (Cardiff C, WBA) 11
Roberts, A. M. 1993 (QPR) 2
Roberts, C. R. J. 2018 (Swansea C, Burnley) 39
Roberts, D. F. 1973 (Oxford U, Hull C) 17
Roberts, G. W. 2000 (Tranmere R) 9
Roberts, I. W. 1990 (Watford, Huddersfield T, Leicester C, Norwich C) 15
Roberts, Jas 1913 (Wrexham) 2
Roberts, J. 1879 (Corwen, Berwyn R) 7
Roberts, J. 1881 (Ruthin) 2
Roberts, J. 1906 (Bradford C) 2
Roberts, J. G. 1971 (Arsenal, Birmingham C) 22

Roberts, J. H. 1949 (Bolton W) 1
Roberts, N. W. 2000 (Wrexham, Wigan Ath) 4
Roberts, P. S. 1974 (Portsmouth) 4
Roberts, R. 1884 (Druids, Bolton W, Preston NE) 9
Roberts, R. 1886 (Wrexham) 3
Roberts, R. 1891 (Rhos, Crewe Alex) 2
Roberts, R. L. 1890 (Chester) 1
Roberts, S. W. 2005 (Wrexham) 1
Roberts, T. D. 2019 (Leeds U) 19
Roberts, W. 1879 (Llangollen, Berwyn R) 6
Roberts, W. 1883 (Rhyl) 1
Roberts, W. 1886 (Wrexham) 4
Roberts, W. H. 1882 (Ruthin, Rhyl) 6
Robinson, C. P. 2000 (Wolverhampton W, Portsmouth, Sunderland, Norwich C, Toronto Lynx) 52
Robinson, J. R. C. 1996 (Charlton Ath) 30
Robson-Kanu, T. H. 2010 (Reading, WBA) 46
Rodon, J. P. 2020 (Swansea C, Tottenham H) 28
Rodrigues, P. J. 1965 (Cardiff C, Leicester C, Sheffield W) 40
Rogers, J. P. 1896 (Wrexham) 3
Rogers, W. 1931 (Wrexham) 2
Roose, L. R. 1900 (Aberystwyth, London Welsh, Stoke, Everton, Stoke, Sunderland) 24
Rouse, R. V. 1959 (Crystal Palace) 1
Rowlands, A. C. 1914 (Tranmere R) 1
Rowley, T. 1959 (Tranmere R) 1
Rush, I. 1980 (Liverpool, Juventus, Liverpool) 73
Russell, M. R. 1912 (Merthyr T, Plymouth Arg) 23

Sabine, H. W. 1887 (Oswestry) 1
Saunders, D. 1986 (Brighton & HA, Oxford U, Derby Co, Liverpool, Aston Villa, Galatasaray, Nottingham F, Sheffield U, Benfica, Bradford C) 75
Savage, R. W. 1996 (Crewe Alex, Leicester C, Birmingham C) 39
Savin, G. 1878 (Oswestry) 1
Sayer, P. A. 1977 (Cardiff C) 7
Scrine, F. H. 1950 (Swansea T) 2
Sear, C. R. 1963 (Manchester C) 1
Shaw, E. G. 1882 (Oswestry) 3
Sheehan, J. L. 2021 (Newport Co, Bolton W) 3
Sherwood, A. T. 1947 (Cardiff C, Newport Co) 41
Shone, W. W. 1879 (Oswestry) 1
Shortt, W. W. 1947 (Plymouth Arg) 12
Showers, D. 1975 (Cardiff C) 2
Sidlow, C. 1947 (Liverpool) 7
Sisson, H. 1885 (Wrexham Olympic) 3
Slatter, N. 1983 (Bristol R, Oxford U) 22
Smallman, D. P. 1974 (Wrexham, Everton) 7
Smith, M. 2018 (Manchester C, Milton Keynes D) 18
Southall, N. 1982 (Everton) 92
Speed, G. A. 1990 (Leeds U, Everton, Newcastle U, Bolton W) 85
Sprake, G. 1964 (Leeds U, Birmingham C) 37
Stansfield, F. 1949 (Cardiff C) 1
Stevenson, B. 1978 (Leeds U, Birmingham C) 15
Stevenson, N. 1982 (Swansea C) 4
Stitfall, R. F. 1953 (Cardiff C) 2
Stock, B. B. 2010 (Doncaster R) 3
Sullivan, D. 1953 (Cardiff C) 17
Symons, C. J. 1992 (Portsmouth, Manchester C, Fulham, Crystal Palace) 37

Tapscott, D. R. 1954 (Arsenal, Cardiff C) 14
Taylor, G. K. 1996 (Crystal Palace, Sheffield U, Burnley, Nottingham F) 15
Taylor, J. 1898 (Wrexham) 1
Taylor, J. W. T. 2015 (Reading) 1
Taylor, N. J. 2010 (Wrexham, Swansea C, Aston Villa) 43
Taylor, O. D. S. 1893 (Newtown) 4
Thatcher, B. D. 2004 (Leicester C, Manchester C) 7
Thomas, B. S. W. 2022 (Huddersfield T) 5
Thomas, C. 1899 (Druids) 2
Thomas, D. A. 1957 (Swansea T) 2
Thomas, D. S. 1948 (Fulham) 4
Thomas, E. 1925 (Cardiff Corinthians) 1
Thomas, G. 1885 (Wrexham) 2
Thomas, G. S. 2018 (Leicester C) 3
Thomas, H. 1927 (Manchester U) 1
Thomas, Martin R. 1987 (Newcastle U) 1
Thomas, Mickey 1977 (Wrexham, Manchester U, Everton, Brighton & HA, Stoke C, Chelsea, WBA) 51
Thomas, R. J. 1967 (Swindon T, Derby Co, Cardiff C) 50
Thomas, T. 1898 (Bangor) 2
Thomas, W. R. 1931 (Newport Co) 2
Thomson, D. 1876 (Druids) 1
Thomson, G. F. 1876 (Druids) 2
Toshack, J. B. 1969 (Cardiff C, Liverpool, Swansea C) 40
Townsend, W. 1887 (Newtown) 2
Trainer, H. 1895 (Wrexham) 3
Trainer, J. 1887 (Bolton W, Preston NE) 20
Trollope, P. J. 1997 (Derby Co, Fulham, Coventry C, Northampton T) 9
Tudur-Jones, O. 2008 (Swansea C, Norwich C, Hibernian) 7
Turner, H. G. 1937 (Charlton Ath) 8
Turner, J. 1892 (Wrexham) 1
Turner, R. E. 1891 (Wrexham) 2
Turner, W. H. 1887 (Wrexham) 5

Van Den Hauwe, P. W. R. 1985 (Everton) 13
Vaughan, D. O. 2003 (Crewe Alex, Real Sociedad, Blackpool, Sunderland, Nottingham F) 42
Vaughan, Jas 1893 (Druids) 4
Vaughan, John 1879 (Oswestry, Druids, Bolton W) 11
Vaughan, J. O. 1885 (Rhyl) 4
Vaughan, N. 1983 (Newport Co, Cardiff C) 10
Vaughan, T. 1885 (Rhyl) 1
Vaulks, W. R. 2019 (Rotherham U, Cardiff C) 7
Vearncombe, G. 1958 (Cardiff C) 2
Vernon, T. R. 1957 (Blackburn R, Everton, Stoke C) 32
Villars, A. K. 1974 (Cardiff C) 3
Vizard, E. T. 1911 (Bolton W) 22
Vokes, S. M. 2008 (Bournemouth, Wolverhampton W, Burnley, Stoke C) 64

Walley, J. T. 1971 (Watford) 1
Walsh, I. P. 1980 (Crystal Palace, Swansea C) 18
Ward, D. 1959 (Bristol R, Cardiff C) 2
Ward, D. 2000 (Notts Co, Nottingham F) 5
Ward, D. 2016 (Liverpool, Leicester C) 26
Warner, J. 1937 (Swansea T, Manchester U) 2
Warren, F. W. 1929 (Cardiff C, Middlesbrough, Hearts) 6
Watkins, A. E. 1898 (Leicester Fosse, Aston Villa, Millwall) 5
Watkins, M. J. 2018 (Norwich C) 2
Watkins, W. M. 1902 (Stoke, Aston Villa, Sunderland, Stoke) 10
Webster, C. 1957 (Manchester U) 4
Weston, R. D. 2000 (Arsenal, Cardiff C) 7
Whatley, W. J. 1939 (Tottenham H) 2
White, P. F. 1896 (London Welsh) 1
Wilcock, A. R. 1890 (Oswestry) 1
Wilding, J. 1885 (Wrexham Olympians, Bootle, Wrexham) 9
Williams, A. 1994 (Reading, Wolverhampton W, Reading) 13
Williams, A. E. 2008 (Stockport Co, Swansea C, Everton) 86
Williams, A. L. 1931 (Wrexham) 1
Williams, A. P. 1998 (Southampton) 2
Williams, B. 1930 (Bristol C) 1
Williams, B. D. 1928 (Swansea T, Everton) 10
Williams, D. G. 1988 (Derby Co, Ipswich T) 13
Williams, D. M. 1986 (Norwich C) 5
Williams, D. R. 1921 (Merthyr T, Sheffield W, Manchester U) 8
Williams, E. 1893 (Crewe Alex) 2
Williams, E. 1901 (Druids) 5
Williams, G. 1893 (Chirk) 6
Williams, G. C. 2014 (Fulham) 7
Williams, G. E. 1960 (WBA) 26
Williams, G. G. 1961 (Swansea T) 5
Williams, G. J. 2006 (West Ham U, Ipswich T) 2
Williams, G. J. J. 1951 (Cardiff C) 1
Williams, G. O. 1907 (Wrexham) 1
Williams, H. J. 1965 (Swansea T) 3
Williams, H. T. 1949 (Newport Co, Leeds U) 4
Williams, J. H. 1884 (Oswestry) 1
Williams, J. J. 1939 (Wrexham) 1
Williams, J. P. 2013 (Crystal Palace, Charlton Ath, Swindon T) 33
Williams, J. T. 1925 (Middlesbrough) 1
Williams, J. W. 1912 (Crystal Palace) 2
Williams, N. S. 2021 (Liverpool) 21
Williams, R. 1935 (Newcastle U) 2
Williams, R. P. 1886 (Caernarvon) 1
Williams, S. G. 1954 (WBA, Southampton) 43
Williams, W. 1876 (Druids, Oswestry, Druids) 11
Williams, W. 1925 (Northampton T) 1

Wilson, H. 2013 (Liverpool, Fulham) 39
Wilson, J. S. 2013 (Bristol C) 1
Witcomb, D. F. 1947 (WBA, Sheffield W) 3
Woodburn, B. 2018 (Liverpool) 11
Woosnam, A. P. 1959 (Leyton Orient, West Ham U, Aston Villa) 17
Woosnam, G. 1879 (Newtown Excelsior) 1
Worthington, T. 1894 (Newtown) 1
Wynn, G. A. 1909 (Wrexham, Manchester C) 11
Wynn, W. 1903 (Chirk) 1

Yorath, T. C. 1970 (Leeds U, Coventry C, Tottenham H, Vancouver Whitecaps) 59
Young, E. 1990 (Wimbledon, Crystal Palace, Wolverhampton W) 21

REPUBLIC OF IRELAND

Aherne, T. 1946 (Belfast Celtic, Luton T) 16
Aldridge, J. W. 1986 (Oxford U, Liverpool, Real Sociedad, Tranmere R) 69
Ambrose, P. 1955 (Shamrock R) 5
Anderson, J. 1980 (Preston NE, Newcastle U) 16
Andrews, K. J. 2009 (Blackburn R, WBA) 35
Andrews, P. 1936 (Bohemians) 1
Arrigan, T. 1938 (Waterford) 1
Arter, H. N. 2015 (Bournemouth) 19

Babb, P. A. 1994 (Coventry C, Liverpool, Sunderland) 35
Bailham, E. 1964 (Shamrock R) 1
Barber, E. 1966 (Shelbourne, Birmingham C) 2
Barrett, G. 2003 (Arsenal, Coventry C) 6
Barry, P. 1928 (Fordsons) 2
Bazunu, G. O. 2021 (Manchester C) 10
Beglin, J. 1984 (Liverpool) 15
Bennett, A. J. 2007 (Reading) 2
Bermingham, J. 1929 (Bohemians) 1
Bermingham, P. 1935 (St James' Gate) 1
Best, L. J. B. 2009 (Coventry C, Newcastle U) 7
Bonner, P. 1981 (Celtic) 80
Boyle, A. 2017 (Preston NE) 1
Braddish, S. 1978 (Dundalk) 2
Bradshaw, P. 1939 (St James' Gate) 5
Brady, F. 1926 (Fordsons) 2
Brady, R. 2013 (Hull C, Norwich C, Burnley) 57
Brady, T. R. 1964 (QPR) 6
Brady, W. L. 1975 (Arsenal, Juventus, Sampdoria, Internazionale, Ascoli, West Ham U) 72
Branagan, K. G. 1997 (Bolton W) 1
Breen, G. 1996 (Birmingham C, Coventry C, West Ham U, Sunderland) 63
Breen, T. 1937 (Manchester U, Shamrock R) 5
Brennan, F. 1965 (Drumcondra) 1
Brennan, S. A. 1965 (Manchester U, Waterford) 19
Brown, J. 1937 (Coventry C) 2
Browne, A. J. 2017 (Preston NE) 23
Browne, W. 1964 (Bohemians) 3
Bruce, A. S. 2007 (Ipswich T) 2
Buckley, L. 1984 (Shamrock R, Waregem) 2
Burke, F. 1952 (Cork Ath) 1
Burke, G. D. 2018 (Shamrock R, Preston NE) 3
Burke, J. 1929 (Shamrock R) 1
Burke, J. 1934 (Cork) 1
Butler, P. J. 2000 (Sunderland) 1
Butler, T. 2003 (Sunderland) 2
Byrne, A. B. 1970 (Southampton) 14
Byrne, D. 1929 (Shelbourne, Shamrock R, Coleraine) 3
Byrne, J. 1928 (Bray Unknowns) 1
Byrne, J. 1985 (QPR, Le Havre, Brighton & HA, Sunderland, Millwall) 23
Byrne, J. 2004 (Shelbourne) 2
Byrne, J. 2020 (Shamrock R) 4
Byrne, P. 1931 (Dolphin, Shelbourne, Drumcondra) 3
Byrne, P. 1984 (Shamrock R) 8
Byrne, S. 1931 (Bohemians) 1

Campbell, A. 1985 (Santander) 3
Campbell, N. 1971 (St Patrick's Ath, Fortuna Cologne) 11
Cannon, H. 1926 (Bohemians) 2
Cantwell, N. 1954 (West Ham U, Manchester U) 36
Carey, B. P. 1992 (Manchester U, Leicester C) 3
Carey, J. J. 1938 (Manchester U) 29
Carolan, J. 1960 (Manchester U) 2
Carr, S. 1999 (Tottenham H, Newcastle U) 44
Carroll, B. 1949 (Shelbourne) 2
Carroll, T. R. 1968 (Ipswich T, Birmingham C) 17
Carsley, L. K. 1998 (Derby Co, Blackburn R, Coventry C, Everton) 39
Cascarino, A. G. 1986 (Gillingham, Millwall, Aston Villa, Celtic, Chelsea, Marseille, Nancy) 88
Chandler, J. 1980 (Leeds U) 2
Chatton, H. A. 1931 (Shelbourne, Dumbarton, Cork) 3
Christie, C. S. F. 2015 (Derby Co, Middlesbrough, Fulham) 30
Clark, C. 2011 (Aston Villa, Newcastle U) 36
Clarke, C. R. 2004 (Stoke C) 2
Clarke, J. 1978 (Drogheda U) 1
Clarke, K. 1948 (Drumcondra) 2
Clarke, M. 1950 (Shamrock R) 1
Clinton, T. J. 1951 (Everton) 3
Coad, P. 1947 (Shamrock R) 11
Coffey, T. 1950 (Drumcondra) 1
Coleman, S. 2011 (Everton) 65
Colfer, M. D. 1950 (Shelbourne) 2
Colgan, N. 2002 (Hibernian, Barnsley) 9
Collins, F. 1927 (Jacobs) 1
Collins, J. S. 2020 (Luton T, Cardiff C) 14
Collins, N. M. 2022 (Burnley) 6
Conmy, O. M. 1965 (Peterborough U) 5
Connolly, A. A. 2020 (Brighton & HA) 8
Connolly, D. J. 1996 (Watford, Feyenoord, Wolverhampton W, Excelsior, Feyenoord, Wimbledon, West Ham U, Wigan Ath) 41
Connolly, H. 1937 (Cork) 1
Connolly, J. 1926 (Fordsons) 1
Conroy, G. A. 1970 (Stoke C) 27
Conway, J. P. 1967 (Fulham, Manchester C) 20
Corr, P. J. 1949 (Everton) 4
Courtney, E. 1946 (Cork U) 1
Cox, S. R. 2011 (WBA, Nottingham F) 30
Coyle, O. C. 1994 (Bolton W) 1
Coyne, T. 1992 (Celtic, Tranmere R, Motherwell) 22
Crowe, G. 2003 (Bohemians) 2
Cullen, J. J. 2020 (West Ham U, Anderlecht) 20
Cummins, G. P. 1954 (Luton T) 19
Cuneen, T. 1951 (Limerick) 1
Cunningham, G. R. 2010 (Manchester C, Bristol C) 4
Cunningham, K. 1996 (Wimbledon, Birmingham C) 72
Curtis, D. P. 1957 (Shelbourne, Bristol C, Ipswich T, Exeter C) 17
Curtis, R. 2019 (Portsmouth) 7
Cusack, S. 1953 (Limerick) 1

Daish, L. S. 1992 (Cambridge U, Coventry C) 5
Daly, G. A. 1973 (Manchester U, Derby Co, Coventry C, Birmingham C, Shrewsbury T) 48
Daly, J. 1932 (Shamrock R) 2
Daly, M. 1978 (Wolverhampton W) 2
Daly, P. 1950 (Shamrock R) 1
Davis, T. L. 1937 (Oldham Ath, Tranmere R) 4
Deacy, E. 1982 (Aston Villa) 4
Delaney, D. F. 2008 (QPR, Ipswich T, Crystal Palace) 9
Delap, R. J. 1998 (Derby Co, Southampton) 11
De Mange, K. J. P. P. 1987 (Liverpool, Hull C) 2
Dempsey, J. T. 1967 (Fulham, Chelsea) 19
Dennehy, J. 1972 (Cork Hibernians, Nottingham F, Walsall) 11
Desmond, P. 1950 (Middlesbrough) 4
Devine, J. 1980 (Arsenal, Norwich C) 13
Doherty, G. M. T. 2000 (Luton T, Tottenham H, Norwich C) 34
Doherty, M. J. 2018 (Woverhampton W, Tottenham H) 29
Donnelly, J. 1935 (Dundalk) 10
Donnelly, T. 1938 (Drumcondra, Shamrock R) 2
Donovan, D. C. 1955 (Everton) 5
Donovan, T. 1980 (Aston Villa) 2
Douglas, J. 2004 (Blackburn R, Leeds U) 8
Dowdall, C. 1928 (Fordsons, Barnsley, Cork) 3
Doyle, C. 1959 (Shelbourne) 1
Doyle, C. A. 2007 (Birmingham C, Bradford C) 4
Doyle, D. 1926 (Shamrock R) 1
Doyle, K. E. 2006 (Reading, Wolverhampton W, Colorado Rapids) 63
Doyle, L. 1932 (Dolphin) 1
Doyle, M. P. 2004 (Coventry C) 1

Duff, D. A. 1998 (Blackburn R, Chelsea, Newcastle U, Fulham) 100
Duffy, B. 1950 (Shamrock R) 1
Duffy, S. P. M. 2014 (Everton, Blackburn R, Brighton & HA) 55
Duggan, H. A. 1927 (Leeds U, Newport Co) 5
Dunne, A. P. 1962 (Manchester U, Bolton W) 33
Dunne, J. 1930 (Sheffield U, Arsenal, Southampton, Shamrock R) 15
Dunne, J. C. 1971 (Fulham) 1
Dunne, L. 1935 (Manchester C) 2
Dunne, P. A. J. 1965 (Manchester U) 5
Dunne, R. P. 2000 (Everton, Manchester C, Aston Villa, QPR) 80
Dunne, S. 1953 (Luton T) 15
Dunne, T. 1956 (St Patrick's Ath) 3
Dunning, P. 1971 (Shelbourne) 2
Dunphy, E. M. 1966 (York C, Millwall) 23
Dwyer, N. M. 1960 (West Ham U, Swansea T) 14

Eccles, P. 1986 (Shamrock R) 1
Egan, J. 2017 (Brentford, Sheffield U) 26
Egan, R. 1929 (Dundalk) 1
Eglington, T. J. 1946 (Shamrock R, Everton) 24
Elliot, R. 2014 (Newcastle U) 4
Elliott, S. W. 2005 (Sunderland) 9
Ellis, P. 1935 (Bohemians) 7
Evans, M. J. 1998 (Southampton) 1

Fagan, E. 1973 (Shamrock R) 1
Fagan, F. 1955 (Manchester C, Derby Co) 8
Fagan, J. 1926 (Shamrock R) 1
Fahey, K. D. 2010 (Birmingham C) 16
Fairclough, M. 1982 (Dundalk) 2
Fallon, S. 1951 (Celtic) 8
Fallon, W. J. 1935 (Notts Co, Sheffield W) 9
Farquharson, T. G. 1929 (Cardiff C) 4
Farrell, P. 1937 (Hibernian) 2
Farrell, P. D. 1946 (Shamrock R, Everton) 28
Farrelly, G. 1996 (Aston Villa, Everton, Bolton W) 6
Feenan, J. J. 1937 (Sunderland) 2
Finnan, S. 2000 (Fulham, Liverpool, Espanyol) 53
Finucane, A. 1967 (Limerick) 11
Fitzgerald, F. J. 1955 (Waterford) 2
Fitzgerald, P. J. 1961 (Leeds U, Chester) 5
Fitzpatrick, K. 1970 (Limerick) 1
Fitzsimons, A. G. 1950 (Middlesbrough, Lincoln C) 26
Fleming, C. 1996 (Middlesbrough) 10
Flood, J. J. 1926 (Shamrock R) 5
Fogarty, A. 1960 (Sunderland, Hartlepools U) 11
Folan, C. C. 2009 (Hull C) 7
Foley, D. J. 2000 (Watford) 6
Foley, J. 1934 (Cork, Celtic) 7
Foley, K. P. 2009 (Wolverhampton W) 8
Foley, M. 1926 (Shelbourne) 1
Foley, T. C. 1964 (Northampton T) 9
Forde, D. 2011 (Millwall) 24
Foy, T. 1938 (Shamrock R) 2
Fullam, J. 1961 (Preston NE, Shamrock R) 11
Fullam, R. 1926 (Shamrock R) 2

Gallagher, C. 1967 (Celtic) 2
Gallagher, M. 1954 (Hibernian) 1
Gallagher, P. 1932 (Falkirk) 1
Galvin, A. 1983 (Tottenham H, Sheffield W, Swindon T) 29
Gamble, J. 2007 (Cork C) 2
Gannon, E. 1949 (Notts Co, Sheffield W, Shelbourne) 14
Gannon, M. 1972 (Shelbourne) 1
Gaskins, P. 1934 (Shamrock R, St James' Gate) 7
Gavin, J. T. 1950 (Norwich C, Tottenham H, Norwich C) 7
Geoghegan, M. 1937 (St James' Gate) 2
Gibbons, A. 1952 (St Patrick's Ath) 4
Gibson, D. T. D. 2008 (Manchester U, Everton) 27
Gilbert, R. 1966 (Shamrock R) 1
Giles, C. 1951 (Doncaster R) 1
Giles, M. J. 1960 (Manchester U, Leeds U, WBA, Shamrock R) 59
Given, S. J. J. 1996 (Blackburn R, Newcastle U, Manchester C, Aston Villa, Stoke C) 134
Givens, D. J. 1969 (Manchester U, Luton T, QPR, Birmingham C, Neuchatel X) 56
Gleeson, S. M. 2007 (Wolverhampton W, Birmingham C) 4

Glen, W. 1927 (Shamrock R) 8
Glynn, D. 1952 (Drumcondra) 2
Godwin, T. F. 1949 (Shamrock R, Leicester C, Bournemouth) 13
Golding, J. 1928 (Shamrock R) 2
Goodman, J. 1997 (Wimbledon) 4
Goodwin, J. 2003 (Stockport Co) 1
Gorman, W. C. 1936 (Bury, Brentford) 13
Grace, J. 1926 (Drumcondra) 1
Grealish, A. 1976 (Orient, Luton T, Brighton & HA, WBA) 45
Green, P. J. 2010 (Derby Co, Leeds U) 20
Gregg, E. 1978 (Bohemians) 8
Griffith, R. 1935 (Walsall) 1
Grimes, A. A. 1978 (Manchester U, Coventry C, Luton T) 18

Hale, A. 1962 (Aston Villa, Doncaster R, Waterford) 14
Hamilton, C. N. 2022 (Blackpool) 1
Hamilton, T. 1959 (Shamrock R) 2
Hand, E. K. 1969 (Portsmouth) 20
Harrington, W. 1936 (Cork) 5
Harte, I. P. 1996 (Leeds U, Levante) 64
Hartnett, J. B. 1949 (Middlesbrough) 2
Haverty, J. 1956 (Arsenal, Blackburn R, Millwall, Celtic, Bristol R, Shelbourne) 32
Hayes, A. W. P. 1979 (Southampton) 1
Hayes, J. 2016 (Aberdeen) 4
Hayes, W. E. 1947 (Huddersfield T) 2
Hayes, W. J. 1949 (Limerick) 1
Healey, R. 1977 (Cardiff C) 2
Healy, C. 2002 (Celtic, Sunderland) 13
Heighway, S. D. 1971 (Liverpool, Minnesota K) 34
Henderson, B. 1948 (Drumcondra) 2
Henderson, W. C. P. 2006 (Brighton & HA, Preston NE) 6
Hendrick, J. P. 2013 (Derby Co, Burnley, Newcastle U) 74
Hennessy, J. 1965 (Shelbourne, St Patrick's Ath) 5
Herrick, J. 1972 (Cork Hibernians, Shamrock R) 3
Higgins, J. 1951 (Birmingham C) 1
Hogan, S. A. 2018 (Aston Villa, Birmingham C) 11
Holland, M. R. 2000 (Ipswich T, Charlton Ath) 49
Holmes, J. 1971 (Coventry C, Tottenham H, Vancouver Whitecaps) 30
Hoolahan, W. 2008 (Blackpool, Norwich C) 43
Horgan, D. J. 2017 (Preston NE, Hibernian, Wycombe W) 17
Horlacher, A. F. 1930 (Bohemians) 7
Houghton, R. J. 1986 (Oxford U, Liverpool, Aston Villa, Crystal Palace, Reading) 73
Hourihane, C. 2017 (Aston Villa) 35
Howlett, G. 1984 (Brighton & HA) 1
Hoy, M. 1938 (Dundalk) 6
Hughton, C. 1980 (Tottenham H, West Ham U) 53
Hunt, N. 2009 (Reading) 3
Hunt, S. P. 2007 (Reading, Hull C, Wolverhampton W) 39
Hurley, C. J. 1957 (Millwall, Sunderland, Bolton W) 40
Hutchinson, F. 1935 (Drumcondra) 2

Idah, A. 2021 (Norwich C) 13
Ireland S. J. 2006 (Manchester C) 6
Irwin, D. J. 1991 (Manchester U) 56

Jordan, D. 1937 (Wolverhampton W) 2
Jordan, W. 1934 (Bohemians) 2
Judge, A. C. 2016 (Brentford, Ipswich T) 9

Kavanagh, G. A. 1998 (Stoke C, Cardiff C, Wigan Ath) 16
Kavanagh, P. J. 1931 (Celtic) 2
Keane, R. D. 1998 (Wolverhampton W, Coventry C, Internazionale, Leeds U, Tottenham H, Liverpool, Tottenham H, LA Galaxy) 146
Keane, R. M. 1991 (Nottingham F, Manchester U) 67
Keane, T. R. 1949 (Swansea T) 4
Keane, W. D. 2022 (Wigan Ath) 4
Kearin, M. 1972 (Shamrock R) 1
Kearns, F. T. 1954 (West Ham U) 1
Kearns, M. 1971 (Oxford U, Walsall, Wolverhampton W) 18
Kelleher, C. O. 2021 (Liverpool) 8
Kelly, A. T. 1993 (Sheffield U, Blackburn R) 34
Kelly, D. T. 1988 (Walsall, West Ham U, Leicester C, Newcastle U, Wolverhampton W, Sunderland, Tranmere R) 26

Kelly, G. 1994 (Leeds U) 52
Kelly, J. 1932 (Derry C) 4
Kelly, J. A. 1957 (Drumcondra, Preston NE) 47
Kelly, J. P. V. 1961 (Wolverhampton W) 5
Kelly, M. J. 1988 (Portsmouth) 4
Kelly, N. 1954 (Nottingham F) 1
Kelly, S. M. 2006 (Tottenham H, Birmingham C, Fulham, Reading) 38
Kendrick, J. 1927 (Everton, Dolphin) 4
Kenna, J. J. 1995 (Blackburn R) 27
Kennedy, M. F. 1986 (Portsmouth) 2
Kennedy, M. J. 1996 (Liverpool, Wimbledon, Manchester C, Wolverhampton W) 34
Kennedy, W. 1932 (St James' Gate) 3
Kenny, P. 2004 (Sheffield U) 7
Keogh, A. D. 2007 (Wolverhampton W, Millwall) 30
Keogh, J. 1966 (Shamrock R) 1
Keogh, R. J. 2013 (Derby Co) 26
Keogh, S. 1959 (Shamrock R) 1
Kernaghan, A. N. 1993 (Middlesbrough, Manchester C) 22
Kiely, D. L. 2000 (Charlton Ath, WBA) 11
Kiernan, F. W. 1951 (Shamrock R, Southampton) 5
Kilbane, K. D. 1998 (WBA, Sunderland, Everton, Wigan Ath, Hull C) 110
Kinnear, J. P. 1967 (Tottenham H, Brighton & HA) 26
Kinsella, J. 1928 (Shelbourne) 1
Kinsella, M. A. 1998 (Charlton Ath, Aston Villa, WBA) 48
Kinsella, O. 1932 (Shamrock R) 2
Kirkland, A. 1927 (Shamrock R) 1
Knight, J. P. 2021 (Derby Co) 15

Lacey, W. 1927 (Shelbourne) 3
Langan, D. 1978 (Derby Co, Birmingham C, Oxford U) 26
Lapira, J. 2007 (Notre Dame) 1
Lawler, J. F. 1953 (Fulham) 8
Lawlor, J. C. 1949 (Drumcondra, Doncaster R) 3
Lawlor, M. 1971 (Shamrock R) 5
Lawrence, L. 2009 (Stoke C, Portsmouth) 15
Lawrenson, M. 1977 (Preston NE, Brighton & HA, Liverpool) 39
Lee, A. D. 2003 (Rotherham U, Cardiff C, Ipswich T) 10
Leech, M. 1969 (Shamrock R) 8
Lenihan, D. P. 2018 (Blackburn R) 3
Lennon, C. 1935 (St James' Gate) 3
Lennox, G. 1931 (Dolphin) 2
Long, K. F. 2017 (Burnley) 17
Long, S. P. 2007 (Reading, WBA, Hull C, Southampton) 88
Lowry, D. 1962 (St Patrick's Ath) 1
Lunn, R. 1939 (Dundalk) 2
Lynch, J. 1934 (Cork Bohemians) 1

Macken, A. 1977 (Derby Co) 1
Macken J. P. 2005 (Manchester C) 1
Mackey, G. 1957 (Shamrock R) 3
Madden, O. 1936 (Cork) 1
Madden, P. 2013 (Scunthorpe U) 1
Maguire, J. 1929 (Shamrock R) 1
Maguire, S. P. 2018 (Preston NE) 11
Mahon, A. J. 2000 (Tranmere R) 2
Malone, G. 1949 (Shelbourne) 1
Mancini, T. J. 1974 (QPR, Arsenal) 5
Manning, R. P. (Swansea C) 6
Martin, C. 1927 (Bo'ness) 1
Martin, C. J. 1946 (Glentoran, Leeds U, Aston Villa) 30
Martin, M. P. 1972 (Bohemians, Manchester U, WBA, Newcastle U) 52
Maybury, A. 1998 (Leeds U, Hearts, Leicester C) 10
McAlinden, J. 1946 (Portsmouth) 2
McAteer, J. W. 1994 (Bolton W, Liverpool, Blackburn R, Sunderland) 52
McCann, J. 1957 (Shamrock R) 1
McCarthy, J. 1926 (Bohemians) 3
McCarthy, J. 2010 (Wigan Ath, Everton, Crystal Palace) 43
McCarthy, M. 1932 (Shamrock R) 1
McCarthy, M. 1984 (Manchester C, Celtic, Lyon, Millwall) 57
McClean, J. J. 2012 (Sunderland, Wigan Ath, WBA, Stoke C, Wigan Ath) 94
McConville, T. 1972 (Dundalk, Waterford) 6
McDonagh, Jacko 1984 (Shamrock R) 3
McDonagh, J. 1981 (Everton, Bolton W, Notts Co, Wichita Wings) 25
McEvoy, M. A. 1961 (Blackburn R) 17
McGeady, A. J. 2004 (Celtic, Spartak Moscow, Everton, Sunderland) 93
McGee, P. 1978 (QPR, Preston NE) 15
McGoldrick, D. J. 2015 (Ipswich T, Sheffield U) 14
McGoldrick, E. J. 1992 (Crystal Palace, Arsenal) 15
McGowan, D. 1949 (West Ham U) 3
McGowan, J. 1947 (Cork U) 1
McGrath, J. T. 2021 (St Mirren) 6
McGrath, M. 1958 (Blackburn R, Bradford) 22
McGrath, P. 1985 (Manchester U, Aston Villa, Derby Co) 83
McGuire, W. 1936 (Bohemians) 1
McKenzie, G. 1938 (Southend U) 9
McLoughlin, A. F. 1990 (Swindon T, Southampton, Portsmouth) 42
McLoughlin, F. 1930 (Fordsons, Cork) 2
McMillan, W. 1946 (Belfast Celtic) 2
McNally, J. B. 1959 (Luton T) 3
McPhail, S. 2000 (Leeds U) 10
McShane, P. D. 2007 (WBA, Sunderland, Hull C, Reading) 33
Meagan, M. K. 1961 (Everton, Huddersfield T, Drogheda) 17
Meehan, P. 1934 (Drumcondra) 1
Meyler, D. J. 2013 (Sunderland, Hull C, Reading) 26
Miller, L. W. P. 2004 (Celtic, Manchester U, Sunderland, Hibernian) 21
Milligan, M. J. 1992 (Oldham Ath) 1
Molumby, J. P. 2021 (Brighton & HA, Wigan Ath) 14
Monahan, P. 1935 (Sligo R) 2
Mooney, J. 1965 (Shamrock R) 2
Moore, A. 1996 (Middlesbrough) 8
Moore, P. 1931 (Shamrock R, Aberdeen, Shamrock R) 9
Moran, K. 1980 (Manchester U, Sporting Gijon, Blackburn R) 71
Moroney, T. 1948 (West Ham U, Evergreen U) 12
Morris, C. B. 1988 (Celtic, Middlesbrough) 35
Morrison, C. H. 2002 (Crystal Palace, Birmingham C, Crystal Palace) 36
Moulson, C. 1936 (Lincoln C, Notts Co) 5
Moulson, G. B. 1948 (Lincoln C) 3
Muckian, C. 1978 (Drogheda U) 1
Muldoon, T. 1927 (Aston Villa) 1
Mulligan, P. M. 1969 (Shamrock R, Chelsea, Crystal Palace, WBA, Shamrock R) 50
Munroe, L. 1954 (Shamrock R) 1
Murphy, A. 1956 (Clyde) 1
Murphy, B. 1986 (Bohemians) 1
Murphy, D. 2007 (Sunderland, Ipswich T, Newcastle U, Sheffield W) 32
Murphy, J. 1980 (Crystal Palace) 3
Murphy, J. 2004 (WBA, Scunthorpe U) 2
Murphy, P. M. 2007 (Carlisle U) 1
Murray, T. 1950 (Dundalk) 1

Newman, W. 1969 (Shelbourne) 1
Nolan. E. W. 2009 (Preston NE) 3
Nolan, R. 1957 (Shamrock R) 10

Obafemi, M. O. 2019 (Southampton, WBA) 4
O'Brien, A. 2007 (Newcastle U) 5
O'Brien, A. A. 2019 (Millwall) 5
O'Brien, A. J. 2001 (Newcastle U, Portsmouth) 26
O'Brien, F. 1980 (Philadelphia F) 3
O'Brien J. M. 2006 (Bolton W, West Ham U) 5
O'Brien, L. 1986 (Shamrock R, Manchester U, Newcastle U, Tranmere R) 16
O'Brien, M. T. 1927 (Derby Co, Walsall, Norwich C, Watford) 4
O'Brien, R. 1976 (Notts Co) 5
O'Byrne, L. B. 1949 (Shamrock R) 1
O'Callaghan, B. R. 1979 (Stoke C) 6
O'Callaghan, K. 1981 (Ipswich T, Portsmouth) 21
O'Cearuill, J. 2007 (Arsenal) 2
O'Connell, A. 1967 (Dundalk, Bohemians) 2
O'Connor, L. P. 2020 (Celtic) 1
O'Connor, T. 1950 (Shamrock R) 4
O'Connor, T. 1968 (Fulham, Dundalk, Bohemians) 7
O'Dea, D. 2010 (Celtic, Toronto, Metalurh Donetsk) 20
O'Dowda, C. J. R. 2016 (Oxford U, Bristol C) 23
O'Driscoll, J. F. 1949 (Swansea T) 3

O'Driscoll, S. 1982 (Fulham) 3
O'Farrell, F. 1952 (West Ham U, Preston NE) 9
O'Flanagan, K. P. 1938 (Bohemians, Arsenal) 10
O'Flanagan, M. 1947 (Bohemians) 1
Ogbene, C. 2021 (Rotherham U) 10
O'Halloran, S. E. 2007 (Aston Villa) 2
O'Hanlon, K. G. 1988 (Rotherham U) 1
O'Hara, K. M. 2020 (Manchester U) 2
O'Kane, E. C. 2016 (Bournemouth, Leeds U) 7
O'Kane, P. 1935 (Bohemians) 3
O'Keefe, E. 1981 (Everton, Port Vale) 5
O'Keefe, T. 1934 (Cork, Waterford) 3
O'Leary, D. 1977 (Arsenal) 68
O'Leary, P. 1980 (Shamrock R) 7
O'Mahoney, M. T. 1938 (Bristol R) 6
Omobamidele, A. A. 2022 (Norwich C) 5
O'Neill, F. S. 1962 (Shamrock R) 20
O'Neill, J. 1952 (Everton) 17
O'Neill, J. 1961 (Preston NE) 1
O'Neill, K. P. 1996 (Norwich C, Middlesbrough) 13
O'Neill, W. 1936 (Dundalk) 11
O'Regan, K. 1984 (Brighton & HA) 4
O'Reilly, J. 1932 (Brideville, Aberdeen, Brideville, St James' Gate) 20
O'Reilly, J. 1946 (Cork U) 2
O'Shea, D. J. 2021 (WBA) 13
O'Shea, J. F. 2002 (Manchester U, Sunderland) 118

Parrott, T. D. 2020 (Tottenham H) 15
Pearce, A. J. 2013 (Reading, Derby Co) 9
Peyton, G. 1977 (Fulham, Bournemouth, Everton) 33
Peyton, N. 1957 (Shamrock R, Leeds U) 6
Phelan, T. 1992 (Wimbledon, Manchester C, Chelsea, Everton, Fulham) 42
Pilkington, A. N. J. 2013 (Norwich C, Cardiff C) 9
Potter, D. M. 2007 (Wolverhampton W) 5

Quinn, A. 2003 (Sheffield W, Sheffield U) 8
Quinn, B. S. 2000 (Coventry C) 4
Quinn, N. J. 1986 (Arsenal, Manchester C, Sunderland) 91
Quinn, S. 2013 (Hull C, Reading) 18

Randolph, D. E. 2013 (Motherwell, West Ham U, Middlesbrough) 50
Reid, A. M. 2004 (Nottingham F, Tottenham H, Charlton Ath, Sunderland, Nottingham F) 29
Reid, C. 1931 (Brideville) 1
Reid, S. J. 2002 (Millwall, Blackburn R) 23
Rice, D. 2018 (West Ham U) 3
Richardson, D. J. 1972 (Shamrock R, Gillingham) 3
Rigby, A. 1935 (St James' Gate) 3
Ringstead, A. 1951 (Sheffield U) 20
Robinson, C. J. 2019 (Preston NE, Sheffield U, WBA) 30
Robinson, J. 1928 (Bohemians, Dolphin) 2
Robinson, M. 1981 (Brighton & HA, Liverpool, QPR) 24
Roche, P. J. 1972 (Shelbourne, Manchester U) 8
Rogers, E. 1968 (Blackburn R, Charlton Ath) 19
Rowlands, M. C. 2004 (QPR) 5
Ryan, G. 1978 (Derby Co, Brighton & HA) 18
Ryan, R. A. 1950 (WBA, Derby Co) 16

Sadlier, R. T. 2002 (Millwall) 1
Sammon, C. 2013 (Derby Co) 9
Savage, D. P. T. 1996 (Millwall) 5
Saward, P. 1954 (Millwall, Aston Villa, Huddersfield T) 18
Scannell, T. 1954 (Southend U) 1
Scully, P. J. 1989 (Arsenal) 1
Sheedy, K. 1984 (Everton, Newcastle U) 46
Sheridan, C. 2010 (Celtic, CSKA Sofia) 3
Sheridan, J. J. 1988 (Leeds U, Sheffield W) 34
Slaven, B. 1990 (Middlesbrough) 7
Sloan, J. W. 1946 (Arsenal) 2
Smyth, M. 1969 (Shamrock R) 1
Squires, J. 1934 (Shelbourne) 1
Stapleton, F. 1977 (Arsenal, Manchester U, Ajax, Le Havre, Blackburn R) 71
Staunton, S. 1989 (Liverpool, Aston Villa, Liverpool, Aston Villa) 102
St Ledger-Hall, S. P. 2009 (Preston NE, Leicester C) 37
Stevens, E. J. 2018 (Sheffield U) 25
Stevenson, A. E. 1932 (Dolphin, Everton) 7
Stokes, A. 2007 (Sunderland, Celtic) 9
Strahan, F. 1964 (Shelbourne) 5
Sullivan, J. 1928 (Fordsons) 1
Swan, M. M. G. 1960 (Drumcondra) 1
Synnott, N. 1978 (Shamrock R) 3

Taylor, T. 1959 (Waterford) 1
Thomas, P. 1974 (Waterford) 2
Thompson, J. 2004 (Nottingham F) 1
Townsend, A. D. 1989 (Norwich C, Chelsea, Aston Villa, Middlesbrough) 70
Travers, M. 2020 (Bournemouth) 3
Traynor, T. J. 1954 (Southampton) 8
Treacy, K. 2011 (Preston NE, Burnley) 6
Treacy, R. C. P. 1966 (WBA, Charlton Ath, Swindon T, Preston NE, WBA, Shamrock R) 42
Tuohy, L. 1956 (Shamrock R, Newcastle U, Shamrock R) 8
Turner, C. J. 1936 (Southend U, West Ham U) 10
Turner, P. 1963 (Celtic) 2

Vernon, J. 1946 (Belfast Celtic) 2

Waddock, G. 1980 (QPR, Millwall) 21
Walsh, D. J. 1946 (Linfield, WBA, Aston Villa) 20
Walsh, J. 1982 (Limerick) 1
Walsh, M. 1976 (Blackpool, Everton, QPR, Porto) 21
Walsh, M. 1982 (Everton) 4
Walsh, W. 1947 (Manchester C) 9
Walters, J. R. 2011 (Stoke C, Burnley) 54
Ward, S. R. 2011 (Wolverhampton W, Burnley) 50
Waters, J. 1977 (Grimsby T) 2
Watters, F. 1926 (Shelbourne) 1
Weir, E. 1939 (Clyde) 3
Westwood, K. 2009 (Coventry C, Sunderland, Sheffield W) 21
Whelan, G. D. 2008 (Stoke C, Aston Villa, Hearts) 91
Whelan, R. 1964 (St Patrick's Ath) 2
Whelan, R. 1981 (Liverpool, Southend U) 53
Whelan, W. 1956 (Manchester U) 4
White, J. J. 1928 (Bohemians) 1
Whittaker, R. 1959 (Chelsea) 1
Williams, D. S. 2018 (Blackburn R) 3
Williams, J. 1938 (Shamrock R) 1
Williams, S. 2018 (Millwall) 3
Wilson, M. D. 2011 (Stoke C, Bournemouth) 25

BRITISH AND IRISH INTERNATIONAL GOALSCORERS 1872–2022

Where two players with the same surname and initials have appeared for the same country, and one or both have scored, they have been distinguished by reference to the club which appears *first* against their name in the international appearances section.
Bold type indicates players who have scored international goals in season 2021–22.

ENGLAND

Abraham, K. O. T. (Tammy) 3
A'Court, A. 1
Adams, T. A. 5
Adcock, H. 1
Alcock, C. W. 1
Alexander-Arnold, T. J. 1
Allen, A. 3
Allen, R. 2
Alli, B. J. (Dele) 3
Amos, A. 1
Anderson, V. 2
Anderton, D. R. 7
Astall, G. 1
Athersmith, W. C. 3
Atyeo, P. J. W. 5

Bache, J. W. 4
Bailey, N. C. 2
Baily, E. F. 5
Baines, L. J. 1
Baker, J. H. 3
Ball, A. J. 8
Bambridge, A. L. 1
Bambridge, E. C. 11
Barclay, R. 2
Barkley, R. 6
Barmby, N. J. 4
Barnes, J. 11
Barnes, P. S. 4
Barry, G. 3
Barton, J. 1
Bassett, W. I. 8
Bastin, C. S. 12
Beardsley, P. A. 9
Beasley, A. 1
Beattie, T. K. 1
Beckham, D. R. J. 17
Becton, F. 2
Bedford, H. 1
Bell, C. 9
Bent, D. A. 4
Bentley, R. T. F. 9
Bertrand, R. 1
Bishop, S. M. 1
Blackburn, F. 1
Blissett, L. 3
Bloomer, S. 28
Bond, R. 2
Bonsor, A. G. 1
Bowden, E. R. 1
Bowers, J. W. 2
Bowles, S. 1
Bradford, G. R. W. 1
Bradford, J. 7
Bradley, W. 2
Bradshaw, F. 3
Brann, G. 1
Bridge, W. M. 1
Bridges, B. J. 1
Bridgett, A. 3
Brindle, T. 1
Britton, C. S. 1
Broadbent, P. F. 2
Broadis, I. A. 8
Brodie, J. B. 1
Bromley-Davenport, W. 2
Brook, E. F. 10
Brooking, T. D. 5
Brooks, J. 2
Broome, F. H. 3
Brown, A. 4
Brown, A. S. 1
Brown, G. 5
Brown, J. 3
Brown, W. 1
Brown, W. M. 1
Buchan, C. M. 4
Bull, S. G. 4
Bullock, N. 2
Burgess, H. 4
Butcher, T. 3
Byrne, J. J. 8

Cahill, G. J. 5
Calvert-Lewin, D. N. 4
Campbell, S. J. 1
Camsell, G. H. 18
Carroll, A. T. 2
Carter, H. S. 7
Carter, J. H. 4
Caulker, S. A. 1
Chadwick, E. 3
Chamberlain, M. 1
Chambers, H. 5
Channon, M. R. 21
Charlton, J. 6
Charlton, R. 49
Chenery, C. J. 1
Chilwell, B. J. 1
Chivers, M. 13
Clarke, A. J. 10
Coady, C. D. 1
Cobbold, W. N. 6
Cock, J. G. 2
Cole, A. 1
Cole, J. J. 10
Common, A. 2
Connelly, J. M. 7
Coppell, S. J. 7
Cotterill, G. H. 2
Cowans, G. 2
Crawford, R. 1
Crawshaw, T. H. 1
Crayston, W. J. 1
Creek, F. N. S. 1
Crooks, S. D. 7
Crouch, P. J. 22
Currey, E. S. 2
Currie, A. W. 3
Cursham, A. W. 2
Cursham, H. A. 5

Daft, H. B. 3
Davenport, J. K. 2
Davis, G. 1
Davis, H. 1
Day, S. H. 2
Dean, W. R. 18
Defoe, J. C. 20
Devey, J. H. G. 1
Dewhurst, F. 11
Dier, E. J. E. 3
Dix, W. R. 1
Dixon, K. M. 4
Dixon, L. M. 1
Dorrell, A. R. 1
Douglas, B. 11
Drake, E. J. 6
Ducat, A. 1
Dunn, A. T. B. 2

Eastham, G. 2
Edwards, D. 5
Ehiogu, U. 1
Elliott, W. H. 3
Evans, R. E. 1

Ferdinand, L. 5
Ferdinand, R. G. 3
Finney, T. 30
Fleming, H. J. 9
Flowers, R. 10
Foden, P. W. 2
Forman, Frank 1
Forman, Fred 3
Foster, R. E. 3
Fowler, R. B. 7
Francis, G. C. J. 3
Francis, T. 12
Freeman, B. C. 3
Froggatt, J. 2
Froggatt, R. 2

Galley, T. 1
Gascoigne, P. J. 10
Geary, F. 3
Gerrard, S. G. 21
Gibbins, W. V. T. 3
Gilliatt, W. E. 3
Goddard, P. 1
Goodall, J. 12
Goodyer, A. C. 1
Gosling, R. C. 2
Goulden, L. A. 4
Grainger, C. 3
Grealish, J. P. 1
Greaves, J. 44
Grovesnor, A. T. 2
Gunn, W. 1

Haines, J. T. W. 2
Hall, G. W. 9
Halse, H. J. 2
Hampson, J. 5
Hampton, H. 2
Hancocks, J. 2
Hardman, H. P. 1
Harris, S. S. 2
Hassall, H. W. 4
Hateley, M. 9
Haynes, J. N. 18
Hegan, K. E. 4
Henderson, J. B. 2
Henfrey, A. G. 2
Heskey, E. W. 7
Hilsdon, G. R. 14
Hine, E. W. 4
Hinton, A. T. 1
Hirst, D. E. 1
Hitchens, G. A. 5
Hobbis, H. H. F. 1
Hoddle, G. 8
Hodgetts, D. 1
Hodgson, G. 1
Holley, G. H. 8
Houghton, W. E. 5
Howell, R. 1
Hughes, E. W. 1
Hulme, J. H. A. 4
Hunt, G. S. 1
Hunt, R. 18
Hunter, N. 2
Hurst, G. C. 24

Ince, P. E. C. 2
Ings, D. 1
Jack, D. N. B. 3
Jagielka, P. N. 3
Jeffers, F. 1
Jenas, J. A. 1
Johnson, A. 2
Johnson, D. E. 6
Johnson, E. 2
Johnson, G. M. C. 1
Johnson, J. A. 2
Johnson, T. C. F. 5
Johnson, W. H. 1

Kail, E. I. L. 2
Kane, H. E. 50
Kay, A. H. 1
Keane, M. V. 1
Keegan, J. K. 21
Kelly, R. 8
Kennedy, R. 3
Kenyon-Slaney, W. S. 2
Keown, M. R. 2
Kevan, D. T. 8
Kidd, B. 1
King, L. B. 2
Kingsford, R. K. 1
Kirchen, A. J. 2
Kirton, W. J. 1

Lallana, A. D. 3
Lambert, R. L. 3
Lampard, F. J. 29
Langton, R. 1
Latchford, R. D. 5
Latheron, E. G. 1
Lawler, C. 1
Lawton, T. 22
Lee, F. 10
Lee, J. 1
Lee, R. M. 2
Lee, S. 2
Lescott, J. 1
Le Saux, G. P. 1
Lindley, T. 14
Lineker, G. 48
Lingard, J. E. 6
Lofthouse, J. M. 3
Lofthouse, N. 30
Hon. A. Lyttelton 1

Mabbutt, G. 1
Macdonald, M. 6
Maguire, J. H. 7
Mannion, W. J. 11
Mariner, P. 13
Marsh, R. W. 1
Matthews, S. 11
Matthews, V. 1
McCall, J. 1
McDermott, T. 3
McManaman, S. 3
Medley, L. D. 1
Melia, J. 1
Mercer, D. W. 1
Merson, P. C. 3
Milburn, J. E. T. 10
Miller, H. S. 1
Mills, G. R. 3
Milner, J. P. 1
Milward, A. 3
Mings, T. D. 2
Mitchell, C. 5
Moore, J. 1
Moore, R. F. 2

Moore, W. G. B.	2
Morren, T.	1
Morris, F.	1
Morris, J.	3
Mortensen, S. H.	23
Morton, J. R.	1
Mosforth, W.	3
Mount, M. T.	4
Mullen, J.	6
Mullery, A. P.	1
Murphy, D. B	1
Neal, P. G.	5
Needham, E.	3
Nicholls, J.	1
Nicholson, W. E.	1
Nugent, D. J.	1
O'Grady, M.	3
Osborne, F. R.	3
Owen, M. J.	40
Own goals	34
Oxlade-Chamberlain, A. M. D.	7
Page, L. A.	1
Paine, T. L.	7
Palmer, C. L.	1
Parry, E. H.	1
Parry, R. A.	1
Pawson, F. W.	1
Payne, J.	2
Peacock, A.	3
Pearce, S.	5
Pearson, J. S.	5
Pearson, S. C.	5
Perry, W.	2
Peters, M.	20
Pickering, F.	5
Platt, D.	27
Pointer, R.	2
Quantrill, A.	1
Ramsay, A. E.	3
Rashford, M.	12
Revie, D. G.	4
Redknapp, J. F.	1
Reynolds, J.	3
Rice, D.	**2**
Richards, M.	1
Richardson, K. E.	2
Richardson, J. R.	2
Rigby, A.	3
Rimmer, E. J.	2
Roberts, F.	2
Roberts, H.	1
Roberts, W. T.	2
Robinson, J.	3
Robson, B.	26
Robson, R.	4
Rooney, W. M.	53
Rowley, J. F.	6
Royle, J.	2
Rutherford, J.	3
Sagar, C.	1
Saka, B. A. T. M.	**4**
Sancho, J. M.	3
Sandilands, R. R.	3
Sansom, K.	1
Schofield, J.	1
Scholes, P.	14
Seed, J. M.	1
Settle, J.	6
Sewell, J.	3
Shackleton, L. F.	1
Sharp, J.	1
Shaw, L. P. H.	**2**
Shearer, A.	30
Shelton, A.	1
Shepherd, A.	2
Sheringham, E. P.	11
Simpson, J.	1
Smalling, C. L.	1
Smith, A.	1
Smith, A. M.	2
Smith, G. O.	11
Smith, Joe	1
Smith, J. R.	2
Smith, J. W.	4
Smith, R.	13
Smith, S.	1
Smith Rowe, E.	**1**
Sorby, T. H.	1
Southgate, G.	2
Southworth, J.	3
Sparks, F. J.	3
Spence, J. W.	1
Spiksley, F.	5
Spilsbury, B. W.	5
Steele, F. C.	8
Stephenson, G. T.	2
Sterling, R. S.	**19**
Steven, T. M.	4
Stewart, J.	2
Stiles, N. P.	1
Storer, H.	1
Stone, S. B.	2
Stones, J.	**3**
Sturridge, D. A.	8
Summerbee, M. G.	1
Tambling, R. V.	1
Taylor, P. J.	2
Taylor, T.	16
Terry, J. G.	6
Thompson, P. B.	1
Thornewell, G.	1
Tilson, S. F.	6
Townley, W. J.	2
Townsend, A. D.	3
Trippier, K. J.	1
Tueart, D.	2
Upson, M. J.	2
Vardy, J. R.	7
Vassell, D.	6
Vaughton, O. H.	6
Veitch, J. G.	3
Viollet, D. S.	1
Waddle, C. R.	6
Walcott, T. J.	8
Walker, W. H.	9
Wall, G.	2
Wallace, D.	1
Walsh, P.	1
Ward-Prowse, J. M. E.	**2**
Waring, T.	4
Warren, B.	2
Watson, D. V.	4
Watson, V. M.	4
Watkins, O. G. A.	**2**
Webb, G. W.	1
Webb, N.	4
Wedlock, W. J.	2
Welbeck D. N. T. M.	16
Weller, K.	1
Welsh, D.	1
Whateley, O.	2
Wheldon, G. F.	6
Whitfield, H.	1
Wignall, F.	2
Wilkes, A.	1
Wilkins, R. G.	3
Willingham, C. K.	1
Wilshaw, D. J.	10
Wilshere J. A.	2
Wilson, C.	1
Wilson, G. P.	1
Winckworth, W. N.	1
Windridge, J. E.	7
Winks, H. B.	1
Wise, D. F.	1
Withe, P.	1
Wollaston, C. H. R.	1
Wood, H.	1
Woodcock, T.	16
Woodhall, G.	1
Woodward, V. J.	29
Worrall, F.	2
Worthington, F. S.	2
Wright, I. E.	9
Wright, M.	1
Wright, W. A.	3
Wright-Phillips, S. C.	6
Wylie, J. G.	1
Yates, J.	3
Young, A. S.	7

NORTHERN IRELAND

Anderson, T.	4
Armstrong, G.	12
Ballard, D. G.	**2**
Bambrick, J.	12
Barr, H. H.	1
Barron, H.	3
Best, G.	9
Bingham, W. L.	10
Black, K.	1
Blanchflower, D.	2
Blanchflower, J.	1
Boyce, L.	2
Brennan, B.	1
Brennan, R. A.	1
Brotherston, N.	3
Brown, J.	1
Browne, F.	2
Brunt, C.	3
Campbell, J.	1
Campbell, W. G.	1
Casey, T.	2
Caskey, W.	1
Cassidy, T.	1
Cathcart, C. G.	2
Chambers, J.	3
Clarke, C. J.	13
Clements, D.	2
Cochrane, T.	1
Condy, J.	1
Connor, M. J.	1
Coulter, J.	1
Croft, T.	1
Crone, W.	1
Crossan, E.	1
Crossan, J. A.	10
Curran, S.	2
Cush, W. W.	5
Dallas, S. A.	3
Dalton, W.	4
D'Arcy, S. D.	1
Darling, J.	1
Davey, H. H.	1
Davis, S.	**13**
Davis, T. L.	1
Dill, A. H.	1
Doherty, L.	1
Doherty, P. D.	3
Dougan, A. D.	8
Dowie, I.	12
Dunne, J.	4
Elder, A. R.	1
Elliott, S.	4
Emerson, W.	1
English, S.	1
Evans, C.	2
Evans, J. G.	**5**
Feeney, W.	1
Feeney, W. J.	5
Ferguson, S. K.	**2**
Ferguson, W.	1
Ferris, J.	1
Ferris, R. O.	1
Finney, T.	2
Gaffkin, J.	4
Gara, A.	3
Gaukrodger, G.	1
Gibb, J. T.	2
Gibb, T. J.	1
Gibson, W.	1
Gillespie, K. R.	2
Gillespie, W.	13
Goodall, A. L.	2
Griffin, D. J.	1
Gray, P.	6
Grigg, W. D.	2
Halligan, W.	1
Hamill, M.	1
Hamilton, B.	4
Hamilton, W. R.	5
Hannon, D. J.	1
Harkin, J. T.	2
Harvey, M.	3
Healy, D. J.	36
Hill, C. F.	1
Hughes, A.	1
Hughes, M. E.	5
Humphries, W.	1
Hunter, A. (Distillery)	1
Hunter, A. (Blackburn R)	1
Hunter, B. V.	1
Irvine, R. W.	3
Irvine, W. J.	8
Johnston, H.	2
Johnston, S.	2
Johnston, W. C.	1
Jones, S. (Distillery)	1
Jones, S. (Crewe Alex)	1
Jones, J.	1
Jones, J. L.	1
Kelly, J.	4
Kernaghan, N.	2
Kirwan, J.	2
Lacey, W.	3
Lafferty, K.	20
Lavery, S. F.	**2**
Lemon, J.	2
Lennon, N. F.	2
Lockhart, N.	3
Lomas, S. M.	3
Magennis, J. B. D.	**9**
Magilton, J.	5
Mahood, J.	2
Martin, D. K.	3
Maxwell, J.	2
McAdams, W. J.	7
McAllen, J.	1
McAuley, G.	9
McAuley, J. L.	1
McCann, A.	1
McCann, G. S.	4
McCartney, G.	1
McCandless, J.	2
McCandless, W.	1
McCaw, J. H.	1
McClelland, J.	1
McCluggage, A.	2
McCourt, P.	2
McCracken, W.	1
McCrory, S.	1
McCurdy, C.	1
McDonald, A.	3
McGarry, J. K.	1
McGrath, R. C.	4
McGinn, N.	6
McIlroy, J.	10
McIlroy, S. B.	5
McKenzie, H	1
McKnight, J.	2
McLaughlin, C. G.	1
McLaughlin, J. C.	6
McMahon, G. J.	2
McMordie, A. S.	3
McMorran, E. J.	4
McNair, P. J. C.	**6**
McParland, P. J.	10
McWha, W. B. R.	1
Meldon, P. A	1
Mercer, J. T.	1

Millar, W. 1
Milligan, D. 1
Milne, R. G. 2
Molyneux, T. B. 1
Moreland, V. 1
Morgan, S. 3
Morrow, S. J. 1
Morrow, W. J. 1
Mulryne, P. P. 3
Murdock, C. J. 1
Murphy, N. 1

Neill, W. J. T. 2
Nelson, S. 1
Nicholl, C. J. 3
Nicholl, J. M. 1
Nicholson, J. J. 6

O'Boyle, G. 1
O'Hagan, C. 2
O'Kane, W. J. 1
O'Neill, J. 2
O'Neill, M. A. 4
O'Neill, M. H. 8
Own goals 10

Paterson, M. A. 3
Patterson, D. J. 1
Patterson, R. 1
Peacock, R. 2
Peden, J. 7
Penney, S. 2
Pyper, James 2
Pyper, John 1

Quinn, J. M. 12
Quinn, S. J. 4

Reynolds, J. 1
Rowland, K. 1
Rowley, R. W. M. 2
Rushe, F. 1

Sheridan, J. 2
Sherrard, J. 1
Sherrard, W. C. 2
Shields, D. 1
Simpson, W. J. 5
Sloan, H. A. de B. 4
Smith, M. 1
Smyth, P. 1
Smyth, S. 5

Spence, D. W. 3
Sproule, I. 1
Stanfield, O. M. 11
Stevenson, A. E. 5
Stewart, I. 2

Taggart, G. P. 7
Thompson, F. W. 2
Torrans, S. 1
Tully, C. P. 3
Turner, A. 1

Walker, J. 1
Walsh, D. J. 5
Ward, J. J. 4
Washington, C. J. 6
Welsh, E. 1
Whiteside, N. 9
Whiteside, T. 1
Whitley, Jeff 2
Whyte, G. 4
Williams, J. R. 1
Williams, M. S. 1
Williamson, J. 1
Wilson, D. J. 1
Wilson, K. J. 6
Wilson, S. J. 7
Wilton, J. M. 2
Young, S. 1

N.B. In 1914 Young goal should be credited to Gillespie W v Wales

SCOTLAND
Adams, C. Z. E. F. 5
Aitken, R. (Celtic) 1
Aitken, R. (Dumbarton) 1
Aitkenhead, W. A. C. 2
Alexander, D. 1
Allan, D. S. 4
Allan, J. 2
Anderson, F. 1
Anderson, W. 4
Andrews, P. 1
Anya, I. 3
Archibald, A. 1
Archibald, S. 4
Armstrong, S. 4

Baird, D. 2
Baird, J. C. 2
Baird, S. 2
Bannon, E. 1
Barbour, A. 1
Barker, J. B. 4
Battles, B. Jr 1
Bauld, W. 2
Baxter, J. C. 3
Beattie, C. 1
Bell, J. 5
Bennett, A. 2
Berra, C. D. 4
Berry, D. 1
Bett, J. 1
Beveridge, W. W. 1
Black, A. 3
Black, D. 1
Bone, J. 1
Booth, S. 6
Boyd, K 7
Boyd, R. 2
Boyd, T. 1
Boyd, W. G. 1
Brackenridge, T. 1
Brand, R. 8
Brazil, A. 1
Bremner, W. J. 3
Broadfoot, K. 1
Brown, A. D. 6
Brown, S. 4
Buchanan, P. S. 1
Buchanan, R. 1
Buckley, P. 1
Buick, A. 2
Burke, C. 2
Burke, O. J. 1
Burley, C. W. 3
Burns, K. 1

Cairns, T. 1
Caldwell, G. 2
Calderwood, C. 1
Calderwood, R. 2
Caldow, E. 4
Cameron, C. 2
Campbell, C. 1
Campbell, John (Celtic) 5
Campbell, John (Rangers) 4
Campbell, J. (South Western) 1
Campbell, P. 2
Campbell, R. 1
Cassidy, J. 1
Chalmers, S. 3
Chambers, T. 1
Cheyne, A. G. 4
Christie, A. J. 1
Christie, R. 4
Clarkson, D. 1
Clunas, W. L. 1
Collins, J. 12
Collins, R. Y. 10
Combe, J. R. 1
Commons, K. 2
Conn, A. 1
Cooper, D. 6
Craig, J. 1
Craig, T. 1
Crawford, S. 4
Cunningham, A. N. 5
Curran, H. P. 1

Dailly, C. 6
Dalglish, K. 30
Davidson, D. 1
Davidson, J. A. 1
Delaney, J. 3
Devine, A. 1
Dewar, G. 1
Dewar, N. 4
Dickov, P. 1
Dickson, W. 4
Divers, J. 1
Dobie, R. S. 1
Docherty, T. H. 1
Dodds, D. 1
Dodds, W. 7
Donaldson, A. 1
Donnachie, J. 1
Dougall, J. 1
Drummond, J. 2
Dunbar, M. 1
Duncan, D. 7
Duncan, D. M. 1
Duncan, J. 1
Dunn, J. 2
Durie, G. S. 7
Dykes, L. J. 6

Easson, J. F. 1
Elliott, M. S. 1
Ellis, J. 1

Ferguson, A. 4
Ferguson, B. 3
Ferguson, J. 6
Fernie, W. 1
Findlay, S. J. 1
Fitchie, T. T. 1
Flavell, R. 2
Fleming, C. 2
Fleming, J. W. 3
Fletcher, D. 5
Fletcher, S. K. 10
Forrest, J. 5
Fraser, M. J. E. 3
Fraser, R. 4
Freedman, D. A. 1

Gallacher, H. K. 23
Gallacher, K. W. 9
Gallacher, P. 1
Galt, J. H. 1
Gemmell, T. (St Mirren) 1
Gemmell, T. (Celtic) 1
Gemmill, A. 8
Gemmill, S. 1
Gibb, W. 1
Gibson, D. W. 3
Gibson, J. D. 1
Gibson, N. 1
Gillespie, Jas. 3
Gillick, T. 3
Gilzean, A. J. 12
Goodwillie, D. 1
Gossland, J. 2
Goudie, J. 1
Gough, C. R. 6
Gourlay, J. 1
Graham, A. 2
Graham, G. 3
Gray, A. 7
Gray, E. 3
Gray, F. 1
Greig, J. 3
Griffiths, L. 4
Groves, W. 4

Hamilton, G. 4
Hamilton, J. (Queen's Park) 3
Hamilton, R. C. 15
Hanley, G. C. 2
Harper, J. M. 7
Hartley, P. J. 1
Harrower, W. 5
Hartford, R. A. 4
Heggie, C. W 4
Henderson, J. G. 1
Henderson, W. 5
Hendry, E. C. J. 3
Hendry, J. W. 2
Herd, D. G. 3
Herd, G. 1
Hewie, J. D. 2
Higgins, A. (Newcastle U) 1
Higgins, A. (Kilmarnock) 4
Highet, T. C. 1
Holt, G.J. 1
Holton, J. A. 2
Hope, R. 1
Hopkin, D. 2
Houliston, W. 2
Howie, H. 1
Howie, J. 2
Hughes, J. 1
Hunter, W. 1
Hutchison, D. 6
Hutchison, T. 1
Hutton, J. 1
Hyslop, T. 1

Imrie, W. N. 1

Jackson, A. 8
Jackson, C. 1
Jackson, D. 4
James, A. W. 4
Jardine, A. 1
Jenkinson, T. 1
Jess, E. 2
Johnston, A. 2
Johnston, L. H. 1
Johnston, M. 14
Johnstone, D. 2
Johnstone, J. 4
Johnstone, Jas. 1
Johnstone, R. 10
Johnstone, W. 1
Jordan, J. 11

Kay, J. L. 5
Keillor, A. 3
Kelly, J. 1
Kelso, R. 1
Ker, G. 10
King, A. 1
King, J. 1
Kinnear, D. 1
Kyle, K. 1

Lambert, P. 1
Lambie, J. 1
Lambie, W. A. 5
Lang, J. J. 2
Latta, A. 2
Law, D. 30
Leggat, G. 8
Lennie, W. 1
Lennox, R. 3
Liddell, W. 6
Lindsay, J. 6
Linwood, A. B. 1
Logan, J. 1
Lorimer, P. 4
Love, A. 1
Low, J. (Cambuslang) 1
Lowe, J. (St Bernards) 1

Macari, L. 5
MacDougall, E. J. 3
MacFarlane, A. 1
MacLeod, M. 1
Mackay, D. C. 4
Mackay, G. 1
MacKenzie, J. A. 1
Mackail-Smith, C. 1

Mackie, J. C. 2
MacKinnon, W. W. 5
Madden, J. 5
Maloney, S. R. 7
Marshall, H. 1
Marshall, J. 1
Martin, C. H. 3
Mason, J. 4
Massie, A. 1
Masson, D. S. 5
McAdam, J. 1
McAllister, G. 5
McArthur, J. 4
McAulay, J. D. 1
McAvennie, F. 1
McCall, J. 1
McCall, S. M. 1
McCalliog, J. 1
McCallum, N. 1
McCann, N. 3
McClair, B. J. 2
McCoist, A. 19
McColl, R. S. 13
McCormack, R. 2
McCulloch, D. 3
McCulloch, L. 1
McDougall, J. 4
McFadden, J.* 15
McFadyen, W. 2
McGhee, M. 2
McGinlay, J. 4
McGinn, J. 13
McGregor, C. W. 2
McGregor, J. 1
McGrory, J. 6
McGuire, W. 1
McInally, A. 3
McInnes, T. 2
McKenna, S. F. 1
McKie, J. 2
McKimmie, S. 1
McKinlay, W. 4
McKinnon, A. 1
McKinnon, R. 1
McLaren, A. 4
McLaren, J. 1
McLean, A. 1
McLean, K. 1
McLean, T. 1
McLintock, F. 1
McMahon, A. 6
McManus, S. 2
McMenemy, J. 5
McMillan, I. L. 2
McNeill, W. 3
McNiel, H. 5
McPhail, J. 3
McPhail, R. 7
McPherson, J. (Kilmarnock) 7
McPherson, J. (Vale of Leven) 1
McPherson, R. 1
McQueen, G. 5
McStay, P. 9
McSwegan, G. 1
McTominay, S. F. 1
Meiklejohn, D. D. 3
Millar, J. 2
Miller, K. 18
Miller, T. 2
Miller, W. 1
Mitchell, R. C. 1
Morgan, W. 4
Morris, D. 1
Morris, H. 3
Morrison, J. C. 3
Morton, A. L. 5
Mudie, J. K. 9
Mulgrew, C. P. 3
Mulhall, G. 1
Munro, A. D. 1
Munro, N. 2
Murdoch, R. 5
Murphy, F. 1
Murray, J. 1

Napier, C. E. 3
Narey, D. 1
Naismith, S. J. 10
Naysmith, G. A. 1
Neil, R. G. 2
Nevin, P. K. F. 5
Nicholas, C. 5
Nisbet, J. 2
Nisbet, K. 1

O'Connor, G. 4
O'Donnell, F. 2
O'Hare, J. 5
Ormond, W. E. 2
O'Rourke, F. 1
Orr, R. 1
Orr, T. 1
Oswald, J. 1
Own goals 21

Parlane, D. 1
Patterson, N. K. 1
Paul, H. McD. 2
Paul, W. 5
Pettigrew, W. 2
Phillips, M. 1
Provan, D. 1

Quashie, N. F. 1
Quinn, J. 7
Quinn, P. 1

Ralston, A. 1
Rankin, G. 2
Rankin, R. 2
Reid, W. 4
Reilly, L. 22
Renny-Tailyour, H. W. 1
Rhodes, J. L. 3
Richmond, J. T. 1
Ring, T. 2
Rioch, B. D. 6
Ritchie, J. 1
Ritchie, M. T. 3
Ritchie, P. S. 1
Robertson, A. (Clyde) 2
Robertson, A. 3
Robertson, J. 3
Robertson, J. N. 8
Robertson, J. T. 2
Robertson, T. 1
Robertson, W. 1
Russell, D. 1
Russell, J. S. S. 1

Scott, A. S. 5
Sellar, W. 4
Shankland, L. 1
Sharp, G. 1
Shaw, F. W. 1
Shearer, D. 2
Simpson, J. 1
Smith, A. 5
Smith, G. 4
Smith, J. 1
Smith, John 13
Snodgrass, R. 7
Somerville, G. 1
Souness, G. J. 4
Souttar, J. 1
Speedie, F. 2
St John, I. 9
Steel, W. 12
Stein, C. 10
Stevenson, G. 4
Stewart, A. 1
Stewart, R. 1
Stewart, W. E. 1
Strachan, G. 5
Sturrock, P. 3

Taylor, J. D. 1
Templeton, R. 1
Thompson, S. 3
Thomson, A. 1
Thomson, C. 4
Thomson, R. 1
Thomson, W. 1
Thornton, W. 1
Tierney, K. 1
Townsend, J. 1

Waddell, T. S. 1
Waddell, W. 6
Walker, J. 2
Walker, R. 7
Walker, T. 9
Wallace, I. A. 1
Wark, J. 7
Watson, J. A. K. 1
Watt, F. 2
Watt, W. W. 1
Webster, A. 1
Weir, A. 1
Weir, D. 1
Weir, J. B. 2
White, J. A. 3
Wilkie, L. 1
Wilson, A. (Sheffield W) 2
Wilson, A. N. (Dunfermline Ath) 13
Wilson, D. (Liverpool) 1
Wilson, D. (Queen's Park) 2
Wilson, D. (Rangers) 9
Wilson, H. 1
Wylie, T. G. 1

Young, A. 5

WALES

Allchurch, I. J. 23
Allen, J. M. 2
Allen, M. 3
Astley, D. J. 12
Atherton, R. W. 2

Bale, G. F. 39
Bamford, T. 1
Barnes, W. 1
Bellamy, C. D. 19
Blackmore, C. G. 1
Blake, D. 1
Blake, N. A. 4
Bodin, P. J. 3
Boulter, L. M. 1
Bowdler, J. C. H. 3
Bowen, D. L. 1
Bowen, M. 3
Boyle, T. 1
Brooks, D. R. 2
Bryan, T. 1
Burgess, W. A. R. 1
Burke, T. 1
Butler, W. T. 1

Chapman, T. 2
Charles, J. 1
Charles, M. 6
Charles, W. J. 15
Church, S. R. 3
Clarke, R. J. 5
Coleman, C. 4
Collier, D. J. 1
Collins, J. 3
Colwill, R. 1
Cotterill, D. R. G. B. 2
Crosse, K. 1
Cumner, R. H. 1
Curtis, A. 6
Curtis, E. R. 3
Davies, B. T. 1
Davies, D. W. 1
Davies, E. Lloyd 1
Davies, G. 2
Davies, L. S. 6
Davies, R. T. 9
Davies, R. W. 6
Davies, Simon 6
Davies, Stanley 5
Davies, W. 6
Davies, W. H. 1
Davies, William 5
Davis, W. O. 1
Deacy, N. 4
Doughty, J. 6
Doughty, R. 2
Durban, A. 2
Dwyer, P. 2

Earnshaw, R. 16
Eastwood, F. 4
Edwards, D. A. 3
Edwards, G. 2
Edwards, R. I. 4
England, H. M. 4
Evans, C. 2
Evans, I. 1
Evans, J. 1
Evans, R. E. 2
Evans, W. 1
Eyton-Jones, J. A. 1

Fletcher, C. 1
Flynn, B. 7
Ford, T. 23
Foulkes, W. I. 1
Fowler, J. 3

Giles, D. 2
Giggs, R. J. 12
Glover, E. M. 7
Godfrey, B. C. 2
Green, A. W. 3
Griffiths, A. T. 6
Griffiths, M. W. 2
Griffiths, T. P. 3

Harris, C. S. 1
Hartson, J. 14
Hersee, R. 1
Hewitt, R. 1
Hockey, T. 1
Hodges, G. 2
Hole, W. J. 1
Hopkins, I. J. 2
Horne, B. 2
Howell, E. G. 3
Hughes, L. M. 16
Huws, E. W. 1

James, D. O. 5
James, E. 2
James, L. 10
James, R. 7
Jarrett, R. H. 3
Jenkyns, C. A. 1
Johnson, B. P. 2
Jones, A. 1
Jones, Bryn 6
Jones, B. S. 2
Jones, Cliff 16
Jones, C. W. 1
Jones, D. E. 1
Jones, Evan 1
Jones, H. 1
Jones, I. 1
Jones, J. L. 1
Jones, J. O. 1
Jones, J. P. 1
Jones, Leslie J. 1
Jones, R. A. 2
Jones, W. L. 6

* *The Scottish FA officially changed Robson's goal against Iceland on 10 September 2008 to McFadden.*

Keenor, F. C. 2
King, A. P. 2
Koumas, J. 10
Krzywicki, R. L. 1

Lawrence, T. M. 3
Ledley, J. C. 4
Leek, K. 5
Lewis, B. 4
Lewis, D. M. 2
Lewis, W. 8
Lewis, W. L. 3
Llewelyn, C. M 1
Lovell, S. 1
Lowrie, G. 2

Mahoney, J. F. 1
Mays, A. W. 1
Medwin, T. C. 6
Melville, A. K 3
Meredith, W. H. 11
Mills, T. J. 1
Moore, G. 1
Moore, K. R. F. 8
Morgan, J. R. 2
Morgan-Owen, H. 1
Morgan-Owen, M. M. 2
Morison, S. 1
Morris, A. G. 9
Morris, H. 2
Morris, R. 1
Morris, S. 2

Nicholas, P. 2
Norrington-Davies, R. L. 1

O'Callaghan, E. 3
O'Sullivan, P. A. 1
Owen, G. 2
Owen, W. 4
Owen, W. P. 6
Own goals 14

Palmer, D. 3
Parry, P. I. 1
Parry, T. D. 3
Paul, R. 1
Peake, E. 1
Pembridge, M. 6
Perry, E. 1
Phillips, C. 5
Phillips, D. 2
Powell, A. 1
Powell, D. 1
Price, J. 4
Price, P. 1
Pryce-Jones, W. E. 3
Pugh, D. H. 2

Ramsey, A. J. 20
Reece, G. I. 2
Rees, R. R. 3
Richards, R. W. 1
Roach, J. 2
Robbins, W. W. 4
Roberts, C. R. J. 3
Roberts, J. (Corwen) 1
Roberts, Jas. 1
Roberts, P. S. 1
Roberts, R. (Druids) 1
Roberts, W. (Llangollen) 2
Roberts, W. (Wrexham) 1
Roberts, W. H. 1
Robinson, C. P. 1
Robinson, J. R. C. 3
Robson-Kanu, T. H. 5
Rush, I. 28
Russell, M. R. 1

Sabine, H. W. 1
Saunders, D. 22
Savage, R. W. 2
Shaw, E. G. 2
Sisson, H. 4
Slatter, N. 2
Smallman, D. P. 1
Speed, G. A. 7
Symons, C. J. 2

Tapscott, D. R. 4
Taylor, G. K. 1
Taylor, N. J. 1
Thomas, M. 4
Thomas, T. 1
Toshack, J. B. 12
Trainer, H. 2

Vaughan, D. O. 1
Vaughan, John 2
Vernon, T. R. 8
Vizard, E. T. 1
Vokes, S. M. 11

Walsh, I. 7
Warren, F. W. 3
Watkins, W. M. 4
Wilding, J. 4
Williams, A. 1
Williams, A. E. 2
Williams, D. R. 2
Williams, G. E. 1
Williams, G. G. 1
Williams, J. P. 2
Williams, N. S. 2
Williams, W. 1
Wilson, H. 5
Woodburn, B. 2
Woosnam, A. P. 3
Wynn, G. A. 1

Yorath, T. C. 2
Young, E. 1

REPUBLIC OF IRELAND

Aldridge, J. 19
Ambrose, P. 1
Anderson, J. 1
Andrews, K. 3

Barrett, G. 2
Bermingham, P. 1
Bradshaw, P. 4
Brady, L. 9
Brady, R. 8
Breen, G. 7
Brown, J. 1
Browne, A. J. 4
Burke, G. D. 1
Byrne, D. 1
Byrne, J. 4

Cantwell, N. 14
Carey, J. 3
Carroll, T. 1
Cascarino, A. 19
Christie, C. S. F. 2
Clark, C. 2
Coad, P. 3
Coleman, S. 1
Collins, J. S. 2
Collins, N. M. 1
Connolly, D. J. 9
Conroy, T. 2
Conway, J. 3
Cox, S. R. 4
Coyne, T. 6
Cummins, G. 5
Curtis, D. 8

Daly, G. 13
Davis, T. 4
Dempsey, J. 1
Dennehy, M. 2
Doherty, G. M. T. 4
Doherty, M. J. 1
Donnelly, J. 4
Donnelly, T. 1
Doyle, K. E. 14
Duff, D. A. 8
Duffy, B. 1
Duffy, S. P. M. 7
Duggan, H. 1
Dunne, J. 13
Dunne, L. 1
Dunne, R. P. 8

Egan, J. 1
Eglington, T. 2
Elliott, S. W. 1
Ellis, P. 1

Fagan, F. 5
Fahey, K. 3
Fallon, S. 2
Fallon, W. 2
Farrell, P. 3
Finnan, S. 2
Fitzgerald, P. 2
Fitzgerald, J. 1
Fitzsimons, A. 7
Flood, J. J. 4
Fogarty, A. 3
Foley, D. 2
Fullam, J. 1
Fullam, R. 1

Galvin, A. 1
Gavin, J. 2
Geoghegan, M. 2
Gibson, D. T. D. 1
Giles, J. 5
Givens, D. 19
Gleeson, S. M. 1
Glynn, D. 1
Grealish, T. 8
Green, P. J. 1
Grimes, A. A. 1

Hale, A. 2
Hand, E. 2
Harte, I. P. 11
Haverty, J. 3
Healy, C. 1
Hendrick, J. P. 2
Holland, M. R. 5
Holmes, J. 1
Hoolahan, W. 3
Horlacher, A. 2
Horgan, D. J. 1
Houghton, R. 6
Hourihane, C. 1
Hughton, C. 1
Hunt, S. P. 1
Hurley, C. 2

Ireland, S. J. 4
Irwin, D. 4

Jordan, D. 1
Judge, A. C. 1

Kavanagh, G. A. 1
Keane, R. D. 68
Keane, R. M. 9
Kelly, D. 9
Kelly, G. 2
Kelly, J. 2
Kennedy, M. 4
Keogh, A. 2
Keogh, R. J. 1
Kernaghan, A. N. 1
Kilbane, K. D. 8
Kinsella, M. A. 3
Knight, J. P. 1

Lacey, W. 1
Lawrence, L. 2
Lawrenson, M. 5
Leech, M. 2
Long, K. F. 1
Long, S. P. 17
Maguire, S. P. 1
Mancini, T. 1
Martin, C. 6
Martin, M. 4
McAteer, J. W. 3
McCann, J. 1
McCarthy, M. 2
McClean, J. J. 11
McEvoy, A. 6
McGeady, A. G. 5
McGee, P. 4
McGoldrick, D. J. 1
McGrath, P. 8
McLoughlin, A. F. 2
McPhail, S. J. P. 1
Miller, L. W. P. 1
Mooney, J. 1
Moore, P. 7
Moran, K. 6
Morrison, C. H. 9
Moroney, T. 1
Mulligan, P. 1
Murphy, D. 3

Obafemi, M. O. 1
O'Brien, A. A. 1
O'Brien, A. J. 1
O'Callaghan, K. 1
O'Connor, T. 2
O'Dea, D. 1
O'Farrell, F. 2
O'Flanagan, K. 3
Ogbene, C. 3
O'Keefe, E. 1
O'Leary, D. A. 1
O'Neill, F. 1
O'Neill, K. P. 4
O'Reilly, J. (Brideville) 2
O'Reilly, J. (Cork) 1
O'Shea, J. F. 3
Own goals 14

Parrott, T. D. 4
Pearce, A. J. 2
Pilkington, A. N. J. 1

Quinn, N. 21

Reid, A. M. 4
Reid, S. J. 2
Ringstead, A. 7
Robinson, C. J. 7
Robinson, M. 4
Rogers, E. 5
Ryan, G. 1
Ryan, R. 3

St Ledger-Hall, S. 3
Sheedy, K. 9
Sheridan, J. 5
Slaven, B. 1
Sloan, J. 1
Squires, J. 1
Stapleton, F. 20
Staunton, S. 7
Strahan, J. 1
Sullivan, J. 1

Townsend, A. D. 7
Treacy, R. 5
Touhy, L. 4

Waddock, G. 3
Walsh, D. 5
Walsh, M. 3
Walters, J. R. 14
Ward, S. R. 3
Waters, J. 1
White, J. J. 2
Whelan, G. D. 2
Whelan, R. 3
Williams, D. S. 1
Williams, S. 1
Wilson, M. D. 1

SOUTH AMERICA

COPA AMERICA 2021

(in Brazil, postponed from 2020)

GROUP A (SOUTH ZONE)

Argentina v Chile 1-1
Paraguay v Bolivia 3-1
Chile v Bolivia 1-0
Argentina v Uruguay 1-0
Uruguay v Chile 1-1
Argentina v Paraguay 1-0
Bolivia v Uruguay 0-2
Chile v Paraguay 0-2
Uruguay v Paraguay 1-0
Bolivia v Argentina 1-4

Group A Table	P	W	D	L	F	A	GD	Pts
Argentina	4	3	1	0	7	2	5	10
Uruguay	4	2	1	1	4	2	2	7
Paraguay	4	2	0	2	5	3	2	6
Chile	4	1	2	1	3	4	–1	5
Bolivia	4	0	0	4	2	10	–8	0

GROUP B (NORTH ZONE)

Brazil v Venezuela 3-0
Colombia v Ecuador 1-0
Colombia v Venezuela 0-0
Brazil v Peru 4-0
Venezuela v Ecuador 2-2
Colombia v Peru 1-2
Ecuador v Peru 2-2
Brazil v Colombia 2-1
Brazil v Ecuador 1-1
Venezuela v Peru 0-1

Group B Table	P	W	D	L	F	A	GD	Pts
Brazil	4	3	1	0	10	2	8	10
Peru	4	2	1	1	5	7	–2	7
Colombia	4	1	1	2	3	4	–1	4
Ecuador	4	0	3	1	5	6	–1	3
Venezuela	4	0	2	2	2	6	–4	2

QUARTER-FINALS

Peru v Paraguay 3-3
Peru won 4-3 on penalties
Brazil v Chile 1-0
Uruguay v Colombia 0-0
Colombia won 4-2 on penalties
Argentina v Ecuador 3-0

SEMI-FINALS

Brazil v Peru 1-0
Argentina v Colombia 1-1
Argentina won 3-2 on penalties

THIRD PLACE PLAY-OFF

Colombia v Peru 3-2

COPA AMERICA 2021 FINAL

Rio de Janeiro, Sunday 11 July 2021

Argentina (1) 1 *(Di Maria 22)*

Brazil (0) 0 7,800

Argentina: Martinez E; Montiel, Romero (Pezzella 79), Otamendi, Acuna, Di Maria (Palacios 79), De Paul, Paredes (Rodriquez 54), Los Celso (Tagliafico 63), Messi, Martinez L (Gonzalez 79).
Brazil: Ederson Moraes; Danilo, Marquinhos, Thiago Silva, Renan Lodi (Emerson 76), Lucas Paqueta (Gabriel Barbosa 76), Casemiro, Fred (Firmino 46), Everton (Vinicius Junior 63), Neymar, Richarlison.
Referee: Esteban Ostojich (Uruguay).

COPA LIBERTADORES 2021

SECOND STAGE – FIRST LEG

Universidad Catolica v Libertad 0-1
Gremio v Ayacucho 6-1
Montevideo Wanderers v Bolivar 1-0
Universidad de Chile v San Lorenzo 1-1
Santos v Deportivo Lara 2-1
Caracas v Junior 1-2
Union Espanola v Independiente del Valle 1-0
Guarani v Atletico Nacional 0-2

SECOND STAGE – SECOND LEG

		(agg)
Libertad v Universidad Catolica	2-2	3-2
Ayacucho v Gremio	1-2	2-8
Bolivar v Montevideo Wanderers	5-0	5-1
San Lorenzo v Universidad de Chile	2-0	3-1
Deportivo Lara v Santos	1-1	2-3
Junior v Caracas	3-1	5-2
Independiente del Valle v Union Espanola	6-2	6-3
Atletico Nacional v Guarani	3-0	5-0

THIRD STAGE – FIRST LEG

Libertad v Atletico Nacional 1-0
Independiente del Valle v Gremio 2-1
Bolivar v Junior 2-1
San Lorenzo v Santos 1-3

THIRD STAGE – SECOND LEG

		(agg)
Atletico Nacional v Libertad	4-1	4-2
Gremio v Independiente del Valle	1-2	2-4
Junior v Bolivar	3-0	4-2
Santos v San Lorenzo	2-2	5-3

GROUP STAGE – GROUP A

Independiente del Valle v Defensa y Justicia 1-1
Universitario v Palmeiras 2-3
Palmeiras v Independiente del Valle 5-0
Defensa y Justicia v Universitario 3-0
Defensa y Justicia v Palmeiras 1-2
Independiente del Valle v Universitario 4-0
Independiente del Valle v Palmeiras 0-1
Universitario v Defensa y Justicia 1-1
Palmeiras v Defensa y Justicia 3-4
Universitario v Independiente del Valle 3-2
Palmeiras v Universitario 6-0
Defensa y Justicia v Independiente del Valle 1-1

Group A Table	P	W	D	L	F	A	GD	Pts
Palmeiras	6	5	0	1	20	7	13	15
Defensa y Justicia	6	2	3	1	11	8	3	9
Independiente del Valle	6	1	2	3	8	11	–3	5
Universitario	6	1	1	4	6	19	–13	4

GROUP B

Always Ready v Internacional 2-0
Deportivo Tachira v Olimpia 3-2
Internacional v Deportivo Tachira 4-0
Olimpia v Always Ready 2-1
Internacional v Olimpia 6-1
Always Ready v Deportivo Tachira 2-0
Deportivo Tachira v Internacional 2-1
Always Ready v Olimpia 1-2
Deportivo Tachira v Always Ready 7-2
Olimpia v Internacional 0-1
Olimpia v Deportivo Tachira 6-2
Internacional v Always Ready 0-0

Group B Table	P	W	D	L	F	A	GD	Pts
Internacional	6	3	1	2	12	5	7	10
Olimpia	6	3	0	3	13	14	–1	9
Deportivo Tachira	6	3	0	3	14	17	–3	9
Always Ready	6	2	1	3	8	11	–3	7

GROUP C

Santos v Barcelona 0-2
The Strongest v Boca Juniors 0-1
Boca Juniors v Santos 2-0
Barcelona v The Strongest 4-0

Santos v The Strongest 5-0
Barcelona v Boca Juniors 1-0
The Strongest v Barcelona 2-0
Santos v Boca Juniors 1-0
The Strongest v Santos 2-1
Boca Juniors v Barcelona 0-0
Boca Juniors v The Strongest 3-0
Barcelona v Santos 3-1

Group C Table	P	W	D	L	F	A	GD	Pts
Barcelona	6	4	1	1	10	3	7	13
Boca Juniors	6	3	1	2	6	2	4	10
Santos	6	2	0	4	8	9	–1	6
The Strongest	6	2	0	4	4	14	–10	6

GROUP D

Fluminense v River Plate 1-1
Junior v Santa Fe 1-1
Santa Fe v Fluminense 1-2
River Plate v Junior 2-1
Santa Fe v River Plate 0-0
Junior v Fluminense 1-1
Fluminense v Santa Fe 2-1
Junior v River Plate 1-1
Fluminense v Junior 1-2
River Plate v Santa Fe 2-1
River Plate v Fluminense 1-3
Santa Fe v Junior 0-0

Group D Table	P	W	D	L	F	A	GD	Pts
Fluminense	6	3	2	1	10	7	3	11
River Plate	6	2	3	1	7	7	0	9
Junior	6	1	4	1	6	6	0	7
Santa Fe	6	0	3	3	4	7	–3	3

GROUP E

Sporting Cristal v Sao Paulo 0-3
Rentistas v Racing 1-1
Racing v Sporting Cristal 2-1
Sao Paulo v Rentistas 2-0
Racing v Sao Paulo 0-0
Rentistas v Sporting Cristal 0-0
Sporting Cristal v Racing 0-2
Rentistas v Sao Paulo 1-1
Sao Paulo v Racing 0-1
Sporting Cristal v Rentistas 2-0
Sao Paulo v Sporting Cristal 3-0
Racing v Rentistas 3-0

Group E Table	P	W	D	L	F	A	GD	Pts
Racing	6	4	2	0	9	2	7	14
Sao Paulo	6	3	2	1	9	2	7	11
Sporting Cristal	6	1	1	4	3	10	–7	4
Rentistas	6	0	3	3	2	9	–7	3

GROUP F

Argentinos Juniors v Nacional 2-0
Atletico Nacional v Universidad Catolica 2-0
Nacional v Atletico Nacional 4-4
Universidad Catolica v Argentinos Juniors 0-2
Universidad Catolica v Nacional 3-1
Atletico Nacional v Argentinos Juniors 0-2
Argentinos Juniors v Universidad Catolica 0-1
Atletico Nacional v Nacional 0-0
Nacional v Universidad Catolica 1-0
Argentinos Juniors v Atletico Nacional 1-0
Nacional v Argentinos Juniors 2-0
Universidad Catolica v Atletico Nacional 2-0

Group F Table	P	W	D	L	F	A	GD	Pts
Argentinos Juniors	6	4	0	2	7	3	4	12
Universidad Catolica	6	3	0	3	6	6	0	9
Nacional	6	2	2	2	8	9	–1	8
Atletico Nacional	6	1	2	3	6	9	–3	5

GROUP G

Velez Sarsfield v Flamengo 2-3
Union La Calera v LDU Quito 2-2
LDU Quito v Velez Sarsfield 3-1
Flamengo v Union La Calera 4-1
Union La Calera v Velez Sarsfield 0-2
LDU Quito v Flamengo 2-3
Union La Calera v Flamengo 2-2
Velez Sarsfield v LDU Quito 3-1
Velez Sarsfield v Union La Calera 2-1
Flamengo v LDU Quito 2-2
Flamengo v Velez Sarsfield 0-0
LDU Quito v Union La Calera 5-2

Group G Table	P	W	D	L	F	A	GD	Pts
Flamengo	6	3	3	0	14	9	5	12
Velez Sarsfield	6	3	1	2	10	8	2	10
LDU Quito	6	2	2	2	15	13	2	8
Union La Calera	6	0	2	4	8	17	–9	2

GROUP H

Deportivo La Guaira v Atletico Mineiro 1-1
America de Cali v Cerro Porteno 0-2
Atletico Mineiro v America de Cali 2-1
Cerro Porteno v Deportivo La Guaira 0-0
Atletico Mineiro v Cerro Porteno 4-0
Deportivo La Guaira v America de Cali 0-0
Deportivo La Guaira v Cerro Porteno 0-1
America de Cali v Atletico Mineiro 1-3
Cerro Porteno v Atletico Mineiro 0-1
America de Cali v Deportivo La Guaira 3-1
Cerro Porteno v America de Cali 1-0
Atletico Mineiro v Deportivo La Guaira 4-0

Group H Table	P	W	D	L	F	A	GD	Pts
Atletico Mineiro	6	5	1	0	15	3	12	16
Cerro Porteno	6	3	1	2	4	5	–1	10
America de Cali	6	1	1	4	5	9	–4	4
Deportivo La Guaira	6	0	3	3	2	9	–7	3

ROUND OF 16 – FIRST LEG

Defensa y Justicia v Flamengo 0-1
Boca Juniors v Atletico Mineiro 0-0
Universidad Catolica v Palmeiras 0-1
Cerro Porteno v Fluminense 0-2
Velez Sarsfield v Barcelona 1-0
Sao Paulo v Racing 1-1
River Plate v Argentinos Juniors 1-1
Olimpia v Internacional 0-0

ROUND OF 16 – SECOND LEG

		(agg)
Flamengo v Defensa y Justicia	4-1	5-1
Atletico Mineiro v Boca Juniors	0-0	0-0
Atletico Mineiro won 3-1 on penalties		
Palmeiras v Universidad Catolica	1-0	2-0
Fluminense v Cerro Porteno	1-0	3-0
Barcelona v Velez Sarsfield	3-1	3-2
Racing v Sao Paulo	1-3	2-4
Argentinos Juniors v River Plate	0-2	1-3
Internacional v Olimpia	0-0	0-0
Olimpia won 5-4 on penalties		

QUARTER-FINALS – FIRST LEG

Olimpia v Flamengo 1-4
River Plate v Atletico Mineiro 0-1
Sao Paulo v Palmeiras 1-1
Fluminense v Barcelona 2-2

QUARTER-FINALS – SECOND LEG

		(agg)
Flamengo v Olimpia	5-1	9-2
Atletico Mineiro v River Plate	3-0	4-0
Palmeiras v Sao Paulo	3-0	4-1
Barcelona v Fluminense	1-1	3-3
Barcelona won on away goals		

SEMI-FINALS – FIRST LEG

Flamengo v Barcelona 2-0
Palmeiras v Atletico Mineiro 0-0

SEMI-FINALS – SECOND LEG

		(agg)
Barcelona v Flamengo	0-2	0-4
Atletico Mineiro v Palmeiras	1-1	1-1
Palmeiras won on away goals		

COPA LIBERTADORES FINAL 2021

Montevideo, Saturday 27 November 2021

Palmeiras (1) 2 *(Raphael Veiga 5, Deyverson 95)*

Flamengo (0) 1 *(Gabriel Barbosa 72)* 55,023

Palmeiras: Weverton; Mayke (Gabriel Menino 105), Gomez, Luan, Piquerez (Melo 113), Danilo (Patrick de Paula 70), Ze Rafael (Danilo Barbosa 82), Dudu (Wesley 77), Raphael Veiga (Deyverson 90), Gustavo Scarpa, Rony.
Flamengo: Diego Alves; Isla (Matheuzinho 79), Rodrigo Caio, David Luiz, Filipe Luis (Rene 32), Willian Arao, Andreas Pereira (Pedro 111), Everton Ribeiro (Michael 63), Arrascaeta (Vitinho 111), Bruno Henrique (Kenedy 90), Gabriel Barbosa.
aet.
Referee: Nestor Pitana (Argentina).

COPA SUDAMERICANA 2021

GROUP A
12 de Octubre v Rosario Central 1-0
San Lorenzo v Huachipato 0-1
Huachipato v 12 de Octubre 0-0
Rosario Central v San Lorenzo 2-0
Huachipato v Rosario Central 1-1
San Lorenzo v 12 de Octubre 1-1
12 de Octubre v Huachipato 1-2
San Lorenzo v Rosario Central 1-2
Rosario Central v Huachipato 5-0
12 de Octubre v San Lorenzo 0-2
Rosario Central v 12 de Octubre 0-0
Huachipato v San Lorenzo 0-3

Group A Table	P	W	D	L	F	A	GD	Pts
Rosario Central	6	3	2	1	10	3	7	11
Huachipato	6	2	2	2	4	10	–6	8
San Lorenzo	6	2	1	3	7	6	1	7
12 de Octubre	6	1	3	2	3	5	–2	6

GROUP B
Montevideo City Torque v Bahia 1-1
Guabira v Independiente 1-3
Bahia v Guabira 5-0
Independiente v Montevideo City Torque 3-1
Bahia v Independiente 2-2
Montevideo City Torque v Guabira 4-0
Montevideo City Torque v Independiente 1-1
Guabira v Bahia 0-1
Independiente v Bahia 1-0
Guabira v Montevideo City Torque 0-4
Independiente v Guabira 1-0
Bahia v Montevideo City Torque 2-4

Group B Table	P	W	D	L	F	A	GD	Pts
Independiente	6	4	2	0	11	5	6	14
Montevideo City Torque	6	3	2	1	15	7	8	11
Bahia	6	2	2	2	11	8	3	8
Guabira	6	0	0	6	1	18	–17	0

GROUP C
Ceara v Jorge Wilstermann 3-1
Bolivar v Arsenal 2-1
Arsenal v Ceara 0-0
Jorge Wilstermann v Bolivar 0-0
Bolivar v Ceara 0-0
Arsenal v Jorge Wilstermann 3-0
Ceara v Arsenal 0-0
Bolivar v Jorge Wilstermann 2-2
Jorge Wilstermann v Arsenal 1-2
Ceara v Bolivar 2-0
Jorge Wilstermann v Ceara 1-0
Arsenal v Bolivar 3-1

Group C Table	P	W	D	L	F	A	GD	Pts
Arsenal	6	3	2	1	9	4	5	11
Ceara	6	2	3	1	5	2	3	9
Bolivar	6	1	3	2	5	8	–3	6
Jorge Wilstermann	6	1	2	3	5	10	–5	5

GROUP D
Metropolitanos v Melgar 2-3
Aucas v Athletico Paranaense 0-1
Athletico Paranaense v Metropolitanos 1-0
Melgar v Aucas 2-0
Metropolitanos v Aucas 3-2
Melgar v Athletico Paranaense 1-0
Metropolitanos v Athletico Paranaense 0-1
Aucas v Melgar 2-1
Athletico Paranaense v Melgar 1-0
Aucas v Metropolitanos 3-0
Athletico Paranaense v Aucas 4-0
Melgar v Metropolitanos 0-0

Group D Table	P	W	D	L	F	A	GD	Pts
Athletico Paranaense	6	5	0	1	8	1	7	15
Melgar	6	3	1	2	7	5	2	10
Aucas	6	2	0	4	7	11	–4	6
Metropolitanos	6	1	1	4	5	10	–5	4

GROUP E
Penarol v Sport Huancayo 5-1
River Plate v Corinthians 0-0
Sport Huancayo v River Plate 1-2
Corinthians v Penarol 0-2
Sport Huancayo v Corinthians 0-3
Penarol v River Plate 3-0
River Plate v Sport Huancayo 2-1
Penarol v Corinthians 4-0
River Plate v Penarol 2-1
Corinthians v Sport Huancayo 5-0
Corinthians v River Plate 4-0
Sport Huancayo v Penarol 0-0

Group E Table	P	W	D	L	F	A	GD	Pts
Penarol	6	4	1	1	15	3	12	13
Corinthians	6	3	1	2	12	6	6	10
River Plate	6	3	1	2	6	10	–4	10
Sport Huancayo	6	0	1	5	3	17	–14	1

GROUP F
Atletico Goianiense v Newell's Old Boys 0-0
Libertad v Palestino 2-0
Palestino v Atletico Goianiense 0-1
Newell's Old Boys v Libertad 1-3
Palestino v Newell's Old Boys 0-1
Libertad v Atletico Goianiense 1-2
Atletico Goianiense v Palestino 0-0
Libertad v Newell's Old Boys 1-0
Atletico Goianiense v Libertad 0-0
Newell's Old Boys v Palestino 3-1
Newell's Old Boys v Atletico Goianiense 1-1
Palestino v Libertad 1-2

Group F Table	P	W	D	L	F	A	GD	Pts
Libertad	6	4	1	1	9	4	5	13
Atletico Goianiense	6	2	4	0	4	2	2	10
Newell's Old Boys	6	2	2	2	6	6	0	8
Palestino	6	0	1	5	2	9	–7	1

GROUP G
Talleres v Emelec 1-2
Red Bull Bragantino v Deportes Tolima 2-1
Deportes Tolima v Talleres 1-1
Emelec v Red Bull Bragantino 3-0
Red Bull Bragantino v Talleres 0-1
Deportes Tolima v Emelec 1-1
Red Bull Bragantino v Emelec 2-0
Talleres v Deportes Tolima 0-0
Talleres v Red Bull Bragantino 0-1
Emelec v Deportes Tolima 2-0
Emelec v Talleres 1-4
Deportes Tolima v Red Bull Bragantino 1-2

Group G Table	P	W	D	L	F	A	GD	Pts
Red Bull Bragantino	6	4	0	2	7	6	1	12
Emelec	6	3	1	2	9	8	1	10
Talleres	6	2	2	2	7	5	2	8
Deportes Tolima	6	0	3	3	4	8	–4	3

GROUP H
Gremio v La Equidad 2-1
Aragua v Lanus 0-1
La Equidad v Aragua 2-1
Lanus v Gremio 1-2
Gremio v Aragua 8-0
La Equidad v Lanus 0-1
Aragua v La Equidad 1-2
Gremio v Lanus 3-1
Lanus v La Equidad 4-1
Aragua v Gremio 2-6
Lanus v Aragua 0-0
La Equidad v Gremio 0-0

Group H Table	P	W	D	L	F	A	GD	Pts
Gremio	6	5	1	0	21	5	16	16
Lanus	6	3	1	2	8	6	2	10
La Equidad	6	2	1	3	6	9	–3	7
Aragua	6	0	1	5	4	19	–15	1

ROUND OF 16 – FIRST LEG
Nacional v Penarol 1-2
Independiente del Valle v Red Bull Bragantino 0-2
Santos v Independiente 1-0
America de Cali v Athletico Paranaense 0-1
LDU Quito v Gremio 0-1
Junior v Libertad 3-4
Deportivo Tachira v Rosario Central 2-2
Sporting Cristal v Arsenal 2-1

ROUND OF 16 – SECOND LEG *(agg)*

Penarol v Nacional	0-1	2-2
Penarol won on away goals		
Red Bull Bragantino v Independiente del Valle	1-1	3-1
Independiente v Santos	1-1	1-2
Athletico Paranaense v America de Cali	4-1	5-1
Gremio v LDU Quito	1-2	2-2
LDU Quito won on away goals		
Libertad v Junior	0-1	4-4
Libertad won on away goals		
Rosario Central v Deportivo Tachira	1-0	3-2
Arsenal v Sporting Cristal	1-1	2-3

QUARTER-FINALS – FIRST LEG

Sporting Cristal v Penarol	1-3
Rosario Central v Red Bull Bragantino	3-4
Santos v Libertad	2-1
LDU Quito v Athletico Paranaense	1-0

QUARTER-FINALS – SECOND LEG *(agg)*

Penarol v Sporting Cristal	1-0	4-1
Red Bull Bragantino v Rosario Central	1-0	5-3
Libertad v Santos	1-0	2-2
Libertad won on away goals		
Athletico Paranaense v LDU Quito	4-2	4-3

SEMI-FINALS – FIRST LEG

Penarol v Athletico Paranaense	1-2
Red Bull Bragantino v Libertad	2-0

SEMI-FINALS – SECOND LEG *(agg)*

Athletico Paranaense v Penarol	2-0	4-1
Libertad v Red Bull Bragantino	1-3	1-5

COPA SUDAMERICANA FINAL 2021

Montevideo, Saturday 20 November 2021

Athletico Paranaense (1) 1 *(Nikao 29)*

Red Bull Bragantino (0) 0 20,000

Athletico Paranaense: Santos; Pedro Henrique, Thiago Heleno, Hernandez (Jose Ivaldo 75), Marcinho, Erick (Fernando Canesin 82), Cittadini (Nicolas 90), Abner, Nikaao, Kayzer (Pedro Rocha 75), Terans (Christian 75).
Red Bull Bragantino: Cleiton; Aderlan, Fabricio Bruno, Ortiz, Edimar (Candido 77), Artur (Leandrinho 88), Jadsom, Cuello (Novaes 82), Helinho, Praxedes (Alerrandro 82), Ytalo (Hurtado 88).
Referee: Andres Matonte (Uruquay).

RECOPA SUDAMERICANA 2022

FINAL – FIRST LEG

Athletico Paranaense v Palmerias	2-2

FINAL – SECOND LEG

Palmerias v Athletico Paranaense	2-0
Palmerias won 4-2 on aggregate.	

NORTH AMERICA

MAJOR LEAGUE SOCCER 2021

**After extra time.*

EASTERN CONFERENCE

	P	W	D	L	F	A	GD	Pts
New England Revolution	34	22	7	5	65	41	24	73
Philadelphia Union	34	14	12	8	48	35	13	54
Nashville	34	12	18	4	55	33	22	54
New York City	34	14	9	11	56	36	20	51
Atlanta U	34	13	12	9	45	37	8	51
Orlando C	34	13	12	9	50	48	2	51
New York Red Bulls	34	13	9	12	39	33	6	48
DC United	34	14	5	15	56	54	2	47
Columbus Crew	34	13	8	13	46	45	1	47
Montreal	34	12	10	12	46	44	2	46
Inter Miami	34	12	5	17	36	53	−17	41
Chicago Fire	34	9	7	18	36	54	−18	34
Toronto	34	6	10	18	39	66	−27	28
FC Cincinnati	34	4	8	22	37	74	−37	20

WESTERN CONFERENCE

	P	W	D	L	F	A	GD	Pts
Colorado Rapids	34	17	10	7	51	35	16	61
Seattle Sounders	34	17	9	8	53	33	20	60
Sporting Kansas City	34	17	7	10	58	40	18	58
Portland Timbers	34	17	4	13	56	52	4	55
Minnesota U	34	13	10	11	42	44	−2	49
Vancouver Whitecaps	34	12	13	9	45	45	0	49
Real Salt Lake	34	14	6	14	55	54	1	48
LA Galaxy	34	13	9	12	50	54	−4	48
Los Angeles	34	12	9	13	53	51	2	45
San Jose Earthquakes	34	10	11	13	46	54	−8	41
FC Dallas	34	7	12	15	47	56	−9	33
Austin	34	9	4	21	35	56	−21	31
Houston Dynamo	34	6	12	16	36	54	−18	30

EASTERN CONFERENCE FIRST ROUND

Philadelphia Union v New York Red Bulls	1-0*
New York City v Atlanta U	2-0
Nashville v Orlando C	3-1

WESTERN CONFERENCE FIRST ROUND

Sporting Kansas City v Vancouver Whitecaps	3-1
Portland Timbers v Minnesota U	3-1
Seattle Sounders v Real Salt Lake	0-0*
Real Salt Lake won 6-5 on penalties	

EASTERN CONFERENCE SEMI-FINALS

Philadelphia Union v Nashville	1-1*
Philadelphia Union won 2-0 on penalties	
New England Revolution v New York City	2-2*
New York City won 5-3 on penalties	

WESTERN CONFERENCE SEMI-FINALS

Colorado Rapids v Portland Timbers	0-1
Sporting Kansas City v Real Salt Lake	1-2

EASTERN CONFERENCE FINAL

Philadelphia Union v New York City	1-2

WESTERN CONFERENCE FINAL

Portland Timbers v Real Salt Lake	2-0

MLS CUP FINAL 2021

Portland, Saturday 11 December 2021

Portland Timbers (0) 1 *(Mora 90)*

New York City (1) 1 *(Castellanos 41)* 25,218

Portland Timbers: Clark; Van Rankin (Valeri 89), Mabiala, Zuparic, Bravo, Chara D, Fochive (Paredes 62), Chara Y, Blanco (Moreno 62), Asprilla (Niezgoda 84), Mora.
New York City: Johnson; Gray, Chanot, Callens, Porarinsson (Amundsen 90), Sands, Morales, Medina (Magno 90), Moralez, Rodriguez (Tajouri-Shradi 80), Castellanos.
Referee: Armando Villarreal.
aet; New York City won 4-2 on penalties.

AFRICA

AFRICAN CUP OF NATIONS 2021 (IN CAMEROON)

** After extra time.*

GROUP A
Cameroon v Burkina Faso 2-1
Ethiopia v Cape Verde Islands 0-1
Cameroon v Ethiopia 4-1
Cape Verde Islands v Burkina Faso 0-1
Cape Verde Islands v Cameroon 1-1
Burkina Faso v Ethiopia 1-1

Group A Table	P	W	D	L	F	A	GD	Pts
Cameroon	3	2	1	0	7	3	4	7
Burkina Faso	3	1	1	1	3	3	0	4
Cape Verde Islands	3	1	1	1	2	2	0	4
Ethiopia	3	0	1	2	2	6	–4	1

GROUP B
Senegal v Zimbabwe 1-0
Guinea v Malawi 1-0
Senegal v Guinea 0-0
Malawi v Zimbabwe 2-1
Malawi v Senegal 0-0
Zimbabwe v Guinea 2-1

Group B Table	P	W	D	L	F	A	GD	Pts
Senegal	3	1	2	0	1	0	1	5
Guinea	3	1	1	1	2	2	0	4
Malawi	3	1	1	1	2	2	0	4
Zimbabwe	3	1	0	2	3	4	–1	3

GROUP C
Morocco v Ghana 1-0
Comoros v Gabon 0-1
Morocco v Comoros 2-0
Gabon v Ghana 1-1
Gabon v Morocco 2-2
Ghana v Comoros 2-3

Group C Table	P	W	D	L	F	A	GD	Pts
Morocco	3	2	1	0	5	2	3	7
Gabon	3	1	2	0	4	3	1	5
Comoros	3	1	0	2	3	5	–2	3
Ghana	3	0	1	2	3	5	–2	1

GROUP D
Nigeria v Egypt 1-0
Sudan v Guinea-Bissau 0-0
Nigeria v Sudan 3-1
Guinea-Bissau v Egypt 0-1
Guinea-Bissau v Nigeria 0-2
Egypt v Sudan 1-0

Group D Table	P	W	D	L	F	A	GD	Pts
Nigeria	3	3	0	0	6	1	5	9
Egypt	3	2	0	1	2	1	1	6
Sudan	3	0	1	2	1	4	–3	1
Guinea-Bissau	3	0	1	2	0	3	–3	1

GROUP E
Algeria v Sierra Leone 0-0
Equatorial Guinea v Ivory Coast 0-1
Ivory Coast v Sierra Leone 2-2
Algeria v Equatorial Guinea 0-1
Ivory Coast v Algeria 3-1
Sierra Leone v Equatorial Guinea 0-1

Group E Table	P	W	D	L	F	A	GD	Pts
Ivory Coast	3	2	1	0	6	3	3	7
Equatorial Guinea	3	2	0	1	2	1	1	6
Sierra Leone	3	0	2	1	2	3	–1	2
Algeria	3	0	1	2	1	4	–3	1

GROUP F
Tunisia v Mali 0-1
Mauritania v Gambia 0-1
Gambia v Mali 1-1
Tunisia v Mauritania 4-0
Gambia v Tunisia 1-0
Mali v Mauritania 2-0

Group F Table	P	W	D	L	F	A	GD	Pts
Mali	3	2	1	0	4	1	3	7
Gambia	3	2	1	0	3	1	2	7
Tunisia	3	1	0	2	4	2	2	3
Mauritania	3	0	0	3	0	7	–7	0

ROUND OF 16
Burkina Faso v Gabon 1-1*
Burkina Faso won 7-6 on penalties
Nigeria v Tunisia 0-1
Guinea v Gambia 0-1
Cameroon v Comoros 2-1
Senegal v Cape Verde Islands 2-0
Morocco v Malawi 2-1
Ivory Coast v Egypt 0-0*
Egypt won 5-4 on penalties
Mali v Equatorial Guinea 0-0*
Equatorial Guinea won 6-5 on penalties

QUARTER-FINALS
Gambia v Cameroon 0-2
Burkina Faso v Tunisia 1-0
Egypt v Morocco 2-1*
Senegal v Equatorial Guinea 3-1

SEMI-FINALS
Burkina Faso v Senegal 1-3
Cameroon v Egypt 0-0*
Egypt won 3-1 on penalties

THIRD PLACE PLAY-OFF
Burkina Faso v Cameroon 3-3
Cameroon won 5-3 on penalties

FINAL
Sunday 6 February 2022

Senegal (0) 0

Egypt (0) 0

Senegal: (433) Mendy E; Sarr B, Koulibaly, Diallo, Ciss; Kouyate (Gueye P 66), Mendy N, Gueye I; Sarr I (Dia 77), Diedhiou (Dieng 77), Mane.
Egypt: (433) Mohamed Abou Gabal; Ahmed Abou El Fotouh, Mahmoud Hamdi, Mohamed Abdelmonem, Emam Ashour; Amr El Soleya (Trezeguet 58), Mohamed Elneny, Hamdi Fathi (Mohanad Lashhen 99); Omar Mahmoush (Zizo 59), Mostafa Mohamed (Marwan Hamdy 59), Mohamed Salah.
aet; Senegal won 4-2 on penalties.

UEFA YOUTH LEAGUE 2021–22

UEFA CHAMPIONS LEAGUE PATH

GROUP A

Manchester C v RB Leipzig 5-1
Club Brugge v Paris Saint-Germain 2-2
RB Leipzig v Club Brugge 1-4
Paris Saint-Germain v Manchester C 1-1
Club Brugge v Manchester C 1-1
Paris Saint-Germain v RB Leipzig 3-0
RB Leipzig v Paris Saint-Germain 1-4
Manchester C v Club Brugge 3-5
Manchester C v Paris Saint-Germain 1-3
Club Brugge v RB Leipzig 4-1
RB Leipzig v Manchester C 0-1
Paris Saint-Germain v Club Brugge 3-2

Group A Table	P	W	D	L	F	A	GD	Pts
Paris Saint-Germain	6	4	2	0	16	7	9	14
Club Brugge	6	3	2	1	18	11	7	11
Manchester C	6	2	2	2	12	11	1	8
RB Leipzig	6	0	0	6	4	21	–17	0

GROUP B

Liverpool v AC Milan 1-0
Atletico Madrid v Porto 1-2
AC Milan v Atletico Madrid 1-1
Porto v Liverpool 1-1
Atletico Madrid v Liverpool 2-0
Porto v AC Milan 3-1
AC Milan v Porto 0-1
Liverpool v Atletico Madrid 2-0
Liverpool v Porto 4-0
Atletico Madrid v AC Milan 3-0
Porto v Atletico Madrid 1-2
AC Milan v Liverpool 1-1

Group B Table	P	W	D	L	F	A	GD	Pts
Liverpool	6	3	2	1	9	4	5	11
Atletico Madrid	6	3	1	2	9	6	3	10
Porto	6	3	1	2	8	9	–1	10
AC Milan	6	0	2	4	3	10	–7	2

GROUP C

Besiktas v Borussia Dortmund 2-3
Sporting Lisbon v Ajax 1-1
Ajax v Besiktas 3-1
Borussia Dortmund v Sporting Lisbon 0-0
Besiktas v Sporting Lisbon 1-3
Ajax v Borussia Dortmund 1-5
Borussia Dortmund v Ajax 0-1
Sporting Lisbon v Besiktas 1-2
Besiktas v Ajax 0-1
Sporting Lisbon v Borussia Dortmund 3-2
Ajax v Sporting Lisbon 2-3
Borussia Dortmund v Besiktas 6-2

Group C Table	P	W	D	L	F	A	GD	Pts
Sporting Lisbon	6	3	2	1	11	8	3	11
Borussia Dortmund	6	3	1	2	16	9	7	10
Ajax	6	3	1	2	9	10	–1	10
Besiktas	6	1	0	5	8	17	–9	3

GROUP D

Sheriff Tiraspol v Shakhtar Donetsk 0-5
Internazionale v Real Madrid 1-1
Shakhtar Donetsk v Internazionale 0-1
Real Madrid v Sheriff Tiraspol 4-1
Shakhtar Donetsk v Real Madrid 3-2
Internazionale v Sheriff Tiraspol 2-1
Real Madrid v Shakhtar Donetsk 1-0
Sheriff Tiraspol v Internazionale 2-4
Internazionale v Shakhtar Donetsk 1-0
Sheriff Tiraspol v Real Madrid 0-1
Shakhtar Donetsk v Sheriff Tiraspol 6-0
Real Madrid v Internazionale 2-1

Group D Table	P	W	D	L	F	A	GD	Pts
Real Madrid	6	4	1	1	11	6	5	13
Internazionale	6	4	1	1	10	6	4	13
Shakhtar Donetsk	6	3	0	3	14	5	9	9
Sheriff Tiraspol	6	0	0	6	4	22	–18	0

GROUP E

Barcelona v Bayern Munich 2-0
Dynamo Kyiv v Benfica 4-0
Benfica v Barcelona 4-0
Bayern Munich v Dynamo Kyiv 0-4
Barcelona v Dynamo Kyiv 0-0
Benfica v Bayern Munich 4-0
Bayern Munich v Benfica 0-2
Dynamo Kyiv v Barcelona 4-1
Dynamo Kyiv v Bayern Munich 2-1
Barcelona v Benfica 0-3
Bayern Munich v Barcelona 3-2
Benfica v Dynamo Kyiv 1-0

Group E Table	P	W	D	L	F	A	GD	Pts
Benfica	6	5	0	1	14	4	10	15
Dynamo Kyiv	6	4	1	1	14	3	11	13
Barcelona	6	1	1	4	5	14	–9	4
Bayern Munich	6	1	0	5	4	16	–12	3

GROUP F

Young Boys v Manchester U 0-1
Villarreal v Atalanta 2-0
Atalanta v Young Boys 3-0
Manchester U v Villarreal 1-4
Young Boys v Villarreal 1-3
Manchester U v Atalanta 4-2
Villarreal v Young Boys 3-3
Atalanta v Manchester U 1-2
Villarreal v Manchester U 1-2
Young Boys v Atalanta 2-3
Atalanta v Villarreal 2-2
Manchester U v Young Boys 2-1

Group F Table	P	W	D	L	F	A	GD	Pts
Manchester U	6	5	0	1	12	9	3	15
Villarreal	6	3	2	1	15	9	6	11
Atalanta	6	2	1	3	11	12	–1	7
Young Boys	6	0	1	5	7	15	–8	1

GROUP G

Sevilla v Red Bull Salzburg 2-0
Lille v VfL Wolfsburg 2-0
Red Bull Salzburg v Lille 3-1
VfL Wolfsburg v Sevilla 1-1
Lille v Sevilla 0-3
Red Bull Salzburg v VfL Wolfsburg 3-0
Sevilla v Lille 0-0
VfL Wolfsburg v Red Bull Salzburg 1-2
Sevilla v VfL Wolfsburg 2-0
Lille v Red Bull Salzburg 1-0
VfL Wolfsburg v Lille 0-3
Red Bull Salzburg v Sevilla 2-0

Group G Table	P	W	D	L	F	A	GD	Pts
Red Bull Salzburg	6	4	0	2	10	5	5	12
Sevilla	6	3	2	1	8	3	5	11
Lille	6	3	1	2	7	6	1	10
VfL Wolfsburg	6	0	1	5	2	13	–11	1

GROUP H

Chelsea v Zenit St Petersburg 3-1
Malmo v Juventus 2-2
Zenit St Petersburg v Malmo 3-2
Juventus v Chelsea 3-1
Zenit St Petersburg v Juventus 0-2
Chelsea v Malmo 4-2
Juventus v Zenit St Petersburg 4-2
Malmo v Chelsea 0-5
Chelsea v Juventus 1-3
Malmo v Zenit St Petersburg 1-3
Zenit St Petersburg v Chelsea 1-1
Juventus v Malmo 4-1

Group H Table	P	W	D	L	F	A	GD	Pts
Juventus	6	5	1	0	18	7	11	16
Chelsea	6	3	1	2	15	10	5	10
Zenit St Petersburg	6	2	1	3	10	13	–3	7
Malmo	6	0	1	5	8	21	–13	1

DOMESTIC CHAMPIONS PATH

FIRST ROUND – FIRST LEG

Pogon Szczecin v Deportivo La Coruna 3-0
MTK Budapest v Sparta Prague 3-1
PAOK v Zilina 1-5
Shkendija v Hajduk Split 0-2

Daugavpils v FC Minsk	0-4
APOEL v Kairat	1-1
Zalgiris Vilnius v Maccabi Haifa	0-3
Cologne v Genk	2-4
Septemvri Sofia v Akademia e Futbollit	3-0
Zvijezda 09 v Trabzonspor	0-1
Domzale v Empoli	1-2
Gabala v AZ Alkmaar	0-4
Miercurea Ciuc v Angers	0-2
Rangers v Hammarby	3-0
Rosenborg v FC Midtjylland	2-4
St Patrick's Ath v Red Star Belgrade	1-2

FIRST ROUND SECOND LEG

		(agg)
Deportivo La Coruna v Pogon Szczecin	4-0	4-3
Sparta Prague v MTK Budapest	3-3	4-6
Zilina v PAOK	2-0	7-1
Hajduk Split v Shkendija	3-1	5-1
FC Minsk v Daugavpils	2-0	6-0
Kairat v APOEL	1-0	2-1
Maccabi Haifa v Zalgiris Vilnius	2-0	5-0
Genk v Cologne	3-1	7-3
Akademia e Futbollit v Septemvri Sofia	1-1	1-4
Trabzonspor v Zvijezda 09	2-0	3-0
Empoli v Domzale	1-1	3-2
AZ Alkmaar v Gabala	7-0	11-0
Angers v Miercurea Ciuc	3-0	5-0
Hammarby v Rangers	1-2	1-5
FC Midtjylland v Rosenborg	10-1	14-3
Red Star Belgrade v St Patrick's Ath	2-0	4-1

SECOND ROUND FIRST LEG

Hajduk Split v FC Minsk	3-0
MTK Budapest v Genk	1-2
Deportivo La Coruna v Maccabi Haifa	5-1
Zilina v Kairat	3-2
Red Star Belgrade v Empoli	1-1
Trabzonspor v FC Midtjylland	2-5
Angers v AZ Alkmaar	0-1
Septemvri Sofia v Rangers	2-4

SECOND ROUND SECOND LEG

		(agg)
FC Minsk v Hajduk Split	1-1	1-4
Genk v MTK Budapest	1-0	3-1
Maccabi Haifa v Deportivo La Coruna	3-0	4-5
Kairat v Zilina	1-0	3-3
Zilina won 3-0 on penalties		
Empoli v Red Star Belgrade	5-0	6-1
FC Midtjylland v Trabzonspor	5-0	10-2
AZ Alkmaar v Angers	0-1	1-1
AZ Alkmaar won 5-4 on penalties		
Rangers v Septemvri Sofia	3-0	7-2

KNOCKOUT PHASE

PLAY-OFFS

Empoli v Borussia Dortmund	3-5
Genk v Chelsea	5-1
AZ Alkmaar v Villarreal	3-3
AZ Alkmaar won 4-3 on penalties	
Zilina v Internazionale	3-1
Hajduk Split v Atletico Madrid	0-0
Atletico Madrid won 3-2 on penalties	
FC Midtjylland v Club Brugge	3-2
Deportivo La Coruna v Dynamo Kyiv	2-2
Dynamo Kyiv won 3-2 on penalties	
Rangers v Sevilla	0-1

ROUND OF 16

Liverpool v Genk	1-1
Liverpool won 4-3 on penalties	
Real Madrid v Atletico Madrid	2-3
AZ Alkmaar v Juventus	0-0
Juventus won 5-4 on penalties	
Dynamo Kyiv v Sporting Lisbon	1-2
Manchester U v Borussia Dortmund	2-2
Borussia Dortmund won 3-1 on penalties	
Zilina v Red Bull Salzburg	1-1
Red Bull Salzburg won 4-3 on penalties	
Paris Saint-Germain v Sevilla	2-0
FC Midtjylland v Benfica	2-3

QUARTER-FINALS

Juventus v Liverpool	2-0
Paris Saint-Germain v Red Bull Salzburg	1-3
Sporting Lisbon v Benfica	0-4
Borussia Dortmund v Atletico Madrid	0-1

SEMI-FINALS

Juventus v Benfica	2-2
Benfica won 4-3 on penalties	
Atletico Madrid v Red Bull Salzburg	0-5

UEFA YOUTH LEAGUE FINAL 2021–22

Nyon, Monday 25 April 2022

Benfica (2) 6 *(Neto 2, Araujo H 15, 57, 89 (pen), N'Dour 53, Semedo 69)*

Red Bull Salzburg (0) 0

Benfica: Gomes; Tome (Ferreira 66), Araujo T, Silva, Rodrigues, N'Dour, Jevsenak (Felix N 80), Neto (Felix H 80), Santos (Marques 80), Araujo H, Moreira (Semedo 59).
Red Bull Salzburg: Stejskal; Atiabou (Pejazic 39), Baidoo, Wallner (Moswitzer 77), Ibertsberger, Agyekum, Kameri (Jano 77), Sahin, Hofer (Reischl 46), Diakite (Berki 86), Simic.
Referee: Harm Osmers (Germany).

UEFA UNDER-17 CHAMPIONSHIP 2021–22

QUALIFYING ROUND

GROUP 1 (MALTA)

Turkey v Malta	6-1
Montenegro v Denmark	0-2
Turkey v Montenegro	1-0
Denmark v Malta	5-1
Denmark v Turkey	3-3
Turkey won 6-5 on penalties and won Group 1	
Malta v Montenegro	0-3

Group 1 Table	P	W	D	L	F	A	GD	Pts
Turkey	3	2	1	0	10	4	6	7
Denmark	3	2	1	0	10	4	6	7
Montenegro	3	1	0	2	3	3	0	3
Malta	3	0	0	3	2	14	–12	0

GROUP 2 (LATVIA)

Sweden v Lithuania	8-0
Latvia v Czech Republic	0-1
Czech Republic v Lithuania	4-0
Czech Republic v Sweden	2-2
Lithuania v Latvia	1-4
Sweden v Latvia	2-2

Group 2 Table	P	W	D	L	F	A	GD	Pts
Czech Republic	3	2	1	0	7	2	5	7
Sweden	3	1	2	0	12	4	8	5
Latvia	3	1	1	1	6	4	2	4
Lithuania	3	0	0	3	1	16	–15	0

GROUP 3 (BELGIUM)

Due to positive Covid tests, all Azerbaijan matches were cancelled. Opponents with awarded a 3-0 win.

Azerbaijan v Norway	0-3
Belgium v Luxembourg	0-1
Norway v Luxembourg	2-2
Belgium v Azerbaijan	3-0
Luxembourg v Azerbaijan	3-0
Norway v Belgium	0-2

Group 3 Table	P	W	D	L	F	A	GD	Pts
Luxembourg	3	2	1	0	6	2	4	7
Belgium	3	2	0	1	5	1	4	6
Norway	3	1	1	1	5	4	1	4
Azerbaijan	3	0	0	3	0	9	–9	0

GROUP 4 (HUNGARY)

Hungary v Estonia	3-0
Georgia v Iceland	1-1

Hungary v Georgia 0-1
Iceland v Estonia 1-2
Iceland v Hungary 0-0
Estonia v Georgia 1-0

Group 4 Table	P	W	D	L	F	A	GD	Pts
Estonia	3	2	0	1	3	4	–1	6
Georgia	3	1	1	1	2	2	0	4
Hungary	3	1	1	1	3	1	2	4
Iceland	3	0	2	1	2	3	–1	2

GROUP 5 (REPUBLIC OF IRELAND)

North Macedonia v Poland 0-0
Republic of Ireland v Andorra 5-0
Poland v Andorra 1-0
Republic of Ireland v North Macedonia 2-0
Andorra v North Macedonia 0-6
Poland v Republic of Ireland 2-2

Group 5 Table	P	W	D	L	F	A	GD	Pts
Republic of Ireland	3	2	1	0	9	2	7	7
Poland	3	1	2	0	3	2	1	5
North Macedonia	3	1	1	1	6	2	4	4
Andorra	3	0	0	3	0	12	–12	0

GROUP 6 (ROMANIA)

Germany v San Marino 11-0
Romania v Russia 0-2
Russia v San Marino 6-1
Germany v Romania 5-0
Russia v Germany 1-2
San Marino v Romania 0-5

Group 6 Table	P	W	D	L	F	A	GD	Pts
Germany	3	3	0	0	18	1	17	9
Russia	3	2	0	1	9	3	6	6
Romania	3	1	0	2	5	7	–2	3
San Marino	3	0	0	3	1	22	–21	0

GROUP 7 (FINLAND)

Bosnia-Herzegovina v Gibraltar 6-1
Finland v Switzerland 1-1
Switzerland v Gibraltar 7-0
Bosnia-Herzegovina v Finland 1-1
Switzerland v Bosnia-Herzegovina 1-0
Gibraltar v Finland 0-4

Group 7 Table	P	W	D	L	F	A	GD	Pts
Switzerland	3	2	1	0	9	1	8	7
Finland	3	1	2	0	6	2	4	5
Bosnia-Herzegovina	3	1	1	1	7	3	4	4
Gibraltar	3	0	0	3	1	17	–16	0

GROUP 8 (GREECE)

France v Moldova 3-0
Cyprus v Greece 0-3
France v Cyprus 1-1
Greece v Moldova 0-0
Greece v France 1-0
Moldova v Cyprus 0-1

Group 8 Table	P	W	D	L	F	A	GD	Pts
Greece	3	2	1	0	4	0	4	7
France	3	1	1	1	4	2	2	4
Cyprus	3	1	1	1	2	4	–2	4
Moldova	3	0	1	2	0	4	–4	1

GROUP 9 (AUSTRIA)

Faroe Islands v Slovenia 0-8
Austria v Kosovo 0-1
Slovenia v Kosovo 1-0
Austria v Faroe Islands 2-0
Kosovo v Faroe Islands 1-0
Slovenia v Austria 4-0

Group 9 Table	P	W	D	L	F	A	GD	Pts
Slovenia	3	3	0	0	13	0	13	9
Kosovo	3	2	0	1	2	1	1	6
Austria	3	1	0	2	2	5	–3	3
Faroe Islands	3	0	0	3	0	11	–11	0

GROUP 10 (SERBIA)

Bulgaria v Croatia 1-0
Serbia v Liechtenstein 11-0
Croatia v Liechtenstein 3-0
Serbia v Bulgaria 0-2
Croatia v Serbia 0-1
Liechtenstein v Bulgaria 0-5

Group 10 Table	P	W	D	L	F	A	GD	Pts
Bulgaria	3	3	0	0	8	0	8	9
Serbia	3	2	0	1	12	2	10	6
Croatia	3	1	0	2	3	2	1	3
Liechtenstein	3	0	0	3	0	19	–19	0

GROUP 11 (PORTUGAL)

Portugal v Kazakhstan 5-0
Wales v Ukraine 3-1
Portugal v Wales 2-0
Ukraine v Kazakhstan 3-0
Ukraine v Portugal 3-2
Kazakhstan v Wales 1-1

Group 11 Table	P	W	D	L	F	A	GD	Pts
Ukraine	3	2	0	1	7	5	2	6
Portugal	3	2	0	1	9	3	6	6
Wales	3	1	1	1	4	4	0	4
Kazakhstan	3	0	1	2	1	9	–8	1

GROUP 12 (NORTHERN IRELAND)

Northern Ireland v Scotland 2-3
Italy v Albania 5-0
Italy v Northern Ireland 2-0
Scotland v Albania 3-2
Scotland v Italy 0-3
Albania v Northern Ireland 2-2

Group 12 Table	P	W	D	L	F	A	GD	Pts
Italy	3	3	0	0	10	0	10	9
Scotland	3	2	0	1	6	7	–1	6
Northern Ireland	3	0	1	2	4	7	–3	1
Albania	3	0	1	2	4	10	–6	1

GROUP 13 (BELARUS)

England v Armenia 7-0
Belarus v Slovakia 0-0
Slovakia v Armenia 5-0
England v Belarus 1-0
Slovakia v England 2-2
Armenia v Belarus 0-2

Group 13 Table	P	W	D	L	F	A	GD	Pts
England	3	2	1	0	10	2	8	7
Slovakia	3	1	2	0	7	2	5	5
Belarus	3	1	1	1	2	1	1	4
Armenia	3	0	0	3	0	14	–14	0

UEFA UNDER-17 ELITE ROUND 2021–22

GROUP 1 (NETHERLANDS)

Netherlands v Hungary 2-0
Slovakia v Greece 1-1
Greece v Hungary 1-1
Netherlands v Slovakia 1-1
Greece v Netherlands 0-0
Hungary v Slovakia 3-1

Group 1 Table	P	W	D	L	F	A	GD	Pts
Netherlands	3	1	2	0	3	1	2	5
Hungary	3	1	1	1	4	4	0	4
Greece	3	0	3	0	2	2	0	3
Slovakia	3	0	2	1	3	5	–2	2

GROUP 2 (DENMARK)

Switzerland v Latvia 1-0
Sweden v Denmark 2-2
Switzerland v Sweden 0-2
Denmark v Latvia 3-2
Denmark v Switzerland 5-0
Latvia v Sweden 0-0

Group 2 Table	P	W	D	L	F	A	GD	Pts
Denmark	3	2	1	0	10	4	6	7
Sweden	3	1	2	0	4	2	2	5
Switzerland	3	1	0	2	1	7	–6	3
Latvia	3	0	1	2	2	4	–2	1

GROUP 3 (SCOTLAND)

Scotland v Czech Republic 2-2
Germany v Georgia 3-0
Germany v Scotland 4-0
Czech Republic v Georgia 1-2
Czech Republic v Germany 2-5
Georgia v Scotland 1-6

Group 3 Table	P	W	D	L	F	A	GD	Pts
Germany	3	3	0	0	12	2	10	9
Scotland	3	1	1	1	8	7	1	4
Georgia	3	1	0	2	3	10	–7	3
Czech Republic	3	0	1	2	5	9	–4	1

GROUP 4 (BOSNIA-HERZOGOVINA)

Spain v Bosnia-Herzegovina 4-1
Belgium v Estonia 8-1
Spain v Belgium 1-0
Estonia v Bosnia-Herzegovina 1-2
Estonia v Spain 0-4
Bosnia-Herzegovina v Belgium 0-6

Group 4 Table	P	W	D	L	F	A	GD	Pts
Spain	3	3	0	0	9	1	8	9
Belgium	3	2	0	1	14	2	12	6
Bosnia-Herzegovina	3	1	0	2	3	11	–8	3
Estonia	3	0	0	3	2	14	–12	0

GROUP 5 (LUXEMBOURG)

FIFA and UEFA suspended Russian clubs and national teams from all competitions due to invasion of Ukraine.

Luxembourg v France 0-2
England v Russia Cancelled
Russia v Luxembourg Cancelled
France v England 3-1
England v Luxembourg 0-2
France v Russia Cancelled

Group 5 Table	P	W	D	L	F	A	GD	Pts
France	2	2	0	0	5	1	4	6
Luxembourg	2	1	0	1	2	2	0	3
England	2	0	0	2	1	5	–4	0
Russia	0	0	0	0	0	0	0	0

GROUP 6 (ITALY)

Kosovo v Ukraine 0-2
Italy v Poland 1-0
Ukraine v Poland 2-3
Italy v Kosovo 1-0
Ukraine v Italy 1-3
Poland v Kosovo 2-1

Group 6 Table	P	W	D	L	F	A	GD	Pts
Italy	3	3	0	0	5	1	4	9
Poland	3	2	0	1	5	4	1	6
Ukraine	3	1	0	2	5	6	–1	3
Kosovo	3	0	0	3	1	5	–4	0

GROUP 7 (SLOVENIA)

Slovenia v Wales 5-0
Serbia v Turkey 3-2
Slovenia v Serbia 2-2
Turkey v Wales 5-2
Turkey v Slovenia 4-3
Wales v Serbia 2-4

Group 7 Table	P	W	D	L	F	A	GD	Pts
Serbia	3	2	1	0	9	6	3	7
Turkey	3	2	0	1	11	8	3	6
Slovenia	3	1	1	1	10	6	4	4
Wales	3	0	0	3	4	14	–10	0

GROUP 8 (PORTUGAL)

Bulgaria v Finland 1-0
Portugal v Republic of Ireland 4-1
Republic of Ireland v Finland 2-3
Bulgaria v Portugal 1-2
Republic of Ireland v Bulgaria 2-2
Finland v Portugal 1-9

Group 8 Table	P	W	D	L	F	A	GD	Pts
Portugal	3	3	0	0	15	3	12	9
Bulgaria	3	1	1	1	4	4	0	4
Finland	3	1	0	2	4	12	–8	3
Republic of Ireland	3	0	1	2	5	9	–4	1

UEFA UNDER-17 FINAL TOURNAMENT (ISRAEL)

GROUP A

Italy v Germany 2-3
Israel v Luxembourg 3-0
Germany v Luxembourg 3-0
Israel v Italy 0-1
Germany v Israel 3-0
Luxembourg v Italy 0-1

Group A Table	P	W	D	L	F	A	GD	Pts
Germany	3	3	0	0	9	2	7	9
Italy	3	2	0	1	4	3	1	6
Israel	3	1	0	2	3	4	–1	3
Luxembourg	3	0	0	3	0	7	–7	0

GROUP B

France v Poland 6-1
Bulgaria v Netherlands 1-3
Netherlands v Poland 2-1
France v Bulgaria 4-0
Netherlands v France 3-1
Poland v Bulgaria 1-1

Group B Table	P	W	D	L	F	A	GD	Pts
Netherlands	3	3	0	0	8	3	5	9
France	3	2	0	1	11	4	7	6
Poland	3	0	1	2	3	9	–6	1
Bulgaria	3	0	1	2	2	8	–6	1

GROUP C

Serbia v Belgium 1-1
Turkey v Spain 0-2
Serbia v Turkey 2-1
Spain v Belgium 2-0
Spain v Serbia 1-1
Belgium v Turkey 3-1

Group C Table	P	W	D	L	F	A	GD	Pts
Spain	3	2	1	0	5	1	4	7
Serbia	3	1	2	0	4	3	1	5
Belgium	3	1	1	1	4	4	0	4
Turkey	3	0	0	3	2	7	–5	0

GROUP D

Denmark v Sweden 1-2
Scotland v Portugal 1-5
Denmark v Scotland 3-1
Portugal v Sweden 4-2
Portugal v Denmark 1-3
Sweden v Scotland 1-0

Group D Table	P	W	D	L	F	A	GD	Pts
Denmark	3	2	0	1	7	4	3	6
Portugal	3	2	0	1	10	6	4	6
Sweden	3	2	0	1	5	5	0	6
Scotland	3	0	0	3	2	9	–7	0

QUARTER-FINALS

Germany v France 1-1
France won 4-3 on penalties
Netherlands v Italy 2-1
Denmark v Serbia 1-2
Spain v Portugal 1-2

SEMI-FINALS

France v Portugal 2-2
France won 6-5 on penalties
Netherlands v Serbia 2-2
Netherlands won 5-3 on penalties

FINAL

Netanya, Wednesday 1 June 2022

France (0) 2 *(Kumbedi 58, 60)*

Netherlands (0) 1 *(Slory 48)*

France: Olmeta; Kumbedi, Mawissa, Bitshiabu, Belocian (Vangi 73), Atanga, Emery, Byar, Doue (Gueguin 64), Saettel (Zidane 86), Tel.
Netherlands: Kuijsten; Rovers (Henry 53), Blokzijl, Huijsen, Breinburg (Agougil 75), Vos (Van Den Heuvel 83), Misehouy, Milambo (Kleijn 46), Slory (Boerhout 83), Van Duiven, Babadi.
Referee: Christian-Petru Ciochirca (Austria)

UEFA UNDER-19 CHAMPIONSHIP 2021–22

QUALIFYING ROUND

GROUP 1 (SWEDEN)

England v Andorra 4-0
Switzerland v Sweden 1-2
England v Switzerland 0-0
Sweden v Andorra 2-0
Andorra v Switzerland 0-6
Sweden v England 0-2

Group 1 Table	P	W	D	L	F	A	GD	Pts
England	3	2	1	0	6	0	6	7
Sweden	3	2	0	1	4	3	1	6
Switzerland	3	1	1	1	7	2	5	4
Andorra	3	0	0	3	0	12	–12	0

GROUP 2 (GREECE)

Germany v Faroe Islands 4-1
Russia v Greece 1-0
Germany v Russia 1-3
Greece v Faroe Islands 0-0
Faroe Islands v Russia 0-5
Greece v Germany 1-1

Group 2 Table	P	W	D	L	F	A	GD	Pts
Russia	3	3	0	0	9	1	8	9
Germany	3	1	1	1	6	5	1	4
Greece	3	0	2	1	1	2	–1	2
Faroe Islands	3	0	1	2	1	9	–8	1

GROUP 3 (HUNGARY)

Austria v Estonia 4-0
Belarus v Hungary 1-2
Austria v Belarus 1-1
Hungary v Estonia 2-0
Estonia v Belarus 0-1
Hungary v Austria 1-1

Group 3 Table	P	W	D	L	F	A	GD	Pts
Hungary	3	2	1	0	5	2	3	7
Austria	3	1	2	0	6	2	4	5
Belarus	3	1	1	1	3	3	0	4
Estonia	3	0	0	3	0	7	–7	0

GROUP 4 (ISRAEL)

Netherlands v Moldova 4-0
Cyprus v Israel 0-1
Netherlands v Cyprus 5-0
Israel v Moldova 6-0
Moldova v Cyprus 2-2
Israel v Netherlands 1-4

Group 4 Table	P	W	D	L	F	A	GD	Pts
Netherlands	3	3	0	0	13	1	12	9
Israel	3	2	0	1	8	4	4	6
Cyprus	3	0	1	2	2	8	–6	1
Moldova	3	0	1	2	2	12	–10	1

GROUP 5 (POLAND)

Ukraine v Malta 4-2
Finland v Poland 3-1
Ukraine v Finland 2-1
Poland v Malta 4-0
Malta v Finland 0-1
Poland v Ukraine 2-2

Group 5 Table	P	W	D	L	F	A	GD	Pts
Ukraine	3	2	1	0	8	5	3	7
Finland	3	2	0	1	5	3	2	6
Poland	3	1	1	1	7	5	2	4
Malta	3	0	0	3	2	9	–7	0

GROUP 6 (BULGARIA)

Bosnia-Herzegovina v Bulgaria 2-0
Republic of Ireland v Montenegro 3-2
Bulgaria v Montenegro 0-1
Republic of Ireland v Bosnia-Herzegovina 1-1
Bulgaria v Republic of Ireland 0-2
Montenegro v Bosnia-Herzegovina 0-4

Group 6 Table	P	W	D	L	F	A	GD	Pts
Bosnia-Herzegovina	3	2	1	0	7	1	6	7
Republic of Ireland	3	2	1	0	6	3	3	7
Montenegro	3	1	0	2	3	7	–4	3
Bulgaria	3	0	0	3	0	5	–5	0

GROUP 7 (ALBANIA)

North Macedonia v Serbia 1-2
France v Albania 4-0
France v North Macedonia 2-0
Serbia v Albania 2-2
Albania v North Macedonia 3-1
Serbia v France 1-2

Group 7 Table	P	W	D	L	F	A	GD	Pts
France	3	3	0	0	8	1	7	9
Serbia	3	1	1	1	5	5	0	4
Albania	3	1	1	1	5	7	–2	4
North Macedonia	3	0	0	3	2	7	–5	0

GROUP 8 (LUXEMBOURG)

Azerbaijan v Belgium 1-5
Spain v Luxembourg 2-1
Belgium v Luxembourg 5-1
Spain v Azerbaijan 6-0
Luxembourg v Azerbaijan 0-2
Belgium v Spain 2-2

Group 8 Table	P	W	D	L	F	A	GD	Pts
Belgium	3	2	1	0	12	4	8	7
Spain	3	2	1	0	10	3	7	7
Azerbaijan	3	1	0	2	3	11	–8	3
Luxembourg	3	0	0	3	2	9	–7	0

GROUP 9 (TURKEY)

Latvia v Romania 0-1
Turkey v San Marino 3-1
Romania v San Marino 5-0
Turkey v Latvia 2-1
San Marino v Latvia 0-2
Romania v Turkey 1-4

Group 9 Table	P	W	D	L	F	A	GD	Pts
Turkey	3	3	0	0	9	3	6	9
Romania	3	2	0	1	7	4	3	6
Latvia	3	1	0	2	3	3	0	3
San Marino	3	0	0	3	1	10	–9	0

GROUP 10 (NORWAY)

Norway v Kosovo 3-0
Wales v Georgia 0-0
Norway v Wales 5-0
Georgia v Kosovo 1-0
Kosovo v Wales 0-3
Georgia v Norway 1-0

Group 10 Table	P	W	D	L	F	A	GD	Pts
Georgia	3	2	1	0	2	0	2	7
Norway	3	2	0	1	8	1	7	6
Wales	3	1	1	1	3	5	–2	4
Kosovo	3	0	0	3	0	7	–7	0

GROUP 11 (CROATIA)

Armenia v Scotland 3-2
Croatia v Gibraltar 7-0
Scotland v Gibraltar 3-0
Croatia v Armenia 2-0
Gibraltar v Armenia 0-1
Scotland v Croatia 1-1

Group 11 Table	P	W	D	L	F	A	GD	Pts
Croatia	3	2	1	0	10	1	9	7
Armenia	3	2	0	1	4	4	0	6
Scotland	3	1	1	1	6	4	2	4
Gibraltar	3	0	0	3	0	11	–11	0

GROUP 12 (SLOVENIA)

Iceland v Slovenia 3-1
Italy v Lithuania 2-0
Slovenia v Lithuania 1-1
Italy v Iceland 3-0
Lithuania v Iceland 1-2
Slovenia v Italy 1-3

Group 12 Table	P	W	D	L	F	A	GD	Pts
Italy	3	3	0	0	8	1	7	9
Iceland	3	2	0	1	5	5	0	6
Lithuania	3	0	1	2	2	5	–3	1
Slovenia	3	0	1	2	3	7	–4	1

GROUP 13 (CZECH REPUBLIC)

Northern Ireland v Denmark 0-2
Czech Republic v Kazakhstan 3-0
Denmark v Kazakhstan 5-2
Czech Republic v Northern Ireland 2-0
Denmark v Czech Republic 1-1
Kazakhstan v Northern Ireland 1-2

Group 13 Table	P	W	D	L	F	A	GD	Pts
Denmark	3	2	1	0	8	3	5	7
Czech Republic	3	2	1	0	6	1	5	7
Northern Ireland	3	1	0	2	2	5	–3	3
Kazakhstan	3	0	0	3	3	10	–7	0

UEFA UNDER-19 ELITE ROUND 2021–22

GROUP 1 (HUNGARY)

Turkey v Scotland 1-2
Israel v Hungary 0-0
Turkey v Israel 1-3
Hungary v Scotland 3-0
Scotland v Israel 0-1
Hungary v Turkey 1-2

Group 1 Table	P	W	D	L	F	A	GD	Pts
Israel	3	2	1	0	4	1	3	7
Hungary	3	1	1	1	4	2	2	4
Scotland	3	1	0	2	2	5	–3	3
Turkey	3	1	0	2	4	6	–2	3

GROUP 2 (FRANCE)

France v Sweden 5-0
Czech Republic v Bosnia-Herzegovina 0-1
France v Czech Republic 0-1
Bosnia-Herzegovina v Sweden 3-2
Sweden v Czech Republic 1-3
Bosnia-Herzegovina v France 1-2

Group 2 Table	P	W	D	L	F	A	GD	Pts
France	3	2	0	1	7	2	5	6
Bosnia-Herzegovina	3	2	0	1	5	4	1	6
Czech Republic	3	2	0	1	4	2	2	6
Sweden	3	0	0	3	3	11	–8	0

GROUP 3 (ENGLAND)

Portugal v Armenia 4-0
Republic of Ireland v England 1-3
England v Armenia 4-0
Portugal v Republic of Ireland 4-1
Armenia v Republic of Ireland 0-4
England v Portugal 2-0

Group 3 Table	P	W	D	L	F	A	GD	Pts
England	3	3	0	0	9	1	8	9
Portugal	3	2	0	1	8	3	5	6
Republic of Ireland	3	1	0	2	6	7	–1	3
Armenia	3	0	0	3	0	12	–12	0

GROUP 4 (CROATIA)

Croatia v Iceland 2-1
Romania v Georgia 5-1
Croatia v Romania 1-2
Georgia v Iceland 1-1
Iceland v Romania 3-0
Georgia v Croatia 1-0

Group 4 Table	P	W	D	L	F	A	GD	Pts
Romania	3	2	0	1	7	5	2	6
Iceland	3	1	1	1	5	3	2	4
Georgia	3	1	1	1	3	6	–3	4
Croatia	3	1	0	2	3	4	–1	3

GROUP 5 (FINLAND)

Italy v Germany 2-2
Finland v Belgium 1-3
Belgium v Germany 2-2
Italy v Finland 4-0
Germany v Finland 0-1
Belgium v Italy 0-2

Group 5 Table	P	W	D	L	F	A	GD	Pts
Italy	3	2	1	0	8	2	6	7
Belgium	3	1	1	1	5	5	0	4
Finland	3	1	0	2	2	7	–5	3
Germany	3	0	2	1	4	5	–1	2

GROUP 6 (NETHERLANDS)

Norway v Ukraine 2-3
Netherlands v Serbia 1-2
Ukraine v Serbia 1-1
Netherlands v Norway 1-1
Serbia v Norway 3-2
Ukraine v Netherlands 2-1

Group 6 Table	P	W	D	L	F	A	GD	Pts
Serbia	3	2	1	0	6	4	2	7
Ukraine	3	2	1	0	6	4	2	7
Norway	3	0	1	2	5	7	–2	1
Netherlands	3	0	1	2	3	5	–2	1

GROUP 7 (SPAIN)

FIFA and UEFA suspended Russian clubs and national teams from all competitions due to invasion of Ukraine.

Spain v Austria 2-2
Russia v Austria Cancelled
Austria v Denmark 2-0
Russia v Spain Cancelled
Denmark v Spain 3-3
Denmark v Russia Cancelled

Group 7 Table	P	W	D	L	F	A	GD	Pts
Austria	2	1	1	0	4	2	2	4
Spain	2	0	2	0	5	5	0	2
Denmark	2	0	1	1	3	5	–2	1
Russia	0	0	0	0	0	0	0	0

UEFA UNDER-19 FINAL TOURNAMENT (SLOVAKIA)

GROUP A

Slovakia v France 0-5
Italy v Romania 2-1
Slovakia v Italy 0-1
Romania v France 1-2
Romania v Slovakia 0-1
France v Italy 4-1

Group A Table	P	W	D	L	F	A	GD	Pts
France	3	3	0	0	11	2	9	9
Italy	3	2	0	1	4	5	–1	6
Slovakia	3	1	0	2	1	6	–5	3
Romania	3	0	0	3	2	5	–3	0

GROUP B

Serbia v Israel 2-2
England v Austria 2-0
Israel v Austria 4-2
England v Serbia 4-0
Israel v England 0-1
Austria v Serbia 3-2

Group B Table	P	W	D	L	F	A	GD	Pts
England	3	3	0	0	7	0	7	9
Israel	3	1	1	1	6	5	1	4
Austria	3	1	0	2	5	8	–3	3
Serbia	3	0	1	2	4	9	–5	1

FIFA U-20 WORLD CUP PLAY-OFF

Slovakia v Austria 1-0

SEMI-FINALS

England v Italy 2-1
France v Israel 1-2

FINAL

Trnava, Friday 1 July 2022

Israel (1) 1 *(Gloch 40)*

England (0) 3 *(Doyle 52, Chukwuemeka 108, Ramsey 116)*

Israel: Zarfati; Israelov, Lemkin, Kancepolsky (Nawi 86), Madmoun, Gloch, Lugassy (Turgeman 86), Revivo, Feingold (Ilay 90), Kassus (Yifrah 86), Ibrahim (Gorno 67).

England: Cox; Doyle, Edwards, Quansah, Devine (Chambers 78), Chukwuemeka, Scarlett (Delap 106), Vale, Oyegoke (Norton-Cuffy 73), Scott (Iroegbunam 73), Bynoe-Gittens (Ramsey 58).

Referee: Antonio Nobre (Portugal).

aet.

UEFA UNDER-21 CHAMPIONSHIP 2021–23

QUALIFYING

GROUP A

Austria v Estonia 2-0
Croatia v Azerbaijan 2-0
Estonia v Finland 0-3
Norway v Austria 3-1
Finland v Croatia 0-2
Austria v Azerbaijan 6-0
Estonia v Norway 0-5
Croatia v Norway 3-2
Azerbaijan v Finland 1-1
Estonia v Austria 0-4
Norway v Estonia 3-0
Azerbaijan v Croatia 1-5
Finland v Austria 3-1
Croatia v Estonia 2-0
Azerbaijan v Austria 0-3
Norway v Finland 3-1
Finland v Estonia 1-0
Azerbaijan v Norway 1-2
Austria v Croatia 1-3
Azerbaijan v Estonia 3-0
Croatia v Austria 0-0
Austria v Norway 2-1
Croatia v Finland 2-3
Norway v Croatia 3-2
Estonia v Azerbaijan 0-5
Austria v Finland 2-3
Finland v Azerbaijan 3-0
Estonia v Croatia 0-4
Finland v Norway 0-2
Norway v Azerbaijan 2-1

Group A Table	*P*	*W*	*D*	*L*	*F*	*A*	*GD*	*Pts*
Norway	10	8	0	2	26	11	15	24
Croatia	10	7	1	2	25	10	15	22
Finland	10	6	1	3	18	13	5	19
Austria	10	5	1	4	22	13	9	16
Azerbaijan	10	2	1	7	12	24	–12	7
Estonia	10	0	0	10	0	32	–32	0

GROUP B

Hungary v Israel 1-2
San Marino v Germany 0-6
Latvia v Poland 0-2
Latvia v Germany 1-3
Poland v Israel 1-2
San Marino v Hungary 0-4
Latvia v San Marino 2-0
Germany v Israel 3-2
Hungary v Poland 2-2
Poland v San Marino 3-0
Hungary v Germany 1-5
Israel v Latvia 2-1
San Marino v Israel 0-4
Hungary v Latvia 1-0
Germany v Poland 0-4
Poland v Latvia 5-0
Germany v San Marino 4-0
Israel v Hungary 3-0
Hungary v San Marino 4-0
Israel v Poland 2-2
Germany v Latvia 4-0
Poland v Hungary 1-1
Israel v Germany 0-1
San Marino v Latvia 0-0
Latvia v Israel 1-0
San Marino v Poland 0-5
Germany v Hungary 4-0
Israel v San Marino 2-0
Latvia v Hungary 0-2
Poland v Germany 1-2

Group B Table	*P*	*W*	*D*	*L*	*F*	*A*	*GD*	*Pts*
Germany	10	9	0	1	32	9	23	27
Israel	10	6	1	3	19	10	9	19
Poland	10	5	3	2	26	9	17	18
Hungary	10	4	2	4	16	17	–1	14
Latvia	10	2	1	7	5	19	–14	7
San Marino	10	0	1	9	0	34	–34	1

GROUP C

FIFA and UEFA suspended Russian clubs and national teams from all competitions due to the Russian invasion of Ukraine. All previous results (shown in italics) were void and remaining fixtures cancelled.

Malta v Northern Ireland 4-1
Slovakia v Lithuania 3-1
Spain v Russia *4-1*
Lithuania v Spain 0-2
Russia v Malta *6-0*
Northern Ireland v Slovakia 1-0
Lithuania v Malta 2-1
Russia v Northern Ireland *1-0*
Spain v Slovakia 3-2
Slovakia v Malta 4-0
Lithuania v Russia *0-3*
Spain v Northern Ireland 3-0
Northern Ireland v Lithuania 4-0
Russia v Slovakia *3-0*
Malta v Spain 0-5
Lithuania v Slovakia 0-2
Russia v Spain *1-0*
Northern Ireland v Malta 0-2
Malta v Russia Cancelled
Slovakia v Northern Ireland 2-1
Spain v Lithuania 8-0
Northern Ireland v Russia Cancelled
Slovakia v Spain 2-3
Malta v Lithuania 1-3
Northern Ireland v Spain 0-6
Russia v Lithuania Cancelled
Malta v Slovakia 1-3
Lithuania v Northern Ireland 1-1
Slovakia v Russia Cancelled
Spain v Malta 7-1

Group C Table	*P*	*W*	*D*	*L*	*F*	*A*	*GD*	*Pts*
Spain	8	8	0	0	37	5	32	24
Slovakia	8	5	0	3	18	10	8	15
Northern Ireland	8	2	1	5	8	18	–10	7
Lithuania	8	2	1	5	7	22	–15	7
Malta	8	2	0	6	10	25	–15	6
Russia	0	0	0	0	0	0	0	0

GROUP D

Greece v Cyprus 0-0
Liechtenstein v Greece 0-5
Belarus v Iceland 1-2
Liechtenstein v Cyprus 0-6
Portugal v Belarus 1-0
Cyprus v Liechtenstein 6-0
Iceland v Greece 1-1
Portugal v Liechtenstein 11-0
Belarus v Greece 0-2
Iceland v Portugal 0-1
Belarus v Liechtenstein 6-0
Greece v Belarus 2-0
Liechtenstein v Iceland 0-3
Cyprus v Portugal 0-1
Greece v Iceland 1-0
Liechtenstein v Belarus 0-4
Portugal v Cyprus 6-0
Greece v Liechtenstein 4-0
Portugal v Iceland 1-1
Cyprus v Belarus 0-1
Cyprus v Iceland 1-1
Greece v Portugal 0-4
Belarus v Cyprus 2-0
Iceland v Liechtenstein 9-0
Belarus v Portugal 1-5
Cyprus v Greece 3-0
Liechtenstein v Portugal 0-9
Iceland v Belarus 3-1
Iceland v Cyprus 5-0
Portugal v Greece 2-1

Group D Table	*P*	*W*	*D*	*L*	*F*	*A*	*GD*	*Pts*
Portugal	10	9	1	0	41	3	38	28
Iceland	10	5	3	2	25	7	18	18
Greece	10	5	2	3	16	10	6	17
Belarus	10	4	0	6	16	15	1	12
Cyprus	10	3	2	5	16	16	0	11
Liechtenstein	10	0	0	10	0	63	–63	0

GROUP E

Wales v Moldova 0-0
Moldova v Bulgaria 0-2
Switzerland v Gibraltar 4-0
Bulgaria v Wales 0-4
Gibraltar v Switzerland 0-4

Netherlands v Moldova 3-0
Moldova v Wales 1-0
Bulgaria v Gibraltar 5-0
Switzerland v Netherlands 2-2
Bulgaria v Switzerland 0-1
Moldova v Gibraltar 1-0
Netherlands v Wales 5-0
Switzerland v Moldova 3-0
Netherlands v Bulgaria 3-1
Gibraltar v Wales 0-7
Gibraltar v Netherlands 0-7
Bulgaria v Moldova 0-0
Wales v Switzerland 0-1
Bulgaria v Netherlands 0-0
Switzerland v Wales 5-1
Gibraltar v Moldova 0-4
Wales v Bulgaria 1-1
Netherlands v Switzerland 2-0
Moldova v Netherlands 0-3
Switzerland v Bulgaria 1-0
Netherlands v Gibraltar 6-0
Moldova v Switzerland 1-1
Wales v Netherlands 0-1
Gibraltar v Bulgaria 1-1
Wales v Gibraltar 2-0

Group E Table	P	W	D	L	F	A	GD	Pts
Netherlands	10	8	2	0	32	3	29	26
Switzerland	10	7	2	1	22	6	16	23
Moldova	10	3	3	4	7	12	–5	12
Wales	10	3	2	5	15	14	1	11
Bulgaria	10	2	4	4	10	11	–1	10
Gibraltar	10	0	1	9	1	41	–40	1

GROUP F

Montenegro v Bosnia-Herzegovina 2-2
Luxembourg v Montenegro 1-2
Sweden v Luxembourg 6-0
Bosnia-Herzegovina v Republic of Ireland 0-2
Italy v Luxembourg 3-0
Montenegro v Sweden 1-3
Luxembourg v Republic of Ireland 1-1
Bosnia-Herzegovina v Sweden 1-1
Italy v Montenegro 1-0
Bosnia-Herzegovina v Italy 1-2
Sweden v Montenegro 3-1
Republic of Ireland v Luxembourg 2-0
Luxembourg v Bosnia-Herzegovina 0-2
Montenegro v Republic of Ireland 2-1
Italy v Sweden 1-1
Sweden v Bosnia-Herzegovina 4-0
Republic of Ireland v Italy 0-2
Bosnia-Herzegovina v Montenegro 2-1
Republic of Ireland v Sweden 1-0
Bosnia-Herzegovina v Luxembourg 1-0
Montenegro v Italy 1-1
Italy v Bosnia-Herzegovina 1-0
Sweden v Republic of Ireland 0-2
Luxembourg v Sweden 0-3
Republic of Ireland v Bosnia-Herzegovina 3-0
Republic of Ireland v Montenegro 3-1
Luxembourg v Italy 0-3
Sweden v Italy 1-1
Montenegro v Luxembourg 3-0
Italy v Republic of Ireland 4-1

Group F Table	P	W	D	L	F	A	GD	Pts
Italy	10	7	3	0	19	5	14	24
Republic of Ireland	10	6	1	3	16	10	6	19
Sweden	10	5	3	2	22	8	14	18
Bosnia-Herzegovina	10	3	2	5	9	16	–7	11
Montenegro	10	3	2	5	14	17	–3	11
Luxembourg	10	0	1	9	2	26	–24	1

GROUP G

Andorra v Albania 0-3
Kosovo v Andorra 2-0
Czech Republic v Slovenia 1-0
Czech Republic v Albania 4-0
Andorra v Slovenia 0-1
England v Kosovo 2-0
Kosovo v Czech Republic 0-1
Slovenia v England 2-2
Albania v Andorra 2-0
Albania v Slovenia 2-0
Andorra v England 0-1
Czech Republic v Kosovo 3-0
England v Czech Republic 3-1
Slovenia v Albania 3-0
Slovenia v Czech Republic 1-1
Kosovo v Albania 2-1
Kosovo v Slovenia 0-0
Albania v Czech Republic 0-1
England v Andorra 4-1
Slovenia v Kosovo 0-0
Andorra v Czech Republic 0-3
Albania v England 0-3
Czech Republic v England 1-2
Andorra v Kosovo 0-3
England v Albania 3-0
Slovenia v Andorra 2-0
Kosovo v England 0-5
Czech Republic v Andorra 7-0
Albania v Kosovo 1-1
England v Slovenia 1-2

Group G Table	P	W	D	L	F	A	GD	Pts
England	10	8	1	1	26	7	19	25
Czech Republic	10	7	1	2	23	6	17	22
Slovenia	10	4	4	2	11	7	4	16
Kosovo	10	3	3	4	8	13	–5	12
Albania	10	3	1	6	9	17	–8	10
Andorra	10	0	0	10	1	28	–27	0

GROUP H

Faroe Islands v Armenia 2-0
Armenia v Faroe Islands 2-0
France v North Macedonia 3-0
Serbia v Ukraine 0-1
Faroe Islands v France 1-1
North Macedonia v Serbia 0-0
Ukraine v Armenia 2-1
Faroe Islands v North Macedonia 1-1
Armenia v Serbia 1-4
France v Ukraine 5-0
Armenia v North Macedonia 1-2
Ukraine v Faroe Islands 1-0
Serbia v France 0-3
North Macedonia v Ukraine 1-1
France v Armenia 7-0
Serbia v Faroe Islands 0-0
Ukraine v Serbia 2-1
North Macedonia v France 0-1
Serbia v North Macedonia 2-1
France v Faroe Islands 2-0
Serbia v Armenia 2-0
North Macedonia v Faroe Islands 0-1
Faroe Islands v Ukraine 0-4
North Macedonia v Armenia 3-1
France v Serbia 2-0
Ukraine v North Macedonia 4-0
Armenia v France 1-4
Faroe Islands v Serbia 1-1
Ukraine v France 3-3
Armenia v Ukraine 0-2

Group H Table	P	W	D	L	F	A	GD	Pts
France	10	8	2	0	31	5	26	26
Ukraine	10	7	2	1	20	11	9	23
Serbia	10	3	3	4	10	11	–1	12
Faroe Islands	10	2	4	4	6	12	–6	10
North Macedonia	10	2	3	5	8	15	–7	9
Armenia	10	1	0	9	7	28	–21	3

GROUP I

Kazakhstan v Belgium 1-3
Turkey v Belgium 0-3
Kazakhstan v Denmark 0-1
Turkey v Scotland 1-1
Scotland v Denmark 0-1
Belgium v Kazakhstan 2-0
Kazakhstan v Turkey 0-1
Belgium v Denmark 1-0
Belgium v Turkey 2-0
Scotland v Kazakhstan 2-1
Turkey v Denmark 1-2
Scotland v Belgium 0-2
Scotland v Turkey 0-2
Kazakhstan v Scotland 2-2
Denmark v Belgium 1-1
Denmark v Kazakhstan 3-0
Belgium v Scotland 0-0
Denmark v Scotland 1-1
Turkey v Kazakhstan 0-0
Denmark v Turkey 3-2

Group I Table	P	W	D	L	F	A	GD	Pts
Belgium	8	6	2	0	14	2	12	20
Denmark	8	5	2	1	12	6	6	17
Turkey	8	2	2	4	7	11	–4	8
Scotland	8	1	4	3	6	10	–4	7
Kazakhstan	8	0	2	6	4	14	–10	2

ENGLAND UNDER-21 RESULTS 1976–2022

EC *UEFA Competition for Under-21 Teams*

Bold type indicates matches played in season 2021–22.

v ALBANIA

Year	Date		Venue	Eng	Alb
EC1989	Mar	7	Shkoder	2	1
EC1989	April	25	Ipswich	2	0
EC2001	Mar	27	Tirana	1	0
EC2001	Sept	4	Middlesbrough	5	0
EC2019	Nov	15	Shkoder	3	0
EC2020	Nov	17	Wolverhampton	5	0
EC2022	**Mar**	**29**	**Elbasan**	**3**	**0**
EC2022	**June**	**7**	**Chesterfield**	**3**	**0**

v ANDORRA

Year	Date		Venue	Eng	And
EC2017	Oct	10	Andorra la Vella	1	0
ec2018	Oct	11	Chesterfield	7	0
EC2020	Oct	7	Andorra la Vella	3	3
EC2020	Nov	13	Wolverhampton	3	1
EC2021	**Oct**	**11**	**Andorra la Vella**	**1**	**0**
EC2022	**Mar**	**25**	**Bournemouth**	**4**	**1**

v ANGOLA

Year	Date		Venue	Eng	Ang
1995	June	10	Toulon	1	0
1996	May	28	Toulon	0	2

v ARGENTINA

Year	Date		Venue	Eng	Arg
1998	May	18	Toulon	0	2
2000	Feb	22	Fulham	1	0

v AUSTRIA

Year	Date		Venue	Eng	Aus
1994	Oct	11	Kapfenberg	3	1
1995	Nov	14	Middlesbrough	2	1
EC2004	Sept	3	Krems	2	0
EC2005	Oct	7	Leeds	1	2
2013	June	26	Brighton	4	0
EC2019	Oct	15	Milton Keynes	5	1
EC2020	Sept	9	Reid	2	1

v AZERBAIJAN

Year	Date		Venue	Eng	Az
EC2004	Oct	12	Baku	0	0
EC2005	Mar	29	Middlesbrough	2	0
2009	June	8	Milton Keynes	7	0
EC2011	Sept	1	Watford	6	0
EC2012	Sept	6	Baku	2	0

v BELARUS

Year	Date		Venue	Eng	Bel
2015	June	11	Barnsley	1	0

v BELGIUM

Year	Date		Venue	Eng	Belg
1994	June	5	Marseille	2	1
1996	May	24	Toulon	1	0
EC2011	Nov	14	Mons	1	2
EC2012	Feb	29	Middlesbrough	4	0

v BOSNIA-HERZEGOVINA

Year	Date		Venue	Eng	B-H
EC2015	Nov	12	Sarajevo Canton	0	0
EC2016	Oct	11	Walsall	5	0

v BRAZIL

Year	Date		Venue	Eng	Bra
1993	June	11	Toulon	0	0
1995	June	6	Toulon	0	2
1996	June	1	Toulon	1	2

v BULGARIA

Year	Date		Venue	Eng	Bul
EC1979	June	5	Pernik	3	1
EC1979	Nov	20	Leicester	5	0
1989	June	5	Toulon	2	3
EC1998	Oct	9	West Ham	1	0
EC1999	June	8	Vratsa	1	0
EC2007	Sept	11	Sofia	2	0
EC2007	Nov	16	Milton Keynes	2	0

v CHINA PR

Year	Date		Venue	Eng	CPR
2018	May	26	Toulon	2	1

v CROATIA

Year	Date		Venue	Eng	Cro
1996	Apr	23	Sunderland	0	1
2003	Aug	19	West Ham	0	3
EC2014	Oct	10	Wolverhampton	2	1
EC2014	Oct	14	Vinkovci	2	1
EC2019	June	24	Serravale	3	3
EC2021	Mar	31	Koper	2	1

v CZECHOSLOVAKIA

Year	Date		Venue	Eng	Cz
1990	May	28	Toulon	2	1
1992	May	26	Toulon	1	2
1993	June	9	Toulon	1	1

v CZECH REPUBLIC

Year	Date		Venue	Eng	CzR
1998	Nov	17	Ipswich	0	1
EC2007	June	11	Arnhem	0	0
2008	Nov	18	Bramall Lane	2	0
EC2011	June	19	Viborg	1	2
2015	Mar	27	Prague	1	0
EC2021	**Nov**	**11**	**Burnley**	**3**	**1**
EC2022	**June**	**3**	**Ceske Budejovice**	**2**	**1**

v DENMARK

Year	Date		Venue	Eng	Den
EC1978	Sept	19	Hvidovre	2	1
EC1979	Sept	11	Watford	1	0
EC1982	Sept	21	Hvidovre	4	1
EC1983	Sept	20	Norwich	4	1
EC1986	Mar	12	Copenhagen	1	0
EC1986	Mar	26	Maine Road	1	1
1988	Sept	13	Watford	0	0
1994	Mar	8	Brentford	1	0
1999	Oct	8	Bradford	4	1
2005	Aug	16	Herning	1	0
2011	Mar	24	Viborg	4	0
2017	Mar	27	Randers	4	0
2018	Nov	20	Esbjerg	5	1

v EQUADOR

Year	Date		Venue	Eng	Eq
2009	Feb	10	Malaga	2	3

v FINLAND

Year	Date		Venue	Eng	Fin
EC1977	May	26	Helsinki	1	0
EC1977	Oct	12	Hull	8	1
EC1984	Oct	16	Southampton	2	0
EC1985	May	21	Mikkeli	1	3
EC2000	Oct	10	Valkeakoski	2	2
EC2001	Mar	23	Barnsley	4	0
EC2009	June	15	Halmstad	2	1
EC2013	Sept	9	Tampere	1	1
EC2013	Nov	14	Milton Keynes	3	0

v FRANCE

Year	Date		Venue	Eng	Fra
EC1984	Feb	28	Hillsborough	6	1
EC1984	Mar	28	Rouen	1	0
1987	June	11	Toulon	0	2
EC1988	April	13	Besancon	2	4
EC1988	April	27	Highbury	2	2
1988	June	12	Toulon	2	4
1990	May	23	Toulon	7	3
1991	June	3	Toulon	1	0
1992	May	28	Toulon	0	0
1993	June	15	Toulon	1	0
1994	May	31	Aubagne	0	3
1995	June	10	Toulon	0	2
1998	May	14	Toulon	1	1
1999	Feb	9	Derby	2	1
EC2005	Nov	11	Tottenham	1	1
EC2005	Nov	15	Nancy	1	2
2009	Mar	31	Nottingham	0	2
2014	Nov	17	Paris	2	3
2016	May	29	Toulon	2	1
2016	Nov	14	Bondoufle	2	3
EC2019	June	18	Cesena	1	2

v GEORGIA

Year	Date		Venue	Eng	Geo
EC1996	Nov	8	Batumi	1	0
EC1997	April	29	Charlton	0	0
2000	Aug	31	Middlesbrough	6	1
2021	**Nov**	**16**	**Batumi**	**2**	**3**

v GERMANY

Year	Date		Venue	Eng	Ger
1991	Sept	10	Scunthorpe	2	1
EC2000	Oct	6	Derby	1	1
EC2001	Aug	31	Frieburg	2	1
2005	Mar	25	Hull	2	2
2005	Sept	6	Mainz	1	1
EC2006	Oct	6	Coventry	1	0
EC2006	Oct	10	Leverkusen	2	0
EC2009	June	22	Halmstad	1	1
EC2009	June	29	Malmo	0	4
2010	Nov	16	Wiesbaden	0	2
2015	Mar	30	Middlesbrough	3	2
2017	Mar	24	Wiesbaden	0	1
EC2017	June	27	Tychy	2	2
2019	Mar	26	Bournemouth	1	2

			v EAST GERMANY	*Eng*	*EG*
EC1980	April	16	Bramall Lane	1	2
EC1980	April	23	Jena	0	1

			v WEST GERMANY	*Eng*	*WG*
EC1982	Sept	21	Bramall Lane	3	1
EC1982	Oct	12	Bremen	2	3
1987	Sept	8	Ludenscheid	0	2

			v GREECE	*Eng*	*Gre*
EC1982	Nov	16	Piraeus	0	1
EC1983	Mar	29	Portsmouth	2	1
1989	Feb	7	Patras	0	1
EC1997	Nov	13	Heraklion	0	2
EC1997	Dec	17	Norwich	4	2
EC2001	June	5	Athens	1	3
EC2001	Oct	5	Blackburn	2	1
EC2009	Sept	8	Tripoli	1	1
EC2010	Mar	3	Doncaster	1	2

			v GUINEA	*Eng*	*Gui*
2016	May	23	Toulon	7	1

			v HUNGARY	*Eng*	*Hun*
EC1981	June	5	Keszthely	2	1
EC1981	Nov	17	Nottingham	2	0
EC1983	April	26	Newcastle	1	0
EC1983	Oct	11	Nyiregyhaza	2	0
1990	Sept	11	Southampton	3	1
1992	May	12	Budapest	2	2
1999	April	27	Budapest	2	2

			v ICELAND	*Eng*	*Ice*
2011	Mar	28	Preston	1	2
EC2011	Oct	6	Reykjavik	3	0
EC2011	Nov	10	Colchester	5	0

			v ISRAEL	*Eng*	*Isr*
1985	Feb	27	Tel Aviv	2	1
2011	Sept	5	Barnsley	4	1
EC2013	June	11	Jerusalem	0	1

			v ITALY	*Eng*	*Italy*
EC1978	Mar	8	Maine Road	2	1
EC1978	April	5	Rome	0	0
EC1984	April	18	Maine Road	3	1
EC1984	May	2	Florence	0	1
EC1986	April	9	Pisa	0	2
EC1986	April	23	Swindon	1	1
EC1997	Feb	12	Bristol	1	0
EC1997	Oct	10	Rieti	1	0
EC2000	May	27	Bratislava	0	2
2000	Nov	14	Monza*	0	0
**Abandoned 11 mins; fog.*					
2002	Mar	26	Valley Parade	1	1
EC2002	May	20	Basle	1	2
2003	Feb	11	Pisa	0	1
2007	Mar	24	Wembley	3	3
EC2007	June	14	Arnhem	2	2
2011	Feb	8	Empoli	0	1
EC2013	June	5	Tel Aviv	0	1
EC2015	June	24	Olomouc	1	3
2016	Nov	10	Southampton	3	2
2018	Nov	15	Ferrara	2	1

			v JAPAN	*Eng*	*Jap*
2016	May	27	Toulon	1	0

			v KAZAKHSTAN	*Eng*	*Kaz*
EC2015	Oct	13	Coventry	3	0
EC2016	Oct	6	Aktobe	1	0

			v KOSOVO	*Eng*	*Kos*
EC2019	Sept	9	Hull	2	0
EC2020	Sept	4	Prishtina	6	0
EC2021	**Sept**	**7**	**Milton Keynes**	**2**	**0**
EC2022	**June**	**10**	**Pristina**	**5**	**0**

			v LATVIA	*Eng*	*Lat*
1995	April	25	Riga	1	0
1995	June	7	Burnley	4	0
EC2017	Sept	5	Bournemouth	3	0
EC2018	Sept	11	Jelgava	2	1

			v LITHUANIA	*Eng*	*Lith*
EC2009	Nov	17	Vilnius	0	0
EC2010	Sept	7	Colchester	3	0
EC2013	Oct	15	Ipswich	5	0
EC2014	Sept	5	Zaliakalnis	1	0

			v LUXEMBOURG	*Eng*	*Lux*
EC1998	Oct	13	Greven Macher	5	0
EC1999	Sept	3	Reading	5	0

			v MALAYSIA	*Eng*	*Mal*
1995	June	8	Toulon	2	0

			v MEXICO	*Eng*	*Mex*
1988	June	5	Toulon	2	1
1991	May	29	Toulon	6	0
1992	May	25	Toulon	1	1
2001	May	24	Leicester	3	0
2018	May	29	Toulon	0	0
2018	June	9	Toulon	2	1

			v MOLDOVA	*Eng*	*Mol*
EC1996	Aug	31	Chisinau	2	0
EC1997	Sept	9	Wycombe	1	0
EC2006	Aug	15	Ipswich	2	2
EC2013	Sept	5	Reading	1	0
EC2014	Sept	9	Tiraspol	3	0

			v MONTENEGRO	*Eng*	*Mon*
EC2007	Sept	7	Podgorica	3	0
EC2007	Oct	12	Leicester	1	0

			v MOROCCO	*Eng*	*Mor*
1987	June	7	Toulon	2	0
1988	June	9	Toulon	1	0

			v NETHERLANDS	*Eng*	*N*
EC1993	April	27	Portsmouth	3	0
EC1993	Oct	12	Utrecht	1	1
2001	Aug	14	Reading	4	0
EC2001	Nov	9	Utrecht	2	2
EC2001	Nov	13	Derby	1	0
2004	Feb	17	Hull	3	2
2005	Feb	8	Derby	1	2
2006	Nov	14	Alkmaar	1	0
EC2007	June	20	Heerenveen	1	1
2009	Aug	11	Groningen	0	0
EC2017	Sept	1	Doetinchem	1	1
EC2018	Sept	6	Norwich	0	0
2019	Nov	19	Doetinchem	1	2

			v NORTHERN IRELAND	*Eng*	*NI*
2012	Nov	13	Blackpool	2	0

			v NORTH MACEDONIA	*Eng*	*M*
EC2002	Oct	15	Reading	3	1
EC2003	Sept	5	Skopje	1	1
EC2009	Sept	4	Prilep	2	1
EC2009	Oct	9	Coventry	6	3

			v NORWAY	*Eng*	*Nor*
EC1977	June	1	Bergen	2	1
EC1977	Sept	6	Brighton	6	0
1980	Sept	9	Southampton	3	0
1981	Sept	8	Drammen	0	0
EC1992	Oct	13	Peterborough	0	2
EC1993	June	1	Stavanger	1	1
1995	Oct	10	Stavanger	2	2
2006	Feb	28	Reading	3	1
2009	Mar	27	Sandefjord	5	0
2011	June	5	Southampton	2	0
EC2011	Oct	10	Drammen	2	1
EC2012	Sept	10	Chesterfield	1	0
EC2013	June	8	Petah Tikva	1	3
EC2015	Sept	7	Drammen	1	0
EC2016	Sept	6	Colchester	6	1

			v PARAGUAY	*Eng*	*Par*
2016	May	25	Toulon	4	0

			v POLAND	*Eng*	*Pol*
EC1982	Mar	17	Warsaw	2	1
EC1982	April	7	West Ham	2	2
EC1989	June	2	Plymouth	2	1
EC1989	Oct	10	Jastrzebie	3	1
EC1990	Oct	16	Tottenham	0	1
EC1991	Nov	12	Pila	1	2
EC1993	May	28	Zdroj	4	1
EC1993	Sept	7	Millwall	1	2
EC1996	Oct	8	Wolverhampton	0	0
EC1997	May	30	Katowice	1	1
EC1999	Mar	26	Southampton	5	0
EC1999	Sept	7	Plock	1	3
EC2004	Sept	7	Rybnik	3	1
EC2005	Oct	11	Hillsborough	4	1
2008	Mar	25	Wolverhampton	0	0
EC2017	June	22	Kielce	3	0
2019	Mar	21	Bristol	1	1

			v PORTUGAL	*Eng*	*Por*
1987	June	13	Toulon	0	0
1990	May	21	Toulon	0	1
1993	June	7	Toulon	2	0
1994	June	7	Toulon	2	0
EC1994	Sept	6	Leicester	0	0

				Eng	*Por*
1995	Sept	2	Lisbon	0	2
1996	May	30	Toulon	1	3
2000	Apr	16	Stoke	0	1
EC2002	May	22	Zurich	1	3
EC2003	Mar	28	Rio Major	2	4
EC2003	Sept	9	Everton	1	2
EC2008	Nov	20	Agueda	1	1
2008	Sept	5	Wembley	2	0
EC2009	Nov	14	Wembley	1	0
EC2010	Sept	3	Barcelos	1	0
2014	Nov	13	Burnley	3	1
EC2015	June	18	Uherske Hradiste	0	1
2016	May	19	Toulon	1	0
EC2021	Mar	28	Ljubljana	0	2

			v QATAR	*Eng*	*Qat*
2018	June	1	Toulon	4	0

			v REPUBLIC OF IRELAND	*Eng*	*RoI*
1981	Feb	25	Liverpool	1	0
1985	Mar	25	Portsmouth	3	2
1989	June	9	Toulon	0	0
EC1990	Nov	13	Cork	3	0
EC1991	Mar	26	Brentford	3	0
1994	Nov	15	Newcastle	1	0
1995	Mar	27	Dublin	2	0
EC2007	Oct	16	Cork	3	0
EC2008	Feb	5	Southampton	3	0

			v ROMANIA	*Eng*	*Rom*
EC1980	Oct	14	Ploesti	0	4
EC1981	April	28	Swindon	3	0
EC1985	April	30	Brasov	0	0
EC1985	Sept	10	Ipswich	3	0
2007	Aug	21	Bristol	1	1
EC2010	Oct	8	Norwich	2	1
EC2010	Oct	12	Botosani	0	0
2013	Mar	21	Wycombe	3	0
2018	Mar	24	Wolverhampton	2	1
EC2019	June	21	Cesena	2	4

			v RUSSIA	*Eng*	*Rus*
1994	May	30	Bandol	2	0

			v SAN MARINO	*Eng*	*SM*
EC1993	Feb	16	Luton	6	0
EC1993	Nov	17	San Marino	4	0
EC2013	Oct	10	San Marino	4	0
EC2013	Nov	19	Shrewsbury	9	0

			v SCOTLAND	*Eng*	*Sco*
1977	April	27	Bramall Lane	1	0
EC1980	Feb	12	Coventry	2	1
EC1980	Mar	4	Aberdeen	0	0
EC1982	April	19	Hampden Park	1	0
EC1982	April	28	Maine Road	1	1
EC1988	Feb	16	Aberdeen	1	0
EC1988	Mar	22	Nottingham	1	0
1993	June	13	Toulon	1	0
2013	Aug	13	Bramall Lane	6	0
EC2017	Oct	6	Middlesbrough	3	1
2018	June	6	Toulon	3	1
EC2018	Oct	16	Tynecastle Park	2	0

			v SENEGAL	*Eng*	*Sen*
1989	June	7	Toulon	6	1
1991	May	27	Toulon	2	1

			v SERBIA	*Eng*	*Ser*
EC2007	June	17	Nijmegen	2	0
EC2012	Oct	12	Norwich	1	0
EC2012	Oct	16	Krusevac	1	0

			v SERBIA-MONTENEGRO	*Eng*	*S-M*
2003	June	2	Hull	3	2

			v SLOVAKIA	*Eng*	*Slo*
EC2002	June	1	Bratislava	0	2
EC2002	Oct	11	Trnava	4	0
EC2003	June	10	Sunderland	2	0
2007	June	5	Norwich	5	0
EC2017	June	19	Kielce	2	1
EC2021	**Oct**	**7**	**Celje**	**2**	**2**
EC2022	**June**	**13**	**Huddersfield**	**1**	**2**

			v SLOVENIA	*Eng*	*Slo*
2000	Feb	12	Nova Gorica	1	0
2008	Aug	19	Hull	2	1
2019	Oct	11	Maribor	2	2

			v SOUTH AFRICA	*Eng*	*SA*
1998	May	16	Toulon	3	1

			v SPAIN	*Eng*	*Spa*
EC1984	May	17	Seville	1	0
EC1984	May	24	Bramall Lane	2	0
1987	Feb	18	Burgos	2	1
1992	Sept	8	Burgos	1	0
2001	Feb	27	St Andrew's	0	4
2004	Nov	16	Alcala	0	1
2007	Feb	6	Derby	2	2
EC2009	June	18	Gothenburg	2	0
EC2011	June	12	Herning	1	1

			v SWEDEN	*Eng*	*Swe*
1979	June	9	Vasteras	2	1
1986	Sept	9	Ostersund	1	1
EC1988	Oct	18	Coventry	1	1
EC1989	Sept	5	Uppsala	0	1
EC1998	Sept	4	Sundvall	2	0
EC1999	June	4	Huddersfield	3	0
2004	Mar	30	Kristiansund	2	2
EC2009	June	26	Gothenburg	3	3
2013	Feb	5	Walsall	4	0
EC2015	Jun	21	Olomouc	1	0
EC2017	June	16	Kielce	0	0

			v SWITZERLAND	*Eng*	*Swit*
EC1980	Nov	18	Ipswich	5	0
EC1981	May	31	Neuenburg	0	0
1988	May	28	Lausanne	1	1
1996	April	1	Swindon	0	0
1998	Mar	24	Brugglifeld	0	2
EC2002	May	17	Zurich	2	1
EC2006	Sept	6	Lucerne	3	2
EC2015	Nov	16	Brighton	3	1
EC2016	Mar	26	Thun	1	1
EC2021	Mar	25	Koper	0	1

			v TURKEY	*Eng*	*Tur*
EC1984	Nov	13	Bursa	0	0
EC1985	Oct	15	Bristol	3	0
EC1987	April	28	Izmir	0	0
EC1987	Oct	13	Bramall Lane	1	1
EC1991	April	30	Izmir	2	2
1991	Oct	15	Reading	2	0
EC1992	Nov	17	Leyton	0	1
EC1993	Mar	30	Izmir	0	0
EC2000	May	29	Bratislava	6	0
EC2003	April	1	Newcastle	1	1
EC2003	Oct	10	Istanbul	0	1
EC2019	Sept	6	Izmir	3	2
EC2020	Oct	13	Wolverhampton	2	1

			v UKRAINE	*Eng*	*Uk*
2004	Aug	17	Middlesbrough	3	1
EC2011	June	15	Herning	0	0
EC2017	Nov	10	Kyiv	2	0
EC2018	Mar	27	Sheffield	2	1

			v USA	*Eng*	*USA*
1989	June	11	Toulon	0	2
1994	June	2	Toulon	3	0
2015	Sept	3	Preston	1	0

			v USSR	*Eng*	*USSR*
1987	June	9	Toulon	0	0
1988	June	7	Toulon	1	0
1990	May	25	Toulon	2	1
1991	May	31	Toulon	2	1

			v UZBEKISTAN	*Eng*	*Uzb*
2010	Aug	10	Bristol	2	0

			v WALES	*Eng*	*Wal*
1976	Dec	15	Wolverhampton	0	0
1979	Feb	6	Swansea	1	0
1990	Dec	5	Tranmere	0	0
EC2004	Oct	8	Blackburn	2	0
EC2005	Sept	2	Wrexham	4	0
2008	May	5	Wrexham	2	0
EC2008	Oct	10	Cardiff	3	2
EC2008	Oct	14	Villa Park	2	2
EC2013	Mar	5	Derby	1	0
EC2013	May	19	Swansea	3	1

			v YUGOSLAVIA	*Eng*	*Yugo*
EC1978	April	19	Novi Sad	1	2
EC1978	May	2	Maine Road	1	1
EC1986	Nov	11	Peterborough	1	1
EC1987	Nov	10	Zemun	5	1
EC2000	Mar	29	Barcelona	3	0
2002	Sept	6	Bolton	1	1

BRITISH AND IRISH UNDER-21 TEAMS 2021–22

▪ *Denotes player sent off.*

ENGLAND

UEFA UNDER-21 CHAMPIONSHIPS QUALIFYING

GROUP G

Tuesday, 7 September 2021

England U21 (2) 2 *(Brewster 10 (pen), Palmer 26)*

Kosovo U21 (0) 0

England U21: (433) Bursik; Aarons, Guehi, Harwood-Bellis, Thomas; Skipp (Doyle 82), Gallagher, Garner; Palmer (John-Jules 72), Brewster (Balogun 65), Madueke (Livramento 82).

Thursday, 7 October 2021

Slovenia U21 (0) 2 *(Spanring 50, Stojinovic 66)*

England U21 (2) 2 *(Gallagher 5, Palmer 14)*

England U21: (433) Bursik; Aarons (Livramento 62), Guehi, Harwood-Bellis, Thomas; Skipp, Gallagher, Ramsey; Smith Rowe, Brewster (Balogun 69), Palmer (John-Jules 69).

Monday, 11 October 2021

Andorra U21 (0) 0

England U21 (0) 1 *(Smith Rowe 67)*

England U21: (433) Green; Livramento, Harwood-Bellis, Guehi, Thomas; Gallagher, Doyle, Garner (Jones 57); Palmer (Gomes 65), Brewster▪, Smith Rowe (Balogun 90).

Thursday, 11 November 2021

England U21 (3) 3 *(Gordon 4, 11, Balogun 30)*

Czech Republic U21 (1) 1 *(Karabec 40 (pen))*

England U21: (433) Bursik; Aarons, Guehi, Harwood-Bellis, Thomas; Skipp, Ramsey, Gallagher (Cresswell 89); Gordon, Balogun (Gibbs-White 77), Palmer (Gomes 72).

Friday, 25 March 2022

England U21 (2) 4 *(Balogun 7, Ramsey 34, Gibbs-White 54, Gordon 80)*

Andorra U21 (0) 1 *(Rosas 62)*

England U21: (433) Bursik; Livramento, Harwood-Bellis, Colwill, Thomas; Doyle, Gibbs-White (Jones 61), Ramsey (Gomes 82); Balogun, Madueke (Gordon 70), Elliott.

Tuesday, 29 March 2022

Albania U21 (0) 0

England U21 (0) 3 *(Balogun 47, 61, Jones 51)*

England U21: (433) Bursik; Johnson, Harwood-Bellis, Colwill, Livramento (Spence 56); Gibbs-White (Gomes 76), Jones, Garner; Balogun, Gordon, Madueke (Lewis-Potter 82).

Friday, 3 June 2022

Czech Republic U21 (0) 1 *(Fila 87)*

England U21 (1) 2 *(Smith Rowe 22, Ramsey 46)*

England U21: (433) Bursik; Aarons, Cresswell, Harwood-Bellis, Johnson; Gibbs-White (Gomes 82), Jones, Garner; Ramsey, Balogun (Archer 68), Smith Rowe (Gordon 65).

Tuesday, 7 June 2022

England U21 (1) 3 *(Balogun 45, 66, Archer 77)*

Albania U21 (0) 0

England U21: (433) Bursik; Johnson (Thomas 83), Harwood-Bellis, Cresswell, Spence; Doyle, Smith Rowe (Gibbs-White 61), Jones (Garner 73); Gordon (Lewis-Potter 83), Balogun (Archer 73), Gomes.

Friday, 10 June 2022

Kosovo U21 (0) 0

England U21 (2) 5 *(Lewis-Potter 3, Gordon 13, Archer 52, 71, Krasniqi I 84 (og))*

England U21: (433) Trafford; Aarons, Hill, Harwood-Bellis (Cresswell 45), Thomas; Ramsey, Elliott (McAtee 72), Doyle; Gordon (Gomes 56), Archer (Balogun 73), Lewis-Potter.

Monday, 13 June 2022

England U21 (0) 1 *(Archer 90)*

Slovenia U21 (1) 2 *(Spence 2 (og), Zabukovnik 64)* 5236

England U21: (433) Bursik; Spence (Aarons 61), Cresswell, Harwood-Bellis, Johnson; Ramsey (Elliott 61), Garner (Lewis-Potter 74), Jones; Gibbs-White, Balogun (Archer 61), Smith Rowe (Gomes 78).

FRIENDLY

Tuesday, 16 November 2021

Georgia U21 (1) 3 *(Guliashvili 24, 47, Gocholeishvili 65)*

England U21 (0) 2 *(Greenwood 81, Guehi 90)*

England U21: (442) Green; Cresswell, Drameh (Aarons 77), Doyle, Garner (Skipp 77); Gibbs-White (Ramsey 66), Gomes (Gordon 66), Mola, Thomas (Guehi 77); Balogun (Greenwood 36), Brewster (Harwood-Bellis 71).

SCOTLAND

UEFA UNDER-21 CHAMPIONSHIPS QUALIFYING

GROUP I

Tuesday, 7 September 2021

Turkey U21 (0) 1 *(Destan 75)*

Scotland U21 (1) 1 *(Middleton 9)*

Scotland U21: (433) Sinclair; Mayo, Welsh, Doig, Ramsay; Williamson, Middleton, Kelly; Kennedy (Rudden 63), Scott (Anderson M 76), Montgomery (Mackay 72).

Thursday, 7 October 2021

Scotland U21 (0) 0

Denmark U21 (1) 1 *(Isaksen 13)*

Scotland U21: (433) Slicker; Ashby, Welsh, Mayo, Doig (Banks 72); Kelly (High 76), Williamson (Leonard 72), Montgomery (Mebude 56); Burroughs, Fiorini, Middleton.

Friday, 12 November 2021

Scotland U21 (1) 2 *(Fiorini 28, Middleton 56)*

Kazakhstan U21 (0) 1 *(Samorodov 71)*

Scotland U21: (433) Mair; Doig, Welsh, Mayo, Ashby (Burroughs 79); Kelly (Williamson 79), High, Fiorini (Clayton 90); Leonard, Mebude (Banks 79), Middleton.

Tuesday, 16 November 2021

Scotland U21 (0) 0

Belgium U21 (1) 2 *(Openda 40 (pen), Raskin 87)*

Scotland U21: (433) Slicker; Burroughs, Welsh (Montgomery 85), Mayo, Doig (Clayton 46); Williamson, Kelly (Banks 86), High; Leonard, Middleton (Mebude 60), Fiorini.

Friday, 25 March 2022

Scotland U21 (0) 0

Turkey U21 (1) 2 *(Bayir 28, Yilmaz K 71)*

Scotland U21: (433) Slicker; Ramsay, Welsh, Mayo, Doig; High (Campbell 46), Fiorini (Henderson 76), Williamson (Smith 81); Banks (Rudden 46), Middleton, Leonard (Barron 46).

Tuesday, 29 March 2022

Kazakhstan U21 (0) 2 *(Seydakhmet 71 (pen), Zhumabek 90)*

Scotland U21 (1) 2 *(Graham 25, Clayton 58)*

Scotland U21: (433) Slicker; Ramsay (Banks 69), Welsh (Clayton 51), Graham, Doig; Barron, Mayo, Campbell; Leonard, Middleton, Burroughs (High 74).

Sunday, 5 June 2022

Belgium U21 (0) 0

Scotland U21 (0) 0

Scotland U21: (433) Sinclair; Welsh (Clayton 84), Mayo, Graham, Burroughs; Freeman, Barron, High; Mebude (Mulligan 88), Leonard (Kelly 71), Anderson E.

Friday, 10 June 2022

Denmark U21 (0) 1 *(Kjaergaard 70)*

Scotland U21 (1) 1 *(Kelly 45)*

Scotland U21: (433) Sinclair; Freeman, Welsh, Mayo, Graham; Burroughs (King 80), Kelly, High; Mulligan, Leonard (Smith 64), Mebude.

WALES

UEFA UNDER-21 CHAMPIONSHIPS QUALIFYING

GROUP E

Tuesday, 7 September 2021

Bulgaria U21 (0) 0

Wales U21 (2) 4 *(Vale 27, 50, 73, Sass-Davies 42)*

Wales U21: (442) Barden; Stevens, Boyes, Sass-Davies, Jones E; Pearson (Huggins 79), Bowen, Williams, Adams (Beck 80); Vale (Davies 83), Hughes.

Friday, 8 October 2021

Moldova U21 (1) 1 *(Ieseanu 21)*

Wales U21 (0) 0

Wales U21: (442) Ratcliffe; Stevens, Boyes, Beck, Cooper; Pearson (Jephcott 67), Bowen (Sass-Davies 90), Williams, Adams; Vale, Hughes.

Tuesday, 12 October 2021

Netherlands U21 (2) 5 *(Ekkelenkamp 7, 54, Botman 35, Stevens 48 (og), Redan 50)*

Wales U21 (0) 0

Wales U21: (442) Ratcliffe; Stevens, Cooper, Sass-Davies, Jones E; Pearson (Beck 70), Taylor, Williams (Hammond 84), Adams; Jephcott (Vale 59), Hughes (Spence 59).

Friday, 12 November 2021

Gibraltar U21 (0) 0

Wales U21 (3) 7 *(Beck 13, Adams 16 (pen), 51, Jephcott 33, Williams 71, Taylor 84, Astley 88)*

Wales U21: (442) Ratcliffe; Astley, Sass-Davies, Cooper (Boyes 59), Beck; Taylor, Pearson (Davies 59), Williams (King 77), Vale; Adams (Hughes 70), Jephcott.

Tuesday, 16 November 2021

Wales U21 (0) 0

Switzerland U21 (0) 1 *(Mambimbi 53)*

Wales U21: (433) Ratcliffe; Astley, Sass-Davies, Cooper, Beck; Adams (Jones E 74), Williams, Taylor; Pearson, Jephcott (Hughes 82), Vale (Davies 77).

Friday, 25 March 2022

Switzerland U21 (3) 5 *(Mambimbi 12, Ndoye 15, 47, Amdouni 20, 50)*

Wales U21 (0) 1 *(Adams 46)*

Wales U21: (4231) Shepperd; Boyes, Astley, Jones E, Stevens; Pearson, Taylor (King 81); Williams, Adams (Hughes 69), Davies; Jephcott (Vale 46).

Tuesday, 29 March 2022

Wales U21 (0) 1 *(Pearson 63)*

Bulgaria U21 (0) 1 *(Nikolov 61)*

Wales U21: (433) Shepperd; Boyes, Jones E, Stevens, Astley; Pearson (Popov 81), Taylor, Williams (King 86); Thorpe (Hughes 68), Davies, Vale.

Saturday, 11 June 2022

Wales U21 (0) 0

Netherlands U21 (0) 1 *(Geertruida 86)*

Wales U21: Shepperd, Beck, Turns, Astley, Stevens, Taylor, King, Thorpe (Jones P 65), Hughes (Hammond 80), Jephcott (Popov 65), Pearson (Adams 75).

Tuesday, 14 June 2022

Wales U21 (1) 2 *(King 1, Hammond 53)*

Gibraltar U21 (0) 0

Wales U21: (433) Webb; Stevens (Hoole 75), Astley, Connolly, Beck; Adams (Ashworth 81), King (Popov 67), Hammond (Sparrow 75); Pearson (Jones P 67), Jephcott, Hughes.

NORTHERN IRELAND

UEFA UNDER-21 CHAMPIONSHIPS QUALIFYING

GROUP C

Friday, 3 September 2021

Malta U21 (3) 4 *(Engerer 24, Veselji 36, 40 (pen), Attard A 84)*

Northern Ireland U21 (0) 1 *(Lane 58)*

Northern Ireland U21: (442) Hughes; Hume, Donnelly, Scott (Anderson 85), McClelland S (McClelland K 46); Balmer, Boyd-Munce (Smyth 46), Galbraith, Johnston (Conn-Clarke 85); Waide, Baggley (Lane 46).

Tuesday, 7 September 2021

Northern Ireland U21 (0) 1 *(Galbraith 54 (pen))*

Slovakia U21 (0) 0

Northern Ireland U21: (433) Hughes; McClelland S, Balmer, Hume, Donnelly; Galbraith, Scott (Cousin-Dawson 90), Lane; Waide (Palmer 82), Boyd-Munce (Smyth 82), Conn-Clarke (Johnston 90).

Tuesday, 12 October 2021

Spain U21 (2) 3 *(Gomez S 26 (pen), 32, Ruiz 56)*

Northern Ireland U21 (0) 0

Northern Ireland U21: (532) Webber; Balmer (McClelland K 67), McClelland S, Donnelly, Hume, Galbraith; Boyd-Munce, Scott (Cousin-Dawson 46), Waide (O'Neill 67); Conn-Clarke (Smyth 46), Lane (McGovern 67).

Friday, 12 November 2021

Northern Ireland U21 (2) 4 *(McCalmont 8, 75, O'Neill 44 (pen), Conn-Clarke 87)*

Lithuania U21 (0) 0

Northern Ireland U21: (433) Hughes; Hume, Balmer, Cousin-Dawson, Donnelly (Charles 82); Smyth, McCalmont, Boyd-Munce (Conn-Clarke 71); Waide (Johnston 82), Lane (Scott 90), O'Neill (McGovern 71).

Tuesday, 16 November 2021

Northern Ireland U21 (0) 0

Malta U21 (0) 2 *(Grima 49, Zammit 89)*

Northern Ireland U21: (433) Hughes; Hume■, Smyth (Boyd-Munce 72), Balmer, Donnelly; McCalmont, Galbraith, Cousin-Dawson; Taylor, Lane (McGovern 72), O'Neill (Waide 72).

Friday, 25 March 2022

Slovakia U21 (1) 2 *(Trusa 37, Kadak 86 (pen))*

Northern Ireland U21 (0) 1 *(Johnston 61)*

Northern Ireland U21: (433) Webber; Charles, Balmer (Price 86), Donnelly, Stewart (Baggley 86); Galbraith, Johnston (Scott 65), McCann; McKee, McCalmont, Taylor (McGovern 71).

Monday 28 March 2022

Russia (1) 1 *(Prokhin 16)*

Northern Ireland U21 (0) 0

Northern Ireland U21: Webber; Hume, Donnelly, Balmer, McClelland S, McCalmont, Galbraith, Scott (Cousin-Dawson 79), Conn-Clarke (Boyd-Munce 63), Waide (O'Neill 63), Lane (McGovern 79).
Russia suspended and match cancelled.

Friday, 3 June 2022

Northern Ireland U21 (0) 0

Spain U21 (1) 6 *(Ruiz 22, Gil Salvatierra 50, 61, Miranda 64, Riquelme 77, Gomez V 87)*

Northern Ireland U21: (433) Mee; Scott, McClelland S, Donnelly, Stewart; Galbraith (Boyle 77), Balmer, Allen (McGuckin 59); McKee (McGovern 59), Taylor, Devlin.

Tuesday, 7 June 2022

Lithuania U21 (0) 1 *(Tutyskinas 90)*

Northern Ireland U21 (1) 1 *(Taylor 17)*

Northern Ireland U21: Mee, Scott (Daws 67), McClelland S, Donnelly, Stewart, Galbraith (Boyle 81), Smyth, Allen, Taylor (McGovern 75), Baggley (Devlin 81), McKee (McGuckin 81).

FRIENDLY

Monday 28 March 2022

France (1) 5 *(Larouci 21, Diop 65, Gouri 66, Caqueret 72, Kalimuendo-Muinga 76)*

Northern Ireland U21 (0) 0

Northern Ireland U21: Berry; Cousin-Dawson, Charles (McCann 63), Balmer (McClelland S 46), Donnelly, Scott, Galbraith (Devlin 46), Smyth (McCausland 46), McCalmont (Price 46), McKee (Taylor 46), McGovern (Baggley 74).

REPUBLIC OF IRELAND

UEFA UNDER-21 CHAMPIONSHIPS QUALIFYING

GROUP F

Friday, 3 September 2021

Bosnia-Herzegovina U21 (0) 0

Republic of Ireland U21 (0) 2 *(Wright 52 (pen), Coventry 73)*

Republic of Ireland U21: (442) Maher; Lyons, O'Brien, McEntee, Ferry (O'Connor 83); Kilkenny, Coventry (Johansson 88), Tierney, Watson (Noss 80); Kayode (Ferguson 83), Wright.

Tuesday, 7 September 2021

Luxembourg U21 (0) 1 *(Nsidjine 84 (pen))*

Republic of Ireland U21 (0) 1 *(Whelan 70)*

Republic of Ireland U21: (4231) Maher; O'Connor, McEntee, O'Brien, Bagan; Kilkenny, Coventry (Johansson 81); Wright, Devoy (Noss 81), Ferry (Moran 67); Ferguson (Whelan 67).

Friday, 8 October 2021

Republic of Ireland U21 (1) 2 *(Kayode 18, Coventry 64 (pen))*

Luxembourg U21 (0) 0

Republic of Ireland U21: (433) Maher; O'Connor, O'Brien, McGuinness, Bagan; Kilkenny (Devoy 87), Coventry, Tierney (Noss 70); Kayode (Ferguson 69), Kerrigan (Gilbert 86), Wright.

Tuesday, 12 October 2021

Montenegro U21 (2) 2 *(Krstovic N 4, Vukcevic I 9)*

Republic of Ireland U21 (0) 1 *(McGuinness 74)*

Republic of Ireland U21: (4231) Maher; O'Connor, McGuinness, O'Brien, Bagan; Kilkenny (Kayode 77), Coventry; Gilbert (O'Neill 60), Tierney (Devoy 77), Ferry; Ferguson (Whelan 61).

Friday, 12 November 2021

Republic of Ireland U21 (0) 0

Italy U21 (1) 2 *(Lucca 31, Cancellieri 90)*

Republic of Ireland U21: (541) Maher; O'Connor, O'Brien, McGuinness, Bagan, Wright; Kilkenny (Tierney 76), Coventry, Smallbone (Devoy 76), Noss (Ebosele 56); Whelan (Kayode 56).

Tuesday, 16 November 2021

Republic of Ireland U21 (0) 1 *(O'Neill 90)*

Sweden U21 (0) 0

Republic of Ireland U21: (3421) Maher; O'Brien, McGuinness, Bagan; O'Connor, Kilkenny, Coventry, Wright (O'Neill 84); Smallbone (Noss 84), Kayode (Ferguson 76); Tierney (Ferry 68).

Tuesday, 29 March 2022

Sweden U21 (0) 0

Republic of Ireland U21 (1) 2 *(Tierney 12, Wright 89)*

Republic of Ireland U21: (433) Maher; McEntee, O'Brien, McGuinness, Bagan; O'Connor, Coventry, Kilkenny; Tierney, Odubeko (Kayode 70), O'Neill (Wright 64).

Friday, 3 June 2022

Republic of Ireland U21 (1) 3 *(Smallbone 16, 81, Odubeko 63)*

Bosnia-Herzegovina U21 (0) 0

Republic of Ireland U21: (442) Maher; O'Connor, McEntee (O'Brien 53), McGuinness, Bagan; Coventry, Kilkenny (Devoy 78), Smallbone, Tierney (O'Neill 64); Odubeko (Ferguson 63), Wright.

Monday, 6 June 2022

Republic of Ireland U21 (1) 3 *(Smallbone 41, Kerrigan 57, Wright 67)*

Montenegro U21 (0) 1 *(Dukanovic 76)*

Republic of Ireland U21: Maher, Adaramola (Lyons 84), McGuinness, Cashin, O'Connor, Wright, Coventry, Noss (Kilkenny 64), Smallbone, Kayode (Ferguson 64), Kerrigan.

Tuesday, 14 June 2022

Italy U21 (2) 4 *(Rovella 20 (pen), Cambiaghi 35, Pellegri 46, Quagliata 86)*

Republic of Ireland U21 (0) 1 *(Coventry 62 (pen))*

Republic of Ireland U21: Maher, Bagan (Lyons 46), McGuinness, Cashin (O'Brien 83), O'Connor, Wright, Kilkenny (Odubeko 62), Coventry, Smallbone, Ferguson (Kayode 74), Kerrigan (Noss 62).

BRITISH UNDER-21 APPEARANCES 1976–2022

Bold type indicates players who made an international appearance in season 2021–22.

ENGLAND

Player	Apps
Aarons, M. J. 2020 (Norwich C)	**18**
Ablett, G. 1988 (Liverpool)	1
Abraham, K. O. T. (Tammy) 2017 (Chelsea)	26
Akpom, C. A. 2015 (Arsenal)	5
Adams, N. 1987 (Everton)	1
Adams, T. A. 1985 (Arsenal)	5
Addison, M. 2010 (Derby Co)	1
Afobe, B. T. 2012 (Arsenal)	2
Agbonlahor, G. 2007 (Aston Villa)	16
Albrighton, M. K. 2011 (Aston Villa)	8
Alexander-Arnold, T. J. 2018 (Liverpool)	3
Alli, B. J. (Dele) 2015 (Tottenham H)	2
Allen, B. 1992 (QPR)	8
Allen, C. 1980 (QPR, Crystal Palace)	3
Allen, C. A. 1995 (Oxford U)	2
Allen, M. 1987 (QPR)	2
Allen, P. 1985 (West Ham U, Tottenham H)	3
Allen, R. W. 1998 (Tottenham H)	3
Alnwick, B. R. 2008 (Tottenham H)	1
Ambrose, D. P. F. 2003 (Ipswich T, Newcastle U, Charlton Ath)	10
Ameobi, F. 2001 (Newcastle U)	19
Ameobi, S. 2012 (Newcastle U)	5
Amos, B. P. 2012 (Manchester U)	3
Anderson, V. A. 1978 (Nottingham F)	1
Anderton, D. R. 1993 (Tottenham H)	12
Andrews, I. 1987 (Leicester C)	1
Archer, C. D. 2022 (Aston Villa)	**4**
Ardley, N. C. 1993 (Wimbledon)	10
Armstrong, A. J. 2018 (Newcastle U)	5
Ashcroft, L. 1992 (Preston NE)	1
Ashton, D. 2004 (Crewe Alex, Norwich C)	9
Atherton, P. 1992 (Coventry C)	1
Atkinson, B. 1991 (Sunderland)	6
Awford, A. T. 1993 (Portsmouth)	9
Bailey, G. R. 1979 (Manchester U)	14
Baines, L. J. 2005 (Wigan Ath)	16
Baker, G. E. 1981 (Southampton)	2
Baker, L. R. 2015 (Chelsea)	17
Baker, N. L. 2011 (Aston Villa)	3
Ball, M. J. 1999 (Everton)	7
Balogun, F. J. 2022 (Arsenal)	**11**
Bamford, P. J. 2013 (Chelsea)	2
Bannister, G. 1982 (Sheffield W)	1
Barker, S. 1985 (Blackburn R)	4
Barkley, R. 2012 (Everton)	5
Barmby, N. J. 1994 (Tottenham H, Everton)	4
Barnes, H. L. 2019 (Leicester C)	4
Barnes, J. 1983 (Watford)	2
Barnes, P. S. 1977 (Manchester C)	9
Barrett, E. D. 1990 (Oldham Ath)	4
Barry, G. 1999 (Aston Villa)	27
Barton, J. 2004 (Manchester C)	2
Bart-Williams, C. G. 1993 (Sheffield W)	16
Batty, D. 1988 (Leeds U)	7
Bazeley, D. S. 1992 (Watford)	1
Beagrie, P. 1988 (Sheffield U)	2
Beardsmore, R. 1989 (Manchester U)	5
Beattie, J. S. 1999 (Southampton)	5
Beckham, D. R. J. 1995 (Manchester U)	9
Bellingham, J. V. W. 2021 (Borussia Dortmund)	4
Berahino, S. 2013 (WBA)	11
Bennett, J. 2011 (Middlesbrough)	3
Bennett, R. 2012 (Norwich C)	2
Bent, D. A. 2003 (Ipswich T, Charlton Ath)	14
Bent, M. N. 1998 (Crystal Palace)	2
Bentley, D. M. 2004 (Arsenal, Blackburn R)	8
Beeston, C 1988 (Stoke C)	1
Benjamin, T. J. 2001 (Leicester C)	1
Bertrand, R. 2009 (Chelsea)	16
Bertschin, K. E. 1977 (Birmingham C)	3
Bettinelli, M. 2015 (Fulham)	1
Birtles, G. 1980 (Nottingham F)	2
Blackett, T. N. 2014 (Manchester U)	1
Blackstock, D. A. 2008 (QPR)	2
Blackwell, D. R. 1991 (Wimbledon)	6
Blake, M. A. 1990 (Aston Villa)	8
Blissett, L. L. 1979 (Watford)	4
Bond, J. H. 2013 (Watford)	5
Booth, A. D. 1995 (Huddersfield T)	3
Bothroyd, J. 2001 (Coventry C)	1
Bowyer, L. D. 1996 (Charlton Ath, Leeds U)	13
Bracewell, P. 1983 (Stoke C)	13
Bradbury, L. M. 1997 (Portsmouth, Manchester C)	3
Bramble, T. M. 2001 (Ipswich T, Newcastle U)	10
Branch, P. M. 1997 (Everton)	1
Bradshaw, P. W. 1977 (Wolverhampton W)	4
Breacker, T. 1986 (Luton T)	2
Brennan, M. 1987 (Ipswich T)	5
Brewster, R. J. 2020 (Liverpool, Sheffield U)	**16**
Bridge, W. M. 1999 (Southampton)	8
Bridges, M. 1997 (Sunderland, Leeds U)	3
Briggs, M. 2012 (Fulham)	2
Brightwell, I. 1989 (Manchester C)	4
Briscoe, L. S. 1996 (Sheffield W)	5
Brock, K. 1984 (Oxford U)	4
Broomes, M. C. 1997 (Blackburn R)	2
Brown, M. R. 1996 (Manchester C)	4
Brown, W. M. 1999 (Manchester U)	8
Buchanan, L. D. 2021 (Derby Co)	2
Bull, S. G. 1989 (Wolverhampton W)	5
Bullock, M. J. 1998 (Barnsley)	1
Burrows, D. 1989 (WBA, Liverpool)	7
Bursik, J. J. 2021 (Stoke C)	**9**
Butcher, T. I. 1979 (Ipswich T)	7
Butland, J. 2012 (Birmingham C, Stoke C)	28
Butt, N. 1995 (Manchester U)	7
Butters, G. 1989 (Tottenham H)	3
Butterworth, I. 1985 (Coventry C, Nottingham F)	8
Bywater, S. 2001 (West Ham U)	6
Cadamarteri, D. L. 1999 (Everton)	3
Caesar, G. 1987 (Arsenal)	3
Cahill, G. J. 2007 (Aston Villa)	3
Callaghan, N. 1983 (Watford)	9
Calvert-Lewin, D. N. 2018 (Everton)	17
Camp, L. M. J. 2005 (Derby Co)	5
Campbell, A. P. 2000 (Middlesbrough)	4
Campbell, F. L. 2008 (Manchester U)	14
Campbell, K. J. 1991 (Arsenal)	4
Campbell, S. 1994 (Tottenham)	11
Cantwell, T. O. 2020 (Norwich C)	4
Carbon, M. P. 1996 (Derby Co)	4
Carr, C. 1985 (Fulham)	1
Carr, F. 1987 (Nottingham F)	9
Carragher, J. L. 1997 (Liverpool)	27
Carroll, A. T. 2010 (Newcastle U)	5
Carroll, T. J. 2013 (Tottenham H)	17
Carlisle, C. J. 2001 (QPR)	3
Carrick, M. 2001 (West Ham U)	14
Carson, S. P. 2004 (Leeds U, Liverpool)	29
Casper, C. M. 1995 (Manchester U)	1
Caton, T. 1982 (Manchester C)	14
Cattermole, L. B. 2008 (Middlesbrough, Wigan Ath, Sunderland)	16
Caulker, S. R. 2011 (Tottenham H)	10
Chadwick, L. H. 2000 (Manchester U)	13
Challis, T. M. 1996 (QPR)	2
Chalobah, N. N. 2012 (Chelsea)	40
Chalobah, T. T. 2020 (Chelsea)	3
Chamberlain, M. 1983 (Stoke C)	4
Chambers, C. 2015 (Arsenal)	22
Chaplow, R. D. 2004 (Burnley)	1
Chapman, L. 1981 (Stoke C)	1
Charles, G. A. 1991 (Nottingham F)	4
Chettle, S. 1988 (Nottingham F)	12
Chilwell, B. J. 2016 (Leicester C)	10
Chopra, R. M. 2004 (Newcastle U)	1
Choudhury, H. D. 2018 (Leicester C)	7
Clark, L. R. 1992 (Newcastle U)	11
Clarke, P. M. 2003 (Everton)	8

Clarke-Salter, J. L. 2018 (Chelsea) 12
Christie, M. N. 2001 (Derby Co) 11
Clegg, M. J. 1998 (Manchester U) 2
Clemence, S. N. 1999 (Tottenham H) 1
Cleverley, T. W. 2010 (Manchester U) 16
Clough, N. H. 1986 (Nottingham F) 15
Clyne, N. E. 2012 (Crystal Palace) 8
Cole, A. 2001 (Arsenal) 4
Cole, A. A. 1992 (Arsenal, Bristol C, Newcastle U) 8
Cole, C. 2003 (Chelsea) 19
Cole, J. J. 2000 (West Ham U) 8
Colwill, L. S 2022 (Chelsea) 2
Coney, D. 1985 (Fulham) 4
Connolly, C. A. 2018 (Everton) 4
Connor, T. 1987 (Brighton & HA) 1
Cook, L. J. 2018 (Bournemouth) 14
Cooke, R. 1986 (Tottenham H) 1
Cooke, T. J. 1996 (Manchester U) 4
Cooper, C. T. 1988 (Middlesbrough) 8
Cork, J. F. P. 2009 (Chelsea) 13
Corrigan, J. T. 1978 (Manchester C) 3
Cort, C. E. R. 1999 (Wimbledon) 12
Cottee, A. R. 1985 (West Ham U) 8
Couzens, A. J. 1995 (Leeds U) 3
Cowans, G. S. 1979 (Aston Villa) 5
Cox, N. J. 1993 (Aston Villa) 6
Cranie, M. J. 2008 (Portsmouth) 16
Cranson, I. 1985 (Ipswich T) 5
Cresswell, C. R. 2022 (Leeds U) 6
Cresswell, R. P. W. 1999 (York C, Sheffield W) 4
Croft, G. 1995 (Grimsby T) 4
Crooks, G. 1980 (Stoke C) 4
Crossley, M. G. 1990 (Nottingham F) 3
Crouch, P. J. 2002 (Portsmouth, Aston Villa) 5
Cundy, J. V. 1991 (Chelsea) 3
Cunningham, L. 1977 (WBA) 6
Curbishley, L. C. 1981 (Birmingham C) 1
Curtis, J. C. K. 1998 (Manchester U) 16

Daniel, P. W. 1977 (Hull C) 7
Dann, S. 2008 (Coventry C) 2
Dasilva, J. R. 2018 (Chelsea) 13
Dasilva, P. J. T. 2021 (Brentford) 5
Davenport, C. R. P. 2005 (Tottenham H) 8
Davies, A. J. 2004 (Middlesbrough) 1
Davies, C. E. 2006 (WBA) 3
Davies, K. C. 1998 (Southampton, Blackburn R, Southampton) 3
Davies, T. 2018 (Everton) 23
Davis, K. G. 1995 (Luton T) 3
Davis, P. 1982 (Arsenal) 11
Davis, S. 2001 (Fulham) 11
Dawson, C. 2012 (WBA) 15
Dawson, M. R. 2003 (Nottingham F, Tottenham H) 13
Day, C. N. 1996 (Tottenham H, Crystal Palace) 6
D'Avray, M. 1984 (Ipswich T) 2
Deehan, J. M. 1977 (Aston Villa) 7
Defoe, J. C. 2001 (West Ham U) 23
Delfouneso, N. 2010 (Aston Villa) 17
Delph, F. 2009 (Leeds U, Aston Villa) 4
Dennis, M. E. 1980 (Birmingham C) 3
Derbyshire, M. A. 2007 (Blackburn R) 14
Diangana, G. G. 2020 (West Ham U) 1
Dichio, D. S. E. 1996 (QPR) 1
Dickens, A. 1985 (West Ham U) 1
Dicks, J. 1988 (West Ham U) 4
Dier, E. J. E. 2013 (Sporting Lisbon, Tottenham H) 9
Digby, F. 1987 (Swindon T) 5
Dillon, K. P. 1981 (Birmingham C) 1
Dixon, K. M. 1985 (Chelsea) 1
Dobson, A. 1989 (Coventry C) 4
Dodd, J. R. 1991 (Southampton) 8
Donowa, L. 1985 (Norwich C) 3
Dorigo, A. R. 1987 (Aston Villa) 11
Dowell, K. O. 2018 (Everton) 17
Downing, S. 2004 (Middlesbrough) 8
Doyle, T. G. 2022 (Manchester C) 6
Dozzell, J. 1987 (Ipswich T) 9
Draper, M. A. 1991 (Notts Co) 3
Drameh, C. C. P. (Leeds U) 1
Driver, A. 2009 (Hearts) 1
Duberry, M. W. 1997 (Chelsea) 5
Dunn, D. J. I. 1999 (Blackburn R) 20
Duxbury, M. 1981 (Manchester U) 7
Dyer, B. A. 1994 (Crystal Palace) 10
Dyer, K. C. 1998 (Ipswich T, Newcastle U) 11
Dyson, P. I. 1981 (Coventry C) 4

Eadie, D. M. 1994 (Norwich C) 7
Ebanks-Blake, S. 2009 (Wolverhampton W) 1
Ebbrell, J. 1989 (Everton) 14
Edghill, R. A. 1994 (Manchester C) 3
Ehiogu, U. 1992 (Aston Villa) 15
Ejaria, O. D. 2018 (Liverpool) 1
Elliott, H. D. J. 2022 (Liverpool) 3
Elliott, P. 1985 (Luton T) 3
Elliott, R. J. 1996 (Newcastle U) 2
Elliott, S. W. 1998 (Derby Co) 3
Etherington, N, 2002 (Tottenham H) 3
Euell, J. J. 1998 (Wimbledon) 6
Evans, R. 2003 (Chelsea) 2
Eze, E. O. 2020 (QPR, Crystal Palace) 8

Fairclough, C. 1985 (Nottingham F, Tottenham H) 7
Fairclough, D. 1977 (Liverpool) 1
Fashanu, J. 1980 (Norwich C, Nottingham F) 11
Fear, P. 1994 (Wimbledon) 3
Fenton, G. A. 1995 (Aston Villa) 1
Fenwick, T. W. 1981 (Crystal Palace, QPR) 11
Ferdinand, A. J. 2005 (West Ham U) 17
Ferdinand, R. G. 1997 (West Ham U) 5
Fereday, W. 1985 (QPR) 5
Fielding, F. D. 2009 (Blackburn R) 12
Flanagan, J. 2012 (Liverpool) 3
Flitcroft, G. W. 1993 (Manchester C) 10
Flowers, T. D. 1987 (Southampton) 3
Foden, P. W. 2019 (Manchester C) 15
Ford, M. 1996 (Leeds U) 2
Forster, N. M. 1995 (Brentford) 4
Forsyth, M. 1988 (Derby Co) 1
Forster-Caskey, J. D. 2014 (Brighton & HA) 14
Foster, S. 1980 (Brighton & HA) 1
Fowler, R. B. 1994 (Liverpool) 8
Fox, D. J. 2008 (Coventry C) 1
Froggatt, S. J. 1993 (Aston Villa) 2
Fry, D. J. 2018 (Middlesbrough) 11
Futcher, P. 1977 (Luton T, Manchester C) 11

Gabbiadini, M. 1989 (Sunderland) 2
Gale, A. 1982 (Fulham) 1
Gallagher, C. J. 2020 (Chelsea) 13
Gallen, K. A. 1995 (QPR) 4
Galloway, B. J. 2017 (Everton) 3
Garbutt, L. S. 2014 (Everton) 11
Gardner, A. 2002 (Tottenham H) 1
Gardner, C. 2008 (Aston Villa) 14
Gardner, G. 2012 (Aston Villa) 5
Garner, J. D. 2022 (Manchester U) 7
Gascoigne, P. J. 1987 (Newcastle U) 13
Gayle, H. 1984 (Birmingham C) 3
Gernon, T. 1983 (Ipswich T) 1
Gerrard, P. W. 1993 (Oldham Ath) 18
Gerrard, S. G. 2000 (Liverpool) 4
Gibbs, K. J. R. 2009 (Arsenal) 15
Gibbs, N. 1987 (Watford) 5
Gibbs-White, M. A. 2019 (Wolverhampton W) 10
Gibson, B. J. 2014 (Middlesbrough) 10
Gibson, C. 1982 (Aston Villa) 1
Gilbert, W. A. 1979 (Crystal Palace) 11
Goddard, P. 1981 (West Ham U) 8
Godfrey, B. M. 2020 (Norwich C, Everton) 9
Gomes, A. A. A. de A. 2022 (Lille) 9
Gomez, J. D. 2015 (Liverpool) 7
Gordon, A. M. 2022 (Everton) 7
Gordon, D. 1987 (Norwich C) 4
Gordon, D. D. 1994 (Crystal Palace) 13
Gosling, D. 2010 (Everton, Newcastle U) 3
Grant, A. J. 1996 (Everton) 1
Grant, L. A. 2003 (Derby Co) 4
Granville, D. P. 1997 (Chelsea) 3
Gray, A. 1988 (Aston Villa) 2
Gray, D. R. 2016 (Leicester C) 26
Grealish, J. 2016 (Aston Villa) 7
Green, E. 2022 (Saint-Etienne) 2
Greening, J. 1999 (Manchester U, Middlesbrough) 18
Greenwood, M. W. J. 2020 (Manchester U) 4

Greenwood, S. 2022 (Leeds U) 1
Griffin, A. 1999 (Newcastle U) 3
Grimes, M. J. 2016 (Swansea C) 4
Guehi, A. K. M.-I. (Marc) 2020 (Chelsea, Crystal Palace) 16
Gunn, A. 2015 (Manchester C, Southampton) 12
Guppy, S. A. 1998 (Leicester C) 1

Haigh, P. 1977 (Hull C) 1
Hall, M. T. J. 1997 (Coventry C) 8
Hall, R. A. 1992 (Southampton) 11
Hamilton, D. V. 1997 (Newcastle U) 1
Hammill, A. 2010 (Wolverhampton W) 1
Harding, D. A. 2005 (Brighton & HA) 4
Hardyman, P. 1985 (Portsmouth) 2
Hargreaves, O. 2001 (Bayern Munich) 3
Harley, J. 2000 (Chelsea) 3
Harrison, J. D. 2018 (Manchester C) 2
Hart, C. J. J. (Joe) 2007 (Manchester C) 21
Harwood-Bellis, T. J. 2022 (Manchester C) 11
Hateley, M. 1982 (Coventry C, Portsmouth) 10
Hause, K. P. D. 2015 (Wolverhampton W) 10
Hayden, I. 2017 (Newcastle U) 3
Hayes, M. 1987 (Arsenal) 3
Hazell, R. J. 1979 (Wolverhampton W) 1
Heaney, N. A. 1992 (Arsenal) 6
Heath, A. 1981 (Stoke C, Everton) 8
Heaton, T. D. 2008 (Manchester U) 3
Henderson, D. B. 2018 (Manchester U) 11
Henderson, J. B. 2011 (Sunderland, Liverpool) 27
Hendon, I. M. 1992 (Tottenham H) 7
Hendrie, L. A. 1996 (Aston Villa) 13
Hesford, I. 1981 (Blackpool) 7
Heskey, E. W. I. 1997 (Leicester C, Liverpool) 16
Hilaire, V. 1980 (Crystal Palace) 9
Hill, D. R. L. 1995 (Tottenham H) 4
Hill, J. C. 2022 (Bournemouth) 1
Hillier, D. 1991 (Arsenal) 1
Hinchcliffe, A. 1989 (Manchester C) 1
Hines, Z. 2010 (West Ham U) 2
Hinshelwood, P. A. 1978 (Crystal Palace) 2
Hirst, D. E. 1988 (Sheffield W) 7
Hislop, N. S. 1998 (Newcastle U) 1
Hoddle, G. 1977 (Tottenham H) 12
Hodge, S. B. 1983 (Nottingham F, Aston Villa) 8
Hodgson, D. J. 1981 (Middlesbrough) 6
Holding, R. S. 2016 (Bolton W, Arsenal) 5
Holdsworth, D. 1989 (Watford) 1
Holgate, M. 2017 (Everton) 6
Holland, C. J. 1995 (Newcastle U) 10
Holland, P. 1995 (Mansfield T) 4
Holloway, D. 1998 (Sunderland) 1
Horne, B. 1989 (Millwall) 5
Howe, E. J. F. 1998 (Bournemouth) 2
Howson, J. M. 2011 (Leeds U) 1
Hoyte, J. R. 2004 (Arsenal) 18
Hucker, P. 1984 (QPR) 2
Huckerby, D. 1997 (Coventry C) 4
Huddlestone, T. A. 2005 (Derby Co, Tottenham H) 33
Hudson-Odoi, C. J. 2020 (Chelsea) 9
Hughes, S. J. 1997 (Arsenal) 8
Hughes, W. J. 2012 (Derby Co) 22
Humphreys, R. J. 1997 (Sheffield W) 3
Hunt, N. B. 2004 (Bolton W) 10

Ibe, J. A. F. 2015 (Liverpool) 4
Impey, A. R. 1993 (QPR) 1
Ince, P. E. C. 1989 (West Ham U) 2
Ince, T. C. 2012 (Blackpool, Hull C) 18
Ings, D. W. J. 2013 (Burnley) 13
Iorfa, D. 2016 (Wolverhampton W) 13

Jackson, M. A. 1992 (Everton) 10
Jagielka, P. N. 2003 (Sheffield U) 6
James, D. B. 1991 (Watford) 10
James, J. C. 1990 (Luton T) 2
James, R. 2020 (Chelsea) 2
Jansen, M. B. 1999 (Crystal Palace, Blackburn R) 6
Jeffers, F. 2000 (Everton, Arsenal) 16
Jemson, N. B. 1991 (Nottingham F) 1
Jenas, J. A. 2002 (Newcastle U) 9
Jenkinson, C. D. 2013 (Arsenal) 14
Jerome, C. 2006 (Cardiff C, Birmingham C) 10
Joachim, J. K. 1994 (Leicester C) 9
John-Jules, T. R. 2022 (Arsenal) 2
Johnson, A. 2008 (Middlesbrough) 19
Johnson, B. A. 2022 (West Ham U) 4
Johnson, G. M. C. 2003 (West Ham U, Chelsea) 14
Johnson, M. 2008 (Manchester C) 2
Johnson, S. A. M. 1999 (Crewe Alex, Derby Co, Leeds U) 15
Johnson, T. 1991 (Notts Co, Derby Co) 7
Johnston, C. P. 1981 (Middlesbrough) 2
Jones, C. J. 2021 (Liverpool) 12
Jones, D. R. 1977 (Everton) 1
Jones, C. H. 1978 (Tottenham H) 1
Jones, D. F. L. 2004 (Manchester U) 1
Jones, P. A. 2011 (Blackburn R) 9
Jones, R. 1993 (Liverpool) 2
Justin, J. M. 2020 (Leicester C) 8

Kane, H. E. 2013 (Tottenham H) 14
Keane, M. V. 2013 (Manchester U, Burnley) 16
Keane, W. D. 2012 (Manchester U) 3
Keegan, G. A. 1977 (Manchester C) 1
Kelly, L. C. 2019 (Bournemouth) 10
Kelly, M. R. 2011 (Liverpool) 8
Kenny, J. 2018 (Everton) 16
Kenny, W. 1993 (Everton) 1
Keown, M. R. 1987 (Aston Villa) 8
Kerslake, D. 1986 (QPR) 1
Kightly, M. J. 2008 (Wolverhampton W) 7
Kilcline, B. 1983 (Notts C) 2
Kilgallon, M. 2004 (Leeds U) 5
King, A. E. 1977 (Everton) 2
King, L. B. 2000 (Tottenham H) 12
Kirkland, C. E. 2001 (Coventry C, Liverpool) 8
Kitson, P. 1991 (Leicester C, Derby Co) 7
Knight, A. 1983 (Portsmouth) 2
Knight, I. 1987 (Sheffield W) 2
Knight, Z. 2002 (Fulham) 4
Konchesky, P. M. 2002 (Charlton Ath) 15
Konsa, E. 2018 (Charlton Ath, Brentford) 7
Kozluk, R. 1998 (Derby Co) 2

Lake, P. 1989 (Manchester C) 5
Lallana, A. D. 2009 (Southampton) 1
Lampard, F. J. 1998 (West Ham U) 19
Lamptey, T. K. N.-L. 2021 (Brighton & HA) 2
Langley, T. W. 1978 (Chelsea) 1
Lansbury, H. G. 2010 (Arsenal, Nottingham F) 16
Lascellas, J. 2014 (Newcastle U) 2
Leadbitter, G. 2008 (Sunderland) 3
Lee, D. J. 1990 (Chelsea) 10
Lee, R. M. 1986 (Charlton Ath) 2
Lee, S. 1981 (Liverpool) 6
Lees, T. J. 2012 (Leeds U) 6
Lennon, A. J. 2006 (Tottenham H) 5
Le Saux, G. P. 1990 (Chelsea) 4
Lescott, J. P. 2003 (Wolverhampton W) 2
Lewis, J. P. 2008 (Peterborough U) 5
Lewis-Potter, K. W. 2022 (Hull C) 4
Lingard, J. E. 2013 (Manchester U) 11
Lita, L. H. 2005 (Bristol C, Reading) 9
Livramento, V. F. 2022 (Southampton) 5
Loach, S. J. 2009 (Watford) 14
Loftus-Cheek, R. I. 2015 (Chelsea) 17
Lookman, A. 2018 (Everton) 11
Lowe, D. 1988 (Ipswich T) 2
Lowe, J. J. 2012 (Blackburn R) 11
Lukic, J. 1981 (Leeds U) 7
Lund, G. 1985 (Grimsby T) 3

McAtee, J. J. 2022 (Manchester C) 1
McCall, S. H. 1981 (Ipswich T) 6
McCarthy, A. S. 2011 (Reading) 3
McDonald, N. 1987 (Newcastle U) 5
McEachran, J. M. 2011 (Chelsea) 13
McEveley, J. 2003 (Blackburn R) 1
McGrath, L. 1986 (Coventry C) 1
MacKenzie, S. 1982 (WBA) 3
McLeary, A. 1988 (Millwall) 1
McLeod, I. M. 2006 (Milton Keynes D) 1
McMahon, S. 1981 (Everton, Aston Villa) 6
McManaman, S. 1991 (Liverpool) 7

McNeil, D. J. M. 2020 (Burnley) 10
McQueen, S. J. 2017 (Southampton) 1
Mabbutt, G. 1982 (Bristol R, Tottenham H) 7
Maddison, J. D. 2018 (Norwich C, Leicester C) 9
Madueke, C. T. (Noni) 2021 (PSV Eindhoven) 4
Maguire, J. H. 2012 (Sheffield U) 1
Maitland-Niles, A. C. 2018 (Arsenal) 4
Makin, C. 1994 (Oldham Ath) 5
Mancienne, M. I. 2008 (Chelsea) 30
March, S. B. 2015 (Brighton & HA) 3
Marney, D. E. 2005 (Tottenham H) 1
Marriott, A. 1992 (Nottingham F) 1
Marsh, S. T. 1998 (Oxford U) 1
Marshall, A. J. 1995 (Norwich C) 4
Marshall, B. 2012 (Leicester C) 2
Marshall, L. K. 1999 (Norwich C) 1
Martin, L. 1989 (Manchester U) 2
Martyn, A. N. 1988 (Bristol R) 11
Matteo, D. 1994 (Liverpool) 4
Mattock, J. W. 2008 (Leicester C) 5
Matthew, D. 1990 (Chelsea) 9
Mawson, A. R. J. 2017 (Swansea C) 6
May, A. 1986 (Manchester C) 1
Mee, B. 2011 (Manchester C) 2
Merson, P. C. 1989 (Arsenal) 4
Middleton, J. 1977 (Nottingham F, Derby Co) 3
Miller, A. 1988 (Arsenal) 4
Mills, D. J. 1999 (Charlton Ath, Leeds U) 14
Mills, G. R. 1981 (Nottingham F) 2
Milner, J. P. 2004 (Leeds U, Newcastle U, Aston Villa) 46
Mimms, R. 1985 (Rotherham U, Everton) 3
Minto, S. C. 1991 (Charlton Ath) 6
Mitchell, J. 2017 (Derby Co) 1
Mola, C. 2022 (VfB Stuttgart) 1
Moore, I. 1996 (Tranmere R, Nottingham F) 7
Moore, L. 2012 (Leicester C) 10
Moore, L. I. 2006 (Aston Villa) 5
Moran, S. 1982 (Southampton) 2
Morgan, S. 1987 (Leicester C) 2
Morris, J. 1997 (Chelsea) 7
Morrison, R. R. 2013 (West Ham U) 4
Mortimer, P. 1989 (Charlton Ath) 2
Moses, A. P. 1997 (Barnsley) 2
Moses, R. M. 1981 (WBA, Manchester U) 8
Moses, V. 2011 (Wigan Ath) 1
Mount, M. T. 2019 (Chelsea) 4
Mountfield, D. 1984 (Everton) 1
Muamba, F. N. 2008 (Birmingham C, Bolton W) 33
Muggleton, C. D. 1990 (Leicester C) 1
Mullins, H. I. 1999 (Crystal Palace) 3
Murphy, D. B. 1998 (Liverpool) 4
Murphy, Jacob K. 2017 (Norwich C) 6
Murray, P. 1997 (QPR) 4
Murray, M. W. 2003 (Wolverhampton W) 5
Musiala, J. 2021 (Bayern Munich) 2
Mutch, A. 1989 (Wolverhampton W) 1
Mutch, J. J. E. S. 2011 (Birmingham C) 1
Myers. A. 1995 (Chelsea) 4

Naughton, K. 2009 (Sheffield U, Tottenham H) 9
Naylor, L. M. 2000 (Wolverhampton W) 3
Nelson, R. L. 2019 (Arsenal) 12
Nethercott, S. H. 1994 (Tottenham H) 8
Neville, P. J. 1995 (Manchester U) 7
Newell, M. 1986 (Luton T) 4
Newton, A. L. 2001 (West Ham U) 1
Newton, E. J. I. 1993 (Chelsea) 2
Newton, S. O. 1997 (Charlton Ath) 3
Nicholls, A. 1994 (Plymouth Arg) 1
Nketiah, E. K. 2018 (Arsenal) 17
Nmecha, L. 2018 (Manchester C) 3
Noble, M. J. 2007 (West Ham U) 20
Nolan, K. A. J. 2003 (Bolton W) 1
Nugent, D. J. 2006 (Preston NE) 14

Oakes, M. C. 1994 (Aston Villa) 6
Oakes, S. J. 1993 (Luton T) 1
Oakley, M. 1997 (Southampton) 4
O'Brien, A. J. 1999 (Bradford C) 1
O'Connor, J. 1996 (Everton) 3
O'Hara, J. D. 2008 (Tottenham H) 7
Ojo, O. B. (Sheyi) 2018 (Liverpool) 1
Oldfield, D. 1989 (Luton T) 1
Olney, I. A. 1990 (Aston Villa) 10
O'Neil, G. P. 2005 (Portsmouth) 9
Onomah, J. O. P. 2017 (Tottenham H) 8
Onuoha, C. 2006 (Manchester C) 21
Ord, R. J. 1991 (Sunderland) 3
Osman, R. C. 1979 (Ipswich T) 7
Owen, G. A. 1977 (Manchester C, WBA) 22
Owen, M. J. 1998 (Liverpool) 1
Oxlade-Chamberlain, A. M. D. 2011 (Southampton, Arsenal) 8

Painter, I. 1986 (Stoke C) 1
Palmer, C. J. 2022 (Manchester C) 4
Palmer, C. L. 1989 (Sheffield W) 4
Palmer, K. R. 2016 (Chelsea) 6
Panzo, J. W. 2020 (Monaco) 5
Parker, G. 1986 (Hull C, Nottingham F) 6
Parker, P. A. 1985 (Fulham) 8
Parker, S. M. 2001 (Charlton Ath) 12
Parkes, P. B. F. 1979 (QPR) 1
Parkin, S. 1987 (Stoke C) 5
Parlour, R. 1992 (Arsenal) 12
Parnaby, S. 2003 (Middlesbrough) 4
Peach, D. S. 1977 (Southampton) 6
Peake, A. 1982 (Leicester C) 1
Pearce, I. A. 1995 (Blackburn R) 3
Pearce, S. 1987 (Nottingham F) 1
Pearce, T. M. 2018 (Leeds U) 2
Pennant, J. 2001 (Arsenal) 24
Pickering N. 1983 (Sunderland, Coventry C) 15
Pickford, J. L. 2015 (Sunderland) 14
Platt, D. 1988 (Aston Villa) 3
Plummer, C. S. 1996 (QPR) 5
Pollock, J. 1995 (Middlesbrough) 3
Porter, G. 1987 (Watford) 12
Potter, G. S. 1997 (Southampton) 1
Powell, N. E. 2012 (Manchester U) 2
Pressman, K. 1989 (Sheffield W) 1
Pritchard, A. D. 2014 (Tottenham H) 9
Proctor, M. 1981 (Middlesbrough, Nottingham F) 4
Prutton, D. T. 2001 (Nottingham F, Southampton) 25
Purse, D. J. 1998 (Birmingham C) 2

Quashie, N. F. 1997 (QPR) 4
Quinn, W. R. 1998 (Sheffield U) 2

Ramage, C. D. 1991 (Derby Co) 3
Ramsdale, A. C. 2018 (Bournemouth) 15
Ramsey, J. M. 2022 (Aston Villa) 7
Ranson, R. 1980 (Manchester C) 10
Rashford, M. 2017 (Manchester U) 1
Redknapp, J. F. 1993 (Liverpool) 19
Redmond, N. D. J. 2013 (Birmingham C, Norwich C, Southampton) 38
Redmond, S. 1988 (Manchester C) 14
Reeves, K. P. 1978 (Norwich C, Manchester C) 10
Regis, C. 1979 (WBA) 6
Reid, N. S. 1981 (Manchester C) 6
Reid, P. 1977 (Bolton W) 6
Reo-Coker, N. S. A. 2004 (Wimbledon, West Ham U) 23
Richards, D. I. 1995 (Wolverhampton W) 4
Richards, J. P. 1977 (Wolverhampton W) 2
Richards, M. 2007 (Manchester C) 15
Richards, M. L. 2005 (Ipswich T) 1
Richards, O. T. C. 2020 (Reading) 1
Richardson, K. E. 2005 (Manchester U) 12
Rideout, P. 1985 (Aston Villa, Bari) 5
Ridgewell, L. M. 2004 (Aston Villa) 8
Riggott, C. M. 2001 (Derby Co) 8
Ripley, S. E. 1988 (Middlesbrough) 8
Ritchie, A. 1982 (Brighton & HA) 1
Rix, G. 1978 (Arsenal) 7
Roberts, A. J. 1995 (Millwall, Crystal Palace) 5
Roberts, B. J. 1997 (Middlesbrough) 1
Robins, M. G. 1990 (Manchester U) 6
Robinson, J. 2012 (Liverpool, QPR) 10
Robinson, P. P. 1999 (Watford) 3
Robinson, P. W. 2000 (Leeds U) 11
Robson, B. 1979 (WBA) 7
Robson, S. 1984 (Arsenal, West Ham U) 8
Rocastle, D. 1987 (Arsenal) 14
Roche, L. P. 2001 (Manchester U) 1
Rodger, G. 1987 (Coventry C) 4

Rodriguez, J. E. 2011 (Burnley) 1
Rodwell, J. 2009 (Everton) 21
Rogers, A. 1998 (Nottingham F) 3
Rosario, R. 1987 (Norwich C) 4
Rose, D. L. 2009 (Tottenham H) 29
Rose, M. 1997 (Arsenal) 2
Rosenior, L. J. 2005 (Fulham) 7
Routledge, W. 2005 (Crystal Palace, Tottenham H) 12
Rowell, G. 1977 (Sunderland) 1
Rudd, D. T. 2013 (Norwich C) 1
Ruddock, N. 1989 (Southampton) 4
Rufus, R. R. 1996 (Charlton Ath) 6
Ryan, J. 1983 (Oldham Ath) 1
Ryder, S. H. 1995 (Walsall) 3

Saka, B. A. T. M. 2021 (Arsenal) 1
Samuel, J. 2002 (Aston Villa) 7
Samways, V. 1988 (Tottenham H) 5
Sansom, K. G. 1979 (Crystal Palace) 8
Scimeca, R. 1996 (Aston Villa) 9
Scowcroft, J. B. 1997 (Ipswich T) 5
Seaman, D. A. 1985 (Birmingham C) 10
Sears, F. D. 2010 (West Ham U) 3
Sedgley, S. 1987 (Coventry C, Tottenham H) 11
Sellars, S. 1988 (Blackburn R) 3
Selley, I. 1994 (Arsenal) 3
Serrant, C. 1998 (Oldham Ath) 2
Sessegnon, K. R. (Ryan) 2018 (Fulham, Tottenham H) 18
Sessegnon, Z. S. (Steven) 2020 (Fulham) 5
Sharpe, L. S. 1989 (Manchester U) 8
Shaw, L. P. H. 2013 (Southampton, Manchester U) 5
Shaw, G. R. 1981 (Aston Villa) 7
Shawcross, R. J. 2008 (Stoke C) 2
Shearer, A. 1991 (Southampton) 11
Shelton, G. 1985 (Sheffield W) 1
Shelvey, J. 2012 (Liverpool, Swansea C) 13
Sheringham, E. P. 1988 (Millwall) 1
Sheron, M. N. 1992 (Manchester C) 16
Sherwood, T. A. 1990 (Norwich C) 4
Shipperley, N. J. 1994 (Chelsea, Southampton) 7
Sidwell, S. J. 2003 (Reading) 5
Simonsen, S. P. A. 1998 (Tranmere R, Everton) 4
Simpson, J. B. 2019 (Bournemouth) 1
Simpson, P. 1986 (Manchester C) 5
Sims, S. 1977 (Leicester C) 10
Sinclair, S. A. 2011 (Swansea C) 7
Sinclair, T. 1994 (QPR, West Ham U) 5
Sinnott, L. 1985 (Watford) 1
Skipp, O. W. 2020 (Tottenham H) 14
Slade, S. A. 1996 (Tottenham H) 4
Slater, S. I. 1990 (West Ham U) 3
Small, B. 1993 (Aston Villa) 12
Smalling, C. L. 2010 (Fulham, Manchester U) 14
Smith, A. 2000 (Leeds U) 10
Smith, A. J. 2012 (Tottenham H) 11
Smith, D. 1988 (Coventry C) 10
Smith, M. 1981 (Sheffield W) 5
Smith, M. 1995 (Sunderland) 1
Smith, T. W. 2001 (Watford) 1
Smith Rowe, E. 2021 (Arsenal) 7
Snodin, I. 1985 (Doncaster R) 4
Soares, T. J. 2006 (Crystal Palace) 4
Solanke, D. A. 2015 (Chelsea, Liverpool, Bournemouth) 18
Sordell, M. A. 2012 (Watford, Bolton W) 14
Spence, D. T. D.-H. 2022 (Middlesbrough) 3
Spence, J. 2011 (West Ham U) 1
Stanislaus, F. J. 2010 (West Ham U) 2
Statham, B. 1988 (Tottenham H) 3
Statham, D. J. 1978 (WBA) 6
Stead, J. G. 2004 (Blackburn R, Sunderland) 11
Stearman, R. J. 2009 (Wolverhampton W) 4
Steele, J. 2011 (Middlesbrough) 7
Stein, B. 1984 (Luton T) 3
Stephens, J. 2015 (Southampton) 8
Sterland, M. 1984 (Sheffield W) 7
Sterling, R. S. 2012 (Liverpool) 8
Steven, T. M. 1985 (Everton) 2
Stevens, G. A. 1983 (Brighton & HA, Tottenham H) 8
Stewart, J. 2003 (Leicester C) 1
Stewart, P. 1988 (Manchester C) 1
Stockdale, R. K. 2001 (Middlesbrough) 1
Stones, J. 2013 (Everton) 12
Stuart, G. C. 1990 (Chelsea) 5
Stuart, J. C. 1996 (Charlton Ath) 4
Sturridge, D. A. 2010 (Chelsea) 15
Suckling, P. 1986 (Coventry C, Manchester C, Crystal Palace) 10
Summerbee, N. J. 1993 (Swindon T) 3
Sunderland, A. 1977 (Wolverhampton W) 1
Surman, A. R. E. 2008 (Southampton) 4
Surridge, S. W. 2020 (Bournemouth) 3
Sutch, D. 1992 (Norwich C) 4
Sutton, C. R. 1993 (Norwich C) 13
Swift, J. D. 2015 (Chelsea, Reading) 13
Swindlehurst, D. 1977 (Crystal Palace) 1

Talbot, B. 1977 (Ipswich T) 1
Tangana, J. M. 2021 (Tottenham H) 2
Targett, M. R. 2015 (Southampton) 12
Taylor, A. D. 2007 (Middlesbrough) 13
Taylor, M. 2001 (Blackburn R) 1
Taylor, M. S. 2003 (Portsmouth) 3
Taylor, R. A. 2006 (Wigan Ath) 4
Taylor, S. J. 2002 (Arsenal) 3
Taylor, S. V. 2004 (Newcastle U) 29
Terry, J. G. 2001 (Chelsea) 9
Thatcher, B. D. 1996 (Millwall, Wimbledon) 4
Thelwell, A. A. 2001 (Tottenham H) 1
Thirlwell, P. 2001 (Sunderland) 1
Thomas, D. 1981 (Coventry C, Tottenham H) 7
Thomas, J. W. 2006 (Charlton Ath) 2
Thomas, L. J. 2022 (Leicester C) 8
Thomas, M. 1986 (Luton T) 3
Thomas, M. L. 1988 (Arsenal) 12
Thomas, R. E. 1990 (Watford) 1
Thompson, A. 1995 (Bolton W) 2
Thompson, D. A. 1997 (Liverpool) 7
Thompson, G. L. 1981 (Coventry C) 6
Thorn, A. 1988 (Wimbledon) 5
Thornley, B. L. 1996 (Manchester U) 3
Thorpe, T. J. 2013 (Manchester U) 1
Tiler, C. 1990 (Barnsley, Nottingham F) 13
Tomkins, J. O. C. 2009 (West Ham U) 10
Tomori, O. O. (Fikayo) 2018 (Chelsea) 15
Tonge, M. W. E. 2004 (Sheffield U) 2
Townsend, A. D. 2012 (Tottenham H) 3
Trafford, J. 2022 (Manchester C) 1
Trippier, K. J. 2011 (Manchester C) 2
Tuanzebe, A. 2018 (Manchester U) 1

Unsworth, D. G. 1995 (Everton) 6
Upson, M. J. 1999 (Arsenal) 11

Vassell, D. 1999 (Aston Villa) 11
Vaughan, J. O. 2007 (Everton) 4
Venison, B. 1983 (Sunderland) 10
Vernazza, P. A. P. 2001 (Arsenal, Watford) 2
Vieria, R. A. 2018 (Leeds U) 3
Vinnicombe, C. 1991 (Rangers) 12

Waddle, C. R. 1985 (Newcastle U) 1
Waghorn, M. T. 2012 (Leicester C) 5
Walcott, T. J. 2007 (Arsenal) 21
Wallace, D. L. 1983 (Southampton) 14
Wallace, Ray 1989 (Southampton) 4
Wallace, Rod 1989 (Southampton) 11
Walker, D. 1985 (Nottingham F) 7
Walker, I. M. 1991 (Tottenham H) 9
Walker, K. 2010 (Tottenham H) 7
Walker-Peters, K. L. 2018 (Tottenham H) 11
Walsh, G. 1988 (Manchester U) 2
Walsh, P. A. 1983 (Luton T) 4
Walters, K. 1984 (Aston Villa) 9
Walton, C. T. 2017 (Brighton & HA) 1
Wan Bissaka, A. 2019 (Crystal Palace) 3
Ward, P. 1978 (Brighton & HA) 2
Ward-Prowse, J. M. E. 2013 (Southampton) 31
Warhurst, P. 1991 (Oldham Ath, Sheffield W) 8
Watmore, D. I. 2015 (Sunderland) 13
Watson, B. 2007 (Crystal Palace) 1
Watson, D. 1984 (Norwich C) 7
Watson, D. N. 1994 (Barnsley) 5
Watson, G. 1991 (Sheffield W) 2
Watson, S. C. 1993 (Newcastle U) 12
Weaver, N. J. 2000 (Manchester C) 10

Webb, N. J. 1985 (Portsmouth, Nottingham F) 3
Welbeck, D. 2009 (Manchester U) 14
Welsh, J. J. 2004 (Liverpool, Hull C) 8
Wheater, D. J. 2008 (Middlesbrough) 11
Whelan, P. J. 1993 (Ipswich T) 3
Whelan, N. 1995 (Leeds U) 2
Whittingham, P. 2004 (Aston Villa, Cardiff C) 17
White, D. 1988 (Manchester C) 6
Whyte, C. 1982 (Arsenal) 4
Wickham, C. N. R. 2011 (Ipswich T, Sunderland) 17
Wicks, S. 1982 (QPR) 1
Wilkins, R. C. 1977 (Chelsea) 1
Wilkinson, P. 1985 (Grimsby T, Everton) 4
Williams, B. P. B. 2021 (Manchester U) 1
Williams, D. 1998 (Sunderland) 2
Williams, P. 1989 (Charlton Ath) 4
Williams, P. D. 1991 (Derby Co) 6
Williams, R. 2021 (Liverpool) 2
Williams, S. C. 1977 (Southampton) 14
Willock, J. G. 2020 (Arsenal) 4
Wilmot, B. L. 2020 (Watford) 4
Wilshere, J. A. 2010 (Arsenal) 7
Wilson, C. E. G. 2014 (Bournemouth) 1
Wilson, J. A. 2015 (Manchester U) 1
Wilson, M. A. 2001 (Manchester U, Middlesbrough) 6
Winks, H. 2017 (Tottenham H) 2
Winterburn, N. 1986 (Wimbledon) 1
Wisdom, A. 2012 (Liverpool) 10
Wise, D. F. 1988 (Wimbledon) 1
Woodcook, A. S. 1978 (Nottingham F) 2
Woodgate, J. S. 2000 (Leeds U) 1
Woodhouse, C. 1999 (Sheffield U) 4
Woodman, F. J. 2017 (Newcastle U) 6
Woodrow, C. 2014 (Fulham) 9
Woods, C. C. E. 1979 (Nottingham F, QPR, Norwich C) 6
Worrall, J. A. 2018 (Nottingham F) 3
Wright, A. G. 1993 (Blackburn R) 2
Wright, M. 1983 (Southampton) 4
Wright, R. I. 1997 (Ipswich T) 15
Wright, S. J. 2001 (Liverpool) 10
Wright, W. 1979 (Everton) 6
Wright-Phillips, S. C. 2002 (Manchester C) 6

Yates, D. 1989 (Notts Co) 5
Young, A. S. 2007 (Watford, Aston Villa) 10
Young, L. P. 1999 (Tottenham H, Charlton Ath) 12

Zaha, D. W. A. 2012 (Crystal Palace, Manchester U) 13
Zamora, R. L. 2002 (Brighton & HA) 6

NORTHERN IRELAND

Allen, C. 2009 (Lisburn Distillery) 1
Allen, C. S. 2022 (Leeds U) 2
Amos, D. 2019 (Doncaster R) 7
Anderson, H. 2022 (Portadown) 1
Armstrong, D. T. 2007 (Hearts) 1

Baggley (Crowe), B. T. 2021 (Fleetwood T) 6
Bagnall, L. 2011 (Sunderland) 1
Bailie, N. 1990 (Linfield) 2
Baird, C. P. 2002 (Southampton) 6
Ball, D. 2013 (Tottenham H) 2
Ball, M. 2011 (Norwich C) 5
Ballard, D. G. 2019 (Arsenal) 3
Balmer, K. 2019 (Ballymena U, Larne) 20
Bansal-McNulty, A. P. S. 2021 (QPR) 2
Beatty, S. 1990 (Chelsea, Linfield) 2
Berry, D. 2022 (Norwich C) 1
Bird, P. M. 2019 (Notts Co) 4
Black, J. 2003 (Tottenham H) 1
Black, K. T. 1990 (Luton T) 1
Black, R. Z. 2002 (Morecambe) 1
Blackledge, G. 1978 (Portadown) 1
Blake, R. G. 2011 (Brentford) 2
Blayney, A. 2003 (Southampton) 4
Bonis, L. 2021 (Portadown) 2
Boyd-Munce, C. S. 2019 (Birmingham C) 19
Boyce, L. 2010 (Cliftonville, Werder Bremen) 8
Boyle, D. M. 2021 (Fleetwood T) 3
Boyle, W. S. 1998 (Leeds U) 7
Braniff, K. R. 2002 (Millwall) 11
Breeze, J. 2011 (Wigan Ath) 4
Brennan, C. 2013 (Kilmarnock) 13
Brobbel, R. 2013 (Middlesbrough) 9
Brotherston, N. 1978 (Blackburn R) 1
Brown, C. M. 2020 (Cardiff C) 4
Browne, G. 2003 (Manchester C) 5
Brunt, C. 2005 (Sheffield W) 2
Bryan, M. A. 2010 (Watford) 4
Buchanan, D. T. H. 2006 (Bury) 15
Buchanan, W. B. 2002 (Bolton W, Lisburn Distillery) 5
Burns, A. 2014 (Linfield) 1
Burns, R. (Bobby) 2018 (Glenavon, Hearts, Barrow) 12
Burns, L. 1998 (Port Vale) 13

Callaghan, A. 2006 (Limavady U, Ballymena U, Derry C) 15
Campbell, S. 2003 (Ballymena U) 1
Camps, C. 2015 (Rochdale) 1
Capaldi, A. C. 2002 (Birmingham C, Plymouth Arg) 14
Carlisle, W. T. 2000 (Crystal Palace) 9
Carroll, R. E. 1998 (Wigan Ath) 11
Carson, J. G. 2011 (Ipswich T, York C) 12
Carson, S. 2000 (Rangers, Dundee U) 2
Carson, T. 2007 (Sunderland) 15
Carvill, M. D. 2008 (Wrexham, Linfield) 8
Casement, C. 2007 (Ipswich T, Dundee) 18
Cathcart, C. 2007 (Manchester U) 15
Catney, R. 2007 (Lisburn Distillery) 1
Chapman, A. 2008 (Sheffield U, Oxford U) 7
Charles, D. 2017 (Fleetwood T) 3
Charles, S. E. 2022 (Manchester C) 3
Clarke, L. 2003 (Peterborough U) 4
Clarke, R. 2006 (Newry C) 7
Clarke, R. D. J. 1999 (Portadown) 5
Clingan, S. G. 2003 (Wolverhampton W, Nottingham F) 11
Close, B. 2002 (Middlesbrough) 10
Clucas, M. S. 2011 (Preston NE, Bristol R) 11
Clyde, M. G. 2002 (Wolverhampton W) 5
Colligan, L. 2009 (Ballymena U) 1
Conlan, L. 2013 (Burnley, Morecambe) 11
Conn-Clarke, C. S. M. 2021 (Fleetwood T) 6
Connell, T. E. 1978 (Coleraine) 1
Cooper, J. 2015 (Glenavon) 5
Coote, A. 1998 (Norwich C) 12
Convery, J. 2000 (Celtic) 4
Cousin-Dawson, F. 2021 (Bradford C) 7

Dallas, S. 2012 (Crusaders, Brentford) 2
Davey, H. 2004 (UCD) 3
Davis, S. 2004 (Aston Villa) 3
Daws, M. 2022 (Bournemouth) 1
Devine, D. 1994 (Omagh T) 1
Devine, D. G. 2011 (Preston NE) 2
Devine, J. 1990 (Glentoran) 1
Devlin, C. 2011 (Manchester U, unattached, Cliftonville) 11
Devlin, T. 2022 (Dungannon Swifts 3
Dickson, H. 2002 (Wigan Ath) 1
Doherty, B. 2018 (Derry C) 4
Doherty, J. E. 2014 (Watford, Leyton O, Crawley T) 6
Doherty, M. 2007 (Hearts) 2
Dolan, J. 2000 (Millwall) 6
Donaghy, M. M. 1978 (Larne) 1
Donnelly, A. 2021 (Nottingham F) 12
Donnelly, L. F. P. 2012 (Fulham, Hartlepool U, Motherwell) 23
Donnelly, M. 2007 (Sheffield U, Crusaders) 5
Donnelly, R. 2013 (Swansea C) 1
Dowie, I. 1990 (Luton T) 1
Drummond, W. 2011 (Rangers) 2
Dudgeon, J. P. 2010 (Manchester U) 4
Duff, S. 2003 (Cheltenham T) 1
Duffy, M. 2014 (Derry C, Celtic) 9
Duffy, S. P. M. 2010 (Everton) 3
Dummigan, C. 2014 (Burnley, Oldham Ath) 18
Dunne, D. 2019 (Cliftonville) 1
Dunwoody, J. 2017 (Stoke C, Derry C, Helsinki IFK) 16

Elliott, S. 1999 (Glentoran) 3
Ervin, J. 2005 (Linfield) 2
Evans, C. J. 2009 (Manchester U) 10
Evans, J. 2006 (Manchester U) 3

Feeney, L. 1998 (Linfield, Rangers) 8
Feeney, W. 2002 (Bournemouth) 8
Ferguson, M. 2000 (Glentoran) 2
Ferguson, S. 2009 (Newcastle U) 11
Ferris, C. 2020 (Portadown) 1
Finlayson, D. 2019 (Rangers) 3
Fitzgerald, D. 1998 (Rangers) 4
Flanagan, T. M. 2012 (Milton Keynes D) 1
Flynn, J. J. 2009 (Blackburn R, Ross Co) 11
Fordyce, D. T. 2007 (Portsmouth, Glentoran) 12
Friars, E. C. 2005 (Notts Co) 7
Friars, S. M. 1998 (Liverpool, Ipswich T) 21

Galbraith, E. S. W. 2019 (Manchester U) 20
Gallagher, C. 2019 (Glentoran) 5
Garrett, R. 2007 (Stoke C, Linfield) 14
Gartside, N. J. 2020 (Derry C) 2
Gault, M. 2005 (Linfield) 2
Gibb, S. 2009 (Falkirk, Drogheda U) 2
Gilfillan, B. J. 2005 (Gretna, Peterhead) 9
Gillespie, K. R. 1994 (Manchester U) 1
Glendinning, M. 1994 (Bangor) 1
Glendinning, R. 2012 (Linfield) 3
Gordon, S. M. 2017 (Motherwell, Partick Thistle) 9
Gorman, D. A. 2015 (Stevenage, Leyton Orient) 13
Gorman, R. J. 2012 (Wolverhampton W, Leyton Orient) 4
Graham, G. L. 1999 (Crystal Palace) 5
Graham, R. S. 1999 (QPR) 15
Graham, S. 2020 (Blackpool) 2
Gray, J. P. 2012 (Accrington S) 11
Gray, P. 1990 (Luton T) 1
Griffin, D. J. 1998 (St Johnstone) 10
Grigg, W. D. 2011 (Walsall) 10

Hall, B. 2018 (Notts Co) 3
Hamilton, G. 2000 (Blackburn R, Portadown) 12
Hamilton, W. R. 1978 (Linfield) 1
Hanley, N. 2011 (Linfield) 1
Harkin, M. P. 2000 (Wycombe W) 9
Harney, J. J. 2014 (West Ham U) 1
Harvey, J. 1978 (Arsenal) 1
Hawe, S. 2001 (Blackburn R) 2
Hayes, T. 1978 (Luton T) 1
Hazard, C. 2019 (Celtic) 12
Hazley, M. 2007 (Stoke C) 3
Healy, D. J. 1999 (Manchester U) 8
Hegarty, C. 2011 (Rangers) 7
Herron, C. J. 2003 (QPR) 2
Higgins, R. 2006 (Derry C) 1
Hodson, L. J. S. 2010 (Watford) 10
Holden, R. 2019 (Bristol C) 2
Holmes, S. 2000 (Manchester C, Wrexham) 13
Howland, D. 2007 (Birmingham C) 4
Hughes, J. 2006 (Lincoln C) 7
Hughes, L. 2020 (Celtic, Liverpool) 6
Hughes, M. A. 2003 (Tottenham H, Oldham Ath) 12
Hughes, M. E. 1990 (Manchester C) 1
Hume, T. 2021 (Linfield, Sunderland) 9
Hunter, M. 2002 (Glentoran) 1

Ingham, M. G. 2001 (Sunderland) 4

Jarvis, D. 2010 (Aberdeen) 2
Johns, C. 2014 (Southampton) 1
Johnson, D. M. 1998 (Blackburn R) 11
Johnson, R. A. 2015 (Stevenage) 13
Johnston, B. 1978 (Cliftonville) 1
Johnston, C. R. 2021 (Fleetwood T) 6
Julian, A. A. 2005 (Brentford) 1

Kane, A. M. 2008 (Blackburn R) 5
Kane, M. 2012 (Glentoran) 1
Kee, B. R. 2010 (Leicester C, Torquay U, Burton Alb) 10
Kee, P. V. 1990 (Oxford U) 1
Kelly, D. 2000 (Derry C) 11
Kelly, J. 2019 (Maidenhead U) 2
Kelly, N. 1990 (Oldham Ath) 1
Kennedy, B. J. 2017 (Stevenage) 8
Kennedy, M. C. P. 2015 (Charlton Ath) 7
Kerr, N. 2019 (Glentoran, Portadown) 6
Kirk, A. R. 1999 (Hearts) 9
Knowles, J. 2012 (Blackburn R) 2

Lafferty, D. 2009 (Celtic) 6
Lafferty, K. 2006 (Burnley) 2
Lane, P. J. 2022 (Fleetwood T) 6
Larkin, R. 2021 (Linfield) 2
Lavery, C. 2011 (Ipswich T, Sheffield W) 7
Lavery, S. 2017 (Everton, Linfield) 13
Lawrie, J. 2009 (Port Vale, AFC Telford U) 9
Lennon, N. F. 1990 (Manchester C, Crewe Alex) 2
Lester, C. 2013 (Bolton W) 1
Lewis, J. 2017 (Norwich C) 1
Lindsay, K. 2006 (Larne) 1
Little, A. 2009 (Rangers) 6
Lowry, P. 2009 (Institute, Linfield) 6
Lund, M. 2011 (Stoke C) 6
Lyttle, G. 1998 (Celtic, Peterborough U) 8

McAlinden, L. J. 2012 (Wolverhampton W) 3
McAllister, M. 2007 (Dungannon Swifts) 4
McArdle, R. A. 2006 (Sheffield W, Rochdale) 19
McAreavey, P. 2000 (Swindon T) 7
McBride, J. 1994 (Glentoran) 1
McCaffrey, D. 2006 (Hibernian) 8
McCallion, E. 1998 (Coleraine) 1
McAlmont, A. J. 2019 (Leeds U) 16
McCann, A. 2020 (St Johnstone) 6
McCann, C. L. 2022 (Rangers) 2
McCann, G. S. 2000 (West Ham U) 11
McCann, L. 2020 (Dunfermline Ath) 5
McCann, P. 2003 (Portadown) 1
McCann, R. 2002 (Rangers, Linfield) 2
McCartan, S. V. 2013 (Accrington S) 9
McCartney, G. 2001 (Sunderland) 5
McCashin, S. 2011 (Jerez Industrial, unattached) 2
McCausland, R. 2022 (Rangers) 1
McChrystal, M. 2005 (Derry C) 9
McClean, J. 2010 (Derry C) 3
McClean, K. 2019 (St Johnstone, Linfield) 7
McClelland, K. 2022 (Rangers) 2
McClelland, S. 2022 (Chelsea) 7
McClure, M. 2012 (Wycombe W) 1
McCourt, P. J. 2002 (Rochdale, Derry C) 8
McCoy, R. K. 1990 (Coleraine) 1
McCreery, D. 1978 (Manchester U) 1
McCullough, L. 2013 (Doncaster R) 8
McDaid, R. 2015 (Leeds U) 5
McDermott, C. 2017 (Derry C) 4
McDonagh, J. D. C. 2015 (Sheffield U, Derry C) 9
McEleney, S. 2012 (Derry C) 2
McElroy, P. 2013 (Hull C) 1
McEvilly, L. R. 2003 (Rochdale) 9
McFlynn, T. M. 2000 (QPR, Woking, Margate) 19
McGeehan, C. 2013 (Norwich C) 3
McGibbon, P. C. G. 1994 (Manchester U) 1
McGivern, R. 2010 (Manchester C) 6
McGlinchey, B. 1998 (Manchester C, Port Vale, Gillingham) 14
McGonigle, J. 2017 (Coleraine) 4
McGovern, J. 2022 (Newry C) 8
McGovern, M. 2005 (Celtic) 10
McGowan, M. V. 2006 (Clyde) 2
McGuckin, C. R. 2022 (Rotherham U) 2
McGurk, A. 2010 (Aston Villa) 1
McIlroy, T. 1994 (Linfield) 1
McKay, W. 2009 (Leicester C, Northampton T) 7
McKee, C. 2022 (Linfied) 4
McKenna, K. 2007 (Tottenham H) 6
McKeown, R. 2012 (Kilmarnock) 12
McKiernan, JJ. 2021 (Watford) 2
McKnight, D. 2015 (Shrewsbury T, Stalybridge Celtic) 5
McKnight, P. 1998 (Rangers) 3
McLaughlin, C. G. 2010 (Preston NE, Fleetwood T) 7
McLaughlin, P. 2010 (Newcastle U, York C) 10
McLaughlin, R. 2012 (Liverpool, Oldham Ath) 6
McLean, B. S. 2006 (Rangers) 1
McLean, J. 2009 (Derry C) 4
McLellan, M. 2012 (Preston NE) 1
McMahon, G. J. 2002 (Tottenham H) 1
McMenamin, L. A. 2009 (Sheffield W) 4

McNair, P. J. C. 2014 (Manchester U) 2
McNally, P. 2013 (Celtic) 1
McQuilken, J. 2009 (Tescoma Zlin) 1
McQuoid, J. J. B. 2009 (Bournemouth) 8
McVeigh, A. 2002 (Ayr U) 1
McVeigh, P. M. 1998 (Tottenham H) 11
McVey, K. 2006 (Coleraine) 8
Magee, J. 1994 (Bangor) 1
Magee, J. 2009 (Lisburn Distillery) 1
Magennis, J. B. D. 2010 (Cardiff C, Aberdeen) 16
Magilton, J. 1990 (Liverpool) 1
Magnay, C. 2010 (Chelsea) 1
Maloney, L. 2015 (Middlesbrough) 6
Marron, C. 2020 (Glenavon) 9
Marshall, R. 2017 (Glenavon) 1
Matthews, N. P. 1990 (Blackpool) 1
Mee, D. 2021 (Manchester U) 4
Meenan, D. 2007 (Finn Harps, Monaghan U) 3
Melaugh, G. M. 2002 (Aston Villa, Glentoran) 11
Millar, K. S. 2011 (Oldham Ath, Linfield) 11
Millar, W. P. 1990 (Port Vale) 1
Miskelly, D. T. 2000 (Oldham Ath) 10
Mitchell, A. 2012 (Rangers) 3
Mitchell, C. 2017 (Burnley) 10
Moreland, V. 1978 (Glentoran) 1
Morgan, D. 2012 (Nottingham F) 4
Morgan, M. P. T. 1999 (Preston NE) 1
Morris, E. J. 2002 (WBA, Glentoran) 8
Morrison, O. 2001 (Sheffield W, Sheffield U) 7
Morrow, A. 2001 (Northampton T) 1
Morrow, S. 2005 (Hibernian) 4
Mulgrew, J. 2007 (Linfield) 10
Mulryne, P. P. 1999 (Manchester U, Norwich C) 5
Murray, W. 1978 (Linfield) 1
Murtagh, C. 2005 (Hearts) 1

Nicholl, J. M. 1978 (Manchester U) 1
Nixon, C. 2000 (Glentoran) 1
Nolan, L. J. 2014 (Crewe Alex, Southport) 4
Norwood, O. J. 2010 (Manchester U) 11

O'Connor, M. J. 2008 (Crewe Alex) 3
O'Hara, G. 1994 (Leeds U) 1
O'Kane, E. 2009 (Everton, Torquay U) 4
O'Mahony, J. 2020 (Glenavon) 1
O'Neill, J. P. 1978 (Leicester C) 1
O'Neill, M. A. M. 1994 (Hibernian) 1
O'Neill, P. 2020 (Glentoran, Cliftonville) 10
O'Neill, S. 2009 (Ballymena U) 4
Owens, C. 2018 (QPR) 2

Palmer, C. 2019 (Rangers, Linfield) 10
Parkhouse, D. 2017 (Sheffield U) 16
Paterson, M. A. 2007 (Stoke C) 2
Patterson, D. J. 1994 (Crystal Palace) 1
Paul, C. D. 2017 (QPR) 3
Peacock-Farrell, B. 2018 (Leeds U) 1
Price, I. J. 2022 (Everton) 2

Quigley, C. 2017 (Dundee) 2
Quinn, S. J. 1994 (Blackpool) 1

Ramsey, C. 2011 (Portadown) 3
Ramsey, K. 2006 (Institute) 1
Reid, J. T. 2013 (Exeter C) 2
Robinson, H. D. 2020 (Motherwell) 1
Robinson, S. 1994 (Tottenham H) 1
Rooney, L. J. 2017 (Plymouth Arg) 1
Roy, A. 2019 (Derry C) 2

Scott, A. 2021 (Larne) 1
Scott, J. 2020 (Wolverhampton W) 14
Scullion, D. 2006 (Dungannon Swifts) 8
Sendles-White J. 2013 (QPR, Hamilton A) 12
Sharpe, R. 2013 (Derby Co, Notts Co) 6
Shiels, D. 2005 (Hibernian) 6
Shields, S. P. 2013 (Dagenham & R) 2
Shroot, R. 2009 (Harrow B, Birmingham C) 4
Simms, G. 2001 (Hartlepool U) 14
Singleton, J. 2015 (Glenavon) 2
Skates, G. 2000 (Blackburn R) 4
Sloan, T. 1978 (Ballymena U) 1
Smylie, D. 2006 (Newcastle U, Livingston) 6
Smyth, O. 2021 (Dunganon Swifts, Oxford U) 9
Smyth, P. 2017 (Linfield, QPR) 12
Stewart, J. 2015 (Swindon T) 2
Stewart, S. 2009 (Aberdeen) 1
Stewart, S. 2021 (Norwich C) 5
Stewart, T. 2006 (Wolverhampton W, Linfield) 19
Sykes, M. 2017 (Glenavon) 10

Taylor, D. 2021 (Nottingham F) 7
Taylor, J. 2007 (Hearts, Glentoran) 10
Taylor, M. S. 1998 (Fuham) 1
Teggart, N. 2005 (Sunderland) 2
Tempest, G. 2013 (Notts Co) 6
Thompson, A. L. 2011 (Watford) 11
Thompson, J. 2017 (Rangers, Blackpool) 13
Thompson, L. 2020 (Blackburn R) 6
Thompson, P. 2006 (Linfield) 4
Toal, E. 2019 (Derry C) 13
Toner, C. 2000 (Tottenham H, Leyton Orient) 17
Tuffey, J. 2007 (Partick Thistle) 13
Turner, C. 2007 (Sligo R, Bohemians) 12

Waide, R. 2021 (Ballymena U) 7
Ward, J. J. 2006 (Aston Villa, Chesterfield) 7
Ward, M. 2006 (Dungannon Swifts) 1
Ward, S. 2005 (Glentoran) 10
Waterman, D. G. 1998 (Portsmouth) 14
Waterworth, A. 2008 (Lisburn Distillery, Hamilton A) 7
Webb, S. M. 2004 (Ross Co, St Johnstone, Ross Co) 6
Webber, O. H. 2021 (Crystal Palace, Portsmouth) 4
Weir, R. J. 2009 (Sunderland) 8
Wells, D. P. 1999 (Barry T) 1
Whitley, J. 1998 (Manchester C) 17
Whyte, G. 2015 (Crusaders) 7
Willis, P. 2006 (Liverpool) 1
Winchester, C. 2011 (Oldham Ath) 13
Winchester, J. 2013 (Kilmarnock) 1
Wylie, B. 2021 (Celtic) 1

SCOTLAND

Adam, C. G. 2006 (Rangers) 5
Adam, G. 2011 (Rangers) 6
Adams, J. 2007 (Kilmarnock) 1
Aitken, R. 1977 (Celtic) 16
Albiston, A. 1977 (Manchester U) 5
Alexander, N. 1997 (Stenhousemuir, Livingston) 10
Allan, S. 2012 (WBA) 10
Anderson, E. 2022 (Newcastle U) 1
Anderson, I. 1997 (Dundee, Toulouse) 15
Anderson, M. 2022 (Dundee) 1
Anderson, R. 1997 (Aberdeen) 15
Andrews, M. 2011 (East Stirlingshire) 1
Anthony, M. 1997 (Celtic) 3
Archdeacon, O. 1987 (Celtic) 1
Archer, J. G. 2012 (Tottenham H) 14
Archibald, A. 1998 (Partick Thistle) 5
Archibald, S. 1980 (Aberdeen, Tottenham H) 5
Archibald, T. V. 2018 (Brentford) 1
Arfield, S. 2008 (Falkirk, Huddersfield T) 17
Armstrong, S. 2011 (Dundee U) 20
Ashby, H. C. 2021 (West Ham U) 4

Bagen, D. 1997 (Kilmarnock) 4
Bain, K. 1993 (Dundee) 4
Baker, M. 1993 (St Mirren) 10
Baltacha, S. S. 2000 (St Mirren) 3
Banks, S. B. 2021 (Crystal Palace) 7
Bannan, B. 2009 (Aston Villa) 10
Bannigan, S. 2013 (Partick Thistle) 3
Bannon, E. J. 1979 (Hearts, Chelsea, Dundee U) 7
Barclay, J. 2011 (Falkirk) 1
Barron, C. 2022 (Aberdeen) 3
Bates, C. 2019 (Hamburg) 4
Beattie, C. 2004 (Celtic) 7
Beattie, J. 1992 (St Mirren) 4
Beaumont, D. 1985 (Dundee U) 1
Bell, D. 1981 (Aberdeen) 2
Bernard, P. R. J. 1992 (Oldham Ath) 15

Berra, C. 2005 (Hearts) 6
Bett, J. 1981 (Rangers) 7
Black, E. 1983 (Aberdeen) 8
Blair, A. 1980 (Coventry C, Aston Villa) 5
Bollan, G. 1992 (Dundee U, Rangers) 17
Bonar, P. 1997 (Raith R) 4
Booth, C. 2011 (Hibernian) 4
Booth, S. 1991 (Aberdeen) 14
Bowes, M. J. 1992 (Dunfermline Ath) 1
Bowie, K. 2021 (Norwich C) 1
Bowman, D. 1985 (Hearts) 1
Boyack, S. 1997 (Rangers) 1
Boyd, K. 2003 (Kilmarnock) 8
Boyd, T. 1987 (Motherwell) 5
Brandon, J. 2019 (Hearts) 2
Brazil, A. 1978 (Hibernian) 1
Brazil, A. 1979 (Ipswich T) 8
Brebner, G. I. 1997 (Manchester U, Reading, Hibernian) 18
Brighton, T. 2005 (Rangers, Clyde) 7
Broadfoot, K. 2005 (St Mirren) 5
Brophy, E. 2017 (Hamilton A, Kilmarnock) 3
Brough, J. 1981 (Hearts) 1
Brown, A. H. 2004 (Hibernian) 1
Brown, S. 2005 (Hibernian) 10
Browne, P. 1997 (Raith R) 1
Bryson, C. 2006 (Clyde) 1
Buchan, J. 1997 (Aberdeen) 13
Burchill, M. J. 1998 (Celtic) 15
Burke, A. 1997 (Kilmarnock) 4
Burke, C. 2004 (Rangers) 3
Burke, O. J. 2018 (WBA) 9
Burley, C. W. 1992 (Chelsea) 7
Burley, G. E. 1977 (Ipswich T) 5
Burns, H. 1985 (Rangers) 2
Burns, T. 1977 (Celtic) 5
Burroughs, J. S. 2021 (Coventry C) 8
Burt, L. 2017 (Rangers) 5

Cadden, C. 2017 (Motherwell) 12
Caddis, P. 2008 (Celtic, Dundee U, Celtic, Swindon T) 13
Cairney, T. 2011 (Hull C) 6
Caldwell, G. 2000 (Newcastle U) 19
Caldwell, S. 2001 (Newcastle U) 4
Cameron, G. 2008 (Dundee U) 3
Cameron, K. M. 2017 (Newcastle U) 3
Campbell, A. 2018 (Motherwell) 24
Campbell, J. 2022 (Hibernian) 2
Campbell, R. 2008 (Hibernian) 6
Campbell, S. 1989 (Dundee) 3
Campbell, S. P. 1998 (Leicester C) 15
Canero, P. 2000 (Kilmarnock) 17
Cardwell, H. 2014 (Reading) 1
Carey, L. A. 1998 (Bristol C) 1
Carrick, D. 2012 (Hearts) 1
Casey, J. 1978 (Celtic) 1
Chalmers, J. 2014 (Celtic, Motherwell) 2
Chalmers, L. 2021 (Dundee U) 3
Christie, M. 1992 (Dundee) 3
Christie, R. 2014 (Inverness CT, Celtic) 9
Clark, R. B. 1977 (Aberdeen) 3
Clarke, S. 1984 (St Mirren) 8
Clarkson, D. 2004 (Motherwell) 13
Clayton, T. 2021 (Liverpool) 5
Cleland, A. 1990 (Dundee U) 11
Cole, D. 2011 (Rangers) 2
Collins, J. 1988 (Hibernian) 8
Collins, N. 2005 (Sunderland) 7
Connolly, P. 1991 (Dundee U) 3
Connor, R. 1981 (Ayr U) 2
Conroy, R. 2007 (Celtic) 4
Considine, A. 2007 (Aberdeen) 5
Cooper, D. 1977 (Clydebank, Rangers) 6
Cooper, N. 1982 (Aberdeen) 13
Coutts, P. A. 2009 (Peterborough U, Preston NE) 7
Crabbe, S. 1990 (Hearts) 2
Craig, M. 1998 (Aberdeen) 2
Craig, T. 1977 (Newcastle U) 1
Crainey, S. D. 2000 (Celtic) 7
Crainie, D. 1983 (Celtic) 1
Crawford, S. 1994 (Raith R) 19
Creaney, G. 1991 (Celtic) 11
Cummings, J. 2015 (Hibernian) 8
Cummings, W. 2000 (Chelsea) 8
Cuthbert, S. 2007 (Celtic, St Mirren) 13

Dailly, C. 1991 (Dundee U) 34
Dalglish, P. 1999 (Newcastle U, Norwich C) 6
Dargo, C. 1998 (Raith R) 10
Davidson, C. I. 1997 (St Johnstone) 2
Davidson, H. N. 2000 (Dundee U) 3
Davidson, M. 2011 (St Johnstone) 1
Dawson, A. 1979 (Rangers) 8
Deas, P. A. 1992 (St Johnstone) 2
Deas, R. 2021 (Inverness CT) 1
Dempster, J. 2004 (Rushden & D) 1
Dennis, S. 1992 (Raith R) 1
Diamond, A. 2004 (Aberdeen) 12
Dickov, P. 1992 (Arsenal) 4
Dixon, P. 2008 (Dundee) 2
Docherty, G. 2017 (Hamilton A) 4
Dodds, D. 1978 (Dundee U) 1
Dods, D. 1997 (Hibernian) 5
Doig, C. R. 2000 (Nottingham F) 13
Doig, J. 2022 (Hibernian) 6
Donald, G. S. 1992 (Hibernian) 3
Donnelly, S. 1994 (Celtic) 11
Doohan, R. 2018 (Celtic) 13
Dorrans, G. 2007 (Livingston) 6
Dow, A. 1993 (Dundee, Chelsea) 3
Dowie, A. J. 2003 (Rangers, Partick Thistle) 14
Duff, J. 2009 (Inverness CT) 1
Duff, S. 2003 (Dundee U) 9
Duffie, K. 2011 (Falkirk) 6
Duffy, D. A. 2005 (Falkirk, Hull C) 8
Duffy, J. 1987 (Dundee) 1
Durie, G. S. 1987 (Chelsea) 4
Durrant, I. 1987 (Rangers) 4
Doyle, J. 1981 (Partick Thistle) 2

Easton, B. 2009 (Hamilton A) 3
Easton, C. 1997 (Dundee U) 21
Edwards, M. 2012 (Rochdale) 1
Elliot, B. 1998 (Celtic) 2
Elliot, C. 2006 (Hearts) 9
Erhahon, E. 2021 (St Mirren) 2
Esson, R. 2000 (Aberdeen) 7

Fagan, S. M. 2005 (Motherwell) 1
Ferguson, B. 1997 (Rangers) 12
Ferguson, D. 1987 (Rangers) 5
Ferguson, D. 1992 (Dundee U) 7
Ferguson, D. 1992 (Manchester U) 5
Ferguson, I. 1983 (Dundee) 4
Ferguson, I. 1987 (Clyde, St Mirren, Rangers) 6
Ferguson, L. 2019 (Aberdeen) 11
Ferguson, R. 1977 (Hamilton A) 1
Feruz, I. 2012 (Chelsea) 4
Findlay, S. 2012 (Celtic) 13
Findlay, W. 1991 (Hibernian) 5
Fiorini, L. 2021 (Manchester C) 5
Fitzpatrick, A. 1977 (St Mirren) 5
Fitzpatrick, M. 2007 (Motherwell) 4
Flannigan, C. 1993 (Clydebank) 1
Fleck, J. 2009 (Rangers) 4
Fleck, R. 1987 (Rangers, Norwich C) 6
Fleming, G. 2008 (Gretna) 1
Fletcher, D. B. 2003 (Manchester U) 2
Fletcher, S. 2007 (Hibernian) 7
Forrest, A. 2017 (Ayr U) 1
Forrest, J. 2011 (Celtic) 4
Foster, R. M. 2005 (Aberdeen) 5
Fotheringham, M. M. 2004 (Dundee) 3
Fowler, J. 2002 (Kilmarnock) 3
Foy, R. A. 2004 (Liverpool) 5
Fraser, M. 2012 (Celtic) 5
Fraser, R. 2013 (Aberdeen, Bournemouth) 10
Fraser, S. T. 2000 (Luton T) 4
Freedman, D. A. 1995 (Barnet, Crystal Palace) 8
Freeman, K. E. 2022 (Dundee U) 2
Fridge, L. 1989 (St Mirren) 2
Fullarton, J. 1993 (St Mirren) 17
Fulton, J. 2014 (Swansea C) 2
Fulton, R. 2017 (Liverpool, Hamilton A) 11
Fulton, M. 1980 (St Mirren) 5

Fulton, S. 1991 (Celtic) 7
Fyvie, F. 2012 (Wigan Ath) 8

Gallacher, K. W. 1987 (Dundee U) 7
Gallacher, P. 1999 (Dundee U) 7
Gallacher, S. 2009 (Rangers) 2
Gallagher, P. 2003 (Blackburn R) 11
Galloway, M. 1989 (Hearts, Celtic) 2
Gardiner, J. 1993 (Hibernian) 1
Gauld, R. 2013 (Dundee U, Sporting Lisbon) 11
Geddes, R. 1982 (Dundee) 5
Gemmill, S. 1992 (Nottingham F) 4
Germaine, G. 1997 (WBA) 1
Gilles, R. 1997 (St Mirren) 7
Gillespie, G. T. 1979 (Coventry C) 8
Gilmour, B. C. 2019 (Chelsea) 13
Glass, S. 1995 (Aberdeen) 11
Glover, L. 1988 (Nottingham F) 3
Goodwillie, D. 2009 (Dundee U) 9
Goram, A. L. 1987 (Oldham Ath) 1
Gordon, C. S. 2003 (Hearts) 5
Gough, C. R. 1983 (Dundee U) 5
Graham, D. 1998 (Rangers) 8
Graham, R. J. 2022 (Dundee U) 3
Grant, P. 1985 (Celtic) 10
Gray, D. P. 2009 (Manchester U) 2
Gray, S. 1987 (Aberdeen) 1
Gray S. 1995 (Celtic) 7
Griffiths, L. 2010 (Dundee, Wolverhampton W) 11
Grimmer, J. 2014 (Fulham) 1
Gunn, B. 1984 (Aberdeen) 9

Hagen, D. 1992 (Rangers) 8
Hamill, J. 2008 (Kilmarnock) 11
Hamilton, B. 1989 (St Mirren) 4
Hamilton, C. 2018 (Hearts) 3
Hamilton, J. 1995 (Dundee, Hearts) 14
Hamilton, J. 2014 (Hearts) 8
Hammell, S. 2001 (Motherwell) 11
Handling, D. 2014 (Hibernian) 3
Handyside, P. 1993 (Grimsby T) 7
Hanley, G. 2011 (Blackburn R) 1
Hanlon, P. 2009 (Hibernian) 23
Hannah, D. 1993 (Dundee U) 16
Hardie, R. 2017 (Rangers) 8
Harper, C. 2021 (Inverness CT) 1
Harper, K. 1995 (Hibernian) 7
Hartford, R. A. 1977 (Manchester C) 1
Hartley, P. J. 1997 (Millwall) 1
Harvie, D. W. 2018 (Aberdeen, Ayr U) 15
Hastie, J. 2019 (Motherwell) 1
Hegarty, P. 1987 (Dundee U) 6
Henderson, E. 2020 (Celtic) 1
Henderson, J. 2022 (St Mirren) 1
Henderson, L. 2015 (Celtic) 9
Hendrie, S. 2014 (West Ham U) 3
Hendry, J. 1992 (Tottenham H) 1
Henly, J. 2014 (Reading) 1
Herron, J. 2012 (Celtic) 2
Hetherston, B. 1997 (St Mirren) 1
Hewitt, J. 1982 (Aberdeen) 6
High, S. J. 2022 (Huddersfield T) 7
Hogg, G. 1984 (Manchester U) 4
Holsgrove, J. 2019 (Reading) 5
Holt, J. 2012 (Hearts) 7
Hood, G. 1993 (Ayr U) 3
Horn, R. 1997 (Hearts) 6
Hornby, F. D. I. 2018 (Everton, Reims) 18
House, B. 2019 (Reading) 1
Howie, S. 1993 (Cowdenbeath) 5
Hughes, R. D. 1999 (Bournemouth) 9
Hughes, S. 2002 (Rangers) 12
Hunter, G. 1987 (Hibernian) 3
Hunter, P. 1989 (East Fife) 3
Hutton, A. 2004 (Rangers) 7
Hutton, K. 2011 (Rangers) 1
Hyam, D. J. 2014 (Reading) 5

Iacovitti, A. 2017 (Nottingham F) 4
Inman, B. 2011 (Newcastle U) 2
Irving, A. 2021 (Hearts) 1
Irvine, G. 2006 (Celtic) 2

Jack, R. 2012 (Aberdeen) 19
James, K. F. 1997 (Falkirk) 1
Jardine, I. 1979 (Kilmarnock) 1
Jess, E. 1990 (Aberdeen) 14
Johnson, G. I. 1992 (Dundee U) 6
Johnston, A. 1994 (Hearts) 3
Johnston, F. 1993 (Falkirk) 1
Johnston, G. 2019 (Liverpool, Feyenoord) 10
Johnston, M. 1984 (Partick Thistle, Watford) 3
Johnston, M. A. 2018 (Celtic) 7
Jones, J. C. 2017 (Crewe Alex) 4
Jordan, A. J. 2000 (Bristol C) 3
Joseph, K. A. 2021 (Wigan Ath) 1
Jules, Z. K. 2017 (Reading) 3
Jupp, D. A. 1995 (Fulham) 9

Kelly, L. A. 2017 (Reading) 11
Kelly, S. 2014 (St Mirren) 1
Kelly, S. 2020 (Rangers) 11
Kennedy, J. 2003 (Celtic) 15
Kennedy, K. A. 2022 (Rangers) 1
Kennedy, M. 2012 (Kilmarnock) 1
Kenneth, G. 2008 (Dundee U) 8
Kerr, B. 2003 (Newcastle U) 14
Kerr, F. 2012 (Birmingham C) 3
Kerr, J. 2018 (St Johnstone) 6
Kerr, M. 2001 (Kilmarnock) 1
Kerr, S. 1993 (Celtic) 10
Kettings, C. D. 2012 (Blackpool) 3
King, A. 2014 (Swansea C) 1
King, C. M. 2014 (Norwich C) 1
King, L. T. 2022 (Rangers) 1
King, W. 2015 (Hearts) 8
Kingsley, S. 2015 (Swansea C) 6
Kinnear, B. 2021 (Rangers) 2
Kinniburgh, W. D. 2004 (Motherwell) 3
Kirkwood, D. 1990 (Hearts) 1
Kyle, K. 2001 (Sunderland) 12

Lambert, P. 1991 (St Mirren) 11
Langfield, J. 2000 (Dundee) 2
Lappin, S. 2004 (St Mirren) 10
Lauchlan, J. 1998 (Kilmarnock) 11
Lavety, B. 1993 (St Mirren) 9
Lavin, G. 1993 (Watford) 7
Lawson, P. 2004 (Celtic) 10
Leighton, J. 1982 (Aberdeen) 1
Lennon, S. 2008 (Rangers) 6
Leonard, M. H. 2022 (Brighton & HA) 7
Levein, C. 1985 (Hearts) 2
Leven, P. 2005 (Kilmarnock) 2
Liddell, A. M. 1994 (Barnsley) 12
Lindsey, J. 1979 (Motherwell) 1
Locke, G. 1994 (Hearts) 10
Love, D. 2015 (Manchester U) 5
Love, G. 1995 (Hibernian) 1
Loy, R. 2009 (Dunfermline Ath, Rangers) 5
Lynch, S. 2003 (Celtic, Preston NE) 13

McAllister, G. 1990 (Leicester C) 1
McAllister, K. 2019 (Derby Co, St Mirren) 2
McAllister, R. 2008 (Inverness CT) 2
McAlpine, H. 1983 (Dundee U) 5
McAnespie, K. 1998 (St Johnstone) 4
McArthur, J. 2008 (Hamilton A) 2
McAuley, S. 1993 (St Johnstone) 1
McAvennie, F. 1982 (St Mirren) 5
McBride, J. 1981 (Everton) 1
McBride, J. P. 1998 (Celtic) 2
McBurnie, O. 2015 (Swansea C) 12
McCabe, R. 2012 (Rangers, Sheffield W) 3
McCall, A. S. M. 1988 (Bradford C, Everton) 2
McCann, K. 2008 (Hibernian) 4
McCann, N. 1994 (Dundee) 9
McCart, J. 2017 (Celtic) 1
McClair, B. 1984 (Celtic) 8
McCluskey, G. 1979 (Celtic) 6
McCluskey, S. 1997 (St Johnstone) 14
McCoist, A. 1984 (Rangers) 1
McConnell, I. 1997 (Clyde) 1
McCormack, D. 2008 (Hibernian) 1
McCormack, R. 2006 (Rangers, Motherwell, Cardiff C) 13
McCracken, D. 2002 (Dundee U) 5

McCrorie, Robby 2018 (Rangers) 7
McCrorie, Ross 2017 (Rangers) 20
McCulloch, A. 1981 (Kilmarnock) 1
McCulloch, I. 1982 (Notts Co) 2
McCulloch, L. 1997 (Motherwell) 14
McCunnie, J. 2001 (Dundee U, Ross Co, Dunfermline Ath) 20
MacDonald, A. 2011 (Burnley) 6
MacDonald, C. 2017 (Derby Co) 2
MacDonald, J. 1980 (Rangers) 8
MacDonald, J. 2007 (Hearts) 11
McDonald, C. 1995 (Falkirk) 5
McDonald, K. 2008 (Dundee, Burnley) 14
McEwan, C. 1997 (Clyde, Raith R) 17
McEwan, D. 2003 (Livingston) 2
McFadden, J. 2003 (Motherwell) 7
McFadzean C. 2015 (Sheffield U) 3
McFarlane, D. 1997 (Hamilton A) 3
McGarry, S. 1997 (St Mirren) 3
McGarvey, F. P. 1977 (St Mirren, Celtic) 3
McGarvey, S. 1982 (Manchester U) 4
McGeough, D. 2012 (Celtic) 10
McGhee, J. 2013 (Hearts) 20
McGhee, M. 1981 (Aberdeen) 1
McGinn, J. 2014 (St Mirren, Hibernian) 9
McGinn, S. 2009 (St Mirren, Watford) 8
McGinnis, G. 1985 (Dundee U) 1
McGlinchey, M. R. 2007 (Celtic) 1
McGregor, A. 2003 (Rangers) 6
McGregor, C. W. 2013 (Celtic) 5
McGrillen, P. 1994 (Motherwell) 2
McGuire, D. 2002 (Aberdeen) 2
McHattie, K. 2012 (Hearts) 6
McInally, J. 1989 (Dundee U) 1
McInroy, K. 2021 (Celtic) 1
McIntyre, T. P. 2019 (Reading) 3
McKay, B. 2012 (Rangers) 4
McKay, B. 2013 (Hearts) 1
McKean, K. 2011 (St Mirren) 1
McKenna, S. 2018 (Aberdeen) 5
McKenzie, R. 2013 (Kilmarnock) 4
McKenzie, R. 1997 (Hearts) 2
McKimmie, S. 1985 (Aberdeen) 3
McKinlay, T. 1984 (Dundee) 6
McKinlay, W. 1989 (Dundee U) 6
McKinnon, R. 1991 (Dundee U) 6
McLaren, A, 1989 (Hearts) 11
McLaren, A. 1993 (Dundee U) 4
McLaughlin, B. 1995 (Celtic) 8
McLaughlin, J. 1981 (Morton) 10
McLean, E. 2008 (Dundee U, St Johnstone) 2
McLean, S. 2003 (Rangers) 4
McLeish, A. 1978 (Aberdeen) 6
McLean, K. 2012 (St Mirren) 11
McLennon, C. 2020 (Aberdeen) 9
MacLeod, A. 1979 (Hibernian) 3
McLeod, J. 1989 (Dundee U) 2
MacLeod, L. 2012 (Rangers) 8
MacLeod, M. 1979 (Dumbarton, Celtic) 5
McManus, D. J. 2014 (Aberdeen, Fleetwood T) 4
McManus, T. 2001 (Hibernian) 14
McMillan, S. 1997 (Motherwell) 4
McMullan, P. 2017 (Celtic) 1
McNab, N. 1978 (Tottenham H) 1
McNally, M. 1991 (Celtic) 2
McNamara, J. 1994 (Dunfermline Ath, Celtic) 12
McNaughton, K. 2002 (Aberdeen) 1
McNeil, A. 2007 (Hibernian) 1
McNichol, J. 1979 (Brentford) 7
McNiven, D. 1977 (Leeds U) 3
McNiven, S. A. 1996 (Oldham Ath) 1
McPake, J. 2021 (Rangers) 1
McParland, A. 2003 (Celtic) 1
McPhee, S. 2002 (Port Vale) 1
McPherson, D. 1984 (Rangers, Hearts) 4
McQuilken, J. 1993 (Celtic) 2
McStay, P. 1983 (Celtic) 5
McWhirter, N. 1991 (St Mirren) 1
MacGregor, R. 2021 (Inverness CT) 1
Mackay, D. 2021 (Inverness CT, Hibernian) 2
Mackay-Steven, G. 2012 (Dundee U) 3
Mackie, S. 2019 (Hibernian) 1
Magennis, K. 2019 (St Mirren) 5
Maguire, B. 2019 (Motherwell) 10
Maguire, C. 2009 (Aberdeen) 12
Main, A. 1988 (Dundee U) 3
Mair, A. 2021 (Norwich C) 2
Malcolm, R. 2001 (Rangers) 1
Mallan, S. 2017 (St Mirren, Barnsley, St Mirren) 9
Maloney, S. 2002 (Celtic) 21
Malpas, M. 1983 (Dundee U) 8
Marr, B. 2011 (Ross Co) 1
Marshall, D. J. 2004 (Celtic) 10
Marshall, S. R. 1995 (Arsenal) 5
Martin, A. 2009 (Leeds U, Ayr U) 12
Mason, G. R. 1999 (Manchester C, Dunfermline Ath) 2
Mathieson, D. 1997 (Queen of the South) 3
May, E. 1989 (Hibernian) 2
May, S. 2013 (St Johnstone, Sheffield W) 8
Mayo, L. 2021 (Rangers) 12
Mebude, A. P. O. A. (Dapo) 2022 (Watford) 5
Meldrum, C. 1996 (Kilmarnock) 6
Melrose, J. 1977 (Partick Thistle) 8
Middleton, G. B. D. 2018 (Rangers) 23
Millar, M, 2009 (Celtic) 1
Miller, C. 1995 (Rangers) 8
Miller, J. 1987 (Aberdeen, Celtic) 7
Miller, K. 2000 (Hibernian, Rangers) 7
Miller, W. 1991 (Hibernian) 7
Miller, W. F. 1978 (Aberdeen) 2
Milne, K. 2000 (Hearts) 1
Milne, R. 1982 (Dundee U) 3
Mitchell, C. 2008 (Falkirk) 7
Money, I. C. 1987 (St Mirren) 3
Montgomery, A. 2022 (Celtic) 3
Montgomery, N. A. 2003 (Sheffield U) 2
Morgan, L. 2017 (Celtic) 9
Morrison, S. A. 2004 (Aberdeen, Dunfermline Ath) 12
Muir, L. 1977 (Hibernian) 1
Mulgrew, C. P. 2006 (Celtic, Wolverhampton W, Aberdeen) 14
Mulligan, J. 2022 (Dundee) 2
Murphy J. 2009 (Motherwell) 13
Murray, H. 2000 (St Mirren) 3
Murray, I. 2001 (Hibernian) 15
Murray, N. 1993 (Rangers) 16
Murray, R. 1993 (Bournemouth) 1
Murray, S. 2004 (Kilmarnock) 2

Narey, D. 1977 (Dundee U) 4
Naismith, J. 2014 (St Mirren) 1
Naismith, S. J. 2006 (Kilmarnock, Rangers) 15
Naysmith, G. A. 1997 (Hearts) 22
Neilson, R. 2000 (Hearts) 1
Nesbitt, A. 2017 (Celtic) 2
Ness, J, 2011 (Rangers) 2
Nevin, P. 1985 (Chelsea) 5
Nicholas, C. 1981 (Celtic, Arsenal) 6
Nicholson, B. 1999 (Rangers) 7
Nicholson, S. 2015 (Hearts) 8
Nicol, S. 1981 (Ayr U, Liverpool) 14
Nisbet, S. 1989 (Rangers) 5
Noble, D. J. 2003 (West Ham U) 2
Notman, A. M. 1999 (Manchester U) 10

O'Brien, B. 1999 (Blackburn R, Livingston) 6
O'Connor, G. 2003 (Hibernian) 8
O'Donnell, P. 1992 (Motherwell) 8
O'Donnell, S. 2013 (Partick Thistle) 1
O'Halloran, M. 2012 (Bolton W) 2
O'Hara, M. 2015 (Kilmarnock, Dundee) 2
O'Leary, R. 2008 (Kilmarnock) 2
O'Neil, B. 1992 (Celtic) 7
O'Neil, J. 1991 (Dundee U) 1
O'Neill, M. 1995 (Clyde) 6
Orr, N. 1978 (Morton) 7

Palmer, L. J. 2011 (Sheffield W) 8
Park, C. 2012 (Middlesbrough) 1
Parker, K. 2001 (St Johnstone) 1
Parlane, D. 1977 (Rangers) 1
Paterson, C. 1981 (Hibernian) 2
Paterson, C. 2012 (Hearts) 12
Paterson, J. 1997 (Dundee U) 9
Patterson, N. K. 2021 (Rangers) 4
Pawlett, P. 2012 (Aberdeen) 7

Payne, G. 1978 (Dundee U) 3
Peacock, L. A. 1997 (Carlisle U) 1
Pearce, A. J. 2008 (Reading) 2
Pearson, S. P. 2003 (Motherwell) 8
Perry, R. 2010 (Rangers, Falkirk, Rangers) 16
Polworth, L. 2016 (Inverness CT) 1
Porteous, R. 2018 (Hibernian) 14
Pressley, S. J. 1993 (Rangers, Coventry C, Dundee U) 26
Provan, D. 1977 (Kilmarnock) 1
Prunty, B. 2004 (Aberdeen) 6

Quinn, P. C. 2004 (Motherwell) 3
Quinn, R. 2006 (Celtic) 9
Quitongo, J. 2017 (Hamilton A) 1

Rae, A. 1991 (Millwall) 8
Rae, G. 1999 (Dundee) 6
Ralston, A. 2018 (Celtic) 5
Ramsay, C. W. 2022 (Liverpool) 3
Reading, P. J. 2020 (Stevenage) 6
Redford, I. 1981 (Rangers) 6
Reid, B. 1991 (Rangers) 4
Reid, C. 1993 (Hibernian) 3
Reid, M. 1982 (Celtic) 2
Reid, R. 1977 (St Mirren) 3
Reilly, A. 2004 (Wycombe W) 1
Renicks, S. 1997 (Hamilton A) 1
Reynolds, M. 2007 (Motherwell) 9
Rhodes, J. L. 2011 (Huddersfield T) 8
Rice, B. 1985 (Hibernian) 1
Richardson, L. 1980 (St Mirren) 2
Ridgers, M. 2012 (Hearts) 5
Riordan, D. G. 2004 (Hibernian) 5
Ritchie, A. 1980 (Morton) 1
Ritchie, P. S. 1996 (Hearts) 7
Robertson, A. 1991 (Rangers) 1
Robertson, A. 2013 (Dundee U, Hull C) 4
Robertson, C. 1977 (Rangers) 1
Robertson, C. 2012 (Aberdeen) 10
Robertson, D. 2007 (Dundee U) 4
Robertson, D. A. 1987 (Aberdeen) 7
Robertson, G. A. 2004 (Nottingham F, Rotherham U) 15
Robertson, H. 1994 (Aberdeen) 2
Robertson, J. 1985 (Hearts) 2
Robertson, L. 1993 (Rangers) 3
Robertson, S. 1998 (St Johnstone) 2
Roddie, A. 1992 (Aberdeen) 5
Ross, G. 2007 (Dunfermline Ath) 1
Ross, N. 2011 (Inverness CT) 2
Ross, T. W. 1977 (Arsenal) 1
Rowson, D. 1997 (Aberdeen) 5
Rudden, Z. A. 2022 (Partick Thistle) 3
Ruddy, J. 2017 (Wolverhampton W) 1
Russell, J. 2011 (Dundee U) 11
Russell, R. 1978 (Rangers) 3

Salton, D. B. 1992 (Luton T) 6
Sammut, R. A. M. 2017 (Chelsea) 3
Samson, C. I. 2004 (Kilmarnock) 6
Saunders, S. 2011 (Motherwell) 2
Scobbie, T. 2008 (Falkirk) 12
Scott, J. R. 2020 (Motherwell, Hull C) 3
Scott, M. 2006 (Livingston) 1
Scott, P. 1994 (St Johnstone) 4
Scougall, S. 2012 (Livingston, Sheffield U) 2
Scrimgour, D. 1997 (St Mirren) 3
Seaton, A. 1998 (Falkirk) 1
Severin, S. D. 2000 (Hearts) 10
Shankland, L. 2015 (Aberdeen) 4
Shannon, R. 1987 (Dundee) 7
Sharp, G. M. 1982 (Everton) 1
Sharp, R. 1990 (Dunfermline Ath) 4
Shaw, O. 2019 (Hibernian) 2
Sheerin, P. 1996 (Southampton) 1
Sheppard, J. 2017 (Reading) 2
Shields, G. 1997 (Rangers) 2
Shinnie, A. 2009 (Dundee, Rangers) 3
Shinnie, G. 2012 (Inverness CT) 2
Simmons, S. 2003 (Hearts) 1
Simpson, N. 1982 (Aberdeen) 11
Sinclair, G. 1977 (Dumbarton) 1
Sinclair, R. 2022 (St Johnstone) 3
Skilling, M. 1993 (Kilmarnock) 2
Slater, C. 2014 (Kilmarnock, Colchester U) 9
Slicker, C. 2021 (Manchester C) 5
Smith, B. M. 1992 (Celtic) 5
Smith, C. 2008 (St Mirren) 2
Smith, C. 2015 (Aberdeen) 1
Smith, C. 2022 (Hearts) 2
Smith, D. 2012 (Hearts) 4
Smith, D. L. 2006 (Motherwell) 2
Smith, G. 1978 (Rangers) 1
Smith, G. 2004 (Rangers) 8
Smith, H. G. 1987 (Hearts) 2
Smith, L. 2017 (Hearts, Ayr U) 12
Smith, L. 2020 (Hamilton A) 1
Smith, S. 2007 (Rangers) 1
Sneddon, A. 1979 (Celtic) 1
Snodgrass, R. 2008 (Livingston) 2
Soutar, D. 2003 (Dundee) 11
Souttar, J. 2016 (Dundee U, Hearts) 11
Speedie, D. R. 1985 (Chelsea) 1
Spencer, J. 1991 (Rangers) 3
Stanton, P. 1977 (Hibernian) 1
Stanton, S. 2014 (Hibernian) 1
Stark, W. 1985 (Aberdeen) 1
St Clair, H. 2018 (Chelsea) 3
Stephen, R. 1983 (Dundee) 1
Stevens, G. 1977 (Motherwell) 1
Stevenson, L. 2008 (Hibernian) 8
Stewart, C. 2002 (Kilmarnock) 1
Stewart, J. 1978 (Kilmarnock, Middlesbrough) 3
Stewart, M. J. 2000 (Manchester U) 17
Stewart, R. 1979 (Dundee U, West Ham U) 12
Stillie, D. 1995 (Aberdeen) 14
Storie, C. 2017 (Aberdeen) 2
Strachan, G. D. 1998 (Coventry C) 7
Sturrock, P. 1977 (Dundee U) 9
Sweeney, P. H. 2004 (Millwall) 8
Sweeney, S. 1991 (Clydebank) 7

Tapping, C. 2013 (Hearts) 1
Tarrant, N. K. 1999 (Aston Villa) 5
Taylor, G. J. 2017 (Kilmarnock) 14
Teale, G. 1997 (Clydebank, Ayr U) 6
Telfer, P. N. 1993 (Luton T) 3
Templeton, D. 2011 (Hearts) 2
Thomas, D. 2017 (Motherwell) 6
Thomas, K. 1993 (Hearts) 8
Thompson, S. 1997 (Dundee U) 12
Thomson, C. 2011 (Hearts) 2
Thomson, J. A. 2017 (Celtic) 1
Thomson, K. 2005 (Hibernian) 6
Thomson, W. 1977 (Partick Thistle, St Mirren) 10
Tolmie, J. 1980 (Morton) 1
Tortolano, J. 1987 (Hibernian) 2
Toshney, L. 2012 (Celtic) 5
Turnbull, D. 2019 (Motherwell) 4
Turner, I. 2005 (Everton) 6
Tweed, S. 1993 (Hibernian) 3

Urain, E. R. 2021 (Athletic Bilbao) 2

Wales, G. 2000 (Hearts) 1
Walker, A. 1988 (Celtic) 1
Walker, J. 2013 (Hearts) 1
Wallace, I. A. 1978 (Coventry C) 1
Wallace, L. 2007 (Hearts) 10
Wallace, M. 2012 (Hudderfield T) 4
Wallace, R. 2004 (Celtic, Sunderland) 4
Walsh, C. 1984 (Nottingham F) 5
Wark, J. 1977 (Ipswich T) 8
Watson, A. 1981 (Aberdeen) 4
Watson, K. 1977 (Rangers) 2
Watt, A. 2012 (Celtic) 9
Watt, E. 2018 (Wolverhampton W) 3
Watt, M. 1991 (Aberdeen) 12
Watt. S. M. 2005 (Chelsea) 5
Webster, A. 2003 (Hearts) 2
Welsh, S. 2021 (Celtic) 10
Whiteford, A. 1997 (St Johnstone) 1
Whittaker, S. G. 2005 (Hibernian) 18
Whyte, D. 1987 (Celtic) 9
Wighton, C. R. 2017 (Dundee) 6
Wilkie, L. 2000 (Dundee) 6
Will, J. A. 1992 (Arsenal) 3

Williams, G. 2002 (Nottingham F) 9
Williamson, B. 2021 (Rangers) 6
Williamson, R. 2018 (Dunfermline) 4
Wilson, D. 2011 (Liverpool, Hearts) 13
Wilson, I. 2018 (Kilmarnock) 7
Wilson, M. 2004 (Dundee U, Celtic) 19
Wilson, S. 1999 (Rangers) 7
Wilson, T. 1983 (St Mirren) 1
Wilson, T. 1988 (Nottingham F) 4
Winnie, D. 1988 (St Mirren) 1
Woods, M. 2006 (Sunderland) 2
Wotherspoon, D. 2011 (Hibernian) 16
Wright, K. 2021 (Rangers) 1
Wright, P. 1989 (Aberdeen, QPR) 3
Wright, Stephen 1991 (Aberdeen) 14
Wright, Scott 2018 (Aberdeen) 5
Wright, T. 1987 (Oldham Ath) 1
Wylde, G. 2011 (Rangers) 7

Young, Darren 1997 (Aberdeen) 8
Young, Derek 2000 (Aberdeen) 5

WALES

Abbruzzese, R. 2018 (Cardiff C) 3
Absolom, K. 2019 (Ostersund) 1
Adams, J. A. 2021 (Brentford, Dundalk) 10
Adams, N. W. 2008 (Bury, Leicester C) 5
Alfei, D. M. 2010 (Swansea C) 13
Aizlewood, M. 1979 (Luton T) 2
Allen, J. M. 2008 (Swansea C) 13
Anthony, B. 2005 (Cardiff C) 8
Ashworth, Z. 2022 (WBA) 1
Astley, R. 2021 (Everton) 7

Babos, A. 2018 (Derby Co) 7
Baddeley, L. M. 1996 (Cardiff C) 2
Baker, A. T. 2019 (Sheffield W) 3
Balcombe, S. 1982 (Leeds U) 1
Bale, G. 2006 (Southampton, Tottenham H) 4
Barden, D. J. 2021 (Norwich C) 2
Barnhouse, D. J. 1995 (Swansea C) 3
Basey, G. W. 2009 (Charlton Ath) 1
Bater, P. T. 1977 (Bristol R) 2
Beck, O. M. 2022 (Liverpool) 7
Beevers, L. J. 2005 (Boston U, Lincoln C) 7
Bellamy, C. D. 1996 (Norwich C) 8
Bender, T. J. 2011 (Colchester U) 4
Birchall, A. S. 2003 (Arsenal, Mansfield T) 12
Bird, A. 1993 (Cardiff C) 6
Blackmore, C. 1984 (Manchester U) 3
Blake, D. J. 2007 (Cardiff C) 14
Blake, N. A. 1991 (Cardiff C) 5
Blaney, S. D. 1997 (West Ham U) 3
Bloom, J. 2011 (Falkirk) 1
Bodin, B. P. 2010 (Swindon T, Torquay U) 21
Bodin, P. J. 1983 (Cardiff C) 1
Bond, J. H. 2011 (Watford) 1
Bowen, J. P. 1993 (Swansea C) 5
Bowen, M. R. 1983 (Tottenham H) 3
Bowen, S. L. 2021 (Cardiff C) 4
Boyes, M. M. 2021 (Liverpool, Livingston) 11
Boyle, T. 1982 (Crystal Palace) 1
Brace, D. P. 1995 (Wrexham) 6
Bradley, M. S. 2007 (Walsall) 17
Bradshaw, T. 2012 (Shrewsbury T) 8
Broadhead, N. P. 2018 (Everton) 17
Brooks, D. R. 2018 (Sheffield U) 3
Brough, M. 2003 (Notts Co) 3
Brown, J. D. 2008 (Cardiff C) 6
Brown, J. R. 2003 (Gillingham) 7
Brown, T. A. F. 2011 (Ipswich T, Rotherham U, Aldershot T) 10
Burns, W. J. 2013 (Bristol C) 18
Burton, R. L. 2018 (Arsenal) 9
Byrne, M. T. 2003 (Bolton W) 1

Cabango, B. 2019 (Swansea C) 5
Calliste, R. T. 2005 (Manchester U, Liverpool) 15
Carpenter, R. E. 2005 (Burnley) 1
Cassidy, J. A. 2011 (Wolverhampton W) 8
Cegielski, W. 1977 (Wrexham) 2
Chamberlain, E. C. 2010 (Leicester C) 9
Chapple, S. R. 1992 (Swansea C) 8
Charles, J. D. 2016 (Huddersfield T, Barnsley) 9
Charles, J. M. 1979 (Swansea C) 2
Christie-Davies, I. 2018 (Chelsea, Liverpool) 4
Church, S. R. 2008 (Reading) 15
Clark, J. 1978 (Manchester U, Derby Co) 2
Clifton, H. L. 2019 (Grimsby T) 6
Coates, J. S. 1996 (Swansea C) 5
Coleman, C. 1990 (Swansea C) 3
Collins, J. M. 2003 (Cardiff C) 7
Collins, L. R. 2021 (Newport Co) 2
Collins, M. J. 2007 (Fulham, Swansea C) 2
Collison, J. D. 2008 (West Ham U) 7
Colwill, R. 2021 (Cardiff C) 1
Connolly, J. 2022 (Cardiff C) 1
Cooper, B. J. 2019 (Swansea C) 14
Cooper, O. J. 2020 (Swansea C) 3
Cornell, D. J. 2010 (Swansea C) 4
Cotterill, D. R. G. B. 2005 (Bristol C, Wigan Ath) 11
Coyne, D. 1992 (Tranmere R) 7
Coxe, C. T. 2018 (Cardiff C, Solihull Moors) 16
Craig, N. L. 2009 (Everton) 4
Critchell, K. A. R. 2005 (Southampton) 3
Crofts, A. L. 2005 (Gillingham) 10
Crowe, M. T. T. 2017 (Ipswich T) 1
Crowell, M. T. 2004 (Wrexham) 7
Cullen, L. J. 2018 (Swansea C) 12
Curtis, A. T. 1977 (Swansea C) 1

Dasilva, C. P. 2018 (Chelsea, Brentford) 3
Davies, A. 1982 (Manchester U) 6
Davies, A. G. 2006 (Cambridge U) 6
Davies, A. R. 2005 (Southampton, Yeovil T) 14
Davies, C. M. 2005 (Oxford U, Verona, Oldham Ath) 9
Davies, D. 1999 (Barry T) 1
Davies, G. M. 1993 (Hereford U, Crystal Palace) 7
Davies, I. C. 1978 (Norwich C) 1
Davies, I. J. 2022 (Cardiff C) 5
Davies, K. E. 2019 (Swansea C) 1
Davies, L. 2005 (Bangor C) 1
Davies, R. J. 2006 (WBA) 4
Davies, S. 1999 (Peterborough U, Tottenham H) 10
Dawson, C. 2013 (Leeds U) 2
Day, R. 2000 (Manchester C, Mansfield T) 11
Deacy, N. 1977 (PSV Eindhoven) 1
De-Vulgt, L. S. 2002 (Swansea C) 2
Dibble, A. 1983 (Cardiff C) 3
Dibble, C. 2014 (Barnsley) 1
Doble, R. A. 2010 (Southampton) 10
Doughty, M. E. 2012 (QPR) 1
Doyle, S. C. 1979 (Preston NE, Huddersfield T) 2
Duffy, R. M. 2005 (Portsmouth) 7
Dummett, P. 2011 (Newcastle U) 3
Dwyer, P. J. 1979 (Cardiff C) 1

Eardley, N. 2007 (Oldham Ath, Blackpool) 11
Earnshaw, R. 1999 (Cardiff C) 10
Easter, D. J. 2006 (Cardiff C) 1
Ebdon, M. 1990 (Everton) 2
Edwards, C. N. H. 1996 (Swansea C) 7
Edwards, D. A. 2006 (Shrewsbury T, Luton T, Wolverhampton W) 9
Edwards, G. D. R. 2012 (Swansea C) 6
Edwards, R. I. 1977 (Chester) 2
Edwards, R. W. 1991 (Bristol C) 13
Evans, A. 1977 (Bristol R) 1
Evans, C. 2007 (Manchester C, Sheffield U) 13
Evans, J. A. J. 2014 (Fulham, Wrexham) 6
Evans, J. M. 2018 (Swansea C) 13
Evans, K. 1999 (Leeds U, Cardiff C) 4
Evans, K. G. 2019 (Swansea C) 2
Evans, L. 2013 (Wolverhampton W) 13
Evans, O. R. 2018 (Wigan Ath) 3
Evans, P. S. 1996 (Shrewsbury T) 1
Evans, S. J. 2001 (Crystal Palace) 2
Evans, T. 1995 (Cardiff C) 3

Fish, N. 2005 (Cardiff C) 2
Fleetwood, S. 2005 (Cardiff C) 5
Flynn, C. P. 2007 (Crewe Alex) 1
Folland, R. W. 2000 (Oxford U) 1
Foster, M. G. 1993 (Tranmere R) 1
Fowler, L. A. 2003 (Coventry C, Huddersfield T) 9
Fox, M. A. 2013 (Charlton Ath) 6
Freeman, K. 2012 (Nottingham F, Derby Co) 15
Freestone, R. 1990 (Chelsea) 1

Gabbidon, D. L. 1999 (WBA, Cardiff C) 17
Gale, D. 1983 (Swansea C) 2
Gall, K. A. 2002 (Bristol R, Yeovil T) 8
Gibson, N. D. 1999 (Tranmere R, Sheffield W) 11
Giggs, R. J. 1991 (Manchester U) 1
Gilbert, P. 2005 (Plymouth Arg) 12
Giles, D. C. 1977 (Cardiff C, Swansea C, Crystal Palace) 4
Giles, P. 1982 (Cardiff C) 3
Graham, D. 1991 (Manchester U) 1
Green, R. M. 1998 (Wolverhampton W) 16
Griffith, C. 1990 (Cardiff C) 1
Griffiths, C. 1991 (Shrewsbury T) 1
Grubb, D. 2007 (Bristol C) 1
Gunter, C. 2006 (Cardiff C, Tottenham H) 8

Haldane, L. O. 2007 (Bristol R) 1
Hall, G. D. 1990 (Chelsea) 1
Hammond, O. J. 2022 (Nottingham F) 3
Harries, C. W. T. 2018 (Swansea C) 7
Harris, M. T. 2018 (Cardiff C) 20
Harrison, E. W. 2013 (Bristol R) 14
Hartson, J. 1994 (Luton T, Arsenal) 9
Haworth, S. O. 1997 (Cardiff C, Coventry C, Wigan Ath) 12
Hedges, R. P. 2014 (Swansea C) 11
Henley, A. 2012 (Blackburn R) 3
Hennessey, W. R. 2006 (Wolverhampton W) 6
Hewitt, E. J. 2012 (Macclesfield T, Ipswich T) 10
Hillier, I. M. 2001 (Tottenham H, Luton T) 5
Hodges, G. 1983 (Wimbledon) 5
Holden, A. 1984 (Chester C) 1
Holloway, C. D. 1999 (Exeter C) 2
Hoole, L. A. 2022 (Bristol R) 1
Hopkins, J. 1982 (Fulham) 5
Hopkins, S. A. 1999 (Wrexham) 1
Howells, J. 2012 (Luton T) 5
Huggins, D. S. 1996 (Bristol C) 1
Huggins, N. J. 2019 (Leeds U, Sunderland) 4
Hughes, D. 2005 (Kaiserslautern, Regensburg) 2
Hughes, D. R. 1994 (Southampton) 1
Hughes, I. 1992 (Bury) 11
Hughes, L. M. 1983 (Manchester U) 5
Hughes, R. 2022 (Everton) 9
Hughes, R. D. 1996 (Aston Villa, Shrewsbury T) 13
Hughes, W. 1977 (WBA) 3
Huws, E. W. 2012 (Manchester C) 6

Isgrove, L. J. 2013 (Southampton) 6

Jackett, K. 1981 (Watford) 2
Jacobson, J. M. 2006 (Cardiff C, Bristol R) 15
James, D. O. 2017 (Swansea C) 11
James, L. R. S. 2006 (Southampton) 10
James, R. M. 1977 (Swansea C) 3
Jarman, L. 1996 (Cardiff C) 10
Jeanne, L. C. 1999 (QPR) 8
Jelleyman, G. A. 1999 (Peterborough U) 1
Jenkins, L. D. 1998 (Swansea C) 9
Jenkins, S. R. 1993 (Swansea C) 2
Jephcott, L. O. 2021 (Plymouth Arg) 12
John, D. C. 2014 (Cardiff C) 9
Johnson, B. P. 2020 (Nottingham F) 4
Jones, C. T. 2007 (Swansea C) 1
Jones, E. 2021 (Stoke C) 7
Jones, E. P. 2000 (Blackpool) 1
Jones, F. 1981 (Wrexham) 1
Jones, G. W. 2014 (Everton) 9
Jones, J. A. 2001 (Swansea C) 3
Jones, L. 1982 (Cardiff C) 3
Jones, M. A. 2004 (Wrexham) 4
Jones, M. G. 1998 (Leeds U) 7
Jones, O. R. 2015 (Swansea C) 1
Jones, P. L. 1992 (Liverpool) 12
Jones, P. S. 2022 (Huddersfield T) 2
Jones, R. 2011 (AFC Wimbledon) 1
Jones, R. A. 1994 (Sheffield W) 3
Jones, S. J. 2005 (Swansea C) 1
Jones, V. 1979 (Bristol R) 2

Kendall, L. M. 2001 (Crystal Palace) 2
Kendall, M. 1978 (Tottenham H) 1
Kenworthy, J. R. 1994 (Tranmere R) 3
King, A. 2008 (Leicester C) 11
King, E. J. 2022 (Cardiff C) 5
Knott, G. R. 1996 (Tottenham H) 1

Law, B. J. 1990 (QPR) 2
Lawless, A. 2006 (Torquay U) 1
Lawrence, T. 2013 (Manchester U) 8
Ledley, J. C. 2005 (Cardiff C) 5
Lemonheigh-Evans, C. 2019 (Bristol C) 3
Letheran, G. 1977 (Leeds U) 2
Letheran, K. C. 2006 (Swansea C) 1
Levitt, D. J. C. 2020 (Manchester U) 1
Lewis, A. 2018 (Swansea C, Lincoln C) 12
Lewis, D. 1982 (Swansea C) 9
Lewis, J. 1983 (Cardiff C) 1
Lewis, J. C. 2020 (Swansea C) 2
Llewellyn, C. M. 1998 (Norwich C) 14
Lockyer, T. A. 2015 (Bristol R) 7
Loveridge, J. 1982 (Swansea C) 3
Low, J. D. 1999 (Bristol R, Cardiff C) 1
Lowndes, S. R. 1979 (Newport Co, Millwall) 4
Lucas, L. P. 2011 (Swansea C) 19

MacDonald, S. B. 2006 (Swansea C) 25
McCarthy, A. J. 1994 (QPR) 3
McDonald, C. 2006 (Cardiff C) 3
Mackin, L. 2006 (Wrexham) 1
Maddy, P. 1982 (Cardiff C) 2
Margetson, M. W. 1992 (Manchester C) 7
Martin, A. P. 1999 (Crystal Palace) 1
Martin, D. A. 2006 (Notts Co) 1
Marustik, C. 1982 (Swansea C) 7
Matondo, R. 2018 (Manchester C) 8
Matthews, A. J. 2010 (Cardiff C) 5
Maxwell, C. 2009 (Wrexham) 16
Maxwell, L. J. 1999 (Liverpool, Cardiff C) 14
Meades, J. 2012 (Cardiff C) 4
Meaker, M. J. 1994 (QPR) 2
Melville, A. K. 1990 (Swansea C, Oxford U) 2
Mepham, C. J. 2018 (Brentford) 4
Micallef, C. 1982 (Cardiff C) 3
Mooney, D. 2019 (Fleetwood T) 4
Morgan, A. M. 1995 (Tranmere R) 4
Morgan, C. 2004 (Wrexham, Milton Keynes D) 12
Morrell, J. J. 2018 (Bristol C) 8
Morris, A. J. 2009 (Cardiff C, Aldershot T) 8
Moss, D. M. 2003 (Shrewsbury T) 6
Mountain, P. D. 1997 (Cardiff C) 2
Mumford, A. O. 2003 (Swansea C) 4

Nardiello, D. 1978 (Coventry C) 1
Neilson, A. B. 1993 (Newcastle U) 7
Nicholas, P. 1978 (Crystal Palace, Arsenal) 3
Nogan, K. 1990 (Luton T) 2
Nogan, L. M. 1991 (Oxford U) 1
Norrington-Davies, R. L. 2018 (Sheffield U) 14
Norton, C. A. 2021 (Stoke C) 1
Nyatanga, L. J. 2005 (Derby Co) 10

Oakley, A. 2013 (Swindon T) 1
O'Brien, B. T. 2015 (Manchester C) 8
Ogleby, R. 2011 (Hearts, Wrexham) 12
Oster, J. M. 1997 (Grimsby T, Everton) 9
O'Sullivan, T. P. 2013 (Cardiff C) 15
Owen, G. 1991 (Wrexham) 8

Page, R. J. 1995 (Watford) 4
Parslow, D. 2005 (Cardiff C) 4
Partington, J. M. 2009 (Bournemouth) 8
Partridge, D. W. 1997 (West Ham U) 1
Pascoe, C. 1983 (Swansea C) 4
Pearce, S. 2006 (Bristol C) 3
Pearson, S. 2021 (Bristol C) 12

Pejic, S. M. 2003 (Wrexham) 6
Pembridge, M. A. 1991 (Luton T) 1
Peniket, R. 2012 (Fulham) 1
Perry, J. 1990 (Cardiff C) 3
Peters, M. 1992 (Manchester C, Norwich C) 3
Phillips, D. 1984 (Plymouth Arg) 3
Phillips, G. R. 2001 (Swansea C) 3
Phillips, L. 1979 (Swansea C, Charlton Ath) 2
Pilling, L. 2018 (Tranmere R) 9
Pipe, D. R. 2003 (Coventry C, Notts Co) 12
Pontin, K. 1978 (Cardiff C) 1
Poole, R. L. 2017 (Manchester U, Milton Keynes D) 23
Popov, C. 2022 (Leicester C) 3
Powell, L. 1991 (Southampton) 4
Powell, L. 2004 (Leicester C) 3
Powell, R. 2006 (Bolton W) 1
Price, J. J. 1998 (Swansea C) 7
Price, L. P. 2005 (Ipswich T) 10
Price, M. D. 2001 (Everton, Hull C, Scarborough) 13
Price, P. 1981 (Luton T) 1
Price, T. O. 2019 (Swansea C) 1
Pritchard, J. P. 2013 (Fulham) 3
Pritchard, M. O. 2006 (Swansea C) 4
Pugh, D. 1982 (Doncaster R) 2
Pugh, S. 1993 (Wrexham) 2
Pugh, T. 2019 (Scunthorpe U) 2
Pulis, A. J. 2006 (Stoke C) 5
Przybek, A. 2020 (Ipswich T) 3

Ramasut, M. W. T. 1997 (Bristol R) 4
Ramsey, A. J. 2008, (Cardiff C, Arsenal) 12
Ratcliffe, G. 2019 (Cardiff C) 10
Ratcliffe, K. 1981 (Everton) 2
Ray, G. E. 2013 (Crewe Alex) 5
Ready, K. 1992 (QPR) 5
Rees, A. 1984 (Birmingham C) 1
Rees, J. M. 1990 (Luton T) 3
Rees, M. R. 2003 (Millwall) 4
Reid, B. 2014 (Wolverhampton W) 1
Ribeiro, C. M. 2008 (Bristol C) 8
Richards, A. D. J. 2010 (Swansea C) 16
Richards, E. A. 2012 (Bristol R) 1
Roberts, A. M. 1991 (QPR) 2
Roberts, C. 2013 (Cheltenham T) 6
Roberts, C. J. 1999 (Cardiff C) 1
Roberts, C. R. J. 2016 (Swansea C) 2
Roberts, G. 1983 (Hull C) 1
Roberts, G. W. 1997 (Liverpool, Panionios, Tranmere R) 11
Roberts, J. G. 1977 (Wrexham) 1
Roberts, N. W. 1999 (Wrexham) 3
Roberts, P. 1997 (Porthmadog) 1
Roberts, S. I. 1999 (Swansea C) 13
Roberts, S. W. 2000 (Wrexham) 3
Roberts, T. W. 2018 (Leeds U) 5
Robinson, C. P. 1996 (Wolverhampton W) 6
Robinson, J. R. C. 1992 (Brighton & HA, Charlton Ath) 5
Robson-Kanu, K. H. 2010 (Reading) 4
Rodon, J. P. 2017 (Swansea C) 9
Rowlands, A. J. R. 1996 (Manchester C) 5
Rush, I. 1981 (Liverpool) 2

Sass-Davies, W. J. 2021 (Crewe Alex) 7
Savage, R. W. 1995 (Crewe Alex) 3
Saunders, C. L. 2015 (Crewe Alex) 1
Sayer, P. A. 1977 (Cardiff C) 2
Searle, D. 1991 (Cardiff C) 6
Sheehan, J. L. 2014 (Swansea C) 12
Shephard, L. 2015 (Swansea C) 2
Shepperd, N. 2021 (Brentford, Dundalk) 4
Slatter, D. 2000 (Chelsea) 6
Slatter, N. 1983 (Bristol R) 6
Smith, D. 2014 (Shrewsbury T) 3
Smith, M. 2018 (Manchester C) 5
Somner, M. J. 2004 (Brentford) 2
Sparrow, T. L. 2022 (Stoke C) 1
Speed, G. A. 1990 (Leeds U) 3
Spence, S. 2021 (Cardiff C, Crystal Palace) 6
Spender, S. 2005 (Wrexham) 6
Stephens, D. 2011 (Hibernian) 7
Stevens, F. J. 2021 (Brentford) 9
Stevenson, N. 1982 (Swansea C) 2
Stevenson, W. B. 1977 (Leeds U) 3
Stirk, R. W. 2020 (Birmingham C) 7
Stock, B. B. 2003 (Bournemouth) 4
Symons, C. J. 1991 (Portsmouth) 2

Tancock, S. 2013 (Swansea C) 6
Taylor, A. J. 2012 (Tranmere R) 3
Taylor, G. F. 1995 (Bristol R) 4
Taylor, J. W. T. 2010 (Reading) 12
Taylor, N. J. 2008 (Wrexham, Swansea C) 13
Taylor, R. F. 2008 (Chelsea) 5
Taylor, T. 2020 (Wolverhampton W, Burton Alb) 12
Thomas, C. E. 2010 (Swansea C) 3
Thomas, D. G. 1977 (Leeds U) 3
Thomas, D. J. 1998 (Watford) 2
Thomas, G. S. 2018 (Leicester C) 8
Thomas, J. A. 1996 (Blackburn R) 21
Thomas, Martin R. 1979 (Bristol R) 2
Thomas, Mickey R. 1977 (Wrexham) 2
Thomas, S. 2001 (Wrexham) 5
Thompson, L. C. W. 2015 (Norwich C) 2
Thorpe E. 2022 (Luton T) 2
Tibbott, L. 1977 (Ipswich T) 2
Tipton, M. J. 1998 (Oldham Ath) 6
Tolley, J. C. 2001 (Shrewsbury T) 12
Touray, M. 2019 (Newport Co, Salford C) 6
Tudur-Jones, O. 2006 (Swansea C) 3
Turns, E. J. 2022 (Brighton & HA) 1
Twiddy, C. 1995 (Plymouth Arg) 3

Vale, J. R. 2020 (Blackburn R) 8
Valentine, R. D. 2001 (Everton, Darlington) 8
Vaughan, D. O. 2003 (Crewe Alex) 8
Vaughan, N. 1982 (Newport Co) 2
Vokes, S. M. 2007 (Bournemouth, Wolverhampton W) 14

Waite, J. 2021 (Cardiff C) 2
Walsh, D. 2000 (Wrexham) 8
Walsh, I. P. 1979 (Crystal Palace, Swansea C) 2
Walsh, J. 2012 (Swansea C, Crawley T) 11
Walton, M. 1991 (Norwich C.) 1
Ward, D. 1996 (Notts Co) 2
Ward, D. 2013 (Liverpool) 6
Warlow, O. J. 2007 (Lincoln C) 2
Webb, L. 2021 (Swansea C) 2
Weeks, D. L. 2014 (Wolverhampton W) 2
Weston, R. D. 2001 (Arsenal, Cardiff C) 4
Wharton, T. J. 2014 (Cardiff C) 1
Whitfield, P. M. 2003 (Wrexham) 1
Wiggins, R. 2006 (Crystal Palace) 9
Williams, A. P. 1998 (Southampton) 9
Williams, A. S. 1996 (Blackburn R) 16
Williams, D. 1983 (Bristol R) 1
Williams, D. I. L. 1998 (Liverpool, Wrexham) 9
Williams D. P. 2021 (Swansea C) 8
Williams, D. T. 2006 (Yeovil T) 1
Williams, E. 1997 (Caernarfon T) 2
Williams, G. 1983 (Bristol R) 2
Williams, G. A. 2003 (Crystal Palace) 5
Williams, G. C. 2014 (Fulham) 3
Williams, J. P. 2011 (Crystal Palace) 8
Williams, M. 2001 (Manchester U) 10
Williams, M. P. 2006 (Wrexham) 14
Williams, M. J. 2014 (Notts Co) 1
Williams, M. R. 2006 (Wrexham) 6
Williams, O. fon 2007 (Crewe Alex, Stockport Co) 11
Williams, R. 2007 (Middlesbrough) 10
Williams, S. J. 1995 (Wrexham) 4
Wilmot, R. 1982 (Arsenal) 6
Wilson, H. 2014 (Liverpool) 10
Wilson, J. S. 2009 (Bristol C) 3
Worgan, L. J. 2005 (Milton Keynes D, Rushden & D) 5
Wright, A. A. 1998 (Oxford U) 3
Wright, J. 2014 (Huddersfield T) 2

Yorwerth, J. 2014 (Cardiff C) 7
Young, S. 1996 (Cardiff C) 5

ENGLAND YOUTH GAMES 2021–22

▪ *Denotes player sent off.*

ENGLAND UNDER-16

FRIENDLIES

Burton, Thursday 3 June 2021

England (0) 6 *(Tezgel 47, 73, 86, Gee 60, Feeney 71, O'Reilly 84)*

Northern Ireland (0) 0

England: Grant (Wooster 46); Jackson (Gee 46), Feeney, Susoho, Scarles (Sousa 46), Taylor (Patterson 46), McGrath (Waldron 46), Castledine (Whitwell 46), Stutter (Lawrence 76), Bellingham (O'Reilly 46), Lawrence (Tezgel 46).
Northern Ireland: McClean (Williamson 46); Jordan (Hamilton 69), Brown (Farley 55), Thompson (Higgins 69), McCloskey, Sousa (Maguire 69), Donnelly, Doherty (Boyd 54), Loughlin (Reid 55), Glenfield (Withers 55), Brennan (Berry 69).

VAL DE MARNE TOURNAMENT

Tuesday 2 November 2021

Italy (0) 0

England (1) 1 *(Oboavwoduo 15)*

England: Curd; Samuel, Samuels-Smith, McAllister, Boniface, Golding (Dyer 59), De Jesus (Amo-Ameyaw 41), Gray, Oboavwoduo (Danns 70), George (Lewis-Skelly 59), Young (Jimoh 40).

Thursday 4 November 2021

England (2) 3 *(Amo-Ameyaw 3, Danns 32, Golding 74)*

Belgium (1) 2 *(Nuozzi 10, Bounida 66 (pen))*

England: Thompson; Meghoma, Samuels-Smith (Samuel 46), Jimoh (Oboavwoduo 67), Parker (Dobson-Ventura 56), McAllister (De Jesus 46), Dyer (Golding 56), Danns (George 46), Amo-Ameyaw (Gray 80), Young (Boniface 56), Lewis-Skelly.

Saturday 6 November 2021

France (1) 2 *(Mbondo 6, Kroupi 90)*

England (1) 3 *(Dobson-Ventura 35, 49, Boniface 68)*

England: Curd; McAllister (De Jesus 72), Samuels-Smith, Boniface (Young 80), Dobson-Ventura (Parker 80), Golding, Amo-Ameyaw (Danns 58), Gray (Jimoh 80), Oboavwoduo (Samuel 81), George (Meghoma 73, Dyer (Lewis-Skelly 46).
England win the tournament.

Sunday 20 December 2021

England (2) 2 *(Dibling 8, George 37)*

Turkey (1) 1 *(Calayir 34)*

England: Proctor (Hammons 57); Samuels-Smith, Roswell (Kamason 73), Meghoma, Akomeah, Dibling (Cardoso 58), Ammo-Ameyaw, Golding, George (Issaka 75), Morgan (Musa 69), Dyer (Lewis-Skelly 58).

Tuesday 22 December 2021

England (0) 3 *(Parker 50, Golding 79, Morgan 88)*

Turkey (0) 1 *(Calayir 47)*

England: Herrick (Proctor 62); Musa (Morgan 64), Cardoso (Dyer 72), Willhoft-King (Golding 63), Meghoma (Samuels-Smith 46), Parker, Renecke, Lewis-Skelly, Issaka (Dibling 72), George (Amo-Ameyaw 46), Kamason.

ALGARVE TOURNAMENT

Sunday 12 February 2022

Germany (1) 5 *(Rahmann 16, Jeltsch 62, Moerstedt 72, Herrmann 79, Preuss 84)*

England (1) 1 *(Morgan 27)*

England: Thompson; Rowe, Meghoma, Renecke, Akomeah, McAllister (Dyer 73), Amo-Ameyaw, Golding, George (Dibling 59), Nwaneri (Orford 59), Morgan (Oboavwoduo 73).

Tuesday 15 February 2022

England (0) 0

Portugal (0) 0

England: Herrick; Samuels-Smith, Samuel, Meghoma, Dibling (Amo-Ameyaw 77), Omoruyi (Akomeah 86), Golding (Orford 61), Jimoh (McAllister 87), Lennon (George 61), Oboavwoduo (Morgan 77), Dyer (Nwaneri 61).
England won 5-3 on penalties.

MONTAIGU TOURNAMENT

12 April 2022

England (0) 1 *(Morgan 58)*

Netherlands (0) 1 *(Bal 70 (pen))*

England: Curd; Acheampong, Abbott, Samuel, Meghoma, Dada-Mascoll (Golding 80), Rigge (Nwaneri 72), Gray, Amo-Ameyaw, George, Morgan (Oboavwoduo 59).

Thursday 14 April 2022

Mexico (0) 0

England (2) 3 *(Dyer 13, Irow 35, Nwaneri 71)*

England: Curd; Samuel, Omoruyi, Akomeah, Renecke, Dyer, Golding, Gray, Oboavwoduo, Irow, Nwaneri.
Substitutes: Dada-Mascoll, Rigge, Proctor, Acheampong, Meghoma, Abbott, Amo-Ameyaw, George, Morgan.

Saturday 16 April 2022

England (0) 0

Brazil (1) 3 *(Guilherme 6, 70, Endrick 72)*

England: Curd; Samuel (Acheampong 69), Abbott, Omoruyi (Renecke 65), Meghoma, Dyer (Oboavwoduo 61), Dada-Mascoll (Golding 46), Gray (Rigge 69), Irow (Nwaneri 61), Amo-Ameyaw (George 69), Morgan.

Monday 18 April 2022

England (0) 1 *(Irow 57 (pen))*

Portugal (1) 1 *(Tome 6)*

England: Proctor; Acheampong, Dada-Mascoll, Akomeah (Abbott 78), Renecke (Meghoma 59), Golding (Gray 58), Rigge (Dyer 46), Nwaneri (Samuel 77), Irow (Morgan 58), Oboavwoduo (Amo-Ameyaw 58), George.
England won 4-1 on penalties.

ENGLAND UNDER-17

SYRENKA CUP

Friday 3 September 2021

England (1) 2 *(Ehibhatioman 35, Castledine 67)*

Romania (0) 0

England: Ombang; Davidson (Barber 75), Gee (Dorrington 46), Feeney (Phillips 83), Scarles (Patterson 62), Rak-Sakyi (Whitwell 75), Kyerematen, Castledine, O'Reilly (Bloxham 83), Ehibhatioman (Stutter 46), Tezgel (Jobe Bellingham 63).

Sunday 5 September 2021

England (0) 2 *(Tezgel 84, 90)*

Portugal (1) 1 *(Joao Goncalves 2)*

England: Grant; Davidson (Ehibhatioman 78), Dorrington (Feeney 46), Phillips, Scarles (O'Reilly 46), Whitwell (Kyerematen 59), Gee (Rak-Sakyi 70), Patterson, Bloxham (Castledine 46), Jobe Bellingham, Stutter (Tezgel 59).

SYRENKA CUP FINAL

Tuesday 7 September 2021

England (0) 2 *(Tezgel 89, 90)*

Netherlands (1) 3 *(Rijkhoff 32, Slory 47, Rust 90)*

England: Grant; Dorrington (Davidson 46), Phillips (Bloxham 83), Feeney, Patterson (Scarles 64), Whitwell (Gee 64), Kyerematen (Ehibhatioman 73), O'Reilley, Castledine, Jobe Bellingham (Stutter 46), Tezgel.

UEFA EUROPEAN U17 CHAMPIONSHIP QUALIFYING (IN BELARUS)

Minsk, Saturday 16 October 2021

England (2) 7 *(Avetisyan 23 (og), Feeney 37, Tezgel 56, Taylor 64, Cozier-Duberry 77, Donley 88 (pen), Mainoo 89)*

Armenia (0) 0

England: Setford; Kyerematen (Rak-Sakyi 62), Feeney, O'Reilly Taylor 61), Jobe Bellingham, Finch (Cozier-Duberry 68), Tezgel (Donley 68), Smith, Ogunneye (Davidson 61), Mainoo, Patterson.

Borisov, Tuesday 19 October 2021

England (1) 1 *(Donley 27)*

Belarus (0) 0

England: Setford; Davidson, Scarles, Kyerematen, Fredricson, Feeney, Castledine (Finch 62), O'Reilly (Jobe Bellingham 90), Donley (Tezgel 62), Taylor (Cozier-Duberry 71), Rak-Sakyi (Mainoo 71).

Borisov, Friday 22 October 2021

England (0) 2 *(Tezgel 71 (pen), O'Reilly 88)*

Slovakia (2) 2 *(Rehus 22, Zahradnik 40)*

England: Ombang; Kyerematen (Rak-Sakyi 57), Feeney, Jobe Bellingham (O'Reilly 73), Donley (Tezgel 57), Finch (Castledine 57), Cozier-Duberry, Smith, Taylor, Ogunneye, Mainoo (Patterson 73).

FRIENDLIES

Tuesday 30 November 2021

England v Portugal

Match postponed.

Friday 3 December 2021

Israel v England

Match postponed.

Monday 6 December 2021

Spain v England

Match postponed.

Oriam, Tuesday 8 February 2022

Scotland (0) 0

England (0) 3 *(Mendel-Idowu 49, 71, Castledine 71)*

Scotland: Pazikas; Kingdon, Doak, McArthur, Lobban (Bruce 63), Luyeye (Murray 46), Sharpe (Reid 46), Gaffney (Moore 63), O'Donnell (Miller 75), Mackenzie (Rice 75), Laidlaw (Harvey 63).
England: Grant; Carrington (Barber 63), Phillips (Wright 72), Feeney, Boniface (Batty 63), Jobe Bellingham (Castledine 63), O'Reilly (Lewis-Skelly 72), Finch (Mendel-Idowu 46), Alves (Cozier-Duberry 72), Rak-Sakyi, Tezgel (Ballard 46).

Oriam, Thursday 10 February 2022

Scotland (2) 2 *(Wilson 10, Harvey 36)*

England (1) 2 *(Mendel-Idowu 31, Tezgel 62)*

Scotland: Pazikas; Murray (McArthur 46), Allen, Reid, Moore (O'Donnell 78), Miller, Bruce, Harvey (Sharpe 60), Wilson, Rice (Kingdon 65), MacLeod (Doak 60).
England: Setford; Phillips (Feeney 46), Ballard (Tezgel 46), Batty, Castledine (Jobe Bellingham 56), Cozier-Duberry (Alves 56), Doyle (O'Reilly 46), Barber (Carrington 56), Lewis-Skelly (Rak-Sakyi 65), Wright (Boniface 72), Mendel-Idowu (Finch 65).

UEFA EUROPEAN U17 CHAMPIONSHIP ELITE ROUND GROUP 5 (LUXEMBOURG)

Wednesday 23 March 2022

England

Russia

FIFA and UEFA suspended Russian clubs and national teams from all competitions due to invasion of Ukraine.. Match cancelled.

Luxembourg, Saturday 26 March 2022

England (1) 1 *(Cozier-Duberry 40)*

France (1) 3 *(Tel 19 (pen), Edoa 83, Byar 86)*

England: Setford; Barber, Feeney, Fredricson, Alves (Castledine 62), Mainoo, Gray (Mendel-Idowu 86), Scanlon, Donley (Tezgel 62), Cozier-Duberry, O'Reilly (Kyerematen 90).

Luxembourg, Tuesday 29 March 2022

Luxembourg (1) 2 *(Flick 31 (pen), Souchard 53)*

England (0) 0

England: Grant; Ogunneye (Scanlon 32), Samuels-Smith, Batty (Donley■ 69), Castledine■, Kyerematen (Ballard 69), Feeney, Mainoo, Mendel-Idowu (Alves 46), O'Reilly (Gray 58), Tezgel.

ENGLAND UNDER-18

FRIENDLIES

Newport, Friday 3 September 2021

Wales (1) 1 *(Harris 20)*

England (0) 1 *(Lewis 76)*

Wales: Hollingshead; Bennett (Karadogan 46), Abbott (Hammond 52), Williams Z, Green (Davies 33), Purcell (Lloyd 46), James (Congreve 73), Williams M (Jewitt-White 46), Harris, Ashford (Roberts M 46 (Wigley 88)), Roberts I (Cotterill 46).
England: Setford (Knightsbridge 57); Lewis, Katongo (Hughes 46), Jonas (Chambers 57), Hackett-Valton (Sturge 10), Braybrooke (Hall L 57), Gyabi (Wells-Morrison 46), Gordon (Olise 76), Perkins (Gore 66), Mather (Olakigbe 46), Emmerson (Pennant 66).

Marbella, Thursday, Wednesday 7 October 2021

England (0) 1 *(Soonsup-Bell 49)*

Norway (0) 2 *(Odegard 70, Flataker 88)*

England: Setford; Lewis, Sturge (Araujo 80), Campbell (Katongo 82), Hughes (Clarridge 82), Braybrooke (Webster 60), Thomas (Olakigbe 46), Wells-Morrison (Hall L 60), Emmerson (Soonsup-Bell 46), Pennant (Perkins 80), Mather (Gore 60).

Marbella, Monday 11 October 2021

England (2) 3 *(Perkins 29, Olakigbe 38, Hall L 54)*

Russia (0) 0

England: Thompson (Hall J 46); Katongo, Soonsup-Bell, Webster, Olakigbe (Mather 71), Perkins (Pennant 70), Hall L (Braybrooke 58), Araujo (Campbell 58), Clarridge (Hughes 85), Robinson (Lewis 58), Gore (Wells-Morrison 71).

Marbella, Friday 25 March 2022

Sweden (0) 2 *(Eklund 56, Omar 89)*

England (2) 3 *(Mabaya 18, Amoran (og) 34, Mubama 73)*

England: Beadle; Walters, Hall L (Sturge 90), Webster (Hall G 65), Miles, Jonas, Mabaya, Gyabi (Braybrooke 90), Cannonier (Bynoe-Gittens 65), Wells-Morrison (Mather 80), Mubama (Perkins 80).

Marbella, Monday 28 March 2022

Denmark (2) 3 *(Christensen 35, 48, Bundgaard 38)*

England (0) 3 *(Perkins 55, Gore 75, Fischer 79 (og))*

England: Thompson (Simkin 72); Lewis, Sturge, Braybrooke, Nelson, Campbell, Mather (Wells-Morrison 87), Hall G, Perkins (Cannonier 72), Gore, Bynoe-Gittens.

PINATAR TOURNAMENT

Pinatar, Thursday 11 November 2021

Netherlands (0) 3 *(Gonzaga 47, Poku 51, Houben 74)*

England (1) 2 *(Perkins 28, Mather 62)*

England: Beadle (Simkin 75); Lewis, Araujo (Norton-Cuffy 75), Nelson (Miles 79), Clarridge, Braybrooke, Perkins, Hall G, Mubama (Olakigbe 89), Gore (Hall L 75), Mather (Akinwale 89).

Pinatar, Saturday 13 November 2021

Belgium (0) 0

England (0) 0

England: Whitworth (Setford 76); Norton-Cuffey, Hughes, Miles, Walters (Lewis 76), Rodney (Hall G 76), Hall L (Braybrooke 76), Wells-Morrison, Olakigbe, Arblaster (Mather 84), Akinwale (Mubama 64).
England won 5-4 on penalties.

Pinatar, Monday 15 November 2021

Portugal (0) 0

England (1) 2 *(Mubama 4, Olakigbe 78)*

England: Simkin (Setford 79); Lewis (Walters 87), Araujo (Norton-Cuffy■ 46), Nelson, Clarridge, Braybrooke, Perkins (Olakigbe 64), Hall G (Hall L), Mubama, Gore (Wells-Morrison 64), Mather (Arblaster 87).

ZAGREB TOURNAMENT

Zagreb, Tuesday 7 June 2022

Austria (1) 2 *(Reischl 22, Ristanic 53)*

England (1) 3 *(Hall G 41, Mubama 47, Arblaster 84)*

England: Beadle; Hughes (Potter 71), Nelson, Hall L (Sturge 82), Walters (Olakigbe 46), Hall G, Braybrooke, Wells-Morrison (Arblaster 82), Small (Araujo 82), Mubama (Soonsup-Bell 62), Pennant (Perkins 62).

Zagreb, Friday 10 June 2022

Wales (0) 0

England (1) 2 *(Soonsup-Bell 24, Perkins 79)*

England: Simkin; Rodney, Sturge (Araujo 46), Ibrahim (Hall G 69), Nelson (Hall L 80), Potter, Olakigbe (Pennant 66), Webster (Braybrooke 69), Soonsup-Bell (Wells-Morrison 66), Perkins (Mubama 80), Arblaster (Small 66).
Wales: Hollingshead (Ridd 65); Godden (Hanks 46), Bennett (Bell 65), Hammond (Ludvigsen 65), Davies, Cotterill (Lloyd 65), Ashford (Purcell 46), Williams (Jewitt-White 65), Colwill (Fish 65), Congreve (Roberts 58), Crole.

Zagreb, Monday 13 June 2022

England (0) 0

Croatia (0) 0

England: Whitworth; Walters, Small (Rodney 61), Braybrooke (Ibrahim 84), Nelson (Hughes 46), Potter, Perkins, Hall G (Webster 84), Mubama (Soonsup-Bell 61), Wells-Morrison (Arblaster 70), Pennant (Olakigbe 70).
England won 4-3 on penalties.
England U18 won the Zagreb Cup.

ENGLAND UNDER-19

FRIENDLIES

St George's Park, Thursday 2 September 2021

England (2) 2 *(Scarlett 10 (pen), Soonsup-Bell 34)*

Italy (0) 0

England: Sharman-Lowe (Cox 46); Baptiste, Fish, Doyle, Oyegoke (Balagizi 87), Scott (John 73), Chukwuemeka (Egan-Riley 87), Vale, Shoretire (Devine 73), Scarlett (Edozie 87), Soonsup-Bell (Jebbison 67).

Frankfurt, Monday 6 September 2021

Germany (0) 1 *(Sieb 59)*

England (0) 1 *(Jebbison 62)*

England: Marschall; Welch (Baptiste 70), Humphreys, Mbete-Tabu (Doyle 70), Egan-Riley (Oyegoke 60), John (Shoretire 83), Devine (Chukwuemeka 60), Norris (Vale 60), Balagizi (Scott 83), Edozie (Scarlett 60), Jebbison.

MARBELLA TOURNAMENT

Marbella, Wednesday 6 October 2021

France (1) 3 *(Toure 26, Edwards 71 (og), Wahi 84)*

England (0) 1 *(Ramsey 67)*

England: Oluwayemi; Oyegoke, Doyle, Ramsey, Edwards, Baptiste, Dobbin (Iling-Junior 72), Scott, Scarlett, Shoretire (Devine 76), Vale.

Marbella, Saturday 9 October 2021

Mexico (1) 1 *(Ambriz 9)*

England (0) 3 *(Ramsey 52, Parra 79 (og), Vale 84)*

England: Davies; Oyegoke (Ramsey 46), Mbete-Tabu, John, Fish, Egan-Riley, Iling-Junior (Baptiste 85), Patino (Balagizi 70), Dobbin (Scarlett 60), Devine, Norris (Vale 60).

Marbella, Tuesday 12 October 2021

England (1) 2 *(Scarlett 27, 67)*

Belgium (0) 3 *(Descotte 51, Engels 61, Bakayoko 79)*

England: Marschall; Baptiste (Mbete-Baptiste-Tabu 46), Chambers, Scott (Shoretire 46), Doyle (Egan-Riley 90), Edwards, Balagizi (John 77), Vale (Devine 77), Scarlett, Ramsey, Iling-Junior.

EUROPEAN CHAMPIONSHIP QUALIFYING ROUND GROUP 3

Stockholm, Wednesday 10 November 2021

England (2) 4 *(Iling-Junior 24, Chukwuemeka 41, Scarlett 55, 66 (pen)*

Andorra (0) 0

England: Oluwayemi; Oyegoke, Chukwuemeka, Samuels-Colwill (Doyle 79), Iling-Junior (Giraud-Hutchinson 63), Scott (John 63), Scarlett (Jebbison 72), Ramsey (Balagizi 72), Vale, Chambers, Edwards.

Stockholm, Saturday 13 November 2021

England (0) 0

Switzerland (0) 0

England: Cox; Oyegoke, Doyle, Chukwuemeka, Samuels-Colwill, Baptiste, Scott, Scarlett, Ramsey, Vale, Chambers (John 71).

Stockholm, Tuesday 16 November 2021

England (1) 2 *(Scarlett 6, Samuels-Colwill 65)*

Sweden (0) 0

England: Cox; Oyegoke, Doyle, Chukwuemeka, Samuels-Colwill, Iling-Junior (John 68), Scott (Webster 85), Scarlett (Soonsup-Bell 85), Ramsey (Chambers 39), Vale (Balagizi 68), Edwards.

EUROPEAN CHAMPIONSHIP ELITE ROUND GROUP 1

Walsall, Wednesday 23 March 2022

England (2) 3 *(Scarlett 5, Chukwuemeka 42, 47))*

Republic of Ireland (0) 1 *(Abankwah 38)* 2688

England: Cox; Norton-Cuffey (Oyegoke 77), Doyle (Humphreys 66), Iroehbunam (Simons 77), Edwards, Quansah, Devine (Edozie 66), Chukwuemeka, Scarlett (Delap 66), Ramsey, Vale.

Rotherham, Saturday 26 March 2022

England (2) 4 *(Devine 6, Manukyan 38 (og), Quansah 58, Edozie 76)*

Armenia (0) 0

England: Cox (Sharman-Lowe 87); Norton-Cuffey (Oyegoke 77), Edwards, Quansah (Norris 73), Humphreys, Chukwuemeka, Simons, Devine (Balagizi 73), Edozie, Vale (Jebbison 46), Delap■.

Chesterfield, Tuesday 29 March 2022

England (2) 2 *(Scarlett 10, 40 (pen))*

Portgual (0) 0 6005

England: Cox; Norton-Cuffey (Oyegoke 71), Quansah, Humphreys, Doyle, Chukwuemeka (Norris 89), Iroehbunam, Devine (Balagizi 46), Ramsey (Simons 76), Vale, Scarlett (Jebbison 76).

EUROPEAN CHAMPIONSHIP FINALS IN SLOVAKIA GROUP B

Banska Bystrica, Sunday 19 June 2022

England (1) 2 *(Chukwuemeka 43, Devine 65)*

Austria (0) 0 1537

England: Cox; Norton-Cuffy (Oyegoke 72), Doyle, Iroegbunam, Edwards, Quansah, Devine (Bynoe-Gittens 80), Chukwuemeka (Iling-Junior (80), Scarlett (Delap 72), Ramsey (Scott 60), Vale.

Banska Bystrica, Wednesday 22 June 2022

England (2) 4 *(Scarlett 5, 40, Chukwuemeka 68, Jebbison 90)*

Serbia (0) 0 2569

England: Cox; Norton-Cuffy (Oyegoke 75), Doyle, Iroegbunam (Devine 60), Quansah, Chukwuemeka, Scarlett (Jebbison 70), Vale (Chambers 75), Scott, Humphreys, Bynoe-Gittens (Ramsey 60).

Ziar nad Hronom, Saturday 25 June 2022

Israel (0) 0

England (1) 1 *(Delap 6)* 933

England: Sharman-Lowe; Edwards (Doyle 46), Quansah (Norton-Cuffy 46), Devine, Chukwuemeka (Ramsey 76), Oyegoke, Scott, Chambers, Humphreys, Iling-Junior, Delap (Jebbison 76).

SEMI-FINALS

Senec, Tuesday 28 June 2022

England (0) 2 *(Scott 58, Quansah 82)*

Italy (1) 1 *(Miretti 12 (pen))* 897

England: Cox; Norton-Cuffy (Oyegoke 56), Doyle, Iroegbunam (Scott 56), Edwards, Quansah, Devine, Chukwuemeka, Scarlett (Jebbison 87), Ramsey (Bynoe-Gittens 56 (Chambers 83)), Vale.

FINAL

Trnava, Friday 1 July 2022

Israel (1) 1 *(Gloch 40)*

England (0) 3 *(Doyle 52, Chukwuemeka 108, Ramsey 116)*

Israel: Zarfati; Israelov, Lemkin, Kancepolsky (Nawi 86), Madmoun), Gloukh, Lugassy (Turgeman 86), Revivo (Gorno 67), Feingold (Tomer 90), Kassus (Yifrah 86), Ibrahim.
England: Cox; Doyle, Edwards, Quansah, Devine (Chambers 78), Chukwuemeka, Scarlett (Delap 106), Vale, Oyegoke (Norton-Cuffy 73), Scott (Iroegbunam 73), Bynoe-Gittens (Ramsey 58).
Referee: Antonio Nobre (Portugal).
aet.

ENGLAND UNDER-20

UEFA ELITE LEAGUE

St George's Park, Monday 6 September 2021

England (2) 6 *(Mola 15, McAtee 23, Gelhardt 52, 81 (pen), Weir 74, Rak-Sakyi 90)*

Romania (0) 1 *(Ghindovean 60)*

England: Trafford; Drameh (Kesler-Hayden 63), Buchanan (Cirkin 46), Bate (Clarkson 46), Wood (Hill 63), Mola (Branthwaite 73), Philogene-Bidace (Gelhardt 13), Azeez (Weir 63), Greenwood (Sibley 73), McAtee (Rak-Sakyi 77), Mighten (Rogers 46).

Chesterfield, Thursday 7 October 2021

England (1) 1 *(Bate 41)*

Italy (1) 1 *(Maldini 33)*

England: Trafford; Drameh, Cirkin (Lawrence 73), Weir, Hill, Wood, McAtee, Bate (Azeez 71), Greenwood (Stansfield 89), Anjorin (Rogers 61), Philogene-Bidace.

Teplice, Monday 11 October 2021

Czech Republic (0) 0

England (1) 5 *(Azeez 15. Stansfield 49, Anjorin 70, Rogers 76, Hill 83)*

England: Trafford (Cox 80); Kesler-Hayden, Lawrence, Clarkson, Wood (Hill 46), Branthwaite, Rak-Sakyi (Philogene-Bidace 56), Azeez, Stansfield (Greenwood 71), Anjorin (Bate 71), Rogers.

Leiria, Thursday 11 November 2021

Portugal (0) 2 *(Couto 52, Cruz 69)*

England (0) 0

England: Trafford; Lawrence (Kesler-Hayden 46), Wilson-Esbrands, Neil (Morton 74), Mengi, Alese (Welch 78), Philogene-Bidace (Rak-Sakyi 64), Bate, Greenwood (Stansfield 78), McAtee (Clarkson 64), Rogers (Archer 64).

Bielsko-Biala, Thursday 24 March 2022

Poland (0) 2 *(Golebiowki 55, Szwedzik 60)*

England (0) 0

England: Cartwright; Kesler-Hayden (Gardner-Hickman 74), Ogbeta, Mola, Wood, Alese, McAtee (Rak-Sakyi 90), Morton (Neil 81), Greenwood (Plange 74), Clarkson (James 90), Dolan (Stansfield 81).

Colchester, Tuesday 29 March 2022

England (1) 3 *(Greenwood 10, McAtee 52, Dolan 62)*

Germany (0) 1 *(Samadvic 87)*

England: Trafford; Gardner-Hickman (Stansfield 85), Ogbeta (Kesler-Hayden 57), Hill, Wood, Mola (Alese 78), McAtee (Rak-Sakyi 78), Neil (Morton 78), Archer (Dolan 57), Clarkson (James 82), Greenwood (Plange 78).

UNIVERSITY FOOTBALL 2021–22

136th UNIVERSITY MATCH

Saturday 26 June 2021, at The Hive, Barnet FC

Oxford (1) 2 *(Coveny 35, Cicale 59)* **Cambridge (0) 0**

Oxford: Way; Song, Rickett, Putland, Clifford, Duxbury, Cicale, Ryan-Phillips, Guy, Smith, Coveney.
Substitutes: Peters, Clark, Suljik, Ratcliff, Hickey.

Cambridge: Wallace; Stacey, Mortimer, Adam, Bull, Wooding, Thomson, Hoffman, Birch, Costapas, Pugh.
Substitutes: Gallagher, Kanwei, Roberts, Oshasha, Sunuwar.

137th UNIVERSITY MATCH

Sunday 13 March 2022, at Abbey Stadium, Cambridge United

Oxford (1) 1 *(Smith 36 (pen))* **Cambridge (0) 0**

Oxford: Way; Song, Barber, Putland, Hudson, Smith, Ryan-Phillips, Hickey (Burton 64), Cicale, Lewis (Downes 70), Lai.

Cambridge: Wallace; McPherson, Bragg, Harris, Adam, Hawthorn (Roberts 88), Cusack (Wooding 63), Linney, La Trobe-Roberts (Pugh 63), Oshasha, Kanwei.

Oxford have won 57 games (2 on penalties), Cambridge 54 games (4 on penalties) and 27 games have been drawn. Oxford have scored 218 goals, Cambridge 208 goals.

SCHOOLS FOOTBALL 2021–22

BOODLES INDEPENDENT SCHOOLS FA CUP 2021–22

**After extra time.*

FIRST ROUND

Abingdon v Harrodian	2-1
ACS Cobham v Bede's	1-6
AKS Lytham v Bolton	1-7
Bedford Modern v Haberdashers'	0-4
Berkhamsted v St John's, Leatherhead	5-0
Bournemouth Collegiate v Brighton College	1-3
Bootham v RGS, Newcastle	2-6
Box Hill v Lancing	0-5
Campbell College, Belfast v Stockport GS	3-5
Chigwell v Norwich	3-1
City of London v Wellington	5-3
Clifton College v Reading Blue Coat	1-6
Colfe's v St Joseph's College, Ipswich	3-2
Culford v St Columba's College	3-2
Dulwich College v Sevenoaks	3-1
Grammar School at Leeds v King's School, Chester	2-1
Ibstock Place v RGS, Guildford	2-0
John Lyon v Mill Hill	0-8
KCS, Wimbledon v Tonbridge	1-0
Kingston GS v Lingfield College	2-1
Merchant Taylors', Crosby v Oswestry	3-0
Milton Abbey v Bristol GS	2-1
Oldham Hulme GS v Rossall	0-4
Princethorpe v University College School	1-2*
Princethorpe won 2-0 on penalties	
Reigate GS v Worth	0-2
Sherborne v Truro	1-7
Taunton v Marlborough	0-3
The Grange v Bury GS	6-3
Trent College v Birkdale	2-3
Trinity v King Edwards, Witley	9-0
Winchester v Bryanston	8-0
Wolverhampton GS v Bromsgrove	0-4

SECOND ROUND

Abingdon v Kingston GS	5-1
Alleyn's v Colfe's	3-1
Bede's v Highgate	5-1
Bolton v The Grange	2-1
Brentwood v Trinity	2-1
Brighton College v Charterhouse	0-3
Brooke House v Birkdale	13-0
Cheadle Hulme v Bromsgrove	4-1
Chigwell v Forest	2-1
City of London v Latymer Upper	4-4*
Latymer Upper won 4-2 on penalties	
Dulwich College v Berkhamsted	0-2
Grammar School at Leeds v Queen Ethelburga's Collegiate	1-1*
Queen Ethelburga's won 5-4 on penalties	
Haberdashers' v Culford	6-0
Harrow v Marlborough	3-1
KCS, Wimbledon v Kimbolton	0-1
Lancing v Worth	7-0
Manchester GS v Stockport GS	2-1
Merchant Taylors', Crosby v Rossall	0-5
Mill Hill v Princethorpe	2-1
Reading Blue Coat v Winchester	3-1
RGS, Newcastle v St Bede's College	3-2
Truro v Milton Abbey	4-0
Westminster v Aldenham	1-10
Whitgift v Ibstock Place	5-1

THIRD ROUND

Alleyn's v Kimbolton	2-1
Bede's v Haberdashers'	1-1*
Haberdashers' won 5-4 on penalties	
Berkhamsted v Bradfield	1-6
Brentwood v Whitgift	1-3
Chigwell v Charterhouse	2-1
Harrow v Aldenham	1-6
Latymer Upper v Hampton	0-6
Millfield v Lancing	2-0
Mill Hill v Ardingly	3-1
Queen Ethelburga's Collegiate v Bolton	0-2
Reading Blue Coat v Eton	0-5
Repton v Cheadle Hulme	4-0
RGS, Newcastle v Manchester GS	1-4
Rossall v Shrewsbury	2-1
Royal Russell v Brooke House	
Match awarded to Royal Russell	
Truro v Abingdon	5-2

FOURTH ROUND

Aldenham v Hampton	0-1
Alleyn's v Whitgift	2-1
Bolton v Manchester GS	0-3
Bradfield v Chigwell	3-0
Eton v Rossall	1-4
Millfield v Haberdashers'	2-0
Royal Russell v Mill Hill	1-1*
Mill Hill won 7-6 on penalties	
Truro v Repton	3-5

FIFTH ROUND

Alleyn's v Bradfield	1-4
Hampton v Repton	3-2*
Manchester GS v Mill Hill	2-1
Rossall v Millfield	2-1

SEMI FINALS

Bradfield v Hampton	4-0
Manchester GS v Rossall	0-3

BOODLES INDEPENDENT SCHOOLS FA CUP FINAL 2021–22

Milton Keynes, Monday 21 March 2022

Bradfield (1) 4 *(McFarlane 7, 56, 67, Ezeanyika 90)*

Rossall (0) 0 1400

Bradfield: S. Negus, G. Brough, H. Ford, J. Owen, Z. Lion-Cachet, J. Buchan, T. Bough, A. Gallagher, T. Morley, C. McFarlane, D. Lowther.

Subs: B. Bagshaw, I. Ezeanyika, H. Stephenson, J. Mason, M. Gilpin.

Rossall: W. Owen, T. Shuttleworth, O. Leggett, Y. Basweiden, S. Maltsev, J. McField, J. Hunter, H. Welles, B. Pearson, J. Michelis, C. Reid.

Subs: I. Natowicz, M. Butz, K. Dewalt, H. Sutton, S. Wong.

Referee: Martin Atkinson.

INDEPENDENT SCHOOLS FA U15 CUP FINAL

Cheadle Hulme v Eton *(at Burton Alb)* 2-1*

INDEPENDENT SCHOOLS FA U13 CUP FINAL

Dulwich College v Manchester GS *(at Burton Alb)* 3-0

NON-LEAGUE TABLES 2021–22

NATIONAL LEAGUE SYSTEM STEP 3

PITCHING IN NORTHERN PREMIER LEAGUE – PREMIER DIVISION

			Home					*Away*					*Total*						
		P	*W*	*D*	*L*	*F*	*A*	*W*	*D*	*L*	*F*	*A*	*W*	*D*	*L*	*F*	*A*	*GD*	*Pts*
1	Buxton	42	14	5	2	48	17	9	7	5	32	21	23	12	7	80	38	42	81
2	South Shields	42	15	2	4	47	21	8	7	6	24	19	23	9	10	71	40	31	78
3	Scarborough Ath¶	42	10	7	4	35	23	11	4	6	26	25	21	11	10	61	48	13	74
4	Matlock T*	42	10	6	5	31	15	11	4	6	28	21	21	10	11	59	36	23	72
5	Warrington T	42	10	5	6	36	24	10	6	5	31	23	20	11	11	67	47	20	71
6	Bamber Bridge	42	9	5	7	35	30	12	1	8	32	29	21	6	15	67	59	8	69
7	Whitby T	42	9	6	6	27	20	10	3	8	30	30	19	9	14	57	50	7	66
8	Stafford Rangers	42	6	8	7	26	18	9	8	4	29	21	15	16	11	55	39	16	61
9	FC United of Manchester	42	12	2	7	38	24	6	5	10	28	33	18	7	17	66	57	9	61
10	Morpeth T	42	12	5	4	35	21	5	5	11	32	38	17	10	15	67	59	8	61
11	Lancaster Ci	42	10	3	8	17	16	7	2	12	27	35	17	5	20	44	51	–7	56
12	Mickleover Sports	42	9	6	6	34	30	6	4	11	20	35	15	10	17	54	65	–11	55
13	Nantwich T	42	8	4	9	24	27	6	6	9	22	25	14	10	18	46	52	–6	52
14	Stalybridge Celtic	42	9	3	9	29	29	6	4	11	22	30	15	7	20	51	59	–8	52
15	Ashton U	42	9	6	6	26	22	4	6	11	24	37	13	12	17	50	59	–9	51
16	Radcliffe	42	10	1	10	34	35	5	5	11	22	38	15	6	21	56	73	–17	51
17	Gainsborough Trinity	42	9	10	2	26	17	3	4	14	14	35	12	14	16	40	52	–12	50
18	Hyde U	42	9	2	10	29	34	5	6	10	23	31	14	8	20	52	65	–13	50
19	Atherton Collieries®	42	7	5	9	20	20	6	4	11	14	25	13	9	20	34	45	–11	48
20	Basford U®	42	5	7	9	17	19	7	2	12	15	30	12	9	21	32	49	–17	45
21	Witton Alb	42	7	2	12	27	37	5	5	11	21	41	12	7	23	48	78	–30	43
22	Grantham T	42	4	4	13	23	39	4	6	11	22	42	8	10	24	45	81	–36	34

*¶Scarborough Ath promoted after play-offs. *Matlock T deducted 1 point for fielding an ineligible player.*
®Atherton Collieries and Basford U reprieved from relegation.

PITCHING IN SOUTHERN PREMIER LEAGUE – CENTRAL DIVISION

		P	*W*	*D*	*L*	*F*	*A*	*W*	*D*	*L*	*F*	*A*	*W*	*D*	*L*	*F*	*A*	*GD*	*Pts*
1	Banbury U	40	15	4	1	44	18	17	2	1	48	14	32	6	2	92	32	60	102
2	Peterborough Sports¶	40	14	2	4	50	17	10	5	5	44	29	24	7	9	94	46	48	79
3	Coalville T	40	14	4	2	52	17	9	5	6	34	30	23	9	8	86	47	39	78
4	Rushall Olympic	40	12	3	5	48	26	8	6	6	32	28	20	9	11	80	54	26	69
5	Alvechurch	40	12	3	5	34	19	6	8	6	23	22	18	11	11	57	41	16	65
6	AFC Rushden & D	40	9	4	7	28	23	10	4	6	29	26	19	8	13	57	49	8	65
7	Leiston	40	11	5	4	28	23	7	1	12	31	42	18	6	16	59	65	–6	60
8	Royston T	40	7	6	7	33	23	10	2	8	32	28	17	8	15	65	51	14	59
9	Hednesford T	40	7	6	7	37	34	7	6	7	29	30	14	12	14	66	64	2	54
10	Tamworth	40	9	5	6	38	26	5	7	8	20	32	14	12	14	58	58	0	54
11	Stourbridge	40	8	6	6	34	29	7	2	11	27	42	15	8	17	61	71	–10	53
12	Needham Market	40	6	8	6	35	28	6	5	9	31	41	12	13	15	66	69	–3	49
13	Stratford T	40	8	4	8	26	28	5	4	11	22	42	13	8	19	48	70	–22	47
14	St Ives T	40	9	3	8	32	47	4	5	11	25	43	13	8	19	57	90	–33	47
15	Redditch U	40	7	5	8	23	26	4	7	9	15	24	11	12	17	38	50	–12	45
16	Nuneaton Bor*	40	4	8	8	21	26	7	2	11	30	36	11	10	19	51	62	–11	42
17	Hitchin T	40	8	3	9	27	31	3	6	11	20	27	11	9	20	47	58	–11	42
18	Bromsgrove Sporting®	40	8	2	10	19	29	2	10	8	17	30	10	12	18	36	59	–23	42
19	Barwell®	40	6	5	9	33	37	4	6	10	24	41	10	11	19	57	78	–21	41
20	Biggleswade T	40	6	8	6	35	26	1	5	14	12	38	7	13	20	47	64	–17	34
21	Lowestoft T	40	6	5	9	27	34	3	1	16	22	59	9	6	25	49	93	–44	33

*¶Peterborough Sports promoted after play-offs. *Nuneaton Bor deducted 1 point for fielding an ineligible player.*
®Bromsgrove Sporting and Barwell reprieved from relegation.

PITCHING IN SOUTHERN PREMIER LEAGUE – SOUTH DIVISION

		P	*W*	*D*	*L*	*F*	*A*	*W*	*D*	*L*	*F*	*A*	*W*	*D*	*L*	*F*	*A*	*GD*	*Pts*
1	Taunton T	42	18	2	1	55	20	10	5	6	28	22	28	7	7	83	42	41	91
2	Hayes & Yeading U	42	16	1	4	58	19	10	7	4	42	20	26	8	8	100	39	61	86
3	Farnborough¶	42	15	3	3	40	16	11	4	6	33	28	26	7	9	73	44	29	85
4	Metropolitan Police	42	10	7	4	32	20	14	2	5	40	26	24	9	9	72	46	26	81
5	Weston-super-Mare	42	11	5	5	37	22	12	4	5	35	19	23	9	10	72	41	31	78
6	Chesham U	42	14	6	1	53	22	8	5	8	27	28	22	11	9	80	50	30	77
7	Yate T	42	8	6	7	30	30	13	3	5	36	18	21	9	12	66	48	18	72
8	Truro C	42	11	5	5	28	22	9	5	7	34	32	20	10	12	62	54	8	70
9	Gosport Bor	42	11	4	6	35	25	8	5	8	30	31	19	9	14	65	56	9	66
10	Poole T	42	13	3	5	40	30	6	4	11	34	39	19	7	16	74	69	5	64
11	Walton Casuals	42	10	7	4	34	29	6	3	12	19	32	16	10	16	53	61	–8	58
12	Swindon Supermarine	42	11	4	6	38	27	5	5	11	25	36	16	9	17	63	63	0	57
13	Tiverton T	42	8	5	8	28	23	7	3	11	33	40	15	8	19	61	63	–2	53
14	Harrow Bor	42	9	5	7	31	32	6	2	13	31	45	15	7	20	62	77	–15	52
15	Salisbury	42	5	5	11	21	36	8	4	9	28	39	13	9	20	49	75	–26	48
16	Hendon	42	10	0	11	33	32	4	5	12	25	38	14	5	23	58	70	–12	47
17	Beaconsfield T	42	7	5	9	46	42	6	2	13	24	50	13	7	22	70	92	–22	46
18	Hartley Wintney	42	10	2	9	27	27	3	3	15	29	48	13	5	24	56	75	–19	44
19	Dorchester T®	42	7	2	12	25	27	5	3	13	16	31	12	5	25	41	58	–17	41
20	Kings Langley®	42	5	6	10	31	27	4	4	13	18	41	9	10	23	49	68	–19	37
21	Merthyr T	42	3	2	16	24	46	3	6	12	23	48	6	8	28	47	94	–47	26
22	Wimborne T	42	3	3	15	20	51	1	4	16	15	55	4	7	31	35	106	–71	19

¶Farnborough promoted after play-offs. ®Dorchester T and King's Langley reprieved from relegation.

PITCHING IN ISTHMIAN LEAGUE – PREMIER DIVISION

			Home					*Away*					*Total*						
		P	*W*	*D*	*L*	*F*	*A*	*W*	*D*	*L*	*F*	*A*	*W*	*D*	*L*	*F*	*A*	*GD*	*Pts*
1	Worthing	42	18	1	2	56	17	13	3	5	44	28	31	4	7	100	45	55	97
2	Bishop's Stortford	42	14	6	1	57	19	11	6	4	32	14	25	12	5	89	33	56	87
3	Enfield T	42	16	2	3	42	20	10	4	7	49	37	26	6	10	91	57	34	84
4	Hornchurch	42	13	3	5	44	19	12	3	6	45	23	25	6	11	89	42	47	81
5	Cheshunt¶	42	9	5	7	31	20	13	5	3	40	20	22	10	10	71	40	31	76
6	Folkestone Invicta	42	11	7	3	44	21	9	5	7	41	41	20	12	10	85	62	23	72
7	Lewes	42	10	5	6	44	30	10	5	6	45	33	20	10	12	89	63	26	70
8	Margate	42	13	3	5	38	28	6	5	10	22	34	19	8	15	60	62	–2	65
9	Bognor Regis T	42	8	6	7	33	33	7	8	6	29	25	15	14	13	62	58	4	59
10	Kingstonian	42	10	5	6	39	30	7	3	11	29	41	17	8	17	68	71	–3	59
11	Horsham	42	8	6	7	38	31	8	3	10	28	27	16	9	17	66	58	8	57
12	Carshalton Ath	42	10	3	8	40	29	5	9	7	25	28	15	12	15	65	57	8	57
13	Potters Bar T	42	8	2	11	28	38	8	3	10	26	36	16	5	21	54	74	–20	53
14	Corinthian-Casuals	42	5	7	9	20	25	8	6	7	31	33	13	13	16	51	58	–7	52
15	Wingate & Finchley	42	7	6	8	34	30	6	4	11	26	44	13	10	19	60	74	–14	49
16	Bowers & Pitsea	42	5	2	14	23	38	7	7	7	31	34	12	9	21	54	72	–18	45
17	Haringey Bor	42	5	11	5	42	40	4	4	13	15	41	9	15	18	57	81	–24	42
18	Brightlingsea Regent	42	7	2	12	24	46	4	4	13	20	46	11	6	25	44	92	–48	39
19	Cray W*®	42	5	4	12	37	44	5	5	11	27	41	10	9	23	64	85	–21	36
20	Leatherhead	42	3	4	14	16	37	6	5	10	27	46	9	9	24	43	83	–40	36
21	East Thurrock U	42	6	6	9	24	37	3	2	16	20	61	9	8	25	44	98	–54	35
22	Merstham	42	6	3	12	28	35	4	0	17	15	49	10	3	29	43	84	–41	33

*¶Cheshunt promoted after play-offs. *Cray W deducted 3 points for fielding an ineligible player.*
®Cray W reprieved from relegation.

NATIONAL LEAGUE SYSTEM STEP 4

PITCHING IN NORTHERN PREMIER LEAGUE – DIVISION ONE EAST

1	Liversedge	36	15	3	0	56	12	14	3	1	42	10	29	6	1	98	22	76	93
2	Marske U¶	36	14	2	2	46	16	14	2	2	48	18	28	4	4	94	34	60	88
3	Cleethorpes T	36	7	6	5	34	25	14	0	4	40	21	21	6	9	74	46	28	69
4	Stockton T	36	11	5	2	41	20	8	4	6	38	21	19	9	8	79	41	38	66
5	Shildon	36	11	4	3	37	16	8	2	8	24	19	19	6	11	61	35	26	63
6	Dunston UTS	36	12	0	6	42	25	5	3	10	25	35	17	3	16	67	60	7	54
7	Brighouse T	36	7	5	6	27	24	8	4	6	32	28	15	9	12	59	52	7	54
8	Worksop T	36	9	3	6	36	29	7	3	8	20	24	16	6	14	56	53	3	54
9	Ossett U	36	11	3	4	27	24	4	5	9	16	35	15	8	13	43	59	–16	53
10	Yorkshire Amateur†	36	9	2	7	27	23	5	3	10	28	40	14	5	17	55	63	–8	47
11	Stocksbridge Park Steels	36	11	2	5	33	24	2	5	11	20	34	13	7	16	53	58	–5	46
12	Pontefract Collieries	36	7	1	10	23	28	6	3	9	18	26	13	4	19	41	54	–13	43
13	Hebburn T	36	7	2	9	26	33	5	4	9	21	23	12	6	18	47	56	–9	42
14	Tadcaster Alb	36	4	4	10	21	34	6	3	9	26	29	10	7	19	47	63	–16	37
15	Bridlington T	36	7	4	7	26	32	2	3	13	14	33	9	7	20	40	65	–25	34
16	Lincoln U®	36	5	6	7	23	34	4	1	13	33	57	9	7	20	56	91	–35	34
17	Sheffield FC®	36	6	4	8	22	28	2	5	11	25	49	8	9	19	47	77	–30	33
18	Frickley Ath	36	4	2	12	16	32	4	4	10	14	35	8	6	22	30	67	–37	30
19	Pickering T*	36	5	2	11	27	50	2	3	13	25	53	7	5	24	52	103	–51	20

*¶Marske U promoted after play-offs. *Pickering T deducted 6 points for fielding an ineligible player.*
®Lincoln U and Sheffield FC reprieved from relegation play-offs. †Yorkshire Amateur relegated to Step 5 for failing ground criteria for Level 4 (appeal dismissed).

PITCHING IN NORTHERN PREMIER LEAGUE – DIVISION ONE WEST

1	Warrington Rylands 1906	38	15	2	2	65	20	11	5	3	30	18	26	7	5	95	38	57	85
2	Workington	38	13	4	2	39	14	12	5	2	33	13	25	9	4	72	27	45	84
3	Leek T	38	11	6	2	41	16	13	1	5	33	20	24	7	7	74	36	38	79
4	Runcorn Linnets	38	11	6	2	40	15	12	1	6	32	24	23	7	8	72	39	33	76
5	Marine¶*	38	13	1	5	33	24	11	4	4	30	16	24	5	9	63	40	23	74
6	Clitheroe	38	13	2	4	50	21	8	6	5	28	23	21	8	9	78	44	34	71
7	Bootle	38	11	0	8	40	30	9	2	8	38	35	20	2	16	78	65	13	62
8	Mossley	38	7	6	6	24	26	10	0	9	36	33	17	6	15	60	59	1	57
9	City of Liverpool	38	7	6	6	16	15	7	5	7	32	36	14	11	13	48	51	–3	53
10	Kidsgrove Ath	38	8	3	8	25	21	6	5	8	26	32	14	8	16	51	53	–2	50
11	Trafford	38	9	4	6	29	24	4	6	9	27	31	13	10	15	56	55	1	49
12	1874 Northwich	38	5	3	11	31	36	8	5	6	28	22	13	8	17	59	58	1	47
13	Widnes	38	8	4	7	27	23	5	4	10	19	22	13	8	17	46	45	1	47
14	Colne	38	6	4	9	14	20	6	4	9	25	34	12	8	18	39	54	–15	44
15	Ramsbottom U	38	10	2	7	34	22	2	4	13	13	40	12	6	20	47	62	–15	42
16	Newcastle T	38	5	4	10	29	30	5	6	8	20	34	10	10	18	49	64	–15	40
17	Glossop North End®	38	6	6	7	26	29	3	7	9	10	26	9	13	16	36	55	–19	40
18	Prescot Cables®	38	8	2	9	30	30	4	1	14	19	40	12	3	23	49	70	–21	39
19	Kendal T*	38	2	3	14	14	41	1	1	17	14	49	3	4	31	28	90	–62	12
20	Market Drayton T	38	2	5	12	12	45	0	1	18	9	71	2	6	30	21	116	–95	12

*¶Marine promoted after play-offs. *Marine deducted 3 points for fielding an ineligible player. ®Glossop North End and Prescot Cables reprieved from relegation play-offs. *Kendal Town deducted 1 point for fielding an ineligible player.*

PITCHING IN NORTHERN PREMIER LEAGUE – DIVISION ONE MIDLANDS

			Home					Away					Total						
		P	W	D	L	F	A	W	D	L	F	A	W	D	L	F	A	GD	Pts
1	Ilkeston T	38	14	2	3	59	24	13	4	2	38	18	27	6	5	97	42	55	87
2	Stamford	38	13	3	3	53	22	13	3	3	42	14	26	6	6	95	36	59	84
3	Halesowen T	38	13	2	4	43	16	12	6	1	49	23	25	8	5	92	39	53	83
4	Chasetown	38	12	5	2	39	19	13	2	4	40	19	25	7	6	79	38	41	82
5	Belper T¶	38	13	2	4	43	21	10	2	7	30	30	23	4	11	73	51	22	73
6	Carlton T	38	12	5	2	39	21	7	6	6	32	27	19	11	8	71	48	23	68
7	Coleshill T	38	8	3	8	34	28	11	1	7	37	21	19	4	15	71	49	22	61
8	Sporting Khalsa	38	11	3	5	46	30	7	3	9	30	38	18	6	14	76	68	8	60
9	Cambridge C	38	6	5	8	32	33	9	4	6	28	25	15	9	14	60	58	2	54
10	Spalding U	38	9	4	6	26	25	6	4	9	21	31	15	8	15	47	56	–9	53
11	Shepshed Dynamo	38	8	6	5	27	23	5	6	8	28	37	13	12	13	55	60	–5	51
12	Bedworth U	38	8	5	6	25	20	5	3	11	22	39	13	8	17	47	59	–12	47
13	Loughborough Dynamo	38	7	4	8	41	37	6	2	11	30	39	13	6	19	71	76	–5	45
14	Yaxley	38	7	3	9	34	45	5	2	12	25	50	12	5	21	59	95	–36	41
15	Corby T	38	7	4	8	26	27	4	3	12	30	39	11	7	20	56	66	–10	40
16	Daventry T	38	6	4	9	25	42	4	5	10	25	38	10	9	19	50	80	–30	39
17	Sutton Coldfield T®	38	7	3	9	21	20	2	7	10	21	42	9	10	19	42	62	–20	37
18	Histon§	38	2	7	10	19	39	3	2	14	18	52	5	9	24	37	91	–54	24
19	Soham Town Rangers	38	3	0	16	16	49	2	6	11	26	42	5	6	27	42	91	–49	21
20	Wisbech T	38	3	2	14	22	44	2	1	16	13	46	5	3	30	35	90	–55	18

¶Belper T promoted after play-offs. ®Sutton Coldfield T reprieved from relegation play-offs.
§Histon relegated after play-offs.

PITCHING IN SOUTHERN LEAGUE – DIVISION ONE CENTRAL

		P	W	D	L	F	A	W	D	L	F	A	W	D	L	F	A	GD	Pts
1	Bedford T	38	16	2	1	54	13	12	5	2	46	15	28	7	3	100	28	72	91
2	Berkhamsted	38	13	3	3	37	14	11	6	2	27	15	24	9	5	64	29	35	81
3	AFC Dunstable	38	12	4	3	37	17	9	6	4	27	16	21	10	7	64	33	31	73
4	Ware	38	10	6	3	53	24	11	2	6	37	23	21	8	9	90	47	43	71
5	Welwyn Garden C†	38	11	6	2	41	19	10	2	7	39	29	21	8	9	80	48	32	71
6	North Leigh¶	38	10	3	6	37	23	9	8	2	32	19	19	11	8	69	42	27	68
7	Harlow T	38	8	7	4	39	24	9	3	7	32	25	17	10	11	71	49	22	61
8	Thame U	38	8	6	5	38	25	8	6	5	26	20	16	12	10	64	45	19	60
9	Biggleswade	38	9	3	7	27	24	9	3	7	35	32	18	6	14	62	56	6	60
10	St Neots T	38	6	6	7	32	30	8	5	6	25	23	14	11	13	57	53	4	53
11	Waltham Abbey	38	8	3	8	33	36	7	4	8	31	28	15	7	16	64	64	0	52
12	FC Romania	38	8	1	10	33	35	7	2	10	38	48	15	3	20	71	83	–12	48
13	Didcot T	38	5	3	11	25	38	8	5	6	25	31	13	8	17	50	69	–19	47
14	Aylesbury U	38	7	3	9	27	26	5	4	10	37	44	12	7	19	64	70	–6	43
15	Barton R	38	5	3	11	17	30	6	5	8	30	33	11	8	19	47	63	–16	41
16	Hertford T	38	7	1	11	29	41	3	5	11	29	41	10	6	22	58	82	–24	36
17	Kidlington	38	4	9	6	27	39	4	2	13	20	47	8	11	19	47	86	–39	35
18	Kempston R§	38	5	3	11	27	47	3	2	14	23	55	8	5	25	50	102	–52	29
19	Colney Heath	38	5	1	13	22	37	2	1	16	13	55	7	2	29	35	92	–57	23
20	Wantage T	38	2	4	13	21	46	3	1	15	16	57	5	5	28	37	103	–66	20

†Welwyn Garden C relegated to Step 5 for failing ground criteria for Level 4 (subject to appeal).
¶North Leigh promoted after play-offs. §Kempston R retained place in league after play-offs.

PITCHING IN SOUTHERN LEAGUE – DIVISION ONE SOUTH

		P	W	D	L	F	A	W	D	L	F	A	W	D	L	F	A	GD	Pts
1	Plymouth Parkway	36	15	2	1	49	11	11	1	6	43	29	26	3	7	92	40	52	81
2	Frome T	36	12	4	2	40	16	11	5	2	36	14	23	9	4	76	30	46	78
3	Cirencester T	36	13	4	1	42	17	10	4	4	33	12	23	8	5	75	29	46	77
4	Winchester C¶	36	10	5	3	48	23	11	3	4	45	24	21	8	7	93	47	46	71
5	Bristol Manor Farm	36	10	5	3	29	16	10	4	4	35	25	20	9	7	64	41	23	69
6	AFC Totton	36	11	2	5	36	18	10	3	5	47	19	21	5	10	83	37	46	68
7	Sholing	36	11	4	3	29	12	8	2	8	30	24	19	6	11	59	36	23	63
8	Melksham T	36	8	5	5	31	31	7	3	8	25	28	15	8	13	56	59	–3	53
9	Paulton R	36	6	4	8	28	28	8	3	7	44	33	14	7	15	72	61	11	49
10	Highworth T	36	8	4	6	28	23	4	2	12	13	36	12	6	18	41	59	–18	42
11	Larkhall Ath	36	5	5	8	26	28	4	7	7	17	20	9	12	15	43	48	–5	39
12	Bideford	36	7	1	10	18	25	4	5	9	18	30	11	6	19	36	55	–19	39
13	Evesham U	36	7	4	7	31	38	4	2	12	19	34	11	6	19	50	72	–22	39
14	Slimbridge	36	7	3	8	35	39	4	2	12	17	44	11	5	20	52	83	–31	38
15	Willand R	36	5	3	10	23	28	5	4	9	31	34	10	7	19	54	62	–8	37
16	Lymington T®	36	5	5	8	26	43	4	4	10	25	47	9	9	18	51	90	–39	36
17	Cinderford T§	36	6	3	9	28	40	2	4	12	26	43	8	7	21	54	83	–29	31
18	Mangotsfield U	36	5	2	11	24	47	2	4	12	18	44	7	6	23	42	91	–49	27
19	Barnstaple T	36	6	0	12	25	59	1	3	14	20	56	7	3	26	45	115	–70	24

¶Winchester C promoted after play-offs. ®Lymington T reprieved from relegation play-offs.
§Cinderford T relegated after play-offs.

PITCHING IN ISTHMIAN LEAGUE – DIVISION ONE NORTH

			Home					*Away*					*Total*						
		P	*W*	*D*	*L*	*F*	*A*	*W*	*D*	*L*	*F*	*A*	*W*	*D*	*L*	*F*	*A*	*GD*	*Pts*
1	Aveley	38	15	3	1	58	17	9	5	5	36	20	24	8	6	94	37	57	80
2	Canvey Island¶	38	13	2	4	58	19	11	4	4	42	23	24	6	8	100	42	58	78
3	Brentwood T	38	12	1	6	33	19	12	2	5	40	22	24	3	11	73	41	32	75
4	Stowmarket T	38	11	6	2	35	15	10	4	5	40	24	21	10	7	75	39	36	73
5	Felixstowe & Walton U	38	12	2	5	28	17	11	1	7	32	28	23	3	12	60	45	15	72
6	Grays Ath	38	12	3	4	40	22	8	5	6	29	16	20	8	10	69	38	31	68
7	AFC Sudbury	38	10	4	5	29	23	8	5	6	28	23	18	9	11	57	46	11	63
8	Hashtag U	38	8	4	7	30	24	10	4	5	30	25	18	8	12	60	49	11	62
9	Maldon & Tiptree	38	10	2	7	30	30	8	4	7	44	33	18	6	14	74	63	11	60
10	Dereham T	38	11	3	5	36	21	8	0	11	27	32	19	3	16	63	53	10	60
11	Heybridge Swifts	38	9	3	7	49	45	7	2	10	28	28	16	5	17	77	73	4	53
12	Bury T	38	7	4	8	32	36	5	4	10	31	35	12	8	18	63	71	–8	44
13	Coggeshall T	38	7	5	7	31	31	4	5	10	22	37	11	10	17	53	68	–15	43
14	Tilbury	38	6	5	8	27	28	5	3	11	30	40	11	8	19	57	68	–11	41
15	Great Wakering R	38	4	6	9	28	39	6	4	9	30	35	10	10	18	58	74	–16	40
16	Hullbridge Sports	38	4	6	9	22	38	6	3	10	21	34	10	9	19	43	72	–29	39
17	Basildon U®	38	2	3	14	11	35	7	5	7	24	25	9	8	21	35	60	–25	35
18	Witham T§	38	1	6	12	11	31	6	6	7	29	40	7	12	19	40	71	–31	33
19	Barking*	38	5	3	11	27	41	4	5	10	24	38	9	8	21	51	79	–28	32
20	Romford	38	1	2	16	12	70	2	2	15	14	69	3	4	31	26	139	–113	13

¶Canvey Island promoted after play-offs. ®Basildon U reprieved from relegation play-offs.
*§Witham T retained place in league after play-offs. *Barking deducted 3 points for breach of rules.*

PITCHING IN ISTHMIAN LEAGUE – DIVISION ONE SOUTH CENTRAL

		P	*W*	*D*	*L*	*F*	*A*	*W*	*D*	*L*	*F*	*A*	*W*	*D*	*L*	*F*	*A*	*GD*	*Pts*
1	Bracknell T	36	15	1	2	45	6	16	2	0	45	6	31	3	2	90	12	78	96
2	Chertsey T	36	9	3	6	37	27	14	4	0	44	13	23	7	6	81	40	41	76
3	Bedfont Sports	36	13	4	1	53	20	9	4	5	33	27	22	8	6	86	47	39	74
4	Hanwell T¶	36	9	6	3	41	22	12	3	3	42	15	21	9	6	83	37	46	72
5	Basingstoke T	36	8	3	7	31	35	13	4	1	34	14	21	7	8	65	49	16	70
6	Uxbridge	36	13	1	4	34	23	6	8	4	30	19	19	9	8	64	42	22	66
7	Marlow	36	12	2	4	35	15	6	5	7	17	25	18	7	11	52	40	12	61
8	Binfield	36	4	7	7	21	25	10	4	4	36	25	14	11	11	57	50	7	53
9	South Park	36	9	5	4	36	19	5	4	9	31	34	14	9	13	67	53	14	51
10	Chipstead	36	6	8	4	27	17	6	4	8	33	35	12	12	12	60	52	8	48
11	Northwood	36	3	5	10	18	38	9	1	8	33	29	12	6	18	51	67	–16	42
12	Thatcham T	36	4	4	10	20	35	6	4	8	28	30	10	8	18	48	65	–17	38
13	Ashford T (Middx)	36	6	0	12	23	34	6	2	10	19	26	12	2	22	42	60	–18	38
14	Guernsey	36	5	6	7	35	36	4	3	11	25	43	9	9	18	60	79	–19	36
15	Tooting & Mitcham U	36	5	4	9	22	24	4	3	11	20	32	9	7	20	42	56	–14	34
16	Westfield	36	5	6	7	20	23	2	7	9	18	31	7	13	16	38	54	–16	34
17	Sutton Common R®	36	5	1	12	23	45	5	3	10	23	37	10	4	22	46	82	–36	34
18	Chalfont St Peter§	36	4	1	13	14	30	2	2	14	17	53	6	3	27	31	83	–52	21
19	Staines T	36	2	1	15	15	71	2	1	15	17	56	4	2	30	32	127	–95	14
20	Whyteleafe*	0	0	0	0	0	0	0	0	0	0	0	0	0	0	0	0	0	0

*¶Hanwell T promoted after play-offs. *Whyteleafe resigned.*
®Sutton Common R reprieved from relegation play-offs. §Chalfont St Peter relegated after play-offs.

PITCHING IN ISTHMIAN LEAGUE – DIVISION ONE SOUTH EAST

		P	*W*	*D*	*L*	*F*	*A*	*W*	*D*	*L*	*F*	*A*	*W*	*D*	*L*	*F*	*A*	*GD*	*Pts*
1	Hastings U	38	13	2	4	42	14	14	2	3	40	19	27	4	7	82	33	49	85
2	Ashford U	38	11	4	4	41	23	11	2	6	38	25	22	6	10	79	48	31	72
3	Herne Bay¶	38	12	2	5	37	17	9	5	5	26	17	21	7	10	63	34	29	70
4	Haywards Heath T	38	10	3	6	23	14	9	7	3	28	19	19	10	9	51	33	18	67
5	Cray Valley PM	38	9	4	6	25	17	10	5	4	45	31	19	9	10	70	48	22	66
6	Ramsgate	38	10	3	6	43	26	10	2	7	37	26	20	5	13	80	52	28	65
7	Burgess Hill T	38	9	6	4	28	19	9	2	8	29	28	18	8	12	57	47	10	62
8	Corinthian	38	7	7	5	20	20	9	4	6	30	19	16	11	11	50	39	11	59
9	VCD Athletic	38	8	5	6	39	25	7	4	8	27	29	15	9	14	66	54	12	54
10	Sittingbourne	38	9	4	6	25	22	6	3	10	22	29	15	7	16	47	51	–4	52
11	Chichester C	38	9	3	7	29	23	4	7	8	19	20	13	10	15	48	43	5	49
12	Faversham T	38	10	3	6	28	23	4	4	11	15	33	14	7	17	43	56	–13	49
13	Sevenoaks T	38	9	1	9	33	33	6	2	11	21	33	15	3	20	54	66	–12	48
14	Three Bridges	38	6	5	8	36	39	5	6	8	24	36	11	11	16	60	75	–15	44
15	East Grinstead T	38	8	5	6	24	29	2	6	11	12	37	10	11	17	36	66	–30	41
16	Whitehawk	38	4	7	8	14	21	5	5	9	25	33	9	12	17	39	54	–15	39
17	Hythe T®	38	3	5	11	19	40	7	4	8	21	32	10	9	19	40	72	–32	39
18	Lancing§	38	5	4	10	19	32	4	5	10	15	33	9	9	20	34	65	–31	36
19	Phoenix Sports	38	4	3	12	21	38	5	3	11	14	26	9	6	23	35	64	–29	33
20	Whitstable T	38	4	4	11	21	31	4	2	13	18	42	8	6	24	39	73	–34	30

¶Herne Bay promoted after play-offs. ®Hythe T reprieved from relegation play-offs.
§Lancing retained place in league after play-offs.

THE BUILDBASE FA TROPHY 2021–22

FIRST QUALIFYING ROUND

Pontefract Collieries v Yorkshire Amateur 1-1
Yorkshire Amateur won 4-2 on penalties
Widnes v Brighouse T 2-0
City of Liverpool v Stockton T 0-0
City of Liverpool won 4-3 on penalties
Dunston UTS v Worksop T 3-2
Sporting Khalsa v Dereham T 6-5
Stamford v Daventry T 0-1
Bedford T v St Neots T 1-0
Kempston R v Newcastle T 2-2
Newcastle T won 4-3 on penalties
Hastings U v AFC Dunstable 3-0
Welwyn Garden City v Hythe T 3-3
Welwyn Garden City won 4-1 on penalties
Ramsgate v Sutton Common R 5-0
Hashtag U v Chipstead 1-4
Stowmarket T v Great Wakering R 1-1
Great Wakering R won 4-3 on penalties
Corinthian v Grays Ath 1-1
Corinthian won 5-4 on penalties
Canvey Island v Coggeshall T 4-1
Ashford U v Chalfont St Peter 1-1
Ashford U won 5-4 on penalties
Chichester C v Whitstable T 4-0
Wantage T v Willand R 1-2
Thame U v Winchester C 3-2

SECOND QUALIFYING ROUND

Mossley v Ossett U 3-1
Bridlington T v Sheffield 3-3
Bridlington T won 5-4 on penalties
Clitheroe v Liversedge 1-1
Liversedge won 10-9 on penalties
Trafford v Bootle 1-1
Bootle won 3-1 on penalties
Prescot Cables v Frickley Ath 0-2
Pickering T v Ramsbottom U 2-1
Tadcaster Alb v Runcorn Linnets 1-5
1874 Northwich v Marine 1-1
Marine won 4-1 on penalties
Stocksbridge Park Steels v Widnes 0-2
Kendal T v Yorkshire Amateur 0-3
Marske U v Glossop North End 3-0
City of Liverpool v Colne 0-1
Cleethorpes T v Shildon 0-2
Warrington Rylands v Hebburn T 0-0
Hebburn T won 3-2 on penalties
Workington v Dunston UTS 0-1
Market Drayton T v Leek T 0-7
Soham T Rangers v Shepshed Dynamo 1-0
Coleshill T v Newcastle T 2-3
Chasetown v Halesowen T 0-0
Chasetown won 4-2 on penalties
Bury T v Wisbech T 0-2
Kidsgrove Ath v Evesham U 4-1
Spalding U v Belper T 3-2
Carlton T v Bedworth U 1-1
Carlton T won 5-4 on penalties
Bedford T v Cambridge C 5-0
Loughborough Dynamo v Sporting Khalsa 3-6
Corby T v Histon 5-3
Lincoln U v Sutton Coldfield T 0-3
Yaxley v Biggleswade 2-0
Daventry T v Ilkeston T 0-0
Ilkeston T won 4-1 on penalties
Chichester C v Great Wakering R 1-2
Westfield v Ramsgate 3-2
Heybridge Swifts v Barking 2-0
Faversham T v Tilbury 3-2
AFC Sudbury v Cray Valley (PM) 0-0
AFC Sudbury won 3-2 on penalties
Maldon & Tiptree v Felixstowe & Walton U 1-1
Felixstowe & Walton U won 7-6 on penalties
Sittingbourne v Herne Bay 1-3
Staines T v Three Bridges 3-1
South Park (walkover) v Whyteleafe
Colney Heath v Basildon U 2-5
VCD Ath v Chertsey T 1-2
Northwood v Haywards Heath T 0-0
Northwood won 4-3 on penalties
Marlow v FC Romania 1-0
Welwyn Garden City v Ashford T (Middlesex) 3-0
East Grinstead T v Waltham Abbey 2-2
Waltham Abbey won 4-2 on penalties
Barton R v Berkhamsted 0-2
Hullbridge Sports v Hanwell T 1-4
Bedfont Sports Club v Romford 3-1
Tooting & Mitcham U v Whitehawk 1-4
Witham T v Lancing 1-0
Burgess Hill T v Sevenoaks T 1-1
Burgess Hill T won 3-1 on penalties
Bracknell T v Hertford T 3-2
Ware v Canvey Island 2-2
Canvey Island won 7-6 on penalties
Corinthian v Brentwood T 1-2
Aveley v Uxbridge 1-2
Hastings U v Ashford U 2-0
Aylesbury U v Chipstead 1-1
Chipstead won 4-2 on penalties
Harlow T v Phoenix Sports 3-1
Bristol Manor Farm v Paulton R 1-2
Melksham T v Basingstoke T 3-2
Didcot T v Frome T 1-5
North Leigh v Binfield 2-2
Binfield won 4-1 on penalties
Willand R v Mangotsfield U 2-1
Cinderford T v Bideford 0-0
Cinderford T won 4-2 on penalties
Cirencester T v Kidlington 5-1
Thame U v Lymington T 3-0
Larkhall Ath v Slimbridge 3-1
Thatcham T v Sholing 1-1
Thatcham T won 3-2 on penalties
AFC Totton v Barnstaple T 6-0
Highworth T v Plymouth Parkway 3-5

THIRD QUALIFYING ROUND

Bridlington T v Marske U 0-7
Marine v South Shields 0-0
Marine won 5-3 on penalties
Hebburn T v Warrington T 0-2
Morpeth T v Pickering T 4-2
Bootle v Widnes 1-1
Bootle won 4-3 on penalties
Stalybridge Celtic v Yorkshire Amateur 4-1
Shildon v Whitby T 0-1
Dunston UTS v Bamber Bridge 2-2
Dunston UTS won 3-2 on penalties
Runcorn Linnets v FC United of Manchester 0-2
Buxton v Colne 1-2
Ashton U v Atherton Collieries 1-0
Witton Alb v Lancaster C 1-2
Hyde U v Mossley 1-2
Radcliffe v Frickley Ath 3-1
Liversedge v Scarborough Ath 4-0
Spalding U v Tamworth 1-1
Tamworth won 4-2 on penalties
Wisbech T v Biggleswade T 0-2
Lowestoft T v Yaxley 2-3
Sutton Coldfield T v Newcastle T 0-0
Sutton Coldfield T won 5-4 on penalties
Hitchin T v Leiston 1-3
Redditch U v Stourbridge 0-1
Gainsborough Trinity v Coalville T 3-0
Mickleover v Grantham T 0-1
Chasetown v Alvechurch 2-1
Hednesford T v Peterborough Sports 2-3
Royston T v Stratford T 2-1
Carlton T v Kidsgrove Ath 2-2
Carlton T won 4-3 on penalties
Sporting Khalsa v Rushall Olympic 1-4
Corby T v Banbury U 0-1
Nantwich T v Barwell 2-1
Soham T Rangers v Nuneaton Bor 0-3
Matlock T v Rushden & D 2-1
St Ives T v Needham Market 0-2
Bedford T v Stafford Rangers 3-1
Bromsgrove Sporting v Ilkeston T 2-0
Basford U v Leek T 2-1
Bishop's Stortford v Lewes 2-0
Faversham T v Leatherhead 2-1

Margate v Beaconsfield T 2-0
Herne Bay v Binfield 0-2
Cray W v Kings Langley 4-1
East Thurrock U v Kingstonian 0-6
Hastings U v Felixstowe & Walton U 1-3
Enfield T v Metropolitan Police 2-1
Witham T v Hanwell T 1-3
Farnborough v Bowers & Pitsea 4-1
Horsham v Carshalton Ath 2-3
Chipstead v Whitehawk 2-1
Corinthian Casuals v Cheshunt 0-1
Merstham v Welwyn Garden City 1-3
Heybridge Swifts v Hayes & Yeading U 2-2
Hayes & Yeading U won 4-1 on penalties
Marlow v Westfield 4-3
Potters Bar T v Haringey Bor 2-0
Chertsey T v Worthing 0-2
South Park v Harrow Bor 0-1
Folkestone Invicta v Hendon 2-1
Walton Casuals v Great Wakering R 2-1
Wingate & Finchley v Hornchurch 1-1
Wingate & Finchley won 5-4 on penalties
Staines T v Brightlingsea Regent 1-0
Bedfont Sports Club v Harlow T 2-1
Brentwood T v AFC Sudbury 3-0
Northwood v Berkhamsted 2-2
Berkhamsted won 6-5 on penalties
Bognor Regis T v Waltham Abbey 5-0
Chesham U v Bracknell T 1-1
Bracknell T won 2-1 on penalties
Uxbridge v Basildon U 2-1
Canvey Island v Burgess Hill T 3-0
Weston-super-Mare v Taunton T 3-2
Thame U v Wimborne T 2-4
AFC Totton v Dorchester T 2-0
Paulton R v Larkhall Ath 1-5
Gosport Bor v Salisbury 1-2
Truro C v Cirencester T 1-0
Yate T v Willand R 0-2
Tiverton T v Swindon Supermarine 1-1
Tiverton T won 5-4 on penalties
Frome T v Poole T 3-2
Plymouth Parkway v Merthyr T 1-0
Cinderford T v Thatcham T 2-2
Cinderford T won 5-4 on penalties
Hartley Wintney v Melksham T 2-1

FIRST ROUND
Radcliffe v Nuneaton Bor 2-0
Marske U v FC United of Manchester 3-2
Rushall Olympic v Matlock T 0-4
Ashton U v Sutton Coldfield T 5-1
Nantwich T v Grantham T 2-1
Warrington T v Chasetown 2-0
Colne v Tamworth 1-1
Tamworth won 4-3 on penalties
Bromsgrove Sporting v Morpeth T 0-0
Morpeth T won 4-3 on penalties
Whitby T v Mossley 5-0
Marine v Dunston UTS 2-2
Marine won 5-4 on penalties
Carlton T v Stourbridge 1-2
Bootle v Stalybridge Celtic 3-3
Stalybridge Celtic won 5-3 on penalties
Gainsborough Trinity v Lancaster C 1-2
Liversedge v Basford U 3-2
Walton Casuals v Uxbridge 2-6
Canvey Island v Yaxley 6-0
Brentwood T v Staines T 4-1
Needham Market v Margate 3-2
Hayes & Yeading U v Worthing 0-3
Bishop's Stortford v Chipstead 2-1
Royston T v Kingstonian 1-1
Kingstonian won 4-3 on penalties
Welwyn Garden City v Carshalton Ath 2-1
Cheshunt v Berkhamsted 1-0
Bedford T v Potters Bar T 0-1
Match abandoned after 93 minutes due to violence between teams and staff. The score was 0-1 to Potters Bar T and the FA decided that the result should stand at 0-1.
Leiston v Harrow Bor 3-0
Biggleswade T v Enfield T 1-2
Felixstowe & Walton U v Peterborough Sports 2-1
Hanwell T v Wingate & Finchley 1-0
Cray W v Bedfont Sports Club 2-1
Folkestone Invicta v Faversham T 2-1
Farnborough v Banbury U 1-0
Marlow v Larkhall Ath 2-2
Larkhall Ath won 6-5 on penalties
Weston-super-Mare v Wimborne T 1-2
Hartley Wintney v Willand R 3-0
Binfield v Cinderford T 3-0
Bracknell T v Tiverton T 1-3
AFC Totton v Frome T 2-2
AFC Totton won 4-2 on penalties
Truro C v Bognor Regis T 1-1
Truro C won 4-2 on penalties
Plymouth Parkway v Salisbury 4-0

SECOND ROUND
Bradford (Park Avenue) v Marine 3-3
Bradford (Park Avenue) won 3-0 on penalties
York C v Blyth Spartans 1-0
Farsley Celtic v Stalybridge Celtic 1-0
Liversedge v Lancaster C 1-3
Ashton U v Guiseley 1-2
Warrington T v Morpeth T 1-1
Morpeth T won 5-3 on penalties
Curzon Ashton v Chester 2-1
Southport v Darlington 1-1
Southport won 5-4 on penalties
Spennymoor T v Chorley 0-0
Spennymoor T won 3-1 on penalties
Radcliffe v Tamworth 5-1
Matlock T v Marske U 3-2
AFC Fylde v Gateshead 1-0
Whitby T v Nantwich T 0-1
Gloucester C v Kettering T 3-0
Needham Market v Welwyn Garden City 3-1
Hereford v Kidderminster H 1-1
Kidderminster H won 5-3 on penalties
Bishop's Stortford v Leiston 5-1
Leamington v Alfreton T 0-3
Braintree T v Potters Bar T 3-1
Chelmsford C v Cheshunt 1-2
Oxford C v St Albans C 1-4
Felixstowe & Walton U v AFC Telford U 0-4
Brackley T v Boston U 1-2
Hemel Hempstead T v Stourbridge 1-1
Stourbridge won 6-5 on penalties
Hungerford T v Welling U 3-2
Cray W v Ebbsfleet U 2-2
Cray W won 5-3 on penalties
Hanwell T v Enfield T 0-2
Slough T v Havant & Waterlooville 1-0
Binfield v Truro C 2-3
Bath C v Dartford 0-0
Dartford won 5-3 on penalties
Concord Rangers v AFC Totton 0-5
Kingstonian v Farnborough 4-1
Plymouth Parkway v Hampton & Richmond Bor 1-0
Canvey Island v Tonbridge Angels 0-1
Eastbourne Bor v Tiverton T 2-1
Brentwood T v Dulwich Hamlet 1-2
Chippenham T v Uxbridge 0-1
Maidstone U v Billericay T 1-1
Maidstone U won 6-5 on penalties
Wimborne T v Larkhall Ath 1-2
Worthing v Dorking W 0-2
Hartley Wintney v Folkestone Invicta 0-2

THIRD ROUND
Boston U v Kidderminster H 4-1
Matlock T v York C 0-1
Stockport Co v Grimsby T 4-0
Stourbridge v AFC Telford U 3-2
Morpeth T v Lancaster C 3-3
Morpeth T won 5-3 on penalties
Chesterfield v Guiseley (walkover)
King's Lynn T v Nantwich T 2-1
Farsley Celtic v Southport 0-3
Wrexham v Gloucester C 5-0
Bradford (Park Avenue) v FC Halifax T 3-3
FC Halifax T won 5-3 on penalties
AFC Fylde v Solihull Moors 0-1
Curzon Ashton v Alfreton T 1-3
Radcliffe v Spennymoor T 0-1
Eastleigh v Enfield T 5-0
Cheshunt v Bishop's Stortford 0-0
Cheshunt won 4-3 on penalties
Aldershot T v Kingstonian 2-1

Cray W v Dartford 1-3
Southend U v Dorking W 2-1
Larkhall Ath v AFC Totton 2-1
St Albans C v Braintree T 0-0
St Albans C won 6-5 on penalties
Dover Ath v Bromley 0-1
Yeovil T v Woking 3-1
Truro C v Dagenham & R 1-1
Dagenham & R won 4-2 on penalties
Slough T v Eastbourne Bor 3-1
Barnet v Boreham Wood 2-3
Tonbridge Angels v Torquay U 2-1
Hungerford T v Weymouth 0-1
Needham Market v Wealdstone 2-1
Folkestone Invicta v Uxbridge 2-0
Plymouth Parkway v Dulwich Hamlet 1-1
Plymouth Parkway won 4-3 on penalties
Maidenhead U v Maidstone U (walkover)

FOURTH ROUND
Alfreton T v FC Halifax T 1-1
FC Halifax T won 3-2 on penalties
Dagenham & R v Southend U 2-0
Wrexham v Folkestone Invicta 5-1
St Albans C v Cheshunt 0-3
York C v Slough T 1-0
Stourbridge v Guiseley 0-0
Stourbridge won 2-0 on penalties
Tonbridge Angels v King's Lynn T 1-1
Tonbridge Angels won 5-4 on penalties
Southport v Solihull Moors 0-3
Notts Co v Eastleigh 2-1
Dartford v Weymouth 1-0
Aldershot T v Bromley 0-2
Boreham Wood v Maidstone U 1-1
Boreham Wood won 5-4 on penalties
Morpeth T v Boston U 4-3
Yeovil T v Needham Market 1-1
Needham Market won 8-7 on penalties
Stockport Co v Larkhall Ath 3-0
Spennymoor T v Plymouth Parkway 3-1

FIFTH ROUND
York C v Morpeth T 3-2
Tonbridge Angels v Bromley 1-1
Bromley won 3-2 on penalties
Needham Market v Dartford 1-0
Stourbridge v Solihull Moors 0-1
Dagenham & R v Spennymoor T 2-0
FC Halifax T v Notts Co 1-2
Wrexham v Boreham Wood 3-0
Stockport Co v Cheshunt 1-0

QUARTER-FINALS
Bromley v Solihull Moors 3-1
Needham Market v Stockport Co 0-3
Notts Co v Wrexham 1-2
Dagenham & R v York C 1-1
York C won 8-7 on penalties

SEMI-FINALS
Wrexham v Stockport Co 2-0
Bromley v York C 3-1

THE BUILDBASE FA TROPHY FINAL 2021–22

Sunday 22 May 2022

(at Wembley, attendance 46,111 combined with FA Vase)

Bromley (0) 1 Wrexham (0) 0

Bromley: Balcombe; Sowunmi (Partington 45), Webster, Bush, Coulson, Bingham (Trotter 75), Vennings, Forster, Whitely, Cheek (Bloomfield 80), Al-Hamadi.
Scorer: Cheek 64.

Wrexham: Dibble; O'Connor (Jarvis 74), Tozer, Cleworth, McAlinden (Hall-Johnson 74), Young (Hyde 85), Davies, Jones J, McFadzean, Palmer, Mullin.

Referee: Thomas Bramall.

ENGLAND C 2021–22

INTERNATIONAL CHALLENGE MATCH

Caernarfon, Wednesday 30 March 2022

Wales C (4) 4 *(Evans W 11, 34, Edwards A 22, 27)*

England C (0) 0 1402

Wales C: Ramsay, Davies M (Phillips 71), Owen, Donohue, Edwards (Thomas 81), Green, McLaggon (Smith 89), Evans (Wood 86), Davies, Lewis, Harling (Price 84).
England C: Loach (Boot 59), Wynter, Beard, Wright (Baines 75), Palmer A, Robinson, Little (Palmer M 73), Mandeville (Sbarra 59), Cheek (Mason-Clark 59), Waters, Roberts.
Referee: Tim Marshall.

THE BUILDBASE FA VASE 2021–22

FIRST QUALIFYING ROUND

Padiham v North Shields	0-4
Chester-le-Street T v Jarrow	1-1
Chester-le-Street T won 3-1 on penalties	
Willington v Tow Law T	3-2
West Allotment Celtic v Steeton	5-5
West Allotment Celtic won 4-3 on penalties	
Carlisle C v Guisborough T	1-0
Whitley Bay v Billingham Synthonia	3-4
Washington v Thornaby	0-5
Squires Gate v Garforth T	1-1
Garforth T won 4-3 on penalties	
Newcastle University v Heaton Stannington	1-1
Heaton Stannington won 4-3 on penalties	
Barnoldswick T v AFC Blackpool	3-3
Barnoldswick T won 9-8 on penalties	
Easington Colliery v Redcar Ath	2-1
Campion v Newton Aycliffe	3-3
Newton Aycliffe won 3-2 on penalties	
Crook T v Eccleshill U	0-2
Sunderland West End v Cleator Moor	2-3
Sunderland RCA v Redcar T	1-2
Bishop Auckland v Ryton & Crawcrook Alb	2-2
Bishop Auckland won 15-14 on penalties	
Ilkley T v Penrith	1-2
Newcastle Benfield v Ashington	3-2
Silsden v Albion Sports	1-2
Litherland Remyca v Wythenshawe T	0-6
Avro v AFC Darwen	2-1
AFC Liverpool v Charnock Richard	5-3
Athersley Recreation v Chadderton	1-5
Brigg T v Cammell Laird 1907	3-2
Runcorn T v Ashton T	4-1
FC St Helens v South Liverpool (walkover)	
Burscough v Hallam	2-1
New Mills v Armthorpe Welfare	1-1
New Mills won 6-5 on penalties	
Bacup Bor v Penistone Church	1-0
St Helens T v Cheadle Heath Nomads	0-4
West Didsbury & Chorlton v Nostell MW	3-2
Northwich Vic v Bury	1-2
Skelmersdale U v Retford	9-1
Maltby Main v Glasshoughton Welfare	1-1
Maltby Main won 5-4 on penalties	
Swallownest v Bottesford T	3-1
FC Humber U v Parkgate	1-4
Selby T v Hemsworth MW	5-2
Winterton Rangers v Macclesfield	3-2
Dronfield T v Barnton	1-0
Worsbrough Bridge Ath v Maine Road	1-2
Handsworth v Golcar U	1-2
Cheadle T v Irlam	0-1
Abbey Hey v Ashton Ath	1-0
Shifnal T v Smethwick Rangers	5-1
Dudley T v Alsager T	2-0
Brocton v Boldmere St Michaels	1-5
Winsford U v Stapenhill	3-1
Hinckley LR v Cradley T	3-0
Shawbury U v Romulus	0-4
Lichfield C v FC Stratford	2-1
Haughmond v Ashby Ivanhoe	2-3
Wem T v Bilston T (walkover)	
Bewdley T v Hereford Lads Club	2-2
Bewdley T won 7-6 on penalties	
Wellington v Nuneaton Griff (walkover)	
Stone Old Alleynians v Heather St Johns	2-3
Uttoxeter T v Littleton	2-0
Atherstone T v Abbey Hulton U	2-1
AFC Bridgnorth v Rocester	2-1
Studley v Paget Rangers	2-0
Whitchurch Alport v Tividale	3-0
Coventry Copsewood v Rugby T	2-8
Gresley R v Dudley Sports	7-0
Stafford T (walkover) v Eccleshall	
St Martins v Hinckley	0-18
Bourne T v Belper U	1-2
Clipstone v St Andrews	1-1
St Andrews won 5-4 on penalties	
Teversal v Eastwood Community	0-2
Saffron Dynamo v Quorn	1-1
Quorn won 4-1 on penalties	
Melton T v West Bridgford	3-0
Sherwood Colliery v Borrowash Vic	1-0
Selston v Barrow T	2-1
Dunkirk v AFC Mansfield	3-0
Leicester Nirvana v Clifton All Whites	4-1
Birstall U v Kirby Muxloe	2-2
Birstall U won 6-5 on penalties	
Hucknall T v Gedling MW	1-3
Ingles v Blackstones	4-1
Boston T v Lutterworth Ath	4-1
Rainworth MW v Heanor T	0-2
Deeping Rangers v Holwell Sports	3-0
Debenham LC v Peterborough Northern Star	1-1
Debenham LC won 4-2 on penalties	
Eynesbury R v Huntingdon T	2-0
Wisbech St Mary v Great Yarmouth T	0-6
Godmanchester R v FC Parson Drove	6-1
Walsham Le Willows v March T U	5-2
UEA v Swaffham T	1-2
Brimsdown v Barkingside	0-1
Whitton U v Enfield Bor	4-3
Takeley v Frenford	2-0
Long Melford v Little Oakley	3-0
St Margaretsbury v Benfleet	0-2
Newbury Forest v Haverhill Bor	1-0
Halstead T v Potton U	1-2
Coggeshall U v Glebe	1-3
Walthamstow v Hadleigh U	0-0
Hadleigh U won 4-3 on penalties	
Woodbridge T v Woodford T	1-1
Woodford T won 5-4 on penalties	
Hoddesdon T v FC Clacton	5-2
Biggleswade U v Southend Manor	0-8
London Lions v St Panteleimon	2-1
Stotfold v White Ensign	1-5
Hackney Wick v New Salamis	1-4
Park View v Sawbridgeworth T	2-2
Sawbridgeworth T won 3-1 on penalties	
Harwich & Parkeston v Ipswich W	1-2
Brantham Ath v Holland	1-2
Sudbury Sports v May & Baker Eastbrook Community (walkover)	
Buckhurst Hill v Enfield	3-0
Windsor v Kensington & Ealing Bor	3-0
British Airways v Dunstable T	2-2
British Airways won 5-3 on penalties	
Chalvey Sports v Rothwell Corinthians	0-2
Cogenhoe U v Harefield U	2-3
Burnham v Bedford	6-1
Amersham T v Winslow U	2-3
Irchester U v Hillingdon Bor	1-5
Holmer Green v Spelthorne Sports	2-0
Buckingham Ath v Rushden & Higham U	4-2
Long Buckby v Tring Ath	2-2
Tring Ath won 4-2 on penalties	
Arlesey T v FC Deportivo Galicia	4-4
FC Deportivo Galicia won 4-2 on penalties	
Risborough Rangers v Edgware T	3-2
London Colney v Leverstock Green	1-1
London Colney won 4-3 on penalties	
Hilltop v Langley	4-2
Ardley U v Burton Park W	5-0
Egham T v Crawley Green	1-1
Egham T won 11-10 on penalties	
Broadfields U v Holyport	1-0
Aylesbury Vale Dynamos v London Tigers	3-1
Wembley v Oxhey Jets	5-1
Camberley T v Long Crendon	1-1
Long Crendon won 5-4 on penalties	
Sheerwater v Roman Glass St George	4-1
Shortwood U v Cove	4-2
Longlevens v Fairford T	3-2
Wokingham & Emmbrook v Moreton Rangers	4-0
Frimley Green v Shrivenham	3-0
Eversley & California v Virginia Water	3-0
Berks Co v Newent T	3-1
Hengrove Ath v Ascot U	0-2
Stonehouse T v Ashton & Backwell U	0-2
Brislington v Fleet T	4-0
Almondsbury v Cheltenham Saracens	1-2
Royal Wootton Bassett T v Knaphill	1-0
Bishop's Cleeve v Thornbury T	4-1
Reading C v Cribbs	1-2

Malmesbury Vic v Tuffley R	2-4
Clanfield 85 v Wallingford T	2-3
Lydney T v Hallen	3-3
Hallen won 5-4 on penalties	
Rochester U v Hollands & Blair	3-2
Canterbury C v FC Elmstead	5-0
Staplehurst Monarchs U v Sporting Bengal U	3-2
Broadbridge Heath v Croydon	3-3
Croydon won 6-5 on penalties	
Erith T v Sporting Club Thamesmead	2-0
AFC Uckfield T v Colliers Wood U	2-3
Westside v Snodland T	1-2
Tunbridge Wells v Roffey	1-1
Tunbridge Wells won 4-3 on penalties	
Abbey Rangers v Horsham YMCA	4-0
Crawley Down Gatwick v Lewisham Bor (Community)	3-1
Eastbourne U v Bridon Ropes	0-3
Greenways v Lydd T	2-2
Greenways won 5-3 on penalties	
Raynes Park Vale v Steyning T Community	3-1
Molesey v Shoreham	0-2
Banstead Ath v Horley T	0-1
Lordswood v Storrington Community	4-0
Eastbourne T v Sheppey U	0-1
Sutton Ath v Newhaven	4-2
East Preston v Redhill	0-5
Lingfield v Erith & Belvedere	1-2
Larkfield & New Hythe v Epsom & Ewell	2-3
Seaford T v Peacehaven & Telscombe	1-1
Seaford T won 4-2 on penalties	
Billingshurst v Forest Hill Park	0-3
Rushtall v Crowborough Ath	0-2
Balham v Tower Hamlets	1-2
Bearsted v Fisher	0-1
Tooting Bec v Jersey Bulls	0-3
Oakwood v Welling T	3-4
Loxwood v Faversham Strike Force	1-0
K Sports v Beckenham T	0-5
Stansfeld v Bagshot	3-1
Horndean v Hamble Club	9-0
Wick v Alton	0-0
Alton won 4-1 on penalties	
Radstock T v Arundel	0-1
Westbury U v Alresford T	1-4
AFC Stoneham v Portland U	4-0
Folland Sports v Corsham T	0-1
Millbrook (Hampshire) v Shaftesbury	0-2
Cowes Sports v Bournemouth	3-4
Amesbury T v Andover New Street	1-4
Baffins Milton R v Andover T	1-3
Selsey v Pagham	0-1
Bradford T v Wincanton T	3-0
Calne T v Whitchurch U	1-4
Sherborne T v Verwood T	5-3
Moneyfields v Totton & Eling	4-0
Ash U v Hythe & Dibden	2-0
Devizes T v Badshot Lea	0-10
Petersfield T v Bashley	0-3
Farnham T v Warminster T	4-0
AFC Portchester v Romsey T	4-0
Ringwood T v Bridport	2-0
Godolphin Atlantic v Bovey Tracey	1-3
Saltash U v Cullompton Rangers	3-1
Exmouth T v Shepton Mallet	0-1
Torpoint Ath v Callington T	1-0
Wadebridge T v AFC St Austell	2-1
Bodmin T v Crediton U	3-3
Bodmin T won 4-3 on penalties	
Ilfracombe T v Bishop Sutton	0-2
Elburton Villa v Welton R	0-4
Torrington v Bishops Lydeard	1-1
Bishops Lydeard won 3-2 on penalties	

SECOND QUALIFYING ROUND

Blyth T v West Allotment Celtic	1-8
Birtley T v Knaresborough T	4-1
Redcar T v Billingham T	2-0
Thackley v Holker Old Boys	2-3
Eccleshill U v Bishop Auckland	2-0
Northallerton T v Penrith	1-2
Cleator Moor v Harrogate Railway Ath	3-2
North Shields v Whickham	0-0
North Shields won 5-4 on penalties	
Garforth T v Garstang	4-0
Chester-le-Street T v Easington Colliery	2-0
Barnoldswick T v Heaton Stannington	1-2
Carlisle C v Esh Winning	4-1
Willington v Thornaby	1-3
Newton Aycliffe (walkover) v Boro Rangers	
Billingham Synthonia v Brandon U	3-1
Albion Sports v Newcastle Benfield	1-8
Maltby Main v Bury	2-2
Bury won 4-3 on penalties	
West Didsbury & Chorlton v Parkgate	0-1
Lower Breck v Swallownest	5-0
Tie awarded to Swallownest after Lower Breck fielded an ineligible player	
Daisy Hill v Atherton LR	0-4
Bacup Bor v Wythenshawe T	3-3
Wythenshawe T won 4-2 on penalties	
Rossington Main v Skelmersdale U	0-3
Golcar U v Wythenshawe Amateurs	4-0
Winterton Rangers v Selby T	2-0
FC Isle of Man v Avro	3-1
Emley v Chadderton	1-1
Emley won 6-5 on penalties	
Grimsby Bor v Cheadle Heath Nomads	3-1
Abbey Hey v Hall Road Rangers	5-2
New Mills v AFC Liverpool	2-5
Goole v Maine Road	4-0
Burscough v Irlam	2-0
South Liverpool v Dronfield T	4-1
Prestwich Heys v Brigg T	7-2
Staveley MW v Barton T	1-1
Barton T won 5-3 on penalties	
Runcorn T v Pilkington	1-4
Heath Hayes v Highgate U	2-3
Stafford T v Studley	0-2
Lichfield C v Uttoxeter T	4-0
Ashby Ivanhoe v Romulus	0-1
Worcester Raiders v Atherstone T	1-2
Sandbach U v Dudley T	2-2
Sandbach U won 3-1 on penalties	
Wolverhampton Casuals v Ellesmere Rangers	4-1
AFC Bridgnorth v Lye T	2-2
AFC Bridgnorth won 4-3 on penalties	
Wednesfield v Hereford Pegasus	2-0
Racing Club Warwick v Chelmsley T	4-1
Heather St Johns v Darlaston T (1874)	3-1
Nuneaton Griff v Bewdley T	0-3
Whitchurch Alport v Pershore T	2-1
Rugby T v AFC Wulfrunians	1-0
Worcester C v Bilston T	3-1
Winsford U v Gresley R	1-3
Boldmere St Michaels v Shifnal T	3-3
Boldmere St Michaels won 3-2 on penalties	
Hinckley LR v Hinckley	1-0
Gedling MW v Kimberley MW	1-3
Birstall U v St Andrews	5-2
Deeping Rangers v Dunkirk	4-0
Harborough T v Sherwood Colliery	2-0
Ingles v Harrowby U	0-2
Heanor T v Eastwood Community	0-2
Lutterworth T v Skegness T	5-1
Boston T v Holbeach U	2-0
Pinchbeck U v Graham St Prims	1-2
Quorn v Leicester Nirvana	2-1
Belper U v Selston	4-1
GNG Oadby T v Loughborough Students	2-3
Melton T v Aylestone Park	1-4
Shirebrook T v Sleaford T	0-1
Ely C v Mildenhall T	0-1
Swaffham T v Eynesbury R	0-3
Sheringham v Thetford T	0-4
Whittlesey Ath v Framlingham T	3-2
Great Yarmouth T v Walsham Le Willows	1-0
Kirkley & Pakefield v Debenham LC	3-0
Newmarket T v Diss T	6-2
Wroxham v Godmanchester R	4-0
Lakenheath v Downham T	3-0
Newbury Forest v Buckhurst Hill	1-7
Redbridge v Hadleigh U	3-0
Saffron Walden T v Southend Manor	3-0
May & Baker Eastbrook Community v Glebe	0-5
Hoddesdon T v Woodford T	4-3
Sawbridgeworth T v Cockfosters	1-3
White Ensign v Ipswich W	1-2
Potton U v Baldock T	1-1
Baldock T won 3-2 on penalties	
Stansted v West Essex	2-2
Stansted won 3-2 on penalties	

Wivenhoe T v Stanway R	2-1
Whitton U v Wormley R	5-1
Benfleet v Holland	6-1
Cornard U v Barkingside	3-2
New Salamis v Takeley	3-2
Langford v Ilford	1-4
Burnham Ramblers v Long Melford	3-4
Haverhill R v London Lions	2-2
London Lions won 5-4 on penalties	
Winslow U v Shefford T & Campton	2-3
Northampton Sileby Rangers v Buckingham Ath	3-4
AFC Hayes v Risborough Rangers	0-3
Wembley v Holmer Green	0-0
Holmer Green won 5-4 on penalties	
FC Deportivo Galicia v Tring Ath	1-4
Egham T v Northampton ON Chenecks	3-2
Hilltop v Broadfields U	3-1
Hillingdon Bor v Bugbrooke St Michaels	1-1
Hillingdon Bor won 5-3 on penalties	
Bedfont & Feltham v Rayners Lane	0-0
Rayners Lane won 7-6 on penalties	
Southall v CB Hounslow U	5-1
British Airways v Desborough T	3-1
Burnham v Aylesbury Vale Dynamos	3-0
Wellingborough Whitworths v Windsor	5-1
Ardley U v Rothwell Corinthians	5-0
Newport Pagnell T v Harpenden T	1-0
Penn & Tylers Green v Harefield U	1-1
Harefield U won 4-3 on penalties	
Easington Sports v London Colney	0-2
Frimley Green v AFC Aldermaston	3-1
Tadley Calleva v Ascot U	1-4
Bitton v Cheltenham Saracens	3-1
Abingdon U v Berks Co	1-10
Brislington v Ashton & Backwell U	1-2
Tuffley R v Fleet Spurs	3-2
Bishop's Cleeve v Wallingford T	4-4
Wallingford T won 4-3 on penalties	
Eversley & California v Oldland Abbotonians	1-2
Bristol Telephones v Chipping Sodbury T	1-6
Longwell Green Sports v Cadbury Heath	0-2
Sheerwater v Tytherington Rocks	1-0
Wokingham & Emmbrook v Hallen	1-1
Wokingham & Emmbrook won 5-4 on penalties	
Keynsham T v Long Crendon	4-1
Cribbs v Shortwood U	1-1
Cribbs won 5-4 on penalties	
Milton U v Woodley U	6-0
Sandhurst T v Longlevens	1-3
Portishead T v Royal Wootton Bassett T	1-3
Raynes Park Vale v Welling T	4-0
AFC Varndeanians v Kent Football U	0-5
Tunbridge Wells v Canterbury C	4-1
Epsom & Ewell v Mile Oak	4-0
Holmesdale v AFC Croydon Ath	4-0
Alfold v Redhill	2-2
Redhill won 4-3 on penalties	
Meridian v Shoreham	1-5
Fisher (walkover) v Little Common	
Rochester U v Chessington & Hook U	1-1
Rochester U won 7-6 on penalties	
Snodland T v Sutton Ath	4-1
Abbey Rangers v Montpelier Villa	4-2
Jersey Bulls v Crowborough Ath	5-0
Hassocks v Beckenham T	1-2
Lordswood v Seaford T	1-1
Lordswood won 4-2 on penalties	
Croydon v Horley T	1-4
Erith T v Sheppey U	2-3
Saltdean U v Bridon Ropes	1-3
Colliers Wood U v Punjab U	1-0
Tower Hamlets v Crawley Down Gatwick	1-3
Hailsham T v Staplehurst Monarchs U	1-2
Greenways v Forest Hill Park	2-3
Athletic Newham v Bexhill U	2-2
Athletic Newham won 7-6 on penalties	
Loxwood v Erith & Belvedere	0-5
Worthing U v Stansfeld	1-5
Midhurst & Easebourne v Alresford T	0-1
Ringwood T v Downton	1-2
Moneyfields v AFC Portchester	2-0
Laverstock & Ford v Fawley	4-0
Whitchurch U v Ash U	2-2
Ash U won 5-3 on penalties	
Godalming T v Badshot Lea	2-2
Badshot Lea won 5-4 on penalties	
Sherborne T v Bemerton Heath Harlequins	3-6
Horndean v Brockenhurst	1-1
Brockenhurst won 4-1 on penalties	
Bournemouth v East Cowes Vic Ath	5-3
Alton v Pagham	2-2
Pagham won 5-3 on penalties	
Andover T v Andover New Street	1-4
AFC Stoneham v Blackfield & Langley	2-3
Arundel v Shaftesbury	0-5
Bradford T v Odd Down	2-0
Corsham T v Hamworthy U	1-1
Hamworthy U won 4-2 on penalties	
Farnham T v Bashley	1-1
Bashley won 7-6 on penalties	
Wendron U v Bishop Sutton	2-1
St Blazey v Dobwalls	2-2
Dobwalls won 6-5 on penalties	
Wadebridge T v Newquay	1-4
Elmore v Helston Ath	1-5
Shepton Mallet v Mousehole	0-1
Launceston v Newton Abbot Spurs	1-2
Sidmouth T v Welton R	2-10
Bovey Tracey v Street	4-6
Porthleven v Liskeard Ath (walkover)	
Bishops Lydeard v Wellington	2-2
Wellington won 4-2 on penalties	
Camelford v Cheddar	3-2
Saltash U v Bodmin T	2-2
Tie awarded to Bodmin T after Saltash U fielded an ineligible player. Saltash had won the original tie 5-4 on penalties,	
Axminster T v Brixham	0-1
Torpoint Ath v Stoke Gabriel	6-1
Ivybridge T v Wells C	1-2

FIRST ROUND

Carlisle C v Chester-le-Street T	5-1
Pilkington v West Allotment Celtic	7-3
Heaton Stannington v Eccleshill U	2-5
Seaham Red Star v Wythenshawe T	0-0
Wythenshawe T won 4-3 on penalties	
Newcastle Benfield v Golcar U	3-2
Abbey Hey v Parkgate	6-0
Prestwich Heys v Penrith	4-2
Swallownest v Birtley T	1-3
Emley v Longridge T	4-1
AFC Liverpool v Newton Aycliffe	2-1
Sunderland RCW v Bury	1-2
Billingham Synthonia v FC Isle of Man	4-2
Holker Old Boys v Skelmersdale U	3-2
Barton T v Cleator Moor	3-1
Thornaby v South Liverpool	4-0
Consett v Atherton LR	2-1
Grimsby Bor v Redcar T	1-1
Redcar T won 4-1 on penalties	
Vauxhall Motors v North Shields	1-2
Winterton Rangers v Goole	5-1
Burscough v Garforth T	1-1
Burscough won 6-5 on penalties	
Bewdley T v Racing Club Warwick	1-3
Wellingborough Whitworths v Highgate U	1-6
Heather St Johns v Atherstone T	1-2
Newark v Deeping Rangers	1-1
Deeping Rangers won 3-1 on penalties	
Gresley R v Harrowby U	7-2
Quorn v Hinckley LR	0-4
Eynesbury R v Sandbach U	1-2
Kimberley MW v Studley	3-2
Boston T v Hanley T	0-1
Belper U v Rugby T	1-2
Radford v Boldmere St Michaels	1-2
Worcester C v Lutterworth T	2-1
Romulus v Harborough T	1-1
Harborough T won 5-4 on penalties	
Whittlesey Ath v Wolverhampton Casuals	1-0
Whitchurch Alport v Sleaford T	2-1
Coventry U v Birstall U	2-1
Graham St Prims v Lichfield C	0-4
Coventry Sphinx v AFC Bridgnorth	9-0
Eastwood Community v Loughborough Students	1-1
Loughborough Students won 4-2 on penalties	
Aylestone Park v Wednesfield	4-0
Whitton U v Cockfosters	2-4
Mildenhall T v Lakenheath	1-2
Saffron Walden T v Kirkley & Pakefield	3-1

Stansted v Wivenhoe T 1-1
Stansted won 4-1 on penalties
Wroxham v Benfleet 6-0
Ipswich W v Milton Keynes Irish 2-0
Buckingham Ath v Cornard U 2-2
Cornard U won 4-2 on penalties
Ilford v Shefford T & Campton 0-1
Norwich U v New Salamis 1-2
London Colney v Newport Pagnell T 0-1
Ampthill T v Norwich CBS 0-4
Ardley U v Tring Ath 1-1
Tring Ath won 4-3 on penalties
Hoddesdon T v Gorleston 0-0
Gorleston won 5-4 on penalties
Great Yarmouth T v Buckhurst Hill 1-5
Risborough Rangers v Long Melford 3-1
Baldock T v Hillingdon Bor 5-1
Holmer Green v Glebe 1-3
Newmarket T v Redbridge 2-1
London Lions v Thetford T 4-2
North Greenford U v Ash U 3-2
Fisher v Badshot Lea 1-2
Rayners Lane v Sheerwater 2-3
Hilltop v Tunbridge Wells 2-3
Southall v Erith & Belvedere 3-0
Fareham T v Jersey Bulls 1-1
Fareham T won 4-3 on penalties
Abbey Rangers v Horley T 2-2
Abbey Rangers won 4-2 on penalties
Littlehampton T v Moneyfields 3-2
British Airways v Epsom & Ewell 4-0
Clapton v Beckenham T 0-2
Pagham v Snodland T 1-1
Pagham won 4-2 on penalties
Wallingford T v Ascot U 2-2
Wallingford T won 6-5 on penalties
Stansfeld v Staplehurst Monarchs U 3-1
Blackfield & Langley v Wokingham & Emmbrook 4-2
Sheppey U v Forest Hill Park 4-0
Chatham T v Alresford T 6-0
Holmesdale v Athletic Newham 1-1
Athletic Newham won 6-5 on penalties
Milton U v Bridon Ropes 2-1
Harefield U v Kent Football U 3-0
Guildford C v Shoreham 4-0
Deal T v Kennington 4-0
Frimley Green v Rochester U 2-1
Berks Co v Burnham 2-1
Crawley Down Gatwick v Lordswood 3-2
Egham T v Colliers Wood U 4-1
Raynes Park Vale v Redhill 2-0
Dobwalls v Bashley 0-3
Royal Wootton Bassett T v Downton 4-0
Wendron U v Bournemouth 4-2
Buckland Ath v Camelford 3-0
Newton Abbot Spurs v Brixham 1-2
Tuffley R v Street 1-4
Cribbs v Andover New Street 1-2
Liskeard Ath v Laverstock & Ford 4-2
Bitton v New Milton T 2-4
Oldland Abbotonians v Helston Ath 2-2
Oldland Abbotonians won 5-3 on penalties
Brimscombe & Thrupp v Welton R 2-1
Mousehole v Wells C 4-0
Brockenhurst v Bodmin T 6-0
Longlevens v Shaftesbury 0-3
Newquay v Keynsham T 2-3
Millbrook (Cornwall) v Wellington 1-2
Ashton & Backwell U v Bemerton Heath Harlequins 0-0
Bemerton Heath Harlequins won 5-4 on penalties
Falmouth T v Bradford T 2-1
Torpoint Ath v Chipping Sodbury T 4-1
Cadbury Heath v Hamworthy U 1-1
Hamworthy U won 6-5 on penalties

SECOND ROUND

Pilkington v Burscough 3-1
AFC Liverpool v Redcar T 2-0
Eccleshill U v Barton T 2-3
Newcastle Benfield v Emley 2-0
Carlisle C v Abbey Hey 0-1
North Shields v North Ferriby 2-2
North Shields won 6-5 on penalties
Bury v Birtley T 3-1
Holker Old Boys v Wythenshawe T 0-3
Billingham Synthonia v West Auckland T 2-1
Thornaby v Consett 1-1
Consett won 4-3 on penalties
Prestwich Heys v Winterton Rangers 3-1
Sandbach U v Hanley T 1-0
Lichfield C v Highgate U 3-0
Tie awarded to Highgate U after Lichfield C fielded an ineligible player
Stourport Swifts v Kimberley MW 3-1
Atherstone T v Long Eaton U 3-1
Rugby T v Hinckley LR 1-0
Loughborough Students v Gresley R 2-0
Racing Club Warwick v Coventry Sphinx 1-3
Aylestone Park v Anstey Nomads 1-5
Boldmere St Michaels v Congleton T 1-1
Congleton T won 4-2 on penalties
Whitchurch Alport v Malvern T 1-1
Whitchurch Alport won 5-3 on penalties
Coventry U v Westfields 1-1
Coventry U won 5-4 on penalties
Harborough T v Wellingborough T 2-0
Whittlesey Ath v Worcester C 0-0
Whittlesey Ath won 7-6 on penalties
Walsall Wood v Deeping Rangers 2-0
Mulbarton W v London Lions 1-2
Shefford T & Campton v Risborough Rangers 1-1
Shefford T & Campton won 5-4 on penalties
Cockfosters v Tring Ath 0-4
Saffron Walden T v Cornard U 5-1
Fakenham T v Stansted 1-1
Fakenham T won 4-2 on penalties
Baldock T v Hadley 2-2
Hadley won 5-4 on penalties
New Salamis v Ipswich W 2-0
Norwich CBS v Lakenheath 0-3
Newport Pagnell T v Leighton T 1-1
Newport Pagnell T won 2-1 on penalties
Gorleston v Buckhurst Hill 2-3
Wroxham v Newmarket T 1-1
Wroxham won 6-5 on penalties
Glebe v Hanworth Villa 1-1
Glebe won 5-3 on penalties
Deal T v Littlehampton T 1-2
Crawley Down Gatwick v British Airways 3-0
Flackwell Heath v Guildford C 0-1
Raynes Park Vale v Blackfield & Langley 6-2
Fareham T v Abbey Rangers 3-5
Milton U v Beckenham T 2-3
Cobham v Egham T 0-3
Frimley Green v United Services Portsmouth 5-1
Stansfeld v Badshot Lea 2-1
Tunbridge Wells v Walton & Hersham 1-0
Southall v Chatham T 2-2
Southall won 3-1 on penalties
Wallingford T v North Greenford U 1-0
Harefield U v Berks Co 2-3
Sheerwater v Sheppey U 2-3
Athletic Newham v Pagham 5-3
Wellington v Christchurch 5-2
Buckland Ath v Falmouth T 3-1
Wendron U v New Milton T 3-6
Andover New Street v Hamworthy U 1-2
Liskeard Ath v Keynsham T 2-3
Royal Wootton Bassett T v Torpoint Ath 2-0
Brixham v Tavistock 1-5
Tie awarded to Brixham after Tavistock fielded an ineligible player
Bemerton Heath Harlequins v Clevedon T 1-4
Bashley v Shaftesbury 2-2
Bashley won 6-5 on penalties
Street v Oldland Abbotonians 1-1
Street won 5-4 on penalties
Bridgwater U v Mousehole 1-0
Brockenhurst v Brimscombe & Thrupp 4-1

THIRD ROUND

AFC Liverpool v Pilkington 1-0
Abbey Hey v Bury 4-1
Newcastle Benfield v Consett 0-4
Barton T v North Shields 2-3
Wythenshawe T v Billingham Synthonia 3-0
Stourport Swifts v Rugby T 2-2
Rugby T won 5-4 on penalties
Loughborough Students v Sandbach U 4-0
Atherstone T v Whitchurch Alport 1-3
Coventry Sphinx v Coventry U 1-0
Prestwich Heys v Harborough T 1-7
Highgate U v Congleton T 0-4

Walsall Wood v Anstey Nomads 1-1
Tie awarded to Anstey Nomads after Walsall Wood fielded an ineligible player. Walsall Wood had won the original tie 4-2 on penalties.
Whittlesey Ath v Newport Pagnell T 0-6
Tring Ath v Saffron Walden T 0-1
London Lions v New Salamis 2-0
Buckhurst Hill v Wroxham 2-3
Lakenheath v Shefford T & Campton 3-2
Fakenham T v Hadley 3-1
Tunbridge Wells v Wallingford T 4-2
Glebe v Beckenham T 0-0
Glebe won 4-3 on penalties
Abbey Rangers v Athletic Newham 1-1
Athletic Newham won 4-2 on penalties
Stansfeld v Frimley Green 3-1
Berks Co v Egham T 1-2
Crawley Down Gatwick v Raynes Park Vale 0-4
Littlehampton T v Sheppey U 1-0
Guildford C v Southall 0-0
Southall won 4-3 on penalties
New Milton T v Keynsham T 0-0
New Milton T won 4-3 on penalties
Bridgwater U v Bashley 2-1
Street v Brockenhurst 1-1
Brockenhurst won 3-2 on penalties
Buckland Ath v Wellington 2-0
Royal Wootton Bassett T v Hamworthy U 1-3
Brixham v Clevedon T 0-6

FOURTH ROUND
Consett v Wythenshawe T 1-2
Abbey Hey v AFC Liverpool 2-2
Abbey Hey won 6-5 on penalties
Harborough T v North Shields 1-1
North Shields won 5-3 on penalties
Whitchurch Alport v Congleton T 2-1
Rugby T v Lakenheath 5-1
Saffron Walden T v Loughborough Students 1-1
Loughborough Students won 6-5 on penalties
Coventry Sphinx v London Lions 6-0
Newport Pagnell T v Fakenham T 3-1
Brockenhurst v New Milton T 2-0
Bridgwater U v Tunbridge Wells 2-2
Tunbridge Wells won 5-3 on penalties
Hamworthy U v Glebe 3-2
Athletic Newham v Littlehampton T 5-0
Tie awarded to Littlehampton T after Athletic Newham fielded an ineligible player
Buckland Ath v Egham T 2-1
Southall v Clevedon T 1-1
Southall won 5-4 on penalties
Raynes Park Vale v Stansfeld 1-2

FIFTH ROUND
Coventry Sphinx v Whitchurch Alport 3-3
Whitchurch Alport won 4-2 on penalties
North Shields v Rugby T 2-0
Loughborough Students v Abbey Hey 3-0
Anstey Nomads v Wythenshawe T 1-1
Wythenshaw T won 3-2 on penalties
Southall v Stansfeld 0-0
Southall won 4-2 on penalties
Hamworthy U v Tunbridge Wells 3-1
Littlehampton T v Brockenhurst 3-3
Littlehampton T won 4-1 on penalties
Newport Pagnell T v Buckland Ath 1-1
Newport Pagnell won 4-3 on penalties

QUARTER-FINALS
Whitchurch Alport v Newport Pagnell T 1-2
Loughborough Students v Wythenshawe T 2-0
Littlehampton T v North Shields 1-0
Hamworthy U v Southall 1-1
Hamworthy U won 7-6 on penalties

SEMI-FINALS
Littlehampton T v Loughborough Students 4-0
Newport Pagnell T v Hamworthy U 1-1
Newport Pagnell T won 6-5 on penalties

THE BUILDBASE FA VASE FINAL 2021–22
Sunday 22 May 2022
(at Wembley, attendance 46,111 combined with FA Vase)
Newport Pagnell T (0) 3 Littlehampton T (0) 0

Newport Pagnall T: Conway, Sage, Smail, Wright (Pryke 73), Powell, Barnes (Ford 68), Shepherd, Watkinson (Burnside 68), Ahmed, Webb, Markey.
Scorers: Barnes 19, Shepherd 55, 63.

Littlehampton T: Binfield; Wiggans, Clarke, Layton (Harris 58), Pattenden, Biggs, Benn, Gaskin (Capon 45), Jarvis, Humphreys (Herbert 58), Jenkins.

Referee: Samuel Barrott.

THE FA YOUTH CUP 2021–22

**After extra time.*

PRELIMINARY ROUND
North Shields v Newcastle Benfield 4-0
Stockton T v Ryton & Crawcrook Alb 3-0
Billingham T v Scarborough Ath 10-1
South Shields (walkover) v Guisborough T
Gateshead (walkover) v Boro Rangers
Blyth Spartans v Darlington 6-0
Workington v Bishop Auckland 1-1
Workington won 4-3 on penalties
Seaham Red Star v Morpeth T 0-4
Hebburn T v Spennymoor T 3-5
Birtley T (walkover) v Billingham Synthonia
Pickering T v Penrith 4-3
Trafford v Glossop North End 4-1
Avro v AFC Fylde 0-6
Macclesfield v Chorley 0-2
Radcliffe v Vauxhall Motors 0-2
Runcorn Linnets v Marine 1-0
St Helens T v Ashton U 8-1
AFC Blackpool (walkover) v Runcorn T
Atherton Collieries (walkover) v Cheadle T
Prestwich Heys v Cheadle Heath Nomads 3-2
Hyde U (walkover) v Sandbach U
City of Liverpool (walkover) v AFC Darwen
Chester v Clitheroe 5-0
West Didsbury & Chorlton (walkover) v Southport
Wythenshawe Amateurs v FC United of Manchester 2-2
Wythenshawe Amateurs won 5-3 on penalties
Bootle v Witton Alb 8-0
Nantwich T v Lancaster C 0-1
AFC Liverpool v Ramsbottom U 4-0
Ashton Ath v South Liverpool (walkover)
Prescot Cables v Buxton (walkover)
Curzon Ashton v Stalybridge Celtic 1-1
Curzon Ashton won 4-3 on penalties
Gainsborough Trinity v North Ferriby 4-1
Brighouse T v Farsley Celtic 2-4
York C (walkover) v Rossington Main
Sheffield v Cleethorpes T 2-2
Sheffield won 3-2 on penalties
Silsden v Stocksbridge Park Steels 3-0
Retford v Tadcaster Alb 1-8
Frickley Ath v Eccleshill U 1-1
Frickley Ath won 4-2 on penalties
Dronfield T v Handsworth 1-3
Worsbrough Bridge Ath v Pontefract Collieries 2-5
Bottesford T v Ossett U 0-7
Emley v Staveley MW 14-1
Lutterworth Ath (walkover) v Pinchbeck U
West Bridgford v Boston U 1-3

Holbeach U v Quorn (walkover)
Harborough T v Ashby Ivanhoe 6-0
Anstey Nomads v AFC Mansfield 2-0
Gresley R v Alfreton T 1-5
Grantham T v Eastwood Community 1-0
Mickleover v Lincoln U 2-0
Dunkirk (walkover) v Bourne T
Long Eaton U v Kirby Muxloe 3-1
Borrowash Vic v Aylestone Park 1-6
Lutterworth T v Leicester Nirvana 2-1
Deeping Rangers v Hinckley LR 4-0
Basford U v Kimberley MW 7-0
Ilkeston T v Stamford 1-6
St Andrews v Coalville T 3-2
Leamington v Paget Rangers 5-3
Dudley Sports v Walsall Wood (walkover)
Lichfield C v Evesham U 0-3
Stratford T v Halesowen T 1-2
Pershore T v Hednesford T 2-2
Pershore T won 3-2 on penalties
Dudley T v Newcastle T 0-2
Bedworth U v Stafford Rangers 2-2
Bedworth U won 4-3 on penalties
Boldmere St Michaels v Haughmond 5-1
Bilston T v Malvern T 7-0
Coventry Sphinx v Kidderminster H 1-6
AFC Telford U v Hereford Pegasus 3-2
Alvechurch v Atherstone T (walkover)
Rushall Olympic v Lye T 4-0
Worcester C v Sutton Coldfield T 1-3
Racing Club Warwick v Stourport Swifts 2-1
Romulus v Stourbridge 2-7
Shawbury U v Tamworth 0-0
Shawbury U won 5-4 on penalties
Tividale v Redditch U 1-4
Hitchin T v Bugbrooke St Michaels 0-6
Wellingborough Whitworths v Huntingdon T 5-1
Rushden & D v Welwyn Garden City 6-1
Newport Pagnell T v Stotfold 1-3
Leighton T v Corby T 5-0
Arlesey T v AFC Dunstable (walkover)
Yaxley v Rothwell Corinthians (walkover)
Dunstable T v Brackley T 1-1
Dunstable T won 4-3 on penalties
Northampton ON Chenecks v St Ives T (walkover)
Biggleswade T v Winslow U 0-6
Ampthill T v Buckingham Ath 3-4
Royston T v Baldock T 1-2
St Neots T v Harpenden T 4-1
Kettering T v Wellingborough T 4-0
Barton R v Cogenhoe U 1-4
Godmanchester R v Milton Keynes Irish 1-0
Long Melford v Dereham T 0-8
Needham Market v AFC Sudbury 1-4
Lakenheath v Gorleston (walkover)
Woodbridge T v Ipswich W 4-3
Stowmarket T v Walsham Le Willows 3-1
Cambridge C v Newmarket T 1-5
Leiston v Framlingham T 2-1
Lowestoft T v Mulbarton W 3-1
Ely C v Histon 2-3
Mildenhall T v March T U 2-2
Mildenhall T won 5-4 on penalties
Swaffham T v Whitton U 1-2
Felixstowe & Walton U (walkover) v Fakenham T
Wroxham (walkover) v Whittlesey Ath
Wisbech St Mary v Brantham Ath 1-4
May & Baker Eastbrook Community v Romford (walkover)
Woodford T v Potters Bar T 5-0
St Albans C v Frenford 4-3
St Margaretsbury v Cheshunt 2-4
Hullbridge Sports v Hadley 1-7
London Colney v Walthamstow 0-3
Tilbury v London Lions 0-5
FC Clacton v Barking 1-7
Enfield T v Brentwood T 2-2
Enfield T won 4-3 on penalties
Billericay T v Hashtag U 3-1
Ilford v Sawbridgeworth T 0-1
Takeley v Buckhurst Hill 2-0
Grays Ath v Little Oakley 10-0
West Essex v Aveley 1-3
Wingate & Finchley v Brimsdown 13-0
Barkingside v Ware (walkover)
Cockfosters v Hackney Wick 3-4

Braintree T v Colney Heath 0-4
Redbridge v Concord Rangers 1-6
Hornchurch v Bishop's Stortford 0-1
Stanway R v Chelmsford C 2-3
Haringey Bor v Southend Manor 4-0
Hampton & Richmond Bor v Kensington & Ealing Bor 2-4
Hemel Hempstead T v Burnham 3-1
Harefield U (walkover) v Chesham U
Wembley v Kings Langley 0-6
London Tigers v Balham (walkover)
Tring Ath v Hendon 1-2
Rayners Lane v Langley 1-8
Edgware T v Chalfont St Peter 1-2
Hillingdon Bor v Berkhamsted 0-7
Hayes & Yeading U (walkover) v Spelthorne Sports
Leverstock Green v Ashford T (Middlesex) 0-2
Beaconsfield T v CB Hounslow U 3-1
Uxbridge v Northwood 4-1
Bedfont Sports Club v Windsor 8-0
Hanwell T v North Greenford U 0-2
Sittingbourne v VCD Ath 4-6
Ebbsfleet U v Croydon 0-3
Sevenoaks T v Welling U 0-1
Chatham T v Erith T 1-2
Folkestone Invicta v Tonbridge Angels 0-7
Faversham T v Phoenix Sports 0-4
Tower Hamlets v Margate 1-1
Tower Hamlets won 5-4 on penalties
Cray W v Fisher 6-1
Maidstone U v Dulwich Hamlet 1-0
Lewisham Bor (Community) v K Sports (walkover)
Lordswood v Whitstable T 3-2
Corinthian v AFC Croydon Ath 3-1
Whyteleafe v Cray Valley (PM) (walkover)
Ashford U v Sheppey U 2-2
Sheppey U won 5-4 on penalties
Erith & Belvedere v Punjab U 1-7
Hollands & Blair v Kent Football U 5-2
Arundel v Tooting & Mitcham U (walkover)
East Preston v Horsham YMCA 0-2
Badshot Lea (walkover) v Raynes Park Vale
Chessington & Hook U v Hastings U 1-3
South Park v Kingstonian 2-9
Ash U v Redhill 0-1
Worthing (walkover) v Guildford C
Pagham v Farnham T 4-6
Crawley Down Gatwick v Alfold 2-7
Burgess Hill T v Chipstead 2-1
Dorking W v East Grinstead T 1-1
Dorking W won 5-4 on penalties
Steyning T Community v Sutton Common R 0-8
Abbey Rangers (walkover) v Broadbridge Heath
Walton & Hersham v Corinthian Casuals 1-5
Three Bridges v Chertsey T 4-0
AFC Uckfield T v Colliers Wood U 1-4
Seaford T v Virginia Water 0-3
Saltdean U v Loxwood 3-0
Leatherhead v Horsham 5-1
Eastbourne Bor v Walton Casuals 9-0
Whitehawk v Eastbourne T 1-1
Whitehawk won 4-2 on penalties
Shoreham v Bexhill U 1-4
Lewes v Worthing U 6-0
Godalming T v Chichester C 1-2
Westfield v Carshalton Ath 3-0
Montpelier Villa v Billingshurst 4-2
Cove (walkover) v Clanfield 85
Holmer Green v Ascot U 0-2
Fleet T (walkover) v Binfield
Camberley T v Hungerford T 3-0
Risborough Rangers v Reading C 0-5
Penn & Tylers Green v Ardley U (walkover)
North Leigh v Bracknell T 2-0
Wokingham & Emmbrook v Aylesbury Vale Dynamos 5-3
Banbury U v Flackwell Heath 2-1
Hartley Wintney v Oxford C (walkover)
Marlow (walkover) v Shrivenham
Abingdon U v Wallingford T 9-1
Thame U v Kidlington 4-2
Thatcham T v Didcot T 5-2
Farnborough v Easington Sports (walkover)
Shaftesbury v Hamworthy U 0-1
Sholing v Bournemouth 8-0
Alton v Andover T 2-0

Dorchester T v Fareham T	12-0
Lymington T v Cowes Sports	0-4
Wimborne T v Moneyfields	3-2
Bemerton Heath Harlequins v Poole T	1-5
AFC Stoneham v Horndean	6-1
Christchurch v United Services Portsmouth	4-1
AFC Portchester v Basingstoke T	1-3
Gosport Bor (walkover) v Romsey T	
Winchester C v Brockenhurst	5-2
Clevedon T v Welton R	1-2
Royal Wootton Bassett T v Paulton R	1-3
Street v Keynsham T	2-1
Tuffley R (walkover) v Newent T	
Mangotsfield U v Bradford T	9-0
Bristol Manor Farm v Bishop's Cleeve	5-1
Shepton Mallet v Devizes T	1-6
Cribbs v Wells C	5-2
Corsham T v Portishead T (walkover)	
Cinderford T v Yate T	5-1
Bitton v Oldland Abbotonians	4-2
Frome T v Bath C	0-9
Radstock T v Bishop Sutton	2-1
Chippenham T v Malmesbury Vic	9-0
Cheltenham Saracens v Weston-super-Mare	3-1
Odd Down v Slimbridge	1-1
Odd Down won 3-2 on penalties	
Brixham v Saltash U	0-2
Tiverton T v Bishops Lydeard	0-4
Barnstaple T v Stoke Gabriel	20-0
Truro C v Elburton Villa	3-2
Elmore (walkover) v AFC St Austell	

FIRST QUALIFYING ROUND

Stockton T v Workington	1-0
Carlisle C v North Shields	0-5
South Shields v Pickering T	5-1
Spennymoor T v Gateshead	1-1
Gateshead won 5-4 on penalties	
Blyth Spartans v Billingham T	2-0
Morpeth T v Birtley T	9-1
Skelmersdale U v Prestwich Heys	1-3
Lancaster C v St Helens T	1-0
City of Liverpool v Trafford	5-0
Bootle v Atherton Collieries	0-3
Wythenshawe Amateurs v Chorley	1-1
Wythenshawe Amateurs won 3-2 on penalties	
West Didsbury & Chorlton v Buxton	0-0
West Didsbury & Chorlton won 9-8 on penalties	
Curzon Ashton v AFC Blackpool	1-3
Runcorn Linnets v AFC Liverpool	3-3
AFC Liverpool won 4-3 on penalties	
Chester v Irlam	2-0
Hyde U v South Liverpool	5-0
AFC Fylde v Vauxhall Motors	3-0
Sheffield v Frickley Ath	3-2
Farsley Celtic v York C	0-3
Gainsborough Trinity v Handsworth	0-3
Bradford (Park Avenue) v Emley	2-2
Bradford (Park Avenue) won 4-3 on penalties	
Guiseley v Tadcaster Alb	4-0
Pontefract Collieries v Ossett U	0-5
Silsden v Grimsby Bor	0-2
Mickleover v Quorn	10-1
Basford U v Deeping Rangers	8-1
Anstey Nomads v Alfreton T	3-1
Harborough T v Long Eaton U	1-5
Aylestone Park v Lutterworth T	10-1
St Andrews v Matlock T	4-0
Stamford v Lutterworth Ath	0-2
Grantham T (walkover) v Shirebrook T	
Boston U v Dunkirk	8-1
Racing Club Warwick v AFC Telford U	2-4
Sutton Coldfield T v Newcastle T	1-1
Newcastle T won 5-3 on penalties	
Rushall Olympic v Rugby T	0-3
Nuneaton Bor v Boldmere St Michaels	0-2
Kidderminster H v Pershore T	4-1
Bedworth U v Shawbury U	5-0
Bilston T v Halesowen T	1-2
Atherstone T v Evesham U (walkover)	
Walsall Wood v Redditch U	1-5
Leamington v Stourbridge	0-2
Dunstable T v Rushden & D	0-5
Kettering T v St Neots T	2-4
Leighton T v AFC Dunstable	2-1
Stotfold v Winslow U	0-3
Buckingham Ath v Baldock T	2-0
Godmanchester R v Crawley Green	3-0
Cogenhoe U v Bugbrooke St Michaels	0-4
Rothwell Corinthians v Kempston R	3-2
Wellingborough Whitworths v St Ives T	3-3
Wellingborough Whitworths won 4-2 on penalties	
Lowestoft T v Gorleston	2-0
Brantham Ath v Wroxham	2-1
Stowmarket T v Newmarket T	0-5
Woodbridge T v Mildenhall T	1-2
Whitton U v Felixstowe & Walton U	0-5
Bury T v Hadleigh U	9-0
Great Yarmouth T v Dereham T	0-5
Leiston v Haverhill R	4-2
AFC Sudbury v Histon	3-1
Grays Ath v Sawbridgeworth T	2-3
Aveley v Enfield T	2-0
Billericay T v Hadley	2-2
Billericay T won 6-5 on penalties	
Chelmsford C v Walthamstow	3-2
St Albans C v Woodford T	2-3
Colney Heath v Bowers & Pitsea	3-2
Hertford T v Wingate & Finchley	0-2
Barking v Cheshunt	5-1
Bishop's Stortford v Concord Rangers	0-4
Takeley v Ware	1-3
London Lions v Hackney Wick	5-3
Romford v Haringey Bor	1-3
Uxbridge v Bedfont Sports Club	1-3
Hanworth Villa v Berkhamsted (walkover)	
Hemel Hempstead T v Kensington & Ealing Bor	2-2
Hemel Hempstead T won 9-8 on penalties	
Ashford T (Middlesex) v Hendon	1-1
Ashford T (Middlesex) won 7-6 on penalties	
Balham v Beaconsfield T	1-4
Harefield U v Kings Langley	1-1
Kings Langley won 4-2 on penalties	
Hayes & Yeading U v Chalfont St Peter	4-0
North Greenford U v Langley	2-4
Punjab U v Lordswood	3-1
Sheppey U v Phoenix Sports	1-2
Cray Valley (PM) v Sutton Ath	7-1
Glebe v Cray W	3-1
K Sports v Tonbridge Angels	1-3
Tower Hamlets v Dartford	0-5
Maidstone U v Erith T	0-1
Corinthian v Welling U	0-3
Croydon v Ramsgate	9-0
VCD Ath v Hollands & Blair	1-1
Hollands & Blair won 5-4 on penalties	
Whitehawk v Abbey Rangers	5-0
Horsham YMCA v Worthing	2-8
Colliers Wood U v Farnham T	1-2
Bexhill U v Chichester C	0-0
Bexhill U won 4-2 on penalties	
Kingstonian v Three Bridges	2-2
Kingstonian won 3-1 on penalties	
Alfold v Peacehaven & Telscombe	5-1
Badshot Lea v Lewes (walkover)	
Leatherhead v Tooting & Mitcham U	1-0
Westfield v Burgess Hill T	1-6
Hastings U v Virginia Water	4-1
Redhill v Sutton Common R	0-5
Metropolitan Police v Dorking W	7-1
Corinthian Casuals v Montpelier Villa	5-0
Eastbourne Bor v Newhaven	7-1
Saltdean U v Bognor Regis T	1-3
Thame U v Thatcham T	2-1
Fleet Spurs v Banbury U	0-3
Ascot U v Cove	6-0
Marlow v Ardley U	12-0
Reading C v Abingdon U	2-0
Fleet T v Camberley T	0-4
Oxford C v Wokingham & Emmbrook	3-0
Easington Sports v North Leigh	1-5
Dorchester T v Poole T	1-2
Sholing v Alton	0-1
Hamworthy U v AFC Stoneham	1-7
Hamble Club v Gosport Bor	0-10
Havant & Waterlooville v Wimborne T	0-1
Christchurch v Basingstoke T	1-3
Cowes Sports v Winchester C	0-6
Cribbs v Street	1-2
Chippenham T v Radstock T	7-0
Mangotsfield U v Bristol Manor Farm	3-1
Tuffley R v Cinderford T	0-4

Bitton v Bath C 1-2
Odd Down v Cirencester T 1-5
Cheltenham Saracens v Welton R 7-0
Devizes T v Gloucester C 2-5
Paulton R v Portishead T 2-0
Truro C v Barnstaple T 2-3
AFC St Austell v Bishops Lydeard 1-8
Saltash U v Bridgwater U 2-1

SECOND QUALIFYING ROUND

North Shields v Morpeth T 6-1
South Shields v Stockton T 4-3
Blyth Spartans v Gateshead 0-0
Blyth Spartans won 4-3 on penalties
West Didsbury & Chorlton v Atherton Collieries 3-2
City of Liverpool v AFC Liverpool 5-3
Chester v Altrincham 2-0
Wrexham v AFC Blackpool 1-1
AFC Blackpool won 4-3 on penalties
Lancaster C v AFC Fylde 0-1
Hyde U v Wythenshawe Amateurs 5-4
Prestwich Heys v Stockport Co 0-1
Grimsby Bor v Guiseley 0-4
Bradford (Park Avenue) v York C 0-1
Ossett U v Sheffield 6-0
Chesterfield v Handsworth 4-0
Grimsby T v FC Halifax T 3-0
Boston U v Mickleover 3-1
Basford U v St Andrews 7-1
Anstey Nomads v Lutterworth Ath 3-1
Grantham T v Long Eaton U 0-3
Notts Co v Aylestone Park 2-3
Newcastle T v Halesowen T 0-3
Kidderminster H v Stourbridge 3-2
Solihull Moors v Evesham U 5-0
Bedworth U v AFC Telford U 2-0
Boldmere St Michaels v Redditch U 2-0
Winslow U v Wellingborough Whitworths 4-2
Rothwell Corinthians v Leighton T 1-5
Bugbrooke St Michaels v Rushden & D 4-4
Bugbrooke St Michaels won 5-3 on penalties
Buckingham Ath v Godmanchester R 2-2
Buckingham Ath won 6-5 on penalties
Rugby T v St Neots T 2-1
Mildenhall T v AFC Sudbury 0-5
Newmarket T v Brantham Ath 1-1
Brantham Ath won 4-1 on penalties
Bury T v Felixstowe & Walton U 2-2
Felixstowe & Walton U won 5-3 on penalties
Leiston v Dereham T 0-1
Lowestoft T v King's Lynn T 1-2
Southend U v Barking 2-0
Chelmsford C v Ware 8-0
Dagenham & R v Concord Rangers 0-10
Wingate & Finchley v Billericay T 0-1
Aveley v Haringey Bor 3-0
Woodford T v Colney Heath 2-4
Sawbridgeworth T v London Lions 1-4
Beaconsfield T v Hayes & Yeading U 4-4
Hayes & Yeading U won 4-3 on penalties
Ashford T (Middlesex) v Boreham Wood 0-1
Hemel Hempstead T v Bedfont Sports Club 3-1
Maidenhead U v Langley 3-4
Barnet v Berkhamsted 0-0
Barnet won 4-3 on penalties
Kings Langley v Wealdstone 4-1
Welling U v Punjab U 1-1
Welling U won 9-8 on penalties
Tonbridge Angels v Croydon 6-0
Hollands & Blair v Bromley 2-4
Dartford v Dover Ath 1-2
Erith T v Glebe 7-2
Cray Valley (PM) v Phoenix Sports 4-2
Corinthian Casuals v Burgess Hill T 6-0
Kingstonian v Lewes 1-3
Leatherhead v Bognor Regis T 4-0
Bexhill U v Alfold 4-3
Whitehawk v Farnham T 2-3
Sutton Common R v Eastbourne Bor 5-1
Worthing v Hastings U 2-1
Woking v Metropolitan Police 5-2
Banbury U v Reading C 0-5
Oxford C v Camberley T 4-0
Marlow v Ascot U 5-2
North Leigh v Thame U 8-0
AFC Stoneham v Eastleigh 2-3
Wimborne T v Weymouth 4-2
Gosport Bor v Poole T 2-0
Aldershot T v Basingstoke T 6-0
Alton v Winchester C 0-3
Bath C v Mangotsfield U 1-3
Cheltenham Saracens v Yeovil T 3-1
Gloucester C v Paulton R 2-2
Gloucester C won 4-2 on penalties
Chippenham T v Street 6-0
Cirencester T v Cinderford T 2-1
Bishops Lydeard v Torquay U 0-5
Barnstaple T v Saltash U 1-1
Saltash U won 6-5 on penalties

THIRD QUALIFYING ROUND

City of Liverpool v North Shields 4-2
Guiseley v Ossett U 3-2
Blyth Spartans v AFC Fylde 4-2
Chester v Grimsby T 0-1
South Shields v York C 1-1
South Shields won 4-3 on penalties
Stockport Co v Hyde U 3-1
West Didsbury & Chorlton v AFC Blackpool 0-2
Bedworth U v Aylestone Park 0-3
Basford U v Halesowen T 2-2
Basford U won 5-3 on penalties
Winslow U v Anstey Nomads 5-4
Kidderminster H v Boldmere St Michaels 2-2
Boldmere St Michaels won 2-1 on penalties
Long Eaton U v Buckingham Ath 1-1
Long Eaton U won 5-4 on penalties
Boston U v Chesterfield 1-0
Rugby T v Solihull Moors 3-1
Bugbrooke St Michaels v Leighton T 4-1
Chelmsford C v Felixstowe & Walton U 8-0
Southend U v Aveley 0-0
Southend U won 6-5 on penalties
London Lions v Concord Rangers 4-0
Billericay T v King's Lynn T 0-1
Dereham T v AFC Sudbury 1-3
Colney Heath v Brantham Ath 2-4
Cray Valley (PM) v Bexhill U 3-2
Aldershot T v Tonbridge Angels 2-0
Dover Ath v Woking 2-3
Hayes & Yeading U v Langley 2-1
Lewes v Hemel Hempstead T 6-0
Boreham Wood v Erith T 0-3
Barnet v Bromley 0-5
Worthing v Kings Langley 3-1
Marlow v Sutton Common R 1-2
Farnham T v Leatherhead 2-5
Welling U v Corinthian Casuals 2-2
Corinthian Casuals won 4-3 on penalties
Oxford C v Torquay U 0-1
Gloucester C v Reading C 1-5
Wimborne T v Chippenham T 0-0
Wimborne T won 4-3 on penalties
Winchester C v Saltash U 4-3
North Leigh v Cirencester T 3-1
Gosport Bor v Cheltenham Saracens 1-0
Eastleigh v Mangotsfield U 0-2

FIRST ROUND

Carlisle U v Oldham Ath 4-4*
Oldham Ath won 5-3 on penalties
City of Liverpool v Morecambe 0-1*
(0-0 at the end of normal time)
Guiseley v Rochdale 2-1
Fleetwood T v Tranmere R 3-3*
Fleetwood T won 4-3 on penalties
South Shields v Stockport Co 1-3
Accrington S v Wigan Ath 4-3*
(3-3 at the end of normal time)
Hartlepool U v Bolton W (walkover)
AFC Blackpool v Harrogate T 1-2
Sunderland v Bradford C 0-2
Salford C v Blyth Spartans 3-0
Basford U v Doncaster R 1-2
Aylestone Park v Lincoln C 4-4*
Aylestone Park won 3-1 on penalties
Burton Alb v Sheffield W 0-3
Long Eaton U v Rugby T 0-2
Walsall v Port Vale 1-1
Port Vale won 3-0 on penalties
Shrewsbury T v Scunthorpe U 0-1

Boston U v Mansfield T	2-5*
(2-2 at the end of normal time)	
Crewe Alex v Grimsby T	3-0
Rotherham U v Boldmere St Michaels	3-0
King's Lynn T v Northampton T	0-3
Brantham Ath v Stevenage	2-4
Ipswich T v Winslow U	7-1
Bugbrooke St Michaels v Colchester U	1-8
Southend U v Cambridge U	1-1*
Cambridge U won 5-4 on penalties	
AFC Sudbury v Chelmsford C	2-3
Milton Keynes D v London Lions	5-0
Worthing v Charlton Ath	1-3
Oxford U v Sutton Common R	4-0
Lewes v Bromley	2-4
Tie ordered to be replayed after serious error by the officials. First tie ended 1-2.	
Reading C v Gosport Bor	1-0
AFC Wimbledon v Woking	7-0
Hayes & Yeading U v Corinthian Casuals	0-1
Erith T v Portsmouth	0-1
Leatherhead v Leyton Orient	1-3
Cray Valley (PM) v Aldershot T	0-1
Sutton U v Gillingham	3-2*
(2-2 at the end of normal time)	
Swindon T v Winchester C	5-1
Wimborne T v Forest Green R	0-7
Bristol R v Exeter C	0-4
Plymouth Arg v Mangotsfield U	2-1
Cheltenham T v North Leigh	3-0
Newport Co v Torquay U	4-3

SECOND ROUND

Northampton T v Stockport Co	3-2
Bradford C v Oldham Ath	1-3
Accrington S v Bolton W	3-2
Fleetwood T v Mansfield T	1-0*
(0-0 at the end of normal time)	
Crewe Alex v Harrogate T	5-3
Scunthorpe U v Guiseley	1-0
Salford C v Port Vale	3-2*
(2-2 at the end of normal time)	
Doncaster R v Rotherham U	1-2*
(1-1 at the end of normal time)	
Aylestone Park v Sheffield W	1-2
Rugby T v Morecambe	2-0
Cheltenham T v Portsmouth	4-3*
(2-2 at the end of normal time)	
Swindon T v Colchester U	0-2
Corinthian Casuals v Cambridge U	1-5
Aldershot T v Ipswich T	1-4
Leyton Orient v Newport Co	6-1
Charlton Ath v AFC Wimbledon	2-0*
(0-0 at the end of normal time)	
Plymouth Arg v Milton Keynes D	3-1
Chelmsford C v Exeter C	0-4
Forest Green R v Bromley	3-4
Stevenage v Sutton U	0-2
Reading C v Oxford U	2-3

THIRD ROUND

Plymouth Arg v Brighton & HA	1-2
WBA v Rotherham U	3-2
Accrington S v Swansea C	1-0*
(0-0 at the end of normal time)	
QPR v Oldham Ath	2-1
Rugby T v Cheltenham T	0-4
Cambridge U v Oxford U	2-2*
Cambridge U won 4-2 on penalties	
Manchester U v Scunthorpe U	4-2
Bromley v Reading	1-3*
(1-1 at the end of normal time)	
Cardiff C v Watford	1-2
Colchester U v Arsenal	3-0
Liverpool v Fleetwood T	4-0
Birmingham C v Blackburn R	1-5
Nottingham F v Bristol C	3-1
Wolverhampton W v Salford C	4-1
Northampton T v Charlton Ath	0-6
Aston Villa v Leicester C	0-2
Burnley v Luton T	3-0
Sutton U v Preston NE	2-2*
Preston NE won 4-2 on penalties	
Exeter C v Bournemouth	0-2
Barnsley v Crystal Palace	1-2
Everton v Fulham	3-2
Crewe Alex v Hull C	1-0
Sheffield U v Millwall	1-1*
Sheffield U won 6-5 on penalties	
West Ham U v Newcastle U	2-3
Middlesbrough v Manchester C	0-3
Derby Co v Peterborough U	0-1
Blackpool v Huddersfield T	1-0
Norwich C v Stoke C	2-3
Tottenham H v Ipswich T	5-1
Southampton v Sheffield W	0-1
Coventry C v Leeds U	1-4
Chelsea v Leyton Orient	4-1

FOURTH ROUND

Liverpool v Burnley	4-1
Peterborough U v Nottingham F	1-2
Crystal Palace v Wolverhampton W	1-1*
Wolverhampton W won 6-5 on penalties	
Leicester C v Crewe Alex	1-0
Brighton & HA v Manchester C	1-0
Everton v Sheffield U	2-1
Watford v Chelsea	2-3*
(2-2 at the end of normal time)	
Blackburn R v Stoke C	3-0
Accrington S v Charlton Ath	1-2
Bournemouth v QPR	2-0
Tottenham H v WBA	6-1
Reading v Manchester U	1-3
Sheffield W v Preston NE	1-0
Newcastle U v Colchester U	3-2
Cheltenham T v Blackpool	1-3
Cambridge U v Leeds U	2-0

FIFTH ROUND

Cambridge U v Nottingham F	0-0*
Nottingham F won 5-3 on penalties	
Bournemouth v Leicester C	1-5
Liverpool v Chelsea	3-4
Blackburn R v Sheffield W	2-1
Blackpool v Newcastle U	3-0
Manchester U v Everton	4-1
Wolverhampton W v Tottenham H	3-0
Charlton Ath v Brighton & HA	0-2

SIXTH ROUND

Blackburn R v Nottingham F	1-3
Wolverhampton W v Brighton & HA	3-1
Manchester U v Leicester C	2-1
Chelsea v Blackpool	3-2

SEMI-FINALS

Manchester U v Wolverhampton W	3-0
Nottingham F v Chelsea	3-1

THE FA YOUTH CUP FINAL 2021–22

Wednesday 11 May 2022

(at Old Trafford, attendance 67,492)

Manchester U (1) 3 Nottingham F (1) 1

Manchester U: Vitek; Jurado, Murray, Jackson, Bennett, Mainoo, Mather (Aljofree 86), Gore, McNeill (Hugill 64), Hansen (Oyedele 64), Garnacho.
Scorers: Bennett 13, Garnacho 78, 90.

Nottingham F: Bott; Abbott, McAdam, Hammond, Johnson, Hanks (Gardner 81), Powell, McDonnell (Korpal 90), Esapa-Osong, Taylor, Collins (Perry 73).
Scorer: Powell 43.

Referee: Josh Smith.

THE FA SUNDAY CUP 2021–22

FIRST ROUND

Peterlee Catholic Club v Sunderland The Lansdowne	2-2
Peterlee Catholic Club won 5-3 on penalties	
Burradon & New Fordley v Hazlerigg Victory	5-1
Newton Aycliffe Iron Horse v Murton Colliery	1-2
Belle Vue R v Boro Walkers	4-0
Middlesbrough Dormans v Chapeltown	1-0
Hartlepool WHTDSOB v Hartlepool Lion O'Mally	3-1
Scawthorpe Ath v RHP Sports & Social	4-0
Main Line Social v Oakenshaw	9-1
LIV Supplies v AFC West Hull Gunners	1-3
Home Bargains v Campfield	0-1
Queens Park v Mayfair	1-6
Pineapple v Custys	0-3
Westwood Park (walkover) v Linthwaite Hounds	
Melling Vic v Dock	2-3
Netherton v Codsall Legion Sundats	2-2
Codsall Legion Sundats won 4-3 on penalties	
Oyster Martyrs (walkover) v SSS Lions	
FC Lizard v Austin Ex Apprentices	0-9
Sileby Ath v Sporting Dynamo	2-3
Sporting Loughborough v Poet Young Boys	1-4
Long Whatton v Birstall Stamford	2-4
Priory Sports (walkover) v Rouge 21	
Baiteze v Borussia Martlesham	0-0
Baiteze won 5-4 on penalties	
Royston R v Falcons	2-3
Wixams W v MK Gallacticos	3-1
Skew Bridge v Highgate Alb (walkover)	
St Josephs (Luton) v Club Lewsey	3-3
Club Lewsey won 5-4 on penalties	
Flaunden v St Josephs (Watford)	1-2
NLO v Greater Leys	6-1
Singh Sabha Slough v Burghfield	3-4
Lambeth All Stars v SE Dons	0-2
Chatham T SR v Banstead R	1-3
Grand Ath (walkover) v North End Cosmos	

SECOND ROUND

Burradon & New Fordley v Murton Colliery	6-2
Hartlepool WHTDSOB v Middlesbrough Dormans	1-1
Middlesbrough Dormans won 5-4 on penalties	
Belle Vue R v Peterlee Catholic Club	0-3
Main Line Social v AFC West Hull Gunners	3-1
Scawthorpe Ath v Westwood Park	2-2
Scawthorpe Ath won 3-1 on penalties	
Mayfair v Custys	3-0
Codsall Legion Sundats v Oyster Martyrs	1-1
Oyster Martyrs won 15-14 on penalties	
Dock v Campfield	3-5
Sporting Dynamo v Poet Young Boys	2-4
Austin Ex Apprentices v Birstall Stamford	0-1
Wixams W v Club Lewsey	0-3
Falcons v Highgate Alb (walkover)	
Baiteze v SE Dons	3-2
Priory Sports v Grand Ath	2-2
Grand Ath won 4-2 on penalties	
St Josephs (Watford) v NLO	3-1
Burghfield v Banstead R	4-1

THIRD ROUND

Burradon & New Fordley v Peterlee Catholic Club	3-0
Middlesbrough Dormans v Main Line Social	3-1
Scawthorpe Ath v Poet Young Boys	4-1
Oyster Martyrs v Campfield	1-2
Mayfair v Birstall Stamford	4-3
Club Lewsey v St Josephs (Watford)	2-0
Grand Ath v Baiteze	1-3
Highgate Alb v Burghfield	2-0

QUARTER-FINALS

Burradon & New Fordley v Mayfair	1-2
Campfield v Middlesbrough Dormans	1-1
Middlesbrough Dormans won 4-2 on penalties	
Scawthorpe Ath v Baiteze	2-4
Highgate Alb v Club Lewsey	6-1

SEMI-FINALS

Highgate Alb v Mayfair	3-2
Baiteze v Middlesbrough Dormans	1-1
Balteze won 3-2 on penalties	

THE FA SUNDAY CUP FINAL 2021–22

Millwall, Sunday 1 May 2022

(at Millwall, attendance 1440)

Baiteze (1) 2 Highgate Alb (0) 0

Baiteze: Otuyo; Pires, Cruickshank, Gibbs, Krans, Napa, Jeremiah (Barnett 80), Hession (Kahie 80), Adenji, Barnwell (Teniola 75), Cole.
Scorers: Barnwell 3, Barnett 86.

Highgate Alb: Gauriloaia (Ward 20); Magwood, Brindle, Sheikh, Riley, Hayes, Edwards (Mukemba 72), Scott, Kennedy, Ofori, Maitland (Tripp 53).

Referee: Lee Swabey.

PREMIER LEAGUE 2 2021–22

**After extra time.*

PREMIER LEAGUE 2 DIVISON ONE

	P	W	D	L	F	A	GD	Pts
Manchester C	26	16	6	4	65	32	33	54
West Ham U	26	15	3	8	59	39	20	48
Arsenal	26	10	11	5	56	48	8	41
Liverpool	26	11	7	8	47	37	10	40
Crystal Palace	26	12	3	11	54	50	4	39
Manchester U	26	11	6	9	46	43	3	39
Tottenham H	26	10	7	9	49	45	4	37
Leicester C	26	10	7	9	38	53	−15	37
Blackburn R	26	9	8	9	50	56	−6	35
Brighton and HA	26	9	7	10	41	41	0	34
Everton	26	8	5	13	33	54	−21	29
Chelsea	26	7	7	12	39	47	−8	28
Leeds U	26	7	6	13	44	49	−5	27
Derby Co	26	4	3	19	31	58	−27	15

PREMIER LEAGUE 2 DIVISON TWO

	P	W	D	L	F	A	GD	Pts
Fulham	26	20	2	4	64	27	37	62
Wolverhampton W	26	14	5	7	46	37	9	47
Stoke C	26	12	7	7	34	36	−2	43
Nottingham F	26	12	6	8	52	31	21	42
Norwich C	26	12	3	11	64	52	12	39
Burnley	26	11	6	9	46	39	7	39
Southampton	26	12	3	11	45	42	3	39
Newcastle U	26	12	2	12	51	56	−5	38
WBA	26	10	5	11	44	54	−10	35
Aston Villa	26	9	5	12	53	51	2	32
Birmingham C	26	7	5	14	34	51	−17	26
Middlesbrough	26	8	2	16	31	50	−19	26
Sunderland	26	7	3	16	35	49	−14	24
Reading	26	5	8	13	32	56	−24	23

PROMOTION PLAY-OFFS SEMI-FINALS

Stoke C v Nottingham F 2-0
Wolverhampton W v Norwich C 1-1
Wolverhampton W won 5-4 on penalties

PROMOTION PLAY-OFFS FINAL

Stoke C v Wolverhampton W 2-0

PROFESSIONAL DEVELOPMENT LEAGUE

GROUP NORTH	P	W	D	L	F	A	GD	Pts
Sheffield U	23	15	3	5	47	23	24	48
Coventry C	23	13	4	6	57	39	18	43
Hull C	23	12	4	7	44	41	3	40
Wigan Ath	23	7	4	12	31	39	−8	25
Crewe Alex	23	7	2	14	27	50	−23	23
Peterborough U	23	5	7	11	36	41	−5	22
Barnsley	23	5	7	11	22	42	−20	22
Sheffield W	23	4	8	11	21	32	−11	20

GROUP SOUTH	P	W	D	L	F	A	GD	Pts
Ipswich T	24	16	3	5	58	27	31	51
Bristol C	24	15	5	4	60	31	29	50
Cardiff C	24	15	2	7	44	30	14	47
Charlton Ath	24	10	6	8	55	46	9	36
Millwall	24	9	3	12	34	45	−11	30
Colchester U	24	8	5	11	35	44	−9	29
Watford	24	6	7	11	28	43	−15	25
Swansea C	24	5	9	10	34	41	−7	24
QPR	24	7	3	14	34	53	−19	24

PREMIER LEAGUE 2 LEAGUE CUP

QUALIFYING ROUND

Salford C v Mansfield T 2-3
Stevenage v Southend U 1-1*
Southend U won 5-4 on penalties
Oxford U v Huddersfield T 3-4
Plymouth Arg v Exeter C 1-2

GROUP STAGE

Group A Table	P	W	D	L	F	A	GD	Pts
WBA	6	4	1	1	18	8	10	13
Arsenal	6	2	2	2	11	12	−1	8
Bournemouth	6	2	2	2	8	9	−1	8
Southampton	6	0	3	3	7	15	−8	3

Group B Table	P	W	D	L	F	A	GD	Pts
Middlesbrough	6	3	0	3	13	10	3	9
QPR	6	3	0	3	15	14	1	9
Blackburn R	6	3	0	3	16	16	0	9
Nottingham F	6	3	0	3	13	17	−4	9

Group C Table	P	W	D	L	F	A	GD	Pts
Derby Co	6	5	1	0	17	9	8	16
Charlton Ath	6	3	1	2	14	6	8	10
Norwich C	6	1	2	3	12	16	−4	5
Reading	6	1	0	5	6	18	−12	3

Group D Table	P	W	D	L	F	A	GD	Pts
Peterborough U	6	3	1	2	13	8	5	10
Sheffield U	6	3	1	2	9	10	−1	10
Everton	6	3	0	3	8	9	−1	9
Burnley	6	2	0	4	8	11	−3	6

Group E Table	P	W	D	L	F	A	GD	Pts
Wigan Ath	6	4	1	1	13	7	6	13
Leeds U	6	2	2	2	10	10	0	8
Sunderland	6	1	3	2	9	13	−4	6
Mansfield T	6	1	2	3	7	9	−2	5

Group F Table	P	W	D	L	F	A	GD	Pts
West Ham U	6	4	1	1	11	5	6	13
Wolverhampton W	6	3	2	1	8	6	2	11
Exeter C	6	1	2	3	9	12	−3	5
Swansea C	6	0	3	3	7	12	−5	3

Group G Table	P	W	D	L	F	A	GD	Pts
Huddersfield T	6	5	1	0	17	3	14	16
Newcastle U	6	3	1	2	9	6	3	10
Watford	6	2	0	4	7	15	−8	6
Birmingham C	6	1	0	5	6	15	−9	3

Group H Table	P	W	D	L	F	A	GD	Pts
Fulham	6	5	1	0	14	4	10	16
Stoke C	6	3	0	3	15	11	4	9
Colchester U	6	1	2	3	8	10	−2	5
Southend U	6	1	1	4	4	16	−12	4

ROUND OF 16

Peterborough U v Charlton Ath 6-2
Fulham v Newcastle U 2-0
Wigan Ath v Wolverhampton W 0-1
WBA v QPR 4-2
Derby Co v Sheffield U 4-3*
Middlesbrough v Arsenal 1-1*
Middlesbrough won 4-3 on penalties
Huddersfield T v Stoke C 1-3
West Ham U v Leeds U 5-1

QUARTER-FINALS

Stoke C v Middlesbrough 1-2
Derby Co v WBA 3-4
Peterborough U v Wolverhampton W 0-1
West Ham U v Fulham 0-1

SEMI-FINALS

WBA v Fulham 2-1
Wolverhampton W v Middlesbrough 3-2

FINAL

WBA v Wolverhampton W 2-2*
WBA won 5-4 on penalties

UNDER-18 PROFESSIONAL DEVELOPMENT LEAGUE 2021–22

U18 PREMIER LEAGUE

NORTH	P	W	D	L	F	A	GD	Pts
Manchester C	26	19	4	3	87	26	61	61
Liverpool	26	16	3	7	85	45	40	51
Manchester U	26	11	9	6	58	47	11	42
Nottingham F	26	12	6	8	36	32	4	42
Blackburn R	26	11	5	10	56	38	18	38
Middlesbrough	26	10	8	8	38	45	–7	38
Burnley	26	10	6	10	40	44	–4	36
Wolverhampton W	26	10	6	10	41	46	–5	36
Leeds U	26	9	7	10	66	70	–4	34
Everton	26	8	7	11	28	37	–9	31
Sunderland	26	8	5	13	39	48	–9	29
Derby Co	26	7	6	13	31	62	–31	27
Stoke C	26	6	4	16	33	56	–23	22
Newcastle U	26	3	8	15	27	69	–42	17

SOUTH	P	W	D	L	F	A	GD	Pts
Southampton	26	20	2	4	80	34	46	62
West Ham U	26	18	4	4	70	25	45	58
Crystal Palace	26	16	5	5	61	31	30	53
Arsenal	26	14	6	6	58	43	15	48
Leicester C	26	14	5	7	47	31	16	47
Fulham	26	14	4	8	53	30	23	46
Chelsea	26	14	4	8	66	49	17	46
Brighton & HA	26	10	3	13	57	58	–1	33
Tottenham H	26	10	1	15	52	66	–14	31
WBA	26	9	2	15	42	63	–21	29
Reading	26	7	3	16	36	62	–26	24
Aston Villa	26	5	5	16	44	69	–25	20
Birmingham C	26	3	5	18	29	76	–47	14
Norwich C	26	3	1	22	20	78	–58	10

U18 PREMIER LEAGUE PLAY-OFF FINAL

Southampton v Manchester C 1-2

U18 PROFESSIONAL DEVELOPMENT LEAGUE

NORTH	P	W	D	L	F	A	GD	Pts
Sheffield U	23	15	8	0	62	21	41	53
Barnsley	23	13	4	6	54	35	19	43
Coventry C	23	10	8	5	40	31	9	38
Sheffield W	23	11	5	7	39	36	3	38
Wigan Ath	23	7	5	11	34	42	–8	26
Crewe Alex	23	7	3	13	42	57	–15	24
Peterborough U	23	5	4	14	40	47	–7	19
Hull C	23	6	1	16	29	61	–32	19

SOUTH	P	W	D	L	F	A	GD	Pts
Charlton Ath	24	17	3	4	77	37	40	54
Colchester U	24	12	5	7	63	47	16	41
Millwall	24	11	3	10	41	45	–4	36
Ipswich T	24	9	7	8	47	49	–2	34
Watford	24	9	6	9	43	46	–3	33
Swansea C	24	9	4	11	45	52	–7	31
Cardiff C	24	8	5	11	46	45	1	29
Bristol C	24	5	8	11	30	50	–20	23
QPR	24	4	5	15	38	69	–31	17

SEMI-FINALS

Charlton Ath v Barnsley 3-2
Sheffield U v Colchester U 5-1

FINAL

Sheffield U v Charlton Ath 2-1

U18 PREMIER LEAGUE CUP

GROUP STAGE

Group A Table	P	W	D	L	F	A	GD	Pts
Leicester C	3	2	0	1	7	4	3	6
Southampton	3	2	0	1	5	4	1	6
Nottingham F	3	1	0	2	5	6	–1	3
Newcastle U	3	1	0	2	3	6	–3	3

Group B Table	P	W	D	L	F	A	GD	Pts
Stoke C	3	2	1	0	6	1	5	7
Fulham	3	2	0	1	8	5	3	6
Leeds U	3	1	0	2	5	7	–2	3
Tottenham H	3	0	1	2	1	7	–6	1

Group C Table	P	W	D	L	F	A	GD	Pts
Manchester C	3	2	1	0	9	4	5	7
Liverpool	3	2	0	1	5	5	0	6
Crystal Palace	3	1	1	1	7	6	1	4
Aston Villa	3	0	0	3	4	10	–6	0

Group D Table	P	W	D	L	F	A	GD	Pts
Chelsea	3	2	1	0	9	7	2	7
Blackburn R	3	2	0	1	6	5	1	6
Derby Co	3	0	2	1	5	6	–1	2
Reading	3	0	1	2	4	6	–2	1

Group E Table	P	W	D	L	F	A	GD	Pts
Brighton & HA	3	2	0	1	6	4	2	6
Sunderland	3	1	1	1	7	5	2	4
Middlesbrough	3	1	1	1	4	3	1	4
Norwich C	3	1	0	2	3	8	–5	3

Group F Table	P	W	D	L	F	A	GD	Pts
Manchester U	3	2	0	1	12	6	6	6
Birmingham C	3	2	0	1	5	8	–3	6
Wolverhampton W	3	1	0	2	7	5	2	3
WBA	3	1	0	2	2	7	–5	3

Group G Table	P	W	D	L	F	A	GD	Pts
Arsenal	3	1	2	0	6	5	1	5
Everton	3	1	1	1	6	5	1	4
Burnley	3	1	1	1	5	6	–1	4
West Ham U	3	1	0	2	4	5	–1	3

QUARTER-FINALS

Brighton & HA v Leicester C 1-2
Chelsea v Manchester U 3-2
Stoke C v Arsenal 2-1
Fulham v Manchester C 2-0

SEMI-FINALS

Leicester C v Fulham 0-2
Stoke C v Chelsea 1-5

FINAL

Fulham v Chelsea 1-2

U18 DEVELOPMENT LEAGUE CUP

GROUP STAGE

Group A Table	P	W	D	L	F	A	GD	Pts
Cardiff C	3	3	0	0	12	0	12	9
Bristol C	3	2	0	1	6	5	1	6
Watford	3	1	0	2	3	8	–5	3
Swansea C	3	0	0	3	0	8	–8	0

Group B Table	P	W	D	L	F	A	GD	Pts
Charlton Ath	3	2	0	1	14	9	5	6
Millwall	3	2	0	1	11	7	4	6
Colchester U	3	2	0	1	10	9	1	6
QPR	3	0	0	3	2	12	–10	0

Group C Table	P	W	D	L	F	A	GD	Pts
Barnsley	3	2	1	0	7	4	3	7
Wigan Ath	3	2	0	1	11	4	7	6
Crewe Alex	3	1	0	2	12	9	3	3
Hull C	3	0	1	2	4	17	–13	1

Group D Table	P	W	D	L	F	A	GD	Pts
Coventry C	3	2	1	0	10	5	5	7
Ipswich T	3	1	1	1	5	8	–3	4
Peterborough U	3	1	0	2	7	6	1	3
Sheffield U	3	0	2	1	3	6	–3	2

QUARTER-FINALS

Ipswich T v Bristol C 3-2
Wigan Ath v Cardiff C 4-3
Millwall v Coventry C 1-2
Charlton Ath v Barnsley 2-0

SEMI-FINALS

Ipswich T v Wigan Ath 1-0
Coventry C v Charlton Ath 1-0

FINAL

Ipswich T v Coventry C 7-0

CENTRAL LEAGUE 2021–22

CENTRAL LEAGUE TABLE 2021–22

	P	W	D	L	F	A	GD	Pts
Preston NE	10	5	4	1	25	17	8	19
Fleetwood T	10	5	3	2	23	10	13	18
Accrington S	10	4	2	4	26	16	10	14
Bolton W	10	3	3	4	15	20	–5	12
Huddersfield T	10	3	2	5	21	20	1	11
Walsall	10	2	2	6	7	34	–27	8

CENTRAL LEAGUE CUP 2021–22

GROUP A

Burnley v Rochdale 3-2
Accrington S v Bolton W 3-3
Burnley v Accrington S 1-0
Rochdale v Bolton W 5-0
Bolton W v Burnley 1-4
Rochdale v Accrington S 0-2

Group A Table	P	W	D	L	F	A	GD	Pts
Burnley	3	3	0	0	8	3	5	9
Accrington S	3	1	1	1	5	4	1	4
Rochdale	3	1	0	2	7	5	2	3
Bolton W	3	0	1	2	4	12	–8	1

GROUP B

Carlisle U v Fleetwood T 2-1
Preston NE v Carlisle U 5-0
Preston NE v Fleetwood T 3-2
Morecambe v Preston NE 1-1
Fleetwood T v Morecambe 0-0
Morecambe v Carlisle U 1-2

Group B Table	P	W	D	L	F	A	GD	Pts
Preston NE	3	2	1	0	9	3	6	7
Carlisle U	3	2	0	1	4	7	–3	6
Morecambe	3	0	2	1	2	3	–1	2
Fleetwood T	3	0	1	2	3	5	–2	1

GROUP C

Rotherham U v Huddersfield T 1-2
Lincoln C v Grimsby T 1-0
Walsall v Huddersfield T 3-0
Grimsby T v Walsall 6-1
Walsall v Rotherham U 0-3
Huddersfield T v Lincoln C 1-0
Huddersfield T v Grimsby T 2-5
Rotherham U v Grimsby T 1-0
Lincoln C v Rotherham U 5-0
Lincoln C v Walsall 8-0

Group C Table	P	W	D	L	F	A	GD	Pts
Lincoln C	4	3	0	1	14	1	13	9
Grimsby T	4	2	0	2	11	5	6	6
Rotherham U	4	2	0	2	5	7	–2	6
Huddersfield T	4	2	0	2	5	9	–4	6
Walsall	4	1	0	3	4	17	–13	3

SEMI-FINALS

Preston NE v Carlisle U 2-1
Burnley v Lincoln C P-P
Match postponed, Lincoln C withdrew.

FINAL

Preston NE v Burnley
To be played next season.

YOUTH ALLIANCE LEAGUE 2021–22

NORTH EAST	P	W	D	L	F	A	GD	Pts
Bradford C	22	17	2	3	71	24	47	53
Grimsby T	22	14	5	3	49	17	32	47
Rotherham U	22	11	2	9	44	43	1	35
Lincoln C	22	11	1	10	46	47	–1	34
Doncaster R	22	10	2	10	38	43	–5	32
Burton Alb	22	9	5	8	40	35	5	32
Scunthorpe U	22	9	4	9	48	52	–4	31
Mansfield T	22	7	4	11	37	42	–5	25
Harrogate T	22	4	2	16	30	59	–29	14
Huddersfield T	22	4	1	17	27	68	–41	13

NORTH WEST	P	W	D	L	F	A	GD	Pts
Preston NE	26	20	3	3	83	25	58	63
Carlisle U	26	17	5	4	61	18	43	56
Blackpool	26	14	6	6	57	29	28	48
Accrington S	26	13	3	10	63	63	0	42
Bolton W	26	11	6	9	54	46	8	39
Shrewsbury T	26	12	2	12	43	36	7	38
Salford C	26	11	4	11	51	40	11	37
Rochdale	26	9	10	7	46	37	9	37
Oldham Ath	26	10	5	11	45	57	–12	35
Fleetwood T	26	10	4	12	40	43	–3	34
Morecambe	26	8	1	17	34	62	–28	25
Tranmere R	26	7	3	16	38	64	–26	24
Port Vale	26	6	3	17	30	84	–54	21
Walsall	26	4	5	17	24	65	–41	17

SOUTH EAST	P	W	D	L	F	A	GD	Pts
AFC Wimbledon	18	12	2	4	54	31	23	38
Southend U	18	10	1	7	36	32	4	31
Cambridge U	18	8	5	5	47	36	11	29
Stevenage	18	8	4	6	44	37	7	28
Gillingham	18	9	1	8	32	32	0	28
Sutton U	18	8	2	8	36	25	11	26
Northampton T	18	7	3	8	29	33	–4	24
Luton T	18	6	5	7	34	35	–1	23
Leyton Orient	18	5	3	10	24	42	–18	18
Milton Keynes D	18	3	2	13	21	54	–33	11

SOUTH WEST	P	W	D	L	F	A	GD	Pts
Bournemouth	18	10	5	3	39	23	16	35
Plymouth Arg	18	10	5	3	40	27	13	35
Exeter C	18	10	2	6	37	28	9	32
Oxford U	18	8	6	4	34	21	13	30
Portsmouth	18	9	2	7	36	31	5	29
Swindon T	18	7	4	7	29	29	0	25
Newport Co	18	5	4	9	21	27	–6	19
Cheltenham T	18	5	4	9	23	32	–9	19
Forest Green R	18	4	2	12	22	42	–20	14
Bristol R	18	3	4	11	16	37	–21	13

MERIT LEAGUE 1	P	W	D	L	F	A	GD	Pts
Plymouth Arg	9	7	1	1	16	3	13	22
Gillingham	9	6	3	0	15	6	9	21
Southend U	9	6	0	3	24	15	9	18
Portsmouth	9	5	1	3	15	13	2	16
Oxford U	9	4	1	4	8	14	–6	13
Bournemouth	9	3	1	5	16	17	–1	10
Cambridge U	9	3	1	5	9	13	–4	10
AFC Wimbledon	9	3	0	6	15	17	–2	9
Exeter C	9	1	3	5	9	19	–10	6
Stevenage	9	1	1	7	10	20	–10	4

MERIT LEAGUE 2	P	W	D	L	F	A	GD	Pts
Luton T	9	8	0	1	31	9	22	24
Leyton Orient	9	6	1	2	19	6	13	19
Newport Co	9	4	2	3	18	17	1	14
Northampton T	9	4	2	3	9	10	–1	14
Sutton U	9	4	1	4	18	20	–2	13
Cheltenham T	9	3	2	4	20	24	–4	11
Bristol R	9	3	1	5	17	19	–2	10
Forest Green R	9	2	3	4	12	18	–6	9
Swindon T	9	2	3	4	14	26	–12	9
Milton Keynes D	9	1	1	7	9	18	–9	4

YOUTH ALLIANCE LEAGUE CUP 2021–22

FIRST ROUND SOUTH

Sutton U v Oxford U 0-1
Leyton Orient v Gillingham 4-1
Stevenage v Southend U 2-4
Bournemouth v Plymouth Arg 0-1

GROUP STAGE NORTH

Group 1 Table	P	W	D	L	F	A	GD	Pts
Salford C	3	2	1	0	9	1	8	7
Huddersfield T	3	2	0	1	7	8	–1	6
Tranmere R	3	0	2	1	6	7	–1	2
Harrogate T	3	0	1	2	5	11	–6	1

Group 2 Table	P	W	D	L	F	A	GD	Pts
Burton Alb	3	2	0	1	3	3	0	6
Shrewsbury T	3	1	2	0	8	5	3	5
Port Vale	3	1	1	1	6	7	–1	4
Walsall	3	0	1	2	2	4	–2	1

Group 3 Table	P	W	D	L	F	A	GD	Pts
Accrington S	3	3	0	0	7	1	6	9
Preston NE	3	2	0	1	4	4	0	6
Bradford C	3	1	0	2	6	6	0	3
Fleetwood T	3	0	0	3	2	8	–6	0

Group 4 Table	P	W	D	L	F	A	GD	Pts
Blackpool	3	3	0	0	11	4	7	9
Rotherham U	3	2	0	1	6	7	–1	6
Carlisle U	3	1	0	2	8	8	0	3
Morecambe	3	0	0	3	3	9	–6	0

Group 5 Table	P	W	D	L	F	A	GD	Pts
Rochdale	3	1	2	0	5	2	3	5
Grimsby T	3	1	2	0	5	3	2	5
Lincoln C	3	1	1	1	5	6	–1	4
Scunthorpe U	3	0	1	2	4	8	–4	1

Group 6 Table	P	W	D	L	F	A	GD	Pts
Bolton W	3	3	0	0	12	2	10	9
Mansfield T	3	1	1	1	4	4	0	4
Doncaster R	3	1	0	2	3	7	–4	3
Oldham Ath	3	0	1	2	3	9	–6	1

SECOND ROUND SOUTH

Bristol R v Newport Co 0-1
Swindon T v Northampton T 1-3
Southend U v Cambridge U 2-0
Exeter C v Plymouth Arg 2-2
Exeter C won 9-8 on penalties
Milton Keynes D v Cheltenham T 1-3
Luton T v Leyton Orient 4-3
Forest Green R v Portsmouth 1-1
Forest Green R won 5-4 on penalties
AFC Wimbledon v Oxford U 2-1

QUARTER-FINALS NORTH

Accrington S v Bolton W 0-2
Salford C v Burton Alb 0-4
Blackpool v Rochdale 6-1
Huddersfield T v Preston NE 1-3

QUARTER-FINALS SOUTH

Newport Co v Exeter C 1-2
Northampton T v Southend U 2-1
Forest Green R v Luton T 1-7
Cheltenham T v AFC Wimbledon 2-3

SEMI-FINALS NORTH

Blackpool v Bolton W 2-2
Bolton W won 4-2 on penalties
Preston NE v Burton Alb 2-1

SEMI-FINALS SOUTH

Luton T v Northampton T 5-2
AFC Wimbledon v Exeter C 2-0

FINAL NORTH

Preston NE v Bolton W 4-1

FINAL SOUTH

AFC Wimbledon v Luton T 2-3

YOUTH ALLIANCE LEAGUE CUP FINAL 2021–22

Luton T v Preston NE 1-4

IMPORTANT ADDRESSES

The Football Association: Wembley Stadium, PO Box 1966, London SW1P 9EQ. *0844 980 8200*

Scotland: Hampden Park, Glasgow G42 9AY. *0141 616 6000*

Northern Ireland (Irish FA): Chief Executive, Donegall Avenue, Belfast, Northern Ireland BT12 6LU. *028 9066 9458*

Wales: 11/12 Neptune Court, Vanguard Way, Cardiff CF24 5PJ. *029 2043 5830*

Republic of Ireland: National Sports Campus, Abbotstown, Dublin 15. *01 8999 500*

International Federation (FIFA): Strasse 20, P.O. Box 8044, Zurich, Switzerland. *00 41 43 222 7777. Fax: 00 41 43 222 7878*

Union of European Football Associations: Secretary, Route de Geneve 46, P.O. Box 1260, Nyon 2, Switzerland. *+41(0) 848 00 2727*

THE LEAGUES

The Premier League: Brunel Building, 57 North Wharf Road, London W2 1HQ. *0207 864 9000*

The Football League: EFL House, 10–12 West Cuff, Preston PR1 8HU. *01772 325 800. Fax 01772 325 801*

The National League: M. Tattersall, 4th Floor, Waterloo House, 20 Waterloo Street, Birmingham B2 5TB. *0121 643 3143*

FA Women's Super League: Wembley Stadium, PO Box 1966, London SW1P 9EQ. *+44 844 980 8200*

Scottish Professional Football League: Hampden Park, Glasgow G42 9DE. *0141 620 4140*

Cymru Premier League: 11/12 Neptune Court, Vanguard Way, Cardiff CF24 5PJ. *029 2043 5830*

Northern Ireland Football League: Mervyn Brown Suite, National Stadium at Windsor Park, Donegall Avenue, Belfast BT12 6LW. *028 9560 7150*

Football League of Ireland: National Sports Campus, Abbotstown, Dublin 15. *00 353 1 8999 500*

Southern League: J. Mills, Suite 3B, Eastgate House, 121–131 Eastgate Street, Gloucester GL1 1PX. *07768 750 590*

Northern Premier League: Ms A. Firth, 23 High Lane, Norton Tower, Halifax, W. Yorkshire HX2 0NW. *01422 410 691*

Isthmian League: Kellie Discipline, PO Box 393, Dartford DA1 9JK. *01322 314 999*

Combined Counties League: A. Constable, 3 Craigwell Close, Staines, Middlesex TW18 3NP. *01784 440 613*

Eastern Counties League: Nigel Spurling, secretary@thurlownunnleague.co.uk. *07855 279 062*

Essex Senior League: Secretary: Ms M. Dorling, 39 Milwards, Harlow, Essex CM19 4SG. *07939 850 627*

Hellenic League: John Ostinelli, 2 Wynn Grove, Hazlemere HP15 7LY. *07900 081 814*

Midland League: N. Wood, 30 Glaisdale Road, Hall Green, Birmingham B28 8PX. *07967 440 007*

North West Counties League: J. Deal, 24 The Pastures, Crossens, Southport PR9 8RH. *01704 212 917*

Northern Counties East: Matt Jones, 346 Heneage Road, Grimsby DN32 9NJ. *07415 068 996*

Northern League: K. Hewitt, 21 Cherrytree Drive, Langley Park, Durham DH7 9FX. *07897 611 640*

South Midlands League: Louise Condon, Century House, Skimpot Lane, Dunstable LU5 4JU. *01582 567 714*

Southern Combination League: T. Dawes, 32 Reynolds Lane, Langney, Eastbourne BN23 7NW. *01323 764 218*

Southern Counties East League: Andy Short, secretary@scefl.com

United Counties League: Ms W. Newey, Nene Valley Community Centre, Candy Street, Peterborough PE2 9RE. *01733 330 056*

Wessex League: Steve Smith, leaguesecretary.wessexleague @gmail.com. *07368 276 984*

Western League: A. Radford, 19 Longney Place, Patchway, Bristol BS34 5LQ. *07872 818 868*

OTHER USEFUL ADDRESSES

Amateur Football Alliance: Jason Kilby, Unit 3, 7 Wenlock Road, London N1 7SL. *0208 733 2613*

Association of Football Badge Collectors: K. Wilkinson, 18 Hinton St, Fairfield, Liverpool L6 3AR. *0151 260 0554*

British Blind Sport (including football): 19 Coventry Road, Cubbington, Leamington Spa CV32 7JN. *01926 424 247*

British Olympic Association: 101 New Cavendish Street, London W1W 6XH. *0207 842 5700*

British Universities and Colleges Sports Association: Vince Mayne, Chief Executive: BUCSA, 20–24 King's Bench Street, London SE1 0QX. *0207 633 5080*

English Schools FA: 4 Parker Court, Staffordshire Technology Park, Stafford ST18 0WP. *01785 785 972*

England Supporters Club: Wembley Stadium, London HA9 0WS. *0800 389 1966*

Football Foundation: 10 Eastbourne Terrace, Paddington, London W2 6LG. *0345 345 4555*

Football Postcard Collectors Club: PRO: John Farrelly, 34 Franche Road, Wolverly, Kidderminster DY11 5TP. Web: www.hobbyist.co.uk/fpcc

Football Safety Officers Association: Peter Houghton, Suite 5, Blackburn Rovers Enterprise Centre, Ewood Park, Blackburn BB2 4JF. *01254 841 771.*

Grassroots Football Limited: Unit 5, St Hilda's Industrial Estate, Station Road, South Shields, Tyne and Wear NE33 1RA. *0191 447 5250*

Institute of Groundsmanship: 28 Stratford Office Village, Walker Avenue, Wolverton, Milton Keynes MK12 5TW. *01908 312 511*

League Managers Association: St George's Park, Newborough Road, Needwood, Burton on Trent DE13 9PD. *0128 357 6350*

National Football Museum: Urbis Building, Cathedral Gardens, Todd Street, Manchester M4 3BG. *0161 605 8200*

Professional Footballers' Association: 20 Oxford Court, Bishopsgate, Off Lower Moseley Street, Manchester M2 3WQ. *0161 236 0575*

Programme Monthly & Football Collectable Magazine: R. P. Matz, 11 Tannington Terrace, London N5 1LE. *020 7359 8687*

Programme Promotions: 21 Roughwood Close, Watford WD17 3HN. *01923 861 468*

Referees' Association: 1A Bagshaw Close, Ryton-on-Dunsmore, Coventry CV8 3EX. *024 7642 0360*

Scottish Football Museum: Hampden Park, Glasgow G42 9BA. *0141 616 6139*

Sir Norman Chester Centre for Football Research: Department of Sociology, University of Leicester, University Road LE1 7RH. *0116 252 2741/5*

Sport England: 21 Bloomsbury Street, London WC1B 3HF. *0345 8508 508*

Sports Grounds Safety Authority: 2–6 Salisbury Square, London EC4Y 8AE. *0207 930 6693*

Sports Turf Research Institute: St Ives Grove, Harden, Bingley, West Yorkshire BD16 1AU. *01274 565 131*

The Football Supporters' Association: 1 Ashmore Terrace, Stockton Road, Sunderland, Tyne and Wear SR2 7DE. *0330 440 0044*

The Ninety-Two Club: Mr M. Kimberley, The Ninety-Two Club, 153 Hayes Lane, Kenley, Surrey CR8 5HP.

Walking Football Association: Kemp House, 160 City Road, London EC1V 2NX. *07517 033248*

Wheelchair Football Association: c/o Birmingham County FA, Ray Hall Lane, Birmingham B43 6JF.

FOOTBALL CLUB CHAPLAINCY

PARSONS IN FOOTBALL

Professional, top-level football certainly owes a big debt to clergymen.The relationship between men in many dressing rooms wearing a white clergyman's collar and all of the players and staff is usually a positive, happy and relaxed one.

Regardless of the calibre of most footballers, they are often in the limelight. Initially at least, they may be unwilling to broadcast an issue which can readily be resolved in a discussion with a reliable and usually experienced friend.

Happily the relationship, however gained, between the cleric and the members of the playing staff is barely ever a source of disgruntlement.

The professional footballers and other members of the playing staff seldom regard the presence in the dressing room or at the training ground with suspicion or irritation, and very often a footballer has been glad to speak confidentially with a football-interested cleric.

Sometimes the player and the clergyman meet up formally or informally to discuss a situation which may be worrying the player.

All things considered, the cleric often becomes a familiar fellow among the footballers – on the team bus, or in an empty dressing room – and many players have been glad of a quiet, personal chat with the chaplain.

THE REV

OFFICIAL CHAPLAINS TO FA PREMIERSHIP AND FOOTBALL LEAGUE CLUBS

Aston Villa – Jon Grant
Barrow – Jonathan Harrison
Barnsley – Peter Amos
Birmingham C – Kirk McAtear
Birmingham C Academy – Tim Atkins
Blackburn R – Ken Howles
Blackpool – Linda Tomkinson
Bolton W – Philip Mason
Bournemouth – Adam Parrett
Bradford C – Oliver Evans
Brentford – Stuart Cashman
Bristol C – Derek Cleave
Bristol R – Wayne Massey
Burton Alb – Phil Pusey
Cambridge U – Leo Orobor
Cardiff C Academy – James Roach
Carlisle U (not SCUK) – Alun Jones
Charlton Ath Academy – Gareth Morgan
Charlton Ath – Matt Baker
Chelsea (not SCUK) – Martin Swan
Cheltenham T – Malcolm Allen
Coventry C – Kieran Joseph
Crawley T – Steve Alliston
Crewe Alex – Phil Howell
Crystal Palace – Chris Roe
Derby Co – Tony Luke
Doncaster R – Barry Miller
Everton – Henry Corbett
Fleetwood T – George Ayoma
Fulham – Gary Piper
Harrogate T – Rob Brett
Hartlepool U – Chris Stuttard
Huddersfield T – Dudley Martin
Ipswich Town – Kevan McCormack
Leeds U – Dave Niblock
Leyton Orient – Steve Opie
Lincoln C – Andrew Vaughan
Liverpool – Bill Bygroves
Manchester C – Pete Horlock
Mansfield T – Kevin Charles
Millwall – Owen Beament
Morecambe – Martin Bateman
Newport Co – Keith Beardmore
Northampton T – Haydon Spenceley
Norwich C – Jon Norman
Norwich C Academy – Tim Henery
Peterborough U – Richard Longfoot
Peterborough U Academy – Jonathan Greenwood
Plymouth Arg – Arthur Goode
Portsmouth – Jonathan Jeffery and Mick Mellows
Port Vale – Ashley Cooper
Preston NE – Chris Nelson
QPR – Joshua Baines
Reading – Steven Prince
Reading Academy – Charlie Baines
Rochdale – Richard Bradley
Rotherham U – Baz Gascoyne
Sheffield U – Delroy Hall
Sheff W – Baz Gascoyne
Sheffield W Wise Old Owls – David Jeans
Shrewsbury T – Phil Cansdale and Andy Ackroyd
Southampton – Jonny Goodchild
Stevenage – Jon Woodrow
Stockport Co – Billy Montgomery
Sunderland – Marc Lyden-Smith
Swansea C – Eirian Wyn
Swindon T – Simon Stevenette
Tranmere R – Buddy Owen
Tranmere R (Stadium) – Matt Graham
Walsall – Lance Blackwood
Watford – Clive Ross
WBA – Christian Wienkamp
West Ham U – Alan Bolding
West Ham U Academy – Philip Wright
Wimbledon – Simon Elliott
Wolverhampton W – David Wright
Wolverhampton W Academy – Steve Davies
Wycombe W – Benedict Musola

CURRENT CHAPLAINS IN WOMEN'S FOOTBALL

Aston Villa – Jon Grant
Birmingham C – Sophie Hardwick
Bristol C – Esther Legg-Bagg
Cambridge U – Victoria Lawrence
Charlton Ath – Kathryn Sales
Crystal Palace – Dotha Blackwood
Derby Co – Sarah Crathorne
Leicester C – Louise Davis
Lewes Academy – Sharon Phillips
London C Lionesses – Angela Wilson
Newcastle U – Dot Lee
Oxford U – Deborah Rooke
Portsmouth – Debs Smart
Reading – Angy King
Watford – Melanie Sills
West Ham U – Jane Quinton

The chaplains hope that those who read this page will see the value and benefit of chaplaincy work in football and will take appropriate steps to spread the word where this is possible. They would also like to thank the editors of the Football Yearbook for their continued support for this specialist and growing area of work.

For further information, please contact: Sports Chaplaincy UK, The Avenue Methodist Church, Wincham Road, Sale, Cheshire M33 4PL. Telephone: 0800 181 4051 or email: admin@sportschaplaincy.org.uk. Website: www.sportschaplaincy.org.uk

OBITUARIES

Jock Aird (Born: Glencraig, Fife, 18 February 1926. Died: Australia, June 2021.) Jock Aird had played just three games for Jeanfield Swifts when Burnley signed him in August 1948. The Clarets quickly converted him to full-back, but it was not until the 1951–52 season that he began to establish himself in the side. He went on to make 143 first-team appearances before losing his place in the side and in September 1955 he emigrated to New Zealand where he played for the Eastern Union club of Gisborne. He was capped four times for Scotland during his time at Turf Moor, featuring for them in the 1954 World Cup finals, and later won two caps for New Zealand.

Barrie Aitchison (Born: Colchester, 15 November 1937. Died: 23 November 2021.) Barrie Aitchison was a winger who impressed in schoolboy football before joining Tottenham Hotspur. He spent 10 years on the books at White Hart Lane, but although he turned out regularly for the reserves, he was unable to win a place in the first team. In August 1964 he signed for Colchester United and did well during his first season at Layer Road but was then injured soon after the start of 1965–66 resulting in a lengthy lay-off. He left the U's in the summer of 1966 and signed for Southern League club Cambridge City.

Alan Anderson (Born: Edinburgh, 21 December 1939. Died: Leith, 28 February 2022.) Half-back Alan Anderson signed for Falkirk from Junior outfit Dalkeith Thistle in June 1958, but the only first-team football he played during his time at Brockville was during a spell on loan to Alloa Athletic. Shortly after the start of the 1959–60 campaign he moved to Millwall and won a regular place in the side, playing in all but four of their Division Four fixtures in 1960–61 when they won the title. He moved on to Scunthorpe United where he found it difficult to make an impact, but his career blossomed after returning to Scotland and signing for Heart of Midlothian in November 1963. He went on to make over 450 appearances during his time at Tynecastle, gaining a Scottish Cup runners-up medal in 1968. He went on the Scottish FA's 1967 world tour and many years later was awarded an international cap for five of these games when they were reclassified as full internationals.

John Anderson (Born: Johnstone, Renfrewshire, 11 January 1937. Died: July 2021.) Winger John Anderson joined Stoke City from Johnstone Burgh Juniors in January 1957 and spent four seasons at the Victoria Ground but was mostly a back-up player for the Potters. He spent the 1961–62 campaign in the Cheshire League with Bangor City and Northwich Victoria before returning to Scotland. After a season each at Morton and Third Lanark, he emigrated to Australia where he played for the South Melbourne and Hakoah clubs. He won five full caps for the Australia national team in 1965 featuring in both of their World Cup qualifying games against North Korea.

John Angus (Born: Warkworth, Northumberland, 2 September 1938. Died: 8 June 2021.) John Angus was a right-back who was a key member of the successful Burnley team which won the Football League championship in 1959–60 and reached the FA Cup final in 1961–62. He signed for the Clarets in 1954, making his first-team debut two years later, and went on to make 521 appearances, a club record for an outfield player, before retiring in the summer of 1972. John, who played for Burnley throughout his career, played for England at youth level and won seven U23 international caps. His sole appearance for the full England team was in May 1961 against Austria in Vienna.

Tom Anthony (Born: Hounslow, Middlesex, 16 August 1943. Died: September 2021.) Full-back Tom Anthony developed in the junior set-up at Brentford, signing a professional contract at the age of 18. He played regularly for the Bees when they won the Fourth Division title in 1962–63, but then lost his place in the team and was mostly a reserve for the next two seasons. He later spent several seasons with Guildford City, with whom he won the Southern League First Division title in 1970–71.

John Archer (Born: Biddulph, Staffordshire, 18 June 1941. Died: Congleton, Cheshire, 12 December 2021.) John Archer was a forward who came up through the ranks with Port Vale where he was still a teenager when he broke into the first team. He was released at the end of the 1960–61 campaign and signed for Bournemouth. He scored for the Cherries in his debut at Lincoln City and enjoyed regular first-team football during a five-year spell at Dean Court, netting 40 goals from 149 appearances. He went on to play for Crewe Alexandra, Huddersfield Town and Chesterfield, where he captained the Spireites to the Fourth Division title in 1969–70.

Len Ashurst (Born: Liverpool, 10 March 1939. Died: 25 September 2021.) Len Ashurst was a left-back who made 458 first-team appearances for Sunderland, a club record for an outfield player, and later had a successful career as a manager. Len was initially at Liverpool, appearing for the England youth team, and then Wolves without making a first-team appearance for either club. He had a brief spell with non-league Prescot Cables before signing for the Black Cats in December 1957 and after making his Football League debut the following year, he was a regular in the team through to the early 1970s. While at Roker Park he won a single cap for the England U23 team. Len was appointed player-manager of Hartlepool United in March 1971 and later managed Gillingham, Sheffield Wednesday, Cardiff City, Newport County and Sunderland as well as the Kuwait and Qatar national teams. He led Newport to promotion in 1979–80 when they also won the Welsh Cup, and the following season took the club to the quarter-finals of the European Cup Winners' Cup. He also took Sunderland to their first Football League Cup final in 1985.

Ray Aspden (Born: Horwich, Lancashire, 6 February 1938. Died: August 2021.) Centre-half Ray Aspden made his first-team debut for Rochdale at the age of 17, at the time making him the club's youngest-ever Football League player. The requirements of National Service disrupted his early career at Spotland, and it was not until midway through the 1958–59 campaign that he established himself in the line-up. He went on to make over 300 first-team appearances for Dale, featuring in both legs of the 1961–62 Football League Cup final defeat by Norwich City. He later returned to the club for a while as manager of the Rochdale AFC Fighting Fund.

Bertie Auld (Born: Glasgow, 23 March 1938. Died: 14 November 2021.) Bertie Auld, who started his career as an outside-left before switching to a midfield role, was a key member of Celtic's 1966–67 Lisbon Lions team that won the European Cup and a domestic treble. He first signed for Celtic in 1955 but six years later was sold to Birmingham City. During his time at St Andrew's he was a member of the Blues team that won the 1963–64 Football League Cup final but returned to Parkhead in January 1965 at the start of a golden period for the Glasgow club. During his second spell with Celtic, he won six consecutive Scottish League titles together with four Scottish Cups and three League Cups. Bertie was capped three times by Scotland in 1959 and he also played twice for the Scottish League representative team. He finished his career at Hibernian and later managed Partick Thistle, Hibernian, Hamilton Academical and Dumbarton.

Doug Baillie (Born: Douglas, Lanarkshire, 27 January 1937. Died: Hamilton, Lanarkshire, 19 February 2022.) Doug Baillie was a robust centre-half who joined Airdrieonians from Douglas Water Thistle in January 1954. He made over 150 first-team appearances for the Diamonds during his time with the club, also playing a single game in the Football League with Swindon Town when he was based in the area on National Service. He enjoyed a lengthy career in Scottish football with further spells at Rangers, Third Lanark, Falkirk and Dunfermline Athletic. He won two caps for Scotland U23s. After retiring as a player he went on to become a journalist for the *Sunday Post* where he held the position of chief football writer for 32 years.

Bobby Bainbridge (Born: York, 22 February 1931. Died: York, 16 October 1921.) Bobby Bainbridge was a local lad who spent three seasons on the books of York City in the 1950s, making four first-team appearances. He was a regular scorer for the club's reserve team and later continued his career in the Midland League with Frickley Colliery and Denaby United.

Keith Bambridge (Born: Rawmarsh, Yorkshire, 1 September 1935. Died: Bramley, South Yorkshire, 15 July 2021.) Keith Bambridge was an outside-left who developed in Rotherham junior football before signing professional terms with Rotherham United in February 1955. He established himself in the Millers' first team the following season and went on to make over 150 Division Two appearances for the club, also featuring in both legs of the inaugural Football League Cup final of 1960–61 when they lost out to Aston Villa. He concluded his senior career with spells at Darlington and Halifax Town and became the first-ever substitute used by the Shaymen in a Football League match.

Geoff Barker (Born: Hull, 7 February 1949. Died: 14 February 2022.) Geoff Barker was a central defender who joined Hull City as an apprentice before graduating to the professional ranks. He never really established himself with the Tigers but went on to make a total of 350 League and Cup appearances during his career with spells at Darlington, Reading and Grimsby Town, assisting the latter two clubs to win promotion from the old Fourth Division.

Jeff Barmby (Born: Hull, 15 January 1943. Died: Hull, 17 July 2021.) Jeff Barmby was a powerful centre-forward who was an amateur on the books of Hull City, making two first-team appearances. He then switched to non-league football with Bridlington Town and Goole Town before becoming a key member of the successful Northern Premier League club Scarborough in the 1970s. His son Nick Barmby and grandson Jack Barmby both played the game professionally.

Tommy Barnett (Born: Muswell Hill, Haringey, London, 12 October 1936. Died: Great Yarmouth, 14 March 2022.) Tommy Barnett was an inside-forward who develop with Chatham Town before stepping up to the senior ranks when he signed for Crystal Palace in December 1958. Although mostly a reserve at Selhurst Park, he stayed three seasons, making 15 first-team appearances and scoring two goals. He later enjoyed a successful career in Southern League football with Margate and Romford, leading the club scoring charts when Romford won the league title in 1966–67.

Bobby Barr (Born: Halifax, 5 December 1969. Died: 14 July 2021.) Bobby Barr was a central defender who signed for Halifax Town as a trainee and was just 17 years old when he made his first-team debut. He made six appearances during his time at The Shay before moving on to non-league Chorley. He later returned to Halifax as coach of the youth team. He was the younger brother of Billy Barr who also played for the Shaymen.

Mick Bates (Born: Armthorpe, Doncaster, 19 September 1947. Died: July 2021.) After coming up through the ranks with Leeds United, midfielder Mick Bates went on to enjoy 12 years as a key squad member of Don Revie's successful team of the 1960s and '70s. Although often a back-up player he made a valuable contribution throughout his time at Elland Road, with a highlight coming in the 1970–71 Inter Cities Fairs Cup final when his equaliser in the first leg away to Juventus helped the Whites secure the trophy on the away goals ruling. He subsequently had spells with Walsall, Bradford City and Doncaster Rovers before leaving senior football.

Joey Beauchamp (Born: Oxford, 13 March 1971. Died: Kidlington, Oxfordshire, 19 February 2022.) Joey Beauchamp was a local lad developed with Oxford United, signing professional terms in May 1989. He made his first-team debut for the U's at the age of 18 but it was not until the 1992–93 campaign that he established himself in the line-up. A skilful right-winger, he was sold to West Ham United in the summer of 1994 but did not settle in East London and within a matter of weeks he had moved on to Swindon Town. In October 1995 he was back at Oxford where he remained until his career was ended by injury, having made over 400 appearances for the club during his two spells.

Brian Bedford (Born: Ferndale, Glamorgan, 24 December 1933. Died: May 2022.) Centre-forward Brian Bedford signed for Reading at the beginning of 1954 while undergoing his National Service with the RAF in London. He scored seven on his debut for the Royals' 'A' team but was unable to win a regular place either at Elm Park, or in a season with Southampton. He established a reputation as a goalscorer with Bournemouth, featuring in their FA Cup run in 1956–57 when they knocked both Wolverhampton Wanderers and Tottenham Hotspur out of the competition. In each of his six seasons with Queens Park Rangers he finished as top scorer, amassing a total of 180 goals from 283 appearances, before concluding his senior career with spells at Scunthorpe United and Brentford.

Jack Bertolini (Born: Alloa, 21 March 1934. Died: Worthing, 21 June 2021.) Jack Bertolini developed with Sauchie Juveniles and, briefly, Alva Albion Rangers before signing for Stirling Albion in November 1951. He made his first-team debut on the wing for the Annfield club at the age of 17 and subsequently signed for Workington, where he was converted to a wing-half and made over 150 senior appearances. In the summer of 1958 he moved to Brighton & Hove Albion where he became a fixture in the line-up, enjoying a run of 193 consecutive first-team games. He remained at the Goldstone Ground before suffering a knee injury in October 1965 which ended his career.

Louis Bimpson (Born: Rainford, Lancashire, 14 May 1929. Died: 13 November 2021.) Louis Bimpson was a big, powerful centre-forward who signed for Liverpool midway through the 1953–53 season after scoring four goals for Burscough against the Reds' 'A' team in a Liverpool Combination match. He stayed at Anfield for almost seven years, but although he regularly scored when given opportunities, he was never able to establish himself in the line-up. He went on to play for Blackburn Rovers, where he gained an FA Cup runners-up medal in 1960, Bournemouth and Rochdale before leaving senior football. He was a member of the Rochdale team that lost out to Norwich City over two legs in the 1961–62 Football League Cup final.

Mike Bottoms (Born: Fulham, 11 January 1939. Died: August 2021.) Mike Bottoms joined Queens Park Rangers from Harrow Town, then members of the Delphian League, in July 1960, but in 18 months at Loftus Road he mostly featured in the reserve team. He made three first-team appearances, all at inside-left, before moving on to spells with Oxford United and then Cambridge United, both members of the Southern League at the time.

Joe Boyden (Born: Willenhall, Staffordshire, 12 February 1929. Died: 2022.) Left-back Joe Boyden was on Walsall's books as an amateur before becoming a part-time professional during the 1948–49 campaign. He remained at Fellows Park for a further four seasons and although mostly a reserve he made four first-team appearances early in 1952–53. Later he played in non-league football in the West Midlands with Brierley Hill Alliance, Bloxwich Strollers and Dudley Town.

Jackie Bridge (Born: Great Wakering, Essex, 30 May 1932. Died: 17 September 2021.) Jackie Bridge was a wing-half and inside-forward who signed for Southend United from local junior club Great Wakering Rovers in August 1950 and went on to make over 50 first-team appearances for the Blues. He later spent several seasons with Gravesend & Northfleet, helping them win the Southern League title in 1957–58.

George Brown (Born: Station Town, near Wingate, Co. Durham, circa 1944. Died: 12 April 2022.) George Brown was a centre-forward who featured in the Northern League for West Auckland Town, Crook Town, Tow Law Town and Durham City. He was a prolific goalscorer, once netting eight goals in a match for Crook against South Bank in November 1965. Later he was a member of the Tow Law team that enjoyed a successful run in the FA Cup in 1967–68, scoring two goals in their 5–1 victory over Mansfield Town. He won a single cap for England Amateurs, appearing against the Netherlands in May 1963.

Peter Bryan (Born. Ashbourne, Derbyshire, 30 April 1944. Died: Laughlin, Nevada, United States, 23 September 2021.) Full-back Peter Bryan joined Oxford United as a teenager for their final season as a Southern League club but was mostly a squad player during his time with the U's. In the summer of 1966 he signed for League of Ireland club Waterford where he enjoyed considerable success, featuring regularly in the team that won the league title on five occasions and experiencing European Cup football. He later moved to the United States where he coached New York Apollo and Los Angeles Skyhawks.

Alan Buck (Born: Colchester, 25 August 1946. Died: Colchester, 25 November 2021.) Goalkeeper Alan Buck made his debut for Colchester United as an 18-year-old, but although he spent four years as a professional with the U's he only featured regularly during the 1966–67 campaign before eventually moving on to Southern League club Poole Town. His twin brother David also played in the Football League for Colchester.

Joe Buick (Born: Broughty Ferry, Dundee, 1 July 1933. Died: Lincoln, 27 November 2021.) Joe Buick was a wing-half who joined Lincoln City from Dundee Junior club Broughty Athletic in October 1955 and spent seven years on the books at Sincil Bank. Although mostly a reserve, he featured regularly in the first half of the 1957–58 season. Later he played in the Southern League for Cheltenham Town and Weymouth. His father Ronald played for Montrose and East Fife in the 1920s.

Mike Burgess (Born: Montreal, Canada, 17 April 1932. Died: Dorset, 17 June 2021.) Mike Burgess joined Leyton Orient in February 1953 and made his debut at left-half before switching to centre-forward where his height proved to be an asset. He later had a brief spell with Newport County before moving on to Bournemouth where he gained regular first-team football, finishing as the club's leading scorer in 1958–59. He then spent two seasons with Halifax Town prior to a move to Gillingham where he switched to playing at centre-half. He was an ever-present in the 1963–64 campaign when the Gills' ultra-defensive team conceded just 30 goals and won the Fourth Division title on goal average from Carlisle United. He concluded his senior career at Aldershot.

Martin Burleigh (Born: Newcastle upon Tyne, 2 February 1951. Died: Durham, 27 September 2021.) Goalkeeper Martin Burleigh was on amateur forms with Newcastle United before signing professional in December 1968. He stayed at St James' Park almost six years making 15 appearances, mostly as deputy to Willie McFaul. He went on to enjoy a useful career in the lower divisions, playing over 250 games in spells with Darlington (twice), Carlisle United and Hartlepool.

Frank Burrows (Born: Larkhall, Lanarkshire, 30 January 1944. Died: 24 November 2021.) Frank Burrows learnt his football with Raith Rovers in the early 1960s and had played almost 100 games in senior football before moving south to sign for Scunthorpe United in June 1965. A tough, uncompromising central defender, he left the Old Showground for Swindon Town in the summer of 1968 after the Iron were relegated and enjoyed the best years of his playing career with the Wiltshire club. He helped the Robins win the Football League Cup and promotion from Division Three in 1968–69 as well as the Anglo Italian Cup Winners' Cup (1969) and Anglo Italian Cup (1970). He later enjoyed a 20-year career in management with Portsmouth, Cardiff City and Swansea City. He won two promotions with Cardiff (1987–88 and 1998–99) and one with Pompey (1979–80).

Steve Burtenshaw (Born: Portslade, Sussex, 23 November 1935. Died: 17 February 2022.) Steve Burtenshaw was a member of the Sussex team that won the FA County Youth Championship in 1951–52 and signed professional forms for Brighton & Hove Albion at the age of 17. He made his senior debut shortly afterwards, but it was not until the 1956–57 season that he featured regularly in the line-up. A tall wing-half and occasional inside-forward, he featured in the 1957–58 promotion team and went on to make over 250 first-team appearances before retiring as a player in December 1966. He subsequently joined the coaching staff at Arsenal and also coached with Everton and Queens Park Rangers, as well as having a spell as manager of Sheffield Wednesday (January 1974 to October 1975).

Paul Cahill (Born: Liverpool, 29 September 1955. Died: 5 June 2021.) Paul Cahill joined Coventry City as an apprentice on leaving school, progressing to become a professional, but it was not until he signed on loan for Portsmouth midway through the 1974–75 season that he experienced first-team football. He made a permanent move to Fratton Park the following summer and went on to make over 100 senior appearances, winning the club's Player of the Season award in 1975–76. He later had spells with Tranmere Rovers and Stockport County before moving to the United States to play for California Surf.

Bill Calder (Born: Glasgow, 28 September 1934. Died: Ramsbottom, Lancashire, 10 November 2021.) Bill Calder was a tall, powerful winger who joined Leicester City from Port Glasgow Juniors in August 1955 while undergoing National Service. He made three first-team appearances during his time at Filbert Street but fared much better in spells at Bury, where he scored 21 goals as the Shakers won the Division Three title in1960–61, and Oxford United. By the time he arrived at the Manor Ground he had switched to playing at centre-forward and he helped the U's to win the Fourth Division in 1964–65. He concluded his senior career at Rochdale, then helped non-league Macclesfield Town reach the FA Cup third round in 1967–68.

Steve Calvert (Born: Barrow in Furness, 2 April 1952. Died: Walney, Barrow in Furness, 2 March 2022.) Steve Calvert developed in local football, signing on amateur forms for Barrow in August 1970. He featured regularly in midfield in the second half of the 1971–72 campaign, making 22 appearances and scoring four goals. The Bluebirds failed to retain their Football League place at the end of the season, but he continued to play for the club in the Northern Premier League in 1972–73 before leaving.

Bobby Cameron (Born: Greenock, 23 November 1932. Died: Newcastle, New South Wales, Australia, 18 February 2022.) Inside-forward Bobby Cameron represented Scotland Schools in 1946–47 and went on to join Queens Park Rangers from Port Glasgow Rovers in June 1950. He won a regular place in the side at Loftus Road from the 1952–53 season and went on to make 273 first-team appearances scoring 62 goals. Later he had three seasons with Leeds United before helping Gravesend & Northfleet reach the FA Cup fourth round in 1962–63. He concluded his senior career at Southend United before emigrating to Australia where he played for the Adamstown Rosebud club.

Walter Cameron (Born: Alloa, 5 June 1942. Died: 28 October 2021.) Walter Cameron was a member of the Gairdoch United team that won the Lord Weir Cup in 1958–59 and signed for Falkirk soon afterwards. He managed 11 appearances in three seasons at Brockville then moved on to Arbroath. He enjoyed the best years of his career with the Red Lichties, playing over 200 games between 1962 and 1969 and assisting in the 1967–68 promotion team. He concluded his senior career with a brief spell at Alloa Athletic.

Neil Campbell (Born: Middlesbrough, 26 January 1977. Died: Yarm, Teesside, 30 April 2022.) Neil Campbell was a tall, well-built striker who progressed through the ranks with York City to sign professional forms at the age of 18. He was mostly a reserve during his time at Bootham Crescent before gaining further experience with Scarborough, where he made almost 50 first-team appearances. He concluded his senior career with a spell at Southend United before joining then non-league club Doncaster Rovers.

Steve Carty (Born: Dunfermline, 12 January 1934. Died: Canada, 29 December 2021.) A product of Fife Junior club Blairhall Colliery, Steve Carty signed for Crewe Alexandra towards the end of the 1956–57 season. He stayed at Gresty Road until the 1960 close season, but with the exception of his first full season, when he turned out regularly at full-back, he rarely featured in the first team. He then emigrated to North America where he played for a number of clubs including Polish White Eagles (from Toronto) and New York Ukrainians.

Davie Cattanach (Born: 27 June 1946. Died: 4 February 2022.) Davie Cattanach was a wing-half who was capped by Scotland at schoolboy international level. After developing with Woodburn Athletic Juveniles he made his senior debut for Stirling Albion at the age of 16. In August 1963 he signed for Celtic but his nine-year spell at Parkhead was mostly spent in the reserves, with just 19 first-team appearances. In January 1972 he moved on to Falkirk where he featured more regularly before leaving senior football.

Gerry Church (Born: Glasgow, 28 January 1928. Died: Winchester on the Severn, Annapolis, Maryland, United States, 17 July 2021.) Full-back Gerry Church won representative honours for Scottish Universities while studying at Glasgow University and also appeared for the RAMC during his National Service. He played with Queen's Park for several seasons, making nine senior appearances, and also won a single cap for Scotland Amateurs against Northern Ireland in February 1956. He emigrated to North America shortly afterwards to pursue a career in medicine.

Billy Cobb (Born: Newark, 29 September 1940. Died: 27 July 2021.) Billy Cobb was a skilful midfield player who progressed from local football with Ransome & Marles to join Nottingham Forest. He made his first-team debut at Preston North End on Boxing Day 1960, but never really established himself at the City Ground, although he had the distinction of scoring the club's first-ever goal in a European competition when he netted in the 5–1 home defeat by Valencia. He went on to play for Plymouth Argyle, Brentford and Lincoln City, making over 200 senior appearances before switching to non-league football with Boston United.

Jacky Coburn (Born: Methven, Perthshire, 11 May 1938. Died: Perth, 13 November 2021.) A product of Methven Rangers and Crieff Earngrove Juniors, Jacky Coburn was a quick centre forward with an eye for goal. He stepped up to senior football with Forfar Athletic in 1960–61, scoring four on his debut against Brechin City and topping the Forfar scoring charts that season with 34 goals. He then moved on to East Stirlingshire, where his goals helped fire the Fir Park club to promotion to the First Division in 1962–63. He also had spells with St Johnstone, Montrose and Ayr United before leaving the senior game. His brother Willie had a lengthy association with St Johnstone.

Frank Connor (Born: Airdrie, 13 February 1936. Died: Uddingston, Lanarkshire, 3 March 2022.) Frank Connor was a goalkeeper who signed for Celtic from Junior football in March 1960, but in two seasons at Parkhead he made just eight first-team appearances. He went on to play for a number of clubs during the 1960s including Portadown, St Mirren, Third Lanark, Derry City and Albion Rovers. He enjoyed success with Derry City, winning both the Gold Cup and the Irish League in 1964–65. He was later manager of Cowdenbeath, where he made an emergency appearance at the age of 40, Berwick Rangers and Raith Rovers, and on the coaching staff of several clubs, notably Celtic and Heart of Midlothian.

Micky Cook (Born: Belmont, Surrey, 25 January 1950. Died: 13 July 2021.) Micky Cook was an inside-forward who served an apprenticeship with Crystal Palace for whom he made his Football League debut in May 1968. This was his only appearance for Palace, and after joining Brentford on loan at the start of the 1969–70 campaign he signed permanently. He played 24 first-team games for the Bees before being released at the end of the season and then played in non-league football for a number of clubs including Folkestone, Kingstonian and Leatherhead.

Robbie Cooke (Born: Rotherham, 16 February 1957. Died: August 2021.) Robbie Cooke developed in the youth set-up at Mansfield Town but received few opportunities and was released in the summer of 1978. He moved on to Southern League club Grantham Town where he proved to be a lively striker with a good scoring record, earning him a move back to the Football League with Peterborough United. He led the scoring charts for the Posh in his first two seasons but then moved up two divisions to sign for Cambridge United. The U's struggled during his time with them but the goals returned after he joined Brentford, for whom he scored in their 3–1 defeat by Wigan Athletic in the 1984–85 Freight Rover Trophy final. He concluded with a brief spell at Millwall, leaving senior football with a career tally of 155 goals.

Terry Cooper (Born: Brotherton, Yorkshire, 12 July 1944. Died: July 2021.) Terry Cooper was one of the cornerstones of Don Revie's successful Leeds United sides of the 1960s and '70s. He joined the club as an outside-left at the age of 18, but it was only after switching to left-back that he established himself as a regular in the line-up in the 1967–68 campaign. That season he scored the winner in the League Cup final against Arsenal, and in 1968–69 he gained a Football League champions medal. He also won the Inter Cities Fairs Cup on two occasions while at Elland Road (1967–68 and 1970–71). He was capped 20 times for England. A quick and combative defender, he suffered a badly broken leg in April 1972 and after eventually returning to action he went on to play for Middlesbrough, Bristol City, Bristol Rovers and Doncaster Rovers. He subsequently enjoyed a successful career in management, winning the Fourth Division title with Exeter City in 1989–90 and gaining promotions with Bristol City (1983–84) and Birmingham City (1991–92). He also took Bristol City to Wembley, winning the Freight Rover Trophy in 1985–86.

Doug Cowie (Born: Aberdeen, 1 May 1926. Died: 26 November 2021.) Half-back Doug Cowie signed for Dundee in September 1945 and went on to become arguably the greatest player in the club's history. He spent 16 seasons at Dens Park and his total of 446 competitive appearances remains an all-time record for the club. He gained two Scottish League Cup final winners' prizes (1951–52 and 1952–53) and was a Scottish Cup runner-up in 1952. He made his debut for Scotland against England in April 1953 and went on to win a total of 20 full caps, featuring in the squads for both the 1954 and 1958 World Cup finals. He was Scotland's oldest surviving internationalist. After being released by Dundee at the end of the 1959–60 season he joined Morton as player-coach and was later manager of Raith Rovers (May 1963 to May 1964).

Bill Cranston (Born: Kilmarnock, 18 January 1942. Died: Blackpool, 10 January 2022.) Bill Cranston won youth international honours for Scotland before moving south to join Blackpool at the age of 20. He made over 30 appearances in top-flight football for Blackpool over three-and-a-half seasons but was rarely a regular in the line-up. He moved on to Preston North End, where he was again mostly a back-up player, but experienced regular first-team football on signing for Oldham Athletic in July 1970. He made over 100 appearances for the Latics and was a near ever-present in the team that won promotion from the old Fourth Division in 1970–71.

Ronnie Curran (Born: Port Glasgow,4 December 1940. Died: November 2021.) Ronnie Curran was a free-scoring inside-forward for Juvenile club Port Glasgow Rangers before stepping up to the Juniors with Irvine Meadow in May 1959. He went straight into the team, gaining a Scottish Junior Cup winners' medal within a month of signing but later converted to centre-half. A second Junior Cup winners' prize followed four years late, earning him a move to Dumbarton. He spent six years at Boghead Park, making over 200 first-team appearances, before moving on to Greenock Juniors.

George Curtis (Born: Dover, 5 May 1939. Died: 17 July 2021.) George Curtis was one of the greatest figures in the post-war history of Coventry City. Signed as a 16-year-old, he was the club's youngest-ever player at the time of his debut and quickly became an established figure in the centre of defence. He spent 14 years on the books at Highfield Road and had the distinction of captaining the Sky Blues to promotions from Division Four (1958–59), Division Three (1963–64) and Division Two (1966–67). He broke his leg in only his second game in top-flight football but recovered and had made over 500 appearances by the time he left for Aston Villa in December 1969, helping Villa win promotion from Division Three in 1971–72. After retiring as a player returned to assist Coventry in a number of capacities before eventually retiring in May 1994.

Peter Darke (Born: Exeter, 21 December 1953. Died: 2021.) Peter Darke was a defender who joined Plymouth Argyle as an apprentice and went on to make over 100 first-team appearances during a six-year stay at Home Park. He moved on to sign for Torquay United in July 1977 where he had two seasons as a regular in the line-up before switching to non-league Minehead. He also had a spell on loan with Exeter City, making him one of the few players to have played senior football for Devon's three Football League clubs.

Terry Darracott (Born: Liverpool, 6 December 1950. Died: 22 March 2022.) A product of Liverpool schools football, Terry Darracott went on to sign for Everton and made his first-team debut against Arsenal in April 1968, making him the club's youngest-ever player at the time. Although often a reserve during a decade at Goodison, he made over 200 appearances and was a member of the team that lost out to Aston Villa in the 1976–77 Football League Cup final. He later had spells with Tulsa Roughnecks in the NASL and Wrexham, before enjoying a lengthy career in coaching including spells with Manchester City, Blackburn Rovers and Wrexham.

Ian Davidson (Born: Goole, 31 January 1947. Died: December 2021.) Ian Davidson was a midfield player who was a product of the Hull City youth set-up, signing professional forms in February 1965. He made his first-team debut as a substitute in November 1966 but struggled to win a place in the Tigers' line-up and after spending most of the 1968–69 campaign on loan to Scunthorpe United he signed permanently for York City in June 1969. He helped the Minstermen win promotion from the Fourth Division in 1970–71, when he also scored twice to knock Bolton Wanderers out of the FA Cup. After an unproductive spell with Bournemouth he returned north, concluding his senior career with two seasons at Stockport County.

Mark Davies (Born: Swansea, 9 August 1972. Died: Cardiff, 15 May 2022.) Mark Davies was a defender who signed for Swansea City as a trainee before progressing to the senior ranks in July 1991. He made his debut for the Swans in a European Cup Winners' Cup tie against Monaco in the 1991–92 season but made just two more first-team appearances before moving on to sign for Merthyr Tydfil. He sadly collapsed and died while playing for Llanelli Town Veterans in the Wales Veterans Over 45s Cup final.

Ally Dawson (Born: Glasgow, 25 February 1958. Died: July 2021.) Defender Ally Dawson joined Rangers on leaving school and went on to make over 300 first-team appearances during his time at Ibrox. He won the Scottish Cup on two occasions and the League Cup four times before eventually leaving to sign for Blackburn Rovers in August 1987. He went on to play for Sligo Rovers and Airdrieonians before concluding his senior career. He won five full caps for Scotland. Later he was manager of Hamilton Academical (August 1999 to July 2002), leading the team to the Division Three title in 2000–01.

Hans-Jürgen Dörner (Born: Görlitz, East Germany, 25 January 1951. Died: Dresden, Germany, 19 January 2022.) Hans-Jürgen Dörner was a defender who played his club football with Dynamo Dresden, with whom he won five national championships in the 1970s. He won 96 caps for East Germany between 1969 and 1985, the second-most capped player for his country. He was a member of the team that won the gold medal at the 1976 Olympic Games.

Rabbie Dow (Born: Cowdenbeath, 29 September 1937. Died: Kirkcaldy, Fife, 3 January 2022.) Rabbie Dow was a lively forward who developed with Cowdenbeath Royals and Crossgates Primrose before stepping up to the seniors with Cowdenbeath. He spent two seasons at Central Park in the late 1950s, making three first-team appearances before returning to the Juniors to sign for Oakley United.

Dave Dunmore (Born: Whitehaven, 8 February 1934. Died: York, 11 July 2021.) Centre-forward Dave Dunmore developed in local junior football before signing for York City as a teenager. He was just 18 when he made a scoring debut against Crewe Alexandra in May 1952 and after topping the club's scoring charts in 1953–54, he was sold to Tottenham Hotspur for what was then a record fee for the Minstermen. However, his career at White Hart Lane was disrupted by National Service, and he was mostly a reserve during his six-year stay. A productive but brief spell with West Ham United followed and he also did well after moving on to Leyton Orient. He was top scorer for the O's in 1961–62 when they won promotion to the First Division, then returned to York to conclude his senior career. In total he scored 131 goals from 369 Football League appearances.

Phil Dwyer (Born: Cardiff, 28 October 1953. Died: 30 November 2021.) Phil Dwyer won representative honours for Wales at schoolboy international level before joining Cardiff City. He went on to become one of the key figures in the club's post-war history and his total of 471 Football League appearances during a 14-year spell at Ninian Park remains an all-time club record. He made his debut at right-back against Orient in October 1972 and quickly established himself in the line-up, winning two promotions (1975–76 and 1982–83) and the Welsh Cup on three occasions. He won 10 full caps for Wales between April 1978 and October 1979 and also represented his country at youth and U23 levels.

Terry Eades (Born: Banbridge, Co. Down, 5 March 1944. Died: Great Shelford, Cambridgeshire, 4 October 2021.) Central defender Terry Eades moved with his family to Essex at an early age and went on to sign for Chelmsford City, winning a regular place in the line-up in the 1963–64 season. He was a member of the team that won the Southern League title in 1967–68 before switching to Cambridge United and helping the U's to become Southern League champions in the next two seasons. He played in Cambridge's first-ever Football League fixture against Lincoln City in August 1970 and made over 250 senior appearances for the club before returning to Chelmsford in 1977.

Allan Ewing (Born: Largs, Ayrshire, 28 September 1968. Died: 25 August 2021.) Allan Ewing was a midfield player who progressed from Beith Juniors to Stranraer in December 1988. He made 81 first-team appearances for Stranraer but was then side-lined for a lengthy period by a knee injury. Once he had recovered, he moved to the Irish League, signing for Coleraine before concluding his senior career with two seasons at Linfield.

Craig Farrell (Born: Middlesbrough, 5 December 1982. Died: May 2022.) Craig Farrell was an enthusiastic striker who came up through the youth ranks with Leeds United and won representative honours for England U16s. In October 2002 he signed for Carlisle United and after netting on his senior debut against Torquay United he went on to finish the campaign as the club's leading scorer with 12 goals. He was joint-top scorer the following season too, but the Cumbrians lost their place in the Football League. He remained at Brunton Park during their season in the Conference, then moved on to Exeter City, then also a non-league club.

Syd Farrimond (Born: Hindley, Wigan, 17 July 1940. Died: 8 May 2022.) Defender Syd Farrimond signed for Bolton Wanderers in January 1958 and made his first-team debut at Preston North End in October of the same year. He went on to establish himself as a first-team regular in the second half of the 1960–61 campaign and made over 400 appearances during his time with the Trotters. After a very brief trial period with Shrewsbury Town he signed for Tranmere Rovers in February 1971 and was a near ever-present during his time at Prenton Park, adding a further 153 appearances. He subsequently turned to coaching with a number of clubs including Halifax Town, Leeds United and Sunderland.

Bert Ferguson (Born: circa 1954. Died: September 2021.) Bert Ferguson was a winger who joined Ayr United from Maybole Juniors in November 1972 and although not always a regular first-teamer did enough to persuade his colleague Alex Ferguson to make him his first signing for St Mirren two years later. He later turned out for Stranraer, bringing his career total of senior appearances to 143, with 30 goals. On leaving Stair Park he returned to the Juniors with Auchinleck Talbot and in April 1984 he was capped for Scotland Juniors against Wales.

Steve Finney (Born: Hexham, Northumberland, 31 October 1973. Died: 2 February 2022.) Striker Steve Finney joined Preston North End as a trainee on leaving school and made a handful of first-team appearances before moving on to Manchester City in February 1993. He continued his career in the Central League team at Maine Road before signing for Swindon Town in the summer of 1995. His career with the Robins got off to a great start when he netted the winner at Hull City on his debut, and he scored regularly until dropping back to the bench in the New Year. In March he suffered a broken leg, and he was never quite the same player afterwards. He went on to play in senior football with Carlisle United, Leyton Orient and Chester City.

Bernard Fisher (Born: York, 23 February 1934. Died: York, 7 April 2022.) Goalkeeper Bernard Fisher was a product of local football in the York district before joining Hull City in August 1955. He made his senior debut for the Tigers two months later but in an eight-year spell at Boothferry Park he was only a regular in the line-up in 1960–61 and 1961–62. Later he spent two seasons with Bradford City and made 65 first-team appearances before emigrating to Australia where he played for the Auburn club of Sydney.

Jack Fisher (Born: Bermondsey, London, 19 June 1925. Died: January 2022.) Jack Fisher was a tough-tackling full-back who joined Millwall in August 1946, but he was mostly a reserve at The Den, making just three appearances. He fared better during a spell with Bournemouth, for whom he played in over 50 first-team games over four seasons before moving on to Kent League club Ramsgate Athletic. His twin brother George was on the books of Millwall with him, while his son-in-law David Webb and grandson Danny Webb both played the game professionally.

Christy Fitzgerald (Died: December 2021.) Christy Fitzgerald was a versatile forward with St Patrick's Athletic during the 1950s. He was a member of two League of Ireland title-winning sides (1954–55 and 1955–56) and was capped for the Republic of Ireland Amateurs against Scotland in May 1954.

Colin Flatt (Born: Blythburgh, Suffolk, 30 January 1940. Died: 7 September 2021.) Colin Flatt was a big, powerful centre-forward who joined Leyton Orient in the summer of 1965 after scoring regularly in the Southern League with Wisbech Town. The O's struggled badly and were relegated in 1965–66 although he finished the campaign as joint-top scorer with eight goals. After a further season in senior football with Southend United, he returned to the Southern League, turning out for a number of clubs including Wisbech, Romford and Barnet (with whom he was an FA Trophy runner-up in 1972).

Ron Flowers, MBE (Born: Edlington, South Yorkshire, 28 July 1934. Died: 12 November 2021.) Ron Flowers was a half-back who won 49 caps for England and was a member of both the 1962 and 1966 World Cup finals squads although he did not play in the 1966 tournament. He also made two appearances for England U23s and played 13 times for the Football League representative team. Ron signed for Wolves in 1952 from their nursery club Wath Wanderers and in a 15-year career at Molineux he made 515 first-team appearances during a period when the club won the Football League championship on three occasions and the FA Cup in 1959–60. After leaving Molineux in 1967 he was player-manager of Northampton Town before managing in non-league football. He was awarded the MBE in 2021.

Alan Fox (Born: Holywell, Flintshire, 10 July 1936. Died: 16 September 2021.) Centre-half Alan Fox was a product of local football who went on to sign for Wrexham, making his senior debut at the age of 17 in April 1954. He spent a decade at the Racecourse Ground, making 385 first-team appearances and was a near ever-present in the team that won promotion from the Fourth Division in 1961–62. Later he had spells with Hartlepools United and Bradford City before becoming player-coach of Dundalk. He won representative honours for the League of Ireland team and assisted Dundalk to the league title in 1966–67, before going on to play for Limerick and Sligo Rovers.

Graham Fyfe (Born: Motherwell, 18 August 1951. Died April 2022.) Graham Fyfe was a lively forward who joined Rangers from school and spent seven seasons on the books at Ibrox. He broke into the first team towards the end of the 1969–70 campaign but was mostly a squad player during his time with the club although he made just short of 100 appearances. After a disappointing season with Hibernian he concluded his career at Dumbarton before moving to the United States to play indoor soccer.

Jimmy Gabriel (Born: Dundee, 16 October 1940. Died: Phoenix, Arizona, United States, 10 July 2021.) Jimmy Gabriel was a combative wing-half who was capped by Scotland Schools before signing for Dundee. He made his senior debut at the age of 17 and was still a teenager when he signed for Everton in March 1960. He spent seven years at Goodison, where he was a near ever-present in the team that won the Football League title in 1962–63 and gained an FA Cup winners' medal in 1966. He subsequently enjoyed a further five seasons in top-flight football with Southampton before winding down his career with spells at Bournemouth and Brentford. He then moved to the United States where he was player-coach of NASL club Seattle Sounders. He won two full caps for Scotland.

Charlie Gallagher (Born: Glasgow, 3 November 1940. Died: 11 July 2021.) Charlie Gallagher was a skilful inside-forward with a powerful shot who made his first-team debut for Celtic in a League Cup tie against Raith Rovers in August 1959. Although never a first-team regular during over a decade at Parkhead, he still made more than 150 first-team appearances, winning the Scottish Cup in 1964–65 and the League Cup the following season. He later joined Dumbarton, helping them win the Division Two title in 1971–72. He won two full caps for the Republic of Ireland.

Andy Geddes (Born: Paisley, 27 October 1959. Died: Great Glen, Leicestershire, 16 March 2022.) Midfielder Andy Geddes was one of several young Scots signed by Jock Wallace when he was manager of Leicester City, but he was unable to break into the first team at Filbert Street and in November 1980 was transferred to Dundee. He played for the Dens Park club in their Scottish League Cup final defeat the following month and made a useful contribution to their success in winning promotion to the top flight later that season. After being affected by injuries he moved to South Africa where he played for Wits University and Kaizer Chiefs.

Andy Gemmell (Born: Greenock, 27 July 1945. Died: Spain, 27 May 2021.) Andy Gemmell was a winger who was on the books of Morton in the mid-1960s without breaking into the first team. He later made three Football League appearances during a brief association with Bradford City at the beginning of 1967, this being the extent of his senior career. He later became a successful businessman and at various times held a place on the board of directors of Dumbarton, Morton and Livingstone.

John Gillen (Born: Glasgow, 24 September 1961. Died 7 October 2021.) John Gillen was a left-sided player who joined Falkirk from Bargeddie Boys' Club in October 1980 and made 23 first-team appearances over the next two seasons. He went on to enjoy a successful seven-year spell with Stenhousemuir for whom he played over 200 senior games, mostly featuring as a left-sided defender. He later played in the Juniors for Port Glasgow.

Jack Gilmour (Born: Dundee circa 1934. Died: 2021.) Jack Gilmour was an outside-left who was briefly attached to Dundee Osborne before moving up to senior football with Brechin City in August 1955. He enjoyed a useful season at Glebe Park, scoring five goals from 21 appearances before leaving the club. He was the son of Jock Gilmour who had played for Dundee and Scotland before the war.

Bill Gourlay (Born: Stoneyburn, West Lothian, 1932. Died: 21 February 2022.) Goalkeeper Bill Gourlay was 19 years old when he made his senior debut for Cowdenbeath against Alloa Athletic and after just 35 appearances for the Fife club he was sold to Manchester City in February 1953. He spent 18 months developing in the Central League team at Maine Road then signed for Cheltenham Town. He spent eight years at Whaddon Road, playing close to 400 games and featuring in the team that defeated Gravesend & Northfleet to win the Southern League Cup final in 1957–58.

Jürgen Grabowski (Born: Wiesbaden, Germany, 7 July 1944. Died: Wiesbaden, Germany, 10 March 2022.) Jürgen Grabowski was an attacking midfield player who made over 400 appearances for Eintracht Frankfurt between 1965 and 1980. He won 44 caps for West Germany between 1966 and 1974 for whom he was part of the squad that won the European Championships in 1972 and a member of the team that defeated the Netherlands to win the World Cup final two years later.

Bill Grant (Born: Spittalfield, Perthshire, 7 October 1933. Died: Hamilton, Ontario, Canada, 29 July 2021.) Bill Grant was a tall, lanky wing-half with a powerful long-range shot. He signed for Brechin City in the summer of 1955 while on National Service at RAF Edzell and featured in 16 first-team games that season. In August 1956 he moved south to sign for Gillingham, but he was mostly a reserve during his stay, making a single first-team appearance in a Division Three South game at Exeter in October 1956.

Bob Gray (Born: Newcastle upon Tyne, 14 December 1923. Died: 8 April 2022.) Goalkeeper Bob Gray made a single wartime appearance for Newcastle United before signing for Gateshead where he made a further 50 appearances in the emergency competitions. He made his Football League debut for the Redheugh Park club in September 1947, and from March 1949 to October 1958 he was the club's first-choice keeper. A highlight came in the 1952–53 season when he was a member of the team that reached the FA Cup quarter-finals. He played a total of 460 peacetime games for Gateshead before joining non-league club North Shields.

Jimmy Greaves, MBE (Born: East Ham, 20 February 1940. Died: 19 September 2021.) Jimmy Greaves was arguably the greatest goalscorer in the post-war English game, scoring a record 357 goals in top-flight football during a career that spanned the period from 1957 to 1971. He was leading scorer in Division One on a record six occasions. By the age of 20 he had scored 100 Football League goals and he remains the youngest player to have done so. Jimmy scored 44 in 57 appearances for England including six hat-tricks which is also a record. He played for England in both the 1962 and 1966 World Cup tournaments and in 1966 appeared in the group games but lost his place through injury and missed out on the final. He also played for England U23s and the Football League representative team. Jimmy began his career with Chelsea, making his debut at the age of 17. During his time at Stamford Bridge he scored 132 goals in 169 games, setting a club record of 41 League goals in 1960–61. He briefly moved to play for AC Milan but returned to England in December 1961 when he signed for Tottenham Hotspur. With Spurs he won the European Cup Winners' Cup and two FA Cup winners medals. He set a club record when he scored 37 goals in the 1962–63 season and in total netted 266 times for Spurs – another record. Jimmy finished his career at West Ham United, retiring in 1971 at the age of 31. He briefly played in non-league football and later found fame as a television pundit. He was awarded the MBE in 2021.

Peter Greenwood (Born: Todmorden, Yorkshire, 11 September 1924. Died: Kendal, 30 November 2021.) Peter Greenwood was a bustling centre-forward who signed for Burnley after being demobilised from the Royal Navy at the end of the Second World War. Although he was unable to break into the first team at Turf Moor, he later spent four seasons with Chester where he made 67 League and Cup appearances before moving on to Witton Albion. He was perhaps better known as a cricketer who played 75 games for Lancashire between 1948 and 1952 and was a member of the team that shared the County Championship title in 1950.

Peter Gunby, OBE (Born: Leeds, 20 November 1934. Died: Leeds, 26 March 2022.) Peter Gunby was a wing-half who was with Leeds United as a youngster before signing for Bradford City in July 1956. As a result of an injury he made just three Football League appearances for the Bantams and left the club a year later. Peter then played for Harrogate Town and went on to become a coach at Huddersfield Town and then back at Leeds where he was a key figure in the development of young players. He twice had spells as caretaker manager of the Whites and was awarded the OBE in 2007 for services to football.

Ken Gunthorpe (Born: Sheffield, 14 November 1938. Died: Rotherham, 15 April 2022.) Ken Gunthorpe was an apprentice turner in an engineering works when he made his senior debut for Rotherham United away to Liverpool in December 1958. The Millers were beaten 4–0 and although he made one further senior appearance later that season he quickly departed from senior football.

Freddy Hall (Born: St George's, Bermuda, 3 March 1985. Died: St George's, Bermuda, 24 April 2022.) Goalkeeper Freddy Hall developed in college soccer in the United States, joining Northampton Town from St George's Colts of the Bermuda Premier Division for the 2011–12 campaign. He made three first-team appearances for the Cobblers, all in the early part of 2012, and later played for a number of clubs including Burton Albion (where he did not make the first team), Chester and Limerick in the League of Ireland. He won 10 full caps for Bermuda.

Hughie Hamilton (Born: Newton Mearns, Renfrewshire, 16 June 1942. Died: May 2022.) Centre-forward Hughie Hamilton stepped up to the seniors with Falkirk in March 1962 but made little progress in his career at Brockville and just over a year later he moved south to sign for Hartlepools United. He mostly featured on the wing for the Fourth Division club and scored seven goals in 41 appearances during his stay. After a spell in the Northern Premier League with Scarborough he joined League of Ireland club Limerick, helping create history when his two late goals won the FAI Cup final replay against Drogheda, the first occasion that the club had won the trophy.

Paul Hampshire (Born: 20 September 1981. Died: Dunbar, East Lothian, 13 March 2022.) Paul Hampshire was a midfield player who joined Raith Rovers from Hutchison Vale in July 1998 and went on to make his debut in senior football two years later. He featured in the club's 2002–03 success in winning the Second Division title and later had spells with Berwick Rangers and East Fife before switching to non-league football with Dunbar United and Newquay, when work commitments took him to Cornwall.

John Harding (Born: Liverpool, circa 1941. Died: 2021.) Defender John Harding won representative honours for British Universities, the FA Amateur XI, the Army, and the Combined Services in a career that spanned the late 1950s and '60s. He made his debut for England Amateurs against Scotland in March 1959 and won a total of four caps for his country. He played for a number of clubs including Oxford University, Pegasus, Kettering Town, Dulwich Hamlet and Corinthian Casuals. After leaving the Army in 1977 he became a football adviser to the Saudi Arabian government.

George Harris (Born: Lambeth, London, 10 June 1940. Died: 9 February 2022.) George Harris was a goalscoring winger who started his career with Newport County. Although a regular in the side, he only stayed a season at Somerton Park before moving on to Watford. In four seasons at Vicarage Road and a further three with Reading he enhanced his reputation for scoring goals and took his career tally beyond the 100-mark. He joined Cambridge United during their final season as a Southern League club, netting a hat-trick on his debut and went on to play for the U's in their first-ever Football League match in August 1970. He finished with a career record of 145 senior goals from 405 appearances.

Jimmy Harris (Born: Birkenhead, 18 August 1933. Died: 17 April 2022.) Jimmy Harris was a centre-forward who signed for Everton in September 1951, but it was only after he returned from spell of National Service that he switched to full-time status. He stepped into the first team early in the 1955–56 campaign and quickly established himself, leading the club's scoring charts in this first season. The best years of his career were spent at Goodison, where he was a regular for six seasons and scored 65 Football League goals. He also won representative honours for England U23s and the Football League XI. He was sold to Birmingham City in December 1960 but after two seasons of regular football he lost his place before winding down his career at Oldham Athletic and, briefly, Tranmere Rovers.

Peter Heathcote (Born: Leicester, 13 November 1932. Died: 17 April 2022.) Peter Heathcote was goalkeeper for the Leicester Boys team that won the English Schools Trophy in 1945–46 and were beaten finalists the following season. He featured for Leicester City 'A' before signing for Southend United as a 17-year-old. He went on to make two first-team appearances for the Blues, following this with a lengthy association with Southern League club Gravesend & Northfleet, where he was an ever-present when they won the league title in 1957–58.

Andy Higgins (Born: Bolsover, Derbyshire, 12 February 1960. Died: Australia, July 2021.) Andy Higgins was a tall central defender who was a trainee with Chesterfield progressing to a professional contract shortly before his 18th birthday. He made just one first-team appearance for the Spireites, then had spells with Port Vale and Hartlepool where he was again mainly a reserve. He fared better with Rochdale (37 appearances) and Chester before emigrating to South Africa where he played for Hellenic. Later he settled in Australia where he turned out for Heidelburg United.

Freddie Hill (Born: Sheffield, 17 January 1940. Died: Bolton, 1 October 2021.) Freddie Hill was a product of Sheffield schools football and went on to make his Football League debut for Bolton Wanderers at the age of 18. He spent over a decade on the books at Burnden Park, making over 400 first-team appearances before moving on to Halifax Town and then Manchester City. His senior career ended with a successful spell at Peterborough United, where he displayed some cultured midfield play and was an ever-present in the team that won the Fourth Division title in 1973–74. He won two full caps for England and a further 10 for the U23s.

Johnny Hills (Born: Northfleet, Kent, 24 February 1934. Died: Brussels, Belgium, 26 November 2021.) Johnny Hills was a full-back who joined the groundstaff at Tottenham Hotspur as a youngster before being sent to develop with Gravesend & Northfleet. A regular in the Spurs reserve and junior teams, he made a total of 23 first-team appearances, memorably featuring in the club's record 13–2 FA Cup victory over Crewe Alexandra in February 1960. In the summer of 1958 he toured West Africa with an FA representative side. He later had brief spells with Bristol Rovers and Margate before injury ended his career.

Paul Hinshelwood (Born: Bristol, 14 August 1956. Died: January 2022.) Paul Hinshelwood was an apprentice with Crystal Palace on leaving school, signing a professional contract in August 1973. He made his first-team debut in an Anglo Italian Cup tie at the age of 16, but it was not until the 1976–77 promotion season that he won a regular place in the line-up. He remained a first choice for the next six seasons, gaining a second promotion in 1978–79 when the Second Division title was won. He was the club's Player of the Season in both 1979–80 and 1980–81 and made over 300 appearances during his time at Selhurst Park before moving on to Oxford United in August 1983. He later concluded his playing career with spells at Millwall and Colchester United. He was from a footballing family and his father (Wally), brother (Martin) and son (Adam) all played in the Football League.

Ivan Hollett (Born: Pinxton, Derbyshire, 22 April 1940. Died: 17 April 2022.) Ivan Hollett began his senior career with Mansfield Town, making his debut at the age of 18. He finished as the Stags' joint-top scorer in 1959–60 with 15 goals from 21 games but was mostly a back-up player during his time at Field Mill. In December 1964 he was transferred to Chesterfield where he flourished at centre-forward, scoring 74 goals in a four-year spell at Saltergate. He went on to play for Crewe Alexandra, Cambridge United and Hereford United, featuring for the Bulls in their first-ever Football League game at Colchester United in August 1972. He later turned to coaching and enjoyed a lengthy spell back at Mansfield working in a number of roles.

Stuart Housley (Born: Doncaster, 15 September 1948. Died: August 2021.) Stuart Housley was a slightly built winger who came up through the ranks with Grimsby Town and was still a teenager when he made his debut for the Mariners in February 1967. Although never a regular first choice he made 38 appearances in three seasons at Blundell Park. He went on to join Southern League club Yeovil Town with whom he made close on 400 appearances in two spells at the club before later being a member of the backroom staff for many years.

Terry Howard (Born: 13 September 1937. Died: September 2021.) Terry Howard was a talented winger who excelled in amateur football in the 1960s, representing Great Britain at the 1960 Olympic Games tournament and winning six England Amateur international caps. He appeared in four FA Amateur Cup finals, scoring the winner for Hendon when they defeated Kingstonian at Wembley in 1960, while in 1967 he played in the Wembley tie but was on the bench when Enfield won the replay. He also featured on the losing side for Enfield (1964) and Sutton United (1969).

Paul Hunt (Born: Hereford, 7 March 1959. Died: 17 April 2022.) Paul Hunt was a versatile player who became an apprentice with Coventry City on leaving school but was released and went on to sign for Hereford United. He made his first-team debut for the Bulls at Stockport on Boxing Day 1978 but although he made over 50 appearances over the next three seasons, he never really established himself in the side. In the summer of 1982 he moved on to join then Football Conference club Trowbridge Town.

Roger Hunt, MBE (Born: Glazebury, Lancashire, 20 July 1938. Died: 27 September 2021.) Roger Hunt was a key member of England's 1966 World Cup-winning team playing in all six games of the tournament and scoring three times in the group games. He was first capped in 1962 and was included in the national team's squad for the World Cup finals later that year but did not make an appearance. In total he was capped 34 times, scoring 18 goals for his country, and also appeared five times for the Football League representative team. Roger's professional career began when he signed for Liverpool in May 1959, and he immediately established himself as a prolific scorer netting 21 League goals in his first season. He was Liverpool's leading scorer in eight consecutive seasons between 1962 and 1969 and in all competitions scored 285 goals in 492 appearances – a total beaten only by Ian Rush. Roger was a member of the Reds' team that won two Football League titles and the FA Cup as well as the Division Two title in the first half of the 1960s. He moved to Bolton Wanderers in December 1969 and remained at Burnden Park until retiring in 1972. He was awarded the MBE in 2000.

Victor Hunter (Born: Sion Mills, Co. Tyrone, 14 February 1937. Died: 31 July 2021.) Goalkeeper Victor Hunter spent most of his playing career with Irish League club Coleraine, making 472 appearances for them and winning the Irish Cup in 1965. He won two full caps for Northern Ireland and played four times for the Irish League representative side, also being capped at youth, Amateur and B international levels.

Alex Ingram (Born: Edinburgh, 2 January 1945. Died: February 2022.) Alex Ingram was a brave centre-forward who began his career with Queen's Park where he became a regular goalscorer and won six caps for Scotland Amateurs. In June 1966 he signed professional terms with Ayr United where he continued to find the net regularly and a total of 66 goals over three-and-a-half seasons helped take the club into the First Division. He won representative honours for the Scottish League XI in November 1969 and soon afterwards he was sold to Nottingham Forest for a substantial fee. He struggled to score in a 12-month spell at the City Ground but after returning to Ayr he rediscovered his form and captained the team that reached the semi-final of the Scottish Cup in 1972–73. His final tally of 117 League and Cup goals makes him the fourth-highest scorer in the history of Ayr United.

Barry Jackson (Born: Askrigg, Yorkshire, 2 February 1938. Died: 7 November 2021.) Barry Jackson developed in local football in York before signing for York City in the summer of 1956. After two seasons in the reserves at Bootham Crescent he stepped up to the first team at the start of the 1958–59 season and went on to remain a first choice in the side for the next decade. He twice won promotion with the Minstermen from Division Four (1958–59 and 1964–65) and established an all-time club record of 539 League and Cup appearances before departing at the end of the 1969–70 season.

Wim Jansen (Born: Rotterdam, Netherlands, 28 October 1946. Died: Kendrk-Ido-Ambacht, Netherlands, 25 January 2022.) Wim Jansen enjoyed a successful playing career with Feyenoord, where he was a member of the team that defeated Celtic in the 1970 European Cup final and then overcame Tottenham Hotspur over two legs to win the UEFA Cup in 1973–74. He also won 65 caps for his country, appearing in the teams that finished runners-up in the World Cup in both 1974 and 1978. He later developed a career in coaching and was head coach of Celtic from July 1997 to May 1998, winning both the Scottish League title and the League Cup in his only season at Parkhead.

Gerry Jones (Born: Newcastle under Lyme, Staffordshire, 30 December 1945. Died: 17 August 2021.) Gerry Jones was an outside-left who joined Stoke City as an apprentice on leaving school and went on to make seven first-team appearances for the Potters before being released at the end of the 1966–67 season. He subsequently enjoyed a lengthy career with Stafford Rangers, where he was a member of the team that defeated Barnet at Wembley to win the FA Trophy final in 1972.

Glyn Jones (Born: Rotherham, 8 April 1936. Died: January 2022.) Glyn Jones was a member of the Sheffield & Hallamshire team that won the FA County Youth Cup in 1952–53 and won England Youth international honours but was initially unable to break into the first team at Rotherham United. He spent four seasons with neighbours Sheffield United where he was mostly a reserve then returned to Millmoor in December 1957, enjoying a short run in the line-up at inside-left. He wound down his senior career at Mansfield where he was a regular in the line-up, making 51 first-team appearances before moving into non-league football.

Rod Jones (Born: Rhiwderin, Monmouthshire, 14 June 1946. Died: May 2022.) Rod Jones was a lively, hard-working striker who developed in local football before joining Newport County from Lovell's Athletic in October 1969. He was a first-team regular at Somerton Park for nine seasons, switching to a defensive role towards the end of his career. He led the club's scoring charts in 1974–75 and finished with a career tally of 71 goals from 306 appearances.

Dennis Keating (Born: Cork, Republic of Ireland, 18 October 1940. Died: July 2021.) Dennis Keating was playing in local football for Saltney Juniors when he signed for Chester in June 1962. He only stayed briefly at Sealand Road, making two first-team appearances at outside-left before moving on to Wellington Town in November of the same year. He later entered the Catholic Church and became a parish priest in Chester.

Paul Kelly (Born: Glasgow, 20 February 1964. Died: Glasgow, 4 November 2021.) Paul Kelly was a midfield player who joined Alloa Athletic from Milngavie Wanderers in the summer of 1984. He was a regular in the team throughout the 1984–85 campaign when they won promotion from the Second Division and went on to have brief spells with Stranraer, Stenhousemuir and East Stirlingshire before switching to the Juniors. He later managed a number of Junior clubs including Ashfield, Petershill and St Rochs, where he was in post at the time of his death.

Johnny Kemp (Born: Clydebank, Dunbartonshire, 11 April 1934. Died: Barrow, 6 March 2022.) A product of Junior club Duntocher Hibs, Johnny Kemp showed great promise on the left wing for Clyde prompting Leeds United to sign him up in December 1957. He had an unfortunate time at Elland Road, with injuries and competition for places restricting him to a single first-team appearance. The best years of his career were spent with Barrow, where he had four years as a first-team regular, scoring 17 goals in the 1961–62 season. He concluded his career with a spell at Crewe Alexandra.

Ray Kennedy (Born: Seaton Delaval, Northumberland, 28 July 1951. Died: 30 November 2021.) Ray Kennedy joined Arsenal as a striker in November 1968 and initially found it difficult to break into the side at Highbury. He came on as a substitute in the first leg of the Inter Cities Fairs Cup final against Anderlecht in April 1970, scoring a vital late goal, and the following season he took advantage of an injury to Charlie George to become a regular as the Gunners went on to win a League and Cup double. In the summer of 1984 he was transferred to Liverpool where he switched to playing in midfield and reignited his career. In eight seasons at Anfield he enjoyed great success, winning the European Cup on three occasions, the Football League five times, the League Cup and the UEFA Cup once each as well as four FA Charity Shields. He made almost 400 appearances for the Reds before winding down his career with spells at Swansea City and Hartlepool United. He won 17 caps for England between 1976 and 1980, scoring on his debut against Wales. In November 1984 he was diagnosed with Parkinson's Disease and was active in promoting awareness of the condition for many years.

Jim Kerray Born: Stirling, 2 December 1935. Died: Larbert, Stirlingshire, 6 November 2021.) Jim Kerray was an inside-forward who made over 400 senior appearances in a career that spanned the period 1956 to 1968. He made his first-team debut for Raith Rovers in August 1957 and scored regularly in the next two-and-a-half seasons, persuading Jock Stein to take him to Dunfermline. However, his stay was very brief and within a few months he was on his way south to Huddersfield Town. He spent three years in English football, also having a spell at Newcastle United before returning north to rejoin Dunfermline. He continued his career with spells at St Johnstone, Stirling Albion and Falkirk before eventually leaving full-time football at the end of 1968.

Pat Kerrins (Born: Fulham, 13 September 1936. Died: 2021.) Outside-left Pat Kerrins starred in West London schoolboy football and went on to join the groundstaff at Queens Park Rangers. He quickly progressed to a professional contract and was only 17 when he made his first-team debut at Exeter in February 1954. Although his career was initially disrupted by

National Service, he became a regular for the R's in the late 1950s, making over 150 first-team appearances. After brief spells with Crystal Palace and Southend United he turned to non-league football, signing for Romford.

George Kinnell (Born: Cowdenbeath, 22 December 1937. Died: 16 October 2021.) George Kinnell was a ball playing centre-half and occasional centre-forward who made over 350 senior appearances in a career that spanned the period from 1959 to 1969. He started at Aberdeen where he established himself in the line-up and was team captain when he was sold to Stoke City midway through the 1963–64 season. He went on to appear for the Potters in their Football League Cup final defeat by Leicester City the following April. Later he had a brief spell with Oldham Athletic before returning to the First Division for a three-year stay at Sunderland. He concluded his senior career at Middlesbrough before emigrating to Australia where he played for the Juventus club of Melbourne.

Joe Laidlaw (Born: Whickham, Gateshead, 12 July 1950. Died: 18 November 2021.) Joe Laidlaw made his debut for Middlesbrough as a centre forward at the age of 17 but was later converted by the club to a midfield role. He enjoyed success with Carlisle United where he was an ever-present in the team that won promotion from the Second Division in 1973–74 and then finished as top scorer in 1974–75, the club's only season in top-flight football. Later he captained Portsmouth to promotion from the Fourth Division in 1979–80. His Football League career spanned the period from 1967 to 1983 and he made over 500 League appearances for six clubs, including more than 100 for Middlesbrough, Carlisle and Doncaster Rovers.

Roy Lambert (Born: Hoyland, Yorkshire, 16 July 1933. Died: 5 February 2022.) Roy Lambert worked in a local colliery on leaving school, later signing for Rotherham United from Thorncliffe Welfare in July 1954. It was not until January 1957 that he made his debut for the Millers, but he soon went on to establish himself as a regular in the line-up at right-half. He featured in both legs of the inaugural Football League Cup final of 1960–61 when Rotherham lost out to Aston Villa and went on to make almost 350 first-team appearances for the Millers before concluding his career with a brief spell at Barnsley.

Billy Lamont (Born: Larkhall, Lanarkshire, 17 May 1936. Died: October 2021.) Goalkeeper Billy Lamont spent over a decade as a regular in Scottish League football with Albion Rovers and Hamilton Academical, with the exception of a season spent at Cheltenham Town in 1962–63. He made over 350 senior appearances and, as an occasional outfield player, scored two goals for Albion. After retiring as a player he turned to management with some success, winning promotion for East Stirlingshire (from the Second Division in 1979–80), Falkirk (from the First Division in 1985–86) and Dumbarton (from the Second Division in 1991–92).

Lex Law (Born: Kirkconnel, Dumfriesshire, 23 October 1946. Died: Whitehaven, 31 March 2022.) Lex Law was an inside-forward who was capped by Scotland at schoolboy and youth international levels before enjoying a lengthy career in the seniors with Queen of the South. He scored on his senior debut in a League Cup tie against East Fife in August 1964 and went on to net 53 goals for Queens from 333 appearances before retiring as a player. He was from a footballing family and both his father, Jackie senior, and brother, Jackie junior played for Queens.

Kirkie Lawson (Born: Glasgow, 4 March 1947. Died: 6 April 2022.) Kirkie Lawson was a lively striker who was a member of the Blantyre Victoria team that won the Scottish Junior Cup in 1970. He went on to sign for Motherwell and scored 28 goals in 99 appearances for the club, but when he found he was no longer a first choice he moved on to sign for Falkirk in October 1973. He led the scoring charts in his first season at Brockville but eventually moved on again to conclude his senior career with Hamilton Academical in 1976–77.

Gordon Lee (Born: Hednesford, Staffordshire, 13 July 1934. Died: Lytham St Annes, Lancashire, 7 March 2022.) Gordon Lee signed for Aston Villa in October 1955, soon after completing his National Service with the RAF. Initially a wing-half, he made his Football League debut in September 1958, but although he later switched to full-back it was not until the 1961–62 season that he claimed a regular place in the side. He appeared in two Football League Cup finals for Villa, as a winner in 1960–61 and a runner-up in 1963. He left the club in the summer of 1966 to become player-coach of Shrewsbury Town and two years later was appointed as manager of Port Vale. He did well in management in the lower divisions, winning promotions with Vale (1969–70) and Blackburn Rovers (1974–75) before stepping up to the First Division at Newcastle United. He later spent four years as manager of Everton, coming close to winning the League Cup in 1976–77 when they were defeated by his former club Villa in the final in a second replay, and also had a spell in charge of Preston North End.

Tommy Leishman (Born: Stenhousemuir, 3 September 1937. Died: Bannockburn, Stirlingshire, 21 July 2021.) Tommy Leishman was a tough-tackling wing-half who developed with Cowie Juveniles and Camelon Juniors before moving up to the seniors with St Mirren. He gained a Scottish Cup winners' medal with the Paisley club in 1958–59 and within a matter of months was his way south, signing for Liverpool. He quickly established himself for the Reds and was a near ever-present in the team that won the Second Division title in 1961–62. Early in 1963 he was on his way to Hibernian where he captained the team that won the Summer Cup the following year. He then enjoyed two seasons as player-manager of Linfield, leading them to a double of the Irish League title and the Gold Cup in 1965–66 and a place in the quarter-finals of the European Cup the following season. He concluded his career with a spell at Stranraer.

Malcolm Lindsay (Born: Ashington, Northumberland, 26 September 1940. Died: 12 March 2022.) Malcolm Lindsay was a striker who was well-known in non-league football in the 1960s and '70s, notably for his goal scoring exploits with King's Lynn Town. Early in his career he made a handful of senior appearances for Berwick Rangers at the start of the 1962–63 season, while he later contributed to Cambridge United's success in winning the Southern League in 1969–70. He went on to feature in the U's first-ever Football League game and scored his only senior goal for the club at Crewe Alexandra in September 1970.

Paul Linger (Born: Stepney, London, 20 December 1974. Died: 1 October 2021.) Paul Linger was a skilful midfield player who was a trainee for Charlton Athletic before progressing to a professional contract. He was mostly on the fringes of the first team during his time with the Addicks but on a rare start at Port Vale in April 1996 he suffered a broken leg. He was released 12 months later and after a brief association with Leyton Orient, featured regularly for Brighton & Hove Albion in the second half of the 1997–98 campaign before moving on to Welling United.

Andy Lochhead (Born: Lenzie, Dunbartonshire, 9 March 1941. Died: Burnley, 18 March 2022.) Andy Lochhead was a big, powerful centre forward who joined Burnley from Renfrew Juniors in December 1958. It was not until August 1962 that he won a regular place in the Clarets' line-up, bursting on the scene by scoring in each of the first six games that season. Thereafter he found the net regularly throughout his time at Turf Moor. He twice scored five goals in a match (against Chelsea in 1964–65 and Bournemouth in the FA Cup the following season), while he also netted four in a memorable 6–1 win over Manchester United on Boxing Day 1963. After losing his place he joined Leicester City, where he gained an FA Cup runners-up medal in 1969. A productive spell with Aston Villa followed, with the Division Three championship won in 1971–72, as well as being losing finalists in the 1971 Football League Cup final. He concluded his career at Oldham Athletic where there was further success when the Latics won the Division Three title in 1973–74.

Terry Long (Born: Tylers Green, Buckinghamshire, 17 November 1934. Died: 19 September 2021.) Wing-half Terry Long joined Crystal Palace from Wycombe Wanderers in the summer of 1955 and quickly progressed to the first team at Selhurst Park. He went on to become a mainstay of the Palace team for over a decade and his total of 442 Football League appearances was a club record for many years. Between September 1956 and March 1961 he did not miss a League game, playing in 214 consecutive matches. He was a member of the promotion teams of 1960–61 and 1963–64 and also made a small contribution in 1968–69 when the club gained top-flight status for the first time. After retiring as a player he remained on the backroom staff for several years and later served Orient and Millwall as a coach.

Wally Lord (Born: Grimsby, 1 November 1933. Died: Grimsby, 27 March 2022.) Wally Lord was a forward who signed for his hometown club Grimsby Town in August 1951 at the age of 17 and marked his Football League debut for the club by scoring against Carlisle United. He made only a handful of further appearances for the Mariners before joining Lincoln City in May 1956. Wally played just once in the Imps first team during his two seasons with the club and went on to play in non-league football.

Frank McCarron (Born: 1 October 1943. Died: 4 November 2021.) Centre-half Frank McCarron captained the Scotland Schools U18 team in April 1962, signing for Celtic soon afterwards. He stayed at Parkhead for five seasons, but his only first-team appearance came against Hibernian in April 1963. He signed for Carlisle United in July 1967 but after making nine appearances in the 1967–68 season his career was ended by a broken leg. His son, Frank junior, played for Montrose in the early 1990s.

Billy McCartney (Born: 5 April 1931. Died: 25 February 2022.) Billy McCartney was a full-back who played for a number of clubs in the Irish League in the years following the Second World War including Glentoran and Linfield. He won a single cap for Ireland Amateurs against Scotland in December 1949.

Billy McDerment (Born: Paisley, 5 January 1943. Died: 13 November 2021.) Half-back Billy McDerment was capped for Scotland Amateurs while with Johnstone Burgh before signing for Leicester City in May 1961. He spent five seasons at Filbert Street where he was regarded as a reliable back-up player but only made 30 first-team appearances. He later made a contribution to Luton Town's Fourth Division championship success in 1967–68, then had an unproductive season with Notts County before returning to Scotland. Here he wound down his career with spells at Morton and St Mirren.

Peter McDonald (Born: Dublin, 6 January 1924. Died: Dublin, 29 March 2022.) Peter McDonald was a forward who played his club football for Bohemians and Transport. He was the last surviving member of the Eire team that took part in the 1948 Olympic Games, losing 3–1 to the Netherlands at Fratton Park in a preliminary round tie.

Billy McEwan (Born: Cleland, Lanarkshire, 20 June 1951. Died: February 2022.) Billy McEwan was a hard-working midfield player who began his senior career with Hibernian where he spent five seasons, mostly on the fringes of the first team. In the summer of 1973 he signed for Blackpool but stayed only a few months before moving on to Brighton & Hove Albion. He then embarked on something of a journey across the lower divisions of the Football League which saw him make over 300 appearances, turning out for Chesterfield, Mansfield Town, Peterborough United and Rotherham United. After retiring as a player he joined the coaching staff at Sheffield United and later served them as manager (March 1986 to January 1988). He went on to further managerial appointments at Rotherham United (April 1988 to January 1991) and Darlington (May 1992 to October 1993) then was on the coaching staff at Derby County before returning to management with York City and Mansfield, both non-league clubs at the time. He led Rotherham to the Fourth Division championship in 1988–89.

Junior McGillivray (Born: Newtongrange, Midlothian, 19 March 1940. Died: Edinburgh, 14 September 2021.) Junior McGillivray won youth international honours for Scotland and developed with Newtongrange Bluebell and Newtongrange Star before stepping up to the seniors with Third Lanark in August 1959. He did well during his time at Cathkin Park, making over 150 appearances and winning a cap for Scotland U23s against England in February 1962. Two years later he was bought by Rangers but in two seasons at Ibrox he never made the first team, and he went on to conclude his career with spells at Bradford Park Avenue and St Johnstone.

Frank Macgregor (Born: Glasgow, 17 January 1937. Died: Glasgow, 9 October 2021.) Full-back Frank Macgregor won four caps for Scotland Amateurs while a student at Jordanhill Training College. He later played for Junior club St Anthony's before signing for Clyde in November 1958. He made two first-team appearances during his time at Shawfield, both in January 1960, before reverting to Junior status. He was later a member of the Johnstone Burgh team that defeated Cambuslang Rangers in a replay to win the Scottish Junior Cup final in 1964.

Ron McIvor (Born: Edinburgh, 23 March 1951. Died: December 2021.) Defender Ron McIvor played in Junior football for Peebles Rovers and Bonnyrigg Rose, appearing for the latter in the 1972 Scottish Junior Cup final at Hampden when he scored, only for his team to lose 3–2 to Cambuslang Rangers in the replayed tie. He went on to play over 200 first-team games for East Fife in a seven-year spell at Methil, then moved south for a season of full-time football at Wigan Athletic. He was mostly a reserve at Springfield Park but made three Football League appearances, scoring on his debut at Doncaster Rovers. Later he moved to Australia where he played for Preston Makedonia.

Peter McNamee (Born: Glasgow, 20 March 1935. Died: 27 August 2021.) Peter McNamee was a traditional outside-left who signed for Peterborough United in January 1955 after being spotted playing in Army football for the Northern Command team. Posh were a Midland League club at the time but he went on to stay with them for a total of 10 seasons, making a total of over 300 first-team appearances including 192 in the Football League. Highlights include the 1960–61 season when he was a near ever-present as Posh ran away with the Fourth Division title at their first attempt, and the FA Cup fourth round victory over Arsenal in January 1965 when he scored late on to earn a historic victory. He left the club shortly after the start of the 1965–66 season and briefly played for King's Lynn before returning to senior football for a short spell with Notts County.

Bobby McPhee (Born: Kirkcaldy, Fife, 23 March 1939. Died: Methil, Fife, 31 October 2021.) Bobby McPhee was a versatile forward who scored regularly during three seasons with Stirling Albion. In April 1960 he signed for East Fife and in December 1960 scored four goals as the black and golds defeated East Stirlingshire 8–1. He later had a brief association with Swindon Town (where he played in the Football Combination team) and then signed for Banbury Spencer while on National Service. He subsequently played for several seasons in South Africa with Addington, Durban City and Bloemfontein City.

Willie McSeveney (Born: Shotts, Lanarkshire, 4 March 1929. Died: 15 December 2021.) Willie McSeveney was a versatile player who developed with Shotts YMCA with whom he won youth international honours for Scotland. After a spell with Wishaw Juniors he signed for Dunfermline Athletic in September 1948, and he went on to make his debut in senior football the following March. After making more than 100 appearances for the Pars he was sold to Motherwell in March 1954, helping them win promotion to the First Division that season. The following October he appeared at left-back in the team beaten by Heart of Midlothian in the League Cup final. He spent 10 seasons at Fir Park, playing 256 first-team games and after retiring as a player he remained with the club in a coaching capacity for many years. At the time of his death he was believed to be Dunfermline's oldest surviving player.

Tony Marchi (Born: Edmonton, Middlesex, 21 January 1933. Died: Chelmsford, 15 March 2022.) Tony Marchi was a wing-half who was capped for England Schools before signing for Tottenham Hotspur. He was only 17 when he made his first-team debut, but it was not until the 1954–55 season that he won a regular place in the side. He captained the team that finished as runners-up in the First Division in 1956–57 and at the end of that season he moved to Italy where he turned out for Lanerossi Vicenza and Torino. Two years later he returned to White Hart Lane, but he was mostly a back-up player to Danny Blanchflower and Dave Mackay in his second spell at the club, although he gained a European Cup Winners' Cup winners' medal when he played in the team that defeated Atletico Madrid in May 1963. He was capped for England B in February 1957, and seven years later played for an FA XI against New Zealand. After leaving Spurs he was player-manager of Cambridge City and then manager of Northampton Town from September 1967 to May 1968.

Paul Mariner (Born: Bolton, 22 May 1953. Died: 9 July 2021.) Paul Mariner was a hard-running and athletic striker who joined Plymouth Argyle from Northern Premier League club Chorley. He scored two on his debut for the Greens and netted 20 goals when they won promotion from the Third Division in 1974–75. His performances attracted the attention of bigger clubs and in September 1976 he signed for Ipswich Town, then one of the leading clubs in the First Division. He spent the best years of his career at Portman Road, winning the FA Cup (1977–78) and UEFA Cup (1980–81), and scoring a total of 135 League and Cup goals from 339 appearances. He went on to play for Arsenal and Portsmouth before leaving senior football. After a spell coaching in the United States he returned to Plymouth for a brief period as head coach (December 2009 to May 2010). He won 35 caps for England between March 1977 and May 1985, scoring 13 goals.

Cliff Marshall (Born: Liverpool, 4 November 1955. Died: 24 November 2021.) Cliff Marshall was a prodigious talent in Merseyside schools football. A pacy winger, he was a member of the Liverpool Boys team that won the English Schools FA U15 Trophy in 1969–70 when just 14 years old and the following season he was capped for England Schools. He went on to join Everton as an apprentice and when he came off the bench for the home game against Leicester City in January 1975, he became the first black player to appear for the Toffees in a Football League match. However, he managed just eight first-team appearances at Goodison before leaving at the end of the 1975–76 season. He spent the summer of 1976 playing in the NASL for Miami Toros, scoring a respectable six goals from 15 appearances then returned to the North West for a final season of senior football with Southport.

Geoff Martin (Born: New Tupton, Derbyshire, 9 March 1940. Died: November 2021.) Geoff Martin was a strong, direct outside-left who joined Chesterfield as a teenager but after a couple of first-team appearances he was released. He signed for Leeds United, a division above the Spireites, but here he was limited to a solitary outing in the Football League Cup. Thereafter he travelled around, playing in turn for Darlington, Carlisle United, Workington and Grimsby Town before ending up back at Chesterfield. He did well in the 1969–70 campaign, but with the club on the way to the Fourth Division championship an injury forced his retirement before the season's end.

Williams Martínez (Born: Montevideo, Uruguay, 18 December 1982. Died: Montevideo, Uruguay, 17 July 2021.) Williams Martínez was a big, powerful central defender who spent the second half of the 2005–06 season on loan to West Bromwich Albion from Uruguayan club Defensor Sporting. He made just two appearances during his stay, coming on as a second-half substitute in the 6–1 defeat at Fulham and playing the full 90 minutes in the 2–2 draw at Everton when he scored his side's second goal. He won a single cap for Uruguay.

John May (Born: 1942, Buckie. Died: 30 July 2021.) Inside-forward John May had trials with Montrose and Forfar Athletic during the 1966–67 season while on the books of Inverurie Loco Works. In the summer of 1967 he signed for Forfar and spent three years at Station Park, combining his football with a career in teaching. He made a total of 85 first-team appearances scoring 12 goals in a three-year stay before leaving the game.

Owen Medlock (Born: Whittlesey, Cambridgeshire, 8 March 1938. Died: 17 October 2021.) Goalkeeper Owen Medlock was playing for Bourne Town reserves when he attended a trial at Chelsea in February 1954 and arising from this, he was invited to join the groundstaff at Stamford Bridge. He signed professional terms in May 1955 but progressed only as far as the reserve team. He later had a short spell with Swindon, making three Football League appearances before signing for Oxford United in December 1959, then members of the Southern League. He was a member of the U's team that won successive Southern League titles in 1960–61 and 1961–62 and then played in their first-ever Football League match against Barrow in August 1962. He later gained a third Southern League winners' medal with Chelmsford City in 1967–68.

Alan Miller (Born: Epping, Essex, 29 March 1970. Died: 3 June 2021.) Goalkeeper Alan Miller came up through the ranks at Highbury and was a member of the Arsenal team that won the FA Youth Cup in 1987–88. He made his debut in senior football in November 1988 while on loan at Plymouth Argyle. He managed a few appearances for the Gunners during his stay but most of his senior experience came in loan spells elsewhere, before he signed for Middlesbrough in August 1994. He enjoyed a successful first campaign at Ayresome Park, where he was a near ever-present in the team that won the First Division title. He went on to play for West Bromwich Albion (1997–2000) and Blackburn Rovers (2000–2003) and had a string of loan spells elsewhere, but injuries affected the later years of his career and eventually led to his retirement.

Jock Miller (Born: Cowdenbeath, circa 1937. Died: 3 November 2021.) Inside-forward Jock Miller represented Scotland in Boys Club internationals and after a good scoring run with Junior club Crossgates Primrose he was called up by Cowdenbeath. He made a scoring debut for the first team at the age of 17 in a Scottish Cup tie against Ayr United in October 1954 and finished the season with 16 goals from 27 appearances. In the summer of 1955 he was sold to Dunfermline Athletic but his time at East End Park was hampered by injuries. He returned to Cowdenbeath in January 1958 and in his first game back he netted a hat-trick in an 8–1 demolition of Stranraer. He later spent a season in the Cheshire League with Rhyl.

Gary Moore (Born: Sedgefield, Co. Durham, 4 November 1945. Died: November 2021.) Centre-forward Gary Moore joined Sunderland on leaving school and was capped for the England Youth team, but with the Black Cats in the First Division he found first-team opportunities few and far between. In February 1957 he dropped into the lower divisions, signing for Grimsby Town, and he later played with success for Southend United, where he was a near ever-present in the team that won promotion from Division Four in 1971–72. He moved on to Chester in the summer of 1974, where he played in both legs of the Football League Cup semi-final against Aston Villa, then wound down his career at Swansea City before injury led to his retirement.

Lol Morgan (Born: Rotherham, 5 May 1931. Died: 14 January 2022.) Lol Morgan played a few games in the First Division for Huddersfield Town as a teenager but was allowed to move to Rotherham United on a free transfer at the end of the 1953–54 season. He was converted to full-back at Millmoor where he became a regular in the line-up, making over 300 first-team appearances. He went on to spend two seasons as player-manager at Darlington with whom he won promotion from the Fourth Division in 1965–66. The success earned him a move to Norwich City where he was manager from June 1966 to April 1969, achieving a respectable mid-table position in Division Two on each occasion.

Marvin Morgan (Born: Manchester, 13 April 1983. Died: 6 December 2021.) Marvin Morgan was a powerful striker who joined Aldershot Town from Woking following the club's promotion to the Football League in 2008. He featured in the Shots' first Football League game against Accrington Stanley and in 2009–10 finished as the club's leading scorer with 16 League and Cup goals. He went on to further spells with Shrewsbury Town and Plymouth Argyle before leaving senior football at the end of the 2014–15 season having scored 52 goals from 256 League and Cup appearances.

Robert Morrow (Born: Glasgow, 29 May 1934. Died: Georgetown, Ontario, Canada, 14 May 2022.) Robert Morrow was on the books of Third Lanark without appearing in the first team and went on to spend the 1953–54 season with Motherwell. He made one senior appearance during his time at Fir Park, lining up at inside-left for the League Cup game at home to Dundee United in August. He later played in the Irish League for Coleraine before emigrating to Canada in 1957.

Alan Morton (Born: Peterborough, 6 March 1942. Died: Lincoln, 14 September 2021.) Alan Morton was an inside-forward who signed for Arsenal shortly before his 17th birthday after previously playing for Peterborough United reserves. He was unable to break into the first team at Highbury and left in the summer of 1961, then had a brief spell playing in Canada before rejoining Peterborough. Alan made his Football League debut while at London Road but was given few further chances and moved on to Lincoln City in July 1963. He scored twice on his debut for the Imps and in his first season finished as leading scorer with 21 goals. Alan had a second season at Sincil Bank and finished his senior career with Chesterfield before playing non-league football.

Keith Morton (Born: Consett, Co. Durham, 11 August 1934. Died: 24 November 2021.) Keith Morton was a versatile forward who had a trial with Crewe Alexandra as a 16-year-old and later signed amateur forms for Crystal Palace while stationed in Kensington with the Army Education Corps on National Service. He scored three goals from five appearances for the Selhurst Park club and also featured for Sutton United, then members of the Athenian League. In the summer of 1954 he returned to the North East, signing professional forms for Sunderland. He featured for the Black Cats' reserves for a season before moving on to Darlington where his career took off. He spent six seasons at Feethams. He was joint-top scorer in 1955–56, while in January 1958 he was a member of the side that memorably drew 3–3 away to Chelsea in an FA Cup third round tie, scoring his team's final goal, although he missed the replay due to injury. He scored 55 goals in 195 appearances for the Quakers before leaving football at the end of the 1960–61 season.

Ernie Moss (Born: Chesterfield, 19 October 1949. Died: 11 July 2021.) Ernie Moss was a strong and powerful striker with an eye for goal who is best remembered for his three spells at Chesterfield. He twice won the Fourth Division with the Spireites (with a 15-year gap between the two) and was the club's all-time record scorer with 162 Football League goals from 469 appearances. In total he made 850 League and Cup appearances in a 20-year career in senior football, turning out for nine different clubs, and was 38 years old when he made his final appearance for Rochdale. Remarkably his career tally of 284 goals did not include a single penalty. In addition to his successes at Saltergate he was a member of the Mansfield Town team that won the Third Division title in 1976–77, and won promotion from Division Four with Doncaster Rovers in 1983–84.

Gerd Müller (Born: Nördlingen, Germany, 3 November 1945. Died: Wolfratshausen, Germany, 15 August 2021.) Gerd Müller was one of the greatest goalscorers in the post-war history of the game. He scored 68 goals in 62 international appearances for West Germany, including the winner in the 1974 World Cup final against the Netherlands, and another two in the European Championship final victory over the USSR in 1972. He was equally successful in club football with Bayern Munich with whom he won the European Cup in three consecutive seasons, the European Cup Winners' Cup once and both the Bundesliga and the DFB Pokal on four occasions. In 1970 he was chosen as the European Footballer of the Year.

Mick Newman (Born: London, Ontario, Canada, 2 April 1932. Died: February 2022.) Mick Newman was an inside-forward who signed for West Ham United in February 1957 after starring with Dagenham in the Delphian League. The last amateur player to feature at first-team level for the Hammers, he made seven first-team appearances during his stay which lasted a little over 12 months. He subsequently continued his career in the Southern League with Dartford.

Brian Nicholas (Born: Cwmaman, Aberdare, 20 April 1933. Died: 14 October 2021.) Defender Brian Nicholas was an England Schools international before joining the groundstaff at Queen's Park Rangers. He made his Football League debut against Leeds United in May 1949 at the age of 16 years and 17 days. He won a regular place in the line-up at Loftus Road during the 1952–53 season and after making over 100 appearances for the R's he was sold to Chelsea in July 1955. He was mostly a reserve during his stint at Stamford Bridge but then enjoyed a more productive time after moving on to Coventry City where he contributed to the club's success in winning promotion from the Fourth Division in 1958–59. He was released at the end of the 1961–62 season and signed for Southern League club Rugby Town.

Neil O'Donnell (Born: Glasgow, 21 December 1949. Died: May 2022.) Midfielder Neil O'Donnell joined Norwich City as a youngster from Scottish Juvenile football in the summer of 1966 and went on to make his senior debut in a League Cup tie at Rotherham 15 months later. He won youth international honours for Scotland and spent seven years at Carrow Road, mostly being on the fringes of the first-team squad. In the summer of 1974 he moved on to Gillingham before following manager Len Ashurst to Sheffield Wednesday in October 1975. He retired from the game through injury in January 1977.

Frank O'Farrell (Born: Cork, Republic of Ireland, 9 October 1927. Died: 6 March 2022.) Frank O'Farrell was a wing-half who won nine full caps for the Republic of Ireland and went on to enjoy a successful career as a manager. He played for Cork United in the League of Ireland before signing for West Ham United in January 1948. During eight years at Upton Park, he made almost 200 Football League appearances before moving to Preston North End where he continued to play regularly until a knee injury led to his retirement in 1961 at the age of 34. He started out in management at Weymouth and was then in charge at Torquay United before being appointed manager of Leicester City in December 1968. He led the Foxes to the 1969 FA Cup final and the 1970–71 Second Division title before taking over from Matt Busby as manager of Manchester United. He had 18 months at Old Trafford and went on to manage Cardiff City, the Iranian national team, whom he guided to the gold medal at the 1974 Asian Games, and had two spells as manager of Torquay sandwiched between a period in charge of the Emirati club Al-Shaab, before retiring. At the time of his death he was the oldest living former West Ham player.

Gerry O'Rourke (Born: Oakbank, West Lothian, 26 December 1938. Died: Newport, Isle of Wight, 10 April 2022.) Gerry O'Rourke was a goalscoring forward and established a reputation as a quality player for Hendon for whom he won three caps for Scotland Amateurs. In the summer of 1964 he joined the newly professional Wimbledon for their first season in the Southern League. He scored 30 goals as the Dons won promotion in 1964–65 and went on to amass a total of 149 in just over 400 games during his time at Plough Lane.

Sam Oji (Born: Westminster, London, 9 October 1985. Died: August 2021.) Sam Oji was a central defender who could also play at right-back. He developed in the youth set-up at Arsenal before signing for Birmingham City in May 2004. He spent three seasons at St Andrew's but his only appearance for the Blues came as a substitute in the FA Cup tie at Reading in February 2006. He gained experience of senior football on loan to Doncaster Rovers and Bristol Rovers and made further appearances in short spells with Leyton Orient and Hereford United before injuries effectively ended his senior career.

Ansah Owusu (Born: Hackney, London, 12 December 1976. Died: Finchley, London, 19 March 2022.) Ansah Owusu was a pacy attacking player who came up through the ranks at Wimbledon. He gained his first experience of senior football during a loan period with Raith Rovers towards the end of the 1999–2000 season, netting three goals from 10 appearances. The following season he made a handful of appearances for the Dons and also gained further experience on loan to Bristol Rovers, but he left Plough Lane in December 2001 and moved into non-league football.

Alf Patrick (Born: York, 25 September 1921. Died: York, 2 November 2021.) Centre-forward Alf Patrick signed for York City during the war and when he returned home following demobilisation was quickly promoted to the first team. He netted on his debut for the Minstermen against Stockport County in November 1946 and led the club's scoring charts in each of the first five post-war seasons. His five-goal haul in the 6–1 win over Rotherham United in November 1948 remains a club record in the Football League. He eventually departed to Scarborough in June 1954 having scored a total of 117 goals from 241 senior appearances.

Steve Peplow (Born: Liverpool, 8 January 1949. Died: December 2021.) After impressing in Merseyside schools football, Steve Peplow came up through the ranks at Liverpool, signing a professional contract at the age of 17. He scored regularly for the Reds' reserve team in 1968–69 and made a couple of first-team appearances the following season before spending 1970–71 on loan to Swindon Town. He went on to sign permanently for the Robins during the summer of 1971 and then had a brief spell with Nottingham Forest before returning to Merseyside in January 1974 when he signed for Tranmere Rovers. He did well during his time at Prenton Park where he was an ever-present in their 1975–76 promotion campaign and made over 250 League and Cup appearances before being released in May 1981.

Davie Phillip (Born: Arbroath, 16 May 1948. Died: Dundee, 27 October 2021.) Goalkeeper Davie Phillip signed for Forfar Athletic in 1967, making his debut at Arbroath on New Year's Day 1968. He spent two-and-a-half years as first choice at Station Park making 83 appearances and lined up in the Scottish Cup tie against Rangers in February 1970 when the ground record attendance was established. He then had a season with Arbroath before returning to Junior football with Arbroath Vics. He later made a further appearance for Alloa Athletic in the 1973–74 season.

Andy Porter (Born: Stewarton, Ayrshire, 21 January 1937. Died: 7 October 2021.) Andy Porter was a wing-half or inside-forward who developed with Darvel in the Ayrshire Juniors before moving south to sign for Watford in the summer of 1959. He made his first-team debut in January 1960 and featured on a handful of occasions as the Hornets won promotion from the old Fourth Division that season. Although never a regular in the line-up he made 80 appearances during his time at Vicarage Road before moving on to join Guildford City.

Eddie Presland (Born: Loughton, Essex, 27 March 1943. Died: Gateshead, 1 August 2021.) Eddie Presland was a defender who came up through the ranks with West Ham United to sign a professional contract in October 1960. He spent seven years with the Hammers but although he scored on his debut against Liverpool in February 1965, he received few first-team opportunities. He did better following a move to Crystal Palace where he was a near ever-present in 1967–68 but although he remained at Selhurst Park for a couple more seasons he was mostly used as a stand-in player. He was later manager of the Dagenham team that won the FA Trophy in 1980. Eddie was also a useful cricketer and played 30 First Class matches for Essex between 1962 and 1970.

Duggie Price (Born: Morriston, Swansea, 17 November 1931. Died: 10 August 2021.) Duggie Price was a lively inside-forward who developed in local football before signing for Swansea Town in April 1950. He had to wait until February 1954 to get a first-team chance, but he was always a back-up player during his time at Vetch Field and eventually moved on to sign for Southend United in January 1958. He did well at Roots Hall, establishing a record as a useful goalscorer and topping the club's scoring charts in 1959–60 with 29 League and Cup goals. Shortly after the start of the following season he was transferred to Hull City, getting off to a good start with two goals on his debut. He stayed at Hull for a further two seasons before concluding his senior career at Bradford City, leaving the game 106 League and Cup goals to his name.

Howard Radford (Born: Abercynon, Glamorgan, 8 September 1930. Died: Poole, 21 January 2022.) Howard Radford was a goalkeeper who first came to notice playing for Penrhiwceiber in the Welsh League in the 1950–51 season. Towards the end of the campaign he received a trial with Bristol Rovers and signed permanently over the summer. He made his debut in October 1951 but although he made a contribution to the team that won the Division Three South title in 1952–53, it was not until the following season that he became first choice. He remained at Eastville until the end of the 1961–62 campaign, leaving when the club were relegated from Division Two having made a career total of 252 senior appearances.

Eddie Rayner (Born: Salford, 13 August 1932. Died: Haslington, Crewe, 5 April 2022.) Eddie Rayner was a wing-half who joined Stoke City from Northwich Victoria in May 1955. He stayed four years at the Victoria Ground but was mostly a reserve during his time with the club, making just four first-team appearances. He later played for a number of non-league clubs including Chelmsford City, Macclesfield Town and Hyde United.

Billy Reid (Born: 31 January 1938. Died: July 2021.) Inside-forward Billy Reid won representative honours for Scotland at schoolboy and youth international levels before signing for Motherwell in January 1955. A hard-tackling midfield player, he spent six seasons at Fir Park making 73 appearances before joining Airdrieonians in October 1961. He stayed a further seven seasons with the Diamonds, taking his total of senior appearances beyond the 200-mark and contributing to their success in gaining promotion to the First Division in 1965–66. His younger brother Sammy Reid was a colleague at Motherwell and also enjoyed a lengthy career in senior football.

Ian Riddell (Born: May 1938. Died: Paisley, 25 September 2021.) Full-back Ian Riddell signed for St Mirren in September 1958 and spent eight seasons on the books of the Paisley club, making over 150 appearances. He won two caps for Scotland U23s, featuring against England on both occasions. He concluded his senior career with Berwick Rangers, where he was a member of the team that memorably eliminated Rangers from the Scottish Cup in January 1967.

Dave Roberts (Born: Plymouth, 8 May 1944. Died: 11 March 2022.) Dave Roberts was a full-back who signed apprenticeship forms for Plymouth Argyle on leaving school. He moved up to the professional ranks in December 1961 and made his first-team debut shortly afterwards at the age of 17. However, although he spent three seasons on the books at Home Park, he was mostly a reserve, making 12 first-team appearances. He later played for South Western League club St Blazey.

Ken Ronaldson (Born: Leith, 27 September 1945. Died: 14 July 2021.) Ken Ronaldson was a versatile attacking player who developed in Juvenile football with Edinburgh Rangers before signing for Aberdeen in July 1963. He made his debut for the Dons in a League Cup game at Ibrox at the age of 18 but was only on the fringes of the first team at Pittodrie before signing for Bristol Rovers. He spent four seasons at Eastville and although injury prone he scored 17 goals from 86 first-team appearances before signing for Gillingham in November 1969. The highlight of his time at Priestfield came when he produced a fine performance in the FA Cup fourth-round tie with Peterborough United in January 1970 as the Gills reached the fifth round of the competition for the first time in their history. He left full-time football in the summer of 1971 and joined the local Police Force, continuing to turn out for Kent Police in the Kent League for several seasons.

Ray Ruffett (Born: Luton, 20 July 1924. Died: Luton, 29 September 2021.) Ray Ruffett was a defensive midfield player who developed in local football and made 20 appearances for Luton Town in the wartime emergency competitions. His only peacetime appearance for the Hatters came at Bury on 2 April 1949 when he suffered a knee injury which led to a lengthy lay off. He joined Abbey United for the 1950–51 season, remaining at the club for five seasons during which they adopted their modern name of Cambridge United and moved up to the Eastern Counties League. In November 1953 he was a member of the U's team that knocked Newport County out of the FA Cup, the first time the club had defeated Football League opposition.

Derek Rutherford (Born: Keith, Banffshire, 23 October 1946. Died: October 2021.) Defender Derek Rutherford played for Aberdeen Juvenile team Banks O'Dee 'A' and had a spell on the groundstaff at Leicester City before moving back to Scotland to sign for Heart of Midlothian in February 1963. He was only 17 when he made his debut in a League Cup tie against Partick Thistle in August 1964 but in a five-year spell at Tynecastle he made just two more first-team appearances. He later joined Partick but rarely featured here too, then moved to South Africa early in 1970 to play for East London Celtic. He was back in Scotland by October 1971 when he signed for Forfar Athletic before ending his senior career with East Stirlingshire.

Keith Rutter (Born: Leeds, 10 September 1931. Died: June 2021.) Keith Rutter was a defender who played for Huddersfield Town 'A' as a youngster, then with junior teams in West Yorkshire before signing for Queens Park Rangers in July 1954. He quickly won a place in the R's line-up, initially at full-back before switching to centre-half, developing into a reliable and uncompromising performer. He remained a first-team regular at Loftus Road for the best part of nine seasons and made over 350 appearances before concluding his senior career with Colchester United. He subsequently appeared in the Southern League with Romford, Ashford Town and Hastings where he was player-manager.

George Ryden (Born: Dumbarton, 14 July 1938. Died: Balmerino, Tayside, 12 December 2021.) George Ryden was a centre-half who joined Dundee from Junior outfit Duntocher Hibs in December 1958, but it was not until October 1962 when Ian Ure moved to Arsenal that he eventually took over the position. The highlight of his career at Dens Park came in April 1964 when he played in front of 120,000 fans at Hampden in the Scottish Cup final when Dundee went down 3–1 to Rangers. He later turned out for both St Johnstone and Stirling Albion before leaving senior football. Two of his brothers, John and Hugh, enjoyed successful careers in the Football League.

Roy Sawyer (Born: Barnsley, 29 March 1940. Died: December 2021.) Roy Sawyer was a centre-half who signed for Barnsley from local club Worsborough Bridge in May 1958. He was mostly a reserve during a five-year stay at Oakwell making just two first-team appearances. He made his debut at Bournemouth in February 1961, and when keeper Don Leeson had to go off injured after 15 minutes he took over in goal, conceding just once in 75 minutes' play as Barnsley held on for a remarkable 2–1 win.

Tony Scott (Born: St Neots, Cambridgeshire, 1 April 1941. Died: Australia, 17 September 2021.) Tony Scott was a winger who played for St Neots Town before joining the groundstaff at West Ham United at the age of 16. The following year he signed professional forms and he went on to gain international honours for England Youths before making his first-team debut against Chelsea in February 1960. He was in and out of the Hammers team, but over the next seven seasons he made 97 first-team appearances before continuing his career in the First Division with Aston Villa. Later his former colleague John Bond signed him for Torquay United and he followed his manager to Bournemouth where he was a key figure in the team that won promotion from the Fourth Division in 1970–71. He concluded his career at Exeter City, where injuries led to his retirement. He emigrated to Australia in 1989 where he remained for the rest of his life.

John Sewell (Born: Brockley, London, 7 July 1936. Died: Sequim, Washington State, United States, 19 November 2021.) John Sewell was a talented all-round sportsman in his schooldays and excelled at rugby union and athletics as well as football. He made two appearances for England U15 schools at rugby against Wales in 1950–51 before focusing on his soccer career. He signed professional forms for Charlton Athletic in January 1955 and after initially appearing in the team at right-half, he switched to right-back and rarely missed a match in a three-year spell before signing for Crystal Palace in October 1963. He helped the Eagles win promotion from Division Three in his first season and then captained the team that won promotion to the First Division for the first time in the club's history in 1968–69. He ended his senior career with a brief spell at Leyton Orient before emigrating to the United States, where he played and then coached St Louis Stars.

Laurie Sheffield (Born: Swansea, 27 April 1939. Died: 9 November 2021.) Centre-forward Laurie Sheffield was capped for Wales at schoolboy international level but then joined Bristol Rovers where he was unable to break into the first team. He dropped into the Southern League with Barry Town but attracted interest after scoring in their 1–1 FA Cup draw with Queens Park Rangers in November 1961 and later that season he signed for Newport County. His goalscoring exploits at Somerton Park earned him a move to Doncaster and he topped the Rovers scoring charts in 1965–66 as they won the Fourth Division championship. Soon afterwards Norwich City bought him as a replacement for the departed Ron Davies and he hit a hat-trick on his Carrow Road debut against Derby County. Thereafter he continued to move around clubs before suffering a broken ankle playing for Peterborough United in November 1970 which ended his career.

Brian Sherratt (Born: Stoke-on-Trent, 29 March 1944. Died: October 2021.) Goalkeeper Brian Sherratt came up through the ranks with Stoke City but made only one senior appearance for the Potters, keeping a clean sheet in the home game with Middlesbrough in April 1962. He moved on to Oxford United in the summer of 1965 and made over 50 appearances for the U's, although he was mostly second choice to Jim Barron in the 1967–68 promotion season. He went on to play for Barnsley and Colchester United before moving into non-league football.

Bill Shipwright (Born: St Pancras, London, 22 December 1932. Died: March 2022.) Bill Shipwright joined the groundstaff at Watford as a 16-year-old, developing in the club's junior teams and with Chesham United before progressing to the professional ranks in April 1953. He became a regular in the half-back line from the start of the 1954–55 season and remained a first choice for three-and-a-half seasons. After losing his place in the side he moved on to Aldershot where he made over 100 first-team appearances before switching to Southern League football with Yiewsley.

John Sillett (Born: Southampton, 20 July 1936. Died: 29 November 2021.) John Sillett signed professional forms for Chelsea at the age of 17 and went on to make his Football League debut at Old Trafford in January 1957, when he partnered his brother Peter at full-back. He went on to have a couple of seasons as a first-team regular at Stamford Bridge and he was capped for the Football League representative team against the League of Ireland in September 1960. In April 1962 he became one of Jimmy Hill's first signings for Coventry City and he missed just a handful of games as the Sky Blues won the Third Division title in 1963–64. He concluded his playing career with Plymouth Argyle before turning to coaching and management. He led Hereford United to the Third Division title in 1975–76 and in April 1986 was appointed as manager of Coventry City where he achieved great success, winning the FA Cup in 1987 and achieving a top-10 position in the First Division in three consecutive seasons, before leaving in October 1990.

Colin Slater, MBE (Born: Bradford, 28 February 1974. Died: 10 January 2022.) Colin Slater was a journalist who became one of the pioneers of local radio broadcasting on the game. He covered over 3,000 Notts County matches for BBC Radio Nottingham from 1968 until he retired in 2017. Previously he reported for the club for the *Nottingham Evening News* and *Evening Post*. He was chairman of Notts County Former Players Association. He was also a magistrate and was elected to the Church of England General Synod in 1990. He was awarded an MBE in 2001 and in 2010 was awarded the Freedom of the Borough of Broxtowe.

Arthur Smith, BEM (Born: Walmersley, Bury, 8 May 1915. Died: Bolton, 21 August 2021.) Arthur Smith was an outside-right who made four appearances for Bury in December 1934. He later signed for Leicester City, where he played eight times in 1938–39 and on two occasions at the start of 1939–40, scoring twice on his debut against Manchester City. The Football League closed down for the war soon afterwards and he did not appear in senior football again. In 2013 he was awarded the British Empire Medal for his long service to Christ Church in Walmersley where he had been the church organist since 1935. He was believed to be the oldest surviving professional footballer at the time of his death.

Billy Smith, MBE (Born: Cumnock, Ayrshire, 12 October 1942. Died: 8 December 2021.) Billy Smith was an inside-forward who won Junior international honours for Scotland against Ireland in March 1965 before joining Sheffield United from Cumnock shortly afterwards. He scored on his first-team debut for the Blades at West Bromwich Albion in February 1967 but played just twice more during his stay at Bramall Lane. He later had a brief association with Preston North End before returning to the Juniors. He worked as a janitor at Cumnock Academy for 30 years and in 2006 was awarded the MBE in the Queen's Birthday Honours List for services to education.

Jimmy Smith (Born: Sheffield, 6 December 1930. Died: January 2022.) Jimmy Smith was a winger who joined Chelsea early in 1951 after service in the Army. He had a couple of good runs in the side in the 1951–52 season but then illness and competition for places restricted his opportunities. In July 1955 he signed for Leyton Orient where he made 39 first-team appearances before suffering a bad knee injury two years later which effectively ended his career.

Mike Smith (Born: Hendon, 1937. Died: July 2021.) Mike Smith was a talented all-round sportsman as a youngster and played trial matches for both Queens Park Rangers 'A' and Brighton 'A' while at school, also featuring for Sussex Second XI at cricket. He combined playing as an amateur for Loughborough Colleges and Corinthian Casuals with a career in teaching before moving into coaching for the Sussex County FA. He went on to join the coaching staff at the FA of Wales, being promoted to become the first full-time manager of the senior national team in July 1974 and remained in post until December 1979 when he became manager of Hull City. The Tigers were relegated to Division Four at the end of his first full season in charge and he left in March 1982. Later he had a spell as coach of the Egypt national team, leading them to victory in the Africa Cup of Nations in 1986.

Walter Smith, OBE (Born: Lanark, 6 February 1948. Died: 26 October 2021.) Walter Smith was a defender who made almost 200 appearances in a playing career with Dundee United and Dumbarton before going on to become one of the most successful managers in Scottish post-war football. Walter joined the Arabs from Junior club Ashfield in November 1966 and won a regular place in the first team from 1971, appearing for the club in the 1974 Scottish Cup final when they lost to Celtic. In September 1975 he was sold to Dumbarton but returned to Tannadice after 18 months. Later.he suffered a pelvic injury which restricted his appearances, and he went on to become United's first-team coach during the most successful period in their history. In April 1986 Walter was appointed as assistant manager at Rangers and five years later took over as manager. He won six consecutive Scottish League titles, including a domestic treble in 1992–93, as well as achieving success in both the Scottish Cup and League Cup before stepping down in 1998. He went on to have four years in charge at Everton and had a short spell as assistant manager at Manchester United before he was appointed manager of the Scotland national team in December 2004. He returned to Rangers in January 2007 and led the club to three more Scottish League titles, two Scottish Cups, three League Cups and a UEFA Cup final. He was the Scottish Football Writers Association manager of the year on seven occasions and in 1997 was awarded an OBE.

Andy Spring (Born: Gateshead, 17 November 1965. Died: Redditch, 13 February 2022.) Andy Spring played for Durham schools before signing professional terms for Coventry City in November 1983. However, he made little progress with his career at Highfield Road and in the summer of 1985 he moved on to Bristol Rovers. He spent a season with the Pirates, making 23 appearances before switching to League of Ireland football where he had spells with Sligo Rovers, Drogheda United and Longford Town.

Bobby Stein (Born: Linlithgow, 19 September 1939. Died: 13 August 2021.) Bobby Stein played in the Juniors for Armadale Thistle and Broxburn Athletic before signing for Raith Rovers in August 1960. He switched to playing at full-back on joining the Kirkcaldy club and went on to make 292 League and Cup appearances over the next nine seasons, helping the team win promotion to the First Division in 1966–67. After spending a season with Montrose he went on to play for East Stirlingshire for another seven seasons before retiring at the age of 37, by which time he had played close on 600 senior games. His younger brother Colin Stein also played the game professionally.

Ron Stephenson (Born: Barrow in Furness, 13 April 1948. Died: Barrow in Furness, 9 March 2022.) Ron Stephenson was a versatile player who developed in local schools and junior football before signing for Barrow. He mostly featured for the club's reserve team but made two first-team appearances, scoring in the second of these away to Mansfield Town in September 1967.

Ian Stirling (Born: Arbroath, 10 October 1942. Died: Arbroath, 9 December 2021.) Ian Stirling joined Arbroath in July 1960 and in his early days at the club he mostly played as a forward before eventually settling into the team at centre-half. He captained the side for several seasons and went on to make a total of 380 League and Cup appearances, leading the team to promotion to the First Division in 1967–68. He retired as a player at the end of the 1970–71 campaign and later served the club as a committee member and then chairman from 1979 to 1987.

Bob Stirrat (Born: Fauldhouse, West Lothian, 1936. Died: Kirkcaldy, Fife, 22 January 2022.) Bob Stirrat attracted plenty of interest from Scottish League clubs for his performances for Whitburn Juniors before signing for East Fife in December 1956. A tall and versatile defender, he eventually settled into the team at full-back and went on to play 290 first-team games during his time at Methil, placing him in 10th position in the club's all-time list of appearances.

Derek Stokes (Born: Normanton, Yorkshire, 13 September 1939. Died: May 2022.) Derek Stokes was a versatile forward who was playing West Yorkshire League football when he signed for Bradford City in May 1956. He scored twice on his debut for the Valley Paraders at Crewe in September 1957 and was a regular scorer throughout his time with the club. He finished as the club's top scorer in the 1959–60 season when he found the net in eight consecutive matches including hat-tricks against Newport and Accrington Stanley. In June 1960 he was sold to Huddersfield Town where he won representative honours for an FA XI against the Army and four caps for England U23s. He was leading scorer four seasons in a row during his time at Leeds Road then returned to Bradford City. He later moved to Dundalk, contributing to their success in winning the League of Ireland title in 1966–67 and appearing for them in the Inter Cities Fairs Cup.

Con Sullivan (Born: Bristol, 22 August 1928. Died: April 2022.) Goalkeeper Con Sullivan was spotted playing in the Bristol Downs League for Horfield Old Boys and after a successful trial period he signed for Bristol City in May 1949. He made his debut against Bournemouth in December 1950 and went on to establish himself as first-choice, playing in all 46 League games in 1951–52. In February 1954 he was sold to Arsenal where he understudied Jack Kelsey, making 32 first-team appearances before injury ended his career.

Trevor Swift (Born: Rotherham, 14 September 1948. Died: February 2022.) Defender Trevor Swift signed for Rotherham United from local club Thurcroft Welfare in September 1965, but it was not until Tommy Docherty was appointed as the Millers' manager that he managed to gain a regular place in the side. He spent the best part of seven seasons as a fixture in the line-up, latterly featuring in a defensive midfield role. He left Millmoor in the summer of 1975, signing for Northern Premier League club Worksop Town.

Trevor Thompson (Born: North Shields, 21 May 1955. Died: December 2021.) Trevor Thompson was a full-back who began his career as an apprentice with West Bromwich Albion, signing a professional contract in January 1974. He made 20 first-team appearances for the Baggies before leaving in 1976 to play for Washington Diplomats in the NASL. He then had a spell with Newport County before signing for Lincoln City in December 1979. He was a member of the Lincoln team which won promotion to Division Three in 1980–81, setting a club record by conceding just 25 League goals in the season. Trevor had a further season with the Imps before continuing his career in non-league football.

Bobby Todd (Born: Goole, Yorkshire, 11 September 1949. Died: Howden, Yorkshire, March 2022.) Bobby Todd was a winger who was an apprentice with Scunthorpe United. After helping the Iron reach the semi-final of the FA Youth Cup in 1966–67 he signed for Liverpool, despite not having appeared in the first team at the Old Showground. He was only a reserve at Anfield and within a matter of months he was on his way to Rotherham United, exchanging one iconic 1960s manager, Billy Shankly, for another, Tommy Docherty. He made his Football League debut for the Millers but again moved on quickly and it was a similar tale at his two other senior clubs, Mansfield Town and Workington. He did better in non-league football, firstly with Wigan Athletic and then Scarborough with whom he played at Wembley in the 1975 FA Trophy final.

Keith Todd (Born: Clydach, Swansea, 2 March 1941. Died: Swansea, 8 January 2022.) Keith Todd was a centre-forward who joined Swansea Town from Welsh League club Clydach United in September 1959. He broke into the first team the following season, scoring in each of his first two Football League appearances. He went on to play for the Swans in their FA Cup semi-final defeat by Preston North End in March 1964 and was a regular in the squad until his departure at the end of the 1967–68 season to play for Pembroke Borough. He was capped for Wales U23s against Northern Ireland in February 1963.

Derek Tomkinson (Born: Stoke-on-Trent, 6 April 1931. Died: Tipton St John, Devon, 27 July 2021.) Derek Tomkinson was a defensive half-back who signed professional forms with Port Vale in December 1952 after a spell with Burton Albion. He was mostly a back-up player during his time at Vale Park, with a highlight coming when he lined-up against West Bromwich Albion in the FA Cup semi-final in March 1954. He spent the 1955–56 campaign with Stafford Rangers in the Cheshire League before concluding his senior career with a season at Crewe Alexandra.

Gary Townend (Born: Kilburn, London, 1 May 1940. Died: 29 May 2022.) Gary Townend was an inside-forward who signed for Millwall from Athenian League club Redhill shortly after the start of the 1960–61 season. He went straight into the Lions' first team but was unable to keep his place in the side and spent most of his time at The Den on the fringes of the squad. He made a total of 51 senior appearances with a highlight coming when he netted a hat-trick at Luton Town in December 1963. He later played in the Southern League for Hillingdon Borough and Chelmsford City.

Wilf Tranter (Born: Pendlebury, Lancashire, 5 March 1945. Died: 2 July 2021.) Wilf Tranter was a member of the Manchester Boys team that won the English Schools Trophy in 1960 and shortly afterwards became an apprentice with Manchester United. His solitary Football League outing for United came at West Ham in March 1964. He made further appearances as a defender for both Brighton & Hove Albion and Fulham but was never a first-team regular with either club. Later he was a member of the St Louis Stars team defeated by New York Cosmos in the NASL championship final in 1972.

David Turner (Born: Derby, 26 December 1948. Died: May 2022.) David Turner was an apprentice with Everton before stepping up to become a professional in October 1966. He made a solitary first-team appearance during his time at Goodison, lining up in the home game with Chelsea in April 1968. He left to sign for Southport in May 1970 and was a near ever-present in his first season at Haig Avenue. However, injuries then disrupted his career, and he left the full-time game at the end of the 1972–73 campaign.

John Varney (Born Oxford, 27 November 1929. Died: Oxford, 23 September 2021.) John Varney was a left-sided player who signed for Hull City after playing for Oxford City and the RAF representative team. He was initially an amateur with the Tigers but signed professional forms in December 1949 after he was demobilised. John made 10 first-team appearances during his time at Boothferry Park and then signed for Lincoln City in the summer of 1951 where he established himself as first-choice left-back before suffering a serious injury. He made a handful of further appearances before rejecting the terms offered to him in the summer of 1953 and returning to his home city of Oxford where he later played for Headington United. At the time of his death, he was Hull City's oldest former player, and was the last surviving member of the Lincoln City team which won the Division Three North championship in 1951–52.

Jamie Vincent (Born: Wimbledon, 18 June 1975. Died: January 2022.) Jamie Vincent was a quick and reliable left-back who played for 10 Football League clubs in a career that spanned the period from 1993 to 2011. A product of the Wimbledon youth set-up, he joined Crystal Palace as a teenager and made his senior debut in November 1994 while on loan at Bournemouth. He later signed permanently for the Cherries and in 1998–99 was chosen as a member of the PFA Second Division Team of the Year. One of his best seasons came in 2006–07, towards the end of his career, when he was a regular in the Swindon Town side that won promotion from League Two. He left senior football at the end of the 2010–11 season having made a total of 495 League and Cup appearances.

Jack Vitty (Born: Chilton, Co. Durham, 19 January 1923. Died: 4 November 2021.) Jack Vitty was a tall left-back who was playing for Boldon Villa when he signed amateur forms for Charlton Athletic during the 1946–47 season. He quickly moved on to sign as a professional, but with the Addicks being in the First Division he made just two first-team appearances. He moved on to Brighton & Hove Albion where he made a greater impact. In December 1951 he scored a remarkable goal for the Seagulls against Exeter City, firing home a free-kick from inside his own half. He concluded his senior career at Workington, where he captained the team and played over 200 first-team games before departing at the end of the 1956–57 season. His younger brother Ron also played in the Football League.

Bobby Waddell (Born: Kirkcaldy, Fife, 5 September 1939. Died: Dundee, 24 August 2021.) Bobby Waddell was a centre-forward who joined Dundee from Juvenile club St Andrew's Swifts in July 1959 and went on to make a scoring first-team debut in a League Cup tie with Rangers the following month. Although rarely a first choice at Dens Park, he made a useful contribution to Dundee's Scottish League title win in 1961–62 then headed south for spells with Blackpool and Bradford Park Avenue. He concluded his career back in Scotland with East Fife and Montrose.

Sid Watson (Born: Pleasley, Mansfield, 12 December 1927. Died: Mansfield, 29 August 2021.) Wing-half Sid Watson was playing for Palterton Welfare and working at Pleasley Colliery as a coal miner when he signed amateur forms for Mansfield Town in November 1948. He turned professional the following January, but it was not until December 1951 that he broke into the first team. He went on to make over 300 first-team appearances for the Stags, remaining with the club until the end of the 1960–61 season when he moved on to Ilkeston Town.

Johnny Watt (Born: Crookedholm, Ayrshire, 17 June 1943. Died: Kilmarnock, 2 March 2022.) Winger Johnny Watt was one of a group of players from Juvenile club Saxone YC who signed for Blackpool in the summer of 1960. Competition for places at Bloomfield Road was fierce and he appeared just five times for the Seasiders before moving on to join Stockport County in July 1963. He did well in two seasons at Edgeley Park, helping the Hatters reach the FA Cup fourth round in 1964–65 when they gained a memorable draw at Anfield in front of a 50,000-plus gate before going out in the replay. He later wound down his career with a spell at Southport before returning to Scotland where he played in the Juniors for Cumnock and Darvel.

Billy Webb (Born: Mexborough, Yorkshire, 7 March 1932. Died: 30 October 2021.) Left-back Billy Webb joined Rochdale from the Wolves nursery club Wath Wanderers towards the end of the 1950–51 season and after appearing for Dale in a Festival of Britain match, he was sold to Leicester City in June 1951. He enjoyed a good run in the side in his first season at Filbert Street but thereafter was mostly a second choice, making 49 appearances over six seasons. After moving on to Stockport County in June 1957 he rarely missed a match over the next five seasons, clocking up over 250 appearances during his stay before eventually moving to non-league Hyde United for the 1963–64 season.

Spencer Whelan (Born: Liverpool, 17 September 1971. Died: June 2021.) Spencer Whelan was a tall central defender who developed in Merseyside schools football and went on to sign professional forms for Liverpool. He moved on to Chester City in April 1990 and after establishing himself in the side at the start of the 1991–92 campaign he went on to make almost 250 first-team appearances for the club, contributing to their success in winning promotion from Division Three in 1993–94. He concluded his career at Shrewsbury Town before injuries forced his retirement.

Jimmy Whitehouse (Born: West Bromwich, 19 September 1934. Died: Tilehurst, Reading, 5 May 2022.) Jimmy Whitehouse was a tall inside-forward who began his career with West Bromwich Albion. Unable to make progress at The Hawthorns, he signed for Reading in June 1956. He scored on his debut for the Royals in the opening game of the 1956–57 campaign and was a regular in the line-up at Elm Park for six seasons, making over 200 first-team appearances. He then moved to Coventry City, where he starred in the team that reached the quarter-finals of the FA Cup in 1962–63 before concluding his senior career at Millwall.

Harold Wilcockson (Born: Sheffield, 23 July 1943. Died: April 2022.) Harold Wilcockson was a full-back who began his career as an amateur with Hillsborough Boys' Club. He spent his entire senior career in South Yorkshire, turning out for Rotherham United in two spells, Sheffield Wednesday and Doncaster Rovers. He made a total of 295 senior appearances between 1964 and 1973, gaining promotion with Doncaster as Fourth Division champions in 1968–69. He later played in non-league football for Goole Town.

Jackie Williamson (Born: 6 September 1932. Died: 3 March 2022.) Jackie Williamson was a half-back who signed for Raith Rovers from Stoneyburn Juniors in February 1952 and made over 150 first-team appearances for the Kirkcaldy club. He moved to Dunfermline Athletic in March 1959, establishing himself as the club's regular left-back under Jock Stein. He played for the Pars against Celtic in the drawn 1961 Scottish Cup final but finished the game hobbling on the wing having suffered a knee injury that forced him to miss the replay. Jackie made five appearances for Dunfermline in their European Cup Winners' Cup campaign, but his knee injury persisted and led to his retirement at the end of 1962–63. He played a total of 111 senior games for Dunfermline.

Johnny Williamson (Born: Manchester, 8 May 1929. Died: 5 August 2021.) Johnny Williamson was a local lad who signed for Manchester City in August 1949 and made his first-team debut at inside-right the following April. He spent seven years at Maine Road, mostly as a reserve, but when called into the first team he proved to be a reliable deputy. His best season was in 1952–53 when he enjoyed a good run in the side and scored 12 goals from 22 games. He left City in March 1956 to conclude his senior career with a spell at Blackburn Rovers. His father, Johnny senior, played for Manchester City, Bury and Crewe Alexandra between the wars.

Alan Woods (Born: Dinnington, Yorkshire, 15 February 1937. Died: 28 September 2021.) Alan Woods was a creative midfield player who was capped by England at youth and schoolboy international levels. He joined the groundstaff at Tottenham Hotspur and went on to earn a professional contract, but apart from a brief run at the start of the 1954–55 season he was unable to win a place in the line-up at White Hart Lane. He later had three seasons with Swansea Town but here too he was mostly a back-up player. His career finally took off on moving to York City in July 1960. He was a regular with the Minstermen for five seasons, playing a key role in 1964–65 when they won promotion from the Fourth Division and making over 250 appearances. Later he switched to non-league football with Boston United. His son Neil Woods and grandson Michael Woods both played in the Football League.

Alan Wooler (Born: Poole, 17 August 1953. Died: March 2022.) Alan Wooler was a left-back who graduated through the youth team at Reading and went on to make 43 appearances before being released at the end of the 1972–73 campaign. He then signed for West Ham United where he spent three seasons but was mostly a stand-in player and rarely featured in the first team. He subsequently joined Aldershot at the end of the 1975–76 where he earned a reputation as a consistent performer and did not miss a match in either the 1979–80 or 1980–81 seasons. He went on to make more than 300 appearances for the Shots before leaving in the summer of 1984.

Stewart Woolgar (Born: Chesterfield, 21 September 1952. Died: 5 August 2021.) Stewart Woolgar was an apprentice with West Bromwich Albion who went on to make his senior debut as a substitute against Manchester United in October 1972. However, he received few opportunities during his time at The Hawthorns and he moved on for a brief spell at Doncaster Rovers. He later played in the Southern League with Dunstable and Wealdstone.

John Wright (Born: 1 May 1945. Died: 11 January 2022.) John Wright was a goalkeeper who signed for Clyde from Petershill Juniors in April 1963 and spent the following season playing for the Shawfield club's reserve team. He eventually stepped up to make his senior debut in a League Cup tie against Rangers in September 1965. He stayed with the Bully Wee until the end of the 1971–72 season, making over 100 first-team appearances, and then had a brief association with Partick Thistle before retiring from the game through injury.

Ian Nannestad

THE FOOTBALL RECORDS

BRITISH FOOTBALL RECORDS

ALL-TIME PREMIER LEAGUE CHAMPIONSHIP SEASONS ON POINTS AVERAGE

	Team	*Season*	*P*	*W*	*D*	*L*	*F*	*A*	*Pts*	*Pts Av*
1	Manchester C	2017–18	38	32	4	2	106	27	100	2.63
2	Liverpool	2019–20	38	32	3	3	85	33	99	2.61
3	Manchester C	2018–19	38	32	2	4	95	23	98	2.58
4	Chelsea	2004–05	38	29	8	1	72	15	95	2.50
5	Chelsea	2016–17	38	30	3	5	85	33	93	2.45
6	Manchester C	2021–22	38	29	6	3	99	26	93	2.45
7	Manchester U	1999–2000	38	28	7	3	97	45	91	2.39
8	Chelsea	2005–06	38	29	4	5	72	22	91	2.39
9	Arsenal	2003–04	38	26	12	0	73	26	90	2.36
	Manchester U	2008–09	38	28	6	4	68	24	90	2.36
11	Manchester C	2011–12	38	28	5	5	93	29	89	2.34
	Manchester U	2006–07	38	28	5	5	83	27	89	2.34
	Manchester U	2012–13	38	28	5	5	86	43	89	2.34
14	Arsenal	2001–02	38	26	9	3	79	36	87	2.28
	Manchester U	2007–08	38	27	6	5	80	22	87	2.28
	Chelsea	2014–15	38	26	9	3	73	32	87	2.28
17	Chelsea	2009–10	38	27	5	6	103	32	86	2.26
	Manchester C	2013–14	38	27	5	6	102	37	86	2.26
	Manchester C	2020–21	38	27	5	6	83	32	86	2.26
20	Manchester U	1993–94	42	27	11	4	80	38	92	2.19
21	Manchester U	2002–03	38	25	8	5	74	34	83	2.18
22	Manchester U	1995–96	38	25	7	6	73	35	82	2.15
23	Leicester C	2015–16	38	23	12	3	68	36	81	2.13
24	Blackburn R	1994–95	42	27	8	7	80	39	89	2.11
25	Manchester U	2000–01	38	24	8	6	79	31	80	2.10
	Manchester U	2010–11	38	23	11	4	78	37	80	2.10
27	Manchester U	1998–99	38	22	13	3	80	37	79	2.07
28	Arsenal	1997–98	38	23	9	6	68	33	78	2.05
29	Manchester U	1992–93	42	24	12	6	67	31	84	2.00
30	Manchester U	1996–97	38	21	12	5	76	44	75	1.97

PREMIER LEAGUE EVER-PRESENT CLUBS

	P	*W*	*D*	*L*	*F*	*A*	*Pts*
Manchester U	1114	703	257	192	2185	1066	2366
Arsenal	1114	619	284	249	2017	1148	2141
Chelsea	1114	618	284	250	1973	1125	2138
Liverpool	1114	609	282	261	2021	1147	2109
Tottenham H	1114	502	281	369	1745	1438	1787
Everton	1114	418	320	414	1491	1481	1574

TOP TEN PREMIER LEAGUE APPEARANCES

1	Barry, Gareth	653	**6**	Speed, Gary	535
2	Giggs, Ryan	632	**7**	Heskey, Emile	516
3	Lampard, Frank	609	**8**	Schwarzer, Mark	514
4	Milner, James	588	**9**	Carragher, Jamie	508
5	James, David	572	**10**	Neville, Phil	505

TOP TEN PREMIER LEAGUE GOALSCORERS

1	Shearer, Alan	260	**6**	Lampard, Frank	177
2	Rooney, Wayne	208	**7**	Henry, Thierry	175
3	Cole, Andrew	187	**8**	Fowler, Robbie	163
4	Aguero, Sergio	184	**9**	Defoe, Jermain	162
5	Harry Kane	183	**10**	Owen, Michael	150

SCOTTISH PREMIER LEAGUE SINCE 1998–99

	P	*W*	*D*	*L*	*F*	*A*	*Pts*
Celtic	900	660	140	100	2098	666	2120
Rangers	747	507	137	103	1573	602	1648
Aberdeen	900	356	211	333	1127	1140	1279
Motherwell	900	318	193	389	1114	1353	1147
Hearts	824	300	198	288	1004	968	1083
Kilmarnock	862	283	215	364	1024	1229	1064
Hibernian	750	261	201	288	984	1023	984
Dundee U	718	224	198	296	874	1071	867

Rangers deducted 10 pts in 2011–12; Hearts deducted 15 pts in 2013–14; Dundee U deducted 3 pts in 2015–16.

DOMESTIC LANDMARKS 2021–22

AUGUST 2021

14 Mo Salah became the first player to score on the opening day of the Premier League season in five successive seasons. He scored Liverpool's third in the 3-0 defeat of newly promoted Norwich C at Carrow Road.

SEPTEMBER 2021

11 Odsonne Edouard became the fastest goalscoring debutant off the substitutes bench in Premier League history. His 84th minute strike against Tottenham H came only 29 seconds after he appeared as a substitute. Edouard scored again in injury time as Palace ran out 3-0 winners against their London rivals at Selhurst Park.

29 Cristiano Ronaldo broke the all-time appearance record for appearances in the Champions League with his 178th appearance. Ronaldo scored the winner for Manchester U in their 2-1 defeat of Villarreal in the Group F match at Old Trafford. The winning goal came in the fifth minute of injury time to see the Reds come back from a goal behind.

OCTOBER 2021

15 Steve Bruce took charge of his 1000th game as manager when Newcastle U entertained Tottenham H at St James' Park. After taking an early lead through Callum Wilson, Newcastle eventually lost 2-3.

19 Mo Salah became Liverpool's all-time Champions League top goalscorer with 2 goals in the Group B match away to Atletico Madrid. Liverpool won 2-3 at the Estadio Metropolitano and Salah's goals took his overall tally to 31 to overtake Steven Gerrard's total of 30.

NOVEMBER 2021

2 Neil Warnock took charge of his 1062nd game as a manager to overtake Dario Gradi's record of 1061. His milestone was achieved as Middlesbrough went down 3-1 away at Luton T with the home side scoring three quick-fire second half goals to come back from being a goal behind.

5 David Moyes took charge of his 1000th game as manager when West Ham U travelled to Genk in the Europa League. An unfortunate late own goal robbed Moyes of a victory in his landmark game, with the match finishing 2-2.

27 Ellen White made her 100th international appearance for England women in the 1-0 FIFA World Cup qualifying victory over Austria at the Stadium of Light. White scored the only goal of the game after 39 minutes.

30 Ellen White became England Women's all-time record goalscorer scoring a hat-trick in the astonishing 20-0 victory over Latvia at the Keepmoat Stadium. The Manchester C striker has 48 goals and has overtaken Kelly Smith's record of 43.

DECEMBER 2021

2 Cristiano Ronaldo scored his 800th career goal in Manchester U's Premier League victory over Arsenal at Old Trafford. He also scored his 801st goal from the penalty spot as United ran out 3-2 winners.

16 Liverpool became the first club in top-flight history to record 2000 league wins. They defeated Newcastle U 3-1 at Anfield.

19 Manchester C broke Liverpool's 1982 record of the most top-flight wins in a calendar year with their 34th victory over Newcastle U at St James' Park. City also scored the most goals in a calendar year with their fourth goal making it 106 for 2021. They also had the most away victories in a calendar year, 18 breaking Tottenham's record of 17 in 1960.

JANUARY 2022

19 Tottenham H became the latest a losing team won a match in their 3-2 defeat of Leicester C at the King Power Stadium. Behind 2-1 after 94 minutes and 52 seconds, 2 goals from Steven Bergwijn gave Spurs the victory.

FEBRUARY 2022

26 Harry Kane and Son Heung-min broke the Premier League record for combined goals and assists. Kane's pass to Son late in the 4-0 victory at Leeds was the 37th time the pair have combined to score in the Premier League, breaking the previous record of 36 set by Didier Droga and Frank Lampard at Chelsea.

MARCH 2022

1 Jamie Vardy broke Ian Wright's record for the most Premier League goals scored by a player over the age of 30. His late goal sealed a 2-0 win for Leicester C at Burnley.

APRIL 2022

23 Oldham Ath relegated from the Football League to the National League and become the first club to have played in the Premier League to drop into non-league football.

MAY 2022

2 Aleksandar Mitrovic scored his 43rd league goal of the season in Fulham's 7-0 victory over Luton at Craven Cottage. His tally exceeded Guy Wittingham's 42 from the 1992–93 season at Portsmouth to break the Championship's 46-game season record.

EUROPEAN CUP AND CHAMPIONS LEAGUE RECORDS

MOST WINS BY CLUB

Real Madrid	14	1956, 1957, 1958, 1959, 1960, 1966, 1998, 2000, 2002, 2014, 2016, 2017, 2018, 2022.
AC Milan	7	1963, 1969, 1989, 1990, 1994, 2003, 2007.
Liverpool	6	1977, 1978, 1981, 1984, 2005, 2019.
Bayern Munich	6	1974, 1975, 1976, 2001, 2013, 2020.
Barcelona	5	1992, 2006, 2009, 2011, 2015.

MOST APPEARANCES IN FINAL
Real Madrid 17; AC Milan 11; Bayern Munich 11.

MOST FINAL APPEARANCES PER COUNTRY
Spain 30 (19 wins, 11 defeats)
Italy 28 (12 wins, 16 defeats)
England 15 (14 wins, 11 defeats)
Germany 18 (8 wins, 10 defeats)

MOST CHAMPIONS LEAGUE/EUROPEAN CUP APPEARANCES
187 Cristiano Ronaldo (Manchester U, Real Madrid, Juventus, Manchester U)
181 Iker Casillas (Real Madrid, Porto)
157 Xavi (Barcelona)
156 Lionel Messi (Barcelona, Paris Saint-Germain)
151 Ryan Giggs (Manchester U)
144 Raul (Real Madrid, Schalke)
142 Karim Benzema (Lyon, Real Madrid)
139 Paolo Maldini (AC Milan)
136 Thomas Muller (Bayern Munich)
132 Andreas Iniesta (Barcelona)
132 Gianluigi Buffon (Parma, Juventus, Paris Saint-Germain)
131 Clarence Seedorf (Ajax, Real Madrid, Internazionale, AC Milan)
130 Paul Scholes (Manchester U)
130 Manuel Neuer (Schalke 04, Bayern Munich)

MOST WINS WITH DIFFERENT CLUBS
Clarence Seedorf (Ajax) 1995; (Real Madrid) 1998; (AC Milan) 2003, 2007.

MOST WINNERS MEDALS
6 Francisco Gento (Real Madrid) 1956, 1957, 1958, 1959, 1960, 1966.

BIGGEST WINS
European Cup
Real Madrid 8, Sevilla 0, 21.1.1958.
Champions League
HJK Helsinki 10, Bangor C 0, 19.7.2011 *(qualifier)*.
Liverpool 8, Besiktas 0, 6.11.2007.
Real Madrid 8, Malmo 0, 8.12.2015.

MOST SUCCESSIVE APPEARANCES
Champions League
Real Madrid (Spain) 25: 1997–98 to 2021–22.
European Cup
Real Madrid (Spain) 15: 1955–56 to 1969–70.

MOST SUCCESSIVE WINS IN THE CHAMPIONS LEAGUE
Bayern Munich (Germany) 15: 18.9.2019 to 25.11.2020.

LONGEST UNBEATEN RUN IN THE CHAMPIONS LEAGUE
Manchester U (England) 25: 2007–08 to 2009 (Final).

MOST GOALS OVERALL
140 Cristiano Ronaldo (Manchester U, Real Madrid, Juventus, Manchester U).
125 Lionel Messi (Barcelona, Paris Saint Germain).
86 Robert Lewandowski (Borussia Dortmund, Bayern Munich).
86 Karim Benzema (Lyon, Real Madrid).
71 Raul (Real Madrid, Schalke).
60 Ruud van Nistelrooy (PSV Eindhoven, Manchester U, Real Madrid).
59 Andriy Shevchenko (Dynamo Kyiv, AC Milan, Chelsea, Dynamo Kyiv).
51 Thierry Henry (Monaco, Arsenal, Barcelona).
50 Filippo Inzaghi (Juventus, AC Milan).
49 Alfredo Di Stefano (Real Madrid).
49 Zlatan Ibrahimovic (Ajax, Juventus, Internazionale, Barcelona, AC Milan, Paris Saint-Germain).
47 Eusebio (Benfica).

MOST GOALS IN CHAMPIONS LEAGUE MATCH
5 Lionel Messi, Barcelona v Bayer Leverkusen (25, 42, 49, 58, 84 mins) (7-1), 7.3.2012.
5 Luiz Adriano, Shaktar Donetsk v BATE (28, 36, 40, 44, 82 mins) (0-7), 21.10.2014.

MOST GOALS IN ONE SEASON
17 Cristiano Ronaldo 2013–14
16 Cristiano Ronaldo 2015–16
15 Cristiano Ronaldo 2017–18
15 Robert Lewandowski 2019–20
14 Jose Altafini 1962–63
14 Ruud van Nistelrooy 2002–03
14 Lionel Messi 2011–12

MOST GOALS SCORED IN FINALS
7 Alfredo Di Stefano (Real Madrid), 1956 (1), 1957 (1 pen), 1958 (1), 1959 (1), 1960 (3).
7 Ferenc Puskas (Real Madrid), 1960 (4), 1962 (3).

HIGHEST SCORE IN A MATCH
European Cup
14 KR Reykjavik (Iceland) 2 Feyenoord (Netherlands) 12 *(First Round First Leg 1969–70)*
Champions League
12 Borussia Dortmund 8, Legia Warsaw 4
(Group Stage 2016–17)

HIGHEST AGGREGATE IN A MATCH
European Cup
Benfica (Portugal) 18, Stade Dudelange (Luxembourg) 0 – 8-0 (h), 10-0 (a) *(Preliminary Round 1965–66)*
Champions League
Bayern Munich (Germany) 12, Sporting Lisbon (Portugal) 1 – 7-1 (h), 5-0 (a) *(Round of 16 2008–09)*

FASTEST GOALS SCORED IN CHAMPIONS LEAGUE

10.12 sec	Roy Makaay for Bayern Munich v Real Madrid, 7.3.2007.
10.96 sec	Jonas for Valencia v Bayer Leverkusen, 1.11.2011.
20.07 sec	Gilberto Silva for Arsenal at PSV Eindhoven, 25.9.2002.
20.12 sec	Alessandro Del Piero for Juventus at Manchester U, 1.10.1997.

YOUNGEST CHAMPIONS LEAGUE GOALSCORER
Ansu Fati for Barcelona v Internazionale 17 years 40 days in 2019–20.

OLDEST CHAMPIONS LEAGUE GOALSCORER
Francesco Totti for Roma v CSKA Moscow 38 years 59 days in 2014–15.

FASTEST HAT-TRICK SCORED IN CHAMPIONS LEAGUE
Bafetimbi Gomis, 8 mins for Lyon in Dinamo Zagreb v Lyon (1-7) 7.12.2011

MOST GOALS BY A GOALKEEPER
Hans-Jorg Butt (for three different clubs)
Hamburg 13.9.2000, Bayer Leverkusen 12.5.2002, Bayern Munich 8.12.2009 – all achieved against Juventus.

LANDMARK GOALS CHAMPIONS LEAGUE
1st Daniel Amokachi, Club Brugge v CSKA Moscow 17 minutes 25.11.1992
1,000th Dmitri Khokhlov, PSV Eindhoven v Benfica 41 minutes 9.12.1998
5,000th Luisao, Benfica v Hapoel Tel Aviv 21 minutes 14.9.2010

HIGHEST SCORING DRAW
Hamburg 4, Juventus 4, 13.9.2000
Chelsea 4, Liverpool 4, 14.4.2009
Bayer Leverkusen 4, Roma 4, 20.10.2015
Chelsea 4, Ajax 4, 5.11.2019

MOST CLUB CLEAN SHEETS IN ONE SEASON
10: Arsenal 2005–06 (995 minutes with two goalkeepers Manuel Almunia 347 minutes and Jens Lehmann 648 minutes).

EUROPEAN CUP AND CHAMPIONS LEAGUE RECORDS – continued

CHAMPIONS LEAGUE ATTENDANCES AND GOALS FROM GROUP STAGES ONWARDS

Season	*Attendances*	*Average*	*Goals*	*Games*
1992–93	873,251	34,930	56	25
1993–94	1,202,289	44,529	71	27
1994–95	2,328,515	38,172	140	61
1995–96	1,874,316	30,726	159	61
1996–97	2,093,228	34,315	161	61
1997–98	2,868,271	33,744	239	85
1998–99	3,608,331	42,451	238	85
1999–2000	5,490,709	34,973	442	157
2000–01	5,773,486	36,774	449	157
2001–02	5,417,716	34,508	393	157
2002–03	6,461,112	41,154	431	157
2003–04	4,611,214	36,890	309	125
2004–05	4,946,820	39,575	331	125
2005–06	5,291,187	42,330	285	125
2006–07	5,591,463	44,732	309	125
2007–08	5,454,718	43,638	330	125
2008–09	5,003,754	40,030	329	125
2009–10	5,295,708	42,366	320	125
2010–11	5,474,654	43,797	355	125
2011–12	5,225,363	41,803	345	125
2012–13	5,773,366	46,187	368	125
2013–14	5,713,049	45,704	362	125
2014–15	5,207,592	42,685	361	125
2015–16	5,116,690	40,934	347	125
2016–17	5,398,851	43,191	380	125
2017–18	5,744,918	45,959	401	125
2018–19	5,746,629	45,973	366	125
2019–20	4,757,233	44,048	386	119
2020–21	No attendances published		366	125
2021–22	4,394,473	35,439	380	125

HIGHEST AVERAGE ATTENDANCE IN ONE EUROPEAN CUP SEASON

1959–60 50,545 from a total attendance of 2,780,000.

GREATEST COMEBACKS

Werder Bremen beat Anderlecht 5-3 after being three goals down in 33 minutes on 8.12.1993. They scored five goals in 23 second-half minutes.

Deportivo La Coruna beat Paris Saint-Germain 4-3 after being three goals down in 55 minutes on 7.3.2001. They scored four goals in 27 second-half minutes.

Liverpool three goals down to FC Basel in 29 minutes on 12.11.2002. They scored three second half goals in 24 minutes to draw 3-3.

Liverpool after being three goals down to AC Milan in the first half on 25.5.2005 in the Champions League Final. They scored three goals in five second-half minutes and won the penalty shoot-out after extra time 3-2.

MOST SUCCESSFUL MANAGER

Carlo Ancelotti 4 wins, 2002–03, 2006–07 (AC Milan), 2013–14, 2021–22 (Real Madrid).

REINSTATED WINNERS EXCLUDED FROM NEXT COMPETITION

Marseille were originally stripped of the title in 1993. This was rescinded but they were not allowed to compete the following season.

INTERNATIONAL LANDMARKS 2021–22

SEPTEMBER 2021

1 Cristiano Ronaldo became the leading international goalscorer in history following his late equaliser for Portugal against Republic of Ireland. It was Ronaldo's 110th international goal, overtaking Iran's Ali Daei who scored 109. Ronaldo scored another in injury time to take his tally to 111 in the 2-1 World Cup qualifying victory at the Estadio Algarve.

1 Andriy Yarmalenko made his 100th international appearance for Ukraine in the Group D World Cup qualifier against Kazakhstan in Nur-Sultan. Two early goals for Ukraine were wiped out by late strikes from Ruslan Valiullin in a 2-2 draw.

5 Romelu Lukaku made his 100th international appearance for Belgium in the Group E World Cup qualifier against Czech Republic in Brussels. Lukaku scored the opening goal in Belgium's 3-0 victory.

5 Birkir Bjarnason made his 100th international appearance for Iceland in the Group J World Cup qualifier against North Macedonia in Reykjavik. Iceland came from 2-0 behind to draw 2-2.

8 Italy set a new world record for the most games undefeated in their World Cup qualifying 5-0 victory against Lithuania. Italy's total of 37 games unbeaten surpasses Brazil's record of 36 games from 1996.

10 Lionel Messi became the South America's top international goalscorer with 79 goals. His total overtook that of Pele who scored 77. Messi scored all three of Argentina's goals in the 3-0 victory over Bolivia in a World Cup qualifier in Buenos Aires.

12 Jose Mourinho recorded his 1000th game as a manager when his Roma side defeated Sassuolo 2-1 at the Stadio Olimpico in Rome. Roma won the Serie A match with an injury-time strike by Stephan El Shaarawy to send Mourinho into his trademark dash down the touchline. He has recorded an impressive 638 wins, with 204 draws and 158 losses.

OCTOBER 2021

9 Andriy Pyatov made his 100th international appearance for Ukraine in the Group D World Cup qualifier against Finland in Helsinki. His side were 2-1 winners.

10 Thiago Silva made his 100th international appearance for Brazil in the World Cup qualifier against Colombia in Barranquilla. The 0-0 draw ended Brazil's winning run of 9 matches in the South American qualifiers.

11 Antoine Griezmann made his 100th international appearance for France in the Nations League Final against Spain in Milan. After Spain had led through a 64th minute goal from Oyarzabal, Karim Benzema and Kylian Mbappe both scored as Les Bleus triumphed.

NOVEMBER 2021

13 Gareth Bale made his 100th international appearance for Wales in the Group E World Cup qualifier against Belarus at the Cardiff City Stadium where Wales completed a comprehensive 5-1 victory. Bale made his international debut in a friendly win over Trinidad and Tobago on 27 May 2006, becoming the youngest player to play for Wales at 16 years, 315 days. That record was beaten by then Liverpool's Harry Wilson in October 2013.

14 Rui Patricio made his 100th international appearances for Portugal in the Goup A World Cup qualifier against Serbia at Estadio da Luz. Serbia won 2-1 with a last-minute goal by Aleksandar Mitrovic.

14 Andre Ayew made his 100th international appearance for Ghana in the World Cup qualifier against in the Cape Coast. Ayew scored a 33rd minute penalty as Ghana ran out 1-0 winners.

15 Xherdan Shaqiri made his 100th international appearance for Switzerland in the Group C World Cup qualifier against Bulgaria in Lucerne. Switzerland won 4-0 with all the goals coming in the second half.

16 Teemu Pukki made his 100th international appearance for Finland in the Group D World Cup qualifier in Helsinki. France won 2-0 with goals from Benzema and Mbappe.

29 Lionel Messi won the Ballon d'Or for a record seventh time. Robert Lewandowski came in second place.

DECEMBER 2021

17 Robert Lewandowski became the highest goalscorer in a calendar year in the Bundesliga with his 87th minute strike against Wolfsburg, his 43rd of 2021.

JANUARY 2022

14 Axel Kei became the youngest player to sign a first-team contract in MLS history. At 14 years and 15 days his signing broke the previous record held by Freddy Adu at DC United.

MARCH 2022

8 Robert Lewandowski scored the earliest hat-trick in Champions League history with his treble against Salzburg at the Allianz Arena. He scored three in 11 minutes, all coming in the first 23 minutes of the match.

29 Wayne Hennessy made his 100th international appearance for Wales in the friendly match against Czech Republic in Cardiff. The match ended in a 1-1 draw.

29 Granit Xhaka made his 100th international appearance for Switzerland in the friendly match against Kosovo. The match ended 1-1 with Jordan Lotomba scoring the equaliser for Switzerland after Milto Rashica had scored for Kosovo.

APRIL 2022

30 Carlo Ancelotti's Real Madrid win 4-0 at home to Espanyol to win La Liga. Ancelotti became the first coach to win league titles in all of Europe's top five leagues.

MAY 2022

28 Carlo Ancelotti became the first manager to win the Champions League four times. His Real Madrid side defeated Liverpool in the Champions League final in Paris. He has now won the Champions League twice with AC Milan (2003, 2007) and twice with Real Madrid (2014, 2022). He also won the competition twice as a player with AC Milan (1989, 1990). Real Madrid have now won the trophy 14 times (twice as many as any other side in history).

TOP TEN AVERAGE ATTENDANCES

1	Manchester U	2006–07	75,826
2	Manchester U	2007–08	75,691
3	Manchester U	2012–13	75,530
4	Manchester U	2011–12	75,387
5	Manchester U	2014–15	75,335
6	Manchester U	2008–09	75,308
7	Manchester U	2016–17	75,290
8	Manchester U	2015–16	75,279
9	Manchester U	2013–14	75,207
10	Manchester U	2010–11	75,109

TOP TEN AVERAGE WORLD CUP FINALS CROWDS

1	In USA	1994	68,991
2	In Brazil	2014	52,621
3	In Germany	2006	52,491
4	In Mexico	1970	50,124
5	In South Africa	2010	49,669
6	In West Germany	1974	49,098
7	In England	1966	48,847
8	In Italy	1990	48,388
9	In Brazil	1950	47,511
10	In Russia	2018	47,371

TOP TEN ALL-TIME ENGLAND CAPS

1	Peter Shilton	125
2	Wayne Rooney	120
3	David Beckham	115
4	Steven Gerrard	114
5	Bobby Moore	108
6	Ashley Cole	107
7	Bobby Charlton	106
	Frank Lampard	106
9	Billy Wright	105
10	Bryan Robson	90

TOP TEN ALL-TIME ENGLAND GOALSCORERS

1	Wayne Rooney	53
2	Harry Kane	50
3	Bobby Charlton	49
4	Gary Lineker	48
5	Jimmy Greaves	44
6	Michael Owen	40
7	Tom Finney	30
	Nat Lofthouse	30
	Alan Shearer	30
8	Vivian Woodward	29
	Frank Lampard	29

GOALKEEPING RECORDS

(without conceding a goal)

FA PREMIER LEAGUE
Edwin van der Sar (Manchester U) in 1,311 minutes during the 2008–09 season.

FOOTBALL LEAGUE
Steve Death (Reading) 1,103 minutes from 24 March to 18 August 1979.

SCOTTISH PREMIER LEAGUE
Fraser Forster (Celtic) in 1,215 minutes from 6 December 2013 to 25 February 2014.

MOST CLEAN SHEETS IN A SEASON

Petr Cech (Chelsea) 24, 2004–05

MOST CLEAN SHEETS OVERALL IN PREMIER LEAGUE

Petr Cech (Chelsea and Arsenal) 202 games.

MOST GOALS FOR IN A SEASON

FA PREMIER LEAGUE		*Goals*	*Games*
2017–18	Manchester C	106	38
FOOTBALL LEAGUE			
Division 4			
1960–61	Peterborough U	134	46
SCOTTISH PREMIER LEAGUE			
2016–17	Celtic	106	38
SCOTTISH LEAGUE			
Division 2			
1937–38	Raith R	142	34

MOST GOALS AGAINST IN A SEASON

FA PREMIER LEAGUE		*Goals*	*Games*
1993–94	Swindon T	100	42
FOOTBALL LEAGUE			
Division 2			
1898–99	Darwen	141	34
SCOTTISH PREMIER LEAGUE			
1999–2000	Aberdeen	83	36
2007–08	Gretna	83	38
SCOTTISH LEAGUE			
Division 2			
1931–32	Edinburgh C	146	38

MOST LEAGUE GOALS IN A SEASON

FA PREMIER LEAGUE		*Goals*	*Games*
1993–94	Andrew Cole (Newcastle U)	34	40
1994–95	Alan Shearer (Blackburn R)	34	42
2017–18	Mohamed Salah (Liverpool)	32	38
FOOTBALL LEAGUE			
Division 1			
1927–28	Dixie Dean (Everton)	60	39
Division 2			
1926–27	George Camsell (Middlesbrough)	59	37
Division 3(S)			
1936–37	Joe Payne (Luton T)	55	39
Division 3(N)			
1936–37	Ted Harston (Mansfield T)	55	41
Division 3			
1959–60	Derek Reeves (Southampton)	39	46
Division 4			
1960–61	Terry Bly (Peterborough U)	52	46
FA CUP			
1887–88	Jimmy Ross (Preston NE)	20	8
LEAGUE CUP			
1986–87	Clive Allen (Tottenham H)	12	9
SCOTTISH PREMIER LEAGUE			
2000–01	Henrik Larsson (Celtic)	35	37
SCOTTISH LEAGUE			
Division 1			
1931–32	William McFadyen (Motherwell)	52	34
Division 2			
1927–28	Jim Smith (Ayr U)	66	38

MOST FA CUP FINAL GOALS

Ian Rush (Liverpool) 5: 1986(2), 1989(2), 1992(1)

SCORED IN EVERY PREMIERSHIP GAME

Arsenal 2001–02: 38 matches

FEWEST GOALS FOR IN A SEASON

FA PREMIER LEAGUE		*Goals*	*Games*
2007–08	Derby Co	20	38
FOOTBALL LEAGUE			
Division 2			
1899–1900	Loughborough T	18	34
SCOTTISH PREMIERSHIP			
2010–11	St Johnstone	23	38
SCOTTISH LEAGUE			
New Division 1			
1980–81	Stirling Alb	18	39

FEWEST GOALS AGAINST IN A SEASON

FA PREMIER LEAGUE		*Goals*	*Games*
2004–05	Chelsea	15	38
FOOTBALL LEAGUE			
Division 1			
1978–79	Liverpool	16	42
SCOTTISH PREMIERSHIP			
2020–21	Rangers	13	38
SCOTTISH LEAGUE			
Division 1			
1913–14	Celtic	14	38

MOST LEAGUE GOALS IN A CAREER

FOOTBALL LEAGUE			
Arthur Rowley	*Goals*	*Games*	*Season*
WBA	4	24	1946–48
Fulham	27	56	1948–50
Leicester C	251	303	1950–58
Shrewsbury T	152	236	1958–65
	434	619	
SCOTTISH LEAGUE			
Jimmy McGrory			
Celtic	1	3	1922–23
Clydebank	13	30	1923–24
Celtic	396	375	1924–38
	410	408	

MOST HAT-TRICKS

Career
37: Dixie Dean (Tranmere R, Everton, Notts Co, England)

Division 1 (one season post-war)
6: Jimmy Greaves (Chelsea), 1960–61

Three for one team in one match
West, Spouncer, Hooper, Nottingham F v Leicester Fosse, Division 1, 21 April 1909
Loasby, Smith, Wells, Northampton T v Walsall, Division 3S, 5 Nov 1927
Bowater, Hoyland, Readman, Mansfield T v Rotherham U, Division 3N, 27 Dec 1932
Barnes, Ambler, Davies, Wrexham v Hartlepools U, Division 4, 3 March 1962
Adcock, Stewart, White, Manchester C v Huddersfield T, Division 2, 7 Nov 1987

MOST CUP GOALS IN A CAREER

FA CUP (pre-Second World War)
Henry Cursham 48 (Notts Co)

FA CUP (post-war)
Ian Rush 43 (Chester, Liverpool)

LEAGUE CUP
Geoff Hurst 49 (West Ham U, Stoke C)
Ian Rush 49 (Chester, Liverpool, Newcastle U)

GOALS PER GAME (Football League to 1991–92)

Goals per game	Division 1		Division 2		Division 3		Division 4		Division 3(S)		Division 3(N)	
	Games	Goals	Games	Goals	Games	Goals	Games	Goals	Games	Goals	Games	Goals
0	2465	0	2665	0	1446	0	1438	0	997	0	803	0
1	5606	5606	5836	5836	3225	3225	3106	3106	2073	2073	1914	1914
2	8275	16550	8609	17218	4569	9138	4441	8882	3314	6628	2939	5878
3	7731	23193	7842	23526	3784	11352	4041	12123	2996	8988	2922	8766
4	6229	24920	5897	23588	2837	11348	2784	11136	2445	9780	2410	9640
5	3752	18755	3634	18170	1566	7830	1506	7530	1554	7770	1599	7995
6	2137	12822	2007	12042	769	4614	786	4716	870	5220	930	5580
7	1092	7644	1001	7007	357	2499	336	2352	451	3157	461	3227
8	542	4336	376	3008	135	1080	143	1144	209	1672	221	1768
9	197	1773	164	1476	64	576	35	315	76	684	102	918
10	83	830	68	680	13	130	8	80	33	330	45	450
11	37	407	19	209	2	22	7	77	15	165	15	165
12	12	144	17	204	1	12	0	0	7	84	8	96
13	4	52	4	52	0	0	0	0	2	26	4	52
14	2	28	1	14	0	0	0	0	0	0	0	0
17	0	0	0	0	0	0	0	0	0	0	1	17
	38164	**117060**	**38140**	**113030**	**18768**	**51826**	**18631**	**51461**	**15042**	**46577**	**14374**	**46466**

Extensive research by statisticians has unearthed seven results from the early years of the Football League which differ from the original scores. These are 26 January 1889 Wolverhampton W 5 Everton 0 (not 4-0), 16 March 1889 Notts Co 3 Derby Co 5 (not 2-5), 4 January 1896 Arsenal 5 Loughborough 0 (not 6-0), 28 November 1896 Leicester Fosse 4 Walsall 2 (not 4-1), 21 April 1900 Burslem Port Vale 2 Lincoln C 1 (not 2-0), 25 December 1902 Glossop NE 3 Stockport Co 0 (not 3-1), 26 April 1913 Hull C 2 Leicester C 0 (not 2-1).

GOALS PER GAME (from 1992–93)

Goals per game	Premier		Championship/Div 1		League One/Div 2		League Two/Div 3	
	Games	Goals	Games	Goals	Games	Goals	Games	Goals
0	955	0	1348	0	1272	0	1326	0
1	2095	2095	3126	3126	3061	3061	3164	3164
2	2820	5640	4200	8400	4159	8318	4099	8198
3	2481	7443	3602	10806	3604	10812	3538	10614
4	1737	6948	2273	9092	2274	9096	2181	8724
5	885	4425	1223	6115	1236	6180	1136	5680
6	406	2436	524	3144	518	3108	456	2736
7	170	1190	186	1302	200	1400	192	1344
8	69	552	58	464	58	464	54	432
9	22	198	11	99	20	180	22	198
10	5	50	7	70	6	60	7	70
11	1	11	2	22	0	0	3	33
	11646	**30988**	**16560**	**42640**	**16408**	**42679**	**16178**	**41193**

New Overall Totals (since 1992)		Totals (up to 1991–92)		Complete Overall Totals (since 1888–89)	
Games	60792	Games	143119	Games	203911
Goals	157500	Goals	426420	Goals	583920
Goals per game	2.59		2.98		2.86

A CENTURY OF LEAGUE AND CUP GOALS IN CONSECUTIVE SEASONS

	League	Cup	Season
George Camsell			
Middlesbrough	59	5	1926–27
(101 goals)	33	4	1927–28

(Camsell's cup goals were all scored in the FA Cup.)

	League	Cup	Season
Steve Bull			
Wolverhampton W	34	18	1987–88
(102 goals)	37	13	1988–89

(Bull had 12 in the Sherpa Van Trophy, 3 Littlewoods Cup, 3 FA Cup in 1987–88; 11 Sherpa Van Trophy, 2 Littlewoods Cup in 1988–89.)

PENALTIES

Most in a season (individual)

Division 1	*Goals*	*Season*
Francis Lee (Manchester C)	13	1971–72

Also scored 2 cup goals.

Most awarded in one game

5 Crystal Palace (1 scored, 3 missed) v Brighton & HA (1 scored), Div 2 1988–89

Most saved in a season

Division 1

Paul Cooper (Ipswich T) 8 (of 10) 1979–80

MOST GOALS IN A GAME

FA PREMIER LEAGUE

4 Mar 1995	Andrew Cole (Manchester U) 5 goals v Ipswich T
19 Sept 1999	Alan Shearer (Newcastle U) 5 goals v Sheffield W
22 Nov 2009	Jermain Defoe (Tottenham H) 5 goals v Wigan Ath
27 Nov 2010	Dimitar Berbatov (Manchester U) 5 goals v Blackburn R
3 Oct 2015	Sergio Aguero (Manchester C) 5 goals v Newcastle U

FOOTBALL LEAGUE

Division 1

14 Dec 1935	Ted Drake (Arsenal) 7 goals v Aston Villa

Division 2

5 Feb 1955	Tommy Briggs (Blackburn R) 7 goals v Bristol R
23 Feb 1957	Neville Coleman (Stoke C) 7 goals v Lincoln C

Division 3(S)

13 Apr 1936	Joe Payne (Luton T) 10 goals v Bristol R

Division 3(N)

26 Dec 1935	Bunny Bell (Tranmere R) 9 goals v Oldham Ath

Division 3

24 Apr 1965	Barrie Thomas (Scunthorpe U) 5 goals v Luton T
20 Nov 1965	Keith East (Swindon T) 5 goals v Mansfield T
16 Sept 1969	Steve Earle (Fulham) 5 goals v Halifax T
2 Oct 1971	Alf Wood (Shrewsbury T) 5 goals v Blackburn R
10 Sept 1983	Tony Caldwell (Bolton W) 5 goals v Walsall
4 May 1987	Andy Jones (Port Vale) 5 goals v Newport Co
3 Apr 1990	Steve Wilkinson (Mansfield T) 5 goals v Birmingham C
5 Sept 1998	Giuliano Grazioli (Peterborough U) 5 goals v Barnet
6 Apr 2002	Lee Jones (Wrexham) 5 goals v Cambridge U

Division 4

26 Dec 1962	Bert Lister (Oldham Ath) 6 goals v Southport

FA CUP

20 Nov 1971	Ted MacDougall (Bournemouth) 9 goals v Margate (*1st Round*)

LEAGUE CUP

25 Oct 1989	Frankie Bunn (Oldham Ath) 6 goals v Scarborough

SCOTTISH LEAGUE

Premier Division

17 Nov 1984	Paul Sturrock (Dundee U) 5 goals v Morton

Premier League

23 Aug 1996	Marco Negri (Rangers) 5 goals v Dundee U
4 Nov 2000	Kenny Miller (Rangers) 5 goals v St Mirren
25 Sept 2004	Kris Boyd (Kilmarnock) 5 goals v Dundee U
30 Dec 2009	Kris Boyd (Rangers) 5 goals v Dundee U
13 May 2012	Gary Hooper (Celtic) 5 goals v Hearts

Division 1

14 Sept 1928	Jimmy McGrory (Celtic) 8 goals v Dunfermline Ath

Division 2

1 Oct 1927	Owen McNally (Arthurlie) 8 goals v Armadale
2 Jan 1930	Jim Dyet (King's Park) 8 goals v Forfar Ath
18 Apr 1936	John Calder (Morton) 8 goals v Raith R
20 Aug 1937	Norman Hayward (Raith R) 8 goals v Brechin C

SCOTTISH CUP

12 Sept 1885	John Petrie (Arbroath) 13 goals v Bon Accord (*1st Round*)

LONGEST SEQUENCE OF CONSECUTIVE DEFEATS

FOOTBALL LEAGUE Division 2	*Team*	*Games*
1898–99	Darwen	18

LONGEST UNBEATEN SEQUENCE

FA PREMIER LEAGUE	*Team*	*Games*
May 2003–Oct 2004	Arsenal	49
FOOTBALL LEAGUE – League 1		
Jan 2011–Nov 2011	Huddersfield T	43

LONGEST UNBEATEN CUP SEQUENCE

Liverpool 25 rounds League Cup 1980–84

LONGEST UNBEATEN SEQUENCE IN A SEASON

FA PREMIER LEAGUE	*Team*	*Games*
2003–04	Arsenal	38
FOOTBALL LEAGUE – Division 1		
1920–21	Burnley	30
SCOTTISH PREMIERSHIP		
2016–17	Celtic	38

LONGEST UNBEATEN START TO A SEASON

FA PREMIER LEAGUE	*Team*	*Games*
2003–04	Arsenal	38
FOOTBALL LEAGUE – Division 1		
1973–74	Leeds U	29
1987–88	Liverpool	29

LONGEST SEQUENCE WITHOUT A WIN IN A SEASON

FA PREMIER LEAGUE	*Team*	*Games*
2007–08	Derby Co	32

FOOTBALL LEAGUE Division 2	*Team*	*Games*
1983–84	Cambridge U	31

LONGEST SEQUENCE WITHOUT A WIN FROM SEASON'S START

FOOTBALL LEAGUE Division 4	*Team*	*Games*
1970–71	Newport Co	25

LONGEST SEQUENCE OF CONSECUTIVE SCORING (individual)

FA PREMIER LEAGUE

Jamie Vardy (Leicester C)	13 in 11 games	2015–16
FOOTBALL LEAGUE RECORD		
Tom Phillipson (Wolverhampton W)	23 in 13 games	1926–27

LONGEST WINNING SEQUENCE

FA PREMIER LEAGUE	*Team*	*Games*
2017–18	Manchester C	18
2019–20	Liverpool	18
FOOTBALL LEAGUE – Division 2		
1904–05	Manchester U	14
1905–06	Bristol C	14
1950–51	Preston NE	14
FROM SEASON'S START – Division 3		
1985–86	Reading	13
SCOTTISH PREMIER LEAGUE		
2003–04	Celtic	25

HIGHEST WINS

Highest win in a First-Class Match
(Scottish Cup 1st Round)

Arbroath	36	Bon Accord	0	12 Sept 1885

Highest win in an International Match

England	13	Ireland	0	18 Feb 1882

Highest win in an FA Cup Match

Preston NE	26	Hyde U	0	15 Oct 1887

(1st Round)

Highest win in a League Cup Match

West Ham U	10	Bury	0	25 Oct 1983
(2nd Round, 2nd Leg)				
Liverpool	10	Fulham	0	23 Sept 1986
(2nd Round, 1st Leg)				

Highest win in an FA Premier League Match

Manchester U	9	Ipswich T	0	4 Mar 1995
Manchester U	9	Southampton	0	2 Jan 2021
Southampton	0	Leicester C	9	25 Oct 2019
Tottenham H	9	Wigan Ath	1	22 Nov 2009

Highest win in a Football League Match

Division 2 – highest home win

Newcastle U	13	Newport Co	0	5 Oct 1946

Division 3(N) – highest home win

Stockport Co	13	Halifax T	0	6 Jan 1934

Division 2 – highest away win

Burslem Port Vale	0	Sheffield U	10	10 Dec 1892

Highest wins in a Scottish League Match

Scottish Premiership – highest home win

Celtic	9	Aberdeen	0	6 Nov 2010

Scottish Division 2 – highest home win

Airdrieonians	15	Dundee W	1	1 Dec 1894

Scottish Premiership – highest away win

Hamilton A	0	Celtic	8	5 Nov 1988

MOST HOME WINS IN A SEASON

Brentford won all 21 games in Division 3(S), 1929–30

RECORD AWAY WINS IN A SEASON

Doncaster R won 18 of 21 games in Division 3(N), 1946–47

CONSECUTIVE AWAY WINS

FA PREMIER LEAGUE
Manchester C 12 games (2020–21)

FOOTBALL LEAGUE
Division 1
Tottenham H 10 games (1959–60 (2), 1960–61 (8))

HIGHEST AGGREGATE SCORES

FA PREMIER LEAGUE

Portsmouth	7	Reading	4	29 Sept 2007

Highest Aggregate Score England
Division 3(N)

Tranmere R	13	Oldham Ath	4	26 Dec 1935

Highest Aggregate Score Scotland
Division 2

Airdrieonians	15	Dundee Wanderers	1	1 Dec 1894

FEWEST WINS IN A SEASON

FA PREMIER LEAGUE		*Wins*	*Games*
2007–08	Derby Co	1	38
FOOTBALL LEAGUE			
Division 2			
1899–1900	Loughborough T	1	34
SCOTTISH PREMIER LEAGUE			
1998–99	Dunfermline Ath	4	36
SCOTTISH LEAGUE			
Division 1			
1891–92	Vale of Leven	0	22

MOST WINS IN A SEASON

FA PREMIER LEAGUE		*Wins*	*Games*
2017–18	Manchester C	32	38
2018–19	Manchester C	32	38
2019–20	Liverpool	32	38
FOOTBALL LEAGUE			
Division 3(N)			
1946–47	Doncaster R	33	42
SCOTTISH PREMIERSHIP			
2016–17	Celtic	34	38
SCOTTISH LEAGUE			
Division 1			
1920–21	Rangers	35	42

UNDEFEATED AT HOME OVERALL

Liverpool 85 games (63 League, 9 League Cup, 7 European, 6 FA Cup), Jan 1978–Jan 1981

UNDEFEATED AT HOME LEAGUE

Chelsea 86 games, Mar 2004–Oct 2008

UNDEFEATED AWAY

Arsenal 19 games, FA Premier League 2001–02 and 2003–04 (only Preston NE with 11 in 1888–89 had previously remained unbeaten away) in the top flight.

MOST POINTS IN A SEASON

(three points for a win)

FA PREMIER LEAGUE		*Points*	*Games*
2017–18	Manchester C	100	38
FOOTBALL LEAGUE			
Championship			
2005–06	Reading	106	46
SCOTTISH PREMIER LEAGUE			
2001–02	Celtic	103	38
SCOTTISH LEAGUE			
League One			
2013–14	Rangers	102	36

MOST POINTS IN A SEASON

(under old system of two points for a win)

FOOTBALL LEAGUE		*Points*	*Games*
Division 4			
1975–76	Lincoln C	74	46
SCOTTISH LEAGUE			
Division 1			
1920–21	Rangers	76	42

FEWEST POINTS IN A SEASON

FA PREMIER LEAGUE		*Points*	*Games*
2007–08	Derby Co	11	38
FOOTBALL LEAGUE			
Division 2			
1904–05	Doncaster R	8	34
1899–1900	Loughborough T	8	34
SCOTTISH PREMIER LEAGUE			
2007–08	Gretna	13	38
SCOTTISH LEAGUE			
Division 1			
1954–55	Stirling Alb	6	30

NO DEFEATS IN A SEASON

FA PREMIER LEAGUE

2003–04	Arsenal	won 26, drew 12

FOOTBALL LEAGUE

Division 1

1888–89	Preston NE	won 18, drew 4

Division 2

1893–94	Liverpool	won 22, drew 6

SCOTTISH LEAGUE

Premiership

2016–17	Celtic	won 34, drew 4
2020–21	Rangers	won 32, drew 6

Division 1

1898–99	Rangers	won 18

League One

2013–14	Rangers	won 33, drew 3

ONE DEFEAT IN A SEASON

FA PREMIER LEAGUE		*Defeats*	*Games*
2004–05	Chelsea	1	38
2018–19	Liverpool	1	38
FOOTBALL LEAGUE			
Division 1			
1990–91	Arsenal	1	38
SCOTTISH PREMIERSHIP			
2001–02	Celtic	1	38
2013–14	Celtic	1	38
SCOTTISH LEAGUE			
Division 1			
1920–21	Rangers	1	42
Division 2			
1956–57	Clyde	1	36
1962–63	Morton	1	36
1967–68	St Mirren	1	36
New Division 1			
2011–12	Ross Co	1	36
New Division 2			
1975–76	Raith R	1	26

MOST DEFEATS IN A SEASON

FA PREMIER LEAGUE		*Defeats*	*Games*
1994–95	Ipswich T	29	42
2005–06	Sunderland	29	38
2007–08	Derby Co	29	38
2020–21	Sheffield U	29	38
FOOTBALL LEAGUE			
Division 3			
1997–98	Doncaster R	34	46
SCOTTISH PREMIERSHIP			
2005–06	Livingston	28	38
SCOTTISH LEAGUE			
New Division 1			
1992–93	Cowdenbeath	34	44

MOST DRAWN GAMES IN A SEASON

FA PREMIER LEAGUE		*Draws*	*Games*
1993–94	Manchester C	18	42
1993–94	Sheffield U	18	42
1994–95	Southampton	18	42
FOOTBALL LEAGUE			
Division 1			
1978–79	Norwich C	23	42
Division 3			
1997–98	Cardiff C	23	46
1997–98	Hartlepool U	23	46
Division 4			
1986–87	Exeter C	23	46
SCOTTISH PREMIER LEAGUE			
1998–99	Dunfermline Ath	16	38
SCOTTISH LEAGUE			
Premier Division			
1993–94	Aberdeen	21	44
New Division 1			
1986–87	East Fife	21	44

SENDINGS-OFF

SEASON

451 (League alone) 2003–04
(Before rescinded cards taken into account)

DAY

19 (League) 13 Dec 2003

FA CUP FINAL

Kevin Moran, Manchester U v Everton	1985
Jose Antonio Reyes, Arsenal v Manchester U	2005
Pablo Zabaleta, Manchester C v Wigan Ath	2013
Chris Smalling, Manchester U v Crystal Palace	2016
Victor Moses, Chelsea v Arsenal	2017
Mateo Kovacic, Chelsea v Arsenal	2020

QUICKEST

FA Premier League

Andreas Johansson, Wigan Ath v Arsenal (7 May 2006) and Keith Gillespie, Sheffield U v Reading (20 January 2007) both in 10 seconds

Football League

Walter Boyd, Swansea C v Darlington, Div 3 as substitute in zero seconds 23 Nov 1999

MOST IN ONE GAME

Five: Chesterfield (2) v Plymouth Arg (3)	22 Feb 1997
Five: Wigan Ath (1) v Bristol R (4)	2 Dec 1997
Five: Exeter C (3) v Cambridge U (2)	23 Nov 2002
Five: Bradford C (3) v Crawley T (2)*	27 Mar 2012

**All five sent off after final whistle for fighting*

MOST IN ONE TEAM

Wigan Ath (1) v Bristol R (4)	2 Dec 1997
Hereford U (4) v Northampton T (0)	6 Sept 1992

MOST SUCCESSFUL MANAGERS

Sir Alex Ferguson CBE
Manchester U
1986–2013, 25 major trophies:
13 Premier League, 5 FA Cup, 4 League Cup, 2 Champions League, 1 Cup-Winners' Cup.

Aberdeen
1976–86, 9 major trophies:
3 League, 4 Scottish Cup, 1 League Cup, 1 Cup Winners' Cup.

Bob Paisley – Liverpool
1974–83, 13 major trophies:
6 League, 3 European Cup, 3 League Cup, 1 UEFA Cup.

Bill Struth – Rangers
1920–54, 30 major trophies:
18 League, 10 Scottish Cup, 2 League Cup.

LEAGUE CHAMPIONSHIP HAT-TRICKS

Huddersfield T	1923–24 to 1925–26
Arsenal	1932–33 to 1934–35
Liverpool	1981–82 to 1983–84
Manchester U	1998–99 to 2000–01
Manchester U	2006–07 to 2008–09

MOST FA CUP WINNERS MEDALS

Ashley Cole 7 (Arsenal 2002, 2003, 2005; Chelsea 2007, 2009, 2010, 2012).

MOST LEAGUE WINNERS MEDALS

Ryan Giggs (Manchester U) 13: 1993, 1994, 1996, 1997, 1999, 2000, 2001, 2003, 2007, 2008, 2009, 2011 and 2013.

MOST SENIOR MATCHES

1,390 Peter Shilton (1,005 League, 86 FA Cup, 102 League Cup, 125 Internationals, 13 Under-23, 4 Football League XI, 20 European Cup, 7 Texaco Cup, 5 Simod Cup, 4 European Super Cup, 4 UEFA Cup, 3 Screen Sport Super Cup, 3 Zenith Data Systems Cup, 2 Autoglass Trophy, 2 Charity Shield, 2 Full Members Cup, 1 Anglo-Italian Cup, 1 Football League play-offs, 1 World Club Championship)

MOST LEAGUE APPEARANCES (750+)

1,005 Peter Shilton (286 Leicester C, 110 Stoke C, 202 Nottingham F, 188 Southampton, 175 Derby Co, 34 Plymouth Arg, 1 Bolton W, 9 Leyton Orient) 1966–97
931 Tony Ford (355 Grimsby T, 9 Sunderland (loan), 112 Stoke C, 114 WBA, 68 Grimsby T, 5 Bradford C (loan), 76 Scunthorpe U, 103 Mansfield T, 89 Rochdale) 1975–2002
909 Graeme Armstrong (204 Stirling A, 83 Berwick Rangers, 353 Meadowbank Thistle, 268 Stenhousemuir, 1 Alloa Ath) 1975–2001
863 Tommy Hutchison (165 Blackpool, 314 Coventry C, 46 Manchester C, 92 Burnley, 178 Swansea C, 68 Alloa Ath) 1965–91
833 Graham Alexander (159 Scunthorpe U, 150 Luton T, 370 Preston NE, 154 Burnley) 1990–2012
824 Terry Paine (713 Southampton, 111 Hereford U) 1957–77
790 Neil Redfearn (35 Bolton W, 10 Lincoln C (loan), 90 Lincoln C, 46 Doncaster R, 57 Crystal Palace, 24 Watford, 62 Oldham Ath, 292 Barnsley, 30 Charlton Ath, 17 Bradford C, 22 Wigan Ath, 42 Halifax T, 54 Boston U, 9 Rochdale) 1982–2004
788 David James (89 Watford, 214 Liverpool, 67 Aston Villa, 91 West Ham U, 93 Manchester C, 134 Portsmouth, 81 Bristol C, 19 Bournemouth) 1988–2013
782 Robbie James (484 Swansea C, 48 Stoke C, 87 QPR, 23 Leicester C, 89 Bradford C, 51 Cardiff C) 1973–94
777 Alan Oakes (565 Manchester C, 211 Chester C, 1 Port Vale) 1959–84
774 Dave Beasant (340 Wimbledon, 20 Newcastle U, 133 Chelsea, 6 Grimsby T (loan), 4 Wolverhampton W (loan), 88 Southampton, 139 Nottingham F, 27 Portsmouth, 1 Tottenham H (loan), 16 Brighton & HA) 1979–2003
771 John Burridge (27 Workington, 134 Blackpool, 65 Aston Villa, 6 Southend U (loan), 88 Crystal Palace, 39 QPR, 74 Wolverhampton W, 6 Derby Co (loan), 109 Sheffield U, 62 Southampton, 67 Newcastle U, 65 Hibernian, 3 Scarborough, 4 Lincoln C, 3 Aberdeen, 3 Dumbarton, 3 Falkirk, 4 Manchester C, 3 Darlington, 6 Queen of the S) 1968–96
770 John Trollope (all for Swindon T) 1960–80†
768 Dean Lewington (29 Wimbledon, 739 Milton Keynes D) 2002-22
764 Jimmy Dickinson (all for Portsmouth) 1946–65
764 Peter Clarke (9 Everton, 13 Port Vale (loan), 139 Blackpool, 5 Coventry C (loan), 126 Southend U, 192 Huddersfield T, 63 Bury, 107 Oldham Ath, 12 Fleetwood T, 98 Tranmere R) 1998-2022
763 Stuart McCall (395 Bradford C, 103 Everton, 194 Rangers, 71 Sheffield U) 1982–2004
761 Roy Sproson (all for Port Vale) 1950–72
760 Mick Tait (64 Oxford U, 106 Carlisle U, 33 Hull C, 240 Portsmouth, 99 Reading, 79 Darlington, 139 Hartlepool U) 1975–97
758 Ray Clemence (48 Scunthorpe U, 470 Liverpool, 240 Tottenham H) 1966–87
758 Billy Bonds (95 Charlton Ath, 663 West Ham U) 1964–88
757 Pat Jennings (48 Watford, 472 Tottenham H, 237 Arsenal) 1963–86
757 Frank Worthington (171 Huddersfield T, 210 Leicester C, 84 Bolton W, 75 Birmingham C, 32 Leeds U, 19 Sunderland, 34 Southampton, 31 Brighton & HA, 59 Tranmere R, 23 Preston NE, 19 Stockport Co) 1966–88
755 Jamie Cureton (98 Norwich C, 5 Bournemouth (loan), 174 Bristol R, 108 Reading, 43 QPR, 30 Swindon T, 52 Colchester U, 8 Barnsley (loan), 12 Shrewsbury T (loan), 88 Exeter C, 19 Leyton Orient, 35 Cheltenham T, 83 Dagenham & R) 1992–2016
753 Andy Millen (71 St Johnstone, 111 Alloa Ath, 119 Hamilton A, 57 Kilmarnock, 51, Hibernian, 18 Raith R, 60 Ayr U, 44 Greenock Morton, 89 Clyde, 114 St Mirren, 19 Queen's Park) 1986–2012
752 Wayne Allison (84 Halifax T, 7 Watford, 195 Bristol C, 101 Swindon T, 74 Huddersfield T, 103 Tranmere R, 73 Sheffield U, 115 Chesterfield) 1987–2008

† *record for one club*

CONSECUTIVE

401 Harold Bell (401 Tranmere R; 459 in all games) 1946–55

YOUNGEST PLAYERS

FA Premier League appearance
Harvey Elliott, 16 years 30 days, Wolves v Fulham, 4.5.2019

FA Premier League scorer
James Vaughan, 16 years 271 days, Everton v Crystal Palace 10.4.2005

Football League appearance
Reuben Noble-Lazarus, 15 years 45 days, Barnsley v Ipswich T, FL Championship 30.9.2008

Football League scorer
Ronnie Dix, 15 years 180 days, Bristol Rovers v Norwich C, Division 3S, 3.3.1928

FA Cup appearance (any round)
Andy Awford, 15 years 88 days as substitute Worcester City v Boreham Wood, 3rd Qual. rd, 10.10.1987

FA Cup goalscorer
Midas Smalls, 16 years, 63 days, Whitton U v Ipswich W (Extra Preliminary Round), 1.9.2021.

FA Cup appearance (competition rounds)
Luke Freeman, 15 years 233 days, Gillingham v Barnet, 10.11.2007

FA Cup Final appearance
Curtis Weston, 17 years 119 days, Millwall v Manchester U, 22.5.2004

FA Cup Final scorer
Norman Whiteside, 18 years 18 days, Manchester United v Brighton & HA, 1983

FA Cup Final captain
David Nish, 21 years 212 days, Leicester C v Manchester C, 1969

League Cup appearance
Harvey Elliott, 15 years and 174 days, Millwall v Fulham (Third Round), 25.9.18.

League Cup goalscorer
Connor Wickham, 16 years 133 days, Ipswich T v Shrewsbury T, 11.8.2009

League Cup Final scorer
Norman Whiteside, 17 years 324 days, Manchester U v Liverpool, 1983

League Cup Final captain
Barry Venison, 20 years 7 months 8 days, Sunderland v Norwich C, 1985

Scottish Premiership appearance
Dylan Reid, 16 years 5 days, St Mirren v Rangers, 6.3.2021

Scottish Football League appearance
Jordan Allan, 14 years 189 days, Airdrie U v Livingston, 26.4.2013

Scottish Premiership scorer
Fraser Fyvie, 16 years 306 days, Aberdeen v Hearts, 27.1.2010

OLDEST PLAYERS

FA Premier League appearance
John Burridge, 43 years 162 days, Manchester C v QPR, 14.5.95

Football League appearance
Neil McBain, 52 years 4 months, New Brighton v Hartlepools U, Div 3N, 15.3.47 (McBain was New Brighton's manager and had to play in an emergency)

Division 1 appearance
Stanley Matthews, 50 years 5 days, Stoke C v Fulham, 6.2.65

INTERNATIONAL RECORDS

MOST GOALS IN AN INTERNATIONAL

Record/World Cup	Archie Thompson (Australia) 13 goals v American Samoa	11.4.2001
England	Howard Vaughton (Aston Villa) 5 goals v Ireland, at Belfast	18.2.1882
	Steve Bloomer (Derby Co) 5 goals v Wales, at Cardiff	16.3.1896
	Willie Hall (Tottenham H) 5 goals v N. Ireland, at Old Trafford	16.11.1938
	Malcolm Macdonald (Newcastle U) 5 goals v Cyprus, at Wembley	16.4.1975
Northern Ireland	Joe Bambrick (Linfield) 6 goals v Wales, at Belfast	1.2.1930
Wales	John Price (Wrexham) 4 goals v Ireland, at Wrexham	25.2.1882
	John Doughty (Newton Heath) 4 goals v Ireland, at Wrexham	3.3.1888
	Mel Charles (Cardiff C) 4 goals v N. Ireland, at Cardiff	11.4.1962
	Ian Edwards (Chester) 4 goals v Malta, at Wrexham	25.10.1978
Scotland	Alexander Higgins (Kilmarnock) 4 goals v Ireland, at Hampden Park	14.3.1885
	Charles Heggie (Rangers) 4 goals v Ireland, at Belfast	20.3.1886
	William Dickson (Dundee Strathmore) 4 goals v Ireland, at Belfast	24.3.1888
	William Paul (Partick Thistle) 4 goals v Wales, at Paisley	22.3.1890
	Jake Madden (Celtic) 4 goals v Wales, at Wrexham	18.3.1893
	Duke McMahon (Celtic) 4 goals v Ireland, at Celtic Park	23.2.1901
	Bob Hamilton (Rangers) 4 goals v Ireland, at Celtic Park	23.2.1901
	Jimmy Quinn (Celtic) 4 goals v Ireland, at Dublin	14.3.1908
	Hughie Gallacher (Newcastle U) 4 goals v N. Ireland, at Belfast	23.2.1929
	Billy Steel (Dundee) 4 goals v N. Ireland, at Hampden Park	1.11.1950
	Denis Law (Manchester U) 4 goals v N. Ireland, at Hampden Park	7.11.1962
	Denis Law (Manchester U) 4 goals v Norway, at Hampden Park	7.11.1963
	Colin Stein (Rangers) 4 goals v Cyprus, at Hampden Park	17.5.1969

MOST GOALS IN AN INTERNATIONAL CAREER

		Goals	*Games*
England	Wayne Rooney (Everton, Manchester U)	53	120
Scotland	Denis Law (Huddersfield T, Manchester C, Torino, Manchester U)	30	55
	Kenny Dalglish (Celtic, Liverpool)	30	102
Northern Ireland	David Healy (Manchester U, Preston NE, Leeds U, Fulham, Sunderland, Rangers, Bury)	36	95
Wales	Gareth Bale (Southampton, Tottenham H, Real Madrid)	39	106
Republic of Ireland	Robbie Keane (Wolverhampton W, Coventry C, Internazionale, Leeds U, Tottenham H, Liverpool, Tottenham H, LA Galaxy)	68	146

HIGHEST SCORES

World Cup Match	Australia	31	American Samoa	0	2001
European Championship	San Marino	0	Germany	13	2006
Olympic Games	Denmark	17	France	1	1908
	Germany	16	Russia	0	1912
Olympic Qualifying Tournament	Vanuatu	46	Micronesia	0	2015
Other International Match	Libya	21	Oman	0	1966
	Abandoned after 80 minutes as Oman refused to play on.				
European Cup	KR Reykjavik	2	Feyenoord	12	1969
European Cup-Winners' Cup	Sporting Lisbon	16	Apoel Nicosia	1	1963
Fairs & UEFA Cups	Ajax	14	Red Boys Differdange	0	1984

GOALSCORING RECORDS

World Cup Final	Geoff Hurst (England) 3 goals v West Germany	1966
World Cup Final tournament	Just Fontaine (France) 13 goals	1958
World Cup career	Miroslav Klose (Germany) 16 goals	2002, 2006, 2010, 2014
Career	Artur Friedenreich (Brazil) 1,329 goals	1910–30
	Pele (Brazil) 1,281 goals	*1956–78
	Franz 'Bimbo' Binder (Austria, Germany) 1,006 goals	1930–50
World Cup Finals fastest	Hakan Sukur (Turkey) 10.8 secs v South Korea	2002

**Pele subsequently scored two goals in Testimonial matches making his total 1,283.*

MOST CAPPED INTERNATIONALS IN BRITAIN AND IRELAND

Republic of Ireland	Robbie Keane	146 appearances	1998–2016
Northern Ireland	Steven Davis	138 appearances	2005–22
England	Peter Shilton	125 appearances	1970–90
Wales	Chris Gunter	109 appearances	2007–2022
Scotland	Kenny Dalglish	102 appearances	1971–86

THE PREMIER LEAGUE AND FOOTBALL LEAGUE FIXTURES 2022–23

All fixtures subject to change.

Community Shield

Saturday, 20 July 2022
Liverpool v Manchester C (17:00)

Premier League

Friday, 5 August 2022
Crystal Palace v Arsenal (20:00)

Saturday, 6 August 2022
Fulham v Liverpool
Bournemouth v Aston Villa
Leeds U v Wolverhampton W
Leicester C v Brentford
Newcastle U v Nottingham F
Tottenham H v Southampton
Everton v Chelsea (17:50)

Sunday, 7 August 2022
Manchester U v Brighton & HA (14:00)
West Ham U v Manchester C (16:30)

Saturday, 13 August 2022
Arsenal v Leicester C
Aston Villa v Everton
Brentford v Manchester U
Brighton & HA v Newcastle U
Chelsea v Tottenham H
Liverpool v Crystal Palace
Manchester C v Bournemouth
Nottingham F v West Ham U
Southampton v Leeds U
Wolverhampton W v Fulham

Saturday, 20 August 2022
Bournemouth v Arsenal
Crystal Palace v Aston Villa
Everton v Nottingham F
Fulham v Brentford
Leeds U v Chelsea
Leicester C v Southampton
Manchester U v Liverpool
Newcastle U v Manchester C
Tottenham H v Wolverhampton W
West Ham U v Brighton & HA

Saturday, 27 August 2022
Arsenal v Fulham
Aston Villa v West Ham U
Brentford v Everton
Brighton & HA v Leeds U
Chelsea v Leicester C
Liverpool v Bournemouth
Manchester C v Crystal Palace
Nottingham F v Tottenham H
Southampton v Manchester U
Wolverhampton W v Newcastle U

Tuesday, 30 August 2022
Bournemouth v Wolverhampton W (19:45)
Arsenal v Aston Villa (19:45)
Fulham v Brighton & HA (19:45)
Leeds U v Everton (19:45)
Leicester C v Manchester U (19:45)
West Ham U v Tottenham H (19:45)
Crystal Palace v Brentford (20:00)

Wednesday, 31 August 2022
Southampton v Chelsea (19:45)
Liverpool v Newcastle U (20:00)
Manchester C v Nottingham F (20:00)

Saturday, 3 September 2022
Aston Villa v Manchester C
Brentford v Leeds U
Brighton & HA v Leicester C
Chelsea v West Ham U
Everton v Liverpool
Manchester U v Arsenal
Newcastle U v Crystal Palace
Nottingham F v Bournemouth
Tottenham H v Fulham
Wolverhampton W v Southampton

Saturday, 10 September 2022
Arsenal v Everton
Bournemouth v Brighton & HA
Crystal Palace v Manchester U
Fulham v Chelsea
Leeds U v Nottingham F
Leicester C v Aston Villa
Liverpool v Wolverhampton W
Manchester C v Tottenham H
Southampton v Brentford
West Ham U v Newcastle U

Saturday, 17 September 2022
Aston Villa v Southampton
Brentford v Arsenal
Brighton & HA v Crystal Palace
Chelsea v Liverpool
Everton v West Ham U
Manchester U v Leeds U
Newcastle U v Bournemouth
Nottingham F v Fulham
Tottenham H v Leicester C
Wolverhampton W v Manchester C

Saturday, 1 October 2022
Arsenal v Tottenham H
Bournemouth v Brentford
Crystal Palace v Chelsea
Fulham v Newcastle U
Leeds U v Aston Villa
Leicester C v Nottingham F
Liverpool v Brighton & HA
Manchester C v Manchester U
Southampton v Everton
West Ham U v Wolverhampton W

Saturday, 8 October 2022
Arsenal v Liverpool
Bournemouth v Leicester C
Brighton & HA v Tottenham H
Chelsea v Wolverhampton W
Crystal Palace v Leeds U
Everton v Manchester U
Manchester C v Southampton
Newcastle U v Brentford
Nottingham F v Aston Villa
West Ham U v Fulham

Saturday, 15 October 2022
Aston Villa v Chelsea
Brentford v Brighton & HA
Fulham v Bournemouth
Leeds U v Arsenal
Leicester C v Crystal Palace
Liverpool v Manchester C
Manchester U v Newcastle U
Southampton v West Ham U
Tottenham H v Everton
Wolverhampton W v Nottingham F

Tuesday, 18 October 2022
Arsenal v Manchester C (19:45)
Bournemouth v Southampton (19:45)
Brentford v Chelsea (19:45)
Brighton & HA v Nottingham F (19:45)
Fulham v Aston Villa (19:45)
Leicester C v Leeds U (19:45)
Crystal Palace v Wolverhampton W (20:00)

Wednesday, 19 October 2022
Newcastle U v Everton (19:45)
Liverpool v West Ham U (20:00)
20:00 Manchester U v Tottenham H

Saturday, 22 October 2022
Aston Villa v Brentford
Chelsea v Manchester U
Everton v Crystal Palace
Leeds U v Fulham
Manchester C v Brighton & HA
Nottingham F v Liverpool
Southampton v Arsenal
Tottenham H v Newcastle U
West Ham U v Bournemouth
Wolverhampton W v Leicester C

Saturday, 29 October 2022
Arsenal v Nottingham F
Bournemouth v Tottenham H
Brentford v Wolverhampton W
Brighton & HA v Chelsea
Crystal Palace v Southampton
Fulham v Everton
Leicester C v Manchester C
Liverpool v Leeds U
Manchester U v West Ham U
Newcastle U v Aston Villa

Saturday, 5 November 2022
Aston Villa v Manchester U
Chelsea v Arsenal
Everton v Leicester C
Leeds U v Bournemouth
Manchester C v Fulham
Nottingham F v Brentford
Southampton v Newcastle U
Tottenham H v Liverpool
West Ham U v Crystal Palace
Wolverhampton W v Brighton & HA

Saturday, 12 November 2022
Bournemouth v Everton
Brighton & HA v Aston Villa
Fulham v Manchester U
Liverpool v Southampton
Manchester C v Brentford
Newcastle U v Chelsea
Nottingham F v Crystal Palace
Tottenham H v Leeds U
West Ham U v Leicester C
Wolverhampton W v Arsenal

Monday, 26 December 2022
Arsenal v West Ham U
Aston Villa v Liverpool
Brentford v Tottenham H

Chelsea v Bournemouth
Crystal Palace v Fulham
Everton v Wolverhampton W
Leeds U v Manchester C
Leicester C v Newcastle U
Manchester U v Nottingham F
Southampton v Brighton & HA

Saturday, 31 December 2022
Bournemouth v Crystal Palace
Brighton & HA v Arsenal
Fulham v Southampton
Liverpool v Leicester C
Manchester C v Everton
Newcastle U v Leeds U
Nottingham F v Chelsea
Tottenham H v Aston Villa
West Ham U v Brentford
Wolverhampton W v Manchester U

Monday, 2 January 2023
Arsenal v Newcastle U
Aston Villa v Wolverhampton W
Brentford v Liverpool
Chelsea v Manchester C
Crystal Palace v Tottenham H
Everton v Brighton & HA
Leeds U v West Ham U
Leicester C v Fulham
Manchester U v Bournemouth
Southampton v Nottingham F

Saturday, 14 January 2023
Aston Villa v Leeds U
Brentford v Bournemouth
Brighton & HA v Liverpool
Chelsea v Crystal Palace
Everton v Southampton
Manchester U v Manchester C
Newcastle U v Fulham
Nottingham F v Leicester C
Tottenham H v Arsenal
Wolverhampton W v West Ham U

Saturday, 21 January 2023
Arsenal v Manchester U
Bournemouth v Nottingham F
Crystal Palace v Newcastle U
Fulham v Tottenham H
Leeds U v Brentford
Leicester C v Brighton & HA
Liverpool v Chelsea
Manchester C v Wolverhampton W
Southampton v Aston Villa
West Ham U v Everton

Saturday, 4 February 2023
Aston Villa v Leicester C
Brentford v Southampton
Brighton & HA v Bournemouth
Chelsea v Fulham
Everton v Arsenal
Manchester U v Crystal Palace
Newcastle U v West Ham U
Nottingham F v Leeds U
Tottenham H v Manchester C
Wolverhampton W v Liverpool

Saturday, 11 February 2023
Arsenal v Brentford
Bournemouth v Newcastle U
Crystal Palace v Brighton & HA
Fulham v Nottingham F
Leeds U v Manchester U
Leicester C v Tottenham H
Liverpool v Everton
Manchester C v Aston Villa
Southampton v Wolverhampton W
West Ham U v Chelsea

Saturday, 18 February 2023
Aston Villa v Arsenal
Brentford v Crystal Palace
Brighton & HA v Fulham
Chelsea v Southampton
Everton v Leeds U
Manchester U v Leicester C
Newcastle U v Liverpool
Nottingham F v Manchester C
Tottenham H v West Ham U
Wolverhampton W v Bournemouth

Saturday, 25 February 2023
Bournemouth v Manchester C
Crystal Palace v Liverpool
Everton v Aston Villa
Fulham v Wolverhampton W
Leeds U v Southampton
Leicester C v Arsenal
Manchester U v Brentford
Newcastle U v Brighton & HA
Tottenham H v Chelsea
West Ham U v Nottingham F

Saturday, 4 March 2023
Arsenal v Bournemouth
Aston Villa v Crystal Palace
Brentford v Fulham
Brighton & HA v West Ham U
Chelsea v Leeds U
Liverpool v Manchester U
Manchester C v Newcastle U
Nottingham F v Everton
Southampton v Leicester C
Wolverhampton W v Tottenham H

Saturday, 11 March 2023
Bournemouth v Liverpool
Crystal Palace v Manchester C
Everton v Brentford
Fulham v Arsenal
Leeds U v Brighton & HA
Leicester C v Chelsea
Manchester U v Southampton
Newcastle U v Wolverhampton W
Tottenham H v Nottingham F
West Ham U v Aston Villa

Saturday, 18 March 2023
Arsenal v Crystal Palace
Aston Villa v Bournemouth
Brentford v Leicester C
Brighton & HA v Manchester U
Chelsea v Everton
Liverpool v Fulham
Manchester C v West Ham U
Nottingham F v Newcastle U
Southampton v Tottenham H
Wolverhampton W v Leeds U

Saturday, 1 April 2023
Arsenal v Leeds U
Bournemouth v Fulham
Brighton & HA v Brentford
Chelsea v Aston Villa
Crystal Palace v Leicester C
Everton v Tottenham H
Manchester C v Liverpool
Newcastle U v Manchester U
Nottingham F v Wolverhampton W
West Ham U v Southampton

Saturday, 8 April 2023
Aston Villa v Nottingham F
Brentford v Newcastle U
Fulham v West Ham U
Leeds U v Crystal Palace
Leicester C v Bournemouth
Liverpool v Arsenal
Manchester U v Everton
Southampton v Manchester C
Tottenham H v Brighton & HA
Wolverhampton W v Chelsea

Saturday, 15 April 2023
Aston Villa v Newcastle U
Chelsea v Brighton & HA
Everton v Fulham
Leeds U v Liverpool
Manchester C v Leicester C
Nottingham F v Manchester U
Southampton v Crystal Palace
Tottenham H v Bournemouth
West Ham U v Arsenal
Wolverhampton W v Brentford

Saturday, 22 April 2023
Arsenal v Southampton
Bournemouth v West Ham U
Brentford v Aston Villa
Brighton & HA v Manchester C
Crystal Palace v Everton
Fulham v Leeds U
Leicester C v Wolverhampton W
Liverpool v Nottingham F
Manchester U v Chelsea
Newcastle U v Tottenham H

Tuesday, 25 April 2023
Everton v Newcastle U (19:45)
Leeds U v Leicester C (19:45)
Nottingham F v Brighton & HA (19:45)
Tottenham H v Manchester U (19:45)
West Ham U v Liverpool (19:45)
Wolverhampton W v Crystal Palace (19:45)
Aston Villa v Fulham (20:00)

Wednesday, 26 April 2023
Chelsea v Brentford (19:45)
Southampton v Bournemouth (19:45)
Manchester C v Arsenal (20:00)

Saturday, 29 April 2023
Arsenal v Chelsea
Bournemouth v Leeds U
Brentford v Nottingham F
Brighton & HA v Wolverhampton W
Crystal Palace v West Ham U
Fulham v Manchester C
Leicester C v Everton
Liverpool v Tottenham H
Manchester U v Aston Villa
Newcastle U v Southampton

Saturday, 6 May 2023
Bournemouth v Chelsea
Brighton & HA v Everton
Fulham v Leicester C
Liverpool v Brentford
Manchester C v Leeds U
Newcastle U v Arsenal
Nottingham F v Southampton
Tottenham H v Crystal Palace
West Ham U v Manchester U
Wolverhampton W v Aston Villa

Saturday, 13 May 2023
Arsenal v Brighton & HA
Aston Villa v Tottenham H
Brentford v West Ham U
Chelsea v Nottingham F
Crystal Palace v Bournemouth
Everton v Manchester C
Leeds U v Newcastle U
Leicester C v Liverpool
Manchester U v Wolverhampton W
Southampton v Fulham

Saturday, 20 May 2023
Bournemouth v Manchester U
Brighton & HA v Southampton
Fulham v Crystal Palace
Liverpool v Aston Villa
Manchester C v Chelsea
Newcastle U v Leicester C
Nottingham F v Arsenal
Tottenham H v Brentford
West Ham U v Leeds U
Wolverhampton W v Everton

Sunday, 28 May 2023
Arsenal v Wolverhampton W (16:00)
Aston Villa v Brighton & HA (16:00)
Brentford v Manchester C (16:00)
Chelsea v Newcastle U (16:00)
Crystal Palace v Nottingham F (16:00)
Everton v Bournemouth (16:00)
Leeds U v Tottenham H (16:00)
Leicester C v West Ham U (16:00)
Manchester U v Fulham (16:00)
Southampton v Liverpool (16:00)

EFL Championship

Friday, 29 July 2022
Huddersfield T v Burnley

Saturday, 30 July 2022
Blackburn R v QPR
Blackpool v Reading
Cardiff C v Norwich C
Hull C v Bristol C
Luton T v Birmingham C
Millwall v Stoke C
Rotherham U v Swansea C
Wigan Ath v Preston NE
Middlesbrough v WBA

Sunday, 31 July 2022
Sunderland v Coventry C

Monday, 1 August 2022
Watford v Sheffield United

Saturday, 6 August 2022
Birmingham C v Huddersfield T
Bristol C v Sunderland
Burnley v Luton T
Coventry C v Rotherham U
Norwich C v Wigan Ath
Preston NE v Hull C
QPR v Middlesbrough
Reading v Cardiff C
Sheffield United v Millwall
Stoke C v Blackpool
Swansea C v Blackburn R
WBA v Watford

Saturday, 13 August 2022
Blackburn R v WBA
Blackpool v Swansea C
Cardiff C v Birmingham C
Huddersfield T v Stoke C
Hull C v Norwich C
Luton T v Preston NE
Middlesbrough v Sheffield United
Millwall v Coventry C
Rotherham U v Reading
Sunderland v QPR
Watford v Burnley
Wigan Ath v Bristol C

Tuesday, 16 August 2022
Birmingham C v Watford
Bristol C v Luton T
Burnley v Hull C
Coventry C v Wigan Ath
Norwich C v Huddersfield T
Preston NE v Rotherham U
QPR v Blackpool
Sheffield United v Sunderland
Swansea C v Millwall
Reading v Blackburn R
Stoke C v Middlesbrough
WBA v Cardiff C

Saturday, 20 August 2022
Birmingham C v Wigan Ath
Bristol C v Cardiff C
Burnley v Blackpool
Coventry C v Huddersfield T
Norwich C v Millwall
Preston NE v Watford
QPR v Rotherham U
Reading v Middlesbrough
Sheffield United v Blackburn R
Stoke C v Sunderland
Swansea C v Luton T
WBA v Hull C

Saturday, 27 August 2022
Blackburn R v Stoke C
Blackpool v Bristol C
Cardiff C v Preston NE
Huddersfield T v WBA
Hull C v Coventry C
Luton T v Sheffield United
Middlesbrough v Swansea C
Millwall v Reading
Rotherham U v Birmingham C
Sunderland v Norwich C
Watford v QPR
Wigan Ath v Burnley

Tuesday, 30 August 2022
Birmingham C v Norwich C
Burnley v Millwall
Cardiff C v Luton T
QPR v Hull C
Watford v Middlesbrough
Wigan Ath v WBA

Wednesday, 31 August 2022
Blackpool v Blackburn R
Bristol C v Huddersfield T
Coventry C v Preston NE
Sheffield United v Reading
Sunderland v Rotherham U
Stoke C v Swansea C

Saturday, 3 September 2022
Blackburn R v Bristol C
Huddersfield T v Blackpool
Hull C v Sheffield United
Luton T v Wigan Ath
Middlesbrough v Sunderland
Millwall v Cardiff C
Norwich C v Coventry C
Preston NE v Birmingham C
Reading v Stoke C
Rotherham U v Watford
Swansea C v QPR
WBA v Burnley

Saturday, 10 September 2022
Birmingham C v Swansea C
Blackpool v Middlesbrough
Bristol C v Preston NE
Burnley v Norwich C
Cardiff C v Hull C
Coventry C v WBA
QPR v Huddersfield T
Sheffield United v Rotherham U
Stoke C v Luton T
Sunderland v Millwall
Watford v Reading
Wigan Ath v Blackburn R

Tuesday, 13 September 2022
Blackburn R v Watford
Huddersfield T v Wigan Ath
Hull C v Stoke C
Middlesbrough v Cardiff C
Preston NE v Burnley
Swansea C v Sheffield United

Wednesday, 14 September 2022
Luton T v Coventry C
Millwall v QPR
Norwich C v Bristol C
Rotherham U v Blackpool
Reading v Sunderland
WBA v Birmingham C

Saturday, 17 September 2022
Birmingham C v Coventry C
Burnley v Bristol C
Huddersfield T v Cardiff C
Luton T v Blackburn R
Middlesbrough v Rotherham U
Millwall v Blackpool
Norwich C v WBA
Preston NE v Sheffield United
QPR v Stoke C
Swansea C v Hull C
Watford v Sunderland
Wigan Ath v Reading

Saturday, 1 October 2022
Blackburn R v Millwall
Blackpool v Norwich C
Bristol C v QPR
Cardiff C v Burnley
Coventry C v Middlesbrough
Hull C v Luton T
Reading v Huddersfield T
Rotherham U v Wigan Ath
Sheffield United v Birmingham C
Stoke C v Watford
Sunderland v Preston NE
WBA v Swansea C

Tuesday, 4 October 2022
Bristol C v Coventry C
Cardiff C v Blackburn R
Luton T v Huddersfield T
Sheffield United v QPR
Sunderland v Blackpool
Reading v Norwich C

Wednesday, 5 October 2022
Burnley v Stoke C
Hull C v Wigan Ath
Middlesbrough v Birmingham C
Preston NE v WBA
Rotherham U v Millwall
Watford v Swansea C

Saturday, 8 October 2022
Birmingham C v Bristol C
Blackburn R v Rotherham U
Blackpool v Watford
Coventry C v Burnley
Huddersfield T v Hull C
Millwall v Middlesbrough
Norwich C v Preston NE
QPR v Reading
Stoke C v Sheffield United
Swansea C v Sunderland
WBA v Luton T
Wigan Ath v Cardiff C

Saturday, 15 October 2022
Bristol C v Millwall
Burnley v Swansea C
Cardiff C v Coventry C
Hull C v Birmingham C
Luton T v QPR
Middlesbrough v Blackburn R
Preston NE v Stoke C
Reading v WBA
Rotherham U v Huddersfield T
Sheffield United v Blackpool
Sunderland v Wigan Ath
Watford v Norwich C

Tuesday, 18 October 2022
Blackburn R v Sunderland
Huddersfield T v Preston NE
Norwich C v Luton T
Swansea C v Reading
Stoke C v Rotherham U
WBA v Bristol C

Wednesday, 19 October 2022
Birmingham C v Burnley
Blackpool v Hull C
Coventry C v Sheffield United
Millwall v Watford
QPR v Cardiff C
Wigan Ath v Middlesbrough

Saturday, 22 October 2022
Blackburn R v Birmingham C
Blackpool v Preston NE
Middlesbrough v Huddersfield T
Millwall v WBA
QPR v Wigan Ath
Reading v Bristol C
Rotherham U v Hull C
Sheffield United v Norwich C
Stoke C v Coventry C
Sunderland v Burnley
Swansea C v Cardiff C
Watford v Luton T

Saturday, 29 October 2022
Birmingham C v QPR
Bristol C v Swansea C
Burnley v Reading
Cardiff C v Rotherham U
Coventry C v Blackpool
Huddersfield T v Millwall
Hull C v Blackburn R
Luton T v Sunderland
Norwich C v Stoke C
Preston NE v Middlesbrough
WBA v Sheffield United
Wigan Ath v Watford

Tuesday, 1 November 2022
Bristol C v Sheffield United
Coventry C v Blackburn R
Hull C v Middlesbrough
Luton T v Reading
Preston NE v Swansea C
WBA v Blackpool

Wednesday, 2 November 2022
Birmingham C v Millwall
Burnley v Rotherham U
Cardiff C v Watford
Huddersfield T v Sunderland
Norwich C v QPR
Wigan Ath v Stoke C

Saturday, 5 November 2022
Blackburn R v Huddersfield T
Blackpool v Luton T
Middlesbrough v Bristol C
Millwall v Hull C
QPR v WBA
Reading v Preston NE
Rotherham U v Norwich C
Sheffield United v Burnley
Stoke C v Birmingham C
Sunderland v Cardiff C
Swansea C v Wigan Ath
Watford v Coventry C

Saturday, 12 November 2022
Birmingham C v Sunderland
Bristol C v Watford
Burnley v Blackburn R
Cardiff C v Sheffield United
Coventry C v QPR
Huddersfield T v Swansea C
Hull C v Reading
Luton T v Rotherham U
Norwich C v Middlesbrough
Preston NE v Millwall
WBA v Stoke C
Wigan Ath v Blackpool

Saturday, 10 December 2022
Blackburn R v Preston NE
Blackpool v Birmingham C
Middlesbrough v Luton T
Millwall v Wigan Ath
QPR v Burnley
Reading v Coventry C
Rotherham U v Bristol C
Sheffield United v Huddersfield T
Stoke C v Cardiff C
Sunderland v WBA
Swansea C v Norwich C
Watford v Hull C

Saturday, 17 December 2022
Birmingham C v Reading
Bristol C v Stoke C
Burnley v Middlesbrough
Cardiff C v Blackpool
Coventry C v Swansea C
Huddersfield T v Watford
Hull C v Sunderland
Luton T v Millwall
Norwich C v Blackburn R
Preston NE v QPR
WBA v Rotherham U
Wigan Ath v Sheffield United

Monday, 26 December 2022
Bristol C v WBA
Burnley v Birmingham C
Cardiff C v QPR
Hull C v Blackpool
Luton T v Norwich C
Middlesbrough v Wigan Ath
Preston NE v Huddersfield T
Reading v Swansea C
Rotherham U v Stoke C
Sheffield United v Coventry C
Sunderland v Blackburn R
Watford v Millwall

Thursday, 29 December 2022
Birmingham C v Hull C
Blackburn R v Middlesbrough
Blackpool v Sheffield United
Coventry C v Cardiff C
Huddersfield T v Rotherham U
Millwall v Bristol C
Norwich C v Reading
QPR v Luton T
Swansea C v Watford
Wigan Ath v Sunderland
Stoke C v Burnley
WBA v Preston NE

Sunday, 1 January 2023
Birmingham C v Middlesbrough
Blackburn R v Cardiff C
Blackpool v Sunderland
Coventry C v Bristol C
Huddersfield T v Luton T
Millwall v Rotherham U
Norwich C v Watford
QPR v Sheffield United
Stoke C v Preston NE
Swansea C v Burnley
WBA v Reading
Wigan Ath v Hull C

Saturday, 14 January 2023
Bristol C v Birmingham C
Burnley v Coventry C
Cardiff C v Wigan Ath
Hull C v Huddersfield T
Luton T v WBA
Middlesbrough v Millwall
Preston NE v Norwich C
Reading v QPR
Rotherham U v Blackburn R
Sheffield United v Stoke C
Sunderland v Swansea C
Watford v Blackpool

Saturday, 21 January 2023
Birmingham C v Preston NE
Blackpool v Huddersfield T
Bristol C v Blackburn R
Burnley v WBA
Cardiff C v Millwall
Coventry C v Norwich C
QPR v Swansea C
Sheffield United v Hull C
Stoke C v Reading
Sunderland v Middlesbrough
Watford v Rotherham U
Wigan Ath v Luton T

Saturday, 28 January 2023
Blackburn R v Blackpool
Huddersfield T v Bristol C
Hull C v QPR
Luton T v Cardiff C
Middlesbrough v Watford
Millwall v Burnley
Norwich C v Birmingham C
Preston NE v Coventry C
Reading v Sheffield United
Rotherham U v Sunderland
Swansea C v Stoke C
WBA v Wigan Ath

Saturday, 4 February 2023
Blackburn R v Wigan Ath
Huddersfield T v QPR
Hull C v Cardiff C
Luton T v Stoke C
Middlesbrough v Blackpool
Millwall v Sunderland
Norwich C v Burnley
Preston NE v Bristol C
Reading v Watford
Rotherham U v Sheffield United
Swansea C v Birmingham C
WBA v Coventry C

Saturday, 11 February 2023
Birmingham C v WBA
Blackpool v Rotherham U
Bristol C v Norwich C
Burnley v Preston NE
Cardiff C v Middlesbrough
Coventry C v Luton T
QPR v Millwall
Sheffield United v Swansea C
Stoke C v Hull C
Sunderland v Reading
Watford v Blackburn R
Wigan Ath v Huddersfield T

Tuesday, 14 February 2023
Birmingham C v Cardiff C
Burnley v Watford
Coventry C v Millwall
Norwich C v Hull C
QPR v Sunderland
Reading v Rotherham U

Wednesday, 15 February 2023
Bristol C v Wigan Ath
Preston NE v Luton T
Sheffield United v Middlesbrough
Swansea C v Blackpool
Stoke C v Huddersfield T
WBA v Blackburn R

Saturday, 18 February 2023
Blackburn R v Swansea C
Blackpool v Stoke C
Cardiff C v Reading
Huddersfield T v Birmingham C
Hull C v Preston NE
Luton T v Burnley
Middlesbrough v QPR
Millwall v Sheffield United
Rotherham U v Coventry C
Sunderland v Bristol C
Watford v WBA
Wigan Ath v Norwich C

Saturday, 25 February 2023
Birmingham C v Luton T
Bristol C v Hull C
Burnley v Huddersfield T
Coventry C v Sunderland
Norwich C v Cardiff C
Preston NE v Wigan Ath
QPR v Blackburn R

Reading v Blackpool
Sheffield United v Watford
Stoke C v Millwall
Swansea C v Rotherham U
WBA v Middlesbrough

Saturday, 4 March 2023
Blackburn R v Sheffield United
Blackpool v Burnley
Cardiff C v Bristol C
Huddersfield T v Coventry C
Hull C v WBA
Luton T v Swansea C
Middlesbrough v Reading
Millwall v Norwich C
Rotherham U v QPR
Sunderland v Stoke C
Watford v Preston NE
Wigan Ath v Birmingham C

Saturday, 11 March 2023
Birmingham C v Rotherham U
Bristol C v Blackpool
Burnley v Wigan Ath
Coventry C v Hull C
Norwich C v Sunderland
Preston NE v Cardiff C
QPR v Watford
Reading v Millwall
Sheffield United v Luton T
Stoke C v Blackburn R
Swansea C v Middlesbrough
WBA v Huddersfield T

Tuesday, 14 March 2023
Blackpool v QPR
Middlesbrough v Stoke C
Millwall v Swansea C
Rotherham U v Preston NE
Watford v Birmingham C
Wigan Ath v Coventry C

Wednesday, 15 March 2023
Blackburn R v Reading
Cardiff C v WBA
Huddersfield T v Norwich C
Hull C v Burnley
Luton T v Bristol C
Sunderland v Sheffield United

Saturday, 18 March 2023
Blackburn R v Burnley
Blackpool v Coventry C
Middlesbrough v Preston NE
Millwall v Huddersfield T
QPR v Birmingham C
Reading v Hull C
Rotherham U v Cardiff C
Sheffield United v WBA
Stoke C v Norwich C
Sunderland v Luton T
Swansea C v Bristol C
Watford v Wigan Ath

Saturday, 1 April 2023
Birmingham C v Blackburn R
Bristol C v Reading
Burnley v Sunderland
Cardiff C v Swansea C
Coventry C v Stoke C
Huddersfield T v Middlesbrough
Hull C v Rotherham U
Luton T v Watford
Norwich C v Sheffield United
Preston NE v Blackpool
WBA v Millwall
Wigan Ath v QPR

Friday, 7 April 2023
Blackburn R v Norwich C
Blackpool v Cardiff C
Middlesbrough v Burnley
Millwall v Luton T
QPR v Preston NE
Reading v Birmingham C
Rotherham U v WBA
Sheffield United v Wigan Ath
Stoke C v Bristol C
Sunderland v Hull C
Swansea C v Coventry C
Watford v Huddersfield T

Monday, 10 April 2023
Birmingham C v Stoke C
Bristol C v Middlesbrough
Burnley v Sheffield United
Cardiff C v Sunderland
Coventry C v Watford
Huddersfield T v Blackburn R
Hull C v Millwall
Luton T v Blackpool
Norwich C v Rotherham U
Preston NE v Reading
WBA v QPR
Wigan Ath v Swansea C

Saturday, 15 April 2023
Blackburn R v Hull C
Blackpool v Wigan Ath
Middlesbrough v Norwich C
Millwall v Preston NE
QPR v Coventry C
Reading v Burnley
Rotherham U v Luton T
Sheffield United v Cardiff C
Stoke C v WBA
Sunderland v Birmingham C
Swansea C v Huddersfield T
Watford v Bristol C

Tuesday, 18 April 2023
Blackpool v WBA
Millwall v Birmingham C
Rotherham U v Burnley
Sheffield United v Bristol C
Sunderland v Huddersfield T
Stoke C v Wigan Ath

Wednesday, 19 April 2023
Blackburn R v Coventry C
Middlesbrough v Hull C
QPR v Norwich C
Swansea C v Preston NE
Watford v Cardiff C
Reading v Luton T

Saturday, 22 April 2023
Birmingham C v Blackpool
Bristol C v Rotherham U
Burnley v QPR
Cardiff C v Stoke C
Coventry C v Reading
Huddersfield T v Sheffield United
Hull C v Watford
Luton T v Middlesbrough
Norwich C v Swansea C
Preston NE v Blackburn R
WBA v Sunderland
Wigan Ath v Millwall

Saturday, 29 April 2023
Blackburn R v Luton T
Blackpool v Millwall
Bristol C v Burnley
Cardiff C v Huddersfield T
Coventry C v Birmingham C
Hull C v Swansea C
Reading v Wigan Ath
Rotherham U v Middlesbrough
Sheffield United v Preston NE
Stoke C v QPR
Sunderland v Watford
WBA v Norwich C

Saturday, 6 May 2023
Birmingham C v Sheffield United
Burnley v Cardiff C
Huddersfield T v Reading
Luton T v Hull C
Middlesbrough v Coventry C
Millwall v Blackburn R
Norwich C v Blackpool
Preston NE v Sunderland
QPR v Bristol C
Swansea C v WBA
Watford v Stoke C
Wigan Ath v Rotherham U

EFL League One

Saturday, 30 July 2022
Accrington S v Charlton Ath
Bristol R v Forest Green R
Cambridge U v Milton Keynes D
Cheltenham T v Peterborough U
Derby Co v Oxford U
Ipswich T v Bolton W
Lincoln C v Exeter C
Morecambe v Shrewsbury T
Plymouth Arg v Barnsley
Port Vale v Fleetwood T
Sheffield W v Portsmouth
Wycombe W v Burton Alb

Saturday, 6 August 2022
Barnsley v Cheltenham T
Bolton W v Wycombe W
Burton Alb v Bristol R
Charlton Ath v Derby Co
Exeter C v Port Vale
Fleetwood T v Plymouth Arg
Forest Green R v Ipswich T
Milton Keynes D v Sheffield W
Oxford U v Cambridge U
Peterborough U v Morecambe
Portsmouth v Lincoln C
Shrewsbury T v Accrington S

Saturday, 13 August 2022
Accrington S v Burton Alb
Bristol R v Oxford U
Cambridge U v Exeter C
Cheltenham T v Portsmouth
Derby Co v Barnsley
Ipswich T v Milton Keynes D
Lincoln C v Forest Green R
Morecambe v Fleetwood T
Plymouth Arg v Peterborough U
Port Vale v Bolton W
Sheffield W v Charlton Ath
Wycombe W v Shrewsbury T

Tuesday, 16 August 2022
Barnsley v Bristol R
Bolton W v Morecambe
Burton Alb v Ipswich T
Charlton Ath v Plymouth Arg
Exeter C v Wycombe W
Fleetwood T v Cheltenham T
Forest Green R v Accrington S
Milton Keynes D v Port Vale
Oxford U v Lincoln C
Peterborough U v Sheffield W
Portsmouth v Cambridge U
Shrewsbury T v Derby Co

Saturday, 20 August 2022
Barnsley v Wycombe W
Bolton W v Sheffield W
Burton Alb v Port Vale
Charlton Ath v Cambridge U
Exeter C v Cheltenham T
Fleetwood T v Derby Co
Forest Green R v Plymouth Arg
Milton Keynes D v Accrington S
Oxford U v Morecambe
Peterborough U v Lincoln C
Portsmouth v Bristol R
Shrewsbury T v Ipswich T

Saturday, 27 August 2022
Accrington S v Exeter C
Bristol R v Shrewsbury T
Cambridge U v Burton Alb
Cheltenham T v Oxford U
Derby Co v Peterborough U
Ipswich T v Barnsley
Lincoln C v Fleetwood T
Morecambe v Milton Keynes D
Plymouth Arg v Bolton W
Port Vale v Portsmouth
Sheffield W v Forest Green R
Wycombe W v Charlton Ath

Saturday, 3 September 2022
Accrington S v Ipswich T
Bolton W v Charlton Ath
Bristol R v Morecambe
Cambridge U v Lincoln C
Derby Co v Plymouth Arg
Exeter C v Milton Keynes D
Fleetwood T v Wycombe W
Forest Green R v Shrewsbury T
Oxford U v Burton Alb
Port Vale v Cheltenham T
Portsmouth v Peterborough U
Sheffield W v Barnsley

Saturday, 10 September 2022
Barnsley v Portsmouth
Burton Alb v Fleetwood T
Charlton Ath v Exeter C
Cheltenham T v Bolton W
Ipswich T v Cambridge U
Lincoln C v Accrington S
Milton Keynes D v Bristol R
Morecambe v Derby Co
Peterborough U v Forest Green R
Plymouth Arg v Sheffield W
Shrewsbury T v Oxford U
Wycombe W v Port Vale

Tuesday, 13 September 2022
Barnsley v Port Vale
Burton Alb v Portsmouth
Charlton Ath v Forest Green R
Cheltenham T v Cambridge U
Ipswich T v Bristol R
Lincoln C v Derby Co
Milton Keynes D v Bolton W
Morecambe v Sheffield W
Peterborough U v Fleetwood T
Plymouth Arg v Oxford U
Shrewsbury T v Exeter C
Wycombe W v Accrington S

Saturday, 17 September 2022
Accrington S v Cheltenham T
Bolton W v Peterborough U
Bristol R v Lincoln C
Cambridge U v Barnsley
Derby Co v Wycombe W
Exeter C v Burton Alb
Fleetwood T v Charlton Ath
Forest Green R v Morecambe
Oxford U v Milton Keynes D
Port Vale v Shrewsbury T
Portsmouth v Plymouth Arg
Sheffield W v Ipswich T

Saturday, 24 September 2022
Barnsley v Charlton Ath
Bristol R v Accrington S
Derby Co v Cheltenham T
Forest Green R v Exeter C
Lincoln C v Milton Keynes D
Morecambe v Cambridge U
Oxford U v Fleetwood T
Peterborough U v Port Vale
Plymouth Arg v Ipswich T
Portsmouth v Bolton W
Sheffield W v Wycombe W
Shrewsbury T v Burton Alb

Saturday, 1 October 2022
Accrington S v Morecambe
Bolton W v Lincoln C
Burton Alb v Forest Green R
Cambridge U v Derby Co
Charlton Ath v Oxford U
Cheltenham T v Shrewsbury T
Exeter C v Bristol R
Fleetwood T v Barnsley
Ipswich T v Portsmouth
Milton Keynes D v Peterborough U
Port Vale v Sheffield W
Wycombe W v Plymouth Arg

Saturday, 8 October 2022
Barnsley v Exeter C
Bristol R v Cambridge U
Derby Co v Port Vale
Forest Green R v Bolton W
Lincoln C v Charlton Ath
Morecambe v Ipswich T
Oxford U v Wycombe W
Peterborough U v Burton Alb
Plymouth Arg v Accrington S
Portsmouth v Fleetwood T
Sheffield W v Cheltenham T
Shrewsbury T v Milton Keynes D

Saturday, 15 October 2022
Accrington S v Derby Co
Bolton W v Barnsley
Burton Alb v Morecambe
Cambridge U v Sheffield W
Charlton Ath v Portsmouth
Cheltenham T v Bristol R
Exeter C v Oxford U
Fleetwood T v Shrewsbury T
Ipswich T v Lincoln C
Milton Keynes D v Plymouth Arg
Port Vale v Forest Green R
Wycombe W v Peterborough U

Saturday, 22 October 2022
Accrington S v Bolton W
Bristol R v Plymouth Arg
Burton Alb v Cheltenham T
Cambridge U v Port Vale
Exeter C v Fleetwood T
Forest Green R v Portsmouth
Ipswich T v Derby Co
Lincoln C v Sheffield W
Milton Keynes D v Wycombe W
Morecambe v Barnsley
Oxford U v Peterborough U
Shrewsbury T v Charlton Ath

Tuesday, 25 October 2022
Barnsley v Lincoln C
Bolton W v Burton Alb
Charlton Ath v Milton Keynes D
Cheltenham T v Morecambe
Derby Co v Exeter C
Fleetwood T v Forest Green R
Peterborough U v Accrington S
Plymouth Arg v Shrewsbury T
Port Vale v Ipswich T
Portsmouth v Oxford U
Sheffield W v Bristol R
Wycombe W v Cambridge U

Saturday, 29 October 2022
Barnsley v Forest Green R
Bolton W v Oxford U
Charlton Ath v Ipswich T
Cheltenham T v Milton Keynes D
Derby Co v Bristol R
Fleetwood T v Accrington S
Peterborough U v Cambridge U
Plymouth Arg v Exeter C
Port Vale v Lincoln C
Portsmouth v Shrewsbury T
Sheffield W v Burton Alb
Wycombe W v Morecambe

Saturday, 12 November 2022
Accrington S v Sheffield W
Bristol R v Fleetwood T
Burton Alb v Charlton Ath
Cambridge U v Bolton W
Exeter C v Peterborough U
Forest Green R v Wycombe W
Ipswich T v Cheltenham T
Lincoln C v Plymouth Arg
Milton Keynes D v Derby Co
Morecambe v Portsmouth
Oxford U v Port Vale
Shrewsbury T v Barnsley

Saturday, 19 November 2022
Barnsley v Milton Keynes D
Bristol R v Peterborough U
Burton Alb v Plymouth Arg
Cambridge U v Accrington S
Cheltenham T v Wycombe W
Exeter C v Ipswich T
Fleetwood T v Bolton W
Lincoln C v Morecambe
Oxford U v Forest Green R
Port Vale v Charlton Ath
Portsmouth v Derby Co
Sheffield W v Shrewsbury T

Saturday, 3 December 2022
Accrington S v Oxford U
Bolton W v Bristol R
Charlton Ath v Cheltenham T
Derby Co v Sheffield W
Forest Green R v Cambridge U
Ipswich T v Fleetwood T
Milton Keynes D v Burton Alb
Morecambe v Exeter C
Peterborough U v Barnsley
Plymouth Arg v Port Vale
Shrewsbury T v Lincoln C
Wycombe W v Portsmouth

Saturday, 10 December 2022
Accrington S v Portsmouth
Bristol R v Port Vale
Burton Alb v Derby Co
Cambridge U v Plymouth Arg
Exeter C v Sheffield W
Forest Green R v Cheltenham T
Ipswich T v Peterborough U
Lincoln C v Wycombe W
Milton Keynes D v Fleetwood T
Morecambe v Charlton Ath
Oxford U v Barnsley
Shrewsbury T v Bolton W

Saturday, 17 December 2022
Barnsley v Burton Alb
Bolton W v Exeter C
Charlton Ath v Bristol R
Cheltenham T v Lincoln C
Derby Co v Forest Green R
Fleetwood T v Cambridge U
Peterborough U v Shrewsbury T
Plymouth Arg v Morecambe
Port Vale v Accrington S
Portsmouth v Milton Keynes D
Sheffield W v Oxford U
Wycombe W v Ipswich T

Monday, 26 December 2022
Accrington S v Barnsley
Bolton W v Derby Co
Burton Alb v Lincoln C
Cambridge U v Shrewsbury T
Charlton Ath v Peterborough U
Cheltenham T v Plymouth Arg
Exeter C v Portsmouth
Fleetwood T v Sheffield W
Ipswich T v Oxford U
Milton Keynes D v Forest Green R
Port Vale v Morecambe
Wycombe W v Bristol R

Thursday, 29 December 2022
Barnsley v Fleetwood T
Bristol R v Exeter C
Derby Co v Cambridge U
Forest Green R v Burton Alb
Lincoln C v Bolton W
Morecambe v Accrington S
Oxford U v Charlton Ath
Peterborough U v Milton Keynes D
Plymouth Arg v Wycombe W
Portsmouth v Ipswich T
Sheffield W v Port Vale
Shrewsbury T v Cheltenham T

Sunday, 1 January 2023
Barnsley v Bolton W
Bristol R v Cheltenham T
Derby Co v Accrington S
Forest Green R v Port Vale
Lincoln C v Ipswich T
Morecambe v Burton Alb
Oxford U v Exeter C
Peterborough U v Wycombe W
Plymouth Arg v Milton Keynes D
Portsmouth v Charlton Ath
Sheffield W v Cambridge U
Shrewsbury T v Fleetwood T

Saturday, 7 January 2023
Accrington S v Plymouth Arg
Bolton W v Forest Green R
Burton Alb v Peterborough U
Cambridge U v Bristol R
Charlton Ath v Lincoln C
Cheltenham T v Sheffield W
Exeter C v Barnsley
Fleetwood T v Portsmouth
Ipswich T v Morecambe
Milton Keynes D v Shrewsbury T
Port Vale v Derby Co
Wycombe W v Oxford U

Saturday, 14 January 2023
Accrington S v Bristol R
Bolton W v Portsmouth
Burton Alb v Shrewsbury T
Cambridge U v Morecambe
Charlton Ath v Barnsley
Cheltenham T v Derby Co
Exeter C v Forest Green R
Fleetwood T v Oxford U
Ipswich T v Plymouth Arg
Milton Keynes D v Lincoln C
Port Vale v Peterborough U
Wycombe W v Sheffield W

Saturday, 21 January 2023
Barnsley v Accrington S
Bristol R v Wycombe W
Derby Co v Bolton W
Forest Green R v Milton Keynes D
Lincoln C v Burton Alb
Morecambe v Port Vale
Oxford U v Ipswich T
Peterborough U v Charlton Ath
Plymouth Arg v Cheltenham T
Portsmouth v Exeter C
Sheffield W v Fleetwood T
Shrewsbury T v Cambridge U

Saturday, 28 January 2023
Barnsley v Sheffield W
Burton Alb v Oxford U
Charlton Ath v Bolton W
Cheltenham T v Port Vale
Ipswich T v Accrington S
Lincoln C v Cambridge U
Milton Keynes D v Exeter C
Morecambe v Bristol R
Peterborough U v Portsmouth
Plymouth Arg v Derby Co
Shrewsbury T v Forest Green R
Wycombe W v Fleetwood T

Saturday, 4 February 2023
Accrington S v Lincoln C
Bolton W v Cheltenham T
Bristol R v Milton Keynes D
Cambridge U v Ipswich T
Derby Co v Morecambe
Exeter C v Charlton Ath
Fleetwood T v Burton Alb
Forest Green R v Peterborough U
Oxford U v Shrewsbury T
Port Vale v Wycombe W
Portsmouth v Barnsley
Sheffield W v Plymouth Arg

Saturday, 11 February 2023
Barnsley v Cambridge U
Burton Alb v Exeter C
Charlton Ath v Fleetwood T
Cheltenham T v Accrington S
Ipswich T v Sheffield W
Lincoln C v Bristol R
Milton Keynes D v Oxford U
Morecambe v Forest Green R
Peterborough U v Bolton W
Plymouth Arg v Portsmouth
Shrewsbury T v Port Vale
Wycombe W v Derby Co

Tuesday, 14 February 2023
Accrington S v Wycombe W
Bolton W v Milton Keynes D
Bristol R v Ipswich T
Cambridge U v Cheltenham T
Derby Co v Lincoln C
Exeter C y Shrewsbury T
Fleetwood T v Peterborough U
Forest Green R v Charlton Ath
Oxford U v Plymouth Arg
Port Vale v Barnsley
Portsmouth v Burton Alb
Sheffield W v Morecambe

Saturday, 18 February 2023
Accrington S v Shrewsbury T
Bristol R v Burton Alb
Cambridge U v Oxford U
Cheltenham T v Barnsley
Derby Co v Charlton Ath
Ipswich T v Forest Green R
Lincoln C v Portsmouth
Morecambe v Peterborough U
Plymouth Arg v Fleetwood T
Port Vale v Exeter C
Sheffield W v Milton Keynes D
Wycombe W v Bolton W

Saturday, 25 February 2023
Barnsley v Derby Co
Bolton W v Port Vale
Burton Alb v Accrington S
Charlton Ath v Sheffield W
Exeter C v Cambridge U
Fleetwood T v Morecambe
Forest Green R v Lincoln C
Milton Keynes D v Ipswich T
Oxford U v Bristol R
Peterborough U v Plymouth Arg
Portsmouth v Cheltenham T
Shrewsbury T v Wycombe W

Saturday, 4 March 2023
Accrington S v Forest Green R
Bristol R v Barnsley
Cambridge U v Portsmouth
Cheltenham T v Fleetwood T
Derby Co v Shrewsbury T
Ipswich T v Burton Alb
Lincoln C v Oxford U
Morecambe v Bolton W
Plymouth Arg v Charlton Ath
Port Vale v Milton Keynes D
Sheffield W v Peterborough U
Wycombe W v Exeter C

Saturday, 11 March 2023
Barnsley v Plymouth Arg
Bolton W v Ipswich T
Burton Alb v Wycombe W
Charlton Ath v Accrington S
Exeter C v Lincoln C
Fleetwood T v Port Vale
Forest Green R v Bristol R
Milton Keynes D v Cambridge U
Oxford U v Derby Co
Peterborough U v Cheltenham T
Portsmouth v Sheffield W
Shrewsbury T v Morecambe

Saturday, 18 March 2023
Accrington S v Milton Keynes D
Bristol R v Portsmouth
Cambridge U v Charlton Ath
Cheltenham T v Exeter C
Derby Co v Fleetwood T
Ipswich T v Shrewsbury T
Lincoln C v Peterborough U
Morecambe v Oxford U
Plymouth Arg v Forest Green R
Port Vale v Burton Alb
Sheffield W v Bolton W
Wycombe W v Barnsley

Saturday, 25 March 2023
Barnsley v Ipswich T
Bolton W v Plymouth Arg
Burton Alb v Cambridge U
Charlton Ath v Wycombe W
Exeter C v Accrington S
Fleetwood T v Lincoln C
Forest Green R v Sheffield W
Milton Keynes D v Morecambe
Oxford U v Cheltenham T
Peterborough U v Derby Co
Portsmouth v Port Vale
Shrewsbury T v Bristol R

Saturday, 1 April 2023
Barnsley v Morecambe
Bolton W v Accrington S
Charlton Ath v Shrewsbury T
Cheltenham T v Burton Alb
Derby Co v Ipswich T
Fleetwood T v Exeter C
Peterborough U v Oxford U
Plymouth Arg v Bristol R
Port Vale v Cambridge U
Portsmouth v Forest Green R
Sheffield W v Lincoln C
Wycombe W v Milton Keynes D

Friday, 7 April 2023
Accrington S v Port Vale
Bristol R v Charlton Ath
Burton Alb v Barnsley
Cambridge U v Fleetwood T
Exeter C v Bolton W
Forest Green R v Derby Co
Ipswich T v Wycombe W
Lincoln C v Cheltenham T
Milton Keynes D v Portsmouth
Morecambe v Plymouth Arg
Oxford U v Sheffield W
Shrewsbury T v Peterborough U

Monday, 10 April 2023
Barnsley v Shrewsbury T
Bolton W v Cambridge U
Charlton Ath v Burton Alb
Cheltenham T v Ipswich T
Derby Co v Milton Keynes D
Fleetwood T v Bristol R
Peterborough U v Exeter C
Plymouth Arg v Lincoln C
Port Vale v Oxford U
Portsmouth v Morecambe
Sheffield W v Accrington S
Wycombe W v Forest Green R

Saturday, 15 April 2023
Accrington S v Fleetwood T
Bristol R v Derby Co
Burton Alb v Sheffield W
Cambridge U v Peterborough U
Exeter C v Plymouth Arg
Forest Green R v Barnsley
Ipswich T v Charlton Ath
Lincoln C v Port Vale
Milton Keynes D v Cheltenham T
Morecambe v Wycombe W
Oxford U v Bolton W
Shrewsbury T v Portsmouth

Tuesday, 18 April 2023
Accrington S v Peterborough U
Bristol R v Sheffield W
Burton Alb v Bolton W
Cambridge U v Wycombe W
Exeter C v Derby Co
Forest Green R v Fleetwood T
Ipswich T v Port Vale
Lincoln C v Barnsley
Milton Keynes D v Charlton Ath
Morecambe v Cheltenham T
Oxford U v Portsmouth
Shrewsbury T v Plymouth Arg

Saturday, 22 April 2023
Barnsley v Oxford U
Bolton W v Shrewsbury T
Charlton Ath v Morecambe
Cheltenham T v Forest Green R
Derby Co v Burton Alb
Fleetwood T v Milton Keynes D
Peterborough U v Ipswich T
Plymouth Arg v Cambridge U
Port Vale v Bristol R
Portsmouth v Accrington S
Sheffield W v Exeter C
Wycombe W v Lincoln C

Saturday, 29 April 2023
Accrington S v Cambridge U
Bolton W v Fleetwood T
Charlton Ath v Port Vale
Derby Co v Portsmouth
Forest Green R v Oxford U
Ipswich T v Exeter C
Milton Keynes D v Barnsley
Morecambe v Lincoln C
Peterborough U v Bristol R
Plymouth Arg v Burton Alb
Shrewsbury T v Sheffield W
Wycombe W v Cheltenham T

Saturday, 6 May 2023
Barnsley v Peterborough U
Bristol R v Bolton W
Burton Alb v Milton Keynes D
Cambridge U v Forest Green R
Cheltenham T v Charlton Ath
Exeter C v Morecambe
Fleetwood T v Ipswich T
Lincoln C v Shrewsbury T
Oxford U v Accrington S
Port Vale v Plymouth Arg
Portsmouth v Wycombe W
Sheffield W v Derby Co

EFL League Two

Saturday, 30 July 2022
AFC Wimbledon v Gillingham
Bradford C v Doncaster R
Carlisle U v Crawley T
Harrogate T v Swindon T
Leyton Orient v Grimsby T
Northampton T v Colchester U
Rochdale v Crewe Alex
Salford C v Mansfield T
Stockport Co v Barrow
Sutton U v Newport Co
Tranmere R v Stevenage
Walsall v Hartlepool U

Saturday, 6 August 2022
Barrow v Bradford C
Colchester U v Carlisle U
Crawley T v Leyton Orient
Crewe Alex v Harrogate T
Doncaster R v Sutton U
Gillingham v Rochdale
Grimsby T v Northampton T
Hartlepool U v AFC Wimbledon
Mansfield T v Tranmere R
Newport Co v Walsall
Stevenage v Stockport Co
Swindon T v Salford C

Saturday, 13 August 2022
AFC Wimbledon v Doncaster R
Bradford C v Newport Co
Carlisle U v Swindon T
Harrogate T v Crawley T
Leyton Orient v Mansfield T
Northampton T v Hartlepool U
Rochdale v Grimsby T
Salford C v Crewe Alex
Stockport Co v Colchester U
Sutton U v Barrow
Tranmere R v Gillingham
Walsall v Stevenage

Tuesday, 16 August 2022
Barrow v Walsall
Colchester U v Bradford C
Crawley T v Northampton T
Crewe Alex v Sutton U
Gillingham v Harrogate T
Grimsby T v Carlisle U
Hartlepool U v Tranmere R
Mansfield T v AFC Wimbledon
Newport Co v Salford C
Stevenage v Rochdale
Swindon T v Leyton Orient
Doncaster R v Stockport Co

Saturday, 20 August 2022
Barrow v Harrogate T
Colchester U v Leyton Orient
Crawley T v AFC Wimbledon
Crewe Alex v Northampton T
Doncaster R v Salford C
Gillingham v Walsall
Grimsby T v Sutton U
Hartlepool U v Bradford C
Mansfield T v Stockport Co
Newport Co v Tranmere R
Stevenage v Carlisle U
Swindon T v Rochdale

Saturday, 27 August 2022
AFC Wimbledon v Barrow
Bradford C v Crewe Alex
Carlisle U v Gillingham
Harrogate T v Newport Co
Leyton Orient v Hartlepool U
Northampton T v Doncaster R
Rochdale v Crawley T
Salford C v Stevenage
Stockport Co v Swindon T
Sutton U v Mansfield T
Tranmere R v Colchester U
Walsall v Grimsby T

Saturday, 3 September 2022
Bradford C v Walsall
Carlisle U v Rochdale
Colchester U v Hartlepool U
Crewe Alex v Stevenage
Doncaster R v Mansfield T
Gillingham v Swindon T
Leyton Orient v Tranmere R
Newport Co v Grimsby T
Northampton T v Barrow
Salford C v Crawley T
Stockport Co v AFC Wimbledon
Sutton U v Harrogate T

Saturday, 10 September 2022
AFC Wimbledon v Leyton Orient
Barrow v Colchester U
Crawley T v Gillingham
Grimsby T v Crewe Alex
Harrogate T v Carlisle U
Hartlepool U v Doncaster R
Mansfield T v Bradford C
Rochdale v Salford C
Stevenage v Sutton U
Swindon T v Newport Co
Tranmere R v Stockport Co
Walsall v Northampton T

Tuesday, 13 September 2022
AFC Wimbledon v Northampton T
Barrow v Doncaster R
Crawley T v Stockport Co
Grimsby T v Gillingham
Harrogate T v Salford C
Hartlepool U v Crewe Alex
Mansfield T v Carlisle U
Rochdale v Leyton Orient
Stevenage v Newport Co
Swindon T v Sutton U
Tranmere R v Bradford C
Walsall v Colchester U

Saturday, 17 September 2022
Bradford C v Stevenage
Carlisle U v AFC Wimbledon
Colchester U v Grimsby T
Crewe Alex v Crawley T
Doncaster R v Swindon T
Gillingham v Mansfield T
Leyton Orient v Walsall
Newport Co v Barrow
Northampton T v Rochdale
Salford C v Tranmere R
Stockport Co v Harrogate T
Sutton U v Hartlepool U

Saturday, 24 September 2022
Barrow v Leyton Orient
Bradford C v AFC Wimbledon
Colchester U v Rochdale
Crewe Alex v Mansfield T
Doncaster R v Crawley T
Grimsby T v Swindon T
Hartlepool U v Gillingham
Newport Co v Carlisle U
Northampton T v Stockport Co
Stevenage v Harrogate T
Sutton U v Salford C
Walsall v Tranmere R

Saturday, 1 October 2022
AFC Wimbledon v Colchester U
Carlisle U v Crewe Alex
Crawley T v Stevenage
Gillingham v Sutton U
Harrogate T v Bradford C
Leyton Orient v Newport Co
Mansfield T v Hartlepool U
Rochdale v Doncaster R
Salford C v Grimsby T
Stockport Co v Walsall
Swindon T v Northampton T
Tranmere R v Barrow

Saturday, 8 October 2022
Barrow v Mansfield T
Bradford C v Stockport Co
Colchester U v Harrogate T
Crewe Alex v Gillingham
Doncaster R v Leyton Orient
Grimsby T v Crawley T
Hartlepool U v Carlisle U

Newport Co v Rochdale
Northampton T v Salford C
Stevenage v Swindon T
Sutton U v Tranmere R
Walsall v AFC Wimbledon

Saturday, 15 October 2022
AFC Wimbledon v Sutton U
Carlisle U v Doncaster R
Crawley T v Newport Co
Gillingham v Stevenage
Harrogate T v Hartlepool U
Leyton Orient v Northampton T
Mansfield T v Walsall
Rochdale v Barrow
Salford C v Bradford C
Stockport Co v Grimsby T
Swindon T v Colchester U
Tranmere R v Crewe Alex

Saturday, 22 October 2022
Carlisle U v Leyton Orient
Crawley T v Mansfield T
Crewe Alex v Doncaster R
Gillingham v Barrow
Grimsby T v Bradford C
Harrogate T v Tranmere R
Newport Co v Colchester U
Rochdale v AFC Wimbledon
Salford C v Stockport Co
Stevenage v Northampton T
Sutton U v Walsall
Swindon T v Hartlepool U

Tuesday, 25 October 2022
AFC Wimbledon v Crewe Alex
Barrow v Grimsby T
Bradford C v Swindon T
Colchester U v Crawley T
Hartlepool U v Salford C
Leyton Orient v Gillingham
Mansfield T v Newport Co
Northampton T v Sutton U
Stockport Co v Carlisle U
Tranmere R v Rochdale
Walsall v Harrogate T
Doncaster R v Stevenage

Saturday, 29 October 2022
AFC Wimbledon v Harrogate T
Barrow v Crewe Alex
Bradford C v Crawley T
Colchester U v Stevenage
Doncaster R v Gillingham
Hartlepool U v Grimsby T
Leyton Orient v Salford C
Mansfield T v Swindon T
Northampton T v Newport Co
Stockport Co v Sutton U
Tranmere R v Carlisle U
Walsall v Rochdale

Saturday, 12 November 2022
Carlisle U v Walsall
Crawley T v Barrow
Crewe Alex v Colchester U
Gillingham v Northampton T
Grimsby T v Doncaster R
Harrogate T v Leyton Orient
Newport Co v Stockport Co
Rochdale v Mansfield T
Salford C v AFC Wimbledon
Stevenage v Hartlepool U
Sutton U v Bradford C
Swindon T v Tranmere R

Saturday, 19 November 2022
Barrow v Hartlepool U
Bradford C v Northampton T
Colchester U v Doncaster R
Grimsby T v Stevenage
Harrogate T v Mansfield T
Newport Co v Gillingham
Salford C v Carlisle U
Stockport Co v Leyton Orient
Sutton U v Rochdale
Swindon T v Crewe Alex
Tranmere R v AFC Wimbledon
Walsall v Crawley T

Saturday, 3 December 2022
AFC Wimbledon v Grimsby T
Carlisle U v Sutton U
Crawley T v Swindon T
Crewe Alex v Newport Co
Doncaster R v Walsall
Gillingham v Salford C
Hartlepool U v Stockport Co
Leyton Orient v Bradford C
Mansfield T v Colchester U
Northampton T v Tranmere R
Rochdale v Harrogate T
Stevenage v Barrow

Saturday, 10 December 2022
Carlisle U v Barrow
Crawley T v Hartlepool U
Crewe Alex v Leyton Orient
Gillingham v Bradford C
Grimsby T v Tranmere R
Harrogate T v Northampton T
Newport Co v Doncaster R
Rochdale v Stockport Co
Salford C v Walsall
Stevenage v Mansfield T
Sutton U v Colchester U
Swindon T v AFC Wimbledon

Saturday, 17 December 2022
AFC Wimbledon v Stevenage
Barrow v Swindon T
Bradford C v Rochdale
Colchester U v Salford C
Doncaster R v Harrogate T
Hartlepool U v Newport Co
Leyton Orient v Sutton U
Mansfield T v Grimsby T
Northampton T v Carlisle U
Stockport Co v Gillingham
Tranmere R v Crawley T
Walsall v Crewe Alex

Monday, 26 December 2022
AFC Wimbledon v Newport Co
Carlisle U v Bradford C
Crawley T v Sutton U
Gillingham v Colchester U
Harrogate T v Grimsby T
Leyton Orient v Stevenage
Mansfield T v Northampton T
Rochdale v Hartlepool U
Salford C v Barrow
Stockport Co v Crewe Alex
Swindon T v Walsall
Tranmere R v Doncaster R

Thursday, 29 December 2022
Barrow v Tranmere R
Bradford C v Harrogate T
Colchester U v AFC Wimbledon
Crewe Alex v Carlisle U
Grimsby T v Salford C
Hartlepool U v Mansfield T
Newport Co v Leyton Orient
Northampton T v Swindon T
Stevenage v Crawley T
Sutton U v Gillingham
Walsall v Stockport Co
Doncaster R v Rochdale

Sunday, 1 January 2023
Barrow v Rochdale
Bradford C v Salford C
Colchester U v Swindon T
Crewe Alex v Tranmere R
Doncaster R v Carlisle U
Grimsby T v Stockport Co
Hartlepool U v Harrogate T
Newport Co v Crawley T
Northampton T v Leyton Orient
Stevenage v Gillingham
Sutton U v AFC Wimbledon
Walsall v Mansfield T

Saturday, 7 January 2023
AFC Wimbledon v Walsall
Carlisle U v Hartlepool U
Crawley T v Grimsby T
Gillingham v Crewe Alex
Harrogate T v Colchester U
Leyton Orient v Doncaster R
Mansfield T v Barrow
Rochdale v Newport Co
Salford C v Northampton T
Stockport Co v Bradford C
Swindon T v Stevenage
Tranmere R v Sutton U

Saturday, 14 January 2023
AFC Wimbledon v Bradford C
Carlisle U v Newport Co
Crawley T v Doncaster R
Gillingham v Hartlepool U
Harrogate T v Stevenage
Leyton Orient v Barrow
Mansfield T v Crewe Alex
Rochdale v Colchester U
Salford C v Sutton U
Stockport Co v Northampton T
Swindon T v Grimsby T
Tranmere R v Walsall

Saturday, 21 January 2023
Barrow v Salford C
Bradford C v Carlisle U
Colchester U v Gillingham
Crewe Alex v Stockport Co
Doncaster R v Tranmere R
Grimsby T v Harrogate T
Hartlepool U v Rochdale
Newport Co v AFC Wimbledon
Northampton T v Mansfield T
Stevenage v Leyton Orient
Sutton U v Crawley T
Walsall v Swindon T

Saturday, 28 January 2023
AFC Wimbledon v Stockport Co
Barrow v Northampton T
Crawley T v Salford C
Grimsby T v Newport Co
Harrogate T v Sutton U
Hartlepool U v Colchester U
Mansfield T v Doncaster R
Rochdale v Carlisle U
Stevenage v Crewe Alex
Swindon T v Gillingham
Tranmere R v Leyton Orient
Walsall v Bradford C

Saturday, 4 February 2023
Bradford C v Mansfield T
Carlisle U v Harrogate T
Colchester U v Barrow
Crewe Alex v Grimsby T
Doncaster R v Hartlepool U
Gillingham v Crawley T
Leyton Orient v AFC Wimbledon
Newport Co v Swindon T
Northampton T v Walsall
Salford C v Rochdale
Stockport Co v Tranmere R
Sutton U v Stevenage

Saturday, 11 February 2023
AFC Wimbledon v Carlisle U
Barrow v Newport Co
Crawley T v Crewe Alex
Grimsby T v Colchester U

Harrogate T v Stockport Co
Hartlepool U v Sutton U
Mansfield T v Gillingham
Rochdale v Northampton T
Stevenage v Bradford C
Swindon T v Doncaster R
Tranmere R v Salford C
Walsall v Leyton Orient

Tuesday, 14 February 2023
Bradford C v Tranmere R
Carlisle U v Mansfield T
Colchester U v Walsall
Crewe Alex v Hartlepool U
Gillingham v Grimsby T
Leyton Orient v Rochdale
Newport Co v Stevenage
Northampton T v AFC Wimbledon
Salford C v Harrogate T
Stockport Co v Crawley T
Sutton U v Swindon T
Doncaster R v Barrow

Saturday, 18 February 2023
AFC Wimbledon v Hartlepool U
Bradford C v Barrow
Carlisle U v Colchester U
Harrogate T v Crewe Alex
Leyton Orient v Crawley T
Northampton T v Grimsby T
Rochdale v Gillingham
Salford C v Swindon T
Stockport Co v Stevenage
Sutton U v Doncaster R
Tranmere R v Mansfield T
Walsall v Newport Co

Saturday, 25 February 2023
Barrow v Stockport Co
Colchester U v Northampton T
Crawley T v Carlisle U
Crewe Alex v Rochdale
Doncaster R v Bradford C
Gillingham v AFC Wimbledon
Grimsby T v Leyton Orient
Hartlepool U v Walsall
Mansfield T v Salford C
Newport Co v Sutton U
Stevenage v Tranmere R
Swindon T v Harrogate T

Saturday, 4 March 2023
AFC Wimbledon v Mansfield T
Bradford C v Colchester U
Carlisle U v Grimsby T
Harrogate T v Gillingham
Leyton Orient v Swindon T
Northampton T v Crawley T
Rochdale v Stevenage
Salford C v Newport Co
Stockport Co v Doncaster R
Sutton U v Crewe Alex
Tranmere R v Hartlepool U
Walsall v Barrow

Saturday, 11 March 2023
Barrow v Sutton U
Colchester U v Stockport Co
Crawley T v Harrogate T
Crewe Alex v Salford C
Doncaster R v AFC Wimbledon
Gillingham v Tranmere R
Grimsby T v Rochdale
Hartlepool U v Northampton T
Mansfield T v Leyton Orient
Newport Co v Bradford C
Stevenage v Walsall
Swindon T v Carlisle U

Saturday, 18 March 2023
AFC Wimbledon v Crawley T
Bradford C v Hartlepool U
Carlisle U v Stevenage
Harrogate T v Barrow
Leyton Orient v Colchester U
Northampton T v Crewe Alex
Rochdale v Swindon T
Salford C v Doncaster R
Stockport Co v Mansfield T
Sutton U v Grimsby T
Tranmere R v Newport Co
Walsall v Gillingham

Saturday, 25 March 2023
Barrow v AFC Wimbledon
Colchester U v Tranmere R
Crawley T v Rochdale
Crewe Alex v Bradford C
Doncaster R v Northampton T
Gillingham v Carlisle U
Grimsby T v Walsall
Hartlepool U v Leyton Orient
Mansfield T v Sutton U
Newport Co v Harrogate T
Stevenage v Salford C
Swindon T v Stockport Co

Saturday, 1 April 2023
AFC Wimbledon v Rochdale
Barrow v Gillingham
Bradford C v Grimsby T
Colchester U v Newport Co
Doncaster R v Crewe Alex
Hartlepool U v Swindon T
Leyton Orient v Carlisle U
Mansfield T v Crawley T
Northampton T v Stevenage
Stockport Co v Salford C
Tranmere R v Harrogate T
Walsall v Sutton U

Friday, 7 April 2023
Carlisle U v Tranmere R
Crawley T v Bradford C
Crewe Alex v Barrow
Gillingham v Doncaster R
Grimsby T v Hartlepool U
Harrogate T v AFC Wimbledon
Newport Co v Northampton T
Rochdale v Walsall
Salford C v Leyton Orient
Stevenage v Colchester U
Sutton U v Stockport Co
Swindon T v Mansfield T

Monday, 10 April 2023
AFC Wimbledon v Salford C
Barrow v Crawley T
Bradford C v Sutton U
Colchester U v Crewe Alex
Doncaster R v Grimsby T
Hartlepool U v Stevenage
Leyton Orient v Harrogate T
Mansfield T v Rochdale
Northampton T v Gillingham
Stockport Co v Newport Co
Tranmere R v Swindon T
Walsall v Carlisle U

Saturday, 15 April 2023
Carlisle U v Northampton T
Crawley T v Tranmere R
Crewe Alex v Walsall
Gillingham v Stockport Co
Grimsby T v Mansfield T
Harrogate T v Doncaster R
Newport Co v Hartlepool U
Rochdale v Bradford C
Salford C v Colchester U
Stevenage v AFC Wimbledon
Sutton U v Leyton Orient
Swindon T v Barrow

Tuesday, 18 April 2023
Carlisle U v Stockport Co
Crawley T v Colchester U
Crewe Alex v AFC Wimbledon
Gillingham v Leyton Orient
Grimsby T v Barrow
Harrogate T v Walsall
Newport Co v Mansfield T
Rochdale v Tranmere R
Salford C v Hartlepool U
Stevenage v Doncaster R
Sutton U v Northampton T
Swindon T v Bradford C

Saturday, 22 April 2023
AFC Wimbledon v Swindon T
Barrow v Carlisle U
Bradford C v Gillingham
Colchester U v Sutton U
Doncaster R v Newport Co
Hartlepool U v Crawley T
Leyton Orient v Crewe Alex
Mansfield T v Stevenage
Northampton T v Harrogate T
Stockport Co v Rochdale
Tranmere R v Grimsby T
Walsall v Salford C

Saturday, 29 April 2023
AFC Wimbledon v Tranmere R
Carlisle U v Salford C
Crawley T v Walsall
Crewe Alex v Swindon T
Doncaster R v Colchester U
Gillingham v Newport Co
Hartlepool U v Barrow
Leyton Orient v Stockport Co
Mansfield T v Harrogate T
Northampton T v Bradford C
Rochdale v Sutton U
Stevenage v Grimsby T

Saturday, 6 May 2023
Barrow v Stevenage
Bradford C v Leyton Orient
Colchester U v Mansfield T
Grimsby T v AFC Wimbledon
Harrogate T v Rochdale
Newport Co v Crewe Alex
Salford C v Gillingham
Stockport Co v Hartlepool U
Sutton U v Carlisle U
Swindon T v Crawley T
Tranmere R v Northampton T
Walsall v Doncaster R

NATIONAL LEAGUE FIXTURES 2022–23

All fixtures subject to change.

Saturday, 6 August 2022
Aldershot T v Solihull Moors
Altrincham v Maidstone U
Barnet v FC Halifax T
Dagenham & R v Gateshead
Dorking W v Chesterfield
Notts Co v Maidenhead U
Scunthorpe U v Yeovil T
Southend U v Boreham Wood
Torquay U v Oldham Ath
Wealdstone v Bromley
Wrexham v Eastleigh
York C v Woking

Saturday, 13 August 2022
Boreham Wood v Notts Co
Bromley v Altrincham
Chesterfield v Aldershot T
Eastleigh v Wealdstone
FC Halifax T v Torquay U
Gateshead v Barnet
Maidenhead U v Scunthorpe U
Maidstone U v York C
Oldham Ath v Dorking W
Solihull Moors v Southend U
Woking v Dagenham & R
Yeovil T v Wrexham

Tuesday, 16 August 2022
Boreham Wood v Aldershot T
Bromley v Torquay U
Chesterfield v Wrexham
Eastleigh v Dagenham & R
FC Halifax T v Southend U
Gateshead v Notts Co
Maidenhead U v Altrincham
Maidstone U v Dorking W
Oldham Ath v Wealdstone
Solihull Moors v York C
Woking v Scunthorpe U
Yeovil T v Barnet

Saturday, 20 August 2022
Aldershot T v Bromley
Altrincham v Yeovil T
Barnet v Woking
Dagenham & R v Maidenhead U
Dorking W v Gateshead
Notts Co v Chesterfield
Scunthorpe U v Solihull Moors
Southend U v Oldham Ath
Torquay U v Boreham Wood
Wealdstone v FC Halifax T
Wrexham v Maidstone U
York C v Eastleigh

Saturday, 27 August 2022
Boreham Wood v Altrincham
Bromley v Scunthorpe U
Chesterfield v Barnet
Eastleigh v Southend U
FC Halifax T v Notts Co
Gateshead v Wealdstone
Maidenhead U v York C
Maidstone U v Torquay U
Oldham Ath v Aldershot T
Solihull Moors v Dorking W
Woking v Wrexham
Yeovil T v Dagenham & R

Monday, 29 August 2022
Aldershot T v Maidstone U
Altrincham v Chesterfield
Barnet v Eastleigh
Dagenham & R v Bromley
Dorking W v Boreham Wood
Notts Co v Solihull Moors
Scunthorpe U v FC Halifax T
Southend U v Maidenhead U
Torquay U v Woking
Wealdstone v Yeovil T
Wrexham v Gateshead
York C v Oldham Ath

Saturday, 3 September 2022
Aldershot T v Barnet
Bromley v Eastleigh
Dagenham & R v Notts Co
Dorking W v Wrexham
Gateshead v Maidstone U
Maidenhead U v FC Halifax T
Oldham Ath v Chesterfield
Scunthorpe U v Boreham Wood
Solihull Moors v Altrincham
Southend U v Torquay U
Wealdstone v Woking
Yeovil T v York C

Saturday, 10 September 2022
Altrincham v Wealdstone
Barnet v Southend U
Boreham Wood v Oldham Ath
Chesterfield v Gateshead
Eastleigh v Scunthorpe U
FC Halifax T v Dorking W
Maidstone U v Solihull Moors
Notts Co v Bromley
Torquay U v Aldershot T
Woking v Yeovil T
Wrexham v Maidenhead U
York C v Dagenham & R

Tuesday, 13 September 2022
Altrincham v Scunthorpe U
Barnet v Dorking W
Boreham Wood v Maidenhead U
Chesterfield v Southend U
Eastleigh v Yeovil T
FC Halifax T v Gateshead
Maidstone U v Wealdstone
Notts Co v Aldershot T
Torquay U v Solihull Moors
Woking v Oldham Ath
Wrexham v Dagenham & R
York C v Bromley

Saturday, 17 September 2022
Aldershot T v FC Halifax T
Bromley v Maidstone U
Dagenham & R v Altrincham
Dorking W v Notts Co
Gateshead v Boreham Wood
Maidenhead U v Woking
Oldham Ath v Eastleigh
Scunthorpe U v York C
Solihull Moors v Barnet
Southend U v Wrexham
Wealdstone v Torquay U
Yeovil T v Chesterfield

Saturday, 24 September 2022
Altrincham v Aldershot T
Bromley v Oldham Ath
Dagenham & R v Barnet
Eastleigh v FC Halifax T
Maidenhead U v Gateshead
Maidstone U v Chesterfield
Scunthorpe U v Dorking W
Wealdstone v Southend U
Woking v Solihull Moors
Wrexham v Torquay U
Yeovil T v Boreham Wood
York C v Notts Co

Saturday, 1 October 2022
Aldershot T v Wealdstone
Barnet v York C
Boreham Wood v Maidstone U
Chesterfield v Maidenhead U
Dorking W v Dagenham & R
FC Halifax T v Woking
Gateshead v Eastleigh
Notts Co v Altrincham
Oldham Ath v Wrexham
Solihull Moors v Bromley
Southend U v Yeovil T
Torquay U v Scunthorpe U

Tuesday, 4 October 2022
Aldershot T v Eastleigh
Barnet v Maidstone U
Boreham Wood v Bromley
Chesterfield v Dagenham & R
Dorking W v Yeovil T
FC Halifax T v York C
Gateshead v Altrincham
Notts Co v Wrexham
Oldham Ath v Scunthorpe U
Solihull Moors v Wealdstone
Southend U v Woking
Torquay U v Maidenhead U

Saturday, 8 October 2022
Altrincham v Dorking W
Bromley v Gateshead
Dagenham & R v Southend U
Eastleigh v Chesterfield
Maidenhead U v Oldham Ath
Maidstone U v FC Halifax T
Scunthorpe U v Aldershot T
Wealdstone v Boreham Wood
Woking v Notts Co
Wrexham v Barnet
Yeovil T v Solihull Moors
York C v Torquay U

Saturday, 22 October 2022
Aldershot T v York C
Barnet v Maidenhead U
Boreham Wood v Wrexham
Chesterfield v Bromley
Dorking W v Wealdstone
FC Halifax T v Dagenham & R
Gateshead v Woking
Notts Co v Maidstone U
Oldham Ath v Yeovil T
Solihull Moors v Eastleigh
Southend U v Scunthorpe U
Torquay U v Altrincham

Tuesday, 25 October 2022
Altrincham v Oldham Ath
Bromley v Barnet
Dagenham & R v Boreham Wood
Eastleigh v Torquay U
Maidenhead U v Solihull Moors
Maidstone U v Southend U
Scunthorpe U v Gateshead
Wealdstone v Notts Co

Woking v Dorking W
Wrexham v FC Halifax T
Yeovil T v Aldershot T
York C v Chesterfield

Saturday, 29 October 2022
Barnet v Scunthorpe U
Chesterfield v Boreham Wood
Dagenham & R v Wealdstone
Dorking W v Aldershot T
FC Halifax T v Oldham Ath
Gateshead v Solihull Moors
Maidenhead U v Bromley
Maidstone U v Yeovil T
Notts Co v Torquay U
Woking v Eastleigh
Wrexham v Altrincham
York C v Southend U

Tuesday, 8 November 2022
Aldershot T v Dagenham & R
Altrincham v Barnet
Boreham Wood v York C
Bromley v Woking
Eastleigh v Maidstone U
Oldham Ath v Gateshead
Scunthorpe U v Wrexham
Solihull Moors v FC Halifax T
Southend U v Notts Co
Torquay U v Dorking W
Wealdstone v Chesterfield
Yeovil T v Maidenhead U

Saturday, 12 November 2022
Aldershot T v Maidenhead U
Altrincham v York C
Boreham Wood v Woking
Bromley v FC Halifax T
Eastleigh v Notts Co
Oldham Ath v Barnet
Scunthorpe U v Maidstone U
Solihull Moors v Dagenham & R
Southend U v Dorking W
Torquay U v Chesterfield
Wealdstone v Wrexham
Yeovil T v Gateshead

Saturday, 19 November 2022
Barnet v Torquay U
Chesterfield v Solihull Moors
Dagenham & R v Scunthorpe U
Dorking W v Bromley
FC Halifax T v Boreham Wood
Gateshead v Southend U
Maidenhead U v Eastleigh
Maidstone U v Oldham Ath
Notts Co v Yeovil T
Woking v Altrincham
Wrexham v Aldershot T
York C v Wealdstone

Saturday, 26 November 2022
Aldershot T v Southend U
Altrincham v Eastleigh
Boreham Wood v Solihull Moors
Chesterfield v Woking
Dorking W v York C
Maidstone U v Maidenhead U
Notts Co v Barnet
Oldham Ath v Dagenham & R
Torquay U v Gateshead
Wealdstone v Scunthorpe U
Wrexham v Bromley
Yeovil T v FC Halifax T

Saturday, 3 December 2022
Barnet v Wealdstone
Bromley v Yeovil T
Dagenham & R v Torquay U
Eastleigh v Boreham Wood
FC Halifax T v Chesterfield
Gateshead v Aldershot T
Maidenhead U v Dorking W
Scunthorpe U v Notts Co
Solihull Moors v Oldham Ath
Southend U v Altrincham
Woking v Maidstone U
York C v Wrexham

Saturday, 10 December 2022
Boreham Wood v Southend U
Bromley v Wealdstone
Chesterfield v Dorking W
Eastleigh v Wrexham
FC Halifax T v Barnet
Gateshead v Dagenham & R
Maidenhead U v Notts Co
Maidstone U v Altrincham
Oldham Ath v Torquay U
Solihull Moors v Aldershot T
Woking v York C
Yeovil T v Scunthorpe U

Tuesday, 13 December 2022
Aldershot T v Boreham Wood
Altrincham v Maidenhead U
Barnet v Yeovil T
Dagenham & R v Eastleigh
Dorking W v Maidstone U
Notts Co v Gateshead
Scunthorpe U v Woking
Southend U v FC Halifax T
Torquay U v Bromley
Wealdstone v Oldham Ath
Wrexham v Chesterfield
York C v Solihull Moors

Monday, 26 December 2022
Aldershot T v Woking
Altrincham v FC Halifax T
Barnet v Boreham Wood
Dagenham & R v Maidstone U
Dorking W v Eastleigh
Notts Co v Oldham Ath
Scunthorpe U v Chesterfield
Southend U v Bromley
Torquay U v Yeovil T
Wealdstone v Maidenhead U
Wrexham v Solihull Moors
York C v Gateshead

Sunday, 1 January 2023
Boreham Wood v Barnet
Bromley v Southend U
Chesterfield v Scunthorpe U
Eastleigh v Dorking W
FC Halifax T v Altrincham
Gateshead v York C
Maidenhead U v Wealdstone
Maidstone U v Dagenham & R
Oldham Ath v Notts Co
Solihull Moors v Wrexham
Woking v Aldershot T
Yeovil T v Torquay U

Saturday, 7 January 2023
Aldershot T v Chesterfield
Altrincham v Bromley
Barnet v Gateshead
Dagenham & R v Woking
Dorking W v Oldham Ath
Notts Co v Boreham Wood
Scunthorpe U v Maidenhead U
Southend U v Solihull Moors
Torquay U v FC Halifax T
Wealdstone v Eastleigh
Wrexham v Yeovil T
York C v Maidstone U

Saturday, 21 January 2023
Boreham Wood v Torquay U
Bromley v Aldershot T
Chesterfield v Notts Co
Eastleigh v York C
FC Halifax T v Wealdstone
Gateshead v Dorking W
Maidenhead U v Dagenham & R
Maidstone U v Wrexham
Oldham Ath v Southend U
Solihull Moors v Scunthorpe U
Woking v Barnet
Yeovil T v Altrincham

Tuesday, 24 January 2023
Boreham Wood v Dorking W
Bromley v Dagenham & R
Chesterfield v Altrincham
Eastleigh v Barnet
FC Halifax T v Scunthorpe U
Gateshead v Wrexham
Maidenhead U v Southend U
Maidstone U v Aldershot T
Oldham Ath v York C
Solihull Moors v Notts Co
Woking v Torquay U
Yeovil T v Wealdstone

Saturday, 28 January 2023
Aldershot T v Oldham Ath
Altrincham v Boreham Wood
Barnet v Chesterfield
Dagenham & R v Yeovil T
Dorking W v Solihull Moors
Notts Co v FC Halifax T
Scunthorpe U v Bromley
Southend U v Eastleigh
Torquay U v Maidstone U
Wealdstone v Gateshead
Wrexham v Woking
York C v Maidenhead U

Saturday, 4 February 2023
Aldershot T v Dorking W
Altrincham v Wrexham
Boreham Wood v Chesterfield
Bromley v Maidenhead U
Eastleigh v Woking
Oldham Ath v FC Halifax T
Scunthorpe U v Barnet
Solihull Moors v Gateshead
Southend U v York C
Torquay U v Notts Co
Wealdstone v Dagenham & R
Yeovil T v Maidstone U

Saturday, 11 February 2023
Barnet v Oldham Ath
Chesterfield v Torquay U
Dagenham & R v Solihull Moors
Dorking W v Southend U
FC Halifax T v Bromley
Gateshead v Yeovil T
Maidenhead U v Aldershot T
Maidstone U v Scunthorpe U
Notts Co v Eastleigh
Woking v Boreham Wood
Wrexham v Wealdstone
York C v Altrincham

Saturday, 18 February 2023
Aldershot T v Wrexham
Altrincham v Woking
Boreham Wood v FC Halifax T
Bromley v Dorking W
Eastleigh v Maidenhead U
Oldham Ath v Maidstone U
Scunthorpe U v Dagenham & R
Solihull Moors v Chesterfield
Southend U v Gateshead
Torquay U v Barnet
Wealdstone v York C
Yeovil T v Notts Co

Tuesday, 21 February 2023
Barnet v Altrincham
Chesterfield v Wealdstone

Dagenham & R v Aldershot T
Dorking W v Torquay U
FC Halifax T v Solihull Moors
Gateshead v Oldham Ath
Maidenhead U v Yeovil T
Maidstone U v Eastleigh
Notts Co v Southend U
Woking v Bromley
Wrexham v Scunthorpe U
York C v Boreham Wood

Saturday, 25 February 2023
Altrincham v Solihull Moors
Barnet v Aldershot T
Boreham Wood v Scunthorpe U
Chesterfield v Oldham Ath
Eastleigh v Bromley
FC Halifax T v Maidenhead U
Maidstone U v Gateshead
Notts Co v Dagenham & R
Torquay U v Southend U
Woking v Wealdstone
Wrexham v Dorking W
York C v Yeovil T

Saturday, 4 March 2023
Aldershot T v Torquay U
Bromley v Notts Co
Dagenham & R v York C
Dorking W v FC Halifax T
Gateshead v Chesterfield
Maidenhead U v Wrexham
Oldham Ath v Boreham Wood
Scunthorpe U v Eastleigh
Solihull Moors v Maidstone U
Southend U v Barnet
Wealdstone v Altrincham
Yeovil T v Woking

Tuesday, 7 March 2023
Aldershot T v Notts Co
Bromley v York C
Dagenham & R v Wrexham
Dorking W v Barnet
Gateshead v FC Halifax T
Maidenhead U v Boreham Wood
Oldham Ath v Woking
Scunthorpe U v Altrincham
Solihull Moors v Torquay U
Southend U v Chesterfield
Wealdstone v Maidstone U
Yeovil T v Eastleigh

Saturday, 11 March 2023
Altrincham v Dagenham & R
Barnet v Solihull Moors
Boreham Wood v Gateshead
Chesterfield v Yeovil T
Eastleigh v Oldham Ath
FC Halifax T v Aldershot T
Maidstone U v Bromley
Notts Co v Dorking W
Torquay U v Wealdstone
Woking v Maidenhead U
Wrexham v Southend U
York C v Scunthorpe U

Saturday, 18 March 2023
Barnet v Notts Co
Bromley v Wrexham
Dagenham & R v Oldham Ath
Eastleigh v Altrincham
FC Halifax T v Yeovil T
Gateshead v Torquay U
Maidenhead U v Maidstone U
Scunthorpe U v Wealdstone
Solihull Moors v Boreham Wood
Southend U v Aldershot T
Woking v Chesterfield
York C v Dorking W

Saturday, 25 March 2023
Aldershot T v Gateshead
Altrincham v Southend U
Boreham Wood v Eastleigh
Chesterfield v FC Halifax T
Dorking W v Maidenhead U
Maidstone U v Woking
Notts Co v Scunthorpe U
Oldham Ath v Solihull Moors
Torquay U v Dagenham & R
Wealdstone v Barnet
Wrexham v York C
Yeovil T v Bromley

Saturday, 1 April 2023
Altrincham v Notts Co
Bromley v Solihull Moors
Dagenham & R v Dorking W
Eastleigh v Gateshead
Maidenhead U v Chesterfield
Maidstone U v Boreham Wood
Scunthorpe U v Torquay U
Wealdstone v Aldershot T
Woking v FC Halifax T
Wrexham v Oldham Ath
Yeovil T v Southend U
York C v Barnet

Friday, 7 April 2023
Aldershot T v Yeovil T
Barnet v Bromley
Boreham Wood v Dagenham & R
Chesterfield v York C
Dorking W v Woking
FC Halifax T v Wrexham
Gateshead v Scunthorpe U
Notts Co v Wealdstone
Oldham Ath v Altrincham
Solihull Moors v Maidenhead U
Southend U v Maidstone U
Torquay U v Eastleigh

Monday, 10 April 2023
Altrincham v Gateshead
Bromley v Boreham Wood
Dagenham & R v Chesterfield
Eastleigh v Aldershot T
Maidenhead U v Torquay U
Maidstone U v Barnet
Scunthorpe U v Oldham Ath
Wealdstone v Solihull Moors
Woking v Southend U
Wrexham v Notts Co
Yeovil T v Dorking W
York C v FC Halifax T

Saturday, 15 April 2023
Aldershot T v Scunthorpe U
Barnet v Wrexham
Boreham Wood v Wealdstone
Chesterfield v Eastleigh
Dorking W v Altrincham
FC Halifax T v Maidstone U
Gateshead v Bromley
Notts Co v Woking
Oldham Ath v Maidenhead U
Solihull Moors v Yeovil T
Southend U v Dagenham & R
Torquay U v York C

Saturday, 22 April 2023
Altrincham v Torquay U
Bromley v Chesterfield
Dagenham & R v FC Halifax T
Eastleigh v Solihull Moors
Maidenhead U v Barnet
Maidstone U v Notts Co
Scunthorpe U v Southend U
Wealdstone v Dorking W
Woking v Gateshead
Wrexham v Boreham Wood
Yeovil T v Oldham Ath
York C v Aldershot T

Saturday, 29 April 2023
Aldershot T v Altrincham
Barnet v Dagenham & R
Boreham Wood v Yeovil T
Chesterfield v Maidstone U
Dorking W v Scunthorpe U
FC Halifax T v Eastleigh
Gateshead v Maidenhead U
Notts Co v York C
Oldham Ath v Bromley
Solihull Moors v Woking
Southend U v Wealdstone
Torquay U v Wrexham

THE SCOTTISH PREMIER LEAGUE AND SCOTTISH LEAGUE FIXTURES 2022–23

All fixtures subject to change.

cinch Premiership

Saturday, 30 July 2022
Livingston v Rangers
Hearts v Ross Co
Kilmarnock v Dundee U
St Johnstone v Hibernian
St Mirren v Motherwell

Sunday, 31 July 2022
Celtic v Aberdeen

Saturday, 6 August 2022
Aberdeen v St Mirren
Dundee U v Livingston
Hibernian v Hearts
Motherwell v St Johnstone
Rangers v Kilmarnock
Ross Co v Celtic

Saturday, 13 August 2022
Aberdeen v Motherwell
Hearts v Dundee U
Kilmarnock v Celtic
Livingston v Hibernian
Rangers v St Johnstone
St Mirren v Ross Co

Saturday, 20 August 2022
Celtic v Hearts
Dundee U v St Mirren
Hibernian v Rangers
Motherwell v Livingston
Ross Co v Kilmarnock
St Johnstone v Aberdeen

Saturday, 27 August 2022
Aberdeen v Livingston
Dundee U v Celtic
Hearts v St Johnstone
Kilmarnock v Motherwell
Rangers v Ross Co
St Mirren v Hibernian

Saturday, 3 September 2022
Celtic v Rangers
Hibernian v Kilmarnock
Livingston v Hearts
Motherwell v Dundee U
Ross Co v Aberdeen
St Johnstone v St Mirren

Saturday, 10 September 2022
Aberdeen v Rangers
Celtic v Livingston
Dundee U v Hibernian
Hearts v St Mirren
Kilmarnock v St Johnstone
Ross Co v Motherwell

Saturday, 17 September 2022
Hibernian v Aberdeen
Livingston v Kilmarnock
Motherwell v Hearts
Rangers v Dundee U
St Johnstone v Ross Co
St Mirren v Celtic

Saturday, 1 October 2022
Aberdeen v Kilmarnock
Celtic v Motherwell
Dundee U v St Johnstone
Hearts v Rangers
Ross Co v Hibernian
St Mirren v Livingston

Saturday, 8 October 2022
Dundee U v Aberdeen
Hibernian v Motherwell
Kilmarnock v Hearts
Livingston v Ross Co
Rangers v St Mirren
St Johnstone v Celtic

Saturday, 15 October 2022
Aberdeen v Hearts
Celtic v Hibernian
Livingston v St Johnstone
Motherwell v Rangers
Ross Co v Dundee U
St Mirren v Kilmarnock

Saturday, 22 October 2022
Hearts v Celtic
Hibernian v St Johnstone
Kilmarnock v Ross Co
Motherwell v Aberdeen
Rangers v Livingston
St Mirren v Dundee U

Saturday, 29 October 2022
Dundee U v Motherwell
Hibernian v St Mirren
Livingston v Celtic
Rangers v Aberdeen
Ross Co v Hearts
St Johnstone v Kilmarnock

Saturday, 5 November 2022
Aberdeen v Hibernian
Celtic v Dundee U
Hearts v Motherwell
Kilmarnock v Livingston
Ross Co v St Mirren
St Johnstone v Rangers

Wednesday, 9 November 2022
Dundee U v Kilmarnock
Hibernian v Ross Co
Livingston v Aberdeen
Motherwell v Celtic
Rangers v Hearts
St Mirren v St Johnstone

Saturday, 12 November 2022
Aberdeen v Dundee U
Celtic v Ross Co
Hearts v Livingston
Kilmarnock v Hibernian
St Johnstone v Motherwell
St Mirren v Rangers

Saturday, 17 December 2022
Aberdeen v Celtic
Hearts v Kilmarnock
Livingston v Dundee U
Motherwell v St Mirren
Rangers v Hibernian
Ross Co v St Johnstone

Saturday, 24 December 2022
Celtic v St Johnstone
Dundee U v Hearts
Hibernian v Livingston
Motherwell v Kilmarnock
Ross Co v Rangers
St Mirren v Aberdeen

Wednesday, 28 December 2022
Dundee U v Ross Co
Hibernian v Celtic
Kilmarnock v Aberdeen
Livingston v St Mirren
Rangers v Motherwell
St Johnstone v Hearts

Monday, 2 January 2023
Aberdeen v Ross Co
Hearts v Hibernian
Kilmarnock v St Mirren
Livingston v Motherwell
Rangers v Celtic
St Johnstone v Dundee U

Saturday, 7 January 2023
Aberdeen v St Johnstone
Celtic v Kilmarnock
Dundee U v Rangers
Motherwell v Hibernian
Ross Co v Livingston
St Mirren v Hearts

Saturday, 14 January 2023
Celtic v St Mirren
Hearts v Aberdeen
Hibernian v Dundee U
Kilmarnock v Rangers
Motherwell v Ross Co
St Johnstone v Livingston

Saturday, 28 January 2023
Dundee U v Celtic
Hibernian v Aberdeen
Livingston v Hearts
Rangers v St Johnstone
Ross Co v Kilmarnock
St Mirren v Motherwell

Wednesday, 1 February 2023
Aberdeen v St Mirren
Celtic v Livingston
Hearts v Rangers
Kilmarnock v Dundee U
Motherwell v St Johnstone
Ross Co v Hibernian

Saturday, 4 February 2023
Aberdeen v Motherwell
Hearts v Dundee U
Livingston v Kilmarnock
Rangers v Ross Co
St Johnstone v Celtic
St Mirren v Hibernian

Saturday, 18 February 2023
Celtic v Aberdeen
Dundee U v St Johnstone
Hibernian v Kilmarnock
Livingston v Rangers
Motherwell v Hearts
St Mirren v Ross Co

Saturday, 25 February 2023
Aberdeen v Livingston
Celtic v Hearts
Hibernian v Rangers
Kilmarnock v Motherwell
Ross Co v Dundee U
St Johnstone v St Mirren

Saturday, 4 March 2023
Dundee U v Aberdeen
Hearts v St Johnstone
Livingston v Hibernian
Rangers v Kilmarnock
Ross Co v Motherwell
St Mirren v Celtic

Saturday, 18 March 2023
Aberdeen v Hearts
Celtic v Hibernian
Dundee U v St Mirren
Kilmarnock v St Johnstone
Livingston v Ross Co
Motherwell v Rangers

Saturday, 1 April 2023
Hibernian v Motherwell
Kilmarnock v Hearts

Rangers v Dundee U
Ross Co v Celtic
St Johnstone v Aberdeen
St Mirren v Livingston

Saturday, 8 April 2023
Aberdeen v Kilmarnock
Celtic v Rangers
Dundee U v Hibernian
Hearts v St Mirren
Motherwell v Livingston
St Johnstone v Ross Co

Saturday, 15 April 2023
Hibernian v Hearts
Kilmarnock v Celtic
Livingston v St Johnstone
Motherwell v Dundee U
Rangers v St Mirren
Ross Co v Aberdeen

Saturday, 22 April 2023
Aberdeen v Rangers
Celtic v Motherwell
Dundee U v Livingston
Hearts v Ross Co
St Johnstone v Hibernian
St Mirren v Kilmarnock

cinch Championship

Saturday, 30 July 2022
Ayr U v Arbroath
Cove Rangers v Raith R
Dundee v Partick Thistle
Hamilton A v Greenock Morton
Inverness CT v Queen's Park

Saturday, 6 August 2022
Arbroath v Inverness CT
Greenock Morton v Cove Rangers
Partick Thistle v Hamilton A
Queen's Park v Ayr U
Raith R v Dundee

Saturday, 13 August 2022
Ayr U v Hamilton A
Dundee v Arbroath
Inverness CT v Cove Rangers
Queen's Park v Partick Thistle
Raith R v Greenock Morton

Saturday, 20 August 2022
Arbroath v Queen's Park
Cove Rangers v Ayr U
Hamilton A v Raith R
Greenock Morton v Dundee
Partick Thistle v Inverness CT

Saturday, 27 August 2022
Ayr U v Dundee
Hamilton A v Arbroath
Inverness CT v Greenock Morton
Partick Thistle v Raith R
Queen's Park v Cove Rangers

Saturday, 3 September 2022
Arbroath v Partick Thistle
Cove Rangers v Hamilton A
Dundee v Queen's Park
Greenock Morton v Ayr U
Raith R v Inverness CT

Saturday, 10 September 2022
Arbroath v Raith R
Ayr U v Partick Thistle
Cove Rangers v Dundee
Inverness CT v Hamilton A
Queen's Park v Greenock Morton

Saturday, 17 September 2022
Dundee v Inverness CT
Hamilton A v Queen's Park
Greenock Morton v Arbroath
Partick Thistle v Cove Rangers
Raith R v Ayr U

Saturday, 1 October 2022
Ayr U v Inverness CT
Cove Rangers v Arbroath
Hamilton A v Dundee
Partick Thistle v Greenock Morton
Queen's Park v Raith R

Saturday, 8 October 2022
Arbroath v Dundee
Ayr U v Queen's Park
Inverness CT v Partick Thistle
Greenock Morton v Hamilton A
Raith R v Cove Rangers

Saturday, 15 October 2022
Cove Rangers v Inverness CT
Dundee v Ayr U
Hamilton A v Partick Thistle
Greenock Morton v Raith R
Queen's Park v Arbroath

Saturday, 22 October 2022
Arbroath v Hamilton A
Ayr U v Cove Rangers
Dundee v Greenock Morton
Inverness CT v Raith R
Partick Thistle v Queen's Park

Saturday, 29 October 2022
Arbroath v Ayr U
Hamilton A v Cove Rangers
Greenock Morton v Inverness CT
Queen's Park v Dundee
Raith R v Partick Thistle

Saturday, 5 November 2022
Ayr U v Greenock Morton
Cove Rangers v Queen's Park
Inverness CT v Arbroath
Partick Thistle v Dundee
Raith R v Hamilton A

Saturday, 12 November 2022
Arbroath v Cove Rangers
Dundee v Raith R
Hamilton A v Ayr U
Greenock Morton v Partick Thistle
Queen's Park v Inverness CT

Saturday, 19 November 2022
Cove Rangers v Greenock Morton
Dundee v Hamilton A
Inverness CT v Ayr U
Partick Thistle v Arbroath
Raith R v Queen's Park

Saturday, 3 December 2022
Arbroath v Greenock Morton
Ayr U v Raith R
Cove Rangers v Partick Thistle
Inverness CT v Dundee
Queen's Park v Hamilton A

Saturday, 17 December 2022
Dundee v Cove Rangers
Hamilton A v Inverness CT
Greenock Morton v Queen's Park
Partick Thistle v Ayr U
Raith R v Arbroath

Saturday, 24 December 2022
Arbroath v Queen's Park
Ayr U v Dundee
Cove Rangers v Hamilton A
Partick Thistle v Inverness CT
Raith R v Greenock Morton

Monday, 2 January 2023
Dundee v Arbroath
Hamilton A v Raith R
Inverness CT v Cove Rangers
Greenock Morton v Ayr U
Queen's Park v Partick Thistle

Saturday, 7 January 2023
Arbroath v Inverness CT
Ayr U v Hamilton A
Partick Thistle v Greenock Morton
Queen's Park v Cove Rangers
Raith R v Dundee

Saturday, 14 January 2023
Ayr U v Arbroath
Cove Rangers v Raith R
Dundee v Partick Thistle
Hamilton A v Greenock Morton
Inverness CT v Queen's Park

Saturday, 28 January 2023
Cove Rangers v Ayr U
Dundee v Queen's Park
Greenock Morton v Arbroath
Partick Thistle v Hamilton A
Raith R v Inverness CT

Saturday, 4 February 2023
Arbroath v Raith R
Hamilton A v Dundee
Inverness CT v Greenock Morton
Partick Thistle v Cove Rangers
Queen's Park v Ayr U

Saturday, 18 February 2023
Ayr U v Partick Thistle
Cove Rangers v Arbroath
Inverness CT v Hamilton A
Greenock Morton v Dundee
Queen's Park v Raith R

Saturday, 25 February 2023
Arbroath v Partick Thistle
Dundee v Inverness CT
Hamilton A v Queen's Park
Greenock Morton v Cove Rangers
Raith R v Ayr U

Saturday, 4 March 2023
Ayr U v Inverness CT
Cove Rangers v Dundee
Hamilton A v Arbroath
Partick Thistle v Raith R
Queen's Park v Greenock Morton

Saturday, 11 March 2023
Cove Rangers v Queen's Park
Dundee v Ayr U
Inverness CT v Arbroath
Greenock Morton v Partick Thistle
Raith R v Hamilton A

Saturday, 18 March 2023
Arbroath v Greenock Morton
Hamilton A v Ayr U
Partick Thistle v Dundee
Queen's Park v Inverness CT
Raith R v Cove Rangers

Saturday, 25 March 2023
Ayr U v Cove Rangers
Dundee v Raith R
Inverness CT v Partick Thistle
Greenock Morton v Hamilton A
Queen's Park v Arbroath

Saturday, 1 April 2023
Arbroath v Ayr U
Cove Rangers v Partick Thistle
Dundee v Hamilton A
Greenock Morton v Inverness CT
Raith R v Queen's Park

Saturday, 8 April 2023
Arbroath v Dundee
Ayr U v Greenock Morton
Hamilton A v Cove Rangers
Inverness CT v Raith R
Partick Thistle v Queen's Park

Saturday, 15 April 2023
Cove Rangers v Inverness CT
Dundee v Greenock Morton
Partick Thistle v Ayr U
Queen's Park v Hamilton A
Raith R v Arbroath

Saturday, 22 April 2023
Arbroath v Cove Rangers
Ayr U v Queen's Park
Hamilton A v Partick Thistle
Inverness CT v Dundee
Greenock Morton v Raith R

Saturday, 29 April 2023
Ayr U v Raith R
Dundee v Cove Rangers
Hamilton A v Inverness CT
Greenock Morton v Queen's Park
Partick Thistle v Arbroath

Friday, 5 May 2023
Arbroath v Hamilton A
Cove Rangers v Greenock Morton
Inverness CT v Ayr U
Queen's Park v Dundee
Raith R v Partick Thistle

cinch League One

Saturday, 30 July 2022
Dunfermline Ath v Alloa Ath
Falkirk v Montrose
Kelty Hearts v FC Edinburgh
Peterhead v Airdrieonians
Queen of the South v Clyde

Saturday, 6 August 2022
Airdrieonians v Falkirk
Alloa Ath v Kelty Hearts
Clyde v Peterhead
FC Edinburgh v Dunfermline Ath
Montrose v Queen of the South

Saturday, 13 August 2022
Alloa Ath v FC Edinburgh
Clyde v Kelty Hearts
Dunfermline Ath v Montrose
Falkirk v Peterhead
Queen of the South v Airdrieonians

Saturday, 20 August 2022
Airdrieonians v Alloa Ath
FC Edinburgh v Falkirk
Kelty Hearts v Dunfermline Ath
Montrose v Clyde
Peterhead v Queen of the South

Saturday, 27 August 2022
Alloa Ath v Peterhead
Dunfermline Ath v Airdrieonians
FC Edinburgh v Clyde
Falkirk v Queen of the South
Montrose v Kelty Hearts

Saturday, 3 September 2022
Airdrieonians v FC Edinburgh
Clyde v Alloa Ath
Kelty Hearts v Falkirk
Peterhead v Montrose
Queen of the South v Dunfermline Ath

Saturday, 10 September 2022
Clyde v Dunfermline Ath
FC Edinburgh v Peterhead
Falkirk v Alloa Ath
Kelty Hearts v Queen of the South
Montrose v Airdrieonians

Saturday, 17 September 2022
Airdrieonians v Clyde
Alloa Ath v Montrose
Dunfermline Ath v Falkirk
Peterhead v Kelty Hearts
Queen of the South v FC Edinburgh

Saturday, 1 October 2022
Dunfermline Ath v Peterhead
Falkirk v Clyde
Kelty Hearts v Airdrieonians
Montrose v FC Edinburgh
Queen of the South v Alloa Ath

Saturday, 8 October 2022
Airdrieonians v Queen of the South
Alloa Ath v Dunfermline Ath
Clyde v Montrose
FC Edinburgh v Kelty Hearts
Peterhead v Falkirk

Saturday, 15 October 2022
Alloa Ath v Airdrieonians
Dunfermline Ath v FC Edinburgh
Kelty Hearts v Clyde
Montrose v Falkirk
Queen of the South v Peterhead

Saturday, 22 October 2022
Clyde v Queen of the South
FC Edinburgh v Airdrieonians
Falkirk v Kelty Hearts
Montrose v Dunfermline Ath
Peterhead v Alloa Ath

Saturday, 29 October 2022
Airdrieonians v Montrose
Alloa Ath v Clyde
Dunfermline Ath v Kelty Hearts
Peterhead v FC Edinburgh
Queen of the South v Falkirk

Saturday, 5 November 2022
Clyde v Airdrieonians
FC Edinburgh v Queen of the South
Falkirk v Dunfermline Ath
Kelty Hearts v Alloa Ath
Montrose v Peterhead

Saturday, 12 November 2022
Airdrieonians v Peterhead
Alloa Ath v Queen of the South
Dunfermline Ath v Clyde
Falkirk v FC Edinburgh
Kelty Hearts v Montrose

Saturday, 19 November 2022
Airdrieonians v Kelty Hearts
Clyde v Falkirk
FC Edinburgh v Alloa Ath
Peterhead v Dunfermline Ath
Queen of the South v Montrose

Saturday, 3 December 2022
Clyde v FC Edinburgh
Dunfermline Ath v Queen of the South
Falkirk v Airdrieonians
Kelty Hearts v Peterhead
Montrose v Alloa Ath

Saturday, 17 December 2022
Airdrieonians v Dunfermline Ath
Alloa Ath v Falkirk
FC Edinburgh v Montrose
Peterhead v Clyde
Queen of the South v Kelty Hearts

Saturday, 24 December 2022
Clyde v Alloa Ath
FC Edinburgh v Peterhead
Falkirk v Queen of the South
Kelty Hearts v Dunfermline Ath
Montrose v Airdrieonians

Monday, 2 January 2023
Airdrieonians v FC Edinburgh
Alloa Ath v Kelty Hearts
Dunfermline Ath v Falkirk
Peterhead v Montrose
Queen of the South v Clyde

Saturday, 7 January 2023
Clyde v Kelty Hearts
FC Edinburgh v Dunfermline Ath
Falkirk v Montrose
Peterhead v Airdrieonians
Queen of the South v Alloa Ath

Saturday, 14 January 2023
Alloa Ath v FC Edinburgh
Dunfermline Ath v Peterhead
Falkirk v Clyde
Kelty Hearts v Airdrieonians
Montrose v Queen of the South

Saturday, 28 January 2023
Airdrieonians v Alloa Ath
Clyde v Dunfermline Ath
FC Edinburgh v Falkirk
Montrose v Kelty Hearts
Peterhead v Queen of the South

Saturday, 4 February 2023
Airdrieonians v Clyde
Alloa Ath v Peterhead
Dunfermline Ath v Montrose
Kelty Hearts v Falkirk
Queen of the South v FC Edinburgh

Saturday, 18 February 2023
Clyde v Peterhead
Dunfermline Ath v Airdrieonians
Falkirk v Alloa Ath
Kelty Hearts v Queen of the South
Montrose v FC Edinburgh

Saturday, 25 February 2023
Airdrieonians v Falkirk
Alloa Ath v Montrose
FC Edinburgh v Clyde
Peterhead v Kelty Hearts
Queen of the South v Dunfermline Ath

Saturday, 4 March 2023
Dunfermline Ath v Alloa Ath
Falkirk v Peterhead
Kelty Hearts v FC Edinburgh
Montrose v Clyde
Queen of the South v Airdrieonians

Saturday, 11 March 2023
Airdrieonians v Kelty Hearts
Clyde v Queen of the South
FC Edinburgh v Alloa Ath
Montrose v Falkirk
Peterhead v Dunfermline Ath

Saturday, 18 March 2023
Airdrieonians v Peterhead
Alloa Ath v Clyde
Dunfermline Ath v FC Edinburgh
Kelty Hearts v Montrose
Queen of the South v Falkirk

Saturday, 25 March 2023
Clyde v Airdrieonians
FC Edinburgh v Queen of the South
Falkirk v Kelty Hearts
Montrose v Dunfermline Ath
Peterhead v Alloa Ath

Saturday, 1 April 2023
Alloa Ath v Airdrieonians
Clyde v Falkirk
Dunfermline Ath v Kelty Hearts
FC Edinburgh v Montrose
Queen of the South v Peterhead

Saturday, 8 April 2023
Airdrieonians v Montrose
Alloa Ath v Queen of the South
Falkirk v Dunfermline Ath
Kelty Hearts v Clyde
Peterhead v FC Edinburgh

Saturday, 15 April 2023
Clyde v FC Edinburgh
Dunfermline Ath v Queen of the South
Falkirk v Airdrieonians
Kelty Hearts v Alloa Ath
Montrose v Peterhead

Saturday, 22 April 2023
Airdrieonians v Dunfermline Ath
Alloa Ath v Falkirk
FC Edinburgh v Kelty Hearts
Peterhead v Clyde
Queen of the South v Montrose

Saturday, 29 April 2023
Airdrieonians v Queen of the South
Dunfermline Ath v Clyde
Falkirk v FC Edinburgh
Kelty Hearts v Peterhead
Montrose v Alloa Ath

Saturday, 6 May 2023
Alloa Ath v Dunfermline Ath
Clyde v Montrose
FC Edinburgh v Airdrieonians
Peterhead v Falkirk
Queen of the South v Kelty Hearts

cinch League Two

Saturday, 30 July 2022
Bonnyrigg Rose Ath v Forfar Ath
Dumbarton v Stirling Alb
Elgin C v East Fife
Stenhousemuir v Albion R
Stranraer v Annan Ath

Saturday, 6 August 2022
Albion R v Dumbarton
Annan Ath v Stenhousemuir
East Fife v Bonnyrigg Rose Ath
Forfar Ath v Stranraer
Stirling Alb v Elgin C

Saturday, 13 August 2022
Albion R v East Fife
Dumbarton v Annan Ath
Forfar Ath v Elgin C
Stirling Alb v Stenhousemuir
Stranraer v Bonnyrigg Rose Ath

Saturday, 20 August 2022
Annan Ath v Stirling Alb
Bonnyrigg Rose Ath v Albion R
East Fife v Forfar Ath
Elgin C v Stranraer
Stenhousemuir v Dumbarton

Saturday, 27 August 2022
Albion R v Annan Ath
Bonnyrigg Rose Ath v Stirling Alb
Dumbarton v Elgin C
Forfar Ath v Stenhousemuir
Stranraer v East Fife

Saturday, 3 September 2022
Annan Ath v Forfar Ath
East Fife v Dumbarton
Elgin C v Bonnyrigg Rose Ath
Stenhousemuir v Stranraer
Stirling Alb v Albion R

Saturday, 10 September 2022
Bonnyrigg Rose Ath v Annan Ath
East Fife v Stenhousemuir
Elgin C v Albion R
Forfar Ath v Stirling Alb
Stranraer v Dumbarton

Saturday, 17 September 2022
Albion R v Forfar Ath
Annan Ath v East Fife
Dumbarton v Bonnyrigg Rose Ath
Stenhousemuir v Elgin C
Stirling Alb v Stranraer

Saturday, 1 October 2022
Bonnyrigg Rose Ath v Stenhousemuir
East Fife v Stirling Alb
Elgin C v Annan Ath
Forfar Ath v Dumbarton
Stranraer v Albion R

Saturday, 8 October 2022
Albion R v Bonnyrigg Rose Ath
Forfar Ath v East Fife
Stenhousemuir v Annan Ath
Stirling Alb v Dumbarton
Stranraer v Elgin C

Saturday, 15 October 2022
Annan Ath v Stranraer
Bonnyrigg Rose Ath v East Fife
Dumbarton v Albion R
Elgin C v Forfar Ath
Stenhousemuir v Stirling Alb

Saturday, 29 October 2022
Albion R v Stenhousemuir
Annan Ath v Dumbarton
East Fife v Elgin C
Stirling Alb v Bonnyrigg Rose Ath
Stranraer v Forfar Ath

Saturday, 5 November 2022
Albion R v Stirling Alb
Bonnyrigg Rose Ath v Elgin C
Dumbarton v Stranraer
Forfar Ath v Annan Ath
Stenhousemuir v East Fife

Saturday, 12 November 2022
East Fife v Albion R
Elgin C v Dumbarton
Forfar Ath v Bonnyrigg Rose Ath
Stirling Alb v Annan Ath
Stranraer v Stenhousemuir

Saturday, 19 November 2022
Albion R v Stranraer
Annan Ath v Elgin C
Dumbarton v Forfar Ath
Stenhousemuir v Bonnyrigg Rose Ath
Stirling Alb v East Fife

Saturday, 3 December 2022
Bonnyrigg Rose Ath v Dumbarton
East Fife v Annan Ath
Elgin C v Stenhousemuir
Forfar Ath v Albion R
Stranraer v Stirling Alb

Saturday, 17 December 2022
Albion R v Elgin C
Annan Ath v Bonnyrigg Rose Ath
Dumbarton v Stenhousemuir
East Fife v Stranraer
Stirling Alb v Forfar Ath

Saturday, 24 December 2022
Annan Ath v Albion R
Bonnyrigg Rose Ath v Stranraer
Dumbarton v East Fife
Elgin C v Stirling Alb
Stenhousemuir v Forfar Ath

Monday, 2 January 2023
Albion R v Dumbarton
East Fife v Bonnyrigg Rose Ath
Forfar Ath v Elgin C
Stirling Alb v Stenhousemuir
Stranraer v Annan Ath

Saturday, 7 January 2023
Annan Ath v Forfar Ath
Bonnyrigg Rose Ath v Albion R
Dumbarton v Stirling Alb
Elgin C v East Fife
Stenhousemuir v Stranraer

Saturday, 14 January 2023
Bonnyrigg Rose Ath v Stirling Alb
East Fife v Stenhousemuir
Elgin C v Annan Ath
Forfar Ath v Dumbarton
Stranraer v Albion R

Saturday, 28 January 2023
Albion R v Forfar Ath
Annan Ath v East Fife
Dumbarton v Bonnyrigg Rose Ath
Stenhousemuir v Elgin C
Stirling Alb v Stranraer

Saturday, 4 February 2023
Bonnyrigg Rose Ath v Annan Ath
East Fife v Stirling Alb
Elgin C v Albion R
Forfar Ath v Stranraer
Stenhousemuir v Dumbarton

Saturday, 11 February 2023
Albion R v East Fife
Dumbarton v Annan Ath
Forfar Ath v Stenhousemuir
Stirling Alb v Elgin C
Stranraer v Bonnyrigg Rose Ath

Saturday, 18 February 2023
Annan Ath v Stirling Alb
Bonnyrigg Rose Ath v Forfar Ath
East Fife v Dumbarton
Elgin C v Stranraer
Stenhousemuir v Albion R

Saturday, 25 February 2023
Albion R v Annan Ath
Bonnyrigg Rose Ath v Stenhousemuir
Dumbarton v Elgin C
Forfar Ath v Stirling Alb
Stranraer v East Fife

Saturday, 4 March 2023
Annan Ath v Stenhousemuir
East Fife v Forfar Ath
Elgin C v Bonnyrigg Rose Ath
Stirling Alb v Albion R
Stranraer v Dumbarton

Saturday, 11 March 2023
Albion R v Stranraer
Annan Ath v Elgin C
Dumbarton v Forfar Ath
Stenhousemuir v East Fife
Stirling Alb v Bonnyrigg Rose Ath

Saturday, 18 March 2023
Bonnyrigg Rose Ath v East Fife
Dumbarton v Albion R
Elgin C v Stenhousemuir
Forfar Ath v Annan Ath
Stranraer v Stirling Alb

Saturday, 25 March 2023
Albion R v Bonnyrigg Rose Ath
Annan Ath v Stranraer
East Fife v Elgin C
Stenhousemuir v Forfar Ath
Stirling Alb v Dumbarton

Saturday, 1 April 2023
Bonnyrigg Rose Ath v Stranraer
Dumbarton v Stenhousemuir
East Fife v Annan Ath
Elgin C v Stirling Alb
Forfar Ath v Albion R

Saturday, 8 April 2023
Albion R v Elgin C
Annan Ath v Dumbarton
Stenhousemuir v Bonnyrigg Rose Ath
Stirling Alb v East Fife
Stranraer v Forfar Ath

Saturday, 15 April 2023
Annan Ath v Albion R
Bonnyrigg Rose Ath v Dumbarton
East Fife v Stranraer
Elgin C v Forfar Ath
Stenhousemuir v Stirling Alb

Saturday, 22 April 2023
Albion R v Stenhousemuir
Dumbarton v East Fife
Forfar Ath v Bonnyrigg Rose Ath
Stirling Alb v Annan Ath
Stranraer v Elgin C

Saturday, 29 April 2023
Annan Ath v Bonnyrigg Rose Ath
East Fife v Albion R
Elgin C v Dumbarton
Stirling Alb v Forfar Ath
Stranraer v Stenhousemuir

Saturday, 6 May 2023
Albion R v Stirling Alb
Bonnyrigg Rose Ath v Elgin C
Dumbarton v Stranraer
Forfar Ath v East Fife
Stenhousemuir v Annan Ath

STOP PRESS

England Women reach quarter-finals of the UEFA Women's Euro Championship, winning their three group matches at an aggregate of 14-0, face Spain in the quarter-finals, but Northern Ireland out ... Rooney off to manage DC United in the USA ... Ronaldo, will he stay or will he go as United tour without him ... Brentford record transfer of £16m for Keane Lewis-Potter but Eriksen leaves for Manchester United ... Jesus to save Arsenal after £45m transfer from Manchester C and the Gunners waiting on Zinchenko.

UEFA WOMEN'S EUROS 2022 – GROUP STAGE RESULTS

GROUP A

England v Austria	1-0
Norway v Northern Ireland	4-1
Austria v Northern Ireland	2-0
England v Norway	8-0
Northern Ireland v England	0-5
Austria v Norway	1-0

Group A Table	P	W	D	L	F	A	GD	Pts
England	3	3	0	0	14	0	14	9
Austria	3	2	0	1	3	1	2	6
Norway	3	1	0	2	4	10	–6	3
Northern Ireland	3	0	0	3	1	11	–10	0

GROUP B

Spain v Finland	4-1
Germany v Denmark	4-0
Denmark v Finland	1-0
Germany v Spain	2-0
Finland v Germany	0-3
Denmark v Spain	0-1

Group B Table	P	W	D	L	F	A	GD	Pts
Germany	3	3	0	0	9	0	9	9
Spain	3	2	0	1	5	3	2	6
Denmark	3	1	0	2	1	5	–4	3
Finland	3	0	0	3	1	8	–7	0

GROUP C

Portugal v Switzerland	2-2
Netherlands v Sweden	1-1
Sweden v Switzerland	2-1
Netherlands v Portugal	3-2
Switzerland v Netherlands	1-4
Sweden v Portugal	5-0

Group C Table	P	W	D	L	F	A	GD	Pts
Sweden	3	2	1	0	8	2	6	7
Netherlands	3	2	1	0	8	4	4	7
Switzerland	3	0	1	2	4	8	–4	1
Portugal	3	0	1	2	4	10	–6	1

GROUP D

Belgium v Iceland	1-1
France v Italy	5-1
Italy v Iceland	1-1
France v Belgium	2-1
Iceland v France	1-1
Italy v Belgium	0-1

Group D Table	P	W	D	L	F	A	GD	Pts
France	3	2	1	0	8	3	5	7
Belgium	3	1	1	1	3	3	0	4
Iceland	3	0	3	0	3	3	0	3
Italy	3	0	1	2	2	7	–5	1

Full coverage of the UEFA Women's Euro 2022 in the next edition.

SELECTED SUMMER TRANSFERS 2022

Reported fees only, otherwise Undisclosed.

4 May: Jayson Molumby Brighton & HA to WBA.

11 May: Jordan Shipley Coventry C to Shrewsbury T.

12 May: Philippe Coutinho Barcelona to Aston Villa £17m.

18 May: James Holden Reading to Cambridge U; Ollie Tanner Lewes to Cardiff C.

20 May: Jake Young Forest Green R to Bradford C.

23 May: Fabio Carvalho Fulham to Liverpool.

25 May: James Bowen Cardiff C to Newport Co; Shaun Rooney St Johnstone to Fleetwood T.

26 May: Brenden Aaronson Red Bull Salzburg to Leeds U £25m; Andre-Frank Zambo Anguissa Fulham to Napoli.

1 June: Diego Carlos Sevilla to Aston Villa £26m.

4 June: Matt Dennis Norwich C to Milton Keynes D; Robin Olsen Roma to Aston Villa.

7 June: Declan Drysdale Coventry C to Newport Co.

8 June: Theo Archibald Lincoln C to Leyton Orient; Patrick Kelly Coleraine to West Ham U; Rasmus Kristensen RB Salzburg to Leeds U; Matt Targett Aston Villa to Newcastle U £15m.

9 June: Rocky Bushiri Norwich C to Hibernian.

10 June: Cameron Carter-Vickers Tottenham H to Celtic; Emmanuel Osadebe Walsall to Bradford C; Nathan Wood Middlesbrough to Swansea C.

13 June: Marquinhos Sao Paulo to Arsenal; Erling Haaland Borussia Dortmund to Manchester C £51.2m.

14 June: Stephen Dooley Rochdale to Harrogate T; Darwin Nunez Benfica to Liverpool £64m.

15 June: Devante Rodney Walsall to Rochdale; Mahlon Romeo Millwall to Cardiff C.

16 June: Dominic Jefferies Brentford to Gillingham; Ryan Williams Oxford U to Perth Glory.

17 June: Gavin Bazunu Manchester C to Southampton £12m; Yves Bissouma Brighton & HA to Tottenham H £25m; Julio Enciso Libertad Asuncion to Brighton & HA; Marc Roca Bayern Munich to Leeds U £10m; Jack Tucker Gillingham to Milton Keynes D.

18 June: Harry Darling Milton Keynes D to Swansea C.

19 June: Calvin Ramsay Aberdeen to Liverpool £4.2m.

20 June: Nayef Aguerd Rennes to West Ham U £30m; Alfie Doughty Stoke C to Luton T; Jayden Richardson Nottingham F to Aberdeen; Tyrell Warren FC Halifax T to Barrow.

21 June: Dan Adshead Norwich C to Cheltenham T; Armel Bella-Kotchap VfL Bochum to Southampton £8.6m; Owen Evans Cheltenham T to Walsall; Cucho Hernandez Watford to Columbus Crew; Danny Hylton Luton T to Northampton T; Kasey Palmer Bristol C to Coventry C; Jordan Rossiter Fleetwood T to Bristol R; Reghan Tumilty Raith R to Hartlepool U; Fabio Viera Porto to Arsenal £34.2m; Jordy de Wijs QPR to Fortuna Dusseldorf; Brendan Wiredu Colchester U to Fleetwood T; Freddie Woodman Newcastle U to Preston NE; Cauley Woodrow Barnsley to Luton T.

22 June: David Ajiboye Sutton U to Peterborough U; Hector Kyprianou Leyton Orient to Peterborough U; Matt Macey Hibernian to Luton T; Sadio Mane Liverpool to Bayern Munich £35m; Callum Morton WBA to Fleetwood T.

23 June: Pipa Huddersfield T to Olympiacos; Richie Bennett Sutton U to Barrow; Ryan Edmondson Leeds U to Carlisle U; Peter Kioso Luton T to Rotherham U; Nick Pope Burnley to Newcastle U; Kane Smith Boreham Wood to Stevenage.

24 June: Simon Adingra FC Nordsjaelland to Brighton & HA; James Connolly Cardiff C to Bristol R; Conor Grant Rochdale to Milton Keynes D; Darragh Lenihan Blackburn R to Middlesbrough; Fran Villalba Birmingham C to Sporting Gijon; Philip Zinckernagel Watford to Olympiacos.

25 June: Taiwo Awoniyi Union Berlin to Nottingham F £17m; Alex Cochrane Brighton & HA to Hearts; Zian Flemming Fortuna Sittard to Millwall; Ross Sykes Accrington S to Union SG.

26 June: Malcolm Ebiowei Derby Co to Crystal Palace; Scott Twine Milton Keynes D to Burnley.

27 June: Alphonse Areola Paris Saint-Germain to West Ham U £10.5m; Jorge Grant Peterborough U to Hearts; Matt Turner New England Revolution to Arsenal; Elliot Watt Bradford C to Salford C.

28 June: Sam Hornby Bradford C to Colchester U; Luke McNally Oxford U to Burnley £1.8m; Takumi Minamino Liverpool to Monaco £15.5m; Ivan Sanchez Birmingham C to Real Valladolid.

29 June: Oli Burke Sheffield U to Werder Bremen; Liam McCarron Leeds U to Stoke C; George Moncur Hull C to Leyton Orient.

30 June: Dan Ballard Arsenal to Sunderland; Omar Bogle Hartlepool U to Newport Co; Saikou Janneh Bristol C to Cambridge U.

1 July: Richarlison Everton to Tottenham H £60m; Sven Botman Lille to Newcastle U £34.5m; Cohen Brammall Lincoln C to Rotherham U; Neill Byrne Hartlepool U to Tranmere R; Lovre Kalinic Aston Villa to Hadjuk Split; Moussa Sissoko Watford to Nantes; Ozan Tufan Fenerbahce to Hull C; Louie Watson Derby Co to Luton T.

2 July: Vakoun Bayo Charleroi to Watford; Akin Odimayo Swindon T to Northampton T.

3 July: Giulian Biancone Troyes to Nottingham F £5m.

4 July: Trezeguet Aston Villa to Trabzonspor; Dan Csoka AFC Wimbledon to Zalaegerszegi; Gabriel Jesus Manchester C to Arsenal £45m; Joao Palhinha Sporting Lisbon to Fulham £17m; Kalvin Phillips Leeds U to Manchester C £45m.

5 July: Samuel Bastien Standard Liege to Burnley; Tyrell Malacia Feyenoord to Manchester U £13m; Brice Samba Nottingham F to Lens; Sam Sherring Bournemouth to Northampton T; Zak Swanson Arsenal to Portsmouth.

6 July: Tyler Adams RB Leipzig to Leeds U £20m; Anel Ahmedhodzic Malmo to Sheffield U; Ross Doohan Celtic to Tranmere R; Akin Famewo Norwich C to Sheffield W; David Kasumu Milton Keynes D to Huddersfield T; Romeo Lavia Manchester C to Southampton £10.5m; Carlton Morris Barnsley to Luton T; Moussa Niakhate Mainz to Nottingham F.

7 July: Flynn Downes Swansea C to West Ham U £12m; Dylan Levitt Manchester U to Dundee U; Luis Sinisterra Feyenoord to Leeds U £21m.

8 July: Steven Bergwijn Tottenham H to Ajax £26m; Jake Taylor Port Vale to Morecambe.

9 July: Joe Aribo Rangers to Southampton; Jack Clarke Tottenham H to Sunderland; Aaron Hickey Bologna to Brentford £15m; Allahyar Sayyadmanesh Fenerbahce to Hull C.

10 July: Omar Richards Bayern Munich to Nottingham F.

11 July: Cheick Doucoure Lens to Crystal Palace; Andreas Pereira Manchester U to Fulham £10m; Neco Williams Liverpool to Nottingham F £17m.

12 July: Tom Clayton Liverpool to Swindon T; Nathan Collins Burnley to Wolverhampton W £20.5m; Josh Cullen Anderlecht to Burnley; Keane Lewis-Potter Hull C to Brentford £16m; Rey Manaj Barcelona to Watford.

13 July: Ronan Darcy Bolton W to Swindon T; Dawson Devoy Bohemians to Milton Keynes D; Raheem Sterling Manchester City to Chelsea £50m.

14 July: Josh Umerah Wealdstone to Hartlepool U.

15 July: Raphinha Leeds U to Barcelona £55m; Aji Alese West Ham U to Sunderland; Marcus Harness Portsmouth to Ipswich T; Wayne Hennessey Burnley to Nottingham F; Remeao Hutton Barrow to Swindon T; Saidou Khan Chesterfield to Swindon T; Jack Rudoni AFC Wimbledon to Huddersfield T; Gabriel Sara Sao Paulo to Norwich C.

16 July: Kalidou Koulibaly Napoli to Chelsea.

18 July: Brandon Aguilera Alajuelense to Nottingham F; Zeno Ibsen Rossi Bournemouth to Cambridge U; Adam Long Wigan Ath to Doncaster R.

19 July: Djed Spence Middlesbrough to Tottenham H £12.5m.